# SOURCES
# OF
# SERIALS

*Sources of Serials* is edited
by R. R. Bowker Company Serials Bibliography Department

Emery I. Koltay, Head of Department;
Louise Valuck, Data Base Production Manager;
Tamas Keri, Data Sources Manager;
Katharine Chibnik, Sharis Duke, Rachel Goldman, Diana
McMorrow, Jacqueline Mullikin and Deborah Waithe, Editors;
Jeanne Bockman, Florentina Hart,
and Anita Zutis, Editorial Assistants;
Leigh C. Yuster, Editorial Coordinator;
Natalia Akkerman, Elizabeth Braham, Evelyn Y. Coleman,
Margaret Davis, Elizabeth Hochberg, Margareta Leon,
Eline van de Poel, Suzanna Simor, Contributing Editors.

Programming and processing was done by the Bowker
Publications Systems Department:
Susan J. Brown, Applications Manager;
Henry N. Lehmann and Laszlo Szabo, Senior Systems
Analysts.

The Bowker Serials Bibliography Department and the
Publications Systems are departments of the Bowker Data
Services and Systems Division, Andrew H. Uszak,
Vice President.

An international publisher and
corporate author directory

# SOURCES

# OF

# SERIALS

First Edition

A Bowker Serials Bibliography

R. R. BOWKER COMPANY

**A Xerox Publishing Company**
**New York & London**

Published by R.R. Bowker Company
(A Xerox Publishing Company)
1180 Avenue of the Americas, New York, N.Y. 10036

International Standard Book Number 0-8352-0855-9
International Standard Serial Number 0000-0523
Library of Congress Catalog Card Number 77-015833

Printed and bound in the United States of America.

# Contents

# Preface

*Sources of Serials* is a Bowker Serials Bibliography international name authority file for all serial publishers and corporate authors included in *Ulrich's International Periodicals Directory, Irregular Serials and Annuals* and *Ulrich's Quarterly*. It includes 63,000 publishers and corporate authors arranged under 181 countries, listing 90,000 current serial titles they publish or sponsor

During the past years, we have developed one of the most sophisticated, perhaps unique, systems for the maintenance of a large machine-readable serials file. Through this system we are in contact with publishers and corporate authors around the world. In addition to keeping us informed on the status of their serials, they were asked and provided us with their official names and addresses. This information is the basis of their listing in *Sources of Serials*.

There is worldwide discordance on serials control. Serials are listed: (a) under author, generally corporate, (b) under title, even if generic, (c) under titles, if distinctive, with all others under corporate body. Obviously these inconsistencies make difficult a cost-effective administration of serials files.

The access to a file such as *Sources of Serials* allowed us, and will allow all serial users from now on, a much better serials control. It enabled us to identify and eliminate hundreds of confusing and duplicate entries, which occurred in a file kept, previously, solely in title sequence.

"Information is one; access to it should be as manifold as the minds that seek it." (Ruth Rains, University of Illinois, Champaign, Ill.) This is what we are offering to all serial users, a new access point to help in their cataloging, collection development, selection, ordering, claiming, etc. The use of *Sources of Serials* is limited solely by the imagination of the user.

All types of publishers and sponsors with innumerable types of publications are listed. A publisher entry includes name and address information, co-publisher information, distributor information, corporate author information and title information. Types of publisher entries included are subdivisions of publishers, publisher imprints and subsidiaries, multinational publishers, government bodies, international organizations, United Nations, European Communities, international conferences, individual publishers and periodical titles as publisher entry. Detailed procedural descriptions are in the User's Guide.

Complete bibliographical description of a title is given in *Ulrich's International Periodicals Directory, Irregular Serials and Annuals* and *Ulrich's Quarterly*. Ordering address information is given for each title as well as for each publisher and sponsoring organization. In cases where an organization edits but does not publish or distribute one or more of its titles, the name of the publisher or distributor is given after these titles.

Although *Sources of Serials* is not an official authority name file according to traditional definitions of library authority files, the directory is a standard name listing that provides the current names of serial publishers and sponsors with 4,000 cross references for variant name formats and for divisions of organizations with a hierarchical structure.

The feature of having all the titles of a learned society listed in one place in alphabetical sequence allows the user to scrutinize and select the most appropriate ones for their collection.

The Bowker Serials Bibliography staff, together with the Publication Systems Department, are making every effort to produce services that meet user's needs. The Ulrich's family—*Ulrich's International Periodicals Directory, Irregular Serials and Annuals, Ulrich's Quarterly*—and *Sources of Serials* are "stand alone" bibliographic tools, but together they constitute the most valuable current serials bibliography reference works for serials management.

Taking stock of all the literature related to current serials control published in the last decade, we consider *Sources of Serials* one of the most outstanding and unmatched accomplishments in the field. Obviously, despite extensive editing and research procedures, there are regrettable omissions in the listings of names and titles which will be amended in our updating service, *Ulrich's Quarterly*, or in future editions.

The update and improvement of such a complex serials bibliography database is a continuous operation. We welcome comments and suggestions, for our updating services and future editions, from users and the authors and publishers listed in this edition.

Emery Koltay
Director, Bowker Serials Bibliography

*From the Bowker Serials Bibliography Department*
*The Ulrich's Family of Directories*

# ULRICH'S INTERNATIONAL PERIODICALS DIRECTORY

No other periodicals reference source is as current and comprehensive as *Ulrich's*, which is one reason why the *American Reference Books Annual* calls it a "truly outstanding reference tool."

The current edition of *Ulrich's International Periodicals Directory* lists some 60,000 periodicals of all kinds from all over the world in some 250 subject areas. Each entry provides title, frequency of publication, publisher name and address, country of publication code, and Dewey Decimal Classification number. Additional bibliographic and buying information provided when available includes: ISSN, subscription price, year first published, language of text, if advertising and book reviews are included, where abstracted or indexed, corporate author, variant forms, whether or not available from a subscription agency, and more. Separate sections include a list of cessations, an index to publications and international organizations, and a title index.

# IRREGULAR SERIALS AND ANNUALS

*An International Directory*

Designed as a companion to *Ulrich's International Periodicals Directory, Irregular Serials and Annuals* is worldwide in scope and provides data on some 30,000 serials, annuals, continuations, conference proceedings, and other publications issued irregularly or less frequently than twice a year. Entries are alphabetically by title under 250 subject headings, and data includes: frequency of issue, publisher, Dewey Decimal number, ISSN number, language of text, year first published, price, and editor.

In addition, the next edition of *Irregular Serials and Annuals* will include an ISSN index. All titles included in the Bowker Serials Bibliography data base, *Ulrich's, Irregular Serials and Annuals* and *Ulrich's Quarterly*, with ISSN are listed in this index.

# ULRICH'S QUARTERLY

*A Supplement to* Ulrich's International Periodicals Directory *and* Irregular Serials and Annuals

This quarterly brings you continuous worldwide, up-to-date information on new serial titles, title changes, and cessations. It gives you all the data you need to keep current between editions of *Ulrich's International Periodicals Directory* and *Irregular Serials and Annuals*. It replaces the *Bowker Serials Bibliography Supplement*. Each issue lists some 2,500 new and newly-added (to our serials database) periodicals, irregular serials and annuals of all kinds from all over the world in all subject areas. It utilizes the same subject arrangement as the base volumes and provides the same full bibliographic annotation for each item.

The *Ulrich's Quarterly* arrangement follows the format of *Ulrich's International Periodicals Directory* and *Irregular Serials and Annuals*. Pagination is continuous within each volume, and title, title changes, and cessations are cumulated in each issue.

**Ulrich's International Periodicals Directory, Irregular Serials and Annuals and Ulrich's Quarterly are "stand alone" bibliographic tools, but together they constitute a unique and valuable current serials bibliography reference work.**

# SOURCES OF SERIALS

*An International Publisher and Corporate Author Directory to* Ulrich's *and* Irregular Serials and Annuals

This directory will provide comprehensive and authoritative *author/publisher* access to the world's periodicals. It enables the user to quickly and easily identify, locate, and contact more than 50,000 publishers of the approximately 90,000 titles listed in the latest editions of *Ulrich's International Periodicals Directory, Irregular Serials and Annuals*, and *Ulrich's Quarterly*.

The arrangement is first by country, then by publisher and/or corporate author. Under each publisher is a complete listing of all serial titles published. The publisher's full name and current address is provided. Cross references from corporate author are included when the publisher is not the corporate author of the serial. A publisher/corporate author index is included.

*Order from*
## R.R. BOWKER ORDER DEPARTMENT
*Box 1807*
*Ann Arbor, Michigan 48106*

# User's Guide

## I   ARRANGEMENT

Over 63,000 publishers and corporate authors with listings of their current serial titles are listed within 181 country sections. Countries are arranged alphabetically by country name. The United Kingdom section includes Great Britain, Scotland, Wales, and Northern Ireland. There are independent sections for the United Nations and for the European Communities. The International Index at the end of the directory lists in alphabetical order all of the *name* headings for publishers and corporate authors, with cross references for variant names. In this index, a country code following the name indicates the country section where the publisher or corporate author entry is listed. A key to country codes and an alphabetical listing of the country sections are given following the User's Guide.

## II   PUBLISHER ENTRY AND CORPORATE AUTHOR REFERENCE ENTRY

There are two types of entries for source-of-serial information: 1) the publisher entry that includes name and address with a listing of the publisher's titles, 2) the corporate author reference entry that gives name, without address, and a listing of the corporate author's titles.

The term *publisher* in this context refers to any organization that publishes a serial title of his own or one that has been sponsored by another organization. Since corporate authors often act as publishers, the term *corporate author* in this context refers to an organization that sponsors, compiles or prepares material for publication but has that material published by another organization.

The corporate author reference entry does not contain the address information or descriptive title information (such as frequency of publication and ISSN) found in the publisher entry. Following each title the corporate author reference entry is the name of the publisher entry where more complete information about that title is listed.

CORPORATE AUTHOR REFERENCE ENTRY

**American Society for Political and Legal Philosophy**
  ● Nomos. (pub. by Lieber-Atherton, Inc.)

PUBLISHER ENTRY

**Lieber-Atherton, Inc.**
  1841 Broadway, New York, NY 10023.
  ● Nomos. a. ISSN 0078-0979 (American Society for
  Political and Legal Philosophy)

If the publisher is not located in the same country as the corporate author, a country code is given after the publisher's name.

PUBLISHER ENTRY

**Africana Publishing Co.**
  (Subsidiary of: Holmes & Meier Publishers, Inc.)
  101 Fifth Ave., New York, NY 10003.
  ● African Bibliography Series. irreg.
  ● African Literature Today. a. ISSN 0065-4000
  (University of Sierra Leone. Fourah Bay College
  SL) (And Heinemann Educational Books, 48
  Charles St., London, England W1X 8AH)
  ● Africana Journal; a bibliographic and review
  quarterly. q. ISSN 0095-1080
  ● International Journal of African Historical Studies.
  q. ISSN 0361-7882 (Boston University. African
  Studies Center)

University of Sierra Leone. Fourah Bay College
Freetown, Sierra Leone.
- African Literature Today. (pub. by Africana
  Publishing Co. US)
- Africana Research Bulletin. s-a. (prep. by its
  Institute of African Studies)

## III  CONTENTS OF PUBLISHER ENTRY

*Publisher name and address information.* The address given directly after the name of the publisher is generally for the editorial office of the publisher. The ordering address, if not the same, is given in parentheses after the editorial address.

If an organization arranges to have one or more of its titles published by another organization, this information is given after each title in a parenthetical note (pub. [published] by . . . ). The publisher entry for the publisher given in parentheses contains address information.

*Co-publisher information.* If a serial is jointly published by two or more organizations, the title is listed only under one publisher entry. The name of the co-publisher is given in parentheses.

*Distributor information.* If all of the publisher's titles are distributed exclusively by another organization, the name and address of the distributor are given in parentheses after the publisher's address. When available, exclusive U.S. distributors are given for titles published outside the U.S.

If only some of the titles of the publishing organization are distributed by another organization, this information will be given in parentheses after each title.

If an organization does original publishing as well as distributing, only the titles actually published by that organization are included in the publishers listing. In the People's Republic of China, Cuba, and a few other Communist countries, some state/central distributors are listed as publishers.

*Corporate author information.* If the publisher is not also the corporate author, the name of the corporate author is given in parentheses. If the corporate author itself issued other titles, these titles are listed under the heading of that corporate author.

PUBLISHER ENTRY

C. V. Mosby Co.
11830 Westline Industrial Dr., St. Louis, MO 63141.
- American Academy of Ophthalmology and Otolaryngology. Selected Proceedings. a.
- American Academy of Orthopaedic Surgeons. Committee on Instructional Courses. Instructional Course Lectures. a. ISSN 0065-6895 (American Academy of Orthopaedic Surgeons)
- American Association of Obstetricians and Gynecologists. Transactions. a. ISSN 0065-728X (American Association of Obstetricians and Gynecologists)
- American Heart Journal; an international publication for the study of the circulation. m. ISSN 0002-8703
- American Journal of Obstetrics and Gynecology. s-m. ISSN 0002-9378 (American Gynecological Society)

American Gynecological Society
c/o Dept. Ob/Gyn., Center for the Health Sciences,
U.C.L.A. School of Medicine, Los Angeles, CA
90024.
- American Gynecological Society. Transactions of the A G S. a. ISSN 0065-8480
- American Journal of Obstetrics and Gynecology. (pub. by C. V. Mosby Co.)

If the corporate author is not located in the same country as the publisher, a country code follows the corporate author name.

If a subdivision responsible for a given title is not in the heading and not in the title, it may be given in a parenthetical note (prep. [prepared] by its) after the title.

If a serial is jointly sponsored by two or more corporate authors, the title is listed in only one publisher main entry. The name(s) of the co-sponsor(s) is given in parentheses.

*Title information.* The following descriptive information, when available, is given after the title: parallel language title (separated from the title by a slash), explanation of abbreviation in the title, when the abbreviation is not explained by the name of the publisher or corporate author, subtitle, frequency of publication, International Standard Serial Number (ISSN).

More complete bibliographic information is given in: *Ulrich's Quarterly* (vol. I, 1977), *Ulrich's International Periodical Directory* (17th edition, 1977), *Irregular Serials and Annuals* (4th edition, 1976).

## IV  TYPES OF PUBLISHER ENTRIES

*Subdivisions of publishers.* If a subdivision is located at an address different from the address of the parent organization, there is a publisher entry for the subdivision, usually listed after the name of the parent organization.

In some cases, there is an entry for the subdivision located at the address of the parent organization because titles issued by the subdivision all relate to a specific subject area or to the specific function of that subdivision. The periodical division of a book publisher may be a publisher main entry. Most university departments are given as publisher entries.

If there is no publisher for a subdivision, the name of a subdivision responsible for the contents of title may be given after that title in a parenthetical note (prep. [prepared] by its . . . ).

If the name of the subdivision is considered distinctive without the name of the parent organization, there is a publisher entry for the subdivision. When there is an independent entry for a subdivision, a cross reference is usually given from the name of parent organization to the distinctive name heading of the subdivision.

*Publisher Imprints and Subsidiaries.* Imprints and subsidiaries of publishing houses are given as publisher entries. The parent publishing organization is given after the name of the imprint or subsidiary in the publisher heading. Imprints and subsidiaries are not listed under the parent publishing organization.

*Multi-National Publishers.* Generally, there is a publisher entry in each country where a multi-national publisher has an office. In these cases, the publisher entry includes the addresses of the publisher's offices in other countries.

In certain cases, the publisher entry for a multi-national publisher appears in only one country section. Cross-references are given from countries where the publisher has offices to the country where the publisher entry is listed. (To facilitate data compiling for this edition, two German publishers, Springer-Verlag and Verlag Chemie International, Inc., are listed in the United States section.)

The user should check both the country sections and the name index for access to all offices of multi-national publishers.

*Governments.* Whenever the address of the issuing government agency of a serial title could be located, the titles are listed under the publisher entry for the issuing agency, not the government printer. In cases where address information for the issuing agency of a government publication could not be located, the publication is listed under the entry for the government printer. U.S. federal government publications are always listed under the issuing agency, and the U.S. Government Printing Office is treated as a distributor. Generally, free single copies are available from the issuing agency, while orders for multiple, priced copies should be directed to the Government Printing Office.

*International organizations* (excluding the United Nations and the European Communities). The International Index of publishers and corporate authors provides the most direct access to international organizations listed in *Sources of Serials*. Specialized centers, national and regional centers of international organizations are listed under the countries where these divisions are located. International organizations that do not have permanent secretariats may be listed under the country where the secretariat general (or other officer) resides or maintains an office. When serial titles of one international organization are published by other organizations or publishing firms, the name heading for that international organization is listed under the countries of the respective publishers.

*The United Nations and the European Communities.* Because of the structural organization of the United Nations and the European Communities, publishing divisions of these international organizations are centralized in independent sections.

Within the section for the United Nations, the divisions of the U.N. and its related agencies are listed. Cross references from the countries where specialized agencies are located to the United Nations section are given. National commissions of the U.N. are listed in the countries in which they are located.

Titles issued by agencies of the European Communities are given under the name of the issuing agency and/or the Official Office of Publications for the European Communities. Names and addresses of regional Information Offices of the European Community are also given in this section.

*International Conferences.* If the international organization that sponsors the conference has a permanent secretariat and is the publisher of the conference reports, the ordering information for the reports is given in the publisher entry for the sponsoring organization.

If the international organization that sponsors the conference has a permanent secretariat but is not the publisher of the conference reports, the name and address of the publisher or distributor of the most recently published proceedings are given.

If a publishing firm regularly publishes the reports of an international conference, ordering information for the reports of the conferences is given in that publisher's entry.

*Individuals as publishers.* If a serial is published by an organization, the publisher is the organization, not the individual who is given as publisher. When an individual acts as both publisher and editor of a serial and is not affiliated with a publishing organization, the publisher entry is for the individual. In these cases, the individual's name is followed by the words Ed. & Pub. (Editor and Publisher).

**Robert M. Bottorff, Ed. & Pub.**
Box 739, Camden, NJ 08102.
• Popular Periodical Index. s-a. ISSN 0092-9727

*Periodical title as publisher entry.* When there is no publisher or organization or individual identified as the publisher of a periodical (as is often the case with small literary and political reviews), the title of the periodical is given as the publisher heading.

**December**
c/o Curt L. Johnson, Ed., 4343 N. Clarendon, Chicago, IL 60613.
• December; a magazine of the arts and opinion. irreg. ISSN 0070-3141

## V  RULES FOR NAME HEADINGS

*Non-governmental organizations.* Names are usually entered as reported by the publisher. Initial articles, however, are usually omitted, but if included are by-passed in filing. In name headings of organizations that begin with proper names and/or initials, titles and personal names are entered in the normal word order of the organization name (e.g. A.K. Smith Library, Sir Thomas Beecham Society.)

If the name of a subdivision is considered distinctive without the name of the parent organization, the name of the parent organization is not included in the name heading; there is a cross-reference from the name of the parent organization and its subdivision to the name heading for the subdivision.

Whenever variant formats were identified, cross-references are given from the variant name formats to the names in the publisher and corporate author entries.

*Governments.* Names of government departments and agencies are entered under the name of the government jurisdiction.

Generally, publisher and author names are for the narrowest, distinctive division of the government department or agency. Cross-references are given to show the hierarchial structures of the departments.

If the name of the government department or agency includes an adjective form of the government jurisdiction, cross-reference is given from the adjective form of the name, e.g. Australian Bureau of Statistics is entered Australia. Australian Bureau of Statistics.

All U.S. federal government names are entered under United States (U.S.) with the exception of quasi-governmental agencies (such as the National Academy of Sciences and the Smithsonian Institution) and independent commissions and committees (such as the Missouri River Basin Commission), which are entered as other publisher and corporate author names.

*Language of name heading.* Names are usually entered in the official language of the country. In Japan and China, in other Asian countries, where non-roman alphabet languages are used, the publisher name is generally given in English. Cross-references are given from the original language name to the English name, wherever this information was available.

In countries where there is more than one official language, cross-references are given from the parallel language names to the names in the publisher entries.

Diacritical marks are not shown. The German umlaut has been replaced by the letter *e* following the vowels *a, o,* and *u.* In Danish, Norwegian, and Swedish names, the letter *å* is entered as *aa* and the letter *ø* as *oe.*

If the publisher or corporate author is an international organization and English is one of the official languages of the organization, the name heading is in English.

## VI FILING RULES

Filing rules for commercial publishing firms differ from filing rules for other organizations.

The name heading for an organization that is *not* a commercial publishing firm is filed under the full name of the organization; initials and proper names, when part of the full names, are used in filing.

Firms in the Netherlands, Belgium, Scandinavia, and Indonesia, which begin with the abbreviations N.V., A.S., A.S.B.L., P.T. are filed according to the first letter of the word following the abbreviation.

If the name of a commercial publishing firm includes a proper name, the heading is filed under the surname. The name heading for an individual who acts as editor and publisher is also filed under the surname.

If the name of a commercial publishing firm begins with a word that designates the function of a publisher (generic terms as *Verlag, editions*), the name heading is filed under the first "distinctive" word following the generic terms. Name headings of this type may also be filed under the generic term if the words immediately following it are adjectives.

Government agencies entered under the name of the government jurisdiction are filed before other non-governmental headings with the same name.

**Connecticut. Treasury Department**
Hartford, CT 06115.
• Connecticut. Treasury Department. Annual Report. a. ISSN 0099-0108

**Connecticut Academy of Arts and Sciences**
• Connecticut Academy of Arts and Sciences. Memoirs. (pub. by Archon Books)
• Connecticut Academy of Arts and Sciences. Transactions. (pub. by Archon Books)

Acronyms and initials are filed at the beginning of each letter of the alphabet with the exceptions of the abbreviations U.N. (United Nations), U.S. (United States), Gt. Brit. (Great Britain), and St. (Saint) which are filed as words.

Initial articles are not considered in filing. Articles and prepositions within entries are filed as words.

## VII ABBREVIATIONS

| | |
|---|---|
| a. | annual |
| approx. | approximately |
| B.R.D. | Federal Republic of Germany |
| bi-m. | every two months |
| c/o | care of |
| Cy. | county |
| d. | daily |
| D.D.R. | German Democratic Republic |
| dist. | distributor, distributed |
| Ed., Eds. | Editor, Editors |
| fortn. | fortnightly |
| ISSN | International Standard Serial Number |
| irreg. | irregular |
| m. | monthly |
| N.S. | New Series |
| Prof. | Professor |
| q. | quarterly |
| s-a. | twice annually |
| s-m. | twice monthly |
| s-w. | twice weekly |
| subscr. | subscription |
| 3 per m. | 3 times a month |
| 3 per yr. | 3 times a year |
| w. | weekly |

# List of Countries and Country Codes

## Country Sequence

AFARS & ISSAS - FT
AFGHANISTAN - AF
ALBANIA - AA
ALGERIA - AE
AMERICAN SAMOA - AS
ANDORRA - AN
ANGOLA - AO
ANTARCTICA - AY
ANTIGUA - AQ
ARGENTINA - AG
ASHMORE & CARTIER ISLANDS - AC
AUSTRALIA - AT
AUSTRIA - AU
BAHAMAS - BF
BAHRAIN - BA
BANGLA DESH - BG
BARBADOS - BB
BELGIUM - BE
BELIZE - BH
BENIN - DM
BERMUDA - BM
BHUTAN - BT
BOLIVIA - BO
BOTSWANA - BS
BRAZIL - BL
BRITISH SOLOMON ISLANDS - BP
BRUNEI - BX
BULGARIA - BU
BURMA - BR
BURUNDI - BD
CAMBODIA - CB
CAMEROON - CM
CANADA - CN
CANAL ZONE - CZ
CAPE VERDE - CV
CAYMAN ISLANDS - CJ
CENTRAL AFRICAN REPUBLIC - CX
CHAD - CD
CHILE - CL
CHINA, MAINLAND - CC
CHINA, REPUBLIC OF - CH
CHRISTMAS ISLAND - XA
COLOMBIA - CK
CONGO (BRAZZAVILLE) - CF
COSTA RICA - CR
CUBA - CU
CYPRUS - CY
CZECHOSLOVAKIA - CS
DENMARK - DK
DOMINICA - DQ
DOMINICAN REPUBLIC - DR
ECUADOR - EC
EGYPT - UA
EL SALVADOR - ES
EQUATORIAL GUINEA - EG
ETHIOPIA - ET
EUROPEAN COMMUNITIES - EI
FAEROE ISLANDS - FA
FALKLAND ISLANDS - FK
FIJI - FJ
FINLAND - FI
FRANCE - FR
FRENCH GUIANA - FG
FRENCH POLYNESIA - FP
GABON - GO
GAMBIA - GM
GERMANY, EAST - GE
GERMANY, WEST - GW
GHANA - GH

GIBRALTAR - GI
GILBERT & ELLICE ISLANDS - GN
GREECE - GR
GREENLAND - GL
GRENADA - GD
GUADELOUPE - GP
GUAM - GU
GUATEMALA - GT
GUINEA - GV
GUINEA-BISSAU - PG
GUYANA - GY
HAITI - HT
HONDURAS - HO
HONG KONG - HK
HUNGARY - HU
ICELAND - IC
INDIA - II
INDONESIA - IO
IRAN - IR
IRAQ - IQ
IRELAND - IE
ISRAEL - IS
ITALY - IT
IVORY COAST - IV
JAMAICA - JM
JAPAN - JA
JORDAN - JO
KENYA - KE
KOREA, NORTH - KN
KOREA, SOUTH - KO
KUWAIT - KU
LAOS - LS
LEBANON - LE
LESOTHO - LO
LIBERIA - LB
LIBYA - LY
LIECHTENSTEIN - LH
LUXEMBOURG - LU
MACAO - MH
MALAGASY REPUBLIC - MG
MALAWI - MW
MALAYSIA - MY
MALDIVE ISLANDS - XC
MALI - ML
MALTA - MM
MARTINIQUE - MQ
MAURITANIA - MU
MAURITIUS - MF
MEXICO - MX
MONACO - MC
MONGOLIA - MP
MONTSERRAT - MJ
MOROCCO - MR
MOZAMBIQUE - MZ
NAMIBIA - SX
NEPAL - NP
NETHERLANDS - NE
NETHERLANDS ANTILLES - NA
NEW CALEDONIA - NL
NEW HEBRIDES - NN
NEW ZEALAND - NZ
NICARAGUA - NQ
NIGER - NG
NIGERIA - NR
NORFOLK ISLAND - NX
NORWAY - NO
OMAN - MK
PAKISTAN - PK

PANAMA - PN
PAPUA NEW GUINEA - PP
PARAGUAY - PY
PERU - PE
PHILIPPINES - PH
PITCAIRN ISLAND - PC
POLAND - PL
PORTUGAL - PO
PORTUGUESE TIMOR - PT
PUERTO RICO - PR
QATAR - QA
REUNION - RE
RHODESIA - RH
RUMANIA - RM
RWANDA - RW
RYUKYU ISLANDS, SOUTHERN - RY
ST. CHRISTOPHER-NEVIS-ANGUILLA - XI
SAINT HELENA - XJ
SAINT LUCIA - XK
SAINT VINCENT - XM
SAN MARINO - SM
SAO TOME E PRINCIPE - SF
SAUDI ARABIA - SU
SENEGAL - SG
SEYCHELLES - SE
SIERRA LEONE - SL
SIKKIM - SK
SINGAPORE - SI
SOMALIA - SO
SOUTH AFRICA - SA
SPAIN - SP
SRI LANKA - CE
SUDAN - SJ
SURINAM - SR
SWAZILAND - SQ
SWEDEN - SW
SWITZERLAND - SZ
SYRIA - SY
TANZANIA - TZ
THAILAND - TH
TOGO - TG
TONGA - TO
TRINIDAD & TOBAGO - TR
TRUST TERRITORY, PACIFIC ISLDS - TT
TUNISIA - TI
TURKEY - TU
TURKS & CAICOS ISLANDS - TC
UGANDA - UG
UNITED ARAB EMIRATES - TS
UNITED KINGDOM - UK
UNITED KINGDOM MISC. ISLANDS - UI
UNITED NATIONS - UN
UNITED STATES - US
UPPER VOLTA - UV
URUGUAY - UY
U S S R - UR
VATICAN CITY - VC
VENEZUELA - VE
VIETNAM - VN
VIRGIN ISLANDS (BRITISH) - VB
VIRGIN ISLANDS (U. S.) - VI
WESTERN SAMOA - WS
YEMEN - YE
YEMEN, SOUTHERN - YS
YUGOSLAVIA - YU
ZAIRE - ZR
ZAMBIA - ZA

# Country Codes Sequence

|  |  | |  |  | |  |  |
|------|---------|---|------|---------|---|------|---------|
| AA | - ALBANIA | | GN | - GILBERT & ELLICE ISLANDS | | PL | - POLAND |
| AC | - ASHMORE & CARTIER ISLANDS | | GO | - GABON | | PN | - PANAMA |
| AE | - ALGERIA | | GP | - GUADELOUPE | | PO | - PORTUGAL |
| AF | - AFGHANISTAN | | GR | - GREECE | | PP | - PAPUA NEW GUINEA |
| AG | - ARGENTINA | | GT | - GUATEMALA | | PR | - PUERTO RICO |
| AN | - ANDORRA | | GU | - GUAM | | PT | - PORTUGUESE TIMOR |
| AO | - ANGOLA | | GV | - GUINEA | | PY | - PARAGUAY |
| AQ | - ANTIGUA | | GW | - GERMANY, WEST | | QA | - QATAR |
| AS | - AMERICAN SAMOA | | GY | - GUYANA | | RE | - REUNION |
| AT | - AUSTRALIA | | HK | - HONG KONG | | RH | - RHODESIA |
| AU | - AUSTRIA | | HO | - HONDURAS | | RM | - RUMANIA |
| AY | - ANTARCTICA | | HT | - HAITI | | RW | - RWANDA |
| BA | - BAHRAIN | | HU | - HUNGARY | | RY | - RYUKYU ISLANDS, SOUTHERN |
| BB | - BARBADOS | | IC | - ICELAND | | SA | - SOUTH AFRICA |
| BD | - BURUNDI | | IE | - IRELAND | | SE | - SEYCHELLES |
| BE | - BELGIUM | | II | - INDIA | | SF | - SAO TOME E PRINCIPE |
| BF | - BAHAMAS | | IO | - INDONESIA | | SG | - SENEGAL |
| BG | - BANGLA DESH | | IQ | - IRAQ | | SI | - SINGAPORE |
| BH | - BELIZE | | IR | - IRAN | | SJ | - SUDAN |
| BL | - BRAZIL | | IS | - ISRAEL | | SK | - SIKKIM |
| BM | - BERMUDA | | IT | - ITALY | | SL | - SIERRA LEONE |
| BO | - BOLIVIA | | IV | - IVORY COAST | | SM | - SAN MARINO |
| BP | - BRITISH SOLOMON ISLANDS | | JA | - JAPAN | | SO | - SOMALIA |
| BR | - BURMA | | JM | - JAMAICA | | SP | - SPAIN |
| BS | - BOTSWANA | | JO | - JORDAN | | SQ | - SWAZILAND |
| BT | - BHUTAN | | KE | - KENYA | | SR | - SURINAM |
| BU | - BULGARIA | | KN | - KOREA, NORTH | | SU | - SAUDI ARABIA |
| BX | - BRUNEI | | KO | - KOREA, SOUTH | | SW | - SWEDEN |
| CB | - CAMBODIA | | KU | - KUWAIT | | SX | - NAMIBIA |
| CC | - CHINA, MAINLAND | | LB | - LIBERIA | | SY | - SYRIA |
| CD | - CHAD | | LE | - LEBANON | | SZ | - SWITZERLAND |
| CE | - SRI LANKA | | LH | - LIECHTENSTEIN | | TC | - TURKS & CAICOS ISLANDS |
| CF | - CONGO (BRAZZAVILLE) | | LO | - LESOTHO | | TG | - TOGO |
| CH | - CHINA, REPUBLIC OF | | LS | - LAOS | | TH | - THAILAND |
| CJ | - CAYMAN ISLANDS | | LU | - LUXEMBOURG | | TI | - TUNISIA |
| CK | - COLOMBIA | | LY | - LIBYA | | TO | - TONGA |
| CL | - CHILE | | MC | - MONACO | | TR | - TRINIDAD & TOBAGO |
| CM | - CAMEROON | | MF | - MAURITIUS | | TS | - UNITED ARAB EMIRATES |
| CN | - CANADA | | MG | - MALAGASY REPUBLIC | | TT | - TRUST TERRITORY, PACIFIC ISLDS |
| CR | - COSTA RICA | | MH | - MACAO | | TU | - TURKEY |
| CS | - CZECHOSLOVAKIA | | MJ | - MONTSERRAT | | TZ | - TANZANIA |
| CU | - CUBA | | MK | - OMAN | | UA | - EGYPT |
| CV | - CAPE VERDE | | ML | - MALI | | UG | - UGANDA |
| CX | - CENTRAL AFRICAN REPUBLIC | | MM | - MALTA | | UI | - UNITED KINGDOM MISC. ISLANDS |
| CY | - CYPRUS | | MP | - MONGOLIA | | UK | - UNITED KINGDOM |
| CZ | - CANAL ZONE | | MQ | - MARTINIQUE | | UN | - UNITED NATIONS |
| DK | - DENMARK | | MR | - MOROCCO | | UR | - U S S R |
| DM | - BENIN | | MU | - MAURITANIA | | US | - UNITED STATES |
| DQ | - DOMINICA | | MW | - MALAWI | | UV | - UPPER VOLTA |
| DR | - DOMINICAN REPUBLIC | | MX | - MEXICO | | UY | - URUGUAY |
| EC | - ECUADOR | | MY | - MALAYSIA | | VB | - VIRGIN ISLANDS (BRITISH) |
| EG | - EQUATORIAL GUINEA | | MZ | - MOZAMBIQUE | | VC | - VATICAN CITY |
| EI | - EUROPEAN COMMUNITIES | | NA | - NETHERLANDS ANTILLES | | VE | - VENEZUELA |
| ES | - EL SALVADOR | | NE | - NETHERLANDS | | VI | - VIRGIN ISLANDS (U. S.) |
| ET | - ETHIOPIA | | NG | - NIGER | | VN | - VIETNAM |
| FA | - FAEROE ISLANDS | | NL | - NEW CALEDONIA | | WS | - WESTERN SAMOA |
| FG | - FRENCH GUIANA | | NN | - NEW HEBRIDES | | XA | - CHRISTMAS ISLAND |
| FI | - FINLAND | | NO | - NORWAY | | XC | - MALDIVE ISLANDS |
| FJ | - FIJI | | NP | - NEPAL | | XI | - ST. CHRISTOPHER-NEVIS-ANGUILLA |
| FK | - FALKLAND ISLANDS | | NQ | - NICARAGUA | | XJ | - SAINT HELENA |
| FP | - FRENCH POLYNESIA | | NR | - NIGERIA | | XK | - SAINT LUCIA |
| FR | - FRANCE | | NX | - NORFOLK ISLAND | | XM | - SAINT VINCENT |
| FT | - AFARS & ISSAS | | NZ | - NEW ZEALAND | | YE | - YEMEN |
| GD | - GRENADA | | PC | - PITCAIRN ISLAND | | YS | - YEMEN, SOUTHERN |
| GE | - GERMANY, EAST | | PE | - PERU | | YU | - YUGOSLAVIA |
| GH | - GHANA | | PG | - GUINEA-BISSAU | | ZA | - ZAMBIA |
| GI | - GIBRALTAR | | PH | - PHILIPPINES | | ZR | - ZAIRE |
| GL | - GREENLAND | | PK | - PAKISTAN | | | |
| GM | - GAMBIA | | | | | | |

# Sources of Serials by Country

## AFARS & ISSAS

**Afars and Issas. Ministry of the Interior**
Box 268, Djibouti, Afars and Issas.
- Reveil de Djibouti. w. ISSN 0034-6276

**Societe d'Etudes de l'Afrique Orientale**
B.P. 677, Djibouti, Afars and Issas.
- Pount. q. ISSN 0554-873X

## AFGHANISTAN

**Afghanistan. Department of Statistics**
Kabul, Afghanistan.
- Statistical Pocket-Book of Afghanistan. irreg.

**Afghanistan. Ministry of Education**
Compilation Dept., Kabul, Afghanistan.
- Bekhan Wa Bedan. m. ISSN 0005-8254

**Afghanistan. Ministry of Information and Culture**
Kabul, Afghanistan.
- Afghanistan Republic Annual. a. ISSN 0304-6133

**Anees Publishing Co.**
Ansari Ave., Kabul, Afghanistan.
- Kochniano Anees/Anees for Children. w. ISSN 0023-2572

**Historical Society of Afghanistan**
Ministry of Information and Culture, Kabul, Afghanistan.
- Afghanistan. q. ISSN 0001-9682
- Aryana. q. ISSN 0004-4164

**Kabul**
Pashtu Tolana, Kabul, Afghanistan.
- Kabul. bi-m.

**Kabul University**
Institute of Geography, Faculty of Letters, Kabul, Afghanistan.
- Geographical Review of Afghanistan. ISSN 0016-7436

## ALBANIA

**Academie des Sciences de la RPA. Institut des Etudes Economiques**
Tirana, Albania.
- Academie des Sciences de la RPA Institut des Etudes Economiques. Probleme Ekonomike. bi-m.

**Albania. Ministere de l'Agriculture**
Tirana, Albania.
- Bujqesia Socialiste. m.

**Albania. Ministere de l'Enseignement et de la Culture**
Tirana, Albania.
- Mesuesi/Instituteur. s-w.
- Sporti Popullor. w.

**Albania. Ministere de la Sante Publique**
Tirana, Albania.
- Shendetesia Popullore. q.

**Croix Rouge Albanaise**
Tirana, Albania.
- Shendeti. bi-m.

**Drejtoria Qendrore e Librit**
Pruga Konferenca e Pezec, Tirana, Albania
(U.S. Subscr. to: F A M Book Service, 69 Fifth Ave., New York, N.Y. 10003)
- Albania Today/Albanie Aujourd'hui. bi-m. ISSN 0044-7072 (Parti du Travail d'Albanie)

**Institut des Etudes Pedagogiques**
Tirana, Albania.
- Revista Pedagogjike. bi-m.

**Parti du Travail d'Albanie**
Tirana, Albania.
- Albania Today/Albanie Aujourd'hui. (pub. by Drejtoria Qendrore e Librit)
- Rruga e Partise. m.

**Union de la Jeunesse du Travail d'Albanie**
Tirana, Albania.
- Pionieri. fortn.
- Zeri i Rinise/La Voix de la Jeunesse. s-w.

**Union des Ecrivains et Artistes d'Albanie**
Tirana, Albania.
- Drita. w.
- Nentori; revue litteraire et artistique. m.

**Union des Femmes d'Albanie**
Tirana, Albania.
- Shqiptarja e Re. m.

**Union des Journalistes d'Albanie**
Tirana, Albania.
- Tribuna e Gazetarit. bi-m.

**Unions Professionnelles d'Albanie**
Tirana, Albania.
- Puna/Travail. s-w.

## ALGERIA

**Algeria. Bibliotheque Nationale**
1 Ave. du Docteur Fanon, Algiers, Algeria.
- Bibliographie de l'Algerie/Al-Bibliyugrafya al-Djazairiyah. s-a. ISSN 0523-2392

**Algeria. Commissariat National a l'Informatique**
4 Boulevard Mohamed V, Algiers, Algeria.
- Informatique et Automatique. bi-m.

**Algeria. Direction des Douanes**
19, rue du Docteur Saadane, Algiers, Algeria.
- Documents Statistiques sur le Commerce Exterieur de l'Algerie. m., q., & a.

**Algeria. Direction des Statistiques**
8-10 rue Desfontaines, Algiers, Algeria.
- Algeria. Direction des Statistiques. Bulletin Trimestriel de Statistique. q.

**Algeria. Institut National Algerien du Commerce Exterieur**
6 Bd. Anatole France, Algeria, Algeria.
- COMEX-Hebdo. w.
- Institut National Algerien du Commerce Exterieur. Annuaire des Exportateurs. a.
- Nouvelles Economiques. m. ISSN 0078-2211

**Algeria. Ministere de l'Industrie et de l'Energie. Direction des Mines et de la Geologie. Service Geologique**
*see* **Algeria. Service Geologique**

**Algeria. Ministere de l'Information et de la Culture**
Algiers, Algeria.
- Maghrib; revue annuelle pour l'archeologie, les masees, les monuments et sites et les arts et traditions populaires. a.

**Algeria. Office Algerien d'Action Economique et Touristique**
40-42 rue Ben M'hidi, Algiers, Algeria.
- Algeria. Office Algerien d'Action Economique et Touristique. Bulletin Economique et Juridique. m.

**Algeria. Office National Algerien du Tourisme**
42 rue Khelifa Boukhalfa, Algiers, Algeria.
- El Djezair. s-a. ISSN 0012-4311

**Algeria. Service Geologique**
Ministere de l'Industrie et de l'Energie, Direction des Mines et de la Geologie, Immeuble Mauretania, Blvd. Colonel Amirouche, Agha, Algeria
(Subscr. address: Librairie Science et Culture, 37 rue Didouche Mourad, Algiers, Algeria)
● Algeria. Service Geologique. Bulletin. irreg., approx. 2 per yr. ISSN 0401-345X

**Algerie Economique**
7Bd. de la Republique, Algiers, Algeria.
● Algerie Economique. s-m.

**Centre Culturel Francais**
7 rue Medecin-Capitaine Kassani Issad, Algiers, Algeria.
● Centre Culturel Francais, Algiers. Rencontres Culturelles. irreg. ISSN 0069-1720

**Centre de Recherches Anthropologiques Prehistoriques et Ethnographiques**
3 rue Franklin Roosevelt, Algiers, Algeria.
● Fiches Typologiques Africaines. irreg., latest issue, 1970. ISSN 0071-4712
● Libyca. (pub. by Flammarion FR)

**Centre de Recherches Oceanographiques et des Peches**
Boite Postale 90, Alger-Bourse, Algeria.
● Pelagos. s-a. ISSN 0031-4137
● Phykos. ISSN 0031-8892

**COMEX**
*see* **Algeria. Institut National Algerien du Commerce Exterieur**

**Djeich**
3 Chemin de Gascogne, Algiers, Algeria.
● Djeich; revue de l'Armee Nationale populare. m.

**Federation Nationale de la Sante**
Maison du Peuple, Place du 1 Mai, Algiers, Algeria.
● Sante. bi-m.

**First Pan African Cultural Festival**
119 rue Didouche Mourad, Algiers, Algeria.
● Algiers; newsbulletin.

**Institut des Sciences Juridiques, Politiques et Administratives. Faculte de Droit et des Sciences Economiques d'Alger**
2 rue M. Didouche, Algiers, Algeria.
● Revue Algerienne des Sciences Juridiques Politiques et Economiques. q. ISSN 0035-0699

**Institut National Algerien du Commerce Exterieur**
*see* **Algeria. Institut National Algerien du Commerce Exterieur**

**Institut Pasteur d'Algerie**
Rue Docteur Laveran, Algiers, Algeria.
● Institut Pasteur d'Algerie. Archives. a. ISSN 0020-2460

**Revolution Africaine**
9 Bd. Khemisti, Algiers, Algeria.
● Revolution Africaine. w. ISSN 0035-0621

**Societe Historique Algerienne**
3 Bd. Zirout Youcef, Algiers, Algeria.
● Revue d'Histoire et de Civilization du Maghreb. irreg. ISSN 0556-7343

**Union General des Travailleurs Algeriens**
Maison du Peuple, Place du 1 Mai, Algiers, Algeria.
● Revolution et Travail. w. ISSN 0484-8365

**Universite d'Alger**
2 rue Didouche-Mourad, Algiers, Algeria.
● Universite d'Alger. Publications Scientifiques. Serie A: Mathematiques. s-a. ISSN 0002-5321
● Universite d'Alger. Publications Scientifiques. Serie B: Sciences Physiques. irreg. ISSN 0002-533X

**Universite d'Alger. Observatoire Astronomique**
Bouzareah, Algiers, Algeria.
● Observatoire Astronomique d'Alger. Annales. irreg. ISSN 0065-6232

## AMERICAN SAMOA

**American Samoa Bar Association**
Box 309, Pago Pago 96799, American Samoa.
● Samoan Pacific Law Journal. q.

## ANGOLA

**Angola. Biblioteca Nacional**
Caixa Postal 2915, Luanda, Angola.
● Biblioteca Nacional de Angola. Novas. irreg.

**Angola. Direccao dos Servicos de Estatistica**
C.P. 1215, Luanda, Angola.
● Angola. Direccao dos Servicos de Estatistica. Anuario Estatistico. a. ISSN 0066-5193
● Angola. Direccao dos Servicos de Estatistica. Boletim Mensal. m. ISSN 0003-3413
● Angola. Direccao dos Servicos de Estatistica. Estatistica dos Veiculos Motorisados. a.
● Angola. Direccao dos Servicos de Estatistica. Estatisticas do Comercio Externo. irreg. ISSN 0066-1848
● Angola. Direccao dos Servicos de Estatistica. Informacoes Estatisticas. a.

**Angola. Direccao Provincial dos Servicos de Geologia e Minas**
C. P. 1260-C, Luanda, Angola.
● Angola. Direccao Provincial dos Servicos de Geologia e Minas. Boletim. irreg. ISSN 0003-3456

**Angola. Imprensa Nacional**
Luanda, Angola.
● Boletim Oficial de Angola. d. ISSN 0067-9631

**Angola. Secretaria Provincial de Saude, Trabalho, Previdencia e Assistencia**
Luanda, Angola.
● Angola. Secretaria Provincial de Saude, Trabalho. Previdencia e Assistencia. Sintese da Actividade dos Servicos e Organismos. irreg; (approx 1 per yr)

**Associacao Industrial de Angola**
Caixa Postal No. 1296-C, Luanda, Angola.
● Associacao Industrial de Angola. Boletim. q.

**Camara Municipal de Luanda**
Av. dos Restauradores de Angola, Luanda, Angola.
● Cidade. m. ISSN 0300-4473

**Camara Municipal du Lobito**
Caixa Postal Tres, Lobito, Angola.
● Divulgacao. a.

**Capricornio**
C.P. 364, Lobito, Angola.
● Cadernos Capricornio. m.

**Companhia do Caminho de Ferro de Benguela**
Box 32, Lobito, Angola.
● Caminho de Ferro de Benguela. Boletim. m. ISSN 0008-2228

**Fundo de Comercializacao**
Box 1338, Luanda (PWA), Angola.
● Actividade Economica de Angola; review of economics, general survey and information. 4 per yr. ISSN 0001-7566

**Instituto de Angola**
C. P. 2767, Luanda, Angola.
● Instituto de Angola. Boletim. 3 per yr. ISSN 0020-3726
● Instituto de Angola. Boletim Analitico. m. ISSN 0020-3734
● Instituto de Angola. Boletim Bibliografico. m. ISSN 0020-3742

**Instituto de Investigacao Agronomica de Angola**
C.P. 406, Nova Lisboa, Angola.
● Instituto de Investigacao Agronomica de Angola. Divisao de Meteorologia Agricola. Anuario. a. (prep. by its Divisao de Meteorologica Agricola)
● Instituto de Investigacao Agronomica de Angola. Relatorio. a. ISSN 0078-2254
● Instituto de Investigacao Agronomica de Angola. Serie Cientifica. irreg.; no. 37, 1974. ISSN 0078-2262
● Instituto de Investigacao Agronomica de Angola. Serie Tecnica. irreg.; no. 44, 1970. ISSN 0078-2270

**Instituto de Investigacao Cientifica de Angola. Departamento de Documentacao e Informacao**
C.P. 3244, Luanda, Angola.
● Arquivos de Angola. q. ISSN 0004-2781
● I I C A. Documentacao; boletim bibliografico. s-m. ISSN 0018-9863

● Instituto de Investigacao Cientifica de Angola. Bibliograficas Tematicas. irreg., 1973, no. 19. ISSN 0074-008X
● Instituto de Investigacao Cientifica de Angola. Boletim. s-a. ISSN 0020-3912
● Instituto de Investigacao Cientifica de Angola. Memorias e Trabalhos. irreg., 1971, no. 8. ISSN 0074-0098
● Instituto de Investigacao Cientifica de Angola. Relatorios e Communicacoes. 1973, no. 25. ISSN 0003-343X

**Instituto do Trabalho, Previdencia e Accao Social de Angola**
Avenida Alvaro Ferreira 5, Luanda, Angola.
● Trabalho. q. ISSN 0564-0342

**Laboratorio de Engenharia de Angola**
P.O. Box 6500, Luanda, Angola.
● Laboratorio de Engenharia de Angola. Boletim Informativo. m. ISSN 0003-3448

**Livrangol Editores**
Ave. dos Restauradores 21-1, Luanda, Angola.
● Coleccao N'gola. a.

**Museu de Dundo**
Dundo, Luanda, Angola.
● Publicacoes Culturais da Companhia. irreg.

**Nova Sociedade Angolana**
R. Padre Antonio Vieira, 107, Luanda, Angola.
● Prisma. m. ISSN 0048-5357

**Organizacao Provincial de Voluntarios e Defesa Civil de Angola**
Rua Cabral de Muncada 134, Caixa Postal 6071, Luanda, Angola.
● Autodefesa.

**Universidade de Luanda**
Caixas Postais 815 & 1350, Luanda, Angola.
● Actualidade Universitaria; noticias e informacoes. m. ISSN 0044-6130 (prep. by its Gabinete de Informacao e Publicacoes)
● Universidade de Luanda. Anuario. a.

**Universidade de Luanda. Faculdade de Ciencias**
Luanda, Angola.
● Universidade de Luanda. Faculdade de Ciencias. Ciencias Biologicas. irreg.

## ARGENTINA

**A L A**
Conesa 1330, Buenos Aires, Argentina.
● A L A; organo de fomento cultural y de circulacion internacional. q. ISSN 0002-4090

**Editorial Abril S.A.**
Leandro N. Alem 896, Buenos Aires, Argentina.
● Nocturno. fortn. ISSN 0029-0866

**Academia Argentina de Farmacia y Bioquimica**
Junin 956, Buenos Aires, Argentina.
● Revista Farmaceutica. 12 nos. in 6 double issues. ISSN 0034-9496

**Academia Argentina de Letras**
Sanchez de Bustamante 2663, Buenos Aires 1425, Argentina.
● Academia Argentina de Letras. Boletin. 2 per yr. ISSN 0001-3757

**Academia Nacional de Bellas Artes**
Sanchez de Bustamante 2663, Buenos Aires, Argentina.
● Academia Nacional de Bellas Artes. Anuario. a.

**Academia Nacional de Ciencias Exactas, Fisicas y Naturales de Buenos Aires**
● Darwiniana. (pub. by Instituto de Botanica Darwinion)

**Academia Nacional de Ciencias Morales y Politicas**
Avda. Corrientes, 1723, Buenos Aires, Argentina.
● Academia Nacional de Ciencias Morales y Politicas. Anales. a.

**Academia Portena del Lunfardo**
● Academia Portena del Lunfardo. Boletin. (pub. by Libreria Pardo)

**Academia Provincial de la Historia**
Avda. Jose I de la Roza, San Juan, Argentina.
● Academia Provincial de la Historia. Boletin. a.
ISSN 0567-6029

**Acta Gastroenterologica Latinoamericana**
Martinez de Hoz y Perdriel, Huedo, Argentina.
● Acta Gastroenterologica Latinoamericana. q. ISSN
0300-9033

**Actualidad Pastoral**
Calle 22 y 31, 6600 Mercedes (B), Argentina.
● Actualidad Pastoral. m.

**Administracion General de Puertos**
Rivadavia 578, Buenos Aires, Argentina.
● Tecnica y Puertos. bi-m.

**Agencia Maritima Internacional S.A.**
Av. Julio Roca 710, 1067 Buenos Aires, Argentina.
● South American Ports Handbook. biennial.

**Agricol de Bianchetti**
Paraguay 1307, Piso 4, Ofic. 41, Buenos Aires,
Argentina.
● Revista de Derecho Deportivo. s-a. ISSN 0034-
7884

**Editorial Francisco de Aguirre S. A.**
Casilla 1653, Correo Central, Buenos Aires,
Argentina.
● Estudios Historicos. q. (Asociaciones
Napoleonicas de Argentina y Chile)
● Estudios Internacionales. q.

**American Chamber of Commerce in Argentina**
Roque Saenz Pena 567, Buenos Aires, Argentina.
● Comments on Argentine Trade. m. ISSN 0010-
2660
● Directory of American Business in Argentina.
irreg.

**Anales de Cirugia**
Calle Paraguay 40, Rosario, Prov. de Santa Fe,
Argentina.
● Anales de Cirugia. irreg. ISSN 0066-1465

**Analisis Confirmado**
Avda. Cordoba 1580, Buenos Aires, Argentina.
● Analisis Confirmado. w.

**Analisis S.A.I.C.**
Bartolome Mitre 226, 4 Piso, Buenos Aires,
Argentina.
● Analisis. w. ISSN 0003-2581
● Bella Gente/Cronopios. m. ISSN 0045-1711
● Pulso; revista semanal para gente de negocios. w.
ISSN 0033-4235

**Antropos**
Rodriguez Pena 557, Buenos Aires, Argentina.
● Antropos. q. ISSN 0003-6137

**Anuario F.H.I. Argentina: Frutas y Hortalizas
Industriarizadas y Frescas**
c/o Riccardo Luchini, 2452 Canning, Buenos Aires,
Argentina.
● Anuario F.H.I. Argentina: Frutas y Hortalizas
Industriarizadas y Frescas/F. H. I. Annual: Fresh
and Industrialized Fruits and Vegetables. a. ISSN
0066-5207

**Apuntes de la Linea**
Diagonal Norte 1142, 2 Piso, Buenos Aires,
Argentina.
● Apuntes de la Linea. irreg.

**Aquario**
Paraguay 647, Buenos Aires, Argentina.
● Aquario; revista internacional de poesia. irreg.
● Hojas de Poesia. irreg.

**Arbo S. A. C. E. I.**
Avda. Martin Garcia 653, Buenos Aires, Argentina.
● Revista Telegrafica Electronica. m. ISSN 0035-
0516

**Archivos Argentinos de Dermatologia**
H. Yrigoyen 2192, Buenos Aires, Argentina.
● Archivos Argentinos de Dermatologia. irreg. ISSN
0066-6750

**Argentina**
Estrada 6647, Santa Fe, Argentina.
● Argentina. q. ISSN 0004-0983

**Argentina. Biblioteca del Congreso**
Rivadavia 1850, Buenos Aires, Argentina.
● Argentina. Biblioteca del Congreso. Boletin. m.
ISSN 0004-1009
● Biblioteca del Congreso de la Nacion. Revista de
Revistas. bi-m.

**Argentina. Caja Federal de Ahorro y Prestamo para
la Vivienda**
Alsina 301 E.P., Buenos Aires, Argentina.
● Argentina. Caja Federal de Ahorro y Prestamo
para la Vivienda. Memoria y Balance. a.

**Argentina. Centro de Investigacion Documentaria**
Casilla de Correo 1359, Buenos Aires, Argentina.
● I N T I. bi-m. ISSN 0019-0225

**Argentina. Centro Nacional de Documentacion e
Informacion Educativa**
Parera 55, Buenos Aires, Argentina.
● Argentina. Centro Nacional de Documentacion e
Informacion Educativa. Informaciones y
Documentos. q.

**Argentina. Comision Nacional de Valores**
250 Hipolito, Oficina 1004, Buenos Aires,
Argentina.
● Argentina. Comision Nacional de Valores. Boletin
Informativo. q.

**Argentina. Consejo Federal de Inversiones**
Alsina 1407, Buenos Aires, Argentina.
● Argentina. Consejo Federal de Inversiones.
Bibliografia Sobre el Desarrollo Economico
Nacional. irreg. ISSN 0066-7005

**Argentina. Consejo Nacional de Desarrollo**
Buenos Aires, Argentina.
● Argentina. Consejo Nacional de Desarollo.
Recursos Humanos. irreg.

**Argentina. Consejo Nacional de Investigaciones
Cientificas y Tecnicas**
Rivadavia 1917, 1033 Buenos Aires, Argentina.
● Consejo Nacional de Investigaciones Cientificas y
Tecnicas. Informaciones. bi-m. ISSN 0010-6364

**Argentina. Departamento de Estudios Historicos
Navales**
Instituto de Publicaciones Navales, Av. Cordoba
547, Buenos Aires, Argentina.
● Argentina. Departamento de Estudios Historicos
Navales. Serie A: Cultura Nautica. irreg. ISSN
0066-703X
● Argentina. Departamento de Estudios Historicos
Navales. Serie B: Historia Naval Argenina. irreg;
no. 18, 1975. ISSN 0066-7048
● Argentina. Departamento de Estudios Historicos
Navales. Serie C: Biografias Navales Argentinas.
irreg; no. 11, 196. ISSN 0066-7056
● Argentina. Departamento de Estudios Historicos
Navales. Serie J: Libros y Impresos Raros. irreg.;
no. 2, 1970. ISSN 0066-7080
● Argentina. Departamento de Estudios Historicos
Navales. Series E: Documentos. irreg.

**Argentina. Departamento de Lecheria**
Buenos Aires, Argentina.
● Argentina. Departamento de Lecheria. Resena
Estadistica. irreg.

**Argentina. Direccion General de Sanidad**
Buenos Aires, Argentina.
● Revista de la Sanidad Militar Argentina. q. ISSN
0048-7716

**Argentina. Direccion Nacional de Asistencia Nacional**
Cangallo 524, Buenos Aires, Argentina.
● Argentina. Direction Nacional de Asistencia
Nacional. DAS. q. ISSN 0004-1025

**Argentina. Direccion Nacional de Energia y
Combustibles. Departamento de Estadistica**
Buenos Aires, Argentina.
● Argentina. Direccion Nacional de Energia y
Combustibles. Departamento de Estadistica
Anuario Estadistico. Combustibles. a.

**Argentina. Direccion Nacional de Migraciones.
Instituto Etnico Nacional**
Buenos Aires, Argentina.
● Argentina. Instituto Etnico Nacional. Anales. a.

**Argentina. Direccion Nacional de Programacion e
Investigacion**
Buenos Aires, Argentina.
● Argentina. Direccion Nacional de Programacion e
Investigacion. Presupuestos Provinciales y
Presupuesto Nacional Distribuidos Por Provincias.
a.
● Argentina. Direccion Nacional de Programacion e
Investigacion. Recursos y Erogaciones
Municipales. irreg.

**Argentina. Division de Estadisticas Sociales**
Buenos Aires, Argentina.
● Argentina. Division de Estadistiças Sociales.
Conflictos del Trabajo. a.

**Argentina. Empresa Nacional de Correos y Telegrafos**
Buenos Aires, Argentina.
● Argentina. Empresa Nacional de Correos y
Telegrafos. s-w.

**Argentina. Instituto Antartico Argentino**
Cerrito 1248, Buenos Aires, Argentina.
● Antartida. a. ISSN 0302-5691
● S. C. A. R. Boletin. 3 per yr. ISSN 0036-1097
(prep. by its Comite Cientifico de Investigaciones
Antarticas) (Co-sponsor: Consejo International de
Uniones Cientificas)

**Argentina. Instituto de Asuntos Tecnicos. Direccion
de Estadistica**
Palacio Municipal, Cordoba, Argentina.
● Argentina. Instituto de Asuntos Tecnicos.
Estadisticas. irreg.

**Argentina. Instituto Forestal Nacional**
Pueyrredon 2446, Buenos Aires, Argentina.
● Argentina. Direccion de Investigaciones
Forestales. Folleto Tecnico Forestal. irreg.; latest
issue, 1974.
● Argentina. Direccion de Investigaciones
Forestales. Notas Silvicolas. irreg. ISSN 0066-
7102
● Argentina. Direccion de Investigaciones
Forestales. Planificacion del Desarrollo Forestal.
irreg.; latest issue, 1970. ISSN 0066-7129
● Argentina. Direccion de Investigaciones
Forrestales. Misceleneas Forestales. irreg; latest
issue, 1973. ISSN 0066-7099
● Argentina. Instituto Forestal Nacional. Anuario de
Estadistica Forestal. a.

**Argentina. Instituto Nacional de Derecho Aeronautico
y Espacial**
Edificio Condor, Comodoro Pedro Zanni 250,
Buenos Aires, Argentina.
● Argentine Republic. Instituto Nacional de
Derecho Aeronautico y Espacial. Publicaciones.
irreg; latest issue, 1974. ISSN 0066-7188

**Argentina. Instituto Nacional de Estadistica y Censos**
Hipolito Yrigoyen 250, Buenos Aires, Argentina.
● Aeronavegacion Comercial Argentina. a.
● Argentina. Instituto Nacional de Estadistica y
Censos. Anuario Estadistico. a.
● Argentina. Instituto Nacional de Estadistica y
Censos. Boletin Estadistico Trimestral. q.
● Argentina. Instituto Nacional de Estadistica y
Censos. Estadistica Mensual. Indice de Precios al
Consumidor. m.
● Argentina. Instituto Nacional de Estadistica y
Censos. Indicadores Industriales. Serie I. irreg.
● Argentina. Instituto Nacional de Estadistica y
Censos. Informe Serie E: Edificacione. irreg.
ISSN 0066-7196
● Argentina. Instituto Nacional de Estadistica y
Censos. Navegacion Commercial Argentina. a.

**Argentina. Instituto Nacional de Planificacion
Economica**
Buenos Aires, Argentina.
● Instituto Nacional de Planificacion Economica.
Boletin Bibliografico. q.

**Argentina. Instituto Nacional de Tecnologia
Agropecuaria**
Rivadavia 1439, Buenos Aires, Argentina.
● Argentina. Instituto Nacional de Tecnologia
Agropecuaria. Suelos. irreg. (prep. by its Centro
de Investigaciones de Recursos Naturales)
● Instituto Nacional de Tecnologia Agropecuaria.
Departamento de Especializacion. Publicacion
Didactica. 3 per yr. ISSN 0020-4161 (prep. by its
Departamento de Especializacion)

**Argentina. Instituto Nacional de Tecnologia Agropecuaria. Estacion Experimental Regional Agropecuaria del Alto Valle**
Casilla de Correo 52, General Roca (Rio Negro), Argentina.
- Boletin Agropecuario del Alto Valle. m. ISSN 0006-6125

**Argentina. Instituto Nacional de Tecnologia Agropecuaria. Estacion Experimental Regional Agropecuaria Pergamino**
C.C.31, Pergamino, Argentina.
- Estacion Experimental Region Agropecuaria Pergamino. Informe Tecnico. 12 per yr. ISSN 0325-1799

**Argentina. Instituto Nacional de Tecnologia Agropecuria. Estacion Experiemntal Agropecuaria Manfredi**
Manfredi (Cordoba), Argentina.
- Argentina. Instituto Nacional de Tecnologia Agropecuria. Estacion Experimental Agropecuria, Cordoba. Serie Informacion Tecnica. irreg., latest issue no. 65. ISSN 0066-7242

**Argentina. Instituto Nacional de Tecnologia Industrial**
Libertad 1235, Buenos Aires, Argentina.
- Instituto Nacional de Tecnologia Industrial. Boletin Tecnico. irreg.

**Argentina. Mercado Nacional de Hacienda**
Buenos Aires, Argentina.
- Argentina. Mercado Nacional de Hacienda. Anuario. a.

**Argentina. Ministerio de Comercio**
Av. Julio A. Roca 851, Buenos Aires, Argentina.
- Exportar es Crecer. bi-m.

**Argentina. Ministerio de Cultura y Educacion**
Avda.Eduardo Madero 235, 1 Piso, Buenos Aires, Argentnia.
- Argentina. Departamento de Estadistica Educativa. Boletin Informativo. a. ISSN 0066-7021 (prep. by its Departamento de Estadistica Educativa)
- Argentina. Ministerio de Cultura y Educacion. Boletin Bibliografico. (pub. by Centro Nacional de Documentacion)
- Bibliografia Argentina de Psicologia. irreg., 1970, no. 5-6. ISSN 0523-1698 (prep. by its Direccion de Bibliotecos)
- Bibliotheca del Planeamiento Educativo. irreg. ISSN 0067-7922 (prep. by its Departamento de Documentacion Informacion Educativa)
- Estadisticas de la Educacion. a. (prep. by its Departamento de Estadistica Educativa)
- Revista de Educacion. q. ISSN 0034-8074
- Umbral 2000. (pub. by Instituto Superior de Bibliotecologia)

**Argentina. Ministerio de Defensa. Escuela de Defensa Nacional**
Maipu 262, Buenos Aires, Argentina.
- Argentina. Escuela de Defensa Nacional. Revista. q.

**Argentina. Ministerio de Economia**
Buenos Aires, Argentina.
- Argentina. Ministerio de Economia. w. (prep. by its Subsecretaria de Coordinacion de Informacion Economica)
- Argentina. Ministerio de Economia. Economic Report. Summary. q.
- Argentina. Ministerio de Economia. Informe Economico. q.
- Argentina. Ministerio de Economia. Informe Economico. Resumen. q.

**Argentina. Ministerio de Economia. Junta Nacional de Carnes**
San Martin 459, Buenos Aires, Argentina.
- Argentina. Junta Nacional de Carnes. Boletin Diario de Informaciones. d.
- Argentina. Junta Nacional de Carnes. Boletin Semanal Sobre Ganados, Carnes y Subproductos. w.
- Argentina. Junta Nacional de Carnes. Exportaciones de Productos Ganaderos. m.
- Argentina. Junta Nacional de Carnes. Sintesis Estadistica. a. ISSN 0066-7269

**Argentina. Ministerio de Economia. Secretaria de Estado de Hacienda**
Buenos Aires, Argentina.
- Argentina. Secretaria de Estado de Hacienda. Memoria. a.

**Argentina. Ministerio de Economia. Secretaria de Estado de Programacion y Coordinacion Economica**
Subsecretaria de Coordinacion de Informacion Economica, Numero Postal 4.340, Buenos Aires, Argentina.
- Economic Information of Argentina. m.

**Argentina. Ministerio de Economia. Secretaria de Recursos Naturales y Ambiente Humano**
Av. Santa Fe 1548, Buenos Aires 1060, Argentina.
- Recursos Hidricos. q. ISSN 0048-6981

**Argentina. Ministerio de Relaciones Exteriores**
Buenos Aires, Argentina.
- Argentina. Ministerio de Relaciones Exteriores y Culto. Revista. q.

**Argentina. Ministerio del Ejercito**
Buenos Aires, Argentina.
- Revista del Suboficial. bi-m. ISSN 0034-9119
- Soldado Argentino. m. ISSN 0038-0954

**Argentina. Oficina de Estudios para la Colaboracion Economica Internacional**
Buenos Aires, Argentina.
- Nivel de la Economia Argentina. a. ISSN 0078-0863

**Argentina. Oficina Sectorial de Desarrollo de Energia. Departamento de Informacion e Investigacion Aplicada**
Av. Julio A. Roca 651, Sector 31, Buenos Aires, Argentina.
- Argentina. Oficina Sectorial de Desarrollo de Energia. Anuarios Estadisticos: Combustible. a. ISSN 0066-7277
- Argentina. Oficina Sectorial de Desarrollo de Energia. Anuarios Estadisticos. Energia Electrica. a. ISSN 0066-7285

**Argentina. Policia Federal Argentina**
- Mundo Policial. (pub. by Editorial Policial)

**Argentina. Santa Fe Centro de Documentacion e Informacion Educativa**
Centro Civico Gubernamental, San Martin 1153 - 2er.P., Santa Fe, Argentina.
- Santa Fe Centro de Documentacion e Informacion Educativa. Boletin de Informacion Educativa. irreg; 1973, no. 15. ISSN 0080-6099

**Argentina. Secretaria de Estado de Agricultura y Ganaderia**
Area de Trabajo de Lecheria, Paseo Colon 922-20, P. Ofic. 232, Argentina.
- Argentina. Area de Trabajo de Lecheria. Resena Estadistica. irreg.
- E A G Publicaciones. (prep. by its Servicio Nacional de Economia y Sociologia Rural)

**Argentina. Secretaria de Estado de Ciencia y Tecnologia**
Av. Cordoba 831, Buenos Aires.
- Guia de Reuniones Cientificas y Tecnicas en Argentina. a. ISSN 0301-7567

**Argentina. Secretaria de Estado de Salud Publica**
Alsina 301, Buenos Aires, Argentina.
- Argentina. Secretaria de Estado de Salud Publica. Programa Nacional de Estadisticas de Salud. irreg.

**Argentina. Secretaria de Estado de Trabajo**
Division Publicaciones y Biblioteca, Julio A. Roca 609, Buenos Aires, Argentina.
- Argentina. Ministerio de Trabajo. Boletin de Biblioteca. s-a. ISSN 0004-1068
- Argentina. Ministerio de Trabajo. Boletin de Legislacion. m. ISSN 0006-6346

**Argentina. Secretaria de Guerra**
Comando en Jefe del Ejercito, Azopardo 250 Planta Baja, Buenos Aires, Argentina.
- Argentina. Secretaria de Guerra. Direccion de Estudios Historicos. Boletin Bibliografico. irreg. ISSN 0066-7293

**Argentina. Servicio de Hidrografia Naval**
Montes de Oca 2124, Buenos Aires, Argentina.
- Argentina. Servicio de Hidrografia Naval. Boletin. 3 per yr. ISSN 0004-1076

**Argentina. Servicio de Inteligencia Naval**
Commando General de la Armada, Buenos Aires, Argentina.
- Revista de Publicaciones Navales. bi-m. ISSN 0034-8775

**Argentina. Servicio de Intelligencia Naval. Bibliotecas de la Armada**
Edificio Libertad, Buenos Aires, Argentina.
- Argentina. Servicio de Inteligencia Naval. Bibliotecas de la Armada. Boletin Bibliografico. a. ISSN 0066-7331

**Argentina. Servicio Nacional de Parques Nacionales**
Buenos Aires, Argentina.
- Argentina. Servicio Nacional de Parques Nacional. Anales. irreg. ISSN 0518-4614

**Argentina. Servicio Nacional de Pesca**
Ministerio de Agricultura y Ganaderia, Buenos Aires, Argentina.
- Argentina. Servicio Nacional de Pesca. Monografias de Recursos Pesqueros. irreg.

**Argentina. Servicio Nacional Minero Geologico**
Biblioteca, Avenida Santa Fe 1548, Buenos Aires, Argentina.
- Argentina. Servicio Nacional Minero Geologico. Anales. irreg. no. 16, 1972. ISSN 0066-7145
- Argentina. Servicio Nacional Minero Geologico. Boletin. irreg. ISSN 0066-7153
- Argentina. Servicio Nacional Minero Geologico. Estadistica Minera. irreg. ISSN 0066-7161
- Argentina. Servicio Nacional Minero Geologico. Informes Tecnicos. irreg; latest no. 153, 1970.
- Argentina. Servicio Nacional Minero Geologico. Revista. irreg. ISSN 0066-717X

**Argentine Science Fiction Review Publications**
Casilla 3869, Correo Central, Buenos Aires, Argentina.
- Argentine Science Fiction Review. 2 per yr. ISSN 0004-1084

**Argentine Society of Angiology**
- Revista Argentina de Angiologia. (pub. by Plantie Talleres Graficos S.A.)

**Argentino**
Unquiza S/N, Cdte. N. Otamendi, Argentina.
- Argentino. w. ISSN 0004-1092

**Argentinos Lietuviu Balsas**
c/o Constantino Norkus & Francisco Ozinskas, J. L. Suarez 5684, Buenos Aires, Argentina.
- Argentinos Lietuviu Balsas/Voz de los Lituanos en la Argentina. s-m. ISSN 0004-1106

**Ediciones Ariadna**
472 Suipacha, Buenos Aires, Argentina.
- Cleo en la Moda. bi-m. ISSN 0009-8728

**Arte Grafico Editorial Argentino S.A.**
Piedras 1743, Buenos Aires, Argentina.
- Clarin Economico. m. ISSN 0009-8256
- Clarin Internacional. w.

**Arte Informa**
Malabia 2765, P. B. A Buenos Aires, Argentina.
- Arte Informa. m.

**Editorial Arte y Letras de America**
Nicaragua 5925, Buenos Aires, Argentina.
- Pluma y Pincel; para la difusion del arte y la cultura latinoamericanos. irreg.

**Asociacion Archivistica Argentina**
Av. Cordoba 1556, Buenos Aires, Argentina.
- Asociacion Archivistica Argentina Boletin. 3 per yr.

**Asociacion Argentina Amigos de la Astronomia**
Av. Patricias Argentinas 550, Buenos Aires 5, Argentina.
- Revista Astronomica. q. ISSN 0044-9253

**Asociacion Argentina Criadores de Cebu**
Arenales 2777, Buenos Aires, Argentina.
- Cebu y Derivados. m. ISSN 0008-8668

**Asociacion Argentina Criadores de Cerdos**
Florida 520, Buenos Aires, Argentina.
- Asociacion Argentina Criadores de Cerdos. Revista. m. ISSN 0004-4741

**Asociacion Argentina de Actores**
Viamonte 1443, Buenos Aires, Argentina.
- Hechos de Mascara. q.

**Asociacion Argentina de Ciencia Politica**
Solis 443, Buenos Aires, Argentina.
- Revista Argentina de Ciencia Politica. irreg' ISSN 0034-7019

**Asociacion Argentina de Mineralogia, Petrologia y Sedimentologia**
Maipu 645-1 Piso, Buenos Aires, Argentina.
- Asociacion Argentina de Mineralogia, Petrologia y Sedimentologia. Revista. s-a.

**Asociacion Argentina de Psiquiatria Social**
Aguero 2259, 8-41, Buenos Aires, Argentina.
- Psiquiatria Social. q. ISSN 0033-2593

**Asociacion Argentina de Quimicos y Coloristas Textiles**
Bulnes 1425, Buenos Aires, Argentina.
- Galaxia. bi-m. ISSN 0016-3996

**Asociacion Argentina de Semiotica**
Tucuman 3748, Buenos Aires, Argentina.
- Lenguajes; revista de linguistica y semiologia. 3 per yr.

**Asociacion Argentina para el Progreso de las Ciencias**
Av. Roque Saenz Pena, 555, Buenos Aires, Argentina.
- Ciencia e Investigacion. m. ISSN 0009-6733

**Asociacion Bioquimica Argentina**
Venezuela 1823-3er. Piso, Buenos Aires, Argentina.
- Asociacion Bioquimica Argentina. Revista. q. ISSN 0004-4768

**Asociacion de Bibliotecarios Profesionales de Rosario**
Rosario de S. Fe, 2000, Argentina.
- Asociacion de Bibliotecarios Profesionales de Rosario. Boletin. irreg. ISSN 0571-3471

**Asociacion de Ex-Alumnos de la Escuela Nacional de Bibliotecarios**
Mexico 564, Buenos Aires, Argentina.
- Asociacion de Ex-Alumnos de la Escuela Nacional de Bibliotecarios. Boletin. q. ISSN 0004-4806

**Asociacion de Industriales Metalurgicos**
Alsina 1607 1 Piso, Buenos Aires, Argentina.
- Metalurgia.

**Asociacion de la Prensa Tecnica Argentina**
- Revista de Ceramica en la Construccion. (pub. by Promocion y Ventes S. A. I. C.)

**Asociacion del Congreso Panamericano de Ferrocarriles**
Av. 9 de Julio 1925, Piso 13, Of.1301, Buenos Aires, Argentina.
- Asociacion del Congreso Panamericano de Ferrocarriles. Boletin de la Comision Permanente. bi-m.

**Asociacion Electrotecnia Argentina**
Posadas 1659, 1112 Buenos Aires, Argentina.
- Revista Electrotecnica. bi-m.

**Asociacion Filatelica de la Republica Argentina**
San Martin 365, Planta Baja, Buenos Aires, Argentina.
- A F R A. Boletin. bi-m. ISSN 0001-1193

**Asociacion Latinoamericana de Ciencias Fisiologicas**
Obligado 2490, Buenos Aires, Argentina.
- Acta Physiologica Latino Americana; fisiologia, farmacologia, bioquimica y ciencias afines. q. ISSN 0001-6764

**Asociacion Medica Argentina**
- Asociacion Medica Argentina. Revista. (pub. by Prensa Medica Argentina, S.R.L.)

**Asociacion Medica de Corrientes y Sociedad de Cirugia**
- Revista Medica de Corrientes. (pub. by Emilie Fenner s.r.l.)

**Asociacion Numismatica Argentina**
Casilla de Correo 496, Buenos Aires, Argentina.
- Asociacion Numismatica Argentina. Revista. s-a. ISSN 0004-4873

**Asociacion Odontologica Argentina**
Junin 959, Buenos Aires, Argentina.
- Asociacion Odontologica Argentina. Revista. 3 per yr. ISSN 0004-4881

**Asociacion Ornitologica del Plata**
25 de Mayo 749, Buenos Aires, Argentina.
- Hornero/Oven Bird. irreg. (approx 2 per year) 1973, vol. 11, no. 3. ISSN 0073-3407

**Asociacion Paleontologica Argentina and Consejo Nacional de Investigaciones Cientificas y Tecnicas**
Avda. Angel Gallardo 470, Buenos Aires, Argentina.
- Ameghiniana. 5 per yr. ISSN 0002-7014

**Asociacion Psicoanalistica Argentina**
Rodriguez Pena 1674, Buenos Aires, Argentina.
- Revista de Psicoanalisis. q. ISSN 0034-8740

**Asociaciones Napoleonicas de Argentina y Chile**
- Estudios Historicos. (pub. by Editorial Francisco de Aguirre S. A.)

**Editorial Atlantida, S. A.**
Azopardo 579, R. 91 Buenos Aires, Argentina.
- Billiken. w. ISSN 0006-2553
- Campo Moderno y Chacra. m.
- Gente y la Actualidad. w.
- Grafico. w. ISSN 0017-291X
- Para Ti. w.

**Automovil Club Argentino**
Av. del Libertador 1850, Buenos Aires, Argentina.
- Autoclub; revista del Automovilismo, turismo e informaciones. bi-m. ISSN 0005-0946

**Autores**
Lavalle 1569 - piso 3o, Buenos Aires, Argentina.
- Autores. fortn.

**Avia Aeroespacial**
Hipolito Yrigoyen 788, Buenos Aires, Argentina.
- Avia Aeroespacial. m. ISSN 0005-2043

**Aviacion y Astronautica**
Av. Belgrano 1735, Buenos Aires, Argentina.
- Aviacion y Astronautica. bi-m. ISSN 0045-1177

**Editorial Axis**
Rosario, Argentina.
- Coleccion Documentos. irreg.

**Banco Central de la Republica Argentina**
Reconquista 266/78, Buenos Aires, Argentina.
- Banco Central de la Republica Argentina. Boletin Estadistico. m. ISSN 0005-4674

**Banco de la Provincia de Buenos Aires**
San Martin 137, Buenos Aires, Argentina.
- Sintesis Informativa Economica y Financiera. m. ISSN 0037-5799

**Banco Ganadero Argentino**
Juncal 735, Buenos Aires, Argentina.
- Produccion Rural Argentina. s-a. ISSN 0079-5852

**Banco Interamericano de Desarrollo. Instituto para la Integracion de America Latina**
Cerrito 264, 1401 Buenos Aires, Argentina.
- Derecho de la Integracion. 3 per yr.
- Integracion Latinoamericana/Latin American Integration. m.
- Inter-American Development Bank. Institute for Latin American Integration. Annual Report. a. ISSN 0538-3110
- Inter-American Development Bank. Institute for Latin American Integration. Memoria Annual. a. ISSN 0538-3129

**Pablo Luis Bardin Ed. & Pub.**
Av. Libertador 3576, Buenos Aires, Argentina.
- Tribuna Musical. bi-m. ISSN 0041-2767

**Bibliograma**
Rivadavia 1255, Casilla de Correo 16-Succursal 2, Buenos Aires, Argentina.
- Bibliograma. q. ISSN 0006-1174

**Biblioteca**
Talcahuano 463, Buenos Aires, Argentina.
- Biblioteca; revista mensual de interes general. m. ISSN 0006-1611
- Coleccion Conocimiento de la Argentina. irreg.

**Biblioteca Argentina para Ciegos**
Lezica 3909, Buenos Aires, Argentina.
- Burbujas. m. ISSN 0007-6015
- Hacia la Luz. m. ISSN 0017-6478

**Biblioteca y Hemeroteca de Servicios Electricos del Gran Buenos Aires**
Balcarce 184, Buenos Aires, Argentina.
- Biblioteca y Hemeroteca de Servicios Electricos del Gran Buenos Aires. Boletin Bibliografico. m. ISSN 0006-1751

**Bolsa de Cereales**
Avenida Corrientes 123, 1043 Buenos Aires, Argentina.
- Bolsa de Cereales. Revista Institucional. m. ISSN 0045-2467
- Bolsa de Cereales. Revista Institucional. Numero Estadistico. a. ISSN 0084-7968

**Bolsa de Comercio de Buenos Aires**
Sarmiento 299, Buenos Aires, Argentina.
- Bolsa de Comercio de Buenos Aires. Boletin. w. ISSN 0006-6923

**Bolsa de Comercio de Mendoza**
Sarmiento 199, Mendoza, Argentina.
- Bolsa de Comercio de Mendoza. Centro de Informaciones. Boletin. m.

**Bolsa de Comercio de Rosario**
Rosario, Santa Fe, Argentina.
- Bolsa de Comercio de Rosario. Boletin Informativo. s-m. (prep. by its Centro de Documentacion para Exportaciones)
- Bolsa de Comercio de Rosario. Revista. a (with monthly supplements) ISSN 0006-6931

**Buenos Aires (Province) Direccion de Vialidad**
Calle 7 No. 1175, La Plata, Argentina.
- D. V. B. A. Publicaciones Tecnicas. 10 per yr. ISSN 0011-5177
- Vialidad. q. ISSN 0042-5028

**Buenos Aires (Province) Direccion Provincial de Cultura**
Roca 250, Viedma, Rio Negro, Argentina.
- Argentina. Direccion Provincial de Cultura. Monografias. a; no. 3, 1973.

**Buenos Aires Musical**
Alsina 912, Buenos Aires 1088, Argentina.
- Buenos Aires Musical. m. ISSN 0007-3113

**Calveiro y Liberatore**
Callao 66, 7 Piso, Buenos Aires, Argentina.
- Tecnica del Frio. m. ISSN 0040-1730 (Camara Argentina de Industrias de Refrigeracion y Aire Acondicionado)

**Camara Argentina de Industrias de Refrigeracion y Aire Acondicionado**
- Tecnica del Frio. (pub. by Calveiro y Liberatore)

**Camara Argentina de la Industria Plastica**
Sarmiento 2494, Buenos Aires, Argentina.
- Plasticos. bi-m. ISSN 0032-1125

**Camara Argentina de Productos Quimicos**
Sanchez de Bustamante 68, 3 Piso, Esc.31, Buenos Aires, Argentina.
- Camara Argentina de Productos Quimicos. Boletin Informativo. m. ISSN 0008-1841

**Camara de Comerciantes en Artefactos para el Hogar**
Bartolome Mitre 2162, Buenos Aires, Argentina.
- Camara de Comerciantes en Artefactos para el Hogar. Revista. irreg.

**Camara de Comercio**
Florida 1 - 4 Piso, Buenos Aires, Argentina.
- Buenos Aires. Camara de Comercio. Informativo Mensual. m.

**Camara de Industria y Comercio Argentino-Alemana**
Calle Maipu 521, Piso 6, Buenos Aires, Argentina.
- Camara de Industria y Comercio Argentino-Alemana. Boletin/Deutsch-Argentinische Industrie-und Handelskammer. Mitteilungen. 10 per yr. ISSN 0008-2112

**Camara de Industriales Graficos de la Argentina**
Avda San Juan 1340, Buenos Aires, Argentina.
- Argentina Grafica. 2 per yr. ISSN 0004-105X

**Camara de Industriales Metalurgicos**
Alsina 1607, Buenos Aires, Argentina.
- Fundidas. bi-m.

**Camara de la Industria Automotriz**
Viamonte 1167, 5 Piso, T.E. 40-4117y 40, 5385 Buenos Aires, Argentina.
- Argentina Automotriz. q. ISSN 0004-0991

**Camara Suecia de Comercio**
Tacuari 147, Buenos Aires, Argentina.
● Noticias de Suecia. bi-m. ISSN 0029-4187

**Capital de la Poesia**
Calle Libertad, Casa 16, Barrio los Olivos, Villa
Dolores (CBA), Argentina.
● Capital de la Poesia. bi-m.

**Ediciones Castaneda**
Biblioteca "Fr. Mamerta Esquiu" Centenario 1399,
San Antonio de Padua, Buenos Aires, Argentina.
● Megafon; revista interdisciplinaria de estudios
latinoamericanos. s-a. (Centro de Estudios
Latinoamericanos)
● Revista de Filosofia Latinoamericana. irreg.

**Centauros**
San Martin 66, Buenos Aires, Argentina.
● Centauros; revista de polo.turf,equitacion,pato &
trote. 6 per yr. ISSN 0008-8986

**Centro de Estudios Economicos Sociales**
Libertad 1050, Buenos Aires, Argentina.
● Dinamica Social. bi-m.

**Centro de Estudios Latinoamericanos**
● Megafon. (pub. by Ediciones Castaneda)

**Centro de Estudios Politicos**
San Nicolas 66, Cordoba, Argentina.
● Estudios Interdisciplinarios. q. ISSN 0302-2420

**Centro de Estudios Procesales**
Dorrego No. 1748, 2000 Rosario, Argentina.
● Revista de Estudios Procesales. q.

**Centro de Estudios Regionales**
Maipu 150, Local F, S. M. de Tucuman, Argentina.
● Cuadrante N.O.A. (Noreste Argentina); revista
del centro de estudios regionale. 3 per yr.

**Centro de Ingenieros Provincia de Buenos Aires**
Calle 53, No. 416 1/2, La Plata, Argentina.
● Revista de Ingenieria. q. ISSN 0484-7113

**Centro de Investigacion de Biologia Marina**
Libertad 1235, Buenos Aires, Argentina.
● Buenos Aires. Centro de Investigacion de Biologia
Marina. Contribucion Cientificia. irreg., 1969, no.
42. ISSN 0068-340X

**Centro de Investigacion y Accion Social**
O'Higgins 1331, Buenos Aires (26), Argentina.
● Centro de Investigacion y Accion Social. Revista.
m. ISSN 0325-1306

**Centro de Investigaciones en Ciencias Agronomicas.**
**Departamento de Genetica**
Casilla de Correo No. 25, 1712 Castelar, Argentina.
● Boletin Genetico. irreg.; no. 9, 1977. ISSN 0067-
9720
● Buenos Aires. Instituto de Fitotecnia. Boletin
Informativo. irreg., 1973, no. 32. ISSN 0068-3418

**Centro de Investigaciones Energeticas**
Av. Belgrano 748, Buenos Aires, Argentina.
● C.I.E. Servicio Informativo. irreg.

**Centro de Investigaciones Sobre China**
Montevideo 666, Oficina 111, Buenos Aires,
Argentina.
● Informes de China. bi-m. ISSN 0020-0875

**Centro de Investigaciones Sociales. Instituto Torcuato**
**di Tella**
1428 Buenos Aires, Argentina.
● Revista Latinoamericana de Sociologia. 3 per
yr.(March, July, Nov.) ISSN 0034-9801

**Centro de la Industria Lechera**
Medrano 281, Buenos Aires, Argentina.
● Industria Lechera. bi-m. ISSN 0046-9181

**Centro de Navegacion Transatlantica**
25 de Mayo 489, Buenos Aires, Argentina.
● Centro de Navegacion Transatlantica. C.N.T.
Handbook. River Plate Handbook for Shipowners
and Agents. a.

**Centro Latinoamericano de Administracion Medica**
Av. Cordoba 2351, Buenos Aires, Argentina.
● Atencion Medica. q.
● Centro Latinoamericano de Administracion
Medica. Traducciones. irreg.

**Centro Nacional de Documentacion**
Av. E. Madero 235, Buenos Aires, Argentina.
● Argentina. Ministerio de Cultura y Educacion.
Boletin Bibliografico. q.

**Centro Naval**
Florida 801, Buenos Aires, Argentina.
● Centro Naval. Boletin. q. ISSN 0009-0123

**Centro Panamericano de Zoonosis**
Casilla 3092, 1000 Correo Central, Buenos Aires,
Argentina.
● Encephalitis Surveillance for the Americas. m.
ISSN 0300-1105
● Vigilancia Epidemiologica. m.

**Editorial Ciclo**
Talcahuano 847, P.B. R.C. 12, Capital Federal,
Argentina.
● Ceramica y Cristal. m. ISSN 0325-0229

**Cineclub Nucleo**
Lavalle 2016, 8 Piso, Of. 17, Buenos Aires,
Argentina.
● Tiempo de Cine. m. ISSN 0040-7283

**Circulo Catolico Polaco en la Republica Argentina**
C.C.C. 1672, Buenos Aires, Argentina.
● Bog i Ojczyzna/Dios y Patria. bi-m. ISSN 0006-
5684

**Circulo de Aeronautica**
Direccion de Publicaciones, Paraguay 748, Buenos
Aires, Argentina.
● Aeroespacio; revista nacional aeronautica y
espacial. bi-m. ISSN 0001-9127

**Circulo Odontologico de Cordoba**
Direccion y Administracion, 27 de Abril 887, T.E.:
46207, Cordoba, Argentina.
● Circulo Odontologico de Cordoba. Revista. a.
ISSN 0045-6942

**Circulo Odontologico de Rosario**
Rioja 2471, Rosario, Argentina.
● Circulo Odontologico de Rosario. Revista. q.
ISSN 0009-7357

**Colegio de Abogados de la Ciudad de Buenos Aires**
Montevideo 640, Buenos Aires, Argentina.
● Colegio de Abogados de la Ciudad de Buenos
Aires/Boletin Informativo. bi-m. ISSN 0010-0560

**Colegio de Bibliotecarios de la Provincia de Buenos**
**Aires**
Casilla de Correo 309, La Plata, Argentina.
● Vinculo. s-a. ISSN 0042-6261

**Colegio de Graduados en Ciencias Economicas**
Viamonte 1582, Buenos Aires, Argentina.
● Administracion. q. ISSN 0325-0814
● Economia. q. ISSN 0325-0830

**Comite Judio Americano**
Oficina Sudamericana, Bartolome Mitre 1943, 1-B,
Buenos Aires, Argentina.
● Cuadernos de Estudios Judios. irreg.

**Compania de Seguros la Franco**
Hipolito Irigoyen 476, Buenos Aires, Argentina.
● Boletin de Informacion Bibliografica. m.

**Conceptos de Matematica**
c/o Jose Banfi, 1949 Paraguay, Buenos Aires,
Argentina.
● Conceptos de Matematica; revista para el maestro,
el profesor y el estudiante. q. ISSN 0010-5147

**Confederacion Argentina de Sordomudos**
Av. Pedro Medrano 1352, Buenos Aires, Argentina.
● Ad Verbum. q. (Co-sponsor: Federacion Mondial
de Sordos)

**Confederacion de Organizaciones Turisticas de la**
**America Latina**
Viamonte 640, 1053 Buenos Aires, Argentina.
● Aqui COTAL. m.
● C O T A L. m. ISSN 0007-8859

**Confederacion General de la Industria.**
Comision Directiva, Rivadavia 1115, Buenos Aires,
Argentina.
● Confederacion General de la Industria. Comision
Directiva. Informe de las Actuaciones Cumplidas.
irreg.
● Confederacion General de la Industria. Memoria y
Balance General. irreg.

**Confederacion General Economica de la Republica**
**Argentina**
Rivadavia 1115, Buenos Aires, Argentina.
● Estudios Sobre la Economia Argentina. q. (prep.
by its Instituto de Investigaciones Economicas y
Financieras)
● Opinion Economica. m. ISSN 0048-198X

**Congreso Judio Latinoamericano**
Pasteur 611, 7 Piso, Buenos Aires, Argentina.
● Congreso Judio Latinoamericano. Boletin
Informativo OJI. w. (World Jewish Congress)

**Conocimiento de la Nueva Era**
Belgrano 624, Buenos Aires, Argentina.
● Conocimiento de la Nueva Era. m. ISSN 0010-
6291

**Consejo Latinoamericano de Ciencias Sociales**
Buenos Aires, Argentina.
● C L A C S O Boletin. q.
● Consejo Latinoamericano de Ciencias Sociales.
Serie Poblacion. Informe de Investigacion. irreg.

**Constructor s.r.l.**
Hipolito Yrigoyen 615, Piso 7, Buenos Aires,
Argentina.
● Constructor. w. ISSN 0010-7018

**Contante y Sonante**
c/o Mario A. Lugue S. A., 462 27 de Abril,
Cordoba, Argentina.
● Contante y Sonante. q. ISSN 0010-7417

**Editorial Contempora s.r.l.**
Sarmiento 643, Buenos Aires, Argentina.
● Casas y Jardines. 10 per yr. ISSN 0008-7203
● Nuestra Arquitectura. 10 per yr. ISSN 0029-5701

**Contracultura**
Casilla de Correo 1332, Buenos Aires, Argentina.
● Contracultura; quarterly Journal and Ecology
Newsletter. q.

**Convencion Evangelica Bautista**
Rivadavia 3476, Buenos Aires, Argentina.
● Expositor Bautista. bi-m. ISSN 0014-522X

**Cooperativa Dental Argentina**
M.T. de Alvear 2167, Buenos Aires, Argentina.
● Cooperador Dental; Cooperativismo, Informacion
y Ciencia Odontologica. irreg. ISSN 0069-9799

**Cooperativa el Hogar Obrero**
Rivadavia 5108, Buenos Aires, Argentina.
● Cooperacion Libre. m.(except Jan. & Feb) ISSN
0010-8316

**Cormoran y Delfin**
F. F. Amador, 1805, Olivos, Buenos Aires,
Argentina.
● Cormoran y Delfin; revista planetaria de poesia. q.
ISSN 0010-8766

**Ediciones Corregidor**
Italcahuano 463, Buenos Aires, Argentina.
● Latinoamericana. 3 per yr.

**Editorial Coyuntura**
San Martin 296, Buenos Aires, Argentina.
● Mercado. w.

**Editorial Criterio s.r.l.**
Alsina 840, Buenos Aires, Argentina.
● Criterio. fortn. ISSN 0011-1473

**Croatian Republican Party**
Casilla de Correo 2959, Buenos Aires, Argentina.
● Republika Hrvatska/Republica Croata. q.

**Cuadernos de Critica**
Charcas 4767, 20 "A" Buenos Aires, Argentina.
● Cuadernos de Critica. q. ISSN 0011-2380

**Cuadernos de la Boca del Riachuelo**
Casilla de Correo 18, Sucursal 32, Buenos Aires,
Argentina.
● Cuadernos de la Boca del Riachuelo. ISSN 0011-
2429

**Cuestionario**
Hipolito Yrigoyen 1394, Buenos Aires, Argentina.
● Cuestionario. m.

**Editorial Cul - Tec s.r.l.**
Independencia 1654, Buenos Aires, Argentina.
● Radio y Television Practica. w. ISSN 0033-8141

**Davke**
Brandsen 1634, Buenos Aires, Argentina.
- Davke; revista Israelita. q.

**Luciano Augusto De Sousa, Ed. & Pub.**
Avenida de Mayo 1365, Buenos Aires, Argentina.
- Ecos de Portugal. m. ISSN 0013-0699

**Carlos Esteban Demalde**
Casilla de Correo 118, Sucursal 16, Buenos Aires, Argentina.
- Generacion 70.

**Devenir Historico**
Correa 2957, Buenos Aires, Argentina.
- Devenir Historico. q. ISSN 0012-1665

**Diana**
Tacuari 237, Buenos Aires, Argentina.
- Diana. m. ISSN 0012-2327

**E.P.I.S.A.**
Rivadavia 825, 2 Piso, Buenos Aires, Argentina.
- Anuario del Comercio Exterior Latino-Americano; guide to the industry and foreign trade of Latin America. a. ISSN 0066-5118 (Latin American Free Trade Association)

**Eco Contemporaneo**
C.C. Central 1933, Buenos Aires, Argentina.
- Eco Contemporaneo; revista de humanologia. q. ISSN 0012-9429

**Editorial Ecro**
Lavalle 2327, Buenos Aires, Argentina.
- Apuntes de Trabajo Social. irreg.

**EDITESA S. A.**
Avda. Pte Rogue Saenz Pena 825, Buenos Aires, Argentina.
- Industria Textil Sud Americana. bi-m. ISSN 0019-7742

**Editora Publicitaria S.A.C.I.F.**
Rivadavia 926, Buenos Aires, Argentina.
- Fotocamara Con Popular Photography. m. ISSN 0015-8771 (Federation Internationale de l'Art Photographique)

**Efluvios**
c/o Graciela B. de Fini, 462 Colon, Monte Grande, Buenos Aires, Argentina.
- Efluvios. m. ISSN 0013-2233

**Editorial Vasca Ekin s.r.l.**
Belgrano 1144, Buenos Aires 1092, Argentina.
- Biblioteca de Cultura Vasca. irreg. (approx. s-a.) ISSN 0067-7396
- Coleccion Aberri ta Azkatasuna. irreg., latest issue, 1972. ISSN 0069-5025
- Euzko Deya; la voz de los Vascos. bi-m.
- Instituto Americano de Estudios Vascos. Boletin. q. ISSN 0020-3637
- Tierra Vasca. m. ISSN 0495-5749

**Elan S.A.**
Uruguay 772-5-55, Buenos Aires, Argentina.
- Zona: Revista de Comercio Latino-Americana. m. ISSN 0044-4995

**Embassy of Greece in Argentina**
Departamento Cultural, Florida 378, Buenos Aires, Argentina.
- Grecia de Ayer, de Hoy y de Siempre. ISSN 0017-3819

**Embassy of Japan in Argentina**
Azcuenaga 1035, Buenos Aires, Argentina.
- Actualidades de Japon. s-m. ISSN 0001-768X

**Embassy of South Africa in Argentina**
Agricultural Counsellor, Marcelo T. de Alvear 590-80 Pnu, Buenos Aires, Argentina.
- Landbou-Rapport. s-a.

**Empresa Editorial s.r.l.**
Cordoba 632, Buenos Aires, Argentina.
- Economista; semanario economico-financiero. w. ISSN 0013-0648

**Encuentro**
Italia 830, Castelar, Buenos Aires, Argentina.
- Encuentro. q. ISSN 0013-7111

**English Language Journal**
c/o Aldo O. Blanco, 224 Parana, 1st Fl., 1017 Buenos Aires, Argentina.
- English Language Journal/Revista de la Lengua Inglesa; for the Latin American teacher of English. q.

**Ensayo Cultural**
Chacabuco 1291 - 2 - B, Buenos Aires, Argentina.
- Ensayo Cultural. q. ISSN 0013-8568

**Escarabajo de Oro**
Maza 1511, 20 C, Buenos Aires, Argentina.
- Escarabajo de Oro. m.

**Editorial Esquiu S. A.**
Sarandi 1067, Buenos Aires, Argentina.
- Esquiu; el mundo en la semana. w. ISSN 0014-0813

**Estacion Experimental Delta del Parana**
Casilla Correo 14, Campana, Buenos Aires, Argentina.
- Delta del Parana. 2 per yr. ISSN 0045-9895

**Nira Etchenique**
Correo Central 3507, Buenos Aires, Argentina.
- Cambio. fortn.

**F.C.N.G.R.**
Casilla de Correo 426, San Carlos de Bariloche, Argentina.
- Suedamerika; Drei-Monatsschrift in deutscher Sprache. q. ISSN 0039-4610

**F I E L**
*see* **Fundacion de Investigaciones Economicas Latinoamericanas**

**Editorial Farbat s.r.l.**
Cangallo 729, 9 Piso, Buenos Aires, Argentina.
- Premisa. m. ISSN 0048-5160

**Federacion Argentina de la Industria del Caucho**
Av. Leandro N. Alem 1069, 1001 Buenos Aires.
- Caucho. bi-m. ISSN 0528-3280

**Federacion Argentina de Periodistas**
Lavalle 1464, Buenos Aires, Argentina.
- Federacion Argentina de Periodistas. Gaceta. a.

**Federacion Argentina de Sociedades de Obstetricia y Ginocologia**
Calle Bernardo de Irigoyen 350, Buenos Aires, Argentina.
- Obstetricia y Ginecologia Latino Americana. bi-m. ISSN 0029-7836 (Co-sponsor: Sociedad Argentina de Fertilidad y Esterilidad)

**Federacion de Especialistas de Analisis Biologicos de la Provincia de BuenosAires**
Calle 48 N. 539, La Plata, Provincia de Buenos Aires, Argentina.
- Bioquimica Clinica. q. ISSN 0006-3533

**Federation Internationale de l'Art Photographique**
- Fotocamara Con Popular Photography. (pub. by Editora Publicitaria S.A.C.I.F.)

**Eugenio Matias Feher**
Espana 635, Castelar. Prov. Bs.As., Argentina.
- Magyar Tortenelmi Szemle/Hungarian Historical Review/Revista Historica Hungara. q. ISSN 0300-3817

**Emilie Fenner s.r.l.**
Sarmiento 575, Rosario, Santa Fe, Argentina.
- Revista Medica de Corrientes. q. ISSN 0034-9895 (Asociacion Medica de Corrientes y Sociedad de Cirugia)

**Ferrocarriles Argentinos**
Avda. Ramos Mejia 1302, Buenos Aires, Argentina.
- Ferrocarriles Argentinos. m. ISSN 0046-3698

**Ediciones Figaro**
Av. Ceballos 274, C.C. 206, 6620 Chivilcoy (BA), Argentina.
- Antologia; revista literaria. q.

**Filcar**
Saavedra 138, Buenos Aires, Argentina.
- Guia Turistica y de Calles de la Ciudad de Mar del Plata. irreg.

**Filippi y Saulino**
Avenida San Martin 427, General Belgrano, F. C. Roca, Argentina.
- Imparcial. 2 per w. ISSN 0019-2902

**First National Bank of Boston, Buenos Aires Branch**
Florida 99, Buenos Aires, Argentina.
- Situation in Argentina. m. ISSN 0037-5934

**Editorial Fotografia Universal**
Muniz 1327/49, Buenos Aires, Argentina.
- Audio Universal. m.
- Foto Cine Guia. a.
- Fotografia Universal. m. ISSN 0015-881X
- Guia de Audio. a.

**Fundacion Acta Fondo para la Salud Mental.**
Malabia 2274 13 a, Buenos Aires, Argentina.
- Acta Psiquiatrica y Psicologica de America Latina. q. ISSN 0001-6896

**Fundacion Bariloche**
Casilla de Correo 138, San Carlos de Bariloche - Rio Negro, Argentina.
- Fundacion Bariloche. Departamento de Biologia. Publicaciones. irreg. (prep. by its Departamento de Biologia)
- Fundacion Bariloche. Departamento de Matematica. Publicaciones. irreg. (prep. by its Departamento de Matematica)
- Fundacion Bariloche. Departamento de Recursos Naturales y Energia. Publicaciones. irreg. (prep. by its Departamento de Recursos Naturales y Energia)
- Fundacion Bariloche. Departamento de Sociologia. Publicaciones. irreg. (prep. by its Departamento de Sociologia)
- Fundacion Bariloche. Memoria Anual. a.
- Fundacion Bariloche. Programa de Transferencia. Publicaciones. irreg. (prep. by its Programa de Transferencia)

**Fundacion de Investigaciones Economicas Latinoamericanas**
Cogtal, Rivadavia 767, Buenos Aires, Rca, Argentina
(Subscriptions to: Esmeralda 320, Piso 4to. Buenos Aires. Rca. Argentina)
- Fundacion de Investigaciones Economicas Latino Americas. Indicadores de Coyuntura. m.
- Fundacion de Investigaciones Economicas Latinoamericanas. Informe Financiero Mensual. m.
- Hojas Industriales; encuestas de coyuntura. q.
- Hojas Industriales. Suplemento Mensual. m.

**Fundacion Dr. Jose Maria Mainetti para el Progreso de la Medicina**
Calle 8, No. 706, La Plata 1900, Argentina.
- Quiron. q.

**Fundacion Miguel Lillo**
Miguel Lillo 205, Tucuman, Argentina.
- Acta Geologica Lilloana. irreg (no. 13, 1976) ISSN 0567-7513
- Acta Zoologica Lilloana. irreg.; no. 32, 1976. ISSN 0065-1729
- Fundacion Miguel Lillo. Miscelanea. irreg.; no. 58, 1977. ISSN 0074-025X
- Lilloa; revista de botanica. irreg., vol. 34, 1976. ISSN 0075-9481
- Opera Lilloana. irreg.; no. 24, 1977. ISSN 0078-5245

**Fundacion Nuestra Historia**
Casilla de Correo No. 50 (Suc. 3), Buenos Aires, Argentina.
- Nuestra Historia; revista de historia de occidente. s-a. ISSN 0029-571X

**Fundacion Romulo Raggio**
Sarmiento 299, Of. 445, Buenos Aires, Argentina.
- Phyton; international journal of experimental botany. s-a. ISSN 0031-9457

**Fundacion Roux-Ocefa**
Montevideo 81, Buenos Aires, Argentina.
- Fundacion Roux-Ocefa. Archivos. q. ISSN 0016-271X (Sociedad Argentina de Neuropatologia)

**Futuro**
Hipolito Yrigoyen 521, Pilar, Argentina.
- Futuro. m. ISSN 0016-3325

**Gaceta Textil**
Av. Roque Saenz Pena, 832, Buenos Aires, Argentina.
- Gaceta Textil. m. ISSN 0046-5364

**Editorial Galerna**
Tucaman 1427, Buenos Aires, Argentina.
- Gaceta Veterinaria. m (10 per yr) ISSN 0367-3812

**Galicia y Rio de la Plata**
Rivadavia 717, Buenos Aires, Argentina.
- Galicia y Rio de la Plata. Compania de Seguros. Memoria y Balance General. a.

**Genesis**
Uruguay 546, Buenos Aires, Argentina.
- Genesis; de un III mundo y su liberacion. fortn.

**Goetheana Periodico Literario**
Casilia Correo 938, Buenos Aires, Argentina.
- Goetheana Periodico Literario. m. ISSN 0017-1522

**Editorial Golova s.r.l.**
Avda. de Mayo 863, Buenos Aires, Argentina.
- Contratista; materiales, metodos, aplicaciones y equipos para la construccion. m. ISSN 0010-7956
- Maquinas y Equipos; resumen de novedades tecnicas para la fabrica y el taller. m. ISSN 0025-2719

**Ediciones Gota de Agua**
Sarmiento 1983, Buenos Aires, Argentina.
- Biblioteca de Secretos Politicos. irreg.

**Habitante**
Chacabuco 1380, Catamarca, Argentina.
- Poesia en la Calle. m. ISSN 0032-1907

**Heraldo Club**
- Heraldo Mercantil Internacional. (pub. by Ed. & Pub. Livio Tiepolo)

**Heraldo del Cine**
Montevideo 443, Buenos Aires, Argentina.
- Heraldo del Cine. fortn. ISSN 0046-7286

**Hispano Americana, S.A.**
Alsina 731, Buenos Aires, Argentina.
- Radio Technica. w. ISSN 0033-8052

**Histonium**
Parana 464, Buenos Aires, Argentina.
- Histonium; en su nueva dimension. m. ISSN 0018-2265

**Editorial Hobby Comercial e Industrial**
Constitucion 2348/50, Buenos Aires, Argentina.
- Hobby. m. ISSN 0046-7650

**Honegger S.A.**
Mexico 4256, Buenos Aires, Argentina.
- Todo es Historia. m. ISSN 0040-8611

**Hospital Municipal Dr. Enrique Tornu. Sociedad de Tisiologia y Neumologia**
Hospital Tornu, Buenos Aires, Argentina.
- Archivos Argentinos de Tisiologia y Neumonologia. q. ISSN 0004-0509

**Editorial Huemul S.A.**
Chacabuco 860, Buenos Aires, Argentina.
- Libro del Ano; almanaque de sucesos argentinos y mundiales. a.

**I N**
Casilla de Correo 323, Correo Central, Buenos Aires, Argentina.
- I N. (Izquierda Nacional) m.

**Iade Argentina S.A.**
Ardoino 140 Ramos Mehia, Buenos Aires, Argentina.
- Iade; electronica - radio - televison. m. ISSN 0019-0934

**Igitur Revista Literaria**
Republica de Israel 115, Cordoba, Argentina.
- Igitur Revista Literaria. q. ISSN 0019-1663

**Iglesia Adventista del Septima Dia**
- Juventud. (pub. by Asociacion Casa Editrice Sudamericana)
- Vida Feliz. (pub. by Asociacion Casa Editrice Sudamericana)

**Iglesia Evangelica del Rio de la Plata**
Esmeralda 162, 1035 Buenos Aires, Argentina.
- Iglesia Evangelica del Rio de la Plata. Revista Parroquial/Evangelischen Kirche Am la Plata. Gemeindeblatt. m. ISSN 0019-1671

**Indupress s.r.l.**
Santiago del Estero 643, Buenos Aires, Argentina.
- I L A Intercambio Latinoamericano. m. ISSN 0018-9952
- Revista Diesel. bi-m. ISSN 0034-9178

**Ingenieria e Industria**
Santiago del Estero 643, Buenos Aires, Argentina.
- Ingenieria e Industria. m. ISSN 0020-1030

**Ingenieria y Ciencia**
c/o Aldo Macchia, 873 Calle Balcarce, Buenos Aires, Argentina.
- Ingenieria y Ciencia; revista de cultura cienfifica. q. ISSN 0020-1103

**Institucion Administrativa de la Iglesia Armenia**
Acevedo 1353, Buenos Aires, Argentina.
- Hay Guetron. m. ISSN 0017-8640

**Instituto Americano de Estudios Vascos**
- Instituto Americano de Estudios Vascos. Boletin. (pub. by Editorial Vasca Ekin s.r.l.)

**Instituto Americano de Investigaciones Economicas, Juridicos y Sociales**
c/o Josue Rizzuto, Maipu 286, Buenos Aires, Argentina.
- Instituto Americano de Investigaciones Economicas, Juridicos y Sociales. Bosquejos Contemporaneos. q. ISSN 0046-9904

**Instituto Argentino de Ciencias Genealogicas**
Circulo Militar, Av. Santa Fe 750, Buenos Aires, Argentina.
- Instituto Argentino de Ciencias Genealogicas. Boletin Interno. m. ISSN 0579-3599

**Instituto Argentino de Cultura Espirita**
Sunchales 520, Buenos Aires, Argentina.
- Universo; revista mensual de ciencia y cultura. m.

**Instituto Argentino de Estudios Estrategicos y de las Relaciones Internationales**
Cordoba 838, Buenos Aires, Argentina.
- Estrategia. 5 per yr. ISSN 0046-2578

**Instituto Argentino de Estudios Municipales**
Jose M. Moreno 437, Buenos Aires, Argentina.
- Selecciones Municipales. 3 per yr. ISSN 0049-0067

**Instituto Argentino de Estudios Politicos**
Mansilla 2698, Buenos Aires, Argentina.
- Revista Argentina de Estudios Politicos. 3 per yr.

**Instituto Croata Latinoamericano**
Cerlos Pellegrini 743, Buenos Aires, Argentina.
- Studia Croatica; revista de estudios politicos y culturales. q. ISSN 0039-3118

**Instituto de Biologia Marina**
Casilla de Correo 175, Mar del Plata, Argentina.
- Instituto de Biologia Marina. Memoria Anual. irreg., 1972 no. 9. ISSN 0076-4310
- Instituto de Biologia Marina. Serie Contribuciones. irreg., 1976, no. 337. ISSN 0076-4302

**Instituto de Botanica Darwinion**
Lavarden y del Campo, San Isidro, Buenos Aires, Argentina.
- Darwiniana. s-a. ISSN 0011-6793 (Academia Nacional de Ciencias Exactas, Fisicas y Naturales de Buenos Aires)

**Instituto de Ciencia Politica Rafael Bielsa. Facultad de Ciencia Politica y Relaciones Internacionales**
Cordoba 2020, Rosario, Argentina.
- Instituto de Ciencia Politica Rafael Bielsa. Anuario. a. ISSN 0074-0063 (prep. by its Division Publicaciones)

**Instituto de Desarrollo Economico y Social**
Guemes 3950, 1425 Buenos Aires, Argentina.
- Desarrollo Economico; revista de ciencias sociales. q. ISSN 0046-001X

**Instituto de Filologia y Literaturas Hispanicas "Dr. Amado Alonso"**
25 de Mayo 217, Buenos Aires, Argentina.
- Filologia. a. ISSN 0071-495X

**Instituto de Filosofia Practica**
Av. de Mayo 1437, Buenos Aires, Argentina.
- Ethos; revista de filosofia practica. a.

**Instituto de Historia del Arte**
Universidad Nacional de Cuyo, Facultad de Filosofia y Letras, Centro Universitario, Parque Gral San Martin, Mendoza, Argentina.
- Cuadernos de Historia del Arte. a. ISSN 0070-1688

**Instituto de Implantodontologia**
Callao 433-3e, Buenos Aires, Argentina.
- Conector. q.

**Instituto de Investigaciones de Historia del Derecho**
- Revista de Historia de Derecho. (pub. by Librart s.r.l.)

**Instituto de Matematica**
Bahia Blanca, Argentina.
- Monografias de Matematica. irreg.

**Instituto de Matematica Beppo Levi**
Avenida Pellegrini 250, Rosario, Argentina.
- Mathematicae Notae. a. ISSN 0025-553X

**Instituto de Maternidad "Alberto Peralata Ramos". Asociacion Medica**
Buenos Aires, Argentina.
- B.I.M. Boletin del Instituto de Maternidad "Alberto Peralta Ramos". irreg.

**Instituto de Publicaciones y Estadisticas S.A.**
Olavarria 1181 20 Piso, Buenos Aires, Argentina.
- Confort. m. ISSN 0010-5708

**Instituto de Terapeutica Purissimus S.A.**
Buenos Aires, Argentina.
- Fichero Medico Terapeutico Purissimus. q. ISSN 0015-0606

**Instituto del Cemento Portland Argentino**
Calle San Martin 1137, Buenos Aires, Argentina.
- Cemento Portland. a. ISSN 0008-8927

**Instituto Latinoamericano de Relacianas Internacionales**
Montevideo 666, Of. 101, Buenos Aires, Argentina (Subscr. to: 23 rue de la Pepiniere, Paris (8e), France)
- Mundo Nuevo. m. ISSN 0027-3333

**Instituto Lucchelli Bonadeo**
Casilla Correo Central 4317, Buenos Aires, Argentina.
- Guia de la Musica Argentina. biennial.

**Instituto Nacional de Estudios de Teatro**
Cordoba 1199, Buenos Aires, Argentina.
- Revista de Estudios de Teatro. 3 per yr. ISSN 0034-8171

**Instituto Nacional de Investigaciones Folkloricas**
Sanchez de Bustamante 2663, Buenos Aires, Argentina.
- Instituto Nacional de Investigaciones Folkloricas. Cuadernos. a.

**Instituto Superior de Bibliotecologia**
Avda. 44 No. 790, La Plata, Argentina.
- Umbral 2000. q. (Argentina. Ministerio de Cultura y Educacion)

**Instituto Torcuato di Tella**
Av. Cordoba 939, Buenos Aires, Argentina.
- Centro de Estudios de Estado y Sociedad. Documentos de Trabajo. irreg.
- Centro de Estudios de Estado y Sociedad. Estudios Sociales. irreg. (prep. by its Centro de Estudios de Estado y Sociedad)
- Instituto Torcuato di Tella. Centro de Estudios Urbanos Regionales. Documentos de Trabajo. irreg. ISSN 0074-0330
- Instituto Torcuato di Tella. Centro de Investigaciones Economicas. Documentos de Trabajo. irreg., 1969, no. 45. ISSN 0074-0349
- Instituto Torcuato di Tella. Centro de Investigaciones Economicas. Informes de Investigacion. irreg.

• Instituto Torcuato di Tella. Centro de
Investigaciones Sociales. Documentos de Trabajo.
irreg., 1973, no. 87. ISSN 0074-0357

**Inter-American Development Bank. Institute for
Latin American Integration**
*see* Banco Interamericano de Desarrollo. Instituto
para la Integracion de America Latina

**International Fertility Association**
c/o Dr. Armando F. Mendizabal, Secretary General,
Vincente Lopez 971, Martinez, Buenos Aires,
Argentina.
• World Congress on Fertility and Sterility.
Proceedings. triennial, 1968, 6th, Tel Aviv. ISSN
0084-1641

**Jazzband**
c/o Alberto Miguel Consiglio, 2291 Yerbal, Buenos
Aires, Argentina.
• Jazzband. bi-m.

**Jockey Club of Buenos Aires**
Cerrito 1353, 2 Piso, Buenos Aires, Argentina
(Subscr. to: Franklin Square Subscription Agency,
545 Cedar Lane Teaneck, NJ 07666)
• Jockey Club. q. ISSN 0021-7115

**Jovenes de la Accion Catolica**
Belgrand 239, Capillaudel Senor, Buenos Aires,
Argentina.
• Revista del Hogar. s-m. ISSN 0034-9070

**Junta de Estudios Historicos de Mendoza**
Calle Montevideo 544, Mendoza, Argentina.
• Junta de Estudios Historicos de Mendoza
(Argentina). Revista. a; latest issue, 1972. ISSN
0076-6380

**Kapelusz Revistas, S.A.I.C.**
Moreno 372, Buenos Aires, Argentina.
• Limen; revista de orientacion didactica. 4 per yr.
ISSN 0024-354X

**Keiron**
Casilla de Correo 2591, Buenos Aires, Argentina.
• Archivos Ethnos. 2 per yr.

**Moises Knaphais, Ed. & Pub.**
Rem. Esc. de San Martin 2670-Dto. C., Buenos
Aires, Argentina.
• Hojas Literarias Ilustradas. bi-m.

**Laboratorio de Ensayo de Materiales e
Investigaciones Technologicas**
La Plata, Argentina.
• L E M I T. Anales.

**Lagrimal Trifurca**
Ocampo 1812, Rosario, Argentina.
• Lagrimal Trifurca. q. ISSN 0023-7280

**Lajouane Import-Export**
San Martin 50, Buenos Aires, Argentina.
• Boletin Bibliografico Lajouane.

**Latin American Free Trade Association**
• Anuario del Comercio Exterior Latino-Americano.
(pub. by E.P.I.S.A.)

**Lealtad**
Sarmiento 672, Quilmes, Buenos Aires, Argentina.
• Lealtad. w. ISSN 0023-9674

**Editorial Victor Leru**
Casilla 1328 Correo Central, Buenos Aires,
Argentina.
• Orientacion Docente. q. ISSN 0030-5251

**Letra Viva**
Coronel Diaz 1837, Buenos Aires, Argentina.
• Imago; revista de psicoanalisis, psiquiatria y
psicologia. q.

**Ediciones la Ley S.A.**
1471 Tucuman, Buenos Aires, Argentina.
• Anales de Legislacion Argentina. issued every ten
days with quarterly cumulative summaries. ISSN
0034-6985
• Ley; revista argentina de jurisprudencia. daily,
with quarterly cummulative summaries. ISSN
0024-1636

**Librart s.r.l.**
Corrientes 127, Buenos Aires, Argentina.
• Archivo de Ciencias Biologicas y Naturales,
Teoricas y Aplicadas. 2 per yr. ISSN 0004-0401

• Asociacion Geologica Argentina. Revista. q. ISSN
0004-4822
• Revista Argentina de Cirugia. bi-m. ISSN 0048-
7600
• Revista de Historia de Derecho. a. (Instituto de
Investigaciones de Historia del Derecho)

**Liga de Almaceneros Minoristas y Afines**
Independencia 10, 231 Berazategui, Argentina.
• L. A. M. Y. A. Revista Mensual. m. ISSN 0023-
6217

**Liga pro Comportamiento Humano**
Maipu 286, Buenos Aires, Argentina.
• Comportamiento Humano. q. ISSN 0010-4329

**Linea Dura**
Alvar Nunez 179, Buenos Aires, Argentina.
• Linea Dura. m.

**Lonja Compania Editora Argentina S.A.C.**
Beruti 2474, Buenos Aires, Argentina.
• Nuestro Holando. m. ISSN 0029-5787

**Luz**
Pasteur 359, Buenos Aires, Argentina.
• Luz; la revista israelita para toda sudamerica.
fortn. ISSN 0024-7693

**Microcritica**
General Hornos 1110, Buenos Aires, Argentina.
• Microcritica; arte-musica-teatro-literatura. bi-m.
ISSN 0026-2676

**Militancia**
c/o Arturo Apicella e Hijo, 319 Esmera Ida, Buenos
Aires, Argentina.
• Militancia; Peronista para la liberacion. s-m.

**Editorial Mirador**
Santiago del Estero 315, Buenos Aires, Argentina.
• Mirador; panorama de la civilizacion industrial.
irreg.

**Alberto Mirkin**
Albarellos 647, Martinez, Buenos Aires, Argentina.
• Aero Mundial; aeronautical weekly letter in
English and Spanish editions. w. ISSN 0001-916X
• Republica Argentina. Transporte Aereo. Noticiero.
fortn. ISSN 0034-5040

**Movimiento de Reconciliacion en la Argentina**
Rivadavia 4044, Buenos Aires, Argentina.
• Reconciliacion. bi-m. ISSN 0034-1460

**Mundo Israelita**
Lavalle 2615, Buenos Aires, Argentina.
• Mundo Israelita; actualidad de la semana en Israel
en el mundo judio. w.

**Mundo Madereru**
Cerrito 446, Buenos Aires, Argentina.
• Mundo Madereru. m. ISSN 0027-3325

**Museo Americanista de Antropologia, Historia,
Numismatica y Ciencias Naturales**
Manuel Castro 254, Lomas de Zamora, Buenos
Aires, Argentina.
• Revista del Museo Americanista. a.

**Museo Argentino de Ciencias Naturales Bernardino
Rivadavia**
Avda. Angel Gallardo 470, Casilla de Correo 10 -
Sucursal 5, Buenos Aires, Argentina.
• Museo Argentino de Ciencias Naturales
Bernardino Rivadavia. Instituto Nacional de
Investigacion de las Ciencias Naturales. Revista.
Botanica. irreg; latest issue, 1974.
• Museo Argentino de Ciencias Naturales
Bernardino Rivadavia. Instituto Nacional de
Investigacion des las Ciencias Naturales. Revista.
Zoologia. (prep. by its Instituto Nacional de
Investigacion de las Ciencias Naturales)
• Museo Argentino de Ciencias Naturales
Bernardino Rivadavia e Instituto Nacional de
Investigaciones de la Ciencias Naturales. Revista y
Communicaciones. irreg. ISSN 0027-3880

**Museo Arqueologico de Cachi**
Cachi, Argentina.
• Estudios de Arqueologia. irreg.

**Museo de Historia Natural de San Rafael**
San Martin No. 127, San Rafael, Mendoza,
Argentina.
• Museo de Historia Natural de San Rafael. Revista
Cientifica de Investigaciones. irreg. ISSN 0027-
3902

**Museo Etnografico Municipal Damaso Aree. Instituto
de Investigaciones Antropologicas**
Olivarria, Buenos Aires, Argentina.
• Etnia. s-a. ISSN 0046-2632 (Co-sponsor: Instituto
de Investigaciones Antropologicas)
• Museo Etnografico Municipal Damaso Aree e
Instituto de Investigaciones Antropologicas.
Monografias. (pub. by Libreria Nueva Vision)

**Museo Social Argentino**
Corrientes 1723, Buenos Aires, Argentina.
• Buenos Aires. Museo Social Argentino. Boletin. q.
ISSN 0045-3331

**Navitecnia S.A.**
Alsina 1360, Buenos Aires, Argentina.
• Navitecnia. m. ISSN 0028-1611

**Editorial del Noroeste, S. A. C. I.**
Pueyrredon 860, 8 Piso, Buenos Aires, Argentina.
• Crisis. m.

**Editorial Norte**
Cuenca 1818, Buenos Aires, Argentina.
• Revista Argentina de Politica. irreg.

**Noticiero del Plastico**
Alsina 971, 5 Piso, Buenos Aires, Argentina.
• Envasamiento. m.
• Noticiero del Plastico-Elastomeros. m. ISSN
0048-0894
• Noticiero Quimico. w. ISSN 0048-0908

**Noticioso Perea**
c/o Dolores Rodriguez Rojo de Perea, 202 Av.
Quintana, Buenos Aires, Argentina.
• Noticioso Perea; organo de la industria de la
construccion. bi-m. ISSN 0029-4276

**Nuestro Anhelo**
Calle Paraguay 419, Piso 3o, Dep. 9, Buenos Aires,
Argentina.
• Nuestro Anhelo. q. ISSN 0029-5760

**Ediciones Nuestro Tiempo**
Rivadavia 1255 4 407, Buenos Aires, Argentina.
• Ahijuna. m. ISSN 0002-2039

**Libreria Nueva Vision**
Viamonte 494, Buenos Aires, Argentina.
• Museo Etnografico Municipal Damaso Aree e
Instituto de Investigaciones Antropologicas.
Monografias. a. ISSN 0074-011X (Co-Sponsor:
Instituto de Investigaciones Antropologicas)

**Nuevos Aires**
Casilla Correo N 11 72. Central, Buenos Aires,
Argentina.
• Nuevos Aires; revista de ficcion y pensamiento
critico. q. ISSN 0048-1092

**Obertura**
San Martin 170, Galeria Guemes, Buenos Aires,
Argentina.
• Obertura. bi-m.

**Obligado Editora s.r.l.**
Chacabuco 1409, Buenos Aires, Argentina.
• Documentos Contemporaneos. 11 per yr.

**Obrero Ferroviario**
c/o Adolfo Medina, Independencia 2880, Buenos
Aires, Argentina.
• Obrero Ferroviario. m. ISSN 0029-7658

**Observatorio Astronomico Municipal de Rosario**
Parque Urquiza, Rosario, Argentina.
• Observatorio Astronomico Municipal de Rosario.
Boletin. irreg.

**Oficina de Informacion Holandesa**
Maipu 66, Buenos Aires, Argentina.
• Cronica de Holanda; organo de informacion para
America Latina. bi-m. ISSN 0011-1791

**Orden de los Frailes Menores Capuchinos**
Esquiu 974, C.C. 14-Suc.37, Buenos Aires, Argentina.
- Nueva Pompeya. m. ISSN 0029-585X (Santuario de la Virgen del Rosario)

**Orelfa Editora**
Ave. Cordoba 2434, Buenos Aires, Argentina.
- Quilates. 5 per yr. ISSN 0033-6459

**Organizacion Universitaria de Intercambio Panamericano**
Tucuman 978, 5 Piso, Of. 10, Buenos Aires, Argentina.
- Argentina Futuro. bi-m. ISSN 0004-1041

**P. S. R. L.**
Tucuman 1452, 2 Piso, Buenos Aires, Argentina.
- Dia Medico. 3 per mo. ISSN 0012-1762

**Editorial Paginas y Tapas s.r.l.**
Peru 689, Buenos Aires, Argentina.
- Paginas y Tapas. m.

**Pan American Railway Congress Associaton**
c/o Lucio A. Hasperue, Secretary-General, Av. 9 de Julio 1925-piso 13, Oficina 1301, Buenos Aires, Argentina.
- Pan American Railway Congress Association. Proceedings of Congress. triennial. ISSN 0078-8872

**Panamerican Federation of Endocrine Societies**
c/o Dr. Noe Altschuler, 25 de Mayo 648, Vicente Lopez, Buenos Aires, Argentina.
- Acta Endocrinologica Panamericana. irreg. ISSN 0065-1192

**Panorama**
Leandro N. Alem 896, Buenos Aires, Argentina.
- Panorama. m. ISSN 0591-2628

**Panorama Bonaerense**
c/o Carlos Herberto Ebeling, Casilla de Correo 322, 1650 San Martin, B.A., Argentina.
- Panorama Bonaerense. w.

**Libreria Pardo**
Defensa 1170, Buenos Aires, Argentina.
- Academia Portena del Lunfardo. Boletin. q. ISSN 0001-3862

**Parroquia "San Roque"**
Calle 40 No.577, La Plata, Argentina.
- Psallite; revista trimestral de Musica Sagrada y cultura musical. q. ISSN 0033-2542

**Parroquia Santisima Trinidad Rufino**
La Misma del Punto (8), Italia 62, Rufino, Argentina.
- Sembrador. s-m. ISSN 0037-1866

**Partido Comunista**
Entre Rios 1031, Buenos Aires, Argentina.
- Nuestra Palabra. w.

**Ediciones Paulinas**
Avenida San Martin 4350, Buenos Aires, Argentina.
- Latinoamerica en Marcha. irreg.

**Paz y Justicia**
c/oAdolfo Perez Esquivel, Espana 890, San Isidro, Argentina.
- Paz y Justicia. m.

**Periodico Delta SCA.**
General Mitre 320, Tigre, Argentina.
- Delta. fortn. ISSN 0011-7978

**Peronismo y Liberacion**
Guise 2064, Piso 3, Sucursal 28, Casilla de Correo Num. 91, Buenos Aires, Argentina.
- Peronismo y Liberacion. 3 per yr.

**Peronismo y Socialismo**
Casilla de Correo Num. 119, Sucursal 25, Buenos Aires, Argentina.
- Peronismo y Socialismo. irreg.

**Peuser S.A.**
Buenos Aires, Argentina.
- Guia Peuser de Turismo Argentina y Sudamericana. irreg.

**Planteo**
Cangallo 1578, Buenos Aires, Argentina.
- Planteo; por la cultura de Occidente. fortn.

**Plantie Talleres Graficos S.A.**
Juan B. Alberdi 571, Buenos Aires, Argentina.
- Revista Argentina de Angiologia. q. ISSN 0034-6993 (Argentine Society of Angiology)

**Editorial Plus Ultra**
Viamonte 1755, Buenos Aires, Argentina.
- Revista Argentina de Ciencias Penales.

**Poesia-Poesia**
Roberto Juarroz & Mario Morales, Mitre 1829, Adrogue, Argentina.
- Poesia-Poesia. q. ISSN 0032-1915

**Editorial Policial**
Casilla Correu 1519 (C.C.), San Martin 353, Piso 8, Buenos Aires, Argentina.
- Mundo Policial. bi-m. ISSN 0030-7955 (Argentina. Policia Federal Argentina)

**Editorial Politea**
Sarmiento 1889, Buenos Aires, Argentina.
- Poder Politico. q. ISSN 0048-4512

**Politica y Economia**
25 de Mayo 486, 5O. Piso, Buenos Aires, Argentina.
- Politica y Economia. m.

**Pontificia Universidad Catolica de Buenos Aires**
Facultad de Filosofia, Calle 24 Entre 65 y 66 la Plata, Argentina.
- Sapientia. q. ISSN 0036-4703

**Por Alquimia**
Casilla de Correo 193, La Plata, Argentina.
- Por Alquimia. q. ISSN 0032-4744

**Pregon Rural**
Garibaldi 55, Buenos Aires, Argentina.
- Pregon Rural; tribuna integral al servicio del agro el comercio y la industria regional. m.

**Prensa Confidencial**
Carlos Pellegrini 1337, Piso 7, Buenos Aires, Argentina
(or Corrientes 1894, 1, Buenos Aires)
- Prensa Confidencial. w. ISSN 0032-7433

**Prensa Medica Argentina, S.R.L.**
Junin 845, Buenos Aires, Argentina.
- Archivos Argentinos de Pediatria. bi-m. ISSN 0325-0075 (Sociedad Argentina de Pediatria)
- Asociacion Medica Argentina. Revista. bi-m. ISSN 0004-4830
- Prensa Medica Argentina. s-m. ISSN 0032-745X

**Editorial Primera Plana s.r.l.**
Peru 367, Floor 12, Buenos Aires, Argentina.
- Primera Plana; la revista de noticias de mayor circulacion. w. ISSN 0032-8375

**Promocion y Ventes S. A. I. C.**
Esmeralda 762, 2 Piso, Buenos Aires, Argentina.
- Revista de Ceramica en la Construccion. bi-m. ISSN 0006-6222 (Asociacion de la Prensa Tecnica Argentina)

**Protexin Americana S.A.**
Parana 140, 2 Flor, Buenos Aires, Argentina.
- En Concreto. m. ISSN 0013-693X

**Punto Omega**
Envios, Gualeguaychu 882, Buenos Aires, Argentina.
- Punto Omega. bi-m. ISSN 0033-4391

**Editorial Dante Quintero S. A.**
Maipu 942-P.8, Capital Federal, Buenos Aires, Argentina.
- Dinamica Rural. m. ISSN 0012-2947

**Radio Chassis Television**
Maipu 391, Buenos Aires, Argentina.
- Radio Chassis Television. m. ISSN 0033-7781

**Ruben A. Ramirez Mitchell, Ed. & Pub.**
Maipu 262, Buenos Aires, Argentina.
- Abstracts of Military Bibliography. q. ISSN 0034-5873

**Repertorio Latinoamericano S.A.**
c/o Francisco R. Bello, Ed., Montevideo 524, Buenos Aires, Argentina.
- Repertorio Latino Americano. q.

**Editorial Replica**
Distribuidora Condor, Av. Independencia, 2744, Buenos Aires, Argentina.
- Redaccion. m.

**Res**
Avda. Roque Saenz Pena 760, 3 Piso, Buenos Aires, Argentina.
- Res; revista illustrada de las carnes argentinas. m. ISSN 0034-5083

**Ressorgiment**
Pergamino 244, Buenos Aires 6, Argentina.
- Ressorgiment; publicacio catalana. m. ISSN 0034-575X

**Review of the River Plate**
Bulnes 44 "a", Buenos Aires, Argentina.
- Review of the River Plate; dealing with Argentine financial, economic, agricultural and shipping affairs. 3 per mo. ISSN 0034-6810

**Revista de Ciencias de la Educacion**
Montevideo 666, Primer Piso, Of. 111, Buenos Aires, Argentina.
- Revista de Ciencias de la Educacion. 3 per yr. ISSN 0048-7686

**Revista de Derecho Laboral**
Calle Uruguay 115, Buenos Aires, Argentina.
- Revista de Derecho Laboral. m.

**Revista de Ferreteria y Ramos Generales**
Avenida de Mayo 963, Buenos Aires, Argentina.
- Revista de Ferreteria y Ramos Generales. m. ISSN 0034-821X

**Revista de Jurisprudencia Argentina**
Talcahuano 650, Buenos Aires, Argentina.
- Revista de Legislacion Argentina. m. ISSN 0034-8481

**Revista de Nutricion y Aterosclerosis**
c/o Mario Campagnoli, Juan B. Alberdi 3255, Buenos Aires, Argentina.
- Revista de Nutricion y Aterosclerosis. bi-m. ISSN 0034-8600

**Revista de Obras Sanitarias de la Nacion**
Rio Bamba 985, Buenos Aires, Argentina.
- Revista de Obras Sanitarias de la Nacion. m. ISSN 0034-8627

**Revista Ilustrade de las Carnes Argentinas**
Avda Roque Saenz Pena 760, 7 Piso, Buenos Aires, Argentina.
- Revista Ilustrade de las Carnes Argentinas. fortn.

**Revista Luterana**
Simbron 4667, Buenos Aires, Argentina.
- Noticiero de la Fe. m. ISSN 0029-425X

**Revista para Jubilados y Pensionados**
Casilla de Correo 4970, Correo Central, Buenos Aires, Argentina.
- Revista para Jubilados y Pensionados. s-m.

**Revista Sur**
Viamonte 494, 8 Buenos Aires, Argentina.
- Sur; fiction, essay, poetry, chronicles. s-a. ISSN 0035-0478

**Ryela, S.A.**
Bme. Mitre 853, Buenos Aires, Argentina.
- Claudia. m. ISSN 0009-8493
- Siete Dias Ilustrados. w. ISSN 0037-4784

**Santa Fe, Argentina. Centro Provincial de Documentacion e Informacion. Educativa,**
San Martin 1153-2 Piso, Santa Fe, Argentina.
- Boletin de Informacion Educativa. s-a. ISSN 0006-632X

**Santiago del Estero, Argentina. Direccion General de Investigaciones Estadistica y Censos**
Palacio de los Tribunales, Santiago del Estero, Argentina.
- Santiago del Estero. Direccion General de Investigaciones Estadistica y Censos. Estadistica Agricola-Ganadera. irreg.
- Santiago del Estero. Direccion General de Investigaciones Estadistica y Censos. Estadisticas Sociales. a.

**Santuario de la Virgen del Rosario**
- Nueva Pompeya. (pub. by Orden de los Frailes Menores Capuchinos)

**Editorial Semanario Israelita S. A.**
Pasteur 341, Buenos Aires, Argentina.
- Semanario Israelita; unabhaengiges juedisches wochenblatt. w. ISSN 0037-1858

**Senales**
Casilla 2484, Correo Central, Buenos Aires, Argentina.
- Senales; revista bibliografica. q. ISSN 0037-2099

**Seyse s.r.l.**
Cordoba 2404, 5 piso, Buenos Aires, Argentina.
- Armas Automaticas Modernas. bi-m.
- Armas y Tiro. bi-m. ISSN 0004-2161

**Sociedad Argentina de Biologia**
Santa Fe 1171, Buenos Aires, Argentina.
- Sociedad Argentina de Biologia. Revista. q. ISSN 0037-8380

**Sociedad Argentina de Cardiologia**
Avda. Xuintana A 3578, Buenos Aires, Argentina.
- Revista Argentina de Cardiologia. bi-m. ISSN 0034-7000

**Sociedad Argentina de Escritores**
Uruguay 1371, Buenos Aires 1016, Argentina.
- Boletin de la S A D E.

**Sociedad Argentina de Estudios Geograficos**
Av. Santa Fe, 1145 Buenos Aires, Argentina.
- Sociedad Argentina de Estudios Geograficos Boletin. irreg; latest issue, 1974.

**Sociedad Argentina de Gastroenterologia**
Santa Fe 1171, Buenos Aires, Argentina.
- Archivos Argentinos Enfermedades del Aparato Digestivo. bi-m. ISSN 0004-0517

**Sociedad Argentina de Investigacion Clinica**
Instituto de Investigaciones Medicas, Donato Alvarez 3000, Buenos Aires, Argentina.
- Medicina. bi-m. ISSN 0025-7680

**Sociedad Argentina de Investigadores en Ciencia de la Ingenieria Quimica y Quimica Aplicada**
Av. 1 No. 867, La Plata, Argentina.
- Revista Latinoamericana de Ingenieria Quimica y Quimica Aplicada/Latin American Journal of Chemical Engineering and Applied Chemistry. s-a. ISSN 0325-0474

**Sociedad Argentina de Leprologia**
Box 2899, Buenos Aires, Argentina.
- Leprologia. s-a. ISSN 0024-1016

**Sociedad Argentina de Metales**
Santa Fe 1145, Buenos Aires, Argentina.
- Metalurgica Moderna. bi-m.

**Sociedad Argentina de Mineria y Geologia**
Av. Sarmiento 2265, Castelar, Buenos Aires, Argentina.
- Revista Mineria, Geologia y Mineralogia. q. ISSN 0035-0176

**Sociedad Argentina de Neuropatologia**
- Fundacion Roux-Ocefa. Archivos. (pub. by Fundacion Roux-Ocefa)

**Sociedad Argentina de Oftalmologia**
Viamonte 1464-1 DTO. 2, Buenos Aires, Argentina.
- Archivos de Oftalmologia de Buenos Aires. bi-m. ISSN 0066-6777

**Sociedad Argentina de Ortodoncia**
Junin 959, Buenos Aires, Argentina.
- Ortodoncia. s-a. ISSN 0030-5936

**Sociedad Argentina de Pediatria**
- Archivos Argentinos de Pediatria. (pub. by Prensa Medica Argentina, S.R.L.)

**Sociedad Argentina de Profesores de Santa Escritura**
Casilla Postal 33-S.25, 1425 Buenos Aires, Argentina.
- Revista Biblica. q. ISSN 0034-7078

**Sociedad Argentina de Radiologia**
Ramon Falcon 1335, Buenos Aires, Argentina.
- Revista Argentina de Radiologia. 3 per yr. ISSN 0048-7619

**Sociedad Argentina de Urologia**
Buenos Aires, Argentina.
- Revista Argentina de Urologia y Nefrologia. bi-m. ISSN 0048-7627

**Sociedad Cientifica Argentina**
Avda. Santa Fe 1145, Buenos Aires, Argentina
- Sociedad Cientifica Argentina. Anales. bi-m. ISSN 0037-8437 (Distr. by: Librart, Casilla Correo Central 5047, Buenos Aires, Argentina)
- Sociedad Cientifica Argentina. Ciclo de Conferencias. irreg.

**Sociedad de Cirugia de Rosario**
Dir. Dr. Mario J. Milano, Italia 663, Rosario, Argentina.
- Sociedad de Cirugia de Rosario. Boletines. m. ISSN 0037-8526

**Sociedad de Historia de Rosario**
1 de Mayo 1082, Rosario, Argentina.
- Revista de Historia de Rosario. a; no. 25, 1974.

**Sociedad de Obstetricia y Ginecologia de Buenos Aires**
Calle Bernardo de Irigoyen 350, Buenos Aires, Argentina.
- Sociedad de Obstetricia y Ginecologia de Buenos Aires. Revista. m. ISSN 0037-8542

**Sociedad Espanola de Socorros Mutuos y Beneficencia**
Rodriquez No. 545, Tandil, Buenos Aires, Argentina.
- Sociedad Espanola de Socorros Mutuos y Beneficencia. Boletin. 4-5 per yr. ISSN 0037-8569

**Sociedad Hebraica Argentina**
Sarmiento 2233, Buenos Aires, Argentina.
- Davar; revista literaria. 4 per yr. ISSN 0011-703X

**Sociedad Neurologica Argentina**
Buenos Aires, Argentina.
- Revista Neurologica Argentina.

**Sociedad Rural Argentina**
Florida 460, Buenos Aires, Argentina.
- Sociedad Rural Argentina. Anales. 4 per yr. ISSN 0037-8631
- Sociedad Rural Argentina. Boletin. fortn. ISSN 0037-864X
- Sociedad Rural Argentina. Memoria. a. ISSN 0081-0630

**Asociacion Casa Editrice Sudamericana**
Avda. San Martin 4555, 1602 Florida, Buenos Aires, Argentina.
- Juventud; la revista de los jovenes de altos ideales. m. ISSN 0022-7196 (Iglesia Adventista del Septima Dia)
- Vida Feliz. m. (Iglesia Adventista del Septima Dia)

**Victor Sulimovich, Ed. & Pub.**
Maipu 645, Buenos Aires, Argentina.
- Petrotecnica. bi-m. ISSN 0031-6598

**Ediciones Summa**
Peru 689, Buenos Aires, Argentina.
- Summa; revista de arquitectura, tecnologia y diseno. m.
- Summarios. irreg.

**T E C O L**
Pueyrredon 1353, Buenos Aires, Argentina.
- Empresas Argentinas. 6-10 per yr.

**Talleres Graficos Amalevi**
Calle Mendoza 1851, Rosario, Santa Fe, Argentina.
- Guia Turistica de Rosario y Sante Fe. irreg.

**Teatro**
Concepcion Arenal 3932, Buenos Aires, Argentina.
- Teatro. m. ISSN 0040-0793

**Tecnica e Industria**
c/o Dante R. Marchesotti, 485 Rodriguez Pena, Buenos Aires, Argentina.
- Tecnica e Industria. m. ISSN 0040-1781

**Tecnologia Alimentaria**
25 de Mayo 786, Buenos Aires, Argentina.
- Tecnologia Alimentaria. bi-m. ISSN 0040-1943

**Editorial Teosofica**
Casilla de Correo 36, Rio Cuarto, Cordoba, Argentina.
- Teosofo. q. (Theosophical Society)

**Theosophical Society**
- Teosofo. (pub. by Editorial Teosofica)

**Ed. & Pub. Livio Tiepolo**
Box 826, Cordoba, Argentina.
- Heraldo Mercantil Internacional. bi-m. ISSN 0018-0548 (Heraldo Club)

**Erwin Toppelberg**
Santiago del Estero 643, Buenos Aires, Argentina.
- Automotor. m. ISSN 0005-1608

**Ediciones la Trenza Loca**
Rodriguez Pena 754, Buenos Aires, Argentina.
- Informacion Meridiana. m.

**Tribuna Odontologica**
Casilla de Correos 2047, Buenos Aires, Argentina.
- Tribuna Odontologica. q. ISSN 0041-2775

**Union Matematica Argentina**
Casilla de Correo 3588, Buenos Aires, Argentina.
- Union Matematica Argentina. Revista. 4 per yr. ISSN 0041-6932

**Union Proprietarios de Talleres Mecanicos de Automoviles**
Alsina 2540, Buenos Aires, Argentina.
- Autotecnica. m.

**Universidad de Belgrano**
Buenos Aires, Argentina.
- Vigencia. m. ISSN 0042-594X

**Universidad de Buenos Aires. Facultad de Derecho y Ciencias Sociales**
Av. Figueroa Alcorta 2263, Buenos Aires, Argentina.
- Lecciones y Ensayos. irreg.

**Universidad de Buenos Aires. Facultad de Filosofia y Letras**
25 de Mayo 217, Buenos Aires, Argentina.
- Buenos Aires. Universidad Nacional. Seccion de Estudios de Filosofia Oriental. Estudios de Filosofia y Religiones del Oriente. 2 per yr. (prep. by its Secion de Estudios de Filosofia Oriental)
- Cuadernos de Filosofia. 2 per yr. (prep. by its Instituto de Filosofia)
- Universidad de Buenos Aires. Gaceta de la Facultad de Filosofia y Letras. m. ISSN 0041-8331

**Universidad de Buenos Aires. Insituto de Sociologia**
Buenos Aires, Argentina.
- Instituto de Sociologia. Boletin. a.

**Universidad de Buenos Aires. Instituto Bibliotecologico**
Departamento de Registros Cientificos, Casilla de Correo 901, 1000buenos Aires, Argentina.
- Guia de Investigaciones en Curso de la Universidad de Buenos Aires. m.
- Tesis Presentadas a la Universidad de Buenos Aires. biennial. ISSN 0325-0245
- Universidad de Buenos Aires, Instituto Bibliotecologico. Boletin Informativo. q. ISSN 0041-834X
- Universidad de Buenos Aires Instituto Bibliotecologico. Publicacion. irreg.; no. 48, 1975. ISSN 0068-3493

**Universidad de Buenos Aires. Instituto de Arte Americano e Investigaciones Esteticas**
Buenos Aires, Argentina.
- Universidad de Buenos Aires. Instituto de Arte Americano e Investigaciones Esteticas. Anales. a.

**Universidad de Buenos Aires. Instituto de Ciencias Antropologicas**
Moreno 350, Buenos Aires, Argentina.
- Runa: Archivo para las Ciencias del Hombre. irreg. ISSN 0080-4843 (prep. by its Facultad de Filosofia y Letras)

**Universidad de Buenos Aires. Instituto de Economia**
Buenos Aires, Argentina.
- Universidad de Buenos Aires. Instituto de Economia. Bibliografia sobre Economia Nacional.

**Universidad de Buenos Aires. Instituto de Historia Antigua Oriental**
25 de Mayo 217, 3er. Piso, Buenos Aires, Argentina.
- Universidad de Buenos Aires. Instituto de Historia Antigua Oriental. Revista. a.

**Universidad del Museo Social Argentina. Estudiantes Universitarios de Psicologia**
Corrientes 1723, Buenos Aires, Argentina.
- Revista Argentina de Psicologia. 2 per yr. ISSN 0034-7027

**Universidad del Norte "San Tomas de Aquino". Facultad de Agronomia y Zootecnia**
Casilla de Correos 125, San Miguel de Tucuman, Argentina.
- Revista Agronomica del Noroeste Argentino. irreg. ISSN 0080-2069

**Universidad del Salvador**
Callao 542, Buenos Aires, Argentina.
- Universidad del Salvador. Anales. a. ISSN 0068-3485

**Universidad del Salvador. Facultad de Psicopedagogia**
Corrientes 4471, Buenos Aires 1195, Argentina.
- Revista de Psicopedagogia. m. (prep. by its Instituto de Investigaciones)

**Universidad del Salvador. Facultades de Filosofia y Teologia**
Avda. Mitre 3226, San Miguel, Argentina.
- Stromata; ciencia y fe. q. ISSN 0049-2353

**Universidad Nacional de Cordoba. Division Publicaciones de la Escuela de Ciencias Politicas y Relaciones Internationales**
Cordoba 2020, Rosario, Argentina.
- Revista de Derecho Internacional y Ciencias Diplomaticas. s-a. ISSN 0034-7892

**Universidad Nacional de Cordoba. Facultad de Ciencias Economicas**
Ciudad Universitaria, Estafeta 32, Cordoba, Argentina.
- Economia de Cordoba. s-a. ISSN 0013-0435
- Revista de Ciencias Administrativas. 3 per yr.
- Revista de Economia y Estadistica. q. ISSN 0034-8066

**Universidad Nacional de Cordoba. Facultad de Ciencias Exactas, Fisicas y Naturales**
Museo Botanico, Casilla de Correo 495, Cordoba, Argentina.
- Lorentzia. irreg. ISSN 0076-0897

**Universidad Nacional de Cordoba. Facultad de Ciencias Medicas**
Ciudad Universitaria, Estafeta 32, 5000 Cordoba, Argentina.
- Facultad de Ciencias Medicas. Revista. q. ISSN 0014-6722

**Universidad Nacional de Cordoba. Facultad de Derecho y Ciencias Sociales**
Direccion de Publicaciones Universitarias, Trejo 242, Cordoba, Argentina.
- Universidad Nacional de Cordoba. Facultad de Derecho y Ciencias Sociales. Boletin. 5 per yr (some double issues)

**Universidad Nacional de Cordoba. Facultad de Filosofia y Humanidades**
Estafeta 32, Cordoba, Argentina.
- Boletin Interamericano de Archivos. a.
- Revista de Humanidades. irreg., 1970, nos. 11-12. ISSN 0080-228X

**Universidad Nacional de Cordoba. Facultad de Odontologia**
Casilla de Correo 458, Cordoba, Argentina.
- Universidad de Cordoba. Facultad de Odontologia. Revista. q. ISSN 0325-1071

**Universidad Nacional de Cordoba. Instituto de Derecho Constitucional**
Cordoba, Spain.
- Cuadernos de los Institutos. irreg.

**Universidad Nacional de Cordoba. Instituto de Economia y Finanzas**
Facultad de Ciencias Economicas, Ciudad Universitaria, Cordoba, Argentina.
- Revista de Compendios de Articulos de Economia. s-a. ISSN 0034-7825

**Universidad Nacional de Cuyo**
Escuela Superior de Artes Plasticas, Centro Universitario, Parque General San Martin, Mendoza, Argentina.
- Boletin de Historia de Arte y Estetica.

**Universidad Nacional de Cuyo. Biblioteca Central**
Centro Universitario-C.C. 420, Mendoza, Argentina.
- Universidad Nacional de Cuyo. Biblioteca Central. Boletin Bibliografico. irreg.; no. 47, 1975. ISSN 0076-6399
- Universidad Nacional de Cuyo. Biblioteca Central. Cuadernos de la Biblioteca. irreg; no. 5, 1970. ISSN 0076-6402

**Universidad Nacional de Cuyo. Facultad de Ciencias Economicas**
Casilla de Correo 594, Mendoza 5500, Argentina.
- Universidad Nacional de Cuyo. Facultad de Ciencias Economicas. Revista. 3 per yr. ISSN 0041-8668

**Universidad Nacional de Cuyo. Facultad de Ciencias Politicas y Sociales**
Canje Biblioteca, Casilla de Correos 182, Mendoza, Argentina.
- Boletin de Ciencias Politicas y Sociales. s-a. ISSN 0045-2394

**Universidad Nacional de Cuyo. Instituto de Arqueologia y Etnologia**
Mendoza, Argentina.
- Anales de Arqueologia y Etnologia. irreg.

**Universidad Nacional de Cuyo. Instituto de Filosofia**
Facultad de Filosofia y Letras, Belgrano 1079, Buenos Aires, Argentina.
- Philosophia. s-a. ISSN 0031-8000

**Universidad Nacional de Cuyo. Instituto de Sociologia**
Patricias Mendocinas 1327, Mendoza, Argentina.
- Investigaciones en Sociologia. s-a. ISSN 0020-9961

**Universidad Nacional de la Plata**
Calle 7 No. 776, La Plata, Argentina.
- Revista de Problemas Argentinos y Americanos. a.

**Universidad Nacional de la Plata. Biblioteca Publica**
Plaza Rocha 137, La Plata, Argentina.
- Bibliografia Argentina Universitaria. q.
- Universidad Nacional de la Plata, Argentina. Revista. s-a. ISSN 0041-8625

**Universidad Nacional de la Plata. Facultad de Agronomia**
Casilla de Correo 31, La Plata, Argentina.
- Universidad Nacional de la Plata. Facultad de Agronomia. Revista. s-a. ISSN 0041-8676

**Universidad Nacional de la Plata. Facultad de Ciencias Economicas**
Calle 53, No. 417, La Plata, Argentina.
- Economica. 3 per yr. ISSN 0013-0419 (prep. by its Instituto de Investigaciones Economicas)

**Universidad Nacional de la Plata. Facultad de Ciencias Economicas-Biblioteca (Hemeroteca)**
Calle 7 No. 776, La Plata, Argentina.
- Sintesis Bibliografica. irreg., 1972, no. 9. ISSN 0080-9772

**Universidad Nacional de la Plata. Facultad de Humanidades y Ciencias de la Educacion**
Calle 46, No. 530, La Plata, Argentina.
- Coleccion Pensamiento Argentino. irreg. ISSN 0069-5149
- Cuadernos de Sociologia. irreg. ISSN 0070-1734

- Revista Humanidades. irreg. ISSN 0080-2387
- Universidad Nacional de la Plata. Facultad de la Educacion. Departamento de Letras. Serie Trabajos. Comunicaciones y Conferencias. irreg; 1972, no. 15. (prep. by its Departamento de Letras)
- Universidad Nacional de la Plata. Instituto de Estudios Sociales y del Pensamiento Argentino. Cuadernos de Extension Universitaria. irreg. ISSN 0075-742X

**Universidad Nacional de la Plata. Instituto de Filosofia**
Facultad de Humanidades y Ciencias de la Educacion, La Plata, Argentina.
- Revista de Filosofia. 9 per yr. ISSN 0034-8228

**Universidad Nacional de la Plata. Instituto de Investigaciones Administrativas**
Facultad de Ciencias Economicas, Casilla de Correo No 376, La Plata, Buenos Aires, Argentina.
- Ciencias Administrativas. q. ISSN 0009-6784

**Universidad Nacional de la Plata. Instituto de la Produccion**
Calle 53, No. 419, La Plata, Argentina.
- Universidad Nacional de la Plata. Instituto de la Produccion. Serie Contribuciones. irreg. ISSN 0457-1673

**Universidad Nacional de Rosario**
Avenida Pellegrini 250, Rosario, Argentina.
- Universidad Nacional de Rosario. Facultad de Ciencias, Ingenieria y Arquitectura. Instituto de Fisiografia y Geologia. Publicaciones. a. ISSN 0041-8684

**Universidad Nacional de Tucuman. Facultad de Ciencias Exactas y Tecnologia**
Avda. Independencia 1700, Tucuman, Argentina.
- Revista de Matematica y Fisica Teorica. Serie A. a. ISSN 0080-2360

**Universidad Nacional de Tucuman. Facultad de Filosofia y Letras**
Tucuman, Argentina.
- Universidad Nacional de Tucuman. Facultad de Filosofia y Letras. Cuadernos de Humanitas. irreg., 1972, no. 40. ISSN 0564-4070

**Universidad Nacional de Tucuman. Instituto de Derecho Publico**
Tucuman, Buenos Aires.
- Revista de Derecho Publico. irreg.

**Universidad Nacional de Tucuman. Instituto de Ingenieria Electrica**
Avda. Independencia 1700, San Miguel de Tucuman, Argentina.
- Universidad Nacional de Tucuman. Instituto de Ingenieria Electrica. Revista. irreg. ISSN 0082-6693

**Universidad Nacional del Litoral**
Boulevar Pellegrini 2750, Santa Fe, Argentina.
- Universidad. q. ISSN 0041-8234

**Universidad Nacional del Litoral. Facultad de Ciencias de la Administracion**
25 de Mayo, 1783, Santa Fe, Argentina.
- Universidad Nacional del Litoral. Facultad de Ciencias de la Administracion. Revista. a.

**Universidad Nacional del Litoral. Facultad de Ciencias Economicas Comerciales y Politicas**
Santa Fe, Argentina.
- Universidad Nacional del Litoral. Facultad de Ciencias Economicas Comerciales y Politicas. irreg.

**Universidad Nacional del Litoral. Facultad de Ciencias Juridicas y Sociales**
Candido Pujato 2751, Sante Fe, Argentina.
- Revista de Ciencias Juridicas Sociales. 4 per yr (2 double issues)

**Universidad Nacional del Nordeste. Facultad de Humanidades**
Av. Las Heras 727, Corrientes, Resistencia, Argentina.
- Nordeste. irreg. ISSN 0029-1242

**Universidad Nacional del Nordeste. Instituto de Geografia**
Las Heras, 727, Resistencia, Argentina.
- Geografica. a.; no. 3, 1974.

**Universidad Nacional del Nordeste. Instituto de Letras**
Resistencia, Chaco, Argentina.
- Cuadernos de Estudios Latinoamericanos. irreg.
- Cuadernos para el Estudio de la Estetica y la Literatura. irreg.

**Universidad Nacional del sur. Centro de Documentacion Bibliotecologica**
Av. Alem 1253, Bahia Blanca, Argentina.
- Bibliografia Bibliotecologica Argentina. irreg. ISSN 0067-656X
- Documentacion Bibliotecologica. irreg; latest issue, 1974. ISSN 0070-6841

**Universidad Nacional del sur. Instituto de Economia**
Avenida Colon, Bahia Blanca, Argentina.
- Estudios Economicos. s-a.

**Universidad Nacional del Sur. Instituto de Matematica**
Bahia Blanca, Argentina.
- Notas de Algebra y Analisis. irreg., 1969, no. 2. ISSN 0078-2009
- Notas de Logica Matematica. irreg. ISSN 0078-2017

**Editorial Universitaria de Buenos Aires**
Rivadivia 1571-73, Buenos Aires, Argentina.
- Hontanar. irreg. ISSN 0073-327X

**Velocidad**
Av. Belgrano 1735, 4-B, Buenos Aires, Argentina.
- Velocidad. bi-m. ISSN 0049-5913

**Venga Que le Cuento...**
Prudan 1330, Buenos Aires, Argentina.
- Venga Que le Cuento; publicacion periodica aleatoria de narradores argentinos. irreg.

**Veritas Editorial S.C.A.**
Maipu 286, T. E. 46-9876, Buenos Aires, Argentina.
- Veritas. m. ISSN 0042-3947

**Vientin S.A.**
Talcahuano 487, Buenos Aires, Argentina.
- Vientin Bibliographic Service. bi-m.

**Voz del Pueblo**
Rivadavia 1237, Tostado, Santa Fe, Argentina.
- Voz del Pueblo; periodico defensor de los intereses del departamento. w. ISSN 0042-9090

**World Jewish Congress**
- Congreso Judio Latinoamericano. Boletin Informativo OJI. (pub. by Congreso Judio Latinoamericano)

**Zona s.r.l**
Bartolome Mitre 1225, Buenos Aires, Argentina.
- GUIPREX. (Guia de Productores y Exportadores Latinoamericanos) a.

**Editorial 2 de Octubre**
Defensa 453, 9 Piso, Buenos Aires, Argentina.
- Dinamis. m.

# AUSTRALIA

**A D C Publications**
P.O. Box 194, Balgowlah, NSW 2093, Australia.
- Australian Drug Compendium. a.

**A.F.E.S. Graduate Fellowship of Australia**
The Business Manager, 2nd Floor, 405-44 Sussex St., Sydney N.S.W. 2000, Australia.
- Interchange. s-a. ISSN 0047-0430

**A.N.A.R.E. Club**
568 St. Kilda Rd., Melbourne, Victoria, 3004, Australia.
- Aurora. 3 per yr. ISSN 0004-8089

**A. S. E. A. Electric Australia Pty. Ltd.**
Beresford Rd., Lilydale, Vic. 3140, Australia.
- A. S. E. A. Action. q.

**Aboriginal Children's Advancement Society**
Box 277, Sutherland, N.S.W. 2232, Australia.
- Kirinari.

**Aboriginal Education Council**
132 St. John's Road, Glebe, N.S.W. 2037, Australia.
- Duran-Duran. irreg.

**Aboriginal Medical Service**
193 Regent St., Redfern, N.S.W. 2016, Australia.
- Aboriginal Medical Service. Newsletter. m. ISSN 0310-8341

**Aboriginal Publications Foundation**
Box M. 931, G. P. O., Perth, W.A. 6001, Australia.
- Aboriginal and Islander Identity. q.

**Aborigines Advancement League (Vic.)**
- Smoke Signals. (pub. by Smoke Signals Publishing Committee)

**Aborigines Advancement League Inc.**
2A Eton Ave., Warradale, S.A. 5046, Australia.
- Aborigines Advancement League. Newsletter. 4 per yr.

**Abyssinian Cat Club of Australasia**
G.P.O. Box 2323, Sydney, N.S.W. 2001, Australia.
- Abyssinian. s-a.

**Accountants and Secretaries Educational Society, Inc. Queensland**
Box 39, Brisbane, Queensland 4001, Australia.
- Accountants and Secretaries Educational Journal. m. ISSN 0044-5916

**Accounting Association of Australia and New Zealand**
Secretary, A. A. A. N. Z., University of New South Wales, P.O. Box 1, Kensington, N.S.W. 2033, Australia.
- Accounting Education. irreg.

**Acorn Publishing Co. Pty. Ltd.**
Box 2186, Sydney, N.S.W. 2001, Australia.
- Australian National Drycleaner. m. ISSN 0045-074X (Australian Institute of Drycleaning)

**Stuart M. Adams Holdings Pty. Ltd.**
77 Pitt St., Sydney, Australia.
- Sydney Tourist Guide. w. ISSN 0039-7601

**Adelaide City Council**
Town Hall, King William St., Adelaide, S.A. 5000, Australia.
- Adelaide City Council Municipal Reference Book. a.

**Adelaide Women's Liberation Movement**
Bloor House, Bloor Court, Adelaide, S.A. 5000, Australia.
- Liberation. irreg. ISSN 0310-964X

**Adis Press Australasia Pty. Ltd.**
559 Sydney Rd., Seaforth, N.S.W. 2092, Australia.
- Clinical Pharmacokinetics. bi-m. ISSN 0312-5963
- Current Therapeutics; journal of clinical pharmacology and therapeutics. m. ISSN 0311-905X

**Administrative and Clerical Officers Association**
75 King St., Sydney, N.S.W. 2000, Australia.
- A C O A. m. ISSN 0044-6289

**Advocate Newspaper Pty. Ltd.**
Box 63, Burnie, Tasmania, Australia.
- Advocate Weekender. w.

**Age Publications**
250 Spencer St, Melbourne, 3000, Victoria, Australia.
- Caravan Manual and Tourist Park Guide. a. ISSN 0069-0295

**Agribusiness Counsellors Pty. Ltd.**
Box 7099, Cloisters Square, Perth, W.A. 6000, Australia.
- Agribusiness Decision. m. ISSN 0311-0370

**Agricultural Engineering Society**
191 Royal Parade, Parkville, Vic. 3052, Australia.
- Agricultural Engineering Australia. ISSN 0044-6807

**Agricultural Societies Council of New South Wales**
Agriculture House, 195 Macquarie Street, Sydney, N.S.W. 2000, Australia.
- Country Shows Annual. a. ISSN 0311-1946

**Agricultural Society of South Australia**
17 Benjamin St., Manningham, S.A. 5086, Australia.
- Bird Keeping in Australia. m. ISSN 0045-2076

**Agricultural Technologists of Australasia, Ltd.**
Box 307, Bathurst, N.S.W. 2795, Australia.
- Agricultural Technologist. q. ISSN 0084-6031

**Agriscene Australia**
Box R 225, Royal Exchange, Sydney, N.S.W. 2000, Australia.
- Agriscene Australia. bi-m. ISSN 0310-0537

**Air Force Association. Victoria Division**
- Contact. (pub. by Air Force Club of Victoria)

**Air Force Club of Victoria**
Air Forces Memorial Centre, 6 Ste. Helens Court, Vermont, Vic. 3133, Australia.
- Contact. irreg. (Air Force Association. Victoria Division)

**Aircraft Owners and Pilots Association of Australia**
Box 2912 G.P.O., Sydney, NSW 2001, Australia.
- A. O. P. A. Magazine. m. ISSN 0002-2691

**Aluminium Development Council of Australia**
99 Elizabeth St., Sydney, N.S.W. 2000, Australia.
- Aluminium Development Council of Australia. Technical Papers. irreg. ISSN 0084-6279
- Standards for Australian Aluminium Mill Products. irreg. ISSN 0085-6657

**Amalgamated Metal Workers' Union**
Commonwealth Headquarters, 126 Chalmers Street, Surry Hills, New South Wales. 2010, Australia.
- A. M. W. U. Journal. m.

**Amalgamated Milk Vendors Association of New South Wales**
King York House, 83 York St., Sydney, N.S.W. 2000, Australia.
- Milk Vendor. m. ISSN 0026-4210

**Amalgamated Wireless (Australasia) Ltd.**
422 Lane Cove Rd., North Ryde, N.S.W. 2113, Australia.
- A W A Technical Review. 2 per yr. ISSN 0001-2920

**Amateur Pistol Shooting Union of Australia Inc.**
Box 47, Eastwood, S. Australia 5063, Australia.
- Australian Pistol Shooters' Bulletin. bi-m. ISSN 0004-9980

**American Chamber of Commerce in Australia**
8Th Floor, 50 Pitt St., Sydney, N.S.W. 2000, Australia.
- American Chamber of Commerce in Australia. Newsletter. m.
- Commerce. bi-m. ISSN 0045-754X

**American Civil War Round Table of Australia**
c/o Barry Crompton, 14 Sunlight Crescent, East Brighton, Vic. 3187, Australia.
- Minie News. irreg. ISSN 0310-3471

**Anarcho Surrealist Insurrectionary Feminists Collective**
P.O. Box 294, Collingwood, Vic. 3066, Australia.
- A S I F. irreg. ISSN 0310-9585

**Anchor Books Pty. Ltd.**
590 George St., Sydney, N.S.W., Australia.
- Film Index. q. ISSN 0015-1289

**Ronald Anderson & Associates**
81 Rokeby St, Collingwood, Vic. 3066, Australia.
- Primary Industry Newsletter. w.
- Primary Industry Survey. m. ISSN 0048-5292
- World Agricultural Report. fortn. ISSN 0049-8017

**Anglican Church in Western Australia**
C.P.O.Box W2067, Perth 6001, Australia.
- Anglican Messenger. m.

**Angora Mohair Association of Australia**
Bank House, 11 Bank Place, Melbourne, Vic. 3000, Australia.
- Herd Book for Angora Goats in Australia. a. ISSN 0310-2971

**Ansett Airlines of Australia**
489 Swanston St., Melbourne 3000, Australia.
- Panorama. m. ISSN 0031-0824

**Anthropological Society of New South Wales**
c/o Dept. of Anthropology, Univ. of Sydney, New South Wales 2006, Australia.
- Mankind. s-a. ISSN 0025-2328

**Antique & Historical Arms Collectors Guild of Victoria**
110 Pellatt St., Beaumaris, Vic. 3193, Australia.
- Caps and Flints. q. ISSN 0045-5695

**Apple & Pear Board**
- Fruit World and Market Grower. (pub. by Fruit World Pty. Ltd.)

**Applied Chemicals Pty. Ltd.**
Domville Ave., Hawthorn, Vic. 3122, Australia.
- Applied Chemical News. irreg.

**Aqua Pura**
c/o R. Fulton, Ed., Box a307, 70 Thorne St., Toronto, N.S.W. 2283, Australia.
- Aqua Pura. bi-m.

**Aquarium Society of New South Wales**
Box 31, Brickfield Hill, N.S.W. 2000, Australia.
- Aquarium Society of New South Wales, Monthly Journal. m. ISSN 0044-8508

**Archaeological Society of Victoria**
Box 98, Caulfield East, Vic. 3145, Australia.
- Artefact. q. ISSN 0044-9075

**Archery Association of Australia**
25 Albert St., Prospect, S.A. 5082, Australia.
- Shooting Lines. bi-m.

**Archives Authority of New South Wales**
Archives Office of New South Wales, Library of New South Wales, Macquarie St., Sydney, N.S.W. 2000, Australia.
- Concise Guide to the State Archives of New South Wales. Supplement. q.

**Arena Publications Association**
Box 36, Greensborough, Victoria 3088, Australia.
- Arena; a marxist journal of criticism and discussion. q. ISSN 0004-0932

**Argus and Australasian Ltd.**
61-73 Flinders Lane, Melbourne 3000, Australia.
- Australasian Post. w. ISSN 0004-8437
- Your Garden. m. ISSN 0044-1031

**Ark**
c/o Susan & Ronald Clarke, 2-159 Herring Rd., North Ryde, N.S.W. 2113, Australia.
- Ark. ISSN 0311-2926

**Armidale and District Historical Society**
c/o J. S. Ryan, Dept. of English, Univ. of New England, Armidale, N.S.W. 2351, Australia.
- Armidale and District Historical Society. Journal and Proceedings. a. ISSN 0084-6732

**Arnall & Jackson Pty. Ltd.**
390 Barkly St., Brunswick, Vic. 3056, Australia.
- Victorian Municipal Directory. s-a. ISSN 0049-6170

**Art Craft Teachers Association**
Room 12, 350 Victoria St., North Melbourne, Vic. 3051, Australia.
- Art Craft Teachers Association Magazine. irreg. (about 8 per yr) ISSN 0311-0087

**Art Dialogue Press**
G.P.O. Box 2426v, Melbourne, Vic. 3001, Australia.
- Art Dialogue. irreg. ISSN 0310-9267

**Art Gallery of South Australia**
North Terrace, Adelaide, S.A. 5000, Australia.
- Art Gallery of South Australia. Special Exhibitions. irreg. ISSN 0066-796X

**Art Teachers Association of Victoria**
Box 121, Parkville 3052, Victoria, Australia.
- Art Teachers Association of Victoria. Journal. m.(exc. Jan.) ISSN 0044-9059

**Arthur Wilson Memorial Foundation**
- Australian and New Zealand Journal of Obstetrics and Gynecology. (pub. by Ramsay, Ware Publishing Pty. Ltd.)

**Artificial Breeding Board of Tasmania**
Box 612, Launceston, Tas. 7250, Australia.
- Artificial Breeding News. q. ISSN 0310-9178

**Artists' Guild of Australia**
156 Banksia St., Pagewood, NSW 2035, Australia.
- Artviews. irreg. ISSN 0311-0095

**Assemblies of God. Australia Foreign Missions Department**
P.O. Box 141, Doncaster, Vic. 3108, Australia.
- Garamut. irreg. ISSN 0311-0362

**Associated Chambers of Manufacturers of Australia**
Industry House, National Circuit, Barton, A. C. T. 2600, Australia.
- Industry News. 8 per yr. ISSN 0310-3064
- Kompass Australia. (pub. by Peter Isaacson Publications)

**Associated Netherlands Societies in Victorian**
P.O. Box 280, Greensborough, Vic. 3088, Australia.
- Dutch Societies Courier. m.

**Associated Pharmaceutical Organisations of Australia**
- Australian Journal of Pharmacy. (pub. by Australasian Pharmaceutical Publishing Co. Ltd.)

**Associated Pulp and Paper Mills Ltd.**
G.P.O. Box 509H, Melbourne, Vic. 3001, Australia.
- Something on Paper. irreg. ISSN 0310-4389

**Association for Children with Aphasic and Perceptual Difficulties**
Box 2, Campsie, N.S.W. 3194, Australia.
- A. C. A. P. Newsletter. m. ISSN 0310-5504

**Association for Christian Social Studies**
6 Park Rd., Mount Evelyn, Vic. 3796, Australia.
- Total Perspective. bi-m.

**Association for Consumer Education**
Box 5043a, Newcastle, N.S.W. 2302, Australia.
- Consumer Impact. q.

**Association for the Journal of Religious History**
- Journal of Religious History. (pub. by Sydney University Press)

**Association of Acrobats**
23 Victor Rd., Brookvale, N.S.W. 2100, Australia.
- World Acrobatics. m.

**Association of Apex Clubs**
39 Milford Road, Miranda, N.S.W. 2228, Australia.
- Apexian. 4 per yr.

**Association of Australian Slovaks**
Box 273, Sydney, N.S.W. 2001, Australia.
- Slovak Shield. m.

**Association of Co-Operative Building Societies of N. S. W. Ltd.**
- Your Home. (pub. by Reville Publishing Co.)

**Association of Foremen and Supervisors**
26 Lancelot St., Blacktown, N.S.W. 2148, Australia.
- Impact. q. ISSN 0310-0316

**Association of Professional Engineers, Australia**
Box 1272L, G.P.O., Melbourne, Vic. 3001, Australia.
- P E News. (Professional Engineer) q.

**Association of Teachers of English as a Foreign Language**
c/o A. Blakeney, 13/7 Hatton St., Ryde, N.S.W. 2112, Australia.
- Association of Teachers of English as a Foreign Language. Bulletin. 3 per yr. ISSN 0310-608X

**Association of Zoo Directors of Australia and New Zealand**
c/o Taronga Zoo, P.O. Box 20, Mosman, N.S.W. 2088, Australia.
- Bulletin of Zoo Management. irreg. ISSN 0084-8182

**Asthma Foundation of New South Wales**
249 Pitt St., Sydney, N.S.W. 2000, Australia.
- Asthma Welfarer. 3 per yr. ISSN 0044-9776

**Astronomical Society of Australia**
c/o Division of Radiophysics, C. S. I. R. O, Epping, N.S.W. 2121, University of Sydney, N.S.W. 2006, Australia.
- Astronomical Society of Australia. Proceedings. irreg., approx. 2 per yr. ISSN 0066-9997

**Astronomical Society of New South Wales**
c/o Box 208, Eastwood, N.S.W. 2122, Australia.
- Universe. m. ISSN 0049-5506

**Astronomical Society of South Australia**
G.P.O. Box, 199, Adelaide 5001, S.A., Australia.
- Astronomical Society of South Australia. Bulletin. m. ISSN 0044-9806

**Astronomical Society of Victoria**
Box 1059 J, G.P.O., Melbourne, Victoria 3001, Australia.
- Astronomical Society of Victoria. Journal. bi-m. ISSN 0044-9814
- Astronomical Society of Victoria. Yearbook. a. ISSN 0067-0006

**Astronomical Society of Western Australia**
83 Blencowe St., West Leederville, W.A. 6007, Australia.
- Astronomical Society of Western Australia. Journal. m.

**Aureal Publications**
91, Brisbane St., Berwick, Victoria 3806, Australia (Subscription Address: Monash University, Dept. of Classical Studies, Clayton, Vic., Australia)
- Ramus; critical studies in Greek and Roman literature. s-a. ISSN 0048-671X

**D. F. Austin Publishing**
Box A-252, Sydney South, N.S.W. 2000, Australia.
- Australian Worker. m. ISSN 0045-0979 (Australian Workers Union)

**Australasian Affiliation of Herpetological Societies**
Box R79, Royal Exchange, N.S.W. 2000, Australia.
- Herpetofauna. s-a.

**Australasian and Pacific Society for Eighteenth-Century Studies**
c/o Department of English, Australian National University, P.O. Box 4, Canberra City, A.C.T. 2601, Australia.
- Australasian and Pacific Society for Eighteenth-Century Studies. Newsletter. irreg.

**Australasian Association of Philosophy**
Philosophy Dept., Australian National University, Canberra, A.C.T.2600, Australia.
- Australasian Journal of Philosophy. 3 per yr. ISSN 0004-8402

**Australasian College of Dermatologists**
271 Bridge Rd., Glebe, N.S.W. 2037, Australia.
- Australasian Journal of Dermatology. 3 per yr. ISSN 0004-8380

**Australasian Commercial Teachers' Association**
20 Napoleon St., Roseberry, N.S.W. 2018, Australia.
- Australasian Commercial Teachers' Association. Journal. a. ISSN 0084-6961

**Australasian Corrosion Association**
16 Ivy St., Chippendale, N.S.W. 2060, Australia.
- Australasian Corrosion Directory. a. ISSN 0067-0715
- Australasian Corrosion Engineering; a technical journal for the control and prevention of corrosion. m. ISSN 0004-833X

**Australasian Institute of Metals**
191 Royal Parade, Parkville, Vic. 3052, Australia.
- Australasian Engineer. m. ISSN 0004-8348 (Co-sponsors: Institute of Diesel Engineers; Society of Mechanical Engineers of Australia)
- Australasian Institute of Metals. Journal. 4 per yr.
- Metals Australasia. 11 per yr.

**Australasian Institute of Mining and Metallurgy**
Clunies Ross House, 191 Royal Parade, Parkville, Vict. 3052, Australia.
- Australasian Institute of Mining and Metallurgy. Proceedings. q. ISSN 0004-8364

**Australasian Institute of Radiography**
- Radiographer. (pub. by Mercedes Publishing Co.)

**Australasian Maritime Historical Society**
Box 33, Magill, S.A. 5072, Australia.
- Australasian Shipping Record. m.

**Australasian Meat Industry Employees Union. Queensland Branch**
Trades Hall, Brisbane, Qld. 4000, Australia.
- Meatworker. irreg. ISSN 0310-6721

**Australasian Meat Industry Employees' Union. W. A. Branch**
- W. A. Meat Worker. (pub. by Western Sun)

**Australasian Medical Publishing Co.**
77 79 Arundel St., Glebe, N.S.W. 2037, Australia.
- A M A Gazette. fortn. ISSN 0300-4708 (Australian Medical Association)

● Australian and New Zealand Journal of Surgery.
  q. ISSN 0004-8682 (Royal Australasian College
  of Surgeons)

**Australasian Methodist Historical Society**
c/o 139 Castlereagh St., Sydney, N.S.W. 2000,
Australia.
● Australasian Methodist Historical Society. Journal
  and Proceedings. irreg. ISSN 0084-6988

**Australasian Pharmaceutical Publishing Co. Ltd.**
35 Walsh St., West Melbourne 3003, Australia.
● Australian Journal of Pharmacy. m. (Associated
  Pharmaceutical Organisations of Australia)

**Australasian Political Studies Association**
c/o Department of Politics, Flinders University,
Bedford Park, S.A. 5042, Australia.
● Politics. s-a. ISSN 0032-3268

**Australasian Security Publishers**
470 Main St., Kangaroo Point, Brisbane, Qld. 4169,
Australia.
● Security and Property Protection. m. (Institute of
  Commerical and Industrial Security Executives)
  (Co-sponsors: Association of Burglary Insurance
  Surveyors Australasia; Security Institute of South
  Australia)

**Australasian Society of Engineers**
422-424 Kent St., Sydney, N.S.W. 2000, Australia.
● Australasian Society of Engineers. Engineers
  Handbook. a. ISSN 0084-6996

**Australasian Society of Engineers. Victorian Branch**
341 Latrobe St., Melbourne, Vic. 3000, Australia.
● Australasian Society of Engineers. A. S. E.
  Journal. bi-m. ISSN 0045-0103

**Australasian Transport Officers' Association**
327-331 Sussex St, Sydney, N.S.W. 2000, Australia.
● Transport Officers' Gazette. bi-m.

**Australasian Union of Jewish Students**
584 St. Kilda Road, Melbourne, Vic. 3004,
Australia.
● Massada. irreg. ISSN 0310-0138

**Australasian Universities Language and Literature
Association**
● A U M L A. (pub. by James Cook University of
  North Queensland)

**Australia. Air Transport Group**
Canberra, Australia.
● Australia. Air Transport Group. Aerodromes and
  Ground Aids. irreg.

**Australia. Atomic Energy Commission**
45 Beach St., Coogee, N.S.W.2034, Australia.
● Atomic Energy in Australia. q. ISSN 0004-7090

**Australia. Atomic Energy Commission. Research
Establishment**
Private Mail Bag, Sutherland N.S.W. 2232,
Australia.
● Australia.Atomic Energy Commission. Research
  Establishment. A A E C/E. irreg., 1970, no. 208.
  ISSN 0067-1657
● Australia. Atomic Energy Commission. Research
  Establishment. A A E C/IP. irreg.
● Australia.Atomic Energy Commission. Research
  Establishment. A A E C/M. irreg. ISSN 0067-
  1665
● Australia. Atomic Energy Commission. Research
  Establishment. List of Report Publications. irreg.

**Australia. Australian Bureau of Statistics**
P.O. Box 10, Belconnen, A.C.T. 2616, Australia
(Subscr. to: Australian Government Publishing
Service, Box 84, Canberra, A.C.T. 2600, Australia)
● Australia. Bureau of Statistics. Apparent
  Consumption of Foodstuffs and Nutrients. a.
● Australia. Bureau of Statistics. Authorities of the
  Australian Government. a.
● Australia. Bureau of Statistics. Balance of
  Payments. a. ISSN 0045-0111
● Australia. Bureau of Statistics. Banking. m.
● Australia. Bureau of Statistics. Bee Keeping. a.
● Australia. Bureau of Statistics. Building and
  Construction Bulletin. a. ISSN 0067-074X
● Australia. Bureau of Statistics. Causes of Death
  Bulletin. a. ISSN 0067-0766
● Australia. Bureau of Statistics. Census of Tourist
  Accomodation Establishments: Australia and
  Australian Capital Territory. a.
● Australia. Bureau of Statistics. Child Care. irreg.

● Australia. Bureau of Statistics. Chronic Illnesses,
  Injuries and Impairments. irreg.
● Australia. Bureau of Statistics. Colleges of
  Advanced Education. a.
● Australia. Bureau of Statistics. Crop Statistics. a.
● Australia. Bureau of Statistics. Dairying Industry.
  a. ISSN 0312-6447
● Australia. Bureau of Statistics. Dairying Industry -
  Australia. a.
● Australia. Bureau of Statistics. Deaths. a.
● Australia. Bureau of Statistics. Digest of Current
  Economic Statistics. m. ISSN 0012-2726
● Australia. Bureau of Statistics. Divorce. a.
● Australia. Bureau of Statistics. Earnings and Hours
  of Employees. a.
● Australia. Bureau of Statistics. Economic
  Censuses: Electricity and Gas Establishments,
  Details of Operations. a.
● Australia. Bureau of Statistics. Employment and
  Unemployment. m. ISSN 0013-6867
● Australia. Bureau of Statistics. Estimates of Gross
  Product by Industry at Current and Constant
  Prices. irreg.
● Australia. Bureau of Statistics. Expenditures on
  Education. irreg.
● Australia. Bureau of Statistics. Finance
  Companies. m.
● Australia. Bureau of Statistics. Foreign Control in
  Manufacturing Industry. a Study of Large
  Enterprise Groups. irreg.
● Australia. Bureau of Statistics. Foreign Ownership
  and Control of Finance Companies. irreg.
● Australia. Bureau of Statistics. Foreign Ownership
  and Control of General Insurance Businesses.
  irreg.
● Australia. Bureau of Statistics. Foreign Ownership
  and Control of Life Insurance Business. irreg.
● Australia. Bureau of Statistics. Foreign Ownership
  and Control of the Mining Industry. a.
● Australia. Bureau of Statistics. Hospitals and
  Nursing Homes. a.
● Australia. Bureau of Statistics. Imports Cleared for
  Home Consumption Bulletin. a. ISSN 0067-0804
● Australia. Bureau of Statistics. Income
  Distribution. irreg.
● Australia. Bureau of Statistics. Instalment Credit
  for Retail Sales. m. ISSN 0519-4997
● Australia. Bureau of Statistics. Labour Mobility.
  irreg.
● Australia. Bureau of Statistics. Labour Report. a.
  ISSN 0067-0812
● Australia. Bureau of Statistics. Labour Turnover.
  irreg.
● Australia. Bureau of Statistics. Life Insurance. m.
  ISSN 0571-9518
● Australia. Bureau of Statistics. Livestock Statistics.
  a.
● Australia. Bureau of Statistics. Manufacturing
  Commodities: Principal Articles Produced. a.
● Australia. Bureau of Statistics. Manufacturing
  Commodities: Principal Materials Used. a.
● Australia. Bureau of Statistics. Marriages. a.
● Australia. Bureau of Statistics. Mineral
  Exploration. a.
● Australia. Bureau of Statistics. Mineral
  Production. a. ISSN 0311-8975
● Australia. Bureau of Statistics. Minerals and
  Mineral Products. m.
● Australia. Bureau of Statistics. Monthly Review of
  Business Statistics. m. ISSN 0027-0539
● Australia. Bureau of Statistics. Motor Vehicle
  Registrations. q.
● Australia. Bureau of Statistics. National Income
  and Expenditure. a. ISSN 0312-6250
● Australia. Bureau of Statistics. Northern Territory
  Statistical Summary. a. ISSN 0067-0855
● Australia. Bureau of Statistics. Outward Overseas
  Cargo: Sea and Air. a.
● Australia. Bureau of Statistics. Overseas and
  Coastal Shipping. a.
● Australia. Bureau of Statistics. Overseas
  Investments: Overseas Borrowings by Companies
  in Australia. irreg. (approx. 1 per yr.)
● Australia. Bureau of Statistics. Overseas Trade
  Bulletin. a. ISSN 0067-0863
● Australia. Bureau of Statistics. Perinatal Deaths. a.
● Australia. Bureau of Statistics. Production
  Statistics. m.
● Australia. Bureau of Statistics. Public Authority
  Finance. Public Authority Estimates. a.
● Australia. Bureau of Statistics. Public Authority
  Finance. State and Local Authorities. a.
● Australia. Bureau of Statistics. Public Authority
  Finance. State Governments: Social Services. a.
● Australia. Bureau of Statistics. Quarterly Estimates
  of National Income and Expenditure. q. ISSN
  0004-8577

● Australia. Bureau of Statistics. Rail, Bus, and Air
  Transport. a.
● Australia. Bureau of Statistics. Road Accident
  Fatalities. m. ISSN 0035-7162
● Australia. Bureau of Statistics. Rural Land Use,
  Improvements, Agricultural Machinery and
  Labour. a.
● Australia. Bureau of Statistics. Seasonally
  Adjusted Indicators. a.
● Australia. Bureau of Statistics. State, Territory and
  Local Government Authorities Finance and
  Government Securities. a. ISSN 0067-0995
● Australia. Bureau of Statistics. Statistical Bulletin:
  Apparent Consumption of Tea and Coffee. a.
● Australia. Bureau of Statistics. Summary of Vital
  and Population Statistics. q.
● Australia. Bureau of Statistics. Survey of Leavers
  from Schools, Universities or Other Educational
  Institutions. a.
● Australia. Bureau of Statistics. Survey of Retail
  Establishments: Australian Capital Territory. a.
● Australia. Bureau of Statistics. Teacher Education.
  a.
● Australia. Bureau of Statistics. the Meat Industry.
  a.
● Australia. Bureau of Statistics. Trade Union
  Statistics. a.
● Australia. Bureau of Statistics. Trade Union
  Statistics: Australia. irreg. ISSN 0312-1437
● Australia. Bureau of Statistics. University
  Statistics. a.
● Australia. Bureau of Statistics. Value of Primary
  Production, Excluding Mining, and Indexes of
  Quantum and Unit Gross Value of Agricultural
  Production. a. ISSN 0312-6242
● Australia. Bureau of Statistics. Wage Rates and
  Earnings. m.
● Australia. Bureau of Statistics. Western Australian
  Office. Building Approvals. m.
● Australia. Bureau of Statistics. Western Australian
  Office. Road Traffic Accident Statistics. q. ISSN
  0004-8569
● Australia. Bureau of Statistics. Wheat Industry. a.
  ISSN 0043-4698
● Australian Capital Territory Statistical Summary.
  a. ISSN 0067-1754
● Australian Exports Bulletin. a. ISSN 0067-186X
● Australian Exports: Country by Commodity. a.
● Australian Imports Bulletin. a. ISSN 0067-1916
● Australian Imports: Country by Commodity. a.
● New South Wales Monthly Summary of Business
  Statistics. m. ISSN 0028-680X
● Official Yearbook of Australia. a. ISSN 0312-4746
● Overseas Trade Bulletin. a.
● Pocket Compendium of Australian Statistics. a.
  ISSN 0079-239X
● Pocket Yearbook of Tasmania. a. ISSN 0085-
  493X

**Australia. Australian Bureau of Statistics. N. S. W.
Office**
Bank House, 315 George St., Sydney, N. S. W.
2000, Australia.
● Australia. Bureau of Statistics. New South Wales
  Office. Education. a.
● Australia. Bureau of Statistics. New South Wales
  Office. Health and Welfare Services. a.
● Australia. Bureau of Statistics. New South Wales
  Office. Law, Order, and Public Safety. a.
● Australia. Bureau of Statistics. New South Wales
  Office. Public Finance. a.
● Australia. Bureau of Statistics. New South Wales
  Office. Trade, Transport and Communication.
  irreg.
● Official Year Book of New South Wales. a. ISSN
  0085-4441
● Pocket Yearbook of New South Wales. a. ISSN
  0085-4921

**Australia. Australian Bureau of Statistics. Queensland
Office**
345 Ann St., Brisbane, Queensland 4000, Australia.
● Australia. Bureau of Statistics. Queensland Office.
  Area and Estimated Population in Each
  Queensland Local Authority Area. irreg.
● Queensland Pocket Yearbook. a. ISSN 0085-5316
● Queensland Statistics; Monthly Summary. m.
  ISSN 0048-6396
● Queensland Yearbook. a. ISSN 0085-5359

**Australia. Australian Bureau of Statistics. South
Australian Office**
Box 2272, Adelaide, S.A. 5001, Australia.
● Australia. Bureau of Statistics. Australian Office.
  Monthly Summary of Statistics. m. ISSN 0047-
  8032
● Australia. Bureau of Statistics. South Australian
  Office. Births. a. ISSN 0067-088X

- Australia. Bureau of Statistics. South Australian Office. Deaths. a. ISSN 0067-0898
- Australia. Bureau of Statistics. South Australian Office. Divisional Statistics. irreg. ISSN 0067-091X
- Australia. Bureau of Statistics. South Australian Office. Divorce. a. ISSN 0067-0901
- Australia. Bureau of Statistics. South Australian Office. Livestock. a. ISSN 0067-0944
- Australia. Bureau of Statistics. South Australian Office. Manufacturing Establishments. a. ISSN 0310-0871
- Australia. Bureau of Statistics. South Australian Office. Marriages. a. ISSN 0067-0952
- Australia. Bureau of Statistics. South Australian Office. Projections of Population. irreg. ISSN 0067-0979
- Australia. Bureau of Statistics. South Australian Office. Rural Production. a. ISSN 0067-0987
- Pocket Year Book of South Australia. a. ISSN 0079-2446
- South Australian Yearbook. a. ISSN 0085-6428

**Australia. Australian Bureau of Statistics. Tasmanian Office**
Box 66A, G.P.O., Hobart, Tasmania 7001, Australia.
- Australia. Bureau of Statistics. Tasmanian Office. Agricultural Industry. a.
- Australia. Bureau of Statistics. Tasmanian Office. Artificial Fertiliser Usage, Size Classification, Tasmania. irreg.
- Australia. Bureau of Statistics. Tasmanian Office. Building Industry. a. ISSN 0067-1010
- Australia. Bureau of Statistics. Tasmanian Office. Demography. a. ISSN 0067-1029
- Australia. Bureau of Statistics Tasmanian Office. Education. a.
- Australia. Bureau of Statistics. Tasmanian Office. Fruit Production, Tasmania. a.
- Australia. Bureau of Statistics. Tasmanian Office. Fruit Statistics. a.
- Australia. Bureau of Statistics. Tasmanian Office. Industrial Accident Statistics. a.
- Australia. Bureau of Statistics. Tasmanian Office. Labour, Wages and Prices. a. ISSN 0067-1045
- Australia. Bureau of Statistics. Tasmanian Office. Local Government Finance. a. ISSN 0312-7850
- Australia. Bureau of Statistics. Tasmanian Office. Potato Statistics. a.
- Australia. Bureau of Statistics. Tasmanian Office. Production of Meat in Tasmania. a.
- Australia. Bureau of Statistics. Tasmanian Office. Public Justice. a. ISSN 0312-1356
- Australia. Bureau of Statistics. Tasmanian Office. Trade and Shipping. a. ISSN 0067-107X
- Australia. Bureau of Statistics. Tasmanian Office. Wool Production Statistics. a.
- Tasmanian Monthly Summary of Statistics. m. ISSN 0039-9833
- Tasmanian Yearbook. a. ISSN 0082-2116

**Australia. Australian Bureau of Statistics. Victorian Office**
Box 2796Y, G.P.O. Melbourne, Victoria 3001, Australia.
- Australia. Bureau of Statisitcs. Victorian Office. Victorian Yearbook. a. ISSN 0067-1223
- Australia. Bureau of Statistics. Victorian Office. Agriculture: Miscellaneous Items. a.
- Australia. Bureau of Statistics. Victorian Office. Apples and Pears in Cool Stores. m. (Mar.-Nov.)
- Australia. Bureau of Statistics. Victorian Office. Building Approvals by Local Government Areas. q. and a.
- Australia. Bureau of Statistics. Victorian Office. Building Operations: Number of New Houses and Other Dwellings: Preliminary Estimates. q.
- Australia. Bureau of Statistics. Victorian Office. Building Operations. q.
- Australia. Bureau of Statistics. Victorian Office. Causes of Death. a. ISSN 0067-1088
- Australia. Bureau of Statistics. Victorian Office. Chicken Hatchings and Poultry Slaughterings. m.
- Australia. Bureau of Statistics. Victorian Office. Demography. a. ISSN 0067-1096
- Australia. Bureau of Statistics. Victorian Office. Estimated Population in Local Government Areas. a.
- Australia. Bureau of Statistics. Victorian Office. General Statistics of Local Government Areas. irreg. ISSN 0067-1118
- Australia. Bureau of Statistics. Victorian Office. Industrial Accidents and Workers Compensation. a.
- Australia. Bureau of Statistics. Victorian Office. Land Utilisation and Crops. a.

- Australia. Bureau of Statistics. Victorian Office. Livestock. a.
- Australia. Bureau of Statistics. Victorian Office. Local Government Finance. a.
- Australia. Bureau of Statistics. Victorian Office. Mortgages of Real Estate Lodged for Registration. q.
- Australia. Bureau of Statistics. Victorian Office. Motor Vehicle Registrations. m.
- Australia. Bureau of Statistics. Victorian Office. Primary and Secondary Education. a. ISSN 0067-1150
- Australia. Bureau of Statistics. Victorian Office. Road Traffic Accidents Involving Casualties. q and a. ISSN 0067-1185
- Australia. Bureau of Statistics. Victorian Office. Value of Primary Commodities Produced. a.
- Australia. Bureau of Statistics. Victorian Office. Victorian Monthly Statistical Review. m. ISSN 0049-6162
- Australia. Bureau of Statistics. Victorian Office. Victorian Pocket Yearbook. a. ISSN 0067-1207
- Australia. Bureau of Statistics. Victorian Office. Victorian Statistical Publications. irreg. ISSN 0067-1215
- Australia Bureau of Statistics. Victorian Office. Building Approvals. m.
- Victorian Yearbook. a.

**Australia. Australian Bureau of Statistics. Western Australian Office**
1-3 St. George's Terrace, Perth, W.A. 6000, Australia.
- Australia. Bureau of Statistics. Western Australian Office. Abstract of Statistics of Local Government Areas. a. ISSN 0067-124X
- Australia. Bureau of Statistics. Western Australian Office. Agricultural and Pastoral Statistics. a. ISSN 0067-1231
- Australia. Bureau of Statistics. Western Australian Office. Building Operations. q. ISSN 0004-8526
- Australia. Bureau of Statistics. Western Australian Office. Census of: Manufacturing Establishments: Summary of Operations by Industry Class. a.
- Australia. Bureau of Statistics. Western Australian Office. Chicks Hatched and Poultry Slaughtered. m.
- Australia. Bureau of Statistics. Western Australian Office. Fisheries. a.
- Australia. Bureau of Statistics. Western Australian Office. Hospital in-Patient Statistics. a.
- Australia. Bureau of Statistics. Western Australian Office. Industrial Accidents. a. ISSN 0067-1266
- Australia. Bureau of Statistics. Western Australian Office. Monthly Statistical Summary. m. ISSN 0004-8542
- Australia. Bureau of Statistics. Western Australian Office. Population, Dwellings and Vital Statistics. a. ISSN 0067-1290
- Australia. Bureau of Statistics. Western Australian Office. Quarterly Statistical Abstract. q. ISSN 0004-8585
- Australia. Bureau of Statistics. Western Australian Office. Rural Land Utilisation. irreg.
- Australia. Bureau of Statistics. Western Australian Office. Sheep, Lambing and Wool Clip. a. ISSN 0312-844X
- Australia. Bureau of Statistics. Western Australian Office. Western Australia: Artificial Fertiliser Used on Rural Holdings. a. ISSN 0312-6269
- Australia. Bureau of Statistics. Western Australian Office. Western Australian Cereal Crop Forecast. a.
- Statistics of Western Australia. a. in parts. ISSN 0081-5187
- Western Australian Pocket Yearbook. a. ISSN 0083-8756
- Western Australian Yearbook. New Series. a. ISSN 0083-8772

**Australia. Australian Government Publishing Service**
P.O. Box 84, Canberra, A.C.T. 2600, Australia.
- Aboriginal News. bi-m. ISSN 0310-723X
- Australia. Advisory Committee on Research and Development in Education. Annual Report. a.
- Australia. Bureau of Meteorology. Bulletin. irreg., no. 49, 1974. ISSN 0067-1312
- Australia. Commission on Advanced Education. Report on Advanced Education. triennial.
- Australia. Department of Science. Antarctic Division. Report. a.
- Australia. Department of Social Security. Annual Report of the Director-General. a.
- Australia. Department of Territories. Territory of Norfolk Island; Report. irreg. ISSN 0572-0494
- Australia. Department of the Treasury. Income Tax Statistics. a. ISSN 0067-1444

- Australia. Department of the Treasury. Round-up of Economic Statistics. irreg. ISSN 0310-4230
- Australia. Department of the Treasury. Taxation Branch. Taxation Statistics. a. ISSN 0519-6035
- Australia. Fishing Industry Research Committee. Annual Report. a.
- Australia. Grants Commission. Grants Commission Report on Financial Assistance for Local Government. irreg.
- Australia. Industries Assistance Commission. Annual Report. a.
- Australia. Insurance Commissioner. Annual Report. a.
- Australia. Ionospheric Prediction Service. Annual Report. a.
- Australia. Metric Conversion Board. Annual Report. a.
- Australia. Public Service Board. Annual Report. a.
- Australia Handbook. a. ISSN 0067-1495
- Australian Government Directory. irreg.
- Australian Government Gazette. w.
- Australian Meteorological Magazine. q. ISSN 0004-9743
- Australian Research Grants Committee. Report. a.
- Australian Shipping and Shipbuilding. a.
- Australian Treaty Series. a.
- Australian Water Resources Council. Hydrological Series. irreg., no. 8, 1974. ISSN 0067-219X
- Australian Water Resources Council. Technical Paper Series. irreg., no. 8, 1974.
- Commonwealth Record. w.
- Compendium of Australian Public Service Information. s-a.
- Developments in Manufacturing Industry. q.
- Directory of Overseas Investment in Australian Manufacturing Industry. every 5 years; latest edition 1976. ISSN 0070-6043
- Quarterly Survey of Manufacturing Activity. q.
- Pesticides Review. s-a. ISSN 0572-0664
- Report on Australian Universities. irreg. ISSN 0085-5510
- Social Science. irreg. ISSN 0310-7353
- Transport Economics and Operational Analysis. irreg.
- Wool Outlook. s-a.

**Australia. Bureau of Agricultural Economics**
P.O. Box 1563, Canberra A.C.T. 2601, Australia.
- Australia. Bureau of Agricultural Economics. Coarse Grains: Situation and Outlook. a. ISSN 0311-0788
- Australia. Bureau of Agricultural Economics. Dairy: Situation and Outlook. a.
- Australia. Bureau of Agricultural Economics. Egg: Situation and Outlook. a.
- Australia. Bureau of Agricultural Economics. Fibre Review. a. ISSN 0311-2950
- Australia. Bureau of Agricultural Economics. Meat: Situation and Outlook. a. ISSN 0311-0885
- Australia. Bureau of Agricultural Economics. Occasional Papers. irreg.
- Australia. Bureau of Agricultural Economics. Oilseeds: Situation and Outlook. a.
- Australia. Bureau of Agricultural Economics. Statistical Handbook of the Meat Industry. a. ISSN 0310-0693
- Australia. Bureau of Agricultural Economics. Wheat: Situation and Outlook. s-a.
- Australia. Bureau of Agricultural Economics. Wool Economic Research Reports. irreg. ISSN 0571-9380
- Quarterly Review of Agricultural Economics. q. ISSN 0033-5754

**Australia. Bureau of Meteorology**
Publications Section, Box 1289 K, Melbourne, Vic. 3001, Australia.
- Australia. Bureau of Meteorology. Meteorological Study. irreg., no. 27, 1974. ISSN 0067-1320
- Australia. Bureau of Meteorology. Technical Report. irreg.

**Australia. Bureau of Mineral Resources, Geology & Geophysics**
Box 378, Canberra, A.C.T. 2601, Australia.
- Australia. Bureau of Mineral Resources, Geology and Geophysics. Bulletin. irreg. ISSN 0084-7089
- Australia. Bureau of Mineral Resources, Geology and Geophysics. Geophysical Observatory Group. Report.
- Australia. Bureau of Mineral Resources, Geology and Geophysics. Open File Circular. irreg.
- Australia. Bureau of Mineral Resources, Geology and Geophysics. Reports. irreg. ISSN 0084-7100

- Australia Mineral Industry Review. a. ISSN 0067-1509
- Australian Mineral Industry. Quarterly Review. q. ISSN 0004-9751
- B M R Journal of Australian Geology and Geophysics. q.

**Australia. Chamber of Industries. Northern Territory**
Director, P.O. Box 1409, Darwin, NT 5794, Australia.
- Australia. Chamber of Industries, Northern Territory. Northern Territory Business Journal. irreg. ISSN 0310-3811

**Australia. Department of Aboriginal Affairs**
Parliament House, Canberra, A.C.T. 2600, Australia.
- Australia. Department of Aboriginal Affairs. Report. irreg.

**Australia. Department of Agriculture**
Canberra, A.C.T. 2600, Australia.
- Australia. Department of Primary Industries. Annual Report on the Operation of the Fishing Industry Act. a. ISSN 0067-1436
- Australian Meat Research Committee. Annual Report. (pub. by Australian Meat Board)

**Australia. Department of Agriculture. Field Crops Division**
Canberra, A.C.T. 2600, Australia.
- Australian Tobacco Grower's Bulletin. irreg. ISSN 0567-1159 (prep. by its Tobacco Secretariat)

**Australia. Department of Agriculture. Fisheries Division**
Canberra, A.C.T. 2600, Australia.
- Australia. Department of Agriculture. Fisheries Report. irreg. ISSN 0084-7151
- Australian Fisheries Paper. irreg. ISSN 0084-7356

**Australia. Department of Construction**
17 Yarra St., Hawthorne, Vic. 3122, Australia.
- Comworks Technical Bulletin. q. ISSN 0310-1967
- Notes on the Science of Building. bi-m. ISSN 0300-371X

**Australia. Department of Defence. Army Office**
Canberra A.C.T. 2600, Australia.
- Defence Force Journal. m.

**Australia. Department of Defence. Defence Standardization Committee**
Victoria Barracks, Melbourne, Vic. 3004, Australia.
- Australia. Department of Defence. Standardization Newsletter. q.

**Australia. Department of Education**
P. O. Box 826, Woden, A.C.T. 2606, Australia.
- Australia. Department of Education. A.C.T. Education Directory. a. ISSN 0067-1355
- Australia. Department of Education. Migrant Education Program. a.
- Education News. bi-m. ISSN 0013-1431
- Hemisphere; Asian-Australian monthly. m. ISSN 0018-0300
- O. E. C. D. Activities in Education. irreg. (seasonal) ISSN 0311-2802

**Australia. Department of Education. Northern Territory Division**
Box 4821, Darwin N.T. 5794, Australia
- Developing Education. bi-m. ISSN 0310-5709 (Subscr. to: Australian Government Publishing Service, Box 364, Kingston, A.C.T. 2604, Australia)

**Australia. Department of Employment and Industrial Relations**
Box 2817AA, Melbourne, Vic. 3001, Australia.
- Australia. Department of Employment and Industrial Relations. Accession List.
- Australia. Department of Employment and Industrial Relations. Monthly Review of the Employment Situation. m.

**Australia. Department of Environment, Housing and Community Development**
Box 1890, Canberra City A.C.T. 2601, Australia.
- Building Industry Quarterly. q.

**Australia. Department of Foreign Affairs**
Canberra, A.C.T. 2600, Australia.
- Australia. Department of Foreign Affairs. International Treaties and Conventions. a. ISSN 0084-7135
- Australia. Department of Foreign Affairs. Select Documents on International Affairs. irreg. ISSN 0519-5950
- Australian Foreign Affairs Record. m. ISSN 0311-7995

**Australia. Department of Health**
Box 100, Woden, A. C. T. 2606, Australia.
- Animal Quarantine. 6 per yr.
- Food and Nutrition Notes and Reviews. bi-m. ISSN 0015-6329
- Health. q. ISSN 0046-7006
- Prescribers' Journal. irreg. ISSN 0085-5103

**Australia. Department of Health. Drugs of Dependence Section**
P.O. Box 100, Woden, A. C. T. 2606, Australia.
- Australia. National Drug Information Service. Technical Information Bulletin. irreg. ISSN 0310-6012

**Australia. Department of Housing and Construction**
Box 690, Canberra City A.C.T. 2601, Australia (Subscr. Address: Australian Government Publishing Service, Box 84, Canberra, A.C.T. 2600, Australia)
- Australia. Department of Housing and Construction. Annual Report. a.
- Australia. Department of Housing and Construction. Civil Works Program. a.
- Housing-Finance; lending terms and conditions. s-a. ISSN 0018-6635

**Australia. Department of Industry and Commerce**
Canberra, A.C.T. 2600, Australia
(Dist. by: Australian Government Publishing Service, Box 84, Canberra, A.C.T. 2600, Australia)
- Australia. Department of Industry and Commerce. Bulletin. irreg.

**Australia. Department of Labor and Immigration**
Canberra, Australia.
- Australian Transport Report. a.

**Australia. Department of Labor and Immigration. Apprenticeship Advisory Committee**
Box 2817 AA, Melbourne, Vic. 3000, Australia.
- Australian Apprenticeship Advisory Committee. Apprenticeship News. q. ISSN 0045-0243

**Australia. Department of Labor and Immigration. Women's Bureau**
Tivoli Court, 239-241 Bourke St., Box 2817AA GPO, Melbourne, Victoria, Australia.
- Comment. q.

**Australia. Department of Labour and National Service**
125 Swanston St., Melbourne C. 1, Vic., Australia.
- Australia. Department of Labour and National Service. Personnel Practice Bulletin. q.

**Australia. Department of National Resources. Australian Water Resources Council**
Box 5, Canberra, A.C.T. 2600, Australia
(Orders to: Australian Government Publishing Service, Box 84, Kingston, A.C.T. 2604, Australia)
- A W R C Activities. a. ISSN 0311-7979
- Australian Water Resources Council. Stream Gauging Information. every 5 years with annual supplement. ISSN 0067-2203
- Australian Water Resources Council. Water Resources Newsletter. bi-m. ISSN 0311-7987
- Inventory of Water Resources Research in Australia. a. after 1972. ISSN 0067-2211
- Review of Australia's Water Resources. irreg. ISSN 0080-1941

**Australia. Department of National Resources. Petroleum Branch**
G.P.O. Box 2831 AA, Melbourne 3001, Australia.
- Australia. Department of National Resources. Petroleum Branch. Petroleum Statistics. s-a.
- Australian Petroleum Statistics.

**Australia. Department of Overseas Trade**
424 St. Kilda Rd., Melbourne, Australia.
- Australian Trader. (pub. by Exportad Pty. Ltd.)
- Overseas Trading. fortn. ISSN 0030-7513

**Australia. Department of Overseas Trade. Central Statistical Section**
424 St. Kilde Rd., Melbourne, Australia.
- Australia. Department of Overseas Trade. Economic Indicators. q.

**Australia. Department of Police and Customs**
Public Relations Section, Barton, A.C.T. 2600, Australia.
- Australia. Department of Police and Customs. Review of Activities. a.

**Australia. Department of Primary Industry**
Canberra, A.C.T. 2600, Australia.
- Australia. Department of Primary Industry. Cotton Market News. m.
- Rural Industry Directory. a. ISSN 0067-2106

**Australia. Department of Primary Industry. Fisheries Division**
Canberra, A.C.T. 2600, Australia.
- Australian Fisheries. m. ISSN 0004-9115

**Australia. Department of Productivity. Human Relations Branch**
P.O. Box 2817AA, Melbourne, Vic. 3000, Australia.
- Work and People. q.

**Australia. Department of Science. Antarctic Division**
- Australia. Department of Science. Antarctic Division. Report. (pub. by Commonwealth Government Printing Office)

**Australia. Department of Social Security**
P.O. Box 1, Woden, A.C.T. 2606, Australia.
- Australian Department of Social Security. Social Security Quarterly. q. ISSN 0310-544X

**Australia. Department of the Capital Territory**
Botanic Gardens, Canberra, A.C.T. 2601, Australia.
- Growing Native Plants. a.

**Australia. Department of the Environment and Conservation**
Canberra, A.C.T. 2600, Australia.
- Australia. Department of the Environment and Conservation. Report. irreg.

**Australia. Department of the Media**
Canberra, Australia.
- Australia. Department of the Media. Annual Report. a.

**Australia. Department of the Navy. Hydrographic Service**
Sydney, Australia.
- Annual Summary of Australian Notices to Mariners. a.

**Australia. Department of the Northern Territory**
Mitchell St., Darwin, N.T. 5790, Australia.
- Australia. Northern Territory Division. Northern Territory Newsletter. m. ISSN 0045-0189

**Australia. Department of the Treasury**
Box 84, Canberra, A.C.T. 2600, Australia.
- Australia. Department of the Treasury. Treasury Economic Paper. a.
- Australian Economy. a. ISSN 0084-733X
- Australia's Overseas Development Assistance. a. ISSN 0312-9217

**Australia. Department of Tourism and Recreation**
8 Martin Place, Sydney, N.S.W. 2000, Australia.
- Australia. Department of Tourism. Farm Holidays. a. ISSN 0310-6276
- Australian Tourist Commission. Annual Report. a.
- National Fitness in Australia. a.

**Australia. Department of Transport. Air Safety Investigation Branch**
Box 1839q, Melbourne, Vic. 3001, Australia (Subscr. to: Australian Government Publishing Service, Box 84, Canberra 2600, Australia)
- Aviation Safety Digest. bi-m. ISSN 0045-1207

**Australia. Department of Transport. Air Transport Group**
Box 1839 Q,G. P.O., Melbourne 3001, Victoria, Australia.
- Australian International Air Transport Statistics. s-a.
- Domestic Air Transport Statistics. s-a.

**Australia. Department of Urban and Regional Development**
Canberra, Australia.
- Australia. Department of Urban and Regional Development. Annual Report. a.

**Australia. Department of Veterans' Affairs**
M. L. C. Tower, Woden, A.C.T. 2606, Australia.
- Medical Research Bulletin. irreg. ISSN 0025-7494

**Australia. Designs Office**
Canberra, A.C.T. 2600, Australia.
- Australia. Designs Office. Registered Owners of Designs and Articles in Respect of Which Designs Have Been Registered Under the Designs Act. irreg.

**Australia. Federal Catholic Education Office**
P.O. Box 1213, Canberra City, A.C.T. 2601, Australia.
- Australia. Federal Catholic Education Office. Information Bulletin. irreg.

**Australia. Fishing Industry Research Committee**
- Australia. Fishing Industry Research Committee. Annual Report. (pub. by Commonwealth Government Printing Office)

**Australia. Forestry and Timber Bureau**
Banks St., Yarralumla A.C.T. 2600, Australia.
- Timber Supply Review. q. ISSN 0040-778X

**Australia. Forestry and Timber Bureau. Division of Forest Research**
Banks St., Yarralumla, A. C. T. 2600, Australia.
- Forest Resources. a.

**Australia. Insurance Commissioner**
- Australia. Insurance Commissioner. Annual Report. (pub. by Commonwealth Government Printing Office)

**Australia. Ionospheric Prediction Service**
- Australia. Ionospheric Prediction Service. Annual Report. (pub. by Commonwealth Government Printing Office)

**Australia. Law Reform Commission**
Box 3708, Sydney, N. S. W. 2001, Australia.
- Australia. Law Reform Commission. Annual Report. a.
- Australia. Law Reform Commission. Report. irreg.
- Reform. q.

**Australia. National Capital Development Commission**
Box 373, Canberra City, A.C.T. 2601, Australia.
- Australia. National Capital Development Commission. Annual Report. a. ISSN 0067-1517
- Australia. National Capital Development Commission. Technical Papers. irreg.

**Australia. National Library of Australia**
Canberra, A.C.T. 2600, Australia.
- Australia. National Library. Acquisitions Newsletter. bi-m.
- Australia. National Library. Annual Report of the Council. a. ISSN 0069-0082
- Australian Books; Select List. a. ISSN 0067-1738
- Australian Government Publications. a. ISSN 0067-1878
- Australian Maps. q. ISSN 0045-0677
- Australian National Bibliography. w. (monthly, four-monthly & annual cumulations) ISSN 0004-9816
- Australian Public Affairs Information Service; subject index to current literature. m. ISSN 0005-0075
- Current Australian Serials. irreg. ISSN 0070-184X
- Guide to Manuscripts Relating to Australia. irreg. ISSN 0072-8578

**Australia. National Library of Australia. Australian Advisory Council on Bibliographical Services**
Canberra, Australia.
- Australian Advisory Council on Bibliographical Services. Library Services for Australia. a.

**Australia. National Library of Australia. Film Division**
Sales & Subscription Unit, Canberra, A.C.T. 2600, Australia.
- Australian Films. q. ISSN 0045-0448

**Australia. National Library of Australia. Resources Organizations and Development Branch**
Sales & Subscription Unit, Canberra, A.C.T. 2600, Australia.
- Australia. National Library. Indonesian Acquisitions. Daftar Permasukan Bahan Indonesia. irreg. (approx 6 per yr.)

**Australia. National Library of Australia. Selection, Acquisition and Processing Section**
Canberra, A.C.T. 2600, Australia.
- Indonesian Acquisitions List. m. ISSN 0310-6659

**Australia. Patent Office**
Canberra, A.C.T. 2600, Australia.
- Australia. Patent Office. Report. a.

**Australia. Post-Master General's Department. Stamps and Philatelic Section**
Australian Post Office Headquarters, Communications House, 199 William Street, Melbourne, Vic 3000., Australia
(Subscriptions to: Philatelic Mailing List, Post Office Box 259, S. Melbourne, Vic. 3205)
- Stamp Preview. irreg.

**Australia. Postmaster General's Department. Research Laboratories**
59 Collins St., Melbourne, Vic. 3000, Australia.
- Australia. Postmaster General's Department. Research Laboratories. Report. irreg.

**Australia. Public Service Board. Personnel Development Branch**
Box 391, Canberra City, A. C. T. 2601, Australia.
- Personnel Development News. bi-m.

**Australia. Repatriation Department**
Central Office, P.O. Box 21, Woden, A.C.T. 2606, Australia.
- Australia. Repatriation Department. Directory of Ex-Service Organisations. a. ISSN 0310-2173

**Australia. Social Welfare Commission**
P.O. Box 732, Queanbeyan, N.S.W. 2620, Australia.
- Australia. Social Welfare Commission. Annual Report. a.

**Australia and New Zealand Banking Group Ltd.**
351 Collins St., Melbourne 3000, Australia.
- A N Z Bank Business Indicators. m. ISSN 0004-850X
- A N Z Bank Quarterly Survey. q. ISSN 0001-2076

**Australia and South Pacific Temperance Council**
c/o T. A. Harwood, Ed., 198 Ann St., Brisbane, Qld. 4000, Australia.
- Australian Temperance Advocate. bi-m. ISSN 0005-0342

**Australia Indonesia Association of New South Wales**
Box 802, G.P.O. Sydney, NSW 2001, Australia.
- Kabar. irreg. ISSN 0311-0419

**Australia International Press**
Box 334, Camberwell 3124, Victoria, Australia.
- Australian Journal of Remedial Education. 4 per yr. ISSN 0311-1954 (Australian Remedial Education Association)

**Australia-Japan Economic Institute**
Suite 719, Australia Square, Sydney, N.S.W. 2000, Australia.
- Economic Bulletin. fortn.

**Australia-Japan Society-Ichido of New South Wales**
G.P.O. Box 3802, Sydney, NSW 2001, Australia.
- Australia-Japan Society-Ichido of New South Wales. irreg.

**Australia Mineral Development Laboratories**
Flemington St., Frewville, S.A. 5063, Australia.
- A M D E L Bulletin. 2 per yr. ISSN 0045-0707

**Australia Party. Victorian Branch**
P.O. Box 96, St. Kilda West, Vic. 3182, Australia.
- Action Report. irreg. ISSN 0311-2527

**Australian Academy of Forensic Sciences**
c/o Butterworths Pty. Ltd., 586 Pacific Highway, Chatswood, N.S.W. 2067, Australia.
- Australian Journal of Forensic Sciences. q. ISSN 0045-0618

**Australian Academy of Science**
Box 783, Civic Square, Canberra, A.C.T. 2608, Australia.
- Australian Academy of Science. Records. a. ISSN 0067-155X
- Australian Academy of Science. Report. irreg., no. 21, 1976. ISSN 0067-1568
- Australian Academy of Science. Science and Industry Forum Reports. irreg., no. 9, 1974. ISSN 0067-1576
- Australian Academy of Science. Year Book. a. ISSN 0067-1584
- Calendar of National and International Scientific Meetings to Be Held in Australia. s-a.

**Australian Academy of Science. National Committee for Antarctic Research**
Box 216, Civic Square, Canberra, A.C.T. 2608, Australia.
- Australian Academy of Science. National Committee for Antarctic Research. Australian Antarctic and Sub-Antarctic Research Programmes. irreg.

**Australian Academy of the Humanities**
- Australian Academy of the Humanities. Proceedings. (pub. by Sydney University Press)

**Australian Accounting Research Foundation**
49 Exhibition St., Melbourne, Vic. 3000, Australia.
- Australian Accounting Research Foundation. Research Studies. irreg. (Co-sponsors: Australian Society of Accountants; Institute of Chartered Accountants in Australia)

**Australian Agricultural Council**
- Australian Journal of Experimental Agriculture and Animal Husbandry. (pub. by C. S. I. R. O.)

**Australian Agricultural Economic Society**
Room 302, 191 Royal Parade, Parkville, 3052 Victoria, Australia.
- Australian Journal of Agricultural Economics. s-a. ISSN 0004-9395

**Australian Amateur Weight Lifting Federation**
P.O. Box 37, Rosanna, Vic. 3084, Australia.
- Australian Weight Lifting Journal. bi-m. ISSN 0310-5903

**Australian-American Association**
39-41 Lower Fort St., Sydney, Australia.
- Australian-American News N.S.W. Annual Edition.
- Pacific Neighbors. m. ISSN 0030-8781

**Australian and New Zealand American Studies Association**
c/o Dept. of American History, La Trobe University, Bundoora, Vic. 3083, Australia.
- A. N. Z. A. S. A. Bulletin. irreg. ISSN 0084-7194

**Australian and New Zealand Association for Medieval and Renaissance Studies**
Australian National University, c/o Dept. of English, School of General Studies, Canberra, A.C.T., Australia.
- Parergon. 3 per yr.

**Australian and New Zealand Association for the Advancement of Science**
Science House, 157 Gloucester St., Sydney, N.S.W. 2000, Australia.
- Search; science, technology and society. m. ISSN 0004-9549

**Australian and New Zealand Association of Bellringers**
25 Broadway, Camberwell, Vic. 3124, Australia.
- Ringing Towers. q.

**Australian and New Zealand College of Psychiatrists**
Maudsley House, 107 Rathdowne St., Carlton, Victoria 3053, Australia.
- Australian & New Zealand Journal of Psychiatry. q. ISSN 0004-8674

**Australian and New Zealand History of Education Society**
c/o B. Bessant, Ed., School of Education, La Trobe University, Bundoora, Vic. 3083, Australia.
- A. N. Z. H. E. S. Journal. s-a. ISSN 0311-3248

**Australian Anglers Association**
Australian Golf Services Pty. Ltd, 263 Oxford St., Darlinghurst N.S.W. 2010, Australia.
- Anglers' Digest. m. ISSN 0003-3235

**Australian Asphalt Pavement Association**
P.O. Box 185, Blackburn, Vic. 3130, Australia.
- A. A. P. A. Newsletter. q.

**Australian Associated Stock Exchanges**
- Australian Stock Exchange Journal. (pub. by Kralco Printing Co. Pty. Ltd.)

**Australian Association for Cultural Freedom**
181 Clarence St., Sydney 2000, Australia.
- Quadrant. m. ISSN 0033-5002

**Australian Association for Research in Education**
School of Education, University of New South Wales, Kensington, N.S.W. 2033, Australia.
- Australian Education Researcher. q.

**Australian Association for the Mentally Retarded**
Box 91, Brighton, S.A. 5048, Australia.
- Australian Citizen Limited. 3 per yr.

**Australian Association for the Teaching of English**
A.A.T.E. Publications Office, 163a Greenhill Rd., Parkside, S.A. 5063, Australia.
- A. A. T. E. Guide to English Books. a. ISSN 0084-7216
- English in Australia. 5 per yr. ISSN 0046-208X

**Australian Association of Adult Education**
Box 1346, P.O. Canberra City, A.C.T. 2601, Australia.
- Australian Association of Adult Education. Monograph. irreg., 1971, no. 2. ISSN 0067-1630
- Australian Association of Adult Education. Proceedings of the National Conference. a. ISSN 0067-1649
- Handbook of Australian Adult Education. triennial. ISSN 0072-971X

**Australian Association of Adult Education. Division of Postgraduate Extension Studies**
Box 1346, Canberra City, A.C.T. 2601, Australia.
- Australian Journal of Adult Education. 3 per yr. ISSN 0004-9387

**Australian Association of Mathematics Teachers**
c/o J. D. Burge, 51 Wattle Rd., Brookvale, N.S.W. 2100, Australia.
- Australian Mathematics Teacher. 4 per yr. ISSN 0045-0685

**Australian Association of Neurologists**
Suite 5, 5th Floor, The North Shore Medical Centre, 66-80 Pacific Highway, St. Leonards N.S.W. 2065, Australia.
- Australian Association of Neurologists Proceedings. a. ISSN 0084-7224

**Australian Association of Permanent Building Societies**
216 Northbourne Avenue, Canberra City, A. C. T. 2601, Australia.
- Australian Association of Permanent Building Societies. National Newsletter. bi-m. ISSN 0310-1045

**Australian Association of Social Workers**
Box 1059, North Richmond, Victoria 3121, Australia.
- Australian Social Work. q. ISSN 0312-407X

**Australian Association of Speech and Hearing**
P.O. Box 342, Carlton South, Victoria 3053, Australia.
- Australian Journal of Human Communication Disorders. s-a.

**Australian Association of Teachers of the Deaf**
- Australian Teacher of the Deaf. (pub. by Training Centre for Teachers of the Deaf)

**Australian Bank Officials Association**
Federal Office, La Trobe St., Melbourne, Vic. 3000, Australia.
- A. B. O. A. Newsletter. irreg. ISSN 0311-1032
- Australian Bank Officer. irreg.

**Australian Bank Officials Association. State Savings Bank of Victoria Division**
Editor, 4th Floor, 623 Collins St., Melbourne, Vic. 3000, Australia.
- Savings Weekly. fortn.

**Australian Bankers' Association. Research Directorate**
224 Queen St., Melbourne, Vic. 3000, Australia.
- Major Trading Bank Statistics. m.

**Australian Baptist Publishing Co.**
75 Bay St., Broadway 2007, New South Wales, Australia.
- Australian Baptist. fortn. ISSN 0004-8739

**Australian Biochemical Society**
c/o M. K. Gould, Biochemistry Dept., Monash University, Clayton, Victoria 3168, Australia.
- Australian Biochemical Society. Proceedings. a. ISSN 0067-1703

**Australian Book Publishers Association**
163 Clarence Street, Sydney, N.S.W. 2000, Australia.
- Guide to Book Outlets in Australia. a. ISSN 0310-2920

**Australian Book Review**
27 Park Rd., Kensington Park, Australia.
- Australian Book Review. m. ISSN 0004-8755

**Australian Boot Trade Employees Federation**
Trades Hall, Melbourne, Vic. 3000, Australia.
- Unity. irreg.

**Australian Brahman Breeders' Association**
P.O. Box 796, Rockhampton, Qld. 4700, Australia.
- Brahman News. q.

**Australian Breeders Service**
P. O. Box 53, Indooroopilly, Qld. 4068, Australia.
- Cattle. m. ISSN 0310-8279

**Australian Broadcasting Commission**
G.P.O. Box 487, Sydney 2001, N.S.W., Australia.
- A B C Radio Guide. w. ISSN 0001-0464
- Scan. fortn.
- T V Times. w. ISSN 0039-8608

**Australian Builder Publishing Co., Pty. Ltd.**
332-334 Albert St., East Melbourne, Australia.
- Australian Builder. m. ISSN 0004-878X (Master Builders Association of Victoria & Builders Exchange)

**Australian Bulletin of Labour**
c/o Joan Marshall, School of Social Sciences, Flinders Univ. of South Australia, Sturt Road, Bedford Park, S.A. 5042, Australia.
- Australian Bulletin of Labour. q.

**Australian Bureau of Statistics**
see **Australia. Australian Bureau of Statistics**

**Australian Catholic Historical Society**
Rev. C.J. Duffy, 108 Campbell St., Surry Hills 2010, Australia.
- Australian Catholic Historical Society. Journal. a. ISSN 0084-7259

**Australian Ceramic Society**
c/o Dept. Ceramic Engineering, University of New South Wales, Box 1, Kensington, N.S.W. 2033, Australia.
- Australian Ceramic Society. Journal. s-a. ISSN 0004-881X

**Australian Chamber of Commerce**
Commerce House, Barton, Canberra, Australia.
- Canberra Comments. m. ISSN 0045-561X

**Australian Chemical Engineering**
Box 250, North Sydney, N.S.W., Australia.
- Australian Chemical Engineering; a technical journal for chemical engineers. m. ISSN 0004-8828

**Australian Chess Federation**
9 Robert St., Belmore, N.S.W. 2192, Australia.
- Chess in Australia. m. ISSN 0009-3343

**Australian Chicken Meat Council**
- Poultry World. (pub. by Horticultural Press Pty. Ltd)

**Australian Chiropractors Association**
Suite 45, Office Tower, Shoppingtown, Indooroopilly, Qld., 4068, Australia.
- Australian Chiropractors Association. Journal. q. ISSN 0045-0359

**Australian Christian Endeavour Union Inc.**
Box 5093 G.P.O., Sydney 2001, New South Wales, Australia.
- A. C. E. (Australian Christian Endeavourer) bi-m. ISSN 0001-0642

**Australian Citrus Growers' Federation**
Room 46, 4th Floor, T & G Bldg., 82 King William St., Adelaide. S.A. 5000, Australia.
- Australian Citrus News. m. ISSN 0004-8283

**Australian Clay Target Association**
Box 2038, G.P.O., Melbourne, Vic. 3000, Australia.
- Australian Clay Target Shooting News. m.

**Australian Coal Industry Research Laboratories Ltd**
P.O. Box 169, Chatswood 2067, N.S.W, Australia.
- Australian Coal Industry Research Laboratories. Annual Report. a. ISSN 0067-1762

**Australian College of Education**
914 Swanston St., Carlton, Victoria 3053, Australia.
- Unicorn. 3 per yr. ISSN 0311-4775

**Australian College of Ophthalmologists**
27 Commonwealth St., Sydney, 2010 N.S.W., Australia.
- Australian Journal of Ophthalmology. a.

**Australian College of Paediatrics**
- Australian Paediatric Journal. (pub. by Royal Children's Hospital)

**Australian Comparative Education Society**
c/o Ron Fitzgerald, Ed., Box 210, Hawthorn, Vic. 3122, Australia.
- Australian Comparative Education Society. Newsletter. m. ISSN 0310-6500

**Australian Computer Society**
Box 63, Watson, A.C.T. 2602, Australia.
- Australian Computer Society. Council. Report. a. ISSN 0067-1819

**Australian Computer Society, Inc. Canberra Branch**
Box 258, Kingston, A.C.T. 2604, Australia.
- Canberra Computer Bulletin. m.

**Australian Computer Society Inc. New South Wales Branch**
P.O. Box N250, Grosvenor St., Sydney, N.S.W. 2000, Australia.
- A. C. S. Newsletter. m.

**Australian Computer Society, Inc. Queensland Branch**
G.P.O. Box 1484, Brisbane, Qld. 4001, Australia.
- Australian Computer Society. Queensland Branch. Newsletter. irreg.

**Australian Computer Society Inc. Victorian Branch**
Box 98, East Melbourne, Vic. 3002, Australia.
- Victorian Computer Bulletin. m. ISSN 0049-6138

**Australian Conservation Foundation**
364 Albert St., East Melbourne, Vic. 3002, Australia.
- A C F Newsletter. m. ISSN 0084-7283
- Australian Conservation Foundation. Annual Report. a. ISSN 0587-5846
- Australian Conservaton Foundation. Conservation Directory. irreg.
- Habitat. q.

**Australian Consolidated Press**
168 Castlereagh St., Sydney, Australia.
- Australian Home Journal; the complete homemaker magazine. m. ISSN 0004-9298
- Australian Women's Weekly. w. ISSN 0005-0458
- Bulletin. w. ISSN 0007-4039
- Cleo. m. ISSN 0310-1797

**Australian Consumers' Association**
26-30 Queen St., Chippendale, N.S.W. 2008, Australia.
- Choice. m. ISSN 0009-496X

**Australian Copyright Council**
252 George St, Sydney, N.S.W. 2000, Australia.
- Australian Copyright Council. Bulletin. irreg. ISSN 0311-2934

**Australian Council for Educational Research**
Box 210, Hawthorne, Vic. 3122, Australia.
- Australian Council for Educational Research. Educational Research Series. irreg.
- Australian Council for Educational Research. Occasional Papers. irreg. ISSN 0067-1835

- Australian Education Index. bi-m(annual cumulative no.) ISSN 0004-9026
- Australian Education Review. irreg.
- Australian Journal of Education. 3 per yr. ISSN 0004-9441
- Bulletin for Psychologists. irreg.
- I. E. A. (Australia) Report. irreg. ISSN 0310-558X
- International Association for the Evaluation of Educational Achievement (Australia). Newsletter. irreg. ISSN 0310-5571
- Serials in Education in Australian Libraries: a Union List. irreg. ISSN 0311-2373

**Australian Council for Educational Standards**
Box 169, Drysdale, Vic. 3222, Australia (Subscription to: Box 123, Parkville, Vic. 3052, Australia)
- A. C. E. S. Review. 10 per yr. ISSN 0310-9569

**Australian Council for Health, Physcial Education and Recreation**
c/o John Miller, Ed., P.O. Box 1, Kingswood S. A. 5062, Australia.
- Australian Journal for Health, Physical Education and Recreation. q. ISSN 0312-827X (Australian Physical Education Association)

**Australian Council for Overseas Aid**
Box 1562, Canberra City, A.C.T. 2601, Australia.
- Development News Digest. q.

**Australian Council of Social Service**
Box 388, Haymarket, N.S.W. 2000, Australia.
- Australian Journal of Social Issues. q. ISSN 0004-9557
- Australian Social Welfare. q.

**Australian Council of Trade Unions**
254 la Trobe St., Melbourne, Vic. 3000, Australia.
- Australian Congress of Trade Unions. Decisions. biennial.

**Australian Council on Ageing**
Box 1817Q, Melbourne, Vic. 3001, Australia.
- Growing Older. q. ISSN 0046-6492

**Australian Council on Awards in Advanced Education**
P.O. Box 826, Woden, A.C.T. 2606, Australia.
- Australian Council on Awards in Advanced Education. Bulletin. irreg. ISSN 0311-3000

**Australian Cricket Society**
- Extra Cover. (pub. by Thomas W. Williams & Associates Pty. Ltd.)

**Australian Cricket Society. A. C. T. Branch**
91 Gouger Street, Torrens, A. C. T. 2607, Australia.
- Cricket Quadrant. irreg. ISSN 0310-9356

**Australian Crime Prevention Council**
No. 1 Carmel Court, Rio Vista, Qld. 4217, Australia.
- Australian Crime Prevention Council. National Conference. Proceedings. biennial.
- Australian Crime Prevention Council. National Newsletter. irreg.

**Australian Croquet Council**
Unit 3, 1 Panmure Place, Woodville North, S.A. 5012, Australia.
- Australian Croquet Gazette. bi-m.

**Australian Dental Association**
116 Pacific Highway, Box 411, North Sydney, N.S.W. 2060, Australia.
- Australian Dental Journal. bi-m. ISSN 0045-0421

**Australian Dental Association. Western Australian Branch**
14 Altona St., West Perth, W.A. 6005, Australia.
- Australian Dental Association. Dental Bulletin. 10 per yr.

**Australian Dried Fruits Association**
Box 4524, Melbourne 3001, Australia.
- Australian Dried Fruit News. 5 per yr.

**Australian Drug Information Services Pty. Ltd.**
P. O. Box 194, Balgowlah, Sydney, NSW 2093, Australia.
- Drugs; international journal of current therapeutics and applied pharmacology reviews, featuring evaluations on new drugs, review articles on drugs and therapy, and drug literature abstracts. m. ISSN 0012-6667

**Australian Electric Traction Association**
Publishing Dept., Box 1017, Sydney, N.S.W. 2001, Australia.
- Electric Traction. m. ISSN 0013-4163

**Australian Entomological Society**
c/o Department of Entomology, University of Queensland, St. Lucia, Qld 4067, Australia.
- Australian Entomological Society. Journal. q. ISSN 0004-9050
- Australian Entomological Society. Miscellaneous Publications. irreg.
- Australian Entomological Society. News Bulletin. q.

**Australian Esperanto Association**
Box 415, Manly, NSW 2095, Australia.
- Australian Esperantist. irreg.

**Australian Farm Management Society**
13th Floor, O'Connell House, 15 Bent Street, Sydney, N.S.W. 2000, Australia.
- Australian Farm Management Society Newsletter. m(10 per yr) ISSN 0311-8665

**Australian Federation of Air Pilots**
136 Albert Rd., South Melbourne, Vic. 3205, Australia.
- Australian Air Pilot. irreg.

**Australian Federation of Modern Languages Teachers Associations**
c/o Language Centre, University of Melbourne, Parkville. 3052, Victoria, Australia.
- Babel. 3 per yr. ISSN 0005-3503

**Australian Federation of University Women**
c/o Women's College, College Rd., St. Lucia, Qld. 4067, Australia.
- Australian Federation of University Women. Newsletter. q.

**Australian Federation of Wizo**
584 St. Kilda Road, Melbourne, Vic. 3004, Australia.
- Wizo Review. irreg.

**Australian Fish Trades Review**
24 Henry St., Carlton N.S.W. 2218, Australia.
- Australian Fish Trades Review. bi-m. ISSN 0004-9107

**Australian Flying Corps and Royal Australian Air Force Association**
213 Clarence St., Sydney, Australia.
- Wings. q. ISSN 0043-5880

**Australian Forest Industries Journal Pty. Ltd.**
243 Elizabeth St., Sydney 2000, Australia.
- Australian Forest Industries Journal. m.

**Australian Forestry Council**
Director-General, Forestry and Timber Bureau, Banks St., Yarralumla, A.C.T. 2600, Australia.
- Australian Forestry Council. Forest Resources Newsletter. a.

**Australian Foundry Institute**
- Castings. (pub. by F. W. Publications)

**Australian Frontier**
Dairy Industry House, 4th Floor, 576 St. Kilda Road, Melbourne, Vic. 3000, Australia.
- Australian Frontier Newsletter. irreg.

**Australian Gas Association**
P.O. Box 155, Civic Square, Canberra, A.C.T. 2608, Australia.
- Australian Gas Journal. q. ISSN 0004-9166
- Directory of the Australian Gas Industry. a.

**Australian Geography Teachers' Association**
C/O Geographical Society of New South Wales, Science House, Gloucester Street, Sydney, 2000, Australia.
- Geographical Education. a. ISSN 0085-0969

**Australian Group for the Scientific Study of Mental Deficiency**
c/o Childrens Cottages, Princess St., Kew, Vic. 3101, Australia.
- Australian Journal of Mental Retardation. q. ISSN 0045-0634

**Australian Guild of Professional Cooks**
Box 1073J, G.P.O., Melbourne, Vic. 3001, Australia.
- Culinary Times. q. ISSN 0011-2739

**Australian Hereford Society Ltd.**
62 Astor Terrace, Brisbane 4001, Australia.
- Hereford Quarterly. q. ISSN 0311-2144

**Australian Hi-Fi Publications Pty. Ltd.**
Box 341, Mona Vale, N.S.W. 2103, Australia.
- Australian Hi-Fi. bi-m.
- Australian Hi-Fi Annual. a. ISSN 0310-8902

**Australian Hockey Association**
c/o Amateur Sports Club, 12-14 McKillop St., Melbourne, Victoria 3000, Australia.
- Hockey Circle. m.(May-Sep.) ISSN 0018-2982

**Australian Honey Board**
647 George St., Sydney, N.S.W., Australia.
- Australian Honey Board. Annual Report. a. ISSN 0067-1894

**Australian Hospital Association**
Herbert St., St. Leonards, N.S.W. 2065, Australia.
- Australian Hospital Newsletter. irreg. ISSN 0084-7410

**Australian Hotels Association**
New South Wales Branch, 60 Clarence St., Sydney 2000, Australia.
- A. H. A. Review. m. ISSN 0001-1398

**Australian Hotels Association. South Australian Branch**
41 King William St., Adelaide, Australia.
- Hotel Gazette of South Australia. m. ISSN 0018-6139

**Australian Hotels Association. Tasmanian Branch**
c/o C.M. Cannan, 82 Harrington St., Hobart, Tas. 7000, Australia.
- Tasmanian Hotel Review. m. ISSN 0049-3023

**Australian Hotels Association. Victoria Branch**
A. H. A. House, 130-132 Flinders St., Melbourne, Vic. 3000, Australia.
- Hotel and Catering. m.

**Australian Hotels Association. Western Australia Branch**
438 Vincent St., Leederville, W.A. 6007, Australia.
- Hotel Review. bi-m. ISSN 0018-6228
- Licensed Retailer. m. ISSN 0024-2780

**Australian Industries Development Association**
P.O. Box 1576, Canberra City, A. C. T. 2601, Australia.
- A. I. D. A. Bulletin. 11 per yr.

**Australian Inland Mission Frontier Service**
Australian Inland Mission, Box 100, Sydney, N.S.W., Australia.
- Frontier News. 3 per yr. ISSN 0016-2108

**Australian Institute of Aboriginal Studies**
Box 553, Canberra 2601, Australia.
- A.I.A.S. Newsletter. s-a. ISSN 0004-9344
- Australian Aboriginal Studies. irreg. ISSN 0004-9344
- Australian Institute of Aboriginal Studies: Research and Regional Studies. irreg.

**Australian Institute of Agricultural Science**
191 Royal Pde., Ro 302, Parkville, Vic. 3052, Australia.
- Australian Institute of Agricultural Science. Journal. q. ISSN 0045-0545
- Australian Society of Animal Production. Proceedings. biennial. ISSN 0067-2149

**Australian Institute of Archaeology**
174 Collins St., Melbourne 3000, Victoria, Australia.
- Buried History; a quarterly journal of biblical archaeology. q. ISSN 0007-6260

**Australian Institute of Building**
- Chartered Builder. (pub. by Magazine Art Pty. Ltd.)

**Australian Institute of Cartographers**
Box 1292, Canberra City, A.C.T. 2601, Australia.
- Cartography. s-a. ISSN 0069-0805

**Australian Institute of Construction Supervisors**
- Construction Supervisor. (pub. by Percival Publishing Co. Pty. Ltd.)

**Australian Institute of Credit Management**
Box 492 H, Melbourne 3001, Australia.
- Credit Review. bi-m.

**Australian Institute of Credit Management. Victorian Division**
c/o Ley Pulford & Co., 37 Swanston St., Melbourne, Vic. 3000, Australia.
- Credit Scene. bi-m. ISSN 0311-029X

**Australian Institute of Criminology**
Box 28, Woden, A.C.T. 2606, Australia.
- Australian Information Bulletin. 4 per yr.

**Australian Institute of Dairy Factory Managers and Secretaries**
14 Rangeview Grove, Mitcham, Vic. 3132, Australia.
- Australian Institute of Dairy Factory Managers and Secretaries. Butter Fats and Solids. q. ISSN 0045-0553

**Australian Institute of Drycleaning**
- Australian National Drycleaner. (pub. by Acorn Publishing Co. Pty. Ltd.)

**Australian Institute of Engineering Associates**
Box 408, North Sydney, N.S.W. 2060, Australia (Subscription to: Box 132, Hamilton, N.S.W. 2303, Australia)
- Engineering Associate. q. ISSN 0311-1008

**Australian Institute of Hospital Administrators**
- Australian Hospital. (pub. by Peter Isaacson Publications)

**Australian Institute of International Affairs**
124-6 Jolimont Rd., East Melbourne, Victoria, Australia.
- Australian Outlook. 3 per yr. ISSN 0004-9913
- Dyason House Papers; Australia, Asia and the World. 5 per yr.

**Australian Institute of Management**
Suite 6, 476 St. Kilda Rd., Melbourne 3004, Australia.
- Management Australia. bi-m. ISSN 0025-1712
- Management Diary. m. ISSN 0045-057X

**Australian Institute of Management. New South Wales Division**
135 Walker St., North Sydney, NSW 2060, Australia.
- A. I. M. News. irreg.

**Australian Institute of Marine and Power Engineers**
14 Quay St., Sydney 2000, Australia.
- On Watch. q. ISSN 0030-2392

**Australian Institute of Metals**
191 Royal Parade, Parkville, Vic. 3052, Australia.
- Australian Institute of Metals. Proceedings of the Annual Conference. a.

**Australian Institute of Navigation**
Box 2250 G.P.O, Sydney, N.S.W, Australia.
- Navigation. a. ISSN 0077-6262

**Australian Institute of Parks & Recreation**
Box 18, Northcote, Victoria 3070, Australia.
- Australian Parks & Recreation. q. ISSN 0311-8223

**Australian Institute of Petroleum Ltd.**
227 Collins St., Melbourne, Vic. 3000, Australia.
- Oil and Australia; the figures behind the facts. a. ISSN 0472-7584
- Petroleum Gazette. q. ISSN 0048-3591
- Petroleum Search in Australia. bienniel. ISSN 0085-4859

**Australian Institute of Physics**
Science Centre, 35-43 Clarence St, Sydney, N.S.W. 2000, Australia.
- Australian Physicist. m. ISSN 0004-9972

**Australian Institute of Political Science**
4Th Floor, Broughton House, 181 Clarence St., Sydney, N.S.W. 2000, Australia.
- Australian Quarterly. q. ISSN 0005-0091

**Australian Institute of Refrigeration, Air Conditioning and Heating, Inc**
- Australian Refrigeration, Air Conditioning and Heating. (pub. by Page Publications Pty. Ltd.)

**Australian Institute of Steel Construction**
118 Alfred St., Milsons Point, N.S.W. 2061, Australia.
- Steel Construction. q. ISSN 0049-2205
- Steel Fabrication Journal. q. ISSN 0311-015X

**Australian Institute of Urban Studies**
P.O. 809, Canberra A.C.T. 2601, Australia.
- Australian Urban Studies. q.
- Bibliography of Urban Studies in Australia. a.

**Australian Institute of Urban Studies. Queensland Division**
c/o Department of Geography, University of Queensland, St. Lucia, Qld. 4067, Australia (Subscription Address: Hon. Secretary, AIUS (Qld Division), G.P.O. Box 1989, Brisbane, Qld. 4001)
- Urban Issues. irreg.

**Australian Institute of Valuers**
Cattra House, 119-123 York St., Sydney, N.S.W. 2000, Australia.
- Valuer. q. ISSN 0042-241X

**Australian Institute of Weights and Measures**
- Weights and Measures Review. (pub. by Thomas W. Williams & Associates Pty. Ltd.)

**Australian Institution of Refrigeration, Air Conditioning and Heating**
- Refrigeration Annual. (pub. by Page Publications Pty. Ltd.)

**Australian Insurance Institute**
87 King St., Melbourne, Vic. 3000, Australia.
- Australian Insurance Institute. Journal. a. ISSN 0084-7453

**Australian Jaycees**
P.O. Box 356, Hawthorn, Vic. 3122, Australia.
- Australian Jaycees National Directory. a.
- Enterprise. 10 per yr.

**Australian Jersey Herd Society**
Box 97, North Melbourne, Vic. 3051, Australia.
- Australian Jersey Journal. m. ISSN 0045-0588

**Australian Jewish Historical Society**
166 Castlereagh St., Sydney 2000 N.S.W, Australia.
- Australian Jewish Historical Society. Journal and Proceedings. s-a. ISSN 0004-9360

**Australian Jewish Times**
c/o Louis Klein, 140 Darlinghurst Rd., Darlinghaust 2010, Australia.
- Australian Jewish Times. w.

**Australian Jewish Welfare and Relief Society**
466 Punt Rd., South Yarra, Vic. 3141, Australia.
- Welcare. bi-m. ISSN 0310-6969

**Australian Jockey Club**
Randwick Racecourse, Alison Rd., Randwick, N.S.W. 2031, Australia.
- Australian Turf Register. a. ISSN 0084-7615

**Australian Journalists' Association**
93 Clarence St., Sydney, 2000 Australia.
- Journalist. m. ISSN 0022-5584

**Australian Journalists' Association. Western Australia District**
104 St. George's Terrace, Perth, WA 6000, Australia.
- Scribe. irreg.

**Australian Labor Party. Australian Capital Territory Branch**
Box 918, Civic Square, Canberra City, A. C. T. 2608, Australia.
- Australian Labor Party. A. C. T. Branch. Newsletter. irreg. ISSN 0310-785X

**Australian Labor Party. New South Wales Branch**
c/o P.B. Westaway, 377-383 Sussex St., Sydney, N.S.W. 2000, Australia.
- Australian Labor Party. A.L.P. 10 per yr. ISSN 0045-0669
- Radical. bi-m.

**Australian Labor Party. Western Australia Branch**
Room 21, Trades Hall, Perth, Australia.
- Western Sun. m. ISSN 0043-423X

**Australian Ladies Golf Union**
Mrs. K. D. Brown, Honorary Secretary, 22 McKay Road, Rowville, Vic. 3178, Australia.
- Australian Ladies Golf Union. Official Yearbook. a.

**Australian Language Research Centre**
University of Sydney, c/o Secretary, Dept. of English, Sydney, N.S.W. 2006, Australia.
- University of Sydney. Australian Language Research Centre. Occasional Papers. irreg. ISSN 0042-0093

**Australian Law Librarians' Group**
c/o Box 1, Kensington, N.S.W. 2033, Australia.
- Australian Law Librarians' Group. Newsletter. bi-m.

**Australian Lead Development Association**
95 Collins St., Melbourne, Vic. 3000, Australia.
- Lead Battery Power. irreg.

**Australian League of Rights**
273 Little Collins St., Melbourne, Victoria 3001, Australia.
- Intelligence Survey. m. ISSN 0047-0406

**Australian Left Review**
Box A247, South P.O., 2000 Sydney N.S.W., Australia.
- Australian Left Review; a Marxist journal of information analysis and discussion. 10 per yr. ISSN 0004-9638

**Australian Legal Aid Review Committee**
187 Macquarie St., Sydney, N.S.W. 2000, Australia.
- Australian Legal Aid Review Committee. Report. a.

**Australian Library Promotions Council**
State Library of Victoria, 328 Swanston St., Melbourne, Vic. 3000, Australia.
- Bookmark. a. ISSN 0310-0391

**Australian Liquified Petroleum Gas Association**
12 O'Connel St., Sydney, N.S.W. 2000, Australia.
- Liquified Petroleum Gas. bi-m. ISSN 0047-4754

**Australian Litho Club**
- Australian Lithographer, Printer, and Packager. (pub. by Prestige Publishing Pty. Ltd.)

**Australian Littoral Society**
Box 82, St. Lucia, Qld. 4067, Australia.
- Operculm. s-a.

**Australian Mammal Society**
c/o Department of Zoology, Australian National University, Canberra, A.C.T. 2600, Australia.
- Australian Mammalogy. irreg. ISSN 0310-0049

**Australian Map Curators Circle**
Melbourne, Vic., Australia.
- Globe. irreg.

**Australian Mathematical Society**
- Australian Mathematical Society. Bulletin. (pub. by University of Queensland. Dept. of Mathematics)
- Australian Mathematical Society. Journal. (pub. by University of Queensland. Dept. of Mathematics)

**Australian Meat Board**
Box 4129, Sydney, N.S.W. 2001, Australia.
- Australian Meat Board. Meat Producer and Exporter. m. ISSN 0045-0693
- Australian Meat Research Committee. Annual Report. a. (Australia. Department of Agriculture)

**Australian Meat Research Committee**
30 Grosvenor St., Sydney, N.S.W. 2000, Australia.
- A. M. R. C. Review. bi-m. ISSN 0311-0842

**Australian Medical Association**
71-79 Arundel St., Glebe, N.S.W. 2037, Australia.
- A M A Gazette. (pub. by Australasian Medical Publishing Co.)
- Medical Journal of Australia. w. ISSN 0025-729X

**Australian Mensa Inc.**
P.O. Box 272, Mascot, N.S.W. 2020, Australia.
- Tableaus. irreg.

**Australian Metal Trades Export Group**
National Office, 105 Walker St., North Sydney, NSW 2060, Australia.
- A M T E G's Export Note Pad. irreg.

**Australian Meteorological Association**
c/o T. G. Keen, 10 Hill St., Burnside, S.A. 5066, Australia
- Monana. irreg. (Dist. by I. Mills, 50 Highland Drive, Bellevue Heights, SA 5050, Australia)

**Australian Mineral Foundation**
Conyngham St., Glenside, S.A., Australia.
- Earth Science and Related Information; selected annotated titles. m.

**Australian Mineral Industries Research Association**
Clunies Ross House, 191 Royal Parade, Parkville, Victoria 30502, Australia.
- Australian Mineral Industries Research Association. Bulletin. irreg., no. 6, 1976.
- Australian Mineral Industries Research Association Limited. Non-Confidential Research Information. a.

**Australian Mining Industry Council**
P. O. Box 363, Dickson, A.C.T. 2602, Australia.
- E Q B. irreg.

**Australian Model Railway Association**
Box 46, Nunawading, Vic. 3131, Australia.
- A.M.R.A. Journal. bi-m. ISSN 0045-0715

**Australian Museum**
6-8 College St., Sydney, N.S.W. 2000, Australia.
- Australian Museum, Sydney. Memoirs. irreg., 1966, no. 12. ISSN 0067-1967
- Australian Museum, Sydney. Records. irreg. ISSN 0067-1975
- Australian Natural History. q. ISSN 0004-9840
- Coral Reef Newsletter. irreg. (Pacific Science Association) (Co-sponsor: Scientific Committee on Coral Reefs)

**Australian National Association for Mental Health**
R.P.A.H. Medical Center, 100 Carillon Ave., Newtown, N.S.W. 2042, Australia.
- Mental Health in Australia. s-a. ISSN 0025-9667

**Australian National Cat Federation**
P.O. Box 135, Claremont, W. A. 6010, Australia.
- National Cat Journal. b-m.

**Australian National Committee on Large Dams**
c/o Australian Department of Housing Construction, Box 2007AA, Melbourne, Vic. 3001, Australia.
- A N C O L D Bulletin. 3 per yr. ISSN 0045-0731

**Australian National University**
Box 4, Canberra A.C.T. 2600, Australia.
- Australian National University News. 3 per yr. ISSN 0004-9832
- Canberra Poetry. s-a.
- Journal of Pacific History. s-a. ISSN 0022-3344 (Published Under the Imprint of: Oxford University Press)

**Australian National University. Centre for Continuing Education**
Box 4, Canberra, A.C.T. 2600, Australia.
- Canberra Papers in Continuing Education. irreg. ISSN 0310-1649

**Australian National University. Computer Centre**
Box 4, Canberra, A.C.T. 2600, Australia.
- Australian National University, Canberra. Computer Centre. Technical Report. irreg., 1970, no. 36. ISSN 0067-2009

**Australian National University. Department of Far Eastern History**
Canberra, A.C.T. 2600, Australia.
- Papers on Far Eastern History. s-a. ISSN 0048-2870

**Australian National University. Department of International Relations**
Canberra, Australia.
- Australian National University, Canberra. Department of International Relations. Documents and Data Paper. irreg. ISSN 0067-2017
- Australian National University, Canberra. Department of International Relations. Workpaper. irreg., no. 10, 1969. ISSN 0067-2025

**Australian National University. Department of Pacific and Southeast Asian History**
Canberra, Australia.
- Asian Studies Association of Australia. Newsletter. 3 per yr.

**Australian National University. Department of Political Science**
Box 4, Canberra, A.C.T. 2600, Australia
(Dist. in U.S. by International Scholarly Book Services, P.O. Box 4347, Portland, Ore. 97208)
- Australian National University, Canberra. Department of Political Science. Occasional Paper. irreg., no. 9, 1974. ISSN 0067-2033

**Australian National University. Department of Pure Mathematics**
P.O. Box 4, Canberra, 2600, Australia.
- Notes in Pure Mathematics. irreg.

**Australian National University. Faculty of Asian Studies**
Box 4, P.O., Canberra City, A.C.T. 2600, Australia.
- Australian National University, Canberra. Asian Publications Series. (pub. by Australian National University Press)
- Australian National University, Canberra. Faculty of Asian Studies. Occasional Papers. irreg. ISSN 0067-2041

**Australian National University. Forestry Department**
Canberra, A.C.T. 2600, Australia.
- Forestry Log. a. (prep. by its Forestry Students Society)

**Australian National University. Geology Department**
Box 4, Canberra, A.C.T. 2600, Australia.
- Australian National University, Canberra. Geology Department. Publication. irreg. ISSN 0084-750X

**Australian National University Gliding Club**
- Soaring in the A.C.T. (pub. by Canberra Gliding Club)

**Australian National University. Historical Society**
Box 1112, Canberra, A.C.T. 2601, Australia.
- A N U Historical Journal. irreg. ISSN 0001-2068

**Australian National University Press**
P.O. Box 4, Canberra A.C.T. 2001, Australia.
- Arthur F. Yencken Memorial Lectures. biennial.
- Australian National University, Canberra. Asian Publications Series. irreg. ISSN 0067-1991
- George Ernest Morrison Lectures in Ethnology. irreg. ISSN 0072-1190 (Dist. in U.S. by: International Scholarly Book Services, Inc., Box 4347, Portland, OR 97208)
- International Gondwana Symposium. Papers. irreg.

**Australian National University. Research School of Biological Sciences**
Box 4, Canberra, A.C.T. 2600, Australia.
- Australian National University, Canberra. Research School of Biological Sciences. Annual Report. irreg.

**Australian National University. Research School of Pacific Studies**
Box 4, P.O., Canberra 2600, Australia
(and University of Papua and New Guinea, Box 1144, Boroko, Papua New Guinea)
- Bulletin of Indonesian Economic Studies. 3 per yr. ISSN 0007-4918
- New Guinea Research Bulletin. 3 per yr. (prep. by its New Guinea Research Unit)
- Pacific Linguistics. Series A: Occasional Papers. irreg., no. 46, 1976. ISSN 0078-7531 (Linguistic Circle of Canberra)
- Pacific Linguistics. Series B: Monographs. irreg., no. 46, 1976. ISSN 0078-754X (Linguistic Circle of Canberra)
- Pacific Linguistics. Series C: Books. irreg., no. 50, 1976. ISSN 0078-7558 (Linguistic Circle of Canberra)
- Pacific Linguistics. Series D: Special Publications. irreg., no. 27, 1976. ISSN 0078-7566 (Linguistic Circle of Canberra)
- Papers in Australian Linguistics. no. 9, 1976. ISSN 0078-9062 (Linguistic Circle of Canberra)
- Papers in Borneo Linguistics. irreg., 1969, no. 1. ISSN 0078-9070 (Linguistic Circle of Canberra)
- Papers in Linguistics of Melanesia. irreg. ISSN 0078-9127 (Linguistic Circle of Canberra)
- Papers in New Guinea Linguistics. irreg., no. 19, 1976. ISSN 0078-9135 (Linguistic Circle of Canberra)
- Papers in Philippine Linguistics. irreg., no. 8, 1976. ISSN 0078-9143 (Linguistic Circle of Canberra)
- Papers in South East Asian Linguistics. irreg., no. 3, 1973. ISSN 0078-9178 (Linguistic Circle of Canberra)
- Waigani Seminar. Papers. a. ISSN 0085-7866

**Australian National University. Research School of Physical Sciences**
Dept. of Engineering Physics, Box 4, Canberra, A.C.T. 2600, Australia.
- Australian National University, Canberra. Department of Engineering Physics. Publication Ep-Rr. irreg. ISSN 0084-7496
- Australian National University, Canberra. Research School of Physical Sciences. Research Paper. irreg. ISSN 0084-7518

**Australian National University. Students' Association**
Canberra, A. C. T. 2600, Australia.
- Woroni. irreg.

**Australian Natives Association**
28 Elizabeth St., Melbourne, Vic. 3000, Australia.
- Anapress. q. ISSN 0044-8206

**Australian Numismatic Society**
Box 3644 G.P.O., Sydney N.S.W. 2001, Australia.
- Australian Numismatic Society. Report. m. ISSN 0004-9883

**Australian Oil & Colour Chemists Association**
c/o D.S. Myles, 44 Beaver St., Malvern East, Vic. 3145, Australia.
- Australian O.C.C.A. Proceedings and News. m. ISSN 0045-0774

**Australian Optometrical Association**
26 Nithsdale St., Sydney, N.S.W. 2000, Australia.
- Australian Journal of Optometry. m. ISSN 0045-0642

**Australian Performing Right Association**
P.O. Box 291, Crows Nest, N.S.W., Sydney 2000, Australia.
- A P R A Journal. s-a. ISSN 0001-2246

**Australian Petroleum Exploration Association**
Box 834, Sydney, N.S.W. 2001, Australia.
- A. P. E. A. Journal. a. ISSN 0084-7534

**Australian Physical Education Association**
- Australian Journal for Health, Physical Education and Recreation. (pub. by Australian Council for Health, Physcial Education and Recreation)

**Australian Physiological and Pharmacological Society (APPS)**
c/o W. Burke, Department of Physiology, University of Sydney, Sydney, N.S.W. 2006, Australia.
- Australian Physiological and Pharmacological Society. Proceedings. 2 per yr. ISSN 0067-2084

**Australian Physiotherapy Association**
- Australian Journal of Physiotherapy. (pub. by A. H. Massina & Co. Pty. Ltd.)

**Australian Pig Breeders' Society**
P.O. Box 189, Kiama, NSW 2533, Australia.
- Australian Stud Pig Herd Book. a.

**Australian Pre-School Association. Victorian Branch**
- Australian Pre-School Association. Victorian Branch. Newsletter. (pub. by Grennan Publication)

**Australian Press Services Pty., Ltd.**
Box E160, Canberra, A.C.T. 2600, Australia.
- Canberra Survey. m. ISSN 0045-5628
- Inside Canberra. w. ISSN 0046-9629
- Money Matters. w.

**Australian Psychological Society**
National Science Centre, 191 Royal Parade, Parkville, Victoria 3052, Australia.
- Australian Journal of Psychology. 3 per yr. ISSN 0004-9530
- Australian Psychologist. (pub. by University of Queensland Press)

**Australian Racing Drivers Club**
360 Norton St., Leichhardt, NSW 2040, Australia.
- Australian Racing Drivers Club Journal. irreg. ISSN 0311-0346

**Australian Railway Historical Society**
Box E129, St. James, N.S.W., Australia.
- Australian Railway Historical Society. Bulletin. m. ISSN 0005-0105

**Australian Railways Union**
- Australian Railways Union. Federal Office News. (pub. by Percival Publishing Co. Pty. Ltd.)

**Australian Remedial Education Association**
- Australian Journal of Remedial Education. (pub. by Australia International Press)

**Australian Road Research Board**
500 Burwood Rd., Vermont, Victoria 3133, Australia.
- Australian Road Research. q. ISSN 0005-0164
- Australian Road Research Board. Proceedings. a. ISSN 0572-1431

**Australian Road Transport Federation**
Third Floor, 19 Hunter St., Sydney, N.S.W. 2000, Australia.
- Australian Road Transport Federation. A. R. T. F. Digest. m. ISSN 0045-0839

**Australian School Library Association**
P.O. Box 118, Carlton, 3053 Australia.
- School Libraries in Australia. q.

**Australian Science Education Research Association**
Faculty of Education, Monash University, Clayton, Vic. 3168, Australia.
- Australian Science Education Research Association. Research in Science Education. a.

**Australian Science Fiction Association**
Box 4440, Sydney, N.S.W. 2001, Australia.
- Science Fiction News. bi-m.

**Australian Science Teachers Association**
c/o ACER, Box 210, Hawthorn, Vic. 3122, Australia.
- Australian Science Teachers' Journal. 3 per yr. ISSN 0045-0855

**Australian Seed Producers Federation**
c/o the Secretary, 69 French St., Hamilton 3300, Australia.
- Australian Seed Producers Review. s-a.

**Australian Shareholders Association**
N.S.W. Branch, Box 5210, G.P.O., Sydney, Australia.
- Shareholder. q. ISSN 0037-3311

**Australian Shipping Officers' Association**
6Th Floor, 249 George St., Sydney, N.S.W. 2000, Australia.
- Manifest. q. ISSN 0310-334X

**Australian Ski Federation**
P.O. Box 21, Paddington 2021, Sydney, N.S.W., Australia.
- Australian Ski Yearbook. a. ISSN 0084-7593

**Australian Small Animal Veterinary Association**
P. O. Box 276, Hurstville, N.S.W. 2220, Australia.
- Australian Veterinary Practitioner. q. ISSN 0310-138X

**Australian Society for Biblical Archaeology**
- Australian Journal of Biblical Archaeology. (pub. by University of Sydney. Department of Semitic Studies)

**Australian Society for Education in Film and Television**
G.P.O. Box 252c, Hobart, Tas. 7001, Australia.
- Australian Society for Education in Film and Television. President's Newsletter. irreg.

**Australian Society for Education Through the Arts**
P.O. Box 1298N, Hobart, Tasmania 7001, Australia.
- A S E A Bulletin. 3 per yr. ISSN 0001-2440

**Australian Society for Historical Archaeology**
Department of Archaeology, University of Sydney, Sydney, N.S.W. 2006, Australia.
- Studies in Historical Archaeology. a. (Co-sponsor: Australian Humanities Research Council)

**Australian Society for Keyboard Music**
43-35-43 Orchard Rd., Chatswood, N.S.W. 2067, Australia.
- Key Vive. q.

**Australian Society for Limnology**
c/o R. T. Buckney, Dept. of Zoology, University of Adelaide, Adelaide, S.A. 5001, Australia.
- Australian Society for Limnology. Bulletin. irreg. ISSN 0084-7607

**Australian Society for Medical Research**
- Australian Society for Medical Research. Proceedings. (pub. by Blackwell Scientific Publications Ltd. UK)

**Australian Society for Music Education**
Ed. Prof. Frank Callaway, Dept. of Music, University of Western Australia, Nedlands, W.A. 6009, Australia.
- Australian Journal of Music Education. s-a. ISSN 0004-9484

**Australian Society for Parasitology**
- International Journal for Parasitology. (pub. by Pergamon Press, Inc. US)

**Australian Society for the Advancement of Anaesthesia and Sedation in Dentistry**
108 Longueville Rd., Land Cove, NSW 2066, Australia.
- Dental Anaesthesia and Sedation. irreg. ISSN 0311-0699

**Australian Society for the Study of Labour History**
Box 1577, Canberra City, A.C.T. 2601, Australia.
- Labour History. s-a. ISSN 0023-6942

**Australian Society of Accountants**
49 Exhibition St., Melbourne, 3000, Australia.
- Australian Accountant. m. ISSN 0004-8631
- Australian Society of Accountants. Bulletin. irreg. ISSN 0005-0261

**Australian Society of Anaesthetists**
Box 525, Potts Point, N.S.W. 2011, Australia.
- Anaesthesia and Intensive Care Journal. q.

**Australian Society of Animal Production**
- Australian Society of Animal Production. Proceedings. (pub. by Australian Institute of Agricultural Science)

**Australian Society of Authors**
24 Alfred St., Milsons Point, N.S.W. 2061, Australia.
- Australian Author. q. ISSN 0045-026X

**Australian Society of Dairy Technology**
Publications Committee, Box 20, Highett, 3190 Victoria, Australia.
- Australian Journal of Dairy Technology. q. ISSN 0004-9433

**Australian Society of Periodontology**
c/o L. G. O'Brien, Ed., 144 Collins St., Melbourne, Vic. 3000, Australia.
- A. S. P. Newsletter. q.

**Australian Society of Soil Science**
c/o K. M. W. Howes, Ed., CSIRO Division of Land Resources Management, Private Bag, P.O., Wembley, W.A. 6014, Australia.
- Soil News. 2 per yr.

**Australian Stevedoring Industry Authority**
Box 556, Sydney, N.S.W. 2001, Australia.
- Australian Stevedoring Industry Authority. Annual Report. a.
- Australian Stevedoring Industry Authority. Monthly Statistics. m. ISSN 0045-0898

**Australian Sugar Producers Association**
Phoenix House, 333 Adelaide St., Brisbane, Queensland, Australia.
- Australian Sugar Journal. m. ISSN 0005-0318

**Australian Table Tennis Association**
P.O. Box 174, Warrnambool, Vic. 3280, Australia.
- Table Tennis Newsletter. irreg.

**Australian Tape Recordists Association, Inc.**
Box 970, G.P.O., Adelaide, S.A. 5001, Australia.
- Atranews. m.

**Australian Taxpayer's Association**
343 Little Collins St., Melbourne, Australia.
- Australian Taxpayer's Association. Annual Taxation Summary. a.
- Taxpayer. fortn. ISSN 0040-0289

**Australian Teachers' Christian Fellowship**
405-411 Sussex St., Sydney 2000, Australia.
- Journal of Christian Education. 3 per yr. ISSN 0021-9657

**Australian Teachers' Federation**
300 Sussex St., Sydney, N. S. W. 2000, Australia.
- A T F Annual Report. a.
- Austfed News. m.

**Australian Telecommunications Employees Association**
10th Floor, 343 Little Collins St., Melbourne, Vic. 3000, Australia.
- Tele-Technician. m. (except Jan.)

**Australian Thoroughbreds Publications Pty. Ltd.**
179 Elizabeth St., Sydney, N.S.W. 2000, Australia.
- Australian Thoroughbreds; Australia's only national magazine devoted to the breeding of thoroughbred horses. bi-m. ISSN 0005-0350

**Australian Track & Field Coaches Association**
1 Fox Ave., Athelstone, S. A. 5076, Australia.
- Modern Athlete and Coach. q. ISSN 0047-7672

**Australian Trotting Council**
- Australian Trotting Register. (pub. by Cabon Publishing Co. Pty Ltd.)

**Australian Union of Students**
97 Drummond St., Carlton, Vic. 3053, Australia.
- National U. Weekly. w.(during University term) ISSN 0028-0321

**Australian Union of Students. Alternate News Service**
97 Drummond St., Carlton, Melbourne 3053, Australia.
- AUS Education Information. 30 per yr. ISSN 0312-8318

**Australian Veterinary Association**
72-76 Parramatta Rd, Camperdown N.S.W. 2050, Australia.
- Australian Veterinary Journal. m. ISSN 0005-0423

**Australian Veterinary Association. Victorian Division**
Veterinary Research Institute, Story Street, Parkville, Vic. 3052, Australia.
- Victorian Veterinary Proceedings. a.

**Australian Veterinary Association. N.S.W. Division**
76 Parramatta Rd., Camperdown, N.S.W. 2050, Australia.
- New South Wales Veterinary Proceedings. a. ISSN 0085-4026

**Australian Water and Wastewater Association**
c/o A. H. Truman, Ed., Davy-Ashmore Pty. Ltd., G.P.O. Box 4709, Melbourne, Vic. 3001, Australia.
- Water. q. ISSN 0310-0367

**Australian Waterski Association**
- Water Skier. (pub. by Modern Magazines (Holdings) Ltd)

**Australian Welding Research Association**
307 Pitt St., Sydney, N.S.W. 2000, Australia.
- Australian Welding Research. bi-m. ISSN 0045-0960
- Australian Welding Research Association. Bulletin. irreg. ISSN 0084-7631

**Australian Wheat Board**
528 Lonsdale St., Melbourne, Vic. 3000, Australia.
- Wheat Australia. irreg. ISSN 0085-8196

**Australian Women Pilots' Association**
c/o Mrs. J. P. Robinson, Paxton Park, Leopold, Vic. 3221, Australia.
- Airnews. q.

**Australian Wool Corporation**
G.P.O. Box 4867, Melbourne, Vic. 3001, Australia (Orders to: Information Officer, 578 Bourke St., Melbourne, Vic. 2000, Australia)
- Australian Wool. a. ISSN 0067-222X
- Australian Wool Corporation. Bi-Monthly Market Report. bi-m. ISSN 0310-1398
- Australian Wool Sales Statistics. Statistical Analyses. irreg. ISSN 0311-9882
- Wool News Digest. irreg.

**Australian Workers' Union**
Box a-252, Sydney S., N. S. W. 2000, Australia.
- Australian Worker. (pub. by D. F. Austin Publishing)
- Australian Workers' Union. Official Report of the Annual Convention.

**Australian World Christian Action. Australian Council of Churches**
P.O. Box J111, Brickfield Hill, NSW 2000, Australia.
- Christian Action News. irreg.

**Australian Writers' Professional Service**
Box 28, Collins St. P.O., Melbourne, Australia.
- Writers' and Photographers' Marketing Guide; Directory of Australian and New Zealand Literary and Photo Markets. biennial. ISSN 0084-2680
- Writers' World. bi-m. ISSN 0043-9576

**Australijas Latvietis**
Box 23, P.O. Kew, Victoria 3101, Australia.
- Australijas Latvietis/Australian Latvian; a Latvian newspaper in Australia. w. ISSN 0005-0482

**Ausztraliai Magyar Ujsaf. Hungarian Weekly**
c/o F. Antal, Ed., P.O. Box 66, Fitzroy, Vic. 3065, Australia.
- Ausztraliai Magyar Ujsaf. Hungarian Weekly. irreg.

**Autistic Children's Association of New South Wales**
545 Pacific Highway, Artarmon, N.S.W. 2064, Australia.
- Breakthrough. q. ISSN 0045-2777

**Automobile Club Publishing Co**
123 Queen St, Melbourne 3000, Australia.
- Royalauto. m.(except Jan.) ISSN 0035-9300 (Royal Automobile Club of Victoria)

**Automotive Industry Matters Pty. Ltd.**
561 Bourke St., Melbourne, Vic. 3000, Australia.
- A I M/Automotive Industry Matters. 22 per yr. ISSN 0044-5681

**Aviation Historical Society of Australia Ltd.**
P.O. Box 212, Footscray, Vic. 3011, Australia.
- Aviation Historical Society of Australia. Journal. q. ISSN 0045-1185

**Avicultural and Wildlife Association**
165 Planet St., Carlisle, W. A. 6101, Australia.
- Aviary-Bird and Wildlife. m.

**Baas Becking Geobiological Laboratory**
c/o Bureau of Mineral Resources, P.O. Box 378, Canberra City A.C.T., 2601, Australia.
- Baas Becking Geobiological Laboratory. Annual Report. a. ISSN 0572-5860

**Bairnsdale Field Naturalists' Club**
13 Turnbull St., Bairnsdale, Vic. 3550, Australia.
- Clematis. a.

**Baking Trade Federation of Australia. South Australian Branch**
- South Australian Baker and Pastrycook. (pub. by Percival Publishing Co. Pty. Ltd.)

**Banana Growers Federation**
Box 31, Murwillumbah, N.S.W., Australia.
- Banana Bulletin. m. ISSN 0045-1398

**Bank of New South Wales**
341 George St., Sydney, N.S.W. 2000, Australia.
- Etruscan; staff magazine. q. ISSN 0014-1909
- Facts About Australia. a.

**Bank of New South Wales. Economic Department**
60 Martin Place, Sydney, NSW 2001, Australia.
- Bank of New South Wales Review. irreg. ISSN 0522-2818

**Bankers' Institute of Australasia**
51 Queen St., Melbourne 3000, Australia.
- Bankers' Magazine of Australasia. bi-m. ISSN 0005-5468

**Bankruptcy Trustees' & Liquidators' Association of Australia**
16th Floor, Commercial Union House, 109 Pitt St., Box 129, G.P.O., Sydney N.S.W., Australia.
- Australian Bankruptcy Bulletin. q. ISSN 0045-0286

**Baptist Union of Victoria**
300 Burwood Rd., Hawthorn, Vic. 3122, Australia.
- Baptist Witness. m. ISSN 0005-5794

**Bayer Australia Ltd.**
47-67 Wilson St., P.O. Box 159, Botany, N.S.W., Australia
(Main Office: Bayer Pflanzenschutz, Leverkusen, W. Germany (B.R.D.))
- Crop Protection Courier (Australia) irreg.

**Beaconsfield Press Pty., Ltd.**
Box 75, Woollahra, N.S.W. 2025, Australia.
- Australian Giftguide. a (plus supplements)

- Earthmover and Civil Contractor. m. (Earthmovers and Road Contractors Association of Australia Ltd.)

**Bell Bryant Pty. Ltd.**
37 Herbert St., St. Leonards, NSW 2065, Australia.
- Bell Bryant News. irreg. ISSN 0310-1444

**Benalla Art Gallery Society**
Kitson Court, Benalla, Vic. 3672, Australia.
- Art Gallery News. irreg.

**Bendigo Field Naturalist Club**
P.O. Box 396, Bendigo, Vic. 3550, Australia.
- Bendigo Naturalist. irreg.

**Bibliographic Services**
Box 2, Mount Waverley, Vic. 3149, Australia.
- Guidelines; a subject guide for Australian libraries. 9 per yr (plus annual cumulation)

**Bibliographical Society of Australia & New Zealand**
c/o Dept. of English, Monash University, Clayton, Vic. 3168, Australia.
- Bibliographical Society of Australia and New Zealand. Bulletin. irreg. ISSN 0084-7852

**Bird Banders' Association of Australia**
Box A313, Sydney, N.S.W. 2000, Australia.
- Australian Bird Bander. q. ISSN 0004-8747

**Bird Observers Club**
Box 2167 T, G. P. O., Melbourne, Victoria 3001, Australia.
- Australian Birdwatcher. q. ISSN 0045-0316

**Bloodhorse Breeder's Association of Australia. South Australian Division**
Box 1695, G.P.O. Adelaide, SA 5001, Australia.
- South Australian Racehorse. irreg.

**Board of Fire Commissioners of New South Wales**
213 Castlereagh St., Sydney, N.S.W. 2000, Australia.
- New South Wales. Fire Service. Fire News. irreg. ISSN 0047-990X

**Bonsai in Australia**
V. Koreshoff, Teffer Rd., Castle Hill, N.S.W. 2154, Australia.
- Bonsai in Australia. bi-m. ISSN 0045-2483

**Book Collectors' Society of Australia**
64 Young St., Cremorne, N.S.W. 2090, Australia.
- Biblionews and Australian Notes and Queries; journal for book collectors. irreg. ISSN 0045-1940

**Bougainville Copper Pty. Ltd.**
95 Collins St., Melbourne, Vic. 3000, Australia.
- Panguna. irreg.

**Bourke & District Historical Society**
Bourke, N.S.W. 2840, Australia.
- Papers on the History of Bourke. irreg. ISSN 0085-4670

**Breda Publications**
Box 2604, Sydney, N.S.W. 2001, Australia.
- Real Estate Agents & Valuers Society. Land and Building. q. ISSN 0085-6312

**Keith Breusch Pty. Ltd.**
Box 268g, 140 Phillips St., Sydney 2000, Australia.
- Australian Commercial Fishing & Marketing. m. ISSN 0010-2997
- Australian Harness Sport. q. ISSN 0004-9263

**Brighton Historical Society**
Box 50, North Brighton, 3186, Victoria, Australia.
- Brighton Newsletter. 3 per yr.

**Brisbane Development Association**
250 Edward St., Brisbane, Qld. 4000, Australia.
- Better Brisbane. irreg.

**Brivais Vards**
32 Parnell St., Strathfield, N.S.W. 2 BJ, Australia.
- Brivais Vards; latviesu preses biedribas bileteiu. q

**Broken Hill Proprietary Co., Ltd**
140 William St., Melbourne 3001, Australia.
- B. H. P. Review. q. ISSN 0005-3066
- B. H. P. Technical Bulletin. s-a. ISSN 0005-3074

**Bromeliad Society of Australia**
c/o D. Johnston, 4 Warrina St., Berowra Heights, N.S.W. 2082, Australia.
- Bromeletter. bi-m. ISSN 0045-3234

**Brotherhood of St Laurence**
67 Brunswick St., Fitzroy, 3065, Victoria, Australia.
- Action. q. ISSN 0300-4678

**Building Industry Congress of Western Australia**
- Building & Construction. (pub. by Shipping Newspapers (W.A.) Ltd.)

**Building Publishing Co. Pty. Ltd.**
122-126 Cleveland St., Chippendale, N.S.W. 2008, Australia.
- Construction. w. ISSN 0010-6674 (Master Builders Association of New South Wales)

**Building Science Forum of Australia**
Box 250, North Sydney, N.S.W., Australia.
- Australian Building Science and Technology. m. ISSN 0004-8798 (Co-sponsor: Australian Modular Society)
- Building Forum. (pub. by West Publishing Corp. Pty. Ltd.)

**Building Workers' Industrial Union of Australia. Victorian Branch**
- Carpenter and Joiner. (pub. by Industrial Printing and Publicity Co. Ltd.)

**Bundaberg Newspaper Co**
Targo St., Bundaberg, Queensland, Australia.
- Queensland Dairyfarmer. m. ISSN 0033-6106 (Queensland Dairymen's Organization)

**Bureau of Sugar Experiment Stations**
Box 292, North Brisbane, Queensland 4000, Australia.
- Cane Growers Quarterly Bulletin. q. ISSN 0008-5553

**Bush Music Club**
Box 433, Sydney, N.S.W. 2001, Australia.
- Singabout; Journal of Australian Folksong. 2 per yr. ISSN 0037-5632

**Bushell Publishing Co. Pty. Ltd.**
Box 14, Haberfield, N.S.W. 2045, Australia.
- A. I. J. Manual of Australasian Life Assurance. (Australasian Insurance Journal) a. ISSN 0084-697X
- Australasian Insurance Journal. m. ISSN 0045-0073

**Butterworths Pty. Ltd.**
586 Pacific Highway, Chatswood, N.S.W. 2067, Australia.
- Australian and New Zealand Journal of Criminology. q. ISSN 0004-8658
- Australian Current Law. m. ISSN 0045-0405
- Australian Law Reports. fortn.
- Australian Yearbook of International Law. irreg. ISSN 0084-7658 (Dist. in U.S. by: Oceana Publications, Inc., Dobbs Ferry, NY 10522)
- Australiasian Tax Reports. fortn. ISSN 0587-2138
- Commonwealth Taxation Board of Review Decisions. fortn.
- New South Wales District Court Reports. irreg. ISSN 0548-6793 (Council of Law Reporting for New South Wales)
- Victorian Reports. m. ISSN 0042-5214
- Western Australian Reports. irreg., with annual cumulation. ISSN 0083-8764

**C C H Australia Ltd.**
P.O. Box 230, North Ryde, NSW 2113, Australia.
- Australian and New Zealand Environmental Report. bi-m. ISSN 0311-0931
- Australian Corporate Affairs Reporter. m. ISSN 0310-8813
- Australian Estate and Gift Duty Reporter. every 3 wks. ISSN 0310-8562
- Australian Federal Tax Reporter. w. ISSN 0310-7817
- Australian Income Tax Assessment Act; including regulations, rates and international agreements. a.
- Australian Master Tax Guide. a.
- Australian Sales Tax Guide. irreg.
- Australian Securities Law Reporter. m. ISSN 0311-0265
- Australian Superannuation and Employee Benefits Planning in Action. irreg. ISSN 0310-1347
- Australian Tax Cases. fortn.
- Australian Trade Practices Reporter. every 3 wks.
- Law for the Australian Businessman. m. ISSN 0310-7876
- New Zealand Income Tax Report. irreg.

**C. S. I. R. O.**
372 Albert St., East Melbourne, Victoria 3002,
Australia.
- Australian Journal of Agricutural Research. bi-m.
  ISSN 0004-9409
- Australian Journal of Biological Sciences. bi-m.
  ISSN 0004-9417
- Australian Journal of Botany. irreg. ISSN 0067-
  1924
- Australian Journal of Chemistry. m. ISSN 0004-
  9425
- Australian Journal of Experimental Agriculture
  and Animal Husbandry. bi-m. ISSN 0045-060X
  (Australian Agricultural Council)
- Australian Journal of Marine and Freshwater
  Research. irreg. ISSN 0067-1940
- Australian Journal of Physics. bi-m. ISSN 0004-
  9506
- Australian Journal of Plant Physiology. 4 per yr.
- Australian Journal of Soil Research. s-a. ISSN
  0004-9573
- Australian Journal of Zoology. 4 per yr. ISSN
  0004-959X
- Australian Science Index; an index of articles
  published in Australian scientific and technical
  periodicals. m. ISSN 0005-0229
- Australian Wildlife Research. s-a. ISSN 0310-7833
- C. S. I. R. O. Directory. a.
- C. S. I. R. O. Film Catalogue. irreg. ISSN 0069-
  7192
- C. S. I. R. O. Food Research Quarterly. q.
- C. S. I. R. O. Index. m. ISSN 0311-5836
- C. S. I. R. O. Sheep and Wool Research. a. ISSN
  0310-8163
- Commonwealth Scientific and Industrial Research
  Organization. Annual Report. a. ISSN 0069-7184
- Commonwealth Scientific and Industrial Research
  Organization. Herbarium Australiense. Brunonia.
  a.
- Commonwealth Scientific and Industrial Research
  Organization. Industrial Research News. bi-m.
  ISSN 0045-7647
- Commonwealth Scientific and Industrial Research
  Organization. Land Research Series. irreg. ISSN
  0069-7648
- Rural Research in C S I R O. q. ISSN 0036-0090

**C. S. I. R. O. Division of Animal Health**
Private Bag No. 1, Parkville 3052, Victoria,
Australia.
- Commonwealth Scientific and Industrial Research
  Organization. Division of Animal Health. Annual
  Report. a. ISSN 0069-7273

**C. S. I. R. O. Division of Animal Production**
P.O. Box 239, Blacktown 2148, N.S.W., Australia.
- Commonwealth Scientific and Industrial Research
  Organization. Division of Animal Production
  Report. a.
- Commonwealth Scientific and Industrial Research
  Organization. Division of Animal Production
  Technical Report. irreg.

**C. S. I. R. O. Division of Applied Geomechanics**
P.O. Box 54, Mt. Waverley 3149, Victoria, Australia
(Subscr. Address: Box 89, East Melbourne, Vic.
3002, Australia)
- Commonwealth Scientific and Industrial Research
  Organization. Division of Applied Geomechanics.
  Abstracts of Published Papers. irreg. ISSN 0310-
  1894
- Commonwealth Scientific and Industrial Research
  Organization. Division of Applied Geomechanics.
  Report. irreg. ISSN 0069-7222
- Commonwealth Scientific and Industrial Research
  Organization. Division of Applied Geomechanics.
  Research Report. irreg. ISSN 0069-7230
- Commonwealth Scientific and Industrial Research
  Organization. Division of Applied Geomechanics.
  Technical Paper. irreg. ISSN 0069-7257
- Commonwealth Scientific and Industrial Research
  Organization. Division of Applied Geomechanics.
  Technical Report. irreg. ISSN 0069-7249

**C. S. I. R. O. Division of Applied Mineralogy**
Box 89, East Melbourne, Vic. 3002, Australia.
- Commonwealth Scientific and Industrial Research
  Organization. Division of Applied Mineralogy.
  Annual Report. a.

**C. S. I. R. O. Division of Atmospheric Physics**
314 Albert St., East Melbourne, Vic. 3002,
Australia.
- Commonwealth Scientific and Industrial Research
  Organization. Division of Atmospheric Physics.
  Annual Report. bienniel. ISSN 0310-1908
- Commonwealth Scientific and Industrial Research
  Organization. Division of Atmospheric Physics.
  Technical Paper. irreg. (approx. 1-3 per yr.)

**C. S. I. R. O. Division of Building Research**
Graham Rd., Highett, Vic. 3190, Australia.
- Commonwealth Scientific and Industrial Research
  Organization. Division of Building Research.
  Technical Paper. irreg.
- Rebuild. bi-m. ISSN 0312-620X

**C. S. I. R. O. Division of Chemical Technology**
69 Yarra Bank R., South Melbourne, Vic. 3205,
Australia.
- Commonwealth Scientific and Industrial Research
  Organization. Division of Chemical Technology.
  Research Review. irreg.

**C. S. I. R. O. Division of Computing Research**
Box 1800, Canberra City, A.C.T. 2601, Australia.
- Commonwealth Scientific and Industrial Research
  Organization. Division of Computing Research.
  Newsletter. m.

**C. S. I. R. O. Division of Entomology**
Box 3, Indooroopilly, Qld. 4068, Australia.
- Commonwealth Scientific and Industrial Research
  Organization. Division of Entomology. Report. a.
  ISSN 0069-732X
- Commonwealth Scientific and Industrial Research
  Organization. Division of Entomology. Technical
  Paper. irreg. ISSN 0069-7338

**C. S. I. R. O. Division of Fisheries and Oceanography**
P.O. Box 21, Cronulla 2230, N.S.W., Australia.
- Commonwealth Scientific and Industrial Research
  Organization. Division of Fisheries and
  Oceanography. Annual Report. a. ISSN 0069-
  7397
- Commonwealth Scientific and Industrial Research
  Organization. Division of Fisheries and
  Oceanography. Circular. irreg., 1971, latest. ISSN
  0519-5659
- Commonwealth Scientific and Industrial Research
  Organization. Division of Fisheries and
  Oceanography. Fisheries Synopsis. irreg. ISSN
  0069-7346
- Commonwealth Scientific and Industrial Research
  Organization. Division of Fisheries and
  Oceanography. Report. irreg. ISSN 0069-7370

**C.S.I.R.O. Division of Food Research**
P.O. Box 52, N. Ryde 2113, N.S.W., Australia.
- Commonwealth Scientific and Industrial Research
  Organization. Division of Food Research.
  Circular. irreg. ISSN 0069-7400
- Commonwealth Scientific and Industrial Research
  Organization. Division of Food Research. Report
  of Research. a. ISSN 0069-7419
- Commonwealth Scientific and Industrial Research
  Organization. Division of Food Research.
  Technical Paper. irreg. ISSN 0069-7427

**C. S. I. R. O. Division of Forest Research**
Banks St., Yarralumla A.C.T. 2600, Australia.
- Australian Forest Research. q. ISSN 0004-914X
- Commonwealth Scientific and Industrial Research
  Organization. Division of Forest Research.
  Bulletins. irreg., 1973, no. 46.
- Commonwealth Scientific and Industrial Research
  Organization. Division of Forest Research.
  Leaflets. irreg., no. 152, 1976.
- Commonwealth Scientific and Industrial Research
  Organization. Division of Forest Research.
  Reprints. Numbered Series. irreg.

**C. S. I. R. O. Division of Horticultural Research**
Box 350, G.P.O., Adelaide 5001, S. Australia.
- Commonwealth Scientific and Industrial Research
  Organization. Division of Horticultural Research.
  Report. biennial. ISSN 0069-7435

**C.S.I.R.O. Division of Irrigation Research**
Private Bag, Griffith N.S.W. 2680, Australia.
- Commonwealth Scientific and Industrial Research
  Organization. Division of Irrigation Research.
  Report. a. ISSN 0069-7443

**C. S. I. R. O. Division of Land Use Research**
314 Albert St., E. Melbourne 3002, Victoria,
Australia.
- Commonwealth Scientific and Industrial Research
  Organization. Division of Land Use Research.
  Technical Paper. irreg. ISSN 0069-746X

**C. S. I. R. O. Division of Mathematical Statistics**
314 Albert St., E. Melbourne 3002, Victoria,
Australia.
- Commonwealth Scientific and Industrial Research
  Organization. Division of Mathematical Statistics.
  Technical Paper. irreg. ISSN 0069-7524

**C. S. I. R. O. Division of Mechanical Engineering**
P.O. Box 26, Highett, Vic. 3190, Australia.
- Commonwealth Scientific and Industrial Research
  Organization. Division of Mechanical
  Engineering. Report. a. ISSN 0069-7508
- Commonwealth Scientific and Industrial Research
  Organization. Division of Mechanical
  Engineering. Circular. irreg. ISSN 0069-7486
- Commonwealth Scientific and Industrial Research
  Organization. Division of Mechanical
  Engineering. Technical Reports. irreg.

**C. S. I. R. O. Division of Plant Industry**
Box 1600, Canberra City, A.C.T. 2601, Australia.
- Australian Plant Introduction Review. irreg. ISSN
  0313-3192
- Commonwealth Scientific and Industrial Research
  Organization. Division of Plant Industry. Field
  Station Record. irreg. ISSN 0015-0738
- Commonwealth Scientific and Industrial Research
  Organization. Division of Plant Industry. Report.
  a. ISSN 0069-7540
- Commonwealth Scientific and Industrial Research
  Organization. Division of Plant Industry.
  Technical Paper. irreg. ISSN 0069-7567

**C. S. I. R. O. Division of Radiophysics**
P.O. Box 76, Epping 2121. N.S.W., Australia.
- Commonwealth Scientific and Industrial Research
  Organization. Division of Radiophysics. Report.
  irreg. ISSN 0069-7575

**C. S. I. R. O. Division of Soils**
Private Bag 2, Glen Osmond, S.A. 5064, Australia.
- Commonwealth Scientific and Industrial Research
  Organization. Division of Soils. Division Report.
  irreg.
- Commonwealth Scientific and Industrial Research
  Organization. Division of Soils. Report. biennial.
  ISSN 0069-7583
- Commonwealth Scientific and Industrial Research
  Organization. Division of Soils. Technical Papers.
  irreg.
- Soils and Land Use Series. irreg. ISSN 0081-1912
  (Subscr. to: CSIRO, Editorial & Publications
  Service, Box 89, East Melbourne, Vic. 3002,
  Australia)

**C. S. I. R. O. Division of Textile Physics**
338 Blaxland Rd., Ryde, N.S.W. 2112, Australia.
- Commonwealth Scientific and Industrial Research
  Organization. Division of Textile Physics. Annual
  Report. a.

**C. S. I. R. O. Division of Tropical Pastures**
314 Albert St., E. Melbourne 3002, Victoria,
Australia.
- Commonwealth Scientific and Industrial Research
  Organization. Division of Tropical Pastures.
  Technical Paper. irreg. ISSN 0069-7613

**C.S.I.R.O. Division of Wildlife Research**
Box 84, Lyneham, A.C.T. 2602, Australia.
- Commonwealth Scientific and Industrial Research
  Organization. Division of Wildlife Research.
  Technical Memorandum. irreg. ISSN 0084-9073
- Commonwealth Scientific and Industrial Research
  Organization. Division of Wildlife Research.
  Technical Paper. irreg. ISSN 0069-763X

**C. S. I. R. O. Forest Products Laboratory**
P. O. Box 310, South Melbourne, Vic. 3205,
Australia.
- Commonwealth Scientific and Industrial Research
  Organization. Forest Products Laboratory. Forest
  Products Newsletter. irreg.

**C. S. I. R. O. Marine Biochemistry Unit**
Building a12, University of Sydney, N.S.W. 2006,
Australia.
- Commonwealth Scientific and Industrial Research
  Organization. Marine Biochemistry Unit Annual
  Report. a. ISSN 0310-1924

**C.S.I.R.O. Minerals Research Laboratories**
Box 136, North Ryde. N.S.W.2113, Australia.
- Commonwealth Scientific and Industrial Research Organization. Minerals Research Laboratories. Investigation Report. irreg. ISSN 0084-8999
- Commonwealth Scientific and Industrial Research Organization. Minerals Research Laboratories. Technical Communication. irreg., approx. 2 per yr.

**C. S. I. R. O. National Measurement Laboratory**
University Grounds, City Road, Chippendale, N.S.W. 2008, Australia.
- Commonwealth Scientific and Industrial Research Organization. National Measurement Laboratory. Biennial Report. biennial.

**C. S. I. R. O. National Standards Laboratory**
314 Albert St., E. Melbourne 3002, Victoria, Australia.
- Commonwealth Scientific and Industrial Research Organization. National Standards Laboratory. Circular. irreg. ISSN 0069-7656
- Commonwealth Scientific and Industrial Research Organization. National Standards Laboratory. Technical Paper. irreg. ISSN 0069-7664

**C. S. I. R. O. Wheat Research Unit**
314 Albert St., E. Melbourne, Vic. 3002, Australia.
- Commonwealth Scientific and Industrial Research Organization. Wheat Research Unit. Report. a. ISSN 0069-7680

**C. S. I. R. O. Wool Research Laboratories**
314 Albert St., E. Melbourne 3002, Victoria, Australia.
- Commonwealth Scientific and Industrial Research Organization. Wool Research Laboratories. CSIRO Wool Textile News. a. ISSN 0069-7672

**C.S.R. Building Materials**
Box 483, Sydney, N.S.W. 2001, Australia.
- Building Ideas. q. ISSN 0045-3412

**Cabon Publishing Co. Pty Ltd.**
107 The Boulevard, Ivanhoe 3079, Victoria, Australia.
- Australian Trotting Register. m. ISSN 0005-0407 (Australian Trotting Council)

**Cairnmillar Institute**
15 Cromwell Road, South Yarra, Vic., Australia.
- Journal of Societal Issues. s-a.
- Turbulence. q.

**Cairns Folk Club**
Holloway Beach, Qld. 4870, Australia.
- National Folk. m. ISSN 0047-8865

**Calmor & Associates Pty. Ltd.**
283 Alfred St., North Sydney, NSW 2060, Australia.
- Australasian Printer; journal of the graphic arts. m. ISSN 0004-8453

**Quentin Cameron, Ed. & Pub.**
5 Rupert Terrace, Ascot, Qld. 4007, Australia (Subscription Address: P.O.B. 376, Hamilton Central, Qld. 4007, Australia)
- Oil Investment Guidelines. irreg.

**Canary Breeders' Association of Australia**
13 Robina Rd., Eaglemont, Vic. 3084, Australia.
- Australian Canary Breeder. m.

**Canberra Alpine Club**
Box 64, G.P.O., Canberra, A.C.T. 2600, Australia.
- Frozen Acres. irreg.

**Canberra & District Historical Society Inc.**
Box 40, Civic Sq., Canberra, A.C.T. 2608, Australia.
- Canberra Historical Journal. s-a. ISSN 0313-5977

**Canberra Bushwalking Club**
Box 160, Canberra City, A.C.T. 2601, Australia.
- It. irreg.

**Canberra College of Advanced Education. Students' Association**
Box 381, Canberra City, A.C.T. 2601, Australia.
- Caesarian. fortn. ISSN 0311-1229

**Canberra Consumers, Inc.**
Box 591, Canberra City, A.C.T. 2601, Australia.
- Canberra Consumer. q. ISSN 0008-5413

**Canberra Gliding Club**
P.O. Box 1130, Canberra City, A.C.T. 2601, Australia.
- Soaring in the A.C.T. (Australian Capital Territory) irreg. ISSN 0310-9399 (Australian National University Gliding Club)

**Canberra Kennel Association**
Box 132, Manuka, A.C.T. 2603, Australia.
- Canberra Kennel Association. Journal. bi-m.

**Canberra Mathematical Association**
Institute of Advanced Studies, Australian National University, P.O Box 4, Canberra City, A.C.T. 2601, Australia.
- Canberra Mathematical Association. Newsletter. irreg.

**Canberra Post**
Box 752, A. C. T., Canberra City, Australia.
- Canberra Post. bi-m. ISSN 0008-5421

**Cantrills Filmnotes**
c/o Arthur and Corinne Cantrill, Eds. & Pubs., Box 1295, G.P.O. Melbourne, Vic. 3001, Australia.
- Cantrills Filmnotes. q.

**Cape Horners - Australia**
8 Hampton St., Hawthorn, S.A. 5062, Australia.
- Cape Horners - Australia. Newsletter. q.

**Carlson Marsh and Associates**
Urch Rd., Roleystone, W.A. 6111, Australia.
- Geographer. 6 per yr. (Jan.-Oct.) ISSN 0046-5666

**Carlton Association**
P.O. Box 52, North Carlton, Vic. 3054, Australia.
- Carlton Newsletter. irreg.

**J. Carroll and Co.**
Ebley St., Bondi Junction, N. S. W. 2022, Australia.
- Modern Building Architecture and Engineering in Australia. bi-m.

**Cat Fanciers' Club of Tasmania**
P.O. Box 114, North Hobart, Tas. 7002, Australia.
- Cat Fanciers' Magazine. irreg.

**Catholic Leader**
Box 228, Brisbane, Qld. 4001, Australia.
- Catholic Leader. w. ISSN 0008-8145

**Catholic Press Newspaper Co. Ltd.**
104 Campbell St., Surry Hills, N.S.W. 2010, Australia.
- Catholic Weekly. w. ISSN 0008-8420

**Catholic Secondary Schools' Association of N.S.W. and A.C.T. Educational Media Committee**
Christian Brothers' High School, 68 the Boulevard, Lewisham, N.S.W. 2049, Australia.
- Audio-Visual Bulletin. irreg.

**Cauldron Collective**
25 Alberta St., Sydney 2000, Australia.
- Cauldron; feminist journal. q.

**Cave Exploration Group (S.A.)**
c/o S.A. Museum, North Terrace, Adelaide, S.A. 5000, Australia.
- Cave Exploration Group. South Australia. Newsletter. q.

**Central Industrial Secretariat**
P.O. Box 11, Hawthorne, Vic. 3122, Australia.
- Economic Newsletter. s-a. ISSN 0310-2246

**Central Publicity**
25 A'beckett St., Melbourne, Vic. 3000, Australia.
- Local Government Administration. bi-m. ISSN 0024-5518 (Institute of Municipal Administration)

**Ceramic Study Group**
G.P.O. Box 5239, Sydney, N.S.W. 2001, Australia.
- Ceramic Study Group. Newsletter. 10 per yr.

**Chamber of Manufacturers of New South Wales**
6 O'Connell St., Sydney, N. S. W. 2000, Australia.
- Manufacturers' Bulletin. fortn.

**Charlie Carter Pty. Ltd.**
- Living Today. (pub. by Living Today News)

**Charolais Society of Australia**
G. P. O. Box 3963, Sydney, N. S. W. 2001, Australia.
- Charolais Newsletter. m.

**Chartered Institute of Transport in Australia**
- Australian Transport. (pub. by Haldane Publishing Co. Pty. Ltd.)

**Checkpoint Council**
P. O. Box 31, Parkville 3052, Victoria, Australia.
- Checkpoint; a journal of liberal opinion. q. ISSN 0009-2118

**Chevalier Press**
Box 13, Kensington, N.S.W. 2033, Australia.
- Annals Magazine. m. (Missionaries of the Sacred Heart)

**Childrens Activities Time Society Inc.**
P.O. Box J3051 G.P.O., Perth, W.A. 6001, Australia.
- C A T S Tales. irreg.

**Children's Book Council of Australia**
c/o Ed. Anne B.Ingram, School Library Service, 35 Mitchell St., North Sydney 2060, Australia.
- Reading Time. q.

**China Stamp Collector's Club of Australasia**
c/o Norman S. Hale, P.O. Box H137, Australia Square, Sydney, N.S.W. 2000, Australia.
- Great Wall. irreg.

**Chinese Buddhist Society of Australia**
2Nd Floor, 56 Dixon St, Sydney, N.S.W. 2000, Australia.
- Buddhist Studies/Fo Hsueh Yen Chiu. q.

**Christian Brothers of the Australian and N.Z. Provinces**
Mount St. Mary College, Strathfield, N.S.W. 2135, Australia.
- Christian Brothers of the Australian and New Zealand Provinces. Our Studies. 2 per yr. ISSN 0045-6780

**Christian Women Concerned**
1 Henry Lawson Avenue, Abbotsford NSW 2046, Australia.
- Magdalene; Christian newsletter for women. bi-m. ISSN 0310-5474

**Christian Women's Conventions International**
Box 285, Strathfield, N.S.W. 2135, Australia.
- Christian Woman. 11 per yr.

**Church Missionary Society of Australia**
93 Bathurst St., New South Wales, Australia.
- Checkpoint. bi-m. ISSN 0311-0737
- Junior News. m. ISSN 0022-667X

**Church of England. Diocese of Adelaide**
Church of England Office, 18 King William Rd., North Adelaide 5006, Australia.
- Adelaide Church Guardian. m. ISSN 0001-8147

**Church of England, Dioceses of Melbourne & Bendigo**
Anglican Information Office, S. Paul's Cathedral Buildings, Flinders Lane, Melbourne, Vic. 3000, Australia.
- See; journal of the Church of England in the Dioceses of Melbourne and Bendigo. m. ISSN 0037-0754

**Church of England Historical Society**
Box 2902, G.P.O. Sydney, N.S.W. 2001, Australia.
- Church of England Historical Society (Diocese of Sydney). Journal. q. ISSN 0009-6490

**Church Press Ltd.**
196 Flinders St, Melbourne, 3000, Australia.
- Church Scene; Australian National Anglican newspaper. fortn. ISSN 0009-6563

**Citadel Press**
502 Albert St., East Melbourne, 3002, Vic., Australia.
- Musician. s-m. (Salvation Army)
- Rally. m. ISSN 0300-3515 (Salvation Army)
- Young Soldier. w. ISSN 0300-3264 (Salvation Army)

**City of Perth**
Perth, W.A., Australia.
- City of Perth. Annual Report. a.

**Clanalder Press**
Havelock, Vic. 3465, Australia.
- Sennachie. q.

**Clarence Publishing Co.**
283 Clarence St., Sydney, N.S.W. 2000, Australia.
- Taxation Record Journal. bi-m. ISSN 0040-0173 (Federated Clerks' Union (Taxation Branch)

**Clean Air Society of Australia & New Zealand**
c/o Department of Chemical Engineering, University of Melbourne, Parkville, Vic. 3052, Australia.
- Clean Air. q. ISSN 0009-8647

**Coast and Mountain Walkers of New South Wales**
29 Sixth Ave., Loftus, N.S.W. 2232, Australia.
- Into the Blue. irreg.

**Combined Victorian Gem Clubs Association**
P. O. 121, Doncaster, Victoria, Australia 3108.
- Pointer. q.

**Commercial Bank of Australia Ltd.**
335 Collins St., Melbourne, Vic. 3000, Australia.
- Commercial Bank of Australia. Economic Review. q. ISSN 0045-7566

**Commercial Publications of S. A. Pty. Ltd.**
86 Franklin St., Adelaide 5000, Australia.
- South Australian Institute of Architects' Monthly Bulletin. m. ISSN 0038-2922

**Commercial Travellers' Guild**
- C. T. G. Gazette. (pub. by Paragon Publications)

**Commissioner of Patents**
Patent Office, Canberra, Australia.
- Australian Official Journal of Patents, Trade Marks, and Designs. w. ISSN 0004-9891

**Committee for Economic Development of Australia**
139 MacQuarie St., Sydney, N.S.W. 2000, Australia.
- Committee for Economic Development of Australia. C E D A Energy Project Position Papers. irreg.
- Committee for Economic Development of Australia. C E D A Growth Series. irreg.
- Committee for Economic Development of Australia. C E D A "M" Series. irreg. (3-4 per yr.)
- Committee for Economic Development of Australia. C E D A Occasional Papers. irreg. (5-8 per yr.) ISSN 0591-0129
- Growth. irreg (2-4 per yr.) ISSN 0085-1280

**Committee of Direction of Fruit and Vegetable Marketing**
Box 19, Brisbane Market Po., Brisbane, Qld. 4106, Australia.
- Queensland Fruit and Vegetable News. fortn. ISSN 0033-6122

**Commonwealth Banking Corp.**
Box 2719, G.P.O., Sydney, Australia.
- Bank Notes. m. ISSN 0005-5131

**Commonwealth Council for Educational Adminstration**
c/o University of New England, Armidale, NSW 2351, Australia.
- C. C. E. A. Newsletter. irreg. ISSN 0310-1878

**Commonwealth Industrial Gases Ltd.**
Box 2244, Sydney, N.S.W. 2001, Australia.
- Practical Welder. q. ISSN 0085-5065

**Commonwealth Parliamentary Association**
Canberra, Australia.
- Australian Parliamentary Seminar. Summary Report of Proceedings. a.

**Commonwealth Police Officers Association**
926A Botany Road, Mascot, N.W.W. 2020, Australia.
- Commonwealth Police Officers' Association Journal. q. ISSN 0310-1886

**Commonwealth Scientific and Industrial Research Organization**
*see* C. S. I. R. O.

**Commonwealth Taxation Board of Review**
- Commonwealth Taxation Board of Review Decisions. (pub. by Butterworths Pty. Ltd.)

**Commonwealth Teaching Service**
- Commonwealth Teaching Service. Annual Report. (pub. by Commonwealth Government Printing Office)

**Communist Party of Australia**
- Wharfie. (pub. by Red Pen Publications)

**Company Directors Association of Australia Limited**
127 MacQuarie Place, Sydney, NSW 2000, Australia.
- Company Directors Association of Australia. Directors Law Reporter. irreg. ISSN 0311-0389

**Company of Master Mariners of Australia**
Box 46, Williamstown, Vic. 3016, Australia.
- Company of Master Mariners of Australia. Journal. a. ISSN 0084-909X

**Computer Sciences of Australia**
CSA Centre, 460 Pacific Highway, St. Leonard's N.S.W. 2065, Australia.
- Computer Sciences of Australia. C S A Report. irreg. (approx 2-3 per yr.)

**Concord Historical Society**
3 Flavelle St., Concord, NSW 2137, Australia.
- Nurungi. irreg. ISSN 0311-1016

**Concrete Masonry Association of Australia**
147 Walker St., North Sydney, N.S.W. 2060, Australia.
- Concrete Masonry Association of Australia. Project Review. irreg. ISSN 0311-1180

**Concrete Publishing Co. Pty. Ltd.**
147 Walker St., N. Sydney, N.S.W. 2060, Australia.
- Constructional Review. q. ISSN 0010-695X

**Conservation Society of New South Wales**
Agriculture House, 195 MacQuarie St., Sydney, N.S.W., Australia.
- Living Earth. q. ISSN 0047-4843

**Consolidated Publications Pty. Ltd.**
468 Ann St., Brisbane 4000 Qld., Australia.
- Bowls in Queensland. m. (Royal Queensland Bowls Association)
- O P A L. q. (One People's Australia League)

**Consumer Association of Victoria**
Box 1121J, Melbourne, Vic. 3000, Australia.
- Consumer Comment. q. ISSN 0045-8236

**Contempa**
Box 115, Armadale, Victoria 3143, Australia.
- Contempa. q.

**Contemporary Art Society of Australia**
G.P.O. Box 3271, Sydney, NSW 2001, Australia.
- Contemporary Art Society of Australia. Broadsheet. irreg.

**Continental Publicity**
Box 937, 500 Adelaide, Australia.
- Nasza Droga; the newspaper for Poles in Australia. fortn. ISSN 0027-8319 (Polish Association of South Australia)

**Coppleson Postgraduate Medical Institute**
University of Sydney, 25 Lucas St., Camperdown, N.S.W. 2050, Australia.
- University of Sydney. Postgraduate Committee in Medicine. Bulletin. m. ISSN 0042-0115

**Cordell Cost Services Pty. Ltd.**
160 Sailors Bay Rd., Northbridge, N. S. W. 2063, Australia.
- Cordell's Building Cost Book and Estimating Guide. New South Wales. q. ISSN 0311-2497

**Correspondence Chess League of Australia**
G.P.O. Box 2360, Sydney, N.S.W. 2001, Australia.
- C. C. L. A. Record. q.

**Council for Civil Liberties**
P.O. Box 201, Glebe, NSW 2037, Australia.
- Civil Liberty. irreg.

**Council for the Defence of Government Schools. NSW Branch**
P.O. Box 236, Haymarket, NSW 2000, Australia.
- D. O. G. S. Newsletter. irreg.

**Council for the Single Mother and Her Child**
23 Tattersall's Lane, Melbourne, Vic. 3000, Australia.
- C. S. M. C. News. bi-m.

**Council of Australian Food Technology Association**
60 York St., Sydney, N.S.W. 2000, Australia.
- Food Technology in Australia. m. ISSN 0015-6647 (Co-sponsor: Australian Institute of Food Science and Technology)

**Council of Law Reporting for New South Wales**
- New South Wales District Court Reports. (pub. by Butterworths Pty. Ltd.)
- New South Wales Law Reports. (pub. by Law Book Co. Ltd.)

**Council of Social Service of the A.C.T.**
P.O. Box 195, Civic Square, A.C.T. 2608, Australia.
- Directory of Social Agencies in the A.C.T. irreg.

**Country & Western Spotlight**
c/o Eddie Birt, Ed., 170 Chataway St., Carina Heights, Brisbane, Qld. 4152, Australia.
- Country & Western Spotlight; a world wide coverage of country music news. q. ISSN 0011-0108

**Country Life Newspaper Co. Ltd.**
10-14 Underwood St., Sydney 2000, N.S.W, Australia.
- Country Life. w. ISSN 0011-0167

**Country Press Ltd.**
44 Pitt St., Sydney, N.S.W., Australia.
- Press Radio and T.V. Guide. irreg. ISSN 0079-5046

**Courrier Australien**
389 George St., Sydney, N.S.W, 2000, Australia.
- Annuaire Francais d'Australie. biennial.
- Courrier Australien; French weekly/hebdomadaire Francais. w. ISSN 0011-0442

**Cowan Investment Survey**
377 Little Collins St., Melbourne, Vic.3000, Australia.
- Cowan Investment Survey. Midas. w.

**Crafts Council of Australia**
27 King St., Sydney, NSW 2000, Australia.
- Craft Australia. biennial. ISSN 0311-046X

**Cramb Tariff Services Pty. Ltd.**
Box E 263, Canberra, A.C.T. 2600, Australia.
- Tariff Brief. fortn.
- Tariff Insight. m. ISSN 0310-9593

**Creche and Kindergarten Association of Queensland**
130 Victoria Park Road, Kelvin Grove, Qld 4059, Australia.
- Knowing Children. irreg.

**Credit Data Corporation of Western Australia**
19 Gordon St., West Perth, W.A. 6005, Australia.
- Business Week in Western Australia. bi-m.

**Creswick Advertiser Pty. Ltd.**
Box 8, Creswick, Victoria 3363, Australia.
- Potato Grower News. w. ISSN 0032-5589 (Victorian Potato Growers Association)

**Croatian Community of Australia**
Box 5335, Sydney, N.S.W. 2001, Australia.
- Spremnost. m.

**Croatian Cultural and Welfare Association**
107 McKean St., Fitzroy North, Vic. 3068,
Australia.
- Free Home/Slobodni Dom. m.

**Cromptons Collection Service**
84 Charles St., Launceston 7250, Tasmania,
Australia.
- T.T.P.I. Trade Gazette. w. ISSN 0011-1716
  (Tasmanian Trade Protective Institute)

**Cruickshank & Partners Pty. Ltd.**
504 Pacific Highway, St. Leonards N. S. W. 2065,
Australia.
- Journal Abstract Service. m.

**Cruising Yacht Club of Australia**
New Beach Head Rd., Darling Point, N. S. W.
2027, Australia.
- Offshore. bi-m.

**Cullen Egan Dell Australia**
220 George St., Sydney, N. S. W. 2000, Australia.
- Quarterly Salary Review. q.

**Customs Officer's Association of Australia. Fourth Division**
- Customs Officer's Association of Australia. Fourth
  Division. Fourth Division Customs Officer. (pub.
  by Percival Publishing Co. Pty. Ltd.)

**Dairy Industry Authority of New South Wales**
Dairy Industry Authority Building, 71-75 Regent
St., Sydney, N.S.W. 2000, Australia.
- New South Wales Dairyman. m. ISSN 0310-3714

**David G. Stead Memorial Wildlife Research Foundation of Australia**
G.P.O. Box 4840, Sydney, N.S.W. 2001, Australia.
- Wildlife Research News. q.
- Your Australian Garden. irreg. ISSN 0085-8382

**Davies and Dalziel Investment Service**
G.P.O. Box 1392m, Melbourne, Vic. 3001,
Australia.
- Directory of Property Investors and Developers.
  irreg.

**Day & Parsonage Publishing Co. Pty. Ltd.**
Box 185, Cammeray, N. S. W. 2062, Australia.
- B. N. I. A. m. ISSN 0310-9534
- Manufacturing News in Australia. m. ISSN 0311-
  2160

**De Luxe & Red Cabs Co-Operative Trading Society Ltd.**
357 Glenmore Road, Paddington, New South Wales
2021, Australia.
- De Luxe & Red Cab News. m.

**Diabetes Federation of Australia**
Pharmacy Bldg., 45 Gawler Place, Adelaide, S.A.
5000, Australia.
- Conquest. q. ISSN 0045-8147

**Dickson and Johnson Pty. Ltd.**
327-341 Chisholm Rd., Auburn, NSW 2144,
Australia.
- Steel Spiel. irreg. ISSN 0310-7582

**Direct Publications Pty. Ltd.**
121 King Williams St., Adelaide, S.A. 5000,
Australia.
- Homemakers Guide. s-a. ISSN 0018-4217
- S.A. Road Transport Journal. m. (S. A. Road
  Transport Association Inc)
- South Australian Road Transport Year Book. a.
  ISSN 0085-641X

**Direct Publications, West Australian Newspapers, Ltd.**
340 High St., West Perth, W.A. 6005, Australia.
- Tectonics. m.
- Transporter (WA) bi-m. (Road Transport
  Association of Western Australia)

**Dove Communications**
203 Darling Rd., Malvern East, 3145 Victoria,
Australia.
- Dialogue; a Catholic journal of education. 3 per
  yr. ISSN 0012-2130
- Teaching Religion Today; supplement to Teachers
  Notes. irreg. ISSN 0310-4605

**Droughtmaster Stud Breeders' Society**
Suite 33, Office Block, Indooroopilly Shopping
Town, Indooroopilly, Qld. 4068, Australia.
- Droughtmaster Digest. m. ISSN 0310-0081

**Dun and Bradstreet (Australia) Pty. Ltd.**
24 Albert St., South Melbourne, Vic. 3205,
Australia.
- Australian Key Business Directory. a. ISSN 0311-
  2667
- Dun's Gazette. w.

**Dutch-Australian Publishing Co. Pty. Ltd.**
381 Pitt St., Sydney, N.S.W. 2000, Australia.
- Dutch-Australian Weekly. w. ISSN 0012-7310

**E. J. Dwyer Pty. Ltd.**
Box 492 P.O., Darlinghurst N.S.W. 2010, Australia.
- Official Directory of the Catholic Church of
  Australia and New Zealand. a. (Episcopal
  Conferences of Australia and New Zealand)

**Earl Heywood Fan Club**
P.O. Box 186, Murwillumbah, N.S.W. 2484,
Australia.
- Country Music Newsletter. q.

**Earth Garden**
Box 378, Epping, N.S.W. 2121, Australia.
- Earth Garden. q. ISSN 0310-222X

**Earthmovers and Road Contractors Association of Australia Ltd.**
- Earthmover and Civil Contractor. (pub. by
  Beaconsfield Press Pty. Ltd.)

**Ecological Society of Australia**
Box 1564, Canberra A.C.T. 2601, Australia.
- Ecological Society of Australia. Memoirs. irreg.
- Ecological Society of Australia. Proceedings.
  biennial. ISSN 0070-8348

**Ecology Action**
P.O. Box C159, Clarence St., Sydney, NSW 4000,
Australia.
- Ecology Action Newsletter. irreg. ISSN 0310-
  9658

**Economic Society of Australia and New Zealand**
Melbourne Univ., Parkville 3052, Victoria,
Australia.
- Economic Record. 4 per yr. ISSN 0013-0249

**Economic Society of Australia and New Zealand. New South Wales and Victorian Branches**
P.O. Box 200, North Sydney, New South Wales
2060, Australia.
- Economic Society of Australia and New Zealand.
  New South Wales and Victorian Branches.
  Economic Papers. 3 per yr. ISSN 0013-0354

**Economic Society of Australia and New Zealand. Queensland Branch**
c/o Dept. of Economics, Univ. of Queensland, St.
Lucia, Qld. 4067, Australia.
- Economic Analysis and Policy. 2 per yr. ISSN
  0046-1199

**Economic Society of Australia and New Zealand Western Australian Branch**
c/o University of Western Australia, Nedlands,
W.A. 6009, Australia.
- Economic Studies. a. ISSN 0070-8674

**Economics and Commercial Teachers' Association of New South Wales**
Box 20, Belfield, N.S.W. 2191, Australia.
- Economics. q.

**Editorial & Publishing Consultants Pty. Ltd.**
29 First Ave., Klemzig, S.A. 5087, Australia.
- Highway Engineering in Australia. bi-m. ISSN
  0046-7391
- Municipal Engineering in Australia. bi-m. ISSN
  0311-354X
- Waste Disposal and Water Management in
  Australia. bi-m. ISSN 0311-3558

**Edward Shann Memorial Fund**
- Edward Shann Memorial Lecture in Economics.
  (pub. by University of Western Australia Press)

**Egg and Egg Pulp Marketing Board of Victoria**
37 Fennell St., Port Melbourne, Victoria 3207,
Australia.
- Egg and Poultry Producer. m. ISSN 0013-2292

**Egg Marketing Board for the State of New South Wales**
Box 43, Lidcombe, N.S.W., Australia.
- Poultry Farmer. w. ISSN 0032-5732

**Eland Publishing Co. Pty. Ltd.**
107 Ballarat Rd., Maidstone, 3012 Vic., Australia.
- Australasian Sportsgoods and Toy Retailer. m.
  ISSN 0004-8488

**Electrical Contractors Association of New South Wales**
258 Castlereagh St., Sydney 2000, Australia.
- Electrical Contractor. m. ISSN 0013-4279

**Electrical Contractors' Association of Queensland**
45 Berwick St., Fortitude Valley, Brisbane,
Queensland 4006, Australia.
- Queensland Electrical Contractor. m. ISSN 0033-
  6114

**Electrical Contractors Association of S.A. Inc.**
213 Greenhill Road, Eastwood 5063, Australia.
- South Australian Electrical Contractor. bi-m.
  ISSN 0038-2892

**Electrical Contractors Federation (Victoria)**
153-155 Wellington Parade South, South Jolimont,
Vic. 3002, Australia.
- Electrical Contractor. 6 per yr. ISSN 0046-1660
- Victorian Electrical Contractor. 6 per yr.

**Electrical Development Association of Victoria**
Box 2105S, Melbourne, Vic. 3001, Australia.
- Electrical Developments Australia Circuit. m.

**Electrical Trade Unions of Australia**
262 Castlereagh St., Sydney, 2001, Australia.
- E. T. U. News. m.

**Employers' Federation of New South Wales**
313 Sussex St, Sydney, Australia.
- Employers' Review. m. ISSN 0013-6832

**English Association. Sydney Branch**
- Southerly. (pub. by Wentworth Press)

**English Teachers Association of N.S.W.**
c/o Ed. G. M. Boardman, Sydney Teachers'
College, University Grounds, Newtown, N.S.W.
2042, Australia.
- Teaching of English. 2 per yr. ISSN 0049-3147

**Entomological Society of Australia (N.S.W.)**
P.O. Box 22, Five Dock, N.S.W. 2046, Australia.
- Entomological Society of Australia (N.S.W.)
  Journal. a. ISSN 0071-0725

**Environment Control News**
c/o W. R. Cooper, Ed., 99 Fox Valley Rd.,
Wahroonga, N.S.W. 2076, Australia.
- Environment Control News. m. ISSN 0310-5725

**Environmental Law Reform Group**
Hobart, Tasmania, Australia.
- Environmental Law Reform Group. Publication.
  irreg.

**Episcopal Conferences of Australia and New Zealand**
- Official Directory of the Catholic Church of
  Australia and New Zealand. (pub. by E. J. Dwyer
  Pty. Ltd.)

**Europa Kurier Pty. Ltd.**
3 Seddon Street, Bankstown, N.S.W. 2200,
Australia.
- Espanol en Australia. w. ISSN 0014-0546
- Woche in Australien; an independent Australian-
  German newspaper. w. ISSN 0043-7123

**Everett Grant Pty. Ltd.**
6 Lang Rd., Earlwood, N.S.W. 2206, Australia.
- Hospital Journal of Australia. m.
- Modern Cleaning. m. ISSN 0311-1806

**Executor and Trustee Institute**
Suite 2, Eton Square, 476 St. Kilda Rd., Melbourne,
Vic. 3004, Australia.
- Trust Topics. 3 per yr.

**Exportad Pty. Ltd.**
Box 409, Darlinghurst, N.S.W. 2010, Australia.
- Australian Trader. q. ISSN 0045-0944 (Australia.
  Department of Overseas Trade)

**Express Newspapers Ltd.**
36 Nithsdale St., Sydney 2000, Australia.
- Century. w. ISSN 0009-0158

**F. W. Publications**
c/o F. M. Weierter, Ed., 310 George St., Sydney, Australia.
- Castings; a journal for the foundryman. bi-m. ISSN 0008-7521 (Australian Foundry Institute)

**John Fairfax & Sons Ltd.**
Box 506, G.P.O. Sydney, N.S.W. 2001, Australia.
- National Times; Australia's national weekly newspaper of business and affairs. w. ISSN 0047-911X

**Family Circle Publications Ltd.**
100 Arthur St., North Sydney, N.S.W. 2060, Australia.
- Australian Family Circle. m. ISSN 0310-1118

**Farmers Union of Western Australia (Inc.)**
- Farmers Weekly. (pub. by Farmers Weekly Newspaper Co. Ltd.)

**Farmers Weekly Newspaper Co. Ltd.**
239 Adelaide Terrace, Perth, W.A. 6000, Australia.
- Farmers Weekly. w. ISSN 0014-8466 (Farmers Union of Western Australia (Inc.))

**Federal Conference of Churches of Christ in Australia**
Box 101, Essendon North, Victoria, 3041, Australia.
- Australian Christian; national journal of Churches of Christ. fortn. ISSN 0004-8852

**Federal Grapegrowers Council of Australia**
- Australian Grapegrower & Winemaker. (pub. by Ryan Publications)

**Federated Brick, Tile and Pottery Industrial Union of Australia. N.S.W. Branch**
1-15 Deane St., Burwood, N.S.W. 2134, Australia.
- New South Wales Clayworker. bi-m. ISSN 0310-3706

**Federated Clerks' Union (Taxation Branch**
- Taxation Record Journal. (pub. by Clarence Publishing Co.)

**Federated Ironworkers' Association of Australia**
- Federated Ironworkers' Association of Australia. Labor News. (pub. by Magazine Printers)

**Federated Municipal and Shire Council Employees' Union of Australia**
Trades Hall, Carlton South, Vic. 3053, Australia.
- Counsellor. q.

**Federated Rubber & Allied Workers Union of Australia**
Box 47 Trades Hall, Carlton, Victoria 3053, Australia.
- Rubber, Plastic and Cable Industries Journal. q. ISSN 0048-8747

**Federated Shipwrights and Ship Constructors Association of Australia**
188 George St., Sydney, N.S.W. 2000, Australia.
- Slipway. q.

**Federation for Junior Deaf Education**
P.O. Box N300, Grosvenor St., Sydney, NSW 2000, Australia.
- Sound News. irreg.

**Federation of Australian Astrologers Co-Operative (Vic.) Ltd.**
5 Gawler Ct., Mont Albert, Vic. 3127, Australia.
- F. A. A. Journal. q. ISSN 0310-0308

**Federation of Australian Commercial Broadcasters. Research and Promotion Division**
Australian Radio Advertising Bureau, 8 Glen St., Milson's Point, N.S.W. 2061, Australia.
- Radio Facts and Figures. a.

**Federation of Australian Universities Staff Associations**
307 Pitt St., Sydney, N.S.W. 2000, Australia.
- Vestes; the Australian Universities' Review. 3 per yr. ISSN 0042-4560

**Federation of Staff Associations of Australian Colleges of Advanced Education**
- Australian Journal of Advanced Education. (pub. by Pandas Publishing and Advertising Service)

**Federation of Victorian Film Societies**
4 Stanley Grove, Canterbury, Vic. 3126, Australia.
- Federation of Victorian Film Societies. Federation News. q. ISSN 0046-3582

**Federazione Cattolica Italiana**
378 Nicholson St., North Fitzroy, Vic. 3068, Australia.
- Messaggero. m.

**Fellowship for Biblical Studies**
c/o Queen's College, Univ. of Melbourne, Parkville, Vic. 3052, Australia.
- Australian Biblical Review. a. ISSN 0045-0308

**Fellowship of Australian Composers**
P.O. Box 522, Strathfield, NSW 2135, Australia.
- Australian Composer. irreg. ISSN 0311-2764

**Fellowship of First Fleeters**
Box 4441, G.P.O., Sydney 2001, Australia.
- First-Fleeters. q. ISSN 0046-3957

**Fiamma Pty. Ltd.**
499 Parramatta Rd., Leichhardt, N.S.W. 2040, Australia.
- Fiamma. 2 per w. ISSN 0015-0479

**Field Naturalists Club of Victoria**
c/o National Herbarium, The Domain, South Yarra 3141, Victoria, Australia.
- Victorian Naturalist. bi-m. ISSN 0042-5184

**Field Naturalists' Society of South Australia, Inc.**
Box 1594, G. P. O., Adelaide 5001, Australia.
- South Australian Naturalist; a quarterly journal of natural history. q. ISSN 0038-2965

**Fish Trades Review**
24 Henry St., Carlton, N.S.W. 2218, Australia.
- Fish Trades Review. m. ISSN 0046-3965

**Fitzroy Ecumenical Centre**
Box 94, Fitzroy, Vic. 3065, Australia.
- Ekstasis. q. ISSN 0310-5857

**Flinders University of South Australia. History and Politics Society**
School of Social Sciences, Bedford Park, S. A. 5042, Australia.
- Flinders Journal of History and Politics. a.

**Flinders University of South Australia. School of Social Sciences**
Director of Asian Studies, Bedford Park, S. A. 5042, Australia.
- Flinders Asian Studies Lecture. a. ISSN 0085-0586

**Folk Lore Society of Victoria**
36 Westbourne St., Victoria 3181, Australia.
- Australian Tradition. 3 per yr. ISSN 0005-0377 (Co-sponsor: Victorian Folk Music Club)

**Forecast**
c/o Roger Randerson, Ed., 36-48 Upper Pitt St., Kirribilli, N.S.W. 2061, Australia.
- Forecast. w.

**Fort Beaufort Advocate**
c/o W. de S. Hendrikz, Ed., Box 2, Adelaide, S.A., Australia.
- Fort Beaufort Advocate. ISSN 0015-802X

**Franciscan Fathers. Slovenian Chaplaincy**
Baraga House, 19 A'beckett St., Kew, Vic. 3101, Australia.
- Misli/Thoughts. m.

**Franciscan House of Formation of Australian - New Zealand Province**
Box 79, Box Hill, Victoria 3128, Australia.
- Sursum Corda; a spiritual review. bi-m. ISSN 0039-6184

**Frank Browne's Things I Hear**
c/o F. Browne, Ed., Box 4674, Sydney, N.S.W. 2001, Australia.
- Frank Browne's Things I Hear. fortn.

**Franklin Carrack Co.**
Box 70, Toorak, Vic. 3142, Australia.
- Fighter. m.

**Fraser Island Defender's Organization, Ltd.**
Box 420, Maryborough, Qld. 4650, Australia.
- Moonbi. 5 per yr. ISSN 0311-032X

**Fred and Eleanor Schonell Educational Research Centre**
- Exceptional Child. (pub. by University of Queensland Press)

**Fremantle Port Authority**
1 Cliff St., Fremantle 6160, Australia.
- Port of Fremantle; quarterly magazine. 3 per yr.

**Friends of the la Trobe Library**
c/o State Library of Victoria, Swanston St., Melbourne 3000, Victoria, Australia.
- La Trobe Library Journal. s-a. ISSN 0041-3151

**Friends of Vietnam (Australia)**
Box E-137, Canberra 2600, Australia.
- Vietnam Digest. 5 per yr. ISSN 0049-6340

**David Frith Publications**
Box 71, St. Ives, N.S.W. 1975, Australia.
- Australian Disc and Tape Review. m. ISSN 0310-5989

**Fruit World Pty. Ltd.**
Box 1944, Melbourne, Vic. 3001, Australia.
- Fruit World and Market Grower. m. ISSN 0016-2280 (Apple & Pear Board)
- Fruit World Annual and Orchardists Guide. a. ISSN 0085-090X
- Seed and Nursery Trader. m. ISSN 0037-0770

**Furnishing Media Pty. Ltd.**
589 Malvern Rd., Toorak 3142, Australia.
- Australian Furnishing Trade Journal. m. ISSN 0045-0456

**Gallery First Nighters' Club**
Box 100, Ashfield, N.S.W. 2131, Australia
- First Nighters' Curtaincall. m. (Orders to: Mrs. G. Fall, 33 Shirley Rd., Roseville, N.S.W. 2069, Australia)

**Gardner Printing and Publishing Pty. Ltd.**
Box 175, Nunawading, Vic. 3131, Australia.
- Irrigation Farmer. q. ISSN 0310-8880

**Gas and Fuel Corporation of Victoria**
171 Flinders St., Melbourne 3000, Australia.
- Gas and Fuel Corporation of Victoria. Annual Report. a. ISSN 0072-0208

**Gay Liberation Press**
Box A76, Sydney 2000 N.S.W., Australia.
- Gay Liberation Press. m.

**Gazzettino Pty. Ltd.**
163-A Parramatta Rd., Annandale, NSW 2038, Australia.
- Settegiorni; Italian weekly newspaper. w. ISSN 0037-2900

**Geelong Historical Society**
23 Cook St., Newtown, Geelong 3220, Vic, Australia.
- Investigator. q. ISSN 0021-0013

**Gegenschein**
c/o Eric B. Lindsay, Ed., 6 Hillcrest Ave., Faulconbridge, N.S.W. 2776, Australia.
- Gegenschein. irreg., no. 20,1975. ISSN 0310-9968

**Gemmological Association of Australia**
Box 149, G. P. O. Sydney N.S.W. 2001, Australia.
- Australian Gemmologist. q. ISSN 0004-9174

**Genealogical Society of Victoria**
Block Arcade, Room 4, First Floor, 98 Elizabeth St., Melbourne, 3000, Australia.
- Ancestor. q. ISSN 0044-8222

**Gentle Folk and Other Creatures**
c/o Jamie Griffen, Union Building, Australian National University, P.O. Box 4, Canberra City, A.C.T. 2601, Australia.
- Gentle Folk and Other Creatures. irreg. ISSN 0310-639X

**Geographical Society of New South Wales**
Science Centre, 35 Clarence St., Sydney, N.S.W. 2000, Australia.
- Australian Geographer. (pub. by Sydney University Press)
- Geographical Society of New South Wales. Geography Bulletin. 4 per yr. ISSN 0046-5704

**Geography Teachers Association of Queensland**
55 Wharton St., Moorooka, Qld. 4105, Australia.
- Geography Teachers Association of Queensland. Journal. irreg. ISSN 0085-0977

**Geography Teachers Association of South Australia**
c/o 163a Greenhill Rd., Parkside, SA 5063,
Australia.
- Taminga. irreg. ISSN 0494-612X

**Geography Teachers Association of Victoria**
Geography Dept., State College of Victoria, Rusden,
Blackburn Rd, Clayton North, Victoria 3168,
Australia.
- Geography Teacher. 2 per yr. ISSN 0016-7509

**Geological Society of Australia**
39 Hunter St., Sydney, N.S.W. 2000, Australia.
- Geological Society of Australia. Journal. q. ISSN
0016-7614
- Geological Society of Australia. Special
Publication. irreg., no. 6, 1976. ISSN 0072-1085

**Geological Survey of Queensland**
Mineral House, 2 Edward St., Brisbane, Queensland
4000, Australia.
- Queensland. Geological Survey. Report. irreg., no.
86, 1974. ISSN 0079-8819

**Geological Survey of Victoria**
Mines Dept., 107 Russell St., Melbourne, Vic. 3000,
Australia.
- Victoria, Australia. Geological Survey. Bulletin.
irreg. ISSN 0085-7750
- Victoria, Australia. Geological Survey. Memoirs.
irreg. ISSN 0085-7769

**Geriatrics Publishing Co.**
457 Pacific Highway, Artarmon, NSW 2064,
Australia.
- Journal of Geriatrics. 10 per yr. ISSN 0047-2476

**Girl Guides Association (N.S.W.)**
Guide House, 201-203 Clarence St., Sydney,
N.S.W., Australia.
- Waratah. m(except Jan.) ISSN 0043-0307

**Girls Brigade**
9 Albion Place, Sydney, N.S.W. 2000, Australia.
- G. B. Digest. q.

**Glass's Dealers Guide Pty. Ltd.**
265 Coventry St., S. Melbourne 3205, Australia.
- Glass's Dealers Guide to Model Identification;
automobile identification manual. a. ISSN 0072-
4653

**Glenvale Publications Pty. Ltd.**
Glenvale Crescent, Mulgrave, Victoria, Australia.
- Australian Hardware Journal. m. ISSN 0004-9255

**Gliding Club of Victoria**
Box 4, Abbotsford, Vic. 3067, Australia.
- Airflow. q.

**Gliding Federation of Australia**
Box 1650 G.P.O., Adelaide, S.A. 5001, Australia.
- Australian Gliding. m. ISSN 0004-9204
- Australian Gliding Yearbook. a. ISSN 0084-7364

**Globe Publishing Co. Pty. Ltd.**
381 Pitt St., Sydney, N.S.W. 2001, Australia.
- Australian Photography. m. ISSN 0004-9964
- Australian Photography Directory. a. ISSN 0067-
2076

**Goat Breeders' Society of Australia**
Showground, Driver Ave., Paddington, N.S.W.
2021, Australia.
- Australian Goat World. bi-m. ISSN 0045-0472

**Goodyear Tyre and Rubber Co. Australia, Ltd.**
Publications Dept., Yurong Street, Sydney, N.S.W.
2000, Australia.
- Industrial Products News. irreg.

**Gordon Technical College**
Fenwick St., Geelong, Vic. 3220, Australia.
- Priorities. q. ISSN 0310-4036

**Grain Elevators Board of New South Wales**
c/o Charles Reid, 7 Macquarie Place, Sydney,
N.S.W. 2000, Australia.
- Bulk Wheat. a.

**Grand United Order of Oddfellows**
Box 1507 G.P.O., Sydney, N.S.W. 2001, Australia.
- Oddfellow. q.

**Grass Roots General Store**
P.O. Box 900, Shepparton, Vic. 3630, Australia.
- Grass Roots. irreg. ISSN 0310-2890

**Grassland Society of Victoria**
191 Royal Parade, Parkville, Vic. 3052, Australia.
- Grassland Society of Victoria. Newsletter. irreg.

**Graziers' Association of New South Wales**
56 Young St., Sydney, N.S.W. 2001, Australia.
- Muster. m. ISSN 0027-4925

**Great Dane Club of Victoria**
74 Rankin Rd., Frentree Gully, Vic. 3156, Australia.
- Dane Digest. irreg. ISSN 0311-0761

**Greater Publications Pty. Ltd.**
Box 2608, G.P.O., Sydney, N.S.W. 2001, Australia.
- B & T; Australia's advertising & media weekly. w.
ISSN 0005-268X
- Broadcasting and Television Year Book. a. ISSN
0084-8093

**Gredzens**
c/o A. Arcans, 53 Conway Rd., Banstown, N. S. W.
2200, Australia.
- Gredzens; Catholic Latvian bulletin. m. ISSN
0310-5938

**Grennan Publication**
317 Little Collins St., Melbourne, Vic. 3000,
Australia.
- Australian Pre-School Association. Victorian
Branch. Newsletter. a.

**Grey Advertising Pty. Ltd.**
89 Berry St., North Sydney, N.S.W. 2060, Australia.
- Grey Matter; Australian edition. irreg.

**Greyhound News Pty. Ltd.**
Box 72, Waverly, N.S.W. 2024, Australia.
- National Greyhound News. m. ISSN 0310-589X

**Greyhound Racing Control Board (Victoria)**
126 Wellington Parade, East Melbourne, Vic. 3002,
Australia.
- Greyhound Adviser. m. (Co-sponsor: National
Coursing Association of Victoria)

**Greyhound Recorder**
72 Carlton Crescent, Summer Hill, N.S.W. 2130,
Australia.
- Greyhound Recorder. w.

**Griffin Press**
Netley, S.A. 5037, Australia.
- Australian Computer Conference. Proceedings.
irreg., 1969, 4th. ISSN 0067-1800
- South Australian Clinics. q. ISSN 0038-2884
(Royal Adelaide Hospital)

**Grow Publishers**
209 a Edgeware Rd., Marrickville, N.S.W. 2204,
Australia.
- Grow Magazine. q. (Recovers and Growers of
Australia)

**Guest and Bell**
446 Collins St., Melbourne, Vic. 3000, Australia.
- Melbourne Investment Review. irreg.

**Gwalwa Daraniki Association**
Box 4751, Darwin, N.T. 5794, Australia.
- Bunji. m.

**Haldane Publishing Co. Pty. Ltd.**
Box a540, Sydney S. 2000, Australia.
- Australian Transport. m. ISSN 0005-0385
(Chartered Institute of Transport in Australia)
- Highway Transport. m. ISSN 0018-1757 (Long
Distance Road Transport Association of
Australia)

**Paul Hamlyn Pty. Ltd.**
176 S. Creek Rd., Dee Why West, N.S.W. 2099,
Australia
- Australia's Heritage; the making of a nation. w.
ISSN 0005-0466 (U.S. Subscr. to: Lucy Carlborg,
598 Madison Ave., 8th Floor, New York, N.Y.
10022)

**Hand Weavers' and Spinners' Guild of Australia**
c/o Ed. Mrs. P. R. McMahon, 4 The Scarp,
Castlecrag, N.S.W. 2068, Australia.
- Australian Hand Weaver and Spinner. q. ISSN
0045-0510

**Harbour Newspaper & Publishing Co. Ltd.**
Box M60, Sydney Mail Exchange, Sydney, N.S.W.
2012, Australia.
- Australian Orchid Review. q. ISSN 0045-0782
(Orchid Society of New South Wales)

- New South Wales Contract Reporter. w. ISSN
0027-7029

**Hardware Retailer Publishing Co.**
P.O. Box 67, Brighton-le-Sands, N.S.W. 2216,
Australia.
- Hardware Retailer News. irreg. (Hardware
Retailers Association of New South Wales)

**Hardware Retailers Association of New South Wales**
- Hardware Retailer News. (pub. by Hardware
Retailer Publishing Co.)

**Hawthorn Press Pty. Ltd.**
601 Little Bourke St., Melbourne, Vic. 3000,
Australia.
- Australian Banknote Catalogue. irreg. ISSN 0313-
9611
- Australian Coin Catalogue. irreg. ISSN 0084-7267
- Australian Coin Review. m. ISSN 0004-8887
- Australian Commonwealth Specialists' Catalogue.
a. ISSN 0313-9603
- Standard Australian Coin Catalogue. irreg. ISSN
0085-6606

**Hazelwood Publishing Pty. Ltd.**
10 the Centre, Suite 4, Forestville, N.S.W. 2087,
Australia.
- Dawsons Guide to Hotels, Motels, and Resorts. a.

**Health Economics Service**
45 MacQuarie St., Sydney, N.S.W. 2000, Australia.
- Health Economics Service Bulletin. m.

**Health Education Council of Western Australia**
514 Hay St., Perth, W.A. 6000, Australia.
- Australian Public Health Association (WA
Branch). Journal. q. ISSN 0300-8088
- Health Education Council of Western Australia
Information Bulletin. m (plus special issues)

**Heart**
47 Williamson Road, Para Hills, S.A. 5096,
Australia.
- Heart. q.

**Hecate**
G.P.O. Box 99, St. Lucia, Queensland 4067,
Australia.
- Hecate; women's interdisciplinary journal. s-a.

**Helictite**
Box 183, Broadway, N.S.W. 2007, Australia.
- Helictite; journal of Australasian cave research. q.
ISSN 0017-9973

**Hellenic Herald Pty. Ltd.**
261 Broadway, Sydney, 2007, N.S.W., Australia.
- Hellenic Herald. 3 per wk. ISSN 0018-0033

**Hellenic Youth Association of Western Australia**
Box J 666, Perth, W. A. 6001, Australia.
- H. Y. A. News. m.

**Henry George League**
32 Allison Ave., Iris, Vic. 3146, Australia.
- Progress. m.

**Herald & Weekly Times, Ltd.**
44-74 Flinders St., Melbourne, Vic. 3000, Australia.
- Aircraft. m. ISSN 0002-2659 (Royal Aeronautical
Society, Australian Division)
- Australian Home Beautiful. m. ISSN 0004-928X
- Listener in T V. w. ISSN 0024-4406
- Miller's Sporting Annual and Athletic Record. a.
ISSN 0075-2053
- Weekly Times. w. ISSN 0043-194X

**Herald Travel Bureau**
Newspaper House, 247 Collins St., Melbourne, Vic.
3000, Australia.
- Herald Caravanning Guide. a. ISSN 0085-1477
- Herald Motel Guide. a. ISSN 0085-1485

**Heraldry Society of Australia**
c/o A. G. Puttock, Ed., 1 Crusader Crescent, Glen
Waverly, Victoria 3150, Australia.
- Escutcheon. q. ISSN 0046-2489

**Herbicide Recommendations**
3A Ipswich St., Toowoomba, Qld 4350, Australia.
- Australian Weed Control Handbook. biennial.

**Hervey Bay Writers' Workshop**
- Moonaboola Quill. (pub. by Maryborough Adult
Education Centre)

**High Times Pty. Ltd.**
Box 77, Carlton, Vic. 3053, Australia.
- Digger. fortn. ISSN 0310-2165

**Hill Group Publications**
69 Draper St., Ormond, Victoria 3204, Australia.
- Concept; man-made environment & commercial interior design. q. ISSN 0010-5112
- Today's House. irreg. ISSN 0085-7270

**History Teachers' Association of New South Wales**
Box 1495 G. P. O., Sydney, N. S. W. 2001, Australia.
- History Teachers Association of New South Wales. Newsletter. irreg. ISSN 0085-1558
- Teaching History. 3 per yr. ISSN 0040-0602

**Hoad's Technical Publications Pty. Ltd.**
Box 55, Mosman, N.S.W. 2088, Australia.
- Hoads Readout. q. ISSN 0018-2877

**Hobart Walking Club**
G.P.O. Box 753h, Hobart, Tas. 7001, Australia.
- Tasmanian Tramp. biennial.

**Holy Name Society**
320 Riversdale Rd., Camberwell, Victoria 3124, Australia.
- Holy Name Monthly. m. (except Jan.) ISSN 0018-3741

**Home Economics Association of Australia**
c/o A. E. Cocksedge, 17 Mardale St., The Grange, Qld. 4051, Australia.
- Home Economics Association of Australia Newsletter. q.

**Horan & Wall**
Box 8, Surry Hills, Australia.
- Alternative Pink Pages. irreg.

**Horological Guild of Australasia. Victorian Branch**
- Watchmakers of Victoria. (pub. by Research Publications Pty. Ltd.)

**Horticultural Press Pty. Ltd.**
8-14 Orr St., Carlton South, Vic. 3053, Australia.
- Australian Garden Lover. m. ISSN 0045-0464 (Royal Horticultural Society of Victoria)
- Australian Rose Annual. a. (National Rose Society of Australia)
- Australian Stamp Monthly. m. ISSN 0005-0296
- Poultry World. m. ISSN 0004-8445 (Australian Chicken Meat Council)

**Horticultural Research Station**
Tatura, Australia.
- Tatura, Australia. Horticultural Research Station. Annual Research Report. a. ISSN 0082-2124

**Housing Australia Publishing Co.**
29 Coventry St., South Melbourne, Vic. 3205, Australia.
- Housing Products & Costing Guide. bi-m. (Housing Industry Association)

**Housing Industry Association**
- Housing Products & Costing Guide. (pub. by Housing Australia Publishing Co.)

**Hoyts Theatres Ltd.**
600 George St., Sydney, N.S.W. 2000, Australia.
- Movie News. m. ISSN 0027-2728

**Hrvatski Dom**
Box 1070J, Melbourne, Vic. 3001, Australia.
- Hrvatski Dom. m. ISSN 0310-6454

**Humes Ltd.**
G. P. O. Box 4534, Melbourne, Vic. 3001, Australia.
- Hume News. m.

**Hungarian Lutheran Conference**
Box A160, Sydney South, N.S.W. 2000, Australia.
- Hitbol Elunk. bi-m.

**Hunter Valley Research Foundation**
Research Centre, Hall St., Maryville, Newcastle, N.S.W. 2300, Australia.
- Hunter Valley Research Foundation. Monographs. irreg. ISSN 0085-1663

**Huon Newspaper Co. Pty. Ltd.**
Franklin, Tasmania 7113, Australia.
- Huon News. w. ISSN 0018-7909
- Tasmanian Fruitgrower & Farmer. m. ISSN 0039-9787

**I P C Business Press (Australia) Pty. Ltd.**
3-13 Queen St., Chippendale, N.S.W. 2008, Australia.
- Australasian Antique Collector. s-a. ISSN 0004-8704
- Australian Hairdressers Journal. m.
- Australian Machinery and Production Engineering. m. ISSN 0004-9719
- Australian Packaging. m. ISSN 0004-9921
- Australian Packaging Buyers Guide. a. (National Packaging Association of Australia)
- Australian Plastics & Rubber. m.
- Australian Plastics & Rubber Buyers Guide. a. ISSN 0084-7542
- Australian Process Engineering. m. ISSN 0310-933X
- Electronic News. m. ISSN 0311-0230
- Industrial and Commercial Photography. bi-m.
- Jeweller, Watchmaker and Giftware. m.
- Pharmacy Trade. m. ISSN 0031-7071
- Travel Consultant. ISSN 0311-2179
- Travel Trade Yearbook. s-a.

**Ian Buchan Fell Research Project on Housing**
Sydney, Australia.
- Directory: Research in Housing - Australia and New Zealand. irreg.

**Igman Pty. Ltd.**
Box 1269L, Melbourne, Vic. 3001, Australia.
- Osvit; croatian weekly. w.

**Illuminating Engineering Society of Australia**
- I. E. S. Lighting Review. (pub. by Thomson Publications (Australia) Pty. Ltd.)

**Immigration Control Association**
P.O.B. 322, Crow's Nest NSW 2065, Australia.
- I C A Viewpoint. bi-m.

**Impact**
Box 145, Camberwell, Vic. 3124, Australia.
- Impact. q. ISSN 0311-0567

**Incorporated Council of Law Reporting for the State of Queensland**
Box 19, Brisbane, North Quay. 4000, Queensland, Australia.
- Queensland Legal Directory. a.

**Index to Australian Innovative Schools**
c/o Kevin R. Smith, Ed., Box 440, Armidale, N.S.W. 2350, Australia.
- Index to Australian Innovative Schools. irreg.

**Indonesia do-It-Yourself**
Palmii 49 Park St., South Yarra, Vic., Australia.
- Indonesia do-It-Yourself. a.

**Industrial Foundation for Accident Prevention**
Box 28, Mosman Park, W.A. 6012, Australia.
- I. F. A. P. News. bi-m. ISSN 0311-0311

**Industrial Printing and Publicity Co. Ltd.**
122 Dover St., Richmond, Vic. 3121, Australia.
- Carpenter and Joiner. irreg. (Building Workers' Industrial Union of Australia. Victorian Branch)

**Industrial Relations Society of Australia**
c/o Faculty of Economics, University of Sydney, N.S.W. 2006, Australia.
- Journal of Industrial Relations. q. ISSN 0022-1856

**Ingos Pty. Ltd.**
175 George St., Sydney N.S.W. 2000, Australia.
- Polish News/Wiadomosci Polskie. w. ISSN 0032-2954 (Polish Communities in Australia and New Zealand)

**Innisfail District Canegrowers' Executive**
Box 32, Innisfail, Queensland, Australia.
- Innisfail Canegrower. m. ISSN 0020-1588

**Inside Advertising and Media Pty Ltd.**
Box 430, Milsons Point, N.S.W. 2061, Australia.
- Adbrief. w. ISSN 0311-2225

**Institute of Actuaries of Australia and New Zealand**
8 Spring St., Sydney, Australia.
- Institute of Actuaries of Australia and New Zealand. Transactions. a. ISSN 0073-8972

**Institute of Australian Geographers**
Flinders University of South Australia, Bedford Park, South Australia 5042, Australia.
- Australian Geographical Studies. s-a. ISSN 0004-9190

**Institute of Australian Photography**
Box 537, Dandenong, Victoria 3175, Australia.
- I.A.P. Professional Photography in Australia. bi-m. ISSN 0046-9742

**Institute of Automotive Mechanical Engineers (Inc.)**
229 Great North Rd., Fivedock, N.S.W. 2046, Australia.
- Australian Automotive Engineering and Equipment. 10 per yr. ISSN 0004-8720

**Institute of Chartered Accountants in Australia**
Box 3921, G.P.O., Sydney, Australia.
- Chartered Accountant in Australia. m. ISSN 0009-1898

**Institute of Chartered Secretaries and Administrators. Australian Division**
10-12 Clarke St., Crows Nest 2065, Australia.
- Chartered Secretary. q. ISSN 0009-1928

**Institute of Club Managers and Secretaries Ltd.**
82 West St., Crow's Nest, N.S.W. 2065, Australia.
- Institute of Club Managers and Secretaries. Club Guide. q. ISSN 0046-9785

**Institute of Commerical and Industrial Security Executives**
- Security and Property Protection. (pub. by Australasian Security Publishers)

**Institute of Directors in Australia**
16 O'Connell St., Sydney 2000, Australia.
- Australian Director. bi-m.

**Institute of Economic Democracy**
Post Office, Kingston, N.S.W. 2350, Australia.
- Enterprise. q.
- Institute of Economic Democracy. Information Bulletin. 9 per yr. ISSN 0310-916X

**Institute of Electrical Inspectors**
Box Q10, Queen Victoria Bldg., Sydney, N.S.W. 2001, Australia.
- Institute of Electrical Inspectors. I. E. I. Journal. m. ISSN 0046-9807

**Institute of Foresters of Australia**
c/o Ed. E. P. Bachelard, Dept. Forestry, P.O. Box 4, Canberra, A.C.T. 2600, Australia (Subscr. Address: Box 73, Canberra, A.C.T. 2600, Australia)
- Australian Forestry. q. ISSN 0004-9158

**Institute of Industrial Engineers**
12 City Rd., Darlington, N.S.W. 2008, Australia.
- Industrial Engineer. 3 per yr.

**Institute of Instrumentation and Control, Australia. (I.I.C.A.)**
- Australian Journal of Instrumentation and Control. (pub. by Research Publications Pty. Ltd.)

**Institute of Medical and Veterinary Science**
Frome Rd, Adelaide, S., Australia.
- Adelaide. Institute of Medical and Veterinary Science. Annual Report of the Council. a. ISSN 0065-1907

**Institute of Municipal Administration**
- Local Government Administration. (pub. by Central Publicity)

**Institute of Municipal Administration. Queensland Division**
151 Porteus Dr., Seven Hills, Brisbane, Qld. 4170, Australia.
- Q I M A. q. ISSN 0048-6078

**Institute of Personnel Management (Australia)**
- Personnel Management. (pub. by West Publishing Corp. Pty. Ltd.)

**Institute of Public Affairs**
289 Flinders Lane, Melbourne 3000, Australia.
- Facts. bi-m. ISSN 0014-6609
- I P A Review. q. ISSN 0019-0268

**Institute of Purchasing and Supply Management**
181 Clarence St., Sydney, N.S.W. 2000, Australia.
- Australian Purchasing. m. ISSN 0005-0083

**Institute of Real Estate Development**
- Developer. (pub. by West Publishing Corp. Pty Ltd.)

**Institute of Social Order**
Belloc House, 12 Sackville St., Kew, Vic. 3101, Australia.
- Social Survey. m. ISSN 0037-8011

**Institution of Engineers, Australia**
157 Gloucester Street, Sydney, N.S.W. 2000, Australia.
- Australia-New Zealand Conference on Geomechanics Proceedings. 3 per yr.
- Australian Geomechanics Journal. (Co-sponsor: Australasian Institute of Mining and Metallurgy)
- Civil Engineering Transactions. 2 per yr.
- Institution of Engineers, Australia. Civil Engineering Transactions. s-a. ISSN 0020-3297
- Institution of Engineers, Australia. Electrical Engineering Transactions. 2 per yr. ISSN 0020-3300
- Institution of Engineers, Australia. Journal. 26 per yr. ISSN 0020-3319
- Institution of Engineers, Australia. Mechanical and Chemical Engineering Transactions. 2 per yr. ISSN 0020-3327

**Institution of Engineers, Australia. Newcastle Division**
Box 238C, Newcastle, N.S.W. 2300, Australia.
- Institution of Engineers, Australia. Newcastle Division. Bulletin. 10 per yr.

**Institution of Engineers, Australia. Queensland Division**
447 Upper Edward St., Brisbane, Qld. 4000, Australia.
- Institution of Engineers, Australia Queensland Division. Technical Papers. m.

**Institution of Engineers, Australia. South Australian Division**
1 Bagot St., North Adelaide, S.A. 5006, Australia.
- Institution of Engineers Australia. South Australian Division. Bulletin. m. (except Jan.) ISSN 0046-9874

**Institution of Radio and Electronics Engineers**
Science House, 157 Gloucester St., Sydney, N.S.W. 2000, Australia.
- Monitor. m.

**Institution of Surveyors, Australia**
252 George Street, Sydney 2000, Australia.
- Australian Surveyor. q. ISSN 0005-0326

**International Federation for Documentation. Commission for Asia and Oceania**
c/o CSIRO, 314 Albert St., East Melbourne, Victoria, Australia
(and Hofweg 7, 2511 AA The Hague Netherlands)
- F I D/C A O Newsletter. irreg.
- International Federation for Documentation, Commission for Asia and Oceania. Newsletter. irreg.

**International Federation for Modern Languages and Literature**
c/o Prof. R. D. Eagleson, Dept. of English, University of Sydney, Sydney, Australia.
- International Federation for Modern Languages and Literature. Congress Reports. triennial; 13th, Sydney, Australia, 1975. ISSN 0074-5855

**International Film Theatre**
P.O. Box 90, Subiaco, W.A. 6008, Australia.
- Sprocket. irreg. (Co-sponsor: Perth Film Society)

**International Information Center**
Box 535, Parramatta, N.S.W. 2150, Australia.
- News Digest - International. q. ISSN 0028-9000

**International Mathematical Union**
c/o Ed. Professor B. H. Neumann, Department of Mathematics, Australian National University, P.O. Box 4, Canberra A.C.T. 2600, Australia.
- I M U Canberra Circular. irreg (4 per yr.-approx) ISSN 0311-0621

**International Police Association. Australian Section**
- Australian Police World. (pub. by Percival Publishing Co. Pty. Ltd.)

**International Public Relations Pty. Ltd.**
117 Collins St., Melbourne, Vic. 3000, Australia.
- Lion. m. (Lions International. Australian Branch)

**International Solar Energy Society. Australian and New Zealand Section**
Box 26, Highett, Victoria 3190, Australia.
- Solar Energy Progress in Australia and New Zealand. irreg. ISSN 0584-0651

**International 505 Association**
- National Water Sport. (pub. by Messenger Publications Pty. Ltd.)

**Intervention Collective**
P.O. Box 104, Carleton, Vic. 3053, Australia.
- Intervention. irreg. ISSN 0311-1989

**Inventors Society of Australia**
Box 3400, Sydney, N.S.W. 2001, Australia.
- Inventus. m.(exc. Dec.) ISSN 0047-133X

**Inverell and District Historical Society**
P.O. Box 396, Inverell, NSW 2360, Australia.
- Tide of Time. a.

**Invicta Publications**
P.O. Box 142, Bentley, Western Australia 6102, Australia.
- Local Government Journal of Western Australia. q. ISSN 0024-5569

**Irrigation Research & Extension Committee**
Private Mail Bag C.S. I.R.O., Div. of Irrigation Research, Griffith, 2680 N.S.W., Australia.
- Farmers Newsletter. 8 per yr. ISSN 0014-844X

**Peter Isaacson Publications**
46-49 Porter St., Prahran, Vic. 3181, Australia.
- Australian Directory of Exports. a. ISSN 0084-7305
- Australian Hospital. m. (Australian Institute of Hospital Administrators) (Co-sponsor: Australian Public Health Association)
- Australian Hospitals and Health Services Yearbook. a. ISSN 0312-5599 (University of New South Wales. School of Health Administration)
- Aviation News. m.
- Hospitality; national fortnightly newspaper of the accommodation and food service industries. fortn. ISSN 0018-5949
- Hospitality Buyers Guide & Diary. a.
- Hotel and Motel Directory. a. ISSN 0085-1612
- Hotel Motel and Restaurant. m. ISSN 0018-6171
- Kompass Australia; register of Australian industry and commerce. a. ISSN 0075-6628 (Associated Chambers of Manufacturers of Australia) (Dist. by Iliffe NTP Inc., 300 E. 42nd St., New York, NY 10017)
- Pacific Computer Weekly. fortn.
- Travelweek; fortnightly newspaper of the travel industry. fortn.

**Istituto Italiano di Cultura**
947 Punt Road, South Yarra, 3141 Vic. Melbourne, Australia.
- Quaderni. irreg., no. 4, 1971.

**Italian Chamber of Commerce in Australia**
First Floor, 255A Castlereagh St., Sydney, N.S.W. 2000, Australia.
- Italian-Australian Bulletin of Commerce. bi-m. ISSN 0047-1658

**Ivimey and Associates Pty. Ltd.**
35 Hume St., Crows Nest, N.S.W. 2065, Australia.
- Australian Boating Industry. m. ISSN 0045-0324

**John Jackson and Associates Pty. Ltd.**
Box A 771, Sydney South, N.S.W. 2000, Australia.
- Jackson Construction Reports. w.
- Marketing Information Bulletin. m. ISSN 0311-2330

**Jaguar Clubs of Australia**
49 Tristania St., Doveton, Vic. 3177, Australia.
- Jaguar Journal of Australia. irreg. ISSN 0310-3137

**James Conran Pty. Ltd.**
Box 3349, G.P.O., Sydney, N.S.W. 2001, Australia.
- Control Systems; measurement automatic control instrumentation. 10 per yr. (Feb.-Nov.) ISSN 0010-8065

**James Cook University of North Queensland**
Townsville 4811, North Queensland, Australia.
- A U M L A; a journal of literary criticism, philology and linguistics. s-a. ISSN 0001-2793 (Australasian Universities Language and Literature Association)
- James Cook University of North Queensland. Research and Publications Report. a.

**James Cook University of North Queensland. Dept. of English**
Townsville 4811, Australia.
- Ling. 3 per yr.

**James Cook University of North Queensland. Department of Geography**
Box 999, Douglas 04811, Australia.
- James Cook University of North Queensland. Department of Geography. Monograph Series. irreg., no. 6, 1974.

**Japan External Trade Organisation**
Japan Trade Centre, 6th Level, Tower Building, Australia Sq., Sydney, N.S.W. 2000, Australia.
- J E T R O Information Bulletin. bi-m. ISSN 0310-8740

**Jay Kay Publications**
Box 56, Croydon, N.S.W. 2132, Australia.
- Australian Lapidary Magazine. m. ISSN 0004-9603

**Jesus Activity Media**
Voice Media, Box 682, Chatswood, N.S.W. 2067, Australia.
- Sydney Town Express. m. ISSN 0310-5466

**Jobson's Publications**
(Subsidiary of: Dun & Bradstreet (Australia) Pty. Ltd.)
G.P.O. Box 5338, Sydney, N.S.W. 2001, Australia.
- Jobson's Mining Year Book. a. ISSN 0075-3777
- Jobson's Year Book of Public Companies of Australia and New Zealand. a. ISSN 0075-3785

**Journal de Conchyliologie**
Ed. Dr. P. H. Fischer, 18/55 Prince Albert Street, Mosman, N.S.W. 2088, Australia.
- Journal de Conchyliologie. q. ISSN 0021-7719

**Kangaroo Protection Committee**
G.P.O. Box 3719, Sydney, N.S.W. 2001, Australia.
- Kangaroo Protection Committee Newsletter. q.

**Khasmik Poetry Quarterly**
26 Breillat St., Sydney 2038, Australia.
- Khasmik Poetry Quarterly. q.

**Ralph W. King & Yuill**
33 Bligh St., Kindersley House, Sydney 2000, Australia.
- Investment Review of Australian Companies. a. ISSN 0075-6075

**Knights of the Southern Cross**
Box 184C. G.P.O., Melbourne, Victoria 3001, Australia.
- Advance Australia. m. ISSN 0001-8619

**Kralco Printing Co. Pty. Ltd.**
G.P.O. Box 3186, 33 Bligh and 20 O'Connell Sts., Sydney, Australia.
- Australian Stock Exchange Journal. m. ISSN 0045-0901 (Australian Associated Stock Exchanges)

**L.W. & T.S. Nominees**
Tootal Park, Tootal Rd., Dingley, Victoria 3172, Australia.
- Australian Motor Cycle News. fortn. ISSN 0004-9786
- Australian Trail & Track. 6-8 per yr.

**La Trobe University. Historical Association**
La Trobe University, Bundoora, Vic. 3083, Australia.
- La Trobe Historical Studies. irreg.

**La Trobe University. Students Representative Council**
Bundoora, Melbourne 3083, Australia.
- Rabelais. s-m.

**Labor Council of New South Wales**
- Australian Labor Party (NSW Branch). Labor Year Book. (pub. by Mass Communications Pty. Ltd.)

**Lamb Publications Pty. Ltd.**
19 Main St., Osborne Park, W.A. 6017, Australia.
- Commerce Industrial and Mining Review. m. ISSN 0010-2865
- West Australian Craftsman; a magazine for Freemasons. m. ISSN 0043-3055

**E. G. A. Lambert & Associates**
Box 78, Artarmon, N.S.W. 2064, Australia.
- Australian Industrial Law Review. irreg. ISSN 0084-7445

**Land Newspaper Ltd.**
Box 1558, Sydney 2001, Australia.
- Land. w. ISSN 0023-7523

**Law Book Co. Ltd.**
301-305 Kent St., Sydney, N.S.W. 2001, Australia.
- Australian Business Law Review. q. ISSN 0310-1053
- Australian Digest; a digest of all the Australian law reports. irreg., vol. 30, 1970. ISSN 0067-1843
- Australian Law Journal. m. ISSN 0004-9611
- Australian Legal Monthly Digest. m. ISSN 0004-9646
- Australian Tax Review. q.
- Commonwealth Law Reports. irreg.(approx. 10 issues per year) ISSN 0069-7133
- Current Australian and New Zealand Legal Literature Index. q.
- Federal Law Reports. irreg. ISSN 0085-0462
- Industrial Arbitration Service. irreg. ISSN 0085-1825
- Land Laws Service. irreg.
- Local Government Reports of Australia. irreg. ISSN 0076-0242
- New South Wales Law Reports. 6-8 per yr. ISSN 0312-1674 (Council of Law Reporting for New South Wales)
- Papua and New Guinea Law Reports. irreg. ISSN 0085-4689
- Practical Forms and Precedents (New South Wales) irreg., 1972, vol. 7. ISSN 0048-508X
- Shire & Municipal Record. m. ISSN 0037-3966
- Tasmanian State Reports. a. ISSN 0085-7106

**Law Book Co. Ltd. Queensland Branch**
27 Turbot St., Brisbane, Qld. 4000, Australia.
- Queensland Lawyer. bi-m. ISSN 0312-1658

**Law Book Co. Ltd. Victoria Branch**
389 Lonsdale St., Melbourne, Vic. 3000, Australia.
- South Australian State Reports. 2 per yr. ISSN 0049-1470
- Town Planning and Local Government Guide. m. ISSN 0040-9995

**Law Council of Australia**
155 Queen St., Melbourne Vic. 3000, Australia.
- Law Council of Australia. Law Council Newsletter. q. ISSN 0047-4177

**Law Institute of Victoria**
465 Little Bourke St., Melbourne, Victoria 3000, Australia.
- Law Institute Journal. m.(except Jan) ISSN 0023-9267

**Law Society of New South Wales**
170 Phillips St., Sydney, N.S.W. 2000, Australia.
- Law Society Journal. 6 per yr. ISSN 0023-9372

**Lawrence Publishing Co. Pty. Ltd.**
13-31 Barrett St., Kensington, Victoria, Australia.
- Australian Food Manufacturer and Distributor. m. ISSN 0004-9131
- Australian Leather Journal, Boot and Shoe Recorder. m. ISSN 0004-962X
- Australian Wine, Brewing & Spirit Review. m. ISSN 0005-044X
- Epicurean. bi-m. ISSN 0013-9548
- Graphic Pictorial of Australian Food and Allied Industry; buyers guide for the food & allied industry. a.
- Graphic Pictorial Shoe and Leather Industry; buyers guide for footwear, leather & allied industry. a.

**Leader Publishing Co.**
2 Dale St., Brookvale, N.S.W., 2100, Australia.
- Australasian Kennel Review and Dog News. m. ISSN 0045-0081

**Learning Exchange**
430 Waverley Rd., East Malvern, Vic. 3145, Australia.
- Learning Exchange. m. ISSN 0310-3242

**Legion Cabs Trading Co-Operative Society Ltd**
77 Foveaux St, Surry Hills N.S.W. 2010, Australia.
- Legionair. m. ISSN 0024-0451

**Leisure Boating and Speedway Magazines Pty. Ltd.**
P. O. Box 319, Avalon Beach, New South Wales 2107, Australia.
- Australian Boating. m.
- Australian Speedway Yearbook. a. ISSN 0310-8368

**Bernard Leser Publications Pty. Ltd.**
(Subsidiary of: Conde Nast Publications Pty. Ltd.)
49 Clarence St., Sydney 2000, Australia.
- Vogue Australia. 10 per yr. ISSN 0042-8019
- Vogue Living. bi-m. ISSN 0042-8035

**Liberal Catholic Church in Australia**
300 Blaxland Rd., Ryde, N.S.W. 2112, Australia.
- Communion. q. ISSN 0004-9662

**Liberal Party of Australia. Federal Secretariat**
Box 21, Canberra, A.C.T. 2600, Australia.
- Australian Liberal. m. ISSN 0004-9654
- Current Politics. irreg. ISSN 0574-7635

**Libraries Board of South Australia**
Box 419 G.P.O., Adelaide, 5001 South Australia.
- Australiana Facsimile Editions. irreg., 1970, Apr., no. 191. ISSN 0067-2246
- Index to Australian Book Reviews. q. ISSN 0019-3968
- Miscellanea Musicologica; Adelaide studies in musicology. irreg. ISSN 0076-9355 (University of Adelaide)
- Occasional Papers in Librarianship. irreg. ISSN 0078-3080
- Pinpointer; a current subject guide to popular periodicals. bi-m. ISSN 0031-9910
- South Australia. Libraries Board. Annual Report. a. ISSN 0081-2633
- South Australia. Libraries Board. Books for Young People; an annotated list. irreg. ISSN 0081-2641
- South Australia. State Library. Reference Services Branch. Reference Services Bibliographies. irreg. ISSN 0311-3078
- South Australiana; a journal for the publication and study of South Australian historical and literary sources. s-a. ISSN 0038-3023

**Library Association of Australia. A.C.T. Branch**
P.O. Box 679, Canberra City, A.C.T. 2601, Australia.
- Acta. irreg.

**Library Association of Australia. Queensland Branch**
Dept. of Education, Box 33, North Quay, Brisbane, Qld. 4000, Australia.
- Quill; Queensland inter-library liason. q. ISSN 0033-6467

**Library Association of Australia. School and Children's Libraries Sections**
24A Llewellyn St., Oatley, N.S.W. 2223, Australia.
- Orana; journal for school and children's librarians. q.

**Library Association of Australia. Universities & College Libraries Section**
c/o D. H. Borehardt, La Trobe University, Bundoora 3083, Australia.
- Australian Academic and Research Libraries. q. ISSN 0004-8623

**Library Automated Systems Information Exchange**
Box 581, Brookvale, N.S.W. 2100, Australia.
- L. A. S. I. E/Library Automated System Information Exchange. bi-m. ISSN 0047-3774

**Library Board of Queensland**
State Library of Queensland, William St., Brisbane, Australia.
- Queensland Heritage. s-a. ISSN 0033-6157

**Library of New South Wales**
Cataloguing Dept., Macquarie St., Sydney, N.S.W. 2000, Australia.
- New South Wales Library Bulletin. m. ISSN 0028-6788
- New South Wales Official Publications Received in the Library of New South Wales. m. ISSN 0028-6796

**Life & Vision Publications**
240 Collins St., Melbourne, Vic. 3000, Australia.
- Health and Vision. bi-m. ISSN 0046-7014

**Lincoln Electric Co. (Australia)**
35 Bryant St., Padstow, N.S.W. 2211, Australia.
- Australian Welder. 3 per yr. ISSN 0084-7623

**Linguistic Circle of Canberra**
- Pacific Linguistics. Series A: Occasional Papers. (pub. by Australian National University. Research School of Pacific Studies)
- Pacific Linguistics. Series B: Monographs. (pub. by Australian National University. Research School of Pacific Studies)
- Pacific Linguistics. Series C: Books. (pub. by Australian National University. Research School of Pacific Studies)
- Pacific Linguistics. Series D: Special Publications. (pub. by Australian National University. Research School of Pacific Studies)
- Papers in Australian Linguistics. (pub. by Australian National University. Research School of Pacific Studies)
- Papers in Borneo Linguistics. (pub. by Australian National University. Research School of Pacific Studies)
- Papers in Linguistics of Melanesia. (pub. by Australian National University. Research School of Pacific Studies)
- Papers in New Guinea Linguistics. (pub. by Australian National University. Research School of Pacific Studies)
- Papers in Philippine Linguistics. (pub. by Australian National University. Research School of Pacific Studies)
- Papers in South East Asian Linguistics. (pub. by Australian National University. Research School of Pacific Studies)

**Lingvologia Revuo**
c/o Emil Hanhiniemi, Box 764, Ingham, Qld. 4850, Australia.
- Lingvologia Revuo. irreg. ISSN 0024-3965

**Linnean Society of N.S.W.**
Science Center, 35-43 Clarence St., Sydney, N.S.W. 2000, Australia.
- Linnean Society of New South Wales. Proceedings. 4 per yr. ISSN 0047-4746

**Lions International. Australian Branch**
- Lion. (pub. by International Public Relations Pty. Ltd.)

**Lipscombe & Associates**
P.O. Box 158, Claremont, W. A. 6010, Australia.
- Executive Briefing. m. ISSN 0310-8651

**Living Today News**
Box B49 G.P.O., Perth, Australia.
- Living Today. m. (Charlie Carter Pty. Ltd.)

**Lloyds Australian Register of Trades & Commerce Pty. Ltd.**
2 Castlereagh, Sydney, Australia.
- Lloyds Australian and New Zealand Trade Register. a. ISSN 0085-2813

**Local Government Association of South Australia**
- Local Government in South Australia. (pub. by Messenger Publications Pty. Ltd.)

**Long Distance Road Transport Association of Australia**
- Highway Transport. (pub. by Haldane Publishing Co. Pty. Ltd)

**H. D. Love & Associates Pty. Ltd.**
7 Peacock St., Middle Brighton, Vic. 3186, Australia.
- Syntec. m. ISSN 0310-4540

**Low Gear Fellowship**
c/o R.G. Shepherd, Ed., 12-18 Tintern Ave., Toorak, Vic. 3142, Australia.
- Low Gear Bulletin. q.

**Philip Luker**
57 Darlinghurst Rd., Kings Cross, N. S. W. 2011, Australia.
- Interprobe. w. ISSN 0310-8465

**Lutheran Church of Australia**
- Lutheran Church of Australia. Yearbook. (pub. by Lutheran Publishing House)
- Lutheran Theological Journal. (pub. by Lutheran Publishing House)

**Lutheran Publishing House**
205 Halifax Street, Adelaide, S.A. 5000, Australia.
- Lutheran Church of Australia. Yearbook. a.
- Lutheran Theological Journal. 3 per yr. ISSN 0024-7553 (Lutheran Church of Australia)

**Lutheran Women of Australia**
10 Kent Ave., Warradale, S.A. 5406, Australia.
- Lutheran Women. bi-m.

**M.G.A. Publications Pty. Ltd.**
Box 109, Rose Bay, N.S.W. 2029, Australia.
- Australasian Athletics. m. ISSN 0310-8783

**McCarron Bird Pty. Ltd.**
594 Lonsdale St., Melbourne, Victoria 3000,
Australia.
- Insurance Record of Australia & New Zealand; a
monthly journal of insurance, banking and
finance. m.

**J. C. McColl & Associates Pty. Ltd., Farm
Management Consultants**
Box 131, Numurkah, Vic. 3636, Australia.
- Modern Management. m.

**Macquarie University. Centre for Advancement of
Teaching**
North Ryde, N.S.W. 2113, Australia.
- C A T Newsletter. q. ISSN 0311-0982

**Macquarie University. School of English & Linguistics**
c/o Prof. Yasmine Gooneratne, North Ryde,
N.S.W. 2113, Australia.
- New Ceylon Writing; creative and critical writing
of Sri Lanka. irreg.

**Macquarie University. School of History, Philosphy
and Politics**
North Ryde, N.S.W. 2113, Australia.
- Ancient Society; Resources for Teachers. 3 per yr.
ISSN 0310-5814

**Macquarie University. School of Modern Languages**
North Ryde ,New South Wales 2113, Australia.
- Macquarie University French Monographs. 4 per
yr.

**Magazine Art Pty. Ltd.**
571 Hampton St., Hampton, Vic. 3188, Australia.
- Chartered Builder. irreg. ISSN 0311-1903
(Australian Institute of Building)

**Magazine Associates**
Box 66, Avalon Beach, N.S.W. 2107, Australia.
- Mine and Quarry Mechanisation. a. ISSN 0085-
3453

**Magazine Printers**
Foveaux St., Sydney 2000, N.S.W., Australia.
- Federated Ironworkers' Association of Australia.
Labor News. m (9 per yr) ISSN 0014-9276

**Makar Press**
P.O. Box 71, St. Lucia 4067, Australia.
- Gargoyle Poets. 6 per yr. (University of
Queensland. English Department)
- Makar. 3 per yr.

**Malacological Society of Australia**
Box 12771, Melbourne, Vic. 3001, Australia.
- Australian Shell News. q. ISSN 0310-1304
- Malacological Society of Australia. Journal. a.
ISSN 0085-2988

**Manufacturer Publishing Co. Pty. Ltd.**
Box 349, Manuka, A.C.T. 2601, Australia.
- Australasian Manufacturer. w. ISSN 0004-8410
- D. C. N. Exporters and Cargo Handling Guide. a.

**Mappin & Curran (Philatelists) Pty. Ltd.**
Shops 30-31 Mutual Arcade, 266 Flinders St.,
Melbourne 3000, Australia
(Box 5027 G.P.O., Melbourne 3000, Australia)
- Australasian Stamp Collector. bi-m. ISSN 0004-
8496

**Marine Board of Hobart**
Franklin Wharf, Tas. 7000, Australia.
- Marine Board of Hobart. Newsletter. irreg. ISSN
0310-9704

**Mark-Tier's Economy Report**
Box 419, Darlinghurst, N.S.W. 2010, Australia.
- Mark-Tier's Economy Report. s-m.

**Market Industries News**
24 Henry St., Carlton, N.S.W. 2218, Australia.
- Market Industries News. bi-m. ISSN 0025-3561

**D. L. Marks**
279 Flinders Lane, Melbourne, Vic. 3000, Australia.
- Audio Visual Australia. 4 per yr. ISSN 0310-0634

**Maryborough Adult Education Centre**
P.O. Box 65, Maryborough, Qld 4650, Australia.
- Moonaboola Quill. irreg. (Hervey Bay Writers'
Workshop)

**Masque Publications**
22 Steam Mill St., Sydney, N.S.W., 2000, Australia
(Subscr. Address: Box 3504, G.P.O., Sydney,
N.S.W. 2001, Australia)
- Masque. bi-m. ISSN 0025-469X

**Mass Communications Pty. Ltd.**
Labor Council Building, 377 Sussex St., Sydney,
NSW 2000, Australia.
- Australian Labor Party (NSW Branch). Labor
Year Book. a. ISSN 0310-5296 (Labor Council of
New South Wales)

**A. H. Massina & Co. Pty. Ltd.**
98 York St., South Melbourne, Vic 3205, Australia.
- Australian Journal of Physiotherapy. q. ISSN
0004-9514 (Australian Physiotherapy Association)

**Master Bakers Association**
23 Museum St., Perth, W.A. 6000, Australia.
- Bread Manufacturer and Pastrycook of Western
Australia. m. ISSN 0045-2750

**Master Builders Association**
- South Australian Builder. (pub. by Sherwood
Publishing Co.)

**Master Builders Association of New South Wales**
- Construction. (pub. by Building Publishing Co.
Pty. Ltd.)

**Master Builders' Association of Tasmania**
G. P. O. 992k, Hobart, Tas. 7001, Australia.
- Tasmanian Building Journal. m.

**Master Builders Association of Victoria & Builders
Exchange**
- Australian Builder. (pub. by Australian Builder
Publishing Co., Pty. Ltd.)

**Master Carriers' Association of New South Wales**
- Freight Carriers. (pub. by Shennen Publishing &
Publicity Co.)

**Master Grocers' Association of Victoria Ltd.**
1464 Ferntree Gully Rd., Knoxfield 3180, Victoria,
Australia.
- Food and Liquor Retailer. m.

**Master Ladies Hairdressers Association**
- Coiffure. (pub. by Research Publications Pty. Ltd)

**Master Ladies Hairdressers' Association of New
South Wales**
Second Floor, 371 Pitt St., Sydney 2000, Australia.
- Hair Fashions. q. ISSN 0046-6727

**Master Pastrycooks Association of New South Wales**
6Th Floor, 58 Margaret St., Sydney, N.S.W. 2000,
Australia.
- Pastrycooks Review; food service journal. m.

**Master Plumbers & Mechanical Services Association**
177 Archer St., North Adelaide 5006, Australia.
- Master Plumber of South Australia. m. ISSN
0025-5068

**Master Plumbers Association of New South Wales**
10 Regent St., 2008 Sydney, Australia.
- Master Plumber. m. ISSN 0025-5041

**Master Plumbers Association of Queensland**
Box 408, Fortitude Valley, Queensland 4006,
Australia.
- Queensland Master Plumber. m. ISSN 0048-637X

**J.J. Masterson, Ed. & Pub.**
89 Highett St., West Richmond, Vic. 3121,
Australia.
- Australian Communist; a journal of Marxism-
Leninism Mao Tse-Tung thought. irreg. ISSN
0084-7275

**Mathematical Association of South Australia**
424 Kensington Rd., Wattle Park, S.A. 5066,
Australia.
- Mobius. 3 per yr.
- Trigon; school maths journal. 3 per yr.

**Mathematical Association of Victoria**
Clunies Ross House, 191 Royal Parade, Parkville,
Vic. 3052, Australia.
- Vinculum. irreg.

**Mathematical Association of Western Australia**
Department of Mathematics, University of Western
Australia, Nedlands, WA 6009, Australia.
- Rhombus. 4 per yr.
- Sigma. 4 per yr.

**Me Jane**
c/o Womens House, 25 Alberta St., Sydney,
N.S.W., Australia.
- Me Jane; a women's liberation, radical Feminist
newspaper. irreg. ISSN 0047-6315

**Meat and Allied Trades Federation of Australia**
33-35 Pitt St., Sydney, N.S.W. 2000, Australia.
- Meat Trades Journal of Australia. m. ISSN 0047-
6366

**Meat and Allied Trades' Federation of Australia.
Tasmanian Division**
P.O. Box 420, Launceston, Tas. 7250, Australia.
- Tasmanian Meat Industry Journal. irreg.

**Meat & Allied Trades Federation of Australia.
Western Australian Division**
Box 141, West Perth, W.A. 6005, Australia.
- Meat and Allied Trades Federation of Australia.
Western Australian Division. Meat Industry. m.
ISSN 0047-6331

**Medico-Legal Society of New South Wales**
10th Floor, 180 Phillip St., Sydney, N.S.W. 2000,
Australia.
- Medico-Legal Society of New South Wales.
Proceedings. triennial. ISSN 0047-6587

**Medico-Legal Society of Victoria**
2 Collins St., Melbourne, Vic. 3000, Australia.
- Medico-Legal Society of Victoria. Proceedings. 5
per yr. ISSN 0047-6595

**Melbourne Amateur Walking and Touring Club**
G.P.O. Box 2446v, Melbourne, Vic. 3001, Australia.
- Melbourne Walker. a.

**Melbourne & Metropolitan Board of Works**
Box 4342 G.P.O. Melbourne, Victoria 3001,
Australia.
- Living City. 2 per yr. ISSN 0047-4835

**Melbourne Bushwalkers**
G.P.O. Box 1751q, Melbourne, Vic. 3001, Australia.
- Walk. a.

**Melbourne Harbor Trust Commissioners**
Port Authority Bldg., 29 Market St., Melbourn, Vic.
3000, Australia.
- Port of Melbourne Quarterly. q. ISSN 0048-4865

**Melbourne University Press**
Box 278, Carlton South, Vic. 3053, Australia
(Dist. by International Scholarly Book Services,
Inc., Box 555, Forest Grove, Ore. 97116)
- Melbourne Studies in Education. a. ISSN 0076-
6275 (University of Melbourne. School of
Education)

**Mercedes Publishing Co.**
240 Chapel St., Prahran, 3181 Victoria, Australia
(Subscriptions to: Box 669, Adelaide, S.A. 5001,
Australia)
- Australian Journal of Hospital Pharmacy. q.
(Society of Hospital Pharmacists of Australia)
- Radiographer. q. ISSN 0033-8273 (Australasian
Institute of Radiography)

**Merchandising Magazines Pty. Ltd.**
142 Clarence St., Sydney 2000, Australia.
- Textile Journal of Australia. m. ISSN 0040-5019

**Mercury-Walch Pty. Ltd.**
5-7 Bowen Road, Moonah, Tasmania 7009,
Australia.
- Tasmanian Almanac. a. ISSN 0083-7016

**Messenger Publications Pty. Ltd.**
254 Commercial Rd., Port Adelaide, S.A. 5015,
Australia.
- Australasian Nurses Journal. m.
- Local Government in South Australia. q. ISSN
0047-4924 (Local Government Association of
South Australia)
- National Water Sport. 12 per yr. (International
505 Association) (Co-sponsors: S. A. Rowing
Association; S. A. Water Skiing Association)
- South Australian Bowler. 10 per yr. (Royal South
Australian Bowling Association)

**Metal Trades Industry Association of Australia**
105 Walker Street, North Sydney, N.S.W. 2060,
Australia.
- M. T. I. A. Annual Report. a. ISSN 0085-3321
- M T I A News Bulletin. bi-m. ISSN 0047-6854

**Methodist Church in New South Wales**
139 Castlereagh St., Sydney 2000, Australia.
- Methodist. m.

**Methodist Church in South Australia**
Epworth Building, 33 Pirie St., Adelaide 5000,
Australia.
- Central Times. fortn. ISSN 0038-2949

**Methodist Church of Victoria & Tasmania**
- New Spectator. (pub. by Methodist Department of
Communication)

**Methodist Department of Communication**
130 Little Collins St., Melbourne, Victoria 3000,
Australia.
- New Spectator. fortn. ISSN 0300-3736 (Methodist
Church of Victoria & Tasmania)

**Methodist Overseas Missions**
Box 100, Sydney 2001, Australia.
- Missionary Review. q. ISSN 0026-6078 (Co-
Sponsors: Presbyterian Church of Australia;
Council for World Missions)

**Military Historical Society of Australia**
c/o K. R. White, Box 67, Lyneham, A.C.T. 2602,
Australia.
- Sabretache. q. ISSN 0048-8933

**Miners Federation of Australia**
Labor Council Building, 377-383 Sussex St., Sydney,
N.S.W. 2000, Australia.
- Common Cause. w.

**Mirror Class Association of Australia**
29 Haines St., Hawthorn, Vic. 3122, Australia.
- Mirror Class Association of Australia. Yearbook.
a.

**Mirror Newspapers Ltd.**
Brunswick & McLachlan Sts., Fortitude Valley,
Brisbane, Queensland, Australia.
- Sunday Sun. w.

**Missionaries of the Sacred Heart**
- Annals Magazine. (pub. by Chevalier Press)

**Mitchell College of Advanced Education. Business and
Administration Society**
Bathurst, NSW 2795, Australia.
- Mitchell Business Review. a. ISSN 0311-2780

**Mitsui and Co. Australia, Ltd.**
Royal Exchange Building, 56 Pitt St., Sydney,
N.S.W. 2000, Australia.
- Mitsui News. irreg. ISSN 0311-0273

**Modern Country Music Association**
P.O. Box 35, North Quay, Qld. 4000, Australia.
- Country Music Times. bi-m.

**Modern Language Teachers' Association of New
South Wales**
c/o School of Modern Languages, Macquarie
University, North Ryde, NSW 2113, Australia.
- M. L. T. A. News. irreg. ISSN 0310-9674

**Modern Language Teachers Association of Victoria**
c/o Department of French, Monash University,
Clayton, Vic. 3168, Australia.
- M. L. Newsletter. bi-m.

**Modern Magazines (Holdings) Ltd.**
Ryrie House, 15 Boundary St., Rushcutter's Bay,
N.S.W. 2011, Australia.
- Audio Trader. m.
- Australian Camera & Cine. m.
- Australian Cricket. m. ISSN 0004-895X
- Australian Cricket Yearbook. a. ISSN 0084-7291
- Australian Golf Instructional. m. ISSN 0311-0400
- Australian Motorcycle Rider. m. ISSN 0311-0141
- Ear for Music. m.
- Electronics Today International. m.
- Modern Boating. m. ISSN 0026-752X
- Modern Fishing. m. ISSN 0026-7732
- Modern Motor. m. ISSN 0026-8143
- Revs Motorcycle News (Revs) fortn. ISSN 0027-
2175
- Rugby League Week. w. ISSN 0035-9742
- Water Skier. m.(9 per yr.) ISSN 0043-1419
(Australian Waterski Association)

**Modern Medicine of Australia Pty. Ltd.**
457 Pacific Highway, Artarmon, N.S.W. 2064,
Australia.
- Modern Medicine. s-m. ISSN 0312-875X

**Modern Teaching Methods Association**
c/o P. L. Jeffery, 22 Boyana Cres., Croydon, Vic.
3136, Australia.
- Modern Teaching. irreg. ISSN 0085-3526

**Monaro Conservation Society**
Box 42, Cooma, N.S.W. 2630, Australia.
- Monaro Conservation Society. Bulletin. 11 per yr.

**Monash University**
Wellington Rd., Clayton, Vic. 3168, Australia.
- Monash Review; what's new in education,
research and community service. q.

**Monash University. Anthropology and Sociology
Society**
Clayton, Victoria 3168, Australia.
- Contradiction. a.

**Monash University. Centre of Southeast Asian
Studies**
Clayton, Victoria 3168, Australia.
- Monash Papers on Southeast Asia. irreg.

**Monash University. Department of Civil Engineering**
Clayton, Vic. 3168, Australia.
- Monash University. Department of Civil
Engineering. Civil Engineering Research Report.
5 per yr.

**Monash University. Department of Classical Studies**
Wellington Road, Clayton, 3168, Victoria, Australia.
- Apeiron. s-a. ISSN 0003-6390

**Monash University. Department of French**
Clayton, Vic. 3168, Australia.
- Australian Journal of French Studies. 3 per yr.
ISSN 0004-9468

**Monash University. Department of Geography**
Clayton, Australia.
- Monash University. Publications in Geography. 3-
6 per yr.

**Monash University. English Department**
Clayton, Victoria 3168, Australia.
- Komos. irreg. ISSN 0047-3642

**Monash University. Faculty of Law**
Clayton, Victoria 3168, Australia.
- Monash University Law Review. s-a. ISSN 0311-
3140

**Monash University. Higher Education Advisory and
Research Unit**
Clayton, Vic. 3168, Australia.
- Monash University. Higher Education Advisory
and Research Unit. Notes on Higher Education.
irreg. ISSN 0310-5695

**Monash University. Monash Engineering Students
Society**
Clayton, Vic. 3168, Australia.
- Apocalypse. irreg. ISSN 0084-666X

**Monash University. Science Fiction Association**
c/o Union, Monash University, Clayton, Vic. 3168,
Australia.
- Cor Serpentis. irreg. ISSN 0311-1245

**Roy Morgan Research Centre Pty. Ltd.**
G.P.O. Box 2282U, Melbourne, Vic. 3001,
Australia.
- Australian Gallup Polls. w.
- Morgan Index on TV and Radio. a.
- Morgan Magazine & Newspaper Survey. s-a.

**Mothers' Union in Australia**
The Rectory, Coffs Harbour, N. S. W. 2450,
Australia
(Orders to: Financial Secretary, P.O. Box 163, Coffs
Harbour, N. S. W. 2450, Australia)
- Mia-Mia. bi-m.

**Motor Traders Association of N.S.W.**
Box 32, Potts Point, N.S.W. 2011, Australia.
- M. T. A. Journal. (Motor Traders Association of
New South Wales) q. ISSN 0047-5297

**Mt. Isa Writers Workshop**
97 Trainor St., Mt. Isa, Qld. 4825, Australia.
- Plain Turkey. irreg. ISSN 0311-0753

**Municipal Association of Tasmania**
57 Collins St., Hobart, Tas. 7000, Australia.
- Municipal Association of Tasmania. Session.
Minutes of Proceedings. a. ISSN 0085-3585

**Municipal Association of Victoria**
15 Queens Rd., Melbourne 3004 Victoria, Australia.
- Australian Municipal Journal. m. ISSN 0004-9808
- Municipal Association of Victoria. Minutes of
Proceedings of Annual Session. a. ISSN 0077-
2143

**Municipal Tramways Trust**
Box 1019 G.P.O., Adelaide 5001, Australia.
- Among Ourselves. bi-m. ISSN 0003-1968

**Murray Goulburn Co-Op Ltd.**
644 Victoria St., North Melbourne, Vic. 3051,
Australia.
- Murray Goulburn News. m.

**Murray Grey Beef Cattle Society**
- Murray Grey World. (pub. by Geoff Phillips &
Associates Pty. Ltd.)

**Murray Park College of Advanced Education.
Department of History and Australian Studies**
15 Lorne Ave., Magill, SA 5072, Australia.
- Cabbages and Kings. irreg. ISSN 0310-1584

**K.G. Murray Publishing Co. Pty. Ltd.**
142 Clarence St., Sydney 2000, Australia.
- Adam Magazine. m. ISSN 0001-8023
- Australian Bride Magazine. q. ISSN 0004-8771
- Australian Country Magazine. m ISSN 0004-8933
- Australian Hot Rodding Review. q. ISSN 0004-
9301
- Australian House and Garden. m. ISSN 0004-
931X
- Australian House and Garden Annual. a. ISSN
0084-7429
- Australian House and Garden Practical Planning
Series. m. ISSN 0084-7437
- Australian Outdoors. m. ISSN 0004-9905
- Australian Seacraft. m. ISSN 0005-0237
- Australian Speedway. a. ISSN 0311-1199
- Building Materials & Equipment. bi-m. ISSN
0007-3512
- Good Gardening. q. ISSN 0046-6123
- Home Improvement Annual. a.
- Power Boat Tests. irreg.
- Sports Car Road Tests. irreg.
- Sports Car World. m. ISSN 0038-8173
- True Confessions. m. ISSN 0041-347X
- True Experience. m. ISSN 0041-3518
- True Love. m. ISSN 0041-3542
- True Romance. m. ISSN 0041-3585
- True Story. m. ISSN 0041-3593
- Two Wheels. m. ISSN 0041-4700
- Wheels. m. ISSN 0043-4779

**Murray Valley Development League**
Box 359, Albury 2640, Australia.
- Riverlander. m. ISSN 0035-5682

**Musicological Society of Australia**
c/o Australia Music Centre, Box N9, Grosvenor St.,
Sydney, N.S.W. 2000, Australia.
- Musicology. a. ISSN 0077-250X

**Narcotics Education Service**
148 Fox Valley Rd., Wahroonga, N.S.W. 2076,
Australia.
- Alert. bi-m. ISSN 0044-7234

**National Acoustic Laboratories**
5 Hickson Rd., Millers Point, N.S.W., Australia.
- National Acoustic Laboratories, Sydney. Annual
Report. a. ISSN 0311-8983

**National Association of Australian State Road
Authorities**
P.O. Box J141, Brickfield Hill, Sydney, N.S.W.
2000, Australia.
- Australian Roads. bi-a. ISSN 0045-0847
- National Association of Australian State Road
Authorities. Guide to the Publications and
Policies of N A A S R A. a.

**National Association of Retail Grocers of Australia
(NARGA)**
- Retail World. (pub. by Retail World Pty. Ltd.)

**National Association of Testing Authorities**
688 Pacific Highway, Chatswood, N.S.W. 2067,
Australia.
- N. A. T. A. Directory. a.

- N. A. T. A. Register of Laboratories. Monthly Amendment Sheets. m.

**National Bank of Australasia Ltd.**
Box 84A, Melbourne 3001, Australia.
- National Bank of Australasia. National Bank Monthly Summary. m.

**National Civic Council**
5 Riversdale Rd., Hawthorn, Vic. 3122, Australia.
- National Civic Council. Facts. irreg. ISSN 0085-3682

**National Council of the Realist Writers Groups**
Box 12, Northbridge, N.S.W. 2063, Australia.
- Realist. q. ISSN 0048-6884

**National Council of Women of Australia**
Box 75, Manuka A.C.T. 2603, Australia.
- National Council of Women of Australia. Bulletin. q. ISSN 0047-8792

**National Council of Wool Selling Brokers of Australia**
4 O'Connell St., Sydney, N.S.W. 2000, Australia.
- National Council of Wool Selling Brokers of Australia. News Bulletin. m.
- Wool Review. a. ISSN 0084-1218

**National Fund Raising Counsel of Australia Pty. Ltd.**
20 Bridge St., Sydney, N.S.W. 2000, Australia.
- Pride. 2 per yr.

**National Gallery of Victoria**
St. Kilda Rd., Melbourne, Victoria, Australia.
- Art Bulletin of Victoria. a. ISSN 0066-7935

**National Heart Foundation of Australia**
P.O. Box 691, Canberra City, A.C.T. 2601, Australia.
- National Heart Foundation of Australia. Research-In-Progress. a. ISSN 0077-4685

**National Heart Foundation of Australia. Victorian Division**
Royal Parade, Parkville, Vic. 3050, Australia.
- Notes on Cardiovascular Diseases. irreg. ISSN 0550-0990

**National Herbarium**
Royal Botanic Gardens, Sydney, N.S.W. 2000, Australia.
- Flora of New South Wales. irreg., vol. 4, 1973. ISSN 0077-8761
- Telopea. irreg.

**National Library of Australia**
see Australia. National Library of Australia

**National Museum of Victoria**
285-321 Russell St., Melbourne 3000, Victoria, Australia.
- Victoria, Australia. National Museum of Victoria. Memoirs. a. plus special issues. ISSN 0083-5986

**National Packaging Association of Australia**
370 St. Kilda Rd., Melbourne, Vic. 3004, Australia.
- Australian Packaging Buyers Guide. (pub. by I P C Business Press (Australia) Pty. Ltd.)
- National Packaging Association of Australia. Environment Newsletter. irreg.
- National Packaging Association of Australia, Legislation and Metrication Newsletter. irreg.

**National Packaging Association of Australia. Queensland Division**
375 Wickham Terrace, Brisbane, Qld 4000, Australia.
- N. P. A. Packaging Extracts. irreg.

**National Parks Association of N.S.W.**
263 Broadway, Sydney, N.S.W. 2007, Australia.
- National Parks Association of New South Wales. National Parks Journal. 8 per yr. ISSN 0047-9012

**National Roads and Motorists Association**
151 Clarence St., Sydney, N.S.W. 2000, Australia.
- Open Road. bi-m. ISSN 0048-1947

**National Rose Society of Australia**
- Australian Rose Annual. (pub. by Horticultural Press Pty. Ltd.)

**National Safety Council of Australia**
343 Little Collins St., Melbourne, Vict. 3000, Australia.
- Australian Family Safety. 4 per yr. ISSN 0004-9077
- Australian Safety News. bi-m. ISSN 0005-0180

**National Safety Council of Western Australia. Road Safety Division**
P.O. Box 42, Mt. Lawley, W.A. 6050, Australia.
- Road Safety and Driver Education News. irreg.

**National Training Council**
Box 2817AA, Melbourne, Vic. 3001, Australia.
- Australian Training News. q.

**National Trust of Australia (New South Wales)**
123 Clarence St., Sydney, Australia.
- National Trust of Australia (New South Wales) National Trust Bulletin. 5 per yr. ISSN 0047-9128

**National Trust of South Australia, Barmera Branch**
1 Langdon Terrace, Barmera, Australia.
- Historical Journal of Barmera and District. m. ISSN 0046-7545

**National Union of Railwaymen of Australia**
399 Illawarra Rd., Marrickville, Sydney, N.S.W. 2204, Australia.
- Railway Advocate. m. ISSN 0033-8818

**National Water Well Association of Australia**
Box 91, St Ives, N.S.W. 2075, Australia.
- National Water Well Association Journal. q. ISSN 0310-3625

**Natural Resources Conservation League of Victoria**
593-615 Springvale Rd., Springvale South, Victoria, Australia.
- Victoria's Resources. q. ISSN 0042-5230

**Nature Conservation Council of New South Wales**
230 Scenic Rd., Killcare Heights (via Hardy's Bay), NSW 2256, Australia.
- Nature Conservation Council of N. S. W. Bulletin. irreg. ISSN 0311-0745

**Nautical Association of Australia**
132 Noble St., Geelong, Vic. 3220, Australia.
- Log. q.

**Neos Kosmos**
219 Russell St., Melbourne, Victoria, Australia.
- Neos Kosmos. s-w. ISSN 0028-2693

**New Journalist**
Box K750, Haymarket N.S.W. 2000, Australia.
- New Journalist. bi-m.

**New South Wales. Attorney-General. Bureau of Crime Statistics and Research**
G.P.O. Box 6, Sydney, N.S.W. 2001, Australia.
- New South Wales. Attorney-General. Bureau of Crime Statistics and Research. Statistical Report. irreg. ISSN 0310-3684

**New South Wales. Attorney General Justice Department**
17th Level, Goodsell Bldg., 8-12 Chifley Square, Sydney, N.S.W. 2000, Australia.
- New South Wales Law Almanac. a. ISSN 0085-3992

**New South Wales. Department of Agriculture**
StateOffice Block, Phillip St., Sydney, N.S.W. 2000, Australia.
- Agricultural Gazette of New South Wales. bi-m. ISSN 0002-1474
- Dairy Topics.
- New South Wales. Department of Agriculture. Science Bulletin. irreg.

**New South Wales. Department of Agriculture. Division of Marketing and Economics**
State Office Block, Phillip St., Sydney, N.S.W. 2000, Australia.
- New South Wales. Department of Agriculture. Commodity Bulletin. m. ISSN 0310-186X
- New South Wales. Department of Agriculture. Weekly Marketing Notes. w.
- Review of Marketing and Agricultural Economics. q. ISSN 0034-6616

**New South Wales. Department of Decentralisation and Development**
Box 4169, G.P.O Sydney 2001 N.S.W., Australia.
- New South Wales Horizons. bi-m. ISSN 0310-5946

**New South Wales. Department of Education**
Box 33, Sydney, N.S.W. 2000, Australia.
- Education Gazette. fortn. (during school year) ISSN 0013-1334
- Home Science for Teachers in Secondary Schools. irreg.

- Inside Education. q.
- Leader. irreg. ISSN 0023-9585
- New South Wales. Department of Education. School Management Bulletin. irreg. ISSN 0085-3976
- Physical Education and Health. irreg.
- Primary Journal. q. ISSN 0311-1342
- Science Bulletin. 2 per yr.

**New South Wales. Department of Labour and Industry**
53 Martin Place, Sydney, N.S.W. 2000, Australia.
- New South Wales. Department of Labour and Industry. Safety. q.
- New South Wales Industrial Gazette. w. ISSN 0028-677X

**New South Wales. Department of Lands**
G.P.O. Box 39, Sydney, NSW 2001, Australia.
- Scope. irreg.

**New South Wales. Department of Main Roads**
Box 198, Haymarket, Sydney, N.S.W. 2000, Australia.
- Main Roads. q. ISSN 0025-0597

**New South Wales. Department of Mines**
State Office Block, Phillip St., Sydney, N.S.W. 2000, Australia.
- New South Wales. Department of Mines. Annual Report. a. ISSN 0077-8664
- New South Wales. Department of Mines. Annual Report. Statistical Supplement. a.
- New South Wales. Department of Mines. Chemical Laboratory. Report. irreg. ISSN 0077-8672
- New South Wales. Department of Mines. Coalfields Branch. Reports. irreg. ISSN 0077-8680
- New South Wales. Geological Survey. Bulletin. irreg.
- New South Wales. Geological Survey. Memoirs: Geology. irreg. ISSN 0077-8710
- New South Wales. Geological Survey. Memoirs: Palaeontology. irreg., no. 17, 1976.
- New South Wales. Geological Survey. Mineral Industry Series. irreg., no. 34, 1975. ISSN 0077-8729
- New South Wales. Geological Survey. Mineral Resources Series. irreg., no. 41, 1975. ISSN 0077-8737
- New South Wales. Geological Survey. Records. irreg., no. 17, 1976.

**New South Wales. Department of Technical Education**
Box K638, Haymarket, N.S.W. 2007, Australia.
- New South Wales. Department of Technical Education. Monthly Review. m.

**New South Wales. Department of Tourism**
A D C York, 95-99 York St., Sydney, N.S.W. 2000, Australia.
- Compass. m.

**New South Wales. Directorate of Aboriginal Welfare**
Box K718, Haymarket N.S.W. 2000, Australia.
- New Dawn; a magazine for the Aboriginal people of New South Wales, Australia. m. ISSN 0028-4513

**New South Wales. Fire Service**
- New South Wales. Fire Service. Fire News. (pub. by Board of Fire Commissioners of New South Wales)

**New South Wales. Forestry Commission**
93 Clarence St., Sydney, N.S.W. 2000, Australia.
- Forest and Timber. 3 per yr. ISSN 0015-7392
- New South Wales. Forestry Commission. Research Notes. irreg. ISSN 0085-3984

**New South Wales. Forestry Commission. Department of Conservation**
93-95 Clarence St., Sydney, N.S.W. 2000, Australia.
- New South Wales Forestry Commission. Handbook of Trees and Shrubs. a.

**New South Wales. Government Printer**
196 Miller St., North Sydney, N.S.W. 2001, Australia.
- New South Wales. Board of Architects. Architects Roll. a. ISSN 0077-8656
- New South Wales, Australia, Government Gazette. w.
- New South Wales Government Publications. Monthly List. m. ISSN 0028-6761

**New South Wales. Health Commission**
9-13 Young St., Sydney, N.S.W. 2000, Australia.
- Health in New South Wales. q. ISSN 0046-7073

**New South Wales. Health Commission. Division of Health Education**
G.P.O. Box 4235, Sydney, NSW 2001, Australia.
- Informed Opinion. irreg. ISSN 0310-8937

**New South Wales. Higher Education Authority**
G.P.O. Box 4368, Sydney, NSW 2001, Australia.
- New South Wales Higher Education Authority. Higher Education Handbook. a. ISSN 0310-0103

**New South Wales. Industrial Commission**
Queen's Sq., Sydney, NSW 2000, Australia.
- Industrial Arbitration Reports, New South Wales. irreg.

**New South Wales. Law Reform Commission**
Goodsell Bldg., 8-12 Chifley Square, Sydney 2000, Australia.
- New South Wales. Law Reform Commission. Report. irreg., 1972, no. 15. ISSN 0085-400X

**New South Wales. Maritime Services Board. Public Relations Section**
G.P.O. Box 32, Sydney, N.S.W. 2001, Australia.
- Ports of New South Wales Journal. irreg.

**New South Wales. Metric Conversion Board**
P. O. Box 587, Crows Nest, N.S.W. 2065, Australia.
- M. C. B. Newsletter. m. ISSN 0310-6462

**New South Wales. National Parks and Wildlife Service**
Adc Building, 189-193 Kent St., Sydney, NSW 2000, Australia.
- New South Wales. National Parks and Wildlife Service. Parks and Wildlife. a. ISSN 0310-6756

**New South Wales. State Fisheries**
Chief Secretary's Dept., Sydney, N.S.W., Australia.
- Fisherman. q. ISSN 0015-2978
- New South Wales. State Fisheries. Research Bulletin. irreg. ISSN 0077-8788

**New South Wales. Supreme Court**
Sydney, Australia.
- Supreme Court Gazette. irreg.

**New South Wales Association of Special Education Teachers**
P.O. Box 282, Strathfield, N.S.W. 2135, Australia.
- A S E T Journal. 2 per yr.

**New South Wales Conservatorium of Music**
Macquarie Street, Sydney NSW 2000, Australia.
- Con Brio. s-a.

**New South Wales Dairy Farmers Association**
75-77 Pitt St., Sydney, N.S.W. 2000, Australia.
- Dairyman's Digest and Primary Producer; a complete coverage of the dairying industry, farm factory & home. m.

**New South Wales Humanist Society**
17 Latona St., Winston Hills, 2153, N.S.W., Australia.
- Viewpoints. m. ISSN 0042-5877

**New South Wales Independent Teachers Association**
Box 560, Chatswood, N.S.W. 2067, Australia.
- Independent Education. bi-m. ISSN 0310-7175

**New South Wales Institute of Freshwater Fishermen**
P.O. Box 195, Lindfield, NSW 2070, Australia.
- Fish and Wildlife Gazette. irreg.

**New South Wales League of Women Voters**
Box 599, Sydney, N.S.W. 2001, Australia.
- Equality. 10 per yr.

**New South Wales Maritime Services Board**
Box 32, G. P. O., Sydney, Australia.
- Ports of New South Wales. 2 per yr. ISSN 0313-4075

**New South Wales Military Historical Society**
c/o R.K. Cooper, 12 Irvine Cres., Ryde, N.S.W. 2112, Australia.
- Despatch. m. ISSN 0046-0079

**New South Wales Nurses Association**
188/192 Goulburn St., Darlinghurst. 2010, Australia.
- Lamp. m. ISSN 0047-3936

**New South Wales Retail Tobacco Traders Association**
1St Floor, Alexander House, 107 Alexander St., Crows Nest, N.S.W. 2065, Australia.
- Australian Retail Tobacconist. m. ISSN 0045-0820

**New South Wales Rugby League**
165 Phillip St., Sydney, N.S.W. 2000, Australia.
- Big League. w. ISSN 0311-175X

**New South Wales Soil Conservation Service**
Box R201 Royal Exchange, Sydney, Australia.
- New South Wales Soil Conservation Service Journal. q. ISSN 0028-6818

**New South Wales Teachers Federation**
300 Sussex St., Sydney N.S.W. 2000, Australia.
- Education. fortn.(during school term) ISSN 0013-1156
- Teacher Feedback. (pub. by Publicity Press Ltd.)

**Newcastle Flora & Fauna Protection Society**
c/o Science Dept., Newcastle College of Advanced Education, P.O. Box 84, Waratah, N.S.W. 2298, Australia.
- Hunter Natural History. q. ISSN 0046-8312

**Newcastle Public Library**
P.O. Box 489g, Newcastle N. S. W. 2300, Australia.
- Newcastle History Monographs. irreg., 1973, no. 7. ISSN 0078-0243

**Newcastle University Philosophy Club**
Department of Philosophy, Univ. of Newcastle, Shortland, N.S.W. 2308, Australia.
- Dialectic. a. ISSN 0084-9804

**Nicholson's Pty. Ltd.**
Box 1589, G.P.O., Sydney, Australia.
- Music Maker. m. ISSN 0027-4399

**Nimrod Publications**
University of Newcastle, Dept. of English, Australia.
- Hunter Valley Poets. irreg.

**North Queensland Naturalists Club**
Cairns, Queensland 4870, Australia.
- North Queensland Naturalist. irreg., 1973, vol. 40, no. 1. ISSN 0078-1630

**O.P. Books Pty. Ltd.**
P.O. Box 591, Brookvale, NSW 2100, Australia.
- Australian and Pacific Book Prices Current. a. ISSN 0310-9879

**Office of the Australian Official Representative**
Cocos (Keeling) Islands, Australia.
- Cocos Clarion. 11 per yr.

**One People's Australia League**
- O P A L. (pub. by Consolidated Publications Pty. Ltd.)

**Open Book**
21 Smith St., Thornbury, Vic. 3071, Australia.
- Open Book. irreg.

**Opticians and Optometrists Association of N.S.W.**
281 Elizabeth St., Sydney, N.S.W. 2000, Australia.
- New South Wales Journal of Optometry. m. ISSN 0047-9918

**Orchid Society of New South Wales**
- Australian Orchid Review. (pub. by Harbour Newspaper & Publishing Co. Ltd.)

**Orff-Schulwerk Association of Queensland**
c/o Keith Smith, Ed., Music Department, Teachers College, Kelvin Grove, Qld. 4059, Australia.
- Orff-Schulwerk Association of Queensland. Bulletin. m.

**Organic Farming & Gardening Society**
Box 2605w, Melbourne, 3001 Victoria, Australia.
- Good Earth. q. ISSN 0017-2030

**Oto-Laryngological Society of Australia**
c/o Dept. O.R.L., Gisborne St., Melbourne 3002, Australia.
- Oto-Laryngological Society of Australia. Journal. a. ISSN 0030-6614

**Overland**
c/o S. Murray-Smith, Ed., B Ox 98a, G.P.O., Melbourne, Australia.
- Overland. q. ISSN 0030-7416

**Overseas Telecommunications Commission (Australia)**
Box 7000, Sydney, N.S.W. 2001, Australia.
- Contact. q.

**P. D. Consultants**
Suite 16, Eton Square, 474 St. Kilda Rd., Melbourne, Vic. 3004, Australia.
- New Products Bulletin. m. ISSN 0311-2381

**Pacific Publications (Australia) Pty. Ltd.**
Box 3408 GPO, Sydney, N.S.W. 2001, Australia.
- Baker & Millers' Journal. m. ISSN 0311-1385
- Handbook of Fiji. irreg., 5th ed., 1977. ISSN 0072-9809
- Pacific Islands Monthly. m. ISSN 0030-8722
- Pacific Islands Year Book. a; 12th ed., 1977. ISSN 0078-7523
- Papua New Guinea Handbook. irreg., 1974, 7th ed.
- Power and Farming. m. ISSN 0311-1911
- Power Farming Technical Annual. a. ISSN 0079-4422
- Soft Drink Journal. m.

**Pacific Science Association**
- Coral Reef Newsletter. (pub. by Australian Museum)

**Pacific Travel Directory**
c/o Pacific Airlines News, Box 1, Surfers Paradise, Qld. 4217, Australia.
- Pacific Travel Directory. a. ISSN 0311-0826

**Pacific Yearbooks**
Box C235, Clarence St., Sydney, N.S.W. 2000, Australia.
- Australian Aviation Yearbook. a. ISSN 0084-7232

**Page Publications Pty. Ltd.**
Box 606, Sydney, N.S.W. 2001, Australia.
- Australian Angler. m. ISSN 0045-0235
- Australian Flying. bi-m. ISSN 0004-9123
- Australian Hot Rod. 4 per yr.
- Australian Refrigeration, Air Conditioning and Heating. m. ISSN 0005-0148 (Australian Institute of Refrigeration, Air Conditioning and Heating, Inc)
- Club Management in Australia. m. ISSN 0045-7205 (Registered Clubs Association of Australia)
- Refrigeration Annual. a. ISSN 0080-0511 (Australian Institution of Refrigeration, Air Conditioning and Heating)
- Sporting Shooter. m. ISSN 0038-8076

**Pandas Publishing and Advertising Service**
c/o Business Manager, 172 Chetwynd St., North Melbourne, Vic. 3051, Australia.
- Australian Journal of Advanced Education. 3 per yr. ISSN 0045-0596 (Federation of Staff Associations of Australian Colleges of Advanced Education)

**Panorama**
c/o Fred P. Stone, Ed., 22 Northcote St., Kilburn, S.A., Australia.
- Panorama. bi-m. ISSN 0031-0832

**Paragon Publications**
79 Silverwater Rd., Auburn, N. S. W. 2144, Australia.
- C. T. G. Gazette. q. (Commercial Travellers' Guild) (Co-sponsor: New South Wales Sales Representatives)

**Paraplegic-Quadraplegic Association of Western Australia**
Selby St., Shenton Park, WA 6008, Australia.
- Para-Quad News. irreg.

**Pastoralist and Graziers Association of W.A. (Inc.)**
Pastoral House, 156 St. George's Terrace, Perth, W.A. 6000, Australia.
- Pastoralist and Grazier. m. ISSN 0031-2819

**Patterns**
Box 161, Glebe NSW 2037, Australia.
- Patterns. 5 per yr.

**Patterson Publishing Pty. Ltd.**
249 Margaret St., Box 29, Toowoomba, Queensland 4350, Australia.
- Pig Farmer. m. ISSN 0031-9740

**Payton Pty. Ltd.**
50 Albion St., Waverly, NSW 2024, Australia.
- Annual Australia. a.

**Peace Plans**
c/o J. M. Zube, Ed., Wilshire St., Berrima, N.S.W. 2577, Australia.
- Peace Plans. irreg., nos. 16-18, 1975. ISSN 0031-3564

**Pegasus Public Relations**
14 Huntingdon Rd., East Bentleigh, Vic.3165, Australia.
- Cargo Handling & Shipbuilding Quarterly. q.

**Pender Bros. Pty. Ltd.**
Elgin St., Maitland, N.S.W. 2320, Australia.
- Australasian Beekeeper. m. ISSN 0004-8313

**Percival Publishing Co. Pty. Ltd.**
862-870 Elizabeth St., Waterloo, N.S.W. 2017, Australia.
- Australian Police World. q. (International Police Association. Australian Section)
- Australian Railways Union. Federal Office News. q.
- Construction Supervisor. bi-m. (Australian Institute of Construction Supervisors)
- Customs Officer's Association of Australia. Fourth Division. Fourth Division Customs Officer. irreg.
- South Australian Baker and Pastrycook. biennial. (Baking Trade Federation of Australia. South Australian Branch)
- Stud and Stable. irreg. ISSN 0311-8215

**Permail Pty. Ltd.**
54-56 Whiting St., Artarmon, NSW 2064, Australia.
- Permail Hospital Book. biennial.

**Permanent Building Societies Association Ltd.**
15th Floor, 33 Bligh St., Sydney, N. S. W. 2000, Australia.
- Coroboree. m.

**Perth City Council**
Council Chambers, Perth, W.A. 6000, Australia.
- Perth, Australia. City Council. Municipal Yearbook. irreg. ISSN 0085-4832

**Perth Observatory**
Bickley, W.A. 6076, Australia.
- Perth Observatory. Communications. irreg., 1970, no. 2. ISSN 0079-1067

**Petranis Press**
103 Leveson St., North Melbourne, Vic. 3051, Australia.
- Athletic Echo. w. ISSN 0300-4600

**Pharmaceutical Society of Victoria**
381 Royal Parade, Parkville, Vic. 3052, Australia.
- Pharmaceutical Society of Victoria. Bulletin. irreg. ISSN 0311-0184

**Philips Electrical Pty. Ltd.**
P.O. Box 34, Artarmon, NSW 2064, Australia.
- Philips Reporter. irreg.

**Geoff Phillips & Associates Pty. Ltd.**
P.O. Box 158, Eltham, Vic. 3095, Australia.
- Murray Grey World. bi-m. ISSN 0310-9666 (Murray Grey Beef Cattle Society)

**Philosophy of Education Society of Australasia**
University of New South Wales, School of Education, Box 1, Kensington 2033, N.S.W., Australia.
- Educational Philosophy and Theory. s-a. ISSN 0013-1857

**Photo Publishing Co.**
381 Pitt St. Box 4689, Sydney N.S.W., Australia.
- Photo Trade News. m. ISSN 0031-8590 (Photographic Industry Council of Australia)

**Photographic Industry Council of Australia**
- Photo Trade News. (pub. by Photo Publishing Co.)

**Pigeon Fancier**
P.O. Box 78, Yagoona, N.S.W. 2199, Australia.
- Pigeon Fancier. 10 per yr.

**Pig's Arse Press**
Box 164, Wentworth Bldg., City Rd., Darlington, N.S.W. 2008, Australia.
- Your Friendly Fascist. irreg.

**Pipe Club of Australia**
Box 4702 G.P.O., Sydney 2001, Australia.
- Pipesmoke. s-a.

**Play**
Main Street, Box 67, Hahndorf, S.A., Australia.
- Play. m. ISSN 0311-4031

**Playfair Publishing Group**
Box 52, Northbridge, N.S.W. 2063, Australia.
- Australian Horse Racing Annual. a. ISSN 0084-7402
- International Telex Directory. International Service. a. ISSN 0310-8031

**Poeticart Club**
P.O. Box 410, Prahran, Vic. 3181, Australia.
- Unknown Poets. irreg. (1-2 per yr)

**Poetry Society of Australia**
Box N110, Grosvenor St. P.O., Sydney 2000, Australia.
- New Poetry. q. ISSN 0028-6478
- Poetry. q. ISSN 0048-458X

**Police Association of N.S.W.**
393 Sussex St., Sydney, N.S.W., Australia.
- New South Wales Police News. m. ISSN 0047-9934

**Police Forces of Australia**
c/o P. T. Peters, Ed., Box 45 G.P.O., Sydney 2001, Australia.
- Australian Police Journal. q. ISSN 0005-0024

**Polish Association of South Australia**
- Nasza Droga. (pub. by Continental Publicity)

**Polish Communities in Australia and New Zealand**
- Polish News/Wiadomosci Polskie. (pub. by Ingos Pty. Ltd.)

**Port Phillip Authority**
480 Collins St., Melbourne 3000, Victoria, Australia.
- Port Phillip Authority. Annual Report. a. ISSN 0079-4007

**Potters' Society of Australia**
48 Burton St., Darlinghurst, N. S. W. 2010, Australia.
- Potters' Society of Australia. Newsletter. m.
- Pottery in Australia. bi-a. ISSN 0048-4954

**Powder**
Box 1806 Q G.P.O., Melbourne, Australia.
- Powder; radical source guide from light, powder and construction works. bi-m.

**Powell Lorkin and Associates Pty. Ltd.**
24 Little Edward St., Brisbane, Qld 4000, Australia.
- Queensland Architect. irreg. ISSN 0310-687X (Royal Australian Institute of Architects. Queensland Chapter, Information Services Division)

**Power**
Box 37, Harbord, N.S.W. 2096, Australia.
- Power. bi-m. ISSN 0048-5039

**Pregled Review**
P.O. Box 23, Brunswick, Melbourne, Vic. 3056, Australia.
- Pregled Review; bulletin of Croatian resistance. bi-m. ISSN 0300-6271

**Presbyterian Church of Australia**
156 Collins Street, Melbourne, Victoria 3000, Australia.
- Australian Presbyterian Life. fortn. ISSN 0005-0059

**Prestige Publishing Pty. Ltd.**
Box 5158, G.P.O., Sydney, N.S.W. 2001, Australia.
- Australian Lithographer, Printer, and Packager. bi-m. (Australian Litho Club)

**Primary Education Pty. Ltd.**
4 the Crofts, Richmond, Vic. 3121, Australia.
- Primary Education. 9 per yr. ISSN 0048-5284

**Primary English Teachers Association of New South Wales**
c/o 96 Chandos St., Ashfield, NSW 2131, Australia.
- Pen. irreg. ISSN 0311-1490

**Prince Publishing Group**
G.P.O. Box 4318, Sydney, N.S.W. 2001, Australia.
- Tracer's Australian Petroleum and Mining Register. irreg., 1973, no. 9. ISSN 0082-5654

**Printers News Pty. Ltd.**
507 Kent St., Sydney, N.S.W. 2000, Australia.
- Printers News. fortn. ISSN 0048-5322 (Printing and Allied Trades Employers' Federation)

**Printing and Allied Trades Employers' Federation**
- Printers News. (pub. by Printers News Pty. Ltd.)

**Printwrite**
52 High St., North Sydney, N.S.W. 2060, Australia.
- Energy. m.

**Prisoners Aid Association of South Australia (Inc.)**
222 Halifax St., Adelaide, S.A. 5000, Australia.
- Release. q.

**Probation Officers' Association of Victoria**
Box 634E, Melbourne, Vic. 3001, Australia.
- Probation Officer. q.

**Productivity Promotion Council of Australia**
339 Swanston St., Melbourne, Vic. 3000, Australia.
- Australian Productivity Action. q.

**Professional Fishermen's Association of Tasmania**
65-67 Davey St., Hobart, Tasmania, Australia.
- Professional Fishermen's Association of Tasmania Magazine. q. ISSN 0033-0094 (Ed. F. J. E. Johnson)

**Professional Officers' Association**
4Th Floor, 132-136 Albert Rd., South Melbourne 3205, Australia.
- Commonwealth Professional. m. ISSN 0045-7639

**Public Service Association of South Australia Inc.**
82 Gilbert St., Adelaide 5000, S.A., Australia.
- Public Service Review. fortn. ISSN 0033-3786

**Publicity Press Ltd.**
29-31 Meagher St., Chippendale, N.S.W. 2008, Australia.
- Teacher Feedback. q. ISSN 0311-2772 (New South Wales. Teachers' Federation)

**Qantas Airways Ltd.**
Qantas House, 70 Hunter St., Sydney, Australia.
- Airways Inflight. bi-m.

**Queen Victoria Museum**
Wellington St., Launceston, Tasmania 7250, Australia.
- Queen Victoria Museum and Art Gallery. Launceston, Tasmania. Records. irreg. ISSN 0085-5278

**Queensland. Air Pollution Council**
- Queensland. Air Pollution Council. Annual Report. (pub. by Commonwealth Government Printing Office)

**Queensland. Bureau of Sugar Experiment Stations**
P.O. Box 292, North Brisbane, Qld. 4000, Australia.
- Queensland. Bureau of Sugar Experiment Stations. Technical Communication. irreg. ISSN 0085-5286

**Queensland. Department of Commercial and Industrial Development**
Box 183 P.O., North Quay, Brisbane, Qld. 4000, Australia.
- Queensland. Department of Commercial and Industrial Development. Annual Report. a.

**Queensland. Department of Education**
Guidance & Special Education Branch, Box 33, North Quay, Qld. 4000, Australia.
- Queensland. Guidance and Special Education Branch. Special Schools Bulletin for Teachers of Exceptional Children. 2 per yr. ISSN 0048-6337
- Quest. s-a.

**Queensland. Department of Education. Information and Publications Branch**
P.O. Box 33, North Quay, Qld. 4000, Australia.
- Queensland. Department of Education. Information and Publications Branch. Document. irreg.

- Queensland. Department of Education. Information and Publications Branch. Information Statement. irreg.

**Queensland. Department of Education. Primary Curriculum Committee**
P.O. Box 33, North Quay, Qld. 4000, Australia.
- Channels. irreg.

**Queensland. Department of Education. Research and Curriculum Branch**
P.O. Box 33, North Quay, Qld. 4001, Australia.
- Queensland. Department of Education. Research and Curriculum Branch. Curriculum Paper. irreg. ISSN 0310-4079
- Queensland. Department of Education. Research and Curriculum Branch. Bulletin. irreg.
- Queensland. Department of Education. Research Branch. Reporting Research. irreg.

**Queensland. Department of Forestry**
G.P.O. Box 944, Brisbane, Qld 4001, Australia.
- Queensland. Department of Forestry. Research Paper. irreg. ISSN 0311-0893

**Queensland. Department of Health**
63-79 George St., Brisbane, Queensland, Australia.
- Queensland'S Health. irreg., 1964, vol. 1, no. 5. ISSN 0079-9041

**Queensland. Department of Mines**
Watkins Place, 288 Edward St., Brisbane, Australia.
- Queensland. Geological Survey. Publications. irreg. ISSN 0079-8800
- Queensland Government Mining Journal. m. ISSN 0033-6149

**Queensland. Department of Primary Industries**
Brisbane, Australia.
- Queensland Agricultural Journal. bi-m. ISSN 0033-6076
- Queensland Journal of Agricultural and Animal Sciences. s-a. ISSN 0033-6173

**Queensland. Department of Primary Industries. Fisheries Branch**
William St., Brisbane, Qld 4000, Australia.
- Queensland. Department of Primary Industries. Fisheries Branch. Fisheries Notes. irreg.

**Queensland. Department of Primary Industries. Marketing Services Branch**
Comalco House, Ann St., Brisbane, Qld. 4000, Australia.
- Queensland. Department of Primary Industries. Report on Production Trends. m.
- Queensland. Department of Primary Industries. Weekly Market Review. w.

**Queensland. Government Printer**
Brisbane, Australia.
- Queensland. Registrar of Co-Operative and Other Societies. Report. a. ISSN 0481-3375

**Queensland. Land Administration Commission**
- Queensland. Land Administration Commission. Annual Report. (pub. by Commonwealth Government Printing Office)

**Queensland. Main Roads Department**
Box 1412, Brisbane, Qld. 4001, Australia.
- Queensland Roads. 2 per yr. ISSN 0048-6388

**Queensland. State Government Insurance Office**
Box 1453 G.P.O., Brisbane, Queensland, Australia.
- Insurance Lines. q. ISSN 0020-4757

**Queensland Automobile Chamber of Commerce Inc.**
14 Cribb St., Milton 4064, Australia.
- Q A C C Motor Trader. m.

**Queensland Chamber of Manufactures**
375 Wickham Terrace, Brisbane, Queensland 4000, Australia.
- Q. Industry. (Queensland Industry) m. ISSN 0033-6165

**Queensland Conservation Council**
Box 59, Toowong, Qld. 4066, Australia.
- Eco Info. bi-m. ISSN 0310-0294

**Queensland Council of State School Organisations**
Box 1741, Brisbane, Queensland, 4001, Australia.
- P. & C. Guide. (Parents & Citizens) q.

**Queensland Country Life Pty. Ltd.**
432 Queen St., Brisbane, Queensland 4000, Australia.
- Queensland Country Life. w. ISSN 0033-6084

**Queensland Country Women's Association**
1St Floor, Ruth Fairfax House, 89-95 Gregory Terrace, Brisbane, Qld. 4000, Australia.
- Queensland Country Woman. m. ISSN 0033-6092

**Queensland Dairymen's Organization**
- Queensland Dairyfarmer. (pub. by Bundaberg Newspaper Co)

**Queensland Historical Review**
c/o History Students' Association, Department of History, University of Queensland, St. Lucia, Qld. 4067, Australia.
- Queensland Historical Review. irreg. ISSN 0085-5308

**Queensland History Teachers Association**
P.O. Box 84, North Brisbane, Queensland 4000, Australia.
- History Teacher. s-a. ISSN 0085-154X

**Queensland Hotels Association**
Q. H. A. House, 437 Upper Edward St., Brisbane, Qld. 4000, Australia.
- Q. H. A. Review. m. ISSN 0048-6345 (Co-Sponsor: Australian Hotels Association (Queensland Branch))

**Queensland Institute for Educational Research**
c/o Research and Curriculum Branch, Department of Education, Box 33, North Quay, Qld 4000, Australia.
- Q. I. E. R. Journal. 3 per yr. ISSN 0311-2349

**Queensland Master Builders Association**
417-419 Wickham Terrace, Brisbane, Qld. 4000, Australia.
- Queensland Master Builder. fortn. ISSN 0048-6361

**Queensland Museum**
Gregory Terrace, Fortitude Valley, Brisbane 4006, Australia.
- Queensland Museum, Brisbane. Memoirs. a. since 1966. ISSN 0079-8835

**Queensland Naturalists' Club**
c/o Miss M. Hawken, 5 Kidston St., Albion 4010, Queensland, Australia.
- Queensland Naturalist. irreg. ISSN 0079-8843

**Queensland Newspapers Pty. Ltd.**
Campbell St., Bowen Hills, Brisbane, Australia.
- Sunday Mail. w. ISSN 0039-5226

**Queensland Police Union of Employees**
c/o M. J. Callaghan, 269 Main St., Kangeroo Point, East Brisbane, Qld. 4169, Australia.
- Queensland Police Journal. m. ISSN 0085-5324

**Queensland Primary Producers' Co-Operative Association**
Box 186, Brisbane, Qld. 4001, Australia.
- Queensland Primary Producers' Co-Operative Association. Primary Producers' Guide. a. ISSN 0085-5332

**Queensland Professional Officers Association**
P.O.A. House, 453 Ann St., Brisbane, 4000, Queensland, Australia.
- Professional Officer. m. ISSN 0048-5454

**Queensland Retail Tobacco Traders' Association**
Box 1635, Brisbane, Qld. 4001, Australia.
- Tobacco Trade Journal. m.

**Queensland Retail Traders' Association**
11-15 Buchanan St., West End, Brisbane, Queensland 4101, Australia.
- Retailer of Queensland. m. ISSN 0034-6144

**Queensland Shopkeepers' Association**
11 Buchanan St., West End, Qld. 4101, Australia.
- Queensland Shopkeeper. m. ISSN 0033-622X

**Queensland Society of Sugar Cane Technologists**
G.P.O. Box 608, Brisbane, Queensland, Australia.
- Queensland Society of Sugar Cane Technologists. Proceedings. a. ISSN 0079-8851

**Queensland Teachers Union**
Box 310, North Brisbane, Qld. 4000, Australia.
- Queensland Teachers' Journal. m(Feb.-Nov) ISSN 0033-6238

**Queensland Writers' Workshop**
P.O. Box 230, North Quay, Qld. 4000, Australia.
- Poets of Australia. a. ISSN 0311-2810

**Quirindi & District Historical Society**
c/o W.A. McNamara, Tamarang Shire Council Chambers, Quirindi, N.S.W. 2343, Australia.
- Quirindi and District Historical Notes. a. ISSN 0085-5375

**R.C.A. North Ryde Pty. Ltd.**
11 Khartoum Road, North Ryde, N.S.W. 2113, Australia.
- Revolution. irreg. ISSN 0310-4176 (Radio Corporation of America, Sydney)

**Racing Car News Pty. Ltd.**
177 Lawson St., Redfern N.S.W. 2016, Australia.
- Racing Car News. m. ISSN 0033-7374

**Radio Corporation of America, Sydney**
- Revolution. (pub. by R.C.A. North Ryde Pty. Ltd.)

**Railways Institute Council**
543 Wellington St., Perth W.A., Australia.
- Railways Institute Magazine. m. ISSN 0033-9040

**Ramsay, Ware Publishing Pty. Ltd.**
8 La Trobe St., Melbourne 3000, Victoria, Australia.
- Australian and New Zealand Journal of Obstetrics and Gynecology. q. ISSN 0004-8666 (Arthur Wilson Memorial Foundation)

**Rationalist Association of Australia Ltd.**
Box 738 F, G.P.O., Melbourne, Australia.
- Rationalist. bi-m. ISSN 0034-0065

**Rationalist Association of N.S.W.**
58 Regent St., Chippendale, N.S.W. 2008, Australia.
- Rationalist News. bi-m.

**Rationalist Society of Australia Ltd.**
Box 19, Malvern Vic., Australia.
- Australian Rationalist. m. ISSN 0005-0113

**Reader's Digest Association Pty. Ltd.**
Reader's Digest Bldg., 26-32 Waterloo St., Surry Hills, Sydney, N.S.W. 2010, Australia.
- Reader's Digest (Australian Edition) m. ISSN 0034-0391
- Reader's Digest (New Zealand Edition) m. ISSN 0034-0448

**Real Estate Agents & Valuers Society**
- Real Estate Agents & Valuers Society. Land and Building. (pub. by Breda Publications)

**Real Estate and Stock Institute of Victoria**
142 Wellington Parade, East Melbourne 3002, Australia.
- Real Estate and Stock Journal. m. ISSN 0034-0669

**Real Estate Institute of New South Wales**
Box A624, Sydney N.S.W. 2000, Australia.
- Real Estate Journal. m. ISSN 0034-074X

**Real Estate Institute of Queensland**
88 Brunswick St., Fortitude Valley, Qld. 4006, Australia.
- Real Estate Institute of Queensland. Real Estate Journal. bi-m. ISSN 0048-685X

**Recovers and Growers of Australia**
- Grow Magazine. (pub. by Grow Publishers)

**Red Comb Co-Operative**
Box 2, Dry Creek, S.A. 5094, Australia.
- Red Comb Journal. m.

**Red Pen Publications**
4 Dixon St., Sydney, N.S.W. 2000, Australia.
- Wharfie. w. (Communist Party of Australia)

**A. H. & A. W. Reed**
53 Myoora Rd., Terrey Hills, N.S.W. 2084, Australia.
- Birds of Australia. irreg.
- Franklin's Guide to Australian First Day Covers. irreg.
- Franklin's Guide to the Stamps of Papua and New Guinea. irreg.

- Handbook of Australian Sea Birds. irreg.
- Map Guide to Modern History. irreg.
- Reducing Your Income Tax. a. ISSN 0080-0414

**Reformed Theological Review**
Box 2587W, Elizabeth St. P.O., Melbourne, Victoria 3001, Australia.
- Reformed Theological Review. 3 per yr. ISSN 0034-3072

**Refractory**
25 Alberta St., Sydney, Australia.
- Refractory; girl-women studies journal. q.

**Registered Clubs Association of Australia**
- Club Management in Australia. (pub. by Page Publications Pty. Ltd.)

**Reldt Pty. Ltd.**
Box 3805, Sydney, N.S.W. 2001, Australia.
- Australian Bridge. bi-m. ISSN 0045-0332

**Reporter Newspapers Co.**
Box 2557 G.P.O., Sydney, Australia.
- New Legislation of the Australian Parliament. irreg.

**Research Publications Pty. Ltd.**
418 Canterbury Rd., Surrey Hills, Victoria 3127, Australia.
- Architectural Science Review. q. ISSN 0003-8628
- Australian Journal of Instrumentation and Control. bi-m. ISSN 0045-0626 (Institute of Instrumentation and Control, Australia. (I.I.C.A.))
- Coiffure. m. ISSN 0010-0331 (Master Ladies Hairdressers Association)
- Science and Technology. bi-m. ISSN 0310-9100
- Watchmakers of Victoria. m. ISSN 0049-6960 (Horological Guild of Australasia. Victorian Branch)

**Reserve Bank of Australia**
65 Martin Place, Box 3947 G.P.O., Sydney, N.S.W. 2001, Australia.
- Reserve Bank of Australia. Annual Report. a. ISSN 0080-1771
- Reserve Bank of Australia. Currency. m. ISSN 0048-7368
- Reserve Bank of Australia. Occasional Papers. irreg. ISSN 0080-178X
- Reserve Bank of Australia. Statistical Bulletin. m. ISSN 0034-5504
- Reserve Bank of Australia. Statistical Bulletin. Supplement. issued irregularly as supplements to monthly bulletin. ISSN 0080-1798

**Retail Grocers and Storekeepers' Association of Western Australia (Inc.)**
3 Hooper St., West Perth, W.A. 6005, Australia.
- Grocers' and Storekeepers' Journal of Western Australia. m. ISSN 0017-4378

**Retail Storekeeper's Association of S.A. Inc.**
329 King William St., Adelaide 5000, Australia.
- South Australian Storekeepers' Journal. m. ISSN 0038-3007

**Retail Tobacco Sellers Association of Victoria**
Box 1780, Melbourne, Vic. 3001, Australia.
- Tobacco Journal. m. (Co-sponsor: Retail Tobacco Traders' Association of Tasmania)

**Retail Traders Association of Tasmania**
160 Brisbane St., Launceston, Tasmania, Australia.
- Tasmanian Trader. m. ISSN 0039-9876

**Retail World Pty. Ltd.**
168 Castlereagh St., Sydney, N.S.W. 2000, Australia.
- Retail World. s-m. ISSN 0034-6136 (National Association of Retail Grocers of Australia (NARGA))

**Retrieval**
P.O. Box 51, Fitzroy, Vic. 3065, Australia.
- Retrieval. m. ISSN 0310-9143

**Returned Services League of Australia. New South Wales Branch**
Anzac House, 26 College Street, Darlinghurst, N.S.W. 2010, Australia.
- Reveille. m. ISSN 0034-6306

**Returned Services League of Australia. Victorian Branch**
Anzac House, 4 Collins St., Melbourne, Vic., Australia.
- Mufti. bi-m.

**Review Publications Pty. Ltd.**
Sterling St., Dubbo, N. S. W. 2830, Australia.
- Stamp News. m. ISSN 0038-9293

**Reville Publishing Co.**
299 Anzac Parade, Kingsford, N. S. W. 2032, Australia.
- Your Home. q. (Association of Co-Operative Building Societies of N. S. W. Ltd.)

**Revolutionary Marxist Group**
Box 13, Balmain, N.S.W. 2041, Australia.
- International. m.

**Ricegrowers' Co-Operative Mills Ltd.**
Wade Ave., Leeton, N.S.W. 2705, Australia.
- Ricemill News. q. ISSN 0048-8275

**R.G. Riddell Pty.Ltd.**
32 Burton St., Milsons Point, N.S.W. 2061, Australia
(Dist. in U.S. by: International Publications Service, 114 E. 32nd St., New York, NY 10016)
- Business Who's Who Australian Buying Reference. s-a.
- Business Who's Who of Australia. a. ISSN 0068-4503

**Road Ahead Publishing Co. Pty Ltd.**
Ann & Boundary Sts., Brisbane, Queensland, Australia.
- Road Ahead. m. ISSN 0035-7170 (Royal Automobile Club of Queensland, Brisbane)

**Road Transport Association of Western Australia**
- Transporter (WA) (pub. by Direct Publications, West Australian Newspapers Ltd.)

**Rotary International in Australia, New Zealand and Pacific**
P.O. Box 779, Parramatta, N.S.W. 2150, Australia.
- Rotary Down Under. m. ISSN 0048-8631

**Rotor Publications Pty. Ltd.**
261 Broadway, Sydney, N.S.W. 2007, Australia.
- N. S. W. Golf. m.

**Royal Adelaide Hospital**
- South Australian Clinics. (pub. by Griffin Press)

**Royal Aeronautical Society, Australian Division**
- Aircraft. (pub. by Herald & Weekly Times, Ltd.)

**Royal Agricultural Society**
Showground, Driver Ave., Paddington, N.S.W. 2021, Australia.
- R A S Kennel Control Journal. m. ISSN 0033-6777

**Royal Agricultural Society of Victoria. Kennel Control Council**
Royal Show Grounds, Epsom Road, Ascot Vale, Vic. 3032, Australia.
- K. C. C. Kennel Gazette. m.

**Royal Australasian College of Physicians**
145 Macquarie St., Sydney, Australia.
- Australian and New Zealand Journal of Medicine. bi-m. ISSN 0004-8291

**Royal Australasian College of Radiologists**
37 Lower Fort St., Millers Point, N.S.W. 2000, Australia.
- Australasian Radiology. q. ISSN 0004-8461

**Royal Australasian College of Surgeons**
- Australian and New Zealand Journal of Surgery. (pub. by Australasian Medical Publishing Co.)

**Royal Australasian Ornithologists Union**
Box 5236 BB, Melbourne, Vic. 3001, Australia.
- Emu. q. ISSN 0046-192X

**Royal Australian Chemical Institute**
Clunies Ross House, 191 Royal Parade, Parkville, Victoria 3052, Australia.
- Royal Australian Chemical Institute. Proceedings. m. ISSN 0035-8746

**Royal Australian College of Dental Surgeons**
229 Macquarie St., Sydney, N.S.W. 2000, Australia.
- Royal Australian College of Dental Surgeons. Annals. triennial. ISSN 0312-7923

**Royal Australian College of General Practitioners**
1St Floor, 70 Jolimont St., Jolimont 3002, Victoria, Australia.
- Australian Family Physician. m. ISSN 0300-8495

**Royal Australian Historical Society**
History House, 133 Macquane St., Sydney, Australia.
- Royal Australian Historical Society. Journal. 4 per yr. ISSN 0035-8762

**Royal Australian Institute of Architects**
Federal Headquarters, 2A Mugga Way, Red Hill,A.C.T. 2603, Australia.
- Architecture Australia. 6 per yr.

**Royal Australian Institute of Architects. Queensland Chapter**
- Queensland Architect. (pub. by Powell Lorkin and Associates Pty. Ltd.)

**Royal Australian Institute of Architects. Western Australian Chapter**
22 Altona St., West Perth 6005, Australia.
- Architect. q. ISSN 0003-8393

**Royal Australian Nursing Federation**
132 Albert Rd., Melbourne, Vic. 3205, Australia.
- Australian Nurses' Journal. 11 per yr. ISSN 0045-0758

**Royal Australian Planning Institute. Queensland Division**
Box 233, North Quay, Qld. 4000, Australia.
- Planner. q. ISSN 0032-0676

**Royal Automobile Association of South Australia Inc.**
41 Hindmarsh Sqe., Adelaide, S.A. 5000, Australia.
- Royal Automobile Association of South Australia. Accommodation Guide. a. ISSN 0085-5782
- South Australian Motor. (pub. by South Australian Motor Pty. Ltd.)

**Royal Automobile Club of Queensland, Brisbane**
- Road Ahead. (pub. by Road Ahead Publishing Co. Pty Ltd.)

**Royal Automobile Club of Tasmania**
Murray & Patrick Sts., Hobart 7001, Tasmania, Australia.
- Tasmanian Motor News. bi-m. ISSN 0039-9841

**Royal Automobile Club of Victoria**
- Royalauto. (pub. by Automobile Club Publishing Co)

**Royal Automobile Club of Western Australia**
Box C140, GPO, Perth 6001, Australia.
- Road Patrol. bi-m. (Co-Sponsor: R. A. C. Insurance Pty. Ltd.)

**Royal Botanic Gardens and National Herbarium**
South Yarra, Victoria 3141, Australia.
- Muelleria; an Australian journal of botany. irreg., 1973, vol. 2, no. 4. ISSN 0077-1813

**Royal Children's Hospital**
Editorial Office, Flemington Rd., Parkville, Vic. 3052, Australia.
- Australian Paediatric Journal. q. ISSN 0004-993X (Australian College of Paediatrics)

**Royal College of Pathologists of Australia**
- Pathology. (pub. by Sydney University Press)

**Royal Commonwealth Society. New South Wales Branch**
Norwich House, 17 Bligh St., Sydney 2000, Australia.
- Commonwealth Outlook. m.

**Royal Far West Children's Health Scheme**
Wentworth St., Manly, N.S.W., Australia.
- Far West Magazine. q. ISSN 0014-763X

**Royal Geographical Society of Australasia. South Australian Branch**
State Library Bldg., North Terrace, Adelaide, S.A. 5000, Australia.
- Royal Geographical Society of Australasia. South Australian Branch. Proceedings. a. ISSN 0085-5790

**Royal Geographical Society of Australia. Queensland Branch**
117 Ann St., Brisbane, Qld 4000, Australia.
- Queensland Geographical Journal. irreg.

**Royal Historical Society of Queensland**
Box 1811, Brisbane, Qld. 4001, Australia.
- Royal Historical Society of Queensland. Journal. a. ISSN 0085-5804
- Royal Historical Society of Queensland Bulletin. m. ISSN 0035-8916

**Royal Horticultural Society of Victoria**
- Australian Garden Lover. (pub. by Horticultural Press Pty. Ltd.)

**Royal Institute of Public Administration. Australian Regional Groups**
c/o B. R. Green, G.P.O. Box 904, Sydney 2001, Australia.
- Australian Journal of Public Administration. q.

**Royal Melbourne Institute of Technology**
Directorate of Student Publications, Box 2476V G.P.O., Melbourne 3000, Vic., Australia.
- Catalyst. w.

**Royal Military College of Australia**
Department of History, Duntroon, A.C.T. 2600, Australia.
- R. M. C. Historical Journal. a. ISSN 0310-4141

**Royal N.S.W. Bowling Association**
61 Wentworth Ave., Sydney, N.S.W. 2010, Australia.
- Bowls in N.S.W. m. ISSN 0006-8454

**Royal Philatelic Society of Victoria**
Box 222, Melbourne, Victoria 3001, Australia.
- Philately from Australia; a chronicle of Australasian stamps and their collectors. q. ISSN 0031-7403

**Royal Queensland Bowls Association**
- Bowls in Queensland. (pub. by Consolidated Publications Pty. Ltd.)

**Royal Society of New South Wales**
Science Centre, 35 Clarence St., Sydney, N.S.W. 2000, Australia.
- Royal Society of New South Wales. Journal and Proceedings. q. ISSN 0035-9173

**Royal Society of Queensland**
Box 50, St. Lucia, Queensland 4067, Australia.
- Royal Society of Queensland, St. Lucia. Proceedings. a. ISSN 0080-469X

**Royal Society of S.A.**
State Library Bldg, North Terrace, Adelaide, S.A. 5000, Australia.
- Royal Society of South Australia. Transactions. a. ISSN 0085-5812

**Royal Society of Tasmania**
G.P.O. Box 1166M, Hobart, Tasmania 7001, Australia.
- Royal Society of Tasmania, Hobart. Papers and Proceedings. a. ISSN 0080-4703

**Royal Society of Victoria**
9 Victoria St., Melbourne 3000, Australia.
- Royal Society of Victoria. Proceedings. a. ISSN 0035-9211

**Royal Society of Western Australia**
c/o Western Australian Museum, Perth, W.A., Australia.
- Royal Society of Western Australia. Journal. q. ISSN 0035-922X

**Royal South Australian Bowling Association**
- South Australian Bowler. (pub. by Messenger Publications Pty. Ltd.)

**Royal South Australian Society of Arts**
Institute Bldg., North Tce., Adelaide, S.A. 5000, Australia.
- Kalori. q. ISSN 0047-312X

**Royal Volunteer Coastal Patrol**
Box 211, Avalon Beach, N. S. W. 2107, Australia.
- Beam Ends. 11 per yr.

**Royal Western Australian Historical Society**
49 Broadway, Nedlands, 6009 WA, Australia.
- Royal Western Australian Historical Society. Journal and Proceedings. a. ISSN 0080-4738

**Royal Western Australian Historical Society.**
Newsletter. 10 per yr. ISSN 0557-4242

**Royal Zoological Society of New South Wales**
Taronga Zoo, Mosman, N.S.W. 2088, Australia.
- Australian Zoologist. irreg. ISSN 0067-2238
- Royal Zoological Society of New South Wales. Proceedings. a. ISSN 0085-5820

**Rural Bank of New South Wales**
Martin Place, Sydney, N.S.W., Australia.
- Trends. 3 per yr. ISSN 0041-2341

**Rural Reconstruction Authority of Western Australia**
Central Government Building, Barrack Street, Perth, W.A. 6000, Australia.
- Rural Reconstruction Authority of Western Australia. Annual Report. a. ISSN 0310-4923

**Russell Fenton Co.**
196 Churchill Ave., Subiaco, Australia.
- Visor; motor sport monthly. m. ISSN 0049-6537 (W.A. Sporting Car Club)

**Ryan Publications**
95 Currie St., Adelaide, Australia.
- Australian Grapegrower & Winemaker. m. (Federal Grapegrowers Council of Australia)

**Ryde District Historical Society**
Old Council Library Bldg., Devlin St., Ryde, Australia.
- Ryde Recorder. bi-m. ISSN 0048-8879

**Rydge Publications Pty. Ltd.**
74 Clarence St., Sydney, N.S.W. 2001, Australia.
- Manufacturers' Monthly. m. ISSN 0025-2530
- Modern Office & Data Management. 11 per yr. ISSN 0311-7731
- Rydge's. m. ISSN 0036-0511
- Rydge's C C E M-Construction, Civil Engineering and Mining. m.
- Rydge's CCEM Industry Report and Buyers Guide. (Construction, Civil Engineering and Mining) a. ISSN 0310-4257
- Rydge's Office Equipment Buyers Guide. a. ISSN 0078-3749
- Rydge's Sales and Marketing Service. m.

**S. A. Road Transport Association Inc**
- S.A. Road Transport Journal. (pub. by Direct Publications Pty. Ltd.)

**S C J**
c/o Ken Quinell & Michael Thornhill, Eds., Box4430, Sydney, N.S.W., Australia.
- S C J/Sydney Cinema Journal. q. ISSN 0036-1135

**S F Commentary**
c/o Bruce Gillespie, Box 5195AA, Melbourne, Vic. 3001, Australia
- S F Commentary. (Science Fiction) q.

**S. K. F. Ball Bearing (Australia) Pty. Ltd.**
168 Kings' Way, South Melbourne, Vic. 3205, Australia.
- Ball Bearing Journal. q. ISSN 0310-6748

**St. Mark's Institute of Theology**
Box 67 P.O., Canberra, A.C.T. 2600, Australia.
- St. Mark's Review. 5 per yr. ISSN 0036-3103

**St. Patrick's College**
Manly N.S.W., Australia.
- Australasian Catholic Record. q. ISSN 0004-8321

**St. Thomas More Society**
Box 282 G.P.O., Sydney, N.S.W. 2001, Australia.
- St. Thomas More Society. Journal. irreg. ISSN 0310-6861

**Salvation Army**
- Musician. (pub. by Citadel Press)
- Rally. (pub. by Citadel Press)
- Young Soldier. (pub. by Citadel Press)

**Santa Gertrudis Breeders' (Australia) Association**
109 Pitt St., Sydney, N.S.W. 2000, Australia.
- Santa Gertrudis Annual. a.

**Saturday Centre**
Box 140, Cammeray, N. S. W. 2062, Australia.
- S C O P P. (Saturday Centre of Prose and Poetry) 3 per yr.

**Save the Kangaroo Committee**
29 Wordsworth Ave., Clayton, Vic. 3168, Australia.
- Save the Kangaroo Committee. Newsletter. q.

**Saving Grace**
Box 286, P.O. South Yarra 3141, Australia.
- Saving Grace. m.

**School Library Association of New South Wales**
French's Forest, N.S.W. 2086, Australia.
- Teacher-Librarian. q. ISSN 0049-3090

**School Library Association of Queensland**
G. P. O. Box 2244, Brisbane, Qld. 4001, Australia.
- School Library Association of Queensland. Journal. q. ISSN 0048-9425

**School Library Association of the Northern Territory**
P.O. Box 3162, Darwin, N.T. 5794, Australia.
- S. L. A. N. T. Newsletter. bi-m.

**School Library Association of Victoria**
P.O. Box 280, East Melbourne 3002, Australia.
- Australian School Librarian. q. ISSN 0005-0199

**Science Foundation for Physics**
Sydney, N.S.W. 2006, Australia.
- Nucleus. a. ISSN 0085-4409 (Co-sponsor: University of Sydney, School of Physics)

**Science Museum of Victoria**
304-328 Swanston St, Melbourne, Victoria 3000, Australia.
- Melbourne. Science Museum of Victoria. Report of Activities. a. ISSN 0076-6240
- Science Museum of Victoria. Report of Activities. a.

**Science Teachers Association of New South Wales**
10 Marion St., Homebush 2140, Australia.
- Science Education News. 5 per yr. ISSN 0048-9603

**Science Teachers Association of Queensland**
c/o J. Sinclair, 17 Indooroopilly Rd., Jaringa, Qld. 4068, Australia.
- Science Teachers Association of Queensland. Newsletter. irreg.

**Science Teachers Association of Tasmania**
Box 170, North Hobart, Tas. 7002, Australia.
- Static. 5 per yr.

**Science Teachers Association of Victoria**
Clunies Ross House, 191 Royal Pde., Parkville, Vic. 3052, Australia.
- Lab-Talk. bi-m. ISSN 0047-3820

**Science Teachers Association of Western Australia**
Box X1501, Perth, W.A. 6000, Australia.
- Scios. q.

**W. D. Scott & Co.**
100 Pacific Highway, North Sydney, N.S.W. 2060, Australia.
- Australian Economy; Business Forecasts. a. ISSN 0084-7348
- Economic Advice to Business. fortn.

**Scout Association of Australia**
Brigadier R. Fullford, National Headquarters, Churchill House, 218 Northbourne Avenue, Braddon, A. C. T. 2601, Australia.
- Scout Association of Australia. Review of Progress. a. ISSN 0310-818X

**Scout Association of Australia. Victoria Branch**
384 Elizabeth St., Melbourne, 3000, Australia.
- Victorian Scout. m.

**Sea Spray**
Box M5, Sydney Mail Exchange, N.S.W. 2012, Australia.
- Australian Sea Spray. fortn. ISSN 0311-7839

**Seamen's Union of Australia**
289A Sussex St., Sydney, N.S.W. 2000, Australia.
- Seamen's Journal. m.

**Second Back Row Press**
Box 197, North Sydney, N.S.W. 2095, Australia.
- Australasian Small Press Review. 3 per yr. ISSN 0312-0112

**Secondary Student Union of Western Australia**
University of Western Australia, Nedlands, W.A. 6009, Australia.
- Nexus. irreg. ISSN 0311-1873

**Secretaries and Managers Association**
Labor Council Bldg., 377-83 Sussex St., Sydney,
2000 N.S.W., Australia.
- Secretaries and Managers Journal of Australia. m.

**Security Education (Australasia) Pub. Co.**
Box 230, Eastwood, N.S.W. 2122, Australia.
- Australian Security Journal. bi-m. ISSN 0045-0871

**Selby's Laboratory News**
P.O. Box 11, Oakleigh, Vic. 3166, Australia.
- Selby's Laboratory News. irreg.

**Serbian Cultural Club "St. Sava" in New South Wales**
Box 183, Cabramatta, N.S.W. 2166, Australia.
- Serbian Struggle.

**Serbian National Defence**
c/o Gvozden Bralovic, Box 236, Canberra City,
A.C.T. 2601, Australia.
- Serbian Bulletin. m. ISSN 0310-740X

**Service Station Association of N.S.W. Ltd.**
504 Darling St., Rozelle N.S.W. 2039, Australia.
- Automotive Service. m. ISSN 0005-1586

**Service to Youth Council Inc.**
128 Glen Osmond Rd., Parkside, S. A. 5063,
Australia.
- Caring. m.

**Seventh-Day Adventists. Australasian Division**
148 Fox Valley Road, Wahroonga, N.S.W. 2076,
Australia.
- Link (N.S.W.) irreg. (prep. by its Department of
Education)

**Shennen Publishing & Publicity Co.**
64 Kippax St., Surry Hills, N.S.W. 2010, Australia.
- Freight & Container Transportation. m (except
Jan.) ISSN 0016-0865
- Freight Carriers. bi-m. (Master Carriers'
Association of New South Wales)
- Truck and Bus Transportation; national road
transport fleetowner monthly. m. ISSN 0041-3380

**Sherwood Publishing Co.**
62 South Tce, Adelaide 5000, Australia.
- South Australian Builder. m. (Master Builders
Association)

**Shiplovers Society of Victoria**
G.P.O. Box 1169K, Melbourne, Victoria, 3001,
Australia.
- Dog Watch. a.

**Shipping Newspapers (W.A.) Ltd.**
171-177 Hay St., Perth, W.A. 6000, Australia.
- Building & Construction. w. ISSN 0007-3342
(Building Industry Congress of Western Australia)

**Showcast**
35 A Rosebery Street, Mosman, N.S.W. 2088,
Australia.
- Showcast. a.

**Slow Learning Childrens Group of W.A.**
1305 Hay St., West Perth, W.A. 6005, Australia.
- Activ News. m.

**Smoke Signals Publishing Committee**
43 Flintoff St., Greensborough, Vic. 3088, Australia.
- Smoke Signals. q. ISSN 0049-0776 (Aborigines
Advancement League (Vic.))

**Snowy Mountains Engineering Corporation**
- Snowy Mountains Engineering Corporation.
Annual Report. (pub. by Commonwealth
Government Printing Office)

**Soccer World Publishing Co. Pty. Ltd.**
54 Renwick St., Marrickville, Australia.
- Soccer World. w. ISSN 0037-7554

**Socialist Party of Australia**
c/o W. Brown, Ed., 111 Sussex St., Sydney, N.S.W.
2000, Australia.
- Australian Marxist Review. bi-m. ISSN 0310-8252

**Socialist Youth Alliance**
c/o Col. Moynard, 6 Uther St., Surry Hills, N.S.W.
2010, Australia.
- S. Y. A. Internal Bulletin. irreg.

**Society for Growing Australian Plants**
860 Henry Lawson Dr., Picnic Point, N.S.W. 2213,
Australia.
- Australian Plants. q. ISSN 0005-0008

**Society for Mass Media and Resource Technology**
Box 44, Ingle Farm, S.A. 5098, Australia.
- Society for Mass Media and Resource
Technology. Journal. q. ISSN 0311-0478

**Society of Australian Genealogists**
413 Riley Street, Surry Hills N.S.W. 2010,
Australia.
- Australian Genealogists' Newsletter. s-a.
- Descent. irreg., (approx 2 issues per yr.) ISSN
0084-9731

**Society of Automotive Engineers-Australasia**
191 Royal Parade, Parkville, Victoria 3052,
Australia.
- S A E - Australasia. bi-m. ISSN 0036-0651

**Society of Hospital Pharmacists of Australia**
- Australian Journal of Hospital Pharmacy. (pub. by
Mercedes Publishing Co.)

**Society of Registered Surveyors**
c/o Regan and Shaw, 79 Eagle Street, 7th Floor
Dalgety House, Brisbane, Qld. 4000, Australia.
- Metes and Bounds. q.

**Sophia**
c/o School of Humanities, Deakin University, P.O.
Box 125, Belmont, Vic. 3216, Australia.
- Sophia; a journal for discussion in philosophical
theology. 3 per yr. ISSN 0038-1527

**Soundtracks Publishing Pty. Ltd.**
Box 281, Broadway, N.S.W. 2007, Australia.
- Tracks. m.

**South Asia Studies Association**
- South Asia; Journal of South Asian Studies. (pub.
by University of Western Australia. Centre for
South & Southeast Asian Studies)

**South Australia. Department of Agriculture**
Box 1671, Adelaide, S.A. 5001, Australia.
- Journal of Agriculture-South Australia. q. ISSN
0021-8626
- South Australia. Department of Agriculture.
Agricultural Record. s-a. ISSN 0081-2625
- South Australia. Department of Agriculture.
Animal Industry Division. Annual Report. a.
ISSN 0081-2617
- South Australia. Department of Agriculture.
Extension Bulletin. irreg. ISSN 0489-8788
- South Australia. Department of Agriculture.
Special Bulletin. irreg.

**South Australia. Department of Agriculture and
Fisheries. Economics Branch**
Box 1671, G.P.O., Adelaide 5001, South Australia,
Australia.
- Farming Forum. q.

**South Australia. Department of Labour and Industry**
G.P.O. Box 297 A, Adelaide, SA 5001, Australia.
- South Australia. Department of Labour and
Industry. Guide to Legislation. irreg. ISSN 0311-0702

**South Australia. Department of Mines**
P.O. Box 151, Eastwood, South Australia 5063,
Australia.
- Mineral Industry Quarterly. q.
- Mineral Resources Review. s-a. ISSN 0026-525X
- Quarterly Geological Notes. q.

**South Australia. Department of Mines. Geological
Survey of South Australia**
Box 151, Eastwood, S. A. 5063, Australia.
- South Australia. Geological Survey. Bulletin. irreg.
ISSN 0016-7673
- South Australia. Geological Survey. Report of
Investigations. irreg. ISSN 0016-7681

**South Australia. Department of Public Health**
158 Rundle St., Adelaide, S.A. 5000, Australia.
- Good Health. irreg. ISSN 0085-1124

**South Australia. Department of Woods and Forests**
135 Waymouth St., Adelaide, South Australia,
Australia.
- South Australia. Department of Woods and
Forests. Bulletin. irreg.

**South Australia. Education Department**
Adelaide, S.A., Australia.
- South Australia. Department of Education.
Education Gazette. m. ISSN 0049-1438

**South Australia. Education Department. School
Libraries Branch**
Box 1152, Adelaide, S.A. 5001, Australia.
- South Australia. Education Department. School
Libraries Branch. Review. q. ISSN 0310-5202

**South Australia. Government Printer**
282 West Beach Road, Netley, S.A. 5037, Australia.
- South Australian Government Gazette. w. ISSN
0038-2906

**South Australia. Highways Department**
Box 19, Walkerville, S.A. 5081, Australia.
- Highway. bi-m. ISSN 0046-7383

**South Australia. State Planning Authority**
G.P.O. Box 1815, Adelaide, S.A. 5001, Australia.
- Planning News. s-a. ISSN 0554-2626

**South Australia Fruitgrowers & Market Gardeners
Association Inc.**
Box 43, Rundle St., Adelaide, S.A. 5000, Australia.
- Grower. m. ISSN 0046-6476

**South Australian Automobile Chamber of Commerce**
50-51 Greenhill Rd., Wayville 5034, S. A.,
Australia.
- Motor Trade Journal. m. ISSN 0027-2035

**South Australian Canine Association**
Box 646, Adelaide, S.A. 5001, Australia.
- South Australian Canine Journal. m. ISSN 0310-7078

**South Australian Chamber of Commerce and Industry**
Industry House, 12 Pirie St., Adelaide, 5000 S.A.,
Australia.
- Journal of Industry. m. ISSN 0022-1872

**South Australian Chess Association**
c/o Lot 8, Esk St., Woodville South, S.A. 5011,
Australia.
- South Australian Chess Bulletin. m.

**South Australian Dairymen's Association**
Aston House, 13 Leigh St., Adelaide, S.A. 5000,
Australia.
- South Australian Dairymen's Journal. bi-m. ISSN
0049-1446

**South Australian Government Tourist Bureau**
18 King William St., Adelaide, S.A. 5000, Australia.
- What's on in Adelaide and South Australia; what's
on and where to go in Adelaide this month. m.

**South Australian Institute of Teachers**
163A Greenhill Rd., 5063 Parkside, S.A., Australia.
- South Australian Teachers Journal. s-m. ISSN
0038-3015

**South Australian Jockey Club Inc.**
Box 1695, G.P.O. Adelaide 5001, Australia.
- South Australian Racing Calendar. m. ISSN 0038-2981

**South Australian Motor Pty. Ltd.**
RAA of SA Bldg., Hindmarsh Square, Adelaide,
S.A. 5000, Australia.
- South Australian Motor. bi-m. ISSN 0038-2957
(Royal Automobile Association of South Australia
Inc)

**South Australian Museum**
North Terrace, Adelaide 5000, S.A., Australia.
- South Australian Museum, Adelaide. Records.
irreg., 1973, vol. 16, no. 14. ISSN 0081-2676

**South Australian Numismatic Society**
Box 80 G.P.O., Adelaide, South Australia, Australia.
- Australian Numismatic Journal; devoted to the
study of coins, tokens, paper money and medals,
particularly the issues of Australia. a. ISSN 0004-9875

**South Australian Ornithological Association**
c/o South Australian Museum, North Terrace,
Adelaide 5000, S.A., Australia.
- South Australian Ornithologist. s-a. ISSN 0038-2973

**South Head Press**
350 Lyons Rd., Five Dock, N. S. W. 2046,
Australia.
- Poetry Australia. q. ISSN 0032-2059

**South Pacific Commission. Publications Bureau**
Box 306, Haymarket 2000 N.S.W., Australia.
- South Pacific Bulletin. q. ISSN 0038-349X

**South Pacific Electric Railway Co-Operative Society Ltd.**
P.O. Box 103, Sutherland, N.S.W. 2232, Australia.
- Trolley Wire. bi-m.

**Southdown Press Pty. Ltd.**
32 Walsh Street, Melbourne, Vic., 3000, Australia.
- New Idea. w. ISSN 0028-5404
- Parade. m. ISSN 0031-1596

**Southeast Asian Research Materials Group**
c/o Ed. B. Muskens, Monash University Library,
Clayton, Victoria 3168, Australia.
- Southeast Asian Research Materials Group. Newsletter. irreg. ISSN 0311-290X

**Southern Caving Society**
Box 121, Moonah, Tas. 7009, Australia.
- Southern Caver. q.

**Southern Cross Model Railway Association**
Box 235, Matraville, N.S.W. 2036, Australia.
- Australasian Model Railroad Magazine. bi-m. ISSN 0045-009X

**Spartacist League of Australia & New Zealand**
G.P.O. Box 3473, Sydney, N.S.W. 2001, Australia.
- Revolutionary Communist Bulletin. irreg.

**Speak**
c/o Audrey Windram, Ed., Conrad St., Longwood,
S. A. 5153, Australia.
- Speak. a.

**Specific Learning Difficulties Association of New South Wales**
Box 94, Mosman, N.S.W. 2088, Australia.
- S P E L D News. q.

**Specific Learning Difficulties Association of Victoria**
Box 146, Camberwell, Vic. 3124, Australia.
- S P E L D. 3 per yr.

**Specific Learning Difficulties Association of Western Australia**
Community Development Centre, Corner Selby Rd.
and Stubbs Terrace, Shenton Park, W. A. 6008,
Australia.
- S P E L D Bulletin. q.

**Speedo Knitting Mills Pty. Ltd.**
Box 25, Artarmon N.S.W. 2064, Australia.
- International Swimmer. m. ISSN 0020-8876

**Sporting Shooters Association of Australia**
Box 12, Elizabeth, South Australia. 5112, Australia.
- Australian Shooters Journal. m. ISSN 0005-0245

**Sportsmen's Association of Australia. Western Australian Division**
G.P.O. Box T 1854, Perth, W. A. 6001, Australia.
- Lindy News. irreg.

**Standards Association of Australia**
Standards House, 80 Arthur St., North Sydney,
NSW 2060, Australia.
- S A A Monthly Information Sheet. m.

**Stanton Library**
234 Miller St., North Sydney, N.S.W. 2060,
Australia.
- List of Books on Architecture, Building, Town Planning and Related Subjects Held in the Stanton Library, Municipality of North Sydney. Supplement. irreg. ISSN 0310-9097

**State College of Victoria at Toorak**
336 Glenferrie Rd., Malvern, Vic. 3144, Australia.
- Probe. 2 per yr. ISSN 0310-4044

**State Library of Tasmania**
91 Murray St., Hobart, Tasmania 7000, Australia.
- Tasmanian Official Publications. q.

**State Planning Authority of New South Wales**
G.P.O. Box 3927, Sydney, N.S.W. 2001, Australia.
- S. P. A. N. (State Planning Authority News) irreg.

**State Rivers and Water Supply Commission**
590 Orrong Rd., Armadale 3143, Victoria, Australia.
- Aqua. s-a. ISSN 0003-7206

**State School Teachers Union of W.A. (Inc.)**
13 Murray St, Perth, Australia.
- Western Teacher. every 3 wks (except Jan. and school holidays)

**Statisical Society of Australia**
c/o Australian National University, Box 4,
Canberra, A.C.T. 2600, Australia.
- Australian Journal of Statistics. 3 per yr. ISSN 0004-9581

**Stock and Land Publishing Co.**
174 Peel St., North Melbourne, Victoria 3051,
Australia.
- Stock and Land. w. ISSN 0039-1565

**Stock Exchange of Melbourne Ltd.**
G.P.O. Box 1784Q, Melbourne, Vic. 3001,
Australia.
- Chart Book of the Melbourne Share Price Index. a. ISSN 0311-3655

**Stock Exchange of Perth**
68 St. George's Tce., Perth, W.A. 6000, Australia.
- Perth. Stock Exchange. Official Record. bi-m. ISSN 0048-3559

**Stock Feed Manufacturer's Association of New South Wales**
6 O'Connell St., Sydney, N.S.W. 2000, Australia.
- Australian Stock Feed Manufacturer's Federal Council. Stock Feed News. irreg.

**Stock Journal Publishers Pty.**
11 Cannon St., Adelaide, S.A. 5000, Australia.
- Stock Journal. w. ISSN 0039-162X

**Stockowners Association of S.A.**
Stockowners House, 63 Waymouth St., Adelaide,
S.A. 5000, Australia.
- Stockowners' Digest. m. ISSN 0049-2280

**Stormtrooper**
G.P.O. 443c, Melbourne, Victoria, Australia.
- Stormtrooper. q.

**Stowarzyszenie Polakow W Queensland**
Box 1808, Brisbane, Qld. 4001, Australia.
- Biuletyn/Bulletin of Polonia. m.

**Strand Publishing Pty. Ltd.**
432 Queen St., Brisbane, Australia.
- Australian Electrical World. m. ISSN 0004-9034
- Australian Sugar Year Book. a. ISSN 0067-2173
- Producers Review. m. ISSN 0032-972X

**Sub-Normal Children's Welfare Association**
8 Junction St., Ryde, N.S.W. 2112, Australia.
- Sub-Normal Children's Welfare Association. Welfare News. q. ISSN 0049-2418

**Sulphide Corporation Pty. Ltd.**
P.O. Box 42, Boolaroo, NSW 2284, Australia.
- Zinc Today. irreg.

**Sungravure Pty. Ltd.**
57-59 Regent St., Chippendale, N.S.W. 2008,
Australia.
- Cosmopolitan. m. ISSN 0310-2076
- Dolly. m.
- Electronics Australia. m. ISSN 0013-5135
- Woman's Day. w. ISSN 0043-7328

**Sunstate Publishers Inc. (Qld.) Pty. Ltd.**
369 George St., Brisbane, Qld. 4000, Australia.
- Queensland Home & Garden. m.

**Suomi**
Box 75, Darra, Qld. 4076, Australia.
- Suomi. fortn.

**Superior Council of Australia**
7 Young St., Sydney N.S.W. 2000, Australia.
- Saint Vincent de Paul Record. q. ISSN 0036-3219

**Sydney Bush Walkers**
Box 4476, G.P.O., Sydney, N. S. W. 2001,
Australia.
- Sydney Bushwalker. m.

**Sydney County Council. Publicity Section**
Box 4009, Sydney, N.S.W. 2001, Australia.
- Contractor. q.

**Sydney Libertarians**
Box 2986, G. P. O., Sydney, Australia.
- Broadsheet. 4-6 per yr. ISSN 0007-2036

**Sydney Medieval and Renaissance Group**
History Department, University of Sydney, Sydney,
NSW 2006, Australia.
- Studium. irreg. ISSN 0311-2233

**Sydney Metropolitan Water Sewerage and Drainage Board**
341 Pitt St., Sydney, N.S.W., Australia.
- Sydney Water Board Journal. s-a. ISSN 0039-761X

**Sydney Observatory**
c/o Government Astronomer, Observatory Park,
Sydney 2000, Australia.
- Sydney Observatory Papers. irreg. ISSN 0085-7009

**Sydney Rugby Union**
Crane Place, Sydney N. S. W. 2000, Australia.
- Rugby News. 40 per yr. ISSN 0035-9750

**Sydney Speleological Society**
P.O. Box 198, Broadway, N.S.W. 2007, Australia.
- Australian Speleo Abstracts. a.
- Sydney Speleological Society. Journal. m.
- Sydney Speleological Society. Occasional Paper. irreg.

**Sydney Stock Exchange**
Research & Statistics Department, 13-15 O'Connell
St., Sydney, Australia.
- Sydney Stock Exchange. Research and Statistical Department. Company Review Service. a.

**Sydney Teachers' College**
P.O. Box 63, Camperdown, New South Wales 2050,
Australia.
- Forum of Education. 3 per yr. ISSN 0015-8542

**Sydney University Press**
Press Bldg., University of Sydney, Sydney 2006,
Australia
(Dist. by: International Scholarly Book Services
Inc., Box 4347, Portland, OR 97208)
- Abacus; a journal of accounting and business studies. s-a. ISSN 0001-3072
- Australian Academy of the Humanities. Proceedings. a. ISSN 0067-1592
- Australian Economic History Review. s-a. ISSN 0004-8992
- Australian Geographer. s-a. ISSN 0004-9182 (Geographical Society of New South Wales)
- Journal of Religious History. s-a. ISSN 0022-4227 (Association for the Journal of Religious History)
- Pathology. q. ISSN 0031-3025 (Royal College of Pathologists of Australia)
- Sources in Ancient History. irreg. ISSN 0081-2110
- Sydney Studies in Literature. irreg., no. 8, 1977. ISSN 0082-0520

**Sydney University Speleological Society**
Box 35, The Union, University of Sydney, NSW
2006, Australia.
- S U S S. irreg.

**David Syme & Co.**
250 Spencer St., Melbourne, Australia.
- Australian Caravan World and Camper Trailering. m.
- Australian Motor Manual. m.

**Tasmania. Department of Agriculture**
Box 192 B, G.P.O., Hobart, Tasmania, Australia.
- Tasmania. Department of Agriculture. Annual Report. a. ISSN 0082-1993
- Tasmania. Department of Agriculture. Bulletin. irreg., no. 47, 1976. ISSN 0082-2000
- Tasmania. Department of Agriculture. Dairy Herd Improvement Scheme. Annual Report. a. ISSN 0082-2019
- Tasmania. Department of Agriculture. Reprint. q. ISSN 0082-2027
- Tasmania. Department of Agriculture. Research Bulletin. irreg., 1968, no. 5. ISSN 0082-2035
- Tasmanian Journal of Agriculture. q. ISSN 0039-9817

**Tasmania. Department of Agriculture. Fisheries Div.**
Box 192b, Hobart, Tas. 7001, Australia.
- Tasmanian Fisheries Research. s-a. ISSN 0049-3015

**Tasmania. Department of Mines**
Box 124B, G.P.O., Hobart, Tasmania, Australia 7001.
- Tasmania. Department of Mines. Geological Survey Bulletins. irreg., 1973, no. 54. ISSN 0082-2043
- Tasmania. Department of Mines. Technical Reports. irreg., no. 19, 1975. ISSN 0082-2078

**Tasmania. Department of Tourism and Immigration**
G.P.O. Box 399D, Hobart 7001, Australia.
- Tasmanian Travelways. bi-m.

**Tasmania. Directorate of Industrial Development & Trade**
152 Macquarie St., Hobart, Tas. 7000, Australia.
- Information about Investment in Tasmania. irreg. ISSN 0082-1985

**Tasmania. Education Department**
2 Edward St., Glebe, Tasmania 7000, Australia.
- Panorama. q.
- Tasmanian Education Gazette. m. ISSN 0039-9760

**Tasmania. Education Department. Curriculum Branch**
181 Elizabeth St., Hobart, Tas. 7000, Australia.
- Tasmania. Education Department. Curriculum Branch. Modern Languages Information Series. irreg.

**Tasmania. Government Printer**
2 Salamanca Place, Hobart 7000, Australia.
- Tasmanian Government Gazette. w. ISSN 0039-9795

**Tasmania. Metropolitan Water Board**
G.P.O. Box 179, Hobart, Tasmania, Australia.
- Tasmania. Metropolitan Water Board. Report. a. ISSN 0082-2094

**Tasmania. Tasmanian Government Printer**
c/o T. J. Hughes, Hobart, Tas., Australia.
- Tasmania. Department of the Treasury. Commonwealth Grants to Tasmania. irreg.
- Tasmania. Department of the Treasury. Consolidated Revenue Fund; summary of estimated expenditure (including expenditure reserved by law) and estimated revenue.

**Tasmanian Association for the Teaching of English**
c/o J. W. Annells, Curriculum Centre, 181 Elizabeth St., Hobart, Tas. 7000, Australia.
- Words and Windmills. 3 per yr. ISSN 0311-1784

**Tasmanian Automobile Chamber of Commerce**
G. P. O. Box 511E, Hobart, Tasmania 7001, Australia.
- Tasmanian Motor Trader. m. ISSN 0039-985X

**Tasmanian Caverneering Club**
Box 641 G, Hobart, Tas. 7001, Australia.
- Speleo-Spiel. 11 per yr.

**Tasmanian Chamber of Industries**
191 Liverpool St., Hobart, Tas. 7000, Australia.
- Tasmanian Chamber of Industries. Service Bulletin. m. ISSN 0310-4575

**Tasmanian Historical Research Association. Dept. of History**
Tasmanian Museum, G.P.O. Box 1164M, Hobart, Tasmania 7001, Australia.
- Tasmanian Historical Research Association. Papers and Proceedings. q. ISSN 0039-9809

**Tasmanian Teachers' Federation**
32 Patrick St, Hobart, Australia.
- Tasmanian Teacher. 8 per yr. ISSN 0039-9868

**Tasmanian Trade Protective Institute**
- T.T.P.I. Trade Gazette. (pub. by Cromptons Collection Service)

**Tasmanian Transport Commission**
G.P.O. Box 1002 K, Hobart 7001, Tasmania, Australia.
- Tasmanian Transport Bulletin. q. ISSN 0310-7531

**Tattersall's Club**
Box 4308, Sydney, N.S.W. 2001, Australia.
- Tattersall's Club Magazine. m.

**Taxation Institute of Australia**
13-15 O'Connell St., Sydney 2000, Australia.
- Taxation in Australia. m.

**Taxi Council of Queensland**
- Taxi News. (pub. by A. Webb & Sons Pty. Ltd.)

**Teachers Central Registry**
Assembly Hall, 44 Margaret St., Sydney, N.S.W. 2000, Australia.
- Australian Teacher. 2 per yr. ISSN 0045-091X (Teachers' Guild of New South Wales)

**Teachers' Guild of New South Wales**
- Australian Teacher. (pub. by Teachers Central Registry)

**Technical Association of the Australian and New Zealand Pulp and Paper Industry**
Clunies Ross House, 191 Royal Pde., Parkville, Victoria 3052, Australia.
- Appita. bi-m. ISSN 0003-6757

**Technical Teachers Association of Australia**
Ed. R. J. Millican, 101 Gap Creek Rd., Brookfield, 4069, Australia.
- Australian Technical Teacher. q. ISSN 0045-0928

**Technical Teachers Association of Victoria**
485 Queensberry St., North Melbourne, Victoria 3051, Australia.
- Technical Teachers Association of Victoria. Associate News. s-m. ISSN 0049-3163

**TecPress Group**
G.P.O. Box 4318, Sydney, N.S.W. 2001, Australia.
- Contracting & Construction Engineer. m. ISSN 0010-7867
- Industrial Technology and Machine Tools. bi-m.
- Oil & Gas, Australasia,.S.E. Asia. m.
- Public Works, Australasia, S.E. Asia & West Pacific. 6 per yr.
- Quarry Mine & Pit. 11 per yr. ISSN 0048-6116

**Telecommunication Society of Australia**
Box 4050, Melbourne 3001, Victoria, Australia.
- A T R (Australian Telecommunication Research) s-a. ISSN 0001-2777
- Australian Telecommunication Monographs. irreg., 1966, no. 3. ISSN 0067-2181
- Telecommunication Journal of Australia. 3 per yr. ISSN 0040-2486

**Television and Electronic Services Associations of Australasia**
- Video-Tronics. (pub. by Video Publishing Co.)

**Testing, Instruments & Controls**
Box 250, North Sydney, Australia.
- Testing, Instruments & Controls; a technical journal for industries using instrumentation. m. ISSN 0040-3997

**Textile Council of Australia**
Accountants House, 5th Floor, 49 Exhibition St., Melbourne, Vic. 3000, Australia.
- Textile Council of Australia. Textile Information Service. irreg.

**Theatre Publications**
7 President Place, New Lambton Heights, N.S.W. 2305, Australia.
- Theatre - Australia. m. ISSN 0313-2080

**Theosophical Society in Australia**
121 Walker St., North Sydney, N.S.W. 2060, Australia.
- Theosophy in Australia. q. ISSN 0049-3694

**Thomson Publications (Australia) Pty. Ltd.**
47 Chippen St., Chippendale, 2008 N.S.W., Australia.
- Australian Advertising Rate and Data Service. m. ISSN 0067-1606
- Australian Electronics Engineering. m. ISSN 0004-9042
- Australian Mining. m. ISSN 0004-976X
- Building Products News. m. ISSN 0007-358X
- C E N/Construction Equipment News. m. ISSN 0007-8247
- Electrical Engineer; power generation, electricity transmission and utilization. m. ISSN 0013-4309
- F E N/Australian Factory Equipment News. m. ISSN 0014-5807
- I. E. S. Lighting Review. bi-m. ISSN 0018-9618 (Illuminating Engineering Society of Australia)
- Mingay's Electrical Supplies Guide. s-a. ISSN 0026-508X
- Mingay's Price Service. q. ISSN 0026-5101
- Mingay's Retailer & Merchandiser; covering sales and service in the home appliance radio and TV market. m.

**P A C E. (Process & Chemical Engineering) m.**
- Tenders. w. ISSN 0040-3113
- Thomsons Travel News. m.

**D. W. Thorpe Pty. Ltd.**
384 Spencer St., Melbourne, Vic. 3003, Australia.
- Australian Audio Visual News. q. ISSN 0312-0716
- Australian Audio-Visual Reference Book. a. ISSN 0311-323X
- Australian Books in Print; bookbuyers reference book. a(biennial until 1968) ISSN 0067-172X
- Australian Bookseller and Publisher. m. ISSN 0004-8763
- Australian Newsagent and Stationer. m. ISSN 0004-9867

**Tidal Publications**
Box 2318 V, G.P.O., Melbourne, Australia.
- Social Crediter; for political and economic realism. m. ISSN 0037-7694

**Timber Development Association (NSW) Ltd.**
525 Elizabeth St., Sydney, NSW 2000, Australia.
- T. D. A. Bulletin. irreg.
- Wood World. 2 per yr. ISSN 0049-7924

**Times of Malta and Australia**
c/o Alfred Ciantar, Ed., 535 Sydney Rd., Brunswick, Vic. 3056, Australia.
- Times of Malta and Australia. (T.O.M.A.) m.

**Timestream**
c/o Richard Coady, Ed., P. O. Box A360, Sydney South 2000, New South Wales, Australia.
- Timestream. bi-m.

**Tomorrow's Business Decisions**
Suite 26, 7 Elizabeth St., Sydney 2000, Australia.
- Tomorrow's Business Decisions. m.

**Town and Country Planning Association of Victoria**
Box 175, Nunawading, Vic. 3131, Australia.
- Space. bi-m. ISSN 0310-0189

**Townsville Writers' Group**
Flat 2, First St., Railway Estate, Townsville, Qld 4810, Australia.
- In Print. a. ISSN 0310-3048

**Trade Directories**
P.O. Box 94, Morningside, Qld 4170, Australia.
- Transport Services Directory. a.

**Trade Union Education Centre**
Rm. 9, Box 9, Trades Hall, Goulburn St., Sydney, N.S.W. 2000, Australia.
- Modern Unionist. q. ISSN 0047-7753

**Trade Unionists' Defence Committee. Union Publicity Council**
42 Errol St., North Melbourne, Vic. 3051, Australia.
- Scope (Melbourne) irreg.

**Trade Winds Publications Pty. Ltd.**
79 1/2 George Street North, Sydney, N.S.W. 2000, Australia.
- Tailor and Men's Wear. m. ISSN 0039-9043

**Trades and Labor Council of Queensland**
Room 1, Trades Hall, Edward Street, Brisbane, Qld. 4000, Australia.
- Trades Union Directory. a.

**Training Centre for Teachers of the Deaf**
Box 100, Croydon Park. N.S.W. 2133., Australia.
- Australian Teacher of the Deaf. a. ISSN 0005-0334 (Australian Association of Teachers of the Deaf)

**Trans-Australia Airlines**
50 Franklin St, Melbourne 3001, Australia.
- Transair. m. ISSN 0041-1043

**Transport Journal of Australia**
c/o Iain Macdougall, Ed., 507 Kent St., Sydney, N.S.W., Australia.
- Transport Journal of Australia. m. ISSN 0041-1493

**Tropical Grassland Society of Australia**
c/o C.S.I.R.O., Mill Rd., St. Lucia, Qld. 4067, Australia.
- Tropical Grasslands. 3 per yr. ISSN 0049-4763

**Tube**
c/o Richard Coady, Ed., 32 Coventry Rd.,
Strathfield, NSW 2135, Australia.
- Tube. irreg. ISSN 0310-6217

**Turk Sesi Pty. Ltd.**
472 William St., Melbourne 3003, Australia.
- Turk Sesi/Turkish News. w.

**Tweed**
c/o Janice M. Bostok, Ed., Box 304, Murwillumbah,
N.S.W. 2484, Australia.
- Tweed. q.

**Ukrainian Womens' Association in Australia**
Private Bag No. 3, Bundoora, Vic. 3083, Australia.
- Nashe Slovo/Our Word. q.

**Ulster Link**
Box 135, South Melbourne, Vic. 3205, Australia.
- Ulster Link. m.

**Ultra Light Aircraft Association of Australia**
Box 41, Bankstown, N.S.W. 2200, Australia.
- Australian Airsport. m.

**Underwater Federation of Australia**
- Australian Skindivers. (pub. by Underwater
Skindivers and Fishermen's Association of
N.S.W.)

**Underwater Skindivers and Fishermen's Association
of N.S.W.**
Box 1192, G.P.O., Sydney 2001, Australia
(Subscr. to: Post Office Box 121, Campbelltown,
N.S.W., 2560 Australia)
- Australian Skindivers. m. ISSN 0005-0253
(Underwater Federation of Australia)

**Unidentified Flying Objects Investigation Centre**
P.O. Box 6, Lane Cove, N.S.W. 2066, Australia.
- U F O I C Newsletter. bi-m.

**Unification Printers & Publishers Pty. Ltd.**
497 Collins St., Melbourne, 3000, Australia.
- Unification/Edinenie; Russian language newspaper
in Australia. w.

**Union of Australian Women**
Room 5, Floor 2A, Block Arcade, Melbourne, Vic.
3000, Australia.
- Union of Australian Women. Newsletter. m.

**United Farmers and Woolgrowers Association**
GPO Box 1576, Sydney 2001, Australia.
- United Farmer. m.

**United Nations Association of Australia**
N.S.W. Division, 11 Loftus Street, Sydney, N.S.W.
2000, Australia.
- United Nations Association of Australia. United
Nations Reporter. irreg. ISSN 0085-7475

**Universal Business Directories (Australia) Pty. Ltd.**
P.O. Box 155, North Ryde, N.S.W. 2113, Australia.
- Register of Companies in New South Wales. a.
ISSN 0085-5456
- Universal Business Directories. ITEMS;
Instrumentation and Control; Tools; Equipment;
Machinery; Supplies and service. a. ISSN 0083-
3738
- Universal Business Directories, Adelaide Business
and Street Directory. a.
- Universal Business Directories, Brisbane and
Suburban Business and Street Directory. a.
- Universal Business Directories, New South Wales
Business and Street Directory. a.
- Universal Business Directories, Northern
Queensland Business and Street Directory. a.
- Universal Business Directories, Southern
Queensland Business and Street Directory. a.
- Universal Business Directories, Sydney and
Suburban Business and Street Directory. a.
- Universal Business Directories, Tasmania Business
and Street Directory. a.

**Universal Business Directories (Vic.) Pty. Ltd.**
159 Eastern Rd., S. Melbourne, Victoria, Australia.
- Universal Business Directories East Victoria
Country Trade Directory. a. ISSN 0083-372X
- Universal Business Directories Melbourne and
Suburban Business and Trade Directory. a. ISSN
0083-3746
- Universal Business Directories West Victoria
Country Business and Trade Directory. a. ISSN
0083-3835

**Universal Business Directories (WA) Pty. Ltd.**
20 Milford St., East Victoria Park, W. Australia,
Australia.
- Universal Business Directories North Territory
Business and Trade Directory. a. ISSN 0083-3754
- Universal Business Directories Perth and
Fremantle and Suburbs Business and Trade
Directory. a. ISSN 0083-3789
- Universal Business Directories Western Australia
Country Business and Trade Directory. a. ISSN
0083-3843

**University of Adelaide**
Adelaide, S. A., Australia.
- Australian Journal of Experimental Biology and
Medical Science. bi-m. ISSN 0004-945X
- Miscellanea Musicologica. (pub. by Libraries
Board of South Australia)

**University of Adelaide. Dental Students Society**
School of Dentistry, Adelaide, Australia.
- Probe. a. ISSN 0079-5631

**University of Adelaide. Department of English**
Adelaide 5000, Australia.
- Southern Review; literary and interdisciplinary
essays. 3 per yr. ISSN 0038-4526

**University of Adelaide. Economics Department**
Adelaide, Australia.
- Australian Economic Papers. s-a. ISSN 0004-
900X (Co-sponsor: Flinders University of South
Australia)

**University of Adelaide. Faculty of Law**
Adelaide, S.A., Australia
(Dist. by: Law Book Co. Ltd., 389 Lonsdale St.,
Melbourne, Vic., Australia)
- Adelaide Law Review. a. ISSN 0065-1915

**University of Adelaide. Graduates Union**
Box 498 D, Adelaide, S. Australia.
- University of Adelaide. Graduates Union.
Monthly Newsletter and Gazette. m. ISSN 0001-
8163

**University of Adelaide. Students Representative
Council**
Adelaide, Australia.
- On Dit. s-m. ISSN 0030-2333

**University of Kensington. School of Librarianship**
P. O. Box 1, Kensington, New South Wales,
Australia.
- University of Kensington. School of Librarianship.
Occasional Paper. irreg.

**University of Melbourne**
Parkville, Victoria 3052, Australia.
- Meanjin Quarterly; a magazine of literature, art
and discussion. q. ISSN 0025-6293
- University of Melbourne. Research Report. a.
ISSN 0543-4262

**University of Melbourne. Department of Civil
Engineering**
Parkville, Vic. 3052, Australia.
- University of Melbourne. Department of Civil
Engineering. Departmental Report. irreg. ISSN
0085-3240

**University of Melbourne. Department of Electrical
Engineering**
Parkville, Vic. 3052, Australia.
- University of Melbourne. Department of Electrical
Engineering. Research Report. irreg. ISSN 0085-
3259

**University of Melbourne. Department of English**
Parkville, Victoria 3052, Australia.
- Critical Review Melbourne. a. ISSN 0070-1548

**University of Melbourne. Department of History**
Parkville, N.2, Victoria, Australia.
- Historical Studies. s-a. ISSN 0018-2559

**University of Melbourne. Department of Middle
Eastern Studies**
Parkville 3052, Victoria, Australia.
- Abr-Nahrain. (pub. by E. J. Brill NE)
- Abr-Nahrain. Supplements. (pub. by E. J. Brill
NE)
- Milla Wa-Milla; the Australian bulletin of
comparative religion. a. ISSN 0076-8790

**University of Melbourne. Department of Political
Science**
Parkville 3052, Victoria, Australia.
- Melbourne Politics Monographs. irreg.

**University of Melbourne. Department of Russian
Language and Literature**
Parkville, Victoria 3052, Australia.
- Melbourne Slavonic Studies. a. ISSN 0076-6267

**University of Melbourne. Faculty of Agriculture and
Forestry**
Parkville, Vic. 3052, Australia.
- Melbourne Notes on Agricultural Extension. irreg.
ISSN 0085-3232 (Co-Sponsor: Victorian
Department of Agriculture)
- University of Melbourne. Faculty of Agriculture
and Forestry. Agricultural Economics Report.
irreg. ISSN 0085-3267

**University of Melbourne. Historical Society**
Parkville, Victoria 3052, Australia.
- Melbourne Historical Journal. a. ISSN 0076-6232

**University of Melbourne. Institute of Applied
Economic and Social Research**
Parkville, Vic. 3052, Australia.
- Australian Economic Review. q. ISSN 0004-9018
- University of Melbourne. Institute of Applied
Economic and Social Research. Monographs.
irreg., no. 7, 1977. ISSN 0076-6283
- University of Melbourne. Institute of Applied
Economic and Social Research. Technical Papers.
irreg., no. 8, 1975. ISSN 0076-6291

**University of Melbourne. Law School**
Parkville 3052, Victoria, Australia
(Subscr. to: Law Book Co. Ltd., 389 Lonsdale St.,
Melbourne 3000, Australia)
- Melbourne University Law Review. s-a. ISSN
0025-8938

**University of Melbourne. Liberal Club**
The Union, Parkville, Vic., Australia.
- Ad Lib. 3 per yr. ISSN 0001-7949

**University of Melbourne. Magazine Society**
Box 120, Union Howe, University of Melbourne,
Parkville 3052, Australia.
- Circus. q.

**University of Melbourne. Philosophy Department**
- Melbourne International Philosophy Series. (pub.
by Martinus Nijhoff NE)

**University of Melbourne. Political Science Society**
Parkville, Vic. 3052, Australia.
- Melbourne Journal of Politics. irreg., no. 6, 1974-
75. ISSN 0085-3224

**University of Melbourne. Registrar**
Parkville, Vic. 3052, Australia.
- University of Melbourne. Gazette. q. ISSN 0085-
3275

**University of Melbourne. School of Education**
- Melbourne Studies in Education. (pub. by
Melbourne University Press)

**University of Melbourne. Students Representative
Council**
Union House, Univ. of Melbourne, Parkville, Vic.
3052, Australia.
- Melbourne University Magazine. a. ISSN 0085-
3283

**University of New England**
Armidale, N.S.W. 2351, Australia.
- U N E Bulletin. a.

**University of New England. Agricultural Business
Research Institute**
Armidale, N.S.W. 2351, Australia.
- Professional Farm Management Guidebook. irreg;
(approx. 1 per yr)

**University of New England. Classical Society**
c/o Dept. of Classics, Univ. of New England,
Armidale, N.S.W. 2351, Australia.
- Camena. a. ISSN 0084-8352

**University of New England. Department of
Accounting & Financial Management**
Accounting Systems Research Centre, Armidale,
N.S.W. 2351, Australia.
- New England Accounting Practice Report. irreg.

**University of New England. Department of Continuing Education**
Armidale, N.S.W. 2351, Australia
(Subscr. to: Connexion, Box 249, St. Marys, N.S.W. 2760, Australia)
- Aboriginal Human Relations Newsletter. irreg. ISSN 0311-0028

**University of New England. Department of External Studies**
Armidale, N.S.W. 2351, Australia.
- External Studies Gazette. bi-m. ISSN 0014-5459

**University of New England. Department of Geography**
Armidale, N.S.W. 2351, Australia.
- University of New England. Department of Geography. Monograph Series in Geography. irreg., 1966, no. 2. ISSN 0066-7706
- University of New England. Department of Geography. Research Series in Applied Geography. irreg., no. 44, 1976. ISSN 0066-7714
- University of New England. Department of Geography. Studies in Applied Geographical Research. irreg.

**University of New England. Exploration Society**
Armidale, N.S.W., Australia.
- University of New England. Exploration Society. Report. irreg., 1966, no. 4. ISSN 0066-7730

**University of New England. Faculty of Education**
Armidale, N.S.W. 2351, Australia.
- Journal of Educational Administration. s-a. ISSN 0022-0639
- New England Papers on Education. irreg., 1972, no. 4. ISSN 0077-8230

**University of New England. Rural Science Undergraduates' Society**
Armidale, N.S.W. 2351, Australia.
- Chiasma. a. ISSN 0084-8735

**University of New England. Student's Representative Council**
Armidale, New South Wales, Australia.
- Neucleus; the voice of New England. fortn.

**University of New South Wales**
Director of Student Publications, Box 1, Kensington, N.S.W. 2033, Australia.
- Tharunka. w.
- University of New South Wales. Australian Journal of Management. s-a.
- University of New South Wales. School of Civil Engineering. U N I C I V Reports. Series I. irreg. ISSN 0077-8796
- University of New South Wales, Kensington. Research and Publications. a. ISSN 0548-6831
- Wool Technology and Sheep Breeding. q. ISSN 0043-7875

**University of New South Wales. Commerce Society**
Box 81, The Union, Univ. of N.S.W., Kensington, N.S.W. 2033, Australia.
- Enterprise. a. ISSN 0085-0268

**University of New South Wales. Democratic Club**
Box 111, the Union, Kensington, N.S.W. 2033, Australia.
- Kundu. w.

**University of New South Wales. Faculty of Law**
Kensington, Sydney, N.S.W. 2033, Australia.
- Lawasia. s-a. ISSN 0047-4207

**University of New South Wales. Library**
P.O. Box 1, Kensington, NSW 2033, Australia.
- University of New South Wales. Library. Information Bulletin. irreg.

**University of New South Wales. Metallurgical Society**
Box 1, Kensington, N.S.W. 2033, Australia.
- University of New South Wales. Metallurgical Society. Metallurgical Review. a. ISSN 0085-4018

**University of New South Wales. School of Civil Engineering**
P.O. Box 1, Kensington, N.S.W. 2033, Australia.
- University of New South Wales. School of Civil Engineering. U N I C I V Reports. Series R. irreg. ISSN 0077-880X

**University of New South Wales. School of Health Administration**
P.O. Box 1, Kensington, N.S.W. 2033, Australia.
- Australian Hospitals and Health Services Yearbook. (pub. by Peter Isaacson Publications)
- Australian Studies in Health Service Administration. irreg., nos. 24-25, 1974. ISSN 0067-2165

**University of New South Wales. School of Sociology**
Box 1, Kensington, N.S.W. 2033, Australia.
- Iconoclast. 3 per yr.

**University of New South Wales. School of Surveying**
P.O. Box 1, Kensington, N.S.W. 2033, Australia.
- Unisurv G; an Australian journal of geodesy, photogrammetry & surveying. s-a.

**University of New South Wales. School of Town Planning**
P.O. Box 1, Kensington, NSW 2033, Australia.
- Urbanology. irreg. ISSN 0310-5601

**University of New South Wales. Water Reference Library**
King St., Manly Vale, N.S.W. 2093, Australia.
- University of New South Wales. Water Reference Library. Current Awareness List. m.

**University of New South Wales. Water Research Laboratory**
King St., Manly Vale, N.S.W. 2093, Australia.
- University of New South Wales. Water Research Laboratory, Manly Vale. Laboratory Research Reports. irreg., 1970, no. 110. ISSN 0077-8818

**University of Newcastle. Board of Environmental Studies**
Newcastle, N.S.W., Australia.
- University of Newcastle. Board of Environmental Studies. Research Papers. 2-3 per yr.

**University of Newcastle. Department of Electrical Engineering**
Shortland, N.S.W. 2308, Australia.
- University of Newcastle. Department of Electrical Engineering. Technical Report EE. irreg. ISSN 0085-4158

**University of Newcastle. Department of History**
Newcastle, N.S.W. 2308, Australia.
- University of Newcastle Historical Journal. a. ISSN 0085-7629

**University of Newcastle. Students Association**
Shortland, N.S.W. 2308, Australia.
- Nimrod. a. ISSN 0085-4204

**University of Queensland**
Brisbane, Qld., Australia.
- University of Queensland. Combined Faculty Directory. irreg.

**University of Queensland. Bushwalking Club**
St. Lucia, Qld. 4067, Australia.
- Heybob. a.

**University of Queensland. Department of Anthropology, Sociology and Geography**
Brisbane, Qld. 4067, Australia.
- Man in Southeast Asia. 2-4 per yr.

**University of Queensland. Department of Education**
St. Lucia, Qld. 4067, Australia.
- Aboriginal Child at School. bi-m (approx) ISSN 0310-5822
- Administrators' Bulletin. (pub. by University of Queensland Press)

**University of Queensland. Department of German**
St. Lucia 4067, Australia
- Queensland Studies in German Language and Literature. biennial. (Vol. 5 Published by: A. Francke AG Verlag, 3000 Bern 26, Switzerland)

**University of Queensland. Dept. of Mathematics**
St. Lucia, Q. 4067, Australia.
- Australian Mathematical Society. Bulletin. 2 vols. per yr.(3 nos. per vol.) ISSN 0004-9727
- Australian Mathematical Society. Journal. 2 vol. per yr. (4 nos. per vol.) ISSN 0004-9735

**University of Queensland. Dept. of Mechanical Engineering**
St. Lucia, 4067 Queensland, Australia.
- Solar Research Notes. irreg., 1973, no. 5. ISSN 0081-1920

**University of Queensland. English Department**
- Australian Literary Studies. (pub. by University of Queensland Press)
- Gargoyle Poets. (pub. by Makar Press)

**University of Queensland. Information Office**
Brisbane, Qld., Australia.
- University of Queensland. Combined Higher Degree Handbook. irreg.

**University of Queensland. Prentice Computer Center**
St. Lucia, Queensland 4067, Australia.
- University of Queensland. Computer Centre. Computer Centre Bulletin. m. ISSN 0041-9958

**University of Queensland Press**
Box 42, St. Lucia, Qld. 4067, Australia.
- Administrators' Bulletin. 8 per yr. (University of Queensland. Department of Education)
- Australian Journal of Politics and History. 3 per yr. ISSN 0004-9522
- Australian Literary Studies. s-a. ISSN 0004-9697 (University of Queensland. English Department)
- Australian Psychologist. 3 per yr. ISSN 0005-0067 (Australian Psychological Society) (Subscr. to: Australian Psychological Society, National Science Centre, 191 Royal Parade, Parkville Vic. 3052, Australia)
- Exceptional Child; the Australian journal on the education of backward children. 3 per yr. (Fred and Eleanor Schonell Educational Research Centre)
- University of Queensland. Computer Centre. Papers. irreg. ISSN 0079-886X
- University of Queensland. Department of Agriculture. Papers. irreg. ISSN 0079-8878
- University of Queensland. Department of Architecture. Papers. irreg. ISSN 0079-8886
- University of Queensland. Department of Botany. Papers. irreg., 1965, vol. 4, no. 16. ISSN 0079-8908
- University of Queensland. Department of Commerce. Papers. irreg., 1973, vol. 2, no. 4.
- University of Queensland. Department of Education. Administrators Bulletin. 8 per yr. ISSN 0048-6418
- University of Queensland. Department of Entomology. Papers. irreg. ISSN 0079-8916
- University of Queensland. Department of Geology. Papers. irreg., 1969, vol. 6. no. 9. ISSN 0079-8932
- University of Queensland. Department of Social Sciences. Papers. irreg., 1972, vol. 1, no. 3. ISSN 0079-8940
- University of Queensland. Department of Zoology. Papers. irreg., 1971, vol. 3, no. 8. ISSN 0079-8959
- University of Queensland. Departments of Government and History. Paper. irreg., 1971, vol. 1, no. 5. ISSN 0079-8924
- University of Queensland. Faculty of Arts. Papers. irreg. ISSN 0079-8975
- University of Queensland. Faculty of Education. Papers. irreg., 1972, vol. 2, no. 1. ISSN 0079-8983
- University of Queensland. Faculty of Law. Papers. irreg. ISSN 0079-8991
- University of Queensland. Faculty of Medicine. Papers. irreg. ISSN 0079-9009
- University of Queensland. Faculty of Veterinary Science. Papers. irreg. ISSN 0079-9017
- University of Queensland. Great Barrier Reef Committee: Heron Island Research Station. Papers. irreg., 1969, vol. 1, no. 4. ISSN 0073-1994
- University of Queensland Inaugural Lectures. irreg. ISSN 0079-9033
- University of Queensland Law Journal. a. ISSN 0083-4041
- World Review. 3 per yr. ISSN 0043-8960

**University of Queensland. Speleological Society**
c/o Student Union, University of Queensland, St. Lucia, Qld. 4067, Australia.
- Down Under. 5 per yr. ISSN 0046-0648

**University of Queensland Union**
Brisbane, Queensland, Australia.
- Gamut. w.

**University of Sydney**
Sydney, New South Wales, Australia 2006.
- Archaeology and Physical Anthropology in Oceania. 3 per yr. ISSN 0003-8121
- Oceania; devoted to the study of the native peoples of Australia, New Guinea and the Islands of the Pacific Ocean. q. ISSN 0029-8077

- University of Sydney. Gazette. s-a. ISSN 0042-0107

**University of Sydney. Archives**
Sydney, N.S.W. 2006, Australia.
- University of Sydney. Archives Record. 3 per yr. ISSN 0310-4729

**University of Sydney. Arts Association**
University of Sydney, Sydney, N.S.W., Australia.
- Arts. irreg. ISSN 0066-8095

**University of Sydney. Arts Society**
Box 54, The Union, Sydney, N.S.W. 2006, Australia.
- Germinal; journal of the social sciences. s-a. ISSN 0300-4139

**University of Sydney. Australian Society for Classical Studies**
Dept. of Greek, Sydney N.S.W. 2006, Australia.
- Antichthon; journal of the Australian Society for Classical Studies. a. ISSN 0066-4774

**University of Sydney. Basser Department of Computer Science**
Sydney 2006, N.S.W., Australia.
- University of Sydney. Basser Department of Computer Science. Technical Report. irreg. ISSN 0082-0547

**University of Sydney. Dental Alumni Society**
Sydney, N. S. W., Australia.
- Apollonia. irreg. ISSN 0066-5339

**University of Sydney. Dental Health Education and Research Foundation**
G.P.O. Box 3834, Sydney, NSW 2001, Australia.
- Dental Outlook. irreg. ISSN 0418-694X

**University of Sydney. Department of Adult Education**
Sydney, N.S.W. 2006, Australia.
- Current Affairs Bulletin. m. ISSN 0011-3182

**University of Sydney. Department of Agricultural Economics**
Sydney, N.S.W. 2006, Australia.
- University of Sydney. Department of Agricultural Economics. Agricultural Extension Bulletin. irreg. ISSN 0313-8704
- University of Sydney. Department of Agricultural Economics. Mimeographed Report. irreg., no. 6, 1977. ISSN 0082-0555
- University of Sydney. Department of Agricultural Economics. Research Bulletin. irreg. ISSN 0082-0563

**University of Sydney. Department of Architectural Science**
Sydney, N.S.W., Australia.
- University of Sydney. Department of Architectural Science. Reports. irreg. ISSN 0082-0571

**University of Sydney. Department of Government and Public Administration**
Sydney, New South Wales 2006, Australia.
- University of Sydney. Department of Government and Public Administration. Occasional Monograph. irreg.

**University of Sydney. Department of History**
Sydney, N.S.W. 2006, Australia.
- Edubba; studies ancient history. a. ISSN 0085-0187

**University of Sydney. Department of Indonesian & Malayan Studies**
Sydney, N.S.W. 2006, Australia.
- Review of Indonesian and Malayan Affairs; a bi-annual survey of political, economic, social and cultural aspects of Indonesia and Malaysia. s-a. ISSN 0034-6594

**University of Sydney. Department of Oriental Studies**
Sydney 2006, Australia.
- Oriental Society of Australia. Journal. a. ISSN 0030-5340

**University of Sydney. Department of Semitic Studies**
Sydney, N.S.W. 2006, Australia.
- Australian Journal of Biblical Archaeology. a. ISSN 0084-747X (Australian Society for Biblical Archaeology)

**University of Sydney. Economics Society**
Box 35, Wentworth Bldg., Sydney, N.S.W. 2006, Australia.
- University of Sydney Economics Society. Economic Review. 3 per yr. ISSN 0085-7025

**University of Sydney. Faculty of Law**
173 Phillip St., Sydney, 2000, Australia.
- Sydney Law Review. a. ISSN 0082-0512

**University of Sydney Geographical Society**
Sydney, N.S.W. 2006, Australia.
- Oondoona. irreg. ISSN 0085-4506

**University of Sydney. Institute of Criminology**
c/o Faculty of Law, 173-175 Phillip St., Sydney, N.S.W. 2000, Australia.
- University of Sydney. Institute of Criminology. Proceedings. irreg. ISSN 0085-7033

**University of Sydney. Law Graduates Association**
173-175 Phillip St., Sydney, N.S.W. 2000, Australia.
- Whiteacre. irreg. ISSN 0085-820X

**University of Sydney. Medical Society**
Blackburn Bldg., University of Sydney, Sydney, Australia.
- Innominate. 4 per yr. ISSN 0020-1618
- University of Sydney Medical Journal. a. ISSN 0085-7041

**University of Sydney. Students Representative Council**
Darlington, N.S.W. 2006, Australia.
- Honi Soit. w.

**University of Sydney Union**
Sydney, N.S.W. 2006, Australia.
- Union Recorder. w (Feb.-Nov.) ISSN 0041-7017

**University of Tasmania. Law Review**
Box 252 C, Hobart, Tas. 7001, Australia.
- University of Tasmania Law Review. a. ISSN 0082-2108

**University of Western Australia**
Nedlands, W. A. 6009, Australia.
- Australian Journal of Higher Education. (pub. by University of Western Australia Press)
- Essays in French Literature. a. ISSN 0071-139X
- Studies in Music. a. ISSN 0081-8267 (Dist. in U.S. by: Theodore Front Musical Literature; Alfred A. Kalmus Ltd., 131 N. Robertson Blvd., Beverly Hills, CA 90211; 2-3 Fareham St., London W.1., England)
- University of Western Australia. Library. Report on the Library. a. ISSN 0083-8713

**University of Western Australia. Centre for Asian Studies**
Nedlands, WA 6009, Australia.
- University of Western Australia. Centre for Asian Studies. Asia Bulletin. a.

**University of Western Australia. Centre for South & Southeast Asian Studies**
Nedlands, W.A. 6009, Australia.
- South Asia; Journal of South Asian Studies. a. ISSN 0085-6401 (South Asia Studies Association) (Co-sponsor: University of Heidelberg, South Asia Institute)

**University of Western Australia. Department of Agricultural Economics**
Nedlands, W.A., Australia.
- Farm Policy. q. ISSN 0014-8075

**University of Western Australia. Department of Anthropology**
Nedlands, W.A. 6009, Australia.
- Anthropological Forum; an international journal of social and cultural anthropology and comparative sociology. a. ISSN 0066-4677

**University of Western Australia. Department of Education**
Nedlands, W.A. 6009, Australia.
- Education Research and Perspectives. s-a.

**University of Western Australia. Department of English**
Nedlands, W. A. 6009, Australia.
- Westerly. q. ISSN 0043-342X (Co-Sponsor: Australia Council)

**University of Western Australia. Department of Music**
Nedlands, W. A. 6009, Australia.
- University of Western Australia. Department of Music. Music Monograph. irreg.

**University of Western Australia. Faculty of Economics and Commerce**
Nedlands W.A., Australia.
- Economic Activity. q. ISSN 0012-9925

**University of Western Australia. Faculty of Law**
Nedlands (Perth), Western Australia.
- University of Western Australia Law Review. s-a. ISSN 0042-0328

**University of Western Australia. Philosophy Department**
Nedlands, W.A. 6009, Australia.
- University of Western Australia. Philosophy Society. Journal. a. ISSN 0085-817X

**University of Western Australia Press**
Nedlands, W.A. 6009, Australia
(Dist. in U.S. by: International Scholarly Book Services, Box 555, Forest Grove, OR 97116)
- Australian Journal of Higher Education. a. (University of Western Australia)
- Edward Shann Memorial Lecture in Economics. a. ISSN 0070-945X (Edward Shann Memorial Fund)
- Lectures in Biblical Studies. a. ISSN 0075-8493
- Octagon Lectures. a. ISSN 0078-3269
- University of Western Australia. Institute of Agriculture. Research Report: Agricultural Economics. irreg., 1968, no. 7. ISSN 0083-8705

**Ure Smith Pty. Ltd.**
176 South Creek Rd., Dee Why West, N.S.W. 2099, Australia.
- Art and Australia. q. ISSN 0004-301X

**V. I. E. W. Clubs of Australia**
Smith Family, 137-153 Crown St., Sydney, N.S.W. 2000, Australia.
- View World. q.

**Vance Media Pty. Ltd.**
P.O. Box 213, Oakleigh, Vic. 3166, Australia.
- Furnishing Cyclopaedia. a. ISSN 0310-2815

**Vegetarian Society, South Australia**
45 Fourth Ave., Klemzig, S.A. 5087, Australia.
- Australian Vegetarian. bi-m.

**Victoria. Department of Agriculture**
P.O. Box 4041, Melbourne, Victoria 3001, Australia.
- Journal of Agriculture. m. ISSN 0021-860X
- Mallee Horticulture Digest. 3 per yr. ISSN 0047-5637
- Vegetable Growers Digest. 3 per yr. ISSN 0085-7718
- Victoria, Australia. Department of Agriculture. Agricultural Economics Branch. Contract Rates. biennial. ISSN 0083-5935
- Victoria, Australia. Department of Agriculture. Agricultural Economics Branch. Farm Credit (Sources and Terms) irreg. ISSN 0083-5943
- Victoria, Australia. Department of Agriculture. Dairyfarming Digest. 4 per yr. ISSN 0049-6103
- Victoria, Australia. Department of Agriculture. Pig Industry Branch. Pig Farm Management Study. a. ISSN 0083-5951
- Victoria, Australia. Department of Agriculture. Poultry Branch. Poultry Farm Management Study. a. ISSN 0083-596X
- Victoria, Australia. Department of Agriculture. Technical Bulletin. irreg. ISSN 0085-770X
- Victorian Horticulture Digest. 3 per yr. ISSN 0049-6146

**Victoria. Department of Agriculture. Agricultural Research Unit**
Box 174, Ferntree Gully, Vic. 3156, Australia.
- Beekeepers' Bulletin. q.

**Victoria. Department of Agriculture. Information Officer**
Treasury Gardens, Melbourne, Victoria 3002, Australia.
- Rutherglen, Australia. Research Station. Digest of Recent Research. a. ISSN 0080-5009

**Victoria. Department of Education**
Treasury Place, Melbourne, Vic. 3002, Australia
- Polycom: a Bulletin for Teachers of Non-English-Speaking Migrant Children. irreg. ISSN 0311-1962 (Subscriptions to: Child Migrant Education, Education Department of Victoria, 234 Queensberry St., Carlton, Vic. 3153)
- Victoria, Australia. Education Department. School Library Bulletin. irreg.

**Victoria. Department of Education. Curriculum & Research Branch**
234 Queensberry St., Carlton, Vic. 3053, Australia.
- Victoria, Australia. Education Department. Curriculum and Research Branch. Research Reports. irreg. ISSN 0085-7726

**Victoria. Department of Education. Publications Branch**
234 Queensberry St., Carlton, Victoria 3053, Australia.
- Educational Magazine; a magazine of educational articles, Australian and overseas, for teachers. m. ISSN 0013-1792
- Pursuit. bi-m.
- Victoria. Department of Education. News Exchange. s-m. ISSN 0310-8198
- Victoria, Australia. Education Department. Curriculum and Research Bulletin. q. ISSN 0011-4030

**Victoria. Department of Youth, Sport and Recreation**
- Victoria, Australia. Department of Youth, Sport and Recreation. Report. (pub. by Commonwealth Government Printing Office)

**Victoria. Forests Commission**
Treasury Place, Melbourne, Vic. 3002, Australia.
- Victoria. Forests Commission. Research Activity. a.
- Victoria, Australia. Forests Commission. Bulletin. irreg. ISSN 0085-7742
- Victoria, Australia. Forests Commission. Forestry Technical Papers. s-a. ISSN 0083-5978

**Victoria. Government Printer**
P.O. Box 203, North Melbourne, Vic. 3051, Australia.
- Education Gazette and Teachers' Aid. fortn. ISSN 0013-1342
- Victoria, Australia. Environment Protection Authority. Annual Report. a.
- Victoria, Australia. National Parks Service. Report. a.
- Victoria Government Gazette. w. ISSN 0042-5095

**Victoria. Ministry for Conservation. Fisheries and Wildlife Division**
Box 41, East Melbourne, Vic. 3002, Australia.
- Fisheries and Wildlife Paper. Victoria. irreg. ISSN 0071-5522
- Fisheries Circular, Victoria. irreg., 1969, no. 19. ISSN 0071-5530
- Fisheries Contribution, Victoria. irreg., no. 30, 1973. ISSN 0071-5549
- Wildlife Circular, Victoria. irreg., 1969, no. 31. ISSN 0084-0149
- Wildlife Contribution, Victoria. irreg.

**Victoria. Ministry of Fuel and Power**
Victoria, Australia.
- Victoria, Australia. Ministry of Fuel and Power. the Petroleum and Gas Industries in Victoria; Statistical Review. irreg.

**Victoria. Ministry of Tourism**
G.P.O. Box 1328L, Melbourne, Vic. 3001, Australia.
- Travel News from Victoria, Australia. m. ISSN 0310-7108

**Victoria. Premier's Department**
1 Treasury Place, Melbourne, Vic. 3000, Australia.
- Victoria. Directory of Government Departments and Authorities. a. ISSN 0310-8546

**Victoria. State Electricity Commission. Herman Central Scientific Laboratory**
Howard St., Richmond, Victoria 3121, Australia.
- Victoria, Australia. State Electricity Commission. Science Report. irreg.

**Victoria. State Rivers & Water Supply Commission**
590 Orrong Rd., Armadale, Vic. 3143, Australia.
- Water Talk. q. ISSN 0049-7010

**Victoria Institute of Colleges**
582 St. Kilda Rd., Melbourne, Vic. 3004, Australia.
- Victoria Institute of Colleges. Newsletter. irreg.

**Victoria Police Force**
Police HQ, Melbourne, Australia.
- Police Life. m. ISSN 0032-2598

**Victoria Promotion Committe**
55 Exhibition Street, Melbourne, Vic. 3000, Australia.
- News from Victoria, Australia. irreg. ISSN 0305-0424

**Victoria Promotion Committee, Melbourne**
- Australia Newsletter. (pub. by Sydney Morrell & Co. Inc. US)

**Victoria State Film Centre**
1 McArthur St., East Melbourne, Vic. 3002, Australia.
- Victoria. State Film Centre. New Films. irreg.

**Victoria Town and Country Planning Board**
235 Queen St., Melbourne, Vic. 3000, Australia.
- Albury/Wodonga. irreg. ISSN 0310-7299

**Victorian Advisory Committee on the Teaching of Social Sciences in Secondary Schools**
534-8 Swanston St., Carlton, Vic. 3053, Australia.
- Study of Society. 3 per yr.

**Victorian Apiarist's Association**
Box 313, Wangaratta, Vic. 3677, Australia.
- Australian Bee Journal. m. ISSN 0045-0294

**Victorian Association for the Teaching of English**
c/o H. Haughton, 185 Lygon St., Carlton, Vic. 3053, Australia.
- Idiom. 7 per yr. ISSN 0046-8568

**Victorian Association of Social Studies Teachers**
59 Stanley St., West Melbourne, Vic. 3003, Australia.
- Ethos. 4 per yr.

**Victorian Autombile Chamber of Commerce**
464 St. Kilda Rd., Melbourne 3004, Austrailia.
- V A C C Journal. m. ISSN 0004-8712

**Victorian Bands League**
c/o G. H. Gearside, Lithgow, N.S.W. 2790, Australia.
- Australasian Bandsman. m. ISSN 0084-6953 (Co-sponsor: Queensland Band Associations)

**Victorian Ceramic Group**
Box 4096, Spencer St., Melbourne, Vic. 3001, Australia.
- Victorian Ceramic Group. Newsletter. m.

**Victorian Chamber of Manufacturers**
Industry House, 370 St. Kilda Rd., Melbourne, Vic. 3004, Australia.
- V. C. M. File. irreg. ISSN 0311-127X

**Victorian Country Press Association**
33 Rathdowne St., Carlton, Vic. 3053, Australia.
- Country Press of Victoria. irreg. ISSN 0084-9391

**Victorian Dairyfarmer Company Pty Ltd.**
576 St. Kilda Rd., Melbourne 3004, Australia.
- Victorian Dairy Farmer. m. (Victorian Dairyfarmers' Association)

**Victorian Dairyfarmers' Association**
- Victorian Dairy Farmer. (pub. by Victorian Dairyfarmer Company Pty Ltd.)

**Victorian Farmers Newspapers Pty Ltd.**
Farrer House, 24-28 Collins St., Melbourne, Victoria, Australia.
- Victorian Farmer. m. ISSN 0042-515X (Victorian Farmers Union)

**Victorian Farmers Union**
- Victorian Farmer. (pub. by Victorian Farmers Newspapers Pty Ltd.)

**Victorian Flute Guild**
9 Hinkler Rd., Glen Waverly, Vic. 3150, Australia.
- Flautist. irreg. ISSN 0311-0559

**Victorian Football League**
VFL House, 82 Jolimont St., Jolimont 3002, Victoria, Australia.
- Football Record. w (30 per yr. Apr.-Sept.) ISSN 0015-6795

**Victorian Historical Association**
85 Howard St., North Melbourne, Vic. 3051, Australia.
- Agora. 5 per yr. ISSN 0044-6726
- Journal of Australian Studies. s-a.
- Journal of History for Senior Students. q.

**Victorian Institute of Educational Research**
c/o Max W. Boyce, Ed., Toorak State College, Box 224, Malvern, Vic. 3144, Australia.
- V. I. E. R. Bulletin. 2 per yr. ISSN 0049-6154

**Victorian Jazz Club**
P. O. Box 2421v, Melbourne, Vic. 3001, Australia.
- Jazzline. q.

**Victorian Labor College**
Box 39, Trades Hall, Carlton South, Vic. 3053, Australia.
- Labor College Review. q.

**Victorian Ladies' Bowling Association**
109 Commercial Rd., South Yarra 3141, Australia.
- Bowls-News and Views. 9 per yr.

**Victorian Music Teachers Association**
3A Ashley St., Box Hill North, Victoria 3129, Australia.
- Music and the Teacher. q. ISSN 0047-8431

**Victorian Potato Growers Association**
- Potato Grower News. (pub. by Creswick Advertiser Pty. Ltd.)

**Victorian Railways Board**
67 Spencer St., Melbourne, Vic. 3000, Australia.
- Victorian Rail Ways. m.

**Victorian Road Transport Association**
17 Raglan St., South Melbourne, Victoria, 3205, Australia.
- Road Transporter of Australia. m.

**Victorian Secondary Teachers Association**
58-60 Jolimont St., Jolimont, Vic. 3002, Australia.
- V. S. T. A. Guide to Victorian State Secondary Schools. irreg.

**Victorian Showmen's Guild**
Box 59, North Melbourne, Vic. 3051, Australia.
- Outdoor Showman. m.

**Victorian Speleological Association**
G.P.O. Box 5425cc, Melbourne, Vic.3001, Australia.
- Nargun. irreg.

**Victorian Teachers' Union**
335 Camberwell Rd., Camberwell, Victoria 3124, Australia.
- Teachers' Journal. fortn. ISSN 0040-0483

**Victorian Tobacco Growers' Association**
Box 255, Myrtleford, Vic. 3737, Australia.
- Victorian Tobacco Grower. bi-m. ISSN 0049-6200

**Victorian U.F.O. Research Society**
P.O. Box 43, Moorabbin 3189, Victoria, Australia.
- Australian U.F.O. Bulletin. q.

**Video Publishing Co.**
88 Chalmers St., Lakemba, N.S.W. 2195, Australia.
- Video-Tronics. bi-m. ISSN 0310-6411 (Television and Electronic Services Associations of Australasia) (Co-sponsor: Television and Electronic Technicians Institute of Australia)

**Voice of Malta**
c/o J. J. Briffa, Ed., 369 Clayton Rd., Clayton, Vic. 3168, Australia.
- Voice of Malta. m. ISSN 0300-3205

**Void**
Box 66, St. Kilda, Vic. 3182, Australia.
- Void. q.

**W.A. Sporting Car Club**
- Visor. (pub. by Russell Fenton Co.)

**Wagga Wagga & District Historical Society**
Box 90, Wagga Wagga, N.S.W. 2650, Australia.
- Wagga Wagga and District Historical Society. Journal. a. ISSN 0085-7858

**Walkers Publicity**
Box 121, Nambour, Queensland 4560, Australia.
- Tourist Time. m. ISSN 0040-9804

**Wallacia (Sales) Pty.**
530 Cantenbury Rd., Campsie, N. S. W. 2194,
Australia.
- Caspa. bi-m. ISSN 0311-0001

**War Resisters International Society**
Melbourne University, Parkville, Victoria, Australia.
- Aquarius. q.

**Warwick Boyce Publishing Pty. Ltd.**
Suite 402, 620 Harris St., Ultimo, N.S.W. 2007,
Australia.
- Australian Careers Guide; for school leavers,
parents and careers advisers. a.
- Australian Hotel, Motel, Club Catering Restaurant
Handbook and Buyers Guide. a.

**Water Research Foundation of Australia Ltd.**
Box 47, Kingsford. N.S.W. 2032, Australia.
- Water Research Foundation of Australia. Bulletin.
irreg. ISSN 0085-8013
- Water Research Foundation of Australia.
Newsletter. m.
- Water Research Foundation of Australia. Reports.
irreg. ISSN 0085-8021

**Waterside Workers' Federation of Australia**
Labor Council Bldg, 377-383 Sussex St, Sydney
N.S.W. 2000, Australia.
- Maritime Worker. 16 per yr. ISSN 0025-3464

**Watervale Press Pty. Ltd.**
P.O. Box 109, North Sydney, N.S.W. 2060,
Australia.
- Materials Handling and Storage. bi-m. ISSN 0047-
6234

**Waugh & Josephson Pty. Ltd.**
Box 83, Alexandria, N. S. W. 2015, Australia.
- Track. bi-m.

**A. Webb & Sons Pty. Ltd.**
60 Baxter St., Fortitude Valley 4006, Australia.
- Taxi News. m. (Taxi Council of Queensland)

**Wedgwood Society of Australia**
26 Blake St., Caulfield, Vic. 3162, Australia.
- Wedgwood News. q. ISSN 0310-7213

**Weed Society of N.S.W.**
P.O. Box K 287, Haymarket, Sydney, N.S.W. 2000,
Australia.
- Weed Society of New South Wales. Proceedings.
a. ISSN 0085-803X

**Wentworth Press**
48 Cooper St., Surry Hills, N.S.W. 2010, Australia.
- Southerly; a review of Australian literature. q.
ISSN 0038-3732 (English Association. Sydney
Branch)

**Wesfarmers**
90 King St., Perth 6000, W.A., Australia.
- Western Farmer and Grazier. w.

**West Australian Chamber of Manufactures**
G.P.O. Box H515, Perth, W.A. 6001, Australia.
- Your Chamber Reporting. irreg. ISSN 0311-1172

**West Australian Newspapers Ltd.**
125 St. George's Terrace, Perth, W.A. 6001,
Australia.
- Countryman. w. ISSN 0011-0264
- Weekend. w. ISSN 0043-180X

**West Australian Petroleum Pty. Ltd.**
Wapet House, 12 St. George's Terrace, Perth, W.A.
6000, Australia.
- W A P E T Journal. a. ISSN 0310-7787

**West Publishing Corp. Pty. Ltd.**
1 Barrack St., Sydney, N.S.W. 2000, Australia.
- Australian Journal of Marketing Research. q.
ISSN 0004-9476
- Building Economist. q. ISSN 0007-3431
- Building Forum. s-a. ISSN 0007-3466 (Building
Science Forum of Australia) (Co-sponsor:
Australian Modular Society)
- Developer. q. ISSN 0012-1525 (Institute of Real
Estate Development)
- Personnel Management. q. ISSN 0048-346X
(Institute of Personnel Management (Australia))
- Royal Australian Planning Institute Journal. q.
ISSN 0004-9999

**Western Australia. Coastal Shipping Commission**
P.O. Box 394, Fremantle, Australia.
- Western Australian Coastal Shipping Commission.
Annual Report. a.

**Western Australia. Committee for the Understanding
of the Environment**
c/o Department of Environmental Protection, Bp
House, Mount St., Perth, WA 6000, Australia.
- Western Australia. Committee for the
Understanding of the Environment. Books and
Films on the Environment. irreg.

**Western Australia. Crown Law Department**
109 William St., Perth, W.A. 6000, Australia.
- Western Australia Law Almanac. a. ISSN 0085-
8161

**Western Australia. Department for Community
Welfare**
Perth, W.A., Australia.
- Western Australia. Department for Community
Welfare. Annual Report. a.

**Western Australia. Department of Agriculture**
Jarrah Rd., South Perth 6151, Australia.
- Journal of Agriculture of Western Australia. q.
ISSN 0021-8618
- Western Australia. Department of Agriculture.
Bulletin. irreg.
- Western Australia. Department of Agriculture.
Technical Bulletin. irreg. ISSN 0083-8675

**Western Australia. Department of Agriculture. Animal
Division**
Perth, W.A., Australia.
- Western Australia. Department of Agriculture.
Animal Division. Annual Report. a.

**Western Australia. Department of Agriculture.
Rangeland Management Section**
Jarrah Rd., South Perth, WA 6151, Australia.
- Western Australia. Department of Agriculture.
Rangeland Management Section. Rangeland
Bulletin. irreg. ISSN 0310-897X

**Western Australia. Department of Agriculture. Rural
Economics and Marketing Section**
Perth, W.A., Australia.
- Western Australia. Department of Agriculture.
Rural Economics and Marketing Section. Report
on the Market Milk Industry in Western
Australia. irreg.

**Western Australia. Department of Agriculture.
Western Australian Herbarium**
Jarrah Rd., South Perth, W.A. 6151, Australia.
- Nuytsia. irreg. ISSN 0085-4417

**Western Australia. Department of Agriculture. Wheat
and Sheep Division**
Perth, W.A., Australia.
- Western Australia. Department of Agriculture.
Wheat and Sheep Division. Annual Report. a.

**Western Australia. Department of Conservation and
Environment**
1 Mount St., Perth, W.A. 6000, Australia.
- Western Australia. Conservation and Environment
Council. Annual Report. a.

**Western Australia. Department of Fisheries and
Wildlife**
108 Adelaide Tce., Perth, W. A. 6000, Australia.
- F. I. N. S. (Fishing Industry News Service) q.
ISSN 0046-2993
- S. W. A. N. S. (State Wildlife Advisory News
Service) q. ISSN 0014-889X
- Western Australia. Department of Fisheries and
Wildlife. Fisheries Research Bulletin. irreg.

**Western Australia. Department of Industrial
Development and Decentralisation**
32 St. George's Terrace, Perth, W.A. 6000,
Australia.
- Enterprise, Western Australia. q.
- Western Australia. Major Investment Projects,
Public and Private, Current and Proposed. a.
ISSN 0511-6910
- Western Australian Manufacturers Directory. a.

**Western Australia. Department of Tourism**
P.O. Box X2261, Perth, W.A. 6000, Australia.
- Travel News from Western Australia. bi-m.

**Western Australia. Director General of Transport**
68 St. George's Terrace, Perth, Australia.
- Western Australia. Office of Director General of
Transport. Annual Report. a. ISSN 0083-8691

**Western Australia. Education Department**
Parliament Place, West Perth, WA 6005, Australia.
- Consequences. irreg. ISSN 0310-8228
- Education. q. ISSN 0046-1369
- Western Australia. Education Department.
Education Circular. m.(exec. Jan.) ISSN 0049-
7312
- Western Australia. Education Department.
Schools & Staffing. a.
- Western Australia. Technical Education Division.
Handbook. a.

**Western Australia. Education Department. Curriculum
Branch**
8 Parliament Place, West Perth, WA 6005,
Australia.
- Filter: a Paper for Science Teachers. irreg. ISSN
0310-6020

**Western Australia. Forests Department**
Conservator of Forests, 4Th Floor, R. & I. Bank
Bldg., Barrack St., Perth, W.A. 6000, Australia.
- Western Australia. Forests Department. Bulletin.
irreg. ISSN 0085-8129
- Western Australia. Forests Department. Forest
Focus. 3 per yr. ISSN 0049-7320
- Western Australia. Forests Department Research
Paper. irreg.

**Western Australia. Geological Survey**
Rm. 501, 66 Adelaide Tce., East Perth, W.A. 6000,
Australia.
- Western Australia. Geological Survey. Bulletin.
irreg. ISSN 0085-8137
- Western Australia. Geological Survey. Report.
irreg. ISSN 0085-8145

**Western Australia. Government Chemical
Laboratories**
30 Plain Street, Perth, W.A. 6000, Australia.
- Western Australia. Government Chemical
Laboratories. Report of Investigations. irreg. ISSN
0085-8153

**Western Australia. Law Reform Commission**
R&I Bank Bldg., 593 Hay St., Perth, W.A.,
Australia.
- Western Australia. Law Reform Commission.
Annual Report. a.

**Western Australia. Main Roads Department**
Waterloo Crescent, East Perth, W.A. 6000,
Australia.
- Western Australia. Main Roads Department.
Technical Report. irreg. ISSN 0310-6330

**Western Australia. Parliamentary Library of Western
Australia**
Parliament House, Perth, W.A. 6000, Australia.
- Official Publications of Western Australia. q. ISSN
0310-7345

**Western Australia. Public Library, Museum and Art
Gallery**
Perth, W. A., Australia.
- Western Australia. Public Library, Museum and
Art Gallery. Record. irreg.

**Western Australia. Road Traffic Safety Authority**
Perth, W.A., Australia.
- Western Australia. Road Traffic Safety Authority.
Report of Activities. irreg.

**Western Australia. State Health Laboratory Services**
Perth, Australia.
- Western Australia. State Health Laboratory
Services. Annual Report. a.

**Western Australia. Transport Commission**
136-138 Stirling Highway, Nedlands, W.A. 6009,
Australia.
- Western Australia. Transport Commission. Annual
Report of the Commissioner of Transport. a.

**Western Australia. Western Australia Government
Printing Office**
Station St., Wembley, W.A. 6014, Australia.
- Western Australia. Department of Corrections.
Annual Report. a.
- Western Australia. Government Gazette. w. ISSN
0043-3489

**Western Australia Horticultural Council**
c/o Secretary of the Council, Rothmans Building,
R.A.S. Showground, Claremont 6010, Australia.
- West Australian Gardener. q. ISSN 0049-7185

**Western Australia Seed Board**
Perth, Australia.
- Western Australia. Seed Board. Chairman's
Report. irreg.

**Western Australia Vegetable Growers' Association, Inc.**
110 Havelock St., West Perth, W. A. 6005,
Australia.
- W. A. Grower. q. ISSN 0042-9465

**Western Australian Automobile Chamber of Commerce**
W.A.A.C.C.S. House, 20 Nicholson Rd., Subiaco,
6008, Australia.
- W. A. A. C. C. S. Motor Industry. m. ISSN 0042-9430

**Western Australian Egg Marketing Board**
P.O. Box 46, Melville, W.A. 6156, Australia.
- Western Australian Egg Marketing Board.
Newsletter. irreg.

**Western Australian Employers' Federation**
188 Adelaide Terrace, Perth, W. A. 6000, Australia.
- Industrial News. m.

**Western Australian Institute of Technology**
Hayman Rd., So. Bentley, W.A. 6102, Australia.
- Western Australian Institute of Technology
Gazette. q. ISSN 0049-7347

**Western Australian Museum**
Perth, W.A., Australia.
- Western Australian Museum, Perth. Information
Series. irreg.
- Western Australian Museum, Perth. Report of the
Museum Board. a. ISSN 0083-8721
- Western Australian Museum, Perth. Special
Publication. irreg. ISSN 0083-873X

**Western Australian Music Teachers Association**
c/o Marjorie C. Wyndham, 1 Colin St., West Perth,
W.A. 6005, Australia.
- Music Teachers Bulletin. 10 per yr.

**Western Australian Naturalists' Club**
Naturalists' Hall, 63-65 Merriwa St., Nedlands, W.
Australia 6009, Australia.
- Western Australian Naturalists' Club, Perth.
Handbook. irreg., 1966, no. 9. ISSN 0083-8748

**Western Australian Potato Marketing Board**
Perth, W.A., Australia.
- Western Australian Potato Marketing Board.
Annual Report. a.

**Western Australian Secondary Teachers' College**
Nedlands, W.A. 6009, Australia.
- Swan. a.

**Western Australian Speleological Group**
Box 67, Nedlands, W.A. 6009, Australia.
- Western Caver. q.

**Western Sun**
1St Floor, Panos House, 249 Adelaide Terrace,
Perth 6000, W.A., Australia.
- W. A. Meat Worker. s-a. (Australasian Meat
Industry Employees' Union. W. A. Branch)

**Weston Studstock Advertising**
11 Bank Place, Melbourne, Vic. 3000, Australia.
- Australian Poll Dorset Journal. bi-m.

**White Mercantile Agency**
240 Queen St., Brisbane, Qld. 4000, Australia.
- White Mercantile Gazette. w.

**Wildlife Preservation Society of Australia**
G.P.O. Box 3428, Sydney, N.S.W. 2001, Australia.
- Australian Wildlife Newsletter. q.

**Wildlife Preservation Society of Queensland**
Box 2030, Brisbane, Queensland 4001, Australia.
- Wildlife in Australia. q. ISSN 0043-5481
- Wildlife Preservation Society of Queensland.
Newsletter. irreg.

**Thomas W. Williams & Associates Pty. Ltd.**
Box 101A, Melbourne, Vic. 3001, Australia.
- Extra Cover. a. (Australian Cricket Society)

- Weights and Measures Review. bi-m. ISSN 0049-7096 (Australian Institute of Weights and Measures)

**Winton Tourist Promotion Association**
P.O. Box 44, Winton, Qld. 4735, Australia.
- Bronze Swagman Book of Bush Verse. a. ISSN
0310-2467

**Wireless Institute of Australia**
Box 150, Toorak Victoria 3142, Australia.
- Amateur Radio. m. ISSN 0002-6859

**Wollongong Teachers College**
Literary Club, Wollongong, N.S.W. 2500, Australia.
- Expression. a. ISSN 0085-039X

**Wollongong University College**
Registrar, Wollongong, N.S.W. 2500, Australia.
- Wollongong University College. Bulletin. irreg.

**Woman's Christian Temperance Union of Australia**
c/o Heather Main, Editor, 16 Karen Ave., Picnic
Point, N.S.W. 2213, Australia.
- White Ribbon Signal. bi-m.

**Womanspeak Collective**
Box 103, Spit Junction, Sydney 2000, Australia.
- Womanspeak. 5 per yr.

**Women's Electoral Lobby**
Secretary, P.O. Box 442, Camberwell, Vic. 3124,
Australia.
- W. E. L. Papers. irreg. ISSN 0310-9496
- Women's Electoral Lobby. Newsletter. m. ISSN
0310-7809

**Women's Studies Group**
25 Alberta St., Sydney, N.S.W. 2000, Australia.
- Refractory Girl. q. ISSN 0310-4168

**Working Kelpie Council**
P.O. Box e31, St. James, Sydney, NSW 2000,
Australia.
- Working Kelpie Council. National Stud Book.
irreg.

**Working Papers in Sex, Science and Culture**
Box 83, Wentworth Bldg., 174 City Rd., Darlington,
2008, Australia.
- Working Papers in Sex, Science and Culture. q.

**World Council of Young Men's Service Clubs**
39 Milford Rd., Miranda N.S.W. 2228, Australia.
- International Forum. m. ISSN 0020-6784

**World Education Fellowship in Australia, Inc.**
265 Castlereagh St., Sydney, N. S. W. 2000,
Australia.
- New Horizons in Education. s-a. ISSN 0028-5382

**World Ship Society. Queensland Branch**
23 Mayled St., Chermside West, Qld. 4032,
Australia.
- Queensland Maritime Bulletin. q.

**Wormald International Ltd**
Alexander and Ernest Streets, Crows Nest, N. S. W.
2065, Australia.
- Alert (Crows Nest N. S. W.) q. ISSN 0044-7242

**Y. W. Heron Sailing Association of Australia**
1 Ethel St., Balgowlah, N. S. W. 2093, Australia.
- Heron Newsletter. q.

**Yaffa Publishing Group**
G.P.O. Box 606, Sydney, N.S.W. 2001, Australia.
- Advertising News. fortn.
- Cycle Australia. 4 per yr.
- Educational Books and Equipment. m. ISSN
0013-1652
- Food Manufacturing News. bi-m.
- Furniture and Furnishings. m.
- Packaging News. m. ISSN 0048-2676
- Popular Mechanics. m. ISSN 0032-454X

**York Press Ltd.**
1-19 Hoddle St., Abbotsford, Vic. 3067, Australia.
- Australian Jewish News. w. ISSN 0004-9379

**Young Labor Association of South Australia**
Trades Hall, 11-16 South Terrace, Adelaide, S.A.
5000, Australia.
- Insight. irreg.

**Youth Hostels Association of N.S.W.**
355 Kent, 1St Floor, Sydney NSW 2000, Australia.
- Hostel Yarn. bi-m.

**Youth Hostels Association of South Australia**
72 South Terrace, Adelaide, S.A. 5000, Australia.
- Hostelling. q.

**Youth Hostels Association of Victoria**
Box 411, Richmond, Vic. 3121, Australia.
- Hosteller. q.

# AUSTRIA

**A B Z Druck und Verlagsanstalt Hamann und Sinek**
Richtergasse 4, A-1071 Vienna, Austria.
- Oesterreichische Buergermeister Zeitung. m. ISSN
0048-1424
- Oesterreichische Foto-Zeitung; fachblatt fuer
Lichtbildner. m. ISSN 0048-1459

**A D E G-Oesterreich Handelsaktiengesellschaft**
Postfach 361, Gaudenzdorfer Guertel 41-45, 1120
Vienna, Austria.
- A D E G - Kaufmann. m. ISSN 0001-8112

**A F - Architekturforum**
Strauebengr. 13, A-1050 Vienna, Austria.
- A F - Architekturforum; Zeitschrift fuer
Architektur, Design und Wohnkultur. bi-m. ISSN
0044-5657

**A M K-Verlag**
Imbergstr. 1, Postfach 12, A-5024 Salzburg, Austria.
- Alte und Moderne Kunst. bi-m. ISSN 0002-6565

**A O E**
Maria Theresien Str. 4, A-6020 Innsbruck, Austria.
- A O E. (Aktion Osterreich Europa
Mitteilungsblatt) q.

**Adalbert Stifter-Institut des Landes Oberoesterreich**
Untere Donaulaende 6, A-4020 Linz, Austria.
- Adalbert Stifter-Institut des Landes
Oberoesterreich. Vierteljahresschrift. s-a. ISSN
0001-799X

**Adyar-Verlagsvereinigung**
Postfach 655, A-8011 Graz, Austria.
- Adyar; Theosophische zeitschrift. q. ISSN 0001-9011 (Theosophische Gesellschaft in Europa)

**Akademie der Wissenschaften. Vienna**
- Akademie der Wissenschaften, Vienna.
Mathematisch-Naturwissenschaftliche Klasse.
Anzeiger. (pub. by Springer-Verlag US)

**Akademische Druck- und Verlagsanstalt**
Auersperggasse 12, A-8010 Graz, Austria.
- Afghanistan Journal. q.
- Anzeiger fuer Slavische Philologie. irreg., 1972
vol. 6. ISSN 0066-5282
- Studien zur Bibliotheksgeschichte. irreg.

**Akademisches Gymnasium. Elternvereinigung**
Buergergasse 15, Graz A-8010, Austria.
- Tummelplatz. 3 per yr. ISSN 0041-4085

**Allgemeine Sparkasse in Linz**
Promenade 11-13, A-4010 Linz, Austria.
- Allgemeine Sparkasse in Linz. Kurz Notiert. m.
ISSN 0002-5933

**Allgemeine Unfallversicherungsanstalt. Unfallverhuetungsdienst**
Adalbert-Stifter-Str. 65, A-1200 Vienna, Austria.
- Betriebssicherheit - B S; Zeitschrift fuer
Unfallverhuetung und Erste Hilfe. bi-m. ISSN
0005-3287
- Sichere Arbeit; Fachzeitschrift fuer
Sicherheitstechnik und Arbeitsmedizin. q. ISSN
0037-4512
- Sicherheitstechniker-Korrespondenz. 6 per
yr.(approx.) ISSN 0037-4547

**Alt-Katholische Kirche Oesterreichs**
Schottenring 17, A-1010 Vienna, Austria.
- Alt-Katholische Kirchenzeitung. m. ISSN 0002-6514

**Pressverband Anstoss und Argumente**
Postfach 296, A-1015 Vienna, Austria.
- Anstoss; Evangelisches Forum der jungen
Generation. m. ISSN 0003-5289

**Anthropologische Gesellschaft in Wien**
Burgring 7, A-1014 Vienna, Austria.
- Anthropologische Gesellschaft, Vienna.
Mitteilungen. (pub. by Verlag Ferdinand Berger
und Soehne OHG)

- Praehistorische Forschungen. irreg. ISSN 0032-6534

**Arbeitsgemeinschaft der Dioezesansekretariate der Cursillo-Bewegung**
Bennogasse 21, A-1080 Vienna, Austria.
- Cursillo; fuer eine Kirche in Bewegung. m. ISSN 0011-4057

**Arbeitsgemeinschaft der Oesterreichischen Gemeinwirtschaft**
- Gemeinwirtschaft. (pub. by Verlag fuer Jugend und Volk)

**Arbeitsgemeinschaft fuer Buch- und Schrifttum der Katholischen Aktion Oesterreichs**
Stephans Platz 6/V, A-1010 Vienna, Austria.
- Die Zeit im Buch. q. ISSN 0044-2089

**Arbeitsgemeinschaft fuer Datenverarbeitung**
Billrothstr. 14, A-1190 Vienna, Austria.
- Data Press; oesterreichische Zeitschrift fuer Datenverarbeitung. q.

**Arbeitsgemeinschaft fuer Finanzwissenschaftliche Forschung und Information**
Maygasse 40, A-1130 Vienna, Austria.
- Der Oeffentliche Sektor; Forschungsmemoranden. q.

**Arbeitsgemeinschaft fuer Historische Sozialkunde**
- Beitraege zur Historischen Sozialkunde. (pub. by Wolfgang Neugebauer)

**Arbeitsgemeinschaft fuer Lebensniveauvergleiche**
Postfach 149, A-1131 Vienna, Austria.
- Arbeitsgemeinschaft fuer Lebensniveauvergleiche. Schriftenreihe. irreg.

**Arbeitsgemeinschaft fuer Psychotechnik in Oesterreich**
- Mensch und Arbeit. (pub. by Psychotechnisches Institut)

**Arbeitsgemeinschaft Landwirtschaftlicher Gefluegelzuechter Oesterreichs**
Kohlgasse 16, A-1050 Vienna, Austria.
- Oesterreichische Gefluegelwirtschaft. m. ISSN 0029-9111

**Arbeitsgemeinschaft Oesterreichischer Entomologen**
Ludo-Hartmann-Platz 7, A-1160 Vienna, Austria.
- Arbeitsgemeinschaft Oesterreichischer Entomologen. Zeitschrift. q. ISSN 0003-7729

**Arbeitskreis fuer Kunst und Sprache**
Lerchenfelder Str. 6, A-1080 Vienna, Austria.
- Blaetter fuer Kunst und Sprache. 4-6 annually.

**Association for the Study of the World Refugee Problems**
- A W R Bulletin. (pub. by Wilhelm Braumueller, Universitaets - Verlagsbuchhandlung GmbH)

**Atlas Copco GmbH**
Csokorgasse 11, A-1111 Vienna, Austria.
- Druckluftttechnik. bi-m.

**Auslandsoesterreicherwerk**
Josefsplatz 6, A-1010 Vienna, Austria.
- Der Auslandsoesterreicher. fortn.

**Austria. Bundesamt fuer Eich- und Vermessungswesen**
- Austria. Bundesamt fuer Eich- und Vermessungswesen. Amtsblatt fuer das Eichwesen. (pub. by Kommissionsverlag der Oesterreichischen Staatsdruckerei)

**Austria. Bundesanstalt fuer Pflanzenschutz**
Trunnerstr. 5, A-1021 Vienna, Austria.
- Pflanzenarzt. (pub. by Oesterreichischer Agrarverlag)
- Pflanzenschutzberichte. irreg., vol. 45, 1976. ISSN 0031-675X

**Austria. Bundesdenkmalamt. Abteilung fuer Bodendenkmalpflege**
Saeulenstiege, Hofburg, A-1010 Vienna, Austria.
- Fundberichte aus Oesterreich. a.

**Austria. Bundeskammer der Gewerblichen Wirtschaft**
Sektion Fremdenverkehr, Stubenring 12, A-1010 Vienna, Austria.
- Austria. Bundeskammer der Gewerblichen Wirtschaft. Statistik und Dokumentation. Information. bi-m. ISSN 0039-0585

- Austria. Bundeskammer fuer Die Gewerblichen Wirtschaft. Bericht ueber Die Entwicklung der Industrie. a. ISSN 0067-2254
- Austrian Economic News. m.

**Austria. Bundeskammer der Gewerblichen Wirtschaft. Abteilung fuer Statistik und Dokumentation**
Stubenring 12, A-1010 Vienna, Austria.
- Arbeitskosten in der Industrie Oesterreichs. triennial.

**Austria. Bundeskammer der Gewerblichen Wirtschaft. Wirtschaftsfoerderungsinstitut (Oesterreichisches Verpackungszentrum)**
Hoher Markt 3, A-1011 Vienna, Austria.
- Besser Verpacken. bi-m. ISSN 0005-9595

**Austria. Bundesministerium fuer Auswaertige Angelegenheiten**
Ballhausplatz 2, A-1014 Vienna, Austria.
- Verzeichnis der Konsularischen Vertretungen in Oesterreich. bi-m.

**Austria. Bundesministerium fuer Bauten und Technik**
- Austria. Bundesministerium fuer Bauten und Technik. Wohnbauforschung. (pub. by Sparkassenverlag Ges. m.b.H.)

**Austria. Bundesministerium fuer Bauten und Technik. Beirat fuer Bauwirtschaft**
Stubenring 1, A-1011 Vienna, Austria.
- Austria. Bundesministerium fuer Bauten und Technik. Abteilung Baukoordinierung. Vorschau. a.

**Austria. Bundesministerium fuer Gesundheit und Umweltschutz**
- Amtliche Veterinaernachrichten. (pub. by Oesterreichische Staatsdruckerei)

**Austria. Bundesministerium fuer Handel, Gewerbe und Industrie**
Am Hof 6a, A-1010 Vienna, Austria.
- Brennstoffstatistik der Waermekraftwerke fuer die Oeffentliche Elektrizitaetsversorgung in Oesterreich. a. ISSN 0520-9048

**Austria. Bundesministerium fuer Justiz**
- Amtsblatt der Oesterreichischen Justizverwaltung. (pub. by Oesterreichische Staatsdruckerei)

**Austria. Bundesministerium fuer Land- und Forstwirtschaft**
Stubenring 1, 1010 Vienna, Austria.
- Austria. Bundesministerium fuer Land- und Forstwirtschaft. Taetigkeitsbericht. a. ISSN 0067-2262
- Berufsbildende Schule Oesterreichs; Beitraege zur Berufspaedagogik. 3 per yr. ISSN 0005-9528
- Foerderungsdienst. (pub. by Oesterreichischer Agrarverlag)
- Holzforschung und Holzverwertung. (pub. by Oesterreichischer Agrarverlag)
- Landjugend. (pub. by Oesterreichischer Agrarverlag)

**Austria. Bundesministerium fuer Land- und Forstwirtschaft. Agrarwirtschaftliches Institut**
- Oesterreichische Landwirtschaft. Monatsberichte. (pub. by Oesterreichischer Agrarverlag)
- Schrifttum der Agrarwirtschaft. (pub. by Oesterreichischer Agrarverlag)

**Austria. Bundesministerium fuer Soziale Verwaltung**
- Austria. Bundesministeriums fuer Soziale Verwaltung. Amtliche Nachrichten. (pub. by Oesterreichische Staatsdruckerei)

**Austria. Bundesministerium fuer Unterricht und Kunst.**
Minoritenplatz 5, A-1010 Vienna, Austria.
- Austria. Bundesministerium fuer Unterricht und Kunst. Erziehung, Wissenschaft, Forschung. irreg. ISSN 0067-2270
- Austria. Bundesministerium fuer Unterricht und Kunst. Jahresbericht. a., not published 1968-1970. ISSN 0067-2289
- Bildungsplanung in Oesterreich/Educational Policy and Planning. Austria/Politique et la Planification de l'Enseignement - Autriche. irreg., no. 4, 1974. ISSN 0067-8589
- Erwachsenenbildung in Oesterreich. (pub. by Oesterreichischer Bundesverlag fuer Unterricht Wissenschaft und Kunst)

**Austria. Bundesministerium fuer Wissenschaft und Forschung**
Minoritenplatz 5, A-1014 Vienna, Austria.
- Austria. Bundesministerium fuer Wissenschaft und Forschung. Bericht der Bundesregierung an den Nationalrat. a. ISSN 0300-2772
- Austria. Bundesministerium fuer Wissenschaft und Forschung. Forschungspolitische Dokumentation. a.
- Austria. Bundesministerium fuer Wissenschaft und Forschung. Hochschulbericht. irreg.
- Transparent. (pub. by Guenther Feurstein, Ed. & Pub.)

**Austria. Bundesstaatliche Hauptstelle fuer Lichtbild und Bildungsfilm**
Zentrum fuer AVM, Plunkergasse 3-5, A-1152 Vienna, Austria.
- Sehen und Hoeren/See & Listen; Beitraege zur Paedagogik der audio-visuellen Bildungsmittel. bi-m. ISSN 0037-0975

**Austria. Hoehere Bundeslehr- und Versuchsanstalt fuer Wein- und Obstbau**
Wienerstr. 74, A-3400 Klosterneuburg, Austria.
- Klosterneuburg. Mitteilungen; Rebe und Wein, Obstbau und Fruechteverwertung. bi-m. ISSN 0007-5922

**Austria. Oesterreichisches Bundesdenkmalamt**
- Oesterreichische Zeitschrift fuer Kunst und Denkmalpflege. (pub. by Verlag Anton Schroll und Co.)

**Austria. Oesterreichisches Patentamt**
Kohlmarkt 8-10, A-1014 Vienna, Austria.
- Oesterreichischer Markenanzeiger. m. ISSN 0029-9782
- Oesterreichisches Patentblatt. m. ISSN 0029-9944

**Austria. Oesterreichisches Statistisches Zentralamt**
Heldenplatz, Neue Burg, Vienna, Austria.
- Austria. Statistisches Zentralamt. Aussenhandel Oesterreichs. (pub. by Carl Ueberreuter)
- Austria. Statistisches Zentralamt. die Natuerliche Bevoelkerungsbewegung. (pub. by Oesterreichische Staatsdruckerei)
- Austria. Statistisches Zentralamt. die Wohnbautaetigkeit. (pub. by Oesterreichische Staatsdruckerei)
- Austria. Statistisches Zentralamt. Ergebnisse der Landwirtschaftlichen Maschinenzaehlung. (pub. by Oesterreichische Staatsdruckerei)
- Austria. Statistisches Zentralamt. Ergebnisse der Landwirtschaftlichen Statistik. (pub. by Oesterreichische Staatsdruckerei)
- Austria. Statistisches Zentralamt. Erhebung der Land-und Forstwirtschaftlichen Arbeitskraefte. (pub. by Kommissionsverlag der Oesterreichischen Staatsdruckerei)
- Austria. Statistisches Zentralamt. Gewerbestatistik. a.
- Austria. Statistisches Zentralamt. Industrie Statistik. a.
- Austria. Statistisches Zentralamt. Jugendwohlfahrtspflege. (pub. by Kommissionsverlag der Oesterreichischen Staatsdruckerei)
- Austria. Statistisches Zentralamt. Mikrozensus; Jahresergebnisse. (pub. by Kommissionsverlag der Oesterreichischen Staatsdruckerei)
- Austria. Statistisches Zentralamt. Oeffentliche Fuersorge. (pub. by Kommissionsverlag der Oesterreichischen Staatsdruckerei)
- Austria. Statistisches Zentralamt. Statistik der Aktiengesellschaften in Oesterreich. (pub. by Carl Ueberreuter)
- Austria. Statistisches Zentralamt. Statistik der Rechtspflege. (pub. by Carl Ueberreuter)
- Austria. Statistisches Zentralamt. Statistische Nachrichten. (pub. by Carl Ueberreuter)
- Beitraege zur Oesterreichischen Statistik. irreg. ISSN 0067-2319
- Bestands-Statistik der Kraftfahrzeuge in Oesterreich. (pub. by Verlag Neue Technik)
- Fremdenverkehr in Oesterreich. (pub. by Carl Ueberreuter)
- Oesterreichische Hochschulstatistik. (pub. by Oesterreichische Staatsdruckerei)
- Oesterreichs Industrie. a. ISSN 0078-3684
- Oesterreichs Volkseinkommen. a. ISSN 0085-4433

- Statistisches Handbuch fuer die Republik Oesterreich. (pub. by Oesterreichische Staatsdruckerei)

**Austria Contact**
Brennerstr. 25, A-4820 Bad Ischl, Austria.
- Austria Contact. bi-m. ISSN 0010-7220

**Austria Presse Agentur (APA)**
Gunoldstrasse 14, A-1199 Vienna, Austria.
- Konjunktur. w.
- Metalle. 5 per wk. ISSN 0026-0762
- Motor und Erdoel. w.
- Nahrungsmittel. 3 per w. ISSN 0027-7703
- Obst-Gemuese. 2 per w. ISSN 0029-778X

**Austria Tabakwerke A.G.**
Porzellangasse 51, A-1091 Vienna, Austria.
- Austria Tabakwerke A. G. Fachliche Mitteilungen. s-a. ISSN 0029-9537
- Tabakpflanzer Oesterreichs. s-a. ISSN 0039-8756

**Austria Today GmbH & Co. KG**
P.O. Box 47 Heldenplatz (Kongresszentrum), A-1014 Vienna, Austria.
- Austria Today; quarterly review of trends and events. q.

**Austrian Chamber of Commerce**
- Industrie Compass Oesterreich. (pub. by Compass-Verlagsgesellschaft Rudolf Hanel & Sohn)

**Austrian National Union of Students**
- Bilanz. (pub. by Oesterreichische Hochschuelerschaft)

**Baeuerlicher Presseverein**
Castellezgasse 20/1, A-1020 Vienna, Austria.
- Oesterreichische Bauernzeitung. m. ISSN 0029-8905

**Bauer's Witwe und Co.**
Gersthofer Str.14, 1180 Vienna, Austria.
- Verband Oesterreichischer Landsmannschaften Nachrichten-und Mitteilungsblatt. m. ISSN 0042-3637

**Baufachverlag Wien Ges. m. b. H.**
Fuerstengasse 1, A-1090 Vienna, Austria.
- Bauforum; Fachzeitschrift fuer Architektur-Bautechnik-Bauwirtschaft-Industrial Design. bi-m. ISSN 0005-6596 (Oesterreichisches Bauzentrum)
- Oesterreichischer Yachtsport; oesterreichische Segler-Zeitung und Motorbootrundschau. 10 per yr. ISSN 0029-9812 (Oesterreichischer Segel-Verband)

**Bausparkasse Wuestenrot**
Postfach 115, Alpenstr. 70, A-5021 Salzburg, Austria.
- Das Wuestenrot-Heim. q. ISSN 0043-9622

**Beirat fuer Wirtschafts und Sozialfragen**
Alser Str. 24, A-1095 Vienna 9, Austria.
- Beirat fuer Wirtschafts und Sozialfragen. a.

**Verlag Ferdinand Berger und Soehne OHG**
Wienerstr. 21-23, A-3580 Horn, Austria.
- Anthropologische Gesellschaft, Vienna. Mitteilungen. a. ISSN 0066-4693
- Naturhistorisches Museum in Wien. Neue Denkschriften. irreg.
- Oesterreichische Schriften zur Entwicklungshilfe. irreg. ISSN 0078-3536
- Oesterreichisches Museum fuer Volkskunde. Kataloge. irreg.
- Oesterreichisches Museum fuer Volkskunde: Veroeffentlichungen. irreg.
- Oesterreichisches Staatsarchiv. Mitteilungen. a. ISSN 0067-2297
- Oesterreichisches Staatsarchiv. Publikationen; Inventare oesterreichischer staatlicher Archive. irreg.
- Orientforschung: Archiv; Internationale Zeitschrift fuer die Wissenschaft vom Vorderen Orient. irreg. ISSN 0066-6440
- Phyton. Annales Rei Botanicae. a. ISSN 0079-2047
- Rudolf Virchow Medical Society in the City of New York. Proceedings. irreg., 1972, no. 27. ISSN 0080-4797
- Sydowia: Annales Mycologici. a. ISSN 0082-0598
- Universum; Monatszeitschrift fuer Natur, Technik, und Wirtschaft. m. (Gesellschaft fuer Natur, Technik und Wirtschaft)

- Wiener Beitraege zur Kulturgeschichte und Linguistik. irreg., 1968, vol. 17. ISSN 0083-9922 (Universitaet Wien. Institut fuer Voelkerkunde)
- Wiener Tieraerztliche Monatsschrift. m. ISSN 0043-535X (Oesterreichische Tieraerzteschaft) (Co-Sponsor: Oesterreichische Gesellschaft der Tieraerzte)

**Bergmann-Kameradschaft 137. Inf. Div.**
- Bergmann-Echo. (pub. by Sepp Sattelberger, Editor)

**Berndorf. Stadtgemeinde Berndorf**
Karl Kislingerplatz 2, A-2560 Berndorf, Austria.
- Gemeindekurier; Mitteilungsblatt der Stadt Berndorf. m. ISSN 0016-6146

**Berufsfoerderungsinstitut**
- Start und Aufstieg. (pub. by Verlag des Oesterreichischen Gewerkschaftbundes GmbH)

**Berufsverband Oesterreichischer Diplomfuersorger**
Arbeitergasse 26, A-1050 Vienna, Austria.
- Sozialarbeit in Oesterreich. 4 per yr.

**Studioverlag Beyer**
Schweglerstr. 20 u 7, A-1150 Vienna, Austria.
- Oesterreichisches Hotel-und Gastronomie-Journal. m. ISSN 0029-988X (Internationaler Genfer Verban - Landesteil Oesterreich)

**Bilder-Zeitung G.m.b.H.**
Pilgrimgasse 13, A-1051 Vienna, Austria.
- Praktiker; die Zeitschrift fuer das technische Hobby. s-m. ISSN 0032-6755

**Bischoefliches Ordinariat Sanct Poelten**
Domplatz 1, A-3100 St. Poelten, Austria.
- St. Poeltner Dioezesanblatt. irreg. ISSN 0036-3162

**Bischoefliches Seelsogeamt Klagenfurt**
Waaggasse 18, A-9010 Klagenfurt, Austria.
- Regenbogen; Zeitung fuer Buben und Maedchen. w.

**Hermann Boehlaus Nachf.**
Schmalzhofgasse 4, Postfach 167, A-1061 Vienna, Austria.
- Gesellschaft fuer Griechische und Hellenistische Rechtsgeschichte. Akten. irreg.
- Institut fuer Oesterreichische Geschichtsforschung. Mitteilungen. s-a (often double issues) ISSN 0073-8484 (Universitaet Wien. Institut fuer Oesterreichische Geschichtsforschung)
- Maske und Kothurn; Internationale Beitraege zur Theaterwissenschaft. 4 per yr. ISSN 0025-4606 (Universitaet Wien. Institut fuer Theaterwissenschaft)
- Wiener Humanistische Blaetter. a. ISSN 0083-9965 (Wiener Humanistische Gesellschaft)
- Wiener Jahrbuch fuer Kunstgeschichte. a. ISSN 0083-9981 (Institut fuer Oesterreichische Kunstforschung) (Co-sponsor: Universitaet Wien. Kunsthistorisches Institut)
- Wiener Slavistisches Jahrbuch / Viennese Slavonic Yearbook. a. ISSN 0084-0041 (Universitaet Wien. Institut fuer Slavische Philologie)
- Wiener Studien. Zeitschrift fuer Klassische Philologie und Patristik. a. ISSN 0084-005X (Universitaet Wien. Institut fuer Klassische Philologie)

**Dr. Julius Boese, Ed. & Pub.**
Schleifmuehlgasse 23/9, A-1040 Vienna, Austria.
- Literaturspiegel. irreg. ISSN 0456-2666

**Bohmann Verlag K.G.**
Canovagasse 5, A-1010 Vienna, Austria.
- C W F. (Oesterreichische Chemischreiniger-Waescher und Faerberzeitschrift) m. ISSN 0029-9367 (Bundesinnung der Chemischreiniger, Waescher und Faerber)
- Eisenbahn; Geschichte, Technik, Aktualitaeten. m. ISSN 0013-2756
- Eisenbahntechnik; oesterreichische Fachzeitschrift fuer modernen Eisenbahnbau. q. ISSN 0013-2829
- Internationale Berg- und Seilbahn-Rundschau / International Aerial Tramway Review. 7 per yr. ISSN 0020-9171 (Organizzazione Internationale dei Trasporti a Fune)
- Lagern und Fordern; Foerdertechnik und Transport. bi-m.
- Oesterreich Florist; Fachzeitschrift der oesterreichischen Blumenbinder. m.
- Die Oesterreichische Feuerwehr. m. ISSN 0029-9030 (Oesterreichischer Bundes-Feuerwehrverband)

- Der Oesterreichische Installateur. m. ISSN 0029-9227 (Bundesinnung und Landesinnungen der Installateure Oesterreichs)
- Output Oesterreich. bi-m.
- Reiseland Oesterreich; the Austrian travel magazine. m.
- Stahlbau-Rundschau; fach- und Informationszeitschrift des Oesterreichischen Stahlverbandes. s-a. ISSN 0561-7855 (Oesterreichischer Stahlbau-Verband)
- Tankstelle und Garage. m.
- Umweltschutz. m. ISSN 0049-5131 (Oesterreichische Gesellschaft fuer Natur- und Umweltschutz)
- Verkehr; internationale Fachzeitung fuer Verkehrswirtschaft. w.

**Johann L. Bondi und Sohn**
Zollergasse 17, A-1071 Vienna, Austria.
- Allgemeine Bau-Zeitung. m. ISSN 0002-5798
- P B S Aktuell. (Papierwaren, Buerobedarf, Schreibwaren) m. ISSN 0030-784X
- Recht und Wettbewerb. irreg. ISSN 0080-0155 (Schutzverband gegen unlauteren Wettbewerb)
- Schuh-Revue. s-m.
- Tisch und Kueche; Oesterreichisches Fachblatt fuer den Glas-Porzellanwaren-Haus- und Kuechengeraetefachhandel. m. ISSN 0040-8123

**Verlag Friedrich Brabec**
Biberstr. 2, A-1010 Vienna, Austria.
- Industrie- und Handelszeitung. m. ISSN 0046-9289 (Verband der Maschinen- und Werkzeughaendler, MAWEV)
- Wiener Boersen-Kurier. w. (Zentralverband der oesterreichischen Aktiengesellschaften)

**Zeitschriftenverlag Dr. Hildegard Braig**
Anton Frankgasse 17, A-1181 Vienna, Austria.
- Holz im Handwerk; oesterreichische moebelzeitschrift. m. ISSN 0018-3776
- Internationaler Holzmarkt. fortn. ISSN 0020-9422

**Wilhelm Braumueller, Universitaets - Verlagsbuchhandlung GmbH**
Servitengasse 5, A-1092 Vienna 9, Austria.
- A W R Bulletin; quarterly on refugee problems. q. ISSN 0001-2947 (Association for the Study of the World Refugee Problems)
- Archiv fuer Voelkerkunde. a. ISSN 0066-6513 (Museum fuer Voelkerkunde)
- Europa Ethnica; Vierteljahresschrift fuer Nationalitaetenfragen. q. ISSN 0014-2492
- Oesterreichische Zeitschrift fuer Aussenpolitik. bi-m. ISSN 0029-960X (Oesterreichische Gesellschaft fuer Aussenpolitik)
- Philologische Beitraege zur Suedost- und Osteuropaforschung. irreg. ISSN 0079-1644
- Salzburger Studien zur Anglistik und Amerikanistik. irreg. ISSN 0080-5718
- Wiener Arbeiten zur Deutschen Literatur. a. ISSN 0083-9906
- Wiener Beitraege zur Englischen Philologie. irreg., 1970, vol. 74. ISSN 0083-9914
- Wiener Forschungen zur Theater und Medienwissenschaft. irreg. (Universitaet Wien. Institut fuer Theaterwissenschaft)
- Wiener Jahrbuch fuer Philosophie. a. ISSN 0083-999X
- Wiener Romanistische Arbeiten. a. ISSN 0084-0033
- Zeitschrift fuer Menschenkunde und Zentralblatt fuer Graphologie, Ausdruckswissenschaft und Charakterkunde. q. ISSN 0044-3085

**Brevillier-Urban Aktiengesellschaft**
Linke Wienzeile 18, Vienna 6, Austria.
- B-U Nachrichten. 6 per yr. ISSN 0005-2698

**Brunner Verlag**
Ringelschmiedgasse 5, A-8600 Bruck/Mur, Austria.
- Gute Nachrichten. 8 per yr. ISSN 0017-5781

**Buchalter-Zeitung**
Zeismannsbrunngasse 1, A-1070 Vienna, Austria.
- Human Industrial Design. irreg. ISSN 0018-7224

**Buddhistisches Kultur- und Meditationszentrum Scheibbs**
- Bodhi Baum/Zeitschrift fuer Buddhismus. (pub. by Octopus Verlag)

**Buecher-Herzog**
Mariahilferstr. 1, A-1060 Vienna, Austria.
- Neues aus der Mariahilfer Strasse. irreg. ISSN 0077-7730

**Bulgarian Social Democratic Party in Exile**
Wiedner Haupstrasse 60 B-11, A-1040 Vienna, Austria.
- Swoboden Narod.

**Hans Bulla und Sohn**
Mollardgasse 1, A-1060 Vienna, Austria.
- Der Oesterreichische Friseur; offizielles Fachorgan der Friseure Oesterreichs. m. ISSN 0029-9065 (Landesinnung Wien der Friseure)

**Bund Demokratischer Sozialisten**
Wienerbergstr. 16-20-32-7, Vienna 12, Austria
- Internationales Freies Wort. q. ISSN 0020-9473 (U.S. Subscr. to: World Socialist Party, 259 Huntington Ave. Boston, Mass. 02115)

**Bund Sozialistischer Akademiker, Intellektueller und Kuenstler**
Boltzmanngasse 21, A-1090 Vienna, Austria.
- Sozialistische Akademiker. m. ISSN 0038-6103

**Bund Sozialistischer Freiheitskaempfer und Opfer des Faschismus**
Loewelstr. 18, A-1014 Vienna, Austria.
- Sozialistische Kaempfer. m. ISSN 0038-6162

**Bundes-Blindenerziehungsinstitut**
Wittelsbachstr. 5, A-1020 Vienna, Austria.
- Johann Wilhelm Klein; literarische Zeitschrift fuer Blinde. m. ISSN 0021-7174

**Bundes- und Landesinnungen der Dachdecker**
- Dach und Wand Abdichtung. (pub. by Oesterreichischer Wirtschaftsverlag)

**Bundes- und Landesinnungen der Glaserer**
- Oesterreichische Glaserzeitung. (pub. by Oesterreichischer Wirtschaftsverlag)

**Bundes- und Landesinnungen des Taxigewerbes**
- Oesterreichischer Personenverkehr. (pub. by Oesterreichischer Wirtschaftsverlag)

**Bundesanstalt fuer Alpenlaendische Landwirtschaft Gumpenstein**
Gumpenstein, Austria.
- Bundesversuchsanstalt fuer Alpenlaendische Landwirtschaft Gumpenstein. Versuchsergebnisse. irreg.

**Bundesanstalt fuer Pflanzenbau und Samenpruefung**
Alliierten Str. 1, Postfach 64, A-1201 Vienna, Austria.
- Bundesanstalt fuer Pflanzenbau und Samenpruefung, Vienna. Jahrbuch. (0-582,4-Au) a. ISSN 0068-421X

**Bundesberufsgruppen des Landmaschinenhandels und Landmaschinenhandwerks Oesterreichs**
- Landmaschinen-Handwerk-Handel. (pub. by Verlag Lorenz)

**Bundesfachgruppe fuer Zahn-,Mund-und Kieferheilkunde**
Weihburgstrasse 10-12, A-1010 Vienna, Austria.
- Oesterreichische Zahnaerzte-Zeitung. m. ISSN 0029-9596

**Bundesholzwirtschaftsrat**
- Holz-Kurier. (pub. by Oesterreichischer Agrarverlag)

**Bundesinnung der Cafetiers**
- Oesterreichisches Cafe Journal. (pub. by Oesterreichischer Wirtschaftsverlag)

**Bundesinnung der Chemischreiniger, Waescher und Faerber**
- C W F. (pub. by Bohmann Verlag K.G.)

**Bundesinnung der Elektrotechniker und Radiomechaniker**
- Elektro Journal. (pub. by Oesterreichischer Wirtschaftsverlag)

**Bundesinnung der Kraftfahrzeugmechaniker**
- K F Z Werkstaette. (pub. by Oesterreichischer Wirtschaftsverlag)

**Bundesinnung der Mechaniker**
- Mechanik. (pub. by Oesterreichischer Wirtschaftsverlag)

**Bundesinnung der Schuhmacher**
- Der Oesterreichische Schuhmarkt. (pub. by Oesterreichischer Wirtschaftsverlag)

**Bundesinnung der Zahntechniker**
- Der Oesterreichische Zahntechniker. (pub. by Oesterreichischer Wirtschaftsverlag)

**Bundesinnung des Wirtschaftlichen Werbewesens**
- Werbung in Oesterreich Intern. (pub. by Thiel, Jost und Co., Ges. m.b.H.)

**Bundesinnung und Landesinnung der Tischler Oesterreichs**
- Tischler. (pub. by Oesterreichischer Wirtschaftsverlag)

**Bundesinnung und Landesinnungen der Installateure Oesterreichs**
- Der Oesterreichische Installateur. (pub. by Bohmann Verlag K.G.)

**Bundeskammer der Gewerblichen Wirtschaft**
Stubenring 12, A-1010 Vienna, Austria.
- Austria Export. (pub. by Internationale Werbegesellschaft m.b.H.)
- Jahrbuch der Oesterreichischen Wirtschaft. a.
- Der Unternehmer. (pub. by Oesterreichischer Wirtschaftsverlag)
- Wirtschaftspolitische Blaetter. (pub. by Oesterreichischer Wirtschaftsverlag)
- Zeitschrift fuer Arbeitsrecht und Sozialrecht. (pub. by Manzsche Verlags- und Universitaetsbuchhandlung)

**Bundeskammer der Tieraerzte Oesterreichs**
Biberstrasse 22, A-1010 Vienna, Austria.
- Oesterreichische Tieraerztezeitung. m. ISSN 0048-1475

**Bundeskonvikt Wien**
Josef Gallg.2, 1020 Vienna, Austria.
- Studio. m. ISSN 0039-4084

**Bundesobstbauverband Oesterreichs**
- Besseres Obst. (pub. by Oesterreichischer Agrarverlag)

**Bundesverband der Erwerbsgaertner Oesterreichs**
- Gartenbauwirtschaft. (pub. by Oesterreichischer Agrarverlag)

**Bundesverband der Weinbautreibenden Oesterreichs**
- Der Winzer. (pub. by Oesterreichischer Agrarverlag)

**Bundesverband Oesterreichischer Widerstandskaempfer und Opfer des Faschismus**
Castellezgasse 35, A-1020 Vienna, Austria.
- Der Neue Mahnruf; Zeitschrift fuer Freiheit, Recht und Demokratie. m. ISSN 0028-3274

**Burgen- und Schloessererhaltungsverein**
Stadtamt, A-2070 Retz, Austria.
- Oesterreichs Bindenschild. bi-m. (Co-Sponsor: Kaerntner Burgen-und Schloessererhaltungsverein)

**Burgenlaendische Gemeinschaft**
Mogersdorf 178, A-7540 Guessing, Austria.
- Burgenlaendische Gemeinschaft. m. ISSN 0007-6228

**Burgenland. Amt der Burgenlaendischen Landesregierung**
Landesarchiv, A-7001 Eisenstadt, Austria.
- Burgenlaendische Forschungen. 2-3 per yr. ISSN 0007-621X
- Burgenlaendische Heimatblaetter. q. ISSN 0007-6236
- Landesamtsblatt fuer das Burgenland. w. ISSN 0023-7876

**Burgenland. Burgenlaendische Landwirtschaftskammer**
Esterhazystr. 15, A-7001 Eisenstadt, Austria.
- Burgenlaendische Landwirtschaftskammer. Mitteilungsblatt. m. ISSN 0007-6244

**Burgenland Verlag, G.m.b.H.**
Postfach 14, A-7001 Eisenstadt, Austria.
- Burgenlaendisches Leben. 8 per yr. ISSN 0007-6252

**Carriere Verlagsgesellschaft m.b.H.**
Stock- Im- Eisen- Platz 3, A-1070 Vienna, Austria.
- Carriere; das Bueromagazin. bi-m.

**Chemiefaser Lenzing AG**
A-4860 Lenzing, Austria.
- Lenzinger Berichte. s-a. ISSN 0024-0907

**Chemisches Forschungsinstitut der Wirtschaft Oesterreichs**
Untere Viadukt 55, Vienna 3, Austria.
- Chemie Kunststoffe Aktuell. Mitteilungen. bi-m. ISSN 0009-2991 (Co-Sponsor: Oesterrcichische Kunstoffinstitut)

**Werk Christliche Innerlichkeit**
Karmelweg 1, A-8630 Mariazell, Austria.
- Christliche Innerlichkeit; Schrift fuer Gebet und gelebtes Christentum. bi-m. ISSN 0009-5796

**Cistercienser in Mehrerau**
6901 Bregenz, A-6901 Bregenz.
- Cistercienser Chronik. q.

**Compass-Verlagsgesellschaft Rudolf Hanel & Sohn**
Wipplingerstrasse 32, A-1010 Vienna, Austria.
- Industrie Compass Oesterreich. a. ISSN 0073-7712 (Austrian Chamber of Commerce)

**Coronelli-Weltbund der Globusfreunde**
Erdbergstr. 32, A-1030 Vienna, Austria.
- Globusfreund. 3 per yr. ISSN 0436-0664

**Creditanstalt-Bankverein**
Schottengasse 6, A-1010 Vienna, Austria.
- Creditanstalt-Bankverein. Wirtschaftsberichte. bi-m. ISSN 0590-0727
- Economic Letter: Austrian Economy in Brief. m.
- Nachrichten aus der Oesterreichischen Wirtschaft Wirtschaftsbrief. m.

**Franz Deuticke**
Helferstorfer Str. 4, A-1010 Vienna, Austria.
- Archaeologia Austriaca; Beitraege zur Palaeanthropologie, Ur- und Fruehgeschichte Oesterreichs. s-a. ISSN 0003-8008 (Universitaet Wien. Institut fuer Ur- und Fruehgeschichte)
- Beitraege zur Gerichtlichen Medizin. a. ISSN 0067-5016

**Deutsche Handelskammer in Oesterreich**
Wiedner Hauptstr. 142, Box 107, A-1103 Vienna, Austria.
- Deutsche Handelskammer in Oesterreich (Bulletin) 9 per yr. ISSN 0012-0251

**Dioecesis St. Poelten**
Linzerstr. 3-7, A-1000 St. Poelten, Austria.
- Kirche Bunt. w.

**Dioeze Linz, Pastoralamt. Sozialreferat**
Seilerstaette 14, A-4020 Linz, Austria.
- Interesse; Soziale Information. q. ISSN 0020-5362

**Musikverlag Ludwig Doblinger**
Dorotheegasse 10, A-1011 Vienna, Austria
(Distr. in U.S: by Associated Music Publishers Inc., 48-02 48th Ave., Woodside, New York NY, 11377)
- Doblinger's News Letter. a.
- Doblingers Verlagsnachrichten. a. ISSN 0070-6795

**Dokumentationsarchiv des Oesterreichischen Widerstandes**
Wipplingerstr. 8, 1010 Vienna, Austria.
- Dokumentationsarchiv des Oesterreichischen Widerstandes. Mitteilungen. bi-m.

**Donaueuropaeisches Institut**
- West-Ost-Journal. (pub. by Jupiter Verlag Gmbh)

**Dorotheum**
Dorotheegasse 11, A 1011 Vienna, Austria.
- Kunst-Katalog: Auktionen. irreg. ISSN 0075-7241

**Julius Dressler Buch- und Zeitschriftenverlag**
Schwindgasse 5, A-1041 Vienna, Austria.
- Kunststoffe in Oesterreich. irreg. (Fachverband der Chemischen Industrie Oesterreichs. Gruppe Kunststoffverarbeitende Industrie) (Co-sponsor: Arbeitsgemeinschaft der Kunststoffverarbeitenden Gewerbebetriebe)
- O L W/Oesterreichische Lederwaren. m. ISSN 0029-7151
- Oesterreichische Buchbinder, Kartonage-, Etui-, Kassetten- und Papierwarenerzeuger. m. ISSN 0029-8964 (Innung der Buchbinder, Kartonagewaren- und Etuierzeuger)
- Oesterreichische Leder- und Haeutewirtschaft. m. ISSN 0029-9286

**Druzba Sv. Mohorja**
Viktringer Ring 26, A-9020 Klagenfurt, Austria.
- Druzina in Dom. m. ISSN 0012-6764

**Josef Ebner, Ed. & Pub.**
Am Aigen 5, A-8046 Graz, Austria.
- Alpengarten. q. ISSN 0002-6344

**Ehe und Familie Zeitschriftenverlagsgesellschaft m.b.H.**
Wollzeila 2, A-1010 Vienna, Austria.
- Ehe und Familie. m. ISSN 0013-2470 (Katholischer Familienverband Oesterreichs)

**Elektrizitaets- und Metallwaren-Industrie Gesellschaft (EUMIG)**
Eumig-Str. 2-8, A-2351 Wiener Neudorf, Austria.
- E U M I G - Lupe. m. ISSN 0014-2301

**Elektron-Verlag**
Postfach 156, A-4010 Linz, Austria.
- Elektron-International; revue fuer Radio-Fernsehen-Elektronik und Elektroakustik. m.

**Technischer Verlag Erb GmbH**
Mariahilfer Str. 71, Postfach 101, A-1061 Vienna, Austria.
- Elektro Radio Handel. m.
- Elektronikschau; Radiotechnik, Fernsehen, Elektronik. m.

**Erdoel - Dienst**
Universitaetsstr. 11, A-1010 Vienna, Austria.
- Erdoel - Dienst; Korrespondenz fuer Erdoel, Erdgas, Chemie und Energetik. s-w. ISSN 0046-242X

**Erste Allgemeine Versicherungs-Aktiengesellschaft**
Brandstaette 7-9, Vienna 1, Austria.
- Fundament; Schulungs- und Mitteilungsblatt. 4 per yr. ISSN 0016-2728

**Der Erste Oesterreichischer Musik-Express**
Waldgasse 5, A-2542 Kottingbrunn, Austria.
- Der Erste Oesterreichischer Musik-Express. irreg.

**Erzabtei St. Peter, Salzburg. Institutum Liturgicum**
- Heiliger Dienst. (pub. by Verlag St. Peter).

**Erzdioezese Wien. Katholische Jugend**
Stephansplatz 6/6/65, A-1010 Vienna, Austria.
- Kontakt und Reflexionen. m. ISSN 0034-3013

**Eskimo-Iglo Ges. m.b.H.**
Industriestr. 2, A-2310 Gross Enzersdorf, Austria.
- Gast und Kueche; zeitschrift fuer Gastronomie und Personalrestaurants. q.

**Europa-Verlag AG**
Altmannsderferstr. 154, A-1232 Vienna, Austria.
- Europaeische Rundschau. m.
- Oesterreichische Zeitschrift fuer Politikwissenschaft. q. (Oesterreichische Gesellschaft fuer Politikwissenschaft)

**Europaeische Foederalistische Bewegung**
Postfach 228, A-8011 Graz, Austria.
- Europastimme. bi-m. ISSN 0014-2727

**Europaeisches Erzieherbund (European Assn. of Teachers)**
Sektion Oesterreich, Palais Palffy, Josefsplatz 6, A-1010 Vienna, Austria.
- Schule und Europa; Zeitschrift fuer Europaeische Erziehung. q. ISSN 0036-7109

**Europahaus Wallersee-Salzburg**
Pfeifergasse 18/11, A-5020 Salzburg, Austria.
- Europaeische Integration; Information und Dokumentation. m. ISSN 0014-2662

**European Malacological Union**
- European Malacological Congress. Proceedings. (pub. by Unitas Malacologica Europaea)

**Europublica Verlagsgesellschaft G.m.b.H.**
Karl Schweighofer-Gasse 3, A-1071 Vienna, Austria.
- Austroflug; die Luft-und Raumfahrtzeitschrift Oesterreichs. m. ISSN 0005-0555

**Verlag Eurosport**
Hutweidengasse 30/32, A-1190 Vienna, Austria.
- EUROFREIZEIT; internationales Magazin fuer den Wintersport. q.

**Evangelische Gemeinde A.B. Wien-Waehring**
Martinstr. 25, A-1180 Vienna, Austria.
- Die Lutherkirche; Pfarrblatt. q. ISSN 0024-7626

**Evangelische Pfarrgemeinde Purkersdorf**
Wintergasse 13-15, A-3002 Purkersdorf, Austria.
- Pfarrbrief; fuer die evangelischen Gemeinden Purkersdorf und Pressbaum. 6 per yr. ISSN 0031-6709

**Evangelischer Bund in Oesterreich**
Martinstr. 25, A-1180 Vienna, Austria.
- Evangelischer Bund in Oesterreich. Schriftenreihe. q. ISSN 0036-6943
- Martin Luther. s-a. (Co-sponsor: Martin Luther-Bund)

**Evangelisches Jugendwerk in Oesterreich**
Liechtensteinstr. 20, A-1090 Vienna, Austria.
- Junge Gemeinde. q. ISSN 0022-6289

**Evangelisches Pfarramt Melk**
Kirchenstr. 15, Postfach 9, A-3390 Melk, Austria.
- Gemeindebrief; fuer die gemeindemitglieder der evangelischen Pfarrgemeinde Melk-Scheibbs. irreg. ISSN 0016-6111

**F K K Vereinigung Gymnasion**
Koestlergasse 4/21, A-1060 Vienna, Austria.
- Das Gymnasion. bi-m. ISSN 0017-5935

**Fachgruppenvereinigung des Krankenpflegepersonals und verwandter Berufe**
Theresiengasse 37, A-1180 Vienna, Austria.
- Soziale Berufe. bi-m. ISSN 0038-6049

**Fachverband der Chemischen Industrie Oesterreichs. Gruppe Kunststoffverarbeitende Industrie**
- Kunststoffe in Oesterreich. (pub. by Julius Dressler Buch- und Zeitschriftenverlag)

**Fachverband der Maschinen und Stahlbauindustrie Oesterreichs**
Bauernmarkt 13, A-1010 Vienna, Austria.
- Machinery and Steel. 10 per yr.
- Maschinen und Stahlbau/Austrian Machinery and Steel Construction Review. m.

**Fachverband der Oesterreichischen Standesbeamten**
Habsburgergasse 5, A-1010 Vienna, Austria.
- Oesterreichisches Standesamt; Fachzeitschrift fuer Personenstands-, Ehe- und Staatsbuergerschaftsrecht. m. ISSN 0029-9952

**Fachvereinigung der Trafikanten im Freien Wirtschaftsverband**
Schottenfeldgasse 24, A-1070 Vienna, Austria.
- Tabakverschleisser Oesterreichs. 10 per yr. ISSN 0039-8772

**Fachverlag fuer das Oesterreichische Bekleidungsgewerbe**
Judenplatz 5, A-1010 Vienna, Austria.
- Oesterreichisches Bekleidungsjournal; Fachtechnik-Mode-Modell-Material. m.

**Facultas Buch- und Zeitschriftenverlag fuer Medizin und Pharmazie GmbH**
Berggasse 4, A-1090 Vienna, Austria.
- Oesterreichische Krankenpflegezeitschrift. m. (Oesterreichischer Krankenpflegeverband)

**Festungsverlag Salzburg**
Mirabellplatz 7, A-5020 Salzburg, Austria.
- Offizieller Salzburger Wochenspiegel. w. ISSN 0030-0586 (Salzburg. Stadtverkehrsbuero Salzburg)

**Guenther Feurstein, Ed. & Pub.**
Wiedner Hauptstr. 40, A-1040 Vienna, Austria.
- Transparent; Manuskripte fuer Architektur, Theorie, Umraum, Kunst. m. ISSN 0041-1302 (Austria. Bundesministerium fuer Wissenschaft und Forschung)

**Filmclub Action**
A-1152 Vienna, Austria.
- Filmclub Action-Mitteilungen. s-m. ISSN 0015-1505

**Firma Dr. Karl Eisenhardt und Soehne**
Schwefel 81, 1070 Vienna, Austria.
- Eisenhardt-Post. 4 per yr. ISSN 0022-6440

**Firma Eisner Baumaschinen Ges. m.b.H.**
Industriezentrum NOe-Sved, Srasse Nr. 1,Objekt 27, A-2351 Wr. Neudorf, Austria.
- Erdbau. m. ISSN 0013-998X

**Verlag Michael Fischer**
Neulerchenfelderstr. 8, A-1160 Vienna, Austria.
- Oesterreichische Naehmaschinen- und Zweirad-Zeitung. 16 per yr. (Verband des Naehmaschinen-und Fahrradhandels und Gewerbes Oesterreichs)
- Schuh-Zeitung. 24 per yr. ISSN 0036-7060 (Verband der Schuhindustrie und dem Schuhhandel)

**Forschungsgesellschaft fuer Wohnen, Bauen und Planen**
Loewengasse 47, A-1030 Vienna 3, Austria.
- W B F O. (Wohnbauforschung in Oesterreich) bi-m. ISSN 0042-9562

**Forstliche Fachvereine und Standesorganisationen Oesterreichs**
- Allgemeine Forstzeitung. (pub. by Oesterreichischer Agrarverlag)

**Forum Stadtpark**
A-8010 Graz, Austria.
- Manuskripte; Zeitschrift fuer Literatur, Kunst, Kritik. 4 per yr. ISSN 0025-2638

**Forumverlag**
Skodagasse 20, A-1080 Vienna, Austria.
- Wiener Buecherbriefe. bi-m. ISSN 0043-5295 (Vienna. Kulturamt der Stadt Wien. Direktion der Staedtischen Buechereien)

**Freiheitliche Partei Oesterreichs**
Kaerntnerstr. 28/I, A-1010 Vienna, Austria.
- Freiheitlicher Pressedienst. s-w.
- N F Z; Neue Freie Zeitung. w.

**Freiheitliche Partei Oesterreichs. Freiheitliche Betriebsorganisation in der Voeest**
Klammstr. 7/1, A-4020 Linz, Austria.
- Voeest-Alpine Betriebeskurier; Mitteilungen der freiheitlichen Betriebsorganisation. m. ISSN 0042-7942

**Freiheitliche Partei Oesterreichs. Landesgruppe Oberoesterreich**
Klammstrasse 7/1, A-4020 Linz, Austria.
- Oberoesterreichische F P O-Nachrichten fuer Freiheit und Recht. m. ISSN 0029-7534

**Freiheitlicher Oberoesterreichischer Landeslehrerverein**
Klammstr. 7-1, A-4020 Linz, Austria.
- Freiheitlicher Oberoesterreichischer Landeslehrerverein Zeitschrift. q. ISSN 0016-0903

**Fremdenverkehrsverband fuer Wien**
Kinderspitalgasse 5, A-1095 Vienna, Austria.
- Programm-Wien/Vienna/Vienne/Viena/Events Manifestations. m.
- Rendezvous Wien. s-a.

**Verlag Georg Fromme und Co.**
Spengergasse 39, A-1051 Vienna, Austria.
- Mikroskopie; Zentralblatt fuer mikroskopische Forschung und Methodik. bi-m. ISSN 0026-3702

**Die Furche Zeitschriften-Betriebsgesellschaft mbH und Co. KG**
Reichsratsstr. 17, A-1010 Vienna, Austria.
- Die Furche; freie kulturpolitische Wochenschrift. w. ISSN 0016-299X

**Verlag die Galerie GmbH**
Linke Wienzeile 36, A-1060 Vienna, Austria.
- Inpho Oesterreich. m. ISSN 0020-1707 (Oesterreichischer Photohaendlerverband)

**Galerie Sanct Lucas**
Josefsplatz 5, Palais Pallavicini, A-1010 Vienna, Austria.
- Galerie Sanct Lucas. Gemaelde Alter Meister. a.

**Gast- und Schankbetriebe**
- Oesterreichische Gastgewerbe-Zeitung. (pub. by Oesterreichischer Wirtschaftsverlag)

**Gazzetta Zeitschriften Ges. mbH**
Moellwaldplatz 5, A-1040 Vienna, Austria.
- Peace and the Sciences. q. ISSN 0031-3513 (International Institute for Peace)

**Gebetsliga**
Strozzigasse 8, A-1080 Vienna, Austria.
- Gebetsliga. Jahrbuch. a. ISSN 0081-5594

**Gemeinschaft der Wohnungseigentuemer**
Wiedner Guertel 1d, A-1100 Vienna, Austria.
• Gemeinschaft der Wohnungseigentuemer-Informationen. 6 per yr. ISSN 0016-6219

**Geographisches Institut der Hochschule fuer Welthandel**
• Wiener Geographische Schriften. (pub. by Verlag Ferdinand Hirt GmbH)

**Geologische Bundesanstalt**
Rasumofskygasse 23, Postfach 154, A-1031 Vienna, Austria.
• Geologische Bundesanstalt, Vienna. Abhandlungen. irreg.
• Geologische Bundesanstalt, Vienna Jahrbuch. s-a. ISSN 0016-7800

**Geologische Gesellschaft in Wien**
Universitaet Str. 7, A-1010 Vienna, Austria.
• Geologische Gesellschaft. Vienna. Mitteilungen. 1-2 per yr. ISSN 0016-7843

**Gerold und Co.**
Graben 31, A-1011 Vienna, Austria
(and E. J. Brill, Antwerpener Str. 6-12, Leiden, Netherlands)
• Wiener Zeitschrift fuer die Kunde Suedasiens und Archiv fuer Indische Philosphie. a. ISSN 0084-0084 (Oesterreichische Akademie der Wissenschaften. Kommission fuer Sprachen und Kulturen Sued- und Ostasiens) (Co-sponsor: Universitaet Wien. Indologisches Institut)

**Geschichtsverein fuer Kaernten**
Museumgasse 2, A-9020 Klagenfurt, Austria.
• Archiv fuer Vaterlaendische Geschichte und Topographie. irreg. ISSN 0003-9462
• Aus Forschung und Kunst. (pub. by Rudolf Habelt Verlag GW)
• Carinthia 1; Zeitschrift fuer geschichtliche Landeskunde von Kaernten. q. ISSN 0008-6606

**Gesellschaft der Freunde Carnuntums**
Mariahilferstr. 1, 1060 Vienna, Austria.
• Verein der Freunde Carnuntums. Mitteilungen. 14 per yr. ISSN 0042-3750

**Gesellschaft der Freunde der Oesterreichischen Nationalbibliothek**
Josefsplatz 1, A-1014 Vienna, Austria.
• Biblos; Oesterreichische Zeitschrift fuer Buch- und Bibliothekswesen, Dokumentation, Bibliographie und Bibliophilie. q. ISSN 0006-2022

**Gesellschaft der Freunde der Stadt Linz**
Bancalariweg 2, A-4020 Linz, Austria.
• Oberoesterreichisches Reise-Journal; Fachzeitschrift fuer Tourismus. bi-m. ISSN 0029-7569

**Gesellschaft der Redakteure der Neuen Freien Presse**
Museumstr. 5, A-1070 Vienna, Austria.
• Neue Freie Presse. m.

**Gesellschaft fuer das Oeffentliche Haushaltswesen**
Herrengasse 11, A-1010 Vienna, Austria.
• Das Oeffentliche Haushaltswesen in Oesterreich. q. ISSN 0029-8581

**Gesellschaft fuer Ganzheitsforschung**
Franz-Klein-Gasse 1, A-1190 Vienna, Austria.
• Schrifttumsspiegel. q.
• Zeitschrift fuer Ganzheitsforschung. q. ISSN 0044-2763

**Gesellschaft fuer Griechische und Hellenistische Rechtsgeschichte**
• Gesellschaft fuer Griechische und Hellenistische Rechtsgeschichte. Akten. (pub. by Hermann Boehlaus Nachf.)

**Gesellschaft fuer Klassische Philologie in Innsbruck**
• Acta Philologica Aenipontana. (pub. by Universitaetsverlag Wagner)

**Gesellschaft fuer Natur, Technik und Wirtschaft**
• Universum. (pub. by Verlag Ferdinand Berger und Soehne OHG)

**Gesellschaft fuer Ost- und Suedostkunde**
Bismarckstr. 5, A-4020 Linz, Austria.
• Ostpanorama. a. ISSN 0078-6896
• Ostpanorama. Sonderausgabe. a.

**Gesellschaft Mariae in Oesterreich und Deutschland**
Scheidlstr. 2, A-1180 Vienna, Austria.
• Marianist. 5 per yr. ISSN 0025-3014

**Gesellschaft zur Foerderung der Kunststofftechnik**
• Oesterreichische Kunststoff-Zeitschrift. (pub. by Verlag Lorenz)

**Gesellschaft zur Foerderung der Unabhaengigen Presse**
Favoritenstr. 56, A-1040 Vienna, Austria.
• Europa-Korrespondenz; Monatsinformationen. m. ISSN 0014-2522

**Gewerbliches Guetertransportwesen Oesterreichs**
• Strassengueterverkehr. (pub. by Oesterreichischer Wirtschaftsverlag)

**Gewerkschaft der Arbeiter in der Land und Forst-Wirtschaft**
Loquaiplatz 9, A-1061 Vienna, Austria.
• Landbote; Fachblatt der Gewerkschaft der Land- und Forstarbeiter. m. ISSN 0023-7744

**Gewerkschaft der Oeffentlich Bediensteten. Bundessektion Hoehere Schule**
Lackierergasse 7, A-1090 Vienna, Austria.
• Handbuch der Allgemeinbildenden Hoeheren Schulen Oesterreichs. biennial.

**Gewerkschaft Druck und Papier**
Seidengasse 15, A-1070 Vienna, Austria.
• Graphische Revue Oesterreichs; Fachzeitschrift fuer das gesamte graphische Gewerbe. bi-m. ISSN 0017-3479
• Vorwaerts. m. ISSN 0042-8930

**Geyer-Edition**
Favoritenstr. 58, A-1040 Vienna, Austria.
• Zeitgeschichte. m.

**Globus-Verlag**
Hoechstaedtplatz 3, A-1200 Vienna, Austria.
• Weg und Ziel; Monatsschrift fuer Theorie und Praxis des Marxismus-Leninismus. m. ISSN 0043-2024

**Glueckstelle Mihalovits**
Wipplingerstr. 21, A-1013 Vienna, Austria.
• Hohe Bruecke. m. ISSN 0018-3245

**Dieter Goeschl Buch- und Zeitschriftenverlag**
Klopstockg. 34, A-1170 Vienna, Austria.
• Handbuch fuer die Sanitaetsberufe Oesterreich. a. ISSN 0073-0181
• Jahrbuch Krankenhaus. a. ISSN 0075-7063
• Oesterreichische Krankenhaus Zeitung. m. ISSN 0029-876X

**Alois Goeschl und Co.**
Trummelhofgasse 12, A-1190 Vienna, Austria.
• Jahrbuch fuer den Oesterreichischen Tierarzt. a. ISSN 0075-2606

**Buch und Offsetdruck W. Goetz**
Franzensbrueckenstr. 9, A-1020 Vienna, Austria.
• Wiener Tagebuch; Zeitschrift fuer Kultur und Politik. m. ISSN 0039-8934 (Verein der Freunde des Wiener Tagebuch)

**Grenzverlag**
Flossgasse 6, A-1025 Vienna, Austria.
• Finanzjournal mit Gebuehren-und Verkehrsteuerrundschau; Informationsorgan fuer Finanzdienst und Wirtschaft. m. ISSN 0015-2250
• Oesterreichische Zoll und Steuer Nachrichten; Informationsorgan fuer den Zoll-und Steuerdienst und fuer die Wirtschaft. s-m. ISSN 0029-9685

**Gruppe Revolutionaere Marxisten**
Postfach 354, A-1011 Vienna, Austria.
• Kommunistische Hefte. q.
• Rotfront. m.

**Dr. Wilhelm Hadmovsky,Ed. & Pub.**
Freyung 6/11, A-1010 Vienna, Austria.
• Oesterreichische Hoehere Schule. 5 per yr. ISSN 0029-9200 (Vereinigung christlicher Lehrer an den hoeheren Schulen Oesterreichs)

**F. M. Hammerle Textilwerke AG**
A-6850 Dornbirn, Austria.
• Dreihammer. bi-m. ISSN 0012-6071

**Handelskammer Niederoesterreich**
Herrengasse 10, A-1014 Vienna, Austria.
• Wirtschaftszahl. irreg. (1-2 per yr) ISSN 0510-5609

**Handelskammer Oberoesterreich**
Hessenplatz, A-4010 Linz, Austria.
• Baeuerlicher Ratgeber; Mitteilungsblatt von Handel und Gewerbe fuer die oberoesterreichische Landwirtschaft. 7 per yr. ISSN 0005-3872

**Franz Hanke, Editor and Publisher**
Laxenburgerstr. 5, 1100 Vienna, Austria.
• Neue Wort. m.

**Harmonikaverband Oesterreichs**
Steingasse 3, A-1030 Vienna, Austria.
• Harmonika. 5 per yr. ISSN 0017-7830 (Cosponsor: Gesellschaft zur Foerderung der Harmonikamusik)

**A. Hartleben**
Postfach 3, A-1014 Vienna, Austria.
• Food und Non- Food. w.

**Hauptverband der Graphischen Unternehmungen Oesterreichs**
Gruenangergasse 4, A-1010 Vienna, Austria.
• Graphische Unternehmungen Oesterreichs. Jahrbuch. a. ISSN 0075-2266

**Hauptverband der Oesterreichischen Sozialversicherungstraeger**
Traungasse 14-16, A-1037 Vienna, Austria.
• Oesterreichische Sozialversicherung. irreg.
• Soziale Sicherheit; Zeitschrift fuer die Oesterreichische Sozialversicherung. m. ISSN 0038-6065
• Statistisches Handbuch der Oesterreichischen Sozialversicherung. irreg.

**Hauptverband der Oesterreichischen Sparkassen**
P.O. Box 256, A-1011 Vienna, Austria.
• Hauptverband der Oesterreichischen Sparkassen. Jahresbericht. a.
• Der Sparefroh. (pub. by Sparkassenverlag Ges. m.b.H.)

**Hauptverband des Oesterreichischen Buchhandels**
Gruenangergasse, A-1010 Vienna, Austria.
• Anzeiger des Oesterreichischen Buchhandels. s-m. ISSN 0003-6277
• Anzeiger des Verbandes der Antiquare Oesterreichs. s-m. ISSN 0042-3610
• Buecher fuer Alle. a. ISSN 0067-0634
• Oesterreichische Bibliographie; Verzeichnis der oesterreichischen Neuerscheinungen. s-m. ISSN 0029-8913
• Das Oesterreichische Buch. a. ISSN 0078-3455

**Heimatland-Verlag**
V Margaretenstr. 114, A-1050 Vienna, Austria.
• Heimatland; Schrifttum aus Oesterreich. bi-m. ISSN 0017-9779
• Kulturgemeinschaft der Kreis. Mitteilungen. q. ISSN 0023-5229

**Verlag Dr. Adolf Heinrich**
Akademiestr. 3, A-1010 Vienna, Austria.
• Handbuch des Oeffentlichen Lebens in Oesterreich. a. ISSN 0440-2103

**Hennessen Verlag KG**
St. Julienstr. 35, A-5020 Salzburg, Austria.
• Oesterreichische Textil-Mitteilungen; Unabhaengige Fachzeitung fuer die gesamte Textilwirtschaft. w. ISSN 0029-9545

**Heraldisch-Genealogische Gesellschaft Adler**
Haarhof 4a, A-1010 Vienna, Austria.
• Adler; review for genealogy and heraldry. q. ISSN 0001-8260
• Heraldisch-Genealogische Gesellschaft Adler. Jahrbuch. irreg. ISSN 0073-1897

**Verlag Herder**
Wollzeile 33, A-1010 Vienna, Austria.
• Merleg; folyoiratok es konyvek szemleje. q. ISSN 0026-0126
• Oesterreichisches Archiv fuer Kirchenrecht. q. ISSN 0029-9820 (Institut fuer Kirchenrecht)
• Zeitschrift fuer katholische Theologie. q. ISSN 0044-2895 (Universitaet Innsbruck. Theologische Fakultaet)

**Verlag W. Herget**
Goldschlagstr. 40, A-1150 Vienna, Austria.
• Oesterreichische Bau-Wirtschaft. q. ISSN 0048-1416

**Herold Vereinigte Anzeigen-Gesellschaft M.B.H.**
Wipplingerstr. 14, A-1013 Vienna, Austria.
- Herold Export-Adressbuch von Oesterreich/
  Austrian Export Directory/Annuaire
  d'Exportation de l'Autriche/Anuario de
  Exportacion de Austria. a. ISSN 0531-5824

**Herz und Co.**
Hetzgasse 20, A-1030 Vienna, Austria.
- Oesterreichische Richterzeitung; organ der Richter
  und Staatsanwaelte Oesterreichs. m. (Vereinigung
  der Oesterreichischen Richter)

**Hilfsgemeinschaft Aller Menschen Guten Willens**
Webgasse 42, A-1060 Vienna, Austria.
- Lebe Dich Gesund; Zeitschrift zur
  Lebenserneuerung. bi-m. ISSN 0023-9879

**Hilfsgemeinschaft der Blinden und Sehschwachen
Oesterreichs**
Treustr. 9, A-1200 Vienna, Austria.
- Unser Schaffen. m. ISSN 0042-0492

**Hinterbruehl. Marktgemeinde Hinterbruehl.
Gemeindeamt**
Hauptstr. 66, A-2371 Hinterbruehl, Austria.
- Gemeindebote. 4-6 per yr. ISSN 0016-609X

**Verlag Ferdinand Hirt GmbH**
Widerhofergasse 8, Postfach 39, A-1094 Vienna,
Austria.
- Wiener Geographische Schriften. irreg., 1972, no.
  36-37. ISSN 0083-9957 (Geographisches Institut
  der Hochschule fuer Welthandel)

**Historischer Verein fuer Steiermark**
Wastlergasse 8, A-8010 Graz, Austria.
- Blaetter fuer Heimatkunde. q. ISSN 0006-4459

**Hochschule fuer Bodenkultur**
- Bodenkultur. (pub. by Oesterreichischer
  Agrarverlag)

**Hochschule fuer Bodenkultur. Forstliche Abteilung**
- Centralblatt fuer das Gesamte Forstwesen. (pub.
  by Oesterreichischer Agrarverlag)

**Hochschule fuer Sozial- und
Wirtschaftswissenschaften, Linz**
A-4045 Linz/Donau, Austria.
- Sozialforschung. Beitraege. a.

**Hochschule fuer Sozial- und
Wirtschaftswissenschaften, Linz. Oesterreichisches
Institut fuer Arbeitsmarkt Politik**
4045 Auhof, A-4045 Linz/Donau.
- Arbeitsmarkt Politik. irreg. ISSN 0587-1689

**Hoehere Graphische Bundes Lehr und
Versuchsanstalt**
Leyserstr. 6, A-1140 Vienna, Austria.
- G L V Mitteilungen. (Graphische Lehr und
  Versuchsanstalt) 1-2 per yr. ISSN 0016-3562

**Hoerbiger Institut**
- Hoerbiger Instituts Mitteilungen. (pub. by
  Emmerich Selinger, Ed. & Pub.)

**Brueder Hollinek**
Landstr. Hauptstr. 163, A-1030 Vienna, Austria.
- Acta Chirurgica Austriaca. 5 per yr. ISSN 0001-
  544X (Oesterreichische Gesellschaft fuer
  Chirurgie)
- Acta Medica Austriaca. m. (Wiener Gesellschaft
  fuer Innere Medizin) (Co-Sponsor:
  Oesterreichische Kardiologische Gesellschaft)
- Codices Manuscripti; Zeitschrift fuer
  Handschriftenkunde. 4 per yr.
- Museion. irreg. ISSN 0077-2208 (Oesterreichische
  Nationalbibliothek)
- Paracelsus; Archiv der praktischen Medizin. m.
  ISSN 0031-157X
- Schul-und Sportstaettenbau. q. ISSN 0036-7095
  (Oesterreichisches Institut fuer Schul-und
  Sportstaettenbau)
- Wiener Medizinische Wochenschrift. w. ISSN
  0043-5341

**Adolf Holzhausens Nachfolger**
Kandlgasse 19, A-1070 Vienna, Austria.
- Oesterreichische Zeitschrift fuer Onkologie. bi-m.

**Holzwarth und Berger**
Borseplatz 6, A-1010 Vienna, Austria.
- Buch und Bildung. bi-m. ISSN 0007-277X

**Hotel Verlag**
Leopold Steinergasse 50, A-1190 Vienna, Austria.
- Modernes Hotel; Hotel und Restaurant im Dienste
  des Fremdenverkehrs. m. ISSN 0026-8704

**Hubertusverlag**
Huetteldorfer Str. 26, A-1150 Vienna, Austria.
- St. Hubertus; aelteste oesterreichische Jagdzeitung.
  m. ISSN 0036-2875

**Illustrierte Rundschau der Gendarmerie**
3 Hauptstr. Nr. 68, A-1031 Vienna, Austria.
- Illustrierte Rundschau der Gendarmerie. m. ISSN
  0019-2511

**Industrie Zeitschriftenverlags Ges. m.b.H.**
Bauernmarkt 13, A-1010 Vienna, Austria.
- Metallbericht. m. ISSN 0047-6889
- Sozialpolitik und Arbeitsrecht. bi-m. ISSN 0038-
  6197 (Vereinigung Oesterreichischer Industrieller)

**Innung der Buchbinder, Kartonagewaren- und
Etuierzeuger**
- Oesterreichische Buchbinder, Kartonage-, Etui-,
  Kassetten- und Papierwarenerzeuger. (pub. by
  Julius Dressler Buch- und Zeitschriftenverlag)

**Institut fuer Angewandte Sozial und
Wirtschaftsforschung**
- Materialien zur Sozial- und Wirtschaftspolitik.
  (pub. by Jupiter Verlag GmbH)

**Institut fuer Bildungs- und Entwicklungsforschung**
Institute of Research in Education and
Development, Schottenbastei 6, A-1010 Vienna,
Austria.
- I B E Bulletin; Bildungsforschung-
  Entwicklungshilfe. q.

**Institut fuer Finanzwissenschaft und Steuerrecht**
Seilerstaette 24, A-1010 Vienna, Austria.
- Institut fuer Finanzwissenschaft und Steuerrecht.
  Mitteilungsblatt. Gelbe Briefe. 8 per yr.
- Steuer-Auslanddienst. irreg., no. 90, 1974.

**Institut fuer Gesellschaftspolitik**
- Institut fuer Gesellschaftspolitik. Mitteilungen.
  (pub. by Sensen-Verlag Ernst Schwarcz)

**Institut fuer Gewerbeforschung**
Tuerkenschanzstr. 18, A-1180 Vienna, Austria.
- Institut fuer Gewerbeforschung, Vienna.
  Taetigkeitsbericht. a. ISSN 0073-8468

**Institut fuer Industrieforschung**
Box 68, A-1014 Vienna, Austria.
- Betrieb und Absatz. q. ISSN 0005-9943

**Institut fuer Kirchenrecht**
- Oesterreichisches Archiv fuer Kirchenrecht. (pub.
  by Verlag Herder)

**Institut fuer Oesterreichische Kunstforschung**
- Wiener Jahrbuch fuer Kunstgeschichte. (pub. by
  Hermann Boehlaus Nachf.)

**Institut fuer Oesterreichkunde**
- Oesterreich in Geschichte und Literatur (mit
  Geographie) (pub. by Carl Ueberreuter)

**Institut fuer Sozialpolitik und Sozialreform (Dr. Karl
Kummer-Institut)**
Ebendorferstr. 6/4, A-1010 Vienna, Austria.
- Gesellschaft und Politik. q. ISSN 0016-9099

**Institut fuer Voelkerkunde**
Universitatstr. 7, A-1010 Vienna, Austria.
- R E/Review of Ethnology. s-m. ISSN 0048-6507

**Institut fuer Wissenschaft und Kunst**
Museumstr. 5, A-1070 Vienna, Austria.
- Institut fuer Wissenschaft und Kunst.
  Mitteilungen. 4 per yr. ISSN 0020-2320

**Institut "Haus der Barmherzigkeit"**
Vinzenzg. 2-6, A-1180 Vienna, Austria.
- Barmherzigkeit; Blaetter fuer die Freunde des
  Hauses der Barmherzigkeit. q. ISSN 0005-5999

**Institute for Advanced Studies, Vienna**
- International Journal of Game Theory. (pub. by
  Physica-Verlag Rudolf Liebing GmbH und Co.
  GW)

**Institutum Canarium**
Postfach 109, A-5400 Hallein, Austria.
- Almogaren. a.

- Institutum Canarium. I. C. Nachrichten. irreg., no.
  17, 1974.

**International Association for Cereal Chemistry**
Schmidgasse 3-7, A-2320 Schwechat, Austria.
- Internatio nal Association for Cereal Chemistry.
  Working and Discussion Meetings Reports.
  biennial; 8th, Vienna, 1974. ISSN 0074-1450

**International Association for the Exchange of
Students for Technical Experience**
c/o Rolf Kratchowill, Secretary, Tuerkenstr. 4/11,
A-1090 Vienna, Austria.
- I A E S T E. Annual Report. irreg. ISSN 0538-
  4427

**International Atomic Energy Agency**
For publications of this agency see section for
UNITED NATIONS

**International Board on Books for Young People**
- Bookbird. (pub. by Verlag fuer Jugend und Volk)

**International Committee on Urgent Anthropological
and Ethnological Research**
c/o Institut fuer Voelkerkunde, Universitaetsstrasse
7, A-1010 Vienna, Austria.
- International Committee on Urgent
  Anthropological and Ethnological Research.
  Bulletin. a. ISSN 0538-5865

**International Egg Commission**
Hietzinger Kai, 125, A-1130 Vienna, Austria.
- International Egg Commission. Market Review
  Situation & Outlook Report. s-a. ISSN 0020-661X
- International Egg Commission. Six-Monthly
  Statistical Bulletin. s-a. ISSN 0020-6628

**International Falcon Movement**
Rauhensteingasse 5, P. O. Box 583, 1011 Vienna,
Austria.
- International Falcon Movement. Conference
  Reports. irreg., 1970, 11th, Germany. ISSN 0074-
  5790

**International Falcon Movement - Socialist
Educational International**
Ruahensteingasse 5, A-1011 Vienna, Austria.
- I F M - S E I Bulletin/International Falcon
  Movement. 10 per yr. ISSN 0018-9715

**International Information Centre for Terminology,
Vienna**
- Infoterm Series. (pub. by Verlag Dokumentation
  GW)

**International Institute for Applied Systems Analysis**
Laxenburg, Austria.
- I I A S A. Annual Report. a.

**International Institute for Children's Literature and
Reading Research**
- Jugend und Buch. (pub. by Karl Werner)

**International Institute for Peace**
- Peace and the Sciences. (pub. by Gazzetta
  Zeitschriften Ges. mbH)

**International Jazz Federation**
Box 671, Andreasgasse 10/17, A-1011 Vienna,
Austria.
- Jazz Forum. bi-m. ISSN 0021-5635 (Co-sponsor:
  Polish Jazz Society)
- Swinging Newsletter. m.

**International Music Centre**
Lothringstr. 20, A-1030 Vienna, Austria.
- I M Z Information. a. ISSN 0538-8783

**International Society for Electrosleep and
Electroanaesthesia**
Chirurgische Univaersitaetsklinik, A-8032 Graz,
Austria.
- I E S A Informations. irreg. ISSN 0539-0230

**International Society for Jazz Research (Graz,
Austria)**
- Jazzforschung/Jazz Research. (pub. by Universal
  Edition AG)

**International Society for Research on the Moors**
Graben 2, Postf. 67, A-4810 Gmunden, Austria.
● International Society for Research on the Moors.
Report of Congress. irreg., 1970, 10th Rome.
ISSN 0074-8471

**International Speleological Union**
c/o Hubert Trimmel, Sec.-Gen., Bundesdenkmalamt,
Hofburg, Saeulenstiege, A-1010 Vienna, Austria.
● U I S Bulletin. (Union Internationale de
Speleologie) s-a.

**International Union of Socialist Youth**
Neustiftgasse, A-1070 Vienna, Austria.
● I U S Y Bulletin. irreg.

**Internationale Lenau-Gesellschaft**
Lerchenfelderstr. 14, A-1080 Vienna, Austria.
● Lenau-Forum; Vierteljahresschrift fuer
vergleichende Literaturforschung. q. ISSN 0024-
0788

**Internationale Stefan Zweig-Gesellschaft**
Sandwirtgasse 21, A-1060 Vienna, Austria.
● Archiv der Internationalen Stefan Zweig-
Gesellschaft. s-a. ISSN 0003-8873

**Internationale Stiftung Mozarteum**
Schwarzstr. 26, Salzburg, Austria.
● Internationale Stiftung Mozarteum. Mitteilungen.
s-a. ISSN 0020-9325
● Mozart-Jahrbuch. (pub. by Baerenreiter-Verlag
GW)

**Internationale Werbegesellschaft m.b.H.**
Hoher Markt 12, A-1010 Vienna, Austria.
● Austria Export. 4 per yr. ISSN 0005-0490
(Bundeskammer der gewerblichen Wirtschaft)

**Internationaler Genfer Verban - Landesteil
Oesterreich**
● Oesterreichisches Hotel-und Gastronomie-Journal.
(pub. by Studioverlag Beyer)

**Internationales Esperanto-Museum in Wien**
Hofburg, A-1010 Vienna, Austria.
● Internacia Esperanto-Muzeo en Wien. Informilo.
q. ISSN 0020-5710

**Internationales Forschungszentrum fuer Grundfragen
der Wissenschaften, Salzburg**
● Internationales Forschungszentrum fuer
Grundfragen der Wissenschaften, Salzburg.
Forschungsgespraeche. (pub. by
Universitaetsverlag Anton Pustet)

**Internationales Institut fuer den Frieden**
Moellwaldplatz 5, A-1040 Vienna, Austria.
● Internationales Institut fuer den Frieden. Cultural
Anniversaries Series. irreg. ISSN 0574-6817

**Internationales Musikzentrum**
Lothringerstr. 20, A-1030 Vienna, Austria.
● I M Z Bulletin. 10 per yr. ISSN 0019-0071

**Internationales Wollsekretariat Geschaeftsstelle fuer
Oesterreich**
Rotenturmstr. 5-9, A-1011 Vienna, Austria.
● Modetelegramm. m. ISSN 0026-8755

**Israelitische Kultusgemeinde Wien**
Bauernfeldgasse 4, A-1190 Vienna, Austria.
● Die Gemeinde. m. ISSN 0021-2334

**Jesuitenkolleg**
Sillgasse 6, A-6021 Innsbruck, Austria.
● Sendbote des Herzens Jesu. m. ISSN 0037-2129

**Joanneum. Abteilung fuer Botanik**
Raubergasse 10, A-8010 Graz, Austria.
● Joanneum. Abteilung fuer Botanik. Mitteilungen.
irreg.

**Joanneum. Abteilung fuer Geologie, Palaeontologie
und Bergbau**
Raubergasse 10, A-8010 Graz, Austria.
● Joanneum. Abteilung fuer Geologie,
Palaeontologie und Bergbau. Mitteilungen. irreg.

**Joanneum. Abteilung fuer Zoologie**
Raubergasse 10, A-8010 Graz, Austria.
● Joanneum. Abteilung fuer Zoologie. Mitteilungen.
irreg; 2-4 per yr.

**Wilfried Josch, Editor and Publisher**
Anton-Anderer-Platz 2/2, A-1210 Vienna, Austria.
● Blaetter fuer Philosophische Ethik. fortn.

**Jugend und Volk Verlagsgesellschaft**
Tiefer Graben 7, A-1014 Vienna, Austria.
● Elternblatt; du und dein Kind. m. ISSN 0013-
6441
● Oesterreichische Gemeinde-Zeitung. s-m. ISSN
0029-912X (Oesterreichischer Staedtebund)
● Ver Sacrum; Neue Hefte fuer Kunst und Literatur.
irreg. ISSN 0083-5463

**Junge Generation in der Volkspartei**
Wollzeile 24, 1010 Vienna, Austria.
● Initiative. bi-m. (prep. by its Jugendklub Innere
Stadt)

**Jupiter Verlag GmbH**
Robertgasse 2, A-1020 Vienna, Austria.
● Austro-Motor; Internationale Auto- und Motor-
Rundschau. m. ISSN 0005-0539
● Austro-Motor-Kalender. a. ISSN 0005-0547
● Handelsregister Oesterreich; mit dem genauen
Wortlaut der amtlichen Protokollierung. a.
● Made in Austria. a. ISSN 0076-2105
● Materialien zur Sozial- und Wirtschaftspolitik.
irreg. ISSN 0506-9122 (Institut fuer Angewandte
Sozial und Wirtschaftsforschung)
● West-Ost-Journal; unabhaengige
wirtschaftspolitische Zeitschrift. 6 per yr. ISSN
0043-2954 (Donaueuropaeisches Institut)

**Kaernten. Amt der Kaerntner Landesregierung**
Arnulfplatz 1, A-9010 Klagenfurt, Austria.
● Kaerntner Gemeindeblatt. (pub. by Kaertner
Druck- und Verlags-Gesellschaft mbH)
● Kaerntner Landes-Zeitung. w. ISSN 0022-7579
● Landesgesetzblatt fuer Kaernten. (pub. by
Kaertner Druck- und Verlags-Gesellschaft mbH)

**Kaernten. Amt der Kaerntner Landesregierung.
Abteilung Landesplanung**
Wulfengasse 13, A-9010 Klagenfurt, Austria.
● Kaerntner Naturschutzblaetter. a. ISSN 0022-7595

**Kaernten. Landesmuseum fuer Kaernten**
Museumgasse 2, A-9020 Klagenfurt, Austria.
● Kaernten, Landesmuseum. Buchreihe. ISSN 0007-
280X
● Kaerntner Heimatleben. ISSN 0022-7560
● Kaerntner Museumsschriften. ISSN 0022-7587

**Kaerntner Jaegerschaft**
Bahnhofstr. 38B, A-9020 Klagenfurt, Austria.
● Kaerntner Jaeger. q.

**Kaertner Druck- und Verlags-Gesellschaft mbH**
Viktringer Ring 28, A-9010 Klagenfurt, Austria.
● Kaerntner Gemeindeblatt. 15 per yr. approx. ISSN
0022-7552 (Kaernten. Amt der Kaerntner
Landesregierung)
● Landesgesetzblatt fuer Kaernten. irreg. ISSN
0023-7892 (Kaernten. Amt der Kaerntner
Landesregierung)

**Zeitungsverlag Kahn und Co. KG**
Wallnerstr. 8, Postfach 66, A-1014 Vienna, Austria.
● Der Neve Kaufmann; das unabhaengige fachblatt
fuer den oesterreichischen handel. s-m. ISSN
0028-324X

**Kammer der Gewerblichen Wirtschaft fuer Salzburg**
Julius-Raab-Platz 1, A-5027 Salzburg, Austria.
● Salzburger Wirtschaft. w. ISSN 0036-3677

**Kammer der Gewerblichen Wirtschaft fuer Vorarlberg**
Wichnergasse 9, 6800 Feldkirch, Austria.
● Vorarlbergs Wirtschaft aktuell. w. (Co-sponsor:
Vorarlberger Handelskammer)

**Kapfenberg. Stadtgemeinde Kapfenberg**
8605 Kapfenberg, Austria.
● Amtsblatt der Stadt Kapfenberg. q. ISSN 0003-
2239

**Kastner und Oehler**
Sackstr. 7-13, 8012 Graz, Austria.
● Kastner & Oehler Firmen-Zeitung. q. ISSN 0022-
9253

**Katechetisches Institut**
Stephanspl. 3-III, A-1010 Vienna, Austria.
● Christlich-Paedagogische Blaetter; Zeitschrift fuer
den katechetischen Dienst. bi-m. ISSN 0009-5761

**Katholische Filmkommission fuer Oesterreich**
Singerstr. 7, Vienna 1, Austria.
● Filmschau. w. ISSN 0015-1696

**Katholische Hochschuljugend Oesterreichs**
Ebendorferstr. 8/3, A-1010 Vienna, Austria.
● Katholische Hochsc..uljugend Oesterreichs-
Blaetter; Zeitschrift fuer studierende. irreg. (8 per
yr.) ISSN 0022-9393

**Katholische Jungschar Oesterreichs**
Johannesgasse 16, A-1010 Vienna, Austria.
● Dynamic. q. ISSN 0014-0317

**Katholische Lehrerschaft Oesterreichs**
Stephansplatz 5-2-4, A-1010 Vienna, Austria.
● K L O E Impulse. q.

**Katholische Oesterreichische Studentenverbindung
"Borussia" im MKV**
Bandgasse 31/8, A-1070 Vienna 7, Austria.
● Borussen-Echo; Monatsblatt mit freier
Meinungsaeusserung. m. ISSN 0006-7865

**Katholischer Familienverband Oesterreichs**
● Ehe und Familie. (pub. by Ehe und Familie
Zeitschriftenverlagsgesellschaft m.b.H.)

**Katholisches Frauenwerk in Oesterreich**
Stephanspl. 6-V, A-1010 Vienna, Austria.
● Katholische Frauenbewegung Oesterreichs.
Fuehrungsblatt. q. ISSN 0022-9377

**Katholisches Jugendwerk Oesterreichs**
● Die Wende. (pub. by Styria Verlag)

**Eugen Ketterl**
Anastasius-Grun-Gasse 43, A-1180 Vienna, Austria.
● Farbenkreis, Oesterreichische Malerzeitung. m.
ISSN 0014-7737 (Landesinnung Wien der Maler,
Anstreicher und Lackierer)

**Verlag A. Kirsch**
Kaiserstr 8-10, A-1072 Vienna, Austria.
● Neue Illustrierte Wochenschau; das Blatt fuer
Alle. w. ISSN 0028-3223
● Perchtoldsdorfer Pfarrbote. m. ISSN 0031-5141
(Pfarre Perchtoldsdorf)
● R Z-Illustrierte Romanzeitung. w. ISSN 0033-
7218

**Verlag Therese Kirschner GmbH**
Singerstr. 27, A-1010 Vienna, Austria.
● Architekt; Zeitschrift oesterreichischer
Architekten. q. ISSN 0044-8672

**Klagenfurt. Magistrat der Landeshauptstadt
Klagenfurt**
Rathaus, A-9010 Klagenfurt, Austria.
● Klagenfurt; mitteilungesblatt der landeshauptstadt.
fortn. ISSN 0023-2017

**Klub der Kinoamateure Oesterreichs**
Neubaugasse 36, A-1070 Vienna, Austria.
● Der Oesterreichische Filmamateur. bi-m. ISSN
0029-9057

**Klub Slovenischer Studenten in Wien**
Albertgasse 48, A-1080 Vienna, Austria.
● Klub Slowenischer Studenten in Wien.
Information. s-a. ISSN 0023-2203

**Manfred Kmoch**
Parkring 45, Bisamberg, Austria.
● Korneuburger Kulturnachrichten; fuer die Bezirke
Korneuburg und Stockerau. irreg. ISSN 0023-
4087

**Ed. & Pub. Horst Knapp**
Bankgasse 1, A-1010 Vienna, Austria.
● Finanznachrichten. w. ISSN 0015-2269

**Kommission fuer Literaturwissenschaft.**
● Oesterreichische Akademie der Wissenschaften.
Kommission fuer Literaturwissenschaft.
Veroeffentlichungen. (pub. by Verlag der
Oesterreichischen Akademie der Wissenschaften)

**Kommissionsverlag der Oesterreichischen
Staatsdruckerei**
Rennweg 12a, A-1037 Vienna, Austria.
● Austria. Bundesamt fuer Eich- und
Vermessungswesen. Amtsblatt fuer das Eichwesen.
irreg (8 per yr.)
● Austria. Statistisches Zentralamt. Erhebung der
Land-und Forstwirtschaftlichen Arbeitskraefte.
irreg.
● Austria. Statistisches Zentralamt.
Jugendwohlfahrtspflege. a.
● Austria. Statistisches Zentralamt. Mikrozensus;
Jahresergebnisse. a.

• Austria. Statistisches Zentralamt. Oeffentliche
  Fuersorge. a.

**Kommunalwissenschaftliches Dokumentationszentrum**
  Linzer Str. 452, A-1140 Vienna, Austria.
• Index Kommunalwissenschaftlicher Literatur:
  Buecher/Index of Publications on Local
  Government and Urban Studies: Books. a.

**Kommunistischer Bund Wien**
  Halbgasse 12, 1070 Vienna, Austria.
• Kommunist; theoretisches Organ des
  Kommunistischen Bundes Wien. irreg.

**Verlag Adolf Kosel**
  Postfach 55, A-1095 Vienna, Austria.
• Austria-Philatelist; Oesterreichische Briefmarken-
  Zeitung. q. ISSN 0005-0512

**Matthias Kraintschan, Ed. & Pub.**
  Stumpergasse 63-14, A-1060 Vienna, Austria.
• Die Ergokratische Schule; fuer Neu
  Testamentliche Denkungsart. bi-m.

**Kriegsopferverband Steiermark**
  Burggasse 4, A-8011 Graz, Austria.
• Steirische Kriegsopfer Zeitung. q. ISSN 0039-1085

**H. Kuchling**
  Linzerstr. 392, A-1014 Vienna, Austria.
• Kontur; Zeitschrift fuer Kunsttheorie. 10 per yr.
  ISSN 0023-3757

**Hubert Fabian Kulterer, Editor and Publisher**
  Unter-Meidlinger Str. 16-18, A-1120 Vienna,
  Austria.
• Eroeffnungen; Magazin fuer Literatur & bildende
  Kunst. q. ISSN 0014-0252

**Kultur**
  Pointengasse 22, A-1170 Vienna, Austria.
• Kultur/Art et Culture; monde-information. m.
  ISSN 0023-5113

**Kunsthistorisches Museum in Wien**
• Kunsthistorische Sammlungen in Wien. Jahrbuch.
  (pub. by Verlag Anton Schroll und Co.)

**Kuratorium fuer Verkehrssicherheit**
  Oelzeltgasse 3, A-1030 Vienna, Austria.
• Kuratorium fuer Verkehrssicherheit. Kleine
  Fachbuchreihe. irreg., no. 12, 1972. ISSN 0075-
  7306

**Kuratorium fuer Verkehrssicherheit.
Verkehrspsychologisches Institut**
  Oelzeltgasse 3, A-1031 Vienna, Austria.
• Verkehrspsychologischer Informationsdienst. 2-3
  per yr. ISSN 0042-4048

**Verlag J. Lachner und Co.**
  Kohlmarkt 11, A-1014 Vienna, Austria.
• Neue Mode - Frau und Mutter; die grosse
  Frauenzeitschrift fuer Oesterreich. fortn. ISSN
  0016-0199

**Musikverlag Elisabeth Lafite**
  Hegelgasse 13/22, 1010 Vienna 1, Austria
  (and Oesterreichischer Bundesverlag,
  Schwarzenbergstr. 5, 1015 Vienna 1, Austria)
• Beitraege zur Harmonikalen Grundlagenforschung.
  irreg., no. 6, 1974. ISSN 0067-5067
• Oesterreichische Komponisten des XX.
  Jahrunderts. irreg. ISSN 0078-3501
• Oesterreichische Musikzeitschrift. m. ISSN 0029-
  9316
• Wiener Musikhochschule. Publikationen. irreg.,
  no. 6, 1974. ISSN 0084-0017

**Landes-Obst-und Weinbauverein fuer Steiermark**
  Hamerlinggasse 3, A-8010 Graz, Austria.
• Obst- und Weinbau. m. ISSN 0029-7771

**Landesinnung Wien der Friseure**
• Der Oesterreichische Friseur. (pub. by Hans Bulla
  und Sohn)

**Landesinnung Wien der Graphischen Gewerbe**
  Gruenangergasse 4, A-1050 Vienna, Austria.
• Das Oesterreichische Graphische Gewerbe. m.
  ISSN 0029-9170

**Landesinnung Wien der Maler, Anstreicher und
Lackierer**
• Farbenkreis, Oesterreichische Malerzeitung. (pub.
  by Eugen Ketterl)

**Landesinnung Wien der Spengler und Kupferschmiede**
  Gruengasse 27, Vienna 5, Austria.
• Oesterreichische Spengler und Kupferschmied;
  offizielles Fachorgan der Bundesinnung. m. ISSN
  0029-9499

**Landestheater**
  Promenade 39, A-4010 Linz, Austria.
• Linzer Theaterzeitung. m. ISSN 0024-4139

**Landesverband der Heimat und Trachtenvereine fuer
Tirol**
  Langstrasse 46, A-6020 Innsbruck, Austria.
• Trachtler. 3 per yr.

**Landesverein fuer Hoehlenkunde in der Steiermark**
  Brandhofgasse 18, A-8010 Graz, Austria.
• Landesverein fuer Hoehlenkunde in der
  Steiermark. Mitteilungen. q.

**Lehrerbund der O V P Steiermark**
  Keplerstr. 92, A-8020 Graz, Austria.
• Beruf und Gesinnung. m.(except July & Aug.)
  ISSN 0005-9471

**Verlag B. M. Leitner**
  Riemergasse 13, A-1010 Vienna, Austria.
• Tafelfreuden; Gastronomie & Gastlichkeit-mit "die
  Gastronomie Oesterreichs". bi-m.

**Industrieverlag Peter Linde GmbH**
  Dominikanerbastei 10, A-1010 Vienna, Austria.
• Oesterreichische Steuer und Wirtschaftskartei;
  Kommunikation, Information, Dokumentation. s-
  m. ISSN 0029-9510

**Linz. Archiv der Stadt Linz**
  Hauptplatz 1, Rathaus, A-4010 Linz, Austria.
• Historisches Jahrbuch der Stadt Linz. biennial.
  ISSN 0440-9736

**Linz. Magistrat**
  Annagasse 2-4, A-4010 Linz, Austria.
• Linzer Woche. (pub. by Rudolf Trauner Verlag)
• Stadt Linz; Amtsblatt der Landeshauptstadt Linz.
  s-m. ISSN 0038-8971

**Verlag Lorenz**
  Ebendorferstr. 10, A-1010 Vienna, Austria.
• Giesserei Rundschau. q. ISSN 0016-979X (Verein
  Oesterreichischer Giessereifachleute) (Co-Sponsor:
  Fachverband der Giessereiindustrie und des
  Oesterreichischen Giesserei Institutes)
• Landmaschinen-Handwerk-Handel. m. ISSN 0023-
  7973 (Bundesberufsgruppen des
  Landmaschinenhandels und
  Landmaschinenhandwerks Oesterreichs)
• Oesterreichische Kunststoff-Zeitschrift. bi-m.
  (Gesellschaft zur Foerderung der
  Kunststofftechnik)

**Ludwig Boltzmann-Institut fuer
Umweltwissenschaften und Naturschutz**
  Peinrichstr. 5, A-8010 Graz, Austria.
• Ludwig Boltzmann-Institut fuer
  Umweltwissenschaften und Naturschutz.
  Mitteilungen. irreg.

**Erika Lux Verlag**
  Mariahilferstr. 62, A-1070 Vienna, Austria.
• Oesterreichischer Wohnungs- Geschaefts- und
  Realitaeten-Anzeiger; Inseratenzeitung fuer alle
  bundeslaender. m. ISSN 0029-9804

**Manzsche Verlags- und Universitaetsbuchhandlung**
  Kohlmarkt 16, Postfach 163, A-1014 Vienna,
  Austria.
• Gesamtregister mit den Rechtssaetzen und
  Fundstellen der Entscheidungen der Zeitschrift
  fuer Verkehrsrecht. irreg.
• Index der Rechtsmittelentscheidungen und des
  Schrifttums. a.
• Oesterreichische Blaetter fuer Gewerblichen
  Rechtsschutz und Urheberrecht. bi-m. ISSN 0029-
  8921 (Oesterreichische Vereinigung fuer
  Gewerblichen Rechtsschutz und Urheberrecht)
• Oesterreichische Juristen-Zeitung. s-m. ISSN
  0029-9251
• Oesterreichische Notariats-Zeitung. m. ISSN
  0029-9340 (Oesterreichische Notariatskammer)
• Oesterreichische Bank-Archiv. m. ISSN 0029-
  9839 (Oesterreichische Bankwissenschaftliche
  Gesellschaft)
• Wiener Rechtswissenschaftliche Studien. irreg., no.
  14, 1974. ISSN 0084-0025 (Universitaet Wien.
  Institut fuer Rechtsvergleichung) (Co-Sponsor:
  Oesterreichische Gesellschaft fuer
  Rechtsvergleichung)

• Zeitschrift fuer Arbeitsrecht und Sozialrecht. bi-m.
  ISSN 0044-2321 (Bundeskammer der
  Gewerblichen Wirtschaft)
• Zeitschrift fuer Rechtsvergleichung. q.
  (Universitaet Wien. Institut fuer
  Rechtsvergleichung) (Co-Sponsor:
  Oesterreichische Gesellschaft fuer
  Rechtsvergleichung)
• Zeitschrift fuer Verkehrsrecht. m. ISSN 0044-3662

**Mariahilf, Pfarre**
  Barnabitengasse 14, 1060 Vienna, Austria.
• Mariahilfer Pfarrbote. q. ISSN 0025-2999

**Marktgemeinde**
  Hauptstr. 17, Leobersdorf, Bezirk Baden, Austria.
• Marktgemeinde Loebersdorf. Amtliches
  Mitteilungsblatt. m. ISSN 0003-2182

**Verlag Wilhelm Maudrich**
  Franz Josefs Kai 23, A-1010 Vienna, Austria.
• Probleme der Ernaehrungs-und
  Lebensmittelwissenschaft. irreg. (Oesterreichische
  Gesellschaft fuer Ernaehrungsforschung)

**Mechitharisten-Congregation in Wien**
  Mechitharistengasse 4, A-1070 Vienna, Austria.
• Handes Amsorya; Zeitschrift fuer armenische
  Philologie. q. ISSN 0017-7377

**Merkur Wechselseitige Versicherungsanstalt**
  Neutorgasse 57, A-8010 Graz, Austria.
• Merkur Magazin fuer Volksgesundheit. q. ISSN
  0026-010X

**Metaphysische Rundschau**
  Fuchtshallergasse 4/25, A-1090 Vienna, Austria.
• Metaphysische Rundschau. irreg. ISSN 0076-6720

**Missionare von Mariannhill**
  Riedegg 1, A-4210 Gallneukirchen, Austria.
• Mariannhill. bi-m. ISSN 0025-3022

**Moorbad Neydharting**
  Pfarrplatz 3-4, A-4010 Linz, Austria.
• Neydhartinger Moorpost. irreg. ISSN 0028-9620

**Mozartgemeinde Wien**
  Metternichgasse 8, A-1030 Vienna, Austria.
• Wiener Figaro. a.

**Verlag Hermann Mucke. Astronomisches Buero**
  Sanettystr. 3, A-1080 Vienna, Austria.
• Der Sternenbote; Monatsschrift fuer Oesterreichs
  Amateurastronomen. m. ISSN 0039-1271

**Otto Mueller Verlag**
  Ernest-Thunstr. 11, A-5021 Salzburg, Austria.
• Bild des Menschen in der Wissenschaft. irreg.
  ISSN 0067-8570
• Kairos; Zeitschrift fuer Religionswissenschaft und
  Theologie. q. ISSN 0022-7757
• Literatur und Kritik. 10 per yr. ISSN 0024-466X

**Mundartfreunde Oesterreichs**
  Liebiggasse 5, A-1010 Vienna, Austria.
• Mundartfreunde Oesterreichs. Mitteilungen. s-a.
  ISSN 0027-3228

**Museum fuer Voelkerkunde**
  Neue Hofburg, A-1014 Vienna, Austria.
• Archiv fuer Voelkerkunde. (pub. by Wilhelm
  Braumueller Universitaets-Verlagsbuchhandlung
  GmbH)
• Wiener Voelkerkundliche Mitteilungen. a. ISSN
  0084-0068 (Oesterreichische Ethnologische
  Gesellschaft)

**Museumsverein Alsergrund**
  Waehringer Str. 43, A-1090 Vienna, Austria.
• Das Heimatmuseum Alsergrund. q. ISSN 0017-
  9809

**N O I International**
  Morrestrasse 13, A-9020 Klagenfurt, Austria.
• N O I International; Mensch, Gesellschaft, Kultur,
  Umwelt. q.

**Naturhistorisches Museum in Wien**
  Burgring 7, A-1014 Vienna, Austria.
• Naturhistorisches Museum in Wien. Annalen. a.
  ISSN 0083-6133
• Naturhistorisches Museum in Wien. Flugblatt.
  irreg. ISSN 0083-6141
• Naturhistorisches Museum in Wien.
  Monatsprogramm. m. ISSN 0028-095X

- Naturhistorisches Museum in Wien. Neue
  Denkschriften. (pub. by Verlag Ferdinand Berger
  und Soehne OHG)

**Naturkundliche Station der Stadt Linz**
Roseggerstr. 22, A-4020 Linz, Austria.
- Apollo. q. ISSN 0003-6528

**Verlag Neue Physik**
Mollardgasse 8, Vienna 6, Austria.
- Neue Physik; Zeitschrift fuer die Gebiete der
  Atom- und Strahlungsphysik. 4 per yr. ISSN
  0028-3312

**Verlag Neue Technik**
Walfischgasse 15, A-1010 Vienna, Austria.
- Bestands-Statistik der Kraftfahrzeuge in
  Oesterreich. a. ISSN 0067-6306 (Austria.
  Oesterreichisches Statistisches Zentralamt)

**Neues Leben**
A-4822 Bad Goisern, Austria.
- Neues Leben; durch Gesundung von Leib und
  Seele. q. ISSN 0028-3657

**Wolfgang Neugebauer**
Alpenstr. 12, Postfach 89, A-5027 Salzburg, Austria.
- Beitraege zur Historischen Sozialkunde. q. ISSN
  0045-1681 (Arbeitsgemeinschaft fuer Historische
  Sozialkunde)

**Neydharting Verlag**
Pfarrplatz 3-4, A-4020 Linz, Austria.
- Oesterreichische Moorforschung. irreg. ISSN
  0078-351X

**Niederlaendische Handelskammer fuer Oesterreich**
Schwarzenbergplatz 10, Postfach 160, A-1041
Vienna, Austria.
- Oesterreich-Nederland. 10 per yr. approx. ISSN
  0029-8751

**Niederoesterreich. Amt der Niederoesterreichische
Landesregierung. Presseabteilung**
Herrengasse 11, A-1014 Vienna, Austria.
- Kulturberichte aus Niederoesterreich. m. ISSN
  0023-5121

**Niederoesterreich. Niederoesterreichische Landes-
Landwirtschaftskammer**
- Die Landwirtschaft. (pub. by Oesterreichischer
  Agrarverlag)
- Niederoesterreichische Landes-
  Landwirtschaftskammer. Amtlicher Marktbericht.
  (pub. by Oesterreichischer Agrarverlag)

**Niederoesterreichischer Landesfeuerwehrverband.
Landesfeuerwehrkommando**
Bankgasse 2, A-1014 Vienna, Austria.
- Brand Aus. m. ISSN 0006-9035

**Niederoesterreichischer Landesjagdverband**
- Oesterreichs Weidwerk. (pub. by Oesterreichischer
  Jagd und Fischerei-Verlag des N-O
  Landesjagdverbandes)

**Oberoesterreich. Kammer der Gewerblichen
Wirtschaft fuer Oberoesterreich**
Hessenplatz, A-4010 Linz, Austria.
- Kammer-Nachrichten; Kammer der gewerblichen
  Wirtschaft fuer Oberoesterreich-Chamber of
  Commerce of Upper Austria. w. ISSN 0022-8184

**Oberoesterreich. Landesinstitut fuer Volksbildung und
Heimatpflege in Oberoesterreich**
Landstr. 31, A-4020 Linz, Austria.
- Oberoesterreichische Heimatblaetter. s-a. ISSN
  0029-7550
- Oberoesterreichisches Volksbildungswerk.
  Mitteilungen. bi-m. ISSN 0026-6922

**Oberoesterreich. Landwirtschaftskammer fuer
Oberoesterreich**
Auf der Gugl 3, A-4027 Linz, Austria.
- Der Bauer; mitteilungsblatt der
  oberoesterreichischen. w. ISSN 0005-6561

**Oberoesterreichischer Gemeindebund**
- Oberoesterreichische Gemeindezeitung. (pub. by
  Oberoesterreichischer Landesverlag (Ried))

**Oberoesterreichischer Landesverlag**
Landstr. 41, A-4010 Linz, Austria.
- Oberoesterreich; Kulturzeitschrift. q.
- Schulpraktische Reihe. irreg. (Paedagogisches
  Institut des Bundes in Oberoesterreich)

- Theologisch-Praktische Quartalschrift. q. ISSN
  0040-5663 (Philosophisch-Theologische
  Hochschule der Dioezese Linz)

**Oberoesterreichischer Landesverlag (Ried)**
Wohlmayrgasse 6, A-4910 Ried, Austria.
- Oberoesterreichische Gemeindezeitung. m. ISSN
  0029-7542 (Oberoesterreichischer Gemeindebund)

**Octopus Verlag**
Postfach 53, A-1236 Vienna, Austria.
- Bodhi Baum/Zeitschrift fuer Buddhismus. q.
  (Buddhistisches Kultur- und Meditationszentrum
  Scheibbs)

**Oesterreichisch - Amerikanische Gesellschaft**
Stallburggasse 2, A-1010 Vienna, Austria.
- Contact. 10 per year. ISSN 0010-7239

**Oesterreichisch-Polnische Gesellschaft**
Biberstr. 4/4, A-1010 Vienna, Austria.
- Oesterreich-Polen, Austria-Polska. q. ISSN 0030-
  6398

**Oesterreichisch-Spanische Gesellschaft**
Maysedergasse 4, A-1010 Vienna, Austria.
- Hispania. m.

**Oesterreichische Aerztekammer. Pressestelle und
Verlag**
Weihburggasse 10-12, A-1010 Vienna, Austria.
- Aerztliche Tonbandzeitung; europaeisches
  kolloquium fuer die aerztliche Fortbildung. m.
  ISSN 0001-9542
- Oesterreichische Aerztezeitung. bi-m. ISSN 0029-
  8786

**Oesterreichische Akademie der Wissenschaften**
- Oesterreichische Akademie der Wissenschaften.
  Almanach. (pub. by Verlag der Oesterreichischen
  Akademie der Wissenschaften)

**Oesterreichische Akademie der Wissenschaften.
Historische Kommission**
- Fontes Rerum Austriacarum. Reihe 1. Scriptores.
  (pub. by Verlag der Oesterreichischen Akademie
  der Wissenschaften)
- Fontes Rerum Austriacarum. Reihe 2.
  Diplomataria et Acta. (pub. by Verlag der
  Oesterreichischen Akademie der Wissenschaften)
- Fontes Rerum Austriacarum. Reihe 3. Fontes
  Juris. (pub. by Verlag der Oesterreichischen
  Akademie der Wissenschaften)
- Oesterreichische Akademie der Wissenschaften.
  Archiv fuer Oesterreichische Geschichte. (pub. by
  Verlag der Oesterreichischen Akademie der
  Wissenschaften)

**Oesterreichische Akademie der Wissenschaften.
Iranische Kommission**
- Oesterreichische Akademie der Wissenschaften.
  Iranische Kommission. Veroeffentlichungen. (pub.
  by Verlag der Oesterreichischen Akademie der
  Wissenschaften)

**Oesterreichische Akademie der Wissenschaften.
Kommission fuer Byzantinistik**
- Oesterreichische Byzantinistik. Jahrbuch. (pub. by
  Verlag der Oesterreichischen Akademie der
  Wissenschaften)

**Oesterreichische Akademie der Wissenschaften.
Kommission fuer die Archaeologische Erforschung**
- Inschriften Griechischer Staedte aus Kleinasien.
  (pub. by Rudolf Habelt Verlag GW)

**Oesterreichische Akademie der Wissenschaften.
Kommission fuer die Tabula Imperii Byzantini**
- Oesterreichische Akademie der Wissenschaften.
  Kommission fuer die Tabula Imperii Byzantini.
  Veroeffentlichungen. (pub. by Verlag der
  Oesterreichischen Akademie der Wissenschaften)

**Oesterreichische Akademie der Wissenschaften.
Kommission fuer Linguistik und
Kommunikationsforschung**
- Oesterreichische Akademie der Wissenschaften.
  Kommission fuer Linguistik und
  Kommunikationsforschung. Veroeffentlichungen.
  (pub. by Verlag der Oesterreichischen Akademie
  der Wissenschaften)

**Oesterreichische Akademie der Wissenschaften.
Kommission fuer Musikforschung**
- Oesterreichische Akademie der Wissenschaften.
  Kommission fuer Musikforschung. Mitteilungen.
  (pub. by Verlag der Oesterreichischen Akademie
  der Wissenschaften)

**Oesterreichische Akademie der Wissenschaften.
Kommission fuer Mykenische Forschung**
- Mykenische Studien. (pub. by Verlag der
  Oesterreichischen Akademie der Wissenschaften)

**Oesterreichische Akademie der Wissenschaften.
Kommission fuer Sozial- und
Wirtschaftswissenschaften**
- Oesterreichische Akademie der Wissenschaften.
  Kommission fuer Sozial- und
  Wirischaftswissenschaften. Veroeffentlichungen.
  (pub. by Verlag der Oesterreichischen Akademie
  der Wissenschaften)

**Oesterreichische Akademie der Wissenschaften.
Kommission fuer Sprachen und Kulturen Sued- und
Ostasiens**
- Wiener Zeitschrift fuer die Kunde Suedasiens und
  Archiv fuer Indische Philosphie. (pub. by Gerold
  und Co.)

**Oesterreichische Akademie der Wissenschaften.
Kommission zur Herausgabe des Corpus der
Lateinischen Kirchenvaeter**
- Oesterreichische Akademie der Wissenschaften.
  Kommission zur Herausgabe des Corpus der
  Lateinischen Kirchenvaeter. Veroeffentlichungen.
  (pub. by Verlag der Oesterreichischen Akademie
  der Wissenschaften)

**Oesterreichische Akademie der Wissenschaften.
Numismatische Kommission**
- Oesterreichische Akademie der Wissenschaften.
  Numismatische Kommission. Veroeffentlichungen.
  (pub. by Verlag der Oesterreichischen Akademie
  der Wissenschaften)

**Oesterreichische Akademie der Wissenschaften.
Philosophisch-Historische Klasse**
- Oesterreichische Akademie der Wissenschaften.
  Philosophisch-Historische Klasse. Anzeiger. (pub.
  by Verlag der Oesterreichischen Akademie der
  Wissenschaften)
- Oesterreichische Akademie der Wissenschaften.
  Philosophisch-Historisch Klasse. Sitzungsberichte.
  (pub. by Verlag der Oesterreichischen Akademie
  der Wissenschaften)

**Oesterreichische Akademie der Wissenschaften.
Praehistorische Kommission**
- Oesterreichische Akademie der Wissenschaften.
  Prahistorische Kommission. Mitteilungen. (pub. by
  Verlag der Oesterreichischen Akademie der
  Wissenschaften)

**Oesterreichische Apotheker-Verlagsgesellschaft**
Spitalgasse 31, A-1094 Vienna, Austria.
- Oesterreichische Apotheker-Zeitung. w. ISSN
  0029-8859
- Scientia Pharmaceutica. q. ISSN 0036-8709
  (Oesterreichische Apothekerkammer)

**Oesterreichische Apothekerkammer**
- Scientia Pharmaceutica. (pub. by Oesterreichische
  Apotheker-Verlagsgesellschaft)

**Oesterreichische Arbeitsgemeinschaft fuer Alm und
Weide**
Museumstr. 5, A-6020 Innsbruck, Austria.
- Alm und Bergbauer. m.

**Oesterreichische Arbeitsgemeinschaft fuer
Rehabilitation**
Barichgasse 28, A-1030 Vienna, Austria.
- Oesterreichische Arbeitsgemeinschaft fuer
  Rehabilitation. Information. 3 per yr. ISSN 0029-
  8867

**Oesterreichische Bankwissenschaftliche Gesellschaft**
- Oesterreichisches Bank-Archiv. (pub. by
  Manzsche Verlags und
  Universitaetsbuchhandlung)

**Oesterreichische Bischofskonferenz.
Dioezesankommission fuer Kirchenmusik**
Stock-im-Eisen Platz 3, A-1010 Vienna, Austria.
- Singende Kirche; Zeitschrift fuer katholische
  Kirchenmusik. q. ISSN 0037-5721

**Oesterreichische Caritaszentrale**
Nibelungengasse 1, A-1011 Vienna, Austria.
- Caritas; fachzeitschrift der caritas oesterreichs. 6
  per yr.

**Oesterreichische Chemie Zeitschrift**
Ebendorferstr. 10, A-1010 Vienna, Austria.
- Oesterreichische Chemie Zeitschrift. m.

**Oesterreichische Dentisten-Kammer**
Kohlmarkt 11, A-1010 Vienna, Austria.
• Oesterreichische Dentisten-Zeitschrift. m. ISSN 0029-9006

**Oesterreichische Ethnologische Gesellschaft**
• Wiener Voelkerkundliche Mitteilungen. (pub. by Museum fuer Voelkerkunde)

**Oesterreichische Exlibris-Gesellschaft**
Tuerkenstr. 17/4, A-1090 Vienna, Austria.
• Oesterreichisches Jahrbuch fuer Exlibris und Gebrauchsgraphik. a. ISSN 0078-3633

**Oesterreichische Foerster Zeitung**
Passauerhof 4, 3001 Mauerbach, Austria
• Oesterreichische Foerster Zeitung. q. ISSN 0029-9502

**Oesterreichische Forschungsstiftung fuer Entwicklungshilfe**
Tuerkenstrasse 3, A-1090 Vienna, Austria.
• Internationale Entwicklung. q.

**Oesterreichische Frauenbewegung. Landesleitung Wien**
Falkestr. 3, A-1010 Vienna, Austria.
• Die Frau in Wien. q.

**Oesterreichische Fremdenverkehrswirtschaft**
• Hotel 2000. (pub. by Oesterreichischer Wirtschaftsverlag)

**Oesterreichische Galerie**
Postfach 12, A-1037 Vienna, Austria.
• Oesterreichische Galerie. Mitteilungen. a. ISSN 0029-909X

**Oesterreichische Geographische Gesellschaft**
Karl Schweighoferg 3, A-1071 Vienna, Austria.
• Oesterreichische Geographische Gesellschaft. Mitteilungen. 3 per yr. ISSN 0029-9138

**Oesterreichische Gesellschaft fuer Absatzwirtschaft**
Franz-Kleing. 1, A-1190 Vienna, Austria.
• Markt; Zeitschrift fuer Absatzwirtschaft und Marketing. q. ISSN 0025-3863

**Oesterreichische Gesellschaft fuer Aussenpolitik**
• Oesterreichische Zeitschrift fuer Aussenpolitik. (pub. by Wilhelm Braumueller, Universitaets - Verlagsbuchhandlung GmbH)

**Oesterreichische Gesellschaft fuer Baumforschung und Raumplanung**
• Oesterreichische Gesellschaft fuer Raumforschung und Raumplanung. Schriftenreihe. (pub. by Springer-Verlag US)

**Oesterreichische Gesellschaft fuer Chirurgie**
• Acta Chirurgica Austriaca. (pub. by Brueder Hollinek)

**Oesterreichische Gesellschaft fuer Dokumentation und Information**
c/o O.P.W.Z., Hohenstaufengasse 3, A-1014 Vienna, Austria.
• O G D I Mitteilungen. q.

**Oesterreichische Gesellschaft fuer Ernaehrungsforschung**
• Probleme der Ernaehrungs-und Lebensmittelwissenschaft. (pub. by Verlag Wilhelm Maudrich)

**Oesterreichische Gesellschaft fuer Filmwissenschaft**
Rauhensteingasse 5, A-1010 Vienna, Austria.
• Filmkunst; Zeitschrift fuer Filmkultur und Filmwissenschaft. q. ISSN 0015-1599
• Oesterreichische Gesellschaft fuer Filmwissenschaft. Mitteilungen. bi-m. ISSN 0029-9146

**Oesterreichische Gesellschaft fuer Holzforschung**
Arsenal-Objekt 212, A-1030 Vienna, Austria.
• Oesterreichische Gesellschaft fuer Holzforschung. Schrifttumskarteidienst. s-m. ISSN 0029-9154

**Oesterreichische Gesellschaft fuer Land- und Forstwirtschaftspolitik**
• Agrarische Rundschau. (pub. by Oesterreichischer Agrarverlag)

**Oesterreichische Gesellschaft fuer Meteorologie**
Hohe Warte 38, A-1190 Vienna, Austria.
• Wetter und Leben; Zeitschrift fuer angewandte Meteorologie. q. ISSN 0043-4450

**Oesterreichische Gesellschaft fuer Musik**
• Oesterreichische Gesellschaft fuer Musik. Beitraege. (pub. by Baerenreiter Verlag GW)

**Oesterreichische Gesellschaft fuer Musikwissenschaft**
Postfach 1461, A-1011 Vienna, Austria.
• Oesterreichische Gesellschaft fuer Musikwissenschaft. Mitteilungen. irreg.

**Oesterreichische Gesellschaft fuer Natur- und Umweltschutz**
• Umweltschutz. (pub. by Bohmann Verlag K.G.)

**Oesterreichische Gesellschaft fuer Politikwissenschaft**
• Oesterreichische Zeitschrift fuer Politikwissenschaft. (pub. by Europa-Verlag AG)

**Oesterreichische Gesellschaft fuer Raumforschung und Raumplanung**
Karlsplatz 13, A-1040 Vienna, Austria.
• Oesterreichische Gesellschaft fuer Raumforschung und Raumplanung. Berichte zur Raumforschung und Raumplanung. bi-m. ISSN 0005-9102

**Oesterreichische Gesellschaft fuer Vogelkunde**
c/o Naturhistorisches Museum, Burgring 7, Postfach 417, A-1014 Vienna, Austria.
• Egretta; vogelkundliche Nachrichten aus Oesterreich. s-a. ISSN 0013-2373

**Oesterreichische Hochschuelerschaft**
Fuehrichgasse 10, A-1010 Vienna, Austria.
• Bilanz; das Oesterreichische Studentenmagazin. 5 per yr. ISSN 0006-2340 (Austrian National Union of Students)

**Oesterreichische Hochschuelerschaft an der Universitaet Salzburg**
Residenzplatz 1, A-5020 Salzburg, Austria.
• Facto. m. ISSN 0014-6536

**Oesterreichische Jungarbeiterbewegung**
Tuchlauben 8, A-1010 Vienna, Austria.
• Der Oesterreichische Jungarbeiter. bi-m. ISSN 0029-9243

**Oesterreichische Kommissionsbuchhandlung**
Maximilianstrasse 17, A-6020 Innsbruck, Austria.
• Forschungen zur Innsbrucker Universitaetsgeschichte. irreg., vol, 10, 1971. ISSN 0429-1573 (Universitaet Innsbruck)
• Innsbrucker Universitaetsreden. irreg., vol. 8, 1974. (Universitaet Innsbruck)
• Studien zur Rechts-, Wirtschafts- und Kulturgeschichte. irreg., vol. 10, 1974. (Universitaet Innsbruck)
• Universitaet Innsbruck. Alpenkundliche Studien. irreg., vol. 10, 1972.
• Universitaet Innsbruck. Alpin-Biologische Studien. irreg., vol. 6, 1974.
• Universitaet Innsbruck. Finanzwissenschaftliche Studien. irreg., vol. 9, 1970.
• Universitaet Innsbruck. Kunstgeschichtliche Studien. irreg.
• Universitaet Innsbruck. Mathematische Studien. irreg.
• Universitaet Innsbruck. Medizinische Fakultaet. Arbeiten. irreg. ISSN 0579-7772
• Universitaet Innsbruck. Theologische Fakultaet. Studien und Arbeiten. irreg., vol. 10, 1974. ISSN 0579-7780
• Volkskundliche Studien. irreg. (Universitaet Innsbruck)

**Oesterreichische Laenderbank A.G.**
Am Hof 2, A-1011 Vienna, Austria.
• Laenderbank Boerseninformationen. m. ISSN 0029-9278
• Mercur; Authentischer Verlosungsanzeiger mit Anzeiger aufgebotener Wertpapiere. m. ISSN 0025-9926

**Oesterreichische Liga fuer Menschenrechte**
Hermanngasse 9/14, A-1070 Vienna, Austria.
• Das Menschenrecht. q. ISSN 0025-9616

**Oesterreichische Mathematische Gesellschaft**
Technische Universitaet, Gusshausstr. 27, A-1040 Vienna, Austria.
• International Mathematical News. 3 per yr. ISSN 0020-7926

**Oesterreichische Mineraloelverwaltung AG**
9 Otto Wagnerplatz 5, A-1091 Vienna, Austria.
• O M V - Zeitschrift. q. ISSN 0029-7194

**Oesterreichische Nationalbank**
Otto-Wagner-Platz 3, A-1090 Vienna, Austria.
• Oesterreichische Nationalbank. Bericht ueber das Geschaeftsjahr mit Rechnungsabschluss. a. ISSN 0078-3528
• Oesterreichische Nationalbank.Mitteilungen des Direktoriums/Austria's Monetary Situation, Survey. m. ISSN 0029-9332

**Oesterreichische Nationalbibliothek**
• Museion. (pub. by Brueder Hollinek)

**Oesterreichische Notariatskammer**
• Oesterreichische Notariats-Zeitung. (pub. by Manzsche Verlags- und Universitaetsbuchhandlung)

**Oesterreichische Numismatische Gesellschaft**
Burgring 5, A-1010 Vienna, Austria.
• Oesterreichische Numismatische Gesellschaft. Mitteilungen. 6 per yr. ISSN 0029-9359

**Oesterreichische Staatsdruckerei**
Rennweg 12a, A-1037 Vienna, Austria.
• Amtliche Veterinaernachrichten. s-m. ISSN 0003-2107 (Austria. Bundesministerium fuer Gesundheit und Umweltschutz)
• Amtsblatt der Oesterreichischen Justizverwaltung. ISSN 0003-2220 (Austria. Bundesministerium fuer Justiz)
• Austria. Bundesministeriums fuer Soziale Verwaltung. Amtliche Nachrichten. m. (Austria. Bundesministerium fuer Soziale Verwaltung)
• Austria. Statistisches Zentralamt. die Natuerliche Bevoelkerungsbewegung. a. ISSN 0067-2335 (Austria. Oesterreichisches Statistisches Zentralamt)
• Austria. Statistisches Zentralamt. die Wohnbautaetigkeit. a. ISSN 0067-2300
• Austria. Statistisches Zentralamt. Ergebnisse der Landwirtschaftlichen Maschinenzaehlung. irreg.
• Austria. Statistisches Zentralamt. Ergebnisse der Landwirtschaftlichen Statistik. a. ISSN 0067-2327
• Oesterreichische Hochschulstatistik. a. ISSN 0067-2343 (Austria. Oesterreichisches Statistisches Zentralamt)
• Statistisches Handbuch fuer die Republik Oesterreich. a. ISSN 0081-5314 (Austria. Oesterreichisches Statistisches Zentralamt)

**Oesterreichische Tieraerzteschaft**
• Wiener Tieraerztliche Monatsschrift. (pub. by Verlag Ferdinand Berger und Soehne OHG)

**Oesterreichische Vereinigung fuer das Gas- und Wasserfach**
Ebendorferstr. 10, A-1010 Vienna, Austria.
• Gas, Wasser, Waerme. m. ISSN 0016-5018 (Co-sponsor: Fachverband der Gas- und Waermeversorgungsunternehmungen)

**Oesterreichische Vereinigung fuer Gewerblichen Rechtsschutz und Urheberrecht**
• Oesterreichische Blaetter fuer Gewerblichen Rechtsschutz und Urheberrecht. (pub. by Manzsche Verlags- und Universitaetsbuchhandlung)

**Oesterreichische Verkehrswissenschaftliche Gesellschaft**
Gauermanngasse 4, Vienna, Austria.
• Oesterreichische Verkehrswissenschaftliche Gesellschaft. Mitteilungen.

**Oesterreichische Volkspartei. Bundesparteileitung**
Kaerntner Str. 51, A-1010 Vienna, Austria.
• Brennpunkt. m. ISSN 0006-9604
• Oesterreichische Monatshefte; Zeitschrift fuer Politik. m. ISSN 0029-9308

**Oesterreichischer Agrarverlag**
Bankgasse 1-3, A-1014 Vienna, Austria.
• Agrarische Rundschau. bi-m. ISSN 0002-0710 (Oesterreichische Gesellschaft fuer Land- und Forstwirtschaftspolitik)
• Allgemeine Forstzeitung. m. ISSN 0002-5879 (Forstliche Fachvereine und Standesorganisationen Oesterreichs)
• Besseres Obst. m. ISSN 0005-9609 (Bundesobstbauverband Oesterreichs)
• Bodenkultur; Journal fuer landwirtschaftliche Forschung. 4 per yr. ISSN 0006-5471 (Hochschule fuer Bodenkultur) (Co-Sponsor: Bundesministerium fuer Land-und Forstwirtschaft)

- Centralblatt fuer das Gesamte Forstwesen. q.
  ISSN 0008-9583 (Hochschule fuer Bodenkultur.
  Forstliche Abteilung) (Co-Sponsor: Forstliche
  Bundesversuchanstalt Mariabrunn in Wien)
- Foerderungsdienst; Zeitschrift fuer Lehr-und
  Beratungskraefte. m. ISSN 0015-525X (Austria.
  Bundesministerium fuer Land-und Forstwirtschaft)
- Gartenbauwirtschaft. m. (Bundesverband der
  Erwerbsgaertner Oesterreichs)
- Holz-Kurier; Forst- und Holzwirtschaftlicher
  Wochendienst. w. ISSN 0018-3784
  (Bundesholzwirtschaftsrat)
- Holzforschung und Holzverwertung; Mitteilungen
  der Oesterreichischen Gesellschaft fuer
  Holzforschung. 6 per yr. ISSN 0018-3849
  (Austria. Bundesministerium fuer Land- und
  Forstwirtschaft)
- Der Land- und Forstwirtschaftliche Betrieb. m.
  ISSN 0023-7558 (Verband Landwirtschaftlicher
  Gutsbetriebe in Oesterreich)
- Landjugend; illustrierter Landkurier. m. ISSN
  0023-7957 (Austria. Landwirtschaftsministerium)
- Die Landwirtschaft; Fachzeitschrift fuer die
  Gesamtinteressen der Land- und Forstwirtschaft.
  ISSN 0047-4010 (Niederoesterreich.
  Niederoesterreichische Landes-
  Landwirtschaftskammer)
- Niederoesterreichische Landes-
  Landwirtschaftskammer. Amtlicher Marktbericht.
  s-m. ISSN 0028-9744
- Oesterreichische Landwirtschaft. Monatsberichte.
  m. ISSN 0026-9220 (Austria. Bundesministerium
  fuer Land- und Forstwirtschaft.
  Agrarwirtschaftliches Institut)
- Pflanzenarzt. m.(2-3 special nos.per yr.) ISSN
  0031-6733 (Austria. Bundesanstalt fuer
  Pflanzenschutz)
- Schrifttum der Agrarwirtschaft. bi-m. ISSN 0036-
  6986 (Austria. Bundesministerium fuer Land- und
  Forstwirtschaft. Agrarwirtschaftliches Institut)
- Der Winzer. m. ISSN 0043-5953 (Bundesverband
  der Weinbautreibenden Oesterreichs)
- Zahlen aus Oesterreichs Land- und
  Forstwirtschaft. a.

**Oesterreichischer Akademikerbund**
Freyung 2, A-1010 Vienna, Austria.
- Politische Perspektiven; Blaetter zur Zeitkritik. m.
  ISSN 0032-3454

**Oesterreichischer Alpenverein**
Akademischen Sektion Graz, Rechbauerstr. 12, A-
8010 Graz, Austria.
- Oesterreichischer Alpenverein. Akademische
  Sektion Graz. Mitteilungen. a. ISSN 0029-8840
- Oesterreichischer Alpenverein. Mitteilungen. bi-m.
  ISSN 0029-9715

**Oesterreichischer Arbeiter-Saengerbund**
Arndtstr. 27, A-1120 Vienna, Austria.
- Chormeister. q.
- Der Oesterreichische Arbeitersaenger. q.

**Oesterreichischer Arbeiter und Angestelltenbund.**
**Bundesfachgruppe Wirtschaftsverwaltung**
Laudong. 16, A-1080 Vienna, Austria.
- Bei Uns. q. ISSN 0005-8009

**Oesterreichischer Arbeitkammertag**
- Arbeit und Wirtschaft. (pub. by Verlag des
  Oesterreichischen Gewerkschaftbundes GmbH)

**Oesterreichischer Auslandsstudentendienst**
Dr. Karl Lueger-Ring 1, A-1010 Vienna, Austria.
- Deutschkurse/German Language Courses. irreg.
  ISSN 0012-1398
- Information/Information for Foreign Students
  Intending to Study at Austrian Universities; fuer
  auslaendische Studienbewerber an
  oesterreichischen Hochschulen. irreg. ISSN 0020-
  0077
- Nota Bene. s-a. ISSN 0029-3822
- Oesterreichischer Auslandsstudentendienst.
  Rechenschaftsbericht. a.
- Scholarships for Foreign Students and University
  Graduates at Austrian Institutions of Higher
  Learning/Stipendien fuer Auslaendische
  Studierende und Akademiker an
  Oesterreichischen Hochschulen. irreg. ISSN 0036-
  6374

**Oesterreichischer Automobil- Motorrad- und Touring-**
**Club**
Schubertring 3, A-1010 Vienna, Austria.
- A. T. Auto Touring; Oesterreichische Kraftfahr-
  Zeitung. s-m. ISSN 0001-2688

**Oesterreichischer Blindenverband**
Mariahilfer Guertel 4, A-1060 Vienna, Austria.
- Oesterreichischer Blindenverband. Mitteilungen.
  bi-m. ISSN 0029-9723

**Oesterreichischer Buchklub der Jugend**
Fuhrmannsgasse 18a, A-1082 Vienna, Austria.
- Die Barke; lehrer-jahrbuch. a. ISSN 0067-4206
- Oesterreichischer Buchklub der Jugend. Jahrbuch.
  a. ISSN 0078-3560
- Schriften zur Jugendlektuere. irreg. ISSN 0080-
  701X
- Schriftenreihe des Buchklubs der Jugend. irreg.
  ISSN 0080-7117

**Oesterreichischer Bundes-Feuerwehrverband**
- Die Oesterreichische Feuerwehr. (pub. by
  Bohmann Verlag K.G.)

**Oesterreichischer Bundesverlag fuer Unterricht**
**Wissenschaft und Kunst**
Schwarzenbergstrasse 5, A-1010 Vienna, Austria.
- Erwachsenenbildung in Oesterreich. m. (Austria.
  Bundesministerium fuer Unterricht und Kunst)
- Erziehung und Unterricht; oesterreichische
  paedagogische Zeitschrift. 10 per yr.(with
  supplement "Heilpaedagogik" 5 per yr.) ISSN
  0014-0325
- Litterae Latinae. 5 per yr.
- Musikerziehung; Zeitschrift der Musikerzieher
  Oesterreichs. 5 per yr. ISSN 0027-4798

**Oesterreichischer Camping Club (OCC)**
Johannesgasse 20, A-1010 Vienna, Austria.
- Oesterreichische Camping Revue. 6 per yr.

**Oesterreichischer Cartell-Verband**
Lerchenfelderstr. 14, A-1080 Vienna, Austria.
- Academia. bi-m. ISSN 0029-8778

**Oesterreichischer Eisenbahner Esperantisten Verband**
Postfach 117, A-1103 Vienna, Austria.
- I F E F, Austria Sekcio. Bulteno. (Federacio
  Esperantista Fervojista) 4-6 per yr. ISSN 0005-
  0504

**Oesterreichischer Fachhandel mit Papier,**
**Bueroartikeln und Schreibwaren**
- Papierhandels-Fachblatt. (pub. by Papier- und
  Buchgewerblicher Verlag)

**Oesterreichischer Fischereiverband**
Scharfling, A-5310 Mondsee, Austria.
- Oesterreichs Fischerei; Zeitschrift fuer die gesamte
  Wirtschafts- und Sportfischerei, fuer
  gewaesserkundliche und
  fischereiwissenschaftlicheFragen. m. ISSN 0029-
  9987

**Oesterreichischer Gewerkschaftsbund**
- Buecherschau. (pub. by Verlag des
  Oesterreichischen Gewerkschaftbundes GmbH)

**Oesterreichischer Gewerkschaftsbund. Gewerkschaft**
**der Eisenbahner**
Margaretenstr. 166, A-1050 Vienna, Austria.
- Eisenbahner. m. ISSN 0013-2799

**Oesterreichischer Handball-und Faustball-Bund**
Hauslabgasse 24, A-1050 Vienna, Austria.
- Handball und Faustball in Oesterreich. irreg. ISSN
  0072-9698

**Oesterreichischer Imkerbund**
Georg-Coch-Platz 3-11 A, A-1010 Vienna, Austria.
- Bienenvater. m. ISSN 0006-2146

**Oesterreichischer Jagd und Fischerei-Verlag des N-O**
**Landesjagdverbandes**
Wickenburggasse 3, A-1080 Vienna, Austria.
- Oesterreichs Weidwerk. m. ISSN 0030-0012
  (Niederoesterreichischer Landesjagdverband)

**Oesterreichischer Kameradschaftsbund.**
**Landesverband Wien, Kameradschaft der Wiener**
**Panzer Division im OEKB Lds. V6**
Postfach 159, A-1061 Vienna, Austria.
- Oesterreichischer Kameradschaftsbund.
  Landesverband Wien. Mitteilungsblatt. q. ISSN
  0029-974X

**Oesterreichischer Komponistenbund**
Baumannstr. 8-10, A-1031 Vienna, Austria.
- Komponist und Musikerzieher. bi-m.

**Oesterreichischer Krankenpflegeverband**
Mollgasse 3a, A-1180 Vienna, Austria.
- Oesterreichische Krankenpflegezeitschrift. (pub. by
  Facultas Buch- und Zeitschriftenverlag fuer
  Medizin und Pharmazie GmbH)
- Oesterreichischer Krankenpflegerverband.
  Fortbildungsprogramm. a.
- Oesterreichischer Schwesternkalender. a.

**Oesterreichischer Luftfahrt Pressedienst**
Karl Schweighofer Gasse 3, A-1071 Vienna, Austria.
- Europublica Combinations Flugplan. s-a. ISSN
  0014-3219
- Oesterreichischer Luftfahrt Pressedienst. w. ISSN
  0029-9774

**Oesterreichischer Naturschutzbund**
Bundesgeschaeftsstelle, Kugelfangweg 15, A-6040
Innsbruck, Austria.
- Natur und Land. bi-m. ISSN 0028-0607

**Oesterreichischer Paddelsport-Verband**
Berggasse 16, A-1090 Vienna, Austria.
- Oesterreichs Paddelsport. 9 per yr(approx) ISSN
  0029-9995

**Oesterreichischer Photohaendlerverband**
- Inpho Oesterreich. (pub. by Verlag die Galerie
  GmbH)

**Oesterreichischer Rundfunk**
Postfach 700, A-1041 Vienna, Austria.
- Der Oesterreichische Schulfunk mit Telespiegel &
  Doig. m. ISSN 0048-1467

**Oesterreichischer Schutzverband der**
**Wertpapierbesitzer**
Schellinggasse 6, A-1010 Vienna, Austria.
- Der Wertpapierbesitzer. m.

**Oesterreichischer Segel-Verband**
- Oesterreichischer Yachtsport. (pub. by
  Baufachverlag Wien Ges. m. b. H.)

**Oesterreichischer Staedtebund**
- Oesterreichische Gemeinde-Zeitung. (pub. by
  Jugend und Volk Verlagsgesellschaft)

**Oesterreichischer Stahlbau-Verband**
- Stahlbau-Rundschau. (pub. by Bohmann Verlag
  K.G.)

**Oesterreichischer Tennisverband**
- Austria Tennis. (pub. by Verlag A. Schendl)

**Oesterreichischer Touristen-Klub**
Baeckerstr. 16, A-1010 Vienna, Austria.
- Oesterreichische Touristenzeitung. m. ISSN 0048-
  1483

**Oesterreichischer Verband Gemeinneutziger Bau-,**
**Wohnungs- und Siedlungsvereinigungen**
Boesendorferstr. 7, A-1010 Vienna, Austria.
- Wohnen und Siedeln; Zeitschrift fuer das
  gemeinnuetzige Wohnungswesen in Oesterreich.
  m. ISSN 0043-7158

**Oesterreichischer Verein fuer Vermessungswesen und**
**Photogrammetrie**
Friedrich-Schmidt-Platz 3, A-1082 Vienna, Austria.
- Oesterreichische Zeitschrift fuer
  Vermessungswesen und Photogrammetrie. 4 per
  yr.

**Oesterreichischer Verlag**
Parkstr. 1, A-8011 Graz, Austria.
- Sonntagspost; die illustrierte unabhaengige
  Wochenzeitung. w. ISSN 0038-139X

**Oesterreichischer Wasserwirtschaftsverband**
Ander Huelben 4, A-1010 Vienna, Austria.
- Wasserwirtschaftliche Mitteilungen. m. ISSN
  0043-0994

**Oesterreichischer Wirtschaftsbund**
Landesleitung Steiermark, A-8010 Graz, 8010 Graz,
Austria.
- Steirische Wirtschaft; Mitteilungsblatt des
  steirischen wirtschaftsbundes. m. ISSN 0039-1107

**Oesterreichischer Wirtschaftsverlag**
Nikolsdorfer Gasse 7-11, A-1051 Vienna, Austria.
- Dach und Wand Abdichtung. m. (Bundes- und Landesinnungen der Dachdecker)
- Elektro Journal. m. (Bundesinnung der Elektrotechniker und Radiomechaniker)
- Fahrzeughandel; Fachzeitschrift fuer den Fahrzeughandel. m. ISSN 0014-6870
- Hotel 2000. m. (Oesterreichische Fremdenverkehrswirtschaft)
- Internationale Wirtschaft; Eildienst fuer den Aussenhandel. w. ISSN 0020-935X
- K F Z Werkstaette. m. ISSN 0022-7323 (Bundesinnung der Kraftfahrzeugmechaniker)
- Lebensmittel-Kaufmann. w. ISSN 0047-4282
- Mechanik. m. ISSN 0029-9294 (Bundesinnung der Mechaniker)
- Metall; Fachblatt fuer Metall- und Landtechnik. m. (Wiener Innung der Schlosser)
- Oesterreichische Bauzeitung. w. ISSN 0029-8891
- Oesterreichische Gastgewerbe-Zeitung. w. ISSN 0029-9103 (Gast- und Schankbetriebe)
- Oesterreichische Glaserzeitung. m. ISSN 0029-9162 (Bundes- und Landesinnungen der Glaserer)
- Oesterreichische Trafikanten-Zeitung. m. ISSN 0029-9561
- Der Oesterreichische Zahntechniker. q. (Bundesinnung der Zahntechniker)
- Oesterreichische Zimmermeister. m. ISSN 0029-9677
- Oesterreichischer Personenverkehr. m. ISSN 0029-9790 (Bundes- und Landesinnungen des Taxigewerbes)
- Der Oesterreichische Schuhmarkt. m. (Bundesinnung der Schuhmacher)
- Oesterreichisches Cafe Journal; Fachblatt fuer Kaffeehaeuser, Caferestaurants, Espressi, Cafekonditoreien. m. ISSN 0029-9847 (Bundesinnung der Cafetiers)
- Sport - Spiel - Freizeit. m.
- Strassengueterverkehr. m. ISSN 0029-9073 (Gewerbliches Guetertransportwesen Oesterreichs)
- Tischler. s-m. ISSN 0040-8131 (Bundesinnung und Landesinnung der Tischler Oesterreichs)
- Der Unternehmer. 8 per yr. ISSN 0042-0581 (Bundeskammer der Gewerblichen Wirtschaft)
- Viehhandel. s-m. ISSN 0049-6308
- Wir und Unsere Welt. m. ISSN 0043-5988
- Wirtschaft; Wochenzeitung fuer oesterreichs Industrie, Handel, Gewerbe, Finanzen. w. ISSN 0043-6100
- Wirtschaftspolitische Blaetter. bi-m. ISSN 0043-6291 (Bundeskammer der Gewerblichen Wirtschaft)

**Oesterreichischer Wohlfahrtsdienst**
Falkestr. 3, A-1010 Vienna, Austria.
- Wohlfahrtsdienst; Monatsschrift fuer Fragen der Wirtschaft und des Sozialen Lebens. m.

**Oesterreichisches Archaeologisches Institut**
Universitaet, Dr. Karl Lueger-Ring, A-1010 Vienna, Austria.
- Oesterreichisches Archaeologisches Institut. Jahreshefte: Grabungen. a. ISSN 0078-3579

**Oesterreichisches Bauzentrum**
- Bauforum. (pub. by Baufachverlag Wien Ges. m. b. H.)

**Oesterreichisches Chemiefaser-Institut**
Ploesslgasse 8, A-1041 Vienna, Austria.
- Oesterreichisches Chemiefaser-Institut. Nachrichten. 4 per yr. ISSN 0027-7401

**Oesterreichisches Forschungsinstitut fuer Sparkassenwesen**
- Oesterreichisches Forschungsinstitut fuer Sparkassenwesen. Schriftenreihe. (pub. by Sparkassenverlag Ges. m.b.H.)

**Oesterreichisches Forschungsinstitut fuer Wirtschaft und Politik**
Sigmund-Haffner-Gasse, Salzburg, Austria.
- Oesterreichisches Forschungsinstitut fuer Wirtschaft und Politik. Berichte und Informationen. w. ISSN 0029-9863

**Oesterreichisches Institut fuer Bauforschung**
Dr. Karl Lueger-Ring 10, A-1010 Vienna, Austria.
- I B Nachrichten. 10 per yr. ISSN 0018-8697

**Oesterreichisches Institut fuer Raumplanung**
Franz Josefs-Kai 27, A-1011 Vienna, Austria.
- Oesterreichisches Institut fuer Raumplanung. Mitteilungen. 6 per yr. ISSN 0029-9707

- Oesterreichisches Institut fuer Raumplanung. Taetigkeitsbericht. a. ISSN 0078-3617
- Oesterreichisches Institut fuer Raumplanung. Veroeffentlichungen. irreg. ISSN 0078-3625

**Oesterreichisches Institut fuer Schul-und Sportstaettenbau**
- Schul-und Sportstaettenbau. (pub. by Brueder Hollinek)

**Oesterreichisches Institut fuer Verpackung**
Hochschule fuer Welthandel, Franz Klein-Gasse 1, A-1190 Vienna, Austria.
- Informationsdienst Verpackung. irreg.

**Oesterreichisches Institut fuer Wirtschaftsforschung**
Arsenal, A-1103 Vienna, Austria.
- Oesterreichisches Institut fuer Wirtschaftsforschung. Monatsberichte. m. ISSN 0029-9898

**Oesterreichisches Jugendrotkreuz**
Gusshausstr. 3, A-1041 Vienna 4, Austria.
- Oesterreichisches Jugendrotkreuz. Arbeitsblaetter. bi-m. ISSN 0029-9901

**Oesterreichisches Kolpingwerk**
Paulanergasse 11, A-1040 Vienna 6, Austria.
- Oesterreichisches Kolpingblatt. bi-m. ISSN 0029-9928

**Oesterreichisches Kuratorium fuer Sicherheit im Bergland**
Prinz Eugen Str. 12, A-1040 Vienna, Austria.
- Fuer die Sicherheit im Bergland; Jahrbuch. a.

**Oesterreichisches Lateinamerika-Institut**
Bartensteingasse 2, A-1010 Vienna, Austria.
- Zeitschrift fuer Lateinamerika Wien. s-a. ISSN 0049-8645

**Oesterreichisches Luftfahrt Archiv**
Dirkensgasse 21, A-1131 Vienna, Austria.
- Flugsport-Informationen. m. ISSN 0015-4598

**Oesterreichisches Museum fuer Volkskunde**
- Oesterreichisches Museum fuer Volkskunde. Kataloge. (pub. by Verlag Ferdinand Berger und Soehne OHG)
- Oesterreichisches Museum fuer Volkskunde: Veroeffentlichungen. (pub. by Verlag Ferdinand Berger und Soehne OHG)

**Oesterreichisches Nationalinstitut**
- Die Republik. (pub. by Styria Verlag)

**Oesterreichisches Ost- und Suedosteuropa Institut**
Josefsplatz 6, A-1010 Vienna, Austria.
- Dokumentation der Gesetze und Verordnungen Osteuropas. 8 per yr. ISSN 0012-5075
- Oesterreichische Osthefte. q. ISSN 0029-9375
- Oesterreichisches Ost- und Suedosteuropa Institut. Schriftenreihe. (pub. by Verlag fuer Geschichte und Politik)
- Presseschau Ostwirtschaft. m. ISSN 0032-7891

**Oesterreichisches Rotes Kreuz**
Gusshausstr. 3, A-1041 Vienna, Austria.
- Das Rote Kreuz. q.

**Oesterreichisches Staatsarchiv**
- Oesterreichisches Staatsarchiv. Mitteilungen. (pub. by Verlag Ferdinand Berger und Soehne OHG)
- Oesterreichisches Staatsarchiv. Publikationen. (pub. by Verlag Ferdinand Berger und Soehne OHG)

**Oesterreichisches Volksliedwerk**
Fuhrmannsgasse 18/5, A-1080 Vienna, Austria.
- Oesterreichisches Volksliedwerk. Jahrbuch. a. ISSN 0473-8624

**Oesterreichisches Wirtschaftsinstitut fuer Strukturforschung und Strukturpolitik**
Hessenplatz, A-4020 Linz, Austria.
- Oesterreichisches Wirtschaftsinstitut fuer Strukturforschung und Strukturpolitik. Schriftenreihe. irreg. ISSN 0078-3595

**Oesterreichisches Zentrum fuer Wirtschaftlichkeit und Produktivitaet (OPWZ)**
Hohenstaufengasse 3, A-1014 Vienna, Austria.
- O P W Z-Dokumentation. m.
- Schluessel. bi-m. ISSN 0036-617X

**Verlag Grac**
Graben 17, A-1014 Vienna, Austria.
- Autorevue. m. ISSN 0005-0830

- Finanzrechtliche Erkenntnisse des Verwaltungsgerichtshofes; Beilage zur Oesterreichischen Steuer-Zeitung. s-m. ISSN 0015-2277
- Oesterreichische Steuer-Zeitung. s-m. ISSN 0029-9529

**Organization of Petroleum Exporting Countries**
Obere-Donaustr. 93, A-1020 Vienna, Austria.
- Organization of Petroleum Exporting Countries. Annual Review and Record. a. ISSN 0474-6317
- Organization of Petroleum Exporting Countries. Annual Statistical Bulletin. a. ISSN 0475-0608
- Selected Documents of the International Petroleum Industry. a. ISSN 0080-858X

**Organizzazione Internazionale dei Trasporti a Fune**
- Internationale Berg- und Seilbahn-Rundschau/ International Aerial Tramway Review. (pub. by Bohmann Verlag K. G.)

**Paedagogisches Institut der Stadt Wien**
7 Burggasse 14-16, A-1070 Vienna, Austria.
- Paedagogisches Institut der Stadt Wien. Mitteilungen. 10 per yr. ISSN 0030-9281 (Distrib. by: Verlag fuer Jugend und Volk, Tiefer Graben 7, 1014 Vienna, Austria)

**Paedagogisches Institut des Bundes in Oberoesterreich**
- Schulpraktische Reihe. (pub. by Oberoesterreichischer Landesverlag)

**Paedagogisches und Berufspaedagogisches Institut des Bundes in Salzburg**
Akademiestrasse 25, A-5020 Salzburg, Austria.
- Paedagogische Mitteilungen. m.

**Panorama Verlagsgesellschaft m.b.H.**
Hamburgerstr. 2, A-1052 Vienna, Austria.
- Mutter. m. ISSN 0027-5131

**Papier- und Buchgewerblicher Verlag**
Georg H. Diezel, Schelleingasse 10, A-1040 Vienna, Austria.
- Oesterreichische Papier-Zeitung. m. ISSN 0029-9391
- Papier- und Buchgewerbe-Rundschau; Fachorgan fuer das Graphische Gewerbe, die Buchbinderei und die Kartonagen-Erzeugung. m. ISSN 0031-1359
- Papierhandels-Fachblatt. s-m. ISSN 0031-1391 (Oesterreichischer Fachhandel mit Papier, Bueroartikeln und Schreibwaren)

**Pensionistenverband Oesterreichs**
Sperrgasse 8, A-1153 Vienna, Austria.
- Rentner und Pensionist. m. ISSN 0034-4540

**Perfekt Verlag**
Gentzgasse 121, A-1181 Vienna, Austria.
- Perfekt Kindermode. s-a. ISSN 0031-5192
- Perfekt Mode. s-a. ISSN 0031-5206

**Pfarre Perchtolsdorf**
- Perchtoldsdorfer Pfarrbote. (pub. by Verlag A. Kirsch)

**Pflanzenschuetzer**
Dr. K. Luegerring 6, A-1010 Vienna, Austria.
- Pflanzenschuetzer. irreg. ISSN 0079-1334

**Philosophisch-Theologische Hochschule der Dioezese Linz**
- Theologisch-Praktische Quartalschrift. (pub. by Oberoesterreichischer Landesverlag)

**Philosophische Gesellschaft Oesterreichs**
Salesianergasse 8, A-1030 Vienna, Austria.
- Philosophischer Zeitspiegel; philosophische Monatsschrift fuer den deutschen Sprachraum. m. ISSN 0031-8167

**Physica-Verlag Rudolf Liebing KG**
Seiler Staette 18, A-1010 Vienna, Austria.
- Metrika; Internationale Zeitschrift fuer theoretische und angewandte Statistik. 1 vol. per yr. (4 nos. per vol.) ISSN 0026-1335

**A. Pichlers Witwe und Sohn**
Rafaelgasse 12-14, A-1200 Vienna, Austria.
- Technik und Betrieb; illustrierte Zeitschrift der gesamten Technik, Maschinenbau, Metallbearbeitung, Elektrotechnik. q. ISSN 0040-1102

**Verlag Piletzky**
Schoenbrunnerstr. 237, A-1120 Vienna, Austria.
- Oesterreichische Fussbodenzeitung. bi-m. ISSN 0029-9081
- Oesterreichische Installateurzeitung. bi-m. ISSN 0029-9235
- Oesterreichische Raumausstatterzeitung. bi-m. ISSN 0029-9405

**G. Pilz**
Stifterstrasse 4a, A-4320 Perg, Austria.
- Eselsohr. 2 per yr.

**Pius-Parsch-Institut**
Stiftsplatz 8, A-3400 Klosterneuburg, Austria.
- Bibel und Liturgie. q. ISSN 0006-064X (Co-Sponsor: Oesterreichisches Katholisches Bibelwerk)

**Metallwerk Plansee AG**
Postfach 74, A-6600 Reutte, Austria.
- Planseeberichte fuer Pulvermetallurgie. q. ISSN 0032-0765

**Verlag der Praktische Arzt**
Trude Schmitt, Kleine Sperlgasse 1, A-1020 Vienna, Austria.
- Der Praktische Arzt; Oesterreichische Monatsschrift fuer Allgemeinmedizin. m. ISSN 0048-5128

**Presbyterium der Evangelischen Gemeinde Wien-Favoriten-Christuskirche**
Triester Str. 1, A-1100 Vienna, Austria.
- Evangelische Pfarrgemeinde A.B. Wien-Favoriten-Christuskirche. Gemeindebrief. q. ISSN 0016-6154

**Promotia-Zeitschriftenverlagsges. m.b.H.**
Trauttmansdorffgasse 41, A-1130 Vienna, Austria.
- A D E G - Kurier; Kundenzeitschrift der Adeg-Kaufleute oesterr. m. ISSN 0001-8120

**Provinzialat der Brueder der Christlichen Schulen**
Anton Boeckgasse 20, A-1215 Vienna, Austria.
- Rundbrief Ehemaliger Schueler und Freunde der Schulbrueder. q. ISSN 0013-2489

**Psychotechnisches Institut**
Vegagasse 4, A-1190 Vienna, Austria.
- Mensch und Arbeit; internationale Zeitschrift fuer Arbeitspaedagogik, Arbeitspsychologie, Arbeitstechnik und Betriebswirtschaft. irreg. (Arbeitsgemeinschaft fuer Psychotechnik in Oesterreich)

**Universitaetsverlag Anton Pustet**
Bergstr. 12, Postschliessfach 144, A-5021 Salzburg, Austria.
- Internationales Forschungszentrum fuer Grundfragen der Wissenschaften, Salzburg. Forschungsgespraeche. irreg. ISSN 0074-980X (Internationales Forschungszentrum fuer Grundfragen der Wissenschaften, Salzburg)
- Oesterreichisches Klerus Blatt. fortn. ISSN 0029-991X (Universitaet Salzburg. Professorenkollegium der Theologischen Fakultaet)
- Salzburger Jahrbuch fuer Philosophie. a. ISSN 0080-5696
- Salzburger Studien zur Philosophie. irreg. ISSN 0080-5726
- Salzburger Universitaetsreden. irreg., no. 60, 1976. ISSN 0080-5734 (Universitaet Salzburg)

**Rampe (Linz)**
Koeglstr. 14, A-4020 Linz, Austria.
- Rampe (Linz) s-a.

**Dr. Herta Ranner**
Zeismannsbrunngasse 1, A-1070 Vienna, Austria.
- B Z; Fachzeitschrift fuer Wirtschaft-Steuer-Datentechnik. m. ISSN 0005-3465
- Der Junge Kaufmann. m. ISSN 0022-6300

**Reformverband Oesterreichischer Hausbesitzer**
Trattnerhof 1, A-1010 Vienna, Austria.
- Oesterreichische Hausbesitz. 11 per yr. ISSN 0029-9189

**Reichsverband Oesterreichischer Kleintierzuechter**
Postfach 14 ., A-4910 Ried im Innkreis, Austria.
- Oesterreichischer Kleintierzuechter; Fachblatt fuer die gesamte Kleintierzucht. m. ISSN 0029-9766

**Verlag Franz Reisinger**
A-4601 Wels, Austria.
- Benediktusbote. m. ISSN 0005-8742

**Residenz Verlag**
Imbergstr. 9, A-5020 Salzburg, Austria.
- Salzburger Festspiele. Offizielles Programm. a. ISSN 0080-5688

**Oskar Riedel, Ed. & Pub.**
Schottenring 28, A-1010vienna, Austria.
- Das Moderne Heim; mit der "Internationalen Bauchronik". a. ISSN 0026-8607

**Ring Freiheitlicher Jugend**
Kaerntnerstrasse 28, Mezzanin, A-1010 Vienna, Austria.
- Tangente. bi-m.

**Roemisches Katholisches Pfarramt Atzgersdorf**
Peter Kirchenplatz 1, A-1230 Vienna, Austria.
- Kontakt Drei und Zwanzig. bi-m. ISSN 0023-3676

**Edition Roetzer**
Haydngasse 41, A-7001 Eisenstadt, Austria.
- Pult; literatur- kunst- kritik. q. ISSN 0033-4251

**F. O. Rothy, Ed. & Pub.**
A-4360 Grein, Austria.
- Radiobote. s-a. ISSN 0033-8214

**Friedrich Rudy**
Florianigasse 21, A-1080 Vienna, Austria.
- Der Wirtschaftstreuhaender. 6 per yr. ISSN 0043-6321 (Vereinigung Oesterreichischer Wirtschaftstreuhaender)

**S O S Kinderdorf**
Stafflerstr. 10a, A-6021 Innsbruck, Austria.
- Kinderdorfbote. q. ISSN 0023-1509
- S O S Messenger. q. ISSN 0036-178X

**S Z**
Ed. Magdalena Troestler, Christian-Coulin Str. 13, Postfach 324, A-4021 Linz, Austria.
- S Z/Sozialwirtschaftliche Korrespondenz. m. ISSN 0036-1585

**Verlag St. Peter**
Postfach 113, A-5010 Salzburg, Austria.
- Heiliger Dienst. q. ISSN 0017-9620 (Erzabtei St. Peter, Salzburg. Institutum Liturgicum)

**Salzburg. Bundesland Salzburg**
Chiemseehof, A-5010 Salzburg, Austria.
- Landesgesetzblatt fuer das Land Salzburg. ISSN 0023-7884

**Salzburg. Stadtverkehrsbuero Salzburg**
- Offizieller Salzburger Wochenspiegel. (pub. by Festungsverlag Salzburg)

**Salzburger Aktiengesellschaft fuer Elektrizitaetswirtschaft**
Schwarzstr. 44, A-5021 Salzburg, Austria.
- S A F E - Nachrichten. q. ISSN 0036-0708

**Sepp Sattelberger, Editor**
Wienerstr. 50, A-3252 Petzenkirchen, Austria.
- Bergmann-Echo. bi-m. ISSN 0005-8947 (Bergmann-Kameradschaft 137. Inf. Div.)

**Schachklub Hietzing**
Cafe Frey, Favoritenstr. 44, A-1040 Vienna, Austria.
- Schachklub Hietzing Nachrichtenblatt. q. ISSN 0036-584X

**Verlag A. Schendl**
Karlsgasse 15, Postfach 29, A-1041 Vienna, Austria.
- Austria Tennis. 10 per yr. (Oesterreichischer Tennisverband)
- Austropack; Zeitschrift fuer alle Gebiete des Verpackungswesens, fuer Transport und Verkehr. m. ISSN 0005-0563

**Reinhold Schmidt Verlag**
Mariahilferstrasse 113, A-1060 Vienna, Austria.
- Bauindustrie. 10 per yr. ISSN 0005-6456
- Maschinenwelt-Elektrotechnik. a. ISSN 0025-4533

**Schriften zur Zeit GmbH**
Museumstr. 5, A-1070 Vienna, Austria.
- Neues Forum; internationale fuer den dialog. m. ISSN 0028-3622

**Verlag Anton Schroll und Co.**
Spengergasse 39, A-1051 Vienna, Austria.
- Kunsthistorische Sammlungen in Wien. Jahrbuch. a. ISSN 0075-2312 (Kunsthistorisches Museum in Wien)

**Oesterreichische Zeitschrift fuer Kunst und**
Denkmalpflege. 5 per yr. ISSN 0029-9626 (Austria. Oesterreichisches Bundesdenkmalamt)

**Schutzverband gegen unlauteren Wettbewerb**
- Recht und Wettbewerb. (pub. by Johann L. Bondi und Sohn)

**Emmerich Selinger, Ed. & Pub.**
Oelweingasse 35, A-1153 Vienna, Austria.
- Erfolgs- und Erwerbspost. m. ISSN 0014-0104
- Hoerbiger Instituts Mitteilungen. a. (Hoerbiger Institut)
- World-Magazine.

**Seminarhilfswerk Innsbruck**
Riedgasse 9, A-6020 Innsbruck-Hoetting, Austria.
- Auftrag/Mandate. s-a. ISSN 0004-7872

**Sensen-Verlag Ernst Schwarcz**
Sensengasse 4, A-1090 Vienna, Austria.
- Institut fuer Gesellschaftspolitik. Mitteilungen. s-a. ISSN 0046-9696
- Wissenschaft und Weltbild; Zeitschrift fuer die Grundfragen der Forschung. q. ISSN 0043-6798

**Shell Austria AG**
Rennweg 12, A-1030 Vienna, Austria.
- Shell Erdoel Informationen. m. ISSN 0037-3567
- Shell Hausnachrichten. m. ISSN 0037-3540

**Der Soldat Zeitungs- und Zeitschriftenverlags-Gesellschaft MbH**
Seidengasse 3, A-1070 Vienna, Austria.
- Der Soldat; Oesterreichische Soldaten-zeitung. s-m. ISSN 0038-0962

**Sonnen-Verlag Bauer und Co.**
Gaertnergasse 1, A-1030 Vienna, Austria.
- Die Sphinx. fortn. ISSN 0017-1654
- Spinx-Magazin. m. ISSN 0038-7436

**Sozialistische Jugend Oesterreichs**
Neustiftgasse 3-4, A-1070 Vienna, Austria.
- Trotzdem; Zeitschrift fuer junge Sozialisten. m. ISSN 0041-3356

**Sozialistische Partei Oberoesterreichs. Landesorganisation**
Landstr. 36, A-4020 Linz, Austria.
- Bildungs-Kurier. bi-m.

**Sozialistische Partei Oesterreichs**
- Zukunft. (pub. by Sozialistischer Verlag GmbH)

**Sozialistische Partei Oesterreichs. Bezirksorganisation Linz-Stadt**
Muldenstr. 5, A-4020 Linz, Austria.
- Die Wahrheit; Betriebszeitung fuer Arbeiter und Angestellte der Voest-Alpine. m. ISSN 0042-9996 (Betriebsektion Voest Alpine)

**Sozialistische Partei Oesterreichs. Bildungszentrale**
Loewelstr. 18, A-1010 Vienna, Austria.
- Sozialistische Erziehung; zeitschrift fuer die Bildungsund Kulturarbeit der sozialistischen Bewegung Oesterreichs. 5 per yr. ISSN 0038-6146

**Sozialistischer Lehrerverein Oesterreichs**
Lange Gasse 20, A-1080 Vienna, Austria.
- Freie Lehrerstimme. bi-m. ISSN 0016-075X

**Sozialistischer Verlag GmbH**
Rechte Wienzeile 97, A-1050 Vienna, Austria.
- Frau. w. ISSN 0016-0121
- Zukunft; Sozialistische Zeitschrift fuer Politik, Wirtschaft und Kultur. fortn. ISSN 0044-5452 (Sozialistische Partei Oesterreichs)

**Sozialwissenschaftliche Studiengesellschaft. Wissenschaftlicher Beirat**
Maria Theresienstrasse 9, A-1090 Vienna, Austria.
- Angewandte Sozialforschung. Journal. q. ISSN 0025-8822

**Sparkassenverlag Ges. m.b.H.**
Grimmelshausengasse 1, A-1030 Vienna, Austria.
- Austria. Bundesministerium fuer Bauten und Technik. Wohnbauforschung. m.
- Oesterreichisches Forschungsinstitut fuer Sparkassenwesen. Schriftenreihe. q. ISSN 0472-5859
- Der Sparefroh; Freund der Sparjugend. 7 per yr. ISSN 0038-6510 (Hauptverband der Oesterreichischen Sparkassen)

**Springer-Verlag**
For publications of this company see section for
UNITED STATES

**Staatlich Genehmigte Gesellschaft der Autoren**
Komponisten und Musikverleger, Baumannstr. 10,
1030 Vienna 3, Austria.
- Oesterreichische Autorenzeitung. q. ISSN 0029-
8883

**Stadl-Paura. Gemeindeamt**
A-4651 Stadl-Paura, Austria.
- Stadlinger Post. q. ISSN 0038-8939

**Stadtmuseum Linz**
Bethlehemstrasse 7, A-4020 Linz/Donau, Austria.
- Naturkundliches Jahrbuch der Stadt Linz. a. ISSN
0470-3901

**Standpunkte und Dokumente**
Post Jach 115, A-1191 Vienna, Austria.
- Standpunkte und Dokumente. q. ISSN 0049-2078

**Steiermaerkischer Gemeindebund**
Burgring 18, A-8010 Graz, Austria.
- Steirische Gemeinde-Nachrichten. m. ISSN 0039-
1050

**Steiermark. Amt der Steiermaerkischen
Landesregierung. Landesamtsdirektion - Referat
Statistik**
Hofgasse 13, A-8010 Graz, Austria.
- Steirische Statistiken. q. ISSN 0039-1093

**Steiermark. Landesjugendreferat der
Steiermaerkischen Landesregierung**
Burg, A-8010 Graz, Austria.
- Der Froehliche Kreis; Vierteljahrsschrift fuer
Volkstanz und Volkstumspflege. q. ISSN 0016-
156X

**Steiermark. Landesstelle fuer Brandverhuetung in
Steiermark**
Roseggerkai 3/III, A-8010 Graz, Austria.
- Brandverhuetung; Mitteilungsblatt der
oesterreichischen Brandverhutungsstellen. bi-m.
ISSN 0029-8956

**Steiermarkische Gebietskrankenkasse fuer Arbeiter
und Angestellte**
Josef-Pongratz-Platz 1, A-1070 Vienna, Austria.
- Krankenversicherung. q. ISSN 0023-4524

**Steiger-Werbung Verlag GmbH**
Kandlgasse 2, 1070 Vienna, Austria.
- Hutmacher-, Modisten- und Schirmmacher-
Zeitung. m. ISSN 0018-8050
- Der Oesterreichische Arzt. 8 per yr. ISSN 0029-
8875 (Vereinigung Oesterreichischer Aerzte)

**Steirische Landesjaegerschaft**
Hartenaugasse 6, A-8010 Graz, Austria.
- Anblick; Zeitschrift fuer Jagd, Fischerei,
Jagdhundwesen und Naturschutz. m. ISSN 0003-
2824

**Steirische Wasserkraft- und Elektrizitaets-AG**
Leonhardguertel 10, A-8011 Graz, Austria.
- STEWEAG-Rundschau. bi-m.

**Steirischer Tonkuenstlerbund**
Joanneumring 11/I, 8010 Graz, Austria.
- Musik aus der Steiermark. 4-6 per yr.

**Steirisches Volksbildungswerk**
Dietrichsteinplatz 15-III, A-8010 Graz, Austria.
- Steirische Berichte. bi-m. ISSN 0039-1042

**Stephanus-Verlag**
Box 303, A-1071 Vienna, Austria.
- Religioese Graphik; Blaetter fuer Freunde
christlicher Gebrauchsgraphik. irreg. (2-3 per yr.)
ISSN 0034-3935

**Stern-Verlagsges MbH.**
Hoechstaedtpl. 5, A-1020 Vienna, Austria.
- Arbeit; Zeitschrift fuer Sozialpolitik, Wirtschaft
und Betrieb. m. ISSN 0003-7605

**Steyr-Daimler-Puch AG**
Kaerntner Ring 7, A-1011 Vienna, Austria.
- Traktor Aktuell. q. ISSN 0041-0985 (Subscr. to:
Morawa und Co., Postfach 159, a-1011 Vienna,
Austria)
- Transport Aktuell. q.

**Leopold Stocker Verlag**
Buergergasse 11, A-8011 Graz, Austria.
- Alpenlaendische Bienenzeitung. m (11 per yr.)
ISSN 0002-6352
- Bienenwelt; Zeitschrift fuer den fortschrittlichen
Imker. m. ISSN 0006-2154
- Der Fortschrittliche Landwirt. s-m. ISSN 0015-
8224

**Ed. & Pub. Eduard Strohmaier**
Waldstr. 75, A-2130 Mistelbach, Austria.
- Heimat und Welt. m.

**P. Adalbert Stummbillig, C. Pp.S.**
Kleinholz-Postfach 7, A-6330 Kufstein, Austria.
- Herold des Kostbaren Blutes. m. ISSN 0018-0815

**Styria Verlag**
Schoenaugasse 64, A-8011 Graz, Austria.
- Entschluss; Zeitschrift fuer plants Praxis und
Theologie. m. ISSN 0017-4602
- Die Republik; staatspolitische Blaetter des
Oesterreichischen Nationalinstituts. q. ISSN 0048-
7287 (Oesterreichisches Nationalinstitut)
- Die Wende; oesterreichs groesste wochenzeitung
fuer junge erwaehsene. w. ISSN 0043-2679
(Katholisches Jugendwerk Oesterreichs)

**Sudetendeutsche Landsmannschaft Oesterreich**
- Sudetenpost. (pub. by Sudetendeutscher
Presseverein)

**Sudetendeutscher Presseverein**
Postfach 405, Obere Donaulaende 7, A-4010 Linz,
Austria.
- Sudetenpost. fortn. ISSN 0039-4556
(Sudetendeutsche Landsmannschaft Oesterreich)

**Suedtirol Verlag**
Defreggerstr. 23, A-6020 Innsbruck, Austria.
- Suedtirol in Wort und Bild. q. ISSN 0039-4629

**Suttner-Gesellschaft, Oesterreichische
Friedensgesellschaft**
Landstr. Hauptstr. 14/5, A-1030 Vienna, Austria.
- Kampf dem Krieg; Blaetter fuer internationale
Verstaendigung. 4 per yr. ISSN 0022-8230

**Technische Universitaet Wien. Institut fuer
Eisenbahnwesen, Spezialbahnen und
Verkehrswirtschaft**
Karlsplatz 13, A-1040 Vienna, Austria.
- Technische Hochschule Wien. Institut fuer
Eisenbahnwesen, Spezialbahnen und
Verkehrswirtschaft. Arbeiten. biennial.

**Technische Universitaet Wien. Institut fuer
Wasserversorgung, Abwassereinigung und
Gewaesserschutz**
A-1040 Vienna, Austria.
- Wiener Mitteilungen-Wasser, Abwasser,
Gewaesser. irreg.

**Technisches Museum fuer Industrie und Gewerbe,
Vienna**
- Blaetter fuer Technikgeschichte. (pub. by Springer-
Verlag US)

**Technopress Fachzeitschriften Verlagsgesellschaft
m.b.H.**
Felix-Mottl-Str. 12, A-1190 Vienna, Austria.
- Baumaschine - Baugeraet - Baustelle;
Fachzeitschrift fuer Bau- und Baunebengewerbe.
14 per yr.
- I T R. (International Transport Revue) 14 per yr.
ISSN 0019-0845
- Maschinen Report International. q.
- Technopress Bau Magazin; fuer baustoffe,
elemente und zubehoer. q.

**Theater der Jugend**
Batthianystiege Hofburg, A-1010 Vienna, Austria.
- Neue Wege; kulturzeitschrift junger menschen. 7-8
per yr. ISSN 0028-3444

**Theater in der Josefstadt. Direktion**
Josefstaedterstr. 26, A-1082 Vienna, Austria.
- Neue Blaetter des Theaters in der Josefstadt. s-m.
ISSN 0028-3096

**Theosophische Gesellschaft in Europa**
- Adyar. (pub. by Adyar-Verlagsvereinigung)

**Thiel, Jost und Co., Ges. m.b.H.**
Margaretenstr. 56, A-1050 Vienna, Austria.
- Werbung in Oesterreich Intern. m. ISSN 0043-
2725 (Bundesinnung des Wirtschaftlichen
Werbewesens)

**Tierschutzaktion "der Blaue Kreis"**
Arsenal Obj. 8c, 1030 Vienna, Austria.
- Kamerad Tier. bi-m. ISSN 0022-8117

**Tiroler Landesmuseum Ferdinandeum, Innsbruck**
Museumstr. 15, A-6010 Innsbruck, Austria.
- Tiroler Landesmuseum Ferdinandeum, Innsbruck.
Veroeffentlichungen. a.

**Tiroler Landestheater**
Rennweg 2, Postfach 134, A-6010 Innsbruck,
Austria.
- Innsbrucker Theater- und Konzertspiegel. m. ISSN
0020-1642

**Rudolf Trauner Verlag**
Koeglstr. 14, A-4020 Linz/Donau, Austria.
- Linzer Woche. m. ISSN 0024-4147 (Linz.
Magistrat)

**Tyrol. Amt der Tiroler Landesregierung**
Landhaus, A 6010 Innsbruck, Tyrol, Austria.
- Bote fuer Tirol; Amtsblatt der Behoerden Aemter
und Gerichte Tirols. w. ISSN 0006-8225

**Tyrol. Institut fuer Verkehr und Tourismus**
Wilhelm-Greil-Str. 14, A-6010 Innsbruck, Austria.
- Tiroler Verkehswirtschaftliche Zahlen. a.

**Tyrol. Tiroler Landesregierung. Kulturreferat**
Neues Landhaus, A-6010 Innsbruck, Austria.
- Das Fenster; tiroler Kulturzeitschrift. s-a. ISSN
0015-0029
- Kulturberichte aus Tirol. q. ISSN 0023-5210

**Ueberparteilicher Aerzteverband Niederoesterreichs**
Helenen Str. 12, A-2500 Baden be, Wien, Austria.
- Arzt in Niederoesterreich. q. ISSN 0004-4180

**Carl Ueberreuter**
Alserstr. 24, A-1095 Vienna, Austria.
- Austria. Statistisches Zentralamt. Aussenhandel
Oesterreichs. ISSN 0004-816X (Austria.
Oesterreichisches Statistisches Zentralamt)
- Austria. Statistisches Zentralamt. Statistik der
Aktiengesellschaften in Oesterreich. a. ISSN
0081-5233 (Austria. Oesterreichisches
Statistisches Zentralamt)
- Austria. Statistisches Zentralamt. Statistik der
Rechtspflege. a.
- Austria. Statistisches Zentralamt. Statistische
Nachrichten. m. ISSN 0029-9960
- Fremdenverkehr in Oesterreich. a. ISSN 0071-
948X (Austria. Oesterreichisches Statistisches
Zentralamt)
- Oesterreich in Geschichte und Literatur (mit
Geographie) bi-m. ISSN 0029-8743 (Institut fuer
Oesterreichkunde)
- Oesterreichische Militaerische Zeitschrift. bi-m.
ISSN 0048-1440
- Truppendienst; Zeitschrift fuer die Ausbildung im
Bundesheer. bi-m. ISSN 0041-3658

**Walter E. Ullmann, Editor and Publisher**
Senefeldergasse 18, A-1100 Vienna, Austria.
- Welt der Diplomatie; die Zeitschrift fuer den
diplomatischen Corps und anspruchsvolle Leser.
bi-m.

**Unitas Malacologica Europaea**
Secretary: Dr. Oliver E. Paget, Burgring 7, A-1010
Vienna, Austria.
- European Malacological Congress. Proceedings.
irreg.; 5th, Milan, 1974. ISSN 0071-2914
(European Malacological Union)

**United Nations Industrial Development Organization**
For publications of this agency see section for
UNITED NATIONS

**United Nations World**
Graben 27, A-1010 Vienna, Austria.
- Eine Welt der Vereinten Nationen/United
Nations World. 4 per yr. ISSN 0013-2640

**United States East-West Trade Center**
Prinz Eugen-Str. 8, A-1041 Vienna, Austria.
- East West Trade Information Bulletin. irreg.

**Universal Edition AG**
Karlsplatz 6, Postfach 130, Vienna A-1015, Austria.
- Jazzforschung/Jazz Research. a. ISSN 0075-3572
(International Society for Jazz Research (Graz,
Austria)) (Co-Sponsors: Hochschule fuer Musik
und Institut fuer Jazz Darstellende Kunst.)

**Universitaet Innsbruck**
- Forschungen zur Innsbrucker Universitaetsgeschichte. (pub. by Oesterreichische Kommissionsbuchhandlung)
- Innsbrucker Universitaetsreden. (pub. by Oesterreichische Kommissionsbuchhandlung)
- Studien zur Rechts-, Wirtschafts- und Kulturgeschichte. (pub. by Oesterreichische Kommissionsbuchhandlung)
- Universitaet Innsbruck. Alpenkundliche Studien. (pub. by Oesterreichische Kommissionsbuchhandlung)
- Universitaet Innsbruck. Alpin-Biologische Studien. (pub. by Oesterreichische Kommissionsbuchhandlung)
- Universitaet Innsbruck. Finanzwissenschaftliche Studien. (pub. by Oesterreichische Kommissionsbuchhandlung)
- Universitaet Innsbruck. Kunstgeschichtliche Studien. (pub. by Oesterreichische Kommissionsbuchhandlung)
- Universitaet Innsbruck. Mathematische Studien. (pub. by Oesterreichische Kommissionsbuchhandlung)
- Universitaet Innsbruck. Medizinische Fakultaet. Arbeiten. (pub. by Oesterreichische Kommissionsbuchhandlung)
- Volkskundliche Studien. (pub. by Oesterreichische Kommissionsbuchhandlung)

**Universitaet Innsbruck. Arbeitsgemeinschaft fuer Wissenschaft und Politik**
Salurnerstr. 15, A-6020 Innsbruck, Austria.
- Universitaet Innsbruck. Arbeitsgemeinschaft fuer Wissenschaft und Politik. Veroeffentlichungen. irreg.

**Universitaet Innsbruck. Theologische Fakultaet**
- Universitaet Innsbruck. Theologische Fakultaet. Studien und Arbeiten. (pub. by Oesterreichische Kommissionsbuchhandlung)
- Zeitschrift fuer katholische Theologie. (pub. by Verlag Herder)

**Universitaet Salzburg**
- Salzburger Universitaetsreden. (pub. by Universitaetsverlag Anton Pustet)

**Universitaet Salzburg. Institut fuer Englische Sprache**
Akademiestr. 24, A-5020 Salzburg, Austria.
- Analecta Cartusiana. irreg.
- Elizabethan and Renaissance Studies. irreg.
- Jacobean Drama Studies. irreg.
- Poetic Drama and Poetic Theory. irreg.
- Romantic Reassessment. irreg.

**Universitaet Salzburg. Institut fuer Romanische Philologie**
Akademiestr. 24, A-5020 Salzburg, Austria.
- Salzburger Romantische Schriften. irreg.

**Universitaet Salzburg. Professorenkollegium der Theologischen Fakultaet**
- Oesterreichisches Klerus Blatt. (pub. by Universitaetenverlag Anton Pustet)

**Universitaet Wien**
- Universitaet Wien. Institut fuer Statistik. Schriftenreihe. Neue Folge. (pub. by Physica-Verlag Rudolf Liebing GmbH und Co. GW)

**Universitaet Wien. Institut fuer Klassische Philologie**
- Wiener Studien. Zeitschrift fuer Klassische Philologie und Patristik. (pub. by Hermann Boehlaus Nachf.)

**Universitaet Wien. Institut fuer Oesterreichische Geschichtsforschung**
- Institut fuer Oesterreichische Geschichtsforschung. Mitteilungen. (pub. by Hermann Boehlaus Nachf.)

**Universitaet Wien. Institut fuer Rechtsvergleichung**
- Wiener Rechtswissenschaftliche Studien. (pub. by Manzsche Verlags- und Universitaetsbuchhandlung)
- Zeitschrift fuer Rechtsvergleichung. (pub. by Manzsche Verlags- und Universitaetsbuchhandlung)

**Universitaet Wien. Institut fuer Slavische Philologie**
- Wiener Slavistisches Jahrbuch/Viennese Slavonic Yearbook. (pub. by Hermann Boehlaus Nachf.)

**Universitaet Wien. Institut fuer Theaterwissenschaft**
- Maske und Kothurn. (pub. by Hermann Boehlaus Nachf.)
- Schauspielfuehrer. (pub. by Anton Hiersemann Verlag GW)

- Wiener Forschungen zur Theater und Medienwissenschaft. (pub. by Wilhelm Braumueller Universitaets-Verlagsbuchhandlung GmbH)

**Universitaet Wien. Institut fuer Ur- und Fruehgeschichte**
Universitaetsstr. 7, A-1010 Vienna, Austria.
- Archaeologia Austriaca. (pub. by Franz Deuticke)
- Oesterreichischen Arbeitsgemeinschaft fuer Ur- und Fruhgeschichte. Mitteilungen. s-a. ISSN 0029-9693

**Universitaet Wien. Institut fuer Voelkerkunde**
- Wiener Beitraege zur Kulturgeschichte und Linguistik. (pub. by Verlag Ferdinand Berger und Soehne OHG)

**Universitaet Wien. Katholisch-Theologische Fakultaet**
- Wiener Beitraege zur Theologie. (pub. by Wiener Dom Verlag)

**Universitaet Wien. Orientalisches Institut**
Universitaets Str. 7/V, A-1010 Vienna, Austria.
- Wiener Zeitschrift fuer die Kunde des Morgenlandes. irreg.    ISSN 0084-0076

**Universitaet Wien. Studienrichtungsvertretung am Germanistischen Institut**
Universitaetsstr. 7, A-1010 Vienna, Austria.
- Beitraege zum Deutschstudium; Zeitschrift fuer Studierende der deutschen Philologie. s-a.

**Universitaetssternwarte zu Wien**
- Universitaetssternwarte zu Wien. Annalen. (pub. by Duemmlers Verlag GW)

**Universitaetsverlag Wagner**
Andreas-Hofer-Str. 13, Postfach 219, A-6010 Innsbruck, Austria.
- Acta Philologica Aenipontana. irreg., vol. 3, 1976. ISSN 0065-1532 (Gesellschaft fuer Klassische Philologie in Innsbruck)

**Ventil**
Piaristengasse 33/2/10, A-1080 Vienna, Austria.
- Ventil; oesterreichische Kulturblatter. q. ISSN 0042-3467

**Verband der Altpfadfindergilden Oesterreichs**
Hetzendorferstr. 73, A-1120 Vienna, Austria.
- Gildenweg. 5 per yr. ISSN 0016-9986

**Verband der Maschinen- und Werkzeughaendler, MAWEV**
- Industrie- und Handelszeitung. (pub. by Verlag Friedrich Brabec)

**Verband der Oesterreichischen Neuphilologen fuer Moderne Sprachen, Literatur und Paedagogik**
Universitaetsstr. 11, A-1010 Vienna 1, Austria.
- Moderne Sprachen. q. ISSN 0026-8666

**Verband der Professoren Oesterreichs**
c/o Dr. Gertraud Christian, Ed., Neue- Weit- Gasse 17, A-1130 Vienna, Austria.
- Professor. m. or bi-m. ISSN 0033-0221

**Verband der Schuhindustrie und dem Schuhhandel**
- Schuh-Zeitung. (pub. by Verlag Michael Fischer)

**Verband der Versicherungsunternehmungen Oesterreichs**
Schwarzenbergplatz 7, A-1030 Vienna, Austria.
- Verband der Versicherungsunternehmungen Oesterreichs. Geschaeftsbericht. a.

**Verband der Wissenschaftlichen Gesellschaften**
Lindengasse 37, A-1070 Vienna, Austria.
- Gesamtverzeichnis Oesterreichischer Dissertationen. a. ISSN 0072-4165
- Oesterreichische Volkskundliche Bibliographie. irreg., no. 6, 1973. (prep. by its Verein fuer Volkskunde)
- Wiener Gesellschaft fuer Theaterforschung. Jahrbuch. irreg.

**Verband des Naehmaschinen-und Fahrradhandels und Gewerbes Oesterreichs**
- Oesterreichische Naehmaschinen- und Zweirad-Zeitung. (pub. by Verlag Michael Fischer)

**Verband fuer Heimatschutz und Heimatpflege in Tirol**
Exlgasse 20, Innsbruck, Austria.
- Tiroler Heimatblaetter. q. ISSN 0040-8115

**Verband Landwirtschaftlicher Gutsbetriebe in Oesterreich**
- Der Land- und Forstwirtschaftliche Betrieb. (pub. by Oesterreichischer Agrarverlag)

**Verband Oesterreichischer Archivare**
Minoritenplatz 1, A-1010 Vienna, Austria. (Subscr. to: Stiftgasse 2, 1070 Vienna, Austria)
- Scrinium. bi-a.

**Verband Oesterreichischer Brieftaubenzuechter**
Josef Oesterreichergasse 18, A-1233 Vienna, Austria.
- Oesterreichischer Brieftaubensport. q. ISSN 0029-9731

**Verband Oesterreichischer Hoehlenforscher**
Obere Donaustr. 99, A-1020 Vienna, Austria.
- Hoehle; Zeitschrift fuer Karst- und Hoehlenkunde. q. ISSN 0018-3091

**Verband Oesterreichischer Landsmannschaften**
- Verband Oesterreichischer Landsmannschaften Nachrichten-und Mitteilungsblatt. (pub. by Bauer's Witwe und Co.)

**Verband Oesterreichischer Philatelisten-Vereine**
Universitaetsstr. 8, Postfach 79, A-1096 Vienna, Austria.
- Briefmarke. m. ISSN 0007-0033

**Verband Oesterreichischer Zeitungsherausgeber und Zeitungsverleger**
Schreyvogelgasse 3, A-1010 Vienna, Austria.
- Oesterreichs Presse, Werbung, Graphik. a. ISSN 0030-0004

**Verband Sozialistischer Mittelschueler**
Lindengasse 32, A-1070 Vienna, Austria.
- Schuelerfront. bi-m.

**Verband Sozialistischer Studenten Oesterreichs**
Werdertorgasse 6, A-1010 Vienna, Austria.
- Alternative; sozialistische Zeitschrift fuer Politik, Wirtschaft und Kultur. bi-m. ISSN 0002-659X
- Neue Alternative; sozialist Zeitschrift fuer Kultur, Wirtschaft, Politik. m. ISSN 0028-3061

**Verein der Freunde der Volksliteratur**
Elisabethstr. 12, A-8010 Graz, Austria.
- Blaetter fuer Volksliteratur. q. ISSN 0006-4483

**Verein der Freunde des Wiener Tagebuch**
- Wiener Tagebuch. (pub. by Buch und Offsetdruck W. Goetz)

**Verein der Oesterreichischen Zementfabrikanten**
Mentergasse 3, A-1070 Vienna, Austria.
- Zement und Beton. a. (Co-Sponsor: Oesterreichischer Betonverein)

**Verein Evangelisches Diakoniewerk Gallneukirchen**
Haupstr. 1, A-4210 Gallneukirchen, Austria.
- Gallneukirchner Bote. q. ISSN 0016-4143

**Verein fuer Denkmal und Stadtbildpflege**
Karlplatz 5, A-1010 Vienna, Austria.
- Steine Sprechen. q. ISSN 0039-1026

**Verein fuer Geschichte der Arbeiterbewegung**
- Archiv. (pub. by Vorwaerts AG)

**Verein fuer Geschichte der Stadt Wien**
Lassingleithnerplatz 3, A-1020 Vienna, Austria.
- Wiener Geschichtsblaetter. q. ISSN 0043-5317

**Verein fuer Heimatpflege Fuerstenfeld**
Wallstr. 24, A-8280 Fuerstenfeld, Austria.
- Fuerstenfelder Grenzlandecho. fortn. ISSN 0016-2469

**Verein fuer Lebenskunde**
Postfach 6, A-5033 Salzburg, Austria.
- Lebensschutz; der stille Weg. 8 per yr.

**Verein fuer Sozial- und Wirtschaftsforschung**
Renngasse 12, A-1010 Vienna, Austria.
- Informationen zu Aktuellen Fragen der Sozial- und Wirtschaftpolitik. irreg. ISSN 0083-6125

**Verein fuer Volkskunde**
Laudongasse 19, A-1080 Vienna, Austria.
- Oesterreichische Zeitschrift fuer Volkskunde. q. ISSN 0029-9669

- Verein fuer Volkskunde in Wien. Sonderschriften. irreg., vol. 2, 1972.
- Volkskunde in Oesterreich. m. ISSN 0042-8531

**Verein Internationale Joseph Haydn Institut, Eisenstadt**
- Haydn Yearbook. Haydn Jahrbuch. (pub. by Universal Edition Sales, Inc. US)

**Verein Oesterreichischer Giessereifachleute**
- Giesserei Rundschau. (pub. by Verlag Lorenz)

**Verein Oesterreichischer Zahnaerzte**
Weihburggasse 10-12, Vienna 1, Austria.
- Oesterreichische Zeitschrift fuer Stomatologie. m. ISSN 0029-9642 (Co-sponsors: Oesterreichische Gesellschaft fuer Zahn- Mund- und Kieferheilkunde; Bundesfachgruppe fuer Zahn-, Mund- und Kieferheilkunde der Oesterreichischen Aerztekammer)

**Verein zur Foerderung der Liberalkatholischen Kirche**
Erdenweg 21, A-1140 Vienna, Austria.
- Kirche; Dioezesanblatt fuer die Kirchenprovinz Mitteleuropa. q. ISSN 0023-1789

**Verein zur Foerderung des Schienenverkehrs**
Oldenburggasse 73, A-1232 Vienna, Austria.
- Der Spurkranz; Unabhaengige Zeitschrift fuer Verkehrspolitik. m. ISSN 0038-870X

**Verein zur Foerderung des Tischtennissports in Oesterreich**
Neulerchenfelderstr. 5-7, A-1160 Vienna, Austria.
- Tischtennis-Schau. 6 per yr. ISSN 0040-814X

**Vereinigte Buehnen Graz**
Burggasse 16, A-8010 Graz, Austria.
- Theater in Graz. 3 per m.

**Vereinigung christlicher Lehrer an den hoeheren Schulen Oesterreichs**
- Oesterreichische Hoehere Schule. (pub. by Dr. Wilhelm Hadmovsky, Ed. & Pub.)

**Vereinigung der Ehemaligen Don Boscos**
Hagenmuellergasse 31, A-1030 Vienna 3, Austria.
- Er Ruft. q. ISSN 0013-9912

**Vereinigung der Oesterreichischen Richter**
- Oesterreichische Richterzeitung. (pub. by Herz und Co.)

**Vereinigung Oesterreichischer Aerzte**
- Der Oesterreichische Arzt. (pub. by Steiger-Werbung Verlag GmbH)

**Vereinigung Oesterreichischer Bibliothekare**
Josefsplatz 1, A-1014 Vienna 1, Austria (Subscription to; Universitaetsbibliothek Graz, Universitaetsplatz 3, A-8010 Graz, Austria)
- Vereinigung Oesterreichischer Bibliothekare. Mitteilungen. q.

**Vereinigung Oesterreichischer Industrieller**
Am Heumarkt 12, A-1030 Vienna, Austria.
- Die Industrie. w. ISSN 0019-896X
- Sozialpolitik und Arbeitsrecht. (pub. by Industrie Zeitschriftenverlags Ges. m.b.H.)

**Vereinigung Oesterreichischer Klubs Berufstaetiger Frauen**
Elisabethstr. 48, A-8010 Graz, Austria.
- Berufstaetige Frau Oesterreichs; die unabhaengige Zeitschrift fuer die moderne frau. bi-m. ISSN 0005-9560

**Vereinigung Oesterreichischer Papierindustrieller**
Gumpendorferstrasse 6, A-1061 Vienna, Austria.
- Oesterreichische Papier. m. ISSN 0473-8322

**Vereinigung Oesterreichischer Wirtschaftstreuhaender**
- Der Wirtschaftstreuhaender. (pub. by Friedrich Rudy)

**Verlag der Oesterreichischen Akademie der Wissenschaften**
Dr. Ignaz Seipel-Platz 2, A-1010 Vienna, Austria.
- Fontes Rerum Austriacarum. Reihe 1. Scriptores. irreg. ISSN 0071-6871 (Oesterreichische Akademie der Wissenschaften. Historische Kommission)
- Fontes Rerum Austriacarum. Reihe 2. Diplomataria et Acta. irreg. ISSN 0071-688X (Oesterreichische Akademie der Wissenschaften. Historische Kommission)

- Fontes Rerum Austriacarum. Reihe 3. Fontes Juris. irreg. ISSN 0071-6898 (Oesterreichische Akademie der Wissenschaften. Historische Kommission)
- Mykenische Studien. irreg. (Oesterreichische Akademie der Wissenschaften. Kommission fuer Mykenische Forschung)
- Oesterreichische Akademie der Wissenschaften. Almanach. a. ISSN 0078-3447
- Oesterreichische Akademie der Wissenschaften. Archiv fuer Oesterreichische Geschichte. irreg. ISSN 0003-9322 (Oesterreichische Akademie der Wissenschaften. Historische Kommission)
- Oesterreichische Akademie der Wissenschaften. Iranische Kommission. Veroeffentlichungen. irreg.
- Oesterreichische Akademie der Wissenschaften. Kommission fuer die Tabula Imperii Byzantini. Veroeffentlichungen. irreg.
- Oesterreichische Akademie der Wissenschaften. Kommission fuer Linguistik und Kommunikationsforschung. Veroeffentlichungen. irreg.
- Oesterreichische Akademie der Wissenschaften. Kommission fuer Literaturwissenschaft. Veroeffentlichungen. irreg.
- Oesterreichische Akademie der Wissenschaften. Kommission fuer Musikforschung. Mitteilungen. irreg. ISSN 0023-3048
- Oesterreichische Akademie der Wissenschaften. Kommission fuer Sozial- und Wirtschaftswissenschaften. Veroeffentlichungen. irreg., no. 9, 1976.
- Oesterreichische Akademie der Wissenschaften. Kommission zur Herausgabe des Corpus der Lateinischen Kirchenvaeter. Veroeffentlichungen. irreg.
- Oesterreichische Akademie der Wissenschaften. Numismatische Kommission. Veroeffentlichungen. irreg.
- Oesterreichische Akademie der Wissenschaften. Philosophisch-Historische Klasse. Anzeiger. a. ISSN 0065-5368
- Oesterreichische Akademie der Wissenschaften. Philosophisch-Historische Klasse. Sitzungsberichte. irreg. ISSN 0029-8832
- Oesterreichische Akademie der Wissenschaften. Prahistorische Kommission. Mitteilungen. irreg., vol. 15 per 16, 1974. ISSN 0065-5376
- Oesterreichische Byzantinistik. Jahrbuch. a. ISSN 0075-2355 (Oesterreichische Akademie der Wissenschaften. Kommission fuer Byzantinistik)
- Oesterreichisches Kulturinstitut, Rom. Abteilung fuer Historische Studien. Publikationen I. Abteilung: Abhandlungen. irreg. ISSN 0078-3641
- Oesterreichisches Kulturinstitut, Rom. Abteilung fuer Historische Studien. Publikationen Ii. Abteilung: Quellen. irreg. ISSN 0078-365X
- Roemische Historische Mitteilungen. a. ISSN 0080-3790 (Oesterreichisches Kulturinstitut, Rom IT)
- Sprachkunst; Beitraege zur Literaturwissenschaft. s-a. ISSN 0038-8483

**Verlag des Oesterreichischen Gewerkschaftsbundes GmbH**
Altmannsdorferstrasse 154-156, A-1232 Vienna, Austria.
- Arbeit und Wirtschaft. m. ISSN 0003-7656 (Oesterreichischer Arbeitkammertag) (Co-Sponsor: Oesterreichischer Gewerkschaftsbund)
- Buecherschau; Zeitschrift fuer Betriebs- und Gewerkschaftsbibliotheken. q. ISSN 0007-3040 (Oesterreichischer Gewerkschaftsbund)
- Start und Aufstieg. m. ISSN 0038-9951 (Berufsfoerderungsinstitut)

**Verlag fuer Geschichte und Politik**
Neulinggasse 26, A-1030 Vienna, Austria.
- Oesterreichisches Ost- und Suedosteuropa Institut. Schriftenreihe. irreg., vol. 5, 1975. ISSN 0078-3439

**Verlag fuer Jugend und Volk**
Tiefer Graben 7, A-1014 Vienna, Austria.
- Aufbau; Fachschrift fuer Planen, Bauen, Wohnen. bi-m. ISSN 0004-7805 (Vienna. Stadtbauamt der Stadt Wien)
- Bookbird; literature for children and young people, news from all over the world, recommendations for translation. q. ISSN 0006-7377 (International Board on Books for Young People) (Co-Sponsor: International Institute for Children's Literature and Reading Research)
- Gemeinwirtschaft. 10 per yr. ISSN 0016-6227 (Arbeitsgemeinschaft der Oesterreichischen Gemeinwirtschaft)
- Volkshochschule Brigittenau. Mitteilungsblatt. m.(Sept.-June) ISSN 0042-8507

**Versicherungsanstalt der Oesterreichischen Eisenbahnen. Unfallverhuetungsdienst**
Linke Wienzeile 48-52, A-1060 Vienna, Austria.
- Sicherheit Zuerst. q. ISSN 0037-4539

**Versuchsstation fuer das Gaerungsgewerbe**
Michaelerstr. 25, A-1182 Vienna, Austria.
- Versuchsstation fuer das Gaerungsgewerbe Wien. Mitteilungen. 10 per yr. ISSN 0042-4390

**Victoria Druck-und Verlag Poech und Co. GmbH**
Millergasse 20, A-1062 Vienna, Austria.
- Allgemeiner Muehlen-Markt; Fach-und Ankuendigungsblatt fuer die Getreide-Muehlen- und Futtermittelwirtschaft. s-m. ISSN 0002-5992

**Vienna. Kulturamt der Stadt Wien. Direktion der Staedtischen Buechereien**
- Wiener Buecherbriefe. (pub. by Forumverlag)

**Vienna. Magistrat der Stadt Wien**
Rathaus, A-1082 Vienna, Austria.
- Wiener Wirtschaftsberichte. 3 per yr.

**Vienna. Magistrat der Stadt Wien. Statistisches Amt**
Volksgartenstr. 3, A-1016 Vienna, Austria
- Vienna. Statistik und Verwaltung. Mitteilungen. q. ISSN 0026-6876 (Subscriptions to: Carl Ueberreuter Druck und Verlag M. Salzer A. G., Alserstr. 24, A-1090 Vienna, Austria)

**Vienna. Magistrat der Stadt Wien. Verein Wiener Jugendkreis**
Friedrich Schmidt-Platz 5, A-1082 Vienna, Austria.
- Wir Blenden Auf; eine Information des Landesjugendreferates Wien. q. ISSN 0043-5961

**Vienna. Stadtbauamt der Stadt Wien**
- Aufbau. (pub. by Verlag fuer Jugend und Volk)

**Vinzenzgemeinschaft**
A 4020 Linz, Austria.
- Dienen und Helfen. q.

**Volksbildungshaus Wiener Urania**
Uraniastr. 1, A-1010 Vienna, Austria.
- Wiener Urania. Mitteilungen. m. ISSN 0026-6906

**Volksbuchverlag GmbH**
Rennweg 1, A-1030 Vienna, Austria.
- Gildenfreund; Mitteilungsblatt fuer Vertrauenspersonen der Buecher- und Schallplattengilde Gutenberg. 5 per yr. ISSN 0016-9978

**Volkshochschule Linz**
Coulinstrasse 18, A-4020 Linz, Austria.
- Nach der Arbeit. 10 per yr. ISSN 0027-7363

**Volkswirtschaftliche Verlagsgesellschaft m.b.H.**
Schottenfeld Gasse 93/6, A-1070 Vienna, Austria.
- Der Oesterreichische Volkswirt. fortn. ISSN 0029-957X

**Voralberg. Landesregierung**
Montfortstr. 12, 6900 Bregenz, Austria.
- Amtsblatt fuer das Land Vorarlberg. w. ISSN 0003-2271
- Montfort. (pub. by Vorarlberger Verlagsanstalt GmbH)

**Vorarlberger Verlagsanstalt GmbH**
6850 Dornbirn, Austria.
- Montfort; Vierteljahresschrift fuer Geschischte und Gegenwart Vorarlbergs. q. ISSN 0027-0148 (Vorarlberg. Landesregierung)

**Vorwaerts AG**
Rechte Wienzeile 97, Vienna 5, Austria.
- Archiv. q. ISSN 0003-8849 (Verein fuer Geschichte der Arbeiterbewegung)

**Wels. Magistrat der Stadt Wels**
A-4600 Wels, Austria.
- Wels, Stadt. Amtsblatt. m. ISSN 0003-2247

**Welser Kulturring**
Alois Auerstr. 13, A-4600 Wels, Austria.
- Kulturring. m. ISSN 0023-527X

**Welt-Spirale**
Willemerstr. 2, A-4020 Linz, Austria.
- Welt-Spirale; Zeitschrift fuer Fortschrift und Welterneuerung. m. ISSN 0043-2555

**Karl Werner**
Bandg. 34, 1071 Vienna, Austria.
- Jugend und Buch. q. ISSN 0022-5916 (International Institute for Children's Literature and Reading Research) (Co-Sponsor: Oesterreichischer Buchklub der Jugend)

**Wiener Bibliophilen Gesellschaft**
Annagasse 18, A-1015 Vienna, Austria.
- Wiener Bibliophilen Gesellschaft. Mitteilungen. irreg. ISSN 0083-9949

**Wiener Boersekammer**
Wipplingerstr. 34, A-1010 Vienna, Austria.
- Amtlich Nicht Notierte Wertpapiere-Geregelter Freiverkehr an der Wiener Boerse. d.(5 per w.) ISSN 0003-2093
- Wiener Boersekammer. Verordnungsblatt. several times a week. ISSN 0042-4250
- Wiener Warenboerse Holz und Kolonialwaren. Amtliches Kursblatt. w. ISSN 0003-2166
- Wiener Warenboerse Rohhaeute und Felle, Leder Treibriemen und Technische Lederartikel. fortn.

**Wiener Dom Verlag**
Postfach 668, A-1011 Vienna, Austria.
- Wiener Beitraege zur Theologie. irreg., 1971, vol. 32. ISSN 0083-9930 (Universitaet Wien. Katholisch-Theologische Fakultaet)

**Wiener Entomologische Gesellschaft**
Rathausstr. 11, A-1010 Vienna, Austria.
- Wiener Entomologische Gesellschaft. Zeitschrift. 12 per yr. ISSN 0043-5309

**Wiener Gesellschaft fuer Innere Medizin**
- Acta Medica Austriaca. (pub. by Verlag Brueder Hollinek)

**Wiener Gesellschaft fuer Theaterforschung**
Batthyanystiege, A-1010 Vienna, Austria.
- Wiener Gesellschaft fuer Theaterforschung. Jahrbuch. a. ISSN 0072-4262

**Wiener Humanistische Gesellschaft**
- Wiener Humanistische Blaetter. (pub. by Hermann Boehlaus Nachf.)

**Wiener Innung der Schlosser**
- Metall. (pub. by Oesterreichischer Wirtschaftsverlag)

**Wiener Institut fuer Internationale Wirtschaftsvergleiche**
Postfach 87, A-1103 Vienna, Austria.
- Wiener Institut fuer Internationale Wirtschaftsvergleiche. Forschungsberichte. irreg.
- Wiener Institut fuer Internationale Wirtschaftsvergleiche. Reprint Serie. irreg., no. 16, 1972.

**Wiener Institut fuer Standortberatung**
Berggasse 16, A-1090 Vienna, Austria.
- Wiener Institut fuer Standortberatung. W I S T-Informationen. 4 per yr. ISSN 0083-9973

**Wiener Katholische Akademie**
Freyung 6, A-1010 Vienna, Austria.
- Religion, Wissenschaft, Kultur. Jahrbuch. a. ISSN 0080-0872
- Wiener Katholische Akademie. Studien. irreg. ISSN 0084-0009

**Wiener Kulturkreis**
Prinz-Eugen Str. 3, A-1030 Vienna, Austria.
- Wiener Kulturkreis. Mitteilungen. bi-m.

**Wiener Medizinische Akademie**
6-8 Stadiongasse, A-1010 Vienna, Austria.
- International Pediatric Association. Proceedings of Congress. triennial, 1971, 13th, Vienna. ISSN 0074-7300

**Wiener Musikhochschule**
- Wiener Musikhochschule. Publikationen. (pub. by Musikverlag Elisabeth Lafite)

**Wiener Neustadt. Magistrat**
Rathaus, A-2700 Wiener Neustadt, A-4020 Linz.
- Wiener Neustadt. Amstblatt der Statutarstadt. m.

**Wiener Neustaedter Denkmalschutzverein**
Zehnergasse 4, A-2700 Wiener Neustadt, Austria.
- Unser Neustadt. q. ISSN 0042-0484

**Wiener Secession**
Friedrichstr. 5, A-1010 Vienna, Austria.
- Zeit und Kunst. q.

**Wirtschafts-Trend Zeitschriftenverlagsgesellschaft mbH**
Marc-Aurel-Str. 12, A-1010 Vienna, Austria.
- Profil; das unabhaengige Magazin Oesterreichs. w.
- Trend; das Oesterreichische Wirtschaftsmagazin. m. ISSN 0049-4623

**Wohnungsaktiengesellschaft Linz**
Dr. Oswald Kratochwill, Stadlerstr. 3, A-4026 Linz, Austria.
- Daheim Bei der W A G; Mieterzeitung. s-a. ISSN 0011-5320

**Ed. & Pub. Alois Wolf**
Wuerffelgasse 6-8, A-1150 Vienna, Austria.
- Kommentare Zum Zeitgeschehen. approx. 10 per yr. ISSN 0023-303X

**Verlag Dr. Ruediger Wurth**
Greiseneckergasse 6, A-1200 Vienna, Austria.
- Wiener Briefmarkenspiegel; oesterreichisches fachblatt fuer philatelistische forschung und postgeschichte. 6 per yr. ISSN 0043-5287

**Zeitschriftenverlag Austria International GmbH**
Wallnerstr. 8, A-1014 Vienna, Austria.
- Die Buehne. m. ISSN 0007-3075

**Zeitungsunternehmen "Sport", GmbH**
Frankenberggasse 11/6, A-1040 Vienna, Austria.
- Trabrennen. irreg. ISSN 0082-5646

**Josef Zelger**
Luis Zuegg Str. 12, A-6020 Innsbruck, Austria.
- Conceptus; Zeitschrift fuer Philosophie. s-a. ISSN 0010-5155

**Zentralanstalt fuer Meteorologie und Geodynamik**
Hohe Warte 38, A-1190 Vienna, Austria.
- Aerologische Berichte/Aerological Report; Radiosondenaufstiege und Hoehenwindmessungen. q. ISSN 0001-9224
- Austria. Zentralanstalt fuer Meteorologie und Geodynamik. Jahrbuch. irreg. ISSN 0067-2351
- Witterung in Oesterreich. Monatsuebersicht. m. ISSN 0043-7077

**Zentralsparkasse der Gemeinde Wien**
Vordere Zollamtsstr. 13, A-1030 Vienna, Austria.
- Summa. m. ISSN 0039-4971
- Zentralsparkasse der Gemeinde Wien. Information. s-m. ISSN 0044-4316

**Zentralverband der Kleingaertner, Siedler und Kleintierzuechter Oesterreichs**
Getreidemarkt 11, A-1060 Vienna, Austria.
- Der Oesterreichische Kleingaertner. m. ISSN 0029-9758

**Zentralverband der oesterreichischen Aktiengesellschaften**
- Wiener Boersen-Kurier. (pub. by Verlag Friedrich Brabec)

**Zentralverband der Oesterreichischen Konsumgenossenschaften Konsumerverband**
Theobaldgasse 19, A-1060 Vienna, Austria.
- Die Konsumgenossenschaft. bi-w.
- Wir vom Konsum. m. ISSN 0508-8445

**Zentralverein der Wiener Lehrerschaft**
Langegasse 20, A-1080 Vienna, Austria.
- Zentralverein der Wiener Lehrerschaft. Mitteilungen. m. ISSN 0044-4324

**Zoologisch-Botanische Gesellschaft**
Burgring 7, A-1010 Vienna, Austria.
- Koleopterologische Rundschau. irreg. ISSN 0075-6547
- Zoologisch-Botanische Gesellschaft, Vienna. Abhandlungen. irreg. ISSN 0084-5639
- Zoologisch-Botanische Gesellschaft, Vienna. Verhandlungen. irreg. ISSN 0084-5647

**Zwiazek Polakow W Austrii**
Schliessfach 67, A-1021 Vienna, Austria.
- Polonia; biuletyn informacyjny dla Polakow w Austrii/Zeitschrift fuer Polen in Oesterreich. ISSN 0032-3683

**3M Oesterreich m.b.h.**
Feldstr. 63, Box 611, 1011 Vienna-Perchtoldsdorf, Austria.
- 3M Panorama. q. ISSN 0040-6554

# BAHAMAS

**Bahama out Islands Promotion Board**
- Bahama Out Islands Tourist News. (pub. by Star-Advertiser Ltd.)

**Bahamas. Department of Statistics**
P.O. Box N 3904, Nassau, Bahamas.
- Bahamas. Department of Statistics. Labour Force and Income Distribution. irreg.

**Bahamas. Ministry of Works**
Nassau, Bahamas.
- Bahamas. Ministry of Works. Annual Report. a.; latest issue, 1973.

**Bahamas Magazine Ltd.**
Box 208, Nassau, Bahamas.
- Bahamas. q. ISSN 0005-3953

**Bahamian Review**
P.O. 494, Nassau, Bahamas.
- Bahamian Review. m. ISSN 0005-397X

**Central Bank of the Bahamas**
P.O. Box N. 4868, Nassau, Bahamas.
- Central Bank of the Bahamas. Annual Report and Statement of Accounts. a.
- Central Bank of the Bahamas Quarterly Review. q.

**Etienne Dupuch, Jr. Publications**
P.O. Box N7513, Nassau, Bahamas.
- Bahamas Handbook and Businessman's Annual. a. ISSN 0067-2912

**Johnson Publications**
P.O. Box N-1505, Nassau, Bahamas.
- International Bahama Life. m.

**Nassau & Paradise Island Promotion Board**
- Nassau and Paradise Island.Tourist News. (pub. by Star- Advertiser Ltd.)

**Star-Advertiser Ltd.**
P.O. Box 4855, Nassau, Bahamas.
- Bahama Out Islands Tourist News. q. (Bahama out Islands Promotion Board)
- Nassau and Paradise Island.Tourist News. q. (Nassau & Paradise Island Promotion Board)

# BAHRAIN

**Arab Markets**
Box 604, Manama, Bahrain.
- Arab Markets. m.

**Bahrain. Ministry of Information**
Box 253, Manama, Bahrain.
- Bahrain. Ministry of Information. Official Gazette/Al-Jiridah al-Rasmiyah. w.
- Bahrain News/Akhbar al-Bahrain. w. ISSN 0408-2133
- Bahrain Today. m.

**Bahrain Chamber of Commerce and Industry**
Box 666, Manama, Bahrain.
- Bahrain Chamber of Commerce and Industry. Commerce Review/Al-Hiyat al Tijariya. m.

**Bahrain Petroleum Co. Ltd.**
Manama, Bahrain.
- Weekly Star/Al-Najmah al Usbuia. w.

**Bahrain Trade Directory**
Box 524, Manama, Bahrain.
- Bahrain Trade Directory. a. ISSN 0408-215X

**Gulf Weekly Mirror**
Box 551, Manama, Bahrain.
- Gulf Weekly Mirror. w.

# BANGLA DESH

**Al Helal Printing and Publishing Co. Ltd.**
Observer House, Motijheel, Dacca, Bangladesh.
  ● Chitrali. w. ISSN 0009-4870

**Asian Trade Publications**
SWA (20) Gulshan Model Town, Dacca 12,
Bangladesh.
  ● Yearbook on Jute. a. ISSN 0084-411X

**Asiatic Society of Bangladesh**
Dacca Museum Bldgs., Ramna, Dacca 2,
Bangladesh.
  ● Asiatic Society of Bangladesh. Journal. 3 per yr.

**Atomic Energy Centre**
Box 164, Ramna, Dacca, Bangladesh.
  ● Nuclear Science and Applications. s-a. ISSN
  0078-2637

**B.C.S.I.R.**
  *see* **Bangladesh Council of Scientific and Industrial
  Research**

**Bangla Academy**
Burdwan House, Dacca 2, Bangladesh.
  ● Bamla Ekademi Gabeshana Patrika. q.
  ● Bangla Academy Journal. s-a.

**Bangladesh. Bureau of Statistics**
Secretariat, Dacca 2, Bangladesh.
  ● Agricultural Statistics of Bangladesh. a. ISSN
  0065-4566
  ● Annual Foreign Trade Statistics of Bangladesh. a.
  ISSN 0071-7371
  ● Statistical Abstract for Bangladesh. a. ISSN 0081-
  4628
  ● Statistical Yearbook of Bangladesh. a.

**Bangladesh. Directorate of Agricultural Marketing**
Dacca, Bangladesh.
  ● Bangladesh. Directorate of Agricultural Marketing.
  Agricultural Marketing Series. irreg. ISSN 0070-
  8143

**Bangladesh. Directorate of Agriculture**
Dacca, Bangladesh.
  ● Bangladesh. Directorate of Agriculture. Season
  and Crop Report. a. ISSN 0070-8151

**Bangladesh. Directorate of Education**
Comilla, Bangladesh.
  ● Bangladesh. Directorate of Education. Report on
  the Pilot Project on Adult Education. a. ISSN
  0070-8135

**Bangladesh. Ministry of Finance**
Economic Adviser's Wing, Bangladesh Secretariat,
Shed No. 27, Dacca 2, Bangladesh.
  ● Bamladesa Arthanaitika Jaripa. a.

**Bangladesh. Ministry of Information and
Broadcasting**
Dacca, Bangladesh.
  ● Bangladesh Sangbad. w.

**Bangladesh. Ministry of Planning. Bureau of
Statistics**
  *see* **Bangladesh. Bureau of Statistics**

**Bangladesh. National Institute of Public
Administration**
Publications Officer, Nilkhet, Dacca 2, Bangladesh.
  ● Administrative Science Review. q. ISSN 0001-
  8406
  ● Dialogue. m. ISSN 0012-219X

**Bangladesh Agricultural University Old Boys'
Association**
c/o Dept. of Genetics and Plant Breeding,
Bangladesh Agricultural University, Mymensingh,
Bangladesh.
  ● Bangladesh Agricultural Sciences Abstracts. a.
  (Co-sponsor: Bangladesh Agricultural Research
  Council)

**Bangladesh Animal Science Association**
Bangladesh Agricultural University, Mymensingh,
Bangladesh.
  ● Bangladesh Journal of Animal Science. s-a.

**Bangladesh Bank**
Motijheel Commercial Area, Dacca 2, Bangladesh.
  ● Bangladesh Bank. Balance of Payments. q. (prep.
  by its Department of Public Relations and
  Publications)
  ● Bangladesh Bank. Bulletin. m. (prep. by its
  Department of Public Relations and Publications)
  ● Bangladesh Bank. Selected Economic Indicators.
  w. (prep. by its Research Department)
  ● Bangladesh Bank. Statistics Department. Annual
  Import Payments. a. (prep. by its Department of
  Public Relations and Publications)
  ● Bangladesh Bank. Statistics Department. Quarterly
  Scheduled Banks Statistics. q. (prep. by its
  Department of Public Relations and Publications)
  ● Economic Trends. m. (prep. by its Department of
  Public Relations and Publications)

**Bangladesh Council of Scientific and Industrial
Research**
Mirpur Road, Dhanmondi, Dacca 5, Bangladesh.
  ● Bangladesh Journal of Scientific and Industrial
  Research. q. (prep. by its B. C. S. I. R.
  Laboratories)

**Bangladesh Geographical Society**
Dept. of Geography, University of Dacca, Ramna,
Dacca 2, Bangladesh.
  ● Oriental Geographer. s-a. ISSN 0030-5308

**Bangladesh Institute of Development Studies**
Adamjee Court, Motijheel Commercial Area, Dacca
2, Bangladesh.
  ● Bangladesh Development Studies. q.

**Bangladesh Jute Industries Corp.**
62-63 Motijheel, Dacca, Bangladesh.
  ● Bangladesh Jute Industries Corp. Quarterly
  Summary of Jute Goods Statistics. q.

**Bangladesh Jute Research Institute**
Sher-e-Bangla Nagar, Dacca 15, Bangladesh.
  ● Jute and Jute Fabrics-Bangladesh. m.

**Bangladesh Management Development Centre**
Mirpur Rd., Dacca 7, Bangladesh.
  ● Management Development. q.

**Bangladesh Medical Association**
B.M.A. House, 15/2 Topkhana Rd., Dacca 2,
Bangladesh.
  ● Bangladesh Medical Journal. q. ISSN 0301-035X

**Bangladesh Pharmaceutical Society**
University of Dacca, Ramna, Dacca 2, Bangladesh.
  ● Bangladesh Pharmaceutical Journal. q.

**Bangladesh Research and Evaluation Centre**
16 B, Rd. No. 7, Dhanmondi, Bangladesh.
  ● Bangladesh Research and Evaluation Centre.
  Report. a. ISSN 0070-8178

**Bangladesh Scout Samity**
National Headquarters, 67-A Purana Paltan, Dacca
2, Bangladesh.
  ● Agradoot. m. ISSN 0002-1040

**Bangladesh Society for Biological and Agricultural
Sciences**
Dept. of Biochemistry, University of Dacca, Ramna,
Dacca 2, Bangladesh.
  ● Bangladesh Journal of Biological and Agricultural
  Sciences. s-a. ISSN 0045-1428

**Bangladesh Tea Research Institute**
Srimangal, Sylhet, Bangladesh.
  ● Tea Journal of Bangladesh. s-a.

**Bangladesh University of Engineering and Technology**
Ramna, Dacca 2, Bangladesh.
  ● Bangladesh University of Engineering and
  Technology, Dacca. Technical Journal. a. ISSN
  0070-8186
  ● Electromagnetic Theory. irreg. ISSN 0070-9794

**Bangladesh Veterinary Association**
Bangladesh Agricultural University, Mymensingh,
Bangladesh.
  ● Bangladesh Veterinary Journal. q.

**Chittagong Port Trust**
Chittagong, Bangladesh.
  ● Chittagong Port Trust. Yearbook of Information.
  a. ISSN 0069-3723

**College of Social Welfare and Research Centre**
Dacca 9, Bangladesh.
  ● Social Horizon. 3 per yr. ISSN 0037-7759

**Commerce & Industry Monthly Journal**
22 B. K. Das Rd., Farashganj, Dacca 1, Bangladesh.
  ● Commerce & Industry Monthly Journal. m. ISSN
  0010-2792

**Concept Publications**
25 Elephant Rd., Dhanmondi, Dacca, Bangladesh.
  ● Concept of Pakistan. m. ISSN 0010-5120

**Council for Islamic Studies and Research**
G.P.O. Box 351, 16-A Larmini St., Wari, Dacca 3,
Bangladesh.
  ● Islam and the Modern World. q.

**Dacca University**
  *see* **University of Dacca**

**Dacca University Geography Association**
Ramna, Dacca 2, Bangladesh.
  ● Upokul. irreg.

**East Pakistan Co-operative Society**
Polwell Building, Naya Paltan, Dacca, Bangladesh.
  ● Detective. s-m.

**Forest Research Institute**
Chittagong, Bangladesh.
  ● Bano Biggyan Patrika. q.

**Hobby International**
26/18 Pand T Colony, Motijheel, Dacca,
Bangladesh.
  ● Penpals. q.

**Institute of Engineers**
Ramma, Dacca 2, Bangladesh.
  ● Institute of Engineers, Dacca. Journal. a. ISSN
  0073-9200
  ● Institute of Engineers, Dacca. Year Book. a. ISSN
  0073-9219
  ● Pakistan Engineer. m. ISSN 0030-9753

**Local Government Institute**
217-B Dhanmandi Residential Area, Rd. No. 15,
Dacca 5, Bangladesh.
  ● Local Government Quarterly. q.

**National Book Centre of Bangladesh**
67-A Purana Paltan, Dacca 2, Bangladesh.
  ● Boi. m. ISSN 0006-5773

**Rajshahi University**
  *see* **University of Rajshahi**

**Soil Science Society of Bangladesh**
c/o Dept. of Soil Science, University of Dacca,
Ramna, Dacca 2, Bangladesh.
  ● Bangladesh Journal of Soil Science. s-a.

**Sujaneshu**
15/16 Goalnagar Lane, Dacca 1, Bangladesh.
  ● Sujaneshu. m.

**University of Dacca**
Ramna, Dacca 2, Bangladesh.
  ● Sonjog. q. ISSN 0038-1381

**University of Dacca. Department of Library Science**
Ramna, Dacca 2, Bangladesh.
  ● Bangladesh Library Science News Bulletin. bi-m.

**University of Dacca. Economics Association**
c/o Dept. of Economics, Ramna, Dacca 2,
Bangladesh.
  ● Economic Review. a. ISSN 0070-8631

**University of Dacca. Institute of Education and
Research**
Ramna, Dacca 2, Bangladesh.
  ● Teacher's World; quarterly journal of education
  and research. q. ISSN 0040-0521

**University of Dacca. Institute of Statistical Research
and Training**
Ramna, Dacca 2, Bangladesh.
  ● Rural Demography. s-a.
  ● University of Dacca. Institute of Statistical
  Research and Training. Bulletin. s-a. ISSN 0020-
  3165

**University of Dacca. Studies Board**
c/o Dacca University Library, Ramna, Dacca 2,
Bangladesh.
  ● Dacca University Studies. Part A: Humanities.
  ISSN 0011-5223
  ● Dacca University Studies. Part B: Science.

**University of Rajshahi**
c/o M. Rahman, Rajshahi, Bangladesh.
- Rajshahi University Studies. a. ISSN 0483-9218

**Zoological Society of Bangladesh**
c/o Dept. of Zoology, University of Dacca, Ramna, Dacca 2, Bangladesh.
- Bangladesh Journal of Zoology. s-a.

# BARBADOS

**Barbados. Government Printing Office**
Bay Street, St. Michael, Barbados, W. Indies.
- Barbados Official Gazette. s-w.

**Barbados. Ministry of Agriculture and Fisheries**
Bridgetown, Barbados, W. Indies.
- Barbados. Ministry of Agriculture and Fisheries. Bulletin. irreg.

**Barbados. Ministry of External Affairs**
Bridgetown, Barbados, W. Indies.
- Barbados Foreign Affairs Bulletin. q.

**Barbados. Ministry of Finance and Planning**
Bay Street, St. Michael, Barbados, W. Indies.
- Barbados. Ministry of Finance and Planning. Financial Statement and Budgetary Proposals. bi-m.

**Barbados. Ministry of Health and Welfare**
Bridgetown, Barbados.
- Barbados. Ministry of Health and Welfare. Chief Medical Officer. Annual Report. a.

**Barbados. Registration Office**
Bridgetown, Barbados, W. Indies.
- Barbados. Registration Office. Report on Vital Statistics & Registrations. a; latest edt., 1971.

**Barbados. Statistical Service**
National Insurance Building, Fairchild St., Bridgetown, Barbados, W. Indies.
- Barbados. Statistical Service. Monthly Digest of Statistics. m.
- Barbados. Statistical Service. Monthly Statistics of Overseas Trade. m.

**Barbados Labour Party**
11 Roebuck Street, Bridgetown, Barbados, W. Indies.
- Beacon. w.

**Barbados Museum and Historical Society**
St. Ann's Garrison, Barbados, W. Indies.
- Barbados Museum and Historical Society. Journal. a. ISSN 0005-5891

**Barbados News**
Carlisle House, Hincks Street, Box 718c, Bridgetown, Barbados, W. Indies.
- Barbados News. bi-m.

**Barbados Public Library**
Bridgetown 2, Barbados, West Indies.
- National Bibliography of Barbados. q.

**Barbados Registered Nurses Association**
Gibson House, Spry Street, Bridgetown, Barbados, W. I.
- Barbados Nursing Journal. a. ISSN 0572-6042

**Barbados Society of Architects**
c/o Ferdinand Hart & Leonard, Chartered Quan. Surveyors, Adulo, Rockley, Christ Church, Barbados, W. I.
- Barbados Society of Architects. Yearbook. a.

**Barbados Tourist Board**
Bridgewater, Barbados, W. Indies.
- Barbados Tourist Board. Annual Report. a.

**Bim**
Ferney, Atlantic Shores, Christ Church, Barbados, W. Indies.
- Bim. s-a. ISSN 0006-2766

**Carib Publicity Co. Ltd.**
Box 718c, Bridgetown, Barbados, W. Indies.
- Bajan & South Caribbean. m. ISSN 0005-4011

**Caribbean Conservation Association**
Savannah Lodge, The Garrison, St. Michael, Barbados, W. Indies.
- Caribbean Conservation News. q.

**Caribbean Consumers Documentation Centre**
Gibson House, Spry Street, St. Michael, Barbados, W. I.
- Caribbean Newsletter. a.

**Caribbean Development Bank. Board of Governors**
Bridgetown, Barbados, W. Indies.
- Caribbean Development Bank. Board of Governors. Annual Meeting of the Board of Governors: Summary of Proceedings. a.

**Caribbean Universities Press**
8 Rock Dundo Heights, Lodge Hill, Eagle Hall 15, Barbados, West Indies
(Subscriptions to Ginn and Company Ltd., 18 Bedford Row, London WC1R 4EJ, Eng.)
- Journal of Caribbean History. s-a. ISSN 0047-2263 (University of the West Indies. Department of History)

**Cedar Press**
Box 616, Bridgetown, Barbados, W.I.
- Challenges in the New Caribbean. irreg.

**Central Bank of Barbados**
Box 1016, Treasury Bldg., Bridgetown, Barbados.
- Central Bank of Barbados. Annual Statistical Digest. a.
- Central Bank of Barbados. Economic and Financial Statistics. m. ISSN 0378-178X
- Central Bank of Barbados. Quarterly Report. q. ISSN 0378-1771

**Library Association of Barbados**
Box 827E, Bridgetown, Barbados, W. Indies.
- Library Association of Barbados. Bulletin. a.
- Library Association of Barbados. Occasional Newsletter. irreg.

**University of the West Indies. Department of History**
- Journal of Caribbean History. (pub. by Caribbean Universities Press)

**University of the West Indies. School of Education**
Cave Hill, Barbados, W. Indies.
- Conference on Teacher Education in the Eastern Caribbean. Report. biennial. ISSN 0069-8695

# BELGIUM

**A M C K**
Conscience Str. 54-56, Antwerp, Belgium.
- A. M. C. K. Mededelingsblad. m. ISSN 0001-1886

**Abbaye de Maredsous**
B-5642 Maredsous, Belgium.
- Revue Benedictine; de critique, d'histoire et de litterature religieuses. 2-4 nos.per year. ISSN 0035-0893

**Abbaye du Mont-Cesar**
202 Mechelse Straat, B-3000 Louvain, Belgium.
- Bulletin de Theologie Ancienne et Medievale. s-a. ISSN 0007-442X
- Recherches de Theologie Ancienne et Medievale. s-a. ISSN 0034-1266

**Academie Internationale de Comptabilite**
- Comptabilite Economique Universelle-Scientifique. (pub. by Cambel)

**Academie Royale d'Archeologie de Belgique**
Hotel de Societes Scientifiques, Rue des Champs Elysees, 43, 1050 Brussels, Belgium.
- Revue Belge d'Archeologie et d'Histoire de l'Art. q. ISSN 0035-077X

**Academie Royale de Langue et de Litterature Francaises**
Palais des Academies, 1 rue Ducale, Brussels, Belgium.
- Academie Royale de Langue et de Litterature Francaises. Annuaires. a. ISSN 0567-6584
- Academie Royale de Langue et de Litterature Francaises. Bulletin.

**Academie Royale de Medecine de Belgique**
43 Ave. des Arts (6e), 1040 Brussels, Belgium.
- Academie Royale de Medecine de Belgique. Bulletin et Memoires. m.

**Academie Royale des Sciences d'Outre-Mer**
Rue Defacqz 1, 1050 Brussels, Belgium.
- Academie Royale des Sciences d'Outre-Mer. Bulletin des Seances/Koninklijke Academie voor Overzeese Wetenschappen. Mededelingen der Zittingen. 4 per yr. ISSN 0001-4176
- Academie Royale des Sciences d'Outre Mer. Revue Bibliographique/Koninklijke Academie voor Overzeese Wetenschappen. Bibliografisch Overzicht. a. ISSN 0567-6592

**Academie Royale des Sciences, des Lettres et des Beaux Arts de Belgique**
Palais des Academies, Rue Ducale 1, B-1000 Brussels, Belgium.
- Academie Royale des Sciences, des Lettres et des Beaux Arts de Belgique. Index Biographique des Membres, Correspondants et Associes. irreg. ISSN 0065-0609

**Academie Royale des Sciences, des Lettres et des Beaux-Arts de Belgique. Classe des Lettres et des Sciences Morales et Politiques**
- Academie Royale des Sciences, des Lettres et des Beaux-Arts de Belgique. Classe des Lettres et Sciences Morales et Politiques. Bulletin. (pub. by Editions J. Duculot a Gembloux, S.A.)
- Academie Royale des Sciences, des Lettres et des Beaux-Arts de Belgique. Classes des Sciences. Bulletin. (pub. by Editions J. Duculot a Gembloux, S.A.)

**Academie Royale des Sciences, des Lettres et des Beaux-Arts de Belgique. Commission Royale d'Histoire**
Palais des Academies, Rue Ducale 1, B-1000 Brussels, Belgium.
- Academie Royale de Belgique. Commission Royale d'Histoire. Bulletin. q. ISSN 0001-415X
- Academie Royale des Sciences, des Lettres et des Beaux Arts de Belgique. Commission Royale d'Histoire. Documents Relatifs au Statut International de la Belgique Depuis 1830. Bescheiden Betreffende Het Internationaal Statut van Belgie Sedert 1830. irreg. ISSN 0065-0617

**Ackroyd Publications S. A.**
25, rue des Minimes, 1000 Brussels, Belgium.
- Bulletin; Belgium's news weekly in English. w. ISSN 0007-4047

**Publications Acta Medica Belgica**
Hotel de Societes Scientifiques, 43 rue des Champs-Elysees, B-1050 Brussels, Belgium.
- Acta Anaesthesiologica Belgica. 4 per yr. ISSN 0001-5164 (Association des Societes Scientifiques Medicales Belges)
- Acta Chirurgica Belgica. 8 per yr. ISSN 0001-5458 (Association des Societes Scientifiques Medicales Belges)
- Acta Gastro-Enterologica Belgica. 8 per yr. ISSN 0001-5644 (Association des Societes Scientifiques Medicales Belges)
- Acta Neurologica Belgica. bi-m. (Association des Societes Scientifiques Medicales Belges)
- Acta Orthopaedica Belgica. bi-m. ISSN 0001-6462 (Association des Societes Scientifiques Medicales Belges)
- Acta Oto-Rhino-Laryngologica Belgica. 6-8 per yr. ISSN 0001-6497 (Association des Societes Scientifiques Medicales Belges)
- Acta Paediatrica Belgica. 4 per yr. ISSN 0001-6535 (Association des Societes Scientifiques Medicales Belges)
- Acta Psychiatrica Belgica. bi-m. (Association des Societes Scientifiques Medicales Belges)
- Acta Stomatologica Belgica. 4 per yr. ISSN 0001-7000 (Association des Societes Scientifiques Medicales Belges)
- Acta Tuberculosea et Pneumologica Belgica. bi-m. ISSN 0001-7078 (Association des Societes Scientifiques Medicales Belges)
- Acta Urologica Belgica. 4 per yr. ISSN 0001-7183 (Association des Societes Scientifiques Medicales Belges)
- Archives Belges de Medecine Sociale, Hygiene, Medecine du Travail et Medecine Legale. 10 per yr. ISSN 0003-9578 (Association des Societes Scientifiques Medicales Belges)
- Journal Belge de Rhumatologie et de Medecine Physique. bi-m. ISSN 0021-7654 (Association des Societes Scientifiques Medicales Belges)

**Action Cinematographique**
- Cine-Dossiers. (pub. by Francis Bolen, Ed. & Pub.)

**Actualite en Copie Conforme S.P.R.L.**
Rue des Drapiers 31, 1050 Brussels, Belgium.
- Special; hebdomadaire d'information. w. ISSN 0038-6693

**Agence de Presse Liberation**
9 rue Goffart, 1050 Brussels, Belgium.
- Agence de Presse Liberation. Bulletin.

**Agence Havas Belge**
13-17 Bd. Adolphe Max, 1000 Brussels, Belgium.
- Annonces de l'Industrie. s-w. ISSN 0003-505X

**Algemeen Belgisch Vlasverbond**
Oude-Vestingsstraat 15, B-8500 Kortrijk, Belgium.
- Fibra; international journal on growing and processing of flax and hemp. 3 per yr. ISSN 0015-0525

**Algemeen Christelijk Werkersverbond**
- Gids Op Maatschappelijk Gebied. (pub. by Arbeiderspers)

**Algemene Pharmaceutische Bond**
Archimedesstraat 11, Brussels 4, Belgium.
- Apothekersblad. m. ISSN 0003-6579

**Alliance Nationale des Mutualites Chretiennes**
121 rue de la Loi, 1040 Brussels, Belgium.
- En Marche. s-m. ISSN 0013-6964

**Antwerp Bibliophile Society**
*see* Vereeniging der Antwerpsche Bibliophielen

**Antwerp Chamber of Commerce and Industry**
*see* Chambre de Commerce et d'Industrie d'Anvers

**Arbeiderspers**
Wetstraat 125, Brussels, Belgium.
- Gids Op Maatschappelijk Gebied; tijdschrift voor sociale cultur. irreg. (Algemeen Christelijk Werkersverbond)

**Archives Internationales de Pharmacodynamie et de Therapie**
De Pintelaan 135, B-9000 Ghent, Belgium.
- Archives Internationales de Pharmacodynamie et de Therapie. m. ISSN 0003-9780

**Armorial Francais**
2 rue Emmanuel Hiel, 1030 Brussels, Belgium.
- Armorial Francais; ou repertoire alphabetique des notices des familles nobles, patriciennes bourgeoises de france. q.

**Ars Medici et Nouveautes Medicales**
59 rue de Fontaine-1'Eveque, 1400 Nivelles, Belgium.
- Ars Medici et Nouveautes Medicales; revue internationale de pharmacotherapie clinique. fortn. ISSN 0004-2900

**Art et Technique**
Rue d'Arlon 25, 1040 Brussels, Belgium.
- Environnement. m. ISSN 0013-9130

**Art History Museums, Antwerp**
*see* Kunsthistorische Musea, Antwerp

**Editions ARTO**
85 Avenue Winston Churchill, 1180 Brussels, Belgium.
- Annuaire General des Beaux-Arts/Algemeen Jaarboek der Schone Kunsten. biennial. ISSN 0066-3174

**Association Belge de Documentation**
Rue Joseph Schols, 62, B-1080 Brussels, Belgium.
- Association Belge de Documentation. Cahiers de Documentation/Bladen voor de Documentatie. q. ISSN 0007-9804

**Association Belge des Editeurs de Journaux**
Rue Belliard 20, B-1040 Brussels, Belgium.
- Presse/Pers. q. ISSN 0478-1546

**Association Belge des Paralyses**
61 rue des Champs Elysees, Brussels 5, Belgium.
- A B P - Association Belge des Paralyses. Bulletin/ B V V - Belgische Vereniging voor Verlamden. Bulletin. q. ISSN 0001-0553

**Association Belge pour l'Etude, l'Essai et l'Emploi des Materiaux**
46, rue C. Franck, B-1050 Brussels, Belgium.
- Association Belge pour l'Etude, l'Essai et l'Emploi des Materiaux. Publication A.B.E.M. irreg. ISSN 0066-8796
- Association Belge pour l'Etude, l'Essai et l'Emploi des Materiaux. Publication Groupement. irreg. ISSN 0066-880X
- Association Belge pour l'Etude, l'Essai et l'Emploi des Materiaux. Proces Verbal de l'Assemblee Generale Ordinaire. a. ISSN 0066-8818

**Association Belge pour le Progres Social**
Rue des Glacis, 141, 4000 Liege, Belgium.
- Progres Social/Maatschappelijke Vooruitgang. bi-m. ISSN 0033-0698

**Association des Archivistes et Bibliothecaires de Belgique**
4 Bd. de l'Empereur, 1000 Brussels, Belgium.
- Archives et Bibliotheques de Belgique/Archief-en Bibliotheekwezen in Belgie. 2-4 per yr. ISSN 0003-9748

**Association des Ecrivains Belges de Langue Francaise**
Maison des Ecrivains, 150 Chaussee de Wavre, Brussels, Belgium.
- Nos Lettres. q. ISSN 0029-3717

**Association des Fabricants Belges et Explosifs**
PRB 4133, Usine de Clermont-S-Huy, Belgium.
- Explosifs. q.

**Association des Ingenieurs de la Faculte Polytechnique de Mons**
Rue de Houdain 9, 7000 Mons, Belgium.
- A. T. B. Trimestrielle Metallurgie Revue. q. ISSN 0001-2696

**Association des Ingenieurs Techniciens Chimistes de St. Ghislain-Hornu**
43 Route d'Eugies, Frameries, Belgium.
- Chimie et Technique. q. ISSN 0009-4366

**Association des Licencies et Ingenieurs Commerciaux**
23 Grand Place, 7000 Mons, Belgium.
- Association des Licencies et Ingenieurs Commerciaux. Etudes Economiques. q.

**Association des Professeurs de Langues Vivantes**
- Revue des Langues Vivantes/Tijdschrift voor Levende Talen. (pub. by Librairie Marcel Didier)

**Association des Societes Scientifiques Medicales Belges**
- Acta Anaesthesiologica Belgica. (pub. by Publications Acta Medica Belgica)
- Acta Chirurgica Belgica. (pub. by Publications Acta Medica Belgica)
- Acta Gastro-Enterologica Belgica. (pub. by Publications Acta Medica Belgica)
- Acta Neurologica Belgica. (pub. by Publications Acta Medica Belgica)
- Acta Orthopaedica Belgica. (pub. by Publications Acta Medica Belgica)
- Acta Oto-Rhino-Laryngologica Belgica. (pub. by Publications Acta Medica Belgica)
- Acta Paediatrica Belgica. (pub. by Publications Acta Medica Belgica)
- Acta Psychiatrica Belgica. (pub. by Publications Acta Medica Belgica)
- Acta Stomatologica Belgica. (pub. by Publications Acta Medica Belgica)
- Acta Tuberculosea et Pneumologica Belgica. (pub. by Publications Acta Medica Belgica)
- Acta Urologica Belgica. (pub. by Publications Acta Medica Belgica)
- Archives Belges de Medecine Sociale, Hygiene, Medecine du Travail et Medecine Legale. (pub. by Publications Acta Medica Belgica)
- Journal Belge de Rhumatologie et de Medecine Physique. (pub. by Publications Acta Medica Belgica)

**Association Generale des Meuniers Belges**
Rue du Midi 165, B-1000 Brussels, Belgium.
- Meunerie Belge/Belgische Maalderij. q. ISSN 0026-1661

**Association Graphique et Artistique**
225 Avenue Moliere, 1060 Brussels, Belgium.
- Excavator. m. ISSN 0014-4002

**Association Homoeopathique Belge**
10 Square Vergote, 1200 Brussels, Belgium.
- Revue Belge d'Homoeopathie. q. ISSN 0035-0885 (Societe Royale Belge d'Homoeopathie)

**Association Internationale de Cybernetique**
*see* International Association for Cybernetics

**Association Internationale de Geodesie**
*see* International Association of Geodesy

**Association Internationale des Etudiants en Sciences Economiques et Commerciales**
*see* International Association of Students in Business and Economics

**Association Internationale pour l'Histoire du Verre**
*see* International Association for the History of Glass

**Association Mars et Mercure**
13 rue Brederode, 1000 Brussels, Belgium.
- Mars et Mercure/Mars en Mercurius. m ( 10 per yr.)

**Association Nationale d'Aide aux Handicapes Mentaux**
12 rue Forestiere, B-1050 Brussels, Belgium.
- Amentia. q. ISSN 0002-7022

**Association Nationale pour la Protection Contre l'Incendie**
Rue de l'Autonomie 4, B-1070 Brussels, Belgium.
- Notice Technique A N P I. q.
- Revue Belge du Feu/Belgisch Brandtijdschrift. q. ISSN 0048-7910

**Association of Archivists and Librarians of Belgium**
*see* Association des Archivistes et Bibliothecaires de Belgique

**Association of Belgian Writers in the French Language**
*see* Association des Ecrivains Belges de Langue Francaise

**Association Permanente des Congres Belges de la Route**
49 Av.d'Auderghem, Brussels 4, Belgium.
- Technique Routiere. q. ISSN 0040-1277

**Association Pharmaceutique Belge**
- Journal de Pharmacie de Belgique. (pub. by Masson FR)

**Association pour l'Encouragement a l'Union des Revues Techniques Belges**
43 rue des Champs-Elysees, 1050 Brussels, Belgium.
- Journal des Ingenieurs. q. ISSN 0021-8065

**Association pour l'Etude Taxonomique de la Flore d'Afrique Tropicale**
19 rue de Decembre, 1200 Brussels, Belgium.
- A.E.T.F.A.I. Index; releve des travaux de phanerogamie systematique et des taxons nouveaux concernant l'Afrique au sud du Sahara et Madascar. a. ISSN 0066-9784

**Association pour l'Information Culturelle**
10 Rue Royale, 1000 Brussels, Belgium.
- Cles; musique-arts-spectacles. m. ISSN 0045-7140

**Association pour la Promotion de l'Etude des Langues Modernes**
- Equivalences. (pub. by Institut Superieur de l'Etat de Traducteurs et d'Interpretes)

**Association pour les Etudes et Recherches de Zoologie Appliquee et de Phytopathologie**
Ave. Marechal Juin 13, B-5800 Gembloux, Belgium.
- Parasitica. q. ISSN 0031-1812

**Association Royale des Anciens Eleves des Ecoles de Brasserie Gand, Bruxelles et Louvain**
- Cerevisia. (pub. by Cerevisia a.s.b.l.)

**Association Scientifique et Technique pour la Recherche en Informatique Documentaire**
Koningin Astridlaan 89, B-9000 Ghent, Belgium.
- Recommended Science Information Sources. a.

**Association Technique de Fonderie de Belgique**
Grote Steenweg Noord, 12, B-9710 Zwijnaarde, Belgium.
- Fonderie Belge. q. ISSN 0015-6108

**Ateliers de Constructions Electriques de Charleroi**
B. P. 4, 6000 Charleroi, Belgium.
- A C E C Review. q. ISSN 0001-0669

**Editions Auto-Magazine**
Avenue Coghen, 135, 1180 Brussels, Belgium.
- Auto-Digest. a.

**Aviation et Astronautique S. P. R. L**
96 Ave. de Tervueren, 1040 Brussels, Belgium.
- Aviastro; mensuel aerospatial du Benelux. m.

**Avocat a la Cour d'Appel**
- Cahiers de Droit Europeen. (pub. by Maison Ferdinand Larcier, S.A.)

**Albert Ayguesparse, Ed. and Pub.**
Bd. General Jacques 159, B-1050 Brussels, Belgium.
- Marginales; revue des idees et des lettres. bi-m. ISSN 0025-293X

**B E N E L U X Documentatie Centrum**
Bosmanslei 5, B-2000 Antwerp, Belgium.
- B E N E L U X International. m. ISSN 0005-3058

**B E N E L U X Economic Union**
Rue de la Regence 39, 1000 Brussels, Belgium.
- Benelux Publikatieblad/Bulletin Benelux. 8 per yr. ISSN 0005-8777
- Benelux Tijdschrift/Revue Benelux. q.

**B E N E L U X Economic Union. Central Economic Council**
21 Avenue de la Joyeuse Entree, 1040 Brussels, Belgium.
- B E N E L U X Economic Union. Conseil Central de l'Economie. Rapport du Secretaraire sur l'Activite du Conseil. biennial.

**Banque Bruxelles Lambert**
B.P. 1469, 1000 Brussels, Belgium.
- Banque Bruxelles Lambert. Bulletin Financier. w.

**Banque de Bruxelles**
Rue de la Regence, 2, 1000 Brussels, Belgium.
- Banque de Bruxelles. Rapport Annuel. a. ISSN 0067-3919

**Banque Nationale de Belgique**
Departement des Etudes, 5 Bd. de Berlaimont, B-1000 Brussels, Belgium.
- Banque Nationale de Belgique. Bulletin. m.(plus s-a supplements) ISSN 0005-5611
- Banque Nationale de Belgique. Rapport sur les Operations. a. ISSN 0067-3978

**Editions du Baucens**
Rue Hector Denis 13, 7490 Braine -le-Compte, Belgium.
- Bibliotheque Internationale d'Etudes Maconniques. irreg.

**N.V. Bayer Gorsac S.A.**
St. Truiden, Belgium
(Main Office: Bayer Pflanzenschutz, Leverkusen, W. Germany (B.R.D.))
- Gorsac Koerier. irreg.

**Belgian Centre for Geochronology**
c/o Museum, Steenweg Op Leuven, 11, B-1980 Tervuren, Belgium.
- Abstracts of Geochronology and Isotope Geology. 5 per yr. ISSN 0304-5935

**Belgian Federation of Food Trade**
see Federation Belge du Commerce Alimentaire

**Belgian Federation of Ironmongers**
- Mars-Magazine. (pub. by Editions "E.G.P.")

**Belgian Geological Society**
see Societe Geologique de Belgique

**Belgian Information and Documentation Institute**
see Institut Belge d'Information et de Documentation

**Belgian Institute of Political Science**
see Institut Belge de Science Politique

**Belgian National Library**
see Bibliotheque Royal Albert 1er

**Belgian Society for Geographical Studies**
see Societe Belge d'Etudes Geographiques

**Belgian Society of Musicology**
see Societe Belge de Musicologie

**Belgian Society of Photogrammetry**
see Societe Belge de Photogrammetrie

**Belgian Society of Tropical Medicine**
see Societe Belge de Medicine Tropicale

**Belgicatom**
1 Heiken, 2840 Haacht, Belgium.
- Belgicatom; atomic space age & electronics. bi-m. ISSN 0005-8408

**Belgisch Instituut Tot Verbetering van de Biet**
see Institut Belge pour l'Amelioration de la Betterave

**Belgisch Instituut voor Voorlichting en Documentatie**
see Institut Belge d'Information et de Documentation

**Belgisch Instituut voor Wetenschap de Politiek**
see Institut Belge de Science Politique

**Belgisch Israelitisch Weekblad**
Pelikaanstraat, 106-108, Antwerp, Belgium.
- Guide Touristique Europeen pour Israelites/ European Travel Guide for Jews. irreg. (Co-sponsor: Belgian National Tourist Office)

**Belgisch Petroleum Instituut**
see Institut Belge du Petrole

**Belgische Boerenbond. Economaat**
Minderbroedersstraat 8, B-3000 Louvain, Belgium.
- Agriculteur. w.
- Alliance Agricole. w. (Subscr. to: 82 rue Joseph II, 1040 Brussels, Belgium)
- Bestuursblad. m. (Katholiek Vormingswerk voor Landelijke Vrouwen)
- Bij de Haard. m. ISSN 0006-2227 (Katholiek Vormingswerk voor Landelijke Vrouwen)
- Boer en de Tuinder. w.
- Brieven aan Gezinnen. bi-m. (Katholiek Vormingswerk voor Landelijke Vrouwen)

**Belgische Duivensport**
Spoorweglaan 1, B-8860 Meulebeke, Belgium.
- Belgische Duivensport. w. ISSN 0005-8459

**Belgische Fruittelersorganisaties**
c/o Storme Georges, Hoger Rijksinstituut voor Tuinbouw, Bursselse Steenweg 165, B-9230 Melle, Belgium.
- Belgische Fruitrevue. m. ISSN 0005-8467 (Vlaamse Pomologische Verenigingen)

**Belgische Nationale Federatie voor Bont en Kleinvel**
see Federation Nationale Belge de la Fourrure et de la Peau en Poil

**Belgische Vereniging voor Documentatie**
see Association Belge de Documentation

**Belgische Vereniging voor Geologie**
see Societe Belge de Geologie

**Belgische Vereniging voor Psychologie**
see Societe Belge de Psychologie

**Belgische Vereniging voor Verlamden**
see Association Belge des Paralyses

**Belgium. Administration de l'Education Physique, des Sports et de la Vie en Plein Air**
4-27 Galerie Ravenstein, B-1000 Brussels, Belgium.
- Sport. 4 per yr. ISSN 0038-7770

**Belgium. Administration de l'Energie**
49-51 rue de Treves, 1040 Brussels, Belgium.
- Belgium. Administration de l'Energie. Bulletin Mensuel de l'Energie Electrique. m.

**Belgium. Administration de la Marine et de la Navigation Interieure**
30 rue Belliard, 1040 Brussels, Belgium.
- Belgium. Administration de la Marine et de la Navigation Interieure. Rapport Annuel sur l'Evolution de la Flotte de Peche. a.
- Liste Officielle des Navires de Mer Belges et de la Flotte de la Force Navale. irreg.

**Belgium. Administration des Eaux et Forets**
Gronendall-Hoilaart, Belgium.
- Belgium. Administration des Eaux et Forets. Station de Recherches des Eaux et Forets. Travaux. Serie D. Hydrobiologie. irreg. ISSN 0067-5369

**Belgium. Administration des Mines**
3 rue Montoyer, 1040 Brussels, Belgium.
- Belgium. Administration des Mines. Statistiques: Houille, Cokes, Agglomeres Metallurgie, Carrieres /Statistieken: Steenkolen, Cokes, Agglomeraten, Metallnijverheid, Groeven. irreg.
- Memoires pour Servir a l'Explication des Cartes Geologiques et Minieres de la Belgique. irreg.

**Belgium. Administration du Commerce. Service de la Propriete Industrielle et Commerciale**
see Belgium. Service de la Propriete Industrielle et Commerciale

**Belgium. Administration Penitentiare**
Direction Etudes et Affaires Generales, 4 Place Poelaert, 1000 Brussels, Belgium.
- Belgium. Administration Penitentiare. Bulletin/ Belgium. Restuur Strafinrichtingen. Bulletin. bi-m. ISSN 0007-4306

**Belgium. Belgische Dienst voor de Buitenlandse Handel**
see Belgium. Office Belge du Commerce Exterieur

**Belgium. Bestuur Strafinrichtingen**
see Belgium. Administration Penitentiaire

**Belgium. Bestuur van het Zeewezen en van de Binnenvaart**
see Belgium. Administration de la Marine et de la Navigation Interieure

**Belgium. Bureau National de Documentation sur le Bois**
Rue Royale 111, 1000 Brussels, Belgium.
- Courrier du Bois. q.

**Belgium. Centre d'Etude de l'Energie Nucleaire**
see Centre d'Etude de l'Energie Nucleaire

**Belgium. Commissariat General au Tourisme**
Gare Centrale, Brussels, Belgium.
- Belgium. Commissariat General au Tourisme. Bulletin. m. ISSN 0032-7859

**Belgium. Conseil National de la Politique Scientifique**
8 rue de la Science, Brussels 8, Belgium.
- Belgium. Conseil National de la Politique Scientifique. Rapport Annuel. a. ISSN 0067-5377

**Belgium. Conseil National du Travail**
Brussels, Belgium.
- Belgium. Conseil National du Travail. Rapport du Secretariat sur l'Activite du Conseil/Belgium. Nationale Arbeidsraad. Verslag van de Secretaris over de Activiteit van de Raad. a. ISSN 0067-5385

**Belgium. Counseil Superieur des Classes Moyennes**
Secretary-General, Rue de la Charite, 24, 1040 Brussels, Belgium.
- Belgium. Conseil Superieur des Classes Moyennes. Rapport Annuel du Secretaire General. a. ISSN 0067-5393

**Belgium. Cour de Cassation**
- Belgium. Cour de Cassation. Bulletin des Arrets. (pub. by Etablissements Emile Bruylant)

**Belgium. Fonds National de la Recherche Scientifique**
Rue d'Egmont 5, 1050 Brussels, Belgium.
- Belgium. Fonds National de la Recherche Scientifique. Liste Bibliographique des Travaux. Bibliografische Lijst van de Werken. biennial.
- Belgium. Fonds National de la Recherche Scientifique. Liste des Beneficiaires d'Une Subvention. a.
- Belgium. Fonds National de la Recherche Scientifique. Rapport Annuel. a. ISSN 0067-5407

**Belgium. Force Navale**
Portbus 17, Oostende 1, Belgium.
- Neptunus; info marine. bi-m. ISSN 0028-2790

**Belgium. Hoge Raad voor de Middenstand**
see Belgium. Conseil Superieur des Classes Moyennes

**Belgium. Institut National d'Assurance Maladie Invalidite**
Avenue de Tervuren 211, B-1150 Brussels, Belgium.
- Belgium. Institut National d'Assurance Maladie Invalidite. I.N.A.M.I. Bulletin d'Information. 6 per yr. ISSN 0046-9726

**Belgium. Institut National d'Assurances Sociales pour Travailleurs Independants**
Bibliotheque - Bureau 7-6 (Wat.), Place Jean Jacobs, 6, 1000 Brussels, Belgium.
- Belgium. Institut National d'Assurances Sociales pour Travailleurs Independants. Rapport Annuel. a.
- Belgium. Institut National d'Assurances Sociales pour Travailleurs Independants. Statistiques des Beneficiaires de Prestations de Retraite et de Survie. a.
- Belgium. Institut National d'Assurances Sociales pour Travailleurs Independants. Statistiques des Personnes Assujetties au Statut Social des Travailleurs Independants. a.
- Statistique des Enfants Beneficiaires d'Allocations Familiales/Statistiek van de Kinderen die Recht Geven Op de Kinderbijslag. a.

**Belgium. Institut National de Statistique**
44 rue de Louvain, 1000 Brussels, Belgium.
- Annuaire Statistique de la Belgique. a. ISSN 0066-3646
- Belgium. Institut National de Statistique. Activities des Aerodromes Belges. a. ISSN 0067-5415
- Belgium. Institut National de Statistique. Annuaire Statistique de Poche. a. ISSN 0067-5431
- Belgium. Institut National de Statistique. Annuaire Statistique de l'Enseignement. a. ISSN 0067-5423
- Belgium. Institut National de Statistique. Bevolkingsstatistieken. irreg.
- Belgium. Institut National de Statistique. Bulletin de Statistique. m. ISSN 0045-1703
- Belgium. Institut National de Statistique. Landbouwstatistieken. m.
- Belgium. Institut National de Statistique. Statistique Annuelle du Trafic International des Ports. a. ISSN 0067-5482
- Belgium. Institut National de Statistique. Statistique de la Navigation du Rhin. a. ISSN 0067-5520
- Belgium. Institut National de Statistique. Statistique de la Navigation Interieure. a. ISSN 0067-5539
- Belgium. Institut National de Statistique. Statistique de la Navigation Maritime. q. ISSN 0039-0615
- Belgium. Institut National de Statistique. Statistique des Accidents de la Circulation sur la Voie Publique. a. ISSN 0067-5504
- Belgium. Institut National de Statistique. Statistique des Vehicules a Moteur Neufs Mis en Circulation/Statisiek van der Nieuwe Tot Het Verkeet Toegelaten Motorvoertuigen. a. ISSN 0067-5555
- Belgium. Institut National de Statistique. Statistique du Commerce. m (10 per yr)
- Belgium. Institut National de Statistique. Statistique du Tourisme et de l'Hotellerie. a. ISSN 0067-5547
- Belgium. Institut National de Statistique. Statistiques Agricoles. m.
- Belgium. Institut National de Statistique. Statistiques de la Construction et du Logement. irreg. (1-2 per yr.)
- Belgium. Institut National de Statistique. Statistiques Demographies. irreg. (2-4 per yr.) ISSN 0067-5490
- Belgium. Institut National de Statistique. Statistiques des Transports. m.
- Belgium. Institut National de Statistique. Statistiques Financieres. 2-3 per yr. approx.
- Belgium. Institut National de Statistique. Statistiques Industrielles. m.
- Belgium. Institut National de Statistique. Statistiques Sociales. irreg. (1-3 per yr.) ISSN 0067-5563
- Comptes Nationaux de la Belgique. irreg. ISSN 0069-8075
- Statistique Criminelle de la Belgique. a. ISSN 0081-5268

**Belgium. Institut National du Logement**
10 Bd. St. Lazare, 1030 Brussels, Belgium.
- Belgium. Institut National du Logement. Bulletin d'Information/Informatiebulletin. m. ISSN 0020-2436
- Belgium. Institut National du Logement. Rapport Annuel. a. ISSN 0067-5652
- Habiter. q.
- Wonen. q.

**Belgium. Institut Royal Meteorologique**
Avenue Circulaire, 3, 1180 Brussels, Belgium.
- Belgium. Institut Royal Meteorologique. Annuaire: Magnetisme Terrestre/Jaarboek: Aardmagnetisme. a. ISSN 0524-7764

- Belgium. Institut Royal Meteorologique. Annuaire: Rayonnement Solaire/Jaarboek: Zonnestraling. irreg., latest 1973. ISSN 0524-7780
- Belgium. Institut Royal Meteorologique de Belgique. Bulletin Quotidien du Temps. d. ISSN 0007-5280
- Belgium. Institut Royal Meteorologique. Observations Climatologiques. m. ISSN 0029-7682
- Belgium. Institut Royal Meteorologique. Observations d'Ozone. q. ISSN 0029-7690
- Belgium. Institut Royal Meteorologique. Observations Geophysiques. m. ISSN 0020-2525
- Belgium. Institut Royal Meteorologique. Observations Ionospheriques et du Rayonnement Cosmique. m. ISSN 0020-2533
- Belgium. Institut Royal Meteorologique. Observations Synoptiques. m. ISSN 0020-2541
- Belgium. Institut Royal Meteorologique. Publications. 5 per yr.(approx.) ISSN 0020-255X

**Belgium. Ministere de l'Agriculture**
Rue de Stassart 36, 1050 Brussels, Belgium.
- Revue de l'Agriculture. bi-m. ISSN 0035-1296

**Belgium. Ministere de l'Agriculture. Administration des Eaux et Forets**
see Belgium. Administration des Eaux et Forets

**Belgium. Ministere de l'Agriculture. Bestuur der Economische Diensten**
Koninginnelaan 59, 8400 Oostende, Belgium.
- Uitkomsten van de Belgische Zeevisserij. a. (prep. by its Dienst voor de Zeevisserij)

**Belgium. Ministere de l'Education Nationale et de la Culture Francaise**
158 Ave. Cortenbergh, 1040 Brussels, Belgium.
- Belgium. Ministere de l'Education Nationale et de la Culture Francaise Revue. 10 per yr.
- Belgium. Ministere de l'Education Nationale et de la Culture Francaise. Rapport Annuel. a. ISSN 0067-5598
- Cahiers J. E. B; jeunesse, education populaire, bibliotheques publiques. q. ISSN 0008-0292

**Belgium. Ministere de l'Education Nationale et de la Culture Francaise. Administration de l'Education Physique, des Sports et de la Vie en Plein Air**
see Belgium. Administration de l'Education Physique, des Sports et de la Vie en Plein Air

**Belgium. Ministere de l'Education Nationale et de la Culture Francaise. Direction Generale de l'Organisation des Etudes**
Cite Administrative de l'Etat, Quartier Arcades, 1010 Brussels, Belgium.
- Belgium. Ministere de l'Education Nationale et de la Culture Francaise. Direction Generale de l'Organisation des Etudes. Revue. m.

**Belgium. Ministere de l'Emploi et du Travail**
Bibliotheque, 53 rue Belliard, 1040 Brussels, Belgium.
- Belgium. Ministere de l'Emploi et du Travail. Bibliotheque. Bulletin Bibliographique Mensuel. m. ISSN 0408-9189
- Revue du Travail. m. ISSN 0035-2705

**Belgium. Ministere de la Defense Nationale**
Service de l'Information, 21 rue de Pepin, 1000 Brussels, Belgium.
- Vox; Hebdomadaire Militaire. w.

**Belgium. Ministere de la Justice. Administration Penitentiaire**
see Belgium. Administration Penitentiaire

**Belgium. Ministere de la Prevoyance Sociale**
123 rue Royale, B-1000 Brussels, Belgium.
- Belgium. Ministere de la Prevoyance Sociale. Rapport General sur la Securite Sociale/Algemeen Verslag over de Sociale Zekerheid. a. ISSN 0067-558X
- Revue Belge de Securite Sociale. 10 per yr. ISSN 0035-0834

**Belgium. Ministere de la Sante Publique et de la Famille**
Cite Administrative de l'Etat, Quartier Vesale, 1010 Brussels, Belgium.
- Annuaire Statistique de la Sante Publique/Statistisch Jaarboek van Volksgezondheid. a. ISSN 0522-7690 (prep. by its Centre de Traitement de l'Information)
- Belgium. Ministere de la Sante Publique et de la Famille. Bulletin. 5 per yr.

- Belgium. Ministere de la Sante Publique et de la Famille. Centrum voor Bevolkings-en Gezinsstudien. Technisch Rapport. irreg.
- Belgium. Ministere de la Sante Publique et de la Famille. Rapport Annuel. a.
- Population et Famille/Bevolking en Gezin. 3 per yr. ISSN 0523-1159 (prep. by its Centrum voor Bevolkings- en Gezinsstudien)

**Belgium. Ministere des Affaires Economiques**
Direction Generale des Etudes et de la Documentation, 16 rue de l'Industrie, 1040 Brussels, Belgium.
- Belgium. Ministere des Affaires Economiques. Bibliotheque Centrale (Fonds Quetelet). Accroissements/Belgium. Ministerie van Economische Zaken. Centrale Bibliotheek (Queteletfonds). Aanwinsten. m. ISSN 0005-8521
- Belgium. Ministere des Affaires Economiques. Direction Generale des Etudes et de la Documentation. Apercu de l'Evolution Economique. m. ISSN 0408-9235
- Belgium. Ministere des Affaires Economiques. Direction Generale des Etudes et de la Documentation. Budget Economique: Estimations Revisees. Economisch Budget: Herziene Ramingen. irreg.
- Belgium. Ministere des Affaires Economiques. Economische en Sociale Documentatie. Referaten /Documentation Economique et Sociale. Resumes Analytiques. q. ISSN 0005-8513
- Investissements Etrangers en Belgique. a. ISSN 0075-0247

**Belgium. Ministere des Affaires Economiques. Administration de l'Energie**
see Belgium. Administration de l'Energie

**Belgium. Ministere des Affaires Economiques. Administration des Mines**
see Belgium. Administration des Mines

**Belgium. Ministere des Affaires Economiques. Institut National de Statistique**
see Belgium. Institut National de Statistique

**Belgium. Ministere des Affaires Economiques. Service de la Metrologie**
see Belgium. Service de la Metrologie

**Belgium. Ministere des Affaires Economiques. Service de la Propriete Industrielle et Commerciale**
see Belgium. Service de la Propriete Industrielle et Commerciale

**Belgium. Ministere des Affaires Etrangeres**
2 rue des Quatre-Bras, 1000 Brussels, Belgium
- Memo from Belgium. 6 per yr. ISSN 0025-908X (For English edition, inquire: Consulate General de Belgique, Information Officer, 50 Rockefeller Plaza, Suite 1104, New York, New York)
- Repertoire des Theses de Doctorat/Reportorium van Doctorale Proefschriften. a.

**Belgium. Ministere des Affaires Etrangeres. Administration des Relations Culturelles**
see Belgium. Administration des Relations Culturelles

**Belgium. Ministere des Communications**
62 rue de la Loi, 1040 Brussels, Belgium.
- Belgium. Ministere des Communications. Bulletin de Documentation/Verkeersdocumentatie Bulletin. m. ISSN 0007-4225
- Echos des Communications. 3 per yr. ISSN 0422-2504

**Belgium. Ministere des Communications. Administration de la Marine et de la Navigation Interieure**
see Belgium. Administration de la Marine et de la Navigation Interieure

**Belgium. Ministere des Finances. Administration Centrale des Contributions**
B-1040 Brussels, Belgium.
- Belgium. Ministere des Finances. Administration Centrale des Contribution. Bulletin des Contributions. m. ISSN 0005-853X

**Belgium. Ministere des Trauvaux Public**
- Annales des Travaux Publics de Belgique/Tijdschrift des Openbare Werken van Belgie. (pub. by Nouvelle Imprimerie Commerciale et Industrielle S.C.)

**Belgium. Ministerie van Economische Zaken**
*see* **Belgium. Ministere des Affaires Economiques**

**Belgium. Ministerie van Landbouw**
*see* **Belgium. Ministere de l'Agriculture**

**Belgium. Ministerie van Nationale Opvoeding en Nederlandse Cultuur**
Kortenberglaan 158, 1040 Brussels, Belgium.
- Agricultura. (pub. by Katholieke Universiteit te Leuven. Fakulteit der Landbouwwetenschappen)
- Open Deur. 10 per yr. ISSN 0030-3399

**Belgium. Ministerie van Verkeerswezen**
*see* **Belgium. Ministere des Communications**

**Belgium. Ministerie van Volksgezondheid en van Het Gezin**
*see* **Belgium. Ministere de la Sante Publique et de la Famille**

**Belgium. Nationaal Arbeidsraad**
*see* **Belgium. Conseil National du Travail**

**Belgium. Nationaal Instituut voor de Huisvesting**
*see* **Belgium. Institut National du Logement**

**Belgium. Nationaal Instituut voor de Statistiek**
*see* **Belgium. Institut National de Statistique**

**Belgium. National Dairy Office**
Froissartstraat 95-99, B-1040 Brussels, Belgium.
- Belgique Laitiere/Belgisch Zuivelbedrijf. 5 per yr. ISSN 0005-8424

**Belgium. Nationale Centrale Landbouw-Service**
Spastraat 8, 1040 Brussels, Belgium.
- Agro-Service/Landbouw Service. m.(alternate nos. in Dutch & French) ISSN 0002-1814

**Belgium. Nationale Dienst voor Opgravingen**
*see* **Belgium. Service National des Fouilles**

**Belgium. Office Belge du Commerce Exterieur**
World Trade Center, 4, Galerie Ravenstein, 1000 Brussels, Belgium.
- Belgium. Office Belge du Commerce Exterieur. Bijvoegsel B B H. Reeks B. irreg. ISSN 0067-561X
- Belgium. Office Belge du Commerce Exterieur. Informations du Commerce Exterieur. 2 per w. ISSN 0037-1416
- Belgium/Economic and Technical Information. ISSN 0005-8491
- Commerce Exterieur de l'U.E.B.L. Avec les Pays d'Afrique. (Union Economique Belgo-Luxembourgeoise) a.
- Commerce Exterieur de l'U.E.B.L. Avec les Pays d'Amerique Latine/Buitenlandse Handel van de B.L.E.U. Met de Landen van Latijns Amerika Bruxelles. a.
- Commerce Exterieur de l'U.E.B.L. Avec les Pays d'Asie/Buitenlandse Handel van de B.L.E.U. Met de Landen van Azie Bruxelles. a.
- Commerce Exterieur de l'U.E.B.L. Avec les Pays de l'Est/Buitenlandse Handel van de B.L.E.U. Met de Oostlanden Bruxelles. a.
- Commerce Exterieur de l'U.E.B.L. Avec les Pays de la C.E.E./Buitlandse Handel van de B.L.E.U. Met de E.E.G.-Lidstaten Bruxelles. a.
- Commerce Exterieur de l'U.E.B.L. avec les Pays Industrialises (Autre Que les Pays de la C.E.E. et l'A.E.L.E.)/Buitenlandse Handel van de B.L.E.U. met de Industrielanden (Niet E.E.G.-en E.V.A.-Lidstaten Bruxelles) a.
- I C E Supplement. Serie C. irreg. ISSN 0067-5628

**Belgium. Office National de l'Emploi**
Bd. de l'Empereur 7, 1000 Brussels, Belgium.
- Belgium. Office National de l'Emploi. Bulletin Mensuel. m. (prep. by its Direction Statistiques-Etudes-Information)
- Belgium. Office National de l'Emploi. Liste des Informations Statistiques et des Publications de l'O N E M. irreg.
- Belgium. Office National de l'Emploi. Rapport Annuel. a. ISSN 0067-5644

**Belgium. Parlement**
Bibliotheque Documentation, Brussels, Belgium.
- Belgium. Parlement. Documentation Parlementaire. Parlementaire Documentatie. irreg.

**Belgium. Regie des Postes Belges**
Centre Monnai 1000, Brussels, Belgium.
- Belgium. Regie des Postes. Rapport d'Activite. irreg.

**Belgium. Rijksinstituut voor Ziekte- en Invaliditeitsverzekering**
*see* **Belgium. Institut National d'Assurance Maladie Invalidite**

**Belgium. Rijksstation voor Landbowtechniek**
Van Gansberghelan 115, B-9220 Merelbeke, Belgium.
- Belgium. Rijksstation voor Landbouwtechniek. Mededelingen. irreg. ISSN 0303-9056

**Belgium. Rijksstation voor Sierplantenteelt**
Caritasstraat 21, B-9230 Melle, Belgium.
- Rijksstation en de Werkgroep voor de Sierplantenteelt. Mededelingen. irreg. ISSN 0303-903X

**Belgium. Rijksstation voor Zeevisserij**
Stadhuis, 4e Verdieping, B-8400 Ostend, Belgium.
- Belgium. Rijksstation voor Zeevisserij. Mededelingen. irreg. ISSN 0303-9072

**Belgium. Service de la Metrologie**
24 rue Demot, Brussels 4, Belgium.
- Bulletin Belge de Metrologie. 6 per yr. ISSN 0007-4136

**Belgium. Service de la Propriete Industrielle et Commerciale**
24-26, rue de Mot, 1040 Brussels, Belgium.
- Recueil des Brevets d'Invention. m. ISSN 0034-1851

**Belgium. Service Geologique de Belgique. Administration des Mines**
*see* **Belgium. Administration des Mines**

**Belgium. Service National des Fouilles**
Parc du Cinquantenaire 1, B-1040 Brussels, Belgium.
- Archaeologische Kaarten van Belgie/Cartes Archeologiques de la Belgique. irreg. ISSN 0066-6025

**Belgium. Service Social des Postes**
Blvd. St.-Lazare, 10, 1030 Brussels, Belgium.
- Revue des Postes Belges. m (10 per yr.)

**Belgium. Services de Programmation de la Politique Scientifique**
Rue de la Science, 8, 1040 Brussels, Belgium.
- Science and Technology Yearbook. a.

**Editions Biblio-Mer**
Ankerstraat 10, 8400 Oostende, Belgium.
- Biblio-Mer. irreg.

**Bibliotheque Africaine**
Place Royale, 7, B-1000 Brussels, Belgium.
- Bibliographie Africaine/Afrikaanse Bibliografie. 10 per yr. ISSN 0006-1298
- Bibliotheque Africaine. Catalogue des Acquisitions. Catologus van de Aanwinsten. a. ISSN 0067-5601
- Bibliotheque Africaine. Liste des Acquisitions. m.

**Bibliotheque Royale Albert 1er**
4 Bd. de l'Empereur, 1000 Brussels, Belgium.
- Bibliographie de Belgique/Belgische Bibliografie. m. ISSN 0006-1336
- Bibliotheque Royale Albert 1er. Acquisitions Majeures/Koninklijke Bibliotheek Albert I. Voorname Aanwinsten. Dienstjaar. a. ISSN 0524-7624
- Bibliotheque Royale Albert 1er. Bulletin. irreg.
- Bibliotheque Royale Albert 1er. Catalogue Collectif des Periodiques Etrangers/Koninklijke Bibliotheek Albert I. Centrale Catalogus van Buitenlandse Tijdschriften. (pub. by Editions "Culture et Civilisation")
- Bibliotheque Royale Albert 1er. Rapport Annuel. a.

**Blankenbergs Literair Archief Trefpunt**
Kerkstraat 41, TE Blankenberge, Belgium.
- Trefpunt. 4 per yr. ISSN 0041-2252

**Bloc de la Liberte Linguistique**
31 rue Duquesnoy, Brussels, Belgium.
- Pays de Bruxelles. m. ISSN 0479-7337

**Blues**
39 rue Chanbery, 1040 Brussels, Belgium.
- Blues. irreg.

**Bobeck Laboratories B E N E L U X**
Morgenrood 10, B-2232 's-Gravenwezel, Belgium.
- Gong. m. ISSN 0017-1980

**Francis Bolen, Ed. & Pub.**
30 rue de l'Etuve, 1000 Brussels, Belgium.
- Cine-Dossiers. bi-m. ISSN 0045-690X (Action Cinematographique)
- Francis Bolen's Newsletter. m. ISSN 0015-9786

**Georges Bouillon, Ed. & Pub.**
"La Dryade", B-6762 Vieux-Virton, Belgium.
- Dryade; revue artistique et litteraire. q. ISSN 0012-6799

**Uitgave van de N.V. Drukkerij de Bouwkroniek**
Zennestraat 37, B-1000 Brussels, Belgium.
- Bouwkroniek; moniteur du batiment et des travaux publics. w.
- Houthandel Fen Nijverheid. w.

**Brabant. Dienst voor Geschiedkundige en Folkloristische Opzoekingen**
*see* **Brabant. Service de Recherches Historiques et Folkloriques**

**Brabant. Service de Recherches Historiques et Folkloriques**
61 rue du Marche-aux-Herbes, 1000 Brussels, Belgium.
- Folklore Brabancon. 4 per yr. ISSN 0015-590X

**P.H. Brans Ltd.**
221 Turnhoutsebaan, 2200 Borgerhout, Belgium.
- Radio Revue TV-Electronique Industrielle. m. ISSN 0033-8028

**Brussels Society for Latin Studies**
*see* **Societe d'Etudes Latines de Bruxelles**

**Etablissements Emile Bruylant**
67 rue de la Regence, 1000 Brussels, Belgium.
- Annales d'Etudes Internationales/Annals of International Studies. a. ISSN 0066-2135 (Universite de Geneve. Institut Universitaire de Hautes Etudes Internationales Alumni Association SZ)
- Annuaire Administratif et Judiciaire de Belgique/Administratief en Gerechtelijk Jaarboek voor Belgie. a. ISSN 0066-2461
- Belgium. Cour de Cassation. Bulletin des Arrets. m.
- Etudes de Logique Juridique. irreg.
- Journal de Droit Fiscal. m.
- Organisation Internationale et Relations Internationales. a. (Centre de Recherches sur les Institutions Internationales)
- Pasicrisie Belge. m. ISSN 0031-2614
- Pasinomie. m. ISSN 0031-2630
- Revue Belge de Droit International/Belgian Review of International Law. s-a. ISSN 0035-0788 (Societe Belge de Droit International)
- Revue Critique de Jurisprudence Belge. m. ISSN 0035-0966
- Revue de Droit International et de Droit Compare. q. ISSN 0035-1105 (Institut Belge de Droit Compare)

**C E D-Samsom, N.V.**
Rue Philippe de Champagne 7, 1000 Brussels, Belgium.
- Orientations; la revue du droit social et de la gestion du personnel. 10 per yr. ISSN 0030-543X
- R G F. (Revue Generale de Fiscalite) 10 per yr.

**Editions C.I.B.**
Rue Charles de Meer 21, 1020 Brussels, Belgium.
- Documentation Commerciale et Comptable; le magazine moderne des affaires. m. ISSN 0012-4621 (Union Professionnelle Reconnue de Comptabilite) (Co-Sponsor: Association des Eleves de l'Institut Professionnel Superieur de Belgique)

**C I D E S A**
*see* **International Centre for African Social and Economic Documentation**

**C I R I E C**
*see* **International Centre of Research and Information on Public and Cooperative Economy**

**C R I C**
*see* **Centre National de Recherches Scientifiques et Techniques pour l'Industrie Cimentiere**

**Cahiers Bruxellois**
c/o Mina Martens, Archives de la Ville de Bruxelles, Hotel de Ville, Brussels, Belgium.
- Cahiers Bruxellois; revue d'histoire urbaine. q. ISSN 0007-9626

**Cambel**
21 rue Ernest Havaux, 1040 Brussels, Belgium.
● Comptabilite Economique Universelle-Scientifique;
revue internationale de sciences economiques co-
ordonnees. m. ISSN 0035-3418 (Academie
Internationale de Comptabilite)

**Campagnie Internationale d'Editions Populaires**
Dekens 5, 1040 Brussels, Belgium.
● Nouvel Europe-Magazine. m.

**Carnegie Endowment for International Peace.**
**European Center**
● Etudes de Cas de Conflits Internationaux. (pub.
by Editions de l'Universite de Bruxelles)

**Casterman, S.A.**
28 rue des Soeurs Noires, B-7500 Tournai, Belgium.
● Nouvelle Revue Theologique. bi-m. ISSN 0029-
4845 (College Philosophique et Theologique S.J.
St.-Albert)
● Revue des Ecoles. m. ISSN 0035-1997

**Catholic Diocese of Tournai**
20 Place de Vannes, Mons, Belgium.
● Dimanche. w. ISSN 0012-2866

**Catholic International Education Office**
60 rue des Eburons, B-1040 Brussels, Belgium.
● Catholic International Education Office. Bulletin
Documentaire. irreg. ISSN 0528-2950
● Catholic International Education Office. Bulletin
Nouvelle Serie/Office International de
l'Enseignement Catholique. Bulletin Nouvelle
Serie. irreg., 1971, no. 13. ISSN 0084-8638
● Catholic International Education Office. Etudes et
Documents. irreg.; latest issue, 1974. ISSN 0590-
6008

**Catholic International Union of Social Service**
50 rue du Gouvernement, B-7000 Mons, Belgium.
● Service Social dans le Monde. q. ISSN 0037-2641

**Catholic University of Louvain**
*see* **Katholieke Universiteit Te Leuven; Universite**
**Catholique de Louvain (The two universities have**
**been separate institutions since 1970)**

**Catholic Workers Movement**
Wetstraat 121, B-1040 Brussels, Belgium.
● Volksmacht; weekblad van de christelijke
arbeidersbeweging. w. ISSN 0042-854X

**Centexbel**
Rue Montoyer 24, 1040 Brussels, Belgium.
● Annales Scientifiques Textiles Belges/Belgische
Wetenschappelijke Textielannalen. s-a. ISSN
0003-4517

**Centrale de l'Industrie du Livre et du Papier**
Galerie du Centre, Bloc 2, 1000 Brussels, Belgium.
● Travailleur du Livre. m. ISSN 0041-1876

**Centrale der Boek- en Papiernijverheid**
*see* **Centrale de l'Industrie du Livre et du Papier**

**Centre Belge d'Etudes et de Documentation des Eaux**
2 rue A. Stevart, 4000 Liege, Belgium
● C E B E D E A U. Tribune. 10 per yr. ISSN
0007-8115 (Subscr. to: 3 Bd. Frere Orban, 4000
Liege, Belgium)

**Centre Belge d'Histoire Rurale**
*see under* **Universite Catholique de Louvain**

**Centre Belgo-Luxembourgeois d'Information de**
**l'Acier**
47 rue Montoyer, B-1040 Brussels, Belgium
● Acier/Stahl/Steel; international review for the
development of the uses of steel. m. ISSN 0001-
4923 (U.S. Subscr. to: Marcel L. Lomont, P.O.B.
70 - Wykagyl Stat. New Rochelle, NY 10804)

**Centre Culturel et d'Animation Cinematographique**
10 rue de l'Orme, Brussels 4, Belgium.
● Amis du Film & de la Television. m. ISSN 0003-
1860

**Centre d'Action Culturelle de la Communaute**
**d'Expression Francaise**
Rue Saintraint 12, 5000 Namur, Belgium.
● C. A. C. E. F. Revue de Presse. 10 per yr. ISSN
0045-6071
● Livres et Disques.
● Rencontres.
● Wallonie Art et Histoire. (pub. by Editions J.
Duculot a Gembloux, S.A.)

**Centre d'Archives Husserl**
● Husserliana. (pub. by Martinus Nijhoff NE)
● Phaenomenologica. (pub. by Martinus Nijhoff NE)

**Centre d'Ecologie Forestiere et Rurale**
59 Ave. de la Faculte d'Agronomie, 5800
Gembloux, Belgium.
● Centre d'Ecologie Forestiere et Rurale.
Communications. irreg., N.S. no. 7, 1974.
● Centre d'Ecologie Forestiere et Rurale. Notes
Techniques Herbageres. irreg., N.S. no. 1-7, 1975.

**Centre d'Education Sanitaire et Nurtritionnelle**
**d'Afrique Centrale**
11 rue Brialmont, 1030 Brussels, Belgium.
● Education Sanitaire et Nurtritionnelle d'Afrique
Centrale. q. ISSN 0004-5144

**Centre d'Etude de l'Energie Nucleaire**
Boeretang 200, B-2400 MOL, Belgium.
● Studiecentrum voor Kernenergie. Annual
Scientific Report. a. ISSN 0081-7155

**Centre d'Etude de la Delinquance Juvenile**
*see* **Studiecentrum voor Jeugdmisdadigheid**

**Centre d'Etude des Pays de l'Est**
*see under* **Universite Libre de Bruxelles**

**Centre d'Etude du Sud-Est Asiatique et de l'Extreme-**
**Orient**
44 Avenue Jeanne, 1050 Brussels, Belgium.
● Asia Quarterly; a journal from Europe. q. ISSN
0035-2683
● Centre d'Etude du Sud-Est Asiatique et de
l'Extreme-Orient. Bibliographie. irreg. ISSN 0069-
181X
● Courrier de l'Extreme-Orient/Berichten uit het
Verne Oosten. m. ISSN 0591-0471

**Centre d'Etudes de Recherche Operationnelle**
*see under* **Universite Libre de Bruxelles**

**Centre d'Etudes et de Documentation Africaines**
7 Place Royale, 1000 Brussels, Belgium.
● Centre d'Etudes et de Documentation Africaines.
Cahiers. m. ISSN 0008-9753

**Centre d'Etudes et de Documentation Sociales**
15, rue du Croisiers, 4000 Liege, Belgium.
● Revue d'Action Sociale; organe interprovincial
d'action sociale de la communaute belge
d'expression francaise. s-a.

**Centre d'Etudes Politiques**
*see under* **Universite Catholique de Louvain**

**Centre d'Etudes Theatrales**
*see under* **Universite Catholique de Louvain**

**Centre d'Histoire et d'Art de la Thudinie**
Rue Louis Cambier No. 7, 6530 Thuin, Belgium.
● Centre d'Histoire et d'Art de la Thudinie.
Publications. irreg.

**Centre d'Information de l'Etain**
56 rue de Marais, B-1000 Brussels, Belgium.
● L'Etain et ses Usages. q. ISSN 0014-1631
(International Tin Research Institute)

**Centre d' Information du Cobalt**
66 rue Royale, 1000 Brussels, Belgium
(Other Cobalt Information Centers: in U.S. c/o
Battelle Memorial Institute, 505 King Ave.,
Columbus, OH 43201; in U.K. 7 Rolls Bldgs., Fetter
Lane, London EC4A 1JA, Eng; in W. Germany,
Elizabethstr. 14, D-4 Dusseldorf)
● Cobalt and Cobalt Abstracts. q.

**Centre de la Pedagogie de l'Histoire**
208 Avenue des 7 Bonniers, 1190 Brussels, Belgium.
● Clio. Cahiers. q.

**Centre de Recherche et d'Information Socio-**
**Politiques**
Rue du Congres 35, 1000 Brussels, Belgium.
● Courrier Hebdomadaire. w.
● Repertoire Permanent des Groupes Financiers et
Industriels. q. ISSN 0034-4583

**Centre de Recherches Metallurgiques\**
47 rue Montoyer, B-1040 Brussels, Belgium
● C R M Metallurgical Reports. q. ISSN 0026-0851

**Centre de Recherches Sociologiques**
*see under* **Universite Catholique de Louvain**

**Centre de Recherches sur les Institutions**
**Internationales**
● Organisation Internationale et Relations
Internationales. (pub. by Etablissements Emile
Bruylant)

**Centre Europeen de Diffusion de la Culture**
137 rue de Livourne, Brussels, Belgium.
● Scarabee. bi-m. ISSN 0036-567X

**Centre Interdisciplinaire d'Etudes Philosophique**
*see under* **Universite de l'Etat a Mons**

**Centre International d'Etudes Poetiques**
Bibliotheque Royale, 4 Bd de l'Empereur, 1000
Brussels, Belgium.
● Centre International d'Etudes Poetiques. Courrier.
6 per yr. ISSN 0011-0531

**Centre International de Documentation Economique**
**et Sociale Africaine**
*see* **International Centre for African Social and**
**Economic Documentation**

**Centre International de l'Actualite Fantastique et**
**Magique**
77, rue Emil Banning, B-1050 Brussels, Belgium.
● Fantasmagie. q. ISSN 0427-9824

**Centre International Rogier**
Bureau 2006, bte. 363, 1000 Brussels, Belgium.
● Vleugel en Wiel/Vleugelen Wiel. q. ISSN 0515-
7935

**Centre Internationale de Dialectologie Generale**
*see under* **Universite Catholique de Louvain**

**Centre Interuniversitaire d'Histoire Contemporaine**
● Centre Interuniversitaire d'Histoire
Contemporaine. Cahiers/Interuniversitair
Centrum voor Hedendaagse Geschiedenis.
Mededelingen. (pub. by Editions Nauwelaerts)

**Centre Interuniversitaire de Formation Permanente**
Bd. Defontaine 10, B-6000 Charleroi, Belgium.
● Actuel. m. ISSN 0001-7833

**Centre National d'Archeologie et d'Histoire du Livre**
c/o Bibliotheque Royale de Belgique, 4, Boulevard
de l'Empereur, Brussels, Belgium.
● Centre National d'Archeologie et d'Histoire du
Livre. Publication. irreg., 1968, vol. 2. ISSN 0069-
1984

**Centre National d'Histoire des Sciences**
Bibliotheque Royale Albert I, Boulevard de
l'Empereur, 4, B-1000 Brussels, Belgium.
● Comite Belge d'Histoire des Sciences. Notes
Bibliographiques/Belgische Komitee voor de
Geschiedenis der Wetenschappen. Bibliografische
Notas. s-a. ISSN 0010-2415

**Centre National de Documentation Scientifique et**
**Technique**
4 Blvd. de l'Empereur, B-1000 Brussels, Belgium.
● Belgian Environmental Research Index. s-a.
● Centre National de Documentation Scientifique et
Technique. Rapport d'Activite. a. ISSN
0069-1968

**Centre National de Recherches Archeologiques en**
**Belgique**
Parc du Cinquantenaire 1, 1040 Brussels, Belgium.
● Archeologie; chronique semestrielle. s-a. ISSN
0003-8210
● Centre National de Recherches Archeologiques en
Belgique. Repertoires Archeologiques. Serie A:
Repertoires Bibliographiques. irreg. ISSN 0069-
1992
● Centre National de Recherches Archeologiques en
Belgique. Repertoires Archeologiques. Serie B:
Repertoires des Collections. irreg. ISSN 0069-
200X
● Centre National de Recherches Archeologiques en
Belgique. Repertoires Archeologiques. Serie C:
Repertoires Divers. irreg. ISSN 0069-2018

**Centre National de Recherches Scientifiques et**
**Techniques pour l'Industrie Cimentiere**
46 rue Cesar Franck, B-1050 Brussels, Belgium.
● C R I C Rapport de Recherche. irreg. ISSN 0069-
2026

**Centre pour l'Etude des Problemes du Monde Musulman Contemporain**
Ave. Jeanne, 44, 1050 Brussels, Belgium.
- Centre pour l'Etude des Problemes de Monde Musulman Contemporain. Initiations. irreg. ISSN 0077-0353
- Correspondance d'Orient. s-a. ISSN 0070-0517

**Centrum voor Onkruidonderzoek**
see under **Rijksuniversiteit Te Gent**

**Centrum voor Ziekenhuiswetenschap**
see under **Katholieke Universiteit Te Leuven**

**Cercle Belge de la Librairie**
111 Ave. du Parc, 1060 Brussels, Belgium.
- Cercle Belge de la Librairie. Annuaire. a.
- Cercle Belge de la Librairie. Journal de la Librairie. m.

**Cercle d'Archeologie et de Folklore du Comte de Jette et des Environs**
35 Avenue de Brouckere, 1080 Brussels, Belgium, Belgium.
- Comte de Jette Bulletin. s-a. ISSN 0010-4914
- Notre Comte/Ons Graafschap. q. ISSN 0048-0924

**Cercle d'Etudes Numismatiques**
4 Boulevard de l'Empereur, B-1000 Brussels, Belgium.
- Cercle d'Etudes Numismatiques. Bulletin. q. ISSN 0009-0344
- Cercle d'Etudes Numismatiques. Travaux. irreg. ISSN 0069-2247
- Vie Numismatique. m. (Co-sponsor: Alliance Europeene Numismatique)

**Cercle d'Histoire et d'Archeologie de Saint-Ghislain et de la Region**
Saint-Ghislain, Belgium.
- Cercle d'Histoire et d'Archeologie de Saint-Ghislain et de la Region. Anales. a.

**Cercle des Officiers de Reserve de Bruxelles**
43 Av. des Traquets, 1160 Brussels, Belgium.
- Vigilo. q.

**Cercle Historique et Archeologique de Wavre et de la Region**
2 rue de l'Escaille, 1300 Wavre, Belgium.
- Wavriensia. 6 per yr. ISSN 0043-1567

**Cerevisia a.s.b.l.**
Avenue Mozart 66, B-1190 Brussels, Belgium.
- Cerevisia. q. (Association Royale des Anciens Eleves des Ecoles de Brasserie Gand, Bruxelles et Louvain)

**Chambre de Commerce de Bruxelles**
112 rue de Treves, 1040 Brussels, Belgium.
- Chambre de Commerce de Bruxelles. Bulletin Officiel. w. ISSN 0009-1197
- Seminaire Belge de Perfectionnement aux Affaires. Exposes. a. ISSN 0080-8792

**Chambre de Commerce et d'Industrie d'Anvers**
Markgravestraat 12, 2000 Antwerp, Belgium.
- Chambre de Commerce et d'Industrie d'Anvers. Bulletin. m.
- Kamer van Koophandel en Nijverheid van Antwerpen. Bulletin. m. ISSN 0022-8087

**Chambre de Commerce Neerlandaise pour la Belgique et le Luxembourg**
93 rue Royale, Bte. 4, B-1000 Brussels, Belgium.
- Chambre de Commerce Neerlandaise pour la Belgique et le Luxembourg. Revue Commerciale/Kamer van Koophandel voor Belgie en Luxembourg. Handelsoverzicht. m. ISSN 0017-7334

**Chambre Syndicale de l'Industrie des Vernis, Peintures, Mastics, Encres d'Imprimerie et Couleurs d'Art**
49 Square Marie-Louise, Brussels, Belgium.
- Digest des Revues Techniques. 11 per yr. ISSN 0012-2718

**Chambre Syndicale des Fabricants de Confections de Belgique**
Av. de la Liberte 104, 1080 Brussels, Belgium.
- Syncobel. m.

**Chambre Syndicale des Grossistes en Confiserie-Chocolaterie-Biscuits et Autres Derives du Sucre**
Rue Botanique 67, B-1020 Brussels, Belgium.
- Chobisco. m.

**Chambre Syndicale des Importateurs et Negociants en Machines - Outils et Outillages en Belgique**
- Inter-Tecniek; Alle Internationale Technische Nieuwigheden. (pub. by Etablissement Dessart)

**Chambre Syndicale du Commerce Automobile de Belgique**
Bd. de la Woluwe 46, 1200 Brussels, Belgium.
- Auto-Moto-Revue. m.
- Cars. a.
- Catalogue General de l'Industrie et du Commerce Automobile de Belgique. a.
- Chambre Syndicale du Commerce Automobile de Belgique. Bulletin Mensuel. m.
- Commercial Vehicles. a.
- Etude du Marche Automobile Belge. a.
- Motorcycles and Mopeds. a.

**Chasovoi**
Boite Postale 31, Ixelles 4, 1050 Brussels, Belgium.
- Chasovoi/Sentinelle; organ svyazi rossiiskovo natzional-novo dvizheniya. m. ISSN 0009-1960

**Chemical Bank**
46 Ave. des Arts, 1040 Brussels, Belgium.
- Report from Europe. 9 per yr.

**CHOBISCO**
see **Chambre Syndicale des Grossistes en Confiserie-Chocolaterie-Biscuits et Autres Derives du Sucre**

**Christelijk Syndicaat van Personeel van Spoorwegen, Posterijen**
R.T.T., Zeewezen, Luchtvaart en B.R.T, Oudergemselaan 26-32, 1040 Brussels, Belgium.
- Rechte Lijn. s-m. ISSN 0048-6949

**Christelijk Vlaams Kunstenaarsverbond**
A. van Daele Lindenlaan 18, B-8880 Tielt, Belgium.
- Vlaanderen; Tijdschrift voor kunst en cultuur. bi-m. ISSN 0042-7683

**Christelijke Arbeidersbeweging**
see **Catholic Workers Movement**

**Christelijke Middenstands- en Burgersvrouwen**
99 Jozef 2-Straat, Brussels, Belgium.
- Vrouw. 10 per yr.

**Cine-Revue S. A.**
Ave. Marechal Foch 7, 1030 Brussels, Belgium.
- Cine Presse; revue professionnelle de la corporation cinematographique. bi-m.
- Cine-Revue. w. ISSN 0045-6918

**Citeaux V.Z.W.**
Cistercian Abbey, B-3581 Achel, Belgium.
- Citeaux; commentarii Cistercienses. q. ISSN 0009-7497

**College d'Europe**
- Cahiers de Bruges/Bruges Quarterly. (pub. by De Tempel)

**College Philosophique et Theologique S.J. St.-Albert**
- Nouvelle Revue Theologique. (pub. by Casterman, S.A.)

**COMAUBEL**
see **Chambre Syndicale du Commerce Automobile de Belgique**

**Comite Belge d'Histoire des Sciences**
- Comite Belge d'Histoire des Sciences. Notes Bibliographiques/Belgische Komitee voor de Geschiedenis der Wetenschappen. Bibliografische Notas. (pub. by Centre National d'Histoire des Sciences)

**Comite Belge de la Distribution**
34 rue Marianne, 1180 Brussels, Belgium.
- Comite Belge de la Distribution. Information Specialisee. q. ISSN 0046-9386
- Distribution d'Aujourd'Hui/Distributie Vandaag; le mensuel des fabricants et commercants dynamiques. m. ISSN 0012-3935

**Comite Central de la Bonneterie Belge**
Frere Orbanlaan 236, 9000 Ghent, Belgium.
- Contact. 25 per yr.

**Comite de Controle de l'Electricite et du Gaz**
Boulevard du Regent 8, 1000 Brussels, Belgium.
- Comite de Controle de l'Electricite et du Gaz. Rapport Annuel. a.

**Comite Maritime International**
see **International Maritime Committee**

**Commission Belge de Bibliographie**
Rue des Tanneurs 80-84, B-1000 Brussels, Belgium.
- Bibliographia Belgica. q. ISSN 0409-3747
- Commission Belge de Bibliographie. Bulletin. q. ISSN 0408-9006
- Commission Belge de Bibliographie, Repertoire Annuel des Comptes-Rendus de Congres Scientifiques. a. ISSN 0080-0937

**Commission de la Bourse**
Palais de la Bourse, B-1000 Brussels, Belgium.
- Commission de la Bourse. Indices et Statistiques. Bulletin Mensuel. m.

**Commission Internationale Technique de Sucrerie**
see **International Commission of Sugar Technology**

**Communication and Cognition**
Blandijnberg 2, 9000 Ghent, Belgium.
- Communication and Cognition. q.

**Compagnie Europeene et d'Outre-Mer**
13, rue de Brederode, Brussels, Belgium.
- Compagnie Europeenne et d'Outre-Mer. Rapports. a.

**Confederation des Brasseries de Belgique**
101 Av. Eugene Demolder, Brussels, Belgium.
- Petit Journal du Brasseur/Kleine Brouwersblad. fortn. ISSN 0031-6253

**Confederation International des Negociants en Oeuvres d'Art**
see **International Confederation of Art Dealers**

**Confederation Internationale des Syndicats Libres**
see **International Confederation of Free Trade Unions**

**Confederation Mondiale du Travail**
see **World Confederation of Labour**

**Confederation Nationale de la Construction**
Lombardstraat 34-42, 1000 Brussels, Belgium.
- Confederation Nationale de la Construction. Annuaire. a. ISSN 0045-8023

**Confederation Nationale des Cadres**
Ave. Josse Goffin 199, B-1080 Brussels, Belgium.
- Inforcadre. m.

**Confederation Royale Horeca**
- New Horeca Belgie. (pub. by Sodedi S.A.)

**Conseil Economique Regional de Wallonie**
16 rue J. Saintraint, 5000 Namur, Belgium.
- Wallonie. bi-m.

**Controle Comite voor de Electriciteit en het Gas**
see **Comite de Controle de l'Electricite et du Gaz**

**Cooperative d'Edition pour les Industries Alimentaires**
Avenue E. Gryzon, B-1070 Brussels, Belgium.
- Ingenieur Chimiste. q. ISSN 0020-1162 (Institut des Industries de Fermentation) (Co-Sponsor: Institut Meurice-Chimie)
- Revue des Fermentations et des Industries Alimentaires. bi-m. ISSN 0035-2071 (Societe Belge de Zymologie Pure et Appliquee)

**Corpus Scriptorum Christianorum Orientalium de Louvain-Washington**
c/o Rene Draguet, Waversebaan 49, 3030 Heverlee-Louvain, Belgium.
- Corpus Scriptorum Christianorum Orientalium: Aethiopica. irreg. ISSN 0070-0398 (Universite Catholique de Louvain) (Co-sponsor: Catholic University of America)
- Corpus Scriptorum Christianorum Orientalium: Arabica. irreg. ISSN 0070-0401 (Universite Catholique de Louvain) (Co-Sponsor: Catholic University of America)
- Corpus Scriptorum Christianorum Orientalium: Armeniaca. irreg. ISSN 0070-041X (Universite Catholique de Louvain) (Co-sponsor: Catholic University of America)
- Corpus Scriptorum Christianorum Orientalium: Coptica. irreg. ISSN 0070-0428 (Universite Catholique de Louvain) (Co-sponsor: Catholic University of America)
- Corpus Scriptorum Christianorum Orientalium: Iberica. irreg. ISSN 0070-0436 (Universite Catholique de Louvain) (Co-Sponsor: Catholic University of America)

- Corpus Scriptorum Christianorum Orientalium: Subsidia. irreg. ISSN 0070-0444 (Universite Catholique de Louvain) (Co-Sponsor: Catholic University of America)
- Corpus Scriptorum Christianorum Orientalium: Syriaca. irreg. ISSN 0070-0452 (Universite Catholique de Louvain) (Co-Sponsor: Catholic University of America)

**Council of European National Youth Committees**
Rue du Cornet 120, 1040 Brussels, Belgium.
- C E N Y C Information. irreg.

**Credit Communal de Belgique**
44 Bd Pacheco, Brussels, Belgium.
- Credit Communal de Belgique. Bulletin Trimestriel. q. ISSN 0011-099X

**CRISP**
*see* **Centre de Recherche et d'Information Socio-Politiques**

**Editions "Culture et Civilisation"**
115 Av. Gabriel Lebon, 1160 Brussels, Belgium.
- Bibliotheque Royale Albert 1er. Catalogue Collectif des Periodiques Etrangers/Koninklijke Bibliotheek Albert I. Centrale Catalogus van Buitenlandse Tidjschriften. irreg. ISSN 0068-2926

**Cultures et Developpement**
c/o A. Lecointre, 62 Tervuurse Vest, 3000 Louvain, Belgium.
- Cultures et Developpement; revue internationale des sciences du developpement. q. ISSN 0011-295X

**Joseph Deghaye**
98 rue Bidaut, Liege, Belgium.
- Nouvelle Etoile. m. ISSN 0029-473X

**J. Dehantschutter**
5 rue de Huldenberg, Brussels 18, Belgium.
- Colombophilie Belge. w. ISSN 0010-1427

**Editions Dereume**
Rue du Marche 69, 1000 Brussels, Belgium.
- Revue des Disques et de la Haute Fidelite. 10 per yr. ISSN 0035-1970

**Editions Derouaux**
10, Place St.-Jacques, Liege, Belgium.
- Dossiers de Demographie de la Belgique. irreg. (Societe Belge de Demographie)

**Desoer S.A.**
21 rue Sainte Veronique, Liege, Belgium.
- Cahiers de Pedagogie et d'Orientation Professionnelle. q. (Universite de Liege. Institut Superieur des Sciences Pedagogiques)

**Etablissement Dessart**
50 rue J. Genot, B-1080 Brussels, Belgium.
- Inter-Tecniek; Alle Internationale Technische Nieuwigheden. m (11 per yr) (Chambre Syndicale des Importateurs et Negociants en Machines - Outils et Outillages en Belgique)

**Dhondt Foundation**
*see* **Fondation Jan Dhondt**

**Librairie Marcel Didier**
Place de la Maison Rouge 1, 1020 Brussels, Belgium.
- Revue des Langues Vivantes/Tijdschrift voor Levende Talen. 6 per yr. ISSN 0035-211X (Association des Professeurs de Langues Vivantes)

**Discotheque National de Belgique**
320 Chaussee de Vleurgat, Brussels, Belgium.
- Discotheque Nationale de Belgique. Catalogue General. irreg. ISSN 0068-2934

**Editions "Distrigraph" s.p.r.l.**
50 Av. Alexandre Bertrand, 1190 Brussels, Belgium.
- Entreprise/Onderneming. m. ISSN 0013-905X

**Editions J. Duculot a Gembloux, S.A.**
Rue de la Postiere 6, 5800 Gembloux, Belgium
- Academie Royale des Sciences, des Lettres et des Beaux-Arts de Belgique. Classe des Lettres et Sciences Morales et Politiques. Bulletin. m. ISSN 0001-4133 (Subscr. to: Office International de Librairie, 30 Av. Marnix, 1050 Brussels, Belgium)
- Academie Royale des Sciences, des Lettres et des Beaux-Arts de Belgique. Classes des Sciences. Bulletin. m. ISSN 0001-4141 (Subscr. to: Office International de Librairie, 30 Av. Marnix, 1050 Brussels, Belgium)

- Wallonie Art et Histoire. 5 per yr. ISSN 0049-6871 (Centre d'Action Culturelle de la Communaute d'Expression Francaise)

**Editions du Dulbea**
50 Ave. F. D. Roosevelt, 1050 Brussels, Belgium.
- Cahiers Economiques de Bruxelles. q. ISSN 0008-0195 (Universite Libre de Bruxelles. Department of Economics)

**Editions Jean Dupuis**
39 rue Destree, 6001 Marcinelle, Belgium.
- Bonne Soiree. w.
- Mimo. w.
- Spirou. w.
- Tele-Moustique. w. ISSN 0027-2647

**Editions "E.G.P."**
Ave. de la Constitution 114, B-1090 Brussels, Belgium.
- Mars-Magazine. m. ISSN 0025-4037 (Belgian Federation of Ironmongers)

**East Flanders. Provinciebestuur**
Kunstpatrimonium, Gouvernementstraat, 24, 9000 Ghent, Belgium.
- Inventaris van Het Kunstpatrimonium van Oost-Vlaanderen. irreg., 1971, no. 8. ISSN 0075-0166

**East-West S.P.R.L.**
13 rue Hobbema, 1040 Brussels, Belgium.
- East European Statistics Service. m.
- East-West. s-m. ISSN 0012-8570
- East-West. Confidential Monthly Report. m.

**S.A. Echo des Bois**
Rue de l'Abattoir 29, B-1000 Brussels, Belgium.
- Echo des Bois. w.

**Ecole des Hautes Etudes Commerciales et Consulaires de Liege. Association des Licencies et Ingenieurs Commerciaux**
c/o Business Information Establishment S.A., 2, rue de la Resistance, 4400 Herstal, Belgium.
- Revue Pratique des Questions Commerciales et Economiques. q. ISSN 0035-3876

**Ecole du Genie**
Rue de Dave, B-5100 Jambes, Belgium.
- Genie. q. ISSN 0016-6804 (Etat-Major General de la Force Terrestre. Direction du Genie)

**Economic Council of Limburg**
*see* **Limburgse Economische Raad**

**Editest**
94 rue General Capiaumont, 1040 Brussels, Belgium.
- International Association of Applied Psychology. Proceedings of Congress. irreg., 1971, 17th, Liege. ISSN 0074-1574 (Inquire: Prof. R. Piret, 47 rue Cesar Franck, 4000 Liege, Belgium)

**Editing Service Group S.A.**
Tabakvest 120, 2000 Antwerp, Belgium.
- E V/Elektro-Verkoop/Electro-Vente. m. ISSN 0012-8066

**Editions de l'Universite de Bruxelles**
Parc Leopold, B-1040 Brussels, Belgium.
- Agglomeration Bruxelloise; approche geographique et sociologigue. irreg. (Universite Libre de Bruxelles. Institut de Sociologie)
- Cahiers d'Etude de Sociologie Culturelle. irreg., 1974, no. 3. (Universite Libre de Bruxelles. Institut de Sociologie)
- Chronologie des Communautes Europeennes. irreg. ISSN 0069-3952 (Universite Libre de Bruxelles. Institut d'Etudes Europeennes)
- Collection "Arguments et Documents". irreg.
- Collection de Sociologie Generale et de Philosophie Sociale. irreg. ISSN 0069-5335 (Universite Libre de Bruxelles. Institut de Sociologie)
- Economie Belge et Internationale/Belgische en Internationale Economie. a. ISSN 0070-8771
- Etudes Africaines. irreg. ISSN 0071-187X (Universite Libre de Bruxelles. Institut de Sociologie)
- Etudes de Cas de Conflits Internationaux. irreg. ISSN 0071-1896 (Carnegie Endowment for International Peace. European Center)
- Etudes Ethnologiques. irreg. ISSN 0071-2035 (Universite Libre de Bruxelles. Institut de Sociologie)
- Faits et les Decisions de la Communaute Economique Europeenne. irreg. (Universite Libre de Bruxelles. Institut d'Etudes Europeennes)

- Problems d'Histoire du Christianisme. a. (Universite Libre de Bruxelles. Institut d'Histoire du Christianisme)
- Universite Libre de Bruxelles. Centre d'Etude des Pays de l'Est. Revue des Pays de l'Est. 2 per yr.
- Universite Libre de Bruxelles. Groupe d'Etude du Dix-Huitieme Siecle. Etudes sur le Dix-Huitieme Siecle. irreg.
- Universite Libre de Bruxelles. Institut d'Etudes Europeennes. Enseignement Complementaire. Nouvelle Serie. irreg. ISSN 0068-2993
- Universite Libre de Bruxelles. Institut d'Etudes Europeennes. Theses et Travaux Economiques. irreg. ISSN 0068-3000
- Universite Libre de Bruxelles. Institut d'Etudes Europeennes. Theses et Travaux Juridiques. irreg. ISSN 0068-3019
- Universite Libre de Bruxelles. Institut de Sociologie. Annee Sociale. a. ISSN 0066-2380
- Universite Libre de Bruxelles. Institut de Sociologie. Cahiers. irreg. ISSN 0068-2985
- Universite Libre de Bruxelles. Institut de Sociologie. Revue. q. ISSN 0020-2215

**N. V. Editions et Regies Nouvelles**
Louis Schmidtlaan 101, 1040 Brussels, Belgium.
- Belgian Business. m.

**Editions Gerard et Co.**
Rue de Limbourg 65, 4800 Verviers, Belgium (Dist. by A.D.P., 955 rue Amherst, Montreal B2 P.Q., Canada)
- Championnat du Monde. Conducteurs. a. ISSN 0069-262X
- Championnat du Monde. Sport Prototype-GT. a. ISSN 0069-2638

**Electronique Professionnelle Belge**
127 Avenue Dailly, 1030 Brussels, Belgium.
- Electronique Professionnelle Belge. m. ISSN 0013-5283

**Epicerie Murillo**
19 rue Murillo, 1040 Brussels, Belgium.
- Contre Champ. bi-m.

**Editions EREL**
16, St. Sebastiaanstraat, 8400 Oostende, Belgium.
- Fastes Hippiques Belges; revue annuelle illustree du sport equestre sur le galop, trot, jumping, elevage, dressage, tourisme equestre. a.
- Festival. w. (July-Aug; Dec-May) ISSN 0015-0363
- Yachting Belge; special illustrated annual revue of sailing, motor and watersports in Belgium. a. ISSN 0084-3237

**Etat-Major General de la Force Terrestre. Direction du Genie**
- Genie. (pub. by Ecole du Genie)

**Etoile de la Foire**
15 rue Vanderlinden, Brussels 3, Belgium.
- Etoile de la Foire. m. ISSN 0014-1895

**Etudes Classiques**
Facultes Notre-Dame de la Paix, Rue de Bruxelles, 61, B-5000 Namur, Belgium.
- Etudes Classiques. q. ISSN 0014-200X

**EUROFINAS**
*see* **European Federation of Finance House Associations**

**Europ-Elite N.V.**
B-1600 Sint-Pieters-Leeuw, Belgium.
- Who's Who in Europe; dictionnaire biographique des personnalites europeenes contemporaines. biennial. ISSN 0083-9515

**European Association of Advertising Agencies**
c/o Nils Faernet, Ave. E. Cambier 19, 1030 Brussels, Belgium.
- E A A A News. irreg. ISSN 0531-2701
- E A A A Reviews. irreg. ISSN 0531-271X
- European Association of Advertising Agencies. Annual Report. irreg. ISSN 0531-2698

**European Association of Neurological Societies**
c/o Dr. J. Brihaye, Clinique Neurochirurgical, 1, rue Heger Bordet, B-1000 Brussels, Belgium.
- European Congress of Neurological Surgery. (Reports) quadrennial, 5th, 1979, Paris. ISSN 0071-268X

**European Banks International**
61 Avenue Louise, B-1000 Brussels, Belgium.
- Key Figures to European Securities. 3 per yr. ISSN 0023-0774

**European Community Institute for University Studies**
200 rue de la Loi, B-1040 Brussels, Belgium.
- Institut de la Communaute Europeenne pour les Etudes Universitaires. Recherche. Research. irreg.

**European Council for Education by Correspondence**
c/o Henri A. Vergrugge, 66 rue Beckers, Brussels 4, Belgium.
- European Council for Education by Correspondence. Yearbook C E C. irreg. ISSN 0531-3414

**European Federation for Intercultural Learning**
12 Bosmanslei, B-2000 Antwerp, Belgium.
- A F S Europa. bi-m.

**European Federation of Finance House Associations**
Ave. de Tervuren 267, 1150 Brussels, Belgium.
- European Federation of Finance House Associations. Annual Report. a. ISSN 0071-2787
- European Federation of Finance House Associations. Conference Proceedings. a. ISSN 0071-2795
- European Federation of Finance House Associations. Newsletter. 10 per yr. ISSN 0300-4252

**European Federation of Purchasing**
c/o J. Hyde, Secretary-General, 1, rue aux Laines, 1000 Brussels, Belgium.
- European Purchasing Conference. (Proceedings) irreg. ISSN 0423-8044

**European League for Economic Cooperation**
Ave. de la Toison d'Or 1-Bte. 11, 1060 Brussels, Belgium.
- European League for Economic Cooperation. Publications. irreg.; no. 51, 1974. ISSN 0071-2884
- European League for Economic Cooperation. Report of the Secretary General on the Activities of E. L. E. C. a. ISSN 0531-7436
- European League for Economic Cooperation. Reports of the International Congress. irreg., 1969, 6th, Brussels. ISSN 0071-2892

**European Organization for the Safety of Air Navigation**
72 rue de la Loi, 1040 Brussels, Belgium.
- Eurocontrol. biennal; vol. 4, no. 3, 1974. ISSN 0531-2248

**European Report**
46 Ave. Albert Elisabeth, 1040 Brussels, Belgium.
- European Intelligence; a review of the European business economy: fornightly report on company initiatives E E C (mergers, affiliations etc.) plus community news and articles. fortn. ISSN 0030-3593

**European Society of Cardiology**
Prof. H. Denolin, 178 Av. Winston Churchill, 1180 Brussels, Belgium.
- European Congress of Cardiology. Abstracts of Papers. irreg., 1976, 7th, The Hague. ISSN 0421-7527
- European Congress of Cardiology. (Proceedings) irreg., 1976, 7th, The Hague. ISSN 0423-7242

**European Transport Law**
19 Justitiestraat, Antwerp, Belgium.
- European Transport Law/Droit Europeen des Transports/Europaeisches Transportrecht/Diritto Europeo dei Trasporti/Europees Vervoerrecht. bi-m. ISSN 0014-3154

**FABRIMETAL**
*see* **Federation des Entreprises de l'Industrie des Fabrications Metalliques**

**Faculte des Sciences Agronomiques de l'Etat a Gembloux**
5800 Gembloux, Belgium.
- Association des Ingenieurs Issus de la Faculte des Sciences Agronomiques de l'Etat a Gembloux. q. ISSN 0303-9099

**Editions Henry Fagne**
Rue Francois Bossaerts 105, B-1038 Brussels, Belgium.
- Nouvelles a la Main, Paris-Bruxelles. q.

**FEBECA**
*see* **Federation Belge du Commerce Alimentaire**

**FEBECOOP**
*see* **Federation Belge des Cooperatives**

**Federatie der Belgische Cooperaties**
*see* **Federation Belge des Cooperatives**

**Federatie der Chemische Nijverheid van Belgie**
*see* **Federation des Industries Chimiques de Belgie**

**Federation Belge d'Education Physique**
33 Bd. de la Sauveniere 33, 4000 Liege, Belgium.
- Revue de l'Education Physique. q. ISSN 0035-1377 (Co-Sponsor: Groupement de Professeurs d'Education Physique)

**Federation Belge des Cooperatives**
28 rue Haute, 1000 Brussels, Belgium.
- Consommateur. bi-m.

**Federation Belge des Exploitants d'Autobus et d'Autocars**
4 Leon Lepagestraat, B-1000 Brussels, Belgium.
- Transport et Tourisme/Transport en Toerisme. m. ISSN 0041-1442

**Federation Belge des Professeurs de Geographie**
Heuvelstraat, 2, St.-Amandsberg, 3045 Blanden, Belgium.
- Aardrijkskunde/Geographie. q. ISSN 0435-382X

**Federation Belge du Commerce Alimentaire**
Rue St. Bernard 60, 1060 Brussels, Belgium.
- Courrier Hebdomadaire. w.

**Federation Belgo-Luxembourgeoise des Industries du Tabac**
Ave. de Cortenbergh, 24, 1040 Brussels, Belgium.
- Federation Belgo-Luxembourgeoise des Industries du Tabac. Bulletin F E D E T A B. m. ISSN 0521-7091

**Federation de l'Enseignement Moyen Officiel du Degre Superieur de Belgique**
Rue Laurent de Koninck 16, 4000 Liege, Belgium.
- Athenee. bi-m (Sept.-June) ISSN 0004-6590

**Federation de l'Industrie Cimentiere**
Rue de Treves 96, 1040 Brussels, Belgium.
- Statistiques de Base de l'Industrie Cimentiere Belge/Basisstatistieken van de Belgische Cementnijverhed. a.

**Federation des Centres Psycho-Medico-Sociaux et d'Orientation Libres**
Avenue de Tervuren 296, Bte. 8, 1150 Brussels, Belgium.
- Bulletin de Psychologie Scolaire et d'Orientation. q. ISSN 0007-4411

**Federation des Editeurs Belges**
111 avenue du Parc, I060 Brussels, Belgium.
- Livres Belges/Boeken Uit Belgie/Buecher aus Belgien/Books from Belgium. a.

**Federation des Entreprises de Belgique**
4 rue Ravenstein, 1000 Brussels, Belgium.
- Federation des Entreprises de Belgique. Bulletin. every 10 days.
- Federation des Entreprises de Belgique. Rapport Annuel. a.

**Federation des Entreprises de l'Industrie des Fabrications Metalliques**
Rue des Drapiers 21, 1050 Brussels, Belgium.
- Apercu Technique-Technisch Overzicht (A T O) fortn. ISSN 0003-6412
- Fabrimetal. fortn.
- Federation des Entreprises de l'Industrie des Fabrications Metalliques. Bulletin d'Information Mensuel. m. ISSN 0014-9330
- Federation des Entreprises de l'Industrie des Fabrications Metalliques. Centre de Recherches Scientifiques et Techniques. Section: Fonderie (FD). Research Reports. irreg., no. 10, 1973.

**Federation des Industries Chimiques de Belgique**
Square Marie Louise 49, B-1040 Brussels, Belgium.
- Federation des Industries Chimiques de Belgique. Annuaire. irreg., latest edition 1975-76. ISSN 0425-9076
- Federation des Industries Chimiques de Belgique. Rapport. a. ISSN 0085-0489

**Federation des Institutions Hospitalieres de Caritas Catholica**
1 rue Guimard, 1040 Brussels, Belgium.
- Hospitalia. q. ISSN 0018-5914

**Federation du Tourisme de la Province de Liege**
Av. Blonden 33, 4000 Liege, Belgium.
- Province de Liege-Tourisme; periodique mensuel d'informations touristiques. m. ISSN 0033-1872

**Federation Europeenne des Associations des Instituts de Credit**
*see* **European Federation of Finance House Associations**

**Federation Internationale de Laiterie**
*see* **International Dairy Federation**

**Federation Internationale des Instituts de Recherches Socio-Religieuses**
*see* **International Federation of Institutes for Social and Socio-Religious Research**

**Federation Internationale des Syndicats Chretiens d'Ouvriers Agricoles**
27 rue de l'Association, Brussels, Belgium.
- Federation Internationale des Syndicats Chretiens d'Ouvriers Agricoles. Travailleur de la Terre. irreg. ISSN 0430-2419

**Federation Nationale Belge de la Fourrure et de la Peau en Poil**
4 rue de l'Autonomie, Bte. 4, 1070 Brussels, Belgium.
- Fourrure et Peau en Poil/Bont en Kleinvel. m. ISSN 0015-9174

**Federation Nationale Belge des Tapissiers-Garnisseurs et Decorateurs d'Interieur**
- Tapissier Decorateur/Woningstoffeerder. (pub. by Publi-Contact)

**Federation Nationale des Chambres Syndicales**
2 Henri Beyaertstraat, B-8500 Kortrijk, Belgium.
- Syndikale Kamer. 2 per mo. (Co-sponsor: National Verbond van de S.K.G.)

**Federation Nationale des Commissaires de Police et Commissaires de Police Adjoints de Belgique**
Rue Vanderborght, 87, B-1090 Brussels, Belgium.
- Officer de Police/Politie Officier. m. ISSN 0030-056X

**Federation Nationale des Infirmieres Belges**
18 rue de la Source, 1060 Brussels, Belgium.
- F.N.I.B/N.V.B.V. bi-m. ISSN 0301-0813

**Federation Nationale des Jeunes Alliances Paysannes**
94-96 rue Dansaert, 1000 Brussels, Belgium.
- Voix des Jeunes. m. ISSN 0504-6556

**Federation Nationale des Poissonniers Detaillants Belges**
- Poissonnier Belge/Belgische Vishandelaar. (pub. by Publi-Contact)

**Federation of Tobacco Manufacturers in Belgium**
*see* **Federation Belgo-Luxembourgeoise des Industries du Tabac**

**Federation Royale Belge du Yachting**
- Sur l'Eau. (pub. by Drukkerij-Uitgeverij Vyncke)

**Federation Royale des Associations Belges d'Ingenieurs Civils et d'Ingenieurs Agronomes**
Square Marie-Louise 28,bte.1, B-1040 Brussels, Belgium.
- F. A. B. I. Revue d'Information. q. ISSN 0014-5548

**Federation Touristique du Brabant**
61 rue du Marche-aux-Herbes, 1000 Brussels, Belgium.
- Brabant. 6 per yr. ISSN 0006-8616

**FEDETAB**
*see* **Federation Belgo-Luxembourgeoise des Industries du Tabac**

**Femmes d'Aujourd'hui**
9 Av. Frans van Kalken, Brussels, Belgium.
- Femmes d'Aujourd'hui. w. ISSN 0014-9950

**Flambeau**
75 Av. Emile de Beco, Brussels 5, Belgium.
- Flambeau; revue belge des questions politiques et litteraires. q. ISSN 0015-3427

**Flemish Association of Gastro-Enterology**
222 Lange Lozanastr, B-2000 Antwerp, Belgium.
- Tijdschrift voor Gastro-Enterologie. bi-m. ISSN 0049-3899

**Foi et le Temps**
51 rue du Chambge, 7500 Tournai, Belgium.
- Foi et le Temps. bi-m.

**Fondation Charles Plisnier**
47 rue des Palais, 1030 Brussels, Belgium.
- Ethnie Francaise. bi-m. ISSN 0014-178X
- Fondation Charles Plisnier. Cahiers. irreg., no. 9,
  1966. ISSN 0428-8815
- Fondation Charles Plisnier. Etudes et Documents.
  irreg., no. 8, 1969. ISSN 0531-9757

**Fondation Egyptologique Reine Elisabeth**
Parc du Cinquantenaire, B-1040 Brussels, Belgium.
- Bibliographie Papyrologique sur Fiches. irreg. (6
  per yr.)
- Bibliotheca Aegyptiaca. irreg. ISSN 0067-7817
- Chronique d'Egypte. s-a. ISSN 0009-6067
- Elkab. irreg. (prep. by its Comite des Fouilles
  Belges en Egypte)
- Monographies Reine Elisabeth. irreg., vol. 3, 1974.
- Monumenta Aegyptiaca. irreg. ISSN 0077-1376
- Papyrologica Bruxellensia. irreg. ISSN 0078-9402

**Fondation Eugene Ysaye**
39 rue de l'Escrime, 1190 Brussels, Belgium.
- Fondation Eugene Ysaye. Bulletin d'Information.
  3 per yr. ISSN 0015-6051

**Fondation Jan Dhondt**
Blandijnberg 2, 9000 Ghent, Belgium.
- Revue Belge d'Histoire Contemporaire/Belgisch
  Tijdschrift voor Nieuwste Geschiedenis. s-a, plus
  supplement. ISSN 0035-0869

**Forum A.S.B.L.**
Caserne Prince Baudouin, Place Dailly, 1030
Brussels, Belgium.
- Forum de la Force Terrestre. q. ISSN 0015-8488

**Foundation Byzantine**
Boulevard de l'Empereur 4, B-1000 Brussels,
Belgium.
- Byzantion; revue internationale des etudes
  Byzantines. s-a.

**Free University of Brussels**
see Universitie Libre de Bruxelles; Vrije
Universiteit Brussel (The two universities have
been separate institutions since 1970)

**Miller Freeman Publications S.A.**
123A, Chaussee de Charleroi, 1060 Brussels,
Belgium.
- Pulp & Paper International. m. ISSN 0033-409X

**Galilee**
B.P. 160, Louvain, Belgium.
- Galilee; la newsletter scientifique Belge. q.

**Editions Gamma**
9 rue Barthelemy Frison, 7500 Tournai, Belgium.
- Humanisme, an 2000. irreg. ISSN 0073-392X

**Geneeskundige Kring van Antwerpen**
Louizastraat 8, 2000 Antwerp, Belgium.
- Annales Collegii Medici Antverpiensis. m. ISSN
  0003-3863

**Gewestelijke Economische Raad voor Vlaanderen**
Hertogsstr. 43, 1000 Brussels, Belgium.
- Gewestelijke Economische Raad voor Vlaanderen.
  Activiteitsverslag. irreg. ISSN 0304-5978

**Imprimerie J. Goemaere**
21 rue de la Limite, Brussels 3, Belgium.
- Annales de Droit; revue trimestrielle de droit
  belge. q. (Universite Catholique de Louvain.
  Association des Anciens Etudiants de la Faculte
  de Droit)

**Groupe de Recherche et d'Information Feministes**
Rue du Musee 14, B-1000 Brussels, Belgium.
- Cahiers du Grif. 5 per yr.

**Groupement Europeen la Recherche Scientifique en
Stomatologie et Odontologie**
- Groupement Europeen pour la Recherche
  Scientifique en Stomatologie et Odontologie.
  Bulletin. (pub. by International Group for
  Scientific Research in Stomatology)

**Groupement International pour la Recherche
Scientifique en Stomatologie**
see International Group for Scientific Research in
Stomatology

**Heideland-Orbis**
Grate Markt 1, B-3500 Hasselt, Belgium.
- Twintig Eeuwen Vlaanderen. irreg.

**Andre Helbo**
Square Sainctelette, 8, B-1000 Brussels, Belgium.
- Degres; revue de synthese a orientation
  semiologique. q.

**Heroldo de Esperanto**
Rue de la Reinette 13, Bte. 28, B-1000 Brussels,
Belgium.
- Heroldo de Esperanto. s-m (18 per yr.) ISSN
  0018-0823

**Hoger Instituut voor Bestuur- en
Handelswetenschappen**
c/o P. Berckx, Trierstraat 94, 1040 Brussels,
Belgium.
- Tijdschrift voor Bestuurswetenschappen en Publiek
  Recht. bi-m. ISSN 0040-7437

**Hoger Instituut voor Grafisch Onderwijs**
Oude Houtlei 38, 9000 Ghent, Belgium.
- Grafiek. 4 per yr. ISSN 0017-2944 (Co-sponsor:
  Hoger Grafisch Studie- en Onderzoekscentrum)

**Hoofdbestur der Belastingen**
Aarlenstraat 80, 1040 Brussels, Belgium.
- Bulletin der Belastingen. bi-m.

**Hopital Universitaire Brugmann. Clinique de
Gynecologie et d'Obstetrique**
Place van Gehuchten 4, 1020 Brussels, Belgium.
- Entretiens d'Actualite. s-a. ISSN 0378-066X

**Uitgeverij J. Hoste N.V.**
Korte Nieuwstraat 28, 2000 Antwerp, Belgium.
- Vlaamse Gids. bi-m. ISSN 0042-7675

**I B P A Electronic Publications**
Leuvensesteenweg 13, 1940 Sint Stevens Woluwe,
Brussels, Belgium.
- Electronic Product News. 11 per yr.

**I E N-Europe S.A.**
Rue Verte 216, 1030 Brussels, Belgium.
- I E N-Europe. (International Equipment News) 10
  per yr.

**I R C A**
see International Railway Congress Association

**ICOMOS**
see International Council of Monuments and Sites

**IDOCET**
see International Documentary Centre for
Electronic Technology

**Impact (Belgium)**
Blvd. Emile Jacqmain 162, 1000 Brussels, Belguim.
- Impact (Belgium); mensuel de la dynamique des
  affairs. m.

**Institut Archeologique du Luxembourg. Bibliotheque**
13, rue des Martyrs, 6700 Arlon, Belgium.
- Institut Archeologique du Luxembourg. Annales.
  irreg.
- Institut Archeologique du Luxembourg. Bulletins;
  archeologie-art-histoire-folklore. q. ISSN 0020-
  2177

**Institut Belge d'Information et de Documentation**
Rue Montoyer 3, B-1040 Brussels, Belgium.
- Belgium Basic Statistics. a.
- Institut Belge d'Information et de Documentation.
  Repertoire de l'Information. a. ISSN 0073-8166
- Interstages. 8 per yr. ISSN 0020-9716
- Vu Par les Belges. bi-m. ISSN 0042-9287

**Institut Belge de Droit Compare**
- Revue de Droit International et de Droit
  Compare. (pub. by Etablissements Emile
  Bruylant)

**Institut Belge de l'Emballage**
15 rue Picard, 1020 Brussels, Belgium.
- I B E-B I V Flash. m.

**Institut Belge de la Soudure**
Rue des Drapiers 21, B-1050 Brussels, Belgium.
- Revue de la Soudure/Lastijdschrift. q. ISSN 0035-
  127X

**Institut Belge de Science Politique**
43 rue des Champs-Elysees, 1050 Brussels, Belgium.
- Institut Belge de Science Politique. Bibliotheque.
  Nouvelle Serie. irreg. ISSN 0073-8131
- Institut Belge de Science Politique. Bibliotheque.
  Serie Documents. irreg. ISSN 0073-814X
- Institut Belge de Science Politique. Documents. a.
  ISSN 0073-8158
- Res Publica. 5 per yr. ISSN 0486-4700

**Institut Belge du Petrole**
4 rue de la Science, 1040 Brussels, Belgium.
- Institut Belge du Petrole. Annales/Belgisch
  Petroleum Instituut. Annalen. q. ISSN 0020-2185

**Institut Belge pour l'Amelioration de la Betterave**
Molenstraat 45, 3300 Tienen, Belgium.
- Institut Belge pour l'Amelioration de la Betterave.
  Bulletin d'Information. m.
- Institut Belge pour l'Amelioration de la Betterave.
  Publication Trimestrielle/Belgisch Instituut tot
  Verbetering van de Biet. Driemaandelijske
  Publikatie. q. ISSN 0303-9145

**Institut Bonnecompagnie**
51 rue Saint-Bernard, 1060 Brussels, Belgium.
- Danses. q. ISSN 0011-6173 (Co-sponsors: Institut
  Mullier; Institut Deschamps)

**Institut d'Aeronomie Spatiale de Belgique**
Ave. Circulaire 3, 1180 Brussels, Belgium.
- Aeronomica Acta. irreg., latest 1975. ISSN 0065-
  3713

**Institut d'Astronomie et de Geophysique Georges
Lemaitre**
Louvain, Belgium.
- Institut d'Astronomie et de Geophysique Georges
  Lemaitre. Publications. irreg.

**Institut d'Etudes Europeenes**
see under Universite Libre de Bruxelles

**Institut d'Etudes Sociales de l'Etat a Bruxelles**
Rue de l'Abbaye 26, 1050 Brussels, Belgium.
- Service Social. q.

**Institut d'Histoire du Christianisme**
see under Universite Libre de Bruxelles

**Institut d'Hygiene des Mines**
Havermarkt 22, B-3500 Hasselt, Belgium.
- Institut d'Hygiene des Mines. Revue/Instituut
  voor Mijnhygiene. Tijdschrift. q.

**Institut de Droit International**
- Institut de Droit International. Annuaire. (pub. by
  S. Karger AG SZ)

**Institut de la Communaute Europeenne pour les
Etudes Universitaires**
see European Community Institute for University
Studies

**Institut de Linguistique de Louvain**
- Institut de Linguistique de Louvain. Cahiers
  (Cours et Documents) (pub. by Editions Peeters
  s.p.r.l.)

**Institut de Pharmacie A. Gilkinet**
see Universite de Liege. Institut de Pharmacie

**Institut de Philosophie de Louvain**
- Bibliotheque Philosophique de Louvain. (pub. by
  Editions Nauwelaerts)

**Institut de Recherches de l'Europe Centrale**
Blijde Inkomstraat 108, B-3000 Louvain, Belgium.
- Documentation sur l'Europe Centrale. q. ISSN
  0419-537X

**Institut des Industries de Fermentation**
- Ingenieur Chimiste. (pub. by Cooperative
  d'Edition pour les Industries Alimentaires)

**Institut Economique Agricole**
Boulevard de Berlaimont 18, 1000 Brussels,
Belgium.
- Institut Economique Agricole. Cahiers/L.E.I.
  Schriften. 10 per yr. ISSN 0303-8971

**Institut Economique et Social des Classes Moyennes**
9 rue Joseph II, 1040 Brussels, Belgium.
- Institut Economique et Social des Classes
  Moyennes. Informations. m. ISSN 0020-2266

**Institut Emile Vandervelde**
13 Bd. de l'Empereur, Brussels 1, Belgium.
● Socialisme. bi-m. ISSN 0037-8127

**Institut Historique Augustinien**
Peres Augustins, Pakenstraat 109, 3030 Heverlee-Louvain, Belgium.
● Augustiniana; revue pour l'etude de Saint Augustin et de l'Ordre des Augustins. q. ISSN 0004-8003

**Institut Historique Belge de Rome**
c/o M. R. Demey, 2-6 rue de Ruysbroeck, B-1000 Brussels, Belgium.
● Analecta Vaticano-Belgica. Deuxieme Serie. Section A: Nonciature de Flandre. irreg. ISSN 0066-1414
● Analecta Vaticano-Belgica. Deuxieme Serie. Section B: Nonciature de Cologne. irreg. ISSN 0066-1422
● Analecta Vaticano-Belgica. Deuxieme Serie. Section C: Nonciature de Bruxelles. irreg. ISSN 0066-1430
● Analecta Vaticano-Belgica. Premiere Serie: Documents Relatifs aux Anciens Dioceses de Cambrai, Liege, Therouanne et Tournai. irreg. ISSN 0066-1449
● Etudes d'Histoire de l'Art. irreg. ISSN 0071-1969
● Etudes d'Histoire Economique et Sociale. irreg. ISSN 0071-1977
● Etudes de Philologie, d'Archeologie et d'Histoire Ancienne. irreg. ISSN 0071-1926
● Institut Historique Belge de Rome. Bibliotheque. irreg. ISSN 0073-8522
● Institut Historique Belge de Rome. Bulletin. a. ISSN 0073-8530

**Institut International d'Etudes sur l'Education**
see **International Institute for Studies on Education**

**Institut Jules Destree pour la Defense et l'Illustration de la Wallonie**
38 rue Chapeau de Cure, 6290 Nalinnes-Lez-Charleroi, Belgium.
● Collection Figures de Wallonie. irreg. ISSN 0069-5386
● Connaitre la Wallonie/To Know Wallony. 2 per yr. ISSN 0010-602X
● Institut Jules Destree pour la Defense et l'Illustration de la Wallonie.Collection: Etudes et Documents sur la Wallonie. irreg. ISSN 0073-8557

**Institut National des Industries Extractives**
200 rue de Chera, B-4000 Liege, Belgium.
● Annales des Mines de Belgique/Annalen der Mijnen van Belgie. (pub. by Imprimerie R. Louis)
● Institut National des Industries Extractives. Fiches de Documentation. 2 per m. ISSN 0020-2428
● Institut National des Industries Extractives. Rapport Annuel. a.

**Institut pour l'Encouragement de la Recherche Scientifique dans l'Industrie et l'Agriculture. Centre d'Ecologie Forestiere et Rurale**
see **Centre d'Ecologie Forestiere et Rurale**

**Institut Royal des Relations Internationales**
Av. de la Couronne 88, 1050 Brussels, Belgium.
● Studia Diplomatica. bi-m.

**Institut Royal du Patrimoine Artistique**
Parc du Cinquantenaire, 1, B-1040 Brussels, Belgium.
● Institut Royal de Patrimoine Artistique. Bulletin/Koninklijk Institut voor Het Kunstpatrimonium. Bulletin. a. ISSN 0085-1892

**Institut Royal Meteorologique de Belgique**
see **Belgium. Institut Royal Meteorologique.**

**Institut Superieur de l'Etat de Traducteurs et d'Interpretes**
Association pour la Promotion de l'Etude des Langues Modernes, Rue J. Hazard 34, 1180 Brussels, Belgium.
● Equivalences. 3 per yr. (Association pour la Promotion de l'Etude des Langues Modernes) (Co-Sponsor: Institut Superieur de l'Etat de Traducteurs et d'Interpretes)

**Institute for the History of Christianity**
see **Universite Libre de Bruxelles. Institut d'Histoire du Christienisme**

**Institute of Applied Linguistics**
see **Instituut voor Toegepaste Linguistiek**

**Instituut voor Franciscaanse Geschiedenis**
Sint-Truiden, Belgium.
● Franciscana; bijdragen tot de geschiedenis van de minderbroeders in de nederlanden. q. ISSN 0015-9840

**Instituut voor Hygiene en Epidemiologie**
14 rue Wytsman, 1050 Brussels, Belgium.
● Instituut voor Hygiene en Epidemiologie. Zwavel-Rook Meetnet. m.

**Instituut voor Staatkundige Vorming**
Boninvest 1, B-8000 Brugge, Belgium.
● Politieke Dokumentatie. bi-m. ISSN 0048-475X

**Instituut voor Toegepaste Linguistick**
Universite Catholique de Louvain, Blijde-Inkomststraat 21, B-3000 Louvain, Belgium.
● I T L Review of Applied Linguistics. q. ISSN 0019-0829

**International Academy of Legal Medicine and Social Medicine**
c/o Armand Andre, Treas., 39, rue dos Fanchon, B-4020 Liege, Belgium.
● Acta Medicinae Legalis et Socialis. irreg. ISSN 0065-1397

**International Actuarial Association**
13 rue des Chevaliers, 1050 Brussels, Belgium.
● International Actuarial Congress. Transactions. quadrennial, 19th, Oslo, 1972. ISSN 0074-1264

**International Association for Cybernetics**
Palais des Expositions, Place Andre Rijckmans, 5000 Namur, Belgium.
● Cybernetica. q. ISSN 0011-4227
● International Congress for Cybernetics. Proceedings. Actes. triennial, 8th, 1976, Namur. ISSN 0074-3380

**International Association for the Advancement of Educational Research**
General Secretariat, Henri-Dunantlaan 1, B-9000 Ghent, Belgium.
● International Association for the Advancement of Educational Research. Congress Proceedings. quadrennial, 1973, 6th, Paris, published 1975. ISSN 0074-1531
● International Association for the Advancement of Educational Research. Congress Reports. quadrennial, 1973, 6th, Paris, published in 1975. ISSN 0074-154X

**International Association for the History of Glass**
Musee du Verre, 13 Quai de Maastricht, 4000 Liege, Belgium.
● International Association for the History of Glass. Bulletin. irreg. ISSN 0447-9823

**International Association of Applied Psychology**
● International Association of Applied Psychology. Proceedings of Congress. (pub. by Editest)

**International Association of Democratic Lawyers**
49 Av. Jupiter, 1190 Brussels, Belgium.
● International Association of Democratic Lawyers. Congress Report. irreg; 1970, 9th. ISSN 0074-1604
● Review of Contemporary Law. s-a. ISSN 0048-7473

**International Association of Geodesy. Commission Permanente des Marees Terrestres**
c/o Observatoire Royal de Belgique, 3 Avenue Circulaire, 1180 Brussels, Belgium.
● International Association of Geodesy. Commission Permanente des Marees Terrestres. Marees Terrestres Bulletin d'Information. irreg. ISSN 0542-6766

**International Association of Lawyers**
Bureau M. 114, Palais de Justice, B-1000 Brussels, Belgium.
● International Congress of Lawyers. Proceedings. biennial; 26th Munich, 1975. ISSN 0074-3739

**International Association of Students in Business and Economics**
International AIESEC Secretariat, Av. Legrand 45, B-1050 Brussels, Belgium.
● International Association of Students in Business and Economics. Compendium. a. ISSN 0074-1752
● LINKletter. q.

**International Association on the Artificial Prolongation of the Human Specific Lifespan**
c/o Dr. H. le Compte, Ed., Fabiolalaan 12, B-8300 Knokke-Zoute, Belgium.
● Rejuvenation. q. (Co-Sponsor: Belgische Vereniging van Geriaters)

**International Bureau for the Study of the Problems in the Teaching of Greek and Latin**
Blandijnberg, B-9000 Ghent, Belgium.
● Acta Colloquii Didacticii Classici; didactica classica gandensia. a.

**International Center of Information on Antibiotics**
32 Bd. Constitution, Liege, Belgium.
● I C I A Information Bulletin. a. ISSN 0018-8948 (Co-sponsor: World Health Organization)

**International Centre for African Social and Economic Documentation**
Place Royale 7, 1000 Brussels, Belgium.
● Bulletin of Information on Current Research on Human Sciences Concerning Africa/Bulletin d'Information sur les Recherches dans les Sciences Humaines Concernant l'Afrique. 2 per yr. ISSN 0007-4926
● Centre International de Documentation Economique et Sociale Africaine. Monographies Documentaires. irreg. ISSN 0069-1763
● Centre International de Documentation et Sociale Africaine. Enquetes Bibliographiques. irreg., 1970, vol.17. ISSN 0069-1755

**International Centre for Religious Education**
● Lumen Vitae. (pub. by Lumen Vitae Press)

**International Centre of Onomastics**
Blijde-Inkomststraat 5, 3000 Louvain, Belgium.
● Onoma; bibliographical and information bulletin. irreg. ISSN 0078-463X

**International Centre of Research and Information on Public and Cooperative Economy**
45 Quai de Rome, 4000 Liege, Belgium.
● Annales de l'Economie Publique, Sociale et Cooperative/Annals of Public and Cooperative Economy. 4 per yr.

**International Commission of Sugar Technology**
c/o Josse Henry, General Secretary-Treasurer, 1 Aandorenstraat, B-3300 Tienen, Belgium.
● International Commission of Sugar Technology. Proceedings of the General Assembly. irreg.; 15th, 1975, Vienna. ISSN 0074-2708
● International Commission of Sugar Technology. Reports of Meetings. irreg; 15th, 1975, Vienna. ISSN 0074-2716

**International Committee of Catholic Nurses**
Square Vergote 43, B-1040 Brussels, Belgium.
● C.I.C.I.A.M.S. News/Nouvelles/Nachrichten. 3 per yr. ISSN 0007-8417

**International Committee of Historical Sciences. Commission for the History of State Assemblies**
● Anciens Pay et Assemblees d'Etats. (pub. by Editions Nauwelaerts)

**International Confederation of Art Dealers**
54 Blvd. de Waterloo, Brussels 1, Belgium.
● International Art Treasures Exhibition. irreg; 1962 no. 3. ISSN 0573-2646

**International Confederation of Free Trade Unions**
37-41 rue Montagne aux Herbes Potageres, 1000 Brussels, Belgium.
● Free Labour World. bi-m. ISSN 0016-0350
● I C F T U Economic & Social Bulletin. 6 per yr. ISSN 0018-8921
● International Confederation of Free Trade Unions. Features. irreg. ISSN 0538-5946
● International Confederation of Free Trade Unions. World Congress Reports. irreg., 11th, 1975, Mexico City. ISSN 0074-2872
● International Trade Union News. fortn. ISSN 0020-899X

**International Coordinating Committee for the Presentation of Science and the Development of out-of-School Scientific Activities**
125 rue de Veeweyde, B-1070 Brussels, Belgium.
● Out of School Scientific and Technical Education. irreg (2-4 per yrs.)

**International Council of Monuments and Sites**
95 Groot Begijnhof, B-3000 Louvain, Belgium.
● Monumentum. s-a. ISSN 0027-0776

**International Customs Tariffs Bureau**
Rue de l'Association 38, B-1000 Brussels, Belgium
(Dist. by: National Bureau of Standards, U.S. Dept.
of Commerce, Wasington, DC 20230)
- International Customs Journal/Bulletin
International des Douanes. irreg.; 14th edt., no.
57. ISSN 0074-4476

**International Dachau Committee**
65 rue de Haerne, 1040 Brussels, Belgium.
- Comite International de Dachau. Bulletin. irreg.
ISSN 0572-9327

**International Dairy Federation**
Square Vergote 41, 1000 Brussels, Belgium.
- International Dairy Federation. Annual Bulletin/
Federation Internationale de Laiterie. Bulletin
Annuel. a; no. 92, 1976. ISSN 0074-4484
- International Dairy Federation. Annual Memento/
Federation Internationale de Laiterie. Memento
Annuel. a; latest issue 1977. ISSN 0538-7078
- International Dairy Federation. Catalogue of I D
F Publications. Catalogue des Publications de la F
I L. a. ISSN 0538-7086
- International Dairy Federation. International
Standard/Federation Internationale de Laiterie.
Norme Internationale. irreg., no. 75, 1976. ISSN
0538-7094

**International Documentation Bureau**
- Selection of International Railway
Documentation/Abrege de Documentation
Ferroviaire Internationale/Auszuege aus der
Internationalen Eisenbahn-Dokumentation/
Resumen de Documentacion Ferroviaria
Internacional. (pub. by International Railway
Congress Association)

**International Federation of Employees in Public
Service**
50, rue Joseph II, 1040 Brussels, Belgium.
- Labor I N F E D O P. m.

**International Federation of Institutes for Social and
Socio-Religious Research**
Batiment S.H. 2, Place Montesquieu 1, Boite 21,
1340 Louvain-la-Neuve, Belgium.
- Social Compass; international review of socio-
religious studies. 4 per yr. ISSN 0037-7686

**International Federation of Trade Unions of
Transport**
Avenue Auderghem, 26, B-1040 Brussels, Belgium.
- Labor-Transport. m.

**International Federation of Translators**
Heiveldstraat 269, B-9000 Ghent, Belgium.
- F I T Newsletter/F I T Nouvelles. irreg.

**International Fellowship of Reconciliation**
Rue van Elewijck 35, 1050 Brussels, Belgium.
- Nonviolence et Societe. bi-m. (Co-sponsor: War
Resisters' International)

**International Group for Scientific Research in
Stomatology**
Institut de Stomatologie, Hopital Universitaire Saint-
Pierre, Rue Haute 322, 1000 Brussels, Belgium.
- Groupement Europeen pour la Recherche
Scientifique en Stomatologie et Odontologie.
Bulletin. q.
- International Group for Scientific Research in
Stomatology. Bulletin. irreg. ISSN 0074-6207

**International Hockey Federation**
55 Bd. du Regent, 1000 Brussels, Belgium
(and 103 Green Lane, Northwood, Middlesex,
England)
- World Hockey. q.

**International Institute for Studies on Education**
Ave. des Arts 1-2, B-1040 Brussels, Belgium.
- I I E E Bulletin. m. ISSN 0046-9718

**International Institute of Administrative Sciences**
25 rue de la Charite, 1040 Brussels, Belgium.
- International Institute of Administrative Sciences.
Reports of the International Congress. triennial
since 1962; 17th, 1977, Abidjan. ISSN 0074-6479
- International Review of Administrative Sciences.
q. ISSN 0020-8523
- Revista Internacional de Ciencias Administrativas.
(pub. by Spain. Boletin Oficial del Estado SP)

**International Institute of Differing Civilizations**
11 Blvd. de Waterloo, 1000 Brussels, Belgium.
- Civilisations. q. ISSN 0009-8140

- International Institute of Differing Civilizations.
(Session Papers) irreg.; 35th, Brussels, 1973. ISSN
0074-6487

**International Iron and Steel Institute**
Place du Champ de Mars 5, B-1050 Brussels,
Belgium.
- International Iron and Steel Institute. Committee
on Economic Studies. I I S I/Econ. q.
- International Iron and Steel Institute. Report of
Conference Proceedings. a.; 8th, Munich, 1974.
ISSN 0074-6630

**International League of Societies for the Mentally
Handicapped**
12 rue Forestiere, B-1050 Brussels, Belgium.
- International League of Societies for the Mentally
Handicapped. (Congress Proceedings) irreg., 1972,
5th, Montreal. ISSN 0074-6754

**International Maritime Committee**
17 Borzestraat, B-2000 Antwerp, Belgium.
- C M I Newsletter.
- International Maritime Committee.
Documentation. irreg.; approx 4 per yr. ISSN
0538-8643

**International Military Sports Council**
Ave. Franklin Roosevelt 230, B-1050 Brussels,
Belgium.
- International Military Sports Council Academy.
Brochure Technique. Technical Brochure. irreg.
ISSN 0538-8732
- Sport International Yearbook. a.

**International Office of Bibliography**
Chaussee de Louvain 696, 1030 Brussels, Belgium.
- Office International de Bibliographie.
Communications Mundaneum. m. ISSN 0027-
321X

**International Office of Cocoa and Chocolate**
Avenue de Cortenbergh 172, 1040 Brussels,
Belgium.
- International Office of Cocoa and Chocolate.
General Assembly of the Members of the Office.
General Report. irreg., latest 1976, Munich. ISSN
0535-1626
- International Office of Cocoa and Chocolate.
Periodic Bulletin. 3 per yr. ISSN 0444-0978 (Co-
sponsor: International Sugar Confectionery
Manufacturers' Association)

**International Organization for Ancient Languages
Analysis by Computer**
110, Boulevard de la Sauveniere, B-4000 Liege,
Belgium.
- Organisation Internationale pour l'Etude des
Langues Anciennes Par Ordinateur. Revue/
International Organization for Ancient Languages
Analysis by Computer. Review. q. ISSN 0030-
4972

**International Railway Congress Association**
85 rue de France, 1070 Brussels, Belgium.
- Rail International. m. ISSN 0020-8442
- Selection of International Railway
Documentation/Abrege de Documentation
Ferroviaire Internationale/Auszuege aus der
Internationalen Eisenbahn-Dokumentation/
Resumen de Documentacion Ferroviaria
Internacional. 10 per yr. ISSN 0037-1424
(International Documentation Bureau)

**International Secretariat for the University Study of
Education**
Baertsoenkaai 3, B-9000 Ghent, Belgium.
- Courrier du Secretariat International de
l'Enseignement Universitaire des Sciences
Pedagogiques. a. ISSN 0011-0558

**International Secretariat of Entertainment Trade
Unions**
c/o Allan J. Forrest, Secretary, C I S L, 37-41 rue
Montagne-aux-Herbes-Potageres, 1000 Brussels,
Belgium.
- International Secretariat of Entertainment Trade
Unions. Newsletter. irreg. ISSN 0538-9755

**International Society for the Study of Medieval
Philosophy**
Kardinaal Mercierplein 2, B-3000 Louvain, Belgium.
- Bulletin de Philosophie Medievale. a. ISSN 0068-
4023
- International Congress of Medieval Philosophy.
Actes. irreg. ISSN 0074-3763

**International Society of Orthopedic Surgery and
Traumatology**
c/o Secretary General, 43 rue des Champs Elysees,
1050 Brussels, Belgium.
- International Orthopaedics. (pub. by Springer-
Verlag US)
- International Society of Orthopedic Surgery and
Traumatology. Proceedings of Congresses.
triennial; 12th, Israel, 1972. ISSN 0074-8552

**International Society of Surgery**
43 rue des Champs Elysees, 1050 Brussels, Belgium.
- International Society of Surgery. Comptes-
Rendus biennial; 25th, Barcelona, 1973.
ISSN 0074-8560
- World Journal of Surgery. (pub. by Springer-
Verlag US)

**International Textile, Garment and Leather Workers'
Federation**
Rue J. Stevens 8, 1000 Brussels, Belgium.
- International Textile, Garment and Leather
Workers' Federation. World Digest. q.

**International Tin Research Institute**
- L'Etain et ses Usages. (pub. by Centre
d'Information de l'Etain)

**International Union for Inland Navigation**
19 rue de la Presse, 1000 Brussels, Belgium.
- International Union for Inland Navigation. Annual
Report. a. ISSN 0074-9311

**International Union for Moral and Social Action**
Rue Brialmont 11, B-1030 Brussels, Belgium.
- U.I.A.M.S. Bulletin Trimestriel. q. ISSN 0579-
5621
- U. I. A. M. S. Informations. q. ISSN 0041-5103

**International Union for the Scientific Study of
Population**
5 rue Forgeur, 4000 Liege, Belgium.
- International Union for the Scientific Study of
Population. Documents du l'Union. irreg.
- International Union for the Scientific Study of
Population. Newsletter. irreg.
- International Union for the Scientific Study of
Population (Proceedings of Conference) (pub. by
Ordina Editions)

**International Union of Academies**
Palais des Academies, 1 rue Ducale, 1000 Brussels,
Belgium.
- Union Academique Internationale. Compte Rendu
de la Session Annuelle du Comite. a.; 48th
Brussels, 1974. ISSN 0074-9346

**International Union of Public Transport**
19, Ave. de l'Uruguay, B-1050 Brussels, Belgium.
- International Statistical Handbook of Urban Public
Transport/Recueil International de Statistiques
des Transports Public Urbains/Internationales
Statistik-Handbuch fuer den Oeffentlichen
Stadtverkehr. irreg. ISSN 0378-1968
- International Union of Public Transport. Reports
and Proceedings of the International Congress.
biennial. ISSN 0074-9494
- International Union of Public Transport. Technical
Reports of the Congresses. biennial. ISSN 0378-
1976
- Metro: a Bibliography. biennial. ISSN 0378-195X
- U I T P Biblio-Index; transport - Verkehr. q. ISSN
0041-5146
- U I T P Revue. q. ISSN 0041-5154

**Interuniversitair Centrum voor Hedendaagse
Geschiedenis**
*see* Centre Interuniversitaire d'Histoire
Contemporaine

**Jardin Botanique National de Belgique**
236 rue Royale, Brussels, Belgium.
- Flore d'Afrique Centrale (Zaire-Rwanda-Burundi)
irreg.
- Jardin Botanique National de Belgique. Bulletin/
Nationale Plantentuin van Belgie. Bulletin. q.
ISSN 0303-9153

**Jonge Muziek**
Van Putlei 33, Antwerp, Belgium.
- Jonge Muziek. q. ISSN 0021-7409

**Kamer van Koophandel en Nyverheid van Antwerpen**
see Chambre de Commerce et d'Industrie d'Anvers

**Katholiek Centrum voor Lectuurinformatie en Bibliotheekvoorziening**
Raapstraat 4, B-2000 Antwerp, Belgium.
- Boekengids; algemeen Nederlands kritisch bibliografisch tijdschrift. m. ISSN 0006-5579
- Jeugdboekengids; kritisch-bibliografisch tydschrift. m. ISSN 0021-6054

**Katholiek Vormingswerk voor Landelijke Vrouwen**
- Bestuursblad. (pub. by Belgische Boerenbond. Economaat)
- Bij de Haard. (pub. by Belgische Boerenbond. Economaat)
- Brieven aan Gezinnen. (pub. by Belgische Boerenbond. Economaat)

**Katholieke Universiteit te Leuven**
see also Universite Catholique de Louvain (the two universities have been separate institutions since 1970)

**Katholieke Universiteit te Leuven**
c/o H. Verdin, Ed., Eikenboslaan 19, B-3200 Kessel-Lo, Belgium.
- Ancient Society. a. ISSN 0066-1619

**Katholieke Universiteit te Leuven. Centrum voor Ziekenhuiswetenschap**
Vital Decosterstraat 102, B-3000 Louvain, Belgium.
- Acta Hospitalia. q. ISSN 0044-6009

**Katholieke Universiteit te Leuven. Department Orientalistiek**
Blijde Inkomststraat 21, B-3000 Louvain, Belgium.
- Orientalia Lovaniensia Periodica. a. ISSN 0085-4522

**Katholieke Universiteit te Leuven. Faculteit der Economische en Toegepaste Economische Wetenschappen**
Van Evenstraat 2B, B-3000 Louvain, Belgium.
- Tijdschrift voor Economie en Management. q.

**Katholieke Universiteit te Leuven. Faculty of Social Science**
Van Evenstraat 2B, B-3000 Louvain, Belgium.
- Politica; sociale wetenschappen en beleid. q.

**Katholieke Universiteit te Leuven. Faculty of Theology**
Naamsestraat 100, 3000 Leuven, Belgium.
- Louvain Studies. s-a. ISSN 0024-6964

**Katholieke Universiteit te Leuven. Fakulteit der Landbouwwetenschappen**
Kardinaal Mercierlaan 92, B-3030 Heverlee, Belgium.
- Agricultura; journal devoted to the management, production and transformation of natural resources. q. ISSN 0044-6785 (Belgium. Ministerie van Nationale Opvoeding en Nederlandse Cultuur)

**Katholieke Universiteit Te Leuven. Instituut voor Middeleeuwse Studies**
- Mediaevalia Lovaniensia. Series I. (pub. by Leuven University Press)

**Katholieke Universiteit te Leuven. Instituut voor Naamkunde**
- Naamkunde. (pub. by Editions Peeters s.p.r.l.)

**Katholieke Universiteit te Leuven. Seminarium Philologiae Humanisticae**
- Humanistica Lovaniensia. (pub. by Leuven University Press)

**Katolieke Filmliga**
Olmstraat 10, 1040 Brussels, Belgium.
- Film en Televisie. 10 per yr. ISSN 0015-1084

**Internationale Drukkerij en Uitgeverij Keesing N.V.**
2-20 Keesinglaan, B-2100 Deurne, Belgium.
- Nouvelles Graphiques/Grafisch Nieuws. s-m. ISSN 0029-4926

**Kompass Belgium S.A.**
Office International de Librairie, Avenue Marnix 30, B-1050 Brussels, Belgium.
- Kompass Belgium/Luxembourg; repertoire de l'economie de la Belgique et du Luxembourg. a. ISSN 0075-6636 (Foundation for Promoting International Economic Information SZ) (Dist. by: Iliffe NTP Inc., 300 E. 42 St., New York, NY 10017)

**Koninklijk Belgisch Instituut voor Natuurwetenschappen**
31 Vautierstraat, B-1040 Brussels, Belgium.
- Giervalk-Gerfaut. q. ISSN 0016-9757

**Koninklijk Instituut voor Het Kunstpatrimonium**
see Institut Royal du Patrimoine Artistique

**Koninklijk Museum voor Midden-Afrika**
see Musee Royal de l'Afrique Centrale

**Koninklijk Natuurwetenschappelijk Genootschap Dodonaea**
Ghent, Belgium.
- Biologisch Jaarboek. a.

**Koninklijke Academie voor Nederlandse Taal- en Letterkunde**
Koningstraat 18, B-9000 Ghent, Belgium.
- Koninklijke Academie voor Nederlandse Taal- en Letterkunde. Jaarboek. a.
- Koninklijke Academie voor Nederlandse Taal-en Letterkunde. Verslagen en Mededeiingen. 2 per yr. ISSN 0023-3404

**Koninklijke Academie voor Overzeese Wetenschappen**
see Academie Royale des Sciences d'Outre-Mer

**Koninklijke Automobiel Club van Belgie**
53 rue d'Arlon, 1040 Brussels, Belgium.
- K. A. C. B. Auto Revue/Royal Auto. m (except Aug.) ISSN 0022-7242

**Koninklijke Bibliotheek Albert I**
see Bibliotheque Royal Albert 1er

**Koninklijke Confederatie Horeca**
see Confederation Royale Horeca

**Koninklijke Maatschappij voor Dierkunde van Antwerpen**
see Societe Royale de Zoologie d'Anvers

**Koninklijke Musea voor Schone Kunsten van Belgie**
see Musees Royaux des Beaux-Arts de Belgique

**Koninklijke Vlaamse Ingenieursvereniging**
Jan van Rijswijcklaan 58, B-2000 Antwerp, Belgium.
- Ingenieursblad. m. ISSN 0020-1235
- International Harbour Congress. Proceedings/ Internationaal Havenkongres. Verslagboek/ Congres Portuaire International. Compte-Rendu/ Internationale Hafentagung. Berichte. irreg, 6th, 1974.
- Journal "A". q.

**Kredietbank**
Arenbergstraat 7, B-1000 Brussels, Belgium.
- Kredietbank. Weekly Bulletin. w. ISSN 0023-4583

**N.V. de Kruidenier-l'Epicier**
Grote Steenweg 519, 2600 Berchem, Belgium.
- Kruidenier/Epicier. m. ISSN 0046-2357

**Kultuurraad voor Vlaanderen**
Jan van Rijswijcklaan 28, B-2000 Antwerp, Belgium.
- Kultuurraad voor Vlaanderen. Verslagboek. irreg., 1969-1971, 5th report. ISSN 0066-4960

**Kunsthistorische Musea, Antwerp**
Rubenshuis, Rubensstraat 9-11, Antwerp 1, Belgium.
- Kunsthistorische Musea, Antwerp. Schone Kunsten. a. ISSN 0066-4979

**Laboratoire de Pedagogie Experimentale**
see under Universite Catholique de Louvain

**Laboratorium voor Experimentele, Differentiele en Genetische Psychologie**
see under Rijksuniversiteit Te Gent

**Maison Ferdinand Larcier S.A.**
Rue des Minimes 39, 1000 Brussels, Belgium.
- Bulletin Legislatif Belge. w.
- Cahiers de Droit Europeen. bi-m. ISSN 0007-9758 (Avocat a la Cour d'Appel)
- Cahiers de Droit Familial. q.
- Codes Larcier. a. ISSN 0010-0188
- Faculte de Droit de Namur. Travaux. irreg. (Societe d'Etudes Morales, Sociales et Juridiques)
- Journal des Tribunaux. w. ISSN 0021-812X
- Journal des Tribunaux du Travail. bi-m.
- Journal Pratique de Droit Fiscal. m.
- Recueil Annuel de Jurisprudence Belge. a.
- Recueil de Jurisprudence du Droit Administratif et du Conseil d'Etat. q.
- Revue de Droit Social/Tijdschrift voor Sociaal Recht. 8 per yr. ISSN 0035-1113
- Revue Juridique du Zaire. 3 per yr.

**Editions de Lejeunia**
Universite de Liege, Departement de Botanique, Sart Tilman, B-4000 Liege, Belgium.
- Lejeunia. irreg. ISSN 0457-4184 (Societe Botanique de Liege)

**Leuven University Press**
Krakenstraat 3, 3000 Louvain, Belgium.
- Humanistica Lovaniensia; journal of neo-latin studies. a. (Katholieke Universiteit te Leuven. Seminarium Philologiae Humanisticae)
- Mediaevalia Lovaniensia. Series I. a. (Katholieke Universiteit Te Leuven. Instituut voor Middeleeuwse Studies)

**Leuvense Bijdragen**
Blijde-Inkomststraat 21, B-3000 Louvain, Belgium.
- Leuvense Bijdragen; Tijdschrift voor Germaanse Filologie. q. ISSN 0024-1482

**Editions Philippe Levie**
210 rue du Trone, Brussels, Belgium.
- Revue Graphique-Imprivaria/Grafisch Tijdschrift-Imprivaria. m. ISSN 0035-323X

**Librairie de Rome**
50 B Avenue Louise, Brussels, Belgium.
- Progres. q. ISSN 0033-0434

**Ligues Pomologiques Wallonnes**
Rue de Waremme 16, B-4391 Berloz, Belgium.
- Fruit Belge. q. ISSN 0016-2248

**Limburg (Province) Culturele Dienst**
Breestraat 15B Bus 3, 3500 Hasselt, Belgium.
- Tijdspiegel; cultureel blad voor Limburg. m. ISSN 0040-764X

**Limburgse Economische Raad**
Thonissenlaan 13, 3500 Hasselt, Belgium.
- Economie in Limburg. q. ISSN 0013-0532

**Lloyd Anversois S.A.**
Eiermarkt 23, B-2000 Antwerp, Belgium.
- Jurisprudence du Port d'Anvers. bi-m. ISSN 0022-6831

**Editions du Lombard**
Avenue Paul-Henri Spaak, 1-11, 1070 Brussels, Belgium.
- Tintin; l'hebdomadaire des super-jeunes de 7 a 77 ans. w.

**Imprimerie R. Louis**
35/43 rue Borrens, 1050 Brussels, Belgium.
- Annales des Mines de Belgique/Annalen der Mijnen van Belgie. m. ISSN 0003-4290 (Institut National des Industries Extractives)

**Louvain Medical**
52, Avenue E. Mounier, B-1200 Brussels, Belgium.
- Louvain Medical. m (except July & Aug) ISSN 0024-6956

**Lumen Vitae Press**
186 rue Washington, B-1050 Brussels, Belgium.
- Lumen Vitae; international review of pastoral work and catechetics. q. ISSN 0024-7324 (International Centre for Religious Education)

**Madrigaal V.Z.W.**
Herestraat 51, 3000 Leuven, Belgium.
- Adem; tweemaandelijks tijdschrift voor muziekkultuur. bi-m. ISSN 0001-8171

**Maison Internationale de la Poesie**
147 Chaussee de Haecht, 1030 Brussels, Belgium.
- Journal des Poetes. m.

**Management Centre Europe**
Ave. des Arts 4, B-1040 Brussels, Belgium.
- Industrial Relations Europe. m.

**Mandragora**
Acacalaan 58, 9620 Zottegem, Belgium.
- Mandragora; tijdschrift voor literatuur en
  beeldende kunsten. q.

**Imprimerie et Publicite du Marais S.A.**
Rue de Flandre 169, 1000 Brussels, Belgium.
- Jeux, Jouets-Puericulture. q.
- Revue Internationale des Deux et Jouets/
  Internationale Tijdschrift voor Spel en Speelgoeol.
  q. ISSN 0021-6232

**Marche**
140 Bd. Lambermont, 1030 Brussels, Belgium.
- Marche; hebdomadaire du dirigeant. w.

**Mariale Werken**
Diestse Vest 119, Leuven, Belgium.
- Orante. 10 per yr. ISSN 0030-4336

**Imprimerie Medicale et Scientifique**
67, rue de l'Orient, 1040 Brussels, Belgium.
- Journal Belge de Radiologie (Monographie) bi-m.
  ISSN 0075-4064 (Societe Royale Belge de
  Radiologie)
- Societe Belge d'Ophtalmologie. Bulletin. q. ISSN
  0081-0746

**Mercure**
135 Bd. Maurice Lemonnier, 1000 Brussels,
Belgium.
- Mercure; hebdomadaire financier, economique et
  politique. w. ISSN 0025-9934

**Meubles et Decors S.A.**
Av. des Mimosas 33, 1150 Brussels, Belgium.
- Decors. bi-m.

**Jean de Mey, Ed. & Pub.**
58 rue de l'Association, 1000 Brussels, Belgium.
- Numismatic Pocket. 3 per yr.

**Monastere Benedictin, Chevetogne**
5395 Chevetogne, Belgium.
- Irenikon. q. ISSN 0021-0978

**Monastere de Saint Andre**
Allee de Clerlande, B-1340 Ottignies, Belgium.
- Art d'Eglise. q. ISSN 0004-3095
- Communautes et Liturgies; revue d'action
  liturgique et paroissiale. 6 per yr.

**Musee de Mariemont**
B-6510 Morlannelz-Mariemont, Belgium.
- Cahiers de Mariemont. a. (prep. by its Service de
  Documentation)

**Musee Royal de l'Afrique Centrale**
13 Steenweg Op Leuven, B-1980 Tervuren, Belgium.
- Africa-Tervuren. q. ISSN 0001-9879
- Africana Linguistica. irreg., 1975, no. 6. ISSN
  0065-4124
- Musee Royal de l'Afrique Centrale. Archives
  d'Anthropologie. irreg.
- Musee Royal de l'Afrique Centrale. Publications
  Linguistiques. irreg. ISSN 0082-2906
- Revue de Zoologie Africaine. q.

**Musees Royaux des Beaux-Arts de Belgique**
Rue de Musee 9, 1000 Brussels, Belgium.
- Musees Royaux des Beaux-Arts de Belgique.
  Bulletin/Koninklijke Musea voor Schone Kunsten
  van Belgie. Bulletin. q. ISSN 0027-3856

**Nationaal Centrum voor Oudheidkundige Navorsingen
in Belgie**
  *see* **Centre National de Recherches Archeologiques
  en Belgique**

**Nationaal Centrum voor Wetenschappelijk en
Technisch Onderzoek der Cementnijverheid**
  *see* **Centre National de Recherches Scientifiques et
  Techniques pour l'Industrie Cimentierre**

**Nationaal Sekretariaat van Het Katholiek Onderwijs**
Guimardstraat, Brussels, Belgium.
- Annuaire et Statistique de l'Enseignement
  Catholique. a. ISSN 0068-2942

**Nationaal Verbond Haarkappers**
- Charm. (pub. by N. Pauwels, Ed. & Pub.)

**Nationaal Verbond voor Volkstuinen**
Koninklijkestraat 55, 1000 Brussels, Belgium.
- Volkstuin; organ werk van akker en volkstuinen.
  m. ISSN 0042-8574

**National Verbond der Textieldetaillanten**
- Navetex. (pub. by N. Pauwels, Ed. & Pub.)

**Nationale Centrale voor Kleine en Middelgrote
Levensmiddellenbedrijven**
Spastraat 8, 1040 Brussels, Belgium.
- Voedingsblad. m. ISSN 0011-0434

**Nationale Confederatie V.D.**
Belgische Textielreiniging, Jezusstraat 16, B-2000
Antwerp, Belgium.
- Belgische Textielreiniging. s-m. ISSN 0005-8475

**Nationale Confederatie van Het Kaderpersoneel**
  *see* **Confederation Nationale des Cadres**

**Nationale Vereniging Tot Voorkoming van
Arbeidsongevallen**
Bischoffsheimlaan 32, B-1000 Brussels, Belgium.
- Promosafe. irreg.

**Natura Mosana**
319 Route de Beaumont, 6030 Marchienne-Au-
Pont, Belgium.
- Natura Mosana. q. ISSN 0028-0666

**Naturalistes Belges a.s.b.l.**
Rue Vautier 31, B-1040 Brussels, Belgium.
- Naturalistes Belges. m. ISSN 0028-0801

**Natuur- en Geneeskundige Vennootschap**
Rozier 44, B-9000 Ghent, Belgium.
- Natuurwetenschappelijk Tijdschrift. 6 per yr.
- Simon Stevin; wis-en natuurkundig tijdschrift. 4
  per yr. ISSN 0037-5454
- Vlaams Diergeneeskundig Tijdschrift/Flemish
  Veterinary Journal. m. ISSN 0303-9021

**Editions Nauwelaerts**
Muntstraat 10, B-3000 Louvain, Belgium.
- Anciens Pay et Assemblees d'Etats. irreg. ISSN
  0066-1589 (International Committee of Historical
  Sciences. Commission for the History of State
  Assemblies)
- Bibliotheque Philosophique de Louvain. irreg.
  ISSN 0067-8430 (Institut de Philosophie de
  Louvain)
- Centre Interuniversitaire d'Histoire
  Contemporaine. Cahiers/Interuniversitair
  Centrum voor Hedendaagse Geschiedenis.
  Mededelingen. irreg., 1972, no. 71. ISSN 0577-
  179X
- Electromyography and Clinical Neurophysiology.
  q.
- Logique et Analyse. 4 per yr. ISSN 0024-5836
- Universite Catholique de Louvain. Ecole des
  Sciences Politiques et Sociales. Collection. irreg.
  ISSN 0076-1214
- Universite Catholique de Louvain. Faculte de
  Philosophie et Lettres. Travaux. irreg. ISSN 0076-
  1222
- Universite Catholique de Louvain. Institut de
  Recherches Economiques, Politiques et Sociales.
  Publications. irreg. ISSN 0076-1303
- Universite Catholique de Louvain. Recueil de
  Travaux d'Histoire et de Philologie. irreg. ISSN
  0076-1311
- Universite Catholique de Louvain. Section de
  Philologie Germanique. Serie Microfiches. irreg.
  ISSN 0076-129X

**Uitgeverij de Nederlandsche Boekhandel**
Kapelsestraat 222, 2080 Kapellen, Belgium.
- Gezelliana. q. (Universitaire Faculteiten Sint
  Ignatius te Antwerpen. Centrum voor
  Gezellestudie)

**North Atlantic Treaty Organization**
Information Service, Distribution Unit, 1110
Brussels, Belgium
(U.S. address: Distribution Services Staff, Office of
Media Services, Dept. of State, Washington D.C.
20520)
- N A T O Handbook. a (English and French
  editions); irreg (other languages) ISSN 0549-7175
- N A T O Review. bi-m editions in Dutch,
  English, French, German and Italian; q. editions
  in Danish, Greek, Portuguese and Turkish.

**North Atlantic Treaty Organization. Committee on
the Challenges of Modern Society**
1110 Brussels, Belgium.
- North Atlantic Treaty Organization. Expert Panel
  on Air Pollution Modeling. Proceedings. a.

**North Atlantic Treaty Organization. Scientific Affairs
Division**
- N A T O Advanced Study Institute Series. C:
  Mathematical and Physical Sciences. (pub. by D.
  Reidel Publishing Co. NE)

**Nouveaux Rythmes du Monde**
Abbaye de Saint-Andre, B-8200 Brugge 2, Belgium.
- Nouveaux Rythmes du Monde; religions, cultures.
  vie sociale-economie. q.

**Nouvelle Imprimerie Commerciale et Industrielle S.C.**
Lousbergskaai 32, 9000 Ghent, Belgium.
- Annales des Travaux Publics de Belgique/
  Tijdschrift des Openbare Werken van Belgie. bi-
  m. (Belgium. Ministere des Trauvaux Public)

**Oeuvre Nationale de l'Enfance**
67 Av. de la Toison d'Or, B-1060 Brussels, Belgium.
- Enfant/Kind. 6 per yr. ISSN 0013-7553

**Office Belge du Commerce Exterieur**
  *see* **Belgium. Office Belge du Commerce Exterieur**

**Office Belge pour l'Accroissement de la Productivite**
60 rue de la Concorde, Brussels 5, Belgium.
- Synopsis. bi-m. ISSN 0039-7830

**Office des Assureurs de Belgique**
25 rue Marie-Therese, B-1040 Brussels, Belgium.
- Petit Moniteur des Assurances; journal
  independant de l'assurance privee. w. ISSN 0031-
  627X

**Office Genealogique et Heraldique de Belgique**
c/o Musees Royaux d'Art et d'Histoire, Parc du
Cinquantenaire 10, B-1040 Brussels, Belgium.
- Parchemin. bi-m.
- Parchemin. Recueil Genealogique et Heraldique.
  a.

**Office International de l'Enseignment Catholique**
  *see* **Catholic International Education Office**

**Office International de Librairie**
Av. Marnix, 30, B-1050 Brussels, Belgium.
- Societes Chimiques Belges. Bulletin. bi-m. ISSN
  0037-9646 (Co-sponsor: Vlaamse Chemische
  Vereniging)

**Office International du Cacao et de Chocalat**
  *see* **International Office of Cocoa and Chocolate**

**Onrea**
Leopoldstraat 25, Anvers, Belgium.
- Revue Internationale de Metaphysique, de
  Sociologie et d'Economie. bi-m.

**Uitgeverij S.M. Ontwikkeling**
Leeuwerikstraat 41, B-2000 Antwerp, Belgium.
- Nieuw Vlaams Tijdschrift. m. ISSN 0028-9868
- Persoon en Gemeenschap; tijdschrift voor
  opvoeding en onderwijs. 10 per yr. ISSN 0031-
  5842
- Vrije Universiteit Brussel. Tijdschrift. q.

**Open Door International**
16 rue Americain, B-1050 Brussels, Belgium.
- Open Door International for the Emancipation of
  the Woman Worker. Report of Congress. irreg.,
  1966, 13th, London. ISSN 0078-5164

**Opticien Belge**
26 rue Capitaine Crespel, 1050 Brussels, Belgium.
- Opticien Belge/Belgische Opticien. 10 per yr.
  ISSN 0030-3976

**Ordina Editions**
Route de Goe 9, Dolhain, Belgium.
- International Union for the Scientific Study of
  Population (Proceedings of Conference) irreg.;
  18th, Accra, Ghana, 1971. ISSN 0074-9338

**Organisation Internationale pour l'Etude des Langues
Anciennes Par Ordinateur**
  *see* **International Organization for Ancient
  Languages Analysis by Computer**

**Ornitologische Vereniging de Wielewaal**
Graatakker 11, B-2300 Turnhout, Belgium.
- Wielewaal. m. ISSN 0043-5260

**Oyez S.A.**
Muntstraat 10, B-3000 Louvain, Belgium.
- Essais Philosophiques. irreg., 1966, no. 8. ISSN 0071-1349 (Universite Catholique de Louvain. Institut Superieur de Philosophie)
- Philosophes Contemporains. irreg. ISSN 0079-1660 (Universite Catholique de Louvain. Institut Superieur de Philosophie)
- Philosophes Medievaux. irreg., 1971, no. 11. ISSN 0079-1679 (Universite Catholique de Louvain. Institut Superieur de Philosophie)
- Recherches de Psychopedagogie et de Pedagogie Experimentale. irreg., 1970, no. 3. ISSN 0080-0066 (Universite Catholique de Louvain. Faculte de Psychologie et des Sciences de l'Education)
- Universite Catholique de Louvain. Institut des Langues Vivantes. Cahiers. irreg., 1972, no. 22. ISSN 0076-1249
- Universite Catholique de Louvain. Institut Superieur de Philosophie. Cours Publies. irreg. ISSN 0076-1273

**P.D.O. de Kesel**
Goede Pers., Averbode, Belgium.
- Zonneland. w. ISSN 0049-8750

**Palais des Beaux-Arts**
10 rue Royal, 1000 Brussels, Belgium.
- Beaux-Arts. w. ISSN 0005-7509
- K & C. (Kunst en Cultuur) bi-m. ISSN 0022-7277

**Paleis voor Schone Kunsten**
*see* **Palais des Beaux Arts**

**N. Pauwels, Ed. & Pub.**
Spastraat 8, 1040 Brussels, Belgium.
- Charm. 6 per yr. ISSN 0009-1804 (Nationaal Verbond Haarkappers)
- Navetex. m.(alternate nos. in Dutch & French) ISSN 0028-1514 (National Verbond der Textieldetaillanten)

**Pauwels Fils**
72 rue des Coteaux, 1030 Brussels, Belgium.
- Revue Medicale de Bruxelles. 10 per yr. ISSN 0035-3639 (Universite Libre de Bruxelles. Association des Medecins Anciens Etudiants)

**Willem Pee, Ed. & Pub.**
Vuurkeienweg 3, Bosvoorde, 1170 Brussels, Belgium.
- Taal en Tongval; tijdschrift voor de studie van de Nederlandse volks-en streektalen. q. ISSN 0039-8691 (Seminarie Vlaamse Dialektologie te Gent) (Co-sponsor: Zuidnederlandse Dialektcentrale te Leuven; Dialectencommissie te Amsterdam)

**Editions Peeters s.p.r.l.**
B.P. 41, B-3000 Louvain, Belgium.
- Ephemerides Theologicae Lovanienses. q. ISSN 0013-9513 (Universite Catholique de Louvain)
- Institut de Linguistique de Louvain. Cahiers (Cours et Documents) q.
- Naamkunde. s-a. (Katholieke Universiteit te Leuven. Instituut voor Naamkunde) (Co-Sponsor: Commissie voor Naamkunde en Nederzettingsgeschiedenis Te Amsterdam)
- Repertoire Bibliographique de la Philosophie. q. ISSN 0034-4567 (Universite Catholique de Louvain. Institut Superieur de Philosophie)
- Revue Philosophique de Louvain. 4 per yr. ISSN 0035-3841 (Universite Catholique de Louvain. Institut Superieur de Philosophie)

**Periscoop**
Nationalestr. 46, 2000 Antwerp, Belgium.
- Periscoop. 11 per yr. ISSN 0048-3397

**Permanent International Association of Navigation Congresses**
155, rue de la Loi, 1040 Brussels, Belgium.
- International Navigation Congress. Proceedings. irreg.; 23rd, Ottawa, 1973.

**Pfizer Europe Management Center**
55 rue du Moulin a Papier, B-1160 Brussels, Belgium.
- Spectrum International. q. ISSN 0038-710X

**Phare**
Rue des Sables 18, 1000 Brussels, Belgium.
- Phare. w. ISSN 0031-6814

**Point du Jazz**
c/o Paul Vande Velde, Rue Emile Delva 34, 1030 Brussels, Belgium.
- Point du Jazz. 3 per yr.

**Pool d'Edition et de Redaction**
Avenue van Volxem, 305, 1190 Brussels, Belgium.
- Science et Paix. q.

**Pourquoi Pas**
95 Bd. Emile Jacqmain, 1000 Brussels, Belgium.
- Pourquoi Pas. w.

**Presse et Loisirs S.A.**
38 rue Marche aux Herbes, 1000 Brussels, Belgium.
- Chasse-Peche-Tir/Hunting & Fishing; hunting, fishing, bullet and clay shooting. m.

**Editions de la Presse Europeenne**
14, Ave. du Suffrage Universel, 1030 Brussels, Belgium.
- Bonjour. w.
- Do Re Mi. bi-m.
- Tremplin. w. ISSN 0041-2279

**Presselec S.P.R.L.**
Ave. Paul Hymans 105, 1200 Brussels, Belgium.
- Panelectronics. bi-m. ISSN 0014-3839
- Paninformatic; all about computers. bi-m.

**Presses Academiques**
Chaussee de Charleroi 98, B-1060 Brussels, Belgium.
- Journal of Computational and Applied Mathematics. q.

**Presses Universitaires de Brussels**
42 Av. Heger, 1050 Brussels, Belgium.
- Dossiers Politiques. m.

**Pro Mundi Vita. Centrum Informationis. Special Notes**
6, rue de la Limite, B-1030 Brussels, Belgium.
- Pro Mundi Vita. Centrum Informationis. Special Notes. irreg. ISSN 0079-5593

**Promovere**
Chaussee de Charleroi 77, 1060 Brussels, Belgium.
- Promovere; revue trimestrielle internationale de socio-criminologie clinique. q.

**Provinces Belge l'Expression Francaise**
73 rue des Ateliers, Morlanwelz, Hainaut, Belgium.
- Savoir et Beaute. q. ISSN 0036-5165

**Provinciale Bibliotheek van Limburg**
Begijnhof, Zuivelmarkt, 3500 Hasselt, Belgium.
- Bibliotheekgids. q. ISSN 0006-1956 (Vlaamse Vereniging van Bibliotheek- en Archiefpersoneel)

**Editions Provinciales**
62 Quai de Rome, 4000 Liege, Belgium.
- Annales des Sciences Economiques Appliquees. 5 per yr. (Universite Catholique de Louvain. Institut des Sciences Economiques Appliquees)

**Publi- Contact**
Blvd. Louis Schmidt, 52, 1040 Brussels, Belgium.
- Photigraf; revue professionelle belge d'information photographique. bi-m.
- Poissonnier Belge/Belgische Vishandelaar. bi-m. ISSN 0032-2385 (Federation Nationale des Poissonniers Detaillants Belges)
- Tapissier Decorateur/Woningstoffeerder. m. ISSN 0039-9582 (Federation Nationale Belge des Tapissiers-Garnisseurs et Decorateurs d'Interieur)

**Publimondex**
58 rue Eugene Smits, 1030 Brussels, Belgium.
- Decoration - Ameublement/Woninginrichting; et revue de tapis et des revetements de sols et murs. m. ISSN 0011-7420 (Union Professionnelle Nationale de la Decoration et de l'Ameublement de Belgique) (Co-sponsor: Groupement des Entreprises de Revetements de Sols et Murs)

**Publitra P.V.B.A.**
Brouwersvliet 33, 2000 Antwerp, Belgium.
- Antwerps Havennieuws/Antwerp Port News. bi-m. ISSN 0003-6188
- Hinterland; periodical of the port of Antwerp. q. ISSN 0018-1978

**Publivog S.P.R.L.**
17 Ave. des Roses, B-9180 Belsele (Waas), Belgium.
- Ami des Fleurs. m.
- Bloemenvriend. m. ISSN 0006-4920

**Ran Tan Plan**
Avenue van Volxem 435, B-1060 Brussels, Belgium.
- Ran Tan Plan. q.

**Reader's Digest S.A.**
12A Grand Place, 1000 Brussels, Belgium.
- Beste uit Reader's Digest (Belgian-Flemish Edition) m. ISSN 0005-8386
- Selection du Reader's Digest (Belgian-French Edition) m. ISSN 0037-1408

**Recherche et Diffusion Economique**
41 Chemin Ducal, 1970 Wezembeek, Belgium.
- Reflets et Perspectives de la Vie Economique. 6 per yr. ISSN 0034-2971

**Relis Namurwes A.S.B.L.**
15 rue Jules Hamoir, 5000 Namur, Belgium.
- Cahiers Wallon. m (10 per yr.)

**Renaissance du Livre S.A.**
12 Place du Petit Sablon, 1000 Brussels, Belgium.
- Moyen Age; revue historique. 4 per yr. ISSN 0027-2841
- Recherches Economiques de Louvain. 4 per yr. ISSN 0034-1274

**Revue Belge de Psychologie et de Pedagogie**
40 Rue du Disque, 1020 Brussels, Belgium.
- Revue Belge de Psychologie et de Pedagogie. q. ISSN 0035-0826

**Revue de Droit Penal et de Criminologie**
Palais de Justice, Brussels, Belgium.
- Revue de Droit Penal et de Criminologie. m. Oct.-Jul. ISSN 0035-4384

**Revue Medicale de Liege**
Hopital de Baviere, Liege, Belgium.
- Revue Medicale de Liege; journal du praticien. bi-m. ISSN 0035-3663

**Revue Nouvelle**
Av. van Volxem 305, B-1190 Brussels, Belgium.
- Revue Nouvelle. 10 per yr. ISSN 0035-3809

**Richard Foncke Gallery**
Ghent, Belgium.
- Richard Foncke Gallery Quarterly Review on Art. q.

**Marc Richter**
Rue Foret de Soignes 3a, 1420 Braine-l'Alleud, Belgium.
- Textures. s-a.

**Rijk der Vrouw**
835 9 Fr. van Kalkenlaan, 1050 Brussels, Belgium.
- Rijk der Vrouw. w. ISSN 0035-5313

**Rijksinstituut Sociale Verzekeringen der Zelfstandigen**
Jan Jacobsplein, 6, 1000 Brussels, Belgium.
- Rijksinstituut Sociale Verzekeringen der Zelfstandigen. Jaarverslag. a.

**Rijksuniversiteit Te Gent**
Blandijnberg 2, B-9000 Ghent, Belgium.
- Didactica Classica Gandensia. a. ISSN 0070-4792
- Documentatio Didactica Classica. a. ISSN 0070-685X
- Philosophica. s-a.

**Rijksuniversiteit Te Gent. Centrale Bibliotheek**
B-9000 Ghent, Belgium.
- Bijdragen Tot de Bibliotheekwetenschap/ Contributions to Library Science. irreg., 1967, no. 3. ISSN 0067-8538

**Rijksuniversiteit Te Gent. Centrum voor Onkruidonderzoek**
Coupure Links 553, B-9000 Ghent, Belgium.
- Rijksuniversiteit Gent. Centrum voor Onkruidonderzoek. Mededeling. s-a.

**Rijksuniversiteit te Gent. Dienst voor Franse Linguistiek**
Blandijnberg 2, 9000 Ghent, Belgium.
- Travaux de Linguistique. irreg. ISSN 0082-6049

**Rijksuniversiteit te Gent. Faculteit Landbouwetenschapen. Centrum voor Onkruidonderzoek**
*see* **Rijksuniversiteit Te Gent. Centrum voor Onkruidonderzoek**

**Rijksuniversiteit Te Gent. Faculteit Landbouwwetenschappen**
Coupure 533, B-9000 Ghent, Belgium.
- International Symposium on Crop Protection. Proceedings. a, 28th, 1976, Ghent.

• Rijksuniversiteit Gent. Faculteit
Landbouwwetenschappen. Mededelingen. q. ISSN
0035-533X

**Rijksuniversiteit te Gent. Faculteit van de
Economische Wetenschappen**
St. Pietersnieuwstraat 25, Ghent, Belgium.
• Rijksuniversiteit te Gent. Faculteit van de
Economische Wetenschappen. Werken. irreg.

**Rijksuniversiteit Te Gent. Geologisch Instituut**
Rozier 44, B-9000 Ghent, Belgium.
• Abstracts of Belgian Geology and Physical
Geography. a. ISSN 0065-0420

**Rijksuniversiteit Te Gent. Laboratorium voor
Experimentele, Differentiele en Genetische
Psychologie**
Blandijnberg, 2, 9000 Ghent, Belgium.
• Rijksuniversiteit Te Gent. Laboratorium voor
Experimentele, Differentiele en Genetische
Psychologie. Mededlingen en Werkdocumenten.
irreg. ISSN 0085-1078

**Rijksuniversiteit Te Gent. Section de Philologie
Romane**
Blandijnberg 2, 9000 Ghent, Belgium.
• Romanica Gandensia. irreg. ISSN 0080-3855

**Rijksuniversiteit Te Gent. Sektie Germaanse
Philologie**
• Studia Germanica Gandensia. (pub. by Studia
Germanica Gandensia)

**Rijksuniversiteit Te Gent. Seminarie voor Musicologie**
Muinkkaai, 45, B-9000 Ghent, Belgium.
• Documenta Musicae Novae; critical edition of
contemporary music sources. biennial.

**Rijksuniversiteit Te Gent. Seminarie voor Sociologie**
Universiteitstraat 14, 9000 Ghent, Belgium.
• Tijdschrift voor Sociale Wetenschappen. 4 per yr.
ISSN 0040-7615

**Rijksuniversiteit te Gent. Seminaries voor Historische
en voor Vergelijkende Pedagogiek**
A. Baertsoenkaai 3, B-9000 Ghent, Belgium.
• Paedagogica Belgica Academica; periodical survey
of the Belgian University Studies in Education. a.
ISSN 0079-0370
• Paedagogica Historica; international journal of the
history of education. s-a. ISSN 0030-9230

**RIjksuniversiteit te Gent. Sterrenkungid
Observatorium**
Krijgslaan 271, B-9000 Ghent, Belgium.
• Rijksuniveristeit te Gent. Sterrenkundig
Observatorium. Mededelingen: Astronomie. irreg.
ISSN 0072-4432
• Rijksuniversiteit te Gent. Sterrenkundig
Observatorium. Mededelingen: Meteorologie en
Geofysica. irreg. ISSN 0072-4440

**Foulek Ringelheim, Ed. & Pub.**
62 rue Emile van Driessche, 1060 Brussels, Belgium.
• Pro Justitia; revue politique de droit. q.

**Rock on Publications**
Postbus 83, 2700 Sint-Niklaas, Belgium.
• Juke Box. fortn. ISSN 0022-6181

**Rossel et Cie, S.A.**
Place de Louvain, 21, 1000 Brussels, Belgium.
• Soir Illustre. w.

**N.V. Roularta**
Tevurenlaan 153, 1040 Brussels, Belgium.
• Knack. w.

**Royal Academy of Dutch Language and Literature**
see Koninklijke Academie voor Nederlandse Taal-
en Letterkunde

**Royal Belgian Society of Political Economy**
see Societe Royale d'Economie Politique de
Belgique

**Royal Flemish Association of Engineers**
see Koninklijke Vlaamse Ingenieursvereniging

**Royale Federation Colombophile Belge**
39 rue de Livourne, 1050 Brussels, Belgium.
• Royale Federation Colombophile Belge. Bulletin
Federal. m. ISSN 0035-9319

**S A B A M**
*see* Societe Belge des Auteurs, Compositeurs et
Editeurs

**Editions S I C**
36 rue du Lombard, B-1000 Brussels, Belgium.
• E T B-T U G. (Equipement Technique du
Batiment-Technische Uitrusting van Het Gebouw)
m.

**Sabena Belgian World Airlines**
35 Cardinale Mercier, B-1000 Brussels, Belgium.
• Sabena Revue. s-a. ISSN 0036-2158

**Uitgegeven voor de St. Pietersabdij van Steenbrugge**
Assebroek, Belgium.
• Librije; bibliografisch bulletijn voor godsdienst,
kunst en kultuur. q. ISSN 0024-2713

**Scientia Paedagogica Experimentalis**
c/o Ed. R. Verbist, Henri Dunantlaan 1, B-9000
Ghent, Belgium.
• Scientia Paedagogica Experimentalis/International
Journal of Experimental Research in Education/
Revue Internationale de Pedagogie
Experimentale/Internationale Zeitschrift fuer
Experimentale Paedagogik. s-a. ISSN 0582-2351

**Scientiarum Historia**
Prinsstraat 5, Antwerp, Belgium.
• Scientiarum Historia; tijdschrift voor de
geschiedenis van de geneeskunde, wiskunde en
natuurwetenschappen. q. ISSN 0036-8725

**Secretariat International de l'Enseignement
Universitaire des Sciences Pedagogiques**
*see* International Secretariat for the University
Study of Education

**Gerd Segers, Ed. & Pub.**
Groenendaallaan 300, 2030 Antwerp, Belgium.
• Revolver/Tijdschrift voor Hedendragse Poezie.
irreg. ISSN 0085-5650

**Seminarie Vlaamse Dialektologie te Gent**
• Taal en Tongval. (pub. by Willem Pee, Ed. &
Pub.)

**Seminaries voor Historische en voor Vergelijkende
Pedagogiek**
*see under* Rijksuniversiteit Te Gent

**Service de Centralisation des Etudes Genealogiques et
Demographiques de Belgique**
Maison des Arts, 147 Chaussee de Haecht, 1030
Brussels, Belgium.
• Intermediaire des Genealogistes/Middelaar Tussen
de Genealogische Navorsers. bi-m. ISSN 0020-
5621

**Editions Services Interentreprises**
38 rue de la Montagne, 1000 Brussels, Belgium.
• Informations Bancaires et Financieres/Inlichtingen
Uit Bank en Financiele Wereld. bi-m. ISSN 0020-
0425

**Uitgeverij de Sikkel N.V.**
Kapelsestraat 222, 2080 Kapellen, Belgium.
• Bevolking en Gezin. 3 per yr. (Nederlands
Interuniversitair Demografisch Instituut NE) (Co-
sponsor: Centrum voor Bevolkings- en
Gezinsstudien) (Co-publisher: Uitgeverij de
Nederlandsche Boekhandel)

**A.S.B.L. Silicates Industriels**
32 rue de Malplaquet, B-7000 Mons, Belgium.
• Silicates Industriels. m. ISSN 0037-5225

**Snoeck-Ducaju en Zoon N.V.**
Begijnhoflaan 440, B-9000 Ghent, Belgium.
• Snoeck's Almanach. a. ISSN 0085-6169
• Snoeck's; Literatuur Kunst Film Toneel Mode
Reizen. a. ISSN 0085-6177

**Sobeli**
23 rue du Boulet, Brussels, Belgium.
• Courrier Industriel et Scientifique. q. ISSN 0011-
0604

**Socialista**
P.S.B.-13 Bd. de l'Empereur, 1000 Brussels,
Belgium.
• Socialista. s-m.

**Societe Adolphe Quetelet**
c/o J. Delince, Laboratoire de Biometrie, Place
Croix du Sud, 2, B-1348 Louvain-la-Neuve,
Belgium.
• Biometrie-Praximetrie. 4 per yr. ISSN 0006-3436

**Societe Belge d'Astronomie, de Meteorologie et de
Physique du Globe**
Av. Circulaire 3, Uccle, Brussels, Belgium.
• Ciel et Terre. bi-m. ISSN 0009-6709

**Societe Belge d'Etude des Phenomenes Spatiaux**
Ave. Paul Janson, 7a, 1070 Brussels, Belgium.
• Inforespace. bi-m.

**Societe Belge d'Etudes Geographiques**
c/o Prof. Dr. M. E. Dumont, 2 Blandijnberg, Ghent,
Belgium.
• Societe Belge d'Etudes Geographiques. Bulletin. s-
a. ISSN 0037-8925

**Societe Belge d'Ophtamologie**
• Societe Belge d'Ophtalmologie. Bulletin. (pub. by
Imprimerie Medicale et Scientifique)

**Societe Belge de Cardiologie**
43 rue des Champs-Elysees, B-1050 Brussels,
Belgium.
• Acta Cardiologica; journal international de
cardiologie. bi-m. ISSN 0001-5385

**Societe Belge de Demographie**
• Dossiers de Demographie de la Belgique. (pub. by
Editions Derouaux)

**Societe Belge de Droit International**
• Revue Belge de Droit International/Belgian
Review of International Law. (pub. by
Etablissements Emile Bruylant)

**Societe Belge de Geologie**
13 rue Jenner, B-1040 Brussels, Belgium.
• Societe Belge de Geologie. Bulletin/Belgische
Vereniging voor Geologie. Bulletin. 3 per yr.

**Societe Belge de Medecine Interne**
Kapucijnenvoer 35, 3000 Leuven, Belgium.
• Acta Clinica Belgica. s-m.

**Societe Belge de Medecine Tropicale**
c/o J. Goemaere, Grensstraat 21, 1030 Brussels,
Belgium.
• Societe Belge de Medecine Tropicale. Annales. bi-
m.

**Societe Belge de Musicologie**
30 rue de la Regence, 1000 Brussels, Belgium.
• Revue Belge de Musicologie/Belgisch Tijdschrift
voor Muziekwetenschap. a.

**Societe Belge de Photogrammetrie**
34 Bd. Pacheco, B-1000 Brussels, Belgium.
• Societe Belge de Photogrammetrie. Bulletin
Trimestriel. q. ISSN 0037-8917

**Societe Belge de Psychologie**
Tiensestraat 100, 3000 Louvain, Belgium.
• Psychologica Belgica. s-a. ISSN 0033-2879

**Societe Belge de Zymologie Pure et Appliquee**
• Revue des Fermentations et des Industries
Alimentaires. (pub. by Cooperative d'Edition pour
les Industries Alimentaires)

**Societe Belge des Auteurs Compositeurs et Editeurs**
61 rue de la Loi, 1040 Brussels, Belgium.
• Cahiers de Droit d'Auteur/Copyright Review.
irreg. ISSN 0068-502X
• Sabam. q. ISSN 0048-8925

**Societe Belge des Ingenieurs des Telecommunications
et d'Electronique**
• Acta Technica Belgica. Revue H F: Electricite
Courants Faibles. Electronique
Telecommunications. (pub. by Union des Revues
Techniques Belges)

**Societe Botanique de Liege**
• Lejeunia. (pub. by Editions de Lejeunia)

**Societe Chimique de Belgique**
• Societes Chimiques Belges. Bulletin. (pub. by
Office International de Librairie)

**Societe Cooperative Agenor**
13 rue Hobbema, Brussels 4, Belgium.
• Agenor; European review/revue europeenne. 8 per
yr. ISSN 0002-080X

**Societe d'Archeologie d'Histoire et de Folklore de Nivelles et du Brabant Wallon**
Musee de Nivelles, 27 rue de Bruxelles, Brussels, Belgium.
- Societe d'Archeologie, d'Histoire et de Folklore de Nivelles et du Brabant Wallon. Annales. irreg, vol. 22, 1973.

**Societe d'Art et d'Histoire du Diocese de Liege**
Rue Bonne Fortune 6, 4000 Liege, Belgium.
- Leodium. s-a.
- Societe d'Art et d'Histoire du Diocese de Liege. Bulletin.

**Societe d'Etudes et d'Expansion**
12 Av. Rogier, 4000 Liege, Belgium.
- Etudes et Expansion. q.

**Societe d'Etudes Latines de Bruxelles**
60 rue Colonel Chaltin, B-1180 Brussels, Belgium.
- Latomus; revue d'etudes latines. q. ISSN 0023-8856

**Societe d'Etudes Morales, Sociales et Juridiques**
- Faculte de Droit de Namur. Travaux. (pub. by Maison Ferdinand Larcier S.A.)

**Societe d'Etudes Ornithologiques Aves.**
16 rue de la Cambre, 1200 Brussels, Belgium.
- Aves. bi-m. ISSN 0005-1993

**Societe de Langue et de Litterature Wallonnes**
Rue M. Beckers, 4634 Soumagne, Belgium.
- Dialectes de Wallonie. a.

**Societe de Traction et Electricite**
Rue de la Science, B-1040 Brussels, Belgium.
- T.E. News. (Traction et Electricite) 3 per yr.

**Societe des Bibliophiles Anversois**
see Vereeniging der Antwerpsche Bibliophielen

**Societe des Bollandistes**
24 Bd. Saint-Michel, 1040 Brussels, Belgium.
- Analecta Bollandiana; revue critique d'hagiographie. s-a. ISSN 0003-2468

**Societe Generale de Banque**
Montagne du Parc 3, B-1000 Brussels, Belgium.
- Conjoncture Boursiere. m.
- Societe Generale de Banque. Rapport. a.

**Societe Generale de Belgique**
Brussels, Belgium.
- Societe Generale de Belgique. Rapport. a. ISSN 0081-1114

**Societe Geographique de Liege**
7, Place du Vingt-Aout, B-4000 Liege, Belgium.
- Societe Geographique de Liege. Bulletin. a. ISSN 0583-8622
- Travaux Geographiques de Liege. s-a. (Co-sponsor: Universite de Liege, Seminaire de Geographie)

**Societe Geologique de Belgique**
Universite de Liege, 7 Place du Vingt-Aout, 4000 Liege, Belgium.
- Societe Geologique de Belgique. Annales. s-a. ISSN 0037-9395

**Societe Internationale de Chirurgie**
see International Society of Surgery

**Societe Internationale pour l'Etude de la Philosophie Medievale**
see International Society for the Study of Medieval Philosophy

**Societe Mathematique de Belgique**
c/o Guy Hirsch, 317 Av. Charles Woeste, 1090 Brussels, Belgium.
- Societe Mathematique de Belgique. Bulletin. q. ISSN 0037-9476

**Societe Medicale Belge de Saint-Luc**
Av. de l'Yser, 19, 1040 Brussels, Belgium.
- Saint-Luc Medical/Sint-Lucas Tijdschrift. q. ISSN 0036-3057

**Societe Nationale des Chemins de Fer Belges**
21 rue de Louvain, 1000 Brussels, Belgium.
- Documentation/Documentatie. m. ISSN 0012-4567
- Rail. m. ISSN 0033-8729
- Societe Nationale des Chemins de Fer Belges. Rapport Annuel. a. ISSN 0081-119X

**Societe pour le Progres des Etudes Philologiques et Historiques**
Bibliotheque Royale, Boulevard de l'Empereur, B-1000 Brussels, Belgium.
- Revue Belge de Philologie et d'Historie. q. ISSN 0035-0818

**Societe Royal Belge d'Entomologie**
31, Rue Vautier, 1040 Brussels, Belgium.
- Societe Royale Belge d'Entomologie. q. ISSN 0049-1128

**Societe Royale Belge d'Anthropologie et de Prehistoire**
31 rue Vautier, 1040 Brussels, Belgium.
- Societe Royale Belge d'Anthropologie et de Prehistoire. Bulletin. irreg.

**Societe Royale Belge d'Homoeopathie**
- Revue Belge d'Homoeopathie. (pub. by Association Homoeopathique Belge)

**Societe Royale Belge de Geographie**
87 Av. Adolphe Buyl, 1050 Brussels, Belgium.
- Revue Belge de Geographie. 3 per yr. ISSN 0035-0796

**Societe Royale Belge de Gynecologie et d'Obstetrique**
309 Ave. Moliere, Brussels 6, Belgium.
- Societe Royale Belge de Gynecologie et d'Obstetrique. Bulletin. bi-m. ISSN 0037-9522

**Societe Royale Belge de Medecine Dentaire**
Avenue de Jette 165, B-1090 Brussels, Belgium.
- Revue Belge de Medecine Dentaire/Belgisch Tijdschrift voor Tandheelkunde. q.

**Societe Royale Belge de Radiologie**
125 Ave. de la Brabanconne, Brussels, Belgium.
- Journal Belge de Radiologie. bi-m. ISSN 0021-7646
- Journal Belge de Radiologie (Monographie) (pub. by Imprimerie Medicale et Scientifique)

**Societe Royale Belge des Electriciens**
Place de Trone 1, B-1000 Brussels, Belgium.
- Societe Royale Belge des Electriciens. Bulletin. q. ISSN 0037-9530 (Co-sponsors: Comite Electrotechnique Belge; Laboratoire Central d'Electricite; Comite National Belge de l'Eclairage)

**Societe Royale Belge des Ingenieurs et des Industriels**
Hotel Ravenstein, 3 rue Ravenstein, B-1000 Brussels, Belgium.
- Societe Royale Belge des Ingenieurs et des Industriels. Revue. 4 per yr. ISSN 0037-9549

**Societe Royale d'Economie Politique de Belgique**
16 rue Royale, 1000 Brussels, Belgium.
- Societe Royale d'Economie Politique de Belgique. Seances. 8 per yr.

**Societe Royale de Botanique de Belgique**
236 rue Royale, B-1030 Brussels, Belgium.
- Societe Royale de Botanique de Belgique. Bulletin. 2 per yr. ISSN 0037-9557

**Societe Royale de Numismatique de Belgique**
22 Avenue Louise, B-1050 Brussels, Belgium.
- Revue Belge de Numismatique et de Sigillographie. a.

**Societe Royale de Zoologie d'Anvers**
Koningin Astridplein 26, B-2000 Antwerp, Belgium.
- Acta Zoologica et Pathologica Antverpiensia. 2-4 per yr. ISSN 0001-7280
- Zoo. q. ISSN 0044-5029

**Societe Royale des Amis du Musee Royal de l'Armee et d'Histoire Militaire**
Parc du Cinquantenaire 3, 1040 Brussels, Belgium.
- Militaria Belgica. q.
- Revue Belge d'Histoire Militaire/Belgisch Tijdschrift voor Militaire Geschiedenis. q. ISSN 0035-0877

**Societe Royale des Bibliophiles et Iconophiles de Belgique**
4 Bd. de l'Empereur, 1000 Brussels, Belgium.
- Livre et l'Estampe. q. ISSN 0024-533X

**Societe Royale des Sciences de Liege**
15 Ave. des Tilleuls, B-4000 Liege, Belgium.
- Societe Royale des Sciences de Liege. Bulletin. 6 per yr. ISSN 0037-9565

- Societe Royale des Sciences de Liege. Memoires in 8. a. ISSN 0085-6282

**Societe Royale Forestiere de Belgique**
Galerie du Centre, Bloc 2, 5e Etage, B-1000 Brussels, Belgium.
- Societe Royale Forestiere de Belgique. Bulletin/ Koninklijke Belgische Bosbouwmaatschappij. Tydschrift. 6 per yr. ISSN 0037-9573

**Societe Royale Zoologique de Belgique**
50 Ave. F. D. Roosevelt, 1050 Brussels, Belgium.
- Societe Royale Zoologique de Belgique. Annales. q. ISSN 0049-1136

**Societe Science et Culture**
Boite Postale 89, 4000 Liege 3, Belgium.
- Science et Culture. bi-m.

**Societe Scientifique de Bruxelles**
Rue de Bruxelles 61, B-5000 Namur, Belgium.
- Revue des Questions Scientifiques. 4 per yr. ISSN 0035-2160
- Societe Scientifique de Bruxelles. Annales. Serie 1: Sciences Mathematiques, Astronomiques et Physiques. 4 per yr. ISSN 0037-959X

**Society for Walloon Language and Literature**
see Societe de Langue et de Litterature Wallonnes

**Socorema**
Rue du Merlo 84a, B-1180 Brussels, Belgium.
- Neuf; architectures nouvelles, materiaux nouveaux. bi-m.

**Sodedi S.A.**
11-13 Ave. Cdt. Lothaire, 1040 Brussels, Belgium.
- New Horeca Belgie. bi-m. (Confederation Royale Horeca)

**SOLEDI**
Rue de la Province 37, B-4000 Liege, Belgium.
- Revue de Psychologie et des Sciences de l'Education. q.

**Editions Soumillion**
28 Av. Massenet, Brussels 19, Belgium.
- Men's Fashions. s-a. ISSN 0025-9497

**Spectator**
Koningsstraat 105, 1000 Brussels, Belgium.
- Spectator. w.

**Standaard**
Emil Jacqmainlaan 127, 1000 Brussels, Belgium.
- Ons Volk; weekblad voor vrouw en gezin. w.

**Standaard-Boekhandel N.V.**
Belgielei 147, 2000 Antwerp, Belgium.
- Dietsche Warande en Belfort; tijdschrift voor letterkunde, kunst en geestesleven. 10 per yr. ISSN 0012-2645
- Nieuwe Maand; tijdschrift voor politieke vernieuwing. 10 per yr. ISSN 0048-0347
- Tijdschrift voor Opvoedkunde. 6 per yr. ISSN 0040-7577

**State University of Ghent**
see Rijksuniversiteit Te Gent

**Stichting Ons Erfdeel**
Murissonstraat 160, B-8530 Rekkem, Belgium.
- De Franse Nederlanden/Pays-Bas Francais. a.
- Ons Erfdeel; algemeen nederlands tweemaandelijks kultureel tijdschrift. 5 per yr. ISSN 0030-2651
- Septentrion; revue de culture neerlandaise. 3 per yr.

**E. Story-Scientia**
Prudens van Duyseplein 8, B-9000 Ghent, Belgium.
- Ktemata. irreg.
- Scriptorium; international review of manuscript studies. s-a. ISSN 0036-9772
- Tijdschrift voor Privaatrecht. q. ISSN 0082-4313

**Streven**
Sanderusstraat 5, B-2000 Antwerp, Belgium.
- Streven. m. ISSN 0039-2324

**Studia Germanica Gandensia**
Blandijnberg 2, B-9000 Ghent, Belgium.
- Studia Germanica Gandensia. a. ISSN 0081-6442 (Rijksuniversiteit Te Gent. Sektie Germaanse Philologie)

**Studiecentrum voor Jeugdmisdadigheid**
Avenue Jeanne 44, 1050 Brussels, Belgium.
- Studiecentrum voor Jeugdmisdadigheid. Publikatie. irreg., no. 40, 1976. ISSN 0585-5721

**Studiecentrum voor Kernenergie**
*see* Centre d'Etude de l'Energie Nucleaire

**Syndicale Kamer Belgische Tuinbouw**
Stationsstraat 29, Ghent, Belgium.
- Belgische Tuinbouw/Horticulture Belge. fortn.; m. Jul.-Aug. ISSN 0005-8483

**Syndicale Kamer der Fabrikanten van Confectie van Belgie**
*see* Chambre Syndicale des Fabricants de Confections de Belgique

**Editions R. Tacoen**
24 Ave. J. S. Bach, 1080 Brussels, Belgium.
- Les Europeens. bi-m.

**Technicien Belge en Prothese Dentaire**
Av. R.Vandendriessche 49, Brussels 15, Belgium.
- Technicien Belge en Prothese Dentaire. q. ISSN 0040-1021

**Technique des Travaux**
196 rue Gretry, 4000 Liege, Belgium.
- Technique des Travaux; revue bimestrielle des procedes modernes de construction. bi-m. ISSN 0040-1218

**Techniques Nouvelles**
80 rue des Deux Gares, 7070 Brussels, Belgium.
- Techniques Nouvelles. m. ISSN 0040-1382

**Telepro**
Rue Saint-Remacle 31, 4800 Verviers, Belgium.
- Telepro; hebdomadaire de programmes de television. w. ISSN 0040-2664

**De Tempel**
37 Tempelhof, Bruges, Belgium.
- Cahiers de Bruges/Bruges Quarterly. q. ISSN 0575-0571 (College d'Europe)

**Textile Magazine**
193 Av. Brugmann, 1180 Brussels, Belgium.
- Textile Magazine. 8 per yr. ISSN 0040-5086

**Tijdschrift voor Filosofie**
Ravenstraat 112, B-3000 Leuven, Belgium.
- Tijdschrift voor Filosofie. q. ISSN 0040-750X

**Tijdschrift voor Geneeskunde A.S.B.L.**
De Pintelaan 135, B-9000 Ghent, Belgium.
- Tijdschrift voor Geneeskunde; orgaan van de Nederlandstalige medische faculteiten in Belgie en van hun alumni-verenigingen. s-m. ISSN 0005-8440

**Tijdschriften Uitgevers Maatschappij N.V.**
Jan Blockxstraat 7, 2000 Antwerp, Belgium (U.S. address: United Dutch Publishing Co., Inc., 55 W. 42nd St., New York, NY 10036)
- Libelle/Rosita. w. ISSN 0024-175X
- Panorama/Ons Land. w.
- Story. w.

**To the Point International N.V.**
Markgravestraat 19-21, 2000 Antwerp, Belgium (U.S. dist. to: Harry C. Thompson, 45 Owenoke Park, Westport, CT 06880)
- To the Point International; world news and commentary. fortn.

**Toison d'Or**
Rue Belliard 220, 1040 Brussels, Belgium.
- Toison d'Or; art, histoire, tourisme, economie, environment. 8 per yr. ISSN 0040-8832

**Top Art S.A.**
Rue de Brochet 62, 1040 Brussels, Belgium.
- Jalons et Actualities des Arts. 10 per yr.

**Touring Club of Belgium**
Rue de la Loi 44, 1040 Brussels, Belgium.
- Autotouring. m. ISSN 0045-1126

**Touring Secours**
Rue de la Loi 411, 1040 Brussels, Belgium.
- Journal de Touring Secours. bi-m.

**Tourist Information Brussels**
Rue de la Colline, 12, 1000 Brussels, Belgium.
- B. B. B. Agenda. w. ISSN 0007-2729

**Trimedia N.V.**
Cuylitsstraat 39, B-2000 Antwerp, Belgium.
- Transport Echo. s-m. ISSN 0009-6083

**UNOR**
10 Avenue de la Cavalerie, 1040 Brussels, Belgium.
- Ares. q.

**Union des Associations Internationales**
*see* Union of International Associations

**Union des Etudiants de l'Ichec**
2 Bd. Brand Whitlock, 1040 Brussels, Belgium.
- Confins. 7-8 per yr. ISSN 0010-5694

**Union des Exploitations Electriques en Belgique**
Galerie Ravenstein 4, Bte. 6, 1000 Brussels, Belgium.
- Electricite/Elektriciteit. s-a. ISSN 0013-4481
- Electricite pour Vous/Elektriciteit voor U. q. ISSN 0013-452X

**Union des Revues Techniques Belges**
Hotel de Societes Scientifiques, Rue des Champs-Elysees 43, 1050 Brussels, Belgium.
- Acta Technica Belgica. Revue A T B: Metallurgie. q.
- Acta Technica Belgica. Revue C: Genie Civil Construction/Bouwkunde Constructie. q.
- Acta Technica Belgica. Revue E: Electricite Courants Forts. Electrotechnique Generale et ses Applications. q.
- Acta Technica Belgica. Revue E P E: Energie Primaire. q.
- Acta Technica Belgica. Revue H F: Electricite Courants Faibles. Electronique Telecommunications. q. ISSN 0035-3248 (Societe Belge des Ingenieurs des Telecommunications et d'Electronique)
- Acta Technica Belgica. Revue M: Mecanique. q.
- Acta Technica Belgica. Revue T: Transport. q.
- Acta Technica Belgica. Revue X. q.

**Union des Villes et Communes Belges**
Rue d'Arlon 53, 1040 Brussels, Belgium.
- Mouvement Communal. m.

**Union International des Avocats**
*see* International Association of Lawyers

**Union Internationale d'Action Morale et Sociale**
*see* International Union for Moral and Social Action

**Union Internationale de la Navigation Fluviale**
*see* International Union for Inland Navigation

**Union Nationale des Entrepreneurs Menuisiers - Charpentiers**
348 Galerie du Centre, Brussels 1, Belgium.
- Entrepreneur Menuisier/Aannemer Schrijnwerker. bi-m. ISSN 0013-9041

**Union Nationale des Ingenieurs Techniciens**
- Ingenieurs: Equipement Industriel/Industrielle Uitrusting. (pub. by Drukkerij-Uitgeverij Vyncke)

**Union of International Associations**
1, rue aux Laines, 1000 Brussels, Belgium.
- Annual International Congress Calendar. a.
- Collection of Documents for the Study of International Non-Governmental Relations. irreg. ISSN 0503-2407
- Congress of International Congress Organizers and Technicians. Proceeding. irreg., 6th, 1977, Kyoto. ISSN 0573-5661
- International Associations/Associations Internationales. 10 per yr. ISSN 0020-6059
- International Congress Science Series. irreg. ISSN 0538-6772
- Yearbook of International Congress Proceedings. irreg. ISSN 0084-3806
- Yearbook of International Organizations. biennial; 16th edt., 1977. ISSN 0084-3814
- Yearbook of World Problems and Human Potential. irreg. ISSN 0304-0089 (Co-sponsor: Mankind 2000)

**Union of the Capitals of the European Community**
10, rue du Chene, Brussels, Belgium.
- Europa des Capitales/Europa of the Capitals. irreg.

**Union Professionnelle Nationale de la Decoration et de l'Ameublement de Belgique**
- Decoration - Ameublement/Woninginrichting. (pub. by Publimondex)

**Union Professionnelle Reconnue de Comptabilite**
- Documentation Commerciale et Comptable. (pub. by Editions C.I.B.)

**United Bible Societies. Europe Regional Center**
Rue du Trone 160, 1050 Brussels, Belgium.
- Practical Papers for the Bible Translator. s-a.
- Technical Papers for the Bible Translator. s-a.

**Editions Universa**
Rue Hoender 24, 9200 Wetteren, Belgium.
- Helinium; revue consacree a l'archeologie des pays-bas, de la Belgique et du Grand-Duche de Luxembourg. 3 per yr. ISSN 0018-0009
- Revue Internationale de Philosophie. q. ISSN 0048-8143

**Universitaire Faculteiten Sint Ignatius te Antwerpen**
Prinsstraat 13, Antwerp, Belgium.
- Bijdragen tot de Geschiedenis; inzonderheid van het oud hertogdom Brabant. q. ISSN 0006-2286

**Universitaire Faculteiten Sint Ignatius te Antwerpen. Centrum voor Gezellestudie**
- Gezelliana. (pub. by Uitgeverij de Nederlandsche Boekhandel)

**Universitaire Faculteiten Sint-Ignatius te Antwerpen. Instituut voor Postuniversitair Onderwijs**
Kipdorp 19, Antwerp 2000, Belgium.
- Economisch en Sociaal Tijdschrift. 6 per yr. ISSN 0013-0575

**Universitas Belgica**
Hotel des Societes Scientifiques, 43 rue des Champs Elysees, 1050 Brussels, Belgium.
- Universitas Belgica. q.
- Universitas Belgica. Feuille d'Avis.

**Universite Catholique de Louvain**
*see also* Katholieke Universiteit te Leuven (the two universities have been separate institutions since 1970)

**Universite Catholique de Louvain**
- Corpus Scriptorum Christianorum Orientalium: Aethiopica. (pub. by Corpus Scriptorum Christianorum Orientalium de Louvain-Washington)
- Corpus Scriptorum Christianorum Orientalium: Arabica. (pub. by Corpus Scriptorum Christianorum Orientalium de Louvain-Washington)
- Corpus Scriptorum Christianorum Orientalium: Armeniaca. (pub. by Corpus Scriptorum Christianorum Orientalium de Louvain-Washington)
- Corpus Scriptorum Christianorum Orientalium: Coptica. (pub. by Corpus Scriptorum Christianorum Orientalium de Louvain-Washington)
- Corpus Scriptorum Christianorum Orientalium: Iberica. (pub. by Corpus Scriptorum Christianorum Orientalium de Louvain-Washington)
- Corpus Scriptorum Christianorum Orientalium: Subsidia. (pub. by Corpus Scriptorum Christianorum Orientalium de Louvain-Washington)
- Corpus Scriptorum Christianorum Orientalium: Syriaca. (pub. by Corpus Scriptorum Christianorum Orientalium de Louvain-Washington)
- Ephemerides Theologicae Lovanienses. (pub. by Editions Peeters s.p.r.l.)
- Universite Catholique de Louvain. Recueil de Travaux d'Histoire et de Philologie. (pub. by Editions Nauwelaerts)

**Universite Catholique de Louvain. Association des Anciens Etudiants de la Faculte de Droit**
- Annales de Droit. (pub. by Imprimerie J. Goemaere)

**Universite Catholique de Louvain. Association des Diplomes en Archeologie et Histoire de l'Art**
Vlamingenstraat 83, B-3000 Louvain, Belgium.
- Revue des Archaeologues et Historiens d'Art de Louvain. a. ISSN 0080-2530

**Universite Catholique de Louvain. Bibliotheque**
Place Mgr. Ladeuze, 3000 Louvain, Belgium.
- Revue d'Histoire Ecclesiastique. q. ISSN 0035-2381

**Universite Catholique de Louvain. Bureau de la Revue d'Histoire Ecclesiastique**
Bibliotheque, Mgr. Ladeuzeplein, Louvain, Belgium.
- Bibliotheque de la Revue d'Histoire Ecclesiastique. irreg. ISSN 0067-8279

**Universite Catholique de Louvain. Centre Belge d'Histoire Rurale**
Blijde-Indomststraat, 29, 3000 Louvain, Belgium.
- Universite Catholique de Louvain. Centre Belge d'Histoire Rurale. Publications. irreg. ISSN 0076-1192

**Universite Catholique de Louvain. Centre d'Etudes Politiques**
2, Place Mgr. Ladeuze, Louvain, Belgium
- Universite Catholique de Louvain. Centre d'Etudes Politiques. Working Group "American Foreign Policy." Cahier. irreg. ISSN 0076-1206 (Dist. in U.S. by: Humanities Press, Inc., 171 First Ave., Atlantic Highlands, NJ 07716)

**Universite Catholique de Louvain. Centre de Recherches Sociologiques**
Batiment Jacques Leclercq, Place Montesquieu, 1 - Bte 10, 1348 Louvain-la-Neuve, Belgium.
- Recherches Sociologiques. 3 per yr.

**Universite Catholique de Louvain. Centre International de Dialectologie Generale**
Blijde-Inkomststraat 21, 3000 Louvain, Belgium.
- Orbis; bulletin international de documentation linquistique. 2 per yr. ISSN 0030-4379
- Universite Catholique de Louvain. Centre International de Dialectologie Generale. Travaux. irreg. ISSN 0577-1765

**Universite Catholique de Louvain. Departement de Archeologie**
Blijde Inkomststraat, 21, B-3000 Louvain, Belgium.
- Acta Archaeologica Lovaniensia. irreg.

**Universite Catholique de Louvain. Ecole des Sciences Politiques et Sociales**
- Universite Catholique de Louvain. Ecole des Sciences Politiques et Sociales. Collection. (pub. by Editions Nauwelaerts)

**Universite Catholique de Louvain. Faculte de Philosophie et Lettres**
- Universite Catholique de Louvain. Faculte de Philosophie et Lettres. Travaux. (pub. by Editions Nauwelaerts)

**Universite Catholique de Louvain. Faculte de Psychologie et des Sciences de l'Educations**
- Recherches de Psychologie Experimentale et Comparee. (pub. by Vander Publishing)
- Recherches de Psychopedagogie et de Pedagogie Experimentale. (pub. by Oyez S.A.)

**Universite Catholique de Louvain. Facultes de Theologie et de Droit Canonique**
Place Croix du Sud, 1, B-1348 Louvain-la-Neuve, Belgium.
- Revue Theologique de Louvain. 4 per yr. ISSN 0080-2654
- Universite Catholique de Louvain. Facultes de Theologie et de Droit Canonique. Dissertationes Ad Gradum Magistri in Facultate Theologica Vel in Facultate Iuris Canonici Consequendum Conscriptae. irreg (series quarta, vol. 1, 1969)
- Universite Catholique de Louvain. Facultes de Theologie et de Droit Canonique. Travaux de Doctorat en Theologie et en Droit Canonique. Nouvelle Serie. irreg., vol. 4, 1974. ISSN 0076-1230

**Universite Catholique de Louvain. Institut de Geographie**
Place Louis Pasteur, 3, 3000 Louvain, Belgium.
- Acta Geographica Lovaniensia. irreg. ISSN 0065-1257

**Universite Catholique de Louvain. Institut de Recherches Economiques. Politiques et Sociale**
- Universite Catholique de Louvain. Institut de Recherches Economiques, Politiques et Sociales. Publications. (pub. by Editions Nauwelaerts)

**Universite Catholique de Louvain. Institut des Langues Vivantes**
- Universite Catholique de Louvain. Institut des Langues Vivantes. Cahiers. (pub. by Oyez S.A.)

**Universite Catholique de Louvain. Institut des Sciences Economiques Appliquees**
- Annales des Sciences Economiques Appliquees. (pub. by Editions Provinciales)

**Universite Catholique de Louvain. Institut Interfacultaire de Mathematique Pure et Appliquee**
Chemi du Cyclotron 2, 1348 Louvain-la-Neuve, Belgium.
- Universite Catholique de Louvain. Institut de Mathematique Pure et Appliquee. Rapport. irreg.

**Universite Catholique de Louvain. Institut Orientaliste**
Redingenstraat 16, 3000 Louvain, Belgium.
- Universite Catholique de Louvain. Institut Orientaliste. Publications. irreg. ISSN 0076-1265

**Universite Catholique de Louvain. Institut Superieur d'Archeologie et d'Histoire de l'Art**
83 Vlamingenstraat, B-3000 Louvain, Belgium.
- Universite Catholique de Louvain. Institut Superieur d'Archeologie et d'Histoire de l'Art. Publications. irreg.

**Universite Catholique de Louvain. Institut Superieur de Philosophie**
- Essais Philosophiques. (pub. by Oyez S.A.)
- Philosophes Contemporains. (pub. by Oyez S.A.)
- Philosophes Medievaux. (pub. by Oyez S.A.)
- Repertoire Bibliographique de la Philosophie. (pub. by Editions Peeters s.p.r.l.)
- Revue Philosophique de Louvain. (pub. by Editions Peeters s.p.r.l.)
- Universite Catholique de Louvain. Institut Superieur de Philosophie. Cours Publics. (pub. by Oyez S.A.)

**Universite Catholique de Louvain. Laboratoire de Pedagogie Experimentale**
Tiense Str. 100, Louvain, Belgium.
- Universite Catholique de Louvain. Laboratoire de Pedagogie Experimentale. Cahiers de Recherches. irreg., 1970, no. 8. ISSN 0076-1281

**Universite Catholique de Louvain. Professors of Romance Literature**
146 Koning Albertlaan, 3040 Korbeek-Lo, Belgium.
- Lettres Romanes. q. ISSN 0024-1415

**Universite Catholique de Louvain. Section de Philologie Germanique**
- Universite Catholique de Louvain. Section de Philologie Germanique. Serie Microfiches. (pub. by Editions Nauwelaerts)

**Universite de l'Etat a Gand**
see **Rijksuniversiteit Te Gent**

**Universite de l'Etat a Mons**
17 Place Warocque, 7000 Mons, Belgium.
- Cahiers Internationaux de Symbolisme. 3 per yr. ISSN 0008-0284
- Revue de Phonetique Appliquee. 4 per yr. ISSN 0035-1660

**Universite de l'Etat a Mons. Centre Interdisciplinaire d'Etudes Philosophique**
17 Place Warocque, B-7000 Mons, Belgium.
- Reseaux; revue interdisciplinaire de philosophie morale et politique. 3-4 per yr.

**Universite de Liege. Association des Classiques**
Place du 20-Aout 7, Liege, Belgium.
- Otia. s-a. ISSN 0030-6584

**Universite de Liege. Centre d'Etudes de Recherches, d'Essais Scientifiques de Genie Civil**
6 Quai Banning, 4000 Liege, Belgium.
- Memoires C.E.R.E.S. irreg. ISSN 0025-9195

**Universite de Liege. Cercle Scientifique des Anciens Eleves de l'Institut A. Gilkinet**
5 rue Fusch, Liege, Belgium.
- Journee Scientifique de Mars. a.

**Universite de Liege. Faculte de Medecine Veterinaire**
45 rue des Veterinaires, B-1070 Brussels, Belgium.
- Annales de Medecine Veterinaire. 8 per yr. ISSN 0003-4118

**Universite de Liege. Faculte de Philosophie et Lettres**
Place du 20-Aout, Liege, Belgium.
- Universite de Liege. Faculte de Philosophie et Lettres. Publications. irreg.

**Universite de Liege. Faculte des Sciences Appliquees**
Commission des Publications, Rue du Val-Benoit, 75, 4000 Liege, Belgium.
- Universite de Liege. Faculte des Sciences Appliquees. Collection des Publications. irreg., 1973, no. 36. ISSN 0075-9333

**Universite de Liege. Institut de Pharmacie**
5 rue Fusch, 4000 Liege, Belgium.
- Universite de Liege. Institut de Pharmacie. Travaux Publies. biennial. ISSN 0075-935X

**Universite de Liege. Institut Superieur des Sciences Pedagogiques**
- Cahiers de Pedagogie et d'Orientation Professionnelle. (pub. by Desoer S.A.)

**Universite de Liege. Laboratoire d'Analyse Statistique des Langues Anciennes**
- Universite de Liege. Laboratoire d'Analyse Statistique des Langues Anciennes. Travaux Publies. (pub. by Mouton Publishers NE)

**Universite Libre de Bruxelles**
see also **Vrije Universiteit Brussel (the two universities have been separate institutions since 1970)**

**Universite Libre de Bruxelles. Association des Medecins Anciens Etudiants**
- Revue Medicale de Bruxelles. (pub. by Pauwels Fils)

**Universite Libre de Bruxelles. Centre d'Etude des Pays de l'Est**
- Universite Libre de Bruxelles. Centre d'Etude des Pays de l'Est. Revue des Pays de l'Est. (pub. by Editions de l'Universite de Bruxelles)

**Universite Libre de Bruxelles. Centre d'Etudes de Recherche Operationnelle**
50 Ave. Franklin Roosevelt, Brussels, Belgium.
- Centre d'Etudes de Recherche Operationnelle. Cahiers. q. ISSN 0008-9737

**Universite Libre de Bruxelles. Cercle des Sciences**
22 Av. Heger, Brussels 5, Belgium.
- Promethee. q. ISSN 0033-1082

**Universite Libre de Bruxelles. Department of Economics**
- Cahiers Economiques de Bruxelles. (pub. by Editions du Dulbea)

**Universite Libre de Bruxelles. Groupe d'Etude de Dix-Huiteme Siecle**
- Universite Libre de Bruxelles. Groupe d'Etude du Dix-Huiteme Siecle. Etudes sur le Dix-Huiteme Siecle. (pub. by Editions de l'Universite de Bruxelles)

**Universite Libre de Bruxelles. Institut d'Etudes Europeennes**
- Chronologie des Communautes Europeennes. (pub. by Editions de l'Universite de Bruxelles)
- Faits et les Decisions de la Communaute Economique Europeenne. (pub. by Editions de l'Universite de Bruxelles)
- Universite Libre de Bruxelles. Institut d'Etudes Europeennes. Enseignement Complementaire. Nouvelle Serie. (pub. by Editions de l'Universite de Bruxelles)
- Universite Libre de Bruxelles. Institut d'Etudes Europeennes. Theses et Travaux Economiques. (pub. by Editions de l'Universite de Bruxelles)
- Universite Libre de Bruxelles. Institut d'Etudes Europeennes. Theses et Travaux Juridiques. (pub. by Editions de l'Universite de Bruxelles)

**Universite Libre de Bruxelles. Institut d'Histoire du Christianisme**
- Problems d'Histoire du Christianisme. (pub. by Editions de l'Universite de Bruxelles)

**Universite Libre de Bruxelles. Institut de Philosophie**
143 Avenue Ad. Buyl, 1050 Brussels, Belgium.
- Universite Libre de Bruxelles. Institut de Philosophie. Annales. a.

**Universite Libre de Bruxelles. Institut de Sociologie**
- Agglomeration Bruxelloise. (pub. by Editions de l'Universite de Bruxelles)
- Cahiers d'Etude de Sociologie Culturelle. (pub. by Editions de l'Universite de Bruxelles)
- Collection de Sociologie Generale et de Philosophie Sociale. (pub. by Editions de l'Universite de Bruxelles)

- Etudes Africaines. (pub. by Editions de
  l'Universite de Bruxelles)
- Etudes Ethnologiques. (pub. by Editions de
  l'Universite de Bruxelles)
- Universite Libre de Bruxelles. Institut de
  Sociologie. Annee Sociale. (pub. by Editions de
  l'Universite de Bruxelles)
- Universite Libre de Bruxelles. Institut de
  Sociologie. Cahiers. (pub. by Editions de
  l'Universite de Bruxelles)
- Universite Libre de Bruxelles. Institut de
  Sociologie. Revue. (pub. by Editions de
  l'Universite de Bruxelles)

**Usines et Industries**
44 Avenue Jean Sobieski, Brussels, Belgium.
- Usines et Industries. bi-m. ISSN 0042-1286

**Imprimerie Vaillant-Carmanne**
4 Place St. Michel, Liege, Belgium.
- Archives de Biologie. 4 per yr. ISSN 0003-9624
- Archives Internationales de Physiologie et de
  Biochimie. 5 per yr. ISSN 0003-9799

**Van Het Belgisch Filmbedryf**
Van Maerlant Straat 71, 2000 Antwerp, Belgium.
- Weekblad Cinema. bi-w. ISSN 0043-177X

**Bureau Vander Haeghen**
63, Ave. de la Toison d'Or, 1060 Brussels, Belgium.
- Revue de Droit Intellectuel l'Ingenieur-Conseil. m.
  ISSN 0035-1083

**Vander Publishing**
Muntstraat 10, B-3000 Louvain, Belgium.
- Cellule; recueil de cytologie et d'histologie. 3 per
  yr. ISSN 0008-8757
- Recherches de Psychologie Experimentale et
  Comparee. irreg., 1973, no. 5. ISSN 0080-0058
  (Universite Catholique de Louvain. Faculte de
  Psychologie et des Sciences de l'Educations)

**Vent - Art**
c/o Jean Schwartz, 36 rue de la Laiterie, Brussels 7,
Belgium.
- Vent - Art. q. ISSN 0042-3440

**Vereeniging der Antwerpsche Bibliophilen**
Museum Plantin-Moretus, Vrijdamarkt 22 B, B-2000
Antwerp, Belgium.
- Gulden Passer/Compas d'Or. a.
- Vereeniging der Antwerpsche Bibliophilen.
  Publications. irreg, 3rd series, no. 4, 1961.

**Vereniging Ter Bevordering van Het Vlaamse
Boekwezen**
Frankrijklei 93, 2000 Antwerp, Belgium.
- Repertorium van Werken, in Vlaanderen
  Uitgegeven, of Door Monopoliehouders
  Ingevoerd. a. ISSN 0080-1224

**Vereniging van Archivarissen en Bibliothecarissen van
Belgie**
*see* **Association des Archivistes et Bibliothecaires
de Belgique**

**Vereniging van Religieus-Wetenschappellijke
Bibliothecarissen**
Minderbroedersstraat 5, 3800 Sint-Truiden, Belgium.
- V.R.B. - Information. q.

**Vereniging voor Studie en Onderzoek over
Fytopathologie en Toegepaste Zoologie**
*see* **Association pour les Etudes et Recherches de
Zoologie Appliquee et de Phytopathologie**

**Editions de la Vie Wallonne**
13 rue Wiertz, 4000 Liege, Belgium.
- Vie Wallonne. q. ISSN 0042-5648

**Vivant Univers**
14 Chaussee de Charleroi, Namur, Belgium.
- Vivant Univers; revue de la promotion humaine et
  chretienne en afrique et dans le monde. bi-m.
  ISSN 0042-7527

**Vlaamse Automobilistenbond**
St.-Jakobsmarkt 45-47, B-2000 Antwerp, Belgium.
- Autotoerist. fortn. ISSN 0005-1772

**Vlaamse Jeugherbergcentrale**
Van Stralenstraat 40, B-2000 Antwerp, Belgium.
- Trekker. bi-m. ISSN 0041-2260

**Vlaamse Pomologische Verenigingen**
- Belgische Fruitrevue. (pub. by Belgische
  Fruittelersorganisaties)

**Vlaamse Toeristenbond**
St.-Jakobsmarkt 45-47, B-2000 Antwerp, Belgium.
- Toerist. fortn. ISSN 0040-8638

**Vlaamse Vereniging van Bibliotheek- en
Archiefpersoneel**
- Bibliotheekgids. (pub. by Provinciale Bibliotheek
  van Limburg)

**Vlaamse Vereniging voor Familiekunde**
Wolstr. 39, B-2000 Antwerp, Belgium.
- Vlaame Stam; tijdschrift voor familiegeschiedenis.
  m (10 per yr)

**Vlaamse Volksbeweging**
Goudbloemstraat 19, 2000 Antwerp, Belgium.
- Doorbraak. fortn. ISSN 0012-5474

**Vrije Universiteit Brussel**
*see also* **Universite Libre de Bruxelles (the two
universities have been separate institutions since
1970)**

**Vrije Universiteit Brussel**
A. Buyllaan 136, B-1050 Brussels, Belgium.
- Dialoog; tijdschrift voor wijsbegeerte. a.
- Vrije Universiteit Brussel. Tijdschrift. (pub. by
  Uitgeverij S.M. Ontwikkeling)

**Vrije Universiteit Brussel. Centrum voor Studie van
de Verlichting**
A. Buyllaan 136, B-1050 Brussels, Belgium.
- Tijdschrift voor de Studie van de Verlichting. q.

**Vrije Universiteit Brussel. Dienst Uitgaven**
Waaglaan 13, 1050 Brussels, Belgium.
- Demografie. irreg.

**Drukkerij-Uitgeverij Vyncke**
Savaanstraat 92, B-9000 Ghent, Belgium.
- Confectie. m.
- Ingenieurs: Equipement Industriel/Industrielle
  Uitrusting. m. (Union Nationale des Ingenieurs
  Techniciens)
- Sur l'Eau. m. ISSN 0039-5994 (Federation Royale
  Belge du Yachting)
- Tex-Textilis. m. (Co-Sponsors: National
  Organisation for Textile Engineers and Directors;
  Association des Ingenieurs de Verviers; Dutch
  Textile Institute)

**War Resisters' International**
Van Elewyckstraat 35, 1050 Brussels, Belgium
- I R G-M I R Bulletin. bi-m. ISSN 0021-0986 (Co-
  sponsor: International Fellowship of
  Reconciliation) (Or 59 rue du Loriot, 1170
  Brussels, Belgium)
- Prisoners for Peace. a. ISSN 0085-5146
- W R I Newsletter. m. ISSN 0085-7882
- War Resistance. 4 per yr. ISSN 0043-0285

**Wereldwijd**
25 Keizerstraat, 2000 Antwerp, Belgium.
- Wereldwijd; tijdschrift over evangelizatie en
  ontwikkeling. m(10 per yr.)

**Wetenschappelijk Onderwijs Limburg**
Universitaire Campus, 3610 Diepenbeek, Belgium.
- Extern; tijdschrift voor omgevingswetenschappen.
  bi-m.

**World Confederation of Labour**
50 rue Joseph II, 1040 Brussels, Belgium.
- Labor Press and Information; revue on trade
  union information and training. bi-m.

## BELIZE

**Belize. Government Information Service**
Belmopan, Belize.
- Belize. Weekly Newsletter. w. ISSN 0522-8603
- New Belize. q.

**Belize Institute of Social Research and Action**
c/o St. John's College, Belize City, Belize.
- Belize Institute of Social Research and Action.
  National Studies; a journal of social research and
  thought. bi-m.

**Journal of Belizean Affairs**
P.O. Box 571, Belize City, Belize.
- Journal of Belizean Affairs. s-a.

## BENIN

**Action Populaire**
c/o Julian Aza, Ed., Boite Postale 215, Cotonou,
Benin.
- Action Populaire. 3 per wk. ISSN 0044-6106

**Association Dahomeene de Geographie**
B.P. 526, Cotonou, Benin.
- Association Dahomeene de Geographie. Bulletin
  de Liaison. q.

**Benin. Institut National de la Statistique et de
l'Analyse Economique**
B.P. 323, Cotonou, Benin.
- Annuaire Statistique de Benin. a.

**Chambre de Commerce et d'Industrie de la
Republique Populaire de Benin**
Avenue du General de Gaulle, Boite Postal 31,
Cotonou, Benin.
- Chambre de Commerce et d'Industrie de la
  Republique Populaire de Benin. Note
  Hebdomadaire. w.

**Institut de Recherches Appliquees du Dahomey**
B.P.6, Porto-Novo, Benin.
- Etudes Dahomeennes. q. ISSN 0014-2018

**Inter-African Council for Philosophy**
P.O. Box 1268, Cotonou, Benin.
- Consequence. s-a.

## BERMUDA

**Bermuda. Finance Department. Statistical Office**
- Bermuda Digest of Statistics. (pub. by Island Press
  Ltd.)

**Bermuda Book Stores**
Hamilton, Bermuda.
- Bermuda Historical Quarterly. q.

**Bermuda Historical Society**
Museum Par La Ville, Hamilton, Bermuda.
- Bermuda Historical Society. Occasional
  Publications. irreg., 1972, no. 8. ISSN 0409-2163

**Bermudian Publishing Co. Ltd.**
Hamilton, Bermuda.
- Bermudian. m. ISSN 0005-9382

**Island Press Ltd.**
Lightbourne Building, Cedar Avenue, Hamilton,
Bermuda.
- Bermuda Digest of Statistics. a. (Bermuda.
  Finance Department. Statistical Office)

**Monetary Research Ltd**
Butterfield Bldg, Front Street, Hamilton, Bermuda.
- Bank Credit Analyst. m.
- International Bank Credit Analyst. m. ISSN 0020-
  6113

**Preview of Bermuda, Ltd.**
Box 266, Hamilton, Bermuda.
- Preview of Bermuda. bi-w. ISSN 0048-5268

## BOLIVIA

**Academia de la Culturas Nativas de Oriente Boliviano**
Casilla 2225, Santa Cruz de la Sierra, Bolivia.
- Jisunu. s-a.

**Andes**
Casilla 4171, La Paz, Bolivia.
- Andes; revista interamericana. ISSN 0003-2948

**Banco Central de Bolivia**
La Paz, Bolivia.
- Banco Central de Bolivia. Boletin Estadistico. q.
  ISSN 0522-0939

**Bolivia. Caja Nacional de Seguridad Social**
Casilla 697, Plaza Murillo, Esquina Ingavi, La Paz,
Bolivia.
- Seguridad Social. m.

**Bolivia. Instituto Nacional de Estadistica**
Ministerio de Planeamiento y Coordinacion, La Paz,
Bolivia.
- Indice de Precios al Consumidor, Ciudad de La
Paz. a.

**Bolivia. Ministerio de Cultura, Informacion y Turismo**
Av. Camacho 1394, 1Er Piso, La Paz, Bolivia.
- Bolivia. bi-m. ISSN 0006-6540

**Bolivia. Ministerio de Defensa Nacional**
La Paz, Bolivia.
- Revista Militar. bi-m. ISSN 0035-0109

**Bolivia. Secretaria General de Deportes**
La Paz, Bolivia.
- Bolivia en el Deporte. q.

**Bolivia. Servicio Geologico de Bolivia**
Casilla 2729, La Paz, Bolivia.
- Bolivia. Servicio Geologico. Boletin. irreg. ISSN
0067-9828
- Bolivia. Servicio Geologico. Circulare. irreg. ISSN
0067-9836
- Bolivia. Servicio Geologico. Informe. a. ISSN
0067-9844
- Bolivia. Servicio Geologico. Serie Mineralogica.
Contribucione. irreg. ISSN 0067-9852

**Bolivia. Servicio Nacional de Caminos**
Av. 20 de Octubre No.311, Casilla No. 1485, La
Paz, Bolivia.
- Bolivia. Servicio Nacional de Caminos. Informe
Anual. a.

**Bolivia. Subsecretaria de Justicia**
La Paz, Bolivia.
- Revista de Justicia. q.

**Bolivia's Bibliographical Society**
- Boletin Bibliografico Boliviano. (pub. by Ediciones
I S L A)

**Camara Nacional de Industrias**
Casilla 611, La Paz, Bolivia.
- Industria Boliviana. s-m.

**Centro de Investigaciones Sociales**
Casilla 6931, La Paz, Bolivia.
- Monografias Urbanas. irreg.

**Centro Nacional de Documentacion Cientifica y
Technologica**
Casilla 3283, La Paz, Bolivia.
- Centro Nacional de Documentacion Cientifica y
Technologica. Actualidades. irreg.

**Corporacion Boliviana de Fomento**
La Paz, Bolivia.
- Corporacion Boliviana de Fomento. Marcha de la
Economia Nacional. Resumen Estadistico. a.

**Corporacion Minera de Bolivia. Dept. de Relaciones
Publicas**
Avda. Mariscal, Casilla 349, Santa Cruz 1092,
Bolivia.
- Estano. bi-m. ISSN 0014-1194

**Embajada del Peru en Bolivia**
Avda. 6 de Agosto 2190, La Paz, Bolivia.
- Peru. m.

**Gaceta Economica**
G. Mercado No. 996, Box 237, La Paz, Bolivia.
- Gaceta Economica. m. ISSN 0016-3767

**Ediciones I S L A**
Casilla N. 4311, La Paz, Bolivia.
- Boletin Bibliografico Boliviano. m. ISSN 0006-
6141 (Bolivia's Bibliographical Society)

**Instituto Boliviano de Estudio y Accion Social**
Casilla 3277, La Paz, Bolivia.
- Estudios Andinos. 3 per yr. ISSN 0014-1429
- I B E A S. m. ISSN 0018-8581

**Instituto Boliviano del Petroleo**
Casilla 4722, La Paz, Bolivia.
- Instituto Boliviano del Petroleo. Boletin. irreg. (1-
2 per year) ISSN 0085-1914

**Instituto de Investigacion Cultural para la Educacion
Popular**
Dpto. de Difusion, Potosi 421, Casilla 525, Bolivia.
- Educacion Popular para el Desarrollo. q.

**Instituto Panamericano de Geografia e Historia**
*see also* **Listings in Ecuador, Mexico and Peru**

**Instituto Panamericano de Geografia e Historia**
Casilla 6003, La Paz, Bolivia.
- Pan American Institute of Geography and
History. Commission on Geophysics. Boletin.
irreg.

**Los Amigos del Libro**
Casilla 450, Cochabamba, Bolivia.
- Bibliografia Boliviana. a. ISSN 0067-6578

**Editora Nacional**
Bolivar 3235, Cochabamba, Bolivia.
- Guia Bolivia; Industria, Comercio, Ganaderia.
irreg.

**Primicia**
Casilla 1844, La Paz, Bolivia.
- Primicia. m. ISSN 0032-8383

**Reportajes: Documentos para la Historia**
Edificio Almarez 50, Casilla Postal 382, La Paz,
Bolivia.
- Reportajes: Documentos para la Historia. s-m.

**Revista Diplomatica e Internacional**
Casilla 1598, La Paz, Bolivia.
- Revista Diplomatica e Internacional. m. ISSN
0034-9194

**Sociedad Boliviana de Historia Natural**
Casilla de Correo 538, Cochabamba, Bolivia.
- Sociedad Boliviana de Historia Natural. Revista.
irreg.

**Universidad Boliviana Gabriel Rene Moreno**
Santa Cruz de la Sierra, Bolivia.
- Universidad Boliviana Gabriel Rene Moreno.
Revista. irreg.

**Universidad Boliviana Juan Misael Saracho**
Tarija, Bolivia.
- Universidad Boliviana Juan Misael Saracho.
Informe de Labores. irreg.

**Universidad Boliviana Mayor de San Andres.
Facultad de Derecho, Ciencias Politicas y Sociales**
Apto. 1925, La Paz, Bolivia.
- Universidad Mayor de San Andres. Facultad da
Derecho. Revista de Derecho. 3 per yr. ISSN
0041-8595

**Universidad Boliviana Mayor de San Andres.
Facultad de Economia, Juridica y Ciencias Sociales**
Casilla Correo s/n, La Paz, Bolivia.
- Dinamica Economica. bi-m. ISSN 0012-2939
- Revista de Derecho. q. ISSN 0034-7868
- Temas Sociales. q. ISSN 0040-2915

**Universidad Boliviana Mayor de "San Simon"**
Cochabamba, Bolivia.
- Revista Juridica. q. (prep. by its Departamento de
Derecho)

**Universidad Boliviana Mayor de "San Simon".
Facultad de Economia, Juridica y Ciencias Sociales**
Instituto de Estudios Sociales y Economicos, Casilla
1392, Cochabamba, Bolivia.
- Universidad Mayor de San Simon. Instituto de
Estudios Sociales y Economicos. Revista. s-a.
ISSN 0041-8617 (prep. by its Departamento de
Economia)

**Universidad Boliviana Tecnica de Oruro. Centro de
Estudiantes de Ciencias Economicas**
Oruro, Bolivia.
- Revista Economica. s-a. ISSN 0034-9283

**Universidad Boliviana Tecnica de Oruro.
Departamento de Extension Cultural**
Oruro, Bolivia.
- Cultura Boliviana. m. ISSN 0011-2763

**Universidad Mayor, Real y Pontificia de San
Francisco Xavier de Chuquisaca**
Apdo. 212, Sucre, Bolivia.
- Archivos Bolivianos de Medicina. 3 per yr. ISSN
0004-0525

**Vertical**
Avenida 1377, 7 Piso, La Paz, Bolivia.
- Vertical. s-a. ISSN 0049-6022

**Vision Boliviana**
Calle Loavza 420, Casilla 2870, La Paz, Bolivia.
- Vision Boliviana. bi-m.

# BOTSWANA

**Botswana. Central Statistics Office**
Ministry of Finance and Development Planning,
Gaborone, Botswana.
- Botswana. Central Statistics Office. Employment
Survey. a.
- Botswana. Central Statistics Office. Statistical
Bulletin. q.
- Botswana. Central Statistics Office. Tourist
Statistics. a.
- National Accounts of Botswana. irreg.

**Botswana. Commissioner of the Police**
Gaborone, Botswana.
- Botswana. Commissioner of the Police. Annual
Report. a. ISSN 0068-046X

**Botswana. Department of Health**
Gaborone, Botswana.
- Botswana. Department of Health. Report. a.

**Botswana. Department of Income Tax**
Gaborone, Botswana.
- Botswana. Department of Income Tax. Annual
Report. a.

**Botswana. Department of Wildlife and National
Parks**
Box 131, Gaborone, Botswana.
- Botswana. Department of Wildlife and National
Parks. Report. a; no. 3, 1971-72.

**Botswana. Forest Department**
Gaborone, Botswana.
- Botswana. Forest Department. Report. a. ISSN
0068-0486

**Botswana. Geological Survey and Mines Department**
Gaborone, Botswana.
- Botswana. Geological Survey and Mines
Department. Annual Reports. irreg.

**Botswana. Government Printer**
Gaborone, Botswana.
- Botswana. Annual Statements of Accounts. a.
ISSN 0068-0451
- Botswana. Estimates of Revenue and Expenditure.
irreg. ISSN 0524-1448

**Botswana. Information Department**
Box 51, Gaborone, Botswana.
- Botswana. s-a. ISSN 0301-9020
- Kutlwano/Mutual Understanding. m. ISSN 0023-
5733

**Botswana. Ministry of Agriculture**
Private Bag 3, Gaborone, Botswana.
- Botswana. Ministry of Agriculture. Annual
Report. a. ISSN 0068-0478

**Botswana. Ministry of Agriculture. Division of Co-
Operative Development**
Gaborone, Botswana.
- Botswana. Ministry of Agriculture. Division of
Co-Operative Development. Annual Report. a.

**Botswana. National Library Service**
Private Bag 0036, Gaborone, Botswana.
- Botswana. National Library Service. Report.
- National Bibliography of Botswana. 3 per yr.
ISSN 0027-8777

**Botswana Development Corporation**
Gaborone, Botswana.
- Botswana Development Corporation. Annual
Report. a.

**Botswana National Library Service**
*see* **Botswana. National Library Service**

**Botswana Society**
Box 71, Gaborone, Botswana.
- Botswana Notes and Records. a. ISSN 0525-5090

**Medical and Dental Association of Botswana**
P.O. Box 798, Gaborone, Botswana.
- Medical and Dental Association of Botswana.
Journal. q.

# BRAZIL

**Editora Abril Ltda.**
Avenida Otaviano de Lima 800, Sao Paulo, Brazil.
- Capricho. fortn. ISSN 0008-5944
- Caricia. m.
- Claudia. 18 per yr. ISSN 0009-8507
- Comercio Exterior. bi-m. (Brazil. Ministerio das Relacoes Exteriores)
- Contigo. fortn. ISSN 0010-7662
- Cosmopolitan Nova. m.
- Documento Abril. irreg.
- Exame. fortn.
- Geracao Pop. m.
- Homen. m.
- Ilusao. fortn. ISSN 0019-2554
- Manequim. 18 per yr. ISSN 0025-2077
- Noturno. 18 per yr. ISSN 0029-4616
- Projeto. a.
- Quatro Rodas. m. ISSN 0033-5908
- Supernovelas. fortn. ISSN 0039-582X
- Veja. w. ISSN 0042-3165

**Academia Brasileira de Ciencias**
Rua Anfilofio de Carvalho 29, Caixa Postal 229, 20000 Rio de Janeiro G.B.ZC-00, Brazil.
- Academia Brasileira de Ciencias. Anais. q. ISSN 0001-3765
- Revista Brasileira de Biologia. q. ISSN 0034-7108

**Academia Brasileira de Neurologia**
c/o Dr. Oswaldo Lange, Caixa Postal 30.657, Sao Paulo, Brazil.
- Arquivos de Neuro-Psiquiatria. q. ISSN 0004-282X

**Academia Campinense de Letras**
Av. Francisco Glicerio 964, Campinas, Brazil.
- Academia Campinense de Letras. Publicacoes. irreg., no. 28, 1974. ISSN 0065-0447

**Academia Nacional de Medicina**
Av. General Justo 364, Rio de Janeiro, Brazil.
- Academia Nacional de Medicina. Boletim. q. ISSN 0001-3838

**Academia Paulista de Direito**
- Academia Paulista de Direito. Revista. (pub. by Universidade de Sao Paulo. Faculdade de Direito)

**Academia Paulista de Letras**
Largo do Arouche 312, Sao Paulo, Brazil.
- Academia Paulista de Letras. Revista. irreg. ISSN 0001-3846

**Academia Pernambucana de Letras**
Av. Rui Barbosa, 1596, Recife, Brazil.
- Academia Pernambucana de Letras. Revista. irreg.

**Academus;**
Praca de Republica 107, S. Paulo, SP, Brazil.
- Academus; democracia e cultura. q. ISSN 0001-4230

**Acares**
Caixa Postal 644, Vitoria, Espirito Santo, Brazil.
- Agricultor; informative mensal da acares a familia rural capixaba. m. ISSN 0002-1318
- Noticiarie a Imprensa Falada e Escrita. w. ISSN 0029-4136

**Editora Almanaque da Paraiba Ltda**
Rua Duque de Caixias, 400, Joao Pessoa, Brazil.
- Almanaque da Paraiba. irreg.

**Amazonas, Brazil. Comissao de Desenvolvimento do Estado do Amazonas. Unidade de Documentacao e Publicacao**
Rua Emilio Moreira, 1308, Manaus, Brazil.
- R A D. (Revista Amazonense de Desenvolvimento) 3 per yr.

**Amazonas, Brazil. Comissao de Desenvolvimento Economico**
Rua Major Gabriel 80, Manaus, Amazonas, Brazil.
- Comissao de Desenvolvimento Economico do Estado do Amazonas. Boletim Informativo. m. ISSN 0010-2407

**American Chamber of Commerce for Brazil**
Avenida Rio Branco 123, Caixa Postal 916-ZC-00, 20.000 Rio de Janeiro, Brazil.
- American Chamber of Commerce for Brazil. Annual Directory. a. ISSN 0065-7662

- Brazilian Business. m. ISSN 0006-9493
- Brazilian News Briefs. w. ISSN 0006-9507

**Companhia Editora Americana**
Rua Visconde de Maranguape, 15-ZC 06, Rio de Janeiro 20.000 GB, Brazil.
- Boletim de Ariel. m.

**ANFAVEA**
Avenida Paulista, Sao Paulo, Brazil.
- Industria Automobilistica Brasileira. a. (Sindicato Nacional da Industria de Tratores, Caminhoes, Automoveis e Veiculos Similares)

**Antenna Edicoes Tecnicas Ltda**
Av. Marechal Floriano 143, C.P. 1131, 20000 Rio de Janeiro, R.J., Brazil.
- Antenna. m. ISSN 0003-5378
- Eletronica Popular. bi-m. ISSN 0013-6085
- Som; selecoes de Revista de Som. a.

**Aonde Vamos**
Av. 13 de Maio, Grupo 1540, Rio de Janeiro, Brazil.
- Aonde Vamos; semanario Judaico independente do Brasil. w.

**APEC Editora S.A.**
Rua Sorocaba 316, Botafogo, Rio de Janeiro, Brazil.
- A P E C. (Analise e Perspectiva Economica) w. ISSN 0001-2181
- Economia Brasileira e suas Perspectivas-APECAO. a.
- Panorama APEC of the Brazilian Economy. m.

**Arquivos Brasileiros de Oftalmologia**
Rua Barao de Itapetininga 297, Caixa 4086, Sao Paulo, Brazil.
- Arquivos Brasileiros de Oftalmologia. bi-m. ISSN 0004-2749

**Artes**
Rua Nestor Pestana 30.21 Conj. 216, Sao Paulo 3 S.P., Brazil.
- Artes. m. ISSN 0004-3486

**Asociacion Latino-Americana de Filosofos Catolicos**
Via Anhanguera, Km. 26, Caixa Postal 11587, Sao Paulo, Brazil.
- Asociacion Latino-Americana de Filosofos Catolicos. Boletin. irreg.

**Assessoria de Servicos Ltda.**
Rua Rodrigo Silva 70, Sao Paulo, Brazil.
- Aves & Ovos; producao-industria-politica-comercio-mercado. m. ISSN 0005-2000

**Associacao Bahiana de Bibliotecarios. Biblioteca Central do Estado**
Rua General Labatut 27, Barris Salvador, Bahia, Brazil.
- Associacao Bahiana de Bibliotecarios. Informa. q. ISSN 0004-5187

**Associacao Brasileira da Industria Farmaceutica**
Av. Beira Mar 262, Rio de Janeiro, Brazil.
- Cadastro Brasileiro de Materias-Primas Farmaceuticas, Por Produto, Por Fabricante. a. ISSN 0068-4775
- Diretorio Brasileiro de Industria Farmaceutica. a. ISSN 0070-6612

**Associacao Brasileira da Industria Grafica**
Rua Marques de Itu 70, 01223 Sao Paulo, Brazil.
- B I G. (Boletim da Industria Grafica) m. ISSN 0006-5862

**Associacao Brasileira de Administracao de Pessoal**
Servicos Editoriais, Rua Cardoso de Almeida 163, Sao Paulo, Brazil.
- R I: Revista dos Recursos Humanos na Empresa. irreg.

**Associacao Brasileira de Antropologia**
- Revista de Antropologia. (pub. by Universidade de Sao Paulo. Faculdade de Filosofia, Letras e Ciencias Humanas)

**Associacao Brasileira de Ceramica**
Praca Cel. Fernando Prestes 110, Vila Mariana, 04013 Sao Paulo, S.P., Brazil.
- Ceramica. 6 per yr.

**Associacao Brasileira de Cimento Portland**
Av. Nilo Pecanha 50, ZC 21 Rio de Janeiro, Brazil.
- Cimento e Concreto. bi-m.

**Associacao Brasileira de Educacao Agricola Superior**
Praia do Flamengo 322, Caixa Postal 16074 ZC01, 20000 Rio de Janeiro, R.J., Brazil.
- Associacao Brasileira de Educacao Agricola Superior. A B E A S Informa. q. ISSN 0044-9369
- Associacao Brasileira de Educao Agricola Superior. Anais de Reuniao Anual. a. (Instituto Interamericano de Ciencias Agricolas)

**Associacao Brasileira de Endodontia, Seccao Sao Paulo**
Rua Humaita, 389, C.E.P. 01321, Caixa Postal 2523, Sao Paulo, Brazil.
- A. B. E. S. P. Boletim. q.

**Associacao Brasileira de Enfermagem**
Av. Franklin Roosevelt 39, Sala 1304, Rio de Janeiro GB, Brazil.
- Revista Brasileira de Enfermagem. q. ISSN 0034-7167

**Associacao Brasileira de Metais**
Av. Paulista 2073 - 15th (Horsa I), P.O. Box 22161, 01311 Sao Paulo, Brazil.
- Metalurgia. m. ISSN 0026-0983

**Associacao Brasileira de Odontologia**
Av. 13 de Maio 13-10 Andar, Salas 1001/6, Rio de Janeiro-Guanabara, Brazil.
- Revista Brasileira de Odontologia. bi-m. ISSN 0034-7272

**Associacao Brasileira de Pesquisas Sobre Plantas Aromaticas e Oleos Essenciais**
Viaduto Dona Paulina 80, Sao Paulo, Brazil.
- Associacao Brasileira de Pesquisas sobre Plantas Aromaticas e Oleos Essenciais. Boletim. 2 per yr.(approx.) ISSN 0004-5195

**Associacao Brasileira de Psiquiatria**
Rua Itapeva 490 Cj. 104, Sao Paulo, Brazil.
- Revista Brasileira de Psiquiatria. q.

**Associacao Brasileira de Reforma Agraria.**
Caixa Postal, 1.596, Campinas Sao Paulo, Brazil.
- Reforma Agraria. m.

**Associacao Brasileira de Refrigeracao, Ar Condicionado, Ventilacao e Aquecimento**
- Revista do Frio. (pub. by Editora Marcos Ltda.)

**Associacao Brasileira de Tecnicos Graficos**
- Remag. (pub. by Editora Metodos Ltda.)

**Associacao Brasileira de Telecomunicacoes**
Rua da Quitanda, 191, Rio de Janeiro, Brazil.
- Autoridades e Executivos. irreg.

**Associacao Brasileira de Teleducacao**
C.P. 56008, Rio de Janeiro, Brazil.
- Revista Brasileira de Teleducacao. irreg.

**Associacao Brasileira dos Distribuidores de Gas Liquefeito de Petroleo**
Av. Paulista 1009-16, Caixa Postal 6132, 01311 Sao Paulo, Brazil.
- Revista do Gas. q.

**Associacao Brasileira dos Supermercados**
- Anuario Brasileiro de Supermercados. (pub. by Publinform Publicacoes Informativas Ltda.)

**Associacao Brasileira para o Desenvolvimento das Industrias de Base**
- Anuario A B D I B. (pub. by Diagrama Comunicacoes)

**Associacao Brasileira para o Estudo Cientifico do Deficiencia Mental**
Rua Itapeva 490, Sao Paulo, Brazil.
- Revista Brasileira de Deficiencia Mental. q. ISSN 0034-7132

**Associacao Comercial de Sao Paulo**
Rua Boa Vista 51, C.P. 8082, Sao Paulo, Brazil.
- Digesto Economico. m.

**Associacao Comercial do Amazona**
Rua Guilherme Moreira 281, Manaus, Amazonas, Brazil.
- Associacao Comercial do Amazonas. Boletim. s-m. ISSN 0004-5217

**Associacao de Credito e Assistencia Rural**
Caixa Postal 900, Belo Horizonte 30000, Minas Gerais, Brazil.
- Extensao em Minas Gerais. fortn. ISSN 0014-5394

**Associacao de Exportadores Brasileiros**
Av. Beira Mar, 200-12o. andar, Rio de Janeiro, Brazil.
- Brasil. a.

**Associacao de Geografia Teoretica**
Caixa Postal 178, 13500 Rio Claro, Brazil.
- Boletim de Geografia Teoretica. s-a.

**Associacao dos Bibliotecarios do Distrito Federal**
Rua Washington Luiz 13, Rio de Janeiro, Brazil.
- A. B. B. Noticias. s-a. ISSN 0001-0332
- Biblioteconomia de Brasilia. s-a. (Co-sponsor: University of Brasilia. Department of Library Science)

**Associacao dos Dirigentes de Vendas do Brasil**
Al. Santos 2326, Sao Paulo, Brazil.
- Marketing. bi-m. ISSN 0025-3634

**Associacao dos Geografos Brasileiros**
Secao Regional de Minas Gerais, Rua Carangola 288, Belo Horizonte MG, Brazil.
- Boletim Mineiro de Geografia. s-a. ISSN 0006-6060

**Associacao dos Geografos Brasileiros. Secao Regional de Sao Paulo**
C.P. 8. 105, Sao Paulo, Brazil.
- Boletim Paulista de Geografia. irreg. ISSN 0006-6079

**Associacao dos Hospitais do Estado de Sao Paulo**
Av. Ipiranga 919- 11, Sao Paulo 01039, Brazil.
- Vida Hospitalar. bi-m. ISSN 0300-3183

**Associacao dos Juizes do Rio Grande do Sul**
- Ajuris. (pub. by Livraria Sulina)

**Associacao Latin Americana di Direito Agrario**
- ALADA. (pub. by Fundacao Getulio Vargas)

**Associacao Medica Brasileira**
Av. Brig. Luiz Antonio 278, 9 Andar, Sao Paulo, Brazil.
- Associacao Medica Brasileira. Boletim. m. ISSN 0004-5225
- Associacao Medica Brasileira. Jornal. w. ISSN 0004-5233
- Associacao Medica Brasileira. Revista. m. ISSN 0004-5241

**Associacao Medica Catarinense**
- Arquivos Catarinenses de Medicina. (pub. by Universidade Federal de Santa Catarina. Faculdade de Medicina)

**Associacao Medica de Goias**
- Revista Goiana de Medicina. (pub. by Imprensa da Universidade Federal de Goias)

**Associacao Medica de Minas Gerais**
C. P. 260, Belo Horizonte, Brazil.
- Associacao Medica de Minas Gerais. Revista. q. ISSN 0004-525X

**Associacao Medica do Rio Grande do Sul**
Av. Salgado Filho 135, 6 Andar, Porto Alegre, RS, Brazil.
- Revista da Amrigs. q.

**Associacao Nacional das Empresas de Transportes Rodoviarios de Carga**
Rua Araujo 216, 1 Andar, Sao Paulo, Brazil.
- B R. (Boletim Rodoviario) m. ISSN 0006-6087
- Guia Nacional do Transporte Rodoviario de Carga. irreg.

**Associacao Paulista de Cirurgioes Dentistas**
Rua Humaita 389, 01321 Sao Paulo -SP, Brazil.
- Associacao Paulista de Cirurgioes Dentistas. Journal. m.
- Associacao Paulista de Cirurgioes Dentistas. Revista. bi-m. ISSN 0004-5276

**Associacao Paulista de Criadores de Bovinos**
- Revista dos Criadores. (pub. by Editora dos Criadores Ltda.)

**Associacao Paulista de Criticos de Artes**
Sao Paulo, Brazil.
- Anuario das Artes. a.

**Associacao Paulista de Hospitais**
Avenida Reboucas 1205, Sao Paulo, Brazil.
- Revista Paulista de Hospitais. m. ISSN 0048-7864

**Associacao Paulista de Medicina**
Av. Brigadeiro Luiz Antonio, 278, C. Postal 2103, Sao Paulo, Brazil.
- Revista Paulista de Medicina. m. ISSN 0035-0362

**Associacao Tecnica Brasileira de Celulose e Papel**
- Papel. (pub. by Editora Orientador Ltda.)

**Ateneu Angrense de Letras e Artes**
Caixa Postal 03, Angra dos Reis, Rio de Janeiro 27300, Brazil.
- Ateneu Angrense de Letras e Artes. Revista. q.

**Atlantis Livros Ltda**
C. P. 3752, 01000 Sao Paulo, Brazil.
- Livros Novos; bibliografia brasileira. m.

**Editora Ave Maria Ltda**
Rua Martim Francisco, 636, Caixa Postal, 615, 01000 Sao Paulo, Brazil.
- A M. (Ave Maria) s-m. ISSN 0005-1934

**Aviacao em Revista Editora Ltda.**
Caixa Postal 1604, ZC-00 Rio de Janeiro, Brazil.
- Aviacao em Revista. bi-m.

**Bahia, Brazil. Centro de Planejamento**
Av. Luis Viana Filho, s/n-Paralela, Salvador, Brazil.
- Bahia. Departamento de Geografia e Estatistica. Provoados do Estado da Bahia.

**Bahia, Brazil. Divisao de Informacao Industrial e Promocao de Investimentos**
Salvador, Bahia, Brazil.
- Bahia, Brazil (State). Divisao de Informacao Industrial e Promocao de Investimentos. Resenha Bimestral. irreg.

**Bahia, Brazil. Fundacao de Pesquisa. Secretaria do Planejamento Ciencia e Tecnologia**
Av. Luiz Filho, CEP 4000 - Salvador, Bahia, Brazil.
- Planejamento. bi-m.

**Bahia, Brazil. Secretaria das Minas e Energia**
Coordenacao de Energia, Av. Centro Administrativo da Bahia, Av. Luiz Viana Filho, 40000 Salvador - Bahia, Brazil.
- Bahia. Secretaria das Minas e Energia. Boletim Estatistico Mensal de Energia Eletrica. m.
- Consumo Industrial de Energia Eletrica No Estado da Bahia. m.

**Bahia, Brazil. Secretaria de Saude**
Av. Sete de Setembro 280, Salvador, Bahia, Brazil.
- Revista Baiana de Saude Publica. q.

**Editora Banas, S.A.**
Av. Presidente Castelo Branco 6241, Sao Paulo, Brazil.
- Banas; revista industrial e financeira. w. ISSN 0005-4585
- Banas: Classificado Industrial Brasileiro/Who Produces What in Brazil. a.
- Brasil Financeiro e Grandes Companhias; Brazil's capital/market. a.
- Brasil Industrial; the great industrial handbook. a. ISSN 0068-0699
- Imagem do Brasil e da America Latina/Brazil and Latin America. a.
- P S-Produtos e Servicos. m.
- Super P S Anual. (Produtos e Servicos) a.

**Banco Bamerindus do Brazil**
Avenida Kennedy 3080, 80000 Curitiba, Parana, Brazil.
- Informativo Bamerindus. m. ISSN 0020-0654

**Banco Central do Brasil S. A.**
Departamento de Administracao Financeira, Edificio Vera Cruz, Setor Comercial Sul, 70000 Brasilia D.F., Brazil.
- Banco Central do Brasil. Boletim. m (11 per yr and annual supplement) ISSN 0005-4763

**Banco da Amazonia. Centro de Documentacao e Biblioteca**
Av. Presidente Vargas, 800 - 16. Andar, Belem, Brazil.
- Banco da Amazonia. Centro de Documentacao e Biblioteca. Contexto Boletim. irreg.

**Banco de Desenvolvimento do Parana, S.A.**
Av. Vicente Machado, 445, Cx. Postal 6042, Curitiba, Parana, Brazil.
- Information on Parana. irreg.
- Revista Paranaense de Desenvolvimento. bi-m. ISSN 0556-6916

**Banco de Nordeste do Brasil**
Rua Senador Pompeu 590, C. P. 628, Fortaleza, Ceara, Brazil.
- Nordeste Conjuntura Industrial. q.

**Banco do Brasil S.A.**
Setor Bancario Sul, Edificio Sede do Banco do Brasil, 70000 Brasilia, Brazil.
- Arquivos Economicos. (pub. by Irmao di Giorgio)
- Banco do Brasil. Annual Report. a.
- Banco do Brasil. Boletim. q. ISSN 0005-4879
- Informacao Semanal; carteira de comercio exterior. w. ISSN 0019-9737

**Banco do Brasil S.A. Departamento Geral de Selecao e Desenvolvimento do Pessoal**
Setor Bancario Sul, Bloco H, Brasilia, Brazil.
- D E S E D. (Departamento Geral de Selecao e Desenvolvimento do Pessoal) bi-m.

**Banco do Estado de Pernambucco**
Cais do Apolo, 222, Recife, Brazil.
- Banco do Estado de Pernambuco. BANDEPE Relatorio. a.

**Banco do Nordeste do Brasil**
Rua Major Facundo 500, Caixa Postal 628, 60000 Fortaleza - Ceara, Brazil.
- Banco do Nordeste do Brasil. Serie Estudos Economicos e Sociais. irreg.
- Revista Economica. q.

**Banco do Nordeste do Brasil. Departamento de Estudos Economicos do Nordeste**
Rua Senador Pompeu, No. 826-1 Andar, Ceara, Fortaleza, Brazil.
- Banco do Nordeste do Brasil. Departamento de Estudos Economicos do Nordeste. Analise Conjuntural da Economia Nordestina.

**Banco Lar Brasileiro S.A.**
Rua do Ouvidor 98, Rio de Janeiro, Brazil.
- Trends and Perspectives of the Brazilian Economy. q.

**Banco Nacional do Desenvolvimento Economico**
Av. Rio Branco 53, Rio de Janeiro, Brazil.
- B N D E Noticias. m.
- Banco Nacional do Desenvolvimento Economico. Plano de Acao/Banco Nacional do Desenvolvimento Economico. Plan of Action. triennial.
- Revista do B I N D E. a.

**Bayer do Brasil Industrias Quimicas S.A.**
C.P. 22-523-ZP-18, 01000 Sao Paulo, Brazil.
- Correio Agricola (Brazil) irreg., no. 3, 1974.

**Biblioteca do Sejur**
- Biblioteca do Sejur. Boletim. (pub. by Petroleo Brasileiro S.A.)

**Bloch Editores S.A.**
Rua Frei Caneca 511, Rio de Janeiro, Brazil.
- Amiga. w. ISSN 0003-1755
- Desfile. m. ISSN 0021-7301
- Ele e Ela; uma revista para ler a dois. m. ISSN 0531-9153
- Fatos & Fotos. w. ISSN 0014-8849
- Geografica Universal. m.
- Manchete. w. ISSN 0025-2042
- Medicina de Hoje. m.
- Pais e Filhos; revista mensal da familia moderna. m. ISSN 0030-9567
- Setimo Ceu. m. ISSN 0037-2862
- Tendencia.

**Editora Edgard Bluecher Ltda.**
Rua Valson Lopes, 101, C.P. 05360-VI, Butante, Sao Paulo, Brazil.
- Revista Brasileira de Geociencias. q. (Conselho Nacional de Pesquisas, Sociedade Brasileira de Geologia)

- Revista Brasileira de Tecnologia. q. ISSN 0048-7643 (Conselho Nacional de Desenvolvimento Cientifico e Tecnologico)

**Editora Boletin de Custos Ltda.**
Rua Dona Mariana, 2, Botafogo, Box 15090, Rio de Janeiro GB-ZC-06, Brazil.
- Boletim de Custos. m. ISSN 0006-5900

**Bolsa de Valores de Sao Paulo**
Pateo do Colegio, Sao Paulo, Brazil.
- Bolsa de Valores de Sao Paulo. Relatorio. a.
- Bolsa de Valores de Sao Paulo. Revista. m. ISSN 0034-7558

**Bolsa de Valores do Rio de Janeiro**
Praca 15 de Novembro, 20, Rio de Janeiro, Brazil.
- Bolsa de Valores do Rio de Janeiro. Resumo Anual. a. ISSN 0557-0506

**Brasil Ilustrado**
Rua da Almirante Goncalvez 23, Rio de Janeiro, Gb, Brazil.
- Brasil Ilustrado. fortn.

**Impressora Brasileira**
c/o Emilio Berla, 46/302 Copacabana, Rio de Janeiro, RJ-20.000, Brazil.
- Ginecologia Brasileira. bi-m. ISSN 0046-5941 (Instituto de Ginecologia)

**Editora Brasileira de Agricultura S.A.**
Rua Aurora 277, 01209 Sao Paulo, Brazil.
- Avicultura Brasileira. m. ISSN 0005-2248

**Empresa Brasileira de Telecomunicacoes**
Av. Presidente Vargas 1012, Rio de Janeiro, Brazil.
- Empresa Brasileira de Telecommunicacoes. Relatorio. a.

**Empresa Brasileira de Turismo**
Praca Maua 7/11 Andar, Rio de Janeiro 20000, Brazil
(Subscr. to: rua Ribeiro 272, 20000 Rio de Janeiro, Brazil)
- Empresa Brasileira de Turismo. Anuario Estatistico. a; 1974 latest edt.

**Brasilia, Brazil. Departamento de Estradas de Rodagem. Diretoria Geral**
Secretaria de Viacao e Obras, Brasilia, Brazil.
- Distrito Federal, Brasil. Departamento de Estradas de Rodagem. Directoria Geral. Relatorio Anual. a.

**Editora Brasiliense**
Rua Barao de Itapetininga 93, 01042 Sao Paulo, Brazil.
- Almanaque; cadernos de literatura e ensaio. irreg.
- Cadernos de Debate. irreg.

**Brazil. Arquivo Nacional**
Praca da Republica 26, Rio de Janeiro, Guanabara, Brazil.
- Brazil. Arquivo Nacional. Serie de Publicacoes. irreg.
- M A N. (Mensario de Arquivo Nacional) m. ISSN 0045-2726

**Brazil. Banco Nacional da Habitacao. Assessoria Tecnica de Documentacao**
Biblioteca, Av. Chile 230, Rio de Janeiro, Brazil.
- Brazil. Banco Nacional da Habitacao. Assessoria Tecnica de Documentacao. Boletim Bibliografico. irreg.

**Brazil. Banco Nacional da Habitacao. Secretaria de Divulgacao**
Rio de Janeiro, Brazil.
- Banco Nacional da Habitacao. Orcamento Plurianual.

**Brazil. Biblioteca Nacional**
Rio Branco 219, 20000 - Rio de Janeiro - RJ, Brazil.
- Biblioteca Nacional, Brazil. Boletim Bibliografico. q.

**Brazil. Camara dos Deputados. Centro de Documentacao e Informacao**
Divisao Publicacoes, Palacio do Congresso Nacional, Brasilia 70000, Brazil.
- Artigos Selecionados; ciencias sociais, direito, economia, politica. 9 per yr. ISSN 0004-3753
- Brazil. Camara dos Deputados. Almanaque dos Funcionarios de Secretaria. biennial.
- Brazil. Camara dos Deputados. Documentacao e Informacao. 3 per yr.

- Estudos Legislativas. s-a.

**Brazil. Comissao Central de Levantamento e Fiscalizacao das Safras Triticolas**
Edificio Planalto, Av. Borges de Medeiros, 328 - 13, Caixa Postal N. 2021, Porto Alegre, Brazil.
- Brazil. Comissao Central de Levantamento e Fiscalizacao das Safras Triticolas. Annuario Estatistico do Trigo: Producao Nacional. a.

**Brazil. Comissao de Financiamento da Producao**
Avda. W-3 Norte Quadra 514, Bloco "B" Lote 7, 70000 Brasilia, D.F., Brazil.
- Brazil. Comissao de Financiamento da Producao. Anuario Estatistico. a.
- Mercado Em Analise. bi-m.

**Brazil. Comissao Executiva do Plano da Lavoura Cacaneira**
Km 22 Rodovia, Ilheus-Itabuna, Bahia, Brazil.
- Cacau Atualidades. q. ISSN 0007-9340

**Brazil. Conselho de Desenvolvimento Economico**
Brasilia, Brazil.
- C D E. irreg.

**Brazil. Conselho Federal de Farmacia**
Brasilia, Brazil.
- Brazil. Conselho Federal de Farmacia. Relatorio. irreg.

**Brazil. Conselho Nacional de Petroleo. Secao de Relacoes Publicas**
Esplanada dos Ministerios - Bloco J, 6 Andar - Sala 606, Brasilia, Brazil.
- Brazil. Conselho Nacional de Petroleo. Atualidades. irreg.; no. 40, 1975.

**Brazil. Departamento Administrativo do Pessoal Civil**
Esplanada dos Ministerios, Bloco 7, Brasilia, Brazil.
- Revista do Servico Publico. q. ISSN 0034-9240

**Brazil. Departamento Estadual de Estatistica**
Rua Carlos Gomes, 111 - 2o. Andar, Salvador, Brazil.
- Bahia, Brazil (State). Departamento Estadual de Estatistica. Comercio Exterior de Bahia: Exportacao Segundo as Firmas e Mercadorias. irreg.
- Boletim do Comercio Exterior da Bahia/Bahia's Foreign Trade Bulletin. irreg.

**Brazil. Departamento Nacional de Mao-de-Obra. Secao de Documentacao**
Rio de Janeiro, Brazil.
- Brazil. Departmento Nacional de Mao-de-Obra. Secao de Documentacao. Serie Bibliografia. q.

**Brazil. Departamento Nacional de Obras Contra as Secas**
Fortaleza, Ceara, Brazil.
- D N O C S-Fins e Atividades. irreg.

**Brazil. Departamento Nacional de Obras Contra as Secas. Centro de Pesquisas Ictiologicas**
Av. Duque de Caxias 1700, Cx. Postal 650, 60000 Fortaleza, Ceara, Brazil.
- Centro de Pesquisas Ictiologicas. Boletim Tecnico. bi-m. ISSN 0068-0796

**Brazil. Departamento Nacional de Obras Contras as Secas. Servico de Piscicultura**
Rio de Janeiro, Brazil.
- Brazil. Servico de Piscicultura. Publicacao. irreg. ISSN 0068-0850

**Brazil. Departamento Nacional de Obras de Saneamenento**
Av. Pres. Vargas 62-11, Z.C. 00 Rio de Janeiro G.B., Brazil.
- Saneamento. q. ISSN 0036-4312

**Brazil. Departamento Nacional de Pesquisa Agropecuaria**
Ministerio da Agricultura, Brasilia, Brazil.
- Brazil. Departamento Nacional de Pesquisa Agropecuaria. Programa Nacional de Pesquisa Agropecuaria. irreg.

**Brazil. Diretoria de Intendencia da Marinha**
Rio de Janeiro, Brazil.
- Revista da Intendencia da Marinha. irreg. (1-2 per yr)

**Brazil. Fundacao Nacional do Indio**
Rua Mata Machado 127, Maracana, 20000 Rio de Janeiro, Brazil.
- Brazil. Fundacao Nacional do Indio. Informativo. q.

**Brazil. Instituto de Pesquisas Agropecuarias do Norte**
Caixa Postal 48, Belem, Para, Brazil.
- Instituto de Pesquisas Agropecuarias do Norte. Circular. irreg. ISSN 0067-5288
- Instituto de Pesquisas Agropecurarias do Norte. Communicado Tecnico. irreg. ISSN 0067-5296

**Brazil. Instituto do Acucar e do Alcool**
Praca Quinze de Novembro 42, Rio de Janeiro, Brazil.
- Plano da Safra Acucar e Alcool. irreg.

**Brazil. Instituto do Acucar e do Alcool. Divisao de Estudo e Planejamento**
Divisao Administrativa, Servico de Documentacao, Caixa Postal 420, Rio de Janeiro, Brazil.
- Brazil. Instituto do Acucar e do Alcool. Conselho Deliberativo. Coletanea de Resolucoes (e) Presidencia. Coletanea de Atos. irreg.

**Brazil. Instituto Nacional de Previdencia Social**
Rua Mexico, 128, ZC-P, Rio de Janeiro-GB, Brazil.
- I N P S. Mensario Estatistico. s-a. ISSN 0019-0195
- Informe I N P S. s-m.
- Instituto Nacional de Previdencia Social. Procuradoria-Geral. Revista. bi-m.

**Brazil. Instituto Nacional de Tecnologia**
Av. Venezuela 82, 20000 Rio de Janeiro, Guanabara, Brazil.
- I. N. T. Informativo. q. ISSN 0019-0233

**Brazil. Instituto Nacional do Livro**
Brasilia, D.F., Brazil.
- Brazil. Instituto Nacional do Livro. Relatorio de Atividades. a.

**Brazil. Ministerio da Aeronautica**
- Aerovisao. (pub. by Centro de Relacoes Publicas da Aeronautica)

**Brazil. Ministerio da Agricultura**
- Informacao Agricola. (pub. by Diarios Associados)
- Pesquisa Agropecuaria Brasileira. Serie Agronomia/Brazilian Journal of Agricultural and Veterinary Research. Agronomy Series. (pub. by Empresa Brasileira de Pesquisa Agropecuaria)
- Pesquisa Agropecuaria Brasileira. Serie Veterinaria-Zootecnia/Brazilian Journal of Agricultural and Veterinary Research. Animal Husbandry Series. (pub. by Empresa Brasileira de Pesquisa Agropecuaria)

**Brazil. Ministerio da Agricultura. Conselho Nacional de Desenvolvimento de Pecuaria**
Rio de Janeiro, Brazil.
- Brazil. Conselho Nacional de Desenvolvimento de Pecuaria. Mercado Atacadista de Gado e Carne: Analise da Variacao dos Precos. irreg.

**Brazil. Ministerio da Agricultura. Departamento de Assistencia ao Cooperativismo**
Rua do Carmo 88, Sao Paulo, Brazil.
- Brazil. Ministerio da Agricultura Departamento de Assistencia ao Cooperativismo Serie Contabilidade. irreg.
- Brazil. Ministerio da Agricultura Departamento de Assistenica ao Cooperativismo. Serie Integracao. irreg.

**Brazil. Ministerio da Agricultura. Departamento Nacional de Producao Animal**
Brasilia, Brazil.
- D N P A. (Departamento Nacional de Producao Animal) irreg.
- Inseminacao Artificial. irreg. (prep. by its Divisao de Fisiopatologia da Inseminacao Artificial)

**Brazil. Ministerio da Agricultura. Escritorio de Estatistica**
Esplanada dos Ministerios, Bloco 8-6 Andar, Rio de Janiero, Brazil.
- Brazil. Escritorio de Estatistica. Pecuaria, Avicultura, Apicultura, Sericicultura. a.
- Brazil. Ministerio da Agricultura. Escritorio de Estatistica. Cadastro das Empresas Produtoras de Oleos, Gorduras Vegetais e Sabprodutos. triennial.
- Brazil. Ministerio da Agricultura. Escritorio de Estatistica. Oleos e Gorduras Vegetais. a.

**Brazil. Ministerio da Agricultura. Instituto Nacional de Colonizacao e Reforma Agraria**
Palacico do Desenvolvimento, Brasilia, Brazil.
- Brazil. Ministerio da Agricultura. Departamento de Desenvolvimento Rural. Instituto Nacional de Colonizacao e Reforma Agraria. Acao Associativista. irreg.
- Brazil. Ministerio da Agricultura. Instituto Nacional de Colonizacao e Reforma Agraria. Encontro Nacional. irreg.
- Instituto Nacional de Colonizacao e Reforma Agraria. Coordenadoria Regional do Parana. Sinopse do Cooperativismo No Parana. irreg.
- Revista de Direito Agrario. q.

**Brazil. Ministerio da Agricultura. Subsecretaria de Planejamento e Orcamento**
Brasilia, Brazil.
- Brazil. Ministerio da Agricultura. Subsecretaria de Planejamento e Orcamento. Producao e Abastecimento, Perspectivas e Proposicoes: Sintese. irreg.

**Brazil. Ministerio da Educacao e Cultura**
Departamento de Documentacao e Divulgacao, Esplanada dos Ministerios, Bloco L, Brasilia, D.F., Brazil.
- Cultura. q.
- Educacao. q. ISSN 0046-1334
- Selecao de Artigo do Boletim do Servico Alemao de Pesquisas. bi-m.

**Brazil. Ministerio da Educacao e Cultura. Campanha de Defesa do Folclore Brasileiro**
Rua do Catete 179, Rio de Janeiro, Brazil.
- Revista Brasileira de Folclore. 3 per yr. ISSN 0034-7213

**Brazil. Ministerio da Educacao e Cultura. Departamento de Assuntos Universitaries**
Esplanada dos Ministerios, Bloco H, Brasilia, Brazil.
- Brazil. Departamento de Assuntos Universitarios. Coordenacao de Avaliacao e Controle. Atividades das Instituicoes Federais de Ensino Superior. a. (prep. by its Coordenacao de Avaliacao e Controle)
- Catalogo dos Cursos de Pos-Graduacao No Brasil. irreg.

**Brazil. Ministerio da Educacao e Cultura. Departamento de Educacao Fisica e Desportos**
Brasilia, Brazil.
- Brazil. Departamento de Educacao Fisica e Desportos. Caderno Cultural. q.

**Brazil. Ministerio da Educacao e Cultura. Directoria do Patromonio Historico e Artistico Nacional**
Esplanada dos Ministerios, Bloco L, Brasilia, D.F., Brazil.
- Brazil. Diretoria do Patrimonio Historico e Artistico Nacional. Revista. irreg. ISSN 0068-0788

**Brazil. Ministerio da Educacao e Cultura. Servico de Estatistica da Educacao e Cultura**
Rua da Imprensa, 16 - 3o. Andar, Rio de Janeiro, Brazil.
- Brazil. Servico de Estatistica da Educacao e Cultura. Ensino Superior. irreg.
- Brazil. Servico de Estatistica da Educacao e Cultura. Estatisticas da Educacao Nacional. irreg.

**Brazil. Ministerio da Fazenda**
Inspetoria-Geral de Financas, Esplanada dos Ministerios, 8 Andar, Brasilia DF, Brazil.
- Brazil. Inspetoria-Geral de Financas. Balancos Gerais da Uniao. a.

**Brazil. Ministerio da Fazenda. Assesoria de Estudos, Planejamento e Avalicao**
Av. Antonio Carlos/926, Rio de Janeiro Gb, Brazil.
- Revista de Politica e Administracao Fiscal. bi-m.

**Brazil. Ministerio da Fazenda. Delegacio no Estado do Rio de Janeiro**
Av. Presidente Antonio Carlos, 375, Rio de Janeiro, R.J., Brazil.
- Ministerio da Fazenda. Boletim Informativo da Secao de Documentacao. m. (prep. by its Secao de Documentacao)

**Brazil. Ministerio da Fazenda. Subsecretaria de Economia e Financas**
Secretaria Geral, Caixa Postal 1580, Rio de Janeiro, Brazil.
- Financas Publicas. q.

**Brazil. Ministerio da Guerra**
Rio de Janeiro, Brazil.
- Defesa Nacional. bi-m. ISSN 0011-7641

**Brazil. Ministerio da Industria e do Comercio. Superintendencia da Borracha**
Avda. Almirante Barroso, 81-4 andar, Rio de Janeiro, GB, Brazil.
- Brazil. Superintendencia da Borracha. Annuario Estatistico. Mercado Nacional. a. ISSN 0572-5542
- Brazil. Superintendencia da Borracha. Annuario Estatistico. Mercado Estrangeiro. a. ISSN 0572-5534
- Mercado da Borracha no Brasil. Boletim Mensal. m. ISSN 0025-9748

**Brazil. Ministerio da Justica**
Servico de Documentacao, Rua Mexico 128, 6, 20000 Rio de Janeiro-RJ, Brazil.
- Brazil. Ministerio da Justica. Arquivos. q.

**Brazil. Ministerio da Marinha. Diretoria de Comunicacoes e Eletronica da Marinha**
Ilha das Cobras, Rio de Janeiro, G.B., Brazil.
- Previsoes Ionosfericas M U F. m. ISSN 0032-812X

**Brazil. Ministerio da Marinha. Servico de Documentacao Geral da Marinha**
Rua Dom Manuel N0. 15, Rio de Janeiro, Brazil.
- Navigator. s-a.
- Revista Maritima Brasileira. q. ISSN 0034-9860

**Brazil. Ministerio da Saude**
Servico de Divulgacao e Informacao, Avenida Brasil 4046, 20.000 Rio de Janeiro, Brazil.
- Revista Brasileira de Malariologia e Doencas Tropicais. q. ISSN 0034-7256 (prep. by its Divisao Tecnica)

**Brazil. Ministerio da Saude. Coordenacao de Assistencia Medica e Hospitalar**
Brasilia, Brazil.
- Brazil. Coordenacao de Assistencia Medica e Hospitalar. Cadastro Hospitalar Brasileiro. irreg.

**Brazil. Ministerio da Saude. Servico Nacional da Enfermidade Mental**
Avda. Pasteur 296, Rio de Janeiro GB, Pasteur 296, Brazil.
- Revista Brasileira de Saude Mental/Brazilian Journal of Mental Health. s-a. ISSN 0034-7337

**Brazil. Ministerio das Minas e Energia. Departamento Nacional da Producao Mineral**
Setor Autarquia Norte, Quadra 1 Bloco B, Brasilia D.F., Brazil.
- Anuario Mineral Brasileiro. a.
- Balanco Energetico Nacional. irreg.
- Brazil. Departamento Nacional da Producao Mineral.. Avulso. irreg.
- Brazil. Departamento Nacional da Producao Mineral. Boletim. irreg.
- Carta Geologica do Brasil Ao Milionesimo. irreg.
- Destaques. irreg.

**Brazil. Ministerio das Relacoes Exteriores**
Brasilia, Brazil.
- Brazil Trade and Industry. s-a.
- Comercio Exterior. (pub. by Editora Abril Ltda.)

**Brazil. Ministerio das Relacoes Exteriores, Biblioteca. Servico de Documentao**
70000 Brasilia, Brazil.
- Brazil. Ministerio das Relacoes Exteriores. Biblioteca. Bibliografia Anual. a. ISSN 0068-0834

**Brazil. Ministerio das Relacoes Exteriores. Divisao de Documentacao Diplomatica. Biblioteca**
70000 Brasilia, D.F., Brazil.
- Brazil. Ministerio das Relacoes Exteriores. Divisao de Documentacao Diplomatica. Biblioteca. Aquisicoes Bibliograficas. irreg.

**Brazil. Ministerio de Educacao e Cultura. Instituto Nacional de Estudos e Pesquisas Educacionais**
Rua Voluntarios da Patria 107, Rio de Janeiro, Brazil.
- Brazil. Instituto Nacional de Estudos e Pesquisas Educacionais. Conferencia Nacional de Educacao. Anais. irreg. ISSN 0068-080X
- Revista Brasileira de Estudos Pedagogicos. q. ISSN 0034-7183 (prep. by its Centro Brasileiro de Pesquisas Educacionais)

**Brazil. Ministerio do Interior**
Brasilia, Brazil.
- Brazil. Ministerio do Interior. Relatorio Sintetico, Andamento do Programa de Irrigacao do Nordeste. irreg.

**Brazil. Ministerio do Interior. Secretaria Geral**
Brasilia, Brazil.
- Brazil. Ministerio do Interior. Relatorio de Atividades. irreg.

**Brazil. Ministerio do Trabalho e Previdencia Social. Centro de Documentacao e Informatica**
Rio de Janeiro, Brazil.
- Brazil. Ministerio do Trabalho e Previdencia Social. Centro de Documentacao e Informatica. Mercado de Trabalho: Flutuacao. irreg.
- Brazil. Ministerio do Trabalho e Providencia Social. Centro de Documentacao e Informatica. Boletim Tecnico. q.

**Brazil. Ministerio do Trabalho, Industria e Comercio**
Caixa Postal 90, Lapa, Rio de Janeiro, Brazil.
- Brazil. Ministerio do Trabalho, Industria e Comercio. Boletim. q.

**Brazil. Ministerio dos Transportes. Departamento Nacional de Estradas de Rodagem**
- Pesquisa Rodoviaria. Documentacao e Informacoes. (pub. by Instituto de Pesquisas Rodoviarias)

**Brazil. Ministerio dos Transportes. Operacao Maua**
- Opema Em Ritmo de Brasil Jovem. (pub. by Editora Promocoes e Publicidade, Assessoria de Relacoes Publicas Ltda.)

**Brazil. Observatorio Nacional**
Rua General Bruce, 586, Sao Cristovao, Rio de Janeiro, G.B., Brazil.
- Observatorio Nacional Rio de Janeiro. Anuario. a.
- Observatorio Nacional, Rio de Janeiro. Relatorios Preliminares. irreg., 1969, no. 5. ISSN 0080-3138

- Observatorio Nacional, Rio de Janeiro. Servico Astronomico. Publicacoes. irreg. ISSN 0080-3146
- Observatorio Nacional, Rio de Janeiro. Servico Gravimetrico. Publicacoes. irreg., 1968, no. 1. ISSN 0080-3154
- Observatorio Nacional, Rio de Janeiro. Servico Magnetico. Publicacoes. irreg. ISSN 0080-3162

**Brazil. Rede Ferroviaria Federal. Departamento Geral de Estadistica**
Rio de Janeiro, Brazil.
- Sistema Ferroviario R F F S A. irreg.

**Brazil. Rede Ferroviaria Federal. Regional do Nordeste**
Rua Dona Maria Cesar 170 1 Andar, Recife, Brazil.
- Informativo RN.

**Brazil. Rede Ferroviaria Federal. Superintendencia Geral de Coordenacao e de Planejamento**
Rio de Janeiro, Brazil.
- Rede Ferroviaria Federal. Lista de Artigos Selecionados. q.

**Brazil. Secretaria da Agricultura. Coordenadoria da Pesquisa de Recursos Naturais**
Secao de Biblioteca, Av. Francisco Matarazzo, 455, 05001 Sao Paulo, S.P., Brazil.
- Instituto de Pesca, Sao Paulo. Boletim. irreg. ISSN 0046-9939 (prep. by its Instituto de Pesca)
- Instituto de Pesca, Sao Paulo. Boletim. Serie de Divulgacao. irreg. (prep. by its Instituto de Pesca)

**Brazil. Secretaria da Agricultura. Instituto de Zootecnia**
Rua Heitor Penteado 56, Caixa Postal 60, 13460 Nova Odessa (SP), Brazil.
- Boletim de Industria Animal. s-a. ISSN 0067-9615
- Zootecnia. q. ISSN 0044-5320

**Brazil. Secretaria da Agricultura. Instituto Florestal**
C.P. 1322, Sao Paulo 01000, Brazil.
- Instituto Florestal. Boletim Tecnico. irreg.

**Brazil. Secretaria da Receita Federal. Centro de Informacoes Economico- Fiscais**
Esplanada dos Ministerios, Bloco 5, 70000 Brasilia, Brazil.
- Brazil. Centro de Informacoes Economico-Fiscais. Imposto Sobre Produtos Industrializados; Arrecadacao Setorial. a.
- Brazil. Secretaria da Receita Federal. Centro de Informacoes Economico-Fiscais. Estatisticas Tributarias Basicas. m.
- Brazil. Secretaria da Receita Federal. Centro de Informacoes Economico-Fiscais. Rendas Aduaneiras. a.

**Brazil. Secretaria de Coordenacao e Planejamento. Fundacao de Economia e Estatistica**
Rua Siqueira Campos 1044, 4 Andar, Box 2355, 90000 Porto Alegre, Brazil.
- Rio Grande do Sul. Secretaria de Coordenacao e Planejamento. Indicadores Sociais R S. s-a. ISSN 0301-8156
- Rio Grande do Sul, Brazil. Fundacao de Economia e Estatistica. Boletim Estatistico do Seite. s-a.

**Brazil. Secretaria de Estado de Educacao de Cultura**
Rua Ulhoa Cintra s/n, Recife-Pernambuco, Brazil.
- Revista de Educacao e Cultura. a. ISSN 0482-5527

**Brazil. Secretaria de Obras Publicas**
Av. Erasmo Braga 118, 16 Andar, C.P. 2536, Rio de Janeiro, GB, Brazil.
- Revista de Engenharia do Estado da Guanabara. q. ISSN 0034-8104

**Brazil. Secretaria de Planejamento da Presidencia da Republica**
Av. Presidente Antonio Carlos 375/604, Brazil.
- Brazil. Secretaria de Planeyamento da Presidencia da Republica. Planejamento & Desenvolvimento. m.

**Brazil. Secretaria de Planejamento. Instituto de Planejamento Economico e Social**
Rua Melvin Jones 5, ZC-00 Centro, Rio de Janeiro, Brazil.
- Boletim Economico. irreg.
- Brazilian Economic Studies. irreg.
- I P E A Serie Monografica. irreg.
- Instituto de Planejamento Economico e Social. Boletim. bi-m.
- Instituto de Planejamento Economico e Social. Estudos para O Planejamento. irreg.
- Instituto de Planejamento Economico e Social. Relatorios de Pesquisa. irreg.
- Pesquisa e Planejamento Economico. 3 per yr.
- Serie Pensamento Economico Brasileiro. irreg.

**Brazil. Secretaria do Saneamento, Habitacao e Obras**
Av. Cruz Cabuga 1111-St. Amaro, Recife, Pernambuco, Brazil.
- Brazil. Secretaria do Saneamento, Habitacao e Obras. Boletim Tecnico. bi-m. ISSN 0006-9469

**Brazil. Secretaria-Geral do Exercito**
Brasilia-DF, SMU, Brazil.
- Revista Militar Brasileira. s-a. ISSN 0035-0125

**Brazil. Senado Federal**
Praca dos Tres Poderes, 7000 Brasilia D.F., Brazil.
- Brazil. Senado Federal. Subsecretaria de Edicoes Tecnicas. Catalogo de Publicacoes. 10 per yr. (prep. by its Subsecretaria de Edicoes Tecnicas)
- Revista de Informacao Legislativa. q. ISSN 0034-835X (prep. by its Subsecretaria de Edicoes Tecnicas)

**Brazil. Servico de Estatistica da Educacao e Cultura**
Rio de Janeiro, Brazil.
- Brazil. Servico de Estatistica da Educacao e Cultura Sinopse Estatistica do Ensino Primario. irreg.

**Brazil. Servico Federal de Processamento de Dados**
Biblioteca, Rua Teixeira de Freitas, 31, Rio de Janerio 20000, Brazil.
- Dados e Ideias. bi-m.

**Brazil. Servico Social do Comercio**
Av. General Justo 307, Rio de Janeiro, Brazil.
- Brazil. Servico Social do Comercio. Boletim Bibliografico. s-a.
- Brazil. Servico Social do Comercio. Boletim de Intercambio. s-a.
- Colecao Bibliografica. a.

**Brazil. Servico Social do Comercio. Administracao Regional do Estado de Sao Paulo**
Rua Dr. Vila Nova, 228, Sao Paulo, Brazil.
- Brazil. Servico Social do Comercio. Administracao Regional do Estado de Sao Paulo. Relatoria Annual. a.

**Brazil. Servico Social do Comercio. Divisao de Documentacao e Intercambio**
Av. General Justo 307, Rio de Janeiro, Brazil.
- Brazil. Servico Social do Comercio. Documento. q.

**Brazil. Superintendencia do Desenvolvimento da Amazonia**
Travessa Antonio Baena 1113, Caixa Postal 874, Belem-Para, Brazil.
- Brazil. Superintendencia do Desenvolvimento da Amazonia. S U D A M Documenta. q. ISSN 0045-2742
- Documentacao Amazonica; catalogo coletivo. irreg. (Prepared by: Rede de Bibliotecas da Amazonia)

**Brazil. Superintendencia do Desenvolvimento da Amazonia. Departamento Administrativo**
Biblioteca, C. Postal 874, Belem, Brazil.
- S U D A M. Biblioteca. Informa. bi-m. ISSN 0036-1992 (prep. by its Servico de Documentacao e Divulgacao)

**Brazil. Superintendencia do Desenvolvimento da Regiao Sul**
Rua Caldas Junior 120-20, Porto Alegre, Rio Grande do Sul, Brazil.
- Centro Regional de Pesquisas Educacionais Jaoa Pinheiro. Boletim Informativo. 3 per yr. ISSN 0009-014X

- Servicio Nacional de Aprendizagem Comercial. Departamento Regional do Parana. Pesquisa do Mercado de Trabalho. (pub. by Servico Nacional de Appendizagem Comerical - SENAC)

**Brazil. Superintendencia do Desenvolvimento do Nordeste**
Edificio Entreposto Federal de Pesca, Cais de Santa Rita, 8 Andar, Recife, Pernambuco, Brazil.
- Boletim de Estudos de Pesca. 3 per yr. ISSN 0006-5927
- Equipe; revista dos servidores da Sudene. m. ISSN 0046-239X
- Sudene Informa. q. ISSN 0039-453X

**Brazil. Superintendencia do Desenvolvimento do Nordeste. Coordenacao de Informatica**
Caixa Postal No. 960, Recife, Brazil.
- Brazil. Superintendencia do Desenvolvimento do Nordeste. Coordenacao de Informatica. Boletim de Informatica. irreg.

**Brazil. Superintendencia do Desenvolvimento do Nordeste. Departamento de Agricultura e Abastecimento**
Av. Professor Moraes Rego, Edificio S U D E N E, 50000 Recife, Pernambuco, Brazil.
- Brazil. S U D E N E. Departamento de Agricultura e Abastecimento. s-a.
- Brazil. Superintendencia do Desenvolvimento do Nordeste. Departamento de Agricultura e Abastecimento. Programa de Trabalho para a Agricultura Nordestina. irreg.
- Plano Anual de Trabalho do D A A. (Plano Anual de Trabalho do Departamento de Agricultura e Abastecimento) a.

**Brazil. Superintendencia do Desenvolvimento do Nordeste. Departamento de Recursos Naturais**
Av. Dantas Barreto. Recife, Pernambuco, Brazil.
- Brazil. Superintendencia do Desenvolvimento do Nordeste. Departamento de Recursos Naturais. Boletim de Recursos Naturais. a.

**Brazil. Superintendencia do Desenvolvimento do Nordeste. Departamento de Servicos Basicos da Sudene**
Av. Prof. Moraes Rego, Edf. da Sudene, Cidade Universitaria, Brazil.
- Brazil. Superintendencia do Desenvolvimento do Nordeste. Departamento de Servicos Basicos da Sudene. Estatistica de Trafego No Nordeste. a.

**Brazil. Superintendencia Nacional da Marinha Mercante. Assessoria de Relacoes Publicas**
Av. Rio Branco, 115 - 5 Andar, Rio de Janeiro, Brazil.
- Marinha Mercante. bi-m.

**Brazil. Supremo Tribunal Federal**
Departamento de Imprensa Nacional, Brasilia, Brazil.
- Brazil. Indices da Legislacao Federal. a.
- Brazil. Supremo Tribunal Federal. Jurisivel do S.T.F. (pub. by Cultural Distribuidora de Livros)
- Revista Trimestral de Jurisprudencia. q. ISSN 0035-0540

**Brazil. Tribunal Regional do Trabalho**
3rd Region, Rua Curitiba, 835, 3 Andar, Belo Horizonte, Brazil.
- Minas Gerais, Brazil. Tribunal Regional do Trabalho. Tercero Region. Revista. biennial. ISSN 0076-8855

**Brazilian College of Angiology**
Caixa Postal 104-07, Copacabana, Rio de Janeiro, Brazil.
- Angiopatias; revista brasileira de angiologia. q. ISSN 0003-3200

**Brazilian Institute of Economic Studies**
- Brazil Development Series/Series Desenvolvimento Brasileiro. (pub. by TELEPRESS Servicos de Imprensa, Ltda.)

**British Chamber of Commerce in Brazil**
Box 1621, Sao Paulo, Brazil.
- British Chamber of Commerce in Brazil. Information Circular. s-m. ISSN 0007-0408

**Empresa C I L U de Jornalismo**
Rua Sen. Paulo Egidio 15, Suite 501, Sao Paulo - 1, Brazil.
- Vigilante. w. ISSN 0042-5982

BRAZIL 95

**Editora C Q, Ltda.**
Avda. Fagundes Filho 343, Caixa Postal 8034, 04004 Sao Paulo, Brazil.
- Atualidades Agroveterinarias. bi-m. (Sociedade Paulista de Medicina Veterinaria)
- Avicultura Industrial. m. ISSN 0009-0905

**Camara Brasileira do Livro. Centro de Catalogacao-na-Fonte**
Av. Ipiranga, 1267, 10 andar, Sao Paulo 01039, Brazil.
- Camara Brasileira do Livro. Centro de Catalogacao-na-Fonte. Oficina de Livros: Novidades Cataloga das na Fonte. irreg.

**Campina Grande, Brazil. Comissao Cultural do Municipio Prefeitura**
Municipal de Campina Grande, Paraiba, Brazil.
- Revista Campinense de Cultura. q. ISSN 0034-7353

**Campinas, Brazil. Instituto Agronomico. Servico de Divulgacao Tecnico-Cientifica**
Caixa Postal 28, 13100 Campinas, Sao Paulo, Brazil.
- Agronomico. bi-m. ISSN 0044-6866

**Campo**
Rua Sao Pedro 733, 3 Andar, Porto Alegre, Brazil.
- Campo; revista mensal de temas agropecuarios. m. ISSN 0008-2465

**Empresa Grafica Carazinhense Ltda.**
C.P. 92, Avenida Flores da Cunha 1603, Carazinho RS, Brazil.
- Noticioso; jornal trissemanal independente. 3 per wk.

**Casa e Jardim**
Avda. Casper Libero 383, Sao Paulo, Brazil.
- Casa e Jardim. m.

**Centrais Eletricas Brazileiras S.A. Assessoria de Relacoes Publicas de Eletrobras**
Avenida Rio Branco 52, 18 Andar, Rio de Janeiro, Brazil.
- Revista Brasileira de Energia Eletrica. q. ISSN 0034-7159

**Centro Academico Piraja da Silva. Faculdade de Ciencias Medicas e Biologicas de Botucatu**
C.P. 102, Botucatu, S.P., Brazil.
- Ciencia. irreg. ISSN 0084-8794

**Centro Brasileiro de Cooperacao e Intercambio de Servicos Socials**
Av. General Justo 305-307, Rio de Janeiro GB ZC-39, Brazil.
- Debates Sociais. s-a.

**Centro Brasileiro de Dinamica Populacional e Reproducao Humana**
Box 1289, Rio de Janeiro, Brazil.
- Journal Brasileiro de Ginecologia.

**Centro Brasileiro de Estudos Demograficos**
- Boletim Demografico CBED. (pub. by Fundacao Instituto Brasileiro de Geografia e Estatistica)

**Centro Brasileiro de Pesquisas Educacionais**
Instituto Nacional de Estudos e Pesquisas Educacionais, Rua Voluntarios da Patria 107, Caixa Postal 1-68 Botafogo, Rio de Janeiro, Brazil.
- Bibliografia Brasileira de Educacao. q. ISSN 0067-6632

**Centro da Industria do Espirito Santo**
- Anuario Industrial do Espirito Santo. (pub. by Federacao das Industrias do Estado do Espirito Santo)

**Centro de Estudos Cientificos**
Caixa Postal 11585, Sao Paulo - SP, Brazil.
- C E C. Revista. m. ISSN 0034-7361

**Centro de Estudos da Clinica Infantil do Ipiranga**
Avda Nazare 1361, Sao Paulo, Brazil.
- Pediatria Pratica; revista de puericultura e clinica infantil. fortn. ISSN 0031-3947 (Sociedade de Pediatria de Sao Paulo)

**Centro de Estudos e Acao Social**
Rua Aristides Novis 101, Salvador, Bahia, Brazil.
- Centro de Estudos e Acao Social. Cadernos do C.E.A.S. bi-m.

**Centro de Estudos Rurais e Urbanos**
Cidade Unversitaria, Caixa Postal 8105, Sao Paulo, Brazil.
- Cadernos de Estudos Rurais e Urbanos. a.

**Centro de Investigacao e Documentacao**
Caixa Postal 23, Petropolis, Rio de Janeiro, Brazil.
- Bibliografia Classificada. bi-m. ISSN 0006-0992

**Centro de Linguistica Aplicada**
Av. 9 de Julho, 3166, Sao Paulo, Brazil.
- Estudos Linguisticos; revista brasileira de linguistica teorica e aplicada. s-a.

**Centro de Orientacao e Selecao Psicotencia**
Rua Jacinto Gomes 540, Porto Algre (R.S.), Brazil.
- Cadernos de Psicologia Aplicada. s-a.

**Centro de Pesquisas Socio-Economicas**
Divisao de Documentacao, Rua Jose Paranagua, 200, Caixa Postal 378, Manaus, Brazil.
- Universidade do Amazonas. Centro de Pesquisas Socio-Economicas. Boletim Tecnico Informativo. irreg.

**Centro de Relacoes Publicas da Aeronautica**
Av. Churchill, No. 157-11o, Rio de Janeiro, Brazil.
- Aerovisao. m. (Brazil. Ministerio da Aeronautica)

**Centro do Comercio de Cafe do Rio de Janeiro**
Rua da Quitanda 191-10 And., Rio de Janeiro, Brazil.
- Revista do Comercio de Cafe. m. ISSN 0034-9224

**Centro dos Inspetores Federais de Ensino do Estado de Sao Paulo**
Praca da Se 108, 5 Andar-Sala 501, Sao Paulo, Brazil.
- Ensino Secundario. ISSN 0013-8614

**Centro Educacional**
Av. Ernai do Amaral Peixoto, 836, Niteroi, Brazil.
- Cadernos Pedagogicos. q.

**Centro Latino Americano de Fisica**
Av. Wenceslau Braz, 71, 20.000 Rio de Janeiro ZC-82, Brazil.
- Centro Latino Americano de Fisica Noticia. m. ISSN 0009-0050

**Centro Latino-Americano de Pesquisas em Ciencias Sociais**
Caixa Postal 12, 20000 ZC-02 Rio de Janeiro RJ, Brazil.
- America Latina. irreg. ISSN 0002-709X

**Centro Nacional de Pesquisas Habitacionais**
Departamento de Documentacao e Intecambio Cientifico, R. Marques de Sao Vicente 225, Rio de Janeiro GB, Brazil.
- C E N P H A. Boletim. bi-m. ISSN 0007-8263

**Editora Chacara e Quintais, Ltda.**
*see* Editora C Q, Ltda.

**Circulo de Estudos Linguisticos**
Universidade Estadual de Londrina, Centro de Ciencias Humanas, Caixa Postal 2003, Londrina, Brazil.
- Boletim de Linquistica. irreg.

**Cleveland Ltda.**
Av. Amaral Peixoto, 207, Gr. 811, Niteroi, Brazil.
- Estado do Rio: Industria & Comercio. (Federacao das Industrias do Estado do Rio de Janeiro)

**Clube de Engenharia**
Av. Rio Branco 124, Rio de Janeiro, Gb, Brazil.
- Grandes Vultos da Engenharia Brasileira. a.

**Clube Naval. Departamento Cultural**
Av. Rio Branco, 180, Rio de Janeiro, Brazil.
- Clube Naval Revista. bi-m.

**Codecri Ltda.**
Rua Saint Romain 142, ZC-37 Copacabana, Brazil.
- Pasquim. w. ISSN 0556-350X

**Colegio Anchieta. Centro de Estudos Sociais**
Nuova Friburgo, Brazil.
- Arquivo Social; revista de cultura social. q.

**Colegio Militar do Rio de Janeiro**
Rua Sao Francisco Xavier 267 - ZC-11, Rio de Janeiro, Brazil.
- Colegio Militar do Rio de Janeiro. Revista Didactica. a. ISSN 0080-3103

**Empresa Jornalistica a Comarca de Suzano**
Travessa Mirambawa 408, Suzano, Sao Paulo, Brazil.
- Comarca de Suzano. w. ISSN 0010-2105

**Comissao de Integracao Eletrica Regional. Sub-Comite de Operacao e Mantencao de Sistemas Eletricos**
Sao Paulo, Brazil.
- Comissao de Integracao Eletrica Regional. Informe do Coordenador Tecnico; operacao e mantencao dos sistemas eletricos nos paises membros da CIER. a.

**Comissao Estadual de Planejamento Agricola**
Paraiba, Brazil.
- Aspectos Gerais e Principais Tendencias da Agropecuaria Paraibana. a.

**Comite Nacional Brasileiro da Conferencia Mundial da Energia**
Av. Presidente Vargas, 642-11 Andar, Rio de Janeiro, Brazil.
- Estatistica Brasileira de Energia/Brazilian Energy Statistics. s-a. ISSN 0512-350X

**Companhia Brasileira de Armazenamento**
Palacio do Desenvolvimento, Brasilia, Brazil.
- Armazenagem. irreg.

**Companhia de Desenvolvimento Industrial e Comercial do Rio Grande do Sul. Departamento de Estudos e Projetos**
Porto Alegre, Rio Grande do Sul, Brazil.
- Perfil da Carne Bovina. irreg.

**Companhia de Eletricidade de Brasilia**
Quadra 04-Bloco A, Lotes 106 e 136, Brasilia-DF, Brazil.
- Companhia de Electricidade de Brasilia. Relatorio das Atividades.

**Companhia Paranaense de Energia Eletrica. Assesoria de Planejamento**
Rua Cel. Dulcidio, 800 Curitiba, 80000 Parana, Brazil.
- C O P E L. Boletim Estatistico Mensal. m.
- Companhia Paranaense de Energia Eletrica. Informe Estatistico Anual. a.

**Companhia Paulista de Force e Luz. Assessoria de Planejamento e Gestao Empresarial**
Avenida Angelica, 2565, Sao Paulo, Brazil.
- Companhia Paulista de Forca e Luz. Assessoria de Planejamento e Gestao Empresarial. Relatorio Estatistico Anual; acompanhamento do mercado de energia eletrica. a.

**Confederacao Brasileira de Desportos**
Rua da Alfandega, 70, Rio de Janeiro, Brazil.
- Confederacao Brasileira de Desportos. Relatorio. irreg.

**Confederacao Nacional da Industria**
Avenida Nilo Pecanha, 50 Ed. "Rodolpho de Paoli", 25 Andar-Grupo 2512, Rio de Janeiro, Guanabara, Brazil.
- Industria & Produtividade. m. ISSN 0019-7718

**Confederacao Nacional da Industria. Departamento Economico**
Rua Santa Luzia 735, Rio de Janeiro, Brazil.
- Estudos Economicos. q.

**Confederacao Nacional do Comercio**
Avenida General Justo 307, 3 Andar, ZC-39, Rio de Janeiro, Brazil.
- Comercio & Mercados. m. ISSN 0010-227X (Co-Sponsors: Servico Social do Comercio, Servico Nacional de Aprendizagem Comercial)
- Confederacao Nacional do Comercio. Assessoria Juridica. Boletim Informativo. w.
- Confederacao Nacional do Comercio. Divisao de Divulgacao. Carta Mensal. bi-m. ISSN 0588-9979

**Confederacao Nacional dos Trabalhadores Em Comunicacoes e Publicidade**
Edificio Serra Dourada, Conj. 705, Brasilia, Brazil.
- Confederacao Nacional dos Trabalhadores Em Comunicacoes e Publicidade. Relatorio Anual. a.

**Congregacao do Santissimo Redentor**
- Santuario de Aparecida. (pub. by Editora Santuario)

**Conselho Estadual de Educacao de Sao Paulo**
Avenida Rio Branco 1260, Caixa Postal 30.630, Sao Paulo, Brazil.
- Conselho Estadual de Educacao de Sao Paulo. Acta. 6 per yr. ISSN 0010-6410

**Conselho Federal de Cultura**
Palacio da Cultura, Rua de Imprensa, 16-70. and., Rio de Janeiro, Brazil.
- Conselho Federal de Cultura. Boletim. q.

**Conselho Nacional de Desenvolvimento Cientifico e Tecnologico**
- Revista Brasileira de Tecnologia. (pub. by Editora Edgard Bluecher Ltda)

**Conselho Nacional de Economia**
Rua SenadorDantas 74, Rio de Janeiro, Brazil.
- Brazil. Conselho Nacional de Economia. Revista. 3 per yr.(approx.) ISSN 0006-937X

**Conselho Nacional de Pesquisas**
Caixa Postal 60, Piracicaba, Sao Paulo, Brazil.
- Revista de Agricultura. 4 per yr. ISSN 0034-7655

**Conselho Nacional de Pesquisas, Sociedade Brasileira de Geologia**
- Revista Brasileira de Geociencias. (pub. by Editora Edgard Bluecher Ltda.)

**Cooperacao Editora Ltda.**
Rua Teodoro Sampaio 2550, Sao Paulo, Brazil.
- Agricultura Brasileira. m. (Cooperativa Agricola de Cotia)

**Cooperativa Agricola de Cotia**
- Agricultura Brasileira. (pub. by Cooperacao Editora Ltda.)

**Cooperativa Central de Laticinios do Estado de Sao Paulo**
Rua Gomes Cardim 532, Sao Paulo, Brazil.
- Balde Branco. m. ISSN 0005-4275

**Coordenadorias de Planejamento e de Acao Regional**
Av. Angelica 2223, 12 Andar, 01227 Sao Paulo 16, Brazil.
- Sao Paulo, Brazil (State). Secretaria de Economia e Planejamento. Conjuntura Regional: 10a. Regiao Administrativa. bi-m.

**Editora dos Criadores Ltda.**
Avenida Pompeia 1214, Fundos B, 05022 Sao Paulo, Brazil.
- Revista dos Criadores. m. ISSN 0034-9259 (Associacao Paulista de Criadores de Bovinos)

**Cruzeiro**
Rua do Livramento 179-203, Rio de Janeiro, Brazil.
- Cruzeiro. w. ISSN 0011-2216

**Cultural Distribuidora de Livros**
Rua Sergipe, No. 1.466, Sao Joaquim da Barra, Brazil.
- Brazil. Supremo Tribunal Federal. Juriscivel do S.T.F. irreg.

**Editora Delta**
Av. Almirante Barroso 263-26 andar, Rio de Janeiro, Brazil.
- Annuario Delta-Larousse. a.

**Diagrama Comunicacoes**
Rua Arthur de Azevedo, Sao Paulo 05405, Brazil.
- Anuario A B D I B. a. (Associacao Brasileira para o Desenvolvimento das Industrias de Base)

**Diarios Associados**
Folha de Goias, Avenida Goias No 17, Goiania-Goias, Brazil.
- Informacao Agricola. w. ISSN 0019-9729 (Brazil. Ministerio da Agricultura)

**Diocese de Petropolis**
Rua Santos Dumont 571, 25600 Petropolis, Rio de Janeiro, Brazil.
- Acao. m. ISSN 0001-4400

**Divulgacao da Pesca Maritima Ltda.**
Box 716, Av. Onze de Junho 370, 04041 Sao Paulo, Brazil.
- Revista Nacional da Pesca. m. ISSN 0035-0214

**Editora Dois Irmaos Ltda**
Rua Caninde 24, 20000 Rio de Janeiro, Brazil.
- Revista Brasileira de Patologia Clinica. bi-m. ISSN 0034-7302 (Sociedade Brasileira de Patologia Clinica)

**Edece-Edicoes Culturais Ltda.**
R. Brasilio Machado, 91, Sao Paulo - SP, Brazil.
- Coopercotia. m. ISSN 0010-8529
- Mundo Economico. m. ISSN 0027-3287

**Edicao S.A.**
Rua Dr. Virgilio de Carvalho Pinto 625, Pinheiros, Sao Paulo, Brazil.
- Movimento. 10 per yr.

**Editora de Guias Ltda.**
Av. Paulista 1776, 01310 Sao Paulo, Brazil.
- Sinal; registro de marcas e simbolos. irreg.

**Editora Ementario Forense Ltda.**
Rua da Lapa 180, Rio de Janeiro, Brazil.
- Ementario Forense; repositorio de jurisprudencia dos triunais brasileiros e de legislacao federal. m. ISSN 0013-6638

**Empreiteiro Ltda**
Caixa Postal 30165, Sao Paulo, Brazil.
- Empreiteiro. irreg.

**Empresa Brasileira de Pesquisa Agropecuaria**
Km 47, 20000 Rio de Janeiro RJ, ZC - 26, Brazil.
- Pesquisa Agropecuaria Brasileira. Serie Agronomia/Brazilian Journal of Agricultural and Veterinary Research. Agronomy Series. s-a. (Brazil. Ministerio da Agricultura)
- Pesquisa Agropecuaria Brasileira. Serie Veterinaria-Zootecnia/Brazilian Journal of Agricultural and Veterinary Research. Animal Husbandry Series. s-a. (Brazil. Ministerio da Agricultura)

**Empresa de Pesquisa Agropecuaria de Minas Gerais**
Rua Espirito Santo, 495-8 andar, 30000 Belo Horizonte, Brazil.
- Informe Agropecuario: Conjuntura e Estatistica. m.

**Empresa de Pesquisa Agropecuaria de Minas Gerais. Biblioteca**
Caixa Postal 515, Belo Horizonte (MG), Brazil.
- Agricolas. s-a.

**Engetec Ltda.**
Rua Nestor Pestana 125, Sao Paulo, Brazil.
- Engenharia Civil. m.
- Engenharia na Industria. m.

**Escola de Administracao de Empresas de Sao Paulo. Servico de Publicacoes**
- Revista de Administracao de Empresas. (pub. by Fundacao Getulio Vargas)

**Escola do Rio de Janeiro. Centro de Estudos da Maternidade**
Av. Almirante Barroso 63, Caixa Postal 1289, ZC 00 - 20000 Rio de Janeiro, Brazil.
- Jornal Brasileiro de Ginecologia. m.

**Editora do Escritor Ltda**
Rua Senador Vlaquer 133, 04744 Sao Paulo, Brazil.
- Colecao Editora do Escritor Em Revista. irreg.

**Espirito Santo. Empresa de Assistencia Tecnica e Extensao Rural**
Rua Afonso Sarlo 160, Bento Ferreira, Caixa Postal 644, 29000 Vitoria E.S., Brazil.
- Agricultor. bi-m.

**Etegil-Edit.Tecn.Graf.Ind.Ltda.**
R. Santa Ifigenia 180, Cx. Postal 30869, Sao Paulo, Brazil.
- Electron; revista de engenharia electronica. bi-m. ISSN 0013-4740
- Electronica. bi-m. ISSN 0013-502X

**Ex-Editora**
Rua Santo Antonio 1043, CP 01314, Sao Paulo, Brazil.
- Ex. irreg.

**Editora Expansao Ltda.**
Rua Livramento 109, Caixa Postal 30329, Sao Paulo, Brazil.
- Atualidades Medicas. m. ISSN 0001-1800
- Clinica Geral; revista de clinica medica. m. ISSN 0009-9015

**Editora F T D**
C.P. 30402, Rua do Lavapes 1023, Sao Paulo, Brazil.
- Constructura. q. (Universidade Catolica do Parana. Departamento de Letras)

**Edicoes F U C M T**
Av. Mato Grosso 491, Caixa Postal 801, Campo Grande, Mato Grosso, Brazil, Brazil.
- Estudos Universitarios. a. (Faculdades Unidas Catolicas de Mato Grosso. Faculdade Dom Aquino de Filosofia, Ciencias e Letras)

**Faculdade de Ciencias Medicas da Santa Casa de Sao Paulo**
Rua Dr. Cesario Motta Jr. 112, 01221 Sao Paulo, Brazil.
- Arquivos dos Hospitais e da Faculdade de Ciencias Medicas da Santa Casa de Sao Paulo. q. ISSN 0018-5442

**Faculdade de Farmacia e Odontologia de Ribeirao Preto**
Caixa Postal 241, 14100 Ribeirao Preto, Sao Paulo, Brazil.
- Faculdade de Farmacia e Odontologia de Ribeirao Preto- Revista. s-a.

**Faculdade de Filosofia, Ciencias e Letras de Araraquara. Cadeira de Politica**
Praca Santos Dumont, Caixa Postal 174, Araraquara, Brazil.
- Faculdade de Filosofia, Ciencias e Letras de Araraquara. Cadeira de Politica. Boletim. m.

**Faculdade de Filosofia, Ciencias e Letras de Araraquara. Cadeira de Sociologia e Fundamentos Sociologicos da Educao**
Praca Santos Dumont, C.P. 174, Araraquara, S.P., Brazil.
- Faculdade de Filosofia, Ciencias e Letras de Araraquara. Cadeira de Sociologia e Fundamentos Sociologicos da Educao. Boletim. irreg.

**Faculdade de Filosofia, Ciencias e Letras de Assis**
Caixa Postal 335, 19800-Assis (S.P.), Brazil.
- Revista de Letras. a. ISSN 0080-2352

**Faculdade de Filosofia, Ciencias e Letras de Assis Departamento de Filosofia**
Caixa Postal 315, CP 19800, Assis, Brazil.
- Transformacao. a.

**Faculdade de Filosofia, Ciencias e Letras de Assis. Departamento de Historia**
Departamento de Historia, Caixa Postal 335, 19800 Assis SP, Brazil.
- Anais de Historia. a.

**Faculdade de Filosofia, Ciencias e Letras de Cataguases**
Praca Santa Rita 340, Cataguases (MG) 36770, Brazil.
- Totem. q.

**Faculdade de Filosofia, Ciencias e Letras de Marilia**
Caixa Postal 420, Marilia, SP, Brazil.
- Alfa. a. ISSN 0002-5216

**Faculdade de Filosofia de Mariana**
Mariana, Brazil.
- Rua Direita. irreg.

**Faculdade de Odontologia de Pernambuco. Biblioteca**
Av. General Newton Cavalcanti, 146, Caixa Postal 3615, Camarajibe, Pernambuco, Brazil.
- Pernambuco, Brazil (State). Faculdade de Odontologia. Revista. s-a. ISSN 0048-3419

**Faculdade Municipal de Ciencias Economicas e Administrativa de Osasco**
- Ciencias Economicas Sociais. (pub. by Editora Revista dos Tribunais)

**Faculdades Integradas Estacio de Sa**
- Lugar em Comunicacao. (pub. by Editora Rio)

**Faculdades Unidas Catolicas de Mato Grosso.**
**Faculdade Dom Aquino de Filosofia, Ciencias e**
**Letras**
- Estudos Universitarios. (pub. by Edicoes F U C M T)

**Federacao Brasileira das Sociedades de**
**Otorinolaringologia e Broncoesofagologia**
Rua Sao Bento 181, Sao Paulo SP, Brazil.
- Revista Brasileira de Oto-Rino-Laringologia. bi-m. ISSN 0034-7299

**Federacao Brasileira de Associacao de Bibliotecarios**
40 rua Avanhandava, Conj. 110, Sao Paulo, Brazil.
- Revista Brasileira de Biblioteconomia e Documentacao. m.

**Federacao Brasileira de Medicina Desportiva. Centro**
**de Documentacao e Informacao Em Ciencias do**
**Esporte**
Av. Sen. Salgado Filho, 135 - 6, 90000 Porto Alegre, R.S., Brazil.
- Medicina do Esporte. q.

**Federacao das Industrias**
Av. Nazare, 759, Belem, Para, Brazil.
- Cadastro Industrial do Para. irreg.

**Federacao das Industrias do Estado da Bahia**
Rua Miguel Calmon 39, Salvador, Bahia, Brazil.
- Cadastro Industrial da Bahia.

**Federacao das Industrias do Estado de Minas Gerais**
Av. Carandai 1115, Belo Horizonte, Brazil.
- Anuario Industrial de Minas Gerais. a. ISSN 0066-5231

**Federacao das Industrias do Estado do Espirito Santo**
Av. Princesa Isabel 54, Vitoria, Espirito Santo, Brazil.
- Anuario Industrial do Espirito Santo. irreg. (Centro da Industria do Espirito Santo)

**Federacao das Industrias do Estado do Rio de Janeiro**
- Estado do Rio: Industria & Comercio. (pub. by Cleveland Ltda.)

**Federacao das Industrias do Estado do Rio Grande do**
**Norte**
Av. Rio Branco, Natal Rio Grande do Norte, Brazil.
- Empresa. m.

**Federacao das Industrias do Estado do Rio Grande do**
**Sul**
Porto Alegre, Brazil.
- Seminario Nacional de Controle de Qualidade. Anais. irreg.

**Federacao dos Trabalhadores na Agricultura do**
**Estado do Parana**
Curitiba, Brazil.
- Federacao dos Trabalhadores na Agricultura do Estado do Parana. Relatorio. irreg.

**Federacao e Centro das Industrias do Estado de Sao**
**Paulo**
Viaduto Dona Paulina 80, Sao Paulo, Brazil.
- Industria e Desenvolvimento. m. ISSN 0019-7602

**Folclore do Maranhao**
Sao Luis, Maranhao, Brazil.
- Folclore do Maranhao. irreg.

**Folha Carioca Editora S.A.**
Rua Juan Cardoso 23, Cep 20000 Rio de Janeiro, Brazil.
- Anuario de Poetas do Brasil. a.

**Editora Fontana Ltda**
Rua Visconde de Piraja 430, Ipanema, ZC 37 Rio de Janeiro, Brazil
(Dist. by: Superbancas Ltda. rua Ubaldino do Amaral 42, Rio de Janeiro, Brazil)
- Jose; literatura-critica-arte. m.

**Fotoptica S-A**
- Novidades Fotoptica. (pub. by Editora Morumbi)

**Foyer Bulgare**
Caixa Postal 14590-ZC-95, Rio de Janeiro, Brazil
(Subscr. Also Through: Bulgarian Historical Institute, Chase Manhattan Bank, National Div., Madison Ave. at 64 St., N.Y. 10021)
- Bulgarian Review. a. ISSN 0007-3946

**Otto Frensel Material para Lacticinios Ltda.**
Caixa Postal 1283-ZC-00, 20000 Rio de Janeiro, R.J., Brazil.
- Boletim do Leite. m. ISSN 0006-5951

**Fundacao Armando Alvares Penteado. Faculdade de**
**Administracao**
Rua Alagoas 903, Sao Paulo, Brazil.
- Revista de Estudos de Administracao. irreg.

**Fundacao Carlos Chagas. Departamento de Pesquisas**
**Educacionais**
Rua Cardeal Arcoverde 1847, CEP05407, Sao Paulo, Brazil.
- Cadernos de Pesquisa. q.
- Fundacao Carlos Chagas. Departamento de Pesquisas Educacionais. Profissoes. irreg.
- Fundacao Carlos Chagas. Departamento de Pesquisas Educacionais. Simposios. a.
- Pesquisas Educacionais. a.

**Fundacao Casa Dr. Blumenau**
Alameda Duque de Caixas 64, Caixa Postal 425, 89100 Blumenau, Santa Catarina, Brazil.
- Blumenau em Cadernos. m. ISSN 0006-5218

**Fundacao Centro de Pesquisas Economicas e Sociais**
**do Piaui**
Teresina, Brazil.
- Fundacao Centro de Pesquisas Economicas e Sociais do Piaui. Relatorio de Atividades. irreg.

**Fundacao Cultural de Curitiba**
Curitiba, Brazil.
- Fundacao Cultural de Curitiba. Relatorio. irreg.

**Fundacao de Assistencia dos Municipios do Estado do**
**Parana**
Rua Mariano Torres, no. 135, Curitiba, Parana, Brazil.
- Fundacao de Assistencia dos Municipios do Estado do Parana. Boletim dos Municipios. irreg.

**Fundacao de Economia e Estatistica**
Rua Sigueira Campos 1044- 4 Andar, Box 2355, 90000 Porto Alegre, Brazil.
- Estudo de Deflatores para a Economia do Rio Grande do Sul. irreg.
- Fundacao de Economia e Estatistica. Indicadores Sociais R S. a.
- Rio Grande do Sul, Brazil. Fundacao de Economia e Estatistica. Indicadores Economicos RS. q.
- Sorgo - Uma Alternativa Economica. a.

**Fundacao Faculdade Catolica de Medicina. Centro**
**Academico XXII de Marco**
Rua Sarmento Leite, 245 S-402, 90000 Porto Alegre, Rio Grande do Sul, Brazil.
- Pesquisa Medica. bi-m. ISSN 0048-3567

**Fundacao Getulio Vargas**
Praia de Botafogo 190, Rio de Janeiro, Brazil
(Orders to: Caixa Postal 9052, Rio de Janeiro, Brazil)
- ALADA. 3 per yr. (Associacao Latin Americana di Direito Agrario)
- Arquivos Brasileiros de Psicologia Aplicada. q. ISSN 0004-2757
- Conjuntura Economica; economics and business conditions in Brazil. m (with semi-annual supplements) ISSN 0010-5945 (Instituto Brasileiro de Economia)
- Correio da Unesco. m.
- Forum Educacional. q. (Instituto de Estudos Avancados en Educacao)
- Fundacao Getulio Vargas. Informativo. m.
- Instituto Brasileiro de Economica. Centro de Estudos Agricolas. Agropecuaria. m.
- Revista Brasileira de Economia. q. ISSN 0034-7140 (Instituto Brasileiro de Economia)
- Revista de Administracao de Empresas. bi-m. ISSN 0034-7590 (Escola de Administracao de Empresas de Sao Paulo. Servico de Publicacoes)
- Revista de Administracao Publica. q. ISSN 0034-7612
- Revista de Ciencia Politica. q. ISSN 0034-8023 (Instituto de Direito Publico e Ciencia Politica)

**Fundacao Getulio Vargas. Servico de Publicacoes**
Praia de Botafogo 188, Rio de Janeiro-GB, Brazil.
- Revista de Direito Administrativo. q. ISSN 0034-8007 (Instituto de Direito Publico e Ciencia Politica)

**Fundacao Instituto Brasileiro de Geografia e**
**Estatistica**
Av. Beira Mar 436, Rio de Janeiro, Brazil.
- Atlas de Relacoes Internacionais. q.
- Boletim Demografico CBED. q. (Centro Brasileiro de Estudos Demograficos)
- Boletim Geografico. q. ISSN 0006-6028
- Brazil. Instituto Brasileiro de Geografia e Estatistica. Registro Industrial. irreg.
- Brazil. Instituto Brasileiro de Geografia e Estatistica. Veiculos Licenciados. a.
- Revista Brasileira de Estatistica. q. ISSN 0034-7175
- Revista Brasileira de Geografia. 4 times a year. ISSN 0034-723X

**Fundacao Instituto Brasileiro de Geografia e**
**Estatistica. Departmento de Estatisticas**
**Industriais, Comerciais e de Servicos**
Av. Franklin Roosevelt No 146a, Rio de Janeiro GB, Brazil.
- Anuario Estatistico do Brasil. a.
- Industrias de Transformacao: Pesquisa Mensal. irreg.
- Instituto Brasileiro de Geografia e Estatistica (IBGE). Departamento de Estatisticas Industriais, Comerciais e de Servicos. Comercio Interestadual, Esportacao Por Vias Internas. a.

**Fundacao Joao Pinheiro**
Equipe de Analise da Conjuntura, Av. Joao Pinheiro 146, Belo Horizonte, Brazil.
- Boletim de Conjuntura. m.

**Fundacao Metropolitana Paulista**
Av. Higienopolis, 890, CEP 01238 Sao Paulo, Brazil.
- Sao Paulo. w. ISSN 0036-4657

**Fundacao Nacional do Bem-Estar do Menor**
R. Visconde de Inhauma 39, C. Postal 3871, Rio de Janeiro, Brazil.
- Brasil Jovem. 4 per yr. ISSN 0006-9191

**Fundacao para o Livro do Cego no Brasil**
- Lente (Inkprint Edition) (pub. by Dorina de Gouvea Nowill)
- Relevo. (pub. by Dorina de Gouvea Nowill)

**Fundacao para o Progresso da Cirugia**
Caixa Postal 1574, Rua Pirapitinqui 80, Sao Paulo, Brazil.
- Anais Paulistas de Medicina e Cirurgia. bi-m. ISSN 0003-245X
- Sanatorio Sao Lucas. Boletim. bi-m. ISSN 0036-4258

**Fundacao Servicos de Saude Publica. Centro de**
**Investigacoes Epidemiologicas**
Av. Rio Branco 251, Rio de Janeiro GB, Brazil.
- Boletim Epidemiologico. s-m.

**Fundacao Zoobotanica do Rio Grande do Sul. Museu**
**de Ciencias Naturais**
Caixa Postal 1188, 90.000 Porto Alegre, Rio Grande do Sul, Brazil.
- Iheringia. Serie Antropologia. irreg., 1972, no. 2. ISSN 0073-4691
- Iheringia. Serie Botanica. irreg.; no. 22, 1977. ISSN 0073-4705
- Iheringia. Serie Divulgacao. irreg.; no. 5, 1976.
- Iheringia. Serie Geologia. irreg., 1971, no. 4. ISSN 0073-4713
- Iheringia. Serie Zoologia. irreg., no. 50, 1977. ISSN 0073-4721
- Natureza em Revista. s-a.

**Gazeta da Farmacia Ltda.**
Caixa Postal 528, Rio de Janeiro, Brazil.
- Gazeta da Farmacia. m. ISSN 0016-5409

**Gazeta de Pinheiros Ltda.**
Teodoro Sampaio 2216, Sao Paulo, Brazil.
- Gazeta de Pinheiros; semanario imparcial. w. ISSN 0016-5425

**Irmao di Giorgio**
Rua Caninde 32, Rio de Janeiro, Brazil.
- Arquivos Economicos. irreg. (Banco do Brasil S.A.)

**Goias, Brazil. Secretaria da Educacao e Cultura. Instituto Goiano de Folclore**
Praca Civica 13, 7400 Goiania, Goias, Brazil.
- Folclorica. q.

**Goias, Brazil. Secretaria da Industria e Comercio**
Praca Civica, Centro Administrativo, 70. Andar, Goiania, Brazil.
- Goias, Brazil. Secretaria da Industria e Comercio. S I C Informativo. fortn.

**Goias, Brazil. Secretaria do Planejamento e Coordenacao**
Goiania, Brazil.
- Goias, Brazil. Secretaria do Planejamento e Coordenacao. Boletim Estadistico.

**Carlos Goncalves Fidalgo, Ed. & Pub**
Rua Riachuelo 414, Rio de Janeiro GB, Brazil.
- Vida Domestica. m.
- Vida Infantil. m.
- Vida Juvenil. m.

**Dorina de Gouvea Nowill**
Rua Dr. Diogo de Foria 558, Sao Paula, Brazil.
- Lente (Inkprint Edition); special review on visually handicapped. q. ISSN 0024-0893 (Fundacao para o Livro do Cego no Brasil)
- Relevo. m. ISSN 0048-7201 (Fundacao para O Livro do Cego No Brasil)

**Editora Gruenwald Ltda.**
Caixa Postal 3798, Sao Paulo, Brazil.
- C & I. (Controle & Instrumentacao/ Automatizacao) m.
- Mundo Electrico. m. ISSN 0027-3295
- Mundo Mecanico. m.

**Guanabara, Brazil. Secretaria de Ciencia e Tecnologia. Instituto de Conservacao da Natureza**
Estrada da Vista Chinesa 741, Caixa Postal 3545, ZC-00 Rio de Janeiro, Brazil.
- Arboreto Carioca. irreg., 1969, no. 4. ISSN 0084-6686

**Editora Guia Aeronautico Ltda**
Rua Joao Alvares 27, 20000 Rio de Janeiro 14 GB, Brazil.
- Guia Aeronautico. m. ISSN 0017-5145

**Editora de Guias Ltda**
Caixa Postal 4724, 01407 Sao Paulo, Brazil
(and Av. Paulista 1776, 01098 Sao Paulo, Brazil)
- Guia de Comunicacao a Distancia. irreg.
- Mercado Comum Brasileiro. irreg.
- Shopping: Opcoes de Compra para a Grande Sao Paulo. irreg.
- Todo. irreg.

**Herbarium. Bradeanum**
C.P. 15005-ZC-06, 2000 Rio de Janeiro-RJ, Brazil.
- Bradea. irreg. ISSN 0084-800X

**Hospital de Juqueri**
Franco da Rocha, Estado de Sao Paulo, Brazil.
- Coordenadoria de Saude Mental, Sao Paulo. Arquivos. irreg. ISSN 0080-6404

**Hospital dos Servidores do Estado**
Rua Sacadura Cabral 178, 20000 Rio de Janeiro, Brazil.
- Revista Medica do HSE. q.

**Editora Imagem Nova**
Rua da Graca, 201, Conj. 41, C.E.P. 01125, Sao Paulo, Brazil.
- Aerospaco. irreg.

**Imprensa Universitaria do Ceara**
2762 Avda. da Universidade, C.P. 1257, Fortaleza BR Ceara, Brazil.
- Universidade Federal do Ceara. Departamento de Ciencias Sociais e Filosofia. Documentos. a. ISSN 0041-8870

**Editora Industrial Teco Ltda**
Rua Dr. Licio de Miranda 451, Box 5632, Sao Paulo, Brazil.
- Revista da Madeira. m. ISSN 0034-7582

**Industrias Graficas Centrograf Ltd**
Rua Alencar Lima, 35- Grupo 903/7, Petropolis, Brazil.
- Revista de Direito do Trabalho. irreg.

**Industrias Graficas Libra**
Rua Visconde de Carandai, 19, Jardim Botanico, Rio de Janeiro, Brazil.
- Vida das Artes. irreg.

**Inodon Editora**
24 Outubro 435, Apto. 202, Porto Alegre, Rio Grande do Sul, Brazil.
- Revista Gaucha de Odontologia. q. ISSN 0034-9542

**Instituto Adolfo Lutz**
Biblioteca, Av. Dr. Arnaldo 355, C.P. 7027, Sao Paulo, Brazil.
- Instituto Adolfo Lutz. Revista. a. ISSN 0073-9855

**Instituto Agronomico. Servicio de Divulgacao Tecnico-Cientifica**
C. Postal 28, 13100 Campinas, Sao Paulo, Brazil.
- Bragantia. 1-2 per yr.(approx) ISSN 0006-8705

**Instituto Bahiano do Fumo**
Rua de Belgica, 2, Edificio Roosevelt, Salvador-Bahia, Brazil.
- Instituto Bahiano do Fumo. Boletim Informativo: Comercio Exterior - Esportacao de Fumo Em Folhas. irreg.

**Instituto Biologico**
Av. Rodrigues Alves 1252, C.P. 4185, Sao Paulo, Brazil.
- Biologico. m. ISSN 0029-6953
- Instituto Biologico. Arquivos. q. ISSN 0020-3653

**Instituto Biologico da Bahia. Secretaria da Agricultura**
C.P. 553, 40000 Salvador, Bahia, Brazil.
- Instituto Biologico da Bahia. Boletim. irreg. ISSN 0020-3661

**Instituto Brasil-Estados Unidos**
Av. N. S. de Copacabana 690, Rio de Janeiro, R.A., Brazil.
- Instituto Brasil-Estados Unidos. Boletim. bi-m. ISSN 0020-367X

**Instituto Brasileiro de Administracao Municipal**
Rua Visconde de Silva 157, Rio de Janeiro, GB, 20000, Brazil.
- Revista de Administracao Municipal. bi-m. ISSN 0034-7604

**Instituto Brasileiro de Bibliografia e Documentacao**
*see under* **Instituto Brasileiro de Informacao Em Ciencia e Tecnologia**

**Instituto Brasileiro de Desenvolvimento Florestal**
Av. Antonio Carlos, 607, Rio de Janeiro, Gb, Brazil.
- Brasil Florestal. s-a. ISSN 0045-270X

**Instituto Brasileiro de Direito Comercial Comparado**
- Revista de Direito Mercantil, Industrial, Economico, e Financeiro. (pub. by Editora Revista dos Tribunais)

**Instituto Brasileiro de Economia**
- Conjuntura Economica. (pub. by Fundacao Getulio Vargas)
- Revista Brasileira de Economia. (pub. by Fundacao Getulio Vargas)

**Instituto Brasileiro de Economica. Centro de Estudos Agricolas**
- Instituto Brasileiro de Economica. Centro de Estudos Agricolas. Agropecuaria. (pub. by Fundacao Getulio Vargas)

**Instituto Brasileiro de Estatistica**
Av. Franklin Roosevelt 166, Rio de Janeiro, GB, Brazil.
- Brazil, Series Estatisticas Retrospectivas. irreg. ISSN 0068-0842
- Instituto Brasileiro de Estatistica. Boletim Bibliografico. q.

**Instituto Brasileiro de Estudos e Pesquisas de Gastroenterologia**
Rua Dr. Seng 320, C.P. 6209 - 01331, Sao Paulo, Brazil.
- Arquivos de Gastroenterologia. q. ISSN 0004-2803

**Instituto Brasileiro de Filosofia**
Rua Barao de Itapetininga 88, 7 Andar, S-701-5, Sao Paulo, Brazil.
- Revista Brasileira de Filosofia. q. ISSN 0034-7205

**Instituto Brasileiro de Informacao Em Ciencia e Tecnologia**
Av. General Justo 171, 4 Andar, 20.000 Rio de Janeiro, GB, Brazil.
- Amazonia - Bibliografia. irreg. ISSN 0100-0977
- Bibliografia Brasileira de Botanica. irreg. ISSN 0067-6586
- Bibliografia Brasileira de Ciencias Agricolas. irreg. ISSN 0067-6594
- Bibliografia Brasileira de Ciencias Sociais. a. ISSN 0067-6608
- Bibliografia Brasileira de Direito. irreg. ISSN 0067-6616
- Bibliografia Brasileira de Documentacao. irreg. ISSN 0067-6624
- Bibliografia Brasileira de Engenharia. a. ISSN 0100-0705
- Bibliografia Brasileira de Fisica. irreg. ISSN 0067-6640
- Bibliografia Brasileira de Matematica. irreg. ISSN 0067-6667
- Bibliografia Brasileira de Medicina. irreg. ISSN 0067-6675
- Bibliografia Brasileira de Quimica e Quimica Tecnologia. irreg. ISSN 0100-0756
- Bibliografia Brasileira de Zoologia. irreg. ISSN 0067-6691
- Ciencia da Informacao. s-a. ISSN 0100-1965
- Congreso Regional Sobre Documentacao. Anais. a., 3rd, Lima, 1971.

**Instituto Brasileiro de Mercado de Capitais**
Av. Beira Mar s/n Anexo AO MAM, Caixa Postal 6.047-ZC00, 20,000 Rio de Janeiro G.B., Brazil.
- Revista Brasileira de Mercado de Capitais. 3 per yr.

**Instituto Brasileiro de Petroleo**
Av. Rio Branco 156, Rio de Janeiro, Brazil.
- Petroleo e Petroquimica. m.

**Instituto Brasileiro de Relacoes Internacionais**
Praia de Botafogo 186, B. 213-217, Rio de Janeiro 2000, Brazil.
- Revista Brasileira de Politica Internacional. s-a. ISSN 0034-7329

**Instituto Brasileiro de Siderurgia**
Rua Araujo Porto Alegre, 36-conj. 707/712, Sao Paulo, Brazil
- Boletim I B S. m. (Orders to: I B S Publishing Division, Orders to: I B S Publishing Division, Av. 13 de Maio 45, Rio de Janeiro, Brazil)

**Instituto Brasileiro do Cafe**
Av. Rodrigues Alves, 129, 20000 Rio de Janeiro Brazil.
- Instituto Brasileiro do Cafe. Cafe: Resultados Obtidos. irreg.
- Instituto Brasileiro do Cafe. Departamento Economico. Anuario Estatistico do Cafe. irreg., 1964, no. 1. ISSN 0073-988X
- Instituto Brasileiro do Cafe. Grupo Executivo de Racionalizacao de Cafeicultura. Relatorio. irreg.
- Instituto Brasileiro do Cafe. Politica Nacional de Cafe. irreg.

**Instituto Brasileiro do Couro, Calcados e Afins**
Caixa Posta, 48, Estancia Velha 93600, Brazil.
- Instituto Brasileiro do Couro, Calcados e Afins. Sistema de Informacao Estatistica para e Industria Nacional de Couros: Boletim de Informacoes. irreg.

**Instituto Brasileiro para Investigacao do Torax**
Caixa Postal 635, Salvador, Bahia, Brazil.
- Arquivos Brasileiros de Tuberculose e Doencas do Torax. q. ISSN 0004-2765

**Instituto Butantan**
Caixa Postal 65, Sao Paulo, Brazil.
- Instituto Butantan, Sao Paulo, Brazil (City) Memorias. a. ISSN 0073-9901

**Instituto Cultural Italo-Brasileiro**
Rua Frei Caneca 1071, Sao Paulo, Brazil.
- Instituto Cultural Italo-Brasileiro. Caderno. irreg.

**Instituto de Botanica**
Caixa Postal 4005, Sao Paulo, Brazil.
- Hoehnea. irreg. ISSN 0073-2877
- Rickia. irreg., 1974, vol. 6. ISSN 0080-3014
- Rickia. Suplemento. irreg., 1971, no 4. ISSN 0080-3022

**Instituto de Ciencias da Informacao**
Rua do Principe 526, Recife, Brazil.
- Instituto de Ciencias da Informacao Comunicacoes & Problemas. q. ISSN 0010-5007

**Instituto de Criminalistica**
Av. Joao Pessoa 2050, Porto Alegre, Rio Grande do Sul, Brazil.
- Revista de Criminalistica do Rio Grande do Sul. s-a. ISSN 0034-7841

**Instituto de Desenvolvimento da Guanabara**
Av. Calogeras, 15 - 3. andar, Rio de Janeiro, Brazil.
- Guanabara: O Balanco Economico. a.

**Instituto de Desenvolvimento Tecnologico**
Caixa Postal 5722, Rua Conde de Porto Alegre 1263, 04608 Sao Paulo, Brazil.
- I D T Abstracts. m.

**Instituto de Direito Publico e Ciencia Politica**
- Revista de Ciencia Politica. (pub. by Fundacao Getulio Vargas)
- Revista de Direito Administrativo. (pub. by Fundacao Getulio Vargas. Servico de Publicacoes)

**Instituto de Endocrinologia**
Santa Casa da Misericordia, Rua Santa Luzia 206 ZC-39, Rio de Janeiro, Brazil.
- Arquivos Brasileiros de Endocrinologia e Metabologia. 3 per yr. ISSN 0004-2730

**Instituto de Engenharia do Parana**
Rua Voluntarios da Patria, 475 - 10 andar, conj, Curitiba 1004, Brazil.
- Instituto de Engenharia do Parana. Revista Tecnica. q.

**Instituto de Estudos Avancados en Educacao**
- Forum Educacional. (pub. by Fundacao Getulio Vargas)

**Instituto de Geografia e Historia Militar do Brazil. Ministerio do Exercito**
Praca Duque de Caxias, Rio de Janeiro, Brazil.
- Instituto de Geografia e Historia Militar do Brasil. Revista. s-a. ISSN 0020-3890

**Instituto de Ginecologia**
- Ginecologia Brasileira. (pub. by Impressora Brasileira)

**Instituto de Matematica Pura e Aplicada**
Rua Luiz de Camoes 68, Rio de Janeiro GB, Brazil.
- Summa Brasiliensis Mathematicae. irreg. ISSN 0039-498X

**Instituto de Medicina Tropical de Sao Paulo**
Ave. Dr. Eneias C. Aguiar 470, Caixa Postal 2921, Sao Paulo 01000, Brazil.
- Sao Paulo. Instituto de Medicina Tropical. Revista. bi-m. ISSN 0036-4665

**Instituto de Nutricao**
Largo da Misericordia, 24, Rio de Janeiro, Brazil.
- Arquivos Brasileiros de Nutricao. irreg. ISSN 0084-6775

**Instituto de Organizacao Racional do Trabalho**
Av. Sao Luiz 131, Sao Paulo, Brazil
(and Praca Dom Jose Gaspar 30, Sao Paulo, Brazil)
- I D O R T; a revista Brasileira de produtividade. bi-m. ISSN 0018-9103

**Instituto de Pesquisa Agropecuaria do l'Este**
Cruz das Almas, Bahia 44380, Brazil.
- Instituto de Pesquisa Agropecuaria do l'Este. Pesquisa e Experimentos. Comunicado Technico. 40 per yr. ISSN 0046-9947

**Instituto de Pesquisa Veterinarias Desiderio Finamor**
Caixa Postal 2076, Porto Alegre-R S, Brazil.
- I. P. V. D. F. Boletim Mensal; dos trabalhos relatados pelos tecnicos. m. ISSN 0019-0411

**Instituto de Pesquisas e Experimentacao Agropecuarias do Norte**
Cx. Postal 48, Belem, Para, Brazil.
- Instituto de Pesquisas Agropecuarias do Norte. Boletim Tecnico. irreg. ISSN 0067-527X

**Instituto de Pesquisas e Experimentacao Agropecuarias do Sul**
Divisao de Informacao e Divulgacao Agricolas, Caixa Postal E, Pelotas, Rio Grande do Sul, Brazil.
- Agrisul. m. ISSN 0002-1784

**Instituto de Pesquisas Rodoviarias**
Rio de Janeiro, Brazil.
- Instituto de Pesquisas Rodoviarias. Relatorio das Atividades. irreg.
- Pesquisa Rodoviaria. Documentacao e Informacoes. s-a. (Brazil. Ministerio dos Transportes. Departamento Nacional de Estradas de Rodagem)

**Instituto de Previdencia do Estado da Guanabara. Servico de Relacoes Publicas**
Av. Pres. Vargas 670, 8 Andar, Rio de Janeiro, Brazil.
- I P E G. Boletim Informativo. m. ISSN 0019-0292

**Instituto de Previdencia e Assistencia dos Servidores do Estado. Divisao de Relacoes Publicas**
Biblioteca, Rua Pedro Lessa 36, 13 Andar, Rio de Janeiro, G B, Brazil.
- I. P. A. S. E. Biblioteca Informa. q. ISSN 0019-0276

**Instituto de Resseguros do Brasil. Assessoria de Relacoes Publicas**
Av. Marechal Camara 171, ZC-00 Rio de Janeiro, Brazil.
- I R B. Revista. q. ISSN 0019-0446

**Instituto de Tecnologia de Alimentos**
Caixa Postal 139, Campinas SP, Brazil.
- Instituto de Tecnologia de Alimentos. Boletin. q.
- Instituto de Tecnologia de Alimentos. Coletanea. a.
- Instituto de Tecnologia de Alimentos. Instrucoes Praticas. irreg.; no. 4, 1974. ISSN 0074-0144
- Instituto de Tecnologia de Alimentos. Instrucoes Praticas. (pub. by Instituto de Tecnologia de Alimentos)
- Instituto de Tecnologia de Alimentos. Instrucoes Tecnicas. irreg. ISSN 0074-0152

**Instituto do Desenvolvimento Economico Social do para**
Av. Nazare 871, Belem, Para, Brazil.
- Instituto do Desenvolvimento Economico-Social do Para. Indicadores Setoriais. q.

**Instituto Estadual de Hematologia Arthur de Siqueira Cavalcanti**
Biblioteca, Rua Frei Caneca 8-30, ZC14-2000 Rio de Janeiro, Brazil.
- Instituto Estadual de Hematologia Arthur de Siqueira Cavalcanti. Boletim. s-a. ISSN 0046-9963

**Instituto Genealogico Brasileiro**
Rua Conselheiro Crispiniano 53, Sao Paulo SP, Brazil.
- Revista Genealogica Latina. s-a. ISSN 0034-9550

**Instituto Geografico e Geologico**
Rua Antonio de Godoi, 122, 80 Andar, Sao Paulo, Brazil.
- O. I. G. G; revista do Instituto Geografico e Geologico. irreg. ISSN 0078-2874

**Instituto Historico e Geografico Brasileiro**
Av. Augusto Severo, 8-10, Rio de Janeiro, Brazil.
- Instituto Historico e Geografico Brasileiro. Revista. q. ISSN 0046-998X

**Instituto Historico e Geografico de Juiz de Fora**
Caixa Postal 438, Juiz de Fora, Minas Gerais, Brazil.
- Instituto Historico e Geografico de Juiz de Fora. q. ISSN 0020-4218

**Instituto Joaquim Nabuco de Pesquisas Sociais**
Rua Dois Irmaos 92, 50000 - Recife - P.E., Brazil.
- Ciencia & Tropico. s-a. ISSN 0304-2685 (prep. by its Departamento de Processamento de Dados e Documentacao)
- Instituto Joaquim Nabuco de Pesquisas Sociais. Serie Cursos e Conferencias. irreg.

- Instituto Joaquim Nabuco de Pesquisas Sociais. Serie Documentos. irreg.
- Instituto Joaquim Nabuco de Pesquisas Sociais. Serie Estudos e Pesquisas. irreg.
- Instituto Joaquim Nabuco de Pesquisas Sociais. Serie Monografias. irreg.

**Instituto Nacional de Pesquisas da Amazonia**
Estrada do Aleixo 1756, Manaus, Amazonas, Brazil.
- Acta Amazonica. 3 per yr. ISSN 0044-5967

**Instituto Nacional de Pesquisas da Amazonia. Museu Paraense Emilio Goeldi**
Belem, Para, Brazil.
- Museu Paraense Emilio Goeldi. Boletim Antropologia. Nova Serie. irreg. ISSN 0522-7291
- Museu Paraense Emilio Goeldi. Boletim Botanica. Nova Serie. irreg. ISSN 0077-2216
- Museu Paraense Emilio Goeldi. Boletim Zoologia. Nova Serie. irreg. ISSN 0077-2224
- Museu Paraense Emilio Goeldi. Publicacoes Avulsas. irreg., no. 28, 1975. ISSN 0077-2240

**Instituto Neo Pitagorico**
P.O.Box 1047, Curitiba, Parana, Brazil.
- A Lampada. q. ISSN 0001-1789

**Instituto Oswaldo Cruz**
Caixa Postal 926, ZC-OO, Rio de Janeiro, Brazil.
- Comunicacoes Bioquimicas. q. ISSN 0010-5015 (prep. by its Biochemical Laboratory)
- Instituto Oswaldo Cruz, Rio de Janeiro. Memorias. irreg. ISSN 0074-0276

**Instituto Paranaense de Botanica**
Caixa Postal 1362, Curitiba, Parana, Brazil.
- Instituto Paranaense de Botanica. Revista. Serie: Flora do Parana. irreg. ISSN 0074-0284

**Instituto Rio Grandese do Arroz**
Av. Julio de Castilhos 585, Porto Alegre RS, Brazil.
- Lavoura Arrozeira. bi-m. ISSN 0023-9143

**Instituto Tecnologico de Aeronautica**
Sao Jose dos Campos, Sao Paulo, Brazil.
- I T A-Engenharia. bi-m. ISSN 0019-0772
- I T A Humanidades. a; vol. 9, 1973. ISSN 0074-0292

**Instituto Tecnologico do Rio Grande do Sul**
Porto Alegre, Brazil.
- Porto Alegre, Brazil. Instituto Tecnologico do Rio Grande do Sul. Publicacao. irreg.

**International Institute of Administrative Sciences**
Avenida Treze de Maio 23, Rio de Janeiro S/1204, Brazil
(or rue de la Charite, 1040 Brussels, Belgium)
- International Institute of Administrative Sciences. Brazilian Section. Serie de Administracao Comparada. ISSN 0535-0956

**Editora Inubia S.A.**
Rua Andre Cavalcante 86, Jardim Botanico, Rio de Janeiro, Brazil.
- Opiniao. w.

**Irmanaultson Realizacoes**
Av. 13 de Maio, 47/S, Rio de Janeiro 1713, Brazil.
- Revista do Musico. m.

**Jornal Brasileiro de Doencas Toracicas**
Rua Araiyo 70, Caixa Postal 1554, Rio de Janeiro, Brazil.
- Jornal Brasileiro de Doencas Toracicas. bi-m. ISSN 0047-2069

**Jornal de Letras**
Rua Barata Ribeiro 774, Copacabana - Rio de Janeiro GB, Brazil.
- Jornal de Letras. 11 per yr. ISSN 0047-2093

**Jornal de Poesia**
Rua Carlos Fernandes 290, Hipdromo, Recife, Brazil.
- Jornal de Poesia. 8-10 per yr. ISSN 0021-7565

**Jornal do Brasil**
Departamento Circulacao, Av. Brasil 500, ZC-00 Rio de Janeiro, Brazil.
- Cadernos de Jornalismo e Comunicacao. bi-m. ISSN 0007-943X

**Empresa Jornalistica**
Rua de Consulacao 2223, Sao Paulo 01301, Brazil.
- Resenha Judaica. irreg.

**Companhia Editora Jorues**
R. Bahia 988, CX Postal 2.591, Sao Paulo, Brazil.
- Correio Agro-Pecuario; o companheiro do productor. bi-m. ISSN 0010-9061

**Editora Juridica Ltda.**
Rua Princesa Isabel 639, Caixa Postal 428, Fortaleza, Ceara, Brazil.
- Jurisprudencia e Doutrina. q. ISSN 0022-684X (Ordem dos Advogados do Brasil) (Co-sponsor: Tribunal de Justica do Est. Ceara)

**Henerik Kocher, Ed. & Pub.**
Rua Baltasar Lisboa 34, ZC-11 Rio de Janeiro GB, Brazil.
- Literatura Kajero; monata kultura kajero en esperanto. m. ISSN 0024-4694

**Livraria Kosmos Editora**
Rua Saradura Cabral 240-A, Rio de Janeiro, Brazil.
- Anuario de Cinema. a. ISSN 0066-5053

**L T R Editora Ltda.**
Rua Xavier de Toledo 114, 1, Sao Paulo, Brazil.
- L T R. Revista. (Legislacao do Trabalho) m. ISSN 0048-7813

**Legiao Brasileira de Assistencia**
Rua Guaianazes 1385, Sao Paulo, Brazil.
- Maternidade e Infancia; arquivos medico-sociais. q. ISSN 0025-5491

**Lex Editoria S. A.**
Machado de Assis, Caixa Postal 12880, Sao Paulo, Brazil.
- Lex; coletanea de legislacao e jurisprudencia. 3 per mo. ISSN 0024-158X

**Liga Alvaro Bahia Contra a Mortalidade Infantil**
Avenida Joana Angelica 75, Salvador, Bahia, Brazil.
- Pediatria e Puericultura. 4 per yr. ISSN 0031-3912

**Liga Brasileira de Esperanto**
Praca da Republica 54, Rio de Janeiro ZC-14, Brazil.
- Brazila Esperantisto. q. ISSN 0006-9477

**Litis**
Rua Sao Salvador, 31, ZC-01 Rio de Janeiro, Brazil.
- Litis; revista trimestral de direito processual. q.

**Loefgrenia**
Caixa Postal 4755, Sao Paulo, Brazil.
- Loefgrenia; comunicacoes avulsas de botanica. irreg.; latest issue, 1975. ISSN 0024-578X

**Empresa Jornalistica Ulrich Loew S.A.**
Box 520, Rua 15 de Novembro 210, 98700 Ijui, RS, Brazil.
- Correio Serrano. 3 per w. ISSN 0010-9088
- Serra-Post. w. ISSN 0037-251X

**Manicomio Judiciario Heitor Carrilho**
R. Frei Caneca 401, Rio de Janeiro-GB, Brazil.
- Manicomio Judiciario Heitor Carrilho. Arquivos. ISSN 0025-214X

**Mapa Fiscal Editora S.A.**
Rua Miguel Teles Jr., 382 a 394, Sao Paulo, Brazil.
- Coordenacao do Sistema de Tributacao, Brazil. Pareceres Normativos. irreg.

**Editora Marcos Ltda.**
Av. Sao Joao 1113, 1 Andar, Sao Paulo-SP, Brazil.
- Revista do Frio. m. ISSN 0044-5762 (Associacao Brasileira de Refrigeracao, Ar Condicionado, Ventilacao e Aquecimento)

**Mato Grosso, Brazil. Servico do Acordo de Classificacao**
Rua Pres. Marques 559, Cuiaba, Brazil.
- A G R I S A C Mato Grosso. ISSN 0001-1363

**Editora Mayo**
Curitiba, Parana, Brazil.
- Parana em Tres Dimensoes. irreg.

**Editora Medica Brasileira Ltda**
Avenida Almirante Barroso 90-12, Rio de Janeiro, Brazil.
- Revista Brasileira de Medicina. m. ISSN 0034-7264

**Editora Medica Ltda**
Rua Pinheiros 504, Sao Paulo, Brazil.
- Pediatria Moderna. m. ISSN 0031-3920
- Revista Brasileira de Clinica e Terapeutica. m.
- Sinopse de Ginecologia e Obstetricia. bi-m.
- Sinopse de Medicina Interna. bi-m.

**Editora Medico-Biologica Brasileira**
Rua Henrique Schaumann 749, 05413 Sao Paulo, Brazil.
- Revista Brasileira de Pesquisas Medicas e Biologicas/Brazilian Journal of Medical and Biological Research. bi-m. ISSN 0034-7310

**J. Ribeiro de Mendonca**
Av. Alfonso de Taunay, 143, Barra de Tijuca, Rio de Janeiro, Brazil.
- Aero. irreg.

**Mercado de Capitais Brasileiro**
Av Sao Luis 50, Edificio Italia, Rio de Janeiro, Brazil.
- Bolsa. m.

**Editora Metodos Ltda**
Av. Gomes Freire 663, Rio de Janeiro RJ, Brazil.
- Embalagem. bi-m. ISSN 0013-6530
- Remag; revista metodos de artes graficas. m. ISSN 0034-4168 (Associacao Brasileira de Tecnicos Graficos)

**Minas Gerais, Brazil. Departamento de Estradas de Rodagem. Servico de Transito**
Av. Andradas, 1120, 30000 Belo Horizonte, Brazil.
- Minas Gerais, Brazil. Departamento de Estradas de Rodagem. Servico de Transito. Estatistica de Trafego. a; latest issue, 1973.
- Minas Gerais, Brazil. Departamento de Estradas de Rodagem. Servico de Transito. Estatistica de Trafego.

**Mineracao Metalurgia**
Av N.S. Copacabana 637, Copacabana, Rio de Janeiro, Brazil.
- Mineracao Metalurgia. m. ISSN 0026-4520

**Editora Morumbi**
Rua E. Goeldi 575, Caixa Postal 2372, Sao Paulo, Brazil.
- Novidades Fotoptica. bi-m. ISSN 0029-5159 (Fotoptica S-A)

**Movimento Familiar Cristao**
Rua Sao Jose 90, Sala 2208, 20000 Rio de Janeiro, Brazil.
- Limiar. q. ISSN 0024-3566

**Mundo Cultural**
Rua Marconi, 53, Sao Paulo, Brazil.
- Mundo Economico, Politico e Social. q

**Museu de Arqueologia e Etnologia**
- Dedalo. (pub. by Universidade de Sao Paulo)

**Museu do Indio**
Biblioteca Marechal Rondon, Rua Mata Machado, 127, Maracana, Rio de Janeiro, Brazil.
- Boletim do Museu do Indio. m.
- Museu do Indio. Documentacao. irreg.

**Museu Nacional**
Quinta da Boa Vista, Rio de Janiero, GB 08, Brazil.
- Flora Ecologica de Restingas do Sudeste do Brasil. irreg., 1970, no. 16. ISSN 0071-5751
- Museu Nacional, Rio de Janeiro. Arquivos. irreg.; latest issue, 1971. ISSN 0080-3111

- Museu Nacional, Rio de Janeiro. Boletim. Nova Serie. Botanica. irreg. ISSN 0080-3197
- Museu Nacional, Rio de Janeiro. Boletim. Nova Serie. Geologie. irreg. ISSN 0080-3200
- Museu Nacional, Rio de Janeiro. Boletim. Nova Serie. Zoologia. irreg., 1969, no. 272. ISSN 0080-312X
- Museu Nacional, Rio de Janeiro. Boletin. Nova Serie. Antropologia. irreg. ISSN 0080-3189

**Empresa de Navegacao de Amazonia, S.A. Setor de Processamento de Dados Estatisticos**
Av. P. Vargas, 41, Cx. Postal, 1068, Belem, Brazil.
- Dados Estatisticos da Movimentacao de Carga e Passageiros. a.

**Sociedade Editora da Revista Neurobiologia**
Largo dos Coelhos s/n, Recife-PE, Brazil.
- Neurobiologia; revista de neurologia psiquiatria e neurocirurgia. q. ISSN 0028-3800 (Sociedade de Neurologia, Psiquiatria e Higiene Mental do Brasil. Hospital das Clinicas Pedro II) (Co-sponsor: Sociedade Brasileira de Neurocirurgia)

**Norma Editora e Publicidade Ltda.**
Av. Princesa Isabel 323, Rio de Janeiro G.B., Brazil.
- Hotelnews. bi-m. ISSN 0018-6333

**Noticiario da Moda**
Rua Dr. Candido Espinheira 349, Rio de Janeiro, Brazil.
- Noticiario da Moda. m.

**Noticias Caninas**
Petropolis, RJ, Brazil.
- Noticias Caninas. m. ISSN 0029-4179

**Observador Economico e Financeiro**
Av. Grace Aranha 182, Rio de Janeiro GB, Brazil.
- Observador Economico e Financeiro. m.

**Ordem dos Advogados do Brasil**
- Jurisprudencia e Doutrina. (pub. by Editora Juridica Ltda.)

**Ordem dos Economistas de Sao Paulo**
Viaduto 9 de Julho, 26, Sao Paulo, Brazil.
- Ciencias Economicas. irreg.

**Editora Orientador Ltda.**
Caixa Postal 1430, Sao Paulo, Brazil.
- Papel; cellulose, papel, impressao. m. ISSN 0031-1057 (Associacao Tecnica Brasileira de Celulose e Papel)

**Parana, Brazil. Secretaria de Estado para os Negocios da Fazenda**
Curitiba, Brazil.
- Parana, Brazil. Secretaria de Estado para os Negocios da Fazenda; estatistica economico-financeira. irreg.

**Parana em Paginas**
Rua Augusto Stellfeld, 70 Curitiba, Parana, Brazil.
- Parana em Paginas. m. ISSN 0031-174X

**Empresa Grafica Editorial Paulista**
Rue Dr. Trajano 572, Caixa Postal 109, Limeira, Estado de Sao Paulo, Brazil.
- Letras da Provincia. bi-m. ISSN 0047-441X

**Editora Paz e Terra**
Rua Andre Cavalcante 86, Rio de Janeiro, Brazil.
- Argumento; revista mensal de cultura. m.
- Paz e Terra; ecumenismo e humanismo, encontro e dialogo. 6 per yr. ISSN 0031-3408

**Pedra e Cal**
Rua Goncalves Maia, 57, Boa Vista, Recife-PE, Brazil.
- Pedra e Cal; informador mensal das construcoes nordestinas. m. ISSN 0048-315X

**Editora Permanencia**
Rua Jardim Botanico 86, Rio de Janeiro, Brazil.
- Permanencia. m. ISSN 0031-5486

**Pernambuco, Brazil. Conselho de Desenvolvimento. Instituto de Desenvolvimento de Pernambuco**
Av. Dantas Barreto 1200, Ed. San Diego, C. Postal 3344, Recife, Pernambuco, Brazil.
- Revista Pernambucana de Desenvolvimento. s-a.

**Pernambuco, Brazil. Governo do Estado**
Rua Debret 23, Room 711, Rio de Janeiro, Guanabara, Brazil.
- Actualides Pernambucanas. w. ISSN 0004-7368

**Editora Pesquisa Brasileiro do Disco**
Rua Timbiras 502, Sao Paulo, Brazil.
- Pesquisa Brasileira do Disco. m.

**Petroleo Brasileiro S.A.**
Servico Juridico, Av. Republica do Chile, 65-17,
20000 Rio de Janeiro R.J., Brazil.
- Biblioteca do Sejur. Boletim. m. ISSN 0006-1662
- Ementario da Legislacao do Petroleo. s-a. ISSN
0013-662X
- Petrobras. q. ISSN 0031-6334
- Petrobras. Consolidated Report. a.

**Petroleo Brasileiro S.A. Centro de Pesquisas e Desenvolvimento**
Divisao de Informacao Tecnica e Propriedade
Industrial, Cidade Universitaria, Quadra 7, Ilha do
Fundao, Rio de Janeiro GB, Brazil.
- Boletim Tecnico da Petrobras. q. ISSN 0006-6117

**Petroleo Brasileiro, S. A. Servicio de Pessoal**
Avenida Republico do Chile, 65 - 7 andar, Rio de
Janeiro, Brazil.
- Petroleo Brasileiro, S. A. Servicio de Pessoal.
Recursos Humanos. q.

**Pia Sociedade Filhas de Sao Paulo**
Rua Domingos de Morais 678, Sao Paulo 04010,
Brazil.
- Familia Crista; revista da paz e do amor - revista
mensal para a familia. m. ISSN 0014-7125

**Editora Pini Ltda.**
Rua Anhaia 964, Bom Retiro, Sao Paulo, Brazil.
- Construcao Em Sao Paulo. w. ISSN 0010-6631
- Construcao - Minas /Centro Oeste. m.
- Construcao - Norte Nordeste. m.
- Construcao-Regiao Sul. m.
- Construcao-Rio de Janeiro. fortn.

**Plasticos em Revista Editora Ltda.**
Rua Marques de Itu 95, Sao Paulo - SP, Brazil.
- Plasticos em Revista. m. ISSN 0032-1133

**Empresa Jornalistico o Poder**
Cx. Postal 3491, Rio de Janeiro, Brazil.
- Poder. irreg.

**Policlinica Geral do Rio de Janeiro**
Av. Nilo Pecanha 38, Rio de Janeiro, Brazil.
- Brasil-Medico; revista de medicina e cirurgia. bi-
m. ISSN 0006-9205

**Polo Petroquimico da Bahia**
Salvador, Bahia, Brazil.
- Polo Petroquimico da Bahia. Situacao das
Empresas. irreg.

**Pontificia Universidade Catolica de Sao Paulo**
Rua Monte Alegre 984, Sao Paulo, Brazil.
- Pontificia Universidade Catolica de Sao Paulo.
Revista. q.

**Pontificia Universidade Catolica do Rio de Janeiro**
Rua Marques de Sao Vicente 209 - Gaveas, ZC-20
Rio de Janeiro GB, Brazil.
- Monographs in Computer Science and Computer
Applications. irreg. ISSN 0077-0817 (prep. by its
Departamento de Informatica)
- Verbum. q. ISSN 0042-3688

**Pontificia Universidade Catolica do Rio de Janeiro. Instituto de Odontologia**
Av. Rio Branco 128, S-1008 Rio de Janeiro, Brazil.
- Revista de Farmacia e Odontologia. m. ISSN
0034-8201

**Pontificia Universidade Catolica do Rio de Janeiro. Nucleo de Estudos Sociais para Habitacao e Urbanismo**
Rua Marques de Sao Vicente 209, 20000 Rio de
Janeiro, Brazil.
- Nucleo de Estudos Sociais para Habitacao e
Urbanismo. irreg.

**Pontificia Universidade Catolica do Rio Grande do Sul**
Av. Ipiranga 6681, Caixa Postal 1429, Porto Alegre,
RS, Brazil.
- I E S P E. Boletim. q. ISSN 0018-9626 (prep. by
its Instituto de Estudos Sociais, Politicos e
Economicos)
- Teocomunicacao. 4 per yr. (prep. by its Instituto
de Teologia)
- Veritas. q. ISSN 0042-3955

**Pontificia Universidade Catolica do Rio Grande do Sul. Centro de Estudos de Lingua Portuguesa**
Av. Ipiranga 6681, Porto Alegre, Rio Grande do
Sul, Brazil.
- Letras de Hoje; estudo e debate de assuntos da
lingua Portuguesa. q. ISSN 0047-4428

**Pontificia Universidade Catolica do Rio Grande do Sul. Pos-Graduacao em Historia da Cultura**
Av. Ipiranga 6681, Porto Alegre, Brazil.
- Estudos Ibero-Americanos. irreg.

**Pool Editorial Ltda.**
Rua Feliciano Gomes 262, Derbi, Brazil.
- Confidencial Economico- N E m.

**Primeira Escola de Tecelagem**
- Revista Textil. (pub. by M. L. Silva Haydu & Cia.
Ltda.)

**Pro Arte-Sociedade de Artes, Letras e Ciencias**
Rua Mexico 74, Sala 601, Rio de Janeiro-20.000
GB, Brazil.
- Intercambio; economia e cultura. q. ISSN 0020-
5184

**Promocao-Da-Familia Editora**
Caixa Postal-1133, Belo Horizonte-MG., Brazil.
- Reino; de deus no mundo dos homens. m. ISSN
0034-3633

**Editora Promocoes e Publicidade, Assessoria de Relacoes Publicas Ltda.**
Av. Beira Mar 406, Grupo 906, Rio de Janeiro,
Brazil.
- Opema Em Ritmo de Brasil Jovem. irreg. (Brazil.
Ministerio dos Transportes. Operacao Maua)

**Editora Propaganda S.A.**
Rua Maranhao 620, Sao Paulo, Brazil.
- Propaganda; revista mensal de publicidade,
promocao de vendas, relacoes publicas e estudios
de mercado. m. ISSN 0033-1244

**Publicacoes Associadas Paulista Ltda**
Avenida Ipiranga 1267, Caixa Postal 30.560, Sao
Paulo, Brazil.
- Revista Imposto Fiscal. 3 per m. ISSN 0034-9666

**Editora de Publicacoes Cientificas Ltda**
Rua do Russel, 450,6 Andar, Rio de Janeiro - GB,
Brazil.
- Jornal Brasileiro de Medicina. m. ISSN 0047-2077

**Publicacoes Executivas Brasileiras Ltda**
Rua dos Ingleses 150, Caixa Postal 30837, CEP
01329 Sao Paulo, Brazil.
- Analise. a.
- Expansao. s-m.

**Publicacoes Informativas Ltda.**
R. de Quitanda, 199, Rio de Janeiro, Brazil.
- Anuario Brasileiro de Media. a.
- Anuario Brasileiro de Propaganda. a. ISSN 0570-
3956

**Editora Publicacoes Technicas Ltda.**
Av. Sao Joao 1113, Sao Paulo, Brazil.
- Anuario Brasileiro do Frio. irreg.

**Publinform Publicacoes Informativas Ltda.**
Vitorino Carmilo, 690, Sao Paulo, Brazil.
- Anuario Brasileiro de Supermercados. a.; latest
issue, 1975. (Associacao Brasileira dos
Supermercados)
- Anuario Brasileiro de Transportes. a.

**Quartel-General de Intendencia do Exercito**
Campo de Sao Cristovao 136-30 Andar, Rio de
Janeiro, Brazil.
- Revista de Intendencia. bi-m. ISSN 0034-8368

**Editora R J Ltda**
Av. Barao de Rio Branco, 389 (Guarulhos), Cx.
Postal 4544, Sao Paulo, Brazil.
- R J. (Relogios e Joias) m. ISSN 0033-6971

**Recife, Brazil. Secretaria de Assuntos Juridicos**
Recife, Brazil.
- Recife, Brazil. Secretaria de Assuntos Juridicos.
Revista. irreg.

**Empresa Jornalistica o Reporter de Santo Andre Ltda.**
Rua Coronel Oliveira Lima, 180, Santo Andre,
Brazil.
- Reporter. s-w. ISSN 0034-4753

**Revista de Cultura Vozes**
Rua Frei Luis 100, Caixa Postal 23, 25600
Petropolis RJ, RJ, Brazil.
- Revista de Cultura Vozes. 10 per yr.

**Revista de Ginecologia e d'Obstetricia**
Rua Frei Caneca 1245, Sao Paulo, SP, Brazil.
- Revista de Ginecologia e d'Obstetricia. bi-m.
ISSN 0034-8287

**Revista do Esporte**
Rua Sao Luiz Gonzaga 601, Rio de Janeiro, Brazil.
- Revista do Esporte. w.

**Revista do Trabalho**
Av. Rio Branco 277, Rio de Janeiro GB, Brazil.
- Revista do Trabalho. m (some special issues)

**Editora Revista dos Tribunais**
Rua Conde do Pinhal 78, Sao Paulo, Brazil.
- Ciencias Economicas Sociais. s-a. (Faculdade
Municipal de Ciencias Economicas e
Administrativa de Osasco)
- R T - Informa. fortn.
- Revista de Direito Civil; imobiliario, agrario e
empresarial. q.
- Revista de Direito do Trabalho. q.
- Revista de Direito Mercantil, Industrial,
Economico, e Financeiro. q. (Instituto Brasileiro
de Direito Comercial Comparado) (Co-Sponsors:
Biblioteca Tullio Ascarelli; Instituto de Direito
Economico e Financeiro)
- Revista de Direito Publico. q. ISSN 0034-8015
(Universidade de Sao Paulo. Instituto de Direito
Publico)
- Revista de Direito Tributario. 2 per yr.
- Revista de Processo. q.
- Revista dos Tribunais. m. ISSN 0034-9275

**Editora Revista Fiscal Ltda.**
Av. Graca Aranha 19, Rio de Janeiro, Brazil.
- Revista Fiscal e de Legislacao de Fazenda. s-m.
ISSN 0034-9534

**Revista Fotoarte Ltda.**
C.P. 1430, Rua Conselheiro Crispiniano 404, 9o
Andar, S.910, Sao Paulo, Brazil.
- Fotoarte. m. ISSN 0046-4791

**Revista Mensal de Exportacao Ltda.**
Rua General Camara 77, 5 Andar, Santos, SP,
Brazil.
- Revista Mensal de Exportacao/Exportation
Monthly Review. m. ISSN 0014-5203

**Revista Odonto-Estomatologica**
Av. Dantas Barreto, No 564, Edificio Inalmar,
Caixa Postal 803, Recife, Pe., Brazil.
- Revista Odonto-Estomatologica. 4 per yr. ISSN
0048-7856

**Revista Tecnica e Informativa Ltda.**
Rua Leandro Martins, ZC 05 - Rio de Janeiro,
Brazil.
- Portos e Navios; revista tecnica e informativa. m.
ISSN 0032-4973

**Francisco Jose Ribeiro de Vasconcellos**
Av. Rio Branco 277, Group 1001, Rio de Janeiro
20.000, Brazil.
- Encontro Com O Folclore. a  ISSN 0013-7049

**Editora Rio**
Rua do Bispo, 83, Rio de Janeiro, Brazil.
- Lugar em Comunicacao. q. (Faculdades Integradas
Estacio de Sa)

**Rio de Janeiro, Brazil  Empresa de Turismo do Municipio**
Rua Sao Jose 90, CEP 20000 Rio de Janeiro, Brazil.
- Riotur. irreg.

**Rio de Janeiro, Brazil. Imprensa Oficial**
Rua Margues de Olinda, Niteroi, Rio de Janeiro,
Brazil.
- Imprensa Oficial do Estado do Rio de Janeiro. d.

**Rio de Janeiro, Brazil. Secretaria de Saude. Departamento de Recursos Humanos**
Praca da Republica 111, ZC-14 Rio de Janeiro,
Brazil.
- Revista Medica do Estado do Rio de Janeiro. q.

**Rio de Janeiro. Servico Social do Comercio**
Av. General Justo, 307, Rio de Janeiro, Brazil.
- Servico Social do Comercio. Unidades
Operacionais: Enderecos. irreg.

**Rio Grande do Sul, Brazil. Departamento Autonomo del Estradas de Rodagem. Divisao de Servicos Especiais**
Av. Borges de Medeiros No 1555, Porto Alegre, Brazil.
- Revista Rodoviaria. m.

**Rio Grande do Sul, Brazil. Departamento da Saude**
Av. Borges de Medeiros 308, 90 Andar S/92 90,000, Porto Alegre, Rio Grande do Sul, Brazil.
- Equipe de Odontologia Sanitaria. Boletim. 4 per yr.

**Rio Grande do Sul, Brazil. Rio Grande do Sul Consultoria-Geral**
Av. Borges Medeiros 417, Porto Alegre 90000, Brazil
- Rio Grande do Sul, Brazil. Consultoria-Geral. Revista. (Subscr. to: Livraria Sulina, Rua Cel. Genuino 290, Porto Alegre 90000 R.S., Brazil)

**Editora e Grafica o Ruralista Ltda.**
Av. dos Andradas 367, Belo Horizonte, MG, Brazil.
- Ruralista; jornal da familia rural. fortn. ISSN 0036-0139

**Santamaria e Correa Ltda.**
Av. Pompeia, 506, 05022 Sao Paulo SP, Brazil.
- Eletronica em Foco. w. ISSN 0046-1814

**Editora Santuario**
Rua Padre Claro Monteiro 342, 12570 Aparecida SP, Brazil.
- Santuario de Aparecida. w. ISSN 0036-4614 (Congregacao do Santissimo Redentor)

**Livraria Sao Jose**
Rua Sao Jose 70, Rio de Janeiro, Brazil.
- Sociedade Brasileira. a.

**Sao Paulo, Brazil (City) Biblioteca Municipal Mario de Andrade**
Sao Paulo, Brazil.
- Sao Paulo. Biblioteca Municipal Mario de Andrade. Boletim Bibliografico. q.

**Sao Paulo, Brazil. Centrais Eletricas. Setor de Estudos de Mercado**
Diretoria de Distribuicao, Sao Paulo, Brazil.
- Estado de Sao Paulo; Amalise e Acompanhemento do Mercado de Energia Electrica dos Autoproductores. irreg.

**Sao Paulo, Brazil. Departamento de Aguas e Energia Eletrica. Secretaria dos Servicos e Obras Publica**
Rua Riachuelo 115, 4 Andar, Sao Paulo, Brazil.
- Revista Aguas e Energia Eletrica de Sao Paulo. q. ISSN 0034-6950

**Sao Paulo, Brazil. Departamento de Edificios e Obras Publicas**
Sao Paulo, Brazil.
- Sao Paulo, Brazil (State). Departamento de Edificios e Obras Publicas. Relatorio de Atividades. irreg.

**Sao Paulo, Brazil. Instituto de Saude. Divisao de Hansenologia e Dermatologia Sanitaria**
Caixa Postal 8027, 01000 Sao Paulo, Brazil.
- Hanseniase-Resumos e Noticias/Hanseniasis-Abstracts and News. s-a. ISSN 0017-7512
- Hansenologia Internationalis. s-a.

**Sao Paulo, Brazil. Secretaria da Agricultura do Estado. Instituto de Economia Agricola**
Av. Miguel Estefano 3900, Caixa Postal 8114, Sao Paulo, Brazil.
- Prognostico Regiao Centro-Sul. a.

**Sao Paulo, Brazil. Secretaria da Agricultura. Instituto de Economia Agricola**
Secretaria da Agricultura do Estado de Sao Paulo, Av. Miguel Estefano, 3900, Caixa Postal 8114, Sao Paulo, SP, Brazil.
- Agricultura em Sao Paulo. q. ISSN 0044-6793
- Informacoes Economicas. m.
- Prognostico da Agricultura Paulista. a.

**Sao Paulo, Brazil. Secretaria de Economia e Planejamento. Coordenadoria de Planejamento**
Av. Angelica 2223, 01227 Sao Paulo S.P., Brazil.
- Planejamento e Conjuntura.

**Sao Paulo, Brazil. Secretaria da Educacao**
Sao Paulo, Brazil.
- Sao Paulo, Brazil (State). Secretaria da Educacao. Atividades Desenvolvidas. irreg.

**Sao Paulo. Servico Social do Comercio. Conselho Tecnico de Economia, Sociologia e Politica**
Rua Dr. Vila Nova 228, 01222 Sao Paulo SP, Brazil.
- Problemas Brasileiros; revista mensal de cultura. m. ISSN 0555-2176

**Sao Paulo, Brazil. Superintendencia de Saneamento Ambiental**
Secretaria de Estado da Saude, Sao Paulo, Brazil.
- Sao Paulo, Brazil (State). Superintendencia de Saneamento Ambiental. Relatorio Anual de Atividades. a.

**Seara Medica Neurocirurgica**
Rua Maestro Cardim 769, Sao Paulo, Brazil.
- Seara Medica Neurocirurgica. 4 per yr. ISSN 0037-0169

**Selecoes do Readers Digest**
Av. Presidente Vargas 62, Rio de Janeiro, Gb, Brazil.
- Selecoes do Readers Digest. m.

**Selecoes Odontologicas Editora e Publicidade Ltda**
Avenida Ipiranga 890, 10, CEP-01040-Sao Paulo, Brazil.
- Selecoes Odontologicas. m. ISSN 0049-0075

**Seminario Nacional de Controle de Qualidade**
- Seminario Nacional de Controle de Qualidade. Anais. (pub. by Federacao das Industrias do Estado do Rio Grande do Sul)

**Servico Nacional de Appendizagem Comerical - SENAC**
Departamento Regional do Parana, Rua Andre de Barros, 750, 80000 Curitiba, Parana, Brazil.
- Servicio Nacional de Aprendizagem Comercial. Departamento Regional do Parana. Pesquisa do Mercado de Trabalho; necessidades de Mao-de-Obra e Formacao Professional. irreg. (Brazil. Superintendencia do Desenvolvimento da Regiao Sul)

**Servico Nacional de Cancer**
Praca Cruz Vermelha 23, Rio de Janeiro, Brazil.
- Revista Brasileira de Cancerologia. q. ISSN 0034-7116

**Servico Social da Industria. Divisao de Orientacao Social**
Praca D. Jose Gaspar 30, Sao Paulo, Brazil.
- Educador Social. bi-m. ISSN 0013-1105

**Servicos de Publicacoes Especializadas Ltda**
Rua Brigadeiro Tobias 356, 6 Sao Paulo, Brazil (Subscr. Address: Caixa Postal, 30.493, Sao Paulo, Brazil)
- G O/Ginecologia e Obstetricia; revista de atualizacao em ginecologia e obstetricia. m. ISSN 0016-3597
- Medico Moderno; revista profesional de medicina. m. ISSN 0025-8180

**Shalom Ltda.**
R. da Graca 201, 7 Andar, C.J.71 Sao Paulo, Brazil.
- Shalom. m.

**Siderurgia Brasileira**
Brasilia, Brazil.
- Siderurgia Brasileira. Relatoria da Diretoria. irreg.

**Editora Signo Ltda**
Cx. Postal 2483-ZC-00, 20000 Rio de Janiero, Brazil.
- Eletronica para Todos. m.
- Mundo Eletronico. m.
- Radio TV Tecnico. m.

**M. L. Silva Haydu & Cia. Ltda.**
Rua Parana 136, P.O.B. 10.675, Sao Paulo, Brazil.
- Revista Textil. m. ISSN 0035-0524 (Primeira Escola de Tecelagem)

**Sindicato da Industria da Construcao Civil do Estado da Guanabara**
Rua do Senado 213, Rio de Janeiro GB, Brazil.
- Revista da Construcao Civil. m(plus supplement) ISSN 0034-7566 (Co-sponsor: Camara Brasileira da Industria da Construcao)

**Sindicato dos Bancarios de Sao Paulo**
*see* Sindicato dos Empregados Em Estabelecimentos Bancarios de Sao Paulo

**Sindicato dos Bancos do Estado da Guanabara. Assessoria Economica**
Av. Rio Branco, 81, Rio de Janeiro, Brazil.
- Panorama Estatistico de Setor Bancaria. q.

**Sindicato dos Empregados em Estabelecimentos Bancarios de Sao Paulo**
Rua Sao Bento, 365, Sao Paulo, Brazil.
- Folha Bancaria. bi-m. ISSN 0015-5446

**Sindicato dos Lojistas do Comercio de Sao Paulo**
Rua Xavier de Toledo, 99-2. andar, Sao Paulo, Brazil.
- Lojas & Lojistas. m.

**Sindicato Nacional da Industria de Tratores, Caminhoes, Automoveis e Veiculos Similares**
- Industria Automobilistica Brasileira. (pub. by ANFAVEA)

**Sindicato Nacional dos Editores de Livros. Centro de Bibliotecnia**
Av. Rio Branco. 37-S/1503/6, 1510-12 Guanabara, Brazil.
- Bibliografia Brasileira de Livros Infantis. a. ISSN 0067-6659
- Guia das Livrarias e Pontos de Venda de Livros No Brasil. irreg.
- Sindicato Nacional dos Editores de Livros. Informativo Bibliografico. m.

**Sociadade Brasileira de Instrucao**
Rua da Matriz, 82, Rio de Janeiro, Brazil.
- Dados. 2 per yr. ISSN 0011-5258

**Sociedade Brasileira de Anestesiologia**
Rua Alfredo Gomes 36, ZC-02 Rio de Janeiro GB, Brazil.
- Revista Brasileira de Anestesiologia. q. ISSN 0034-7094

**Sociedade Brasileira de Angiologia**
Rua Dna. Veridiana 661, Caixa Postal, Sao Paulo 01238, Brazil.
- Revista Brasileira Cardiovascular. q. ISSN 0048-7635

**Sociedade Brasileira de Cardiologia**
Rua Itapeva, Sao Paulo, Brazil.
- Arquivos Brasileiros de Cardiologia. 6 per yr. ISSN 0066-782X

**Sociedade Brasileira de Cultura**
Alameda Eduardo Prado 705, C. P. 30004, 01218 Sao Paulo, Brazil.
- Convivium; investigacao e cultura. bi-m.

**Sociedade Brasileira de Dermatologia**
Rua Santa Luzia, 206, Caixa Postal 389, Rio de Janeiro, Brazil.
- Anais Brasileiros de Dermatologia. q. ISSN 0003-2433

**Sociedade Brasileira de Direito Internacional**
Palacio Itamaraty, Rio de Janeiro, Brazil.
- Sociedade Brasileira de Direito Internacional. Boletim. 2 per yr.

**Sociedade Brasileira de Economistas Rurais**
Rua Anchieta, 41, 10 Andar, Sao Paulo, Brazil.
- Sociedade Brasileira de Economistas Rurais. Anais da Reuniao. irreg.

**Sociedade Brasileira de Educacao**
Rua Bambina 115, ZC-02 Rio de Janeiro GB, Brazil.
- Sintese. q.

**Sociedade Brasileira de Entomologia**
Caixa Postal 9063, Sao Paulo, Brazil.
- Revista Brasileira de Entomologia. a. ISSN 0085-5626

**Sociedade Brasileira de Estudos Sobre Discos Voadores**
Postal 16-017, Correio Largo do Machado, Rio de Janeiro, Brazil.
- Sociedade Brasileira de Estudos Sobre Discos Voadores. Boletim. s-a. ISSN 0037-8666

**Sociedade Brasileira de Filosofos Catolicos**
Via Anhanguera, Km. 26, Caixa Postal 11.587, Sao Paulo, Brazil.
- Presenca Filosofica. irreg.

**Sociedade Brasileira de Fisica**
Universidade de Sao Paulo, Instituto di Fisica,
Caixa Postal 20553, 01000 Sao Paulo, Brazil.
• Revista Brasileira de Fisica. 3 per yr.

**Sociedade Brasileira de Geografia**
Praca da Republica, 54, 1 And., Rio de Janeiro-GB
20.000 ZC-14, Brazil.
• Sociedade Brasileira de Geografia. Boletim. q.
ISSN 0037-8674

**Sociedade Brasileira de Matematica**
Rua Luiz de Camoes, 68, Rio de Janeiro, Brazil.
• Sociedade Brasileira de Matematica. Boletim. s-a.

**Sociedade Brasileira de Medicina Tropical**
Rua Laura de Araujo 36, P.O. Box 1859, Rio de
Janeiro, Brazil.
• Sociedade Brasileira de Medicina Tropical.
Revista. bi-m. ISSN 0037-8682

**Sociedade Brasileira de Microbiologia**
c/o Ed. Joao S. Furtado, Instituto de Botanica,
Caixa Postal 4005, 01000 Sao Paulo SP, Brazil.
• Revista de Microbiologia. q. ISSN 0001-3714

**Sociedade Brasileira de Oftalmologia**
Rua Sao Salvador, 107, Rio de Janeiro ZC 01,
Brazil.
• Revista Brasileira de Oftalmologia. q. ISSN 0034-
7280

**Sociedade Brasileira de Patologia Clinica**
• Revista Brasileira de Patologia Clinica. (pub. by
Editora Dois Irmaos Ltda)

**Sociedade Brasileira de Pediatria**
Avda. Franklin Roosevelt 39, Grupos 1112/1113,
Rio de Janeiro, Brazil.
• Jornal de Pediatria. bi-m. ISSN 0021-7557

**Sociedade Brasileira para o Progresso da Ciencia**
Caixa Postal 11.008, Sao Paulo, Brazil.
• Ciencia e Cultura. m. ISSN 0009-6725

**Sociedade Brasileira para Professores de Linguistica**
• Revista Brasileira de Linguistica. (pub. by Editora
Vozes Ltda)

**Sociedade Civil de Bem-Estar Familiar No Brasil**
Rua das Laranjeiras 308, Rio de Janeiro, Brazil.
• Bemfam. irreg.

**Sociedade de Farmacia e Quimica de Sao Paulo**
Avda. Brigadeiro Luis Antonio 393, 7 Sao Paulo,
Brazil.
• Anais de Farmacia e Quimica de Sao Paulo. bi-m.
ISSN 0003-2441

**Sociedade de Medicina e Cirurgia de Sao Jose do Rio
Preto**
Rua Spinola s/n, Sao Jose da Rio Preto 15100,
Brazil.
• Sociedade de Medicina e Cirurgia de Sao Jose do
Rio Preto. Revista. q.

**Sociedade de Medicina e Cirurgia do Rio de Janeiro**
Av. Almirante Barroso, 63, 20.000 - Rio de Janeiro
(GB), Brazil.
• Folha Medica. m. ISSN 0015-5454
• Revista Brasileira de Cirurgia. bi-m. ISSN 0034-
7124

**Sociedade de Neurologia, Psiquiatria e Higiene
Mental do Brasil. Hospital das Clinicas Pedro II**
• Neurobiologia. (pub. by Sociedade Editora da
Revista Neurobiologia)

**Sociedade de Pediatria de Sao Paulo**
• Pediatria Pratica. (pub. by Centro de Estudos da
Clinica Infantil do Ipiranga)

**Sociedade de Psicologia de Sao Paulo**
Caixa Postal 8105, Sao Paulo, Brazil.
• Boletim de Psicologia. s-a. ISSN 0006-5943

**Sociedade Entomologica do Brasil**
c/o Sr. Joao Manuel de Abreu, Centro de Pesquisas
do Cacau, C.P. 7, 45600 Itabuna, Bahia, Brazil.
• Sociedade Entomologica do Brasil. Anais. a.

**Sociedade Nacional de Agricultura**
General Justo 171, Rio de Janeiro, Brazil.
• Lavoura. bi-m. ISSN 0023-9135

**Sociedade Paranaense de Matematica**
Caixa Postal 1611, Curitiba, Parana, Brazil.
• Sociedade Paranaense de Matematica. Boletim. 3
per yr. ISSN 0037-8712

**Sociedade Paulista de Medicina Veterinaria**
• Atualidades Agroveterinarias. (pub. by Editora C
Q, Ltda.)

**Sociedade Paulista de Ortodontia**
R. Humaita, 389, 01321 Sao Paulo, SP, Brazil.
• Ortodontia. 3 per yr. ISSN 0030-5944

**Sociedade Visconde de Sao Leopoldo**
Rue Euclides de Cunha, 241, 11100 Santos, Brazil.
• Leopoldianum. 3 per yr.

**Grupo Editorial Spagat**
Av. Ipiranga 84, 01046 Sao Paulo, SP, Brazil.
• Flap Internacional; revista Latinoamericana de
aviacao. m. ISSN 0046-404X

**Sugestoes Literarias**
Caixa Postal 3422, Sao Paulo, Brazil.
• Vox Juris Trabalhista. m.

**Livraria Sulina**
Av. Borges de Medeiros, 1030, Porto Alegre, Brazil.
• Ajuris. irreg. (Associacao dos Juizes do Rio
Grande do Sul)
• Revista Juridica. 1-3 per yr. ISSN 0034-9739

**Summer Institute of Linguistics. Departamento de
Estudos Tecnicos**
C.P. 14-2221, Brasilia 70000, Brazil.
• Summer Institute of Linguistics. Serie Linguistica.
irreg.

**Syntex Brasil S.A., Industria e Comercio**
Caixa Postal 951, Sao Paulo, Brazil.
• Pinheiros Farmaceutico. bi-m. ISSN 0031-9899

**Editora Tecnica Ltda**
Rua Barao de Itapetininga 273, Sao Paulo SP,
Brazil.
• Elastomeros. s-a.

**Oyama Pereira Teixeira e Ronaldo Boucas Teixeira,
Eds. and Pubs.**
Caixa Postal 2291, ZC-00 Rio de Janeiro, Brazil.
• Revista Bancaria Brasileira. m. ISSN 0034-706X

**Telecommunicacoes do Rio de Janeiro S.A.**
Av. Nilo Pecanha 50, Sala 209, Rio de Janeiro,
Brazil.
• Sino Azul. bi-m. ISSN 0037-5764

**Teleplan S-A**
Rua Siqueira Campos 244, Rio de Janeiro GB,
Brazil.
• Agente; a revista da habitacao. m. ISSN 0002-
0834

**TELEPRESS Servicos de Imprensa, Ltda.**
Rua Albuquergue Lins, 1315, 01230 Sao Paulo,
S.P., Brazil.
• Brazil Development Series/Series
Desenvolvimento Brasileiro. a. (Brazilian Institute
of Economic Studies)

**Titular S.A. Distribuidora de Titulos e Valores
Mobiliarios**
Pca. Ramos de Azevedo 209-1, Sao Paulo, Brazil.
• Titular. w. ISSN 0040-8212

**Trabalho e Seguro Social**
Rua Sao Jose 85, Rio de Janeiro, Brazil.
• Trabalho e Seguro Social. 6 per yr (double issues)

**Empresa Jornalistica dos Transportes**
Rua Mexico 41 S-904, Rio de Janeiro ZC-00, Brazil.
• Revista dos Transportes. m. ISSN 0034-9267
• Revista Ferroviaria. m. ISSN 0034-950X

**Editora Tres Ltda.**
Av. Paulista 2006, 15 andar, Caixa Postal 1481, Sao
Paulo, Brazil.
• Mais. m.

**Tribunal de Justica**
Rua D. Manuel 29, 3 Andar, Guanabara, Brazil.
• Tribunal Justica Estado da Guanabara. Biblioteca.
Boletim. m. ISSN 0006-1670

**Tribunal de Justica do Estado do Rio Grande do Sul**
Palacio da Justica, Porto Alegre -RS, Brazil.
• Tribunal de Justica do Estado do Rio Grande do
Sul. Revista de Jurisprudencia; doutrina,
jurisprudencia, legislacao. bi-m. ISSN 0041-2805

**Tribunal Federal de Recursos**
Praca dos Trubunais Superiores, Brasilia, D.F.,
Brazil
• Tribunal Federal de Recursos. Revista. q. ISSN
0041-2813 (Subscr. to: Imprensa Nacional, Secao
de Vendas, Avenida Rodrigues Alves, No. 1, Rio
de Janeiro)

**Editora Trofeu Ltda.**
Av. Republica do Libano, 2131, Caixa Postal 8222,
C.E.P. 04501 Sao Paulo, Brazil.
• Trofeu. m.

**Unidade Executiva de Pesquisa Agropecuaria
Estadual- RS**
Caixa Postal E, Pelotas, Rio Grande do Sul, Brazil.
• Rio Grande do Sul. Unidade Executiva de
Pesquisa Agropecuaria Estadual. Boletim
Bibliografico. m.

**Unisinos**
Praca Tiradentes 35, 93000 Sao Leopoldo RS,
Brazil.
• Estudos Juridicos. 3 per yr. (Universidade do Vale
do Rio dos Sinos)
• Estudos Leopoldenses. 3 per yr. ISSN 0014-1607
(Universidade do Vale do Rio dos Sinos)
• Estudos Tecnologicos. 3 per yr. (Universidade do
Vale do Rio dos Sinos)
• Perspectiva Economica. 2 per yr. (Universidade
do Vale do Rio dos Sinos)
• Perspectiva Teologica. 3 per yr. (Universidade do
Vale do Rio dos Sinos)
• Pesquisas: Publicacoes de Antropologia. irreg.
ISSN 0553-8467 (Universidade do Vale do Rio
dos Sinos. Instituto Anchietano de Pesquisas)
• Pesquisas: Publicacoes de Botanica. irreg. ISSN
0553-8475 (Universidade do Vale do Rio dos
Sinos. Instituto Anchietano de Pesquisas)
• Pesquisas: Publicacoes de Historia. irreg. ISSN
0553-8491 (Universidade do Vale do Rio dos
Sinos. Instituto Anchietano de Pesquisas)
• Pesquisas: Publicacoes de Zoologia. irreg. ISSN
0553-8505 (Universidade do Vale do Rio dos
Sinos. Instituto Anchietano de Pesquisas)

**Universidade Catolica de Campinas**
Rua Marechal Deodoro 1099, Campinas, Sao Paulo,
Brazil.
• Universidade Catolica de Campinas. Revista. q.

**Universidade Catolica de Campinas. Dept. of
Geography**
Caixa Postal 317, 13100 Campinas, Brazil.
• Noticia Geomorfologica. s-a. ISSN 0029-4128

**Universidade Catolica de Goias. Gabinete de
Arqueologia**
Caixa Postal, 86, Goiania 74000, Brazil.
• Universidade Catolica de Goias. Gabinete de
Arqueologia. Anuario de Divulgacao Cientifica. a.

**Universidade Catolica de Minas Gerais. Escola de
Servico Social**
Av. Dom Jose Gaspar 500, Belo Horizonte 30000,
Minas Gerais, Brazil.
• Critica Social. irreg.

**Universidade Catolica de Pernambuco. Biblioteca
Central**
Rua do Principe, 526, 5000 Recife, Brazil.
• Symposium. 2 per yr. ISSN 0039-7695

**Universidade Catolica do Parana. Departamento de
Letras**
• Constructura. (pub. by Editora F T D)

**Universidade de Brasilia. Departamento de
Biblioteconomia**
Caixa Postal 15-2833, Brasilia, Brazil.
• Universidade de Brasilia. Departamento de
Biblioteconomia. Revista. s-a. (Co-sponsor:
Associacao dos Bibliotecarios do Distrito Federal)

**Universidade de Mackenzie. Centro de Radio-
Astronomia e Astrofisica**
Sao Paulo, Brazil.
• Universidade de Mackenzie. Centro de Radio-
Astronomia e Astrofisica. Relatoria Anual. a.

**Universidade de Sao Paulo**
C.P. 8105, Sao Paulo, Brazil.
- Dedalo. s-a. ISSN 0011-7455 (Museu de Arqueologia e Etnologia)

**Universidade de Sao Paulo. Centro de Studos Portugueses**
Sao Paulo, Brazil.
- Universidade de Sao Paulo. Centro de Studos Portugueses. Boletim Informativo. irreg.

**Universidade de Sao Paulo. Departamento de Engenharia de Electricidade**
Cidade Universitaria, "Armando de Salles Oliveira", C.P.8191, Sao Paulo, Brazil.
- Boletim de Engenharia de Producao. irreg. ISSN 0067-9607

**Universidade de Sao Paulo. Departamento de Fisiologia Geral de Zoologia**
Caixa Postal 11,230, Sao Paulo ZC9, Brazil.
- Boletim de Zoologia e Biologia Marinha. Nova Serie. a. ISSN 0067-9623 (Co-sponsor: Instituto de Biologia Marinha)

**Universidade de Sao Paulo. Escola de Enfermagem**
Caixa Postal 5751, 01000 Sao Paulo, Brazil.
- Universidade de Sao Paulo. Escola de Enfermagem. Revista. q. ISSN 0080-6234

**Universidade de Sao Paulo. Escola de Engenharia de Sao Carlos**
Centro de Processamento de Dados e Estudos de Sistemas, Av. Dr. Carlos Botelho 1465, C.P. 378, Sao Carlos 13560, Brazil.
- Sistemas. bi-m.

**Universidade de Sao Paulo. Escola de Saude Publica**
Caixa Postal 8191, Cidade Universitaria, Sao Paulo, Brazil.
- Noticiario-Odontologia. 2 per yr. ISSN 0029-4144

**Universidade de Sao Paulo. Escola Superior de Agricultura "Luis de Queiroz"**
Library, P.O. Box 9, 13400 Piracicaba, Sao Paulo, Brazil.
- Escola Superior de Agricultura "Luiz de Queiroz." Anais. a. ISSN 0071-1276
- Escola Superior de Agricultura "Luiz de Queiroz." Boletim de Divulgacao. irreg., 1973, no. 18. ISSN 0071-1292
- Escola Superior de Agricultura "Luiz de Queiroz." Boletim Didatico. irreg., 1971, no. 23. ISSN 0071-1284
- Escola Superior de Agricultura "Luiz de Queiroz." Boletim Tecnico/Cientifico. irreg., 1973, no. 36. ISSN 0071-1306

**Universidade de Sao Paulo. Faculdade de Ciencias Farmaceuticas**
Biblioteca, Caixa Postal 30786, Sao Paulo, Brazil.
- Universidade de Sao Paulo. Revista de Farmacia e Bioquimica. s-a. ISSN 0014-6676

**Universidade de Sao Paulo. Faculdade de Direito**
Largo de Sao Francisco, 95, Sao Paulo, Brazil.
- Academia Paulista de Direito. Revista. irreg.
- Universidade de Sao Paulo. Faculdade de Direito. Revista. a. ISSN 0080-6250

**Universidade de Sao Paulo. Faculdade de Economia e Administracao**
Cidade Universitaria Armando de Salles Oliveira, C.P. 11498, 01000 Sao Paulo, Brazil.
- Universidade de Sao Paulo. Faculdade de Economia e Administracao. Biblioteca. Boletim. irreg.

**Universidade de Sao Paulo. Faculdade de Filosofia, Ciencias e Letras**
Cidade Universitaria, "Armando de Salles Oliveira", Caixa Postal 8105, Sao Paulo, Brazil.
- Sociologia II. irreg. ISSN 0081-1742
- Zoologia. irreg. ISSN 0084-5582

**Universidade de Sao Paulo. Faculdade de Filosofia, Letras e Ciencias Humanas**
Ciudade Universitaria, C. P. 8105, Sao Paulo, Brazil.
- Lingua e Literatura. a. ISSN 0047-4711
- Revista de Antropologia. a. ISSN 0034-7701 (Associacao Brasileira de Antropologia)
- Revista de Historia. q. ISSN 0034-8309
- Revista de Pedagogia. q.

**Universidade de Sao Paulo. Faculdade de Medicina**
Caixa Postal 2921, Sao Paulo, Brazil.
- Folia Clinica et Biologica. q. ISSN 0015-5519 (prep. by its Departamento de Anatomia)

- Revista de Medicina. q. ISSN 0034-8554 (prep. by its Centro Academico "Oswaldo Cruz")

**Universidade de Sao Paulo. Faculdade de Medicina de Ribeirao Preto**
Rua Bernardino de Campos, 1000, Caixa Postal 572, Ribeirao Preto, Sao Paulo, Brazil.
- Medicina. s-a. ISSN 0076-6046 (prep. by its Centro Academico Rocha Lima)

**Universidade de Sao Paulo. Faculdade de Odontologia**
Rua Tres Rios 363, Sao Paulo, Brazil.
- Bibliografia Brasileira de Odontologia. biennial.
- Sumarios de Odontologia. bi-m. ISSN 0039-4947
- Universidade de Sao Paulo. Faculdade de Odontologia. Revista. s-a. ISSN 0041-879X

**Universidade de Sao Paulo. Faculdade de Odontologia de Bauru**
C.P. 73, 17100 Bauru, Sao Paulo, Brazil.
- Estomatologia e Cultura. s-a. ISSN 0014-1364

**Universidade de Sao Paulo. Faculdade de Saude Publica**
Av. Dr. Arnaldo 715, Caixa Postal 8099, Sao Paulo, Brazil.
- Revista de Saude Publica. q. ISSN 0034-8910

**Universidade de Sao Paulo. Hospital das Clinicas**
Caixa Postal 4066, Sao Paulo, Brazil.
- Arquivos de Cirurgia Clinica e Experimental. irreg. ISSN 0066-7846
- Universidade de Sao Paulo. Faculdade de Medicina.Hospital das Clinicas.Revista. bi-m. ISSN 0041-8781

**Universidade de Sao Paulo. Instituto Astronomico e Geofisico**
Universidade de Sao Paulo, C. P. 30627, 01000-Sao Paulo, Brazil.
- Previsoes de Radio Propagacao para Sao Paulo. m.
- Universidade de Sao Paulo. Instituto Astronomico e Geofisico. Anuario Astronomico. a.

**Universidade de Sao Paulo. Instituto de Direito Publico**
- Revista de Direito Publico. (pub. by Editora Revista dos Tribunais)

**Universidade de Sao Paulo. Instituto de Estudos Brasileiros**
Caixa Postal 11 154, Sao Paulo, Brazil.
- Instituto de Estudos Brasileiros. Revista. 2-4 per yr. ISSN 0020-3874
- Seminario de Estudos Brasileiros. Anais. irreg.

**Universidade de Sao Paulo. Instituto de Geociencias y Astronomia**
Cidade Universitaria "Armando de Salles Oliveira", Bloco, 19, Sao Paulo, Brazil.
- Universidade de Sao Paulo. Instituto de Geociencias y Astronomia. Boletim. irreg.

**Universidade de Sao Paulo. Instituto de Geografia, Sedimentologia e Pedologia**
Cidade Universitaria, C.P. 20715, 05508 Sao Paulo-SP, Brazil.
- Universidade de Sao Paulo. Instituto de Geografia, Sedimentologia e Pedologia. irreg; (approx. 2-3 per yr)

**Universidade de Sao Paulo. Instituto de Pesquisas Economicas**
Cidade Universitaria, Caixa Postal 11.498, Sao Paulo, Brazil.
- Estudos Economicos. 3 per yr.
- Universidade de Sao Paulo. Instituto de Pesquisas Economicas. Trabalho para Discussao. irreg.

**Universidade de Sao Paulo. Instituto Oceanografico**
Cidade Universitaria, Butanta, 05508 Sao Paulo, SP, Brazil.
- Boletim Climatologico. irreg.; no. 3, 1974. ISSN 0067-9585
- Universidade de Sao Paulo. Instituto Oceanografico. Boletim. a. ISSN 0080-6331
- Universidade de Sao Paulo. Instituto Oceanografico. Publicacao Especial. irreg.

**Universidade de Sao Paulo. Museu de Arte Contemporanea**
Caixa Postal 22031, Sao Paulo, Brazil.
- Universidade de Sao Paulo. Museu de Arte Contemporanea. Boletim Informativo. s-m. ISSN 0041-8803

**Universidade de Sao Paulo. Museu de Zoologia**
Caixa Postal 7172, Sao Paulo, Brazil.
- Arquivos de Zoologia. irreg. ISSN 0066-7870
- Papeis Avulsos de Zoologia. irreg. ISSN 0031-1049

**Universidade de Sao Paulo. Museu Paulista**
C.P. 42.503, 04263 Sao Paulo, Brazil.
- Museu Paulista. Anais. a. ISSN 0080-6374
- Museu Paulista. Colecao. irreg. ISSN 0080-6382
- Museu Paulista. Revista. a. ISSN 0080-6390

**Universidade de Sao Paulo. Servico de Documentacao**
Cidade Universitaria, Sao Paulo, Brazil.
- U. S. P. Boletim Informativo; servico de documentacao. ISSN 0041-8013

**Universidade de Uberlandia. Faculdade de Direito**
Av. Joao Pinheiro, 556, Uberlandia 38400, Brazil.
- Universidade de Uberlandia. Faculdade de Direito. Revista. s-a.

**Universidade do Estado do Rio de Janeiro**
Av Turf Club 5, Maracana ZC 11 C E P 20000, Rio de Janeiro, Guanabara, Brazil.
- Boletim U E R J. m.

**Universidade do Rio Grande do Norte**
Av. Hermes da Fonseca 780, Natal, Rio Grande, Brazil.
- Universidade Federal do Rio Grande do Norte. Instituto de Biologia Marinha. Boletim. ISSN 0041-8927

**Universidade do Vale do Rio dos Sinos**
- Estudos Juridicos. (pub. by Unisinos)
- Estudos Leopoldenses. (pub. by Unisinos)
- Estudos Tecnologicos. (pub. by Unisinos)
- Perspectiva Economica. (pub. by Unisinos)
- Perspectiva Teologica. (pub. by Unisinos)

**Universidade do Vale do Rio dos Sinos. Instituto Anchietano de Pesquisas**
- Pesquisas: Publicacoes de Antropologia. (pub. by Unisinos)
- Pesquisas: Publicacoes de Botanica. (pub. by Unisinos)
- Pesquisas: Publicacoes de Historia. (pub. by Unisinos)
- Pesquisas: Publicacoes de Zoologia. (pub. by Unisinos)

**Universidade Estadual de Campinas. Faculdade de Odontologia de Piracicaba**
Sao Paulo, Brazil.
- Boletim de Materiais Dentarios. s-a. ISSN 0045-2378

**Universidade Estadual de Londrina. Centro de Ciencias Humanas**
Brazil.
- Estudos de Psicanalise. a. ISSN 0014-1593 (prep. by its Circulo de Estudos Linguisticos)

**Universidade Estadual de Maringa**
Maringa, Brazil.
- Revista UNIMAR. irreg.

**Universidade Estadual Paulista. Faculdade de Filosofia, Ciencias e Letras de Presidente Prudente**
Rua Roberto Simonsen 305, C.P. 957, Presidente Prudente, Brazil.
- Faculdade de Filosofia, Ciencias e Letras de Presidente Prudente. Departamento de Educacao. Boletim.
- Faculdade de Filosofia, Ciencias e Letras de Presidente Prudente. Departamento de Geografia. Boletim. a.

**Universidade Estadual Paulista "Julio de Mesquita Filho". Faculdade de Farmacia e Odontologia de Araraquara**
Rua Expedicionarios do Brasil 1621, Caixa Postal 331, 14800 Araraquara (SP), Brazil.
- Universidade Estadual Paulista "Julio de Mesquita Filho." Faculdade de Farmacia e Odontologia de Araraquara. s-a.

**Universidade Estadual Paulista "Julio de Mesquito Filho". Faculdade de Filosofia, Ciencias e Letras de Marilia**
Avda. Vicente Ferreira 1278, Caixa Postal 420, 17500 Marilia, S.P., Brazil.
• Estudos Historicos. irreg. (prep. by its Departamento de Historia)

**Universidade Federal da Bahia**
Parque Universitario da Federacao, 40000 - Salvador, Bahia, Brazil.
• Universitas. q. ISSN 0041-9052

**Universidade Federal da Bahia. Centro de Estudos Afro-Orientais**
Rua A. Viana s/n, Salvador, Bahia, Brazil.
• Afro-Asia. irreg. ISSN 0002-0591

**Universidade Federal da Bahia. Centro Editorial e Didatico**
Rua A. Viana s/n, Canela, Salvador, Bahia, Brazil.
• Estudos Baianos. irreg.

**Imprensa da Universidade Federal de Goias**
Caixa Postal 9-Goiania, Goias, Brazil.
• Revista Goiana de Medicina. q. ISSN 0034-9585 (Associacao Medica de Goias) (Co-sponsor: Faculdade de Medicina da Universidade Federal de Goias)

**Universidade Federal de Minas Gerais**
Belo Horizonte MG 30000, Brazil.
• Revista Brasileira de Estudos Politicos. s-a. ISSN 0034-7191

**Universidade Federal de Minas Gerais. Escola de Biblioteconomia**
Caixa Postal 1906, Belo Horizonte MG 30000, Brazil.
• Universidade Federal de Minas Gerais. Escola de Biblioteconomia. Revista. s-a.

**Universidade Federal de Minas Gerais. Escola de Engenharia**
Rua Espirito Santo 35, 4 Andar-Sala 7, Belo Horizonte, Minas Gerais, Brazil.
• Universidade Federal de Minas Gerais. Escola de Engenharia. Revista. s-a. ISSN 0041-8838

**Universidade Federal de Minas Gerais. Escola de Veterinaria**
C.P. 567, Belo Horizonte, Minas Gerais, Brazil.
• Universidade Federal de Minas Gerais. Escola de Veterinaria. Arquivos. q. ISSN 0076-8863 (prep. by its Centro de Pesquisas Veterinarias)

**Universidade Federal de Minas Gerais. Faculdade de Letras**
Rua Carangola, 288 - 7 Andar, Caixa Postal 905, Belo Horizonte, Brazil.
• Phasis.

**Universidade Federal de Minas Gerais. Faculdade de Medicina**
C.P. 1621, 30000 Belo Horizonte, Minas Gerais, Brazil.
• Universidade Federal de Minas Gerais. Faculdade de Medincina. Anais. a.

**Universidade Federal de Minas Gerais. Faculdade de Odontologia**
Rua Conde Linhares 141, Belo Horizonte, Minas Gerais, Brazil.
• Universidade Federal de Minas Gerais. Curso de Odontologia. Arquivos do Centro de Estudos. s-a. ISSN 0004-2838

**Universidade Federal de Minas Gerais. Instituto de Pesquisas Radioativas**
Belo Horizonte, MG, Brazil.
• Universidade Federal de Minas Gerais. Instituto de Pesquisas Radioativas. Relatorios Anuais. a. ISSN 0067-5687

**Universidade Federal de Minas Gerais. Servicio de Relacoes Universitarias**
Caixa Postal 1621, Cidade Universitaria, 30000 Belo Horizonte, Minas Gerais, Brazil.
• Revista Literaria do Corpo Discente da Universidade Federal de Minas Gerais. a ISSN 0079-9327

**Universidade Federal de Pelotas. Faculdade de Agronomie "Eliseu Maciel"**
C.P.15, Pelotas, Rio Grande do Sul, Brazil.
• Instituto Agronomico do Sul. Escola de Agronomia Eliseu Maciel. Arquivos de Entomologia. Serie A & Serie B. s-a. ISSN 0020-3629

**Universidade Federal de Pernambuco**
Biblioteca Central, Cidade Universitaria, Recife, Pernambuco, Brazil.
• Catalogo de Pesquisas Concluidas e Em Desenvolvimento. (pub. by Editora Universitaria)
• Edicoes Cadernos Culturais. (pub. by Editora Universitaria)
• Universidade Federal de Pernambuco. Relatorio das Attividades Universitias. a.

**Universidade Federal de Pernambuco. Assessoria da Area de Informacao**
Cidade Universitaria, Av. Prof. Morais Rego, Recife, Pernambuco, Brazil.
• Universidade Federal de Pernambuco. Anuario Estatistico. a (with supplement)

**Universidade Federal de Pernambuco. Instituto de Antibioticos**
Recife, Pernambuco, Brazil.
• Universidade Federal de Pernambuco. Instituto de Antibioticos. Revista. irreg. ISSN 0080-0228

**Universidade Federal de Pernambuco. Instituto de Biologia Maritima e Oceanografia**
Recife, Pernambuco, Brazil.
• Universidade Federal de Pernambuco. Instituto de Biologie Maritima e Oceanografia. Trabalhos Oceanograficos. irreg.; vol. 14, 1975. ISSN 0080-0236

**Universidade Federal de Pernambuco. Instituto de Geociencias**
Recife, PE, Brazil.
• Universidad Federal de Pernambuco. Instituto de Geosciencias. Serie B: Estudos e Pesquisas. irreg. ISSN 0080-0244

**Universidade Federal de Pernambuco. Instituto de Matematica**
Cidade Universitaria, Caixa Postal 2672, Recife. Pernambuco, Brazil.
• Universidade Federal de Pernambuco. Instituto de Matematica. Notas e Communicacoes de Matematica. irreg. ISSN 0085-5413

**Universidade Federal de Santa Catarina. Faculdade de Medicina**
Rua Ferrira Lima 26, Florianopolis, Santa Catarina, Brazil.
• Arquivos Catarinenses de Medicina. s-a. ISSN 0004-2773 (Associacao Medica Catarinense)

**Universidade Federal de Santa Catarina. Museu de Antropologia**
Cx. Postal 476, Trinidade, Florianopolis, Santa Catarina, Brazil.
• Universidade Federal de Santa Catarina. Museu de Antropologia. Anais. irreg. ISSN 0581-6076

**Universidade Federal de Santa Maria. Centro de Ciencias Rurais**
97.100 Santa Maria, Rio Grande do Sul, Brazil.
• Universidade Federal de Santa Maria. Centro de Ciencias Rurais. Revista. irreg. ISSN 0085-5901

**Universidade Federal de Santa Maria. Centro de Estudos Antonio Pimenta**
Rio Grande do Sul, Brazil.
• Universidade Federal de Santa Maria. Centro de Estudos Antonio Pimenta. Curso de Odontologia de Santa Maria. Boletim. s-a. ISSN 0014-6706

**Universidade Federal de Santa Maria. Faculdade de Farmacie e Bioquimica**
Caixa Postal 124, Santa Maria R. G. S., Brazil.
• Universidade Federal de Santa Maria. Faculdade de Farmacie e Bioquimica. Revista. s-a. ISSN 0041-8846

**Universidade Federal de Vicosa**
Vicosa, Minas Gerais, Brazil.
• Ceres; publicacao de ensinamentos teoricos e praticos sobre, agricultura, veterinaria, industrias rurais. bi-m. ISSN 0034-737X
• Experientiae. s-m. ISSN 0014-4762

**Universidade Federal de Vicosa. Directorio Central dos Estudantes**
Vicosa, MG, Brazil.
• Seiva. q. ISSN 0037-1122

**Universidade Federal do Ceara**
Faculdade de Letras, Av. da Universidade, Fortaleza, Ceara, Brazil.
• Cabore. 3 per yr. ISSN 0007-9316
• Fortaleza, Brazil. Universidade do Ceara. Boletim. bi-m. ISSN 0046-4678

**Universidade Federal do Ceara. Centro de Ciencias Agrarias**
Avda. Mister Hull s/n, Caixa Postal 354, 6000 Fortaleza-Ceara, Brazil.
• Ciencia Agronomica. s-a. ISSN 0045-6888

**Universidade Federal do Ceara. Departamento de Ciencias Sociais e Filosofia**
C.P. 1257, Fortaleza, Ceara, Brazil.
• Revista de Ciencias Sociais. s-a. ISSN 0041-8862
• Universidade Federal do Ceara. Departamento de Ciencias Sociais e Filosofia. Documentos. (pub. by Imprensa Universitaria do Ceara)

**Universidade Federal do Ceara. Escola de Agronomia**
Departamento de Filotecnia, Caixa Postal 354, Fortaleza, Ceara 60000, Brazil.
• Universidade Federal do Ceara. Escola de Agronomia. Departamento de Fitotecnia. Relatoria Tecnico. irreg. ISSN 0084-8646

**Universidade Federal do Ceara. Faculdade de Medicina**
Caixa Postal 688 Fortaleza, Ceara, Brazil.
• Universidade Federal do Ceara. Faculdade de Medicina. Revista de Medicina/Federal University of Ceara School of Medicine. Journal of Medicine. s-a.

**Universidade Federal do Ceara. Laboratorio de Ciencias do Mar**
Avenida da Abolicao 3207 (Meireles), Caixa Postal 1072, Fortaleza, Ceara, Brazil.
• Arquivos de Ciencias do Mar. s-a. ISSN 0041-8854
• Boletim de Ciencias do Mar. irreg.; no. 25, 1974. ISSN 0067-9593

**Universidade Federal do Espirito Santo. Sub Reitoria de Planejamento e Desenvolvimento**
Vitoria, Espirito Santo, Brazil.
• Universidad Federal do Espirito Santo. Comissao de Planejamento. Documentario Estatistico Sobre a Situacao Educacional. Supplemento. irreg. ISSN 0085-0292
• Universidade Federal do Espirito Santo. Comissao de Planejamento. Documentario Estatistico Sobre a Situacao Educacional. irreg. ISSN 0085-0284

**Universidade Federal do Para**
Av. Governador Jose Malcher 1192, 66000 Belem-para, Brazil.
• Universidade Federal do Para. Revista. s-a. ISSN 0301-6722

**Universidade Federal do Parana**
Curitiba, Parana, Brazil.
• Curitiba. Universidade do Parana. Departamento de Historia. Boletim. irreg., 1969, no. 8. ISSN 0070-1815

**Universidade Federal do Parana. Centro de Estudos Portugueses**
Caixa Postal 441, 80000 Curitiba, Parana, Brazil.
• Universidade Federal do Parana. Centro de Estudos Portugueses. Arquivos; publicacao semestral para a divulgacao da cultura portuguesa. s-a.

**Universidade Federal do Parana. Centro de Pesquisas Florestais**
Rua Bom Jesus 650, P.O. Box 2959, Curitiba, Parana, Brazil.
• Floresta. s-a. ISSN 0015-3826

**Universidade Federal do Parana. Departamento de Letras Neolatinas**
Curitiba, Brazil.
• Cadernos de Neolatinas. s-a.

**Universidade Federal do Parana. Faculdade de Farmacia**
Rua Coronel Dulcidio 638, Caixa Postal 888, Curitiba, Parana, Brazil.
• Tribuna Farmaceutica. s-a. ISSN 0049-4631

**Universidade Federal do Parana. Instituto de Biologia**
Cx. Postal 888, Curitiba, Parana, Brazil.
- Acta Biologica Paranaense. 1-2 per yr. (prep. by its Departamento de Botanica)

**Universidade Federal do Parana. Museu de Arqueologia e Artes Populares**
Rua 15 de Novembro, No. 567, Paranagua, Brazil.
- Universidade Federal do Parana. Museu de Arqueologia e Artes Populares. Cadernos de Artes e Tradicoes Populares. irreg.

**Universidade Federal do Parana. Setor de Ciencias Humanas, Letras e Artes**
Curitiba, Parana, Brazil.
- Revista Letras. s-a.

**Universidade Federal do Parana. Setor de Tecnologia**
80000 Curitiba, Parana, Brazil.
- Boletim Paranaense de Geociencias. irreg.; nos. 28-29, 1970 per 71. ISSN 0067-964X

**Universidade Federal do Rio de Janeiro. Coordenacao dos Programas de Pos-Graduacao de Engenharia**
Rio de Janeiro- RJ, Brazil.
- C O P P E Noticiario. bi-m.

**Universidade Federal do Rio de Janeiro. Faculdade de Odontologia**
Avenida Pasteur N.438, Praia Vermelha, Rio de Janeiro, Guanabara, Brazil.
- Universidade Federal do Rio de Janeiro. Faculdade de Odontologia. Anais. ISSN 0041-8919

**Universidade Federal do Rio de Janeiro. Forum de Ciencia e Cultura.**
Av. Pasteur 250, Praia Vermelha, Rio de Janeiro, Brazil.
- Cadernos de Estudos Brasileiros. irreg.

**Universidade Federal do Rio de Janeiro. Instituto de Geociencias**
Biblioteca, Cidade Universitaria-Ilha do Funado, 2000 Rio de Janeiro, GB, Brazil.
- Boletim de Geologia. a. ISSN 0566-1765

**Universidade Federal do Rio de Janeiro. Instituto de Matematica**
C.P. 1835-ZC-00, 20000 Rio de Janeiro, RJ, Brazil.
- Universidade Federal de Rio de Janeiro. Instituto de Matematica. Memorias de Matematica. irreg. (approx. 12 per yr), no. 58, 1975.

**Universidade Federal do Rio de Janeiro. Instituto de Neurologia**
Av. Venceslau Bras 95, Rio de Janeiro, Brazil.
- Jornal Brasileiro de Neurologia. ISSN 0021-7514

**Universidade Federal do Rio de Janeiro. Instituto de Psiciatria**
Av. Venceslau Braz, 71, Rio de Janeiro 20000, Brazil.
- Jornal Brasileiro de Psiquiatria. q. ISSN 0047-2085

**Universidade Federal do Rio Grande do Norte. Instituto de Antropologia "Camara Cascudo"**
Av. Hermes da Fonseca 1398, Natal, Rio Grande do Norte, Brazil.
- Instituto de Antropologia "Camara Cascudo". Arquivos. irreg.

**Universidade Federal do Rio Grande do Sul**
Porto Alegre, Brazil.
- Colecao Teatro. irreg.

**Universidade Federal do Rio Grande do Sul. Centro de Investigacao do Gondwana**
Rua Gen. Vitorino 255, Porto Alegre, Brazil.
- Gondwana Newsletter. irreg., 1969, no. 1. ISSN 0072-4998

**Universidade Federal do Rio Grande do Sul. Faculdade de Agronomia e Veterinaria**
Bento Goncalves 7712, P.O. Box 776, 90000 Porto Alegre, R.S., Brazil.
- Universidade Federal do Rio Grande do Sul. Faculdade de Agronomia e Veterinaria. Revista.

**Universidade Federal do Rio Grande do Sul. Faculdade de Medicina**
Rua Sarmento Leite s/n, 90000 Porto Alegre, R.S., Brazil.
- Revista de Psiquiatria Dinamica. q. ISSN 0034-8767 (Co-sponsor: Associacao Encarnacion Blava)

- Universidade Federal do Rio Grande do Sul. Faculdade de Medicina. Anais. irreg. ISSN 0085-042X

**Universidade Federal do Rio Grande do Sul. Instituto de Biociencias**
Porto Alegre, Rio Grande do Sul, Brazil.
- Universidade Federal do Rio Grande do Sul. Instituto Central de Biociencias. Boletim. irreg.; no. 32, 1974.

**Universidade Federal do Rio Grande do Sul. Instituto de Ciencias Naturais**
Santa Maria, Rio Grande do Sul, Brazil.
- Universidade Federal do Rio Grande do Sul. Instituto de Ciencias Naturais. Boletim. irreg. ISSN 0080-6129

**Universidade Federal do Rio Grande do Sul. Instituto de Filosofia e Ciencias Humanas**
Porto Alegre, Rio Grande do Sul, Brazil.
- Universidade Federal do Rio Grande do Sul. Instituto de Filosofia e Ciencias Humanas. Revista. irreg.

**Universidade Federal do Rio Grande do Sul. Instituto de Geosciencias**
Rua Ge. Vitotino, 255, Porto Alegre, Brazil.
- Universidade Federal do Rio Grande do Sul. Instituto de Geosciencias. Pesquisas. irreg.

**Universidade Federal Fluminense. Faculdade de Odontologia**
Rua Sao Paulo 28, Niteroi, Rio de Janeiro, Brazil.
- Arquivos Fluminenses de Odontologia. q. ISSN 0044-8982

**Universidade Federal Fluminense. Instituto de Matematica**
Niteroi, Brazil.
- Boletim de Analise e Logica Matematica. irreg.

**Universidade Federal Fluminense. Secao de Referencia Legislativa**
R. Miguel de Frias 9, Caixa Postal 1108, Niteroi, Brazil.
- Universidade Federal Fluminense. Secao de Referencia Legislativa. Boletim de Referencia Legislativa. s-m.

**Universidade Mackenzie. Centro Academico Horacio Lane**
149 rua Itambe, C.P. 8792, Sao Paulo, Brazil.
- Revista de Engenharia Mackenzie. s-a. ISSN 0034-8112

**Editora Universitaria**
Recife, Brazil.
- Catalogo de Pesquisas Concluidas e Em Desenvolvimento. irreg. (Universidade Federal de Pernambuco)
- Edicoes Cadernos Culturais; uma revista de cultura do nordeste para o Brasil. irreg. (Universidade Federal de Pernambuco)

**Editora Vecchi, S.A.**
Rua do Resende 144, Rio de Janeiro, Brazil.
- Figurino Moderno. m. ISSN 0015-0851
- Grande Hotel. w. ISSN 0017-3142

**Vertente Editora Ltda.**
Rua Monte Alegre 1434, 05014 Sao Paulo, Brazil.
- Escrita. m.

**Vida Rural e Economica**
Rua do Rosario, 371, Porto Alegre, Brazil.
- Vida Rural e Economica. m. ISSN 0042-5273

**Visao S.A. Editorial**
Afonso Celso 243, 04119 Sao Paulo, Brazil.
- Dirigente Construtor. m. ISSN 0012-3358
- Dirigente Industrial. m. ISSN 0012-3366
- Dirigente Municipal. bi-m. ISSN 0419-3911
- Dirigente Rural. bi-m. ISSN 0012-3374
- Perfil da Administracao Federal. s-a.
- Visao. s-m. ISSN 0042-6873

**Editora Vozes Ltda.**
Caixa Postal 23, 25600 Petropolis, Rio de Janeiro, Brazil.
- Grande Sinal. 10 per yr. ISSN 0046-6271
- Poetas Modernos do Brasil. irreg.
- Revista Brasileira de Linguistica. s-a. (Sociedade Brasileira para Professores de Linguistica)
- Revista Eclesiastica Brasileira. q.
- S E D O C/Servico de Documentacao. m. ISSN 0036-1267

- Studia Entomologica; revista internacional de entomologia. a. ISSN 0585-5098

# BRITISH SOLOMON ISLANDS

**British Solomon Islands. Department of Posts and Telecommunications**
Honiara, British Solomon Islands.
- British Solomon Islands. Department of Posts and Telecommunications. Annual Report. a. ISSN 0068-2535
- Solomon Islands Stamp Magazine. irreg., 1970, no. 5. ISSN 0081-198X

**Solomon Islands Museum Association**
Box 313, Honiara, British Solomon Islands.
- Solomon Islands Museum Association. Journal. a.

# BRUNEI

**Brunei. State Secretariat. Information Service**
Brunei, Brunei.
- Brunei Annual Report. a. ISSN 0084-8123

**Brunei Museum**
Kota Batu, Bandar Seri Begawan, Brunei.
- Brunei Museum. Special Publication/Muzium Brunei. Penerbitan Khas. irreg., 1972, no. 7. ISSN 0084-8131
- Brunei Museum Journal. a. ISSN 0068-2918

**Language and Literature Bureau**
Jalan Elizabeth II, Bandar Seri Begawan, Brunei.
- Bahana. q. ISSN 0005-3988

# BULGARIA

**Akademiia na Selskostopanskite Nauki**
- Abstracts of Bulgarian Scientific Literature. Agriculture and Forestry. Veterinary Medicine. (pub. by Publishing House of the Bulgarian Academy of Sciences)
- Agrofizichni Izsledovaniia. (pub. by Publishing House of the Bulgarian Academy of Sciences)
- Genetika i Selektsiia. (pub. by Publishing House of the Bulgarian Academy of Sciences)
- Gorskostopanska Nauka/Forestry Science. (pub. by Publishing House of the Bulgarian Academy of Sciences)
- Gradinarska i Lozarska Nauka/Horticultural and Viticultural Science. (pub. by Publishing House of the Bulgarian Academy of Sciences)
- Pochvoznanie i Agrokhimiia. (pub. by Publishing House of the Bulgarian Academy of Sciences)
- Rastenievudni Nauki. (pub. by Publishing House of the Bulgarian Academy of Sciences)
- Selskostopanska Tekhnika. (pub. by Publishing House of the Bulgarian Academy of Sciences)
- Zhivotnovudni Nauki. (pub. by Publishing House of the Bulgarian Academy of Sciences)

**American Embassy**
1, Aleksandur Stamboliiski Blvd., Sofia, Bulgaria.
- Directory of Key Bulgarian Government and Party Officials.

**Bulgaria. Ministerstvo na Finansite**
Sofia, Bulgaria
(Dist. by: Hemus, 6, Rouski Blvd., 1000 Sofia, Bulgaria)
- Finansi I Kredit. 10 per yr. ISSN 0015-2137 (Co-sponsor: Bulgarska Narodna Banka)

**Bulgaria. Ministerstvo na Informatsiiata i Suobshteniiata**
8, Ul. Graf Ignatiev, Sofia, Bulgaria
(Dist. by: Hemus, 6, Rouski Blvd., 1000 Sofia, Bulgaria)
- Bulgaria. Ministerstvo na Informatsiiata i Suobshteniiata. Suobshteniia; nauchno i proizvodstveno-tekhnichesko spisanie. m.
- Filatelen Pregled. m. (Co-sponsor: Suiuz na Bulgarski Filatelisti)
- Statisticheski Godishnik na Narodna Republika Bulgaria. (pub. by Izdatelstvo Nauka i Izkustvo)
- Statisticheski Izvestiia. m. (Co-sponsor: Tsentralno Statistichesko Upravlenie)
- Statisticheski Spravochnik. a. (Co-sponsor: Tsentralno Statistichesko Upravlenie)
- Tseni. a. (Co-sponsor: Tsentralno Statistichesko Upravlenie)

- Turizum/Turism. irreg. (Co-sponsor: Tsentralno Statistichesko Upravlenie)

**Bulgaria. Ministerstvo na Khimicheska Promishlenost**
Sofia, Bulgaria
(Dist. by: Hemus, 6, Rouski Blvd., 1000 Sofia, Bulgaria)
- Tseluloza i Khartiia. bi-m. (Co-sponsor: Nauchno-Tekhnicheski Suiuz po Khimicheska Promishlenost)

**Bulgaria. Ministerstvo na Lekata Promishlenost**
Sofia, Bulgaria
(Dist. by: Hemus, 6, Rouski Blvd., 1000 Sofia, Bulgaria)
- Kozharska i Obuvna Promishlenost. 8 per yr.
- Tekstilna Promishlenost. 10 per yr. (Co-sponsor: Nauchno- Tekhnicheski Suiuz po Tekstil i Obleklo)

**Bulgaria. Ministerstvo na Mashinostroeneto i Metalurgiiata**
8, Ul. Slavianska, Sofia, Bulgaria
(Dist. by: Hemus, 6, Rouski Blvd., 1000 Sofia, Bulgaria)
- Elektropromishlenost i Priborostroene. 10 per yr. ISSN 0013-5763 (Co-sponsor: Ministerstvo na Elektronikata i Elektrotekhnikata)
- Mashinostroene. m. ISSN 0025-455X (Co-Sponsor: Nauchno-Tekhnicheski Suiuz po Mashinostroene)
- Rudodobiv. m. (Co-sponsor: Nauchno-Tekhnicheski Suiuz po Minno Delo, Geologiia i Metalurgiia)

**Bulgaria. Ministerstvo na Narodnata Otbrana**
- Armeiski Pregled. (pub. by Durzhavno Voenno Izdatelstvo)

**Bulgaria. Ministerstvo na Narodnoto Zdrave**
- Dermatologiia i Venerologiia. (pub. by Izdatelstvo Meditsina i Fizkultura)
- Farmatsiia. (pub. by Izdatelstvo Meditsina i Fizkultura)
- Ftiziatriia. (pub. by Izdatelstvo Meditsina i Fizkultura)
- Khigiena i Zdraveopazvane. (pub. by Izdatelstvo Meditsina i Fizkultura)
- Khirurgiia. (pub. by Izdatelstvo Meditsina i Fizkultura)
- Nevrologiia, Psikhiatriia i Nevrokhirurgiia. (pub. by Izdatelstvo Meditsina i Fizkultura)
- Onkologiia. (pub. by Izdatelstvo Meditsina i Fizkultura)
- Pediatriia. (pub. by Izdatelstvo Meditsina i Fizkultura)
- Rentgenologiia i Radiologiia. (pub. by Izdatelstvo Meditsina i Fizkultura)
- Suvremenna Meditsina. (pub. by Izdatelstvo Meditsina i Fizkultura)

**Bulgaria. Ministerstvo na Stroezhite i Arkhitekturata**
Sofia, Bulgaria
(Dist. by: Hemus, 6, Rouski Blvd., 1000 Sofia, Bulgaria)
- Stroitelni Materiali i Silikatna Promishlenost. m.
- Stroitelstvo. m. (Co-sponsor: Nauchno-Tekhnicheski Suiuz po Stroitelstvo)

**Bulgaria. Ministerstvo na Transporta**
Sofia, Bulgaria
(Dist. by: Hemus, 6, Rouski Blvd., 1000 Sofia, Bulgaria)
- Korabostroene i Koraboplavane/Shipbuilding and Shipping. m. (Co-sponsor: Bulgaria. Ministerstvo na Mashinostroeneto i Metalurgiiata)

**Bulgaria. Ministerstvo na Transporta. Glavno Upravlene na Putushtata**
Sofia, Bulgaria
(Dist. by: Hemus, 6, Rouski Blvd., 1000 Sofia, Bulgaria)
- Putishta. m. (Co-sponsor: Nauchno - Tekhnicheski Suiuz po Stroitelstvo)

**Bulgaria. Ministerstvo na Vutreshnita Turgoviia i Uslugite**
Sofia, Bulgaria
(Dist. by: Hemus, 6, Rouski Blvd., 1000 Sofia, Bulgaria)
- Lada. m.

**Bulgaria. Ministerstvo na Zemedelieto i Khranitelna Promishlenost**
- Gradinarstvo. (pub. by Izdatelstvo Profizdat)
- Lozarstvo i Vinarstvo. (pub. by Izdatelstvo Profizdat)
- Rastitelna Zashtita. (pub. by Izdatelstvo Profizdat)

- Ribno Stopanstvo. (pub. by Izdatelstvo Profizdat)

**Bulgarreklama Agency**
42, Ul. Parchevich, Sofia, Bulgaria
(Dist. by: Hemus, 6, Rouski Blvd., 1000 Sofia, Bulgaria)
- Bulgarian Foreign Trade. bi-m. ISSN 0007-392X (Bulgarska Turgovska Promishlena Palata)

**Bulgarska Akademiia na Naukite**
- Abstracts of Bulgarian Scientific Literature. Biology and Biochemistry. (pub. by Publishing House of the Bulgarian Academy of Sciences)
- Abstracts of Bulgarian Scientific Literature. Economics and Law. (pub. by Publishing House of the Bulgarian Academy of Sciences)
- Abstracts of Bulgarian Scientific Literature. Geology and Geography. (pub. by Publishing House of the Bulgarian Academy of Sciences)
- Abstracts of Bulgarian Scientific Literature. Mathematics, Physics, Astronomy, Geophysics, Geodesy. (pub. by Publishing House of the Bulgarian Academy of Sciences)
- Abstracts of Bulgarian Scientific Literature. Philosophy, Sociology, Science of Sciences, Psychology and Pedagogics. (pub. by Publishing House of the Bulgarian Academy of Sciences)
- Academie Bulgare des Sciences. Comptes Rendus. (pub. by Publishing House of the Bulgarian Academy of Sciences)
- Acta Mikrobiologika, Virologika et Immunologica. (pub. by Publishing House of the Bulgarian Academy of Sciences)
- Acta Morfologika. (pub. by Publishing House of the Bulgarian Academy of Sciences)
- Acta Physiologica et Pharmacologica Bulgarica. (pub. by Publishing House of the Bulgarian Academy of Sciences)
- Astrofizicheskie Issledovaniia. (pub. by Publishing House of the Bulgarian Academy of Sciences)
- Bulgarian Academic Books. (pub. by Publishing House of the Bulgarian Academy of Sciences)
- Bulgarian Historical Review/Revue Bulgare d'Histoire. (pub. by Publishing House of the Bulgarian Academy of Sciences)
- Bulgarian Journal of Physics/Bolgarskii Fizicheskii Zhurnal. (pub. by Publishing House of the Bulgarian Academy of Sciences)
- Bulgarska Akademiia na Naukite. Spisanie. (pub. by Publishing House of the Bulgarian Academy of Sciences)
- Bulgarska Etnografiia. (pub. by Publishing House of the Bulgarian Academy of Sciences)
- Bulgarski Folklor. (pub. by Publishing House of the Bulgarian Academy of Sciences)
- Bulgarsko Geologichesko Druzhestvo. Spisanie. (pub. by Publishing House of the Bulgarian Academy of Sciences)
- Bulletin d'Analyses de la Litterature Scientifique Bulgare. Linguistique et Litterature. (pub. by Publishing House of the Bulgarian Academy of Sciences)
- Ekologiia. (pub. by Publishing House of the Bulgarian Academy of Sciences)
- Fiziko-Khimicheska Mekhanika/Physico-Chemical Mechanics. (pub. by Publishing House of the Bulgarian Academy of Sciences)
- Fiziologiia na Rasteniiata. (pub. by Publishing House of the Bulgarian Academy of Sciences)
- Geokhimiia, Mineralogiia i Petrologiia. (pub. by Publishing House of the Bulgarian Academy of Sciences)
- Geologica Balcanica. (pub. by Publishing House of the Bulgarian Academy of Sciences)
- Geotektonika, Tektonofizika i Geodinamika. (pub. by Publishing House of the Bulgarian Academy of Sciences)
- Hydrobiology. (pub. by Publishing House of the Bulgarian Academy of Sciences)
- Iaderna Energiia/Nuclear Energy. (pub. by Publishing House of the Bulgarian Academy of Sciences)
- Istoriia na Bulgarskoto Izobrazitelno Izkustvo. (pub. by Publishing House of the Bulgarian Academy of Sciences)
- Linguistique Balkanique. (pub. by Publishing House of the Bulgarian Academy of Sciences)
- Materialoznanie i Tekhnologiia. (pub. by Publishing House of the Bulgarian Academy of Sciences)
- Molekulna Biologiia. (pub. by Publishing House of the Bulgarian Academy of Sciences)

- Neftena i Vuglishtna Geologiia/Petroleum and Coal Geology. (pub. by Publishing House of the Bulgarian Academy of Sciences)
- Obshta i Sravnitelna Patologiia. (pub. by Publishing House of the Bulgarian Academy of Sciences)
- Okeanologiia. (pub. by Publishing House of the Bulgarian Academy of Sciences)
- Priroda. (pub. by Publishing House of the Bulgarian Academy of Sciences)
- Problemi na Khelminthologiiata. (pub. by Publishing House of the Bulgarian Academy of Sciences)
- Problemi na Tekhnicheskata Kibernetika. (pub. by Publishing House of the Bulgarian Academy of Sciences)
- Rudoobrazuvatelni Protsesi i Mineralni Nakhodishta. (pub. by Publishing House of the Bulgarian Academy of Sciences)
- Serdika; Bulgarsko Matematichesko Spisanie/ Serdica; Bulgaricae Mathematicae Publicationes. (pub. by Publishing House of the Bulgarian Academy of Sciences)
- Tekhnicheska Misul. (pub. by Publishing House of the Bulgarian Academy of Sciences)
- Vissha Geodeziia. (pub. by Publishing House of the Bulgarian Academy of Sciences)
- Zentralblatt der Bulgarischen Wissenschaftlichen Literatur. Geschichte, Archaeologie und Ethnographie. (pub. by Publishing House of the Bulgarian Academy of Sciences)

**Bulgarska Akademiia na Naukite. Mikrobiologicheski Institut**
- Bulgarska Akademiia na Naukite, Sofia. Mikrobiologicheski Institut. Izvestiia. (pub. by Publishing House of the Bulgarian Academy of Sciences)

**Bulgarska Akademiia na Naukite. Arkheologicheski Institut i Muzei**
- Arkheologiia. (pub. by Publishing House of the Bulgarian Academy of Sciences)
- Bulgarska Akademiia na Naukite, Sofia. Arkheologicheski Institut. Izvestiia. (pub. by Publishing House of the Bulgarian Academy of Sciences)

**Bulgarska Akademiia na Naukite. Botanicheski Institut**
- Bulgarska Akademiia na Naukite, Sofia. Botanicheski Institut. Izvestiia. (pub. by Publishing House of the Bulgarian Academy of Sciences)

**Bulgarska Akademiia na Naukite. Fizicheski i Matematicheski Institut**
- Fiziko-Matematichesko Spisanie. (pub. by Publishing House of the Bulgarian Academy of Sciences)

**Bulgarska Akademiia na Naukite. Geofizichni Institut**
- Bulgarska Akademiia na Naukite, Sofia. Geofizichni Institut. Izvestiia. (pub. by Publishing House of the Bulgarian Academy of Sciences)

**Bulgarska Akademiia na Naukite. Geografski Institut**
- Bulgarska Akademiia na Naukite, Sofia. Geografski Institut. Izvestiia. (pub. by Publishing House of the Bulgarian Academy of Sciences)

**Bulgarska Akademiia na Naukite. Geologicheski Institut**
- Inzhenerna Geologiia i Khidrogeologiia. (pub. by Publishing House of the Bulgarian Academy of Sciences)
- Paleontologiia, Stratigrafiia i Litologiia. (pub. by Publishing House of the Bulgarian Academy of Sciences)

**Bulgarska Akademiia na Naukite. Ikonomicheski Institut**
- Ikonomicheska Misul. (pub. by Publishing House of the Bulgarian Academy of Sciences)

**Bulgarska Akademiia na Naukite. Institut po Filosofiia**
- Bulgarska Akademiia na Naukite, Sofia. Institut po Filosofiia. Izvestiia. (pub. by Publishing House of the Bulgarian Academy of Sciences)
- Filosofska Misul. (pub. by Publishing House of the Bulgarian Academy of Sciences)

**Bulgarska Akademiia na Naukite. Institut po Istoriia**
- Izsledovaniia po Bulgarska Istoriia. (pub. by Publishing House of the Bulgarian Academy of Sciences)

**Bulgarska Akademiia na Naukite. Institut po Khidrologiia i Meteorologiia**
- Bulgarska Akademiia na Naukite, Sofia. Institut po Khidrologiia 1 Meteorologiia. Izvestiia. (pub. by Publishing House of the Bulgarian Academy of Sciences)

**Bulgarska Akademiia na Naukite. Institut po Mikrobiologiia**
- Prilozhna Mikrobiologiia/Applied Microbiology. (pub. by Publishing House of the Bulgarian Academy of Sciences)

**Bulgarska Akademiia na Naukite. Institut po Morfologiia**
- Bulgarska Akademiia na Naukite, Sofia. Institut po Morfologiia. Izvestiia. (pub. by Publishing House of the Bulgarian Academy of Sciences)

**Bulgarska Akademiia na Naukite. Institut po Obshta i Sravnitelna Patalogiia**
- Bulgarska Akademia na Naukite, Sofia. Institut po Obshta i Sravnitelna Patalogiia. Izvestiia. (pub. by Publishing House of the Bulgarian Academy of Sciences)

**Bulgarska Akademiia na Naukite. Institut po Sotsiologiia**
- Sotsiologicheski Problemi. (pub. by Publishing House of the Bulgarian Academy of Sciences)

**Bulgarska Akademiia na Naukite. Institut po Tekhnicheska Kibernetika**
- Bulgarska Akademiia na Naukite, Sofia. Institut po Tekhnicheska Kibernetika. Izvestiia. (pub. by Publishing House of the Bulgarian Academy of Sciences)

**Bulgarska Akademiia na Naukite. Institut po Vodni Problemi**
- Vodni Problemi. (pub. by Publishing House of the Bulgarian Academy of Sciences)

**Bulgarska Akademiia na Naukite. Institut za Balkanistika**
- Etudes Balkaniques. (pub. by Publishing House of the Bulgarian Academy of Sciences)

**Bulgarska Akademiia na Naukite. Institut za Bulgarski Ezik**
- Bulgarska Akademiia na Naukite, Sofia. Institut za Bulgarski Ezik. Izvestiia. (pub. by Publishing House of the Bulgarian Academy of Sciences)
- Bulgarski Etimologichen Rechnik. (pub. by Publishing House of the Bulgarian Academy of Sciences)
- Bulgarski Ezik. (pub. by Publishing House of the Bulgarian Academy of Sciences)

**Bulgarska Akademiia na Naukite. Institut za Istoriia**
- Bulgarska Akademiia na Naukite, Sofia. Institut za Istoriia. Izvestiia. (pub. by Publishing House of the Bulgarian Academy of Sciences)
- Istoricheski Pregled. (pub. by Publishing House of the Bulgarian Academy of Sciences)
- Metodologicheski i Istoriografski Problemi na Istoricheskata Nauka. (pub. by Publishing House of the Bulgarian Academy of Sciences)

**Bulgarska Akademiia na Naukite. Institut za Izkustvoznanie**
- Problemi na Izkustvoto/Problems of Arts. (pub. by Publishing House of the Bulgarian Academy of Sciences)

**Bulgarska Akademiia na Naukite. Institut za Literatura**
- Literaturna Misul. (pub. by Publishing House of the Bulgarian Academy of Sciences)

**Bulgarska Akademiia na Naukite. Institut za Muzikoznanie**
- Bulgarska Akademia na Naukite, Sofia. Institut za Muzikoznanie. Izvestiia. (pub. by Publishing House of the Bulgarian Academy of Sciences)

**Bulgarska Akademiia na Naukite. Institut za Pravni Nauki**
- Bulgarska Akademiia na Naukite, Sofia. Institut za Pravni Nauki. Izvestiia. (pub. by Publishing House of the Bulgarian Academy of Sciences)
- Pravna Misul. (pub. by Publishing House of the Bulgarian Academy of Sciences)

**Bulgarska Akademiia na Naukite. Nauchnoizsledovatelski Tsentur za Africa i Aziia**
- Afrikano-Aziatski Problemi. (pub. by Publishing House of the Bulgarian Academy of Sciences)

**Bulgarska Akademiia na Naukite. Sektsiia po Astronomiia**
- Astronomicheski Kalendar na Observatoriiata v Sofia. (pub. by Publishing House of the Bulgarian Academy of Sciences)

**Bulgarska Akademiia na Naukite. Tsentralna Biblioteka**
- Bulgarska Akademiia na Naukite, Sofia. Tsentralna Biblioteka. Izvestiia. (pub. by Publishing House of the Bulgarian Academy of Sciences)

**Bulgarska Akademiia na Naukite. Tsentralna Khelmintologichna Laboratoriia**
- Bulgarska Akademiia na Naukite, Sofia. Tsentralna Khelmintologichna Laboratoriia. Izvestiia. (pub. by Publishing House of the Bulgarian Academy of Sciences)

**Bulgarska Akademiia na Naukite. Tsentralna Laboratoriia po Biomekhanika**
- Biomekhanika/Biomechanics. (pub. by Publishing House of the Bulgarian Academy of Sciences)

**Bulgarska Akademiia na Naukite. Tsentralna Laboratoriia po Geodeziia**
- Geodesy. (pub. by Publishing House of the Bulgarian Academy of Sciences)

**Bulgarska Akademiia na Naukite. Zoologicheski Institut**
- Acta Zoologica Bulgarica. (pub. by Publishing House of the Bulgarian Academy of Sciences)

**Bulgarska Turgovska Promishlena Palata**
11-a, Stamboliiski Blvd., Sofia, Bulgaria.
- Bulgarian Foreign Trade. (pub. by Bulgarreklama Agency)
- Economic News of Bulgaria. m. ISSN 0013-0176

**Bulgarski Profesionalni Suiuzi**
- Bulgarian Trade Unions. (pub. by Izdatelstvo Profizdat)

**Bulgarsko Istorichesko Druzhestvo**
- Bulgarsko Istorichesko Druzhestvo. Izvestiia. (pub. by Publishing House of the Bulgarian Academy of Sciences)

**Cinematography Committee**
8A, Rouski Blvd., Sofia, Bulgaria
(Dist. by: Hemus, 6, Rouski Blvd., 1000 Sofia, Bulgaria)
- Bulgarian Films. 8 per yr. ISSN 0007-3911 (Co-sponsor: Suiuz na Kinodeitsite)

**Druzhestvo na Psikholozite**
8, Ul. Bialo More, Sofia, Bulgaria
(Dist. by: Hemus, 6, Rouski Blvd., 1000 Sofia, Bulgaria)
- Psikhologiia. q.

**Durzhavno Voenno Izdatelstvo**
12, Ul. Ivan Vazov, Sofia, Bulgaria
(Dist. by: Hemus, 6, Rouski Blvd., 1000 Sofia, Bulgaria)
- Armeiski Pregled. m. ISSN 0004-2285 (Bulgaria. Ministerstvo na Narodnata Otbrana)
- Bulgaro-Suvetska Druzhba. m. (Obshtonarodna Komitet za Bulgaro-Suvetska Druzhba)
- Bulgarski Voenen Knigopis. bi-m. (Institut po Voena Istoriia)

**Glavno Politichesko Upravlenie na Narodnata Armiia**
1, Ul. Sofiiska Komuna, Sofia, Bulgaria
(Dist. by: Hemus, 6, Rouski Blvd., 1000 Sofia, Bulgaria)
- Bulgarski Voin. m. ISSN 0007-4004

**Institut po Voena Istoriia**
- Bulgarski Voenen Knigopis. (pub. by Durzhavno Voenno Izdatelstvo)

**Komitet za Izkustvo i Kultura**
39, Dondukov Blvd., Sofia, Bulgaria
(Dist. by: Hemus, 6, Rouski Blvd., 1000 Sofia, Bulgaria)
- Bulgarsko Foto; a journal of photographic art, technique, and photojournalism. 10 per yr. ISSN 0007-4012
- Chitalishte. (pub. by Izdatelstvo Natsionalen Suvet na Otechestveniia Front)
- Kinoizkustvo. m. (Co-sponsors: Suiuz na Kinodeitsite; Suiuz na Bulgarskite Pisatel)
- Obzor; Bulgarian quarterly review of literature & the arts. q. ISSN 0029-7852 (Co-sponsor: Suiuz na Bulgarski Pisateli)

- Tantsovo Izkustvo. (pub. by Izdatelstvo Nauka i Izkustvo)
- Teatur. m. (Co-sponsor: Suiuz na Artistite)

**Komitet za Nauka, Tekhnicheski Progres i Visshe Obrazovanie**
16, Ul. Gurko, Sofia, Bulgaria.
- Abstracts of Bulgarian Scientific Literature. Industry, Building and Transport. q.

**Komitet za Otdikh i Turizum**
- Resorts in Bulgaria. (pub. by Sofia-Press Agency)

**Komitet za Televiziia i Radio**
4, Dragan Tsankov Blvd., Sofia, Bulgaria
(Dist. by: Hemus, 6, Rouski Blvd., 1000 Sofia, Bulgaria)
- Televiziia. Radio. w.

**Izdatelstvo Meditsina i Fizkultura**
11, Pl. Slaveikov, Sofia, Bulgaria
(Dist. by: Hemus, 6, Rouski Blvd., 1000 Sofia, Bulgaria)
- Dermatologiia i Venerologiia. q. (Bulgaria. Ministerstvo na Narodnoto Zdrave) (Co-sponsor: Nauchno Druzhestvo na Dermatolozite)
- Farmatsiia. bi-m. (Bulgaria. Ministerstvo na Narodnoto Zdrave) (Co-sponsor: Nauchno Druzhestvo na Farmatsevtite)
- Ftiziatriia. q. (Bulgaria. Ministerstvo na Narodnoto Zdrave) (Co-sponsor: Nauchno Druzhestvo na Ftiziatrite)
- Khigiena i Zdraveopazvane. bi-m. ISSN 0018-8247 (Bulgaria. Ministerstvo na Narodnoto Zdrave) (Co-sponsor: Nauchno Druzhestvo na Khigienisti, Epidemiolozi, Mikrobiolozi, Infektsionisti i Organizatori na Zdraveopazvaneto)
- Khirurgiia. bi-m. (Bulgaria. Ministerstvo na Narodnoto Zdrave) (Co-sponsor: Nauchno Druzhestvo na Khirurzite)
- Nevrologiia, Psikhiatriia i Nevrokhirurgiia. bi-m. (Bulgaria. Ministerstvo na Narodnoto Zdrave) (Co-sponsor: Nauchno Druzhestvo na Nevrolozi, Psikhiatri i Nevrokhirurzi)
- Onkologiia. q. (Bulgaria. Ministerstvo na Narodnoto Zdrave) (Co-sponsor: Nauchno Druzhestvo na Onkolozite)
- Pediatriia. bi-m. (Bulgaria. Ministerstvo na Narodnoto Zdrave) (Co-sponsor: Nauchno Druzhestvo na Pediatrite)
- Rentgenologiia i Radiologiia. q. (Bulgaria. Ministerstvo na Narodnoto Zdrave) (Co-sponsor: Nauchno Druzhestvo na Rentgenolozite 1 Radiolozite)
- Suvremenna Meditsina. m. (Bulgaria. Ministerstvo na Narodnoto Zdrave)

**Narodna Biblioteka "Kiril i Metodii"**
11, Tolbukhin Blvd., 1504 Sofia, Bulgaria
(Dist. by: Hemus, 6, Rouski Blvd., 1000 Sofia, Bulgaria)
- Bibliografia na Bulgarskata Bibliografiia/ Bibliography of Bulgarian Bibliographies. a.
- Bibliotekar; spisanie za bibliotechno delo. m. ISSN 0006-1794
- Bibliotekoznanie, Bibliografiia, Knigoznanie, Nauchna Informatsiia. a.
- Bulgaria v Chuzhdata Literatura/Bulgaria in Foreign Literature. a.
- Bulgarski Gramofonni Plochi. a.
- Bulgarski Knigopis. Seriia 1: Knigi, Notni, Graficheski i Kartografski. s-m. ISSN 0007-3997
- Bulgarski Knigopis. Seria 2: Sluzhebni Izdaniia i Disertatsii. m.
- Bulgarski Periodichen Pechat/Bulgarian Periodicals; vestnitsi, spisaniia, biuletini i periodichni sbornitsi. a.
- Letopis na Statiite ot Bulgarskite Spisaniia i Sbornitsi/Articles from Bulgarian Journal and Collections. s-m.
- Letopis na Statiite ot Bulgarskite Vestnitsi/ Articles from Bulgarian Newspapers; mesechen bibliografski biuletin. m.
- Statisticheski Danni za Bibliotekite v Bulgaria/ Statistical Data on Libraries in Bulgaria. a.

**Izdatelstvo Natsionalen Suvet na Otechestveniia Front**
32, Dondukov Blvd., Sofia, Bulgaria
(Dist. by: Hemus, 6, Rouski Blvd., 1000 Sofia, Bulgaria)
- Chitalishte. m. ISSN 0009-4862 (Komitet za Izkustvo i Kultura)
- Nauchen Zhivot. 5 per yr. ISSN 0028-1123 (Suiuz na Nauchni Rabotnitsi v Bulgaria)

**Izdatelstvo Nauka i Izkustvo**
6, Rouski Blvd., Sofia, Bulgaria.
- Sofiiski Universitet. Geologo-Geografski Fakultet. Geografiia. Godishnik. irreg.
- Sofiiski Universitet. Geologo-Geografski Fakultet. Geologiia. Godishnik. irreg.
- Statisticheski Godishnik na Narodna Republika Bulgaria. a. (Bulgaria. Ministerstvo na Informatsiiata i Suobshteniiata)
- Tantsovo Izkustvo. m. (Komitet za Izkustvo i Kultura)

**Obshtonarodna Komitet za Bulgaro-Suvetska Druzhba**
- Bulgaro-Suvetska Druzhba. (pub. by Durzhavno Voenno Izdatelstvo)

**Pharmachim**
3, Ul. Ivan Vazov, 1000 Sofia, Bulgaria.
- M B I. (Medico-Biologic Information) q.

**Izdatelstvo Profizdat**
82, Dondukov Blvd., Sofia, Bulgaria
(Dist. by: Hemus, 6, Rouski Blvd., 1000 Sofia Bulgaria)
- Bulgarian Trade Unions. bi-m. ISSN 0007-3954 (Bulgarski Profesionalni Suiuzi)
- Bulgarski Tiutiun. m. ISSN 0521-6680
- Gradinarstvo. m. (Bulgaria. Ministerstvo na Zemedelieto i Khranitelna Promishlenost)
- Lozarstvo i Vinarstvo. 8 per yr. (Bulgaria. Ministerstvo na Zemedelieto i Khranitelna Promishlenost)
- Rabotnichka. bi-m.
- Rastitelna Zashtita. m. (Bulgaria. Ministerstvo na Zemedelieto i Khranitelna Promishlenost)
- Ribno Stopanstvo. 8 per yr. (Bulgaria. Ministerstvo na Zemedelieto i Khranitelna Promishlenost) (Co-sponsor: Durzhavno Stroitelno Obedinenie Ribno Stopanstvo)

**Publishing House of the Bulgarian Academy of Sciences**
Ul. Akad. G. Bonchev, 1113 Sofia, Bulgaria
(Dist. by: Hemus, 6, Rouski Blvd., 1000 Sofia, Bulgaria)
- Abstracts of Bulgarian Scientific Literature. Agriculture and Forestry. Veterinary Medicine. q. ISSN 0001-3463 (Akademiia na Selskostopanskite Nauki)
- Abstracts of Bulgarian Scientific Literature. Biology and Biochemistry. q. ISSN 0001-3471 (Bulgarska Akademiia na Naukite)
- Abstracts of Bulgarian Scientific Literature. Economics and Law. q. ISSN 0001-348X (Bulgarska Akademiia na Naukite)
- Abstracts of Bulgarian Scientific Literature. Geology and Geography. s-a. ISSN 0001-3498 (Bulgarska Akademiia na Naukite)
- Abstracts of Bulgarian Scientific Literature. Mathematics, Physics, Astronomy, Geophysics, Geodesy. s-a. ISSN 0001-351X (Bulgarska Akademiia na Naukite)
- Abstracts of Bulgarian Scientific Literature. Philosophy, Sociology, Science of Sciences, Psychology and Pedagogics. s-a. (Bulgarska Akademiia na Naukite)
- Academie Bulgare des Sciences. Comptes Rendus. m. ISSN 0001-3978 (Bulgarska Akademiia na Naukite)
- Acta Mikrobiologika, Virologika et Immunologica. s-a. (Bulgarska Akademiia na Naukite)
- Acta Morfologica. s-a. (Bulgarska Akademiia na Naukite)
- Acta Physiologica et Pharmacologica Bulgarica. q. (Bulgarska Akademiia na Naukite)
- Acta Zoologica Bulgarica. q. (Bulgarska Akademiia na Naukite. Zoologicheski Institut)
- Afrikano-Aziatski Problemi. irreg. (Bulgarska Akademiia na Naukite. Nauchnoizsledovatelski Tsentur za Africa i Aziia)
- Agrofizichni Izsledovaniia. irreg., vol. 2, 1975. (Akademiia na Selskostopanskite Nauki)
- Arkheologiia. q. ISSN 0004-1912 (Bulgarska Akademiia na Naukite. Arkheologicheski Institut i Muzei)
- Astrofizicheskie Issledovaniia. irreg. (Bulgarska Akademiia na Naukite)
- Astronomicheski Kalendar na Observatoriiata v Sofia. a. ISSN 0068-3639 (Bulgarska Akademiia na Naukite. Sektsiia po Astronomiia)
- Biomekhanika/Biomechanics. irreg. (Bulgarska Akademiia na Naukite. Tsentralna Laboratoriia po Biomekhanika)
- Bulgarian Academic Books. a. (Bulgarska Akademiia na Naukite)
- Bulgarian Historical Review/Revue Bulgare d'Histoire. q. (Bulgarska Akademiia na Naukite)

- Bulgarian Journal of Physics/Bolgarskii Fizicheskii Zhurnal. bi-m. (Bulgarska Akademiia na Naukite)
- Bulgarska Akademia na Naukite, Sofia. Institut po Obshta i Sravnitelna Patalogiia. Izvestiia. irreg. ISSN 0068-3841
- Bulgarska Akademiia na Naukite, Sofia. Institut za Muzikoznanie. Izvestiia. ISSN 0068-3965
- Bulgarska Akademiia na Naukite. Spisanie. bi-m. ISSN 0007-3989
- Bulgarska Akademiia na Naukite, Sofia. Arkheologicheski Institut. Izvestiia. irreg. ISSN 0068-3620
- Bulgarska Akademiia na Naukite, Sofia. Botanicheski Institut. Izvestiia. a. ISSN 0068-3655
- Bulgarska Akademiia na Naukite, Sofia. Geofizichni Institut. Izvestiia. a. ISSN 0068-3736
- Bulgarska Akademiia na Naukite, Sofia. Geografski Institut. Izvestiia. irreg. ISSN 0068-3744
- Bulgarska Akademiia na Naukite, Sofia. Institut po Filosofiia. Izvestiia. irreg. ISSN 0068-3973
- Bulgarska Akademiia na Naukite, Sofia. Institut po Khidrologiia I Meteorologiia. Izvestiia. irreg. ISSN 0068-3876
- Bulgarska Akademiia na Naukite, Sofia. Institut po Morfologiia. Izvestiia. irreg. ISSN 0068-3817
- Bulgarska Akademiia na Naukite, Sofia. Institut po Tekhnicheska Kibernetika. Izvestiia. irreg. ISSN 0068-385X
- Bulgarska Akademiia na Naukite, Sofia. Institut za Bulgarski Ezik. Izvestiia. a. ISSN 0068-3787
- Bulgarska Akademiia na Naukite, Sofia. Institut za Istoriia. Izvestiia. irreg. ISSN 0068-3779
- Bulgarska Akademiia na Naukite, Sofia. Institut za Pravni Nauki. Izvestiia. irreg. ISSN 0068-3884
- Bulgarska Akademiia na Naukite, Sofia. Mikrobiologicheski Institut. Izvestiia. irreg. ISSN 0068-3957
- Bulgarska Akademiia na Naukite, Sofia. Tsentralna Biblioteka. Izvestiia. ISSN 0068-3671
- Bulgarska Akademiia na Naukite, Sofia. Tsentralna Khelmintologichna Laboratoriia. Izvestiia. a. ISSN 0068-371X
- Bulgarska Etnografiia. irreg. (Bulgarska Akademiia na Naukite)
- Bulgarski Etimologichen Rechnik. irreg. (Bulgarska Akademiia na Naukite. Institut za Bulgarski Ezik)
- Bulgarski Ezik. bi-m. ISSN 0005-4283 (Bulgarska Akademiia na Naukite. Institut za Bulgarski Ezik)
- Bulgarski Folklor. irreg. (Bulgarska Akademiia na Naukite)
- Bulgarsko Geologichesko Druzhestvo. Spisanie. 3 per yr. ISSN 0007-3938 (Bulgarska Akademiia na Naukite)
- Bulgarsko Istorichesko Druzhestvo. Izvestiia. irreg. ISSN 0081-1122 (Co-sponsor: Bulgarska Akademiia na Naukite)
- Bulletin d'Analyses de la Litterature Scientifique Bulgare. Linguistique et Litterature. s-a. ISSN 0001-3501 (Bulgarska Akademiia na Naukite)
- Ekologiia. irreg. (Bulgarska Akademiia na Naukite)
- Etudes Balkaniques. q. ISSN 0014-1976 (Bulgarska Akademiia na Naukite. Institut za Balkanistika)
- Filosofska Misul. m. ISSN 0015-184X (Bulgarska Akademiia na Naukite. Institut po Filosofiia)
- Fiziko-Khimicheska Mekhanika/Physico-Chemical Mechanics. irreg. (Bulgarska Akademiia na Naukite)
- Fiziko-Matematichesko Spisanie. q. ISSN 0015-3265 (Bulgarska Akademiia na Naukite. Fizicheski i Matematicheski Institut)
- Fiziologiia na Rasteniiata. q. (Bulgarska Akademiia na Naukite) (Co-sponsor: Akademiia na Selskostopanskite Nauki)
- Genetika i Selektsiia. bi-m. ISSN 0016-6766 (Akademiia na Selskostopanskite Nauki)
- Geodesy. a. (Bulgarska Akademiia na Naukite. Tsentralna Laboratoriia po Geodeziia)
- Geokhimiia, Mineralogiia i Petrologiia. 3 per yr. (Bulgarska Akademiia na Naukite)
- Geologica Balcanica. q. (Bulgarska Akademiia na Naukite)
- Geotektonika, Tektonofizika i Geodinamika. 3 per yr. (Bulgarska Akademiia na Naukite)
- Gorskostopanska Nauka/Forestry Science. bi-m. ISSN 0017-2286 (Akademiia na Selskostopanskite Nauki)
- Gradinarska i Lozarska Nauka/Horticultural and Viticultural Science. 8 per yr. (Akademiia na Selskostopanskite Nauki)
- Hydrobiology. (Bulgarska Akademiia na Naukite)
- Iaderna Energiia/Nuclear Energy. s-a. (Bulgarska Akademiia na Naukite)

- Ikonomicheska Misul. 10 per yr. ISSN 0013-2993 (Bulgarska Akademiia na Naukite. Ikonomicheski Institut)
- Inzhenerna Geologiia i Khidrogeologiia. 3 per yr. (Bulgarska Akademiia na Naukite. Geologicheski Institut)
- Istoricheski Pregled. bi-m. ISSN 0021-2636 (Bulgarska Akademiia na Naukite. Institut za Istoriia)
- Istoriia na Bulgarskoto Izobrazitelno Izkustvo. irreg. (Bulgarska Akademiia na Naukite)
- Izsledovaniia po Bulgarska Istoriia. irreg. (Bulgarska Akademiia na Naukite. Institut po Istoriia)
- Linguistique Balkanique. q. ISSN 0075-9678 (Bulgarska Akademiia na Naukite)
- Literaturna Misul. 8 per yr. ISSN 0024-4813 (Bulgarska Akademiia na Naukite. Institut za Literatura)
- Materialoznanie i Tekhnologiia. irreg. (Bulgarska Akademiia na Naukite)
- Metodologicheski i Istoriografski Problemi na Istoricheskata Nauka. biennial. (Bulgarska Akademiia na Naukite. Institut za Istoriia)
- Molekulna Biologiia. s-a. (Bulgarska Akademiia na Naukite)
- Neftena i Vuglishtna Geologiia/Petroleum and Coal Geology. irreg. (Bulgarska Akademiia na Naukite)
- Obshta i Sravnitelna Patologiia. s-a. (Bulgarska Akademiia na Naukite)
- Okeanologiia. irreg. (Bulgarska Akademiia na Naukite)
- Paleontologiia, Stratigrafiia i Litologiia. 3 per yr. (Bulgarska Akademiia na Naukite. Geologicheski Institut)
- Pochvoznanie i Agrokhimiia. bi-m. (Akademiia na Selskostopanskite Nauki)
- Pravna Misul. bi-m. ISSN 0032-6968 (Bulgarska Akademiia na Naukite. Institut za Pravni Nauki)
- Prilozhna Mikrobiologiia/Applied Microbiology. s-a. (Bulgarska Akademiia na Naukite. Institut po Mikrobiologiia)
- Priroda. bi-m. ISSN 0032-8731 (Bulgarska Akademiia na Naukite)
- Problemi na Izkustvoto/Problems of Arts. q. ISSN 0032-9371 (Bulgarska Akademiia na Naukite. Institut za Izkustvoznanie)
- Problemi na Khelminthologiiata. s-a. (Bulgarska Akademiia na Naukite)
- Problemi na Tekhnicheskata Kibernetika. irreg. (Bulgarska Akademiia na Naukite)
- Rastenievudni Nauki. 10 per yr. (Akademiia na Selskostopanskite Nauki)
- Rudoobrazuvatelni Protsesi i Mineralni Nakhodishta. 3 per yr. (Bulgarska Akademiia na Naukite)
- Selskostopanska Tekhnika. 8 per yr. ISSN 0037-1718 (Akademiia na Selskostopanskite Nauki)
- Serdika; Bulgarsko Matematichesko Spisanie/ Serdica; Bulgaricae Mathematicae Publicationes. q. (Bulgarska Akademiia na Naukite)
- Sofiiski Universitet. Biologicheski Fakultet. Godishnik. irreg., vol. 63, 1970. ISSN 0081-1823
- Sofiiski Universitet. Fakultet po Matematika i Mekhanika. Godishnik/L'Universite de Sofia. Faculte des Mathematiques et de Mecanique. Annuaire. irreg. vol. 67, 1972 per 73. ISSN 0081-1858
- Sofiiski Universitet. Fakultet po Slavianska Filologiia. Godishnik. irreg., vol. 63, 1970. ISSN 0081-1831
- Sofiiski Universitet. Fakultet po Zapadni Filologii. Godishnik/L'Universite de Sofia. Faculte des Lettres. Annuaire. irreg. vol. 70, 1975. ISSN 0584-0252
- Sofiiski Universitet. Filosofski Fakultet. Godishnik/L'Universite de Sofia. Faculte de Philosophie. Annuaire. vol. 67, 1973. ISSN 0081-184X
- Sofiiski Universitet. Iuridicheski Fakultet. Godishnik. irreg., vol. 61, 1970. ISSN 0081-1866
- Sotsiologicheski Problemi. bi-m. ISSN 0038-1683 (Bulgarska Akademiia na Naukite. Institut po Sotsiologiia) (Co-sponsor: Bulgarska Sotsiologicheska Asotsiatsiia)
- Studia Balcanica. irreg., 1970, no. 3. ISSN 0081-6329
- Tekhnicheska Misul. bi-m. ISSN 0040-2168 (Bulgarska Akademiia na Naukite)
- Vissha Geodeziia. irreg. (Bulgarska Akademiia na Naukite)
- Vodni Problemi. irreg. (Bulgarska Akademiia na Naukite. Institut po Vodni Problemi)
- Zentralblatt der Bulgarischen Wissenschaftlichen Literatur. Geschichte, Archaeologie und Ethnographie. s-a. ISSN 0044-4014 (Bulgarska Akademiia na Naukite)

- Zhivotnovudni Nauki. 8 per yr. ISSN 0514-7441
(Akademiia na Selskostopanskite Nauki)

**Sofia-Press Agency**
1, Ul. Levski, Sofia, Bulgaria
(Dist. by: Hemus, 6, Rouski Blvd., 1000 Sofia,
Bulgaria)
- Bulgaria Today; social politics. m. ISSN 0007-
3903
- Resorts in Bulgaria. bi-m. (Komitet za Otdikh i
Turizum)
- Sofia News; weekly for politics, culture and
tourism.

**Sofiiski Universitet. Biologicheski Fakultet**
- Sofiiski Universitet. Biologicheski Fakultet.
Godishnik. (pub. by Publishing House of the
Bulgarian Academy of Sciences)

**Sofiiski Universitet. Fakultet po Matematika i
Mekhanika**
- Sofiiski Universitet. Fakultet po Matematika i
Mekhanika. Godishnik/L'Universite de Sofia.
Faculte des Mathematiques et de Mecanique.
Annuaire. (pub. by Publishing House of the
Bulgarian Academy of Sciences)

**Sofiiski Universitet. Fakultet po Slavianski Filologii**
- Sofiiski Universitet. Fakultet po Slavianska
Filologiia. Godishnik. (pub. by Publishing House
of the Bulgarian Academy of Sciences)

**Sofiiski Universitet. Fakultet po Zapadni Filologii**
- Sofiiski Universitet. Fakultet po Zapadni Filologii.
Godishnik/L'Universite de Sofia. Faculte des
Lettres. Annuaire. (pub. by Publishing House of
the Bulgarian Academy of Sciences)

**Sofiiski Universitet. Filosofski Fakultet**
- Sofiiski Universitet. Filosofski Fakultet.
Godishnik/L'Universite de Sofia. Faculte de
Philosophie. Annuaire. (pub. by Publishing House
of the Bulgarian Academy of Sciences)

**Sofiiski Universitet. Geologo-Geografski Fakultet**
- Sofiiski Universitet. Geologo-Geografski Fakultet.
Geografiia. Godishnik. (pub. by Izdatelstvo Nauka
i Izkustvo)
- Sofiiski Universitet. Geologo-Geografski Fakultet.
Geologiia. Godishnik. (pub. by Izdatelstvo Nauka
i Izkustvo)

**Sofiiski Universitet. Iuridicheski Fakultet**
- Sofiiski Universitet. Iuridicheski Fakultet.
Godishnik. (pub. by Publishing House of the
Bulgarian Academy of Sciences)

**Suiuz na Arkhitektite v Bulgaria**
11, Ul. D. Polianov, Sofia, Bulgaria
(Dist. by: Hemus, 6, Rouski Blvd., 1000 Sofia,
Bulgaria)
- Arkhitektura. 10 per yr. ISSN 0003-8644 (Co-
sponsor: Ministerstvo na Stroezhite i
Arkhitekturata)

**Suiuz na Bulgarski Filatelisti**
Sofia, Bulgaria
(Dist. by: Hemus, 6, Rouski Blvd., 1000 Sofia,
Bulgaria)
- Numizmatika. q.

**Suiuz na Bulgarski Kompozitori**
52, Ul. Alabin, Sofia, Bulgaria.
- Music News Bulletin. m. ISSN 0566-9197

**Suiuz na Bulgarski Pisateli**
5, Ul. Angel Kanchev, Sofia, Bulgaria
(Dist. by: Hemus, 6, Rouski Blvd., 1000 Sofia,
Bulgaria)
- Plamuk; spisanie za literatura, izkustvo i
publitsistika. m. ISSN 0032-0528

**Suiuz na Nauchni Rabotnitsi v Bulgaria**
- Nauchen Zhivot. (pub. by Izdatelstvo Natsionalen
Suvet na Otechestveniia Front)

**Tsentur za Nauchno-Meditsinska Informatsiia**
8, Ul. Bialo More, Sofia 27, Bulgaria.
- Abstracts of Bulgarian Scientific Medical
Literature. q. ISSN 0001-3536

**Vissh Finansovo- Stopanski Institut**
Svishtov, Bulgaria
(Dist. by: Hemus, 6, Rouski Blvd., 1000 Sofia,
Bulgaria)
- Narodnostopanski Arkhiv/Archives of National
Economy. q.

# BURMA

**Burma Medical Association**
249 Theinbyu Rd., Rangoon, Burma.
- Burma Medical Journal. q. ISSN 0007-6295

# BURUNDI

**Banque de la Republique du Burundi**
B.P. 705, Bujumbra, Burundi.
- Banque de la Republique du Burundi. Bulletin
Trimestriel. q.
- Banque de la Republique du Burundi. Rapport
Annuel. a. ISSN 0067-3935

**Burundi. Departement de la Presse**
6 Ave. de la Poste, B. P. 1400, Bujumbura, Burundi.
- Flash-Infor; bulletin quotidien d'information. m.

**Burundi. Secretariat General a la Presidence Charge
du Bureau Technique d'Etudes. Department des
Etudes et Statistiques**
B. P. 1156, Bujumbura, Burundi.
- Burundi. Secretariat General a la Presidence
Charge du Bureau Technique d'Etudes.
Departement des Etudes et Statistiques. Bulletin.
q.

**Conference des Ordinaires du Rwanda et Burundi**
B.P. 1390, Bujumbura, Burundi
(Subscr. to: Presses Lavigerie, B.P. 1640,
Bujumbura, Burundi)
- Au Coeur de l'Afrique. bi-m. ISSN 0563-4245

# CAMEROON

**Association des Historiens Africains**
B.P. 309, Yaounde, Cameroon.
- Afrika Zamani; revue d'histoire africaine. s-a.

**Association Nationale des Poetes et Ecrivains
Camerounais**
B.P. 2180, Yaounde-Messa, Cameroon.
- Cameroun Litteraire. m. ISSN 0045-4087

**Au Large**
B.P. 504, Yaounde, Cameroon.
- Au Large/Go Ahead; magazine of young
Cameroonian students. m.

**Cameroon. Bureau Information Presse de Forces
Armees**
B. P. 1191, Yaounde, Cameroon.
- Honneur et Fidelite; bulletin de liaison des forces
armees. q. ISSN 0046-7855

**Cameroon. Department of Statistics and National
Accounts**
Ministere du Plan et de l'Amenagement du
Territoire, Boite Postale 660, Yaounde, Cameroon.
- Cameroon. Department of Statistics and National
Accounts. Note Annuelle de Statistique. a.
- Comptes Nationaux du Cameroun. Principaux
Tableaux. irreg. (prep. by its Sous-Direction des
Syntheses Economiques)

**Cameroon. Direction des Affaires Culturelle**
Ministere de l'Education, de la Culture et de la
Formation Professionelle, Yaounde, Cameroon.
- Culture Camerounaise/Cameroonian Culture.
irreg, vol. 2, 1971.

**Cameroon. Direction des Mines et de la Geologie**
Ministere des Mines et de l'Energie, Yaounde,
Cameroon.
- Activites Mineres au Cameroun. a. ISSN 0575-
7258

**Cameroon. Regie Nationale des Chemins de Fer**
Douala, Cameroon.
- Cameroon. Regie Nationale des Chemins de Fer.
Statistiques. irreg.

**Cameroon. Service d'Hydrometeorologie**
Yaounde, Cameroon.
- Cameroon. Service d'Hydrometeorologie.
Pluviometrie Mensuelle et Annuelle. a.

**Cameroon Development Corporation**
Bota, Victoria, Cameroon.
- Cameroon Development Corporation. Annual
Report and Accounts/Rapport Annuel et Compte-
Rendu Financier. a.

**Centre de Litterature Evangelique**
- Abbia. (pub. by Editions CLE)
- Afrique Urbaine/Urban Africa. (pub. by Editions
CLE)
- Flambeau. (pub. by Editions CLE)

**Centre Technique Forestier Tropical du Cameroun**
B.P. 832, Douala, Cameroon.
- Centre Technique Forestiere Tropical du
Cameroun. Rapport Annuel. a.

**Chambre de Commerce, d'Industrie et des Mines du
Cameroun**
Box 4011, Douala, Cameroon.
- Chambre de Commerce, d'Industrie et des Mines
du Cameroun. Bulletin. m. ISSN 0008-2198
- Chambre de Commerce, d'Industrie et des Mines
du Cameroun. Compte-Rendu d'Activites. irreg.
- Chambre de Commerce, d'Industrie et des Mines
du Cameroun. Rapport Annuel. a. ISSN 0069-
2530

**Editions CLE**
B. P. 1501, Yaounde, Cameroon.
- Abbia; revue culturelle Camerounaise. q. ISSN
0001-3102 (Centre de Litterature Evangelique)
- Afrique Urbaine/Urban Africa; West African
edition. q. ISSN 0002-0559 (Centre de Litterature
Evangelique) (Co-sponsor: All Africa Conference
of Churches)
- Flambeau; revue trimestrielle de theologie pour
l'engagement de l'eglise dans le monde africain. q.
ISSN 0015-3435 (Centre de Litterature
Evangelique)

**Le Griot**
Boite Postale 23, Yaounde, Cameroom.
- Le Griot; hebdomadaire des spectacles, du cinema
et de la culture. w.

**Institut Panafricain pour le Developpement**
*see* Pan-African Institute for Development

**Inter-African Phyto-Sanitary Commission**
B.P. 4170, Yaounde, Cameroon.
- Inter-African Phyto-Sanitary Bulletin/Bulletin
Interafricain d'Informations Phytosanitaires. irreg.
- Inter-African Phyto-Sanitary Commission.
Publication. irreg. ISSN 0534-4859

**Pan-African Institute for Development**
Box 4078, Douala, Cameroon.
- Institut Panafricain pour le Developpement.
Bulletin de Liaison des Anciens Etudiants. q.
ISSN 0046-9734
- Institut Panafricain pour le Developpement.
Travaux Manuscrits. irreg.

**Syndicat des Industries du Cameroun**
B. P. 673, Douala, Cameroon.
- Industrie Camerounaise. a.

**United Publishers**
P.O. Box 200, Victoria, Cameroon.
- Cameroon Year Book. a.

**Universite de Yaounde**
P.O. Box 337, Yaounde, Cameroon
(Dist. by: Service Central des Bibliotheques,
Services des Publications, B. P. 1312, Yaounde,
Cameroon)
- Guide Bibliographique du Monde Noir/
Bibliographic Guide to the Negro World. irreg.

**Universite de Yaounde. Ecole Normale Superieure**
B.P. 47, Yaounde, Cameroon.
- Revue Camerounaise de Pedagogie/Cameroon
Review of Education. q. ISSN 0556-7262 (prep.
by its Institut Pedagogique National)

**Universite de Yaounde. Faculte des Sciences**
Box 337, Yaounde, Cameroon
(Dist. by: Service Central des Bibliotheques,
Services des Publications, B. P. 1312, Yaounde,
Cameroon)
- Universite de Yaounde. Faculte des Sciences.
Annales. irreg. ISSN 0566-201X

**West Cameroon. Service Statistique**
B. P. 93, Buea, Cameroon.
- West Cameroon Monthly Digest of Statistics. m.
ISSN 0043-3098

**Les 4 Points Cardinaux**
B.P. 513, Douala, Cameroon.
- Republique Unie du Cameroun: Annuaire International/United Republic of Cameroon International Year Book. a.

# CANADA

**Abbaye Benedictine de Mont-Laurier**
Mont Laurier, Que., Canada.
- Musique Liturgique. irreg. ISSN 0384-5133

**Academic Publishing Co.**
Box 42, Snowdon Sta., Montreal, Que., Canada.
- Economic Planning; journal for agriculture and related industries. bi-m. ISSN 0013-0222

**Academie Canadienne-Francaise**
163a Est, rue Saint-Paul, Montreal-127, Canada.
- Academie Canadienne-Francaise. Cahiers. a. ISSN 0065-0528

**Academie des Sciences Morales et Politiques**
- Academie des Sciences Morales et Politiques, Montreal. Travaux et Communications. (pub. by Editions Paulines)

**Academy of Medicine, Toronto**
288 Bloor St. W., Toronto M5S 1V8, Canada.
- Academy of Medicine, Toronto. Bulletin. m. ISSN 0001-4311

**Acadia University. Associated Alumni**
Box 520, Wolfville, N. S., Canada.
- Acadia Bulletin. 3 per yr. ISSN 0044-5843

**Acadia University. Student's Union**
Box 40, Box 698, Wolfville, N. S. BOP 1XD, Canada.
- Athenaeum. w.(during school term) ISSN 0004-6566

**Achdut Ha-Avoda-Poale Zion of Canada**
272 Codsell Ave., Downsview, Ont., Canada.
- Undzer Veg. q.

**Ackermann Advertising and News Service Ltd.**
Box 2033, Vancouver B.C. V6B 3R6, Canada
(U.S. Address: Box 0-1, Blaine, WA 98230)
- Pazifische Rundschau/Pacific Review. fortn. ISSN 0048-3095

**Acta Press**
P. O. Box 3243, Postal Station B, Calgary, Alta. T2M 4L8, Canada.
- Automatic Control Theory and Applications. 3 per yr. ISSN 0315-8934 (International Association of Science and Technology for Development)

**Actualite Agricole**
2120 Est, Rue Sherbrooke, Montreal 133, Canada.
- Actualite Agricole; agricole francais au Canada. m. ISSN 0015-0045

**Actualite Magazine Quebec Ltd.**
4059 Hochelaga St., Montreal, Canada.
- Actualite. m. ISSN 0001-7698

**Addiction Research Foundation of Ontario**
33 Russell St., Toronto, Ontario M5S 2S1, Canada.
- Addiction Research Foundation of Ontario. Annual Report. a.
- Addiction Research Foundation of Ontario. Bibliographic Series. irreg. ISSN 0065-1885
- Addiction Research Foundation of Ontario. Journal. m. ISSN 0044-6203
- Addictions. q. ISSN 0001-8082
- Brookside Monographs. (pub. by University of Toronto Press)

**Affairs Publishing Ltd.**
1118 Melville, Vancouver, B.C., Canada.
- B. C. Affairs Quarterly. irreg. ISSN 0315-3355

**Afterthought**
157 James St., No. 4, Ottawa, Ont., Canada.
- Afterthought. every 6 wks. ISSN 0044-670X

**Agence de Publicite Media Ltee.**
1460 Ave. Union, Montreal, Que., Canada.
- Quebec Library Association. Newsletter. irreg. ISSN 0079-8428

**Agence du Livre Francais**
1249 Ouest, rue Bernard Outrem, Montreal, Que., Canada.
- Socialisme Quebecois. q. ISSN 0049-0938

**Agricultural Institute of Canada**
151 Slater St., Suite 907, Ottawa, Ont. K1P 5H4, Canada.
- Agricultural Institute of Canada. Membership Directory/Institut Agricole du Canada. Liste des Membres. triennial. ISSN 0083-9744
- Agrologist. q. ISSN 0044-684X
- Canadian Journal of Animal Science. q. ISSN 0008-3984 (Canadian Society of Animal Production)
- Canadian Journal of Plant Science. q. ISSN 0008-4220
- Canadian Journal of Soil Science. q. ISSN 0008-4271

**Agricultural Pesticide Society**
c/o Plant Products Division, Canada Agriculture, Ottawa, Ont. K1A 0C5, Canada.
- Agricultural Pesticide Society. Annual Meeting. Proceedings. a. ISSN 0065-4485

**Agricultural Publishing Co.**
10 St. Mary St., Suite 300, Toronto, Ont. M4Y 1R1, Canada.
- Farm and Country. s-m. ISSN 0046-3299 (Ontario Federation of Agriculture)
- Hog Marketplace Quarterly; serving Canada's leading hog farmers. q. (Pork Producers Marketing Board)

**Agriculture Canada**
*see* Canada. Agriculture Canada

**Agriculture Economic Research Council of Canada**
55 Parkdale Ave., Ottawa, Ontario K1Y 1E5, Canada.
- Agriculture Economic Research Council of Canada. Publication Series. irreg., no. 28, 1972.

**Air Canada**
1 Place Ville Marie, Montreal, Quebec Province, Canada.
- Air Canada. Annual Report. a. ISSN 0568-3424
- EnRoute. (pub. by Southam-Murray)
- Horizons. s-m.

**Air Transport Association**
116 Albert St., Ottawa 4, Ont., Canada.
- Air Transport Association of Canada. Annual Report. a. ISSN 0065-485X

**Alberta. Alberta Council on Aging**
503, 10012 Jasper Ave., Edmonton, Alta. T5J 1R7, Canada.
- Alberta Council on Aging News. q.

**Alberta. Alcoholism & Drug Abuse Commission**
112 Professional Centre, 10050 112 St., Edmonton, Alta. T5K 2J1, Canada.
- Rapport. bi-m.

**Alberta. Bureau of Statistics**
48 Terrace Bldg., Edmonton, Alta. T5K 2C3, Canada.
- Alberta Statistical Review; a monthly statistical summary. m. ISSN 0317-3925
- Alberta Statistical Review. a.

**Alberta. Business Development and Tourism. Business Services Branch**
1629 Centennial Bldg., Edmonton, Alta. T5J 0H4, Canada.
- Alberta Trade Index of Alberta Manufacturers and Manufactured Products. a. ISSN 0065-6011

**Alberta. Department of Agriculture**
Edmonton, Alberta, Canada.
- Alberta. Department of Agriculture. Annual Report. a. ISSN 0065-597X

**Alberta. Department of Agriculture. Horticultural Research Center**
Communications Branch, 9718-107th St., Edmonton, Alta. T5K 2C8, Canada.
- Alberta. Horticultural Research Center. Annual Report. a.

**Alberta. Department of Agriculture. Market Analysis Branch**
9718-107 St., Edmonton, Alta. T5K 2C8, Canada.
- Alberta Farm Market Analysis. q.

**Alberta. Department of Education**
Executive Bldg., 10105 109th St., Edmonton, Alta. T5J 2V2, Canada.
- Alberta. Department of Education. Annual Report. a.
- Alberta. Department of Education. Annual Review, Alberta Education. a.

**Alberta. Department of Health and Social Development**
Petroleum Plaza, 9945 108 St., Edmonton T5K 1G8 Alberta, Canada.
- Alberta. Department of Health and Social Development. Annual Report. a. ISSN 0084-6163

**Alberta. Department of Industry and Commerce**
Economic Research and Analysis Branch, Rm. 1629 Centennial Bldg., Edmonton, Alta., Canada.
- Alberta. Economic Research and Analysis Branch. Executive Report: a Mid-Year Economic Forecast. a.
- Alberta Industry and Resources. irreg.

**Alberta. Department of Recreation, Parks and Wildlife. 4-H and Junior Forest Ranger Branch**
Edmonton, Alberta, Canada.
- Clover Leaflet. irreg. ISSN 0381-3932

**Alberta. Department of the Environment**
9820 106th St., Edmonton, Alta. T5K 2J6, Canada.
- Alberta. Department of the Environment. Annual Report. a. ISSN 0383-3739

**Alberta. Department of the Environment. Communications Branch**
9820 106th St., Edmonton, Alta. T5K 2J6, Canada.
- Environment News. m. ISSN 0319-3608

**Alberta. Energy Resources Conservation Board**
603 Sixth Ave. S.W., Calgary, Alta. T2P 0T4, Canada.
- Conservation in Alberta. a.
- Summary of Monthly Statistics of the Alberta Energy Resource Industries. m.
- Weekly Production and Drilling Statistics. w. ISSN 0032-9827

**Alberta. Environment Conservation Authority**
2100 College Plaza Tower 3, 8215 112Th St., Edmonton, Alta. T6G 2M4, Canada.
- Alberta. Environment Conservation Authority. Annual Report. a. ISSN 0380-450X

**Alberta Association for the Mentally Retarded**
12225-105 Ave., Edmonton, Alberta T5N 0Y3, Canada.
- New Horizon. q. ISSN 0028-5366

**Alberta Association of Registered Nurses**
10256-112 St., Edmonton, Alta. T5K 1M6, Canada.
- A. A. R. N. Newsletter. 11 per yr. ISSN 0001-0197

**Alberta Association of Registered Nursing Orderlies**
10112 124th St., Edmonton, Alberta T5N 1P6, Canada.
- Registered Nursing Orderly. q. ISSN 0380-1861

**Alberta Bowhunters and Archers Association**
c/o William A. Gillespie, Ed., 10129-90 St., Edmonton, Alta. T5H 1R5, Canada.
- Alberta Bowhunter and Archer. 6 per yr. ISSN 0044-7080

**Alberta Certified Nursing Aide Association**
No. 2, 10830-107 Ave., Edmonton, Alta., Canada.
- Alberta Certified Nursing Aide Association. Newsletter. q. ISSN 0044-7102

**Alberta Chamber of Commerce**
No. 212, 10201-104th St., Edmonton, Alta., Canada.
- Enterpriser. q. ISSN 0046-2136

**Alberta Disaster Services Agency**
10320 146th St., Edmonton T5N 3A2, Alta., Canada.
- Alberta Disaster Services News & Notes. q.

**Alberta Federation of Labour**
15104 Stony Plain Rd., Edmonton, Alta, Canada.
- Alberta Labour. bi-m. ISSN 0002-4813

**Alberta Genealogical Society**
Box 3151, Sta. A, Edmonton, Alta. T5J 2G9, Canada.
- Alberta Genealogical Society. Surnames Register. q.

- Relatively Speaking. q.

**Alberta Government Telephones**
Rm. 3158 Alberta Telephone Tower, 10020-100 St., Edmonton, Alberta T5J 0N5, Canada.
- Alberta Calls. fortn. ISSN 0002-4740

**Alberta Hail and Crop Insurance Corporation**
1110 First Street, S.W., Calgary, Alberta T2R OV2, Canada.
- Alberta Hail and Crop Insurance Corporation. Annual Report. a. ISSN 0319-3535

**Alberta Hog Producers Marketing Board**
6113 101 Ave., Edmonton, Alta. T6C 4G2, Canada.
- Alberta Hog Journal. q. ISSN 0315-3800

**Alberta Home Economics Association**
Box 1052, Calgary, Alta, Canada.
- A H E A Newsletter. 4 per yr. ISSN 0044-7137

**Alberta Hospital Association**
10025 108th St., Edmonton, Alta. T5J 1K9, Canada.
- Hospitalta. m.

**Alberta Information Retrieval Association. Western Canada Chapter of A.S.I.S.**
c/o Research Council of Alberta, 11315 - 87th Ave., Edmonton, Alta. T6G 2C2, Canada.
- A. I. R. A.-Wes-Can. A. S. I. S. Newsletter. irreg. ISSN 0382-4969

**Alberta Landrace Swine Association**
c/o N. Helfrich, Box 250, Rockford, Alberta, Canada.
- Alberta Landrace Association. Newsletter. irreg. ISSN 0044-7145

**Alberta Motor Association**
Box 3740, 11230 110th St., Edmonton, Alberta, Canada.
- Alberta Motorist. q. ISSN 0002-4856

**Alberta Native Communications Society**
11427 Jasper Ave, Edmonton 11, Alta., Canada.
- Native People. w. ISSN 0047-9144

**Alberta Opportunity Co.**
14th Floor, Capitol Square, 10065 Jasper Ave., Edmonton, Alta. T5J 0H4, Canada.
- Alberta Opportunity Company. Annual Report. a. ISSN 0318-3971

**Alberta Pharmaceutical Association**
9901 108th St., Edmonton, Alta. TSK 1G8, Canada.
- Alberta Pharmaceutical Association. A. Ph. A. Communications. q.

**Alberta Research Council**
11315 87th Ave., Edmonton, Alberta T6G 2C2, Canada.
- Alberta Research Council. Annual Report. a. ISSN 0080-1526
- Alberta Research Council. Atmospheric Sciences Reports. irreg.
- Alberta Research Council. Bulletins. irreg. ISSN 0034-5172
- Alberta Research Council. Contribution Series. irreg. ISSN 0080-1534
- Alberta Research Council. Earth Science Reports. irreg.
- Alberta Research Council. Highway Research. irreg. ISSN 0065-5988
- Alberta Research Council. Information Series. irreg. ISSN 0034-5180
- Alberta Research Council. List of Publications. a. ISSN 0080-1569
- Alberta Research Council. Memoirs. irreg. ISSN 0080-1577
- Alberta Research Council. Preliminary Reports. Soil Surveys. irreg. ISSN 0080-1593
- Alberta Research Council. Reports. irreg.
- Alberta Research Council. River Engineering and Surface Hydrology Reports. irreg.

**Alberta School Trustees Association**
311 Royal Alex Pl., 10106 111 Ave., Edmonton, Alta., Canada.
- Alberta School Trustee. 4 per yr. ISSN 0002-4880

**Alberta Teachers' Association**
11010-142 St., Edmonton Alta. T5N 2R1, Canada.
- A T A Magazine. q.
- A T A News. fortn. ISSN 0001-267X
- Alberta English. irreg. (approx. 3-4 per yr.) ISSN 0382-5191

- Alberta Modern Language Journal. 3 per yr. ISSN 0318-5176
- Alberta Science Education Journal. q.
- Alberta Teachers' Association. Learning Resources Council. Newsletter. irreg. ISSN 0380-8491
- Alberta Teachers Association. Mathematics Monograph. a. ISSN 0317-8579
- Challenge in Educational Administration. 4 per yr. ISSN 0045-625X
- Delta-K; Mathematics Council newsletter. 4 per yr. ISSN 0025-5688
- Early Childhood Education. s-a. ISSN 0012-8171
- F A C T A Newsletter. (Fine Arts Council of the Alberta Teachers' Association) irreg., 3-4 per yr. ISSN 0014-5556
- Fine. s-a. ISSN 0015-2293
- H P E C Runner. 3 per yr. ISSN 0318-0433
- Home Ec News. 4 per yr. ISSN 0018-4004
- Home Echoes. 2-3 per yr. ISSN 0018-4012
- Synoptic. 4 per yr. ISSN 0049-2760

**Alberta Teachers' Association. Professional Development Department**
Barnett House, 11010-142 St., Edmonton, Alta. T5N 2R1, Canada.
- P D B. (Professional Development Bulletin) irreg. ISSN 0384-0972

**Alberta Trucking Association**
5112-3 St. S.E., Box 5520, Sta. A, Calgary, Alta. T2H 1X9, Canada.
- A T A News Bulletin. m. ISSN 0380-8920
- Alberta Motor Transport Directory. a. ISSN 0084-6171

**Alberta-Westmorland-Kent Regional Library. Extension Department**
Box 708, Moncton, N.B. E1C 8M9, Canada.
- Alberta-Westmorland-Kent Regional Library. Extension Department. News. irreg. ISSN 0315-355X

**Alcan Canada Products**
Box 269, Toronto Dominion Centre, Toronto, Ont. M5K 1K1, Canada.
- Alcan News. m. ISSN 0002-4996

**Alcan Smelters and Chemicals Ltd.**
P.O. Box 1800, Kitimat, B.C. V8C 2H2, Canada.
- Ingot. fortn.

**Alchemist**
Box 123, Lasalle, Quebec, Canada.
- Alchemist. q. ISSN 0384-8523

**Alcohol and Drug Concerns Inc.**
15 Gervais Dr., No. 603, Don Mills, Ont. M3C 1Y8, Canada.
- Concerns. q. ISSN 0045-799X

**Alcoholism and Drug Addiction Research Foundation of Ontario**
*see* **Addiction Research Foundation of Ontario**

**Alcuin Society**
P.O. Box 94108, Richmond, B.C. V6Y 2A2, Canada.
- Amphora. q. ISSN 0003-200X

**Publications Alerte**
25 av. Royale, Ste-Petronille I.O., Quebec G0A 4C0, Canada.
- Alerte au Quebec. m. ISSN 0319-6984

**All Seasons Publishing Co.**
1437 College Dr., Saskatoon, Sask. S7N OW6, Canada.
- Chelsea Journal; Canadian periodical of social comment, literature and religion. bi-m. ISSN 0317-2147

**Allergy Information Association**
3 Powburn Pl., Weston, Ont. M9R 2C5, Canada.
- Allergy Information. q. ISSN 0044-7331

**Alliance Chorale Canadienne**
1052 Avenue Laurien Ouest, Montreal, Que. H2V 2K8, Canada.
- Bouscueil; bulletin d'information de l'Alliance Chorale Canadienne. irreg. ISSN 0382-5604

**Alliance des Professeurs de Montreal**
4455 rue St-Hubert, Montreal, P. Q., Canada.
- Alliance. s-m. ISSN 0002-6034

**Alpine Club of Canada**
P.O. Box 1026, Banff, Alberta T0L 0C0, Canada.
- Canadian Alpine Journal. a. ISSN 0068-8207

**Alpine Club of Canada. Edmonton Section**
Edmonton, Alta., Canada.
- Mountain Breeze. irreg. ISSN 0383-2694

**Alternative to Alienation**
Box 46 Station M, Toronto, Ontario M65 4T2, Canada.
- Alternative to Alienation. m.

**Amateur Radio League of Alberta**
Box 1226, Bonnyville T0A 0L0, Alta., Canada.
- V E 6. m. ISSN 0049-5778

**American Dialect Society**
c/o H. R. Wilson, Exec. Sec., Department of English, University of Western Ontario, London, Ont. N6A 3K7, Canada.
- American Dialect Society Newsletter. 3 per yr. ISSN 0002-8193

**Americans Exiled in Canada**
Box 189, Sta. P, Toronto, Ont. M5S 2S7, Canada.
- A M E X Canada. bi-m.

**Amis de l'Histoire de la Perade**
Case Postale 157, Sainte-Anne de la Perade, Quebec, Canada.
- Amis de l'Histoire de la Perade. Collection "Nos Vielles Familles". irreg.

**Amish Church**
- Family Life. (pub. by Pathway Publishing Corporation)
- Young Companion. (pub. by Pathway Publishing Corporation)

**Amnesty International (Toronto Group)**
Toronto, Ont., Canada.
- Amnesty International (Toronto Group) Newsletter. irreg. ISSN 0382-6295

**Ampersand Publishing Services**
95 Thorncliffe Park Dr., Suite 2012, Toronto, Ont. M4H 1L7, Canada.
- Book Publishers in Canada. a.

**Anchor Press**
1434 St. Catherine St. W., Suite 504, Montreal, Que. H3G 1R4, Canada.
- Containerization and Material Handling Annual. a.
- Great Lakes Navigation. a.
- Marine Equipment Directory. a.
- Mirabel Airport Directory. a.
- Montreal Port Guide & Directory. a.
- Ports Annual. a.
- Shipping Register and Shipbuilder. bi-m. ISSN 0037-3923

**Anglican Church of Canada**
600 Jarvis St., Toronto, Ont., Canada.
- Anglican Church of Canada. Bulletin. irreg. ISSN 0381-6079
- Canadian Churchman. m. ISSN 0008-3216

**Anglican Church of Canada. Diocese of Caledonia**
Dawson Creek, B.C., Canada.
- Caledonia Diocesan Times. m. ISSN 0383-6509

**Anglican Church of Canada. General Synod**
600 Jarvis Street, Toronto, Ont. M4Y 2J6, Canada.
- Anglican Church of Canada. General Synod. Journal of Proceedings. biennial. ISSN 0380-2469
- Anglican Year Book. a.

**Anglo-Jewish Publishers**
3285 Heather St, Vancouver 9, B.C., Canada.
- Jewish Western Bulletin. w. ISSN 0021-6879 (Jewish Community of British Columbia)

**Animal Defence League of Canada**
Box 713, Ottawa, Ont. K1P 5P8, Canada.
- Animal Defence League of Canada. News Bulletin. q. ISSN 0044-829X

**Anthol Publications**
Box 208, 71 Pardo Ave., Pointe Claire, Que., Canada.
- Anthol. a. ISSN 0316-2583

**Anthropological Association of Canada**
1575 Forlan Drive, Ottawa, Ont. K2C OR8, Canada.
- Anthropological Journal of Canada/Journal Anthropologique du Canada. q. ISSN 0003-5475

**Antonson Publishing Co., Ltd.**
P.O. Box 157, New Westminster, B.C. V3L 4Y4, Canada.
- Canadian Frontier; Canada's national history magazine. a. ISSN 0315-0062

**Apex Publishers & Publicity Ltd.**
59 Front St. E., Toronto, Ont. M5E 1B3, Canada.
- Dogs in Canada. m. ISSN 0012-4915

**Apostles of Infinite Love**
Sanctuary of the Magnificat, Box 308, Saint Jovite JOT 2H0, Que., Canada.
- Magnificat. m. ISSN 0025-0007

**Apostleship of Prayer**
833 Broadview Ave., Toronto M4K 2P9, Ont., Canada.
- Canadian Messenger of the Sacred Heart. m. ISSN 0008-4425

**Applegarth Follies**
Box 40, Sta. B, London, Ont. N6A 4V3, Canada.
- Applegarth's Folly. irreg. ISSN 0316-1412
- Brick: a Journal of Reviews. 3 per yr.
- Twelfth Key: a Poetry Journal. 3 per yr.

**Appraisal Institute of Canada Inc.**
502-177 Lombard Ave., Winnipeg 2, Man., Canada.
- A I M Magazine. q. ISSN 0044-846X
- Appraisal Institute Digest. s-a. ISSN 0003-7079

**Arab League Information Centre**
170 Laurier Avenue, W., Suite 709, Ottawa, K1P 5V5, Ontario, Canada.
- Arab Review. q.

**Arbutus Publications Ltd.**
P.O. Box 35466 Station E, Vancouver, B.C. V6M 4G8, Canada.
- British Columbia Insurance Directory. Insurance Companies, Agents and Adjusters. a. ISSN 0068-1598

**Arch-Way Publishers Ltd.**
7560 Lawrence Dr., Burnaby, B. C. V5A 1T6, Canada.
- Playboard; professional stage magazine. m. ISSN 0048-4415

**Archaeological Society of B. C.**
c/o Centennial Museum, 1100 Chestnut, Vancouver, B.C., Canada.
- Midden. bi-m. ISSN 0047-7222

**Archai**
21 N. Grosvenor Ave., N. Burnaby 2, B.C., Canada.
- Archai. irreg.

**Archdiocese of Montreal**
Bible Centre, 2000 Sherbrooke West, Montreal, Que. H3H 1G4, Canada.
- Discover the Bible. w(except July & Aug.) ISSN 0018-912X
- Parole-Dimanche. w (except Jul.& Aug.)

**Archeveque Catholique Romain de Quebec**
Grand Seminaire (3317), Cite Universitaire, Quebec G1K 7P4, Canada.
- Pastorale-Quebec; revue de l'eglise de Quebec. s-w.

**Archives of Vancouver Society**
City Hall, Vancouver, B.C., Canada.
- Vancouver Historical Journal. irreg. ISSN 0506-3973

**Arctic Institute of North America**
University Library Tower, 2920 24th Ave. N.W., Calgary, Alta. T2N 1N4, Canada
(U.S. Address: 3426 N. Washington Blvd., Arlington, VA 22201)
- Arctic. q. ISSN 0004-0843
- Arctic Institute of North America. Annual Report. a. ISSN 0066-6955
- Arctic Institute of North America. Library. Accessions List. bi-m.
- Arctic Institute of North America. Newsletter. irreg. ISSN 0066-6963
- Arctic Institute of North America. Northern Libraries Colloquy. Proceedings. irreg.

- Arctic Institute of North America. Research Paper. irreg., 1970, no. 68. ISSN 0066-6971
- Arctic Institute of North America. Technical Paper. irreg., no. 27, 1974. ISSN 0066-698X
- Man in the North Project. Technical Reports. irreg.

**Armenian Evangelical Church**
34 Glenforest Rd., Toronto, Ont. M4N 1H8, Canada.
- Canada Armenian Press. Newsletter. q.

**Armenian Youth Federation. Simon Zavarian Chapter**
18 Dupont St., Toronto, Ont. M5R 1V2, Canada.
- Echo/Artzakank. m. ISSN 0046-1040

**Army, Navy and Air Force Veterans Association in Canada**
Scarborough, Ont., Canada.
- A. N. & A. F. Journal. irreg. ISSN 0315-0224

**Art and Literary Society**
c/o Lakehead University Student Union, Oliver Rd., Thunderbay, Ont., Canada.
- Art and Literary Review. s-a.
- Muskeg Review. a.

**Art Gallery of Greater Victoria**
1040 Moss St., Victoria, B. C., Canada.
- Arts Victoria. 10 per yr. ISSN 0317-2031

**Art Gallery of Hamilton**
Forsythe Avenue, Hamilton, Ontario, Canada.
- Hamilton, Ontario. Art Gallery. Annual Exhibition. a. ISSN 0072-9639

**Art Gallery of Ontario**
Grange Park, Toronto, Ont. M5T 1G4, Canada.
- Art Gallery of Ontario. Annual Report. a. ISSN 0082-5018
- Art Gallery of Ontario. Coming Events. q. ISSN 0044-9024

**Art Magazine Inc.**
Suite 403, 234 Eglinton Ave. E., Toronto, Ont. M4P 1K5, Canada.
- Artmagazine. bi-m. ISSN 0318-6644

**Art Official Inc.**
241 Yonge St. Third Floor, Toronto, Ont. M5B 1N8, Canada.
- File. s-a. ISSN 0315-2456

**Arteditorial Co.**
Box 261, Station z, Toronto, Ont. M5N 2Z4, Canada.
- Onion. s-m. ISSN 0380-285X

**Arthurs Publications Ltd.**
Suite 204, 5200 Dixie Rd., Mississauga, Ont. L4W 1E4, Canada.
- Beverage Canada. 6 per yr.
- Canadian Boating. 10 per yr. ISSN 0045-4494
- Canadian Hairdresser; Canada's professional beauty magazine. 10 per yr (except Aug. & Dec.) ISSN 0008-3720
- Marine and Outdoor Trades. q. ISSN 0047-5939

**Arum Holdings Ltd.**
11615 Edinboro Rd., Edmonton 61, Alta., Canada.
- Canadian Sports Digest. m. ISSN 0045-5385

**Aslin Advertising Co.**
P.O. Box 481, Halifax, N.S. B3J 2R7, Canada.
- Metro Guide. Halifax-Dartmouth Current Events. m. ISSN 0047-6935 (Halifax Visitors and Convention Bureau)

**Assocation des Editeurs Canadiens**
- Vient de Paraitre. (pub. by Edi-Quebec Inc.)

**Associate Committee on the National Building Code.**
- N B C /N F C. (pub. by National Research Council of Canada)

**Association Canadienne d'Education de Langue Francaise**
3, Place Jean-Talon, Quebec G1K 7N8, Canada.
- Association Canadienne d'Education de Langue Francaise. Revue. irreg. (3-4 per yr.) ISSN 0315-3088

**Association Canadienne de la Construction**
*see* **Canadian Construction Association**

**Association Canadienne des Bibliothecaires des Langue Francaise (ASTED)**
360, Rue le Moyne, Montreal H2Y 1Y3, Canada.
- Association pour l'Avancement des Sciences et des Techniques de la Documentation. Rapport des Travaux du Congres. a. ISSN 0316-098X

**Association Canadienne des Ecoles Universitaires de Musique. Department of Music**
c/o Yves Chartier, Ed., Dept. of Music, Ottawa K1N 6N5, Canada.
- Canadian Association of University Schools of Music. Journal. s-a. ISSN 0315-3541

**Association Canadienne-Francaise pour l'Avancement des Sciences**
C.P. 6060, Montreal H3C 3A7, Que., Canada.
- Association Canadienne-Francaise pour l'Avancement des Sciences. A C F A S; Resumes des Communications; congres annuel-annales de l'ACFAS. a.
- Association Canadienne-Francaise pour l'Avancement des Sciences. Annales. a. ISSN 0066-8842
- Association Canadienne-Francaise pour l'Avancement des Sciences. Bulletin. irreg. ISSN 0066-8850

**Association Culturelle Franco-Canadienne de la Saskatchewan**
2604 rue Centrale, Regina, Sask. S4N 2N9, Canada.
- Ficelle; la publication des Francophones de la Saskatchewan. m (approx.) (Co-sponsor: Family Life Assurance Co.)

**Association de la Construction de Montreal et du Quebec**
4970 Place de la Savane, Montreal, Quebec H4P 1Z6, Canada.
- Association de la Construction de Montreal et du Quebec. Nouvelles. q.

**Association des Archivistes du Quebec**
C.P. 159, Haute-Ville, Que. G1R 4P3, Canada.
- Archives. q. ISSN 0044-9423

**Association des Assureurs-Vie du Canada**
41 Chemin Lesmill, Don Mills, Ont. M3B 2T3, Canada.
- Guide de Reussite dans le Carriere d'Assureur-Vie. a. ISSN 0317-2678

**Association des Demographes du Quebec**
2041 rue Dallaire, Ste-Foy, Que. G1V 1N5, Canada.
- Cahiers Quebecois de Demographie. 4 per yr. ISSN 0380-1721

**Association des Diplomes de Polytechniques**
c/o Ecole Polytechnique, Box 6079, Sta. A, Montreal, Que. H3C 3A7, Canada.
- Ingenieur. bi-m. ISSN 0020-1138

**Association des Editeurs Canadiens**
- Repertoire de l'Edition au Quebec. (pub. by Edi-Quebec Inc.)

**Association des Educateurs Specialises pour Inadaptes du Quebec**
8147 Est, rue Sherbrooke, Montreal, Que. H1L 1A7, Canada.
- Adaptation (Montreal); revue d'education specialisee. q. ISSN 0380-4194

**Association des Eglises Baptistes Evangeliques**
230 rue Lupien, Cap-De-la Madeleine, Que., Canada.
- Phare. m. ISSN 0031-7187

**Association des Enseignants Franco-Ontariens**
1427 Chemin Ogilvie, Suite 202, Ottawa, Ont. K1J 8M7, Canada.
- Entre Nous. 6 per yr. ISSN 0319-1788

**Association des Guides Catholiques du Canada**
3827, rue St.-Hubert, Montreal, Que. H2L 4A4, Canada.
- Brasier. irreg. ISSN 0381-596X

**Association des Infirmieres Catholiques du Canada**
108, 13e rue, Quebec G1L 2K3 P.Q., Canada.
- Bulletin des Infirmieres Catholiques du Canada. q. ISSN 0007-4470

**Association des Maitres Imprimeurs de Montreal**
480 Est, Ave Mont-Royal, Ch.22, Montreal, Que. H2J 1W4, Canada.
- Maitre Imprimeur. m. ISSN 0025-0996

**Association des Medecins de Langue Francaise du Canada**
5064 Ave. du Parc, Montreal 152, Canada.
- Association des Medecins de Langue Francaise du Canada. Bulletin. bi-m. ISSN 0004-539X

**Association des Photographes Professionnelle de la Province de Quebec**
2210 Boul. Pie IX, Montreal 403, Que., Canada.
- Photographe Professionnel. bi-m. ISSN 0048-3990

**Association des Professeurs d'Arts Plastiques du Quebec**
Box 424, Station Youville, Montreal,Que. H2P 2V6, Canada.
- Vision. irreg. ISSN 0382-0424

**Association des Professionnels de l'Activite Physique du Quebec**
1415 Est, rue Jarry, Montreal, H2E 2Z7 Que., Canada.
- Association des Professionnels de l' Activite Physique du Quebec. Actua. 11 per yr.
- Mouvement. q. ISSN 0047-827X

**Association des Technologistes Agricoles Inc.**
B. P. 308, St. Hyacinthe, Que., Canada.
- Quebec Horticole. m. ISSN 0048-6264
- Quebec Laitier et Alimentaire. m. ISSN 0048-6272

**Association des Traducteurs et Interpretes de l'Ontario**
457A Sussex, Ottawa, Ontario K1N 6Z4, Canada.
- Association des Traducteurs et Interpretes de l'Ontario. Annuaire. a. ISSN 0066-9016
- Association des Traducteurs et Interpretes de l'Ontario. Informatio. irreg. ISSN 0381-5781
- Association des Traducteurs et Interpretes de l'Ontario. Translatio. irreg. ISSN 0381-9965

**Association des Universites Partiellement Ou Entierement de Langue Francaise**
Universite de Montreal, B.P. 6128, Montreal, Que. H3C 3J7, Canada.
- A U P E L F. Bulletin de Nouvelles Breves. 4 per yr. ISSN 0007-4373
- A U P E L F. Revue. 2 per yr. ISSN 0001-2807
- Etudes Francaises dans le Monde. q. ISSN 0316-2672
- I D E E S. (Innovations, Demarches, Experiences dans l'Enseignement Superier) 3 per yr. ISSN 0382-0769
- Nouvelles Universitaires Africaines. 4 per yr.

**Association du Diabete du Quebec Inc.**
934 Est, rue Ste-Catherine, Suite 240, Montreal, Que. H2L 2E9, Canada.
- Plein Soleil. q.

**Association Feminine d'Education et d'Action Sociale**
515 Viger, Montreal H2L 2P2, Canada.
- A.F.E.A.S. Bulletin. 10 per yr. ISSN 0044-9458

**Association for Media and Technology in Education in Canada**
Duncan McArthur Hall, Queens University, Kingston, Ont., Canada.
- Media Message. q.

**Association for Preservation Technology**
Box 2487, Station D, Ottawa, Ontario K1P 5W6, Canada.
- Association for Preservation Technology. Bulletin. q. ISSN 0044-9466

**Association for Protection of Fur-Bearing Animals**
P.O. Box 274, Station A, Vancouver, B.C. V6C 2M7, Canada.
- Association for Protection of Fur-Bearing Animals. Annual Report. a. ISSN 0066-913X

**Association Forestiere Quebecoise**
915 St. Cyrille Ouest, Quebec G1S 1T8, Canada.
- Foret-Conservation. m. ISSN 0380-321X

**Association Generale des Etudiants de l'Universite de Sherbrooke**
Universite de Sherbrooke, Centre Social, Cite' Universitaire, Sherbrooke, P.Q., Canada.
- Campus Estrien. w. ISSN 0008-2511

**Association in Canada Serving Organizations for Human Settlements**
Box 48360, Bentall Centre, Vancouver, Canada.
- Habitat Forum News. q.

**Association of Canadian Archivists**
c/o Public Archives of Canada, Rm. 349, 395 Wellington St., Ottawa, Ont. K1A 0N3, Canada.
- Archivaria. s-a. ISSN 0318-6954

**Association of Canadian Community Colleges**
1750 Finch Ave. E., Willowdale, Ont. M2N 5T7, Canada.
- Association of Canadian Community Colleges. Yearbook. a.

**Association of Canadian Faculties of Dentistry**
c/o Faculty of Dentistry, University of Alberta, Edmonton T6G 2E1, Alta., Canada.
- Association of Canadian Faculties of Dentistry. Newsletter. q. ISSN 0044-9555

**Association of Canadian Law Teachers**
c/o Faculty of Law, Queen's University, Kingston, Ont., Canada.
- Directory of Law Teachers/Annuaire des Professeurs de Droit. a. ISSN 0383-8358

**Association of Canadian Map Libraries**
c/o National Map Collection, Public Archives of Canada, 395 Wellington St., Ottawa, Ont. K2P 0H6, Canada.
- Association of Canadian Map Libraries. Annual Conference. Proceedings. a. ISSN 0066-9474
- Association of Canadian Map Libraries. Bulletin. irreg.
- Directory of Canadian Map Collections. irreg. ISSN 0070-5217

**Association of Canadian Medical Colleges**
151 Slater St., Ottawa K1P 5H3 Ont., Canada.
- A C M C Forum. bi-m. ISSN 0317-5006

**Association of Canadian Television and Radio Artists (ACTRA)**
105 Carlton St., Toronto, Ont. M5B 1M2, Canada.
- Actrascope News. q. ISSN 0315-484X

**Association of Canadian University Teachers of English**
- English Studies in Canada. (pub. by University of Toronto Press)

**Association of Consulting Engineers of Canada**
130 Albert St., St. 616, Ottawa K1P 5G4, Canada.
- Consulting Engineers-Canada-Ingenieurs-Conseils. irreg. ISSN 0317-6525

**Association of Faculties of Pharmacy of Canada**
c/o Dr. A. M. Goodeve, Faculty of Pharmaceutical Sciences, University of British Columbia, Vancouver 8, B.C., Canada.
- Association of Faculties of Pharmacy of Canada. Proceedings. a. ISSN 0066-9555

**Association of Kinsmen Clubs**
Box 40, 55 Glencameron Rd., Suite 7, Thornhill, Ont. L3T 1P2, Canada.
- Kin. 6 per yr. ISSN 0023-1436

**Association of Mary Immaculate**
17 Graham Ave., Ottawa, Ont. K1S 0B6, Canada.
- Oblate Mission. q.

**Association of New Brunswick Land Surveyors**
P.O. Box 22, Fredericton, New Brunswick E3B 4Y2, Canada.
- Association of New Brunswick Land Surveyors.Annual Report. a.

**Association of Ontario Land Surveyors**
6070 Yonge St., Willowdale, Ont. M2M 3Z3, Canada.
- Association of Ontario Land Surveyors. Annual Report. a.

**Association of Professional Engineers, Geologists & Geophysicists of Alberta**
215 One Thornton Court, Edmonton, Alta., Canada.
- Pegg/Professional Engineer, Geologist, Geophysicist. 4 per yr. ISSN 0030-7912

**Association of Professional Engineers of British Columbia**
2210 W. 12th Ave., Vancouver V6K 2N6, B.C., Canada.
- B. C. Professional Engineer. m. ISSN 0005-2906

**Association of Professional Engineers of Manitoba**
710-177 Lombard Ave., Winnipeg 2, Man., Canada.
- Manitoba Professional Engineer. q. ISSN 0025-2271

**Association of Professional Engineers of Newfoundland**
Box 8414, Sta. A, St. John's, Nfld. A1B 3N7, Canada.
- Newfoundland and Labrador Engineer. irreg. ISSN 0384-1898

**Association of Professional Engineers of Nova Scotia**
Box 129, Halifax, N.S. B3J 2M4, Canada.
- Professional Engineer in Nova Scotia. 3 per yr. ISSN 0033-0086

**Association of Professional Engineers of Saskatchewan**
No. 220, 2220 12th Ave., Regina, Sask., Canada.
- Saskatchewan Professional Engineer. irreg. ISSN 0080-6579

**Association of Registered Professional Foresters of New Brunswick**
P.O. Box 23, Fredericton, N.B., Canada.
- Association of Registered Professional Foresters of New Brunswick. Papers and Reports. a. ISSN 0066-9644

**Association of Universities and Colleges of Canada**
151 Slater St., Ottawa K1P 5N1, Ont., Canada.
- Association of Universities and Colleges of Canada. Annual Meeting. Proceedings. a. ISSN 0066-9725
- Canadian Directory to Foundations and Other Granting Agencies. irreg. ISSN 0068-9947
- Financing Higher Education in Canada/ Financement de l'Enseignement Superieur au Canada. irreg. ISSN 0071-5166
- Select Bibliography on Higher Education. q. ISSN 0049-0091
- Universities and Colleges of Canada. a. ISSN 0083-3932 (Co-sponsor: Statistics Canada)
- University Affairs/Affaires Universitaires. 10 per yr.(including supplement listing academic and administrative vacancies in Canadian universities) ISSN 0041-9257

**Association pour l'Avancement des Sciences et des Techniques de la Documentation**
360 rue le Moyne, Montreal, Que., Canada.
- A. S. T. E. D. Nouvelles.
- Association pour l'Avancement des Sciences et des Techniques de la Documentation. Nouvelles de l'A S T E D. 6 per yr. ISSN 0316-0963
- Association pour l'Avancement des Sciences et des Techniques de la Documentation. Rapport. a. ISSN 0316-0955
- Documentation et Bibliotheques. q. ISSN 0315-2340

**Association pour la Protection Automobile**
292 ouest, Bd. St. Joseph, Box 117, Succursale E., Montreal, Que. H2V 3A7, Canada.
- Communique aux Consommateurs. irreg. ISSN 0380-7193

**Association Professionnelle des Meuniers du Quebec**
915 Bd. St. Cyrille Ouest, L-105, C.P. 247, Sillery, Quebec G1T 2R1, Canada.
- Meunier Quebecois. m. (except July & Aug.)

**Association Quebecoise des Pharmaciens Proprietaries**
5115 St. Denis St., Montreal, Que. H2J 2M1, Canada.
- Quebec Pharmacie. m. ISSN 0048-6280

**Association Quebecoise des Techniques de l'Eau**
6065 rue Sherbrooke Ouest, Ste. 4, Montreal, Que. H4A 1Y2, Canada.
- Eau du Quebec. q. ISSN 0315-2081

**Association Quebecoise du Transport et des Routes Inc.**
C.P. 218, Succ. Montreal-Nord, Montreal, Que. H1H 5L2, Canada.
- Routes et Transports. q.

**Association Quebecoise pour l'Etude Comparative du Droit**
5451 Durocher, Montreal, Quebec, Canada.
- Revue de Droit Compare. a. ISSN 0080-2514

**Association U F O-Quebec**
P.O. Box 53, Dollard-des-Ormeaux, Que. H9G 2H5, Canada.
- U F O - Quebec; recherches et informations. q. ISSN 0317-9311

**Associes de Neuve-France**
6463 St. Dominique, Montreal, Canada.
- Nouvelle France; revue du Canada francais. q.
ISSN 0029-4756

**Athletica Press**
Box 4981, Vancouver, B.C. V6B 4A6, Canada.
- Athletica; canadian track & field magazine/revue
canadienne d'athletisme. m. ISSN 0382-4438

**Atkinson College Students' Association**
Rm. 253, Atkinson College, York University, 4700
Keele St., Downsview M3J IP3 Ont., Canada.
- Atkinson Balloon. 9 per yr.

**Atlantic and Pacific Publications**
Box 297, Pointe Claire-Lorval 700, Que., Canada.
- Photography North; Canada's national photo
magazine. q. ISSN 0048-4016

**Atlantic Canada Economics Association**
c/o Dept. of Economics, Mount Allison University,
Sackville, N.B. E0A 3C0, Canada.
- Atlantic Canada Economics Association. Annual
Conference: A C E A Papers. a. ISSN 0319-003X

**Atlantic Provinces Economic Council**
One Sackville Place, Halifax, N.S. B3J 1K1,
Canada.
- Atlantic Provinces Economic Council. Annual
Report. a. ISSN 0067-0162
- Atlantic Provinces Economic Council. Newsletter.
m. ISSN 0044-989X
- Atlantic Provinces Economic Council. Pamphlet
Series. irreg. ISSN 0067-0170
- Atlantic Report. q. ISSN 0004-6841

**Atlantic Provinces Inter-University Committee on the Sciences**
Box 24, Halifax, N.S., Canada.
- Atlantic Provinces Inter-University Committee on
the Sciences. Newsletter. m. ISSN 0004-6825
- Atlantic Provinces Interuniversity Committee on
the Sciences. Annual Report. a. ISSN 0067-0197

**Atlantic Provinces Library Association**
c/o School of Library Service, Dalhousie University,
Halifax, N.S. B3H 4H8, Canada.
- A P L A Bulletin. q. ISSN 0001-2203
- Atlantic Provinces Checklist. a. ISSN 0571-7817

**Atlantic Provinces Numismatic Association**
25 Honeydale Cresc., Halifax, N. S., Canada.
- Atlantic Provinces Numismatic Association.
Newsletter. m. ISSN 0044-9903

**Atlantic Provinces Psychological Association**
c/o Dept of Psychology, Memorial University of
Newfoundland, St. John's, Nfld., Canada.
- Atlantic Psychologist. s-a. ISSN 0004-6833

**Atlantic Provinces Transportation Commission**
Box 577, Moncton, N.B. E1C 8L9, Canada.
- Atlantic Provinces Transportation Commission.
Tips & Topics. irreg. ISSN 0381-9345

**Atlantic Provinces Trucking Association**
Hartland, N.B., Canada.
- Atlantic Truck Transport Review. m. ISSN 0004-
6868

**Atlantic Region German Shepherd Dog Club**
Truro, N.S., Canada.
- Atlantic Shepherd. irreg. ISSN 0044-9938

**Atlantic Salmon Association**
1405 Peel St., Ste. 200, Montreal, Que. H3A 1S5,
Canada.
- Atlantic Salmon Journal. q. ISSN 0044-992X

**Atlas Copco Canada Ltd.**
Box 745, Point Claire-Dorval, Quebec H9R 4S8,
Canada.
- Canadian Air Comments; commentary on the
applications of compressed air. q. ISSN 0045-
4338

**Atomic Energy of Canada Ltd.**
Technical Information Branch, S.D.D.O., Station 14,
Chalk River, Ont. K0J 1J0, Canada.
- A E C L Review. m. ISSN 0001-1029
- Atomic Energy of Canada. A E C L Report
Series. irreg. ISSN 0067-0367
- Atomic Energy of Canada. Annual Report. a.
ISSN 0067-0383
- Atomic Energy of Canada. List of Publications.
irreg. ISSN 0067-0405
- Materials Research in A E C L. a.

**Auctioneers Association of Alberta**
1306 15th St. S.W., Calgary, Alta, Canada.
- Auctioneer. m. ISSN 0382-4942

**Editions Aujourd'hui**
Montreal, Que., Canada.
- Digeste Francais. m. ISSN 0383-2066

**Australia New Zealand Association**
3 West 8th Ave., Vancouver, B.C., Canada.
- A N z A News. m. ISSN 0045-0170

**Australian Trade Commission**
1155 Dorchester Blvd. W., Ste. 811, Montreal H3B
1H8, Canada.
- Australian Trading News. m.

**Avala Printing and Publishing**
1297 Drouillard Rd., Windsor, Ont. N8Y 2R6,
Canada.
- Glas Kanadskin Srba/Voice of Canadian Serbs. w.
ISSN 0046-5992 (Serbian National Shield
Society)

**Automotive Retailers' Publishing Co. Ltd.**
1687 W. Broadway, Vancouver 9, B. C., Canada.
- Automotive Retailer. m. ISSN 0005-1578

**Axiom Publications Ltd.**
Box 1525, Halifax, N.S., Canada.
- Axiom; Atlantic Canada's magazine. m. ISSN
0316-7747

**Ayrshire Breeders' Association**
1160 Carling Ave., Ottawa 3, Ont., Canada.
- Canadian Ayrshire Review. m. ISSN 0008-2961

**B. C. Teachers' Federation**
105-2235 Burrard St., Vancouver B.C. V6J 3H9,
Canada.
- B. C. Science Teacher. ( British Columbia
Science Teachers Association)
- B. C. Teacher. 5 per yr. ISSN 0005-2957
- British Columbia Art Teachers' Association.
Journal.
- British Columbia Association of Teachers of
Classics. Newsletter.
- British Columbia English Teachers' Association.
Journal.
- British Columbia Music Educator. ( British
Columbia Music Educators' Association)
- British Columbia School Counsellors' Association.
Newsletter.
- British Columbia Teachers' Federation.
Newsletter. 18-20 per yr. ISSN 0005-2965
- Exploration. ( British Columbia Social
Studies Teachers Association)
- Horizon. ( British Columbia Social Studies
Teachers Association)
- Intermediate Teacher. ( Provincial
Intermediate Teachers)
- Prime Areas. ( British Columbia Primary
Teachers' Association)
- Pro Motion. ( British Columbia Physical
Education Teachers Association)
- T H E S A Journal. ( Teachers of Home
Economics Specialist Association)
- Teaching Mathematics. ( British Columbia
Association of Mathematics Teachers)
- Vector. ( British Columbia Association of
Mathematics Teachers)
- Vexillum. ( British Columbia Association
of Teachers of Classics)

**B M I Canada Limited**
41 Valleybrook Dr., Don Mills, Ont. M3B 2S6,
Canada.
- Music Scene. bi-m. ISSN 0380-5131
- Yes, There Is Canadian Music/Oui, Notre
Musique Existe. m (with cum. editions) ISSN
0381-579X

**Baltic Philatelist Club**
Box 5, Roxboro, Que., Canada.
- Baltic Philatelist-Numismatist. m.
- Filatelists. 2-3 per yr. ISSN 0046-3779

**Banff Centre Press**
Box 1020, Banff, Alta. T0L 0C0, Canada.
- Centre Stage. 6 per yr. ISSN 0319-4728

**Bank of Canada**
Distribution Section, Secretary's Department,
Ottawa, Ont. K1A 0G9, Canada.
- Bank of Canada. Annual Report. a. ISSN
0067-3587
- Bank of Canada. Review/Banque du Canada.
Revue. m. ISSN 0045-1460
- Bank of Canada. Staff Research Studies.
irreg. ISSN 0067-3595
- Bank of Canada Weekly Financial Statistics. w.
ISSN 0005-5158

**Bank of Montreal**
Head Office, Box 6002, Montreal, Que. H3C 3B1,
Canada.
- Bank of Montreal Business Review. m. ISSN
0005-531X

**Bank of Nova Scotia**
Economics Dept., General Office, 44 King St.W.,
Toronto, Ont. M5H 1E2, Canada.
- Bank of Nova Scotia. Monthly Review. m. ISSN
0005-5328

**Banque Canadienne Nationale**
500 Place d'Armes, Montreal, Que., Canada.
- Banque Canadienne Nationale. Bulletin Mensuel.
m. ISSN 0045-1533

**Banque de Commerce Canadienne Imperiale**
Bureau Regional, Montreal, Que. H3C 3B2,
Montreal, Que., Canada.
- Banque de Commerce Canadienne Imperiale.
Lettre Commerciale. irreg.

**Baptist Convention of Ontario and Quebec**
217 St. George St., Toronto M5R 2M2, Ont.,
Canada.
- Canadian Baptist. m. ISSN 0008-2988 (Co-
sponsor: Baptist Union of Western Canada)

**Baptist Union of Western Canada**
4404 16 St. S.W., Calgary, Alta. T2T 4H9, Canada.
- Baptist Union of Western Canada. Year Book. a.
ISSN 0067-4087

**Barnet Rifle Club**
8550 Barnet Hwy, Barnet P.O., B.C., Canada.
- Barnet Marksman. q. ISSN 0045-155X

**Pascal Barrasso**
1081 Bas l'Assomption Nord, Montreal, Que.,
Canada
(Subscription Address: 2125 rue Jean Talon Est,
Montreal, Que., Canada)
- Ciao; l'unica rivista italiana edita in nord america.
m.

**Barreau du Quebec. Revue**
1, Est, Notre Dame St., Bureau 9.80, Montreal,
Que. H2Y 1B6, Canada.
- Barreau du Quebec. Revue. m.(Sept-June) ISSN
0005-6065

**Murray Isaac Barrett**
1498 Yonge St., Suite 7, Toronto, Ont. M4T 1Z6,
Canada.
- Jewish Dialogue. q. ISSN 0315-2685

**Barristers' Society of New Brunswick**
Fredericton, N.B., Canada.
- Legal Aid New Brunswick Annual Report/
Assistance Judiciaire Nouveau-Brunswick Rapport
Annuel. a. ISSN 0381-2049

**Basilian Press**
95 St. Joseph St., Toronto 5, Ont., Canada.
- Basilian Historical Bulletins. irreg., no. 8, 1972.
- Beacon; Ukrainian rite monthly. bi-m. ISSN 0382-
6384 (Order of Saint Basil-The-Great)
- Svitlo/Light; Ukrainian Catholic monthly. m.
ISSN 0039-7164 (Order of Saint Basil-the-Great)

**Nancy Bauer, Ed. & Pub.**
252 Stanley St., Fredericton, N.B. E3B 3A3,
Canada.
- New Brunswick Chapbooks. irreg; (approx 3-4 per
yr)

**Baxter Publishing Co.**
401, 150 King St. W., Toronto, Ont., Canada.
- Canadian Travel Press. fortn. ISSN 0045-5490
- Personnel Guide to Canada's Travel Industry. s-a.
ISSN 0048-3451

**Mahlon F. Beach, Ed. & Pub.**
1330 Danforth Ave., Toronto, Ont. M4J 1M9,
Canada.
- Freemason; Canada's national Masonic magazine.
  bi-m. ISSN 0016-0660

**Colin Beale, Ed. & Pub.**
1512-925 W. Georgia St., Vancouver, B.C. V6C
IR5, Canada.
- Beal's Letter. 26 per yr. ISSN 0315-0917

**Beaux-Arts**
3625 St. Laurent, Montreal, P.Q. H2X 2V5,
Canada.
- Beaux-Arts. irreg.

**Beaverbrook Art Gallery**
P. O. Box 605, Fredericton, N. B., Canada.
- Beaverbrook Art Gallery. q. ISSN 0045-1592

**Bedford Institute of Oceanography**
Dartmouth, N.S. B2Y 4A2, Canada.
- Bedford Institute of Oceanography. Biennial
  Review. biennial. ISSN 0067-480X
- Bedford Institute of Oceanography. Collected
  Contributions of the Bedford Institute of
  Oceanography. a. ISSN 0067-4818
- Bedford Institute of Oceanography. Computer
  Note. irreg.
- Bedford Institute of Oceanography. Data Report.
  irreg., 1970, no. 04-D.
- Bedford Institute of Oceanography. Report. irreg.,
  1970, no.o-3.
- Maritime Sediments. 3 per yr. ISSN 0025-3456

**Bell-Northern Research Ltd.**
Box 3511 Sta. C, Ottawa, Ont. K1Y 4H7, Canada.
- Telesis. 6 per yr. ISSN 0040-2710

**Bell Publishers**
Box 532, Calgary, Alta., Canada.
- Alberta Transport Reporter. q. ISSN 0002-4902

**Bell Telephone Company of Canada**
1050 Beaver Hall Hill, Montreal Que., Canada.
- Bell Telephone Company of Canada. Annual
  Statistical Report. a.

**Editions Bellarmin**
8100 Blvd. Saint Laurent, Montreal, Quebec H2P
2L9, Canada.
- Philosophiques. s-a.
- Relations. m. ISSN 0034-3781 (Peres de la
  Compagnie de Jesus)
- Science et Esprit. 3 per yr.

**Bellrock Press Association**
2050 Mackay St., Montreal, Que. H3G 2J1,
Canada.
- Journal of Canadian Fiction. q. ISSN 0047-2255

**Bent**
1111 Bewdley Avenue, Victoria, B. C., Canada.
- Bent. irreg., 1971, no. 7. ISSN 0067-5733

**Bernard Amtmann Inc.**
1529 Sherbrooke W., Montreal, Canada.
- Canadian Art Auction Record. irreg. ISSN 0317-
  7920

**Bible Holiness Movement**
Box 223, Sta. A, Vancouver, B.C. V6C 2M3,
Canada.
- Truth on Fire. bi-m.

**Bibliographical Society of Canada**
32 Lowther Ave., Toronto, Ont. M5R 1C6, Canada.
- Bibliographical Society of Canada. Bulletin. s-a.
- Bibliographical Society of Canada. Facsimile
  Series. irreg. ISSN 0067-687X
- Bibliographical Society of Canada. Monographs.
  irreg. ISSN 0067-6888
- Bibliographical Society of Canada. Papers. a. ISSN
  0067-6896
- Bibliography of Canadian Bibliographies. irreg.,
  2nd ed. ISSN 0067-7175

**Bibliotheca Polyglotta**
P.O. Box 202, Postal Station A, Montreal, P.Q.
H3C 2S1, Canada.
- Library Innovator. irreg.

**Bibliotheque Nationale du Quebec**
1700 rue Saint-Denis, Montreal, Que. H2X 3K6,
Canada.
- Bibliographie du Quebec. m. ISSN 0006-1441
- Quebec. Bibliotheque Nationale. Bulletin. q. ISSN
  0045-1967

**Biographies Canadienness-Francaises, Ltee.**
4246 E. rue Jean-Talon, Suite 15, Montreal, 452,
P.Q., Canada.
- Biographies Canadiennes-Francaises/Who's Who
  in Quebec. irreg.

**Biomass Energy Institute**
301-870 Cambridge St., Winnipeg., Manitoba R3M
3H5, Canada.
- Biomass Energy Institute. Newsletter. 3 per yr.

**Bishops University. Students' Executive Council**
Lennoxville, Que., Canada.
- Campus (Lennoxville) w. ISSN 0008-2481
- New Mitre; students' literary magazine. a.

**Blackfish**
1851 Moore St., Burnaby 2, B.C. Canada.
- Blackfish. 3 per yr. ISSN 0045-2270

**Bluenose Rambler**
Box 32, Western Shore, Nova Scotia BOJ 3MU,
Canada.
- Bluenose Rambler. q.

**Blues**
Box 585, Station P, Toronto M5S 2T1, Canada.
- Blues. bi-m.

**Blyth Standard**
Box 10, Blyth, Ontario, Canada.
- Village Squire. m. ISSN 0382-0203

**Bonanza Press Ltd.**
133 Besserer St., Ottawa, Ont., Canada
(Subscr. to: 578 Pleasant Park Rd., Ottawa, Ont.
K1H 5N1, Canada)
- Canadian Dancers News. q. ISSN 0315-3959

**Boreal**
Box 262, Victoria Station, Montreal 215 P.Q.,
Canada.
- Boreal; poesia espanola en el Canada. 2 per yr.
  ISSN 0006-7717

**Boreal Institute for Northern Studies**
University of Alberta, Edmonton, Alberta T6G 2E9,
Canada.
- Boreal Institute, Edmonton. Annual Report. a.
  ISSN 0068-0281
- Boreal Institute, Edmonton. Miscellaneous
  Publications. irreg. ISSN 0068-029X
- Boreal Institute, Edmonton. Occasional
  Publications. irreg. ISSN 0068-0303

**Eli Bornstein, Ed. & Pub.**
Box 378, Sub. P.O. 6, University of Saskatchewan,
Saskatoon, Sask. S7N 0W0, Canada
- Structurist. a. ISSN 0081-6027 (Dist. in U.S. by:
  Wittenborn, 1018 Madison Ave., New York, NY
  10021)

**Boundary Historical Society**
12 Street, S.E., Grand Forks, B.C., Canada.
- Boundary Historical Society. Report. every four or
  five years. ISSN 0068-0524

**Bowes Publishers Ltd.**
215 Adelaide St., London, Ont., Canada.
- Western Ontario Farmer. w. ISSN 0049-7460

**Bradley Publications Ltd.**
210-1808 Smith St., Regina Sask. S4P 2N4, Canada.
- Farm Light & Power. 10 per yr. ISSN 0014-8032

**Branstead Press**
Carlisle, Ont., Canada.
- Modicum. w. ISSN 0381-0739

**Bratstvo**
345 Dovercourt Rd., Toronto, Ont. M6J 3E4,
Canada.
- Bratstvo; casopis za jacanje nacionalno-politickog
  jedinstva Srba pravoslavnih i muslimana u
  emigraciji. m. ISSN 0006-9264

**Brave Beaver Pressworks Ltd.**
81A Front St. E., Toronto, Ont. M5E 1B8, Canada.
- Cycle Canada. m. ISSN 0319-2822

**Brewing and Malting Barley Research Institute**
206 Grain Exchange Bldg., Winnipeg, Manitoba,
Canada.
- Brewing and Malting Barley Research Institute.
  Annual Report. a. ISSN 0068-094X

**British America Publishing Co. Ltd.**
Canadian Orange Hdqs., 94 Sheppard Ave. W.,
Willowdale, Ont. M2N 1M5, Canada.
- Sentinel (Willowdale) 10 per yr. ISSN 0049-0202
  (Grand Orange Lodge of Canada)

**British Canadian Trade Association**
- New (Toronto) (pub. by Pendragon House Ltd.)

**British Columbia. Alcohol and Drug Commission**
Parliament Bldgs., Victoria, B.C., Canada.
- British Columbia. Alcohol and Drug Commission.
  Annual Report. a.

**British Columbia. Bureau of Economics and Statistics**
Victoria B.C., Canada.
- Selected Forest Industry Statistics of British
  Columbia. a. ISSN 0080-8598

**British Columbia. Cancer Foundation**
2656 Heather St., Vancouver, B.C. V5Z 3J3,
Canada.
- British Columbia. Cancer Foundation. Annual
  Report. a. ISSN 0068-1423

**British Columbia. Department of Human Resources**
Parliament Buildings, Victoria, British Columbia,
Canada.
- Services for People; annual report of the
  Department of Human Resources. a. ISSN 0317-
  4670

**British Columbia. Department of Labour. Research
Branch**
Victoria, B.C., Canada.
- British Columbia. Department of Labour.
  Research Branch. Working Conditions in British
  Columbia Industry. irreg.

**British Columbia. Department of Lands, Forests and
Water Resources. Water Resources Service**
Victoria, B.C., Canada.
- British Columbia. Department of Lands, Forests
  and Water Resources. Water Resources Service.
  Report. a. ISSN 0068-1873

**British Columbia. Department of Recreation and
Conservation**
Parliament Buildings, Victoria, B.C., Canada.
- British Columbia. Department of Recreation and
  Conservation. Annual Report. a. ISSN 0068-1458

**British Columbia. Department of Travel Industry**
Parliament Buildings, Victoria B.C. V8V 1X4,
Canada, Parliament Buildings.
- Beautiful British Columbia. q. ISSN 0005-7460

**British Columbia. Energy Commission**
1177 West Hastings St, Vancouver, B. C. V 6E 2L7,
Canada.
- British Columbia. Energy Commission. Annual
  Report. a.

**British Columbia. Environment and Land Use
Committee**
Victoria, B.C., Canada.
- Land; B.C. resource magazine. q. ISSN 0318-7446

**British Columbia. Forest Service**
Information Division, Parliament Building, Victoria,
B.C., Canada.
- British Columbia. Forest Service. Annual Report.
  a. ISSN 0068-1490
- British Columbia. Forest Service. Forest
  Management Notes. irreg., 1966, no. 5. ISSN
  0068-1504
- British Columbia. Forest Service. Forest Survey
  Notes. irreg., 1966, no. 7. ISSN 0068-1512
- British Columbia. Forest Service. Research Notes.
  irreg., 1970, no. 54. ISSN 0068-1520
- British Columbia. Forest Service. Research
  Review. a. ISSN 0068-1539
- British Columbia. Forest Service. Technical
  Publications. irreg. ISSN 0068-1547
- Conservation Topics. (pub. by Canadian Forestry
  Association of B.C.)

**British Columbia. Library Development Commission**
Parliament Buildings, Victoria, British Columbia,
Canada.
- British Columbia. Library Development
  Commission. Public Libraries, Statistics. a. ISSN
  0084-8034

**British Columbia. Ministry of Economic Development**
Victoria, B.C. V8V 4R9, Canada.
- B.C. Market News. q.

British Columbia. Department of Economic
Development. Monthly Bulletin of Business
Activity. m.
- British Columbia Economic Outlook Survey. irreg.
- Summary of Economic Activity in British
Columbia. a.

**British Columbia. Ministry of Labour. Research and Planning Branch**
Victoria, B.C., Canada.
- British Columbia. Ministry of Labour. Labour
Research Bulletin. m.

**British Columbia. Ministry of Mines and Petroleum Resources**
Parliament Bldgs, Victoria, B.C. V8V 1X4, Canada.
- British Columbia. Department of Mines and
Petroleum Resources. Bulletin. irreg. ISSN 0068-
144X
- British Columbia. Minister of Mines and
Petroleum Resources. Annual Report. a.
- Geology, Exploration, and Mining in British
Columbia. a. ISSN 0085-1027

**British Columbia. Ministry of Recreation and Conservation**
Parliament Bldgs., Victoria, B.C., Canada.
- Wildlife Review. q. ISSN 0511-9510

**British Columbia. Ministry of the Environment. Water Investigation Branch**
Parliament Bldgs., Victoria, B.C. V8V 1X5, Canada.
- British Columbia Snow Survey Bulletin. 6 per yr.
ISSN 0045-303X

**British Columbia. Provincial Archives. Aural History**
Victoria, B.C. V8V 1X4, Canada.
- Sound Heritage. q. ISSN 0316-2516

**British Columbia. Royal Commission on Family and Children's Law**
Vancouver, B.C., Canada.
- British Columbia. Royal Commission on Family
and Children's Law. Report. irreg.

**British Columbia Art Teachers Association**
No. 105, 2235 Burrard St., Vancouver, B. C. V6J
3H9, Canada.
- British Columbia Art Teachers' Association.
Journal. q. ISSN 0316-1544 (pub. by B. C.
Teachers' Federation)

**British Columbia Association for the Mentally Retarded**
No. 221 119 W. Pender, Vancouver, B. C. V6B 1S5,
Canada.
- British Columbia Reporter. q.

**British Columbia Association of Mathematics Teachers**
105-2235 Burrard St., Vancouver, B.C. V6J 3H9,
Canada.
- Teaching Mathematics. irreg. ISSN 0382-5493
(pub. by B. C. Teachers' Federation)
- Vector. irreg. ISSN 0382-0718 (pub. by
B. C. Teachers' Federation)

**British Columbia Association of Teachers of Classics**
No. 105, 2235 Burrard St., Vancouver, B.C. V6J
3H9, Canada.
- British Columbia Association of Teachers of
Classics. Newsletter. 3 per yr. ISSN 0045-2912
(pub. by B. C. Teachers' Federation)
- Vexillum. irreg. ISSN 0316-2508 (pub. by
B. C. Teachers' Federation)

**British Columbia Bond Dealers Association**
- British Columbia Municipal Yearbook. (pub. by
Sanderson Publications Ltd.)

**British Columbia Civil Liberties Association**
206-207 W. Hastings, Vancouver, B.C. V6B 1H7,
Canada.
- Democratic Commitment. bi-m. ISSN 0045-9909

**British Columbia English Teachers' Association**
105-2235 Burrard St., Vancouver, B. C. V6J 3H9,
Canada.
- British Columbia English Teachers' Association.
Journal. 3 per yr. ISSN 0316-0173 (pub. by B. C.
Teachers' Federation)

**British Columbia Federation of Labour**
517 East Broadway, Vancouver, B.C., Canada.
- British Columbia Federation of Labour.
Proceedings of the Convention. a. ISSN 0068-
1482
- Labour Statesman. w. ISSN 0381-0585

**British Columbia Fruit Growers Association**
1473 Water Street, Kelowna, B.C. V1Y 7N6,
Canada.
- British Columbia Fruit Growers Association.
Horticultural Conference Proceedings. a. ISSN
0068-1555
- British Columbia Fruit Growers Association.
Minutes of the Proceedings of the Annual
Convention. a. ISSN 0068-1563

**British Columbia Genealogical Society**
Box 94371, Richmond, V6Y 2A8, B.C., Canada.
- British Columbia Genealogist. q. ISSN 0315-3835

**British Columbia Health Association**
440 Cambie, Vancouver, B.C., Canada.
- B. C. Health Association. Proceedings of the
Annual Conference. a.

**British Columbia Historical Association**
3450 W. 20th Ave., Vancouver 8, B. C., Canada.
- British Columbia Historical News. q. ISSN 0045-
2963

**British Columbia Institute for Economic Policy**
- British Columbia Institute for Economic Policy
Analysis Series. (pub. by University of British
Columbia Press)

**British Columbia Library Association**
Box 46378, Sta. G., Vancouver, B.C. V6R 4G6,
Canada.
- B C L A Reporter. 10 per yr. ISSN 0005-2876

**British Columbia Medical Association**
1807 W. Tenth Ave., Vancouver, B.C. V6J 2A9,
Canada.
- British Columbia Medical Journal. m. ISSN 0007-
0556

**British Columbia Mountaineering Club**
Box 2674, Vancouver, B.C., Canada.
- British Columbia Mountaineer. m. ISSN 0045-
2998

**British Columbia Museums Association**
c/o B. C. Provincial Museum, Victoria, B.C. V8W
1A1, Canada.
- British Columbia Museums Association. Museum
Round-Up. q. ISSN 0045-3005

**British Columbia Music Educators' Association**
105-2235 Burrard St., Vancouver, B.C. V6J 3H9,
Canada.
- British Columbia Music Educator. s-a. ISSN 0007-
0564 (pub. by B. C. Teachers' Federation)

**British Columbia Native Indian Teachers' Association**
- Indian Education Newsletter. (pub. by Indian
Education Resources Centre)

**British Columbia Physical Education Teachers Association**
105-2235 Burrard St., Vancouver, B.C. V6J 3H9,
Canada.
- Pro Motion. s-a. ISSN 0048-5381 (pub. by
B. C. Teachers' Federation)

**British Columbia Primary Teachers' Association**
105-2235 Burrard St., Vancouver, B.C. V6J 3H9,
Canada.
- Prime Areas. 2-3 per yr. ISSN 0032-8359 (pub.
by B. C. Teachers' Federation)

**British Columbia Provincial Judges' Association**
Vancouver, B.C., Canada.
- British Columbia Provincial Judges' Association.
Annual Conference. a. ISSN 0317-297X

**British Columbia Research Council**
3650 Wesbrook Cresc., Vancouver, B. C. V6S 2L2,
Canada.
- B. C. Research. Annual Report. a.

**British Columbia School Counsellors' Association**
2235 Burrard St., Vancouver, B. C. V6J 3H9, Canada.
- British Columbia School Counsellors' Association.
Newsletter. 5 per yr. (pub. by B. C. Teachers'
Federation)

**British Columbia School Trustees Association**
1155 West 8th Ave., Vancouver 6,B.C., Canada.
- British Columbia School Trustees Association.
Newsletter. irreg. ISSN 0381-5978
- Education B.C; British Columbia's educational
news magazine. m. ISSN 0046-1393

**British Columbia Science Teachers Association**
Suite 105, 2235 Burrard St., Vancouver, B. C. V6J
3H9, Canada.
- B. C. Science Teacher. m ISSN 0381-6036
(pub. by B. C. Teachers' Federation)

**British Columbia Social Studies Teachers Association**
105-2235 Burrard St., Vancouver, B.C. V6J 3H9,
Canada.
- Exploration. irreg. (approx. 2 per yr.) ISSN 0014-
4959 (pub. by B. C. Teachers' Federation)
- Horizon. q. ISSN 0315-8527 (pub. by
B. C. Teachers' Federation)

**British Columbia Society for Crippled Children**
1345 S.W. Marine Drive, Vancouver, B.C., Canada.
- B. C. Rehabilitation News. irreg. ISSN 0382-5485
(Co-Sponsor: Rehabilitation Foundation of British
Columbia)

**British Columbia Thoroughbred Breeders Society**
4023 E. Hastings St., Burnaby, B.C. V5C 2J1,
Canada.
- British Columbia Thoroughbred. m. ISSN 0045-
3064

**British Columbia Tuberculosis Christmas Seal Society**
906 W. Broadway, Vancouver 9, B.C., Canada.
- Your Health. q. ISSN 0044-104X

**British Columbia Voice of Women**
P.O. Box 235, Nanaimo, B.C. V9R 5K9, Canada.
- B.C. Voice. 6 per yr. ISSN 0045-3080

**British Israel World Federation (Canada) Inc.**
313 Sherbourne St., Toronto, Ont., Canada.
- Prophetic Expositor. m. ISSN 0048-5578

**British North America Philatelic Society**
c/o Robert F. Boudignon, Circ. Mgr., Box 639,
Copper Cliff, Ont. P0M 1N0, Canada.
- B N A Topics. bi-m. ISSN 0045-3129

**Brock University. Department of Geological Sciences**
Merrittville Highway, St. Catharines, Ont. L2S 3AI,
Canada.
- Brock University. Department of Geological
Sciences. Research Report Series. irreg., approx 5
per yr.

**Brome County Historical Society**
Knowlton, Que., Canada.
- Brome County Historical Society. Publication.
irreg. ISSN 0381-6206

**Brotherhood of Railway Running Trades**
London, Ont., Canada.
- Brotherhood of Railway Running Trades.
Communique. irreg. ISSN 0383-9486

**Bruce County Historical Society**
c/o Mrs. George Downey, Eskadale Farm, Tiverton,
Ontario N0G 2T0, Canada.
- Bruce County Historical Society. Year Book. a.
ISSN 0084-8115
- Pioneer Days. irreg., 3rd ed. 1975. (Subscr. to:
Mrs. James McClure, Box 82, Chesley, Ont.,
Canada)

**Bryant Press**
Toronto, Ont., Canada.
- Canadian Practitioner and Review. m. ISSN 0382-
7453

**Buckingham Publishing Co.**
Box 927, Sta. F, Toronto 5, Ont., Canada.
- National Horse Journal. m. ISSN 0047-8873

**Building Owners Managers Association**
- Building Management Maintenance News. (pub.
by Logan Brown Communications)

**Louis Burke**
518 26th St. S., Lethbridge, Alta, Canada.
- Canadian Short Story. q.

**Burnard Printing Co.**
6424-1A St. S. W., Calgary, Alta., Canada.
- Dinny's Digest; magazine for animal lovers. q.
ISSN 0046-029X (Calgary Zoological Society)

**Bust Press**
Box 367, Sta. F, Toronto, Ont., Canada.
- Bust. irreg. ISSN 0045-3676

**Butterworth & Co.(Canada) Ltd.**
2265 Midland Ave., Scarborough, Toronto, Ont., Canada.
- Canadian Income Tax. w.
- Canadian Legal Manual Series. irreg.
- Canadian Legal Studies Series. irreg. ISSN 0576-5625
- Canadian Weekly Law Sheet. w. ISSN 0008-5308
- Modern Trends in Oncology. irreg.
- New Law Journal. w. ISSN 0306-6479

**Buyers Market of Canada**
P. O. Box 87, 400 Paris Bldg., Winnipeg 2, Man., Canada.
- Buyers' Market. 2 per yr. ISSN 0045-3684

**Byelorussian Literary Association**
24 Tarlton Rd., Toronto, Ont. M5P 2MC, Canada.
- Bayavaya Uskalos; Byelorussian literary magazine. a. ISSN 0005-6952

**Byers Associates**
1885 Wilson Ave., Weston, Ont. M9M IA2, Canada.
- Byers National Industrial Directory. a. ISSN 0068-4600
- Byers Trade Directory. a. ISSN 0068-4619
- Byers Western Industrial Directory. a. ISSN 0068-4627
- Canadian Merchandise Mart. a. ISSN 0068-9238

**C A E Industries Ltd.**
Box 30, Royal Bank Plaza, Toronto, Ont. M5J 2J1, Canada.
- C A E News. q. ISSN 0007-7739

**Editions C A S C**
Montreal, Que., Canada.
- Auto Revue (Montreal) irreg. ISSN 0382-5825

**C B Media Limited**
1080 Beaver Hall Hill, Montreal, Que. H2Z 1T2, Canada.
- Canadian Business. m. ISSN 0008-3100

**C C F Publishing and Printing Co. Ltd.**
1630 Quebec St., Regina, Sask., Canada.
- Commonwealth. fortn. ISSN 0010-3357

**C C H Canadian Ltd.**
6 Garamond Ct., Don Mills, Ontario M3C 1Z5, Canada.
- British Columbia Corporations Law Guide. m.
- British Columbia Tax Reports. m. ISSN 0045-3056
- Canada Business Corporations Act with Regulations. irreg. ISSN 0317-6649
- Canada Income Tax Guide. 18 per yr. ISSN 0008-2694
- Canadian Depreciation Guide. irreg., 13th ed., 1974. ISSN 0068-8649
- Canadian Environmental Control Newsletter. s-m.
- Canadian Government Programs and Services. m. ISSN 0045-4893
- Canadian Industrial Relations and Personnel Developments. w. ISSN 0045-4966
- Canadian Insurance Law Reports. m. ISSN 0045-4990
- Canadian Labor Law Reports. s-m. ISSN 0008-4328
- Canadian Labour Terms. a. ISSN 0068-905X
- Canadian Sales and Credit Law Guide. m. ISSN 0045-5318
- Canadian Sales Tax Reports. m. ISSN 0045-5326
- Canadian Securities Law Reports. m. ISSN 0045-5342
- Canadian Tax Reports. w. ISSN 0008-5138
- Canadian Workmen's Compensation. a., 18th ed., 1975 per 6. ISSN 0069-004X
- Dominion Companies Law Reports. m. ISSN 0046-0559
- Dominion Report Service. m.
- Dominion Tax Cases. 3 per mo. ISSN 0046-0567
- Loi de l'Impot sur le Revenu, Canadienne. a. ISSN 0076-048X

- Manitoba and Saskatchewan Tax Reports. m.
- Maritime Tax Reports. m. ISSN 0047-5971
- Ontario Corporations Law Guide. m.
- Ontario Real Estate Law Guide. m. ISSN 0382-5906
- Ontario Tax Reports. m. ISSN 0048-1866
- Provincial Inheritance and Gift Tax Reports. m.
- Quebec Tax Reports. m. ISSN 0048-6299
- View from Ottawa. w. ISSN 0049-6383

**C F F S Index Committee**
1762 Carling Avenue, Toronto 13, Ontario, Canada.
- Index of Feature Length Films. irreg.

**C F P Publications, Ltd.**
Box 208, Station "J", 685 Danforth Ave., Toronto 6, Ontario, Canada.
- Canadian Free Press. w.
- Kanadai Fuggetlen Hirlap. w. ISSN 0047-3146

**C O P A**
- Canadian Flight. (pub. by Canadian Flight Publishing Co.)

**C T R Publications**
Downsview, Ont., Canada.
- Canadian Theatre Review Yearbook. a.

**C V 2**
Box 32, University Centre, University of Manitoba, Winnipeg, Man. R3T 1E0, Canada.
- C V 2. (Contemporary Verse Two) q. ISSN 0319-6879

**Cactus Inc.**
873 St.-Jean, Quebec City, Canada.
- Cactus. irreg. ISSN 0409-7734

**Editions le Caducee, Inc.**
1440 West St. Catherine St., Suite 1100, Montreal, Que. H3G 1R8, Canada.
- Medecin du Quebec. m. ISSN 0025-6692

**Calendar Magazines Ltd.**
65 Front St. East, Toronto, Ont. M5E 1B6, Quebec H2Y 2B6.
- Montreal Calendar Magazine; digest of things to do for people who live in Montreal. m. ISSN 0315-0534
- Toronto Calendar Magazine. m. ISSN 0040-9537
- Vancouver Calendar Magazine; the digest of things to do for people who live in Vancouver. m. ISSN 0049-5816

**Calgary Aquarium Society**
Box 6116, Sta. D, Calgary 2, Alta., Canada.
- Calquarium. m. ISSN 0045-4052

**Calgary Fish and Game Association**
2A-351-13 Ave. S.W., Calgary 3, Alta., Canada.
- Our Vanishing Heritage. irreg. ISSN 0078-706X

**Calgary Indian Friendship Centre**
140-2 Ave. S.W., Calgary, Alta., Canada.
- Elbow Drums. m.

**Calgary Livestock Market Journal**
Rm. 203, Alberta Stockyards Bldg., Calgary, Alta. T2G4 M8, Canada.
- Calgary Livestock Market Journal. m. ISSN 0045-3889

**Calgary Sports Car Club**
Box 844, Calgary, Alta., Canada.
- Broken Spoke. m. ISSN 0045-3226

**Calgary Zoological Society**
- Dinny's Digest. (pub. by Burnard Printing Co.)

**Canada. Agriculture Canada. Animal Research Institute**
Ottawa, Ont. K1A 0C6, Canada.
- Canada. Agriculture Canada. Animal Research Institute. Research Report. a. ISSN 0066-1899

**Canada. Agriculture Canada. Economics Branch**
Ottawa K1A OC5, Canada.
- Animal and Products Outlook.
- Canadian Farm Economics/Economie Agricole au Canada. bi-m. ISSN 0008-3518

**Canada. Agriculture Canada. Experimental Farm**
L'Assomption, Que., Canada.
- Canada. Experimental Farm, L'Assomption. Rapport de Recherches. a. ISSN 0068-7464

**Canada. Agriculture Canada. Information Division**
Ottawa K1A 0C7, Ont., Canada.
- Canada Agriculture. q. ISSN 0008-2554
- Directory of Farmers' Organizations and Marketing Boards in Canada. a. ISSN 0070-5527
- Farm Letter/Lettre au Cultivateur. m. ISSN 0014-8024
- Lighter/Briquet. q. ISSN 0024-340X

**Canada. Agriculture Canada. International Liaison Service**
Ottawa, Canada.
- Agriculture Abroad; a bi-monthly digest of agricultural policies and programs in various countries. bi-m. ISSN 0002-1717
- Spot News from Abroad. w. ISSN 0038-8343

**Canada. Agriculture Canada. Library**
Ottawa, K1A 0C5, Canada.
- Canada. Department of Agriculture. Library. Current Periodicals. Periodiques en Cours. irreg. ISSN 0084-8379

**Canada. Agriculture Canada. Market Information Service**
Ottawa, Canada.
- Dairy Produce Market Report. w.

**Canada. Agriculture Canada. Pesticide Technical Information Office**
K. W. Neatby Bldg., Ottawa, Ont. K1A 0C6, Canada.
- Canada. Committee on Pesticide Use in Agriculture. Pesticide Research Report. a. ISSN 0068-7898

**Canada. Agriculture Canada. Research Branch**
Central Experimental Farm, Ottawa, Ont. K1A 0C6, Canada.
- Aphidologists' Newsletter. irreg., vol. 13, 1974. ISSN 0066-5304
- Canada. Department of Agriculture. Engineering Research Service, Ottawa. Research Report. a. ISSN 0068-7294
- Canada. Department of Agriculture. Forage Crops Division. Forage Notes. q. ISSN 0045-4168
- Canadian Plant Disease Survey. q. ISSN 0008-476X
- E R D A. (Engineering Research and Development in Agriculture) q. ISSN 0012-7892 (prep. by its Engineering Research Service)

**Canada. Agriculture Canada. Research Institute**
University Sub Post Office, London, Ont. N6A 3KO, Canada.
- Canada. Agriculture Canada. Research Institute. Research Branch Report. a., since 1966.

**Canada. Agriculture Canada. Research Program Services**
Ottawa K1A 0C5, Canada.
- Canadian Agricultural Insect Pest Review. a. ISSN 0068-8185

**Canada. Agriculture Canada. Research Station**
Box 1240, Melfort, Sask., Canada.
- Canada. Research Station, Melfort, Saskatchewan. Research Highlights. Annual Publications. a. ISSN 0068-7472

**Canada. Air Pollution Control Directorate**
Ottawa, Ont. K1A 0H3, Canada.
- Canada. Air Pollution Control Directorate. Annual Summary: National Air Pollution Surveillance. a.

**Canada. Anti-Dumping Tribunal**
Ottawa, Ont. K1A 0S9, Canada.
- Canada. Anti-Dumping Tribunal. Annual Report. a.

**Canada. Atmospheric Environment Service**
4905 Dufferin St., Downsview, Ont. M3H 5T4, Canada
(Subscr. to: Supply & Services Canada, Printing & Publishing, Ottawa, Ont. K1A 0S9, Canada)
- Canada Atmospheric Environment Service. Climatological Studies. irreg. ISSN 0068-7715
- Canada. Atmospheric Environment Service. Ice Observations: Canadian Arctic. irreg. ISSN 0068-7723
- Canada. Atmospheric Environment Service. Ice Observations: Canadian Inland Waterways. a. ISSN 0068-7731
- Canada. Atmospheric Environment Service. Ice Observations: Eastern Canadian Seaboard. irreg. ISSN 0068-774X

- Canada. Atmospheric Environment Service. Ice Summary and Analysis, Canadian Arctic. a. ISSN 0068-7758
- Canada. Atmospheric Environment Service. Ice Summary and Analysis, Eastern Canadian Seaboard. a. ISSN 0068-7766
- Canada. Atmospheric Environment Service. Ice Summary and Analysis, Hudson Bay and Approaches. a. ISSN 0068-7774
- Canada. Atmospheric Environment Service. Meteorological Translations. irreg., no. 30, 1976. ISSN 0068-7782
- Canada. Atmospheric Environment Service. Monthly Record. m.
- Canada. Atmospheric Environment Service. Snow Cover Data. Canada. a. ISSN 0068-7790
- Canada. Atmospheric Environment Service. Technical Memoranda. irreg., ISSN 0068-7804
- Canadian Meteorological Memoirs. irreg., no. 29, 1973. ISSN 0068-9246
- Canadian Meteorological Research Reports. irreg.
- Canadian Weather Review/Revue du Temps au Canada. m. ISSN 0008-5294
- Monthly Radiation Summary/Sommaire du Rayonnement Mensuel. m. ISSN 0027-0482
- Monthly Record of Meteorological Observations in Canada. m. ISSN 0026-1157
- Ozone Data for the World. bi-m (plus supplements and annual cummulative catalog) ISSN 0030-7777

**Canada. Bureau of Intellectual Property**
Ottawa, Ont., Canada.
- Canada. Bureau of Intellectual Property. Annual Report /Rapport Annuel. a.

**Canada. Canadian Penitentiary Service. National Parole Service**
340 Laurier Ave. West, Ottawa, Ontario K1A 0P9, Canada.
- Discussion. q. ISSN 0384-2126

**Canada. Centre for Geoscience Data**
580 Booth St., Ottawa, Ontario K1A 0E8, Canada (Dist. by the Queen's Printer, Ottawa, Canada)
- Canadian Index to Geoscience Data. Alberta. irreg. ISSN 0084-8441
- Canadian Index to Geoscience Data. British Columbia. irreg. ISSN 0084-845X
- Canadian Index to Geoscience Data. Manitoba. irreg. ISSN 0084-8468
- Canadian Index to Geoscience Data. New Brunswick/P.E.I. irreg. ISSN 0084-8476
- Canadian Index to Geoscience Data. Newfoundland. irreg. ISSN 0084-8484
- Canadian Index to Geoscience Data. Nova Scotia. irreg. ISSN 0084-8492
- Canadian Index to Geoscience Data. Offshore Canada. irreg. ISSN 0084-8506
- Canadian Index to Geoscience Data. Ontario (South) & Ontario (North) irreg. ISSN 0084-8514
- Canadian Index to Geoscience Data. Quebec (North and East) & Quebec (West) irreg. ISSN 0084-8522
- Canadian Index to Geoscience Data. Saskatchewan. irreg. ISSN 0084-8530
- Canadian Index to Geoscience Data. Thesaurus. irreg. ISSN 0084-8549
- Canadian Index to Geoscience Data. Yukon Territory & Northwest Territories. irreg. ISSN 0084-8557

**Canada. Centre for Inland Waters**
867 Lakeshore Road, Box 5050, Burlington, Ontario L7R 4A6, Canada.
- Canada. Centre for Inland Waters. Annual Report. a.

**Canada. Centre for Mineral and Energy Technology**
555 Booth St., Ottawa, Ont. K1A 0GI, Canada.
- Canada. Centre for Mineral and Energy Technology. CANMET Report. m.
- Canada. Centre for Mineral and Energy Technology. Mines Memo; annual review of research investigations of the Mines Branch. a.
- Canada. Centre for Mineral and Energy Technology. Technology Series Reports. a.

**Canada. Commissioner of Official Languages**
Ottawa, Ont. K1A OT8, Canada.
- Canada. Commissioner of Official Languages. Annual Report. a.

**Canada. Correctional Investigator**
Box 950, Sta. B, Ottawa, Ont. K1P 5R1, Canada.
- Canada. Correctional Investigator. Annual Report. a. ISSN 0383-4379

**Canada. Department of Agriculture**
Ottawa, Ont., Canada.
- Canada. Department of Agriculture. Hatchery Outlook. q.
- Canada. Department of Agriculture. Livestock Market Review. a. ISSN 0068-7324
- Canada. Department of Agriculture. Market Commentary. m.

**Canada. Department of Agriculture. Economics Branch**
Ottawa, Canada.
- Canada. Department of Agriculture. Economics Branch. Trade in Agricultural Products. a. ISSN 0068-7286
- Food Outlook. m. ISSN 0015-6507
- Marketing Boards in Canada/Offices de Commercialisation au Canada. a. ISSN 0527-6624

**Canada. Department of Agriculture. Food Research Institute**
Ottawa, Canada.
- Canada. Department of Agriculture. Food Research Institute, Ottawa. Research Report. irreg. ISSN 0068-7308

**Canada. Department of Agriculture. Health of Animals Branch**
Ottawa, Canada.
- Canada. Department of Agriculture. Health of Animals Branch. Bovine Tuberculosis and Brucellosis. a. ISSN 0068-7316

**Canada. Department of Agriculture. Information Division**
Ottawa, Ontario, Canada.
- Canada. Department of Agriculture. Publication. irreg. ISSN 0068-7340

**Canada. Department of Agriculture. Microbiology Research Institute**
Ottawa, Canada.
- Canada. Department of Agriculture. Microbiology Research Institute, Ottawa. Research Report. irreg. ISSN 0068-7332

**Canada. Department of Agriculture. Poultry Division & Markets Information Section**
Ottawa, Ont., Canada.
- Poultry Market Review. a. ISSN 0032-5775

**Canada. Department of Communications. Engineering Support Division**
1241 Clyde Ave., Ottawa K2C 1Y3, Canada.
- Canadian Ionospheric Data. m. ISSN 0045-5024

**Canada. Department of Communications. Information Services**
Ottawa, Ontario K1A 0C8, Canada.
- In Search/En Quete. q.

**Canada. Department of Consumer & Corporate Affairs**
Place du Portage, Ottawa-Hull K1A OC9, Canada.
- Canada. Department of Consumer & Corporate Affairs. Annual Report. a.
- Trade Marks Journal/Journal des Marquesde Commerce; consumer and corporate affairs. w. ISSN 0041-0438

**Canada. Department of Consumer and Corporate Affairs. Patent Office**
Ottawa-Hull, Ont. K1A 0E1, Canada
- Patent Office Record (Canada)/Gazette du Bureau des Brevets. w. ISSN 0008-4670 (Subscr. to: Information Canada)

**Canada. Department of Energy, Mines and Resources**
Ottawa, Ont. K1A 0G1, Canada.
- Canada. Oceanographic Data Centre. Data Record Series. irreg. ISSN 0068-8061
- Canadian Rock Mechanics Symposium. Proceedings. irreg. ISSN 0375-605X
- Canadian Tide and Current Tables. a. ISSN 0068-9882
- Geos; quarterly concerned with the earth's resources. q.

**Canada. Department of Energy, Mines and Resources. Energy Policy Sector**
Ottawa, Ontario, Canada.
- Coal in Canada, Supply and Demand. irreg.

**Canada. Department of Energy, Mines and Resources. Mineral Development Sector**
Publication Distribution Office, Ottawa, Ont. K1A 0E4, Canada.
- Canada. Mineral Development Sector. Mineral Information Bulletin. irreg.
- Canada. Mineral Development Sector. Mineral Report. irreg.
- Canada. Mineral Development Sector. Mineral Survey. irreg.
- Canadian Mineral Reviews. irreg. ISSN 0068-9262
- Canadian Minerals Yearbook/Annuaire des Mineraux du Canada. a. ISSN 0068-9270
- Ceramic Plants in Canada. a. ISSN 0069-2220
- Coal Mines in Canada. a. ISSN 0069-4894
- Metallurgical Works in Canada, Nonferrous and Precious Metals. a. ISSN 0076-6704
- Metallurgical Works in Canada, Primary Iron and Steel. a. ISSN 0076-6712
- Natural Gas Processing Plants in Canada. a. ISSN 0077-6041
- Petroleum Refineries in Canada. a. ISSN 0079-1296

**Canada. Department of External Affairs**
Information Division, Ottawa, Ont. K1A 0G2, Canada.
- Canada. Department of External Affairs. Reference Papers. irreg.
- Canada. Department of External Affairs. Statements and Speeches. irreg.
- Canada Weekly. w. ISSN 0384-2312
- Canadian Foreign Relations. a.
- Diplomatic Corps and Consular and Other Representatives in Canada. Corps Diplomatique et Representants Consulaires et Autres au Canada. irreg. ISSN 0486-4514
- Hebdo Canada. w.
- International Perspectives/Perspectives Internationales. bi-m.
- Noticiario de Canada. s-m. ISSN 0384-2282
- Profil Kanada. s-w. ISSN 0384-2290

**Canada. Department of Finance.**
160 Elgin St., Ottawa, Ont. K1A 0G5, Canada.
- Canada. Department of Finance. Economic Review. a.

**Canada. Department of Indian and Northern Affairs**
400 Laurier Ave. West, Ottawa, Ont. K1A 0H4, Canada
(Orders to: Supply and Services Canada, Printing and Publishing, 270 Albert St., Ottawa, Ont. K1A 0S9, Canada)
- Canada. Department of Indian and Northern Affairs. Mines and Minerals Statistics: North of 60/Statistiques Minieres et Minerales: au Nord du 60e. m.
- Canada. Department of Indian and Northern Affairs. Oil and Gas Land and Exploration Section. Oil and Gas Activities. North of 60. a.
- Canada. Northern Natural Resources and Environment Branch. Schedule of Wells, Oil and Gas North of 60. a.
- Canadian Historic Sites/Lieux Historiques Canadiens; occasional papers in archaeology and history. q.
- Indian News. m. ISSN 0019-6029
- Inuttituut; the Eskimo way. q. ISSN 0020-9872
- North/Nord. bi-m. ISSN 0029-2362
- Tawow; Canadian Indian cultural magazine. 4 per yr. ISSN 0039-9930

**Canada. Department of Industry, Trade and Commerce**
Ottawa, Ont., Canada.
- Canada. Department of Industry, Trade and Commerce. Annual Report. a.
- Canada. Department of Industry, Trade and Commerce. Revue Annuelle-Industrie et Commerce. a.
- Canada Commerce. m.
- Canada Courier. m.(English edt.); q.(French, German, Japanese & Spanish edts.) ISSN 0008-2635
- Canadian Chemical Register. a.
- Trade and Industry Bulletin. m.

**Canada. Department of Industry, Trade and Commerce. Office of Design**
Ottawa, Ont. K1A 0H5.
- Canadian Design. 6 per yr.

**Canada. Department of Labour**
Ottawa K1A OJ2, Canada.
- Canada. Department of Labour. Economics and
  Research Branch. Provisions in Major Collective
  Agreements. Dispositions de Grandes
  Conventions Collectives. irreg. ISSN 0068-7421
- Canada. Department of Labour. Wage Rates,
  Salaries and Hours of Labour. a. ISSN 0068-743X
- Changes in Labour Relations Legislation in
  Canada/Changements dans les Lois sur les
  Relations du Travail au Canada. a. ISSN 0069-
  2670
- Changes in Workmen's Compensation Laws in
  Canada/Changements dans la Reparation des
  Accidents du Travail au Canada. a. ISSN 0069-
  2689
- Industrial Relations Research in Canada. a. ISSN
  0073-7593
- Labour Gazette. m. ISSN 0023-6926
- Labour Organizations in Canada. Organisations de
  Travailleurs au Canada. a. ISSN 0075-7578
- Labour Standards in Canada. Normes du Travail
  au Canada. a. ISSN 0075-7586
- Strikes and Lockouts in Canada. Greves et
  Lockout au Canada. a. ISSN 0081-5985
- Teamwork in Industry/Travail d'Equipe dans
  l'Industrie. m. ISSN 0040-0718
- Working Conditions in Canadian Industry/
  Conditions de Travail dans l'Industrie
  Canadienne. a. ISSN 0084-1307

**Canada. Department of Labour. Collective Bargaining
Division**
Ottawa K1A OJ2, Ont, Canada.
- Collective Bargaining Review. m. ISSN 0010-0803

**Canada. Department of Labour. Women's Bureau**
Ottawa K1A OJ2, Ont., Canada.
- Canada. Department of Labour. Women's Bureau.
  Women in the Labour Force: Facts and Figures.
  a. ISSN 0068-7448

**Canada. Department of Manpower and Immigration**
Information Service, 305 Rideau St., Ottawa, Ont.
K1A OJ9, Canada.
- Canada. Department of Manpower and
  Immigration. Quarterly Immigration Bulletin. q.
  ISSN 0576-1174
- Canada Manpower and Immigration Review. q.
  ISSN 0318-4099

**Canada. Department of Manpower and Immigration.
Economic Analysis and Forecasts Branch**
Ottawa, Ont. K1A OJ9, Canada.
- Annuaire des Employeurs des Nouveaux
  Diplomes de College. a. ISSN 0381-3711
- Employers of New University Graduates:
  Directory. a. ISSN 0381-372X
- Manpower and Immigration Review: Quebec
  Region/Revue de la Main d'Oeuvre: Region du
  Quebec. q.

**Canada. Department of Manpower and Immigration.
Pacific Region Office**
Royal Centre, Box 11145, Vancouver, B.C. V6E
2P8, Canada
- Manpower Review, Pacific Region. q.

**Canada. Department of Manpower and Immigration.
Regional Economic Services Branch**
Halifax, N.S., Canada.
- Canada. Department of Manpower and
  Immigration. Manpower and Immigration
  Review/Revue de la Main - d'Oeuvre et de
  l'Immigration. Region de l'Atlantique. q.

**Canada. Department of Manpower and Immigration.
Strategic Planning and Research**
325 Dalhousie St., Ottawa, Ont., Canada.
- Canada. Department of Manpower and
  Immigration. Strategic Planning and Research.
  Supply, Demand and Salaries: New Graduates of
  Universities and Community Colleges. Offre,
  Demande et Salaires.: Nouveaux Diplomes
  d'Universites et de Colleges. irreg. ISSN 0317-
  4697

**Canada. Department of National Defence**
Ottawa, Ont., Canada.
- Canada. Department of National Defence.
  Defence. a.
- Canada. Department of National Defence.
  Directorate of History. Occasional Paper. irreg.
- Sentinel (Ottawa) 9 per yr. ISSN 0037-2315
- Sentinelle; revue des forces armees Canadiennes. 9
  per yr. ISSN 0037-2358

**Canada. Department of National Health and Welfare**
Ottawa, Ont. K1A OK9, Canada.
- Canada. Department of National Health and
  Welfare. Annual Report. a. ISSN 0068-7456
- Canada Diseases Weekly Report/Rapport
  Hebdomadaire des Maladies au Canada. w.
- Emergency Health Services Newsletter. q. ISSN
  0013-6646
- Health Education/Education Sanitaire. q. ISSN
  0017-8950
- Living/Visa-Vie. q. ISSN 0317-4522
- Rehabilitation in Canada. irreg. ISSN 0080-0716

**Canada. Department of National Health and Welfare.
Fitness and Amateur Sport Branch**
Journal Bldg., 365 Laurier Ave. W., Ottawa, Ont.
K1A OX6, Ontario, Canada.
- Calendar of Sports Events. q. ISSN 0008-0772
- Recreation Research Bulletin. irreg.

**Canada. Department of National Health and Welfare.
Health Programs Branch**
Ottawa K1A 1B4, Canada.
- Canada's Mental Health/Hygiene Mentale au
  Canada. q. ISSN 0008-2791

**Canada. Department of National Health and Welfare.
Library**
Ottawa, Ont., Canada.
- Canada. Department of National Health and
  Welfare. Library. Acquisitions. irreg.

**Canada. Department of National Revenue. Customs
and Excise Branch**
48 Besserer St., Ottawa, Ont. K1A OL5, Canada.
- Canada. Department of National Revenue. Excise
  News/Nouvelles de l'Accise. q.
- Canada. Department of National Revenue.
  Report: Customs, Excise and Taxation. a.

**Canada. Department of Regional Economic Expansion**
Information Division, Ottawa, Ontario, Canada.
- Canada. Department of Regional Economic
  Expansion. Annual Report on Prairie Farm
  Rehabilitation and Related Activities/Rapport
  Annuel: Retablissement Agricole des Prairies et
  Travaux Connexes. a.

**Canada. Department of Transport. Marine
Telecommunications & Electronics Branch**
Ottawa, Ont., Canada
- Radio Aids to Marine Navigation. q. ISSN 0033-
  7692

**Canada. Department of Transport. Public Affairs
Branch**
Ottawa, Canada.
- Transport Canada. bi-m.

**Canada. Department of Veterans Affairs**
Ottawa, Canada.
- Canada. Pension Review Board. Reports/Recueil
  des Arrets du Conseil de Revision des Pensions.
  q. ISSN 0382-1587

**Canada. Earth Physics Branch. Division of
Seismology**
Carling Ave., Ottawa, Ont., Canada.
- Canada. Earth Physics Branch. Seismological
  Series. a. ISSN 0084-8387

**Canada. Eastern Forest Products Laboratory**
Ottawa, Ont., Canada.
- Canada. Eastern Forest Products Laboratory,
  Ottawa. Program Review. biennial. ISSN 0068-
  7596

**Canada. Fisheries and Environment Canada**
Ottawa, Ont. K1A OS9, Canada.
- Canada. Environment Canada. Annual Report/
  Rapport Annuel. a.
- Canada. Fisheries and Environment Canada.
  Occasional Paper. irreg.
- Canada. Fisheries and Environment Canada.
  Report of Operations Under the Canada Water
  Act. a.

**Canada. Fisheries and Environment Canada. Canadian
Environmental Advisory Council**
Ottawa K1A OH3, Canada.
- Canadian Environmental Advisory Council.
  Annual Review. a.
- Canadian Environmental Advisory Council.
  Reports. irreg.

**Canada. Fisheries and Environment Canada. Canadian
Forestry Service**
Ottawa, Ont. K1A OH3, Canada.
- Canada. Department of the Environment. Forest
  Insect and Disease Survey. Annual Report. a.
  ISSN 0068-7588
- Canada. Forestry Service. Bi-Monthly Research
  Notes. bi-m. ISSN 0317-6908

**Canada. Fisheries and Environment Canada. Canadian
Wildlife Service**
Ottawa, Ont. K1A OE7, Canada
(Dist. by: Dept. of Supply and Services, Ottawa,
Ont. K1A OS6, Canada)
- Canadian Wildlife Service. Monograph Series.
  irreg.,no. 5, 1972. ISSN 0069-0015
- Canadian Wildlife Service. Occasional Papers.
  irreg; no. 29, 1976.
- Canadian Wildlife Service. Progress Notes/Service
  Canadien de la Faune. Cahiers de Biologie. irreg.,
  no. 69, 1976. ISSN 0069-0023
- Canadian Wildlife Service. Report Series. irreg.,
  no. 39, 1976. ISSN 0069-0031

**Canada. Fisheries and Environment Canada. Fisheries
and Marine Service**
116 Lisgar, Ottawa, Ont. K1A OH3, Canada
(Avail. from: Supply and Services Canada, Printing
and Publishing, Ottawa, Ont. K1A OS9, Canada)
- Annual Statistical Review of Candian Fisheries/
  Revue Statistique Annuelle des Peches
  Canadiennes. a.
- Canada. Fisheries and Marine Service. Biological
  Station, St. Andrews, New Brunswick. General
  Series Circular. irreg. ISSN 0068-7510
- Canada. Fisheries and Marine Service Bulletin
  Series. irreg., no. 197, 1976. ISSN 0068-7537
- Canada. Fisheries and Marine Service. Pacific
  Region. Annual Summary of British Columbia
  Catch Statistics. a.
- Canada. Fisheries and Marine Service.
  Recreational Fisheries Branch. Statistics on Sales
  of Sport Fishing Licences in Canada. a. (prep. by
  its Recreational Fisheries Branch)
- Canada. Fisheries and Marine Service. Resource
  Management Branch-Central Region. Annual
  Report. a.
- Canada. Fisheries and Marine Service. Technical
  Report Series. irreg., no. 651, 1976. ISSN 0068-
  7553
- Canada. Fisheries Research Board Annual. a.
- Canada. Fisheries Research Board. Journal. m.
  ISSN 0008-2686
- Canada. Fisheries Research Board. Miscellaneous
  Special Publication Series. irreg., no. 33, 1976.
- Canada. Hydrographic Service. Water Levels. a.
  ISSN 0068-7669
- Fisheries Fact Sheet. irreg.

**Canada. Fisheries and Environment Canada. Fisheries
Management**
Vancouver, B.C., Canada.
- Canada. Department of Fisheries. Analysis of
  Gross Returns from Salmon Fishing in British
  Columbia by Seiners, Gillnetters and Trollers. a.
  ISSN 0068-7367
- Canada. Fisheries and Environment Canada.
  Annual Report. a. ISSN 0068-7375

**Canada. Fisheries and Environment Canada. Forest
Fire Research Institute**
240 Bank St., Ottawa, Ont. K2P 1X4, Canada.
- Canada. Forest Fire Research Institute.
  Bibliography. Supplement. a. ISSN 0068-7561
- Canada. Forest Fire Research Institute.
  Information Report (FF-X) irreg. ISSN 0068-
  757X
- Forest Fire Control Abstracts/Precis de
  Repression des Feux de Forets. q. ISSN 0015-
  7414

**Canada. Fisheries and Environment Canada. Forest Management Institute**
Ottawa, Ont. K1A OH3, Canada.
- Canada. Department of the Environment. Forest Management Institute. Program Review. biennial. ISSN 0071-7495

**Canada. Fisheries and Environment Canada. Inland Waters Directorate**
Ottawa, Ont. K1A 0S9, Canada.
- Canada. Inland Waters Directorate. Historical Streamflow Summary: Alberta. triennial.
- Canada. Inland Waters Directorate. Historical Streamflow Summary: Atlantic Provinces. triennial.
- Canada. Inland Waters Directorate. Historical Streamflow Summary: British Columbia. triennial.
- Canada. Inland Waters Directorate. Historical Streamflow Summary: Manitoba. triennial.
- Canada. Inland Waters Directorate. Historical Streamflow Summary: Ontario. triennial.
- Canada. Inland Waters Directorate. Historical Streamflow Summary: Saskatchewan. triennial.
- Canada. Inland Waters Directorate. Historical Streamflow Summary: Yukon Territory and Northwest Territories. triennial.
- Canada. Inland Waters Directorate. Water Resources Research Support Program Programme de Subvention a la Recherche sur les Ressources en Eau. irreg.
- Canada. Water Survey. Surface Water Data: British Columbia. a.
- Canadian National Committee for the International Hydrological Decade. Canadian Progress Report. a. ISSN 0068-936X
- Electric Power in Canada. Publications. a. ISSN 0070-962X
- Sediment Data for Selected Canadian Rivers. a. ISSN 0080-8482

**Canada. Fisheries and Environment Canada. Insect Pathology Research Institute**
1195 Queen St., Box 490, Sault Ste. Marie, Ont. P6A 5M7, Canada.
- Canada. Department of the Environment. Insect Pathology Research Institute. Program Review. biennial. ISSN 0073-8093

**Canada. Fisheries and Environment Canada. Lands Directorate**
Ottawa, Ont. K1A 0E7, Canada.
- Canada Land Inventory. Report. irreg. ISSN 0068-7693

**Canada. Fisheries and Environment Canada. Maritimes Regional Library**
Box 550, Halifax, N.S. B3J 2S7, Canada.
- Atlantic Salmon References. a.

**Canada. Fisheries and Environment Canada. Northern Forest Research Centre**
5320-122 St., Edmonton, Alta. T6H 3S5, Canada.
- Canada. Northern Forest Research Centre. Forestry Report. irreg. (approx 5-6 per yr.)
- Canada. Northern Forest Research Centre. Information Report. irreg. (approx. 100 per yr.)

**Canada. Fisheries and Environment Canada. Western Forest Products Laboratory**
6620 Northwest Marine Drive, Vancouver, B.C. V6T 1X2, Canada.
- Canada. Western Forest Products Laboratory. Information Reports. irreg. ISSN 0045-429X
- Canada. Western Forest Products Laboratory. Program Review. biennial.
- Wood Research Notes. q.

**Canada. Food Prices Review Board**
Box 1540, Station B, Ottawa, Ont. KIP 5z5, Canada.
- Canada. Food Prices Review Board. Quarterly Report. q.

**Canada. Geological Survey of Canada**
601 Booth St., Ottawa, Ont. K1A OE8, Canada
(Dist. by: Supply and Services Canada, Ottawa, Ont. K1A 0S9, Canada)
- Canada. Geological Survey. Abstracts of Publications. a.
- Canada. Geological Survey. Bulletin. irreg. ISSN 0068-7626
- Canada. Geological Survey. Index of Publications of the Geological Survey of Canada. a.

- Canada. Geological Survey. Memoir. irreg. ISSN 0068-7634
- Canada. Geological Survey. Miscellaneous Report. irreg. ISSN 0068-7642
- Canada. Geological Survey. Monthly Information Circular. m.
- Canada. Geological Survey. Paper. irreg. ISSN 0068-7650

**Canada. Grain Commission. Economics and Statistics Division**
747-303 Main St., Winnipeg, Man. R3C 3H5, Canada.
- Canada. Grain Commission. Economics and Statistics Division. Canadian Grain Exports. a.
- Canada. Grain Commission. Economics and Statistics Division. Exports of Canadian Grain and Wheat Flour. m.
- Canada. Grain Commission. Economics and Statistics Division. Visible Grain Supplies and Disposition. a.

**Canada. Grains Council**
400-177 Lombard Avenue, Winnipeg, Man R3B OW5, Canada.
- Canada. Grains Council. Annual Report. a.
- Canada. Grains Council. Statistical Handbook. a.
- Canadian Grains for Beef Cattle. irreg.
- Canadian Grains for Dairy Cattle. irreg.
- Canadian Grains for Pigs. irreg.
- Canadian Grains for Poultry. irreg.
- Open Door. 6 per yr.

**Canada. Health and Welfare Canada**
Brooke Claxton Bldg., Ottawa, Ont. K1A OK9, Canada.
- Venereal Diseases in Canada. a. ISSN 0319-0382

**Canada. Labour Canada**
Ottawa, Ont. K1A 0J2, Canada
- Gazette du Travail. m. ISSN 0317-834X (Subscr. to: Information Canada, Publishing Div., 171 Slater St., Ottawa, Ont. K1A 0S9, Canada)

**Canada. Labour Canada. Public Relations Branch**
340 Laurier Ave. W., Ottawa, Ont. K1A 0J2, Canada.
- Canada. Labour Canada. Annual Report. a.

**Canada. Law Reform Commission**
130 Albert St., Ottawa, Ont. K1A 0L6, Canada.
- Canada. Law Reform Commission. Annual Report. a.
- Canada. Law Reform Commission. Study Report. irreg.
- Canada. Law Reform Commission. Working Paper. irreg.

**Canada. Marine Environmental Data Service**
Ottawa, Ont., Canada.
- Canada. Marine Environmental Data Service. Monthly and Yearly Mean Water Levels with 10 Year and All Time Averages. irreg.

**Canada. Marine Sciences Directorate. Pacific Region**
1230 Government St., Victoria, B.C, Canada.
- Canada. Marine Sciences Directorate. Pacific Region. Pacific Marine Science Report. irreg.

**Canada. Maritimes Forest Research Centre**
P.O. Box 4000, Fredericton, N.B., Canada.
- Canada. Maritimes Forest Research Centre, Fredericton, New Brunswick. Information Report M-X. irreg., 1973, M-X 36. ISSN 0068-7618

**Canada. Marketing and Trade Division**
Ottawa, Ont. K1A 0C5, Canada.
- Canada. Marketing and Trade Division. Animal and Animal Products; Outlook. irreg.

**Canada. Ministere de l'Industrie et du Commerce**
171 rue Slater, Ottawa, Ont. K1A 0S9, Canada.
- Produits Chimiques Canadiens. irreg.

**Canada. Ministry of State for Science and Technology**
Ottawa, Canada.
- Canada. Ministry of State for Science and Technology. Annual Report/Rapport Annuel. a.

**Canada. Ministry of State for Urban Affairs**
Ottawa, Ont., Canada.
- Canada. Ministry of State for Urban Affairs. Annual Report. a. ISSN 0317-4867

**Canada. Ministry of Transport. Canadian Air Transportation Administration**
Transport Canada Bldg., Ottawa, Ont. K1A 0N8, Canada
- Air Navigation Radio Aids. q. ISSN 0002-2454 (Subscr. to: Information Canada)

**Canada. Ministry of Treasury, Economics and Intergovernmental Affairs**
Office of Information Services, 5Th Floor, Frost Bldg. South, Queen's Park, Toronto, Ont., Canada.
- Background. irreg.

**Canada. National Energy Board**
Ottawa, Ont., Canada.
- Canada. National Energy Board. Annual Report. a. ISSN 0068-7901
- Canada. National Energy Board. Reports to the Governor in Council. irreg.
- Canada. National Energy Board. Staff Papers. irreg. ISSN 0068-791X

**Canada. Northern Administration Branch. Resources Division**
Ottawa, Ont., Canada.
- Canada. Northern Administration Branch. Resources Division. Schedule of Wells, Northwest Territories and Yukon Territory. a. ISSN 0068-8053

**Canada. Parks Canada**
Ottawa, Ont. K1A OH4, Canada.
- Canada. Parks Canada. C O R D Study Technical Note. irreg.
- Conservation Canada. q.

**Canada. Permanent Committee on Geographical Names. Surveys and Mapping Branch**
c/o Dept. of Energy, Mines and Resources, Ottawa, Ont., Canada.
- Gazetteer of Canada. irreg. ISSN 0576-1999

**Canada. Radio-Television and Telecommunications Commission**
100 Metcalfe St., Ottawa, Ont. K1A ON2, Canada.
- Canada. Radio-Television and Telecommuncations Commission. Annual Report. a.

**Canada. Research Station**
Beaverlodge, Alta., Canada.
- Canada. Research Station, Beaverlodge, Alberta. Research Report. biennial. ISSN 0068-8096

**Canada. Road and Motor Vehicle Traffic Safety Branch**
Ottawa, Ont. K1P 5R1, Canada
- Canada. Road and Motor Vehicle Traffic Safety Branch. Road Safety Annual Report. Rapport Annuel, Securite Routiere. a. ISSN 0317-8196 (Order from: Information Canada, Ottawa K1P 5R1)

**Canada. Statistics Canada**
Ottawa, Ont. K1A 0T6, Canada
(and Publications Distribution, Bureau of Statistics, Ottawa, Canada)
- Canada. Aviation Statistics Centre. Service Bulletin. irreg. ISSN 0068-7057
- Canada. Statistics Canada. Aggregate Productivity Trends/Tendances de la Productivite des Agregats. a. ISSN 0068-7073
- Canada. Statistics Canada. Air Carrier Financial Statements/Transporteurs Aeriens Etats Financiers. a.
- Canada. Statistics Canada. Air Carrier Operations in Canada. q. ISSN 0008-2570
- Canada. Statistics Canada. Air Passenger Origin and Destination. Canada-United States Report/ Origine et Destination des Passagers Aeriens. a.
- Canada. Statistics Canada. Annual Report of Notifiable Diseases/Rapport Annuel sur les Malades a Declaration Obligatoire. a.
- Canada. Statistics Canada. Annual Report/ Rapport Annuel. a.
- Canada. Statistics Canada. Asbestos Mines/Mines d'Amiante. a.
- Canada. Statistics Canada. Awards for Graduate Study and Research. irreg. ISSN 0576-6311

- Canada. Statistics Canada. Biscuits and Confectionery. q. ISSN 0008-2600
- Canada. Statistics Canada. Boatbuilding and Repair/Construction et Reparation d'Embarcations. a.
- Canada. Statistics Canada. Breweries/Brasseries. m.
- Canada. Statistics Canada. Building Permits. m.
- Canada. Statistics Canada. Building Permits. Annual Summary. a.
- Canada. Statistics Canada. Canadian Statistical Review. m. ISSN 0008-509X
- Canada. Statistics Canada. Canadian Statistical Review. Annual Supplement to Section 1/ Supplement Annuel de la Section 1. a. ISSN 0575-8084
- Canada. Statistics Canada. Canadian Statistical Review. Weekly Supplement. w. ISSN 0300-0273
- Canada. Statistics Canada. Cane and Beet Sugar Processors/Traitement du Sucre de Canne et de Betteraves. a.
- Canada. Statistics Canada. Canned and Frozen Processed Foods (Selected Items) Aliments, Conditionnes en Boites et Congeles. a.
- Canada. Statistics Canada. Canvas Products and Cotton and Jute Bag Industries/Industrie des Articles en Grosse Toile et des Sacs de Coton et de Jute. a.
- Canada. Statistics Canada. Carpet, Mat and Rug Industry/Industrie des Tapis, des Carpettes et de la Moquette. a. ISSN 0527-4893
- Canada. Statistics Canada. Causes of Death, Provinces by Sex and Canada by Sex and Age/ Causes de Deces, Par Provinces Selon le Sexe et le Canada Selon le Sexe et l'Age. a. ISSN 0380-7533
- Canada. Statistics Canada. Coal and Coke Statistics/Statistique du Charbon et du Coke. m. ISSN 0380-6847
- Canada. Statistics Canada. Coal Mines/Mines de Charbon. a. ISSN 0068-709X
- Canada. Statistics Canada. Coarse Grains Review. q. ISSN 0009-9996
- Canada. Statistics Canada. Coffin and Casket Industry/Industrie des Cercueils. a. ISSN 0527-4915
- Canada. Statistics Canada. Commercial Failures Under the Bankruptcy and Winding up Acts. q. ISSN 0380-6928
- Canada. Statistics Canada. Communications Equipment Manufactures/Fabricants d'Equipement de Telecommunication. a.
- Canada. Statistics Canada. Community Antenna Television/Services de Television a Antenne Collective. a.
- Canada. Statistics Canada. Concrete Products Manufacturers/Fabricants de Produits en Beton. a. ISSN 0382-0971
- Canada. Statistics Canada. Consolidated Government Finance; revenue and expenditure and assets and liabilities of federal, provincial and local governments. a. ISSN 0575-8254
- Canada. Statistics Canada. Construction Division. Investment Statistics; Service Bulletin. irreg. ISSN 0380-7053
- Canada. Statistics Canada. Construction Price Statistics. Quarterly Report/Statistiques des Prix de la Construction Rapport Trimestriel. q. ISSN 0319-8251 (Information Canada., Ottawa, Ont., Canada)
- Canada. Statistics Canada. Consumer Credit. m.
- Canada. Statistics Canada. Consumer Prices and Price Indexes. q. ISSN 0380-691X
- Canada. Statistics Canada. Consumption of Containers and Other Packaging Supplies by the Manufacturing Industries /Consommation de Contenants et Autres Matieres d'Emballage, Par Industrie Manufacturiere. a.
- Canada. Statistics Canada. Consumption, Production and Inventories of Rubber. m. ISSN 0008-2651
- Canada. Statistics Canada. Continuing Education. Part 1: Elementary-Secondary Level/Education Permanente. Partie 1: Niveau Primaire-Secondaire. a.
- Canada. Statistics Canada. Continuing Education. Part 2: Post-Secondary Level/Education Permanente. Partie 2: Niveau Postsecondaire. a.
- Canada. Statistics Canada. Contract Drilling for Petroleum and Other Contract Drilling/Forage de Puits de Petrole a Forfait et Autre Forage a Forfait. a.
- Canada. Statistics Canada. Cordage and Twine Industry /Corderie et Ficellerie (Fabrication) a.
- Canada. Statistics Canada. Corrugated Box Manufacturers/Fabricants de Boites en Carton Ondule. a. ISSN 0575-8912

- Canada. Statistics Canada. Cotton Yarn and Cloth Mills/Filature et Tissage du Coton. a. ISSN 0527-5016
- Canada. Statistics Canada. Crops Section. Production and Value Estimate of Honey. s-a.
- Canada. Statistics Canada. Crude Petroleum and Natural Gas Industry/Industrie du Petrole Brut et du Gaz Naturel. a. ISSN 0068-7103
- Canada. Statistics Canada. Dairy Statistics/ Statistique Laitiere. a. ISSN 0068-7111
- Canada. Statistics Canada. Direct Selling in Canada/Vente Directe au Canada. a. ISSN 0590-5702
- Canada. Statistics Canada. Distilleries. a. ISSN 0527-5024
- Canada. Statistics Canada. Educational Staff in Community Colleges. a. ISSN 0382-411X
- Canada. Statistics Canada. Electric Lamp and Shade Manufacturers/Industrie des Lampes Electrique et des Abat-Jour. a.
- Canada. Statistics Canada. Electric Power Statistics. Volume 1: Annual Electric Power Survey of Capability and Load. a. ISSN 0575-8351
- Canada. Statistics Canada. Electrical Contracting Industry/Entrepreneurs d'Installation Electriques. a.
- Canada. Statistics Canada. Employment, Earnings and Hours, Seasonally-Adjusted Series. a.
- Canada. Statistics Canada. Estimated Population of Canada by Province/Population Estimative du Canada Par Province. a.
- Canada. Statistics Canada. Estimates of Labour Income/Estimations du Revenu du Travail. q. ISSN 0318-9007
- Canada. Statistics Canada. Estimates of Production and Disappearance of Meats/ Estimations de la Production et de la Disparition des Viandes. a. ISSN 0575-8440
- Canada. Statistics Canada. Family Incomes (Census Families) /Revenus de Familles (Familles de Recensement) a.
- Canada. Statistics Canada. Farm Income and Prices Section. Farm Cash Receipts. a.
- Canada. Statistics Canada. Farm Net Income/ Revenu Net Agricole. a. ISSN 0068-712X
- Canada. Statistics Canada. Federal Government Activities in the Human Sciences/Activites de l'Administration Federale en Sciences Humaines. a.
- Canada. Statistics Canada. Federal Government Activities in the Natural Sciences/Activites de l'Administration Federale en Sciences Naturelles. a.
- Canada. Statistics Canada. Federal Government Employment/Emploi dans l'Administration Publique Federale. q. ISSN 0014-9098
- Canada. Statistics Canada. Federal Government Employment in Metropolitan Areas/Effectifs de l'Administration Federale dans les Regions Metropolitaines. a.
- Canada. Statistics Canada. Federal Government Finance/Finances de l'Administration Publique Federale. a. ISSN 0575-8521
- Canada. Statistics Canada. Feldspar and Quartz Mines/Mines de Feldspath et de Quartz. a.
- Canada. Statistics Canada. Felt and Fibre Processing Mills/Industrie du Feutre et du Traitement des Fibres. a.
- Canada. Statistics Canada. Field Crop Reporting Series. seasonal, 20 per yr. ISSN 0575-8548
- Canada. Statistics Canada. Fish Products Industry/Industrie de la Transformation du Poisson. a. ISSN 0527-5172
- Canada. Statistics Canada. Flour and Breakfast Cereal Products Industry/Meunerie et Fabrication de Cereales de Table. a.
- Canada. Statistics Canada. For-Hire Trucking Survey/Enquete sur le Transport Routier de Marchandises pour Compte d'Autrui et en Location. a.
- Canada. Statistics Canada. Foundation Garment Industry/Industrie des Corsets et Soutiens-Gorge. a. ISSN 0575-8599
- Canada. Statistics Canada. Fruit and Vegetable Crop Reports. F.V.R. irreg.
- Canada. Statistics Canada. Fruit and Vegetable Industries/Preparation de Fruits et de Legumes. a.
- Canada. Statistics Canada. Gas Utilities (Transport and Distribution Systems) /Services de Gaz (Reseaux de Transport et de Distribution) a.
- Canada. Statistics Canada. General Review of the Mineral Industries/Revue Generale sur les Industries Minerales; mines, quarries and oil wells/mines, carrieres et puits de petrole. a.
- Canada. Statistics Canada. Glass and Glass Products Manufacturers/Fabricants de Verre et d'Articles en Verre. a.

- Canada. Statistics Canada. Grain Milling Statistics/Statistiques de Mouture des Grains. m. ISSN 0410-5389
- Canada. Statistics Canada. Guide to Federal Government Labour Statistics/Guide de la Statistique du Travail du Gouvernement Federal. irreg.
- Canada. Statistics Canada. Gypsum Products/ Produits de Gypse. m. ISSN 0380-7223
- Canada. Statistics Canada. Hardwood Flooring Plants/Fabrication de Parquets en Bois Dur. a.
- Canada. Statistics Canada. Health Manpower Section. Annual Salaries of Hospital Nursing Personnel. biennial. ISSN 0576-016X
- Canada. Statistics Canada. Highway, Road, Street and Bridge Contracting Industry/Entrepreneurs de Grande Route, Chemin, rue et Pont. a.
- Canada. Statistics Canada. Historical Labour Force Statistics, Actual Data, Seasonal Factors, Seasonally Adjusted Data/Statistiques Chronologiques sur la Population Active, Chiffres Reels, Facteurs Saisonniers et Donnees Desaisonnalisees. a.
- Canada. Statistics Canada. Horticultural Crops Unit. Survey of Canadian Nursery Trades Industry. a. ISSN 0318-5184
- Canada. Statistics Canada. Hospital Statistics: Preliminary Annual Report/Statistique Hospitaliere: Rapport Annuel Preliminaire. a.
- Canada. Statistics Canada. Hospitals Section. Canadian Hospitals and Related Facilities. a. ISSN 0319-8014
- Canada. Statistics Canada. Household Facilities and Equipment. a. ISSN 0318-5273
- Canada. Statistics Canada. Household Facilities by Income and Other Characteristics. irreg.
- Canada. Statistics Canada. Household Furniture Manufacturers/Industrie des Meubles de Maison. a. ISSN 0527-5407
- Canada. Statistics Canada. Housing Starts and Completions. m.
- Canada. Statistics Canada. Income Distributions by Size in Canada: Preliminary Estimates/ Repartition du Revenu au Canada Selon la Taille du Revenu: Premieres Estimations. a. ISSN 0317-5405
- Canada. Statistics Canada. Income Distributions by Size in Canada/Repartition du Revenu au Canada Selon la Taille du Revenu. a.
- Canada. Statistics Canada. Index Numbers of Farm Prices of Agricultural Products/Nombres - Indices des Prix des Produits Agricoles. m 270can. ISSN 0380-7541
- Canada. Statistics Canada. Index of Farm Production/Indexe de la Production Agricole. a. ISSN 0068-7146
- Canada. Statistics Canada. Industrial Corporations Financial Statistics/Societes Industrielles Statistique Financiere. q.
- Canada. Statistics Canada. Industrial Organization and Concentration in the Manufacturing, Mining, and Logging Industries/Organisation des Industries et Concentration dans le Secteur de la Fabrication, des Mines, et de l'Abattage. irreg.
- Canada. Statistics Canada. Industrial Research and Development Expenditures in Canada/Depenses au Titre de la Recherche et du Developpement Industriels au Canada. a. ISSN 0575-8807
- Canada. Statistics Canada. Infomat. w.
- Canada. Statistics Canada. Inter-Corporate Ownership/Liens de Parente Entre Firmes. biennial. ISSN 0575-8823
- Canada. Statistics Canada. Investissements Prives et Publics au Canada: Perspectives. a.
- Canada. Statistics Canada. Iron and Steel Mills/ Siderurgie. a.
- Canada. Statistics Canada. Knitting Mills/ Bonneterie. a.
- Canada. Statistics Canada. Labour Costs in Canada. a. ISSN 0380-2108
- Canada. Statistics Canada. Labour Costs in Canada: Finance, Insurance and Real Estate/ Couts de la Main-d'Oeuvre au Canada: Finances, Assurances, et Immeuble. a.
- Canada. Statistics Canada. Labour Force/ Population Active. m.
- Canada. Statistics Canada. Law Enforcement, Judicial and Correctional Statistics Service Bulletin. 20 per yr.
- Canada. Statistics Canada. Leather Glove Factories/Fabriques de Gants en Cuir. a.
- Canada. Statistics Canada. Livestock and Animal Product Statistics/Statistique du Betail et des Produits Animaux. a. ISSN 0068-7154
- Canada. Statistics Canada. Livestock and Animal Products Section. Head, Dairy & Cold Storage Units. m.

- Canada. Statistics Canada. Local Government Finance: Revenue and Expenditure, Assets and Liabilities, Actual/Finances des Administrations Locales: Recettes et d'Epenses, Actif et Passif, Chiffres Reels. a.
- Canada. Statistics Canada. Manufacturers of Electric Wire and Cable/Fabricants de Fils et de Cables Electriques. a.
- Canada. Statistics Canada. Manufacturers of Industrial Chemicals/Fabricants de Produits Chimiques Industriels. a.
- Canada. Statistics Canada. Manufacturers of Soap and Cleaning Compounds/Fabricants de Savon et de Produits de Nettoyage. a.
- Canada. Statistics Canada. Manufacturing and Primary Industries Division. Interprovincial and Foreign Shipments of Paper Boxes, and Paper and Plastic Bags/Livraisons Interprovinciales et a l'Etranger des Boites en Papier et Sacs en Papier et en Plastique. irreg.
- Canada. Statistics Canada. Manufacturing and Primary Industries Division. Miscellaneous Non-Metallic Mineral Product Industries. a. ISSN 0381-9256
- Canada. Statistics Canada. Manufacturing Industries Division. Potash Mines. a.
- Canada. Statistics Canada. Manufacturing Industries of Canada: Type of Organization and Size of Establishment. a. ISSN 0076-4248
- Canada. Statistics Canada. Mechanical Contracting Industry/Les Entrepreneurs d'Installations Mecaniques. a.
- Canada. Statistics Canada. Men's Clothing Industries/Industrie des Vetements pour Hommes. a. ISSN 0527-5679
- Canada. Statistics Canada. Merchandising and Services Division. Wholesale Trade/Commerce de Gros. m. ISSN 0380-7894
- Canada. Statistics Canada. Merchandising Inventories/Stocks Commerciaux. m. ISSN 0380-7177
- Canada. Statistics Canada. Mineral Wool/Laine Minerale. m. ISSN 0380-8203
- Canada. Statistics Canada. Miscellaneous Clothing Industries/Industries Diverses de l'Habillement. a.
- Canada. Statistics Canada. Miscellaneous Food Processors/Industries Alimentaires Diverses. a.
- Canada. Statistics Canada. Miscellaneous Leather Products Manufacturers/Fabricants d'Articles Divers en Cuir. a.
- Canada. Statistics Canada. Miscellaneous Manufacturing Industries/Industries Manufacturieres Diverses. a.
- Canada. Statistics Canada. Miscellaneous Metal Mines/Mines Metalliques Diverses. a.
- Canada. Statistics Canada. Miscellaneous Non-Metal Mines/Mines Non Metalliques Diverses. a.
- Canada. Statistics Canada. Miscellaneous Non-Metallic Mineral Products Industries/Industries des Produits Mineraux Non Metalliques Divers. a.
- Canada. Statistics Canada. Motion Picture Theatres and Film Distributors/Cinemas et Distributeurs de Films. a. ISSN 0380-6294
- Canada. Statistics Canada. Motor Vehicle, Part 2, Motive Fuel Sales/Vehicules a Moteur, Partie 2, Ventes des Carburants. a. ISSN 0527-5830
- Canada. Statistics Canada. Motor Vehicle, Part 3, Registrations/Vehicules a Moteur, Partie 3, Immatriculations. a. ISSN 0575-9110
- Canada. Statistics Canada. Motor Vehicle Traffic Accidents/Accidents de la Circulation Routiere. a. ISSN 0527-5865
- Canada. Statistics Canada. Moving and Storage Household Goods. a. ISSN 0575-9137
- Canada. Statistics Canada. Murder Statistics/Statistique de l'Homicide. a. ISSN 0575-917X
- Canada. Statistics Canada. Music Competition Festivals/Festivals de Concours de Musique. irreg.
- Canada. Statistics Canada. National Income and Expenditure Accounts/Comptes Nationaux des Revenus et des Depenses. q.
- Canada. Statistics Canada. New Manufacturing Establishments in Canada/Nouveaux Etablissements Manufacturiers au Canada. s-a. ISSN 0527-5881
- Canada. Statistics Canada. New Surveys/Nouvelles Enquetes. q.
- Canada. Statistics Canada. Non-Ferrous Scrap Metal. a. ISSN 0029-1013
- Canada. Statistics Canada. Non-Institutional Special Care Facilities and Programs/Centres Non-Institutionnels de Soins et Services Speciaux. irreg.
- Canada. Statistics Canada. Non-Residential General Building Contracting Industry/Entrepreneurs Generaux en Batiments Non Residentiels. a.

- Canada. Statistics Canada. Office Furniture Manufacturers/Industrie des Meubles de Bureau. a. ISSN 0527-5903
- Canada. Statistics Canada. Oils and Fats/Huiles et Corps Gras. m. ISSN 0527-5911
- Canada. Statistics Canada. Ornamental and Architectural Metal Industry/Industrie des Produits Metalliques d'Architecture et d'Ornement. a.
- Canada. Statistics Canada. Passenger Bus Statistics/Statistique du Transport de Voyageurs Par Autobus. a. ISSN 0527-6012
- Canada. Statistics Canada. Payrolls, and Labour Income Section. Employment Earnings and Hours. m.
- Canada. Statistics Canada. Petroleum Refineries/Raffineries de Petrole. a. ISSN 0068-7162
- Canada. Statistics Canada. Placer Gold Mines, Gold Quartz Mines and Copper-Gold-Silver Mines/Placers d'Or, Mines de Quartz Aurifere et Mine de Cuivre-or-Argent. a. ISSN 0068-7138
- Canada. Statistics Canada. Police Administration Statistics/Statistique de l'Administration Policiere. a.
- Canada. Statistics Canada. Population Estimates by Marital Status, Age and Sex, for Canada and Provinces/Estimations de la Population Selon l'Etat Matrimonial, l'Age et le Sexe, Canada et Provinces. a. ISSN 0575-934X
- Canada. Statistics Canada. Principal Taxes in Canada. a. ISSN 0382-0998
- Canada. Statistics Canada. Private and Public Investment in Canada. Outlook and Regional Estimates/Investissements Prives et Publics au Canada. Perspectives et Estimates d'Ordre Regional. a.
- Canada. Statistics Canada. Private and Public Investment in Canada. Outlook, Mid-Year Review, and Regional Estimates/Investissements Prives et Publics au Canada. Perspectives, Revue de la Mi-Annee, et Estimates d'Ordre Regional. a.
- Canada. Statistics Canada. Production of Canada's Leading Minerals. m. ISSN 0008-2619
- Canada. Statistics Canada. Production of Maple Products and Value of Maple Products/Production et Valeur des Produits de l'Erable. a. ISSN 0317-9672
- Canada. Statistics Canada. Production of Poultry and Eggs/Production de Volaille et d'Oeufs. a. ISSN 0068-7189
- Canada. Statistics Canada. Products Shipped by Canadian Manufacturers. a.
- Canada. Statistics Canada. Provincial Government Employment/L'Emploi dans les Administrations Publiques Provinicales. q. ISSN 0527-608X
- Canada. Statistics Canada. Provincial Government Enterprise Finance/Finances des Entreprises Publiques Provinciales. a. ISSN 0575-9463
- Canada. Statistics Canada. Provincial Government Finance, Assets, Liabilities, Sources and Uses of Funds/Finances des Administrations Publiques Provinciales, Actif, Passif, Sources et Utilisations des Fonds. a. ISSN 0318-8876
- Canada. Statistics Canada. Provincial Government Finance, Revenue and Expenditure (Estimates) / Finances des Administrations Publiques Provinciales, Recettes et Depenses (Previsions) a. ISSN 0575-9501
- Canada. Statistics Canada. Public Health Section. Surgical Procedures and Treatments Interventions Chirurgicales et Traitements; report on surgical operations and non surgical procedures performed on inpatients in Canadian hospitals. a. ISSN 0317-3720
- Canada. Statistics Canada. Pulp and Paper Mills/Usines de Pates et Papiers. a.
- Canada. Statistics Canada. Quarterly Bulletin of Agricultural Statistics. q. ISSN 0033-5320
- Canada. Statistics Canada. Quarterly Survey of Trusted Pensions Plans. q.
- Canada. Statistics Canada. Radio and Television Broadcasting/Radiodiffusion et Television. a.
- Canada. Statistics Canada. Railway Carloadings/Chargements Ferroviaires. m.
- Canada. Statistics Canada. Railway Freight Traffic/Trafic Marchandises Ferroviaire. a.
- Canada. Statistics Canada. Railway Operating Statistics/Statistique de l'Exploitation Ferroviaire. m.
- Canada. Statistics Canada. Railway Transport. a. ISSN 0410-5796
- Canada. Statistics Canada. Refined Petroleum Products/Produits Petroliers Raffines. m.
- Canada. Statistics Canada. Report on Fur Farms/Rapport sur les Fermes d'Animaux a Fourrures. a.

- Canada. Statistics Canada. Report on Livestock Surveys: Cattle, Sheep, Horses/Rapport des Enquetes sur le Betail: Bovins, Moutons, Chevaux. s-a.
- Canada. Statistics Canada. Research and Development Expenditure in Canada/Depenses au Titre de la Recherche et du Developpement au Canada. biennial.
- Canada. Statistics Canada. Restaurant Statistics. m. ISSN 0008-2627
- Canada. Statistics Canada. Retail Chain Stores/Magasins de Detail a Succursales. a. ISSN 0380-7878
- Canada. Statistics Canada. Review of Foreign Trade. irreg. ISSN 0068-7219
- Canada. Statistics Canada. Road and Street Mileage and Expenditure/Voies Publiques: Longueur et Depenses. a. ISSN 0410-5869
- Canada. Statistics Canada. Salaries and Qualifications of Teachers in Public Elementary and Secondary Schools/Traitements et Qualifications des Enseignants des Ecoles Publiques Elementaires et Secondaires. a.
- Canada. Statistics Canada. Sales Financing/Financement des Ventes. a. ISSN 0410-5877
- Canada. Statistics Canada. Sales of Toilet Preparations in Canada. a.
- Canada. Statistics Canada. Sawmills and Planing Mills and Shingle Mills/Scieries et Ateliers de Rabotage et Usines de Bardeaux. a.
- Canada. Statistics Canada. Scientific and Professional Equipment Industries/Fabrication de Materiel Scientifique et Professionnel. a.
- Canada. Statistics Canada. Scrap Iron and Steel/Dechets de Fer et d'Acier. a. ISSN 0380-8238
- Canada. Statistics Canada. Security Transactions with Non-Residents. m.
- Canada. Statistics Canada. Selected Financial Statistics of Charitable Organizations. a. ISSN 0318-8787
- Canada. Statistics Canada. Service Bulletin. Energy Statistics. 40 per yr. ISSN 0008-266X
- Canada. Statistics Canada. Shipbuilding and Repair/Construction et Reparation de Navires. a. ISSN 0527-6144
- Canada. Statistics Canada. Shipping Report. Part 1: International Seaborne Shipping (by Country) / Transport Maritime. Partie 1: Transport Maritime International (Par Pays) a.
- Canada. Statistics Canada. Shipping Report. Part 2: International Seaborne Shipping (by Port) / Transport Maritime. Partie 2: Transport Maritime International (Par Port) a.
- Canada. Statistics Canada. Shipping Report. Part 3: Coastwise Shipping/Transport Maritime. Partie 3: Navigation Nationale. a.
- Canada. Statistics Canada. Shipping Report. Part 4: Origin and Destination for Selected Ports/Transport Maritime. Partie 4: Orgine et Destination pour Certains Ports. a. ISSN 0575-9757
- Canada. Statistics Canada. Shipping Report. Part 5: Origin and Destination for Selected Commodities/Transport Maritime. Partie 5: Origine et Destination de Certaines Marchandises. a.
- Canada. Statistics Canada. Shipping Statistics/Statistiques Maritime. m.
- Canada. Statistics Canada. Shopping Centers in Canada/Centres Commerciaux au Canada. a.
- Canada. Statistics Canada. Shorn Wool Production/Production de Laine Tondue. a.
- Canada. Statistics Canada. Silver-Cobalt Mines and Silver-Lead-Zinc Mines/Mines d'Argent-Cobalt et Mines d'Argent-Plomb-Zinc. a.
- Canada. Statistics Canada. Slaughtering and Meat Processors/Abattage et Conditionnement de la Viande. a.
- Canada. Statistics Canada. Smelting and Refining/Fonte et Affinage. a.
- Canada. Statistics Canada. Sporting Goods and Toy Industries/Fabrication d'Articles de Sport et de Jouets. a. ISSN 0575-979X
- Canada. Statistics Canada. Statistics of Criminal and Other Offences/Statistique de la Criminalite. a.
- Canada. Statistics Canada. Stocks of Frozen Meat Products/Stocks de Viandes Congelees. m.
- Canada. Statistics Canada. Stone Quarries/Carrieres. a. ISSN 0575-9846
- Canada. Statistics Canada. Survey of Education Finance. a.
- Canada. Statistics Canada. Survey of Elementary and Secondary Education/Releve de l'Enseignement Elementaire et de l'Enseignement Secondaire/Clientele Scolaire aux Ecoles Elementaires et Secondaires au Canada. a.

- Canada. Statistics Canada. Survey of Libraries. Part 1: Public Libraries/Releve des Bibliotheques. Partie 1: Bibliotheques Publiques. a.
- Canada. Statistics Canada. Survey of Libraries. Part 2: Academic Libraries/Releve des Bibliotheques. Partie 2: Bibliotheques Scolaires. a.
- Canada. Statistics Canada. Survey of Production. System of National Accounts. Domestic Product by Industry. a. ISSN 0068-7227
- Canada. Statistics Canada. Telecommunications Statistics/Statistique des Telecommunications. a.
- Canada. Statistics Canada. Therapeutic Abortions. a.
- Canada. Statistics Canada. Tobacco Products Industries/Industrie du Tabac. a.
- Canada. Statistics Canada. Training in Industry/ Formation dans l'Industrie. irreg.
- Canada. Statistics Canada. Training Schools/ Etablissements de Protection de la Jeunesse. a.
- Canada. Statistics Canada. Transportation and Communications Division. Service Bulletin: Communications. irreg.
- Canada. Statistics Canada. Travel, Tourism and Outdoor Recreation /Voyages, Tourisme et Loisirs de Plein Air. a.
- Canada. Statistics Canada. Trusteed Pension Plans-Financial Statistics/Regimes de Pensions en Fiduci--Statistique Financiere. a. ISSN 0575-9978
- Canada. Statistics Canada. Tuberculosis Statistics. Volume 1: Tuberculosis Morbidity and Mortality. a.
- Canada. Statistics Canada. Tuberculosis Statistics. Volume 2: Institutional Facilities, Services and Finances. a.
- Canada. Statistics Canada. Vegetable Oil Mills/ Moulins a Huile Vegetale. a. ISSN 0527-6403
- Canada. Statistics Canada. Vending Machine Operators/Exploitants de Distributeurs Automatiques. a.
- Canada. Statistics Canada. Warehousing/ Entreposage; general merchandise and refrigerated goods/entrepots de marchandises et installations frigorifiques. a.
- Canada. Statistics Canada. Water Transportation/ Transport Par Eau. a.
- Canada. Statistics Canada. Women's and Children's Clothing Industries/Industries des Vetements pour Dames et pour Enfants. a. ISSN 0527-6446
- Canada. Statistics Canada. Wooden Box Factories/Fabriques de Boites en Bois. a. ISSN 0576-0070
- Canada. Statistics Canada. Wool Production and Supply/Production et Stocks de Laine. a. ISSN 0300-0265
- Canada. Statistics Canada. Wool Yarn and Cloth Mills/Filature et Tissage de la Laine. a. ISSN 0300-1202
- Canada: Official Handbook of Present Conditions and Recent Progress/Revue Officielle de la Situation Actuelle et des Progres Recents. a.
- Canada Yearbook. a. ISSN 0068-8142
- Canada's International Investment Position. a.
- Canada's Mineral Production. a. ISSN 0380-7797
- Canadian Community Colleges and Related Institutions/Colleges Communautaires Canadiens et Institutions Connexes. a.
- Canadian Universities: Income and Expenditure. a.
- Construction in Canada/Construction au Canada. a. ISSN 0527-4974
- Control and Sale of Alcoholic Beverages in Canada/Coutrole et la Veut des Boissous Alcooliques au Canada. a.
- Education in Canada/Education au Canada; statistical review/revue statistique. a.
- Grain Trade of Canada/Commerce des Grains au Canada. a. ISSN 0072-5358
- Hospital Indicators/Indicateurs des Hopitaux. q. ISSN 0046-7995
- Manufacturing Industries of Canada: Geographical Distribution/Industries Manufacturieres du Canada: Repartition Geographique. a.
- Pension Plans in Canada. biennial.
- Trade of Canada. Vol. 2: Exports/Commerce du Canada. Vol. 2: Exportations. a.
- Trade of Canada. Vol. 3: Imports/Commerce du Canada. Vol. 3: Importations. a.
- Travel Between Canada and Other Countries/ Voyages Entre le Canada et les Autres Pays. a. ISSN 0380-2094
- University and College Libraries in Canada/ Bibliotheques des Universites et des Colleges du Canada. a. ISSN 0318-7179

**Canada. Supply and Services Canada**
Publications Division, Ottawa, Ont. K1A 0S9, Canada.
- Actualite Terminologique. 10 per yr. ISSN 0001-7779
- British Columbia Water and Waste Association. Proceedings of the Annual Conference. a.
- Canada. Department of Insurance. Report. Co-Operative Credit Associations. a. ISSN 0068-7383
- Canada. Department of Insurance. Report. Loan and Trust Companies. a. ISSN 0068-7391
- Canada. Department of Insurance. Report of the Superintendent of Insurance. a. ISSN 0068-7405
- Canada. Department of Insurance. Report. Small Loans Companies and Money-Lenders. a. ISSN 0068-7413
- Canada. Hydrographic Service. Annual Report. a.
- Canada. Northern Natural Resources and Environment Branch. Mining Section. North of 60: Mines and Minerals, Activities. a.
- Canada. Northern Natural Resources and Environment Branch. Oil and Mineral Division. North of 60: Oil and Gas Technical Reports. irreg.
- Canada Gazette: Part 1: Government, Divorce, Bankruptcy Notices, Etc. w. ISSN 0045-4192
- Canada Gazette: Part 2: Statutory Orders and Regulations. s-m. ISSN 0045-4206
- Canadian Government Publications Monthly Catalog; a comprehensive listing of all Government publications with index. m. ISSN 0008-3690
- Canadian Historic Sites; Occasional Papers in Archaeology and History. irreg.
- Directory of Canadian Women's Groups/Annuaire Canadien des Groupes de Femmes. a.
- Index to Current Legal Research in Canada. a. ISSN 0319-5880
- List of Broadcasting Stations in Canada. a.
- Optimum. q. ISSN 0475-1906

**Canada. Supreme Court**
Ottawa, Ont. K1A 0J1, Canada.
- Canada Supreme Court Reports/Recueil des Arrets de la Cour Supreme du Canada. irreg., 1971, pt. 8. ISSN 0045-4230

**Canada. Transport Commission**
275 Slater St., Ottawa, Ont. K1A 0N9, Canada (Subscr. to: Supply and Services Canada, Publications Division, Ottawa, Ont. K1A 0S9, Canada)
- Canada. Transport Commission. Annual Report. a. ISSN 0068-9912
- Canada. Transport Commission. Decisions and Orders Summary. m.

**Canada. Tax Review Board**
Ottawa, Ont., Canada.
- Canada. Tax Review Board. Annual Report/ Rapport Annuel. a.

**Canada. Treasury Board Secretariat**
160 Elgin St., Ottawa, Ont. K1A 0G5, Canada.
- Canada. Treasury Board Secretariat. Estimates/ Budget des Depenses. a.

**Canada. Unemployment Insurance Commission**
c/o Public Relations, 222 Nepean, Ottawa K1A 0J5, Canada.
- Unemployment Insurance Canada. Annual Report/Assurance-Chomage Canada. Rapport Annuel. a. ISSN 0576-4157

**Canada Council**
151 Sparks St., Ottawa K1P 5V8, Canada.
- Canada Council. Touring Office. Bulletin. q.
- Canada Council Annual Report. a. ISSN 0576-4300
- Touring Directory of the Performing Arts in Canada. a. ISSN 0317-5960

**Canada Institute for Scientific and Technical Information**
Ottawa, Ont. K1A 0S2, Canada.
- Directory of Federally Supported Research in Universities. a. ISSN 0316-0297 (Co-sponsor: National Research Council)

**Canada Japan Trade Council**
No. 903, 75 Albert St., Ottawa K1P 5E7 Ont, Canada.
- Canada Japan Trade Council. Newsletter. m. ISSN 0045-4214

**Canada Jaycees-Jaycees du Canada**
39 Leacock Way, Kanata, Ont. K2K 1T1, Canada.
- Canadian Jaycee. 5 per yr. ISSN 0008-3895

**Canada Law Book Ltd.**
80 Cowdray Court, Agincourt, Ont. M1S 1S5, Canada.
- Canadian Business Law Journal. q.
- Canadian Criminal Cases. w. ISSN 0008-3348
- Canadian Criminal Cases. Annotation Service. a. ISSN 0380-2582
- Canadian Law List. a. ISSN 0084-8573
- Canadian Patent Reporter. m. ISSN 0008-4689
- Criminal Law Quarterly. q. ISSN 0011-1333
- Dominion Law Reports. w. ISSN 0012-5350
- Estates and Trusts Quarterly. q. ISSN 0381-8888
- Labour Arbitration Cases. m. ISSN 0023-690X
- Land Compensation Reports. bi-m (with semi-annual cumulations) ISSN 0380-4208
- Ontario Annual Practice. a.
- Ontario Reports. w. ISSN 0030-3089
- Ontario Statute Citator. 4 per yr. ISSN 0030-3127

**Canada-Mongolia Society**
c/o Far Eastern Studies, University of Saskatchewan, Saskatoon, Sask, S7N 0W0, Canada.
- Canada-Mongolia Review/Revue Canada-Mongolie; a journal of Mongolian studies. 2-3 per yr. ISSN 0383-2813

**Canada Rides Publications Ltd.**
1347 12th Ave., Calgary, Alta. T3C 0P6, Canada.
- Canada Rides; Canada's international horse magazine. bi-m. ISSN 0300-4511

**Canada Safety Council**
1765 St. Laurent Blvd., Ottawa Ont., K1G 3V4, Canada.
- Safety Canada. m. ISSN 0048-8968

**Canada Ski Magazine**
145 Prince Edward Ave., Box 180, Pointe Claire, Dorval, Que. H9R 4N9, Canada.
- Canada Ski. 4 per yr. ISSN 0045-4222

**Canada West Publications**
Box 995, Summerland, B.C. V0H 1Z0, Canada.
- Canada West. q. ISSN 0590-7853

**Canada's Foundry Journal**
85 Bellefair Ave., Toronto, Canada.
- Canada's Foundry Journal. m.

**Canada's Wings**
Box 393, Stittsville, Ont. K0A 3G0, Canada.
- Canada's Wings. irreg.

**Canadian Aberdeen Angus Association**
- Canadian Aberdeen-Angus News. (pub. by R. H. Turner, Ed. & Pub.)

**Canadian Aeronautics and Space Institute**
c/o Mrs. Gladys Hanley, 77 Metcalfe St., Ottawa, Ont. K1P 5L6, Canada.
- Canadian Aeronautics and Space Journal. bi-m. ISSN 0008-2821

**Canadian Air Traffic Control Association, Inc.**
Suite 1216, 1 Nicholas St., Ottawa, K1N 7B7, Canada.
- C A T C A Journal. s-a. ISSN 0007-7860

**Canadian Amateur Boxing Association**
333 River Rd., Place Vanier, Vanier City, Ont. K1L 8B9, Canada.
- Canadian Amateur Boxing News. m. 10 per yr. ISSN 0315-0909

**Canadian Amateur Radio Federation Inc.**
Box 356, Kingston, Ont. K7L 4W2, Canada.
- Canadian Amateur; Canadian amateur radio from coast to coast. m. (except. Jul. and Aug.) ISSN 0318-0867
- Canadian Amateur Certificate Study Guide. a.
- Canadian Amateur Radio Regulations Handbook. a.

**Canadian Amateur Softball Association**
333 River Rd., Vanier, Ont. K1L 8B9, Canada.
- Grand Slam. bi-m.

**Canadian Anaesthetists' Society**
178 St.George St., Toronto, Ont. M5R 2M7,
Canada.
- Canadian Anaesthetists' Society. Journal. bi-m.
ISSN 0008-2856

**Canadian Analyst Ltd.**
32 Front St. W., Suite 237, Toronto, Ont. M5J 1C5,
Canada.
- Canadian Daily Stock Charts. w. ISSN 0045-4656
- Canadian Stock Market Point and Figure
Summary. w. ISSN 0045-5407
- Graphoscope. bi-m. ISSN 0046-631X
- Point and Figure Digest. q. ISSN 0048-4636

**Canadian Appaloosa Horse Association**
Centre St., Calgary, Alta, Canada.
- Canadian Appaloosa Journal. m.

**Canadian Arabian Horse Registry**
Box 5242 Station A, Calgary, Alta. T2H 1X6,
Canada.
- Canadian Arabian News. m. ISSN 0008-2864

**Canadian Arctic Resources Committee**
46 Elgin St., Rm. 11, Ottawa, Ont. K1P 5K6,
Canada.
- Northern Perspectives. m.

**Canadian Arthritis and Rheumatism Society**
45 Charles St., East, Toronto Ont. M4Y 1S3,
Canada.
- Canadian Arthritis and Rheumatism Society. C.
A. R. Scope. irreg., approx. 6-7 per year. ISSN
0068-8258

**Canadian Association for Adult Education**
238 St. George St., Toronto M5R 2P3, Ont.,
Canada.
- C A A E Annual Report. a. ISSN 0068-8274

**Canadian Association for American Studies**
University of Manitoba, Winnipeg, Man. R3T 2N2,
Canada.
- Canadian Review of American Studies. s-a. ISSN
0007-7720

**Canadian Association for Children with Learning
Disabilities**
1390 Sherbrooke St. W., Montreal, Que. H3G 1K2,
Canada.
- Post. irreg. ISSN 0380-7967

**Canadian Association for Health, Physical Education
& Recreation**
10th Floor, 333 River Rd., Vanier City, Ontario
K1L 8B9, Canada.
- C A H P E R Journal. bi-m. ISSN 0008-2899

**Canadian Association for Laboratory Animal Science**
St. Lawrence College of Applied Arts and
Technology, Box 6000, Kingston, Ont. K7L 5A6,
Canada.
- Canadian Association for Laboratory Animal
Science Newsletter. bi-m. ISSN 0045-4354

**Canadian Association for Publishing in Philosophy**
- Canadian Journal of Philosophy. (pub. by
University of Alberta)

**Canadian Association for South Asian Studies**
- Contributions to Asian Studies. (pub. by E. J. Brill
NE)

**Canadian Association for the Mentally Retarded**
Kinsmen NIMR Bldg., York Univ., 4700 Keele St.,
Toronto M3J 1P3, Ont., Canada.
- Deficience Mentale/Mental Retardation. q. ISSN
0011-7668

**Canadian Association in Support of the Native People**
251 Laurier Ave. W., Suite 904, Ottawa, Ont. K1P
5J6, Canada.
- C. A. S. N. P. Bulletin. irreg. (approx. 4 per yr.)
ISSN 0073-6341

**Canadian Association of Administrative Sciences**
School of Business, Queen's University at Kingston,
Kingston, Ont., Canada.
- Canadian Association of Administrative Sciences.
Proceedings, Annual Conference/Rapport, la
Conference Annuelle. irreg. ISSN 0318-5036

**Canadian Association of African Studies**
Department of Geography, Carleton University,
Ottawa, Ont. K1S 5B6, Canada.
- Canadian Association of African Studies. Bulletin.
s-a.

- Canadian Journal of African Studies/Revue
Canadienne des Etudes Africaines. 3 per yr. ISSN
0008-3968

**Canadian Association of College and University
Libraries**
151 Sparks St., Ottawa K1P 5E3, Canada.
- C A C U L Newsletter. irreg. ISSN 0068-8290

**Canadian Association of College and University
Student Services**
Box 810, Truro, N.S., Canada.
- Canadian Association of College and University
Student Services. Bulletin. 6 per yr (during
academic year)

**Canadian Association of Departments of Extension
and Summer School**
Saskatoon, Sask, Canada.
- Canadian Correspondence Courses for University
Credit. a. ISSN 0068-855X

**Canadian Association of Exhibitions**
1253 Wellington St., Port Coquitlam, B.C., Canada.
- Canadian Association of Exhibitions. Ex-Site. m.
ISSN 0045-4362

**Canadian Association of Geographers**
McGill University, P.O. Box 6070, Montreal H3C
3G1, Canada.
- Canadian Association of Geographers. Newsletter.
a. ISSN 0068-8312
- Canadian Geographer/Geographe Canadien. (pub.
by University of Toronto Press)

**Canadian Association of Geographers. Education
Committee**
McGill Univ., Burnside Hall, P.O. Box 6070,
Montreal H3C 3G1, Canada.
- Canadian Association of Geographers. Educational
Committee. Educational Bulletin. irreg. ISSN
0068-8304

**Canadian Association of Geographers. Western
Division**
- British Columbia Geographical Series: Occasional
Papers in Geography. (pub. by Tantalus Research
Ltd.)

**Canadian Association of Information Science**
Box 158, Terminal A, Ottawa, Ont. K1N 8V2,
Canada.
- Canadian Journal of Information Science/Revue
Canadienne des Sciences de Information. a. ISSN
0380-9218

**Canadian Association of Law Libraries**
c/o Rosemary McCormick, Ed., Law Society of
Upper Canada, Osgoode Hall, 130 Queen St. W.,
Toronto, Ont. M5H 2N6, Canada.
- Canadian Association of Law Libraries.
Newsletter. q.

**Canadian Association of Management Consultants**
Box 289, Toronto-Dominion Centre, Toronto Ont.
M5K 1K2, Canada.
- Canadian Association of Management
Consultants. Annual Report. a. ISSN 0068-8320

**Canadian Association of Marine Equipment Industries**
Suite 1401, 67 Yonge St., Toronto 1, Ont., Canada.
- Canadian Association of Marine Equipment
Industries. Newsletter. irreg. ISSN 0045-4370

**Canadian Association of Music Libraries**
c/o National Library of Canada, 395 Wellington St.,
Ottawa, Ont. K1A 0N4, Canada.
- C A M L Newsletter/A C B M Nouvelles. irreg.
ISSN 0383-1299

**Canadian Association of Occupational Therapists**
4 New St., Toronto, M5R 1P6, Ont., Canada.
- Canadian Journal of Occupational Therapy/Revue
Canadienne d'Ergotherapie. q. ISSN 0008-4174

**Canadian Association of Optometrists**
Suite 2001, 210 Gladstone, Ottawa, Ont. K2P OY6,
Canada.
- Canadian Journal of Optometry/Revue
Canadienne d'Optometrie. q. ISSN 0045-5075

**Canadian Association of Physicists**
151 Slater St. No. 903, Ottawa, Ont. K1P 5H3,
Canada.
- Canadian Association of Physicists. Annual
Report/Association Canadienne des Physiciennes.
Rapport Annuel. a. ISSN 0068-8339

- Physics in Canada/Physique au Canada. 7 per yr.
ISSN 0031-9147

**Canadian Association of Radiologists**
1440 St. Catherine St. W. Suite 806, Montreal, P.Q.
H3G 1R8, Canada.
- Canadian Association of Radiologists. Journal. q.
ISSN 0008-2902

**Canadian Association of Rehabilitation Personnel**
Toronto, Ont., Canada.
- Comeback. q. ISSN 0383-641X

**Canadian Association of Schools of Social Work**
151 Slater, Ottawa, Ont. K1P 5H3, Canada.
- Canadian Journal of Social Work Education/
Revue Canadienne d'Education en Service Social.
3 per yr. ISSN 0316-8565

**Canadian Association of Slavists**
c/o B. Harasymiw, Sec. Treas., Dept. of Political
Science, University of Calgary, Calgary, Alta. T2N
1N4, Canada.
- Canadian Association of Slavists Newsletter. 3 per
yr. ISSN 0008-2910

**Canadian Association of Slavists. Ottawa Branch**
c/o Carter Elwood, Ed., 256 Paterson Hall,
Carleton Univ., Ottawa, Ont. K1S 5B6, Canada.
- Canadian Slavonic Papers/Revue Canadienne des
Slavistes. q. ISSN 0008-5006

**Canadian Association of Social Workers**
55 Parkdale Ave., No. 400, Ottawa, Ont. K1Y 1E5,
Canada.
- Canadian Association of Social Workers.
Newsletter. 6-8 per yr. ISSN 0045-4419
- Social Worker/Travailleur Social. q. ISSN 0037-
8089

**Canadian Association of Special Libraries &
Information Services**
151 Sparks St., Ottawa, K1P 5E3, Canada.
- Agora: Bulletin of the Canadian Association of
Special Libraries and Information Services. irreg.,
approx. 3-4 per year; 1970, vol.3, no.4. ISSN
0065-4310

**Canadian Association of Sport Sciences**
333 River Rd., Vanier City, Ont. K1L 8B9, Canada.
- Canadian Journal of Applied Sport Sciences/
Journal Canadien des Sciences Appliquees au
Sport. 4 per yr.

**Canadian Association of University Teachers**
75 Albert St., Suite 1001, Ottawa, Ont. K1P 5E7,
Canada.
- C. A. U. T. Bulletin/A. C. P. U. Bulletin. m.
ISSN 0007-7887

**Canadian Association of University Teachers of
German**
- Seminar. (pub. by University of Toronto Press)

**Canadian Authors Association**
Box 120, Niagara-on-the-Lake, Ont. L0S 1J0,
Canada.
- Canadian Author & Bookman. q. ISSN 0008-2937

**Canadian Authors Association. Edmonton Branch**
13104 - 136 Ave., Edmonton, Alta. T5L 4B3,
Canada.
- Alberta Poetry Yearbook. a. ISSN 0065-5996

**Canadian Automobile Association**
150 Gloucester St., Ottawa, Ont. K2P 0A6, Canada.
- Canadian Automobile Association. Communique.
q (approx.) ISSN 0380-6987

**Canadian Aviation Historical Society**
Box 224 Sta. A, Willowdale Ont. M2N 5S8,
Canada.
- C. A. H. S. Journal. q. ISSN 0007-7771

**Canadian Band Directors Association**
21 Tecumseh St., Brantford, Ont. N3S 2B3, Canada.
- Canadian Band Directors Association. Newsletter.
bi-m. ISSN 0381-9159

**Canadian Bankers Association**
Box 282, Toronto Dominion Centre, Toronto, Ont.
M5K 1K2, Canada.
- Bank Directory of Canada. (pub. by Houston
Standard Publications Ltd.)
- Canadian Banker and I C B Review. 6 per yr.
ISSN 0315-6230
- Canadian Bankers Association. C. B. A. Bulletin.
4-5 per yr. ISSN 0045-4435

- Factbook: Chartered Banks of Canada. a.

**Canadian Bar Association**
Suite 1700, 130 Albert St., Ottawa, Ont. K1A 0L6,
Canada.
- Canadian Bar National. m. ISSN 0315-2286
- Canadian Bar Review. q. ISSN 0008-3003

**Canadian Bar Association. British Columbia Branch**
1010-777 Hornby St., Vancouver, B.C. V6Z 1S4,
Canada.
- Canadian Bar Association. British Columbia
Branch. Program Report. irreg. ISSN 0384-5753

**Canadian Bar Association. Toronto Branch**
801-80 Richmond St. W., Toronto, Ont. M5H 2A4,
Canada.
- Philanthropist. s-a.

**Canadian Book Publishers' Council**
45 Charles St., East, Suite 701, Toronto 5, Ontario,
Canada.
- Canadian Book Publishers' Council. Directory of
Members and Agencies. irreg.
- Canadian Books in Print. (pub. by University of
Toronto Press)

**Canadian Botanical Association**
c/o Dr. J. K. Morton, Ed., Univ. of Waterloo, Dept.
of Biology, Waterloo Ont. N2L 3G1, Canada.
- Canadian Botanical Association. Bulletin. q. ISSN
0008-3046

**Canadian Broadcasting Corporation**
7925 Cote St. Luc Rd., Montreal, P.Q. H4W 1R5,
Canada.
- C B C Engineering Review/Revue Technique de
Radio-Canada. a. ISSN 0068-8401

**Canadian Brotherhood of Railway, Transport and
General Workers**
2300 Carling Avenue, Ottawa, Ont., Canada.
- Canadian Transport. m. ISSN 0045-5466

**Canadian Bureau for International Education**
151 rue Slater, Suite 408, Ottawa, Ont. K1P 5H3,
Canada.
- Communications. m.

**Canadian Cable Television Association**
Suite 405, 85 Albert St., Ottawa, Ont. K1P 6A4,
Canada.
- C C T A Communique. bi-m.

**Canadian Cancer Society**
1926 West Broadway, Vancouver, B.C. V6J 1Z2,
Canada.
- Canadian Cancer Society. British Columbia and
Yukon Division. Provincial News. 4 per yr. ISSN
0045-4516
- Progress against Cancer/Progres Contre le
Cancer. q. ISSN 0033-0604

**Canadian Canoe Association**
333 River Rd., Vanier City, Ont. K1L 8B9, Canada.
- Canoe (Vanier City) q.

**Canadian Catholic Historical Association**
c/o P. Bolger, St. Dunstan's University,
Charlottetown, P. E. I., Canada.
- Canadian Catholic Historical Association. Annual
Report. irreg.

**Canadian Caver Magazine**
Dept. of Geography, University of Alberta,
Edmonton, Alta. T6G 2H4, Canada.
- Canadian Caver. s-a.

**Canadian Century Publishers**
Box 129, Lancaster, Ont. K0C 1N0, Canada.
- Arctic and Northern Development Digest. bi-m.
ISSN 0315-4785

**Canadian Century Publishing Co.**
Box 10, Victoria Sta., Montreal, Que. H3Z 2V4,
Canada.
- Canadian Century and Canadian Life &
Resources. w. ISSN 0382-6376

**Canadian Ceramic Society**
2175 Sheppard Ave. E., Suite 110, Willowdale, Ont,
Canada.
- Canadian Ceramic Society. Journal. a. ISSN 0068-
8444
- Canadian Clay & Ceramics. (pub. by Taylor
Enterprises)

**Canadian Certified General Accountants' Association**
Suite 800 - 535 Thurlow St., Vancouver, B.C. V6E
3L2, Canada.
- C G A Magazine. 9 per yr. ISSN 0318-742X

**Canadian Chamber Concerts Press**
Toronto, Ont., Canada.
- Chamber Pot. irreg. ISSN 0382-845X (New
Chamber Orchestra of Canada)

**Canadian Children's Literature Association**
- Canadian Children's Literature. (pub. by Canadian
Children's Press)

**Canadian Children's Magazine**
c/o Evelyn Samuel, Ed., 4150 Bracken Ave.,
Victoria, B.C. V8X 3N8, Canada.
- Canadian Children's Magazine. q. ISSN 0384-
5184

**Canadian Children's Press**
Box 335, Guelph, Ontario, Canada.
- Canadian Children's Literature. q. (Canadian
Children's Literature Association)

**Canadian Chiropractic Association**
1900 Bayview Ave., Toronto M4G 3E6, Ont.,
Canada.
- Canadian Chiropractic Association. Journal. q.
ISSN 0008-3194

**Canadian Church Historical Society**
67 Victoria Ave. S., Hamilton, Ont. L8N 2S8,
Canada.
- Canadian Church Historical Society Journal. q.
ISSN 0008-3208

**Canadian Circulations Audit Board, Inc.**
165 Bloor St. E., Toronto, Ont. M4W 1C8, Canada.
- C C A B Circulate. q.

**Canadian Coin News**
1567 Sedlescomb Dr., Mississauga, Ont. L4X 1M5,
Canada.
- Canadian Coin News. fortn.

**Canadian College of Teachers**
Box 483, Sillery, Quebec G1T 2R8, Canada.
- Canadian College of Teachers. Papers Presented
at the Conference. a. ISSN 0068-8460

**Canadian Commission for Unesco**
255 Albert St., Box 1047, Ottawa, Ont. K1P 5V8,
Canada.
- Canadian Commission for UNESCO. Annual
Report. a. ISSN 0068-8479
- Canadian Commission for UNESCO. Bulletin/
Commission Canadienne pour UNESCO. Bulletin.
4 per yr. ISSN 0008-4557

**Canadian Communist League (Marxist-Leninist)**
C.P. 346, Station Place d'Armes, Montreal, Que.,
Canada.
- Forge. fortn.

**Canadian Comparative Literature Association**
- Canadian Review of Comparative Literature/
Revue Canadienne de Litterature Comparee. (pub.
by University of Toronto Press)

**Canadian Conference of Catholic Bishops.
Publications Service**
90 Parent Ave, Ottawa, Ontario K1N 7BI, Canada.
- Canadian Conference of Catholic Bishops.
National Bulletin on Liturgy. bi-m.

**Canadian Conference of the Arts**
3 Church St., Suite 47, Toronto, Ontario M5E 1M2,
Canada.
- Canadian Conference of the Arts. Bulletin. 7 per
yr. ISSN 0380-5506
- Canadian Conference of the Arts. Miscellaneous
Reports. irreg. ISSN 0068-8487

**Canadian Construction Association**
Centre de la Construction, 151, rue O'Connor,
Ottawa, Ont. K2P 1T2, Canada.
- Canadian Construction Association.
Documentation de Reference. irreg. ISSN 0316-
9375

**Canadian Cooperative Wool Growers Ltd.**
Box 9, Carleton Place, Ontario K0A 1J0, Canada.
- Canadian Wool Grower. s-a.

**Canadian Copper and Brass Development Association**
55 York St., Toronto M5J 1R7, Ont., Canada.
- Canadian Copper/Cuivre Canadien. q. ISSN
0008-3291

**Canadian Corporation for Studies in Religion**
- Studies in Religion/Sciences Religieuses. (pub. by
Wilfrid Laurier University Press)

**Canadian Council of Christians and Jews**
c/o J. Kotick, Rm. 506, 229 Yonge St., Toronto,
Ont., Canada.
- Scope/Envergure. s-a. ISSN 0381-8187

**Canadian Council of Churches**
40 St. Clair Ave. E., Toronto, Ont. M4T 1M9,
Canada.
- Canadian Council of Churches. Council
Communicatior. q. ISSN 0045-4605

**Canadian Council of Professional Engineers**
116 Albert St., Ottawa 4, Canada.
- Canadian Council of Professional Engineers. News
Brief/Communique. m. ISSN 0008-3313

**Canadian Council of Teachers of English**
237 Yonge Blvd., Toronto, Ont. M5M 3J1, Canada.
- Canadian Council of Teachers of English.
Newsletter. 5-6 per yr. ISSN 0045-4613
- English Quarterly. q. ISSN 0013-8355

**Canadian Council of the Blind**
96 Ridout St. S., London, Ont N6C 34, Canada.
- C C B Outlook (Braille Edition) q.
- C C B Outlook (Inkprint Edition); information for
and by sightless Canadians. q. ISSN 0007-7984

**Canadian Council on Social Development**
55 Parkdale Ave., Box 3505, Sta. C, Ottawa, Ont.
K1Y 4G1, Canada.
- Canadian Conference on Social Development.
Proceedings/Compte Rendu. biennial.
- Canadian Council on Social Development. Annual
Report/Rapport Annuel. a. ISSN 0068-8584
- Canadian Welfare. 6 per yr. ISSN 0008-5332
- Digeste Social. 5 per yr.
- Directory of Canadian Community Funds and
Councils/Repertoire des Federations et Conseils
des Oeuvres du Canada. irreg. ISSN 0084-9863
(Community Funds and Councils of Canada)
- Directory of Canadian Welfare Services/
Repertoire des Services Sociaux Canadiens.
biennial (quarterly update) ISSN 0084-9871
- Housing and People/Habitation et les Citoyens. 4
per yr. ISSN 0018-6562
- Social Development. irreg. (approx 4-5 per yr.)
ISSN 0316-313X

**Canadian Council on Urban and Regional Research**
Suite 1100, 251 Laurier Ave. W., Ottawa K1P 5J6,
Ont., Canada.
- Canadian Council on Urban and Regional
Research. Urban and Regional References.
Annual Supplement. a. ISSN 0068-8606
- Urban Forum/Colloque Urbain. bi-m.

**Canadian Criminology and Corrections Association**
55 Parkdale Ave., Ottawa, Ont. K1Y 1E5, Canada.
- Canadian Criminology and Corrections
Association. Annual Report/Societe Canadienne
de Criminologie. Rapport Annuel. a.
- Canadian Criminology and Corrections
Association. Bulletin/Societe Canadienne de
Criminologie. Bulletin. q. ISSN 0045-463X
- Canadian Journal of Criminology and Corrections.
q.
- Correctional Literature Published in Canada/
Ouvrages de Criminologie Publies au Canada. a.
ISSN 0070-0509
- Directory of Correctional Services in Canada/
Repertoire des Services de Correction du Canada.
a. ISSN 0070-5381

**Canadian Cultural Society of the Deaf in Canada**
1475 Pacific Ave. W., Winnipeg, Man. R2E 1H1,
Canada.
- Cultural Horizons of the Deaf in Canada. irreg.
ISSN 0382-8832

**Canadian Curling News**
1112 Centre St. N., Calgary, Alta. T2E 2R2,
Canada.
- Canadian Curling News. m. ISSN 0045-4648

**Canadian Daily Quotation Service Ltd.**
Box 518, Station K, Toronto, Ont. M4P 2G9,
Canada.
- Bond Record. a.

● Canadian Financial E-Z Directory. a.

**Canadian Dental Association**
1815 Alta Vista Drive, Ottawa, Ont. K1G 3Y6,
Canada.
● Canadian Dental Association. Directory. a. ISSN
0068-8622
● Canadian Dental Association. Journal. m. ISSN
0008-3372
● Canadian Dental Association. Transactions. a.
ISSN 0068-8630

**Canadian Dental Hygienists Association**
10560 Milford Drive, Richmond, B.C. V7A 4J7,
Canada.
● Canadian Dental Hygienist/Hygieniste Dentaire
du Canada. q. ISSN 0008-3380

**Canadian Diabetic Association**
1491 Yonge St., Toronto 7, Canada.
● C D A Newsletter. q. ISSN 0007-8018

**Canadian Dietetic Association**
Suite 215, 1393 Yonge St., Toronto, Ont. M4T 1Y4,
Canada.
● Canadian Dietetic Association. Journal. q. ISSN
0008-3399

**Canadian Economics Association**
● Canadian Journal of Economics/Revue
Canadienne d'Economique. (pub. by University of
Toronto Press)

**Canadian Education Association**
252 Ouest rue Bloor, Toronto, Ont. M5S 1V5,
Canada.
● Association Canadienne d'Education. Bulletin. 9
per yr. ISSN 0004-5306
● C E A Handbook/Ki-es-Ki. a. ISSN 0068-8657
● Canadian Education Association. Newsletter. 9
per yr. ISSN 0008-3445
● Canadian Education Association. Proceedings of
the Convention. a.
● Canadian Education Association. Research
Report. irreg.
● Canadian Education Index/Repertoire Canadien
sur l'Education; an index appearing five times a
year to books, reports, pamphlets and periodical
articles on educational publishing in Canada. 5
per yr. ISSN 0008-3453
● Directory of Education Studies in Canada/
Annuaire d'Etudes en Education au Canada. a.
ISSN 0070-5454
● Education Canada. q. ISSN 0013-1253
● Education Studies in Progress in Canadian
Universities. irreg.
● Requirements for Teaching Certificates in Canada.
irreg. ISSN 0080-1437

**Canadian Educational Programmes**
35 Madison Ave., Toronto, Ont. M5R 2S2, Canada.
● Family Involvement; the family resource
magazine. 5 per yr.

**Canadian Egg Producers' Council**
● Canada Poultryman. (pub. by Farm Papers Ltd.)

**Canadian Electrical Distributors Association**
● C E D A Current. (pub. by Kerrwil Publications
Ltd.)

**Canadian Engineering Publications Ltd.**
32 Front St. West, Suite 501, Toronto, Ont. M5J
2H9, Canada.
● Engineering Digest. 10 per yr. ISSN 0013-7901
● Environmental Engineering Newsletter. m. ISSN
0315-0011
● New Equipment News. m. ISSN 0028-4971

**Canadian Environmental Law Research Foundation**
Suite 303, 1 Spadina Crescent, Toronto, Ontario
M5S 1L1, Canada.
● Canadian Environmental Law News. bi-m.

**Canadian Export Association**
Suite 1020, 1080 Beaver Hall Hill, Montreal,
Quebec H2Z 1T7, Canada.
● Canadian Export Association. Review & Digest
Bulletin. m.
● Canadian Export Association Export News
Bulletin. m.
● U S News. q.

**Canadian Family Camping Federation**
Box 397, Rexdale M9W 5L4, Ont., Canada.
● Canadian Camper. 6 per yr. ISSN 0316-280X

**Canadian Federation of Biological Societies**
University of Western Ontario, Department of
Pharmacology, London, Ont. N6A 5C1, Canada.
● Canadian Federation of Biological Societies.
Canadian Federation News of the Annual
Meeting. a. ISSN 0068-8681
● Canadian Federation of Biological Societies.
Proceedings. a. ISSN 0068-869X
● Canadian Federation of Biological Societies.
Programme of the Annual Meeting. a. ISSN
0068-8703

**Canadian Federation of Business and Professional
Women's Clubs**
No. 320, 56 Sparks St., Ottawa Ont. K1P 5A9,
Canada.
● Business and Professional Woman. 5 per yr. ISSN
0045-3587

**Canadian Federation of Humane Societies**
900 Pinecrest Road, Ottawa K2B 6B3, Canada.
● Canadian Federation of Humane Societies.
Newsletter. q.

**Canadian Federation of Mayors and Municipalities**
Suite 600, 220 Saurier Ave. W., Ottawa, Ont. KIP
5A9, Canada.
● Canadian Federation of Mayors and
Municipalities. Annual Conference Proceedings. a.
ISSN 0068-8711

**Canadian Federation of Music Teachers' Association**
c/o Florence Duggan, Ed., 135 32nd Ave. N.W.,
Calgary, Alta. T2M 2P7, Canada.
● Canadian Music Teacher. 4 per yr.

**Canadian Fiction**
c/o Geoffrey Hancock, Ed., Box 46422, Sta. G.,
Vancouver, B.C. V6R 4G7, Canada.
● Canadian Fiction. q. ISSN 0045-477X

**Canadian Field Hockey Council**
333 River Rd., Vanier, Ontario, Canada.
● Canadian Field Hockey News. 3 per yr. ISSN
0045-4788

**Canadian Figure Skating Association**
333 River Rd., Ottawa, Ontario, K1L 8B9, Canada.
● Canadian Skater. 4 per yr (since 1974) ISSN
0068-9637

**Canadian Figure Skating Association. Central Ontario
Section**
R.R.   2, Seagrave, Ont. L0C 1G0, Canada.
● C O S S I P. (Central Ontario Section Speaks in
Print) 6 per yr. ISSN 0045-4796

**Canadian Film Archives**
1762 Carling, Ottawa, Ont. K2A 2H7, Canada.
● Canadian Filmography Series. irreg., 1970, no. 6.
ISSN 0068-872X

**Canadian Film Development Corporation**
800 Place Victoria, Bureau 912, Montreal, Canada.
● C F D C Annual Report. a.

**Canadian Film Institute**
75 Albert St., Suite 611, Ottawa, Ont. K1P 5E7,
Canada.
● Film Canadiana: The Canadian Film Institute
Yearbook of Canadian Cinema. a.
● Guide to Film and Television Courses in Canada.
a.

**Canadian Flight Publishing Co.**
Rm. 605, 77 Metcalfe St., Ottawa, Ont., Canada.
● Canadian Flight; the pilot's magazine. bi-m. ISSN
0008-3577 (C O P A)

**Canadian Folk Music Society**
c/o St. Francis Xavier University, Dept. of Music,
Antigonish, N.S., Canada.
● Canadian Folk Music Journal. a. ISSN 0068-8746
● Canadian Folk Music Society. Newsletter. s-a.
ISSN 0576-5234

**Canadian Forces Base**
Cold Lake, Box 2350, Medley, Alta. T0A 2M0,
Canada.
● C F B Cold Lake Courier. fortn. ISSN 0045-8872

**Canadian Forces Base Edmonton**
Lancaster Park, Edmonton T0A 2H0, Alta., Canada.
● Sealandair. fortn. ISSN 0048-9883

**Canadian Forces Base Montreal**
St. Hubert, Que. J3Y 5T4, Canada.
● Parapet. m. ISSN 0384-0417

**Canadian Forces Base Winnipeg**
Westwin, Manitoba R2R OTO, Canada.
● Voxair. s-m. ISSN 0300-3213

**Canadian Forces Headquarters**
Ottawa K1A OK 2, Ont., Canada.
● Canadian Forces Dental Services Quarterly. q.
ISSN 0045-4850

**Canadian Forces Headquarters - Directorate of Flight
Safety**
● Flight Comment. (pub. by Queen's Printer,
Canada)

**Canadian Foresters Life Insurance Society**
Box 850, Brantford, Ont. N3T 5S3, Canada.
● Canadian Forester. 4 per yr.

**Canadian Forestry Association**
185 Somerset St. W., Ottawa, Ont. K2P 0J2,
Canada.
● C. F. A. News. q. ISSN 0045-4869

**Canadian Forestry Association of B.C.**
Vancouver, B.C., Canada.
● Conservation Topics. irreg. ISSN 0573-715X
(British Columbia. Forest Service)

**Canadian Forwarder**
3440 Trenholme Ave., Montreal H4b 1x9, Canada.
● Canadian Forwarder. bi-w. ISSN 0045-4877

**Canadian Fruit Wholesalers Association**
1568 Carling Ave., Ottawa K1Z 7M5, Ont.,
Canada.
● Canadian Fruit Wholesalers' Association.
Yearbook. a. ISSN 0068-8770

**Canadian Gas Association**
55 Scarsdale Rd., Don Mills, Ont., Canada.
● Canadian Gas Association. Manufacturers'
Section. Manufacturers Directory. a. ISSN 0068-
8797
● Canadian Gas Association. Membership
Directory. irreg.
● Canadian Gas Association. Statistical Summary of
the Canadian Gas Industry. a. ISSN 0068-8800
● Canadian Gas Facts. irreg.
● Canadian Gas Utilities Directory. a. ISSN 0576-
5269

**Canadian Gay Activists Alliance**
P.O. Box 284, Sta. a, Vancouver 1, B.C., Canada.
● Gay Canadian. m.

**Canadian Gladiolus Society**
1274 129 A St., Ocean Park, B.C., Canada.
● Canadian Gladiolus Society. Annual. a.

**Canadian Government Office of Tourism**
Room 900, 150 Kent St., Ottawa K1A OH6,
Canada.
● Canada Travel Digest. q. ISSN 0045-4265
● Sportfishing. biennial.

**Canadian Gregg Association**
● Canadian Gregg News. (pub. by Gregg Publishing
Co.)

**Canadian Guernsey Breeders Association**
368 Woolwich St., Guelph, Ont., Canada.
● Canadian Guernsey Breeders' Journal. 9 per yr.
ISSN 0045-4907

**Canadian Guild of Organists**
Toronto, Ont., Canada.
● Canadian Guild of Organists. Journal. s-a. ISSN
0382-7003

**Canadian Gypsum Co. Ltd.**
Box 4034, Terminal A, Toronto, Ont. M5W 1K8,
Canada.
● Canadian Building News. q. ISSN 0045-4508

**Canadian H & G Publishing Ltd.**
Suite 200, 200 Consumers Rd., Willowdale, Ont.
M2J 1P8, Canada.
● Home. bi-m. ISSN 0383-5030

**Canadian Hackney Horse Society**
c/o Canadian National Live Stock Records, Ottawa,
Ont., Canada.
● Canadian Hackney Stud Book. irreg. ISSN 0382-
5795

**Canadian Health Record Association**
187 King St. E., Oshawa, Ont. L1H 1C3, Canada.
● Canadian Health Record Association. Recorder. 4 per yr.

**Canadian Hearing Society**
60 Bedford Rd., Toronto, Ont., Canada.
● Canadian Hearing Review. irreg. ISSN 0381-6389

**Canadian Heart Foundation**
Suite 1200, One Nicholas St., Ottawa, Ont. K1N 7B7, Canada.
● Canadian Heart Foundation. Annual Report. a. ISSN 0068-8851

**Canadian Hemophilia Society**
Chedoke Hospital, Patterson Bldg., Box 590, Hamilton, Ont. L8N 3L6, Canada.
● Hemophilia Today. q. ISSN 0046-7251

**Canadian Hemophilia Society. Ontario Chapter**
No. 510, 30 Bloor St. W., Toronto, Ont. M4W 1A2, Canada.
● Canadian Hemophilia Society. Ontario Chapter. Bulletin. q. ISSN 0045-4923

**Canadian Historical Association**
c/o Public Archives of Canada, 395 Wellington St., Ottawa, Ontario K1A 0N3, Canada.
● Canada. Public Archives. Register of Post Graduate Dissertations in Progress in History and Related Subjects. a. ISSN 0068-8088
● Canadian Historical Association. Historical Booklets. Brochures Historiques. irreg. ISSN 0068-886X
● Canadian Historical Association. Historical Papers; a selection from the papers presented at the annual meeting. a. ISSN 0068-8878
● Canadian Historical Association. Newsletter. 4 per yr.

**Canadian Home Economics Association**
151 Slater St., 901 Burnside Bldg., Ottawa, Ont., Canada.
● Canadian Home Economics Journal. q. ISSN 0008-3763

**Canadian Horticultural Council**
1568 Carling Ave., Ottawa, Ont. K1Z 7M5, Canada.
● Canadian Horticultural Council. Annual Meeting Reports. a. ISSN 0068-8908
● Canadian Horticultural Council. Committee on Horticultural Research. Annual Reports. a. ISSN 0068-8916

**Canadian Hospital Association**
25 Imperial St., Toronto M5P 1C1, Canada.
● Canadian Hospital Directory/Annuaire des Hopitaux du Canada. a. ISSN 0068-8932
● Dimensions in Health Service. m. ISSN 0317-7645

**Canadian Imperial Bank of Commerce**
Toronto, Ont, Canada.
● Canadian Imperial Bank of Commerce. Commercial Letter. m. ISSN 0008-381X

**Canadian Importers Association, Inc.**
2180 Yonge St., Suite 602, Toronto M4S 2B9 Ont., Canada.
● Canadian Importers Association. Importers' Bulletin. w. ISSN 0045-494X
● Importfile. 2-3 per yr. ISSN 0383-6304

**Canadian Indemnity Co.**
333 Main St., Winnipeg 1, Manitoba, Canada.
● Service and Indemnity. m. ISSN 0037-2552

**Canadian Independent Adjusters' Conference**
55 Queen St. E., Suite 1404, Toronto, Ont. M5C 1R6, Canada.
● Canadian Independent Adjuster. q. ISSN 0008-3828

**Canadian Industrial Traffic League**
Ste. 708, 67 Yonge St., Toronto M5E 1J8, Ont., Canada.
● Canadian Industrial Traffic League. Traffic Notes. w. ISSN 0045-4974

**Canadian Industries Ltd.**
P.O. Box 10, Montreal H3C 2R3, Canada.
● C I L Contact. 17 per yr. ISSN 0384-8701

**Canadian Information Processing Society**
Ste. 214, 212 King St. W., Toronto, Ont. M5H 1Ks, Canada.
● C I P S Review. bi-m.
● Canadian Information Processing Society. Canadian Salary Survey. a.
● Canadian Information Processing Society. Computer Census. a.
● Canadian Information Processing Society. Software Survey. a.

**Canadian Institute of Chartered Accountants**
250 Bloor St. E., Toronto, Ont. M4W 1G5, Canada.
● C A Magazine. m. ISSN 0317-6878
● C I C A Dialogue. 6 per yr. ISSN 0045-4982
● C I C A Handbook. irreg. ISSN 0068-8983
● Canadian Institute of Chartered Accountants. Final Examinations and Approaches to Answering the Uniform Final Examinations. a.
● Directory of Canadian Chartered Accountants. a. ISSN 0527-9275
● Financial Reporting in Canada. biennial. ISSN 0071-5115

**Canadian Institute of Food Science and Technology**
Suite 10, 46 Elgin St., Ottawa K1P 5K6, Ont., Canada.
● Canadian Institute of Food Science and Technology Journal/Institut Canadien de Science et Technologie Alimentaire. Journal. q. ISSN 0315-5463

**Canadian Institute of Forestry**
Box 5000, Macdonald College, Quebec H0A 1C0, Canada.
● Canadian Institute of Forestry. Annual Report. irreg. ISSN 0068-8991
● Forestry Chronicle. 6 per yr. ISSN 0015-7546

**Canadian Institute of International Affairs**
15 King's College Circle, Toronto, Ont. M5S 2V9, Canada.
● Behind the Headlines. 6 per yr. ISSN 0005-7983
● International Canada. m. ISSN 0027-0512
● International Journal. q. ISSN 0020-7020
● Wellesley Papers. irreg.

**Canadian Institute of Mining & Metallurgy**
400-1130 Sherbrooke West, Montreal, Que. H3A 2M8, Canada.
● C I M Bulletin. m.
● C. I. M. Directory. a. ISSN 0068-9009
● Journal of Canadian Petroleum Technology. q. ISSN 0021-9487

**Canadian Institute of Onomastic Sciences**
Box 3504, Sta. B, Winnipeg, Canada.
● Onomastica Canadiana. a. ISSN 0078-4656

**Canadian Institute of Planners**
46 Elgin St., Ste. 30, Ottawa, Ont. K1P 5K6, Canada.
● Forum. m.
● Plan. 3-4 per yr. ISSN 0032-0544

**Canadian Institute of Quantity Surveyors**
Suite 401, 8 Colborne St., Toronto, Ontario, Canada.
● Cipher. m. ISSN 0045-6934

**Canadian Institute of Surveying**
Box 5378, Sta. F, Ottawa, Ont. K2C 3J1, Canada.
● Canadian Surveyor/Geometre Canadien. q. ISSN 0008-5103

**Canadian Institute of Timber Construction**
200 Cooper St., Ottawa, Ont. K2P 0G1, Canada.
● Treated Wood Perspectives/Perspectives des Bois Traites. irreg.

**Canadian Intelligence Publications**
Box 130, Flesherton, Ont., Canada.
● Canadian Intelligence Service. m.
● On Target. w.

**Canadian International Development Agency**
Information Division, 122 Bank St., Ottawa, Ont. K1A 0G4, Canada.
● Action. q.
● C I D A Annual Review. a.
● Canadian International Development Agency. Thoughts on International Development/Canada. Agence Canadienne de Developpement International. Reflexions sur le Developpement International. irreg (2 per yr)
● Contact. m.
● Cooperation Canada. bi-m.

● Thoughts on International Development. irreg., no. 11, 1976.

**Canadian International DX Radio Club**
169 Grandview Ave., Winnipeg, Man. R2G 0L4, Canada.
● C I D X Messenger. m. ISSN 0045-3706

**Canadian Jersey Cattle Club**
c/o C. Honderich, Ed., 343 Waterloo Ave., Guelph, Ont. N1H 3K1, Canada.
● Canadian Jersey Breeder. m. ISSN 0008-3909
● Canadian Jersey Herd Record. irreg. ISSN 0382-6406

**Canadian Jewish Magazine**
6077 Coolbrook Ave., Montreal 252, Que., Canada.
● Canadian Jewish Magazine. 4 per yr. ISSN 0045-5040

**Canadian Jewish News**
Ed. & Pub. Ralph Hyman, 22 Balliol Ave., Suite 15, Toronto M451C1, Ont., Canada.
● Canadian Jewish News. w. ISSN 0008-3941

**Canadian Jewish Outlook**
Box 65, Sta. B, Toronto, Ont. M5T 2T2, Canada.
● Canadian Jewish Outlook. m. ISSN 0045-5059

**Canadian Journal of Neurological Sciences, Inc.**
1516-233 Kennedy St., Winnipeg R3C 3J5, Man., Canada.
● Canadian Journal of Neurological Sciences. q. ISSN 0317-1671

**Canadian Journalism Foundation, Inc.**
454 King St. W., Rm. 302, Toronto, Ont. M5V 1L6, Canada.
● Last Post. 8 per yr. ISSN 0023-8651

**Canadian Labour Congress**
2841 Riverside Drive, Ottawa, Ont. K1V 8X7, Canada.
● Canadian Labour/Travailleur Canadien. q. ISSN 0008-4336
● Canadian Labour Comment/Information Syndicale. fortn. ISSN 0316-4780

**Canadian Ladies' Golf Association**
333 River Road, Ottawa, Ontario, KIL 8B9, Canada.
● Canadian Ladies' Golf Association. Year Book. a. ISSN 0084-8565

**Canadian Lawn Tennis Association**
643 Yonge St., Toronto M4Y 2A2, Ontario, Canada.
● Racquets Canada. bi-m.

**Canadian Library Association**
151 Sparks St., Ottawa K1P 5E3, Canada.
● C.L.A. Feliciter. 12 per yr.
● C L A Organization Handbook and Membership List. irreg. ISSN 0068-9130
● Canadian Library Association. Annual Reports. a. ISSN 0068-9068
● Canadian Library Association. Geographical List and Index of C L A Microfilms. irreg. ISSN 0068-9076
● Canadian Library Association. Occasional Papers. irreg. ISSN 0068-9092
● Canadian Library Association. Proceedings. a. ISSN 0068-9106
● Canadian Library Journal. bi-m. ISSN 0008-4352
● Canadian Materials. 3 per yr.
● Canadian Periodical Index. m(annual cumulation) ISSN 0008-4719

**Canadian Library Association. Microfilm Project**
151 Sparks St., Ottawa, Ontario K1P 5E3, Canada.
● Canadian Library Association. Microfilm Project. News Notes. irreg. ISSN 0527-9445

**Canadian Library Trustees' Association**
151 Sparks St., Ottawa, Ont. K1P 5E3, Canada.
● Canadian Library Trustees' Association. Newsletter. irreg. ISSN 0068-9149

**Canadian Life Insurance Association**
44 King St. W., Toronto M5H 1E9, Canada.
● Canadian Life Insurance Facts; an authoritative source of factual information about life insurance in Canada. a. ISSN 0068-9157

**Canadian Limousin Association**
● Limousin Leader: International Edition. (pub. by Sage Brush Ventures)

**Canadian Linguistic Association**
English Dept., Queens University, Kingston, Ont. K1L 3N6, Canada.
- C L A Membership Directory and Data Book Memento. irreg. ISSN 0084-8581
- Canadian Journal of Linguistics/Revue Canadienne de Linguistique. s-a. ISSN 0008-4131

**Canadian Livestock Feed Board**
Ottawa, Ont., Canada.
- Grain Facts. s-w. ISSN 0381-2472

**Canadian Manufacturers Association**
167 Yonge St., Toronto, Ont. M5E 1J9, Canada.
- Canadian Manufacturers' Association. Bulletin. irreg. ISSN 0382-6635
- Canadian Manufacturers Association. Report. a. ISSN 0068-9173
- Canadian Trade Index. a. ISSN 0068-9904

**Canadian Mass Publications**
Suite 204, 920 Alness St., Downsview, Ont. M3J 2H7, Canada.
- Horse Racing Magazine. m. ISSN 0380-2779

**Canadian Mathematical Congress**
3421 Drummond, Suite 15, Montreal, Que. H3G 1X7, Canada.
- Canadian Journal of Mathematics/Journal Canadien de Mathematiques. (pub. by University of Toronto Press)
- Canadian Mathematical Bulletin/Bulletin Canadien de Mathematiques. 5 per yr. ISSN 0008-4395
- Canadian Mathematical Congress. Notes, News and Comments. 8 per yr. ISSN 0045-5164
- Canadian Mathematical Congress. Proceedings of the Biennial Seminar. biennial.

**Canadian Mathematical Congress. Research Committee**
3421 Drummond St., Montreal, Que. H3G 1X7, Canada.
- Canadian Mathematical Congress. Research Committee. Report. a. ISSN 0380-5921

**Canadian Medical Association**
1867 Alta Vista Dr., Box 8650, Ottawa, Ont. K1G 0G8, Canada.
- Canadian Journal of Surgery/Journal Canadien de Chirurgie. bi-m. ISSN 0008-428X (Co-sponsor: Royal College of Physicians and Surgeons of Canada)
- Canadian Medical Association Journal/Association Medicale Canadienne. Journal. s-m. ISSN 0008-4409

**Canadian Mental Health Association**
2160 Yonge Street, Toronto, Ont. M4S 2Z3, Canada.
- Canadian Mental Health Association. Annual Report/Association Canadienne pour la Sante Mentale. Rapport Annuel. a. ISSN 0068-9211

**Canadian Meteorological Society**
Dept. of Meteorology, McGill University, Box 6070, Montreal, Que. H3C 3G1, Canada.
- Atmosphere. (pub. by University of Toronto Press)
- Canadian Meteorological Society. Annual Congress. a. ISSN 0068-9254

**Canadian Mime Theatre**
Niagara-on-the-Lake, Ontario L0S 1J0, Canada.
- Speaking of Mime. irreg. ISSN 0381-9035

**Canadian Miner Publishing Co.**
Toronto, Ont., Canada.
- Canadian Miner. w. ISSN 0382-8042

**Canadian Mobile Home Association**
Suite 512, 55 York St., Toronto, Ont., Canada.
- Canadian Mobile Home. m. ISSN 0527-9542

**Canadian Motorist**
2 Carlton St, Toronto, Ont. M5B 1K4, Canada.
- Canadian Motorist. q. ISSN 0008-4530

**Canadian Murray Grey Association**
- Murray Grey Journal. (pub. by Idlewilde International Publishing Ltd.)

**Canadian Museums Association**
Suite 505, 56 Sparks St., Ottawa, Ont. K1P 5A9, Canada.
- C M A Gazette/A M C. Gazette. 4 per yr. ISSN 0007-859X

**Canadian Music Centre**
1263 Bay Street, Toronto M5R 2C1, Ontario, Canada.
- Canadian Music Council. Annual Meeting and Conference. Proceedings. a. ISSN 0068-9327

**Canadian Music Council**
Box 156, Sta. E, Montreal, Que. H2T 3A7, Canada
- Canada Music Book/Cahiers Canadiens de Musique. s-a. ISSN 0007-9634 (Subscr. to: Periodica, 7045 Ave. du Parc, Montreal, Que. H3N 1X8)

**Canadian Music Educators Association**
P.O. Box 1461, St. Catharines, Ont. L2R 7J8, Canada.
- Canadian Music Educator. q. ISSN 0008-4549
- Canadian Music Educators Association. Newsletter. q. ISSN 0045-5172

**Canadian Musical News Co.**
Toronto, Ont., Canada.
- Canadian Musical News. irreg. ISSN 0383-1027

**Canadian National Institute for the Blind**
1929 Bayview Ave, Toronto, Ont. M4G 3E8, Canada.
- Canadian National Institute for the Blind. National Report. a. ISSN 0068-9378
- Dots and Taps; Canada's national magazine for the deaf-blind. 5 per yr. ISSN 0012-5679
- National News of the Blind. s-a. ISSN 0027-9781

**Canadian National Railways**
P.O. Box 8100, Montreal, Que. H3C 3N4, Canada.
- Au Fil du Rail. m(10 per yr) ISSN 0004-7376

**Canadian Nationalist Party**
Winnipeg, Man., Canada.
- Canadian Nationalist. irreg. ISSN 0382-6147

**Canadian Native Friendship Centre**
10176 117th St., Edmonton, Alta, Canada.
- Edmonton Native News. m. ISSN 0046-1296

**Canadian Nature Federation**
46 Elgin St., Ottawa, Ont. K1P 5K6, Canada.
- Canadian Conservation Directory/Guide de la Conservation du Canada. irreg. ISSN 0318-2789
- Nature Canada. q. ISSN 0374-9894

**Canadian Negro Publishing Association**
Toronto, Ont., Canada.
- Canadian Negro. irreg. ISSN 0382-6171

**Canadian News Synthesis Project**
Box 6300, Station A, Toronto, Canada.
- Synthesis. m.

**Canadian Newspaper Services International Ltd.**
96 Eglinton Ave. E., Toronto, Ont. M4P 1C5, Canada.
- Blue Book of Canadian Business. a.

**Canadian Notes & Queries**
c/o William F. E. Morley, Ed., Douglas Library, Queen's University, Kingston, Ont. K7L 5C4, Canada.
- Canadian Notes & Queries/Questions & Reponses Canadiennes. 2 per yr. ISSN 0576-5803

**Canadian Nuclear Association**
65 Queen St. West, Toronto M5H 2M5, Ont., Canada.
- Canadian Annual International Conferences on Atomic Energy. Proceedings. irreg.
- Nuclear Canada/Canada Nucleaire. m. ISSN 0029-5469

**Canadian Numismatic Research Society**
10 Wesanford Place, Hamilton, Ont. L8P 1N6, Canada.
- Canadian Numismatic Research Society. Transactions. q. ISSN 0045-5202

**Canadian Nursery Trades Association**
1568 Carling Ave., Ottawa, Ont. K1Z 7M5, Canada.
- Landscape/Paysage Canada. 6 per yr. ISSN 0315-4874

**Canadian Nurses' Association**
50 the Driveway, Ottawa K2P 1E2, Ont., Canada.
- Canadian Nurse. m. ISSN 0008-4581
- Canadian Nurses' Association. Biennial Meeting. Folio of Reports. biennial. ISSN 0068-9386
- Canadian Nurses' Association. Library. Periodical Holdings. a.

- Infirmiere Canadienne. m. ISSN 0019-9605

**Canadian Office Machine Dealers Association**
Box 117, Markham, Ont. L3P 3J5, Canada.
- C O M D A Key. bi-m. ISSN 0045-5210

**Canadian Opera Company**
35-39 Front St. E., Toronto, Ont. M5E 1B3, Canada.
- Canadian Opera Guild. Overtures. q.

**Canadian Ophthalmological Society**
Box 8650, Ottawa, Ont. K1G 0G8, Ottawa Ont., Canada.
- Canadian Journal of Ophthalmology/Journal Canadien d'Ophthalmologie. q. ISSN 0008-4182

**Canadian Oral History Association**
c/o Public Archives Canada, Sound Archives Section, 395 Wellington St., Ottawa, Ont. K1A 0N3, Canada.
- Canadian Oral History Association. Bulletin. irreg. ISSN 0383-6576

**Canadian Orienteering Federation**
1B, 445 Gallard Blvd., Dorval, Que., Canada.
- C O F Newsletter. irreg. ISSN 0382-8255

**Canadian Osteopathic Association**
126/3545 Cote des Neiges Rd., Montreal, Que. H3H 1V1, Canada.
- Canadian D. O. Newsletter. irreg. ISSN 0084-8433

**Canadian Otolaryngological Society**
- Journal of Otolaryngology. (pub. by O R L Publications Ltd.)

**Canadian Paper Money Society**
Box 356, Fredericton, N.B. E3B 4Z9, Canada.
- Canadian Paper Money Journal. q. ISSN 0045-5237

**Canadian Paraplegic Association**
520 Sutherland Dr., Toronto, Ont. M4G 3V9, Canada.
- Caliper. q. ISSN 0045-4001
- Canadian Paraplegic Association. Annual Report. a. ISSN 0068-9424

**Canadian Paraplegic Association. British Columbia Division**
780 S. W. Marine Dr., Vancouver 14, B. C., Canada.
- Paragraphic. q. ISSN 0048-2935

**Canadian Paraplegic Association. Central Western Division**
825 Sherbrooke St., Winnipeg 2, Man., Canada.
- Paratracks. bi-m. ISSN 0048-296X

**Canadian Paraplegic Association. New Brunswick Division**
212 Queen St., Rm. 302, Fredericton, N.B., Canada.
- Para Elite. bi-m. ISSN 0031-1545

**Canadian Parks Recreation Association**
- Recreation Canada. (pub. by Maclean-Hunter Ltd.)

**Canadian Peace Research Institute**
25 Dundana Ave., Dundas, Ont. L9H 4E5, Canada.
- Peace Research; a quarterly journal of original research on the problem of war. q. ISSN 0008-4697
- Peace Research Abstracts Journal. m. ISSN 0031-3599
- Peace Research Reviews. irreg. ISSN 0553-4283

**Canadian Petroleum Association**
Calgary, Alta., Canada.
- Canadian Petroleum Association. Statistical Yearbook. a. ISSN 0068-9432

**Canadian Pharmaceutical Association**
175 College St., Toronto, Ont. M5T 1P8, Canada.
- Canadian Journal of Pharmaceutical Sciences. q. ISSN 0008-4190
- Compendium of Pharmaceuticals and Specialties. a. ISSN 0069-7966

**Canadian Philosophical Association**
1390 Sherbrooke St. W., Montreal, Que. H3G 1K2, Canada.
- Dialogue; Canadian philosophical review/revue Canadienne de philosophie. q. ISSN 0012-2173

**Canadian Photopress Publishing Ltd.**
Box 113, Sta. M., Toronto, Ont. MGS 4T2, Canada.
- Krzyk/Outcry; the North American magazine in Polish. m. ISSN 0317-5545

**Canadian Physiological Society**
Dept. of Physiology, Queen's University, Kingston, Ont. K7L 3N6, Canada.
- Physiology Canada. 3 per yr. ISSN 0048-4067

**Canadian Physiotherapy Association**
25 Imperial St., Toronto M5P 1B9, Ont., Canada.
- Physiotherapy Canada/Physiotherapie. 5 per yr. ISSN 0300-0508

**Canadian Phytopathological Society**
c/o Dr. H. W. Johnston, Research Station, Agricultural Canada, Box 1210, Charlottetown, P.E.I. C1A 7M8, Canada.
- Canadian Phytopathological Society. Proceedings. a. ISSN 0068-9440

**Canadian Plains Research Center**
University of Regina, Regina, Sask. S4S 0A2, Canada.
- Prairie Forum. s-a. ISSN 0317-6282

**Canadian Podiatry Association**
c/o Dr. R. Steiner, Ed., Main Sq., Suite 10, 2615 Danforth Ave., Toronto, Ont. M4C 1L6, Canada.
- Canadian Podiatrist. q. ISSN 0008-4786

**Canadian Political Science Association**
c/o Queens University, Dept. of Political Studies, Kingston, Ontario, Canada.
- Canadian Journal of Political Science/Revue Canadienne de Science Politique. (pub. by Wilfrid Laurier University Press)
- Canadian Political Science Association. Theses in Canadial Political Studies, Completed and in Progress. biennial.

**Canadian Postmasters Association**
130 Albert St., Suite 1204, Ottawa K1P 5G4, Ont., Canada.
- Canadian Postmaster/Maitre de Poste Canadien. 8 per yr. ISSN 0008-4794

**Canadian Psychiatric Association**
225 Lisgar St., Suite 103, Ottawa, Ont. K2P 0C6, Canada.
- Canadian Psychiatric Association Journal. 8 per yr. ISSN 0008-4824

**Canadian Psychological Association**
1390 Sherbrooke St. W., Montreal 109, Que., Canada.
- Canadian Journal of Behavioural Science/Revue Canadienne des Sciences du Comportement. q. ISSN 0008-400X
- Canadian Journal of Psychology/Revue Canadienne de Psychologie. (pub. by University of Toronto Press)
- Canadian Psychological Association. Directory. biennial. ISSN 0068-9475

**Canadian Public Health Association**
1335 Carling Ave., Suite 210, Ottawa, Ont. K1Z 8N8, Canada.
- Canadian Journal of Public Health. bi-m. ISSN 0008-4263
- Canadian Public Health Association. Annual Report. a. ISSN 0068-9483

**Canadian Pulp and Paper Association**
2300 Sun Life Building, Montreal, Que. H3B 2X9, Canada.
- Canadian Pulp and Paper Association. Annual Newsprint Supplement. a. ISSN 0316-4241
- Canadian Pulp and Paper Association. Newsprint Data; statistics of world demand and supply. a. ISSN 0068-9491
- Canadian Pulp and Paper Association. Pulp and Paper Report. a. ISSN 0068-9505
- Canadian Pulp and Paper Association. Technical Section. Proceedings. a. ISSN 0068-9521
- Canadian Pulp & Paper Association. Technical Section. Transactions. q. ISSN 0317-882X
- Canadian Pulp and Paper Association. Woodlands Section. Publications. irreg. ISSN 0068-9548
- Pulp & Paper Canada. (pub. by National Business Publications Ltd.)

**Canadian Quarter Horse Association**
- Canadian Quarter Horse Journal. (pub. by Golden Arc Publishing and Typesetting Ltd.)

**Canadian Railroad Historical Association**
Box 22, Sta. B, Montreal, Que. H3B 3J5, Canada.
- Canadian Rail/Rail Canadien. m. ISSN 0008-4875

**Canadian Railway Club, Inc.**
Box 162, Station A, Montreal, Que. H3C 1C5, Canada.
- Canadian Railway Club. Official Proceedings. s-a. ISSN 0008-4883

**Canadian Real Estate Association**
99 Duncan Mill Rd, Don Mills, Ont, Canada.
- C R E A Reporter; official organ of real estate in Canada. m. ISSN 0315-3843

**Canadian Red Book**
481 University Ave., Toronto Ont. M5W 1A7, Canada.
- Canadian Red Book; official used car valuations. m. ISSN 0045-527X

**Canadian Red Cross Society**
National Headquarters, 95 Wellesley St. E., Toronto, Ont M4Y 1H6, Canada.
- Canadian Red Cross Society. Annual Report. a. ISSN 0068-9572
- Canadian Red Cross Society. Ontario Division. News Bulletin. q. ISSN 0045-5288
- Despatch. q. ISSN 0046-0087

**Canadian Red Cross Society. Alberta - Northwest Territories Division**
1504 First St. S.E., Calgary, Alberta, Canada.
- Action. q. ISSN 0382-4527

**Canadian Rehabilitation Council for the Disabled**
Suite 2110, One Yonge St., Toronto, Ont. M5E 1E8, Canada.
- Canadian Rehabilitation Council for the Disabled. Annual Report. a. ISSN 0068-9580
- Canadian Rehabilitation Council for the Disabled. Employment Bulletin. bi-m. ISSN 0315-3525
- Rehabilitation Digest. q. ISSN 0048-7139

**Canadian Religious Conference**
324 Laurier E, Ottawa, Ont. K1N 6P6, Canada.
- Donum Dei. a. ISSN 0070-7104
- Vita Evangelica. irreg., nos. 8, 9, 1976. ISSN 0082-7304

**Canadian Research Centre for Anthropology**
223 Main St., Ottawa, Ont. K1S 1C4, Canada.
- Anthropologica. s-a. ISSN 0003-5459 (Saint Paul University)

**Canadian Retail Hardware Association**
290 Merton St., Toronto M4S 1B2, Ont., Canada.
- C R H A Reporter. m. ISSN 0045-5296

**Canadian Review of Studies in Nationalism, Inc.**
Charlottetown, P. E. I., Canada.
- Canadian Review of Studies in Nationalism. s-a.

**Canadian Rodeo Cowboys' Association**
- Canadian Rodeo News. (pub. by Canadian Rodeo News Ltd.)

**Canadian Rodeo News Ltd.**
315A-36th Ave. S.E., Calgary, Alta. T2G 1W1, Canada.
- Canadian Rodeo News. bi-m. ISSN 0008-4964 (Canadian Rodeo Cowboys' Association)

**Canadian Rose Society**
c/o M. A. Cadsby, Q.C., 28 Hilltop Rd., Toronto 10, Ont., Canada.
- Canadian Rose Annual. a. ISSN 0068-9602

**Canadian Scene**
Suite 305, 2 College St., Toronto M5G 1K3, Ont., Canada.
- Canadian Scene. fortn. ISSN 0045-5334

**Canadian Schizophrenia Foundation**
2135 Albert St., Regina, Sask. S4P 2V1, Canada.
- Huxley Institute-C.S.F. Newsletter. q. (Co-Sponsor: Huxley Institute for Biosocial Research)
- Journal of Orthomolecular Psychiatry. q. ISSN 0317-0209

**Canadian School Library Association**
151 Sparks St., Ottawa, Ont., K1P 5E3, Canada.
- Canadian School Library Association. Basic Book List for Canadian Schools. Elementary Division. irreg.
- Canadian School Library Association. Basic Book List for Canadian Schools. Junior Division.

- Canadian School Library Association. Basic Book List for Canadian Schools. Senior Division.
- Moccasin Telegraph. q. ISSN 0076-9878

**Canadian Seed Growers Association**
P.O. Box 8455, Ottawa, Ont. K1G 3T1, Canada.
- Canadian Seed Growers Association. Annual Report. a. ISSN 0068-9610
- Seed Scoop. q. ISSN 0049-0040

**Canadian Semiotics Research Association**
- Canadian Journal of Research in Semiotics/Journal Canadien de Recherche Semiotique. (pub. by University of Alberta. Department of Romance Languages)

**Canadian Shorthorn Association**
Gummer Bldg., Guelph, Ont., Canada.
- Shorthorn News. bi-m. ISSN 0037-427X

**Canadian Ski Association**
c/o T. Whelpton, 643 Yonge St., Toronto, Ontario MyY 2A1, Canada.
- Ski Canada Journal. bi-m.

**Canadian Slovak Benefit Society**
P. O. Box 61, Station C, Toronto 145, Ont., Canada.
- Slovensky Hlas/Slovak Voice. m. ISSN 0037-7015

**Canadian Slovak League**
400-A Queen St. W., Toronto 2-B, Ont., Canada.
- Kanadsky Slovak/Canadian Slovak. w. ISSN 0047-3154

**Canadian Society for Asian Studies**
209C rue Slater, Ottawa, Ont. K1P 5H3, Canada.
- C S A S Newsletter. q. ISSN 0382-4772

**Canadian Society for Chemical Engineering**
151 Slater St., Ottawa, Ont., K1P 5H3, Canada.
- Canadian Journal of Chemical Engineering. (pub. by Chemical Institute of Canada)
- Canadian Society for Chemical Engineering Symposium Series. (pub. by Plenum Publishing Corp. US)
- Directory of Chemical Engineering Research in Canadian Universities. a. ISSN 0070-525X

**Canadian Society for Education Through Art**
112 Oakdale Ave., St. Catherines, Ont. L2P 3J9, Canada.
- Canadian Society for Education through Art. Annual Journal. a. ISSN 0068-9645
- Canadian Society for Education through Art. Newsletter. q. ISSN 0045-5369

**Canadian Society for Immunology**
McMaster University Medical Centre, Dept. of Medicine, Hamilton, Ont., Canada.
- Canadian Society for Immunology. Bulletin. irreg. ISSN 0068-9653

**Canadian Society for Legal History**
c/o York University Law Library, 4700 Keele St., Downsview, Ont. M3T 1P3, Canada.
- Canadian Society for Legal History. Newsletter. irreg. ISSN 0317-543X

**Canadian Society for Mechanical Engineering**
c/o Ste 700, EIC Building, 2050 Mansfield St., Montreal, H3A 1Y9, Canada.
- Canadian Society for Mechanical Engineering. Transactions. q. ISSN 0315-8977

**Canadian Society for the Study of Education**
Box 1000, Faculty of Education, University of Alberta, Edmonton, Alta. T6G 2G5, Canada.
- C S S E Yearbook. a. ISSN 0315-727X
- Canadian Journal of Education/Revue Canadienne de l'Education. q. ISSN 0380-2361

**Canadian Society for the Study of Higher Education**
Suite 8039, 130 St. George St., Toronto M5S 2T4, Ontario, Canada.
- Canadian Journal of Higher Education/Revue Canadienne d'Enseignement Superieur. s-a. ISSN 0316-1218

**Canadian Society of Agricultural Engineering**
151 Slater St., Ottawa, Ont. K1P 5H4, Canada.
- Canadian Agricultural Engineering. s-a. ISSN 0045-432X

**Canadian Society of Agronomy**
c/o A. I. C., 151 Slater St., Ottawa 4, Ont., Canada.
- Canadian Society of Agronomy. Annual Meeting. Proceedings. a. ISSN 0068-9688

**Canadian Society of Animal Production**
No. 907, 151 Slater St., Ottawa 4, Ont., Canada.
- Canadian Journal of Animal Science. (pub. by Agricultural Institute of Canada)
- Canadian Society of Animal Production. Proceedings. a. ISSN 0068-9696

**Canadian Society of Biblical Studies**
Religious Studies, University of Calgary, Calgary, Alta, T2N 1N4, Canada.
- Canadian Society of Biblical Studies. Bulletin/ Societe Canadienne des Etudes Bibliques. Bulletin. a. ISSN 0068-970X

**Canadian Society of Clinical Chemists**
151 Slater St., Suite 906, Ottawa, Ont. K1P 5H3, Canada.
- Clinical Biochemistry. 6 per yr. ISSN 0009-9120

**Canadian Society of Creative Leathercraft**
c/o Mrs. G. F. Bottrill, 107 Donald St., Barrie, Ont. L4N 1E6, Canada.
- Canadian Leathercraft. q. ISSN 0045-5121

**Canadian Society of Environmental Biologists**
Box 962 Sta. F, Toronto, Ont. M4Y 2N9, Canada.
- Canadian Society of Environmental Biologists Newsletter. q.

**Canadian Society of Exploration Geophysicists**
Box 117, Calgary, Alta. T2P 2G9, Canada.
- Canadian Society of Exploration Geophysicists. Journal. q. ISSN 0008-5022

**Canadian Society of Forensic Science**
P.O. Box 9051, Ottawa, Ont. K1G 3T8, Canada.
- Canadian Society of Forensic Science Journal/ Societe Canadienne des Sciences Judiciaires Journal. q. ISSN 0008-5030

**Canadian Society of Hospital Pharmacists**
Pharmacy Dept., University Hospital, Saskatoon, Sask. S7N 0W8, Canada.
- Canadian Journal of Hospital Pharmacy. bi-m. ISSN 0008-4123

**Canadian Society of Immunology**
- Canadian Society for Immunology. International Symposium. Proceedings. (pub. by S. Karger AG SZ)

**Canadian Society of Laboratory Technologists**
Box 830, Hamilton L8N 3N8, Ont., Canada.
- Canadian Journal of Medical Technology. bi-m. ISSN 0008-4158
- Canadian Society of Laboratory Technologists. Bulletin/Association Canadienne des Technologistes de Laboratoire. Bulletin. bi-m. ISSN 0045-5377

**Canadian Society of Petroleum Geologists**
612 Lougheed Bldg, Calgary, Alta. T2P 1M7, Canada.
- Bulletin of Canadian Petroleum Geology. q. ISSN 0007-4802
- C S P G Memoirs. irreg.
- C S P G Newsletter. m. ISSN 0318-577X
- Canadian Society of Petroleum Geologists. Bulletin. q.

**Canadian Society of Radiological Technicians**
Ste. 410, 280 Metcalfe St., Ottawa, Ont. K2P 1R7, Canada.
- Canadian Journal of Radiography, Radiotherapy, Nuclear Medicine. bi-m. ISSN 0319-4434

**Canadian Society of Respiratory Technologists**
203-818 Portage Ave., Winnipeg, Manitoba R3G 0N4, Canada.
- Respiratory Technology. q.

**Canadian Society of Rural Extension**
Agricultural Institute of Canada, No. 907, 151 Slater St., Ottawa 4, Ont. K1P 5H4, Canada.
- Canadian Society of Rural Extension. Meeting and Convention. Proceedings. a. ISSN 0068-9718

**Canadian Sociology and Anthropology Association**
Box 878, Montreal, Que., Canada.
- Canadian Review of Sociology and Anthropology/ Revue Canadienne de Sociologie et d'Anthropologie. q. ISSN 0008-4948

- Canadian Sociology and Anthropology Association. Bulletin. 3 per yr. ISSN 0008-5049
- Guide to Departments of Sociology and Anthropology in Canadian Universities/Annuaire des Departements de Sociologie et d'Anthropologie au Canada. a. ISSN 0315-0895

**Canadian Speech and Hearing Association**
University of Alberta, Corbett Hall, Edmonton, Alta. T6G 2G4, Canada.
- Human Communications. 3 per yr.

**Canadian Sport Parachuting Association**
Box 848, Burlington, Ont. L7R 3Y7, Canada.
- Canadian Parachutist. 8 per yr. ISSN 0045-5245

**Canadian Stage and Arts Publications, Ltd.**
52 Avenue Rd., 2nd floor, Toronto M5R 2G3, Ont., Canada.
- Performing Arts in Canada. q. ISSN 0031-5230

**Canadian Standards Association**
178 Rexdale Blvd., Rexdale, Ont. M9W 1R3, Canada.
- C S A and the Consumer; a guide. q. ISSN 0011-2313
- C S A Quarterly Review. q. ISSN 0007-9065
- Canadian Standards Association. Annual Report. a.
- Canadian Standards Association. Standards Catalogue. a.
- Standards/Canada. q. ISSN 0038-965X

**Canadian Tax Foundation**
100 University Ave., Toronto, Ont. M5J 1V6, Canada.
- Canadian Tax Foundation. Provincial and Municipal Finances. biennial. ISSN 0317-946X
- Canadian Tax Journal. bi-m. ISSN 0008-5111
- Canadian Tax Papers. irreg. ISSN 0008-512X
- Corporate Management Tax Conference. a. ISSN 0070-0282
- National Finances; an Analysis of the Revenues and Expenditures of the Government of Canada. a. ISSN 0077-4529
- Tax Memo. irreg.

**Canadian Teachers' Federation**
110 Argyle Ave., Ottawa, Ont. K2P 1B4, Canada.
- Canadian Teachers' Federation. Bibliographies in Education. irreg.

**Canadian Technical Asphalt Association**
P.O. Box 1387, Victoria, B.C., Canada.
- Canadian Technical Asphalt Association. Proceedings of the Annual Conference. a. ISSN 0068-984X

**Canadian Technical Publications Ltd.**
Station F, 36B Prince Arthur Ave., Toronto, Ont. M5R 1A9, Canada.
- Engineering. m. ISSN 0013-7774

**Canadian Textile Journal Publishing Co. Ltd.**
4920 de Maisonneuve Blvd. W., Suite 307, Montreal, Que. H3Z 1N1, Canada.
- Canadian Cleaner & Launderer. m. ISSN 0008-3224
- Canadian Textile Journal. ISSN 0008-5170
- Manual of the Textile Industry of Canada. a. ISSN 0076-4183
- Textile Manual. a.

**Canadian Theatre Review Publications**
222 Admin Studies, York University, Downsview, Ont. M3J 1P3, Canada.
- Canada on Stage: Canadian Theatre Review Yearbook. a. ISSN 0380-9455

**Canadian Theological College**
Regina, Sask., Canada.
- Foreign Focus. irreg. ISSN 0315-8691

**Canadian Toy Manufacturers Association**
Box 294, Kleinburg, Ont. L0J 1C0, Canada.
- Toy and Decoration Fair. a. ISSN 0317-9443

**Canadian Tribune**
924 King St. W., Toronto, Ont. M5V 1P5, Canada.
- Canadian Tribune. w.

**Canadian Trotting Association**
233 Evans Ave., Toronto, Ont. M8Z 1J6, Canada.
- Trot. m.

**Canadian Tuberculosis and Respiratory Disease Association**
345 O'Connor St., Ottawa, Ont. K2P 1V9, Canada.
- Canadian Tuberculosis and Respiratory Disease Association. Annual Report. a. ISSN 0068-9939
- Canadian Tuberculosis and Respiratory Disease Associaton Bulletin. q. ISSN 0008-5235

**Canadian Union of General Employees**
81 Haig Ave., Scarborough 714, Ont., Canada.
- Independence; Canadian independent Labour news. m. ISSN 0046-8835

**Canadian Union of Public Employees**
Suite 800, 233 Gilmour St., Ottawa, Ont. K2P 0P5, Canada.
- C U P E Convention Report. irreg. ISSN 0380-7789
- Canadian Union of Public Employees. Journal. m. ISSN 0045-5512

**Canadian University Service Overseas**
151 Slater St., 10th Floor, Ottawa, Ont. K1P 5H5, Canada.
- C U S O Forum. bi-m. ISSN 0318-6830

**Canadian Urban Transit Association**
1138 Bathurst St., Toronto, Ont. M5R 3H2, Canada.
- Transit Fact Book. a. ISSN 0082-5913

**Canadian Veterinary Medical Association**
360 Bronson Ave., Ottawa K1R 6J3, Ont., Canada.
- Canadian Journal of Comparative Medicine/ Revue Canadienne de Medecine Comparee. q. ISSN 0008-4050
- Canadian Veterinary Journal/Revue Veterinaire Canadienne. m. ISSN 0008-5286

**Canadian Vocational Association**
251 Bank St., Suite 608, Ottawa, Ont. K2P 1X3, Canada.
- Canadian Vocational Journal. q. ISSN 0045-5520

**Canadian Volleyball Association**
- Volleyball Technical Journal. (pub. by Canadian Volleyball Publications)

**Canadian Volleyball Publications**
78 Tedford Drive, Scarborough, Ont. M1R 1M4, Canada.
- Volleyball Technical Journal. 3 per yr. ISSN 0315-0887 (Canadian Volleyball Association)

**Canadian War Records Office**
London, Ont., Canada.
- Canadian Daily Record. irreg. ISSN 0308-6461

**Canadian Wheelmen's Association**
London, Ont., Canada.
- Canadian Wheelman. m. ISSN 0383-137X (Co-sponsor: Cyclists' Touring Club in Canada)

**Canadian Wild Horse Society**
1120 Bird Rd., Richmond, B.C. V6X 1N8, Canada.
- Cayuse Conserver. q. ISSN 0045-6012

**Canadian Wildlife Federation**
1673 Carling Ave., Ottawa, Ont. K2A 1C4, Canada.
- Ottawa Report. bi-m.
- Wildlife Crusader. 7 per yr. ISSN 0043-5457 (Co-sponsors: Manitoba Game and Fish Association; Saskatchewan Fish and Game Association)
- Wildlife Report: the Canadian Scene. bi-m.

**Canadian Woodmen of the World**
Suite 711, 200 Queens Ave., London, Ont. N6A 1J3, Canada.
- Canadian Woodman. 3 per yr. ISSN 0045-558X

**Canadian Youth Hostels Association, North West Region**
10922 88th Ave., Edmonton, Alta. T6G 0Z1, Canada.
- Pathfinder. 3 per yr. ISSN 0031-2940

**Canadian Youth Hostels Association Region. Pacific Region**
1557 W. Broadway, Vancouver, B.C. V6J 1W6, Canada.
- Pacific Hosteller. q. ISSN 0030-8692

**Canvet Publications Ltd.**
Legion House, Suite 504, 359 Kent St., Ottawa, Ont. K2P 0R6, Canada.
- Legion. m. ISSN 0024-0435

**Canyouth Publications**
Box 5112, Postal Stn. F, Ottawa, Ont. K2C 3G7, Canada.
- Canadian Leader. 10 per yr. ISSN 0036-9462

**Capilano College**
2055 Purcell Way, N. Vancouver, B.C. V7J 3H5, Canada.
- Capilano Review. s-a. ISSN 0315-3754

**Ronald Caplan, Ed. & Pub.**
Wreck Cove, Cape Breton, Nova Scotia, Canada.
- Cape Breton's Magazine; devoted to history, natural history & future of Cape Breton Island. bi-m.

**Caribook Ltd.**
1255 Yonge St., Toronto, Ont. M4T 1W6, Canada.
- Caribbean Business News. m. ISSN 0045-5792
- West Indies and Caribbean Year Book. a. ISSN 0083-8233

**Carleton Board of Education**
c/o Mary Curry, Ed., 133 Greenbank Rd., Ottawa, Ont. K2H 6L3.
- Carleton Education Bulletin. 8 per yr. ISSN 0045-5830

**Carleton Press**
Box 184, Kamloops, B.C., Canada.
- Columbia Pictorial. m. ISSN 0384-0093

**Carleton University**
Ottawa, Ont. K1S 5B6, Canada.
- Carleton University, Ottawa. Department of Geology. Geological Papers. irreg. ISSN 0069-0619
- Russian Language Journal. 3 per yr. ISSN 0036-0252 (Co-sponsor: Michigan State University)

**Carleton University. Department of German**
Ottawa K1S 5B6, Canada.
- Carleton Germanic Papers. a.

**Carleton University. Department of Mathematics**
Ottawa, Ont. K1S 5B6, Canada.
- Carleton Lecture Note Series. irreg.
- Carleton Mathematical Series. irreg. ISSN 0069-0600

**Carleton University. Norman Paterson School of International Affairs**
Ottawa, Ont. K1S 5B6, Canada.
- Carleton University, Ottawa. Norman Paterson School of International Affairs. Bibliography Series. irreg. (1-2 per yr) ISSN 0383-2848
- Current Comment; comments of controversial topics in international affairs. irreg. (approx. 5 per yr.)

**Carleton University. School of Journalism**
Ottawa, Ont. K1S 5B6, Canada.
- Hello Ottawa. a. ISSN 0383-6363

**Carleton University Students Association, Inc.**
Carleton University, Ottawa K1S 5B6, Canada.
- Charlatan. w. ISSN 0315-1859

**Carswell Co. Ltd.**
2330 Midland Ave., Agincourt, Ont. M1S 1P7, Canada.
- Canadian Bankruptcy Reports. m (2 vols per year) ISSN 0068-8347
- Canadian Current Law. m. ISSN 0008-3356
- Queen's Law Journal. 2 parts per year. (Queen's University Law School)
- Western Weekly Reports. w (6 vols per year) ISSN 0049-7525

**E. Graydon Carter, Ed. & Pub.**
Cooper House, 251 Cooper St., Ottawa, Ont. K2P 0G2, Canada.
- Canadian Review; feature newsmagazine of the arts, politics, science, current affairs, sports and entertainment. m. ISSN 0315-1190

**Cash Crop Farming Publications Ltd.**
222 Argyle Ave., Delhi, Ont., Canada.
- Canadian Fruitgrower. 9 per yr. ISSN 0045-4885
- Canadian Tobacco Grower. 10 per yr. ISSN 0008-5189
- Cash Crop Farming. 10 per yr. ISSN 0008-7297

**Catholic Children's Aid Society of Metropolitan Toronto**
26 Maitland St., Toronto M4Y 1C6, Ont., Canada.
- Partners in Child Care. q. ISSN 0048-3052

**Catholic Church Extension Society of Canada**
67 Bond St., Toronto, Ont. M5B 1X6, Canada.
- Catholic Register. w.

**Catholic Health Association**
312 Daly Ave., Ottawa 2, Ont, K1N 6G7, Canada.
- Catholic Hospital. bi-m. ISSN 0008-8099

**Catholic Hospital Association of Canada**
312 Daly St., Ottawa K1N 6G7, Canada.
- Catholic Hospital Association of Canada. Directory. a. ISSN 0380-8475

**Cavell Enterprises Ltd.**
Box 834, Iroquois Falls "A", Ont., Canada.
- Enterprise. w. ISSN 0013-8657

**Centennial Commission**
- Canadian Local Histories to 1950. A Bibliography. Histoires Locales et Regionales Canadiennes des Origines A 1950. (pub. by University of Toronto Press)

**Central Fraser Valley Star Publications**
Box 220, Aldergrove, B. C., Canada.
- British Columbia Rancher. m. ISSN 0045-3021

**Central Mortgage and Housing Corporation**
Montreal Road, Ottawa, Ont. K1A OP7, Canada.
- Canadian Housing Statistics. a with monthly supplements. ISSN 0068-8940
- Habitat. bi-m. ISSN 0017-6370

**Centrale de l'Enseignement du Quebec**
2336 Chemin Ste-Foy, Quebec 10, Que., Canada.
- Ligne Directe. m. ISSN 0315-4998

**Centre Canadien des Recherches Genealogiques**
C.P. 845, Haute-Ville, Que. G1R 4S7, Canada.
- French Canadian and Acadian Genealogical Review. q. ISSN 0016-1047

**Centre d'Animation de Developpement et de Recherche en Education**
1940 est, Henri-Bourassa, Montreal, Que. H2B 1S2, Canada.
- Association des Colleges du Quebec Annuaire. a.
- Association des Institutions d'Enseignement Secondaire. Annuaire. a. ISSN 0066-8990
- Federation des Colleges d'Enseignement General et Professionnel. a. ISSN 0084-649X
- Prospectives. 4 per yr. ISSN 0033-1511

**Centre d'Etudes et de Documentation Europeenees**
Universite de Montreal, 5255 Avenue Decelles, Montreal H3T 1V6, Canada.
- Centre d'Etudes et de Documentation Europeennes. Bulletin d'Information Documentaire. q.

**Centre de Recherche en Civilisation Canadienne-Francaise**
- Centre de Recherche en Civilisation Canadienne-Francaise. Bulletin. (pub. by University of Ottawa Press)

**Centre de Recherches en Relations Humaines**
Montreal, Quebec, Canada.
- Contributions a l'Etude des Sciences de l'Homme. irreg. ISSN 0589-5820

**Centre Quebecois de Relations Internationales**
Faculte des Sciences Sociales, Universite Laval, Quebec G1K 7P4, Canada
(Subscr. Address: les Presses de l'Universite Laval, Box 2447, Quebec-Terminus, P. Q., G1K 7R4, Canada)
- Etudes Internationales. q. ISSN 0014-2123
- Informations Universitaires en Relations Internationales et Etudes Etrangeres. irreg. ISSN 0046-9467

**Cercles des Jeunes Naturalistes**
4101 E. Rue Sherbrooke, Montreal, Que. H1X 2B2, Canada.
- Cercles des Jeunes Naturalistes. Feuillets du Club. m. ISSN 0045-6179
- Naturaliste. 10 per yr. ISSN 0028-078X

**Publications Chabanel**
Montreal, Que., Canada.
- Evasion. m. ISSN 0381-8349

**Chambre de Commerce du District de Montreal**
1080 Beaver Hall Hill, Montreal, Que. H2Z 1T1, Canada.
- Commerce Montreal. s-m.

**Chambre de Commerce Francaise au Canada**
1080 Cote du Beaver Hall, Bureau 826, Montreal, Que. H2Z 1S8, Canada.
- Action Canada France. 10 per yr. ISSN 0318-7306

**Chambre des Notaires du Quebec**
C.P. 130, Outremont, Que. H2V 4M8, Canada.
- Revue du Notariat. m.(except July & Aug.) ISSN 0035-2632

**Barry Chamish & Harry Peters, Eds. & Pubs.**
1-277 River Ave., Winnepeg R3L 0B6, Canada.
- Split Level. s-a.

**Champlain Regional College**
Lennoxville, Que. J1M 2A1, Canada.
- Simgames; a guide to simulation & gaming. q. ISSN 0384-0425

**Champlain Society**
Royal York Hotel, 100 Front St. W., Toronto, Ont., M5J 1E3, Canada.
- Champlain Society, Toronto. Report. a. ISSN 0069-2646
- Ontario Series. (pub. by University of Toronto Press)

**Chantiers Pedagogiques**
140 Ouest, 94 rue, Charlesbourg, Quebec 7, Canada.
- Chantiers Pedagogiques. 8 per yr. ISSN 0009-1618

**Charlottetown Group Publishers**
35 Britian St., Toronto Ont., Canada.
- City Magazine. bi-m.

**Charters Publishing Co., Ltd.**
Henderson Ave., Brampton, Ont., Canada.
- Ontario Shade Tree Council. Newsletter. q. ISSN 0048-1858

**Chemical Institute of Canada**
151 Slater St. Suite 906, Ottawa, Ont. K1P 5H3, Canada.
- Canadian Journal of Chemical Engineering. 6 per yr. ISSN 0008-4034 (Canadian Society for Chemical Engineering)
- Canadian Wood Chemistry Symposium. Abstracts. irreg. ISSN 0576-6435
- Chemistry in Canada. 11 per yr. ISSN 0009-3114

**Chesswood House Publishing Ltd.**
542 Mt. Pleasant Rd., Suite 103, Toronto, Ont. M4S 2M7, Canada.
- Canadian Training Methods. bi-m.

**Chevaliers du Colomb du Quebec**
3565 Berri, Montreal H2L 4G5, Que., Canada.
- Colombien. m. ISSN 0384-0298

**Chien d'Or**
c/o Editor, English Department, Carleton University, Ottawa, Ont., Canada.
- Chien d'Or/Golden Dog. irreg. ISSN 0315-467X

**Child Guidance Clinic of Greater Winnipeg**
700 Elgin Ave., Winnipeg, Man. R3E 1B2, Canada.
- Winnipeg. Child Guidance Clinic. Annual Report. a. ISSN 0084-036X

**Children's Aid Society of Metropolitan Toronto**
33 Charles St., E. Toronto M4Y 1R9 Ont., Canada.
- Our Children. 3 per yr. ISSN 0030-6800

**Children's Aid Society of Ottawa**
1370 Bank St., Ottawa, Ont. K1H 7Y3, Canada.
- Children's Aid Society of Ottawa. Information Bulletin. q. (prep. by its Foster Parent Association)
- Communique. q.

**Children's Apparel Manufacturers Association**
No. 304, 8235 Mountain Sights Ave., Montreal 308, Que., Canada.
- Children's Apparel Merchandising Aids. q. ISSN 0045-6691

**Chimo Media Ltd.**
21 Prince Andrew Place, Don Mills, Ont. M3C 2H2, Canada.
- Audio Preview. a.
- Sound Canada. 12 per yr.

**Chinese-Canadian Press**
3289 Main St., Vancouver 10, B.C., Canada.
- Chinese-Canadian Bulletin. m.

**Chinese Publicity Bureau Ltd.**
459 E. Hastings St., Vancouver, B.C. V6A 1P5, Canada.
- Chinatown News. s-m. ISSN 0009-4501

**Chinese Voice Publishing & Printing Co. Ltd**
233 Main St., Vancouver 4, B.C., Canada.
- Chinese Voice. d. ISSN 0009-4641

**Chinook Chemicals Corp.**
- E C O/L O G Information Services. (pub. by Corpus Publishers Services Ltd.)

**Christian Nationalist Party**
c/o K. H. von Harten, Toronto, Ont., Canada.
- Christian Nationalist Party News. irreg. ISSN 0383-624X

**Christian Press Ltd.**
159 Henderson Hwy., Winnipeg, Man. R2L 1L4, Canada.
- Mennonite Brethren Herald. fortn. ISSN 0025-9349 (Conference of Mennonite Brethren Churches of Canada)
- Mennonitische Rundschau/Mennonite Review. w. ISSN 0025-9314 (Mennonite Brethren Conference of Canada)

**Christian Reformed Immigration Societies in Canada**
- Calvinist Contact. (pub. by Guardian Publishing)

**Christian Transportation Inc. Bus Division**
Toronto, Ont., Canada.
- Christian Bus Driver. irreg. ISSN 0382-8727

**Church Army in Canada**
397 Brunswick Ave., Toronto, Ont. M5R 2Z2, Canada.
- Crusader (Toronto) irreg. ISSN 0382-4314

**Cie de Publication Rurale**
5670 rue Chauveau, Montreal, Que. H1N 1H2, Canada.
- Bulletin des Agriculteurs. m. ISSN 0007-4446

**Ciments Canada Lafarge Ltd.**
Sales Promotion and Advertising Dept., 606 rue Cathcart, Montreal, Que. H3B 7K9, Canada.
- Liaison. irreg. ISSN 0318-1340

**Cinema-Canada (Montreal)**
C.P. 398, Outremont Sta., Montreal, Que. H2V 4N3, Canada.
- Cinema/Canada (Montreal) 10 per yr.

**Cinema-Quebec**
C.P. 309, Sta. Outremont, Montreal, Que. H2V 4N1, Canada.
- Cinema-Quebec. 10 per yr.

**CIRIEC Canada**
Dept. of Economics, Sir George Williams Univ., 1455 Boul de Maisonneuve, Montreal 107, Canada.
- Canadian Journal of Public and Cooperative Economy/Revue Canadienne d'Economie Publique et Cooperative. s-a.

**Citoyens du Cosmos**
B.P. 3, Jonquiere, Que. G7X 7V8, Canada.
- Nouveau Cosmos-Express. m. ISSN 0319-4345

**City of Ottawa Coin Club**
Box 6094, Sta. J, Ottawa, Ont. K2A 1T2, Canada.
- City of Ottawa Coin Club. Monthly Bulletin. m. ISSN 0045-7019 (Co-sponsor: Canadian Numismatic Association)

**Civic Garden Centre**
777 Lawrence Avenue East, Don Mills, Ontario M3C 1P2, Canada.
- Trellis. m.

**Clan Donald Association of Nova Scotia**
c/o St. Francis Xavier University, Antigonish, N.S., Canada.
- Clan Donald Bulletin. q.

**Clarke Institute of Psychiatry**
- Clarke Institute of Psychiatry. Monograph Series. (pub. by University of Toronto Press)

**Clarke, Irwin & Co., Ltd.**
791 St. Clair Ave. West, Toronto, Ont., M6C 1B8, Canada.
- Canadian Portraits. irreg.

**Classical Association of Canada**
Dept. of Classical Studies, Univ. of Ottawa, Ottawa K1M 1R3, Ont, Canada.
- Echos du Monde Classique/Classical News and Views. 3 per yr. ISSN 0012-9356
- Phoenix. (pub. by University of Toronto Press)

**Clay Publishing Co. Ltd.**
1 Oak St., Bewdley K0L 1E0, Ont., Canada.
- Canadian Recreational Vehicle Industry. bi-m.
- Fur Trade Journal. m.
- Ontario Cottager. 6 per yr.
- Outdoor Careers. q. ISSN 0316-3431
- Rabbits in Canada. m. ISSN 0033-7242

**Cloudburst Press**
c/o General Delivery, Argenta, B.C., Canada.
- Smallholder. m.

**Club des Ornithologues du Quebec, Inc.**
8191 Avenue du Zoo, Orsainville, Quebec G1G 4Gu, Canada.
- Bulletin Ornithologique. q. ISSN 0007-5256

**Coach House Press**
401 (rear) Huron Street, Toronto 181, Ontario, Canada.
- Image Nation. irreg.
- Open Letter. 4 per yr. ISSN 0048-1939
- Story So Far. irreg.

**Coda Publications**
Box 87, Station J, Toronto M4J 4X8, Canada.
- Coda; Canada's jazz magazine. 6 per yr. ISSN 0010-017X

**College Ahuntsic**
9155 rue St. Hubert, Montreal H2M 1YB, Canada.
- Critere. irreg. ISSN 0384-0174

**College of Family Physicians of Canada**
4000 Leslie St., Willowdale, Ont., Canada.
- Canadian Family Physician/Medecin de Famille Canadien. m. ISSN 0008-350X

**College of New Caledonia**
2001 Central St., Prince George, B.C. V2N 1P8, Canada.
- Caledonian. ISSN 0381-856X

**College of Physicians and Surgeons of British Columbia**
1807 W. 10th Ave., Vancouver, B.C. V6J 2A9, Canada.
- College of Physicians and Surgeons of British Columbia. Medical Directory. a. ISSN 0069-5726

**College of Physicians and Surgeons of Ontario**
64 Prince Arthur Ave., Toronto, Ont., Canada.
- College of Physicians and Surgeons of Ontario. Semi-Annual Report. s-a. ISSN 0045-7388

**College Universitaire de Hearst**
see **University College of Hearst**

**James H. Collyer**
23 McNider, Outremont, Que., Canada.
- Elan Image. q.

**Color Photographic Association of Canada**
New Westminster, B.C., Canada.
- Color Spotlight. irreg. ISSN 0383-9672

**Comac Communications Ltd.**
2300 Yonge St., Toronto, Ont. M4P 1E4, Canada.
- Homemakers's Magazine/Madame au Foyer. 9 per yr. ISSN 0018-4209
- Quest; Canadas urban magazine. 6 per yr.

**Comite Canada-Israel**
1310 Avenue Green, Suite 906, Montreal 215, Que, Canada.
- Regards sur Israel. m. ISSN 0384-9120

**Comite d'Actor Cinematographique**
360 rue McGill, C.H. 212 Montreal, Quebec H2Y 2E9, Canada.
- Comite d'Actor Cinematographique. Cahiers. irreg.

**Commercial Magazine Co.**
Montreal, Quebec, Canada.
- Commercial Monthly. m. ISSN 0383-9648

**Publications Commerciales Francaises**
5020 de Salaberry, Suite 3, Montreal H4J 1H9, Que., Canada.
- Automobile. m. ISSN 0005-1330

**Commission de la Carte Geologique du Monde**
c/o R. D. Russell, Department of Geophysics, University of British Columbia, 2075 Wesbrook Place, Vancouver V6T 1W5, Canada.
- Commission for the Geological Map of the World. Bulletin. irreg.; (approx 2 per year); no. 18, 1974. ISSN 0074-9427

**Committee for an Independent Canada**
36 Chinook Crescent, Ottawa, Ontario K2H 7E2, Canada.
- Independencer. bi-m.

**Committee on Canadian Labour History**
Department of History, Dalhousie University, Halifax, N.S., Canada.
- Labour/Travailleur. a (plus s-a bulletin)

**Commonwealth Parliamentary Association**
Canadian Branch, P.O. Box 950 Confederation Bldg., House of Commons, Ottawa, Ont., Canada.
- Commonwealth Parliamentary Association. Canadian Regional Conference. Report of the Proceedings. a. ISSN 0069-715X

**Communist Party of Canada (Marxist- Leninist)**
Box 666, Station C, Montreal, Que., Canada (Subscr. to: National Publications Centre, P.O. Box 727, Adelaide Station, Toronto, Ont., Canada)
- Mass Line. irreg. ISSN 0047-6110

**Community Funds and Councils of Canada**
- Directory of Canadian Community Funds and Councils/Repertoire des Federations et Conseils des Oeuvres du Canada. (pub. by Canadian Council on Social Development)

**Community Health Co-Operative Federation Ltd.**
455-2nd Ave. N., Saskatoon, Sask., Canada.
- Focus: Social and Preventive Medicine. m. ISSN 0015-5195

**Community Improvement Corporation**
297 Queen St., Fredericton, N.B., Canada.
- Community Improvement Corporation. Annual Report/Societe d'Amenagement Regional. Rapport Annuel. a. ISSN 0069-7842

**Community Planning Association of Canada**
No. 801 318 Homer St., Vancouver, B.C. V6B 2V3, Canada.
- Community Planning in British Columbia. irreg. ISSN 0045-7779
- Community Planning Review/Revue Canadienne d'Urbanisme. m. ISSN 0010-387X

**Compagnie de Publication la Reforme Ltd.**
460 Gilford, Montreal 176, Que., Canada.
- Electeur. 4 per yr. ISSN 0070-9603 (Parti Liberal du Quebec)

**Compagnie des Editions Horlogeres Canadiennes Limitee**
2950 Est rue Masson, Suite 205, Montreal H1Y 1X4, Que., Canada.
- Bijou. m. ISSN 0006-2316

**Comparative and International Education Society of Canada**
Althouse College, University of Western Ontario, London, Ont. N6G 1G7, Canada.
- Canadian and International Education/Education Canadienne et Internationale. s-a. ISSN 0315-1409

**Composers Authors & Publishers Association of Canada**
- Canadian Composer/Compositeur Canadien. (pub. by Creative Arts Co.)

**Concern International**
Box 2086, Thunder Bay, Ont. P7B 5E7, Canada.
- Concern International. bi-m.

**Concorde-Canada**
247 First Ave. N., Saskatoon, Sask. S7K 4H5, Canada.
- Shepherd. m. (Evangelical Lutheran Church of Canada)

**Conference Board in Canada**
Suite 1800, 333 River Rd., Ottawa, Ont. K1L 8B9, Canada.
- Canadian Business Review. q. ISSN 0317-4026
- Canadian Business Trends. m.
- Conference Board. Canadian Office. Canadian Studies. irreg. ISSN 0069-8342

- Financial Post Survey of Consumer Buying Intentions. q. (Contemporary Research Centre Ltd.)

**Conference Catholique Canadienne. Office National de Liturgie**
1225 Est. Boul St. Joseph, Montreal, Que. H2J 1L7, Canada.
- Conference Catholique Canadienne. Bulletin National de Liturgie. irreg. ISSN 0384-5087

**Conference of Mennonite Brethren Churches of Canada**
- Mennonite Brethren Herald. (pub. by Christian Press Ltd.)

**Conference on Scottish Studies**
c/o Dept. of History, Univ. of Guelph, Guelp, Ontario, Canada.
- Scottish Tradition. s-a.

**Conseil d'Expansion Economique Inc.**
3637 Est Rd. Metropolitain, Suite 1405, Montreal 455, Que., Canada.
- Prosperite. bi-m. ISSN 0033-1554

**Conseil de l'Hotellerie et de la Restauration**
Room 410 1500 Stanley St., Montreal. P.Q., Canada.
- Hotellerie Magazine; official organ of hotel-keepers. m. ISSN 0018-6309

**Conseil des Affaires Sociales et de la Famille**
- Family and Social Affairs Council. Objectifs dans le Domaine des Affaires Sociales et de la Famille. (pub. by Editeur Officiel du Quebec)

**Conseil des Arts du Canada. Office des Tournees**
Ottawa, Ont., Canada.
- Tournees de Spectacles. a. ISSN 0317-5979

**Conseil des Recherches Agricoles du Quebec**
Ministere de l'Agriculture, Quebec, Canada.
- Recherches Agronomiques Sommaire des Resultats. a.

**Conseil des Sciences du Canada**
Kent-Albert Bldg., 150 Kent St., Ottawa, Ont. K1P 5P4, Canada.
- Aspects de la Politique Scientifique du Canada. irreg. ISSN 0318-532X

**Conseil du Quebec de l'Enfance Exceptionnelle**
2765 Chemin Cote Ste. Catherine, Montreal 250, Que., Canada.
- Enfant Exceptionnel. q. ISSN 0046-1970

**Conseil Superieur du Livre**
3405 St. Denis, Montreal, Quebec, Canada.
- Conseil Superieur du Livre. Annuaire. (pub. by Edi-Quebec Inc.)
- French Canadian Books in Print. irreg.

**Conservation Council of Ontario**
45 Charles St. E., 6th fl., Toronto, Ont. M4Y 1S2, Canada.
- Conservation Council of Ontario. Bulletin. q. ISSN 0045-8155
- Conservation Council of Ontario. Conference Proceedings. irreg.
- Conservation Council of Ontario. Reports. irreg.
- Ontario Conservation News. m. ISSN 0383-6479

**Constructon Specifications Canada**
1027 Yonge St., Suite 301, Toronto, Ont. M4W 2K9, Canada.
- Specification Associate. bi-m. ISSN 0038-691X

**Consumer Press Ltd.**
401 - 22nd St. East, Saskatoon, Sask. S7K 3M9, Canada.
- Co-Operative Consumer. s-m.

**Consumers Association of Canada**
801-251 Laurier Ave. W., Ottawa, Ont. K1P 5Z7, Canada.
- Canadian Consumer. bi-m. ISSN 0008-3275
- Consommateur Canadien. bi-m.

**Contemporary Research Centre Ltd.**
- Financial Post Survey of Consumer Buying Intentions. (pub. by Conference Board in Canada)

**Content Publishing**
22 Laurier Ave., Toronto, Ont. M4X 1S3, Canada.
- Content. m.

**Contrast Publications Limited**
28 Lennox St., Toronto M6G 1J4, Canada.
- Contrast. w.

**Conventual Franciscan Friars**
15 Chestnut Park Rd., Toronto, Ont. M4W 1W5, Canada.
- Companion of St. Francis and St. Anthony. m.(Sept-Jun); bi-m(July-Aug) ISSN 0010-4000

**R. J. Cooke Publishing**
451 Beaconsfield Blvd., Beaconsfield, Que., Canada.
- Macdonald Journal. m. ISSN 0047-5335

**Cooke Publishing Co.**
Montreal, Que., Canada.
- Canadian Writer and Editor. m. ISSN 0383-1590

**Cooperative Union of Canada**
111 Sparks St., Ottawa 4, Ont., Canada.
- Co-Op Commentary. m. ISSN 0045-7221

**Co-Operatives Unies de l'Ontario**
Weston, Ont., Canada.
- U C O Nouvelles. bi-m. ISSN 0381-1131

**Copp Clark Publishing, Co.**
517 Wellington St. W., Toronto Ontario M5V 1G1, Canada
(U.S. address: Pitman Publishing Corp., 6 E. 43rd St., New York, NY 10017)
- Canadian Almanac and Directory. a. ISSN 0068-8193
- Directory of Canadian Governments: Municipal, Provincial, Federal. irreg. (Richard de Boo Ltd.)

**Copperfield**
Box 421, Temagami, Ont., Canada.
- Copperfield. irreg. ISSN 0069-9942

**Corporation des Bibliothecaires Professionnels du Quebec**
360 Lemoyne, Montreal, Que. H2Y 1Y3, Canada.
- Argus. bi-m. ISSN 0315-9930

**Corporation des Createurs Artisans de l'Est du Quebec**
C.P. 425, Rimouski, Que. G5L 7C3, Canada.
- Ecornifleux. m. ISSN 0380-8890

**Corporation des Electroniciens du Quebec**
2222 Est, rue Beaubien, Montreal, Que H2G 1M7, Canada.
- Electronicien. bi-m. ISSN 0013-5062

**Corporation of Master Electricians of Quebec**
2675 Masson St., Montreal 405, P.Q., Canada.
- Maitre Electricien. m. ISSN 0025-0988

**Corporation of Professional Social Workers**
5757 Decelles Ave., Suite 114, Montreal, Que., Canada.
- Intervention. q. ISSN 0047-1321

**Corporation of the National Museums of Canada**
- Masterpieces in the National Gallery of Canada/Chefs-d'Oeuvre de la Galerie Nationale du Canada. (pub. by National Gallery of Canada)
- National Gallery of Canada. Annual Revue/Galerie Nationale du Canada. Revue Annuelle. (pub. by National Gallery of Canada)

**Corporation Professionnelle des Conseillers d'Orientation du Quebec**
1895 de la Salle Ave., Montreal, Que. H1V 2K4, Canada.
- Orientation Professionnelle/Vocational Guidance. 4 per yr. ISSN 0030-5413

**Corporation Professionnelle des Medecins du Quebec**
1440 ouest, St. Catherine W., Suite 914, Montreal, Que. H3G 1S5, Canada.
- Corporation Professionnelle des Medecins du Quebec. Annuaire Medical. a. ISSN 0315-226X
- Corporation Professionnelle des Medecins du Quebec. Bulletin. irreg. (10-15 per yr.) ISSN 0315-2979

**Corpus Publishers Services Ltd.**
151 Bloor St. W., Toronto, Ont. M5S 1S4, Canada.
- C P I Management Service. w. ISSN 0315-257X
- Corpus Administrative Index. bi-m.
- Corpus Almanac of Canada. a.
- E C O/L O G Information Services. m. (Chinook Chemicals Corp.)
- E C O /L O G Week.
- Electric Power Communicator. w.
- Energy Analects. w. ISSN 0315-1654

- Polyfacts. w. ISSN 0315-2588

**Correio Portugues**
793 Ossington Ave., Toronto, Ont. M6G 3T8, Canada.
- Correio Portugues. s-m. ISSN 0045-8643

**Correo Hispano-Americano**
Box 25, Station E, Toronto, Ont. M6H 4E1, Canada.
- Correo Hispano-Americano. w. ISSN 0045-8651

**Corvus Publishing Group Ltd.**
Suite 203, 2003 McKnight Blvd., Calgary, Alta. T2E 6L2, Canada.
- Wings Magazine of Canada. m. (Nor-Rand Publishing Ltd.)

**Costume Society of Ontario**
c/o A. Suddon, 209 Brunswick Ave., Toronto, Ont. M5S 2M4, Canada.
- Costume Society of Ontario. Newsletter. irreg. ISSN 0383-4239

**Richard L. Coulton, Ed. & Pub.**
Bentley, Alberta, Canada.
- Canadian Steam. q. ISSN 0045-5393
- R. L. C.'s Museum Gazette. irreg. ISSN 0035-7154
- Western Canadian Steam Locomotive Directory. biennial. ISSN 0085-8188

**Council for Exceptional Children. Canadian Committee**
c/o D. Muir, 1 Danforth Ave., Toronto, Ont. M4K 1M8, Canada.
- Special Education in Canada. q. ISSN 0381-9124

**Council of Ontario Universities**
130 St. George St., Suite 8039, Toronto, Ont. M55 2T4, Canada.
- Council of Ontario Universities. Monthly Review. m.
- Council of Ontario Universities. Research Division. Application Statistics. a. ISSN 0382-912X
- Council of Ontario Universities Biennial Review. biennial. ISSN 0084-8972

**Council of the Forest Industries of B.C.**
1055 W. Hastings St., Vancouver 1, B.C., Canada.
- Wood World. q.

**Council on the Study of Religion**
Wilfrid Laurier University, Waterloo, Ont. N2L 3C5, Canada.
- Council on the Study of Religion. Bulletin. 5 per yr. ISSN 0002-7170
- Religious Studies Review; a quarterly review of publications in the field of religion and related disciplines. q. ISSN 0319-485X

**Countdown**
Box 278, Postal Sta. K., Toronto 12, Ont., Canada.
- Countdown. 10 per yr. ISSN 0383-6436

**Country Life Ltd.**
Dominion Bldg., 207 W. Hastings St., Vancouver V6B 1J8, B.C., Canada.
- Country Life in British Columbia. m. ISSN 0011-0183

**Courier Publications Ltd.**
6900 St-Denis, Montreal, Que. H2S 2S2, Canada.
- Corriere Italiano. w. ISSN 0010-9274

**Couvoiriers du Quebec Inc**
Box 207, Beloeil J3G 4T1, Canada.
- Aviculteur Quebecois. m. ISSN 0005-2221

**Creative Arts Co.**
40 St. Clair Ave. W., Toronto, Ont. M4V 1M2, Canada.
- Canadian Composer/Compositeur Canadien. 10 per yr(approx) ISSN 0008-3259 (Composers Authors & Publishers Association of Canada)

**Creative Generation**
1220 Yonge St., Ste. 200, Toronto, Ont. M4T 1W1, Canada.
- Today's Generation. 9 per yr. ISSN 0384-1405

**Credit Union National Association**
Box 800, Toronto 18, Ont. M8Z 5R2, Canada
(and Box 431, Madison, WI 53701)
• Everybody's Money. q. ISSN 0046-287X

**Croatian Republicans**
Postal Station "M", Box 78, Toronto, Ont. M6S
4T2, Canada.
• Hrvatski Put/Croatian Way. m.

**John S. Crosbie, Ed. & Pub.**
Box 5040, Toronto, Ont. M5W 1N4, Canada.
• Canada Report. w. ISSN 0384-9252

**Cruikshank Communications, Ltd.**
P.O. Box 91045, West Vancouver, B.C. V7V 3N3,
Canada.
• Gastown and Vancouver Today. m.

**Crux**
Scarborough College, University of Toronto, West
Hill, Ont. M1C 1A4, Canada.
• Crux; journal of Christian thought. irreg. ISSN
0011-2186

**Culture Vulture Publishing Ltd.**
Box 1784, Edmonton, Alta. T5J 2P2, Canada.
• Edmonton Culture Vulture. m. ISSN 0380-5123

**Phillip J. Currie, Ed. & Pub.**
8198 Ave. de l'Epee, Montreal, Que. H3N 2G1,
Canada.
• Erbivore. irreg., 1972, no. 5. ISSN 0071-1071

**Daisons Press Ltd.**
1000 Lawrence W., Toronto 19, Ont., Canada.
• Corriere Canadese/Canadian Courier. d. ISSN
0045-866X

**Dalhousie Gazette Publishing Society**
Halifax, N.S. B3H 4J2, Canada.
• Atlantic Issues.
• Dalhousie Gazette; Canada's oldest college
newspaper. w. ISSN 0011-5819 (Dalhousie
University)
• Dalhousie International. m.

**Dalhousie University**
Information Office, Old Law Bldg., Halifax, N. S.,
Canada.
• Dalhousie Gazette. (pub. by Dalhousie Gazette
Publishing Society)
• Dalhousie University, Halifax. University News.
fortn. ISSN 0045-9534

**Dalhousie University. Computer Centre**
Halifax, N.S. B3H 4H8, Canada.
• Dalhousie University. Computer Centre.
Newsletter. irreg.

**Dalhousie University. Faculty of Law**
Halifax, N.S. B3H 4H8, Canada
(Subscr. to: Carswell Co. Ltd., 2330 Midland Ave.,
Agincourt, Ont. M1S 1P7, Canada)
• Dalhousie Law Journal. 3 per yr.

**Dalhousie University. Institute of Public Affairs**
Halifax, N.S. B3H 3J5, Canada.
• Dalhousie University, Halifax, N.S. Institute of
Public Affairs. Regional Studies Series. irreg.
• Environmental Management for the Public Health
Inspector. a. ISSN 0316-0661 (Co-sponsors:
Departments of Health-Nova Scotia-New
Brunswick-Prince Edward Island-Newfoundland)
• Nova Scotia Labour-Management Study
Conference. Proceedings. irreg.

**Dalhousie University Press Ltd.**
Dalhousie Univ., Izaak Killam Mem. Library, Rm.
4413, Halifax, N.S. B3H 4H8, Canada.
• Dalhousie Review; a Canadian quarterly of
literature and opinion. q. ISSN 0011-5827

**Dalhousie University. School of Library Service**
Halifax, Nova Scotia B3H 4H8, Canada.
• Dalhousie University. School of Library Service.
Newsletter. s-a. ISSN 0315-0054

**Dalhousie University. Sir James Dunn Law Library**
Halifax, N.S., Canada.
• Current Index to Commonwealth Legal
Periodicals. m. ISSN 0382-5027

**Dalton Printing Co. Ltd.**
1407-50 St., Edmonton, Alta. T5W 3B5, Canada.
• Beverly Page.

**Daniel J. Cillis Associates**
Box 5438, Ottawa, Ont. K2C 3J1, Canada.
• Canadian Layman. bi-m. ISSN 0315-3452

**Data Processing Management Association of Toronto**
Box 116, Sta. F, Toronto, Ont. M4Y 2L4, Canada.
• Data Processing Management Association.
Magazine. m. (10 per yr.) ISSN 0045-9690

**Daugavas Vanags Publishing Ltd.**
125 Broadview Ave., Toronto, Ont. M4M 2E9,
Canada.
• Daugavas Vanagu Menesraksts. bi-m. ISSN 0418-
4297 (Latvian Relief Society of Canada
(Daugavas Vanagi))

**Dellcrest Children's Centre**
1651 Sheppard Ave. W., Downsview, Ont. M3M
2X4, Canada.
• Dellcrest Children's Centre Newsletter. q.

**Democrat Publishing Co., Ltd.**
64-8th St., New Westminster, B.C. V3M 3P1,
Canada.
• Democrat. m. ISSN 0070-3346 (New Democratic
Party of British Columbia)

**Descant**
Box 314, Station P, Toronto, Ont. M5S 2S8,
Canada.
• Descant. 3 per yr. ISSN 0382-909X

**Deutsche Katholik in Kanada**
131 McCaul St., Toronto, Ont. M5T 1W3, Canada.
• Deutsche Katholik in Kanada. m. ISSN 0381-8950

**Development Publications Ltd.**
Box 84, Sta. A., Willowdale, Ont. M2N 5S7,
Canada.
• Careers for Graduates/Carrieres pour Diplomes. a.
ISSN 0318-6229
• Short Courses and Seminars; a compendium of
short management & technical courses. s-a.
• Training Aids Action Service. s-a. ISSN 0318-
6210

**Digest Reporting Service Ltd.**
1-1311 Portage Ave., Winnipeg, Man. R3G 0V3,
Canada.
• Digest, Business & Law Journal. w.

**Diocese of Churchill Hudson's Bay**
Box 10, Churchill, Manitoba R0B 0EO, Canada.
• Eskimo. s-a. ISSN 0318-7551

**N. Divinsky, Ed. & Pub.**
c/o Dept. of Math., University of British Columbia,
Vancouver 8, B.C., Canada.
• Canadian Chess Chat. irreg. (6-12 per yr.) ISSN
0045-4540

**Dominion Astrophysical Observatory**
Observatories Branch, Victoria, B.C., Canada.
• Victoria, British Columbia. Dominion
Astrophysical Observatory. Publications. irreg.
ISSN 0078-6950

**Dominion Engineering Works Ltd.**
Box 220, Montreal, Canada.
• Dominion Engineer. 1-2 per yr. ISSN 0012-5342

**Dominion Life Assurance Co.**
Advertising and Field Services Dept., Waterloo,
Ont., Canada.
• Dominionaire. m. ISSN 0046-0575

**Donovan Ltd.**
6 Adelaide St. E., Suite 904, Toronto M5C 1H6,
Canada.
• Holstein-Friesian Journal. m. ISSN 0018-3687
(Holstein-Friesian Association of Canada)

**Editions J. M. Dore, Inc.**
562 Rue Dollard, Quebec, Que. G1N 1P4, Canada.
• Journal du Bricoleur. 6 per yr. ISSN 0047-2204

**Doubleday Canada Ltd.**
105 Bond St., Toronto, Ont., Canada.
• Canadian History Series. irreg., 1967, vol. 6. ISSN
0068-8894

**Douglas College. English and Communications Division**
Box 2503, New Westminster, B.C. V3L 5B2,
Canada.
• Event. s-a. ISSN 0315-3770

**Walter Drobich, Pub.**
170 Wychwood Ave., Toronto, Ont. M6C 2T3,
Canada.
• Chess Canada. m. ISSN 0045-6578

**Drug Merchandising**
c/o Robert D. Reid, 481 University Ave., Toronto
2, Ont., Canada.
• Cosmetics Handbook/Guide des Cosmetiques. a.
ISSN 0084-9324

**Drum Publishers Ltd.**
c/o Tom Butters, Box 1069, Inuvik, N.W.T. X0E
0T0, Canada.
• Drum. w. ISSN 0012-6721

**Ducks Unlimited (Canada)**
1495 Pembina Hwy., Winnipeg, Man., Canada.
• Duckological. 8 per yr. ISSN 0046-0788

**Dun & Bradstreet of Canada**
84 Carlton St., Toronto, Ont. M5B 1L6, Canada.
• Canadian Key Business Directory. a.

**Dutch Canadian Association**
Box 1468, Place Bonaventure, Montreal, Que. H5A
1H5, Canada.
• Nieuwe Weg (Montreal) irreg. ISSN 0383-1329

**Dutch Canadian Toronto Credit Union**
Box 1100, Willowdale M2N 5T5, Ont., Canada.
• Duca-Post. m. ISSN 0012-6934

**E.C. Boone Advertising Ltd.**
St. John's, N.F., Canada.
• Newfoundland and Labrador Who's Who. irreg.
ISSN 0078-0286

**E M Publications**
Box 306, Oakville, Ont., Canada.
• Modersmaalet/Mother Tongue. w. ISSN 0047-
7788
• Scandinavian Canadian Businessman. m. ISSN
0048-928X

**E R C Publishing Co.**
204-1760 Marine Dr., West Vancouver, B.C. V7V
1J4, Canada.
• World Market Perspective. m.

**Early Childhood Education Council, Manitoba**
Winnipeg, Man., Canada.
• Early Childhood Education Council. Newsletter.
irreg. ISSN 0316-2079

**Earth Research**
Box 1209, Wolfville, Nova Scotia, Canada.
• Earth Research. m.

**Eastern Canada Association of the Deaf, Inc.**
27 Elmwood Drive, Amherst, N.S., Canada.
• Deaf Herald. bi-m. ISSN 0382-8980

**Eastern Canada Centre of Slavists and East European Specialists**
5601 Ave. des Cedres, Montreal H1T 2V4, Canada
(Subscr. to: 256 Paterson Hall, Carleton Univ.,
Ottawa, Ont. K1S 5B6)
• Cahiers Culturels. a.

**Eastern Ontario Regional Library System**
Suite 6, 200 Cooper St., Ottawa, Ont. K2P 0G1,
Canada.
• Dialogue (Ottawa) 6 per yr. ISSN 0700-3048
• Triangle. 3-4 per yr.

**Publications Eclair Ltee**
9393 Ave. Edison, Montreal, Quebec H1J 1T5,
Canada.
• Almanach Moderne. a. ISSN 0569-096X
• Horoscope Quotidien Eclair. m. ISSN 0018-5124

**Ecole des Haute Etudes Commerciales**
5255 Ave. Decelles, Montreal, Que. H3C 1V6,
Canada.
• Actualite Economique. q. ISSN 0001-771X
(Societe Canadienne de Science Economique)

**Economic Council of Canada**
Ottawa, Ontario, Canada.
• Economic Council of Canada. Annual Report. a.
ISSN 0070-847X
• Economic Council of Canada. Annual Review. a.
ISSN 0070-8488
• Economic Council of Canada. Economic and
Social Indicators. a. ISSN 0317-6789
• Economic Council of Canada. Medium-Term
Capital Investment Survey. irreg.

**Edi-Quebec Inc.**
436 Est rue Sherbrooke, Montreal, Que. H2L 1J6, Canada.
- Conseil Superieur du Livre. Annuaire. a. ISSN 0084-9197
- Repertoire de l'Edition au Quebec. biennial. (Association des Editeurs Canadiens) (Co-sponsors: Societe des Editeurs de Manuals Scolaires du Quebec; Conseil Superieur du Livre)
- Vient de Paraitre; bulletin du livre au Canada Francais. q. ISSN 0042-5656 (Assocation des Editeurs Canadiens) (Co-Sponsor: Societe des Editeurs de Manuels Scolaires du Quebec)

**Editeur Officiel du Quebec**
1283 Bd. Charest ouest, Quebec G1N 2C9, Canada.
- Annuaire du Quebec. a. ISSN 0066-3018 (Quebec (Province) Bureau of Statistics)
- Collection l'Etat et le Citoyen. irreg.
- Exportations Internationales du Canada Chargees au Quebec et Dedouanees dans Differentes Regions Canadiennes, Par Produits. a ISSN 0071-3538
- Exportations Internationales du Canada Chargees au Quebec et Dedouanees dans Differentes Regions Canadiennes, Par Pays. a. ISSN 0071-352X
- Family and Social Affairs Council. Objectifs dans le Domaine des Affaires Sociales et de la Famille. irreg. (Conseil des Affaires Sociales et de la Famille)
- Merite du Defricheur. Rapport de l'Ordre du Merite du Defricheur. a. ISSN 0076-6577
- Quebec (Province) Bureau of Statistics. Analyse Budgetaire. Municipalities du Quebec. a. ISSN 0079-8436
- Quebec (Province) Bureau of Statistics. Conditions de Travail dans les Industries de la Province de Quebec. Working Conditions in the Industries in the Province of Quebec. a. ISSN 0079-8460
- Quebec (Province) Bureau of Statistics. Finances Municipales. a. ISSN 0079-8479
- Quebec (Province) Bureau of Statistics. Mines d'Argent, Plomb, Zinc/Silver, Lead, Zinc Mines. a.
- Quebec (Province) Bureau of Statistics. Mines de Feldspath et de Quartz/Feldspar and Quartz Mines. a.
- Quebec (Province) Bureau of Statistics. Pecheries Commerciales/Commercial Fisheries. a. ISSN 0079-8673
- Quebec (Province) Bureau of Statistics. Repertoire des Municipalites et des Commissions Scolaires. Guide of School Boards. a. ISSN 0079-8681
- Quebec (Province) Bureau of Statistics. Repertoire des Municipalites et des Commissions Scolaires. Municipal Guide. a. ISSN 0079-869X
- Quebec (Province) Bureau of Statistics. Statistiques des Produits Forestiers. a. ISSN 0079-8703
- Quebec (Province) Bureau of Statistics. Statistiques sur l'Hotellerie. a. ISSN 0317-6940
- Quebec Official Gazette. w. ISSN 0033-5983
- Repertoire des Cooperatives du Quebec. a. ISSN 0080-097X
- Revue Statistique du Quebec/Quebec Statistical Review. a. ISSN 0039-0550

**Editions de l'Universite d'Ottawa**
65 Hastey Ave., Ottawa, Ont. K1N 6N5, Canada.
- Bibliographies du Canada Francais. irreg.

**Editions Derives**
C.P. 398 Succ., Montreal, Que. H1V 3M5, Canada.
- Derives; Tiers-Monde/Quebec une nouvelle conjoncture culturelle. 6 per yr.

**Editions du Jour**
5705 Est, rue Sherbrooke, Montreal, Que. H1N 1L7, Canada.
- Cahiers de Cite Libre. irreg. ISSN 0009-7489
- Collection Litterature du Jour. irreg.
- Collections: Les Idees du Jour. irreg. ISSN 0069-5513

**Editions Quebecoises**
Montreal, Ont., Canada.
- Gens du Quebec. a. ISSN 0381-8063

**Edmonton Antique Car Club**
Box 102, Edmonton 15, Alta., Canada.
- Running Board. m. ISSN 0048-8771

**Edmonton Business Development Department**
1328-10025 Jasper Ave., Edmonton T5J 1S6, Alta., Canada.
- Edmonton Report on Business and Industrial Development. 10 per yr. ISSN 0046-130X

**Edmonton Public Library**
7. Sir Winston Churchill Square, Edmonton, Alta. T5J 2V4, Canada.
- Connection. bi-m. ISSN 0319-2156

**Edmonton Stamp Club**
Box 399, Edmonton, Alta., Canada.
- Edmonton Stamp Club Bulletin. bi-m. ISSN 0046-1318

**Education Nouvelle Inc.**
260 Ouest Faillon, Montreal 327, Que., Canada.
- Pedagogie Dynamique. 5 per yr. ISSN 0048-3125

**Effective Communications Ltd.**
9 Manorpark Court, Willowdale, Ont. M2J 1A1, Canada.
- Conventions & Meetings-Canada. a.

**Eglise Catholique. Diocese de Chicoutimi**
Office des Communications Sociales, Chicoutimi, Quebec, Canada.
- En Eglise. m. ISSN 0317-851X

**Eglise Catholique. Diocese de Saint-Jean-de-Quebec**
c/o G. Roy, 740, Boul. Ste-Foy, C.P.40, Longueuil, Que. J4K 4X8, Canada.
- Rhythme de Notre Eglise. bi-m. ISSN 0383-0152

**Ego Publishing, Inc.**
5445 de Gaspe Ave., Suite 101, Montreal, Que., Canada.
- Ego; the men's fashion scene in Canada/la mode Canadienne pour les hommes. q. ISSN 0315-3037

**Elder Citizens in British Columbia**
- Elder Statesman. (pub. by Bryon Lawes, Ed. & Pub.)

**Electrical and Electronic Manufacturers Association**
One Yonge St., Suite 1608, Toronto, Ont. M5E 1R1, Canada.
- E E M A C Newsletter. m.

**Robert J. Elias, Ed. & Pub.**
737 8th Ave. S.W., Calgary, Alta. T2P 1H5, Canada.
- Petroleum Land Journal. bi-w.

**R. C. Ellis**
17 Dundonald St., Toronto, Ont., Canada.
- Directory of Broadcast Executives. irreg. ISSN 0419-2273

**Emergency Librarian**
697 Wellington Crescent, Winnipeg. Man. R3M 0A7, Canada.
- Emergency Librarian. bi-m. ISSN 0315-8888

**Empire Life Insurance Co.**
Head Office, Box 1000, Kingston, Ont., Canada.
- Builder. m. ISSN 0045-3382

**Empire Stamp Corporation Ltd.**
1150 Yonge St., Toronto, Ont. M4W 2M2, Canada.
- Philatopic Magazine. bi-m. ISSN 0048-3737

**James G. Endicott, Ed. & Pub.**
232 Wychwood Ave., Toronto, Ont. M6C 2T3, Canada.
- Canadian Far Eastern Newsletter. m. ISSN 0045-4737

**Energy Resources Conservation Board**
603 6th Ave., S.W., Calgary, T2P 0T4, Alta, Canada.
- Cumulative Annual Statistics: Alberta Coal Industry. a.
- Energy Resources Conservation Board. Cumulative Annual Statistics: Alberta Electric Industry. a.

**Engineering Institute of Canada**
2050 Mansfield St., Montreal H3A 1Y9, Canada.
- Engineering Institute of Canada. Transactions. m. ISSN 0013-8002
- Engineering Journal. m. ISSN 0013-8010

**Enseignants**
8350 Dulaus, Saint-Leonard, Montreal 457, Que., Canada.
- Enseignants; mensuel independant d'information pedagogique. m. ISSN 0046-2101

**Entertainment Publications, Inc.**
Box 5696, Postal Stn. A, Toronto, Ont., Canada.
- Beetle. m.

**Entomological Society of Canada**
1320 Carling Ave., Ottawa K1Z 7K9, Ont., Canada.
- Canadian Entomologist. m. ISSN 0008-347X
- Entomological Society of Canada. Bulletin. q. ISSN 0071-0741
- Entomological Society of Canada. Memoirs. irreg.(1-8 per year) ISSN 0071-075X
- Entomological Society of Canada. Proceedings. m.

**Entomological Society of Manitoba**
25 Dagoe Rd., Winnipeg, Man. R3T 2M9, Canada.
- Manitoba Entomologist. a. ISSN 0076-3810

**Entomological Society of Ontario**
University of Guelph, Dept. of Environmental Biology, Graham Hall, Guelph, Ont., Canada.
- Entomological Society of Ontario. Proceedings; annual publication of entomological research in Ontario. a. ISSN 0071-0768

**Entomological Society of Quebec**
*see* Societe Entomologique du Quebec

**Estonian Publishing Co. Toronto Ltd.**
Estonian House, 958 Broadview Ave., Toronto, Ont. M4K 2R6, Canada.
- Meie Elu/Our Life. w. ISSN 0047-665X

**Estuaire**
Box 828, Haute-Ville, Quebec 4, Que., Canada.
- Estuaire. q.

**Eternal Network**
101 Kendal Ave., Toronto, Ont. M5R 1L8, Canada.
- Is. s-a. ISSN 0047-1526

**Evangelical Lutheran Church of Canada**
- Shepherd. (pub. by Concorde-Canada)

**Evangelical Voice**
Box 39, Sta. A, Toronto, Ont. M6P 3J5, Canada.
- Ievanhel's'kyi Holos. q. ISSN 0383-2538

**Evangelistic Enterprises Society**
Box 600, Beaverlodge, Alta. T0H OcO, Canada.
- Communicate. m. excetp aug.

**R. W. Evans Associates Ltd.**
P.O. Box 1127, Station B, Weston, Ont. M9L 2R8, Canada.
- E D P in-Depth Reports. m.

**Events Publications Inc. Ltd.**
1721 Main Street, Winnipeg, Manitoba R2V 1Z4, Canada.
- Events. m. ISSN 0046-2861 (Manitoba Tourist Association)

**Evert Communications Ltd.**
Box 3158, Ottawa, Ont. K1Y 4J4, Canada.
- Electronics Communicator. 48 per yr. ISSN 0046-1733

**Exile & Exile Editions**
Box 546, Downsview, Ontario, Canada.
- Exile. q.

**Fabian Chemical Co.**
Chemical Information Service, Box 154, Sta. G, Montreal 130, Que., Canada.
- Total Translation in Science. q. ISSN 0040-9715

**Farm Credit Corporation**
Box 6309, Postal Station -J, Ottawa, Ont. K2A 3W9, Canada.
- Farm Credit Corporation. Annual Report. a. ISSN 0071-3864
- Farm Credit Corporation. Federal Farm Credit Statistics/Statistiques du Credit Agricole Federal. a. ISSN 0071-3872

**Farm Papers Ltd.**
605 Royal Ave, New Westminster, B.C., Canada.
- Canada Poultryman. m. ISSN 0008-2732 (Canadian Egg Producers' Council) (Cosponsors: Canadian Broiler Council; Canadian Turkey Marketing Agency)
- Canada Who's Who of the Poultry Industry. a. ISSN 0068-8134

**Fashion Textiles Mode Publishing Ltd.**
Bureau 311, 1396 ouest, rue Ste-Catherine, Montreal, Que. H3G 1P9, Canada.
- Fashion Textiles Mode. q. ISSN 0318-8701

- Fem Ego. q. ISSN 0318-871X

**Fax Publishing Inc.**
225 Roy Street, Montreal H2W 1M5, Canada.
- Best True Fact Detective. bi-m.
- Wrestling Monthly. m.

**Federation Canadienne des Maires et des Municipalites**
Box 5738, Succ. F, Ottawa, Ont., Canada.
- Courrier Municipal. w. ISSN 0381-0976

**Federation des Admistrateurs des Services de Sante et des Services Sociaux du Quebec**
- Administration Hospitaliere et Sociale. (pub. by Jean Seguin & Associates)

**Federation des Caisses Populaires Desjardins**
150 Ave. des Commandeurs, Levis, Que., Canada.
- Revue Desjardins. irreg. ISSN 0035-2284

**Federation des Commissions Scolaires Catholiques du Quebec**
1001 Begon Ave., Sainte-Foy, Que. G1V 4C7, Canada.
- Revue Scolaire. m. ISSN 0035-4104

**Federation des Femmes Canadiennes Francaises**
1 Nicholas St., Rm. 1404, Ottawa, Ont. K1N 7B6, Canada.
- Femme d'Action. q.

**Federation des Pompiers Professionnels du Quebec**
2600 Boul. St. Joseph Ch. 206, Montreal, Que., Canada.
- Protection. 4 per yr. ISSN 0048-5616

**Federation Nationale des Enseignants Quebecois**
1001 St.Denis, Montreal 129, Quebec, Canada.
- Nouveau Pouvoir. irreg., (approx. 10-12 per yr.)

**Federation of Arab Canadian Societies**
Box 416, Sta. K, Toronto, Ont., Canada.
- Arab Dawn. bi-m. ISSN 0383-087X

**Federation of British Columbia Naturalists**
Box 33797, Stn. D, Vancouver, B.C. V6j 4L6, Canada.
- Federation of British Columbia Naturalists. Newsletter. q. ISSN 0046-3566

**Federation of Canadian Archers**
c/o Joan McDonald, 244 Cranbrooke Ave., Toronto, Ont. M5M 1M7, Canada.
- Canadian Archer. m. ISSN 0319-2571

**Federation of Free Byelorussian Journalists**
c/o Marian Ziniak, 24 Tarlton Rd., Toronto, Ont. M5P 2MY, Canada.
- Bielaruski Holas/Byelorussian Voice/Voix Bielarusienne. m.

**Federation of Ontario Naturalists**
1262 Don Mills Rd., Don Mills, Ont., Canada.
- Ontario Naturalist. 5 per yr. ISSN 0030-3046

**Federation of Saskatchewan Indians**
1114 Central Ave., Prince Albert, Sask, Canada.
- Indian Outlook. irreg. ISSN 0384-1901
- Saskatchewan Indian. m. ISSN 0048-9204

**Federation of Women Teachers Associations of Ontario**
207 Queen's Quay W., Suite 315, Toronto, Ont. M5J 1A7, Canada.
- Educational Courier. 7 per yr. ISSN 0013-1687 (Co-sponsor: Ontario Public School Men Teachers Federation)

**Federation Quebecoise de la Faune**
6424 Rue St. Denis, Montreal 326, Que., Canada.
- Federation Quebecoise de la Faune. Nouvelles. q. ISSN 0046-3590

**Fellowship of Evangelical Baptist Churches in Canada**
74 Sheppard Ave. W., Willowdale M2N 1M3, Ont., Canada.
- Evangelical Baptist. m. ISSN 0014-3324
- Evangelical Baptist Churches in Canada. Fellowship Yearbook. a. ISSN 0317-266X
- Intercom. irreg. ISSN 0383-6061

**Rev. M. Fesenko, Ed. & Pub.**
26 Robina Ave., Toronto, Ont. M6C 3Y6, Canada.
- Evangelical Truth. bi-m. ISSN 0014-3375

**Editions Fides**
235 E. Dorchester Blvd., Montreal H2X 1N9, Que., Canada.
- Archives des Lettres Canadiennes. irreg. ISSN 0066-6572 (University of Ottawa. Centre de Recherches de Litterature Canadienne-Francaise)
- Collection d'Histoire Economique et Social du Canada Francais. irreg.
- Collection Foi et Liberte. irreg.
- Eglise Canadienne; documents et informations. m. ISSN 0013-2322

**Film Publications of Canada, Ltd.**
175 Bloor St. E., Toronto 5, Ontario, Canada.
- Yearbook of the Canadian Entertainment Industry. a. ISSN 0513-5141

**Financial Post**
481 University Ave., Toronto, Ont. M5W 1A7, Canada.
- Meetings, Conferences & Conventions: a Financial Post Guide. a.
- Survey of Markets and Business Year Book. a. ISSN 0071-5077

**Financial Publishing Company of Canada**
P. O. Box 250, Montreal, Que. HC3 2S1, Canada.
- Canadian Earnings Estimator. m. ISSN 0045-4680

**Financial Times of Canada**
1885 Leslie St., Don Mills, Ont. M3B 3J4, Canada.
- Financial Times of Canada. w. ISSN 0015-2056
- Industrial Locations in Canada. a. ISSN 0073-7569
- Perspective on Money. q.

**Finnish Pentacostal Churches of the U.S. and Canada**
1179 Commerical Dr., Vancouver, B.C. V5L 3X3, Canada.
- Totuuden Todistaja. m (except Jul. and Nov.)

**Fisheries Association of British Columbia**
Rm.400, 100 W. Pender St., Vancouver, B.C. V6B 1R8, Canada.
- Facts on Fish. m. ISSN 0046-3140

**Fisheries Council of Canada**
Suite 603, 77 Metcalfe St., Ottawa, Ont. K1P 5L6, Canada.
- Fisheries Council of Canada. Bulletin. m. ISSN 0046-3973

**Fisherman Publishing Society**
138 E. Cordova St., Vancouver, B.C. V6A 1K9, Canada.
- Fisherman. fortn. ISSN 0015-2986

**Five Windsors Publishing Co. Ltd.**
P.O. Box 775, Oakville, Ontario L6J 5C1, Canada.
- Production Machinery & Equipment. bi-m. ISSN 0315-2057

**Fleet Publications Canada Ltd.**
Box 1679, Winnipeg, Manitoba R3C 2Z6, Canada.
- Opportunity in Northern Canada. q.

**Forges**
2095 Sylvain, Trois-Rivieres, Quebec, Canada.
- Collection les Rouges Gorges. irreg.

**Forum House Publishing Co.**
90 Ronson Dr., Rexdale, Ont., M9W 1C1, Canada.
- Canadian Writers and Critics. irreg.

**Foundation for Coast to Coast Opera Publication**
366 Adelaide St. E., Suite 533, Toronto, Ont. M5A 1N4, Canada.
- Opera/Canada. 4 per yr. ISSN 0030-3577

**Four Decades**
231 Lonsmount Drive, Toronto, Ontario M5P 2Y9, Canada.
- Four Decades; of poetry 1890-1930. s-a. ISSN 0308-0889

**Fourth Estate**
Box 3184, Sta. C, Ottawa, Ont. K1Y 4J4, Canada.
- Fourth Estate; Canada's national press journal. m. ISSN 0015-9190

**Editions du Franc-Canada**
1849 Avenue Cristophe Colomb, Montreal, Que., Canada.
- Cahiers de la Decolonisation du Franc-Canada. irreg. ISSN 0575-0709

**Fraser Group**
University of British Columbia, Vancouver, B.C., Canada.
- Bias. 8 per yr. ISSN 0045-1835

**Fraser Valley Milk Producers' Association**
Box 9100, Vancouver, B.C. V6B 4G4, Canada.
- Butter-Fat. bi-m. ISSN 0007-7275

**Dr. H. T. Fredeen, Ed. & Pub.**
Lacombe, Alberta, Canada.
- Canadian Lacombe Breeders Association. Newsletter. 3-4 per yr. ISSN 0008-4344

**Free Press Publications (Western) Ltd.**
300 Carlton St., Winnipeg 2, Man., Canada.
- Free Press Report on Farming. w.

**Friends of N U S G W U E**
3564 B Clark Street, Montreal, Quebec, Canada.
- About Unions. bi-m. ISSN 0315-9922

**Friends of Osler Library**
- Osler Library Newsletter. (pub. by McGill University. Osler Library)

**Fullerton Publishing Co.**
Toronto, Ont., Canada.
- Canadian Music and Radio Trades. m. ISSN 0383-0713

**Fundy Group Publications Ltd.**
Box 128, Yarmouth, N.S., Canada.
- Atlantic Sport News. w. ISSN 0315-7466
- Farm Focus. s-m.
- Halifax Board of Trade. Commercial News. m. ISSN 0046-6735
- Sou'wester; voice of Atlantic provinces fishing industry. bi-m. ISSN 0049-1705
- Viking. 8 per yr. ISSN 0049-6448

**G.K. Chesterton Society**
c/o Dept. of English, St. Thomas More College, 1437 College Drive, Saskatoon, Sask. S7N 0W6, Canada.
- Chesterton Review. s-a.

**W. J. Gage, Ltd.**
1500 Birchmount Rd., Scharborough 4, Ont., Canada.
- Book of Canadian Prose. irreg., vol. 2, 1973.

**Gallery Publications Ltd.**
1165 Green Ave., Montreal, Que. H3Z 2A2, Canada.
- Arrow. ISSN 0382-4500 (Geography Club, Montreal)
- Seaports and the Shipping World; information magazine of marine activities and personalities in Canada. m. ISSN 0037-0150
- Seaports and the Shipping World. Annual Issue. a. ISSN 0080-8423

**Gam on Yachting**
29 Colborne St., Rm. 309, Toronto, Ont. M5E 1E2, Canada.
- Gam on Yachting. 10 per yr. ISSN 0016-4259

**Ganglia Press**
c/o The Village Bookstore, 239 Queen St. W., Toronto, Ont. M5V 1Z4, Canada.
- Gronk. m. ISSN 0017-453X

**Garage & Service Station News Publishing Co.**
No. 204, 260 Raymur Ave., Vancouver 6, B.C., Canada.
- Garage & Service Station News. m.

**Genetics Society of Canada**
151 Slater St., Suite 907, Ottawa, Ont. K1P 5H4, Canada.
- Canadian Journal of Genetics and Cytology/ Journal Canadien de Genetique et de Cytologie. q. ISSN 0008-4093

**Geography Club, Montreal**
- Arrow. (pub. by Gallery Publications Ltd.)

**Geological Association of Canada**
111 Peter Street, Toronto 1, Canada.
- Geoscience Canada. q. ISSN 0315-0941
- Geological Association of Canada. Guidebooks. irreg.
- Geological Association of Canada. Special Paper. a. ISSN 0072-1042

**Geological Survey of Canada**
*see* Canada. Geological Survey of Canada

**Georgia Straight Publishing Ltd.**
2110 W. 4th Ave., Vancouver, B.C. V6K 1N6, Canada.
● Georgia Straight; Vancouver free press. w. ISSN 0016-8432

**Georgian Bay Regional Library System**
30 Morrow Rd., Barrie, Ont. L4N 3V8, Canada.
● Georgian Bay Regional Library System. Directory-Member Libraries. irreg. ISSN 0380-8068

**German Philatelic Society**
374 Hazel St., Waterloo, Ont., Canada.
● Germany Stamp News. m. ISSN 0016-8963

**German Publications Ltd.**
Box 278, Pickering, Ont., L1V 2R4, Canada.
● Torontoer Zeitung. w. ISSN 0049-4240

**German Society of Winnipeg**
121 Charles St., Winnipeg, Man. R2W 4A6, Canada.
● Deutsche Vereinigung von Winnipeg. Mitteilungen. m. ISSN 0046-0141

**Gideons International in Canada**
501 Imperial Rd., Guelph, Ont. N1H 7A2, Canada.
● Canadian Gideon. bi-m. ISSN 0316-2907

**Gerry Gilbert, Ed. & Pub.**
Box 48884, Vancouver, B. C., Vancouver 5, B.C., Canada.
● British Columbia Monthly. 1-7 per yr. ISSN 0382-5272

**Gilmore Publications**
320 19th St., S.E., Calgary, Alberta T2E 6J6, Canada.
● Canadian Hereford Digest. m. ISSN 0008-3739

**Girl Guides of Canada**
Manitoba Council, 200-267 Edmonton St., Winnipeg, Man. R3C 1S2, Canada.
● Buffalo. irreg. ISSN 0045-334X
● Canadian Guider. 6 per yr.

**Gladney Publishing Group Ltd.**
43 Eglinton Ave. E., 706, Toronto, Ont. M4P 1A2, Canada.
● Government Purchasing Guide. bi-m. ISSN 0046-6220

**Glenbow Alberta Institute**
9Th Ave. & First St. S.E., Calgary, Alta. T2G 0P3, Canada.
● Glenbow Foundation. Archives Series. irreg. ISSN 0436-0605

**Globe and Mail Ltd.**
444 Front St. W., Toronto, Ont. M5V 2S9, Canada.
● Globe and Mail Report on Business. d. ISSN 0017-1212

**Globe Communications Corp.**
1440 St. Catherine St. West, Montreal, Quebec H3G 1S2, Canada.
● Startling Detective. bi-m. ISSN 0038-996X

**Glossa Society**
Dept. of Modern Languages, Simon Fraser University, Burnaby V5A 1S6, B.C., Canada.
● Glossa; an international journal of linguistics. s-a. ISSN 0017-1271

**Go Publishing Ltd.**
Box 2675, Sta. A, Edmonton, Alta., Canada.
● Go; going places, doing things in Edmonton. s-m. ISSN 0046-6042

**Goathair Press**
Box 251, Station B, Toronto, Ont. M5T 2W1, Canada.
● Queen Street. m.

**K. Godzinski, Ed. & Pub.**
Box 86, Toronto 9, Canada.
● Cine World. bi-m. ISSN 0009-6997

**Golden Arc Publishing and Typesetting Ltd.**
Box 65, Ancaster, Ont., Canada.
● Canadian Quarter Horse Journal. m. (Canadian Quarter Horse Association)
● Canadian Rider. m.

**Golden Temple Enterprises**
1962 W. 4th Avenue, Vancouver, B.C., Canada.
● New Directions. m. ISSN 0384-9147 (Humanity Foundation)

**C. W. Gonick**
Box 1413, Winnipeg 1, Man., Canada.
● Canadian Dimension; an independent journal of socialist opinion. 8 per yr. ISSN 0008-3402

**Gontran Trottier**
260 Quest rue Faillon, Montreal 327, Que., Canada.
● Interlex; revue internationale de droit compare generale et special. m.

**Good Neighbours Retired Citizens Association**
25 Palmer St., Truro, N.S. B2N 4E8, Truro, Nova Scotia B2N 3W4, Canada.
● Tidbits. irreg., 8th ed. 1976.

**Gospel Herald Foundation**
Box 94, Beamsville, Ontario L0R 1B0, Canada.
● Gospel Herald. m.

**Gospel Mission Publishers**
132 High Park Ave., Toronto, Ont., Canada.
● Ievanhelyst. m. ISSN 0383-2651

**Grand Manan Historical Society**
c/o Secretary, Grand Manan, New Brunswick EOG ILO, Canada.
● Grand Manan Historian. a.

**Grand Orange Lodge of Canada**
● Sentinel (Willowdale) (pub. by British America Publishing Co. Ltd.)

**Publications des Grands Lacs Inc.**
2418 Avenue Central, Windsor, Ont. N8W 4J3, Canada.
● Rempart. fortn. ISSN 0034-4273

**Great Western Press Ltd.**
9537-76 Ave., Edmonton, Alta. T6C 4H7, Canada.
● Western Catholic Reporter. w. ISSN 0512-5235

**Dr. Jerry Green, Ed. & Pub.**
32 Sullivan St., Toronto M5T 1B9, Canada.
● Critical List; issue in health and the illness business. q.

**Greencrest Industrial Publications**
Vancouver, British Columbia, Canada.
● Green Leaves: British Columbia Edition; directory of suppliers. s-a. ISSN 0380-8572

**Greenwich Meridian**
516 Ave. K. South, Saskatoon, Sask., Canada.
● Crosscurrents. irreg.

**Greey de Pencier Publications**
59 Front St. E., Toronto M5E 1B3, Ont., Canada.
● Canadian Publishers Directory. 2 per yr. ISSN 0008-4859
● Quill and Quire; the magazine of the Canadian book industry. 17 per yr. ISSN 0033-6491

**Gregg Publishing Co.**
Toronto, Ont., Canada.
● Canadian Gregg News. irreg. ISSN 0381-7008 (Canadian Gregg Association)

**Grimsby Independent**
Grimsby, Ontario, Canada.
● Silhouette. w. ISSN 0037-5217

**Growing Room Collective**
1918 Waterloo St., Vancouver, B.C. V6R 3G6, Canada.
● Room of One's Own; a feminist journal of literature and criticism. q. ISSN 0316-1609

**Guardian Publishing**
Box 312, Station B, Hamilton, Ont. L8L 7V7, Canada.
● Calvinist Contact. w. ISSN 0410-3882 (Christian Reformed Immigration Societies in Canada)

**Guide Publishing**
Box 3074, Station P, Thunder Bay, Ont. P7B 5E8, Canada.
● Thunder Bay Camping Guide. irreg. ISSN 0380-6197

**Gut**
c/o 10 Wascana Ave, Toronto, Ontario, Canada.
● Gut; magazine of prose, reviews, poetry, satire, graphics, cartoons. bi-m.

**H. B. Publishers**
1240 West Pender St., Vancouver, B.C. V6E 2S8, Canada.
● Hiballer Contractor. q.

**H.V. Chapman and Associates Ltd.**
Suite 700, 2 Bloor St. W., Toronto, Ont. M4W 1A1, Canada.
● Management Compensation in Canada. a.

**Haiku Press**
61 Macdonell Ave., Toronto, Ont. MGR 2A3, Canada.
● Haiku. q. ISSN 0017-6656

**A. M. Hakkert Ltd.**
554 Spadina Cresc., Toronto, Ont. M5S 2J9, Canada.
● Canadian War Museum. Historical Publications. irreg, no. 8, 1973.
● Case Studies in Community Action. irreg, vol. 3, 1973.
● McMaster Association for 18th Century Studies. Publications. irreg (approx. 1 per yr)
● Modern Drama. q. ISSN 0026-7694 (University of Toronto. Graduate Centre for Study of Drama)

**Robert G. Halford, Ed. & Pub.**
Box 669, Streetsville, Ont., Canada.
● Canadian Aircraft Operator; Canada's general aviation newspaper. s-m. ISSN 0008-2848

**Halifax Board of Trade**
● Halifax Board of Trade. Commercial News. (pub. by Fundy Group Publications Ltd.)

**Halifax Visitors and Convention Bureau**
● Metro Guide. Halifax-Dartmouth Current Events. (pub. by Aslin Advertising Co.)

**Halifax Wildlife Association**
Box 313, Halifax, N. S., Canada.
● Halifax Wildlife Association. Wildlife News. m. ISSN 0046-6743

**Hamilton Naturalists' Club**
Box 182, Sta. E., Hamilton, Ont. L8S 4L5, Canada.
● Wood Duck. 9 per yr. ISSN 0049-7886

**Harlequin Enterprises Ltd.**
240 Duncan Mill Rd., Don Mills, Ont. M3B 1Z4, Canada.
● Harlequin. m. ISSN 0319-0595

**Paul T. Harris, Ed. & Pub.**
Box 116, Terminal A, Besserer St., Ottawa, Ont. K1N 8V1, Canada.
● Catholic Book Review. 6 per yr. ISSN 0008-7920

**Rick Harris, Ed. & Pub.**
Box 5268, Terminal a, Toronto, Ont. M5W 1N5, Canada.
● Pulse. m. ISSN 0316-3857

**Harvest House, Ltd.**
4795 St. Catherine St., W., Montreal, Quebec H3Z 2B9, Canada.
● French Writers of Canada.

**Julius Hayman Ltd.**
Suite 507, 8 Colborne St., Toronto, Ont. M5E 1E1, Canada.
● Canadian Clothing Journal. bi-m. ISSN 0008-3232
● Jewish Standard. s-m. ISSN 0021-6739

**Health Culture Inc.**
10-158 Kennedy Road, South Brampton, Ontario, Canada.
● Muscle Mag International. q.

**Health League of Canada**
76 Avenue Rd., Toronto, Ont. M5R 2H1, Canada.
● Health. q. ISSN 0017-8837

**Heraldry Society of Canada**
1922 Alta Vista Drive, Ottawa, Ont. K1H 7K6, Canada.
● Heraldry in Canada/Heraldique au Canada. q. ISSN 0441-6619

**Highway Book Shop**
300,000 Yonge St., Cobalt, Ont. P0J 1C0, Canada
● Lifeline. s-m. ISSN 0316-0602 (Subscr. to: Pentamus Ltd., 29 Jutland Rd., Toronto, Ont., Canada)

**Historical and Scientific Society of Manitoba**
190 Rupert Ave., Winnipeg, Man. 53B 0N2,
Canada.
- Historical and Scientific Society of Manitoba.
  Transactions. irreg. ISSN 0382-9014
- Manitoba Pageant. 4 per yr (previously annual)
  ISSN 0025-2263

**Historical Society of Alberta**
95 Holmwood Ave. N.W., Calgary, Alta. T2K 2G7,
Canada.
- Alberta History. q.

**Historical Society of Alberta. Whoop up Country
Chapter**
P.O. Box 974, Lethbridge, Alberta T1J 4A2,
Canada.
- Historical Society of Alberta Newsletter. bi-m.

**Historical Society of Mecklenburg Upper Canada**
42 Noranda Drive, Toronto, Ont. M6M 2x9,
Canada.
- German-Canadian Yearbook/Deutschkanadisches
  Jahrbuch. a. ISSN 0316-8603

**History and Social Science Teacher Inc.**
1137 Western Rd., London, Ont. N6G 1G7,
Canada.
- History and Social Science Teacher. q. ISSN
  0316-4969 (University of Western Ontario.
  Faculty of Education)

**Hockey Illustrated Ltd.**
Box 901, Montreal, Que., Canada.
- Hockey Pictorial. 7 per yr. ISSN 0018-3024

**E. M. Hoffman, Ed. & Pub.**
Box 750, Chetwynd, B.C., Canada.
- Chetwynd Echo. w.

**Hollinger Mines Ltd.**
Suite 601, Commerce Court E., Box 221, Toronto,
Ont. M5L 1E8, Canada.
- Hollinger Mines Limited. Annual Report. a. ISSN
  0382-0734

**Holstein-Friesian Association of Canada**
- Holstein-Friesian Journal. (pub. by Donovan Ltd.)

**Holt Rinehart and Winston of Canada, Ltd.**
55 Horner Ave., Toronto, Ont. M8Z 4X6, Canada.
- Books for Young People. s-a. ISSN 0045-2548
- Canadian History Through the Press Series. irreg.

**Homersham Advertising Agency**
215 11802 124th St., Edmonton, Alta., Canada.
- Western Livestock & Agricultural News. m. ISSN
  0383-2058

**Homin Ukrainy Publishing Co.**
140 Bathurst St., Toronto, Ont. M5V 2R3, Canada.
- Almanakh Gomonu Ukrainy. irreg. ISSN 0441-
  1196
- Homin Ukrainy/Ukrainian Echo. w. ISSN 0018-
  4284

**Hopital Chicoutimi, Inc.**
Chicoutimi, Que., Canada.
- Saguenay Medical. q. ISSN 0036-2581

**Hopkins Quarterly**
English Dept., University of Guelph, Guelph, Ont.
N1G 2W1, Canada
- Hopkins Quarterly. q. ISSN 0094-9086

**Horticulture Publications Ltd.**
Box 697, Streetsville, Ont., Canada.
- Canadian Florist, Greenhouse and Nursery. fortn.
  ISSN 0008-3585

**Hospital for Sick Children**
Toronto, Ont., Canada.
- Toronto. Hospital for Sick Children. Research
  Institute. Annual Report. a. ISSN 0082-5034
- What's New. m. ISSN 0049-7533

**Houston Standard Publications Ltd.**
30 Duncan, Toronto, Ont. M5V 2C3, Canada.
- Bank Directory of Canada. a., with loose-
  supplements. ISSN 0045-1436 (Canadian Bankers
  Association)

**C. D. Howe Research Institute**
2064 Sun Life Bldg., Montreal, Que. H3B 2X7,
Canada.
- C. D. Howe Research Institute. Canadian
  Economic Policy Committee. (Publication) irreg.

- C. D. Howe Research Institute. Policy Review
  and Outlook. a.
- Canadian Economic Policy Committee Report.
  irreg.
- H R I Observation. 6 per yr. ISSN 0381-5250

**Howes Waldon Associates Ltd.**
399 Berry St., Winnipeg 1, Man., Canada.
- Winnipeg World. q. ISSN 0049-769X

**Hudson's Bay Co.**
Hudson's Bay House, Winnipeg 1, Man., Canada.
- Beaver; a magazine of the North. q. ISSN 0005-
  7517

**Huguenot Society of Canada**
c/o Mrs. Lela F. Common, 145 Kent St., Hamilton,
Ont. L8P 3Z2, Canada.
- Huguenot Trails. q. ISSN 0441-6910

**Humanities Association of Canada**
c/o P. W. Rogers, Ed., Queens Univ., Kingston,
Ont., Canada.
- Humanities Association Review/Association des
  Humanites. Revue. q. ISSN 0018-7542

**Humanities Research Council of Canada**
151 Slater St., Ottawa K1P 5H3, Canada.
- Humanities Research Council of Canada. Report.
  a. ISSN 0073-3946

**Humanity Foundation**
- New Directions. (pub. by Golden Temple
  Enterprises)

**Hungarian Readers' Service Inc.**
908-1356 Meadowlands Drive E., Ottawa, Ont.,
Canada.
- Canadian American Review of Hungarian Studies.
  s-a. ISSN 0317-204X

**Hungarian Turul Society Inc.**
Box 67, West-Hill, Ont., Canada.
- Crusader: Justice for Hungary. q. ISSN 0045-9143

**J. L. Hunt Publications Ltd.**
37 Hanna Ave., Toronto, Ont. M6K 1X4, Canada.
- Best Wishes. q. ISSN 0005-965X
- Young Family; the magazine for parents. q.

**Hydro-Quebec**
75 Dorchester West, Montreal, Que., Canada.
- Hydro-Presse. s-m.

**I N F O R Journal**
P.O. Box 2225, Station D, Ottawa, Canada.
- I N F O R Journal/C O R S; Canadian journal of
  operational research and information processing. 3
  per yr. ISSN 0315-5986

**I. S. P. of Canada**
2322 Cypress St., Vancouver V6J 3M8, Canada.
- International Skyline. q.

**Icelandic Canadian Club**
868 Arlington St., Winnipeg Man., R3E 2E4,
Canada.
- Icelandic Canadian. q. ISSN 0046-8452

**Iconomatrix**
Box 2, Postal Station A, Fredricton, N.B. E3B 4Y2,
Canada.
- Iconomatrix; polemical and iconoclastic quarterly.
  q. ISSN 0382-876X

**Idlewilde International Publishing Ltd.**
Box 6566, Stn. D, Calgary, Alta., Canada.
- Horses in Canada. m. ISSN 0046-7944
- Murray Grey Journal. m. ISSN 0317-1418
  (Canadian Murray Grey Association)

**Imperial Oil Ltd.**
111 St Clair Ave. W., Toronto, Ont. M5W 1K3,
Canada.
- Imperial Oil Fleet News. q.
- Imperial Oil Limited. Review. bi-m. ISSN 0380-
  903X

**Imperial Order Daughters of the Empire**
111 Eglinton E., Toronto 12, Canada.
- Echoes. q. ISSN 0012-9321

**Impulse**
Box 901, Station Q, Toronto, Ont. M4T 2P1,
Canada.
- Impulse. q.

**Independent Lithuanian Printing Co. Ltd.**
7722 George Street, La Salle 690, Quebec.
- Nepriklausoma Lietuva. w. ISSN 0047-9357

**Independent Order of Foresters**
789 Don Mills Rd., Don Mills, Ont. M3C IT9,
Canada.
- Independent Forester. bi-m.

**Independent Petroleum Association of Canada**
No. 270, 700-6 Ave. S. W., Calgary T2P 0T8,
Alberta, Canada.
- I P A C Petroleum News. irreg. ISSN 0073-5760

**Independent Survey Co. Ltd.**
Box 6000, Vancouver, B.C. V6B 4B9, Canada.
- Canadian Weekly Stock Charts: Industrials. m.
  ISSN 0383-2945
- Canadian Weekly Stock Charts: Mines & Oils. m.
  ISSN 0383-2953

**Indian & Metis Friendship Centre**
465 Alexander Ave., Winnipeg, Man. R3A 0N7,
Canada.
- New Nation. m.

**Indian Education Resources Centre**
c/o Brock Hall 106, University of British Columbia,
Vancouver, B.C. V6T 1W5, Canada.
- Indian Education Newsletter. irreg. (British
  Columbia Native Indian Teachers' Association)

**Indian Homemakers Association**
201-423 West Broadway, Vancouver, B.C. V5Y
1R4, Canada.
- Indian Voice. m.

**Indian News Media**
Box 58, Standoff, Alta., Canada.
- Kainai News. bi-m. ISSN 0047-3081

**Indian People's Association in North America**
Box 37, Westmount Post Office, Montreal, Que.,
Canada.
- New India Bulletin. bi-m.

**Indo-Canadian**
903 No. 5 Rd, Richmond, B.C., Canada.
- Indo-Canadian. q. ISSN 0019-722X

**Industrial Accident Prevention Association**
c/o Jack Oldham, 2 Bloor Street E., Toronto, Ont.
M4W 3C2, Canada.
- Accident Prevention. m. ISSN 0044-5878
- Industrial Accident Prevention Association.
  Annual Report. a. ISSN 0073-7305
- Industrial Accident Prevention Association. Guide
  to Safety. a. ISSN 0073-7313

**Industrial Accident Prevention Association of Quebec**
50 Place Cremalie, Suite 812, Montreal, Que. H2P
2T5, Canada.
- Prevention. m. ISSN 0048-5233

**Industrial Enterprises Inc.**
Charlottetown, P.E.I., Canada.
- Industrial Enterprises Incorporated. Annual
  Report. a.

**Information Access**
Box 34, Station S, Toronto, Ontario M5M 4L6,
Canada.
- Canadian Business Periodicals Index. m. ISSN
  0318-6717
- Canadian Newspaper Index. m (with annual
  cumulation) ISSN 0384-983X

**Information and Referral Centre of Greater Montreal**
759 Victoria Square, Suite 54, Montreal H2Y 2J7,
Canada.
- Directory of Community Services of Greater
  Montreal; welfare-health-recreation. biennial.

**Information Medicale et Paramedicale Inc.**
Boite Postale 219, Westmount-215, Montreal, Que.
H3Z 2T2, Canada.
- Information Medicale et Paramedicale. s-m. ISSN
  0020-014X

**Institut Canadien d'Education des Adultes**
506 Est, Rue Ste-Catherine, Suite 800, Montreal,
Que. H2L 2C7, Canada.
- I C E A; bulletin de liaison. bi-m.
- I. C. E. A. Cahiers. irreg. ISSN 0018-8891

**Institut d'Action Politique Pelerins de Saint Michel**
Rougemont (Rouville), Que., Canada.
- Vers Demain. bi-m. ISSN 0042-434X

**Institut d'Histoire de l'Amerique Francaise**
261 Avenue Bloomfield, Montreal, Que. H2V 3R6,
Canada.
- Revue d'Histoire de l'Amerique Francaise. q.
ISSN 0035-2357

**Institut de Pastorale**
2715 Chemin de la Cote Sainte-Catherine,
Montreal, P.Q. H3T 1B6, Canada.
- Communaute Chretienne. bi-m. ISSN 0010-3454

**Institut de Recherches Psychologiques, Inc.**
34 Fleury Street West, Montreal 357, P.Q., Canada.
- Here and Now; a brief of news from the IPR.
irreg. ISSN 0085-1493

**Institut des Assureurs-Vie Agrees du Canada**
41, Chemin Lesmill, Don Mills, Ont. M3B 2T3,
Canada.
- Commentaires (Don Mills) bi-m. ISSN 0382-7046

**Institute Chartered Life Underwriters**
- C L U Comment. (pub. by Life Underwriters
Association of Canada)

**Institute of Applied Metaphysics**
RR No. 3, Tweed, Ont., Canada.
- I AM Magazine. s-a.

**Institute of Association Executives**
Suite 309, 185 Bay St., Toronto, Ont. M5J 1K6,
Canada.
- Canadian Association Executive. bi-m. ISSN
0380-2264

**Institute of Chartered Secretaries and Administrators.**
**Canadian Division**
119 Adelaide St. W., Toronto, Ont., Canada.
- Institute of Chartered Secretaries &
Administrators. Canadian Division. Newsletter.
irreg. ISSN 0382-5833

**Institute of Municipal Assessors of Ontario**
180 Yorkland Blvd., Willowdale, Ont. M2J 1R5,
Canada.
- Assessors Review. m. ISSN 0044-9342

**Institute of Power Engineers**
c/o S. W. T. Gilbert, Ed., 2555 W. 15th Ave.,
Vancouver, B. C. 9, Canada.
- B. C. Power Engineer. q. ISSN 0005-2892

**Institute of Power Engineers, Toronto**
Toronto, Ont., Canada.
- Canadian Power Engineer. m. ISSN 0384-1677

**Institute of Public Administration of Canada**
1205 Fewster Dr., Unit 14, Mississauga, Ont. L4W
1A2, Canada.
- Canadian Public Administration/Administration
Publique du Canada. q. ISSN 0008-4840

**Institute of Social and Economic Research**
Memorial Univ. of Newfoundland, St. John's, Nfld.
a1C 5S7, Canada.
- Memorial University of Newfoundland. Institute
of Social and Economic Research . I S E R
Papers. irreg. ISSN 0078-0332
- Memorial University of Newfoundland. Institute
of Social and Economic Research. I S E R
Studies. irreg. ISSN 0078-0324

**Insurance Brokers Association of the Province of**
**Quebec**
300 Leo-Pariseau St., Montreal, Que. H2W 2N1,
Canada.
- Foresight. bi-m. ISSN 0384-5958

**Insurance Institute of Canada**
220 Bay St., Toronto, Ont. M5J 1P3, Canada.
- Insurance Institute of Canada. Newsletter. q.
- Insurance Institute of Canada. Report. a. ISSN
0074-0721

**Inter City Publishing Co.**
Montreal, Que., Canada.
- Canadian Mining and Financial News. irreg. ISSN
0382-7712

**International Air Transport Association.**
Box 550, International Aviation Square, 1000
Sherbrooke St., Montreal, Que. H3A 2R4, Canada.
- I A T A Review. irreg.
- International Air Transport Association. Annual
General Meeting Reports and Proceedings. a.
- State of the Air Transport Industry. a. ISSN 0081-
4571

**International Al Jolson Society**
Box 399, Brownsburg, Quebec, Canada.
- Jolson Journal. 3 per yr.

**International Alliance of Hospital Volunteers**
Suite 323, 1117 St. Catherine St. W., Montreal,
P.Q. H3B 1H9, Canada.
- Vistas for Volunteers. a, no. 14, 1974.

**International Association for Cross-Cultural**
**Psychology**
c/o J. W. Berry, Psychology Dept., Queen's
University, Kingston, Ont. K7L 3N6, Canada.
- International Association for Cross-Cultural
Psychology. Newsletter. 6 per yr.

**International Association of Master Penmen and**
**Teachers of Handwriting**
- Penmen's News Letter. (pub. by Eileen
Richardson, Ed. & Pub.)

**International Association of Meteorology and**
**Atmospheric Physics**
- International Conference on Cloud Physics.
Proceedings. (pub. by International Commission
on Cloud Physics)

**International Association of Microbiological Societies**
c/o Gen. Sec., National Research Council, Division
of Biosciences, Sussex Dr., Ottawa 2, Ont., Canada.
- International Congress for Microbiology.
Proceedings. irreg., 10th, 1970, Mexico. ISSN
0074-3410

**International Association of Science and Technology**
**for Development**
- Automatic Control Theory and Applications. (pub.
by Acta Press)

**International Atlantic Salmon Foundation**
P.O. Box 429, St. Andrews, N.B., EG0 2X0,
Canada.
- International Atlantic Salmon Foundation.
Newsletter. bi-m.
- International Atlantic Salmon Foundation. Special
Publication Series. irreg.

**International Civil Aviation Organization**
For publications of this agency see section for
UNITED NATIONS

**International Commission for the Northwest Atlantic**
**Fisheries**
P.O. Box 638, Dartmouth, N.S. B2Y 3Y9, Canada.
- International Commission for the Northwest
Atlantic Fisheries. Annual Report. a. ISSN 0303-
4151
- International Commission for the Northwest
Atlantic Fisheries. Guide to I C N A F Papers.
Supplement. a.
- International Commission for the Northwest
Atlantic Fisheries. List of Fishing Vessels.
triennial. ISSN 0074-2635
- International Commission for the Northwest
Atlantic Fisheries. Research Bulletin. a. ISSN
0074-2651
- International Commission for the Northwest
Atlantic Fisheries. Redbook. a. ISSN 0074-2643
- International Commission for the Northwest
Atlantic Fisheries. Selected Papers. irreg. ISSN
0380-4933
- International Commission for the Northwest
Atlantic Fisheries. Special Publications. irreg.
ISSN 0074-2678
- International Commission for the Northwest
Atlantic Fisheries. Statistical Bulletin. a. ISSN
0074-266X

**International Commission on Cloud Physics**
Inquire: Prof. W. Hitschfeld, Sec., Dept. of
Meteorology, McGill University, Montreal 110,
Que, Canada.
- International Conference on Cloud Physics.
Proceedings. irreg., 1968, 14th, Toronto. ISSN
0074-3011 (International Association of
Meteorology and Atmospheric Physics)

**International Commission on the History of**
**Mathematics**
c/o Dept. of Mathematics, University of Toronto,
Toronto, Ont. M5S 1A1, Canada.
- Historia Mathematica. q. ISSN 0315-0860

**International Council for Adult Education**
29 Prince Arthur Ave., Toronto, Ont. M5R 1B2,
Canada.
- Convergence/Convergencia; international journal
of adult education. q. ISSN 0010-8146

**International Development Research Centre. Devsis**
**Study Team**
Box 8500, Ottawa K1S 3H9, Canada.
- Devsis Newsletter. (Development Sciences
Information System) irreg. ISSN 0303-9544

**International Fiction Association**
Dept of German & Russian, University of New
Brunswick, Fredericton, N. B., Canada.
- International Fiction Review. s-a. ISSN 0315-4149

**International Folk Music Council**
Department of Music, Queen's University, Kingston,
Ont. K7L 3N6, Canada.
- International Folk Music Council. Bulletin. s-a.
ISSN 0020-6768
- International Folk Music Council. Yearbook. a.
ISSN 0074-6096

**International Group for Research on Women**
c/o Dept. of Sociology, O.I.S.E., 252 Bloor St. W.,
Toronto, Ont. M5S 1V6, Canada.
- Canadian Newsletter of Research on Women. 3
per yr. ISSN 0319-4477

**International Harvester Company of Canada Ltd**
1190 Blair Rd., Burlington, Ont. L7M 1K9, Canada.
- Canadian Farming. 4 per yr. ISSN 0045-4753

**International Joint Commission. Great Lakes**
**Regional Office**
100 Quellette Ave., Windsor, Ontario N9A 6T3,
Canada.
- Great Lakes Focus on Water Quality. q.

**International Joint Commission. Great Lakes**
**Research Advisory Board**
100 Quellette Ave., Windsor, Ont. N9A 6T3,
Canada.
- Great Lakes Research Advisory Board. Annual
Report. a.

**International Microwave Power Institute**
Box 1556, Edmonton, Alta. T5J 2N7, Canada.
- Journal of Microwave Power. q. ISSN 0022-2739
- Microwave Energy Applications Newsletter. bi-m.
ISSN 0026-2889
- Microwave Power Symposium. Proceedings. a.

**International Nickel Company of Canada Ltd.**
Toronto Dominion Centre, Toronto 1, Ont.,
Canada.
- I N C O Nickel News. q.
- International Nickel Company of Canada. Annual
Report. a. ISSN 0383-1264

**International North Pacific Fisheries Commission**
6640 N.W. Marine Dr., Vancouver, B.C. V6T 1X2,
Canada.
- International North Pacific Fisheries Commission.
Annual Report. a. ISSN 0074-7165
- International North Pacific Fisheries Commission.
Bulletin. irreg. ISSN 0074-7157

**International Organization of Supreme Audit**
**Institutions**
Box 1138, Postal Station Q, Toronto, Ont. M4T
2P4, Canada.
- International Journal of Government Auditing/
Journal International des Institutions Superieures
de Controle/Revista Internacional de Entidades
Fiscalizadoras Superiores. q. ISSN 0047-0724

**International Pacific Salmon Fisheries Commission**
New Westminster, B.C., Canada.
- International Pacific Salmon Fisheries
Commission. Annual Report. a. ISSN 0074-7254
- International Pacific Salmon Fisheries
Commission. Bulletin. irreg. ISSN 0074-7262
- International Pacific Salmon Fisheries
Commission. Progress Report. irreg. ISSN 0074-
7270

**International Plastic Modellers Society-Canada**
Box 626, Stn.B, Ottawa, Ont. K1P 5P7, Canada.
- Random Thoughts. m. ISSN 0380-8114

**International Political Science Association**
c/o University of Ottawa, Ottawa, Ont. K1N 6N5,
Canada.
- International Political Science Association. World
Congress. triennial, 10th, 1976. Edinburgh.
- Participation. 3 per yr. (plus annual supplement)

**International Press Journal**
Box 758, Station F, Toronto, Ont., Canada.
- International Press Journal; international press
news and views. bi-m. ISSN 0020-837X

**International Press Ltd.**
643 Yonge St., Toronto, Ont. M4Y 2A2, Canada.
- Who's Who in Canada. biennial. ISSN 0083-9450

**International Railway Publishing Co. Ltd.**
480 Lagauchetiere St. W., Montreal, Que. H2Z 1E3, Canada.
- Canadian Guide; Canada's Up-to-the-Minute Gazetteer & Shipper's Directory. m. ISSN 0008-3712

**International Review**
2 Carlton St., Suite 919, Toronto, Ont., Canada.
- International Review. fortn. ISSN 0047-1186

**International Society of Educational Planners**
c/o Dept. of Educational Planning, OISE, 252 Bloor St. W., Toronto M5S 1V6, Ont., Canada, MN 56001.
- Educational Planning. q. ISSN 0315-9388

**International Union of Geodesy and Geophysics**
University of Toronto, Geophysics Laboratory, Toronto 5, Canada.
- International Union of Geodesy and Geophysics. Monograph. irreg. ISSN 0539-1016

**International Union of Pure and Applied Physics**
c/o Prof. L. Kerwin, Sec.-Gen., Universite Laval, Quebec, P.Q. G1K 7P4, Canada.
- International Conference on Atomic Masses. Proceedings. (pub. by University of Manitoba Press)
- International Conference on High Energy Physics and Nuclear Structure. Proceedings. irreg., 3rd, 1970.
- International Congress on Acoustics. Reports. irreg., 1968, 6th, Tokyo. ISSN 0074-400X

**International Union of Pure and Applied Physics. Commission on Atomic and Molecular Physics and Spectroscopy**
c/o Prof. L. Kerwin, Universite Laval, Quebec, P.Q. G1K 7P4, Canada.
- International Conference on the Physics of Electronic and Atomic Collisions. Papers. irreg., 1971, no. 7, publisher varies for each number. ISSN 0074-333X

**International Woodworkers of America. Regional Council No. 1**
2859 Com. Dr., Vancouver 12, B. C., Canada.
- Western Canadian Lumber Worker. m. ISSN 0049-7371

**Interpress Publications Ltd.**
1132 Hamilton St., Vancouver, B.C., Canada.
- Pacific Yachting. m. ISSN 0030-8986

**Interprovincial School for the Deaf**
Box 308, Amherst, N.S., Canada.
- New Scotian. bi-m.(Sept-June) ISSN 0028-6672

**Inter-Union Commission on Geodynamics**
c/o R. D. Russell, Department of Geophysics, University of British Columbia, 2075 Wesbrook Place, Vancouver V6T 1W5, Canada.
- Geodynamic Highlights. irreg (1-4 per yr)
- Inter-Union Commission on Geodynamics Report/Commission Inter-Unions de Geodynamique Report. irreg. (approx. 1-2 per yr.)

**Interuniversity Centre for European Studies**
P.O. Box 8888, Montreal, Quebec H3C 3P8, Canada.
- Interuniversity Centre for European Studies. International Colloquium Proceedings. irreg.
- Interuniversity Centre for European Studies. Newsletter. s-m. ISSN 0319-1095

**Inummart**
Igloolik, Northwest Territories, Canada.
- Inummart. q.

**Italian Chamber of Commerce of Toronto**
159 Bay St., Suite 313, Toronto, Ont. M5J 1J7, Canada.
- Italy Canada Trade. q. ISSN 0021-3098

**Italian Cultural Institute**
- Yearbook of Italian Studies. (pub. by Casalini Libri IT)

**Japan External Trade Organization**
- J E T R O Communique. (pub. by Japan Trade Centre)

**Japan Trade Centre**
151 Bloor St. West, Toronto, Ont. M5S 1T7, Canada.
- J E T R O Communique; a digest of business news from Japan. (Japan External Trade Organization)

**Jardin Botanique de Montreal**
Bibliotheque, 4101 E. rue Sherbrooke, Montreal 406, Que., Canada.
- Jardin Bontanique de Montreal. Annuelles et Legumes. a. ISSN 0077-1317
- Jardin Botanique de Montreal. Annuelles et Legumes: Resultats des Cultures d'Essai. irreg. ISSN 0319-3098
- Jardin Botanique de Montreal. Memoire. irreg. ISSN 0077-1325

**Jewish Chronicle Enterprises, Inc.**
4781 van Horne, Montreal, Que. H3W 1J1, Canada.
- Canadian Jewish Chronicle Review. m. ISSN 0008-3925

**Jewish Community Council of Ottawa**
151 Chapel St., Ottawa, Ont. K1N 7Y2, Canada.
- Ottawa Jewish Bulletin and Review. m.

**Jewish Community of British Columbia**
- Jewish Western Bulletin. (pub. by Anglo-Jewish Publishers)

**Jewish Public Library**
Cote St. Catherine Rd., Montreal H3W 1M6, Canada.
- Jewish Public Library Bulletin/Bibliotheque Publique Juive Bulletin. m.

**John Coutts Library Service Ltd.**
4290 Third Ave., Niagara Falls, Ont. L2E 4K7, Canada.
- Current Canadian Imprints Catalogued. m.

**Bruce Johnston**
80 Brock St. E., Tillsonburg, Ont. N4G 4H6, Canada.
- Canadian Sportsman; devoted to the interests of harness horse breeding and racing. w.(May-Oct.) fortn.(Nov-April) ISSN 0008-5073

**Joint Fire Prevention Publicity Committee Inc.**
196 Bronson Ave., Suite 111, Ottawa, Ont. K1R 6H4, Canada.
- Fire Prevention News. a. ISSN 0071-5395 (Co-sponsors: Canadian Association of Fire Chiefs; Association of Fire Commissioners and Fire Marshalls)

**Jonah Publishing Ltd.**
46 Park Hill Rd., Toronto, Ont. M6C 3N1, Canada.
- Chitty's Law Journal. m.(except July & Aug.) ISSN 0009-4889
- Legal Medical Quarterly. q.

**Journal Constructo**
Service de Gestion Industrielle, C. P. 157, Longueuil, Que., Canada.
- Journal Constructo. w. ISSN 0047-2115

**Journal of Commerce Ltd.**
2000 W. 12th Ave., Vancouver B. C., Canada.
- British Columbia Lumberman; truck logging, saw milling, plywoods, general forestry (regional) m. ISSN 0007-0548
- British Columbia Lumberman's Greenbook. a. ISSN 0068-1601
- Construction West. m. ISSN 0010-6941
- Journal of Commerce. s-w. ISSN 0021-9819

**Journal of Rheumatology**
920 Yonge St., Suite 420, Toronto, Ont. M4W 3J7, Canada.
- Journal of Rheumatology. q. ISSN 0315-162X

**JR Rider**
c/o Mrs. Jan Fewster, Ed., R.R. 1 Kemptville, Ontario K0G 1J0, Canada.
- JR Rider. 4 per yr.

**Judaica Post**
c/o A. Ben David, 3018 Bathurst St., Toronto, Ont., Canada.
- Judaica Post. bi-m.

**Junior League of Halifax**
Box 3380, Halifax South Post Office, Halifax, N.S. B3J 3J1, Canada.
- Ahoy; an Atlantic magazine for children. 3 per yr.

**K-W Probe News**
University of Waterloo, Waterloo, Ont., Canada.
- K-W Probe. irreg. ISSN 0079-3124

**Kanada Esperanto-Asocio**
5B Commercial Centre, Box 174, Roxboro, Que. H8Y 3E9.
- Lumo. q. ISSN 0024-7367

**Kenroy Publishers Ltd.**
Harpell Press Bldg., 1 Pacific, Ste. Anne de Bellevue, Que. H9X 1C5, Canada.
- Bakers Journal; the national business publication serving the Canadian bakery industry. bi-m. ISSN 0005-4097
- Canadian Beverage Review; serving the vending, brewing, soft-drink, distilling and wine industries. bi-m. ISSN 0008-3011

**Kent Historical Society**
Chatham, Ont., Canada.
- Kent Historical Society. Papers and Addresses. irreg.

**Kerrwil Publications Ltd.**
20 Holly St., Suite 201, Toronto, Ont. M4S 2E8, Canada.
- C E D A Current. 6 per yr. (Canadian Electrical Distributors Association)
- Electrical Business. m. ISSN 0013-4244
- Monde de l'Electricite. m. ISSN 0026-9379

**Key Publishers Ltd.**
59 Front St. E., Toronto, Ont. M5E 1B3, Canada.
- Key to Toronto. m. ISSN 0023-0863
- Toronto Life. m. (plus two quarterly supplements) ISSN 0049-4194

**Kildonan Promotions Ltd.**
1155 Henderson Hwy., North Kildonan 16, Man., Canada.
- Examiner; a community newspaper. w. ISSN 0014-3979

**Killaly Press**
764 Dalkeith Ave., London, Ontario N5X 1R8, Canada.
- Killaly Chapbooks. irreg.
- Stuffed Crocodile. q. ISSN 0315-0496

**Kindness Club**
13 Brant Ave., Mississauga, Ont. L5G 3N9, Canada.
- Fur & Feathers. q. ISSN 0016-2906

**Kingston Arts Council**
246 Phillips St., Kingston, Ont. K7M 3A2, Canada.
- Arts-Kingston. irreg.

**Kingston Field Naturalists**
Box 831, Kingston, Ont. K7L 4X6, Canada.
- Blue Bill. q. ISSN 0382-5655

**KMW Commodity Consultants Ltd.**
85 Bloor St. E., 4th Floor, Toronto, Ont. M4W 1A9, Canada.
- Foodservice & Hospitality; Canada's hospitality business magazine. m. ISSN 0007-8972

**Kobzar Publishing Co. Ltd.**
1164 Dundas St. W., Toronto 3, Ont., Canada.
- Ukrainian Canadian; window on a cultural heritage. m. ISSN 0049-5077

**Mykola Kolankiwsky, Ed. & Pub.**
c/o Niagara Falls Art Gallery and Museum, Queen Elizabeth Way, R.R.2., Niagara Falls, Ont. L2E 6S5, Canada.
- My i Svit/We and the World. ISSN 0027-5417

**Kontakt**
Box 1339, Postal Sta. A, Toronto 1, Ont., Canada.
- Kontakt. 6 per yr. ISSN 0023-365X

**L S M Information Center**
P.O. Box 94338, Richmond, B.C. V6Y 2A8, Canada.
- Life Histories from the Revolution. irreg.

**Editions La Presse**
7 rue St. Jacques, Montreal, Que. H2Y 1K9,
Canada.
- Ecrits du Canada Francais. 3 per yr. ISSN 0013-0729

**Labor Challenge Publications**
Box 5595, Sta. A., Toronto 1, Ont., Canada.
- Labor Challenge. fortn. ISSN 0047-3847

**Labor Zionist Movement of Canada**
4770 Kent Ave., Suite 300, Montreal 252, Que.,
Canada.
- Viewpoints; Canadian Jewish quarterly. q. ISSN 0042-5818

**Labour Canada**
see Canada. Labour Canada

**Bruce & Ruth J. Lahti, Ed. & Pub.**
Box 2418, Postal Station P, Thunder Bay, Ont. P7B
5E9, Canada.
- Canadan Uutiset. w. ISSN 0008-2775

**Lake Erie Regional Library System**
380 Saskatoon Street, London, Ont. N5W 4R3,
Canada.
- Intralogue. m (except Jul. & Aug.) ISSN 0700-463X

**Lakehead University. Art and Literary Society**
c/o Keith Muncaster, Oliver Rd., Thunder Bay N,
Ont., Canada.
- Muskeg Review. a.

**Lakehead University. Student Union**
Thunder Bay, Ont., Canada.
- Argus. w. ISSN 0004-1165

**Lance Publishing Co. Ltd.**
20 Dakota St., Winnipeg, Man., Canada.
- Whiteshell Echo. m. ISSN 0043-5015 (Whiteshell
District Association)

**Lancelot Press, Windsor, N.S. Canada**
- Canadian Directory of Railway Museums and
Displays. a.

**Lapidary Rock & Mineral Society of British
Columbia**
941 Wavertree Rd., North Vancouver, B. C.,
Canada.
- Canadian Rockhound. bi-m. ISSN 0008-4956

**Latin American Working Group**
Box 2207, Station P, Toronto, Ont. M5S 2T2,
Canada.
- L A W G Letter. 8 per yr. ISSN 0316-3393

**Latvian Relief Society of Canada (Daugavas Vanagi)**
- Daugavas Vanagu Menesraksts. (pub. by Daugavas
Vanags Publishing Ltd.)
- Latvija Amerika. (pub. by Latvija Amerika
Publishing Ltd.)

**Latvija Amerika Publishing Ltd.**
125 Broadview Ave., Toronto, Ont. M4M 2E9,
Canada.
- Latvija Amerika; latvian newspaper. s-w. ISSN
0023-8902 (Latvian Relief Society of Canada
(Daugavas Vanagi))

**Laurentian University**
Sudbury, Ontario P3E 2C6, Canada.
- Laurentian University Review/Revue de
l'Universite Laurentienne. 2 per yr. ISSN 0023-9011

**Law Society of Upper Canada**
Osgoode Hall, Toronto M5H 2C9, Ont., Canada
(Subscr. To: John Honsberger, Rm. 501, 85
Richmond St. W., Toronto 1, Ont., Canada)
- Law Society Gazette. q. ISSN 0023-9364
- Law Society of Upper Canada. Special Lectures. a.
ISSN 0316-5310

**Bryon Lawes, Ed. & Pub.**
No. 34, 2625 Hemlock St., Vancouver, B.C. V6H
2V6, Canada.
- Elder Statesman. bi-m. ISSN 0013-4074 (Elder
Citizens in British Columbia)

**Frederic Leach, Ed. & Pub.**
Berens River, Manitoba R0B 0AO, Canada.
- Northern Lights. m.

**Stephen Leacock Associates**
P. O. Box 854, Orilla, Ont., Canada.
- Newspacket. q. ISSN 0384-1642

**League of Canadian Poets. Executive Committee**
10181 149th St., Surrey, B.C. V3R 6A1,
Canada.
- League of Canadian Poets. Newsletter. irreg. ISSN
0319-6658

**Leech Printing Ltd.**
Brandon, Man., Canada.
- Canadian Gunner. a. ISSN 0068-8843 (Royal
Regiment of Canadian Artillery)
- Shilo Stag. s-m. ISSN 0037-3729

**Leisurability Publications Inc.**
Box 281, Ottawa, Ontario K1N 8V2, Canada.
- Journal of Leisurability. q.

**J. H. Leonard**
Toronto, Ont., Canada.
- Canadian Gem and Family Visitor. m. ISSN
0382-5809

**Publications Les Affaires Inc.**
635 Henri-Bourassa E., Montreal, P.Q. H2C 1E4,
Canada.
- Affaires. w. ISSN 0044-6459

**Letters of Interest Associates**
Box 181, Don Mills, Ont., Canada.
- Interest. m. ISSN 0381-7857

**Liberal Party in Alberta**
912 McLeod Bldg., Edmonton, Alberta, Canada.
- Alberta Liberal. irreg. ISSN 0382-5345

**Liberal Party in Ontario**
15 Duncan St., Toronto 1, Ontario, Canada.
- Liberal. bi-m. ISSN 0024-1784

**Libertarian Enterprises of Canada**
Box 603 Station F, Toronto, Ont. M4Y 2L8,
Canada.
- Option; Canada's international magazine for free
enterprise & civil liberty. bi-m.

**Librairie Beauchemin Limitee**
450 Avenue Beaumont, Montreal, Que. H3N 1T8,
Canada.
- Almanach du Peuple. a. ISSN 0065-650X
- Union Medicale du Canada. m. ISSN 0041-6959

**Library Association of Alberta**
1122 Crescent Rd N.W., Calgary 41, Alberta,
Canada.
- Library Association of Alberta. Occasional Papers.
irreg. ISSN 0075-904X

**Editions Lidec**
1083 Ave. van Horne, Montreal 154, Quebec,
Canada.
- Collection Panorama. irreg. ISSN 0530-8836

**Life Underwriters Association of Canada**
41 Lesmill Rd., Don Mills, Ont. M3B 2T3, Canada.
- C L U Comment. 6 per yr. ISSN 0382-7038
(Institute Chartered Life Underwriters)
- Forum. 10 per yr.
- Guide to a Successful Life Insurance Career. a.
ISSN 0381-6532
- L U A C Monitor. irreg. ISSN 0318-8116

**Ligue Antituberculeuse de Quebec**
261 W. Rue St-Vallier, Quebec 8, Canada.
- Ligue Antituberculeuse de Quebec. Rapport. a.
ISSN 0075-9465

**Ligue d'Action Nationale**
82 ouest, rue Sherbrooke, Montreal, Que. H2X 1X3,
Canada.
- Action Nationale. 10 per yr. ISSN 0001-7469

**Ligue des Jeune Socialistes**
226 Est rue Ste-Catherine, Montreal, Que., Canada.
- Jeune Garde. bi-m. ISSN 0021-5759

**Lillooet District Historical Society**
Box 441, Lillooet, B.C. V0K 1V0, Canada.
- Lillooet District Historical Society. Bulletin. irreg.
ISSN 0383-9133

**Linguistic Research Inc.**
Box 5677, Sta. L., Edmonton, Alta. T6C 4G1,
Canada.
- International Review of Slavic Linguistics. irreg.
(Co-sponsor: Vanek Institute of Canadian
Languages and Cultures)

**Lions International District "A"**
1407 Yonge St., Toronto 7, Ont., Canada.
- Lionage. q.

**Livre Canadien**
4635 rue de Lorimer, Montreal, Que. H2H 2B4,
Canada.
- Livre Canadien. 10 per yr. ISSN 0384-7446

**Editions Lizon**
Montreal, Que., Canada.
- Tricot Journal. irreg. ISSN 0381-9485

**Lloyd Publications of Canada**
Box 262, West Hill, Ont. M1E 4R5, Canada.
- Canadian Chemical, Pharmaceutical and Product
Directory. a. ISSN 0068-8452
- Canadian Engineering & Industrial Year Book. a.
ISSN 0068-8665
- Canadian Food and Packaging Directory. a. ISSN
0068-8754
- Canadian Footwear & Leather Directory. a. ISSN
0068-8762
- Canadian Furniture & Furnishings Directory. a.
ISSN 0068-8789
- Canadian Hardware, Electrical & Building Supply
Directory. a. ISSN 0456-3867
- Canadian Hotel, Restaurant, Institution & Store
Equipment Directory. a. ISSN 0381-5765
- Canadian Jewellery & Giftware Directory. a. ISSN
0068-9041
- Canadian Music Directory. a. ISSN 0381-5730
- Canadian Sporting Goods & Playthings. Directory.
a. ISSN 0316-7771
- Canadian Textile Directory. a. ISSN 0068-9858
- Canadian Variety & Merchandise Directory. a.
ISSN 0068-9955

**Logan Brown Communications**
56 Esplanade, Suite 504, Toronto, Ont. M5E 1A7,
Canada.
- Building Management Maintenance News. bi-m.
(Building Owners Managers Association) (Co-
sponsor: Canadian Sanitation Standards
Association)
- Curler; Canada's national curling magazine. 4 per
yr.
- Decor; the Canadian journal for decorating
retailers. 6 per yr.

**Logberg-Heimskringla Publishing Co. Ltd.**
67 St. Anne's Rd., Winnipeg, Man. R2M 2Y4,
Canada.
- Logberg-Heimskringla. 39 per yr. ISSN 0047-4967

**Long Time Coming**
Box 128, Station G, Montreal, Que., Canada.
- Long Time Coming. bi-m. ISSN 0382-5868

**Longmans Canada, Ltd.**
55 Barber Greene Rd., Don Mills, Ont., M3C 2A1,
Canada.
- Canadian Social Problems Series. irreg.

**Henri Longpre**
2673 de la Ronde Quebec 3, Que., Canada.
- Courrier du Francais-Cadre. m. except Jul.-Aug.

**Loto-Quebec**
Bureau 2100, 500 Place d'Armes, Montreal, Que.
H2Y 3J4, Canada.
- Loto-Quebec. Rapport Annuel. a.

**Loyola Students Association**
6931 Sherbrooke St. W., Montreal 262, Que,
Canada.
- Loyola News. w. ISSN 0024-7073

**Lutheran Church in America. Eastern Canada Synod**
251 King St. W., Kitchener, Ont., Canada.
- Canada Lutheran. 10 per yr. ISSN 0008-2716

**Lutheran Church in America. Western Canada Synod**
9901 107Th Street, Edmonton, Alberta T5K 1G4,
Canada.
- Lutheran Church in America. Western Canada
Synod. Minutes of the Annual Convention. a.
ISSN 0460-024X

**Lutheran Council in Canada**
Division of Information Services, 500-365 Hargrave St., Winnipeg, Man. R3B 2K3, Canada.
- Lutheran Churches in Canada. Directory. a. ISSN 0316-800X

**R. W. Lyman (Canada Co.)**
Box 23, Station V, Toronto, Ont. M6R 3A4, Canada.
- Lyman's Canada-British North America Postage Stamp Retail Catalogue. a. ISSN 0085-2910

**Lyone Publications Ltd.**
508-606 Victoria Avenue, Saskatoon, Sask. 57N 0Z1, Canada.
- Who's Who in Alberta. irreg.

**M D Publications (Canada) Ltd.**
1310 Greene Ave., Westmount 215, Que., Canada.
- M D of Canada. m. ISSN 0047-5246

**M. P. I. Publishers (Motive Power International)**
Box 39, Port Moody, B.C. V3H 3E1, Canada.
- Motive Power International. q. ISSN 0381-9868

**Maccan Publishing Co.**
702 Weston Rd., Suite 203, Toronto, Ont. M6N 3R2, Canada.
- Modern Dairy. bi-m. ISSN 0026-7651

**McGill Medical Undergraduate Society**
McIntyre Medical Sciences Centre, Montreal, Que, Canada.
- McGill Medical Journal. 4 per yr. ISSN 0024-905X

**McGill-Queen's University Press**
1020 Pine Ave. W., Montreal, Quebec H3A 1A2, Canada.
- Keith Callard Lecture Series. irreg. ISSN 0541-623X (McGill University. Centre for Developing - Area Studies)
- Transcultural Psychiatric Research Review. s-a. ISSN 0041-1108

**McGill University**
P. O. Box 6070, Montreal, Que. 101, Canada
(Dist. by McGill Sub-Arctic Research Laboratory, P.O. Box 790, Schefferville, Que. Canada)
- McGill Sub-Arctic Research Papers. irreg., 1970, no. 25. ISSN 0076-1982
- McGill University, Montreal. Axel Heiberg Island Research Reports. irreg. ISSN 0076-1850
- McGill University, Montreal. Marine Sciences Centre. Manuscript Report. irreg. (approx. 2 per yr.)

**McGill University. Brace Research Institute**
Ste. Anne de Bellevue, Que. H0A 1C0, Canada.
- McGill University, Montreal. Brace Research Institute. Annual Report. a. ISSN 0076-1877
- McGill University, Montreal. Brace Research Institute, Barbados. Do-It-Yourself Leaflets. irreg., 1969, no. 9. ISSN 0076-1869

**McGill University. Centre for Developing-Area Studies**
Montreal, Que. H3A 1W7, Canada.
- Keith Callard Lecture Series. (pub. by McGill-Queen's University Press)
- McGill University, Montreal. Centre for Developing-Area Studies. Annual Report. a. ISSN 0076-1893
- McGill University, Montreal. Centre for Developing-Area Studies. Bibliography Series. irreg., no. 7, 1977. ISSN 0316-6570
- McGill University, Montreal. Centre for Developing-Area Studies. Occasional Paper Series. irreg., no. 11, 1975. ISSN 0076-1907
- McGill University, Montreal. Centre for Developing-Area Studies. Reprint Series. irreg., no. 40, 1975. ISSN 0076-1915
- McGill University, Montreal. Centre for Developing-Area Studies. Working Papers. irreg., no. 18, 1976. ISSN 0384-059X
- Manpower and Unemployment Research. s-a.

**McGill University. Dental Students' Society**
Montreal, Quebec, Canada.
- McGill Dental Review. irreg. ISSN 0024-9025

**McGill University. Department of Classics**
855 Sherbrooke St. W., Montreal, Que. H3A 2T7, Canada.
- Teiresias; a review and continuing bibliography of boiotian studies. s-a (plus supplements) ISSN 0381-9361

**McGill University. Department of Geography**
805 Sherbrooke St. West, Montreal, Que. H3A 2K6, Canada.
- McGill University, Montreal. Department of Geography. Climatological Bulletin. s-a. ISSN 0541-6256
- McGill University, Montreal. Department of Geography. Climatological Research Series. irreg. ISSN 0076-1931
- Publications in Tropical Geography Savanna Research Series. irreg. ISSN 0079-7758

**McGill University. Department of Meteorology**
P.O. Box 6070, Montreal, Que. H3C 3G1, Canada.
- McGill University, Montreal. Department of Meteorology. Publication in Meteorology. irreg. ISSN 0076-1842

**McGill University. Department of Physics**
Eaton Lab., Rm 115, Po Box 6070, Station a, Montreal H3C 3G1, Que., Canada.
- Eaton Electronics Research Laboratories. Technical Report. irreg. ISSN 0070-8275

**McGill University. Engineering Undergraduate Society**
Engineering Bldg., P.O. Box 6070, Montreal 101 H3C 3G1, Canada.
- McGill Engineer. a. ISSN 0076-1826

**McGill University. Faculty of Education**
3700 McTavish St., Montreal 112, Que., Canada.
- McGill Journal of Education. s-a. ISSN 0024-9033

**McGill University. Faculty of Law**
Chancellor Day Hall, 3644 Peel St., Montreal, Que. H3A 1W9, Canada.
- McGill Law Journal. 4 per yr. ISSN 0024-9041
- W. C. J. Meredith Memorial Lectures. (pub. by Wilson et Lafleur Ltee)

**McGill University. Graduate Business Students' Society**
Box 6070, Montreal, Que. H3C 3G1, Canada.
- McGill Journal of Business. q. ISSN 0541-6159

**McGill University. Graduates' Society**
3605 Mountain St., Montreal, P.Q. H3G 2M1, Canada.
- McGill News. q. ISSN 0024-9068

**McGill University. Industrial Relations Centre**
1001 Sherbrooke St. W., Montreal 110 P.Q., Canada.
- McGill University, Montreal. Industrial Relations Centre. Annual Conference Proceedings. a. ISSN 0076-194X
- McGill University, Montreal. Industrial Relations Centre. Review. 3 per yr. ISSN 0024-9076

**McGill University. Institute of Air and Space Law**
McGill University Press, Montreal, Que., Canada.
- Yearbook of Air and Space Law/Annuaire de Droit Aerien et Spatial. a. ISSN 0084-3636

**McGill University. Macdonald Physics Laboratory**
Montreal, Que. H3C 3G1, Canada.
- McGill University, Montreal. Macdonald Physics Laboratory. Ice Research Project. Annual Report. irreg. ISSN 0076-1796

**McGill University. Marine Sciences Centre**
Box 6070, Station a, Montreal H3C 3G1, Canada.
- McGill University, Montreal. Marine Sciences Centre. Annual Report. a. ISSN 0541-6299

**McGill University. Mechanical Engineering Department**
P.O. Box 6070, Sta. A, Montreal, Que. H3A 2K6, Canada.
- McGill University, Montreal. Mechanical Engineering Research Laboratories. Report. irreg. ISSN 0076-1966
- McGill University, Montreal. Mechanical Engineering Research Laboratories. Technical Note. irreg. ISSN 0076-1974

**McGill University. Osler Library**
McIntyre Medical Sciences Bldg., Montreal, Que. H3G 1Y6, Canada.
- Osler Library Newsletter. 3 per yr. ISSN 0085-4557 (Friends of Osler Library)

**McGill University. Redpath Museum**
Montreal, Que., Canada.
- McGill University, Montreal. McGill University Museums. Publications. irreg. ISSN 0076-1958

**McGill University, Montreal. Redpath Museum.**
Bulletin. irreg. ISSN 0085-5448

**McGill University. School of Nursing**
3506 University St., Montreal H3A 2A7, Que., Canada.
- Nursing Papers: Perspectives on Nursing. q. ISSN 0318-1006

**McGraw-Hill Information Systems Company of Canada Ltd.**
330 Progress Ave., Scarborough, Ontario, Canada.
- Sweet's Canadian Construction Catalogue File. a. ISSN 0082-0431

**McIntish Publishing Co. Ltd.**
Box 430, North Battleford, Sask. S9R 2Y5, Canada.
- Western Canada Outdoors. m. (Saskatchewan Wildlife Federation) (Co-sponsor: Alberta Fish and Game Association)

**Maclean-Hunter Ltd.**
481 University Ave., Toronto, Ont. M5W 1A7, Canada.
- Acheteur. m. ISSN 0001-4885
- Audio Retailer. q.
- AudioScene Canada; Canadian electronics, hi-fi, hobby, servicing. m.
- Batiment. m. ISSN 0005-6278
- Building Supply Dealer. m. ISSN 0007-3687
- Bureau. bi-m. ISSN 0007-604X
- Bus and Truck Transport. m. ISSN 0007-635X
- Canada & the World; the magazine for students of current events. m.(Sept.-May) ISSN 0043-8170
- Canadian Automotive Trade. m. ISSN 0008-2945
- Canadian Aviation. m. ISSN 0008-2953
- Canadian Building. m. ISSN 0008-3070
- Canadian Controls & Instrumentation. m. ISSN 0008-3283
- Canadian Controls and Instrumentation. Control/Instrumentation Buyers' Guide. a. ISSN 0068-8525
- Canadian Datasystems. m. ISSN 0008-3364
- Canadian Driver/Owner. q.
- Canadian Electronics Engineering. m. ISSN 0008-3461
- Canadian Electronics Engineering Components and Equipment Directory. a.
- Canadian Grocer. m. ISSN 0008-3704
- Canadian Hotel & Restaurant. m. ISSN 0008-3801
- Canadian Industry Shows and Exhibitions. a. ISSN 0068-8967
- Canadian Interiors. m. ISSN 0008-3887
- Canadian Jeweller. m. ISSN 0008-3917
- Canadian Machinery and Metalworking. m. ISSN 0008-4379
- Canadian Packaging. m. ISSN 0008-4654
- Canadian Paint and Finishing. m. ISSN 0008-4662
- Canadian Photo Annual. a.
- Canadian Photography. m. ISSN 0031-8582
- Canadian Printer and Publisher. m. ISSN 0008-4816
- Canadian Pulp and Paper Industry. m. ISSN 0008-4867
- Canadian Research. bi-m. ISSN 0319-1974
- Canadian Service Data Book. a. ISSN 0068-9629
- Canadian Shipping and Marine Engineering. m. ISSN 0008-4980
- Canadian Special Truck Equipment Manual; directory of truck equipment. a. ISSN 0068-9734
- Canadian Travel Courier. fortn. ISSN 0008-5219
- Chatelaine. m. ISSN 0009-1995
- Civic; public works magazine. m.
- Civic Municipal Reference Manual and Purchasing Guide. a. ISSN 0069-4258
- Construction Today - Middle East. m.
- Design Engineering. m. ISSN 0011-9342
- Drug Merchandising. m. ISSN 0012-6586
- Educational Digest. m (except July) ISSN 0046-1482
- Electrical Contractor and Maintenance Supervisor. m. ISSN 0013-4287
- Epicier. m. ISSN 0013-9521
- Financial Post Directory of Directors. a. ISSN 0071-5042
- Financial Post Magazine; Canada's national weekly of business, investment and public affairs. w.(plus monthly nos) ISSN 0384-0360
- Financial Post Survey of Funds. a.
- Financial Post Survey of Industrials. a. ISSN 0071-5050
- Financial Post Survey of Markets. a. ISSN 0071-5077
- Financial Post Survey of Mines. a. ISSN 0071-5085
- Financial Post Survey of Oils. a. ISSN 0071-5093
- Food in Canada. m. ISSN 0015-6442

- Fraser's Canadian Trade Directory. a. ISSN 0071-9277
- Hardware Merchandising. m. ISSN 0017-7717
- Hardware Merchandising's Hardware Handbook. a. ISSN 0073-036X
- Heavy Construction News. bi-m. ISSN 0017-9426
- Home Goods Retailing. m. ISSN 0018-4055
- Investor's Digest of Canada. s-m. ISSN 0047-1356
- Maclean's; Canada's national magazine. s-m. ISSN 0024-9262
- Market Research Facts and Trends. m. ISSN 0025-360X
- Marketing; Canada's weekly newspaper for advertising and sales executives. w. ISSN 0025-3642
- Materials Management & Distribution. m. ISSN 0025-5343
- Mechanical Contracting & Engineering. m.
- Medical Post. bi-w. ISSN 0025-7435
- Men's Wear of Canada. m. ISSN 0025-9535
- Miss Chatelaine; fashion magazine for young women in their late teens and early twenties. 7 per yr. ISSN 0026-5918
- Modern Power & Engineering. m. ISSN 0026-8313
- Modern Purchasing. m. ISSN 0026-833X
- National List of Advertisers. a. ISSN 0077-5177
- Office Equipment & Methods. m. ISSN 0030-0179
- Pharmacien. m. ISSN 0031-692X
- Plant Management and Engineering. m. ISSN 0315-9183
- Quincaillier. m.
- Real Estate Development Annual. a.
- Recreation Canada. bi-m. ISSN 0031-2231 (Canadian Parks Recreation Association)
- Revue-Moteur. m. ISSN 0035-371X
- SONO; sonorisation au canada. q.
- Stationery & Office Products. m. ISSN 0383-0640
- Style; the Canadian women's and children's wear newspaper. m. ISSN 0039-4246
- T A D. (Teaching Aids Digest) s-a. ISSN 0040-0556
- University of Toronto Undergraduate Dental Journal. a. ISSN 0042-0255

**Maclean-Hunter Ltd. (Calgary)**
200-918-6th Ave. S.W., Calgary, Alta T2P 0V5, Canada.
- Oilweek. w. ISSN 0030-1515

**Maclean-Hunter Ltd. (Montreal)**
625, Ave. du President Kennedy, Montreal, Que. H3A 1K5, Canada.
- Actualite. m.
- Quebec Industriel. m. ISSN 0033-5975
- Transport Commercial. m. ISSN 0041-140X

**McLelland & Stewart**
Toronto, Ont., Canada.
- Canadian Book Prices Current. irreg. ISSN 0576-470X

**Dan Macleod, Ed. & Pub.**
2527 W. 37th Ave., Vancouver 13, B.C., Canada.
- Tish. m. ISSN 0040-8158

**McMaster Association for 18th Century Studies**
- McMaster Association for 18th Century Studies. Publications. (pub. by A. M. Hakkert Ltd.)

**McMaster University**
- Whidden Lectures. (pub. by Oxford University Press US)

**McMaster University. Department of Anthropology**
Hamilton, Ont. L8S 4L9, Canada.
- Journal of Anthropology at McMaster. s-a.

**McMaster University. Institute for Materials Research**
1280 Main St. W., Hamilton Ont. L8S 4M1, Canada.
- McMaster University, Hamilton, Ontario. Institute for Materials Research. Annual Report. a. ISSN 0076-2059

**McMaster University Library Press**
Mills Memorial Library, Hamilton, Ont. L8S 4L6, Canada.
- McMaster University Library Research News. irreg. ISSN 0024-9270
- Russell: The Journal of the Bertrand Russell Archives. q. ISSN 0036-0163
- Stratford Papers. irreg. ISSN 0381-159X

**MacMillan Bloedel Ltd.**
1075 W. Georgia St., Vancouver, B.C. V6E 3R9, Canada.
- MacMillan Bloedel Building Materials News. q.

**McMullin Publishers Ltd.**
417 St. Pierre St., Montreal, Que. H2Y 2M4, Canada.
- McGoldrick's Handbook of Canadian Customs Tariff and Excise Duties. a. ISSN 0076-1990

**Madawaska Limitee**
20 rue Saint-Francois, Edmundston, N.B., Canada.
- Brayon. q. (Societe Historique du Madawaska)

**Madoc-Tweed Art & Writing Centre**
Tweed, Ont., Canada.
- Canada Publishing Company. q.

**Madonna House Apostolate**
Combermere, Ont. K0J 1L0, Canada.
- Restoration. m.

**John Magor, Ed. & Pub.**
Box 758, Duncan, B.C. V9L 3Y1, Canada.
- Canadian U F O Report. q. ISSN 0008-5243

**Mainmise**
1589 rue St. Denis, Montreal 129, Canada.
- Mainmise. m.

**Makara Publishing & Design Co-Operative**
1011 Commercial Drive, Vancouver, B. C. V5L 3X1, Canada.
- Makara. bi-m.

**Malta Service Bureau**
Box 826 Station B, Ottawa, Ont. K1P 5P9, Canada.
- Maltese Directory: Canada, United States. irreg.

**Manila Bay Co.**
6 Lansing Square, Willowdale, Ontario, Canada (Subscriptions to: Box 918, Postal Station Q, Toronto 7, Ontario, Canada)
- Philippine Tribune. m.

**Manitoba. Bureau of Statistics**
Fifth Floor, 213 Notre Dame, Winnipeg, Man. R3B 2C7, Canada.
- Manitoba Statistical Review. m.

**Manitoba. Department of Agriculture**
Winnipeg, Man., Canada.
- Manitoba Grassland Projects; provincial report. irreg.
- Vegetable Growers Association of Manitoba. Technical and Scientific Papers Presented at Horticultural Industry Days. a.
- Yearbook of Manitoba Agriculture. a. ISSN 0084-3865

**Manitoba. Department of Co-Operative Development**
Winnipeg, Man., Canada.
- Manitoba. Department of Co-Operative Development. Report. Rapport. irreg.

**Manitoba. Department of Education**
311-1181 Portage Avenue, Winnipeg R3G 0T3, Manitoba, Canada.
- Education Manitoba. 10 per yr.

**Manitoba. Department of Health and Social Development**
501-177 Lombard Ave., Winnipeg, Man. R3B 0W5, Canada.
- Manitoba. Department of Health and Social Development. Annual Report. a. ISSN 0381-310X
- Manual of Social Services in Manitoba. irreg. ISSN 0318-5427

**Manitoba. Department of Industry and Commerce**
Norquay Bldg., Winnipeg. Man. R3C 0P8, Winnipeg 1, Man., Canada.
- Manitoba. m. ISSN 0025-2182
- Manitoba Community Reports. a.
- Manitoba Trade Directory. (pub. by Sanford Evans Publishing Ltd.)

**Manitoba. Department of Labour**
Room 608, Norquay Bldg., Winnipeg, Man. R3C 0P8, Canada.
- Manitoba Labour-Management Review Committee. Annual Report. a. ISSN 0076-3853

**Manitoba. Department of Mines, Resources and Environment. Exploration & Geological Survey Branch**
Mines Branch, Winnepeg, Man., Canada.
- Manitoba. Department of Mines, Resources and Environmental Management. Mines Branch. Geological Publications. irreg.
- Manitoba. Mines Branch. Geological Paper. irreg. ISSN 0076-387X
- Manitoba. Mines Branch. Publication. irreg. ISSN 0085-3070
- Manitoba. Mines Branch. Summary of Geological Field Work. irreg. ISSN 0085-3089

**Manitoba. Department of Tourism, Recreation and Cultural Affairs**
Archives Bldg., 200 Vaughan St., Winnipeg, Man. R3C 1T5, Canada.
- Manitoba Moods. q. ISSN 0319-7697

**Manitoba. Department of Tourism, Recreation and Cultural Affairs. Research and Planning Branch**
200 Vaughan St., Winnipeg, Man. R3C 1T5, Canada.
- Manitoba. Department of Tourism, Recreation and Cultural Affairs. Park Statistics. irreg.

**Manitoba. Environmental Council**
Box 139, 139 Tuxedo Avenue, Winnipeg, Manitoba R3N 0H6, Canada.
- Manitoba. Environmental Council. Annual Report. a.

**Manitoba. Health Services Commission**
Box 925, 599 Empress St., Winnipeg Man. R3C 2Tc, Canada.
- Manitoba. Health Services Commission. Annual Report. a. ISSN 0076-3837
- Manitoba. Health Services Commission. Statistical Supplement to the Annual Report. a. ISSN 0076-3845

**Manitoba. Horse Racing Commission**
Winnipeg, Man., Canada.
- Manitoba. Horse Racing Commission. Annual Report. a.

**Manitoba. Land Value Appraisal Commission**
1301 Ellice Ave., Winnipeg, Man. R3G 0G1, Canada.
- Manitoba. Land Value Appraisal Commission. Annual Report. a.

**Manitoba. Lotteries Commission**
415-155 Carlton St., Winnipeg, Man. RC3 3H8, Canada.
- Manitoba. Lotteries Commission. Annual Report. a.

**Manitoba. Police Commission**
300-55 Donald St., Winnipeg, Man. R3C 1L8, Canada.
- Manitoba. Police Commission. Annual Report. a.

**Manitoba. Public Library Services**
Room 313, Legislative Building, Winnipeg, Manitoba, Canada.
- Directory of Libraries in Manitoba. biennial. ISSN 0317-8536

**Manitoba. Welfare Advisory Committee**
430 Edmonton Street, Winnipeg, Man. R3B 2M3, Canada.
- Manitoba. Welfare Advisory Committee. Annual Report. a.

**Manitoba Archaeological Society**
Box 1171, Winnipeg R3C 2Y4, Canada.
- Manitoba Archaeological Quarterly. q.

**Manitoba Association of Registered Nurses**
647 Broadway Ave., Winnipeg, Man. R3C 0X2, Canada.
- Nurscene. 8 per yr.

**Manitoba Association of Teachers of English**
191 Harcourt St., Winnipeg, Man. R3S 3H2, Canada.
- Classmate. 3 per yr. ISSN 0315-906X

**Manitoba Cancer Treatment and Research Foundation**
700 Bannatyne Ave., Winipeg R3E 0V9, Man, Canada.
- Manitoba Cancer Treatment and Research Foundation. Report. a. ISSN 0076-3802

**Manitoba Classic and Antique Auto Club**
Box 1031, Winnipeg R3C 2W2, Man., Canada.
● Sidemount Reporter. m. ISSN 0037-4601

**Manitoba Dental Association**
308 Kennedy St., Winnipeg R3B 2M6, Canada.
● Manitoba Dental Association. Bulletin. q. ISSN 0025-2247

**Manitoba Educational Research Council**
140 Rupert Ave., Winnipeg, Man. R3B 0N2, Canada.
● Manitoba Journal of Education. s-a. ISSN 0047-5769

**Manitoba Historical Society**
190 Rupert Ave., Winnipeg 2, Man. R3B 0N2, Canada.
● Manitoba Historical Society. Transactions. a. ISSN 0076-3829

**Manitoba Library Association**
c/o St. Vital Public Library, 6 Fermor Avenue W., Winnipeg Man. R2M 0Y2, Canada.
● Manitoba Library Association Bulletin. q. ISSN 0542-559X

**Manitoba Museum of Man and Nature**
190 Rupert Ave., Winnipeg 2, Man., Canada.
● Manitoba Museum of Man and Nature. Biennial Report. irreg. ISSN 0076-3888

**Manitoba Naturalists' Society**
214 - 190 Rupert Ave., Winnipeg, Man. R3B 0N2, Canada.
● Manitoba Nature. q. ISSN 0315-5064 (Co-sponsor: Zoological Society of Manitoba)

**Manitoba Pool Elevators**
220 Portage Ave., Winnipeg R3C 0A5, Man., Canada.
● Manitoba Co-Operator. w. ISSN 0025-2239

**Manitoba Record Society**
500 Dysart Rd., Winnipeg, 19, Manitoba, Canada.
● Manitoba Record Society. Publications. a. ISSN 0076-3896

**Manitoba School Library Audio Visual Association**
c/o Manitoba Teachers' Society, Ed. Margaret Foran, Winnipeg, Man. R3J 3H2, Canada.
● Manitoba School Library Audio Visual Association Journal. 3-4 per yr. ISSN 0315-9124

**Manitoba Society of Radiological Technologists Inc.**
294 Duffield St., Winnipeg, Man. R3J 2J9, Canada.
● K. V. P. News. q. ISSN 0022-7439

**Manitoba Teachers' Society**
191 Harcourt St., Winnipeg, Man. R3J 3H2, Canada.
● E. F. M. Revue des Educateurs Franco-Maitobains. q. ISSN 0315-8683
● Manitoba Teacher. m. (except Jul. & Aug.) ISSN 0025-228X

**Manitoba Telephone System**
489 Empress St., Winnipeg R3C 0A2, Canada.
● Telephone Echo. fortn. ISSN 0381-4556

**Manitoba Theatre Centre**
174 Market Ave., Winnipeg, Maintoba, R3B 0P8, Canada.
● Manitoba Theatre Centre. House Programme. 6 per yr.

**Manitoba Tourist Association**
● Events. (pub. by Events Publications Inc. Ltd.)

**Manitoba Water Services Board**
693 Taylor Ave, Winnipeg, Manitoba R3M 2K2, Canada.
● Manitoba Water Services Board. Annual Report. a.

**George Mannion, Ed. & Pub.**
39 Trianon Rd., Rigaud, Que. J0P 1P0, Canada.
● Clansman. bi-m.

**Manoir Notre-Dame de Grace**
5319 Av. Notre Dame de Grace, Montreal H4A 1L2, P.Q., Canada.
● Manoir-Echo. m.

**Maple Creek News Ltd.**
P.O. Box 1360, Maple Creek, Sask. S0N 1N0, Canada.
● Saskatchewan Stockgrower. m.

**Marcel Quellet**
10,549 Parthenais St., Montreal 360, P.Q., Canada.
● Quebec Medical. 10 per yr. ISSN 0027-0717

**Editions du Marchand Quebecois**
Bureau 203, 6841 St.-Hubert, Montreal H2S 2M8, Que., Canada.
● Alimentation au Quebec. m. ISSN 0002-5410

**Maritime Co-Operative Printers, Ltd.**
Box 1178, Antigonish, Nova Scotia, Canada.
● Maritime Co-Operator. m. ISSN 0025-3405

**Maritime Command**
Halifax, N.S., Canada.
● Maritime Command Trident. s-m. ISSN 0025-3413

**Maritime Folk Music Society**
Box 3, Moncton, N.B., Canada.
● Moonshine Can. m. ISSN 0027-092X

**Maritime Law Book Co.**
Box 302, Fredericton, N.B. E3B 4Y9, Canada.
● National Reporter. irreg. (2 bound vols. per year)
● Nova Scotia Reports. 3 vols. per year. ISSN 0048-0983

**Maritime Lumber Bureau**
Box 459, Amherst, N.S., Canada.
● M. L. B. Log. m. ISSN 0024-8231
● Maritime Lumber Bureau Annual Report Book. a.

**Maritime Professional Photographers Association**
● Maritime Professional. (pub. by Maritime Professional Publishing Co.)

**Maritime Professional Publishing Co.**
Halifax, N.S., Canada.
● Maritime Professional. irreg. ISSN 0383-610X (Maritime Professional Photographers Association)

**Mark II**
2175 Sheppard Ave. East, Willowdale, Ont. M2J 1W8, Canada.
● Mark II; the sales & marketing management magazine. 8 per yr.

**Harold Markusoff**
P.O. Box 3777, Sta. B, Winnipeg, R2W 3R6, Canada.
● Jewish Post. w.

**Marpep Publishing Ltd.**
700-133 Richmond St. W., Toronto, Ont. M5H 3M8, Canada.
● Blue Book of CBS Stock Reports. fortn. ISSN 0384-7802
● Canadian Business Service Investment Reporter. w.
● Canadian News Facts; the indexed digest of Canadian current events. s-m. ISSN 0008-4565

**Editions Marquis Ltee**
305 E. Boul. Tache, Montmagny, Que., Canada.
● Quebec-Histoire. bi-m. ISSN 0048-6256

**Mayday**
Box 69403, Sta. K, Vancouver, B.C. V5K 4W6, Canada.
● Mayday. 3 per yr. ISSN 0380-2531

**Meadowlark Publishing Ltd.**
Box 696, Maple, Ont. L0J 1E0, Canada.
● Country Estate Magazine. q. ISSN 0315-2154

**Meat Packers Council of Canada**
5233 Dundas St. W., Islington, Ont. M9B 1A6, Canada.
● Canada's Meat Industry. triennial. ISSN 0068-8150
● Meat Packers Council of Canada. Facts, Figures, Comment. s-m. ISSN 0047-6358

**Media Public Relations Ltd.**
Box 2929, Vancouver 3, B.C., Canada.
● Star Serviceman. m. ISSN 0038-9889

**Media Research Society**
500 Brand St., North Vancouver 278, B.C., Canada.
● Focus. bi-m. ISSN 0015-4946

**Medical Research Council**
Tunney's Pasture, Ottawa, Ont. K1A 0W9, Canada.
● Medical Research Council Newsletter/Conseil de Recherches Medicales. Actualites. q. ISSN 0047-6560

● Medical Research Council of Canada. Grants and Awards Guide/Guide de Subventions et Bourses. a.
● Medical Research Council of Canada. Report of the President. a.

**Medical Society of Nova Scotia**
Sir Charles Tupper Medical Bldg., University Ave., Halifax, Nova Scotia, Canada.
● Nova Scotia Medical Bulletin. bi-m. ISSN 0029-5094

**Megamedia Corp.**
902 Lilac Crescent, Whitby, Ont., Canada.
● Communications and Cable TV Business. m.
● Government and Military Business. bi-m.

**Memorial University. Folklore and Language Archives**
St. John's, Newfoundland, Canada.
● R L S: Regional Language Studies... Newfoundland. irreg. ISSN 0079-9335

**Memorial University. Marine Sciences Research Laboratory.**
St. John's, Newfoundland, Canada.
● Memorial University, St. John's, Newfoundland. Marine Sciences Research Laboratory. M.S.R.L. Bulletin. irreg.

**Memorial University of Newfoundland. Library**
St. John's, Nfld. A1C 5S7, Canada.
● Serials Holdings in the Libraries of Memorial University of Newfoundland, St. John's Public Library and College of Trades and Technology. a. ISSN 0316-6597

**Mennonite Brethren Conference of Canada**
● Mennonitische Rundschau/Mennonite Review. (pub. by Christian Press Ltd.)

**Mennonite Literary Society**
203-818 Portage Ave., Winnipeg, Man. R3G 0N4, Canada.
● Mennonite Mirror. 10 per yr. ISSN 0315-8101

**Mennonite Publishing Service**
Waterloo, Ont. N2L 3G6, Canada.
● Mennonite Reporter. fortn. ISSN 0380-0121

**Mental Patients Association**
2146 Yew St., Vancouver, British Columbia V6K 3G7, Canada.
● In a Nutshell. irreg. ISSN 0380-2892

**Mercury Publications Ltd.**
200-633 Portage Ave, Winnipeg, Man. R3B 2Z9, Canada.
● Western Construction & Industry. m. ISSN 0043-3624
● Western Grocer and Food Store Manager. bi-m. ISSN 0043-3780
● Western Motor Fleet. bi-m. ISSN 0043-3950

**Merlin Publishing Co.**
1800 Parthenais St., Montreal, Que. H2V 2Z1, Canada.
● Allo Police. w.

**Merton Publications Ltd.**
R. R 3, London, Ont. N6A 4B7, Canada.
● Scope/Recreational Vehicle and Camping News; Canada's national camping, trailering and recreational vehicle magazine. m (bi-m Aug-Mar) ISSN 0048-9743
● Scope /Wheelers Canadian Campground Guide. irreg. ISSN 0380-8343

**Messagers Catholiques de la Bible**
● Je Crois. (pub. by Editions le Renouveau Inc.)

**Metiers d'Art du Quebec Inc.**
1637 rue St-Denis, Montreal, Canada.
● Metier d'Art du Quebec. m. ISSN 0047-6927
● Signe. 10 per yr.

**Metric Commission**
301 Elgin St., Ottawa, Ontario K15 5G8, Canada.
● Metric Monitor. m.

**Metro-Sud**
937 Bd. Taschereau, Longueil, Que. J4K 2X2, Canada.
● Metro-Sud. w. ISSN 0381-5080

**Metropolitan Pensioners Welfare Association**
Box 2929, Vancouver 3, B. C., Canada.
● Metropolitan Pensioner. m. ISSN 0026-1556

**Metropolitan Toronto Library Board**
789 Yonge St., Toronto, Ont. M4W 2G8, Canada.
- Continuing Education Directory for Metropolitan Toronto. a. ISSN 0045-8384
- Guide to Periodicals and Newspapers in the Public Libraries of Metropolitan Toronto. a. ISSN 0315-7288
- Sixteen Mm Films Available in the Public Libraries of Metropolitan Toronto. a. ISSN 0315-7326
- Talking Books in the Public Library Systems of Metropolitan Toronto. irreg. ISSN 0380-2973

**Metropolitan Toronto Library Board. Theatre Section**
214 College St., Toronto, Ont. M5T 1R3, Canada.
- Metropolitan Toronto Library Board. Theatre Section. Selected List of Acquisitions for Reference Use. irreg. ISSN 0383-2929

**Micromedia Ltd.**
Box 34, Station S, Toronto, Ont. M5M 4L6, Canada.
- Profile Index to Canadian Provincial and Municipal Government Publications. m with annual cumulation. ISSN 0316-4608
- Publicat Index to Canadian Federal Publications. m (with annual cumulation) ISSN 0384-9813
- Urban Canada/Canada Urbaine. q (with annual cumulation) ISSN 0384-9821

**Middlesex County Library**
Arva, Ont., Canada.
- Town and Country Librarian. s-a. ISSN 0382-0912

**Midnight Publishing Corp. Ltd.**
1440 St. Catherine St. W., Suite 625, Montreal, Que. H3G 1S2, Canada.
- Midnight. w.

**Mil-Mac Publications Ltd.**
203 Adelaide St. W., Toronto 1, Ont., Canada.
- Toronto Symphony News. 7 per yr. ISSN 0049-4224

**Mineralogical Association of Canada**
c/o Royal Ontario Museum, 100 Queen's Park, Toronto, Ont. M5S 2C6, Canada.
- Canadian Mineralogist; crystallography, geochemistry mineralogy, petrology, mineral deposits. q. ISSN 0008-4476

**Mining Association of Canada**
20 Toronto St., 9th Floor, Toronto, Ont. M5C 2C2, Canada.
- Mining in Canada - Facts & Figures. a.

**Ministikok**
Box 209, Moose Factory, Ontario, Canada.
- Ministikok. m(except July & Aug.) ISSN 0300-3876

**Mirror**
Box 339, Sooke, B.C. V0S 1N0, Canada.
- Mirror; a community newspaper. w. ISSN 0026-5837

**Missionaires de la Consolata**
2381 W. Bd. Gouin, Montreal H3M 1B5, Que., Canada.
- Reveil Missionnaire. bi-m. ISSN 0034-6284

**Missionnaires du Sacre-Coeur**
C.P. 400, Sillery, Quebec, P. Q. G1T 2R7, Canada.
- R N D. (Revue Notre Dame) m. ISSN 0035-3795

**Missions des Peres des Sainte-Croix**
4961 Coronet, Montreal, Que. H3V 1C9, Canada.
- Orient. bi-m. ISSN 0472-0490

**Mississauga Public Library**
110 Dundas St. W., Mississauga, Ont. L5B IH3, Canada.
- I S M. (Information Services Mississauga) bi-m. ISSN 0046-841X

**George Mitchell, Ed. & Pub.**
10519-128a Ave., Edmonton, Alta. T5E 0K2, Canada.
- Alberta Fishing Guide. a. (Railton Publications Ltd.)

**Mobile Publications Ltd.**
Box 3097, Station B, Calgary, Alta T2M 4L6, Canada.
- Mobile Living in Canada. m. ISSN 0026-7201

**Modernist Studies: Literature and Culture, 1920-1940**
c/o Eds. Shirley Rose and Ernest Griffin, Dept. of English, University of Alberta, Edmonton, Alta. T6G 2E1, Canada.
- Modernist Studies: Literature and Culture, 1920-1940. 3 per yr.

**Publications Mon Bebe**
Suite 203, 6841 rue St. Hubert, Montreal H2S 2M8, Canada.
- Mon Bebe. s-a. ISSN 0384-0816

**Monarch International - Gold and Silver Exchange**
Suite 406-402, West Pender St., Vancouver, B.C., Canada.
- Depression Reporter. m.

**Monarchist League of Canada**
2 Wedgewood Crescent, Ottawa, Ont. K1B 4B4, Canada.
- Monarchy Canada. bi-m. ISSN 0319-4019

**Montfort Fathers**
5875 Est rue Sherbrooke, Montreal H1N 1B6, Canada.
- Regard de Foi; revue mariale d'actualite. bi-m. ISSN 0025-3065

**Montreal Baseball Club Ltd.**
P.O. Box 500, Sta. R, Montreal, Que. H2S 3G7, Canada.
- Baseball/Revue du Baseball. 4 per yr.

**Montreal Catholic School Commission**
3737 Sherbrooke St. E., Montreal, Canada.
- Trans-Parents/Focus. q.

**Montreal Children's Hospital**
2300 Tupper St., Montreal 108, Que., Canada.
- Montreal Children's Hospital. Children's News. q. ISSN 0047-8059

**Montreal General Hospital**
Rm. 635, 1650 Cedar Ave., Montreal, Que. H3G 1A4, Canada.
- Montreal General Hospital News. q. ISSN 0027-0709

**Montreal International Airport**
Box 486, Dorval, Que. H4Y 1B3, Canada.
- Airport News. irreg. ISSN 0382-4276

**Montreal Museum of Fine Arts**
3400 Avenue du Musee, Montreal H3G 1K3, Que., Canada.
- Montreal. Museum of Fine Arts. Quarterly Review. 4 per yr. ISSN 0027-0725

**Montreal Standard Publishing Co.**
231 St. James St., W., Montreal, Que., Canada.
- Weekend Magazine. w. ISSN 0043-1826

**Montreal Stock Exchange**
800 Place Victoria, Montreal, Que. H4Z 1A9, Canada.
- Montreal. Stock Exchange. Monthly Review. m. ISSN 0047-8075

**Montreal Teachers Association**
5585 Monkland Ave., Suite 135, Montreal, Que. H4A 1E1, Canada.
- M T A the Teacher. 8 per yr.

**Montreal Urban Community Policemen's Brotherhood Inc.**
480 Rue Gilford, Montreal H2J 1N3, Que., Canada.
- Revue des Agents de Police/Police Constables Review. m. ISSN 0035-1903

**Mosaic Press**
Box 1032, Oakville, Ont. L6J 5E9, Canada.
- Current Soviet Leaders. s-a.

**Motion Canada Media Productions Ltd.**
c/o Peter M. Evanchuck, Ed., Box 5490, Sta. A, Toronto, Ont. M5W 1N7, Canada.
- Motion. bi-m. ISSN 0315-6966

**Motor Transport Fact Book**
1089 W. Broadway, No. 202, Vancouver, 9, B.C., Canada.
- Motor Transport Fact Book. a. ISSN 0077-1627

**Mount Allison University**
Rm. 302, University Centre, Sackville, N. B. e0A 3C0.
- Argosy Weekly. w. ISSN 0044-8818

**Mount Allison University. Federated Alumni**
Sackville, N.B., Canada.
- Mount Allison Record. q. ISSN 0027-2485

**Mouvement Eucharistique du Canada**
116 ouest, rue Notre Dame, Montreal, Que. H2Y 1T2, Canada.
- Avec "Lui". m. ISSN 0382-4365

**Multiscience Publications Ltd.**
Box 1464, Sta. B, Montreal, Que., H3B 3L2, Canada.
- Canadian Journal of Spectroscopy. bi-m. ISSN 0045-5105 (Spectroscopy Society of Canada)
- Canadian Spectroscopic News. 3 per yr. (Spectroscopy Society of Canada)

**Municipal Forms Ltd.**
Farnham, Que. J2N 2R6, Canada.
- F M Compilation of the Statutes of Canada. a. ISSN 0380-2639

**Municipal World Ltd.**
Box 399, St. Thomas, Ont. N5P 3V3, Canada.
- Municipal World. m. ISSN 0027-3589

**Municipality of Metropolitan Toronto**
Clerk's Dept., Toronto, Ont., Canada.
- Metropolitan Toronto. a. ISSN 0076-7093

**Ahmad Eed Murad, Ed. & Pub.**
Box 1234, Edmonton, Alta. T5J 2M4, Canada.
- Source. fortn. ISSN 0038-1896

**Muscular Dystrophy Association of Canada**
Room 203, 387 Bloor St. E., Toronto, Ont. M4W 1H8, Canada.
- Muscular Dystrophy Reporter. q. ISSN 0580-2512

**Musee d'Art Contemporain**
Cite du Havre, Montreal, Que. H3C 3R4, Canada.
- Ateliers. 6 per yr. ISSN 0382-5124 (Quebec (Province) Ministere des Affaires Culturelles)

**Musee National des Sciences Naturelles**
- Musee National des Sciences Naturelles. Collection d'Histoire Naturelle. (pub. by National Museum of Man)

**Museum Restoration Service**
Box 390, Bloomfield, Ont. K0K 1G0, Canada.
- Arms Collecting; the Canadian journal. q.
- Arms Study Series. irreg., no. 8, 1975.
- Historical Arms Series. irreg. ISSN 0440-9221

**Myasthenia Gravis Foundation**
Alvin Abram, 53 Sunnycrest Rd., Willowdale, Ont., Canada.
- Myasthenia Gravis Foundation. Newsletter. m. ISSN 0027-5506

**Myriad Publishing**
Box 108, S U B, University of British Columbia, Vancouver 8, B. C., Canada.
- Thursday's Child. irreg. ISSN 0082-4291

**Mythical Press**
Windsor, Ont., Canada.
- Connexion. irreg. ISSN 0383-9982

**N R C Publishing Co.**
Ottawa, Ont., Canada.
- N R C - Nouvelle Revue Canadienne. irreg. ISSN 0547-0749

**Editions Naaman**
C.P. 697, Sherbrooke, Que. J1H 5K5, Canada.
- Collection "Atlas". irreg.

**Nan-Sea Publications**
Box 459, Port Stanley, Ont. Canada.
- Bright Leaf Tobacco Journal. 7 per yr. ISSN 0007-0114
- Great Lakes Fisherman. m.
- Port Stanley Beacon. m.

**Nanaimo Old Time Bottle Association**
Nanaimo, B.C., Canada.
- Digger's Digest. m. ISSN 0315-9396

**Nathanael Literature Distributors**
64 Hills Rd., Ajax, Ont. L1S 2W4, Canada.
- Come and See. bi-m. ISSN 0316-3040

**National Action Committee on the Status of Women**
40 St. Clair Ave. E., Suite 300, Toronto, Ont. M5R 2G3, Canada.
- Status of Women News. q. ISSN 0381-9418

**National Arts Centre**
Ottawa, Ont. Canada.
- National Arts Centre. Calendar of Events. m. ISSN 0033-1023

**National Association for Photographic Art**
10 Shaneen Blvd., Scarborough M1R 1B5 Ont., Canada.
- Camera Canada. q. ISSN 0008-2090

**National Association of Friendship Centres**
200 Cooper St., Suite 2, Ottawa, Ont. K2P 0G1, Canada.
- Native Perspective. 10 per yr. ISSN 0381-7717

**National Auto Research Canada**
67 Ellesmere Rd., Ste. 1A, Scarborough, Ont. M1R 4B8, Canada.
- Canadian Black Book; official used car market guide. fortn.

**National Business Publications Ltd.**
310 Victoria Ave., Westmount, P.Q. H3Z 2M9, Canada.
- Canadian Doctor. m. ISSN 0008-3429
- Canadian Mining Journal. m. ISSN 0008-4492
- Canadian Mining Journal's Reference Manual & Buyers' Guide. a. ISSN 0315-9140
- Pulp & Paper Canada. m. ISSN 0316-4004 (Canadian Pulp & Paper Association)
- Pulp & Paper Canada's Business Directory. a. ISSN 0317-3550
- Pulp and Paper, Canada's Reference Manual & Buyers' Guide. a.

**National Cancer Institute of Canada**
25 Adelaide St. E., Toronto, Ont. M5C 1Y2, Canada.
- National Cancer Institute of Canada. Report. a. ISSN 0077-3689

**National Chinchilla Breeders of Canada**
Box 64, Carleton Place, Ont. K7C 3P3, Canada.
- National Chinchilla Breeders of Canada. Bulletin. m. ISSN 0027-8963

**National Conference of Canadian Universities and Colleges Committee**
- Studies in Higher Education in Canada. (pub. by University of Toronto Press)

**National Dairy Council of Canada**
365 Laurier Ave. W., Ottawa, Ont. K1P 5K2, Canada.
- National Dairy Council of Canada. Resume. m.

**National Defence Headquarters**
DGMEO, Ottawa, Ont. K1A OK2, Canada.
- Canadian Military Engineer. s-a. ISSN 0008-445X

**National Drug & Chemical Co. of Canada Ltd.**
Box 758, Winnipeg, Man, Canada.
- Western Horizons; a quarterly magazine for Western Canadian Pharmacists. q. ISSN 0043-3829

**National Emergency Planning Establishment**
3Rd Floor, Tower B. Lester B. Pearson Bldg., 125 Sussex Drive, Ottawa, Ont., K1A 0W6, Canada.
- Emergency Planning Digest/Revue Plans des Mesures d'Urgence. bi-m.

**National Farmers Union**
250-C 2nd Ave. S., Saskatoon, Sask. S7K 2MI, Canada.
- Union Farmer. m. ISSN 0041-6878

**National Film Board**
1 Lombard Street, Toronto, Ontario M5C 1J6, Canada.
- Pot Pourri. q.

**National Gallery of Canada**
Publications Division, Ottawa, Ont. K1A 0M8, Canada
(Order from: National Museums of Canada, Marketing Services Division, Ottawa, Ont. K1A 0M8, Canada)
- Artists in Canada. a.
- Masterpieces in the National Gallery of Canada/ Chefs-d'Oeuvre de la Galerie Nationale du Canada. irreg. (Corporation of the National Museums of Canada)
- National Gallery of Canada. Annual Revue/ Galerie Nationale du Canada. Revue Annuelle. a. ISSN 0078-6977 (Corporation of the National Museums of Canada)
- National Gallery of Canada. Bulletin. s-a. ISSN 0027-9323
- National Gallery of Canada. Library. Canadiana in the Library of the National Gallery of Canada: Supplement. irreg. ISSN 0078-6985

**National Harbours Board**
Ottawa, Ont., Canada.
- Canada. National Harbours Board. Port Directory. a.

**National Hockey League**
920 Sun Life Building, Montreal, Quebec, Canada.
- National Hockey League. Guide. a. ISSN 0316-8174
- National Hockey League. Official Rule Book. a.

**National Library of Canada**
Ottawa, Ont. K1A ON4, Canada
(Subscr. to: Supply & Services Canada, Printing and Publishing Division, Ottawa, Ont. K1A 0S9, Canada)
- Canadian Theses/Theses Canadiennes. a. ISSN 0068-9874
- Canadiana. m.(Annual cumulations) ISSN 0008-5391
- National Library News/Bibliotheque Nationale. Nouvelles. bi-m. ISSN 0027-9633
- National Library of Canada. Annual Report. a. ISSN 0078-7000

**National Museum of Man**
Ottawa, Ont. K1A 0M8, Canada.
- Archaeological Survey of Canada. Mercury Series. Papers. (pub. by National Museums of Canada)
- Canada. National Museums, Ottawa. Publications in Ethnology/Canada. Musees Nationaux. Publications d'Ethnologie. (pub. by National Museums of Canada)
- Canada. National Museums, Ottawa. Publications in Folk Culture. (pub. by National Museums of Canada)
- Canada. National Museums, Ottawa. Publications in History/Canada. Musees Nationaux. Publications d'Histoire. (pub. by National Museums of Canada)
- Canadian War Museum. Historical Publications. (pub. by National Museums of Canada)
- Musee National des Sciences Naturelles. Collection d'Histoire Naturelle. irreg.

**National Museum of Man. History Division**
Ottawa, Ont. K1A 0M8, Canada
(Subscr. to: 491 Bank St., Ottawa. Ont., K2P 1Z2 Canada)
- Urban History Review/Revue d'Histoire Urbaine. 3 per yr. (Co-Sponsor: Canadian Historical Association)

**National Museum of Natural Sciences**
- Canada. National Museums, Ottawa. Publications in Biological Oceanography. (pub. by National Museums of Canada)
- Canada. National Museums, Ottawa. Publications in Botany/Canada. Musees Nationaux. Publications de Botanique. (pub. by National Museums of Canada)
- Canada. National Museums, Ottawa. Publications in Palaeontology/Canada, Musees Nationaux. Publications de Paleontologie. (pub. by National Museums of Canada)
- Canada. National Museums, Ottawa. Publications in Zoology/Canada. Musees Nationaux. Publications de Zoologie. (pub. by National Museums of Canada)
- National Museum of Natural Sciences. Natural History Series. (pub. by National Museums of Canada)
- National Museum of Natural Sciences. Syllogeus. (pub. by National Museums of Canada)
- Publications in Mineral Sciences/Publications de Sciences Minerales. (pub. by National Museums of Canada)

**National Museums of Canada**
Ottawa, Ont. K1A 0M8, Canada.
- Archaeological Survey of Canada. Mercury Series. Papers. irreg.,no.65,1977. (National Museum of Man)
- Canada. National Museums, Ottawa. Publications in Biological Oceanography. irreg. ISSN 0068-7995 (National Museum of Natural Sciences)
- Canada. National Museums, Ottawa. Publications in Botany/Canada. Musees Nationaux. Publications de Botanique. irreg. ISSN 0068-7987 (National Museum of Natural Sciences)
- Canada. National Museums, Ottawa. Publications in Ethnology/Canada. Musees Nationaux. Publications d'Ethnologie. irreg. ISSN 0068-8002 (National Museum of Man)
- Canada. National Museums, Ottawa. Publications in Folk Culture. irreg. (National Museum of Man)
- Canada. National Museums, Ottawa. Publications in History/Canada. Musees Nationaux. Publications d'Histoire. irreg. ISSN 0068-8010 (National Museum of Man)
- Canada. National Museums, Ottawa. Publications in Palaeontology/Canada, Musees Nationaux. Publications de Paleontologie. irreg. ISSN 0068-8029 (National Museum of Natural Sciences)
- Canada. National Museums, Ottawa. Publications in Zoology/Canada. Musees Nationaux. Publications de Zoologie. irreg. ISSN 0068-8037 (National Museum of Natural Sciences)
- Canadian Conservation Institute Newsletter/ Institut Canadien de Conservation. Nouvelles. q.
- Canadian War Museum. Historical Publications. irreg. (National Museum of Man)
- National Museum of Natural Sciences. Natural History Series. irreg. ISSN 0317-5642
- National Museum of Natural Sciences. Syllogeus. irreg.
- Publications in Mineral Sciences/Publications de Sciences Minerales. irreg. ISSN 0079-7693 (National Museum of Natural Sciences)

**National Police Gazette**
1434 St. Catherine St. W., Montreal 107, Que., Canada.
- National Police Gazette. m. ISSN 0047-9039

**National Publishers Ltd.**
462 Hargrave St., Winnipeg 2, Man., Canada.
- Canadian Farmer Annual. a. ISSN 0068-8673

**National Research Council of Canada**
Ottawa, Ont. K1A OR6, Canada.
- Air Cushion Technology in Canada. a.
- Better Building Bulletin. irreg. ISSN 0067-642X
- Canadian Geotechnical Journal/Revue Canadienne de Geotechnique. q. ISSN 0008-3674 (Co-sponsor: Canadian Geotechnical Society)
- Canadian Journal of Biochemistry/Journal Canadien de Biochimie. m. ISSN 0008-4018
- Canadian Journal of Botany/Journal Canadien de Botanique. 2 per m. ISSN 0008-4026
- Canadian Journal of Chemistry/Journal Canadien de Chimie. s-m. ISSN 0008-4042
- Canadian Journal of Civil Engineering/Revue Canadienne de Genie Civil. q. ISSN 0315-1468 (Co-sponsor: Canadian Society of Civil Engineers)
- Canadian Journal of Earth Sciences/Journal Canadien des Sciences de la Terre. m. ISSN 0008-4077 (Co-sponsor: Geological Association of Canada)
- Canadian Journal of Forest Research. q. ISSN 0045-5067
- Canadian Journal of Microbiology/Journal Canadien de Microbiologie. m. ISSN 0008-4166
- Canadian Journal of Physics/Journal Canadien de Physique. s-m. ISSN 0008-4204
- Canadian Journal of Physiology and Pharmacology/Journal Canadien de Physiologie et Pharmacologie. bi-m. ISSN 0008-4212
- Canadian Journal of Zoology/Journal Canadien de Zoologie. m. ISSN 0008-4301
- International Towing Tank Conference. Proceedings. a.
- Muskeg Research Conference. Proceedings. irreg., usually a. ISSN 0541-4393
- N B C /N F C. (National Building Code / National Fine Code) irreg. ISSN 0380-8599
- National Research Council, Canada. Man-Computer Communications Conference. Proceedings. irreg.
- National Research Council, Canada. National Aeronautical Establishment. Aeronautical Report (L R Series) irreg. ISSN 0077-5541
- National Research Council, Canada. National Aeronautical Establishment. Mechanical Engineering Reports. irreg. ISSN 0077-555X
- National Research Council, Canada. National Aeronautical Establishment. Publications List and Supplements. irreg. ISSN 0077-5568
- National Research Council, Canada. Publications. irreg. ISSN 0077-5584
- National Research Council, Canada. Space Research Facilities Branch. Report. (SRFB Series) irreg. ISSN 0077-5592
- National Research Council, Canada. Technical Translation. irreg. ISSN 0077-5606
- National Research Council of Canada. Report of the President/Rapport du President. a.
- Problems of the North. irreg. ISSN 0079-5771

**National Research Council of Canada. Associate
Committee on Air Cushion Technology**
Ottawa K1A 0R6, Canada.
- National Research Council, Canada. Associate
  Committee on Air Cushion Technology.
  Newsletter. 3 per yr.

**National Research Council of Canada. Associate
Committee on Geotechnical Research**
Ottawa, Ontario K1A 0R6, Canada.
- National Research Council, Canada. Associate
  Committee on Geotechnical Research. Technical
  Memorandum. irreg. ISSN 0077-5428

**National Research Council of Canada. Associate
Committee on Scientific Criteria for Environmental
Quality**
Ottawa, Ont., Canada.
- National Research Council, Canada. Associate
  Committee on Scientific Criteria for
  Environmental Quality. Status Report/Conseil
  National de Recherches, Canada, Comite Associe
  sur les Criteres Scientifiques. Rapport d'Activite.
  irreg.

**National Research Council of Canada. Canada
Institute for Scientific and Technical Information
(CISTI)**
Publications Section, Ottawa, K1A 0S2, Canada.
- Canadian Locations of Journals Indexed in Index
  Medicus/Bibliotheques Canadiennes Detenant les
  Periodiques Repertories dans l'Index Medicus. a.
  ISSN 0316-3938
- Directory of Canadian Scientific and Technical
  Periodicals/Repertoire des Periodiques
  Scientifiques et Techniques Canadiens. biennial.
  ISSN 0012-3269
- National Science Library. Health Sciences
  Resources Centre. Conference Proceedings in the
  Health Sciences Held by the National Science
  Library/Comptes Rendus des Conferences sur les
  Sciences de la Sante Qui Se Trouvent a la
  Bibliotheque Scientifique Nationale. a.
- National Science Library of Canada. Annual
  Report/Bibliotheque Scientifique Nationale du
  Canada. Rapport Annuel. a. ISSN 0077-5576
- Union List of Scientific Serials in Canadian
  Libraries/Catalogue Collectif des Publications
  Scientifiques dans les Bibliotheques Canadiennes.
  irreg., 5th ed., 1973. ISSN 0082-7657

**National Research Council of Canada. Canadian
National Committee for the I.U.G.G.**
Ottawa, Ont. K1A 0R6, Canada.
- Canadian Geophysical Bulletin. a. ISSN 0068-
  8819

**National Research Council of Canada. Division of
Building Research**
Ottawa, Ont. K1A 0R6, Canada.
- Building Research News. 3 per yr. ISSN 0007-
  361X
- Canadian Building Abstracts. a. ISSN 0008-3089
- Canadian Building Digest. m. ISSN 0008-3097
- Canadian Building Series. (pub. by University of
  Toronto Press)
- National Research Council, Canada. Division of
  Building Research. Bibliography. irreg. ISSN
  0085-3828
- National Research Council, Canada. Division of
  Building Research. Building Research Note. irreg.
  ISSN 0077-5460
- National Research Council, Canada. Division of
  Building Research. Computer Program. irreg.
  ISSN 0077-5479
- National Research Council, Canada. Division of
  Building Research. Research Program. a. ISSN
  0077-5517

**National Research Council of Canada. Division of
Mechanical Engineering**
Montreal Rd., Ottawa, Ont. K1A 0R6, Canada.
- National Research Council, Canada. Division of
  Mechanical Engineering and National
  Aeronautical Establishment. Quarterly Bulletin. q.
  ISSN 0047-9055

**National Research Council of Canada. Office of
Grants & Scholarships**
Ottawa, Ont. K1A 0R6, Canada.
- National Research Council, Canada. Annual
  Report on Scholarships and Grants in Aid of
  Research/Conseil National de Recherches du
  Canada. Compte Rendu Annuel des Bourses et
  Subventions d'Aide a la Recherche. a. ISSN 0316-
  4047

**National Research Council of Canada. Public
Information Branch**
Ottawa, Ont. K1A 0R6, Canada.
- Science Dimension. 6 per yr. ISSN 0036-830X

**National Unity Party of Canada**
Box 120, Sta. R, Montreal, P.Q., Canada.
- Serviam. 10 per yr. ISSN 0037-2536

**Native Brotherhood of British Columbia and Raven
Society**
- Native Voice. (pub. by Native Voice Publishing
  Society)

**Native Communications Society of Nova Scotia**
Box 961, Sydney, N.S., Canada.
- Mic Mac News. m. ISSN 0026-2528

**Native Communications Society of the Western
N.W.T.**
P.O. Box 1992, Yellowknife, N.W.T. X0E 1H0,
Canada.
- Native Press. s-m.

**Native Council of Canada**
Rm. 1010, 77 Metcalf St., Ottawa, Ont. K1P 5L6,
Canada.
- Forgotten People/Oublies. m. ISSN 0315-4459

**Native Voice Publishing Society**
517 Ford Bldg, 193 E. Hasting St., Vancouver, B.C.
V6A 1N7, Canada.
- Native Voice. m. ISSN 0028-0542 (Native
  Brotherhood of British Columbia and Raven
  Society)

**Eric Neal, Ed. & Pub.**
3500 Henri-Bourassa Blvd. E. Apt 106, Montreal
459, Que., Canada.
- Advance Weather Forecasts. m. ISSN 0015-7104
- Weather Timetable. m. ISSN 0049-7053

**Nebula Press**
509 Lakeshore Drive, North Bay, Ont. P1A 2E3,
Canada.
- Nebula. q.

**New Brunswick. Correctional Program**
Fredericton, N.B., Canada.
- New Brunswick. Correctional Program. Annual
  Report of the Director. a. ISSN 0077-8028

**New Brunswick. Department of Agriculture and Rural
Development**
Box 6000, Fredericton, N.B. E3B 5H1, Canada.
- Agriculture News Notes. m. ISSN 0002-1768

**New Brunswick. Department of Agriculture & Rural
Development. Horticulture Division**
Plant Industry Branch, Fredericton, N.B., Canada.
- Vegetables Newsletter. irreg. ISSN 0042-3092

**New Brunswick. Department of Agriculture and Rural
Development. Plant Industry Branch**
Box 6000, Fredericton, N.B. E3B 5H1, Canada.
- New Brunswick. Plant Industry Branch. Selected
  Potato Statistics. a.
- New Brunswick, Department of Agriculture and
  Rural Development. Plant Industry Branch.
  Agricultural Report. irreg. ISSN 0041-218X

**New Brunswick. Department of Fisheries**
Box 600, Fredericton, N.B. e3B 5H1, Canada.
- New Brunswick Department of Fisheries. Annual
  Report. a. ISSN 0077-8036

**New Brunswick. Department of Health**
Centennial Building, Fredericton, New Brunswick,
Canada.
- New Brunswick. Department of Health. Annual
  Report. a.

**New Brunswick. Department of Labour**
Fredericton, New Brunswick, Canada.
- New Brunswick. Department of Labour. Annual
  Report. a. ISSN 0077-8052

**New Brunswick. Department of Municipal Affairs**
Fredericton, New Brunswick, Canada.
- New Brunswick. Department of Municipal Affairs.
  Report. a. ISSN 0077-8060

**New Brunswick. Department of Natural Resources**
Mines Division, Fredericton, N.B., Canada.
- New Brunswick. Beach Resources-Eastern New
  Brunswick. irreg.

- New Brunswick. Mineral Resources Branch.
  Mineral Resources Reports. irreg. ISSN 0077-
  8095
- New Brunswick. Mineral Resources Branch.
  Report of Investigations. irreg. ISSN 0077-8109
- New Brunswick. Wetlands-Peatlands Resources.
  irreg.

**New Brunswick. Department of Youth**
Fredericton, N.B., Canada.
- New Brunswick. Department of Youth. Report. a.
  ISSN 0077-8079

**New Brunswick. Economic Advisor's Office**
Box 6000, Fredericton, N.B. e3B 5H1, Canada.
- New Brunswick Economic Statistics. 3 per yr.
  ISSN 0028-4351

**New Brunswick. Field Services Branch**
Box 1030, Fredericton, N.B. e3B 5C3, Canada.
- New Brunswick. Field Services Branch. Provincial
  Park Statistics. irreg.

**New Brunswick. Health Services Advisory Council**
Fredericton, N.B., Canada.
- New Brunswick. Health Services Advisory
  Council. Annual Report/Rapport Annuel. a.

**New Brunswick. Liquor Control Commission**
Fredericton, N.B., Canada.
- New Brunswick. Liquor Control Commission.
  Report. a. ISSN 0077-8087

**New Brunswick. Research and Productivity Council**
Fredericton, N. B., Canada.
- New Brunswick. Research and Productivity
  Council. Record. irreg. ISSN 0077-8125
- New Brunswick. Research and Productivity
  Council. Report. a. ISSN 0077-8117
- New Brunswick. Research and Productivity
  Council. Research Note. irreg. ISSN 0077-8133

**New Brunswick Development Corporation**
238 Waterloo Rd., Fredericton, N.B. E3B 4Y2,
Canada.
- New Brunswick Development Corporation.
  Annual Report. a. ISSN 0548-4065

**New Brunswick Electric Power Commission**
Box 2000, Fredericton, N.B. e3B 4X1, Canada.
- Current Events (Fredericton) bi-m. ISSN 0011-
  3468
- Electricity Today. bi-m. ISSN 0383-3402

**New Brunswick Federation of Naturalists**
277 Douglas Ave., Saint John, N. B., Canada.
- New Brunswick Naturalist. 5 per yr. ISSN 0047-
  9551

**New Brunswick Home Economics Association**
Bathurst, N.B., Canada.
- New Brunswick Home Economics Association.
  Newsletter. irreg. ISSN 0548-4081

**New Brunswick Industrial Safety Council**
Saint John, N.B., Canada.
- Working Safely. bi-m. ISSN 0381-3975

**New Brunswick Information Service**
Fredericton, N.B., Canada.
- Nouveau-Brunswick. q. ISSN 0381-3150

**New Brunswick Museum**
277 Douglas Ave., Saint John, N. B., Canada.
- New Brunswick Museum, Saint John. Annual
  Report. a. ISSN 0080-5475

**New Brunswick Public Employees Association**
Box 95, 238 King St., Fredericton, N.B., Canada.
- New Brunswick Public Employees Association.
  News Letter. irreg. ISSN 0381-7970
- Public Employees Journal/Journal des Employes
  Publics. a. ISSN 0381-7962

**New Brunswick Teachers' Association**
Box 752, Fredericton, N.B. E3B 5B4, Canada.
- Teaching Positions Available. 3-4 per yr. ISSN
  0380-1462

**New Canadian Publisher**
479 Queen St., Toronto M5V 2A9, Ont., Canada.
- New Canadian. s-w(Tues. & Fri.) ISSN 0028-4394

**New Chamber Orchestra of Canada**
- Chamber Pot. (pub. by Canadian Chamber
  Concerts Press)

**New Democratic Party of British Columbia**
- Democrat. (pub. by Democrat Publishing Co., Ltd.)

**New Hellas**
1555 Louvain St., West Montreal 355, P.Q., Canada.
- New Hellas/Nouvelle Hellas. q. ISSN 0047-9721

**New Leaf Publications**
52 St. Clair Ave., Toronto, Ont. M4T 1N4, Canada.
- Saturday Night; Canada's leading magazine of comment and opinion. m. ISSN 0036-4975

**New Pathway Publishing Co. Ltd**
184 Alexander Ave., Winnipeg, Manitoba 2, Manitoba R3C 2N4.
- Novy Shliakh/New Pathway; Ukrainian weekly. w. ISSN 0029-5310

**New Review Books**
Box 31, Post. Sta. E, Toronto 4, Ont., Canada.
- New Review of East-European History. q.

**New Statements**
Suite 1000, 151 Slater St., Ottawa 4, Ont., Canada.
- New Statements. 3 per yr.

**New Women's Magazine Society**
Box 4098, Edmonton, Alta T6E 4S8, Canada.
- Branching out. ISSN 0382-5264

**Newest Press**
Edmonton, Alberta, Canada.
- Newest Review. 10 per yr. ISSN 0380-2817

**Newfoundland. Department of Fisheries**
St. John's, Newfoundland, Canada.
- Newfoundland. Department of Fisheries. Annual Report. a.

**Newfoundland. Department of Mines and Energy**
Mineral Development Division, St. John's, Newfoundland, Canada.
- Newfoundland. Geological Survey. Bulletin. irreg. ISSN 0078-0308
- Newfoundland. Mineral Development Division. Information. irreg. ISSN 0078-0340
- Newfoundland. Mineral Development Division. Information Circular. irreg. ISSN 0078-0359
- Newfoundland. Mines Branch. Annual Report Series. a. ISSN 0078-0367
- Newfoundland. Mines Branch. Geological Survey of Newfoundland. Bulletin Series. irreg. ISSN 0078-0375
- Newfoundland. Mines Branch. Geological Survey of Newfoundland. Report Series. irreg. ISSN 0078-0383
- Newfoundland and Labrador. Bulletin. irreg.
- Newfoundland and Labrador. Geological Report. irreg.
- Newfoundland and Labrador. Mineral Resources Report. irreg.

**Newfoundland. Department of Social Services**
St. John's, Newfoundland, Canada.
- Newfoundland. Department of Social Services. Annual Report. a. ISSN 0078-0294

**Newfoundland Association of Public Employees**
Box 1085, St. John's, Nfld. A1C 5M5, Canada.
- N A P E Journal. irreg. ISSN 0381-6826

**Newfoundland Medical Association**
O'Mara-Martin Bldg., St. John's, Nfld., Canada.
- Newfoundland Medical Association. Newsletter. 4 per yr. ISSN 0048-0193

**Newfoundland Medical Board**
Registrar, 47 Queen's Rd., St. John's Nfld., A1C 2A7, Canada.
- Newfoundland Medical Directory. a. ISSN 0078-0316

**Newfoundland Outdoors**
Box 219, Holyrood, C.B., Newfoundland A0A 2R0, Canada.
- Newfoundland Outdoors. m.

**Newfoundland Public Libraries Board. Public Library Services**
St. John's, Nfld., Canada.
- Newfoundland and Labrador Provincial Libraries. Newsletter. q. ISSN 0381-2022

**Newfoundland Teachers Association**
3 Kenmount Rd., St. John's, Nfld. a1B 1W1, Canada.
- N T A Journal. s-a. ISSN 0027-7037

**Newman Foundation of Toronto**
89 St. George St., Toronto M5S 2E8, Canada.
- Ontario Catholic Directory. a. ISSN 0078-4702

**Next Year Country Magazine Inc.**
Box 3446, Regina, Saskatchewan, Canada.
- Next Year Country; Saskatchewan's news magazine. bi-m. ISSN 0315-758X

**Niagara Parks Commission**
Toronto, Ont., Canada.
- Niagara Parks Commission. Annual Report. a. ISSN 0078-0502

**Nickle Publications Co. Ltd.**
Suite 110, 330 Ninth Ave. S.W., Calgary. Alta. T2P 1K8, Canada.
- Canadian Oil Register. a. ISSN 0068-9394

**Nimrod Publications Ltd**
Box 737, Regina, Sask. S4P 3A8, Canada.
- Fish and Game Sportsman. q. ISSN 0015-2897

**Nor-Rand Publishing Ltd.**
- Wings Magazine of Canada. (pub. by Corvus Publishing Group Ltd.)

**Publications Norco Inc.**
5890 Monkland, Suite 306, Montreal H4A 1G2, Canada.
- Aqua-Mag.
- Ski-Mag. 5 per yr ( Nov. - Mar.)

**Norman Bethune Institute of Ideological Studies**
Box 727, Adelaide Station, Toronto M5C 2J8 Ont., Canada
(Subscr. to: National Publications Centre, P.O. Box 727, Adelaide Station, Toronto, Ont., Canada)
- New Literature and Ideology. q.

**Norman Mackenzie Art Gallery**
Regina, Sask., Canada.
- N M A G Review. irreg. ISSN 0384-1022

**P. G. Normandin**
P. O. Box 3455, Station C, Ottawa, Canada.
- Canadian Parliamentary Guide. a.

**Norrona Publishing Co.**
8594 Sunbury Pl., Delta, B.C. V4C 3Y7, Canada.
- Norrona/Norseman. s-m. ISSN 0048-0568

**North American Trackless Trolley Association**
Box 5, Oshawa, Ont. L1H 7L9, Canada.
- Trolley Coach News. q.

**North Shore Numismatic Society**
P.O. Box 86241, North Vancouver, British Columbia V7L 4J8, Canada.
- Shore Line. m. ISSN 0380-8866

**Northeastern Regional Library System**
6 Al Wende St., Kirkland Lake, Ont. P2N 3G9, Canada.
- N. E. R. L. S. Newsletter. irreg. ISSN 0380-2841

**Northern Miner Press Ltd.**
77 River St, Toronto, Ont. M5A 3P2, Canada.
- Canadian Mines Handbook. a. ISSN 0068-9289
- Canadian Mines Register of Dormant and Defunct Companies. irreg. ISSN 0068-9297
- Canadian Mines Register of Dormant and Defunct Companies. Supplement. irreg., 3rd. 1976. ISSN 0068-9300
- Northern Miner; devoted to the mining industry of Canada. w. ISSN 0029-3164

**Northern Neighbors Ltd.**
Box 1000, Gravenhurst, Ont. P0C 1G0, Canada.
- Northern Neighbors. m. ISSN 0029-3199

**Northern News Services**
Yellowknife, N.W.T., Canada.
- Arctic in Colour. 3 per yr. ISSN 0382-0467

**Northwest Digest Ltd.**
Box 900, Station A, Surrey, B.C. V3S 4P4, Canada.
- B C Outdoors. (British Columbia) bi-m. ISSN 0045-3013

**Nouvelle Barre du Jour**
1-55th Ave., Bois-des-Filion J6Z 2P5, Que., Canada.
- Nouvelle Barre du Jour. m.

**Nova Scotia. Department of Agriculture and Marketing**
- Nova Scotia Farm News. (pub. by Nova Scotia Communications and Information Centre)

**Nova Scotia. Department of Agriculture and Marketing. Horticulture and Biology Services Branch**
Halifax, N.S., Canada.
- Nova Scotia Lowbush Blueberries Newsletter. irreg.

**Nova Scotia. Department of Development**
Halifax, Nova Scotia, Canada.
- Nova Scotia. Department of Development. Annual Report. a.

**Nova Scotia. Department of Education**
Box 578, Halifax, N. S. B3J 2S9, Halifax Nova Scotia, Canada.
- Adult Education in Nova Scotia. 4 per yr. ISSN 0001-8511 (prep. by its Adult Education Program)
- Education Nova Scotia. fortn.
- Journal of Education. 4 per yr. ISSN 0022-0566

**Nova Scotia. Department of Education. Health and Physical Education Office**
Box 578, Halifax, N.S. B3J 2S9, Canada.
- Inform. bi-m.

**Nova Scotia. Department of Labour**
Economics and Research Division, P.O. Box 697, Halifax, Nova Scotia, Canada.
- Labour Organizations in Nova Scotia. a.
- Nova Scotia. Department of Labour. Economics and Research Division. Wage Rates, Salaries and Hours of Labour in Nova Scotia. a. ISSN 0550-1741
- Nova Scotia. Fire Marshal. Annual Report. a. ISSN 0085-4395
- Trends in Collective Bargaining Settlements in Nova Scotia. a. ISSN 0381-3258

**Nova Scotia. Department of Labour. Economics and Research Division**
Box 697, Halifax, N.S., Canada.
- Selected Labour Statistics for Nova Scotia. a.

**Nova Scotia. Department of Public Health**
Halifax, N.S., Canada.
- Nova Scotia. Department of Bacteriology. Annual Report. a. ISSN 0078-2319
- Nova Scotia. Department of Pathology. Annual Report. a. ISSN 0078-2351
- Nova Scotia. Department of Public Health. Nutrition Division. Annual Report. a. ISSN 0078-236X

**Nova Scotia. Department of Recreation**
5151 George St., P.O. Box 864, Halifax, N.S. B3J 2V2, Canada.
- Nova Scotia. Department of Recreation. Annual Report. a.

**Nova Scotia. Department of Social Services**
Halifax, Nova Scotia, Canada.
- Social Services in Nova Scotia. a. ISSN 0317-4336

**Nova Scotia. Emergency Measures Organization**
Box 1502, Halifax, Nova Scotia, Canada.
- E M O Bulletin. q. ISSN 0012-7779
- Nova Scotia. Emergency Measures Organization. Report. a. ISSN 0078-2378

**Nova Scotia. Environmental Control Council**
Halifax, N.S., Canada.
- Nova Scotia. Environmental Control Council. Annual Report. a. ISSN 0317-3526

**Nova Scotia. Office of the Ombudsman**
Halifax, Nova Scotia, Canada.
- Nova Scotia. Office of the Ombudsman. Annual Report. a.

**Nova Scotia Bird Society**
c/o Nova Scotia Museum, 1747 Summer St., Halifax, N.S. B3H 3A6, Canada.
- Nova Scotia Bird Society. Newsletter. irreg. ISSN 0383-9567

**Nova Scotia College of Art & Design**
Halifax, N.S., Canada.
- Universities Art Association of Canada. Journal/ Association d'Art des Universites du Canada. Journal. q. ISSN 0315-940X

**Nova Scotia Communications and Information Centre**
Truro, Nova Scotia, Canada.
- Nova Scotia Farm News. ISSN 0029-5086 (Nova Scotia. Department of Agriculture and Marketing)

**Nova Scotia Drama League**
c/o St. Mary's University, Sub. 4th, Halifax, N.S. B3H 3C3, Canada.
- Callboard. 4 per yr. ISSN 0045-4044

**Nova Scotia Fruit Growers Association**
Kentville, N. S., Canada.
- Nova Scotia Fruit Growers Association. Annual Report and Proceedings. a. ISSN 0078-2386

**Nova Scotia Historical Society**
1271 Edward St., Halifax, N.S., Canada.
- Nova Scotia Historical Society. Collections. irreg. ISSN 0383-8420

**Nova Scotia Land Surveyors Association**
Box 1541, Halifax, N.S., Canada.
- Nova Scotian Surveyor. q. ISSN 0380-9242

**Nova Scotia Museum**
1747 Summer St., Halifax, N. S., Canada.
- Nova Scotia Museum, Halifax. Occasional Papers. irreg. ISSN 0078-2424

**Nova Scotia Power Corporation**
P.O. Box 910, Halifax, N.S., Canada.
- Nova Scotia Power Corporation. Annual Report. a. ISSN 0078-2459

**Nova Scotia Research Foundation**
Box 790, Dartmouth, N.S. B2Y 3Z7, Canada.
- Nova Scotia Research Foundation. Bulletin. irreg. ISSN 0078-2483

**Nova Scotia Springhill Penitentiary**
Box 2140, Springhill, Canada.
- Communicator. bi-m.

**Nova Scotia Teachers Union**
106 Dutch Village Rd., Box 1060 Armdale, Halifax, Nova Scotia, Canada.
- Teacher. m. ISSN 0382-408X

**Nova Scotia Technical College. School of Architecture**
Box 1000, Halifax, Nova Scotia, Canada.
- Nova Scotia Technical College. School of Architecture. Report Series. irreg. ISSN 0078-2491

**Nova Scotian Institute of Science**
Science Library Dalhousie University, Halifax., N.S. Canada.
- Nova Scotian Institute of Science. Proceedings. irreg. ISSN 0078-2521

**Novy Domov**
978 Queen St., W., Toronto, Ont. M6J 1H1, Canada.
- Novy Domov/New Homeland. w.

**Nowi Dni Publications Ltd.**
28 Northcliffe Blvd., Toronto, Ont. M6H 3G1, Canada.
- Nowi Dni; universal illustrated monthly. m. ISSN 0048-1017

**O R L Publications Ltd.**
Suite 405, Mount Sinai Hospital, 600 University Ave., Toronto, Ont. M5G 1X5, Canada.
- Journal of Otolaryngology. bi-m. (Canadian Otolaryngological Society)

**Oberon Press**
555 Maple Lane, Ottawa, Ont. K1M 0N7, Canada.
- New Canadian Stories. a. ISSN 0316-7518

**Oblate Fathers**
1301 Wellington Crescent, Winnipeg, Man. R3Q 0A9, Canada.
- Indian Record. bi-m. ISSN 0019-6282

**Oblate Fathers of St. Mary's Province of Canada**
Box 249, Battleford, Sask. S0M 0E0, Canada.
- Our Family; Canada's Catholic family monthly magazine. m. ISSN 0030-6843

**Observatoire de Geophysique**
College Jean-De-Brebeuf, 3200 Chemin Ste-Catherine, Montreal, Que. H3T 1C1, Canada.
- Bulletin de Geophysique. s-a. ISSN 0007-4284

**Ob'yednannya Demokratychnoyi Ukrayins'koyi Molodi. Tzentral'nyi Komitet**
Postal Station M, Box 40, Toronto, Ont. M6S 4T2, Canada.
- Moloda Ukrayina/Young Ukraine; zhurnal ukrayins' koyi demokvatychnoyi molodi. m. ISSN 0026-9042

**Office des Communications Sociales**
4635 rue de Lorimer, Montreal, Que. H2H 2B4, Canada.
- Films a l'Ecran. fortn. ISSN 0046-3825
- Inter; information et documentation sur les moyens de communication sociale. m. ISSN 0020-4927
- Office des Communications Sociales, Montreal. Cahiers d'Etudes et de Recherches. irreg. ISSN 0078-3722
- Office des Communications Sociales, Montreal. Selection de Films pour Cine-Clubs. irreg. ISSN 0078-3730
- Recueil des Films. a. ISSN 0085-543X

**Old Nun Publications**
129 Seaton St., Toronto, Ont. M5A 2T2, Canada.
- Old Nun. bi-m.
- Poetry Toronto Newsletter. m.

**Ontario. Division of Mines. Geological Branch**
Room 2309, Whitney Block, Queen's Park, Toronto, Ont., Canada.
- Ontario. Division of Mines. Geochemical Reports. irreg., 1-2 per yr.
- Ontario. Division of Mines. Geological Reports. irreg., 10-12 per yr.
- Ontario. Division of Mines. Geophysical Reports. irreg., 1-2 per yr.
- Ontario. Division of Mines. Guide Books. irreg., 1-2 per yr.
- Ontario. Division of Mines. Industrial Mineral Reports. irreg., 3-4 per yr.
- Ontario. Division of Mines. Mineral Resource Circulars. irreg., 1-2 per yr.
- Ontario. Division of Mines. Miscellaneous Papers. irreg., 3-4 per yr.

**Ontario. Government Services**
Parliament Bldgs., Toronto, Ont. M7A 1N8, Canada.
- Ontario Gazette. w. ISSN 0030-2937

**Ontario. Labour Relations Board**
Toronto, Ont., Canada.
- Ontario. Labour Relations Board. Decisions. 3 per yr. ISSN 0472-9986

**Ontario. Ministry of Agriculture and Food**
Extension Branch, Parliament Bldgs., Toronto M7A 1B2 Ont., Canada.
- Junior Farmer and 4-H Enthusiast. bi-m. ISSN 0022-6572
- Ontario. Agricultural Research Institute. Report. a. ISSN 0078-4664
- Ontario. Ministry of Agriculture and Food. Monthly Crop and Live Stock Report. m. ISSN 0027-0342
- Ontario. Ministry of Agriculture and Food. Monthly Dairy Report. m. ISSN 0030-2872
- Ontario. Ministry of Agriculture and Food. Seasonal Fruit and Vegetable Report. m (annual supplement) ISSN 0474-1560

**Ontario. Ministry of Colleges and Universities**
Toronto, Ont., Canada.
- Ontario. Ministry of Colleges and Universities. Public Library Statistics. irreg.

**Ontario. Ministry of Community and Social Services**
Toronto, Ont., Canada.
- Ontario. Ministry of Community and Social Services. Social Assistance Review Board. Annual Report of the Chairman. a.

**Ontario. Ministry of Consumer and Commercial Relations**
Toronto, Canada.
- Ontario. Ministry of Consumer and Commercial Relations. Statistical Review. irreg. ISSN 0317-8161

**Ontario. Ministry of Culture and Recreation. Provincial Library Service**
Parliament Bldgs., Toronto, Ont. M7A 2R9, Canada.
- In Review; Canadian books for children. q. ISSN 0019-3259
- Ontario Library Review. q. ISSN 0030-2996

**Ontario. Ministry of Education**
Toronto, Ont. M7A 1L2, Toronto, Ont. M7A 1L4, Canada
(Orders to: Publications Centre, Ministry of Government Services, 3B7 MacDonald Block, Queen's Park, Toronto, Ont., M7A 1N8, Canada)
- Directory of Education. a. ISSN 0316-8549
- Ontario Education Dimensions. m. ISSN 0317-0349

**Ontario. Ministry of Energy**
Toronto, Ontario, Canada.
- Ontario Ministry of Energy. a.

**Ontario. Ministry of Government Services. Printing Services Branch**
3B7 Macdonald Block, Queen's Park, Toronto, Ont. M7A 1N8, Canada.
- Ontario Government Publications, Monthly Checklist. m. ISSN 0316-1617

**Ontario. Ministry of Housing**
56 Wellesley St. W., 2nd Floor, Toronto, Ont. M7A 2K4, Canada.
- Housing Ontario. 8 per yr.
- Housing Ontario. s-a. ISSN 0318-4552
- Ontario. Ministry of Housing. Annual Report. a. ISSN 0078-4885

**Ontario. Ministry of Industry and Tourism**
900 Bay St., 9th Fl., Toronto M7A 1T2, Ontario, Canada.
- Ontario Trade and Export Journal. bi-m.

**Ontario. Ministry of Labour. Research Library**
400 University Library, Toronto, Ont. M7A 1T8, Canada.
- Ontario. Ministry of Labour. Research Library. Library Selections. 3 per m. ISSN 0319-8316

**Ontario. Ministry of Natural Resources.**
Toronto, Ont., Canada.
- Ontario. Ministry of Natural Resources. Natural Resources Mineral Review. a.
- Ontario. Ministry of Natural Resources. Statistics. irreg.
- Ontario. Petroleum Resources Branch. Drilling and Production Report, Oil and Natural Gas. a. ISSN 0078-5059
- Ontario Fish and Wildlife Review. q. ISSN 0030-2929
- Ontario Mineral Review. a.

**Ontario. Ministry of Natural Resources. Division of Forests**
Research Branch, Parliament Bldgs., Toronto, Ont., Canada.
- Ontario. Ministry of Natural Resources. Research Library. Research Report. irreg., 1973, no. 93. ISSN 0078-4753

**Ontario. Ministry of the Environment**
135 St. Clair Ave. W., Toronto, Ontario, Canada.
- Environment Ontario Legacy. bi-m.
- Ontario. Ministry of the Environment. Annual Report. a.

**Ontario. Ministry of the Environment. Information Services Branch**
135 St. Clair Ave. W., Toronto, Ont. M4V 1P5, Canada.
- Ontario. Water Resources Commission. Ground Water Bulletin. irreg. ISSN 0078-5156
- Selected Streamflow Data for Ontario. a.

**Ontario. Ministry of the Environment. Water Resources Branch**
135 St. Clair Ave. W., Toronto, Ont. M4V 1P5, Canada.
- Ontario. Ministry of the Environment, Pollution Control Branch. Research Paper. irreg. ISSN 0078-513X
- Ontario. Ministry of the Environment. Pollution Control Branch. Research Publication. irreg. ISSN 0078-5148
- Ontario. Ministry of the Environment. Water Resources Report. irreg.
- Ontario Industrial Waste Conference. Proceedings. a. ISSN 0078-4893
- Water Quality Data for Ontario Streams & Lakes. a.

**Ontario. Ministry of Transportation and Communications**
1201 Wilson Ave., Downsview, Ont. M3M 1J8, Canada.
- Ontario. Ministry of Transportation and Communications. Motor Vehicle Accident Facts. a.
- Ontario. Ministry of Transportation and Communications. Research and Development Division. Research Report. irreg. ISSN 0078-4745

**Ontario. Ministry of Treasury, Economics and Intergovernmental Affairs. Ontario Statistical Centre**
Toronto M7A 1Z1, Ont., Canada.
- Ontario Statistics. a.

**Ontario Archaeological Society**
Box 241, Station P, Toronto, Ont. M5S 2S8, Canada.
- Ontario Archaeology. 2 per yr. ISSN 0078-4672

**Ontario Archaeological Society. Ottawa Chapter**
Box 70, Greely, Ont. K0A 1Z0, Canada.
- Archaic Notes. 10 per yr. ISSN 0381-8357

**Ontario Association for Curriculum Development**
1260 Bay St., 6th Floor, Toronto 5, Ontario, Canada.
- Ontario Association for Curriculum Development. Annual Conference (Report) a. ISSN 0078-4680

**Ontario Association for Emotionally Disturbed Children**
511 Church St, Toronto 5, Ont., Canada.
- E D C/Emotionally Disturbed Children. 10 per yr. ISSN 0012-7507

**Ontario Association for Geographic and Environmental Education**
32 Holywell Dr., Weston, Ont. M9R 1K1, Canada.
- Ontario Association for Geographic & Environmental Education. Monograph. q.

**Ontario Association for Mathematics Education**
c/o Arn Harris, Althouse College, University of Western Ontario, 1137 Western Rd., London, Ont. M6G 1G7, Canada.
- Ontario Mathematics Gazette. 3 per yr. ISSN 0030-3011

**Ontario Association of Children's Aid Societies**
663 Yonge St., Toronto, Ont. M4Y 2A4, Canada.
- Ontario Association of Children's Aid Societies. Journal. m. except July & Aug. ISSN 0030-283X

**Ontario Bird Banding Association**
277 Arthur St. N., Guelph, Ont., Canada.
- Ontario Bird Banding. a. ISSN 0475-025X

**Ontario Cancer Treatment and Research Foundation**
7 Overlea Blvd., Toronto, Ont. M4H 1A8, Canada.
- Cancer in Ontario. a. ISSN 0315-9884

**Ontario College of Pharmacists**
483 Huron St., Toronto, Ont. M5R 2R4, Canada.
- On Continuing Practice. q. ISSN 0315-1042

**Ontario Crafts Council**
346 Dundas St. W., Toronto, Ont. M5T 1G5, Canada.
- Craftnews. bi-m. ISSN 0319-7832
- Craftsman. bi-m. ISSN 0319-7840

**Ontario Criminal Injuries Compensation Board**
454 University Avenue, Room 201, 2 Toronto, Ont., Canada.
- Ontario. Criminal Injuries Compensation Board. Report.

**Ontario Dental Association**
230 St. George St., Toronto, Ont. M5R 2P1, Canada.
- Ontario Dental Association. Journal. (pub. by Scholar House Publishing)
- Ontario Dentist. m.

**Ontario Dental Hygienists' Association**
Box 264, Maxville, Ont., Canada.
- Ontario Dental Hygienist. s-a.

**Ontario Educational Association**
Ste. 904, 252 Bloor St. W., Toronto, Ont. M5S 1V7, Canada.
- O E A Review. 3 per yr.

**Ontario Educational Research Council**
1260 Bay St., Toronto, Ont. M5R 2B1, Canada.
- Reporting Classroom Research. q.

**Ontario Energy Board**
14 Carlton St., Toronto M5B 1K5, Ontario, Canada.
- Ontario Energy Board. Annual Report. a.

**Ontario English Catholic Teachers Association**
Suite 228, 1260 Bay St., Toronto 5, Ont., Canada.
- O. E. C. T. A. Reporter. 10 per yr.

**Ontario Federation of Agriculture**
- Farm and Country. (pub. by Agricultural Publishing Co.)

**Ontario Federation of Labour**
15 Gervais Drive, Don Mills, Ont., Canada.
- O F L Facts and Figures. a.
- Ontario Federation of Labour. Legislative Proposals. Submission to the Premier and Other Ministers of the Government of Ontario. a. ISSN 0078-4818
- Ontario Federation of Labour. Report of Proceedings. a. ISSN 0078-4826

**Ontario Film Association Inc.**
Box 521, Barrie, Ont., Canada.
- Newsletter Called Fred. m.

**Ontario Folk Dance Association**
43 Cynthia Road, Toronto, Ont. M6N 2P8, Canada.
- Ontario Folkdancer. m (10 per yr) ISSN 0384-5052

**Ontario Forest Information Service**
No. 708, Essex House, 185 Bay St., Toronto 1, Ont., Canada.
- Forest Scene. q. ISSN 0046-4589

**Ontario Forestry Association**
150 Consumers Rd., Willowdale, Ont. M2J 1P9, Canada.
- Ontario Forests. q. ISSN 0048-1785

**Ontario Fruit and Vegetable Growers Association**
303 Ontario Food Terminal, 165 The Queensway, Toronto, Ont. M8Y 1H8, Canada.
- Grower. m. ISSN 0017-4777

**Ontario Genealogical Society**
Box 66, Station Q, Toronto, Ont. M4T 2L7, Canada.
- Families. q. ISSN 0030-2945
- Ontario Genealogy Society. Newsleaf. 3 per yr. ISSN 0380-1616

**Ontario Handgun Association**
135 Centre St. E., Richmond Hill, Ont. L4C 1A5, Canada.
- Canadian Handgun. bi-m. ISSN 0045-4915

**Ontario Historical Society**
1466 Bathurst St., Toronto, Ont. M5R 3J3, Canada.
- Ontario Historical Society. Bulletin. s-a. ISSN 0078-4869
- Ontario History. q. ISSN 0030-2953

**Ontario Hog Producers Association**
4198 Dundas St. W., Toronto, Ont., Canada.
- O H P A Market Place. m. ISSN 0315-9523

**Ontario Hospital Association**
150 Ferrand Drive, Don Mills, Ont. M3C 1H6, Canada.
- Hospital Highlights. 4 per yr. ISSN 0018-5701

**Ontario Human Rights Commission**
Ministry of Labour, 400 University Ave., Toronto, Ont. M7A 1T7, Canada.
- Human Relations. a. ISSN 0441-4128

**Ontario Hydro**
700 University Ave., Toronto, Ont. M5G 1X6, Canada.
- Ontario Hydro. Statistical Yearbook. irreg.
- Ontario Hydro Research Quarterly. q. ISSN 0030-2988

**Ontario Institute for Studies in Education**
252 Bloor St. W., Toronto, Ont. M5S 1V6, Canada.
- Degree Research in Adult Education in Canada. a.
- Interchange; a journal of educational studies. q. ISSN 0020-5230
- O I S E Monograph Series. irreg., no. 15, 1977. ISSN 0078-5016
- O I S E Occasional Papers. irreg., no. 17, 1977. ISSN 0078-5024

- O I S E Profiles in Practical Education Series. irreg., no. 10, 1976.
- O I S E Symposium Series. irreg., no. 8, 1977.
- Ontario Institute for Studies in Education. Board of Governors. Annual Report. a. ISSN 0078-4915
- Ontario Institute for Studies in Education. Department of Curriculum. Curriculum Series. irreg., no. 26, 1977. ISSN 0078-4923
- Ontario Institute for Studies in Education. Department of Educational Planning. Educational Planning Occasional Papers. irreg. ISSN 0078-494X
- Ontario Institute for Studies in Education. Department of Measurement and Evaluation. Test Development Paper. irreg. ISSN 0078-4966
- Ontario Institute for Studies in Education. Enrollment Projections Series. irreg. ISSN 0078-4974
- Ontario Population Reports. irreg. ISSN 0078-5075
- Orbit; ideas about teaching and learning. 5 per yr. ISSN 0030-4433

**Ontario Insurance Adjusters Association**
c/o C. W. Gibula, Ed., 55 Devins Dr., Aurora, Ont. L4G 2Z3, Canada.
- Without Prejudice. 10 per yr.(Sept.-June) ISSN 0043-700X

**Ontario Insurance Agents and Brokers Association. Consumer Liaison Committee**
Toronto, Ontario, Canada.
- O I A B A Consumer Liaison Committee. Bulletin. irreg. ISSN 0384-1766

**Ontario Library Association**
2397a Bloor St. W., M6S 1P6, Canada.
- O L A Focus. m.

**Ontario Lung Association**
157 Willowdale Ave., Willowdale, Ont. M2N 4Y7, Canada.
- O L A Report. m.

**Ontario Medical Association**
240 St. George St., Toronto M5R 2P4, Canada.
- Ontario Medical Review. m. ISSN 0030-302X

**Ontario Medical Wives Association**
240 St. George St., Toronto M5R 2P4, Ont., Canada.
- Ontario Doctor's Wife. 4 per yr. ISSN 0030-2880

**Ontario Metis & Non-Status Indian Association**
5300 Yonge St., Suite 208, Willowdale, Ont. M2N 5R2, Canada.
- Dimensions. m.

**Ontario Milk Marketing Board**
Box 4027 Sta. A, Toronto, Ont. M5W 1K2, Canada.
- Ontario Milk Producer. m. ISSN 0030-3038

**Ontario Modern Language Teachers' Association**
4 Oakmount Road, Welland, Ont. L3C 4X8, Canada.
- Canadian Modern Language Review. q. ISSN 0008-4506

**Ontario Motor League. Ottawa Club**
1354 Richmond Rd., Ottawa, Ont. K2B 7Z3, Canada.
- Accelerator. q. ISSN 0315-3339

**Ontario Numismatist**
Box 33, Waterloo, Ont., Canada.
- Ontario Numismatist. m. ISSN 0048-1815

**Ontario Petroleum Institute Inc.**
Box 396, Chatham, Ont., Canada.
- Ontario Petroleum Institute. Annual Conference Proceedings. a. ISSN 0078-5040

**Ontario Plumbing Inspectors Association**
Box 1118, 22 Frederick St, Kitchener, Ont., Canada.
- Ontario Plumbing Inspectors Association. Bulletin. bi-m. ISSN 0048-1823

**Ontario Progressive Conservative Association**
Government Members' Services, Rm. 425,
Legislative Bldg., Queen's Park, Toronto, Ont. M7A
1A2, Canada.
- Momentum. m.

**Ontario Psychological Association**
c/o G. Brooker, 245 Old Forest Hill Rd., Toronto
M6C 2H5, Canada.
- Ontario Psychologist. q. ISSN 0030-3054

**Ontario Public School Trustees Association**
Suite 303, 4195 Dundas St. W., Toronto M8X 1Y4,
Ont., Canada.
- Ontario Education. 5 per yr. ISSN 0030-2902

**Ontario Puppetry Association**
c/o Kenneth McKay, Sec., 10 Skyview Crescent,
Willowdale Ont. M2J 1B8, Canada.
- Opal. 6 per yr. ISSN 0030-3062

**Ontario Report**
Box 6851, Sta. A, Toronto, Ont., Canada.
- Ontario Report. bi-m.

**Ontario Research Foundation**
Dept. of Marketing Services, Sheridan Park, Ont.
L5K 1B3, Canada.
- Ontario Research Foundation. Annual Report. a.
ISSN 0078-5083
- Technology Today. bi-m.

**Ontario Retail Gasoline and Automotive Service
Association**
312 Dolomite Drive, Suite 210, Downsview, Ont.
M3J 2N2, Canada.
- Voice of the Ontario Gasoline Retailer. m.

**Ontario Review**
6000 Riverside Drive E., Windsor, Ont. N8S 1B6,
Canada.
- Ontario Review; North American journal of the
arts. s-a. ISSN 0316-4055

**Ontario Secondary School Teachers' Federation**
60 Mobile Drive, Toronto, Ont. M4A 2P3, Canada.
- O S S T F. Forum. bi-m(during school year)

**Ontario Securities Commission**
555 Yonge St., Toronto, Ont. M4Y 1Y7, Canada.
- Ontario Securities Commission. Monthly Bulletin.
m. ISSN 0030-3097
- Ontario Securities Commission. Weekly Summary.
w. ISSN 0030-3100

**Ontario Shade Tree Council**
- Ontario Shade Tree Council. Newsletter. (pub. by
Charters Publishing Co., Ltd.)

**Ontario Showcase Publishing Co. Ltd.**
Box 1000, Ridgetown, Ont., Canada.
- Ontario Showcase; the magazine for antique
collectors. m. ISSN 0030-3119

**Ontario Society of Medical Technologists**
96 Eglinton Ave., Suite 400, Toronto, Ont. M4P
1C5, Canada.
- Ontario Society of Medical Technologists.
Newsletter. q. ISSN 0380-1888

**Ontario Speech and Hearing Association**
c/o Association House, 191 College St., Toronto,
Ont. M5T 1P7, Canada.
- Ontario Speech and Hearing Association. Journal.
4 per yr. ISSN 0078-5105

**Ontario Status of Women Council**
Toronto, Canada.
- Ontario. Status of Women Council. Annual
Report. a.

**Ontario Teachers' Federation**
1260 Bay St., Toronto M5R 2B5, Ont., Canada.
- O T F Interaction. 4 per yr.

**Ontario Trucking Association**
555 Dixon Road, Rexdale, Ontario M9W 1H8,
Canada.
- O T A News Round-up; highway transport board
bulletin. w.

**Oratoire Saint-Joseph du Mont-Royal**
3800 Chemin Reine-Marie, Montreal H3V 1H6,
Canada.
- Cahiers de Josephologie. s-a. ISSN 0007-9774
- Oratoire. bi-m. ISSN 0030-4344

**Order of Agrologists of Quebec**
262 Henri-Bourassa Blvd. W., Montreal, Que. H3L
1N6, Canada.
- Agriculture. q. ISSN 0002-1687
- Agro-Nouvelles. irreg. ISSN 0065-4655

**Order of Engineers of Quebec**
1100-2075 University Street, Montreal, Quebec
H3A 1K8, Canada.
- Interplan. 18 per yr.
- PLAN. m. ISSN 0032-0536

**Order of Nurses of Quebec**
4200 Dorchester Blvd. West, Montreal, Quebec
H3Z 1V4, Canada.
- Order of Nurses of Quebec. News and Notes/
Rdre des Infirmieres et Infirmiers du Quebec.
Notes et Nouvelles. 5 per yr. ISSN 0319-2636

**Order of Saint Basil-The-Great**
- Beacon. (pub. by Basilian Press)
- Svitlo/Light. (pub. by Basilian Press)

**Ordre des Architectes du Quebec**
1825 W. Blvd. Dorchester, Montreal, Que. H3H
1R4, Canada.
- Ordre des Architectes du Quebec. Bulletin/Order
of Architects of Quebec. Bulletin. m.

**Ordre des Arpenteurs-Geometres du Quebec**
917, Mgr Grandin, Ste-Foy, Que. G1V 3X8,
Canada.
- Revue de l'Arpenteur-Geometre. q.

**Ordre des Dentistes du Quebec**
Suite 303, 801 est, rue Sherbrooke, Montreal, Que.,
Canada.
- Journal Dentaire du Quebec. m. ISSN 0021-7999

**Ordre Professionnelle des Ingenieurs Forestiers du
Quebec**
C.P. 57, Sillery, Que. G1T 2P7, Canada.
- Ordre des Ingenieurs Forestiers du Quebec.
Congres Annuel. Texte des Conferences. a.

**Orhanizatsiia Ukra Inok Kanady**
18 Leland Ave., Toronto M8Z 2X5, Canada.
- Zhinochyi Svit/Woman's World. m. ISSN 0513-
9856

**Origins Publications**
Box 5072, Sta. E, Hamilton, Ont. L8S 4K9, Canada.
- Origins. q. ISSN 0048-2234

**Other Woman Collective**
Box 928, Station Q, Toronto 7, Ont., Canada.
- Other Woman. bi-m.

**Ottawa. Board of Trade**
88 Argyle Ave., Ottawa, Ont. K2P 1B4, Canada.
- Ottawa. Board of Trade. Annual Report. a. ISSN
0078-6934

**Ottawa Civil Service Recreational Association**
2451 Riverside Dr., Ottawa 8, Ont., Canada.
- R A News. 8 per yr. ISSN 0033-6734

**Ottawa Field-Naturalists' Club**
Box 3264, Postal Station C, Ottawa K1Y 4J5,
Canada.
- Canadian Field-Naturalist. q. ISSN 0008-3550
- Trail and Landscape. 5 per yr. ISSN 0041-0748

**Ottawa Public Library**
120 Metcalfe St., Ottawa, Ont. K1P 5M2, Canada.
- New Books for Young Adults/Nouveau Livres
pour Adolescents. m.

**Ottawa Valley Western Horse Association**
P.O. Box 2685, Station D, Ottawa, Ontario,
Canada.
- Horsing Around. a. ISSN 0073-3423

**Our Generation Press**
3934 rue St. Urbain, Montreal, P.Q., Canada.
- Black Rose Books. irreg.
- Our Generation. q. ISSN 0030-686X

**Outdoor Canada Magazine Limited**
Suite 201, 181 Eglinton Ave. E., Toronto, Ont.
M4P 1J9, Canada.
- Outdoor Canada. 7 per yr.

**Outdoors Unlittered**
c/o A. van Ween & Associates, 1-9930 106th St.,
Edmonton, Alta. T5K 1C8, Canada.
- Newslitter. m. ISSN 0383-9168

**OVO Photo**
C.P. 1431, Succursale A, Montreal, Quebec H3C
2Z9, Canada.
- OVO Photo. q. ISSN 0315-9507

**Owl's Head Press**
Concordia University, H-543, 1455 de Maisonneuve
Blvd., Montreal, Que., Canada.
- Journal of Canadian Art History/Annales
d'Histoire de l'Art Canadien. s-a. ISSN 0315-
4297

**Oxford University Press**
70 Wynford Dr., Don Mills, Ontario M3C 1J9,
Canada.
- Canadian Lives. irreg.

**P R Productions**
Bay 26, 1865 Sargent Ave, Winnipeg, Man. R: H
0E4, Canada.
- Driveway Reporter. m. ISSN 0046-0729

**P. W. P.**
Box 7186, Sandwich, Windsor, Ont. N9C 3Z1,
Canada.
- P. W. P. 3 per yr.

**Pacific Northwest Humanist Publications**
Box 157, Victoria, B.C. V8W 2M6, Canada.
- Humanist in Canada. q. ISSN 0018-7402

**Pacific Trollers' Association**
Box 94336, Richmond, B.C., Canada.
- Pacific Trollers Association Newsletter. irreg.
ISSN 0078-7663

**Pacific West Publications Ltd.**
1008-Hornby St., Vancouver, B.C. V6Z 1V7,
Canada.
- Vancouver. m.

**G. P. Page Publications**
380 Wellington St., Toronto, Ont. M5V 1E3,
Canada.
- Canada Crafts. bi-m.
- Sporting Goods Trade. irreg. ISSN 0381-9280
- Toys & Games. irreg. ISSN 0381-9930

**Pageant**
1229 Mountain St., Montreal, Que. H3G 1Z2,
Canada.
- Pageant. m. ISSN 0030-9370

**Palestine National Liberation Movement**
- Fateh. (pub. by Solidarity Committee with the
People of Palestine)

**Paper Jacks**
25 Torbay Rd., Markham, Ont., L3R 1H1, Canada.
- Canadian Critical Issues Series. irreg.

**Parachute Publications**
Box 1471, Peterborough, Ont., Canada.
- Parachute. q.

**Parent Cooperative Preschools International**
International Office, Whiteside Taylor Center for
Cooperative Education, 20551 Lakeshore Road,
Baie d'Urfe, Quebec H9X 1R3, Canada.
- Parent Cooperative Preschools International.
Directory. irreg.

**P. E. Parent, Ed. & Pub.**
Suite 8, 3450 Durocher, Montreal H2X 2E1, Que.,
Canada.
- Canadian Military Journal/Revue Militaire
Canadienne. 4 per yr. ISSN 0008-4468

**J. N. Parenteau, Ed. & Pub.**
C.P. 660, East Angus, Compton, Que., Canada.
- Journal de Compton News. w. ISSN 0021-7700
- Missisquoi. w. ISSN 0026-6140

**Gerard Parizeau & Cie, Inc.**
410 rue St-Nicolas, Montreal, Canada.
- Assurances; Revue trimestrielle consacree a
l'etude theorique et pratique de l'assurance au
Canada. q. ISSN 0004-6027

**Parkdale Young Liberal Association**
41 Westminster Ave., Toronto 3, Ont., Canada.
- Parkdalian. m.(Sept-May) ISSN 0031-2177

**Parkins Publishing Co. Ltd.**
222 Argyle Ave., Delhi, Ont. N4B 2Y2, Que.,
Canada.
- Canadian Occupational Safety. bi-m. ISSN 0008-
4611

● Fire Fighting in Canada. bi-m. ISSN 0015-2595

**Parkway Printing and Publishing Ltd.**
122 40th St., Toronto 510, Ont., Canada.
● Bit and Bridle. bi-m. ISSN 0006-3851

**Parti Liberal du Quebec**
● Electeur. (pub. by Compagnie de Publication la
Reforme Ltd.)

**Patent and Trademark Institute of Canada**
P.O. Box 553, Station B, Ottawa 4, Ont., Canada.
● Patent and Trademark Institute of Canada.
Annual Proceedings. a. ISSN 0079-015X

**Pathfinder Travel Parks**
Box 6360, Postal Station A, Toronto, Ont., Canada.
● Pathfinder Travel Parks Directory. s-a. ISSN
0315-3584

**Pathway Publishing Corporation**
R.R.4, Aylmer, Ont., Canada.
● Blackboard Bulletin. m (10 per yr.) ISSN 0006-
4327
● Family Life. m (11 per yr.) ISSN 0014-7303
(Amish Church)
● Young Companion. m. (Amish Church)

**Patria Publishing Co. Ltd.**
6 Alcina Ave., Toronto, Ont. M6G 2E8, Canada.
● Magyar Elet/Hungarian Life. w. ISSN 0047-5513

**Editions Paulines**
250nord, Boul. St. Francois, Sherbrooke, Quebec,
Canada.
● Academie des Sciences Morales et Politiques,
Montreal. Travaux et Communications. irreg.
● Presence Francophone. s-a. ISSN 0048-5195
(Universite de Sherbrooke. Centre d'Etude des
Litteratures d'Expression Francaise)
● Video-Presse. m. ISSN 0315-3975

**Peak Publications Society**
Simon Fraser Univ., Burnaby 2, B.C., Canada.
● Peak. s-w. ISSN 0031-3629

**Pendejo Press**
3358 W. First Ave., Vancouver, Canada.
● Ballsout. ISSN 0005-4399

**Pendragon House Ltd.**
69 Bathurst St., Toronto, Ont. M5V 2P7, Canada.
● New (Toronto) q. ISSN 0028-4130 (British
Canadian Trade Association)

**Editions Penelope**
1200 Avenue Allan, Chomedey, Que. H7W 1G9,
Canada.
● Revue des Fermieres. irreg. ISSN 0381-8225

**Barry Penhale**
12 Crescent Town Rd., Unit 210, Toronto, Ont.
M4C 5L3, Canada.
● Rocks & Minerals in Canada. 6 per yr. ISSN
0035-7537

**Penstock Publications**
75 Thomas St., Oakville, Ont. L6J 3A3, Canada.
● Scott's Industrial Directory. Western
Manufacturers. irreg. ISSN 0317-879X

**Pentamas Ltd.**
29 Jutland Rd., Toronto, Ont., Canada.
● Lifeline. s-m.

**Pentecostal Assemblies of Canada**
10 Overlea Blvd., Toronto, Ont. M4H 1A5, Canada.
● Pentecostal Testimony. m. ISSN 0031-4927
● Real Living. q. ISSN 0034-0847

**People's Alternative Press**
Box 701, Kingston, Ont., Canada.
● This Paper Belongs to the People. s-m. ISSN
0040-6260

**Peres de la Compagnie de Jesus**
● Relations. (pub. by Editions Bellarmin)

**Peres Montfortains**
665 Church St., Dorval, Que. H9S 1R4, Canada.
● Notres. q. ISSN 0029-4578

**Periodiques Reader's Digest Ltee.**
215 Redfern Ave., Montreal, Que. H3Z 2V9,
Canada.
● Selection du Reader's Digest (Canadian-French
Edition) m. ISSN 0037-1378

**A. Perrault**
1700 des Cascades St., St.-Hyacinthe, Que. J2S 3J1,
Canada.
● Adagio. bi-m. ISSN 0380-2914

**Peter Perry Publishing Ltd.**
1658 Victoria Park Ave., Scarborough, Ont. M1R
1P7, Canada.
● Canadian Funeral Director. m. ISSN 0319-3225

**Peter Martin Associates**
35 Britain St., Toronto M5A 1R7, Canada.
● Canadian Book Review Annual. a.

**Petheric Press Ltd.**
Box 1102, Halifax, N.S., Canada.
● Nova Scotia Historical Quarterly. q. ISSN 0300-
3728

**Philips Electron Devices**
116 Vanderhoof, Toronto 17, Ontario, Canada.
● Semiconductors and Integrated Circuits. a. ISSN
0080-8776

**Photo-Memo**
383 rue Belanger, Montreal, 327 Quebec, Canada.
● Photo-Memo. m. ISSN 0048-3974

**A. Pidhainy**
Box 31, Postal Sta. E, Toronto, Ont. M6H 4E1,
Canada.
● New Review of East-European History. irreg.
ISSN 0381-9140

**Jean-Guy Pilon, Ed. & Pub.**
5724 Chemin de la Cote Saint-Antoine, Montreal,
Que. H4A 1R9, Canada.
● Liberte. bi-m. ISSN 0024-2020

**Pilote**
Casier Postal 58, St. Hubert, P.Q., Canada.
● Pilote. m.

**Pink Triangle Press**
Box 639, Sta. A, Toronto, Ont. M5W 1E4, Canada.
● Body Politic. m. ISSN 0315-3606

**Planning Institute of British Columbia**
Box 24835 Stn. C., Vancouver, B.C. V5T 4E9,
Canada.
● P I B C News. 10 per yr. ISSN 0048-4326

**Plast-Ukrainian Youth Organization**
2150 Bloor Street West, Toronto, Ont. M6S 1M8,
Canada.
● Hotuys/Be Prepared. m. ISSN 0046-8061
● Yunak. m. ISSN 0044-1384

**Publications Plein Air**
3580 rue Masson, Montreal, Quebec H1X 1S2,
Canada.
● Quebec Chasse et Peche. m. ISSN 0315-260X

**Poemes Inedits**
198 Ave. Royale, St. Pierre, Ile d'Orleans, Que.,
Canada.
● Poemes Inedits. q. ISSN 0048-4520

**Poetry - Windsor - Poesie**
Box 6, Sandwich P.O., Windsor, Ontario N9C 3Y6,
Canada.
● Poetry - Windsor - Poesie. 3 per yr.

**Polish Press Ltd.**
1150 Main St., Winnipeg, Man. R2W 3S6, Canada.
● Czas/Polish Times. w. ISSN 0045-9445

**Polish Voice Publishing Co.**
1089 Queen St. W., Toronto, Ont. M6J 1H5,
Canada.
● Glos Polski-Gazeta Polska/Polish Voice Gazette.
w. ISSN 0046-6034

**R. L. Polk & Co. Ltd.**
2485 Bd. St. Anne, Quebec City, Que. G1J 1Y4,
Canada.
● Annuaire Polk de Granby, Quebec. a. ISSN 0317-
1515
● Annuaire Polk de St. Hyacinthe. irreg. ISSN
0380-1551

**Polysar Ltd.**
Vidal St., Sarnia, Ont. N7T 7M2, Canada.
● Polysar Progess. Rubber & Latex Edition. bi-m.
● Polysphere. q. ISSN 0032-4043

**Pontifical Institute of Mediaeval Studies**
59 Queen's Park Crescent E., Toronto, Ont.M5S
2C4, Canada.
● Mediaeval Studies. a. ISSN 0076-5872
● Pontifical Institute of Mediaeval Studies. Studies
and Texts. irreg. ISSN 0082-5328
● Toronto Mediaeval Latin Texts. irreg. ISSN 0082-
5050

**Porcupine's Quill**
Erin, Ont., Canada.
● Essays on Canadian Writing. 3 per yr. ISSN 0316-
0300

**Pork Producers Marketing Board**
● Hog Marketplace Quarterly. (pub. by Agricultural
Publishing Co.)

**Post Printing and Publishing Co.**
Ottawa, Ont., Canada.
● Ottawa Saturday Post. w. ISSN 0384-0670

**Potters Guild of British Columbia**
c/o Community Arts Council, 315 West Cordova
St., Vancouver, B.C. V6B 1E5, Canada.
● Western Potter. irreg. ISSN 0049-7495

**Prairie Bible Institute**
Three Hills, Alberta, Canada.
● Prairie Harvesters. q. ISSN 0383-7653

**Prairie Provinces Water Board**
305 Brent Building, 2505 11th Ave, Regina, Sask.,
Canada.
● Prairie Provinces Water Board Annual Report. a.

**William B. Prentice & Associates**
30 Longwood Dr., Don Mills, Ont., Canada.
● Canadian Athletic Director and Coach. 6 per yr.
ISSN 0045-4427

**Prentice-Hall of Canada, Ltd.**
1870 Birchmont Rd., Scarborough, Ont., M1P 2J7,
Canada.
● Canadian Historical Controversies. irreg.

**Presbyterian Church in Canada**
General Assembly, 50 Wynford Dr., Don Mills
M3C 1J7, Ont., Canada.
● Presbyterian Church in Canada. General
Assembly. Acts and Proceedings. a. ISSN 0079-
4996
● Presbyterian Record. m. ISSN 0032-7573

**Presbyterian Comment**
c/o the Editor, P3-120 Edinburgh Rd. S., Guelph,
Ont. N1H 5P7, Canada.
● Presbyterian Comment. bi-m. ISSN 0383-7645

**Presse Ltee.**
7 St. James St. W., Montreal H2Y 1K9, Que.,
Canada.
● Tele Presse. w. ISSN 0049-3252

**Presses de l'Universite de Montreal**
C.P. 6128, Succ. A, Montreal, Que. H3C 3J7,
Canada.
● Bibliotheque des Lettres Quebecoises. irreg.
● Collection du Prix de la Revue Etudes Francaises.
irreg.
● Collection Lignes Quebecoises. Serielles. irreg.
● Collection Lignes Quebecoises. Textuelles. irreg.
● Criminologie. a. ISSN 0316-0041
● Etudes Francaises; revue des lettres Francaises et
Canadiennes-Francaises. s-a. ISSN 0014-2085
● Meta. q. ISSN 0026-0452
● Revue Canadienne de Biologie. q. ISSN 0035-
0915
● Revue de Geographie de Montreal. q. ISSN 0035-
1148
● Sociologie et Societes. s-a. ISSN 0038-030X

**Presses de l'Universite du Quebec**
C.P. 250, Succ.N., Montreal 129, Quebec H3C 3P8,
Canada.
● Cahier de Linguistique. s-a.
● Cahiers des Etudes Anciennes. irreg.
● Voix et Images. 3 per yr. ISSN 0318-9201

**Presses de l'Universite Laval**
B.P. 2447, Quebec, P.Q. G1K 7R4, Canada.
● Cahiers de Droit. q. ISSN 0007-974X (Universite
Laval)

- Cahiers de Geographie de Quebec. 3 per yr. ISSN 0007-9766
- Cahiers de Psychomecanique de Langage. irreg. ISSN 0068-5070 (Universite Laval. Department de Linguistique)
- Etudes Litteraires. 3 per yr. ISSN 0014-214X
- Lange et Litterature Francaises au Canada. ISSN 0384-5710 (Quebec (Province) Ministere des Affaires Culturelles)
- Laval Theologique et Philosophique. 3 per yr. ISSN 0023-9054
- Livres et Auteurs Quebecois. a. ISSN 0076-0153
- Naturaliste Canadien. bi-m. ISSN 0028-0798
- Recherches Sociographiques. 3 per yr. ISSN 0034-1282 (Universite Laval. Department de Sociologie)
- Relations Industrielles/Industrial Relations. q. ISSN 0034-379X
- Service Social. 3 per yr. ISSN 0037-2633
- Universite Laval. Archives de Folklore. irreg., 1972, no. 14. ISSN 0085-5243
- Universite Laval. Centre d'Etudes Nordiques. Travaux et Documents. irreg., 1970, no. 5. ISSN 0079-8347
- Universite Laval. Departement de Geographie. Travaux. irreg (approx. biennial)
- Universite Laval. Institut d'Histoire. Cahiers. irreg. ISSN 0079-8398

**Prestige Books of Canada**
99 Vaugham Rd., Toronto, Ont., Canada.
- National Publishing Directory. biennial. ISSN 0077-5347

**Prince Edward Island. Civil Service Commission**
Charlottetown, Canada.
- Prince Edward Island. Civil Service Commission. Annual Report. a.

**Prince Edward Island. Department of Agriculture**
P.O. Box 2000, Charlottetown, P.E.I. C1A 7N8, Canada.
- Prince Edward Island. Economics, Marketing & Statistics Branch. Agricultural Statistics. a. (Co-sponsor: Statistics Canada)

**Prince Edward Island. Department of Community Services**
Box 2000, Charlottetow, P.E.I. C1A 7N8, Canada.
- Prince Edward Island. Department of Community Services. Annual Report. a.

**Prince Edward Island. Department of Development**
Charlottetown, Prince Edward Island, Canada.
- Prince Edward Island. Department of Development. Annual Report. a.

**Prince Edward Island. Department of Environment**
Charlottetown, Prince Edward Island, Canada.
- Prince Edward Island. Environmental Control Commission. Annual Report. a.
- Prince Edward Island Environmental Control Commission. Annual Report. a. ISSN 0085-5138

**Prince Edward Island. Department of Fisheries**
Charlottetown, P.E.I., Canada.
- Prince Edward Island. Department of Fisheries. Report. a. ISSN 0079-5143

**Prince Edward Island. Department of Health**
Charlottetown, Canada.
- Prince Edward Island. Department of Health. Annual Report. a.

**Prince Edward Island. Department of Industry and Commerce**
P.O. Box 2000, Charlottetown, P.E.I. C1A 7N8, Canada.
- Prince Edward Island. Department of Industry and Commerce. Annual Report. a.

**Prince Edward Island. Department of Labour**
Box 2000, Charlottetown, Prince Edward Island, Canada.
- Prince Edward Island. Department of Labour. Annual Report. a. ISSN 0085-512X

**Prince Edward Island. Department of the Environment and Tourism**
Box 2000, Charlottetown, P.E.I. C1A 7N8, Canada.
- Prince Edward Island. Department of the Environment and Tourism. Annual Report. a.

**Prince Edward Island . Land Development Corporation**
Charlottetown, P.E.I., Canada.
- Prince Edward Island Land Development. Annual Report. a.

**Prince Edward Island. Public Utilities Commission**
Box 577, Charlottetown P.E.I. C1A 2N3, Canada.
- Prince Edward Island. Public Utilities Commission. Annual Report. a. ISSN 0079-5151

**Prison Arts Foundation**
43 5th Ave., Brantford, Ont. N3S 1A3, Canada.
- Catalyst (Brantford) irreg. ISSN 0381-5005
- Words from Inside. a.

**Professional Corporation of Nursing Assistants of Quebec**
1380 rue Gilford - Suite 201, Montreal 177, P.Q., Canada.
- Revue des Infirmieres et Infirmiers Auxiliairs du Quebec. m.

**Professional Institute of the Public Service of Canada**
786 Bronson Ave., Ottawa, Ont. K1S 4G4, Canada.
- Professional Institute of the Public Service of Canada. Communications. every three weeks. ISSN 0318-0646
- Professional Institute of the Public Service of Canada. Journal. m.

**Professional Photographers of Canada**
c/o Peter Jansen, Ed., Box 3719, Sta. B, Winnipeg, Man. R2W 3R6, Canada.
- P P O C National News. bi-m. ISSN 0048-5462

**Progress Books**
487 Adelaide St. West, Toronto M5V 1T4, Ont., Canada.
- Communist Viewpoint. bi-m. ISSN 0010-3756
- World Marxist Review; problems of peace and socialism. m. ISSN 0043-8642

**Progress Printing & Publishing Co. Ltd.**
418 Aberdeen Ave., Winnipeg 4, Man., Canada.
- Progress/Pustup. w. ISSN 0033-054X (Ukrainian Catholic Archdiocese of Winnipeg)

**Progress Publishing Company, Ltd.**
355 Burrard St., Vancouver, B.C. V6C 2G6, Canada.
- A B C British Columbia Lumber Trade Directory and Year Book. biennial. ISSN 0065-0013
- Harbour and Shipping. m. ISSN 0017-7636

**Progressive Conservative Association of Alberta**
No. 32, 9912-106th St., Edmonton, Alta. T5K 1C5, Canada.
- Progressive Conservative Association of Alberta. Progress Bulletin. 4-5 per yr.

**Progressive Conservative Party of Ontario**
73 Richmond W., Toronto, Ont., Canada.
- Young Conservative Action. irreg.

**Progressive Students for Israel**
Ross Bldg. CS 106, York University, Downsview, Ont., Canada.
- Masada. s-m. ISSN 0025-4428

**Progressive Workers Movement**
35 E. Hastings St., Vancouver 4, B.C., Canada.
- Progressive Worker. m. ISSN 0033-0841

**Proscope**
6344 rue St. Hubert, Montreal 326, Que., Canada.
- Proscope; pour l'homme du Quebec. m. ISSN 0048-5586

**Provincial Association of Catholic Teachers of Quebec**
5767 Monkland Ave., Montreal, Que. H4A 1E8, Canada.
- P A C T. m (9 per yr) ISSN 0384-1006

**Provincial Bank of Canada. Economic Research Department**
215 St-Jacques Street, Montreal, Que. H2Y 1M6, Canada.
- Economic Review. bi-m. ISSN 0319-8685
- Provincial Bank of Canada. Economic Review. bi-m.

**Provincial Intermediate Teachers**
105-2235 Burrard St., Vancouver, B.C. V6J 3H9, Canada.
- Intermediate Teacher. q. ISSN 0020-563X (pub. by B. C. Teachers' Federation)

**Provoker**
St. Catharines, Ontario, Canada.
- Provoker. bi-m. ISSN 0033-1937

**Pryde Publications**
130 Bloor St. W., Suite 301, Toronto, Ont. M4W 1A2, Canada.
- Cable Communications. m. ISSN 0318-0069

**Psychiatric Nurses Association of Canada**
871 Notre Dame Ave., Winnipeg R3E OM4, Man., Canada.
- Canadian Journal of Psychiatric Nursing. bi-m. ISSN 0008-4247

**Public Press Ltd.**
1760 Ellice Ave., Winnipeg, Man. R3H 0B6, Canada.
- Cattlemen; the beef magazine. m. ISSN 0008-3143
- Corn-Soy Guide. s-a.
- Country Guide; the farm magazine. m. ISSN 0011-0140
- Crops Guide. a.
- Dairy Guide. bi-m. ISSN 0011-5606
- Hog Guide. bi-m. ISSN 0018-3199

**Public Service Alliance of Canada**
233 Gilmour St., Ottawa K2P 0P1, Canada.
- Argus-Journal. m. ISSN 0004-1211
- Civil Service Review/Revue du Service Civil. q. ISSN 0009-8035

**Public Service Commission**
Personnel Psychology Centre, 14th Floor, Tower A, Place de Ville, Ottawa, Ont. K1A 0M7, Canada.
- Studies in Personnel Psychology/Etudes en Psychologie du Personnel. s-a. ISSN 0081-8364

**Publications du Nord-Ouest**
167 Dallaire, c.p. 490, Rouyn, Que. J9X 4T3, Canada.
- Journal du Nord-Ouest. d. ISSN 0380-2051

**Publicite B. M. Inc.**
450 Beaumont Ave, Montreal, Que. H3N 1T8, Canada.
- Annuaire de l'Eglise du Quebec. a.

**Pulp and Paper Research Institute of Canada**
570 St. John's Road, Pointe Claire, Que. H9R 3J9, Canada.
- Pulp and Paper Research Institute of Canada. Annual Report. a. ISSN 0079-7960
- Pulp and Paper Research Institute of Canada. Logging Research Reports. irreg. ISSN 0316-4853
- Pulp and Paper Research Institute of Canada. Woodlands Papers. irreg. ISSN 0043-7743
- Trend. 1-2 per yr. ISSN 0041-2295

**Pulp Press**
Box 48806, Station Bental, Vancouver, B. C. V7X 1A6, Canada.
- 3-Cents Pulp. s-m.

**Purchasing Management Association of Canada. British Columbia District**
- Purchasing in Western Canada. (pub. by Western Miner Press Ltd.)

**Quarry**
Box 1061, Kingston, Ontario, Canada.
- Quarry. q. ISSN 0033-5266

**Quarterbacks, Delta Canada**
351 Gerald Street, Lasalle, Quebec H8P 2A4, Canada.
- Quarterbacks. irreg.

**Quebec (Province) Bureau of Statistics**
Production Statistics Service, Crops Division, Quebec, P.Q., Canada.
- Annuaire du Quebec. (pub. by Editeur Officiel du Quebec)
- Quebec (Province). Bureau of Statistics. Agriculture Section. Area of the Principal Field Crops. a.
- Quebec (Province) Bureau of Statistics. Agriculture Section.Mink Breeding/Elevage de Visons. a.
- Quebec (Province) Bureau of Statistics. Agriculture Section. Statistiques Agricoles. Agricultural Statistics. a. ISSN 0079-8444
- Quebec (Province) Bureau of Statistics. Analyse Budgetaire. Municipalites du Quebec. (pub. by Editeur Officiel du Quebec)
- Quebec (Province) Bureau of Statistics. Conditions de Travail dans les Industries de la Province de Quebec. Working Conditions in the Industries in the Province of Quebec. (pub. by Editeur Officiel du Quebec)
- Quebec (Province) Bureau of Statistics. Finances Municipales. (pub. by Editeur Officiel du Quebec)

- Quebec (Province) Bureau of Statistics. Mines d'Argent, Plomb, Zinc/Silver, Lead, Zinc Mines. (pub. by Editeur Officiel du Quebec)
- Quebec (Province) Bureau of Statistics. Mines de Feldspath et de Quartz/Feldspar and Quartz Mines. (pub. by Editeur Officiel du Quebec)
- Quebec (Province) Bureau of Statistics. Pecheries Commerciales/Commercial Fisheries. (pub. by Editeur Officiel du Quebec)
- Quebec (Province) Bureau of Statistics. Repertoire des Municipalities et des Commissions Scolaires. Guide of School Boards. (pub. by Editeur Officiel du Quebec)
- Quebec (Province) Bureau of Statistics. Repertoire des Municipalities et des Commissions Scolaires. Municipal Guide. (pub. by Editeur Officiel du Quebec)
- Quebec (Province) Bureau of Statistics. Statistiques des Produits Forestiers. (pub. by Editeur Officiel du Quebec)
- Quebec (Province) Bureau of Statistics. Statistiques Financieres, Gouvernement du Quebec/Financial Statistics, Government of Quebec. a.
- Quebec (Province) Bureau of Statistics. Statistiques sur l'Hotellerie. (pub. by Editeur Officiel du Quebec)
- Revue Statistique du Quebec/Quebec Statistical Review. (pub. by Editeur Officiel du Quebec)

**Quebec (Province) Bureau of Statistics. Division des Peches**
Quebec, Quebec, Canada.
- Peche Hauturiere au Quebec. irreg.

**Quebec (Province) Bureau of Statistics. Service du Travail et de la Main d'Oeuvre**
Hotel du Gouvernement, Quebec, P.Q., Canada.
- Conditions de Travail au Quebec des Activites Economiques Choisies. a.

**Quebec (Province) Centrale des Bibliotheques**
1685 Est, rue Fleury, Montreal, Que, Canada.
- Information C B. 3 per yr.
- Periodex; index analytique de periodiques de langue Francaise. m. ISSN 0300-3663

**Quebec (Province). Commission des Services Juridiques**
1170 Square Beaver Hall, Montreal H38 3C6, Quebec, Canada.
- Quebec (Province). Commission des Services Juridiques. Rapport Annuel. a.

**Quebec (Province) Department of Agriculture**
Quebec, Que., Canada.
- Quebec (Province). Department of Agriculture. la Conjoncture de l'Economie Agricole du Quebec. irreg.

**Quebec (Province) Department of Intergovernmental Affairs**
1225 Place Georges V, Quebec G1R 4Z7, Canada.
- Quebec at a Glance. m.

**Quebec (Province) Department of Natural Resources**
Distribution et Documentation, 1620 Bd. de l'Entente, Quebec G1S 4N6, Canada.
- Index de References: Inventaire des Stations Hydrometriques. irreg.
- Quebec (Province) Department of Natural Resources. Geological Reports. irreg. ISSN 0079-8738

**Quebec (Province) Department of Tourism, Fish and Game**
Quebec, P.Q., Canada.
- Quebec (Province). Department of Tourism, Fish and Game. Annual Report. a. ISSN 0481-2786

**Quebec (Province) Health Insurance Board**
Case Postale 6600, Quebec, Que. G1A 7T3, Canada.
- Quebec (Province) Health Insurance Board. Annual Statistics/Regie de l'Assurance Malade. Statistiques Annuelles. a.

**Quebec (Province) Ministere de l'Industrie et du Commerce**
Direction de la Recherche, 2700 Einstein, Quebec G1P 3W8, Canada.
- Quebec (Province) Direction Generale des Peches Maritimes Cahiers d'Information. irreg., no. 80, 1977.

- Quebec (Province). Direction Generale des Peches Maritimes. Direction de la Recherche. Rapport Annuel. a. ISSN 0318-8779
- Travaux sur les Pecheries du Quebec. irreg., no. 45, 1976. ISSN 0082-609X

**Quebec (Province) Ministere des Affaires Culturelles**
- Ateliers. (pub. by Musee d'Art Contemporain)
- Lange et Litterature Francaises au Canada. (pub. by Presses de l'Universite Laval)

**Quebec (Province) Ministere des Communications**
Quebec, Canada.
- Quebec (Province). Ministere des Communications. Rapport Annuel. a.

**Quebec (Province) Ministere des Consommateurs, Cooperatives et Institutions Financieres**
Edifice Place Hauteville, 700 Bd. St-Cyrille est., Quebec G1R 5A9, Canada.
- Protegez-Vous. irreg.

**Quebec (Province) Ministere des Richesses Naturelles**
Distribution et Documentation, 1620 Bd. l'Entente, Quebec G1S 4N6, Canada.
- Quebec (Province) Department of Natural Resources. Repertoire des Publications. irreg.
- Quebec (Province) Ministere des Richesses Naturelles. a.
- Quebec (Province) Service Geologique. Travaux sur le Terrain. Field Work. a. ISSN 0079-8746

**Quebec (Province) Ministere des Terres et Forets**
Service de la Recherche, 2700 rue Einstein, Complexe Scientifique, Sainte-Foy G1P 3W8, Canada.
- Quebec (Province) Ministere des Terres et Forets. Service de la Recherche. Guide. irreg.
- Quebec (Province) Ministere des Terres et Forets. Service de la Recherche. Memoire/Quebec (Province) Department of Lands and Forests. Research Service. Memoire. irreg.
- Quebec (Province) Ministere des Terres et Forets. Service de la Recherche. Note. irreg.
- Quebec (Province) Ministere des Terres et Forets. Service de la Recherche. Rapport d'Activites. irreg.

**Quebec (Province) Ministere des Terres et Forets. Conseil Consultatif des Reserves Ecologiques**
200 B, chemin Ste-Foy, Quebec, Canada.
- Quebec (Province) Ministere des Terres et Forets. Conseil Consultatif des Reserves Ecologiques. Rapport Annuel. a.

**Quebec (Province) Ministere du Travail et de la Main d'Oeuvre**
Direction Generale de la Recherche, 600 rue St. Amable, Quebec G1R 4Z1, Canada.
- Quebec (Province) Ministere du Travail et de la Main d'Oeuvre. Jurisprudence en Droit du Travail: Tribunal du Travail. q.
- Quebec/Travail. bi-m. ISSN 0033-5991

**Quebec (Province) National Assembly**
Quebec, Canada.
- Quebec (Province). National Assembly. Proces-Verbaux/Votes and Proceedings. irreg.

**Quebec (Province) National Assembly. Parliamentary Documents Service**
Parliament Bldgs., Quebec G1A 1A7, Canada.
- Quebec (Province). National Assembly. Journal des Debats. irreg.
- Quebec (Province). National Assembly. Journal des Debats: Commissions Parlementaires.

**Quebec (Province) Office de la Langue Francaise**
Quebec, P.Q., Canada.
- Neologie en Marche. Serie A. Langue Generale. irreg. ISSN 0380-9366
- Quebec (Province) Office de la Langue Francaise. Cahiers. irreg, 1973, no. 20. ISSN 0079-8770

**Quebec (Province) Office de la Protection du Consommateur**
800 Carre d'Youville, Quebec G1R 4Y5, Canada.
- Quebec (Province). Office de la Protection du Consommateur. Rapport d'Activites. a.

**Quebec (Province) Pension Board**
Quebec, Canada.
- Quebec (Province). Pension Board. Regimes Supplementaires de Rentes - Caracteristiques et Participation; Statistiques/Supplemental Pension Plans - Characteristics and Membership; Statistics. irreg.

**Quebec (Province) Service de Consultation et Assistance en Toxicomanies**
Quebec G1S 1T5, Canada.
- Toxicomanies. 4 per yr. ISSN 0041-0098

**Quebec (Province) Service de l'Hydrometrie**
Quebec, Que, Canada.
- Quebec (Province) Service de l'Hydrometrie. Annuaire Hydrologique. a.

**Quebec Automobile Club**
871 St. Louis Rd., Quebec City 6, Que., Canada.
- Autoclub. 5 per yr. ISSN 0005-0954

**Quebec Camping Association**
952 Cherrier St., Montreal, Que. H2L 1H7, Canada.
- Directory of Accredited Camps. a. ISSN 0316-1226

**Quebec Federation of Home and School Associations**
4795 St. Catherine St. W., Montreal, Que. H3Z 1S8, Canada.
- Quebec Home & School News. 5 per yr. during school yr. ISSN 0033-5967

**Quebec Forest Industries Association**
500 E. Grande Allee, Suite 508, Quebec, P.Q. G1R 2J7, Canada.
- Papetier. bi-m. ISSN 0048-2889

**Quebec Industrial Development Corporation**
1126 St. Louis Rd., Sillery, Que., Canada.
- Quebec Industrial Development Corporation. Annual Report/Rapport Annuel. a.

**Quebec Society for the Protection of Plants**
c/o Leon Tartier, Sec., Station de Recherches, C.P. 70, St-Hyacinthe, Que. J2S 7B3, Canada.
- Phytoprotection. 3 per yr. ISSN 0031-9511

**Queen Alexandra Solarium for Crippled Children Society**
2400 Arbutus Road, Victoria, British Columbia, Canada.
- Queen Alexandra Hospital for Children. Annual Report. a.

**Queen Charlotte Islands Musuem Society**
Box 130, Masset, B.C. V0T 1M0, Canada.
- Charlottes. a.

**Queen's Printer, Alberta**
Edmonton, Alta., Canada.
- Alberta Gazette. s-m. ISSN 0002-4775

**Queen's Printer, Canada**
Ottawa, Ontario, Canada.
- Canada. Experimental Farm, St. John's West, Newfoundland. Research Report. a. ISSN 0068-7480
- Canada. Parliament. House of Commons. Special Committee on Trends in Food Prices. Minutes of Proceedings and Evidence/Proces-Verbaux et Temoignages. s-w.
- Flight Comment. bi-m. ISSN 0015-3702 (Canadian Forces Headquarters - Directorate of Flight Safety)
- Statement of the Assets and Liabilities of the Chartered Banks of Canada. m. ISSN 0049-2167

**Queen's Printer, Newfoundland**
Box 967, St. John's, Nfld. a1C 5M3, Canada.
- Newfoundland Gazette. w. ISSN 0028-8888

**Queen's Printer, Prince Edward Island**
Charlottetown, Prince Edward Island, Canada.
- Royal Gazette. w. ISSN 0035-8908

**Queen's Printer, Saskatchewan**
Regina, Sask., Canada.
- Saskatchewan Gazette. w. ISSN 0036-4894

**Queen's University**
Aesculapian Society, Kingston, Ontario, Canada.
- Queen's Medical Review. a. ISSN 0079-8789
- Queen's Quarterly; a Canadian review. q. ISSN 0033-6041
- Queen's University at Kingston. Douglas Library. Occasional Papers. irreg. ISSN 0075-6113

**Queen's University. Department of Electrical Engineering**
Kingston, Ontario, Canada.
- Queen's University at Kingston. Department of Electrical Engineering. Research Report. irreg. ISSN 0075-6091

**Queen's University. Department of Mathematics**
Kingston, Ontario, Canada.
- Queen's Papers on Pure and Applied
  Mathematics. irreg. ISSN 0079-8797

**Queen's University. Engineering Society**
Kingston, Ontario, Canada.
- Queen's University. Engineering Society.
  Proceedings. a. ISSN 0075-6121

**Queen's University. Industrial Relations Centre**
Kingston, Ont. K7L 3N6, Canada.
- Current Industrial Relations Scene in Canada. a.
  ISSN 0318-952X
- Queen's University. Industrial Relations Centre.
  Research and Current Issues Series. irreg., no. 34,
  1976. ISSN 0317-2546
- Queen's University at Kingston. Industrial
  Relations Centre. Bibliography Series. irreg., no.
  6, 1975. ISSN 0075-613X
- Queen's University at Kingston. Industrial
  Relations Centre. Report of Activities. a. ISSN
  0075-6148
- Queen's University at Kingston. Industrial
  Relations Centre. Reprint Series. irreg., no. 37,
  1977. ISSN 0075-6156

**Queen's University. Institute for Economic Research**
Kingston, Ont., Canada.
- Queen's University. Institute for Economic
  Research. Discussion Paper. irreg. ISSN 0316-
  5078

**Queen's University. Institute of Local Government**
Kingston, Ont. K7L 3N6, Canada.
- Urban Focus. bi-m. ISSN 0315-0143

**Queen's University Law School**
- Queen's Law Journal. (pub. by Carswell Co. Ltd.)

**Queen's University. Law Students Society**
Sir John A. Macdonald Hall, Kingston, Ont.,
Canada.
- Queen's Law Journal. s-a.

**Quest**
RR 1, Inwood, Ont., Canada.
- Quest. q.

**Don Quick Publications**
227 Morrish Rd., West Hill, Ont. M1C 1E9,
Canada.
- Furniture Production and Design Meubles. bi-m.
- Molten Metal. 6 per yr.
- Truck Canada. 9 per yr.

**R.G. Lewis & Co. Ltd.**
77 River St., Toronto, Ont. M5A 3P2, Canada.
- Broadcaster. m.(plus semi-annual directory nos.)
  ISSN 0008-3038

**R. M. Bucke Memorial Society**
4453 Maisonneuve Blvd. W., Montreal, Que. H3Z
1L8, Canada.
- R. M. Bucke Memorial Society for the Study of
  Religious Experience. Newsletter-Review. irreg.
  ISSN 0079-9343
- R. M. Bucke Memorial Society for the Study of
  Religious Experience. Proceedings of the
  Conference. irreg., vol. 7, 1974. ISSN 0079-9351

**R P M Music Publications Ltd.**
6 Brentcliffe Road, Toronto, M4G 3Y2, Ont.,
Canada.
- Canadian Music Industry Directory. a. ISSN
  0068-9335
- R P M Weekly. (Records-Promotion-Music);
  music, television, radio, film, records, theatre. w.
  ISSN 0033-7064

**Radio Society of Ontario, Inc.**
P. O. Box 334, Toronto, Ont. M8Z 5P7, Canada.
- Ontario Amateur. bi-m. ISSN 0048-1734

**Ragtime Society**
Box 520, Station A, Weston Ont. M9N 3N3, Ont.,
Canada.
- Ragtimer. bi-m. ISSN 0033-8672

**Railton Publications Ltd.**
125 Talisman Ave., Vancouver, B. C. V5Y 2L6,
Canada.
- Alberta Fishing Guide. (pub. by George Mitchell,
  Ed. & Pub.)
- B. C. Salt Water Salmon Guide. a.
- British Columbia's Fresh Water Fishing Guide. a.

**Raincoast Historical Society**
Box 119, Madeira Park, B.C. V0N 2H0, Canada.
- Raincoast Chronicles. q.

**Rapeseed Association of Canada**
G-11, 355 Burrard St., Vancouver, B.C. V6C 2G6,
Canada.
- Rapeseed Digest. m. ISSN 0048-6728

**Reader's Club of Canada Ltd.**
35 Britain St., Toronto, Ont. M5A 1R7, Canada.
- Canadian Reader. m. ISSN 0008-4891

**Reader's Digest Magazines Ltd.**
215 Redfern Ave., Montreal, Que. H3Z 2V9,
Canada.
- Reader's Digest (Canadian-English Edition) m.
  ISSN 0034-0413

**Real Estate Board of Greater Vancouver**
1101 W. Broadway, Vancouver, B.C. V6H 1G2,
Canada.
- Real Estate Trends in Metropolitan Vancouver. a.
  ISSN 0085-5405

**Red Deer College. Learning Resources Centre**
Red Deer, Alberta, Canada.
- Red Deer College. Learning Resources Centre.
  What's the Use...? a. ISSN 0380-5727

**Red Maple Publishing Co.**
3 Church St., Suite 401, Toronto, Ont. M5E 1M2,
Canada.
- This Magazine: Education, Culture, Politics. bi-m.
  ISSN 0381-3746

**Redeemer's Voice**
165 Catherine St., Yorkton, Sask., Canada.
- Redeemer's Voice/Holos Spasytelya. m. ISSN
  0034-2122

**Redemptorist Fathers. Ste-Anne de Beaupre Province**
Basilica of Ste. Anne, Quebec G0A 3C0, Canada.
- Annals of Good St. Anne. m. ISSN 0003-4797

**Regie de l' Assurance-Maladie du Quebec**
200 Chemin Ste-Foy, Quebec, P.Q. G1K 7T3,
Canada.
- Regie de l'Assurance Maladie du Quebec.
  Bulletin. m.

**Registered Nurses Association of British Columbia**
2130 W. 12th Ave., Vancouver, B.C., Canada.
- R N A B C News. 8 per yr. ISSN 0048-7104

**Registered Nurses Association of Nova Scotia**
6035 Coburg Road, Halifax, N.S. B3H 1Y8,
Canada.
- R N A N S Bulletin. bi-m.

**Registered Nurses Association of Ontario**
33 Price St., Toronto M4W 1Z2 Ont., Canada.
- R N A O News. bi-m. ISSN 0048-7112

**Rendez-Vous**
1440 Ste. Catherine West, Rm. 625, Montreal, Que,
Canada.
- Rendez-Vous. bi-m. ISSN 0034-4370

**Editions le Renouveau Inc.**
C.P. 1815, Quebec, G1K 7K7, Canada.
- Je Crois; magazine populaire Catholique. m. ISSN
  0021-5740 (Messagers Catholiques de la Bible)

**Reporter**
Box 130, Newcastle, Ont. L0A 1H0, Canada.
- Reporter. w. ISSN 0034-4761

**Repository Press**
R.R. 7 Buckhorn Road, Prince George, B.C. V2N
2J5, Canada.
- Repository. q. ISSN 0317-0845

**Research Institute of Northern Canada**
Box 188, Yellowknife, N.W.T. X0E 1H0, Canada.
- Canada North Almanac. irreg.

**Research Society for Victorian Periodicals**
Dept. of English, University College, University of
Toronto, Toronto, Ont. M5S 1A1, Canada.
- Victorian Periodicals Newsletter. q. ISSN 0049-
  6189

**Resort & Motel Administration**
451 Beaconsfield Blvd, Beaconsfield 870, Que.,
Canada.
- Resort & Motel Administration. q. ISSN 0034-
  5628

**Retail Council of Canada**
74 Victoria St., Suite 723, Toronto, M5G 2A5,
Ont., Canada.
- Retail Council of Canada. Operating Results of
  Independent Specialty and Department Stores.
  biennial. ISSN 0085-5588
- Retail Wages and Salaries in Canada. a. ISSN
  0080-1860

**Retail Merchants Association of Canada
(Saskatchewan) Inc.**
Retailers' Trust Bldg., Third Ave. & 22nd St.,
Saskatoon S7K 2H6, Saskatchewan, Canada.
- National Retailer. bi-m. ISSN 0028-002X
- R.M.A. Retailers' Group Service Bulletin. q. (Co-
  Sponsor: Norfolk and Retailers Trust and Savings
  Co.)

**Revista Canadiense de Estudios Hispanicos**
Box 857, Station B, Ottawa K1P 5A0, Ont.,
Canada.
- Revista Canadiense de Estudios Hispanicos. q.

**Revue Action Canada France Inc.**
1080 Beaver Hall, Suite 826, Montreal, Que. H2Z
1S8, Canada.
- Action Canada France. 10 per yr. ISSN 0318-
  7306

**Revue Commerce**
1080 Beaver Hall Hill, Montreal, Que. H2Z 1T1,
Que., Canada.
- Commerce. m. ISSN 0010-2725
- Commerce. le Point; une revue annuel de
  l'economie du Quebec. a.

**Revue Hippique**
185 Je Me Souviens, Ste-Rose, Que., Canada.
- Revue Hippique. m.

**Revue Municipale Inc.**
6841 St-Hubert Suite 203, Montreal, Que. H2S
2M8, Canada.
- Revue Municipale. m. ISSN 0035-3728

**Rexwood Publications Ltd.**
48 Belfield Rd., Rexdale, Ont. M9W 1G1, Canada.
- Canadian Horse. m. ISSN 0008-378X

**Richard de Boo Ltd.**
70 Richmond St. E., Toronto M5C 2M8, Ont.,
Canada.
- Canada Labour Service. m. ISSN 0008-2708
- Canada Tax Cases. s-m. ISSN 0008-2740
- Canada Tax Service; a loose-leaf tax information
  service. 3 per m. ISSN 0008-2759
- Directory of Canadian Governments: Municipal,
  Provincial, Federal. (pub. by Copp Clark
  Publishing Co.)

**Eileen Richardson, Ed. & Pub.**
34 Broadway Ave., Ottawa K1S 2V6 Ont., Canada.
- Penmen's News Letter. 6 per yr. ISSN 0031-4315
  (International Association of Master Penmen and
  Teachers of Handwriting)

**Riegel Publications**
10623 Kingsway Ave., Edmonton, Alta. T5G 2Z6,
Canada.
- Curling Review. m (Oct.-Apr.) ISSN 0011-3115

**Rikka Publishing House**
Box 6031, Sta. A., Toronto, Ont. M5W 1P4,
Canada.
- Rikka. q.

**Riviera Printers & Publishers Inc.**
6896 St. Lawrence Blvd., Montreal 327, Que.,
Canada.
- Cittadino Canadese. w. ISSN 0009-7667

**Roads and Transportation Association of Canada**
1765 St. Laurent Bd., Ottawa, Ont. K1G 3Va,
Canada.
- Nation on the Move. a. ISSN 0073-215X
- Roads and Transportation Association of Canada.
  Proceedings. a. ISSN 0080-3324
- Transportation Research in Canada. a. ISSN
  0381-8284

**R. D. Robinson Publishing Co.**
Corner Crown & Union Sts., Saint John, N.B.,
Canada.
- Maritime Farmer and Co-Operative Dairyman. s-
  m. ISSN 0025-343X

**Rod & Gun Publishing Corp. Ltd.**
1219 Hotel de Ville, Montreal, Que., Canada.
• Au Grand Air. irreg. ISSN 0004-7384

**Rodney Publications Ltd.**
2 St. Clair Ave. W., Toronto M4V 1L5, Ont,
Canada.
• Canadian Travel News Weekly. w.

**Roundstone Council for the Arts.**
546 Richmond St. W., Toronto, Ont. M5V 1Y4,
Canada.
• Canadian Artists in Exhibition/Artistes
Canadiens: Expositions. a.

**Editions Rousseau**
No. 201, 3009 Boul. de la Concorde, Duvernay,
Laval, Que., Canada.
• Magazine de l'Autoneige. 6 per yr. ISSN 0047-
5459

**Publications Rowe**
2995 Chemin du Portage, Carignan, Chambly, Que.,
Canada.
• Barrique. m. ISSN 0315-0399

**Royal Astronomical Society of Canada**
124 Merton St., Toronto, Ont. M4S 2Z2, Canada.
• Royal Astronomical Society of Canada. Journal.
bi-m. ISSN 0035-872X
• Royal Astronomical Society of Canada. Observer's
Handbook. a. ISSN 0080-4193

**Royal Bank of Canada**
Monthly Letter Dept., Box 6001, Montreal, Que.
H3C 3A9, Canada.
• Royal Bank of Canada. Monthly Letter. m. ISSN
0035-8770

**Royal Botanical Gardens**
Box 399, Hamilton, Ont. L8N 3H8, Canada.
• Hamilton, Ontario. Royal Botanical Gardens.
Gardens' Bulletin. bi-m. ISSN 0046-6751
• Royal Botanical Gardens, Hamilton, Ont. Special
Bulletin. a. ISSN 0072-9647
• Royal Botanical Gardens, Hamilton, Ont.
Technical Bulletin. irreg. ISSN 0072-9655

**Royal Canadian Academy of Arts**
40 University Ave., Suite 1112, Toronto, Ont.,
Canada.
• Royal Canadian Academy of Arts. Annual
Exhibition. Catalogue. a. ISSN 0080-4290

**Royal Canadian Air Force Association**
424 Metcalfe, Ottawa, Ont. K2P 2C3, Canada.
• Airforce. q.

**Royal Canadian Geographical Society**
488 Wilbrod St., Ottawa K1N 6M8, Canada.
• Canadian Geographical Journal. bi-m. ISSN 0315-
1824

**Royal Canadian Institute**
191 College Street, Toronto 2b, Ontario, Canada.
• Royal Canadian Institute. Proceedings. a. ISSN
0080-4304
• Royal Canadian Institute. Transactions. irreg.
ISSN 0080-4312

**Royal Canadian Mounted Police**
Ottawa, Ont. K1A 0R2, Canada.
• R. C. M. P. Quarterly/G R C. Revue
Trimestrielle. q. ISSN 0033-6858

**Royal College of Physicians & Surgeons of Canada**
74 Stanley, Ottawa, Ont. K1M 1P4, Canada.
• Royal College of Physicians and Surgeons of
Canada. Annals/College Royal des Medecins et
Chirurgiens du Canada. Annales. q. ISSN 0035-
8800

**Royal Military College of Canada**
Kingston, Ont., Canada.
• Marker. 8 per yr.(Sept-May) ISSN 0025-3529

**Royal Ontario Museum**
100 Queen's Park, Toronto M5S 2C6, Ont.,
Canada.
• Rotunda. q. ISSN 0035-8495
• Royal Ontario Museum. Annual Report. a. ISSN
0082-5115
• Royal Ontario Museum. Archaeology
Monographs. irreg. ISSN 0316-1285
• Royal Ontario Museum. Ethnography Monograph.
irreg.
• Royal Ontario Museum. History, Technology and
Art Monographs. irreg.

• Royal Ontario Museum. Life Sciences
Contributions. irreg. ISSN 0082-5085
• Royal Ontario Museum. Life Sciences Division.
Miscellaneous Publications. irreg. ISSN 0082-
5093
• Royal Ontario Museum. Life Sciences Division.
Occasional Papers. irreg., no. 27, 1975. ISSN
0082-5107

**Royal Philatelic Society of Canada**
Box 4195, Sta. E, Ottawa, Ont. K1S 5B2, Canada.
• Canadian Philatelist. bi-m. ISSN 0045-5253

**Royal Regiment of Canadian Artillery**
• Canadian Gunner. (pub. by Leech Printing Ltd.)

**Royal Society of Canada**
De Koninck Hall, Laval University, Quebec G1K
7P4, Canada.
• Royal Society of Canada. Transactions. a. ISSN
0035-9122

**Royal Winnipeg Ballet**
289 Portage Ave., Winnipeg, Man. R3B 2B4,
Canada.
• Ballet-Hoo. 6 per yr. ISSN 0045-1347

**Ryerson Polytechnical Institute. Student's Union**
380 Victoria, Toronto, Ont. M5B 1W7, Canada.
• Eyeopener. w (during academic year) ISSN 0014-
5513

**Sage Brush Ventures**
Suite 201, 5920 MacLeod Trail S.W., Calgary Alta.
T2H 0K2, Canada.
• Limousin Leader: International Edition. m. ISSN
0381-503X (Canadian Limousin Association)

**St. Bernard Charities**
2 Lakeview Square, 175 Carlton St., Winnipeg,
Man. R3C 3H9, Canada.
• Challenge (Winnipeg) irreg. ISSN 0382-8409

**St. Francis Xavier University**
Antigonish, Nova Scotia, Canada.
• Antigonish Review. q. ISSN 0003-5661
• St. Francis Xavier University Contemporary and
Alumni News. q. ISSN 0036-2824
• Xaverian Weekly. w. 22 per yr. ISSN 0043-9886

**St. Mary's University. Division of Continuing
Education**
Halifax, N.S. B3H 3C3, Canada.
• Atlantic Provinces Book Review. q.

**St. Mary's University. English Department**
Halifax, N.S., Canada.
• Sift. ISSN 0380-6693

**St. Mary's University Student Council**
Saint Mary's University, Halifax, N.S., Canada.
• Saint Mary's University Journal. w. ISSN 0036-
3138

**Saint Paul Society**
223 Main St., Ottawa K1S 1C4, Canada.
• Christian Communications. q. ISSN 0009-5303

**Saint Paul University**
Faculty of Theology, 223 Main St., Ottawa K1S
1C4, Ont., Canada.
• Anthropologica. (pub. by Canadian Research
Centre for Anthropology)
• Eglise et Theologie. 3 per yr. ISSN 0013-2349
• Studia Canonica; a Canadian canon law review. s-
a. ISSN 0039-310X

**Saint Paul University. Institute of Mission Studies**
223 Main St., Ottawa K1S 1C4, Ont., Canada.
• Kerygma. s-a. ISSN 0023-0693

**St. Peter's Abbey**
• Prairie Messenger. (pub. by St. Peter's Press)

**St. Peter's Press**
Muenster, Sask. S0K 2Y0, Canada.
• Prairie Messenger. w. ISSN 0032-664X (St.
Peter's Abbey)

**St. Thomas More College**
University of Saskatchewan, 1437 College Dr.,
Saskatoon, Sask. S7N 0W6, Canada.
• History Collection: Canadian Catholic Church/
Collection d'Histoire: l'Eglise Catholique
Canadienne. irreg. ISSN 0315-3371

**Salvation Army. Canada Territorial Headquarters**
20 Albert St., Toronto, Ont. M5G 1A6, Canada.
• Canadian Home Leaguer. m. ISSN 0008-3771
• War Cry. w. ISSN 0043-0218

**T. J. Samuel, Ed. & Pub.**
161 Dalhousie St., Ottawa, Ont. K1H 7C3, Canada.
• Canadian India Times. s-m. ISSN 0045-4958

**Sanderson Publications Ltd.**
204-2182 W. 12th Ave., Vancouver, B.C. V6K 2N4,
Canada.
• British Columbia Municipal Yearbook. a. ISSN
0068-161X (British Columbia Bond Dealers
Association)

**Sanford Evans Publishing Ltd.**
1077 St. James St., Box 6900, Winnipeg, Man. R3C
3B1, Canada.
• Canadian Welder & Fabricator. m. ISSN 0008-
5324
• Energy Processing/Canada. 6 per yr.
• Feed and Farm Supply Dealer. m. ISSN 0046-
3604
• Manitoba Trade Directory. a. ISSN 0076-390X
(Manitoba. Department of Industry and
Commerce)
• Motor in Canada; in the interests of the
automotive trade in Western Canada. m. ISSN
0027-190X
• Propane/Canada. q. ISSN 0033-1260
• Trade and Commerce. m. ISSN 0049-4321

**Saskatchewan. Alcoholism Commission**
2134 Hamilton Street, Regina, Saskatchewan,
Canada.
• Saskatchewan. Alcoholism Commission. Annual
Report. a.

**Saskatchewan. Bureau of Statistics**
Rm. 129, Legislative Bldg., Regina, Sask. S4S 0B3,
Canada.
• Saskatchewan Economic Review. a. ISSN 0558-
6976
• Saskatchewan Monthly Statistical Review. m.

**Saskatchewan. Department of Agriculture. Family
Farm Improvement Branch**
1318 Winnipeg St., Regina, Sask. S4R 1J6, Canada.
• Saskatchewan. Department of Agriculture. Family
Farm Improvement Branch. Technical Bulletin.
irreg. ISSN 0080-648X

**Saskatchewan. Department of Culture and Youth**
Regina, Sask., Canada.
• Saskatchewan. Department of Culture and Youth.
Annual Report. a.

**Saskatchewan. Department of Finance**
119 Legislative Bldg., Regina, Saskatchewan,
Canada.
• Saskatchewan's Financial and Economic Position.
biennial. ISSN 0080-6676

**Saskatchewan. Department of Highways**
1610 Park St., Regina, Sask. S4N 2G1, Canada.
• Saskatchewan. Department of Highways.
Technical Report. 3 per yr.

**Saskatchewan. Department of Highways and
Transportation. Planning Branch**
Administration Bldg., Regina, Sask. S4S 0B1,
Canada.
• Travel on Saskatchewan Highways. a. ISSN 0581-
8079

**Saskatchewan. Department of Industry and
Commerce**
S.P.C. Bldg., 7th Floor, Regina, Sask. S4P 2Y9,
Canada.
• Business Forum. bi-m.
• Saskatchewan. Department of Industry and
Commerce. Business Forum. bi-m.
• Saskatchewan. Department of Industry and
Commerce. Report for the Fiscal Year. a. ISSN
0080-6498
• Saskatchewan Manufacturers Guide. biennial.
ISSN 0080-6536

**Saskatchewan. Department of Labour. Research and
Planning Division**
2350 Albert St., Regina, Sask., Canada.
• Saskatchewan Labour Report. irreg. ISSN 0317-
7335

**Saskatchewan. Department of Mineral Resources**
1914 Hamilton Street, P.O. Box 5114, Regina,
Saskatchewan S4P 3P5, Canada.
- Saskatchewan Mineral Spotlight. m. ISSN 0036-4932

**Saskatchewan. Department of Mineral Resources.
Mineral Records Branch**
Toronto-Dominion Bank Bldg., 13th Floor, 1914
Hamilton St., Regina, Sask. S4P 3N6, Canada.
- Saskatchewan. Department of Mineral Resources.
Core Index. irreg., 1964, vol. 3. ISSN 0080-6501
- Saskatchewan. Department of Mineral Resources.
Petroleum and Natural Gas Reservoir Annual. a.
- Saskatchewan. Department of Mineral Resources.
Statistical Yearbook. a. ISSN 0080-651X

**Saskatchewan. Department of the Environment**
Regina, Sask., Canada.
- Saskatchewan. Department of the Environment.
Annual Report. a.

**Saskatchewan. Department of Tourism and
Renewable Resources**
1825 Lorne St., Regina, Sask. S4P 3N1, Canada.
- Aquaculture Review. a.
- Saskatchewan. Department of Tourism and
Renewable Resources. Annual Report. a.
- Saskatchewan. Department of Tourism and
Renewable Resources. Technical Bulletins. irreg.
- Saskatchewan. Game Surveys Unit. Aerial
Antelope Survey Report. a.
- Saskatchewan. Game Surveys Unit. Sex and Age
Ratios of Sharp-Tailed Grouse and Gray
(Hungarian) Partridge. a.
- Saskatchewan. Game Surveys Unit. Spring Survey
of Sharp-Tailed Grouse and Cock Pheasant. a.
- Saskatchewan. Game Surveys Unit. Winter Mule
Deer Survey in Southwestern Saskatchewan. a.

**Saskatchewan. Highway Traffic Board**
- Saskatchewan Government Insurance Office.
Province of Saskatchewan Motor Vehicle Traffic
Accidents, Annual Report. (pub. by Saskatchewan
Government Insurance Office)

**Saskatchewan. Medical Care Insurance Commission**
Provincial Health Bldg., 3211 Albert St., Regina,
Sask. S4S 0A8, Canada.
- Saskatchewan. Medical Care Insurance
Commission. Annual Report. a. ISSN 0080-6544

**Saskatchewan Archaeological Society**
c/o Saskatchewan Museum of Natural History,
Wascana Park, Regina, Saskatchewan, Canada.
- Saskatchewan Archaeology Newsletter. q. ISSN
0036-4878

**Saskatchewan Archives Board**
Saskatchewan Archives Office, Univ. of
Saskatchewan, Saskatoon S7N 0W0, Sask., Canada.
- Saskatchewan History. 3 per yr. ISSN 0036-4908

**Saskatchewan Association for the Mentally Retarded.
Regina Branch**
1602 12th Ave., Regina, Sask., Canada.
- Trust. irreg. ISSN 0381-9612

**Saskatchewan Association of Educational Media
Specialists**
- Medium. (pub. by Saskatchewan Teachers'
Federation)

**Saskatchewan Association of Housing and Nursing
Homes**
Box 442, Saskatoon, Sask., Canada.
- Saskatchewan Care. 4 per yr. ISSN 0048-9166

**Saskatchewan Association of Rural Municipalities**
c/o Lorne Wilkinson, Sec., 2075 Hamilton St.,
Regina, Sask. S4P 2E1, Canada.
- Rural Councillor. m.(except Jan. & July) ISSN
0036-0007

**Saskatchewan Centre of the Arts**
200 Lakeshore Drive, Regina, Sasketchewan,
Canada.
- Saskatchewan Centre of the Arts. Annual Report.
a.

**Saskatchewan Council of Social Studies Teachers**
- Perspectives. (pub. by Saskatchewan Teachers'
Federation)

**Saskatchewan Council on Educational Administration**
- Administrative Scene. (pub. by Saskatchewan
Teachers' Federation)

- Saskatchewan Administrator. (pub. by
Saskatchewan Teachers' Federation)

**Saskatchewan Educational Research Association**
c/o W. Toews, Ed., Faculty of Education,
University of Regina, Regina, Sask. S4S 0AZ,
Canada.
- Saskatchewan Journal of Educational Research
and Development. s-a. ISSN 0048-9212

**Saskatchewan English Teachers Association**
2317 Arlington Ave., Saskatoon, Saskatchewan,
Canada.
- Skylark. q.

**Saskatchewan Farmstart Corporation**
Regina, Sask., Canada.
- Saskatchewan FarmStart Corporation. Annual
Report. a.

**Saskatchewan Genealogical Society**
Box 1894, Regina S4P 3E1, Sask., Canada.
- Saskatchewan Genealogical Society. Bulletin. q.
ISSN 0048-9182

**Saskatchewan Government Employees' Association**
1440 Broadway Ave., Regina, Sask. S4P 1E2,
Canada.
- Dome. bi-m. ISSN 0316-8433
- News News News. fortn.

**Saskatchewan Government Insurance Office**
Regina, Saskatchewan, Canada.
- Saskatchewan Government Insurance Office.
Province of Saskatchewan Motor Vehicle Traffic
Accidents, Annual Report. a. (Saskatchewan.
Highway Traffic Board)

**Saskatchewan Guidance and Counseling Association**
- Saskatchewan Guidance and Counseling
Association. Guidelines. (pub. by Saskatchewan
Teachers' Federation)

**Saskatchewan Gun Collectors Association**
Box 1334, Regina S4P 0A0, Sask., Canada.
- Gun Talk. q. ISSN 0017-5625

**Saskatchewan Home Economics Teachers' Association**
- Vista. (pub. by Saskatchewan Teachers'
Federation)

**Saskatchewan Housing Corporation**
Regina, Saskatchewan, Canada.
- Saskatchewan Housing Corporation. Annual
Report. a.

**Saskatchewan Industrial Education Association**
- Insite. (pub. by Saskatchewan Teachers'
Federation)

**Saskatchewan Library Association**
Box 3388, Regina, Sask. S4P 3H1, Canada.
- Saskatchewan Library. s-a. ISSN 0036-4924

**Saskatchewan Motor Club**
200 Albert St. N., Regina, Sask., Canada.
- Saskatchewan Motorist. bi-m. ISSN 0036-4940

**Saskatchewan Natural History Society**
Box 1321, Regina, Sask. S4P 3B8, Canada.
- Blue Jay. q. ISSN 0006-5099
- Saskatchewan Natural History Society.
Newsletter. q. ISSN 0581-8443
- Saskatchewan Natural History Society. Special
Publications. irreg. ISSN 0080-6552

**Saskatchewan Oil and Gas Corporation**
303 Financial Building, Scarth & 13th Avenue,
Regina, Saskatchewan, Canada.
- Saskatchewan Oil and Gas Corporation. Annual
Report. a.

**Saskatchewan Poetry Society**
3104 College Avenue, Regina, Saskatchewan S4T
1V7, Canada.
- Saskatchewan Poetry Book. biennial. ISSN 0080-6560

**Saskatchewan Provincial Library**
1352 Winnipeg St., Regina, Sask. S4R 1J9,
Canada.
- Focus on Saskatchewan Libraries. m.(except July)
ISSN 0015-5179

**Saskatchewan Registered Nurses' Association**
2066 Retallack Street, Regina, Saskatchewan, S4T
2K2, Canada.
- Saskatchewan Registered Nurses' Association.
Bulletin. bi-m.

**Saskatchewan Research Council**
Industrial Services Division, 30 Campus Drive,
Saskatoon, Sask., Canada.
- Catalyst (Saskatchewan) m. ISSN 0008-7653
- Industrial Business Management. 12 per yr. ISSN
0319-8294

**Saskatchewan Research Council Library**
30 Campus Drive, Saskatoon Sask S7N 0X1,
Canada.
- Saskatchewan. Research Council. Annual Report.
a. ISSN 0080-6587

**Saskatchewan School Trustees Association**
570 Avord Tower, Regina, Sask. S4P 0R7, Canada.
- School Trustee. 5 per yr. ISSN 0036-6854

**Saskatchewan Science Teachers' Society**
- Accelerator. (pub. by Saskatchewan Teachers'
Federation)

**Saskatchewan Society for Education Through Art**
c/o S.T.F. Building, P.O. Box 1108, Saskatchewan,
Canada.
- Discovery Through Art.

**Saskatchewan Teachers' Federation**
2317 Arlington Ave., Saskatoon, Saskatchewan,
Canada.
- Accelerator. 4 per yr. ISSN 0001-446X
(Saskatchewan Science Teachers' Society)
- Administrative Scene. m. ISSN 0044-6300
(Saskatchewan Council on Educational
Administration)
- Insite. s-a. ISSN 0020-2029 (Saskatchewan
Industrial Education Association)
- Medium. q. (Saskatchewan Association of
Educational Media Specialists)
- Perspectives. q. ISSN 0316-3334 (Saskatchewan
Council of Social Studies Teachers)
- Saskatchewan Administrator. 5 per yr. ISSN
0048-914X (Saskatchewan Council on
Educational Administration)
- Saskatchewan Bulletin. fortn. ISSN 0036-4886
- Saskatchewan Guidance and Counseling
Association. Guidelines. q. ISSN 0048-9190
- Tema. q.
- Vista. irreg. ISSN 0382-0289 (Saskatchewan
Home Economics Teachers' Association)

**Saskatchewan Teachers' Federation. Early Childhood
Education Council**
Box 1108, Saskatoon, Sask, S7K 3N3, Canada.
- Venture Forth. q. ISSN 0315-2235

**Saskatchewan Telecommunications**
2350 Albert St., Regina, Sask. S4P 2Y4, Canada.
- Sask Tel News. m. ISSN 0036-4851
- Saskatchewan Telecommunications. Annual
Report. a. ISSN 0080-6633

**Saskatchewan Tourist Association**
P.O. Box 184, Regina, Sask., Canada.
- Tourist Talks. m.

**Saskatchewan Trucking Association**
1335 Wallace St., Regina, Sask. S4N 3Z5, Canada.
- Saskatchewan Motor Transport Guide. a.
- This Business of Trucking. bi-m.

**Saskatchewan Water Supply Board**
2345 Broad St., Regina, Sask. S4P 1Y1, Canada.
- Saskatchewan Water Supply Board Annual
Report. a.

**Saskatchewan Wildlife Federation**
- Western Canada Outdoors. (pub. by McIntish
Publishing Co. Ltd.)

**Saskatchewan Writers Guild**
Box 1885, Saskatoon, Sask., Canada.
- Grain. 3 per yr. ISSN 0315-7423

**Satellite Video Exchange Society**
261 Powell St., Vancouver, B.C., Canada.
- Video Exchange Directory. a.

**Scandinavian News Co.**
Box 653, Sta. F, Toronto, Ont. M1R 4J2, Canada.
- Canada-Svensken/Swedish Canadian. s-m. ISSN
0045-4249

**Scarboro Foreign Mission Society**
2685 Kingston Rd., Scarborough, Ont. M1M 1M4,
Canada.
- Scarboro Missions. m.

**Scarborough College. Students Council**
c/o Dennis Schilling, Ed., 1265 Military Trail, West
Hill, Ont. M1C 1A4, Canada.
- Balcony Square. 15 per yr. ISSN 0005-4267

**Scholar House Publishing**
234 St. George St., Toronto, Ont., Canada.
- Ontario Dental Association. Journal. m. ISSN
0030-2864

**Science Council of Canada**
150 Kent St., Ottawa, Ont. K1P 5P4, Canada.
- Food Production in the Canadian Environment.
irreg.
- Issues in Canadian Science Policy. ISSN 0318-
5311
- Science Council of Canada. Annual Report. a.
ISSN 0080-7478
- Science Council of Canada. Background Studies.
irreg.
- Science Council of Canada. Reports. irreg. ISSN
0080-7486

**Scotian Pen Guild**
Box 173, Dartmouth, N.S., Canada.
- Amber. q. ISSN 0318-5753
- Marsh and Maple. q.

**Scruncheons**
English Dept., Arts and Administration Bldg.,
Memorial Univ., St. John's, Newfoundland, Canada.
- Scruncheons; review of creative writing published
in Newfoundland.

**Seafarers International Union of Canada**
634 St. James St. W., Montreal, Que., Canada.
- Canadian Sailor. m. ISSN 0008-4972

**Jean Seguin & Associates**
601 Cote Vertu, Ville St-Laurent, Que. H4L 1X8,
Canada.
- Administration Hospitaliere et Sociale. 10 per yr.
ISSN 0317-3739 (Federation des Admistrateurs
des Services de Sante et des Services Sociaux du
Quebec)

**Senate of Canada**
Ottawa, Ont., Canada
- Canada. Parliament. Senate. Standing Senate
Committee on Agriculture. Proceedings. irreg.
(Dist. by: Information Canada, Ottawa, Ont. K1A
0S9, Canada)

**Seneca College**
1750 Finch Ave. E., Willowdale, Ont. M2N 5T7.
- Canadian Speech Communication Journal. a.

**Sentinel Publishing Co.**
27 Central St., LaSalle, Que. H8R 2J1, Canada.
- Canadian Fisherman & Ocean Science. bi-m. ISSN
0317-2023

**Sept-Jours Inc.**
112 Leacock Rd., Pointe Claire, Que., Canada.
- Auto-Neige. m. ISSN 0045-1002

**Sequences**
4635 rue de Lorimier, Montreal, Que. H2H 2B4,
Canada.
- Sequences. 4 per yr. ISSN 0037-2412

**Serbian League of Canada**
335 Britannia Ave., Hamilton, Ont. L8H 1Y4,
Canada.
- Kanadski Srbobran/Canadian Srbobran
w. ISSN 0022-829X

**Serbian National Shield Society**
- Glas Kanadskin Srba/Voice of Canadian Serbs.
(pub. by Avala Printing and Publishing)

**Service Monde-Ami. Secretariat National**
25 Ouest rue Jarry, Montreal H2P 1S6, Canada.
- Amigo. bi-m. ISSN 0318-5729
- Amisol. bi-m. ISSN 0318-5737

**Shaver Poultry Breeding Farms, Ltd**
Box 400, Cambridge, Ont. N1R 5V9, Canada.
- Shaver Focus. q. ISSN 0315-6915

**Shell Canada Ltd.**
505 University Ave., Toronto, Ont. M5G 1X4,
Canada.
- Sphere. bi-m.

**Shipyard General Workers' Federation of British
Columbia**
1219 Nanaimo St., Vancouver, B.C., Canada.
- Main Deck. irreg. ISSN 0383-7769

**Shooting Federation of Canada**
333 River Rd., Vanier, Ont. K1L 8B9, Canada.
- Aim. bi-m. ISSN 0382-4373

**Showbill Publications Ltd.**
105 Davenport Rd., Suite 219, Toronto, Ont. M5R
1H6, Canada.
- Showbill. bi-m.

**Sigalert Enterprises Ltd.**
Box 3026, Vancouver, B. C. V6B 3X5, Canada.
- Precious Metals Investment Report. s-m.

**Silayan Filipino Community Center**
520 Sherbourne St., Toronto, Ont. M4X 1K9,
Canada.
- Silahis. irreg. ISSN 0381-9027

**Geo. Alex. Simon**
1585 Barrington St., Halifax, N. S., Canada.
- Atlantic Review. m. ISSN 0044-9911

**Simon & Schuster of Canada, Ltd.**
330 Steelcase Rd., Markham, Ont. L3R 2M1,
Canada
(and 630 Fifth Ave., New York, N.Y. 10020)
- Pro Hockey. a. ISSN 0079-5569

**Simon Fraser University**
Burnaby, B.C., Canada.
- West Coast Review; a quarterly magazine of the
arts. 4 per yr. ISSN 0043-311X

**Sir George Williams University Day Students
Association**
Concordia Univ., Sir George Williams Campus,
1455 de Maisonneuve St. West, Montreal H3G
1M8, Canada.
- Georgian. 2 per wk. ISSN 0016-8467

**Sir James Whitney School**
Belleville, Ont., Canada.
- Canadian. m. ISSN 0008-2805

**Sisters of Service**
10 Montcrest Blvd., Toronto, Ontario M4K 2J7,
Canada.
- Field at Home. q.

**Slesse News**
Box 320, Chilliwack, B. C., Canada.
- Slesse News. m. ISSN 0049-0717

**Slovak Jesuit Fathers in Canada**
Box 600, Cambridge, Ont. N1R 5W3, Canada.
- Slovenski Jezuiti V Kanade. Year Book. a. ISSN
0085-6134

**Slovenian National Federation of Canada**
c/o V. Mauko, Ed., 646 Euclid Ave., Toronto 4,
Ont., Canada.
- Slovenska Drzava; for a free Slovenia. m. ISSN
0037-6957

**Smith Publishing Company**
Scarborough, Ont., Canada.
- Canadian Footwear News. irreg. ISSN 0045-4842

**Social Science Research Council of Canada**
151 Slater St., Ottawa K1P 5H3, Canada.
- Atlantic Provinces Studies. (pub. by University of
Toronto Press)
- Canadian Studies in History and Government.
(pub. by University of Toronto Press)
- Social Science Research Council of Canada.
Report. a. ISSN 0081-0452
- Social Sciences in Canada. 3-4 per yr. ISSN 0049-
092X
- Studies in the Structure of Power: Decision
Making in Canada. (pub. by University of
Toronto Press)

**Socialist Labor Party of Canada**
Box 123, Adelaide St., Toronto, Ont. M5C 2J1,
Canada.
- Socialist Press Bulletin. m. ISSN 0049-0954

**Societe Canadienne d'Orientation et de Consultation**
Faculty of Education, University of Ottawa, Ottawa,
Ont. K1H 6K9, Canada.
- Canadian Counsellor/Conseiller Canadien. q.
ISSN 0008-333X
- Cognica. 8 per yr.

**Societe Canadienne de Science Economique**
- Actualite Economique. (pub. by Ecole des Haute
Etudes Commerciales)

**Societe d'Astronomie de Montreal**
3860 est, rue Rachel, Montreal, Que., Canada.
- Quebec Astronomique. m. ISSN 0318-0492

**Societe d'Edition de la Revue Forces**
1450 City Councillors, Montreal, Que. H3A 2E6,
Quebec, Canada.
- Forces. q. ISSN 0015-6957

**Societe d'Histoire de Matane**
616 St. Redempteur, Local 1603, Matane, Que.,
Canada.
- Histoire au Pays de Matane. s-a. ISSN 0046-7499

**Societe de Conservation de la Region de Quebec-
Mauricie**
126, rue St-Pierre, C.P. 35, Station B, Quebec 2,
Canada.
- Societe de Conservation de la Region de Quebec-
Mauricie. Annual Report. a. ISSN 0075-8183

**Societe de Recherches Amerindiennes au Quebec**
4050 Berri, Montreal, Que. H2L 2R1, Canada.
- Recherches Amerindiennes au Quebec. 5 per yr.

**Societe des Alcools du Quebec**
C. P. 1058, Place d'Armes, Montreal, P. Q.,
Canada.
- Societe des Alcools du Quebec. Rapport Annuel.
a.

**Societe des Bernier d'Amerique Inc.**
1205 Champigny, Duvernay, Que. H7E 4M3,
Canada.
- Journal Historique des Bernier; voix des Bernier
d'Amerique. q. ISSN 0021-8006

**Societe des Ecrivains Canadiens**
454 Ave. Willowdale, No. 8, Montreal 257, Que.,
Canada.
- Societe des Ecrivains Canadiens. Bulletin. q. ISSN
0049-1055

**Societe des Missions-Etrangeres**
60 rue Desnoyers, Pont-Viau, Ville de Laval H7G
1A4, Que., Canada.
- Missions-Etrangeres. bi-m. ISSN 0026-6116

**Societe des Poetes Canadiens Francais**
917. Mgr. Grandin, Suite 300, Quebec-10, Canada.
- Poesie. q. ISSN 0032-1923

**Societe du Timbre de Noel du Quebec, Inc.**
264 rue Chenier, Quebec G1K 1R2 P.Q., Canada.
- Poumons. 4 per yr.

**Societe Entomologique du Quebec**
c/o Michel Letendre, Sec., Scientific Complex D-
159, 2700 Einstein, Ste-Foy, Que. G1P 3W8,
Canada.
- Societe Entomologique du Quebec. Annales. 3 per
yr. ISSN 0037-9301
- Societe Entomologique du Quebec. Memoires.
irreg. ISSN 0071-0784

**Societe Genealogique Canadienne-Francaise**
Case Postale 335, Place d'Armes, Montreal, Que.
H2Y 3H1, Canada.
- Societe Genealogique Canadienne-Francaise.
Memoires. q. ISSN 0037-9387

**Societe Historique Acadienne**
C. P. 2363, Stn. A, Moncton, N.B. E1C 8J3,
Canada.
- Societe Historique Acadienne. Cahiers. 4 per yr.
ISSN 0049-1098

**Societe Historique de l'Ouest du Quebec**
C.P. 7, Hull, Que., Canada.
- Asticou. irreg. ISSN 0066-992X

**Societe Historique de la Gaspesie**
Case Postale 680, Gaspe, Quebec, Canada.
- Revue d'Histoire et de Traditions Populaires de la
Gaspesie. q.

**Societe Historique de Quebec**
C.P. 460, Quebec, P.Q. G1R 4R7, Canada.
• Societe Historique de Quebec. Textes. irreg. ISSN
0081-1130

**Societe Historique du Madawaska**
• Brayon. (pub. by Madawaska Limitee)

**Societe Historique du Saguenay**
C.P. 456, 930, rue Jacques-Cartier, Chicoutimi,
Canada.
• Saguenayensia. bi-m. ISSN 0581-295X

**Societe Historique Nicolas Denys Revue d' Histoire**
Case 6, Site 19, Bertrand, N.B. E0B 1J0, Canada.
• Societe Historique Nicolas Denys Revue d'
Histoire. q. ISSN 0381-9388

**Societe la Vie des Arts**
360 rue McGill, Montreal, Que. H2Y 2E9, Canada.
• Vie des Arts. q. ISSN 0042-5435

**Societe Medicale des Trois-Rivieres**
Box 667, 1563 Royale, Trois-Rivieres, Que.,
Canada.
• Mauricien Medical. 4 per yr. ISSN 0025-6048

**Societe pour Vaincre la Pollution**
B.P. 65, Place d'Armes, Montreal, Que., Canada.
• Bulletin - S V P. irreg. ISSN 0382-5302

**Societe Radio Canada**
C. P. 6000, Montreal, Que. H3C 3A8, Canada.
• Ici Radio Canada Television. w. ISSN 0046-8460

**Societe Rencesvals. American-Canadian Branch**
c/o John R. Allen, Ed., Dept. of French & Spanish,
University of Manitoba, Winnipeg, Man. R3T 2N2,
Canada.
• Olifant. q. ISSN 0381-9132

**Societe Saint-Jean-Baptiste de Montreal**
1182 rue Saint-Laurent, Montreal 18,Que., Canada.
• Societe Saint-Jean-Baptiste de Montreal.
Information Nationale. irreg. ISSN 0537-6211

**Societe Vega, Engraver**
Roxton Pond (Shefford) Que., Granby, Que.,
Canada.
• Entre-Nous. q. ISSN 0046-2144 (Societes des
Eleveurs des Bovins et des Chevaux Canadiens)

**Societe Zoologigue de Quebec, Inc.**
8191 Av du Zoo, Orsainville, Que. G1G 4G4,
Canada.
• Carnets de Zoologie. q. ISSN 0008-669X

**Societes des Eleveurs des Bovins et des Chevaux
Canadiens**
• Entre-Nous. (pub. by Societe Vega, Engraver)

**Society for Art Publications**
3 Church St., Toronto, Ont. M5E 1M2, Canada.
• Artscanada. bi-m. ISSN 0004-4113

**Society for Indian and Northern Education**
Univ. of Saskatchewan, Saskatoon S7N 0W0, Sask.,
Canada.
• Northian. q. ISSN 0029-3253

**Society for the Promotion of Art History Publications
in Canada**
c/o Dr. Harold D. Kalman, 236 Queen Elizabeth
Drive, Ottawa, Ont. K1S 3M4, Canada.
• R A C A R. (Revue d'Art Canadienne/Canadian
Art Revue) s-a.

**Society of Industrial Accountants of Canada**
154 Main St. E., Hamilton, Ont. L8N 1G9, Ont.,
Canada.
• Cost and Management. bi-m. ISSN 0010-9592

**Soft Press**
1050 Saint David St., Victoria, B.C. V8S 4Y8,
Canada.
• Vancouver Island Poems; cloud nine. a.

**Sokuedit Ltee**
C.P. 310, Sta. B, Quebec, G1K 7B1, Canada.
• Semaine Commerciale; l'organe officiel des
interets commerciaux et financiers du grand
Quebec. w. ISSN 0037-1750

**Solar Energy Society of Canada**
P.O. Box 1353, Winnipeg, Man. R3C 2Z1, Canada.
• SOL Newsletter. 6 per yr.

**Editions Solidarite Inc.**
2030 Blvd. Pere Lelievre, Que. G1P 2X1, Canada.
• Ensemble; journal d'information cooperative. bi-m.
ISSN 0013-8592

**Solidarity Committee with the People of Palestine**
Box 93, Sta. G, Montreal 130, Que., Canada.
• Fateh. s-m. ISSN 0014-8792 (Palestine National
Liberation Movement)

**Sono Nis Press**
c/o Dept. of Creative Writing, University of British
Columbia, Vancouver, B.C., Canada.
• Contemporary Poetry of British Columbia. irreg.
ISSN 0384-0433

**Sons of Temperance of Nova Scotia**
c/o F. Payne, 1745 Vernon St., Halifax, N. S.,
Canada.
• Forward. m.

**Sound Publishing**
126 14th St. West, Owen Sound, Ont., Canada.
• Canadian Coin Box. m. ISSN 0045-4575
• Canadian Vending; the voice of automatic vending
in Canada. bi-m. ISSN 0008-5278

**South of Tuk**
c/o K. Vaughn, Box 1267 Station A, Toronto, Ont.
M5W 1G7, Canada.
• South of Tuk. irreg. ISSN 0382-8522

**Southam Business Publications Ltd.**
1450 Don Mills Rd., Don Mills, Ont. M3B 2X7,
Canada.
• Administrative Digest. m. ISSN 0001-835X
• Architecture Concept. m. ISSN 0003-8687
• Canadian Architect. m. ISSN 0008-2872
• Canadian Architecture Yearbook. a. ISSN 0068-
8231
• Canadian Chemical Processing. m. ISSN 0008-
3186
• Canadian Consulting Engineer; a magazine for
professional engineers in private practice. m.
ISSN 0008-3267
• Canadian Farm Equipment Dealer. m. ISSN 0008-
3526
• Canadian Forest Industries; Canada's only
national publication serving saw and pulpwood
logging, sawmilling and allied activities. m. ISSN
0008-3623
• Canadian Industrial Equipment News; reader
service on new, improved and redesigned
industrial equipment & supplies. s-m. ISSN 0008-
3836
• Canadian Medical Directory. a. ISSN 0068-9203
• Canadian Office Products and Stationery. bi-m.
ISSN 0008-462X
• Canadian Petroleum. m. ISSN 0008-4735
• Canadian Plastics Directory and Buyer's Guide. a.
ISSN 0068-9459
• Canadian Plastics Magazine. m. ISSN 0008-4778
• Canadian Ports and Seaways Directory. a. ISSN
0068-9467
• Canadian Transportation and Distribution
Management. m. ISSN 0008-5200
• Chemical Buyers Guide. a. ISSN 0069-2891
• Construction and Aggregates Production
Industries Directory. a.
• Electrical Equipment News. m. ISSN 0013-4333
• Electronics and Communications; the engineering
journal of the Canadian electronics industry. 7 per
yr. ISSN 0013-5100
• Engineering and Contract Record. m. ISSN 0013-
7804
• Executive. m. ISSN 0014-4509
• Farm Equipment Directory/Annuaire. a. ISSN
0071-3899
• Furniture and Furnishings. m. ISSN 0046-5313
• Genie Construction. m. ISSN 0016-6820
• Good Farming. 10 per yr. ISSN 0017-2049
• Heating, Plumbing, Air Conditioning. m. ISSN
0017-9418
• Hospital Administration in Canada. m. ISSN
0018-554X
• Laboratory Guide. a. ISSN 0075-7500
• Laboratory Product News. bi-m. ISSN 0047-3855
• Modern Medicine of Canada; the journal of
diagnosis and treatment. m. ISSN 0026-8097
• Operations Forestieres et de Scierie. m. ISSN
0030-3631
• Oral Health; clinical journal devoted to the
advancement of the dental profession. m. ISSN
0030-4204
• Plomberie-Chauffage et Climatisation. m. ISSN
0032-1591
• Pools, Parks & Rinks. bi-m.
• Shoe and Leather Journal. m. ISSN 0037-4032

• Shop; national newspaper of used & new
equipment. m.
• Southam Building Guide. m. ISSN 0038-3597
• Southam Business. irreg. ISSN 0383-9745
• T. V. Times. w.
• Water and Pollution Control. m. ISSN 0043-1117
• Water & Pollution Control Directory. irreg. ISSN
0511-3555

**Southam-Murray**
2973 Weston Rd., Weston, Ont., Canada.
• EnRoute. 10 per yr. (Air Canada)

**Southern Alberta Institute of Technology. Students
Association**
1301 16th Ave. N.W., Calgary, Alta. T2M 0L4,
Canada.
• Emery Weal. w.

**Sovereign Publishing Co.**
110 Church St., Toronto 1, Ont., Canada.
• Ontario Journal and Tax Sale Register. every 8
wks. ISSN 0048-1807
• Tax Sale Register. Ontario Region. m.

**Sovremennik Publishing Association Inc.**
9 Garnet Ave., Toronto, Ont. M6G 1V6, Canada.
• Sovremennik; zhurnal russkoi kul'tury i
natzional'noi mysli. q. ISSN 0038-5948

**Soyuz Dukhovnykh Obshchin Krista**
Box 760, Grand Forks, B.C., Canada.
• Iskra. fortn. ISSN 0021-1761

**Spear Publications Ltd.**
1532 Eglinton Ave. W., Toronto, Ont. M6E 2G7,
Canada.
• Spear; Canadian magazine of truth and soul. m.
ISSN 0315-0208

**Special Libraries Association, Montreal Chapter**
Box 10, Jardins Sta., Montreal, Que. H5B 1C8,
Canada.
• Directory of Special Libraries in Montreal.
biennial. ISSN 0070-6396
• Special Libraries Association. Montreal Chapter.
Bulletin. q. ISSN 0381-9833

**Spectroscopy Society of Canada**
• Canadian Journal of Spectroscopy. (pub. by
Multiscience Publications Ltd.)
• Canadian Spectroscopic News. (pub. by
Multiscience Publications Ltd.)

**Spiritual Press**
Box 464, Don Mills, Ont. M3C 2T3, Canada.
• Journal of Automatic Writing. m.

**Square Dance Federation of Manitoba. Eastern
Division**
1177 Corydon Ave., Winnipeg, Mb. R3M OX5,
Canada.
• Manisquare. 9 per yr. ISSN 0383-6037

**Squatchberry Press**
Box 205, Geraldton, Ont. P0T 1M0, Canada.
• Squatchberry Journal. s-a.

**Stanstead County Historical Society**
Box 210, Stanstead, Que. J0B 3E0, Canada.
• Stanstead County Historical Society. Journal.
biennial. ISSN 0081-4369

**Statistical Science Association of Canada**
c/o Department of Mathematics, McGill University,
Burnside Hall, 805 Sherbrooke St. W., Montreal,
Que. H3A 2K6, Canada.
• Canadian Journal of Statistics/Revue Canadienne
de Statistique. s-a. ISSN 0319-5724

**Statistics Canada**
*see* **Canada. Statistics Canada**

**Steel Company of Canada, Ltd.**
Hamilton, Ont. L8N 3T1, Canada.
• S T E L C O - Scope. q. ISSN 0036-1976

**Stereogrammetry Ltd**
• West Canadian Research Publications of Geology
and Related Sciences. (pub. by West Canadian
Research Publications)

**Ted Stevens Publications Ltd.**
50 Erimea Street, Guelph, Ontario N1H 2Y6,
Canada.
• Canadian Road Knight. m. ISSN 0315-0682

**Stimulus Publishing Co. Ltd.**
67 Yonge St., Suite 721, Toronto, Ont. M5E 1J8, Canada.
- Stimulus. bi-m. ISSN 0039-1514

**Stock Market News & Comment Ltd.**
Suite 1614 8 King St. East, Toronto, Ont. M5C 1B5, Canada.
- Stock Market News & Comment. w.

**Stone and Cox Ltd.**
100 Simcoe St., Toronto, Ont. M5H 3G2, Canada.
- Canadian Insurance. m. ISSN 0008-3879
- Canadian Insurance. Annual Statistical Issue. a. ISSN 0068-9025
- Canadian Insurance Law Bulletin Service. irreg(issued as frequently as required) ISSN 0068-9033
- Corporate Insurance in Canada. a.
- Provincial Results in Canada of General Insurance Companies. a.
- Stone and Cox General Insurance Register. a.
- Stone and Cox Life Insurance Tables. a. ISSN 0081-5780
- Underwriting Results in Canada. a. ISSN 0082-7452
- Uniform Life Accident & Sickness Insurance Act of Canada. irreg., latest issue 1972.

**Strange Faeces Press**
Box 81, Sta. N.D.G., 5751 Sherbrooke W., Montreal, P.Q. H4A 3P4, Canada.
- Strange Faeces. q.

**Strategie**
C.P. 124, Ucc.Beaubien, Mlt P.2 H2G 3L8, Canada.
- Strategie; lutte ideologique. q. ISSN 0315-3673

**Stratford Shakespearean Festival Foundation of Canada**
Festival Theatre, Box 520, Stratford, Ont. N5A 6V2, Canada.
- Fanfares. q. ISSN 0046-3256
- Stratford Festival; souvenir book. a. ISSN 0085-6770
- Stratford Festival Story. a. ISSN 0085-6789

**Student Mathematics**
c/o W. W. Sawyer, Ed., Faculty of Education, Rm. 373, University of Toronto, 371 Bloor St. West, Toronto M5S 2R7, Canada.
- Student Mathematics. a. ISSN 0085-6800

**Sudan Interior Mission**
10 Huntingdale Blvd., Scarborough, Ont. M1W 2S5, Canada.
- Africa Now. bi-m. ISSN 0044-6513

**Sun Life Assurance Company of Canada**
Sales Promotion Department, Dominion Square, Montreal, Que., Canada.
- Sunbeat/Echo Soleil. m.

**Sunyata**
P.O.Box 1012, Montreal 3, Que., Canada.
- Sunyata; a Buddhist magazine of poetry. 4 per yr. ISSN 0039-5463

**Survival Foundation**
3 Church St., Suite 401, Toronto, Ont. M5E 1M2, Canada.
- Canadian Forum. m. ISSN 0008-3631

**Svetovy Kongres Slovakov**
4 King St., Toronto, Ont., Canada.
- Svetovy Kongres Slovakov. Bulletin. irreg. ISSN 0317-4018

**Swiss Club Toronto**
Box 823, Station Q, Toronto, Ont. M4T 2N7, Canada.
- Swiss Canadian News. m. ISSN 0049-2728

**Synod of the Diocese of Ontario. Board of Parish Services**
90 Johnson St., Kingston, Ont., Canada.
- Ontario Churchman. m. ISSN 0030-2848

**T. C. Publishing Ltd.**
Box 6103, Sta. A, Toronto, Ont. M5W 1P5, Canada.
- Transit Canada. bi-m. ISSN 0045-4559

**T I O Communications Limited**
318 Berkeley St., Toronto, Ont. M5A 2X5, Canada.
- This Is Ontario. 4 per yr. during summer.

**T V-Film Filebook**
2533 Gerrard St. E., Scarborough, Ont., Canada.
- T V-Film Filebook; information on Canadian TV-film industry. a. ISSN 0082-1365

**T V Guide Ltd.**
9393 Edison Ave., Montreal H1J 1T5, Que., Canada.
- T V Hebdo. w. ISSN 0039-8551

**Tab Publishing**
43 Victoria St., Toronto, Ont. M5C 2A3, Canada.
- Tab International. irreg. ISSN 0380-2604

**Jean-Pierre Tadros, Ed. & Pub.**
C.P. 309, Station Outremont, Montreal 154, Que., Canada.
- Cinema Quebec. irreg. (approx. 10 per yr.)

**Tall-Taylor Publishing Co. Ltd.**
532 Cleveland Cresc. S.E., Calgary, Alta., Canada.
- Taylor's Leisure Wheels. m. ISSN 0318-3467
- Taylor's Trade Index. a. ISSN 0082-6170

**Talonbooks**
201-1019 E. Cordova St., Vancouver 6, B.C., Canada.
- Magenta Frog. irreg. ISSN 0076-2350

**Tamarack Review**
Box 159, Postal Sta. K, Toronto, Canada.
- Tamarack Review. 4 per yr. ISSN 0039-9256

**Tantalus Research Ltd.**
P.O. Box 34248, Vancouver, B.C. V6J 4N8, Canada.
- British Columbia Geographical Series: Occasional Papers in Geography. irreg. ISSN 0068-1571 (Canadian Association of Geographers. Western Division)
- Canadian Culture Series. irreg.

**Taylor Enterprises**
Suite 110, 2175 Sheppard Ave. E., Willowdale, Ont. M2J 1W8, Canada.
- Canadian Clay & Ceramics. m. ISSN 0009-8566 (Canadian Ceramic Society)

**Teachers of Home Economics Specialist Association**
105-2235 Burrard St., Vancouver, B.C. V6J 3H9, Canada.
- T H E S A Journal. a. (pub. by B. C. Teachers' Federation)

**Technical Information-Documentation Consultants Ltd.**
Suite 2-A, 1509 Sherbrooke St. W., Montreal-109, P.Q., Canada.
- Canadian Technical and Scientific Information News Journal. fortn.

**Technocracy Inc.**
3642 Kingsway, Vancouver V5R 5M2, B.C., Canada.
- Technocracy Digest. q. ISSN 0040-1587

**Tegwar Press**
1119-13th Ave. N.W., Moose Jaw, Sask., Canada.
- Salt; A Little Magazine of Contemporary Writing. irreg. ISSN 0085-5863

**Editions Tele Semaine Inc.**
C.P. 908, Succursale H, Montreal, Que. H3G 2L6, Canada.
- TeleSemaine. w. ISSN 0380-6073

**Terry Art Ltd.**
643 Yonge St., Toronto, Ont. M4Y 2A2, Canada.
- Know Canada. q. ISSN 0023-2459

**Textile Technical Federation of Canada**
4999 St. Catherine St. W., Suite 446, Montreal H3Z 1T3, Que., Canada.
- Canadian Textile Seminar. Book of Papers. biennial. ISSN 0068-9866

**Textile Workers Union of America**
AFL-CIO, CLC, 15 Gervais Dr., Don Mills, Ont., Canada.
- Textile Labour/Canadian Edition. 8 per yr. ISSN 0049-3562

**That's Showbusiness Inc.**
191 Church St., Toronto M5B 1Y7, Canada.
- That's Showbusiness. s-m.

**Theatre du Nouveau Monde**
84 Ouest, rue Ste-Catherine, Montreal, Que. H2X 1Z6, Canada.
- Envers du Decor; la vie du theatre. bi-m.

**Editions Themis**
C.P. 6201, Succursale A, Montreal, Que. H3C 3T1, Canada.
- Revue Juridique Themis. 3 per yr. ISSN 0556-7963

**Theosophical Society in Canada**
Box 5051, Postal Sta. A, Toronto, Ont. M5W 1N4, Canada.
- Canadian Theosophist. bi-m. ISSN 0045-544X

**J. D. Thomson Tourist Promotions Ltd.**
RR No. 5 Dresden, Ontario NOP 1MD, Canada.
- Bluewater Vacation Guide; Lake Huron and Georgian Bay. a.

**Thorne Riddell Associates Ltd.**
Royal Trust Tower, Toronto Dominion Center, Box 260, Toronto, Ont. M5K 1J9, Canada.
- Fringe Benefit Costs in Canada. biennial. ISSN 0071-9625

**Thunder Bay Museum**
219 S. May St., Thunder Bay, Ont. P7E 1B5, Canada.
- Thunder Bay Historical Museum Society. irreg. ISSN 0082-4283

**Charles Tidler, Ed. & Pub.**
Box 14, Ganges, B.C., Canada.
- Empty Belly; a magazine of poetry and communication. a. ISSN 0316-9529

**Titmouse Review**
720 W. 19th Ave., Vancouver 9, B.C., Canada.
- Titmouse Review. a. ISSN 0315-0720

**J. B. Tompkins, Ed. & Pub.**
202-1089 West Broadway, Vancouver, B.C., Canada.
- Westrade Traffic Directory. irreg.

**Toronto Board of Trade**
P.O. Box 60, 3 First Canadian Place, Toronto, Ont. M5X 1C1, Canada.
- Metropolitan Toronto Board of Trade. Journal. m. ISSN 0040-9510

**Toronto Boys and Girls House**
Toronto Public Library, 40 St. George St., Toronto 5, Ont., Canada.
- Toronto Boys and Girls House Subscription Reviews. q. ISSN 0040-9529

**Toronto Bureau of Municipal Research**
2 Toronto St. Suite 306, Toronto, Ont. M5C 2B6, Canada.
- Civic Affairs. q. ISSN 0045-7027
- Directory of Governments in Metropolitan Toronto. biennial. ISSN 0084-9944

**Toronto Dominion Bank**
Dept. of Economic Research, Box 1, Toronto-Dominion Centre, Toronto M5K 1A2, Ont., Canada.
- Canada's Business Climate; charts with commentary. q. ISSN 0045-4303

**Toronto Field Naturalists' Club**
c/o Mary Robson, Sec., 49 Craighurst Ave., Toronto, Ont. M4R 1J9, Canada.
- Ontario Field Biologist. s-a. ISSN 0078-4834

**Toronto Free Press Publications Ltd.**
196 Bathurst St., Toronto, Ont. M5T 2R8, Canada.
- Vilne Slovo; Ukrainian weekly. fortn.
- Vilne Slovo Annual. biennial.

**Toronto Home Builders Association**
5218 Yonge St., Willowdale, Ont., Canada.
- New Homes and Apartment Guide. s-a.

**Toronto Jewish Press**
Box 142, Downsview, Ont., M3M 3A3, Canada.
- Toronto Jewish Press. w. ISSN 0049-4186

**Toronto Public Library**
40 St. Clair Ave. E., Toronto M4T 1M9, Ont., Canada.
- T. P. L. News. m. ISSN 0039-8470

**Toronto Railway Club**
Box 8, Postal Terminal Station "A", Toronto M5W
1A2, Canada.
- Toronto Railway Club. Official Proceedings. 5 per
  yr. ISSN 0040-9553

**Toronto Ski Club**
8 Colborne St., Toronto 1, Ont., Canada.
- Ski Runner. 6 per yr. ISSN 0037-6221

**Toronto Stock Exchange**
234 Bay St., Toronto, Ont. M5J 1R1, Canada.
- Toronto Stock Exchange Review. m. ISSN 0049-
  4216

**Toronto Vegetarian Association**
28 Walker Ave., Toronto M4V 1G2, Ont., Canada.
- Toronto Vegetarian Association. Newsletter. bi-m.
  ISSN 0049-4232

**Toronto Wages for Housework Committee**
745 Danforth Avenue, Suite 301, Toronto, Ontario,
Canada.
- Women in Struggle Series. irreg.

**T. Toth, Ed. & Pub.**
1608 Eglinton Ave. W., Toronto, Ont. M6E 2G8,
Canada.
- Earth and You; vehicle of current ideas for
  modern men. a. ISSN 0085-011X

**Town Talk Publications**
89 Oriole Parkway, Toronto M5P 2G7, Ont.,
Canada.
- Town Talk about Toronto. q. ISSN 0041-0039

**Traditional Studies Press**
Box 984, Adelaide St. Sta., Toronto, Ont. M5C
2K4, Canada.
- Journal of Our Time. irreg. ISSN 0381-6524

**Trans-Canada Matchcover Club**
58 Purvis Drive, Hamilton, Ont. L8S 2S4, Canada.
- Saddle and Striker. 5 per yr. ISSN 0048-895X

**Trans-Global Enterprises Ltd.**
Box 2321, New Westminster, B. C., Canada.
- Action Sports. m.

**Transition Society**
308 Glengarry Bldg., 245 3rd Ave. So., Saskatoon,
Sask, Canada.
- Transition. bi-m. ISSN 0382-0750

**Translators' Society of Quebec**
1010 St. Catherine St. W., Montreal, Que. H3B
3R5, Canada.
- Antenne; bulletin d'information de la Societe des
  Traducteurs du Quebec. 10 per yr.

**Transport Routier du Quebec**
8575 Pascal Gagnon Blvd., Montreal 458, Que.,
Canada.
- Transport Routier du Quebec. m. ISSN 0049-
  447X

**Transportation Safety Association of Ontario**
9Th Floor, 2 Bloor St. E., Toronto, Ont. M4W 3C2,
Canada.
- Transportation Safety Association of Ontario.
  Bulletin. m. ISSN 0049-4518
- Transportation Safety Association of Ontario.
  Driver's News Letter. m. ISSN 0049-4526

**Travcom Inc.**
111 Pears Ave., Toronto, Ontario M5R 1S9,
Canada.
- Selling Travel. m.

**Travel Alberta**
Suite 320, the Boardwalk, 10310-102 Ave.,
Edmonton, Alta., Canada.
- Travel Alberta-Annual Review. a.

**Travel Industry Association of Alberta**
105 8th Avenue, S.E., Calgary, Alberta T2G 0K4,
Canada.
- Voice of Tourism. q. ISSN 0380-5476

**Travel Industry Association of Canada**
Suite 1016, 130 Albert St., Ottawa, Ont. K1P 5G4,
Canada.
- T I A C Newsletter. bi-m.
- Travel Industry Association of Canada.
  Convention Report. a. ISSN 0082-612X

**Tree of Peace**
Box 2667, Yellowknife, Northwest Territories, XOE
1HO, Canada.
- Ts'igonde/Tree Speaks; community voice. s-m.

**Trent University**
Peterborough, Ontario, Canada.
- Alternatives: Perspectives on Society and
  Environment. q. ISSN 0002-6638
- Catalyst (Peterborough) s-a. ISSN 0008-7661
- Journal of Canadian Studies/Revue d'Etudes
  Canadiennes. q. ISSN 0021-9495

**Trent University. Student Union**
Peterborough, Ont., Canada.
- Arthur; the undergraduate weekly. w. ISSN 0044-
  9091

**Tribuna Italiana**
257 Dante St., Montreal 327, Que., Canada.
- Tribuna Italiana. w. ISSN 0049-464X

**Tribune Press Ltd.**
Sackville, N.B., Canada.
- Tribune-Post. w. ISSN 0049-4658

**Tribune Publishing Co. Ltd.**
101-1416 Commercial Dr., Vancouver, B.C. V5L
3X9, Canada.
- Pacific Tribune. w. ISSN 0030-896X

**Trident Press Ltd.**
840 Main Street, Winnipeg R2W 2X5, Manitoba,
Canada.
- Canadian Farmer/Kanadiysky Farmer. w. ISSN
  0045-4745
- Ukrainian Voice. w. ISSN 0041-6037

**TRIUMF**
University of British Columbia, Vancouver 8, B.C.,
Canada.
- TRIUMF, Vancouver, British Columbia. Report. a.
  ISSN 0082-6367

**Trust Companies Association of Canada**
Suite 400, Board of Trade Bldg., 11 Adelaide St.,
W., Toronto, Ont. M5H 1L9, Canada.
- Directory of Canadian Trust Companies. a. ISSN
  0070-5225

**Tuatara**
759 Helvetia Cres, Victoria, B.C., Canada.
- Tuatara. s-a. ISSN 0041-3852

**R. H. Turner, Ed. & Pub.**
Box 277, Lethbridge, Alta. T1J 3Y7, Canada.
- Canadian Aberdeen-Angus News. 9 per yr. ISSN
  0045-4311 (Canadian Aberdeen Angus
  Association)

**W. Tyrrell**
Toronto, Ont., Canada.
- Book Commentator. irreg. ISSN 0382-5590

**Ukrainian Canadian Committee**
456 Main St., Winnipeg, Man. R3B 1B6, Canada.
- Komitet' Ukrainstsiv Kanady. Biuleten' q. ISSN
  0503-1036

**Ukrainian Catholic Archdiocese of Winnipeg**
- Progress/Pustup. (pub. by Progress Printing &
  Publishing Co. Ltd.)

**Ukrainian Catholic Mission of the Most Holy
Redeemer**
Catherine St., Yorkton, Sask., Canada.
- Lohos; bohoslov'kyi kvartal'nyk. q. ISSN 0024-
  5895

**Ukrainian Language Association**
Box 3504, Winnipeg, Man., Canada.
- Slovo na Storozhi/Word on Guard. a. ISSN 0583-
  6263

**Ukrainian News Publishers Ltd.**
10967-97 St., Edmonton, 18 Alta, Canada.
- Ukrainian News/Ukrainski Visti. w. ISSN 0041-
  6002

**Unicorn Publishing Corporation**
Box 1778, Sta. B, Montreal H3B 3L3, Que.,
Canada.
- Take One; the film magazine. m. ISSN 0039-9132

**Unifarm**
9934-106 St., Edmonton T5K 1E1, Alta., Canada.
- Farm Trends. m.

**Union des Producteurs Agricoles**
515 Viger Ave., Montreal, Que. H2L 2P2, Canada.
- Terre de Chez Nous. w. ISSN 0040-3830

**Union Internationale des Ouvriers du Vetement pour
Dames**
405 rue Concord, Montreal 111 P.Q., Canada.
- Justice. irreg. ISSN 0075-4595

**Union Nationale Francaise**
429 Av. Viger, Montreal, Que., Canada.
- Courrier Francais de Montreal; organe de la
  colonie francaise de Montreal. m. ISSN 0384-
  028X

**Union of British Columbia Municipalities**
No. 204, 604 Blackford St., New Westminster, B.C.,
Canada.
- Union of British Columbia Municipalities. Minutes
  of Annual Convention. a. ISSN 0082-7746

**Union of Nova Scotia Municipalities**
Suite 132, 136 Roy Bldg., 1657 Barrington St.,
Halifax, N.S. B3J 2A1, Canada.
- Union of Nova Scotia Municipalities. Proceedings
  of the Annual Convention. a. ISSN 0082-7762

**Union of Vietnamese in Canada**
Box 220, Station G, Montreal, Que. H2W 2M9,
Canada.
- Vietnam Report. irreg. ISSN 0382-0122

**United Baptist Convention of the Atlantic Provinces**
112 Princess St., Saint John, N.B., Canada.
- United Baptist Convention of the Atlantic
  Provinces. Yearbook. a. ISSN 0082-7843

**United Baptist Convention of the Atlantic Provinces.
Nova Scotia Branch**
Board of Publication, Box 756, Kentville, N.S. B4N
3X9, Canada.
- Atlantic Baptist. m. ISSN 0004-6752

**United Church of Canada**
85 St. Clair Ave. E., Toronto, Ont. M4T 1M8,
Canada.
- Issue. irreg.
- United Church Observer. m. ISSN 0041-7238
- United Church of Canada. Committee on
  Archives. Bulletin. Records and Proceedings. a.
  ISSN 0082-786X
- United Church of Canada. General Council.
  Record of Proceedings. biennial. ISSN 0082-7878
- United Church of Canada. Year Book. a. ISSN
  0082-7886

**United Co-operatives of Ontario**
151 City Centre Drive, Mississauga, Ont., Canada.
- U C O Leader. m. ISSN 0382-7070
- U C O News. irreg. ISSN 0049-5328

**United Electrical Radio and Machine Workers of
America**
10 Codeco Court, Don Mills, Ont., Canada.
- U E News. s-w. ISSN 0041-5049

**United Empire Loyalists Association of Canada**
Dominion Headquarters, 23 Prince Arthur Ave.,
Toronto, Ont M5R 1B2, Canada.
- Loyalist Gazette. s-a. ISSN 0047-5149

**United Flowers-by-Wire Canada Ltd.**
Penthouse Floor, 350 Bay St., Toronto, Ont. M5H
3N9, Canada.
- United Flowers-by-Wire Canada Journal. m.

**United Grain Growers Ltd.**
Box 6600, Winnipeg, Man. R3C 3A7, Canada.
- Grain Grower; farm business digest for prairie
  farmers. m. ISSN 0046-6255
- Grainews. m.
- Unifeed Beef Letter. m.

**United Nurses Inc.**
345 Victoria Ave., Suite 200, Montreal, P.Q. H3Z
2N1, Canada.
- Dialogue. q. ISSN 0316-2060

**United Radomer Relief for U.S. and Canada**
c/o A. Glass, Apt. 201, 4415 Bathurst St.,
Downsview, Ont., Canada.
- Voice of Radom. 10 per yr. ISSN 0382-0327

**United Senior Citizens of Ontario**
105 4th St., Toronto, Ont. M8V 2Y4, Canada.
- Voice of United Senior Citizens of Ontario. m
(except Jul. & Aug.) ISSN 0382-0068

**United Steelworkers of America**
Local 6500, 92 Frood Rd., Sudbury, Ont., Canada.
- Searcher. m. ISSN 0037-041X
- United Steelworkers of America. Information. bi-
m. ISSN 0566-0963

**Universite de Moncton**
Moncton, N.B., Canada.
- Universite de Moncton. Revue. 3 per yr. ISSN
0316-6368

**Universite de Montreal**
5255 Ave. Decelles, Montreal, Que. H3T 1V6,
Canada.
- Centre d'Etudes et de Documentation
Europeennes. Cahiers. Annals. irreg., 1969, no. 2.
ISSN 0069-1844
- Industrialization Forum; building: systems,
construction, analysis research. 5 per yr. ISSN
0019-8927 (Co-Sponsors: Harvard University;
Massachusetts Institute of Technology;
Washington University)

**Universite de Montreal. Association des Diplomes**
2910 Edouard-Montpetit, Bureau 3, Montreal, Que.
H3T 1JT, Canada.
- Interdit. 6 per yr. ISSN 0300-3965

**Universite de Montreal. Ecole de Bibliotheconomie**
C.P. 6128, Montreal 101, Canada.
- Universite de Montreal. Ecole de
Bibliotheconomie. Publications. irreg. ISSN 0077-
1341

**Universite de Montreal. Ecole de Medecine
Veterinaire**
C.P. 6128, Montreal, Que., Canada.
- Universite de Montreal. Ecole de Medecine
Veterinaire. Annuaire. a. ISSN 0383-8455

**Universite de Montreal. Faculte de Medecine
Veterinaire**
C.P. 5000, St. Hyacinthe, Que., Canada.
- Information Veterinaire. irreg. ISSN 0581-3263

**Universite de Montreal. Industrialization Forum
Team**
C.P. 6128, Montreal, Que. H3C 3J7, Canada.
- I.F. (Industrialization Forum) 5 per yr.

**Universite de Montreal. Institut Botanique**
4101 rue Sherbrooke E., Montreal 406, Que.,
Canada.
- Universite de Montreal. Institute Botanique.
Contributions. irreg. ISSN 0041-9168

**Universite de Montreal. Institut d'Etudes Medievales**
C.P. 6128, Montreal 101, P.Q., Canada.
- Computers and Medieval Data Processing. 2 per
yr. ISSN 0384-5060

**Universite de Sherbrooke. Centre d'Etude des
Litteratures d'Expression Francaise**
- Presence Francophone. (pub. by Editions Paulines)

**Universite de Sherbrooke. Departement d'Economique**
Sherbrooke, Que., Canada.
- Universite de Sherbrooke. Departement
d'Economique. Cahiers de la Cooperation. irreg.
- Universite de Sherbrooke. Departement
d'Economique. Dossiers sur les Cooperatives.
irreg.

**Universite de Sherbrooke. Faculte de Droit**
Sherbrooke, Que J1K 2R1, Canada.
- Universite de Sherbrooke. Revue de Droit. a.

**Universite de Sherbrooke. Faculte des Arts**
Box 10, Sherbrooke, Que., Canada.
- Ellipse. 3 per yr. ISSN 0046-1830

**Universite du Quebec**
Box 250, Sillery, Que. G1T 2R1, Canada.
- Quebec Science. m. ISSN 0021-6127
- Universite du Quebec (Province). Rapport Annuel.
a.

**Universite du Quebec a Chicoutimi. Department des
Sciences Humaines**
930 rue Jacques-Cartier E., Chicoutimi, Que.,
Canada.
- Protee. s-a. ISSN 0300-3523

**Universite du Quebec a Montreal**
Pavillon Emile-Gerard, B.P. 8888, Montreal, P.Q.
H3C 3P8, Canada.
- Sarracenia. irreg., no. 15, 1972. ISSN 0080-6463

**Universite du Quebec a Trois-Rivieres. Centre de
Recherches en Histoire des Religions et de la
Pensee**
C.P. 500, Trois-Rivieres, Que., Canada.
- Cahiers d'Archeologie Quebecoise. ISSN 0007-
9707

**Universite Laval**
- Cahiers de Droit. (pub. by Presses de l'Universite
Laval)

**Universite Laval. Association des Etudiants en
Sciences**
Pavillon Vachon, Cite Universitaire, Que., Canada.
- Eprouvette. s-m. ISSN 0046-2373

**Universite Laval. Cartotheque, Bibliotheque Generale**
Quebec G1K 7P4, Canada.
- Cartologica. bi-m. ISSN 0045-5881

**Universite Laval. Centre d'Etudes Nordiques**
Quebec C1K 7P4, Canada.
- Nordicana. irreg. (approx. 3-5 nos. per year) ISSN
0078-1053

**Universite Laval. Centre de Recherches sur les
Atomes et les Molecules**
Quebec, Que. G1K 7P4, Canada.
- Universite Laval. Centre de Recherches sur les
Atomes et les Molecules. Rapport Annuel;
physics and chemistry of atoms and molecules. a.

**Universite Laval. Department de l'Anthropologie**
Quebec 10, Canada
- Yearbook of Symbolic Anthropology. a. (Subscr.
to: C. Hurst & Co., Seager Bldg., Brookmill Road,
London S.E. 8, England)

**Universite Laval. Department de Linguistique**
- Cahiers de Psychomecanique de Langage. (pub. by
Presses de l'Universite Laval)

**Universite Laval. Department de Sociologie**
- Recherches Sociographiques. (pub. by Presses de
l'Universite Laval)

**Universite Laval. Faculte de Foresterie**
Quebec, Que, Canada.
- Universite Laval. Departement d'Exploitation et
Utilisation des Bois. Note de Recherches. irreg.
ISSN 0079-8355
- Universite Laval. Departement d'Exploitation et
Utilisation des Bois. Note Technique. irreg. ISSN
0079-8363

**Universite Laval. Faculte de Medecine**
Suite 0447, Cite Universitaire, Quebec, Que. G1K
7P4, Canada.
- Vie Medicale au Canada Francais; Canadian
journal of continuing medical education. m. ISSN
0301-1534 (Vie Medicale Inc.)

**Universite Laval. Faculte des Sciences de
l'Administration**
Cite Universitaire, Ste-Foy, Que. 10, Canada.
- Laval Administration. q. ISSN 0023-9038

**Universite Laval. Fonds de Recherches Forestieres**
Cite Universitaire, Quebec 10, P.Q., Canada.
- Universite Laval. Fonds de Recherches
Forestieres. Bulletin. 2-3 per yr. ISSN 0041-9214
- Universite Laval. Fonds de Recherches
Forestieres. Contribution. irreg. ISSN 0079-838X

**Universite Laval. Public Relations Department**
Quebec, P.Q. G1K 7P4, Canada.
- Bulletin du Comite de Terminologie. 4-5 per yr.

**Universities Art Association of Canada**
- Universities Art Association of Canada. Journal/
Association d'Art des Universites du Canada.
Journal. (pub. by Nova Scotia College of Art &
Design)

**University and College Placement Association**
Box 356, Markham, Ont. L3P 3J8, Canada.
- Who's Who in Canadian Placement. a. ISSN
0083-9469

**University of Alberta**
Edmonton, Alta. T6G 2H4, Canada.
- Canadian Journal of Philosophy. q. ISSN 0045-
5091 (Canadian Association for Publishing in
Philosophy)
- New Trail. 3 per yr. ISSN 0028-6907

**University of Alberta. Department of Agricultural
Economics and Rural Sociology**
Edmonton, Alta., Canada.
- University of Alberta. Department of Agricultural
Economics and Rural Sociology. Bulletin. irreg.

**University of Alberta. Department of Animal Science**
326 Assiniboia Hall, Edmonton, Alta. T6G 2E1,
Canada.
- University of Alberta. Department of Animal
Science. Annual Feeders' Day Report. a. ISSN
0084-618X

**University of Alberta. Department of Anthropology**
Edmonton, Alta T6G 2H4, Canada.
- Western Canadian Journal of Anthropology. 4 per
yr. ISSN 0008-5340

**University of Alberta. Department of Chemistry**
Edmonton, Alta T6G 2G2, Canada.
- University of Alberta. Department of Chemistry.
Division of Theoretical Chemistry. Technical
Report. irreg. (5-10 per yr.) ISSN 0041-9370

**University of Alberta. Department of Computing
Science**
Edmonton 7, Alberta, Canada.
- University of Alberta. Department of Computing
Science. Technical Reports. irreg. ISSN 0316-
4683

**University of Alberta. Department of Educational
Administration**
Edmonton, Alta. T6G 2G5, Canada.
- Canadian Administrator. m.(Oct-May) ISSN
0008-2813
- University of Alberta. Department of Educational
Administration. College Administration Project
Colleges. Occasional Paper. irreg. ISSN 0318-
8582

**University of Alberta. Department of Educational
Foundations**
5-109, Education N, Edmonton, Alta. T6G 2G5,
Canada.
- Indian-Ed. q. ISSN 0318-8647

**University of Alberta. Department of Educational
Psychology**
Edmonton, Alta. T6G 2G5, Canada.
- Education for the Disadvantaged Child. q.

**University of Alberta. Department of Elementary
Education**
Edmonton, Alta. T6G 2G5, Canada.
- Elements; translating theory into practice. m.
ISSN 0046-1792

**University of Alberta. Department of English**
Edmonton, Alta. T6G 2E5, Canada.
- Nineteenth Century Theatre Research. s-a. ISSN
0316-5329

**University of Alberta. Department of Entomology**
Edmonton, Alta. T6G 2E3, Canada.
- Entomological Society of Alberta. Proceedings. a.
ISSN 0071-0709
- Quaestiones Entomologicae; a periodical record of
entomological investigation. 4 per yr. ISSN 0033-
5037

**University of Alberta. Department of Geography**
Edmonton, Alta. T6G 2H4, Canada.
- Albertan Geographer. a. ISSN 0065-6097
- University of Alberta. Studies in Geography.
Bibliographies. irreg.
- University of Alberta. Studies in Geography.
Monographs. irreg.
- University of Alberta. Studies in Geography.
Occasional Papers. irreg.

**University of Alberta. Department of Romance Languages**
Edmonton, Alberta T6G 2E1, Canada.
- Canadian Journal of Research in Semiotics/ Journal Canadien de Recherche Semiotique. 3 per yr. ISSN 0316-7917 (Canadian Semiotics Research Association)

**University of Alberta. Department of Sociology**
Tory Building, University of Alberta, Edmonton, Alberta, Canada.
- University of Alberta. Department of Sociology. Population Research Laboratory. Alberta Series Report. irreg. ISSN 0317-3119 (prep. by its Population Research Laboratory)

**University of Alberta. Faculty of Agriculture**
Edmonton, Alta. T6G 2G4, Canada.
- University of Alberta. Agriculture and Forestry Bulletin. q.

**University of Alberta. Faculty of Business Administration and Commerce**
Edmonton 7, Alberta, Canada.
- University of Alberta. Faculty of Business Administration and Commerce. Research Studies in Business. irreg. ISSN 0065-6070

**University of Alberta. Faculty of Education**
Edmonton, Alta. T6G 2G5, Canada.
- Alberta Journal of Educational Research. q. ISSN 0002-4805

**University of Alberta. Faculty of Law**
Edmonton 7, Alta., Canada.
- Alberta Law Review. 3 per yr. ISSN 0002-4821

**University of Alberta Library. Special Collections Division**
Edmonton, Alta. TG6 2J8, Canada.
- News from the Rare Book Room. irreg., no. 15, 1975. ISSN 0085-4166

**University of Alberta. Students Union**
Students' Union Bldg., Edmonton, Alta., Canada.
- Gateway. 2 per wk. ISSN 0016-5190

**University of British Columbia**
2075 Wesbrook Pl., Vancouver, B.C. V6T 1W5, Canada.
- B. C. Studies. q. ISSN 0005-2949
- Canadian Congress of Applied Mechanics. Proceedings. biennial, 6th, 1977.
- Canadian Literature/Litterature Canadienne; a quarterly of criticism and review. q. ISSN 0008-4360
- Pacific Affairs; an international review of Asia and the Pacific. q. ISSN 0030-851X

**University of British Columbia. Alumni Association**
Cecil Green Park, 6251 Cecil Green Park Rd., Vancouver, B.C. V6T 1X8, Canada.
- U B C Alumni Chronicle. q. ISSN 0041-4999

**University of British Columbia. Animal Resource Ecology Library**
2075 Wesbrook Place, Vancouver, B.C. V6T 1W5, Canada.
- H. R. MacMillan Lectures in Fisheries. irreg. ISSN 0072-9132

**University of British Columbia. Botanical Garden**
Vancouver, B.C. V6T 1W5, Canada.
- Davidsonia. q. ISSN 0045-9739

**University of British Columbia. Center for Continuing Education**
Vancouver 8, B.C., Canada.
- University of British Columbia. Center for Continuing Education. Occasional Papers in Continuing Education. irreg. ISSN 0068-1695

**Univ. of British Columbia. Creative Writing Department**
2075 Westbrook Pl., Vancouver 8, B.C., Canada.
- Prism International; a journal of contemporary writing. 2 per yr. ISSN 0032-8790

**University of British Columbia. Department of Civil Engineering**
Vancouver 8, B.C., Canada.
- First Canadian Conference on Earthquake Engineering. Proceedings. quadrennial.
- University of British Columbia. Department of Civil Engineering. Report. Soil Mechanics Series irreg. ISSN 0068-1709

**University of British Columbia. Department of Economics**
2075 Wesbrook Place, Vancouver, B.C. V6T 1W5, Canada.
- University of British Columbia. Department of Economics. Resources Paper. irreg. ISSN 0381-0410

**University of British Columbia. Department of Geological Sciences**
Vancouver, B. C. V6T 1W5, Canada.
- University of British Columbia. Department of Geological Sciences. Report. irreg., no. 15, 1975.

**University of British Columbia. Department of Geophysics and Astronomy**
Vancouver, B.C. V6T 1W5, Canada.
- University of British Columbia. Department of Geophysics and Astronomy. Annual Report. a. ISSN 0068-1725
- University of British Columbia. Department of Geophysics and Astronomy. Publications. a. ISSN 0068-1431

**University of British Columbia. Department of Psychiatry**
Vancouver 8, B.C., Canada.
- T V in Psychiatry Newsletter. irreg. ISSN 0082-139X

**University of British Columbia. Electrical Engineering Department**
Vancouver, B.C. V6T 1W5, Canada.
- Electrical Engineering Research Abstracts. Canadian Universities. a. ISSN 0070-9662

**University of British Columbia. Faculty of Commerce and Business Administration**
Vancouver, B.C. V6T 1W5, Canada.
- Journal of Business Administration. s-a. ISSN 0021-941X
- Logistics and Transportation Review. q. ISSN 0047-4991

**University of British Columbia. Faculty of Forestry**
Vancouver, B.C. V6t 1w5, Canada.
- H. R. Macmillan Lectureship in Forestry. irreg. ISSN 0072-9140
- University of British Columbia. Faculty of Forestry. Bulletin. irreg. ISSN 0068-1776
- University of British Columbia. Faculty of Forestry. Research Notes. irreg. ISSN 0068-1784
- University of British Columbia. Faculty of Forestry. Research Papers. irreg. ISSN 0068-1792
- University of British Columbia. Faculty of Forestry. Translations. irreg. ISSN 0068-1806
- University of British Columbia. Research Forest Annual Report. a. ISSN 0084-8069

**University of British Columbia. Faculty of Law**
Vancouver, B.C. V6T 1W5, Canada.
- University of British Columbia Law Review. s-a. ISSN 0068-1849

**University of British Columbia. Library**
2075 Westbrook Mall, Vancouver, B.C. V6T 1W5, Canada.
- University of British Columbia Library. Reference Publication. irreg. ISSN 0068-1857

**University of British Columbia Library. Asian Studies Division**
Vancouver, B. C. V6T 1W5, Canada.
- University of British Columbia Library. Asian Studies Division. List of Catalogued Books. 3 per yr. ISSN 0041-9427
- University of British Columbia Library. Asian Studies Division. List of Catalogued Books. Supplement. irreg., 1972, no. 4. ISSN 0068-1687

**University of British Columbia Press**
2075 Wesbrook Place, Vancouver, B.C. V6T 1W5, Canada.
- British Columbia Institute for Economic Policy Analysis Series. irreg.
- Canadian Yearbook of International Law/ Annuaire Canadien de Droit International. a. ISSN 0069-0058

**University of British Columbia. School of Community and Regional Planning**
Vancouver 8, B.C., Canada.
- University of British Columbia. School of Community and Regional Planning. Regional Planning Report. irreg., no. 12, 1975. ISSN 0084-8042

**University of British Columbia. Westwater Research Centre**
Vancouver, B.C. V6T 1W5, Canada.
- Westwater; notes on water research in western Canada. q. ISSN 0315-3010

**University of Calgary**
Rm 219 Social Sciences 1 Bldg., 2920 24th Ave. N.W., Calgary, Alta T2N 1N4, Canada.
- University of Calgary Gazette. bi-w. Sept. to Apr.; m. May-August. ISSN 0300-4333

**University of Calgary. Archaeological Association**
Department of Archaeology, Calgary, Alta. T2N 1N4, Canada.
- University of Alberta. Archaeological Association. Paleo-Environmental Workshop. Proceedings. a. ISSN 0068-5437

**University of Calgary. Computer Services**
2920 - 24th Ave N. W., Calgary, Alberta, Canada.
- Big Byte. m. ISSN 0045-1991

**University of Calgary. Department of Archaeology**
Calgary, Alta, Canada.
- Calgary Archaeologist. a.

**University of Calgary. Department of Civil Engineering**
Calgary T2N 1N4, Alta, Canada.
- University of Calgary. Department of Civil Engineering Research Report. irreg (25 per yr)

**University of Calgary. Department of English**
D630 Calgary Hall, Calgary, Alberta, Canada.
- Ariel; a review of international English literature. q. ISSN 0004-1327

**University of Calgary. Department of History**
2920 24th Ave., Calgary, Alta. T2N 1N4, Canada.
- University of Calgary Studies in History. irreg.

**University of Calgary. Department of Mathematics and Computing Science**
Calgary, Alta, Canada.
- University of Calgary. Department of Mathematics and Computing Science. Research Papers. irreg. ISSN 0575-206X
- University of Calgary. Department of Mathematics, Statistics and Computing Sciences. Research Report. irreg., 1970, no. 104. ISSN 0068-5445

**University of Calgary. Department of Sociology**
2920 24th Ave. N.W., Calgary, Alta. T2N 1N4, Canada.
- Journal of Comparative Family Studies. 3 per yr. ISSN 0047-2328

**University of Calgary. Faculty of Education**
Rm. 514, Education Tower, Calgary Alberta T2N 1N4, Canada.
- Journal of Educational Thought. 3 per yr. ISSN 0022-0701

**University of Guelph. Center for Resources Development**
Guelph, Ont. N1G 2W1, Canada.
- University of Guelph. Center for Resources Development. Annual Report. a.

**University of Guelph. Department of Geography**
Guelph, Ont., Canada
(Sole Distributor: Geo Abstracts Ltd., University of East Anglia, Norwich N0R 88C, England)
- Guelph. University. Department of Geography. Geographical Publication. irreg.

**University of Guelph. Department of Land Resource Science**
Guelph, Ontario, Canada.
- University of Guelph. Department of Land Resource Science. Progress Report. a. ISSN 0085-1329

**University of Guelph. Interdepartmental Committee on Scottish Studies**
Guelph, Ont., Canada.
- Colloquium on Scottish Studies. Proceedings. a. ISSN 0069-5823

**University of Manitoba**
- Algebra Universalis. (pub. by Birkhaeuser Verlag SZ)

**University of Manitoba. Alumni Association**
139 University Center, Winnipeg, Man., Canada.
- University of Manitoba Alumni Journal. q. ISSN 0041-980X

**University of Manitoba. Center for Transportation Studies**
Rm. 513, University Centre, Winnipeg, Manitoba R3T 2N2, Canada.
- University of Manitoba. Center for Transportation Studies. Annual Report. a.
- University of Manitoba. Center for Transportation Studies. Occasional Paper. irreg. ISSN 0076-3977
- University of Manitoba. Center for Transportation Studies. Research Report. irreg. ISSN 0076-3985
- University of Manitoba. Center for Transportation Studies. Seminar Series on Transportation. Proceedings. a. ISSN 0076-3993

**University of Manitoba. Department of Agricultural Economics and Farm Management**
Winnipeg, Manitoba R3T 2N2, Canada.
- University of Manitoba. Department of Agricultural Economics and Farm Management. Occasional Papers. irreg. ISSN 0076-4000

**University of Manitoba. Department of Anthropology**
Winnipeg, Manitoba R3T 2N2, Canada.
- University of Manitoba Anthropology Papers.

**University of Manitoba. Department of Geography**
Winnipeg, Manitoba, Canada.
- Manitoba Geographical Studies. 2-3 per yr.

**University of Manitoba. Department of Slavic Studies**
Winnipeg, Man. R3T 2N2, Canada.
- University of Manitoba. Department of Slavic Studies. Readings in Slavic Literature. irreg. ISSN 0076-4035

**University of Manitoba. Faculty of Agriculture**
Winnipeg, Man., Canada.
- University of Manitoba. Faculty of Agriculture. Progress Report on Agricultural Research and Experimentation. a. ISSN 0076-4051

**University of Manitoba. Faculty of Arts**
Winnipeg, Man. R3T 2N2, Canada.
- Linguistic Circle of Manitoba and North Dakota. Proceedings. approx. a. ISSN 0075-9597

**University of Manitoba. Faculty of Education**
Winnipeg, Man., Canada.
- Manitoba Educational Research Council. Newsletter. q. ISSN 0383-6096

**University of Manitoba. Faculty of Law**
Winnipeg, Man. R2M 1C3, Canada.
- Manitoba Law Journal. q. ISSN 0076-3861

**University of Manitoba Press**
Box 35, Winnipeg, Man. R3T 2N2, Canada.
- International Conference on Atomic Masses. Proceedings. irreg., 1967, 3rd, Winnipeg, Canada. ISSN 0074-3003 (International Union of Pure and Applied Physics)
- International Economic History Association. Congress Proceedings. every 4 years.
- Mosaic; a journal for the comparative study of literature and ideas. q. ISSN 0027-1276
- Northern Light. s-a.

**University of Manitoba. Students' Architectural Society**
Faculty of Architecture, Winnipeg, Man. 53T 2N2, Canada.
- Perspective. irreg. ISSN 0079-0966

**University of Manitoba. Students' Union**
UMSU Bldg., Winnipeg, Man. R3T 2N2, Canada.
- Manitoban. 2 per wk. ISSN 0025-2298

**University of New Brunswick**
c/o the Observatory, Fredericton, N.B. E3B 5A3, Canada.
- Fiddlehead. q. ISSN 0015-0630 (Co-Sponsors: Canada Council; University of New Brunswick; Provincial Government; Saint Thomas University)

**University of New Brunswick. Department of English**
Fredericton, N.B., Canada.
- Studies in Canadian Literature. s-a.

**University of New Brunswick. Department of History**
Fredericton, N.B., Canada.
- Acadiensis: Journal of the History of the Atlantic Region. s-a. ISSN 0044-5851

**University of New Brunswick. Faculty of Forestry**
Box 440, Fredericton, N. B.E3B SA3, Canada.
- Megadrilogica. irreg. ISSN 0380-9633

**University of New Brunswick. Faculty of Law**
Ludlow Hall, Fredericton, N.B., Canada
- University of New Brunswick. Law Journal. a. ISSN 0077-8141 (Subscr. to: Carswell Co. Ltd., 2330 Midland Ave., Agincourt Ont., Canada)

**University of New Brunswick. Student Union**
Fredericton, N.B., Canada.
- Brunswickan. w. ISSN 0007-2699

**University of New Brunswick. Students Representative Council**
Tucker Park, Saint John, N.B., Canada.
- Equinox. bi-w. ISSN 0046-2381

**University of Ottawa**
- Social Science Studies. (pub. by University of Ottawa Press)

**University of Ottawa. Centre de Recherches de Litterature Canadienne-Francaise**
- Archives des Lettres Canadiennes. (pub. by Editions Fides)

**University of Ottawa. Department of English**
Faculty of Arts, Ottowa 2, Ont., Canada.
- Inscape. 3 per yr. ISSN 0020-1782

**University of Ottawa. Department of Geography and Regional Planning**
Ottawa, Ont. K1N 6N5, Canada.
- Geoscope. s-a. ISSN 0046-581X
- University of Ottawa. Department of Geography and Regional Planning. Notes de Recherches/ Research Notes. irreg.

**University of Ottawa. Department of History**
Ottawa, Ont. K1G 6N5, Canada.
- Canadian Ethnic Studies Association Bulletin/ Societe Canadienne d'Etudes Ethniques. Bulletin. q. ISSN 0315-8705

**University of Ottawa. Department of Slavic Studies**
Ottawa 2, Canada.
- Etudes Slaves. irreg. ISSN 0071-2183

**University of Ottawa. Faculty of Law**
Common Law Section, Ottawa, Ont. K1N 5N5, Canada.
- Monographies Juridiques. (pub. by University of Ottawa Press)
- Ottawa Law Review. 3 per yr. ISSN 0048-2331
- Revue Generale de Droit. s-a. ISSN 0035-3086

**University of Ottawa. General Library**
65 Hastey, Ottawa, Ont. K1N 6N5, Canada.
- University of Ottawa. Library. Annual Report. a. ISSN 0078-7027

**University of Ottawa Press**
65 Hastey Ave., Ottawa, Ont. K1N 6N5, Canada.
- Cahiers Canadiens Claudel. irreg. ISSN 0068-4961
- Cahiers de Sciences Sociales. a. ISSN 0068-5097
- Centre de Recherche en Civilisation Canadienne-Francaise. Bulletin. s-a. ISSN 0045-608X
- Co-Incidences; revue litteraire. 3 per yr. ISSN 0019-3402
- Collection Philosophica. irreg.
- Collection Presence. irreg.
- French-Canadian Civilization Research Center. Cahiers/Centre de Recherche en Civilisation Canadienne-Francaise. Cahiers. irreg. ISSN 0069-1771
- Histoire Sociale. 2 per yr. ISSN 0018-2257
- International Symposia on Comparative Law. Proceedings/Colloques Internationaux de Droit Compare. Travaux. irreg. ISSN 0074-8722
- Journal of Psychiatry of the University of Ottawa. q.
- Monographies Juridiques. irreg. ISSN 0077-0728 (University of Ottawa. Faculty of Law)
- Social Science Studies. irreg. ISSN 0081-0460 (University of Ottawa)
- Universite d'Ottawa. Revue. q. ISSN 0041-9206
- University of Ottawa. Department of Geography. Occasional Papers. irreg.

**University of Ottawa Students' Federation**
85 Hastey Ave., Rm. 07, Ottawa, Ont. K1N 5N6, Canada.
- Fulcrum/Rotonde. w. ISSN 0016-2604

**University of Regina**
Regina Campus, Regina, Sask., Canada.
- Wascana Review. s-a. ISSN 0043-0412

**University of Regina. Department of English**
Regina, Saskatchewan S4s 0a2, Canada.
- Sphinx; a magazine of literature and society. s-a.

**University of Regina. Students' Union**
Regina Campus, Regina, Sask., Canada.
- Carillon. w. ISSN 0008-6576

**University of Saskatchewan**
Saskatoon, Sask. S7N 0W0, Canada.
- Canadian Journal of History/Annales Canadiennes d'Histoire. 3 per yr. ISSN 0008-4107
- Saskatchewan University. University News. 6 per yr. ISSN 0042-0026

**University of Saskatchewan. Alumni Association**
Saskatoon, Saskatchewan S7N 0W0, Canada.
- Green and White. q. ISSN 0017-3924

**University of Saskatchewan. College of Law**
Saskatoon, Sask, Canada.
- Saskatchewan Law Review. s-a. ISSN 0036-4916

**University of Saskatchewan. Department of Anthropology and Archaeology**
Senior Anthropology Students, Saskatoon, Sask., Canada.
- Napao: A Saskatchewan Anthropology Journal. irreg. ISSN 0077-2755

**University of Saskatchewan. Extension Division**
Saskatoon, Sask., Canada.
- Agricultural Science. irreg. ISSN 0381-5927

**University of Saskatchewan. Institute for Northern Studies**
Saskatoon, Sask. S7N 0W0, Canada.
- Musk-Ox; a journal on the North. 2 per yr. ISSN 0077-2542
- News from the Canadian North. m.
- Saskatchewan. University. Institute for Northern Studies. Northern Research Conference. Proceedings. irreg. ISSN 0080-6641
- University of Saskatchewan. Institute for Northern Studies. Annual Report. a. ISSN 0080-665X

**University of Toronto. Centre for Medieval Studies**
- Toronto Medieval Bibliographics. (pub. by University of Toronto Press)

**University of Toronto. Centre of Criminology**
- Canadian Studies in Criminology. (pub. by University of Toronto Press)

**University of Toronto. Commerce Club**
Toronto, Ont., Canada.
- Commerce Journal. a. ISSN 0383-9737

**University of Toronto. Department of Computer Science**
Toronto, Ont. M5S 1A7, Canada.
- Computernews. m. ISSN 0315-4661
- University of Toronto. Department of Computer Science. Technical Reports. 12 per yr (approx) ISSN 0042-0204

**University of Toronto. Department of Electrical Engineering**
Toronto, Ont., Canada.
- University of Toronto. Department of Electrical Engineering. Research Report. irreg. ISSN 0082-514X

**University of Toronto. Department of Geography**
Toronto, Ont. M5S 1A1, Canada.
- University of Toronto. Department of Geography. Discussion Paper Series. irreg.
- University of Toronto. Department of Geography. Research Publications. (pub. by University of Toronto Press)

**University of Toronto. Department of Information Services**
45 Willcocks St., Toronto M5S 1A1, Ont., Canada.
- University of Toronto Graduate. q. ISSN 0042-0212

**University of Toronto. Department of Mathematics**
Toronto, Ont., Canada.
- World Directory of Historians of Mathematics. irreg. ISSN 0315-1700

**University of Toronto. Department of Mechanical Engineering**
Toronto, Ont., Canada.
- University of Toronto. Department of Mechanical Engineering. Technical Publication Series. irreg. ISSN 0082-5182

**University of Toronto. Department of Romance Languages**
- University of Toronto Romance Series. (pub. by University of Toronto Press)

**University of Toronto. Department of Urban & Regional Planning**
Toronto, Ont. M5S 1A1, Canada.
- University of Toronto. Department of Urban & Regional Planning. Papers on Planning & Design. irreg.

**University of Toronto. Engineering Society**
2Nd Floor Engineering Annex, 2Nd Floor Engineering Annex, 10 King's College Rd., Toronto, Ont. M5S 1A4, Canada.
- Toike Oike. 9 per yr. ISSN 0049-4038

**University of Toronto. Erindale College**
Mississauga, Ont. L5L 1C6, Canada.
- Renaissance and Reformation/Renaissance et Reforme. s-a. ISSN 0034-429X

**University of Toronto. Faculty of Education**
Guidance Centre, Suite 304, Toronto, Ont. M4W 2K8, Canada.
- Comment on Education. 4 per yr. ISSN 0315-4351
- Teacher Education. a. ISSN 0082-2205

**University of Toronto. Faculty of Forestry**
Toronto, Ont., Canada.
- University of Toronto. Faculty of Forestry. Technical Reports. irreg. ISSN 0082-5190

**University of Toronto. Faculty of Law**
Toronto, Ont. M5S 1A1, Canada.
- Advocate. irreg. ISSN 0382-456X

**University of Toronto. Faculty of Management Studies**
246 Bloor St. W., Toronto, Ont. M5S 1V4, Canada.
- University of Toronto. Faculty of Management Studies. Working Paper Series. irreg.

**University of Toronto. Graduate Centre for Study of Drama**
- Modern Drama. (pub. by A. M. Hakkert Ltd.)

**University of Toronto. Great Lakes Institute**
Toronto 5, Ont., Canada.
- University of Toronto. Institute of Environmental Sciences and Engineering. Great Lakes Division. Report. irreg. ISSN 0082-5220

**University of Toronto. Guidance Centre**
1000 Yonge St., Toronto, Ont. M4W 2K8, Canada.
- School Guidance Worker. bi-m. ISSN 0048-9409

**University of Toronto. Institute for Aerospace Studies**
4925 Dufferin St., Downsview, Ont. M3H 5T6, Canada.
- University of Toronto. Institute for Aerospace Studies. Progress Report. irreg. ISSN 0082-5239
- University of Toronto. Institute for Aerospace Studies. Report. irreg. ISSN 0082-5255
- University of Toronto. Institute for Aerospace Studies. Review. irreg. ISSN 0082-5247
- University of Toronto. Institute for Aerospace Studies. Technical Note. irreg. ISSN 0082-5263

**University of Toronto. Institute for Policy Analysis**
150 St. George St., Toronto, Ont. M5S 1A1, Canada.
- University of Toronto. Institute for Policy Analysis. Annual Report. irreg.
- University of Toronto. Institute for Policy Analysis. Policy Paper Series. irreg.
- University of Toronto. Institute for Policy Analysis. Reprint Series. irreg.
- University of Toronto. Institute for Policy Analysis. Working Paper Series. irreg.

**University of Toronto. Library**
Toronto, Ont., Canada.
- University of Toronto. Library. Annual Report. a. ISSN 0082-531X

**University of Toronto. Medical Society**
Medical Sciences Bldg., Toronto, Ont. M5W 1A1, Canada.
- University of Toronto Medical Journal. 5 per yr. ISSN 0042-0239

**University of Toronto Press**
Front Campus, Toronto, Ont. M5S 1A6, Canada (U.S. Address: 33 East Tupper St., Buffalo, NY 14203)
- Alexander Lectures. irreg. ISSN 0065-616X
- Atlantic Provinces Studies. irreg. ISSN 0067-0200 (Social Science Research Council of Canada)
- Atmosphere. q. ISSN 0004-6973 (Canadian Meteorological Society)
- Brookside Monographs. irreg. ISSN 0068-2853 (Addiction Research Foundation of Ontario)
- Canada in the Atlantic Economy. irreg. ISSN 0068-7677
- Canadian Annual Review of Politics and Public Affairs. a. ISSN 0315-1433
- Canadian Biographical Studies/Etudes Biographiques Canadiennes. irreg. ISSN 0045-4486
- Canadian Books in Print. a. ISSN 0068-8398 (Canadian Book Publishers' Council) (Co-sponsors: Canadian Booksellers' Assn.; Canadian Library Assn)
- Canadian Building Series. irreg., 1970, no. 4. ISSN 0068-841X (National Research Council of Canada. Division of Building Research)
- Canadian Essay and Literature Index. a.
- Canadian Geographer/Geographe Canadien. q. ISSN 0008-3658 (Canadian Association of Geographers)
- Canadian Government Series. irreg. ISSN 0068-8835
- Canadian Historical Review. q. ISSN 0008-3755
- Canadian Journal of Economics/Revue Canadienne d'Economique. q. ISSN 0008-4085 (Canadian Economics Association)
- Canadian Journal of Mathematics/Journal Canadien de Mathematiques. bi-m. ISSN 0008-414X (Canadian Mathematical Congress)
- Canadian Journal of Psychology/Revue Canadienne de Psychologie. q. ISSN 0008-4255 (Canadian Psychological Association)
- Canadian Local Histories to 1950. A Bibliography. Histoires Locales et Regionales Canadiennes des Origines A 1950. irreg. ISSN 0068-9165 (Centennial Commission)
- Canadian Play Series. irreg.
- Canadian Public Policy/Analyse de Politiques. q.
- Canadian Review of Comparative Literature/Revue Canadienne de Litterature Comparee. 3 per yr. (Canadian Comparative Literature Association)
- Canadian Serials Directory/Repertoire des Publications Seriees Canadiennes. a.
- Canadian Studies in Criminology. irreg. ISSN 0068-9777 (University of Toronto. Centre of Criminology)
- Canadian Studies in History and Government. irreg. ISSN 0068-9793 (Social Science Research Council of Canada)
- Clarence M. Hincks Memorial Lectures. a.
- Clarke Institute of Psychiatry. Monograph Series. irreg. ISSN 0069-441X
- Collected Works of Erasmus. irreg. (approx. 2 per yr.)
- Creative Canada. irreg. ISSN 0315-3290 (University of Victoria. McPherson Library)
- Dictionary of Canadian Biography. irreg. ISSN 0070-4717
- Directory of Associations in Canada. a. ISSN 0316-0734
- English Studies in Canada. q. (Association of Canadian University Teachers of English)
- Erasmus in English. irreg.(approx. a) ISSN 0071-1063
- Mathematical Expositions. irreg. ISSN 0076-5333
- Near and Middle East Series. irreg. ISSN 0077-6300
- Ontario Series. irreg. ISSN 0078-5091 (Champlain Society)
- Phoenix. q. ISSN 0031-8299 (Classical Association of Canada) (Order from the Association, Dept. of Classics, University College, Univ. of Toronto, Toronto, Ont. M5S 1A1)
- Phoenix. Supplementary Volumes. irreg. ISSN 0079-1784
- Political Economy Series. irreg. ISSN 0381-1603
- Resolutions and Decisions of the Communist Party of the Soviet Union. irreg.
- Scholarly Publishing. q. ISSN 0036-634X
- Science Forum; a Canadian journal of science and technology/revue Canadienne des sciences pures et appliquees. bi-m. ISSN 0036-8393

- Seminar; a journal of Germanic studies. 3 per yr. ISSN 0037-1939 (Canadian Association of University Teachers of German) (Co-Sponsor: Australasian Universities Language and Literature Association, Germanic Section)
- Social History of Canada. irreg. ISSN 0085-6207
- Studies in Higher Education in Canada. irreg. ISSN 0081-7988 (National Conference of Canadian Universities and Colleges Committee)
- Studies in Irish History. irreg. ISSN 0081-8097
- Studies in Social History. irreg. ISSN 0081-850X
- Studies in the Structure of Power: Decision Making in Canada. irreg. ISSN 0081-8690 (Social Science Research Council of Canada)
- Subject Guide to Canadian Books in Print. a.
- Toronto Medieval Bibliographies. irreg. ISSN 0082-5042 (University of Toronto. Centre for Medieval Studies)
- Toronto Semitic Texts and Studies. irreg. ISSN 0082-5123
- University of Toronto. Department of Geography. Research Publications. irreg., 1970, no. 5. ISSN 0082-5174
- University of Toronto Law Journal. q. ISSN 0042-0220
- University of Toronto Quarterly; a Canadian journal of the humanities. q. ISSN 0042-0247
- University of Toronto Romance Series. irreg. ISSN 0082-5336

**University of Toronto. Students Administrative Council**
91 St. George St., Toronto, Ont., Canada.
- Varsity. 63 per yr. ISSN 0042-2789

**University of Toronto. Victoria College**
Dept. of English, Toronto M5S 1K7, Canada.
- Mill News Letter. s-a. ISSN 0026-4253

**University of Toronto-York University Joint Program in Transportation**
c/o Centre for Urban & Community Studies, 150 St. George St., University of Toronto, Toronto, Ont. M5S 1A1, Canada.
- University of Toronto-York University. Joint Program in Transportation. Annual Report. a.
- University of Toronto-York University Joint Program in Transportation. Newsletter. 4-5 per yr.

**University of Victoria**
Box 1700, Victoria, B.C. V8W 2Y2, Canada.
- Malahat Review. q. ISSN 0025-1216

**University of Victoria. Alma Mater Society**
Box 1700, Victoria, B.C., Canada.
- Martlet. w. (Sept.-April)

**University of Victoria. Department of Geography**
Victoria, B.C. V8W 2Y2, Canada.
- Western Geographical Series. irreg. (approx. 2-4 per yr.) ISSN 0315-2022

**University of Victoria. McPherson Library**
- Creative Canada. (pub. by University of Toronto Press)

**University of Waterloo**
Waterloo, Ont. N2L 3Gl, Canada.
- International Newsletter on Migration. irreg. ISSN 0383-2767

**University of Waterloo. Department of Biology**
Waterloo, Ont. N2L 3Gl, Canada.
- University of Waterloo Biology Series. irreg. ISSN 0317-3348

**University of Waterloo. Department of Chemistry**
Waterloo, Ont. N2L 3Gl, Canada.
- Chem Thirteen News. 9 per yr.

**University of Waterloo. Department of English**
Waterloo, Ont. N2L 3Gl, Canada.
- Canadian Drama/Art Dramatique Canadien. s-a. ISSN 0317-9044

**University of Waterloo. Department of Germanic and Slavic Languages and Literature**
Waterloo, Ont. N2L 3Gl, Canada.
- Germano-Slavica. s-a.

**University of Waterloo. Department of History**
Waterloo, Ontario N2L 36F, Canada.
- Historical Reflections/Reflexions Historiques. s-a. ISSN 0315-7997

**University of Waterloo. Department of Physics**
Waterloo, Ont. N2L 3G1, Canada.
- Phys 13 News. 5 per yr.

**University of Waterloo. Department of Political Science**
Waterloo, Ont., Canada.
- Past & Present. irreg.

**University of Waterloo. Faculty of Environmental Studies**
Waterloo, Ont., Canada.
- Contact in Urban and Regional Affairs. q. ISSN 0045-8309

**University of Waterloo. Faculty of Mathematics**
- Aequationes Mathematicae. (pub. by Birkhaeuser Verlag SZ)

**University of Waterloo. Information Services Department**
Waterloo, Ont. N2L 3G1, Canada.
- University of Waterloo. Gazette. w. ISSN 0042-031X

**University of Waterloo. Solid Mechanics Division**
Waterloo, Ont. N2L 3G1, Canada.
- University of Waterloo. Solid Mechanics Division. Technical Notes. irreg.

**University of Waterloo. Undergraduate Engineering Society "B"**
Waterloo, Ont., Canada.
- Focus (Waterloo) irreg. ISSN 0430-8247

**University of Western Ontario**
London, Ontario, Canada.
- Ontario Geography. irreg. ISSN 0078-4850
- University of Western Ontario. Center for Radio Science. Annual Report. a. ISSN 0076-0587
- University of Western Ontario Series in Philosophy of Science. (pub. by D. Reidel Publishing Co. NE)

**University of Western Ontario. D. B. Weldon Library**
London, Ont., Canada.
- University of Western Ontario. D. B. Weldon Library. Library Bulletin. irreg., no. 8, 1970. ISSN 0076-0595

**University of Western Ontario. Department of Alumni Affairs**
London, Ont. N6A 5B9, Canada.
- University of Western Ontario. Alumni Gazette. 4 per yr. ISSN 0042-0344

**University of Western Ontario. Faculty of Education**
- History and Social Science Teacher. (pub. by History and Social Science Teacher Inc.)

**University of Western Ontario. Faculty of Law**
London, Ont., Canada.
- Western Ontario Law Review. a. ISSN 0083-8950

**University of Western Ontario. Library**
London, Ont., Canada.
- Western Ontario Historical Notes. s-a. ISSN 0382-0157

**University of Western Ontario. Medical School**
London, Ont., Canada.
- University of Western Ontario Medical Journal. 4 per yr. ISSN 0042-0336

**University of Western Ontario. Office of International Education**
London, Ont. N6A 5B9, Canada.
- View. irreg. ISSN 0382-036X

**University of Western Ontario. School of Business Administration**
London, Ont., Canada.
- Business Quarterly. q. ISSN 0007-6996

**University of Western Ontario. School of Library and Information Science**
London, Ontario N6A 5B9, Canada.
- S L I S Newsletter. q. ISSN 0380-8041

**University of Windsor**
Windsor, Ontario, Canada.
- Generation (Windsor); creative work by the students of the University of Windsor. s-a.
- Seminar on Canadian-American Relations (Papers) a. ISSN 0080-8814

**University of Windsor. Faculty of Human Kinetics**
Windsor, Ont., Canada.
- Canadian Journal of History of Sport and Physical Education. s-a. ISSN 0008-4115 (Co-Sponsor: Canadian Association for Health, Physical Education & Recreation)

**University of Windsor Press**
Windsor, Ont., Canada.
- University of Windsor Review. s-a. ISSN 0042-0352

**University of Windsor. Students' Administrative Council**
Windsor, Ont. N9B 3P4, Canada.
- Lance. w. ISSN 0023-7493

**University of Winnipeg. Institute of Urban Studies**
515 Portage Ave., Winnipeg, Man. R3B 2E9, Canada.
- Urban Issues (Winnipeg) irreg.

**University of Winnipeg. Students Association**
Room 230 Lockhart Hall, 515 Portage Ave., Winnipeg 2, Man., Canada.
- Uniter. w. ISSN 0041-817X

**University Press of New Brunswick Ltd.**
Gleaner Bldg., Phoenix Sq., Fredericton, N.B., Canada.
- Atlantic Advocate. m. ISSN 0004-6744
- Atlantic Yearbook; incorporating Atlantic Almanac. a. ISSN 0067-0219

**Up the Tube with One I (Open)-Pomes**
4875 Albert St., North Burnaby, B. C., Canada.
- Up the Tube with One I (Open)-Pomes. irreg. ISSN 0083-4602

**Urban Social Redevelopment**
3553 rue St. Urbain, Montreal 130, Que., Canada.
- Up to the Neck-Action; non-profit citizens paper. m. ISSN 0315-8624

**Ursa Major Press**
302, 60 High St., Nelson, B.C. V1L 3Z4, Canada.
- Inside. irreg. ISSN 0380-2957

**Utilitas Mathematica Publications**
University Centre, University of Manitoba, Winnipeg, Man. R3T 2N2, Canada.
- British Combinatorial Conference. Proceedings. irreg., latest 1975.
- Manitoba Conference on Numerical Mathematics. Proceedings. a.
- Utilitas Mathematica; Canadian journal of applied mathematics, computer science, and statistics. s-a. ISSN 0315-3681

**Vancouver. Social Planning Department**
Vancouver City Hall, 453 West 12th Ave., Vancouver, B.C. V5Y 1V4, Canada.
- Urban Reader. bi-m. ISSN 0382-5205

**Vancouver Archdiocese**
Archibishop James Carney, 150 Robson St., Vancouver, B.C. V6B 2A7, Canada.
- British Columbia Catholic. w. ISSN 0007-0483

**Vancouver Art Gallery**
1145 Georgia St., Vancouver, B. C. V6E 3H2, Canada.
- Vancouver Art Gallery. Annual Report. a. ISSN 0083-5161
- Vanguard. 10 per yr.

**Vancouver Ballet Society**
3694 W. 16th Ave., Vancouver 8, B.C., Canada.
- Ballet - Who. q. ISSN 0005-4348

**Vancouver Board of Trade**
1177 W. Hastings, Vancouver, B.C., Canada.
- Vancouver. Board of Trade. Annual Report. a. ISSN 0083-517X

**Vancouver Community College**
Langara, 100 W. 49th Ave., Vancouver, B.C. V5Y 2Z6, Canada.
- Savant. w.(Sept.-April) ISSN 0036-5084

**Vancouver Community Press**
2504 York St., Vancouver 9, B.C., Canada.
- Vancouver Community Press. Writing Series. irreg.

**Vancouver Historical Society**
Vancouver, B.C., Canada.
- Focus on Vancouver. irreg. ISSN 0383-2708

- Vancouver Historical Society. Newsletter. m. ISSN 0042-2487
- Vancouver Historical Society. Occasional Papers. irreg.

**Vancouver Natural History Society**
c/o Miss E. Wayne, 604-6026 Tisdall St., Vancouver, B. C. V5Z 3N3, Canada.
- Discovery. q.

**Vancouver Neurological Centre**
645 W. Broadway, Vancouver, B.C. V5Z 1G6, Canada.
- Vancouver Neurological Centre. Annual Reports. a. ISSN 0083-5196

**Vancouver Numismatic Society**
Box 2467, Vancouver 3 B. C., Canada.
- Vancouver Numismatic Society. News Bulletin. m. (except July-Aug.) ISSN 0049-5824

**Vancouver Poetry Society**
c/o 4602 Prospect Rd., North Vancouver, B. C., Canada.
- Full Tide. s-a. ISSN 0046-5267

**Vancouver Public Aquarium Association**
Stanley Park, Box 3232, Vancouver, B.C. V6B 3X8, Canada.
- Vancouver Public Aquarium Newsletter. bi-m. ISSN 0042-2495

**Vancouver Stock Exchange**
536 Howe St., Vancouver, B.C. V6C 2E1, Canada.
- Vancouver Stock Exchange. Annual Report. a. ISSN 0083-520X
- Vancouver Stock Exchange Review. m. ISSN 0049-5832

**Vancouver Weather Office**
115-416 Cowley Cres, Int'l Airport South, Vancouver, B.C., Canada.
- Canada. Meteorological Branch. Annual Meteorological Summary. a. ISSN 0068-7707

**Vanier Institute of the Family**
151 Slater St., Ottawa, Ont., Canada.
- Transition. 5 per yr. ISSN 0049-4429

**W. Venner**
London, Ont., Canada.
- Canadian Science Digest. m. ISSN 0383-0381

**Vernon Directories**
Hamilton, Ont., Canada.
- Vernon's City of Guelph (Ontario) Directory. a. ISSN 0317-2961

**Versatile Publishing Co. Ltd.**
151 W. Hastings, Vancouver, B.C. V6B 1H4, Canada.
- Canadian Library Progress: a Selection of the Best Writings from Canadian Library Publications/ Progress des Bibliotheques Canadiennes: Une Selection des Meilleures Oeuvres de Publications Canadiennes de Bibliotheconomie. a. ISSN 0315-2693

**Victorian Order of Nurses for Canada**
5 Blackburn Ave., Ottawa, Ont. K1N 8A2, Canada.
- Victorian Order of Nurses for Canada. National Office. Newsletter. q.

**Vie Medicale Inc.**
- Vie Medicale au Canada Francais. (pub. by Universite Laval. Faculte de Medecine)

**Vie Montante. Edition Canadienne**
21, rue Ste-Elisabeth, Longueuil, Que., J4H 1J3, Canada.
- Vie Montante. Edition Canadienne. irreg. ISSN 0382-4926

**Voce d'Italia in Canada**
6736 Monk Blvd., Montreal 206, Que., Canada.
- Voce d'Italia in Canada. s-m. ISSN 0049-6634

**Vochenblatt Association**
209-430 King St. W., Toronto, Ont. M5V 1L5, Canada.
- Canadian Jewish Weekly/Vochenblatt. fortn. ISSN 0008-395X

**Vorosvary Publishing Co. Ltd.**
412 Bloor St. W, Toronto 4-Ont., Canada.
- Kanadai Magyarsag/Canadian Hungarians. w. ISSN 0022-8281

**W.C.C. Publishing Ltd.**
1434 St. Catherine St. W., Montreal, Que. H3G
1R7, Canada.
- Canadian Football News. m. 4 per yr. ISSN 0045-4834
- Hockey News; the international hockey weekly. w. (m. Jun.-Sep.) ISSN 0018-3016
- Hockey Pictorial World; the international hockey magazine. m.

**W 3 Publishing Co.**
10 Pine Ave. W., No. 110, Montreal, Que., Canada.
- Woman's World Weekly. w. ISSN 0049-7789

**Wadham Publications Ltd.**
109 Vanderhoof Ave., Toronto, Ont. M4G 2J2, Canada.
- Automotive Mass Marketer. s-a. ISSN 0067-2572
- Bodyshop. bi-m. ISSN 0045-2319
- Canadian Risk Management & Business Insurance. bi-m. ISSN 0045-530X
- Canadian Underwriter. m. ISSN 0008-5251
- Environment. m.
- Jobber News; for Canadian automotive wholesalers and salesmen warehouse distributors and automotive rebuilders. m. ISSN 0021-7050
- Life Insurance in Canada. bi-m.
- Motor Truck. m. ISSN 0027-2108
- Service Station & Garage Management. m. ISSN 0037-2668

**Wagtail**
111 N. Victoria St., Sarnia, Ont., Canada.
- Wagtail. 4 per yr. ISSN 0042-9988

**Wapiti Regional Library**
145-12 St. E., Prince Albert, Sask. S6V 0K7, Canada.
- Northern Air. q. ISSN 0048-0754

**Wargamer**
8635 Gilley Ave., Burnaby, B.C. V5J 4Z1, Canada.
- Wargamer. bi-m.

**Waterloo Historical Society**
c/o 131 William St. W., Waterloo, Ont. N2L 1K2, Canada.
- Waterloo Historical Society. Report. a. ISSN 0083-7733

**Waterloo-Wellington Flying Club**
Breslau, Ont., Canada.
- Tailspinner. irreg. ISSN 0316-2494

**Wedge Publishing Foundation**
229 College St., Toronto, Ont. M5T 1R4, Canada.
- Vanguard. 6 per yr. ISSN 0009-5680

**West Canadian Research Publications**
P.O. Box 997, Calgary, Alta, Canada.
- West Canadian Research Publications of Geology and Related Sciences. irreg., ser. 2, no. 3, 1972. ISSN 0083-8195 (Stereogrammetry Ltd)

**Western Canada Water and Sewage Conference**
c/o D. A. Shillabeer, P.O. Box 3212, Postal Station D, Edmonton, Alta., Canada.
- Western Canada Water and Sewage Conference. Papers Presented at Annual Convention. a. ISSN 0083-8799

**Western Canadian Society for Horticulture**
Plant Science Dept., University of Manitoba, Winnipeg, Man. R3T 2N2, Canada.
- Western Canadian Society for Horticulture. Report of Proceedings of Annual Meeting. a. ISSN 0083-8810

**Western Fish & Game Magazine Ltd.**
205-1591 Bowser Ave., N. Vancouver, B. C., Canada.
- Western Angling. m.

**Western Guard Party**
Box 193, Station J, Toronto, Ont. M4J 4Y1, Canada.
- Straight Talk. m. ISSN 0039-209X

**Western Institute for the Deaf**
2125 W. 7th Ave., Vancouver, B.C. V6K 1X9, Canada.
- W I D News. m. ISSN 0049-7436

**Western Jewish News**
P.O. Box 87, Winnipeg, Manitoba, Canada.
- Western Jewish News. w.

**Western Miner Press Ltd.**
305-1200 W. Pender St., Vancouver, B.C. V6E 2T4, Canada.
- Purchasing in Western Canada. m. ISSN 0033-4464 (Purchasing Management Association of Canada. British Columbia District)
- Western Miner. m. ISSN 0043-3934

**Western Producer Publications**
P.O. Box 2500, Saskatoon S7K 2C4, Sask., Canada.
- Western Producer. w. ISSN 0043-4094

**Western Publishers**
Box 30193 Sta. B, Calgary, Alta., Canada.
- Ethnic Directory of Canada. irreg.

**Western Thoroughbred**
727-33A St. N. W., Calgary, Alta., Canada.
- Western Thoroughbred. a. ISSN 0083-9000

**Westminster Abbey Ltd.**
Mission City, British Columbia, Canada.
- Pax Regis. s-a. ISSN 0031-3335

**Westmorland Historical Society**
c/o F. McManus, 291 Highfield St., Moncton, N.B., Canada.
- Westmorland Historical Society. Newsletter. irreg. ISSN 0382-0831

**Westworld Publications Ltd.**
999 W. Broadway, Vancouver, B.C. V5Z 1K5, Canada.
- Interlude. bi-m. ISSN 0381-0569
- Westworld. bi-m.

**What's on Publishing Co.**
77 Maclaren St., Ottawa K2P OK5, Canada.
- What's on in Ottawa/Voici Ottawa. m. ISSN 0043-468X

**Wheelspin News Inc.**
3057 Universal Dr., Mississauga, Ont., Canada.
- Autosport Canada. m.
- Wheelspin News. m.(Oct.-Feb.) bi-w.(Mar.-Sep.) ISSN 0020-9104

**White Pelican**
8918 Windsor Rd., Edmonton 61, Alberta, Canada.
- White Pelican; a quarterly review of the arts. q. ISSN 0049-7584

**Whiteshell District Association**
- Whiteshell Echo. (pub. by Lance Publishing Co. Ltd.)

**Whitsed Publishing Ltd.**
2 Bloor St. W., Toronto, Ont. M4W 3G1, Canada.
- Canadian Campus Career Directory. a.
- Canadian Office. m.

**Who's Who Canadian Publications**
171 Yonge St., Toronto, Ont. M5C 2N4, Canada.
- Who's Who, the Canadian. triennial, vol. 13, 1973-75. ISSN 0068-9963

**Gary Wilcox, Ed. & Pub.**
Box 24954, Station C, Vancouver, B. C. VST 4G3, Canada.
- Photographer. q.

**Wilfrid Laurier University**
75 University Ave. W, Waterloo, Ont. N2L 3C5, Ont., Canada.
- Laurier Campus. 4 per yr.

**Wilfrid Laurier University Press**
75 University Ave., Waterloo, Ont. N2L 3C5, Canada.
- Canadian Journal of Political Science/Revue Canadienne de Science Politique. q. ISSN 0008-4239 (Canadian Political Science Association)
- Philosophy of the Social Sciences. q. ISSN 0048-3931
- Studies in Religion/Sciences Religieuses. q. ISSN 0008-4298 (Canadian Corporation for Studies in Religion)

**William M. Mercer Ltd.**
7 King Street E., Toronto, Ont. M5C 1A5, Canada.
- Mercer Actuarial Bulletin. m. ISSN 0025-9845

**Williams Publishers Ltd.**
1420 Mountain Ave., Kelowna, B.C. V1Y 7H5, Canada.
- Teleguide. w. ISSN 0049-3295

**Willow Beach Field Naturalist Club**
18 Fraser St., Port Hope, Ont., Canada.
- Curlew. 10 per yr.(Sept-June) ISSN 0011-3093

**Wilson et Lafleur Ltee**
39 Notre Dame Ouest, Montreal 126, Que., Canada.
- Rapports de Pratique de Quebec. bi-m. ISSN 0384-6970
- Revue du Droit du Travail. 5 per yr. ISSN 0035-256X
- Revue Legale. m. ISSN 0035-3604
- W. C. J. Meredith Memorial Lectures. irreg. ISSN 0509-5166 (McGill University. Faculty of Law)

**Windsor Sportsmen's Club**
2401 Dougall Rd., Box 452, Windsor, Ont., Canada.
- Windsor Sportsmen's News. m. ISSN 0049-7681

**Winnipeg Economic Development Board**
515-305 Broadway, Winnipeg, Man. R3C 3J7, Canada.
- Winnipeg Industrial Topics. bi-m. ISSN 0316-3458

**Winters College Council**
York University, 4700 Keele St., Downsview, Ont. M3J 1P3, Canada.
- Seer. 9 per yr.

**Women's Liberation Movement of Montreal**
3837 St. Lawrence Blvd., Montreal, Que., Canada.
- Montreal Women's Liberation Newsletter. irreg. ISSN 0077-1368

**Women's Missionary Society (WD)**
Presbyterian Church in Canada, 50 Wynford Dr., DonMills, Ont., Canada.
- Glad Tidings. m. ISSN 0017-0720

**Woodland Indian Cultural Educational Centre**
184 Mohawk St., Box 1506, Brantford, Ont. N3T 5V6, Canada.
- Tekawennake; Six Nations-New Credit reporter. s-m. ISSN 0300-3159

**Words Unlimited Writers Group**
Miss Gladys Willison, 11575 University Avenue, Edmonton, Alberta, Canada.
- Alberta Writers Speak Overland to the Klondike. biennial. ISSN 0065-6089

**Workers' Compensation Board of British Columbia**
Information Services, 5255 Heather St., Vancouver 13, B. C., Canada.
- British Columbia. Workers' Compensation Board. Workers' Compensation Reporter. irreg.

**World Federation for Mental Health**
Dept. of Psychiatry, University of British Columbia, Vancouver, B.C. V6O 1W5, Canada.
- World Federation for Mental Health. Proceedings of Annual Meetings. a. ISSN 0084-1757

**World Federation of Hemophilia**
c/o Frank Schnabel, Suite 106, 1420 St. Mathieu, Montreal 108, Canada.
- World Federation of Hemophilia. Proceedings of Congress. irreg., 1975, 11th, Helsinki. ISSN 0084-1765

**Writ**
c/o Innis College, University of Toronto, Toronto, Ont. M5S 1J5, Canada.
- Writ. irreg. ISSN 0316-3768

**Yale Book Co. Ltd.**
34 Butternut St., Toronto M4K 1T7, Ont., Canada.
- Res Gestae; a news sheet in Latin. s-m(Oct. to May) ISSN 0034-5091

**Yasodhara Ashram Society**
Box 9, Kootenay Bay, B.C. V0B 1X0, Canada.
- Ascent. 3 per yr. ISSN 0315-8179

**Yellowknife Publishing Co. Ltd.**
P.O. Box 68, Yellowknife, N.W.T. XOE 1HE, Canada.
- News of the North. w.

**Yiddish Press**
P.O. Box 3616, 230 Cathedral Ave., Winnipeg 4, Man., Canada.
- Yiddish Press/Yiddische Wort. w. ISSN 0049-8300

**York Pioneer and Historical Society**
P.O. Box 481, Station "K", Toronto, Ont. M4P 2G9, Canada.
- York Pioneer. a. ISSN 0084-4233

**York University**
Downsview, Ont., Canada.
- Canadian Theatre Review. q. ISSN 0315-0836
- Waves; York University magazine. 3 per yr. ISSN 0315-3932

**York University. Department of Geography**
Downsview, M3J 1P3 Ont., Downsview, Ont., Canada.
- Canadian Cartographer. s-a. ISSN 0008-3127
- Cartographica; monographs on cartography. s-a. ISSN 0317-7173

**York University. Department of Sociology**
- International Journal of Comparative Sociology. (pub. by E. J. Brill NE)

**York University. Faculty of Administrative Studies**
Rm 111, Administrative Studies Bldg., 4700 Keele St., Downsview, Ontario M3J 2R6, Canada.
- Administrator. irreg. ISSN 0065-1974

**York University. Glendon College**
Student Union, 2275 Bayview Ave., Toronto, Ont. M4N 3M6, Canada.
- Pro Tem. w (Sep.-Mar.) ISSN 0032-9134

**York University. Osgoode Hall Law School**
Downsview, Ont., Canada.
- Continuum. irreg. ISSN 0381-0925
- Obiter Dicta. 25 per yr. ISSN 0029-7585
- Osgoode Hall Law Journal. 3 per yr. ISSN 0030-6185

**Young Men's Christian Association of Canada. National Council**
Toronto, Ont., Canada.
- Canadian Manhood. irreg. ISSN 0382-6031
- Y Canada. irreg. ISSN 0315-095X

**Young People's Societies Eastern Ontario League**
75 Garden St., R. R. 1 Brockville, Ottawa, Ont., Canada.
- Eastern Light. 11 per yr (approx.) ISSN 0383-1418

**Young Socialist**
Box 517, Station a, Toronto, Ont., Canada.
- Young Socialist. irreg. ISSN 0044-0884

**Young Worker Publishing Co.**
24 Cecil St., Toronto, Ont., Canada.
- Young Worker. irreg. ISSN 0382-4047

**Youth Science Foundation**
151 Slater St., Ste. 302, Ottawa, Ont., Canada.
- Science Affairs. q. ISSN 0036-813X

**Yukon News Ltd.**
c/o D. H. Robertson, 112 Wood St., Whitehorse, Yukon, Canada.
- Yukon News. w. ISSN 0044-1376

**Barrie Zwicker, Ed. & Pub.**
22 Laurier Ave., Toronto, Ont. M4X 1S3, Canada.
- Content; Canada's national news media magazine. m. ISSN 0045-835X

## CAPE VERDE

**Cape Verde. Direccao Nacional de Informacao**
Caixa Postal 118, Praia, Sao Tiago, Cape Verde Islands.
- Voz di Povo. w.

**Centro de Estudos de Cabo Verde**
Praia, Sao Tiago, Cape Verde Islands.
- Centro de Estudos de Cabo Verde. Revista: Serie de Ciencias Humanas. irreg.

## CAYMAN ISLANDS

**Cayman Islands. Currency Board**
Grand Cayman, Cayman Islands, B.W.I.
- Cayman Islands. Currency Board. Report. a.

**Cayman Islands. Department of Finance and Development**
Georgetown, Grand Cayman, Cayman Islands, B.W.I.
- Cayman Islands. Department of Finance and Development. Estimates of Gross Domestic Product and Related Aggregates. a.
- Statistical Abstract of the Government of the Cayman Islands. 2 per yr.
- Statistical Abstract of the Government of the Cayman Islands. a.

**Cayman Islands. Department of Tourism**
- Cayman Islands Holiday Guide. (pub. by Northwester Company Ltd.)

**Cayman Islands. Education Department**
Grand Cayman, Cayman Islands, B.W.I.
- Cayman Islands. Education Department. Report of the Chief Education Officer. a.

**Cayman Islands. Legislative Assembly**
Box 243, Georgetown, Grand Cayman, Cayman Islands, B.W.I.
- Cayman Gazette. fortn.
- Cayman Islands. Legislative Assembly. Minutes. q.

**International Management Services**
P.O. Box 61, Grand Cayman, Cayman Islands, B.W.I.
- International Wealth Protection Letter. 22 per yr.

**Northwester Company Ltd.**
P.O. Box 243, George Town, Grand Cayman, B.W.I.
- Cayman Islands Handbook and Businessman's Guide. a.
- Cayman Islands Holiday Guide. s-a. (Cayman Islands. Department of Tourism)
- Cayman Islands Nor'wester. m.

## CENTRAL AFRICAN REPUBLIC

**Central African Republic. Direction de la Statistique Generale et des Etudes Economiques**
B.P. 732, Bangui, Central African Republic.
- Central African Republic. Direction de la Statistique Generale et des Etudes Economiques. Bulletin Mensuel de Statistique. m.

**Organisation Commune Africaine et Mauricienne**
B. P. 965, Bangui, Cameroon.
- Nations Nouvelles; nouvelle serie. q. ISSN 0028-050X

**Organization of African Unity. Inter- African Bureau for Soils**
B.P. 1352, Bangui, Central African Republic.
- Organization of African Unity. Inter- African Bureau for Soils. Bibliographie. irreg. ISSN 0538-2769
- Sols Africains/African Soils. q. ISSN 0038-1209

**Terre Africaine**
B.P. 373, Bangui, Central African Republic.
- Terre Africaine. w. ISSN 0049-3473

## CHAD

**Chad. Direction du Plan et du Developpement. Sous-Direction de la Statistique**
N'djamena, Chad.
- Annuaire Statistique du Tchad. a. ISSN 0577-5000

**Chad. Ministere de l'Economie Moderne, du Plan, du Commerce et de la Cooperation Internationale**
B. P. 453, N'djamena, Chad.
- Chad. Ministere de l'Economie Moderne, du Plan, du Commerce et de la Cooperation Internationale. Rapport Economique Annuel. a.
- Commerce Exterieur de la Republique du Chad. a. ISSN 0069-6617

**Chad. Ministere de l'Economie Moderne, du Plan, du Commerce et de la Cooperation International. Direction du Plan et du Developpement. Sous-Direction de la Statistique**
see Chad. Direction du Plan et du Developpement. Sous-Direction de la Statistique

**Institut National des Sciences Humaines**
B. P. 503, N'djamena, Chad.
- Etudes et Documents Tchadiens. Serie A. irreg.
- Etudes et Documents Tchadiens. Serie B. irreg.

**Tchad et Culture**
B.P. 456, N'djamena, Chad.
- Tchad et Culture. m. Nov.-Jun. ISSN 0049-3066

## CHILE

**Ediciones A U C A**
Villavicencio 378, Santiago, Chile.
- A U C A; arquitectura, urbanismo, construccion y arte. 3-4 per yr. ISSN 0567-428X

**Armada de Chile**
Correo 21, Santiago, Chile.
- Revista de Marina. bi-m. ISSN 0034-8511

**Banco Central de Chile**
Direccion de Operaciones en Moneda Extranjera, Casilla 967, Santiago, Chile.
- Balanza de Pagos de Chile. a. ISSN 0067-3013
- Banco Central de Chile. Boletin Mensual. m. ISSN 0005-464X
- Banco Central de Chile, Santiago. Memoria Anual. a. ISSN 0067-3196

**Banco de Chile. Gerencia de Estudios**
Ahumada 251, Casilla 151D, Santiago, Chile.
- Estudios Monetarios. irreg.

**Caja Central de Ahorros y Prestamos. Seccion Estadistica**
Agustinas 1357, Casilla 9254, Santiago, Chile.
- Caja Central de Ahorros y Prestamos. Seccion Estadistica. Informativo Estadistico. m.

**Carrion and Sons, Co.**
Calle Madrid 2058, Santiago, Chile.
- Revista Dental de Chile. bi-m. ISSN 0034-9143 (Sociedad Odontologica de Chile)

**Centro de Documentacion de la Corporacion de Promocion Universitaria**
Miguel Claro, 1460, Casilla 1056 correo 9, Santiago, Chile.
- Universidad y Desarrollo. q.

**Centro de Investigacion y Desarrollo de Educacion**
Casilla 13608, Santiago 1, Chile.
- Cuadernos de Educacion. irreg.
- Resumenes Analiticos en Educacion. q.

**Centro Interdisciplinario de Desarrollo Urbano Regional**
Nueva de Lyon, 150, Santiago, Chile.
- Cuadernos de Desarrollo Urbano Regional. q.

**Centro Latinoamericano de Demografia**
For publications of this agency see section for UNITED NATIONS

**Centro Nacional de Informacion y Documentacion**
Casilla 297-V, Santiago, Chile.
- C E N I D. Notas Informativas. 4 per yr. ISSN 0029-3873

**Centro para el Desarrollo Economico y Social de America Latina**
Carmen Silva 2542, Casilla 9990, Santiago, Chile.
- Pensamiento y Accion. q.

**Chile. Ferrocarriles del Estado**
Oficina de Publicacones y Propaganda, Casilla 1173, Santiago, Chile.
- En Viaje. m. ISSN 0013-6972

**Chile. Fuerza Aerea**
Galvez 390, Department a, Santiago, Chile.
- Revista de la Fuerza Aerea. bi-m. ISSN 0034-8414

**Chile. Instituto de Investigaciones Agropecuarias**
Casilla 5427, Santiago, Chile.
- Chile. Instituto de Investigaciones Agropecuarias. Agricultura Tecnica. q.
- Investigacion y Progreso Agricola. irreg. (2-3 per yr) ISSN 0539-239X

**Chile. Instituto Nacional de Estadisticas**
Casilla 7597-Correo 3, Santiago, Chile.
- Agricultura e Industrias Agropecuarias y Pesca. a; latest edition, 1974-75.

- Chile. Instituto Nacional de Estadisticas.
  Comercio Exterior. a.
- Chile. Instituto Nacional de Estadisticas.
  Compendio Estadistico. biennial.
- Chile. Instituto Nacional de Estadisticas.
  Estadisticas de Salud. irreg; latest 1973.
- Chile. Instituto Nacional de Estadisticas. Indice
  de Precios al Consumidor. irreg.
- Chile. Instituto Nacional de Estadisticas. Indice
  de Salarios y Sueldos. q.
- Chile. Instituto Nacional de Estadisticas.
  Informativo Estadistico. bi-m.

**Chile. Ministerio de Agricultura. Servicio Agricola y Ganadero**
Santiago, Chile.
- Biologia Pesquera. irreg., 1973, no. 6. ISSN 0067-
  8767 (prep. by its Div. Pesca y Caza)
- Chile. Division de Pesca y Caza. Departamento
  Estadistica. Anuario Estadistico de Pesca. a. ISSN
  0069-3537

**Chile. Ministerio de Educacion Publica. Centro de Documentacion Pedagogica**
Morande 322, Santiago, Chile.
- Chile. Centro de Documentacion Pedagogica.
  Bibliografia de la Educacion Chilena. irreg.

**Chile. Ministerio de Hacienda. Direccion de Presupuestos**
Teatinos 120, Piso 12, Of. 27, Santiago, Chile.
- Chile. Departamento de Estudios Financieros.
  Finanzas Publicas. a.
- Chile. Ministerio de Hacienda. Direccion de
  Presupuestos. Calculo de Entradas de la Nacion.
  a.
- Chile. Ministerio de Hacienda. Direccion de
  Presupuestos. Exposicion Sobre el Estado de la
  Hacienda Publica. a.
- Chile. Ministerio de Hacienda. Direccion de
  Presupuestos. Instruccions para la Ejecucion de la
  Ley de Presupuestos. a.
- Chile. Ministerio de Hacienda. Direccion de
  Presupuestos. Ley de Presupuestos. a.

**Chile. Ministerio del Trabajo y Prevision Social. Superintendencia de Seguridad Social**
Santiago, Chile.
- Chile. Superintendencia de Seguridad Social.
  Seguridad Social: Estadisticas. irreg.
- Seguridad Social. s-a.

**Chile. Oficina de Planificacion Nacional. Departamento de Estudios y Planificacion Urbano**
Santiago, Chile.
- Revista de Planificacion; vivienda, ciudad, region.
  irreg. ISSN 0034-8694

**Chile. Servicio Nacional de Salud**
Sub-Departamento Proteccion Salud, Maciver 541,
Santiago, Chile.
- Notificacion de las Principales Enfermedades
  Transmisibles. w. ISSN 0029-4284

**Chile. Superintendencia de Bancos**
Santiago, Chile.
- Chile. Superintendencia de Bancos. Boletin
  Estadistico. m.
- Estadistica Bancaria; resumen de los estados de
  situacion balances generales. 4 per yr. ISSN 0014-
  1143

**Colegio de Dentistas de Chile**
Avda. Santa Maria 1990, Casilla 252-V, Santiago,
Chile.
- Odontologia Chilena. q. ISSN 0029-8417

**Comision Permanente del Pacifico Sur**
Casilla 16,199, Santiago 9, Chile.
- Revista Pacifica Sur. a.

**Comite de Investigaciones Tecnologicas de Chile**
Avda. Santa Maria 6500, Casilla 667, Santiago,
Chile.
- Comite de Investigaciones Tecnologicas de Chile.
  biennial.

**Corporacion del Cobre. Departamento Estudios y Analisis de Mercados**
Morande 239, Santiago, Chile.
- Indicadores del Cobre y Sub Productos; boletin
  estadistico anual. a.

**Economic Commission for Latin America**
For publications of this agency see section for
UNITED NATIONS

**Sociedad Editora Revista Ercilla Ltda.**
Quebec 497, Casilla 63-D.T., Santiago, Chile.
- Ercilla. w. ISSN 0013-9971

**Escuela Latinoamericana de Ciencia Politica y Administracion Publica**
Casilla 3213, Santiago, Chile.
- Revista Latinoamericana de Ciencia Politica. 3 per
  yr. ISSN 0048-783X

**Escuela Latinoamericana de Sociologia**
Casilla 3213, Santiago, Chile.
- E L A S. Boletin. s-a. ISSN 0012-7698

**Estado Mayor del Ejercito**
Seccion Historica, Santiago, Chile.
- Chile. Ejercito. Anexo Historico. Memorial. bi-m.
  ISSN 0009-4242

**Food and Agriculture Organization of the United Nations. Regional Office for Latin America**
For publications of this agency see section for
UNITED NATIONS

**Fundacion Educacional Roberto Bellarmino**
- Revista Mensaje. (pub. by Fernando Montes
  Matte S. J.)

**Instituto Antartico Chileno**
Luis Thayer Ojeda 814, Casilla 16521, Correo 9
Prov., Santiago, Chile.
- Instituto Antartico Chileno. Boletin. irreg., no. 9,
  1976. ISSN 0073-9863
- Instituto Antartico Chileno. Contribution. Serie
  Cientifica. irreg. vol. 2, no. 29, 1972. ISSN 0073-
  9871

**Instituto Bacteriologico de Chile**
Casillo 48, Santiago, Chile.
- Instituto Bacteriologico de Chile. Boletin. 2 per
  yr.

**Instituto de Ciencias Penales**
Huerfanos 1147, Oficina 546, Santiago de Chile,
Chile.
- Revista de Ciencias Penales. s-a.

**Instituto de Fomento Pesquero**
Jose Domingo Canas 2277, Santiago, Chile.
- Instituto de Fomento Pesquero. Informes
  Pesquero. irreg., no. 60, 1975.
- Serie Investigacion Pesquera. irreg., no. 20, 1975.

**Instituto de Ingenieros de Minas de Chile**
Alam. B. O'Higgins 1170, 9 Piso, Of. 919, Casilla
14668, Correo 21, Santiago, Chile.
- Minerales. q. ISSN 0026-458X

**Instituto de Investigacion de Recursos Naturales**
Santiago de Chile, Chile.
- Instituto de Investigacion de Recursos Naturales.
  Publicacion. irreg. ISSN 0538-0898

**Instituto de Investigaciones Geologicas**
Agustinas 785, Santiago, Chile
(Subscr. to: Biblioteca, Instituto de Investigaciones
Geologicas, Casilla 10465, Santiago, Chile)
- Instituto de Investigaciones Geologicas Boletin.
  irreg. ISSN 0020-3939
- Revista Geologica de Chile. irreg; latest 1976, no.
  3.

**Instituto de la Patagonia**
Casilla de Correo 102-D, Punta Arenas, Magallanes,
Chile.
- Instituto de la Patagonia. Anales. a. ISSN 0085-
  1922
- Instituto de la Patagonia. Serie Monografias. irreg.

**Instituto de Neurocirugia e Investigaciones Cerebrales**
Casilla 3717, Santiago, Chile.
- Neurocirugia. 4 per yr. ISSN 0047-9411

**Instituto Forestal. Division Estudios Economicos**
Casilla 3085, Santiago, Chile.
- Instituto Forestal. Boletin Estadistico. a.

**Instituto Latinoamericano de Planificacion Economica y Social**
For publications of this agency see section for
UNITED NATIONS

**Instituto Latinoamericano del Fierro y el Acero**
Casilla 16065, Santiago 9, Chile.
- Siderurgia Latinoamericana. m.

**Editorial Juridica de Chile**
Casilla 4256, Santiago, Chile.
- Revista de Derecho Procesal. s-a. (Universidad de
  Chile. Facultad de Ciencias Juridicas y Sociales.
  Departamento de Derecho Procesal)

**Latin American Institute for Economic and Social Planning**
For publications of this agency see section for
UNITED NATIONS

**Liga Maritima de Chile**
Box 117-V, Valparaiso, Chile.
- Mar. s-a. ISSN 0047-5866

**Mensaje**
Casilla 10445, Santiago, Chile.
- Mensaje. 10 per yr. ISSN 0025-956X

**Fernando Montes Matte S. J.**
Casilla 10445, Santiago, Chile.
- Revista Mensaje; mensaje cristiana para el mundo
  de hoy. m. ISSN 0034-9968 (Fundacion
  Educacional Roberto Bellarmino)

**Museo Nacional de Historia Natural**
Casilla 787, Santiago, Chile.
- Museo Nacional de Historia Natural. Boletin.
  ISSN 0027-3910
- Museo Nacional de Historia Natural. Noticiario
  Mensual. m. ISSN 0027-3945

**Nacional Quimantu Ltda.**
Avda. Santa Maria 076, Casilla 10155, Santiago,
Chile.
- Quinta Rueda. m.

**Orfeo**
Casilla 14139, Santiago, Chile.
- Orfeo; revista de poesia y teoria poetica. 10 per
  yr. ISSN 0030-4875

**Dr. Hector Orrego Puelma, Ed. & Pub.**
J.M. Infante 717, Santiago de Chile, Chile.
- Enfermedades del Torax y Tuberculosis. s-a. ISSN
  0013-7588

**Miguel Poradowski**
Casilla 261, Santiago, Chile.
- Estudios Sobre el Communismo. q. ISSN 0014-
  1550

**Prensa Latinoamericana S.A.**
Av. Espana 620, Santiago, Chile.
- Sociedad y Desarrollo. q.

**Prensachil Ltda**
Estado 115, Oficina, 505, Santiago de Chile, Chile.
- Prensa Chilena y Sus Comentarios. s-m. ISSN
  0048-5179

**Reader's Digest Chile Limitada**
Calle Huelen 95, Casilla 3141, Santiago, Chile.
- Selecciones del Reader's Digest (Chilean Edition)
  m. ISSN 0037-1203

**Regional Center for Demographic Training and Research in Latin America**
For publications of this agency see section for
UNITED NATIONS

**Revista Continente: Chile Hacia el Mundo**
Serrano 20, Casilla 11840, Santiago, Chile.
- Revista Continente: Chile Hacia el Mundo. bi-m.

**Imprenta San Jose**
Casilla 30-D, Santiago, Chile.
- Revista Catolica. q.

**Sociedad Agronomica de Chile**
Casilla 4109, Santiago, Chile.
- Simiente. 4 per yr. ISSN 0037-5403

**Sociedad Chilena de Historia y Geografia**
Casilla 1386, Santiago, Chile.
- Revista Chilena de Historia Y Geografia. a. ISSN
  0080-2093

**Sociedad Chilena de Obstetricia y Ginecologia**
Esmeralda 678, Piso 2, Of. 236, Casilla 23-D,
Santiago, Chile.
- Revista Chilena de Obstetrica y Ginecologia. bi-
  m. ISSN 0048-766X

**Sociedad Chilena de Otorrinolaringologia**
Huelen 23, Santiago, Chile.
- Revista de Otorrinolaringologia. 3 per yr. ISSN
  0034-8643

**Sociedad Chilena de Pediatria**
Esmeralda 678, 2 Piso, Santiago, Chile.
- Revista Chilena de Pediatria. bi-m. ISSN 0034-7396

**Sociedad Chilena de Quimica**
Casilla 2613, Concepcion, Chile.
- Sociedad Chilena de Quimica. Boletin/Chilean Chemical Society. Bulletin. q.

**Sociedad Chilena Entomologia**
Casilla 21132, Santiago (15), Chile.
- Revista Chilena de Entomologia. irreg. ISSN 0034-740X

**Sociedad de Biologia de Concepcion**
- Sociedad de Biologia de Concepcion. Boletin. (pub. by Universidad de Concepcion)

**Sociedad de Fomento Fabril**
Moneda 759, Santiago de Chile, Chile.
- Industria. m (with annual supplement) ISSN 0019-7386

**Sociedad de Medicina Veterinaria de Chile**
Clasificador 740, Santiago, Chile.
- Sociedad de Medicina Veterinaria de Chile. Revista. s-a (with special nos.) ISSN 0037-8534

**Sociedad de Neurologia. Psiquiatria y Neurocirugia**
Casilla 6504, Santiago, Chile.
- Revista Chilena de Neuropsiquiatria. q. ISSN 0034-7388

**Sociedad Medica de Santiago**
Casilla 23, D, Santiago, Chile.
- Revista Medica de Chile. m. ISSN 0034-9887

**Sociedad Medica de Valparaiso**
Av. Brazil 1689, Valparaiso, Chile.
- Revista Medica de Valparaiso. q. ISSN 0034-9917

**Sociedad Nacional de Agricultura**
Tenderini 187, Casilla 40-D, Santiago, Chile.
- Campesino. m. ISSN 0008-2341

**Sociedad Odontologica de Chile**
- Revista Dental de Chile. (pub. by Carrion and Sons, Co.)

**Trilce de Poesia**
Casilla 695, Valdivia, Chile.
- Trilce de Poesia. bi-m. ISSN 0041-297X

**Unesco. Regional Office for Education in Latin America and the Caribbean**
For publications of this agency see section for UNITED NATIONS

**United Nations. Centro Latinoamericano de Demografia**
For publications of this agency see section for UNITED NATIONS

**United Nations Economic Commission for Latin America**
For publications of this agency see section for UNITED NATIONS

**United Nations. Regional Center for Demographic Training and Research in Latin America**
For publications of this agency see section for UNITED NATIONS

**Universidad Austral de Chile. Facultad de Ciencias Agrarias**
Valdivia, Chile.
- Agro sur. s-a.

**Universidad Austral de Chile. Facultad de Filosofia y Letras**
- Estudios Filologicos. (pub. by Editorial Universitaria, S.A.)

**Universidad Austral de Chile. Instituto de Filologica**
Valdivia, Chile.
- Estudios Filologicos. Anejo. irreg., 1972, no. 4. ISSN 0071-1721 (prep. by its Instituto de Filologia)
- Seminario de Investigacion y Esnenanza de la Linguistica. Actas. irreg.

**Editorial Universidad Catolica de Chile**
Diagonal Oriente 3300, Santiago, Chile.
- Taller de Letras. a. (Universidad Catolica. Instituto de Letras)

**Universidad Catolica de Chile. Centro de Estudios de la Realidad Nacional**
Alameda 341, Santiago, Chile.
- Cuadernos de la Realidad Nacional. q.

**Universidad Catolica de Chile. Escuela Artes de la Comunicacion**
Diagonal Oriente 3300, Santiago, Chile.
- Revista Artes de la Comunicacion. s-a.

**Universidad Catolica de Chile. Escuela de Teatro, Cine y Television**
Biblioteca, Diagonal Oriente 3300, Casilla 114 D, Santiago, Chile.
- Apuntes. s-a.
- Revista E A C. s-a. ISSN 0302-8003

**Universidad Catolica de Chile. Escuela de Trabajo Social**
Diagonal Oriente, 3300 Santiago, Chile.
- Trabajo Social. s-a.

**Universidad Catolica de Chile. Facultad de Agronomia**
Casilla 114-D, Santiago, Chile.
- Ciencia e Investigacion Agraria. q.

**Universidad Catolica de Chile. Facultad de Teologia**
Casilla 114-D, Santiago, Chile.
- Chile. Universidad Catolica, Santiago. Facultad de Teologia. Anales. irreg.; vol. 24, 1971. ISSN 0069-3596
- Teologia y Vida. q. ISSN 0049-3449

**Universidad Catolica de Chile. Instituto de Economia**
Casilla 114-D, Santiago, Chile.
- Cuadernos de Economia. 3 per yr. ISSN 0011-2399

**Universidad Catolica de Chile. Instituto de Estetica**
Diagonal Oriente 3.300, Santiago, Chile.
- Aisthesis; revista chilena de investigaciones esteticas. irreg. no. 9, 1976. ISSN 0568-3939

**Universidad Catolica de Chile. Instituto de Historia**
Casilla 114-D, Santiago, Chile.
- Historia. a. ISSN 0073-2435

**Universidad Catolica de Chile. Instituto de Matematicas**
Casilla 114-D, Santiago, Chile
(Subscr to: Instituto de Matematica. Vicuna Mackenna 4860, Santiago Chile )
- Notas Matematicas/Mathematical Notes. irreg; no. 3, 1974.

**Universidad Catolica de Chile. Instituto de Planificacion del Desarrollo Urbano**
Los Navegantes 1919, Casilla 16002-Correo 9, Santiago, Chile.
- Revista Latinoamericana de Estudios Urbano-Regionales. 3 per yr. ISSN 0048-7821

**Universidad Catolica de Chile. Seminario Latinoamericano**
Casilla 114 D, Santiago, Chile.
- Fe de Un Pueblo. irreg. (prep. by its Centro de Documentacion)
- Panorama de la Teologia Latinoamericana. a. (prep. by its Centro de Documentacion)

**Universidad Catolica de Valparaiso**
Casilla 4059, Valparaiso, Chile.
- Boletin Informativo. m. ISSN 0006-6389

**Universidad Catolica de Valparaiso. Centro de Investigaciones del Mar**
- Investigaciones Marinas. (pub. by Ediciones Universitarias de Valparaiso)

**Universidad Catolica de Valparaiso. Instituto de Geografia**
- Revista Geografica de Valparaiso. (pub. by Ediciones Universitarias de Valparaiso)

**Universidad Catolica de Valparaiso. Instituto de Lenguas y Literatura**
- Revista Signos. (pub. by Ediciones Universitarias de Valparaiso)

**Universidad Catolica. Instituto de Letras**
- Taller de Letras. (pub. by Editorial Universidad Catolica de Chile)

**Universidad de Chile**
Casa Central Universitaria, Casilla 10 D, Santiago, Chile.
- Universidad de Chile. Boletin. 9 per yr. ISSN 0041-8374

**Universidad de Chile. Centro de Estudios Antropologicos**
Av. J.P. Alessandri 774, Santiago, Chile.
- Antropologia. s-a.

**Universidad de Chile. Centro de Publicaciones Biologicas**
Casilla 12967, Santiago, Chile.
- Archivos de Biologia y Medicina Experimentales. a. ISSN 0004-0533

**Universidad de Chile. Departamento de Astronomia**
Santiago, Chile.
- Universidad de Chile. Departamento de Astronomia. Publicaciones. irreg., 1969, vol. 1, no. 8. ISSN 0069-3553

**Universidad de Chile. Departamento de Bibliotecologia**
Santiago, Chile.
- Revista Chilena de Bibliotecologia y Documentacion. s-a.

**Universidad de Chile. Departamento de Ciencia de los Materiales**
Instituto de Investigaciones y Ensayes de Materiales, Plaza Ercilla 883, Casilla 1420, Santiago de Chile, Chile.
- Revista del Idiem. 3 per yr. ISSN 0034-9089

**Universidad de Chile. Departamento de Economia**
Santiago, Chile.
- Estudios de Economia. s-a.

**Universidad de Chile. Departamento de Geologia**
Casilla 13518, Correo 21, Santiago, Chile.
- Universidad de Chile. Departamento de Geologia. Serie Communicaciones. irreg.; 1976 no. 19. ISSN 0069-357X
- Universidad de Chile. Departamento de Geologia. Serie Publicaciones. irreg.; no. 45, 1976. ISSN 0069-3588

**Universidad de Chile. Departamento de Linguistica y Filologia**
Valparaiso, Chile.
- Alpha; revista de linguistica y filologia. s-a.

**Universidad de Chile. Departamento de Oceanologia**
Casilla 13 D., Vina del Mar, Chile.
- Revista de Biologia Marina. irreg; vol. 15, no. 1, 1973. ISSN 0080-2115

**Universidad de Chile. Departamento de Pediatria**
Zanartu 1085, Santiago, Chile.
- Pediatria. q. ISSN 0031-3882

**Universidad de Chile. Departamento de Psicologia**
Jose Pedro Alessandri 862, Santiago, Chile.
- Cuadernos de Psicologia.

**Universidad de Chile. Dept. of Microbiology and Parasitology**
Casilla No. 9183, Santiago, Chile.
- Boletin Chileno de Parasitologia. s-a. ISSN 0006-6176

**Universidad de Chile. Facultad de Ciencias Economicas y Administrativas**
Departamento de Economia, Distribucion y Venta, Av. Condell 362, Santiago, Chile.
- Comentarios de la Situaccion Economica. s-a.
- Estudios de Economia. s-a.
- Ocupacion y Desocupacion en el Gran Santiago. q.
- Universidad de Chile. Facultad de Ciencias Economicas y Administrativas. Desarrollo. irreg.

**Universidad de Chile. Facultad de Ciencias Fisicas y Matematicas**
Departamento de Geologia, Santiago, Chile.
- Universidad de Chile. Departamento de Geologia. Serie Apartado. irreg., 1969, no. 22. ISSN 0069-3561

**Universidad de Chile. Facultad de Ciencias Juridicas y Sociales**
- Revista de Derecho Procesal. (pub. by Editorial Juridica de Chile)

**Universidad de Chile. Facultad de Ciencias y Artes Musicales y de la Representacion**
Compania 1264, Casilla 2100, Santiago, Chile.
- Revista Musical Chilena. q. ISSN 0035-0192

**Universidad de Chile. Facultad de Filosofia y Letras**
Casilla 147, Santiago, Chile.
- Boletin de Filologia. a. ISSN 0067-9674 (prep. by its Departamento de Linguistica y Filologia)
- Revista de Filosofia. 3 per yr. ISSN 0034-8236

**Universidad de Chile. Instituto de Economia**
Casilla 3861, Santiago, Chile.
- Universidad de Chile. Biblioteca Instituto de Economia. Boletin Bibliografico; libros y folletos recibidos, articulos seleccionados. bi-m. ISSN 0041-8366

**Universidad de Chile. Instituto de Investigaciones Musicales**
Casilla 2100, Santiago, Chile.
- Antologia del Folklore Musical Chileno. irreg. ISSN 0066-4928

**Universidad de Chile. Instituto de Investigaciones Oceanologicas**
Casilla 1240, Antofagasta, Chile.
- Apuntes Oceanologicos. irreg.

**Universidad de Chile. Instituto de Quimica Fisologica y Patologica**
Santiago, Chile.
- Conferencias de Bioquimica. a. ISSN 0069-8784

**Universidad de Chile-Zona Norte**
Casilla 1240, Antofagasta, Chile.
- Ancora; Revista de Cultura Universitaria. s-a. ISSN 0003-2883
- Zonarida. irreg. ISSN 0084-554X

**Universidad de Concepcion**
Casilla 1367, Concepcion, Chile.
- Sociedad de Biologia de Concepcion. Boletin. s-a. ISSN 0037-850X (Sociedad de Biologia de Concepcion)

**Universidad de Concepcion. Colegio de Dentistas**
Concepcion, Chile.
- Revista Odontologica de Concepcion. q. ISSN 0035-0265

**Universidad de Concepcion. Escuela de Derecho**
Casilla 26C, Concepcion, Chile
- Revista de Derecho. q. (Subscr. to: Biblioteca Central, Canje y Donacion, Casilla 1807, Concepcion, Chile)

**Universidad de Concepcion. Escuela de Economia y Administracion**
Casilla 1987, Concepcion, Chile.
- Economia y Administracion. q. ISSN 0012-9887

**Universidad de Concepcion. Instituto Central de Biologia**
Casilla 301, Concepcion, Chile
- Gayana: Botanica. irreg (3-4 per yr.); no. 27, 1974. ISSN 0016-5301
- Gayana: Zoologica. 4 per yr. ISSN 0016-531X

**Universidad de Concepcion. Instituto Central de Lenguas**
Casilla 1807, Concepcion, Chile.
- R L A; revista de linguistica teorica y aplicada. a. ISSN 0033-698X

**Universidad del Norte. Departamento de Agricultura**
Arica, Chile.
- Idesia. irreg. ISSN 0073-4675

**Universidad del Norte. Museo de Arqueologia**
San Pedro de Atacama, Chile.
- Estudio Atacamenos. irreg.
- Universidad del Norte. Museo de Arqueologia. Documentos para la Investigacion. irreg.

**Universidad Tecnica del Estado**
Avda. Ecuador 3469, Correo 2, Santiago, Chile.
- Universidad Tecnica del Estado. Revista. irreg.

**Universidad Tecnica Federico Santa Maria**
Casilla 110-V, Valparaiso, Chile.
- Scientia; revista cientifica y tecnologica. q. ISSN 0036-8679

**Editorial Universitaria, S.A.**
Alameda B. O' Higgins, Casilla 10220, Santiago, Chile.
- Estudios Filologicos. a. ISSN 0071-1713 (Universidad Austral de Chile. Facultad de Filosofia y Letras)
- Estudios Internacionales. q. ISSN 0014-1518
- Mapocho. q. ISSN 0025-2689
- Orbita. q. ISSN 0030-445X
- Panorama Economico. m. ISSN 0031-093X
- Revista Chilena de Literatura. 3 per yr. ISSN 0048-7651
- Revista del Pacifico. q. ISSN 0034-9100

**Ediciones Universitarias de Valparaiso**
Yungay 2872, Of. 2, Casilla 1415, Valparaiso, Chile.
- Investigaciones Marinas. 15 per yr. ISSN 0020-997X (Universidad Catolica de Valparaiso. Centro de Investigaciones del Mar)
- Revista Geografica de Valparaiso. s-a. ISSN 0034-9577 (Universidad Catolica de Valparaiso. Instituto de Geografia)
- Revista Signos; estudios de lengua y literatura. s-a. ISSN 0035-0451 (Universidad Catolica de Valparaiso. Instituto de Lenguas y Literatura)

## CHINA, MAINLAND

**Academia Sinica. Institute of Geophysics and Meteorology**
Peking, Peoples Republic of China
(Dist. by Guozi Shudian (China Publications Centre), Box 399, Peking, Peoples Republic of China)
- Acta Geophysica Sinica. q. ISSN 0001-5733
- Acta Meteorologica Sinica. q. ISSN 0001-6179

**Academia Sinica. Institute of Vertebrate Paleontology and Paleoanthropology**
Science Press, Peking, Peoples Republic of China.
- Vertebrata Palasiatica (China) q. ISSN 0042-4404

**Academia Sinica. Institute of Zoology**
Zoological Society of China, Peking, Peoples Republic of China
(Dist. by Guozi Shudian (China Publications Centre), Box 399, Peking, People's Republic of China)
- Acta Zoologica Sinica/Tung Wu Hsueh Pao. q. ISSN 0001-7302

**China Welfare Institute**
- China Reconstructs. (pub. by Guozi Shudian (China Publications Centre))

**Chinese Medical Association**
- Chinese Medical Journal. (pub. by Guozi Shudian (China Publications Centre))

**Cina Esperanto Ligo**
P.O. Kesto 77, Peking, People's Republic of China
- Popola Cinio. m. ISSN 0032-4361 (Dist. by Guozi Shudian, P.O. Box 399, Peking, People's Republic of China)

**Guozi Shudian (China Publications Centre)**
Box 399, Hsitan Bldg., Peking, Peoples Republic of China.
- China Pictorial. m. ISSN 0009-4420
- China Reconstructs. m. ISSN 0009-4447 (China Welfare Institute)
- Chinese Medical Journal. bi-m. (Chinese Medical Association)

**Institute of Scientific and Technological Information of China**
Box 640 A, 117 Chao Yang Men St., Peking, Peoples Republic of China
(Dist. by: Guozi Shudian (China Publications Centre), Box 399, Peking, Peoples Republic of China)
- Acta Geologica Sinica. q. ISSN 0001-5717
- Acta Microbiologica Sinica/Wei Sheng Wu Hsueh Pao. q. ISSN 0001-6209
- Acta Palaeontologica Sinica. s-a. ISSN 0001-6616 (Dist. by Guozi Shudian, P.O. Box 399, Peking, People's Republic of China)

**Kexue Chuban She**
Chaoyang Men Nei da Jie 117, Peking, Peoples Republic of China
(Dist. by Guozi Shudian (China Publications Centre), Box 399, Peking, People's Republic of China)
- Acta Astronomica Sinica. s-a. ISSN 0001-5245
- Kexue Tongbao. m. ISSN 0023-074X

**Ko Hsueh Chu Pan She. Chung-Kuo Kuo Chi Shu Tien**
P.X. Box 399, Peking, China.
- Chung-Kuo Ko Hsueh. q.

**Pai Wan Chuang**
Peking 37, Peoples' Republic of China
(Dist. by Guozi Shudian (China Publications Centre), Box 399, Peking, People's Republic of China)
- Peking Review; a magazine of Chinese news and views. w. ISSN 0031-4129

**Sun Yat-Sen University**
Canton, Peoples Republic of China.
- Sun Yat-Sen University. Journal: Social Sciences. 4 per yr.

**Szechuan University**
Chengtu, Peoples Republic of China.
- Szechuan University Journal: Social Sciences Edition. 4 per yr.

**University of Peking**
Peking, Hopei, Peoples Republic of China.
- University of Peking. Human Sciences. Journal. 4 per yr.

## CHINA, REPUBLIC OF

**Academia Sinica. Institute for Advanced Chinese Studies**
Box 12, Yang Ming Shan, Taiwan, Republic of China.
- Chinese Culture. q. ISSN 0009-4544

**Academia Sinica. Institute of Botany**
Nankang, Taiwan, Republic of China.
- Botanical Bulletin of Academia Sinica. s-a. ISSN 0006-8063

**Academia Sinica. Institute of Chemistry**
Taipei, Taiwan, Republic of China.
- Academia Sinica. Institute of Chemistry. Bulletin. a. ISSN 0001-3927

**Academia Sinica. Institute of Ethnology**
Nankang, Taipei, Taiwan, Republic of China.
- Academia Sinica. Institute of Ethnology. Bulletin. s-a. ISSN 0001-3935

**Academia Sinica. Institute of History and Philology**
Taipei, Taiwan, Republic of China.
- Academia Sinica. Institute of History and Philology. Bulletin.

**Academia Sinica. Institute of Mathematics**
Taipei, Taiwan, Republic of China.
- Academia Sinica. Institute of Mathematics. Bulletin/Chung Yang Yen Chiu y Uan Shu Hs Ueh Yen Chiu So. s-a.

**Academia Sinica. Institute of Modern History**
Nankang, Taipei, Taiwan, Republic of China.
- Academia Sinica. Institute of Modern History. Bulletin/Chung Yang Yen Chiu Yuan. Chiu Tai Shih Yen Chiu So Chi K'an. irreg.

**Academia Sinica. Institute of Zoology**
Nankang, Taipei, Taiwan, Republic of China.
- Academia Sinica.Institute of Zoology.Bulletin. s-a. ISSN 0001-3943

**Agricultural Association of China**
14 Weng-Chow St., Taipei 107, Taiwan, Republic of China.
- Agricultural Association of China. Journal. q. ISSN 0300-550X

**Asian and Pacific Council**
Food and Fertilizer Technology Center, 4Th Fl., 116 Huaining St., Taipei, Taiwan.
- Asian and Pacific Council. Food and Fertilizer Technology Center. Technical Bulletin. bi-m.

**Asian Cultural Center**
c/o Dr Chang Pe-Chin, Cathay Sung Chiang Bldg., 5th Fl., 129 Sung Chiang Road, Taipei, Taiwan, Republic of China.
- Asian Culture Quarterly. q.

**Asian Outlook**
Box 22992, Taipei, Taiwan, Republic of China.
- Asian Outlook; the Asian peoples' Anti-Communist League, Republic of China. m. ISSN 0004-4628

**Asian Peoples' Anti-Communist League - Republic of China**
1, Tsiangtao E. Road, Sec. 1, Taipei, Taiwan, Republic of China.
- Asian Peoples' Anti-Communist League. China. Pamphlet. irreg. (10-12 per yr) ISSN 0571-2920

**Association for Asian Studies**
P.O. Box 22048, Taipei 100, Taiwan, Republic of China
(U.S. Subscr. to: Chinese Materials Center Inc., 809 Taraval St., San Francisco, CA 94116)
- Annotated Guide to Taiwan Periodical Literature. ISSN 0066-2445

**Association of Obstetrics and Gynecology of the Republic of China**
No.1 Chang-Te St., Taipei, Taiwan, Republic of China.
- Journal of Obstetrics and Gynecology of the Republic of China. q.

**Atomic Energy Council**
6Th Floor, BCC Building, 53, Jen Ai Road, Section 3, Taipei, Taiwan 106, Republic of China.
- Chinese A E C Bulletin. bi-m.

**Bank of Communications**
91 Heng Yang Road, Taipei, Taiwan, Republic of China.
- Chiao T'ung Yin Hang. Annual Report. a.

**Bank of Taiwan**
Chungking Rd. South, Taipei, Taiwan, Republic of China
- Bank of Taiwan Quarterly. q. ISSN 0005-5344 (Chung-Hwa Book Co., Ltd., 94 Sectional Chungking Rd. South, Box 3942, Taipei, Taiwan, Republic of China)

**Board of Foreign Trade**
1 Hu Kou St., Taipei, Taiwan, Republic of China.
- Taiwan Exports. irreg. ISSN 0494-5336

**Business and Industry: Taiwan**
P. O. Box 30-332, Taipei, Taiwan, Republic of China.
- Business and Industry: Taiwan. w.

**Central Bank of China**
Taipei, Taiwan, Republic of China.
- Central Bank of China, T'ai-Pei. Annual Report. a. ISSN 0069-150X
- Graphical Survey of the Economy of Taiwan, the Republic of China. a.

**Central Bank of China. Economic Research Department**
Taipei, Taiwan, Republic of China.
- Taiwan Financial Statistics Monthly/T'ai-Wan Chin Jung T'ung Chi Yueh Pao. m. ISSN 0496-7046

**Prof. Chien-Fu Chen, Ed. & Pub.**
Box 22239, Taipei, Taiwan, Republic of China.
- Hsin Ju Chia/New Confucians. m. ISSN 0018-6937

**China Academy**
- Institute of Pacific Research. Journal. (pub. by Hwa-Kang Publishing Co.)

**China Development Corporation**
131 Nanking East Road, Section 5, Taipei, Taiwan, Republic of China.
- China Development Corporation. Annual Report. a.

**China Economic News Service**
555 Chunghsiao E. Road, Sec. 4, Taipei 105, Taiwan, Republic of China.
- Taiwan Products. m.

**China External Trade Development Council**
10th Floor, 201 Tun Hwa N. Road, Taipei 105, Taiwan, Republic of China.
- Exports of the Republic of China. a. ISSN 0301-9217
- Imports of the Republic of China. a.
- Trade Opportunities in Taiwan. (pub. by Far East Trade Service, Inc.)

**China Forum Incorporation**
7 Lin Shen North Rd., Taipei, Taiwan, Republic of China.
- China Forum. s-a.

**China Philatelic Society**
Box 18, Taipei 231, Taiwan, Republic of China.
- China Philatelic Magazine. q.

**China Productivity Center**
P.O. Box 769, 62 Sining South Road, Taipei, Taiwan, Republic of China.
- Taiwan Buyers' Guide; alphabetical and classified lists of 12,000 Taiwan manufacturers, importers, exporters, and services representatives. biennial. ISSN 0082-1470

**China Publishing Company**
Box 337, Taipei, Taiwan, Republic of China
(U.S. Subscr. to: Chinese Information Office, 159 Lexington Ave., New York, N.Y. 10016)
- Sinorama. m.
- Vista. bi-m. ISSN 0042-7101

**China, Republic. Department of Social Affairs**
Nan-Tou Hsien, Taiwan, Republic of China.
- Social Affairs Statistics of Taiwan/Chung-Hua Min Kuo Tai-Wan Sheng She Hui Shih Yeh Tung Chi. a.

**China, Republic. Directorate-General of Budget, Accounting and Statistics**
Taiwan, Republic of China.
- China (Republic). Directorate-General of Budget, Accounting, and Statistics. Report on the Survey of Personal Income Distribution in Taiwan Area. a.
- China (Republic). Monthly Bulletin of Statistics. m.
- Statistical Yearbook of the Republic of China. a.

**China, Republic. Economic Planning Council**
- Industry of Free China. (pub. by Publishing Committee of Industry of Free China)

**China, Republic. Ministry of Communications. Tourism Bureau**
P.O. Box 1490, Taipei, Taiwan, Republic of China.
- Kuan Kuang Tzu Liao/Monthly Report on Tourism, Republic of China. m.

**China, Republic. Ministry of Economic Affairs. Industrial Development & Investment Center**
5Th Floor, Hwianing Bldg., 53 Hwaining St., Taipei, Taiwan, Republic of China.
- Taiwan Industrial Panorama. m. ISSN 0039-9108

**China, Republic. Ministry of Finance. Department of Statistics**
Taipei, Taiwan, Republic of China.
- China (Republic) Dept. of Statistics. Monthly Statistics of Exports and Imports. m.

**China, Republic. Ministry of the Interior**
Taipei, Taiwan, Republic of China.
- Taiwan Demography Monthly. m.

**China, Republic. Telecommunications Laboratories**
Ministry of Communications, Box 71, Chung-Li, Taiwan, Republic of China.
- China, Republic. Telecommunication Laboratories. Technical Reports. q.

**China Society**
- China Society Journal. (pub. by Chung Tai Publishing Co.)

**Chinese Chemical Society**
Box 609, Taipei, Taiwan, Republic of China.
- Chinese Chemical Society. Journal. q. ISSN 0009-4536

**Chinese Institute of Chemical Engineers**
c/o Ed. Min-San Hsieh, Dept. of Chemical Engineering, Republic of China, Taipei 107, Taiwan, Taiwan.
- Chinese Institute of Chemical Engineers. Journal. s-a.

**Chinese Institute of Civil and Hydraulic Engineering**
P.O. Box No. 499, Taipei, Taiwan, Republic of China
- Journal of Civil and Hydraulic Engineering. q. (Dist. by: Kiji Publishing Co., 185 po Ai Rd., 2nd Fl., Taipei 100, Taiwan)

**Chinese Institute of Mining & Metallurgical Engineers. Industrial Technology Research Institute**
- Mining Technical Digest. (pub. by Mining Research & Service Organization)

**Chinese Petroleum Corporation. Exploration Division**
46 Chung Cheng Rd., Miaoli, Taiwan, Republic of China.
- Petroleum Geology of Taiwan/T'aiwan Shih Yu Ti Chih. a.

**Chinese Physiological Society**
Department of Biophysics, Box 7432, National Defense Medical Center, Taipei, Taiwan, Republic of China.
- Chinese Journal of Physiology. a.

**Chinese Psychological Association**
c/o Department of Psychology, National Taiwan University, Taipei, Taiwan, Republic of China.
- Acta Psychologica Taiwanica. a. ISSN 0065-1613

**Chinese Society of Microbiology**
National Taiwan University, College of Medicine, Taipei, Taiwan, Republic of China.
- Chinese Journal of Microbiology. q. ISSN 0009-4587

**Ching Sui Printing Works Co., Ltd.**
71 Chung Shan Rd. Section 1, Box 1108 Musa, Taipei, Taiwan, Republic of China.
- African Studies. a. (National Chengehi University. Program of African Studies)

**Chung Hwa Information Service**
Box 337, Taipei, Taiwan, Republic of China
(U.S. Subscr. to: Chinese Information Service, 159 Lexington Ave., New York, NY 10016)
- Free China Review. m. ISSN 0016-030X
- Free China Weekly. w. ISSN 0016-0318
- What's Happening on the Chinese Mainland. fortn. ISSN 0512-5278

**Chung-Kuo Tai Chi Chuan Hsueh Shu Yen Chiu Hui**
Taipei, Taiwan, Republic of China.
- Tai Chi Chuan Yen Chiu Chuan Chi. m.

**Chung Tai Publishing Co.**
Box 1637, Taipei, Taiwan, Republic of China.
- China Society Journal. a.

**Confucius-Mencius Society of the Republic of China**
45, Nan Hai Rd., Taipei, Taiwan, Republic of China.
- Confucius & Mencius Society of the Republic of China Journal. s-a.

**Cooperative Bank of Taiwan**
75-1 Kuan Chien Rd., Taipei, Taiwan, Republic of China.
- Cooperative Bank of Taiwan. Annual Report/Tai-Wan Shena Ho Tso Chin Ku. Annual Report. a.
- Co-Operatives Quarterly. q. ISSN 0009-9856

**Echo Magazine Co.**
5-2 Pa Teh Rd., Sec. 4, Lane 72, Alley 16, Taipei, Taiwan, Republic of China.
- Echo; of things Chinese. m. (11 per yr) ISSN 0012-9135

**Epoch Publicity Agency**
8 Nanking East Rd., Section 1, Taipei, Taiwan, Republic of China.
- Free China. a. ISSN 0071-9315

**Evensongs Association**
- Evensongs/Yeh Ko. (pub. by Tamkang College of Arts & Sciences)

**Family Planning Association of China**
1 Lane 160 Fu Hsing S. Rd., Sec. 2, Taipei 106, Taiwan, Republic of China.
- F P A C Monthly Report. m.

**Far East Trade Service, Inc.**
10th Floor, 201 Tun Hwa North Rd., Taipei 105, Taiwan, Republic of China.
- Trade Opportunities in Taiwan. every 10 days. (China External Trade Development Council)

**Farmers' Friend**
Box 16, Nei-Hsin, Taichung, Taiwan, Republic of China.
- Farmers' Friend. m. ISSN 0014-8415

**Fen Tou**
Cultural Building, 5th Floor, Sec. 1, Hsin i Road, Taipei, Taiwan, Republic of China.
- Struggle/Fen Tou. m.

**Formosan Association for Advancement of Science**
341 Hwa Cheng Rd., Hsin Chuang Chen, Taipei, Taiwan, Republic of China.
- Formosan Science. q. ISSN 0015-7791

**Formosan Medical Association**
No. 1, Sect. 1, Jen-Ai Rd., Taipei, Taiwan, Republic of China.
- Formosan Medical Association. Journal. m. ISSN 0015-7783

**Fu-Min Geographical Institute of Economic Development**
Taipei, Taiwan, Republic of China.
- Geography and Industries. s-a. ISSN 0016-7495

**Fukien Humanities Society**
22 Lane 113, Amoy St., Taipei, Taiwan (Formosa), Republic of China.
- Journal of Fukien History. q. ISSN 0022-1228

**Good Earth Press**
P.O. Box 697, Taipei, Taiwan, Republic of China.
- Taiwan Sugar. irreg. ISSN 0492-1712

**Harvest Farm Magazine**
14, Wenchow St., Taipai, Taiwan, Republic of China.
- Harvest Farm Magazine. s-m. ISSN 0017-8195

**Jeng Herney-Shorng, Ed. & Pub.**
61, Lane 813 Chung Chen Rd., Chu 1 Village, Chu-Pei, Hsinchu, Taiwan, Republic of China.
- Guide to Chinese Periodicals. irreg.

**Hwa-Kang Publishing Co.**
Yangmingshan, Taiwan, Republic of China
(Subscr. Address: P.O. Box 2, Yangmingshan, Taipei, Republic of China)
- Institute of Pacific Research. Journal. s-a. ISSN 0020-3025 (China Academy)

**Importers & Exporters Association of Taipei**
3D Floor, Traders' Bldg., 65, Nanking East Rd., Section 3, Taipei, Taiwan, Republic of China.
- Taiwan International Trade. m.
- Taiwan Trade Directory. a.

**Inspectorate General of Customs. Statistical Department**
85, Hsin-Sheng S. Rd. Sec., 1, Taipei, Taiwan, Republic of China.
- Trade of China. a. ISSN 0082-5778

**Institute for the Study of Chinese Communist Problems**
Box 351, Taipei, Taiwan, Republic of China.
- Chung Kung Yen Chiu/Studies on Chinese Communism. m. ISSN 0014-9667

**Institute of International Relations**
Box 1189, Taipei, Taiwan, Republic of China.
- Fei-Ching Yueh-Pao/Chinese Communist Affairs Monthly. m. ISSN 0014-9675
- Issues & Studies. m. ISSN 0021-2377

**Institute of Sino-American Relations**
College of Chinese Culture, Hwa Kang, Taiwan 13, Republic of China.
- Sino-American Relations. q.

**International Commercial Bank of China**
15 Chungshan Rd., N., Section 2, 104, Taipei, Taiwan, Republic of China.
- International Commercial Bank of China. Annual Report. a.

**International Commercial Bank of China. Head Office-Economic Research Dept.**
100 Chi-Lin Rd., Taipei, Taiwan 104, Republic of China.
- Economic Review. bi-m. ISSN 0013-029X
- International Commerical Bank of China. Monthly Economic Survey. m.

**International P. E. N. Taipei Chinese Center**
277 Roosevelt Road, Section 3, Taipei, Taiwan, Republic of China.
- Chinese Pen. q.

**Jeng-Yih Lin**
12 Lane 28, Tung Hwa St., Taipei, Taiwan, Republic of China.
- Modern Printing. bi-m.

**Kwang Wen Book Co.**
9-3 Roosevelt Rd., Section 2, Taipei, Taiwan, Republic of China.
- Ch'ing Documents/Ku-Kung Wen Hsien. q. ISSN 0009-465X (National Palace Museum)

**Land Bank of Taiwan. Research Dept.**
Taipei, Taiwan, Republic of China.
- Quarterly Journal of Taiwan Land Credit. q. ISSN 0033-5665

**Mining Research & Service Organization**
No. 1, Tun-Hwa S. Rd., Sec.3, Taipei, Taiwan, Republic of China.
- Mining Technical Digest. m. ISSN 0300-3760 (Chinese Institute of Mining & Metallurgical Engineers. Industrial Technology Research Institute)

**National Central Library**
43 Nan Hai Road, Taipei 107, Taiwan, Republic of China.
- Chinese National Bibliography. m.
- Index to Chinese Periodicals. m.
- National Central Library. Bulletin. s-a. ISSN 0027-8947
- Republic of China. National Central Library. Newsletter. q. ISSN 0034-5016

**National Central Library. Bureau of International Exchange of Publications**
43 Nan-Hai Rd., Taipei 107, Taiwan, Republic of China.
- Directory of the Cultural Organizations of the Republic of China. ISSN 0419-3733

**National Chengchi University**
Center for Public and Business Administration Education, No. 187-1, Chin-Hua St., Taipei, Taiwan, Republic of China.
- Chinese Journal of Administration. s-a. ISSN 0009-4579

**National Chengehi University. Program of African Studies**
- African Studies. (pub. by Ching Sui Printing Works Co., Ltd.)

**National Palace Museum**
Wai-Shuang-Hsi, Shih-Lin, Taipei, Taiwan, Republic of China.
- Ch'ing Documents/Ku-Kung Wen Hsien. (pub. by Kwang Wen Book Co.)
- National Palace Museum Bulletin. bi-m. ISSN 0027-9846
- National Palace Museum Newsletter. m. ISSN 0027-9854
- National Palace Museum Quarterly. q.

**National Press Council of the Republic of China**
c/o Independence Evening Post, 4th Floor, 15 Chinan Road, Section 2, Taipei (100), Taiwan, Republic of China.
- P C O T Bulletin. irreg.

**National Science Council of the Republic of China**
2 Canton St., Taipei, 108 Taiwan, Republic of China.
- N S C Review. a.

**National Taiwan Normal University. Department of Social Education**
Taipei, Taiwan, Republic of China
(U.S. Subscr. to: Chinese Culture Service, Inc., Box 444, Oak Park, IL 60303)
- Journal of Library & Information Science. s-a.

**National Taiwan Normal University. Graduate Institute of Education**
East Ho-Ping Road, Taipei, Taiwan, Republic of China.
- National Taiwan Normal University. Graduate Institute of Education. Bulletin. a.

**National Taiwan University. College of Agriculture**
Taipei, Taiwan, Republic of China.
- National Taiwan University. College of Agriculture. Memoirs. irreg. ISSN 0077-5819

**National Taiwan University. College of Engineering**
Taipei, Taiwan, Republic of China.
- National Taiwan University. College of Engineering. Memoirs. irreg. ISSN 0077-5827

**National Taiwan University. College of Law**
Taipei, Taiwan, Republic of China.
- National Taiwan University. College of Law. Journal of Social Science. irreg., 1973, no. 22. ISSN 0077-5835

**National Taiwan University. College of Medicine**
Taipei, Taiwan, Republic of China.
- National Taiwan University. College of Medicine. Memoirs. 2 per yr. ISSN 0028-0275

**National Taiwan University. College of Science**
Taipei, Taiwan, Republic of China.
- Taiwania. 2-3 per yr. ISSN 0065-1125

**National Taiwan University. Department of Agricultural Chemistry**
Taipei, Taiwan, Republic of China.
- Chinese Agricultural Chemical Society. Journal. q.

**National Taiwan University. Department of Archaeology and Anthropology**
Taipei, Taiwan, Republic of China.
- National Taiwan University. Department of Archaeology and Anthropology. Bulletin. s-a. ISSN 0077-5843

**National Taiwan University. Department of Geography**
Taipei Taiwan, Republic of China.
- National Taiwan University. Department of Geography. Science Reports. irreg.

**National Taiwan University. Department of Geology**
Taipei, Taiwan, Republic of China.
- Acta Geologica Taiwanica. a. ISSN 0065-1265

**National Taiwan University. Department of Sociology**
21 Hsu-Chow Road, Taipei, Taiwan 100, Republic of China.
- National Taiwan University Journal of Sociology/Tai-Wan ta Hsueh She Hui Hsueh K'an. a. ISSN 0077-5851

**National Taiwan University. Graduate Institute of Electrical Engineering**
Taipei, Taiwan, Republic of China.
- Journal of Electrical Engineering. a.

**National Taiwan University. Institute of Fishery Biology**
Taipei, Taiwan 107, Republic of China.
- National Taiwan University. Institute of Fishery Biology. Report. biennial.

**National Taiwan University. Institute of Oceanography**
Taipei, Taiwan, Republic of China.
- Acta Oceanographica Taiwanica. a.

**New China Publication Service**
Cultural Bldg., Fifth Floor, No. 3 Hsin 1 Road, Sec 1, Taipei, Taiwan, Republic of China.
- Torch of Victory. m. ISSN 0582-9860

**Nuclear Energy Society**
6th Floor, BCC Bldg., 53 Jen Ai Rd. Section 3, Taipei, Taiwan 106, Republic of China.
- Nuclear Science Journal. q. ISSN 0029-5647

**Nurses Association of the Republic of China**
89 Neichiang, Taipei, Republic of China.
- Journal of Nursing/Hu Li Tsa Chih. q. ISSN 0047-262X

**Opthalmological Society of the Republic of China**
c/o National Taiwan University Hospital, Department of Ophthalmology, 1 Chan-Teh St., Taipei 100, Taiwan, Republic of China.
- Ophthalmological Society of the Republic of China. Transactions. a.

**Pediatric Association of the Republic of China**
Dept. of Pediatrics, National Taiwan Univ. Hospital, 1 Chang Te St., Taipei, Taiwan, Republic of China.
- Acta Paediatrica Sinica. q. ISSN 0001-6578

**Plant Protection Center**
Chung Cheng Rd., Wuffeng, Taichung Hsien, Taiwan, Republic of China.
- Plant Protection Center. Annual Report. a.

**Prophet Press, Taipei**
Ed. Dr. Thaddeus Hang, 51 Roosevelt Rd., 5Th
Section, Taipei, Taiwan, Republic of China.
● Chieh-Hsueh Yu Wen-Hua. (Universitas)/
Universitas; monthly review of philosophy and
culture. m.

**Publishing Committee of Industry of Free China**
118 Hwai Ning St., Taipei, Taiwan, Republic of
China.
● Industry of Free China. m.(2 vols. per yr.) ISSN
0019-946X (China, Republic. Economic Planning
Council)

**Shih Chieh Wen Wu Kung Ying She Tsung Ching
Hsiao**
37 O-Mei St., 4Th Fl. 100, Taipei, Taiwan, Republic
of China.
● Jen Yu She Hui. bi-m.

**Sino-American Cultural and Economic Association**
Liang Han-Chao, 8 Fst. Sec. Chung Hslao Rd.,
Taipei, Taiwan, Republic of China.
● West & East. m. ISSN 0043-3047

**Social Education Society of China**
c/o Social Education Dept, Ministry of Education,
Chungshan S. Rd., Taipei, Taiwan, Republic of
China.
● Social Education Yearly. a.

**Soochow University**
Wai Shuang Hsi, Shihlin, Taipei, Taiwan, Republic
of China.
● Soochow University Journal of Chinese Art
History. irreg.

**Student Book Co. Ltd.**
298, Roosevelt Road, 3Rd Section, Taipei, Taiwan,
Republic of China.
● Bibliography Quarterly/Shu Mo Chi Kan. q. ISSN
0006-1581

**Sun-Lin-Sheng**
123 Wenchou St., Taipei, Taiwan, Republic of
China.
● New World. m. ISSN 0028-7032

**Sun Yat-Sen Cultural Foundation**
23 Lane 13, Yung Kang St., Taipei 106, Taiwan,
Republic of China.
● Chung Shan Hsueh Shu Wen Hua Chi Kan. s-a.
ISSN 0009-6288
● Sun Yat-Sen Cultural Foundation Bulletin. s-a.
ISSN 0300-3302

**Taipei City Department of Information**
Department of Information, 39 Chang An West Rd.,
Taipei, Taiwan, Republic of China.
● Taipei Pictorial. m. ISSN 0039-9051

**Taipei Public Health Teaching and Demonstration
Center**
7-2, Kung-Yuan Rd., Taipei, Taiwan, Republic of
China
(Dist. in U.S. by China Medical Board of New
York, Inc., 420 Lexington Ave., New York, N.Y.
10017)
● Taipei Public Health Teaching and Demonstration
Center. Annual Report. a. ISSN 0082-1462

**Taipei Tourism Bureau**
Box 1490, Taipei, Taiwan, Republic of China.
● Annual Report on Tourism Statistics, Republic of
China. a.

**Taiwan Agricultural Research Institute**
Taipei, Taiwan, Republic of China.
● Journal of Taiwan Agricultural Research. q. ISSN
0022-4847
● Taiwan Agricultural Research Institute. Bulletin.
m.

**Taiwan Enterprise Press**
Box 73--4, Taipei, Taiwan, Republic of China.
● Taiwan Enterprise. m.

**Taiwan Fisheries Research Institute**
199 Hou-Ih Rd., Keelung, Taiwan, Republic of
China.
● Taiwan. Fisheries Research Institute, Keelung.
Bulletin. irreg. , 1973, no. 22. ISSN 0082-1489
● Taiwan. Fisheries Research Institute, Keelung.
Laboratory of Fishery Biology. Report. irreg.,
1973, no. 23. ISSN 0082-1497

**Taiwan Fisheries Research Institute. Tungkang
Marine Laboratory**
Tungkang, Pingtung, Taiwan, Republic of China.
● Aquiculture. irreg.

**Taiwan Museum**
No. 2 Siangyand Rd., Taipei, Taiwan, Republic of
China.
● Taiwan Museum. Quarterly Journal. q. ISSN
0039-9116

**Taiwan Pictorial Society**
Box 1919, 20 Chungking South Rd., Sec. 2 Taipei,
Taiwan, Republic of China.
● Taiwan. m. ISSN 0039-9086

**Taiwan Provincial Labor Force Survey and Research
Institute**
75-2, Sect. 3 Hjin-Yi Road, Taipei, Taiwan,
Republic of China.
● Taiwan Provincial Labor Force Survey and
Research Institute Quarterly Report on the Labor
Force Survey in Taiwan. q.

**Taiwan Railway Administration**
Taipei, Taiwan, Republic of China.
● Taiwan Railway. irreg.

**Taiwan Sheng Cheng Fu Chiao Tung Chu**
Nan-Tou Hsien, Taiwan, Republic of China.
● Taiwan Annual Statistical Report of
Transportation/Tai-Wan Sheng Chiao Tung Tung
Chi Nien Pao. a.

**Taiwan Sugar Research Institute. Tai-Wan Tang Yeh
Yen Chiu So**
Tainan, Taiwan, Republic of China.
● Taiwan Sugar Research Institute. Annual Report.
a.

**Taiwan ta Hsueh Nung Tai Hui**
Taipei, Taiwan, Republic of China.
● Chu Chen. irreg.

**Taiwan Telecommunications Administration**
Ministry of Communications, 42 Jen Ai Road,
Taipei, Taiwan, Republic of China.
● Taiwan Telecommunications Technical Quarterly.
q.

**Tamkang College of Arts & Sciences**
English Department Evening School, No. 5, Lane
199, Kinghua St., Taipei, Taiwan, Republic of
China.
● Evensongs/Yeh Ko. irreg., no. 12, 1975.

**Tamkang College of Arts & Sciences. Graduate
Institute of Western Languages and Literature**
King-Hua St., Taipei, Taiwan 106, Republic of
China.
● Tamkang Review; a journal mainly devoted to
comparative studies between Chinese and foreign
literatures. s-a. ISSN 0049-2949

**Tamkang College of Arts & Sciences. Research
Institute of Mathematics**
Tamsui, Taipei, Taiwan, Republic of China.
● Tamkang Journal of Mathematics. s-a. ISSN 0049-
2930

**Tattler**
P. O. Box 362, Tai-Nan, Taiwan, Republic of China.
● Tattler/Ku Chin T'an. m.

**Thought and Word Association**
28-1 Park Rd., 3rd Floor, Taipei, Taiwan, Republic
of China.
● Thought and Word/Ssu Yu Yen. bi-m.

**Times Enterprise Corp.**
Fl. 10 No. 219 Hsi Ning South Rd., Taipei, Taiwan,
Republic of China.
● Shih Tai Chi Yeh/Times Enterprise. m.

**Tong-Hsing Culture Press**
P.O. Box 3377, Taipei, Republic of China.
● Businessman's Directory, The Republic of China.
a.

**Trade Winds, Inc.**
P. O. Box 7-179, Taipei, Taiwan, Republic of China.
● Trade Winds. w.

**Tsai Cheng Pu Tung Chi Chu**
Taipei, Taiwan, Republic of China.
● China (Republic). Yearbook of Tax Statistics/Fu
Shui Tung Chi Shou Tse. a.

**United Nations Association of the Republic of China**
15 Chuan Chow St., Taipei, Taiwan, Republic of
China.
● United Nations Association of the Republic of
China News Letter. m.

**Wen i Yueh K'an She**
Taipei, Taiwan, Republic of China.
● Literature and Art/Wen i Yueh K'an. m.

**Wen-Tsal-Lee**
162 Section 1, Hoping East Rd., Taipei, Taiwan,
Republic of China.
● Sinological Studies. bi-m.

**World Enterprise**
247 San Ming Road, Tai - Chung, Taiwan, Republic
Jf China.
● China (Republic). Machinery and Electrical
Apparatus Industry Yearbook/Chung-Hua Min
Kuo Chi Chi Yu Tien Kung Chi Tsai Nien Chien.
a.

# COLOMBIA

**Editorial A B C**
Apartado Aereo No. 28454, Bogota, Colombia.
● Revista Latinoamericana de Psicologia. 3 per yr.
ISSN 0034-978X

**Academia Colombiana de Historia**
Calle 10, No. 8-95, Bogota, Colombia.
● Boletin de Historia y Antiguedades. q. ISSN
0006-6303

**Academia Colombiana de la Lengua Espanola**
Carrera 3-A, Numero 17-34, Bogota, Colombia.
● Academia Colombiana. Boletin. q. ISSN 0001-
3773

**Academia de Medicina de Medellin. Facultad de
Medicina**
Apartado Aereo 52278 y Nacional, 3301 Medellin,
Colombia.
● Antioquia Medica. 10 per yr. ISSN 0044-8389

**Accion Cultural Popular**
● Campesino. (pub. by Editora Dosmil)

**Eduardo Acevedo, Ed. & Pub.**
Apdo. Nal. 2584, Bogota, Colombia.
● Sociedad Geografica de Colombia. Boletin. q.
ISSN 0037-8577

**Agrosintesis**
Apartado Aereo 24.215, Bogota, Colombia.
● Agrosintesis. w. ISSN 0044-6882

**Alvaro Aldana y Cia Ltd.**
Calle 37 No. 17-27, Bogota, Colombia.
● Industria y Desarrollo Internacional. bi-m.

**Antioquia, Colombia. Departamento Administrativo de
Planeacion Biblioteca**
Oficina 107, Medellin, Colombia.
● Planeacion Regional. q.

**Antioquia, Colombia. Secretaria de Educacion y
Cultura**
Medellin, Antioquia, Colombia.
● Antioquia. Secretaria de Educacion y Cultura.
Revista Cultura. q.

**Aquarimantima**
Apartado Aereo 3845, Medelin, Colombia.
● Aquarimantima. irreg.

**Asociacion Colombiana de Archivistas. Archivo
Nacional**
Calle 24, No. 5-60 40 Piso, Bogota, D.E., Colombia.
● Carta de Archivo. q.

**Asociacion Colombiana de Facultades de Medicina**
Calle 45a No. 9-77 Piso 8, Bogota, D. E., Colombia.
● Indice de la Literatura Medica Colombiana. irreg.

**Asociacion Colombiana para al Estudio Cientifico de
la Poblacion**
Carrera 18 No. 33-95, Canal Ramirez - Antares,
Bogota, Colombia.
● Estudios de Planificacion Familiar. 2 per yr.

**Asociacion Nacional de Enfermeras de Colombia**
Apartado Aereo No. 15031, Bogota, D.E.,
Colombia.
● A N E C. 3 per yr. ISSN 0044-930X

**Asociacion Nacional de Industriales**
Centro Coltejer, P. 8, Apartado Aereo 997,
Medellin, Colombia.
- Asociacion Nacional de Industriales. Revista
  Bimestral. bi-m.
- Industria y Exportacion. bi-m.

**Asociacion Nacional de Instituciones Financieras**
Calle 35, No. 4-89, Apdo. Aereo 29677, Bogota,
Colombia.
- Derecho Financiero. irreg.

**Bancas y Bancarios de Colombia**
Avenida Jimenez 4-49, Apdo. Aereo 94-18, Bogota,
Colombia.
- Bancas y Bancarios de Colombia. q. ISSN 0408-
  4012

**Banco de la Republica. Departamento de
Investigaciones Economicas**
Carrera 7A No. 14-78, Apdo. Postal 402, Bogota,
Colombia.
- Banco de la Republica. Registros de Exportacion e
  Importacion. a.
- Colombia. Banco de la Republica. Revista. m.
  ISSN 0005-4828

**Bogota, Colombia. Camara de Comercio**
Carrera 9, No. 16-21, Piso 7, Apartado Aereo
29824, Bogota, Colombia.
- Camara de Comercio de Bogota. Boletin. m. ISSN
  0008-185X
- Camara de Comercio de Bogota. Departamento de
  Promocion y Desarrollo. Indicadores Economicos.
  irreg. (prep. by its Departamento de Promocion y
  Desarrollo)
- Camara de Comercio de Bogota. Revista. q.
- Camara de Comercio de Bogota. Servicio
  Informativo Quincenal. bi-w.

**Bucaramanga, Colombia. Camara de Comercio**
Edificio Camara de Comercio-2-Piso, Apdo. Aereo
973, Bucaramanga, Colombia.
- Noticiero Mercantil. m.

**Libreria Buchholz**
Av. Jimenez de Quesada 8-40, Bogota, Colombia.
- Eco; revista de la cultura de occidente. m. ISSN
  0012-9410

**Caja de Credito Agrario, Industrial y Minero**
Bogota, Colombia.
- Caja de Credito Agrario, Industrial y Minero.
  Financiamento de la Pequena y Mediana
  Industria. a.

**Camara Colombiana de la Construccion**
Aptdo Aero 9983, Bogota D.E., Colombia.
- Camara Colombiana de la Construccion. Boletin
  Mensual de Estadistica. m.
- Camara Colombiana de la Construccion Boletin
  Trimestral. q.

**Camara de Comercio Colombo-Americana**
Carrera 7 No. 32-16, Suite 701, Bogota, Colombia.
- Comercio Colombo Americano/Columbian
  American Business. bi-m. ISSN 0010-2288

**Cano Isaza & Cia**
Avenida el Espectador, Bogota, Colombia.
- Espectador. d. ISSN 0014-0589

**Capitulo Colombiano de la Academia Americana de
Pediatria**
Apartado 606, Bogota, Colombia.
- Revista Colombiana de Pediatria y Puericultura. 6
  per yr. ISSN 0034-7442

**Juan Caro & Asociados Ltda.**
Aptdo Aero 090914, Bogota, Colombia.
- Legal Bulletin; monthly service
  containing...laws..regulations affecting business in
  Colombia. m. ISSN 0458-9564

**Eliecer Celnik, Ed. & Pub.**
Apartado Aereo 9081, Bogota, Colombia.
- Menorah. m. ISSN 0025-939X

**Centro de Estudios e Investigaciones Sobre Mercados
Agropecuario**
Unidad de Documentacion e Intercambio, Calle 23,
No. 4-47, Of. 201, Bogota D. E., Colombia.
- C E I M A. Adquisiciones Recienta. bi-m. (Co-
  Sponsor: Universidad Jorge Tadeo Lozano)

**Centro de Estudios para el Desarrollo e Integracion
de America Latina**
Calle 17 No. 4-68, Apartamento 401, Apartado
20134, Bogota D.E. 1, Colombia.
- Tierra Nueva. q.

**Centro de Investigacion y Accion Social**
Carrera 5, No. 11-53, Aptdo. Aereo 25916, Bogota,
Colombia.
- Congreso Internacional de Vivienda Popular.
  (Servicio Latino-Americano y Asiatico de
  Vivienda Popular)

**Centro Internacional de Agricultura Tropical**
Office of Publication Services, Apartado Aereo 67-
13, Cali, Colombia.
- International Center of Tropical Agriculture.
  Annual Report. a.
- International Center of Tropical Agriculture.
  Information Bulletin. irreg.
- International Center of Tropical Agriculture.
  Reference Bulletins. irreg., 1973 no. 2.
- International Center of Tropical Agriculture.
  Technical Bulletin. irreg.

**Centro Nacional de Documentacion e Informacion
Pedagogica**
Apartado Aereo: 52976, Bogota, Colombia.
- Informacion Bibliografica Educativa. q. (Co-
  sponsor: Instituto Colombiano de Pedagogia)

**Centro Nacional de Investigaciones de Cafe. Seccion
de Publicaciones y Relaciones Publicas**
Chinchina, Caldas, Colombia.
- Cenicafe. q. ISSN 0008-8951

**Centro Regional para el Fomento del Libro en
America Latina**
Calle 70 No. 9-52, Bogota, Colombia.
- C E R L A L. Boletin Bibliografico. q. ISSN
  0120-1204
- Noticias CERLAL. q. ISSN 0120-1158

**Colegio Antioqueno de Abogados**
Edificio Bolsa de Medellin, Cra. 50, No. 50-48 - Of.
700, Medellin, Colombia.
- COLEGAS. irreg.

**Colegio de Abogados de Medellin**
Apartado Nacional 3446, Medellin, Colombia.
- Derecho. ISSN 0301-9063

**Colombia. Corporacion Nacional de Turismo**
Apartado Aereo 8400, Bogota, Colombia.
- Corporacion Nacional de Turismo de Colombia.
  Boletin de Investigaciones e Informacion
  Turistica. irreg.; latest issue, 1974.

**Colombia. Departamento Administrativo Nacional de
Estadistica. Banco Nacional de Datos**
Apdo Nacional 80043, Bogota D.E., Colombia.
- Colombia. Departamento Administrativo Nacional
  de Estadistica. Anuario Demografico. a.
- Colombia. Departamento Administrativo Nacional
  de Estadistica. Anuario de Estadisticas Fiscales y
  Financieras. a.
- Colombia. Departamento Administrativo Nacional
  de Estadistica. Anuario General de Estadistica -
  Justicia.
- Colombia. Departamento Administrativo Nacional
  de Estadistica. Boletin Mensual de Estadistica. m.
  ISSN 0010-1370
- Colombia. Departamento Administrativo Nacional
  de Estadistica. Educacion Superior; estadisticas
  basicas. irreg.
- Colombia. Departamento Administrativo
  Nacional. Division Politico-Administrativa de
  Colombia. irreg.
- Colombia. Departamento Administrativo Nacional
  de Estadistica. Anuario General de Estadistica -
  Transportes y Comunicaciones.

**Colombia. Departamento Nacional de Planeacion**
- Revista de Planeacion y Desarrollo. (pub. by
  Colombiana de Impresos)

**Colombia. Direccion General del Presupuesto**
Bogota, Colombia.
- Colombia. Direccion General del Presupuesto.
  Proyecto de Presupuesto. a. ISSN 0588-3598

**Colombia. Escuela Superior de Guerra. Fuerzas
Militares de Colombia**
Avenida 81 No. 45a-40, Apdo. Aereo 4403, Bogota,
D. E., Colombia.
- Revista de las Fuerzas Armadas. 3 per yr. ISSN
  0016-2485

**Colombia. Fuerza Aerea**
Apartado Aereo 51097, Bogota, D.E., Colombia.
- Revista Aeronautica; al servicio de la aviacion
  colombiana. q. ISSN 0034-6942

**Colombia. Instituto Colombiana de Seguros Sociales**
Transversal 17, no. 25-39, Bogota, Colombia.
- Seguridad Social. q.

**Colombia. Ministerio de Agricultura**
Bogota, Colombia.
- Colombia. Ministerio de Agricultura. (Informa
  Sobre las Actividades)
- Colombia. Ministerio de Agricultura. Programas
  Agricolas. (prep. by its Unidad de Estadistica)

**Colombia. Ministerio de Defensa**
Bogota D.E., Colombia.
- Colombia. Ministerio de Defensa. Boletin. ISSN
  0010-1389

**Colombia. Ministerio de Educacion Nacional. Division
de Educacion de Adultos**
Bogota, Colombia.
- Colombia. Ministerio de Educacion Nacional.
  Educacion para Desarrollo. irreg.

**Colombia. Ministerio de Educacion Nacional.
Instituto Colombiano de Antropologia**
Apdo. Nacional 407, Bogota, Colombia.
- Revista Colombiana de Folclor. s-a.

**Colombia. Ministerio de Educacion Nacional.
Instituto Colombiano para el Fomento de la
Educacion Superior**
Division de Documentacion y Fomento
Bibliotecario, Bogota, Colombia.
- Indice de Articulos de Publicaciones Periodicas en
  el Area de Ciencias Sociales y Humanidades.
  irreg.

**Colombia. Ministerio de Educacion Nacionial.
Extension Cultural**
Bucaramanga, Colombia.
- Revista de Santander. ISSN 0034-8902

**Colombia. Ministerio de Gobierno. Instituto
Linguistico de Verano**
Lomalinda, Meta, Colombia.
- Articulos en Linguistica y Campos Afines. irreg.
  (prep. by its Division Operativa de Asuntos
  Indigenas)

**Colombia. Ministerio de Minas y Energia**
Bogota, Colombia.
- Colombia. Ministerio de Minas y Energia.
  Memoria al Congreso de la Republica. irreg.
- Colombia. Ministerio de Minas y Energia.
  Officina de Planeacion. Indicadores de la
  Industria del Petroleo. irreg. (prep. by its Oficina
  de Planeacion)

**Colombia. Ministerio de Trabajo y Seguridad Social**
Bogota, Colombia.
- Colombia. Ministerio de Trabajo y Seguridad
  Social. Memoria. a.

**Colombia. Ministerio del Trabajo**
Oficina No. 42, Bogota, Colombia.
- Trabajo. irreg.

**Colombia. Policia Nacional**
Carrera 15, No. 10-41, Bogota, Colombia.
- Estadistica de Criminalidad. a.

**Colombia. Servicio Colombiano de Meteorologia e
Hidrologia**
Apartado Aereo 20032, Bogota, Colombia.
- Meteoros. irreg.

**Colombia. Superintendencia Bancaria**
Bogota, Colombia.
- Colombia. Superintendencia Bancaria. Revista. q.

**Colombiana de Impresos**
Carrera 13 26-45, Mezzanine, Of. 4, Bogata, D. E.,
Colombia.
- Revista de Planeacion y Desarrollo. irreg. ISSN
  0034-8686 (Colombia. Departamento Nacional de
  Planeacion)

**Compania de Seguros Bolivar**
Medellin, Colombia.
- Bolivar. q.

**Confederacion Colombiana de Camaras de Comercio**
Carrera 9a No.16-21, Bogota, Colombia.
- Confederacion Colombiana de Camaras de Comercio. Asamblea General. Informe Final. irreg.
- Confederacion Colombiana de Camaras de Comercio. Sintesis Mensual. m.

**Compania Editoria Continente**
Edificio Morulanda, Carrera 6a, 14-74, Bogota, Colombia.
- Economia. irreg.

**Corporacion Financiera Colombiana S.A. Departamento Tecnico-Economico**
Carrera 13 Nos. 26-45, Apdo. Aereo 11843, Bogota, Colombia.
- Corporacion Financiera Colombiana. Informativo Mensual. m.

**Corporacion Hotelera de Colombia**
Calle 19 No. 4-88, Piso 14, Apartado Aereo 29692, Bogota, Colombia.
- Corporacion Hotelera de Colombia. Boletin Informativo. m.
- Hoteles de Colombia. m. ISSN 0018-6279

**Cromos**
Calle 20 No. 4-55, Apartado Aereo 14860, Bogota, Colombia.
- Cromos; la actualidad ilustrada. w. ISSN 0011-1708

**Cuadernos Colombianos**
Apartado Aereo 51968, Medellin, Colombia.
- Cuadernos Colombianos. bi-m.

**Departamento del Valle del Cauca**
Cali, Colombia.
- Cespedesia; boletin cientifico del Departamento del Valle del Cauca. irreg.

**Desarrollo Indoamericano**
Apdo. Aereo 15122, Barranquilla, Colombia.
- Desarrollo Indoamericano. bi-m.

**Editora Dosmil**
Cra 39 A. No. 15-11, Bogota, Colombia.
- Campesino; semanario para la cultura y dignificacion del pueblo rural. w. ISSN 0008-235X (Accion Cultural Popular)

**E C O C Ltda.**
Calle 31, No. 10-41, Of. 702, Apartado Aereo 15964, Bogota, Colombia.
- Directorio Nacional de Profesionales. irreg.

**Escuela de Administracion y Finanzas y Tecnologias. Centro de Investigaciones**
Apartado Aereo 3300, Medellin, Colombia.
- Revista E A F I T - Temas Administrativos. q. ISSN 0120-033X

**Escuela Superior de Administracion Publica**
A.A. 29745, Bogota, Colombia.
- Administracion y Desarrollo. irreg. ISSN 0001-8309

**Esparavel**
Apartado Aereo 2670, Cali, Colombia.
- Esparavel; gaceta de poesia. 10 per yr. ISSN 0014-0562

**Fedemetal**
Av. Caracas No. 37-15, Bogota, Colombia.
- Metal. a.

**Federacion Latinoamericana de Bancos**
Calle 17, No. 7-35, Apartado Aereo 13997, Bogota, Colombia.
- Revista FELABAN. q.

**Federacion Nacional de Cafeteros de Colombia**
Apartado de Correos, Bogota, Colombia.
- Boletin de Informacion Estadistica Sobre Cafe. a. ISSN 0084-7941 (prep. by its Division de Investigaciones Economicas)
- Economia Cafetera. m. ISSN 0046-1148 (prep. by its Division de Investigaciones Economicas)
- Federacion Nacional de Cafeteros de Colombia. Informe de Labores de los Comites Departamentales de Cafeteros. irreg.
- Revista Cafetera de Colombia. bi-m.

**Federacion Odontologica Colombiana**
Calle 71 No. 11-10, Apdo. Aereo 52925, Bogota, Colombia.
- Federacion Odontologica Colombiana. Revista. 4 per yr. ISSN 0046-354X

**Fondo Colombiano de Investigaciones Cientificas**
Bogota, Colombia.
- Coleccion: Documentos e Historia de la Ciencia en Colombia. irreg.

**Editora Guadalupe Ltda.**
Apdo. Aereo 854, Bogota, Colombia.
- America Latina 2001; revista latinoamericana de ciencia, tecnologia y futurologia. q.

**Heraldo Dental**
Carrera 18, No. 34-34, Bucaramanga, Colombia.
- Heraldo Dental. irreg. ISSN 0073-1900

**Ideologia y Sociedad**
Apdo. Aero 51 181, Bogota 2, D. E., Colombia.
- Ideologia y Sociedad. q.

**Instituto Caro y Cuervo**
Apartado Aereo 20002, Bogota, Colombia.
- Anuario Bibliografico Colombiano. a. ISSN 0570-393X
- Archivo Epistolar Colombiano. irreg.; latest issue, no. 10, 1976. ISSN 0066-6734
- Biblioteca Colombiana. irreg., no. 11, 1974.
- Clasicos Colombianos. irreg. 1972, no. 6. ISSN 0069-4444
- Filologos Colombianos. irreg., 1972, no. 7. ISSN 0071-4976
- Instituto Caro y Cuervo. Noticias Culturales. m. ISSN 0020-370X
- Instituto Caro y Cuervo. Publicaciones. irreg; latest 1975, no. 36.
- Instituto Caro y Cuervo. Serie Bibliografica. irreg.; no. 12, 1976. ISSN 0073-991X
- Instituto Caro y Cuervo. Serie Granada Entreabierta. irreg.; no. 15, 1976.
- Instituto Caro y Cuervo. Series Minor. irreg.; no. 20, 1975. ISSN 0073-9928
- Thesaurus. 3 per yr. ISSN 0040-604X

**Instituto Colombiana de Cultura**
Bogota, Colombia.
- Gaceta; revista internacional de cultura. irreg.

**Instituto Colombiano Agropecuario**
Apartado Aereo 7984, Bogota, D.E., Colombia.
- Indice Agricola Colombiano. a. ISSN 0073-7151
- Instituto Colombiano Agropecuario. I C A Informa. m. ISSN 0046-9920 (prep. by its Division de Comunicacion Rural)
- Instituto Colombiano Agropecuario. Revista I C A. q. ISSN 0018-8794 (prep. by its Division de Comunicacion Rural)
- Instituto Colombiano Agropecuario. Temas Didacticos. bi-m. (prep. by its Division de Comunicacion Rural)

**Instituto Colombiano de Comercio**
Cra. 40 No. 22c-67, Bogota, Colombia.
- Comercio Exterior. m.

**Instituto Colombiano de Investigaciones Sociales**
Carrera 50, No. 50-48, Oficina 402, Apto. 2021, Medellin, Colombia.
- Ciencias Sociales; economia - sociologia - derecho. bi-m. ISSN 0009-6806

**Instituto de Anthropologia e Historia del Estado Carabobo**
Caracas, Colombia.
- Instituto de Anthropologia e Historia del Estado Carabobo. Boletin. a.

**Instituto de Ciencias Naturales**
Apartado Aereo 7495, Bogota, Colombia.
- Mutisia; acta botanica Colombiana. ISSN 0027-5123

**Instituto de Desarrollo de los Recursos Naturales Renovables. Oficina de Planeacion**
Bogota, Columbia.
- Instituto de Desarrollo de los Recursos Naturales Renovables. Oficina de Planeacion. Estadisticas Pesqueras. a.

**Instituto de Investigaciones Tecnologicas**
Apdo Aereo 7031, Av. 30, 52-A-77, Bogota D. E., Colombia.
- I I T Tecnologia. bi-m. ISSN 0018-9901

**Instituto de Sociologia. Facultad de Ciencias Sociales**
Apartado Nacional 109, Apartado No.1178, Medellin, Colombia.
- Revista de Sociologia. s-a. ISSN 0034-8945

**Instituto Geografico "Agustin Codazzi"**
Carrera 30, No. 48-51, Apartado Aereo 6721, Aero 6721, Bogota, Colombia.
- Colombia Geografica. s-a.
- Instituto Geografico Agustin Codazzi. Informe de Labores. irreg.

**Instituto Nacional de Investigaciones Geologico Mineras**
Carrera 30 No. 51-59, Bogota D.E., Colombia.
- Boletin Geologico. a. ISSN 0067-9739

**International Federation for Documentation. Comision Latinoamericana**
c/o Instituto Colombiano para el Fomento de la Educacion Superior, Apartado Aereo No. 6319, Bogota, Colombia
(and Hofweg 7, 2511 AA The Hague, Netherlands)
- Informaciones F I D/C L A. q. ISSN 0014-5866

**Legislacion Economica Ltda.**
Aptdo. Aero 8646, Bogota, Colombia.
- Carta de Gerencia. s-a.

**Letras Nacionales**
Carrera No. 5, N. 17-69, Bogota, Colombia.
- Letras Nacionales. bi-m. ISSN 0459-1356

**Manual de Impuestos - Regimen Legal Tributario**
Avda. Jimenez No. 4-49, Aptdo Aero 14965, Bogota, Colombia.
- Manual de Impuestos - Regimen Legal Tributario. a.

**Carlos Martinez**
Calle 13, No. 9-20 Of. 425, Bogota, Colombia.
- Proa; urbanismo, arquitectura, industrias. 10 per yr. ISSN 0032-9150

**Corporacion Editora Medica del Valle**
Apartado Aereo 8025 Cali, Colombia.
- Acta Medica del Valle. 4 per yr. ISSN 0044-6017

**Mujer de America**
Apdo. 10634, Bogota, Colombia.
- Mujer de America; revisto paro el mundo femenino. m. ISSN 0027-3066

**Nova**
Apartado Aereo 15858, Bogota, Colombia.
- Nova; revista de arte y literatura. bi-m. ISSN 0029-4969

**Observatorio Astronomico Nacional**
Aptdo. Aereo 2584, Bogota, Colombia.
- Observatorio Astronomico Nacional. Anuario. a. ISSN 0067-950X
- Observatorio Astronomico Nacional. Publicaciones. (pub. by Universidad Nacional de Colombia. Facultad de Ciencias)

**Editorial Pacifico**
Apdo. Aereo 2188, Cali, Colombia.
- Lenguaje. q. (Universidad del Valle. Division de Humanidades. Oficina de Publicaciones)

**Panamerican Federation of Associations of Medical Schools**
Carrera 7 No. 29-34, Bogota, Colombia.
- Federacion Panamericana de Associaciones de Facultades de Medicina. Boletin. bi-m. ISSN 0533-0327

**Ediciones Paulinas**
Calle 12 No.6-11, Bogota, Colombia.
- Pastoral Popular. q.

**Editorial Pax**
Carrera 7, No. 40-62, Bogota, D.E., Colombia.
- Universitas; ciencias juridicas y socio-economicas. s-a. ISSN 0041-9060 (Pontificia Universidad Javeriana. Facultad de Derecho)

**Joaquin Pineros Corpus**
Carrera 7A, No. 17-01 Oficina 712, Bogota, Colombia.
- Colombia Ilustrada; revista de coltejer al servicio de la cultura Colombiana. q.

**J. Plaza, Ed. & Pub.**
Apartado Aereo 27765, Bogota, Colombia.
- Anuario de la Arquitectura en Colombia. a. (Sociedad Colombiana de Arquitectos)

**Pluma**
Apartado Aero 16416, Bogota, Colombia.
- Pluma; politica, economia, literatura, arte. m.

**Pontificia Universidad Javeriana**
Carrera 6, No. 10-72, 2 Piso, Apartado Aereo
24773, Bogota, Colombia.
- Javeriana. m. Feb.-Nov. ISSN 0021-5562

**Pontificia Universidad Javeriana. Facultad de Derecho**
- Universitas. (pub. by Editorial Pax)

**Pontificia Universidad Javeriana. Facultad de Medicina**
Bogota D.E., Colombia.
- Universitas Medica. s-a' ISSN 0041-9095

**Pontificia Universidad Javeriana. Facultad de Teologia**
Carrera 10, No. 65-48, Bogota 2 D.E., Colombia.
- Theologica Xaveriana. q.

**Editorial Presencia Ltda**
Calle 11 No. 5-10, Bogota, Colombia.
- Presencia. m.

**Provincia Occidental Claretianos de Colombia**
Apdo Aereo 51-841, Medellin, Colombia.
- Mysterium. q. ISSN 0027-5638

**Revista Colombiana del Trabajo**
Carrera 7a, 14-35, Edificio Augustin Nieto, Apdo.
Postal 2-6-8, Bogota, Colombia.
- Revista Colombiana del Trabajo. m.

**Revista Manizales**
Ed. J. B. Jaramillo Meza, Manizales, Caldas,
Colombia.
- Revista Manizales; al servicio de la cultura
Colombiana y Americana. m. ISSN 0034-9852

**Servicio Latino-Americano y Asiatico de Vivienda Popular**
- Congreso Internacional de Vivienda Popular. (pub.
by Centro de Investigacion y Accion Social)

**Sociedad Americana de Oftalmologia y Optometria**
Apartado aereo 091019, Bogota, D. E. 8, Colombia.
- Sociedad Americana de Oftalmologia y
Optometria. Archivos/American Society Fo
Ophthalmology and Optometry. Archives. q.
ISSN 0037-8364

**Sociedad Antioquena de Ingenieros**
Calle 54 No. 50-12, Of. 301, Medellin, Colombia.
- Sociedad Antioquena de Ingenieros. Boletin. q.
ISSN 0037-8372

**Sociedad Colombiana de Arquitectos**
- Anuario de la Arquitectura en Colombia. (pub. by
J. Plaza, Ed. & Pub.)

**Sociedad Colombiana de Arquitectos. Seccional de Antioquia**
Calle 49-B, No. 63-21, Piso 4, Apartado Aereo
1197, Medellin, Colombia.
- Ingenieria Arquitectura Construccion. q. ISSN
0020-1014

**Sociedad Colombiana de Economistas**
Apdo. Aereo 8429, Bogota, Colombia.
- Sociedad Colombiana de Economistas. Revista. 3
per yr.

**Sociedad Colombiana de Matematicas**
Apartado Aereo No. 25-21, Apartado Nacional No
25-21, Bogota, Colombia.
- Revista Colombiana de Matematicas. q. ISSN
0034-7426

**Sociedad Colombiana de Obstetricia y Ginecologia y Federacion Colombiana de Sociedades de Obstetricia y Ginecologia**
Carrera 9a No.20-13, Apartado Aereo 14961,
Bogota, Colombia.
- Revista Colombiana de Obstetricia y Ginecologia.
bi-m. ISSN 0034-7434

**Sociedad Colombiana de Ortodoncia**
Carrera 9a, No. 52A-46, Bogota D.E., Colombia.
- Sociedad Colombiana de Ortodoncia. Revista. q.
ISSN 0037-8453

**Sociedad Colombiana de Planificacion**
Apartado Aereo 12029, Bogota, Colombia.
- Sociedad Colombiana de Planificacion. Cuadernos.
irreg.

**Sociedad Colombiana de Psiquiatria**
Carrera 18, No. 8487, Ap. 203, Bogota, Colombia.
- Revista Colombiana de Psiquiatria. q. ISSN 0034-
7450

**Sociedad Colombiana de Quimicos Farmaceuticos**
c/o Dir. Dr. Carles Ballestas, Apartade Aereo 6300,
Cali, Colombia.
- Sociedad Colombiana de Quimicos Farmaceuticos.
Boletin. m. ISSN 0037-8461

**Sociedad de Agricultores de Colombia**
Carrera 10a, No. 14-56, Piso 3, Bogota, Colombia.
- Revista Nacional de Agricultura. m. ISSN 0035-
0222

**Sociedad Odontologica Antioquena**
Carrera 54 Nos. 48-49, Medellin, Colombia.
- Temas Odontologicos. q. ISSN 0040-2907

**Temas de Orientacion Agropecuaria**
Av. Jimenez No. 4-49, Apdo. Aereo 13169, Bogota,
Colombia.
- Temas de Orientacion Agropecuaria; conviertase
en un agricultor o ganadero progesistas. m. ISSN
0049-3333

**Ediciones Tercer Mundo**
Apdo. Aereo No. 4817, Bogota, Colombia.
- Tierra; revista de economia agraria. q. ISSN 0040-
7321

**Ediciones Testimonio**
Apartado Aereo 8213, Bogota, Colombia.
- Acteon; revista de creacion y critica. m. ISSN
0001-7337

**Ediciones Tiempo Presente**
Bogota, Colombia.
- Serie Economia Colombiana. irreg.

**Universidad Autonoma Latinoamericana**
Carrera 55 No. 49-51, Apdo. Aereo 3455, Medellin,
Colombia.
- U N A U L A. s-a.

**Universidad de Antioquia**
Apartado Aereo 1226, Medellin, Colombia.
- Actualidades Biologicas. q. ISSN 0304-3584 (prep.
by its Departamento de Biologia)
- Escuela Interamericana de Bibliotecologia.
Estadisticas. a. ISSN 0071-1314
- Indice Economico Colombiano; literatura
economica colombiana. a. ISSN 0019-7033 (prep.
by its Escuela Interamericana de Bibliotecologia)
- Indice Medico Colombiano. a. ISSN 0019-705X
(prep. by its Escuela Interamericana de
Bibliotecologia)
- Medellin. Universidad de Antioquia. Asociacion
de Profesionales de la Educacion. Estudios
Educativos. q. (prep. by its Oficina de Extension
Cultural)
- Medellin. Universidad de Antioquia. Facultad de
Ciencias Economicas. Empresa. q. (prep. by its
Facultad de Ciencias Economicas)
- Medellin. Universidad de Antioquia. Facultad de
Derecho y Ciencias Politicas. Estudios de
Derecho. s-a. (prep. by its Facultad de Derecho)
- Medellin. Universidad de Antioquia. Revista. q.
(prep. by its Oficina de Extension Cultural)
- Universidad de Antioquia. Centro de
Investigaciones Economicas. Boletin Bibliografico.
irreg. (prep. by its Centro de Investigaciones
Economicas)
- Universidad de Antioquia. Departamento de
Antropologia. Boletin de Antropologia. q. (prep.
by its Departamento de Antropologia)
- Universidad de Antioquia. Escuela Interamericana
de Bibliotecologia. Publicaciones. Serie:
Legislacion Bibliotecaria. irreg.

**Universidad de Antioquia. Facultad de Derecho y Ciencias Politicas**
Medellin, Colombia.
- Estudios de Derecho. s-a. ISSN 0014-1461

**Universidad de Bogota Jorge Tadeo Lozano. Museo del Mar**
Calle 23 No. 4-47, Bogota, Colombia.
- Museo del Mar. Boletin. a.
- Museo del Mar. Informe. irreg.

**Universidad de los Andes**
Calle 18A Carrera 1e, Apdo. Aereo 4976, Bogota,
Colombia.
- C.E.D.E. Documentos de Trabajo. m. (prep. by its
Centro de Estudios sobre Desarrollo Economico)

- Razon y Fabula. irreg. ISSN 0048-6841 (prep. by
its Comite de Investigaciones y Publicaciones)
- Universidad de los Andes. Cuadernos de Ciencia
Politica. irreg.
- Universidad de los Andes. Cuadernos de Letras.
irreg.

**Universidad de Medellin. Facultad de Ciencias Administrativas**
Calle 31, No. 83b-150, Medellin, Colombia.
- Medellin. Universidad. Facultad de Ciencias
Administrativas, Revista. q. ISSN 0465-4773

**Universidad de Narino. Biblioteca Central**
Apartado Aereo 505, Nal. 75, Narino, Colombia.
- Universidad de Narino. Biblioteca Central. Boletin
Informativo y Bibliogroficas. bi-m. ISSN 0041-
848X

**Universidad de Narino. Facultad de Derecho**
Apdo. Aereo 505, Pasto, Narino, Colombia.
- Foro Universitario. ISSN 0040-9502

**Universidad de San Buenaventura**
Calle 73 No. 10-45, Apdo. Aereo 52312, Bogota 2,
Colombia.
- Franciscanum; revista de las ciencias del espiritu.
3 per yr. ISSN 0015-9859

**Universidad del Atlantico. Instituto de Investigacion Etnologica**
Carrera 43, No. 50-53, Apdo. Aereo 1890,
Barranquilla, Colombia.
- Divulgaciones Etnologicas. s-a.

**Universidad del Cauca. Archivo Central del Cauca**
Popayan, Colombia.
- Popoyan. q. ISSN 0032-4388

**Universidad del Valle. Departamento de Bibliotecas**
Apartado Aereo 6641, Cali, Colombia, Colombia.
- Universidad del Valle. Departamento de
Biliotecas. Boletin de Adquisiciones. q.

**Universidad del Valle. Division de Ciencias Sociales y Economicas**
Apdo. Aereo 1738, Cali, Colombia.
- Sociedad Interamericana de Planificacion. Revista.
q. (Co-sponsor: Sociedad Interamericana de
Planificacion)

**Universidad del Valle. Division de Humanidades**
Cali, Colombia.
- Lenguaje. (pub. by Editorial Pacifico)
- Universidad del Valle. Division de Humanidades.
Revista. s-a.

**Universidad Externado de Colombia**
Calle 12 No. 1-17 Este, Bogota, Colombia.
- Documentos de Trabajo. q. (prep. by its Centro de
Investigaciones Sociales)
- Universidad Externado de Colombia. Revista. 3
per yr. ISSN 0041-8544

**Universidad Industrial de Santander**
Apdo Aereo 678, Bucaramanga, Santander,
Colombia.
- Universidad Industrial de Santander. Boletin de
Geologia. m. ISSN 0041-8560 (prep. by its
Facultad de Ingenieria de Petroleos)
- Universidad Industrial de Santander. Revista. 2
per yr. ISSN 0041-8587 (prep. by its Centro de
Documentacion y Bibliografia)

**Universidad Javeriana. Facultad de Teologia**
Carrera 10, No. 65-48, Bogota 2, D.E., Colombia.
- Universidad Javeriana. Facultad de Teologia.
Coleccion Profesores. irreg.

**Universidad La Gran Colombia**
Apartado Aereo No. 7909, Bogota, Colombia.
- Revista Universidad La Gran Colombia. irreg.

**Universidad Nacional de Colombia**
Apdo. Aere 1080, Manizales, Colombia.
- Aleph. bi-m. ISSN 0120-0216

**Universidad Nacional de Colombia. Biblioteca Central**
Aereo No. 14490, Bogota. D.E., Colombia.
- Universidad Nacional de Colombia. q. ISSN 0010-
1400
- Universidad Nacional de Colombia. Biblioteca
Central. Boletin de Adquisiciones. irreg., latest
issue, 1974.

**Universidad Nacional de Colombia. Departamento de Farmacia**
Apdo Nacional 1467, Bogota, Colombia.
- Revista Colombiana de Ciencias Quimico Farmaceuticas. 3 per yr. ISSN 0034-7418

**Universidad Nacional de Colombia. Departamento de Geologia**
Apartado Aereo 7495, Bogota, D.E., Columbia.
- Geologia Colombiana. irreg.; no. 7, 1970. ISSN 0072-0992

**Universidad Nacional de Colombia. Dept. de Filosofia y Humanidades**
Bogota, Colombia.
- Ideas y Valores. 3 per yr. ISSN 0019-140X

**Universidad Nacional de Colombia. Facultad de Artes**
Conservatorio de Musica, Bogota, Colombia.
- Universidad Nacional de Colombia. Centro de Estudios Folkloricos. Monografias. irreg.; latest issue, 1973. ISSN 0067-9534
- Universidad Nacional de Colombia. Centro de Estudios Folkloriques. Annuairo. a; latest issue, 1973. ISSN 0067-9526

**Universidad Nacional de Colombia. Facultad de Ciencias**
Aptdo. Aereo 2584, Bogota, Colombia.
- Observatorio Astronomico Nacional. Publicaciones. irreg.; no. 3, 1970. ISSN 0067-9518 (Observatorio Astronomico Nacional)

**Universidad Nacional de Colombia. Facultad de Ciencias Agropecuarias**
Apartado 237, Palmira, Colombia.
- Acta Agronomica. q. ISSN 0044-5959

**Universidad Nacional de Colombia. Facultad de Ciencias Humanas**
Departamento de Historia, Ciudad Universitaria, Apartado Nacional, Bogota, D.E., Colombia.
- Anuario Colombiano de Historia Social y de la Cultura. a. ISSN 0066-5045

**Universidad Nacional de Colombia. Facultad de Ingenieria**
Secretario, Apartado Nal. 1537, Bogota, Colombia.
- Ingenieria. Boletin Informativo. irreg. ISSN 0073-7992

**Universidad Nacional de Colombia. Facultad de Odontologia**
Bogota, Colombia.
- Odontologia. 3 per yr. ISSN 0029-8409

**Universidad Nacional de Colombia. Facultad Nacional de Minas**
Apdo. Aereo 1027, Apdo. Nacional 47, Medellin, Colombia.
- Dyna. s-a. ISSN 0012-7353

**Universidad Nacional de Colombia. Instituto de Ciencias Naturales**
Aptdo. Aereo 7495, Bogota, Colombia.
- Lozania; Acta Zoologica Colombiana. irreg. ISSN 0085-2899

**Universidad Pedagogica y Tecnologica de Colombia. Fundo Especial de Publicaciones y Ayudas Educativas**
Apartado Nacional 34, Tunja, Boyaca, Columbia.
- Pensamiento y Accion. bi-m. ISSN 0031-4765

**Universidad Pontificia Bolivariana. Facultad de Filosifia y Letras**
Facultad de Filosfia y Letras, Aptdo 1178, Medellin, Colombia.
- Escritos. q.

**Universidad Tecnologica del Magdalena**
Apartado Aereo No. 731, Santa Marta, Colombia.
- Universidad Tecnologica del Magdalena. UTEMAGD. q.

**Uno en Dos**
Apdo. 5685, Medellin, Colombia.
- Uno en Dos. q. ISSN 0049-5565

**Viga en el Ojo**
Apdo. Aereo 788, Pereira, Colombia.
- Viga en el Ojo; revista de vanguardia literatura y arte. m. ISSN 0042-5931

**Editorial 8 de Junio**
Apdo. 51694, Medellin, Colombia.
- Partido Comunista de Colombia. Documentos. irreg.

## CONGO (BRAZZAVILLE)

**Centre d'Enseignement Superieur de Brazzaville**
B.P. 69, Brazzaville, Congo.
- Centre d'Enseignement Superieur de Brazzaville. Annales. a.

**Congo. Service de la Statistique**
B.P. 2031, Brazzaville, Congo.
- Congo. Service de la Statistique. Bulletin Mensuel de Statistique. m. ISSN 0010-5805

**Universite de Brazzaville**
B. P. 69, Brazzaville, Congo.
- Universite de Brazzaville. Annales. a. ISSN 0302-4814

**World Health Organization. Regional Office for Africa**
For publications of this agency see section for UNITED NATIONS

## COSTA RICA

**Asociacion Costarricense de Bibliotecarios**
Apartado 3308, San Jose, Costa Rica.
- Anuario Bibliografico Costarricense. irreg. ISSN 0066-5010
- Asociacion Costarricense de Bibliotecarios. Boletin. irreg. ISSN 0004-4784

**Asociacion de Medicos Especialistas de la Salud Publica de Costa Rica**
Apdo. 978, San Jose, Costa Rica.
- Revista Medica de Costa Rica. q. ISSN 0034-9909

**Asociacion Demografica Costarricense**
San Jose, Costa Rica.
- Asociacion Demografica Costarricense. Informe de Labores. irreg.

**Asociacion Interamericana de Bibliotecarios y Documentalistas Agricolas**
Instituto Interamericana de Ciencias Agricolas de la OEA, Turrialba, Costa Rica.
- A I B D A. Boletin Informativo. q. ISSN 0001-1495
- Asociacion Interamericana de Biblietecarios y Documentalistas Agricolas. Boletin Tecnico. irreg., no. 16, 1976. ISSN 0074-0756
- Asociacion Interamericana de Bibliotecarios y Documentalistas. irreg., no. 17, 1977. ISSN 0074-0748

**Banco Central de Costa Rica**
San Jose, Costa Rica.
- Banco Central de Costa Rica. Boletin Estadistico Mensual. m.
- Banco Central de Costa Rica. Memoria Anual. a; latest issue, 1973. ISSN 0067-320X

**Banco Central de Costa Rica. Departamento Monetario**
San Jose, Costa Rica.
- Banco Central de Costa Rica. Departamento Monetario. Credito y Cuentas Monetarias. irreg.

**Banco Central de Costa Rica. Division de Asuntos Economicas**
San Jose, Costa Rica.
- Banco Central de Costa Rica. Informacion Economica Semanal. w. ISSN 0408-3172

**Camara de Comercio de Costa Rica**
Apdo. 1114, San Jose, Costa Rica.
- Comercio. q.

**Central American Institute of Public Administration**
*see* **Instituto Centroamericano de Administracion Publica**

**Centro Interamericano de Documentacion e Informacion Agricola**
*see under* **Instituto Interamericano de Ciencias Agricolas de la OEA**

**Colegio de Abogados**
Apartado 3161, San Jose, Costa Rica.
- Colegio de Abogados. Revista. 3 per yr. ISSN 0010-0587

**Colegio de Farmaceuticos de Costa Rica**
Aptdo 396, San Jose, Costa Rica.
- Revista Ciencias Farmaceuticas. a.

**Colegio de Medicos y Cirujanos**
Apdo 4054, San Jose, Costa Rica.
- Acta Medica Costarricense. 3 per yr. ISSN 0001-6012

**Confederacion Universitaria Centro-Americana**
Ciudad Universitaria, Rodrigo Facio, Apdo. 37, San Jose, Costa Rica.
- Estudios Sociales Centroamericanos. 3 per yr.

**Consejo Superior Universitario Centroamericano**
Apdo. 37, Ciudad Universitaria Rodrigo Facio, San Jose, Costa Rica.
- Repertorio Centroamericano. q. ISSN 0034-4613

**Editorial Costa Rica**
Apdo. 10010, San Jose, Costa Rica.
- Anuario del Cuento Costariccense. a. ISSN 0587-5196

**Costa Rica. Archivo Nacional**
Calle 7, Ave. 4, Apdo. 5028, San Jose, Costa Rica.
- Archivo Nacional de Costa Rica. Revista. q. ISSN 0034-9003

**Costa Rica. Direccion General de Estadistica y Censos**
San Jose, Costa Rica.
- Accidentes de Transito en Costa Rica. a. ISSN 0525-8693
- Costa Rica. Direccion General de Estadistica y Censos. Inventario de las Estadisticas Nacionales. irreg. ISSN 0589-8544
- Costa Rica. Revista de Estudios y Estadisticas. Serie Demografica. a.

**Costa Rica. Ministerio de Cultura, Juventud y Deportes**
Departamento de Publicaciones, Apdo 10227, San Jose, Costa Rica.
- Papel Impreso. m. ISSN 0048-2854
- Serie Estudios Literarios. irreg.

**Costa Rica. Ministerio de Educacion Publica. Direccion General de Artes y Letras**
c/o Litografia Costa Rica, Ave. San Martin, Calle Central-Calle 2, San Jose, Costa Rica.
- Artes/Letras. q. ISSN 0004-3524

**Costa Rica. Ministerio de Hacienda. Oficina del Presupuesto**
San Jose, Costa Rica.
- Costa Rica. Ministerio de Hacienda Oficina del Presupuesto. Informe. a. ISSN 0070-0576

**Costa Rica. Ministerio de Obras Publicas y Transportes. Instituto Geografico Nacional**
Ap. 2272, San Jose, Costa Rica.
- Institute Geografico Nacional, Costa Rica. Informe Semestral. s-a. ISSN 0045-8740

**Institute of In-Depth Evangelism**
Apartado 1307, San Jose, Costa Rica.
- In-Depth Evangelism Around the World. q.

**Instituto Centroamericano de Administracion Publica**
Apartado 10025, San Jose, Costa Rica.
- Administracion, Desarrollo, Integracion. q. ISSN 0044-6262
- I C A P Lista de Nuevas Adquisiciones. irreg. ISSN 0487-1596 (prep. by its Departamento de Biblioteca)
- Instituto Centroamericano de Administracion Publica. Serie 100. Aspectos Humanos de la Administracion. irreg. ISSN 0073-9944
- Instituto Centroamericano de Administracion Publica. Serie 200. Ciencia de la Administracion. irreg. ISSN 0073-9952
- Instituto Centroamericano de Administracion Publica. Serie 300: Investigacion. irreg. ISSN 0073-9960
- Instituto Centroamericano de Administracion Publica. Serie 400: Economia y Finanzas. irreg. ISSN 0073-9979
- Instituto Centroamericano de Administracion Publica. Serie 600: Informes de Seminarios. irreg. ISSN 0073-9995
- Instituto Centroamericano de Administracion Publica. Serie 700: Materiales de Informacion. irreg. ISSN 0074-0004
- Instituto Centroamericano de Administracion Publica. Serie 800: Metodologia de la Administracion. irreg. ISSN 0074-0012

- Instituto Centroamericano de Administracion Publica. Serie 900: Miscelaneas. irreg. ISSN 0074-0020

**Instituto Costarricense de Cultura Hispanica**
Apartado 4860, San Jose, Costa Rica.
- Instituto Costarricense de Cultura Hispanica. Publicacion. irreg. ISSN 0074-0039

**Instituto Costarricense de Electricidad**
Apto. 10032, San Jose, Costa Rica.
- Boletin Hidrologico. irreg.; latest issue, 1973. ISSN 0067-9747
- Informe de Operacion de las Principales Empresas Productoras y Distribuidoras de Energia Electrica de Costa Rica. a. ISSN 0074-0047 (prep. by its Direccion de Electrificacion)

**Instituto Costarricense de Turismo**
San Jose, Costa Rica.
- Instituto Costarricense de Turismo.. Memoria Anual. a.

**Instituto Interamericano de Ciencias Agricolas de la O E A. Centro Interamericano de Documentacion e Informacion Agricola**
Apartado 74, Turrialba, Costa Rica.
- Boletin para Bibliotecas Agricolas. q.
- Desarrollo del Tropico Americano. q. ISSN 0300-4317
- Documentacion e Informacion para el Desarrollo Agricola. q. ISSN 0304-2839

**Instituto Interamericano de Ciencias Agricolas de la O E A. Secretariado**
Apartado 10281, San Jose, Costa Rica.
- Desarrollo Rural en las Americas. 3 per yr. ISSN 0046-0028
- I I C A en America; boletin sobre el desarrollo rural. q. ISSN 0304-0100
- Indice Agricola de America Latina y el Caribe. q. ISSN 0304-0119
- Instituto Interamericano de Ciencias Agricola de la OEA. Hemispheric and Humanistic Projection: I I C A Report. irreg.
- Instituto Interamericano de Ciencios Agricolas de la O E A. Documentos Oficiales. irreg.
- Inter-American Centre for Agricultural Documentation and Information. Documentacion e Informacion Agricola. irreg. ISSN 0301-438X
- Inter-American Institute of Agricultural Sciences. Informe Anual. a. ISSN 0538-3277
- Turrialba; revista interamericana de ciencias agricolas. q. ISSN 0041-4360

**Instituto Interamericano de Ciencias Agricolas de la O E A. Technical Advisory Council**
Apartado 10281, San Jose, Costa Rica.
- Inter-American Institute of Agricultural Sciences. Technical Advisory Council. Report of the Meeting. irreg.

**Instituto Nacional de Seguros**
San Jose, Costa Rica.
- Instituto Nacional de Seguros. Memoria Annal I.N.S. a.

**Instituto Nacional de Seguros. Division de Mercadeo**
Apartado 10061, San Jose, Costa Rica.
- Libre Crezca Fecundo. s-a.

**Inter-American Institute of Agricultural Sciences**
*see* Instituto Interamericano de Ciencias Agricolas de la OEA

**Museo Nacional de Costa Rica**
P.O. Box 749, San Jose, Costa Rica.
- Brenesia. irreg., approx. s-a. (prep. by its Departamento de Historia Natural)
- Museo Nacional de Costa Rica. Informe Rendido al Minsterio de Educacion Publica. a.
- Vinculos. irreg. (prep. by its Departamento de Antropologia e Historia)

**Revista Agropecuaria**
Apartado 5645, San Jose, Costa Rica.
- Revista Agropecuaria; al servicio de la agricultura y la ganaderia centroamericana. bi-m. ISSN 0048-7597

**Tropical Science Center**
Calle 1, No. 442, San Jose, Costa Rica.
- Tropical Science Center, Costa Rica. Occasional Paper. irreg.; no. 11, 1974. ISSN 0069-2107

**Editorial Universidad de Costa Rica**
Ciudad Universitaria, San Jose, Costa Rica.
- Agronomia Costarricense. s-a. ISSN 0377-9424

- Anuario de Estudios Centroamericanos. a. ISSN 0377-7316
- Kanina; revista de artes y letras. s-a. ISSN 0378-0473
- Revista de Biologia Tropical. s-a (with supplements) ISSN 0034-7744
- Revista de Ciencias. s-a.
- Revista de Ciencias Juridicas. s-a. ISSN 0034-7787
- Revista de Ciencias Sociales. s-a. ISSN 0482-5276
- Revista de Filologia y Linguistica. s-a. ISSN 0377-628X
- Universidad de Costa Rica. Revista. s-a. ISSN 0041-8382
- Universidad de Costa Rica. Revista de Filosofia. s-a. ISSN 0034-8252

**Universidad de Costa Rica. Centro Estudios Sociales y Poblacion**
Apartado 49, Ciudad Universitaria Rodrigo Facio, San Jose, Costa Rica.
- Dialogo. q.

**Universidad de Costa Rica. Departamento de Lenguas Modernas**
San Jose, Costa Rica.
- Universidad de Costa Rica. Departamento de Lenguas Modernas. Anales. irreg.

**Universidad de Costa Rica. Instituto de Estudios Centroamericanos**
San Jose, Costa Rica.
- Revista de Poesia Centroamericana. q.
- Revista Historico: Critica de Literatura Centroamericana.

**Vista Femenina Centroamericana**
Apdo. 3087, San Jose, Costa Rica.
- Vista Femenina Centroamericana. m. ISSN 0049-6545

**Zenith**
Apdo 40, Heredia, Costa Rica.
- Zenith; revista literaria internacional. m. ISSN 0034-9828

**15 Dias en Costa Rica**
Casa Presidencial, San Jose, Costa Rica.
- 15 Dias en Costa Rica. m.

# CUBA

**Academia de Ciencias de Cuba. Instituto de Documentacion e Informacion Cientifica y Tecnica**
Havana, Cuba.
- Academia de Ciencias de Cuba. Instituto de Documentacian e Informacion Cientifica y Tecnica Boletin. q ISSN 0020-3831
- Academia de Ciencias de Cuba. Instituto de Documentacion e Informacion Cientifica y Tecnica. Actualidades de la Informacion Cientifica y Tecnica. m.

**Academia de Ciencias de Cuba. Instituto de Etnologia y Folklore**
Havana, Cuba.
- Etnologia y Folklore. 2 per yr.

**Academia de Ciencias de Cuba. Instituto de Geologia**
Havana, Cuba.
- Academia de Ciencias de Cuba. Instituto de Geologia. Resumenes, Communicaciones y Notas del Consejo Cientifico. irreg.
- Academia de Ciencias de Cuba. Instituto de Geologia. Serie Geologica. 3-4 per yr.

**Academia de Ciencias de Cuba. Instituto de Investigaciones de la Cana de Azucar**
Av. van Troi 17203, R. Boyeros, Havana, Cuba.
- Serie Cana de Azucar. irreg.

**Academia de Ciencias de Cuba. Instituto de Investigaciones Tropicales**
Santiago de las Vega, Havana, Cuba.
- Revista de Agricultura. ISSN 0034-7671

**Academia de Ciencias de Cuba. Instituto de Oceanologia**
Ave. 1ra No. 18406, Havana 16, Cuba.
- Academia de Ciencias de Cuba. Instituto de Oceanologia. Serie Oceanologica. irreg. ISSN 0567-5782
- Academia de Ciencias de Cuba. Instituto de Oceanologia. Tablas de Mareas. irreg.

**Academia de Ciencias de Cuba. Instituto de Zoologia**
Havana, Cuba.
- Academia de Ciencias de Cuba. Instituto de Zoologia. Miscelanea Zoologica. irreg.
- Poeyana. irreg.

**Asociacion Cubano de las Naciones Unidas**
Calle J y 25 Vedado, Havana, Cuba.
- Association Cubano de las Naciones Unidas. Boletin. s-a.

**Asociacion de Tecnicos Azucareros de Cuba**
- A T A C. (pub. by Instituto Cubano del Libro (Distrib.))

**Asociacion Nacional de Agricultores Pequenos. Secretaria Ideologica**
- A N A P. (pub. by Instituto Cubano del Libro (Distrib.))

**Avances de l'Information Scientifique**
Casilla 351, Vedado, Havana, Cuba.
- Avances de l'Information Scientifique. m.

**Ballet Nacional de Cuba**
- Cuba en el Ballet. (pub. by Instituto Cubano del Libro (Distrib.))

**Biblioteca Nacional Jose Marti**
No. 3 Plaza de la Revolucion, Havana, Cuba.
- Anuario Martiano. a. ISSN 0066-524X
- Biblioteca Nacional Jose Marti. Revista. 3 per yr. ISSN 0006-1727 (Subscr. to: Instituto Cubano del Libro, Belascoain y Desague, Havana, Cuba)

**Biblioteca Nacional Jose Marti. Departamento de Coleccion Cubana**
Plaza de la Revolucion, Havana, Cuba
- Bibliografia Cubana. a. ISSN 0067-6705 (Subscr. to: Instituto Cubano del Libro, Departamento de Relaciones Internationales, Belascoain y Desague, Havana, Cuba)

**Biblioteca Nacional Jose Marti. Departamento de Hemeroteca e Informacion de Humanidades**
Plaza de la Revolucion, Havana, Cuba
- Indice General de Publicaciones Periodicas Cubanas. irreg. (Subscr. to: Instituto Cubano del Libro, Departamento de Relaciones Internacionales, Belascoain y Desague, Havana, Cuba)

**Casa de las Americas. Departamento de Teatro**
G y Tercera, el Vedado, Havana, Cuba.
- Conjunto. q. ISSN 0010-5937

**Central Committee of the Communist Party of Cuba**
Av. Suarez y Territorial, Plaza de la Revolucion, Havana, Cuba.
- Granma. w. ISSN 0017-3223

**Centro de Automatizacion Industrial**
Paseo No. 452, Esq. 19, Vedado, Havana, Cuba.
- Control Cibernetica y Automatizacion. q. (Co-Sponsor: Academia de Ciencias de Cuba, Instituto de Matematica Cibernetica y Computacion)

**Centro de Documentacion e Informacion Tecnica de la Construccion**
Monserrate 258 Entre Animas y Neptuno, Havana 1, Cuba
- Arquitectura/Cuba. 3 per yr. (Subscr. to: Instituto Cubano del Libro, Departamento de Exportacion, O'Reilly 407, Apdo. 605, Havava 1, Cuba)
- Revista Referativa de la Construccion. bi-m. ISSN 0035-0427

**Centro de Informacion y Documentacion Agropecuaria**
Calle 13 No 959, Havana 4, Cuba.
- Informacion Express Agricola. m.
- Informacion Express Pecuaria. s-m.
- Revista Cubana de Ciencias Veterinarias. 2 per yr. ISSN 0048-7678 (Co-sponsor: Consejo Cientifico Veterinario)

**Centro Tecnico Superior de la Construccion**
Ave. de Belgica (Monserrate) No. 258 Entre Animas y Neptuno, Havana, Cuba.
- Ingenieria Civil. bi-m. ISSN 0020-1022

**Cine Cubano**
Calle 23, No. 1155, Apdo. 55, Havana, Cuba.
- Cine Cubano. m. ISSN 0009-6946

**Comision de Estudios Juridicos**
- Revista Cubano de Derecho. (pub. by Instituto Cubano del Libro (Distrib.)

**Consejo de Direccion**
Palacio de Justicia, Plaza de la Revolucion-Jose
Marti, Havana, Cuba.
- Revista Cubana de Jurisprudencia. m.

**Cuba. Camara de Comercio**
Calle 21 No. 701, Havana, Cuba.
- Cuba Noticias Economicas. m. ISSN 0011-2607

**Cuba. Centro Nacional de Investigaciones Cientificas**
Universidad de la Habana, Havana, Cuba
- C E N I C. Revista. Ciencias Biologicas. s-a.
(Subscr. to: Instituto de Libro, Departamento de
Exportaciones, O'Reilly No. 407, Apto. 605,
Havana, Cuba)
- C E N I C. Revista. Ciencias Fisicas. s-a. (Subscr.
to: Instituto de Libro, Departamento de
Exportaciones, O'Reilly No. 407, Apto 605,
Havana, Cuba)

**Cuba. Comite Estatal de Estadisticas**
Havana, Cuba.
- Economia Cubana. a.

**Cuba. Comite Estatal de Estadisticas. Direccion de
Informacion y Relaciones Internacionales**
Gaveta Postal 6016, Havana, Cuba.
- Anuario Estadistico de Cuba. a. ISSN 0574-6132
- Censo de Poblacion y Viviendas. a.

**Cuba. Consejo Nacional de Cultura. Direccion
Nacional de Bibliotecas**
Biblioteca Nacional Jose Marti, Plaza de la
Revolucion, Havana, Cuba.
- Bibliotecas. bi-m. ISSN 0006-176X

**Cuba. Direccion Nacional de Zoologicos y Acuarios**
Apartado de Correos 7097, Havana, Cuba.
- Torreia. s-a. ISSN 0563-9425

**Cuba. Ministerio de Comunicaciones. Centro de
Informacion de Comunicaciones**
- C I C - Informacion Tecnica. (pub. by Instituto
Cubano del Libro (Distrib.))
- Comunicaciones - Revista Tecnica. (pub. by
Instituto Cubano del Libro (Distrib.))

**Cuba. Ministerio de Cultura**
Calle O'Reilly esq. a Tacon, Havana 1, Cuba
- Revolucion y Cultura. m. (Subscr. to: Instituto
Cubano del Libro, Departamento de
Exportaciones, O'Reilly No. 407 Apdo. 605,
Havana 1, Cuba)

**Cuba. Ministerio de Educacion**
Obispo 160, Havana, Cuba.
- Educacion. q.

**Cuba. Ministerio de Educacion. Departamento de
Bibliotecas Escolares y Servicios Audiovisuales**
Calle 76 y Avenida 29-e, Mariano 14, Havana,
Cuba.
- Boletin para las Bibliotecas Escolares. bi-m.

**Cuba. Ministerio de Industria Basica**
Avda. Carlos III No. 666, Havana, Cuba.
- Revista Tecnologica. bi-m. ISSN 0029-5736

**Cuba. Ministerio de la Industria Alimenticia**
Ave. 41 No 4455, Marianao, Havana, Cuba.
- Industria Alimenticia. q. ISSN 0019-7459

**Cuba. Ministerio de la Industria Azucarera**
Aptdo. Postal 6565, Havana, Cuba.
- Cuba Azucar. q. ISSN 0590-2916

**Cuba. Ministerio de la Industria Quimica. Centro de
Automatizacion Industrial**
- Control, Cibernetica y Automatizacion. (pub. by
Instituto Cubano del Libro (Distrib.))

**Cuba. Ministerio de Salud Publica**
c/o Gregorio Delgado Garcia, Apartado 97, Havana
1, Cuba.
- Cuadernos de Historia de la Salud Publica. q.
ISSN 0045-9178

**Cuba. Ministerio de Salud Publica. Centro Nacional
de Informacion de Ciencias Medicas**
Calle 23 No. 177, Vedado, Apdo. 6520, Havana,
Cuba
- Medicina Tropical. 3 per yr. ISSN 0025-794X
(Orders to: Instituto Cubano del Libro,
Departamento de Exportaciones, O'Reilly 407,
Apdo. 605, Havana, Cuba)
- Revista Cubana de Administracion de Salud. bi-m.
- Revista Cubana de Cirugia. bi-m. ISSN 0034-7493

- Revista Cubana de Estomatologia. bi-m. ISSN
0034-7507 (Orders to: Instituto Cubano del Libro,
Departamento de Exportaciones, O'Reilly 407,
Apdo 605, Havana, Cuba)
- Revista Cubana de Farmacia. 3 per yr. ISSN
0034-7515 (Orders to: Instituto Cubano del Libro,
Departamento de Exportaciones, O'Reilly 407,
Apdo. 605, Havana, Cuba)
- Revista Cubana de Higiene y Epidemiologia. 3 per
yr. (Orders to: Instituto Cubano del Libro,
Departamento de Exportaciones, O'Reilly 407,
Apdo. 605, Havana, Cuba)
- Revista Cubana de Medicina. bi-m. ISSN 0034-
7523
- Revista Cubana de Obstetricia y Ginecologia. 3
per yr.
- Revista Cubana de Pediatria. bi-m. ISSN 0034-
7531

**Cuba. Ministerio del Commercio Exterior**
16 Infanta, Havana, Cuba.
- Cuba. Ministerio del Commercio Exterior.
Revista. q. ISSN 0026-5292

**Cuba. Oficina Nacional de Invenciones, Informacion
Tecnica y Marcas**
Tte. Rey No. 405, Esq. a Cristo, Havana 1, Cuba.
- Cuba. Oficina Nacional de Invenciones,
Informacion Tecnica y Marcas. Boletin Oficial. q.
ISSN 0011-2615

**Cuba Internacional**
Havana 1, Cuba
- Cuba Internacional. m. ISSN 0011-2593 (Distrib.:
Instituto Cubano del Libro, Direccion de
Comercio International, O'Reilly 407, Apdo. 605,
Havana, Cuba)

**Desarrollo Agropecuario del Pais. Grupo Hidraulico**
Humboldt No. 106, Havana 4, Cuba
- Voluntad Hidraulica. q. ISSN 0505-9461 (Instituto
Cubano del Libro, Departamento de
Exportaciones, O'Reilly 407, Apdo. 605, Havana,
Cuba)

**Federacion de Ajedrez de Cuba**
15 y C Vedado, Havana, Cuba.
- J M. (Jacque Mate) m. ISSN 0021-3683

**Federacion de Mujeres Cubanas**
Infanta y Penalver, Havana, Cuba.
- Mujeres. m. ISSN 0581-2011

**Federacion Filatelica Cubano**
- Filatelia Cubana. (pub. by Instituto Cubano del
Libro (Distrib.))

**Fuerzas Armadas Revolucionarias**
Avenida de Independencia y San Pedro, Aptdo
6916, Havana, Cuba.
- Verde Olivo. w. ISSN 0506-6913

**Hospital Psiquiatrico de la Habana**
- Hospital Psiquiatrico de la Habana. Revista. (pub.
by Instituto Cubano del Libro (Distrib.))

**Instituto Cubano de Investigaciones de los Derivados
de la Cana de Azucar**
Apdo. 4026, Havana 1, Cuba.
- Sobre los Derivados de la Cana de Azucar. 3 per
yr. ISSN 0049-0849

**Instituto Cubano del Libro (Distrib.)**
Departamento de Exportacion, Apdo. 605, Havana
1, Cuba.
- A N A P. m. ISSN 0514-9797 (Asociacion
Nacional de Agricultores Pequenos. Secretaria
Ideologica)
- A T A C. bi-m. (Asociacion de Tecnicos
Azucareros de Cuba)
- Bohemia. w.
- C I C - Informacion Tecnica. s-a. (Cuba.
Ministerio de Comunicaciones. Centro de
Informacion de Comunicaciones)
- Casa de las Americas. q. ISSN 0008-7157
- Comunicaciones - Revista Tecnica. s-a. ISSN
0588-9545 (Cuba. Ministerio de Comunicaciones.
Centro de Informacion de Comunicaciones)
- Constructores. m. (Union de Jovenes Comunistas.
Sector de la Construccion)
- Control, Cibernetica y Automatizacion. q. (Cuba.
Ministerio de la Industria Quimica. Centro de
Automatizacion Industrial) (Co-sponsor: Instituto
do Matematica, Cibernetica y Computacion)
- Cuba en el Ballet. 3 per yr. (Ballet Nacional de
Cuba)

- Deporte-Derecho del Pueblo. m. (Instituto
Nacional de Deportes, Educacion Fisica y
Recreacion)
- Economia y Desarrollo. bi-m. (Universidad de la
Habana. Instituto de Economica)
- Filatelia Cubana. 3 per yr. (Federacion Filatelica
Cubano)
- Hospital Psiquiatrico de la Habana. Revista. 3 per
yr. (Hospital Psiquiatrico de la Habana)
- Juventud Tecnica. m. ISSN 0449-4555 (Union de
Jovenes Comunistas. Movimiento de Brigadas
Tecnicas)
- L P V- Listos para Vencer. w. ISSN 0458-5674
(Instituto Nacional de Deportes, Educacion,
Fisica y Recreacion)
- Pensamiento Critico. m.
- Revista Cubana de Derecho. s-a.
- Revista Cubano de Derecho. w. (Comision de
Estudios Juridicos)
- Romances. m.
- Seminaria Pa'lante. w.
- Signos. q. (Las Villas, Cuba. Consejo Nacional de
Cultura)

**Instituto de Ciencia Animal**
Tulipan No. 1011 e 47 y Loma, Nuevo Vedado,
Havana, Cuba
- Revista Cubana de Ciencia Agricola. 3 per yr.
ISSN 0034-7485 (Dist. by: Empresa Comercio
Exterior de Publicaciones, Subscr. Dept., Box 605,
Havana 1, Cuba)
- Revista de Divulgacion Agropecuaria. 3 per yr.
ISSN 0048-7872 (Empresa Comercio Exterior de
Publicaciones, Subscr. Dept., Box 605, Havana 1,
Cuba)

**Instituto de Estudios Financieros**
Zanja No. 352, Esq. Escobar, Havana, Cuba.
- Finanzas al Dia; revista financiero-economica de
Cuba. q. ISSN 0015-2226

**Instituto Nacional de Deportes, Educacion Fisica y
Recreacion**
- Deporte-Derecho del Pueblo. (pub. by Instituto
Cubano del Libro (Distrib.))
- L P V- Listos para Vencer. (pub. by Instituto
Cubano del Libro (Distrib.))

**Instituto Nacional de la Pesca de Cuba**
San Ignacio 303, Havana, Cuba.
- Mar y Pesca; la revista del hombre de mar. m.
ISSN 0025-2735

**Instituto Nacional de la Pesca de Cuba. Centro de
Investigaciones Pesqueras**
Av. Primera y 26, Miramar, Marianao, Havana,
Cuba.
- Instituto Nacional de la Pesca de Cuba. Centro de
Investigaciones Pesqueras. Revista de
Investigaciones. q.

**Inter-Continental Press Guide**
c/o Angelica P. Rayner:, 270 Industria St., Havana,
Cuba.
- Inter-Continental Press Guide; a directory of the
leading newspapers and magazines in Latin
America, the Islands and possessions throughout
the Caribbean area. m (2 complete semi-annual
cumulations) ISSN 0020-501X

**Las Villas, Cuba. Consejo Nacional de Cultura**
- Signos. (pub. by Instituto Cubano del Libro
(Distrib.))

**Marina de Guerra**
Havana, Cuba.
- Dotacion; boletin tecnico informativo. s-m. ISSN
0012-5652

**Mosca Profana**
Apartado 87, Matanzas, Cuba.
- Mosca Profana. bi-m. ISSN 0047-8148

**Organizacion Continental Latino Americana de
Estudiantes**
Calle 36 No. 710 Entre 7a. y 9a., Miramar, Havana,
Cuba.
- O C L A E Revista. m. ISSN 0029-6961

**Organization of Solidarity of the Peoples of Asia,
Africa and Latin America**
- Magazine Tricontinental. (pub. by Tricontinental
Publications)

**Partido Unido de la Revolucion Socialista Cubana**
Prado y Teniente Rey, Havana, Cuba.
- Cuba Socialista. m.

**Sindicato Nacional de Trabajadores de la Aviacion**
Palacio de los Trabajadores, San Carlos y Penalver, Havana, Cuba.
- Aerovoz. m. ISSN 0001-9461

**Sociedad Cubana de Historia de la Medicina**
Apartado de Correos97, Havana, Cuba.
- Sociedad Cubana de Historia de la Medicina. Revista. q. ISSN 0037-847X

**Sociedad Cubana de Ingenieros**
Ave. de Belgica 258, Havana, Cuba.
- Sociedad Cubana de Ingenieros. Revista. bi-m. ISSN 0037-8488

**Tricontinental Publications**
Box 4224, Havana, Cuba.
- Magazine Tricontinental. bi-m. ISSN 0049-4682 (Organization of Solidarity of the Peoples of Asia, Africa and Latin America)

**Unesco. Regional Cultural Bureau for Latin America and the Caribbean**
For publications of this agency see section for UNITED NATIONS

**Union de Escritores y Artistas de Cuba**
Calle 17 y Vedado, Havana, Cuba.
- Gaceta de Cuba. m.
- Union. q. ISSN 0041-6770

**Union de Jovenes Comunistas. Movimiento de Brigadas Tecnicas**
- Juventud Tecnica. (pub. by Instituto Cubano del Libro (Distrib.))

**Union de Jovenes Comunistas. Sector de la Construccion**
- Constructores. (pub. by Instituto Cubano del Libro (Distrib.))

**Union de Periodistas de Cuba**
Calle 23, No. 452, Havana, Cuba.
- U P E C. irreg.

**Universidad Central de las Villas. Faculty of Humanities**
Santa Clara, L.V., Cuba.
- Islas. 3 per yr. ISSN 0047-1542

**Universidad de la Habana. Centro de Informacion Cientifica y Tecnica**
Havana, Cuba.
- Actualidades de la Ingenieria Agronomica. irreg.; 1971, no. 23.
- Cuadernos de Informacion Cientifica. 2-3 per yr. ISSN 0045-9194
- Sobre Educacion Superior. s-a. ISSN 0037-752X
- Universidad de la Habana. Centro de Informacion Cientificas y Tecnica. Ciencias. Serie 9. Antropologia y Prehistoria. irreg.
- Universidad de la Habana. Publicacion. 3 per yr. ISSN 0041-8420

**Universidad de la Habana. Direccion de Extension Universitaria**
Edificio Julio A. Mella, Calle L No. 353, Havana, Cuba.
- Universidad de la Habana. Revista. q.

**Universidad de la Habana. Escuela de Matematica**
Havana, Cuba.
- Universidad de la Habana. Escuela de Matematica. Investigacion Operacional.

**Universidad de la Habana. Escuela de Periodismo**
10 de Mayo, No. 14, Havana, Cuba.
- Despegue. m.

**Universidad de la Habana. Instituto de Economica**
- Economia y Desarrollo. (pub. by Instituto Cubano del Libro (Distrib.))

**Universidad de Oriente. Direccion de Extension Universitaria**
Santiago de Cuba, Cuba
- Santiago. q. ISSN 0048-9115 (Subsc. to: Instituto Cubano del Libro, Departamento de Exportacion, Apdo. 605, Havana, Cuba)

**Universidad de Oriente. Escuela de Letras**
Santiago de Cuba, Cuba.
- Taller. Literario. q.

# CYPRUS

**Central Bank of Cyprus**
P.O. Box 1087, Nicosia, Cyprus.
- Central Bank of Cyprus. Annual Report. a. ISSN 0069-1518
- Central Bank of Cyprus. Bulletin. q. ISSN 0008-9230

**Cosmos Press Ltd.**
Cosmos Press Bldg., Apostolos Varnavas St., Box 1491, Nicosia, Cyprus.
- Kypros; Pancyprian newspaper. w. ISSN 0023-611X

**D. Couvas & Sons Ltd.**
P.O. Box 35, Limasol, Cyprus
(Dist. by: International Publications Service, 114 E. 32nd St., New York, NY 10016)
- Cyprus Chamber of Commerce and Industry Directory; guide to commerce, industry, tourism and agriculture. irreg., 1970, 2nd ed. ISSN 0070-2331

**Cyprus. Agricultural Research Institute**
Nicosia, Cyprus.
- Cyprus. Agricultural Research Institute. Agricultural Economics Report. irreg.
- Cyprus. Agricultural Research Institute. Report. a. ISSN 0070-2307
- Cyprus. Agricultural Research Institute. Technical Bulletin. irreg., no. 18, 1974. ISSN 0070-2315

**Cyprus. Department of Agriculture. Soils and Plant Nutrition Section**
Nicosia, Cyprus.
- Cyprus. Department of Agriculture. Soils and Plant Nutrition Section. Report. biennial. ISSN 0070-234X

**Cyprus. Department of Antiquities**
Nicosia, Cyprus.
- Cyprus. Department of Antiquities. Annual Report. a. ISSN 0070-2374
- Cyprus. Department of Antiquities. Monographs. irreg., 1971, no. 11. ISSN 0070-2366

**Cyprus. Department of Social Welfare Services**
c/o Director, Nicosia, Cyprus.
- Cyprus. Department of Social Welfare Services. Annual Report. a. ISSN 0070-2404

**Cyprus. Department of Statistics and Research**
Ministry of Finance, Nicosia, Cyprus.
- Analysis of Cyprus Foreign Trade. a. ISSN 0526-5053
- Cyprus. Department of Statistics and Research. Agricultural Survey. a.
- Cyprus. Department of Statistics and Research. Analysis of Wholesale and Retail Trade. a.
- Cyprus. Department of Statistics and Research. Annual Industrial Production Survey. a. ISSN 0590-4854
- Cyprus. Department of Statistics and Research. Construction and Housing Report. a.
- Cyprus. Department of Statistics and Research. Demographic Report. a. ISSN 0590-4846
- Cyprus. Department of Statistics and Research. Economic Report. a. ISSN 0070-2412
- Cyprus. Department of Statistics and Research. Imports and Exports Statistics. m. ISSN 0011-4472
- Cyprus. Department of Statistics and Research. Index Numbers of Industrial Production. a.
- Cyprus. Department of Statistics and Research. Motor Vehicles and Road Accidents. a. ISSN 0574-8399
- Cyprus. Department of Statistics & Research. Quarterly Statistical Digest. q. ISSN 0011-4464
- Cyprus. Department of Statistics and Research. Road Motor Transport Sample Survey. a.
- Cyprus. Department of Statistics and Research. Services Survey. a.
- Cyprus. Department of Statistics and Research. Shipping and Aviation Statistics. a. ISSN 0070-2439
- Cyprus. Department of Statistics and Research. Short-Term Industrial Indicators. m.
- Cyprus. Department of Statistics and Research. Statistical Abstract. a. ISSN 0590-4862
- Cyprus. Department of Statistics and Research. Statistical Summary. m. ISSN 0526-5096
- Cyprus. Department of Statistics and Research. Statistics of Imports and Exports. a. ISSN 0070-2420

- Cyprus. Department of Statistics and Research. Tourism, Migration and Travel Statistics. m.
- Cyprus. Department of Statistics and Research. Wages, Salaries and Hours of Work. a.
- Financial Statistics of Education in Cyprus. a.
- Sales of Vine Products Manufactured in Cyprus. a.
- Statistics of Education in Cyprus. a.

**Cyprus. Geological Survey Department**
Nicosia, Cyprus.
- Cyprus. Geological Survey Department. Annual Report. a. ISSN 0574-8267
- Cyprus. Geological Survey Department. Bulletin. irreg.
- Cyprus. Geological Survey Department. Memoirs. irreg. ISSN 0574-8259

**Cyprus. Government Printing Office**
Nicosia, Cyprus.
- Cyprus. Budget: Estimates of Revenue and Expenditure. a. ISSN 0070-2323
- Cyprus. Development Estimates. a. ISSN 0084-9510

**Cyprus. Ministry of Education**
c/o Paedagogical Academy, Nicosia, Cyprus.
- Cyprus Today. q. ISSN 0045-9429

**Cyprus. Ministry of Education. Nicosia School Committee**
Nicosia, Cyprus.
- Mathitiki Estia. 1-2 per yr. ISSN 0025-5904

**Cyprus. Ministry of Finance. Department of Statistics and Research**
see Cyprus. Department of Statistics and Research

**Cyprus. Ministry of Labour and Social Insurance**
Nicosia, Cyprus.
- Cyprus. Ministry of Labour and Social Insurance. Annual Report. a. ISSN 0070-2390
- Cyprus. Ministry of Labour and Social Insurance. Quarterly Review. m. ISSN 0011-4480

**Cyprus. Public Information Office**
Nicosia, Cyprus.
- Agrotis/Countryman. bi-m. ISSN 0002-1997
- Cyprus Bulletin. w. ISSN 0011-4456

**Cyprus Educational Research Association**
Nicosia, Cyprus.
- Bulletin of Paedagogical Research/Deltion Paedagogikon Erevnon. s-a. ISSN 0007-5019

**Cyprus Geographical Association**
P.O. Box 3656, Nicosia, Cyprus.
- Geographika Chronika/Geographical Chronicles. s-a.

**Cyprus Research Centre**
Box 1436, Nicosia, Cyprus.
- Kentron Epistemonikon Ereunion. Epeteris/Cyprus Research Center. Annual. a. ISSN 0071-0954

**Geographikos Homilos Kyprou**
see Cyprus Geographical Association

**Laographike Kypros**
P.O. Box 1034, Leukosia, Cyprus.
- Laographike Kypros. q.

**M A M**
Box 1722, Nicosia, Cyprus.
- Kosmos Tou Kypriakou Vivliou/World of Cypriot Books. m.

**PAN Publishing House**
Corner Makarios-Xenopoullos Str., Box 1209, Nicosia, Cyprus.
- Welcome to Cyprus. m. ISSN 0044-0698

**School for Parents**
A. D. Christodoulides, Ed., Teachers Building, Nicosia, Cyprus.
- Family and School/Oikogeneia Kai Scholeio. bi-m. ISSN 0014-7192

**Society of Cypriot Studies**
P.O. Box 1436, Nicosia, Cyprus.
- Society of Cypriot Studies. Bulletin/Kypriakai Spoudai. a. ISSN 0081-1580

# CZECHOSLOVAKIA

**A-Press**
Markusova 7, Bratislava, Czechoslovakia
(Subscr. to: Slovart, Gottwaldovo nam. 48, 805 32 Bratislava)
- Projekt; revue slovenskej architektury. 10 per yr. (Zvaz Slovenskych Architektov)

**Academia, Publishing House of the Czechoslovak Academy of Sciences**
Vodickova 40, 112 29 Prague 1, Czechoslovakia
- Acta Entomologica Bohemoslovaca. bi-m. ISSN 0001-5601 (Ceskoslovenska Akademie Ved. Entomologicky Ustav) (Distributor in Western countries; Dr. W. Junk B.V., 13, van Stolkweg, The Hague, Netherlands)
- Aplikace Matematiky/Applied Mathematics. bi-m. ISSN 0003-6501 (Ceskoslovenska Akademie Ved. Matematicky Ustav) (Distributor in Western countries: Plenum Publishing Co. Ltd., Davis House, 8 Scrubs Lane, London NW10 6SE, England)
- Archeologicke Rozhledy/Archaeological Review. bi-m. ISSN 0044-8605 (Ceskoslovenska Akademie Ved. Archeologicky Ustav) (Distributor in Western countries: John Benjamins B.V., Amsteldijk 44, Amsterdam (Z.), Netherlands)
- Archiv Orientalni/Oriental Archives; quarterly journal of African and Asian studies. q. ISSN 0044-8699 (Ceskoslovenska Akademie Ved. Orientalni Ustav) (Distributor in Western countries: John Benjamins B.V., Amsteldijk 44, Amsterdam (Z.), Netherlands)
- Biologia Plantarum; journal for experimental botany. bi-m. ISSN 0006-3134 (Ceskoslovenska Akademie Ved) (Distributor in Western countries: Dr. W. Junk B.V., 13, van Stolkweg, The Hague, Netherlands)
- Biologicke Listy/Biological Review. q. (Ceskoslovenska Akademie Ved) (Distributor in Western countries: John Benjamins B.V., Amsteldijk 44, Amsterdam (Z.), Netherlands)
- Bulletin of the Astronomical Institutes of Czechoslovakia. bi-m. ISSN 0004-6248 (Ceskoslovenska Akademie Ved. Astronomicky Ustav) (Distributor in Western countries: Academic Press Inc. Ltd., 24-28 Oval Rd., London NW1 7DX, England)
- Bulletin of the Czechoslovak Seismological Stations: Pruhonice, Praha and Kasperske Hory. s-a. (Ceskoslovenska Akademie Ved. Geofyzikalni Ustav) (Subscr. to: Ceskoslovenska Akademie Ved, Geofyzikalni Ustav, Bocni 11, 141 31 Prague 4)
- Byzantinoslavica; international journal of Byzantine studies. s-a. ISSN 0007-7712 (Ceskoslovenska Akademie Ved. Kabinet pro Studia Recka, Rimska a Latinska) (Distributor in Western countries: John Benjamins B.V., Amsteldijk 44, Amsterdam (Z.), Netherlands)
- Casopis pro Mineralogii a Geologii/Journal of Mineralogy and Geology. q. ISSN 0008-7378 (Ceskoslovenska Spolecnost pro Mineralogii a Geologii) (Distributor in Western countries: John Benjamins B.V., Amsteldijk 44, Amsterdam (Z.), Netherlands)
- Casopis pro Pestovani Matematiky/Journal for the Cultivation of Mathematics. q. ISSN 0008-7394 (Ceskoslovenska Akademie Ved. Matematicky Ustav) (Distributor in Western countries: Kubon & Sagner, P.O.B. 68, 8000 Munich 34, W. Germany (B.R.D.))
- Ceska Literatura/Czech Literature; casopis pro literarni vedu. bi-m. ISSN 0009-0468 (Ceskoslovenska Akademie Ved. Ustav pro Ceskou Literaturu) (Distributor in Western countries: John Benjamins B.V., Amsteldijk 44, Amsterdam (Z.), Netherlands)
- Ceska Mykologie/Czech Mycology. q. ISSN 0009-0476 (Ceskoslovenska Vedecka Spolecnost pro Mykologii) (Distributor in Western countries: John Benjamins B.V., Amsteldijk 44, Amsterdam (Z.), Netherlands)
- Ceskoslovenska Akademie Ved. Acta Technica. bi-m. ISSN 0001-7043 (Distributor in Western countries: John Benjamins B.V., Amsteldijk 44, Amsterdam (Z.), Netherlands)
- Ceskoslovenska Akademie Ved. Rozpravy. MPV: Rada Matematickych a Prirodnich Ved. irreg., vol. 85, 1975. ISSN 0069-228X
- Ceskoslovenska Akademie Ved. Rozpravy. SV: Rada Spolecenskych Ved. irreg., vol. 85, 1975. ISSN 0069-2298

- Ceskoslovenska Akademie Ved. Rozpravy. TV: Rada Technickych Ved. irreg., vol. 85, 1975. ISSN 0069-2301
- Ceskoslovenska Akademie Ved. Ustredni Archiv. Archivni Zpravy. 1-2 per yr.
- Ceskoslovenska Akademie Ved. Vestnik. bi-m. ISSN 0009-0492 (Distributor in Western countries: Kubon & Sagner, P.O.B. 68, 8000 Munich 34, W. Germany (B.R.D.))
- Ceskoslovenska Fysiologie/Czechoslovak Physiology. bi-m. ISSN 0009-0557 (Ceskoslovenska Akademie Ved. Fysiologicky Ustav) (Distributor in Western countries: John Benjamins B.V., Amsteldijk 44, Amsterdam (Z.), Netherlands)
- Ceskoslovenska Psychologie/Czechoslovak Psychology. bi-m. ISSN 0009-062X (Ceskoslovenska Akademie Ved. Psychologicky Ustav) (Distributor in Western countries: John Benjamins B.V., Amsteldijk 44, Amsterdam (Z.), Netherlands)
- Ceskoslovenska Rusistika/Journal of Czechoslovak Russian Studies; casopis pro jazyky a literaturу slovanskych narodu SSSR. 5 per yr. ISSN 0009-0638 (Ceskoslovenska Akademie Ved) (Distributor in Western countries: John Benjamins B.V., Amsteldijk 44, Amsterdam (Z.), Netherlands)
- Ceskoslovenska Spolecnost Zemepisna. Sbornik. q. ISSN 0036-5254 (Distributor in Western countries: John Benjamins B.V., Amsteldijk 44, Amsterdam (Z.), Netherlands)
- Ceskoslovenska Spolecnost Zoologicka. Vestnik. q. ISSN 0042-4595 (Distributor in Western countries: John Benjamins B.V., Amsteldijk 44, Amsterdam (Z.), Netherlands)
- Ceskoslovensky Casopis Historicky/Czechoslovak Historical Journal. bi-m. ISSN 0045-6187 (Ceskoslovenska Akademie Ved. Historicky Ustav) (Distributor in Western countries: John Benjamins B.V., Amsteldijk 44, Amsterdam (Z.), Netherlands)
- Ceskoslovensky Casopis pro Fyziku. Sekce A/ Czechoslovak Journal of Physics. Section A. bi-m. ISSN 0009-0700 (Ceskoslovenska Akademie Ved. Ustav Fysiky Pevnych Latek) (Distributor in Western countries: John Benjamins B.V., Amsteldijk 44, Amsterdam (Z.), Netherlands)
- Cesky Lid/Czech People. q. ISSN 0009-0794 (Ceskoslovenska Akademie Ved. Ustav pro Etnografii a Folkloristiku) (Distributor in Western countries: Kubon & Sagner, P.O.B. 68, 8000 Munich 34, W. Germany (B.R.D.))
- Chemicke Listy/Journal of Chemistry. m. ISSN 0009-2770 (Ceskoslovenska Spolecnost Chemicka) (Distributor in Western countries: Kubon & Sagner, P.O.B. 68, 8000 Munich 34, W. Germany (B.R.D.))
- Collection of Czechoslovak Chemical Communications. m. ISSN 0010-0765 (Ceskoslovenska Akademie Ved) (Distributor in Western countries: Academic Press Inc. Ltd., 24-28 Oval Rd., London NW1 7DX, England)
- Czechoslovak Economic Papers. irreg. ISSN 0590-5001 (Ceskoslovenska Akademie Ved. Ekonomicky Ustav)
- Czechoslovak Journal of Physics. Europhysics Journal. m. (Ceskoslovenska Akademie Ved. Ustav Fysiky Pevnych Latek) (Distributor in Western countries: Plenum Publishing Co. Ltd., Davis House, 8 Scrubs Lane, London NW10 6SE, England)
- Czechoslovak Mathematical Journal. q. ISSN 0011-4642 (Ceskoslovenska Akademie Ved. Matematicky Ustav) (Distributor in Western countries: Kubon & Sagner, P.O.B. 68, 8000 Munich 34, W. Germany (B.R.D.))
- De Musica Disputationes Pragenses. irreg. (Ceskoslovenska Akademie Ved. Ustav pro Teorii a Dejiny Umeni)
- Dejiny Ved a Techniky/History of Sciences and Technology. q. ISSN 0300-4414 (Ceskoslovenska Spolecnost pro Dejiny Ved a Techniky) (Distributor in Western countries: Kubon & Sagner, P.O.B. 68, 8000 Munich 34, W. Germany (B.R.D.))
- Ekonomicko-Matematicky Obzor/Review of Econometrics. q. ISSN 0013-3027 (Ceskoslovenska Akademie Ved. Ekonomicky Ustav) (Distributor in Western countries: John Benjamins B.V., Amsteldijk 44, Amsterdam (Z.), Netherlands)
- Estetika/Aesthetics. q. ISSN 0014-1291 (Ceskoslovenska Akademie Ved. Ustav pro Teorii a Dejiny Umeni) (Distributor in Western countries: John Benjamins B.V., Amsteldijk 44, Amsterdam (Z.), Netherlands)

- Filosoficky Casopis/Philosophical Journal. bi-m. ISSN 0015-1831 (Ceskoslovenska Akademie Ved. Ustav pro Filosofii a Sociologii) (Distributor in Western countries: John Benjamins B.V., Amsteldijk 44, Amsterdam (Z.), Netherlands)
- Folia Biologica. bi-m. ISSN 0015-5500 (Ceskoslovenska Akademie Ved) (Distributor in Western countries: Academic Press Inc. Ltd., 24-28 Oval Rd., London NW1 7DX, England)
- Folia Geobotanica et Phytotaxonomica. q. ISSN 0015-5551 (Ceskoslovenska Akademie Ved. Botanicky Ustav) (Distributor in Western countries: Dr. W. Junk B.V., 13, van Stolkweg, The Hague, Netherlands)
- Folia Microbiologica. bi-m. ISSN 0015-5632 (Ceskoslovenska Akademie Ved. Mikrobiologicky Ustav) (Co-sponsor: Ceskoslovenska Spolecnost Mikrobiologicka) (Distributor in Western countries: Academic Press Inc. Ltd., 24-28 Oval Rd., London NW1 7DX, England)
- Folia Morphologica. q. ISSN 0015-5640 (Ceskoslovenska Akademie Ved. Embryologicky Ustav) (Distributor in Western countries: Plenum Publishing Co. Ltd., Davis House, 8 Scrubs Lane, London NW10 6SE, England)
- Folia Parasitologica. q. ISSN 0015-5683 (Ceskoslovenska Akademie Ved. Parasitologicky Ustav) (Distributor in Western countries: Dr. W. Junk B.V., 13. van Stolkweg, The Hague, Netherlands)
- Hudebni Veda/Musicology. q. ISSN 0018-7003 (Ceskoslovenska Akademie Ved. Ustav pro Teorii a Dejiny Umeni. Sekce Hudebni Vedy) (Distributor in Western countries: John Benjamins B.V., Amsteldijk 44, Amsterdam (Z.), Netherlands)
- International Congress of Acarology. Proceedings. quadrennial, 3rd, 1973, Prague. ISSN 0074-3445 (Inquiries to:, K. Samsinak, Sec. of Congress)
- International Symposium on the Continuous Cultivation of Microorganisms. Proceedings. biennial, 4th, 1968, Prague. ISSN 0074-8927 (Dist. by: Academic Press Inc., 111 Fifth Ave., New York, NY 10003, U.S.A.)
- Krystalinikum; contributions to the geology and petrology of crystalline complexes. a.
- Kybernetika/Cybernetics. bi-m. ISSN 0023-5954 (Czechoslovak Cybernetic Association) (Distributor in Western Countries: John Benjamins B.V., Amsteldijk 44, Amsterdam (Z.), Netherlands)
- Lide a Zeme/People and Countries. m. ISSN 0024-2896 (Ceskoslovenska Akademie Ved) (Subscr. to: Artia, Ve Smeckach 30, 111 27 Prague 1)
- Listy Filologicke/Journal of Philology. q. ISSN 0024-4457 (Ceskoslovenska Akademie Ved. Kabinet pro Studia Recka, Rimska a Latinska) (Distributor in Western countries: John Benjamins B.V., Amsteldijk 44, Amsterdam (Z.), Netherlands)
- Metodicke Prirucky Experimentalni Botaniky/ Methods of Experimental Botany. irreg., no. 3, 1974. ISSN 0076-6984 (Ceskoslovenska Akademie Ved)
- Nase Rec/Our Language. 5 per yr. ISSN 0027-8203 (Ceskoslovenska Akademie Ved. Ustav pro Jazyk Cesky) (Distributor in Western countries: Kubon & Sagner, P.O.B. 68, 8000 Munich 34, W. Germany (B.R.D.))
- Novy Orient/New Orient. 10 per yr. ISSN 0029-5302 (Ceskoslovenska Akademie Ved. Orientalni Ustav) (Subscr. to: Artia, Ve Smeckach 30, 111 27 Prague 1)
- Pamatky Archeologicke/Archaeological Memoirs. s-a. ISSN 0031-0506 (Ceskoslovenska Akademie Ved. Archeologicky Ustav) (Distributor in Western countries: John Benjamins B.V., Amsteldijk 44, Amsterdam (Z.), Netherlands)
- Pedagogika/Pedagogy; casopis pro pedagogicke vedy. bi-m. ISSN 0031-3815 (Ceskoslovenska Akademie Ved. Pedagogicky Ustav J. A. Komenskeho) (Distributor in Western Countries: John Benjamins B. V., Amsteldijk 44, Amsterdam (Z.), Netherlands)
- Philologica Pragensia. q. ISSN 0048-3885 (Ceskoslovenska Akademie Ved. Kabinet Cizich Jazyku) (Co-sponsor: Ceskoslovenska Akademie Ved. Ustav Ceske a Svetove Literatury) (Distributor in Western countries: John Benjamins B.V., Amsteldijk 44, Amsterdam (Z.), Netherlands)
- Photosynthetica; international journal for photosynthesis research. q. ISSN 0300-3604 (Ceskoslovenska Akademie Ved. Institute of Experimental Botany) (Distributor in Western countries: Dr. W. Junk B.V., 13, van Stolkweg, The Hague, Netherlands)

- Physiologia Bohemoslovaca. bi-m. ISSN 0031-9309 (Ceskoslovenska Akademie Ved. Fysiologicky Ustav) (Distributor in Western countries: Academic Press Inc. Ltd., 24-28 Oval Rd., London NW1 7DX, England)
- Pokroky Matematiky, Fyziky a Astronomie/Progress in Mathematics, Physics and Astronomy. bi-m. ISSN 0032-2423 (Jednota Ceskoslovenskych Matematiku a Fyziku) (Distributor in Western countries: John Benjamins B.V., Amsteldijk 44, Amsterdam (Z.), Netherlands)
- Politicka Ekonomie/Journal of Political Economy. m. ISSN 0032-3233 (Ceskoslovenska Akademie Ved. Ekonomicky Ustav) (Distributor in Western countries: John Benjamins B.V., Amsteldijk 44, Amsterdam (Z.), Netherlands)
- Prameny Ceske a Slovenske Lingvistiky. Rada Ceska. irreg. ISSN 0079-4902 (Ceskoslovenska Akademie Ved)
- Pravnehistoricke Studie. irreg., vol. 18, 1974. ISSN 0079-4929 (Ceskoslovenska Akademie Ved)
- Pravnik/Lawyer. m. (Ceskoslovenska Akademie Ved. Ustav Prava) (Distributor in Western countries: John Benjamins B.V., Amsteldijk 44, Amsterdam (Z.), Netherlands)
- Preslia. q. ISSN 0032-7786 (Ceskoslovenska Botanicka Spolecnost) (Distributor in Western countries: John Benjamins B.V., Amsteldijk 44, Amsterdam (Z.), Netherlands)
- Prirodovedne Prace Ustavu C S A V v Brne/Acta Scientarum Naturalium Academiae Scientiarum Bohemoslovacae Brno. m. ISSN 0032-8758 (Ceskoslovenska Akademie Ved)
- Silikaty/Silicates. q. ISSN 0037-5241 (Ceskoslovenska Akademie Ved) (Distributor in Western countries: John Benjamins B.V., Amsteldijk 44, Amsterdam (Z.), Netherlands)
- Slavia; casopis pro slovanskou filologii. q. ISSN 0037-6736 (Ceskoslovenska Akademie Ved) (Distributor in Western countries: John Benjamins B.V., Amsteldijk 44, Amsterdam (Z.), Netherlands)
- Slezsky Sbornik/Acta Silesiaca; ctvrtletnik pro vedy o spolecnosti. q. ISSN 0037-6833 (Ceskoslovenska Akademie Ved. Slezsky Ustav) (Distributor in Western countries: John Benjamins B.V., Amsteldijk 44, Amsterdam (Z.), Netherlands)
- Slovanske Historicke Studie. irreg., vol. 10, 1974. ISSN 0081-007X (Ceskoslovenska Akademie Ved)
- Slovansky Prehled/Slavonic Review. bi-m. ISSN 0037-6922 (Ceskoslovenska Akademie Ved. Ceskoslovensko-Sovetsky Institut) (Distributor in Western countries: John Benjamins B.V., Amsteldijk 44, Amsterdam (Z.), Netherlands)
- Slovo a Slovesnost/Word and Writing; casopis pro otazky teorie a kultury jazyka. q. ISSN 0037-7031 (Ceskoslovenska Akademie Ved. Ustav pro Jazyk Cesky) (Distributor in Western countries: John Benjamins B.V., Amsteldijk 44, Amsterdam (Z.), Netherlands)
- Sociologicky Casopis/Sociological Review. bi-m. ISSN 0038-0288 (Ceskoslovenska Akademie Ved. Ustav pro Filosofii a Sociologii) (Distributor in Western countries: John Benjamins B.V., Amsteldijk 44, Amsterdam (Z.), Netherlands)
- Studia Geophysica et Geodaetica; a journal of geophysics, geodesy, meteorology and climatology. q. ISSN 0039-3169 (Ceskoslovenska Akademie Ved. Geofyzikalni Ustav) (Distributor in Western countries: Plenum Publishing Co. Ltd., Davis House, 8 Scrubs Lane, London NW10 6SE, England)
- Umeni/Arts. bi-m. ISSN 0049-5123 (Ceskoslovenska Akademie Ved) (Distributor in Western countries: John Benjamins B.V., Amsteldijk 44, Amsterdam (Z.), Netherlands)
- Ustredni Ustav Geologicky. Vestnik. bi-m. ISSN 0042-1359 (Distributor in Western countries: John Benjamins B.V., Amsteldijk 44, Amsterdam (Z.), Netherlands)
- Vesmir/Universe. m. ISSN 0042-4544 (Ceskoslovenska Akademie Ved) (Subscr. to: Artia, Ve Smeckach 30, 111 27 Prague 1)
- Zdravotni Technika a Vzduchotechnika/Sanitary and Air Technics. bi-m. ISSN 0044-1988 (Ceskoslovenska Spolecnost pro Vedu a Techniku) (Distributor in Western countries: John Benjamins B.V., Amsteldijk 44, Amsterdam (Z.), Netherlands)
- Ziva; casopis pro biologickou praci. bi-m. ISSN 0044-4812 (Ceskoslovenska Akademie Ved) (Subscr. to: Artia, Ve Smeckach 30, 111 27 Prague 1)

- Zoologicke Listy/Folia Zoologica. q. ISSN 0044-5142 (Ceskoslovenska Akademie Ved) (Distributor in Western countries: Plenum Publishing Co. Ltd., Davis House, 8 Scrubs Lane, London NW10 6SE, England)

**Aeroklub CSSR**
Prague, Czechoslovakia
(Subscr. to: Artia, Ve Smeckach 30, 111 27 Prague 1)
- Letectvi a Kosmonautika. fortn. ISSN 0024-1156

**Albatros, Nakladatelstvi pro Deti a Mladez**
Na Perstyne 1, 110 01 Prague 1, Czechoslovakia
(Subscr. to: Artia, Ve Smeckach 30, 111 27 Prague 1)
- Zlaty Maj; casopis o detske literature. m(10 per yr) ISSN 0044-4871 (Co-publisher: Mlade Leta)

**Alfa**
Hurbanovo nam. 3, 893 31 Bratislava, Czechoslovakia
(Subscr. to: Slovart, Gottwaldovo nam 48, 805 32 Bratislava)
- Agrochemia/Agricultural Chemicals. m. ISSN 0002-1830 (Vyzkumny Ustav Agrochemicke Technologie)
- Drevo/Wood. m. ISSN 0012-6144 (Czechoslovakia. Ministerstvo Priemyslu Slovenskej Socialistickej Republiky)
- Ekonomika Stavebnictva/Economics of Civil Engineering. m. ISSN 0013-3108 (Vyskumny Ustav Ekonomiky a Organizacie Stavebnictva)
- Informacne Systemy.
- Inzinierske Stavby/Civil Engineering. m. ISSN 0021-0277 (Czechoslovakia. Ministerstvo Stavebnictva Slovenskej Socialistickej Republiky)
- Mechanizacia. m. ISSN 0025-6595
- Urob - Udelej si Sam. q.
- Zvaranie/Welding. m. ISSN 0044-5525 (Czechoslovakia. Federalni Ministerstvo Hutnictvi a Tezkeho Strojirenstvi)

**Amaterska Scena**
Vinohradska 2, 120 00 Prague 2, Czechoslovakia
- Amaterska Scena; ochotnicke divadlo. m. ISSN 0002-6786

**Amaterske Radio**
Lubljanska 57, 120 00 Prague 2, Czechoslovakia
- Amaterske Radio. m.

**Americke Velvyslanectvi**
Trziste 15, 125 48 Prague 1, Czechoslovakia.
- Spektrum.

**Artia**
Ve Smeckach 30, 111 27 Prague 1, Czechoslovakia.
- Czech Books in Print. m.

**Association of Czechoslovak Plastic Surgeons**
Legerova 63, 120 00 Prague 2, Czechoslovakia
(Distributor in Western countries: Karger Libri A G, Petersgraben 31, 4001 Basel, Switzerland)
- Acta Chirurgiae Plasticae; international journal of plastic surgery. q. ISSN 0001-5423

**Avicenum, State Health Publishing House**
Tomasska 1, 118 02 Prague 1, Czechoslovakia
- Acta Chirurgiae Orthopaedicae et Traumatologiae Cechoslovaca. bi-m. ISSN 0001-5415 (Ceskoslovenska Spolecnost pro Ortopedickou Chirurgii a Traumatologii) (Co-sponsor: Ceskoslovenska Lekarska Spolecnost J. Ev. Purkyne) (Subscr. to: Artia, Ve Smeckach 30, 111 27 Prague 1)
- Activitas Nervosa Superior; interdisciplinary journal for the study of higher nervous activity. q. ISSN 0001-7604 (Ceskoslovenska Spolecnost pro Studium Vyssi Nervove Cinnosti) (Co-sponsor: Ceskoslovenska Lekarska Spolecnost J. Ev. Purkyne) (Distributor in Western countries: Karger Libri A G, Petersgraben 31, 4011 Basel, Switzerland)
- Balneologia Bohemica. q. (Vyzkumny Ustav Balneologicky)
- Biochemia Clinica Bohemoslovaca. q. (Ceskoslovenska Spolecnost pro Klinickou Biochemii) (Co-sponsor: Ceskoslovenska Lekarska Spolecnost J. Ev. Purkyne) (Subscr. to: Slovart, Gottwaldovo nam. 48, 805 32 Bratislava)
- Casopis Lekaru Ceskych. w. ISSN 0008-7335 (Ceskoslovenska Lekarska Spolecnost J. Ev. Purkyne) (Subscr. to: Artia, Ve Smeckach 30, 111 27 Prague 1)

- Ceskoslovenska Dermatologie. bi-m. ISSN 0009-0514 (Ceskoslovenska Dermato-Venerologicka Spolecnost) (Co-sponsor: Ceskoslovenska Lekarska Spolecnost J. Ev. Purkyne) (Subscr. to: Artia, Ve Smeckach 30, 111 27 Prague 1)
- Ceskoslovenska Epidemiologie, Mikrobiologie, Imunologie. bi-m. ISSN 0009-0522 (Ceskoslovenska Mikrobiologicka-Epidemiologicka Spolecnost) (Co-sponsor: Ceskoslovenska Lekarska Spolecnost J. Ev. Purkyne) (Subscr. to: Artia, Ve Smeckach 30, 111 27 Prague 1)
- Ceskoslovenska Farmacie. 10 per yr. ISSN 0009-0530 (Ceskoslovenska Farmaceuticka Spolecnost) (Co-sponsor: Ceskoslovenska Lekarska Spolecnost J. Ev. Purkyne) (Subscr. to: Artia, Ve Smeckach 30, 111 27 Prague 1)
- Ceskoslovenska Gastroenterologie a Vyziva. 8 per yr. ISSN 0009-0565 (Ceskoslovenska Spolecnost pro Gastroenterologii a Vyzivu) (Co-sponsor: Ceskoslovenska Lekarska Spolecnost J. Ev. Purkyne) (Subscr. to: Artia, Ve Smeckach 30, 111 27 Prague 1)
- Ceskoslovenska Gynekologie. 10 per yr. ISSN 0069-231X (Ceskoslovenska Spolecnost Gynekologicka a Porodnicka) (Co-sponsor: Ceskoslovenska Lekarska Spolecnost J. Ev. Purkyne) (Subscr. to: Artia, Ve Smeckach 30, 111 27 Prague 1)
- Ceskoslovenska Hygiena. 10 per yr. ISSN 0009-0573 (Ceskoslovenska Spolecnost Hygienicka) (Co-sponsor: Ceskoslovenska Lekarska Spolecnost J. Ev. Purkyne) (Subscr. to: Artia, Ve Smeckach 30, 111 27 Prague 1)
- Ceskoslovenska Neurologie a Neurochirurgie. bi-m. ISSN 0301-0597 (Ceskoslovenska Neurologicka Spolecnost) (Co-sponsor: Ceskoslovenska Lekarska Spolecnost J. Ev. Purkyne) (Subscr. to: Artia, Ve Smeckach 30, 111 27 Prague 1)
- Ceskoslovenska Oftalmologie. bi-m. ISSN 0009-059X (Ceskoslovenska Oftalmologicka Spolecnost) (Co-sponsor: Ceskoslovenska Lekarska Spolecnost J. Ev. Purkyne) (Subscr. to: Artia, Ve Smeckach 30, 111 27 Prague 1)
- Ceskoslovenska Otolaryngologie/Acta Otolaryngologica Cechoslovaca. bi-m. ISSN 0009-0603 (Ceskoslovenska Otolaryngologicka Spolecnost) (Co-sponsor: Ceskoslovenska Lekarska Spolecnost J. Ev. Purkyne) (Subscr. to: Artia, Ve Smeckach 30, 111 27 Prague 1)
- Ceskoslovenska Patologie. q. ISSN 0009-0611 (Ceskoslovenska Spolecnost Patologicka) (Co-sponsor: Ceskoslovenska Lekarska Spolecnost J. Ev. Purkyne) (Subscr. to: Artia, Ve Smeckach 30, 111 27 Prague 1)
- Ceskoslovenska Pediatrie. m. ISSN 0069-2328 (Ceskoslovenska Pediatricka Spolecnost) (Co-sponsor: Ceskoslovenska Lekarska Spolecnost J. Ev. Purkyne) (Subscr. to: Artia, Ve Smeckach 30, 111 27 Prague 1)
- Ceskoslovenska Psychiatrie. bi-m. ISSN 0069-2336 (Ceskoslovenska Psychiatricka Spolecnost) (Co-sponsor: Ceskoslovenska Lekarska Spolecnost J. Ev. Purkyne) (Subscr. to: Artia, Ve Smeckach 30, 111 27 Prague 1)
- Ceskoslovenska Radiologie. bi-m. ISSN 0069-2344 (Ceskoslovenska Radiologicka Spolecnost) (Co-sponsor: Ceskoslovenska Lekarska Spolecnost J. Ev. Purkyne) (Subscr. to: Artia, Ve Smeckach 30, 111 27 Prague 1)
- Ceskoslovenska Stomatologie. bi-m. ISSN 0009-0654 (Ceskoslovenska Stomatologicka Spolecnost) (Co-sponsor: Ceskoslovenska Lekarska Spolecnost J. Ev. Purkyne) (Subscr. to: Artia, Ve Smeckach 30, 111 27 Prague 1)
- Ceskoslovenske Zdravotnictvi. m. ISSN 0009-0689 (Ceskoslovenska Spolecnost pro Socialni Zdravotnictvi) (Co-sponsor: Ceskoslovenska Lekarska Spolecnost J. Ev. Purkyne) (Subscr. to: Artia, Ve Smeckach 30, 111 27 Prague 1)
- Cor et Vasa; international journal of cardiology. q. ISSN 0010-8650 (Distributor in Western countries: Karger Libri A G, Petersgraben 31, 4011 Basel, Switzerland)
- Fysiatricky a Reumatologicky Vestnik. bi-m. ISSN 0072-0038 (Ceskoslovenska Fysiatricka Spolecnost) (Co-sponsor: Ceskoslovenska Lekarska Spolecnost J. Ev. Purkyne) (Subscribe to: Artia, Ve Smeckach 30, 111 27 Prague 1)
- Journal of Hygiene, Epidemiology, Microbiology and Immunology. q. ISSN 0022-1732 (Institut Hygieny a Epidemiologie) (Co-sponsor: Czechoslovakia. Ministerstvo Zdravi Ceske Socialisticke Republiky) (Distributor in Western countries: Karger Libri A G, Petersgraben 31, 4011 Basel, Switzerland)

- Pracovni Lekarstvi. 10 per yr. ISSN 0032-6291 (Ceskoslovenska Spolecnost pro Pracovni Lekarstvi) (Co-sponsor: Ceskoslovenska Lekarska Spolecnost J. Ev. Purkyne) (Subscr. to: Artia, Ve Smeckach 30, 111 27 Prague 1)
- Prakticke Zubni Lekarstvi. 10 per yr. ISSN 0032-6720 (Ceskoslovenska Stomatologicka Spolecnost) (Co-sponsor: Ceskoslovenska Lekarska Spolecnost J. Ev. Purkyne) (Subscr. to: Artia, Ve Smeckach 30, 111 27 Prague 1)
- Prakticky Lekar. s-m. ISSN 0032-6739 (Ceskoslovenska Lekarska Spolecnost J. Ev. Purkyne) (Subscr. to: Artia, Ve Smeckach 30, 111 27 Prague 1)
- Review of Czechoslovak Medicine. q. ISSN 0034-6497 (Ceskoslovenska Lekarska Spolecnost J. Ev. Purkyne) (Subscr. to: Artia, Ve Smeckach 30, 111 27 Prague 1)
- Rozhledy v Chirurgii. m. ISSN 0035-9351 (Ceskoslovenska Chirurgicka Spolecnost) (Co-sponsor: Ceskoslovenska Lekarska Spolecnost J. Ev. Purkyne) (Subscr. to: Artia, Ve Smeckach 30, 111 27 Prague 1)
- Studia Pneumologica et Phtiseologica Cechoslovaca. 10 per yr. (Ceskoslovenska Pneumologicka a Ftizeologicka Spolecnost) (Co-sponsor: Ceskoslovenska Lekarska Spolecnost J. Ev. Purkyne) (Subscr. to: Artia., Ve Smeckach 30, 111 27 Prague 1)
- Vnitrni Lekarstvi. m. ISSN 0042-773X (Ceskoslovenska Spolecnost pro Vnitrni Lekarstvi) (Co-sponsor: Ceskoslovenska Lekarska Spolecnost J. Ev. Purkyne) (Subscr. to: Artia, Ve Smeckach 30, 111 27 Prague 1)
- Vyziva Lidu. m. ISSN 0042-9414 (Spolecnost pro Racionalni Vyzivu) (Subscr. to: Artia, Ve Smeckach 30, 111 27 Prague 1)
- Zdravotnicka Pracovnice. m. ISSN 0049-8572 (Subscr. to: Artia, Ve Smeckach 30, 111 27 Prague 1)

**Cerveny Kvet**
Tyrsova 9, Ostrava 1, Czechoslovakia.
- Cerveny Kvet; literatura, umeni, zivot. m. ISSN 0009-0441

**Ceska Statni Pojistovna**
Spalena 16, 113 04 Prague 1, Czechoslovakia (Subscr. to: Artia, Ve Smeckach 30, 111 27 Prague 1)
- Pojistny Obzor. m. ISSN 0032-2393
- Zabrana Skod; damage prevention: fire prevention, road safety, work safety, agriculture and industry protection. m. ISSN 0044-1708

**Ceskoslovenska Akademie Ved**
- Biologia Plantarum. (pub. by Academia, Publishing House of the Czechoslovak Academy of Sciences)
- Biologicke Listy/Biological Review. (pub. by Academia, Publishing House of the Czechoslovak Academy of Sciences)
- Ceskoslovenska Akademie Ved. Acta Technica. (pub. by Academia, Publishing House of the Czechoslovak Academy of Sciences)
- Ceskoslovenska Akademie Ved. Rozpravy. MPV: Rada Matematickych a Prirodnich Ved. (pub. by Academia, Publishing House of the Czechoslovak Academy of Sciences)
- Ceskoslovenska Akademie Ved. Rozpravy. SV: Rada Spolecenskych Ved. (pub. by Academia, Publishing House of the Czechoslovak Academy of Sciences)
- Ceskoslovenska Akademie Ved. Rozpravy. TV: Rada Technickych Ved. (pub. by Academia, Publishing House of the Czechoslovak Academy of Sciences)
- Ceskoslovenska Akademie Ved. Vestnik. (pub. by Academia, Publishing House of the Czechoslovak Academy of Sciences)
- Ceskoslovenska Rusistika/Journal of Czechoslovak Russian Studies. (pub. by Academia, Publishing House of the Czechoslovak Academy of Sciences)
- Collection of Czechoslovak Chemical Communications. (pub. by Academia, Publishing House of the Czechoslovak Academy of Sciences)
- Folia Biologica. (pub. by Academia, Publishing House of the Czechoslovak Academy of Sciences)
- Lide a Zeme/People and Countries. (pub. by Academia, Publishing House of the Czechoslovak Academy of Sciences)
- Metodicke Prirucky Experimentalni Botaniky/ Methods of Experimental Botany. (pub. by Academia, Publishing House of the Czechoslovak Academy of Sciences)
- Prague Studies in Mathematical Linguistics. (pub. by University of Alabama Press US)

- Prameny Ceske a Slovenske Lingvistiky. Rada Ceska. (pub. by Academia, Publishing House of the Czechoslovak Academy of Sciences)
- Pravnehistoricke Studie. (pub. by Academia, Publishing House of the Czechoslovak Academy of Sciences)
- Prirodovedne Prace Ustavu C S A V v Brne/Acta Scientarum Naturalium Academiae Scientiarum Bohemoslovacae Brno. (pub. by Academia, Publishing House of the Czechoslovak Academy of Sciences)
- Silikaty/Silicates. (pub. by Academia, Publishing House of the Czechoslovak Academy of Sciences)
- Slavia. (pub. by Academia, Publishing House of the Czechoslovak Academy of Sciences)
- Slovanske Historicke Studie. (pub. by Academia, Publishing House of the Czechoslovak Academy of Sciences)
- Umeni/Arts. (pub. by Academia, Publishing House of the Czechoslovak Academy of Sciences)
- Vesmir/Universe. (pub. by Academia, Publishing House of the Czechoslovak Academy of Sciences)
- Ziva. (pub. by Academia, Publishing House of the Czechoslovak Academy of Sciences)
- Zoologicke Listy/Folia Zoologica. (pub. by Academia, Publishing House of the Czechoslovak Academy of Sciences)

**Ceskoslovenska Akademie Ved. Archeologicky Ustav**
- Archeologicke Rozhledy/Archaeological Review. (pub. by Academia, Publishing House of the Czechoslovak Academy of Sciences)
- Pamatky Archeologicke/Archaeological Memoirs. (pub. by Academia, Publishing House of the Czechoslovak Academy of Sciences)

**Ceskoslovenska Akademie Ved. Astronomicky Ustav**
- Bulletin of the Astronomical Institutes of Czechoslovakia. (pub. by Academia, Publishing House of the Czechoslovak Academy of Sciences)

**Ceskoslovenska Akademie Ved. Botanicky Ustav**
- Folia Geobotanica et Phytotaxonomica. (pub. by Academia, Publishing House of the Czechoslovak Academy of Sciences)

**Ceskoslovenska Akademie Ved. Ceskoslovensko-Sovetsky Institut**
- Slovansky Prehled/Slavonic Review. (pub. by Academia, Publishing House of the Czechoslovak Academy of Sciences)

**Ceskoslovenska Akademie Ved. Ekonomicky Ustav**
- Czechoslovak Economic Papers. (pub. by Academia, Publishing House of the Czechoslovak Academy of Sciences)
- Ekonomicko-Matematicky Obzor/Review of Econometrics. (pub. by Academia, Publishing House of the Czechoslovak Academy of Sciences)
- Politicka Ekonomie/Journal of Political Economy. (pub. by Academia, Publishing House of the Czechoslovak Academy of Sciences)

**Ceskoslovenska Akademie Ved. Embryologicky Ustav**
- Folia Morphologica. (pub. by Academia, Publishing House of the Czechoslovak Academy of Sciences)

**Ceskoslovenska Akademie Ved. Entomologicky Ustav**
- Acta Entomologica Bohemoslovaca. (pub. by Academia, Publishing House of the Czechoslovak Academy of Sciences)

**Ceskoslovenska Akademie Ved. Fysiologicky Ustav**
- Ceskoslovenska Fysiologie/Czechoslovak Physiology. (pub. by Academia, Publishing House of the Czechoslovak Academy of Sciences)
- Physiologia Bohemoslovaca. (pub. by Academia, Publishing House of the Czechoslovak Academy of Sciences)

**Ceskoslovenska Akademie Ved. Geofyzikalni Ustav**
- Bulletin of the Czechoslovak Seismological Stations: Pruhonice, Praha and Kasperske Hory. (pub. by Academia, Publishing House of the Czechoslovak Academy of Sciences)
- Studia Geophysica et Geodaetica. (pub. by Academia, Publishing House of the Czechoslovak Academy of Sciences)

**Ceskoslovenska Akademie Ved. Geograficky Ustav, Brno**
Mendlovo nam. 1, 662 82 Brno, Czechoslovakia.
- Ceskoslovenska Akademie Ved. Geograficky Ustav, Brno. Zpravy. 8 per yr.

**Ceskoslovenska Akademie Ved. Historicky Ustav**
- Ceskoslovensky Casopis Historicky/Czechoslovak Historical Journal. (pub. by Academia, Publishing House of the Czechoslovak Academy of Sciences)

**Ceskoslovenska Akademie Ved. Institute of Experimental Botany**
- Photosynthetica. (pub. by Academia, Publishing House of the Czechoslovak Academy of Sciences)

**Ceskoslovenska Akademie Ved. Kabinet Cizich Jazyku**
- Philologica Pragensia. (pub. by Academia, Publishing House of the Czechoslovak Academy of Sciences)

**Ceskoslovenska Akademie Ved. Kabinet Mezinarodniho Prava**
Narodni tr. 18, Prague 1, Czechoslovakia.
- Casopis pro Mezinarodni Pravo/Czechoslovak Journal of International Law. q. ISSN 0008-736X

**Ceskoslovenska Akademie Ved. Kabinet pro Studia Recka, Rimska a Latinska**
- Byzantinoslavica. (pub. by Academia, Publishing House of the Czechoslovak Academy of Sciences)
- Listy Filologicke/Journal of Philology. (pub. by Academia, Publishing House of the Czechoslovak Academy of Sciences)

**Ceskoslovenska Akademie Ved. Matematicky Ustav**
- Aplikace Matematiky/Applied Mathematics. (pub. by Academia, Publishing House of the Czechoslovak Academy of Sciences)
- Casopis pro Pestovani Matematiky/Journal for the Cultivation of Mathematics. (pub. by Academia, Publishing House of the Czechoslovak Academy of Sciences)
- Czechoslovak Mathematical Journal. (pub. by Academia, Publishing House of the Czechoslovak Academy of Sciences)

**Ceskoslovenska Akademie Ved. Mikrobiologicky Ustav**
- Folia Microbiologica. (pub. by Academia, Publishing House of the Czechoslovak Academy of Sciences)

**Ceskoslovenska Akademie Ved. Orientalni Ustav**
- Archiv Orientalni/Oriental Archives. (pub. by Academia, Publishing House of the Czechoslovak Academy of Sciences)
- Novy Orient/New Orient. (pub. by Academia, Publishing House of the Czechoslovak Academy of Sciences)

**Ceskoslovenska Akademie Ved. Parasitologicky Ustav**
- Folia Parasitologica. (pub. by Academia, Publishing House of the Czechoslovak Academy of Sciences)

**Ceskoslovenska Akademie Ved. Pedagogicky Ustav J. A. Komenskeho**
- Pedagogika/Pedagogy. (pub. by Academia, Publishing House of the Czechoslovak Academy of Sciences)

**Ceskoslovenska Akademie Ved. Psychologicky Ustav**
- Ceskoslovenska Psychologie/Czechoslovak Psychology. (pub. by Academia, Publishing House of the Czechoslovak Academy of Sciences)

**Ceskoslovenska Akademie Ved. Slezsky Ustav**
- Slezsky Sbornik/Acta Silesiaca. (pub. by Academia, Publishing House of the Czechoslovak Academy of Sciences)

**Ceskoslovenska Akademie Ved. Ustav Fysiky Pevnych Latek**
- Ceskoslovensky Casopis pro Fyziku. Sekce A/ Czechoslovak Journal of Physics. Section A. (pub. by Academia, Publishing House of the Czechoslovak Academy of Sciences)
- Czechoslovak Journal of Physics. Europhysics Journal. (pub. by Academia, Publishing House of the Czechoslovak Academy of Sciences)

**Ceskoslovenska Akademie Ved. Ustav Prava**
- Pravnik/Lawyer. (pub. by Academia, Publishing House of the Czechoslovak Academy of Sciences)

**Ceskoslovenska Akademie Ved. Ustav pro Ceskou Literaturu**
- Ceska Literatura/Czech Literature. (pub. by Academia, Publishing House of the Czechoslovak Academy of Sciences)

**Ceskoslovenska Akademie Ved. Ustav pro Etnografii a Folkloristiku**
- Cesky Lid/Czech People. (pub. by Academia, Publishing House of the Czechoslovak Academy of Sciences)

**Ceskoslovenska Akademie Ved. Ustav pro Filosofii a Sociologii**
Jilska 1, 110 00 Prague 1, Czechoslovakia.
- Filosoficky Casopis/Philosophical Journal. (pub. by Academia, Publishing House of the Czechoslovak Academy of Sciences)
- Sociologicky Casopis/Sociological Review. (pub. by Academia, Publishing House of the Czechoslovak Academy of Sciences)
- Teorie Rozvoje Vedy. q. (Co-sponsor: Ceskoslovenske Akademie Ved. Ustav pro Ekonomiku a Rizeni Vedeckotechnickeho Rozvoje)

**Ceskoslovenska Akademie Ved. Ustav pro Jazyk Cesky**
- Nase Rec/Our Language. (pub. by Academia, Publishing House of the Czechoslovak Academy of Sciences)
- Slovo a Slovesnost/Word and Writing. (pub. by Academia, Publishing House of the Czechoslovak Academy of Sciences)

**Ceskoslovenska Akademie Ved. Ustav pro Teorii a Dejiny Umeni**
- De Musica Disputationes Pragenses. (pub. by Academia, Publishing House of the Czechoslovak Academy of Sciences)
- Estetika/Aesthetics. (pub. by Academia, Publishing House of the Czechoslovak Academy of Sciences)
- Hudebni Veda/Musicology. (pub. by Academia, Publishing House of the Czechoslovak Academy of Sciences)

**Ceskoslovenska Akademie Ved. Ustav pro Vyzkum Obratlovcu**
Kvetna 8, 603 65 Brno, Czechoslovakia.
- Vertebratologicke Zpravy/Notulae Vertebratologicae. a. ISSN 0506-7847

**Ceskoslovenska Akademie Ved. Ustredni Archiv**
- Ceskoslovenska Akademie Ved. Ustredni Archiv. Archivni Zpravy. (pub. by Academia, Publishing House of the Czechoslovak Academy of Sciences)

**Ceskoslovenska Akademie Zemedelska. Ustav Vedeckotechnickych Informaci pro Zemedelstvi**
Slezska 7, 120 56 Prague 2, Czechoslovakia.
- Agricultural Literature of Czechoslovakia. q. ISSN 0002-1520 (prep. by its Ustredni Zemedelska a Lesnicka Knihovna)
- Dokumentacni Listkova Sluzba/Card Documentation Service. m. ISSN 0032-7352 (prep. by its Ustredni Zemedelska a Lesnicka Knihovna)
- Lesnictvi/Forestry; vedecky casopis-scientific journal. m. ISSN 0024-1105 (prep. by its Ustredni Zemedelska a Lesnicka Knihovna) (Subscr. to: Artia, Ve Smeckach 30, 111 27 Prague 1)
- Metodiky pro Zavadeni Vysledku Vyzkumu do Praxe/Methods for the Application of Research Results into Practice. 25 per yr. ISSN 0026-1319 (prep. by its Ustredni Zemedelska a Lesnicka Knihovna)
- Prehled Lesnicke a Myslivecke Literatury/Review of Literature on Forestry and Game Management. m. ISSN 0032-7336 (prep. by its Ustredni Zemedelska a Lesnicka Knihovna) (Subscr. to: Artia, Ve Smeckach 30, 111 27 Prague 1)
- Rostlinna Vyroba/Plant Production. m. ISSN 0035-8371 (prep. by its Ustredni Zemedelska a Lesnicka Knihovna) (Subscr. to: Artia, Ve Smeckach 30, 111 27 Prague 1)
- Sbornik UVTIZ - Genetika a Slechteni/Journal of ISTI - Genetics and Breeding; vedecky casopis-scientific journal. q. ISSN 0036-5378 (prep. by its Ustredni Zemedelska a Lesnicka Knihovna) (Subscr. to: Artia, Ve Smeckach 30, 111 27 Prague 1)
- Sbornik UVTIZ - Meliorace/Journal of ISTI - Irrigation and Drainage; vedecky casopis-scientific journal. s-a. ISSN 0036-5386 (prep. by its Ustredni Zemedelska a Lesnicka Knihovna) (Subscr. to: Artia, Ve Smeckach 30, 111 27 Prague 1)
- Sbornik UVtIZ - Ochrana Rostlin/Journal of ISTI - Plant Protection; vedecky casopis-scientific journal. m. ISSN 0036-5394 (prep. by its Ustredni Zemedelska a Lesnicka Knihovna) (Subscr. to: Artia, Ve Smeckach 30, 111 27 Prague 1)
- Sbornik UVTIZ - Sociologie a Historie Zemedelstvi/Journal of ISTI - Sociology and History of Agriculture; vedecky casopis-scientific journal. s-a. (prep. by its Ustredni Zemedelska a Lesnicka Knihovna) (Subscr. to: Artia, Ve Smeckach 30, 111 27 Prague 1)
- Sbornik UVTIZ - Zahradnictvi/Journal of ISTI - Horticulture; vedecky casopis-scientific journal. q. (prep. by its Ustredni Zemedelska a Lesnicka Knihovna) (Subscr. to: Artia, Ve Smeckach 30, 111 27 Prague 1)
- Scientia Agriculturae Bohemoslovaca; vedecky casopis-scientific journal. q. ISSN 0582-2343 (prep. by its Ustredni Zemedelska a Lesnicka Knihovna) (Subscr. to: Artia, Ve Smeckach 30, 111 27 Prague 1)
- Veterinarni Medicina; vedecky casopis. m. (prep. by its Ustredni Zemedelska a Lesnicka Knihovna) (Subscr. to: Artia, Ve Smeckach 30, 111 27 Prague 1)
- Zemedelska Ekonomika/Agricultural Economy. m. (prep. by its Ustredni Zemedelska a Lesnicka Knihovna) (Subscr. to: Artia, Ve Smeckach 30, 111 27 Prague 1)
- Zemedelska Informatika; metodicky zpravodaj. bi-m. ISSN 0026-1300 (prep. by its Ustredni Zemedelska a Lesnicka Knihovna)
- Zemedelska Technika/Agricultural Technology; vedecky casopis. m. ISSN 0044-3883 (prep. by its Ustredni Zemedelska a Lesnicka Knihovna) (Subscr. to: Artia, Ve Smeckach 30, 111 27 Prague 1)
- Zivocisna Vyroba/Animal Production; vedecky casopis. m. ISSN 0044-4847 (prep. by its Ustredni Zemedelska a Lesnicka Knihovna) (Subscr. to: Artia, Ve Smeckach 30, 111 27 Prague 1)

**Ceskoslovenska Botanicka Spolecnost**
- Preslia. (pub. by Academia, Publishing House of the Czechoslovak Academy of Sciences)

**Ceskoslovenska Chirurgicka Spolecnost**
- Rozhledy v Chirurgii. (pub. by Avicenum, State Health Publishing House)

**Ceskoslovenska Dermato-Venerologicka Spolecnost**
- Ceskoslovenska Dermatologie. (pub. by Avicenum, State Health Publishing House)

**Ceskoslovenska Farmaceuticka Spolecnost**
- Ceskoslovenska Farmacie. (pub. by Avicenum, State Health Publishing House)

**Ceskoslovenska Fysiatricka Spolecnost**
- Fysiatricky a Reumatologicky Vestnik. (pub. by Avicenum, State Health Publishing House)

**Ceskoslovenska Lekarska Spolecnost J. Ev. Purkyne**
- Casopis Lekaru Ceskych. (pub. by Avicenum, State Health Publishing House)
- Prakticky Lekar. (pub. by Avicenum, State Health Publishing House)
- Review of Czechoslovak Medicine. (pub. by Avicenum, State Health Publishing House)

**Ceskoslovenska Mikrobiologicka-Epidemiologicka Spolecnost**
- Ceskoslovenska Epidemiologie, Mikrobiologie, Imunologie. (pub. by Avicenum, State Health Publishing House)

**Ceskoslovenska Neurologicka Spolecnost**
- Ceskoslovenska Neurologie a Neurochirurgie. (pub. by Avicenum, State Health Publishing House)

**Ceskoslovenska Obchodni Komora**
- Czechoslovak Foreign Trade. (pub. by Rapid, Foreign Trade Publicity Corporation)
- Czechoslovak Heavy Industry. (pub. by Rapid, Foreign Trade Publicity Corporation)
- Czechoslovak Motor Review. (pub. by Rapid, Foreign Trade Publicity Corporation)
- For You from Czechoslovakia. (pub. by Rapid, Foreign Trade Publicity Corporation)
- Glass Review. (pub. by Rapid, Foreign Trade Publicity Corporation)
- Kovoexport-Investa. (pub. by Rapid, Foreign Trade Publicity Corporation)
- Obchod-Prumysl-Hospodarstvi. (pub. by Rapid, Foreign Trade Publicity Corporation)

**Ceskoslovenska Oftalmologicka Spolecnost**
- Ceskoslovenska Oftalmologie. (pub. by Avicenum, State Health Publishing House)

**Ceskoslovenska Otolaryngologicka Spolecnost**
- Ceskoslovenska Otolaryngologie/Acta Otolaryngologica Cechoslovaca. (pub. by Avicenum, State Health Publishing House)

**Ceskoslovenska Pediatricka Spolecnost**
- Ceskoslovenska Pediatrie. (pub. by Avicenum, State Health Publishing House)

**Ceskoslovenska Pneumologicka a Ftizeologicka Spolecnost**
- Studia Pneumologica et Phtiseologica Cechoslovaca. (pub. by Avicenum, State Health Publishing House)

**Ceskoslovenska Psychiatricka Spolecnost**
- Ceskoslovenska Psychiatrie. (pub. by Avicenum, State Health Publishing House)

**Ceskoslovenska Radiologicka Spolecnost**
- Ceskoslovenska Radiologie. (pub. by Avicenum, State Health Publishing House)

**Ceskoslovenska Spolecnost Chemicka**
- Chemicke Listy/Journal of Chemistry. (pub. by Academia, Publishing House of the Czechoslovak Academy of Sciences)

**Ceskoslovenska Spolecnost Gynekologicka a Porodnicka**
- Ceskoslovenska Gynekologie. (pub. by Avicenum, State Health Publishing House)

**Ceskoslovenska Spolecnost Hygieniku**
- Ceskoslovenska Hygiena. (pub. by Avicenum, State Health Publishing House)

**Ceskoslovenska Spolecnost Mikrobiologicka**
Vinicna 5, 128 44 Prague 2, Czechoslovakia.
- Ceskoslovenska Spolecnost Mikrobiologicka. Bulletin. bi-m. ISSN 0009-0646

**Ceskoslovenska Spolecnost Patologicka**
- Ceskoslovenska Patologie. (pub. by Avicenum, State Health Publishing House)

**Ceskoslovenska Spolecnost pro Dejiny Ved a Techniky**
- Dejiny Ved a Techniky/History of Sciences and Techncology. (pub. by Academia, Publishing House of the Czechoslovak Academy of Sciences)

**Ceskoslovenska Spolecnost pro Gastroenterologii a Vyzivu**
- Ceskoslovenska Gastroenterologie a Vyziva. (pub. by Avicenum, State Health Publishing House)

**Ceskoslovenska Spolecnost pro Klinickou Biochemii**
- Biochemia Clinica Bohemoslovaca. (pub. by Avicenum, State Health Publishing House)

**Ceskoslovenska Spolecnost pro Mineralogii a Geologii**
- Casopis pro Mineralogii a Geologii/Journal of Mineralogy and Geology. (pub. by Academia, Publishing House of the Czechoslovak Academy of Sciences)

**Ceskoslovenska Spolecnost pro Ortopedickou Chirurgii a Traumatologii**
- Acta Chirurgiae Orthopaedicae et Traumatologiae Cechoslovaca. (pub. by Avicenum, State Health Publishing House)

**Ceskoslovenska Spolecnost pro Pracovni Lekarstvi**
- Pracovni Lekarstvi. (pub. by Avicenum, State Health Publishing House)

**Ceskoslovenska Spolecnost pro Socialni Zdravotnictvi**
- Ceskoslovenske Zdravotnictvi. (pub. by Avicenum, State Health Publishing House)

**Ceskoslovenska Spolecnost pro Studium Vyssi Nervove Cinnosti**
- Activitas Nervosa Superior. (pub. by Avicenum, State Health Publishing House)

**Ceskoslovenska Spolecnost pro Vedu a Techniku**
- Zdravotni Technika a Vzduchotechnika/Sanitary and Air Technics. (pub. by Academia, Publishing House of the Czechoslovak Academy of Sciences)

**Ceskoslovenska Spolecnost pro Vnitrni Lekarstvi**
- Vnitrni Lekarstvi. (pub. by Avicenum, State Health Publishing House)

**Ceskoslovenska Spolecnost Zemepisna**
- Ceskoslovenska Spolecnost Zemepisna. Sbornik. (pub. by Academia, Publishing House of the Czechoslovak Academy of Sciences)

**Ceskoslovenska Spolecnost Zoologicka**
- Ceskoslovenska Spolecnost Zoologicka. Vestnik. (pub. by Academia, Publishing House of the Czechoslovak Academy of Sciences)

**Ceskoslovenska Stomatologicka Spolecnost**
- Ceskoslovenska Stomatologie. (pub. by Avicenum, State Health Publishing House)
- Prakticke Zubni Lekarstvi. (pub. by Avicenum, State Health Publishing House)

**Ceskoslovenska Televize. Studijni Odbor**
Jindrisska 16, 111 50 Prague 1, Czechoslovakia.
- Vyberova Anotovana Bibliografie Studijnich Materialu. a. (prep. by its Oddeleni Dokumentace a Odborne Informace)

**Ceskoslovenska Tiskova Kancelar**
Opletalova 5, 111 44 Prague 1, Czechoslovakia.
- Dokumentacni Prehled CTK. w., plus 2-3 supplements per yr. ISSN 0590-501X (prep. by its Dokumentacni Redakce)
- Moderni Rizeni. m. ISSN 0026-8720 (Co-sponsor: Institut Rizeni) (Subscr. to: Ceskoslovenska Tiskova Kancelar, Obchodni Odbor, Hastalska 14, 115 21 Prague 1)
- Revue Prumyslu a Obchodu. m. (Subscr. to: Artia, Ve Smeckach 30, 111 27 Prague 1)
- Rizeni Ekonomiky v Socialistickych Zemich; mesicni vyber z ceskoslovenskeho a zahranicniho tisku. m. ISSN 0035-7146 (prep. by its Ekonomicka Redakce) (Co-sponsor: Institut Rizeni) (Subscr. to: Ceskoslovenska Tiskova Kancelar, Obchodni Odbor, Hastalska 14, 115 21 Prague 1)

**Ceskoslovenska Vedecka Spolecnost pro Mykologii**
- Ceska Mykologie/Czech Mycology. (pub. by Academia, Publishing House of the Czechoslovak Academy of Sciences)

**Ceskoslovenske Hudebni Nastroje**
Skroupova 9, 501 97 Hradec Kralove, Czechoslovakia
(Subscr. to: Artia, Ve Smeckach 30, 111 27 Prague 1)
- Hudebni Nastroje. bi-m.

**Ceskoslovensky Cerveny Kriz. Slovensky Ustredni Vybor**
- Zdravie. (pub. by Obzor)

**Ceskoslovensky Filmovy Ustav**
Narodni 40, 110 00 Prague 1, Czechoslovakia
(Subscr. to: Artia, Ve Smeckach 30, 111 27 Prague 1)
- Filmovy Prehled. w. ISSN 0015-1645
- Panorama. q. ISSN 0031-0859

**Ceskoslovensky Rozhlas**
Vinohradska 12, 120 99 Prague 2, Czechoslovakia.
- Ceskoslovensky Rozhlas a Televize. w. ISSN 0009-0735
- Rozhlasova Prace; casopis pro teorii a praxi rozhlasu. m. ISSN 0035-9335

**Ceskoslovensky Svaz Novinaru**
- Novinar. (pub. by Novinar)

**Ceskoslovensky Svaz Telesne Vychovy**
- Atletika. (pub. by Olympia)
- Ceskoslovensky Sach. (pub. by Olympia)
- Gymnastika. (pub. by Olympia)
- Lyzarstvi. (pub. by Olympia)
- Telovychovny Pracovnik. (pub. by Olympia)
- Teorie a Praxe Telesne Vychovy. (pub. by Olympia)
- Turista. (pub. by Olympia)
- Vodni Sporty. (pub. by Olympia)
- Zakladni a Rekreacni Telesna Vychova. (pub. by Olympia)

**Ceskoslovensky Svaz Telesne Vychovy. Ceskoslovensky Svaz Cyklistiky**
- Cyklistika. (pub. by Olympia)

**Ceskoslovensky Svaz Telesne Vychovy. Cesky Ustredni Vybor**
- Stadion. (pub. by Olympia)

**Ceskoslovensky Vybor pro Turism**
- Welcome to Czechoslovakia. (pub. by Made In...Publicity)

**Ceskoslovensky Vybor Zen**
Panska 7, Prague 1, Czechoslovakia.
- Czechoslovak Woman. q. ISSN 0011-4677

**Ceskoslovensky Vyzkumny Ustav Prace a Socialnich Veci**
- Synteza. (pub. by Praca, Publishing House of the Slovak Trade Unions Council)

**Ceskoslovensky Zavod Gumarenskeho Prumyslu**
- Plasty a Kaucuk. (pub. by Statni Nakladatelstvi Technicke Literatury)

**Cesky Geologicky Urad**
- Geologicky Pruzkum/Geologicky Prieskum/Geological Surveying. (pub. by Statni Nakladatelstvi Technicke Literatury)

**Cesky Rybarsky Svaz**
- Ceskoslovenske Rybarstvi. (pub. by Statni Zemedelske Nakladatelstvi)

**Cesky Svaz Myslivcu a Ochrancu Prirody**
Husova 7, 115 25 Prague 1, Czechoslovakia
(Subscr. to: Artia, Ve Smeckach 30, 111 27 Prague 1)
- Myslivost. m.

**Cesky Svaz Novinaru**
- Svet v Obrazech. (pub. by Novinar)

**Cesky Svaz Zen**
- Prakticka Zena. (pub. by Mona)

**Cesky Urad pro Geodesii a Kartografii**
- Geodeticky a Kartograficky Obzor. (pub. by Statni Nakladatelstvi Technicke Literatury)

**Christian Peace Conference**
Jungmannova 9, 110 00 Prague 1, Czechoslovakia (Subscr. to: Artia, Ve Smeckach 30, 111 27 Prague 1)
- Christian Peace Conference. 4-6 per yr. ISSN 0009-5567 (prep. by its International Secretariat)

**Comenius Faculty of Protestant Theology (Ecumenical Institut)**
Jungmannova 9, 110 00 Prague 1, Czechoslovakia (Subscr. to: Artia, Ve Smeckach 30, 111 27 Prague 1)
- Communio Viatorum; a theological quarterly. q. ISSN 0010-3713

**Czech Ecumenical Council**
Jungmannova 9, 110 00 Prague 1, Czechoslovakia.
- Czech Ecumenical News; ecumenical information from C S R. bi-m. ISSN 0013-077X

**Czech Music Fund. Music Information Centre**
Besedni 3, 118 00 Prague 1, Czechoslovakia.
- Music News from Prague. 10 per yr. ISSN 0027-4410

**Czech Union of Fire Brigades**
Borivojova 21, 130 00 Prague 3, Czechoslovakia (Subscr. to: Artia, Ve Smeckach 30, 111 27 Prague 1)
- Pozarni Ochrana. m. ISSN 0032-6127

**Czechoslovak Cybernetic Association**
- Kybernetika/Cybernetics. (pub. by Academia, Publishing House of the Czechoslovak Academy of Sciences)

**Czechoslovak Filmexport**
Vaclavske nam. 28, 111 45 Prague 1, Czechoslovakia
- Czechoslovak Film. q. ISSN 0011-4588 (Subscr. to: Artia, Ve Smeckach 30, 111 27 Prague 1)
- Film News. m.

**Czechoslovakia. Archivni Sprava**
Obrancu miru 133, Prague 6, Czechoslovakia (Subscr. to: Artia, Ve Smeckach 30, 111 27 Prague 1)
- Archivni Casopis. q. ISSN 0004-0398
- Sbornik Archivnich Praci. s-a. ISSN 0036-5246

**Czechoslovakia. Ceskoslovenska Atomova Komise**
- Jaderna Energie/Nuclear Energy. (pub. by Statni Nakladatelstvi Technicke Literatury)

**Czechoslovakia. Ceskoslovenska Lidova Armada. Hlavni Politicka Sprava**
Jungmannova 24, 113 66 Prague 1, Czechoslovakia (Subscr. to: Artia, Ve Smeckach 30, 111 27 Prague 1)
- Ceskoslovensky Vojak. fortn. ISSN 0009-0751

**Czechoslovakia. Federalni Ministerstvo Dopravy**
Na prikope 33, Prague 1, Czechoslovakia.
- Doprava/Transport. (pub. by Nakladatelstvi Dopravy a Spoju)
- Prepravni a Tarifni Vestnik. w. ISSN 0032-7514
- Zeleznicni Technika. (pub. by Nakladatelstvi Dopravy a Spoju)

**Czechoslovakia. Federalni Ministerstvo Financi**
Letenska 15, Prague 7, Czechoslovakia.
- Federalni Ministerstvo Financi. Vestnik. irreg. ISSN 0042-4641
- Finance a Uver. (pub. by Statni Nakladatelstvi Technicke Literatury)

**Czechoslovakia. Federalni Ministerstvo Hutnictvi a Tezkeho Strojirenstvi**
- Automobil/Automobile. (pub. by Statni Nakladatelstvi Technicke Literatury)
- Hutnicke Listy/Metallurgical Journal. (pub. by Statni Nakladatelstvi Technicke Literatury)
- Slevarenstvi/Foundry Industry. (pub. by Statni Nakladatelstvi Technicke Literatury)
- Strojirenstvi. (pub. by Statni Nakladatelstvi Technicke Literatury)
- Zvaranie/Welding. (pub. by Alfa)

**Czechoslovakia. Federalni Ministerstvo Kultury**
- Czechoslovak Life. (pub. by Orbis)

**Czechoslovakia. Federalni Ministerstvo Narodni Obrany. Hlavni Politicka Sprava**
Prague, Czechoslovakia.
- Ceskoslovenska Armada. fortn. ISSN 0009-0506
- Vitezna Kridla. ISSN 0042-7497

**Czechoslovakia. Federalni Ministerstvo Paliv a Energetiky**
- Energetika/Power Engineering. (pub. by Statni Nakladatelstvi Technicke Literatury)

**Czechoslovakia. Federalni Ministerstvo Prace a Socialnich Veci**
- Socialni Politika. (pub. by Obzor)

**Czechoslovakia. Federalni Ministerstvo pro Technicky a Investicni Rozvoj**
- Investicni Vystavba. (pub. by Statni Nakladatelstvi Technicke Literatury)

**Czechoslovakia. Federalni Ministerstvo Spoju**
- Federalni Ministerstvo Spoju. Vestnik. (pub. by Nakladatelstvi Dopravy a Spoju)
- P T T Revue. (pub. by Nakladatelstvi Dopravy a Spoju)
- Telekomunikace. (pub. by Nakladatelstvi Dopravy a Spoju)

**Czechoslovakia. Federalni Ministerstvo Vnitra**
- Silnicni Obzor. (pub. by Nakladatelstvi Dopravy a Spoju)

**Czechoslovakia. Federalni Ministerstvo Zemedelstvi a Vyzivy**
- Mezinarodni Zemedelsky Casopis. (pub. by Statni Zemedelske Nakladatelstvi)
- Zahradnicke Listy. (pub. by Statni Zemedelske Nakladatelstvi)

**Czechoslovakia. Federalni Statisticky Urad**
Sokolovska 142, 186 13 Prague 8, Czechoslovakia.
- Czechoslovakia. Federalni Statisticky Urad. Statisticka Rocenka. (pub. by Statni Nakladatelstvi Technicke Literatury)
- Demografie. (pub. by Orbis)
- Demosta; bulletin pro demografii a statistiku. q. ISSN 0011-8338
- Statistika. (pub. by Orbis)

**Czechoslovakia. Ministerstvo Kultury Ceske Socialisticke Republiky**
- Ctenar. (pub. by Orbis)
- Knihovnictvi a Bibliografie. (pub. by Orbis)
- Tanecni Listy. (pub. by Orbis)

**Czechoslovakia. Ministerstvo Lesniho a Vodniho Hospodarstvi Ceske Socialistike Republiky**
- Ochrana Ovzdusi/Air Conservation. (pub. by Statni Zemedelske Nakladatelstvi)
- Vodni Hospodarstvi. Serie A/Water Management. Series A. (pub. by Statni Zemedelske Nakladatelstvi)
- Vodni Hospodarstvi. Serie B/Water Management. Series B. (pub. by Statni Zemedelske Nakladatelstvi)

**Czechoslovakia. Ministerstvo Obchodu Ceske Socialisticke Republiky**
- Socialisticky Obchod. (pub. by Merkur)

**Czechoslovakia. Ministerstvo Priemyslu Slovenskej Socialistickej Republiky**
- Drevo/Wood. (pub. by Alfa)

**Czechoslovakia. Ministerstvo Prumyslu Ceske Socialisticke Republiky**
- Podnikova Organizace/Enterprise Organization. (pub. by Statni Nakladatelstvi Technicke Literatury)

**Czechoslovakia. Ministerstvo Skolstva Slovenskej Socialistickej Republiky**
- Predskolska Vychova. (pub. by Slovenske Pedagogicke Nakladatelstvo)

**Czechoslovakia. Ministerstvo Skolstvi Ceske Socialisticke Republiky**
Karmelitska 7, Prague 1, Czechoslovakia
(Subscr. to: Artia, Ve Smeckach 30, 111 27 Prague 1)
- Cesky Jazyk a Literatura. (pub. by Statni Pedagogicke Nakladatelstvi)
- Cizi Jazyky ve Skole. (pub. by Statni Pedagogicke Nakladatelstvi)
- Matematika a Fyzika ve Skole. (pub. by Statni Pedagogicke Nakladatelstvi)
- Prirodni Vedy ve Skole. (pub. by Statni Pedagogicke Nakladatelstvi)
- Rozhledy Matematicko-Fyzikalni. (pub. by Statni Pedagogicke Nakladatelstvi)
- Rusky Jazyk. (pub. by Statni Pedagogicke Nakladatelstvi)
- Socialisticka Skola. 10 per yr. ISSN 0037-8291 (Co-sponsor: Ministerstvo Skolstva Slovenskej Socialistickej Republiky)
- Telesna Vychova Mladeze. (pub. by Statni Pedagogicke Nakladatelstvi)

**Czechoslovakia. Ministerstvo Spravedlnosti Ceske Socialisticke Republiky**
Vysehradska 16, 128 10 Prague 2, Czechoslovakia
(Subscr. to: Artia, Ve Smeckach 30, 111 27 Prague 1)
- Socialisticka Zakonnost; casopis pro pravni praxi. 10 per yr. ISSN 0037-8305

**Czechoslovakia. Ministerstvo Stavebnictva Slovenskej Socialistickej Republiky**
- Inzinierske Stavby/Civil Engineering. (pub. by Alfa)

**Czechoslovakia. Ministerstvo Stavebnictvi Ceske Socialisticke Republiky**
Spalena 51, 113 02 Prague 1, Czechoslovakia
- Pozemni Stavby/Construction Engineering. m. ISSN 0477-8685 (Subscr. to: Artia, Ve Smeckach 30, 111 27 Prague 1)

**Czechoslovakia. Ministerstvo Zemedelstvi a Vyzivy Ceske Socialisticke Republiky**
Mostecka 1067, 438 19 Zatec, Czechoslovakia
(Subscr. to: Artia, Ve Smeckach 30, 111 27 Prague 1)
- Chmelarstvi. m. ISSN 0009-4927
- Prumysl Potravin/Food Industry. (pub. by Statni Zemedelske Nakladatelstvi)

**Czechoslovakia. Nejvyssi Soud**
Nam. Hrdinu 1300, Prague 4, Czechoslovakia.
- Sbirka Soudnich Rozhodnuti a Stanovisek. 10 per yr. ISSN 0036-522X

**Czechoslovakia. Statni Banka Ceskoslovenska**
Na prikope 28, 110 03 Prague 1, Czechoslovakia.
- Statni Banka Ceskoslovenska. Bulletin. a. ISSN 0081-539X

**Czechoslovakia. Statni Knihovna**
Klementinum 190, 110 01 Prague 1, Czechoslovakia
- Bibliograficky Katalog C S S R: Ceske Hudebniny a Gramofonove Desky. q. (Subscr. to: Artia, Ve Smeckach 30, 111 27 Prague 1)
- Bibliograficky Katalog C S S R: Ceske Knihy. w. (Subscr. to: Artia, Ve Smeckach 30, 111 27 Prague 1)
- Bibliograficky Katalog C S S R: Ceske Knihy. Bibliograficke Listky. 40 per yr. (Subscr. to: Artia, Ve Smeckach 30, 111 27 Prague 1)
- Bibliograficky Katalog C S S R: Ceske Knihy. Zvlastni Sesit. q. (Subscr. to: Artia, Ve Smeckach 30, 111 27 Prague 1)
- Bibliograficky Katalog C S S R: Clanky v Ceskych Casopisech. m. ISSN 0006-1115 (Subscr. to: Artia, Ve Smeckach 30, 111 27 Prague 1)

- Ceska Bibliografie. a.
- Novinky Knihovnicke Literatury. 5 per yr. (Subscr. to: Artia, Ve Smeckach 30, 111 27 Prague 1)
- Novinky Literatury; prehledy informativni literatury. m. ISSN 0029-5191 (Subscr. to: Artia, Ve Smeckach 30, 111 27 Prague 1)
- Novinky Literatury: Biologie. q. (Subscr. to: Artia, Ve Smeckach 30, 111 27 Prague 1)
- Novinky Literatury: Chemie. q. (Subscr. to: Artia, Ve Smeckach 30, 111 27 Prague 1)
- Novinky Literatury: Ekonomie. m. (Subscr. to: Artia, Ve Smeckach 30, 111 27 Prague 1)
- Novinky Literatury: Filosofie. q. (Subscr. to: Artia, Ve Smeckach 30, 111 27 Prague 1)
- Novinky Literatury: Geologie, Geografie. q. (Subscr. to: Artia, Ve Smeckach 30, 111 27 Prague 1)
- Novinky Literatury: Historie. q.
- Novinky Literatury: Matematika-Fyzika. q. (Subscr. to: Artia, Ve Smeckach 30, 111 27 Prague 1)
- Novinky Literatury: Psychologie. q. ISSN 0029-523X (Subscr to: Artia, Ve Smeckach 30, 111 27 Prague 1)
- Novinky Literatury: Sociologie. q. ISSN 0029-5213 (Subscr. to: Artia, Ve Smeckach 30, 111 27 Prague 1)
- Novinky Literatury: Stat a Pravo. q. (Subscr. to: Artia, Ve Smeckach 30, 111 27 Prague 1)

**Czechoslovakia. Statni Pedagogicka Knihovna Komenskeho - Ustredni Pedagogicka Knihovna C S S R**
Mikulandska 5, Prague 1, Czechoslovakia
(Subscr. to: Artia, Ve Smeckach 30, 111 27 Prague 1)
- Prehled Pedagogicke Literatury. 10 per yr. ISSN 0032-7344

**Czechoslovakia. Statni Planovaci Komise**
- Planovane Hospodarstvi/Planned Economy. (pub. by Orbis)

**Czechoslovakia. Statni Ustav pro Zdravotnickou a Dokumentacni Sluzbu**
Sokolska 31, 121 32 Prague 2, Czechoslovakia.
- Bibliographia Medica Cechoslovaca. a. ISSN 0067-6802
- Novinky Literatury: Zdravotnictvi. 10 per yr. ISSN 0029-5205 (Subscr. to: Artia, Ve Smeckach 30, 111 27 Prague 1)
- Referatovy Vyber z Anestesiologie a Resuscitace/ Abstracts of Anesthesiology and Resuscitation. bi-m. ISSN 0034-2688
- Referatovy Vyber z Chirurgie/Abstracts of Surgery. bi-m. ISSN 0034-2696
- Referatovy Vyber z Chorob Infekcnich/Abstracts of Infectious Diseases. q. ISSN 0034-270X
- Referatovy Vyber z Dermatovenerologie a Pribuznych Oboru/Abstracts of Dermatology, Venereology and Related Subjects. bi-m. ISSN 0034-2718
- Referatovy Vyber z Endokrinologie/Abstracts of Endocrinology. q. ISSN 0034-2726
- Referatovy Vyber z Fysiologie/Abstracts of Physiology. s-a. ISSN 0034-2734
- Referatovy Vyber z Gastroenterologie/Abstracts of Gastroenterology. bi-m. ISSN 0034-2742
- Referatovy Vyber z Gerontologie a Geriatrie/ Abstracts of Gerontology and Geriatrics. s-a. ISSN 0034-2750
- Referatovy Vyber z Kardiologie, Fysiologie a Patologie Obehoveho Ustroji/Abstracts of Cardiology and Physiology and Pathology of the Circulation System. bi-m. ISSN 0034-2769
- Referatovy Vyber z Lekarenstvi. bi-m. ISSN 0034-2777
- Referatovy Vyber z Lekarskeho Tisku o Vychove a Doskolovani Zdravotnickych Pracovniku/ Abstracts of Medical Postgraduate Training and Education. q. ISSN 0034-2785
- Referatovy Vyber z Neurologie/Abstracts of Neurology. q. ISSN 0034-2793
- Referatovy Vyber z Oftalmologie/Abstracts of Ophthalmology. q. ISSN 0034-2807
- Referatovy Vyber z Onkologie/Abstracts of Oncology. q. ISSN 0034-2815
- Referatovy Vyber z Ortopedie, Traumatologie a Pribuznych Oboru/Abstracts of Orthopedics, Traumatology and Related Subjects. bi-m. ISSN 0034-2823
- Referatovy Vyber z Otorhinolaryngologie a Foniatrie/Abstracts of Otorhinolaryngology and Phoniatrics. bi-m. ISSN 0034-2831
- Referatovy Vyber z Patologicke Anatomie/ Abstracts of Pathology. q. ISSN 0034-284X

- Referatovy Vyber z Pediatrie/Abstracts of Pediatrics. bi-m. ISSN 0034-2858
- Referatovy Vyber z Pneumologie a Tuberkulosy/ Abstracts of Pneumology and Tuberculosis. bi-m. ISSN 0034-2890
- Referatovy Vyber z Porodnictvi a Gynekologie/ Abstracts of Obstetrics and Gynecology. bi-m. ISSN 0034-2866
- Referatovy Vyber z Rentgenologie/Abstracts of Radiology. bi-m. ISSN 0034-2874
- Referatovy Vyber z Revmatologie/Abstracts of Rheumatology. bi-m. ISSN 0034-2882
- Referatovy Vyber ze Sportovni Mediciny/ Abstracts of Sports Medicine. s-a. ISSN 0034-2904
- Zdravotnicka Dokumentace. bi-m.

**Divadelni Ustav**
Valdstejnske nam. 3, Prague 1, Czechoslovakia.
- Divadelni Ustav. Zpravy. m. ISSN 0044-5363
- Scenografie; vyber clanku ze zahranicnich casopisu. q. ISSN 0036-5815

**Evangelicka Cirkev Ceskobratrska**
Jungmannova 9, 110 00 Prague 1, Czechoslovakia
(Subscr. to: Artia, Ve Smeckach 30, 111 27 Prague 1)
- Cesky Bratr. 10 per yr. ISSN 0009-0778 (prep. by its Rada)

**Hollar, Skupina Ceskoslovenskych Umelcu-Grafiku**
- Hollar. (pub. by Nakladatelstvi Svazu Ceskych Vytvarnych Umelcu)

**Hydrometeorologicky Ustav**
Holeckova 8, 151 29 Prague 5, Czechoslovakia.
- Hydrometeorologicky Ustav. Sbornik Predpisu. irreg.
- Hydrometeorologicky Ustav. Vyrocni Zprava. a.
- Meteorologicke Zpravy. (pub. by Statni Nakladatelstvi Technicke Literatury)
- Rocenka Povetrnostnich Pozorovani Observatore Karlov. a. ISSN 0554-9221
- Rocenka Znecisteni Ovzdusi na Uzemi C S R. a.

**Hydrometeorologicky Ustav, Bratislava**
- Hydrometeorologicky Ustav, Bratislava. Zbornik Prac. (pub. by Slovenske Pedagogicke Nakladatelstvo)

**IMADOS (Institut Mantpulacnich, Dopravnich, Obalovych a Skladovacich Systemu)**
- Manipulace, Skladovani, Baleni/Material Handling, Storage Packaging. (pub. by Statni Nakladatelstvi Technicke Literatury)

**Institut Hygieny a Epidemiologie**
- Journal of Hygiene, Epidemiology, Microbiology and Immunology. (pub. by Avicenum, State Health Publishing House)

**Institut pre Dalsie Vzdelavanie Lekarov a Farmaceutov**
Kramare, Limbova ul. 17, 809 46 Bratislava, Czechoslovakia
(Subscr. to: Slovart, Gottwaldovo nam. 48, 805 32 Bratislava)
- Farmaceuticky Obzor. m. ISSN 0014-8172
- Rehabilitacia. bi-m. ISSN 0033-8680

**Institut Prumysloveho Designu**
Na Porici 24, Prague 1, Czechoslovakia.
- Design v Teorii a Praxi/Design in Theory and Practice. m.

**Institute for Application of Computing Technique in Control**
Revolucni 24, Prague 1, Czechoslovakia.
- Lormatic; informacni bulletin. irreg.

**Instituti Archaeologici Nitriensis Academiae Scientiarum Slovacae**
- Archaeologica Slovaca. Catalogi. (pub. by Rudolf Habelt Verlag GW)
- Archaeologica Slovaca. Fontes. (pub. by Rudolf Habelt Verlag GW)

**International Chess Federation**
- World Student Chess Team Championship. Results. (pub. by International Union of Students)

**International Organization of Journalists**
Parizska 9, 110 10 Prague 1, Czechoslovakia
(Subscr. to: Artia, Ve Smeckach 30, 111 27 Prague 1)
- Democratic Journalist. m. ISSN 0011-8214
- Journalists' Affairs. fortn.

**International Radio and Television Organization**
U Mrazovky 15, 151 13 Prague 5, Czechoslovakia.
- O I R T Information. m. ISSN 0029-7097
- Radio - Television. bi-m. ISSN 0033-7676

**International Trade Union of Miners**
Opletalova 57, Prague 1, Czechoslovakia.
- Miners' International News; studies and information. q. ISSN 0026-4687

**International Union of Students**
17th November St., 110 01 Prague 1, Czechoslovakia.
- African Bulletin. m.
- Arab Bulletin. m.
- Asian Bulletin. m.
- D E; I U S magazine on the democratization and reform of education. q.
- D E - Bulletin. (Democratization of Education) m.
- I U S Sports Bulletin/Bulletin Sportif de l' U. I. E/Boletin Deportivo de la U. I. E. q. ISSN 0038-7789 (prep. by its Physical Education and Sports Department)
- International Union of Students. Congress Resolutions. irreg., 11th, 1974, Budapest. ISSN 0074-9532
- International Union of Students. News Service. s-m. ISSN 0539-1199
- Latin American Bulletin. bi-m.
- World Student Chess Team Championship. Results. irreg., 20th, 1974, Teesside. (International Chess Federation)
- World Student News/Etudiants du Monde. m. ISSN 0014-2255
- Young Cinema and Theatre/Jeune Cinema et Theatre; cultural magazine of the I U S. q.

**Jednota Ceskoslovenskych Matematiku a Fyziku**
- Pokroky Matematiky, Fyziky a Astronomie/ Progress in Mathematics, Physics and Astronomy. (pub. by Academia, Publishing House of the Czechoslovak Academy of Sciences)

**Komunisticka Strana Ceskoslovenska**
- Dikobraz. (pub. by Rude Pravo)
- Otazky Miru a Socialismu. (pub. by Rude Pravo)

**Kostnicka Jednota**
- Krestanska Revue. (pub. by Ustredni Cirkevni Nakladatelstvi)

**Litomerice (Okres) Okresni Muzeum**
Mirove nam. 171, Litomerice, Czechoslovakia.
- Litomericko. a. ISSN 0075-9988

**Made In...Publicity**
Opletalova 5, 111 44 Prague 1, Czechoslovakia
(Subscr. to: Artia, Ve Smeckach 30, 111 27 Prague 1)
- Welcome to Czechoslovakia. q. ISSN 0043-2210 (Ceskoslovensky Vybor pro Turism) (Co-sponsor: Ceskoslovenska Tiskova Kancelar)

**Magnet**
Vladislavova 26, Prague 1, Czechoslovakia
(Subscr. to: Artia, Ve Smeckach 30, 111 27 Prague 1)
- Svet Motoru. w. ISSN 0039-7016

**Matica Slovenska**
Mudronova 35, 036 52 Martin, Czechoslovakia.
- Bibliograficky Zbornik. a. ISSN 0067-6780
- Biograficke Studie. a. ISSN 0067-8724
- Citatel; mesacnik pre jednotnu sustavu kniznic. m. ISSN 0009-7438 (Subscr. to: Slovart, Gottwaldovo nam. 48, 805 32 Bratislava)
- Knizna Kultura. a.
- Kniznice a Vedecke Informacie. q. (Subscr. to: Slovart, Gottwaldovo nam. 48, 805 32 Bratislava)
- Kniznicny Zbornik/Library Studies. a. ISSN 0075-6369
- Literarno-Muzejny Letopis. a.
- Literarny Archiv. a. ISSN 0075-9872
- Slovaci v Zahranici. a. ISSN 0081-0061
- Slovenska Narodna Bibliografia. Seria C: Clanky. 13 per yr. (Subscr. to: Slovart, Gottwaldovo nam. 48, 805 32 Bratislava)
- Vlastivedny Zbornik. irreg.

**Meopta, n.p., Prerov**
- Jemna Mechanika a Optika/Fine Mechanics and Optics. (pub. by Statni Nakladatelstvi Technicke Literatury)

**Merkur**
Nam. M. Gorkeho 20, 115 69 Prague 1, Czechoslovakia
(Subscr. to: Artia, Ve Smeckach 30, 111 27 Prague 1)
- Socialisticky Obchod. m. ISSN 0037-8321 (Czechoslovakia. Ministerstvo Obchodu Ceske Socialisticke Republiky) (Co-sponsor: Ministerstvo Obchodu Slovenskej Socialistickej Republiky)

**Mezinarodni Politika**
Nekazanka 7, 111 21 Prague 1, Czechoslovakia.
- Mezinarodni Politika. m.

**Mlada Fronta**
Panska 8, 112 22 Prague 1, Czechoslovakia
(Subscr. to: Artia, Ve Smeckach 30, 111 27 Prague 1)
- Materidouska; casopis pro nejmladsi ctenare. m. ISSN 0025-5440 (Socialisticky Svaz Mladeze)
- Sedmicka Pionyru; cteni pro chlapce a devcata na 7 dni. w. (Socialisticky Svaz Mladeze. Pionyrska Organizace. Ceska Ustredni Rada)

**Mona**
Panska 7, 110 00 Prague 1, Czechoslovakia
(Subscr. to: Artia, Ve Smeckach 30, 111 27 Prague 1)
- Prakticka Zena. m. (Cesky Svaz Zen)

**Moravske Muzeum**
Nam. 25. unora 8, 659 37 Brno, Czechoslovakia.
- Acta Musei Moraviae. Scientia Naturales 3: Folia Mendeliana. a.
- Anthropologie. 3 per yr. ISSN 0003-553X
- Anthropologie. (pub. by Rudolf Habelt Verlag GW)
- Anthropos. (pub. by Rudolf Habelt Verlag GW)
- Ethnographica. (pub. by Rudolf Habelt Verlag GW)

**Moravske Muzeum. Numismaticke Oddeleni**
Kapucinske nam. 5, Brno 1, Czechoslovakia.
- Moravske Numismaticke Zpravy. irreg., no. 13, 1973. ISSN 0077-152X (Co-sponsor: Ceska Numismaticka Spolecnost)
- Numismatica Moravica. irreg., no. 4, 1974. ISSN 0078-2726 (Co-sponsor: Ceska Numismaticka Spolecnost)
- Studia Numismatica et Medailistica. irreg. ISSN 0081-6779 (Co-sponsor: Ceska Numismaticka Spolecnost)

**Nakladatelstvi Dopravy a Spoju**
Hybernska 5, 115 78 Prague 1, Czechoslovakia.
- Ceskoslovensko. irreg. (Postovni Filatelisticka Sluzba)
- Doprava/Transport; odborna technicko-ekonomicka revue pro vsechna dopravni odvetvi. q. ISSN 0012-5520 (Czechoslovakia. Federalni Ministerstvo Dopravy) (Subscr. to: Artia, Ve Smeckach 30, 111 27 Prague 1)
- Federalni Ministerstvo Spoju. Vestnik. w. (Subscr. to: Artia, Ve Smeckach 30, 111 27 Prague 1)
- Letecky Obzor. bi-m. (Subscr. to: Artia, Ve Smeckach 30, 111 27 Prague 1)
- P T T Revue. (Posta, Telegraf, Telefon) bi-m. (Czechoslovakia. Federalni Ministerstvo Spoju) (Subscr. to: Artia, Ve Smeckach 30, 111 27 Prague 1)
- Silnicni Obzor; mesicnik pro technicke, technologicke a ekonomicke otazky automobilove a mestske dopravy a silnichniho hospodarstvi. m. (Czechoslovakia. Federalni Ministerstvo Vnitra) (Subscr. to: Artia, Ve Smeckach 30, 111 27 Prague 1)
- Telekomunikace; casopis pro pracovniky provozu, udrzby a vystavby telefonu, telegrafu, rozhlasu po drate a radiokomunikaci. m. ISSN 0040-2591 (Czechoslovakia. Federalni Ministerstvo Spoju) (Subscr. to: Artia, Ve Smeckach 30, 111 27 Prague 1)
- Vyzkumny Ustav Spoju. Sbornik Praci. 2-3 per yr. (Subscr. to: Artia, Ve Smeckach 30, 111 27 Prague 1)
- Zeleznicni Technika. q. ISSN 0513-9295 (Czechoslovakia. Federalni Ministerstvo Dopravy) (Subscr. to: Artia, Ve Smeckach 30, 111 27 Prague 1)

**Nakladatelstvi Svazu Ceskych Vytvarnych Umelcu**
Vorsilska 10, Prague 2, Czechoslovakia.
- Hollar. q. ISSN 0018-3628 (Hollar, Skupina Ceskoslovenskych Umelcu-Grafiku)

**Naprstkovo Muzeum Asijskych, Africkych a Americkych Kultur**
Betlemske nam. 1, 110 00 Prague 1, Czechoslovakia.
- Naprstkovo Muzeum Asijskych, Africkych a Americkych Kultur. Annals. a. ISSN 0554-9256
- Naprstkovo Muzeum Asijskych, Africkych a Americkych Kultur. Anthropological Papers. irreg.

**Narodni Fronta**
- Prager Volkszeitung. (pub. by Rude Pravo)

**Narodni Muzeum**
Vaclavske nam. 1700, 115 79 Prague 1, Czechoslovakia.
- Acta Entomologica. a. (prep. by its Prirodovedecke Muzeum)
- Fontes Archaeologici Pragenses. 1-2 per yr. ISSN 0015-6183 (prep. by its Historicke Muzeum)
- Lynx; novitates mammaliologicae. 1-2 per yr. ISSN 0024-7774 (prep. by its Prirodovedecke Muzeum)
- Narodni Muzeum. Casopis: Oddil Historicky. q. ISSN 0008-7343 (prep. by its Historicke Muzeum) (Subscr. to: Artia, Ve Smeckach 30, 111 27 Prague 1)
- Narodni Muzeum. Casopis: Oddil Prirodovedny. q. ISSN 0008-7351 (prep. by its Prirodovedecke Muzeum) (Subscr. to: Artia, Ve Smeckach 30, 111 27 Prague 1)
- Narodni Muzeum. Sbornik. Rada A: Historie/ Acta Musei Nationalis Pragae. q. ISSN 0036-5335 (prep. by its Historicke Muzeum) (Subscr. to: Artia, Ve Smeckach 30, 111 27 Prague 1)
- Narodni Muzeum. Sbornik. Rada B: Prirodni Vedy/Acta Musei Nationalis Pragae. q. ISSN 0036-5343 (prep. by its Prirodovedecke Muzeum) (Subscr. to: Artia, Ve Smeckach 30, 111 27 Prague 1)
- Narodni Muzeum. Sbornik. Rada C: Literarni Historie/Acta Musei Nationalis Pragae. q. ISSN 0036-5351 (Subscr. to: Artia, Ve Smeckach 30, 111 27 Prague 1)

**Narodni Muzeum. Ustredni Muzeologicky Kabinet**
- Muzejni a Vlastivedna Prace. (pub. by Orbis)

**Narodni Technicke Muzeum**
Kostelni 42, 170 78 Prague 7, Czechoslovakia.
- Dejiny Vyrobnich Sil. irreg.
- Narodni Technicke Muzeum. Bibliografie. Prameny. irreg.
- Narodni Technicke Muzeum. Catalogues of Collections. irreg.
- Narodni Technicke Muzeum. Rozpravy. 5-6 per yr (approx) ISSN 0035-9378

**Narodni Vybory**
Loretanska 9, Prague, Czechoslovakia.
- Narodni Vybory; casopis pro poslance a pracovniky narodnich vyboru. s-m. ISSN 0027-8009

**Nase Vojsko, Publishing House of the Czechoslovak Army**
Na Dekance 3, 128 12 Prague 1, Czechoslovakia.
- Nase Vojsko. w. ISSN 0027-8211

**Novinar**
Narodni tr. 17, Prague 1, Czechoslovakia.
- Novinar. m. ISSN 0029-5167 (Ceskoslovensky Svaz Novinaru)
- Svet v Obrazech; obrazkovy tydenik. w. ISSN 0039-7032 (Cesky Svaz Novinaru) (Subscr. to: Artia, Ve Smeckach 30, 111 27 Prague 1)

**Noviny Vnitrniho Obchodu**
Vaclavske nam. 28, Prague 1, Czechoslovakia
- Noviny Vnitrniho Obchodu. w. ISSN 0029-5248

**Numismaticke Listy**
Vaclavske nam. 68, Prague 1, Czechoslovakia
- Numismaticke Listy. bi-m. ISSN 0029-6074

**Obzor**
Ceskoslovenskej armady 35a, 893 36 Bratislava, Czechoslovakia
- Financne Studie. q. ISSN 0046-3906 (Subscr. to: Slovart, Gottwaldovo nam. 48, 805 32 Bratislava)
- Kulturnopoliticky Kalendar. a.

- Priroda a Spolocnost. fortn. (Socialisticka Akademia Slovenskej Socialistickej Republiky) (Subscr. to: Slovart, Gottwaldovo nam. 48, 805 32 Bratislava)
- Ropa a Uhlie. m. ISSN 0035-8231 (Research Institute of Crude Oil and Hydrocarbon Gases) (Subscr. to: Slovart, Gottwaldovo nam. 48, 805 32 Bratislava)
- Socialni Politika. m. ISSN 0049-0962 (Czechoslovakia. Federalni Ministerstvo Prace a Socialnich Veci) (Subscr. to: Artia, Ve Smeckach 30, 111 27 Prague 1)
- Vytvarnictvo, Fotografia, Film; mesacnik pre zaujmovu umelecku cinnost. m. ISSN 0042-9392 (Osvetovy Ustav) (Subscr. to: Slovart, Gottwaldovo nam. 48, 805 32 Bratislava)
- Zdravie; popularno-zdravotnicky casopis moderneho cloveka. m. ISSN 0044-1953 (Ceskoslovensky Cerveny Kriz. Slovensky Ustredni Vybor) (Subscr. to: Slovart, Gottwaldovo nam. 48, 805 32 Bratislavia)

**Ochrana Prirody**
Valdstejnske nam. 1, Prague 1, Czechoslovakia
- Ochrana Prirody. 10 per yr. ISSN 0029-8204

**Odborovy Svaz Pracovniku Hornictvi a Energetiky**
- Ceskoslovensky Hornik a Energetik. (pub. by Ustredni Rada Odboru)

**Odborovy Svaz Pracovniku Potravinarskeho Prumyslu**
- Potravinar. (pub. by Ustredni Rada Odboru)

**Odborovy Svaz Pracovniku Statnich Organu, Peneznictvi a Zahranicniho Obchodu**
Nam. M. Gorkeho 23, 118 82 Prague 1, Czechoslovakia
(Subscr. to: Artia, Ve Smeckach 30, 111 27 Prague 1)
- Sluzba Lidu. s-m. ISSN 0037-7082

**Odborovy Svaz Pracovniku Stavebnictvi a ve Vyrobe Stavebnich Hmot**
- Stavebnik. (pub. by Prace, Publishing House of the Trade Union Movement)

**Odborovy Svaz Pracovniku Zemedelstvi**
- Zemedelsky a Lesni Zamestnanec. (pub. by Ustredni Rada Odboru)

**Odeon, Nakladatelstvi Krasne Literatury a Umeni**
Narodni tr. 36, 115 86 Prague 1, Czechoslovakia
(Subscr. to: Artia, Ve Smeckach 30, 111 27 Prague 1)
- Svetova Literatura; revue zahranicnich literatur. bi-m. ISSN 0039-7075

**Olympia**
Klimentska 1, 115 88 Prague 1, Czechoslovakia
(Subscr. to: Artia, Ve Smeckach 30, 111 27 Prague 1)
- Atletika. m. (Ceskoslovensky Svaz Telesne Vychovy)
- Ceskoslovensky Sach. m. ISSN 0009-0743 (Ceskoslovensky Svaz Telesne Vychovy)
- Cyklistika. m. ISSN 0011-4413 (Ceskoslovensky Svaz Telesne Vychovy. Ceskoslovensky Svaz Cyklistiky)
- Gymnastika. m. (Ceskoslovensky Svaz Telesne Vychovy)
- Lyzarstvi. m. (Ceskoslovensky Svaz Telesne Vychovy)
- Stadion. w. ISSN 0038-8920 (Ceskoslovensky Svaz Telesne Vychovy. Cesky Ustredni Vybor)
- Telovychovny Pracovnik. s-m. ISSN 0040-2850 (Ceskoslovensky Svaz Telesne Vychovy)
- Teorie a Praxe Telesne Vychovy. m. ISSN 0040-358X (Ceskoslovensky Svaz Telesne Vychovy)
- Turista; mesicnik na cestu. m. ISSN 0496-4845 (Ceskoslovensky Svaz Telesne Vychovy)
- Vodni Sporty. m. (Ceskoslovensky Svaz Telesne Vychovy)
- Zakladni a Rekreacni Telesna Vychova. m. (Ceskoslovensky Svaz Telesne Vychovy)

**Opus**
Bratislava, Czechoslovakia.
- Dychova Hudba. irreg, vol. 17, 1976.
- Melodie pre Vas. irreg, vol. 7, 1974.
- Slovenske Ludove Piesne Pre Akordeon. irreg., vol. 3, 1974.

**Orbis**
Vinohradska 46, 120 41 Prague 2, Czechoslovakia
- Akvarium a Terarium; casopis cs. akvaristu a teraristu. bi-m. ISSN 0002-3930 (Subscr. to Artia, Ve Smeckach 30, 111 27 Prague 1)

- Amatersky Film. m. ISSN 0002-6794 (Subscr. to Artia, Ve Smeckach 30, 111 27 Prague 1)
- Ceskoslovenska Fotografie/Czechoslovak Photography; casopis pro ideovou a odbornou vychovu fotografickych pracovniku. m. ISSN 0009-0549 (Subscr. to Artia, Subscr. to: Artia, Ve Smeckach 30, 111 27 Prague 1)
- Ctenar; mesicnik pro praci s knihou. m. ISSN 0011-2321 (Czechoslovakia. Ministerstvo Kultury Ceske Socialisticke Republiky) (Subscr. to Artia, Subscr. to: Artia, Ve Smeckach 30, 111 27 Prague 1)
- Czechoslovak Life. m. ISSN 0011-4634 (Czechoslovakia. Federalni Ministerstvo Kultury) (Subscr. to Artia, Subscr. to: Artia, Ve Smeckach 30, 111 27 Prague 1)
- Demografie. q. ISSN 0011-8265 (Czechoslovakia. Federalni Statisticky Urad) (Subscr. to Artia, Subscr. to: Artia, Ve Smeckach 30, 111 27 Prague 1)
- Film a Doba. m. ISSN 0015-1068 (Subscr. to Artia, Ve Smeckach 30, 111 27 Prague 1)
- Fotografie; review of art photography. q. ISSN 0015-8828 (Subscr. to Artia, Ve Smeckach 30, 111 27 Prague 1)
- Interscaena/Acta Scaenographica. bi-m. (Scenograficky Ustav) (Subscr. to Artia, Ve Smeckach 30, 111 27 Prague 1)
- Judaica Bohemiae. s-a. ISSN 0022-5738 (Statni Zidovske Museum) (Subscr. to Artia, Ve Smeckach 30, 111 27 Prague 1)
- Knihovnictvi a Bibliografie. bi-m. (Czechoslovakia. Ministerstvo Kultury Ceske Socialisticke Republiky) (Subscr. to Artia, Ve Smeckach 30, 111 27 Prague 1)
- Melodie; monthly for jazz and pop music. m. ISSN 0025-8997 (Subscr. to Artia, Ve Smeckach 30, 111 27 Prague 1)
- Mezinarodni Vztahy; ceskoslovenska revue pro mezinarodni politiku a ekonomiku. q. (Ustav pro Mezinarodni Politiku a Ekonomii) (Subscr. to Artia, Ve Smeckach 30, 111 27 Prague 1)
- Muzejni a Vlastivedna Prace. 5 per yr. ISSN 0027-5255 (Narodni Muzeum. Ustredni Muzeologicky Kabinet) (Subscr. to Artia, Ve Smeckach 30, 111 27 Prague 1)
- Planovane Hospodarstvi/Planned Economy. m. ISSN 0032-0749 (Czechoslovakia. Statni Planovaci Komise) (Subscr. to Artia, Ve Smeckach 30, 111 27 Prague 1)
- Rise Hvezd. m. ISSN 0035-5550 (Subscr. to Artia, Ve Smeckach 30, 111 27 Prague 1)
- Statistika. m. ISSN 0039-0593 (Czechoslovakia. Federalni Statisticky Urad) (Subscr. to Artia, Ve Smeckach 30, 111 27 Prague 1)
- Tanecni Listy. 10 per yr. ISSN 0039-937X (Czechoslovakia. Ministerstvo Kultury Ceske Socialisticke Republiky) (Subscr. to Artia, Ve Smeckach 30, 111 27 Prague 1)

**Osveta**
Skultetyho 1, 036 54 Martin, Czechoslovakia.
- Fontes. irreg. (Slovenske Narodne Muzeum. Archeologicky Ustav)

**Osvetovy Ustav**
- Vytvarnictvo, Fotografia, Film. (pub. by Obzor)

**Pamatnik Narodniho Pisemnictvi**
Strahovska nadv. 132, Prague 1, Czechoslovakia.
- Strahovska Knihovna. a. ISSN 0081-5896

**Pamatnik Terezin**
- Terezinske Listy. (pub. by Severoceske Nakladatelstvi)

**Pedagogicka Fakulta, Presov. Kabinet pre Vyskum Krajiny**
Leninovo nam. 6, Presov, Czechoslovakia.
- Geograficke Prace. s-a.

**Pedagogicka Fakulta v Ostrave**
- Pedagogicka Fakulta v Ostrave. Matematika, Fyzika. (pub. by Statni Pedagogicke Nakladatelstvi)

**Pedagogicka Fakulta v Usti nad Labem**
- Pedagogicka Fakulta v Usti nad Labem. Sbornik: Rada Bohemisticka. (pub. by Statni Pedagogicke Nakladatelstvi)
- Pedagogicka Fakulta v Usti nad Labem. Sbornik: Rada Chemicka. (pub. by Statni Pedagogicke Nakladatelstvi)

**Pivovary a Sladovny**
- Kvasny Prumysl/Fermentation Industry. (pub. by Statni Nakladatelstvi Technicke Literatury)

**Postovni Filatelisticka Sluzba**
- Ceskoslovensko. (pub. by Nakladatelstvi Dopravy a Spoju)

**Praca, Publishing House of the Slovak Trade Unions Council**
Moskovska 17, 897 17 Bratislava, Czechoslovakia
(Subscr. to: Slovart, Gottwaldovo nam. 48, 805 32 Bratislava)
- Kalendar Odborara. a. (Slovenska Odborova Rada)
- Rocenka Odborara. a. ISSN 0557-1693 (Slovenska Odborova Rada)
- Synteza; casopis pre teoriu a metody vied o praci. bi-m. ISSN 0586-3260 (Ceskoslovensky Vyzkumny Ustav Prace a Socialnich Veci)

**Praca Skolna**
Fucikova 19, Cesky Tesin, Czechoslovakia.
- Praca Skolna. 10 per yr. ISSN 0032-6194

**Prace, Publishing House of the Trade Union Movement**
Vaclavske nam. 17, 112 58 Prague 1, Czechoslovakia
(Subscr. to: Artia, Ve Smeckach 30, 111 27 Prague 1)
- Bezpecnost a Hygiena Prace/Safety and Hygiene of Work. m. ISSN 0006-0453
- Prace a Mzda. 13 per yr. ISSN 0032-6208
- Stavebnik. s-m. ISSN 0039-0798 (Odborovy Svaz Pracovniku Stavebnictvi a ve Vyrobe Stavebnich Hmot)

**Pragopress Feature Service**
Slavickova 5, 160 43 Prague 6, Czechoslovakia
- Czechoslovak Digest. w. (Subscr. to: Ceskoslovenska Tiskova Kancelar, Obchodni Odbor, Hastalska 14, 115 21 Prague 1)
- Czechoslovak Economic Digest; commentaries, essays. 8 per yr. ISSN 0045-9461 (Subscr. to: Ceskoslovenska Tiskova Kancelar, Obchodni Odbor, Hastalska 14, 115 21 Prague 1)
- Tschechoslowakische Wirtschaftsrundschau. 8 per yr.

**Pravda. Publishing House of the Central Committee of the Communist Party of Slovakia**
Gundulicova 12, 882 05 Bratislava, Czechoslovakia
(Subscr. to: Slovart, Gottwaldovo nam. 48, 805 32 Bratislava)
- Stop; auto-moto revue. m.

**Pravoslavna Cirkev Ceskoslovenska**
V jame 6, 110 00 Prague 1, Czechoslovakia.
- Pravoslavny Theologicky Sbornik. irreg., no. 4, 1974. ISSN 0079-4937

**Priroda**
Krizkova 9, 894 17 Bratislava, Czechoslovakia
(Subscr. to: Slovart, Gottwaldovo nam. 48, 805 32 Bratislava)
- Domova Pokladnica. a.
- Ekonomika Polnohospodarstva. m.
- Magazin Polovnika. a. ISSN 0541-8836

**Radiovy Konstrukter**
Lublanska 57, 120 00 Prague 2, Czechoslovakia
- Radiovy Konstrukter. bi-m. ISSN 0033-8516

**Rapid, Foreign Trade Publicity Corporation**
Ul. 28. rijna 13, 112 79 Prague 1, Czechoslovakia
- Czechoslovak Foreign Trade. m. ISSN 0011-460X (Ceskoslovenska Obchodni Komora) (Subscr. to Artia, Ve Smeckach 30, 111 27 Prague 1)
- Czechoslovak Heavy Industry; Czechoslovak scientific, technical monthly for engineering and heavy industry. m. ISSN 0011-4618 (Ceskoslovenska Obchodni Komora) (Subscr. to: Artia, Ve Smeckach 30, 111 27 Prague 1)
- Czechoslovak Motor Review. m. ISSN 0011-4650 (Ceskoslovenska Obchodni Komora) (Subscr. to: Artia, Ve Smeckach 30, 111 27 Prague 1)
- For You from Czechoslovakia; information on Czechoslovak textiles, glass, ceramics, jewelry, etc. q. ISSN 0015-6892 (Ceskoslovenska Obchodni Komora) (Subscr. to: Artia, Ve Smeckach 30, 111 27 Prague 1)
- Glass Review; Czechoslovak glass and ceramics magazine. m. (Ceskoslovenska Obchodni Komora) (Subscr. to: Artia, Ve Smeckach 30, 111 27 Prague 1)
- Kovoexport-Investa; Czechoslovak export magazine. m. (Ceskoslovenska Obchodni Komora) (Subscr. to: Artia, Ve Smeckach 30, 111 27 Prague 1)
- Obchod-Prumysl-Hospodarstvi. q. (Ceskoslovenska Obchodni Komora)

**Research Institute of Crude Oil and Hydrocarbon Gases**
- Ropa a Uhlie. (pub. by Obzor)

**Rodina a Skola**
Lazarska 8, Prague 2, Czechoslovakia
- Rodina a Skola; casopis pro rodinu a skolu. m. ISSN 0035-7766

**Rozvoj Mistniho Hospodarstvi**
Hybernska 10, Prague 1, Czechoslovakia
- Rozvoj Mistniho Hospodarstvi; odborny ctrnactidenik pro potreby podniku mistniho hospodarstvi a vyrobnich druzstev. s-m. ISSN 0035-9416

**Rude Pravo**
Na Porici 30, 112 86 Prague 1, Czechoslovakia
(Subscr. to: Artia, Ve Smeckach 30, 111 27 Prague 1)
- Dikobraz; satiricky tydenik. w. ISSN 0012-284X (Komunisticka Strana Ceskoslovenska. Ustredni Vybor)
- Kvety. w. ISSN 0023-5849
- Otazky Miru a Socialismu; teoreticky a informacni casopis komunistickych a delnickych stran. m. ISSN 0030-655X (Komunisticka Strana Ceskoslovenska)
- Prager Volkszeitung; Das Wochenblatt der deutschen Werktatigen in der CSSR. w. ISSN 0032-6569 (Narodni Fronta. Ustredni Vybor)

**Scenograficky Ustav**
- Interscaena/Acta Scaenographica. (pub. by Orbis)

**Sdruzeni Ceskoslovenskych Filatelistu**
Celetna 26, 110 00 Prague 1, Czechoslovakia
(Subscr. to: Artia, Ve Smeckach 30, 111 27 Prague 1)
- Filatelie. s-m. ISSN 0015-0959

**Sdruzeni pro Odbyt Dehtovych Barviv**
Na Porici 24, Prague 2, Czechoslovakia.
- Ceskoslovensky Kolorista. 3-4 per yr. ISSN 0009-0727

**Severoceske Nakladatelstvi**
Velka Hradebni 33, 400 21 Usti nad Labem, Czechoslovakia.
- Terezinske Listy. a. (Pamatnik Terezin)

**Signal**
Jungmannova 24, Prague 1, Czechoslovakia
- Signal; ilustrovany tydenik. w. ISSN 0037-492X

**Slovak Engineering Society**
Stefanikova 39, Bratislava, Czechoslovakia
(Subscr. to: Slovart, Gottwaldovo nam. 48, 805 32 Bratislava)
- Technicka Praca/Engineering. m. ISSN 0040-1056

**Slovenska Akademia Vied**
- Acta Botanica. (pub. by Veda, Publishing House of the Slovak Academy of Sciences)
- Biologia. (pub. by Veda, Publishing House of the Slovak Academy of Sciences)
- Bratislavske Lekarske Listy. (pub. by Veda, Publishing House of the Slovak Academy of Sciences)
- Elektrotechnicky Casopis/Electrotechnical Journal. (pub. by Veda, Publishing House of the Slovak Academy of Sciences)
- Endocrinologia Experimentalis. (pub. by Veda, Publishing House of the Slovak Academy of Sciences)
- Flora Slovenska. (pub. by Veda, Publishing House of the Slovak Academy of Sciences)
- Geograficky Casopis/Geographical Review. (pub. by Veda, Publishing House of the Slovak Academy of Sciences)
- Geologicky Zbornik. (pub. by Veda, Publishing House of the Slovak Academy of Sciences)
- High Energy Particle Physics. (pub. by Veda, Publishing House of the Slovak Academy of Sciences)
- Kovove Materialy/Metal Materials. (pub. by Veda, Publishing House of the Slovak Academy of Sciences)
- Kultura Slova/Culture of the Word. (pub. by Veda, Publishing House of the Slovak Academy of Sciences)
- Lekarske Prace. (pub. by Veda, Publishing House of the Slovak Academy of Sciences)
- Matematicky Casopis. (pub. by Veda, Publishing House of the Slovak Academy of Sciences)
- Nauka o Zemi. Seria Geographica. (pub. by Veda, Publishing House of the Slovak Academy of Sciences)

- Neoplasma. (pub. by Veda, Publishing House of the Slovak Academy of Sciences)
- Polnohospodarstvo. (pub. by Veda, Publishing House of the Slovak Academy of Sciences)
- Prace Astronomickeho Observatoria na Skalnatom Plese/Activities of the Astronomical Observatory on Skalnate Pleso. (pub. by Veda, Publishing House of the Slovak Academy of Sciences)
- Problemy Biologie Krajiny. (pub. by Veda, Publishing House of the Slovak Academy of Sciences)
- Slovenska Akademia Vied. Biologicke Prace/Treatises on Biology. (pub. by Veda, Publishing House of the Slovak Academy of Sciences)
- Slovenska Numizmatika. (pub. by Veda, Publishing House of the Slovak Academy of Sciences)
- Slovenske Divadlo/Slovak Theater. (pub. by Veda, Publishing House of the Slovak Academy of Sciences)
- Studia Psychologica. (pub. by Veda, Publishing House of the Slovak Academy of Sciences)
- Vodohospodarsky Casopis. (pub. by Veda, Publishing House of the Slovak Academy of Sciences)
- Zivotne Prostredie. (pub. by Veda, Publishing House of the Slovak Academy of Sciences)

**Slovenska Akademia Vied. Archeologicky Ustav**
- Slovenska Archeologia/Slovak Archeology. (pub. by Veda, Publishing House of the Slovak Academy of Sciences)

**Slovenska Akademia Vied. Ekonomicky Ustav**
- Ekonomicky Casopis/Economic Journal. (pub. by Veda, Publishing House of the Slovak Academy of Sciences)

**Slovenska Akademia Vied. Filozoficky Ustav**
- Filozofia/Philosophy. (pub. by Veda, Publishing House of the Slovak Academy of Sciences)

**Slovenska Akademia Vied. Fyzikalny Ustav**
- Acta Physica Slovaca. (pub. by Veda, Publishing House of the Slovak Academy of Sciences)

**Slovenska Akademia Vied. Geofyzikalny Ustav**
- Bulletin of the Slovak Seismographic Stations: Bratislava, Srobarova, Hurbanovo and Skalnate Pleso. (pub. by Veda, Publishing House of the Slovak Academy of Sciences)
- Slovenska Akademia Vied. Geofyzikalny Ustav. Contributions. (pub. by Veda, Publishing House of the Slovak Academy of Sciences)

**Slovenska Akademia Vied. Geologicky Ustav D. Stura**
- Slovenska Akademia Vied. Geologicky Ustav D. Stura: Zbornik: Zapadne Karpaty. (pub. by Veda, Publishing House of the Slovak Academy of Sciences)

**Slovenska Akademia Vied. Historicky Ustav**
- Historicke Studie. (pub. by Veda, Publishing House of the Slovak Academy of Sciences)
- Historicky Casopis/Journal of History. (pub. by Veda, Publishing House of the Slovak Academy of Sciences)
- Slovanske Studie. (pub. by Veda, Publishing House of the Slovak Academy of Sciences)

**Slovenska Akademia Vied. Jazykovedny Ustav L. Stura**
- Jazykovedne Studie. (pub. by Veda, Publishing House of the Slovak Academy of Sciences)
- Jazykovedny Casopis. (pub. by Veda, Publishing House of the Slovak Academy of Sciences)
- Slovenska Rec. (pub. by Veda, Publishing House of the Slovak Academy of Sciences)

**Slovenska Akademia Vied. Kabinet Orientalistiky**
- Asian and African Studies. (pub. by Veda, Publishing House of the Slovak Academy of Sciences)

**Slovenska Akademia Vied. Literarnovedny Ustav**
- Slovenska Literatura. (pub. by Veda, Publishing House of the Slovak Academy of Sciences)

**Slovenska Akademia Vied. Narodopisny Ustav**
- Acta Ethnologica Slovaca. (pub. by Veda, Publishing House of the Slovak Academy of Sciences)
- Slovensky Narodopis/Slovak Ethnography. (pub. by Veda, Publishing House of the Slovak Academy of Sciences)

**Slovenska Akademia Vied. Sociologicky Ustav**
- Sociologia. (pub. by Veda, Publishing House of the Slovak Academy of Sciences)

**Slovenska Akademia Vied. Umenovedny Ustav**
- Musicologica Slovaca. (pub. by Veda, Publishing House of the Slovak Academy of Sciences)

**Slovenska Akademia Vied. Ustav Dendrobiologie**
- Folia Dendrologica. (pub. by Veda, Publishing House of the Slovak Academy of Sciences)

**Slovenska Akademia Vied. Ustav Experimentalnej Farmakologie**
- Slovenska Akademia Vied. Ustav Experimentalnej Farmakologie. Zbornik Prac a Studii. (pub. by Veda, Publishing House of the Slovak Academy of Sciences)

**Slovenska Akademia Vied. Ustav Mechaniky Strojov**
- Strojnicky Casopis/Mechanical Periodic. (pub. by Veda, Publishing House of the Slovak Academy of Sciences)

**Slovenska Akademia Vied. Ustav Slovenskej Literatury**
- Literaria. (pub. by Veda, Publishing House of the Slovak Academy of Sciences)

**Slovenska Akademia Vied. Ustav Statu a Prava**
- Pravnicke Studie. (pub. by Veda, Publishing House of the Slovak Academy of Sciences)
- Pravny Obzor/Law Review. (pub. by Veda, Publishing House of the Slovak Academy of Sciences)

**Slovenska Akademia Vied. Ustav Stavebnictva a Architektury**
- Architektura a Urbanizmus/Architecture and Urbanism. (pub. by Veda, Publishing House of the Slovak Academy of Sciences)
- Stavebnicky Casopis. (pub. by Veda, Publishing House of the Slovak Academy of Sciences)

**Slovenska Akademia Vied. Ustav Svetovej Literatury a Jazykov**
- Slavica Slovaca. (pub. by Veda, Publishing House of the Slovak Academy of Sciences)

**Slovenska Akademia Vied. Ustav Teorie a Dejin Umenia**
- Ars. (pub. by Veda, Publishing House of the Slovak Academy of Sciences)

**Slovenska Akademia Vied. Ustav Vlastnosti Hornin**
- Banicke Listy/Folia Montana. (pub. by Veda, Publishing House of the Slovak Academy of Sciences)

**Slovenska Akademia Vied. Virologicky Ustav**
- Acta Virologica. (pub. by Veda, Publishing House of the Slovak Academy of Sciences)

**Slovenska Chemicka Spolocnost**
- Slovenska Chemicka Spolocnost. Chemical Papers/Chemicke Zvesti. (pub. by Veda, Publishing House of the Slovak Academy of Sciences)

**Slovenska Entomologicka Spolocnost**
- Entomologicke Problemy. (pub. by Veda, Publishing House of the Slovak Academy of Sciences)

**Slovenska Narodna Galeria**
Razusovo nabr. 2, 890 13 Bratislava, Czechoslovakia.
- Ars Populi. s-a.

**Slovenska Odborova Rada**
- Kalendar Odborara. (pub. by Praca, Publishing House of the Slovak Trade Unions Council)
- Rocenka Odborara. (pub. by Praca, Publishing House of the Slovak Trade Unions Council)

**Slovenska Spolocnost pre Racionalnu Vyzivu**
Leningradska 19, Bratislava, Czechoslovakia
(Subscr. to: Slovart, Gottwaldovo nam. 48, 805 32 Bratislava)
- Vyziva a Zdravie/Nutrition and Health; journal for rational nutrition. m. ISSN 0042-9406

**Slovenske Narodne Muzeum**
Vajanskeho nabr. 2, 885 36 Bratislava,
Czechoslovakia
- Musikethnologische Jahresbibliographie Europas/
  Annual Bibliography of European
  Ethnomusicology. a. ISSN 0077-2534 (Distributor
  in Western countries: International Folk Music
  Council, Department of Music, Queen's
  University, Kingston, Ontario, Canada)
- Muzeum; metodicky, studijny a informacny
  material. q. ISSN 0027-5263 (prep. by its
  Muzeologicky Kabinet)
- Selected Bibliography of Museological Literature.
  a. (prep. by its Muzeologicky Kabinet)
- Slovenske Narodne Muzeum. Muzeologicky
  Kabinet. Vyrocne Spravy o Cinnosti Slovenskych
  Muzei. a. (prep. by its Muzeologicky Kabinet)

**Slovenske Narodne Muzeum. Archeologicky Ustav**
- Fontes. (pub. by Osveta)

**Slovenske Pedagogicke Nakladatelstvo**
Sasinkova 5, 891 12 Bratislava, Czechoslovakia.
- Hydrometeorologicky Ustav, Bratislava. Zbornik
  Prac. irreg.
- Jednotna Skola; journal for pedagogical theory and
  praxis and psychology. 10 per yr. ISSN 0021-
  5805 (Subscr. to: Slovart, Gottwaldovo nam. 48,
  805 32 Bratislava)
- Predskolska Vychova; casopis pre pracovniky
  jasiel a materskych skol. m. ISSN 0032-7220
  (Czechoslovakia. Ministerstvo Skolstva Slovenskej
  Socialistickej Republiky) (Subscr. to: Slovart,
  Gottwaldovo nam. 48, 805 32 Bratislava)
- Psychologia a Skola. irreg, vol. 3, 1974.
- Universitas Comeniana. Acta Pharmaceuticae. 1-2
  nos. per yr. ISSN 0041-9087 (Univerzita
  Komenskeho. Farmaceuticka Fakulta) (Subscr. to:
  Univerzita Komenskeho, Farmaceuticka Fakulta,
  Ustredna Kniznica, Odbojarov 12, 880 34
  Bratislava)
- Univerzita Komenskeho. Pedagogicka Fakulta v
  Trnave. Prirodne Vedy: Biologia-Genetika. a.

**Slovensky Muzicky Fond**
Fucikova 29, Bratislava, Czechoslovakia.
- Slovenska Hudba. m. ISSN 0037-6965 (Svaz
  Ceskych a Slovenskych Skladatelu)

**Slovensky Spisovatel**
Leningradska 2, 801 00 Bratislava, Czechoslovakia
(Subscr. to: Slovart, Gottwaldovo Nam. 48, 805 32
Bratislava)
- Slovenske Pohlady na Literaturu a Umenie. m.
  ISSN 0037-7007 (Zvaz Slovenskych Spisovatelov)

**Socialisticka Akademia Slovenskej Socialistickej
Republiky**
- Priroda a Spolocnost. (pub. by Obzor)

**Socialisticke Zemedelstvi**
Ve Smeckach 33, Prague 1, Czechoslovakia.
- Socialisticke Zemedelstvi; casopis pro vyrobni
  zemedelske spravy a organizatory vyroby. fortn.
  ISSN 0037-8313

**Socialisticky Svaz Mladeze**
- Materidouska. (pub. by Mlada Fronta)

**Socialisticky Svaz Mladeze. Pionyrska Organizace**
Nam. M. Gorkeho 24, 116 47 Prague 1,
Czechoslovakia
(Subscr. to: Artia, Ve Smeckach 30, 111 27 Prague
1)
- Ohnicek. s-m. ISSN 0030-1272
- Pionyr; zabavny mesicnik pro mladez. m. ISSN
  0042-4919
- Sedmicka Pionyru. (pub. by Mlada Fronta)

**SPOFA, Spojene Podniky pro Zdravotnickou Vyrobu.
Vyzkumny Ustav pro Biofaktory a Veterinarni
Leciva**
254 49 Jilove u Prahy, Czechoslovakia.
- Veterinaria SPOFA; journal for veterinary
  pharmacotherapy. bi-m. (prep. by its Odbor
  Vedeckych Informaci)

**Spolecnost pro Racionalni Vyzivu**
- Vyziva Lidu. (pub. by Avicenum, State Health
  Publishing House)

**Spolek Ceskych Vcelaru**
Kremencova 8, Prague 2, Czechoslovakia
(Subscr. to: Artia, Ve Smeckach 30, 111 27 Prague
1)
- Vcelarstvi. m. ISSN 0042-2924

**Sport, Publishing House of the Central Committee of
the Slovak Physical Culture Organization**
Fucikova 14, 893 44 Bratislava, Czechoslovakia.
- Album Slavnych Sportovcov. irreg, vol. 4, 1976.

**Statni Filharmonie Brno**
Komenskeho nam. 8, 602 00 Brno, Czechoslovakia
(Subscr. to: Artia, Ve Smeckach 30, 111 27 Prague
1)
- Opus Musicum. 10 per yr. (Co-sponsor: Svaz
  Ceskych a Slovenskych Skladatelu)

**Statni Nakladatelstvi Technicke Literatury**
Spalena 51, 113 02 Prague 1, Czechoslovakia
(Subscr. to: Artia, Ve Smeckach 30, 111 27 Prague
1)
- Automatizace/Automation. m. ISSN 0005-125X
  (Subscr. to: Artia, Ve Smeckach 30, 111 27
  Prague 1)
- Automobil/Automobile. m. ISSN 0404-3529
  (Czechoslovakia. Federalni Ministerstvo Hutnictvi
  a Tezkeho Strojirenstvi) (Subscr. to: Artia, Ve
  Smeckach 30, 111 27 Prague 1)
- Ceskoslovenska Informatika/Czechoslovak
  Information Journal. m. (Ustredi Vedeckych,
  Technickych a Ekonomickych Informaci. Statni
  Technicka Knihovna) (Subscr. to: Artia, Ve
  Smeckach 30, 111 27 Prague 1)
- Chemicky Prumysl/Chemical Industry. m. ISSN
  0009-2789 (Vyzkumny Ustav Technicko-
  Ekonomicky Chemickeho Prumyslu) (Subcr. to:
  Artia, Ve Smeckach 30, 111 27 Prague 1)
- Czechoslovakia. Federalni Statisticky Urad.
  Statisticka Rocenka. a. ISSN 0070-248X
- Domov. bi-m. ISSN 0012-5369 (Subscr. to: Artia,
  Ve Smeckach 30, 111 27 Prague 1)
- Elektrotechnicky Obzor/Elektrotechnical Review.
  m. ISSN 0013-5798 (Subscr. to: Artia, Ve
  Smeckach 30, 111 27 Prague 1)
- Elektrotechnik/Electrotechnician. m. (Subscr. to:
  Artia, Ve Smeckach 30, 111 27 Prague 1)
- Energetika/Power Engineering; technical monthly
  for electric power engineering, thermal power
  stations and utilizations of power. m. ISSN 0013-
  7286 (Czechoslovakia. Federalni Ministerstvo
  Paliv a Energetiky) (Subscr. to: Artia, Ve
  Smeckach 30, 111 27 Prague 1)
- Finance a Uver. m. ISSN 0015-1920
  (Czechoslovakia. Federalni Ministerstvo Financi)
  (Co-sponsors: Statni Banka Ceskoslovenska;
  Federalni Cenova Komise) (Subscr. to: Artia, Ve
  Smeckach 30, 111 27 Prague 1)
- Geodeticky a Kartograficky Obzor. m. ISSN
  0016-7096 (Cesky Urad pro Geodesii a
  Kartografii) (Co-sponsor: Slovensky Urad pre
  Geodeziu a Kartografiu) (Subscr. to: Artia, Ve
  Smeckach 30, 111 27 Prague 1)
- Geologicky Pruzkum/Geologicky Prieskum/
  Geological Surveying. m. ISSN 0016-772X
  (Cesky Geologicky Urad) (Co-sponsor: Slovensky
  Geologicky Urad) (Subscr. to: Artia, Ve
  Smeckach 30, 111 27 Prague 1)
- Hutnicke Listy/Metallurgical Journal. m. ISSN
  0018-8069 (Czechoslovakia. Federalni
  Ministerstvo Hutnictvi a Tezkeho Strojirenstvi)
  (Subscr. to: Artia, Ve Smeckach 30, 111 27
  Prague 1)
- Hutnik. m. (Subscr. to: Artia, Ve Smeckach 30,
  111 27 Prague 1)
- Investicni Vystavba; casopis pro popularizaci
  technickoekonomickych poznatku v oboru
  investicni cinnosti. m. ISSN 0020-9937
  (Czechoslovakia. Federalni Ministerstvo pro
  Technicky a Investicni Rozvoj) (Subscr. to: Artia,
  Ve Smeckach 30, 111 27 Prague 1)
- Jaderna Energie/Nuclear Energy. m.
  (Czechoslovakia. Ceskoslovenska Atomova
  Komise) (Subscr. to: Artia, Ve Smeckach 30, 111
  27 Prague 1)
- Jemna Mechanika a Optika/Fine Mechanics and
  Optics. m. ISSN 0447-6441 (Meopta, n.p.,
  Prerov) (Subscr. to: Artia, Ve Smeckach 30, 111
  27 Prague 1)
- Kozarstvi/Leather Industry; odborny casopis pro
  prumysl kozedelny, obuvnicky a gumove obuvi.
  m. ISSN 0023-4338 (Subscr. to: Artia, Ve
  Smeckach 30, 111 27 Prague 1)
- Kvasny Prumysl/Fermentation Industry; odborny
  mesicnik pro pracovniky v kvasnem a napojovem
  prumyslu. m. ISSN 0023-5830 (Pivovary a
  Sladovny) (Subscr. to: Artia, Ve Smeckach 30,
  111 27 Prague 1)
- Listy Cukrovarnicke/Sugar Journal. m. ISSN
  0024-4449 (Vyzkumny Ustav Prumyslu
  Cukrovarnickeho) (Subscr. to: Artia, Ve
  Smeckach 30, 111 27 Prague 1)

- Manipulace, Skladovani, Baleni/Material
  Handling, Storage Packaging. m. (IMADOS
  (Institut Mantpulacnich, Dopravnich, Obalovych a
  Skladovacich Systemu)) (Subscr. to: Artia, Ve
  Smeckach 30, 111 27 Prague 1)
- Meteorologicke Zpravy. bi-m. ISSN 0026-1173
  (Hydrometeorologicky Ustav)
- Mlynsko-Pekarensky Prumysl a Technika
  Skladovani Obili/Milling and Baking Industry and
  Storage Techniques of Grain. m. ISSN 0026-7058
  (Subscr. to: Artia, Ve Smeckach 30, 111 27
  Prague 1)
- Papir a Celuloza. m. ISSN 0031-1421 (Vyskumny
  Ustav Papiera a Celulozy) (Subscr. to: Artia, Ve
  Smeckach 30, 111 27 Prague 1)
- Plasty a Kaucuk. m. (Ceskoslovensky Zavod
  Gumarenskeho Prumyslu) (Subscr. to: Artia, Ve
  Smeckach 30, 111 27 Prague 1)
- Plyn/Gas; manufacture, distribution and utilization
  of gas. m. ISSN 0032-1761 (Subscr. to: Artia, Ve
  Smeckach 30, 111 27 Prague 1)
- Podnikova Organizace/Enterprise Organization;
  casopis pro organizaci, rizeni a ekonomiku
  prumyslu. m. ISSN 0032-1869 (Czechoslovakia.
  Ministerstvo Prumyslu Ceske Socialisticke
  Republiky) (Subscr. to: Artia, Ve Smeckach 30,
  111 27 Prague 1)
- Rudy. m. ISSN 0035-9688 (Subscr. to: Artia, Ve
  Smeckach 30, 111 27 Prague 1)
- Sdelovaci Technika/Telecommunications
  Engineering. m. ISSN 0036-9942 (Subscr. to:
  Artia, Ve Smeckach 30, 111 27 Prague 1)
- Sklar a Keramik/Glass and Ceramics Maker;
  odborny casopis pro prumysl sklarsky a jemne
  keramiky. m. ISSN 0037-637X (Statni Vyzkumny
  Ustav Sklarsky) (Co-sponsor: Ceska Silikatova
  Spolecnost) (Subscr. to: Artia, Ve Smeckach 30,
  111 27 Prague 1)
- Slaboproudy Obzor/Electronics and
  Telecommunications Review. m. ISSN 0037-668X
  (Subscr. to: Artia, Ve Smeckach 30, 111 27
  Prague 1)
- Slevarenstvi/Foundry Industry; casopis pro
  slevarensky prumysl. m. ISSN 0037-6825
  (Czechoslovakia. Federalni Ministerstvo Hutnictvi
  a Tezkeho Strojirenstvi) (Subscr. to: Artia, Ve
  Smeckach 30, 111 27 Prague 1)
- Stavivo/Building Materials. m. ISSN 0039-0801
  (Subscr. to: Artia, Ve Smeckach 30, 111 27
  Prague 1)
- Strojirenska Vyroba/Engineering Production. m.
  ISSN 0039-2456 (Subscr. to: Artia, Ve Smeckach
  30, 111 27 Prague 1)
- Strojirenstvi. m. ISSN 0039-2464 (Czechoslovakia.
  Federalni Ministerstvo Hutnictvi a Tezkeho
  Strojirenstvi) (Subscr. to: Artia, Ve Smeckach 30,
  111 27 Prague 1)
- Technicka Knihovna/Technical Library. m. ISSN
  0049-3171 (Ustredi Vedeckych, Technickych a
  Ekonomickych Informaci. Statni Technicka
  Knihovna) (Subscr. to: Artia, Ve Smeckach 30,
  111 27 Prague 1)
- Textil/Textile; technical monthly dealing with
  textile and clothing industry. m. ISSN 0040-4829
  (U B O K) (Subscr. to; Artia, Ve Smeckach 30,
  111 27 Prague 1)
- Uhli/Coal. m. ISSN 0041-5812 (Subscr. to: Artia,
  Ve Smeckach 30, 111 27 Prague 1)

**Statni Pedagogicke Nakladatelstvi**
Ostrovni 30, 113 02 Prague 1, Czechoslovakia.
- Acta Veterinaria. q, and occasional supplements.
  ISSN 0001-7213 (Vysoka Skola Veterinarni, Brno)
- Cesky Jazyk a Literatura; casopis pro metodiku.
  10 per yr. ISSN 0009-0786 (Czechoslovakia.
  Ministerstvo Skolstvi Ceske Socialisticke
  Republiky) (Subscr. to: Artia, Ve Smeckach 30,
  111 27 Prague 1)
- Cizi Jazyky ve Skole; casopis pro vyucovani cizim
  jazykum krome rustiny, zejmena nemcine,
  anglictine, francouzstine, spanelstine a latine. 10
  per yr. ISSN 0009-8205 (Czechoslovakia.
  Ministerstvo Skolstvi Ceske Socialisticke
  Republiky) (Co-sponsor: Ministerstvo Skolstva
  Slovenskej Socialistickej Republiky) (Subscr. to:
  Artia, Ve Smeckach 30, 111 27 Prague 1)
- Esteticka Vychova. 10 per yr. ISSN 0014-1283
  (Subscr. to: Artia, Ve Smeckach 30, 111 27
  Prague 1)
- Matematika a Fyzika ve Skole. 10 per yr.
  (Czechoslovakia. Ministerstvo Skolstvi Ceske
  Socialisticke Republiky) (Co-sponsor: Ministerstvo
  Skolstva Slovenskej Socialistickej Republiky)
  (Subscr. to: Artia, Ve Smeckach 30, 111 27
  Prague 1)
- Ogoniok. 10 per yr. ISSN 0030-073X (Subscr. to:
  Artia, Ve Smeckach 30, 111 27 Prague 1)

- Pedagogicka Fakulta v Ostrave. Matematika, Fyzika. irreg.
- Pedagogicka Fakulta v Usti nad Labem. Sbornik: Rada Bohemisticka. irreg.
- Pedagogicka Fakulta v Usti nad Labem. Sbornik: Rada Chemicka. irreg.
- Prirodni Vedy ve Skole. 10 per yr. ISSN 0032-8766 (Czechoslovakia. Ministerstvo Skolstvi Ceske Socialisticke Republiky) (Co-sponsor: Ministerstvo Skolstva Slovenskej Socialistickej Republiky) (Subscr. to: Artia, Ve Smeckach 30, 111 27 Prague 1)
- Rozhledy Matematicko-Fyzikalni. 10 per yr. ISSN 0035-9343 (Czechoslovakia. Ministerstvo Skolstvi Ceske Socialisticke Republiky) (Co-Sponsor: Jednota Ceskoslovenskych Matematiku a Fyziku) (Subscr. to: Artia, Ve Smeckach 30, 111 27 Prague 1)
- Rusky Jazyk; casopis pro vyucovani rustine na ceskoslovenskych skolach. 10 per yr. ISSN 0036-0155 (Czechoslovakia. Ministerstvo Skolstvi Ceske Socialisticke Republiky) (Co-sponsor: Ministerstvo Skolstva Slovenskej Socialistickej Republiky) (Subscr. to: Artia, Ve Smeckach 30, 111 27 Prague 1)
- Telesna Vychova Mladeze; mesicnik pro telesnou a brannou vychovu ve skole. 10 per yr. ISSN 0040-2729 (Czechoslovakia. Ministerstvo Skolstvi Ceske Socialisticke Republiky) (Subscr. to: Artia, Ve Smeckach 30, 111 27 Prague 1)
- Universita Palackeho. Filosoficka Fakulta. Slavica. irreg.
- Universita Palackeho. Pedagogicka Fakulta. Sbornick Praci: Rusky Jazyk a Literatura. irreg.
- Univerzita Palackeho. Pedagogicka Fakulta. Sbornik Praci: Cesky Jazyk a Literatura. irreg, vol. 2, 1973.
- Vysoka Skola Banska. Sbornik Vedeckych Praci: Rada Hutnicka/Institute of Mining and Metallurgy. Transactions: Metallurgical Series. 2-8 per yr. ISSN 0042-3726
- Vysoka Skola Banska. Sbornik Vedeckych Praci: Rada Strojni. irreg., vol. 20, 1974.

**Statni Plemenna Stanice**
Prague-Repy, Czechoslovakia
(Subscr. to: Artia, Ve Smeckach 30, 111 27 Prague 1)
- Nas Chov; casopis pro zivocisnou vyrobu. m. ISSN 0027-8068

**Statni Ustav Tesnopisny**
Dusni 7, Prague 1, Czechoslovakia
(Subscr. to: Artia, Ve Smeckach 30, 111 27 Prague 1)
- Sekretarska Praxe. 5 per yr. ISSN 0037-1149

**Statni Vedecka Knihovna. Universitni Knihovna**
Leninova 5-7, 601 87 Brno, Czechoslovakia.
- Statni Vedecka Knihovna. Universitni Knihovna. Vyber Novinek. Serie A: Prirodni Vedy, Zemedelstvi. m.
- Statni Vedecka Knihovna. Universitni Knihovna. Vyber Novinek. Serie B: Lekarstvi. m.
- Statni Vedecka Knihovna. Universitni Knihovna. Vyber Novinek. Serie C: Clovek a Spolecnost. m.
- Statni Vedecka Knihovna. Universitni Knihovna. Vyber Novinek. Serie D: Ekonomika. m.
- Statni Vedecka Knihovna. Universitni Knihovna. Vyber Novinek. Serie F: Pedagogika, Psychologie. m.
- Statni Vedecka Knihovna. Universitni Knihovna. Vyber Novinek. Serie G: Technika. m.
- Statni Vedecka Knihovna Universitni Knihovna. Vyber Novinek. Serie E: Kultura. m.

**Statni Vyzkumny Ustav Ochrany Materialu G. V. Akinova**
U mestanskemo pivovaru 4, Prague 7, Czechoslovakia.
- Koroze a Ochrana Materialu. 5 per yr. ISSN 0023-4095

**Statni Vyzkumny Ustav Sklarsky**
- Sklar a Keramik/Glass and Ceramics Maker. (pub. by Statni Nakladatelstvi Technicke Literatury)

**Statni Zemedelske Nakladatelstvi**
Vaclavske nam. 47, 113 78 Prague 1, Czechoslovakia
(Subscr. to: Artia, Ve Smeckach 30, 111 27 Prague 1)
- Ceskoslovenske Rybarstvi. m. ISSN 0009-0670 (Cesky Rybarsky Svaz)
- Chatar. m.
- Chovatel. m.
- Lesnicka Prace/Forestry. m.

- Mezinarodni Zemedelsky Casopis; vedeckovyrobni casopis pro vymenu vysledku vedy a pokrokovych zkusenosti v zemedelstvi clenskych zemi Rady Vzajemne Hospodarske Pomoci. bi-m. (Czechoslovakia. Federalni Ministerstvo Zemedelstvi a Vyzivy)
- Ochrana Ovzdusi/Air Conservation. m. (Czechoslovakia. Ministerstvo Lesniho a Vodniho Hospodarstvi Ceske Socialistike Republiky)
- Prumysl Potravin/Food Industry; technika a ekonomika prumyslove vyroby potravin. m. ISSN 0033-1988 (Czechoslovakia. Ministerstvo Zemedelstvi a Vyzivy Ceske Socialisticke Republiky)
- Statni Statky. m. ISSN 0039-0704
- Vodni Hospodarstvi. Serie A/Water Management. Series A. m. (Czechoslovakia. Ministerstvo Lesniho a Vodniho Hospodarstvi Ceske Socialisticke Republiky)
- Vodni Hospodarstvi. Serie B/Water Management. Series B. m. (Czechoslovakia. Ministerstvo Lesniho a Vodniho Hospodarstvi Ceske Socialisticke Republiky)
- Zahradkar; casopis cs. ovocnaru a zahradkaru. m.
- Zahradnicke Listy. m. ISSN 0044-1694 (Czechoslovakia. Federalni Ministerstvo Zemedelstvi a Vyzivy)

**Statni Zidovske Museum**
- Judaica Bohemiae. (pub. by Orbis)

**Statny Drevarsky Vyskumny Ustav**
Lamacska cesta 1, 891 29 Bratislava, Czechoslovakia.
- Drevarska Dokumentacia.
- Drevarsky Vyskum. q. ISSN 0012-6136 (Subscr. to: Slovart, Gottwaldovo nam. 48, 805 32 Bratislava)
- Prehlad Lesnickej, Drevarskej, Celulozovej a Papiernickej Literatury. 10 per yr. ISSN 0032-7328 (Subscr. to: Slovart, Gottwaldovo nam. 48, 805 32 Bratislava)

**Stredisko Technickych Informaci Potravinarskeho Prumyslu**
Nam. M. Gorkeho 32, Prague 1, Czechoslovakia.
- Prehledy Potravinarske Literatury/Survey of Food Literature. 10 per yr. ISSN 0032-7379

**Svaz Architektu C S R**
Letenska 5, 118 45 Prague 1, Czechoslovakia
(Subscr. to: Artia, Ve Smeckach 30, 111 27 Prague 1)
- Architektura C S R. 10 per yr. ISSN 0300-5305
- Ceskoslovensky Architekt. fortn. ISSN 0009-0697

**Svaz Ceskoslovensko-Sovetskeho Pratelstvi**
Smetanovo nabr. 18, 115 65 Prague 1, Czechoslovakia
- Praha - Moskva; revue pro ceskoslovensko-sovetskou kulturni, vedeckou a technickou spolupraci. bi-m. ISSN 0032-6593 (Subscr. to: Artia, Ve Smeckach 30, 111 27 Prague 1)
- Sestina Sveta v Obrazech. m. ISSN 0037-2846
- Svet Socialismu. w. (Subscr. to: Artia, Ve Smeckach 30, 111 27 Prague 1)

**Svaz Ceskoslovenskych Divadelnich a Rozhlasovych Umelcu**
Valdstejnske nam. 3, Prague 1, Czechoslovakia.
- Divadelni Noviny. fortn. ISSN 0012-4141 (Co-sponsor: Divadelni Ustav)

**Svaz Ceskoslovenskych Spisovatelu**
Narodni tr. 11, 111 47 Prague 1, Czechoslovakia
(Subscr. to: Artia, Ve Smeckach 30, 111 27 Prague 1)
- Literarni Mesicnik. 10 per yr. (Co-sponsor: Czechoslovakia. Ministerstvo Kultury Ceske Socialisticke Republiky)

**Svaz Ceskych a Slovenskych Skladatelu**
Valdstejnske nam. 1, 118 00 Prague 1, Czechoslovakia
(Subscr. to: Artia, Ve Smeckach 30, 111 27 Prague 1)
- Hudebni Rozhledy. m. ISSN 0018-6996
- Slovenska Hudba. (pub. by Slovensky Muzicky Fond)

**Svaz Druzstevnich Rolniku**
Ve Smeckach 33, 110 00 Prague 1, Czechoslovakia
(Subscr. to: Artia, Ve Smeckach 30, 111 27 Prague 1)
- Beseda Nasi Vesnice. w. ISSN 0045-1770

**Svepomoc, Publishing House of the Central Cooperative Council**
Tesnov 5, 110 06 Prague 1, Czechoslovakia.
- Czechoslovak Cooperator. q. (Ustredni Rada Druzstev)

**Trade Unions International of Agricultural Forestry and Plantataion Workers**
Opletalova 57, 115 70 Prague 1, Czechoslovakia.
- T. U. I. A. F. P. W. Information. bi-m.

**Trade Unions International of Transport Workers**
Opletalova 57, 115 70 Prague 1, Czechoslovakia.
- Transport Workers of the World Review. q.

**Trade Unions International of Workers in Commerce**
Opletalova 57, 115 70 Prague 1, Czechoslovakia.
- Trade Unions International of Workers in Commerce. Bulletin. q. ISSN 0049-433X

**U B O K**
- Textil/Textile. (pub. by Statni Nakladatelstvi Technicke Literatury)

**Universita J. E. Purkyne**
Komenskeho nam. 2, 662 43 Brno, Czechoslovakia.
- Archivum Mathematicum. q. ISSN 0044-8753

**Universita J. E. Purkyne. Filosoficka Fakulta**
A. Novaka 1, 602 00 Brno, Czechoslovakia.
- Brno Studies in English. irreg.
- Universita J. E. Purkyne. Filosoficka Fakulta. Sbornik Praci. a. ISSN 0068-2705

**Universita J. E. Purkyne. Lekarska Fakulta**
Komenskeho nam. 2, 662 43 Brno, Czechoslovakia.
- Scripta Medica/Universita J. E. Purkyne. Lekarska Fakulta. Spisy. 8 per yr. ISSN 0036-9721

**Universita J. E. Purkyne. Prirodovedecka Fakulta**
Kotlarska 2, 611 37 Brno, Czechoslovakia.
- Folia Facultatis Scientiarum Naturalium Universitatis Purkynianae Brunensis: Biologia. irreg (7-12 per yr.)
- Folia Facultatis Scientiarum Naturalium Universitatis Purkynianae Brunensis: Chemia. irreg (7-12 per yr.)
- Folia Facultatis Scientiarum Naturalium Universitatis Purkynianae Brunensis: Geologia. irreg (7-12 per yr.)
- Folia Facultatis Scientiarum Naturalium Universitatis Purkynianae Brunensis: Geographia. irreg (7-12 per yr.)
- Folia Facultatis Scientiarum Naturalium Universitatis Purkynianae Brunensis: Physica. irreg (7-12 per yr.)
- Scripta Facultatis Scientiarum Naturalium Universitatis Purkynianae Brunensis: Biologia. 10 per yr.
- Scripta Facultatis Scientiarum Naturalium Universitatis Purkynianae Brunensis: Chemia. 10 per yr.
- Scripta Facultatis Scientiarum Naturalium Universitatis Purkynianae Brunensis: Geologia. 10 per yr.
- Scripta Facultatis Scientiarum Naturalium Universitatis Purkynianae Brunensis: Geographia. 10 per yr.
- Scripta Facultatis Scientiarum Naturalium Universitatis Purkynianae Brunensis: Mathematica. 10 per yr.
- Scripta Facultatis Scientiarum Naturalium Universitatis Purkynianae Brunensis: Physica. 10 per yr.

**Universita Karlova**
Ovocny trh 5, Prague 1, Czechoslovakia
(Subscr. to: Artia, Ve Smeckach 30, 111 27 Prague 1)
- Acta Universitatis Carolinae: Geographica. s-a. ISSN 0300-5402

**Universita Karlova. Centrum Numericke Matematiky**
Malostranske nam. 25, Prague 1, Czechoslovakia.
- Prague Bulletin of Mathematical Linguistics. s-a. ISSN 0032-6585

**Universita Karlova. Fakulta Matematiky a Fyziky**
Ke Karlovu 3, 121 16 Prague 2, Czechoslovakia
(Subscr. to: Artia, Ve Smeckach 30, 111 27 Prague 1)
- Acta Universitatis Carolinae: Mathematica et Physica. s-a. ISSN 0001-7140

**Universita Karlova. Fakulta Vseobecneho Lekarstvi**
Katerinska 19, 120 00 Prague 2, Czechoslovakia.
- Acta Universitatis Carolinae: Medica. 8 per yr. ISSN 0567-8250 (Subscr. to: Artia, Ve Smeckach 30, 111 27 Prague 1)
- Sbornik Lekarsky. m. ISSN 0036-5327 (Subscr. to: Artia, Ve Smeckach 30, 111 27 Prague 1)
- Universita Karlova. Fakulta Vseobecneho Lekarstvi. Pobocka v Hradci Kralove. Sbornik Vedeckych Praci. 5 per yr. ISSN 0049-5514 (prep. by its Pobocka v Hradci Kralove)
- Universita Karlova. Fakulta Vseobecneho Lekarstvi. Pobocka v Hradci Kralove. Sbornik Vedeckych Praci: Supplementum. 5 per yr. ISSN 0049-5522 (prep. by its Pobocka v Hradci Kralove)

**Universita Karlova. Filosoficka Fakulta**
Nam. Krasnoarmejcu 1, 116 38 Prague 1, Czechoslovakia.
- Lingvisticke Citanky/Readings in Linguistics. a.
- Miscellanea Musicologica. a. ISSN 0544-4136 (prep. by its Katedra Dejin Hudby, Divadla a Filmu)

**Universita Karlova. Matematicky Ustav**
Sokolovska 83, Prague 8, Czechoslovakia.
- Commentationes Mathematicae Universitatis Carolinae. q. ISSN 0010-2628

**Universita Karlova. Prirodovedecka Fakulta**
Vinicna 5, 128 44 Prague 2, Czechoslovakia.
(Subscr. to: Artia, Ve Smeckach 30, 111 27 Prague 1)
- Acta Universitatis Carolinae: Biologica. 5-6 per yr. ISSN 0001-7124 (prep. by its Katedra Biologie)

**Universita Karlova. Psychologicky Ustav**
Hradcanske nam. 5, Prague 1, Czechoslovakia
(Subscr. to: Artia, Ve Smeckach 30, 111 27 Prague 1)
- Psychologie v Ekonomicke Praxi/Applied Industrial Psychology. q. ISSN 0033-300X

**Universita Karlova. Ustav Geologickych Ved**
Albertov 6, 128 43 Prague 2, Czechoslovakia
(Subscr. to: Artia, Ve Smeckach 30, 111 27 Prague 1)
- Acta Universitatis Carolinae: Geologica. q. ISSN 0001-7132

**Univerzita Komenskeho. Farmaceuticka Fakulta**
- Universitas Comeniana. Acta Pharmaceuticae. (pub. by Slovenske Pedagogicke Nakladatelstvo)

**Univerzita Komenskeho. Filozoficka Fakulta**
Gondova 2, 806 01 Bratislava, Czechoslovakia.
- Univerzita Komenskeho. Filozoficka Fakulta. Zbornik: Ethnologia Slavica. a. ISSN 0083-4106
- Univerzita Komenskeho. Filozoficka Fakulta. Zbornik: Graecolatina et Orientalia. a. ISSN 0083-4114
- Univerzita Komenskeho. Filozoficka Fakulta. Zbornik: Historica. a. ISSN 0083-4122
- Univerzita Komenskeho. Filozoficka Fakulta. Zbornik: Musaica. a. ISSN 0083-4130
- Univerzita Komenskeho. Filozoficka Fakulta. Zbornik: Paedagogica. a. ISSN 0083-4165
- Univerzita Komenskeho. Filozoficka Fakulta. Zbornik: Philologica. a. ISSN 0083-4173
- Univerzita Komenskeho. Filozoficka Fakulta. Zbornik: Philosophica. a. ISSN 0083-4181
- Univerzita Komenskeho. Filozoficka Fakulta. Zbornik: Psychologica. a. ISSN 0083-419X
- Univerzita Komenskeho. Filozoficka Fakulta. Zbornik: Zurnalistika. a. ISSN 0083-422X

**Univerzita Komenskeho. Lekarska Fakulta**
- Folia Facultatis Medicae Universitatis Comenianae Bratislaviensis. (pub. by Veda, Publishing House of the Slovak Academy of Sciences)

**Univerzita Komenskeho. Oddelenie Liecebnej a Specialnej Pedagogiky**
Skolska ul., 800 00 Bratislava, Czechoslovakia.
- Univerzita Komenskeho. Oddelenie Liecebnej a Specialnej Pedagogiky. Zbornik: Paedagogica Specialis. a. ISSN 0083-4211

**Univerzita Komenskeho. Pedagogicka Fakulta v Trnave**
- Univerzita Komenskeho. Pedagogicka Fakulta v Trnave. Prirodne Vedy: Biologia-Genetika. (pub. by Slovenske Pedagogicke Nakladatelstvo)

**Univerzita Komenskeho. Ustav Marxizmu-Leninizmu**
Safarikovo nam. 12, Bratislava, Czechoslovakia.
- Univerzita Komenskeho. Ustav Marxizmu-Leninizmu. Zbornik: Dejiny Robotnickeho Hnutia. irreg.
- Univerzita Komenskeho. Ustav Marxizmu-Leninizmu. Zbornik: Marxisticka Filozofia. irreg.

**Univerzita Palackeho. Filosoficka Fakulta**
Krizkovskeho 10, 771 80 Olomouc, Czechoslovakia.
- Russica Olomucensia. a. (prep. by its Katedra Rusistiky)
- Universita Palackeho. Filosoficka Fakulta. Slavica. (pub. by Statni Pedagogicke Nakladatelstvi)

**Univerzita Palackeho. Lekarska Fakulta**
Hnevotinska 3, Olomouc, Czechoslovakia.
- Acta Universitatis Palackianae, Facultatis Medicae. q. ISSN 0001-7167

**Univerzita Palackeho. Pedagogicka Fakulta**
- Univerzita Palackeho. Pedagogicka Fakulta. Sbornik Praci: Cesky Jazyk a Literatura. (pub. by Statni Pedagogicke Nakladatelstvi)
- Univerzita Palackeho. Pedagogicka Fakulta. Sbornick Praci: Rusky Jazyk a Literatura. (pub. by Statni Pedagogicke Nakladatelstvi)

**Univerzitna Kniznica**
Michalska 1, 885 17 Bratislava, Czechoslovakia.
- Zahranicne Periodika v C S S R. a. (Co-sponsor: Czechoslovakia. Statni Knihovna)

**Urad pro Normalizaci a Mereni**
Vaclavske nam. 19, 113 47 Prague 1, Czechoslovakia.
- Seznam Platnych Ceskoslovenskych Statnich a Oborovych Norem. a.
- Urad pro Normalizaci a Mereni. Vestnik. m. ISSN 0042-4714 (Subscr. to: Artia, Ve Smeckach 30, 111 27 Prague 1)

**Urad pro Vynalezy a Objevy**
Vaclavske nam. 19, 113 47 Prague 1, Czechoslovakia
(Subscr. to: Postovni Novinova Sluzba, Jindrisska 14, 125 05 Prague 1)
- Vynalezy a Zlepsovaci Navrhy/Inventions and Improvement Suggestions. m.

**Ustav Bytove a Odevni Kultury**
see U B O K

**Ustav pro Mezinarodni Politiku a Ekonomii**
- Mezinarodni Vztahy. (pub. by Orbis)

**Ustredi Vedeckych, Technickych a Ekonomickych Informaci**
Konviktska 5, 113 57 Prague 1, Czechoslovakia.
- Metodicky Zpravodaj Cs. Soustavy Vedeckych, Technickych a Ekonomickych Informaci. irreg. ISSN 0322-7243

**Ustredi Vedeckych, Technickych a Ekonomickych Informaci. Statni Technicka Knihovna**
Klementinum, Nam. Dr. V. Vacka 5, 3113 07 Prague 1, Czechoslovakia.
- Ceskoslovenska Informatika/Czechoslovak Information Journal. (pub. by Statni Nakladatelstvi Technicke Literatury)
- Czechoslovak Scientific and Technical Periodicals Contents. 10 per yr. ISSN 0045-9488
- Prumyslove Informace. bi-m. ISSN 0322-9564
- Technicka Knihovna/Technical Library. (pub. by Statni Nakladatelstvi Technicke Literatury)

**Ustredna Ekonomicka Kniznica**
Palisady 22, 886 32 Bratislava, Czechoslovakia.
- Eko-Index; prehlad ekonomickej literatury. q. ISSN 0042-1340
- Ustredna Ekonomicka Kniznica. Informacny Zpravodaj. q.

**Ustredni Cirkevni Nakladatelstvi**
Snemovni 9, 118 01 Prague 1, Czechoslovakia
(Subscr. to: Artia, Ve Smeckach 30, 111 27 Prague 1)
- Krestanska Revue. 10 per yr. ISSN 0023-4613 (Kostnicka Jednota)

**Ustredni Rada Druzstev**
Tesnov 5, Prague 1, Czechoslovakia.
- Coop News. m.
- Czechoslovak Cooperative Movement in Figures. a.

- Czechoslovak Cooperator. (pub. by Svepomoc, Publishing House of the Central Cooperative Council)

**Ustredni Rada Odboru**
Nam. Gustava Klimenta 2, 113 59 Prague 3, Czechoslovakia.
- Ceskoslovensky Hornik a Energetik. w. ISSN 0009-0719 (Odborovy Svaz Pracovniku Hornictvi a Energetiky)
- Potravinar. s-m. ISSN 0032-566X (Odborovy Svaz Pracovniku Potravinarskeho Prumyslu) (Subscr. to: Artia, Ve Smekach 30, 111 27 Prague 1)
- Technicky Tydenik; casopis pro novou techniku a otazky zlepsovatelskeho a vynalezcovskeho hnuti. w. ISSN 0040-1064 (Subscr. to: Artia, Ve Smekach 30, 111 27 Prague 1)
- Zemedelsky a Lesni Zamestnanec. s-m. ISSN 0044-3891 (Odborovy Svaz Pracovniku Zemedelstvi) (Subscr. to: Artia, Ve Smekach 30, 111 27 Prague 1)

**Ustredni Ustav Geologicky**
Malostranske nam 19, 118 21 Prague 1, Czechoslovakia
(Subscr. to: Artia, Ve Smeckach 30, 111 27 Prague 1)
- Geo-Index. q.
- Sbornik Geologickych Ved: Antropozoikum/Journal of Geological Sciences: Anthropozoic. irreg. ISSN 0036-5270
- Sbornik Geologickych Ved: Geologie/Journal of Geological Sciences: Geology. 1-3 per yr. ISSN 0581-9172
- Sbornik Geologickych Ved: Hydrogeologie, Inzenyrska Geologie/Journal of Geological Sciences: Hydrogeology, Engineering Geology. irreg. ISSN 0036-5289
- Sbornik Geologickych Ved: Loziskova Geologie, Mineralogie/Journal of Geological Sciences: Economic Geology, Mineralogy. irreg. ISSN 0581-9180
- Sbornik Geologickych Ved: Paleontologie/Journal of Geological Sciences: Paleontology. irreg. ISSN 0036-5297
- Sbornik Geologickych Ved: Technologie, Geochemie/Journal of Geological Sciences: Technology, Geochemistry. irreg. ISSN 0036-5300 (Co-sponsor: Ustav Nerostnych Surovin, Kutna Hora)
- Sbornik Geologickych Ved: Uzita Geofyzika/Journal of Geological Sciences: Applied Geophysics. irreg. ISSN 0036-5319 (Co-sponsor: Geofyzika, n.p. Brno)
- Ustredni Ustav Geologicky. Rozpravy. irreg.
- Ustredni Ustav Geologicky. Vestnik. (pub. by Academia, Publishing House of the Czechoslovak Academy of Sciences)
- Ustredni Ustav Geologicky. Vyzkumne Prace. irreg.

**Veda, Publishing House of the Slovak Academy of Sciences**
Klemensova 19, 895 30 Bratislava, Czechoslovakia.
- Acta Botanica. irreg. (Slovenska Akademia Vied)
- Acta Ethnologica Slovaca. irreg. (Slovenska Akademia Vied. Narodopisny Ustav)
- Acta Physica Slovaca. q. (Slovenska Akademia Vied. Fyzikalny Ustav) (Subscr. to: Slovart, Gottwaldovo nam. 48, 805 32 Bratislava)
- Acta Virologica; international journal. bi-m. ISSN 0001-723X (Slovenska Akademia Vied. Virologicky Ustav) (Distributor in Western countries: Academic Press Inc. Ltd., 24-28 Oval Rd., London NW1 7DX, England)
- Architektura a Urbanizmus/Architecture and Urbanism. q. ISSN 0044-8680 (Slovenska Akademia Vied. Ustav Stavebnictva a Architektury) (Distributor in Western countries: John Benjamins B.V., Amsteldijk 44, Amsterdam (Z.), Netherlands)
- Ars. s-a. ISSN 0044-9008 (Slovenska Akademia Vied. Ustav Teorie a Dejin Umenia) (Distributor in Western countries: John Benjamins B.V., Amsteldijk 44, Amsterdam (Z.), Netherlands)
- Asian and African Studies. a. ISSN 0571-2742 (Slovenska Akademia Vied. Kabinet Orientalistiky)
- Banicke Listy/Folia Montana. irreg. (Slovenska Akademia Vied. Ustav Vlastnosti Hornin)
- Biologia. m. ISSN 0006-3088 (Slovenska Akademia Vied) (Subscr. to: Slovart, Gottwaldovo nam. 48, 805 32 Bratislava)
- Bratislavske Lekarske Listy. m. ISSN 0006-9248 (Slovenska Akademia Vied) (Subscr. to: Slovart, Gottwaldovo nam. 48, 805 32 Bratislava)

- Bulletin of the Slovak Seismographic Stations: Bratislava, Srobarova, Hurbanovo and Skalnate Pleso. a. (Slovenska Akademia Vied. Geofyzikalny Ustav)
- Ekonomicky Casopis/Economic Journal. 10 per yr. ISSN 0013-3035 (Slovenska Akademia Vied. Ekonomicky Ustav) (Distributor in Western countries: John Benjamins B.V., Amsteldijk 44, Amsterdam (Z.), Netherlands)
- Elektrotechnicky Casopis/Electrotechnical Journal. 10 per yr. ISSN 0013-578X (Slovenska Akademia Vied) (Subscr. to: Slovart, Gottwaldovo nam. 48, 805 32 Bratislava)
- Endocrinologia Experimentalis. q. ISSN 0013-7200 (Slovenska Akademia Vied) (Subscr. to: Slovart, Gottwaldovo nam. 48, 805 32 Bratislava)
- Entomologicke Problemy. a. ISSN 0071-0792 (Slovenska Entomologicka Spolocnost)
- Filozofia/Philosophy. bi-m. ISSN 0046-385X (Slovenska Akademia Vied. Filozoficky Ustav) (Distributor in Western countries: John Benjamins B.V., Amsteldijk 44, Amsterdam (Z.), Netherlands)
- Flora Slovenska. irreg. ISSN 0071-5859 (Slovenska Akademia Vied)
- Folia Dendrologica. irreg, vol. 3, 1977. (Slovenska Akademia Vied. Ustav Dendrobiologie) (Co-sponsor: Arboretum Mlynany)
- Folia Facultatis Medicae Universitatis Comenianae Bratislaviensis. s-a. ISSN 0430-8611 (Univerzita Komenskeho. Lekarska Fakulta)
- Folia Veterinaria. s-a. ISSN 0015-5748 (Vysoka Skola Veterinarska v Kosiciach)
- Geograficky Casopis/Geographical Review. q. ISSN 0016-7193 (Slovenska Akademia Vied) (Distributor in Western countries: John Benjamins B.V., Amsteldijk 44, Amsterdam (Z.), Netherlands)
- Geologicky Zbornik. s-a. ISSN 0016-7738 (Slovenska Akademia Vied) (Subscr. to: Slovart, Gottwaldovo nam. 48, 805 32 Bratislava)
- High Energy Particle Physics. irreg, vol. 2, 1976. (Slovenska Akademia Vied)
- Historicke Studie. irreg., vol. 22, 1977. ISSN 0440-9515 (Slovenska Akademia Vied. Historicky Ustav) (Distributor in Western Countries: John Benjamins B.V., Amsteldijk 44, Amsterdam (Z.), Netherlands)
- Historicky Casopis/Journal of History. q. ISSN 0018-2575 (Slovenska Akademia Vied. Historicky Ustav) (Distributor in Western countries: John Benjamins B.V., Amsteldijk 44, Amsterdam (Z.), Netherlands)
- International Symposium on Geophysical Interpretation Methods. Proceedings. irreg., latest 1974, Bratislava.
- Jazykovedne Studie. irreg., vol. 13, 1976. ISSN 0448-9241 (Slovenska Akademia Vied. Jazykovedny Ustav L. Stura) (Distributor in Western countries: John Benjamins B.V., Amsteldijk 44, Amsterdam (Z.), Netherlands)
- Jazykovedny Casopis. s-a. ISSN 0021-5597 (Slovenska Akademia Vied. Jazykovedny Ustav L. Stura) (Distributor in Western countries: John Benjamins B.V., Amsteldijk 44, Amsterdam (Z.) Netherlands)
- Kovove Materialy/Metal Materials. bi-m. ISSN 0023-432X (Slovenska Akademia Vied) (Subscr. to: Slovart, Gottwaldovo nam. 48, 805 32 Bratislava)
- Kultura Slova/Culture of the Word. 10 per yr. ISSN 0023-5202 (Slovenska Akademia Vied) (Distributor in Western countries: John Benjamins B.V., Amsteldijk 44, Amsterdam (Z.), Netherlands)
- Lekarske Prace. irreg., approx. s-a; vol. 10, no. 2, 1973. ISSN 0075-8736 (Slovenska Akademia Vied)
- Literaria. irreg, vol. 16, 1973. (Slovenska Akademia Vied. Ustav Slovenskej Literatury)
- Matematicky Casopis. q. ISSN 0025-5173 (Slovenska Akademia Vied) (Subscr. to: Slovart, Gottwaldovo nam. 48, 805 32 Bratislava)
- Musicologica Slovaca. a. ISSN 0581-0558 (Slovenska Akademia Vied. Umenovedny Ustav)
- Nauka o Zemi. Seria Geographica. irreg. (Slovenska Akademia Vied)
- Neoplasma. bi-m. ISSN 0028-2685 (Slovenska Akademia Vied) (Subscr. to: Slovart, Gottwaldovo nam. 48, 805 32 Bratislava)
- Polnohospodarstvo. m. (Slovenska Akademia Vied) (Subscr. to: Slovart, Gottwaldovo nam. 48, 805 32 Bratislava)
- Prace Astronomickeho Observatoria na Skalnatom Plese/Activities of the Astronomical Observatory on Skalnate Pleso. irreg, vol. 8, 1977. (Slovenska Akademia Vied)

- Pravnicke Studie. q. ISSN 0551-9039 (Slovenska Akademia Vied. Ustav Statu a Prava) (Distributor in Western countries: John Benjamins B.V., Amsteldijk 44, Amsterdam (Z.), Netherlands)
- Pravny Obzor/Law Review. 10 per yr. ISSN 0032-6984 (Slovenska Akademia Vied. Ustav Statu a Prava) (Distributor in Western countries: John Benjamins B.V., Amsteldijk 44, Amsterdam (Z.), Netherlands)
- Problemy Biologie Krajiny. irreg, vol. 20, 1977. (Slovenska Akademia Vied)
- Slavica Slovaca. q. ISSN 0037-6787 (Slovenska Akademia Vied. Ustav Svetovej Literatury a Jazykov) (Distributor in Western countries: John Benjamins B.V., Amsteldijk 44, Amsterdam (Z.), Netherlands)
- Slovanske Studie. a. ISSN 0583-564X (Slovenska Akademia Vied. Historicky Ustav) (Distributor in Western countries: John Benjamins B.V., Amsteldijk 44, Amsterdam (Z.), Netherlands)
- Slovenska Akademia Vied. Biologicke Prace/Treatises on Biology. m. ISSN 0037-6930
- Slovenska Akademia Vied. Geofyzikalny Ustav. Contributions. irreg. ISSN 0586-4607
- Slovenska Akademia Vied. Geologicky Ustav D. Stura: Zbornik: Zapadne Karpaty. 1-2 per yr. ISSN 0036-1372
- Slovenska Akademia Vied. Ustav Experimentalnej Farmakologie. Zbornik Prac a Studii. irreg.
- Slovenska Archeologia/Slovak Archeology. s-a. ISSN 0037-6949 (Slovenska Akademia Vied. Archeologicky Ustav) (Distributor in Western countries: John Benjamins B.V., Amsteldijk 44, Amsterdam (Z.), Netherlands)
- Slovenska Chemicka Spolocnost. Chemical Papers/Chemicke Zvesti. m. ISSN 0037-6906
- Slovenska Literature; revue pre literarnu vedu a kritiku. bi-m. ISSN 0037-6973 (Slovenska Akademia Vied. Literarnovedny Ustav) (Distributor in Western countries: John Benjamins B.V., Amsteldijk 44, Amsterdam (Z.), Netherlands)
- Slovenska Numizmatika. biennial. ISSN 0081-0088 (Slovenska Akademia Vied)
- Slovenska Rec; casopis pre vyskum a kulturu slovenskeho jazyka. bi-m. ISSN 0037-6981 (Slovenska Akademia Vied. Jazykovedny Ustav L. Stura) (Distributor in Western countries: John Benjamins B.V., Amsteldijk 44, Amsterdam (Z.), Netherlands)
- Slovenske Divadlo/Slovak Theater. q. ISSN 0037-699X (Slovenska Akademia Vied) (Distributor in Western countries: John Benjamins B.V., Amsteldijk 44, Amsterdam (Z.), Netherlands)
- Slovensky Narodopis/Slovak Ethnography. q. ISSN 0037-7023 (Slovenska Akademia Vied. Narodopisny Ustav) (Distributor in Western countries: John Benjamins B.V., Amsteldijk 44, Amsterdam (Z.), Netherlands)
- Sociologia. bi-m. ISSN 0049-1225 (Slovenska Akademia Vied. Sociologicky Ustav) (Distributor in Western Countries: John Benjamins B.V., Amsteldijk 44, Amsterdam (Z.), Netherlands)
- Stavebnicky Casopis. m. ISSN 0039-078X (Slovenska Akademia Vied. Ustav Stavebnictva a Architektury) (Subscr. to: Slovart, Gottwaldovo nam. 48, 805 32 Bratislava)
- Strojnicky Casopis/Mechanical Periodic. bi-m. ISSN 0039-2472 (Slovenska Akademia Vied. Ustav Mechaniky Strojov) (Co-sponsor: Ceskoslovenska Akademie Ved) (Subscr. to: Slovart, Gottwaldovo nam. 48, 805 32 Bratislava)
- Studia Psychologica; journal for basic research in psychological sciences. q. ISSN 0039-3320 (Slovenska Akademia Vied) (Distributor in Western countries: John Benjamins B.V., Amsteldijk 44, Amsterdam (Z.), Netherlands)
- Vodohospodarsky Casopis; journal for hydrology and hydromechanics. bi-m. ISSN 0042-790X (Slovenska Akademia Vied) (Co-sponsor: Ceskoslovenska Akademie Ved) (Subscr. to: Slovart, Gottwaldovo nam. 48, 805 32 Bratislava)
- Zivotne Prostredie. 6 per yr. ISSN 0044-4863 (Slovenska Akademia Vied) (Distributor in Western countries: John Benjamins B.V., Amsteldijk 44, Amsterdam (Z.), Netherlands)

**Vinohrad**
Suvorovova 16, Bratislava, Czechoslovakia
- Vinohrad. m. ISSN 0042-6326

**Vojensky Historicky Ustav**
Hradcanske nam. 2, Prague 1, Czechoslovakia
(Subscr. to: Artia, Ve Smeckach 30, 111 27 Prague 1)
- Historie a Vojenstvi. bi-m. ISSN 0018-2583

**Vychodoslovenske Muzeum**
- Historica Carpatica. (pub. by Vychodoslovenske Vydavatelstvo)

**Vychodoslovenske Vydavatelstvo**
Garbanova 11, 040 01 Kosice, Czechoslovakia.
- Historica Carpatica. irreg., vol. 6, 1975. ISSN 0441-8026 (Vychodoslovenske Muzeum)

**Vyskumny Ustav Chemickych Vlaken**
Svit, Okr. Poprad, Czechoslovakia.
- Chemicke Vlakna. bi-m. ISSN 0528-9432

**Vyskumny Ustav Ekonomiky a Organizacie Stavebnictva**
- Ekonomika Stavebnictva/Economics of Civil Engineering. (pub. by Alfa)

**Vyskumny Ustav Inzinierskych Stavieb**
Bratislava, Bratislava, Czechoslovakia.
- European Civil Engineering/Europaeische Ingenieurbau. bi-m. ISSN 0014-2883

**Vyskumny Ustav Papiera a Celulozy**
- Papir a Celuloza. (pub. by Statni Nakladatelstvi Technicke Literatury)

**Vysoka Skola Banska**
- Vysoka Skola Banska. Sbornik Vedeckych Praci: Rada Hutnicka/Institute of Mining and Metallurgy. Transactions: Metallurgical Series. (pub. by Statni Pedagogicke Nakladatelstvi)
- Vysoka Skola Banska. Sbornik Vedeckych Praci: Rada Strojni. (pub. by Statni Pedagogicke Nakladatelstvi)

**Vysoka Skola Veterinarni, Brno**
- Acta Veterinaria. (pub. by Statni Pedagogicke Nakladatelstvi)

**Vysoka Skola Veterinarska v Kosiciach**
- Folia Veterinaria. (pub. by Veda, Publishing House of the Slovak Academy of Sciences)

**Vysoka Skola Zemedelska**
Zemedelska 1, 662 65 Brno, Czechoslovakia.
- Acta Universitatis Agriculturae. Ser. Facultas Agroeconomica. q.
- Acta Universitatis Agriculturae. Ser. Facultas Agronomica. q.
- Acta Universitatis Agriculturae. Ser. Facultas Silviculturae. q.
- Vysoka Skola Zemedelska. Library and Documentation Bulletin. q.

**Vyzkumny a Zkusebni Letecky Ustav**
Beranovych 130, 199 05 Prague 9 - Letnany, Czechoslovakia.
- A R T I Reports. (Aeronautical Research and Test Institute) 4-6 per yr.
- Prehledy Leteckotechnicke Literatury/Abstracts from Aeronautical Literature. m. ISSN 0032-7360
- Zpravodaj VZLU. bi-m. ISSN 0044-5355

**Vyzkumny Ustav Agrochemicke Technologie**
- Agrochemia/Agricultural Chemicals. (pub. by Alfa)

**Vyzkumny Ustav Automacnich Prostredku**
Ul. 1. pluku 12a, Prague 8, Czechoslovakia (Subscr. to: Artia, Ve Smeckach 30, 111 27 Prague 1)
- Mereni a Regulace/Measurement and Control. bi-m. ISSN 0539-3973

**Vyzkumny Ustav Balneologicky**
- Balneologia Bohemica. (pub. by Avicenum, State Health Publishing House)

**Vyzkumny Ustav Energeticky**
Partyzanska 7A, Prague 7, Czechoslovakia.
- E G U Bulletin. bi-m. ISSN 0007-4594

**Vyzkumny Ustav Prumyslu Cukrovarnickeho**
- Listy Cukrovarnicke/Sugar Journal. (pub. by Statni Nakladatelstvi Technicke Literatury)

**Vyzkumny Ustav Rybarsky a Hydrobiologicky**
Vodnany, Czechoslovakia.
- Vyzkumny Ustav Rybarsky a Hydrobiologicky. Bulletin. q. ISSN 0007-389X

**Vyzkumny Ustav Spoju**
- Vyzkumny Ustav Spoju. Sbornik Praci. (pub. by Nakladatelstvi Dopravy a Spoju)

**Vyzkumny Ustav Technicko-Ekonomicky Chemickeho Prumyslu**
- Chemicky Prumysl/Chemical Industry. (pub. by Statni Nakladatelstvi Technicke Literatury)

**Vyzkumny Ustav Vystavby a Architektury**
Letenska 3, 118 45 Prague 1, Czechoslovakia.
- Building Abstracts Service C I B. 2-4 per yr. ISSN 0007-3326
- Vystavba a Architektura. 20 per yr. ISSN 0042-9376

**World Federation of Teachers' Unions**
Opletalova 57, 115 70 Prague 1, Czechoslovakia.
- International Teachers News. 8 per yr. ISSN 0020-8884
- Teachers of the World; international pedagogical and trade union review. q. ISSN 0492-4134

**World Federation of Trade Unions**
Nam. Curieovych 1, 116 88 Prague 1, Czechoslovakia.
- Flashes from the Trade Unions. w.
- World Federation of Trade Unions. Session of the General Council. a. ISSN 0512-2910
- World Trade Union Congress. Reports. quadrennial since 1961; 8th, 1973, Varna. ISSN 0084-2370

**Zdravotnicke Noviny**
Sokolska 54, Prague 2, Czechoslovakia
- Zdravotnicke Noviny; tydenik pracovniku ve zdravotnictvi. w. ISSN 0044-1996

**Zemedelska Skola**
Na prikope 12, Prague 1, Czechoslovakia
- Zemedelska Skola. 10 per yr. ISSN 0044-3875

**Zoologicka Zahrada v Praze**
Troja 120, 170 00 Prague 7, Czechoslovakia.
- Zoologicka Zahrada v Praze. Vyrocni Zprava/ Annual Report. a.

**Zvaz Slovenskych Architektov**
- Projekt. (pub. by A-Press)

**Zvaz Slovenskych Spisovatelov**
- Slovenske Pohlady na Literaturu a Umenie. (pub. by Slovensky Spisovatel)

# DENMARK

**Aarhus Frimaerkehandel**
Bruunsgade 42, 8000 Aarhus C, Denmark.
- A F A Oesteuropa Frimaerkekatalog. irreg.
- A F A Vesteuropa Frimaerkekatalog. irreg.
- Populaer Filateli. m. ISSN 0032-4418

**Aarhus Universitet. Botanical Institute**
DK-8240 Risskov, Denmark.
- Lindbergia. irreg. (Nordic Bryological Society) (Co-Sponsor: Dutch Bryological Society)

**Aarhus Universitet. Institut for Jysk Sprog- og Kulturforskning**
Aarhus, Denmark.
- Sprog og Kultur. irreg. ISSN 0038-8645

**Aarhus Universitet. Matematisk Institut**
Ny Munkegade, 8000 Aarhus C, Denmark.
- Aarhus Universitet. Matematisk Insitut. Lecture Notes Series. irreg., no. 47, 1976. ISSN 0065-017X
- Aarhus Universitet. Matematisk Institut. Memoirs. irreg.
- Aarhus Universitet. Matematisk Institut. Various Publications Series. irreg., no. 26, 1977. ISSN 0065-0188
- Mathematica Scandinavica. 4 per yr.(in 2 vols.) ISSN 0025-5521

**Akademiet for de Tekniske Videnskaber**
Lundtoftevej 266, 2800 Lyngby, Denmark.
- Akademiet for de Videnskaber. Handbog. irreg.

**Akademisk Forlag**
8 St. Kannikestraede, DK 1169 Copenhagen, Denmark.
- Danmarks Folkeminder. irreg. ISSN 0070-2765
- Folk og Kultur. a. (Danmarks Fulkeminder)
- Kopenhagener Beitrage zur Germanistischen Linguistik. irreg. ISSN 0105-0257 (Koebenhavns Universitet)
- Nordisk Psykologi. 4-6 per yr. ISSN 0029-1463

- Revue Romane. s-a. ISSN 0035-3906 (Koebenhavns Universitet. Institut d'Etudes Romanes)

**Forlaget Aktuel Viden A-S**
Flaarupved 18, 4960 Holeby, Denmark.
- Aktuel Grafisk Information. m (11 per yr)

**Aldrig Mere Krig**
Thorsgade 79, 2200 Copenhagen N, Denmark.
- Ikkevold; tidsskrift for antimilitarisme og fredsarbejde. m (10 per yr.) ISSN 0046-8584 (Co-sponsor: Forsoningsforbundet)

**Aller Press A-S**
Vigerslev Alle 18, 2500 Copenhagen Valby, Denmark.
- Familie Journalen. w. ISSN 0014-7133
- Femina. ISSN 0014-9853
- Se og Hoer. fortn.
- Ude og Hjemme. w. ISSN 0041-5669

**Almindelige Danske Laegeforening**
Kristianiagade 12 A, 2100 Copenhagen, Denmark
- Bibliotek for Laeger. irreg. (4-6 per yr.) ISSN 0006-1786 (Subscr. to: Munksgaard, 35 Noerre Soegade, DK-1370 Copenhagen, Denmark)
- Danish Medical Bulletin. 8 per yr. ISSN 0011-6092
- Ugeskrift for Laeger. w. ISSN 0041-5782

**Aluminiumraadet**
Park Alle 345, 2600 Glostrup, Denmark.
- Aluminium. q.

**Amtsraadsforningen i Danmark**
- Danmarks Amstraad. (pub. by Teknisk Forlag A-S)

**Amtsvejinspektoerforeningen i Danmark**
- Dansk Vejtidsskrift. (pub. by Teknisk Forlag A-S)

**Andelsbogtrykkeriet**
Hestehaven 3, 5260 Odense S, Denmark.
- Hojskolebladet. w. ISSN 0018-3334

**Andelsudvalget**
Vester Farimagsgade 3, 1606 Copenhagen V, Denmark.
- Andelsbladet. fortn. ISSN 0003-2913

**Arbejdsgiversammenslutningen Dansk Snedker- og Toemrerhaandverk, Moebel og Bygningsindustri**
Slotsgade 5, 5000 Odense, Denmark.
- Snedker- og Toemrermestrene. 8 per yr.

**Arena Forfatternes Forlag**
Hald Hovedgaard, 8800 Viborg, Denmark.
- Mal & Maele. q.

**Arkitektens Forlag**
Nyhavn 43, DK-1051 Copenhagen K, Denmark.
- Arkitekten. 23 per yr. ISSN 0004-198X (Federation of Danish Architects)
- Arkitektur DK. 8 per yr.
- Byplan. 6 per yr. ISSN 0007-7658
- Landskap. 8 per yr. ISSN 0023-8066 (Association of Danish Landscape Architects)

**Arktisk Institut**
- Acta Arctica. (pub. by C. A. Reitzels Forlag)

**Arnamagnaean Institute**
Njalsgade 76, DK-2300 Copenhagen S, Denmark.
- Arnamagnaean Institute. Bulletin. irreg. ISSN 0066-7765
- Bibliotheca Arnamagnaeana; consilio et auctoritate legati Arnamagnaeani. irreg. ISSN 0067-7841 (Dist. by: C. A. Reitzels Boghandel A-S, Noerregade 20, DK-1165 Copenhagen K, Denmark)
- Bibliotheca Arnamagnaeana. Supplementum. irreg. ISSN 0067-785X (Dist. by: C. A. Reitzels Boghandel A-S, Noerregade 20, DK-1165 Copenhagen K, Denmark)
- Early Icelandic Manuscripts in Facsimile. (pub. by Rosenkilde og Bagger Forlag)
- Editiones Arnamagnaeanae. Series A. irreg. ISSN 0070-9069 (Dist. by: C. A. Reitzels Boghandel A-S, Noerregade 20, DK-1165 Copenhagen K, Denmark)
- Editiones Arnamagnaeanae. Series B. irreg. ISSN 0070-9077 (Dist. by: C. A. Reitzels Boghandel A-S, Noerregade 20, DK-1165 Copenhagen K, Denmark)

- Editiones Arnamagnaeanae. Supplementum. irreg. ISSN 0070-9085 (Dist. by: C. A. Reitzels Boghandel A-S, Noerregade 20, DK-1165 Copenhagen K, Denmark)

**Artilleriofficersforeningen**
Postbox 1, DK-6800 Varde, Denmark.
- Dansk Artilleri-Tidsskrift. 6 per yr. ISSN 0011-6203

**Asfaltindustriens Oplysningskontor for Vejbygning**
Stamholmen 91, 2650 Hvidovre, Denmark.
- Asfalt. q. ISSN 0004-4318

**Asons Forlaget ApS**
Slagelsesgade 1, 2100 Copenhagen, Denmark.
- Kantinen. m. ISSN 0022-8885 (Kantineledernes Landsklub)

**Association of Danish Landscape Architects**
- Landskap. (pub. by Arkitektens Forlag)

**Association of Scandinavian Slavicists and Baltologists**
- Scando-Slavica. (pub. by Munksgaard)
- Scando-Slavica. Supplementum. (pub. by Munksgaard)

**Astrologisk Akademi**
Postbox 932, 2400 Copenhagen NV, Denmark.
- Occulta; den skjulte verden. m.

**Astronomisk Selskab**
Copenhagen University, Oester Voldgade 3, 1350 Copenhagen K, Denmark.
- Astronomisk Tidsskrift. 4 per yr. ISSN 0004-6345

**Athene A-S**
Roedovrevej 224, DK-2610 Roedovre, Denmark.
- Fiskehandleren. m. ISSN 0015-3109 (Fiskehandlerforeningen for Koebenhavn og Omegn)

**Forlaget Audio A-S**
St. Kongensgade 72, DK-1264 Copenhagen K, Denmark.
- Hi Fi Aarbogen. a. ISSN 0441-5833
- High Fidelity. m.

**Auto- Tilbehoers Grossist- Forening**
- AUTIG. (pub. by Harlang og Toksvig Bladforlag A-S)

**Automobil-Importoerernes Sammenslutning**
Ryvangs Alle 68, 2900 Hellerup, Denmark.
- Bilismen i Danmark. a.
- Statistik over Registrering af Nye Automobile i Danmark. m.
- Vejtransporten i Tal og Tekst. a. ISSN 0083-5358

**Avistidsskrifterne A-S**
Gartnervaenget 79, 3520 Farum, Denmark.
- Foto-Avisen. m. ISSN 0046-4775

**Joergen Beck, Ed. & Pub.**
Hoejdevangs Alle 30, 2300 Copenhagen, Denmark.
- Aftenskolelaereren. m. ISSN 0002-0680

**Bedste fra Reader's Digest ApS**
61 Oestergade, DK-1010 Copenhagen, Denmark.
- Bedste fra Reader's Digest (Danish Edition) m. ISSN 0005-7681

**Forlaget Beilin og Johansen ApS**
Rosenborggade 1, DK-1130 Copenhagen K, Denmark.
- Dansk Teknisk Tidsskrift/Danish Technical Magazine. m (10 per yr) ISSN 0011-6505
- Levnedsmiddelbladet-Supermarkedet/Foodstuff Magazine-The Supermarket; skandinavisk tidsskrift for fabrikation og handel med levnedsmidler. m (11 per yr.)
- Nordisk Tidsskrift for Rensning og Vask/ Scandinavian Magazine for Cleaning and Washing. m (10 per yr.) ISSN 0029-1536 (Norsk Renseriforbund) (Co-sponsor: Norske Vaskeriers Forening; Industri-Vaskeriernes Forbund)

**Sigurd Troels Berg**
Skippervaeget 5-A, DK-2791 Dragoer, Denmark.
- Nordisk Tidsskrift for Specialpaedagogik. q. ISSN 0048-0509 (Nordisk Forbund for Special Paedagogik)

**Berlingske Forlag**
Pilestraede 52, DK-1147 Copenhagen K, Denmark.
- Billed Bladet. w. ISSN 0006-2537

- Populaer Radio; Maanedsbladet for populaer elektronik og high fidelity. m.
- Soendags-B. T. w. ISSN 0038-0512

**Bibliotekarforbundet**
Hyskenstraede 2, 1207 Copenhagen K, Denmark.
- Bibliotek 70. 22 per yr. ISSN 0006-1824

**Bibliotekscentralen**
Telegrafvej 5, 2750 Ballerup, Denmark.
- Avis-Kronik-Index. m. ISSN 0005-2280
- Scandinavian Public Library Quarterly. q. ISSN 0036-5602

**Bit**
Kronprinsensgade 14, DK-1114 Copenhagen K, Denmark.
- Bit; nordisk tidskrift for informationsbehandling. q. ISSN 0006-3835

**Boerne- og Ungdomspaedagogernes Landsorganisation**
Skt. Hans Torv 26, 2200 Copenhagen N, Denmark.
- Boern & Unge. w. ISSN 0006-5633

**Forlaget Boersen A-S**
Vognmagergade 2, Box 2103, 1120 Copenhagen K, Denmark.
- Danshore. bi-m.

**Boligselskabernes Landsforening**
Lindevangs Alle 6, 2000 Copenhagen F, Denmark.
- Beboerbladet Boligen. q.
- Boligen. m (10 per yr)

**Borgens Forlag**
Mynstersvej 19, DK 1827 Copenhagen V, Denmark.
- Hvedekorn. 4 per yr. ISSN 0018-8093

**Bruel og Kjaer Industri A-S**
Naerum, Denmark.
- Bruel & Kjaer Technical Review. q. ISSN 0007-2621

**Bygge Fagene**
Torvevangsvej 74, 3460 Birkeroed, Denmark.
- Bygge Fagene. ISSN 0007-747X

**Forlaget Cahier**
Postboks 81, 3050 Humlebaek, Denmark.
- Huset Ude og Inde. m (11 per yr.)

**Carlsberg Foundation. Marinbiogisk Laboratorium Charlottenlund**
H. C. Andersens Boulevard 35, DK-1553 Copenhagen, Denmark.
- Dana-Report. irreg.; 1973, no. 83. ISSN 0070-2668

**Carlsberg Laboratorium**
- Carlsberg Research Communications. (pub. by Springer-Verlag US)

**Centralforeningen af Benzinforhandlere i Danmark**
24 Nordkrog, 2900 Hellerup, Denmark.
- Benzin & Olie Bladet. m. (except Jul.) ISSN 0005-8858

**Centralforeningen af Hotelvaerter og Restauratoerer i Danmark**
Vodroffsvej 46, 1900 Copenhagen V, Denmark.
- Hotel & Restaurant. fortn. ISSN 0018-6201

**Centralforeningen af Murermestre i Danmark**
Tyrrestrupvej 6, Hoejbjerg, Denmark.
- Murermesteren. ISSN 0027-3651

**Centralforeningen af Tolvmandsforeninger og Stoerre Landbrugere i Danmark**
Axelborg, DK-1611 Copenhagen V, Denmark.
- Tolvmandsbladet. m. ISSN 0040-9111

**Centralforeningen for Stampersonel**
Farvergade 10, 4, DK-1463 Copenhagen K, Denmark.
- Stampersonel. m.

**Centralinstitut for Nordisk Asienforskning**
*see* **Scandinavian Institute of Asia Studies**

**Chauffoerernes Forbund i Danmark**
Buelowsvej 48, 1870 Copenhagen V, Denmark.
- Chauffoeren. m.

**Communist Party of Denmark**
Dronningens Tvaergade 3, DK-1260 Copenhagen K, Denmark.
- Tiden; verden rundt. 12 per yr. ISSN 0040-6740

**Conseil International pour l'Exploration de la Mer**
*see* **International Council for the Exploration of the Sea**

**Copenhagen. Statistical Office**
Nyropsgade 7, Copenhagen V, Denmark
- Kobenhavns Statistiske Aarbog; statistisk arbog for Kobenhavn, Frederiksberg og Gentofte samt omegnskommumerne. a. (Subscr. to: DBK, Siljangade 6-8, 2300 Copenhagen S, Denmark)

**Copenhagen Handelsbank**
Holmens Kanal 2, DK-1091 Copenhagen, Denmark.
- Copenhagen Handelsbank. Annual Report. a.
- Denmark Quarterly Review. q. ISSN 0011-8427
- Setting up in Denmark; a survey of economic, legal and financial aspects of foreign investment in Denmark. biennial.

**D I S A Elektronik A-S**
Mileparken 22, DK-2740 Skovlunde, Denmark.
- D I S A Information. Measurement and Analysis. irreg. ISSN 0070-6639

**DAGROFA**
Mileparken 28, 2730 Herlev, Denmark.
- Impuls. 20 per yr. ISSN 0019-3097

**William Dams Bookshop**
3700 Roenne, Bornholm, Denmark.
- Bornholmske Samlinger. irreg. ISSN 0084-7976

**Danatom**
Tingvej 7, DK-4690 Haslev, Denmark.
- Kort Nyt Om Atomenergi/Short News on Atomic Energy. m.

**Danfoss A-S**
DK-6430 Nordborg, Denmark.
- Danfoss Journal; automatic controls design and practice. q. ISSN 0011-6076

**Danish Camping Union**
Gammel Kongevej 74, DK-1850 Copenhagen, Denmark.
- Camping. m. ISSN 0045-4125

**Danish Cement Works**
Technical Information Office, Roerdalsvej 165, DK-9100 Aalborg, Denmark.
- Beton-Litteratur Referater. q. ISSN 0409-2694

**Danish Colonial Grocers**
*see* **DAGROFA**

**Danish Farmers' Union**
Vester Farimagsgade 6, 1606 Copenhagen V, Denmark.
- Landsbladet. w.

**Danish General Aviation A-S**
Copenhagen Airport, DK-4000 Roskilde, Denmark.
- Flyv. m. ISSN 0015-492X (Kongelig Dansk Aeroklub)

**Danish International Development Agency**
*see* **Denmark. Danida**

**Danish Medical Association**
*see* **Almindelige Danske Laegeforening**

**Danish National Institute of Building Research**
20 Borgergade, Copenhagen, Denmark.
- Scandinavian Building Research. biennial. ISSN 0581-9423 (Scandinavian Building Research Congress)

**Danish Ophthalmological Society**
Rigshospitalet, Eye Department, Blegdamsvej 9, DK-2100 Copenhagen, Denmark.
- Danish Ophthalmological Society. Transactions. a.

**Danish Producers of Compressed Gasses**
- Svejsetidende. (pub. by Teknisk Forlag A-S)

**Danish Public Health Authorities**
Oesterbrogade 115 A, 2100 Copenhagen OE, Denmark.
- Helse; familiens laegeblad. bi-m. ISSN 0018-0149

**Danish Technical Press**
*see* **Teknisk Forlag A-S**

**Danish Union of Dental Laboratories**
- Dental Laboratorie Bladet. (pub. by Petersen Public Relations)

**Danish United Nations Association**
Kronprinsensgade 9, 1114 Copenhagen K, Denmark.
- F. N. Orientering. 8 per yr. ISSN 0014-5998 (Co-Sponsor: Ministry of Foreign Affairs)

**Danmarks Apotekerforening**
Hammerichsgade 14, 1611 Copenhagen V, Denmark.
- Archiv for Pharmaci og Chemi. fortn. ISSN 0003-8938
- Archiv for Pharmaci og Chemi. Scientific Edition. bi-m. ISSN 0302-248X

**Danmarks Biblioteksforening**
Trekronergade 15, DK-2500 Copenhagen V, Denmark.
- Biblioteksaarbog. a. ISSN 0084-957X
- Bogens Verden; tidsskrift for dansk biblioteksvaesen. 10 per yr. ISSN 0006-5692
- Danmarks Biblioteksforening. Biblioteksvejviser/ Guide of Danish Libraries. a.

**Danmarks Biblioteksskole**
Birketinget 6, 2300 Copenhagen S, Denmark.
- Biblioten. m.
- Danmarks Biblioteksskole. Skrifter. a. ISSN 0069-9861
- Danmarks Bilioteksskole. Studier. irreg. (8-10 per yr.)

**Danmarks Bridgeforbund**
Korsgade 62, 2200 Copenhagen N, Denmark
(Suscr. to: Baunebjergvej 448, DK-3050 Humlebaek, Denmark)
- Dansk Bridge. m. ISSN 0011-6238

**Danmarks Cafeteriaforening**
Vesterbrogade 18, Copenhagen, Denmark.
- Cafeteria Bladet. m.

**Danmarks Fulkeminder**
- Folk og Kultur. (pub. by Akademisk Forlag)

**Danmarks Institut for International Udveksling**
*see* **Denmark. I.D.E., Danmarks Institut for International Udveksling**

**Danmarks Isenkraemmerforening**
Naverland 34, DK-2600 Glostrup, Denmark.
- Forbrugsgoder. fortn. (18 per yr.)

**Danmarks Jordbrugsvidenskabelige Kandidatforbund**
Gammeltorv 22, Box 2172, DK-1017 Copenhagen K, Denmark.
- Ugeskrift for Agronomer, Hortonomer Forstkandidater og Licentiater. w. (Co-sponsors: Dansk Agronomforening; Dansk Hortonomforening)

**Danmarks Jurist og Oekonomforbund**
Gothersgade 133, 1123 Copenhagen K, Denmark.
- Juristen og Oekonomen; debat og orientering. s-m.
- Tidsskrift for Groenlands Retsvaesen. q. ISSN 0040-6880

**Danmarks Laererforening**
Kompagnistraede 32, 1208 Copenhagen K, Denmark.
- Folkeskolen. w. ISSN 0015-5837

**Danmarks Nationalbank**
5 Havnegade, 1093 Copenhagen K, Denmark.
- Danmarks Nationalbank. Monetary Review. q. ISSN 0011-6149

**Danmarks Naturfredningsforening**
Frederiksberg Runddel 1, 2000 Copenhagen F, Denmark.
- Natur og Miljoe. q.

**Danmarks Psoriasis Forening**
Albertslund, Denmark.
- Dansk Psoriasis Tidsskrift. q. ISSN 0105-0370

**Danmarks Skohandlerforening**
H. C. Andersens Boulevard 48, 1553 Copenhagen V, Denmark.
- Sko-Magasinet. m. ISSN 0037-6388

**Danmarks Skolebiblioteksforening**
Vejlemosevej 21, 2840 Holte, Denmark.
- Born og Boger. 8 per yr. ISSN 0006-7792

**Danmarks Smedemesterforeninger**
Vestergade 5, DK-4300 Holbaek, Denmark.
- Dansk Smede-Tidende. w. ISSN 0011-6483

**Danmarks Sparekasseforening**
- Sparekassen. (pub. by Harlang og Toksvig Bladforlag A-S)

**Danmarks Sportsfiskerforbund**
Worsaaesgade 1, 1, 7100 Vejle, Denmark.
- Sportsfiskeren. m. ISSN 0038-8211

**Danmarks Textiltekniske Forening**
Fredericiavej 99, DK-7100 Vejle, Denmark.
- Teknisk Tidsskrift for Textil og Beklaedning. 10 per yr. ISSN 0049-3236 (Co-sponsors: Dansk Textilindustrie Mesterforening; Dansk Beklaednings Industri; Lonkonfektionsindustriens Sammenslutning)

**Dansk Amatoer- Musik Union**
Holbaekvej 34, 4571 Grevinge, Denmark.
- Dansk Amatoermusik. bi-m.

**Dansk Arbejdsgiverforening**
113 Vester Voldgade, 1503 Copenhagen V, Denmark.
- Arbejdsgiveren. s-m. ISSN 0003-7818
- Dansk Arbejdsgiverforening. Statistikken. q.

**Dansk Badminton Forbund**
Idraettens Hus, Broendby Station, 2600 Glostrup, Denmark.
- Badminton. 12 per yr. ISSN 0005-3791

**Dansk Bladforlag K-S**
Holbergsgade 20, DK-1057 Copenhagen K, Denmark.
- Brygmesteren. m. ISSN 0007-2737 (Dansk Brygmester Forening) (Co-sponsors: Norsk Bryggerlaug; Sveriges Bryggeritekniker Foerening)
- Legetoejs-Tidende. m (11 per yr.)
- Scandinavian Refrigeration. bi-m. ISSN 0048-9301 (Koeletekniske Foreninger i Skandinavien)
- Skandinavisk Tidskrift for Faerg och Lack. m. ISSN 0037-6094 (Federation of Scandinavian Paint and Varnish Technicians)
- Skandinavisk Tidskrift for Faerg och Lack. Aarsbok. a. ISSN 0085-6126 (Federation of Scandinavian Paint and Varnish Technicians)
- Tidsskrift for Danske Sygehuse. 10 per yr. ISSN 0040-702X (Foreningen af Sygehusadministratorer i Danmark)

**Dansk Blomsterhandlerforening**
Floras Alle 19, 2720 Vanloese, Denmark.
- Blomster; Nordisk tidsskrift for binderi og blomster. m. ISSN 0006-4955

**Dansk Bogforlag**
Box 770, Boerstenbindervej 4, 5230 Odense M, Denmark.
- Sundhedsbladet. 6 per yr. ISSN 0039-5366 (Nordisk Filantropisk Selskab)

**Dansk Botanisk Forening**
Gothersgade 130, DK-1123 Copenhagen K, Denmark.
- Botanisk Tidsskrift. q. ISSN 0006-8187
- Dansk Botanisk Arkiv. irreg. ISSN 0011-6211

**Dansk Brandinspektrforening**
Nygaards Plads 9, DK-2610 Roedovre, Denmark.
- Brandvaern. m. (Co-sponsor: Dansk Brandvaerns-Komite)

**Dansk Brygmester Forening**
- Brygmesteren. (pub. by Dansk Bladforlag K-S)

**Dansk Cubansk Forening**
Gothersgade 8 B, 1, 1123 Copenhagen K, Denmark.
- Cuba-Bladet. q.

**Dansk Ejendomsmaeglerforening**
Stormgade 16, 1470 Copenhagen K, Denmark.
- Ejendomsmaegleren. m. ISSN 0013-2896

**Dansk Erhvervsfrugtavl**
Vindegade 72, 5000 Odense, Denmark.
- Frugtavleren. m.

**Dansk Erhvervsgartnerforening**
Anker Heegaards Gade 2, Postbox 3073, 1508 Copenhagen V, Denmark.
- Gartner Tidende. w.

**Dansk Etnografisk Forening**
Nationalmuseet, DK-1471 Copenhagen K, Denmark.
- Folk; Dansk Etnografisk Tidsskrift. a. ISSN 0085-0756

**Dansk Exlibris Selskab**
Postbox 1519, DK 2700 Copenhagen, Denmark.
- Exlibris-Nyt. 4 per yr. ISSN 0014-4681
- Nordisk Exlibris Tidsskrift. 4 per yr. ISSN 0029-1323

**Dansk Fagpresseforening**
Borgergade 32, Copenhagen K, Denmark.
- Dansk Fagpresse. 4 per yr.

**Dansk Farmaceutforening**
Stormgade 20, DK-1555 Copenhagen V, Denmark.
- Farmaceutisk Tidende. w. ISSN 0014-8199

**Dansk Farmacihistorisk Selskab**
Farmacilaboratorium, Universistetsparken 2, DK-2100 Copenhagen, Denmark.
- Theriaca; samlinger til farmaciens og medicinens historie. irreg., no. 17, 1974. ISSN 0082-4003

**Dansk Fiskeriforening**
Studiestraede 3, 2, 1455 Copenhagen K, Denmark.
- Dansk Fiskeritidende. w ISSN 0011-6270 (Co-sponsor: Danmarks Havfiskeriforening)

**Dansk Forsikrings Tidende-Assurandoeren**
10 Amaliegade, DK-1256 Copenhagen K, Denmark.
- Tidskriftet "Forsikring". fortn.

**Dansk Fotografisk Forening**
Valdemarsgade 19, DK-1665 Copenhagen V, Denmark.
- Dansk Fotografisk Tidsskrift. 6 per yr.

**Dansk Frisioerforbund**
Lersoe Parkalle 21, DK-2100 Copenhagen OE, Denmark.
- Spejlet. m. ISSN 0038-7266

**Dansk Geologisk Forening**
Oester Voldgade 5-7, 1350 Copenhagen K, Denmark.
- Dansk Geologisk Forening. Arsskrift. a.
- Geological Society of Denmark. Bulletin/Dansk Geologisk Forening. Bulletin. (pub. by C.A. Reitzels Forlag)

**Dansk Golf Union**
- Golf. (pub. by Forlaget Sabroe A-S)

**Dansk Historisk Faellesforening**
Postbox 213, DK-4000 Roskilde, Denmark.
- Dansk Historisk Aarsbibliografi. a. (Co-sponsor: Kongelige Bibliotek)
- Fortid og Notid. s-a.

**Dansk Ingenioer Forening**
- Ingenioeren. (pub. by Teknisk Forlag A-S)
- Management/Virksomhedsstyring. (pub. by Teknisk Forlag A-S)

**Dansk Institutions Tidsskrift**
Brandmosevej 57, DK-2750 Ballerup, Denmark.
- Dansk Institutions Tidsskrift/Journal for Danish Institutions. m. ISSN 0011-6319

**Dansk Interlingua Union**
c/o Information Interlingua, Juvelvej 25, DK-5210 Odense NV, Denmark.
- Actualitates. q.

**Dansk Israelsk Selskab**
Ny Kongensgade 6, 1472 Copenhagen K, Denmark.
- Israel. q. ISSN 0021-194X (Co-sponsor: Dansk Zionistforbund; DAKIV)

**Dansk Jagtforening**
Bredgade 47, 1260 Copenhagen K, Denmark.
- Dansk Jagt. m. ISSN 0011-6327

**Dansk Jernbane-Klub**
Holmevej 8, 4340 Toelloese, Denmark.
- Jernbanen. bi-m.

**Dansk Konfektureforening**
Hambros Alle 3, 2900 Hellerup, Denmark.
- Konfekturehandleren. m. ISSN 0047-3553

**Dansk Kulturhistorisk Museumsforening**
Postbox 26, DK-4000 Roskilde, Denmark.
- Dansk Kulturhistorisk Museumsforening. Museumsregister. a.

**Dansk Maskinhandlerforening**
Aboulevard 48, 2200 Copenhagen V, Denmark.
- Dansk Maskinhandlerforening. Handbog. irreg.

**Dansk Mejeristforening**
Hestehaven 3, Hjallese, Denmark.
- Maelkeritidende. w. ISSN 0024-9645

**Dansk Metalarbejderforbund**
Nyropsgade 38, 1602 Copenhagen V, Denmark
(Subscr. to: Vester Soegade 12,4, DK-1601 Copenhagen V, Denmark)
- Metal. fortn. ISSN 0026-0517

**Dansk Missionraad**
Vendersgade 28, DK-1363 Copenhagen K, Denmark.
- Mission; Nordisk missions tidsskrift. q.

**Dansk Moellerforening**
Moellegade 3, Herning, Denmark.
- Moellen. m. ISSN 0026-8852

**Dansk Musiker Forbund**
Vendersgade 25, 1363 Copenhagen K, Denmark.
- Dansk Musiker Tidende. m (11 per yr)

**Dansk Musikhandlerforening**
Enghavevej 70, 1674 Copenhagen 5, Denmark.
- Musik og Handel. m. ISSN 0027-4739

**Dansk Orienterings Forbund**
Brondby-Station 20, DK-2600 Glostrup, Denmark.
- O-Posten. bi-m.

**Dansk Ornithologisk Forening**
Faelledvej 9, DK-2200 Copenhagen N, Denmark.
- Dansk Ornithologisk Forenings Tidsskrift. 2-4 per yr. ISSN 0011-6394
- Feltornithologen. q. ISSN 0046-3647

**Dansk Paedagogisk Tidsskrift**
Noerrebred 196, Vallensbaek, DK-2620 Albertslund, Denmark.
- Dansk Paedagogisk Tidsskrift/Danish Journal of Education. 9 per yr. ISSN 0011-6408

**Dansk Pelsdyravlerforening**
Langagervej 60, DK-2600 Glostrup, Denmark.
- Dansk Pelsdyravl. m. ISSN 0011-6424

**Dansk Politiforbund**
N.J. Fjords Alle 8, 1957 Copenhagen V, Denmark.
- Tidsskrift for Dansk Politi. 18 per yr. (Co-sponsors: Dansk Kriminalpolitiforening; Rigspolitichefen; Foreningen af Politimestre i Danmark)

**Dansk Ponyavlsforbund**
- Hippologisk Tidsskrift. (pub. by Landsbladet)

**Dansk Provins Bogtrykkerforening**
Bogtrykkernes Hus, Helgavej 26, 5230 Odense M, Denmark.
- Bogtrykkerbladet. m. ISSN 0006-5730

**Dansk Psykologforening**
Skt. Peders Stradede 34-36, DK-1453 Copenhagen K, Denmark.
- Dansk Psykolognyt. s-m. ISSN 0011-6432

**Dansk Samvirke**
Kristianiagade 8, DK-2100 Copenhagen OE, Denmark.
- Danmarksposten; a magazine for Danes abroad. bi-m. ISSN 0011-6157

**Dansk Selskab for Bygningsstatik**
Bygning 118, Lundtoftevej 100, 2800 Lyngby, Denmark.
- Bygningsstatiske Meddelelser. irreg.(approx. 4 per yr.)

**Dansk Selskab for Oldtids og Middelalderforskning**
- Classica et Mediaevalia. (pub. by Gyldendalske Boghandel-Nordisk Forlag A-S)

**Dansk-Skaansk Forening**
Strandboulevard 35, Box 827, 2100 Copenhagen, Denmark.
- Sundet Rundt. bi-m. ISSN 0049-2531

**Dansk Skak Union**
Postboks 8, DK-4180 Soroe, Denmark.
- Dansk Skak Union. Presse-Service. fortn.
- Skakbladet. 10 per yr. ISSN 0037-6043

**Dansk Skovforening**
Vester Voldgade 86, Copenhagen, Denmark.
- Dansk Skovforenings Tidsskrift. q. ISSN 0011-6475
- Skoven. m.

**Dansk Socialraadgiverforening**
Noerrebrogade 12, 4, DK-2200 Copenhagen N,
Denmark.
- Socialraadgiveren. s-m.

**Dansk Standardiseringsraad**
Box 77, DK-2900 Hellerup, Denmark.
- Standard Nyt. bi-m.

**Dansk Stenografisk Forening**
Sjaellandsgade 24, 8900 Randers, Denmark
- Stenografisk Tidsskrift. 8 per yr. ISSN 0039-1166
  (Subscr. to: Bent Kelstrup, 7321 Gadbjerg,
  Denmark)

**Dansk Strandjagtforening**
Skoleparken 77, 7500 Holstebro, Denmark.
- Strandjaegeren. m. ISSN 0039-212X (Co-sponsor:
  Danske Strandjaegeres Motorbaadsunion)

**Dansk Sygeplejeraad**
Vimmelskaftet 38, Postbox 1084, DK-1008
Copenhagen K, Denmark.
- Sygeplejersken. w. ISSN 0049-3856

**Dansk Tandlaegeforening**
Oslo Plads 14, Copenhagen OE, Denmark.
- Tandlaegebladet/Danish Dental Journal. 22 per
  yr. ISSN 0039-9353

**Dansk Taxi Forbund**
Taebyvej 15-17, 2610 Roedovre, Denmark.
- Dansk Taxi Tidende. m.

**Dansk Tennis Forbund**
Broenby Stadion 20, 2600 Glostrup, Denmark.
- Tennis. bi-m.

**Dansk Toldtjenestemands Forbund**
Tjenestemaendenes Hus, Bredgade 21, DK-1260
Copenhagen K, Denmark.
- Toldbladet. m. ISSN 0040-9049

**Dansk Ungdom Faellesraad**
Raadmandsgade 55, DK-2200 Copenhagen,
Denmark.
- D U Bladet. m (10 per yr.)

**Dansk Urmager og Optiker Centralforening**
Bornholmsgade 1, DK-1266 Copenhagen K,
Denmark.
- Urmager-Tidende. m. ISSN 0042-1081

**Dansk V V S -Installatoer Forening**
Hoejnaesej 75, 2610 Roedovre, Denmark.
- V V S-Installatoeren. m.

**Dansk Vandteknisk Forening**
Vilh. Becks Vej 60, 8260 Viby J, Denmark.
- Vandteknik. bi-m.

**Dansk Vaskeri Forening**
Noerre Voldgade 22, DK-1358 Copenhagen K,
Denmark.
- Vask-Rens-Rengoering. m. (Co-Sponsor: Dansk
  Renseri Forening)

**Danske Advokatsamfund**
Kronprinsessegade 28, 1306 Copenhagen K,
Denmark.
- Advokatbladet. s-m.

**Danske Bagerstands Faellesorganisation**
c/o Nyhedsbureauet News Express A/S,
Hovedvejen 118, DK-2600 Glostrup, Denmark.
- Bager-Konditor. m. (Co-sponsors: Danmarks
  Konditorforening; Koebenhavns Konditorlaug)

**Danske Boghandler-Medhjaelperforening**
Siljangade 6-8, DK-2300 Copenhagen S, Denmark.
- Bogormen. 4 per yr. ISSN 0006-5706

**Danske Boghandlerforening**
Noerre Soegade 35 A, 1370 Copenhagen K,
Denmark.
- Danske Bogmarked. 8 per yr. ISSN 0011-6556
  (Co-Sponsor: Danske Forlaggerforening)

**Danske Dagblades Udgiverforening**
Pressens Hus, Skindergade 7, 1159 Copenhagen K,
Denmark.
- Dansk Presse. m (11 per yr) (Co-sponsor: Danske
  Dagblades Faellesrepraesentation)

**Danske Dyrlaegeforening**
Alhambravej 15, DK-1826 Copenhagen V,
Denmark.
- Acta Veterinaria Scandinavica. q. ISSN 0044-
  605X (Societatum Veteranariarum
  Scandanivacarum)
- Acta Veterinaria Scandinavica. Supplementum.
  irreg., vol. 18, 1977. ISSN 0065-1699 (Societatum
  Veteranariarum Scandanivacarum)
- Dansk Veterinaertidsskrift/Danish Veterinary
  Journal. s-m.
- Nordisk Veterinaermedicin/Scandinavian Journal
  of Veterinary Science. m. ISSN 0029-1579

**Danske Elvaerkers Forening**
Vodroffs Vej 59, 1900 Copenhagen, Denmark.
- Dansk Elvaerksstatistik. a. ISSN 0070-2803
- Elektroteknikeren. m. ISSN 0013-5879

**Danske Filminstitut**
Store Soendervoldstraede, DK-1419 Copenhagen,
Denmark.
- Danish Films. a. ISSN 0418-3304

**Danske Filmmuseum**
Store Sondervoldstraede, 1419 Copenhagen K,
Denmark.
- Kosmorama. 4 per yr. ISSN 0023-4222
- Nye Boeger Om Film/New Books on Film. s-a.
  ISSN 0048-1238

**Danske Forlaeggerforening**
Sekretariat, Vesterbrogade 41 B, 1620 Copenhagen
V, Denmark.
- Danske Forlaeggerforening. Faelleslagerkatalog. s-
  a. ISSN 0070-282X (Co-sponsor: Danske
  Boghandlerforening)

**Danske Gymnastik- og Ungdomsforeninger**
Brummersvej 10, DK-7100 Vejle, Denmark.
- Dansk Ungdom og Idraet. w. ISSN 0045-9631

**Danske Handelsforenings Faelles-Organisation**
Ehlersvej 9, 2900 Hellerup, Denmark.
- Danmarks Handels Tidende. 8 per yr. ISSN 0045-
  9585

**Danske Hedeselskab**
Viborg, Denmark.
- Hedeselskabets Tidsskrift. 8 per yr. ISSN 0017-
  9507

**Danske Husmandsforeninger**
Vester Farimagsgade 6, 1606 Copenhagen V,
Denmark.
- Landbrugsmagasinet Husmandshjemmet. w.

**Danske Laegestuderendes Landsraad**
Rigshospitalet, Blegdamsvej 13, 2100 Copenhagen
OE, Denmark.
- Stud. Med. 8 per yr. ISSN 0039-2634

**Danske Landinspektoerforening**
- Landinspektoeren. (pub. by Teknisk Forlag A-S)

**Danske Landmandsbank**
12, Holmens Kanal, DK-1092 Copenhagen K,
Denmark.
- Danske Landmandsbank. Annual Report. a. ISSN
  0070-2838

**Danske Missionsselskab**
Strandagervej 24, DK-2900 Hellerup, Denmark.
- Dansk Missionsblad. m. ISSN 0011-6378

**Danske Praesteforening**
Rosenvaengets Hovedvej 19, 2100 Copenhagen,
Denmark.
- Praesteforeningens Blad. w (50 per yr.)

**Danske Radioamatorer**
Postbox 79, 1003 Copenhagen K, Denmark.
- O Z; tidsskrift for amator radio. m.

**Danske Realskoleforening**
- Tidens Skole. (pub. by O. Mygind)

**Danske Reklamebureauers Brancheforening**
GL Strand 44, DK-1202 Copenhagen, Denmark.
- Danske Reklamebureauers Brancheforening.
  Oplagstal og Markedstal. a. ISSN 0070-2854
- Media Scandinavia; a Scandinavian advertising
  directory. a. ISSN 0076-5821
- Orientering. m (10 per yr.) ISSN 0030-5499

**Danske Selskab**
2 Kultorvet, DK-1175 Copenhagen K, Denmark.
- Contact with Denmark. 1-2 per yr.

- Musical Denmark. 1-2 per yr. ISSN 0027-4585

**Danske Skovteknikeres Landsforening**
Klempegaardsvej 26, 4140 Borup, Denmark.
- Skovbrugstidende. m.

**Danske Skytte- , Gymnastik- og Idraetsforeninger**
Strandgade 8, 1401 Copenhagen K, Denmark.
- Dansk Idraet. s-m.

**Danske Slagtermestres Landsforening**
Postboks 709, DK-5230 Odense M, Denmark.
- Koedbranchen. s-m.

**Danske Studerendes Faellesraad**
Knabrostraede 3, Copenhagen K, Denmark.
- Danske Studerendes Faellesraad. Studenterbladet.
  20 per yr. ISSN 0039-2839

**Denmark. Atomenergikommissionen Forsoegsanslaeg
Risoe**
DK-4000 Roskilde, Denmark.
- Denmark. Atomenergikommissionens
  Forsoegsanslaeg, Risoe. Risoe Report. irreg., no.
  321, 1975. ISSN 0418-6443

**Denmark. Boligministeriet**
Copenhagen, Denmark.
- Bygge- og Boligpolitiske Udvikling. irreg.

**Denmark. Danida**
Amaliegade 7, DK-1256 Copenhagen K, Denmark.
- Denmark's Development Assistance. Annual
  Report. a.
- Udvikling Danmark og U-Landen. bi-m.

**Denmark. Danmarks Fiskeri- og Havundersoegelser**
Charlottenlund Slot, 2920 Charlottenlund,
Denmark.
- Denmark. Danmarks Fiskeri- og
  Havundersoegelser. Meddeleser. irreg. ISSN 0070-
  3435
- Fisk og Hav. a. ISSN 0070-3443

**Denmark. Danmarks Geologiske Undersoegelse**
- Danmarks Geologiske Undersoegelse/Geological
  Survey of Denmark. (pub. by C. A. Reitzels
  Forlag)

**Denmark. Danmarks Statistik**
Sejroegade 11, 2100 Copenhagen OE, Denmark
- Danmarks Skibe og Skibsfart/Danish Ships and
  Shipping. a. ISSN 0070-3486
- Danmarks Vareindfoersel og- Udfoersel/Foreign
  Trade of Denmark. a. ISSN 0070-2781
- Denmark. Danmarks Statistik. Arbejdsloesheden/
  Unemployment. a. ISSN 0070-346X
- Denmark. Danmarks Statistik. Befolkningens
  Bevaegelser. a. ISSN 0070-3478
- Denmark. Danmarks Statistik. Ejendoms- og
  Selskabsbeskatningen i Skatteaaret. a.
- Denmark. Danmarks Statistik. Ejendomssalg/Sales
  of Real Property. a. ISSN 0070-3508
- Denmark. Danmarks Statistik. Faerdselsuheld. a.
  ISSN 0070-3516
- Denmark. Danmarks Statistik. Handelsstatistiske
  Meddelelser. Maanedsstatistik over
  Udenrigshandelen. Monthly Bulletin of Foreign
  Trade. m. ISSN 0017-7342
- Denmark. Danmarks Statistik. Industristatistik/
  Industrial Statistics. a. ISSN 0070-3532
- Denmark. Danmarks Statistik. Konjunkturo.
  Versigt/Economic Trends. irreg.
- Denmark. Danmarks Statistik. Kriminalstatistik. a.
  ISSN 0070-3540
- Denmark. Danmarks Statistik. Kvartalsstatistik for
  Industrien. q.
- Denmark. Danmarks Statistik. Kvartalsstatistik
  over Udenrigshandelen/Quarterly Bulletin of
  Foreign Trade. q.
- Denmark. Danmarks Statistik. Landbrugsstatistik
  Herunder Gartneri og Skovbrug/Statistics on
  Agriculture, Gardening and Forestry. a. ISSN
  0070-3559
- Denmark. Danmarks Statistik. Statistik Tiars-
  Oversigt. a. ISSN 0070-3583
- Denmark. Danmarks Statistik. Statistisk Aarbog/
  Statistical Yearbook. a. ISSN 0070-3567
- Denmark. Danmarks Statistik. Statistisk
  Tabelvaerk/Statistical Tables. irreg. ISSN 0039-
  0658
- Denmark. Danmarks Statistik. Statistiske
  Efterretninger. irreg. ISSN 0039-0674
- Denmark. Danmarks Statistik. Statistiske
  Meddelelser. irreg.

- Denmark. Danmarks Statistik. Statistiske
Undersogelser. irreg. ISSN 0039-0682
- Denmark Danmarks Statistik. Indkomster og
Formuer ved Slutligningen. a.

**Denmark. Danske Statsbaner**
Soelvgade 40, DK-1349 Copenhagen K, Denmark.
- D S B Bladet. m.

**Denmark. Direktoratet for Kriminalforsorgen**
Justitsministeriet, Klareboderne 1, DK-1115
Copenhagen K, Denmark.
- Denmark. Direktoratet for Kriminalforsorgen.
Kriminalforsorgen. a.

**Denmark. Direktoratet for Toldvaesenet**
Straudgade 29, 1401 Copenhagen K, Denmark.
- Denmark. Direktoratet for Toldvaesenet.
Toldvaesenet. irreg; latest 1974.

**Denmark. Farvandsdirektoratet. Nautisk Afdeling**
Esplanaden 19, 1263 Copenhagen K, Denmark.
- Tidevandstabeller for Groenland. a.

**Denmark. Fiskeriministeriet Forsoegslaboratorium**
Bldg. 221, 2800 Lyngby, Denmark.
- Denmark. Fiskeriministeriet Forsoegslaboratorium.
Aarsberetning. a. ISSN 0070-3605

**Denmark. Folketing**
- Denmark. Folketinget. Folketingsaarbog. (pub. by
J. H. Schultz Forlag)

**Denmark. Forskningssekretariatet**
Holmens Kanal 7, 1060 Copenhagen K, Denmark.
- Denmark. Forskningensekretariatet. Forskningen
og Samfundet. m.

**Denmark. Groenlands Geologiske Undersogelse**
Oestervoldgade 10, DK-1350 Copenhagen K,
Denmark.
- Groenlands Geologiske Undersogelse. Report/
Geological Survey of Greenland. Report. irreg.

**Denmark. I.D.E., Danmarks Institut for International
Udveksling**
Amaliegade 38, 1256 Copenhagen K, Denmark
- Bibliografi over Danmarks Offentlige
Publikationer. a. ISSN 0067-6543 (Sold on
commission by Bibliotekscentralen, Telegrafvej 5,
DK-2750 Ballerup, Denmark)
- Theses and Other Publications of the University
of Copenhagen. a.

**Denmark. Jordfordelingssekretariatet**
Sankt Ann Plads 19, 1250 Copenhagen, Denmark.
- Denmark. Jordfordelingssekretariatet.
Arsbereining. a.

**Denmark. Justitsministeriet. Direktoratet for
Kriminalforsorgen**
*see* Denmark. Direktoratet for Kriminalforsorgen

**Denmark. Kommissionen for Videnskabelige
Undersogelser i Groenland**
- Meddelelser om Groenland. (pub. by Nyt Nordisk
Forlag)

**Denmark. Kongelige Bibliotek**
8 Christians Brygge, DK-1219 Copenhagen K,
Denmark.
- Bibliography of Old Norse-Icelandic Studies. a.
ISSN 0067-7213
- Bidrag til H. C. Andersens Bibliografi. irreg.,
1973, vol. 6. ISSN 0067-8473
- Dania Polyglotta; literature on Denmark in
languages other than Danish and books of Danish
interest published abroad. a. ISSN 0070-2714
- Dansk Periodicafortegnelse. Supplement/Danish
National Bibliography. Serials. Supplement. a.
ISSN 0084-9596
- Denmark. Kongelige Bibliotek. Fund og
Forskning. a. ISSN 0069-9896
- Musikalier i Danske Biblioteker/Music in Danish
Libraries; accesionskatalog/union catalogue. a.
ISSN 0085-3623

**Denmark. Landoekomiske Driftsbureau**
Valby Langgade 19, 2500 Valby, Denmark.
- Denmark. Landoekonomiske Driftsbureau.
Meddelese. irreg; (approx. 1-2 per yr.) ISSN
0460-1424

**Denmark. Landsnaevnet for Boerne- og
Ungdomsforsorg**
Rosenvaengets Alle 16-18, 2100 Copenhagen,
Denmark.
- Denmark. Landsnaevnet for Boerne- og
Ungdomsforsorg. Beretning for Boerne- og
Ungdomsforsorgen. a. ISSN 0070-3613 (Co-
sponsor: National Council of Child and Youth
Welfare Services)

**Denmark. Ministeriet for Groenland. Statistisk
Kontor**
Copenhagen, Denmark.
- Denmark. Ministeriet for Groenland. Statistisk
Kontor. Meddelelser. irreg.

**Denmark. Ministry of Foreign Affairs**
*see* Denmark. Udenrigsministeriet

**Denmark. Nationalmuseet**
Oplysningsafdelingen, Ny Vestergade 10, 1471
Copenhagen K, Denmark.
- Denmark. Nationalmuseet. Arbejdsmarkt. a. ISSN
0084-9308
- Tools and Tillage; a journal on the history of the
implements of cultivation and other agricultural
processes. a. ISSN 0563-8887

**Denmark. Nationalmuseet. Nationaldiskoteket**
Ny Vestergade 10, 1417 Copenhagen K, Denmark.
- Danske Grammofonplader. m.

**Denmark. Nordisk Statistisk Sekretariat**
Postbox 2550, DK-2100 Copenhagen OE, Denmark.
- Nordisk Statistisk Skriftserie/Statistical Reports of
the Nordic Countries. irreg., no. 28, 1974. ISSN
0078-1096

**Denmark. Planlaegningsraadet**
Forskningssekretariatet, Copenhagen, Denmark.
- Denmark. Planlaegningsraadet for Forskningen.
Beretning. a.

**Denmark. Post- og Telegrafvaesenet**
Kannikegade 16, DK-8000 Aarhus C, Denmark.
- Teleteknik. Danish Edition. 4 per yr. ISSN 0040-
2753 (Co-sponsor: Concessionary Telephone
Companies in Denmark)

**Denmark. Rigsarkivet**
Rigsdagsgaarden 9, 1218 Copenhagen K, Denmark.
- Arkiv; tidsskrift for arkivforskning. s-a. ISSN
0004-203X
- Diplomatarium Danicum. irreg. ISSN 0070-4938

**Denmark. Rigsbibliotekarembedet**
Christians Brygge 8, DK-1219 Copenhagen K,
Denmark.
- Denmark. Rigsbibliotekarembedet.
Accessionskatalog. a. ISSN 0084-9715
- Information for Forskningsbiblioteker. 10 per yr.
(Co-sponsor: Forskningsbibliotekernes
Faellesraad)

**Denmark. Socialforskningsinstituttet**
Borgergade 28, DK-1300 Copenhagen, Denmark.
- Denmark. Socialforskningsinstituttet. Beretning
Om Socialforskningsinstituttet Virksomhed.
biennial. ISSN 0081-0584

**Denmark. Socialstyrelsen**
Copenhagen, Denmark.
- Denmark. Socialstyrelsen. Revalideringsstatistik. a.

**Denmark. Statens Bygningsfredningsfond**
2 Nybrogade, DK-1203 Copenhagen K, Denmark.
- Denmark. Statens Bygningsfredningsfond.
Beretning. a.

**Denmark. Statens Filmcentral**
27 Vestergade, 1456 Copenhagen K, Denmark.
- Denmark. Statens Filmcentral. S F C Film. irreg.,
approx. a. ISSN 0070-3621

**Denmark. Statens Forstlige Forsoegsvaesen**
Springforbivej 4, 2930 Klampenborg, Denmark.
- Forstlige Forsoegsvaesen i Danmark. irreg., 1972,
vol. 33. ISSN 0085-0837

**Denmark. Statens Husdyrbrugsudvalg**
Rolighedsvej 25, 1958 Copenhagen V, Denmark.
- Denmark. Statens Husdyrbrugsudvalg. Beretning.
irreg.

**Denmark. Statens Husholdningsraad**
56 Amagerfaelledvej, DK-2300 Copenhagen S,
Denmark.
- Denmark. Statens Husholdningsraad. Pjecer. 4 per
yr.
- Denmark. Statens Husholdningsraad. Raad og
Resultater Med Tekniske Meddelelser. 8 per yr.
ISSN 0033-748X

**Denmark. Statens Kunstmuseumsnaevn**
Nybrogade 2, DK-1203 Copenhagen K, Denmark.
- Denmark. Statens Kunstmuseumsnaevn. Beretning.
quadrennial.

**Denmark. Statens Planteavlsudvalg**
Kongevejen 83, 2800 Lyngby, Denmark.
- Tidsskrift for Planteavl. 4-5 per yr. ISSN 0040-
7135

**Denmark. Udenrigsministeriet**
Christiansborg, DK-1218 Copenhagen K, Denmark.
- Danish Journal. q. ISSN 0011-6084
- Denmark Review. q. ISSN 0418-6745

**Denmark. Udenrigsministeriet. Handelsafdelingen**
Amaliegade 18, DK-1256 Copenhagen K, Denmark.
- Danmarks Eksportmarkeder. irreg.
- U T. (Udenrigsministeriets Tidsskrift for
Udenrigsoekonomi) w.

**Denmark. Undervisningministeriet. Oekonomisk-
Statistiske Konsulent**
Copenhagen, Denmark.
- Denmark. Undervisningministeriet. Oekonomisk-
Statistiske Konsulent. Statistik de Videregaende
Uddannelser. irreg.

**Denmark. Vildtbiologisk Station**
Kalo, 8410 Ronde, Denmark.
- Danish Review of Game Biology. irreg. ISSN
0070-2730

**Detail-Papirhandlerforeningen i Danmark**
Stoltenbergsgade 3, 1576 Copenhagen V, Denmark.
- Papirhandleren. m. ISSN 0031-143X

**Dybfrost Instituttet**
Kastelvej 11, 2100 Copenhagen, Denmark.
- Frozen Foods in Denmark. a.

**Dyrefondet**
Nansensgade 90, 1366 Copenhagen, Denmark.
- Hunde-Journalen; monthly magazine for animal
friends. m.

**E L-Information ELRA**
Vodroffsvej 59, 1900 Copenhagen V, Denmark.
- Elnyt. 3 per yr.

**Editions Nordiques**
P.O. Box 1521, DK-8220 Brabrand, Denmark.
- Nordisk Mellemoesten Institut. Bulletin/Nordic
Middle East Institute. Bulletin. q.

**Eget Forlag**
Karl Andersensvej 37, 6700 Esbjerg, Denmark.
- Bygd. 4 per yr. ISSN 0007-7445 (Fiskeri- og
Soefartsmuseet. Saltvandsakvariet)

**Christian Ejlers Forlag A-S**
Brolaeggerstraede 4, 1211 Copenhagen K, Denmark.
- Bogvennen. 3 per yr. ISSN 0006-5749 (Forening
for Boghaandvaerk)

**Elbiom Forlagsaktieselskab**
C. N. Petersenvej 26, 2000 Copenhagen F,
Denmark.
- Skov og So; tidsskrift for fiskeri, jagt og friluftsliv.
m. ISSN 0037-6582

**Entomologisk Forening**
Universitetsparken 15, 2100 Copenhagen OE,
Denmark.
- Entomologiske Meddelelser. 3 nos. per yr. ISSN
0013-8851

**Erhvervenes Forlag**
Skovbogaards Alle 11, 2500 Valby, Denmark.
- Tidsskrift for Soevaesen. m. ISSN 0040-7186
(Soe-Lieutenant-Selskabet)

**Erhvervs-Bladet**
Vesterbrogade 12, DK-1620 Copenhagen V,
Denmark.
- Erhvervs-Bladet; industri, handel, transport,
ekonomi, ledelse, rationalisering, emballage,
markedsfoering. d. ISSN 0014-0155

**Express-Trykkeriet**
Raadhustorvet 4, 8900 Randers, Denmark.
- Danmarks Bilruter. m.

**F D M-Huset**
Blegdamsvej 124, DK-2100 Copenhagen, Denmark.
- Motor. fortn. ISSN 0047-8199 (Forenede Danske Motorejere)

**F T A**
Risager 1, 8270 Hoejbjerg, Denmark.
- Dansk Arbejde. m. ISSN 0011-6181 (Landsforeningen Dansk Arbejde)

**Faellesforeningen for Danmarks Brugsforeninger**
c/o Aage Buechert, Roskildevej 65, DK-2620 Albertslund, Denmark.
- Samvirke. m. ISSN 0036-3944

**Faellesraadet for Markedsfoering**
- Markedsfoering. (pub. by Specialbladsforlaget)

**Faellesrepraesentationen for Danmarks Biografteatre**
Nygade 3, 1164 Copenhagen K, Denmark.
- Biograf-Bladet. m. ISSN 0006-3045

**Faellesrepraesentationen for Funktionaerer ved Koebenhavns Havnevaesen**
7 Nordre Toldbod, DK-1259 Copenhagen K, Denmark.
- Koebenhavns Havneblad. 10 per yr. ISSN 0023-2629

**Faellesudralget Mellem Erhvervsvejledningsraadet og Folkeskolens Laeseplansudvalg**
Adelgade 13, 1304 Copenhagen K, Denmark.
- Uddannelse og Erhverv Katalog. irreg.

**Federation of Danish Architects**
- Arkitekten. (pub. by Arkitektens Forlag)

**Federation of Scandinavian Paint and Varnish Technicians**
- Skandinavisk Tidskrift for Faerg och Lack. (pub. by Dansk Bladforlag K-S)
- Skandinavisk Tidskrift for Faerg och Lack. Aarsbok. (pub. by Dansk Bladforlag K-S)

**Ferskvandsfiskeriforeningen for Denmark**
Sct. Nikolajgade 2, 8800 Viborg, Loegstrup, Denmark.
- Ferskvandsfiskeribladet. m. ISSN 0015-0223

**Finanstidende**
Store Kannikestraede 16, DK-1169 Copenhagen K, Denmark.
- Finanstidende. w. ISSN 0015-2153

**Fiskehandlerforeningen for Koebenhavn og Omegn**
- Fiskehandleren. (pub. by Athene A-S)

**Fiskeri- og Soefartsmuseet. Saltvandsakvariet**
- Bygd. (pub. by Eget Forlag)

**Flyvevaabnets Soldaterforening**
c/o B. Aalbaek-Nielsen, Ed., Aeblevadsvej 5, DK-5883 Oure, Denmark.
- Propel; tidsskrift for civil og militaer flyvning. m. (except June, July & Dec.) ISSN 0033-1279

**Folkeligt Oplysnings Forbund**
Palaegade 5, 1261 Copenhagen K, Denmark.
- Folk og Fritid. s-m. ISSN 0015-5810

**Folkevirke**
Solsortvej 1, 2000 Copenhagen F, Denmark.
- Folkevirke; social og polistisk oplysning. q. ISSN 0015-5845

**Forenede Danske Motorejere**
- Motor. (pub. by F D M-Huset)

**Forenedetidsskrifters Forlag**
Klosterstaede 23, 1157 Copenhagen K, Denmark.
- Fyring. 9 per yr. (Teknologisk Institut. Afdeling for Varme- og Installationsteknik)
- Varme. bi-m. (Teknologisk Institut. Afdeling for Varme- og Installationsteknik)

**Forening for Boghaandvaerk**
- Bogvennen. (pub. by Christian Ejlers Forlag A-S)

**Foreningen af Arbejdsledere i Danmark**
Vermlandsgade 67, 2300 Copenhagen S, Denmark.
- Arbejdslederen. m. ISSN 0003-7826

**Foreningen af Danske Civiloekonomer**
Boersen, Indgang B, Slotsholmsgade, DK-1216 Copenhagen K, Denmark.
- Civiloekonomen. m. (except Jan & Jul)
- Erhversoekonomisk Tidsskrift. (pub. by Harlang og Toksvig Bladforlag A-S)

**Foreningen af Danske Medicinfabrikker**
Landemaerket 25, DK-1119 Copenhagen K, Denmark.
- Medicinsk Forum. 6 per yr. ISSN 0025-8040

**Foreningen af Kioskejere i Danmark**
c/o Aage Kock Petersen, Banegaardsplads 20, 8000 Aarhus C, Denmark.
- Kioskejer-Bladet. m. ISSN 0023-172X

**Foreningen af Registrerede Revisorer**
Skjulhoej Alle 57, 2720 Vanloese, Denmark.
- Revisorbladet. 8 per yr.

**Foreningen af Statsautoriserede Revisorer**
Kronprinsessegade 8, DK-1306 Copenhagen, Denmark.
- Revision og Regnskabsvaesen; tidsskrift for Erhvervsoekonomi og Skatteforhold. m. ISSN 0034-6918

**Foreningen af Sygehusadministratorer i Danmark**
- Tidsskrift for Danske Sygehuse. (pub. by Dansk Bladforlag K-S)

**Foreningen Dansk Erhvervsfjerkrae**
Stenlosevej 361, DK-5260 Hjallese, Denmark.
- Dansk Erhvervsfjerkrae. fortn.

**Foreningen til Soefartens Fremme**
Dampfaergevej 3, DK-2100 Copenhagen OE, Denmark.
- Soefart. m. ISSN 0038-0520

**Foreningen til Svampekundskabens Fremme**
Thorvaldsensvej 40, 1871 Copenhagen V, Denmark.
- Friesia; Nordisk mykologisk tidsskrift. 1-2 nos.per year. ISSN 0016-1403

**Frederiksberg Frimaerke Forening**
16 Lindevang, DK-2660 Broendby Strand, Denmark.
- Frimaerkesamleren. m. ISSN 0016-1438

**Fremad A-S**
c/o Lasse Budtz, Ed., Christiansborg, 1218 Copenhagen, Denmark.
- Ny Politik. m. ISSN 0029-6759 (Social Democratic Party)

**Frit Nordens Forlag**
P.O. Box 525, DK-8100 Aarhus C, Denmark.
- Frit Norden. 10-12 per yr.

**Arne Frost-Hansens Forlag**
Gammel Torv 16, Copenhagen, Denmark.
- Tidsskrift for Udenrigspolitik og Udenrigshandel. q.

**G M T**
9293 Korgerslev, Denmark.
- Historievidenskab; tidsskrift for historisk forskning. q.

**Poul Gammelbo, Ed. & Pub.**
Kloverstykket 7, Postbox 17, 2791 Dragor, Denmark.
- CRAS, Tidsskrift for Kunst & Kultur. q.

**Geological Society of Denmark**
*see* Dansk Geologisk Forening

**Geological Survey of Greenland**
*see* Denmark. Groenlands Geologiske Undersoegelse

**Geoteknisk Institut**
1 Maglebjergvej, DK-2800 Lyngby, Denmark.
- Geoteknisk Institut, Copenhagen. Bulletin. irreg. ISSN 0069-987X

**Jul. Gjellerups Boghandel A-S**
Soelvgade 87-89, DK-1307 Copenhagen K, Denmark.
- Fysisk Tidsskrift. 4 per yr. ISSN 0016-3392 (Selskabet for Naturlaerens Udbredelse)

**J. Gjellerups Forlag A-S**
Roemersgade 11, DK-1362 Copenhagen K, Denmark.
- NY Selecta; Gjellerups tvaerfaglige sprogtidsskrift. 2 per yr.

- Paedagogik. q.

**Glarmesterlauget i Danmark**
Gothersgade 160, DK-1123 Copenhagen K, Denmark.
- Glarmestertidende. m. ISSN 0017-0755

**Groenlands Geologiske Undersogelse**
*see* Denmark. Groenlands Geologiske Undersogelse

**Groenlands Landsraad**
- Atuagagdliutit/Groenlandsposten. (pub. by Harlang og Toksvig Bladforlag A-S)

**Groenlandske Selskab**
L.E. Bruunsvej 10, Charlottenlund, Denmark.
- Groenland. 10 per yr. ISSN 0017-4556

**Guldsmedefagets Faellesraad**
Ryvangs Alle 26, DK-2100 Copenhagen OE, Denmark.
- Guldsmedebladet. m. ISSN 0017-5544

**Gutenberghus Bladene**
Vognmagergade 11, 1148 Copenhagen K, Denmark.
- Alt for Damerne. w. ISSN 0002-6506
- Dansk Familieblad. w. ISSN 0011-6262
- Hendes Verden. w.
- Hjemmet. w. ISSN 0046-7626

**Gyldendalske Boghandel-Nordisk Forlag A-S**
Klareboderne 3, DK-1001 Copenhagen K, Denmark.
- Classica et Mediaevalia; revue Danoise de philologie et d'histoire. a. (Dansk Selskab for Oldtids og Middelalderforskning)
- Excerpta Historica Nordica. irreg, no. 8, 1975. ISSN 0085-0365
- Gyldendals Magasin. q.

**Gymnasieskolernes Laererforening**
Magistrenes Hus, Lyngbyvej 32, 2100 Copenhagen OE, Denmark
- Gymnasieskolen. bi-w. ISSN 0017-5927 (Subscr. to: Lundgren Beck, Herlufsholm, 4700 Noestved, Denmark)

**Handels- og Soefartsmuseet paa Kronborg**
DK-3000 Helsingoer, Denmark.
- Handels- og Soefartsmuseet paa Kronborg. Aarbog. a. ISSN 0085-1418

**Handelshoejskolen i Koebenhavn. Instituttet for Udenrigshandel**
1925 Copenhagen, Denmark.
- Handelshoejskolen i Koebenhavn. Instituttet for Udenrigshandel. Smaaskrifter. irreg. ISSN 0069-9888

**Hans Christian Andersens Hus**
Hans Christian Andersen Museum, Odense Bys Museer, 5000 Odense, Denmark.
- Anderseniana. a. ISSN 0084-6465

**Harlang og Toksvig Bladforlag A-S**
Dr. Tvaergade 30, 1302 Copenhagen K, Denmark.
- Atuagagdliutit/Groenlandsposten. fortn. ISSN 0004-7341 (Groenlands Landsraad)
- AUTIG. m. (Auto- Tilbehoers Grossist-Foreningen)
- Auto-Orientering. m. (Royal Danish Automobile Club)
- Erhversoekonomisk Tidsskrift. q. ISSN 0014-0147 (Foreningen af Danske Civiloekonomer)
- Jagt og Fiskeri. m. ISSN 0021-3977 (Landsjagtforeningen)
- Militaert Tidsskrift. m. ISSN 0026-3850 (Krigsvidenskabelige Selskab)
- Nordisk Medicin. 10 per yr. ISSN 0029-1420
- Sparekassen. m. (Danmarks Sparekasseforening)

**Hestesport**
Jenseous Ivarvei 18, 2920 Charlottenfind, Denmark.
- Hestesport; organ for Dansk ridesport. m. ISSN 0018-1110

**Historisk Samfund for Als og Sundeved**
Soenderborg Slot, DK-6400 Soenderborg, Denmark.
- Fra Als og Sundeved. irreg., 1971, no. 50. ISSN 0085-0845

**Historisk Samfund for Fyns Stift**
c/o H. H. Jacobsen, Hyrdinden 5, 5270 Naesby, Denmark.
- Fynske Aarboeger. ISSN 0085-0918

**Historisk Samfund for Holback**
Holback Museum, DK-4340 Toelloese, Denmark.
- Fra Holback Amt. Historiske Aarboeger. a.

**Historisk Samfund for Ribe Amt**
6870 Oelgod, Denmark.
- Fra Ribe Amt. a. ISSN 0046-4864

**Historisk Samfund for Ringkoebing Amt**
c/o Kr. Bjerregaard, Holstebro Bibliotek, 7500
Holstebro, Denmark.
- Hardsyssels Aarbog. a. ISSN 0046-6840

**Historisk Samfund for Skive og Omegn**
Folkebiblioteket, Skive, Denmark.
- Historisk Aarbog for Skive og Omegn. a. ISSN
  0046-7588

**Historisk Samfund for Soenderjylland**
Landsarkivet, 6200 Aabenraa, Denmark.
- Soenderjysk Maanedsskrift. m. ISSN 0049-125X

**Historisk Samfund for Vendsyssel**
Sct.Annavej 3, DK-9800 Hjoerring, Denmark.
- Vendsyssel Aarbog. a. ISSN 0085-7645

**Historisk Samfund for Viborg Amt**
Landsarkivet, 8800 Viborg, Denmark.
- Fra Viborg Amt. Aarbog. a. ISSN 0085-0853

**Historisk-Topografisk Selskab for Soelleroed
Kommune**
Soelleroed Kommunebiblioteker, Biblioteksalleen 1-
5, 2850 Naerum, Denmark.
- Soelleroedbogen. a. ISSN 0085-6339

**Hjemkundskabslaererforeningen**
Leos Alle 48, DK-6270 Toender, Denmark.
- Hjemkundskab. m (10 per yr.)

**Hjemmevaernsbladet**
Generalstok, Kastellet 2100, Denmark.
- Hjemmevaernsbladet. m.

**Joergen Holst, AD Promotion-Forlag**
Fjordhoej, Egebjergvej, Atterup, 4571 Grevinge,
Denmark.
- Renhold Vedligehold. bi-m.

**Hovedorganisationen af Officerer af a-Linien**
Rosenvaengets Alle 33, 2100 Copenhagen,
Denmark.
- Linieofficeren. m. ISSN 0024-3973

**Hovedsorganisationen af Mesterforeninger i
Byggefagne i Danmark**
Reklame- Centret, P. Bangsvej 109, 2000
Copenhagen F, Denmark.
- Byggehaandvaerket. ISSN 0007-7496

**Hus og Hjem**
Kronprinsensgade 1, 1116 Copenhagen K, Denmark.
- Hus og Hjem. w. ISSN 0018-795X

**Husholdningslaereren (Vaeloese)**
Skovbovaenget 114, Vaeloese, Denmark.
- Husholdningslaereren (Vaeloese) m. ISSN 0018-
  0866

**Husholdningslaererforeningen**
Kompagnistraede 6, 1208 Copenhagen K, Denmark.
- Husholdningslaereren (Copenhagen) 18 per yr.
  ISSN 0046-8347

**Hvidvarebranchens Faellesraad**
Rosenborggade 5, 1130 Copenhagen K, Denmark.
- Hvidvare - Nyt. m. ISSN 0018-8107

**I. D. E., Danmarks Institut for International
Udveksling**
see Denmark. I. D. E., Danmarks Institut for
International Udveksling

**Industriraadet**
Aldersrogade 20, DK-2200 Copenhagen N,
Denmark.
- Dansk Industri. m. ISSN 0045-9623

**Institut for Dansk Dialektforskning**
St. Kannikestraede 13, 1169 Copenhagen K,
Denmark.
- Danske Folkemaal. a.

**Institute Danois des Echanges**
see Denmark. I.D.E., Danmarks Institut for
International Udveksling

**Institutet for Lederskab og Loensomhed**
Lyshojgardsvej 45, Copenhagen Valby, Denmark.
- Lederskab og Loensomhed. 8 per yr.

**International Antonio Vivaldi Society**
c/o Istituto Italiano de Cultura, Gjoerlingsvej 11,
DK-2900 Hellerup, Denmark.
- Vivaldi Informations. a.

**International Association of Oral Surgeons**
- International Journal of Oral Surgery. (pub. by
  Munksgaard)

**International Council for the Exploration of the Sea**
Charlottenlund Slot, DK-2920 Charlottenlund,
Denmark
(Subscr. to: C. A. Reitzels Forlag, Noerre Soegade
35, 1370 Copenhagen K, Denmark)
- I C E S Oceanographic Data Lists and
  Inventories. irreg.
- International Council for the Exploration of the
  Sea. Annales Biologiques. a. ISSN 0074-4301
- International Council for the Exploration of the
  Sea. Bulletin Statistique. a; no. 58, 1976. ISSN
  0074-4344
- International Council for the Exploration of the
  Sea. Cooperative Research Reports. irreg. ISSN
  0074-431X
- International Council for the Exploration of the
  Sea. Journal du Conseil. 3 per yr. ISSN 0020-
  6466
- International Council for the Exploration of the
  Sea. Rapports et Proces-Verbaux des Reunions.
  irreg, no. 170, 1977. ISSN 0074-4336

**International Grafik**
Box 109, 9900 Frederikshavn, Denmark.
- International Grafik; original graphics review. s-a.
  ISSN 0020-6830

**International Movement of Radical Anthropologists.
Etnografisk Afdeling**
Moesgaard, DK-8270 Hoejbjerg, Denmark.
- Marxistisk Antropologi. q.

**International Society for Experimental Hematology**
- Experimental Hematology. (pub. by Munksgaard)

**International Union of Crystallography**
- International Union of Crystallography. Abstracts
  of the Triennial Congress. (pub. by Munksgaard)
- Journal of Applied Crystallography. (pub. by
  Munksgaard)

**International Union of Theoretical and Applied
Mechanics**
c/o F. Niordson, Sec., Technical University of
Denmark, Department of Solid Mechanics, Building
404, DK-2800 Lyngby, Denmark.
- International Union of Theoretical and Applied
  Mechanics. Proceedings of Symposia. irreg., 1974,
  14th, Moscow. ISSN 0074-9559

**International Work Group for Indigenous Affairs**
Frederiksholms Kanal 4A, DK-1220 Copenhagen K,
Denmark.
- I W G I A Documents; documentation of
  oppression of ethnic groups in various countries.
  q.

**Jysk Selskab for Historie**
Erhvervsarkivet, Vester Alle 12, DK-8000 Aarhus
C, Denmark.
- Historie; jyske samlinger. s-a. ISSN 0046-7561
- Nyt Fra Historien. 4 per yr. ISSN 0029-6848

**Kabel- og Liniemesterenforeningen**
Moellegangen 3, 8240 Risskov, Denmark.
- Kabel- og Liniemesteren. m.

**Kalk- og Teglvaerksforeningen**
Noerre Voldgade 34, 1358 Copenhagen K,
Denmark.
- Lerindustrien. bi-m. ISSN 0024-1040 (Nordens
  Samvirkende Teglvaerksforeninger)

**Kalkmaleriregistranten**
Kobmagergade 44-46, DK-1150 Copenhagen K,
Denmark.
- Ico-den iconographiske Post; et nordisk blad om
  billeder. q.

**Kamptroppernes Tidsskrift**
Panserskolen, 6840 Oksbol, Denmark.
- Kentaur. q. ISSN 0023-0057

**Kantineledernes Landsklub**
- Kantinen. (pub. by Asons Forlaget ApS)

**Kjoebenhavns Handelsbank**
see Copenhagen Handelsbank

**Koebenhavns Bogtrykkerforening**
Landemaerket 11, DK-1119 Copenhagen K,
Denmark.
- Grafiske Fag. m. ISSN 0017-2995 (Co-sponsors:
  Bogbinderlauget i Danmark; Reprolauget i
  Danmark)

**Koebenhavns Cykelhandler Forening**
Ny Kongensgade 20, 1557 Copenhagen V,
Denmark.
- Styret. fortn. ISSN 0039-4319

**Koebenhavns Philatelist Klub**
Groennegade 41, Copenhagen, Denmark.
- Nordisk Filatelistisk Tidsskrift. 6 per yr.

**Koebenhavns Universitet**
Pilestraede 58, 1112 Copenhagen, Denmark.
- Atlantide Report. Scientific Results of the Danish
  Expedition to the Coasts of Tropical West Africa.
  (pub. by Scandinavian Science Press Ltd.)
- Kopenhagener Beitrage zur Germanistischen
  Linguistik. (pub. by Akademisk Forlag)
- Universitetsavisen. fortn.

**Koebenhavns Universitet. Arnamagnaeanske Institut**
see Arnamagnaean Institute

**Koebenhavns Universitet. Centralinstitut for Nordisk
Asienforskning**
see Scandinavian Institute of Asia Studies

**Koebenhavns Universitet. Geologisk Centralinstitut**
Oester Voldgade 5-7, 1350 Copenhagen K,
Denmark.
- Koebenhavns Universitet. Geologisk
  Centralinstitut. Aarsberetning. a.

**Koebenhavns Universitet. Historisk Institut**
Bispetorvet 3, DK-1167 Copenhagen K, Denmark.
- 1066 Tidsskrift for Historisk Forskning. bi-m.

**Koebenhavns Universitet. Institut d'Etudes Romanes**
- Revue Romane. (pub. by Akademisk Forlag)

**Koebenhavns Universitet. Institut for Anvendt og
Matematisk Lingvistik**
1168 Copenhagen, Denmark.
- Koebenhavns Universitet. Institut for Anvendt og
  Matematisk Lingvistik. Skrifter. irreg.

**Koebenhavns Universitet. Institut for Filmvidenskab**
1168 Copenhagen, Denmark.
- Koebenhavns Universitet. Institut for
  Filmvidenskab. Skrifter. irreg.

**Koebenhavns Universitet. Institut for Matematisk
Statistik**
5 Universitetsparken, 2100 Copenhagen OE,
Denmark.
- University of Copenhagen. Institute of
  Mathematical Statistics. Lecture Notes. irreg.

**Koebenhavns Universitet. Institute of Art History**
Frue Plads, Copenhagen, Denmark.
- Hafnia; Copenhagen Papers in the History of Art.
  biennial. ISSN 0085-1361

**Koebenhavns Universitet. Marinbiologisk Institut**
Strandpromenaden, DK-3000 Helsingoer, Denmark.
- Ophelia. a.(approx.) ISSN 0078-5326

**Koebenhavns Universitet. Medicinsk-Historiske
Institut og Museum**
Bredgade 62, DK-1260 Copenhagen, Denmark.
- Dansk Medicinhistorisk Aarbog/Yearbook of
  Danish Medical History. a. ISSN 0084-9588

**Koebenhavns Universitet. Sociologisk Institut**
22 Linnegade, 1361 Copenhagen K, Denmark.
- Sociological Microjournal. a.
- Sociologiske Meddelelser; a Danish sociological
  journal. 2 per yr. ISSN 0038-0350

**Koeletekniske Foreninger i Skandinavien**
- Scandinavian Refrigeration. (pub. by Dansk
  Bladforlag K-S)

**Kolonihaveforbundet for Danmark**
Frederikssundsvej 308 B, 2700 Broenshoej,
Denmark.
- Havebladet. bi-m. ISSN 0017-8497

**Kommunernes Landsforening**
Gyldenlovesgade 11, DK-1600 Copenhagen V,
Denmark.
- Danske Kommuner. fortn. ISSN 0011-6572

**Forlaget Kompas-Denmark**
Landskornagade 70, DK-2100 Copenhagen,
Denmark.
- Kompas Danmark; indeks over Danmarks industri
og Naegringsliv. a. ISSN 0075-661X (Foundation
for Promoting International Economic
Information SZ)

**Kongelig Dansk Aeroklub**
- Flyv. (pub. by Danish General Aviation A-S)

**Kongelige Danske Geografiske Selskab**
Haraldsgade 68, DK-2100 Copenhagen OE,
Denmark.
- Folia Geographica Danica. irreg., (approx. 1 per
year) ISSN 0071-6693
- Geografisk Tidsskrift. s-a. ISSN 0016-7223
- Kulturgeografiske Skrifter. ISSN 0023-5245

**Kongelige Danske Landhusholdningsselskab**
Rolighedsvej 26, 1958 Copenhagen V, Denmark.
- Tidsskrift for Landokonomi. q. ISSN 0040-7119

**Kongelige Danske Selskab for Faedrelandets Historie**
Vester Voldgade 92, 1552 Copenhagen 5, Denmark.
- Danske Magazin. a. ISSN 0070-2846

**Kongelige Danske Videnskabernes Selskab**
Dantes Plads 5, DK-1556 Copenhagen V, Denmark
(Orders to: Munksgaard, 35 Noerre Soegade, DK
1370 Copenhagen K, Denmark)
- Kongelige Danske Videnskabernes Selskab.
Biologiske Meddelelser. irreg.
- Kongelige Danske Videnskabernes Selskab.
Biologiske Skrifter. irreg (3-6 per yr.) ISSN 0006-
3320
- Kongelige Danske Videnskabernes Selskab.
Historisk-Filosofiske Meddelelser. irreg (3-5 per
yr.)
- Kongelige Danske Videnskabernes Selskab.
Historisk-Filosofiske Skrifter. irreg. ISSN 0023-
3307
- Kongelige Danske Videnskabernes Selskab.
Matematisk-Fysiske Meddelelser. irreg., vol. 39,
1974. ISSN 0023-3323
- Kongelige Danske Videnskabernes Selskab
Matematisk-Fysiskeskrifter. irreg. ISSN 0023-
3331
- Kongelige Danske Videnskabernes Selskab.
Oversigt over Selskabets Virksomhed. a. ISSN
0023-3315

**Kongelige Veterinaer- og Landbohoejskole**
Bulowsvej 13, DK-1870 Copenhagen V, Denmark.
- Kongelige Veterinaer- og Landbohoejskole.
Aarskrift. a. ISSN 0045-852X

**Kongeriget Danmarks Handels-Kalender**
Postbox 84, Mollergade 17-19, 5700 Svendborg,
Denmark.
- Kongeriget Danmarks Handels-Kalender. a. ISSN
0302-5403

**Kooperative Faellesforbund i Danmark**
Reventlowsgade 14, 2, 1651 Copenhagen V,
Denmark.
- Kooperationen. m (10 per yr.) ISSN 0023-382X

**Korrosionscentralen, ATV**
Park Alle 345, DK-2600 Glostrup, Denmark.
- Scandinavian Corrosion Congress. Proceedings.
irreg. ISSN 0581-9431

**Krak**
Nytorv 17, DK-1450 Copenhagen K, Denmark.
- Kraks Vejviser; industrial and trade directory for
Denmark. a.

**Krigsvidenskabelige Selskab**
- Militaert Tidsskrift. (pub. by Harlang og Toksvig
Bladforlag A-S)

**Kroghs Skolehandbog**
Gl. Landevej 13, 7100 Vejle, Denmark.
- Arbog for Erhvervsuddannelserne i Danmark. a.

**Kunstakademiets Bibliotek**
Kongens Nytorv 1, DK-1050 Copenhagen K,
Denmark.
- Bibliografi over Dansk Kunst. a.

**Laedervarehandlerforeningen for Danmark**
Hovedvejen 3, DK-2600 Glostrup, Denmark.
- Laedervare-Nyt. m.

**Landbohistorisk Selskab**
H. C. Andersens Boulevard 38, DK-1553
Copenhagen K, Denmark.
- Aeldre Danske Tingboeger. irreg. ISSN 0065-3667
- Bol og By. irreg., no. 1, 1977 (n.s.) ISSN 0067-
9550

**Forlaget Landbonyt**
Tullinsgade 1, DK-1618 Copenhagen V, Denmark.
- Landbonyt. m. ISSN 0047-3960

**Landsarkivet for Sjaelland**
Jagtvej 10, 2200 Copenhagen N, Denmark.
- Nordisk Arkivkunskab. irreg (approx. a)

**Landsbladet**
V. Farimagsgade 6, 1606 Copenhagen, Denmark.
- Hippologisk Tidsskrift. m. ISSN 0018-201X
(Dansk Ponyavlsforbund) (Co-sponsors: Dansk
Sportsheste Avlsforbund; Sportsrideklubben i
Koebenhavn, Danish Equestrian Federation)

**Landsforeningen af Danske Fodterapeuten**
Bjelkes Alle 43, 2200 Copenhagen, Denmark.
- Fodterapeuten. m (10 per yr)

**Landsforeningen af Vanfoere**
Kollektivhuset, Hans Knudsens Plads 1,10, 2100
Copenhagen OE, Denmark.
- Vanfoerebladet. m. ISSN 0042-2541

**Landsforeningen Dansk Arbejde**
- Dansk Arbejde. (pub. by F T A)

**Landsforeningen Dansk Faareavl**
Lillering, 8462 Harlev J, Denmark.
- Tidsskrift for Faareavl. m (10 per yr.) ISSN 0040-
7038

**Landsforeningen Danske Maskinstationer**
L. P. Bechs Vej 29, 8240 Risskov, Denmark.
- Maskinstationen og Landbrugslederen. m. (Co-
sponsor: Selskabet Landbrugslederen)

**Landsforeningen Danske Vognmaend**
Jens Kofodsgade 1, 1268 Copenhagen K, Denmark.
- Danske Vognmaend. m. ISSN 0011-6629
- L D V Bogen. a.

**Landsforeningen Eksperimenterende Danske
Radioamatoerer**
Postbox 79, DK-1003 Copenhagen K, Denmark.
- OZ; tidsskrift for amatoer-radio. m.

**Landsforeningen for Bedre Horelse**
Tordenskjoldsgade 11, Copenhagen K, Denmark.
- Horelsen. m. ISSN 0018-4934

**Landsjagtforeningen**
- Jagt og Fiskeri. (pub. by Harlang og Toksvig
Bladforlag A-S)

**Landsorganisation af Frugt- og Blomsterhandlere**
Hambros Alle 3, 2900 Hellerup, Denmark.
- Frugt. m.
- Frugt, Groent og Blomster. s-m. ISSN 0046-5224
(Co-sponsor: Frugthandlerforeningen af 1889)

**Landsorganisationen i Danmark**
Rosenoerns Alle 14, Copenhagen V, Denmark.
- LO-Bladet. s-m.

**Landssammenslutningen af Hospitalslaboranter**
Nannasgade 28, 2200 Copenhagen N, Denmark.
- Nyt for Hospitalslaboranter. fortn. ISSN 0029-
683X

**Lejernes Landsorganisation**
Reventlowsgade 14,3, 1651 Copenhagen V,
Denmark.
- Bolignyt. q. ISSN 0006-6524

**Lepidopterologisk Forening**
Rodkildevej 14, 2400 Copenhagen NV, Denmark.
- Lepidoptera. irreg (approx. s-a) ISSN 0075-8787

**Forlaget Levende Billeder A-S**
Sct. Peders Straede 28 B,2, 1453 Copenhagen V,
Denmark.
- L B Levende Billeder; et maanedsblad om film og
TV. m.

**Linguistic Circle of Copenhagen**
- Acta Linguistica Hafniensia. (pub. by
Munksgaard)

**Louisiana**
Gl. Strandvej 13, 3050 Humlebaek, Denmark.
- Louisiana-Revy. 3 per yr. ISSN 0024-6891

**Lynge og Soen**
Loevstraede 10, DK-1152 Copenhagen K, Denmark.
- Aarboeger for Nordisk Oldkyndighed og Historie.
irreg. ISSN 0084-585X

**Lysteknisk Selskab**
Herlev Hovedgade 188, DK-2730 Herlev, Denmark.
- Lampetten. 4-5 per yr. ISSN 0023-7442 (Co-
sponsor: Lysteknisk Laboratorium)

**Maanedsskrift for Praktisk Laegegerning**
Vendersgade 4, 1363 Copenhagen K, Denmark.
- Maanedsskrift for Praktisk Laegegerning; tidsskrift
for praktiserende laegers efteruddannelse. m.
ISSN 0024-8789

**Malmborg og Hedstroem Forlag A-S**
Mikkelbryggersgade 10, 1460 Copenhagen K,
Denmark.
- Kryds-Avisen. ISSN 0047-3715

**Maskinmestrenes Forening**
Sankt Annae Plads 16, DK-1250 Copenhagen K,
Denmark.
- Maskinmesteren. m. ISSN 0047-6102

**Medicinsk-Historisk Institut og Museum**
*see under* **Koebenhavns Universitet**

**Mellemfolkeligt Samvirke**
Hejrevel 38, 2400 Copenhagen NV, Denmark.
- M S Biblioteksnyt. irreg.

**Ole Miller, Ed. & Pub.**
Wiehesvej 12, 2900 Hellerup, Denmark.
- Mediakontakt; orientation-planning-buying of
media. m (11 per yr.)

**Mobilia Press A-S**
Staget 12, 3070 Snekkersten, Denmark.
- Mobilia. 8 per yr. ISSN 0026-7228

**Morsingboernes Forening**
Aadalsparkvej 61, DK-2970 Hoersholm, Denmark.
- Morsingboen. m. ISSN 0027-1195

**Mosaisk Troessamfund**
Ny Kongensgade 6, 1472 Copenhagen K, Denmark.
- Joedisk Orientering. m. ISSN 0021-7131

**Munksgaard**
Noerre Soegade 35, DK-1370 Copenhagen K,
Denmark.
- Acta Allergologica. bi-m. ISSN 0001-5148
(Northern Society of Allergology) (Co-sponsor:
European Academy of Allergology)
- Acta Allergologica. Supplementum. irreg. ISSN
0065-096X (Northern Society of Allergology)
(Co-sponsor: European Academy of Allergology)
- Acta Anaesthesiologica Scandinavica. 6 per yr.
ISSN 0001-5172
- Acta Anaesthesiologica Scandinavica.
Supplementum. irreg. ISSN 0515-2720
- Acta Archaeologica. a. ISSN 0065-101X
- Acta Chemica Scandinavica. Series A: Physical
and Inorganic Chemistry. 10 per yr. ISSN 0302-
4377
- Acta Chemica Scandinavica. Series B: Organic
Chemistry and Biochemistry. 10 per yr.
- Acta Chemica Scandinavica. Supplementum. irreg.
ISSN 0065-1133
- Acta Crystallographica. Section A: Crystal
Physics, Diffraction, Theoretical and General
Crystallography. bi-m. ISSN 0567-7394
- Acta Crystallographica. Section B: Structural
Crystallography and Crystal Chemistry. m. ISSN
0567-7408
- Acta Linguistica Hafniensia; international journal
of general linguistics. 2 per yr. ISSN 0374-0463
(Linguistic Circle of Copenhagen)
- Acta Neurologica Scandinavica. m. ISSN 0001-
6314
- Acta Neurologica Scandinavica. Supplementum.
irreg. ISSN 0065-1427
- Acta Orientalia. a.
- Acta Orthopaedica Scandinavica. bi-m. ISSN
0001-6470 (Scandinavian Orthopaedic
Association)
- Acta Orthopaedica Scandinavica. Supplementum.
irreg. (Scandinavian Orthopaedic Association)
- Acta Pathologica et Microbiologica Scandinavica.
Section A: Pathology. bi-m. ISSN 0365-4184

- Acta Pathologica et Microbiologica Scandinavica. Section A: Pathology. Supplementum. irreg. ISSN 0365-5571
- Acta Pathologica et Microbiologica Scandinavica. Section B: Microbiology. bi-m. ISSN 0304-131X
- Acta Pathologica et Microbiologica Scandinavica. Section B: Microbiology. Supplementum. irreg. ISSN 0105-0656
- Acta Pathologica et Microbiologica Scandinavica. Section C: Immunology. bi-m. ISSN 0304-1328
- Acta Pharmacologica et Toxicologica. 10 per yr. ISSN 0001-6683
- Acta Pharmacologica et Toxicologica. Supplementum. irreg. ISSN 0065-1508
- Acta Philologica Scandinavica; tidsskrift for nordisk sprogforskning. 2 per yr. ISSN 0001-6691
- Acta Psychiatrica Scandinavica. 10 per yr. ISSN 0001-690X
- Acta Psychiatrica Scandinavica. Supplementum. irreg. ISSN 0065-1591
- Alfred Benzon Symposium. Proceedings. irreg., 1973, 5th, Copenhagen. ISSN 0065-6186 (Dist. in U.S. by: Academic Press Inc., 171 First Ave., Atlantic Highlands, NJ 07716)
- Centaurus; international magazine of the history of mathematics, science and technology. 4 per yr. ISSN 0008-8994
- Clinical Genetics; an international journal of genetics in medicine. m. ISSN 0009-9163
- Community Dentistry and Oral Epidemiology. bi-m. ISSN 0301-5661
- Contact Dermatitis; environmental and occupational dermatitis. bi-m. ISSN 0105-1873
- Danish Yearbook of Philosophy. a. ISSN 0070-2749 (Dist. in U.S. by Humanities Press, Inc., 171 First Ave., Atlantic Highlands, NJ 07716)
- Experimental Hematology. bi-m. ISSN 0301-472X (International Society for Experimental Hematology)
- Immunological Reviews. irreg.
- International Journal of Oral Surgery. bi-m. ISSN 0300-9785 (International Association of Oral Surgeons)
- International Journal of Peptide and Protein Research. 10 per yr. ISSN 0020-7551
- International Union of Crystallography. Abstracts of the Triennial Congress. triennial since 1960; 1975, 10th General Assembly, Amsterdam. ISSN 0074-9389
- Journal of Applied Crystallography. bi-m. ISSN 0021-8898 (International Union of Crystallography)
- Journal of Clinical Periodontology. q. ISSN 0303-6979
- Journal of Cutaneous Pathology. bi-m. ISSN 0303-6987
- Journal of Oral Pathology. bi-m. ISSN 0300-9777
- Journal of Periodontal Research. 6 per yr. ISSN 0022-3484
- Journal of Periodontal Research. Supplementum. irreg. ISSN 0075-4331
- Kulturgeografi; tidsskrift for befolkningsgeografi. 2 per yr. ISSN 0023-5237
- Libri; International Library Review. q. ISSN 0024-2667
- Oekonomi og Politik. q. ISSN 0030-1906 (Selskabet for Historie og Samfundsoekonomi)
- Oikos; Acta Oecologica Scandinavica. 4-6 per yr. ISSN 0030-1299
- Orbis Litterarum; international review of literary studies. 4 per yr. ISSN 0030-4409
- Physiologia Plantarum. 12 per yr. ISSN 0031-9317 (Scandinavian Society for Plant Physiology)
- Scandinavian Journal of Dental Research. 6 per yr. ISSN 0029-845X (Nordiska Odontologiska Foreningen)
- Scandinavian Journal of Haematology. 10 per yr. ISSN 0036-553X
- Scandinavian Journal of Haematology. Supplementum. irreg. ISSN 0080-6722
- Scandinavian Journal of Respiratory Diseases. 6 per yr. ISSN 0036-5572
- Scandinavian Journal of Respiratory Diseases. Supplementum. irreg. ISSN 0080-6730
- Scando-Slavica. a. ISSN 0080-6765 (Association of Scandinavian Slavicists and Baltologists)
- Scando-Slavica. Supplementum. irreg. (Association of Scandinavian Slavicists and Baltologists)
- Tellus; a journal of geophysics. bi-m. ISSN 0040-2826 (Svenska Geofysiska Foerening SW)
- Tissue Antigens. 10 per yr. ISSN 0001-2815
- Zoology of Iceland. irreg. ISSN 0084-5655

**Murerfagets Oplysningsraad**
Peblinge Dossering 36, 2200 Copenhagen N, Denmark.
- Tegl. q. ISSN 0040-2141

**O. Mygind**
Duevej 3, 9352 Dybrad, Denmark.
- Tidens Skole. 21 times per year. (Danske Realskoleforening) (Co-sponsor: Frie Grundskolers Laererforening)

**Narayananda Universal Yoga Ashrama**
DK-8773 Gylling, Denmark.
- Yoga; tidsskrift for universel religion /magazine for the universal religion. 4 per yr. ISSN 0044-0485

**Nationaloekonomisk Forening**
Danmarks Nationalbank, Havnegade 5, DK-1093 Copenhagen K, Denmark.
- Nationaloekonomisk Tidsskrift. 3 per yr. ISSN 0028-0453

**Naturhistorisk Forening for Jylland**
Natural History Museum, DK-8000 Aarhus C, Denmark.
- Flora og Fauna. q. ISSN 0015-3818

**Naturhistorisk Museum**
DK-8000 Aarhus C, Denmark.
- Natur og Museum. q. ISSN 0028-0585
- Natura Jutlandica. irreg. ISSN 0077-6033

**Navigatoerenes Faellesforening**
Navigatoernes Hus, 55 Havnegade, DK-1058 Copenhagen K, Denmark.
- Nyt Navigatoer-Navigatoer Nyt/New Navigator. m.

**Nordens Samvirkende Teglvaerksforeninger**
- Lerindustrien. (pub. by Kalk- og Teglvaerksforeningen)

**Nordeuropaeisk Mejeri-Tidsskrift**
Box 1648, DK-2720 Vanloese, Denmark.
- Nordeuropaeisk Mejeri-Tidsskrift/North European Dairy Journal/Nordeuropaeische Molkerei-Zeitschrift. m.

**Nordic Bryological Society**
- Lindbergia. (pub. by Aarhus Universitet. Botanical Institute)

**Nordic Data Union**
Kronprinsensgade 14, DK-1114 Copenhagen K, Denmark.
- Data; Nordic journal of electronic data processing. 10 per yr.

**Nordic Optical Council**
34 Holbaekvej, 4571 Grevinge, Denmark.
- Nordisk Tidsskrift for Special-Optikere. bi-m. ISSN 0029-1544

**Nordic Statistical Secretariat**
see Denmark. Nordisk Statistisk Sekretariat

**Nordisk Filantropisk Selskab**
- Sundhedsbladet. (pub. by Dansk Bogforlag)

**Nordisk Forbund for Special Paedagogik**
- Nordisk Tidsskrift for Specialpaedagogik. (pub. by Sigurd Troels Berg)

**Nordisk Institut for Teoretisk Atomfysik**
Blegdamsvej 17, DK 2100 Copenhagen, Denmark.
- Nordisk Institut for Teoretisk Atomfysik. Virksomhedsberetning/Nordita Report. irreg.

**Nordisk Mellemoesten Institut**
- Nordisk Mellemoesten Institut. Bulletin/Nordic Middle East Institute. Bulletin. (pub. by Editions Nordiques)

**Nordisk Numismatisk Union**
c/o Royal Collection of Coins and Medals, National Museum, DK-1220 Copenhagen K, Denmark.
- Nordisk Numismatisk Union. Medlemsblad. 10 per yr. ISSN 0025-8539

**Nordisk Raad**
Christiansborg Ridebane 10, DK-1218 Copenhagen, Denmark.
- Nordiska Samarbetsorgan. irreg.

**Nordisk Statistisk Sekretariat**
see Denmark. Nordisk Statistisk Sekretariat

**Nordisk Tidsskrift for Tale og Stemme**
Tjoernevej 6, Risskov, Denmark.
- Nordisk Tidsskrift for Tale og Stemme/Scandinavian Review of Speech and Voice. 3 per yr. ISSN 0029-1552

**Nordiska Institutet Foer Faergforskning**
Odensegade 14, DK-2100 Copenhagen OE, Denmark.
- Environmental Control Literature Review. m (10 per yr.) (Co-sponsor: Verfinstituut T N O, Netherlands)
- Nordiska Institutet Foer Faergforskning. Litteraturoversigt. m. ISSN 0029-1587

**Nordiska Odontologiska Foreningen**
- Scandinavian Journal of Dental Research. (pub. by Munksgaard)

**Nordiske Administrative Forbund**
c/o Indenrigsministeriet, Slotsholmsgade 6, DK-1216 Copenhagen K, Denmark.
- Nordisk Administrativt Tidsskrift. q. ISSN 0029-1285

**NORDITA**
see Nordisk Institut for Teoretisk Atomfysik

**Norsk Renseriforbund**
- Nordisk Tidsskrift for Rensning og Vask/Scandinavian Magazine for Cleaning and Washing. (pub. by Forlaget Beilin og Johansen ApS)

**Northern Society of Allergology**
- Acta Allergologica. (pub. by Munksgaard)
- Acta Allergologica. Supplementum. (pub. by Munksgaard)

**Ny Carlsberg Glyptotek**
Dantes Plads 1556, Copenhagen V, Denmark.
- Ny Carlsberg Glyptotek. Meddelelser. a. ISSN 0085-3208

**Forlaget Ny Teknik A-S**
Kjaerbovaenge 52, 3520 Farum, Denmark.
- Automatik; industrial automation. m (8 per yr.) ISSN 0105-0168
- Teknik & Miljoe. m.

**Anders Nyborg A-S**
Internationalt Forlag, Rungstedvej 13, 2970 Hoersholm, Denmark.
- Key to Finland. a. ISSN 0085-2511
- Kunstmedaljen. s-a.
- North Atlantic. a.
- Welcome to Finland. a. ISSN 0085-8048
- Welcome to Norway. a. ISSN 0105-2454

**Forlaget P.E. Nygaard**
Holgey Danskesvej 69, 2000 Copenhagen F, Denmark.
- Radiotelegrafen. m. ISSN 0033-8508 (Radiotelegrafistforenigen)
- Skandinavisk Skibsfart. m.

**Nyt Nordisk Forlag**
49 Koebmagergade, DK-1150 Copenhagen K, Denmark.
- Meddelelser om Groenland. 10-15 nos. per yr. ISSN 0025-6676 (Denmark. Kommissionen for Videnskabelige Undersogelser i Groenland)

**Nyt Presse Bureau**
Postboks 56, 2830 Virum, Denmark.
- Moentsamlernyt; Scandinavian coin collectors magazine/zeitschrift fuer Muenzensammler in Skandinavien. m (10 per yr.)

**Odense Universitet. Universitetsbibliotek**
Niels Bohrs Alle 75, 5230 Odense M, Denmark.
- Odense Universitet. Universitetsbibliotek. Musiklitteratur og Musikalier. Nyanskaffelser. q.

**Odense University Press**
36 Pjentedamsgade, DK-5000 Odense, Denmark.
- Acta Historica Scientiarum Naturalium et Medicinalium. irreg., 1969, vol. 21. ISSN 0065-1311
- Analecta Romana Instituti Danici. irreg., vol. 5, 1969. ISSN 0066-1392
- Analecta Romana Instituti Danici. Supplementum. irreg. ISSN 0066-1406
- Mediaeval Scandinavia. a. ISSN 0076-5864
- Odense University Classical Studies. irreg.
- Odense University Slavic Studies. irreg. ISSN 0078-3277
- Odense University Studies in Art History. irreg. ISSN 0078-3285
- Odense University Studies in English. irreg. ISSN 0078-3293
- Odense University Studies in History and Social Sciences. irreg. ISSN 0078-3307

- Odense University Studies in Linguistics. irreg., 1968, vol. 2. ISSN 0078-3315
- Odense University Studies in Literature. irreg. ISSN 0078-3323
- Odense University Studies in Philosophy. irreg.
- Odense University Studies in Psychiatry and Medical Psychology. irreg.
- Odense University Studies in Scandinavian Languages and Literatures. irreg. ISSN 0078-3331
- Universite d'Odense. Etudes Romanes. irreg.

**Paul C. Olrik, Ed. & Pub.**
Postbox 1, 3460 Birkeroed, Denmark.
- Stop; magazine for reflective smokers. bi-m. ISSN 0039-1808

**Ostehandlerforeningen for Danmark**
Peblinge Dosseringen 36, DK-2200 Copenhagen N, Denmark.
- Ostehandleren. m. ISSN 0030-6355

**Palle Fogtdals A-S**
Noerre Farimagsgade 49, DK-1364 Copenhagen K, Denmark.
- Eva. m. ISSN 0014-3278
- Mad fra A til Z. s-m.
- Motor-Journalen Bilen. m. (Royal Danish Automobile Club)

**Bo Torp Pedersen, Ed. and Pub.**
Hans Egedesgade 7, 3, 2200 Copenhagen N, Denmark.
- Spotlight. q.

**C. F. Pederson**
Listedvej 84, Kastrup, Denmark.
- Nordisk Flaggskrift. irreg.

**Periodica**
Skolegade 12, DK-2500 Copenhagen V, Denmark.
- Acta Endocrinologica. m. ISSN 0001-5598
- Acta Endocrinologica Congress. Advance Abstracts. irreg, 1974 latest edt.

**Petersen og Bratvolds Bladforlag**
Vimmelskaftet 42 A, 1161 Copenhagen K, Denmark.
- Bygmesteren; fagblad for arkitekter og byggehandvaerker. m. ISSN 0007-7623

**Petersen Public Relations**
Falkehusene 56, DK-2620 Albertslund, Denmark.
- Dental Laboratorie Bladet. 10 per yr. ISSN 0070-3672 (Danish Union of Dental Laboratories)

**Photographic Workers Union**
Grafisk Forbundshus, Lygten 16, DK-2400 Copenhagen NV, Denmark.
- Fotograferne. m. except Jul., Dec. ISSN 0015-8798

**Physiognomy**
c/o David Gould, Ed., Asgard, Ydby, 7760 Hurup Thy, Denmark.
- Physiognomy. 3 per yr.

**Politiken Weekly**
Raadhuspladsen 37, 1585 Copenhagen V, Denmark.
- Politiken Weekly. w.

**Polyteknisk Forening**
Polytekniske Laereanstalt, Danmarks Tekniske Hoejskole, DK-2800 Lyngby, Denmark.
- Polyteknikeren. m. ISSN 0032-4124

**Polytekniske Laereanstalt, Danmarks Tekniske Hoejskole**
Bygning 115, DK-2800 Lyngby, Denmark.
- Nordic Hydrology; an international journal. q. ISSN 0029-1277

**Polytekniske Laereanstalt, Danmarks Tekniske Hoejskole. Afdelingen for Baerende Konstruktioner**
Bldg. 118, DK-2800 Lyngby, Denmark.
- Polytekniske Laereanstalt, Danmarks Tekniske Hoejskole. Afdelingen for Baerende Konstruktioner. Rapport R. irreg.

**Polytekniske Laereanstalt, Danmarks Tekniske Hoejskole. Laboratoriet for Elektronik**
Bygning 344, 2800 Lyngby, Denmark.
- Polytekniske Laereanstalt, Danmarks Tekniske Hoejskole. Laboratoriet for Elektronik. Beretning. a.

**Radikale Venstre**
Christiansborg, 1218 Copenhagen K, Denmark.
- Fremsyn. fortn. ISSN 0016-1012

**Radiobranchens Informationstjeneste**
Onsgaardsvej 35, DK-2900 Hellerup, Denmark.
- Radiobranchen. m. (Co-sponsor: Radiobranchens Faellesraad)

**Radiotelegrafistforenigen**
- Radiotelegrafen. (pub. by Forlaget P.E. Nygaard)

**Rederiforeningen for Mindre Skibe**
Valmuevej 4, 9380 Vestbjerg, Denmark.
- Skipperen. m.

**Redstockings**
Kvindehuset, Prinsessegade 7, DK-1422 Copenhagen, Denmark.
- Kvinder. bi-m.

**C. A. Reitzels Forlag**
35 Noerre Soegade, DK-1370 Copenhagen K, Denmark.
- Acta Arctica. irreg. ISSN 0065-1028 (Arktisk Institut)
- Danmarks Geologiske Undersoegelse/Geological Survey of Denmark. 6 per yr. ISSN 0011-6114 (Denmark. Danmarks Geologiske Undersoegelse)
- Geological Society of Denmark. Bulletin/Dansk Geologisk Forening. Bulletin. 4 per yr. ISSN 0011-6297 (Dansk Geologisk Forening)

**Restaurator Press**
Box 96, DK-1004 Copenhagen K, Denmark.
- Restaurator; international journal for the preservation of library and archival material. 3 per yr. ISSN 0034-5806
- Restaurator. Supplement. irreg. ISSN 0080-1836

**Retsforbundets Presse**
Kroghsgade 1, 2100 Copenhagen OE, Denmark.
- Vejen Frem; retspolitisk ugeblad. w. ISSN 0042-3173

**Retsvideustabelige Institut**
Set. Pedersstraede 19, 1453 Copenhagen K, Denmark
- Nordisk Tidsskrift for International Ret/Acta Scandinavica Juris Gentium. q. ISSN 0029-151X (U.S. dist.: Stechert Hafner, 31 E. 10 St., New York, NY 10003)

**Revolutionaere Socialisters Forbund**
Vendersgade 9 Kld., DK-1363 Copenhagen K, Denmark.
- Klassekampen; revolutionaert marxistisk tidsskrift. s-m. ISSN 0023-2025

**Rhodos, International Science and Art Publishers**
Strandgade 36 D, DK-1401 Copenhagen K, Denmark.
- Naturens Verden. m. ISSN 0028-0895

**Klaus Roedel, Ed. & Pub.**
P.O. Box 109, DK-9900 Frederikshavn, Denmark.
- Bibliografi over Europaeiske Kunstneres Ex Libris/Europaeische Ex Libris/European Book Plates/Ex Libris d'Europe. a.

**Roedovre Avis**
Roskildeve 288, DK-2610 Roedovre, Denmark.
- Roedovre Avis. w. ISSN 0035-7782

**Rosenkilde og Bagger Forlag**
3 Kron-Prinsens-Gade, Copenhagen K, Denmark.
- Anglistica. irreg., vol. 20, 1974. ISSN 0066-1805
- Danske Bogauktioner med en Oversigt over Bogpriserne/Danish Book Auctions with an Outline of the Book Prices. irreg. ISSN 0070-2811
- Early English Manuscripts in Facsimile. irreg, vol. 19, 1974. ISSN 0070-7856 (Dist. in U. S. and Canada by: Johns Hopkins University Press, Baltimore, MD 21218)
- Early Icelandic Manuscripts in Facsimile. irreg., 1972, vol. 10. ISSN 0070-7899 (Arnamagnaean Institute)
- Mediaeval Manuscripts from the Low Countries in Facsimile. irreg. ISSN 0076-5848

**Royal Danish Academy of Sciences and Letters**
*see* Kongelige Danske Videnskabernes Selskab

**Royal Danish Agricultural Society**
*see* Kongelige Danske Landhusholdningsselskab

**Royal Danish Automobile Club**
- Auto-Orientering. (pub. by Harlang og Toksvig Bladforlag A-S)
- Motor-Journalen Bilen. (pub. by Palle Fogtdals A-S)

**Royal Danish Geographical Society**
*see* Kongelige Danske Geografiske Selskab

**Forlaget Sabroe A-S**
Grundtvigsvej 25, 1864 Copenhagen V, Denmark.
- Golf. m. (Dansk Golf Union)

**Saddlers and Upholsterer's Guild**
Fortunstraede 5, 1065 Copenhagen K, Denmark.
- Sadelmager-og Tapetserer Tidende. m. ISSN 0036-228X

**Samfundet for Dansk Genealogi og Personalhistorie**
c/o Hans Worsoe, Stenshoej 12, Bruunshaab, DK-8800 Viborg, Denmark.
- Personalhistorisk Tidsskrift. s-a. ISSN 0300-3655

**Sammenslutningen af Lokalhistoriske Arkiver**
c/o Dorte Haahr Carlsen, Esbjerg Byhistoriske Arkiv, Teglvaerksgade 1 B, 6700 Esbjerg, Denmark.
- Lokalhistorisk Journal. 4 per yr. (Co-sponsor: Sammenslutningen af Lokalhistoriske Foreninger)

**Samvirkende Danske Haveselskaber**
Rolighedsvej 26, DK-1958 Copenhagen, Denmark.
- Haven. m. ISSN 0017-8500

**Samvirkende Koebmandsforeninger i Danmark**
Fenrisvej 11, 8230 Aabyhoej, Denmark.
- Dansk Handelsblad. w. ISSN 0045-9615

**Scandinavian Building Research Congress**
- Scandinavian Building Research. (pub. by Danish National Institute of Building Research)

**Scandinavian Institute of Asian Studies**
2 Kejsergade, DK-1155 Copenhagen K, Denmark.
- Scandinavian Institute of Asian Studies. Annual Newsletter. a. ISSN 0069-1704
- Scandinavian Institute of Asian Studies. Monograph Series. irreg., no. 25, 1976. ISSN 0069-1712 (Outside Scandinavia, orders to: Curzon Press, 88 Gray's Inn Rd., London W.C.1., England)

**Scandinavian Media Ltd.**
Krystalgade 3, DK-1172 Copenhagen, Denmark.
- Scandinavian Shipping Gazette; the international review. m. ISSN 0036-5629
- Take Off-Trafik og Turisme; travel trade magazine for Scandinavian agents. m (11 per yr.)

**Scandinavian Orthopaedic Association**
- Acta Orthopaedica Scandinavica. (pub. by Munksgaard)
- Acta Orthopaedica Scandinavica. Supplementum. (pub. by Munksgaard)

**Scandinavian Science Press Ltd.**
Christiansholms Parallelvej 2, DK-2930 Klampenborg, Denmark.
- Atlantide Report. Scientific Results of the Danish Expedition to the Coasts of Tropical West Africa. biennial. ISSN 0067-0227 (Koebenhavns Universitet) (Co-sponsor: British Museum)
- Fauna Entomologica Scandinavica. irreg. (2-5 per yr.)

**Scandinavian Society for Economic and Social History and Historical Geography**
University of Odense, DK-5000 Odense, Denmark.
- Scandinavian Economic History Review. s-a. ISSN 0036-5491

**Scandinavian Society for Plant Physiology**
- Physiologia Plantarum. (pub. by Munksgaard)

**J. H. Schultz Forlag**
Vognmagergade 2, 1120 Copenhagen K, Denmark.
- Danmarks Adels Aarbog. biennial. ISSN 0084-9561
- Denmark. Folketinget. Folketingsaarbog. a. ISSN 0084-9707
- Kongelig Dansk Hof- og Statskalender; Statshaandbog for Kongeriget Danmark. a. ISSN 0085-2589
- Ministerialtidende for Kongeriget Danmark: Section A & B. m. ISSN 0085-3461

**Forlaget Scriptor**
Gasvaerksvej 15, DK-1565 Copenhagen K, Denmark.
- Acta Ophthalmologica. bi-m. ISSN 0001-639X
- Acta Ophthalmologica. Supplementum. irreg. ISSN 0065-1451

**Selektiv Reklame A-S**
Kroghsgade 1, 2100 Copenhagen, Denmark.
- Vi med Hus og Have. 5 per yr.

**Selskabet for Dansk Skolehistorie**
Lersoe Parkalle 101, DK-2100 Copenhagen OE, Denmark.
- Aarbog for Dansk Skolehistorie. a. ISSN 0065-0145

**Selskabet for Historie og Samfundsoekonomi**
- Oekonomi og Politik. (pub. by Munksgaard)

**Selskabet for Naturlaerens Udbredelse**
- Fysisk Tidsskrift. (pub. by Jul. Gjellerups Boghandel A-S)

**Selskabet for Stuekulturer i Danmark**
Buddingevej 244-F, DK-2860 Soeborg, Denmark.
- Stuekulturer; naturen og hjemmet. m. ISSN 0039-4165

**Selvejende Institution Politisk Revy**
Skt. Pederstraede 28 B 1, 1453 Copenhagen K, Denmark.
- Politisk Revy. fortn. ISSN 0551-3464

**Skandinavisk Motor Presse**
Gladsaxe Moellevej 26, 2860 Soeborg, Denmark.
- Motorsporten. a.

**Skandinavisk U F O Information**
Lunagervej 23, 2650 Hvidovre, Denmark.
- U F O-Nyt. bi-m. ISSN 0049-4976

**Skolepsykologernes Landsforening**
c/o Bjoern Glasel, Skelvej 7, 3450 Alleroed, Denmark.
- Skolepsykologi/Journal of School Psychology; tidsskrift for paedagogisk psykologi og raadgivning. 6 per yr. plus monographs. ISSN 0037-6493

**Forlaget Skribella A-S**
Egegaardsvej 15, 2610 Roedovre, Denmark.
- Kontor-Nyt. 27 per yr. ISSN 0023-3714
- Licitationen; dagbladet for bygge-og anlaegsvirksomhed. d. ISSN 0024-287X

**Social Democratic Party**
- Ny Politik. (pub. by Fremad A-S)

**Social Tidsskrift**
Sankt Peters Straede 45, Copenhagen, Denmark.
- Social Tidsskrift. m.

**Societatum Veteranariarum Scandanivacarum**
- Acta Veterinaria Scandinavica. (pub. by Danske Dyrlaegeforening)
- Acta Veterinaria Scandinavica. Supplementum. (pub. by Danske Dyrlaegeforening)

**Soe-Lieutenant-Selskabet**
- Tidsskrift for Soevaesen. (pub. by Erhvervenes Forlag)

**Soft Machine Productions**
c/o Dan Turell, Ed., Forhabningsholms Alle 18, 1904 Copenhagen 5, Denmark.
- Soft Machine Productions. q.

**Forlaget Solidaritet**
Radhusstrade 13, 3 Sal, DK-1466 Copenhagen, Denmark.
- International Bulletin. 10 per yr.

**Specialbladsforlaget**
Ravnsborggade 12, 2200 Copenhagen N, Denmark
- Foto og Smalfilm. m (11 per yr.) (Or Forlaget Sabroe A-S, Grundtvigsvej 25, 1864 Copenhagen V, Denmark)
- Kamera. s-a. (Or Forlaget Sabroe A-S, Grundtvigsvej 25, 1864 Copenhagen V, Denmark)
- Markedsfoering. m. (Faellesraadet for Markedsfoering)
- Vi Unge. m.

**Stadsingenioerforeningen i Danmark**
- Stads & Havneingenioeren/Municipal Engineer. (pub. by Teknisk Forlag A-S)

**Statens Humanistiske Forskningsraad**
Holmens Kanal 7, 1060 Copenhagen K, Denmark.
- Humaniora. irreg.

**Niels Steensens Forlag**
Bredgade 67 A, DK-1717 Copenhagen V, Denmark.
- Lumen; Katolsk teologisk tidsskrift. 3 per yr. ISSN 0047-5173

**Finn Suenson Forlag**
Rosenoerns Alle 18, 1970 Copenhagen V, Denmark.
- Danske Skolehaandbog. a.

**Teknisk Forlag A-S**
Bredgade 67 A, DK-1717 Copenhagen V, Denmark.
- Byggeindustrien; Tidsskrift for bygningsteknik. m. ISSN 0007-750X
- Danmarks Amstraad. fortn. ISSN 0011-6106 (Amtsraadsforningen i Danmark)
- Danmarks 1000 Stoerste Virksomheder/1000 Largest Companies in Denmark. a.
- Dansk-Kemi. m. ISSN 0011-6335
- Dansk Vejtidsskrift. m. ISSN 0011-6548 (Amtsvejinspektoerforeningen i Danmark)
- Effektivt Landbrug. fortn. ISSN 0013-2187
- Elektronik. m. ISSN 0013-5631
- Elektronikindustriens Indkoebsbog. a.
- Emballage/Packaging. m. ISSN 0013-6549
- Ingenioeren. w. (Dansk Ingenioer Forening) (Co-sponsor: Ingenioer Sammenslutningen)
- Ingenioeren Indkoebsbog. a. ISSN 0446-2491
- Landinspektoeren. bi-m. (Danske Landinspektoerforening)
- Management/Virksomhedsstyring. m. ISSN 0025-1631 (Dansk Ingenioer Forening)
- Moderne Jordflytning/Modern Earthmoving. 8 per yr. ISSN 0026-8623
- S M E A Maskin-Industrien. (Smith-Machine-Electrical and Automotive Workshops) fortn. ISSN 0036-164X
- Stads & Havneingenioeren/Municipal Engineer. m. ISSN 0038-8947 (Stadsingenioerforeningen i Danmark)
- Svejsetidende. 4 per yr. (Danish Producers of Compressed Gasses)
- Trae og Industri. m(10 per yr) (Traeindustriens Fabrikantforening) (Co-sponsors: Traeindustriens Faellesrepraesentation; Traeraadet)
- Transport; the periodical rallying all transport interests. m. ISSN 0041-1361 (Transportoekonomisk Forening)
- V V S; Tidsskrift for varme, ventilation, sanitet. m. ISSN 0042-1944
- Vand/Water; Tidsskrift for Vandkvalitet. q. ISSN 0042-2509

**Teknisk Skoleforening**
Rebslagervej 11, DK-2400 Copenhagen NV, Denmark.
- Teknisk Skoletidende. m. ISSN 0040-2338

**Teknologisk Institut. Afdeling for Varme- og Installationsteknik**
- Fyring. (pub. by Forenedetidsskrifters Forlag)
- Varme. (pub. by Forenedetidsskrifters Forlag)

**Thomson Communications (Scandinavia) A-S**
Hestemoellestraede 6, 1464 Copenhagen K, Denmark.
- Agro Nyt. m.
- Elektronik Nyt. m.
- Elektronik Nyt Buyers Guide. a.
- Materialehaandtering og Transport Nyt. m. ISSN 0025-5297
- Produktions Nyt/Vaerksteds Nyt. fortn.
- Teknisk Nyt. w. ISSN 0040-232X
- Teknisk Nyt Buyers Guide. a.
- Trae Nyt. fortn. ISSN 0041-0624
- Trae Nyt Buyers Guide. a.
- Varme & Sanitets Nyt. fortn. ISSN 0042-2770
- Varme og Sanitets Nyt. m. ISSN 0007-7488
- Virksomheds Nyt. m (11 per yr.)

**Thorvaldsen Museum**
Porthusgade 2, 1213 Copenhagen K, Denmark.
- Thorvaldsen Museum. Meddelelser. irreg. ISSN 0085-7262

**Tiderne Skrifter**
Moellelodden 4, 2791 Draegor, Denmark.
- Hug! bi-m.

**Tidsskriftsforlaget**
Tordenskjoldsgade 29, 1055 Copenhagen K, Denmark.
- Dansk Bygge Journal; orienterende tidsskrift for offentligt. m. ISSN 0045-9593

**Traeindustriens Fabrikantforening**
- Trae og Industri. (pub. by Teknisk Forlag A-S)

**Traktor- og Landbrugsbladet**
Praestoevej 19, Faxe, Denmark.
- Traktor- og Landbrugsbladet. m. ISSN 0041-0977

**Translatoerforeningen**
Bornholmsgade 1, DK-1266 Copenhagen K, Denmark.
- Translatoeren. 5 per yr. ISSN 0041-1264

**Transportoekonomisk Forening**
- Transport. (pub. by Teknisk Forlag A-S)

**Transropa Press**
Noerre Soegade 7, DK-1370 Copenhagen K, Denmark.
- Kontorbladet; tidsskrift for erhverv og kontor. m. ISSN 0026-8631

**Udenrigs Handel & Industri Information**
Vesterbrogade 42, DK-1620 Copenhagen V, Denmark.
- Udenrigs Handel & Industri Information. s-a. ISSN 0041-5677

**Udenrigspolitiske Selskab**
Vandkunsten 8, 1467 Copenhagen K, Denmark.
- Fremtiden. q. ISSN 0016-1020
- Oekonomisk Kronik. m. ISSN 0029-8646
- Udenrigspolitiske Skrifter. q. ISSN 0041-5693

**Vaabenhistorisk Selskab**
Danish Arms and Armour Society, "Brobyvang", Freerslev, DK-3400 Hilleroed, Denmark.
- Vaabenhistoriske Aarboeger. a.

**Forlaget John Vabroe A-S**
Svanemoellevej 34, DK-2100 Copenhagen OE, Denmark.
- Scanodont. 6 per yr.

**Venstres Landsorganisation**
Soelleroedvej 30, 2840 Holte, Denmark.
- Liberal. 8 per yr. ISSN 0047-4460

**Viborg Stiftsmuseum**
DK-8800 Viborg, Denmark.
- M I V: Museerne i Viborg Amt. a.
- N A A. (Nordic Archaeological Abstracts) a.

**Vikingens Forlag**
Christiansborggade 1, 1558 Copenhagen V, Denmark.
- Sejl og Motor; tidsskrift for Dansk sejl- og motorbaadssport. m. (Oct.-April) bi-m (May-Sept.) ISSN 0037-1130

**Julia Voldan, Ed. & Pub.**
Frederiksborgvej 60, DK-3450 Alleroed, Denmark.
- Tidsskriftet Ny Tid og Vi. 10 per yr. ISSN 0040-7224

**Williams Forlag A-S**
Box 39, 2880 Bagsvaerd, Denmark.
- Mit Livs Novelle. fortn.

**World Health Organization. Regional Office for Europe**
For publications of this agency see section for UNITED NATIONS

**World Pictures A-S**
Martinsvej 8, 1926 Copenhagen V, Denmark.
- Architecture from Scandinavia; engineering-construction-materials. biennial.
- Design from Scandinavia; a Scandinavian production in furniture, textiles, illumination, arts and crafts and industrial design. ISSN 0011-9369

**Kristian Zarp, Ed. & Pub.**
Kalvebod Brygge 20, DK-1560 Copenhagen V, Denmark.
- Danmarks Handels- og Soefarts-Tiedende/Danish Journal of Commerce and Shipping. w. ISSN 0011-6122

# DOMINICA

**Dominica. House of Assembly**
Government Headquarters, Dominica, West Indies.
- Dominica Official Gazette. w.

**Dominica. Ministry of Agriculture, Trade and Natural Resources**
Roseau, Dominica, West Indies.
- Dominica. Registrar of Co-Operative Societies. Report. irreg.

**Dominica. Treasury Department**
Roseau, Dominica, West Indies.
- Dominica. Treasury Department. Annual Overseas Trade Report. a. ISSN 0417-9382

**Dominica Agricultural and Industrial Development Bank**
Roseau, Dominica, West Indies.
- Dominica Agricultural and Industrial Development Bank. Annual Report and Financial Statements. a.

**New Chronicle Printery Ltd.**
7 Queen Mary St., Roseau, Dominica, West Indies (Subscr. to: Box 124, Roseau, Dominica, W.I.)
- New Chronicle. w.

# DOMINICAN REPUBLIC

**Academia Dominicana de la Historia**
Calle de las Mercades, 50, Santo Domingo, Dominican Republic.
- Clio. 3 per yr. ISSN 0009-9376

**Publicaciones Ahora**
Apartado Postal 1402, San Martin 236, Santo Domingo, Dominican Republic.
- Ahora. w. ISSN 0002-2047
- Eva. m. ISSN 0014-3286

**Asociacion Dominicana pro Bienestar de la Familia**
Apdo. Postal 1053, Santo Domingo, Dominican Republic.
- Asociacion Domincana pro Bienestar de la Familia. Boletin. bi-m.

**Banco Central de la Republica Dominicana**
Santo Domingo, Dominican Republic.
- Banco Central de la Republica Dominicana. Boletin Mensual. m. ISSN 0005-4682

**Camara Oficial de Comercio, Agricultura e Industria del Distrito Nacional**
Distrito Nacional, Arz. Nouel No. 52, Santo Domingo, Dominican Republic.
- Comercio y Produccion. m. ISSN 0010-2342

**Editoria del Caribe**
Ciudad Trujillo, Dominican Republic.
- Revista Juridica Dominicana. q (some double issues) (Dominican Republic. Secretaria de Estado de Justicia y Trabajo)

**Colegio Dominicano de Ingenieros, Arquitectos y Agrimensores**
Ave. Ortega y Gasset Esq., Padre Fantino Falco. Ens. Naco, Santo Domingo, Dominican Republic.
- C O D I A. bi-m. ISSN 0045-7310

**Dominican Republic. Centro Dominicano de Promocion de Exportaciones**
Edificio del Archivo General de la Nacion, Calle Modesto Diaz Esq. Huascar Tejeda, Apartado 199-2, Santo Domingo, Dominican Republic.
- Dominican Republic. Centro Dominicano de Promocion de Exportaciones. Informe de Labores. irreg.

**Dominican Republic. Centro Nacional de Investigaciones Agropecuarias. Laboratorio de Sanidad Vegetal**
San Cristobal, Dominican Republic.
- Dominican Republic. Centro Nacional de Investigaciones Agropecuarias. Laboratorio. de Sanidad Vegetal. Sanidad Vegetal. irreg. (5-6 per yr.)

**Dominican Republic. Direccion General de Bellas Artes**
Santo Domingo, Dominican Republic.
- Dominican Republic. Direccion General de Bellas Artes. Catalogo de la Bienal de Artes Plasticas. irreg.

**Dominican Republic. Ejercito Nacional**
Ciudad Trujillo, Dominican Republic.
- Revista Militar. ISSN 0035-0117

**Dominican Republic. Oficina Nacional de Presupuesto**
Santo Domingo, Dominican Republic.
- Dominican Republic. Oficina Nacional del Presupuesto. Ejecucion del Presupuesto. irreg.

**Dominican Republic. Secretaria de Estado de Agricultura y Colonisacion**
Santo Domingo, Dominican Republic.
- Agricultura. m.

**Dominican Republic. Secretaria de Estado de Industria y Comercio**
Santo Domingo, Dominican Republic.
- Dominican Republic. Secretaria de Estado de Industria y Comercio. Revista. 2 per yr.

**Dominican Republic. Secretaria de Estado de Justicia y Trabajo**
- Revista Juridica Dominicana. (pub. by Editoria del Caribe)

**Dominican Republic. Secretaria de Estado de las Fuerzas Armadas**
Apartado de Correos 1350, Santo Domingo, Dominican Republic.
- Revista de las Fuerzas Armadas. m. ISSN 0034-8457

**Dominican Republic. Secretaria de Estado de Obras Publicas y Comunicaciones**
c/o Director General de Programacion y Proyectos, Santo Domingo, Dominican Republic.
- Dominican Republic Secretaria de Estado de Obras Publicas y Comunicaciones. OPC. irreg.

**Eco Dominicana, S. A.**
Av. Independencia 103, Santo Domingo, Dominican Republic.
- Economia Dominicana; revista independiente de informacion economica. 8-10 per yr. ISSN 0012-9763

**Fondo Cultural de la Cuna de America**
Jose Reyes 50, Santo Domingo Dominican Republic.
- Helios. q.

**Fundacion Dominicana de Desarrollo**
Calle Mercedes 4, Santo Domingo, Z. P. No. 1, Dominican Republic.
- Fundacion Dominicana de Desarrollo. a.
- Notas de Desarrollo. q.

**Iglesia Evangelica Dominicana**
Apartado 727, Santo Domingo, Dominican Republic.
- Nuestro Amigo. m. ISSN 0029-5752

**Instituto Montecristeno de Arqueologia**
Montecristi, Dominican Republic.
- Instituto Montecristeno de Arqueologia. Boletin. s-a.

**Museo del Hombre Dominicano**
Calle Pedro Henriquez Urena, Santo Domingo, Dominican Republic.
- Museo del Hombre Dominicano. Boletin. irreg.

**Puerta del Sol**
Calle Jose Reyes, 36 Esq. A. el Conde, Apts. 301-303, Box 650, Santo Domingo, Dominican Republic.
- Renovacion. s-m. ISSN 0034-446X

**Ruta Dominicana**
Apartamiento 313, Edificio Baquero, Calle Elconde, Santo Domingo, Dominican Republic.
- Ruta Dominicana. s-m. ISSN 0036-0422

**Sociedad Dominicana de Geografia**
Calle Mercedes 50, Santo Domingo, Dominican Republic.
- Sociedad Dominicana de Geografia Boletin. 3 per yr. ISSN 0049-0997

**Sociedad Dominicana de Pediatria**
El Vergel 3, Santo Domingo, Dominican Republic.
- Archivos Dominicanos de Pediatria. 3 per yr. ISSN 0004-0606 (Co-sponsors: Academia Americana de Pediatria (Capitulo Dominicano); Hospital de Ninos de Santo Domingo)

**Imprenta de Universidad Autonoma de Santo Domingo**
Edificio Dr. Defillo, Ciudad Universitaria, Dominican Republic.
- Universidad Autonoma de Santo Domingo. Direccion de Investigaciones. D I C Boletin. m.

**Universidad Autonoma de Santo Domingo. Biblioteca Central**
Santo Domingo, Dominican Republic.
- Universidad Autonoma de Santo Domingo. Biblioteca Central. Buletin de Adquisiciones. bi-m. ISSN 0041-8277

**Universidad Autonoma de Santo Domingo. Comision para el Desarrollo y Reforma Universitarios**
Ciudad Universitaria, Apdo. 1355, Santo Domingo, Dominican Republic.
- Universidad Autonome de Santo Domingo. Comision para el Desarrollo y Reforma Universitarios. irreg.

**Universidad Autonoma de Santo Domingo. Direccion de Investigaciones Cientificas**
Santo Domingo, Dominican Republic.
- Ciencia. q.

**Universidad Autonoma de Santo Domingo. Direccion de Investigaciones**
- Universidad Autonoma de Santo Domingo. Direccion de Investigaciones. D I C Boletin. (pub. by Imprenta de Universidad Autonoma de Santo Domingo)

**Universidad Autonoma de Santo Domingo. Escuela de Ciencias de la Informacios Publica**
Santo Domingo, Dominican Republic.
- Universitario. s-m. ISSN 0041-9044

**Universidad Autonoma de Santo Domingo. Facultad de Ciencias Economicas y Sociales**
Santo Domingo, Dominican Republic.
- Revista de Ciencias Economicas y Sociales. q.

**Universidad Autonoma de Santo Domingo. Facultad de Humanidades**
Santo Domingo, Dominican Republic.
- Pequeno Universo. q.

**Universidad Catolica Madre y Maestra. Centro de Estudios Dominicanos**
Santiago de los Caballeros, Dominican Republic.
- Eme Eme; estudios Dominicanos. irreg.

**Universidad Nacional "Pedro Henriquez Urena"**
Santo Domingo, Dominican Republic.
- Aula. q.
- Fisica y Tecnologia. q.

# ECUADOR

**Archivo Historico del Guayas**
Casilla 1333, Guayaquil, Ecuador.
- Archivo Historico del Guayas. Revista. s-a.

**Banco Central del Ecuador**
Quito, Ecuador.
- Banco Central del Ecuador. Boletin. 3 per yr. ISSN 0005-4739
- Banco Central del Ecuador. Memoria del Gerente General. a; latest issue, 1973. ISSN 0067-3277

**Banco Central del Ecuador. Biblioteca**
Aptdo.Postal 339, Quito, Ecuador.
- Banco Central del Ecuador. Biblioteca. General Lista de Canje. q.

**Banco Nacional de Fomento**
Casa Matriz: Ante 107y, 10 de Agosto - Aptdo 685, Quito, Ecuador.
- B N F Bulletin. bi-m.

**C O F I E C**
Av. 10 de Agosto No. 1564, P.O. Box 411, Quito, Ecuador.
- C O F I E C. Annual Report. a.

**Camara de Comercio de Quito**
Diego de Almagro No. 1170 y La Nina, Apdo 202, Quito, Ecuador.
- Comercio Ecuatoriano. q. ISSN 0010-2296

**Casa de la Cultura Ecuatoriana**
Avda. 6 de Diciembre 332, Apdo. 67, Quito, Ecuador.
- Arnahis; archivo nacional de historia. s-a.
- Casa de la Cultura Ecuatoriana. Revista. ISSN 0008-7149
- Coleccion Letras del Ecuador. irreg.
- Letras del Ecuador. m. ISSN 0024-1237
- Revista de Antropologia. q.
- Revista Ecuatoriana de Education. s-a. ISSN 0034-9305

- Revista Ecuatoriana de Medicina y Ciencias
  Biologicas. q. ISSN 0034-9313

**Comerciante**
Av. Olmedo 414, Guayquil, Ecuador.
- Comerciante. m. ISSN 0008-1868

**Corporacion de Estudios y Publicaciones**
Edificio Alvarez, Orellana y 6 de Deciembre, Quito,
Ecuador.
- Revista de Derecho. q. ISSN 0556-5693

**Economica**
Av. America 3747, Quito, Ecuador.
- Economica. bi-m.

**Compania Editora del Ecuador**
Salinas 841, Casilla 3358, Quito, Ecuador.
- Carta Economomica del Ecuador. w (with special
  nos.) ISSN 0528-1865

**Ecuador. Centro de Desarrollo Industrial del Ecuador**
Av. Orellana 1297, Box 2321, Quito, Ecuador.
- Centro de Desarrollo Industrial del Ecuador.
  Boletin Industrial. bi-m. ISSN 0045-611X
- Centro de Desarrollo Industrial del Ecuador
  (CENDES) Informe de Labores. a; latest issue,
  1973. ISSN 0070-8887
- Centro de Desarrollo Industrial del Ecuador.
  Noticias Tecnicas. a.

**Ecuador. Comision de Valores. Corporacion
Financiera Nacional**
Robles 731 y Amazonas, Quito, Ecuador.
- C V-C F N News Bulletin. m.
- Ecuador. Comision de Valores. Corporacion
  Financiera Nacional. Memoria. a. ISSN 0589-
  7688

**Ecuador. Direccion de Aviacion Civil**
Box 2077, Quito, Ecuador.
- Ecuador. Direccion de Aviacion Civil. Estadisticas
  de Trafico Aereo. m.
- Ecuador. Direccion de Aviacion Civil.
  Mathematics. m.

**Ecuador. Instituto Nacional de Estadistica**
Junta Nacional de Planificacion y Coordinacion
Economica, Quito, Ecuador.
- Ecuador. Division de Estadistica y Censos.
  Estadisticas del Trabajo. q. ISSN 0070-8917
- Ecuador. Instituto Nacional de Estadistica.
  Anuario de Estadisticas del Transporte. a.
- Ecuador. Instituto Nacional de Estadistica.
  Anuario de Estadisticas Educacionales
  (Ensenanza Primaria y Media)
- Ecuador. Instituto Nacional de Estadistica.
  Anuario de Estadisticas Hospitalarias. a. ISSN
  0070-8895
- Ecuador. Instituto Nacional de Estadistica.
  Anuario de Estadisticas Vitales. a. ISSN 0070-
  8909
- Ecuador. Instituto Nacional de Estadistica.
  Encuesta de Manufactura y Mineria. a.
- Ecuador. Oficina de los Censos Nacionales.
  Compendio de Informacion Socio-Economica de
  las Provincias del Ecuador. a. (prep. by its Oficina
  de los Censos Nacionales)
- Indice de Precios del Consumo. m. ISSN 0019-
  7025

**Ecuador. Instituto Nacional de Higiene "Leopoldo
Izquieta Perez"**
Casilla de Correos No. 3961, Guayaquil, Ecuador.
- Revista Ecuatoriana de Higiene y Medicina
  Tropical. 2 per yr. ISSN 0048-7775

**Ecuador. Instituto Nacional de Meteorologia e
Hidrologia**
Daniel Hidalgo No. 132 y 10 de Agosto, Quito,
Ecuador.
- Ecuador.Instituto Nacional de Meteorologia e
  Hidrologia. Anuario Hidrologico. a.
- Ecuador. Instituto Nacional de Meteorologia e
  Hidrologia. Anuario Meteorologico. a.
- Ecuador. Instituto Nacional de Meteorologia e
  Hidrologia. Boletin Climatologico. m.

**Ecuador. Instituto Nacional de Pesca del Ecuador**
Box 5918, Guayaquil, Ecuador.
- Instituto Nacional de Pesca del Ecuador. Boletin
  Cientifico y Tecnico. s-a. ISSN 0020-4153

**Ecuador. Instituto Nacional de Prevision**
Casilla 2640, Quito, Ecuador.
- Boletin de Informaciones y de Estudios Sociales y
  Economicos. s-a.

**Ecuador. Ministerio de Defensa Nacional.
Comandancia General de Marina**
Apdo. 2095, Quito, Ecuador.
- Revista de Marina. ISSN 0034-852X

**Ecuador. Ministerio de Finanzas. Direccion General
de Recaudaciones**
Quito, Ecuador.
- Ecuador. Ministerio de Finanzas. Direccion
  General de Recaudaciones. Boletin. irreg.

**Ecuador. Ministerio de Industrias, Comercio e
Integracion**
Quito, Ecuador.
- Ecuador. Ministerio de Industrias, Comercio e
  Integracion. Boletin de Informacion de las
  Empresas Acogidas a la Ley de Fomento
  Industrial. a.
- Ecuador. Ministerio de Industrias Comercio e
  Integracion. Documento. a.
- Ecuador. Ministerio de Industrias, Comercio e
  Integracion. Empresas Acogidas a la Ley de
  Fomento Industrial. Directorio Industrial. irreg.
- Ecuador. Ministerio de Industrias, Comercio e
  Integracion. Informe a la Nacion. a.

**Ecuador. Ministerio de Recursos Naturales y
Energeticos**
Quito, Ecuador.
- Ecuador. Ministerio de Recursos Naturales y
  Energeticos. Informe de Labores. irreg.

**Ecuador. Ministerio de Recursos Naturales y
Energeticos. Direccion General de Geologia y
Minas**
Apartado 23-a, Quito, Ecuador.
- Ecuador. Ministerio de Recursos Naturales y
  Energeticos. Direccion General de Geologia y
  Minas. Revista.

**Ecuador. Ministerio de Relaciones Exteriores**
Quito, Ecuador.
- Ecuador; carta semanal de noticias. w.

**Ecuador. Ministerio de Salud Publica. Departamento
Nacional de Poblacion**
Quito, Ecuador.
- Informe Anual de las Actividades de las Unidades
  Operativas de Salud en el Programa de
  Planificacion Familiar del Ministerio de Salud. a.

**Ecuador. Superintendencia de Bancos**
10 de Agosto, 251, Casilla 424, Quito, Ecuador.
- Ecuador. Superintendencia de Bancos. Boletin. bi-
  m.
- Ecuador. Superintendencia de Bancos.
  Conferencia Bancaria Nacional. Memoria. irreg.

**Escuela Politecnica Nacional**
Apdo. 2759, Quito, Ecuador.
- Politecnica; revista de informacion tecnico -
  cientifica. a. ISSN 0032-3055

**Instituto Ecuatoriano de Ciencias Naturales**
Apartado 408, Quito, Ecuador.
- Flora. ISSN 0015-380X
- Instituto Ecuatoriano de Ciencias Naturales.
  Contribuciones. s-a. ISSN 0010-7972

**Instituto Ecuatoriano de Folklore**
Casilla 2140, Quito, Ecuador.
- Revista del Folklore Ecuatoriano. irreg. ISSN
  0556-6436

**Instituto Otavaleno de Antropologia. Centro de
Documentacion**
Seccion Canje, Casilla 1478, Otavalo, Ecuador.
- Sarance. 3 per yr.

**Instituto Panamericano de Geografia e Historia**
*see also* Listings in- Bolivia, Mexico and Peru

**Instituto Panamericano de Geografia e Historia**
Casa de la Cultura Ecuatoriana, Quito, Ecuador.
- Revista de Historia de las Ideas. irreg. ISSN 0556-
  5987

**Laboratorios "Life"**
Apdo. 458, Quito, Ecuador.
- Terapia. q. ISSN 0040-3679

**Museo Antropologico "Antonio Santiana"**
Universidad Central, Quito, Ecuador.
- Humanitas; boletin Ecuatoriano de antropologia.
  irreg. ISSN 0018-7453

**Editores Nacionales**
Aguirre 724, Casilla 1239, Guayaquil, Ecuador.
- Estadio. q.
- Hogar; la revista de la familia ecuatoriana. m.
  ISSN 0018-3210
- Vistazo. m. ISSN 0042-7128

**Nueva**
Apdo. 3224, Quito, Ecuador.
- Nueva.

**Padres Jesuitas de la Iglesia de San Jose**
Eloy Alfaro 505, Apdo 76, Guayaquil, Ecuador.
- Catolicismo; revista de informacion, cultura y
  orientacion. w. ISSN 0008-8528

**Ediciones Paralelo Cero**
Box 1135, Av. 12 de Octubre 186, Quito, Ecuador.
- Artistas Ecuatorianos. irreg.

**Pontificia Universidad Catolica del Ecuador.
Departamento de Historia y Geografia**
Apdo. 2184, Quito, Ecuador.
- Quitumbe. a; no. 2, 1972.

**Semanario Sabado**
Vargas 219, Quito, Ecuador.
- Pantuflas del Obispo; teatro - cuento. ISSN 0031-
  1022

**Universidad Central del Ecuador**
Box 2349, Quito, Ecuador.
- Revista de Derecho Social Ecuatoriano. irreg.
  ISSN 0484-6923

**Universidad Central del Ecuador. Biblioteca General**
Quito, Ecuador.
- Universidad Central del Ecuador. Biblioteca
  General. Bibliografia Ecuatoriana. bi-m.

**Universidad Central del Ecuador. Facultad de
Ciencias Economicas y Administrativas**
Casilla 166, Quito, Ecuador.
- Economia. s-a. ISSN 0012-9704

**Universidad Central del Ecuador. Instituto de
Ciencias Naturales**
Casilla 633, Quito, Ecuador.
- Ciencia y Naturaleza. s-a. ISSN 0009-6768

**Universidad Central del Ecuador. Instituto de
Criminologia**
Apdo. de Correos No. 185, Quito, Ecuador.
- Archivos de Criminologia, Neuro-Psiquiatria y
  Disciplinas Conexas. q. ISSN 0004-0541

**Universidad Central del Ecuador. Instituto de
Derecho Comparado**
Editorial Universitaria, Quito, Ecuador.
- Instituto de Derecho Comparado. Boletin. s-a.

**Universidad Central del Ecuador. Instituto de
Estudios Administrativos**
Av. 9 de Octubre 955 y Cordero, Quito, Ecuador.
- Desarrollo Administrativo. q. ISSN 0011-9202

**Universidad Central del Ecuador. Instituto de
Investigaciones Economicas**
Casilla 1088, Quito, Ecuador.
- Boletin Trimestral de Informacion Economica.
  irreg.
- Ecuador Economico. a. ISSN 0070-8925

**Universidad Central del Ecuador. Instituto
Ecuatoriano de Derecho Internacional**
Apdo. 1025, Quito, Ecuador.
- Anuario Ecuatoriano de Derecho Internacional. a.
  ISSN 0570-4251

**Universidad de Cuenca**
Apdo. 168, Ciudad Universitaria, Cuenca, Ecuador.
- Universidad de Cuenca. Anales. q. ISSN 0041-
  8390

**Universidad de Guayaquil**
Box 3637, Guayaquil, Ecuador.
- Universidad de Guayaquil. Facultad de Ciencias
  Medicas. Revista. s-a. ISSN 0041-8412

**Universidad de Guayaquil. Escuela de Diplomacia**
Guayaquil, Ecuador.
- Universidad de Guayaquil. Escuela de Diplomacia.
  Revista. irreg.

**Universidad de Guayaquil. Instituto de Investigaciones
Economicas y Politicas**
Guayaquil, Ecuador.
- Difusion Economica. 3 per yr. ISSN 0012-2696

**Weekly Analysis of Ecuadorian Issues**
Box 4925, Guayaquil, Ecuador.
- Weekly Analysis of Ecuadorian Issues. w.

# EGYPT

**A B C - Arab Trade Reference: Arab & Middle East Countries**
99 Shari Ramsis, Al-Qahirah, Egypt.
- A B C - Arab Trade Reference: Arab & Middle East Countries. irreg.

**African Society**
5 Ahmed Hishmat Street, Zamalek, Cairo, Egypt.
- Africa News Letter. m.

**Afro-Asian Organization for Economic Co-Operation**
Cairo Chamber of Commerce Bldg., Midan el Falaky, 4, Cairo, Egypt.
- Afro Asian Economic Review. bi-m. ISSN 0002-0613

**Afro-Asian Peoples' Solidarity Organization**
89 Abdel Aziz al- Saoud St., Manial, Cairo, Egypt.
- Afro-Asian Peoples' Conference. Proceedings. irreg., 1965, 4th, Winneba, Ghana. ISSN 0065-4191
- Afro-Asian Peoples' Solidarity Organization. Council. Documents of the Session. irreg, 12th, 1975, Moscow. ISSN 0078-6233
- Afro-Asian Publications. irreg. ISSN 0515-6327
- Afro-Asian Woman's Bulletin. irreg. ISSN 0065-4205
- Solidarity. m.

**Al-Ahram Newspaper. Al-Ahram Organization and Microfilming Centre**
Al-Galaa St., Cairo, Egypt.
- Al-Ahram Index. m. ISSN 0303-2728

**Al-Ahram Organization and Microfilming Centre**
*see under* **Al-Ahram Newspaper**

**Ain Shams Clinical and Scientific Society**
Ain Shams University, Cairo, Egypt.
- Ain Shams Medical Journal. bi-m. ISSN 0002-2144

**Akhbar el Yom Publishing House**
6 Sahafa Str., Cairo, Egypt.
- Akhbar el Yom. w. ISSN 0002-3647
- Akher Saa. w. ISSN 0002-3655

**Al-Akhbar Printing Establishment**
8 Hoda Shaarawy St., Cairo, Egypt.
- Doctor; health education magazine. m. ISSN 0012-4435

**Alamal Magazine**
42 Elgomhoriah St., P.O. 1862, Cairo, Egypt.
- Labour. s-a.

**Alexandria Medical Association**
4 G. Carducci St., Alexandria, Egypt.
- Alexandria Medical Journal. q. ISSN 0516-5849

**American University in Cairo**
113 Sharia Kasr el-Aini, Cairo, Egypt.
- American University in Cairo. Annual Report. a.

**American University in Cairo. Division of Public Service**
28 Falaki St. Bab el-Louk, Cairo, Egypt.
- Journal of Modern Education/Majallat Al-Tarbeya Al-Haditha. q. ISSN 0022-2798

**Arab Book Information Centre**
P.O. Box 1509, Cairo, Egypt.
- Arab Book Annual/Al-Kitab Al-Arabi Fi Aam. a. ISSN 0066-5630

**Arab Federation of Petroleum Mining & Chemical Workers**
5 Zaki St., Cairo, Egypt.
- Arab Petroleum. m. ISSN 0003-7443

**Arab Lawyers Union**
13, rue Itehad el Mohameen el Arab, Garden City, Cairo, Egypt.
- Droit/Al-Haqq. 3 per yr.

**Arab League Educational Scientific and Cultural Organization**
Cairo, Egypt.
- A L E S C O Newsletter. bi-m.

**Arab Veterinary Medical Association**
8 Sh 26 July, Cairo, Egypt.
- Arab Veterinary Medical Association. Journal. q. ISSN 0003-746X

**Association of the Graduates of the Institutes and Faculties of Education**
13 Tahrir Square, Cairo, Egypt.
- Sahifat Al-Tarbiya. q. ISSN 0036-2654

**Al-Azhar University**
Cairo, Egypt.
- Majallat al-Azhar. m.

**Banque de Port-Said**
18 Rue Talaat Harb, Alexandria, Egypt.
- Banque de Port-Said. Revue Economique Trimestrielle. q. ISSN 0005-5603

**Botanical Society of Egypt**
- Egyptian Journal of Botany. (pub. by National Information and Documentation Centre)

**Cairo Chamber of Commerce**
4 Midan Ealaky, Cairo, Egypt.
- Cairo Chamber of Commerce. Journal/Gharfet el Hahira. m.

**Central Bank of Egypt**
31 Sharia Kasr-el Nil, Cairo, Egypt.
- Central Bank of Egypt. Board of Directors. Report/Al-Bank Al-Markazi Al-Misri. Board of Directors. Report. a. ISSN 0069-1526
- Central Bank of Egypt. Economic Review. ISSN 0008-9249

**Centre de Documentation d'Etudes Juridiques, Economiques et Sociales**
French Embassy, Cairo, Egypt.
- Centre de Documentation d'Etudes Juridiques, Economiques et Sociales. Bulletin. s-a.

**Centre de Documentation et de Recherches**
Administration de l'Information, 22 rue Talaat Harb, Cairo, Egypt.
- Encyclopedie Politique Arabe. Documents et Notes. s-a. ISSN 0013-7146

**Cotton Exporters Association**
Box 291, Alexandria, Egypt.
- Egyptian Cotton Gazette. 3 per yr. ISSN 0013-2403

**Deutsch-Arabische Handelskammer**
2 Sheif Str., Cairo, Egypt.
- German Arab Trade. irreg. ISSN 0072-1433

**Drug Research & Control Centre**
6, Abou-Hazem St., Pyramids Ave., Box 29, Cairo, Egypt.
- Journal of Drug Research. 3 per yr. ISSN 0085-2406

**Egypt. Central Agency for Public Mobilisation & Statistics**
Nasr City, Cairo, Egypt.
- Egypt. Central Agency for Public Mobilisation and Statistics. Monthly Bulletin of Foreign Trade. m. ISSN 0027-0237
- Statistical Handbook of Egypt. a.

**Egypt. Meteorological Authority**
Kubri- el Qubbeh, Cairo, Egypt.
- Egypt. Meteorological Authority. Meteorological Research Bulletin. irreg.
- Egypt. Meteorological Authority. Monthly Weather Report. m.

**Egypt. Ministry of Tourism**
5 Adly St., Cairo, Egypt.
- Egypt. Ministry of Tourism. Statistical Bulletin. q. ISSN 0041-4948 (prep. by its Planning and Research Department, Statistical Studies Section)
- Egypt Travel Magazine. q. ISSN 0013-2381

**Egypt. Service des Antiquites**
- Egypt. Service des Antiquites. Annales. (pub. by Egyptian National Museum)

**Egyptian Chamber of Commerce**
4 Midan Falaki, Cairo, Egypt.
- Egyptian Chamber of Commerce. Bulletin. m.

**Egyptian Chemical Society**
- Egyptian Journal of Chemistry. (pub. by National Information and Documentation Centre)

**Egyptian Dental Association**
Dar el Hekma, 42 Kasr el-Aini St., Cairo, Egypt.
- Egyptian Dental Journal. q. ISSN 0070-9484

**Egyptian Horticultural Society**
- Egyptian Journal of Horticulture. (pub. by National Information and Documentation Centre)

**Egyptian Medical Association**
42 Kasr-El-Aini St., Cairo, Egypt.
- Egyptian Medical Association. Journal. m. ISSN 0013-2411

**Egyptian National Museum**
Midan - el - Tahrir, Kasr el-Nil, Cairo, Egypt.
- Egypt. Service des Antiquites. Annales. irreg. ISSN 0082-7835
- Egyptian National Museum. Library. Catalogue. irreg. ISSN 0068-5275

**Egyptian Orthopaedic Association**
Box 4, Alexandria, Egypt.
- Egyptian Orthopaedic Journal. q. ISSN 0013-242X

**Egyptian Physical Society**
- Egyptian Journal of Physics. (pub. by National Information and Documentation Centre)

**Egyptian Physiological Society**
- Egyptian Journal of Physiological Science. (pub. by National Information and Documentation Centre)

**Egyptian Phytopathological Society**
- Egyptian Journal of Phytopathology. (pub. by National Information and Documentation Centre)

**Egyptian Public Health Association**
Shousha Bldg., Bloc A, Apt. 116, 31 Sharia 26 July, Cairo, Egypt.
- Egyptian Public Health Association Journal. 6 per yr. ISSN 0013-2446

**Egyptian School Library Association**
35 al-Galaa St., Cairo, Egypt.
- Egyptian Library Journal/Sahifat al Makta-Bah. q. ISSN 0531-6723

**Egyptian Society of Animal Production**
- Egyptian Journal of Animal Production. (pub. by National Information and Documentation Centre)

**Egyptian Society of Dairy Science**
National Research Centre, Cairo, Egypt.
- Egyptian Journal of Dairy Science. s-a.

**Egyptian Society of Endocrinology and Metabolism**
42 Sharia Kasr el-Aini, Cairo, Egypt.
- Egyptian Society of Endocrinology and Metabolism. Journal. irreg. ISSN 0070-9506

**Egyptian Society of Genetics**
c/o University of Alexandria, Department of Genetics, Alexandria, Egypt.
- Egyptian Journal of Genetics and Cytology. s-a. ISSN 0046-161X

**Egyptian Society of International Law**
16 Ramses St., Cairo, Egypt
(Dist. by Oceana Publications Inc., 40 Cedar St., Dobbs Ferry, N.Y. 10522)
- Revue Egyptienne de Droit International. a. ISSN 0080-259X

**Egyptian Society of Political Economy, Statistics and Legislation**
16 Ave. Ramses, Box 732, Cairo, Egypt.
- Egypte Contemporaine. q. ISSN 0013-239X

**Egyptian Society of Population Research**
Tharwat St., Giza, Cairo, Egypt.
- Egyptian Population and Family Planning Review. s-a.

**Egyptian Society of Tropical Medicine and Parasitology**
- Egyptian Journal of Bilharziasis. (pub. by National Information and Documentation Centre)

**Egyptian Surgical Society**
Dar el Hekma, 42 Kasr el-Aini St., Cairo, Egypt.
- Egyptian Surgical Society Quarterly Review. q. ISSN 0013-2454

**Entomological Society of Egypt**
B.P. 430, Cairo, Egypt.
- Societe Entomologique d'Egypte. Bulletin/ Entomological Society of Egypt. Bulletin. a. ISSN 0081-0983
- Societe Entomologique d'Egypte. Bulletin. Economic Series. a. ISSN 0081-0991

**Federation of Egyptian Industries**
26 A Sherif St., Cairo, Egypt.
- Federation of Egyptian Industries. Monthly Bulletin. m.
- Industrial Egypt Quarterly. q.
- Ittihad al-Sinaat al-Misriyah. Yearbook. a.

**French Institute of Oriental Archaeology**
see Institut Francais d'Archeologie Orientale

**Geological Society of Egypt**
- Egyptian Journal of Geology. (pub. by National Information and Documentation Centre)
- Geological Society of Egypt. Annual Meeting. Abstracts of Papers. (pub. by National Information and Documentation Centre)

**Margaret Hosni, Ed. & Pub.**
Box 847, Alexandria, Egypt.
- Economiste Egyptien. w. ISSN 0013-0672

**Institut Francais d'Archeologie Orientale**
37 rue Mourira, Cairo, Egypt
- Annuaire de l'Egyptologie. irreg. (Subscr. to: Leila Bookshop, 17 Gawad Hosni St., Cairo, Egypt)

**Institute of Statistical Studies and Research**
see under University of Cairo

**International Confederation of Arab Trade Unions**
Ramses Bldg., Ramses Square, Cairo, Egypt.
- I C A T U Review. m. ISSN 0018-8816

**Ittihad al-Sinaat al-Misriyah**
see Federation of Egyptian Industries

**Kasr el-Aini Clinical Society. Faculty of Medicine**
23 Sharia Abdul Khalek Tharwat, Cairo, Egypt.
- Kasr el-Aini Clinical Society. Faculty of Medicine. Gazette. q.

**Kasr-El-Aini Journal of Surgery**
c/o Prof. I. Mehrez, 33 Sarwat Pasha St., Cairo, Egypt.
- Kasr-El-Aini Journal of Surgery. q. ISSN 0022-9237

**Library World**
Box 1509, Cairo, Egypt.
- Library World/Alam Al-Maktabat. bi-m. ISSN 0024-2608

**Medicine and Medicaments Courier**
32 Talaat Harb St. (Ex-Soliman Pasha), Cairo, Egypt.
- Medicine and Medicaments Courier. bi-m. ISSN 0025-7982

**Middle East News Agency**
11 Sharia Samafa, Cairo, Egypt.
- Arab Observer. w. ISSN 0570-5258
- M. E. N. Economic Weekly. w. ISSN 0024-8118

**Middle East Observer**
8 Chawarby St., Cairo, Egypt.
- Middle East Observer. w. ISSN 0047-7257

**Middle Eastern Regional Radioisotope Centre for the Arab Countries**
Sh. Malaeb el Gamaa, Dokki, Cairo, Egypt.
- Isotope and Radiation Research. a. ISSN 0021-1907

**N I D O C**
see National Information and Documentation Centre

**Nadi al-Tijarah**
11 Shari Marrayn, Al-Qahirah, Egypt.
- Al-Mal Wa-al-Tijarah. m. (Co-Sponsor: al-Ghurfah al-Tijariyah Bi-al-Minufiyah)

**National Bank of Egypt**
24 Sharia Sherif Pasha, Cairo, Egypt.
- National Bank of Egypt. Economic Bulletin. q. ISSN 0027-8742 (prep. by its Research Department)

**National Center for Social and Criminological Research**
Gezira P.O.B., Cairo, Egypt.
- National Review of Criminal Sciences. 3 per yr. ISSN 0028-0054
- National Review of Social Sciences. 3 per yr. ISSN 0028-0062

**National Information and Documentation Centre**
24 Sharia Sherif Pasha, Dokki, Cairo, Egypt.
- Egyptian Journal of Animal Production. s-a. ISSN 0302-4520 (Egyptian Society of Animal Production. Research Department)
- Egyptian Journal of Bilharziasis. s-a. (Egyptian Society of Tropical Medicine and Parasitology. Research Department) (Co-sponsor: General Society for Combat of Bilharziasis)
- Egyptian Journal of Botany. 3 per yr. (Botanical Society of Egypt. Research Department)
- Egyptian Journal of Chemistry. 6 per yr. ISSN 0449-2285 (Egyptian Chemical Society. Research Department)
- Egyptian Journal of Food Science. s-a. (Society of Food Science and Technology. Research Department)
- Egyptian Journal of Geology. s-a. (Geological Society of Egypt. Research Department)
- Egyptian Journal of Horticulture. s-a. (Egyptian Horticultural Society. Research Department)
- Egyptian Journal of Microbiology. s-a. (Society of Applied Microbiology. Research Department)
- Egyptian Journal of Pharmaceutical Sciences. 4 per yr. ISSN 0301-5068 (Pharmaceutical Society of Egypt. Research Department)
- Egyptian Journal of Physics. s-a. (Egyptian Physical Society. Research Department)
- Egyptian Journal of Physiological Science. s-a. (Egyptian Physiological Society. Research Department)
- Egyptian Journal of Phytopathology. a. (Egyptian Phytopathological Society. Research Department)
- Egyptian Journal of Soil Science. s-a. (Society of Soil Science. Research Department)
- Geological Society of Egypt. Annual Meeting. Abstracts of Papers. a. ISSN 0446-4648

**Ophthalmological Society of Egypt**
Dar el Hekma, 42 Kasr el-Aini St., Cairo, Egypt.
- Ophthalmological Society of Egypt. Bulletin. a. ISSN 0078-5342

**Peres Jesuits**
1 rue Boustan El Maksi, Faggalah, Cairo, Egypt.
- Etudes Medicales. q. ISSN 0025-6714
- Etudes Scientifiques. q. ISSN 0041-9036

**Permanent Bureau of Afro-Asian Writers**
104 Kasr El-Aini St., Cairo, Egypt.
- Lotus; Afro-Asian writings. q. ISSN 0002-0664

**Pharmaceutical Society of Egypt**
- Egyptian Journal of Pharmaceutical Sciences. (pub. by National Information and Documentation Centre)

**Scientific Society of the Medical Care Organization**
375 Ramses St., Abbassieh, Cairo, Egypt.
- Hospital Medical Practice. q. ISSN 0046-8010

**Societe d'Archeologie Copte**
see Society for Coptic Archaeology

**Societe Entomologique d'Egypte**
see Entomological Society of Egypt

**Society for Coptic Archaeology**
222 rue Ramses, Cairo, Egypt.
- Societe d'Archeologie Copte. Bibliotheque de Manuscrits. irreg., latest issue in print: no. 3, no. 4 in preparation. ISSN 0068-5283
- Societe d'Archeologie Copte. Bulletin. irreg. ISSN 0068-5291
- Societe d'Archeologie Copte. Textes et Documents. irreg., latest issue, in print: no. 15, no. 16 in preparation. ISSN 0068-5305

**Society of Applied Microbiology**
- Egyptian Journal of Microbiology. (pub. by National Information and Documentation Centre)

**Society of Food Science and Technology**
- Egyptian Journal of Food Science. (pub. by National Information and Documentation Centre)

**Society of Islamic Studies**
Cairo, Egypt.
- Journal of Islamic Studies. 2-3 per yr. ISSN 0022-2046

**Society of Soil Science**
- Egyptian Journal of Soil Science. (pub. by National Information and Documentation Centre)

**Supreme Council for Islamic Affairs**
42, Saad Zaghloul St., Cairo, Egypt.
- Minbar al Islam. q.

**University of Alexandria. Faculty of Agriculture**
Alexandria, Egypt.
- Alexandria Journal of Agricultural Research. 3 per yr. ISSN 0044-7250

**University of Alexandria. Faculty of Medicine**
Alexandria, Egypt.
- Alexandria Faculty of Medicine Bulletin. q.

**University of Cairo. Botany Department**
Herbarium, Giza, Egypt.
- University of Cairo. Herbarium. Publications. a. ISSN 0068-5313

**University of Cairo. Faculty of Commerce**
Cairo, Egypt.
- Accountancy, Business & Insurance Review. 2 per yr. ISSN 0001-4680

**University of Cairo. Faculty of Law**
Cairo, Egypt.
- Al Qanoun Wal Iqtisad/Droit et Economy Politique. q.

**University of Cairo. Faculty of Medicine**
Clinical Society Office, Manyal Hospital, Kasr el Aini Post, Cairo, Egypt.
- University of Cairo. Faculty of Medicine. Medical Journal. q. ISSN 0045-3803

**University of Cairo. Institute of Statistical Studies and Research**
5 el-Goheiny St., Dokki, Cairo, Egypt.
- E P F P R. (Egyptiam Population and Family Planning Review) s-a.
- Egyptian Computer Journal. s-a.

**World Health Organization. Regional Office for the Eastern Mediterranean**
For publications of this agency see section for UNITED NATIONS

# EL SALVADOR

**Asociacion General de Archivistas de el Salvador**
Casa de Cultura, 11 Avenida Sur, No. 223, Aptdo. Pastal 664, San Salvador, El Salvador.
- Archivo. q. ISSN 0518-3618

**Ateneo**
San Salvador, El Salvador.
- Ateneo; ubi scientia, ibi patria. s-a. ISSN 0004-6515

**Banco Central de Reserva de el Salvador**
Apdo. Postal (06) 106, San Salvador, El Salvador.
- Banco Central de Reserva de el Salvador. Memoria. a.
- Banco Central de Reserva de El Salvador. Revista Mensual. m. ISSN 0005-4704

**Colegio Medico de El Salvador**
Final Pasaje 10, Col. Miramonte, San Salvador, El Salvador.
- Colegio Medico de El Salvador. Archivas. q. ISSN 0010-0641

**Consejo Superior Universitaria Centroamericano**
- Consejo Superior Universitario Centroamericano. Actas de la Reunion Ordinaria. (pub. by Editorial Universitaria)

**Editorial Universitaria**
5A. Calle Oriente No. 220, San Salvador, El Salvador.
- Universidad. bi-m. ISSN 0041-8242

**El Salvador. Consejo Nacional de Planificacion y Coordinacion Economica**
San Salvador, Salvador.
- El Salvador, Informe Economico y Social.

**El Salvador. Direccion General de Economia y Planificacion Agropecuaria**
Ministerio de Agricultura y Ganaderia, San Salvador, El Salvador.
- El Salvador. Direccion General de Economia y Planificacion Agropecuaria. Anuario de Estadisticas Agropecuarias. a.

**El Salvador. Direccion General de Estadistica y Censos**
San Salvador, El Salvador.
- El Salvador. Direccion General de Estadistica y Censos. Anuario Estadistico. a. ISSN 0080-5661
- El Salvador. Direccion General de Estadistica y Censos. Boletin Estadistico. q. ISSN 0013-404X
- Indice de Precios al Consumidor Obrero para San Salvador Mejicanos y Villa Delgado. m. ISSN 0019-7009

**El Salvador. Ministerio de Agricultura y Ganaderia. Direccion General de Economia Agropecuaria**
San Salvador, El Salvador.
- El Salvador. Departamento de Estadisticas Agropecuarias. Pronostico de Zafra. irreg.
- El Salvador. Ministerio de Agricultura y Ganaderia. Departamento de Estadisticas Agropecuarias. Pronostico de Algodon. irreg. (prep. by its Departamento de Estadisticas Agropecuarias)

**El Salvador. Ministerio de Agricultura y Ganaderia. Direccion General de Recursos Naturales Renovables**
23 Ave. Norte No 114, San Salvador, El Salvador.
- Almanaque Salvadoreno. a. ISSN 0084-6236 (prep. by its Servicio Meteorologico)

**El Salvador. Ministerio de Economia. Instituto de Estudios Economicos**
San Salvador, El Salvador.
- Revista de Economia de El Salvador. q.

**El Salvador. Ministerio de Educacion**
Direccion General de Publicaciones, Pasaje Contreras 145, San Salvador, El Salvador.
- Cultura. q. ISSN 0011-2755

**El Salvador. Ministerio de Planificacion y Coordinacion del Desarrollo Economico y Social. Seccion de Investigaciones Estadisticas**
Casa Presidencial, San Salvador, El Salvador.
- El Salvador. Ministerio de Planificacion y Coordinacion del Desarrollo Economico y Social. Indicadores Economicos y Sociales. a. ISSN 0581-4111

**El Salvador. Servicio e Investigaciones Hidrologicas.**
San Salvador, El Salvador.
- El Salvador. Servicio e Investigaciones Hidrologicas. Anuario Hidrologico. a.

**El Salvador. Superintendencia de Bancos y Otras Instituciones Financieras**
Junta Monetaria, San Salvador, El Salvador.
- El Salvador. Superintendencia de Bancos y Otras Instituciones Financieras. Estadisticas: Seguros, Fianzas, Capitalizacion. irreg. ISSN 0067-3234

**Instituto de Investigaciones Medicas**
Hospital Rosales, Calle Arce No 1441, San Salvador, El Salvador.
- Instituto de Investigaciones Medicas. Revista. q.

**Instituto Salvadoreno de Cultura Hispanica**
San Salvador, El Salvador.
- Cultura Hispanica. q. ISSN 0011-278X

**Instituto Salvadoreno de Turismo**
4A Avda. Norte No. 220 Altos, Aptdo Postal No. 98, San Salvador, El Salvador.
- Travelers' Courier. m.

**Sociedad Dental de el Salvador**
5 Avenida Sur, No. 4, San Salvador, El Salvador.
- Revista Dental. q. ISSN 0048-7767

**Sociedad Salvadorena de Odontologia Infantil**
- Centro America Odontologica. (pub. by Editorial Zavaleta)

**Universidad Centroamericana "Jose Simeon Canas"**
c/o Sebastian Mantilla, Apdo. 668, San Salvador, El Salvador.
- Estudios Centro Americanos. m. ISSN 0014-1445

**Universidad de El Salvador. Associacion de Estudiantes de Derecho**
Ciudad Universitaria, San Salvador, El Salvador.
- Ciencias Juridicas y Sociales. s-a.

**Universidad Nacional Autonoma de El Salvador. Instituto de Estudios Economicas**
Facultad de Ciencias Economicas, Ciudad Universitaria, San Salvador, El Salvador.
- Economia Salvadorena. a. ISSN 0012-9860

**Editorial Universitaria**
5 Calle Oriente 220, San Salvador, El Salvador.
- Consejo Superior Universitario Centroamericano. Actas de la Reunion Ordinaria. irreg. ISSN 0589-4301

**Editorial Zavaleta**
23 Av. N. 1214, San Salvador, El Salvador.
- Centro America Odontologica. q. ISSN 0008-9907 (Sociedad Salvadorena de Odontologia Infantil)

# ETHIOPIA

**Addis Ababa University**
University College, Addis Ababa, Ethiopia.
- Something. s-a. ISSN 0584-1070

**Addis Ababa University. College of Technology**
Box 518, Addis Ababa, Ethiopia.
- Addis Ababa University. College of Technology. Library Bulletin. q. ISSN 0017-6680

**Addis Ababa University. Educational Research Centre**
Faculty of Education, Box 1176, Addis Ababa, Ethiopia.
- Ethiopian Journal of Education. s-a. ISSN 0425-4414

**Addis Ababa University. Faculty of Law**
Box 1176, Addis Ababa, Ethiopia.
- African Law Digest. 3 per yr. ISSN 0002-0052

**Addis Ababa University. Geophysical Observatory**
Box 1176, Addis Ababa, Ethiopia.
- Addis Ababa University. Geophysical Observatory. Contributions. irreg. ISSN 0072-9345

**Addis Ababa University. Institute of Development Research**
P.O. Box 1176, Addis Ababa, Ethiopia.
- Ethiopian Journal of Development Research. s-a.

**Addis Ababa University. Institute of Ethiopian Studies**
Box 1176, Addis Ababa, Ethiopia.
- Addis Ababa University. Institute of Ethiopian Studies. Qene Collections. irreg; latest issue, 1975. ISSN 0072-9361
- Ethiopian Publications: Books, Pamphlets, Annuals and Periodical Articles. a. ISSN 0071-1772
- Journal of Ethiopian Studies. s-a. ISSN 0022-0922 (Subscr. to: Oxford University (East African Branch), Box 72532, Church House, Government Rd., Nairobi, Kenya)
- List of Current Periodical Publications in Ethiopia. irreg. ISSN 0459-5009

**Addis Ababa University. University Testing Center**
P.O. Box 1176, Addis Ababa, Ethiopia.
- Addis Ababa University. University Testing Center. Technical Report. irreg., 1971, no. 5. ISSN 0072-9388

**Arussi Rural Development Unit**
Box 3376, Addis Ababa, Ethiopia.
- A R D U Publication. irreg.

**Association for the Advancement of Agricultural Sciences in Africa**
P.O. 30087-M.A., Addis Ababa, Ethiopia.
- Association for the Advancement of Agricultural Sciences in Africa. Journal/Association pour l'Avancement en Afrique des Sciences de l'Agriculture. Journal. 3 per yr. ISSN 0044-9482

**Centre for Entrepreneurship and Management**
Box 3246, Addis Ababa, Ethiopia.
- Manager and Entrepreneur. irreg, latest 1974, vol. 3. ISSN 0580-8898

**Chamber of Commerce, Industry and Agriculture of Eritrea**
Box 856, Asmara, Ethiopia.
- Chamber of Commerce, Industry and Agriculture of Eritrea. Trade and Development Bulletin. irreg.

**Commercial Bank of Ethiopia**
Box 255, Addis Ababa, Ethiopia.
- Commercial Bank of Ethiopia. Annual Report. a. ISSN 0588-6694
- Commercial Bank of Ethiopia. Market Report. m. ISSN 0045-7574 (prep. by its Business Development Division)
- Commercial Bank of Ethiopia. Trade Directory. irreg.

**Desert Locust Control Organization for Eastern Africa**
P.O. Box 4255, Addis Ababa, Ethiopia.
- Desert Locust Control Organization for Eastern Africa. Report. a. ISSN 0418-761X

**Economic Commission for Africa**
For publications of this agency see section for UNITED NATIONS

**Ethiopia. Central Statistical Office**
Addis Ababa, Ethiopia.
- Ethiopia. Central Statistical Office. Information P. m.

**Ethiopia. Civil Aviation Administration. Climatological Branch**
P.O. Box 1090, Addis Ababa, Ethiopia.
- Ethiopia. Civil Aviation Administration. Climatological Branch. Monthly Weather Reports. m.

**Ethiopia. Customs Head Office**
P.O. Box 3248, Addis Ababa, Ethiopia.
- Ethiopia. Customs Head Office. External Trade Statistics. a. ISSN 0425-4309

**Ethiopia. Department of Labour and Employment**
Addis Ababa, Ethiopia.
- Addis Ababa Employment Survey. s-a. (prep. by its Employment and Statistics Division)
- Ethiopia. Department of Labour and Employment. Employment and Manpower Division. Employment Service Information. q.

**Ethiopia. Public Employment Administration**
Ministry of National Community Development and Social Affairs, Addis Ababa, Ethiopia.
- Ethiopia. Public Employment Administration. Labour Exchange Information. q.

**Ethiopia. Smallpox Eradication Programme**
Ministry of Public Health, Box 3061, Addis Ababa, Ethiopia.
- Smallpox Surveillance in Ethiopia. m.

**Ethiopian Chamber of Commerce**
Box 517, Addis Ababa, Ethiopia.
- Business Spectator. fortn.
- Ethiopian Chamber of Commerce. Directory of Agriculture. s-a.
- Ethiopian Chamber of Commerce. Directory of Industry. s-a.
- Ethiopian Chamber of Commerce. Statistical Digest. a.
- Trade Directory and Guide Book to Ethiopia. a. ISSN 0564-0490

**Ethiopian Library Association**
Box 30530, Addis Ababa, Ethiopia.
- Ethiopian Library Association. Bulletin. ISSN 0014-1747

**Ethiopian Manuscript Microfilm Library**
Box 30274, Addis Ababa, Ethiopia.
- Bulletin of Ethiopian Manuscripts. a.
- Ethiopian Manuscripts Microfilm Library. Bulletin. q.

**Ethiopian Medical Association**
P.O. Box 3472, Addis Abada, Ethiopia.
- Ethiopian Medical Journal. 4 per yr. ISSN 0014-1755

**Ethiopian Tourist Office**
Box 2183, Addis Ababa, Ethiopia.
- Discovering Ethiopia. q.

**Ethiopian Wildlife and Natural History Society**
P.O. Box 1160, Addis Ababa, Ethiopia.
- Walia. a; no. 7, 1976. ISSN 0083-7059

**Ethiopian Women's Welfare Association**
Box 2418, Addis Ababa, Ethiopia.
- Azeb. q.

**Institute of Agricultural Research**
Box 2003, Addis Ababa, Ethiopia.
- Institute of Agricultural Research. Projects. a.
- Institute of Agricultural Research. Report.

**National Bank of Ethiopia**
c/o Research Library, Box 5550, Addis Ababa, Ethiopia.
- National Bank of Ethiopia. Economic Research Department. Local Prices. irreg., May 1970, no. 4. ISSN 0077-3506
- National Bank of Ethiopia. Quarterly Bulletin. q. ISSN 0027-8750 (prep. by its Economic Research Department)

**Novosti Press Agency in Ethiopia**
Box 239, Addis Ababa, Ethiopia.
- Keste Damena/Rainbow; illustrated monthly. m. ISSN 0047-3391

**Organization of African Unity. Health, Sanitation and Nutrition Commission**
Box 3243, Addis Ababa, Ethiopia.
- Organization of African Unity. Health, Sanitation and Nutrition Commission. Proceedings and Report. a. ISSN 0473-3657

**Teachers Association of Ethiopia**
Box 1639, Addis Ababa, Ethiopia.
- Yememhiran Dimts/Teachers' Voice of Ethiopia. q. ISSN 0044-0310

**Teachers Association of Ethiopia. Eritrea Branch**
Box 954, Asmara - Eritrea, Ethiopia.
- Yememhiran Melkt/Teachers' Message. ISSN 0044-0329

**United Nations Economic Commission for Africa**
For publications of this agency see section for UNITED NATIONS

# EUROPEAN COMMUNITIES

**Association of International Libraries**
c/o C E C A, 2 Place de Metz, Luxembourg.
- A I L/Doc. irreg. ISSN 0571-6357
- A I L Newsletter. (pub. by Commission of the European Communities Library)

**Banque Europeene d'Investissement**
see European Investment Bank

**Bureau Euristop**
Rue de la Loi 200, 1049 Brussels, Belgium.
- Bureau Euristop. Cahiers d'Information. irreg.; latest issue, 1975.
- Bureau Euristop. Informations Technico-Economiques. irreg.; latest issue, 1975.

**C E C A**
see European Coal and Steel Community. Consultative Committee

**C E E A**
see European Atomic Energy Community

**Comite Consultatif (CECA)**
see European Coal and Steel Community. Consultative Committee

**Comite Economique et Social des Communautes Europeenes**
see Economic and Social Committee of the European Communities

**Commission des Communautes Europeennes**
see Commission of the European Communities

**Commission Generale de la Securite et de la Salubrite dans la Siderurgie**
see General Commission on Safety and Health in the Iron and Steel Industry

**Commission of the European Communities**
Services de Renseignement et de Diffusion des Documents, Rue de la Loi 200, 1049 Brussels, Belgium
(Dist. in the U.S. by: European Community Information Service, 2100 M St., NW, Suite 707, Washington, DC 20037)
- Bulletin of the European Communities. (pub. by Office for Official Publications of the European Communities)
- Bulletin of the European Communities. Supplement. (pub. by Office for Official Publications of the European Communities)
- Commission of the European Communities. Annual Reports on the Progress of Research Work Promoted by the ECSC. a.
- Commission of the European Communities. Cahiers de Reconversion Industrielle. (pub. by Office for Official Publications of the European Communities)
- Commission of the European Communities. Centre for Information and Documentation. Annual Report: Program Biology-Health Protection. (pub. by Office for Official Publications of the European Communities)
- Commission of the European Communities. Collection d'Economie du Travail. (pub. by Office for Official Publications of the European Communities)
- Commission of the European Communities. Collection d'Economie et Politique Regionale. (pub. by Office for Official Publications of the European Communities)
- Commission of the European Communities. Collection d'Hygiene et de Medecine du Travail. (pub. by Office for Official Publications of the European Communities)
- Commission of the European Communities. Collection du Droit du Travail. (pub. by Office for Official Publications of the European Communities)
- Commission of the European Communities. Collection Objectifs Generaux Acier. (pub. by Office for Official Publications of the European Communities)
- Commission of the European Communities. Collection Physiologie et Psychologie du Travail. (pub. by Office for Official Publications of the European Communities)
- Commission of the European Communities. Community Law. a. ISSN 0590-6563
- Commission of the European Communities. Conjoncture Energetique dans la Communaute. (pub. by Office for Official Publications of the European Communities)
- Commission of the European Communities. Directory. (pub. by Office for Official Publications of the European Communities)
- Commission of the European Communities. Documentation Bulletin. s-m.
- Commission of the European Communities. Etudes: Serie Aide au Developpement. (pub. by Office for Official Publications of the European Communities)
- Commission of the European Communities. Etudes: Serie Concurrence - Rappochement des Legislations. (pub. by Office for Official Publications of the European Communities)
- Commission of the European Communities. Etudes: Serie Energie. (pub. by Office for Official Publications of the European Communities)
- Commission of the European Communities. Etudes: Serie Industrie. (pub. by Office for Official Publications of the European Communities)
- Commission of the European Communities. Etudes: Serie Informations Internes sur l'Agriculture. (pub. by Office for Official Publications of the European Communities)
- Commission of the European Communities. Etudes: Serie Politique Sociale. (pub. by Office for Official Publications of the European Communities)
- Commission of the European Communities. Expose Annuel sur les Activities d'Orientation Professionnelle dans la Communaute. (pub. by Office for Official Publications of the European Communities)
- Commission of the European Communities. Expose Annuel sur les Activities des Services de Main-d'Ouvre des Etats Membres de la Communaute. (pub. by Office for Official Publications of the European Communities)
- Commission of the European Communities. Expose sur l'Evolution Sociale dans la Communaute. (pub. by Office for Official Publications of the European Communities)

- Commission of the European Communities. Financial Report. a. ISSN 0590-6571
- Commission of the European Communities. Investments in the Community Coalmining and Iron and Steel Industries. Report on the Survey. (pub. by Office for Official Publications of the European Communities)
- Commission of the European Communities. Marches Agricoles: Serie "Prix". Produits Animaux. 6-9 per yr.
- Commission of the European Communities. Marches Agricoles: Serie "Prix". Produits Vegetaux. 6-9 per yr.
- Commission of the European Communities. Recueils de Recherches Charbon. (pub. by Office for Official Publications of the European Communities)
- Commission of the European Communities. Report on Competition Policy/Rapport sur la Politique de Concurrence. (pub. by Office for Official Publications of the European Communities)
- Commission of the European Communities. Studies: Agricultural Series. (pub. by Office for Official Publications of the European Communities)
- Commission of the European Communities. Studies: Economic and Financial Series. (pub. by Office for Official Publications of the European Communities)
- Commission of the European Communities. Studies: Transport Series. (pub. by Office for Official Publications of the European Communities)
- Documentation Europeenne - Serie Agricole. irreg. ISSN 0537-6297
- Documentation Europeenne - Serie Syndicale et Ouvriere. irreg.
- Etudes Universitaires sur l'Integration Europeenne/University Studies on European Integration. a. ISSN 0071-2213 (European Community Institute for University Studies)
- European Community. (pub. by Office for Official Publications of the European Communities)
- General Report on the Activities of the European Communities. a. ISSN 0069-6749
- Information Service of the European Communities. Trade Union News. irreg.; (approx. 4 per yr) ISSN 0073-7909
- Joint Nuclear Research Center, Ispra, Italy. Annual Report. a.
- Nouvelles Universitaires Europeennes. 9 per yr. ISSN 0029-4950
- Official Journal of the European Communities. C Series: Information and Notices. (pub. by Office for Official Publications of the European Communities)
- Results of the Business Survey Carried out Among Heads of Enterprises in the Community. (pub. by Office for Official Publications of the European Communities)
- Transatom Bulletin. (pub. by Office for Official Publications of the European Communities)

**Commission of the European Communities. Centre d'Information et de Documentation**
29 rue Aldringen, Luxembourg, Luxembourg.
- Commission of the European Communities. Bibliographie. irreg.; 1971, no. 12. ISSN 0588-6880

**Commission of the European Communities. Commission Generale de la Securite et de la Salubrite dans la Siderurgie**
see General Commission on Safety and Health in the Iron and Steel Industry

**Commission of the European Communities. Directorate General for Press and Information. Division for Industrial and Scientific Information**
see Commission of the European Communities. Division for Industrial and Scientific Information

**Commission of the European Communities. Directorate General for Social Affairs. Vocational Guidance and Training Division**
see Commission of the European Communities. Vocational Guidance and Training Division

**Commission of the European Communities. Directorate of Taxation**
- Commission of the European Communities. Directorate of Taxation. Inventory of Taxes. (pub. by Office for Official Publications of the European Communities)

**Commission of the European Communities. Division for Industrial and Scientific Information**
Directorate General for Press and Information, Rue de la Loi 200, 1040 Brussels, Belgium.
• Industry and Society. w.

**Commission of the European Communities. Dublin Office**
Information Office, 29 Merrion Square, Dublin 2, Ireland.
• Commission of the European Communities. Dublin Office. Community Report. m.

**Commission of the European Communities. General Commission on Safety and Health in the Iron and Steel Industry**
see **General Commission on Safety and Health in the Iron and Steel Industry**

**Commission of the European Communities Library**
European Centre, Kirchberg, Luxembourg.
• A I L Newsletter. 4 per yr. ISSN 0001-1606 (Association of International Libraries)

**Commission of the European Communities. Terminology Office**
Monterey Palace, Av. Monterey, Luxembourg, Luxembourg.
• Commission of the European Communities. Terminology Office. Terminology Bulletin/Bulletin de Terminologie. irreg.; latest issue, no. 24, 1975.

**Commission of the European Communities. Vocational Guidance and Training Division**
Directorate General for Social Affairs, Rue de la Loi 200, Brussels 1049, Belgium.
• Vocational Training Information Bulletin. q.

**Common Market**
Popular name for EUROPEAN ECONOMIC COMMUNITY

**Communaute Europeene de l'Energie**
see **European Atomic Energy Community**

**Communaute Europeene du Charbon et de l'Acier**
see **European Coal and Steel Community**

**Council of Ministers of the European Communities**
see **Council of the European Communities**

**Council of the European Communities**
• Council of the European Communities. Review of the Council's Work. (pub. by Office for Official Publications of the European Communities)

**Court of Justice of the European Communities**
• Bibliographie de Jurisprudence Europeene Concernant les Decisions Judiciares Relatives aux Traites Instituant les Communautes Europeenes. Supplement. (pub. by Office for Official Publications of the European Communities)
• Court of Justice of the European Communities. Recueil de la Jurisprudence. (pub. by Office for Official Publications of the European Communities)
• Publications Juridiques Concernant l'Integration Europeenne; Bibliographie Juridique. Supplement. (pub. by Office for Official Publications of the European Communities)

**E A E C**
see **European Atomic Energy Community**

**E C S C**
see **European Coal and Steel Community**

**E E C**
see **European Economic Community**

**E I B**
see **European Investment Bank**

**E U R A T O M**
see **European Atomic Energy Community**

**E U R O S T A T**
see **Statistical Office of the European Communities**

**Economic and Social Committee of the European Communities**
Service Presse et Information, 2 rue Ravenstein, 1000 Brussels, Belgium.
• Economic and Social Committee of the European Communities. Annuaire. irreg.

• Economic and Social Committee of the European Communities. Bulletin d'Information. q. ISSN 0010-2423

**Euratom**
see **European Atomic Energy Community**

**Europaeische Gemeinschaft fuer Kohle und Stahl**
see **European Coal and Steel Community**

**Europaeisches Parlament**
see **European Parliament**

**European Atomic Energy Community**
• Central Nucleaire Ardennes. (pub. by Office for Official Publications of the European Communities)
• Centrale Elletronucleare Latina. Relazione Annuale. (pub. by Office for Official Publications of the European Communities)
• Centrale Nucleare Garigliano. Relazione Annuale. (pub. by Office for Official Publications of the European Communities)
• Euro Abstracts Section 1. Euratom and EEC Research. (pub. by Office for Official Publications of the European Communities)
• European Atomic Energy Community. Contamination Radioactive des Denrees Alimentaires dans les Pays de la Communaute. (pub. by Office for Official Publications of the European Communities)
• European Atomic Energy Community. Resultats des Mesures de la Radioactivite Ambiante dans les Pays de la Communaute: Air-Retombee-Eaux. (pub. by Office for Official Publications of the European Communities)
• Kernenergiecentrale van 50 MWE; Doodeward. Jaarverslag. (pub. by Office for Official Publications of the European Communities)
• Kernkraft Lingen. Jahresbericht. (pub. by Office for Official Publications of the European Communities)
• Kernkraft Zentrale, Gundremmingen. Jahresberichte. (pub. by Office for Official Publications of the European Communities)
• Kernkraftwerk Obrigheim. Jahresbericht. (pub. by Office for Official Publications of the European Communities)
• Niveaux de Contamination Radioactive du Milieu Ambiant et de la Chaine Alimentaire. (pub. by Office for Official Publications of the European Communities)
• Studies on the Radioactive Contamination of the Sea. Annual Report. (pub. by Office for Official Publications of the European Communities)

**European Atomic Energy Community. Bureau Euristop**
see **Bureau Euristop**

**European Coal and Steel Community. Consultative Committee**
Secretariat, 3 bld. Joseph-II, Luxembourg, Luxembourg.
• European Coal and Steel Community. Consultative Committee. Annuaire. a. ISSN 0423-6831
• European Coal and Steel Community. Consultative Committee. Handbook. a.; 16th edt., 1971.
• Organe Permanent pour la Securite et la Salubrite dans les Mines de Houille. Rapport. a. ISSN 0588-702X

**European Communities**
Collective name for the EUROPEAN COAL AND STEEL COMMUNITY, the EUROPEAN ECONOMIC COMMUNITY, and the EUROPEAN ATOMIC ENERGY COMMUNITY

**European Communities. Economic and Social Committee**
see **Economic and Social Committee of the European Communities**

**European Communities Information Office**
Publications of the European Communities can be purchased from the Central Sales Office of the European Communities, Case Postale 1003, Luxembourg, Luxembourg, or the following Information Offices:

**European Communities Information Office, Belgium**
Rue de la Loi 200, 1040 Brussels, Belgium

**European Communities Information Office, Chile**
Torres de Tajamar, Torre A, Apt. 404, Casilla Postal 10094, Santiago, Chile

**European Communities Information Office, Denmark**
Gammel Torv 4, 1004 Copenhagen K., Denmark

**European Communities Information Office, France**
61 rue des Belles-Feuilles, 75782 Paris Cedex 16, France

**European Communities Information Office, Germany**
Zitelmainnstrasse 22, 53 Bonn, W. Germany (B.R.D.)

**European Communities Information Office, Ireland**
29 Merrion Square, Dublin 2, Ireland

**European Communities Information Office, Italy**
Via Poli 29, 00187 Rome, Italy

**European Communities Information Office, Japan**
Kowa 25, 8-7 Sanban-cho, Chiyoda-ku, Tokyo 102, Japan

**European Communities Information Office, Luxembourg**
Centre Europeen, Luxembourg-Kirchberg, Luxembourg

**European Communities Information Office, Netherlands**
Lange Voorhout 29, the Hague, Netherlands

**European Communities Information Office, Switzerland**
37-39 rue de Vermont, 1202 Geneva, Switzerland

**European Communities Information Office, Turkey**
13 Bogaz Sokak, Kavaklidere, Ankara, Turkey

**European Communities Information Office, United Kingdom**
20 Kensington Palace Gardens, London W8 4QQ, England

**European Communities Information Office, United States**
2100 M St., N. W., Suite 707, Washington, D.C. 20037

**European Communities Information Office, Uruguay**
Bartolome Mitre 1337, Casilla Postal 641, Montevideo

**European Community**
Variant name for EUROPEAN COMMUNITIES

**European Communities Institute for University Studies**
• Etudes Universitaires sur l'Integration Europeenne/University Studies on European Integration. (pub. by Commission of the European Communities)

**European Economic Community Savings Bank Group**
92-94 Square E. Plasky, 1040 Brussels, Belgium.
• E E/Epargne Europe. 3 issues per mon. ISSN 0046-0869
• European Economic Community Savings Bank Group. Report. biennial.

**European Investment Bank**
2 Place de Metz, Luxembourg, Luxembourg (Dist. in U.S. by: European Community Information Service, 2100 M St., NW, Suite 707, Washington, DC 20037)
• European Investment Bank. Annual Report. a. ISSN 0071-2868

**European Parliament**
Secretariat, Centre Europeen, Case Postale 1601, Luxembourg, Luxembourg.
• Debates of the European Parliament. (pub. by Office for Official Publications of the European Communities)
• European Parliament. Bulletin. w. ISSN 0423-7846
• European Parliament. Documents de Seance. (pub. by Office for Official Publications of the European Communities)
• European Parliament. Informations. irreg.; issued in relation to its sessions. ISSN 0531-4321
• European Parliament. Selected Documents. (pub. by Office for Official Publications of the European Communities)
• Terminological Information. s-a. (prep. by its Terminology Office)

**European Social Fund**
- European Social Fund. Annual Report on the Activities of the New European Social Fund. (pub. by Office for Official Publications of the European Communities)

**Eurostat**
*see* **Statistical Office of the European Communities**

**General Commission on Safety and Health in the Iron and Steel Industry**
Rue de la Loi 200, 1040 Brussels, Belgium.
- General Commission on Safety and Health in the Iron and Steel Industry. Report. a.

**High Authority**
*see* **Commission of the European Communities**

**Information Office of the European Communities**
*see* **European Communities Information Office**

**Joint Nuclear Research Center, Ispra, Italy**
- Joint Nuclear Research Center, Ispra, Italy. Annual Report. (pub. by Commission of the European Communities)

**Office des Publications Officielles des Communautes Europeennes**
*see* **Office for Official Publications of the European Communities**

**Office for Official Publications of the European Communities**
C.P. 1003, Luxembourg 1, Luxembourg
(Dist. in the U.S. by: European Community Information Service, 2100 M St., NW, Suite 707, Washington, DC 20037)
- Bibliographie de Jurisprudence Europeene Concernant les Decisions Judiciares Relatives aux Traites Instituant les Communautes Europeenes. Supplement. a. ISSN 0590-7233 (Court of Justice of the European Communities)
- Bulletin of the European Communities. m. ISSN 0007-5116 (Commission of the European Communities)
- Bulletin of the European Communities. Supplement. irreg. ISSN 0068-4120 (Commission of the European Communities)
- Central Nucleaire Ardennes. a. (European Atomic Energy Community)
- Centrale Elletronucleare Latina. Relazione Annuale. a. ISSN 0591-1044 (European Atomic Energy Community)
- Centrale Nucleare Garigliano. Relazione Annuale. ISSN 0591-1036 (European Atomic Energy Community)
- Commission of the European Communities. Cahiers de Reconversion Industrielle. irreg., 1971, no. 17.
- Commission of the European Communities. Centre for Information and Documentation. Annual Report: Program Biology-Health Protection. a.
- Commission of the European Communities. Collection d'Economie du Travail. irreg. 1968, vol. III. ISSN 0531-3015
- Commission of the European Communities. Collection d'Economie et Politique Regionale. irreg. ISSN 0531-3023
- Commission of the European Communities. Collection d'Hygiene et de Medecine du Travail. irreg., 1917, no. 14. ISSN 0530-749X
- Commission of the European Communities. Collection du Droit du Travail. irreg. ISSN 0423-6955
- Commission of the European Communities. Collection Objectifs Generaux Acier. irreg.; 1971, no. 4. ISSN 0531-3198
- Commission of the European Communities. Collection Physiologie et Psychologie du Travail. irreg. 1969, no. 6. ISSN 0425-4937
- Commission of the European Communities. Conjoncture Energetique dans la Communaute. a. ISSN 0531-304X
- Commission of the European Communities. Directorate of Taxation. Inventory of Taxes. irreg.
- Commission of the European Communities. Directory. a. ISSN 0591-1745
- Commission of the European Communities. Etudes: Serie Aide au Developpement. irreg.; 1969, no. 3. ISSN 0069-6692
- Commission of the European Communities. Etudes: Serie Concurrence - Rappochement des Legislations. irreg.; no. 18 in prep. ISSN 0069-6706
- Commission of the European Communities. Etudes: Serie Energie. irreg. ISSN 0069-6714

- Commission of the European Communities. Etudes: Serie Industrie. irreg.; 1971, no. 6. ISSN 0591-1737
- Commission of the European Communities. Etudes: Serie Informations Internes sur l'Agriculture. irreg. ISSN 0069-6722
- Commission of the European Communities. Etudes: Serie Politique Sociale. irreg. ISSN 0069-6730
- Commission of the European Communities. Expose Annuel sur les Activities d'Orientation Professionnelle dans la Communaute. a. ISSN 0588-6953
- Commission of the European Communities. Expose Annuel sur les Activities des Services de Main-d'Ouvre des Etats Membres de la Communaute. a. ISSN 0591-0110
- Commission of the European Communities. Expose sur l'Evolution Sociale dans la Communaute. a. ISSN 0531-3724
- Commission of the European Communities. Investments in the Community Coalmining and Iron and Steel Industries. Report on the Survey. a. ISSN 0069-6757
- Commission of the European Communities. Recueils de Recherches Charbon. irreg; 1971, no. 40.
- Commission of the European Communities. Report on Competition Policy/Rapport sur la Politique de Concurrence. a.
- Commission of the European Communities. Studies: Agricultural Series. irreg. ISSN 0069-6765
- Commission of the European Communities. Studies: Economic and Financial Series. irreg. ISSN 0069-6773
- Commission of the European Communities. Studies: Transport Series. irreg. ISSN 0069-679X
- Council of the European Communities. Review of the Council's Work. a.
- Court of Justice of the European Communities. Recueil de la Jurisprudence. a. ISSN 0070-1386
- Debates of the European Parliament. irreg. ISSN 0071-3015 (European Parliament)
- E U R O N O R M. irreg.
- Economic Situation in the Community. 3 per yr. ISSN 0013-0346
- Euro Abstracts Section 1. Euratom and EEC Research. m. (European Atomic Energy Community)
- European Atomic Energy Community. Contamination Radioactive des Denrees Alimentaires dans les Pays de la Communaute. a.
- European Atomic Energy Community. Resultats des Mesures de la Radioactivite Ambiante dans les Pays de la Communaute: Air-Retombee-Eaux. a.
- European Community. m. ISSN 0014-2891 (Commission of the European Communities)
- European Documentation - a Survey. m. ISSN 0014-2905
- European Parliament. Documents de Seance. irreg. ISSN 0071-3023
- European Parliament. Selected Documents. irreg.
- European Social Fund. Annual Report on the Activities of the New European Social Fund. a.
- Fontes et Aciers/Ghise ed Acciai/Roheisen und Stahlerzeugnisse/Ruwijer en Stallprodukten. a. (incl. 7-11 inserts per yr.) ISSN 0531-3120
- Graphs and Notes on the Economic Situation in the Community. m. ISSN 0017-3487
- Joint Meeting of the Members of the Consultative Assembly of the Council of Europe and of the Members of the European Parliamentary Assembly. Official Report of Debates. a. ISSN 0447-8452
- Kernenergiecentrale van 50 MWE; Doodeward. Jaarverslag. a. (European Atomic Energy Community)
- Kernkraft Lingen. Jahresbericht. a. (European Atomic Energy Community)
- Kernkraft Zentrale, Gundremmingen. Jahresberichte. a. ISSN 0453-767X (European Atomic Energy Community)
- Kernkraftwerk Obrigheim. Jahresbericht. a. (European Atomic Energy Community)
- Niveaux de Contamination Radioactive du Milieu Ambiant et de la Chaine Alimentaire. a. (European Atomic Energy Community)
- Official Journal of the European Communities. C Series: Information and Notices. d. (Commission of the European Communities)
- Official Journal of the European Communities. L Series: Legislation. d.
- Publications Juridiques Concernant l'Integration Europeenne; Bibliographie Juridique. Supplement. a. (Court of Justice of the European Communities)

- Results of the Business Survey Carried out Among Heads of Enterprises in the Community. 3 per yr. ISSN 0034-5857 (Commission of the European Communities)
- Studies on the Radioactive Contamination of the Sea. Annual Report. a. (European Atomic Energy Community)
- Transatom Bulletin; a monthly guide to eastern nuclear literature in translation. m. ISSN 0041-1086 (Commission of the European Communities)

**Office Statistique des Communautes Europeenes**
*see* **Statistical Office of the European Communities**

**Parlement Europeen**
*see* **European Parliament**

**Press and Information Service of the European Communities**
224 rue de la Loi, 1004 Brussels, Belgium.
- Information Service of the European Communities. Newsletter on the Common Agricultural Policy. irreg.(approx. 20 nos. per year) ISSN 0073-7895

**Publications Office of the European Communities**
*see* **Office for Official Publications of the European Communities**

**Service d'Information des Communautes Europeennes**
D.E.P.P., 2 rue Merimee, 75 Paris 16e, France.
- 30 Jours d'Europe. m.

**Statistical Office of the European Communities**
B.P. 1907, Luxembourg, Luxembourg
(Dist. in the U.S. by: European Community Information Service, 2100 M St., NW, Suite 707, Washington, DC 20037)
- Eurostat. Agriculture. Monthly Statistics. Eggs. m.
- Eurostat News.
- Statistical Office of the European Communities. Associes Statistique du Commerce Exterieur. Annuaire. a. ISSN 0081-4857
- Statistical Office of the European Communities. Aussenhandel: Analitische Ubersichten. Foreign Trade: Analytical Tables. a. ISSN 0586-4925
- Statistical Office of the European Communities. Balances of Payments Yearbook. a. ISSN 0081-4865
- Statistical Office of the European Communities. Basic Statistics. a. ISSN 0081-4873
- Statistical Office of the European Communities. Commerce Exterieur: Nomenclature des Pays. a.
- Statistical Office of the European Communities. Commerce Exterieur: Products C E C A. a. ISSN 0081-4881
- Statistical Office of the European Communities. Energy Statistics. Yearbook. a. ISSN 0081-489X
- Statistical Office of the European Communities. Foreign Trade: Monthly Statistics. 11 per yr. ISSN 0039-0453
- Statistical Office of the European Communities. Foreign Trade: Standard Country Classification. a. ISSN 0081-4903
- Statistical Office of the European Communities. General Statistical Bulletin. 11 per yr. ISSN 0039-0461
- Statistical Office of the European Communities. Industrial Statistics. q. ISSN 0039-047X
- Statistical Office of the European Communities. Iron & Steel. bi-m. ISSN 0021-1532
- Statistical Office of the European Communities. Monthly Bulletin of General Statistics. m.
- Statistical Office of the European Communities. National Accounts. Yearbook. a. ISSN 0081-4911
- Statistical Office of the European Communities. Overseas Associates. Annuaire Statistiques des Etats Africaines et Malgache. a. ISSN 0081-492X
- Statistical Office of the European Communities. Quarterly Bulletin of Energy Statistics. q. ISSN 0585-1580
- Statistical Office of the European Communities. Recettes Fiscales. Annuaire. a. ISSN 0081-4938
- Statistical Office of the European Communities. Siderurgie Annuaire. a. ISSN 0081-4954
- Statistical Office of the European Communities. Social Statistics. 6 per yr. ISSN 0039-0488
- Statistical Office of the European Communities. Statistical Studies and Surveys. 4 per yr.
- Statistical Office of the European Communities. Statistique Agricole. irreg., 6-8 issues per yr. ISSN 0081-4946
- Statistical Office of the European Communities. Statistiques des Transports. Annuaire. a. ISSN 0081-4962
- Statistical Office of the European Communities. Statistiques Industrielles Annuaire. a. ISSN 0081-4970

- Statistical Office of the European Communities. Statistiques Sociales. Annuaire. a. ISSN 0081-4989
- Statistical Office of the European Communities. Yearbook Regional Statistics. a. ISSN 0081-4997

## FAEROE ISLANDS

**Foeroya Frodskaparfelag**
DK-3800 Torshavn, Faeroe Islands.
- Frodskaparrit; Annales Societatis Scientiarum Faeroensis. a. ISSN 0085-0896 (Mentunargrunner Foeroya Loegtings)
- Frodskaparrit; Annales Societatis Scientiarum Faeronsis. Supplementa. irreg. ISSN 0429-7539 (Mentunargrunner Foeroya Loegtings)

**Mentunargrunner Foeroya Loegtings**
- Frodskaparrit; Annales Societatis Scientiarum Faeroensis. (pub. by Foeroya Frodskaparfelag)
- Frodskaparrit; Annales Societatis Scientiarum Faeronsis. Supplementa. (pub. by Foeroya Frodskaparfelag)

## FALKLAND ISLANDS

**Falkland Islands Journal**
Government Printing Press, Stanley, Falkland Islands, South Atlantic.
- Falkland Islands Journal. a.

## FIJI

**Fiji. Bureau of Statistics**
Government Bldgs., Suva, Fiji.
- Fiji. Bureau of Statistics. Annual Statistical Abstract. a. ISSN 0071-4828
- Fiji. Bureau of Statistics. Consumer Prices Index. m.
- Fiji. Bureau of Statistics. Current Economic Statistics. q. ISSN 0015-0894
- Fiji. Bureau of Statistics. Fiji Household Income and Expenditure Survey. a.
- Insurance Statistics of Fiji. a.
- Statistics on Tourism and Hotel Industry in Fiji. a.

**Fiji. Central Monetary Authority. Minister of Finance**
YMCA Building, Stinson Parade, Suva, Fiji.
- Fiji. Central Monetary Authority. Annual Report. a.

**Fiji. Department of Agriculture**
Suva, Fiji.
- Fiji. Department of Agriculture. Annual Report. a. ISSN 0071-4844
- Fiji. Department of Agriculture. Annual Research Report. a.
- Fiji. Department of Agriculture. Bulletin. irreg.
- Fiji Agricultural Journal. s-a. ISSN 0015-0886

**Fiji. Department of Forestry**
Suva, Fiji.
- Fiji Timbers and Their Uses. irreg.

**Fiji. Government Printing Department**
Box 98, Suva, Fiji.
- Fiji. Government Printing Department Publications Bulletin. s-a. ISSN 0015-0916
- Fiji. Printing Department Report. a.
- Fiji Information. a.
- Fiji Royal Gazette. w.

**Fiji. Housing Authority**
Suva, Fiji.
- Fiji. Housing Authority. Report. a.

**Fiji. Ministry of Education. Youth and Sport**
Suva, Fiji.
- Fiji. Ministry of Education. Youth and Sport. Report. a.

**Fiji. Ministry of Lands and Mineral Resources. Mineral Resources Division**
P.M. Bag, Suva, Fiji.
- Fiji. Mineral Resources Division. Memoir. irreg., latest issue, no. 3.

**Fiji. Office of the Ombudsman**
Suva, Fiji.
- Fiji. Office of the Ombudsman. Annual Report of the Omsbudsman. a.

**Fiji Library Association**
Box 1168, Suva, Fiji.
- Fiji Library Directory. a. (Co-sponsor: Library Service of Fiji)

**Fiji Times & Herald Ltd.**
20 Gordon St., Suva, Fiji.
- Fiji Holiday. m.

**Pacific Daily Ltd.**
50 High St., Suva, Fiji.
- Pacific Review. 3 per wk. ISSN 0030-8862

**Pacific Peoples' Action Front in Suva**
Box 534, Suva, Fiji.
- Povai/War Club. bi-m.

**Pacific Periodicals Ltd.**
Box 9, Nadi, Fiji.
- Jagriti; only tri-weekly Hindi in Pacific. 3 per wk. ISSN 0021-3969

**South Pacific Creative Arts Society**
Box 5083, Suva, Fiji.
- Mana Annual of Creative Writing. a.

**South Pacific Social Sciences Association**
Box 5083, Suva, Fiji.
- Pacific Perspective. s-a.
- South Pacific Social Sciences Association. Publication. irreg.

**University of the South Pacific**
Library, G.P.O. Box 1168, Suva, Fiji.
- University of the South Pacific. Library. Pacific Collection. Accession List. q. with annual cum. as 4th issue.

## FINLAND

**A-Lehdet Oy**
Hitsaajankatu 10, 00810 Helsinki 81, Finland (Subscr. to: Valiolehdet Oy, Postilokero 530, 00101 Helsinki 10, Finland)
- Anna. w. ISSN 0003-374X
- Avotakka. m. ISSN 0355-2950
- Nakke. w.

**Aabo Akademi**
Domkyrkotorget 3, 20500 Aabo 50, Finland.
- Acta Academiae Aboensis. Series A: Humaniora. irreg.
- Acta Academiae Aboensis, Series B: Mathematics, Science and Technology. irreg. ISSN 0001-5105

**Aabo Akademi. Statsvetenskapliga**
Domkyrkotorget 3, 20500 Aabo 50, Finland.
- Aabo Akademi. Statsvetenskapliga Fakulteten. Meddelanden. Serie A. irreg.
- Aabo Akademi. Statsvetenskapliga Fakulteten: Meddelanden. Serie B. irreg.

**Aabo Swedish University School of Economics. Institute of Commercial Geography**
see Handelshoegskolan vid Aabo Akademi. Ekonomisk-Geografiska Institutionen

**Academia Scientiarum Fennica**
see Suomalainen Tiedeakatemia

**Academic Temperance Federation in Finland**
Laivurinrinne 1A, Helsinki 12, Finland.
- Alkoholikysymys/Problem of Alcoholism. 4 per yr. ISSN 0002-5526

**Agricultural Research Centre**
see Maatalouden Tutkimuskeskus

**Agronomien Yhdistys**
P. Makasiinikatu 6 A 8, 00130 Helsinki 13, Finland.
- Maatalous. m (10 per yr) ISSN 0024-8827

**Akademin Foer Tekniska Vetenskaper**
see Teknillisten Tieteiden Akatemia

**Kustannusosakeyhtio Apulehti**
Hitsaajankatu 10, 00810 Helsinki 81, Finland.
- Apu. w. ISSN 0003-7184
- Eevaneule. bi-m. ISSN 0355-3027
- Elamani Tarina. m. ISSN 0355-2977
- Help! m. ISSN 0355-3949
- Katso. w. ISSN 0355-2969
- Kauneus Ja Terveys. m. ISSN 0047-3308
- Rakennusviesti. m. ISSN 0355-5062
- Ravi ja Ratsastus. m. ISSN 0355-3000
- Tuulilasi. m. ISSN 0041-4468

- U M: Uusi Maailma. fortn. ISSN 0355-3043
- Uusi Eeva. m. ISSN 0355-2985

**Artists' Association of Finland**
see Suomen Taiteilijaseura

**Association of Business Archives**
see Likearkistoyhdistys

**Association of Finnish Chemical Societies**
P. Hesperiankatu 3 B 10, 00260 Helsinki 26, Finland.
- Finnish Chemical Letters; short chemical and biochemical communications. 8 per yr. ISSN 0303-4100
- Kemia-Kemi/Finnish Chemistry. (pub. by Kemian Kustannus Oy)

**Association of Finnish Civil Engineers**
- Rakennustekniikka. (pub. by Kustannus Oy Rakennustekniikka)

**Association of Ophthalmic Opticians in Finland**
see Suomen Silmaoptikkojen Liitto

**Association of Private Telephone Companies in Finland**
see Puhelinlaitosten Liitto

**Autoliitto r.y.**
Fabianinkatu 14, 00100 Helsinki 10, Finland.
- Autolla Ulkomaille. a. ISSN 0355-2896
- Moottori/Motor. m. ISSN 0027-0970

**Kustannusliike Autotieto Oy**
Arkadiankatu 15 C 16, SF-00100 Helsinki 10, Finland.
- Suomen Autolehti; the automobile magazine of Finland. m. ISSN 0355-2691

**Bank of Finland**
see Suomen Pankki

**Cancer Society of Finland**
see Suomen Syopayhdistys

**Central Association of Finnish Forest Industries**
see Suomen Metsateollisuuden Keskusliitto

**Central Association of Finnish Photographic Organizations**
see Suomen Valokuvajarjestojen Keskusliitto Finnfoto

**Central Union for Child Welfare in Finland**
see Lastensuojelun Keskusliitto

**Centrallaget Foer Handelslagen i Finland**
see Suomen Osuuskauppojen Keskuskunta

**Centralskogsnaemnden Skogskultur**
Kajsaniemigatan 1 A, 00100 Helsinki 10, Finland.
- Skogsbruket. m. ISSN 0037-6434

**Co-Operative Union**
see Kulutusosuuskuntien Keskusliitto (KK) r.y.

**Disabled War Veterans Association of Finland**
- Sotainvalidi. (pub. by Veljesliitto)

**Economic Society of Finland**
see Ekonomiska Samfundet i Finland

**Ekonomiska Samfundet i Finland**
Arkadiagatan 22, Helsinki 10, Finland.
- Ekonomiska Samfundets Tidskrift/Economic Society of Finland. Journal. q. ISSN 0013-3183

**Elektroingenjoersfoerbundet**
Daavitsaasen 27, 02180 Esbo 18, Finland.
- Sahko-Elektriciteten: Finland. m. ISSN 0036-2670

**Entomological Society of Finland**
P. Rautatiekatu 13, 00100 Helsinki 10, Finland.
- Acta Entomologica Fennica. irreg. ISSN 0001-561X (Co-sponsor: Societas Entomologica Helsingforsiensis)
- Annales Entomologici Fennici/Suomen Hyonteistieteellinen Aikakauskirja. 4 per yr. ISSN 0003-4428 (Co-sponsor: Societas Entomologica Helsingforsiensis)

**Federation of Finnish Film Societies**
Etelaaranta 4 B, Helsinki 13, Finland.
- Projektio. a. ISSN 0079-6964

Federation of the Friends of History
see Historian Ystavain Liitto

Finland. Central Statistical Office
see Finland. Tilastokeskus

Finland. Elinkeinohallitus. Competition Bureau
Haapaniemenkatu 4, Box 53009, 00531 Helsinki 53,
Finland.
• Kilpailunvapauslehti/Konkurrensfrihetsbladet. bi-
m. ISSN 0023-1401

Finland. General Direction of Posts and Telegraphs
see Finland. Posti- ja Lennatinlaitos

Finland. Ilmatieteen Laitos
Box 503, SF-00101 Helsinki 10, Finland.
• Finnish Meteorological Institute. Contributions.
irreg., no. 84, 1976. ISSN 0071-5190
• Finnish Meteorological Institute. Observations of
Radioactivity. a. ISSN 0071-5220
• Finnish Meteorological Institute.Observations of
Satellites. a; no. 17, 1976. ISSN 0355-2004
• Finnish Meteorological Institute. Soil Temperature
Measurements. irreg. ISSN 0071-5239
• Finnish Meteorological Institute. Studies on Earth
Magnetism. irreg., no. 25, 1976. ISSN 0081-783X
• Finnish Meteorological Institute. Tiedonantoja.
irreg. ISSN 0071-5204
• Finnish Meteorological Institute. Tutkimusseloste;
ilmansuojelu, ilmatiede, geomagnetismi ja
aeronomia. irreg. ISSN 0355-1717
• Finnish Meterological Institute. Technical Report.
irreg. ISSN 0355-1733
• Kuukausikatsaus Suomen Ilmastoon/
Maanadsoeversikt Oever Finlands Klimat. m.
ISSN 0303-2485
• Magnetic Results from Nurmijarvi Geophysical
Observatory. a. ISSN 0071-5212
• Meteorological Yearbook of Finland. Part 1A:
Climatological Data. a. ISSN 0076-6747
• Meteorological Yearbook of Finland. Part 1B:
Climatological Data from Jokioinen and
Sodankyla Observatories. a. ISSN 0076-6739
• Meteorological Yearbook of Finland. Part 2:
Precipitation and Snow Cover Data. a. ISSN
0076-6755
• Meteorological Yearbook of Finland. Part 4:
Measurements of Radiation and Bright Sunshine.
a. ISSN 0076-6763

Finland. Kansanelakelaitos
Pohjoinen Hesperiank. 15, 00260 Helsinki, Finland.
• Finland. Kansanelakelaitos. Julkaisuja. Sarja A.
irreg. (approx 1-2 per yr)
• Finland. Kansanelakelaitos. Kertomus. a.
• Finland. Kansanelakelaitos. Tilastollinen
Vuosikirja/Statistisk Aarsbok/Statistical
Yearbook. a. ISSN 0071-5247

Finland. Maatilahallitus. Statistics Office
Mariankatu 23, 00170 Helsinki 17, Finland.
• Finland. National Board of Agriculture. Statistics
Office. Monthly Review of Agricultural Statistics.
m.

Finland. Merentutkimuslaitos
Box 166, SF-00141 Helsinki 14, Finland
(Orders to: Government Printing Centre, Annankatu
44, SF-00100 Helsinki 10, Finland)
• Merentutkimuslaitoksen Julkaisu/
Havsforskningsinstitutets Skrift. irreg, no. 240,
1975. ISSN 0025-9985

Finland. Metsantutkimuslaitos
Unioninkatu 40 A, SF-00170 Helsinki 17, Finland.
• Folia Forestalia. 30 per yr. ISSN 0015-5543
• Metsatilastollinen Vuosikira/Yearbook of Forest
Statistics.

Finland. Ministeriet for Inrikesarendena
Sodra Esplanaden 10, Helsinki 13, Finland.
• N K B Skrift. (Nordiske Komite for
Bygningsbestemmelsei) irreg., no. 20, 1975. ISSN
0078-1126 (Co-sponsor: Nordiske Komite for
Bygningsbestemmelsei)

Finland. Ministry of Foreign Affairs
see Finland. Ulkoasiainministerio

Finland. Ministry of Labour
see Finland. Tyovoimaministerio

Finland. Ministry of Social Affairs and Health
see Finland. Sosiaali- Ja Terveysministerio

Finland. National Board of Agriculture. Statistics
Office
see Finland. Maatilahallitus. Statistics Office

Finland. National Board of Building
see Finland. Rakennushallituksen Tutkimus-ja
Kehitystoiminnan

Finland. National Board of Social Welfare
see Finland. Sosiaalihallitus

Finland. National Board of Trade and Consumers
Interests
see Finland. Elinkeinohallitus

Finland. Patentti- ja Rekisterihallitus
Bulevardi 21, 00180 Helsinki 18, Finland.
• Finland. Patentti- ja Rekisterihallitus.
Mallioikeuslehti/Moensterraettstidning. m. ISSN
0355-4481
• Finland. Patentti- ja Rekisterihallitus.
Patenttilehti/Patenttidning. m. ISSN 0031-2916
• Finland. Patentti- ja Rekisterihallitus.
Tavaramerkkilehti/Varumarkestidning. fortn.
ISSN 0039-9922

Finland. Posti-Ja Lennatinlaitos
Mannerheimintie 11, SF-00100 Helsinki 10,
Finland.
• Finland. Posti- Ja Lennatinlaitos. Kotimaisten
Sanomalehtien Hinnasto. Inhemsk Tidningstaxa. a.
ISSN 0071-5298
• Finland. Posti- Ja Lennatinlaitos. Ulkomaisten
Sanomalehtien Hinnasto. Utlandsk Tidningstaxa.
a. ISSN 0071-5301

Finland. Rakennushallitus. Tutkimus-ja
Kehitystoiminnan
Siltasaarenkatu 18A, Helsinki 53, Finland.
• Finland. Rakennushallitus. Tutkimus-ja
Kehitystoiminnan. Tiedote. irreg. ISSN 0071-
531X

Finland. Social Security Institution
see Finland. Kansanelakelaitos

Finland. Sosiaali- Ja Terveysministerio
Korkeavuorenkatu 21, 00130 Helsinki 13, Finland
(Subscr. to: Government Printing Centre, Box 516,
SF-00100 Helsinki 10, Finland)
• Finland. Sosiaali- Ja Terveysministerio. Sosioalisia
Erikoistutkimuksia/Special Social Studies. irreg.
ISSN 0071-5336
• Sosiaalinen Aikakauskirja/Social Tidskrift. 6 per
yr. ISSN 0038-1594

Finland. Sosiaalihallitus
Siltasaarenkatu 18 C, Helsinki, Finland.
• Finland. Sosiaalihallitus. Sosiaalihuoltotilaston
Vuosikirja/Finalnd. National Board of Social
Welfare. Yearbook of Social Welfare Statistics/
Finland. Socialstyrelsen. Socialvaardsstatistisk
Aarsbok. a. ISSN 0071-5328

Finland. Statistikcentrale
see Finland. Tilastokeskus

Finland. Tilastokeskus
Annakatu 44, SF-00100 Helsinki 10, Finland
(Subscr. to: Government Printing Centre, Box 516,
SF-00100 Helsinki 10,, Finland)
• Finland. Tilastokeskus. Asuntotuotanto/Finland.
Statistikcentralen. Bostadsproduktionen/Finland.
Central Statistical Office. Production of
Dwellings. a. ISSN 0355-2152
• Finland. Tilastokeskus. Indeksitiedotus RK.
Rakennuskustannusindeski/
Byggnadskostnadsindex/Building Cost Index. m.
• Finland. Tilastokeskus. Kansanedustajain Vaalit/
Finland. Statistikcentralen. Ridsdagsmannavalen/
Finland. Central Statistical Office. Parliamentry
Elections. irreg. ISSN 0355-2209
• Finland. Tilastokeskus. Kasikirjoja/Finland.
Statistikcentralen. Handboecker/Finland. Central
Statistical Office. Handbooks. irreg. ISSN 0355-
2063
• Finland. Tilastokeskus. Korkeakoulut/Finland.
Statistikcentralen. Hoegskolora/Finland. Central
Statistical Office. Higher Education. a. ISSN
0355-2225
• Finland. Tilastokeskus. Kunnallisvaalit/Finland.
Statistikcentralen. Kommunalvalen/Finland.
Central Statistical Office. Municipal Elections.
irreg. ISSN 0355-2217

• Finland. Tilastokeskus. Kuntien Finanssitilasto/
Finland. Statistikcentralen. Kommunal
Finansstatistik/Finland. Central Statistical Office.
Communal Finances. a. ISSN 0430-5566
• Finland. Tilastokeskus. Kuolemansyyt/Finland.
Statistikcentralen. Doedsorsaker/Finland. Central
Statistical Office. Causes of Death in Finland. a.
ISSN 0355-2144
• Finland. Tilastokeskus. Kuolleisuus- Ja
Eloonjaamistauluja/Finland. Statistikcentralen.
Doedlighets- och Livslaengdstabeller/Finland.
Central Statistical Office. Life Tables. irreg. ISSN
0355-2128
• Finland. Tilastokeskus. Liikennetilastollinen
Vuosikirja/Finland. Statistikcentralen.
Samfaerdselstatistiskaarsbok/Finland. Central
Statistical Office. Yearbook of Transport
Statistics. a. ISSN 0430-5272
• Finland. Tilastokeskus. Pankit/Finland.
Statistikcentralen/Finland. Central Statistical
Office. Commercial Banks and Mortgage Banks.
a. ISSN 0355-2454
• Finland. Tilastokeskus. Talonrakennustilasto/
Finland. Statistikcentralen. Husbyggnadsstatistik/
Finland. Central Statistical Office. House
Construction Statistics. a. ISSN 0430-5604
• Finland. Tilastokeskus. Teollisuustilasto/Finland.
Statistiska Centralbyraan/Finland. Central
Statistical Office. Industrial Statistics. a. ISSN
0071-5344
• Finland. Tilastokeskus. Tilastokatsauksia/Finland.
Statistiska Centralbyraan. Statistiska Oeversikter/
Finland. Central Statistical Office. Bulletin of
Statistics. m. ISSN 0015-2390
• Finland. Tilastokeskus. Tilastollisia Tiedonantoja/
Finland. Statistikcentralen. Statistiska
Meddelanden/Finland. Central Statistical Office.
Statistical Surveys. irreg. ISSN 0355-208X
• Finland. Tilastokeskus. Tilastotiedotus/Finland.
Statistikcentralen. Statistisk Rapport/Finland.
Central Statistical Office. Statistical Reports. 4-40
per yr. ISSN 0071-5352
• Finland. Tilastokeskus. Tulo- Ja Omaisuustilasto/
Finland. Statistikcentralen. Inkomst- och
Foermoegenhetstatistik/Finland. Central
Statistical Office. Statistics of Income and
Property. a. ISSN 0355-211X
• Finland. Tilastokeskus. Tuomioistuinten Toiminta/
Finland. Statistikcentralen. Domstolarnas
Verksamhet/Finland. Central Statistical Office.
Function of Courts. a. ISSN 0355-2187
• Finland. Tilastokeskus. Tutkimuksia/Finland.
Statistikcentralen. Undersoekningar/Finland.
Central Statistical Office. Studies. irreg.
• Finland. Tilastokeskus. Tutkimustoiminta/Finland.
Statistikcentralen. Forskningsverksamheten/
Finland. Central Statistical Office. Research
Activity. a. ISSN 0355-2233
• Finland. Tilastokeskus. Vaestolaskenta/Finland.
Statistikcentralen. Folkraekningen/Finland.
Central Statistical Office. Population Census. irreg
(every 10 years) ISSN 0355-2136
• Finland. Tilastokeskus. Vaestonmuutokset/
Finland. Statistikcentralen. Befolkningsroerelsen/
Finland. Central Statistical Office. Vital Statistics.
a. ISSN 0430-5612
• Finland. Tilastokeskus. Yleissivistavat
Oppilaitokset/Finland. Statistikcentralen.
Allmaenbildande Laeroanstalter/Finland. Central
Statistical Office. General Education. a. ISSN
0355-2446
• Suomen Tilastollinen Vuosikirja/Statistisk Aarsbok
Foer Finland/Statistical Yearbook of Finland. a.
ISSN 0081-5063

Finland. Tullihallitus
Helsinki, Finland
• Finland. Tullihallitus. Ulkomaankauppa/
Utrikeshandel/Foreign Trade. m. (Subscr. to:
Valtion Painatuskeskus, Annankatu 44, 00100
Helsinki 10, Finland)

Finland. Tyovoimaministerio
Helsinki, Finland
• Finland. Tyovoimaministerio. Tyovoimakatsaus/
Labour Reports. irreg.

Finland. Ulkoasiainministerio
Lonnrotinkatu 4, Helsinki 12, Finland.
• Finland. Ulkoasiainministerio. Ulkopolititisija
Lausuntoja ja Asiakirjoja. s-a. ISSN 0071-528X
• Suomen Osallistuminen Yhdistyneiden
Kansakuntien Toimintaan. a. ISSN 0081-9441

**Finland. Valtion Painatuskeskus**
Annankatu 44, Helsinki 10, Finland.
- Finland. Kansantalousosasto. Kansantalouden
Kehitysarvio. Summary: National Budget. a. ISSN
0071-5255
- Finland. Kansantalousosasto. Taloudellinen
Katsaus. Economic Survey. a. ISSN 0071-5271
- Finland. Valtioneuvoston Kanslian. Julkasuja.
1rreg.

- Finland. Vestientutkimuslaitos. Julkasuja.
Publications. irreg.

**Finland. Valtionrautatiet**
P.O. Box 488, SF-00101 Helsinki, Finland.
- Finnish State Railways. a. ISSN 0506-3876

**Finlands Arkitektfoerbund**
Unioninkatu 30, Helsinki 10, Finland.
- Arkkitehti/Finnish Architectural Review. 8 per yr.
ISSN 0004-2129

**Finlands Bank**
*see* Suomen Pankki

**Finlands Forstmaestarefoerbund**
*see* Suomen Metsanhoitajaliitto

**Finlands Fysioterapeutfoerbund**
*see* Suomen Laakintavoimistelijaliitto

**Finlands Husdjursavelsfoerening**
*see* Suomen Kotielainjalostusyhdistys

**Finlands Journalistfoerbund**
*see* Suomen Sanomalehtimiesten Liitto

**Finlands Juristfoerbund**
*see* Suomen Lakimiesliitto

**Finlands Svenska Koepmannafoerbund**
Kaserngatan 23 A, 00130 Helsinki 13, Finland.
- Koepmannen. 8 per yr. ISSN 0023-3862

**Finlands Utrikeshandelsfoerbund**
*see* Finnish Foreign Trade Association

**Finlands Vetenskapliga Bibliotekssamfund**
*see* Suomen Tieteellinen Kirjastoseura

**Finnfacts Instituutii**
Yrjonkatu 13, 00120 Helsinki 12, Finland
(U.S. address: Suite 1602, 711 Third Ave., New
York, NY 10017)
- Finnfacts. m. ISSN 0015-2412

**Finnish Academy of Science and Letters**
*see* Suomalainen Tiedeakatemia

**Finnish Academy of Technical Sciences**
*see* Teknillisten Tieteiden Akatemia

**Finnish Aeronautical Association**
*see* Suomen Ilmailuliitto

**Finnish Animal Breeding Association**
*see* Suomen Kotielainjalostusyhdistys

**Finnish Boat and Motor Association**
Mariankatu 26 B 19, 00170 Helsinki 17, Finland.
- Finnish Boatbuilding Industry. irreg. (approx. 1
per yr.)

**Finnish Broadcasting Company. Section for Long-
Range Planning**
Kesakatu 2, 00260 Helsinki 26, Finland.
- Finnish Broadcasting Company. Section for Long-
Range Planning. Research Reports. irreg., 1971,
no. 11. ISSN 0084-4225

**Finnish Co-Operative Wholesale Society**
*see* Suomen Osuuskauppojen Keskeskunta

**Finnish Cultural Foundation**
- Parnasso. (pub. by Yhtyneet Kuvalehdet Oy)

**Finnish Dental Society**
*see* Suomen Hammaslaakariseura

**Finnish Economic Association**
*see* Kansantaloudellinen Yhdistys

**Finnish Electric Workers' Union**
*see* Suomen Sahkoalantyontekijian Liitto

**Finnish Employers' Confederation**
*see* Suomen Tyonantajain Keskuslitto

**Finnish Federation of Nurses**
*see* Suomen Sairaanhoitajaliitto

**Finnish Federation of Physical Therapists**
*see* Suomen Laakintayoimistelaliitto

**Finnish Fisheries Association**
*see* Suomen Kalastusyhdistys

**Finnish Foreign Trade Association**
Olavinkatu 1, 00100 Helsinki 10, Finland.
- Designed in Finland. a. ISSN 0418-7717
- Finnische Handelsrundschau. 3 per yr. ISSN
0015-2420
- Finnish Trade Review. 8 per yr. ISSN 0015-2463
- Finskij Torgovyj Zurnal. 2 per yr. ISSN 0015-
251X

**Finnish Forest Research Institute**
*see* Finland. Metsantutkimuslaitos

**Finnish Game and Fisheries Research Institute**
Unioninkatu 45 B, 00170 Helsinki 17, Finland.
- Finnish Game Research/Riistatieteellisia
Julkaisuja. 1-2 per yr. ISSN 0015-2447

**Finnish Game and Fisheries Research Institute.
Fisheries Division**
Box 193, SF-00131 Helsinki 13, Finland.
- Finnish Fisheries Research. irreg.
- Riista- Ja Kalatalouden Tutkimuslaitos.
Kalantutkimusosasto.Tiedonantoja. irreg.
- Suomen Kalatalous. irreg., vol. 47, 1974. ISSN
0085-6940

**Finnish Geodetic Institute**
*see* Suomen Geodeettinen Laitos

**Finnish Hard of Hearing Union**
*see* Kuulonhuoltoliitto

**Finnish Hardware and Builders' Merchants
Association**
*see* Suomen Rauta- ja Koneliikkeiden Yhdistys

**Finnish Historical Society**
*see* Suomen Historiallinen Seura

**Finnish Hotel and Restaurant Association**
- Hotelli- Ja Ravintolalehti/Hotell och
Restaurangtidningen. (pub. by Oy Ravintolalehti)

**Finnish Institute of International Affairs**
*see* Ulkopoliittinen Instituutti

**Finnish Insurance Society**
Bulevardi 28, 00120 Helsinki, Finland.
- Suomen Vakuutusvuosikirja/Foersaekringsaarsbok
Foer Finland/Finnish Insurance Yearbook. a.

**Finnish Literature Society**
*see* Suomalaisen Kirjallisuuden Seura

**Finnish Materials Management Association**
- Osta ja Materiaalitalous. (pub. by Kustannusliike
Liikejulkaisut Oy)

**Finnish Medical Association**
*see* Suomen Laakariliitto

**Finnish Medical Society Duodecim**
Runeberginkatu 47 A, 00260 Helsinki 26, Finland.
- Annales Chirurgiae et Gynaecologiae Fenniae. bi-
m. ISSN 0003-3855
- Annals of Clinical Research. bi-m. ISSN 0003-
4762
- Annals of Clinical Research. Supplementum. irreg.
ISSN 0066-2291
- Duodecim; laaketieteellinen aikakauskirja. s-m.
ISSN 0012-7183
- Medical Biology. bi-m. ISSN 0302-2137
- TH-Kotilaakari. (pub. by Yhtyneet Kuvalehdet
Oy)

**Finnish Music Teachers Association**
Runeberginkatu 15 A 11, 00100 Helsinki 10,
Finland.
- Rondo Musiikkilehti. 10 per yr.

**Finnish Musicians Union**
*see* Suomen Muusikkojen Liitto

**Finnish Newspaper Publishers Association**
*see* Sanomalehtien Liitto

**Finnish Oriental Society**
*see* Suomen Itamainen Seura

**Finnish Ornithological Society**
*see* Suomen Lintutieteellinen Yhdistys

**Finnish Packaging Association**
*see* Suomen Pakkausyhdistys

**Finnish Paper and Timber Journal Publishing Co.**
Pietarinkatu 1 C, Helsinki 14, Finland.
- Finnish Paper and Timber. 8 per yr. ISSN 0015-
2455 (Suomen Metsateollisuuden Keskusliitto)
- Paperi Ja Puu/Papper och Tra/Paper and Timber.
m. ISSN 0031-1243 (Suomen Metsateollisuuden
Keskuslitto) (Co-sponsors: Finnish Woodworking
Engineers' Association; Finnish Paper Engineers'
Association)
- Suomen Puutalous. m. ISSN 0039-5617 (Suomen
Metsateollisuuden Keskusliitto)

**Finnish Political Science Association**
c/o Hannu Nurmi, Department of Political Science,
University of Turku, Kasarmikatu 6/24, SF-20500
Turku 50, Finland.
- Politiikka. q. ISSN 0032-3365

**Finnish Population and Family Welfare Federation**
*see* Vaestontutkimuslaitos

**Finnish Research Library Association**
*see* Suomen Tieteellinen Kirjastoseura

**Finnish Road Association**
*see* Suomen Tieyhdistys

**Finnish Tourist Board**
Box 625, 00101 Helsinki 10, Finland.
- Look at Finland. q. ISSN 0024-6379 (Co-sponsor:
Finnish Ministry of Foreign Affairs, Press
Section)

**Finnish Union of Chemists**
*see* Suomen Kemistiliitto

**Finnish Union of Survey Engineers**
Ojahaantie 8 A 13, 01600 Vantaa 60, Finland.
- Maankaytto. q. (Co-sponsors: Finnish Union of
Surveyor Tecnikers; Finnish Union of
Mapmakers)

**Finnlands Aussenhandelsverband**
*see* Finnish Foreign Trade Association

**Finska Jaern- och Maskinaffaererernas Foerening**
*see* Suomen Rauta- ja Koneliikkeiden Yhdistys

**Finska Laekaresaellskapet**
Snellmansgatan 9-11, 00170 Helsinki 17, Finland.
- Finska Laekaresaellskapet. Handlingar. 4 per yr.
ISSN 0015-2501

**Fiskerifoereningen i Finland**
*see* Suomen Kalastusyhdistys

**Foereningen Granskaren**
- Finsk Tidskrift. (pub. by Foerlags AB
sydvaestkusten)

**Foerlagsfoereningen Forum**
Alexandersgatan 19 A, 00100 Helsinki 10, Finland.
- Forum Foer Ekonomi och Teknik. fortn.

**Foundation for Psychiatric Research in Finland**
- Psychiatria Fennica/Finnish Psychiatry/
Suomalaista Psykiatriaa. (pub. by Psychiatria
Fennica)
- Psychiatria Fennica. Julkaisuserja/Psychiatria
Fennica. Reports. (pub. by Psychiatria Fennica)
- Psychiatria Fennica. Monografiasarja/Psychiatria
Fennica. Monographs. (pub. by Psychiatria
Fennica)

**Friendship Society Finland - USSR**
Hameentie 8, Helsinki, Finland.
- Maailma ja Me/M M. m. ISSN 0024-8541

**Genealogical Society of Finland**
*see* Suomen Sukututkimusseura

**Genealogiska Samfundet i Finland**
*see* Suomen Sukututkimusseura

**Geografiska Saellskapet i Finland**
*see* Suomen Maantieteelinen Seura

**Geographical Society of Finland**
see Suomen Maantieteellinen Seura

**Geological Society of Finland**
see Suomen Geologinen Seura

**Handelshoegskolan Vid Aabo Akademi. Ekonomisk-Geografiska Institutionen**
Henriksgatan 7, 20500 Aabo 50, Finland.
• Handelshoegeskolan Vid Aabo Akademi.
Ekonomisk-Geografiska Instititionen. Memoranda.
irreg., no. 24, 1976.
• Handelshoegeskolan Vid Aabo Akademi.
Ekonomisk-Geografiska Institutionen.
Meddelanden. irreg., no. 10, 1977. ISSN 0564-5409

**Helsingen Kauppakorkeakoulu. Kirjasto**
Runeberginkatu 22-24, 00100 Helsinki 10, Finland.
• Helsingen Kauppakorkeakoulu. Kirjasto.
Julkaisusarja/Helsinki School of Economics.
Library. Publications. irreg., 1973, no. 14.

**Helsingin Yliopisto. Kasvatustieteen Laitos**
Fabianinkatu 28, SF-00100 Helsinki 10, Finland.
• Helsingin Yliopisto. Kasvatustieteen Laitos.
Research Bulletin. irreg. ISSN 0073-179X

**Helsingin Yliopisto. Kirjasto**
Box 312, 00100 Helsinki 10, Finland.
• Books from Finland. q. ISSN 0006-7490
• Suomen Kirjallisuus/Finnish National
Bibliography/Finlands Litteratur. m. ISSN 0355-001X (Avail. from: Valtion Painatuskeskus,
Annankatu 44, 00100 Helsinki 10, Finland)

**Helsingin Yliopisto. Seismologian Laitos**
Et. Hesperiankatu 4, Helsinki 10, Finland.
• Publications in Seismology. irreg. ISSN 0079-774X

**Helsingin Yliopisto. Tahtitieteellinen Observatorio**
Helsinki, Finland.
• Visual Observations of Artificial Earth Satellites in
Finland. a.

**Helsinki. City Statistical Center**
Tooloontorinkatu 2 B, 00260 Helsinki 26, Finland.
• Tilastollisia Kuukaustietietoja Helsingista/Statistika
Maanadsuppifter over Helsingfors/Helsinki. City
Statistical Center. Monthly Review. m. ISSN
0040-7658

**Helsinki School of Economics**
see Helsingin Kauppakorkeakoulu

**Historian Ystavain Liitto**
Museokatu 46 B 42, 00100 Helsinki 10, Finland.
• Historian Aitta. irreg. (approx. every 2-3 yrs.)
ISSN 0439-2183

**Historiska Foereningen**
c/o Historiska Institutionen, Regeringsgatan 15, SF-00100 Helsinki 10, Finland.
• Historisk Tidskrift Foer Finland. q. ISSN 0046-7596

**Kustannus Oy Infopress**
P. Hesperiankatu 37 A, 00260 Helsinki 26, Finland.
• Elektroniikkauutiset/Electronics News. 22 per yr.

**Informa Oy**
Annankatu 18, 00120 Helsinki 12, Finland.
• Kompass/Suomen Talouselaman Kakemisto/
Handbok over Finlands Industri och Naeringsliv/
Register of Finnish Industry and Commerce/
Informationswerk fuer die Finnische Wirtschaft/
Repertoire General de l'Economie Finlandaise. a.

**Ingenjoersfoerlaget AB**
see Insinoorilehdet Oy

**Insinoorilehdet Oy**
Yrjonkatu 30, SF-00100 Helsinki 10, Finland.
• Elektroniikka. 22 per yr. ISSN 0355-4503
• Insinooriuutiset/Ingenjoersnytt. w. ISSN 0020-2010
• Konepajamies; Finnish journal of metalworking
production. 10 per yr. ISSN 0023-3277 (Suomen
Metalliteollisuusyhdistys)
• Muoviuutiset; ajankohtaista muovialalta. m.
• Tekniikka. m. ISSN 0040-2303

**Institute for Migration**
Turku, Finland.
• Institute for Migration, Turku. Migration Studies.
irreg.

**Institute of Marine Research**
see Finland. Merentutkimuslaitos

**International Federation of Medical Students' Associations**
Stenbaeckinkatu 9, SF-00290 Helsinki 29, Finland.
• International Federation of Medical Students'
Associations. Reports of General Assembly. a.
ISSN 0074-6037

**International Peace Research Association**
Box 70, 33101 Tampere 10, Finland.
• Bulletin of Peace Proposals. (pub. by
Universitetsforlaget NO)
• I P R A Studies in Peace Research. irreg., no. 6,
1975. ISSN 0074-7289
• International Peace Research Association.
Proceedings of the Conference. biennial, 5th,
1974, Varanasi, India. ISSN 0074-7297
• International Peace Research Newsletter. bi-m.
ISSN 0020-8213

**International Peace Research Institute**
Box 70, 33101 Tampere, Finland.
• International Peace Research Institute. Basic
Social Science Monographs. irreg. ISSN 0522-4497
• Journal of Peace Research. (pub. by
Universitetsforlaget NO)

**International Peat Society**
Bulevardi 31, 00180 Helsinki 18, Finland.
• International Peat Society. Bulletin/Internationale
Moor- und Torf-Gesellschaft. Mitteilungen. a.

**Invalidiliitto r.y.**
Kumpulantie 1, SF-00510 Helsinki 51, Finland.
• Suomen Invalidi. m. ISSN 0049-2566

**Juridiska Foereningen i Finland**
c/o Hannes Snellman, Alexandersgt. 48 A, 00100
Helsinki 10, Finland.
• Juridiska Foereningen i Finland. Tidskrift. bi-m.
ISSN 0040-6953

**Jyvaskylan Yliopisto. Department of Physics**
SF-40100 Jyvaskyla 10, Finland.
• Jyvaskylan Yliopisto. Department of Physics.
Research Report. irreg. ISSN 0075-465X

**Jyvaskylan Yliopisto. Kasvatustieteiden Tutkimuslaitos**
SF-40100 Jyvaskyla 10, Finland.
• Kasvatus; Suomen kasvatustieteellinen
aikakauskirja. 5 per yr. ISSN 0022-927X

**Jyvaskylan Yliopisto. Kirjasto**
Seminaarinkatu 15, 40100 Jyvaskyla 10, Finland.
• Jyvaskyla Studies in Education, Psychology and
Social Research. irreg., no. 35, 1977. ISSN 0075-4625
• Jyvaskyla Studies in the Arts. irreg. ISSN 0075-4633
• Studia Historica Jyvaskylaensia. irreg. ISSN 0081-6523

**Jyvaskylan Yliopisto. Matematiikan Laitos**
Sammonkatu 6, SF-40100 Jyvaskyla 10, Finland.
• Jyvaskylan Yliopisto. Matematiikan Laitos.
Report. irreg., 1969, no. 5. ISSN 0075-4641

**Kameraseura r.y.**
Kalevankatu 21 A 5, 00100 Helsinki 10, Finland.
• Kameralehti. 10 per yr. ISSN 0022-8133

**Kansallis-Osake-Pankki**
Aleksanterinkatu 42, SF-00101 Helsinki 10, Finland.
• Kansallis-Osake-Pankki. Economic Review. s-a.
ISSN 0022-8419

**Kansantaloudellinen Yhdistys**
Helsingen Kauppakorkeakoulu, Runeberginkatu 22-24, 00100 Helsinki 10, Finland.
• Kansantaloudellinen Aikakauskirja/Finnish
Economic Journal. q. ISSN 0022-8427

**Kansanvalistusseura**
Museokatu 18 A 2, 00100 Helsinki 10, Finland.
• Adult Education in Finland. 4 per yr. ISSN 0001-8503

**Kauppa Koti Oy**
Fabianinkatu 23, 00130 Helsinki 13, Finland.
• Kauppa ja Koti. m (11 per yr.) ISSN 0022-9490
• Myyntineuvoja. 13 per yr. ISSN 0355-3256

**Kauppateknikko**
Bulevardi 17 A 5, 00120 Helsinki 12, Finland.
• Kauppateknikko. 6 per yr. ISSN 0047-3316

**Kauppiaitten Kustannus Oy**
Rauhankatu 15, 00170 Helsinki 17, Finland.
• Kauppias. fortn. ISSN 0355-3078
• Pirkka. m. ISSN 0032-0242
• Rautaviesti. m. ISSN 0022-7404

**Kayttokirjat Oy**
Kauppiaankatu 10 B 10, 00160 Helsinki 16, Finland.
• Teollisuustekniikka. m. ISSN 0040-3547

**Kemian Kustannus Oy**
P. Hesperiankatu 3 B 10, 00260 Helsinki 26,
Finland.
• Kemia-Kemi/Finnish Chemistry. m. ISSN 0355-1628 (Association of Finnish Chemical Societies)
(Co-sponsor: Federation of Finnish Chemical
Industry)

**Klassillis - Filologinen Yhdistys**
Hallituskatu 11-13, Helsinki 17, Finland.
• Arctos; Acta Philological Fennica. a. ISSN 0066-6998

**Koneviestin Ammattilehdet Oy**
Malminrinne 1 B, Helsinki 18, Finland.
• Mootoriviesti; riippumaton auto- ja moottorilehti.
m. ISSN 0027-0962

**Konstnaersgillet i Finland**
see Suomen Taiteilijaseura

**Konsumtionsandelslagens Centralfoerbund**
see Kulutusosuuskuntien Keskusliitto (KK) r.y.

**Kotikielen Seura**
Fabianinkatu 33, 00170 Helsinki 17, Finland.
• Virittaja. q. ISSN 0042-6806

**Kotitalousopettajien Liitto**
Ruusulankatu 19 A 16, 00250 Helsinki 25, Finland.
• Kotitalous. m. ISSN 0047-3685 (Co-sponsors:
Kotitalousopetusseure, Kotitalouden Kandidaatit)

**Kotiteollisuuden Keskusliitto r.y.**
Temppelikatu 15 A 5, 00100 Helsinki 10, Finland.
• Kotiteollisuus/Vaar Hemsloejd/Finnish
Handicraft. bi-m. ISSN 0355-7421

**Kulttuurikeskus Kriittisen Korkeakoulun Kannatusyhdistys r.y.**
Lehtikuusentie 6, 00270 Helsinki 27, Finland.
• Katsaus. bi-m. ISSN 0022-9458

**Kulutusosuuskuntien Keskusliitto (KK) r.y.**
Box 740, 00101 Helsinki 10, Finland.
• E.
• Maamies.
• Me. bi-m. ISSN 0025-6269

**Kuulonhuoltoliitto**
Makipellontie 15, 00320 Helsinki 32, Finland.
• Kuuloviesti. m. ISSN 0023-5741

**Oy Laivastolehti**
Annankatu 25 A 52, 00100 Helsinki 10, Finland.
• Navigator; marine monthly in Finland. m. ISSN
0355-7871

**Lapin Tutkimusseura**
Oulu, Finland.
• Pohjois-Suomen Bibliografia. irreg, vol. 3, 1975.

**Lastensuojelun Keskusliitto**
Armfeltintie 1, 00150 Helsinki 15, Finland.
• Lapset Ja Yhteiskunta. m. ISSN 0355-3736

**Lehtimiehet Oy**
Fredrikinkatu 48 A, 00010 Helsinki 10, Finland
• Hymylehti. m. ISSN 0018-8298 (Orders to:
Puutarhakatu 16, Tampere, Finland)
• Vene; vencilijan lehti. 10 per yr. ISSN 0042-3343

**Library Association of Finland**
see Suomen Kirjastoseura

**Liikearkistoyhdistys r.y.**
Box 271, 00101 Helsinki 10, Finland.
• Liikearkisto. 2-4 per yr.

**Kustannusliike Liikejulkaisut Oy**
Sakottajankatu 2 F, 00520 Helsinki 52, Finland.
• Osta ja Materiaalitalous. m. (Finnish Materials
Management Association)

**Liiketaloudellinen**
Runeberginkatu 22-24, 00100 Helsinki 10, Finland.
- Liiketaloudellinen Aikakauskirja/Finnish Journal of Business Economics. q. ISSN 0024-3469

**Maanmittaustieteiden Seura r.y.**
Tkk/M-Os, 02150 Otaniemi, Finland.
- Maanmittaus. s-a. ISSN 0047-5319

**Maanpudustuslehden Kustannus Oy**
P. Hesperiankatu 15 A, Helsinki 26, Finland.
- Suomalainen. q. ISSN 0039-548X

**Maarakentajain Kustannus Oy**
Arkadiankatu 16 B, 00100 Helsinki 10, Finland.
- Maarakennus Ja Kuljetus. m(11 per yr) ISSN 0024-8819

**Maatalouden Tutkimuskeskus**
Erottajank. 15-17, Helsinki, Finland.
- Annales Agriculturae Fenniae. 4-6 per yr. ISSN 0570-1538

**Mainoshoitajain Yhdistys**
Mariankatu 26 B 5, 00170 Helsinki 17, Finland.
- Mainosuutiset. 10 per yr. ISSN 0025-0864

**Mallasjuomalehti Oy**
Elintarviketeollisuusliitto, Unioninkatu 14, SF-00721 Helsinki 112, Finland.
- Mallas ja Olut. 6 per yr. ISSN 0356-3014

**Markkinointijarjestojen Yheistyoelin**
Fabianinkatu 4 B, 00130 Helsinki 13, Finland.
- Markkinointi. 6 per yr.

**Marttaliitto r.y.**
Uudenmaank. 24, Helsinki 12, Finland.
- Emantalehti. m. ISSN 0013-6522

**Matemaattisten Aineiden Opettajien Liitto**
Parantolankata 8 B, Hyvinkaa, Finland.
- Matemaattisten Aineiden Aikakauskirja. bi-m. ISSN 0025-5149

**Medical Society of Finland**
see Finska Laekaresaellskapets

**Meriupseeriyhdistys**
Merivoimien Esikunta, 00160 Helsinki 16, Finland.
- Suomi Merella. a. ISSN 0039-5633

**Merkonomiliitto r.y.**
Lutherinkatu 6 A 5, 00100 Helsinki 10, Finland.
- Merkonomi. m(10 per yr) ISSN 0026-0088

**Metsastajain Keskusjarjesto**
Fredrikinkatu 47 A, Helsinki 10, Finland.
- Metsastaja. q. ISSN 0047-6986

**Metsataloudellinen Aikakauskirja Oy**
Hietaniemenkatu 19, SF-00100 Helsinki 10, Finland.
- Metsa Ja Puu. m. ISSN 0026-1602

**Mining and Metallurgical Society of Finland**
see Vuorimiesyhdistys

**Modern Language Society**
see Uusfilologinens Yhdistys

**Moniposti**
Box 150, SF-15111 Lahti, Finland.
- Signal International; for penpals, collectors and traders. q. ISSN 0037-4970

**N Y A Argus**
Postbox 100, 00251 Helsinki 25, Finland.
- N Y A Argus. 20 per yr. ISSN 0027-7126

**National Association of Persons Handicapped by Tuberculosis and Other Pulmonary Diseases**
see Tuberkuloosi ja Keuhkovammaisten Liitto

**National Federation of Finnish Master Painters**
see Suomen Maalarimestariliitto

**Neste Oy**
PL 432, 00100 Helsinki 10, Finland.
- Oljyposti. irreg.

**Nordic Institute of Folklore**
Henrikinkatu 3, 20500 Turku 50, Finland.
- N I F Newsletter. q. ISSN 0355-0206

**Nuorten Keskus R.Y.**
Liisankatu 27 A 5, 00170 Helsinki 17, Finland.
- Pistis. m (10 per yr.)

**Nykylehdet Oy**
Italahdenkatu 20, 00210 Helsinki 21, Finland.
- Jermu. m. ISSN 0355-2764
- Seksi; facts about sexuality. m. ISSN 0355-2772

**Nykytekstiili Oy**
Liisankatu 27 A 7, 00170 Helsinki 17, Finland.
- Nykytekstiili. m. ISSN 0029-6813
- Ulkoilu- Ja Urheiluvaline. bi-m. ISSN 0041-6169

**Occupational Health Foundation**
Haartmaninkatu 1, 00290 Helsinki 29, Finland.
- Tyo- Terveys- Turvallisuus/Work-Health-Safety. m. ISSN 0041-4816

**Odontologiska Samfundets i Finland**
c/o Heijke Tallroth, Bergmansg. 11 D, SF-00140 Helsinki 14, Finland.
- Odontologiska Samfundet i Finland. Aarsbok. a. ISSN 0078-3358

**Opettajien Ammattijarjesto**
Rautatielaisenkatu 6, SF-00520 Helsinki 52, Finland.
- Opettaja. w.

**Osuuskunta Kirjapainotaito**
Revontulentie 8, 02100 Espoo 21, Finland.
- Kirjapainotaito-Graafikko. 8 per yr. ISSN 0017-2731

**Kustannusosakeyhtio Otava**
Uudenmaankatu 10, SF-00120 Helsinki 12, Finland.
- Kuka Kukin On/Who's Who in Finland. every 4 yrs.

**Paikallislehtien Liitto**
Arkadiankatu 12 B 34, 00100 Helsinki 10, Finland.
- Paikallislehdisto. 7 per yr. ISSN 0030-9443

**Paloalan Jarjestot**
Neitsytpolku 3 A, 00140 Helsinki 14, Finland.
- Palontorjunta/Brandvaern; trade journal of the fire safety field in Finland. 10 per yr. ISSN 0031-0468
- Palontorjunta-Tekniikka; the trade journal of structural fire safety. 4 per yr. ISSN 0031-0476

**Pellervo-Seura**
Simonkatu 6, 00100 Helsinki 10, Finland.
- Pellervo. 20 per yr. ISSN 0031-4188
- Suomen Osuustoimintalehti. bi-m. ISSN 0039-5609

**Pienteollisuuden Keskusliitto**
Kansakoulukatu 10 A 21, Helsinki 10, Finland.
- Kasityo ja Teollisuus. m. ISSN 0022-9229

**Pioneerikilta r.y.**
Kirja-ja Kivipaina, Kouvolan, Finland.
- Hakku. bi-m. ISSN 0017-6796

**Poiken Keskus r.y.**
Box 345, 00101 Helsinki 10, Finland.
- J P: Joka Poika; monthly paper for boys and girls. m. ISSN 0355-4201

**Poliisimies**
Pursimiehenkatu 5 A 15, 00150 Helsinki 15, Finland.
- Poliisimies. m. ISSN 0048-4725

**Psychiatria Fennica**
Arkadiankatu 35 B 37, 00100 Helsinki 10, Finland.
- Psychiatria Fennica/Finnish Psychiatry/Suomalaista Psykiatriaa. a. ISSN 0079-7227 (Foundation for Psychiatric Research in Finland)
- Psychiatria Fennica. Julkaisuserja/Psychiatria Fennica. Reports. irreg., no. 27, 1977. ISSN 0355-7693 (Foundation for Psychiatric Research in Finland)
- Psychiatria Fennica. Monografiasarja/Psychiatria Fennica. Monographs. irreg., no. 8, 1977. ISSN 0355-7707 (Foundation for Psychiatric Research in Finland)

**Puhelinlaitosten Liitto R.Y.**
Fredrikinkatu 61, 00100 Helsinki 10, Finland.
- Puhelin. bi-m. ISSN 0048-5977

**Puumiesten Liitto**
Rajakatu 32 B, 40200 Jyvaskyla 20, Finland.
- Puumies/Timbermen. m. ISSN 0355-953X

**Radioliikkeiden Liitto**
Iso Roobertinkatu 1 B, 00120 Helsinki 12, Finland.
- Radiokauppias. 10 per yr. ISSN 0355-6735

**Rakennusmestarien Keskusliitto**
Fredrikinkatu 53 A, 00100 Helsinki 10, Finland.
- Rakennuslehti. (pub. by Rakentajain Tiedotus r.y.)
- Rakennustaito. bi-w. ISSN 0048-6663
- Rakentajain Kalenteri. a. ISSN 0355-550X

**Kustannus Oy Rakennustekniikka**
Meritullinkatu 16 A 5, 00170 Helsinki 17, Finland.
- Rakennustekniikka; Finnish civil engineering journal. 8 per yr. ISSN 0033-913X (Association of Finnish Civil Engineers)

**Rakentajain Tiedotus r.y.**
Ratakatu 5 A 14, 00120 Helsinki 12, Finland.
- Rakennuslehti. w. ISSN 0033-9121 (Rakennusmestarien Keskusliitto) (Co-sponsor: Suomen Rakennusinsinoorien Liitto-Association of Finnish Civil Engineers)

**Oy Rastor AB**
Vanha Victortic 16, 00300 Helsinki 30, Finland.
- Tehokas Yritys. m.

**Rationalisointiliitto**
Maurinkatu 4, 00170 Helsinki 17, Finland.
- Tuottavuus. irreg. (Co-sponsor: Konttorirationalisointiyhdistys)

**Rautatievirkamiesliitto**
Rautatiehallitus, Vilhonkatu 13, 00100 Helsinki 10, Finland.
- Rautatieliikenne. m (11 per yr.) ISSN 0048-6833

**Oy Ravintolalehti**
Eerikinkatu 16 A 3, 00100 Helsinki 10, Finland.
- Hotelli- Ja Ravintolalehti/Hotell och Restaurangtidningen. m.(except Jan. & July) ISSN 0018-6317 (Finnish Hotel and Restaurant Association)

**Reader's Digest AB**
see Valitut Palat

**Sairaalatalousyhdistys r.y**
Pihlajatie 7 A 3, 00270 Helsinki 27, Finland.
- Sairaala. m. ISSN 0036-326X

**Sanoma Osakeyhtio**
Ludviginkatu 2-10, SF-00130 Helsinki 13, Finland.
- Aku Ankka. w.
- Kodin Kuvalehti. s-m. ISSN 0023-2610
- Me Naiset. w. ISSN 0025-6277
- Suuri Kasityokerho. m.

**Sanomalehtien Liitto**
Mannerheimintie 18 A, 00100 Helsinki 10, Finland.
- Suomen Lehdisto/Finlands Press. m. ISSN 0039-5587

**Oy Scan-Auto AB**
Sturenkatu 27, 00550 Helsinki 55, Finland.
- A J A. bi-m.

**Scientific Agricultural Society of Finland**
see Suomen Maataloustieteellinen Seura

**Scout Union of Finland**
Heikkilantie 10, 00200 Helsinki 20, Finland.
- Partiojohtaja/Scoutledaren. irreg. ISSN 0085-4794 (Co-sponsor: Union of Finnish Girl Guides)

**Siipikarjanhoitajain Liito**
Kanakouluntie 1, 13100 Hameenlinna 10, Finland.
- Siipikarja. m. ISSN 0037-5098

**Societas Biologica Fennica Vanamo**
Snellmaninkatu 9-11, SF-00170 Helsinki 17, Finland
- Annales Botanici Fennici. q. ISSN 0003-3847 (Subscr. to: Akateeminen Kirjakauppa (Academic Bookstore), Keskuskatu 1, SF-00170 Helsinki 10, Finland or Tieto Ltd., 5 Elton Rd., Clevedon, Avon BS21 7RA, England)
- Annales Zoologici Fennici. q. ISSN 0003-455X (Subscr. to: Akateeminen Kirjakauppa (Academic Bookstore), Keskuskatu 1, SF-00100 Helsinki 10, Finland or Tieto Ltd., 5 Elton Rd., Clevedon, Avon BS 21 7RA, England)
- Atlas Florae Europaeae. irreg, vol. 3, 1976. (Co-sponsor: Committee for Mapping the Flora of Europe) (Subscr. to Akateeminen Kirjakauppa (Academic Bookstore), Keskuskatu 1, SF-00100 Helsinki 10, Finland or Tieto Ltd., 5 Elton Rd., Clevedon, Avon BS21 7RA, England)
- Luonnon Tutkija. 5 per yr. ISSN 0024-7383

**Societas Entomologica Helsingforsiensis**
Zoological Museum, N. Jarnvagsgatan 13, SF-00100
Helsinki 10, Finland.
- Notulae Entomologicae. 4 per yr. ISSN 0029-4594

**Societas Gerontologica Fennica**
Siltavuurendenger 20-A, Helsinki 17, Finland.
- Geron. irreg. ISSN 0072-4157

**Societas Orientalis Fennica**
see **Suomen Itamainen Seura**

**Societas pro Fauna et Flora Fennica**
Snellmaninkatu 9-11, 00170 Helsinki 17, Finland
- Acta Botanica Fennica. 4 per yr.(approx.) ISSN
0001-5369 (Subscr. to: Akateeminen Kirjakauppa
(Academic Bookstore), Keskuskatu 1, SF-00100
Helsinki 10, Finland)
- Acta Zoologica Fennica. 4 per yr.(approx.) ISSN
0001-7299 (Subscr. to: Akateeminen Kirjakauppa
(Academic Bookstore), Keskuskatu 1, SF-00100
Helsinki 10, Finland)
- Fauna Fennica. irreg.(2 per yr.) ISSN 0071-4054
- Societas pro Fauna et Flora Fennica. Memoranda.
2 per yr. ISSN 0373-6873

**Societas Scientiarum Fennica**
Snellmansgatan 9-11, SF-00170 Helsinki 17,
Finland.
- Bidrag till Kaennedom av Finlands Natur och
Folk. irreg. ISSN 0067-8481
- Commentationes Biologicae. irreg. ISSN 0069-
6579
- Commentationes Humanarum Litterarum. irreg.
ISSN 0069-6587
- Commentationes Physico-Mathematicae. q. ISSN
0069-6609
- Commentationes Scientiarum Socialium. irreg.
ISSN 0355-256X

**Society for Finnish Philology**
see **Kotikielen Seura**

**Society of Finnish Jurists**
see **Suomalainen Lakimiesyhdistys**

**Society of Forestry in Finland**
see **Suomen Metsatieteellinen Seura**

**Sokeritautiliitto r.y.**
Kauppakatu 7 A, 33200 Tampere 20, Finland.
- Diabetes. m. ISSN 0046-0192

**Sosialistinen Aikakauslehti**
Paasivuorenkatu 3 B 10, Helsinki, Finland.
- Sosialistinen Aikakauslehti. 10 per yr. ISSN 0038-
1616

**Soumalais-Ugrilainen Seura**
Snellmaninkatu 9-11, 00170 Helsinki 17, Finland.
- Suomalais-Ugrilaisen Seura. Aikakauskirja/Societe
Finno-Ougrienne. Journal. a.

**Suomalainen Kirjakauppa**
Postilokero 10 105, Helsinki 10, Finland.
- Sprache und Denken; Finnische Beitrage zur
Philosophie und Sprachwissenschaft. irreg. ISSN
0081-3818

**Suomalainen Laakariseura Duodecim**
see **Finnish Medical Society Duodecim**

**Suomalainen Lakimiesyhdistys**
Dobelninkatu 5 B, Helsinki 26, Finland.
- Lakimies. 8 per yr. ISSN 0023-7353

**Suomalainen Tiedeakatemia**
Snellmaninkatu 9-11, 00170 Helsinki 17, Finland.
- Academia Scientiarum Fennica. Proceedings/
Sitzungsberichte. a. ISSN 0065-0501
- Annales Academiae Scientiarum Fennicae. Series
A, 1: Mathematica. irreg. ISSN 0066-1953
- Annales Academiae Scientiarum Fennicae. Series
A, 2: Chemica. irreg. ISSN 0066-1961
- Annales Academiae Scientiarum Fennicae. Series
A, 3: Geologica-Geographica. irreg. ISSN 0066-
197X
- Annales Academiae Scientiarum Fennicae. Series
A, 4: Biologica. irreg. ISSN 0066-1988
- Annales Academiae Scientiarum Fennicae. Series
A, 5: Medica. irreg. ISSN 0066-1996
- Annales Academiae Scientiarum Fennicae. Series
A, 6: Physica. irreg. ISSN 0066-2003
- Annales Academiae Scientiarum Fennicae. Series
B. irreg. ISSN 0066-2011
- F F Communications. (Folklore Fellows) 2-5 per
yr. ISSN 0014-5815

**Suomalaisen Kirjallisuuden Seura**
Hallituskatu 1, 00170 Helsinki 17, Finland.
- Studia Fennica: Revue de Linguistique et
d'Ethnologie Finnoises. irreg. ISSN 0085-6835

**Suomen Adventikirkko**
PL 94, 33101 Tampere 10, Finland.
- Terveys. m. ISSN 0040-3911

**Suomen Ampujainliitto**
Aurorankatu 9 B, SF-00100 Helsinki 10, Finland.
- Ampujainlehti. 10 per yr. ISSN 0001-1940

**Suomen Arkkitehtiliitto**
Unioninkatu 30 A, 00100 Helsinki 10, Finland.
- Arkkitehtiuutiset/Arkitektnytt. m. ISSN 0044-
8915

**Suomen Bensiinikauppiaitten Liitto r.y.**
Mannerheimintie 40 D 86, 00100 Helsinki 10,
Finland.
- Bensiini Uutiset. m. ISSN 0045-1738

**Suomen Betoniteollisuuden Keskusjarjesto**
Lapinlahdenkatu 1 A 8, 00180 Helsinki 18, Finland.
- Betonituote. 4 per yr. ISSN 0005-9919

**Suomen Biologian Seura Vanamo**
see **Societas Biologica Fennica Vanamo**

**Suomen Dieselliitto**
Box 176, 00170 Helsinki 17, Finland.
- Diesel-Lehti. m. ISSN 0012-2629

**Suomen Elainlaakariliitto**
Hameentie 78 A 1, 00550 Helsinki 55, Finland.
- Suomen Elainlaakarilehti/Finsk Veterinartidskrift.
m. ISSN 0039-5501

**Suomen Farmisialiitto**
Rautatielaisenkatu 6, 00520 Helsinki 52, Finland.
- Semina. s-m. ISSN 0049-0164

**Suomen Filatelistiliitto r. y.**
Box 202, 00101 Helsinki 10, Finland.
- Philatelia Fennica; stamp journal. m.

**Suomen Fyysikkoseura**
Siltavuorenpenger 20 C, SF-00170 Helsinki 17,
Finland.
- Arkhimedes. q. ISSN 0004-1920 (Co-sponsor:
Finnish Mathematical Society)

**Suomen Geodeettinen Laitos**
Pasilankatu 43A, SF-00240 Helsinki, Finland.
- Suomen Geodeettisen Laitoksen. Julkaisuja/
Finnish Geodetic Institute. Publications/Finnische
Geodaetische Institut. Veroeffentlichungen. irreg.
ISSN 0085-6932

**Suomen Geologinen Seura**
Kivimiehentie 1, SF-02150 Espoo 15, Finland.
- Geologi. 10 per yr. ISSN 0046-5720

**Suomen Hammaslaakariseura**
Akavatalo, Rautatielaisenkatu 6, SF-00520 Helsinki
52, Finland.
- Suomen Hammaslaakariseura. Toimituksia/Finnish
Dental Society. Proceedings. bi-m. ISSN 0039-
551X

**Suomen Historiallinen Seura**
Snellmaninkatu 9-11, 00170 Helsinki 17, Finland.
- Historiallinen Aikakauskirja. q. ISSN 0018-2362
(Co-sponsor: Historian Ystavain Liitto)
- Historiallinen Arkisto. irreg., no. 70, 1975. ISSN
0081-9409
- Historiallisia Tutkimuksia. irreg., more than 1 per
year. ISSN 0073-2559
- Studia Historica. irreg., 1965, no. 7. ISSN 0081-
6493
- Suomen Historiallinen Seura. Kasikirjoja. irreg;no.
8, 1975. ISSN 0081-9417
- Suomen Historian Laehteitae/Source Material of
Finnish History. irreg., 1973, no. 8. ISSN 0081-
9425

**Suomen Ilmailuliitto**
Malmi Airport, 00700 Helsinki 70, Finland.
- Ilmailu. m. ISSN 0019-252X

**Suomen Itamainen Seura**
Snellmanink 9-11, 00170 Helsinki 17, Finland.
- Studia Orientalia. irreg. ISSN 0039-3282

**Suomen Jalkineliikkeenharjoittajain Liitto r.y.**
Iso-Roobertinkatu 24 C 21, Helsinki 12, Finland.
- Jalkine. 6 per yr. ISSN 0021-4078

**Suomen Kahertajatyonantajaliitto**
Makelankatu 54 A, 00510 Helsinki 51, Finland.
- Kahertaja. 7 per yr. ISSN 0022-7714

**Suomen Kalamiesten Keskusliitto**
Suvilahdenkatu 3-5 B 22, 00500 Helsinki 50,
Finland.
- Kalamies. 10 per yr. ISSN 0085-2449

**Suomen Kalastusyhdistys**
Urheilukatu 14 A 10, SF-00250 Helsinki 25,
Finland.
- Fiskeritidskrift Foer Finland. bi-m. ISSN 0015-
3125
- Kalastuspaikkaopas. irreg.(approx. biennial) ISSN
0075-4684
- Suomen Kalastuslehti. 8 per yr. ISSN 0039-5528

**Suomen Katiloliitto**
Dagmarinkatu 8 B, 00100 Helsinki 10, Finland.
- Katilolehti/Tidskrift Foer Barnmorskor. m. ISSN
0022-9415

**Suomen Kaupunki Liitto**
Eduskuntakatu 4, 00100 Helsinki 10, Finland.
- Suomen Kunnallislehti/Finlands
Kommunaltidskrift. 17 per yr. (Finnish edt.); 10
per yr. (Swedish edt.) ISSN 0039-5544

**Suomen Kelloseppaliito**
Vuorikatu 4 A, 00100 Helsinki 10, Finland.
- Kelloseppaa. 8 per yr.

**Suomen Kemistiliitto**
Rautatielaisenkatu 6, 00520 Helsinki 52, Finland.
- Kemisti/Kemisten. bi-m. ISSN 0022-9865
- Kemistin Kalenteri. a.

**Suomen Kirjastoseura**
Museokatu 18 A 4, 00100 Helsinki 10, Finland.
- Kirjastolehti. m. ISSN 0023-1843

**Suomen Kotielainjalostusyhdistys**
Box 40, 01301 Vantaa 30, Finland.
- Nautakarja/Cattle. 5 per yr. ISSN 0028-131X
- Sika/Pig. 5 per yr. ISSN 0037-5101

**Suomen Kotiseutuliitto**
Simonkatu 12 B 13, 00100 Helsinki 10, Finland.
- Kotiseutu. 6 per yr. ISSN 0047-3677

**Suomen Kultaseppien Liitto r. y.**
Vuorikatu 3 A, 00100 Helsinki 10, Finland.
- Kultaseppien Lehti. irreg. ISSN 0085-2600

**Suomen Kunnallisteknillinen Yhdistys r.y.**
Box 51, 00131 Helsinki, Finland.
- Kunnallistekniikka/Kommunalteknik. 6 per yr.
ISSN 0023-5385

**Suomen Kuorma- Autoliitto r.y.**
Nuijamiestentie 5 C, 00400 Helsinki 40, Finland.
- Ammattiautoilija. m.

**Suomen L V I- Yhdistys**
Lonnrotinkatu 22A, 00120 Helsinki 12, Finland.
- L V I-Lehti. (Lampo-, Vesi- Ja Ilmastointi) bi-m.

**Suomen Laakariliitto**
Ruoholandenkatu 4, 00180 Helsinki 18, Finland.
- Suomen Laakarilehti/Finlands Lakartidning. 3 per
mo. ISSN 0039-5560

**Suomen Laakintavoimistelijaliitto**
Asemamiehenkatu 4, 00520 Helsinki 52, Finland.
- Laakintavoimistelija/Fysioterapeuten. 8 per yr.
ISSN 0039-5579

**Suomen Lakimiesliitto**
Rautatielaisenkatu 6, 00520 Helsinki 52, Finland.
- Lakimiesuutiset/Juristbladet. m. ISSN 0023-7361

**Suomen Leipuriliitto r.y.**
Atomitie 1, Helsinki 37, Finland.
- Leipuri. m. ISSN 0024-0699

**Suomen Liikunnanopettajain Liitto**
Mannerheimintie 87 B, 00270 Helsinki 27, Finland
(Subscr. to: Vesalantie 51, 00940 Helsinki 94,
Finland)
- Liikuntakasvatus. 5-6 per yr. (Co-sponsor:
Koululiikuntaliitto)

**Suomen Lintutieteellinen Yhdistys**
c/o Olavi Hilden, Ed., University of Helsinki,
Department of Zoology, P. Rautiekatu 13, SF-00100
Helsinki 10, Finland.
- Ornis Fennica. q. ISSN 0030-5685

**Suomen Maalarimestariliitto**
Niittylantie 4, Helsinki 62, Finland.
- Maalarilehti. m. ISSN 0024-8568

**Suomen Maantieteellinen Seura**
Snellmaninkatu 9-11, 00170 Helsinki 17, Finland.
- Fennia. q. ISSN 0015-0010
- Terra. q. ISSN 0040-3741

**Suomen Maarakentajien Keskusliitto**
Lastenkodinkuja 1 A, 00180 Helsinki 18, Finland.
- Maansiirto/Earthmoving; maa-ja
  vesirakennusteknillinen aikakauslehti. 8 per yr.
  ISSN 0047-5327

**Suomen Maataloustieteellinen Seura**
Rukkila 00001, SF-00710 Helsinki 71, Finland.
- Scientific Agricultural Society of Finland. Journal.
  4-6 per yr. ISSN 0024-8835

**Suomen Matkailuliitto**
Suvilahdenkatu 6 B, 00500 Helsinki 50, Finland.
- Leirinta ja Retkeily/Camping and Hiking. 10 per
  yr. ISSN 0356-0805
- Matkailumaailma/World of Travel. 8 per yr. ISSN
  0025-5963

**Suomen Metalliteollisuusyhdistys**
- Konepajamies. (pub. by Insinoorilehdet Oy)

**Suomen Metsanhoitajaliitto**
Akavatalo, Rautatielaisenkatu 6, 00520 Helsinki 52,
Finland.
- Metsanhoitaja. m(except July & Aug.)

**Suomen Metsateollisuuden Keskusliitto**
- Finnish Paper and Timber. (pub. by Finnish Paper
  and Timber Journal Publishing Co.)
- Paperi Ja Puu/Papper och Tra/Paper and Timber.
  (pub. by Finnish Paper and Timber Journal
  Publishing Co.)
- Suomen Puutalous. (pub. by Finnish Paper and
  Timber Journal Publishing Co.)

**Suomen Metsatieteellinen Seura**
Unioninkatu 40 B, SF-00170 Helsinki 17, Finland.
- Acta Forestalia Fennica. 8-12 per yr. ISSN 0001-
  5636
- Silva Fennica. 4 per yr. ISSN 0037-5330

**Suomen Muusikkojen Liitto**
00120 Helsinki 12, Finland.
- Muusikko/Musician. m.

**Suomen Naishammaslaakarit Ryhma**
Helsinki, Finland.
- Suomen Naishammaslaakarit Ryhma. Julkaisu. a.
  ISSN 0081-9433

**Suomen Osuuskauppojen Keskuskunta**
Vilhonkatu 7, 00100 Helsinki 10, Finland.
- Handelslaget. m. ISSN 0017-7318 (Co-sponsor:
  Yleinen Osuuskauppojen Liitto)
- Osuuskauppalehti. m. ISSN 0030-6533 (Co-
  sponsor: Yleinen Osuuskauppojen Liitto)
- Samarbete. w. ISSN 0036-3715 (Co-sponsor:
  Yleinen Osuuskauppojen Liitto)
- Yhteishyva. w. ISSN 0044-0396 (Co-sponsor:
  Yleinen Osuuskauppojen Liitto)

**Suomen Pakkausyhdistys**
Ritarikatu 3 A, 00170 Helsinki 17, Finland.
- Pakkaus. m. ISSN 0031-0131

**Suomen Pankki**
Information and Publications Department, Box 160,
SF-00101 Helsinki 10, Finland.
- Bank of Finland. Annual Statement. a. ISSN
  0081-945X
- Bank of Finland. Monthly Bulletin. m. ISSN
  0005-5174
- Bank of Finland Year Book. a. ISSN 0081-9468
- Suomen Pankki. Series A. irreg., no. 42, 1976.
  ISSN 0355-6034
- Suomen Pankki. Series B. irreg., no. 31, 1969.
  ISSN 0081-9484
- Suomen Pankki. Series C. irreg., no. 6, 1969.
  ISSN 0081-9492
- Suomen Pankki. Series D. irreg., no. 41, 1976.
  ISSN 0081-9506
- Suomen Pankki. Series Kasvututkimuksia/Studies
  on Finland's Economic Growth. irreg; no. 7, 1976.
  ISSN 0355-6050

**Suomen Partiolaiset**
Heikkilaantie 10, 00210 Helsinki 21, Finland.
- Partio. m (10 per yr.) ISSN 0556-3488

**Suomen Rauta- ja Koneliikkeiden Yhdistys**
Keskuskatu 3, Helsinki 10, Finland.
- Rautakaupan Uutiset. m. (except Jan., July &
  Aug.) ISSN 0034-012X

**Suomen Saastopankkiliitto**
Postilokero 10479, Helsinki 10, Finland.
- Kymppi. q. ISSN 0023-5989
- Saastopankki. m. ISSN 0036-2123 (Co-sponsor:
  Samerka Oy)

**Suomen Sahat r.y.**
Saastopankinranta 4 C 24, SF-00530 Helsinki 53,
Finland.
- Sahamies. 9 per yr. ISSN 0036-262X

**Suomen Sahkoalantyontekijain Liitto**
Hameenkatu 17 A, 33200 Tampere 20, Finland.
- Vasama. fortn. ISSN 0049-5883

**Suomen Sahkourakoitsijaliitto**
Nordenskioldinkatu 3 A 19, 00250 Helsinki 25,
Finland.
- Sahkourakoitsija. 10 per yr. ISSN 0048-8984 (Co-
  sponsor: Sahkotyonantajain Liitto r. y.)

**Suomen Sairaanhoitajaliitto**
Asemamiehenkatu 4, 00520 Helsinki 52, Finland.
- Sairaanhoitaja Sjukskoterskan. 24 per yr. ISSN
  0036-3278

**Suomen Sanomalehtimiesten Liitto**
Yrjonkatu 11 A 2, Helsinki 12, Finland.
- Sanomalehtimies/Journalisten. 25 per yr. ISSN
  0036-4479

**Suomen Silmaoptikkojen Liitto**
Mariank. 26 E, 00170 Helsinki 17, Finland.
- Optikko. bi-m. ISSN 0048-2021

**Suomen Sukututkimusseura**
Snellmaninkatu 9-11, 00170 Helsinki 17, Finland.
- Genos. q. ISSN 0016-6898

**Suomen Syopayhdistys**
Liisankatu 21 B, 00170 Helsinki 17, Finland.
- Syopa/Cancer. 6 per yr.

**Suomen Taiteilijaseura**
Ainonkatu 3, 00100 Helsinki 10, Finland.
- Taide. bi-m. ISSN 0039-8977

**Suomen Tekstiiliteknillinen Liitto r. y.**
Vallerinkatu 13-15 B, 33270 Tampere 27, Finland.
- Tekstiililehti. 6 per yr. ISSN 0040-2370

**Suomen Teollisuusliitto**
Etelaranta 10, PL 220, 00131 Helsinki 13, Finland.
- Suomen Teollisuusliitto. Jasenluettelo/Finlands
  Industrifoerbund. Medlemsfoerteckning/
  Federation of Finnish Industries. List of
  Members. irreg.

**Suomen Tieteellinen Kirjastoseura**
Hotelli- Ja Ravintolaopiston Kirjasto,
Nuijamiestentie 10, 00400 Helsinki 40, Finland.
- Signum. m.

**Suomen Tieyhdistys r.y.**
Vironkatu 6, 00170 Helsinki 17, Finland.
- Tie Ja Liikenne. m. (except Jan. & Jul.)

**Suomen Tiiliteollisuusliitto r.y.**
Iso Roobertinkatu 20, 00120 Helsinki 12, Finland.
- Tiili. 4 per yr. ISSN 0040-7402

**Suomen Tuberkuloosin Vastustamisyhdistys**
Kalevankatu 9, 00100 Helsinki 10, Finland.
- Tuberkuloosi ja Keuhkosairaudet Vuosikirja/
  Tuberculosis and Respiratory Diseases Yearbook/
  Tuberkulos och Lungsjukdomar Aarsbok. 2-3 per
  yr. (1 vol. per yr.) ISSN 0355-5011

**Suomen Tyonantajain Keskusliitto**
Etelaranta 10, Helsinki, Finland.
- Teollisuuslehti. 12 per yr. ISSN 0040-3539

**Suomen Ulkomaanpauppaliitto**
see Finnish Foreign Trade Association

**Suomen Vaatturiliitto r.y.**
Vuorikatu 4 A 8, 00100 Helsinki 10, Finland.
- Vaatturi. bi-m.

**Suomen Valokuvajarjestojen Keskusliitto Finnfoto**
Korkeavuorenkatu 2 B F 72, SF-00140 Helsinki 14,
Finland.
- Valokuva. m. ISSN 0355-1466

**Suomen Valokuvataiteen Museon Saatio**
Helsinki, Finland.
- Valokuvauksen Vuosikirja/Finnish Photographic
  Yearbook/Finsk Fotografisk Arsbok. irreg.

**Suomen Yhdyspankki**
P.B. 868, 00101 Helsinki 10, Finland.
- Union Bank of Finland. Annual Report. a.
- Unitas; illustrating economic conditions in
  Finland. q. ISSN 0041-7130 (prep. by its
  Economic Research Department)

**Suomen 4-H Liitto**
Bulevardi 28, 00120 Helsinki 12, Finland.
- Nuorten Sarka. m.(10 per yr) ISSN 0029-6139
- 4H -Tiedotuksia. q.

**Suomi-Seura r.y.**
Mariankatu 8, 00170 Helsinki 17, Finland.
- Suomen Silta. bi-m. ISSN 0039-5625

**Suoseura**
Unioninkatu 40 B, 00170 Helsinki 17, Finland.
- Suo. 5 per yr. ISSN 0039-5471

**Svenska Finlands Laerarfoerbund R.F.**
Jaernvaegsmannag. 6, 00520 Helsinki 52, Finland.
- Laeraren. fortn.

**Svenska Kvinnofoerbundet**
Bulevarden 7 A, 00120 Helsinki 12, Finland.
- Astra. m. ISSN 0004-6094

**Svenska Lantbruksproducenternas Centralfoerbund**
Loennrotsgatan 35 D, 00180 Helsinki 18, Finland.
- Landsbygdens Folk. w. ISSN 0023-8015

**Svenska Litteratursaellskapet i Finland**
Snellmansg. 9-11, 00170 Helsinki 17, Finland.
- Folklivsstudier. irreg., no. 10, 1974. ISSN 0085-
  0764
- Historiska och Litteraturhistoriska Studier. a.
  ISSN 0073-2702
- Svenska Litteratursaellskapet i Finland. Skrifter.
  irreg (4-8 per yr.) ISSN 0039-6842

**Svenska Traedgaardsfoerbundet**
Elisabetsgatan 21 B, 00170 Helsinki 17, Finland.
- Traedgaardsnytt. s-m. ISSN 0049-4356

**Swedish Literary Society of Finland**
see Svenska Litteratursaellskapet i Finland

**Swedish University of Aabo**
see Aabo Akademi

**Sydantautiliitto r.y.**
Fredrikinkatu 20 B, Helsinki 12, Finland.
- Sydan. 8 per yr. ISSN 0039-7571

**Foerlags AB Sydvaestkusten**
Slottsgatan 23, Aabo, Finland.
- Finsk Tidskrift; kultur-ekonomi-politik. 10 per yr.
  ISSN 0015-248X (Foereningen Granskaren)

**Syndicate Press Oy**
Laivanvarustajankatu 5, 00140 Helsinki 14, Finland.
- Tahti. 8 per yr.

**Tampere Peace Research Institute**
Tammelanpuistokatu 58 B, Tampere, Finland.
- Instant Research on Peace and Violence. q. ISSN
  0046-967X

**Technical Research Centre of Finland**
see Valtion Teknillinen Tutkimuskeskus

**Teknillisten Tieteiden Akatemia**
Lonnrotinkatu 37, SF-00180 Helsinki 18, Finland.
- Acta Polytechnica Scandinavica. Applied Physics
  Series. irreg.(2-3 per yr.) ISSN 0355-2721
- Acta Polytechnica Scandinavica. Chemistry
  Including Metallurgy Series. irreg (2-3 per yr.)
  ISSN 0001-6853
- Acta Polytechnica Scandinavica. Civil Engineering
  and Building Construction Series. irreg. (2-3 per
  yr.) ISSN 0355-2705
- Acta Polytechnica Scandinavica. Electrical
  Engineering Series. irreg (2-3 per yr.) ISSN 0001-
  6845
- Acta Polytechnica Scandinavica. Mathematics and
  Computer Science Series. irreg. (2-3 per yr.) ISSN
  0355-2713
- Acta Polytechnica Scandinavica. Mechanical
  Engineering Series. irreg. (2-3 per yr.) ISSN 0001-
  687X

**Tekstiilikauppiaiden Liitto r. y.**
Mariankatu 26 B 14, 00170 Helsinki 17, Finland.
• Teksi. m (10 per yr.)

**Telefoninraettningarnas Foerbund**
*see* Puhelinlaitosten Liitto

**Teollisuuden Keskusliitto**
Mariankatu 26 B 9, SF-00170 Helsinki 17, Finland.
• Teollisuussanomat/Industrial Magazine. m. ISSN
0300-3124

**Teologinen Julkaisuseura r.y.**
Neitsytpolku 1 B, Helsinki, Finland.
• Teologinen Aikakauskirja/Teologisk Tidskrift. bi-
m. ISSN 0040-3555

**Tidningarnas Foerbund**
*see* Sanomalehtien Liitto

**Toimiupseeriliitto**
Olkkolankatu 7, 50100 Mikkeli, Finland.
• Toimiupseeri. m. ISSN 0355-726X

**Trade Unions International of Workers of the**
**Building, Wood and Building Materials Industries**
Box 281, 00101 Helsinki 10, Finland.
• International Trade Conference of Workers of the
Building, Wood and Building Materials Industries.
(Brochure) irreg, 7th, 1975.
• U I T B B Information. q.

**Tuberkuloosi ja Keuhkovammaisten Liitto**
Siltasaarenkatu 12 A, Postilokero 20, 00531
Helsinki 53, Finland.
• Jousi. m. ISSN 0047-2948

**Turun Hammaslaaketieteenkandidaattiseura**
Lemminkaisenkatu 2, 20520 Turku 52, Finland.
• Hammaslaaketieteenkandidaattiseuran. q. ISSN
0023-5717

**Turun Historiallinen Yhdistys**
Turun Yliopisto, SF-20500 Turku 20, Finland.
• Turun Historiallinen Arkisto. irreg., vol. 30, 1975
(approx. a) ISSN 0085-7440

**Turun Yliopisto**
SF-20500 Turku 50, Finland.
• Turun Yliopisto. Julkaisuja. Sarja A. I.
Astronomica-Chemica-Physica-Mathematica.
irreg. ISSN 0082-7002
• Turun Yliopisto. Julkaisuja. Sarja A. II. Biologica-
Geographica- Geologica. irreg. ISSN 0082-6979
• Turun Yliopisto. Julkaisuja. Sarja B. Humaniora.
irreg. ISSN 0082-6987
• Turun Yliopisto. Julkaisuja. Sarja C. Scripta
Lingua Fennica Edita. irreg. ISSN 0082-6995
• Turun Yliopisto. Julkaisuja. Sarja D. Medica-
Odontologica. irreg.

**Turun Yliopisto. Kirjasto**
SF-20500 Turku 50, Finland.
• Suomen Aikakauslehti-Indeksi/Index to Finnish
Periodicals. a. ISSN 0081-9395
• Turun Yliopisto. Kirjasto. Julkaisuja. irreg; no. 11,
1975. ISSN 0082-7010

**Turun Yliopisto. Klassillisen Filologian Laitos**
SF-20500 Turku 50, Finland.
• Turun Yliopisto. Klassillisen Filologian Laitos.
Opera Ex Instituto Philologiae Classicae
Universitatis Turkuensis Edita. irreg., 1973, no. 3.
ISSN 0082-7029

**Turun Yliopisto. Poliittisen Historian Laitos**
SF-20500 Turku 50, Finland.
• Finland; books and publications in politics,
political history and international relations. a.

**Turun Yliopisto. Psykologian Laitos**
Yliopistonk 23 A, SF-20500 Turku 50, Finland.
• Turun Yliopisto. Psykologian Laitos. Reports.
irreg., 1970, no. 34. ISSN 0082-7037

**Ulkopoliittinen Instituutti**
Museokatu 18 A 9, SF-00100 Helsinki, Finland.
• Yearbook of Finnish Foreign Policy. a.

**Union Bank of Finland**
*see* Suomen Yhdyspankki

**Union of Journalists in Finland**
*see* Suomen Sanomalehtimiesten Liitto

**Union of Swedish Agricultural Producers**
*see* Svenska Lantbruksproducenternas
Centralfoerbund

**University of Helsinki**
*see* Helsingin Yliopisto

**University of Jyvaskyla**
*see* Jyvaskylan Yliopisto

**University of Turku**
*see* Turun Yliopisto

**Upseeriliitto**
Fredrikinkatu 16 A 11, 00120 Helsinki 12, Finland.
• Sotilasaikakauslehti. m. ISSN 0038-1675

**Uusfilologinen Yhdistys**
Porthania, Helsinki University, 00100 Helsinki 10,
Finland
• Neuphilologische Mitteilungen. q. ISSN 0028-
3754 (Subscr. to: Modern Language Society, c/o
Tieto Ltd., 5 Elton Rd., Clevedon, Bristol BS21
7RA, England)

**Vaasa School of Economics**
*see* Vaasan Kauppakorkeakoulu

**Vaasan Kauppakorkeakoulu**
Raastuvank. 31, 65100 Vaasa 10, Finland.
• Acta Wasaensia/Geography. a.

**Vaestontutkimuslaitos**
Bulevardi 28, 00120 Helsinki 12, Finland.
• Yearbook of Population Research in Finland.
biennial. ISSN 0506-3590

**Valio Meijerien Keskusosuusliike**
Koydenpunojankatu 7 A, 00180 Helsinki 18,
Finland.
• Karjantuote; meijeritaloudellinen aikakauslehti. m.
ISSN 0047-3243
• Karjatalous. m. ISSN 0047-3251

**Oy Valitut Palat**
Uudenmaankatu 16A, Helsinki 12, Finland.
• Valitut Patat/Reader's Digest (Finnish edition) m.
ISSN 0042-2290

**Valtion Teknillinen Tutkimuskeskus**
Vuorimiehentie 5, SF-02150 Espoo 15, Finland.
• Bygglitteratur; building abstract service. 4 per yr.
ISSN 0007-7542
• Rakennusalan Suomalaisen Kirjallisuuden
Kuukausikatsaus. 12 per yr. ISSN 0355-5534
(prep. by its Rakennusalan Suomalaisen
Kirjallisuuden Kuukausikatsaus)
• Technical Research Centre of Finland. Julkaisu.
irreg.
• Technical Research Centre of Finland.
Publication. Building Technology and Community
Development. irreg. ISSN 0355-337X
• Technical Research Centre of Finland.
Publication. Electrical and Nuclear Technology.
irreg. ISSN 0355-3396
• Technical Research Centre of Finland.
Publication. Materials and Processing Technology.
irreg. ISSN 0355-3388
• Technical Research Centre of Finland.
Tiedonanto. irreg.

**Valtionyhtioiden Toimisto**
Aleksanterinkatu 10, Helsinki 17, Finland.
• Valtionyhtiot. a.

**Veljesliitto**
Kasarmikatu 34, 00130 Helsinki 13, Finland.
• Sotainvalidi. m. ISSN 0049-1349 (Disabled War
Veterans Association of Finland)

**Vesihuoltomiitto**
Arkadiankatu 15 C 19, 00100 Helsinki 10, Finland.
• Vesitalous; Finnish journal of water economy,
hydraulic and agricultural engineering. bi-m. (Co-
sponsor: Maa- Ja Vesitekniikan Tuki)

**Vesiyhdistys r.y.**
P.O. Box 721, 00101 Helsinki 10, Finland.
• Aqua Fennica. a.

**Viraleinen Lehti**
PL 516, 00101 Helsinki 10, Finland.
• Kaupparekisteri/Handelsregister. w. ISSN 0022-
9504

**Vuorimiesyhdistys**
c/o Martti Sulonen, Ed., Teknillinen Korkeakoulu,
Vuoriteollisuusosasto, 02150 Espoo 15, Finland.
• Vuoriteollisuus/Bergshanteringen. s-a. ISSN 0042-
9317

**Weltfriedensrates**
Box 18114, Helsinki, Finland.
• Friedenskurier. m.

**Workers Educational Association**
Paasivuorenkatu 5b, 00053 Helsinki 53, Finland.
• Aikamerkki. 8 per yr. ISSN 0044-6920

**World Peace Council**
Lonnretinkatu 25 A, Helsinki 18, Finland.
• Peace Courrier. m. ISSN 0031-594X

**World Peace Council. Presidential Committee**
P.O. Box 19114, Helsinki, Finland.
• New Perspectives. bi-m.

**Yhtyneet Kuvalehdet Oy**
Hietalahdenranta 13, 00180 Helsinki 18, Finland.
• Kanava. 9 per yr. ISSN 0355-0303
• Kasari. bi-m. ISSN 0047-3286
• Kaytannon Maamies. m. ISSN 0022-9571
• Kotiliesi. s-m. ISSN 0023-4281
• Metsastys Ja Kalastus. m. ISSN 0026-1629
• Muoti & Kauneus. 6 per yr. ISSN 0355-192X
• Non Stop. fortn.
• P.S. m.
• Parnasso. 8 per yr. ISSN 0031-2320 (Finnish
Cultural Foundation)
• Pientalo-Omakoti. m (10 per yr.)
• Suomen Kuvalehti. w. ISSN 0039-5552
• Suur-Seura. w. ISSN 0355-189X
• Tee Itse. bi-m. ISSN 0355-1873
• TH-Kotilaakari. m. ISSN 0355-1903 (Finnish
Medical Society Duodecim)

**Yliopiston Farmasiakunta r.y.**
Hallituskatu 9, 00170 Helsinki 17, Finland.
• M D S. 6 per yr. ISSN 0024-8045

**Yritystieto Oy**
P.O. Box 274, 00531 Helsinki, Finland.
• Business Contacts in Finland. irreg.

# FRANCE

**A. D. P.**
24, Place Malesherbes, 75017-Paris, France.
• Cadeau et l'Entreprise; les techniques de
stimulation des ventes. a.

**A.D.P.S.**
63 rue de Villiers, 92209 Neuilly, France.
• Architecture de Lumiere Courrier du Verre. q.

**A. E. C. R.**
Box 350R9, 67009 Strasbourg Cedex, France.
• Ktema; civilisations de l 'Orient, de la Grece et de
Rome Antiques. a. (Universite de Strasbourg II.
Groupe de Recherche d'Histoire Romaine)

**A. F. E. R. L. A.**
254 rue Saint-Jacques, Paris (5e), France.
• Revue Generale de l'Enseignement des Deficients
Auditifs. 4 per yr. ISSN 0035-3124

**A.I.F. Services**
10 Rue de Calais, Paris (9e), France.
• Revue de la Securite. m. ISSN 0035-1261

**A.N.F.A.N.O.M.A.**
156 Av. Victor-Hugo, 75116 Paris, France.
• France-Horizon. m (10 per yr) ISSN 0429-5412

**A. R. E. P.- Aime Reboul Editions Publicite**
6, rue Soffrey - Calignon, B.P. 337, 38509 Voiron,
France.
• Economie et Prospective de la Montagne. 5 per
yr.

**Editions A. T. D. Science et Service**
122, Avenue du General Leclerc, 95480 Pierrelaye,
France.
• Feuille de Route. m. (Aide a Toute Detresse)

**Abbaye de Lerins**
B.P. 157, F 06403 Cannes, France.
• Lerins. q.

**Editions de l' Abbaye de Solesmes**
F 72300 Sable, France.
- Etudes Gregoriennes. a. (approx.) vol. 15, 1975. ISSN 0071-2086

**Abeille de France, S.A.R.L.**
11, Rue. Gaillon, 75002 Paris, France.
- Abeille de France et l'Apiculteur. m. (Syndicat National d'Apiculture) (Co-Sponsor: Societe Centrale d'Apiculture)

**Abeilles et Fleurs**
42 rue du Faubourg la Grappe, Chartres - 28, France.
- Abeilles et Fleurs. m. ISSN 0001-3145

**Academia Nissarda**
Villa Massena, 67 rue de France, Nice (A.M.), France.
- Nice Historique. ISSN 0028-9698

**Academie d'Agriculture de France**
18 rue de Bellechasse, Paris (7e), France.
- Academie d'Agriculture de France./Comptes Rendus des Seances. s-m(except Aug-Sept) ISSN 0001-3986

**Academie d'Architecture, Paris**
6-bis rue Danton, Paris 6e, France.
- Academie d'Architecture, Paris. Annuaire. irreg. ISSN 0084-5876

**Academie d'Histoire, Paris**
23 rue Louis-le-Grand, F 75, Paris 2, France.
- Academie d'Histoire, Paris. Cahiers. q.

**Academie de Chirurgie**
- Chirurgie. (pub. by Masson)

**Academie de Chirurgie Dentaire**
- Academie de Chirurgie Dentaire. Bulletin. (pub. by Julien Prelat)

**Academie de Pharmacie**
- Annales Pharmaceutiques Francaises. (pub. by Masson)

**Academie de Philatelie de Paris**
c/o M. de Fontaines, 7 rue Chalgrin, F 75116 Paris, France.
- Documents Philateliques. q.

**Academie des Inscriptions et Belles-Lettres**
- Academie des Inscriptions et Belles-Lettres. Comptes Rendus des Seances. (pub. by Editions Klincksieck)
- Academie des Inscriptions et Belles-Lettres. Etudes et Commentaires. (pub. by Editions Klincksieck)
- Annee Epigraphique; Revue des Publications Epigraphiques Relatives a l'Antiquite Romaine. (pub. by Presses Universitaires de France)
- Journal des Savants. (pub. by Editions Klincksieck)
- Recueil des Historiens de la France. (pub. by Editions Klincksieck)

**Academie des Marches**
c/o Jean Darwell, Saint-Pee-sur Nivelle, 64310 Ascain, France.
- Courrier des Marches et d'Outre Mer. q.

**Academie des Sciences**
- Academie des Sciences. Annuaire. (pub. by Centrale des Revues Dunod Gauthier- Villars)
- Academie des Sciences. Comptes Rendus Hebdomadaires des Seances. Series A: Sciences Mathematiques. (pub. by Centrale des Revues Dunod Gauthier-Villars)
- Academie des Sciences. Comptes Rendus Hebdomadaires des Seances. Serie B: Sciences Physiques. (pub. by Centrale des Revues Dunod Gauthier-Villars)
- Academie des Sciences. Comptes Rendus Hebdomadaires des Seances. Series C: Sciences Chimiques. (pub. by Centrale des Revues Dunod Gauthier-Villars)
- Academie des Sciences. Comptes Rendus Hebdomadaires des Seances. Series D: Sciences Naturelles. (pub. by Centrale des Revues Dunod Gauthier-Villars)
- Academie des Sciences. Index Biographique des Membres et Correspondants. (pub. by Centrale des Revues Dunod Gauthier--Villars)

**Academie des Sciences, Belles-Lettres et Arts de Clermont-Ferrand**
19 rue Bardoux, 63000 Clermont-Ferrand (Puy-de-Dome), France.
- Bulletin Historique et Scientifique de l'Auvergne. q. ISSN 0007-4659

**Academie des Sciences d'Outre-Mer, Paris**
15 rue La Perouse, 75116 Paris, France.
- Academie des Sciences d'Outre-Mer, Paris. Annuaire. a. ISSN 0078-9461
- Academie des Sciences d'Outre-Mer, Paris. Comptes Rendus des Seances. q. ISSN 0001-4044

**Academie des Sports, Paris**
34 rue de Penthievre, 75008 Paris, France.
- Academie des Sports, Paris. Annuaire. irreg. ISSN 0065-0579

**Academie et Societe Lorraines de Sciences (a Nancy) Faculte des Sciences**
C.O. 140, 54037 Nancy Cedex, France.
- Academie et Societe Lorraines de Sciences. Bulletin. q.

**Academie Francaise**
23 Quai de Conti, Paris 6e, France.
- Academie Francaise. Annuaire; documents et notices sur les membres de l'Academie. irreg. ISSN 0065-0587

**Academie Nationale de Medecine**
- Academie Nationale de Medecine. Bulletin. (pub. by Masson)

**Academie Populaire de Litterature et de Poesie**
12 rue Racine, La Courneuve (Seine), France.
- Lettres et Poesie. bi-m. ISSN 0024-1385

**Academie Vauclusienne des Amis de Petrarque**
Villa Petrarque, 36 Bd. Pasteur, Bellevue, Villeneuve-les-Avignon, France.
- Courrier Vauclusien. 3 per yr. ISSN 0011-0639

**Achkhar**
24 rue Albert de Mun, 92 Asnieres, France.
- Achkhar/World. s-w. ISSN 0004-4342

**Acopsis**
42, rue Boileau, 75016 Paris, France.
- Acopsis. bi-m.

**Action Catholique Generale Feminine**
98 rue de l'Universite, 75007 Paris, France.
- En Equipe au Service de l'Evangile. q. ISSN 0395-1766

**Action Chretienne en Orient**
7 rue du General-Offenstein, Strasbourg, France.
- Levant Morgenland. bi-m. ISSN 0024-1490

**Action Municipale**
18 rue Duphot, 75001 Paris, France.
- Action Municipale; organe de defense et d'information des mairies. m. ISSN 0001-7450

**Editions Action Poetique**
Librairie "la Repetition", 27, rue Saint-Andre-des-Arts, 75006 Paris, France.
- Action Poetique. q. ISSN 0001-7477

**Activites Musicales**
Immeuble Pleyel, 252 Faubourg Saint Honore, 75008 Paris, France.
- Activites Musicales. m.

**Actualite Fiduciaire**
2 bis rue de Villiers, 92309 Levallois, France.
- Actualite Fiduciaire. 11 per yr. ISSN 0044-6157

**Actualite Juridique: Edition Droit Administratif**
91 rue de Faubourg-St Honore, Paris (8e), France.
- Actualite Juridique: Edition Droit Administratif. m. ISSN 0001-7728

**SARL Actualites Agricoles**
12 rue du Colonel Driant, Paris (1e), France.
- Actualites Agricoles. w.

**Aeroport de Paris**
291 Bd. Raspail, 75675 Paris 14, France.
- Aeroport de Paris. Rapport du Conseil d'Administration. a. ISSN 0065-3721
- Aeroport de Paris. Service Statistique. Statistique de Trafic. ISSN 0078-947X
- Propos en l'Air. 11 per yr. ISSN 0033-1384
- Trafic des Principaux Aeroports Mondiaux/Traffic at Major World Airports. irreg.

**Affiches d'Alsace et de Lorraine-Moniteur des Soumissions et des Ventes de Bois de l'Est**
20 rue des Charpentiers, B.P. 238/R6, 67006 Strasbourg Cedex, France.
- Affiches d'Alsace et de Lorraine-Moniteur des Soumissions et des Ventes de Bois de l'Est. 2 per wk. ISSN 0001-9666

**Africa Podium**
400 rue Saint Homore, Paris (1e), France.
- Africa Podium; mensuel sportif africain. m.

**Africaine**
23 rue Daubenton, 75005 Paris, France.
- Africaine. m.

**Africasia**
22 rue de la Banque, 75002 Paris, France.
- Africasia. fortn. ISSN 0002-0338

**Afrique Agriculture**
11, rue de Teheran, 75008 Paris, France
- Afrique Agriculture; mensuel d'informations agricoles. m.

**Afrique Industrie Infrastructures**
11 rue de Teheran, 75008 Paris, France
- Afrique Industrie Infrastructures; bi-mensuel d'informations industrielles et economiques. bi-m. ISSN 0301-8520 (Dist. in U.S. by Powers International Inc., 551 Fifth Ave, New York, N.Y. 10017)

**Afrique Service**
23 rue de Cheroy, Paris (17e), France.
- Afrique Service. bi-m. ISSN 0002-0540

**Agence d'Informations Europeenes**
26 rue du Bouloi, Paris I, France.
- Agence d'Informations Europeennes. Bulletin. w. ISSN 0002-0761

**Agence de Cooperation Culturelle et Technique**
21 rue de Constantine, 75007 Paris, France.
- Almanach Africain. biennial. ISSN 0569-0870

**Agence de Diffusion et de Publicite**
24 Place Malesherbes, 75017 Paris, France.
- Annuaire des Fournisseurs de Laboratoires Pharmaceutiques et Cosmetiques. a. ISSN 0396-0625

**Agence de Marketing et d'Etudes Publicitaires**
37, rue du General Foy, 75008 Paris, France.
- Bois d'Aujourd'hui. q.

**Agence France-Presse**
13 Place de la Bourse, 75002 Paris, France.
- Africa. s-w. ISSN 0001-9739
- Bulletin Quotidien d'Afrique. d. ISSN 0007-5264
- Bulletin Quotidien d'Informations Textiles. 6 per wk. ISSN 0007-5272
- Cacaos, Cafes, Sucres. w. ISSN 0007-9332
- Cahiers de l'Afrique Occidentale et de l'Afrique Equatoriale. s-m. ISSN 0007-9855
- Sahara; bulletin d'information. bi-m. ISSN 0036-2638
- Sept Jours de l'Economie Francaise. w. ISSN 0037-2404

**Agence Internationale de Documentation Contemporaine Pharos**
2 Bd. Montmartre, Paris 9, France.
- Evenements de Notre Temps. irreg. ISSN 0531-4895

**Agence Legislative**
22 rue de Chateaudun, Paris 11e, France.
- Vie des Affaires; bulletin consacre a l'analyse des avis emis par les dirigeants d'entreprise a l'egard du droit economique et des politiques gouvernementales. irreg. ISSN 0083-6095

**Agence Nationale de Valorisation de la Recherche**
13, rue Madeleine Michelis, 92522 Neuilly, France.
- Marche de l'Innovation. q.

**Agence Nationale pour le Developpement de l'Education Permanente (A D E P)**
- Education Permanente. (pub. by Documentation Francaise)

**Agence Publiclair**
38, rue des Mathurins, 75008 Paris, France.
- Gazette de Jean Primus. m (11 per yr)

**Agence Transcontinentale de Presse**
28 rue Navarin, Paris (9e), France.
- Coulisse Diplomatique. w. ISSN 0010-986X
- Flash Actualite. w. ISSN 0015-3516

**Agepe**
31 rue Paul- Chenavard, 69001 Lyon, France.
- Maisons, Fermettes et Chalets. m.

**Agri-Editions**
92 rue du Dessous des Berges, Paris 13e, France.
- Dictionnaire-Annuaire de l'Agriculture;
  organismes-dirigeants-fournisseurs. a.

**Agri-Pick-Up**
6 rue Henri Barbusse, 91210 Draveil, France.
- Agri-Pick-Up; hebdomadaire d'information
  agricole. w. ISSN 0002-1199

**Agri-Scop**
64 et 64 bis, rue la Boetie, 75008 Paris, France.
- Agriculture; revue mensuelle technique &
  economique. m.(11 per yr.) ISSN 0002-1709
  (Societe d'Editions des Ingenieurs Agricoles)

**Agrofilm**
11 rue Ferdinand-Gambon, Paris 20e, France.
- Cri du Peuple. irreg. ISSN 0070-1483

**Aide a Toute Detresse**
122 Ave. du General-Leclerc, 95480 Pierrelaye,
France.
- Feuille de Route. (pub. by Editions A. T. D.
  Science et Service)
- Igloos; le quatrieme monde. 3 per yr. ISSN 0019-
  168X

**Aide Inter-Monasteres**
7 rue d'Issy, 92170 Vanves, France.
- A. I. M. Bulletin. s-a. ISSN 0007-4314

**L'Aile et la Plume**
c/o M. Ange Merlo, 8 rue Miollis, Nice 06000,
France.
- L'Aile et la Plume. q.

**Edition Air et Cosmos**
6, rue Anatole-de-la-Forge, 75002 Paris, France.
- Aeronautique et l'Astronautique. bi-m. ISSN
  0001-9275

**Editions Albatros**
14 rue de l'Armorique, Paris (15e), France.
- Cahiers de l'Est. q.

**Alexanor**
45 Rue de Buffon, Paris (5e), France.
- Alexanor; revue des lepidopteristes francais. q.
  ISSN 0002-5208

**Alliance des Jeunes pour le Socialisme**
87 rue du Faubourg Saint-Denis, Paris (10e),
France.
- Jeune Revolutionnaire. m. ISSN 0021-6100

**Alliance Israelite Universelle en France**
45 rue la Bruyere, 75009 Paris, France.
- Alliance Israelite Universelle en France. Cahiers.
  (pub. by Ecole Normale Israelite Orientale)
- Alliance Israelite Universelle en France. Oeuvre
  Scolaire. Nouveaux Cahiers. q. ISSN 0029-4705

**Alliance Marxiste Revolutionnaire**
21 Quai St. Michel, Paris (5e), France.
- Internationale - A. M. R. m. ISSN 0020-9163

**Alliance Syndicaliste, Paris**
21 rue Jean Robert, 75018 Paris, France.
- Solidarite Ouvriere. m. ISSN 0049-1292

**Editions Alsatia**
10 rue Bartholdi, 68001 Colmar, France.
- Archives d'Anatomie, d'Histologie et
  d'Embryologie. s-a. ISSN 0003-9586

**Amateur d'Art**
1 Cite Bergere, 6 Fg. Montmartre, Paris (9e),
France.
- Amateur d'Art. fortn. ISSN 0002-6824

**Ambassade de la Republique Socialiste du Vietnam en
France**
Rue le Verrier No.2, 75006 Paris, France.
- Bulletin du Vietnam. q.

**American Chamber of Commerce in France**
21 Av. George V, 75008 Paris, France.
- American Chamber of Commerce in France.
  Directory. a.
- Commerce in France; U. S. participation in the
  French economy by trade and direct investment.
  bi-m. ISSN 0010-2849
- List of American Firms in France. a.
- List of European Headquarters of American
  Firms. a.

**American College in Paris**
31 Av Bosquest, 75007 Paris, France.
- Latin American Yearly Review. a.

**Ami du Charcutier, du Boucher et du Salaisonnier**
39-41 rue Etienne Marcel, 75015 Paris, France.
- Ami du Charcutier, du Boucher et du
  Salaisonnier. m. ISSN 0044-8117

**Ami du Peuple**
6 rue Finkmatt, 67 Strasbourg, France.
- Ami du Peuple/Volksfreund. w. ISSN 0003-1704

**Amicale Anciens Fonctionnaires de Police Francais
Maroc**
95 Montmorency, Paris, France.
- Lien. bi-m. ISSN 0024-2918

**Amici Thomae Mori**
- Moreana. (pub. by Moreana Publications)

**Amis de la Tradition Celticum**
2 rue Leonard-de-Vinci, Postbox 2, Rennes, France.
- Ogam. q. ISSN 0030-0691

**Amis de Pezenas**
Boutique du Barbier Gely, Marche au Bled,
Pezenas, France.
- Etudes sur Pezena et Sa Region. q.

**Amis de Rimbaud**
c/o Mme Suzanne Briet, 24 rue Gutenberg, 92100
Boulogne, France.
- Rimbaud Vivant. q.

**Amis de Svedectvi**
6 rue du Pont de Lodi, Paris (6e), France.
- Svedectvi. q. ISSN 0039-6419

**Amis des Cahiers Haut-Marnais**
B.P. 167, Chaumont, France.
- Cahiers Haut-Marnais; revue d'histoire, de lettres
  et d'art. q. ISSN 0008-025X

**Amis des Cahiers Libres de Leon Emery**
c/o F. Giraud, 240 Cours Emile Zola, 69100
Villeurbanne, France.
- Cahiers Libres de Leon Emery. q. ISSN 0008-
  0322

**Amis du Lexique Francais**
81 bis rue Lauriston, 75116 Paris, France.
- Mots en Liberte, Bulletin d'Etudes Lexicales. q.
  ISSN 0337-5978

**Amis du Vieux Calais**
c/o Ed. Mme. F. Mulard, 18, Chemin des Regniers,
Calais, France.
- Bulletin Historique et Artistique du Calais. q.
  ISSN 0521-713X

**Amitie Judeo-Arabe**
B.P. 12408, 75008 Paris, France.
- Amitie Judeo- Arabe. Bulletin. m.

**Amities Internationales Napoleoniennes**
1, rue Puits Gaillot, 69001 Lyon, France.
- Courrier de l'Amite: Information et
  Documentation Historiques. s-a.

**Amities Philosophiques Internationales**
187 bis, Promenade des Anglais, Nice, France.
- Amities Philosophiques Internationales. Bulletin.
  irreg. ISSN 0066-1252

**Amities Spirituelles**
5 rue de Savoie, Paris (6e), France.
- Amities Spirituelles. Bulletin. q. ISSN 0003-1909

**Editions Ampere**
46, rue Ampere, 75017 Paris, France.
- Fils-Tubes-Bandes & Profils. 6 per yr.
- Qualite. Revue Pratique de Controle Industriel. 6
  per yr. ISSN 0033-5142
- Qui Fabrique et Fournit Quoi. irreg.
- Surfaces; finition et protection. 8 per yr. ISSN
  0585-9840

**Editions de l' An 2000**
5 rue Viollet-Le-Duc, 75009 Paris, France.
- Jeunesse an Deux Mille. m. ISSN 0021-6194

**Ancienne Maison l'Homme et Argy**
9 rue Lagrange, 75005 Paris, France.
- Annuaire de la Papeterie; France, Allemagne,
  Belgique, Espagne Italie et Pays-bas. biennial.
- Papeterie; revue technique et commerciale. m.
  ISSN 0031-1308

**Editions Andrillon**
6 Avenue du General Leclerc, B.P. 80, 02203
Soissons Cedex, France.
- Actualite de la Medecine Officielle et Medecine
  Naturelle. bi-m. ISSN 0044-6149

**Ange Gardien**
28 rue du Bon Pasteur, 69241 Lyon Cedex 1,
France.
- Ange Gardien. 6 per yr. ISSN 0003-3030

**Annales de Normandie**
Logis des Gouverneurs, Chateau de Caen, 14000
Caen, France.
- Annales de Normandie; revue d'etudes regionales.
  q. ISSN 0003-4134

**Annales Homeopathiques Francaises**
Chateau d'Arros, 64800 Nay, France.
- Annales Homeopathiques Francaises. bi-m. ISSN
  0003-4444

**Annuaire Catholique de France**
17 Bd. Poissonniere, 75002 Paris, France.
- Annuaire Catholique de France. biennial. ISSN
  0066-2488

**Annuaire de l'Education Nationale**
Service d'Edition et de Vente des Publications de
l'Education Nationale, 13 rue du Four, 75-Paris 6e,
France.
- Annuaire de l'Education Nationale. a. ISSN 0071-
  8831

**Annuaire de la Presse et de la Publicite**
24, Place Malesherbes, Paris 17, France.
- Annuaire de la Presse et de la Publicite. a. ISSN
  0066-2585

**Annuaire des Architectes**
53 rue de Rennes, 75 Paris 6e, France.
- Annuaire des Architectes. a. ISSN 0066-2747

**Annuaire des Communautes d'Enfants**
145 Bd. Magenta, 75010 Paris, France.
- Annuaire des Communautes d'Enfants. a. ISSN
  0069-7761

**Annuaire du Spectacle**
Centre du Spectacle, 7 rue du Helder, 75009 Paris,
France.
- Annuaire du Spectacle. a. ISSN 0066-3026

**Annuaire General de la Pharmacie Francaise**
c/o Mme. Boiscourt, Ed., 47 rue de la Victoire,
Paris 9e, France.
- Annuaire General de la Pharmacie Francaise. a.
  ISSN 0066-3158

**Annuaire Paris: Bijoux**
62 rue Beaubourg, Paris 3e, France.
- Annuaire Paris: Bijoux. a. ISSN 0066-3581

**Editions Anthropos**
15 rue Racine, 75006 Paris, France.
- Utopie. s-a.

**L'Arc**
Chemin de Repentance, 13100-Aix-en-Provence,
France.
- L'Arc. 4 per yr. ISSN 0003-7974

**Arcadie**
61 rue du Chateau-d'Eau, 75010 Paris, France.
- Arcadie; revue litteraire et scientifique. m. ISSN
  0003-7990

**Archeveche de Bourges**
4 Av. du 95e de Ligne, B.P. 95, 18002 Bourges
(Cher), France.
- Vie Catholique du Berry. w. ISSN 0042-5362

**Archeveche de Lyon**
1 Place de Fourviere, F-69321 Lyon, France.
- Annuaire de Diocese de Lyon. a.

**Archeveche de Toulouse**
1 Place Stes Scarbes, 31000 Toulouse, France.
- Foi et Vie de l'Eglise au Diocese de Toulouse; semaine catholique de Toulouse. bi-m. ISSN 0015-5365

**Editions de l' Archipel**
3 rue d'Hauteville, 75010 Paris, France.
- Annuaire Philatelique. a. ISSN 0066-359X

**Archistra: Archives-Histoire-Traditions**
c/o Ed. Pierre Salies, 42 rue Capus, 31000 Toulouse, France.
- Archistra: Archives-Histoire-Traditions; journal d'informations sur l'histoire de la France meridionale. bi-m.

**Architecture-France**
17, Rue d'Uzes, 75002 Paris, France.
- Architecture-France; recherche-formes interieures-arts-urbanisme. m.

**Archives de Meurthe et Moselle**
54, rue de la Monnaie, Nancy, France.
- Cercle Genealogique de Lorraine. Bulletin. q.

**Archives Internationales Claude Bernard**
Coussac- Bonneval, 87500 Saint- Yrieix, France.
- Archives Internationales Claude Bernard. q. ISSN 0302-2358

**Archives Medicales de l'Ouest**
c/o J. C. Renier, 1 Ave de l'Hotel-Dieu, 49000 Angers, France.
- Archives Medicales de l'Ouest. m. ISSN 0570-6955

**Editions d' Argenson**
11, Avenue Delcasse, 75008 Paris, France.
- Auto-Club. bi-m.

**Argout Editions**
32, rue d'Argout, 75002 Paris, France.
- Gazette des Armes. m (11 per yr) (Societe d'Editions de Revues d'Armes)

**Argus des Pharmaciens**
26 rue Brey, Paris (17), France.
- Argus des Pharmaciens; journal professionnel et documentaire. s-m. ISSN 0004-1203

**Argus du Livre**
19 Bld. Montmartre, 75002 Paris, France.
- Fichiers-Presse. s-a.

**L. Armand, Ed. & Pub.**
Box 15, Herblay 95220, France.
- Facettes; lien des curieux, chercheurs. m. ISSN 0014-6285

**Armee du Salut**
78 rue de Rome, 75008 Paris, France.
- En Avant. w. ISSN 0013-6921

**Librairie Arnette**
2 rue Casimir Delavigne, Paris (6e), France.
- Cahiers d'Anesthesiologie. 8 per yr. ISSN 0007-9685
- Revue Francaise de Transfusion et Immuno-Hematologie. q. ISSN 0338-4535 (Societe Nationale de Transfusion)

**Ars Una**
3 rue Danielle Casanova, 75001 Paris, France.
- Ars Una. m. ISSN 0004-2943

**Art Chretien**
38 Av. de Chatillon, Paris (14e), France.
- Art Chretien. q. ISSN 0004-3087

**Editions de l' Art de Vivre**
57, Av. d'Iena, 75116 Paris, France.
- L'Estampille; art antiquites et artisanat. m.

**Art et Maitrise Publicite**
9, rue de Trevise, 75009 Paris, France.
- Mur Vivant. q.

**Art Press**
43 rue de Montmorency, 75003 Paris, France.
- Art Press. bi-m.

**Art Vivant**
c/o Aime Maeght, 26 rue Treilhard, Paris (8e), France.
- Art Vivant. bi-m. ISSN 0004-3338

**Editions H. Artese**
B.P. M, 47001 Agen, France.
- Selections Avicoles; aviculture, colombiculture, cuniculture. m (11 per yr.)

**Editions B. Arthaud**
6 rue de Mezieres, Paris 6e, France.
- En Direct Avec l'Histoire. irreg. ISSN 0071-0156
- Reportages Fantastiques. irreg. ISSN 0080-133X
- Semainier Beaux Pays de France. a. ISSN 0080-8768
- Vade-Mecum. irreg. ISSN 0083-5072
- Voix dans le Monde. irreg. ISSN 0083-6826

**Artistes et Varietes**
2 bis rue de la Baume, 75008 Paris, France.
- Artistes et Varietes; revue de l'accordeoniste et des instrumentistes de rythme. 8 per yr. ISSN 0004-3907

**Editions d' Artrey**
17 rue de la Rochefoucauld, Paris (9e), France.
- Francais Moderne; revue de linguistique francaise. q. ISSN 0015-9409
- Revue Internationale d'Onomastique. q. ISSN 0048-8151

**Arts Asiatiques**
22 Av. President Wilson, Paris (16e), France
- Arts Asiatiques. s-a. ISSN 0004-3958

**Arts et Objets du Maroc**
8, rue Saint-Marc, 75002 Paris, France.
- Arts et Objets du Maroc. irreg.

**Arts, Lettres et Progres**
7 rue Riboutte, Paris 9e, France.
- Collection d'Arts, Lettres et Progres. irreg. ISSN 0069-5327

**Assemblee des Presidents des Conseils Generaux**
- Departements et Communes. (pub. by Association des Maires de France)

**Assemblee Permanente des Chambres de Commerce et d'Industrie**
45, Ave. d'Iena, 75116 Paris, France.
- Annuaire des Chambres de Commerce et d'Industrie. a. (approx.) ISSN 0066-2798

**Assembly of Western European Union**
43 Av. du President Wilson, 75775 Paris 16, France (Dist. in U.S. by Manhattan Publishing Co., 225 Lafayette St., New York, N.Y. 10012)
- Assemblee de l'Union de l'Europe Occidentale. Bulletin Mensuel d'Information/Assembly of Western European Union, Monthly Information Bulletin on European Parliamentary Activity in the Seven Member States of WEU; sur l'activite parlementaire europeenne des sept etats membres del'u.e.o. m. ISSN 0041-6827
- Assembly of Western European Union. Proceedings. a. ISSN 0083-8853

**Association al Liamm**
c/o P. le Bihan, 16 rue des Fours a Chaux, 35400 St-Malo, France.
- Liamm. bi-m. ISSN 0024-1733

**Association amicale des Anciens Combattants du 27e Dragons**
34 Avenue Franklin Roosevelt, 94300 Vincennes, France.
- Marjolaine; bulletin trimestriel. q. ISSN 0025-3480

**Association Amicale des Anciens Eleves de l'Ecole Superieure d'Optometrie**
91140 Bures sur Yvette, France.
(U.S. Subscr. Address: 21 Oak Rise, Irvington on Hudson, NY 10533)
- Optometrie. q. ISSN 0030-4115

**Association Amicale des Anciens Eleves des Ecoles de Maitres-Sondeurs et des Sessions de Perfectionnement Forage Production de l'Institut Francais du Petrole (A.E.M.S.-I.F.P.)**
1 et 4, Avenue de Bois-Preau, B.P. No. 311, 92506 Rueil-Malmaison Cedex, France.
- Forages. a. ISSN 0046-4481

**Association Amicale des Eleves et Anciens Eleves de l'Ecole Nationale Superieure des PTT**
46 rue Barrault, 75634 Paris Cedex-13, France.
- Courrier: Cahiers d'Etudes et d'Informations. q. ISSN 0011-0469

**Association Auvergne Economique**
- Auvergne Economique. (pub. by France Diffusion Presse)

**Association Christus de Recherches Ignatiennes**
12 rue d'Assas, 75006 Paris, France.
- Christus; revue de pratique evangelique. q. ISSN 0009-5834
- Croire Aujourd'hui; revue pour la formation permanente de la foi. m.

**Association Culturelle de Cuxa. Centre Permanent de Recherches et d'Etudes Pre-Romanes et Romanes**
Abbaye de Saint-Michel de Cuxa, Prades-Codalet, France
(Subscr. Address: c/o Andre Delteil, 4, rue Louis Esparre, 66000 Perpignan, France)
- Cahiers de Saint-Michel de Cuxa. irreg. ISSN 0068-5089

**Association Culturelle des Membres de la Legion d'Honneur, Palmes Academiques, Arts et Lettres**
c/o Michel Beau, 12 Avenue Foch, 93150 Blanc-Mesnil, France.
- Visages du Vingtieme Siecle; revue de "La Legion Violette". 5 per yr.

**Association Culturelle Louise Michel**
24 rue Paul Albert, Paris (18e), France.
- La rue; revue culturelle et litteraire d'expression anarchiste. q. ISSN 0035-970X

**Association d'Acridologie**
105 Bd. Raspail, 75-Paris(6), France.
- Acrida. q. ISSN 0300-4686

**Association d'Amitie Franco-Vietnamienne**
37, rue Ballu, 75009 Paris, France.
- Cahiers Amitie Franco-Vietnamienne. a. ISSN 0084-8220

**Association d'Etude pour l'Expansion de l'Enseignement Superieur**
173 Bd. St. Germain, Paris 5e, France.
- Cahiers des Universites Francaises. irreg. ISSN 0068-5119

**Association d'Etudes et d'Informations Politiques Internationales**
86 Bd. Haussmann, Paris 75008, France.
- Est et Ouest/Este e Oeste. fortn. ISSN 0014-1267

**Association d'Etudes et de Documentation de Droit Aerien**
- Revue Francaise de Droit Aerien. (pub. by Editions Sirey)

**Association d'Etudes Normandes**
21 rue de Crosne, Rouen 76000, France.
- Etudes Normandes. q. ISSN 0014-2158 (Co-Sponsor: Universite de Haute-Normandie)

**Association de Botanique Tropicale. Laboratoire de Phanerogamie**
16 rue Buffon, 75005 Paris, France.
- Adansonia. q. ISSN 0001-804X

**Association de Developpement et d'Industrialisation de la Region Alsace**
13 Avenue de Lattre de Tassigny, 68 Colmar, France.
- Conjoncture Alsacienne. q.

**Association de Geographes Francais**
191 rue St. Jacques, Paris (5e), France.
- Association de Geographes Francais. Bulletin. bi-m. ISSN 0004-5322

**Association de l'Ecole Nationale Superieure des Bibliothecaires**
17-21 Bd. du 11 Novembre, 69621 Villeurbanne, France.
- Association de l'Ecole Nationale Superieure des Bibliothecaires. Annuaire. irreg. ISSN 0066-8877

**Association de la Revue d'Orthopedie Dento-Faciale**
- Revue d'Orthopedie Dento-Faciale. (pub. by Julien Prelat)

**Association de Pedagogie Cybernetique**
29 rue d'Ulm, Paris, 5e, France.
- Cybernetique et Pedagogie Cybernetique. q. ISSN 0011-4251

**Association de Solidarite France-Arabe**
12-14 rue Augereau, 75007 Paris, France.
- France - Pays Arabes. m. ISSN 0533-0866

**Association des Amis d'Alain**
Secretariat, 16 rue Lacuee, Paris (12e), France.
● Association des Amis d'Alain. Bulletin. s-a. ISSN 0004-5330

**Association des Amis d'Alfred de Vigny**
6 Av. Constant-Coquelin, Paris 7e, France.
● Association des Amis d'Alfred de Vigny. Bulletin. irreg. ISSN 0066-8893

**Association des Amis d'Andre Gide**
● Amis d'Andre Gide. Bulletin. (pub. by Universite de Lyon II. Centre d'Etudes Gidiennes)
● Cahiers Andre Gide. (pub. by Editions Gallimard)

**Association des Amis de Jean Cocteau**
● Cahiers Jean Cocteau. (pub. by Editions Gallimard)

**Association des Amis de l'Assistance Publique**
7 Rue des Minimes, Paris (3e), France.
● Hopital a Paris. bi-m. ISSN 0018-4861

**Association des Amis de l'E.N.S.B.A.N.A.**
Bd. Gabriel 21, Dijon, France.
● Amis de l'E.N.S.B.A.N.A. irreg.

**Association des Amis de la Comedie de l'Ouest**
9B. Avenue Janvier, 35000 Rennes, France.
● Courrier Dramatique de l'Ouest. 5 per yr.

**Association des Amis de la Polynesie Francaise**
9-11 Avenue Franklin-Roosevelt, 75008 Paris, France.
● Ectto du Lagon; bulletin de l'Association de la Polynesie Francaise. q. ISSN 0339-0861

**Association des Amis de la Radiesthesie**
B.P.6-10, 12 rue du Terrage, Paris (10e), France.
● Amis de la Radiesthesie. bi-m. ISSN 0003-1798

**Association des Amis de la Revue de Geographie de Lyon**
74 rue Pasteur, 69007 Lyon, France.
● Revue de Geographie de Lyon. q. ISSN 0035-113X

**Association des Amis de Milosz**
● Amis de Milosz. (pub. by Editions Andre Silvaire)

**Association des Amis de Pierre Teilhard de Chardin**
38 rue Geoffroy-Saint-Hilaire, 75005 Paris, France.
● Association des Amis de Pierre Teilhard de Chardin. Bulletin. a. ISSN 0066-8907

**Association des Amis de Vergy**
Mairie de L"Etang-Vergy, 21220 Gevrey-Chambertin, France.
● Cahiers de Vergy. s-a.

**Association des Amis du Musee des Beaux-Arts**
Palais St. Pierre, 20 Place des Terreaux, 69001 Lyon, France.
● Musees et Monuments Lyonnais. Bulletin. q. ISSN 0027-3848 (Musee de Beaux Arts)

**Association des Amis du Musee International des Hussards**
Jardin Massey, 65000 Tarbes, France.
● Vivat Hussar. a.

**Association des Amis et Ancien Eleves du Laboratoire de Geologie, I**
Faculte de Science, Tour 14-15-16, 4 Etage, 9 Quai St. Bernard, Paris (5e), France.
● Cahiers Geologiques. q. ISSN 0008-0241

**Association des Anatomistes**
31 Rue Lionnois, Nancy, France.
● Association des Anatomistes. Bulletin. irreg. ISSN 0066-8915

**Association des Anciens Eleves de l'Ecole Centrale des Arts et Manufactures**
8 rue Jean-Goujon, Paris (8e), France.
● Arts et Manufactures. 10 per yr. ISSN 0004-3990

**Association des Anciens Eleves de l'Ecole Francaise des Attaches de Presse**
61 rue Pierre-Charron, Paris 8e, France.
● Ecole Francaise des Attaches de Presse. Association des Anciens Eleves. Annuaire. a. ISSN 0070-8321

**Association des Anciens Eleves de l'Ecole Nationale d'Administration**
56 rue des Saints-Peres, 75007 Paris, France.
● Promotions. s-a.

**Association des Anciens Eleves de l'Ecole Superieur de Commerce de Paris**
79 Avenue de la Republique, Paris 11, France.
● Millesime; the point about management consultants. a. ISSN 0076-8812

**Association des Anciens Eleves de l'Ecole Superieure de Fonderie**
● Association des Anciens Eleves de l'Ecole Superieure de Fonderie. Bulletin. (pub. by Edima)

**Association des Anciens Eleves de l'Ecole Technique d'Aeronautique et de Construction Automobile**
1 rue Boutebrie, 75005 Paris, France.
● Anciens Eleves de l'Ecole Technique d'Aeronautique et de Construction Automobile. Annuaire. a.
● De l'Automobile et de l'Aeronautique. (pub. by E.T.A.C.A.)

**Association des Anciens Eleves de l'Institut d'Oenologie de Bordeaux**
351 Cours de la Liberation, 33405 Talence, France.
● Connaissance de la Vigne et du Vin. q. ISSN 0010-597X

**Association des Anciens Eleves des Facultes des Lettres de Paris**
77 rue de Villiers, 92523 Neuilly, France.
● Humanisme et Entreprise; cahiers du Centre d'Etudes et de Recherches. bi-m. ISSN 0018-7372

**Association des Anesthesiologistes Francais**
● Annales de l'Anesthesiologie Francaise. (pub. by Doin Editeurs)

**Association des Archives Spartacus**
● Cahiers Spartacus. (pub. by Rene Lefeuvre)

**Association des Archivistes Francais**
60 rue des Francs-Bourgeois, 75141 Paris Cedex 03, France.
● Association des Archivistes Francais. Gazette des Archives. q. ISSN 0016-5522

**Association des Bibliothecaires Francais**
65 rue de Richelieu, 75002 Paris, France.
● Association des Bibliothecaires Francais. Bulletin d'Informations. q. ISSN 0004-5365
○ Documents A B F. irreg. ISSN 0066-894X

**Association des Bibliotheques Ecclesiastiques de France**
6 rue du Regard, Paris 6e, France.
● Association des Bibliotheques Ecclesiastiques de France. Bulletin de Liaison. q. ISSN 0066-8958

**Association des Chefs d'Entreprises Libres (A.C.E.L.)**
● Informateur des Chefs d'Entreprises Libres. (pub. by Publistyl)

**Association des Cineastes de Marseille-Provence**
55 Bd. Rodocanachi, Marseille (8e), France.
● Cameral. m. ISSN 0008-218X

**Association des Diplomes de Microbiologie de la Faculte de Pharmacie de Nancy**
B.P.403, Nancy, France.
● Microbia (Nancy) q.

**Association des Eleves de l'Ecole Centrale de Lyon**
36, Route de Dardilly, 69130 Ecully, France.
● Engrenage. bi-m.

**Association des Eleves de l'Ecole Speciale des Travaux Publics**
57 Bd. St. Germain, Paris (5e), France.
● Bloc. bi-m. ISSN 0006-4890

**Association des Etudes Tsiganes**
5 rue Las-Cases, 75007 Paris, France.
● Etudes Tsiganes. q. ISSN 0014-2247

**Association des Francais Libres**
6 rue du General de Larminat, 6, 75015 Paris, France.
● Revue de la France Libre. bi-m. ISSN 0035-1210

**Association des Hautes Etudes Hospitalieres**
17/19 rue Danton, 94270 le Kremlin Bicetre, France.
● Techniques Hospitalieres, Medico-Sociales et Sanitaires. 10 per yr. ISSN 0040-1374

**Association des Ingenieurs Anciens Eleves de l'Institut National Polytechnique de Grenoble**
6, rue de Castellane, 75008 Paris, France.
● Ingenieurs I. N. P. G. bi-m.

**Association des Ingenieurs de Chauffage et de Ventilation de France**
● Chauffage - Ventilation - Conditionnement. (pub. by P Y C Edition)

**Association des Ingenieurs des Postes et Telecommunications**
M. Delhaye, 20 Av. de Segur, Paris 7e, France.
● Annuaire du Corps Interministeriel des Ingenieurs des Telecommunications. a. ISSN 0066-2976

**Association des Ingenieurs des Villes de France**
● I V F - Ingenieurs des Villes de France. (pub. by P Y C-Edition)

**Association des Ingenieurs et Anciens Eleves de l'Ecole Superieure d'Ingenieurs et Techniciens pour l'Agriculture (E.S.IT.P.A.)**
38, rue des Ecoles, 75005 Paris, France.
● Association des Ingenieurs et Anciens Eleves de l' E. S. I. T. P. A. Annuaire. a.
● Hommes et Agriculture; technique et pratique agricoles. q.

**Association des Jeunes Romanistes**
● Bulletin des Jeunes Romanistes. (pub. by Editions Klincksieck)

**Association des Joueurs d'Echecs Par Correspondance**
5, Place Gambetta, 24700 Montpon-Menesterol, France.
● Courrier des Echecs; revue mensuelle d'Echecs par correspondance. m. ISSN 0011-0507

**Association des Juifs Originaires d'Algerie Installes en France**
78 Ave. des Champs Elysees, Paris (8e), France.
● Information Juive. m. ISSN 0020-0107

**Association des Maires de France**
89 Av Niel, 75017 Paris, France.
● Departements et Communes. m. ISSN 0045-9984 (Assemblee des Presidents des Conseils Generaux)

**Association des Maitres-Cuisiniers de France**
8 rue de Rome, Paris 8e, France.
● Maitres-Cuisiniers de France. m. ISSN 0076-2822

**Association des Medecins Israelites de France**
2, rue Pigalle, 75009 Paris, France.
● A. M. I. F. 10 per yr. ISSN 0400-132X

**Association des Officiers de la Ville de Paris**
Bureau 485, Hotel de Ville, 75 Paris (4e), France.
● Seine et Paris. q. ISSN 0037-1041

**Association des Paralyses de France**
Bd. Auguste Blanqui, 75013 Paris, France.
● Faire Face; journal des handicapes moteurs et des parents d'enfants handicapes moteurs. m. ISSN 0014-6951

**Association des Peintres Officiels de la Marine**
Musee de la Marine, Palais de Chaillot, 2 rue Royale, 475016 Paris, France.
● Art et la Mer; revue d'action culturelle et d'esthetique maritime. q.

**Association des Pharmaciens Directeurs de Laboratoires d'Analyses Biologiques**
10, rue du 8-Mai-1945, 75010 Paris, France.
● Pharmacien Biologiste. bi-m. ISSN 0553-9323

**Association des Pharmacologistes**
● Journal de Pharmacologie. (pub. by Masson)

**Association des Professeurs de Mathematiques de l'Enseignement Public. Regionale Parisienne**
129 Av. du General-Leclerc, 91120 Palaiseau, France.
● Chantiers de Pedagogie Mathematique. irreg. ISSN 0395-7837

**Association des Professeurs de Philosophie de l'Enseignement Public**
1 rue des Petits Carreaux, 75002 Paris, France.
● Revue de l'Enseignement Philosophique. bi-m. ISSN 0035-1393

**Association des Reeducateurs de la Parole et du Langage Oral et Ecrite (A.R.P.L.O.E.)**
10 rue de l'Arrivee, 75015 Paris, France.
● Reeducation Orthophonique. 6 per yr. ISSN 0034-222X

**Association des Sages-Femmes de l'Ecole d'Accouchement de la Maternite de Nancy**
Rue de Docteur-Heydendreich, 54000 Nancy, France.
- Association des Sages-Femmes de la Maternite de Nancy. Bulletin. q.

**Association des Scouts de France**
- Scouts Louveteaux, Rangers, Pionniers. (pub. by Scouts de France)

**Association des Secretaires Generaux des Parlements**
see **Association of Secretaries General of Parliaments**

**Association des Services Geologiques Africains**
74 rue de la Federation, 75015 Paris, France.
- Association des Services Geologiques Africains. Bulletin d'Information et de Liaison. Information and Liaison Bulletin. q.

**Association des Societes et Fonds Francais d'Investissement**
1 rue d'Astorg, Paris 8e, France.
- Association des Societes et Fonds Francais d'Investissement. Annuaire. biennial. ISSN 0066-9008

**Association des Techniciens d'Animaux de Laboratoire**
Centre d'Experimentation Animale et de Recherches Chirurgicales, 6 rue du General-Sarrail, 94000 Creteil, France.
- S.T.A.L: Sciences et Techniques de l'Animal de Laboratoire. q. ISSN 0339-722X

**Association des Viticulteurs d'Alsace**
44 Ave. de la Republique, Colmar 68000, France.
- Vins d'Alsace; revue viticole et vinicole mensuelle. m. ISSN 0042-6334

**Association du Magnificat**
Clemery Par Nomeny, C.C.P. Strasbourg, France.
- Magnificat - la Verite. m.

**Association du Theatre pour l'Enfance et la Jeunesse**
98 Bd. Kellermann, 75013 Paris, France.
- Theatre Enfance et Jeunesse. q. ISSN 0049-3597

**Association Economie et Humanisme**
- Economie et Humanisme. (pub. by Centre d'Etude des Complexes Sociaux)

**Association en Biologie Appliquee**
50 Rue Gauthier-De-Chatillon, Lille, France.
- Bio-Information. irreg. ISSN 0067-866X

**Association Evangile et Liberte**
27, Avenue Paul Cezanne, 13100 Aix en Provence, France.
- Evangile et Liberte. bi-m.

**Association Francaise d'Etudes Americaines**
1, Place de l'Odeon, 75006 Paris, France.
- Revue Francaise d'Etudes Americaines. s-a.

**Association Francaise d'Experts de la Cooperation Technique Internationale**
150 Champs Elysees, 75008 Paris, France.
- Association Francaise d'Experts de la Cooperation Technique Internationale. Annuaire. a. ISSN 0066-9288

**Association Francaise d'Hygiene et de Medecine Scolaires et Universitaires**
- Revue d'Hygiene et Medecine Scolaire et Universitaire. (pub. by Doin Editeurs)

**Association Francaise de Chirurgie**
27 Bd. Raspail, 75007 Paris, France.
- Forum Chirurgical; revue de l'Association Francaise de Chirurgie. q. ISSN 0395-2096

**Association Francaise de Criminologie**
- Instantes Criminologiques. (pub. by Centre Francais de Criminologie)

**Association Francaise de l'Eclairage**
52 Bd. Malesherbes, 75008 Paris, France.
- Annuaire de l'Eclairage. a. ISSN 0066-264X
- Lux. (pub. by Editions Lux)

**Association Francaise de Normalisation (AFNOR)**
Tour Europe - Cedex 7, 92080 Paris la Defense, France.
- Bulletin Mensuel de la Normalisation Francaise. m. ISSN 0300-1164
- Catalogue des Normes Francaises. a.

- Courrier de la Normalisation. bi-m. ISSN 0011-0485
- Guide de l'Acheteur NF; equipement menager. a. ISSN 0335-394X
- Repertoire de Materiaux et Elements Controles du Batiment. a. ISSN 0335-3559

**Association Francaise des Amis d'Albert Schweitzer**
BP 25208, 75364 Paris Cedex 08, France.
- Association Francaise des Amis d'Albert Schweitzer. Cahiers. s-a.

**Association Francaise des Amis des Chemins de Fer**
Gare de l'Est, Paris (10e), France.
- Chemins de Fer. bi-m. ISSN 0009-2924

**Association Francaise des Banques**
18 rue la Fayette, 75009 Paris, France.
- Banque; revue du banquier, de son personnel et de sa clientele. m. ISSN 0005-5581

**Association Francaise des Collectionneurs et Amis d'Ex Libris (A.F.C.E.L)**
Palais Ducal, Grande rue, 5400 Nancy, France.
- Ex Libris Francais. q.

**Association Francaise des Documentalistes et des Bibliothecaires Specialises**
63 bis, rue du Cardinal-Lemoine, 75005 Paris, France.
- A D B S Annuaire. a. ISSN 0066-9210
- Documentaliste; sciences de l'information. bi-m. ISSN 0012-4508

**Association Francaise des Enseignants de Francais**
1, Avenue Leon Journault, 92310 Sevres, France.
- Francais Aujourd'hui. q.

**Association Francaise des Femmes Diplomees des Universites**
4, rue de Chevreuse, 75-Paris (6e), France.
- Diplomees. q.

**Association Francaise des Ingenieurs du Caoutchouc et des Plastiques**
9 Av. Hoche, Paris (8e), France.
- Association Francaise des Ingenieurs du Caoutchouc et des Plastiques. Annuaire. irreg. ISSN 0066-9229

**Association Francaise des Ingenieurs et Chefs d'Entretien**
- Association Francaise des Ingenieurs et Chefs d'Entretien. Annuaire. (pub. by Entreprise Moderne d'Edition)

**Association Francaise des Ophtalmologistes Praticiens**
94 rue Felix Faure, 92700 Colombes, France.
- Ophtalmologiste Praticien. q.

**Association Francaise des Relations Publiques**
8 rue Jean Goujon, 75008 Paris, France.
- Association Francaise des Relations Publiques. Annuaire. a. ISSN 0066-9253
- Maison de Verre; nouvelles breves. m.

**Association Francaise des Techniciens des Peintures, Vernis, Encres d'Imprimerie, Colles et Adhesifs**
- Double Liaison. (pub. by Presses Continentales)

**Association Francaise des Techniciens du Petrole**
- Association Francaise des Techniciens du Petrole. Annuaire. (pub. by EDIREP)
- Petrole et Techniques. (pub. by EDIREP)

**Association Francaise des Techniciens et Ingenieurs de Securite et des Medecins du Travail**
- Association Francaise des Techniciens et Ingenieurs de Securite et des Medecins du Travail. Annuaire. (pub. by Imprimerie Rouille)

**Association Francaise du Froid**
- Revue Generale du Froid. (pub. by Editions Geographiques Professionnelles)

**Association Francaise pour l'Avancement des Sciences**
250 rue Saint-Jacques, Paris 5e, France.
- Sciences. irreg. ISSN 0080-763X

**Association Francaise pour l'Etude des Eaux**
21, rue de Madrid, 75008 Paris, France.
- Information Eaux. 11 per yr. ISSN 0012-9003

**Association Francaise pour l'Etude du Cancer**
- Bulletin du Cancer. (pub. by Masson)

**Association Francaise pour l'Etude du Quaternaire**
Laboratoire de Geologie 1, Tour 16, 4e Etage, 4 Place Jussieu, 75230 Paris 5, France.
- Association Francaise pour l'Etude du Quaternaire. Bulletin. q. ISSN 0004-5500

**Association Francaise pour l'Etude du Sol**
CNRA, Route de Saint-Cyr Versailles 78000, France.
- Association Francaise pour l'Etude du Sol. Bulletin/Science du Sol. q. ISSN 0335-1653

**Association Francaise pour la Cybernetique Economique et Technique**
156, Boulevard Pereire, 75017 Paris, France.
- Association Francaise pour la Cybernetique Economique et Technique. Annuaire. irreg.
- Automatisme. (pub. by Centrale des Revues Dunod Gauthier- Villars)
- Revue Francaise d'Automatique, d'Informatique et de Recherche Operationnelle. (pub. by Centrale des Revues Dunod Gauthier Villars)

**Association Francaise pour la Sauvegarde de l'Enfance et de l'Adolescence**
28 Place Saint-Georges, 75442 Paris, France.
- Sauvegarde de l'Enfance. bi-m(5 per yr) ISSN 0036-5041

**Association Francaise pour le Controle Industriel de Qualite**
Tour Europe Cedex 7, 92080 Paris la Defense, France.
- A F C I Q. Bulletin; qualite et fiabilite. q. ISSN 0033-4782

**Association Francaise pour le Developpement de l'Enseignement Technique**
61 Avenue du President Wilson, 94230 Cachan, France.
- Technique, Art, Science; revue des enseignements techniques et professionnels. q.

**Association Francaise pour les Recherches et Etudes Camerounaises**
75 Cours d'Alsace Lorraine, 33 Bordeaux, France.
- Association Francaise pour les Recherches et Etudes Camerounaises. Bulletin. s-a. ISSN 0004-5489

**Association France Etats Unis**
6 Bd.de Grenelle, Paris (15e), France.
- France-U.S.A; journal des relations Franco-Americaines. m. ISSN 0015-9751

**Association France-Malte**
9 rue du Quatre-Septembre, 75002 Paris, France.
- Association France-Malte. irreg. ISSN 0339-705X

**Association Franco Ukrainienne**
26 Villa Auguste Blanqui, 75013 Paris, France.
- Revue Franco-Ukrainienne Echanges; revue Franco-Ukrainienne. bi-m.

**Association Generale des Conservateurs, des Collections Publiques de France**
Pavillon Mollien, Palais du Louvre, Paris (1e), France.
- Musees et Collections Publiques de France. q. ISSN 0027-383X

**Association Generale des Etudiants Guadeloupeens**
85 rue Beaubourg, Paris (3e), France.
- Patriote Guadeloupeen. m.

**Association Generale des Hygienistes et Techniciens Municipaux**
9 rue de Phalsbourg, 75017 Paris, France.
- Techniques et Sciences Municipales/Eau; l'eau - terres et eaux. m. ISSN 0040-134X

**Association Generale des Medecins de France**
30 Boulevard Pasteur, 75740 Paris Cedex 15, France.
- Association Generale des Medecins de France.Bulletin. m. ISSN 0004-5519

**Association Geographes de l'Est**
23 Bd. Albert (1e), 54 Nancy, France.
- Revue Geographique de l'Est. q. ISSN 0035-3213

**Association Guillaume Bude**
- Association Guillaume Bude. Bulletin. (pub. by Societe d'Edition les Belles Lettres)

**Association H.E.C.**
164 Faubourg St.-Honore, 75008 Paris, France.
- Hommes et Commerce. q.

Association Internationale d'Information Scolaire
Universitaire et Professionnelle
see International Association for Educational and
Vocational Information

Association Internationale de Bibliophilie
• Bulletin du Bibliophile. (pub. by Bibliotheque
Nationale)

Association Internationale de Broncho-Pneumologie
see International Broncho-Pneumologic Association

Association Internationale de Presse pour l'Etude des
Problems d'Outre-Mer
c/o Henri Bonnefont, Secretary, 41 rue de la
Bienfaisance, 75008 Paris, France.
• Association Internationale de Presse pour l'Etude
des Problemes d'Outre-Mer. Annuaire. a. ISSN
0587-2006

Association Internationale des Docteurs (Lettres) de
l'Universite de Paris
29 rue d'Ulm, 75005 Paris, France.
• Annuaire des Docteurs (Lettres) de l'Universite de
Paris et Autres Universites Francaises;
bibliographie analytique des theses. a. ISSN 0066-
281X

Association Internationale des Etudes Francaises
11 Place Marcelin-Berthelot, 75005 Paris, France.
• Association Internationale des Etudes Francaises.
Cahiers. a. ISSN 0571-5865

Association Internationale des Numismates
Professionnels
see International Association of Professional
Numismatists

Association Internationale des Parlementaires de
Langue Francaise
54 Avenue de Saxe, 75015 Paris, France.
• Revue des Parlementaires de Langue Francaise. q.

Association Internationale des Societes d'Assurance
Mutuelle
see International Association of Mutual Insurance
Companies

Association Internationale des Travailleurs
c/o A. Lamela, 20 rue Jeanne d'Arc, 63 Clermont-
Ferrand, France.
• A. I. T. Bulletin d'Information. m.

Association Internationale du Film d'Animation
see International Animated Film Association

Association Internationale Futuribles
see International Association Futuribles

Association Internationale Permanente des Congres
de la Route
see Permanent International Association of Road
Congresses

Association Internationale pour la Recherche
Medicale
4 rue de Seze, 75009 Paris, France
(Orders to: 38 Avenue William Ponty, Dakar,
Senegal)
• Medecine d'Afrique Noire. m. ISSN 0047-6404

Association Interprofessionnelle des Centres
Medicaux et Sociaux de la Region Parisienne
• Cahiers de Medecine Interprofessionnelle. (pub.
by Editions Docis)

Association Interprofessionnelle pour l'Etude du
Travail
• Etude du Travail. (pub. by Editions
d'Organisation)

Association Jean-Favard pour le Developpement de la
Linguistique Quantitative
St Sulpice Favieres 91910, France
(Dist. by Editions Dunod, 92 rue Bonaparte, 75278
Paris, France)
• Documents de Linguistique Quantitative. 3 per yr.
ISSN 0085-4786

Association "l'Education"
2, rue Chauveau - Lagarde, 75008 Paris, France.
• Education. w. ISSN 0013-1423

Association l'Eglise Reformee Vous Parle
15 rue Grignan, 13006 Marseille, France.
• Echanges; journal de l'eglise reformee...Provence,
Cote d'Azur, Corse. m. ISSN 0397-0736

Association Laitiere Francaise
17 rue de Valois, Paris 75001, France.
• Revue Laitiere Francaise. m. ISSN 0035-3590

Association le Christianisme au 20th Siecle
8 Villa du Parc Montsouris, 75014 Paris, France.
• Christianisme au Vingtieme Siecle. w. ISSN 0009-
5729

Association les Amis de l'Homme
22 rue David d'Angers, 75 Paris (19e), France.
• Moniteur du Regne de la Justice; journal bi-
mensuel, philanthropique et humanitaire pour le
relevement moral et social. 2 per m. ISSN 0026-
9727

Association les Amis de Napoleon 3rd
54 rue Carnot, Levallois Perret-92, France.
• Amis de Napoleon 3rd. Bulletin Interne. m. ISSN
0003-1828

Association Litteraire et Artistique Internationale
see International Literary and Artistic Association

Association Mondiale des Corses
100, rue Saint-Lazare, Paris, France.
• Annuaire Mondial des Corses. a.

Association Mutualiste de l'Industrie Hoteliere
192 Boulevard Haussmann, 775008 Paris, France.
• Amphitryon; revue technique d'enseignment
professionnel. bi-m.

Association Nationale d'Economie
Boite Postale 364-08, 75365 Paris Cedex 08,
France.
• Vie et Sciences Economiques. q.

Association Nationale de la Meunerie Francaise
• Meunerie Francaise. (pub. by Societe d'Edition et
de Publicite Agricoles, Industrielles et
Commerciales (SEPAIC))

Association Nationale de la Presse Mutualiste
10 rue Desaix, 75015 Paris, France.
• France Mutualite. m. ISSN 0015-9670

Association Nationale de la Recherche Technique
44, rue Copernic, 75116 Paris, France.
• Association Nationale de la Recherche Technique.
Information et Documentation. bi-m. ISSN 0066-
9318
• Recherche Technique. q.

Association Nationale de Lutte Contre les Fleaux
Atmospheriques
52, rue Alfred-Dumeril, 31400 Toulouse, France.
• Association Nationale de Lutte Contre les Fleaux
Atmospheriques. Rapport de Campagne. a.

Association Nationale des Anciennes Deportees et
Internees de la Resistance
241 Bd Saint-Germain, Paris (7e), France.
• Voix et Visages. bi-m. ISSN 0042-8396

Association Nationale des Assistants de Service Social
3 rue de Stockholm, 75 Paris(8e), France.
• Revue Francaise de Service Social. q.

Association Nationale des Chasseurs de Gibier d'Eau
11, rue Villebois Mareuil, 75017 Paris, France.
• Sauvagine et Sa Chasse. m.

Association Nationale des Docteurs en Droit
38 bis, rue Fabert, Paris (7e), France.
• Droit et Economie. q. ISSN 0012-639X (Co-
Sponsor: Club International du Droit et de
l'Economie)

Association Nationale des Docteurs es-Sciences
Economiques
Universite de Paris, Faculte de Droit et des Sciences
Economiques, B.P. 364.08, 75008 Paris, France.
• Vie et Sciences Economiques. q.

Association Nationale des Maitres Agricoles
2, rue des Maillets, 72000 le Mans, France.
• Education Rurale. m (10 per yr) ISSN 0395-7691

Association Nationale des Parents d'Enfants Aveugles
74 rue de Sevres, Paris 75007, France.
• Comme les Autres. q. ISSN 0010-2520

Association Nationale des Polios de France
23 rue de la Cerisaie, Paris 75004, France.
• Polio-France. bi-m. ISSN 0032-2741

Association Nationale des Veuves Civiles Chefs de
Famille
c/o Mme. Marchand, Ed., 28 Place St. Georges,
75442 Paris Cedex 09, France.
• Solidaires. q. ISSN 0338-1757

Association Nationale "Notre-Dame des Gitans"
99, rue du Bac, 75-Paris (7e), France.
• Monde Gitan. q. ISSN 0026-9417

Association Nationale pour l'Etude de la Communaute
de la Loire et de ses Affluents
23 Place du Martroi, 45044 Orleans, France.
• Bulletin de l'ANECLA. m. ISSN 0587-5560

Association Nationale pour la Defense de la Qualite
Francaise
18 rue Volney, Paris 2e, France.
• Catalogue des Produits Agrees Par Qualite-France.
irreg. ISSN 0069-1100

Association Nationale pour la Formation
Professionnelle des Adultes (A.F.P.A.)
13, Place de Villiers, 93108 Montreuil, France.
• Objectif Formation. q.

Association Nationale pour le Developpement des
Techniques de Marketing (ADETEM)
30 rue d'Astorg, 75008 Paris, France.
• Annuaire du Marketing. a. ISSN 0066-300X
• Revue Francaise du Marketing. (pub. by Centrale
des Revues Dunod Gauthier Villars)

Association Normandie Protestante
2 rue Lemaistre, 76 le Havre, France.
• Nord-Normandie. m.

Association of Secretaries General of Parliaments
c/o Assemblee Nationale, 75355 Paris, France.
• Constitutional and Parliamentary Information. q.
ISSN 0010-6623 (Interparliamentary Union SZ)

Association Pax Christi
89 rue du Cherche-Midi, 75006 Paris, France.
• Journal de la Paix - Pax Christi. m. 10 per yr.
ISSN 0021-7794 (Pax Christi International.
French Section)

Association Peinture
c/o Ed. Marc Devade, 10 rue Toullier, 75005 Paris,
France.
• Peinture/Cahiers Theoriques. q.

Association Poesie Vivante France
B.P.8, 01210 Ferney-Voltaire, France.
• Argus de la Poesie Francaise. irreg. ISSN 0066-
734X

Association pour Defendre la Memoire du Marechal
Petain
6 rue Marengo, Paris (1e), France.
• Marechal. q. ISSN 0025-2891

Association pour l'Etude des Problemes d'Outre Mer
154 Bd. Haussmann, Paris (8e), France.
• Association pour l'Etude des Problemes d'Outre
Mer. Documentation-Developpement. 8 per yr.

Association pour l'Histoire de Belle Ile-En-Mer
4 Rue Joseph le Brix, 56360 le Palais, France.
• Association pour l'Histoire de Belle-Ile-En-Mer.
Bulletin Trimestriel. q. ISSN 0044-9709

Association pour l'Histoire des Sciences de la Nature
38 rue Geoffroy Saint-Hilaire, Paris 5, France.
• Histoire et Nature. s-a.

Association pour la Connaissance de l'Allemagne
d'Aujourd'hui
8, rue Faraday, F 75017 Paris, France.
• Allemagnes d'Aujourd'hui; revue francaise
d'information sur l'Allemagne. bi-m. ISSN 0002-
5712

Association pour la Democratie et l'Education Locale
et Sociale (A D E L S)
94 rue Notre Dame des Champs, 75006 Paris,
France.
• Correspondance Municipale. m.

Association pour la Diffusion de la Documentation
Hydraulique
5 Chemin des Marronniers, Box 356, 38008
Grenoble Cedex, France.
• Houille Blanche; revue internationale de l'eau. 8
per yr. ISSN 0018-6368 (Societe Hydrotechnique
de France)

**Association pour la Diffusion de la Pensee Francaise**
21 bis, rue la Perouse, 75116 Paris, France.
- Bulletin Critique du Livre Francais. m. ISSN 0007-4209
- Courrier Musical de France. q. ISSN 0011-0620
- Nouvelles de France. fortn.

**Association pour la Diffusion et l'Animation Musicales en Aquitaine**
13 rue d'Aviau, 33 Bordeaux, France.
- A.D.M.A: la Vie Musicale en Aquitaine. q. ISSN 0395-9295

**Association pour la Diffusion et l'Usage de la Langue Latine**
- Vita Latina. (pub. by Aubanel S.A.)

**Association pour la Promotion de l'Orgue dans la Region Grenobloise**
c/o H. Bin, Institution du S. C., 38340 Voreppe, France.
- Plein-Jeu. q.

**Association pour la Promotion de la Couture Personnelle**
64 Bd. Sebastopol, 75003 Paris, France.
- Couture Personnelle. bi-m. ISSN 0339-1094

**Association pour la Promotion Industrie-Agriculture**
35, rue du General Foy, 75008 Paris, France.
- C D I U P A. Bulletin Bibliographique. m. ISSN 0007-8026 (Centre de Documentation Internationale des Industries Utilisatrices de Produits Agricoles)

**Association pour la Promotion Sociale et la Formation Professionelle dans les Transports Routiers**
124 Av. de la Republique, Paris 11e, France.
- Promotrans. irreg. ISSN 0079-6972

**Association pour la Recherche et Intervention Psychosociologiques**
- Connexions Psychosociologie Sciences Humaines. (pub. by E. P. I. S. A. Editeurs)

**Association pour la Traduction Automatique et la Linguistique Appliquee**
- T.A. Documents. (pub. by Editions Klincksieck)
- T. A. Informations. (pub. by Editions Klincksieck)

**Association pour le Bon Usage du Francais dans l'Administration**
54 Avenue de Sax, 75015 Paris, France.
- Service Public et Bon Langage. s-a.

**Association pour le Developpement des Bibliotheques de Religieuses-A D B R**
71 rue Notre Dame des Champs, 75006 Paris, France.
- Elements de Bibliographie. m. ISSN 0424-8775

**Association pour le Developpement des Oeuvres Sociales des Sapeurs-Pompiers de Paris**
1 Place Jules Renard, 75823 Paris Cedex 17, France (Subscriptions to: Brigade de Sapeurs-Pompiers de Paris, 2e Bureau, Service de Presse et de Relations Publiques, 1 Place Jules Renard, 75017 Paris, France)
- Allo Dix-Huit. m. ISSN 0044-7358

**Association pour le Developpement des Techniques de Transport, d'Environnement et de Circulation (A.T.E.C.)**
11, Place Adolphe Cherioux, 75015 Paris, France.
- T. E. C. (Transport Environment Circulation) bi-m.

**Association pour le Developpement et la Diffusion de l'Information Militaire**
6, rue Saint-Charles, 75015 Paris, France.
- Armees d'Aujourd'hui. 10 per yr.
- Cols-Bleus. w. ISSN 0010-1834
- Freres d'Armes; organe de Liaison des Forces Armees Francaises, Africaines et Malgaches. bi-m. ISSN 0016-1144
- Medecine et Armees. 10 per yr. ISSN 0300-4937
- T A M; periodique des forces armees. bi-m. ISSN 0018-8395

**Association pour le Developpment Industriel de l'Ouest Atlantique**
Immeuble Neptune, 44000 Nantes, France.
- Connaissance e l'Quest. irreg. ISSN 0396-2024

**Association pour le Perfectionnement et l'Expansion de la Chocolaterie et de la Confiserie de France**
- Chocolaterie Confiserie de France. (pub. by Societe d'Edition et de Publicite Agricoles, Industrielles et Commerciales (SEPAIC))

**Association pour le Rayonnement des Lettres, des Arts et des Sciences**
c/o Andre Leclere, 80, rue de Miromesnil, Paris (8e), France
(Subscr. Address: c/o J. de Ravinel, 32 rue de Viller, 54300 Luneville, France)
- Terre Lorraine. 3 per yr.

**Association pour les Aveugles**
106 rue de la Pompe, Paris (16e), France.
- Et la Lumiere Fut. m (11 per yr.) ISSN 0046-2586

**Association pour les Espaces Naturels**
21 rue Conseiller Collignon, 75016 Paris, France.
- Amenagement et Nature. q. ISSN 0044-7463

**Association pour Une Libre Vie de l'Esprit**
4 Rue Grande Chaumiere, Paris (6e), France.
- Triades; revue de culture humaine. q. ISSN 0041-252X

**Association pour Une Meilleure Connaissance de l'Asie**
54 rue de Varenne, 75007 Paris, France.
- France-Asie/Asia; revue bilingue des problemes asiatiques et de synthese culturelle. q.

**Association Professionnelle des Dessinateurs et Techniciens du Batiment et des Travaux Publics**
68 rue de la Chausee-d'Antin, Paris (9e), France.
- Dessinateurs de France. m. ISSN 0011-9504

**Association Psychanalytique de France**
24 Place Dauphine, 75006 Paris, France.
- Documents et Debats. 4-5 per yr. ISSN 0012-477X

**Association Reconnue d'Utilite Publique**
93 rue de l'Universite, 75007 Paris 7, France.
- Vieilles Maisons Francaises. q. ISSN 0049-6316

**Association Regionale pour l'Etude et la Recherche Scientifiques**
21 rue de Universite, Reims, France.
- A R E R S. q. ISSN 0001-2297

**Association Reparatrice**
c/o Willibrord Chr. van Dyk, Ed., 32 rue Boissonade, 75014 Paris, France.
- Action Reparatrice Envers la Ste. Trinite. q.

**Association Saint-Ambroise**
85, rue de Paris, 03000 Moulins, France.
- Eglise Qui Chante. 8 per yr. ISSN 0013-2357

**Association Saint-Yves**
3 Place Andre-Leroy, 49005 Angers Cedex, France.
- Impacts. bi-m. ISSN 0019-2899 (Universite Catholique de l'Ouest)

**Association Scientifique de la Precontrainte**
1, Place Genevieres, 59000 Lille, France.
- Association Scientifique de la Precontrainte. Sessions d'Etudes. irreg. ISSN 0066-9792

**Association Spiritus**
- Spiritus. (pub. by Revue Spiritus)

**Association Stenographique Unitaire**
83 Boulevard de Magenta, Paris (10e), France.
- Unite Stenographique; organe prevost-de launiste d'information. m. ISSN 0041-7157

**Association Strasbourgeoise des Periodiques de Sciences Humaines**
- Recherches Anglaises et Americaines. (pub. by Universite de Strasbourg II)

**Association Syndicale des Cadres de l'Edition et de la Librairie Francaise**
117 Bld. Saint-Germain, Paris 6e, France.
- La Lettre. irreg. ISSN 0075-8906

**Association Technique de Fonderie**
- Hommes et Fonderie. (pub. by E D I M A)

**Association Technique de l'Industrie du Gaz en France**
c/o Jacques Bardoux, Secretaire General, 62, rue de Courcelles, 75008 Paris, France.
- Association Technique de l'Industrie du Gaz en France. Bulletin Bibliographique Mensuel. m.
- Association Technique de l'Industrie du Gaz en France. Compte Rendu du Congres. 90th, Nice, 1973. ISSN 0066-9806
- Gaz d'Aujourd'Hui. (pub. by Societe du Journal des Usines a Gaz)

**Association Technique de l'Industrie Papetiere**
154 Bd. Haussmann, Paris (8e), France.
- Association Technique de l'Industrie Papetiere. Revue. 10 per yr. ISSN 0004-5896

**Association Technique Maritime et Aeronautique**
47 rue de Monceau, 75008 Paris, France.
- Association Technique Maritime et Aeronautique, Paris. Bulletin. a. ISSN 0066-9814

**Association Valentin Hauy pour le Bien des Aveugles**
7 & 9 rue Duroc, Paris (7e), France.
- Louis Braille. bi-m. ISSN 0024-6727

**Association Viticole Champenoise**
5 rue Henri- Martin, 51200 Epernay, France.
- Vigneron Champenois; organe de la vigne et du vin de champagne. m (11 per yr) ISSN 0049-643X

**Associations des Anciens Eleves des Ecoles des Mines**
- Revue des Ingenieurs. (pub. by G. E. D. I. M.)

**Assurances Generales de France**
87 rue de Richelieu, Paris 2e, France.
- Assurances Generales de France. Informations. irreg. ISSN 0066-989X

**Editions Asteria**
5, rue Greffulhe, 75-Paris (8e), France.
- Enseignes et Lumiere; eclairage-decoration. bi-m.
- Intermode; blanc/decor textile. ISSN 0047-0503
- Maroquinerie-Voyage-Parapluie-Chaussure. m. ISSN 0025-3898 (Federation Nationale de la Maroquinerie)
- Techniques de l'Habillement. m.(11 per yr.) ISSN 0040-1315 (Centre d'Etude Technique des Industries de l'Habillement (CETIH))

**Astrado Prouvencalo**
2 rue Vincent Allegre, 83100 Toulon, France.
- Astrado; revue bilingue de Provence. a. ISSN 0004-6116

**Editions de l' Atalante**
60 Avenue Simon Bolivar, 75019 Paris, France.
- Ecran. m.

**Atelier du Coeur- Meurtry**
Abbaye Ste. Marie de la Pierre-Qui-Vire, F 89830 St. Leger Vauban, France.
- Zodiaque. q. ISSN 0044-4952

**Atelier du Monastere Sainte Catherine**
c/o Editor Rene Luneau, 20 rue des Tanneries, 75013 Paris, France.
- Afrique et Parole; bulletin de correspondance pour une meilleure expression de la parole de dieu dans les cultures africaines. s-a. ISSN 0044-6661 (Co-Sponsor: Conseil du Secteur Dominicain d'Afrique de l'Ouest)

**Atelier Parisien d'Urbanisme**
17, Boulevard Morland, 75004 Paris, France.
- Paris Project. s-a.

**Ateliers Proteges**
7, Boulevard Chastenet-de-Gery, 96270 le Kremlin-Bicetre, France.
- Ateliers Proteges. q.

**Athenes-Presse Libre**
c/o Richard Someritis, Ed., 23 rue Brezin, 75014 Paris, France.
- Athenes-Presse Libre. w. ISSN 0044-9865

**Atlantic Institute for International Affairs**
120 rue de Longchamps, 75116 Paris, France.
- Atlantic Papers. q. ISSN 0571-7795

**Atlantic Treaty Association**
c/o Pierre Mahias, Secretary General, 185 rue de la Pompe, 75016 Paris, France.
- Atlantic Mail. irreg. ISSN 0519-3125

**Atlas Copco France S.A.**
326 rue du General-Leclerc, 95130 Franconville, France.
- Air Comprime. 3-4 per yr. ISSN 0002-225X

**Aubanel S.A.**
7 Place St. Pierre, 84 Avignon, France.
- Vita Latina. 4 per yr. ISSN 0042-7306 (Association pour la Diffusion et l'Usage de la Langue Latine)

**Editions Aujourd'hui**
8 rue de la Michodiere, 75002 Paris, France.
- Cheval Hebdo; journal hebdomadaire d'information. w. ISSN 0339-9052

**Automobile-Club d'Alsace**
- Alsace Automobile. (pub. by S O P I C)

**Automobiliste**
42, rue du Bac, 75007 Paris, France.
- Automobiliste. bi-m.

**Editions de l' Avant Scene**
27 rue Saint Andre des Arts, 75006 Paris, France
- Avant-Scene Cinema. 20 per yr. ISSN 0045-1150
- Avant-Scene Opera. 6 per yr.
- Avant Scene Theatre. 20 per yr. ISSN 0045-1169
- R I H C (Revue Internationale d'Histoire du Cinema) q.

**Editions de l' Avenir**
18, Av. de la Marne, 92600 Asnieres, France.
- Assure Social. bi-m. ISSN 0587-3746 (Union Nationale pour l'Avenir de la Medecine)
- Profils Medico-Sociaux. w. (Union Nationale pour l'Avenir de la Medecine)

**Aviation 2000**
c/o Claude Alleigre, 49, Avenue Marceau, 75116 Paris, France.
- Aviation 2000. bi-m.

**B. I. E. P.**
3, rue Tronchet, 75008, Paris, France.
- Allo Paris. w.

**B.I.R.E. Entreprise de Presse**
6 rue Fremicourt, Paris (15e), France.
- B. I. R. E; buletin de informatie pentru Romani in Exil/bulletin d'information pour les Roumaines en Exil. s-m. ISSN 0005-3163

**B.R.E.S.**
30 rue Bergere, Paris 9e, France.
- Ordre National des Veterinaires. Revue. q.

**J. B. Bailliere et Fils**
19 rue Hautefeuille, 75279 Paris Cedex 06, France.
- Archives des Maladies du Coeur et des Vaisseaux. m. ISSN 0003-9683
- Coeur et Medecine Interne. 4 per yr. ISSN 0010-0234
- Information Geographique; revue illustree paraissant tous les deux mois pendant la periode scolaire. 5 per yr. ISSN 0020-0093
- Information Historique. 5 per yr. ISSN 0046-9351
- Information Litteraire; revue illustree paraissant tous les deux mois pendant la periode scolaire. 5 per yr. ISSN 0020-0123
- Revue du Praticien. 59 per yr. ISSN 0035-2640

**Banco di Roma**
5, Avenue du Coq, F-750009 Paris, France.
- Euro Cooperation; Economic Studies on Europe. (Co-Sponsors: Commerzbank; Credit Lyonnais)

**Banque Centrale des Etats de l'Afrique Equatoriale et du Cameroun**
29 rue du Colisee, 75008 Paris, France.
- Banque Centrale des Etats de l'Afrique Equatoriale et du Cameroun. Etudes et Statistiques. m.

**Banque de France**
Service de l'Information, 43 rue de Valois, 75 Paris 1 Er, France.
- Banque de France. Bulletin Trimestriel. q.
- Banque de France. Compte- Rendu. a. ISSN 0067-3927
- Banque de France. Direction de la Conjoncture. Structure et Evolution Financiere des Regions de Province. a. ISSN 0522-3199
- Banque de France. Enquete Mensuelle de Conjoncture. m.

**Banque de l'Union Europeenne**
4, rue Gaillon B.P. 89, 75060 Paris Cedex 02, France.
- Banque de l'Union Europeenne. Chiffres et Commentaires. irreg.

**Banque des Etats de l'Afrique Centrale**
29, rue du Colisee, Paris (8e), France.
- Banque des Etats de l'Afrique Centrale. Etudes et Statistiques. 10 per yr. ISSN 0014-2069
- Banque des Etats de l'Afrique Centrale. Rapport d'Activite. a. ISSN 0067-3900

**Banque Francaise et Italienne**
12 rue Halevy, Paris (9e), France.
- Banque Francaise et Italienne. Etudes Economiques. m. ISSN 0014-2042
- Evolution de l'Economie des Pays Sud-Americains. a. ISSN 0071-3252

**Banque Nationale de Paris**
16 Bd. des Italiens, Paris (9e), France.
- Banque Nationale de Paris. Revue. q. ISSN 0005-562X

**Editions Bartheye et Cie**
54 Av. Marceau, 75008 Paris, France.
- Entropie; revue internationale de thermodynamique et de techniques avancees. bi-m. ISSN 0013-9084

**Publicite Stephane Batard**
21 Rue Saint-Fiacre, Paris 2e, France.
- Societe d'Ophtalmologie de France. Bulletin. irreg. ISSN 0081-1270

**Bati-Flash**
23 Bd. Bonne Nouvelle, 75002 Paris, France.
- Bati-Flash. bi-m.

**Editions A. Bauer**
51 Av. des Gobelins, 75013 Paris, France.
- Argus des Collectivites. m. ISSN 0004-119X
- Joint. m(9 per yr.)

**Bayard Presse**
3-5, rue Bayard, 75380 Paris Cedex 08, France.
- Belles Histoires de Pomme d'Api. m.
- Bible et Terre Sainte. 10 per yr. ISSN 0006-0712
- Croix; l'evenement. d.
- Documentation Catholique. s-m. ISSN 0012-4613
- Documents Service Adolescence. 8 per yr.
- Foi Aujourd'hui. m.
- J'aime Lire. m.
- Notre Temps; journal de la retraite heureuse. m(11 per yr) ISSN 0029-456X
- Okapi. bi-m.
- Panorama Aujourd'hui; revue de reflexion chretienne. m.
- Pelerin du Vingtieme Siecle. w. ISSN 0031-4145
- Points de Repere. 7 per yr. (Centre National de l'Enseignement Religieux (C.N.E.R.))
- "Pomme d'Api". m.
- Presse Actualite. 9 per yr. ISSN 0032-7832
- Promesses. 6 per yr. ISSN 0033-1066
- Record. m. ISSN 0048-6957
- Vivante Eglise. 10 per yr.

**Bayer Phytochim**
53 rue du General Leclerc, 92-130 Issy les Moulineauz, France
(Main office: Bayer Pflanzenschutz, Leverkusen, W. Germany (B.R.D.))
- Courrier Bayer Phytochim. irreg.

**Pierre Bearn, Editor and Publisher**
60 rue Monsieur Lc Prince, 75006 Paris, France.
- Passerelle; revue litteraire et trimestrielle a sens unique. q. ISSN 0031-2711

**Editons Beauchesne**
72 rue des Saints Peres, 75007 Paris, France.
- Archives de Philosophie; recherches et documentation. q. ISSN 0003-9632

**Laboratoires Beaufour**
18 Place Doguereau, 28 Dreux, France.
- Gastro-Enterologie Quotidienne. 3 per yr. ISSN 0016-5077

**Editions Beaulieu**
76-78 Champs-Elysees, 75008 Paris, France.
- Cuisine Chez Sol. irreg. ISSN 0339-7963
- Photoroman d'Amour. m. ISSN 0339-1493

**Beauterama**
29, rue de Versailles, 78460 Chevreuse, France.
- Beauterama. bi-m. ISSN 0408-7496

**Editions P. Belfond**
3Bis Passage de la Petite-Boncherie, Paris 6, France.
- Sciences Secretes. irreg. ISSN 0080-7672

**Bella**
36, rue du General-de-Gaulle, 95880 Enghien-les-Bains, France.
- Bella; le magazine de la femme noire. m. ISSN 0399-2322

**Editions Bellefaye**
1 Av. de l'Abbe Roussel, 75016 Paris, France.
- Annuaire du Cinema et Television. a. ISSN 0066-2968

**Editions Henri Belouze**
7, Rue Cacheux, 92100 Boulogne, France.
- Hebdo de la Blanchisserie-Teinturerie. w. ISSN 0046-7154

**Editions Jacques Bereny**
107, rue de l'Universite, 75007 Paris, France.
- Air Cargo. q.

**Imprimerie et Librairie Berger-Levrault**
18 rue des Glaces, 54 Nancy, France.
- Annales de l'Est. q. (Universite de Nancy II)
- Annuaire du Tiers Monde. a.
- Bulletin Technique du Genie (1960) q.
- Documentation Communale. q.
- Tiers-Monde en Marche. irreg.

**Editions de Berne et Cie**
11 Bd. des Batignolles, Paris (8e), France.
- Pensez Plastiques. published in monthly, quarterly and semi-annual editions. ISSN 0031-4803

**Raoul Bertolo, Pub.**
50D rue de Dole, 25000 Besancon, France.
- Europe-Echecs. m.(Nov.-Aug.); bi-m.(Sept.-Oct.) ISSN 0014-2794

**Beton Arme**
57 Ave. du Maine, Paris (14e), France.
- Beton Arme; revue. de traductions internationales. m. ISSN 0005-9854

**Bibliotheque des Ecoles Francaises d'Athenes et de Rome**
- B E F A R. Publication. (pub. by Diffusion de Boccard)

**Bibliotheque Historique de la Ville de Paris**
29 Allec Etienne Dolet, 93190 Livry-Gargan, France.
- Bulletin Folklorique d'Ile-De-France. q. ISSN 0007-4616 (Federation Folklorique d'Ile-de-France)

**Bibliotheque Interuniversitaire de Bordeaux**
Section des Sciences, Ancien Chemin Bernos, 33-Talence, France.
- Societe des Sciences Physiques et Naturelles de Bordeaux. Memoires. irreg.; 1968, vol. 5.

**Bibliotheque Interuniversitaire de Medecine et de Pharmacie. Bibliotheque de Medecine et de Pharmacie**
B.P. 33, 63001 Clermont Ferrand, France.
- Catalogue des Theses de Pharmacie Soutenues en France. a; quinquennial cumulation. ISSN 0069-4665
- Index Alphabetique Annuel des Sujets Traites dans les Theses de Medecine; soutenues en France, a Abidjan, a Alger et a Dakar. a (plus quinquennial cumulations)

**Bibliotheque Nationale**
58 rue de Richelieu, 75084 Paris Cedex 02, France.
- Bibliotheque Nationale. Bulletin. q. ISSN 0338-4446
- Bulletin d'Histoire Economique et Sociale de la Revolution Francaise. a. ISSN 0068-4058 (France. Commission d'Histoire Economique et Sociale de la Revolution Francaise)
- Bulletin des Bibliotheques de France. m. ISSN 0006-2006
- Bulletin du Bibliophile. 4 per yr. ISSN 0399-9742 (Association Internationale de Bibliophilie)
- Comite des Travaux Historiques et Scientifiques. Section de Geographie. Actes du Congres National des Societes Savantes. a., 1976, 99th Besancon, France. ISSN 0071-8424
- France. Comite des Travaux Historiques et Scientifiques. Bulletin Archeologique. a. ISSN 0071-8394

- France. Comite des Travaux Historiques et Scientifiques. Bulletin Philologique et Historique (Jusqu'a 1610) irreg. ISSN 0071-8408
- France. Comite des Travaux Historiques et Scientifiques. Section d'Archeologie. Actes du Congres National des Societes Savantes. a., 1971, 96th, Toulouse, France. ISSN 0071-8416
- France. Comite des Travaux Historiques et Scientifiques. Section de Geographie. Bulletin. irreg. vol. 81, 1968-1974. ISSN 0071-8432
- France. Comite des Travaux Historiques et Scientifiques. Section d'Histoire Moderne et Contemporaine. Actes du Congres National des Societes Savantes. a., 1975, 100th, Paris, France. ISSN 0071-8440
- France. Comite des Travaux Historiques et Scientifiques. Section d'Histoire Moderne et Contemporaine. Bulletin. irreg., 1975, no. 9. ISSN 0071-8459
- Nouvelles du Livre Ancien. q. ISSN 0335-752X (prep. by its Service du Livre Ancien)

**Bibliotheque Nationale. Cabinet des Estampes**
58 rue de Richelieu, 75084 Paris Cedex 02, France.
- Nouvelles de l'Estampe. 6 per yr. ISSN 0029-4888 (Comite National de la Gravure Francaise)

**Bibliotheque Nationale. Departement de la Phonotheque Nationale et de l'Audiovisuel**
2 rue Louvois, Paris 2eme, France.
- Phonotheque Nationale. Bulletin. irreg. ISSN 0031-840X

**Bibliotheque Universitaire, Grenoble**
Saint-Martin-d'Heres, 38401 Grenoble, France.
- Bibliotheque Universitaire, Grenoble. Publications. irreg. ISSN 0072-7520

**Editions Biere**
18-22 rue du Peugue, 33000 Bordeaux, France.
- Bulletin Hispanique. q. ISSN 0007-4640 (Ecole des Hautes Etudes Hispaniques)
- Revue Economique du Sud-Ouest. q. (Universite de Bordeaux I. Faculte de Droit et des Sciences Economiques)

**Biologia Gabonica**
c/oP. P. Grasse, Ed., 105 Bd. Raspail, 75006 Paris, France.
- Biologia Gabonica. q. ISSN 0006-3118

**Biologie Medicale**
Spacia, 26 Av. de l'Observatoire, Paris (14e), France.
- Biologie Medicale. 2 per yr. ISSN 0006-3266

**Librairie Bloud et Gay**
3 rue Garanciere, Paris 6e, France.
- Collection PSI. irreg. ISSN 0069-5440

**Blues and Swing**
Parc Ste Anne 10, Bd. de la Fabrique 42, Marseille 13009, France.
- Blues and Swing. irreg.

**Diffusion de Boccard**
1 rue de Medicis, Paris 6e, France
(U.S. Subscr. to: Institute for the Arts, Rice University, Box 1892, Houston, Tx 77001)
- B E F A R. Publication. irreg. (1-2 per yr) (Bibliotheque des Ecoles Francaises d'Athenes et de Rome)
- Bibliographie Analytique de l'Afrique Antique. a.
- Bulletin de Correspondance Hellenique. a (in two fascicules) ISSN 0007-4217 (Ecole Francaise d'Athenes GR)
- Casa de Velazquez, Madrid. Melanges/Casa de Velasquez, Madrid. Miscellanies. a. ISSN 0076-230X

**Andre-Pierre Body, Ed. & Pub.**
42 rue la Bruyere, 75009 Paris, France.
- Initiatives. bi-m. ISSN 0339-1019 (Mouvement Rural de Jeunesse Chretienne)

**Editions Boileau**
9 rue Clauzel, Paris (9e), France.
- Guide Medical et Hospitalier. a. ISSN 0072-8144

**Bois**
4 Av. de l'Opera, Paris (1er), France.
- Bois; l'officiel du bois et des industries du bois. bi-m. ISSN 0006-5781

**Editions du Boisbaudry**
35, rue Carnot, 35000 Rennes, France.
- Eleveur de Porcs. m.

**Michel Bongrand S.A.**
17 Av. Hoche, 75008 Paris, France.
- Annuaire de l'Industrie du Caoutchouc et de ses Derives. biennial. ISSN 0066-2674
- Revue Francaise de Bridge. m. ISSN 0035-2861 (Federation Francaise de Bridge)

**Bonne Table et Tourisme**
9 Square Moncey, 75009 Paris, France.
- Bonne Table et Tourisme; revue de la gastronomie et du tourisme dans le monde. 5 per yr.

**Bonneterie-Mercerie-Habillement**
39 rue du General-Foy, Paris 8, France.
- Bonneterie-Mercerie-Habillement. a. ISSN 0068-0079

**Bordeaux Chirurgical**
Prof. L. Masse, 11 rue Albert-de Mun, Bordeaux, France.
- Bordeaux Chirurgical. q. ISSN 0006-7660

**Bordeaux Medical**
153 rue de Pessac, 33000 Bordeaux, France.
- Bordeaux Medical. 30 per yr. ISSN 0021-7867

**Editions Edouard Boucherit**
10 rue de la Pepiniere, 75380 Paris, France.
- Modes & Travaux; le guide indispensable de la femme elegante et pratique. m. ISSN 0026-8739

**Pierre Boujut, Pub.**
16200-Jarnac (Charente), France.
- Tour de Feu; revue internationaliste de creation poetique. q. ISSN 0040-9731

**G.F. Boullier, Ed. & Pub.**
21 rue Mademoiselle, 75015 Paris, France.
- Petromonde. w.
- Techniques Petrole Petrochimie. m.

**Claude Boumendil**
Repro 2000, 11, rue Gutenberg, 06000 Nice, France.
- Belisane; bulletin de philosophie et d'histoire traditionnelles. q. ISSN 0339-8498

**C. Bourgeois, Editeur**
8 rue Garanciere, Paris 6e, France.
- Dans le Fantastique. irreg. ISSN 0070-279X

**Bouteille a la Mer**
c/o Ed. Marc Beigbeder, 8 rue Theo- Renaudot, 75015 Paris, France.
- Bouteille a la Mer. q.

**Boutiques de France**
16, Boulevard Saint-Denis, 75010 Paris, France.
- Boutiques de France. bi-m.

**British Chamber of Commerce**
6 rue Halevy, 75009 Paris, France.
- British Chamber of Commerce in France. Year Book. a. ISSN 0068-1415
- Cross Channel Trade. bi-m.

**Brud Nevez**
c/oM. Mevel, Ed., 14 Impasse Breiz Izel, 29N Brest, France.
- Brud Nevez. m.

**Brulot**
30b rue Moliere, 93 Bagnolet, France.
- Brulot. m. ISSN 0007-2672

**Editions Brunier**
Bayer, rue Bellocier, Sens, France.
- Syndromes de la Douleur. irreg. ISSN 0082-1098

**Bulletin Biologique de la France et de la Belgique**
105 Bd. Raspail, Paris 75006, France.
- Bulletin Biologique de la France et de la Belgique. 4 per yr. ISSN 0007-4187

**Bulletin de l'Antiquaire et du Brocanteur**
18, rue de Provence, 75009 Paris, France.
- Bulletin de l'Antiquaire et du Brocanteur. m (10 per yr.)

**Bulletin de l'Oeuvre d'Orient**
20 rue du Regard, Paris (6e), France.
- Bulletin de l'Oeuvre d'Orient. bi-m. ISSN 0007-4349

**Bulletin de Paris**
20 Avenue Franklin D. Roosevelt, Paris(8e), France.
- Bulletin de Paris. bi-w. ISSN 0007-4381

**Bulletin Europeen de Physiopathologie Respiratoire**
Inserm U14, Case Officielle N 10, F-54500 Vandoeuvre-les-Nancy, Annexe 2, France.
- Bulletin Europeen de Physiopathologie Respiratoire. bi-m. ISSN 0395-3890

**Editions des Bulletins Reunis**
18 rue Volney, 75002 Paris, France
(Subscr. Address: 34 Fg. de Pierre, 67 Strasbourg, France)
- Tribune Juive. w.

**Bureau a Tours**
25 Rue du Rempart, Tours, France.
- Chantecoq; informations et techniques de l'elevage. bi-m. ISSN 0009-1553

**Bureau d'Etudes Cooperatives et Communautaires**
7 Ave. Franco-Russe, 75 Paris (7e), France.
- Archives Internationales de Sociologie de la Cooperation et du Developpement. s-a. ISSN 0003-9802 (Centre de Recherches Cooperatives)

**Bureau d'Etudes et de Recherches Theoriques (BERTHE)**
124, Avenue de la Republique, 75011 Paris, France.
- Chronique du Transporteur. m.

**Bureau d'Informations et de Previsions Economiques (B. I. P. E.)**
122 Av. Charles de Gaulle, 92522 Neuilly-sur-Seine, France.
- Tableau de Bord des Industries Francaises. q. ISSN 0039-8802

**Bureau des Relations Exterieures et Sociales**
30 rue Bergere, Paris 9e, France.
- Transtelel; Transmissions, Telecommunications, Electronique en France. biennial. ISSN 0082-5980

**Bureau et Informatique**
14, rue du Champ-de-Mars, 75007 Paris, France.
- Bureau et Informatique; revue de l'actualite de l'informatique et de l'organisation du bureau. bi-m.

**Bureau International de l'Heure**
Observatoire de Paris, 61, Ave. de l'Observatoire, 75014- Paris, France.
- Bureau International de l'Heure. Rapport Annuel. a. ISSN 0068-4236

**Bureau International de Liaison et de Documentation**
50 rue de Laborde, Paris (8e), France.
- Bureau International de Liaison et de Documentation. Documents; revue des questions allemandes. bi-m. ISSN 0007-6139

**Bureau International de Relations Publiques**
123 Avenue Charles de Gaulle, 92000 Neuilly, France.
- Nuclelec. s-w. ISSN 0029-5663

**Bureau International des Containers**
38, Cours Albert 1er, Paris (8e), France.
- B I C-Code. a.

**Bureau International des Poids et Mesures**
Pavillon de Breteuil, 92310 Sevres, France.
- Bureau International des Poids et Mesures Recueil de Travaux. irreg, 1973-74, no. 4. ISSN 0525-2113
- Comite International des Poids et Mesures. Comite Consultatif d'Electricite. (Rapport et Annexes) irreg.; 14th session, 1975.
- Comite International des Poids et Mesures. Comite Consulatif de Thermometrie. (Rapport et Annexes) irreg.; 10th session, 1974.
- Comite International des Poids et Mesures. Comite Consultatif de Photometrie et Radiometrie.(Rapport et Annexes) irreg; 1975, 8th session. ISSN 0588-621X
- Comite International des Poids et Mesures. Comite Consultatif des Unites (Rapport et Annexes) irreg.; 5th session 1976.
- Comite International des Poids et Mesures. Comite Consultatif pour la Definition de la Seconde. (Rapport et Annexes) irreg. ISSN 0588-6228
- Comite International des Poids et Mesures. Comite Consultatif pour la Definition du Metre (Rapport et Annexes) irreg.; 5th session, 1973. ISSN 0588-6236
- Comite International des Poids et Mesures. Comite Consultatif pour la Definition du Metre. Travaux. irreg.; 5th edt., 1973. ISSN 0069-6498

- Comite International des Poids et Mesures. Comite Consultatif pour les Etalons des Mesure des Radiations Ionisantes (Rapport et Annexes) irreg.; 6th session, 1975. ISSN 0588-6244

**Bureau International des Societes Gerant les Droits d'Enregistrement et de Reproduction Mecanique**
12 rue Ballu, 75009 Paris, France.
- Bureau International des Societes Gerant les Droits d'Enregistrement et de Reproduction Mecanique. Bulletin. irreg. ISSN 0572-7529

**Bureau Universitaire de Recherche Operationnelle**
4 Place Jussieu, 75230 Paris, France.
- Bureau Universitaire de Recherche Operationnelle, Paris. Cahiers. ISSN 0078-950X

**Bureau Veritas**
58 bis, rue Paul Vaillant-Couturier, 92300 Levallois-Perret, France.
- Bureau Veritas. Bulletin Technique. 12 per yr (French edt.); 3 per yr (English edt. ISSN 0007-5752
- Registre Aeronautique International. a. ISSN 0080-066X
- Registre International de Classification de Navires et d'Aeronefs. a. ISSN 0080-0678

**Eric Burmann, Ed. & Pub.**
Boite Postale 18, 37005 Tours Cedex, France.
- Imbuvable. m.

**Butterfly**
Box 1350, 76065 le Havre, France.
- Butterfly; English-French magazine. m. ISSN 0007-7291

**Editions C A M**
B.P. 51, 78190 Trappes, France.
- Techniques de l'Air Comprime. bi-m. ISSN 0040-1307

**Editions C A M S**
23 Boulevard de Bonne-Nouvelle, 75002 Paris, France.
- Bacchus International; la revue de la sommellerie. bi-m.

**C. E. D. I.**
79 Ave. Denfert Rochereau, 75014-Paris, France.
- Extension. m.

**C.E.L.**
B.P. 282, 06403 Cannes Cedex, France.
- Cahiers Pedagogiques. m. ISSN 0008-042X

**C. E. P.**
*see* **Compagnie Europeenne d'Editions**

**C. E. R. B. O. M.**
*see* **Centre d'Etudes et de Recherches de Biologie et d'Oceanographie Medicale (C. E. R. B. O. M.)**

**C.E.T.I.A.T.**
B.P. 19, 91402 Orsay, France.
- Informations Aerauliques et Thermiques. q; temporarily suspended in 1975. ISSN 0046-9416

**C F D T**
26 rue de Montholon, 75439 Paris Cedex 09, France.
- Syndicalisme. w. ISSN 0039-7741

**C. F. E.**
*see* **Compagnie Francaise d'Editions**

**C. I. B.**
7 rue Darboy, Paris (11e), France.
- Cinema. m. ISSN 0045-6926
- Connaissance des Plastiques. m. ISSN 0010-6003
- Cycle; cyclomoteurs-scooters. m. ISSN 0011-426X

**C I D E L T**
32 Avenue du President Kennedy, Paris 16, France.
- Equipement, Logement, Transports. bi-m.
- France Transports. bi-m. ISSN 0395-9600

**Editions C.N.C.**
62, rue Guy Moquet, 75017 Paris, France.
- Construction-Amenagement. q. ISSN 0589-4735

**C. N. D. P. - Documentation Migrants**
4, rue de Stockholm, 75008 Paris, France.
- Migrants Formations. bi-m. ISSN 0335-0894
- Migrants Nouvelles. m. ISSN 0397-944X

**C. N. R. A.**
Route de St. Cyr, 78-Versailles, France.
- Phytiatrie-Phythopharmacie. 4 per yr. ISSN 0031-8876 (Societe Francaise de Phytiatrie et de Phytopharmacie)

**C O R E S T A**
53 Quai d'Orsay, Paris (7e), France.
- C O R E S T A; bulletin d'information. q. ISSN 0010-8723

**C. R. E. E.**
51 rue Pierre Charron, 75008 Paris, France.
- C. R. E. E. (Creations et Recherches Esthetiques Europeenes) 7 per yr. ISSN 0591-048X

**C. R. E. S.**
B. P. 446, 75830 Paris, France.
- Communisme. 3 per yr.

**C. T. I. C. M.**
*see* **Centre Technique Industrial de la Construction Metallique**

**Caducee**
18, Avenue de la Marne, 92600 Asnieres, France.
- Caducee. m. ISSN 0007-9480

**Cahier de l'Humanisme Libertaire**
Ed. Gaston Leval, 33 Blvd. Edgar Quinet, Paris, France
- Cahier de l'Humanisme Libertaire; revue mensuelle d'etudes sociologiques. m. ISSN 0007-957X

**Cahiers Bretons**
29 rue des Meulieres, 77260 la Ferte-Sous-Jouarre, France.
- Cahiers Bretons/Ar Gwyr. irreg. ISSN 0068-4953

**Cahiers de l'Homme Espirit**
5 Avenue du General-de-Gaulle, 06240 Beausoleil, France.
- Cahiers de l'Homme Espirit. q.

**Editions des Cahiers de la Ceramique**
Boite Postale 5, 75562 Paris, France.
- Cahiers de la Ceramique, du Verre et des Arts du Feu. q. ISSN 0007-9790

**Cahiers de la Cinematheque**
Palais des Congress, 66000 Perpignan, France.
- Cahiers de la Cinematheque. Bulletin d'Information. q.

**Editons Cahiers de la Republique**
25 rue de Louvre, Paris (1e), France.
- Courrier de la Republique. m. ISSN 0011-0493

**Cahiers de Litterature et de Poesie: Poetes et Leurs Amis**
7 rue des Wallons, 75013 Paris, France.
- Cahiers de Litterature et de Poesie: Poetes et Leurs Amis. q. ISSN 0032-1974

**Cahiers des Ingenieurs Agronomes**
5 Quai Voltaire, 75007paris, France.
- Cahiers des Ingenieurs Agronomes. m(10 per yr) ISSN 0035-2179

**Cahiers du Medecin Specialiste**
144 rue de Rivoli, Paris (1e), France.
- Cahiers du Medecin Specialiste. q. ISSN 0008-0144

**Cahiers du Yachting**
43, Boulevard Barbes, 75018 Paris, France.
- Cahiers du Yachting. 4 per yr.

**Cahiers Fiscaux Europeens**
51 Avenue Victoria, 06000 Nice, France.
- Fiscalite Europeenne. q.
- Tableaux Fiscaux Europeens. a.

**Cahiers Franco-Ecossais de Normandie**
c/o Rene Soyer, Ed., Residence Jeanne-d'Arc, 43 Route d'Ifs, Caen-14, France.
- Cahiers Franco-Ecossais de Normandie.

**Cahiers Medicaux de France**
6 rue Ed.-Detaille, Paris (17e), France.
- Cahiers Medicaux de France. m. ISSN 0008-0349

**Cahiers Pierre Loti**
66 rue Pargaminieres, 31000 Toulouse, France.
- Cahiers Pierre Loti. s-a. ISSN 0008-0438

**Caisse Nationale des Monuments Historiques**
62 rue Saint-Antoine, Paris 4, France.
- Monuments Historiques de la France. bi-m.

**Editions Calmann-Levy**
3, rue Auber, 75009 Paris, France.
- Annee du Football. a.
- Annee du Rugby. a.
- Perspectives de l'Economique. Serie 1. les Fondateurs de l'Economie. irreg. ISSN 0079-0982
- Perspectives de l'Economique. Serie 2. Economie Contemporaine. irreg.
- Perspectives de l'Economique. Serie 3. Critique. irreg.

**Paul Camelio, Pub.**
Marine Blanche K, 13014 Marseille, France.
- Camouflage Air Journal. bi-m. ISSN 0300-452X

**Canoe Kayak Club de France**
47 Quai Fuber, 94360 Bry sur Marne, France.
- Riviere. q. ISSN 0035-5720

**Editions Caracteres**
7 rue de l'Arbalete, 75005 Paris, France.
- Caracteres; revue internationale de poesie. q. ISSN 0008-6134
- Collection "Chants des Peuples". irreg.

**Editions G. N. Carre**
36, rue de Malte, 75011 Paris, France.
- Annonces. w.

**Carrefour**
114 Champs Elysees, 75363 Paris, France.
- Carrefour. w. ISSN 0008-6886

**Madame Carrington**
127 rue Saint-Germain, 27 Louviers, France.
- Scenes et Pistes. m. ISSN 0036-5793

**Editions du Cartel**
2 rue de Florence, 75008 Paris, France.
- Catalogue National du Genie Climatique-Chauffage et Conditionnement d'Air/National Catalogue of Heating and Air Conditioning/Nazionaler Katalog der Heizung und Klimatisierung. a. ISSN 0069-1127
- Traitements de Surface. m.

**Editions Casterman**
66 rue Bonaparte, Paris 6e, France.
- Dossiers du Cinema. irreg., latest issues--1974-75. ISSN 0070-7155

**Catalogue des Catalogues Automobile**
1 Avenue Felix-Faure, Paris 15, France.
- Catalogue des Catalogues Automobile. a. ISSN 0069-1097

**Causse et Cie**
7 rue Dom-Vaissette, Montpellier, France.
- Journee du Batiment; et des trauvaux publics. w. ISSN 0022-5630

**Editions du Cedre**
13 rue Mazarine, 75006 Paris, France.
- Pensee Catholique; cahiers de synthese. bi-m. ISSN 0031-4781

**Centrale des Revues Dunod Gauthier- Villars**
B. P. 119, 93104 Montreuil Cedex, France.
- Academie des Sciences. Annuaire. a. ISSN 0065-0552
- Academie des Sciences. Comptes Rendus Hebdomadaires des Seances. Series A: Sciences Mathematiques. w. ISSN 0302-8429
- Academie des Sciences. Comptes Rendus Hebdomadaires des Seances. Serie B: Sciences Physiques. w. ISSN 0302-8437
- Academie des Sciences. Comptes Rendus Hebdomadaires des Seances. Series C: Sciences Chimiques. w. ISSN 0567-6541
- Academie des Sciences. Comptes Rendus Hebdomadaires des Seances. Series D: Sciences Naturelles. w. ISSN 0567-655X
- Academie des Sciences. Index Biographique des Membres et Correspondants. irreg. ISSN 0065-0560
- Atlas d'Attraction Urbaine. irreg. ISSN 0067-026X (Ecole Pratique des Hautes Etudes. Centre d'Etudes des Techniques Economiques Modernes)
- Automatisme. m. ISSN 0005-1241 (Association Francaise pour la Cybernetique Economique et Technique)
- Bulletin des Sciences Mathematiques. q. ISSN 0007-4497 (Ecole Pratique des Hautes Etudes)

- Cahiers de l'Analyse des Donnees. q. (Co-Sponsor: Centre National de la Recherche Scientifique)
- Centre d'Etudes Pratiques d'Informatique et d'Automatique. Collection. irreg. ISSN 0069-1852
- Consommation. q. ISSN 0010-6593 (Centre de Recherches et de Documentation sur la Consommation)
- Construction; revue mensuelle du batiment et des travaux publics. m. ISSN 0010-6682
- Ecole Normale Superieure. Annales Scientifiques. q. ISSN 0012-9593
- France. Commissariat a l'Energie Atomique. Bulletin d'Informations Scientifiques et Techniques. m. ISSN 0007-4543
- French Railway Techniques. q. ISSN 0016-1101 (Federation des Industries Ferroviaires)
- Institut Henri Poincare. Annales. Section A: Physique Theorique. 8 per yr.(4 nos. per vol.) ISSN 0020-2339 (Universite de Paris VI (Pierre et Marie Curie). Institut Henri Poincare)
- Institut Henri Poincare. Annales. Section B: Calcul des Probabilites et Statistiques. q. ISSN 0020-2347 (Universite de Paris VI (Pierre et Marie Curie). Institut Henri Poincare)
- Journal de Mathematiques Pures et Appliquees. q. ISSN 0021-7824
- Journal de Mecanique. 5 per yr. ISSN 0021-7832
- Journal de Mecanique Appliquee. q.
- Journal Francais de Biophysique et Medecine Nucleaire. q. (Societe Francaise de Physique Biologique)
- Journal International de Psychologie/International Journal of Psychology. q. ISSN 0020-7594 (International Union of Psychological Science)
- Manuels Pratiques d'Economie. irreg. ISSN 0076-4205
- Materiaux & Constructions/Materials & Structures. bi-m. ISSN 0025-5432 (International Union of Testing and Research Laboratories for Materials and Structures)
- Mathematiques et Sciences Humaines. q. ISSN 0025-5815 (Centre de Mathematique Sociale et de Statistique)
- Memoires des Sciences Mathematiques. irreg. ISSN 0025-9187
- Nouveau Journal de Chimie. 6 per yr. (Centre National de la Recherche Scientifique)
- Oecologia Plantarum. q. ISSN 0029-8557
- Oenologie Pratique. irreg. ISSN 0078-3412
- Physiologie Vegetale. q. ISSN 0031-9368 (Societe Francaise de Physiologie Vegetale)
- Radioprotection. q. ISSN 0033-8451 (Societe Francaise de Radioprotection)
- Revue d'Ecologie et de Biologie du Sol. 4 per yr. ISSN 0035-1822
- Revue de Chimie Minerale. 6 per yr. ISSN 0035-1032
- Revue Francaise d'Automatique, d'Informatique et de Recherche Operationnelle. q. ISSN 0035-3035 (Association Francaise pour la Cybernetique Economique et Technique)
- Revue Francaise du Marketing. 6 per yr. ISSN 0035-3051 (Association Nationale pour le Developpement des Techniques de Marketing (ADETEM)
- Revue Generale des Chemins de Fer. 11 per yr. ISSN 0035-3183 (Societe Nationale des Chemins de Fer Francais)
- Sciences de l'Education. irreg. ISSN 0080-7648
- Techniques Economiques Modernes. Espace Economique. irreg. ISSN 0082-2485 (Ecole Pratique des Hautes Etudes. Centre d'Etudes des Techniques Economiques Modernes)
- Techniques Economiques Modernes. Histoire et Pensee Economique. irreg. ISSN 0082-2493 (Ecole Pratique des Hautes Etudes. Centre d'Etudes des Techniques Economiques Modernes)
- Techniques Economiques Modernes. Production et Marches. irreg. ISSN 0082-2507 (Ecole Pratique des Hautes Etudes. Centre d'Etudes des Techniques Economiques Modernes)

**Centrale du Livre Protestant**
- Annuaire Protestant; la France Protestante et les Eglises de Langue Francaise. (pub. by Librairie Fischbacher)

**Centre Africain de Promotion Universitaire**
9 Rue Victor Consin, Paris (5e), France.
- Afrique & Culture. q. ISSN 0002-046X

**Centre Algerien de Documentation et d'Information**
3 rue Joseph Sansboeuf, Paris (8e), France.
- Algerien en Europe. bi-m. ISSN 0002-5313

**Centre Auvergne Gadz'arts**
- Centre Auvergne Gadz'arts. Bulletin Trimestriel des Ingenieurs Arts et Metiers de la Region Auvergne. (pub. by Societe des Arts et Metiers)

**Centre Catholique des Intellectuels Francais**
61 rue Madame, 75006-Paris, France.
- Centre Catholique des Intellectuels Francais. Recherches et Debats. 4 per yr. ISSN 0008-9605

**Centre Catholique des Medecins Francais**
14 bis, rue d'Assas, 75006 Paris, France.
- Medecine de l'Homme. m (10 per yr.) ISSN 0543-2243

**Centre Chretien des Patrons et Dirigeants d'Entreprise**
24 rue Hamelin, 75 Paris (16e), France.
- Professions et Entreprises. m. ISSN 0033-0213

**Centre Communautaire International**
- Communaute Humaine. (pub. by Fleurus Presse International)

**Centre Culturel du Belvedere**
94350 Villiers S/Marne, France.
- Societe Historique de Villiers sur Marne et de la Brie Francaise. Revue. a.

**Centre Culturel et Sportif de Vulaines**
Rue Riche, Vulaines S/Seine 77870, France.
- Courrier-Expression. s-a.

**Centre Culturel International de Cerisy-la-Salle**
- Centre Culturel International de Cerisy-La-Salle. Decades. Nouvelle Serie. (pub. by Mouton Publishers NE)

**Centre d'Amitie Internationale**
212 rue de Vaugirard, Paris (15e), France.
- Centre d'Amitie Internationale. Revue d'Art-Tourisme-Culture. ISSN 0008-9613

**Centre d'Analyse et de Recherche Documentaires pour l'Afrique Noire**
20 rue de la Baume, Paris 8, France.
- C A R D A N. Bulletin d'Information et de Liaison. (pub. by Ecole des Hautes Etudes en Sciences Sociales)
- Sciences Humaines Africanistes. a. ISSN 0078-9577 (prep. by its Centre d'Etudes Africaines)

**Centre d'Archives et de Documentation**
86 Bd. Haussmann, Paris (8e), France.
- Informations Politiques et Sociales; service hebdomadaire de documentation politique et sociale. s-w. ISSN 0046-9440

**Centre d'Entr'aide Genealogique**
- France Genealogique. (pub. by J. Dell'Acquo-Bascourt)

**Centre d'Entrainement a l'Economie**
14 Boulevard Poissonniere, 75009 Paris, France.
- C E N E C O Bulletin. s-a.

**Centre d'Etude des Complexes Sociaux**
99 Quai Clemenceau, 69 Caluire (Rhone), France.
- Economie et Humanisme. bi-m. ISSN 0013-0516 (Association Economie et Humanisme)

**Centre d'Etude des Litteratures d'Expression Graphique**
6 rue Gaguer-Gabillot, Paris (15e), France.
- Giff - Wiff; la revue de la bande dessinee. bi-m. ISSN 0016-9838

**Centre d'Etude des Matieres Plastiques**
65, rue de Prony, 75854 Paris Cedex 17, France.
- Centre d'Etude des Matieres Plastiques. Bulletin de Documentation. m. ISSN 0008-9702

**Centre d'Etude des Revenus et des Couts**
- Centre d'Etude des Revenus et des Couts. Documents. (pub. by Documentation Francaise)

**Centre d'Etude du Commerce et de la Distribution**
2 Place de la Bourse, 75002 Paris, France.
- Commerce Moderne; urbanisme commercial. w. & q. issues. ISSN 0396-714X
- F I T; Feuilles, Informations, Techniques; conseils pratiques aux detaillants. m.

**Centre d'Etude et d'Enseignement de la Methode Naturelle en Medecine**
27 rue Casimir Perier, 75007 Paris, France.
- Cahiers de la Methode Naturelle en Medecine; ancienne Revue Naturiste. q.

**Centre d'Etude et de Promotion de la Lecture**
114 Champs Elysees, Paris (8e), France.
- Psychologie. m. ISSN 0032-1583

**Centre d'Etude Technique des Industries de l'Habillement (CETIH)**
- Techniques de l'Habillement. (pub. by Editions Asteria)

**Centre d'Etudes Compostellanes**
- Compostelle. (pub. by Societe des Amis de St-Jacques de Compostelle)

**Centre d'Etudes, de Documentation, d'Information et d'Action Sociales**
5 rue Las-Cases, 75007-Paris, France.
- Vie Sociale. m. ISSN 0042-5605

**Centre d'Etudes de Documentation et de Recherches**
11 rue Quentin-Bauchard, Paris (8e), France.
- Cahiers de Bibliographie Therapeutique Francaise. Edition Medicale. 10 per yr. ISSN 0007-9715

**Centre d'Etudes de Politique Etrangere**
6 rue Ferrus, 75014 Paris, France.
- Politique Etrangere. 6 per yr. ISSN 0032-342X
- Strategie. q. ISSN 0039-2235 (Institut Francais d'Etudes Strategiques)

**Centre d'Etudes des Plantes Medicinales**
Bd. Daviers, 49 Angers, France.
- Plantes Medicinales et Phytotherapie. q. ISSN 0032-0994

**Centre d'Etudes des Questions Actuelles**
- Ecrits de Paris. (pub. by Societe Parisienne d'Editions et de Publications)

**Centre d'Etudes et d'Editions Patronales**
Palais Consulaire, B.P. 1506, Toulouse, France.
- Nouvelles Industrielles et Commerciales et de Midi-Pyrenees. m. ISSN 0029-4934

**Centre d'Etudes et d'Experimentation du Machinisme Agricole Tropical (C.E.E.M.A.T.)**
Parc de Tourvoie, 92160 Antony (Hauts de Seine), France.
- Machinisme Agricole Tropical. q. ISSN 0024-9246

**Centre d'Etudes et de Documentation sur l'Amerique Latine**
- Problemes d'Amerique Latine. (pub. by Documentation Francaise)

**Centre d'Etudes et de Productivite des Industries des Papiers, Cartons et Celluloses**
154, Boulevard Haussmann, 75008 Paris, France.
- Statistiques de l'Industrie Francaise des Pates, Papiers et Cartons. irreg.

**Centre d'Etudes et de Promotion de la Lecture**
- Dictionnaires du Savoir Moderne. (pub. by Editions Denoel)

**Centre d'Etudes et de Recherches de Biologie et d'Oceanographie Medicale (C.E.R.B.O.M.)**
Parc de la Cote, 1 Av. Jean-Lorrain, 06300 Nice, France.
- Revue Internationale d'Oceanographie Medicale. q. ISSN 0035-3493 (France. Institut National de la Sante et de la Recherche Medicale)

**Centre d'Etudes et de Recherches de l'Industrie des Liants Hydrauliques**
23 Rue de Cronstadt, 75015 Paris, France.
- C. E. R. I. L. H. Bulletin Analytique. m. ISSN 0007-8301
- Centre d'Etudes et de Recherches de l'Industrie des Liants Hydrauliques, Paris. Rapport d'Activite. irreg.
- Ciments, Betons, Platres, Chaux. (pub. by SEPTIMA)

**Centre d'Etudes et de Recherches des Problemes de l'Enfance**
13 rue du Lieutenant Heitz, 94300 Vincennes, France.
- Dossiers de Puericulture Information. irreg. ISSN 0339-8617

**Centre d'Etudes et de Recherches Economiques et Sociale**
146 rue du Fg. Poissonniere, Paris (10e), France.
- Pensee; revue du bon rationalisme moderne. bi-m. ISSN 0031-4773

**Centre d'Etudes et Recherches des Charbonnages de France**
32 Rue de la Baume, 75008 Paris, France.
- Bulletin Bibliographique de Documentation Technique du Groupement des Industries Extractives. m.
- Charbonnages de France. Publications Techniques. 6-7 per yr. ISSN 0009-1685
- Charbonnages de France. Rapport d'Activite. a.

**Centre d'Etudes Foreziennes**
34 rue Francis-Baulier, Saint-Etienne, France.
- Etudes Foreziennes. a. ISSN 0071-206X

**Centre d'Etudes Geographiques de Metz**
Faculte des Lettres et Sciences Humaines, Ile du Saulcy, 57000 Metz, France.
- Mosella. q. ISSN 0047-8164

**Centre d'Etudes Germaniques**
- Revue d'Allemagne et des Pays de Langue Allemande. (pub. by Societe d'Etudes Allemandes)

**Centre d'Etudes Islamiques et Orientales d'Histoire Comparee**
- Documents d'Histoire Maghrebine. (pub. by Librairie Orientaliste Paul Geuthner)

**Centre d'Etudes Istina**
45 rue de la Glaciere, 75013 Paris, France.
- Istina. q. ISSN 0021-2423

**Centre d'Etudes Litteraires Traditionnelles**
- Question de Spiritualite, Tradition, Litteratures. (pub. by Editions Retz)

**Centre d'Etudes Pedagogiques**
15 Rue Louis-David, 75016 Paris, France.
- Parents et Maitres. 5 per yr. ISSN 0031-1901

**Centre d'Etudes Pratiques d'Informatique et d'Automatique**
- Centre d'Etudes Pratiques d'Informatique et d'Automatique. Collection. (pub. by Centrale des Revues Dunod Gauthier-Villars)

**Centre d'Etudes Superieures de Civilisation Medievale**
Hotel Berthelot, 24 rue de la Chaine, 86000 Poitiers, France.
- Cahiers de Civilisation Medievale. q. ISSN 0007-9731
- Repertoire International des Medievistes. irreg. ISSN 0080-1151

**Centre d'Histoire Economique et Sociale de la Region Lyonnaise**
c/o Maurice Garden, Ed., 86 rue Pasteur, 69365 Lyon Cedex 2, France.
- Centre d'Histoire Economique et Sociale, de la Region Lyonnaise. Bulletin. q.

**Centre d'Histoire Militaire**
Montpellier, France.
- Etudes Militaires. irreg.

**Centre d'Information Civique**
164 rue de Vaugirard, Paris (15e), France.
- Centre d'Information Civique, Paris. Etudes. q. ISSN 0008-9788

**Centre d'Information des Services Medicaux d' Entreprises et Interentreprises**
31 rue Mederic, 75821 Paris Cedex 17, France.
- Centre d'Information des Services Medicaux d'Entreprises et Interentreprises. Annuaire. irreg. ISSN 0069-1879

**Centre d'Information Sociale des Employeurs de l'Ile-de-France**
47 rue de l'Universite, 75007 Paris, France.
- Documentation Sociale; revue mensuelle de legislation et d'economie sociales. m. ISSN 0012-4699

**Centre d'Informations des Industries Lorraines**
56 Avenue de Wagram, Paris (17e), France.
- Actualites Industrielles Lorraines. bi-m. ISSN 0044-6165

**Centre de Creativite**
B.P. 237-02, 75-Paris R.P., France.
- Lettrisme. m. ISSN 0024-1423

**Centre de Demographie et Sociologie Medicales**
60 Boulevard de Latour-Maubourg, 75007 Paris (7e), France.
- Cahiers de Sociologie et de Demographie Medicales. q. ISSN 0007-9995

**Centre de Documentation de l'Armement**
26 Bd. Victor, 75996 Paris Armees, France.
- Recapitulatif Mensuel des Signalements d'Origine CEDOCAR. Series 1: Documents Rediges en Langue Francaise. m.
- Recapitulatif Mensuel des Signalements d'Origine CEDOCAR. Series 2: Documents d'Origine Etrangere. m.

**Centre de Documentation de Recherche et de Diffusion des Sciences et des Techniques Astronautiques, C.R.A.**
1 bis rue Friant, Paris(14e), France.
- Espace; techniques et informations spatiales. q. ISSN 0026-6000

**Centre de Documentation des Archives des Alpes-Maritimes**
Archives Departementales, 5 Ave. Edith Cavell, 06052 Nice, France.
- Centre de Documentation des Archives des Alpes-Maritimes. Recherches Regionales. q.

**Centre de Documentation et d'Etudes d'Histoire de l'Art Contemporain**
Musee d'Art et d'Industrie, 2 Place Louis Comte, 42, Saint-Etienne, France.
- Cahiers d'Histoire de l'Art Contemporain. Documents. 3 per yr.

**Centre de Documentation et de Recherche sur l'Asie du Sud-Est et le Monde Insulindien**
- Asie du Sud-Est et Monde Insulindien. (pub. by Mouton Publishers NE)

**Centre de Documentation et Musee Audois des Arts et Traditions Populaires**
24 rue du Palais, Carcassonne, France.
- Folklore; revue d'ethnographie meridionale. q. ISSN 0015-5888

**Centre de Documentation Internationale des Industries Utilisatrices de Produits Agricoles**
- C D I U P A. Bulletin Bibliographique. (pub. by Association pour la Promotion Industrie-Agriculture)

**Centre de Documentation Juive Contemporaine**
17 rue Geoffroy-l'Asnier, 75004 Paris, France.
- Monde Juif. q. ISSN 0026-9425

**Centre de Documentation Siderurgique**
6 rue de Lota, 75116 Paris, France.
- Centre de Documentation Siderurgigue. Bulletin Analytique. m. ISSN 0007-4063
- Centre de Documentation Siderurgique. Circulaire d'Informations Techniques. m. ISSN 0008-963X

**Centre de Formation des Journalistes**
29 rue du Louvre, Paris (2e), France.
- Centre de Formation des Journalistes. Feuillets. q. ISSN 0008-9648

**Centre de l'Industrie Francaise des Travaux Publics**
3 rue de Berri, Paris (8e), France.
- T P Annales. m. ISSN 0039-8462 (Federation Nationale des Travaux Publics et des Syndicats Affilies)

**Centre de Mathematique, Methodologie, Informatique**
Institut de l'Environnement, 14-20 rue Erasme, Paris 75005, France.
- Notes Methodologiques en Architecuture et en Urbanisme. 5 per yr.

**Centre de Mathematique Sociale et de Statistique**
- Mathematiques et Sciences Humaines. (pub. by Centrale des Revues Dunod Gauthier Villars)

**Centre de Perfectionnement pour les Industries du Bois. Service d'Observation Economique**
10, Avenue de Saint Mande, 75012 Paris, France.
- S.O.E.-Bois; service d'observation economique des industries du bois. m.

**Centre de Presse d'Information et de Promotion**
8, Rue St Marc, 75002 Paris, France.
- A B C Decor. m.(10 per yr.) ISSN 0044-5614

**Centre de Productivite dans l'Industrie des Moules et Modeles**
15 rue Beaujon, 75008 Paris, France.
- Moules et Modeles. q. (Syndicat National des Constructeurs de Moules et Modeles)

**Centre de Recherche et d'Action Sociale**
14 rue d'Assas, 75 Paris (6e), France.
- Cahiers de l'Actualite Religieuse et Sociale. bi-m. ISSN 0007-9669
- Projet. m. ISSN 0033-0884

**Centre de Recherche et de Documentation Pedagogiques, Bordeaux**
75, Cours d'Alsace- et- Lorraine, 33075 Bordeaux, France.
- Centre Regional de Documentation Pedagogique de Bordeaux. Messages. s-a.
- SELICAV; selection d'informations pour la communication audio-visuelle. 5 per yr.

**Centre de Recherche pour Un Tresor de la Langue Francaise**
- Bulletin Analytique de Linguistique Francaise. (pub. by Editions Klincksieck)

**Centre de Recherches Cooperatives**
- Archives Internationales de Sociologie de la Cooperation et du Developpement. (pub. by Bureau d'Etudes Cooperatives et Communautaires)

**Centre de Recherches de Politique Criminelle**
- Archives de Politique Criminelle. (pub. by Editions A. Pedone)

**Centre de Recherches et d'Etudes de Psychologie des Peuples et de Sociologie Economique**
56 rue Anatole-France, Le Havre 76600, France.
- Ethnopsychologie; revue de psychologie des peuples. 4 per yr. ISSN 0046-2608

**Centre de Recherches et d'Etudes Oceanographiques**
73-77, rue de Sevres, 92100 Boulogne-sur-Seine, France.
- Centre de Recherches et d'Etudes Oceanographiques. Travaux. q. ISSN 0008-9680
- Corrosion Marine - Fouling. s-a.
- Lithoclastia. s-a.

**Centre de Recherches et de Documentation Cartographiques et Geographiques**
- Annuaire des Geographes de la France et de l'Afrique Francophone. (pub. by Institut de Geographie, Paris. Bibliotheque)

**Centre de Recherches et de Documentation sur la Consommation**
- Consommation. (pub. by Centrale des Revues Dunod Gauthier-Villars)

**Centre de Recherches Science et Vie**
2 rue de la Baume, 75008 Paris, France.
- Centre de Recherches Science et Vie. Cahiers. q.

**Centre de Recherches sur l'URSS et les Pays de l'Est**
- Annuaire de l'URSS et des Pays Socialistes Europeens. (pub. by Librairie Istra)

**Centre de Relations Internationales Culturelles (C.R.I.C.)**
3 rue Pasteur, 78800 Houilles, France.
- Ambiance de Paris. w. (except Jul. & Aug.) ISSN 0002-6948

**Centre des Democrates Sociaux**
- Democratie Moderne. (pub. by Editions et Publicite France-Etranger)

**Centre Europeen d'Information et de Documentation du Vehicule**
53 Avenue Charles-de-Gaulle, 92200 Neuilly, France.
- Information du Vehicule. m.

**Centre Francais de Criminologie**
12 Avenue Rockfeller, 69 Lyon (8e), France.
- Instantanes Criminologiques. q. ISSN 0020-2134 (Association Francaise de Criminologie)

**Centre Francais du Commerce Exterieur**
- M.O.C.I. (pub. by Societe d'Edition de Documentation Economique et Commerciale (S. E. D. E. C))

**Centre Genealogique de Midi-Provence**
13110 Port-de-Bouc, France.
- Centre Genealogique de Midi-Provence Annuaire. Bulletin; liaisons et information. q.
- Centre Genealogique de Midi-Provence. Cahier Genealogique; travaux de membres. irreg.

**Centre Hospitalier**
B.P. 24, 76083 le Havre, France.
- Archives Medicales de Normandie. 10 per yr. ISSN 0044-8702

**Centre Information Europeen**
66 Route d'Olivet, 45100- Orleans, France.
- Ressac; bulletin d'information inter-europeen. bi-m. ISSN 0034-5741

**Centre International d'Etude des Textiles Anciens**
34 rue de la Charite, Lyon (2e), France.
- Centre International d'Etude des Textiles Anciens. Bulletin de Liaison. s-a. ISSN 0008-980X

**Centre International de Documentation Arachnologique**
61 rue de Buffon, Paris 5e, France.
- Annuaire des Arachnologistes Mondiaux; acarologistes exceptes. triennial. ISSN 0066-2739
- Centre International de Documentation Arachnologique. Liste des Travaux Arachnologiques. a. ISSN 0085-2783

**Centre International de l'Enfance**
see **International Children's Centre**

**Centre International de Liaison des Ecoles de Cinema et de Television**
92 Champs Elysees, Paris, France.
- Centre International de Liaison des Ecoles de Cinema et de Television. Bulletin d'Informations. irreg. ISSN 0528-4759

**Centre International de Synthese**
- Revue d'Histoire des Sciences et de Leurs Applications. (pub. by Presses Universitaires de France)
- Revue de Synthese. (pub. by Editions Albin Michel)

**Centre International de Synthese du Baroque**
30 rue de la Banque, Montauban, France.
- Baroque; revue internationale. biennial. ISSN 0067-4222

**Centre Lyonnais d'Acupuncture de Saint-Luc**
- Centre Lyonnais d'Acupuncture de Saint-Luc. Bulletin de Liaison. (pub. by Auguste Nguyen)

**Centre National d'Art et de Culture. Centre de Creation Industrielle**
- Traverses. (pub. by Editions de Minuit)

**Centre National d'Etudes et d'Experimentation de Machinisme Agricole**
Parc de Tourvoie, 92160 Antony, France.
- Bulletin Bibliographique International du Machinisme Agricole/International Farm Machinery Abstracts. 10 per yr. with quarterly supplements. ISSN 0007-4160 (International Commission of Agricultural Engineering)
- C. N. E. E. M. A. Bulletin d'Information. 10-12 per yr. ISSN 0007-8727
- C. N. E. E. M. A. Etudes. 10-12 per yr. ISSN 0007-8735
- C N E E M A Nouvelles. 5 per yr. ISSN 0007-8743

**Centre National d'Etudes Spatiales**
129 rue de l'Universite, 75007 Paris, France.
- Centre National d'Etudes Spatiales, Paris. Rapport d'Activite. a. ISSN 0069-2034

**Centre National d'Information pour la Readaptation**
10, rue de Sevres, 75007 Paris, France.
- Readaptation. m(10 per yr) (Co-sponsor: Office National d'Information sur les Enseignements et les Professions)

**Centre National de l'Enseignement Religieux (C.N.E.R.)**
- Points de Repere. (pub. by Bayard Presse)

**Centre National de la Cinematographie**
12 rue de Lubeck, 75784 Paris Cedex 16, France.
- Centre National de la Cinematographie. Bulletin d'Information. 5 per yr. ISSN 0008-9834

**Centre National de la Recherche Scientifique**
15 Quai Anatole France, 75700 Paris, France (Orders to: Ed. Max Vachon, 61 rue de Buffon, 75005 Paris, France)
- Acarologia. q. ISSN 0044-586X (Co-Sponsor: Museum National d'Histoire Naturelle)
- Animaux de Laboratoire. Revue Bibliographique. m. ISSN 0003-3650
- Annales de Geophysique. q. ISSN 0003-4029
- Annales de la Nutrition et de l'Alimentation. s-a. ISSN 0003-4037
- Annuaire de l'Afrique du Nord. a. ISSN 0066-2607
- Annuaire de Legislation Francaise et Etrangere. a. ISSN 0066-2658 (Service de Recherches Juridiques Comparatives)
- Annuaire Francais de Droit International. a. ISSN 0066-3085 (Academie de Droit International de la Haye. Groupe Francais des Anciens Auditeurs NE)
- Antiquites Africaines. a. ISSN 0066-4871
- Archives de Sciences Sociales des Religions. s-a. (Groupe de Sociologie des Religions)
- Archives de Zoologie Experimentale et Generale. q. ISSN 0003-9667
- Bibliographie Annuelle de l'Histoire de France. a. ISSN 0067-6918
- Bibliographie Geographique Internationale. irreg., 1973, vol. 79. ISSN 0067-6993 (International Geographical Union)
- Bulletin Signaletique. Part 530: Repertoire d'Art et d'Archeologie. Nouvelle Serie. a. ISSN 0080-0953 (Centre National de la Recherche Scientifique. Centre de Documentation Sciences Humaines) (Co-sponsor: Comite Francaise d'Histoire de l'Art)
- Cahiers de Micropaleontologie. irreg. ISSN 0068-5054 (Ecole Pratique des Hautes Etudes. Laboratoire de Micropaleontologie)
- Cahiers Nepalais. irreg. ISSN 0068-5194
- Centre Geologique et Geophysique de Montpellier. Publications. Serie Geologie. irreg.
- Centre National de la Recherche Scientifique. Colloques Internationaux. Sciences Humaines. irreg; several a. year. ISSN 0069-1976
- Centre National de la Recherche Scientifique. Colloques Internationaux. Sciences Mathematiques, Physiques, Chimiques, Biologiques et Medicales. irreg.
- Centre National de la Recherche Scientifique. Rapport d'Activite. a. ISSN 0071-8327
- Centre National de la Recherche Scientifique. Rapport National de Conjoncture Scientifique. a. ISSN 0071-8335
- Centre National de la Recherche Scientifique. Tableau de Classement des Chercheurs. irreg. ISSN 0071-8351
- Courrier du C.N.R.S. q.
- Droit de l'Espace. (pub. by Editions Techniques et Economiques)
- Economie de l'Energie. m. ISSN 0046-1202
- Etudes Anglaises. (pub. by Librairie Marcel Didier)
- Etudes Celtiques. (pub. by Societe d'Edition les Belles Lettres)
- France. Centre National de Coordination des Etudes et Recherches sur la Nutrition et l'Alimentation. Cahiers Techniques. irreg., 1972, no. 16. ISSN 0071-8297
- France. Centre National de la Recherche Scientifique. Colloques Nationaux. irreg., 1975, no. 933. ISSN 0071-8319
- France. Service de Documentation et de Cartographie Geographiques. Memoires et Documents. irreg. ISSN 0071-8262
- Gallia; fouilles et monuments archeologiques en France metropolitaine. s-a. ISSN 0016-4119
- Gallia. Supplement. irreg., 1974, no. 27. ISSN 0072-0119
- Gallia Prehistoire; fouilles et monuments archeologiques en France metropolitaine. s-a. ISSN 0016-4127
- Gallia Prehistoire. Supplement. irreg., 1973, no. 7. ISSN 0072-0100
- Monographies Francaises de Psychologie. irreg., 1974, no. 27. ISSN 0077-071X
- Nouveau Journal de Chimie. (pub. by Centrale des Revues Dunod Gauthier-Villars)
- Protistologica. q. ISSN 0033-1821
- Recueil des Instructions Donnees aux Ambassadeurs et Ministres de France. irreg., 1970, vol. 29. ISSN 0080-0333
- Revue d'Etudes Comparatives Est-Ouest; economies et techniques de planification - droit et sciences sociales. q.
- Revue de l'Art. q. ISSN 0035-1326 (Comite Francais d'Histoire de l'Art)
- Revue Francaise de Sociologie. q. ISSN 0035-2969

**Centre National de la Recherche Scientifique. Centre d'Etudes Sociologiques**
Societe des Amis, 82 rue Cardinet, Paris (17e), France.
- Centre d'Etudes Sociologiques. Travaux et Documents. irreg. ISSN 0071-8289

**Centre National de la Recherche Scientifique. Centre de Documentation Scientifique et Technique**
Service des Abonnements, 26 rue Boyer, 75971 Paris 20, France.
- Bulletin Signaletique. Part 101: Sciences de l'Information. Documentation. m. ISSN 0301-0309
- Bulletin Signaletique. Part 110: Informatique - Automatique - Recherche Operationnelle - Gestion. m. ISSN 0301-3537
- Bulletin Signaletique. Part 120: Astronomie - Physique Spatiale - Geophysique. m. ISSN 0007-5337
- Bulletin Signaletique. Part 130: Physique Mathematique; optique, acoustique, mecanique, chaleur. m. ISSN 0397-7757
- Bulletin Signaletique. Part 140: Electrotechnique. m. ISSN 0301-3308
- Bulletin Signaletique. Part 145: Electronique. m. ISSN 0301-3316
- Bulletin Signaletique. Part 160: Physique de l'Etat Condense. m. ISSN 0301-3332
- Bulletin Signaletique. Part 161: Cristallographie. m. ISSN 0301-3340
- Bulletin Signaletique. Part 165: Atomes et Molecules. Physique des Fluides et Plasmas. m. ISSN 0398-9968
- Bulletin Signaletique. Part 170: Chimie. m. ISSN 0007-5396
- Bulletin Signaletique. Part 310: Genie Biomedical. Informatique Biomedicale. m. ISSN 0398-9941
- Bulletin Signaletique. Part 330: Sciences Pharmacologiques - Toxicologie. m. ISSN 0007-5442
- Bulletin Signaletique. Part 340: Microbiologie-Virologie-Immunologie. m. ISSN 0007-5450
- Bulletin Signaletique. Part 346: Ophtalmologie. m. ISSN 0301-3324
- Bulletin Signaletique. Part 347: Oto-Rhino-Laryngologie, Stomatologie, Pathologie Cervicofaciale. m. ISSN 0301-3375
- Bulletin Signaletique. Part 348: Dermatologie - Venereologie. m. ISSN 0301-3383
- Bulletin Signaletique. Part 349: Anesthesie. Reanimation. Choc. m. ISSN 0301-133X
- Bulletin Signaletique. Part 351: Revue Bibliographique Cancer. m. ISSN 0007-5477 (Institut Gustave Roussy)
- Bulletin Signaletique. Part 352: Maladies de l'Appareil Respiratoire du Coeur et des Vaisseaux - Chirurgie Thoracique et Vasculaire. m. ISSN 0301-3391
- Bulletin Signaletique. Part 354: Maladies de l'Appareil Digestif. Chirurgie Abdominale. m. ISSN 0301-3405
- Bulletin Signaletique. Part 355: Maladies des Reins et des Voies Urinaires - Chirurgie de l'Appareil Urinaire. m. ISSN 0301-3413
- Bulletin Signaletique. Part 356: Maladies du Systeme Nerveux Myopathies-Neurochirurgie. m. ISSN 0301-3421
- Bulletin Signaletique. Part 357: Maladies des Os et des Articulations - Chirurgie Orthopedique - Traumatologie. m. ISSN 0301-343X
- Bulletin Signaletique. Part 359: Maladies du Sang. m. ISSN 0301-3448
- Bulletin Signaletique. Part 360: Biologie Animale. Physiologie et Pathologie des Protozoaires et des Invertebres. Ecologie. m. ISSN 0397-7730
- Bulletin Signaletique. Part 361: Endocrinologie et Reproduction. m. ISSN 0007-5493
- Bulletin Signaletique. Part 362: Diabete - Maladies Metaboliques. m. ISSN 0007-5507
- Bulletin Signaletique. Part 363: Genetique. m. ISSN 0301-3464
- Bulletin Signaletique. Part 365: Physiologie des Vertebres. m. ISSN 0301-3472
- Bulletin Signaletique. Part 370: Biologie et Physiologie Vegetales. m. ISSN 0007-5515
- Bulletin Signaletique. Part 380: Agronomie - Zootechnie - Phytopathologie - Industries Alimentaires. m. ISSN 0007-5523
- Bulletin Signaletique. Part 390: Psychologie - Psychopathologie - Psychiatrie. m. ISSN 0007-5531
- Bulletin Signaletique. Part 730: Combustibles - Energie. m. ISSN 0007-5647

- Bulletin Signaletique. Part 740: Metaux -
  Metallurgie. m. ISSN 0007-5655
- Bulletin Signaletique. Part 745: Soudage, Brasage
  et Techniques Connexes. m. ISSN 0301-3480
- Bulletin Signaletique. Part 761: Microscopie
  Electronique-Diffraction Electronique. m. ISSN
  0007-5663
- Bulletin Signaletique. Part 780: Polymeres.
  Peintures. Bois. Cuirs. m. ISSN 0397-7730
- Bulletin Signaletique. Part 880: Genie Chimique -
  Industries Chimique et Parachimique. m. ISSN
  0007-568X
- Bulletin Signaletique. Part 885: Nuisances. m.
  ISSN 0301-3499
- Bulletin Signaletique. Part 890: Industries
  Mecaniques-Batiment-Travaux Public-Transports.
  m.
- Bulletin Signaletique. Part 900: Bulletin des
  Traductions. Traductions Effectuees dans les
  Services et Centres Francais et Canadiens de
  Documentation. m. ISSN 0301-3502
- Bulletin Signaletique-Bibliographie des Sciences de
  la Terre. Section 220. Cahier A. Mineralogie,
  Geochimie, Geologie Extraterrestre. m. ISSN
  0300-9262 (France. Bureau de Recherches
  Geologiques et Minieres)
- Bulletin Signaletique-Bibliographie des Sciences de
  la Terre. Section 221. Gisements Metalliques et
  Non Metalliques. m. ISSN 0304-1301 (France.
  Bureau de Recherches Geologiques et Minieres)
- Bulletin Signaletique-Bibliographie des Sciences de
  la Terre. Section 222. Cahier C. Roches
  Cristallines. m. ISSN 0300-9289 (France. Bureau
  de Recherches Geologiques et Minieres)
- Bulletin Signaletique-Bibliographie des Sciences de
  la Terre. Section 223. Cahier D. Roches
  Sedimentaires, Geologie Marine. m. ISSN 0300-
  9297 (France. Bureau de Recherches Geologiques
  et Minieres)
- Bulletin Signaletique-Bibliographie des Sciences de
  la Terre. Section 224. Cahier E. Stratigraphie,
  Geologie Regionale et Generale. m. ISSN 0300-
  9300 (France. Bureau de Recherches Geologiques
  et Minieres)
- Bulletin Signaletique-Bibliographie des Sciences de
  la Terre. Section 225. Cahier F. Tectonique. m.
  ISSN 0300-9319 (France. Bureau de Recherches
  Geologiques et Minieres)
- Bulletin Signaletique-Bibliographie des Sciences de
  la Terre. Section 226. Cahier G. Hydrologie,
  Geologie de l'Ingenieur, Formations Superficielles.
  m. ISSN 0300-9327 (France. Bureau de
  Recherches Geologiques et Minieres)
- Bulletin Signaletique-Bibliographie des Sciences de
  la Terre. Section 227. Cahier H. Paleontologie. m.
  ISSN 0300-9335 (France. Bureau de Recherches
  Geologiques et Minieres)

**Centre National de la Recherche Scientifique. Centre
de Documentation Sciences Humaines**
54 Bd. Raspail, 75260- Paris, France.
- Bulletin Signaletique. Part 519: Philosophie. q.
  ISSN 0007-554X
- Bulletin Signaletique. Part 520: Sciences de
  l'Education. q. ISSN 0007-5558
- Bulletin Signaletique. Part 521: Sociologie -
  Ethnologie. q. ISSN 0007-5566
- Bulletin Signaletique. Part 522: Histoire des
  Sciences et des Techniques. q. ISSN 0007-5574
- Bulletin Signaletique. Part 523: Histoire et Science
  de la Litterature. q. ISSN 0007-5582
- Bulletin Signaletique. Part 524: Sciences du
  Langage. q. ISSN 0007-5590
- Bulletin Signaletique. Part 525: Prehistoire. q.
  ISSN 0007-5604
- Bulletin Signaletique. Part 526: Art et
  Archeologie; proche-Orient, Asie, Amerique. q.
  ISSN 0007-5612
- Bulletin Signaletique. Part 527: Sciences
  Religieuses. q. ISSN 0007-5620
- Bulletin Signaletique. Part 528: Science
  Administrative. q. ISSN 0007-5639
- Bulletin Signaletique. Part 530: Repertoire d'Art
  et d'Archeologie. Nouvelle Serie. (pub. by Centre
  National de la Recherche Scientifique)

**Centre National de la Recherche Scientifique. Centre
de Geomorphologie**
Caen, France.
- Centre de Geomorphologie, Caen. Bulletin. irreg.
  ISSN 0068-4791

**Centre National de la Recherche Scientifique.
Seminaire d'Econometrie**
15 Quai Anatole-France, 75700 Paris, France.
- Centre National de la Recherche Scientifique.
  Seminaire d'Econometrie. Cahiers. irreg. ISSN
  0071-8343

- Centre National de la Recherche Scientifique.
  Seminaire d'Econometrie. Monographies. irreg.
  ISSN 0071-8270

**Centre National de Prevention et de Protection**
5 rue Daunou, 75002 Paris, France.
- Face au Risque. m. ISSN 0014-6269

**Centre National des Vocations Francais**
106 rue du Bac, 75341 Paris, France.
- Annuaire des Instituts de Religieuses en France.
  irreg., latest issue, 1970. ISSN 0066-2860
- Semailles; fond commun. q. ISSN 0037-1734
- Vocation. q. ISSN 0042-7756

**Centre National du Commerce Exterieur**
10 Av. d'Iena, Paris 16e, France.
- Centre National du Commerce Exterieur.
  Annuaire. a. ISSN 0071-836X
- Fiches Analytiques de la Presse Technique
  Francaise. irreg. ISSN 0071-4704

**Centre National Esperanto**
46 bis, Bld. Alexandre-Martin, B.P. 2002, 45010
Orleans, France.
- Gazeto. irreg. ISSN 0072-0356

**Centre Regional d'Etudes Occitanes-Provence**
6 Traverse Cas, 13004 Marseille, France.
- Centre Regional d'Etudes Occitanes-Provence.
  Bulletin Pedagogique. q.

**Centre Regional de Documentation Pedagogique**
92 rue d'Antrain, 35000 Rennes, France.
- Centre Regional de Documentation Pedagogique.
  Studi. 4 per yr.

**Centre Regional de Documentation Pedagogique de
Poitiers**
Laboratoire Geologie-Mineralogie, Facultes des
Sciences, 40 Av. Recteur Pineau, Poitiers, France.
- Bulletin des Sciences de la Terre. irreg., 1969, no.
  10. ISSN 0068-404X

**Centre Regional de Documentation Pedagogique de
Reims**
47 rue Simon, 51063 Reims, France.
- Centre Regional de Documentation Pedagogique
  de Reims. Bulletin. irreg. ISSN 0084-8670

**Centre Regional de Documentation Pedagogique de
Toulouse**
3 rue Roquelaine, Toulouse, France.
- Centre Regional de Documentation Pedagogique
  de Toulouse. Annales; dossier d'information et de
  Perfectionnement (Francais-Mathematiques) irreg.
  ISSN 0069-2069

**Centre Regional de la Productivite et des Etudes
Economiques. Faculte de Droit et des Sciences
Economiques**
39 rue de l'Universite, 34060 Montpellier, France.
- Revue de l'Economie Meridionale. q. ISSN 0035-
  1369

**Centre Regional de Recherche et de Documentation
Pedagogique de Besancon**
B.P. 1153, 16-17 Rue Renan, 25003 Besancon
Cedex, France.
- Centre Regional de Recherche et de
  Documentation Pedagogique de Besancon.
  Bulletin de Liaison des Professeurs d'Allemand. 2
  per yr.
- Centre Regional de Recherche et de
  Documentation Pedagogique de Besancon.
  Bulletin de Liaison des Professeurs de Biologie et
  de Geologie. 2 per yr.
- Centre Regional de Recherche et de
  Documentation Pedagogique de Besancon.
  Bulletin de Liaison des Professeurs de
  Technologie. 2 per yr.
- Centre Regional de Recherche et Documentation
  Pedagogique de Besancon. Bulletin de Liaison des
  Professeurs d'Education Physique et Sportive. 2
  per yr.

**Centre Regional de Recherche et de Documentation
Pedagogiques de Lyon**
47-49 rue Philippe-De-Lassalle, 69 Lyon (4e),
France.
- Centre Regional de Recherche et de
  Documentation Pedagogiques de Lyon. Annales.
  irreg. ISSN 0069-2050

**Centre Saint Irenee**
2 Place Gailleton, 69002 Lyon, France.
- Foyers Mixtes; informations et reflexions pour un
  oecumenisme vecu. q. ISSN 0015-9239

**Centre Scientifique et Technique du Batiment**
4 Av. du Recteur Poincare, 75782 Paris Cedex 16,
France.
- Centre Scientifique et Technique du Batiment.
  Cahiers. 10 per yr. ISSN 0008-9850
- Centre Scientifique et Technique du Batiment.
  Repertoire des Cahiers et des Avis Techniques
  Publies. a.

**Centre Soeren Kierkegaard**
- Exister. (pub. by Publications Periodiques
  Specialisees)

**Centre Technique de la Teinture et du Nettoyage
(CTTN)**
Avenue Gambetta, 69250 Neuville-Sur-Saone,
France.
- Entretien des Textiles. m. ISSN 0046-2179

**Centre Technique de Publications**
8 rue de Berri, 75008 Paris, France.
- Revetements Sols et Murs. q. ISSN 0034-6314

**Centre Technique des Tuiles et Briques**
- Terre Cuite. (pub. by Editions R. Franck)

**Centre Technique du Bois**
10 Av. de Saint Mande, 75012-Paris, France.
- Centre Technique du Bois. Bulletin
  Bibliographique. 5 per yr. ISSN 0008-9869
- Centre Technique du Bois. Bulletin d'Informations
  Techniques. q. ISSN 0008-9877
- Centre Technique du Bois. Cahiers. 3-6 nos.per.
  yr. ISSN 0008-9885
- Courrier de l'Exploitant Forestier et du Scieur. q.
- Courrier de l'Industriel du Bois et de
  l'Ameublement. q.

**Centre Technique du Cuir**
DIF 181, Avenue Jean-Jaures, B.P. No. 1, 69342
Lyon, France.
- Centre Technique du Cuir. Bibliographie
  Analytique et Signaletique. m. ISSN 0006-1328
- Technicuir. (pub. by S. E. T. I. C.)

**Centre Technique du Papier**
175X Centre de Tri, 38042 Grenoble, France.
- Centre Technique du Papier. Fueillets
  Bibliographiques. m.

**Centre Technique du Zinc**
34 rue Collange, 92307 Levallois-Perret, France.
- Centre Technique du Zinc. Bulletin Analytique. q.

**Centre Technique Forestier Tropical**
45 bis, Ave. de la Belle Gabrielle, 94-Nogent sur
Marne, France.
- Bois et Forets des Tropiques. bi-m. ISSN 0006-
  579X

**Centre Technique Industriel de la Construction
Metallique**
20 rue Jean Jaures, 92807 Puteaux, France.
- CTICM-Construction Metallique. q.

**Editions du Centurion**
17 rue du Babylone, Paris 7e, France.
- Religion et Sciences de l'Homme. irreg. ISSN
  0080-0864

**CERCHAR**
*see* Centre d'Etudes et Recherches des
Charbonnages de France

**Cercle Culturel et Artisanal de Bonaguil**
Chateau de Bonaguil, Saint Front sur Lemance,
47500 Fumel, France.
- Barbacane; revue des pierres et des hommes. a.

**Cercle de la Librairie**
117, Bd Saint-Germain, 75279 Paris Cedex 06,
France.
- Amicale des Cadres de l'Imprimerie. q.
- Bibliographie de la France. (Biblio); journal officiel
  du livre francais. w. (with monthly and quarterly
  supplements) ISSN 0006-1344
- Guide des Prix Litteraires. irreg., 1965, 5th ed.
  ISSN 0072-8020 (Syndicat des Industries du
  Livres)
- Livres de l'Annee/BIBLIO. a. ISSN 0076-0145
- Repertoire International des Editeurs et Diffuseurs
  de Langue Francaise. a.

**Cercle du Bibliophile**
22 rue de Cocherel, Evreux, France.
- Classiques Immortels. irreg. ISSN 0069-455X
- Grandes Heures de l'Histoire. irreg. ISSN 0072-
  5412

- Humoresque. irreg. ISSN 0073-3954
- Livres Qui Ont Fait le Monde. irreg. ISSN 0076-0161

**Cercle Ernest-Renan**
3 rue Recamier, 75341 Paris Cedex 07, France.
- Cercle Ernest-Renan. Cahiers. bi-m. ISSN 0008-0098

**Cercle Europe de la Faculte de Droit et des Sciences Economiques de Paris**
92 rue d'Assas, Paris 6e, France.
- Europa. Revue de Presse Europeenne. irreg. ISSN 0071-2299

**Cercle Europeen du Livre**
213 bis Boulevard Saint-Germain, 7500 Paris, France.
- Chefs-d'Oeuvre Interdits. irreg. ISSN 0069-2859

**Cercle Fustec de Coulanges**
4 Avenue de Louvois, 92 Chaille, France.
- Cercle Fustec de Coulanges. Documents. s-a.

**Cercle International de la Pensee et des Arts Francais**
58310 St. Amand-en-Puisaye, France.
- Presence des Lettres et des Arts. bi-m. ISSN 0032-7654

**Cercle Occitan d'Auvergne**
29 Bd Gergovia, 63037 Clermont-Ferrand, France.
- Biza Neira (Bise Noire); sur l'auvergne et la civilisation d'oc. q. ISSN 0398-9453

**Cercle Rene Schickele**
31 rue Oberlin, 67000 Strasbourg, France.
- Cahiers du Bilinguisme/Land und Sproch. 6 per yr. ISSN 0045-3773

**Editions du Cerf**
29 Bd. Latour-Maubourg, Paris (7e), France.
- Bible et Son Message. 10 per yr. ISSN 0006-0704
- Fetes et Saisons. 10 per yr. ISSN 0015-0371
- Maison-Dieu; revue de Pastorale Liturgique. q. ISSN 0025-0937
- Le Supplement. q.
- Vie Spirituelle. 6 per yr. ISSN 0042-5613

**Cethedec**
26 Bd. Victor, 75996 Paris Armees, France.
- Revue du Cethedec. bi-m. ISSN 0035-2535

**Editions de Chabassol**
30 rue de Gramont, 75002 Paris, France.
- Annuaire Dentaire. a. ISSN 0066-2712
- Industries Nautiques. q. ISSN 0019-9389 (Federation des Industries Nautiques)
- Syndicat General des Industries Medico - Chirurgicales et Dentaires. Annuaire. a. ISSN 0396-0382

**Chaillot Theatre National**
Place du Trocadero, 75116 Paris, France.
- Journal de Chaillot. 8 per yr.

**Chambefort Edition**
B.P. 1244, 69607 Villeurbanne, France.
- Institut Pasteur de Lyon. Revue. q. ISSN 0020-2487

**Chambre de Commerce Britannique**
see **British Chamber of Commerce**

**Chambre de Commerce et d'Industrie d'Angers**
8, Bd du Roi-Rene, 49000 Angers, France.
- Anjou Economique. m.

**Chambre de Commerce et d'Industrie d'Auxerre. Informations Economiques**
2 bis, Boulevard Davout, 89000 Auxerre, France.
- Chambre de Commerce et d'Industrie d'Auxerre. Documentation Economique. m.

**Chambre de Commerce et d'Industrie de Cambrai**
Place de la Republique, 59407 Cambrai, France.
- Bulletin Economique du Cambresis. q. ISSN 0007-4578

**Chambre de Commerce et d'Industrie de Dunkerque**
1, Quai Freycinet, 59140 Dunkerque, France.
- Inter 8000. q.

**Chambre de Commerce et d'Industrie de Marseille**
Palais de la Bourse, 13231 Marseille Cedex 1, France.
- Centre de Conjoncture Africaine et Malgache. Bulletin d'Information. m. ISSN 0008-9621

- Chambre de Commerce et d'Industrie de Marseille. Cahiers de Documentation. 5 per yr. ISSN 0009-1200
- Commerce Exterieur des Regions Provence, Cote d'Azur et Corse. a.

**Chambre de Commerce et d'Industrie de Meurthe-et-Moselle**
40 rue Henri-Poincare, 54042 Nancy, France.
- Chambre de Commerce et d'Industrie de Meurthe-et-Moselle. Bulletin Mensuel. m. ISSN 0009-1189

**Chambre de Commerce et d'Industrie de Paris**
27 Av. de Friedland, 75008 Paris, France.
- Annuaires Francais et Listes d'Adresses Susceptibles d'Interesser le Commerce et l'Industrie. irreg. ISSN 0066-3743
- Chambre de Commerce et d'Industrie de Paris. Bulletin Mensuel. m. ISSN 0009-1219
- Chambre de Commerce et d'Industrie de Paris. Contribution des Employeurs a l'Effort de Construction. irreg.

**Chambre de Commerce et d'Industrie de Rouen**
Boite Postale 641, 76 Rouen, France.
- Chambre de Commerce et d'Industrie de Rouen. Bulletin Economique. m. ISSN 0009-1227

**Chambre de Commerce et d'Industrie de Strasbourg**
10, Place Gutenberg, 67081 Strasbourg, France.
- Point Economique. m.

**Chambre de Commerce et d'Industrie de Toulouse-Midi-Pyrenee**
2 rue d'Alsace-Lorraine, 31000 Toulouse, France.
- Bulletin Economique du Midi. s-m.

**Chambre de Commerce et d'Industrie du Doubs**
7 rue Charles Nodier, 25042 Besancon, France.
- Realities Franc-Comtoises. m.

**Chambre de Commerce France-Canada**
9 Ave. Franklin D. Roosevelt, 75008 Paris, France.
- Informations Canadiennes; les relations economiques Franco-Canadiennes. m. ISSN 0020-0433

**Chambre de Commerce France-Israel**
47 Faubourg Saint-Honore, 75008 Paris, France.
- Revue Francaise de Cooperation Economique Avec Israel. bi-m. ISSN 0080-2506

**Chambre de Commerce Franco-Asiatique**
94 rue St. Lazare, 75009 Paris, France.
- Asie Nouvelle. w. ISSN 0004-4725
- Chambre de Commerce Franco-Asiatique. Annuaire des Membres. a. ISSN 0069-2557

**Chambre de Commerce Franco-Neerlandaise**
109 Bld. Malesherbes, 75008 Paris, France.
- France Pays-Bas Informations Rapides. 1-5 per mo. ISSN 0046-4945

**Chambre de Commerce Franco-Sovietique**
22, Avenue Franklin-D.-Roosevelt, 75008 Paris, France.
- Commerce et Cooperation. q.

**Chambre de Commerce Italienne de Paris**
134 rue du Faubourg Saint-Honore, Paris 8e, France.
- Annuaire Franco-Italien. biennial. ISSN 0066-3115

**Chambre de Commerce Suedoise en France**
125 Av. des Champs-Elysees, Paris 8e, France.
- Chambre de Commerce Suedoise en France. Annuaire. a. ISSN 0069-2573

**Chambre de Commerce Suisse en France**
16 Av. de l'Opera, 75001 Paris, France.
- Annuaire Franco-Suisse. biennial. ISSN 0066-3123
- Revue Economique Franco Suisse. q. ISSN 0035-2799

**Chambre de Metiers de l'Ain**
3, rue P.-Piola, Bourg (Ain), France.
- Metiers. bi-m.

**Chambre de Metiers Departementale**
- Guide-Annuaire Officiel de l'Artisanat et des Metiers. (pub. by Union Francaise d'Annuaires Professionnels)
- Guide de l'Artisan. (pub. by Union Francaise d'Annuaires Professionnels)

**Chambre de Metiers du Rhone**
58, Av. Marechal Foch, 69453 Lyon Cedex 3, France.
- Carrefour des Metiers. m.

**Chambre des Ingenieurs-Conseils de France**
3 rue Leon Bonnat, 75016 Paris, France.
- Chambre des Ingenieurs-Conseils de France. Annuaire. a. ISSN 0069-2611
- Societe des Ingenieurs-Conseils de France en Genie Civil. Bulletin d'Information SICOFEG. q.

**Chambre Officielle Franco Allemande de Commerce et d'Industrie**
91 rue de Miromesnil, 75008 Paris, France.
- Chambre Officielle Franco Allemande de Commerce et d'Industrie. Liste des Membres/ Offizielle Deutsch-Franzoesische Industrie- und Handelskammer. Mitgliederliste. a. ISSN 0069-2581
- Guide Annuaire du Commerce Franco-Allemand/ Jahrbuch fuer den Deutsch-Franzoesischen Handel. irreg., 1965, 2nd ed. ISSN 0072-7962
- Revue Economique Franco-Allemande/Zeitschrift der Deutsch-Franzoesischen Wirtschaft. 6 per yr. ISSN 0048-8038

**Chambre Regionale de Commerce et d'Industrie d'Alsace**
10, Place Gutenberg, 67081 Strasbourg, France.
- Chambre Regionale de Commerce et d'Industrie d'Alsace. Rapport sur les Activites. a.

**Chambre Regionale de Commerce et d'Industrie de Haute-Normandie**
Palais des Consuls, Quai de la Bourse, Rouen, France.
- Activite Economique de la Haute-Normandie. a. ISSN 0065-1788
- Moyens de la Recherche Scientifique et Technique en Haute-Normandie. a. ISSN 0077-1775
- Qui Vend et Achete Quoi; annuaire economique de Haute Normandie. a. ISSN 0079-9270

**Chambre Regionale de Commerce et d'Industrie de Picardie**
36, rue des Otages, 80037 Amiens Cedex, France.
- Picardie Information. q.

**Chambre Syndicale des Agents de Change**
- Bourse de Paris. Statistiques Mensuelles. (pub. by Societe de Documentation et d'Analyses Financieres (D.A.F.S.A.))

**Chambre Syndicale des Constructeurs de Navires et de Machines Marines**
47, rue de Monceau, 75008 Paris, France.
- Construction Navale; rapport du conseil d'administration, assemblee generale ordinaire. irreg.

**Chambre Syndicale des Editeurs d'Annuaires**
28 rue du Docteur-Finlay, 75015 Paris, France.
- Annuaire des Annuaires. a. ISSN 0066-2720

**Chambre Syndicale des Mines de Fer de France**
15 bis, rue de Marignan, 75008 Paris, France.
- Chambre Syndicale des Mines de Fer de France. Bulletin Technique. q. ISSN 0009-126X
- Chambre Syndicale des Mines de Fer de France. Rapport d'Activite. a. ISSN 0069-259X

**Chambre Syndicale Generale de la Corderie**
- Corderie Francaise. (pub. by Editeur R. Weiss)

**Chambre Syndicale Nationale des Electriciens et Specialistes de l'Automobile**
- Chambre Syndicale Nationale des Electriciens et Specialistes de l'Automobile. Annuaire. (pub. by Electricite Automobile)

**Chambre Syndicale Nationale des Entreprises et Industries de l'Hygiene Publique**
22 rue du General-Foy, 75008 Paris, France.
- Chambre Syndicale Nationale des Entreprises et Industries de l'Hygiene Publique. Annuaire. biennial. ISSN 0069-2603

**Chambre Syndicale Nationale des Representants Agents et Cadres de la Vente Exterieure**
30 Bd. Bonne Nouvelle, Paris (10e), France.
- Tribune Libre. m. ISSN 0041-2872

**Chambre Syndicale Nationale du Commerce et de la Reparation Automobile**
75, rue Voltaire, 92300 Levallois, France.
- Commerce-Reparation Automobile. w.

**Chambre Syndicate des Producteurs de Fer-Blanc et de Fer-Noir**
5, rue Paul-Cezanne, 75008 Paris, France.
• Fer-Blanc en France et dans le Monde. a. ISSN 0085-0519

**Librairie Honore Champion**
7 Quai Malaquais, 75006 Paris, France.
• Provence Historique. q. ISSN 0033-1856 (Federation Historique de Provence)

**Champion d'Afrique**
23 rue Daubenton, 75005 Paris, France.
• Champion d'Afrique. bi-m.

**Chancerel Editions**
4 rue Aumont- Thieville, 75017 Paris, France.
• Prevention Routiere. m. ISSN 0032-8022

**Changer le Cinema**
15 rue des Ursulines, 75005 Paris, France.
• Changer le Cinema. m. ISSN 0339-8978

**Chantemerle**
31 rue Frederic Mistral, 26110 Nyons, France.
• Monde Alpin et Rhodanien; revue regionale d'ethnologie. q.

**Chantiers du Cardinal**
106 rue du Bac, Paris (7e), France.
• Chantiers du Cardinal. q. ISSN 0009-160X

**Editions Chasse Sports**
28 rue de l'Ermitage, Paris (20e), France.
• Nos Chasses. m. ISSN 0048-0835

**Editions du Chastaing**
23 Quai Penthievre-B.P. 51, 45110 Chateauneuf sur Loire, France.
• Arboriculture Fruitiere. m. ISSN 0003-794X

**Publicite Paul Chatelain**
63 rue de la Republique, 69288 Lyon Cedex 1, France.
• Lyon Medical. fortn. ISSN 0024-7790 (Societe Medicale des Hopitaux de Lyon) (Co-Sponsor: Societe Medico-Chirurgicale des Hospitaux de Saint-Etienne)
• Lyon Pharmaceutique. bi-m. ISSN 0024-7804

**F. Chatillon, Pub.**
Palais de l'Universite, France.
• Revue du Moyen Age Latin. irreg.

**Chaussons et Petits Rats**
10 rue Huguenot, 34000 Montpellier, France.
• Pour la Danse. bi-m.

**Chemin**
Parc Saint-Maur, B4 Av General Gouraud 83, Toulon, France.
• Chemin. q. ISSN 0009-2908

**Choix Artistique et Litteraire**
c/o Jean Aubert Ed., 3, Place de la Liberation, 95 Groslay, France.
• Choix Artistique et Litteraire. q. ISSN 0009-5001

**Chretiens dans le Monde Rural**
21, rue du Faubourg-Saint-Antoine, 75541 Paris, France.
• Eglise Aujourd'hui; en monde rural. m.

**Chronique des Lettres Francaises**
33 rue de Verneuil, Paris 7e, France.
• Bibliographie des Auteurs Modernes de Langue Francaise. irreg.

**Chronique Sociale de France**
7, rue du Plat, 69288 Lyon Cedex 1, France.
• A l'Ecoute du Monde Chronique Sociale. m.

**Cie Electro-Mecanique**
37 rue du Rocher, 75383 Paris, France.
• Techniques C E M. q. ISSN 0040-1293

**Cimaise**
c/o J. R. Arnaud, Ed., 212 Bd. Saint-Germain, Paris (7e), France.
• Cimaise; art et architecture actuels. bi-m. ISSN 0009-6830

**Cinethique**
B.P. 65, 75722 Paris Cedex 15, France.
• Cinethique. q.

**Civilisation Libertaire**
c/o Gaston Leval, 33, Bd. Edgar-Quinet, 75014 Paris, France
• Civilisation Libertaire; cahiers d'etudes sociologiques. bi-m.

**Civitec**
1134 rue de Rivoli, 75 Paris (1er), France.
• Nouvelles de Chretiente; notes, documents. w. ISSN 0029-487X

**Claude Bernard Guide Europeen de l'Immobilier**
Champigny-La-Futelaye, France.
• Guide Europeen de l'Immobilier. irreg. ISSN 0072-808X

**Editions Clayton**
99, rue de Richelieu, 75002 Paris, France.
• Revue Francaise Immobiliere. bi-m.

**La Cle des Champs**
Valbonne (Alpes-Maritimes), France.
• Kryptadia: Journal of Erotic Folklore. approx. a. ISSN 0075-7160

**Editions de Clermont**
38 Bd. Raspail, Paris (7e), France.
• Design Industrie. bi-m. ISSN 0011-9385

**Club Alpin Francais**
7 rue la Boetie, Paris (8e), France.
• Montagne et Alpinisme. 4 per yr. ISSN 0047-7923

**Club Alpin Francais. Section Rhone-Alpes**
• Revue Alpine. (pub. by Publications Periodiques Specialisees)

**Club du Cirque**
11Rue Ch-Silvestri, 94300 Vincennes, France.
• Cirque dans l'Univers. q. ISSN 0009-7373

**Club du Griffon, d'Arret a Poil Dur Korthals**
1 Ave. Alphonse 13th, Paris (16e), France.
• Club du Griffon d'Arret a Poil Dur Korthal. Bulletin. q. ISSN 0009-9546

**Club Francais de la Medaille**
• Club Francais de la Medaille. (pub. by Monnaie de Paris)

**Club Pleins Feux**
22 rue de Montpensier, 75001 Paris, France.
• Specialement Votre; votre journal, vos vedettes. m. ISSN 0395-2894

**Librairie Armand Colin**
103 Bd. St-Michel, Paris (5e), France.
• Annales de Geographie. 6 per yr. ISSN 0003-4010 (Societe Geographie)
• Annales-Economies, Societes, Civilisations. 6 per yr. ISSN 0003-441X
• Bibliographie de la Litterature Francaise du Moyen Age a Nos Jours. a. ISSN 0067-6942
• Collection U. Serie Droit des Affaires et de l'Economie. irreg. ISSN 0069-5467
• Collection U. Serie Droit des Communautes Europeennes. irreg. ISSN 0069-5475
• Collection U. Serie Etudes Allemandes. irreg. ISSN 0069-5483
• Collection U. Serie Histoire Ancienne. irreg. ISSN 0069-5491
• Collection U. Serie Relations et Institutions Internationales. irreg. ISSN 0069-5505
• Ecole et la Vie. m.(10 per yr) ISSN 0012-9577
• Ecole Maternelle Francaise. m.(10 per yr.) ISSN 0012-9585
• International Bibliography of Historical Sciences. irreg., ISSN 0074-2015
• Revue d'Histoire Litteraire de la France. 6 per yr. ISSN 0035-2411 (Societe d'Histoire Litteraire de la France)
• Revue de Metaphysique et de Morale. q. ISSN 0035-1571
• Societe Francaise de Philosophie. Bulletin. 4 per yr. ISSN 0037-9352

**Collectif Jeune Cinema**
63 rue Desnonettes, 75015 Paris, France.
• Cinema Different; bulletin de liaison. m. ISSN 0339-8943

**Collections et Monnaies**
P.O. Box 15, 95220 Herblay, France.
• Collections et Monnaies. bi-m. ISSN 0339-0608

**Collectivites-Express**
26 Bd. Poissonniere, Paris 75009, France.
• Collectivites-Express. s-m. ISSN 0010-0811

**College de France. Institut des Hautes Etudes Chinoises**
• College de France. Institut des Hautes Etudes Chinoises. Memoirs. (pub. by Presses Universitaires de France)

**College de Pataphysique**
Vrigny, 51140 Jonchery-sur-Vesle, France.
• Subsidia Pataphysica. q. ISSN 0039-4386

**College Francais de Medecine Interne**
• Medecine Interne. (pub. by Nouvelles Editions Medicales Francaises (NEMF))

**College Francais de Pathologie Vasculaire**
• Journal des Maladies Vasculaires. (pub. by Masson)

**Combat pour l'Homme**
c/o Georges Krassovsky, Ed., 7 rue Boucicaut, 75015 Paris, France.
• Combat pour l'Homme. q. ISSN 0045-7469

**Combattants d'Algerie, Tunisie, Maroc**
46 rue Copernic, 75782 Paris 16, France.
• Combattant Lorrain. bi-m.

**Comedie Francaise**
Place Colette, 75001 Paris, France.
• Comedie Francaise. 10 per yr.

**Editions Comindus**
1 rue Descombes, Paris 17e, France.
• Annuaire National de l'Aviculture. a. ISSN 0066-3328
• Annuaire National des Industries de la Conserve. a. ISSN 0084-652X
• Annuaire National du Lait. a. ISSN 0084-6538

**Comite Anciens Combattants de la Resistance**
B. P. 59, 33008 Bordeaux, France.
• Cahiers de la Resistance. q. ISSN 0526-7994

**Comite Catholique des Amities Francaises dans le Monde**
99 rue de Rennes, Paris(6e), France.
• Amities Catholiques Francaises. q. ISSN 0003-1895

**Comite Central des Armateurs de France**
73 Bld. Haussmann, 75008 Paris, France.
• Annuaire de la Marine Marchande. a. ISSN 0066-2550
• Transport Maritime: Etudes et Statistiques. a.

**Comite d'Action de la Resistance**
10 rue de Charenton, 75012 Paris, France.
• Voix de la Resistance. q (plus special edts.) ISSN 0049-6685

**Comite d'Etablissement Air France-Orly Sud**
Extension Est, Batiment CRP, Aerogare d'Orly, France.
• Regards sur le Comite d'Etablissement d'Orly Sud. q. ISSN 0034-320X

**Comite d'Etudes de Defense Nationale**
c/o General M. de Brebisson, 1 Place Joffre, 75700 Paris, France.
• Defense Nationale; problemes politiques, economiques, scientifiques, militaires. m. ISSN 0035-1075

**Comite d'Etudes et d'Informations Pedagogiques de l'Education Physique et du Sport**
11 Av. du Tremblay, 75012 Paris, France.
• Education Physique et Sport. bi-m. ISSN 0013-1474

**Comite d'Organisation des Recherches Appliquees sur le Developpement Economique et Social (C O R D E S)**
• Comite d'Organisation des Recherches Appliquees sur la Developpement Economique Social. Recherches Economiques et Sociales. (pub. by Documentation Francaise)

**Comite des Travaux Historiques et Scientifiques**
61 rue de Richelieu, 75002 Paris, France.
• Liste des Societes Savantes et Litteraires. irreg. ISSN 0457-9976

**Comite du Folklore Champenois**
13 rue de l'Arquebuse, 51000 Chalons-sur-Marne, France.
- Comite du Folklore Champenois. Bulletin. q. ISSN 0413-9593

**Comite Francais d'Histoire de l'Art**
- Revue de l'Art. (pub. by Centre National de la Recherche Scientifique)

**Comite Francais de Cartographie**
39 Ter rue Gay-Lussac, Paris (5e), France.
- Comite Francais de Cartographie. Bulletin. q.

**Comite Francais UNICEF**
35, rue Felicien David, Paris (16e), France.
- Enfants du Monde. q. ISSN 0013-757X

**Comite Historique du Centre-Est**
86 rue Pasteur, 69365 Lyon Cedex 2, France, France.
- Cahiers d'Histoire. q. ISSN 0008-008X

**Comite Horticole et Maraicher**
3, Place de la Petite-Hollande, 44-Nantes, France.
- Ouest Horticole et Maraicher. m.

**Comite Interministeriel pour l'Information**
- Politique Interieure de la France. (pub. by Documentation Francaise)

**Comite International de Coordination des Recherches Nationales en Demographie**
27 rue du Commandeur, 75675 Paris Cedex 14, France.
- Annuaire des Centres de Recherche Demographique. a.
- C I C R E D Bulletin. q.
- Comite International de Coordination des Recherches Nationales en Demographie. Actes des Seminaires. a.

**Comite International de Medecine et de Pharmacie Militaire**
see **International Committee of Military Medicine and Pharmacy**

**Comite International des Science Historiques**
see **Internaional Committee for Historical Science**

**Comite Internationale de l'Histoire de l'Art**
see **International Committee on the History of Art**

**Comite Intersyndical des Biologistes Francais**
- Feuillets de Biologie. (pub. by Editions Varia)

**Comite National Contre le Tabagisme**
- Tabac et Sante. (pub. by N E T A)

**Comite National de Defense Contre l'Alcoolisme**
20 rue Saint-Fiacre, 75002 Paris, France.
- A Votre Sante. q. ISSN 0001-2912
- Alcool ou Sante. bi-m. ISSN 0002-5054

**Comite National de l'Enfance**
- Medecine Infantile. (pub. by Librairie Maloine)

**Comite National de l'Organisation Francaise**
119 rue de Lille, F-75007 Paris, France.
- Comite National de l'Organisation Francaise. Annuaire. a. ISSN 0069-651X

**Comite National de la Gravure Francaise**
- Nouvelles de l'Estampe. (pub. by Bibliotheque Nationale. Cabinet des Estampes)

**Comite National de Propagande pour la Consommation des Produits de la Mer**
11 rue Anatole de la Forge, Paris (17e), France.
- Maree de France. m. ISSN 0025-2905

**Comite National du Secours Routiers Francais**
99 Bd. Arago, Paris (14e), France.
- Route. q. ISSN 0035-8568

**Comite National Francais de Geodesie et Geophysique**
c/o M. Georges Laclavere, 53, Avenue de Breteuil, 75007 Paris, France.
- Comite National Francais de Geodesie et Geophysique. Comptes-Rendus. a. ISSN 0069-6528
- Comite National Francais de Geodesie et Geophysique. Rapport National Francais a l'U G G I. quadrennial. ISSN 0069-6536

**Comite Professionnel du Petrole**
51 Bd. de Courcelles, 75008 Paris, France.
- Bulletin Analytique Petrolier. s-m. ISSN 0007-4101
- Comite Professionnel du Petrole. Bulletin Mensuel - Statistiques Petrolieres. m.
- Petrole; activite de l'industrie petroliere. a. ISSN 0069-6552

**Comites de Lutte des Handicapes**
18 rue de Cambrai, 75019 Paris, France.
- Handicapes Mechants; journal des comites de lutte des handicapes. bi-m. ISSN 0338-9529

**Commerce Editions**
2 rue des Petits-Peres, 75002 Paris, France.
- France Alimentaire; le bi-mensuel du magasin de proximite. bi-m. ISSN 0015-9484

**Commission Francaise des Archives Juives**
87 rue Vieille du Temple, 75003 Paris, France.
- Archives Juives. q. ISSN 0003-9837

**Commission Internationale des Industries Agricoles et Alimentaires**
see **International Commission for Agricultural Industries**

**Committee for International Coordination of National Research in Demography**
see **Comite International de Coordination des Recherches Nationales en Demographie**

**Committee on Space Research**
51 Bd. de Montmorency, 75016 Paris, France.
- COSPAR Information Bulletin. (pub. by Pergamon Press Ltd. UK)
- COSPAR Technique Manual. irreg. ISSN 0084-9332
- COSPAR Transactions. irreg. ISSN 0084-9340
- Life Sciences and Space Research. (pub. by North Holland Publishing Co. NE)
- Space Research. (pub. by North Holland Publishing Co. NE)

**Communaute de Taize**
71460 Taize-Communaute, France
- Communion/Verbum Caro; cahiers trimestriels. q. ISSN 0042-370X (Subscr. to: 2150 Almaden Rd. 114, San Jose, CA 95125)

**Communaute Non Violente**
50 rue d'Illiers, 4500 Orleans, France.
- Combat Non Violent. w.

**Compagnie d'Editions et de Propagande du Journal "la Vie Claire"**
4 Pl. du General de Gaulle, Perigny-sur-Yerres, 94520 Mandres-les-Roses, France.
- Vie Claire. m.

**Compagnie des Dirigeants d'Approvisionnement et Acheteurs de France**
- Compagnie des Dirigeants d'Approvisionnement et Acheteurs de France. Annuaire. (pub. by Edirep)

**Compagnie des Ecrivains Mediterraneens et des Amis des Lettres**
11 rue Bourrelly, 34000 Montpellier, France.
- Compagnie des Ecrivains Mediterraneens et des Amis des Lettres. Bulletin. q. ISSN 0010-3950

**Compagnie Europeenne d'Editions**
15, rue Bleue, Paris (9), France.
- Usine Nouvelle; technology and economics. w. ISSN 0042-126X

**Compagnie Europeenne d'Expansion**
59, rue Galilee, 75008 Paris, France.
- Ingenieurs et Cadres de France. m. ISSN 0020-1219 (Federation Nationale des Syndicats d'Ingenieurs et de Cadres)

**Compagnie Francaise d'Editions**
Service Abonnements Techniques, 40 rue du Colisee, 75008 Paris, France.
- Alimentation Moderne; revue de la conserve. m.
- Bureaux de France. 9 per yr. ISSN 0007-6074
- Caractere; revue des industries graphiques. m. ISSN 0008-6126
- Chantiers. m.
- Chimie Actualites; le bimensuel de l'industrie chimique. fortn. ISSN 0009-4323
- Collectivites-Gestion-Equipement. m. ISSN 0013-9858
- Composants Mecaniques, Electriques et Electroniques. 10 per yr.
- Emballages; conditionnement, presentation, vente. 11 per yr. ISSN 0013-6573
- Equipement Mecanique, Carrieres et Materiaux. 9 per yr.
- Formage et Traitements des Metaux; assemblage parachevement. m. ISSN 0015-7732
- Guide de l'Environment et des Techniques Antipollution. a.
- Guide du Travail des Metaux. irreg.
- Industries et Techniques; le magazine de l'innovation technique. q. ISSN 0019-9354
- Ingenieur-Constructeur. m. ISSN 0046-9513 (Societe des Ingenieurs Diplomes E.T.P)
- Inter Electronique; revue hebdomadaire-economie et technique industries electroniques. w. ISSN 0020-5036
- M T D. (Manutention/Transport/Distribution); le magazine de la logistique industrielle. m.
- Maison Francaise. 10 per yr. ISSN 0025-0953
- Maison Francaise-Plaisir de France Couplage. m.
- Mesures Regulation Automatisme. 10 per yr. ISSN 0026-0193
- Nuisances et Environnement. m.
- Papier Carton et Cellulose. 10 per yr. ISSN 0031-1367
- Petrole Informations. fortn. ISSN 0031-6377
- Plastiques Modernes et Elastomers. m. ISSN 0032-1303
- Revue du Bois et de ses Applications. m. ISSN 0035-2519 (Institut National de Bois)
- Revue Vinicole Internationale/International Wine Review. 8 per yr. ISSN 0035-4368
- Vetir. 10 per yr. ISSN 0030-0489

**Compagnie Francaise de Journaux**
14 rue d'Uzes, 75081 Paris Cedex 02, France.
- Spectacle du Monde. m. ISSN 0038-6944
- Valeurs Actuelles. w. ISSN 0049-5794

**Compagnie Generale de Developpement**
Service Abonnements, 11, rue Godefroy-Cavaignac, 75011 Paris, France.
- Action Veterinaire. bi-m. ISSN 0001-7523
- Elevage. m.
- Elevage Bovin. q.
- Officiel des Transporteurs; l'hebdomadaire du transport routier. w.

**Compagnie Generale Maritime**
Tour Winterthur, Cedex 18, 92085 Paris la Defense, France.
- Compagnie Generale Maritime. Courrier. q.

**Compagnie Nationale des Commissaries aux Comptes**
6, rue de l'Amiral de Coligny, 75001 Paris, France.
- Conseil National des Commissaires aux Comptes Bulletin. q.

**Compagnie Regionale de Publications Specialisees**
8 rue Chalutier la Tanche, 56100 Lorient, France.
- Maisons et Decors de l'Ouest. 10 per yr.
- Maisons et Decors du Sud-Ouest. bi-m.

**Compagnie Renaud-Barrault**
- Cahiers Renaud Barrault. (pub. by Editions Gallimard)

**Concours Medical**
37 rue de Bellefond, 75441 Paris, France.
- Concours Medical. w. ISSN 0010-5309

**Editions Conde Nast S. A.**
4 Place du Palais Bourbon, 75007 Paris, France.
- Maison et Jardin. 10 per yr. ISSN 0025-0945
- Vogue. 10 per yr.

**Confederation des Industries Ceramiques de France**
44 rue Copernic, 75116 Paris, France.
- Confederation des Industries Ceramiques de France. Annuaire. biennial. ISSN 0069-830X

**Confederation des Industries du Traitement des Produits des Peches Maritimes**
3 rue de Logelbach, Paris 17e, France.
- Congres National des Peches et Industries Maritimes. Compte Rendu. irreg. ISSN 0069-889X

**Confederation des Travailleurs Intellectuels de France**
1 rue de Courcelle, Paris (8e), France.
- Cahiers du Travailleur Intellectuel. q. ISSN 0045-3781

**Confederation Force Ouvriere**
198 Ave. du Maine, Paris (14e), France.
- Force Ouvriere Hebdo. w. ISSN 0046-4511

**Confederation Francaise de l'Harmonica**
21 rue Van Loo, Paris(16e), France.
- Harmonica Accordeon et Musique. q. ISSN 0017-7806

**Confederation Francaise de la Photographie**
116 Place Vendone, 75001 Paris, Francc.
- Annuaire de la Photographie Professionnelle. a. ISSN 0084-6481

**Confederation Francaise des Travailleurs Chretiens**
13 rue des Ecluses Saint-Martin, F75010 Paris, France.
- Syndicalisme C F T C. m. ISSN 0039-775X

**Confederation Generale des Aveugles Sourds, Grands Infirmes et Personnes Agees**
13, rue Blaise-Pascal, 78800 Houilles, France.
- Mieux-Vivre. bi-m.

**Confederation Generale des Cadres**
30 rue de Gramont, 75002 Paris, France.
- Cadres et Maitrise. s-m.

**Confederation Generale du Travail**
213 rue Lafayette, 75010 Paris, France
(Orders to: Antoinette, 50 rue Edouard Pailleron, 75019 Paris, France)
- Antoinette. m. ISSN 0402-6233
- Peuple. s-m. ISSN 0031-661X

**Confederation Internationale des Cinemas d'Art et d'Essai**
see **International Experimental and Art Film Theatres Confederation**

**Confederation Internationale des Societes d'Auteurs et Compositeurs**
see **International Confederation of Societies of Authors and Composers**

**Confederation Kendalc'h**
4, Allee des Ormeaux, 44-la Baule, France.
- Breiz. m.

**Confederation Mondiale des Activites**
see **World Underwater Federation**

**Confederation Nationale des Commerces de Gros**
48, Avenue de Villiers, 75017 Paris, France.
- Commerces de Gros. bi-m. ISSN 0414-0265

**Confederation Nationale des Groupes Autonomes de l'Enseignement Public**
6 rue de Trevise, 75009 Paris, France.
- Universite Autonome. 8-10 per yr. ISSN 0083-3924

**Confederation Nationale des Groupes Folkloriques Francais**
81 rue de Barcelone, 30000 Nimes, France.
- Folklore de France. bi-m. ISSN 0015-5918

**Confederation Nationale des Reserves**
Paris, France.
- Armee Francaise. m. ISSN 0004-2250

**Confederation Nationale des Syndicats de Fabricants de Glaces, Sorbets et Cremes Glacees**
- Glacier Francais. (pub. by Societe d'Editions et de Publicite Professionnelles et Interprofessionnelles)

**Confederation Nationale des Syndicats Dentaires**
22 Av. de Villiers, 75017 Paris, France.
- Chirurgien-Dentiste de France. w. ISSN 0009-4838

**Confederation Nationale du Commerce Charbonnier**
4 rue de Berri, Paris 8e, France.
- Annuaire des Negociants en Combustibles. a. ISSN 0066-2909

**Confederation Nationale du Travail**
39 Rue de la Tour d'Auvergue, Paris (9e), France.
- Combat Syndicaliste. s-m. ISSN 0045-7477

**Editions de la Confiserie**
48 Avenue de Villiers, 75847 Paris Cedex 17, France.
- Confiserie. 8 per yr. (Salon International de la Confiserie Chocolaterie Biscuiterie)

**Congres de Psychiatrie et de Neurologie de Langue Francaise**
- Congres de Psychiatrie et de Neurologie de Langue Francaise. Rapport/French-Language Congress of Psychiatry and Neurology. Report. (pub. by Masson)

**Connaissance des Hommes**
23 Rue de la Haute Bercelle, 77210 Avon, France.
- Connaissance des Hommes; arts - sciences - technique. bi-m. ISSN 0010-5996

**Conseil de l'Europe**
see **Council of Europe**

**Conseil des Musees Nationaux**
10 rue de l'Abbaye, Paris (6e), France.
- Revue du Louvre et des Musees de France. bi-m. ISSN 0035-2608

**Conseil International de l'Action Sociale**
see **International Council on Social Welfare**

**Conseil International de la Langue Francaise**
105 Ter rue de Lille, Paris 75007, France.
- Cle des Mots; cahiers de terminologie scientifique et technique. 11 per yr. ISSN 0395-0026
- Langues et Terminologies. bi-m.

**Conseil International des Machines a Combustion**
see **International Council on Combustion Engines**

**Conseil National des Economies Regionales et de la Productivite (C.N.E.R.P.)**
219 Blvd. Saint-Germain, 75007 Paris, France.
- Cahiers de l'Expansion Regionale; amenagement equipement productivite. q. ISSN 0014-4711

**Conseil National du Mouvement de la Paix**
35 rue de Clichy, 75009 Paris, France.
- Combat pour la Paix. 8 per yr. ISSN 0045-7450

**Conseil National du Patronat Francais**
- Conseil National du Patronat Francais. Annuaire. (pub. by Union Francaise d'Annuaires Professionnels)
- Patronat Francais. (pub. by Editions Techniques Patronales)

**Conseil Regional de Paris de l'Ordre des Architectes**
140 Avenue Victor Hugo, 75116 Paris, France.
- Architectes. 10 per yr. ISSN 0066-6122

**Conseil Superieur de la Peche**
Le Paraclet, B.P. No. 5, F-80440 Boves, France.
- Bulletin Francais de Pisciculture. q. ISSN 0373-0514

**Conseiller des Assurances et de la Finance**
129 Bd. St. Michel, Paris (5e), France.
- Conseiller des Assurances et de la Finance. m.

**Conservatoire National des Arts et Metiers**
292 rue Saint-Martin, Paris 3e, France.
- Annuaire des Chercheurs Francais du Fonds de Bourses de Recherche Scientifique et Technique de l'Organisation du Traite de l'Atlantique Nord. irreg. ISSN 0066-2771

**Consistoire Israelite de Paris**
17 rue St.-Georges, Paris (9e), France.
- Journal des Communautes. s-m. ISSN 0021-8022 (Co-Sponsor: Consistoire Central)

**Contact-Editions**
5 rue Robert-Estienne, Paris 8e, France.
- Annuaire Biographique du Cinema et de la Television en France et en Belgique. irreg. ISSN 0066-247X

**Contacts**
c/o John J. Balzon & Germaine Revault d'Allones, 43 rue du Fer-a-Moulin, 75005 Paris, France.
- Contacts; revue francaise de l'Orthodoxie. q. ISSN 0045-8325

**Containers Actualities**
6 rue Saint-Saens, 75015 Paris, France.
- Containers Actualities. m.

**Contraception-Fertilite-Sexualite**
125, rue de l'Universite, 75007 Paris, France.
- Contraception-Fertilite-Sexualite. 8 per yr. ISSN 0301-861X

**Editions Contraste**
32 rue des Annelets, 75019 Paris, France.
- Cahiers Critiques de la Litterature. q.

**Contre Attaque**
52 rue Victor Hugo, 80002 Amiens, France.
- Contre Attaque. bi-m.

**Contre Reforme Catholique**
Maison Saint-Joseph, 10260-Saint-Parres-les-Vaudes, France.
- Catholic Counter-Reformation in the XXth Century. m.

**Contrepoint**
4 rue Cassette, 75006 Paris, France.
- Contrepoint. q. ISSN 0010-7964

**Cooperation Mediterraneene pour l'Energie Solaire**
- Revue Internationale d'Heliotechnique. (pub. by Estrel Editions)

**Cooperation pour la Nature (COOP-NAT)**
158 rue Pasteur, 91700 Ste. Genevieve des Bois, France.
- Courrier d'Utopie; experimentation realiste du pays ideal, publication ecologique. m.

**Editions Copernic**
B.P. 129, 75326 Paris Cedex 07, France.
- Nouvelle Ecole. bi-m. ISSN 0048-0967

**SARL Editions du Coq Heron**
48 rue Sainte Anne, 75002 Paris, France.
- Faire. m. ISSN 0339-3070

**Couleurs**
26 Rue du Bosquet, 91 Savigny-Sur-Orge, France.
- Couleurs. q. ISSN 0010-9851

**Council of Europe**
Publications Section, 67006 Strasbourg, France
(Dist. in U. S. by Manhattan Publishing Co., 225 Lafayette St., New York, N. Y. 10012)
- Council of Europe. Committee of Independent Experts on the European Social Charter. Conclusions. biennial.
- Council of Europe. Committee on Cooperation in Municipal and Regional Matters. Study Series: Local and Regional Authorities in Europe. irreg.
- Council of Europe. Concise Handbook. irreg. ISSN 0589-9508
- Council of Europe. Council for Cultural Cooperation. Annual Report. a. ISSN 0589-9478 (Co-sponsor: Cultural Fund)
- Council of Europe. Directorate of Legal Affairs. Newsletter on Legislative Activities. 6 per yr. (approx)
- Council of Europe. Documentation Section and Library. Bulletin de Bibliographie. Serie: Affaires Juridiques. q.
- Council of Europe. Documentation Section and Library. Bulletin de Bibliographie. Serie: Affaires Politiques et Economiques. s-m.
- Council of Europe. Documentation Section and Library. Bulletin de Bibliograhie. Serie: Affaires Sociales. 18 per yr.
- Council of Europe. European Treaty Series. irreg., no. 92, 1977. ISSN 0070-105X
- Council of Europe. Exchange of Information Between the Member States on Their Legislative Activity and Regulations (New Series) irreg; no. 6, 1972. ISSN 0589-9362
- Council of Europe. Information Bulletin on Social Policy/Bulletin d'Information sur la Politique Sociale. s-a.
- Council of Europe. Parliamentary Assembly. Documents; Working Papers/Documents de Seance. a.
- Council of Europe. Parliamentary Assembly. Orders of the Day, Minutes of Proceedings/ Ordres du Jour, Proces Verbaux. a.
- Council of Europe. Parliamentary Assembly. Texts Adopted by the Assembly/Textes Adoptes Par l'Assemblee. a.
- Council of Europe. Standing Committee on the European Convention on Establishment (Individuals). Periodical Report. irreg.
- Council of Europe Film Weeks. a. ISSN 0589-9591 (prep. by its Film and Television Division)
- Education and Culture. 3 per yr. ISSN 0013-1229 (prep. by its Council for Cultural Cooperation)
- Education in Europe. Section 1: Higher Education and Research. irreg. ISSN 0070-9182 (prep. by its Council for Cultural Cooperation)
- Education in Europe. Section 2: General and Technical Education. irreg. ISSN 0070-9190 (prep. by its Council for Cultural Cooperation)
- Education in Europe. Section 3: Out-Of-School Education. irreg. ISSN 0070-9204 (prep. by its Council for Cultural Cooperation)
- Education in Europe. Section 4 (General) irreg. ISSN 0070-9212 (prep. by its Council for Cultural Cooperation)

- European Art Exhibitions. Catalog. irreg. ISSN 0071-2426
- European Aspects, Social Studies Series; a collection of studies relating to European integration. irreg. ISSN 0531-2663
- European Co-Operation. irreg. ISSN 0589-9575
- European Convention on Human Rights. Yearbook. (pub. by Martinus Nijhoff NE)
- European Curriculum Studies. irreg. ISSN 0071-2728
- European Yearbook. (pub. by Martinus Nijhoff NE)
- Exchange of Information on Research in European Law/Echange d'Informations sur les Recherches en Droit Europeen. a. (prep. by its Directorate of Legal Affairs)
- Folklore Europeen. (pub. by Editions G. P. Maisonneuve et Larose)
- Forward in Europe. 4 per yr. ISSN 0015-8631

**Council of Europe. Documentation Centre for Education in Europe**
see **Documentation Centre for Education in Europe**

**Council of Europe. European Commission of Human Rights**
see **European Commission of Human Rights**

**Council of Europe. European Committee on Crime Problems**
see **European Committee on Crime Problems**

**Council of Europe. European Conference of Local Authorities**
see **European Conference of Local Authorities**

**Council of Europe. European Information Centre for Nature Conservation**
see **European Information Centre for Nature Conservation**

**Editions de Courcelles**
97 Bd. Arago, 75014 Paris, France.
- Papetier Libraire. m. ISSN 0031-1332

**Courrier de Politique Etrangere**
229 rue du Faubourg St. Honore, Paris (8e), France.
- Courrier de Politique Etrangere. bi-m. ISSN 0045-8880

**Courrier des Tapis, Textiles et Decors**
44 rue de Provence, 75009 Paris, France.
- Courrier des Tapis, Textiles et Decors; hebdomadaire des tapis, revetements de sols et de murs. w. ISSN 0339-106X

**Courrier du Meuble**
44, rue de Provence, Paris (9e), France.
- Courrier du Meuble. w.

**Courrier Roumain**
c/o Ed. C. H. Arsene, 6 rue Troyon, Paris (17e), France.
- Courrier Roumain. bi-m. ISSN 0027-4194

**Courrier Union**
12 rue Duphot, 75001 Paris, France.
- Courrier de l'Informatique. d.

**Edition Courses Hippiques**
33 rue du Buisson-Saint-Louis, 75010 Paris, France.
- Courses Hippiques; informations hippiques. w. ISSN 0395-3599

**Creations, Editions et Productions Publicitaires (C.E.P.P.)**
1 Place d'Estienne d'Orves, 75009 Paris, France.
- France-Peinture. biennial. ISSN 0071-9048
- France Plastiques. a. ISSN 0071-9056
- France-Sports. biennial. ISSN 0071-9102
- Jouets et Jeux. a. ISSN 0075-4056

**Crepin Leblond et Cie**
12 rue Duguay Trouin, 75006 Paris, France.
- Cibles. 11 per yr. ISSN 0009-6679
- Plaisirs de la Chasse. m. ISSN 0048-427X
- Plaisirs Equestre; la revue de l' homme de cheval. 8 per yr. ISSN 0032-051X
- Vie Canine. m. ISSN 0042-5346

**Editions du Creuset**
79 Ave. de Segur, 75 Paris (15e), France.
- Moniteur des Pharmacies et des Laboratoires. w. ISSN 0026-9689

**Croisade des Aveugles**
15 rue Mayet, Paris (6e), France.
- Lux Vera. bi-m. ISSN 0024-7685

**Croissance des Jeunes Nations**
163 Bd Malesherbes, Paris (17e), France.
- Croissance des Jeunes Nations. m. ISSN 0011-1686

**Editions du Croissant**
6 Avenue Delcasse, 75008 Paris, France.
- Votre Maison; l'officiel de la maison individuelle et de la decoration. bi-m. ISSN 0042-8973

**Croix-Rouge Francaise**
17 rue Quentin Bauchart, 75384 Paris Cedex 08, France.
- Presence Croix-Rouge. m. ISSN 0301-0260

**Editions Cujas**
4,6,8, rue de la Maison Blanche, 75013 Paris, France.
- Civilisation Malgache. irreg. ISSN 0578-3917 (Universite de Madagascar. Faculte des Lettres et Sciences Humaines MG)
- Croissance Urbaine et Progres des Nations. irreg. ISSN 0070-1572
- Histoire et Civilisation Arabe. irreg. ISSN 0073-2400
- Initiation. Serie Textes, Bibliographies. irreg. ISSN 0073-8034
- Theorie de la Production. irreg., 2-3 per yr. ISSN 0082-3988 (Institut de Recherches en Economie de la Production)

**Culture, Arts et Loisirs**
114, Av. des Champs-Elysees, Paris 8e, France.
- Histoire des Personnages Mysterieux et des Societes Secretes. irreg. ISSN 0073-2389

**Culture Francaise**
96 Bd. Raspail, 75272 Paris, France.
- Culture Francaise. 4 per yr. ISSN 0011-2925

**Curiospress International**
c/o Ed. Pierre Birukoff, c/o INFOS al International, B.P. 127, 75563 Paris 12, France.
- Curiospress International; annuaire international des editeurs de publications etranges et curieuses. biennial.

**Cyclotouriste**
19 rue du Boeuf, 69005 Lyon, France.
- Cyclotouriste; sports, culture et tourisme. 8 per yr.

**Cyrano de Paris**
26 Rue du Delta, Paris (9e), France.
- Cyrano de Paris. 10 per yr. ISSN 0011-4499

**D.U.L.J.V.A.**
Sac Postal 18, 59650 Villeneuve d'Ascq, France.
- Revue du Nord. q. ISSN 0035-2624 (Universite de Lille III (Sciences Humaines, Lettres et Arts))

**DAFSA Documentation**
125 rue Montmartre, 75081-Paris, France.
- Liaisons Financieres des Entreprises Francaises. a. ISSN 0075-8957

**R. Daillie, Pub.**
Jean-Pierre Geay, le Besignoles "B", Route des Nines, 07000-Privas, Issirac, France.
- Solaire. q.

**Imprimerie Dalex a Montrouge**
5 et 7 rue Victor-Basch, Montrouge, France.
- Lien Entre Meres et Peres de Pretres. q. ISSN 0024-2926 (Diocese de Paris)

**Danse Perspective**
c/o Antoine Livio, Ed., 24, Bd Poissonniere, 75009 Paris, France.
- Danse Perspective. m.

**Dargaud Editeur**
Service des Abonnements, 12 rue Blaise Pascal, 92200 Neuilly-sur-Seine, France.
- Pilote. m.
- Rustica. w.

**Editions G. De Bussac**
2 Cours Sablon, Clermont-Ferrand, France.
- Auvergne Litteraire; artistique et historique. q. ISSN 0005-1845

**De l'Atlantique au Pacifique**
B.P. 3016, Paris 16e, France.
- De l'Atlantique au Pacifique; mensuel de documentation et d'etudes geopolitiques. m. ISSN 0396-4817

**Decennie**
11 rue Tronchet, 75 Paris (8e), France.
- Decennie; magazine illustre de l'afrique moderne. m. ISSN 0045-981X

**Pierre Decoulx, Ed. & Pub.**
229 Blvd. de la Liberte, Lille, France.
- Lille Chirurgical. 6 per yr. ISSN 0024-3493 (Societe de Chirurgie de Lille)

**Defense de l'Occident SARL**
13 rue des Montiboeufs, Paris 20e., France (Orders to: Francois Duprat, Bp 3, 76580 le Trait, France)
- Defense de l'Occident. 10 per yr. ISSN 0011-7552
- Revue d'Histoire du Fascisme. q.

**Defense des Distillateurs Ambulants et des Bouilleurs de Cru**
44 bis rue de la Victoire, 37, Tours 01, France.
- Defense des Distillateurs Ambulants et des Bouilleurs de Cru; organe d'informations professionnelles, commerciales et fiscales. q. ISSN 0011-7560

**Defense des Libertes Scolaires et Familiales**
10 rue Jules-Dauban, Angers, France.
- Echo de la Liberte de l'Ouest; organe mensuel independant de Defense des Libertes Scolaires et Familiales. m. ISSN 0012-9224

**Editions Jean Deit**
14 rue de la Somme, Cachan (Seine), France.
- Organisation Gestion des Enterprises. m. ISSN 0030-4964

**Editions Jean Pierre Delarge**
10, rue Mayet, Paris 6e, France.
- Psychotheque. irreg. ISSN 0079-7448

**Delegation a l'Amenagement du Territoire et a l'Action Regionale**
- 2000. (pub. by Documentation Francaise)

**Delirante**
26 rue de Picpus, Paris 12, France.
- Delirante; revue de poesie. 2-4 per yr. ISSN 0011-7889

**J. Dell'Acquo-Bascourt**
Les Frenes 52, 55 Bd. de Charonne, 75011-Paris, France.
- France Genealogique. bi-m. ISSN 0046-4929 (Centre d'Entr'aide Genealogique)

**Editions J. Delmas et Cie**
13 rue de l'Odeon, Paris (6e), France.
- Richesses de France; revue du tourisme, de l'economie et des arts. q. ISSN 0035-5097

**Editions Denoel**
14 rue Amelie, Paris 7e, France.
- Dictionnaires du Savoir Moderne; les idees, les oeuvres, les hommes. irreg. ISSN 0073-4640 (Centre d'Etudes et de Promotion de la Lecture)
- Etudes Freudiennes. 3 per yr. ISSN 0014-2107

**Dentoscope**
27 rue de l'Ecole de Medecine, 75006 Paris, France.
- Dentoscope. bi-m. ISSN 0045-9968

**Depeche Commerciale et Agricole**
5 bis rue de Louvre, Paris (1e), France.
- Depeche Commerciale et Agricole; l'hebdomadaire de l'economie agricole. w. ISSN 0011-8931

**Depeche Mode**
3 rue de Teheran, Paris (8e), France.
- Depeche Mode. m. ISSN 0011-8958

**Editions Jean Derrier S A R L**
15 rue Ronchaux, 25015 Besancon, France.
- Informations Laitieres. w. ISSN 0046-9432

**Desclee de Brouwer**
76 bis, rue des Saints-Peres, Paris 7e, France
- Bibliotheque de Sciences Religieuses. irreg. ISSN 0067-8295 (also from: Aubier-Montaigne & Editions du Cerf, Paris or Delachaux & Niestle, Switzerland)
- Revue Thomiste; revue doctrinale de theologie et de philosophie. q. ISSN 0035-4295

**Dessin et Technique**
163 rue Saint-Maur, 75 Paris (11e), France.
- Dessin et Technique. bi-m.

**Diana**
C. C. P. de la Diana, 2631-02 Lyon, France.
- Diana. q.

**Diapason S. A.**
6, rue Jules Simon, 92100 Boulogne, France.
- Diapason. 11 per yr.

**Editions de la Diaspora Francaise**
203, Bd de la Republique, 06400 Cannes, France.
- Fer de Lance /Rythmes et Couleurs; fer de lance. q. ISSN 0557-5737

**Librairie Marcel Didier**
15 rue Cujas, 75005 Paris, France
- Cahiers d'Allemand; Revue de Linguistique et de Pedagogie. s-a. ISSN 0068-4996
- Etudes Anglaises. q. ISSN 0014-195X (Centre National de la Recherche Scientifique) (and Chilton Books, Educ. Div., 401 Walnut St., Philadelphia. PA 19106)
- Etudes de Linguistique Appliquee. q. ISSN 0071-190X (Universite de Besancon. Centre de Linguistique Appliquee)
- Etudes Germaniques. q. ISSN 0014-2115
- Revue de Litterature Comparee. q. ISSN 0035-1466

**Societe Didot Bottin**
28 rue du Docteur Finlay, 75738 Paris Cedex 15, France.
- Bottin Administratif. a.
- Bottin de l'Auto et du Cycle. a.
- Bottin du Transport; le transport des marchandises en france, et relations entre la france et l'etranger. irreg.
- Bottin Europe. a. ISSN 0524-1561
- Bottin International. a. ISSN 0068-0494
- Bottin Mondain; Tout Paris-Toute la France. a.
- Bottin Professions. a. (6 vols.)

**Dietetique d'Aujourd'hui**
15 rue Avenue Gourgaud, 75017 Paris, France.
- Dietetique d'Aujourd'hui. 11 per yr. ISSN 0012-2637

**Diffusion Artistique et Graphique**
76 rue de Rivoli, 75004 Paris, France.
- Annuaire des Agents et Representants de l'Industrie et du Commerce des Pays du Marche Commun Europeen. triennial.

**Diffusion de la Pensee Francaise**
Chire-En-Montreuil, 86190 Vouille, France.
- Lecture et Tradition; bulletin litteraire, contrerevolutionnaire. bi-m. ISSN 0024-0125

**Diffusions et Relations Officielles**
50 Rue Championnet, 75018 Paris, France.
- Revue Technique du Batiment; et des constructions industrielles. bi-m. ISSN 0048-8186

**Diloutremer**
15 rue du Louvre, Paris 1e, France.
- Guid'Ouest Africain. a. ISSN 0072-8950

**Diners Club de France**
- Signature. (pub. by Editions Revue Signature)

**Diocese de Paris**
- Lien Entre Meres et Peres de Pretres. (pub. by Imprimerie Dalex a Montrouge)

**Direction des Journaux Officiels**
26, rue Desaix, Paris 75732, France.
- France. Ministere de l'Amenagement du Territoire, de l'Equipement, du Logement et des Transports. Bulletin Officiel. irreg.

**Direction du Pelerinage de Lisieux**
33 rue du Carmel B.P. 205, 14102 Lisieux, France.
- Sainte Therese de Lisieux. Annales. m. ISSN 0036-3243

**Editions Docis**
31 rue Mederic, Paris (17e), France.
- Cahiers de Medecine Interprofessionnelle. q. ISSN 0007-9936 (Association Interprofessionnelle des Centres Medicaux et Sociaux de la Region Parisienne)

**Documentation Agricole**
110 rue Hopital Militaire, 59000 Lille, France.
- Cultivar; mensuel technique agricole. m (10 per yr) ISSN 0045-9216

**Documentation Centre for Education in Europe**
Publications Section, 67006 Strasbourg, France
(Dist. in U. S. by Manhattan Publishing Co., 225 Lafayette St., New York, N. Y. 10012)
- Documentation Centre for Education in Europe. Information Bulletin/Bulletin d'Information. 3 per yr.
- Documentation Centre for Education in Europe. Newsletter. 4-6 per yr.
- Educational Research Policy in European Countries.

**Documentation Francaise**
29-31 Quai Voltaire, 75340 Paris Cedex 07, France.
- Afrique Contemporaine; documents d'Afrique noire et de Madagascar. bi-m. ISSN 0002-0478
- Bibliographie Selective des Publications Officielles Francaise. s-m. ISSN 0045-1894
- Biographies de Personnalites Francaises Vivantes. a. ISSN 0067-8740
- Cahiers Francais. 5 per yr. ISSN 0008-0217
- Centre d'Etude des Revenus et des Couts. Documents. 4 per yr.
- Comite d'Organisation des Recherches Appliquees sur la Developpement Economique Social. Recherches Economiques et Sociales; notes critiques et debats. 4 per yr.
- D F Actualites. m. ISSN 0338-4187
- 2000; amenagement du territoire, innovation, avenir. 4 per yr. ISSN 0012-1509 (Delegation a l'Amenagement du Territoire et a l'Action Regionale)
- Diagonal. 6 per yr. (France. Direction de l'Amenagement Foncier et de l'Urbanisme)
- Documentation Photographique. 6 per yr.
- Documents d'Actualite Internationale. w. (France. Ministere des Affaires Etrangeres)
- Economie et Sante. s-a. (France. Ministere de la Sante)
- Education Permanente. 5 per yr. (Agence Nationale pour le Developpement de l'Education Permanente (A D E P))
- Emploi et Formation. 4 per yr.
- Enquete Economique des Societes de Service et Conseil en Informatique. a. (France. Delegation a l'Informatique)
- France. Commission Nationale de l'Amenagement du Territoire. Rapport. irreg., 1971, no. 2. ISSN 0071-8491
- France. Delegation Generale a la Recherche Scientifique et Technique. Recherche dans le Domaine de l'Eau: Repertoire des Laboratoires. irreg. ISSN 0071-853X
- France. Delegation Generale a la Recherche Scientifique et Technique. Repertoire des Scientifiques Francais. Tome 3: Biologie. irreg. ISSN 0080-1038
- France. Delegation Generale a la Recherche Scientifique et Technique. Repertoire des Scientifiques Francais. Tome 4: Chimie. irreg. ISSN 0080-1046
- France. Delegation Generale a la Recherche Scientifique et Technique. Repertoire des Scientifiques Francais. Tome 5: Physique. irreg. ISSN 0080-1062
- France. Delegation Generale a la Recherche Scientifique et Technique. Repertoire National des Chercheurs: Sciences Sociales et Humaines. Tome 1: Ethnologie, Linguistique, Psychologie, Psychologie Sociale, Sociologie. irreg. ISSN 0080-116X
- France. Delegation Generale a la Recherche Scientifique et Technique. Repertoire National des Laboratoires; la Recherche Universitaire; Sciences Exactes et Naturelles. Tome 1: Physique. irreg. ISSN 0071-8572
- France. Delegation Generale a la Recherche Scientifique et Technique. Repertoire National des Laboratoires; la Recherche Universitaire; Sciences Exactes et Naturelles. Tome 2: Biologie. irreg. ISSN 0071-8548
- France. Delegation Generale a la Recherche Scientifique et Technique. Repertoire National des Laboratoires; la Recherche Universitaire; Sciences Exactes et Naturelles. Tome 3: Chimie. irreg. ISSN 0071-8556
- France. Delegation Generale a la Recherche Scientifique et Technique. Repertoire National des Laboratoires; la Recherche Universitaire; Sciences Exactes et Naturelles. Tome 4: Mathematiques, Sciences de l'Espace et de la Terre. irreg. ISSN 0071-8564
- France. Delegation Generale a la Recherche Scientifique et Technique. Repertoire Permanent de l'Administration Francaise. a. ISSN 0080-1186

- France. Direction de la Documentation. Catalogue des Publications Editees Ou Diffusees Par la Documentation Francaise. a.
- France. Direction de la Documentation. Documents d'Etudes. irreg (10-14 per yr)
- France. Direction de la Documentation. Notes et Etudes Documentaires. irreg. ISSN 0071-8602
- France. Direction de la Prevision. Rationalisation des Choix Budgetaires. 4 per yr.
- France. Direction du Batiment, des Travaux Publics et de la Conjoncture. Statistiques de la Construction. 11 per yr.
- France. Direction du Batiment et des Travaux Publics et de la Conjoncture. Etudes Statistiques de l'Equipment. 8 per yr (plus supplements)
- France. Mediateur. Rapport Annuel du Mediateur. a.
- France. Ministere de l'Amenagement du Territoire, de l'Equipement et des Transports. Tableau de Bord Conjoncturel du Batiment et des Travaux Publics. 4 per yr.
- France. Ministere de l'Amenagement du Territoire, de l'Equipement et des Transports. Tableau de Bord Conjoncturel du Logement. 4 per yr.
- France. Ministere de la Sante. Bulletin de Statistiques de Sante, Securite Sociale. 6 per yr. (Co-sponsor: Ministere du Travail)
- France. Ministere de la Sante. Tableaux Sante et Securite Sociale. biennial.
- France. Ministere du Travail. Bulletin de Statistiques du Travail. Supplement. 12 per yr. (Co-Sponsor: Ministere de la Sante)
- France. Ministere du Travail. Bulletin Mensuel des Statistiques du Travail. m. (Co-sponsor: Ministere de la Sante)
- France. Secretariat d'Etat au Tourisme. Statistiques du Tourisme. q.
- Lettre 101. 20 per yr (plus supplements) (France. Ministere de l'Industrie et de la Recherche)
- Maghreb, Machrek, Monde Arabe. q. ISSN 0336-6324 (Fondation Nationale des Politiques et Direction de la Documentation)
- Notes et Etudes Documentaires. w. ISSN 0029-4004
- Politique Interieure de la France. q. (Comite Interministeriel pour l'Information)
- Problemes d'Amerique Latine; collection des notes et etudes documentaires. q. (Centre d'Etudes et de Documentation sur l'Amerique Latine)
- Problemes Economiques; selection de textes francais et etrangers. w. ISSN 0032-9304
- Problemes Politiques et Sociaux; articles et documents d'actualite mondiale. fortn. ISSN 0015-9743
- Progres Scientifique. 6 per yr. ISSN 0033-0469 (France. Delegation Generale a la Recherche Scientifique et Technique)
- Propriete Industrielle Bulletin Documentaire. 24 per yr. ISSN 0033-1430
- Regards sur l'Actualite; mensuel de la vie publique en France. 10 per yr.
- Revue Francaise des Affaires Sociales. q. ISSN 0035-2985 (France. Ministere de la Sante)
- Terres Australes et Antarctiques Francaises. q. ISSN 0040-389X (France. Ministre d'Etat Charge des Departements et Territories d'Outre-Mer)

**Documentation Professionnelle**
12 rue Richer, 75009 Paris, France.
- Catalogue General. Radio, Television, Electrophones, Magnetophones, Haute-Fidelite, Stereophonie, Audio-Visuel; guide officiel de l'archeteur. a. ISSN 0069-1119

**Documentations Industrielles et Techniques**
11 rue de Madrid, 75 Paris 8, France.
- Genie Industriel; Catalogue de l'Engineering. a. ISSN 0072-0844
- Genie Industriel: Revue; engineering actualites. m.

**Doin Editeurs**
8 Place de l'Odeon, 75006 Paris, France
- Annales d'Oculistique. m. ISSN 0003-4371
- Annales de l'Anesthesiologie Francaise. m. ISSN 0003-4061 (Association des Anesthesiologistes Francais)
- Archives Francaises de Pediatrie. 10 per yr. ISSN 0003-9764
- Broncho-Pneumologie (les Bronches); revue internationale de broncho-pneumologie. 6 per yr. (International Broncho-Pneumologic Association) (Co-publisher: Il Pensiero Scnentifico, via Panama 48, Rome, Italy)
- Encephale. Nouvelle Serie; revue de psychiatrie biologique et therapeutique. irreg.

- Espace Geographique. q. ISSN 0046-2497
- Homeopathie Francaise. 10 per yr. ISSN 0018-4225
- Revue d'Hygiene et Medecine Scolaire et Universitaire. q. ISSN 0035-2446 (Association Francaise d'Hygiene et de Medecine Scolaires et Universitaires)
- Revue d'Oto-Neuro-Ophtalmologie. 5 per yr. ISSN 0035-2497
- Therapie. 6 per yr. ISSN 0040-5957 (Societe Francaise de Therapeutique et de Pharmacodynamie)

**Dokumente-Verlag**
50, rue de Laborde, 75008 Paris, France.
- Documents; revue des questions allemandes. bi-m.

**Droit de Vivre**
40 Rue de Paradis, Paris 10e, France.
- Droit de Vivre. bi-m. ISSN 0012-6373

**Editions Duc**
10 rue de Lancry, 75010 Paris, France.
- Annuaire de la Mercerie, Nouveautes, Bonneterie, Lingerie, Confections. a.

**Editions Dujarric**
79 Av. des Champs-Elysees, 75008 Paris, France.
- Technicien du Film; magazine d'information des professionnels du cinema, de la television, de l'audio-visuel. m. ISSN 0040-103X

**Dulac et Cie**
8 rue Lamartine, Paris (9e), France.
- Institut de Science Financiere et d'Assurances. Bulletin des Actuaires Diplomes. s-a. ISSN 0007-4438
- Institut des Actuaires Francais. Bulletin Trimestriel. q. ISSN 0020-2223

**Publications Paul Dupont**
38 rue Croix des Petits Champs, Paris (1), France.
- Bulletin Annote des Lois et Decrets. m. ISSN 0007-411X
- Memorial des Percepteurs et Receveurs des Communes. m. ISSN 0025-9179

**E D I M A**
7. Villa du Hameau, 78400 Chatou, France.
- Hommes et Fonderie. m. ISSN 0018-4357 (Association Technique de Fonderie)

**E. G. C. M.**
41 rue Volta, 75003 Paris, France.
- Genie Civil; revue generale des techniques. s-m. ISSN 0016-6812 (Societe des Editions du Genie Civil et de la Metallurgie)
- Metallurgie et la Construction Mecanique. m. (Societe des Editions du Genie Civil et de la Metallurgie)

**Editions E.G.E.**
23, rue Chalopin, 69007 Lyon, France.
- Bouliste. m. ISSN 0336-8424
- Cent Blagues. m. ISSN 0045-6047
- Eclats de Rire. m. ISSN 0337-8659

**E. G. P.**
9 rue Coetlogon, 75006 Paris, France.
- Annuaire du Froid, du Conditionnement d'Air et de l'Electro-Menager. a. ISSN 0066-2984
- Musique et Instruments; la revue des editeurs de musique et des facteurs d'instruments. bi-m. ISSN 0027-4852

**Editions E.L.T.A.**
9 rue Saint Fiacre, Paris (2e), France.
- Tourisme Informations; journal technique des professions du tourisme. m. ISSN 0040-9782

**E. P. C. I.**
132 Faubourg Poissonniere, Paris (10e), France.
- Relations Publiques Informations. w. ISSN 0034-3811

**E. P. I. S.A. Editeurs**
68, rue de Babylone, 75007 Paris, France.
- Connexions Psychosociologie Sciences Humaines. q. ISSN 0337-3126 (Association pour la Recherche et Intervention Psychosociologiques)
- Topique - Revue Freudienne. s-a. ISSN 0040-9375

**E. S. T. E. C.**
127 Bd. Saint Michel, 75005 Paris, France.
- Genie Medical; symbiose medico-artistique. m. ISSN 0016-6839
- N. G. M. (Nouveau Genie Medical) bi-m.

**E.T.A.C.A.**
1 rue Bouterie, 75005 Paris, France
(Orders to: J. Argoud, 61 bis Av. J. B. Clement, 92140 Clamart, France)
- De l'Automobile et de l'Aeronautique. q. (Association des Anciens Eleves de l'Ecole Technique d'Aeronautique et de Construction Automobile)

**E. T. A. I.**
20 rue de la Saussiere, 92100 Boulogne Billancourt, France.
- Auto Expertise. bi-m.
- Revue Technique Automobile. m. ISSN 0017-307X
- Revue Technique Diesel. bi-m. ISSN 0037-2579

**Echo Africain**
15 rue du Faubourg, Montmartre 75, Paris (9e), France.
- Echo Africain; revue economique sociale culturelle de liaison eurafricaine. q. ISSN 0012-9178

**Echo de la Finance**
9 Bd. des Italiens, Paris (2e), France.
- Echo de la Finance. w. ISSN 0012-9208

**Echo de la Timbrologie**
37 rue des Jacobins, 80036 Amiens, France.
- Echo de la Timbrologie; revue mensuelle de philatelie. m. ISSN 0012-9240

**Echos de Brehat**
Maryvonne a Jouve-Quemarec, Ed., Ile de Brehat 22870, France.
- Echos de Brehat; la vie d'une ile. bi-m.

**Eclaireuses et Eclaireurs Unionistes de France**
15, rue Klock, 92110 Clichy, France.
- A. E. I. O. U. 5 per yr.

**Eclecta**
44, rue Etienne Marcel, 75002 Paris, France.
- G. A. M. (Grands Articles du Mois) m (10 per yr)

**Editions de l' Ecole**
11 rue de Sevres, Paris 6e, France.
- Dossiers d'Education Familiale. irreg. ISSN 0070-7139

**Ecole Biblique et Archeologique de Jerusalem**
- Revue Biblique. (pub. by J. Gabalda et Cie)

**Ecole d'Alfort**
- Recueil de Medecine Veterinaire d'Alfort. (pub. by Editions Vigot Freres)

**Ecole de Specialisation de l'Artillerie Anti-Aerienne**
Nimes (Gard), France.
- Ecole de Specialisation de l'Artillerie Anti-Aerienne. Bulletin d'Information. q. ISSN 0012-9550

**Ecole des Hautes Etudes en Sciences Sociales**
54 Bd. Raspail, Paris 75006, France.
- Actes de la Recherche en Sciences Sociales. bi-m. ISSN 0335-5322 (Co-sponsor: Maison des Sciences de l'Homme)
- C A R D A N. Bulletin d'Information et de Liaison; etudes africaines. q. ISSN 0034-1231 (Centre d'Analyse et de Recherche Documentaire pour l'Afrique Noire)
- Cahiers d'Etudes Africaines. (pub. by Mouton Publishers NE)
- Connaissance et Langage. (pub. by Mouton Publishers NE)

- Documents pour Servir a l'Histoire de l'Afrique Equatoriale Francaise. Deuxieme Serie. Brazza et la Fondation du Congo Francaise. (pub. by Mouton Publishers NE)
- Etudes Rurales. (pub. by Mouton Publishers NE)
- Histoire des Sciences et des Techniques. (pub. by Mouton Publishers NE)
- Homme. (pub. by Mouton Publishers NE)
- Materiaux pour le Manuel de l'Histoire des Song. (pub. by Mouton Publishers NE)
- Nova Americana. (pub. by Mouton Publishers NE)
- Oeuvre Sociologique. (pub. by Mouton Publishers NE)
- Recherche Urbaine. (pub. by Mouton Publishers NE)
- Savoir Geographique. (pub. by Mouton Publishers NE)
- Savoir Historique. (pub. by Mouton Publishers NE)

**Ecole des Hautes Etudes en Sciences Sociales. Centre d'Etudes Chinoise**
- Revue Bibliographique de Sinologie. (pub. by Mouton Publishers NE)

**Ecole des Hautes Etudes en Sciences Sociales. Section des Sciences Economiques et Sociales**
- Ecole des Hautes Etudes en Sciences Sociales. Section des Sciences Economiques et Sociales. Memoires et Travaux. (pub. by Mouton Publishers NE)

**Ecole des Hautes Etudes Hispaniques**
- Bulletin Hispanique. (pub. by Editions Biere)

**Ecole des Parents**
4, rue Brunel, 75 Paris 17e, France.
- Ecole des Parents. m (10 per yr.)

**Ecole Francaise d'Extreme-Orient**
- Ecole Francaise d'Extreme-Orient.Bulletin. (pub. by Librairie Adrien Maisonneuve)

**Ecole Moderne Francaise - Pedagogie Freinet**
Place Bergia, 06403 Cannes, France.
- B T/Bibliotheque de Travail. 15 per yr. ISSN 0005-335X
- B T J. (Bibliotheque de Travail Junior) 15 per yr. ISSN 0005-3120
- B T 2/Bibliotheque de Travail 2d Degre. m. ISSN 0005-3414
- Educateur. 15nos. per school yr. (s-m) ISSN 0013-113X
- S B T. (Bibliotheque de Travail Supplement) s-m. ISSN 0036-1062

**Ecole Nationale du Genie Rural, des Eaux et des Forets**
14 rue Girardet, 54042 Nancy, France.
- Revue Forestiere Francaise. bi-m (plus special issue) ISSN 0035-2829

**Ecole Nationale Superieure de Techniques Avancees**
32, Boulevard Victor, 75015 Paris, France.
- Ecole Nationale Superieure de Techniques Avancees, Paris. Activities Recherche. irreg.

**Ecole Nationale Superieure des Bibliotheques**
2, rue de Louvois, Paris 2e, France.
- Enseignements Professionnels.

**Ecole Normale Israelite Orientale**
45 rue la Bruyere, 75009 Paris, France.
- Alliance Israelite Universelle en France. Cahiers; paix et droit. m. ISSN 0002-6050

**Ecole Normale Veterinaire d'Alfort**
c/o Professeur Guilhon, 7 Av. Gal de Gaulle, 94701 Maisons Alfort, France.
- Academie Veterinaire de France. Bulletin. 6 per yr. ISSN 0001-4192

**Ecole Pratique des Hautes Etudes**
45-47 rue des Ecoles, Paris 5e, France.
- Bulletin des Sciences Mathematiques. (pub. by Centrale des Revues Dunod Gauthier-Villars)
- Cahiers du Monde Russe et Sovietique. (pub. by Editions Mouton et Cie)
- Colloques Internationaux d'Histoire Maritime. Travaux. irreg., 1967, 9th. ISSN 0069-5815
- Documents et Recherches sur l'Economie des Pays Byzantins, Islamiques et Slaves et Leurs Relations Commerciales au Moyen Age. (pub. by Editions Mouton et Cie)
- Materiaux pour l'Etude de l'Extreme-Orient Moderne et Contemporain. Etudes Linguistiques. (pub. by Editions Mouton et Cie)

- Materiaux pour l'Etude de l'Extreme-Orient Moderne et Contemporain. Textes. (pub. by Editions Mouton et Cie)
- Materiaux pour l'Etude de l'Extreme-Orient Moderne et Contemporain. Travaux. (pub. by Editions Mouton et Cie)
- Materiaux pour l'Histoire du Socialisme International. Deuxieme Serie. Essais Bibliographiques. (pub. by Editions Mouton et Cie)
- Materiaux pour l'Histoire du Socialisme International. Premiere Serie. Textes et Documents. (pub. by Editions Mouton et Cie)
- Memoires de Photo-Interpretation. (pub. by France. Institut National de Recherche et de Documentation Pedagogiques)
- Methodes de la Sociologie. (pub. by Editions Mouton et Cie)

**Ecole Pratique des Hautes Etudes. Centre d'Etudes Arctiques et Finno-Scandinaves**
- Bibliotheque Arctique et Antarctique. (pub. by Editions Mouton et Cie)

**Ecole Pratique des Hautes Etudes. Centre d'Etudes de Planification Socialiste**
17 rue des Feuillantines, 75005 Paris, France.
- Ecole Pratique des Hautes Etudes, Paris. Problemes de Planification. irreg. ISSN 0078-9542

**Ecole Pratique des Hautes Etudes. Centre d'Etudes des Communications de Masse**
- Communications. (pub. by Editions du Seuil)

**Ecole Pratique des Hautes Etudes. Centre d'Etudes des Techniques Economiques Modernes**
1 rue Therese, 75001 Paris, France.
- Atlas d'Attraction Urbaine. (pub. by Centrale des Revues Dunod Gauthier-Villars)
- Techniques Economiques Modernes. Analyse Economique. irreg. ISSN 0082-2477
- Techniques Economiques Modernes. Espace Economique. (pub. by Centrale des Revues Dunod Gauthier-Villars)
- Techniques Economiques Modernes. Histoire et Pensee Economique. (pub. by Centrale des Revues Dunod Gauthier-Villars)
- Techniques Economiques Modernes. Production et Marches. (pub. by Centrale des Revues Dunod Gauthier-Villars)

**Ecole Pratique des Hautes Etudes. Centre d'Etudes Pre- et Protohistoriques**
- Archeocivilisation. (pub. by Editions A. et J. Picard)

**Ecole Pratique des Hautes Etudes. Centre de Documentation sur l'Extreme-Orient (Section Chine)**
VIeme Section, 54 boulevard Raspail, Paris (6e), France.
- Bulletin de Liaison pour les Etudes Chinoises en Europe/Newsletter for Chinese Studies in Europe. a. ISSN 0525-4361

**Ecole Pratique des Hautes Etudes. Centre de Documentation sur l'U.R.S.S. et les Pays Slaves**
- Courrier des Pays de l'Est. (pub. by Groupe d'Etudes Prospectives Internationales du C.F.C.E.)
- Etudes sur l'Histoire, l'Economie et la Sociologie des Pays Slaves. (pub. by Editions Mouton et Cie)

**Ecole Pratique des Hautes Etudes, Centre de Mathematique Sociale**
- Mathematiques et Sciences de l'Homme. (pub. by Editions Mouton et Cie)

**Ecole Pratique des Hautes Etudes. Centre de Psychiatrie Sociale**
- Ecole Pratique des Hautes Etudes, Paris. Centre de Psychiatrie Sociale. Publications. (pub. by Editions Mouton et Cie)

**Ecole Pratique des Hautes Etudes, Centre de Recherches**
- Recherches Cooperatives. (pub. by Editions Mouton et Cie)

**Ecole Pratique des Hautes Etudes. Centre de Recherches d'Histoire et de Philologie**
- Ecole Pratique des Hautes Etudes. Quatrieme Section. Historiques et Philologiques. Annuaire. (pub. by Librarie Droz SZ)
- Hautes Etudes du Monde Greco-Romain. (pub. by Librarie Droz SZ)
- Hautes Etudes Islamiques et Orientales d'Histoire Comparee. (pub. by Librarie Droz SZ)

- Hautes Etudes Medievales et Modernes. (pub. by Librarie Droz SZ)
- Hautes Etudes Numismatiques. (pub. by Librarie Droz SZ)
- Hautes Etudes Orientales. (pub. by Librarie Droz SZ)
- Histoire et Civilisation du Livre. (pub. by Librarie Droz SZ)

**Ecole Pratique des Hautes Etudes. Centre de Recherches Historiques**
29 rue d'Ulm, 75230 Paris, France.
- Affaires et Gens d'Affaires. (pub. by France. Institut National de Recherche et de Documentation Pedagogiques)
- Archeologie et Civilisation. (pub. by France. Institut National de Recherche et de Documentation Pedagogiques)
- Civilisations et Societes. (pub. by Editions Mouton et Cie)
- Demographie et Societes. (pub. by France. Institut National de Recherche et de Documentation Pedagogiques)
- Ecole Pratique des Hautes Etudes, Paris. Centre des Recherches Historiques. Oeuvres Etrangeres. irreg., 1965, no. 5. ISSN 0078-9607
- Hommes et la Terre. (pub. by France. Institut National de Recherche et de Documentation Pedagogiques)
- Industrie et Artisanat. (pub. by Editions Mouton et Cie)
- Monnaies, Prix, Conjoncture. (pub. by France. Institut National de Recherche et de Documentation Pedagogiques)

**Ecole Pratique des Hautes Etudes. Centre de Sociologie Europeenne**
- Ecole Pratique des Hautes Etudes, Paris. Centre de Sociologie Europeenne. Cahiers. (pub. by Editions Mouton et Cie)

**Ecole Pratique des Hautes Etudes. Centre International de Recherches d'Histoire des Sciences et des Techniques**
- Histoire de la Pensee. (pub. by Editions Hermann)

**Ecole Pratique des Hautes Etudes. Division des Aires Culturelles**
- Ecole Pratique des Hautes Etudes, Paris. Division des Aires Culturelles. Congres et Colloques. (pub. by Editions Mouton et Cie)
- Etudes Europeennes. (pub. by Editions Mouton et Cie)
- Etudes Juives. (pub. by Editions Mouton et Cie)
- Livre et Societes. (pub. by Editions Mouton et Cie)
- Monde d'Outre-Mer, Passe et Present. 1 Serie: Etudes. (pub. by Editions Mouton et Cie)
- Monde d'Outre-Mer, Passe et Present. 2 Serie: Documents. (pub. by Editions Mouton et Cie)
- Monde d'Outre-Mer, Passe et Present. 3 Serie: Essais. (pub. by Editions Mouton et Cie)
- Monde d'Outre-Mer, Passe et Present. 4 Serie: Bibliographies et Instruments de Travail. (pub. by Editions Mouton et Cie)
- Recherches Mediterraneennes. Serie 1. Etudes. (pub. by Editions Mouton et Cie)
- Recherches Mediterraneennes. Serie 2 Documents. (pub. by Editions Mouton et Cie)
- Recherches Mediterraneennes. Serie 3: Textes et Etudes Linguistiques. (pub. by Editions Mouton et Cie)
- Societe Mouvements Sociaux et Ideologies. 1 Serie: Etudes. (pub. by Editions Mouton et Cie)
- Societe Mouvements Sociaux et Ideologies. 2 Serie: Documents et Temoignages. (pub. by Editions Mouton et Cie)
- Societe Mouvements Sociaux et Ideologies. 3 Serie: Bibliographies. (pub. by Editions Mouton et Cie)
- Textes de Sciences Sociales. (pub. by Editions Mouton et Cie)

**Ecole Pratique des Hautes Etudes. Laboratoire d'Anthropologie**
- Cahiers de l'Homme. Nouvelle Serie. (pub. by Editions Mouton et Cie)

**Ecole Pratique des Hautes Etudes. Laboratoire d'Anthropologie Sociale**
- Cahiers des Etudes Rurales. (pub. by Editions Mouton et Cie)

**Ecole Pratique des Hautes Etudes. Laboratoire de Micropaleontologie**
- Cahiers de Micropaleontologie. (pub. by Centre National de la Recherche Scientifique)

**Ecole Speciale Militaire de Saint-Cyr**
56210 Coetquidan, France.
- Triomphe; plaquette annuelle des promotions de l'ecole speciale militaire de st. cyr et de l'ecole militaire interarmes. a. ISSN 0036-2794 (Co-sponsor: Ecole Militaire Interarmes)

**Ecole Superieure d'Agriculture I.T.P.A.**
38 rue des Ecoles, Paris (5e), France.
- Hommes et Agriculture; technique et pratique agricoles. q.

**Ecole Superieure des Sciences Economiques et Commerciales**
10 rue de Copenhague, 75008 Paris, France.
- Essor Economique et Commercial. q. ISSN 0012-8015

**Ecoles Nationales Veterinaires de Lyon et de Toulouse**
23 Chemin des Capelles, 31076 Toulouse, France.
- Revue de Medecine Veterinaire. m. ISSN 0035-1555

**Economie**
26 rue du Bouloi, 75001 Paris, France.
- Economie; journal d'information economique et politique. bi-m. ISSN 0013-0478

**Economie et Politique**
8, Cite d'Hauteville, 75010 Paris, France.
- Economie et Politique; revue Marxiste d'economie. m.

**Edi-Clef**
9 Ter, rue Lucien-Sampaix, 75010 Paris, France.
- Fers et Quincaillerie. m.

**Edi-Monde**
7, Square Thiers, 75784 Paris Cedex 16, France.
- Confidences. w.
- Journal de Babar. m.
- Journal de Mickey. w.
- Mickey Poche. m.
- Picsou. m.

**Edi-Publi-France**
8 rue Blanche, 75009 Paris, France.
- Annuaire Medical de l'Hospitalisation Francaise. a. ISSN 0066-3298

**Ediafric - la Documentation Africaine**
57 Avenue d'Iena, 75783 Paris Cedex 16, France.
- Bulletin de l'Afrique Noire. w. ISSN 0045-3501
- Economie Ivoirienne. a.
- Hommes et Organisations d'Afrique Noire. bi-m. ISSN 0018-4373
- Penant; revue du droit des pays d'Afrique. q. ISSN 0336-1551
- Revue Juridique et Politique, Independance et Cooperation. q. ISSN 0035-3574
- Societes et Fournisseurs d'Afrique Noire et de Madagascar. Guide Economique Noria. a. ISSN 0081-1289
- Travail et Profession d'Outre- Mer. m. ISSN 0564-1500

**Edibat Publicite**
106 Boulevard Haussmann, 75008 Paris, France.
- Art du Sol et des Murs; ceramique batiment. bi-m. ISSN 0004-3117
- Reflets et Nuances. q.

**EDICEF**
93, rue Jeanne d'Arc, 75623 Paris Cedex 13, France.
- Guide de la Famille. bi-m.

**Ediciones Catalanes de Paris**
18 rue Jobbe-Duval, Paris, France.
- Frontera Oberta. irreg. ISSN 0071-9633

**Editions Edifor**
49 rue St. Andre-des-Arts, Paris 75006, France.
- European Journal of Toxicology/Journal Europeen de Toxicologie. 6 per yr. ISSN 0021-8219
- Journal de Pharmacologie Clinique. q.

**Edima**
7 Villa du Hameau, Chatou (S 20), France.
- Association des Anciens Eleves de l'Ecole Superieure de Fonderie. Bulletin. q. ISSN 0004-5357

**Edinat S.A.R.L.**
Route des Piles, 24000 Perigueux, France.
- Combat Nature; maisons et paysages - mieux vivre. q.

**Ediregie**
3, Cite d'Hauteville, 75010-Paris, France.
- Caravanier. 7 per yr.
- L'Officiel des Terrains de Camping et de Caravaning. 5 per yr.

**EDIREP**
6, rue de Leningrad, 75008 Paris, France.
- Air Industriel; la pneumatique industrielle: production, traitements et applications de l'air comprime. bi-m.
- Assemblages; soudage,colles et adhesifs, fixations mecaniques. bi-m.
- Association Francaise des Techniciens du Petrole. Annuaire. a. ISSN 0066-9261
- Compagnie des Dirigeants d'Approvisionnement et Acheteurs de France. Annuaire. a.
- Hebdocuir. w.
- Petrole et Techniques. bi-m. (Association Francaise des Techniciens du Petrole)
- Revue Generale des Transmissions Mecaniques, Hydrauliques, Pneumatiques, Commandes et Asservissements. 8 per yr.
- Technique Chaussure. m. ISSN 0040-1196

**Edisport**
176 Quai de Jemmapes, 75010 Paris, France
- Bleu et Rouge; le sport a Paris. 6 per yr. ISSN 0045-2289 (Bleu et Rouge, 2 rue de Commandant-Guilbaud)

**Editem**
1, Avenue Niel ., 75017 Paris, France.
- Expomat Actualites; etudes, chantiers, materiels. bi-m.

**Editeurs de Presse Associes**
46 rue Ampere, Paris (17e), France.
- Revue du Jouet. 5 per yr. ISSN 0035-2594

**Edition Collection Scientifique-Progres de l'Homme**
16 rue de la Convention, Paris 15e, France.
- Reanimation et Organes Artificiels. Revue Internationale de Physiologie, Medecine, Chirugie et des Techniques Appliquees aux Sciences Biologiques. irreg. ISSN 0079-9904

**Editions Caracteres**
7 rue de l'Arbalete, 75005 Paris, France.
- Chants des Peuples. irreg. ISSN 0395-7845

**Editions Commerciales Europeennes**
Boite Postale 55, Evreux, France.
- Transports France-Europe. Annuaire Prive National. a. ISSN 0082-5972

**Editions Commerciales Francaises**
64, rue de Paris, 03 Vichy Allier, France.
- France Affaires; guide commercial et immobilier. m. ISSN 0015-9468

**Editions d'Informatique**
82 rue Lauriston, 75116 Paris, France.
- Informatique Nouvelle. m. ISSN 0337-6729

**Editions d'Organisation**
8 rue Alfred de Vigny, 75008 Paris, France.
- Etude du Travail. m. (Association Interprofessionnelle pour l'Etude du Travail)

**Editions d'Utovie**
64260 Lys, France.
- Encyclopedie d'Utovie; revue mensuelle de science populaire. m. ISSN 0396-4957

**S.A.R.L. Editions de la Francite**
20 rue du Louvre, 75001 Paris, France.
- Spectra 2000; recherche analyse controle. m.

**Editions de la Publicite**
A. Brimond, 44 Rue Blanche, Paris (9e), France.
- Journal de la Publicite et des Techniques de la Promotion et Publi-Magazine. s-m. ISSN 0047-214X

**Editions de la Tete de Feuille**
3 rue Crebillon, Paris 6e, France.
- Delphica. irreg. ISSN 0070-3338

**Editions de la Vie Medicale**
133 bis, rue de l'Universite, 75007 Paris, France.
- Revue de Geriatrie. bi-m.

**Editions de Presse**
11 Bis, Rue Leopold-Bellan, Paris (2e), France.
- Promotion des Affaires; information, publicite, relations publiques. m. ISSN 0033-1120

**Editions des Cahiers Astrologiques**
7 rue Condorcet, 75009 Paris, France.
- Cahiers Astrologiques; revue d'astrologie traditionnelle. 6 per yr. ISSN 0007-9596

**Editions du C.N.R.S**
*see* **Centre National de la Recherche Scientifique**

**Editions du Centre de Psychologie Appliquee**
48 Av. Victor Hugo, 75783 Paris, France.
- Revue de Psychologie Appliquee. q. ISSN 0035-1709

**Editions du Genie Civil et de la Metallurgie**
*see* **E.G.C.M.**

**Editions E.L.T.A.**
9 rue Saint-Fiacre, Paris (2e), France.
- Revue des Tabacs; organe international de la culture, de l'industrie et de la vente du tabac. q. ISSN 0035-225X

**Editions et Techniques**
37 rue Raymond Poincare, 10000 Troyes, France.
- Motorisation Agricole; la premiere revue technique d l'agriculture moderne. m.(10 per yr.) ISSN 0027-2272

**Editions Europeennes**
11 bis Ave. de la Providence, 92 Antony, France.
- Revue de Bio-Mathematique/Biomathematics. q. ISSN 0035-1024 (Societe Internationale de Bio-Mathematique)

**Editions Europeennes Thermique et Industrie**
2 Rue des Tanneries, 75013 Paris, France.
- Revue Generale de Thermique; combustibles, energie, equipements thermiques. m. ISSN 0035-3159 (Institut Francais des Combustibles et de l'Energie)

**Editions Financieres Alphabetiques**
3 Av. Trudaine, 75009 Paris, France.
- Repertoire Complementaire Alphabetique des Valeurs Mobilieres Francaises et Etrangeres Non Cotees en France. a. ISSN 0080-0945
- Repertoire General Alphabetique des Valeurs Cotees en France et des Valeurs Non Cotees. a. ISSN 0080-1127

**Editions Geographiques Professionnelles**
9, rue Coetlogon, 75006 Paris, France.
- Revue Generale du Froid. m. ISSN 0035-3205 (Association Francaise du Froid)

**Editions Internationales de Radio-Television**
L'Hotellerie, 14100 Lisieux, France.
- Dossiers Audio-Visuels; revue internationals de radio et television. q.

**Editions Juridiques Lefebvre**
48 rue Cardinet, Paris (17e), France.
- Documentation Rapide du Chef d'Entreprise. bi-m. ISSN 0012-4680
- Memento Pratique des Societes Commerciales. a.

**Editions Legislatives et Administratives**
19 rue Peclet, 75739 Paris 15, France.
- Dictionnaire Permanent de la Construction. m. ISSN 0012-2467
- Dictionnaire Permanent Droit des Affaires. fortn. ISSN 0012-2475
- Dictionnaire Permanent Entreprise Agricole. m. ISSN 0012-2483
- Dictionnaire Permanent Fiscal. w. ISSN 0012-2491
- Dictionnaire Permanent Rural (Droit, Social, Agricole) m.
- Dictionnaire Permanent Social. fortn. ISSN 0012-2513

**Editions Maconniques de France**
16 rue Cadet, Paris(9e), France.
- Humanisme. bi-m. ISSN 0018-7364 (Grand Orient de France)

**Editions Maritimes**
190 Boulevard Haussmann, 75008 Paris, France.
- Annuaire de l'Armement a la Peche; guide de la peche francaise. a. ISSN 0066-2623
- Annuaire de la Maree. a. ISSN 0066-2542
- Peche Maritime. m. ISSN 0031-3726

**Editions Maritimes et d'Outre-Mer**
17 rue Jacob, Paris 6e, France.
- Au Large l'Aventure. irreg. ISSN 0067-0413
- Romans de la Mer. irreg. ISSN 0080-3901
- Sports. irreg. ISSN 0081-3796

**Editions Medicales D.H.R.**
6, Avenue de Camoens, 78150 Rocquencourt-Parly 2, France.
- Actualites d'Angeiologie et de Pathologie Vasculaire. 6 per yr. (Syndicat National des Angeiologues)
- Actualites Psychiatriques. 7 per yr.
- Mises a Jour Cardiologiques. m. ISSN 0300-0702
- Mises a Jour d'Hepato-Gastro-Enterologie. bi-m. (Societe d'Etude et d'Information Medicales)

**Editions Metaux**
32 rue du Marechal-Joffre, Saint-Germain-en Laye, France.
- Metaux; corrosion-industries. m. ISSN 0026-1084

**Editions Mondiales**
2 rue des Italiens, Paris 9e, France.
- Modes de Paris. w. ISSN 0026-8747
- Nous Deux Presente. m. ISSN 0029-4632
- Romans Illustres de Nous Deux. m. ISSN 0035-8134

**Editions Municipales**
38, rue Croix-des-Petits-Champs, Paris (1e), France.
- Paris District. Journal des Communes. q. ISSN 0031-2002
- Paris-Sud; organe d'information des arrondissements sud de paris. m. ISSN 0031-2045

**Editions Ouvrieres**
12 Av. Soeur-Rosalie, Paris (13e), France.
- Mouvement Social. q. ISSN 0027-2671 (Institut Francais d'Histoire Sociale)

**Editions Parisiennes**
4 rue Charles-Divry, 75014 Paris, France.
- Chaud-Froid-Plomberie. m. ISSN 0009-2010

**Editions Professionnelles Francaises et Europeennes**
19 bis, rue de la Republique, 78600 le Mesnil-le-Roi, France.
- Revue Chien 2000. m.

**Editions, Publicites, Recherches et Inventions**
126 Bd. Blanqui, 75013 Paris, France.
- Societe Francaise de Cardiologie. Bulletin d'Informations. q. ISSN 0395-403X (Societe Francaise de Cardiologie)

**Editions Rationalistes**
16 rue de l'Ecole Polytechnique, Paris (5e), France.
- Cahiers Rationalistes. m. ISSN 0008-0462 (Union Rationaliste)
- Raison Presente. q. ISSN 0033-9075

**Editions S.O.S.P.**
59-61 Avenue de la Grande Annee, 75782 Paris Cedex 16, France.
- Autocatalogue; guide technique de mecanique automobile. a. ISSN 0067-2424
- Motocyclo Catalogue; guide technique du cycle et du motocycle. a. ISSN 0077-1570

**Editions S I M**
14 Bd Poissonniere, Paris (9e), France.
- Fiches Medicales; revue de therapeutique et de documentation pratique. m. ISSN 0015-0614

**Editions Sous-Marines**
Building Club Mediterranee, 10 rue de la Bourse, Paris (2e), France.
- Aventure Sous-Marine; techniques et exploration. bi-m. ISSN 0005-1977

**Editions Sportives Francaises**
10 rue du Fg. Montmartre, 75009 Paris, France.
- Athletisme; l'equipe magazine. m. (Equipe)
- Basket Magazine. 8 per yr.
- Cyclisme. m.
- Football Magazine. 12 per yr.
- Rugby. 8 per yr.

**Editions Techniques**
123 rue d'Alesia, 75014 Paris, France.
- Instantanes Medicaux. m. ISSN 0020-2142 (Encyclopedie Medico Chirurgicale)
- Journal du Droit International. q. ISSN 0021-8170
- Recueil Periodique des Juris-Classeurs: Droit Civil. irreg.
- Semaine Juridique; juris-classeur periodique. w. ISSN 0049-0156

**Editions Techniques des Industries de la Fonderie**
12 Av. Raphael, 75016 Paris, France.
- Fonderie. m. ISSN 0015-6094
- Fondeur d'Aujourd'hui. 10 per yr. ISSN 0015-6116

**Editions Techniques des Industries des Corps Gras**
5 Bd. de Latour- Marbourg, 75007 Paris, France.
- Revue Francaise des Corps Gras. m. ISSN 0035-3000 (Institut des Corps Gras (ITERG))

**Editions Techniques et Artistiques**
22 rue Le Brun, 75013 Paris, France.
- Ceramique Moderne. m. ISSN 0009-0336

**Editions Techniques et Economiques**
3, rue Soufflot, 75005 Paris, France.
- Droit de l'Espace; bulletin d'analyses et d'informations. a. ISSN 0419-747X (Centre National de la Recherche Scientifique)
- Revue de Droit Rural. m.
- Revue de l'Energie. m. ISSN 0303-240X
- Revue du Marche Commun. m. ISSN 0035-2616
- Transports. m. ISSN 0564-1373

**Editions Techniques Europeennes**
16 quai de la Marne, 75019 Paris, France.
- Cinema Pratique; cinema pratique chez soi. every 7 wks. ISSN 0009-7128

**Editions Techniques Marseillaises (E.D.I.T.E.M.)**
1 Bd Garibaldi, B. P. 249, 13211 Marseille Cedex 1, France.
- Travaux Publics et Batiment du Midi. w.

**Editions Techniques Patronales**
31 Av. Pierre-Ier-de-Serbie, Paris (16e), France.
- Patronat Francais. m. ISSN 0031-3165 (Conseil National du Patronat Francais)

**Editions Techno-Loisirs**
3 rue Sivel, 75014 Paris, France.
- Techno-Loisirs; guide international annuel de la construction et de l'Equipment pour le sport et les loisirs. biennial.

**Editions Touristiques**
40, rue du Colisee, 75008 Paris, France.
- Echo Touristique. bi-m.
- Voyages et Affaires. q.

**Edito**
23 Bd. Bonne Nowelle, 75002 Paris, France.
- BREF-Peintures. bi-m.

**Education et Developpement**
11 rue de Clichy, 75009 Paris, France.
- Education et Developpement. m. ISSN 0013-1318

**Education Musicale**
3 rue des Ecoles, 77590 Bois-Le-Roi, France.
- Education Musicale; revue culturelle et pedagogique de tout l'enseignement de la musique. 10 per yr. ISSN 0013-1415

**Eglise Chretienne Universelle**
7, la Pepiniere, Ave. Saint-Ruf, 84000 Avignon, France.
- Lumiere. s-m. ISSN 0024-7332
- Messidor; la tribune de Dieu-revue de la vie totale. m. ISSN 0026-0401

**Eglise de la Confession d'Ausburg**
- Messager Evangelique. (pub. by Librairie Oberlin)

**Eglise Evangelique Lutherienne de France**
16 rue Chauchat, 75009 Paris, France.
- Positions Lutheriennes. q. ISSN 0032-5228

**Eglise Orthodox Catholique de France**
96 Bd. Auguste-Blanqui 75, Paris (13e), France.
- Presence Orthodoxe. q. ISSN 0032-4922

**Eglises Reformees Evangeliques Independants de France**
7 rue Godin, 30000 Nimes, France.
- Christ et France-sur le Roc. m. ISSN 0009-5052

**Electricite Automobile**
59, rue du Faubourg Poissonniere, 75009-Paris, France.
- Chambre Syndicale Nationale des Electriciens et Specialistes de l'Automobile. Annuaire. a.
- Electricite Automobile. m.

**Electricite de France**
Direction des Etudes et Recherches, Centre de Documentation, 1, Av. du General de Gaulle, 92140 Clamart, France.
- Documentation Technique. m.
- Electricite de France. Direction des Etudes et Recherches. Bulletin. Serie A: Nucleaire, Hydraulique, Thermique. (pub. by Houille Blanche)
- Electricite de France. Direction des Etudes et Recherches. Bulletin. Serie B: Reseaux Electriques, Materiels Electriques. (pub. by Houille Blanche)
- Electricite de France. Direction des Etudes et Recherches. Bulletin. Serie C: Mathematiques-Informatique. (pub. by Houille Blanche)
- Electricite de France. Rapport d'Activite. a. ISSN 0070-9735
- Electricite de France. Statistiques de la Production et de la Consommation. a. ISSN 0070-9751

**Elle**
100 rue Reaumur, 75002 Paris, France.
- Elle. w. ISSN 0013-6298

**Email Metal**
16, Avenue Hoche, 75008 Paris, France.
- Email Metal. q.

**Embassy of the Philippines**
26 Ave. Georges Mandel, Paris 16e, France.
- Breves Nouvelles des Philippines. bi-m.

**Editions Emer**
50, rue Quai de l'Hotel-de-Ville, Paris, France.
- Guide Europeen de l'Amateur d'Art, de l'Antiquaire et du Bibliophile. biennial. ISSN 0066-3069

**Encres Vives**
c/oMichel Cosem, Ed., Engomer, 09800-Castillon, France.
- Encres Vives. q. ISSN 0013-7103

**Encyclopedie Medico Chirurgicale**
- Instantanes Medicaux. (pub. by Editions Techniques)

**Editions de l' Energumene**
c/o Gerald Julien Salvy, Ed., 31 rue Victor Duruy, Paris 75015, France.
- Energumene. q.

**Engins Matra, S. A.**
47 Av. Louis Breguet, Velizy, France.
- Performances. q.

**Entr'Acte**
29 Bd. Voltaire, Paris(11e), France.
- Entr'Acte; la revue des theatres lyriques. s-m. ISSN 0013-8975

**Entreprise Moderne d'Edition**
4 rue Cambon, 75001 Paris, France
(Subscr. Address: 9 rue du Roussillon-Zone Industrielle, 91220 Bretigny-sur-Orge, France)
- Association Francaise des Ingenieurs et Chefs d'Entretien. Annuaire. a. ISSN 0066-9237
- Documents-Bureau-Progres. 10 per yr.
- Entretien et Travaux Neufs. irreg.
- Informatheque. irreg., 22 titles published as of 1975. ISSN 0073-7836
- Ingenieurs d'Entretien. 9 per yr.
- Les Dossiers CADRECO. bi-m. ISSN 0007-9464

**Editions Entreprises et Techniques**
5 Av. Friedland, Paris 75008, France.
- Travail et Methodes; revue des techniques nouvelles au service de l'entreprise. m. ISSN 0041-185X

**Editions de l' Epargne**
174 Bld. Saint-Germain, Paris 6e, France.
- Annuaire des Caisses d'Epargne; France et Outre-Mer. biennial. ISSN 0066-278X

**Epta**
41, Avenue de Friedland, 75008 Paris, France.
- Ciments et Beton. m.

**Equipe**
- Athletisme. (pub. by Editions Sportives Francaises)

**Equipes d'Action Contre la Traite des Femmes et des Enfants**
21, rue Sainte Croix de la Bretonnerie, 75004 Paris, France.
- Esclavage; document social. q.

**Equipes Enseignantes**
18, rue Ernest Lacoste, 75012 Paris, France.
- Equipes Enseignantes. bi-m.
- Vivante Education. bi-m. ISSN 0042-7535

**Escola Occitana**
31 rue de la Fonderie, 31068 Toulouse, France.
- Gai Saber. q.

**Espaces**
7 rue Cesar Franck, 75015 Paris, France.
- Technique Moderne. 11 per yr. ISSN 0040-1250

**Espaces et Societes**
15 rue Racine, Paris(6e), France.
- Espaces et Societes; revue critique internationale de l'amenagement de l'architecture et de l'urbanisation. q. ISSN 0014-0481

**Esperanto-Editions**
24 Ave de Riedisheim, F-68 Mulhouse, France.
- Esperanto-Lingvo Internacia. q. ISSN 0014-066X

**Esprit et Vie**
Boite Postale 4, 52-Langres, France.
- Esprit et Vie. w. ISSN 0014-0775

**Esprit Libre**
c/o Ed. Georges Krassovsky, 7 rue Boucicaut, 75 Paris (15e), France.
- Esprit Libre. q. ISSN 0014-0783

**Editions Esprit S.A.R.L.**
c/o Paul Thibaud, Ed., 19 rue Jacob, Paris (6e), France.
- Esprit. m. ISSN 0014-0759

**Estrel Editions**
Le Moulin de la Garde, Route de Grasse, 06270 Villeneuve-Loubet, France.
- Revue Internationale d'Heliotechnique. irreg. (Cooperation Mediterraneene pour l'Energie Solaire)

**Editions ETAPE**
19 Ave. George V, 75008 Paris, France.
- Dirigeant. m (10 per yr)

**Etoile Promotion**
3 rue Troyon, 75017 Paris, France.
- Actua. Special Enfants. bi-m. ISSN 0065-180X

**S. A. les Etudes**
15 rue Monsieur, 75007 Paris, France.
- Etudes. m. ISSN 0014-1941
- Recherches de Science Religieuse. q. ISSN 0034-1258

**Etudes Sociales et Syndicales**
86 Bd. Hausmann, Paris (7e), France.
- Etudes Sociales et Syndicales. m. ISSN 0014-2212

**Etudes Sovietiques**
8, rue de Prony, 75017-Paris, France
- Etudes Sovietiques; revue mensuelle d'informations. m. (Subscr. to: C. D. L. P., 146 rue de Fg- Poissonniere, 75010 Paris, France)

**Etudiants Catholiques de la Region Parisienne**
Centre Richelieu, 75005 Paris, Paris(5e), France.
- Paraboles. 5 per yr. ISSN 0031-1561

**Etudiants de la Restauration Nationale**
10 rue Croix-Des-Petits-Champs, 75001 Paris, France.
- Action Francaise Etudiante. m.

**Eureka**
c/oJean LaPlace, Ed., 10 rue Kuss, Paris (13e), France.
- Eureka. m. ISSN 0046-2667

**Europautomation**
83-85 Avenue d'Italie, Paris (13e), France.
- Europautomation. q.

**Europe**
21 rue de Richelieu, Paris (1er), France.
- Europe. m. ISSN 0014-2751
- Vision/Europe. m. ISSN 0042-6954

**Europe Orientale**
26 rue Cadet, 75009 Paris, France.
- Europe Orientale; mensuel d'informations economiques. m. ISSN 0014-2832

**European and Mediterranean Plant Protection Organization**
1, rue le Notre, 75016 Paris, France.
- European and Mediterranean Plant Protection Organization. E P P O Bulletin/Bulletin O E P P. irreg. ISSN 0071-2388
- European and Mediterranean Plant Protection Organization. Publications. Series B: Plant Health Newsletter. irreg., 1973, no. 75. ISSN 0071-2396

**European Association for Micro-Processing and Micro-Programming**
P.B. 233, 6206 Compiegne, France
- Euromicro Newsletter. q. (Subscr. Address: North-Holland Publishing Co., P.O. Box 211 Amsterdam, Netherlands)

**European Association for Personnel Management**
20, rue des Fosses St. Jacques, 75005 Paris, France.
- European Association for Personnel Management. Congress Reports. biennial, 1973, 6th, Portugal. ISSN 0071-2493

**European Cement Association**
2, rue Saint Charles, Paris 15, France.
- European Symposium on Concrete Pavements. Reports. irreg.; 2nd, Berne, 1973.

**European Ceramic Association**
44, rue Copernic, 75 Paris 16e, France.
- International Ceramic Congress. Proceedings. irreg., 1974, 13th, Amsterdam. ISSN 0074-218X

**European Commission of Human Rights**
67006 Strasbourg, France
(Dist. in U. S. by Manhattan Publishing Co., 225 Lafayette St., New York, N. Y. 10012)
- European Commission of Human Rights. Annual Review/Compte Rendu Annual. a.
- European Commission of Human Rights. Collection of Decisions/Recueil de Decisions. irreg., 1973, vol. 41. ISSN 0071-2566
- European Commission of Human Rights. Report. a.

**European Committee for Concrete**
Secretariat Permanent, 6 rue Lauriston, 75116 Paris, France.
- Comite Europeen du Beton. Bulletin d'Information. irreg. ISSN 0071-2574

**European Committee on Crime Problems**
Publications Section, Strasbourg, France
(Dist. in U.S. by Manhattan Publishing Co., 225 Lafayette St., New York, N.Y. 10012)
- Criminology, Criminal Law, Penology. a.
- European Committee on Crime Problems. Bulletin on Legislative Activities. a.

**European Confederation for Physical Therapy**
9 rue des Petits-Hotels, 75 Paris 10e, France.
- Confederation Europeene pour la Therapie Physique (Physiotherapists). Congress Reports. irreg., 1971, 14th, Strasbourg. ISSN 0071-2817

**European Conference of Local Authorities**
Publications Section, Strasbourg, France
(Dist. in U.S. by Manhattan Publishing Co., 225 Lafayette St., New York, N.Y. 10012)
- European Conference of Local Authorities. Documents. irreg. ISSN 0071-2612
- European Conference of Local Authorities. Official Reports of Debates. biennial. ISSN 0071-2620
- European Conference of Local Authorities. Texts Adopted. biennial. ISSN 0071-2639

**European Conference of Ministers of Transport**
- Recherche en Matiere d'Economie des Transports/Research on Transport Economics. (pub. by Organization for Economic Cooperation and Development)

**European Council of Jewish Community Services**
14 rue Georges Berger, 75017 Paris, France.
- European Council of Jewish Community Services. Exchange. irreg.
- Hamore; revue trimestrielle des enseignants juifs. q. ISSN 0046-676X

**European Cultural Foundation. Council for Cultural Co-Operation**
- Paedagogica Europaea. (pub. by Georg Westermann Verlag GW)

**European Information Centre for Nature Conservation**
Publications Section, 67006 Strasbourg, France
(Dist. in U.S. by Manhattan Publishing Co., 225 Lafayette St., New York, N.Y. 10012)
- Conservation of Nature and Natural Resources. a. ISSN 0069-9144
- European Information Centre for Nature Conservation. Newsletter. Nature. m.
- Naturopa. q.

**European Institute of Business Administration**
Bld. de Constance, Fontainebleau, France
(British Address: INSEAD, 1 Cranley Gardens, London N10 3AA, Eng.)
- Institut Europeen d'Administration des Affaires. Annuaire/I N S E A D Address Book. a. ISSN 0073-831X

**European Organization for Civil Aviation Electronics**
16 rue des Presles, 75740 Paris, France.
- European Organisation for Civil Aviation Electronics. General Assembly. Annual Report. a.; latest issue, 1973. ISSN 0531-7444

**European Space Agency**
8-10 rue Mario Nikis, 75738 Paris Cedex 15, France.
- E S A Bulletin. q.
- E S A Journal. q.

**European University News**
2 rue Merimee, 75782- Paris, France.
- European University News. 8 per yr. ISSN 0014-3170

**Europinion**
2 rue Michel Ange, Paris 16e, France.
- Europinion; revue annuelle. a. ISSN 0071-3155

**Euroviande**
34, rue Laroche, 33-Bordeaux, France.
- Euroviande; le courrier des abattoirs viandes. bi-m.

**Exarchat du Patriarche de Moscou**
26 rue Preclet, 75015 Paris, France.
- Messager de l'Exarchat du Patriarche Russe en Europe Occidentale. q. ISSN 0026-0266

**Excelsior Publications**
5 rue de la Baume, 75008 Paris, France.
- Action Automobile et Touristique. m. ISSN 0001-7418
- Limonadier de Paris. m. ISSN 0024-3612 (Syndicat Patronal des Cafes)
- Science et Vie. m. ISSN 0036-8369

**Exchangiste Universel**
7 rue Dr. Belot, 76600 le Havre, France.
- Exchangiste Universel. m. ISSN 0014-4479

**Expansion Scientifique**
15 rue Saint Benoit, 75278 Paris Cedex 06, France.
- Actualite Rhumatologique, Presentee au Praticien; cahier annuel d'informations et de renseignements. a. ISSN 0065-1818
- Annales d'Urologie. 4 per yr. ISSN 0003-4401
- Annales de Biologie Clinique. 6 per yr. ISSN 0003-3898
- Annales de Cardiologie et d'Angeiologie. 7 per yr. ISSN 0003-3928
- Annales de Chirurgie Thoracique et Cardio-Vasculaire. 4 per yr. ISSN 0066-2054 (Societe de Chirurgie Thoracique de Langue Francaise)
- Annales de Gastroenterologie et d'Hepatologie. 6 per yr. ISSN 0066-2070
- Annales de Genetique. Monographs. irreg. ISSN 0066-2089
- Annales de Medecine de Reims Champagne-Ardennes. 6 per yr. ISSN 0301-4444
- Annuaire des Stations Thermales et Climatiques et des Etablissements Medicaux Francais. a.
- Assises de Medecine. a.
- Europa Medica. q. ISSN 0014-2549
- Guide Rosenwald: Annuaire Medical et Pharmaceutique. a. ISSN 0072-8209
- Journal de Medecine de Besancon. 6 per yr. ISSN 0021-7859 (Faculte de Medecine de Besancon)
- Journal de Medecine de Caen. q. ISSN 0021-7875 (Faculte Medicine de Caen)
- Journal de Medecine de Strasbourg. m. ISSN 0021-7905

- Journee de Reeducation. a. ISSN 0075-4420
- Ouest Medical. 20 per yr. ISSN 0048-2366
- Phlebologie. q. ISSN 0031-8280 (Societe Francaise de Phlebologie)
- Presse Thermale et Climatique. 4 per yr. ISSN 0032-7875 (Societe Francaise d'Hydrologie et de Climatologie Medicales)
- Problemes Actuels d'Endocrinologie et de Nutrition. a. ISSN 0079-5666
- Revue de l'Infirmiere. 10 per yr.
- Revue de Medecine de Limoges. 4 per yr.
- Revue de Neuropsychiatrie Infantile et d'Hygiene Mentale de l'Enfance. 8 per yr. ISSN 0035-1628
- Revue du Rhumatisme et des Maladies Osteoarticulaires. 10 per yr. ISSN 0035-2659 (Societe Francaise de Rhumatologie)
- Revue Francaise d'Allergologie et d'Immunologie. q. (Societe Francaise d'Allergie)
- Revue Francaise de Gynecologie et d'Obstetrique. 10 per yr. ISSN 0035-290X
- Semaine des Hopitaux. w.
- Semaine des Hopitaux. Informations. w.
- Societe Francaise de Chirurgie Orthopedique et Traumatologique. Conferences d'Enseignement. irreg. ISSN 0081-1033

**Express**
25 rue de Berri, 75008 Paris, France.
- Express. w. ISSN 0014-5270

**Express Documents**
61 rue de Malte, 75541 Paris Cedex 11, France.
- Affaires. m. ISSN 0001-9615
- Express Documents; juridique fiscal & social. w. ISSN 0014-5289
- Service Economique & Financier "Secofi". w. ISSN 0037-2595

**F N C E T A**
13 Square Gabriel Faure, 75017 Paris, France.
- Enterprises Agricoles. m (10 per yr.) ISSN 0046-2152

**Faculte de Medecine de Besancon**
- Journal de Medecine de Besancon. (pub. by Expansion Scientifique)

**Faculte de Medecine de Marseille**
- Mediterranee Medicale. (pub. by Sud-Regie)

**Faculte de Pharmacie de Strasbourg**
2 rue St. George, Strasbourg, France.
- Societe de Pharmacie de Strasbourg. Bulletin. s-a. ISSN 0037-9131

**Faculte de Philosophie et de Theologie**
- Revue des Sciences Philosophiques et Theologiques. (pub. by Librairie Philosophique J. Vrin)

**Faculte des Sciences**
Tour 15-4 Et., 9 Quai St. Bernard, 75230 Paris Cedex 05, France.
- Revue de Micropaleontologie. q. ISSN 0035-1598

**Faculte des Sciences de Paris. Laboratoire de Geographie Physique**
- Revue de Geographie Physique et de Geologie Dynamique. (pub. by Masson)

**Faculte Medicine de Caen**
- Journal de Medecine de Caen. (pub. by Expansion Scientifique)

**Facultes Catholiques de Lille**
60 Bd. Vauban, 59046 Lille, France.
- Melanges de Science Religieuse. q. ISSN 0025-8911

**Faims et Soifs des Hommes**
2 Avenue de la Liberte, 94220 Chareuton, France.
- Faims et Soifs des Hommes. m. ISSN 0014-6889

**Editions Georges Fall**
15 Rue Paul Fort, 75014 Paris, France.
- Opus International. bi-m. ISSN 0048-2056

**Fasquelle Editeurs**
61 rue Saints-Peres, Paris(6e), France.
- Cahiers Naturalistes. a. ISSN 0008-0365 (Societe Litteraire des Amis d'Emile Zola)

**Librairie Fayard**
6 rue Casimir Delavigne, Paris 6e, France.
- Aventure des Civilisations. irreg. ISSN 0067-2629
- Management, Fonctions, Methodes, Experiences. irreg. ISSN 0076-3616

**Federation Anarchiste**
3 rue Ternaux, 75011 Paris, France.
● Monde Libertaire. m. ISSN 0026-9433

**Federation Archeologique Septentrion**
50, rue de la Colonne, 62200-Saint-Martin-Boulogne, Calais, France.
● Septentrion; revue archeologique trimestrielle. q.

**Federation d'Associations de Techniciens des Industries des Peintures, Vernis, Emaux et Encres d'Imprimerie de l'Europe Continentale**
Maison de la Chimie, 28 rue Saint Dominique, 75007 Paris, France.
● Congress F A T I P E C. biennial, 11th congress, Milan, 1972. ISSN 0430-2222
● Federation d'Associations de Techniciens des Industries des Peintures, Vernis, Emaux et Encres d'Imprimerie de l'Europe Continentale. Annuaire Officiel. Official Yearbook. Amtliches Jahrbuch. biennial. ISSN 0071-416X

**Federation de l'Education Nationale**
10, rue de Solferino, 75341 Paris Cedex 07, France.
● Enseignement Public. 8 per yr.
● FEN Informations. m.

**Federation Departementale des Combattants Republicains**
25 Ave. De. Bonfflers, Nancy 54, France.
● Poilu Lorrain. 6 per yr. ISSN 0032-2288

**Federation des Amicales Regimentaires et d'Anciens Combattants**
28 Bd. de Strasbourg, 75010-Paris, France.
● Amicales Regimentaires. q.

**Federation des Amputes de Guerre de France**
74 Boulevard Haussmann, Paris(8e), France.
● Ampute de Guerre. m. ISSN 0044-815X

**Federation des Associations des Proprietaires Urbains et Ruraux de la Bretagne et de l'Ouest de la France**
6. R. Saint-Louis, 35000 Rennes, France.
● Bretagne Immobiliere. m.

**Federation des Associations et Societes Francaises d'Ingenieurs Diplomes**
19 rue Blanche, 75009 Paris, France.
● I.D. (Ingenieurs Diplomes) q. ISSN 0536-1362

**Federation des Chambres Syndicales de l'Industrie du Verre**
Office d'Etudes Publicitaires, 23 rue Galvani, Paris 7e, France.
● Annuaire National du Verre. irreg. ISSN 0066-3557 (Co-sponsor: Federation des Christalleries Verreries a la Main et Mixtes)

**Federation des Comites d'Alliance Ouvriere**
88 bis, Ave. Parmentier, 75011 Paris, France.
● Federation des Comites d'Alliance Ouvriere. Informations Ouvrieres. w. ISSN 0020-0484

**Federation des Conseils de Parents d'Eleves**
49 rue Isabey, 54 Nancy, France.
● Guide des Parents d'Eleves. q. ISSN 0017-5250

**Federation des Conseils de Parents d'Eleves des Ecoles Publiques (FCPE)**
209 Bd. Saint-Germain, 75007 Paris, France.
● Pour l'Enfant Vers l'Homme; la revue des parents. m. ISSN 0048-4997

**Federation des Debitants de Tabac de l'Etat**
47, rue Carnot, 88-Raon l'Etape, France.
● Herbe a Nicot. m. ISSN 0018-0610

**Federation des Debitants de Tabac de l'Ile-de-France**
● Federation des Debitants de Tabac de l'Ile-de-France. Annuaire Officiel. (pub. by Pym Editeur)

**Federation des Dirigeants Commerciaux et Economiques de France et d'Expression Francaise**
30 rue d'Astorg, 75008 Paris, France.
● Annuaire Europeen des Directeurs Commerciaux et de Marketing. a. ISSN 0066-3077

**Federation des Francs et Franches Camarades**
66 rue de Chausse d'Antin, Paris 9, France.
● Camaraderie. q.
● Jeunes Annees. 8 per yr. ISSN 0021-6143

**Federation des Hautes Pyrenees du Parti Socialiste Unifie**
6 rue du 4 Septembre, Lannemezan, France.
● Reveil Socialiste de Lannemezan. m. ISSN 0034-6292

**Federation des Industries Electriques et Electroniques**
● Industries Electriques et Electroniques. (pub. by Editions Indelec)

**Federation des Industries Electriques et Electroniques. Syndicat General de la Construction Electrique**
● Syndicat General de la Construction Electrique. Annuaire. (pub. by Union Francaise d'Annuaires Professionnels)

**Federation des Industries Ferroviaires**
● French Railway Techniques. (pub. by Centrale des Revues Dunod Gauthier-Villars)

**Federation des Industries Mecaniques et Transformatrices des Metaux**
● Annuaire de la Mecanique. (pub. by Union Francaise d'Annuaires Professionnels)
● Annuaire Technique de la Sous - Traitance Mecanique. (pub. by Union Francaise d'Annuaires Professionnels)
● Industries Mecaniques. (pub. by Editions Sedom)

**Federation des Industries Mecaniques et Transformatrices des Metaux. Syndicat National de l'Estampage et de la Forge**
● Estampage, Forge, Extrusion et Techniques Connexes. (pub. by Union Francaise d'Annuaires Professionnels)

**Federation des Industries Nautiques**
● Industries Nautiques. (pub. by Editions de Chabassol)

**Federation des Maisons Familiales de Vacances**
28 Place St-Georges, 75442 Paris 9, France.
● Nos Maisons Familiales de Vacances. q. ISSN 0048-0843

**Federation des Parents d'Eleves de l'Enseignement Publique**
91 Bd. Berthier, Paris (17e), France.
● Voix des Parents. q. ISSN 0049-6693

**Federation des Societes d'Histoire Naturelle de Franche-Comte**
c/o M. Tavant, Faculte des Sciences, 25030 Besancon Cedex, France.
● Federation des Societes d'Histoire Naturelle de Franche-Comte. Bulletin. q. ISSN 0014-9357

**Federation des Societes de Croix-Marine**
59 rue de Chateaudun, Clermont-Ferrand, France.
● Revue Pratique de Psychologie de la Vie Sociale et d'Hygiene Mentale. q.

**Federation des Societes Musicales Dauphinoises**
c/o M. Malfait, 1 rue du Serre de l'Aure, 05000 Gap, France.
● Musicien d'Auphinois. bi-m.

**Federation des Societes Philateliques Francaises**
7 rue Saint-Lazare, 75009 Paris, France.
● Philatelie Francaise. m.

**Federation des Syndicats d'Epiciers Detaillants de France**
16, rue Bachaumont, 75002 Paris, France.
● Nouvel Epicier. m.

**Federation des Syndicats Pharmaceutiques de France**
13 rue Ballu, 75009 Paris, France.
● Pharmacien de France; organe d'informations scientifiques et professionnelles. bi-m. ISSN 0031-6938

**Federation des Travaux Publics et des Transports**
78 rue de l'Universite, Paris (7e), France.
● Federation des Travaux Publics et des Transports, Paris. Revue. q. ISSN 0046-3523

**Federation du Cinema Educatif et des Techniques Audio-Visuelles Agree**
27, rue de Poissy, 75005 Paris, France.
● Films et Documents. m.

**Federation Europeenne de la Construction**
● Entreprise Europeenne. (pub. by Societe d'Editions et de Publications Internationales du Batiment et des Travaux Publics)

**Federation Europeenne des Societes Theosophiques**
● Lotus Bleu. (pub. by Societe Theosophique de France)

**Federation Familiale Nationale pour l'Enseignement Agricole Priv e**
227 rue St.-Jacques, 75005 Paris, France.
● Presence de l'Enseignement Agricole Prive. q. ISSN 0339-0055

**Federation Folklorique d'Ile-de-France**
● Bulletin Folklorique d'Ile-De-France. (pub. by Bibliotheque Historique de la Ville de Paris)

**Federation Francaise a Voile**
70, rue Saint-Lazare, 75009 Paris, France.
● Yachting a Voile. bi-m.

**Federation Francaise d'Athletisme**
10 rue Faubourg Poissonniere, 75480 Paris Cedex 10, France.
● Athletisme Francais. a. ISSN 0067-012X

**Federation Francaise d'Education Physique et de Gymnastique Volontaire**
2, rue de Valois, 75001 Paris, France.
● Gymnastique Volontaire. 5 per yr. ISSN 0335-2986

**Federation Francaise de Bridge**
● Revue Francaise de Bridge. (pub. by Michel Bongrand S.A.)

**Federation Francaise de Judo et Disciplines Associees**
● Judo. (pub. by Publijudo)

**Federation Francaise de Motocyclisme**
36 rue d'Hauteville, 75010 Paris, France.
● F. F. M. Annuaire Officiel. a. ISSN 0071-4186

**Federation Francaise de Natation**
148 Av. Gambetta, Paris 20e, France.
● Federation Francaise de Natation. Annuaire. a. ISSN 0071-4194

**Federation Francaise de Ski**
34, rue Eugene Flachat, 75017 Paris, France.
● Ski Francais. bi-m.

**Federation Francaise de Sports pour Handicapes Physiques**
1 Av. Pierre-Grenier, 92100 Boulogne, France.
● Federation Francaise de Sports pour Handicapes Physiques. Informations. irreg. ISSN 0395-7594
● Second Souffle. q. ISSN 0048-9972

**Federation Francaise de Tennis de Table**
84, Avenue Wagram, 75017 Paris, France.
● France Tennis de Table. m(10 per yr)

**Federation Francaise des Agences de Presse**
4 Bis, Rue de Clery, 75002 Paris, France.
● Federation Nationale des Agences de Presse. Annuaire. a. ISSN 0071-4305

**Federation Francaise des Cadres de la Fonction Publique**
30, rue de Gramont, 75002 Paris, France.
● Voix des Cadres de la Fonction Publique. bi-m.

**Federation Francaise des Cineclubs**
6, rue Ordener, 75018 Paris, France.
● Cinema. m. ISSN 0578-2945

**Federation Francaise des Clubs de Femmes de Carrieres Liberales et Commerciales et de Professions Diverses**
c/o Mme. Kraemer-Bach, 75 rue de Longchamp, Paris 16e, France.
● Union Professionnelle Feminine. Annuaire. a. ISSN 0082-7770

**Federation Francaise des Equipes Saint-Vincent**
67 rue de Sevres, Paris 6, France.
● Equipes St Vincent. 3 per yr.

**Federation Francaise des Fabricants de Caisses Emballages en Bois**
36 Avenue Hoche, 75 Paris(8e), France.
● Caisses et Emballages en Bois. 2 per mo. ISSN 0045-3811

**Federation Francaise des Industries Transformatrices des Plastiques**
- Repertoire Technique de la Sous-Traitance des Industries Plastiques. (pub. by Union Francaise d'Annuaires Professionnels)

**Federation Francaise des Maitres-Nageurs Sauveteurs**
23, rue de la Sourdiere, 75001 Paris, France.
- Nager Sauver. q.

**Federation Francaise des Masseurs-Kinesitherapeutes Reeducateurs.**
9 rue des Petits-Hotels, 75010 Paris, France.
- Annuaire National des Masseurs Kinesitherapeutes. a. ISSN 0337-5935

**Federation Francaise des Papetiers Specialistes**
48, rue de la Bienfaisance, 75008-Paris, France.
- L'Officiel des Papetiers Specialistes. m.

**Federation Francaise des Societes d'Aviron**
93, rue Saint Lazare, 75009-Paris, France.
- Aviron. 10 per yr.

**Federation Francaise des Societes de Sciences Naturelles**
- Annee Biologique. (pub. by Masson)

**Federation Francaise des Sports Equestres**
164 Fg. Saint - Honore, 75008 Paris, France.
- Sports Equestres; revue officielle de la Federation Francaise des Sports Equestres. m. ISSN 0395-3491

**Federation Francaise du Jeu de Dames**
25 rue de l'Ermitage, 75020 Paris, France.
- L'Effort; jeu de dames. bi-m. ISSN 0013-2225

**Federation Francaise et Europeenne du Commerce de l'Industrie et de l'Epargne**
44 rue de Reuilly, Paris (12e), France.
- Federation Francaise et Europeenne du Commerce, de l'Industrie et de l'Epargne. Revue. irreg. ISSN 0071-4240

**Federation Historique de Provence**
- Provence Historique. (pub. by Librairie Honore Champion)

**Federation Hospitaliere de France**
83-87, Avenue d'Italie, 75013 Paris, France.
- Revue Hospitaliere de France. m (10 per yr.)

**Federation Internationale Culturelle Feminine**
*see* Women's International Cultural Federation

**Federation Internationale de la Presse Cinematographique**
*see* International Federation of the Cinematographic Press

**Federation Internationale de Medaille**
46 rue de Rennes, 75006 Paris, France.
- Medailles. s-a. ISSN 0025-6625

**Federation Internationale de Rugby Amateur**
*see* International Amateur Rugby Federation

**Federation Internationale des Editeurs de Journaux et Publications**
*see* International Federation of Newspaper Publishers

**Federation Internationale des Organisations de Donneurs de Sang**
c/o Secretary General, Pierre Pelletier, Boite Postale 100, F 39108 Dole, France.
- Don Universel du Sang. q. ISSN 0012-5407

**Federation Internationale des Producteurs Agricoles**
*see* International Federation of Agricultural Producers

**Federation Internationale des Producteurs de Jus de Fruits**
*see* International Federation of Fruit Juice Producers

**Federation Internationale des Professeurs de Francais**
Centre International d'Etudes Pedagogiques, 1 Ave. Leon Journault, 92310 Sevres, France.
- Federation Internationale des Professeurs de Francais. Bulletin. s-a

**Federation Interprofessionnelle de la Congelation Ultra-Rapide**
3 rue de Logelbach, 75847 Paris 17, France.
- Surgelation. m. ISSN 0049-2647

**Federation Interprofessionnelle de la Region Parisienne**
23, rue Philippe-de-Girard, 75010 Paris, France.
- Paris Service Information. m.

**Federation Intersyndicale des Maisons de Sante Privees de France et d'Outremer**
71, Avenue Victor Hugo, 75116 Paris, France.
- Hospitalisation Privee. m. ISSN 0439-6162

**Federation Mondiale des Villes-Cites Unies**
*see* United Towns Organization

**Federation Nationale d'Habitat Rural**
27 rue La Rochefoucauld, Paris 9e, France.
- Annuaire des Organismes d'Habitat Rural. a. ISSN 0066-2917

**Federation Nationale de Commercants de France**
29 rue Fortuny, Paris (17e), France.
- Betail. fortn. ISSN 0005-9765

**Federation Nationale de l'Industrie de la Chaussure de France**
30 Ave. George V., 75008 Paris, France.
- Federation Nationale de l'Industrie de la Chaussure de France. Annuaire. irreg. ISSN 0071-4291

**Federation Nationale de l'Industrie Laitiere**
140 Bd. Haussmann, Paris 8e, France.
- Federation Nationale de l'Industrie Laitiere. Bulletin d'Information. s-m. ISSN 0014-939X

**Federation Nationale de la Coiffure**
- Coiffeur de France. (pub. by S.E.I.D.)
- Voix de la Coiffure Francaise. (pub. by S.E.I.D.)

**Federation Nationale de la Maroquinerie**
- Maroquinerie-Voyage-Parapluie-Chaussure. (pub. by Editions Asteria)

**Federation Nationale de la Presse Francaise**
6 Bis rue Gabriel-Laumain, Paris (10e), France.
- Cahiers de la Presse Francaise. 10 per yr. ISSN 0300-4538

**Federation Nationale de la Propriete Agricole**
5 rue Quentin Bauchart, 75008 Paris, France.
- Propriete Agricole. m.

**Federation Nationale des Agents Commerciaux**
23 rue des Mathurins, 75008 Paris, France.
- Agent Commercial. bi-m. ISSN 0002-0826

**Federation Nationale des Anciens Combattants et Caolets des Transmissions**
60 Quai Michelet, Levallois 92, France.
- Federation Nationale des Anciens Combattants et Caolets des Transmissions. Liason des Transmissions. bi-m. ISSN 0024-1709

**Federation Nationale des Anciens Combattants, Prisonniers, Deportes, Resistants et Victimes de Guerre des Chemins de Fer Francais (ENCAC)**
61, rue d'Anjou, 75008 Paris, France.
- Voix du Cheminot Ancien Combattant. q.

**Federation Nationale des Anciens des Forces Francaises en Allemagne et en Autriche, Rhenanie, Ruhr & Tyrol**
39 rue de Caumartin, Paris (9e), France.
- Ceux des F F A. q. ISSN 0009-0808

**Federation Nationale des Artisans Electriciens**
11, rue des Petites Ecuries, 75010 Paris, France.
- Revue de l'Artisan Electricien. m.

**Federation Nationale des Boissons**
49, rue de la Glaciere, 75013 Paris, France.
- Boissons de France "Saines et Legeres". m. ISSN 0006-5803

**Federation Nationale des Clubs**
B.P. 100-07, 75326 Paris Cedex 07, France.
- Federation Nationale des Clubs "Perspectives et Realites". m. ISSN 0031-5974

**Federation Nationale des Clubs Automobiles de France**
8 Pl. de la Corcorde, Paris 8e, France.
- Federation Nationale des Clubs Automobiles de France. Annuaire. a. ISSN 0071-4321

**Federation Nationale des Combattants Prisonniers de Guerre et Combattants d'Algerie, Tunisie, Maroc.**
46 rue Copernic, Paris (16e), France.
- C A T M. (Combattants d'Algerie, Tunisie, Maroc) m.

**Federation Nationale des Comites de Vigilance**
9 Cite Trevise, Paris (9e), France.
- Tribune de l'Enfance. ISSN 0041-283X

**Federation Nationale des Compagnies de Theatre et d'Animation**
12 Chaussee d'Antin, 75441 Paris Cedex 09, France.
- Theatre et Animation; revue triemestrielle des spectacles non-professionnels et des techniques d'expression et de animation. q. ISSN 0398-0049 (Co-sponsor: Federation Catholique du Theatre Amateur Francais)

**Federation Nationale des Conseils Juridiques et Fiscaux**
16 Pl. de la Madeleine, Paris 8e, France.
- Federation Nationale des Conseils Juridiques et Fiscaux. Cahiers. irreg. ISSN 0071-4348

**Federation Nationale des Cooperatives de Consommation**
c/o Roger Kerinec, 89 rue la Boetie, 75008 Paris, France.
- Annuaire de la Cooperation F.N.C.C. (pub. by Societe Cooperative d'Edition et de Librairie)
- Cooperateur de France. 2 per mo. ISSN 0045-8457

**Federation Nationale des Cooperatives Ouvrieres de Production du Batiment, des Travaux Publics et des Activites Annexes**
88 rue de Courcelles, Paris (8e), France.
- Chantiers Cooperatifs. m. ISSN 0009-1596

**Federation Nationale des Foyers Ruraux de France**
96 rue de Javel, 75015 Paris, France.
- Federation Nationale des Foyers Ruraux de France. Bulletin d'Information. bi-m.

**Federation Nationale des Groupements de Protection des Cultures**
64, rue la Boetie, 75008 Paris, France.
- Defense des Vegetaux; revue des groupements de protection des cultures. bi-m. ISSN 0011-7579

**Federation Nationale des Groupements des Entreprises Francaises dans la Lutte Contre le Cancer**
4 rue Auber, Paris 8e, France.
- Groupement des Entreprises Francaises dans la Lutte Contre le Cancer. Bulletin National de Liaison. irreg., 1970, no. 4. ISSN 0072-7806

**Federation Nationale des Industries Electroniques**
11 rue Hamelin, 75783 Paris 16, France.
- Electronique Francaise. irreg.
- Industrie Electronique Francaise. irreg.
- Syndicat des Industries de Materiel Professionnel Electronique et Radioelectrique. Annuaire. irreg. ISSN 0082-1020

**Federation Nationale des Medecins Omnipraticiens Francais**
30 rue de Londres, Paris (9e), France.
- Omnipraticien Francais. m. ISSN 0030-2287

**Federation Nationale des Mineurs CFDT**
35, rue des Ferronniers, 59500 Douai, France.
- Journal du Mineur. m. ISSN 0397-1511

**Federation Nationale des Negociants en Materiaux de Construction**
215 Boulevard Saint Germain, 75007 Paris, France.
- Federation Nationale des Negociants en Materiaux de Construction. Bulletin d'Informations. bi-m.

**Federation Nationale des Organisations Sanitaires Apicoles Departementales**
149 rue de Bercy, 75579 Paris Cedex 12, France.
- Sante de l'Abeille. q. ISSN 0036-4568

**Federation Nationale des Plus Grands Invalides de Guerre**
13, Avenue de la Motte-Picquet, 75007 Paris, France.
- Grand Invalide. m.

**Federation Nationale des Producteurs de l'Horticulture et des Pepinieres.**
- Annuaire Federal de l'Horticulture et des Pepinieres. (pub. by Regitec, J. de Vaubernier et Cie)

**Federation Nationale des Promoteurs-Constructeurs (F. N. P. C.)**
106 rue de l'Universite, 75007 Paris, France.
- Promotion Immobiliere; hommes et logements. bi-m. with 2 special nos.

**Federation Nationale des Republicains Independants.**
195, Bd Saint-Germain, Paris (7e), France.
- France Moderne. m.

**Federation Nationale des Sapeurs-Pompiers Francais**
27 rue de Dunkerque, Paris (10e), France.
- Sapeur-Pompier. 6 per yr. ISSN 0036-469X

**Federation Nationale des Societes Cooperatives d'H.L.M.**
20 rue de Richelieu, 75001 Paris, France.
- Coop-Habitat; revue de l'habitat familial. q. ISSN 0010-8308

**Federation Nationale des Societes d'Economie Mixte de Construction, d'Amenagement et de Renovation**
66 Bld. Malesherbes, 75008 Paris, France.
- Federation Nationale des Societes d'Economie Mixte de Construction, d'Amenagement et de Renovation. Annuaire. triennial. ISSN 0081-1262

**Federation Nationale des Syndicats. Departement des Medicins Electro- Radiologistes Qualifies**
60 Bld. Latour Maubourg, 75327 Paris, France.
- Medecin Electro-Radiologiste Qualifie de France. Annuaire. a. ISSN 0076-5813

**Federation Nationale des Syndicats d'Exploitants Agricoles**
8 Av. Marceau, Paris (8e), France.
- Information Agricole. m. ISSN 0019-994X

**Federation Nationale des Syndicats d'Ingenieurs et de Cadres**
30, rue de Gramont, 75 Paris (2e), France.
- Elites et Responsabilites; cahiers du Centre Economique et Social de Perfectionnement des Cadres. 3 per yr. ISSN 0013-6239
- Ingenieurs et Cadres de France. (pub. by Compagnie Europeenne d'Expansion)

**Federation Nationale des Syndicats de Droguistes**
- Droguerie Francaise la Couleur. (pub. by Editions P.B.M.)

**Federation Nationale des Syndicats de Proprietaires Forestiers**
6 rue de la Tremoille, Paris (8e), France.
- Forets de France et Action Forestiere. 8 per yr. ISSN 0046-4619

**Federation Nationale des Syndicats de Societes de Commerce Exterieur**
31avenue Pierre-Ier-de-Serbie, 75784 Paris Cedex 16, France.
- Repertoire des Societes de Commerce Exterieur Francaises. irreg. ISSN 0080-1070

**Federation Nationale des Travaux Publics**
- Travaux. (pub. by Science et Industrie)

**Federation Nationale des Travaux Publics et des Syndicats Affilies**
- T P Annales. (pub. by Centre de l'Industrie Francaise des Travaux Publics)

**Federation Nationale du Batiment**
33, Av. Kleber, Paris 16e, France.
- Federation Nationale du Batiment. Mensualisation des Ouvriers du Batiment. irreg.

**Federation Nationale du Commerce des Engrais et Produits Connexes**
216 Bourse du Commerce, 75040 Paris 1, France.
- Engrais; la fertilisation, la protection des vegetaux. m. (10 per yr.)

**Federation Nationale du Commerce et de l'Artisanat Automobile**
- Officiel de l'Automobile. (pub. by Societe S.L.O.C.A.M.)

**Federation Nationale du Commerce et de la Reparation du Cycle & Motocycle**
- Officiel du Cycle, du Motocycle et de la Motoculture. (pub. by Societe S.L.O.C.A.M.)

**Federation Nationale du Credit Agricole**
10 rue Magellan, Paris 8e, France.
- Federation Nationale du Credit Agricole. Annuaire du Credit Agricole Mutuel. a. ISSN 0071-4380

**Federation Nationale "les Fils des Tues"**
25, rue Lavoisier, 75008 Paris, France.
- Journal des Orphelins de Guerre. m.

**Federation Nationale Teinture et Apprets**
- Teinture et Apprets. (pub. by Societe d'Edition Technique de l'Ennoblissement Textile)

**Federation pour le Respect de l'Homme et de l'Humanite (F.R.H.)**
20, rue Lafitte, 75009 Paris, France.
- Federation pour le Respect de l'Homme et de l'Humanite. Selections Mensuelles. m.
- Homme et l'Humanite. q.

**Federation Protestante de France**
47 rue de Clichy, Paris 9e, France.
- Federation Protestante de France. Centre d'Etudes et de Documentation. Bulletin. 10 per yr. ISSN 0008-9842 (prep. by its Centre d'Etudes et de Documentation)
- Service Protestant Francais de Presse et d'Information. w. ISSN 0037-2625

**Federation Sportive et Culturelle de France**
5 rue Cernuschi, Paris (17e), France.
- Jeunes. s-m. ISSN 0021-6135

**Federation Sportive et Gymnique du Travail**
24, rue Yves-Toudic, 75010 Paris, France.
- Sport et Plein Air. m (11 per yr)

**Federation Unie des Auberges de Jeunesse**
11 bis, Rue de Milan, Paris (9e), France.
- Jeunes des Auberges. q. ISSN 0021-616X

**Femme Pratique**
352 rue Saint-Honore, 75001-Paris, France.
- Femme Pratique. m. ISSN 0014-9926

**Femmes Chefs d'Entreprise**
25 Rue de Mouzaia, Paris, France.
- Femmes Chefs d'Entreprise. q' ISSN 0014-9942

**Fenix**
1 rue de Grand Saint Jean, Montpellier 34(Herault), France.
- Fenix. 4 per yr. ISSN 0014-9993

**Fermes Modernes**
15-17, rue Godefroy-Cavaignac, 75541 Paris Cedex 11, France.
- Fermes Modernes; la revue de l'equipement agricole. m.

**Feuille Anarchiste**
122 Ave. de Choisy, Paris (13e), France.
- Feuille Anarchiste. q. ISSN 0015-041X

**Feuille Internationale d'Architecture**
29, Bd Edgar-Quinet, 75014 Paris, France.
- Carre Bleu. q. ISSN 0008-6878

**Feuillets du Praticien**
18 rue de l'Universite, Paris (7e), France.
- Feuillets du Praticien. m. ISSN 0015-0452

**Figaro Litteraire**
14 Rond-Point des Champs-Elysees, Paris (8e), France.
- Figaro Litteraire. w. ISSN 0015-0843

**Publications Filipacchi**
65 Champs Elysees, 75008 Paris, France.
- Une Semaine de Paris-Pariscope. w. ISSN 0049-5190

**Fin de Siecle**
43 rue du Moulin Vert, 75014 Paris, France.
- Fin de Siecle. 5 per yr.

**Librairie Fischbacher**
33 rue de Seine, 75-Paris 6, France.
- Annuaire International des Ventes. a. ISSN 0066-3263
- Annuaire Protestant; la France Protestante et les Eglises de Langue Francaise. a. ISSN 0066-362X (Centrale du Livre Protestant)
- Dictionnaire des Valeurs des Meubles et Objets d'Art. irreg. ISSN 0070-4776
- Ecrits Libres. irreg., 1973, no. 16. ISSN 0070-8860

- Esprit et Liberte; Protestantisme liberal. irreg., 1973, no. 24. ISSN 0071-1330
- Grands Courants de la Pensee Mondiale Contemporaine. irreg. ISSN 0072-5455
- Histoire de l'Europe. irreg. ISSN 0073-2354
- Histoire de la Philosophie Europeenne. irreg. ISSN 0073-2370
- Rudolf Steiner Publications. irreg. ISSN 0080-4789 (Rudolf Steiner Nachlassverwaltung)

**Flammarion**
Service des Periodiques, 26 rue Racine, 75006 Paris, France.
- Libyca; anthropologie, prehistoire, ethnographie. a. ISSN 0459-3030 (Centre de Recherches Anthropologiques, Prehistoriques et Ethnographiques AE)

**Flammarion Medecine Sciences**
20 rue de Vaugirard, 75006 Paris, France (U.S. subscr. address: c/o M. Juery, S. M. P. F., 14 East 60 St., New York, NY 10022)
- Actualites Nephrologiques. a. ISSN 0073-3326 (Hopital Necker. Clinique Nephrologique)
- Annee en Reanimation. irreg.
- Institut Pasteur de Lille. Annales. irreg. ISSN 0073-8573
- Journees Annuelles de Diabetologie de l'Hotel Dieu. a. ISSN 0075-4439 (Hotel-Dieu. Clinique Medico-Sociale du Diabete et des Maladies Metaboliques)
- Journees Parisiennes de Pediatrie. a. ISSN 0075-4471 (Hopital des Enfants Malades. Centre d'Estudes sur les Maladies du Metabolisme Chez l'Enfant)

**Flammes Vives**
50 rue de Montreuil, Paris (11e), France.
- Flammes Vives. q. ISSN 0015-3486

**Fleurus-Presse International**
31 rue de Fleurus, 75260 Paris Cedex 06, France.
- Christiane; pour les jeunes filles de 15 a 20 ans. m. ISSN 0009-5710 (Union des Oeuvres Catholiques de France)
- Communaute Humaine. irreg. ISSN 0069-7753 (Centre Communautaire International)
- Dans la Lumiere. m. (9 per yr.) (Union des Oeuvres Catholiques de France)
- Djin. w. (Union des Oeuvres Catholiques de France)
- Enjeu. 9 per yr. (Union des Oeuvres Catholiques de France)
- Formule 1; pour les garcons de 12 a 15 ans. w. ISSN 0021-3802 (Union des Oeuvres Catholiques de France)
- Fripounet-Marisette. w. ISSN 0016-1446 (Union des Oeuvres Catholiques de France)
- Perlin et Pinpin. w. ISSN 0031-546X (Union des Oeuvres Catholiques de France)

**Foi et Vie**
139 Bd. Montparnasse, 75006 Paris 6, France.
- Foi et Vie. 6 per yr. ISSN 0015-5357

**Fondation Calouste Gulbenkian**
- Poetes et Prosateurs du Portugal. (pub. by Presses Universitaires de France)

**Fondation Francaise d'Etudes Nordiques**
- Inter-Nord; Revue Internationale d'Etudes Arctiques et Nordiques. (pub. by Editions Mouton et Cie)

**Fondation Nationale des Politiques et Direction de la Documentation**
- Maghreb, Machrek, Monde Arabe. (pub. by Documentation Francaise)

**Fondation Nationale des Sciences Politiques**
- Bibliographies Francaises de Sciences Sociales. (pub. by Presses de la Fondation Nationale des Sciences Politiques)
- Bulletin Analytique de Documentation Politique, Economique et Sociale Contemporaine. (pub. by Presses de la Fondation Nationale des Sciences Politiques)
- Fondation Nationale des Sciences Politiques. Cahiers. (pub. by Presses de la Fondation Nationale des Sciences Politiques)
- Fondation Nationale des Sciences Politiques. Textes et Documents de Sciences Sociales. (pub. by Presses de la Fondation Nationale des Sciences Politiques)
- Fondation Nationale des Sciences Politiques. Traavaux et Recherches de Sciences Economiques. (pub. by Presses de la Fondation Nationale des Sciences Politiques)

- Fondation Nationale des Sciences Politiques.
  Trauvaux et Recherches de Science Politique.
  (pub. by Presses de la Fondation Nationale des
  Sciences Politiques)
- Fondation Nationale des Sciences Politiques,
  Paris. Catalogue General des Periodiques Recus.
  (pub. by Librarie Jean Touzot)
- Guide Sommaire des Ouvrages de Reference en
  Sciences Sociales. (pub. by Presses de la
  Fondation Nationale des Sciences Politiques)
- Revue Francaise de Science Politique. (pub. by
  Presses de la Fondation Nationale des Sciences
  Politiques)

**Fondation Nationale pour l'Enseignement de la
Creativite**
4 rue Lefevre, 78390 Bois d'Arcy, France.
- Lettre Culturelle. m, with supplements.

**Fondation Nationale pour l'Enseignement de la
Gestion des Entreprises**
155, Boulevard Haussmann, 75008 Paris, France.
- Enseignement et Gestion. q.

**Fondation pour la Recherche Sociale**
14 rue Saint-Benoit, Paris(6e), France.
- Recherche Sociale. q. ISSN 0034-124X

**Fondation Singer-Polignac**
43 Avenue Georges Mandel, 75, Paris 16e, France.
- Cahiers du Pacifique. irreg. ISSN 0068-5143

**Foret Privee**
61, Avenue de la Grande Armee, 75782 Paris 16,
France.
- Foret Privee; revue forestiere europeenne. bi-m.
  ISSN 0046-4600

**Editions du Forum**
13 rue Giacierre, Paris 13e, France.
- Repertoire General des Clubs Sportifs de France.
  irreg. ISSN 0080-1135

**Francaise d'Edition et de Publication**
172 rue du Jardin-Public, 33300 Bordeaux, France.
- Hetero; la revue des hommes et des femmes
  libres. m. ISSN 0395-2126
- Sapho; le magazine de la femme liberee. m. ISSN
  0339-0713

**Editions de France**
18 rue Theodore Deck, 75015 Paris, France.
- Judo Kokokan/Budo Magazine. 10 per yr. ISSN
  0022-5843
- Karate Cinema. m. ISSN 0395-4382
- Secrets de l'Histoire. m. ISSN 0339-0047

**France. Archives Nationales**
Services de Renseignements, 60 rue des Francs-
Bourgeois, Paris 3e, France.
- France. Archives Nationales. Centre d'Information
  de la Recherche Historique en France. Bulletin. a.
  ISSN 0071-819X

**France. Bibliotheque Nationale**
*see* Bibliotheque Nationale

**France. Bureau de Documentation Miniere. Division
de Documentation**
4, rue las Cases, 75700 Paris, France
(Orders to G. E. D. I. M; 19, rue du Grand-Moulin,
42 Saint-Etienne, France)
- Annuaire de l'Administration et du Corps des
  Mines. a. ISSN 0071-822X

**France. Bureau de Recherches Geologiques et
Minieres**
Departement de Documentation, B.P. 6009, 45018
Orleans Cedex, France.
- Bulletin Signaletique-Bibliographie des Sciences de
  la Terre. Section 220. Cahier A. Mineralogie,
  Geochimie, Geologie Extraterrestre. (pub. by
  Centre National de la Recherche Scientifique.
  Centre de Documentation Scientifique et
  Technique)
- Bulletin Signaletique-Bibliographie des Sciences de
  la Terre. Section 221. Gisements Metalliques et
  Non Metalliques. (pub. by Centre National de la
  Recherche Scientifique. Centre de Documentation
  Scientifique et Technique)
- Bulletin Signaletique-Bibliographie des Sciences de
  la Terre. Section 222. Cahier C. Roches
  Cristallines. (pub. by Centre National de la
  Recherche Scientifique. Centre de Documentation
  Scientifique et Technique)

- Bulletin Signaletique-Bibliographie des Sciences de
  la Terre. Section 223. Cahier D. Roches
  Sedimentaires, Geologie Marine. (pub. by Centre
  National de la Recherche Scientifique. Centre de
  Documentation Scientifique et Technique)
- Bulletin Signaletique-Bibliographie des Sciences de
  la Terre. Section 224. Cahier E. Stratigraphie,
  Geologie Regionale et Generale. (pub. by Centre
  National de la Recherche Scientifique. Centre de
  Documentation Scientifique et Technique)
- Bulletin Signaletique-Bibliographie des Sciences de
  la Terre. Section 225. Cahier F. Tectonique. (pub.
  by Centre National de la Recherche Scientifique.
  Centre de Documentation Scientifique et
  Technique)
- Bulletin Signaletique-Bibliographie des Sciences de
  la Terre. Section 226. Cahier G. Hydrologie,
  Geologie de l'Ingenieur, Formations Superficielles.
  (pub. by Centre National de la Recherche
  Scientifique. Centre de Documentation
  Scientifique et Technique)
- Bulletin Signaletique-Bibliographie des Sciences de
  la Terre. Section 227. Cahier H. Paleontologie.
  (pub. by Centre National de la Recherche
  Scientifique. Centre de Documentation
  Scientifique et Technique)
- Chronique de la Recherche Miniere. 6 per yr.
- France. Bureau de Recherches Geologiques et
  Minieres. Bulletin. Section 1: Geologie de la
  France. q. ISSN 0007-6104
- France. Bureau de Recherches Geologiques et
  Minieres. Bulletin. Section 2: Geologie des Gites
  Mineraux. 9 per yr.
- France. Bureau de Recherches Geologiques et
  Minieres. Bulletin. Section 3: Hydrogeologie-
  Geologie de l'Ingenieur. q. ISSN 0300-936X
- France. Bureau de Recherches Geologiques et
  Minieres. Bulletin. Section 4: Geologie Generale.
  q. ISSN 0007-6112
- France. Bureau de Recherches Geologiques et
  Minieres. Memoires. irreg. (2-4 per yr.), 1976, no.
  87. ISSN 0071-8246
- France. Bureau de Recherches Geologiques et
  Minieres. Resume des Principaux Resultats
  Scientifiques et Techniques. irreg.

**France. Bureau National d'Information Scientifique et
Technique**
97 rue de Grenelle, 75007 Paris, France
(Orders to: Imprimerie Nationale, 39 rue de la
Convention, Paris 15e, France)
- France. Bureau National d'Information
  Scientifique et Technique. Bulletin d'Information.
  q.

**France. Caisse Nationale de Credit Agricole**
91-93 Boulevard Pasteur, 75015 Paris, France.
- France. Caisse Nationale de Credit Agricole.
  Rapport sur le Credit Agricole Mutuel. a. ISSN
  0071-8254

**France. Caisse Nationale de l'Assurance Maladie des
Travailleurs Salaries**
44-46, Boulevard de Grenelle, 75015 Paris, France.
- France. Caisse Nationale de l'Assurance Maladie
  des Travailleurs Salaries. Statistiques de l'Annee.
  a.

**France. Caisse Nationale des Allocations Familiales**
63, Bd Haussmann, Paris 8, France.
- France. Caisse National des Allocations
  Familiales. Action Sociale. a.
- France. Caisse Nationale des Allocations
  Familiales. Prestations Familiales. Resultats
  Generaux: Recettes, Depenses, Beneficiaires. a.

**France. Centre de Diffusion et d'Informations
Administratives**
10, Boulevard Bonne Nouvelle, Paris 10, France.
- Guide Pratique de l'Usager des Prefectures. irreg.

**France. Centre de Documentation et Informations**
22 rue du Sergent Bauchat, 75012 Paris, France.
- France. Centre de Documentation et Informations.
  Information Fiscale et Sociale. m.

**France. Centre de Recherches sur les Zones Arides**
- Centre Geologique et Geophysique de
  Montpellier. Publications. Serie Geologie. (pub. by
  Centre National de la Recherche Scientifique)

**France. Centre National d'Etudes des
Telecommunications**
Service des Abonnements, 38-40 rue du General
Leclerc, 92131 Issy-les-Moulineaux, France.
- Annales des Telecommunications. bi-m. ISSN
  0003-4347 (prep. by its Service de Documentation
  Interministerielle)

- Bulletin Signaletique des Telecommunications. m.
  ISSN 0007-5302 (prep. by its Service de
  Documentation Interministerielle)
- Echo des Recherches. 4 per yr. ISSN 0012-9283
  (Co-Sponsor: Ecole Nationale Superieure des
  Telecommunications)

**France. Centre National d'Etudes des
Telecommunications. Departement Mesures
Ionespheriques et Radioelectriques**
Route de Tregastel, 22301 Lannion, France.
- France. Centre National d'Etudes des
  Telecommunications. Previsions pour la
  Propagation Ionospherique des Ondes
  Radioelectriques. 10 per yr.

**France. Centre National de Coordination des Etudes
et Recherches sur la Nutrition et l'Alimentation**
- France. Centre National de Coordination des
  Etudes et Recherches sur la Nutrition et
  l'Alimentation. Cahiers Techniques. (pub. by
  Centre National de la Recherche Scientifique)

**France. Centre National de la Recherche Scientifique**
*see* Centre National de la Recherche Scientifique

**France. Centre National pour l'Exploitation des
Oceans**
B.P. 107, 75783 Paris Cedex 16, France.
- France. Centre National pour l'Exploitation des
  Oceans. Publications. Serie: Resultats des
  Campagnes a la Mer. irreg.

**France. Comite des Travaux Historiques et
Scientifiques**
- Comite des Travaux Historiques et Scientifiques.
  Section de Geographie. Actes du Congres
  National des Societes Savantes. (pub. by
  Bibliotheque Nationale)
- France. Comite des Travaux Historiques et
  Scientifiques. Bulletin Archeologique. (pub. by
  Bibliotheque Nationale)
- France. Comite des Travaux Historiques et
  Scientifiques. Bulletin Philologique et Historique
  (Jusqu'a 1610) (pub. by Bibliotheque Nationale)
- France. Comite des Travaux Historiques et
  Scientifiques. Section d'Archeologie. Actes du
  Congres National des Societes Savantes. (pub. by
  Bibliotheque Nationale)
- France. Comite des Travaux Historiques et
  Scientifiques. Section de Geographie. Bulletin.
  (pub. by Bibliotheque Nationale)
- France. Comite des Travaux Historiques et
  Scientifiques. Section d'Histoire Moderne et
  Contemporaine. Actes du Congres National des
  Societes Savantes. (pub. by Bibliotheque
  Nationale)
- France. Comite des Travaux Historiques et
  Scientifiques. Section d'Histoire Moderne et
  Contemporaine. Bulletin. (pub. by Bibliotheque
  Nationale)

**France. Comite Monetaire de la Zone Franc**
39, rue Croix-des-Petits-Champs, Paris 75049,
France.
- La Zone Franc. a.

**France. Commision Centrale pour la Navigation du
Rhin**
Palais du Rhin, Strasbourg, France.
- France. Commission Centrale pour la Navigation
  du Rhin. Rapport Annuel. a.

**France. Commissariat a l'Energie Atomique**
29-33, rue de la Federation, Paris (15e), France.
- France. Commissariat a l'Energie Atomique.
  Activites Scientifiques et Techniques.
- France. Commissariat a l'Energie Atomique.
  Annual Report. a. ISSN 0071-8467
- France. Commissariat a l'Energie Atomique.
  Bulletin d'Informations Scientifiques et
  Techniques. (pub. by Centrale des Revues Dunod
  Gauthier- Villars)
- France. Commissariat a l'Energie Atomique.
  Notes d'Information. m. ISSN 0029-3997
- France. Commissariat a l'Energie Atomique.
  Revue de la Presse Francaise.
- Index de la Litterature Nucleaire Francaise. m.
  ISSN 0019-3836 (Co-Sponsor: Association
  Francaise de Documentation et d'Information
  Nucleaires)

**France. Commission d'Histoire Economique et Sociale
de la Revolution Francaise**
- Bulletin d'Histoire Economique et Sociale de la
  Revolution Francaise. (pub. by Bibliotheque
  Nationale)

**France. Commission des Operations de Bourse**
Direction des Journaux Officiels, 26, rue Desaix,
C.C.P. 9063-13, Paris 75732, France.
- France. Commission des Operations de Bourse.
  Rapport au President de la Republique. a.

**France. Commission Nationale de l'Amenagement du
Territoire**
- France. Commission Nationale de l'Amenagement
  du Territoire. Rapport. (pub. by Documentation
  Francaise)

**France. Commission Technique des Ententes**
41 Quai Branly, Paris, France.
- France. Commission Technique des Ententes.
  Economiques Rapports. a. ISSN 0071-8505

**France. Conseil National de la Comptabilite**
20, rue Notre-Dame des Victoires, 75002 Paris,
France.
- France. Conseil National de la Comptabilite.
  Rapport d'Activite. irreg., 1975, no. 8. ISSN
  0071-8513

**France. Delegation a l'Informatique**
- Enquete Economique des Societes de Service et
  Conseil en Informatique. (pub. by Documentation
  Francaise)

**France. Delegation Generale a la Recherche
Scientifique et Technique**
- France. Delegation Generale a la Recherche
  Scientifique et Technique. Recherche dans le
  Domaine de l'Eau: Repertoire des Laboratoires.
  (pub. by Documentation Francaise)
- France. Delegation Generale a la Recherche
  Scientifique et Technique. Repertoire des
  Scientifiques Francais. Tome 3: Biologie. (pub. by
  Documentation Francaise)
- France. Delegation Generale a la Recherche
  Scientifique et Technique. Repertoire des
  Scientifiques Francais. Tome 4: Chimie. (pub. by
  Documentation Francaise)
- France. Delegation Generale a la Recherche
  Scientifique et Technique. Repertoire des
  Scientifiques Francais. Tome 5: Physique. (pub. by
  Documentation Francaise)
- France. Delegation Generale a la Recherche
  Scientifique et Technique. Repertoire National des
  Chercheurs: Sciences Sociales et Humaines. Tome
  1: Ethnologie, Linguistique, Psychologie,
  Psychologie Sociale, Sociologie. (pub. by
  Documentation Francaise)
- France. Delegation Generale a la Recherche
  Scientifique et Technique. Repertoire National des
  Laboratoires; la Recherche Universitaire; Sciences
  Exactes et Naturelles. Tome 1: Physique. (pub. by
  Documentation Francaise)
- France. Delegation Generale a la Recherche
  Scientifique et Technique. Repertoire National des
  Laboratoires; la Recherche Universitaire; Sciences
  Exactes et Naturelles. Tome 2: Biologie. (pub. by
  Documentation Francaise)
- France. Delegation Generale a la Recherche
  Scientifique et Technique. Repertoire National des
  Laboratoires; la Recherche Universitaire; Sciences
  Exactes et Naturelles. Tome 3: Chimie. (pub. by
  Documentation Francaise)
- France. Delegation Generale a la Recherche
  Scientifique et Technique. Repertoire National des
  Laboratoires; la Recherche Universitaire; Sciences
  Exactes et Naturelles. Tome 4: Mathematiques,
  Sciences de l'Espace et de la Terre. (pub. by
  Documentation Francaise)
- France. Delegation Generale a la Recherche
  Scientifique et Technique. Repertoire Permanent
  de l'Administration Francaise. (pub. by
  Documentation Francaise)
- Progres Scientifique. (pub. by Documentation
  Francaise)

**France. Departement des Statistiques de Transport.
Service des Affaires Economiques et
Internationales**
19-21, rue Maturin-Regier, 75015 Paris, France.
- France. Departement des Statistiques de
  Transport. Memento de Statistiques des
  Transports. irreg.

**France. Direction de l'Amenagement Foncier et de
l'Urbanisme**
- Diagonal. (pub. by Documentation Francaise)

**France. Direction de l'Equipement et des Transports.
Bureau A2**
Paris, France.
- France. Direction de l'Equipement et des
  Transports. Bureau A 2. Statistiques: Batiments,
  Transports. irreg.

**France. Direction de la Documentation**
- D F Actualites. (pub. by Documentation
  Francaise)
- France. Direction de la Documentation. Catalogue
  des Publications Editees Ou Diffusees Par la
  Documentation Francaise. (pub. by
  Documentation Francaise)
- France. Direction de la Documentation.
  Documents d'Etudes. (pub. by Documentation
  Francaise)
- France. Direction de la Documentation. Notes et
  Etudes Documentaires. (pub. by Documentation
  Francaise)

**France. Direction de la Prevision**
27 rue des Pyramides, 75001 Paris, France.
- Bibliographie Economique et Financiere Francaise
  et Etrangere. m.
- France. Direction de la Prevision. Rationalisation
  des Choix Budgetaires. (pub. by Documentation
  Francaise)

**France. Direction des Journaux Officiels**
*see* **Direction des Journaux Officiels**

**France. Direction du Batiment, des Travaux Publics
et de la Conjoncture**
- France. Direction du Batiment, des Travaux
  Publics et de la Conjoncture. Statistiques de la
  Construction. (pub. by Documentation Francaise)
- France. Direction du Batiment et des Travaux
  Publics et de la Conjoncture. Etudes Statistiques
  de l'Equipment. (pub. by Documentation
  Francaise)

**France. Direction du Gaz, de l'Electricite et du
Charbon**
24, rue de l'Universite, 75700 Paris, France.
- Statistiques de l'Industrie Gaziere en France.
  irreg.

**France. Direction General de la Concurrence et des
Prix**
26, rue Desaix, 75732 Paris, France.
- France. Direction Generale de la Concurrence et
  des Prix. Bulletin Officiel des Services des Prix.
  irreg. ISSN 0071-870X

**France. Direction Generale a l'Aviation Civile**
246, rue Lecourbe, 75732 Paris Cedex 15, France.
- France. Direction Generale a l'Aviation Civile.
  Annuaire. triennial. ISSN 0071-9072
- France. Direction Generale a l'Aviation Civile.
  Bulletin Statistique. irreg.
- France. Direction Generale a l'Aviation Civile.
  Revue. q.

**France. Direction Generale de la Protection de la
Nature**
15, rue du Docteur-Juliand, Chambery. 73000,
France.
- Parc National de la Vanoise. Travaux Scientifique.
  irreg.

**France. Direction Generale des Douanes et Droits
Indirects**
Paris, France.
- Donnees Statistiques Essentielles sur le Commerce
  Exterieur de la France. a. ISSN 0070-7090
- France. Direction Generale des Douanes et Droits
  Indirects. Annuaire Abrege de Statistiques. (pub.
  by Imprimerie Nationale)
- France. Direction Generale des Douanes et Droits
  Indirects. Annuaire. (pub. by Imprimerie
  Nationale)
- France. Direction Generale des Douanes et Droits
  Indirects. Commentaires Annuels des Statistiques
  du Commerce Exterieur. (pub. by Imprimerie
  Nationale)
- France. Direction Generale des Douanes et Droits
  Indirects. Statistiques du Commerce Exterieur et
  des Transports. (pub. by Imprimerie Nationale)
- France. Direction Generale des Douanes et Droits
  Indirects. Statistiques du Commerce Exterieur:
  Importations- Exportations. Nomenclature:
  N.G.P. (Nomenclature Generale des Produits)
  (pub. by Imprimerie Nationale)
- France. Direction Generale des Douanes et Droits
  Indirects. Statistiques du Commerce Exterieur.
  Transit Direct. (pub. by Imprimerie Nationale)

**France. Direction Nationale des Douanes et
Droits Indirects. Tableau General des Transports.**
(pub. by Imprimerie Nationale)
- France. Direction Nationale des Douanes et
  Droits Indirects. Transport du Commerce
  Exterieur. (pub. by Imprimerie Nationale)

**France. Direction Generale des Impots**
17 rue Scribe, 75436 Paris Cedex 09, France.
- France. Direction Generale des Impots. Bulletin
  Officiel d'Annonces des Domaines. s-m. (prep. by
  its Service des Domaines)

**France. Documentation Francaise**
*see* **Documentation Francaise**

**France. Imprimerie Nationale**
*see* **Imprimerie Nationale**

**France. Inspection Generale des Finances**
- France. Inspection Generale des Finances.
  Annuaire. (pub. by Imprimerie Nationale)

**France. Institut National d'Etudes Demographiques**
27 rue du Commandeur, Paris 14e, France.
- Demographie et Sciences Humaines. (pub. by
  Presses Universitaires de France)
- France. Institut National d'Etudes
  Demographiques. Cahiers de Travaux et
  Documents. irreg. ISSN 0071- 8823
- Population. bi-m. ISSN 0032-4663
- Population et Societes; bulletin mensuel
  d'informations demographiques, economiques,
  sociales. m.
- Rapport sur la Situation Demographique de la
  France. a.

**France. Institut National de Gestion Previsionnelle et
de Controle de Gestion**
22 Avenue de la Grande Armee, Paris (17e),
France.
- Direction et Gestion des Entreprises. bi-m. ISSN
  0012-320X

**France. Institut National de la Propriete Industrielle**
26bis, rue de Leningrad, 75800 Paris, France
(Single copies available: S.E.V.P.O., Imprimerie
Nationale, 39, rue de la Convention, 75732 Paris
Cedex 15, France)
- Bulletin Officiel de la Propriete Industrielle. ISSN
  0007-5183

**France. Institut National de la Recherche
Agronomique**
Service des Publications, Route de St. Cyr, 78350
Jouy en Josas, France
(Orders to: Secretariat A.B.A.B.B., 78350 Jouy en
Josas, France, or to Pergamon Press Inc., Maxwell
House, Fairview Park, Elmsford, Ny 10523, U.S.A.)
- Annales Agronomiques. bi-m. ISSN 0003-3839
- Annales d'Hydrobiologie. s-a. ISSN 0046-4937
- Annales de Biologie Animale, Biochimie,
  Biophysique. bi-m. ISSN 0003-388X
- Annales de Genetique et de Selection Animale. q.
  ISSN 0003-4002
- Annales de l'Amelioration des Plantes. bi-m. ISSN
  0003-4053
- Annales de Phytopathologie. q. ISSN 0003-4177
- Annales de Recherches Veterinaires/Annals of
  Veterinary Research. q. ISSN 0003-4193
- Annales de Technologie Agricole. q. ISSN 0003-
  4223
- Annales de Zoologie- Ecologie Animale. q. ISSN
  0003-4231
- Annales de Zootechnie. q. ISSN 0003-424X
- Annales des Sciences Forestieres. q. ISSN 0003-
  4312
- Apidologie. q. ISSN 0044-8435 (Co-Sponsor:
  Deutscher Imkerbund)

**France. Institut National de la Recherche
Agronomique. Departement d'Economie et de
Sociologie Rurales**
4 rue de Lasteyrie, 75016 Paris, France
(Orders to: Service des Publications, I.N.R.A.,
Route de Saint-Cyr, 78 Versailles, France)
- Annales d'Economie et de Sociologie Rurales.
  irreg, 2-3 per year.

**France. Institut National de la Sante et de la
Recherche Medicale**
101 rue de Tolbiac, 75645 Paris Cedex 13, France.
- France. Institut National de la Sante et de la
  Recherche Medicale. Bulletin d'Information. q.

- Revue Internationale d'Oceanographie Medicale. (pub. by Centre d'Etudes et de Recherches de Biologie et d'Oceanographie Medicale (C.E.R.B.O.M.))

**France. Institut National de la Statistique et des Etudes Economiques**
18, Bd A. Pinard, F 75675 Paris 14, France.
- Annuaire Statistique de la France. a. ISSN 0066-3654
- Annuaire Statistique des Territoires d'Outre Mer. a. ISSN 0071-8793
- Chiffres pour l' Alsace. q.
- Comptes Economiques de la Guadeloupe. a.
- Comptes Economiques de la Martinique. a.
- Comptes Economiques du Territoire Francais des Afars et des Issas. irreg.
- Documentation Economique; revue bibliographique. 6 per yr. ISSN 0012-4648 (Co-Sponsor: Association de Documentation Economique et Sociale)
- France. Institut National de la Statistique et des Etudes Economiques. Annales. 3 per yr. ISSN 0019-0209
- France. Institut National de la Statistique et des Etudes Economiques. Bulletin Bibliographique. bi-m. ISSN 0020-2398
- France. Institut National de la Statistique et des Etudes Economiques. Bulletin Mensuel de Statistique. m. ISSN 0007-4713
- France. Institut National de la Statistique et des Etudes Economiques. Collections. Comptes et Planification. 4 per yr.
- France. Institut National de la Statistique et des Etudes Economiques. Collections. Demographie et Emploi. 8 per yr.
- France. Institut National de la Statistique et des Etudes Economiques. Collections. Menages. 6 per yr.
- France. Institut National de la Statistique et des Etudes Economiques. Collections. Serie C.D.E.M.R. 24 per yr.
- France. Institut National de la Statistique et des Etudes Economiques. Donnees Sociales. a.
- France. Institut National de la Statistique et des Etudes Economiques. Economie et Statistique. m.
- France. Institut National de la Statistique et des Etudes Economiques. Enquete sur l'Emploi. a.
- France. Institut National de la Statistique et des Etudes Economiques. Indicateurs Associes au Sixieme Plan. q.
- France. Institut National de la Statistique et des Etudes Economiques. Informations Statistiques Rapides. m.
- France. Institut National de la Statistique et des Etudes Economiques. l'Enseignement dans les Departments d'Outre-Mer. irreg.
- France. Institut National de la Statistique et des Etudes Economiques. Mouvement de la Population; Statistiques Annuelles. a. ISSN 0071-8807
- France. Institut National de la Statistique et des Etudes Economiques. Tendances de la Conjoncture. m. ISSN 0071-8815
- Point Economique de l'Auvergne. m.
- Statistique et Developpement. Pays de la Loire. q. with irreg. supplements.
- Tableaux de l'Economie Francaise. irreg. (2 per yr?)

**France. Institut National de Recherche et de Documentation Pedagogiques**
29 rue d'Ulm, 75230 Paris, France
- Affaires et Gens d'Affaires. irreg. ISSN 0065-3799 (Ecole Pratique des Hautes Etudes, Centre de Recherches Historiques) (Orders to: I.N.R.D.P., Service des Publications et de la Diffusion, 91 Avenue Ledru-Rollin, B.P. 36 511, 75526 Paris Cedex 11, France)
- Archeologie et Civilisation. irreg., 1963, no. 1. ISSN 0066-6068 (Ecole Pratique des Hautes Etudes, Centre de Recherches Historiques) (Orders to: I.N.R.D.P., Service des Publications et de la Diffusion, 91 Avenue Ledru-Rollin, B.P. 36 511, 75526 Paris Cedex 11, France)
- Demographie et Societes. irreg. ISSN 0070-3362 (Ecole Pratique des Hautes Etudes, Centre de Recherches Historiques) (Orders to: I.N.R.D.P., Service des Publications et de la Diffusion, 91 Avenue Ledru-Rollin, B.P. 36 511, 75526 Paris Cedex 11, France)
- France. Institut National de Recherche et de Documentation Pedagogiques. Cahiers de Documentation. bi-a. (Orders to: I.N.R.D.P. Service des Publications et de la Diffusion, 91 Avenue Ledru-Rollin, B.P. 36 511, 75526 Paris Cedex 11, France)

- France. Institut National de Recherche et de Documentation Pedagogiques. Repertoire d'Etablissements Publics d'Enseignement et de Services. a. ISSN 0071-8963 (Orders to: I.N.R.D.P. Service des Publications et de la Diffusion, 91 Avenue Ledru- Rollin, B. P. 36511, 75526 Paris Cedex 11, France)
- France. Institut National de Recherche et de Documentation Pedagogiques. Textes et Documents pour la Classe. s-m. ISSN 0040-4799 (Orders to: I.N.R.D.P. Service des Publications et de la Diffusion, 91 Avenue Ledru- Rollin, B. P. 36511, 75526 Paris Cedex 11, France)
- Hommes et la Terre. irreg. ISSN 0073-3202 (Ecole Pratique des Hautes Etudes, Centre de Recherches Historiques) (Orders to: I.N.R.D.P., Service des Publications et de la Diffusion, 91 Avenue Ledru-Rollin, B.P. 36 511, 75526 Paris Cedex 11, France)
- Langues Modernes. 6 per yr. ISSN 0023-8376 (Orders to: I.N.R.D.P., Service des Publications et de la Diffusion, 91 Avenue Ledru-Rollin, B.P. 36 511, 75526 Paris Cedex 11, France)
- Livres; bulletin bibliographique mensuel. m. ISSN 0024-5348 (Orders to: I.N.R.D.P., Service des Publications et de la Diffusion, 91 Avenue Ledru-Rollin, B.P. 36 511, 75526 Paris Cedex 11, France)
- Memoires de Photo-Interpretation. irreg 1970, no. 7. ISSN 0076-6364 (Ecole Pratique des Hautes Etudes) (Orders to: I.N.R.D.P., Service des Publications et de la Diffusion, 91 Avenue Ledru-Rollin, B.P. 36 511, 75526 Paris Cedex 11, France)
- Monnaies, Prix, Conjoncture. irreg., 1968, no. 7. ISSN 0077-0434 (Ecole Pratique des Hautes Etudes. Centre de Recherches Historiques) (Orders to: I.N.R.D.P., Service des Publications et de la Diffusion, 91 Avenue Ledru-Rollin, B.P. 36 511, 75526 Paris Cedex 11, France)
- Revue Francaise de Pedagogie. q. ISSN 0556-7807
- Statistiques des Enseignements. m. ISSN 0020-0506 (Orders to: I.N.R.D.P.-Service des Publications et de la Diffusion, 91 Avenue Ledru-Rollin, B.P. 36 511, 75526 Paris Cedex 11, France)
- Techniques Economiques. m. ISSN 0040-1331 (Orders to: I.N.R.D.P., Service des Publications et de la Diffusion, 91 Avenue Ledru-Rollin, B.P. 36 511, 75526 Paris Cedex 11, France)
- Techniques Industrielles. m. ISSN 0013-8576 (Orders to: I.N.R.D.P.-Service des Publications et de la Diffusion, 91 Avenue Ledru-Rollin, B.P. 36 511, 75526 Paris Cedex 11, France)

**France. Institut National de Recherche et de Securite pour la Prevention des Accidents du Travail et des Maladies Professionelles**
30 rue Olivier-Noyer, 75680 Paris Cedex 14, France.
- France. Institut National de Recherche et de Securite pour la Prevention des Accidents du Travail et des Maladies Professionelles. Cahiers de Notes Documentaires; securite et hygiene du travail. q. ISSN 0007-9952
- Travail et Securite. m.

**France. Laboratoire Central des Ponts et des Chaussees**
58 Blvd. Lefebre, 75732 Paris Cedex 15, France.
- France. Laboratoire Central des Ponts et des Chaussees. Rapport de Recherche. irreg., 1971, no. 16. ISSN 0085-2643

**France. Ministere de l'Agriculture et du Developpement Rural**
Sous-Direction de l'Information, des Relations Publiques et de la Documentation, 78, rue de Varenne, 75700 Paris 7e, France.
- Annuaire de la France Rurale dans le Marche Commun. (pub. by Editions Publicitaires Waltz P.R. et M. Puget)
- France. Ministere de l'Agriculture et du Developpement Rural Bulletin d'Information. w.
- France. Ministere de l'Agriculture et du Developpement Rural Bulletin Technique d'Information. m.

**France. Ministere de l'Agriculture et du Developpement Rural. Service Central des Enquetes et Etudes Statistiques**
5 rue Casimir Perier, Paris 7e, France.
- France. Ministere de l'Agriculture et du Developpement Rural. Cahiers de Statistiques Agricoles. bi-m.
- France. Service Central des Enquetes et Etudes Statistiques. Statistique Agricole Annuelle. a. (2 vols.) ISSN 0071-9080
- Situation Agricole en France. m. ISSN 0037-5918

**France. Ministere de l'Agriculture et du Developpement Rural. Service des Forets**
1 Ter. Ave. de Lowendal, 75007 Paris, France.
- France. Service des Forets. Production de la Branche Exploitation Forestiere et Production des Branches Science et Carbonisation en Foret. a.
- France. Service des Forets. Rapport sur le Fonds Forestier National; rapport au Comite de Controle pour l'annee. a.

**France. Ministere de l'Agriculture et du Developpement Rural. Service Regional de Statistique Agricole**
*see* **France. Service Regional de Statistique Agricole**

**France. Ministere de l'Amenagement du Territoire, de l'Equipement du Logement et des Transports**
- France. Ministere de l'Amenagement du Territoire, de l'Equipement, du Logement et des Transports. Bulletin Officiel. (pub. by Direction des Journaux Officiels)
- France. Ministere de l'Amenagement du Territoire, de l'Equipement et des Transports. Tableau de Bord Conjoncturel du Logement. (pub. by Documentation Francaise)
- France. Ministere de l'Amenagement du Territoire, de l'Equipement et des Transports. Tableau de Bord Conjoncturel du Batiment et des Travaux Publics. (pub. by Documentation Francaise)

**France. Ministere de l'Amenagement du Territoire, de l'Equipement du Logement et des Transports. Direction du Batiment et des Travaux Public et de la Conjoncture**
*see* **France. Direction du Batiment et des Travaux Public et de la Conjoncture**

**France. Ministere de l'Economie et des Finances**
Paris, France
(Subscription Address: 29-31 Quai Voltaire, 75340 Paris Cedex 07, France)
- Fonds de Developpment Economique et Social. Conseil de Direction. Rapport. (pub. by Imprimerie Nationale)
- France. Administration Centrale de l'Economie et des Finances. Bulletin. q. ISSN 0532-338X
- France. Ministere de l'Economie et des Finances. Balance des Paiements Entre la France et l'Exterieur. a. ISSN 0071-8890 (prep. by its Direction du Tresor)
- France. Ministere de l'Economie et des Finances. Budget. a. ISSN 0071-8904
- France. Ministere de l'Economie et des Finances. Bulletin Administratif des Assurances. irreg.
- France. Ministere de l'Economie et des Finances. Rapport du Conseil de Direction du Fonds de Developpement Economique et Social. a. ISSN 0071-8920
- France. Ministere de l'Economie et des Finances. Statistiques et Etudes Financieres. m. ISSN 0015-9654
- Nomenclature des Entreprises Nationales a Caractere Industriel Ou Commercial et des Societes d'Economie Mixte d'Interet National. (pub. by Imprimerie Nationale)

**France. Ministere de l'Economie et des Finances. Commission Centrale des Marches**
41, Quai Branly, 75700 Paris, France
(Subscr. Address: Direction des Journaux Officiels, 26 rue Desaix, 75732 Paris, Cedex 15, France)
- France. Commission Centrale des Marches. Guide du Fournisseur de l'Etat et des Collectivites Locales. (pub. by Moniteur des Travaux Publics et du Batiment)
- Marches Publics. 8 per yr. ISSN 0542-6685

**France. Ministere de l'Economie et des Finances. Direction de la Prevision**
*see* **France. Direction de la Prevision**

**France. Ministere de l'Economie et des Finances. Direction du Tresor**
*see* **France. Direction du Tresor**

**France. Ministere de l'Economie et des Finances. Direction Generale des Impots**
*see* **France. Direction Generale des Impots**

**France. Ministere de l'Economie et des Finances. Direction General de la Concurrence et des Prix**
*see* **France. Direction Generale de la Concurrence et des Prix**

**France. Ministere de l'Education Nationale. Office Francais des Techniques Modernes d'Education**
*see* **France. Office Francais des Techniques Modernes d'Education**

**France. Ministere de l'Industrie et de la Recherche**
85, Boulevard de Montparnasse, 75270 Paris Cedex 06, France.
- Annales des Mines. (pub. by G E D I M)
- France. Ministere de l'Industrie et de la Recherche. Service du Traitement de l'Information et des Statistiques Industrielles. Bulletin Mensuel de Statistique Industrielle. m.
- France. Service du Traitement de l'Information et des Statistiques Industrielles. Annuaire de Statistique Industrielle. a. ISSN 0071-8211
- Lettre 101. (pub. by Documentation Francaise)
- Structures Industrielles Francaises. a.

**France. Ministere de l'Industrie et de la Recherche. Service de Relations Publiques et d'Information**
101 rue de Grenelle, 75007 Paris, France.
- France. Ministere de l'Industrie et de la Recherche. Service de Relations Publiques et d'Information. Bibliotheque Centrale. Liste Mensuelle d'Acquisitions d'Ouvrages. Selection Hebdomadaire d'Articles Economiques. w. (prep. by its Bibliotheque Centrale)

**France. Ministere de l'Interieur. Service d'Information et de Relations Publiques (S.I.R.P.)**
1 bis Place des Saussies, 75008 Paris, France.
- Journal de la Police Nationale; informations generales de la police Francaise. m. ISSN 0047-2131
- Revue de la Police Nationale. bi-m. ISSN 0035-1237

**France. Ministere de la Cooperation**
20, rue Monsieur, 75007 Paris, France.
- Cooperation Entre la France et les Etats Francophones d'Afrique Noire et de l'Ocean Indien. a.

**France. Ministere de la Defense Nationale**
231 Bd. St. Germain, Paris 7e, France.
- France. Ministere de la Defense Nationale. Bulletin d'Information Technique et Scientifique. q. ISSN 0015-9719
- France. Ministere de la Defense Nationale. Bulletin Officiel. w. ISSN 0015-9727

**France. Ministere de la Defense Nationale. Antenne Air**
26, Boulevard Victor, 75996 Paris Armees, France.
- Air Actualites. bi-m. ISSN 0002-2152

**France. Ministere de la Protection de la Nature et de l'Environment**
Paris, France.
- France. Ministere de la Protection de la Nature et de l'Environment. Bilan d'Activite des Agences Financieres de Bassin. irreg.

**France. Ministere de la Sante**
1 Place de Fontenoy, 75700 Paris, France.
- Economie et Sante. (pub. by Documentation Francaise)
- France. Ministere de la Sante. Bulletin de Statistiques de Sante, Securite Sociale. (pub. by Documentation Francaise)
- France. Ministere de la Sante. Note d'Information. irreg. ISSN 0071-8882
- France. Ministere de la Sante. Tableaux Sante et Securite Sociale. (pub. by Documentation Francaise)
- Revue Francaise des Affaires Sociales. (pub. by Documentation Francaise)

**France. Ministere des Affaires Culturelles**
- Inventaire General des Monuments et des Richesses Artistiques de la France. (pub. by Imprimerie Nationale)

**France. Ministere des Affaires Etrangeres**
37, Quai d'Orsay, Paris 7e, France.
- Documents d'Actualite Internationale. (pub. by Documentation Francaise)
- France. Ministere des Affaires Etrangeres. Recueil des Traites et Accords de la France. a. ISSN 0071-8971
- France Informations. m. ISSN 0015-959X

**France. Ministere des Affaires Etrangeres. Department of Cultural, Scientific and Technical Relations**
21 bis, rue la Perouse, Paris 16e, France.
- News Briefs from France. w.

**France. Ministere des Affaires Etrangeres. Direction du Personnel et de l'Administration Generale**
37 Quai d'Orsay, Paris 7e, France
- Annuaire Diplomatique et Consulaire de la Republique Francaise. a. ISSN 0066-295X (Subs to: l'Imprimerie Nationale, 27, rue de la Convention, 75015 Paris, France)

**France. Ministere des Armees**
14 rue St. Dominique, 75997 Paris, France.
- France. Ministere des Armees. Bulletin Bibliographique des Armees. q.
- France. Ministere des Armees. Bulletin Officiel des Armees. (pub. by Editions Charles Lavauzelle et Cie.)
- Revue Historique de l'Armee. q. ISSN 0035-3299

**France. Ministere des Postes et Telecommunications**
20avenue de Segur, 75700 Paris, France.
- Revue des P T T de France. bi-m. ISSN 0035-2152

**France. Ministere du Travail**
- France. Ministere du Travail. Bulletin de Statistiques du Travail. Supplement. (pub. by Documentation Francaise)
- France. Ministere du Travail. Bulletin Mensuel des Statistiques du Travail. (pub. by Documentation Francaise)

**France. Ministre d'Etat Charge des Departements et Territoires d'Outre-Mer**
- Terres Australes et Antarctiques Francaises. (pub. by Documentation Francaise)

**France. Office des Cooperatives et des Collectivites**
49 rue de Richelieu, 75001 Paris, France.
- Annuaire General des Cooperatives Francaises et de Leurs Fournisseurs; France, Afrique et Marche Commun. a. ISSN 0066-3182
- France-Collectivites: Guide National des Chefs des Services d'Achats et des Fournisseurs de Collectivites. a. ISSN 0071-8386

**France. Office Francais des Techniques Modernes d'Education**
29 rue d'Ulm, F 75230 Paris (5e), France.
- Media; techniques modernes d'education. m. (10 per yr) ISSN 0025-6889

**France. Office National d'Etudes et de Recherches Aerospatiales**
29 Av. Division Leclerc, 92320 Chatillon, France
- France. Office National d'Etudes et de Recherches Aerospatiales. Activities. a. ISSN 0078-3773
- France. Office National d'Etudes et de Recherches Aerospatiales. Notes Techniques. irreg.(about 20 per year) ISSN 0078-3781
- France. Office National d'Etudes et de Recherches Aerospatiales. Publications. irreg. (about 5 per year) ISSN 0078-379X
- Recherche Aerospatiale. bi-m. ISSN 0034-1223 (English translation Avail. from NTIS, Springfield, VA 22161, U.S.A.)

**France. Office National d'Immigration. Section Documentation-Statistiques**
Paris, France.
- France. Office National d'Immigration. Statistiques de l'Immigration. a. ISSN 0071-903X

**France. Office National d'Information sur les Enseignements et les Professions**
B.P. 102-05, 75225 Paris Cedex 05, France.
- Avenirs. 10 per yr. ISSN 0005-1969

**France. Office National de Publications Culturelles**
3 bis Cite d'Hauteville, Paris (10e), France.
- Guide National de l'Education Permanente. biennial.

**France. Parlement. Assemblee Nationale**
Service des Informations Parlementaires, Palais-Bourbon, Paris, France.
- France. Parlement. Assemblee Nationale. Bulletin. w.

**France. Secretariat d'Etat a la Marine**
2 rue Royale, 75200 Paris Naval, France.
- France. Secretariat d'Etat a la Marine. Bulletin d'Information de la Marine Nationale. w. ISSN 0015-9735

**France. Secretariat d'Etat au Tourisme**
- France. Secretariat d'Etat au Tourisme. Statistiques du Tourisme. (pub. by Documentation Francaise)

**France. Secretariat d'Etat aux Affaires Etrangeres Charge de la Cooperation. Direction de l'Aide au Developpement**
20, rue Monsieur, 75700 - Paris, France.
- France. Secretariat d'Etat aux Affaires Etrangeres Charge de la Cooperation. Direction de l'Aide au Developpement. Mali. Dossier d'Information Economique. irreg.
- France. Secretariat d'Etat aux Affaires Etrangeres Charge de la Cooperation. Direction de l'Aide au Developpement. Niger. Dossier d'Information Economique. irreg.
- France, Secretariat d'Etat aux Affaires Etrangeres Charge de la Cooperation. Direction de l'Aide au Developpement. Cote d'Ivoire. Dossier d'Information Economique. irreg.

**France. Secretariat d'Etat aux Postes et Telecommunications. Service de l'Information et de Relations Publiques**
20 Avenue de Segur, 75700 Paris, France.
- Messages des Postes et Telecommunications. m.

**France. Secretariat d'Etat aux Universites. Service des Bibliotheques**
61 rue de Richelieu, 75002 Paris, France.
- France. Secretariat d'Etat aux Universites. Service des Bibliotheques. Division de la Cooperation et de l'Automatisation. Bulletin de la DICA. 10 per yr. ISSN 0338-5922 (prep. by its Division de la Cooperation et de l'Automatisation)

**France. Secretariat des Missions d'Urbanisme et d'Habitat**
11, rue Chardin, 75016-Paris, France.
- Planification, Habitat, Information. q.

**France. Service de Documentation et de Cartographie Geographiques**
- France. Service de Documentation et de Cartographie Geographiques. Memoires et Documents. (pub. by Centre National de la Recherche Scientifique)

**France. Service des Forets**
*see* **France. Ministere de l'Agriculture et du Developpement Rural. Service des Forets**

**France. Service Hydrographique et Oceanographique de la Marine**
3, Avenue Octave Greard, 75200 Paris Naval, France
(Subscr. Address: Route du Bergot, 29283 Brest Cedex, France)
- Annales Hydrographiques. 2-3 yr.
- Annuaire des Marees pour l'An... Tome 1. Ports de France. a.
- Avis aux Navigateurs.

**France. Service Regional de Statistique Agricole**
47 rue de la Cathedrale, 86020 Poitiers, France.
- France. Service Regional de Statistique Agricole. Bulletin de Statistique Agricole. 3 per yr.

**France a Table**
11 rue Quentin-Bauchart, Paris (8e), France.
- France a Table. 8 per yr. ISSN 0015-9441

**France Catholique-Ecclesia**
12 rue Edmond-Valentin, Paris (7e), France.
- France Catholique-Ecclesia. w.

**France Diffusion Presse**
71 rue Reaumur, 75002 Paris, France
(Orders to: M. Michel Aubin 102 bis Av. Joseph
Claussat 63400 Chamalieres, France)
- Auvergne Economique. q. ISSN 0045-1142
(Association Auvergne Economique)

**France Dimanche**
31-33, rue du Louvre, 75002 Paris, France.
- France Dimanche. w. ISSN 0015-9549

**Editions France-Empire**
68 rue Jean-Jacques Rousseau, Paris 7e, France.
- Homme Face a la Nature. irreg. ISSN 0073-3180

**Editions et Publicite France-Etranger**
207 Bd. Saint-Germain, 75007 Paris, France.
- Democratie Moderne; l'hebdomadaire des
democrates sociaux. w. ISSN 0011-8222 (Centre
des Democrates Sociaux)

**France Europe Publicitec**
2 rue Laure Surville, 75015 Paris, France.
- Officiel des Residences Mobiles et Prefabriquees.
q.
- Technologie et Materiaux; produits - procedes -
applications - recherches - equipement. bi-m.
- Tribune des Coiffeurs. m.

**France Expansion**
336, rue Saint-Honore, 75001 - Paris, France
- Douze Mois d'Edition Francophone. a. with 3
quarterly updating indexes.
- Edition de Langue Francaise-Catalogue Cumulatif.
a.
- Fichier General des Editeurs de Langue Francaise.
a.
- Repertoire des Livres Disponibles. a. ISSN 0080-
1003 (Union des Editeurs de Langue Francaise)
(Dist in U. S. by R. R. Bowker Co., P. O. Box
1807, Ann Arbor, MI 48106)

**France Forum**
6 rue Paul Louis Courier, 75007 Paris, France.
- France Forum. 8 per yr. ISSN 0046-4910

**France-Iberie Recherche. Theses et Documents.
Institut d'Etudes Hispaniques, Hispanoamericaines**
109 bis, rue Vauquelin, 31081 Toulouse Cedex,
France.
- Universite de Toulouse-le Mirail. France-Iberie
Recherche. Theses et Documents. irreg. ISSN
0082-5417

**France Lafayette**
10 rue Bleue, Paris 9e, France.
- Agenda Memento des Cadres et Maitrises de
l'Imprimerie, de l'Edition et des Industries
Graphiques. a. ISSN 0084-6023 (Syndicat des
Cadres et Agents de Maitrise de l'Imprimerie, des
Arts Graphiques et du Cartonnage)

**Editions de la France Libre**
217 Faubourg St. Honore, 75 Paris (8e), France.
- Constellation; le monde vu au Francais. m. ISSN
0010-6615

**France Pharmacie**
c/o Dir. Jean Valby, 9 Square Moncey, 75009 Paris,
France.
- France Pharmacie; revue generale des laboratoires
et de documentation pharmaceutique. m. ISSN
0015-9697

**France Protestante**
c/o Pasteur F. Delforge, Ed., 47 rue de Clichy,
Paris (9e), France.
- France Protestante. a. ISSN 0071-9064

**France-Selection**
9-13 rue du Departement, 75923 Paris Cedex 19,
France.
- Guide du Feu. a. ISSN 0337-5781
- Protection Civile et Securite Industrielle. m. ISSN
0033-1724

**France U. R. S. S. Magazine**
8 Bd. de Menilmontant, 75020 Paris, France.
- France U. R. S. S. Magazine. m (10 per yr)

**France Viticole**
156, rue Paul Rimbaud, 34000 Montpellier, France.
- France Viticole; revue mensuelle d'information
viti-vinicole. m.

**Editions de Francia**
118 bis rue d'Assas, Paris (6e), France.
- Photo-Revue. m.

**Editons R. Franck**
13 rue du Sentier, Paris (2e), France.
- Habitation. m. ISSN 0017-6400
- Terre Cuite; informations techniques et
scientifiques. q. ISSN 0040-3822 (Centre
Technique des Tuiles et Briques)

**Librairie le Francois**
91 Bd. Saint-Germain, Paris (6e), France.
- Entomophaga. q. ISSN 0013-8959 (International
Organization for Biological Control of Noxious
Animals and Plants)

**Fraternites du Saint-Esprit**
30 rue Lhomond, 75005 Paris, France.
- Esprit Saint; revue de spiritualite. q. ISSN 0396-
969X

**Jean Fremon**
9 rue de Belfort, 92 Asnieres, France.
- Strophes; revue litteraire. q. ISSN 0039-2537

**Front Portugais de Liberation**
c/o DaSilva, B.P. 90, 75962 Paris, France.
- Faits et Idees. irreg.

**Front Rouge**
Bp 47, Lyon Prefecture, France.
- Front Rouge; journal de combat Marxiste-
Leniniste. m. ISSN 0046-5208

**Editions Fructidor**
20 bis Avenue des Deux-Routes, Avignon
(Vaucluse), France.
- Annuaire Fructidor; annuaire international des
fruits, legumes, primeurs, derives et industries
annexes. a. ISSN 0066-3131
- Papetier de France; revue professionnelle des
papetiersdetaillants et specialistes du stylo. m.
ISSN 0031-1324
- Revue Europeenne des Papiers Cartons-
Complexes; revue profesionnelle d'impression,
transformation commerce du papier. s-m. ISSN
0035-2802

**Fructidor International**
14 Boulevard Montmartre, Paris, France.
- Fructidor International. a.

**Editions Fruits et Primeurs**
12 rue Tronchet, Ed. Jean-Claude Fouquin, France.
- Marches Europeens des Fruits et Legumes. s-w.
ISSN 0047-5890

**Fueri-Lamy**
21 rue Paradis, 13 Marseille, France.
- Annee Therapeutique et Clinique en
Ophtalmologie. a. ISSN 0301-4495

**G E D I M**
19 rue du Grand Moulin, 42029 Saint Etienne
Cedex, France.
- Annales des Mines; developpement et
environnement industriels-technologie-energie-
sous-sol. m. ISSN 0003-4282 (France. Ministere
de l'Industrie et de la Recherche)
- Revue des Ingenieurs; des ecoles nationales
superieures des mines (Paris, Saint-Etienne,
Nancy) bi-m. (Associations des Anciens Eleves
des Ecoles des Mines)

**G.I.E. Gedimat**
76, rue de Monceau, 75008 Paris, France.
- Gedimat Actualite. 3 per yr.

**G.I.E. Informatique et Gestion**
54 rue Saint Lazare, 75009 Paris, France.
- Informatique et Gestion. m. ISSN 0020-062X

**G. R. E. C. E.**
see **Groupement de Recherche et d'Etudes pour la
Civilisation Europeenne**

**J. Gabalda et Cie**
90 rue Bonaparte, 75006 Paris, France.
- Revue Biblique. q. ISSN 0035-0907 (Ecole
Biblique et Archeologique de Jerusalem)
- Revue de Qumran. s-a. ISSN 0035-1725

**Galerie. Jardin des Arts**
106 rue de Richelieu, 75002 Paris, France.
- Galerie. Jardin des Arts. m.

**Galerie Raymond Creuze**
12 rue Beaujon, 75008 Paris, Paris (8e), France.
- Galerie Raymond Creuze. Bulletin. irreg. ISSN
0016-4046

**Gallard, Johanet & Cie.**
7 rue Lauriston, Paris (16e), France.
- Maroquinerie, Sellerie et Bagages de France. q.
ISSN 0025-3901

**Editions Gallimard**
5, rue Sebastien Bottin, Paris 7, France
- Cahiers Albert Camus. irreg. ISSN 0068-4929
- Cahiers Andre Gide. a. ISSN 0068-4937
(Association des Amis d'Andre Gide)
- Cahiers du Chemin. 3 per yr. ISSN 0008-0101
- Cahiers Jean Cocteau. irreg. ISSN 0068-5178
(Association des Amis de Jean Cocteau)
- Cahiers Marcel Proust. Nouvelle Serie. irreg.
ISSN 0068-5186
- Cahiers Renaud Barrault. 4 per yr. ISSN 0008-
0470 (Compagnie Renaud-Barrault)
- Connaissance de l'Orient. Collection Unesco
d'Oeuvres Representatives. ISSN 0589-3496
(Unesco UN)
- Etudes Proustiennes. irreg.
- Nouvelle Revue de Psychanalyse. q.
- Nouvelle Revue Francaise. m. ISSN 0029-4802

**S.A.R.L. Galvano**
79 Champs-Elysees, Paris (8e), France.
- Galvano-Organo; traitements et finitions des
surfaces. m. (Societe Galvano)

**Ganterie-Vetements de Peau**
7 Place Antoninponcet, 69288 Lyon 1, France.
- Ganterie-Vetements de Peau. bi-m. ISSN 0016-
4518

**Editions Garnier Freres**
19,rue des Plantes, 75014 Paris, France.
- Annee Balzacienne. a. ISSN 0084-6473 (Groupe
d'Etudes Balzaciennes)
- Critiques de Notre Temps Et... irreg. ISSN 0070-
1556
- Dix-Huitieme Siecle. a. ISSN 0070-6760 (Societe
Francaise d'Etude du Dix Huitieme Siecle)

**Editions Robert Garouel et Adaut**
6 Place de la Madeleine, 75 Paris(8e), France.
- Mouvement. bi-m. ISSN 0027-2663

**Gastronomie Magazine: l'Art Culinaire**
10, Grande rue, 42540 St. Just-la-Pendue, France.
- Gastronomie Magazine: l'Art Culinaire;
restaurants, hotellerie, tourisme. 10 per yr.

**Editions Gautier-Languereau**
18, rue Jacob, 75006 Paris, France.
- Veillees des Chaumieres. w.

**Gaz de France**
- Gaz de France. Rapport Annuel. (pub. by Editions
Mercure)

**Gaz de France. Departement Profor**
5 Av. de Friedland, Paris (8e), France.
- Gaz de France. Secretariat General. Schema
d'Organisation Profor. a. ISSN 0072-0321

**Gaz de France. Direction Commerciale**
23 rue Philibert-Delorme, 75840 Paris Cedex 17,
France.
- G; Documentation Technique et Commerciale des
Vendeurs de Gaz. irreg. ISSN 0072-0046

**Gaz de France. Direction Regionale de la Distribution
Paris**
23 rue de Vienne, 75008 Paris, France.
- Gaz Relations; direction regionale de la
distribution Paris. s-a.

**La Gazette**
7 rue Jacquemars-Gielee, 59015 Lille Cedex,
France.
- Gazette de la Region du Nord. 3 per w. ISSN
0016-5514
- Plein Nord; revue economique, historique et
culturelle du Nord de la France. 3 per w.

**Gazette Apicole**
20 rue de Montevideo, 75116 Paris, France.
- Gazette Apicole; annales mensuelles de
l'apiculture mondiale. m. ISSN 0016-5506

**Gazette du Palais et du Notariat**
3, Boulevard du Palais, 75180 Paris, France.
● Gazette du Palais et du Notariat. 3 per wk.

**Gazette Medicale de France**
33 Avenue Mozart, 75016 Paris, France.
● Gazette Medicale de France. w. ISSN 0016-5557

**Editions GEAD**
79 Rue de Faubourg Poisonniere, Paris (9e), France.
● Souder; revue pratique du soudage. 9 per yr. ISSN 0038-1748

**Gerontologie**
16 rue Oberkampf, 75011 Paris, France.
● Gerontologie. q. ISSN 0016-9005

**Gerpresse**
3 Cite d'Hauteville, 75010 Paris, France
(Orders to: 43 Bd. Barbes, 75018 Paris, France)
● Peche et les Poissons. m. ISSN 0031-3718
● Revue Nationale de le Chasse. m. ISSN 0035-3752
● Sport-Auto; la revue 100' dans la course. m. ISSN 0038-7827

**Gestions Hospitalieres**
2 rue Jules Verne, 78200 Mantes-La-Jolie, France.
● Gestions Hospitalieres. 10 per yr. ISSN 0016-9218

**Librairie Orientaliste Paul Geuthner**
12, rue Vavin, 75006 Paris, France.
● Documents d'Histoire Maghrebine. irreg. (Centre d'Etudes Islamiques et Orientales d'Histoire Comparee)
● Ethnographie. irreg. (Societe d'Ethnographie de Paris)
● Journal Asiatique. 4 per yr. ISSN 0021-762X (Societe Asiatique)
● Syria; revue d'art oriental et d'archeologie. 2 double nos. per yr. ISSN 0039-7946 (Institut Francais d'Archeologie de Beyrouth)

**GIROD**
144, rue Marcadet, 75018 Paris, France.
● Cahiers de Sophrologie. q.

**Editions Spes: Jean-Paul Gisserot**
Rue Pierre de Roux, 75007 Paris, France.
● Modele Magazine; revue des modeles d'avions. m. ISSN 0026-7392

**Publications Paul Goebel**
39 rue Taitbout, Paris (9e), France.
● Bulletin Bi-Mensuel des Tirages. s-m. ISSN 0007-4144
● Cote des Coupons. s-m. ISSN 0010-969X

**Editions du Gonfalon**
80 Route de Dourdan, 91670 Angerville (Essonne), France.
● Annuaire des Boissons et des Liquides Alimentaires/Jahrbuch des Getraenke und Fluessigen Nahrmittel. a. ISSN 0066-2763

**Editions Gaston Gorde**
43 Avenue Paul-Doumer, 06190 Roquebrune Cap Martin, France.
● Maisons d'Enfants et d'Adolescents de France. Album-Annuaire National; publication documentaire illustree des etablissements de vacances, de repos, de soins, de cure et de prevention pour enfants et adolescents. alatest edition 28th, 1976. ISSN 0076-2814

**G. Gourdon, Ed. and Pub.**
10, rue de Crussol, 75011 Paris, France.
● Astres. m.

**Editions Gozlan**
94 rue Saint-Lazare, 75442 Paris 9, France.
● Annuaire General Automobile. a. ISSN 0066-314X
● Annuaire National des Transports. a. ISSN 0066-3549
● Annuaire Tractocatalogue; guide technique de mecanique agricole. a. ISSN 0082-5662
● Transporanonces; revue mensuelle d'annonces specialisees pour le transport. m.

**Grand Orient de France**
● Humanisme. (pub. by Editions Maconniques de France)

**Grandremy**
6, rue du Chevalier de la Barre, 93320 Pavillion Sous Bois, France.
● Assistante et le Prothesiste Dentaires. bi-m.

**Grange Bateliere S.A.**
10 rue Chauchat, Paris (9e), France.
● Atlas; geographie physique et humaine - decouverte de l'homme et de la nature. m. ISSN 0004-6922

**Editions Bernard Grasset**
61, rue des Saints-Peres, 75006 Paris, France.
● Cahiers Jean Giraudoux. a.

**Grive**
c/oJean-Paul Vaillant, Ed., 33 Av. Forest, 08100 Charleville-Mezieres, France.
● Grive. q. ISSN 0017-4335

**Sergio Grossu, Ed. & Pub.**
B. P. 79, F-92405 Courbevoie, France.
● Catacombes; messager supraconfessionel de l'eglise du silence. m.

**Groupe Creations**
40, rue de Chabrol, 75010 Paris, France.
● Creations Lingerie. q.
● Creations Pret-a-Porter. q.

**Groupe d'Acoustique Musicale**
Universite Paris VI, Tour 66, 4 Place Jussieu, Paris 5, France.
● Groupe d'Acoustique Musicale. Bulletin. bi-m.

**Groupe d'Etudes Balzaciennes**
● Annee Balzacienne. (pub. by Editions Garnier Freres)

**Groupe d'Etudes de Psychiatrie Psychologie et Sciences Sociales**
● Perspectives Psychiatriques. (pub. by Publicat)

**Groupe d'Etudes Prospectives Internationales du C.F.C.E.**
5 Avenue Pierre-1er-de Serbie, 75783 Paris Cedex 16, France.
● Courrier des Pays de l'Est. m. ISSN 0590-0239 (Ecole Pratique des Hautes Etudes. Centre de Documentation sur l'U.R.S.S. et les Pays Slaves)

**Groupe de Sociologie des Religions**
● Archives de Sciences Sociales des Religions. (pub. by Centre National de la Recherche Scientifique)

**Groupe Expansion**
67, Avenue de Wagram, 75017 Paris, France.
● Expansion. m. ISSN 0014-4703
● Lettre de l'Expansion. w.

**Groupe Intersyndical de l'Industrie Nucleaire**
15, rue Beaujon, Paris 8e, France.
● Annuaire de l'Activite Nucleaire Francaise. irreg. ISSN 0066-2593

**Groupe J.A.**
51 Avenue des Ternes, 75017 Paris, France.
● Dossiers bis. s-a.
● Economia. m.
● Jeune Afrique. w. ISSN 0021-6089

**Groupe L.C.C.E**
7, rue Joubert, F 75009 Paris, France.
● Annuaire des Centrales et Groupements d'Achats; le livre d'or de la distribution francaise. biennial.
● Hyperguide des Hypermarches.

**Groupe, Union, Defense**
● Vaincre. (pub. by S.O.E. (Societe Occidentale d'Edition))

**Groupement d'Edition et d'Information Technique, Economique et Culturelle**
18 rue de Varenne, 75007 Paris, France.
● Actuel Developpement. bi-m. ISSN 0395-9481 (Society for International Development)

**Groupement de Recherche et d'Etudes pour la Civilisation Europeenne**
130 rue de la Pompe, 75116 Paris, France.
● Elements; pour la civilisation Europeenne. bi-m.
● Etudes et Recherches; les cahiers trimestriels du G.R.E.C.E. q.

**Groupement des Associations de Proprietaires d'Appareils a Vapeur et Electriques**
66 rue de Rome, Paris (8e), France.
● A. P. A. V. E. Revue; revue technique du groupement des associations de proprietaires d'appareils a vapeur et electriques. q. ISSN 0001-2122

**Groupement des Directeurs Publicitaires de France**
9 rue Leo-Delibes, 75116 Paris, France.
● Groupement des Directeurs Publicitaires de France. Annuaire. a. ISSN 0072-7792

**Groupement des Industries Francaises Aeronautiques et Spatiales (G.I.F.A.S)**
6 rue Galilee, 75116 Paris, France.
● Informations Aeronautiques et Spatiales. w.

**Groupement des Societes Immobilieres d'Investissement**
18, rue de Vienne, 75008paris, France.
● Groupement des Societes Immobilieres d'Investissement. Annuaire. a. ISSN 0066-2933

**Groupement Genealogique de la Region du Nord**
271 Grand rue, 59100 Roubaix, France.
● Nord Genealogie. q.

**Groupement Medical d'Etudes sur l'Alcoolisme**
● Revue de l'Alcoolisme. (pub. by Masson)

**Groupement National pour l'Organisation de la Medecine Auxiliaire**
12, rue Grange-Bateliere, 75009 Paris, France.
● Therapeutiques Naturelles; revue francaise de vulgarisation. bi-m. ISSN 0396-7107

**Groupement pour l'Etude des Transports Urbains Modernes**
173 rue Armand Silvestre, F-92400 Courbevoie, France.
● Transports Urbains; revue d'information et de documentation. q. ISSN 0397-6521

**Guepes**
B.P. 331, Paris (13e), France.
● Guepes. bi-m. ISSN 0017-5080

**Guerre de Classes**
B.P. 20, 37005 Tours, France.
● Guerre de Classes. m.

**H. Guichou, Ed. & Pub.**
5 bis rue du Louvre, Paris (1er), France.
● Petit Meunier. w. ISSN 0031-6261

**Guide des Ports: France, Maghreb, Algerie, Tunisie, Maroc, Afrique Noire**
13 rue Flegier, Marseille, France.
● Guide des Ports: France, Maghreb, Algerie, Tunisie, Maroc, Afrique Noire. a. ISSN 0072-8012

**Guide des Relais Routiers**
6 rue de l'Isly, 75008 Paris, France.
● Guide des Relais Routiers. a.

**Guide International de l'Energie Atomique et des Etudes Spatiales**
252 rue de Faubourg Saint - Honore, Paris 8, France.
● Guide International de l'Energie Atomique et des Etudes Spatiales. triennial. ISSN 0072-8128

**Guides Equestres**
38 rue Parmentier, 92200 Neuilly-sur-Seine, France.
● Ou Monter a Cheval. a. ISSN 0078-7035

**Guitare et Musique Chansons Poesie**
92 rue de Richelieu, Paris (2e), France.
● Guitare et Musique Chansons Poesie. 10 per yr. ISSN 0017-548X

**Librairie Hachette**
79 Bld. Saint-Germain, 75261 Paris Cedex 06, France.
● Etudes d'Anglais. irreg. ISSN 0071-1888
● Feu Vert. m. (during school year) ISSN 0015-0398
● Francais dans le Monde. 8 per yr. ISSN 0015-9395
● Methodes Mathematiques des Sciences de l'Homme. irreg. ISSN 0076-6798
● Passe-Partout. m(during school year) ISSN 0031-269X
● Quoi de Neuf. m.(during school yr.) ISSN 0033-6645
● Recherches Historiques et Litteraires. irreg. ISSN 0080-0082

**Harangue**
19 rue Raffet, Paris (16), France.
● Harangue. q. ISSN 0017-758X

**Librarie A. Hatier**
8 rue d'Assas, Paris 6e, France.
- Collection d'Histoire Contemporaine. irreg. ISSN 0069-5343
- Documents et Recherches. m (10 per yr.)
- Documents et Recherches-Sciences. m.

**Haute Coiffure Francaise**
35 Av. de l'Opera, Paris 2e, France.
- Haute Coiffure Francaise. irreg. ISSN 0073-0920

**Heimdal**
B.P. 332, 14014 Caen, France.
- Heimdal

**Hellequin**
B.P. 332, 14014 Caen, France.
- Hellequin; revue litteraire Normande. q.

**Editions Hennessen**
61 rue de Malte, Paris (11e), France.
- Journal du Textile. w. ISSN 0021-8197

**Herd Book Charolais**
8, rue de Lourdes, B.P. 107, 58002 Nevers, France.
- Charolais. q. ISSN 0395-8183

**Herd Book F.F.P.N.**
3 Place du Marechal Leclerc, 59405 Cambrai, France.
- Francaise Frisonne Pie Noire. q. ISSN 0046-4872

**Editions Hermann**
293 rue Lecourbe, 75015 Paris, France.
- Collection Formation des Enseignants. irreg.
- Elements de Mathematique. irreg. ISSN 0070-9999
- Histoire de la Pensee. irreg., 1972, no. 17. ISSN 0073-2362 (Ecole Pratique des Hautes Etudes. Centre International de Recherches d'Histoire des Sciences et des Techniques)

**Heugel**
56-62 Galerie Montpensier, 75001 Paris, France.
- Revue de Musicologie. s-a. ISSN 0035-1601 (Societe Francaise de Musicologie)

**Hispania**
Ed. Santiago Sanchez, 11 Rue des Aubepines, 86 Poitiers, France.
- Hispania; revue mensuelle pour tous ceux qui apprennent l'espagnol. m. ISSN 0046-7480

**Historama**
58 rue Perronet, 92523 Neuilly S/Seine, France.
- Historama. m. ISSN 0018-2273

**Homme Libre**
Boite Postale 282, 42006-St. Etienne, France.
- Homme Libre; fils de la terre. q. ISSN 0018-4314

**Homme Nouveau**
1 Place Saint-Sulpice, 75006 Paris, France.
- Homme Nouveau. bi-m. ISSN 0018-4322

**Publications Michel Hommell**
7 rue de Lille, 75007 Paris, France.
- Echappement. m.
- Moto. m.

**Hommes et Migrations**
6 rue Barye, 75017 Paris, France.
- Hommes et Migrations. bi-m. ISSN 0018-4365

**Editions Hommes et Techniques**
2, rue Benoit Malon, B.P. 128, 92154 Suresnes, France.
- Hommes et Techniques. m. ISSN 0018-4381

**Hommes Libres**
36 rue du Commerce, Paris (15e), France.
- Hommes Libres; organe interallie des evades, passeurs, filieristes et prisonniers. bi-m. ISSN 0018-4403

**Hommes Volants**
28 rue de Navarin, Paris (9e), France.
- Hommes Volants. bi-m. ISSN 0018-4411

**Hopital Boucicaut-Paris. Laboratoire d'Eutonologie**
- Agressologie. (pub. by Service de Presse, Edition, Information)

**Hopital des Enfants Malades. Centre d'Estudes sur les Maladies du Metabolisme Chez l'Enfant**
- Journees Parisiennes de Pediatrie. (pub. by Flammarion Medecine-Sciences)

**Hopital, Information Therapeutique**
44 rue du Colisee, 75 Paris (8e), France.
- Hopital, Information Therapeutique. 6 per yr. ISSN 0020-028X

**Hopital Necker. Clinique Nephrologique**
- Actualites Nephrologiques. (pub. by Flammarion Medecine Sciences)

**Editions Horizons de France**
34, rue de Laborde, 75008 Paris, France.
- Hommes et Civilisations. irreg. ISSN 0073-3199
- Plante et l'Homme. irreg. ISSN 0079-2268

**Horizons du Fantastique**
153 Bd. Voltaire, 92 Asnieres sur Seine, France.
- Horizons du Fantastique. m. ISSN 0046-7901

**Hot Club de France. Bulletin**
Hughes Panassie, Toulouse 390-45, France.
- Hot Club de France. Bulletin; fort sur le jazz. 10 per yr.

**Hotel-Dieu. Clinique Medico-Sociale du Diabete et des Maladies Metaboliques**
- Journees Annuelles de Diabetologie de l'Hotel Dieu. (pub. by Flammarion Medecine Sciences)

**Hotels de la France**
15 Faubourg Montmartre, 75009 Paris, France.
- Hotels de la France et d'Outre-Mer. a. ISSN 0073-3539

**Houille Blanche**
5 Chemin des Marronniers, 38100 Grenoble, France.
- Electricite de France. Direction des Etudes et Recherches. Bulletin. Serie A: Nucleaire, Hydraulique, Thermique. 4 per yr.plus supplements. ISSN 0013-449X
- Electricite de France. Direction des Etudes et Recherches. Bulletin. Serie B: Reseaux Electriques, Materiels Electriques. 4 per yr. ISSN 0013-4503
- Electricite de France. Direction des Etudes et Recherches. Bulletin. Serie C: Mathematiques-Informatique. s-a. ISSN 0013-4511

**Houilleres du Bassin du Nord et du Pas-De-Calais**
Service des Centrales Electriques, B.P. 75, 59505 Douai Cedex, France.
- Bulletin d'Information des Centrales Electriques. q. ISSN 0007-4535

**Houilleres du Centre-Midi**
135, rue Paradis, 13006 Marseille, France.
- Mineur d'Auvergne. bi-m. ISSN 0026-5063

**Hudson Research Europe Ltd.**
54, rue de Varenne, 75007 Paris, France.
- Hudson Letter. 22 per yr.

**Humanite Rouge**
Boite Postale 61, 75861 Paris Cedex 18, France.
- Humanite Rouge; quotidien des Communistes Marxistes-Leninistes de France. d. ISSN 0018-750X

**I. F. C. E.**
3 rue Henri-Heine, Paris (16e), France.
- Actualite, Combustibles, Energie. m. ISSN 0337-4092

**I.F.P.**
12 rue des Fosses Saint-Marcel, 75005 Paris, France.
- Revue de Medecine Aeronautique et Spatiale. 4 per yr. ISSN 0035-1520 (Societe de Physiologie et de Medecine Aeronautiques et Cosmonautiques)

**I.L.A.R.I.**
23 rue de la Pepiniere, Paris (8e), France.
- Aportes; revista de estudios latinoamericanos. q. ISSN 0003-6544

**I.N.R.S**
9 Ave. Montaigne, Paris (8e), France.
- Risques du Metier. bi-m. ISSN 0048-8321

**I.P.E.C.**
59 rue de Billancourt, 92100 Boulogne, France.
- Domicible. bi-m.
- Points de Vente. m.

**I R F E D**
47 rue de la Glaciere, 75013 Paris, France.
- Developpement et Civilisations. q. ISSN 0012-1657

**Ici-Paris**
162 rue du Fg. St. Honore, 75380 Paris Cedex 08, France.
- Ici Paris. w.
- Nostra; hebdomadaire de l'actualite mysterieuse. w. ISSN 0337-8888
- Nostradamus. w.

**Idees pour Tous**
33 rue Auguste-Bosc, 30000 Nimes, France.
- Idees pour Tous. w, m, q. ISSN 0019-1434

**Idees-Service**
Avenue de Berlincan 33, Saint Medard en Jalles, France.
- Discours Social. q. ISSN 0012-3595 (Institut de Litterature et de Techniques Artistiques de Masse)

**Images du Transport**
45, Avenue du Roule, 92 Neuilly- sur- Seine, France.
- Images du Transport. bi-m. ISSN 0046-8665

**Editions de l' Impossible**
29 rue de Bellefond, 75009 Paris, France.
- Impossible. m.

**Imprimerie du Messager S.A.**
22 Avenue General de Gaulle, 74210 Thonon les Bains, Haute-Savoie, France.
- Messager de la Haute Savoie. w. ISSN 0026-0258

**Imprimerie du Sud-Est**
Saint-Remy-De-Provence, France.
- Collection Poetique Monclart. irreg. ISSN 0069-5424

**Imprimerie Nationale**
S.E.V.P.O., 39 rue de la Convention, 75732 Paris Cedex 15, France.
- Fonds de Developpment Economique et Social. Conseil de Direction. Rapport. a. ISSN 0071-6847 (France. Ministere de l'Economie et des Finances)
- France. Direction Generale des Douanes et Droits Indirects. Annuaire. irreg. ISSN 0071-8629
- France. Direction Generale des Douanes et Droits Indirects. Annuaire Abrege de Statistiques. irreg. ISSN 0071-8637
- France. Direction Generale des Douanes et Droits Indirects. Commentaires Annuels des Statistiques du Commerce Exterieur. irreg. ISSN 0071-8645
- France. Direction Generale des Douanes et Droits Indirects. Statistiques du Commerce Exterieur et des Transports. a. ISSN 0071-867X
- France. Direction Generale des Douanes et Droits Indirects. Statistiques du Commerce Exterieur: Importations- Exportations. Nomenclature: N.G.P. (Nomenclature Generale des Produits) a. ISSN 0071-8688
- France. Direction Generale des Douanes et Droits Indirects. Statistiques du Commerce Exterieur. Transit Direct. irreg. ISSN 0071-8661
- France. Direction Nationale des Douanes et Droits Indirects. Tableau General des Transports. a. ISSN 0071-8726
- France. Direction Nationale des Douanes et Droits Indirects. Transport du Commerce Exterieur. a. ISSN 0071-8718
- France. Imprimerie Nationale. Annuaire. a. ISSN 0078-9666
- France. Inspection Generale des Finances. Annuaire. a. ISSN 0071-8742
- Inventaire General des Monuments et des Richesses Artistiques de la France. irreg. ISSN 0075-0018 (France. Ministere des Affaires Culturelles)
- Memorial de l'Artillerie Francaise; sciences et techniques de l'armement. q. ISSN 0025-9160
- Nomenclature des Entreprises Nationales a Caractere Industriel ou Commercial et des Societes d'Economie Mixte d'Interet National. irreg. ISSN 0078-0960 (France. Ministere de l'Economie et des Finances)

**Societe des Editions de l' Imprimerie Nouvelle**
89 Rue Barrault, 75013 Paris, France.
- Imprimerie Nouvelle; mensuel technique. 11 per yr. ISSN 0019-302X
- J'emballe. a.
- Mafogra. a.
- Materiel Graphique. a.

- Metiers Graphiques. 3 per mo.; 33 per yr. ISSN 0026-1289
- Quatre Mille Imprimeries Francaises. a. ISSN 0066-3638

**Imprimerie Siciliano**
1Rue General Camp 1, Ajaccio, Corsica, France.
- Journal de la Corse Agricole. m. ISSN 0021-7778 (Mutualite Sociale Agricole de la Corse)

**Editions Indelec**
13 rue Hamelin, 75783 Paris, France.
- Industries Electriques et Electroniques. irreg. (Federation des Industries Electriques et Electroniques)

**Editions Indicateur Bertrand**
11 et 13 rue du Louvre, 75001 Paris, France.
- Indicateur Bertrand; la revue conseil en immobilier. s-m. ISSN 0019-6886
- Locations & Ventes. w. ISSN 0024-5666
- Locations Vacances. s-a. ISSN 0024-5674

**Indiscret de Paris**
BP 104, 94100 St-Maur, France.
- Indiscret de Paris; lettre politique d'information. w. ISSN 0019-7114

**Editions de l' Industrie Textile**
36 rue Ballu, 75009 Paris, France.
- Industrie Textile. m. ISSN 0019-9176

**Industries Sante**
2, rue du 8 Mai-1945, 92700 Colombes, France.
- Industries Sante. 9 per yr.

**Information Dentaire**
20, rue Godot de Mauroy, 75442 Paris Cedex 09, France.
- Information Dentaire; hebdomadaire independant. w. ISSN 0020-0018

**Information du Spectacle**
10 rue de la Chaussee d'Antin, 75-Paris (9e), France.
- Information du Spectacle. m(11 per yr.)

**Information Hippique**
c/o Ed. Robert Louis Thomas, 174 Av. Charles-de-Gaulle, Neuilly-sur-Seine, France.
- Information Hippique. m(11 per yr.)

**Information Promotion et Culture, S.A.R.L.**
17 rue de la Felicite, Paris (17e), France.
- Livres-Actualite. m. ISSN 0024-5356

**Information-Promotion Francaises**
12 rue des Fosses St. Marcel, 75005 Paris, France.
- Revue Radiodiffusion et Television. 5 per yr. (Telediffusion de France)

**Information Transports**
64 rue de Soissons, 33000 Bordeaux (Gironde), France.
- Information Transports; periodique bi-mensuel de documentation et d'information des transports ferroviaires, routiers, fluviaux et maritimes. s-m. ISSN 0020-0298

**Informations Rapides de l'Administration Francaise**
27 rue Jasmin, 75016 Paris, France.
- Gouvernement et les Cabinets Ministeriels. 6 per yr.
- Informations Rapides de l'Administration Francaise. frequency varies per section. ISSN 0020-0492

**Informations Techniques des Services Veterinaires**
5 rue Ernest Renan, 92130 Issy-Les-Moulineaux, France.
- Informations Techniques des Directions des Services Veterinaires. 4 per yr. ISSN 0020-0522 (Syndicat National des Services Veterinaires)

**Ingenierie-Information**
108, rue Saint-Honore, 75001 Paris, France.
- Ingenierie-Information. bi-m. ISSN 0337-2731

**Ingenieurs et Techniciens**
30 rue Tronchet, Paris (9e), France.
- Ingenieurs et Techniciens; revue des progres. m. ISSN 0020-1227

**Institut Appert**
44, rue d'Alesia, 75014 Paris, France.
- Institut Appert. Bulletin Analytique. q.

**Institut Armoricain de Recherches Historiques**
- Institut Armoricain de Recherches Historiques, Rennes. (Publication) (pub. by Editions Klincksieck)

**Institut Catholique d'Arts et Metiers de Lille**
6 rue Auber, Lille, France.
- I C A M Annuaire. a. ISSN 0066-8982

**Institut Catholique de Paris**
21, rue d'Assas, 75270 Paris Cedex 06, France.
- Institut Catholique de Paris. Annuaire. a.

**Institut Catholique de Toulouse**
31 rue de la Fonderie, 31068 Toulouse Cedex, France.
- Bulletin de Litterature Ecclesiastique. q. ISSN 0007-4322

**Institut Collegial Europeen**
Logis Royal de Loches, Loches, France.
- Institut Collegial Europeen. Bulletin. a. ISSN 0073-8174

**Institut d'Amenagement et d'Urbanisme de la Region d'Ile de France**
21-23 rue Miollis, 75732 Paris Cedex 15, France.
- Informations d'Ile de France. bi-m.
- Institut d'Amenagement et d'Urbanisme de la Region d'Ile de France. Cahiers. 4 vols. per yr.

**Institut d'Art et d'Archeologie**
3 rue Michelet, Paris 75006, France.
- International Congress on the History of Art. Proceedings. quinquennial, 1968, 22nd, Budapest. ISSN 0074-4190 (International Committee on the History of Art)

**Institut d'Economie Regionale Bourgogne Franche-Comte**
4 Bd. Gabriel, 21000 Dijon (Cote d'Or), France.
- Revue de l'Economie du Centre-Est. q. ISSN 0035-1350

**Institut d'Embryologie et Teratologie Experimentales**
49 Bis Avenue de la Belle Gabrielle, 94 Nogent-Sur-Marne, France.
- Institut d'Embryologie et Teratologie Experimentales. Activite et Travaux. a. ISSN 0071-8750

**Institut d'Emission d'Outre Mer, Paris.**
233 Boulevard St.-Germain, Paris 7e, France.
- Institut d'Emission d'Outre Mer, Paris. Rapport d'Activite. a. ISSN 0073-8247

**Institut d'Etude du Developpement Economique et Social**
- Tiers Monde. (pub. by Presses Universitaires de France)

**Institut d'Etudes Americaines**
1 Place de Odeon, Paris 6e, France.
- Association Francaise d'Etudes Americaines. s-a.

**Institut d'Etudes et de Recherches Inter-Culturelles**
- Ethnies. (pub. by Editions Mouton et Cie)

**Institut d'Etudes Hispaniques, Paris**
Centre de Recherche, 31 rue Gay-Lussac, Paris 5e, France.
- Etudes Hispaniques Appliquees. irreg., 1974, latest edition. ISSN 0071-2094

**Institut d'Etudes Politiques de Paris**
- Institut d'Etudes Politiques de Paris. Livret. (pub. by Librarie Vuibert)

**Institut d'Etudes Savoisiennes**
Centre Universitaire de Savoie, B.P. 143, 73000 Chambery, France.
- Etudes Savoisiennes. irreg. (Co-Sponsor: Societe Savoisienne d'Histoire et d'Archeologie)

**Institut d'Etudes Semitiques**
11 rue St Sulpice, Paris (6e), France.
- Semitica. a. ISSN 0085-6037

**Institut d'Etudes Slaves, Paris**
9 rue Michelet, F 75006 Paris, France.
- Bibliotheque d'Etudes Balkaniques. irreg., 1965, vol. 8. ISSN 0067-8325
- Guide du Slaviste. irreg. ISSN 0072-8071
- Institut d'Etudes Slaves, Paris. Annuaire. a. ISSN 0078-9968
- Institut d'Etudes Slaves, Paris. Bibliotheque Russe. irreg., vol. 40, 1977. ISSN 0078-9976

- Institut d'Etudes Slaves, Paris. Collection de Grammaires. irreg.; 1972, vol. 6. ISSN 0078-9984
- Institut d'Etudes Slaves, Paris. Collection de Manuels. irreg., vol. 7, 1976. ISSN 0078-9992
- Institut d'Etudes Slaves, Paris. Collection Historique. irreg., vol. 24, 1977. ISSN 0079-0001
- Institut d'Etudes Slaves, Paris. Documents Pedagogiques. irreg; 1977, vol. 18. ISSN 0300-2594
- Institut d'Etudes Slaves, Paris. Textes. irreg., 1968, vol. 8. ISSN 0079-001X
- Institut d'Etudes Slaves, Paris. Travaux. irreg.; 1970, vol. 30. ISSN 0079-0028
- Revue des Etudes Slaves. a. ISSN 0080-2557

**Institut d'Etudes Socialistes, Paris**
25 rue du Louvre, Paris 1er, France.
- Informations et Etudes Socialistes. irreg. ISSN 0073-7925

**Institut d'Odontostomatologie**
20 Cours de la Marne, 33 Bordeaux, France.
- Revue d'Odonto-Stomatologie du Midi de la France. 4 per yr. ISSN 0035-2470

**Institut d'Optique. Centre de Documentation**
3/5 Boulevard Pasteur, 75015 Paris, France.
- Bulletin Vision. bi-m.

**Institut de Botanique, Strasbourg**
8 rue Goethe, Strasbourg, France.
- Informations Annuelles de Caryosystematique et Cytogenetique. a. ISSN 0073-7917

**Institut de Cancerologie et d'Immunogenetique**
- Biomedecine. (pub. by Masson)

**Institut de Ceramique Francaise**
6 Grande Rue, 92310 Sevres, France.
- CERINDEX: Bulletin de Documentation Ceramique. s-m. (prep. by its Service de Documentation)

**Institut de Formation et d'Etudes Psycho-Sociologiques et Pedagogiques**
3 rue Marcoz, Chambery, France.
- I F E P P Informations. q. ISSN 0046-9688

**Institut de France**
23 Quai de Conti, Paris 6e, France.
- Institut de France. Annuaire. a. ISSN 0073-8190

**Institut de France. Academie des Inscriptions et Belles-Lettres**
see Academie des Inscriptions et Belles-Lettres

**Institut de France. Academie des Sciences**
see Academie des Sciences

**Institut de France. Academie Francaise**
see Academie Francaise

**Institut de Geographie Alpine**
Rue M. Gignoux, 38031 Grenoble Cedex, France.
- Revue de Geographie Alpine. q. ISSN 0035-1121

**Institut de Geographie, Paris. Bibliotheque**
191 rue Saint-Jacques, Paris, France.
- Annuaire des Geographes de la France et de l'Afrique Francophone. a. ISSN 0066-2844 (Centre de Recherches et de Documentation Cartographiques et Geographiques)

**Institut de Litterature et de Techniques Artistiques de Masse**
- Discours Social. (pub. by Idees-Service)
- Institut de Litterature et de Techniques Artistiques de Masse. Travaux et Recherches. (pub. by Mouton Publishers NE)

**Institut de Medecine Legale et de Medecine Sociale**
Place Theo Varlet, 59000 Lille, France.
- Institut de Medecine Legale et de Medecine Sociale. Archives. irreg; latest 1966. ISSN 0075-9473

**Institut de Medecine Tropicale**
Parc du Pharo, 13007 Marseille, France.
- Medecine Tropicale. bi-m. ISSN 0025-682X

**Institut de Promotion Internationale**
45 rue de la Procession, 75015 Paris, France.
- Soins. 24 per yr. ISSN 0038-0814

**Institut de Recherche en Informatique et Automatique**
Domaine de Voluceau B.P. No. 105, 78150 le
Chesnay, Rocquencourt, France.
- Bulletin de Liaison de la Recherche en
  Informatique et Automatique. m. ISSN 0303-1276
- Guide Europeen des Produits Logiciels. s-a. ISSN
  0395-2061

**Institut de Recherche et d'Histoire des Textes, Paris**
15, Quai Anatole- France, 75700 Paris, France.
- Institut de Recherche et d'Histoire des Textes,
  Paris. Documents, Etudes et Repertoires. irreg.,
  1976, vol. 22. ISSN 0073-8212

**Institut de Recherches Agronomiques Tropicales et
des Cultures Vivrieres**
110 rue de l'Universite, 75340 Paris, France.
- Agronomie Tropicale. q. ISSN 0002-1946

**Institut de Recherches du Coton et des Textiles
Exotiques**
34 rue des Renaudes, 75017 Paris, France.
- Coton et Fibres Tropicales. q. ISSN 0010-9711
- Coton et Fibres Tropicales. Bulletin
  Bibliographique. ISSN 0010-972X

**Institut de Recherches en Economie de la Production**
- Theorie de la Production. (pub. by Editions Cujas)

**Institut de Recherches pour les Huiles et Oleagineux**
11, Square Petraque, Paris 75016, France.
- Oleagineux; revue internationale des corps gras.
  m. ISSN 0030-2082

**Institut de Recherches sur les Fruits et Agrumes
(IRFA)**
6 Rue du General-Clergerie, 75116 Paris, France.
- Fruits; fruits d'outre mer, culture, industrie,
  economie. m. ISSN 0016-2299

**Institut de Science Financiere**
- Institut de Science Financiere et d'Assurances.
  Bulletin des Actuaires Diplomes. (pub. by Dulac
  et Cie)

**Institut de Sciences Mathematiques et Economiques
Appliquees, Paris**
11 Bd. de Sebastopol, 75001 Paris, France
- Economie Appliquee. irreg. ISSN 0013-0494
  (and Editions DROZ, 11 rue Massot, 1211 Geneva
  12, Switzerland)
- Economies et Societes. Serie AB. Economie du
  Travail. irreg., 1969, latest issue. ISSN 0068-4821
- Economies et Societes. Serie AF. Histoire
  Quantitative de l'Economie Francaise. irreg. ISSN
  0068-4864
- Economies et Societes. Serie AG. Progres et
  Agriculture. irreg., 1974, latest issue. ISSN 0068-
  4899
- Economies et Societes. Serie F. Developpement,
  Croissance, Progres des Pays en Voie de
  Developpement. irreg. ISSN 0068-4813
- Economies et Societes. Serie G. Economie
  Planifiee. irreg. ISSN 0068-483X
- Economies et Societes. Serie L. Economie
  Regionale. irreg. ISSN 0068-4848
- Economies et Societes. Serie M. Philosophie -
  Sciences Sociales Economie. irreg. ISSN 0068-
  4880
- Economies et Societes. Serie P. Relations
  Economiques Internationales. irreg., 1974, latest
  issue. ISSN 0068-4902
- Economies et Societes. Serie S. Etudes de
  Marxologie. irreg. ISSN 0068-4856
- Economies et Societes. Serie T. Information -
  Recherche Innovation. irreg., 1974, latest issue.
  ISSN 0068-4872
- Institut de Sciences Mathematiques et
  Economiques Appliquees. Rapport d'Activite. a.
- Mondes en Developpment. q.

**Institut de Soudure**
- Soudage et Techniques Connexes. (pub. by
  Publications de la Soudure Autogene)

**Institut des Actuaires Francais**
- Institut des Actuaires Francais. Bulletin
  Trimestriel. (pub. by Dulac et Cie)

**Institut des Corps Gras (ITERG)**
- Revue Francaise des Corps Gras. (pub. by
  Editions Techniques des Industries des Corps
  Gras)

**Institut des Etudes Augustiniennes**
8 rue Francois 1er, 75008 Paris, France.
- Revue des Etudes Augustiniennes. q. ISSN 0035-
  2012

**Institut des Hautes Etudes de l'Amerique Latine**
28 rue Saint-Guillaume, 75007 Paris, France.
- Cahiers' des Ameriques Latines. Serie - Sciences
  de l'Homme. s-a. ISSN 0008-0020
- Institut des Hautes Etudes de l'Amerique Latine.
  Cahiers. irreg., 1968, no. 8. ISSN 0073-8271
- Institut des Hautes Etudes de l'Amerique Latine.
  Centre d'Etudes Politiques, Economiques et
  Sociales. Publications Multigraphiees. irreg., 1973,
  no. 14. ISSN 0073-828X
- Institut des Hautes Etudes de l'Amerique Latine.
  Travaux et Memoires. irreg., 1976, no. 28, 29.
  ISSN 0073-8298

**Institut des Hautes Etudes Scientifiques, Paris**
- Institut des Hautes Etudes Scientifiques, Paris.
  Publications Mathematiques. (pub. by Presses
  Universitaires de France)

**Institut des Sciences Humaines Appliquees, Paris**
17, rue Richer, Paris (9e), France
(or 12 rue Cujas, Paris (5e) France)
- Informatique et Sciences Humaines. 4 per yr.

**Institut du Transport Aerien, Paris**
4 rue de Solferino, Paris (7e), France.
- I T A Bulletin. w.(except Aug) ISSN 0019-0748
- I T A Studies. bi-m. ISSN 0019-0780

**Institut du Verre**
34 rue Michel-Ange, 75016 Paris, France.
- Verres et Refractaires. bi-m. ISSN 0042-4331

**Institut Europeen d'Enseignement Culturel et
Professionnel**
Bis rue Lemoine, 92 Boulogne, France.
- Europe Culture. m. ISSN 0046-2691

**Institut Francais d'Archeologie d'Istanbul**
- Institut Francais d'Archeologie d'Istanbul.
  Bibliotheque Archeologique et Historique. (pub.
  by Librairie Adrien Maisonneuve)

**Institut Francais d'Archeologie de Beyrouth**
- Syria. (pub. by Librairie Orientaliste Paul
  Geuthner)

**Institut Francais d'Etude et d'Information Culturelles
et Techniques**
4 bis rue de Clery, Paris (2e), France.
- Voix de l'Edition de la Presse et de l'Audiovision;
  le journal de la promotion culturelle. m. ISSN
  0042-8345

**Institut Francais d'Etudes Strategiques**
- Strategie. (pub. by Centre d'Etudes de Politique
  Etrangere)

**Institut Francais d'Histoire Sociale**
- Mouvement Social. (pub. by Editions Ouvrieres)

**Institut Francais de la Cooperation**
7 Av. Franco-Russe, 75 Paris (7e), France.
- Revue des Etudes Cooperatives; diffusion de la
  doctrine cooperative. q. ISSN 0035-2020

**Institut Francais de Navigation**
3 Ave. Octave Greard, Paris (7e), France.
- Navigation; revue technique de navigation
  maritime aerienne et spatiale. q. ISSN 0028-1530

**Institut Francais des Combustibles et de l'Energie**
- Revue Generale de Thermique. (pub. by Editions
  Europeennes Thermique et Industrie)

**Institut Francais des Experts Comptables**
139 rue du Faubourg Saint-Honore, 75008 Paris,
France.
- Economie et Comptabilite; gestion des entreprises.
  q.
- Institut Francais des Experts Comptables. Cahiers.
  irreg., approx 2 per yr.

**Institut Francais du Cafe, du Cacao et Autres Plantes
Stimulantes**
34 rue des Renaudes, Paris (17e), France.
- Cafe, Cacao, The. q. ISSN 0007-9510

**Institut Francais du Petrole**
1 et 4 Avenue de Bois-Preau, B.P. No. 311, 92506
Rueil-Malmaison Cedex, France.
- Institut Francais du Petrole. Collection Colloques
  et Seminaires. (pub. by Editions Technip)
- Institut Francais du Petrole. Rapport Annuel. a.
  ISSN 0073-8379
- Institut Francais du Petrole. Revue. (pub. by
  Editions Technip)

**Institut Franco-Iranien. Departement d'Iranologie**
- Bibliotheque Iranienne. (pub. by Adrien
  Maisonneuve)

**Institut Geographique National. Service de la
Documentation Geographique**
2, Avenue Pasteur, 94160-Saint-Mande, France.
- Institut Geographique National. Bulletin
  Bibliographique. bi-m.

**Institut Gustave Roussy**
- Bulletin Signaletique. Part 351: Revue
  Bibliographique Cancer. (pub. by Centre National
  de la Recherche Scientifique. Centre de
  Documentation Scientifique et Technique)

**Institut Henri Poincare**
*see under* Universite de Paris VI

**Institut International d'Administration Publique**
2 Avenue de l'Observatoire, Paris (6e), France.
- Revue Francais d'Administration Publique. q.

**Institut International de Recherches Graphologiques**
13 Av. Robert Schuman, 92 Boulogne-sur-Seine,
France.
- Tribune Graphologique; l'annuaire de la
  graphologie. a. ISSN 0041-2864

**Institut J. Solomides**
56 rue de la Marne, 92-Sceaux (Hauts de Seine),
France.
- Remedes; organe de defense des malades en peril.
  3 per mo. ISSN 0048-7228

**Institut Jupiter**
4 Ave Docteur Brouardel, 75007 Paris, France.
- Droit et Affaires-CEE International. bi-m.

**Institut Litteraire**
91 Av. de Poissy, 78600 Maisons-Laffitte, France.
- Kultura; szkice, opowiadania, sprawozdania. m.
  ISSN 0023-5148
- Zeszyty Historyczne. q. ISSN 0044-4391

**Institut Maurice Thorez**
64 Boulevard Auguste Blanqui, 75013 Paris, France.
- Institut Maurice Thorez. Cahiers d'Histoire. q.
- Institut Maurice Thorez. Conferences. 5 per yr
  (approx) ISSN 0579-5109

**Institut Metaphysique International**
1 Place Wagram, 75017 Paris, France.
- Revue Metapsychique. a. ISSN 0484-8934

**Institut Michael Pacha. Laboratoire Maritime de
Physiologie**
Tamaris-sur-Mer, France.
- Institut Michel Pacha. Annales. irreg. ISSN 0073-
  8565

**Institut National d'Etude du Travail et d'Orientation
Professionnelle**
41 rue Gay Lussac, 75005 Paris, France.
- Orientation Scolaire et Professionnelle. q.

**Institut National de Bois**
- Revue du Bois et de ses Applications. (pub. by
  Compagnie Francaise d'Editions)

**Institut National des Appellations d'Origine des Vins
et Eaux-de-Vie.**
138 Ave. des Champs Elysees, Paris (8e), France.
- Institut National des Appellations d'Origine des
  Vins et Eaux-de-Vie. Bulletin. q. ISSN 0020-2401

**Institut National des Langues et Civilisations
Orientales**
2 rue de Lille, 75007 Paris, France.
- Institut National des Langues et Civilisations
  Orientales. Livret de l'Etudiant. a.

**Institut Oceanographique**
- Institut Oceanographique. Annales. (pub. by
  Masson)

**Institut Pasteur**
28 rue du Docteur-Roux, Paris 15e, France.
- Annales de Microbiologie. (pub. by Masson)
- Institut Pasteur. Bulletin. (pub. by Masson)
- Societe Francaise de Microbiologie. Annuaire.
  triennial. ISSN 0081-1068

**Institut Pasteur de Lille**
- Institut Pasteur de Lille. Annales. (pub. by
  Flammarion Medecine-Sciences)

**Institut Pasteur de Lyon**
- Institut Pasteur de Lyon. Revue. (pub. by Chambefort Edition)

**Institut Protestant de Theologie**
13 rue Louis-Perrier, F 34000 Montpellier, France.
- Etudes Theologiques et Religieuses. q. ISSN 0014-2239

**Institut Scientifique et Technique des Peches Maritimes**
Rue de l'Ile-d'Yeu, B.P. 1049, 44037 Nantes Cedex, France.
- Institut Scientifique et Technique des Peches Maritimes. Revue des Travaux. q. ISSN 0020-2231
- Science et Peche; bulletin d'information et de documentation. m. ISSN 0036-8350

**Institut Superieur des Carrieres Artistiques**
48 rue Monsieur-Le-Prince, Paris 6e, France.
- I C K R T. Bulletin d'Information. irreg. ISSN 0073-8581

**Institut Technique de l'Aviculture (ITAVI)**
28, rue du Rocher, 75008 Paris, France.
- Nouvelles de l'Aviculture. bi-m.

**Institut Technique de l'Elevage Ovin et Caprin**
- Chevre. (pub. by Societe de Presse et d'Edition Ovine et Caprine (S.P.E.O.C.))
- Patre. (pub. by Societe de Presse et d'Edition Ovine et Caprine (S.P.E.O.C.))

**Institut Technique de la Vigne et du Vin**
3, rue de Rigny, 75008 Paris, France.
- Vignes et Vins. m.

**Institut Technique des Administrations Publiques**
26 rue Fabert, Paris (7e), France.
- I. T. A. P. q.

**Institut Technique du Batiment et des Travaux Publics. Annales**
9 rue la Perouse, 75784 Paris 16, France.
- Institut Technique du Batiment et des Travaux Publics. Annales. 11 per yr. ISSN 0020-2568

**Institut Textile de France**
35, rue des Abondances, 92100 Boulogne sur Seine, France.
- Institut Textile de France. Bulletin Scientifique; documentation et recherche. q. ISSN 0020-2576

**Institut y Solomides**
56 rue de Marne, 92 - Sceaux, France.
- Remedes. 3 per yr.

**Instituto Latinoamericano de Relaciones Internacionales (I.L.A.R.I)**
23 rue de la Pepiniere, Paris (8e), France.
- Instituto Latinoamericano de Relaciones Internacionales. Trabajos. 3-4 per yr. ISSN 0020-4099

**Inter Auto-Route-Inter Auto-Ecoles de France**
75, rue Voltaire, 92-Levallois, France.
- Inter Auto-Route-Inter Auto-Ecoles de France. m.

**Interedi, SARL**
185, Av. Charles-de-Gaulle, 92521 Neuilly, France.
- Cosmopolitan; magazine de la femme moderne. m.

**Inter-Europeenne de Presse**
127, rue du Faubourg-Poissonniere, 75009 Paris, France.
- Journal de la Mer. m. ISSN 0399-2209

**Intergovernmental Council of Copper Exporting Countries**
177 Avenue du Roule, 92200 Neuilly-sur-Seine, France.
- Intergovernmental Council of Copper Exporting Countries. Quarterly Review. q.

**Inter-Groupe Folklore. Region Parisienne**
56 rue Raynouard, 75016 Paris, France.
- Interfolk. s-a. ISSN 0339-3275

**Intermediaire des Chercheurs et Curieux**
64 rue Richelieu, 75002 Paris, France.
- Intermediaire des Chercheurs et Curieux; de questions et responses historiques, litteraires, artistiques et sur toutes autres curiosites. m. ISSN 0020-5613

**International Abolitionist Federation**
28 Place Saint-George, 75009-Paris, France.
- International Abolitionist Federation. (Report of Congress) irreg., 1972, 25th, New Delhi. ISSN 0074-1221

**International Aeronautic Federation**
6, rue Galilee, Paris 75016, France.
- International Aeronautic Federation. General Conference Minutes (of the) Business Meetings. irreg. ISSN 0534-6509
- International Aeronautic Federation. Latest World Records/Federation Aeronautique Internationale. Records du Monde. a; no. 113, 1974.

**International Agency for Research on Cancer**
For publications of this agency see section for UNITED NATIONS

**International Amateur Rugby Federation**
7 Cite d'Antin, 75009 Paris, France.
- Federation Internationale de Rugby Amateur. Annuaire. a. ISSN 0071-4267

**International Animated Film Association**
21 rue de la Tour d'Auverge, Paris, France.
- International Animated Film Association. Bulletin. irreg. ISSN 0538-4281

**International Association for Educational and Vocational Information**
20 rue de l'Estrapade, 75005 Paris, France.
- Informations Universitaires et Professionnelles Internationales. q. ISSN 0020-0530

**International Association Futuribles**
10 rue Cernuschi, 75017 Paris, France.
- Futuribles; analyse-prevision-prospective. m.

**International Association of Bibliophiles**
*see* Association Internationale de Bibliophie

**International Association of Chain Stores**
Dr. Gen. Frederic C. Treidell, 61 Quai d'Orsay, 75007 Paris, France.
- International Association of Chain Stores. Report of Plenary Session. irreg., 1976, 19th, Rio de Janeiro. ISSN 0074-1582

**International Association of French Studies**
*see* Association Internationale des Etudes Francaises

**International Association of Geodesy**
39 Ter - rue Gay-Lussac, 75005 - Paris, France.
- Bulletin Geodesique. q. ISSN 0007-4632

**International Association of Hydrogeologists**
74 rue de la Federation, 75-Paris (15e), France.
- International Association of Hydrogeologists. Memoires. irreg. ISSN 0579-6733

**International Association of Lighthouse Authorities**
43 Avenue du President Wilson, Paris 16, France.
- International Association of Lighthouse Authorities. I.A.L.A. Bulletin/Association Internationale de Signalisation Maritime. Bulletin de l' A I S M. q.
- International Conference on Lighthouses and Other Aids to Navigation. (Reports) quinquennial. ISSN 0538-6128

**International Association of Mutual Insurance Companies**
114 rue la Boetie, 75 Paris (8e), France.
- Mutualite/Gegenseitigkeit/Mutualismo/Mutuality. s-a. ISSN 0027-5239

**International Association of Philatelic Journalists**
c/o Secretary General Henri Trachtenberg, 115 rue Hoche, 94200 Ivry, Seine, France.
- A. I. J. P. Yearbook. a. ISSN 0074-1698
- International Association of Philatelic Journalists. Bulletin. approx. a. ISSN 0074-1701
- International Association of Philatelic Journalists. Minutes of Annual Congresses. a. ISSN 0074-171X

**International Association of Professional Numismatists**
c/o Michael Kampmann, 49 rue de Richelieu, 75001 Paris, France.
- Association Internationale des Numismates Professionels. Bulletin-Circular. ISSN 0004-5543

**International Association of Thalasso-Theraphy**
c/o Professeur D. Leroy, 6, rue Lafayette, 35000 Rennes, France.
- International Association of Thalassotherapy. Congress Reports. triennial; 1975, 16th, Opatija, Yugoslavia. ISSN 0074-1760

**International Association of Universities**
1 rue Miollis, 75732 Paris Cedex 15, France.
- International Association of Universities. Bulletin/ Association Internationale des Universites. Bulletin. q. ISSN 0020-6032
- International Association of Universities. Cahiers. irreg. ISSN 0538-4702
- International Association of Universities. Papers. irreg. ISSN 0538-4737
- International Association of Universities. Report of the General Conference. quinquennial. ISSN 0074-1779
- International Handbook of Universities and Other Institutions of Higher Education. triennial. ISSN 0074-6215
- World List of Universities, Other Institutions of Higher Education and University Organizations. biennial. ISSN 0084-1889

**International Association of Workers for Maladjusted Children**
66 Chaussee d'Antin, Paris 9e, France.
- International Association of Workers for Maladjusted Children. Congress Reports. irreg., 1970, 7th, Versailles. ISSN 0074-1787

**International Broncho-Pneumologic Association**
- Broncho-Pneumologie (les Bronches) (pub. by Doin Editeurs)

**International Bureau of Weights and Measures**
*see* Bureau International des Poids et Mesures

**International Centre of Films for Children and Young People**
92 Champs Elysees, Paris (8e), France.
- International Centre of Films for Children and Young People. News/Centre International du Film pour l'Enfance et la Jeunesse. Nouvelles. 3 per yr. ISSN 0047-0643

**International Chamber of Commerce**
38 Cours Albert 1er, 75008 Paris, France.
- I. C. C. Information. 6 per yr.
- International Chamber of Commerce. Handbook. irreg.

**International Children's Centre**
Chateau de Longchamp, Bois de Boulogne, 75016 Paris, France.
- Children in the Tropics. 10 per yr. (Co-Sponsor: Institut de Pediatrie Sociale de l'universite de Dakar (Senegal))
- Enfant en Milieu Tropical. 10 per yr. ISSN 0013-7561 (Co-sponsor: Institut de Pediatrie Sociale de l'Universite de Dakkar (Senegal))
- International Children's Center. Courrier; revue medico-sociale de l'enfance. bi-m. ISSN 0538-5482
- International Children's Centre. Paris. Report of the Director-General to the Executive Board. irreg. ISSN 0538-5490
- International Children's Centre. Paris. Travaux et Documents. irreg. ISSN 0534-8021

**International Christian Gypsy Movement**
Vie et Lumiere, 12rue Henri-Bar Busse, Le Mans 72100, France.
(U.S. Subscr. Address: 4260 147th Ave. S.E., Bellevue, WN 98006)
- Gypsies for Christ. q. ISSN 0017-6095

**International Commission for Agricultural Industries**
18 Avenue de Villars, Paris 7e, France.
- Annales des Falsifications et de l'Expertise Chimique; recueil d'etudes et de recherches analytiques, de legislation et de jurisprudence appliquees a l'expertise chimique. m. ISSN 0003-4274
- Revue Internationale des Industries Agricoles. Bulletin Analytique. m. ISSN 0035-3442

**International Commission for the Scientific Exploration of the Mediterranean Sea**
Banyuls-sur-Mer, France.
- International Commission for the Scientific Exploration of the Mediterranean Sea. Bulletin de Liaison des Laboratoires. irreg. ISSN 0538-5687

**International Commission of Agricultural Engineering**
10-12 rue du Capitaine Menard, 75-Paris 15e,
France.
- Bulletin Bibliographique International du
  Machinisme Agricole/International Farm
  Machinery Abstracts. (pub. by Centre National
  d'Etudes et d'Experimentation de Machinisme
  Agricole)
- International Commission of Agricultural
  Engineering. Reports of Congress. irreg., 1969,
  7th, Baden-Baden. ISSN 0074-2694

**International Commission on Illumination**
4 Av.du Recteur Poincare, 75782 Paris 8e, France.
- International Commission on Illumination.
  Proceedings. quadrennial, 1971. 17th, Barcelona.
  ISSN 0074-2724

**International Committee for Historical Science**
Michel Francois, Sec. Gen., 75014paris, Paris 14,
France.
- International Committee for Historical Science.
  Bulletin d'Information. irreg. ISSN 0074-2783

**International Committee of Military Medicine and
Pharmacy**
- Revue Internationale des Services de Sante des
  Armees de Terre, de Mer et de l'Air/International
  Review of the Army, Navy and Air Force
  Medical Services. (pub. by Service de Presse,
  Edition, Information)

**International Committee on the History of Art**
- International Congress on the History of Art.
  Proceedings. (pub. by Institut d'Art et
  d'Archeologie)

**International Communist Party**
- Communist Program. (pub. by Editions
  Programme)
- Programme Communiste. (pub. by Editions
  Programme)
- Proletaire. (pub. by Editions Programme)

**International Confederation of Societies of Authors
and Composers**
11 rue Keppler, 75116 Paris, France.
- Interauteurs. a. ISSN 0020-515X
- International Confederation of Societies of
  Authors and Composers. irreg., no. 186, 1976.
  ISSN 0074-2899

**International Conference on Large High Voltage
Electric Systems**
112 Boulevard Haussman, 75008 Paris, France.
- Electra. bi-m. ISSN 0424-7701
- International Conference on Large High Voltage
  Electric Systems. Proceedings. biennial, 1976.
  26th. ISSN 0074-3151

**International Conference on Sociology of Religion**
39 rue de la Monnaie, 59042 Lille, France.
- International Conference on Sociology of Religion.
  Proceedings. biennial, 1972, 12th, The Hague.
  ISSN 0074-297X

**International Council for Educational Media**
Office Francais des Techniques Modernes
d'Education, 29 rue d'Ulm, 75 Paris (Se), France.
- I C E M Review. q.

**International Council for Philosophy and Humanistic
Studies**
c/o Maison de l'Unesco, 1 rue Miollis, 75732 Paris,
France.
- International Council for Philosophy and
  Humanistic Studies. General Assembly. Compte
  Rendu. irreg., 1973, 11th, Rio de Janeiro. ISSN
  0074-4298

**International Council of Museums (ICOM)**
c/o Maison de l'Unesco, 1 rue Miollis, 75732 Paris,
France.
- I C O M News/I C O M. Nouvelles. q. ISSN
  0018-8999

**International Council of Scientific Unions**
51 Bd. de Montmorency, 75016 Paris, France.
- I C S U Bulletin. q. ISSN 0536-132X
- International Council of Scientific Unions. Year
  Book. a. ISSN 0074-4387

**International Council of Scientific Unions.
Abstracting Board**
17 rue Mirabeau, 75016 Paris, France.
- Survey of the Activities of Scientific Unions;
  Special and Scientific Committees of I C S U in
  the Field of Information. biennial.

**International Council of Scientific Unions. Committee
on Data for Science and Technology**
51 Bd. de Montmorency, 75016 Paris, France.
- CODATA Bulletin. irreg.

**International Council of Sport and Physical
Education. Research Committee**
Unesco House, Place de Fontenoy, 75007 Paris,
France.
- International Seminar on Biomechanics. biennial,
  1971, 3rd, Rome. ISSN 0074-7912

**International Council of Women**
13 rue Caumartin, 75 Paris 9e, France
(Subscription Address: Amro Bank, Markt 7,
Middelburg, Netherlands)
- International Council of Women. Newsletter/
  Conseil International des Femmes. Newsletter. bi-
  m.

**International Council on Archives**
60 rue des Francs Bourgeois, 75003 Paris, France.
- Archivum: Revue Internationale des Archives.
  (pub. by Verlag Dokumentation GW)
- International Congress of Archives. Proceedings.
  irreg., 1968, vol. 18, 6th Congress, Madrid. ISSN
  0074-3518
- International Council on Archives. Microfilm
  Committee. Bulletin. a.

**International Council on Combustion Engines**
10 Avenue Hoche, 75008 Paris, France.
- International Congress on Combustion Engines.
  Proceedings. irreg., 1975, 11th, Barcelona. ISSN
  0074-4077

**International Council on Social Welfare**
Regional Office for Europe, Middle East and
Mediterranean Area, 9 rue Chardin, 75016 Paris,
France.
- International Council on Social Welfare. European
  Symposium. Proceedings. biennial, 8th, 1975,
  Opatija, Yugoslavia. ISSN 0074-4425

**International Criminal Police Organization-Interpol**
26 rue Armengaud, 92 St. Cloud, France.
- Revue Internationale de Police Criminelle. 10 per
  yr. ISSN 0035-3396

**International Experimental and Art Film Theatres
Confederation**
c/o Jean Leseure, Secretary General, 22 rue
d'Artois, 75008 Paris, France.
- C.I.C.A.E. Bulletin d'Information. (Confederation
  Internationale des Cinemas d'Art et d'Essai) irreg.
  ISSN 0526-6513

**International Federation for Home Economics**
64, Avenue Edouard-Vaillant, 92100 Boulogne,
France.
- Economie Familiale/Home Economics. q.
- International Congress of Home Economics.
  Report. quadrennial; 1976, 13th, Ottawa. ISSN
  0074-3712

**International Federation of Agricultural Producers**
1, rue d'Hauteville, 75010 Paris, France.
- I F A P News/F I P A Nouvelles. m. ISSN 0018-
  9650
- International Federation of Agricultural Producers.
  General Conference Proceedings. approx. every
  18 months; 22nd, Helsinki, Finland, 1977. ISSN
  0074-5863
- World Agriculture/Agriculture dans le Monde. q.
  ISSN 0043-8227

**International Federation of Blood Donors
Organizations**
*see* **Federation Internationale des Organisations de
Donneurs de Sang**

**International Federation of Catholic Universities**
Secretariat Permanent, 77 bis rue de Grenelle,
75007 Paris, France.
- International Federation of Catholic Universities.
  General Assembly. (Report) irreg., 1975, 11th
  Assembly, New Delhi. ISSN 0579-3866

**International Federation of Fruit Juice Producers**
10, rue de Liege, 75009 Paris, France.
- Annuaire International des Jus de Fruits. a. ISSN
  0066-3255
- International Federation of Fruit Juice Producers.
  Proceedings. Berichte. Rapports. irreg. ISSN
  0535-0182

**International Federation of Fruit Juice Producers.**
Proceedings of Congress. Compte-Rendu du
Congres. irreg., 1968, 7th, Cannes. ISSN 0074-
5952

**International Federation of Journalists and Travel
Writers**
c/o Jean Hureau, 2 Residence du Parc, Massy,
France.
- International Federation of Journalists and Travel
  Writers. Official List. Repertoire Officiel. irreg.
  ISSN 0074-5979

**International Federation of Newspaper Publishers**
6, rue du Faubourg Poissonniere, 75010 Paris,
France.
- F. I. E. J. Bulletin. (Federation Internationale des
  Editeurs de Journaux et Publications) q. ISSN
  0046-3531

**International Federation of Ophthalmological
Societies**
- Acta Concilium Ophthalmologicum. (pub. by
  Masson)

**International Federation of Secondary Education
Teachers**
120 rue du President Roosevelt, Escalier C., 78100
Saint Germain en Laye, France.
- International Federation of Secondary Education
  Teachers. International Bulletin/Federation
  Internationale des Professeurs de l'Enseignement
  Secondaire Officiel, Bulletin International/
  Internationale Vereinigung der Lehrer an
  Offentlichen Hoheren Schulen. Internationale
  Zeitschrift. q.

**International Federation of Teachers of French**
*see* **Federation Internationale des Professeurs de
Francais**

**International Federation of the Cinematographic
Press**
c/o Marcel Martin, Secretary-General, 2 rue
Leopold-Robert, 75014 Paris, France.
- Bulletin FIPRESCI. 3-4 per yr. ISSN 0007-4608

**International Geographical Union**
- Bibliographie Geographique Internationale. (pub.
  by Centre National de la Recherche Scientifique)

**International Gravimetric Bureau**
9, Quai Saint-Bernard-Tour 14, 75005 Paris, France.
- International Gravimetric Bureau. Bulletin
  d'Information. s-a.

**International Hotel Association**
89 Faubourg Saint-Honore, 75008 Paris, France.
- Directory of Travel Agencies. a. ISSN 0070-6515
- International Hotel Guide. a. ISSN 0074-624X

**International Institute for Educational Planning**
For publications of this agency see section for
UNITED NATIONS

**International Institute of Philosophy**
173 Boulevard St. Germain, 75272 Paris, France.
- Bibliographie de la Philosophie/Bibliography of
  Philosophy. (pub. by Librairie Philosophique J.
  Vrin)
- International Institute of Philosophy. Actes. a.;
  20th, Dubrovnik, 1974. ISSN 0074-6525

**International Institute of Refrigeration**
177 Bd. Malesherbes, 75017 Paris, France.
- Institut International du Froid. Bulletin/
  International Institute of Refrigeration. Bulletin.
  bi-m. ISSN 0020-6970
- International Institute of Refrigeration.
  Proceedings of Commission Meetings. irreg. ISSN
  0074-6541

**International Institute of Space Law**
250 rue Saint-Jacques, 75-Paris (5e), France.
- Worldwide Bibliography of Space Law and
  Related Matters/Bibliographie Mondiale de Droit
  Spatiale et Matieres Connexes. a.; latest issue,
  1973. ISSN 0538-7965

**International Literary and Artistic Association**
c/o A. Francon, 55 rue des Mathurins, 75008 Paris,
France.
- International Literary and Artistic Association.
  Proceedings and Reports of Congress. irreg.,
  1972, 54th, Paris. ISSN 0074-6819

**International Medical Association for the Study of Living Conditions and Health**
c/o J. de Castro, 165, Av Charles de Gaulle, 92200 Neuilly-sur-Seine, France.
- Acta Medica et Sociologica. irreg., 1972, 6th, Varna. ISSN 0515-2925

**International Organization for Biological Control of Noxious Animals and Plants**
- Entomophaga. (pub. by Librairie le Francois)

**International Permanent Committee on Canned Foods. French Delegation**
3, rue de Logelbach, 75 Paris 17, France.
- International Congress on Canned Foods. Texts of Papers Presented and Resolutions/Congres International de la Conserve. Textes des Communications. irreg.; 6th, Paris, 1972. ISSN 0534-9257

**International Plant Breeders Association for the Protection of New Varieties**
101, rue Saint-Lazare, 75009 Paris, France.
- International Plant Breeders Association for the Protection of New Varieties. Congress Reports. a, 1975, 24th, Belgium. ISSN 0074-7408

**International Political Science Association**
27 rue Saint-Guillaume, 75341 Paris, Cedex 07, France.
- International Political Science Abstracts/ Documentation Politique Internationale. bi-m. ISSN 0020-8345

**International Puppeteers Union. French Section**
c/o M. Andre Tahon, Ed., 7, rue du Helder, 75009 Paris, France.
- Unima France. q. ISSN 0503-2032

**International Rayon and Synthetic Fibres Committee**
29 rue de Courcelles, 75008 Paris, France.
- International Rayon and Synthetic Fibres Committee. Statistical Yearbook. a. ISSN 0074-7599
- International Rayon and Synthetic Fibres Committee. Technical Conference. Reports. irreg. ISSN 0074-7602
- International Rayon and Synthetic Fibres Committee. World Congress. Report. irreg., 1971, 3rd, Munich. ISSN 0074-7610

**International Real Estate Federation**
68, rue des Archives, 75003 Paris, France.
- International Real Estate Federation. Reports of Congress. a, 1976, 27th, San Francisco. ISSN 0074-7637

**International Scientific Film Association**
38, Avenue des Ternes, Paris 17, France.
- Science Film. 4 per yr. ISSN 0397-6491

**International Serials Data System. International Centre**
20 rue Bachaumont, 75002 Paris, France.
- I S D S Bulletin. b-m. ISSN 0300-3000

**International Silk Association**
55, Montee de Choulans, 281 Lyons, France.
- International Silk Association. Bulletin. q. ISSN 0020-8698

**International Society for Performing Arts, Libraries and Museums**
1 rue de Sully, 75 Paris 4e, France.
- International Society for Performing Arts, Libraries and Museums. Congress Proceedings. irreg., 1974. ISSN 0074-7882

**International Society of Art and Psychopathology**
c/o Dr. C. Wiart, Clinique de la Faculte, 100 rue de la Sante, 75 Paris 14, France.
- International Congress of Psychopathological Art. Program. Programme. irreg. ISSN 0534-9168

**International Society of Blood Transfusion**
c/o J. P. Soulier, 6 rue Alexandre Cabanel, 75015 Paris, France.
- International Society of Blood Transfusion. Proceedings of the Congress. irreg., 1975, 14th, Helsinki. ISSN 0074-8528

**International Society of Criminology**
4 rue Mondovi, Paris (1er), France.
- Annales Internationales de Criminologie/ International Annals of Criminology/Anales Internacionales de Criminologia. s-a. ISSN 0003-4452

- International Society of Criminology. Bulletin. irreg. ISSN 0539-032X

**International Society of History of Medicine**
22 rue Durand, 3400 Montpellier, France.
- International Congress of History of Medicine. Proceedings. biennial, 24th, Budapest, 1974. ISSN 0074-3704

**International Society of Soil Science**
c/o Dr. M. Bouche, Station de Recherches sur la Faune du Sol, 7 rue Sully, 21 Dijon, France.
- Biologie du Sol/Soil Biology/Bodenbiologie. irreg. ISSN 0067-8805

**International Society of Urology**
c/o Prof. Rene Kuess, 63 Ave. Niel, 75017 Paris, France
- International Society of Urology. Reports of Congress. irreg., 1975, 17th, Madrid. ISSN 0074-8579 (Reports Published in Host Country)

**International Sporting Press Association**
124 rue Reamur, Paris, France.
- International Sporting Press Association. Bulletin. N.S. irreg.; 1967, no. 15. ISSN 0539-0370

**International Superphosphate Manufacturers' Association Ltd.**
28 rue Marbeuf, 75008 Paris, France.
- Phosphorus in Agriculture/Phosphore et Agriculture. 3 per yr. ISSN 0031-8434

**International Theatre Institute**
1 rue Miollis, 75015paris, France.
- International Theatre. q. ISSN 0020-8930

**International Union Against Tuberculosis**
3 rue Georges Ville, 75116 Paris, France.
- International Union against Tuberculosis. Bulletin. irreg. ISSN 0074-9249
- International Union against Tuberculosis. Conference Proceedings. (pub. by Excerpta Medica NE)
- Tuberculosis "T". q.

**International Union of Angiology**
4 rue Pasquier, 75008 Paris, France.
- International Congress of Angiology. Proceedings. irreg., 1974, 9th, Florence. ISSN 0074-347X

**International Union of Architects**
see Union Internationale des Architectes

**International Union of Physiological Sciences**
c/o Dr. J. Scherrer, Department of Physiology, U E R Pitie-Salpetriere, 91 Blvd. de l'Hospital, 75634 Paris Cedex 13, France.
- International Union of Physiological Sciences. Proceedings of Congress. irreg., 27th, 1977, Paris. ISSN 0074-946X

**International Union of Geodesy and Geophysics**
Publications Office, 39 rue Gay-Lussac, F-75 Paris (5e), France.
- I. U. G. G. Chronicle. q. ISSN 0047-1259
- International Union of Geodesy and Geophysics. Proceedings of the General Assembly. quadrennial. ISSN 0074-9419

**International Union of Producers and Distributors of Electrical Energy**
39 Ave. de Friedland, 75008 Paris, France.
- Economie Electrique/Electricity Supply. 3 per yr. ISSN 0013-0508
- Elektrizitaetsverwertung/Electrique/Electrical Service. (pub. by Elektrowirtschaft SZ)
- International Union of Producers and Distributors of Electrical Energy. (Congress Proceedings) triennial, 1973, 16th, The Hague. ISSN 0074-9486

**International Union of Psychological Science**
- Journal International de Psychologie/International Journal of Psychology. (pub. by Centrale des Revues Dunod Gauthier- Villars)

**International Union of Pure and Applied Physics**
c/o J. Bok, Groupe de Physique des Solides, Ecole Normale Superieure, 24, rue Lhomond, Paris 75, France
(U.S. dist.: Four Continent Book Corp., 156 Fifth Ave., New York, NY 10010)
- International Conference on Physics of Semiconductors. Proceedings. irreg., 1974, 20th, Stuttgart. ISSN 0074-3240

**International Union of Railways**
14-16, rue Jean Rey, Paris 15, France.
- International Railway Statistics. Statistics of Individual Railways. irreg. ISSN 0074-7580

**International Union of School and University Health and Medicine**
Chateau de Longchamp, Bois de Boulogne, 75016 Paris, France.
- International Union of School and University Health and Medicine. Congress Reports. quadrennial, 1975, 7th, Mexico City. ISSN 0074-9524

**International Union of Testing and Research Laboratories for Materials and Structures**
- Materiaux & Constructions/Materials & Structures. (pub. by Centrale des Revues Dunod Gauthier Villars)

**International Vine and Wine Office**
see Office International de la Vigne et du Vin

**Interpol**
see International Criminal Police Organization-Interpol

**Librairie Istra**
15 rue des Juifs, 67001 Strasbourg Cedex, France.
- Annuaire de l'URSS et des Pays Socialistes Europeens. a. (Centre de Recherches sur l'URSS et les Pays de l'Est)
- Recueil Juridique de l'Est Securite Sociale; doctrine jurisprudence, documents administratifs. bi-m. ISSN 0034-1878
- Saisons d'Alsace; toute la vie culturelle de l'Alsace. q. ISSN 0048-9018

**Itineraires**
4 rue Garanciere, Paris (6e), France.
- Itineraires; chroniques et documents. m. ISSN 0021-3187

**Jean Jachymiak, Pub.**
6 Square de la Dordogne, Paris 17e, France.
- L.S.I. irreg. ISSN 0335-9190

**Editions Jacquemart**
19 rue des Pretres-Saint-Germain-l'Auxerrois, Paris (1e), France.
- Charivari. q. ISSN 0009-1731
- Echo de la Presse et de la Publicite. w. ISSN 0012-9232
- Echo des Depositaires des Libraires et des Marchands de Journaux. s-m. ISSN 0012-9267
- Repertoire Pratique de la Publicite. a. ISSN 0080-1194
- Sonovision. w&m.

**Jazz Hot**
14 rue Chaptal, 75009 Paris, France.
- Jazz Hot. 11 per yr. ISSN 0021-5643

**Jegu S.A.**
27 rue de Rome, 75008 Paris, France.
- Corset de France. q. ISSN 0010-9436
- Votre Ligne les Dessous Elegants. q.

**Jeunesse et Orgue**
c/o Ed. Christiane Trieu - Colleney, Residence Ophelia B2, 98 Avenue J. Jaures, 33600 Pessac, France.
- Jeunesse et Orgue. q. ISSN 0021-6208

**Jeunesse Ouvriere Chretienne**
12, Ave. Soeur Rosalie, 75621 Paris Cedex 13, France.
- De Nos Mains. bi-m. ISSN 0045-9747
- Equipe Ouvriere. m.
- Jeunesse Ouvriere; journal fait par et pour les jeunes de la classe ouvrier. m. ISSN 0047-1984

**Jeunesses Litteraires de France**
117 Bd. St.-Germain, Paris (6e), France.
- Cahiers d'Action Litteraire. 6 per yr. ISSN 0007-9650

**Editions Louis Johanet**
68 rue Boursault, Paris 17e, France.
- Annuaire de l'Ameublement. a. ISSN 0066-2615
- Annuaire de la Chapellerie et de la Mode. a. ISSN 0066-2518
- Annuaire de la Chaussure et des Cuirs. a. ISSN 0066-2526
- Annuaire National de la Kinesitherapie. a. ISSN 0066-3301
- Annuaire O. G. M. a. ISSN 0066-3565 (Office General de la Musique)

**Pierre Johanet et ses Fils**
7. Av. Franklin-D.-Roosevelt, 75008 Paris, France.
- Eau et l'Industrie. m.
- Revue de la Protection; securite des ouvriers dans les usines en Francais. m. ISSN 0035-1253
- Revue des Industries d'Art - "Offrir". m. ISSN 0035-2101
- Revue Francaise des Bijoutiers Horlogers. m. ISSN 0035-2993

**Jour-Azur S.A.**
210 rue du Faubourg St. Antoine, 75012 Paris, France.
- Nouveau Guide Gault-Millau. m.

**Journal de la Marine Marchande, S.A.**
190 Bd. Haussmann, 75008 Paris, France.
- Droit Maritime Francais. m. ISSN 0012-642X
- Journal de la Marine Marchande. w. ISSN 0021-7786
- Marine Marchande. a. ISSN 0076-4485
- Navires Ports & Chantiers. m. ISSN 0028-159X
- Nouveautes Techniques Maritimes. a. ISSN 0078-2157

**Journal de Medecine de Lyon**
4 rue Gentil, Lyons 2, France.
- Journal de Medecine de Lyon; organe de Professeurs, agreges, medecins des hospitaux et medecins praticiens de Lyon. s-m. ISSN 0021-7883

**Journal de Medecine et de Chirurgie Pratiques**
15 rue Saint-Benoit, Paris (6e), France.
- Journal de Medecine et de Chirurgie Pratiques. s-m. ISSN 0021-7913

**Journal des Combattants**
80 rue des Prairies, 75020 Paris, France.
- Journal des Combattants. w. ISSN 0021-8014

**Journal des Communes**
38 rue Croix des Petits Champs, Paris (1e), France.
- Journal des Communes. m. ISSN 0021-8030

**Journal des Finances**
122 rue Reaumur, Paris, France.
- Journal des Finances. w. ISSN 0021-8049

**Journal des Mots Croises S.A.**
12 rue Coquilliere, 75 Paris (Ie), France.
- Journal des Mots Croises. w. ISSN 0021-809X

**Journal des Notaires et des Avocats**
6, rue de Mezieres, 75006 Paris, France.
- Journal des Notaires et des Avocats. bi-m.

**Journal des Oiseaux du Monde**
Louis Bouille, 59 rue du Faubourg-Poissonniere, Paris 9e, France.
- Journal des Oiseaux du Monde. irreg. ISSN 0075-4080

**Journal des Sciences Medicales de Lille**
8, rue Nicolas Leblanc, 59-Lille, France.
- Journal des Sciences Medicales de Lille. m. ISSN 0021-8111

**Journal du Batiment et des Travaux Publics**
Grand Palais, Batiment 15, Quai Achille-Lignon, 69459 Lyons, France.
- Journal du Batiment et des Travaux Publics. w.

**Journee Vinicole**
7 rue Dom-Vaissette, 34000 Montpellier (Herault), France.
- Journee Vinicole. d. ISSN 0022-5649

**Journee Vinicole Export**
7, rue Dom Vaissette, 34000 Montpellier (Herault), France.
- Journee Vinicole Export. m.

**Editions Julliard**
8 rue Garanciere, Paris 6e, France.
- Lieux et les Dieux. irreg. ISSN 0075-9376

**Jurisprudence Generale Dalloz**
11, rue Soufflot, 75240 Paris Cedex 05, France.
- Bulletin Legislatif Dalloz. s-m.
- Recueil Dalloz-Sirey. w. ISSN 0034-1835

**David Kaisergruber**
77 bis rue Logendre, 75017 Paris, France.
- Dialectiques. q.

**Kendalch Keltiek**
C.C.P. des Bordes 1493-79, C Nantes, France.
- Kendalch Keltiek.

**Editons Kerfan**
115 Ave. Semeria, B.P. 5, 06290 St. Jean Cap Ferrat, France.
- Argus du Bateau et de Tout le Materiel Nautique. q.
- Cote Inter-Europe du Bateau d'Occasion. 4 per yr.
- Marche Europeen. q.

**Editions du Kiosque**
14, rue Chaptal, 75-Paris (9e), France.
- Rock & Folk; pop music, rhythm & blues, jazz chanson. m. ISSN 0048-8445

**Editions Klincksieck**
11 rue de Lille, Paris 7, France.
- Academie des Inscriptions et Belles-Lettres. Comptes Rendus des Seances. 4 per yr. ISSN 0065-0536
- Academie des Inscriptions et Belles-Lettres. Etudes et Commentaires. irreg., 1970, no. 87. ISSN 0065-0544
- Archeologie Mediterraneenne. irreg. ISSN 0066-6084
- Bibliotheque des Cahiers Archeologiques. irreg. ISSN 0068-8309
- Bibliotheque Francaise et Romane. Serie A: Manuels et Etudes Linguistiques. irreg. ISSN 0067-8341 (Universite de Strasbourg II. Centre de Philologie et de Litteratures Romanes)
- Bibliotheque Francaise et Romane. Serie B: Editions Critiques de Textes. irreg. ISSN 0067-835X (Universite de Strasbourg II. Centre de Philologie et de Litteratures Romanes)
- Bibliotheque Francaise et Romane. Serie C: Etudes Litteraires. irreg. ISSN 0067-8368 (Universite de Strasbourg II. Centre de Philologie et de Litteratures Romanes)
- Bibliotheque Francaise et Romane. Serie D: Initiation, Textes et Documents. irreg. ISSN 0067-8376 (Universite de Strasbourg II. Centre de Philologie et de Litteratures Romanes)
- Bibliotheque Francaise et Romane. Serie E: Langue et Litterature Francaises au Canada. irreg, 1973, no. 8. ISSN 0067-8384 (Universite de Strasbourg II. Centre de Philologie et de Litteratures Romanes)
- Bulletin Analytique de Linguistique Francaise. 6 per yr. ISSN 0007-408X (Centre de Recherche pour Un Tresor de la Langue Francaise)
- Bulletin des Jeunes Romanistes. irreg. ISSN 0068-4031 (Association des Jeunes Romanistes) (Co-sponsor: Universite de Strasbourg, Centre de Philologie Romane)
- Cahiers du Vingtieme Siecle. s-a. (Societe d'Etude du Vingtieme Siecle)
- Etudes Finno-Ougriennes. irreg. ISSN 0071-2051 (Universite de Paris X (Paris-Nanterre). Centre d'Etudes Finno-Ougriennes)
- Etudes Gobiniennes. a. ISSN 0071-2078 (Universite de Strasbourg II. Centre de Philologie et de Litteratures Romanes)
- Etudes Linguistiques. irreg. ISSN 0071-2124
- Femmes en Literature. irreg.
- Initiation a la Linguistique. Serie A. Lectures. irreg. ISSN 0073-8018
- Initiation a la Linguistique. Serie B. Problemes et Methodes. irreg. ISSN 0073-8026
- Institut Armoricain de Recherches Historiques, Rennes. (Publication) irreg. ISSN 0073-8220
- Journal des Savants. q. ISSN 0021-8103 (Academie des Inscriptions et Belles-Lettres)
- Karthago. biennial. ISSN 0453-3429 (Universite de Paris I (Pantheon-Sorbonne). Centre d'Etudes Archeologiques de la Mediterranee Occidentale)
- Karthago. Collection Epigraphique. irreg. ISSN 0075-5184 (Universite de Paris I (Pantheon-Sorbonne). Centre d'Etudes Archeologiques de la Mediterranee Occidentale)
- Recueil des Historiens de la France. irreg., 1974, latest issue. ISSN 0080-0325 (Academie des Inscriptions et Belles Lettres)
- Revue d'Egyptologie. a. ISSN 0035-1849
- Revue de Philologie, de Litterature et d'Histoire Anciennes. s-a. ISSN 0035-1652
- Revue des Etudes Armeniennes. a. ISSN 0080-2549
- Revue Hitite et Asiatique. a. ISSN 0080-2603
- Societe d'Histoire de France. Annuaire. a. ISSN 0081-0940
- Societe de Linguistique de Paris. Bulletin. s-a. ISSN 0037-9069

- T.A. Documents. irreg. ISSN 0066-9776 (Dist. by: University of Alabama Press, Drawer 2877, University, AL 35486)
- T. A. Informations; revue internationale des applications de l'automatisme au language. s-a. ISSN 0039-8217 (Association pour la Traduction Automatique et la Linguistique Appliquee)
- Theatre d'Aujourd'hui. irreg.
- Travaux de Linguistique et de Litterature. 2 vols. per yr. ISSN 0082-6057 (Universite de Strasbourg II. Centre de Philologie et de Litteratures Romanes)
- Turcica; Revue d'Etudes Turques. a. ISSN 0082-6847

**Kodak-Pathe. Division Marches et Graphiques**
8 et 14 rue Villiot, 75580 Paris Cedex 12, France.
- Courrier Technique Arts Graphiques. irreg., no. 26, 1975.

**Editions L E P S**
40 rue de Colisee, (8) Paris (2e), France.
- Radio Pratique. m. ISSN 0033-7978

**Labo-France**
239, rue la Fayette, 75010 Paris, France.
- Revue Francaise des Fournisseurs de Laboratoires. m (10 per yr.)

**Editions Labo Pharma**
19 rue Louis le Grand, 75002 Paris, France
- Labo-Pharma; revue d'etudes et de documentation pharmaceutiques. m. ISSN 0023-6470
- Revue d'Odonto-Stomatologie. bi-m. ISSN 0300-9815 (Societe Odontologique de Paris) (Subscription Address: S.O.P. 11, Cite Charles-Godon, 75009 Paris, France)

**Laboratoire Central des Industries Electriques**
33 Ave. du General Leclerc, F-92260 Fontenay aux Roses, France.
- Laboratoire Central des Industries Electriques. Bulletin d'Information. 4-6 per yr. ISSN 0023-6675

**Laboratoire d'Information et de Documentation en Geographie "Intergeo"**
191 rue Saint-Jacques, 75005 Paris, France.
- Intergeo-Bulletin. q. ISSN 0396-5880

**Laboratoire de Biologie Vegetale Appliquee du Museum**
61, rue de Buffon, 75005 Paris, France.
- Revue de Cytologie et de Biologie Vegetales. a. (in 4 parts) ISSN 0035-1067

**Laboratoire de Psychobiologie de l'Enfant**
41 rue Gay-Lussac, Paris (5e), France.
- Enfance; psychologie, pedagogie, neuro-psychiatrie, sociologie. bi-m. ISSN 0013-7545

**Laboratoire de Recherche des Musees de France**
- Laboratoire de Recherche des Musees de France. Annales. (pub. by Services Techniques et Commerciaux de la Reunion des Musees Nationaux)

**Laboratoire des Recherches et de Controle du Caoutchouc**
12, rue Carves, 92120 Montrouge, France.
- L R C C Bulletin Bibliographique. m.

**Laboratoires Biotherax**
58 rue du Landy, La Plaine-Saint-Denis, France.
- Gaster; l'Annuaire de Gastro-Enterologie. biennial. ISSN 0072-0291

**Laboratoires d'Electronique et de Physique Appliquee**
3 Av. Descartes, 94450 Limeil-Brevannes, France.
- Acta Electronica. q. ISSN 0001-558X

**Laboratoires H. Faure**
B.P. 131, 07104 Annonay Cedex, France.
- Revue Internationale du Trachome. q. ISSN 0301-5017

**Editions Lafayette**
3 rue de Montyon, 75429 Paris 9, France.
- Migrations. m. ISSN 0026-3591

**Editions R. Laffont**
6 Place Saint-Sulpice, Paris 6e, France.
- Ailleurs et Demain; Classiques. irreg. ISSN 0065-4787
- Ombres de l'Histoire. irreg. ISSN 0078-4591
- Science Nouvelle. irreg., 1970, no. 8. ISSN 0080-7540

**Editions Jacques Lafitte**
12 rue de l'Arcade, 75008 Paris, France.
- Who's Who in France/Qui Est Qui en France.
  biennial. ISSN 0083-9531

**S.A.R.L. le Lait**
48 Av. President Wilson, 75116 Paris, France.
- Lait; revue generale des questions laitieres. bi-m.
  ISSN 0023-7302

**Lamarre-Poinat**
4 rue Antoine-Dubois, 75006 Paris, France.
- Infirmiere Francaise; revue d'enseignment
  technique et de developpement professionnel.
  m.(Oct-July) ISSN 0019-9613

**LAMY S.A.**
c/o L. Brunat, 38, rue Lantiez, 75017 Paris, France.
- Bulletin des Transports. w. ISSN 0007-4519

**Lancette Francaise**
49 Rue Saint- Andre- Des- Arts, Paris(6e), France.
- Hopitaux Civils et Militaires. Gazette. 36 per yr.
  ISSN 0018-487X

**Langage Total**
21 rue de la Paix, 42 Saint-Etienne, France.
- Langage Total. q. ISSN 0023-8228

**Librairie Lardanchet**
10 rue President Carnot, 69002 Lyon, France.
- Bulletin des Lettres; revue de critique et
  d'information litteraire et bibliophilique: (cercle de
  selection) m. ISSN 0007-4489

**Editions Lariviere**
15-17 Quai de l'Oise, 75019 Paris, France.
- Fanatique de l'Aviation. m.
- Moto Revue. w. ISSN 0047-8180

**Larousse**
17, rue du Montparnasse, 75280 Paris Cedex 06
- Bref. q. (Universite Francois Rabelais, Tours)
- Bulletin de Recherche sur l'Enseignement de
  Francais. q.
- Langages; semiotiques textuelles. q.
  (and Librairie Marcel Didier, 15 rue Cujas, 75005
  Paris, France)
- Langue Francaise. q. ISSN 0023-8368
- Litterature. q. ISSN 0047-4800
- Poche-Couleurs Larousse. irreg. ISSN 0079-2373
- Techniques d'Aujourd'Hui. irreg. ISSN 0082-2469

**Publicite Larrey**
73 bis Avenue de Wagram, 75017 Paris, France.
- Luminaires et Eclairage. q.

**Ed. & Pub. J. Lassieur**
B.P. 64, 64200 Biarritz, France.
- Hotellerie de Plein Air; bulletin d'informations
  professionnelles et techniques. bi-m.

**Editions Charles Lavauzelle et Cie**
20 rue de Leningrad, 75008 Paris, France.
- Dictionnaire des Communes. quadrenially.
- France. Ministere des Armees. Bulletin Officiel
  des Armees. bi-w.

**Librairie Lavoisier**
11 rue Lavoisier, 75008 Paris, France.
- Documentation - Technique, Scientifique et
  Commerciale; revue d'information de l'edition
  francaise et etrangere. 8 per yr. ISSN 0012-4583

**Editions Lecerf**
22 rue des Bons Enfants, Rouen, France.
- Normandie Industrielle. q. ISSN 0029-1803
  (Societe Industrielle de Rouen)

**Lectures Francaises**
27 rue de l'Abbe-Gregoire, Paris (6e), France.
- Lectures Francaises; revue de la politique
  francaise. m. ISSN 0024-0133

**Editions Christian Ledoux**
9 rue Condorcet, 94800 Villejuif, France.
- Piscines. 4 per yr. ISSN 0032-0285

**Rene Lefeuvre**
5 rue Ste-Croix-De-La-Bretonnerie, Paris(4e),
France.
- Cahiers Spartacus. 8 per yr. ISSN 0045-379X
  (Association des Archives Spartacus)

**Jean Pascal Legen**
15 rue de Saint Senoch, Paris 75017, France.
- Clivages. q.

**Editions Olivier Lesourd**
252 rue du Faubourg Saint-Honore, 75008 Paris,
France.
- Guide de l'Organisation de 'linformatique et de la
  Formation. a.
- Guide du Petrole, Gaz, Petrochimie. a.
- Hydrocarbure. q.
- Industrie du Petrole dans le Monde-Gaz-
  Petrochimie. m. ISSN 0337-2219

**Lettres Francaises**
5 rue du Fbg. Poissonniere, Paris (9e), France.
- Lettres Francaises. w. ISSN 0024-1393

**Editions du Levain**
1 rue de l'Abbe-Gregoire, 75006 Paris, France.
- Assemblee Nouvelle. q. ISSN 0335-5012
- Famille Nouvelle. q. ISSN 0014-7184

**Liaisons Sociales**
5 Avenue de la Republique, 75541 Paris Cedex 11,
France.
- Intersocial; Liaisons Sociales/international. m.
- Liaisons Sociales. bi-w. ISSN 0024-1725

**Librairie Ancienne et Moderne. Bulletin**
117 Bd. Saint-Germain, 75006 Paris, France.
- Librairie Ancienne et Moderne. Bulletin. 10 per
  yr. ISSN 0024-2128

**Librairie de la Faculte de Sciences**
12, rue Pierre et Marie Curie, 75005 Paris, France
- Bibliographie Cartographique Internationale. a.
  ISSN 0067-6934 (Distributor: Kraus-Thomson
  Organization Ltd., Nendeln, Liechtenstein)

**Librairie des Cinq Continents**
18 rue de Lille, Paris 7e, France.
- Inedits Russes. irreg. ISSN 0073-7828

**Librairie des Facultes de Medecine et de Pharmacie**
174 Bd. St. Germain, 75280 Paris Cedex 06,
France.
- "R" (Rhumatologie) q.
- Sciences Medicales; revue des universites
  nouvelles. 6 per yr. ISSN 0048-9727

**Librairie Generale de Droit et de Jurisprudence**
20 rue Soufflot, 75005 Paris, France.
- Revue de Science Financiere. q. ISSN 0035-1741
- Revue du Droit Public et de la Science Politique
  en France et a l'Etranger. bi-m. ISSN 0035-2578
- Revue Generale des Assurances Terrestres. q.
  ISSN 0035-3167
- Universite de Lyon III. Faculte de Droit. Annales.
  irreg. ISSN 0336-1357

**Librairie Generale de l'Enseignement**
4 Rue Dante, 75005 Paris, France.
- Revue Generale de Botanique. q. ISSN 0048-8097

**Librairie Mariale et Franciscaine**
9 rue de Vauguois, 41 Blois, France.
- Etudes Franciscaines. 4 per yr. ISSN 0014-2093

**Librairie Sociale et Economique**
3 rue Soufflot, 75005 Paris, France.
- Droit Social. m. ISSN 0012-6438
- Institut International d'Etudes Sociales. Cahiers.
  irreg. ISSN 0537-8184 (International Institute for
  Labour Studies UN)

**Editions Ligel**
77 rue de Vaugirard, 75006 Paris, France.
- Temps et Paroles; revue de pedagogie religieuse. 5
  per yr.

**J. Liger, Ed. & Pub.**
190 rue Beauvoisine, Rouen, France.
- Revue des Societes Savantes de Haute
  Normandie. q. ISSN 0035-2241

**Ligne Creatrice**
c/o J. Tarkieltaub, 69 rue d'Hauteville, Paris,
France.
- Ligne Creatrice. irreg., 14 nos. published through
  1975.

**Ligo Internacia de Blindaj Esperantistoj**
20 Av. de Saint Exupery, 69100 Villeurbanne,
France.
- Esperanta Ligilo. 10 per yr. ISSN 0014-0600

**Ligue des Droits de l'Homme**
27 rue Jean Dolent, 75014 Paris, France.
- Apres - Demain; journal mensuel de
  documentation politique. m. ISSN 0003-7176

**Ligue Francaise de l'Enseignement et de l'Education Permanente**
3, rue Recamier, 75341 Paris, France.
- Pourquoi. 10 per yr. ISSN 0048-5004
- Revue du Cinema/Image et Son; revue culturelle
  de cinema. m. ISSN 0019-2635

**Ligue Francaise du Coin de Terre et du Foyer**
11 rue Saint-Romain, Paris(6e), France.
- Jardin Ouvrier de France. bi-m. ISSN 0021-5465

**Ligue Francaise pour les Auberges de la Jeunesse**
38 Bd. Raspail, Paris (7e), France.
- Auberge de la Jeunesse. m. ISSN 0004-7392

**Ligue Nationale Francaise Contre le Cancer**
90 rue d'Assas, 75006 Paris, France.
- Lutte Contre le Cancer. q. ISSN 0024-7642

**Ligue Nationale pour la Liberte des Vaccinations**
4 rue Saulnier, 75009 Paris, France.
- Sante, Liberte et Vaccination. bi-m. ISSN 0036-
  4584

**Ligue Urbaine et Rurale**
274, Blvd. St. Germain, 75 Paris 7e, France.
- Ligue Urbaine et Rurale Cahiers. q.

**Louis Lippens, Ed. & Pub.**
31 rue Foch, 59126 Linselles, France.
- Elan; poetique, litteraire et pacifiste. q. ISSN
  0013-4066

**Lissot**
105 rue Isambard, 27120 Pacy sur Eure, France.
- Courrier Avicole. w. ISSN 0011-0450

**Livre Contemporain et les Bibliophiles Francosuisses**
3 rue Keppler, Paris 16e, France.
- Livre Contemporain et les Bibliophiles
  Francosuisses. irreg. ISSN 0076-0102

**Loco-Revue**
c/o Jean Fournereau, Jr., Ed., B.P.9, Le Sablen,
56400 Auray (Morbihan), France.
- Loco-Revue; pour les modelistes et amateurs de
  chemins de fer. m. ISSN 0024-5739

**Marcel Locquin, Ed. & Pub.**
Le Village-St. Clement, 89100 Sens, France.
- Odimy/Observations et Disputationes
  Mycologicae. 4 per yr. (Societe Mycologique de
  France) (Co-Sponsor: Mycotaxon)

**Editions Logitec**
43 rue Beaubourg, Paris (3e), France.
- Elements, Produits, Services. 10 per yr. ISSN
  0013-6026

**Loisirs & Nature**
1, rue Jules Simon, 75015 Paris, France.
- Loisirs & Nature. m.

**Loisirs Nautiques**
71 rue Amedee St. Germain, 33800 Bordeaux,
France.
- Loisirs Nautiques; voile et motonautisme
  architecture et construction navale. m. ISSN
  0047-5017

**Lou Pais**
c/o M. Olivier Alle, 2 rue Four des Flammes, 34
Montpellier, France.
- Lou Pais; revue regionaliste. m. ISSN 0024-6697

**Publications Louchel**
8 rue Halevy, 75009 Paris, France.
- Collections - Femme Chic. q. ISSN 0010-0773
- Couture. 4 per yr. ISSN 0011-0655
- Decoration. 5 per yr.
- Femme Chic. q. ISSN 0014-9896
- Mariages. q. ISSN 0025-2980

**Lumiere et Vie**
2, Place Gailleton, 69002 Lyon, France.
- Lumiere et Vie; revue de reflexion et de formation
  chretiennes. 5 per yr. ISSN 0024-7359

**Lutte Ouvriere**
B.P. 233, 75865 Paris Cedex 18, France.
- Lutte de Classe/Class Struggle; pour la
  reconstruction de la quatrieme internationale. m.
  ISSN 0458-5143
- Lutte Ouvriere. w. ISSN 0024-7650

**Editions Lux**
52 Bd. Malesherbes, 75008 Paris, France.
- Lux; la revue de l'eclairage. 5 per yr. ISSN 0024-7669 (Association Francaise de l'Eclairage)

**M. O. D. E. F.**
43, Avenue de Cognac, 16-Angouleme, France.
- Exploitant Familial. m.

**M.R.A.**
see **Societe Nouvelles des Publications M. R. A.**

**Macula**
c/o Pierre Brochet, 313, rue Lecourbe, 75015 Paris, France.
- Macula. q.

**Madure-Madagascar**
79 Avenue de Breteuil, 75015 Paris, France.
- Madure-Madagascar. q.

**Maeght Editeur**
13, rue de Teheran, 75008 Paris, France.
- Argile. q.
- Derriere le Miroir. 5-6 per yr. ISSN 0011-9113

**Magazine-Expansion**
40, rue des Saints-Peres, Paris (7e), France.
- Magazine Litteraire. m. ISSN 0024-9807

**Magelan S.A.R.L.**
Boite Postale 130-10, 75463 Paris, France.
- Israel & Palestine; monthly review. m.

**Editions Magnard**
122, Bd St. Germain, 75006 Paris, France.
- Preparons l'Avenir. bi-m (5 per yr.)

**Magyar Muhely**
7 Bd. St. Marcel, 75013 Paris, France.
- D'Atelier. q. ISSN 0045-9712
- Magyar Muhely; revue litteraire. bi-m. ISSN 0025-0201

**Maille, SARL**
60, rue de Richelieu, 75002 Paris, France.
- Moniteur de la Maille. m.

**Maison de la Chasse et de la Nature**
60, rue des Archives, 75003 Paris, France.
- Maison de la Chasse et de la Nature. Bulletin d'Information. q.

**Maison de Marie Claire**
51 rue Pierre-Charron, 75380 Paris, France
- Maison de Marie Claire. m. ISSN 0542-1594

**Maison des Sciences de l'Homme**
- Atlas des Structures Agraires au Sud du Sahara. (pub. by Mouton Publishers NE)
- Atlas des Structures Agraires de Madagascar. (pub. by Mouton Publishers NE)
- Canadiana Avant 1867. (pub. by Mouton Publishers NE)
- Maison des Sciences de l'Homme. Collection de Reeditions. (pub. by Mouton Publishers NE)
- Recherches Mediterraneennes. Bibliographies. (pub. by Mouton Publishers NE)
- Service d'Echange d'Informations Scientifiques. Serie A: Bibliographies. (pub. by Mouton Publishers NE)
- Service d'Echange d'Informations Scientifiques. Serie B: Guides et Repertoires. (pub. by Mouton Publishers NE)
- Service d'Echange d'Informations Scientifiques. Serie C: Catalogues et Inventaires. (pub. by Mouton Publishers NE)
- Service d'Echange d'Informations Scientifiques. Serie D: Methodes et Techniques. (pub. by Mouton Publishers NE)

**Adrien Maisonneuve**
11 rue Saint-Sulpice, 75006 Paris, France.
- Bibliotheque Iranienne. irreg. (Institut Franco-Iranien. Departement d'Iranologie) (Co-Sponsor: Institut d'Etudes Iraniennes de l'Universite de Paris)
- Ecole Francaise d'Extreme-Orient.Bulletin. a.(approx.)vol. 59, 1972.
- Institut Francais d'Archeologie d'Istanbul. Bibliotheque Archeologique et Historique. irreg. ISSN 0537-779X

**Editions Maisonneuve et Larose**
11 rue Victor-Cousin, Paris 5e, France.
- Erotisme Populaire. irreg. ISSN 0071-1225
- Ethnologie Francaise/French Ethnology. q. ISSN 0046-2616

- Folklore Europeen. irreg. ISSN 0430-8867 (Council of Europe)

**Maisons d'Enfants et d'Adolescents de France**
- Maisons d'Enfants et d'Adolescents de France. Album-Annuaire National. (pub. by Editions Gaston Gorde)

**Librairie Maloine**
27 rue de l'Ecole-De-Medecine, 75006 Paris, France.
- Acquisitions Nouvelles en Pathologie Cardio-Vasculaire. bi-m. ISSN 0001-5008
- Cahiers de Kinesitherapie; revue d'enseignement post-scolaire et de documentation technique. bi-m. ISSN 0007-9782
- Coeur; revue de cardiologie medico-chirurgicale. bi-m. ISSN 0010-0226
- Feuillets d'Electroradiologie. bi-m. ISSN 0015-0444
- Medecine Infantile; revue de clinique, de therapeutique et d'hygiene sociale de l'enfance. m. ISSN 0025-6773 (Comite National de l'Enfance)
- Nouveaux Echos de la Medecine. ISSN 0336-8653

**Mammalia**
M. Jean Dorst, 55 rue Buffon, Paris 5e, France.
- Mammalia. q. ISSN 0025-1461

**A. Manoury**
12 bis Place Henri Bergson, 75008 Paris, France (Orders to: Office Universitarie de Presse, 15 rue Tiphaine, 75015 Paris, France)
- Diagnostics. 22 per yr.

**Manteia**
39 Allees Leon Gambetta, 13 Marseille (1e), France.
- Manteia. q. ISSN 0025-2492

**Maquettes-Plastiques**
21 Rue des Jeuneurs, Paris (2e), France.
- Maquettes-Plastiques. q. ISSN 0047-5858

**Editions Marechal**
173 rue St. Honore, 75001 Paris, France.
- Canard Enchaine; journal satirique paraissant le mercredi. w. ISSN 0008-5405

**Marian Association for Young Girls**
67 rue de Sevres, Paris (6e), France.
- Rayons. 10 per yr. ISSN 0034-0197

**Marie-Claire**
51 rue Pierre-Charron, 75380 Paris, France
- Marie-Claire. m. ISSN 0025-3049

**Editions Marigny**
6 Rue Montalivet, Paris (8e), France.
- Propos Utiles aux Medecins. w. ISSN 0033-1392

**Laboratoires Martinet**
222 Bd. Pereire, 75848 Paris Cedex 17, France.
- Clinique Ophtalmologique. q. ISSN 0009-9368

**Librairie Francois Maspero**
1 Place Paul-Painleve, 75005 Paris, France.
- Bibliotheque d'Anthropologie. irreg. ISSN 0067-8252
- Cahiers du Forum Histoire. 3 per yr.
- Critiques de l'Economie Politique. q. ISSN 0045-9097
- Herodote. q.

**Editions Richard Masse**
7 Place Saint Sulpice, Paris (6e), France.
- Revue Musicale; revue d'esthetique musicale. q. ISSN 0035-3736

**Editions Charles Massin et Cie**
2 rue de l'Echelle, Paris (1e), France.
- Art et Decoration; la revue de la maison. 7 per yr. ISSN 0004-3168
- Techniques Artisanales Modernes. irreg. ISSN 0082-2442

**Masson**
120 Bd. Saint-Germain, 75280 Paris Cedex 06, France
- Academie Nationale de Medecine. Bulletin. 9 per yr. ISSN 0001-4079
- Acta Concilium Ophthalmologicum. quadrennial, 1974, 22nd, Paris. ISSN 0065-115X (International Federation of Ophthalmological Societies)

- Analusis; chimie analytique - methodes physiques d'analyse. 10 per yr.
- Anesthesie, Analgesie, Reanimation. 6 per yr. ISSN 0003-3014 (Societe Francaise d'Anesthesie, d'Analgesie et de Reanimation)
- Annales d'Anatomie Pathologique. q. ISSN 0003-3871
- Annales d'Endocrinologie. 6 per yr. ISSN 0003-4266 (Societe d'Endocrinologie et Societe Belge d'Endocrinologie)
- Annales d'Immunologie; an international journal. bi-m. ISSN 0300-4910 (Societe Francaise d'Immunologie)
- Annales d'Oto-Laryngologie et de Chirurgie Cervico Faciale. 8 per yr. ISSN 0003-438X (Societe de Laryngologie des Hopitaux de Paris)
- Annales de Chimie. 6 per yr. ISSN 0003-3936
- Annales de Chirurgie Infantile. 6 per yr. ISSN 0003-3952 (Societe Francaise de Chirurgie Infantile)
- Annales de Dermatologie et de Venereologie. 10 per yr. (Societe Francaise de Dermatologie et de Syphiligraphie)
- Annales de Kinesitherapie. 10 per yr. ISSN 0302-427X (Societe de Kinesitherapie)
- Annales de Limnologie. 3 per yr. ISSN 0003-4088 (Universite Paul Sabatier (Toulouse). Station Biologique du Lac d'Oredon)
- Annales de Medecine Interne. 10 per yr. ISSN 0003-410X (Societe Medicale des Hopitaux de Paris)
- Annales de Microbiologie. 8 per yr. ISSN 0300-5410 (Institut Pasteur)
- Annales de Paleontologie. q. ISSN 0003-4142
- Annales de Parasitologie Humaine et Comparee. 6 per yr. ISSN 0003-4150
- Annales de Physique. 6 per yr. ISSN 0003-4169
- Annales des Sciences Naturelles. Botanique et Biologie Vegetale. 4 per yr. ISSN 0003-4320
- Annales des Sciences Naturelles. Zoologie et Biologie Animale. 4 per yr. ISSN 0003-4339
- Annales Medico-Psychologiques. 10 per yr. ISSN 0003-4487 (Societe Medico-Psychologique)
- Annales Pharmaceutiques Francaises. 8 per yr. ISSN 0003-4509 (Academie de Pharmacie)
- Annee Biologique. 6 per yr. ISSN 0003-5017 (Federation Francaise des Societes de Sciences Naturelles)
- L'Anthropologie. 4 per yr. ISSN 0003-5521
- Archives d'Anatomie Microscopique et de Morphologie Experimentale. 4 per yr. ISSN 0003-9594
- Archives d'Ophtalmologie. 10 per yr. ISSN 0003-973X
- Archives des Maladies Professionnelles de Medecine du Travail et de Securite Sociale. 8 per yr. ISSN 0003-9691 (Societes de Medecine du Travail de France)
- Autrement. q.
- Biochimie. 10 per yr. ISSN 0300-9084 (Societe de Chimie Biologique)
- Biologie du Comportement/Biology of Behaviour. q. ISSN 0397-7153
- Biomedecine; European journal of biological and clinical research. 16 per yr. ISSN 0300-0893 (Institut de Cancerologie et d'Immunogenetique)
- Bulletin d'Ecologie. q. ISSN 0395-7217 (Societe d'Ecologie)
- Bulletin de Medecine Legale et de Toxicologie Medicale. 6 per yr. ISSN 0007-4365 (Co-Sponsors: Groupement Francais de Centre de Lutte Contre les Intoxications; Association Lyonnaise de Medecine Legale; Association Lyonnaise d'Economie Medicale)
- Bulletin du Cancer. 4 per yr. ISSN 0007-4551 (Association Francaise pour l'Etude du Cancer)
- Chirurgie. 12 per yr. ISSN 0001-4001 (Academie de Chirurgie)
- Congres de Psychiatrie et de Neurologie de Langue Francaise. Rapport/French-Language Congress of Psychiatry and Neurology. Report. a. ISSN 0071-9501
- Diabete & Metabolisme. q. ISSN 0338-1684
- Dossiers d'Histoire Pierre Goubert. irreg. ISSN 0070-7147
- Droit et Pratique du Commerce International. q. ISSN 0335-5047
- Ecole Nationale Superieure des Techniques Avancees, Paris, Collection. irreg. ISSN 0078-9526
- Entretiens de Chize. Serie Ecologie et Ethologie. irreg. ISSN 0071-0814
- Gastro-Enterologie Clinique et Biologique. 10 per yr. (Societe Nationale Francaise de Gastro-Enterologie)
- Geologie des Aires Oceaniques. irreg. ISSN 0072-1107
- Insectes Sociaux. q. ISSN 0020-1812

- Institut Oceanographique. Annales. s-a. ISSN 0078-9682
- Institut Pasteur. Bulletin. q. ISSN 0020-2452
- International Trade-Law & Practice. q. ISSN 0335-5047
- Journal d'Urologie et de Nephrologie. 10 per yr. ISSN 0021-8200 (Societe Francaise d'Urologie) (Co-sponsors: Societe d'Urologie du Sud-Est et du Sud-Ouest; Association Francais d'Urologie)
- Journal de Chirurgie. 10 per yr. ISSN 0021-7697
- Journal de Gynecologie Obstetrique et Biologie de la Reproduction. 8 per yr.
- Journal de Neuroradiologie/Journal of Neuroradiology. q. (Societe Francaise de Neuroradiologie)
- Journal de Pharmacie de Belgique. 6 per yr. ISSN 0047-2166 (Association Pharmaceutique Belge BE)
- Journal de Pharmacologie. 4 per yr. ISSN 0021-793X (Association des Pharmacologistes)
- Journal de Physiologie. 8 per yr. ISSN 0021-7948
- Journal de Radiologie. d'Electrologie et de Medecine Nucleaire. 10 per yr. ISSN 0021-7964 (Societe Francaise d'Electroradiologie Medicale et Filiales)
- Journal des Maladies Vasculaires. q. (College Francais de Pathologie Vasculaire)
- Journal of Optics. 6 per yr.
- Lyon Chirurgical. 6 per yr. ISSN 0024-7782 (Societe de Chirurgie de Lyon)
- Maitrise de Mathematiques. irreg. ISSN 0339-879X
- Neuro-Chirurgie. 9 per yr. ISSN 0028-3770 (Societe de Neuro-Chirurgie de Langue Francaise)
- Nouvelle Presse Medicale. 44 per yr. ISSN 0301-1518
- Nouvelle Revue Francaise d'Hematologie. 3 per yr. ISSN 0029-4810
- Onde Electrique. m. ISSN 0030-2430 (Societe des Electriciens, Electroniciens et Radioelectriciens SEE)
- Ordre National des Medecins. Bulletin. q. ISSN 0030-4565
- Regards sur l'Allemagne. irreg. ISSN 0080-052X
- Reunion des Endocrinologistes de Langue Francaise. Rapports/Association for French-Language Endocrinologists. Reports of Meetings. biennial, 1973, 12th, Paris. ISSN 0066-9113
- Revue d'Electroencephalographie et de Neurophysiologie Clinique. q. ISSN 0035-1857 (Societe d'EEG et de Neurophysiologie Clinique de Langue Francaise)
- Revue d'Epidemiologie, Medecine Sociale et Sante Publique. 8 per yr. ISSN 0035-2438
- Revue de Chirurgie Orthopedique et Reparatrice de l'Appareil Moteur. 9 per yr. ISSN 0035-1040
- Revue de Geographie Physique et de Geologie Dynamique. 5 per yr. ISSN 0035-1164 (Faculte des Sciences de Paris. Laboratoire de Geographie Physique)
- Revue de l'Alcoolisme. 4 per yr. ISSN 0035-130X (Groupement Medical d'Etudes sur l'Alcoolisme)
- Revue de Stomatologie et de Chirurgie Maxillo-Faciale. 8 per yr. ISSN 0035-1768 (Societe de Stomatologie et de Chirurgie Maxillo-Faciale de France)
- Revue Francaise des Maladies Respiratoires. 12 per yr. ISSN 0301-0279 (Societe Francaise de Tuberculose) (Co-sponsor: Comite National de Defense Contre la Tuberculose)
- Revue Internationale des Hautes Temperatures et des Refractaires. 4 per yr. ISSN 0035-3434
- Revue Neurologique. 12 per yr. ISSN 0035-3787 (Societe Francaise de Neurologie)
- Societe Chimique de France. Bulletin. 12 per yr. ISSN 0037-8968
- Societe de Biologie et de ses Filiales. Comptes Rendus des Seances. m. ISSN 0037-9026
- Societe de Pathologie Exotique et de ses Filiales. Bulletin. 6 per yr. ISSN 0037-9085
- Societe Francaise de Mineralogie et de Cristallographie. Bulletin. 6 per yr. ISSN 0037-9328
- Thomson C S F. Revue Technique; electronique. 4 per yr. ISSN 0040-6341
- Vie et Milieu; periodique d'ecologie generale. 4 per yr. ISSN 0042-5516 (Universite de Paris VI (Pierre et Marie Curie). Laboratoire Arago de Biologie Marine)

**Masson Services**
15, rue de Savoie, 75006 Paris, France.
- Cahiers Integres de Medecine. 24 per yr. ISSN 0008-0268

**Master Wineletter**
Drawer N., le Vendome, 38 bis, rue Bernardines, Aix-en-Provence, France.
- Master Wineletter. 8 per yr.

**Materiel d'Entreprise**
2, Cite du Cardinal Lemoine, 75005 Paris, France.
- Materiel d'Entreprise. 10 per yr. ISSN 0025-5467

**Editions d'Art Lucien Mazenod**
33 rue de Naples, Paris 8, France.
- Art et les Grandes Civilisations. irreg., 1974, vol. 5. ISSN 0066-7951

**Medecine Actuelle**
c/o Docteur Pennec, 5 Avenue Alphonse Mas, Beziers 34501 Herault, France.
- Medecine Actuelle; revue d'information medicale et scientifique. m.

**Medecine du Sport**
17, rue du 8 Mai 1945, 75010 Paris, France.
- Medecine du Sport. bi-m. ISSN 0025-6722

**Editions de Medecine Pratique**
2 rue du 8 Mai 1945, 92700 Colombes, France.
- Cahiers de la Puericultrice. q. ISSN 0007-9820
- Clinique; revue du medecin practicien. m. ISSN 0009-935X (Societe Medicale des Praticiens)
- Information Dietetique. 4 per yr. ISSN 0020-0034
- Revue Francaise d'Endocrinologie Clinique, Nutrition et Metabolisme. bi-m. ISSN 0048-8062

**Medecine, Sciences et Documents**
3 Av. Hoche, 75008 Paris, France.
- Medecine, Sciences et Documents; mensuel d'informations medicales et generales. m. ISSN 0395-7349

**Editions Medicale Pratique**
2, rue 8 Mai 1945, 92700 - Colombes, France.
- Angeiologie. bi-m. ISSN 0003-3049

**Mediscope**
13 rue Beethoven, 75016 Paris, France.
- Mediscope. m.

**Editions Mercure**
Place Franz Liszt, Paris, Paris 17e, France
(Editorial Address: 23 rue Philibert Delorme, 75840 Paris 17 France)
- Gaz de France. Rapport Annuel. a. ISSN 0072-0313

**Editions Mericourt**
23 rue d'Antin, 75002 Paris, France.
- Best; la meilleure actualite de l'evolution musicale. m.

**Messageries M.B.P.**
5 Avenue de la Paix, 92120 Montrouge, France
(Orders to: 21 rue du Fbg. Saint- Antoine, 75541 Paris Cedex 11)
- Panorama Aujourd'hui; le journal des chretiens d'aujourd'hui. m. ISSN 0048-2838

**Editions la Metallurgie Francaise**
B.P. 100, 37021 Tours Cedex, France.
- Guide d'Achats Jardin. a.
- Journal de la Quincaillerie. m. ISSN 0048-6477

**Editions Meteore**
48, rue de la Bienfaisance, 75008 Paris, France.
- Revue Technique de la Viande et de l'Alimentation Carnee; des veterinaires hygienistes de l'alimentation. m.

**METRA**
16/20 rue Barbes, 92128 Montrouge, France.
- Marketing Industriel; bulletin de marketing industriel. irreg.

**Editions Albin Michel**
22 rue Huyghens, Paris (14e), France.
- Revue de Synthese. q. ISSN 0035-1776 (Centre International de Synthese)

**Michelin**
Services de Tourisme, 46 Ave. de Breteuil, F 75341 Paris 7e, France
(U.S. subscr. address: Box 5022, New Hyde Park NY 11040)
- Camping, Caravaning in France. a. ISSN 0076-7735
- Michelin Green Guide Series: Austria. irreg.
- Michelin Green Guide Series: Brittany. irreg.
- Michelin Green Guide Series: Chateau of the Loire. irreg.

- Michelin Green Guide Series: French Riviera. irreg.
- Michelin Green Guide Series: Germany. irreg.
- Michelin Green Guide Series: Italy. irreg.
- Michelin Green Guide Series: Londres. irreg.
- Michelin Green Guide Series: Maroc. irreg.
- Michelin Green Guide Series: New York (City) irreg.
- Michelin Green Guide Series: Normandy. irreg.
- Michelin Green Guide Series: Paris. irreg.
- Michelin Green Guide Series: Portugal. irreg.
- Michelin Green Guide Series: Spain. irreg.
- Michelin Green Guide Series: Switzerland. irreg.
- Michelin Red Guide Series: Benelux. a. ISSN 0076-7743
- Michelin Red Guide Series: France. a. ISSN 0076-7778
- Michelin Red Guide Series: Germany. a. ISSN 0076-7751
- Michelin Red Guide Series: Great Britain and Ireland. a.
- Michelin Red Guide Series: Greater London. a.
- Michelin Red Guide Series: Italy. a. ISSN 0076-7786
- Michelin Red Guide Series: Paris. a. ISSN 0076-7794
- Michelin Red Guide Series: Spain & Portugal. a. ISSN 0076-776X

**Midiscope Pyrenees**
16 Chemin Marial, Fonsorbes 31470, France.
- Midiscope Pyrenees. m.

**Militant**
44 Quai de Jemmapes, 75010 Paris, France.
- Militant; revue nationaliste d'action europeenne. m. ISSN 0026-3877

**Societe d'Editions Millot et Cie**
20 rue Gambetta, 25014 Besancon Cedex, France.
- France Horlogere; revue de l'horlogerie, bijouterie, orfevrerie cadeaux. m. ISSN 0015-9573

**Lettres Modernes (Minard)**
73, rue du Cardinal Lemoine, 75005 Paris, France.
- Andre Gide; la revue des lettres modernes. a.
- Archives Claudeliennes. irreg. ISSN 0066-6556
- Archives des Lettres Modernes; etudes de critique et d'histoire litteraire. 6-10 per yr. ISSN 0003-9675
- Avant-Siecle. irreg., no. 14, 1974. ISSN 0067-2610
- Barbey d'Aurevilly. a.
- Bibliotheque Introuvable. irreg. ISSN 0067-8422
- Circe. irreg. ISSN 0069-4177
- Etudes Bernanosiennes. a. ISSN 0425-4791
- Etudes Cinematographiques. irreg. ISSN 0014-1992
- Guillaume Apollinaire. a. ISSN 0072-8993
- Interferences, Arts, Lettres. irreg. ISSN 0074-1140
- Jean Giono. a.
- Langues et Styles. irreg., no. 5, 1974. ISSN 0075-7985
- Nouvelle Bibliotheque Nervalienne. irreg. ISSN 0078-2165
- Paralogue. irreg. ISSN 0078-9429
- Paul Valery. irreg.
- Revue des Lettres Modernes; histoire des idees et des litteratures. irreg. ISSN 0035-2136
- Siecle Eclate: Dada, Surrealisme et les Avant-Gardes. a.

**Editions de Minuit**
7 rue Bernard-Palissy, 75006 Paris, France
- Actes de la Recherche en Sciences Sociales. bi-m. (Orders to: Maison des Sciences de l'Homme, 54 Bd. Raspail, 75270 Paris Cedex 06, France)
- Critique; revue generale des publications francaises et etrangeres. m. ISSN 0011-1600
- Minuit. bi-m.
- Traverses. q. ISSN 0336-9730 (Centre National d'Art et de Culture. Centre de Creation Industrielle)

**Mise en Page**
8 rue de Nesle, Paris (6e), France.
- Mise en Page. q.

**Missi**
6 rue d'Auvergne, 69287 Lyon Cedex 1, France.
- Missi; magazine d'information spirituelle et de solidarite internationale. m. ISSN 0026-5977

**Missionaires Volontaires Adventistes**
130 Bd. de l'Hopital, Paris (13e), France.
- Jeunesse. 10 per yr. ISSN 0021-6178

**Missionnaires Oblats de Marie Immaculee**
36 rue de Trion, 69322 Lyon Cedex 1, France.
- Pole et Tropiques; revue apostolique des missionnaires oblats. m. ISSN 0032-2504

**Mode International**
48, rue Sainte-Anne, 75002 Paris, France.
- Mode International. bi-m.

**Modelisme**
94 Bd. de Sebastopol, 75 Paris (3e), France.
- Modelisme; automobile internationel. bi-m. ISSN 0047-7648

**Mon Jardin et Ma Maison**
31 Route de Versailles, 78560 le Port-Marly, France.
- Mon Jardin et Ma Maison. m. ISSN 0026-9166

**Monde**
5 Rue des Italiens, 75427 Paris Cedex 09, France.
- Monde. w. ISSN 0026-9360
- Monde de l'Education. m.
- Monde des Philatelistes; officiel de la philatelie. m. ISSN 0026-9387
- Monde Diplomatique. m. ISSN 0026-9395

**Mondes Asiatiques**
54 rue de Varenne, 75007 Paris, France.
- Mondes Asiatiques. q.

**Moniteur des Travaux Publics et du Batiment**
91, rue du Faubourg Saint Honore, 75383 Paris 8, France.
- France. Commission Centrale des Marches. Guide du Fournisseur de l'Etat et des Collectivites Locales. irreg. ISSN 0071-8483 (France. Ministere de l'Economie et des Finances. Commission Centrale des Marches)

**Monnaie de Paris**
11 Quai de Conti, 75270 Paris Cedex 05, France.
- Club Francais de la Medaille. 3 per yr. ISSN 0009-9570

**Monographies de l'Industrie et du Commerce en France**
24 Place Malesherbes, Paris 17e, France.
- Monographies de l'Industrie et du Commerce en France. irreg. ISSN 0077-0701

**Editions Montchrestien**
160 rue St.-Jacques, Paris 5, France.
- Bibliographie en Langue Francaise d'Histoire du Droit. a. since 1962. ISSN 0067-6985

**Publications Paul Montel**
189 rue Saint Jacques, 75005 Paris, France.
- Nouveau Photocinema; magazine des photographes et cineastes amateurs. m.
- Photographe. bi-m.

**Moreana Publications**
B.P. 858, 49005 Angers, France.
- Moreana; time trieth truth. q. ISSN 0047-8105 (Amici Thomae Mori)

**Rene Moreux et Cie**
190 Boulevard Haussmann, 75008 Paris, France.
- Annuaire des Entreprises d'Outre-Mer des Organismes Officiels et Professionnels d'Outremer, des Organismes de Cooperation Francais, Etrangers et Internationaux. a. ISSN 0066-2828
- Industries et Travaux d'Outre-Mer. m. ISSN 0019-9362
- Marches Tropicaux et Mediterraneens. w. ISSN 0025-2859
- Navis; annuaire de la marine merchande, de la construction navale et des ports. a. ISSN 0077-6270

**Editions Mouton et Cie**
7, rue Dupuytren, 75006 Paris, France (and B.P. 482, the Hague, Netherlands)
- Bibliotheque Arctique et Antarctique. irreg., 1964, no. 2. ISSN 0067-8244 (Ecole Pratique des Hautes Etudes. Centre d'Etudes Arctiques et Finno-Scandinaves)
- Cahiers de l'Homme. Nouvelle Serie. irreg., 1968, no. 8. ISSN 0068-5046 (Ecole Pratique des Hautes Etudes. Laboratoire d' Anthropologie)
- Cahiers des Etudes Rurales. irreg., no. 2, 1964. ISSN 0071-2175 (Ecole Pratique des Hautes Etudes. Laboratoire d'Anthropologie Sociale)
- Cahiers du Monde Russe et Sovietique. q. ISSN 0008-0160 (Ecole Pratique des Hautes Etudes)

- Civilisations et Societes. irreg., 1969, no. 14. ISSN 0069-4290 (Ecole Pratique des Hautes Etudes. Centre des Recherches Historiques)
- Documents et Recherches sur l'Economie des Pays Byzantins, Islamiques et Slaves et Leurs Relations Commerciales au Moyen Age. irreg., 1969, no. 9. ISSN 0070-6957 (Ecole Pratique des Hautes Etudes)
- Ecole Pratique des Hautes Etudes, Paris. Centre de Psychiatrie Sociale. Publications. irreg., 1967, no. 4. ISSN 0078-9593
- Ecole Pratique des Hautes Etudes, Paris. Centre de Sociologie Europeenne. Cahiers. irreg., 1969, no. 6. ISSN 0078-9615
- Ecole Pratique des Hautes Etudes, Paris. Division des Aires Culturelles. Congres et Colloques. irreg., 1967, no. 11. ISSN 0078-9631
- Environment and Social Sciences/Environnement et Sciences Sociales. irreg. (United Nations UN) (Co-Sponsor: Ecole Pratique des Hautes Etudes)
- Ethnies; linguistique et relations interethniques. irreg. ISSN 0073-4667 (Institut d'Etudes et de Recherches Inter-Culturelles)
- Etudes Europeennes. irreg., 1967, no. 5. ISSN 0071-2043 (Ecole Pratique des Hautes Etudes. Division des Aires Culturelles)
- Etudes Juives. irreg., 1968, no. 14. ISSN 0071-2116 (Ecole Pratique des Hautes Etudes. Division des Aires Culturelles)
- Etudes sur l'Histoire, l'Economie et la Sociologie des Pays Slaves. irreg., 1968, no. 13 ISSN 0071-2205 (Ecole Pratique des Hautes Etudes. Centre de Documentation sur l'U.R.S.S. et les Pays Slaves)
- Industrie et Artisanat. irreg., 1968, no. 5. ISSN 0073-7739 (Ecole Pratique des Hautes Etudes. Centre des Recherches Historiques)
- Inter-Nord; Revue Internationale d'Etudes Arctiques et Nordiques. a(in 2 pts) ISSN 0074-1035 (Fondation Francaise d'Etudes Nordiques)
- Livre et Societes. irreg., 1969, no. 3. ISSN 0076-0129 (Ecole Pratique des Hautes Etudes. Division des Aires Culturelles)
- Materiaux pour l'Etude de l'Extreme-Orient Moderne et Contemporain. Etudes Linguistiques. irreg., 1967, no. 2. ISSN 0076-5252 (Ecole Pratique des Hautes Etudes) (Co-sponsor: Maison des Sciences de l'Homme)
- Materiaux pour l'Etude de l'Extreme-Orient Moderne et Contemporain. Textes. irreg., 1968, no. 6. ISSN 0076-5260 (Ecole Pratique des Hautes Etudes) (Co-sponsor: Maison des Sciences de l'Homme)
- Materiaux pour l'Etude de l'Extreme-Orient Moderne et Contemporain. Travaux. irreg., 1968, no. 3. ISSN 0076-5279 (Ecole Pratique des Hautes Etudes) (Co-sponsor: Maison des Sciences de l'Homme)
- Materiaux pour l'Histoire du Socialisme International. Deuxieme Serie. Essais Bibliographiques. irreg., 1968, no. 2. ISSN 0076-5287 (Ecole Pratique des Hautes Etudes)
- Materiaux pour l'Histoire du Socialisme International. Premiere Serie. Textes et Documents. irreg., 1969, no. 2. ISSN 0076-5295 (Ecole Pratique des Hautes Etudes)
- Mathematiques et Sciences de l'Homme. irreg., 1969, no. 9. ISSN 0076-5406 (Ecole Pratique des Hautes Etudes, Centre de Mathematique Sociale) (Co-Publisher: Gauthier Villars)
- Methodes de Sociologie. irreg., 1966, no. 2. ISSN 0076-678X (Ecole Pratique des Hautes Etudes) (Co-sponsor: Maison des Sciences de l'Homme)
- Monde d'Outre-Mer, Passe et Present. 1 Serie: Etudes. irreg., 1969, no. 33. ISSN 0077-0310 (Ecole Pratique des Hautes Etudes. Division des Aires Culturelles)
- Monde d'Outre-Mer, Passe et Present. 2 Serie: Documents. irreg., 1966, no. 10. ISSN 0077-0329 (Ecole Pratique des Hautes Etudes. Division des Aires Culturelles)
- Monde d'Outre-Mer, Passe et Present. 3 Serie: Essais. irreg., 1968, no. 8. ISSN 0077-0337 (Ecole Pratique des Hautes Etudes. Division des Aires Culturelles)
- Monde d'Outre-Mer, Passe et Present. 4 Serie: Bibliographies et Instruments de Travail. irreg., 1966, no. 7. ISSN 0077-0345 (Ecole Pratique des Hautes Etudes. Division des Aires Culturelles)
- Recherches Cooperatives. irreg., 1968, no. 4. ISSN 0080-004X (Ecole Pratique des Hautes Etudes, Centre de Recherches)
- Recherches Mediterraneennes. Serie 1. Etudes. irreg., 1966, no. 8. ISSN 0080-0104 (Ecole Pratique des Hautes Etudes. Division des Aires Culturelles) (Co-sponsor: Maison des Sciences de l'Homme)

- Recherches Mediterraneennes. Serie 2 Documents. irreg., 1969, no. 4. ISSN 0080-0112 (Ecole Pratique des Hautes Etudes. Division des Aires Culturelles)
- Recherches Mediterraneennes. Serie 3: Textes et Etudes Linguistiques. irreg., 1964, no. 3. ISSN 0080-0120 (Ecole Pratique des Hautes Etudes. Division des Aires Culturelles) (Co-sponsor: Maison des Sciences de l'Homme)
- Regional Planning. irreg.; 1972, vol. 5. (United Nations Research Institute for Social Development UN)
- Societe Mouvements Sociaux et Ideologies. 1 Serie: Etudes. irreg., 1966, no. 8. ISSN 0081-1157 (Ecole Pratique des Hautes Etudes. Division des Aires Culturelles)
- Societe Mouvements Sociaux et Ideologies. 2 Serie: Documents et Temoignages. irreg. ISSN 0081-1165 (Ecole Pratique des Hautes Etudes. Division des Aires Culturelles)
- Societe Mouvements Sociaux et Ideologies. 3 Serie: Bibliographies. irreg. ISSN 0081-1173 (Ecole Pratique des Hautes Etudes. Division des Aires Culturelles)
- Textes de Sciences Sociales. irreg. (Ecole Pratique des Hautes Etudes. Division des Aires Culturelles)

**Mouvement contre le Racisme l'antisemitisme et pour la Paix**
- Droit et Liberte. (pub. by Societe Droit et Liberte)

**Mouvement de la Condition Masculine**
2 rue de la Convention, 75015 Paris, France.
- Mouvement de la Condition Masculine. Revue. bi-m. ISSN 0339-1140

**Mouvement des Cadres, Ingenieurs et Dirigeants Chretiens (M.C.C.)**
18, rue de Varenne, 75007 Paris, France.
- Responsables. m.

**Mouvement des Sionistes Originaires. d'A.F.N. (Afrique Francaise du Nord)**
10 Square Alboni, 75016 Paris, France.
- SIONA Information. q. ISSN 0395-3661

**Mouvement Federaliste European**
Ed. Jean-Lue Prevel, 12 rue A. Bollier, 69007 Lyon, France.
- Federalisme Europeen. bi-m.

**Mouvement Federaliste Francaise**
3 rue Chauveau Lagarde, Paris (8e), France.
- Vingtieme Siecle Federaliste. q.

**Mouvement International de la Reconciliation**
5 rue Thorel, 75002 Paris, France.
- Cahiers de la Reconciliation. m. ISSN 0007-9839

**Mouvement Missionnaire Interieur Laique**
44 rue Beranger, 62400 Bethune, France.
- Etandard de la Bible. bi-m.

**Mouvement pour le Desarmement, la Paix et la Liberte**
25 rue de la Reynie, 75 Paris (1er), France.
- Alerte Atomique; contre toutes les bombes. bi-m. ISSN 0002-5186

**Mouvement Rural de Jeunesse Chretienne**
- Initiatives. (pub. by Andre-Pierre Body, Ed. & Pub.)

**Musee de Beaux Arts**
- Musees et Monuments Lyonnais. Bulletin. (pub. by Association des Amis du Musee des Beaux-Arts)

**Musee de l'Homme**
Palais de Chaillot, Place du Trocadero, 75116 Paris, France.
- Musee de l'Homme, Paris. Catalogues. Serie B: Afrique Blanche et Levant. irreg. ISSN 0553-2507
- Musee de l'Homme, Paris. Catalogues. Serie C: Afrique Noire. irreg.
- Musee de l'Homme, Paris. Catalogues. Serie E: Polynesie. irreg.
- Musee de l'Homme, Paris. Catalogues. Serie F: Madagascar. irreg.
- Musee de l'Homme, Paris. Catalogues. Serie G: Arctiques. irreg. ISSN 0553-2515
- Musee de l'Homme, Paris. Catalogues. Serie H: Amerique. irreg.
- Musee de l'Homme, Paris. Catalogues. Serie K: Asie. irreg.

- Objets et Mondes; la revue du Musee de l'Homme. q. ISSN 0029-7615

**Musee de l'Hotel Gouin**
25 rue du Commerce, 25 Tours, France.
- Societe Archeologique de Touraine. Memoires. irreg.

**Musee Guimet. Paris**
- Recherches et Documents d'Art et d'Archeologie. (pub. by Presses Universitaires de France)

**Musee National des Arts et Traditions Populaires**
6, Route de Madrid, 75116 Paris, France.
- Archives d'Ethnologie Francaise. irreg. ISSN 0066-6580

**Musee Pyreneen du Chateau-Fort de Lourdes. Societe des Amis de Musee**
Place de l'Eglise, Lourdes, France.
- Pyrenees. q. ISSN 0033-474X

**Museum National d'Histoire Naturelle**
38 rue Geoffroy-Saint-Hilaire, Paris 5e, France.
- Museum National d'Histoire Naturelle, Paris. Annuaire. a. ISSN 0078-9720
- Museum National d'Histoire Naturelle, Paris. Archives. irreg. ISSN 0078-9739
- Museum National d'Histoire Naturelle, Paris. Bulletin. (pub. by Librairie Thomas)
- Museum National d'Histoire Naturelle, Paris. Memoires. Nouvelle Serie. Serie A. Zoologie. irreg. ISSN 0078-9747
- Museum National d'Histoire Naturelle, Paris. Memoires. Nouvelle Serie. Serie B. Botanique. irreg. ISSN 0078-9755
- Museum National d'Histoire Naturelle, Paris. Memoires. Nouvelle Serie. Serie C. Sciences de la Terre. irreg. ISSN 0078-9763
- Museum National d'Histoire Naturelle, Paris. Memoires. Nouvelle Serie. Serie D. Sciences Physico-Chimiques. irreg. ISSN 0078-9771

**Museum National d'Histoire Naturelle. Association de Botanique Tropicale**
16 rue Buffon, 75005 Paris, France.
- Flore du Cambodge, du Laos et du Vietnam. irreg., 1977, no. 16. ISSN 0071-5867
- Flore du Cameroun. irreg., no. 20, 1977. ISSN 0071-5875
- Flore du Gabon. irreg., no. 24, 1977. ISSN 0071-5883

**Museum National d'Histoire Naturelle. Bibliotheque Centrale**
38 rue Geoffroy Saint Hilaire, Paris V, France.
- Museum National d'Histoire Naturelle, Paris. Bibliotheque Centrale. Liste des Periodiques Francais et Etrangers.Supplement. a. ISSN 0085-476X

**Museum National d'Histoire Naturelle. Laboratoire d'Ethnobotanique**
57 rue Cuvier, 75005 Paris, France.
- Journal d'Agriculture Tropicale et de Botanique Appliquee. 12 per yr. ISSN 0021-7662
- Museum National d'Histoire Naturelle, Paris. Laboratoire d'Ethnobotanique. Publications Diverses. irreg.

**Museum National d'Histoire Naturelle. Laboratoire de Palynologie**
c/o Ed. Dir. Madeleine van Campo, Universite des Sciences et Techniques du Languedoc, 34060 Montpellier, France.
- Pollen et Spores. 4 per yr. ISSN 0032-3616

**Mutualite Sociale Agricole de la Corse**
- Journal de la Corse Agricole. (pub. by Imprimerie Siciliano)

**Mutuelle Generale de la Police Francaise**
30-32, rue Amelot, 75011 Paris, France.
- Police Mutualite. m.

**Mutuelle Nationale des Etudiants de France**
16 Av Raspail, 94250 Gentilly, France.
- Recherches Universitaires. s-a.

**M. Myogo, Pub.**
8 rue Chabannais, Paris 2e, France.
- Annuaire de l'Industrie et du Commerce France-Afrique. a. ISSN 0066-2690

**N. C. R. A.**
4 rue Pasteur, B.P. No. 7, 14011 Caen Cedex, France.
- Basse Normandie Automobile. m. ISSN 0005-6197

**N.E.B. Editions Scientifiques**
B.P.3, 78350 Jouy-en-Josas, France.
- Journees de Physiologie Appliquee au Travail Humain. irreg. ISSN 0075-4455 (Societe d'Ergonomie de la Langue Francaise)

**N. E. I. D. Informations**
103 Bd. Haussmann, 75008 Paris, France.
- N. E. I. D. Informations; l'information des vins et spiriteux. m (10 per yr.)

**N. E. M. F.**
see **Nouvelles Editions Medicales Francaise (NEMF)**

**N E T A**
19 rue Bergere, 75009 Paris, France.
- Tabac et Sante; tabagisme. bi-m. (Comite National Contre le Tabagisme)

**Librairie Fernand Nathan**
9 rue Mechain, 75680 Paris Cedex 14, France.
- Documentation Par l'Image; revue des activites d'eveil. 9 per yr. ISSN 0046-0478
- Education Enfantine; revue des ecoles maternelles, classes enfantines, cours preparatoires. 9 per yr. ISSN 0013-1288
- Journal des Instituteurs et des Institutrices; nouvelle presentation. m(Sep-June) ISSN 0021-8073

**National China and Glass Federation of France**
- Table et Cadeau. (pub. by Editions G. M. Perrin)

**Nationless Worldwide Assn.**
67 Avenue Gambetta, Paris 20e, France.
- Sennacieca Revuo. a. ISSN 0080-8903

**Naturalistes Parisiens**
57 rue Cuvier, Paris (5e), France.
- Cahiers des Naturalistes. q. ISSN 0008-0039

**Editions de la Navigation du Rhin**
7, Quai du General Koenig, 67085 Strasbourg Cedex, France.
- Revue de la Navigation Fluviale Europeenne, Ports et Industries. s-m.(Sept-July) ISSN 0028-1549

**M. J. Negre, Pub.**
5 rue Bourdaloue, Paris, France.
- Entomologiste; revue d'amateurs. q. ISSN 0013-8886

**Auguste Nguyen**
Hopital St. Luc, 20 Quai Claude-Bernard, 69007 Lyon, France.
- Centre Lyonnais d'Acupuncture de Saint-Luc. Bulletin de Liaison. 2 per yr. ISSN 0338-7070

**Nichiren Shoshu Francaise**
64 rue du Lycee, 92 Sceaux, France.
- Troisieme Civilisation. bi-m. ISSN 0049-4739

**Editions NM**
75440 Paris, France
(U.S. addr.: French National Railroads, 610 Fifth Ave., New York, NY 10020)
- Vie du Rail. w. ISSN 0042-5478

**Nobiliaire**
c/oM. Martin & Miss J. Koenig, 120 Avenue du Roule, 92200 Neuilly-sur-Seine, France.
- Annuaire de la Noblesse de France et d'Europe. ISSN 0066-2569

**Nord Economique**
113 rue Nationale, 59044 Lille Cedex, France.
- Nord Economique; Agricole, Commercial, Maritime. w. ISSN 0029-120X

**Nord Transports S.A.R.L.**
48, rue Nicolas-Leblanc, Lille (Nord), France.
- Nord-Transports. m (11 per yr.)

**Norois**
8 rue Rene-Descartes, 86000 Poitiers, France.
- Norois; revue geographique de l'ouest et des pays de l'atlantique nord. q. ISSN 0029-182X (Co-Sponsor: Universites de l'Ouest (Angers, Brest, Caen, Limoges, Nantes, Orleans, Poitiers, Rennes, Rouen, Tours))

**Notre Dame de Sion**
71 rue Notre-Dame-Des-Champs, 75006 Paris, France.
- Encounter Today; Judaism and Christianity in the contemporary world. q. ISSN 0013-709X

**Notre Voix**
52 rue Rene Boulanger, 75010 Paris, France.
- Notre Voix. bi-m.

**Nouveau Quartier Latin**
78 Bd. St. Michel, 75006 Paris, France.
- Nouveau Commerce. q.
- Nouveau Commerce de la Lecture. q.

**Nouvel Observateur**
11 rue d'Aboukir, 75002 Paris, France
- Nouvel Observateur. w. ISSN 0029-4713

**Editions de la Nouvelle Critique**
168 rue du Temple, 75003 Paris, France.
- Nouvelle Critique. m(10 per yr.) ISSN 0029-4721
- Recherches Internationales a la Lumiere du Marxisme. bi-m. ISSN 0486-1345

**Nouvelle Frontiere**
105 rue de Grenelle, 75-Paris 7e, France.
- Nouvelle Frontiere. q. ISSN 0029-4764

**Nouvelle Hygiene**
24 rue Chaptal, Paris (9e), France.
- Nouvelle Hygiene. bi-m. ISSN 0029-4772

**Nouvelle Revue Franc-Comtoise**
c/oDir. H. Chazelle, Ed., 13 rue Pasteur, 39-Dole (Jura), France.
- Nouvelle Revue Franc-Comtoise. q. ISSN 0029-4799

**Nouvelle Revue Socialiste**
12, Cite Malesherbes, 75009 Paris, France.
- Nouvelle Revue Socialiste. m (10 per yr.)

**Nouvelle Societe Anonyme la Vie Ouvriere**
33, rue Bouret, 75940 Paris Cedex 19, France.
- Vie Ouvriere; l'hebdomadaire de la C.G.T. w.

**Nouvelle Societe Presence Africaine**
25 bis, rue des Ecoles, Paris (5e), France.
- Presence Africaine; revue culturelle du monde noir. q. ISSN 0032-7638

**Nouvelles du Monde**
13 rue de Liege, 75009 Paris, France.
- Equipment Industriel-Achats et Entretien. m.
- Revue Technique des Hotels, Restaurants, Bars, Brasseries, Limonadiers, Tabacs, Habitats Collectifs. m. ISSN 0035-4228

**Nouvelles Editions de la Publicite**
9, rue Leo-Delibes, 75016 Paris, France.
- Publi 10. fortn.

**Nouvelles Editions de Publications Agricoles**
10 rue Martel, 75480 Paris, France.
- France Agricole. w. ISSN 0046-4899

**Nouvelles Editions Latines**
1 rue Palatine, 75006 Paris, France.
- Demain d'Avantage Qu'hier. 15 per yr.

**Nouvelles Editions Medicales Francaises (NEMF)**
20, rue du Bouquet de Longchamp, 75116 Paris, France.
- Allergie et Immunologie. q.
- Cahiers de Sexologie Clinique.
- Medecine et Gastronomie; revue des medicins gastronomes. q. ISSN 0025-6730
- Medecine Interne; revue francaise de medecine interne. m. ISSN 0025-6781 (College Francais de Medecine Interne)

**Nouvelles Editions Musicales Modernes et Cie**
63 Champs-Elysees, Paris (8e), France.
- Jazz Magazine. m. ISSN 0021-566X

**Nouvelles Etudes Marxistes**
87 rue du Faubourg Saint Denis, Paris (10e),
France.
- Nouvelles Etudes Marxistes. 5 per yr. ISSN 0029-4918

**Nouvelles Litteraires, Arts, Sciences, Spectacles**
Rue Rene- Boulanger, 75010 Paris, France.
- Nouvelles Litteraires, Arts, Sciences, Spectacles.
  w. ISSN 0029-4942

**Editions Nova**
24 Ave de Riedisheim, F-68 Mulhouse, France.
- Esperanto - Interlangue Universelle. q. ISSN
  0046-2500

**Editions Nuit et Jour**
103 rue Lauriston, 75116 Paris, France.
- Detective. w. ISSN 0046-0095
- Horoscope. m.

**Numismatique & Change**
Louppy sur Chee, 55000 Bar le Duc, France.
- Numismatique & Change. m. ISSN 0335-1971

**O.D.E.G.E. Presse S.A.**
26, rue des Carmes, Paris 5e, France.
- Univers des Sciences et Techniques. w. ISSN
  0566-8654

**O. G. P. P.**
48 rue de la Bienfaisance, Paris 75008, France.
- Eurotechniques de l'Ameublement. bi-m.
- Officiel de la Droguerie; la revue des points de
  vente dynamiques. m. ISSN 0030-0411

**O. N. I. S. E. P**
see under **France. Office National d'Information
sur les Enseignements et les Professions**

**O. P. E. R. A.**
81, rue Pouchet, 75017 Paris, France.
- Societe Paul Claudel. Bulletin. q. ISSN 0037-9506

**Librairie Oberlin**
19- rue des Francs-Bourgeois, F-67 Strasbourg,
France.
- Messager Evangelique. w. ISSN 0026-0274 (Eglise
  de la Confession d'Ausburg) (Co-sponsor: Eglise
  Reforme d'Alsace et de Lorraine)

**Observateur des Assurances**
6 Route de Rueil, Versailles, France.
- Observateur des Assurances. w. ISSN 0029-7666

**Observatoire de Besancon**
41 bis Avenue de l'Observatoire, F25000, France.
- Annales Francaises de Chronometrie et de
  Micromecanique. a. ISSN 0066-2143 (Societe
  Chronometrique de France)

**Observatoire de Nice**
06300 Nice, France.
- Association pour le Developpement International
  de l'Observatoire de Nice. Bulletin d'Information.
  ISSN 0004-5861

**Observatoire de Paris**
61 Avenue l'Observatoire, Paris 14e, France.
- Cartes Synoptiques de la Chromosphere Solaire.
  biennial. ISSN 0085-4778

**Observatoire de Strasbourg**
11, rue de l'Universite, 67000 Strasbourg, France.
- Observatoire de Strasbourg. Centre de Donnees
  Stellaires. Information Bulletin. irreg.
- Observatoire de Strasbourg. Publication. irreg.
  ISSN 0081-590X

**Occitania Passat e Present**
11 Av. du Mas Ensoleille, 06600 Antibes, France.
- Occitania Passat e Present. bi-m.

**Oceans**
4, rue Luce, 13008 Marseille, France.
- Oceans. m(11 per yr.) ISSN 0475-171X

**Oeil**
10, rue Guichard, 75016 Paris, France.
- Oeil; revue d'art. m. (10 per yr) ISSN 0473-7954

**Oeuvre Apostolique pour les Missions de Fondation
Francaise a l'Etranger**
8 Av. Daniel Lesueur, Paris (7e), France.
- Bulletin de l'Oeuvre Apostolique. q. ISSN 0007-4330

**Oeuvre de Saint Pierre Apotre**
12 rue Sala, 69287 Lyon, France.
- Lumiere du Monde. q. ISSN 0024-7340 (Societe
  Presse et Publications Missionnaires)

**Office Central de la Cooperation a l'Ecole**
101 Bis rue du Ranelagh, 75016 Paris, France.
- Amis-Coop; magazine des cooperatives scolaires.
  m. ISSN 0003-1771

**Office Central des Chemins de Fer d'Outremer**
38 rue la Bruyere, 75009 Paris, France.
- Vie du Rail Outremer. m. ISSN 0049-6278

**Office de Justification de la Diffusion**
29 rue des Recollets, 75481 Paris, France.
- Terre; hebdomadaire paysan du parti communiste
  Francais. w. ISSN 0040-3814

**Office de la Recherche Scientifique et Technique
Outre-Mer. Service des Publications**
70-74 Route d'Aulnay, 93140 Bondy, France.
- Bulletin Analytique d'Entomologie Medicale et
  Veterinaire. 12 per yr. ISSN 0007-4098
- Cahiers ORSTOM. Serie Biologie. q. ISSN 0068-5208
- Cahiers ORSTOM. Serie Entomologie Medicale et
  Parasitologie. q. ISSN 0029-7224
- Cahiers ORSTOM. Serie Geologie. s-a. ISSN
  0029-7232
- Cahiers ORSTOM. Serie Hydrobiologie. q. ISSN
  0029-7240
- Cahiers ORSTOM. Serie Hydrologie. q. ISSN
  0008-0381
- Cahiers ORSTOM. Serie Oceanographie. q. ISSN
  0008-039X
- Cahiers ORSTOM. Serie Pedologie. q. ISSN
  0029-7259
- Cahiers ORSTOM. Serie Sciences Humaines. q.
  ISSN 0008-0403
- Memoires ORSTOM. irreg. ISSN 0071-9005
- Office de la Recherche Scientifique et Technique
  Outre-Mer. Initiations Documentations Techniques.
  irreg. ISSN 0071- 9021
- Office de la Recherche Scientifique et Technique
  Outre-Mer. Rapport d'Activite. irreg. ISSN 0071-9013
- ORSTOM. Annales Hydrologiques. a. ISSN 0071-8998

**Office de Publicite et d'Edition Lutetia**
1, Cite Bergere, 6 Faubourg Montmartre, 75009-
Paris, France.
- Journal des Tirages Financiers. fortn.

**Office de Tourisme de Paris**
- Paris Selection. (pub. by Societe de Presse et
  d'Editions Saint-Honore-Vacances 365 Jours)

**Office de Vulgarisation Pharmaceutique**
11 rue Quentin Bauchart, 75008-Paris, France.
- Dictionnaire Vidal. a. ISSN 0419-1153

**Office des Nouvelles Internationales**
12 rue de Miromesnil, 75008 Paris, France.
- Gazette Officielle de la Peche. 3 per m. ISSN
  0046-5542
- Gazette Officielle du Livre. 3 per mo.
- Gazette Officielle du Spectacle. 3 per m. ISSN
  0046-5550
- Gazette Officielle du Tourisme; bulletin
  d'information et de documentation sur le
  tourisme. every 10 days. ISSN 0016-5573

**Office Diocesain d'Information**
16 rue Brulee, 67081 Strasbourg, France.
- Eglise en Alsace. m. ISSN 0013-2330

**Office Francais de Presse Specialisee**
7, rue Rougemont, 75009 Paris, France.
- Developpement; marketing et communication. m.

**Office General de la Musique**
- Annuaire O. G. M. (pub. by Editions Louis
  Johanet)

**Office General de Presse et de Publicite**
48, rue de la Bienfaisance, 75008 Paris, France.
- Betons Industriels. q.

**Office International de la Vigne et du Vin**
11 rue Roquepine, 75008 Paris, France.
- Bulletin de l'O.I.V. m. ISSN 0029-7119
- Memento de l'O.I.V. quinquennial. ISSN 0085-221X

**Office International Oeuvres Formation Civique**
49 rue des Renaudes, Paris (17e), France.
- Permanences. 10 per yr. ISSN 0031-5478

**Office Publicitaire du Centre**
14 Place Jourdan, 87003 Limoges, France.
- Miroir du Centre; agricole, artistique, economique,
  universitaire. m. ISSN 0026-5810

**Office Technique pour l'Utilisation de l'Acier**
129 Avenue Charles de Gaulle, 92200 Neuilly,
Seine, France.
- Acier dans le Monde. bi-m. ISSN 0001-4931

**Office Universitaire de Recherche Socialiste**
86 rue de Lille, Paris 7e, France.
- Office Universitaire de Recherche Socialiste.
  Cahiers. m. ISSN 0078-3803

**Officiel de la Couture et de la Mode de Paris S.A.**
226 rue du Faubourg St. Honore, Paris, France.
- Officiel de la Couture et de la Mode de Paris. 10
  per yr. ISSN 0030-0403
- Officiel - Hommes (Men) bi-m.

**Officiel de la Photographie et du Cinema**
c/oCharles Vandamme, Ed., 7Bd. Anatole France,
92 Boulogne, France.
- Officiel de la Photographie et du Cinema. m.
  ISSN 0030-0438

**Officiel des Galeries**
15 rue du Temple, 75004 Paris, France.
- Officiel des Galeries. m.

**Officiel des Spectacles**
100 Champs-Elysees, Paris(8e), France.
- Officiel des Spectacles; cette semaine. w. ISSN
  0030-0500

**Officiel Francais des Guides d'Achets Professionnels**
138, Bd. Diderot, 75012 Paris, France.
- Guide d'Achats du Pret-a-Porter. q(public ed.); s-
  a(professional ed.)

**Officiel S.A.**
3-5 Allee Felix Eboue-l'Echat 951, 94024 Creteil
Cedex, France.
- Officiel; hebdomadaire de l'equipement menager.
  w. ISSN 0335-9956

**Oise Peasants Organizations**
7 rue du Musee, 60021 Beauvais, France.
- Oise Agricole. w. ISSN 0030-1523

**Opera, Subtitle**
16, bis rue Res Plantes, 75014 Paris, France.
- Opera, Subtitle; concert, disque, danse, son. bi-m.

**Diffusion Ophrys**
10 rue de Nesle, 75006 Paris, France.
- Collection Etudes et Travaux de la Revue
  "Mediterranee". irreg. ISSN 0069-5378
  (Universite d'Aix-Marseille I (Universite de
  Provence). Institut de Geographie)
- Presence Linguistique.
- Universite d'Aix-Marseille I. Centre d'Etudes des
  Societes Mediterraneennes. Cahiers. a. ISSN
  0065-4949
- Universite d'Aix-Marseille I. Centre d'Etudes et
  de Recherches Helleniques. Publications. irreg.
  ISSN 0065-4981
- Universite d'Aix-Marseille I. Faculte des Lettres
  et Sciences Humaines. Annales. a. ISSN 0065-4973

**Editions Opta**
39 rue d'Amsterdam, 75008 Paris, France.
- Positif. m. ISSN 0048-4911

**Oratoire de France**
75 rue de Vaugirard, Paris (6e), France.
- Oratoriana. s-a. ISSN 0030-4352

**Ordre des Architectes**
Conseil Superieur, 10 rue Portalis, Paris 8e, France.
- Dictionnaire National des Architectes. irreg. ISSN
  0078-5598

**Ordre des Experts Comptables et des Comptables
Agrees. Conseil Superieur**
109, Bd Malesherbes, 75008 Paris, France.
- Revue Francaise de Comptabilite. m. ISSN 0484-8764

**Ordre des Geometres Experts**
40 Av. Hoche, Paris (8e), France.
- Geometre. m. ISSN 0016-7967

- Ordre des Geometres-Experts. Annuaire. a. ISSN 0078-5601

**Ordre National des Chirurgiens- Dentistes. Conseil National**
22, rue Emile-Menier, Paris-16c, France.
- Ordre National des Chirurgiens- Dentistes. Conseil National. Bulletin Officiel. irreg.

**Ordre National des Medecins**
- Ordre National des Medecins. Bulletin. (pub. by Masson)

**Ordre National des Medicins. Conseil Departemental des Hauts-de-Seine**
- Ordre National des Medicins. Conseil Departemental des Hauts- de- Seine. Bulletin. (pub. by Societe d'Edition Medicale Europeenne)

**Organisakous Agricole**
30 rue Paul Ligneul, 72000 le Mans, France.
- Femmes au Village. m. ISSN 0014-9934

**Organisation Francaise du Mouvement Europeen**
24 rue Feydeau, 75 Paris (2e), France.
- Courrier Europeen. m. ISSN 0011-0574

**Organisation Revolutionnaire Anarchiste**
33 rue des Vignoles, Paris 20, France.
- Front Libertaire des Luttes de Classes. m.

**Organisation Sioniste de France**
47 rue de Chabrol, Paris, France.
- Sioniste. m. ISSN 0049-061X

**Organisme Professionnel de Prevention du Batiment et des Travaux Publiques**
2 Bis, rue Michelet, 92130 Issy-les-Moulineaux, France.
- Comites de Prevention du Batiment et des Travaux Publics. Cahiers. bi-m. ISSN 0010-244X
- Sauvegarde des Chantiers. bi-m. ISSN 0036-505X

**Organization for Economic Cooperation and Development**
2 rue Andre-Pascal, 75775 Paris 16, France
(U.S. orders to: O.E.C.D. Publications Center, 1750 Pennsylvania Ave. N.W., Washington, DC 20006)
- Annual Reports on Competition Policy in O E C D Member Countries. irreg. ISSN 0300-1547
- Directory of Development Research and Training Institutes. irreg. (prep. by its Development Centre)
- Directory of Water Pollution Research Laboratories. irreg. ISSN 0419-3865 (prep. by its Central Service for International Cooperation in Scientific Research)
- Educational Statistics Yearbook. a.
- Engineering Industries in O E C D Member Countries: New Basic Statistics. a.
- Food Consumption in the O. E. C. D. Countries/ Consommation de Denrees Alimentaires dans les Pays de l'O.C.D.E. irreg. ISSN 0474-537X
- Hides, Skins and Footwear Industry in O E C D Countries/Industrie des Cuirs et Peaux et de la Chassure dans les Pays de l'OCDE. irreg. ISSN 0474-585X
- List of Research Institutes and Scientists in O. E. C. D. Member Countries. irreg. ISSN 0078-6292
- News from O E C D.
- O E C D Economic Outlook. s-a. ISSN 0029-7011
- O E C D Financial Statistics/Statistiques Financieres de l'OCDE. a. with 5 updating supplements and monthly supplements on interest rates. ISSN 0048-2188
- O E C D Informatics Studies Series. irreg.
- O E C D Observer. bi-m. ISSN 0029-7054
- Organization for Economic Cooperation and Development. Activities of O E C D: Report by the Secretary General. a.
- Organization for Economic Cooperation and Development. Annual Reports on Consumer Policy in O E C D Member Countries. a.
- Organization for Economic Cooperation and Development. Catalogue of Publications. biennial. ISSN 0474-5086
- Organization for Economic Cooperation and Development. Cement Industry. Industrie du Ciment. irreg. ISSN 0474-5493
- Organization for Economic Cooperation and Development. Committee for Scientific Research. Bulletin. irreg. ISSN 0474-5647

- Organization for Economic Cooperation and Development. Council. Code de la Liberation des Mouvements de Capitaux. Code of Liberalisation of Capital Movements. irreg. ISSN 0474-5655
- Organization for Economic Cooperation and Development. Development Assistance Committee. Report by the Chairman on the Annual Review. a. ISSN 0474-5663
- Organization for Economic Cooperation and Development. Development Cooperation; efforts and policies of the members of the Development Assistance Committee. a.
- Organization for Economic Cooperation and Development. Development Centre. Employment Series. irreg.
- Organization for Economic Cooperation and Development. Economic Surveys: Australia. irreg.
- Organization for Economic Cooperation and Development. Economic Surveys: Austria. irreg. ISSN 0474-5124
- Organization for Economic Cooperation and Development. Economic Surveys: Belgium-Luxembourg Economic Union. irreg. ISSN 0474-5132
- Organization for Economic Cooperation and Development. Economic Surveys: Canada. irreg. ISSN 0474-5140
- Organization for Economic Cooperation and Development. Economic Surveys: Denmark. irreg. ISSN 0474-5159
- Organization for Economic Cooperation and Development. Economic Surveys: France. irreg. ISSN 0474-5167
- Organization for Economic Cooperation and Development. Economic Surveys: Greece. irreg. ISSN 0474-5183
- Organization for Economic Cooperation and Development. Economic Surveys: Germany. ISSN 0474-5175
- Organization for Economic Cooperation and Development. Economic Surveys: Ireland. irreg. ISSN 0474-5205
- Organization for Economic Cooperation and Development. Economic Surveys: Iceland. a. ISSN 0474-5191
- Organization for Economic Cooperation and Development. Economic Surveys: Italy. irreg. ISSN 0474-5213
- Organization for Economic Cooperation and Development. Economic Surveys: Japan. irreg. ISSN 0474-5221
- Organization for Economic Cooperation and Development. Economic Surveys: Norway. irreg. ISSN 0474-5248
- Organization for Economic Cooperation and Development. Economic Surveys: Netherlands. irreg. ISSN 0474-523X
- Organization for Economic Cooperation and Development. Economic Surveys: Portugal. irreg. ISSN 0474-5256
- Organization for Economic Cooperation and Development. Economic Surveys: Socialist Federal Republic of Yugoslavia. irreg. ISSN 0474-5264
- Organization for Economic Cooperation and Development. Economic Surveys: Spain. irreg. ISSN 0474-5272
- Organization for Economic Cooperation and Development. Economic Surveys: Sweden. irreg. ISSN 0474-5280
- Organization for Economic Cooperation and Development. Economic Surveys: Switzerland. irreg. ISSN 0474-5299
- Organization for Economic Cooperation and Development. Economic Surveys: Turkey. irreg. ISSN 0474-5302
- Organization for Economic Cooperation and Development. Economic Surveys: United Kingdom. irreg. ISSN 0474-5310
- Organization for Economic Cooperation and Development. Economic Surveys: United States. irreg. ISSN 0474-5329
- Organization for Economic Cooperation and Development. Electricity Supply Industry. l'Industrie de l'Electricite. irreg. ISSN 0474-5477
- Organization for Economic Cooperation and Development. Employment of Special Groups. irreg. ISSN 0474-5337
- Organization for Economic Cooperation and Development. Guide to Legislation on Restrictive Business Practices. Supplements. 2 per yr.
- Organization for Economic Cooperation and Development. Historical Statistics. Statistiques Retrospectives. irreg. ISSN 0474-5442
- Organization for Economic Cooperation and Development. Industrial Production. Production Industrielle. irreg. ISSN 0474-5450

- Organization for Economic Cooperation and Development. Industrial Statistics. Statistiques Industrielles. irreg. ISSN 0474-5469
- Organization for Economic Cooperation and Development. Inter-Regional Dry Cargo Movements/Mouvements Interregionaux de Cargaisons Seches. irreg.
- Organization for Economic Cooperation and Development. Labour Force Statistics. Statistiques de la Population Active. irreg. ISSN 0474-5515
- Organization for Economic Cooperation and Development. Liaison Bulletin Between Research and Training Institutes. q. ISSN 0029-7038
- Organization for Economic Cooperation and Development. Library. Catalogue of Periodicals/ Catalogue des Periodiques. a.
- Organization for Economic Cooperation and Development. Library. Ouvrages et Periodiques Nouveaux Catalogues a la Bibliotheque/New Books and Periodicals Catalogued at the Library. m.
- Organization for Economic Cooperation and Development. Library. Special Annotated Bibliography; Automation. Bibliographie Speciale Analytique. irreg. ISSN 0474-5868
- Organization for Economic Cooperation and Development. Main Economic Indicators/ Principaux Indicateurs Economiques. m. ISSN 0029-7046
- Organization for Economic Cooperation and Development. Maritime Transport Committee. Maritime Transport. irreg. ISSN 0474-5884
- Organization for Economic Cooperation and Development. Provisional Oil Statistics/ Statistiques Petrolieres Provisoires. q. ISSN 0029-7062
- Organization for Economic Cooperation and Development. Revenue Statistics of OECD Member Countries. a.
- Organization for Economic Cooperation and Development. Reviews of Manpower and Social Policies. irreg. ISSN 0473-6788
- Organization for Economic Cooperation and Development. Social Affairs Division. Developing Job Opportunities. irreg. ISSN 0474-5892
- Organization for Economic Cooperation and Development. Social Affairs Division. Employment of Special Groups. irreg. ISSN 0474-5922
- Organization for Economic Cooperation and Development. Special Committee for Iron and Steel. Iron and Steel Industry. irreg. ISSN 0474-5973
- Organization for Economic Cooperation and Development. Special Committee for Oil. Oil Statistics. Supply and Disposal. irreg. ISSN 0474-6007
- Organization for Economic Cooperation and Development. Statistics of Energy. a.
- Organization for Economic Cooperation and Development. Statistics of Foreign Trade. Series A: Monthly Bulletin/Statistiques du Commerce Exterieur. Serie A: Bulletin Mensuel. m.
- Organization for Economic Cooperation and Development. Statistics of Foreign Trade. Series B: Trade by Commodities. Country Summaries/ Statistiques du Commerce Exterieur. Serie B: Exchanges Par Produits Resume Par Pays. q.
- Organization for Economic Cooperation and Development. Statistics of Foreign Trade. Series C: Trade by Commodities. Market Summaries. Imports and Exports/Statistiques du Commerce Exterieur. Serie C: Exchanges Par Produits. Resume Par Marches. Importations et Exportations. a.
- Organization for Economic Cooperation and Development. Tourism Committee. Tourism Policy and International Tourism in OE C D Member Countries. irreg.
- Organization for Economic Cooperation and Development. Wages and Labour Mobility Supplement. irreg. ISSN 0474-5620
- Pulp and Paper Industry in the O E C D Member Countries and Finland/Industrie des Pates et Papiers dans les Pays Membres de l'OCDE et la Finlande. irreg. ISSN 0474-5485
- Recherche en Matiere d'Economie des Transports/Research on Transport Economics. s-a. ISSN 0048-6922 (European Conference of Ministers of Transport)
- Review of Fisheries in OECD Member Countries. a. ISSN 0078-6241
- Textile Industry in O E C D Countries. irreg. ISSN 0474-6023

**Organization for Economic Cooperation and Development. Nuclear Energy Agency**
38 Bd. Suchet, 75016 Paris, France
(U.S. Orders to: O.E.C.D. Publications Centers, Suite 1207, 1750 Pennsylvania Ave., Washington, DC 20006)
- Nuclear Law Bulletin. s-a. ISSN 0550-3132
- O E C D. Newsletter on Isotopic Generators and Batteries; information bulletin on isotopic generators and batteries. irreg.
- O E C D Halden Reactor Project. a. no report in 1963. ISSN 0078-6284
- O E C D High Temperature Reactor Project Dragon. a. ISSN 0078-6276
- Organization for Economic Cooperation and Development. Nuclear Energy Agency. Activity Report. a. ISSN 0078-625X
- Uranium: Resources, Production and Demand. irreg. ISSN 0474-5833 (Co-Sponsor: International Atomic Energy Agency)

**Orphelinat Mutualiste de la Police Nationale**
19, rue du Renard, 75004 Paris, France.
- Orphelinat. m.

**Ouest Industriel, Maritime, Agricole et Commercial**
106 Blvd Malesherbes, Paris (17e), France.
- Ouest Industriel, Maritime, Agricole et Commercial. m. ISSN 0030-6754

**Editions Ouranos**
12bis, rue Jean-Jaures, 92807 Puteaux, France.
- Medecine et Chirurgie Digestives. 8 per yr. ISSN 0047-6412

**Editions P.B.M.**
164, Faubourg Saint-Honore, 75-Paris (8e), France.
- Droguerie Francaise la Couleur. m. (Federation Nationale des Syndicats de Droguistes)

**P. C. M.**
17, Faubourg Montmartre, 75009 Paris, France.
- Mr. q.
- Officiel des Textiles (Ameublement) s-a.
- Officiel des Textiles (Habillement) s-a.
- Officiel du Pret a Porter. q. ISSN 0040-5221

**P E M F**
B.P. 282, 06403 Cannes Cedex, France.
- Art Enfantin. q. ISSN 0004-3133

**P.R.E.E.S.**
17 Faubourg Montmartre, Paris 9, France.
- Art et la Mode. q.

**P Y C Edition**
254 rue de Vaugirard, 75740 Paris Cedex 15, France.
- Chauffage - Ventilation - Conditionnement. 9 per yr. ISSN 0009-2029 (Association des Ingenieurs de Chauffage et de Ventilation de France)
- Genie Rural; revue de l'amenagement et de l'equipement du milieu, rural. m. ISSN 0016-6847
- I V F - Ingenieurs des Villes de France. m. ISSN 0336-4410 (Association des Ingenieurs des Villes de France)
- Revue Pratique du Froid et du Conditionnement d'Air. fortn., 22 per yr.
- Traitement Thermique/Heat Treatment. m. ISSN 0041-0950
- Travail des Metaux Par Deformation; forge-formage-emboutissage-techniques annexes. bi-m.

**Imprimerie F. Paillart**
B.P. 107, 75022 Paris Cedex 01, France
- Revue Francaise d'Histoire d'Outre-Mer. q. (Societe Francaise d'Histoire d'Outre-Mer) (Subscr.to: Librairie Orientaliste Paul Geuthner, 12 rue Vavin, Paris, France)

**Palaeovertebrata**
Laboratoire de Paleontologie, Place E. Bataillon, 34060 Montpellier, France.
- Palaeovertebrata. q. ISSN 0031-0247

**Palais de la Decouverte**
Avenue Franklin-Roosevelt, 75008 Paris, France.
- Palais de la Decouverte, Paris. Revue. m.

**Librairie Palestine**
24 rue de la Reunion, Paris 75020, France.
- Palestine Informations. w.

**Panorama de la Mode**
29, rue de Versailles, 78460 Chevreuse, France.
- Panorama de la Mode. q.

**Panorama de la Musique**
20, Avenue Kleber, 75116 Paris, France.
- Panorama de la Musique et des Instruments. m.

**Par les Loisirs et le Tourisme**
12, rue du Parc-Royal, 75003 Paris, France.
- Tourisme-Loisirs-Environnement. m (10 per yr)

**Paris-Bijoux Exportation**
62 rue Beaubourg, Paris 3e, France.
- Paris-Bijoux Exportation. a. ISSN 0078-9496

**Paris-Cote-d'Azur**
2, rue Auber, 06400 Cannes, France.
- Paris-Cote-d'Azur. bi-m.

**Paris Match**
63, Champs-Elysees, 75360 Paris Cedex 08, France.
- Paris Match. w.

**Paris Regie**
28 rue du Sentier, 75002 Paris, France.
- Journal des Medecins du Nord & de l'Est. 11 per yr. ISSN 0021-8081

**Pariser Kurier**
42 Avenue George V, 75008 Paris, France.
- Pariser Kurier; Deutsche Zeitung in Frankreich periodique Allemand bilingue. fortn. ISSN 0031-2053

**Parti Communiste Francais. Comite Central**
2, Place du Colonel Fabien, Paris 19e, France.
- Cahiers du Communisme. 11 per yr. ISSN 0008-0136

**Parti Nationaliste Occitan**
B.P. 232, 87006 Limoges, France.
- Lu Lugar. q.

**Parti Socialiste et Cercle d'Etudes Socialistes Jean Jaures**
E. Weill-Raynal, 16 rue Vigee-Lebrun, Paris (15e), France.
- Revue Socialiste; revue de culture politique et sociale. m. ISSN 0035-4139

**Parti Socialiste Unifie**
9 Rue Borromee, Paris (15e), France.
- Critique Socialiste. (pub. by Editions Syrus)
- Tribune Socialiste. w. ISSN 0049-4674

**Particulier**
21 Bd. Montmartre, 75082 Paris 2, France.
- Particulier; la documentation pratique des chefs de famille. 2 per m. ISSN 0031-2495

**Partir**
c/o Ed. Michel Burton, 32 rue d'Hauteville, 75010 Paris, France.
- Partir. m.

**Pax Christi International. French Section**
- Journal de la Paix - Pax Christi. (pub. by Association Pax Christi)

**Editions Payot**
106 Bd. Saint-Germain, Paris 6e, France.
- Bibliotheque Historique. irreg.

**Paysan du Midi**
B.P.1098, 34007 Montpellier, France.
- Bulletin d'Information des Piziculteurs de France. q.

**Pecheurs d'Hommes**
6 Place Bellecour, Lyon (2e), France.
- Pecheurs d'Hommes; lien d'apostolat par l'amitie. q. ISSN 0031-3742

**Pediatre Parisien SARL**
20, rue Valiton, 92110 Clichy, France.
- Pediatre. q. (Co-Sponsors: Groupement des Pediatres; Cercle d'Etudes Pediatriques)

**Editions A. Pedone**
13, rue Soufflot, 75005 Paris, France.
- Annales Africaines. a. ISSN 0066-202X
- Annee Africaine. a. ISSN 0570-1937 (Universite de Bordeaux III. Centre d'Etude d'Afrique Noire)
- Archives de Politique Criminelle. irreg. (Centre de Recherches de Politique Criminelle)
- Petite Histoire des Consulats. irreg. ISSN 0079-1261
- Revue d'Histoire Diplomatique. q. ISSN 0035-2365
- Revue des Droits de l'Homme/Human Rights Journal. q. ISSN 0035-1989

- Revue Generale de Droit International Public; droit des gens, histoire diplomatique, droit penal, droit fiscal, droit administratif. q. ISSN 0035-3094
- Serie Afrique Noire. irreg. ISSN 0080-8938

**Pense et Lutte**
8 Place Jacques-Bonsergent, Paris (10e), France.
- Pense et Lutte. m.

**Pensee Nationale**
4 bis rue Antoine, Bourdelle, 75015 Paris, France.
- Pensee Nationale. bi-m.

**Pepinieristes Horticulteurs Maraichers**
59 rue du Faubourg Poissonniere, Paris (9e), France.
- P.H.M.-Revue Horticole. 10 per yr.
- Pepinieristes Horticulteurs Maraichers; revue horticole. 10 per yr. ISSN 0031-5087

**Periodiques Parisiens**
150 Champs Elysees, 75008 Paris, France.
- Annuaire Deschaliers. a.

**Permanent and International Committee of Underground Town Planning and Construction**
94 rue Saint-Lazare, 75 Paris 9e, France.
- International Congress on Underground Techniques and Town-Planning. Reports. irreg., 1969, 5th, Madrid. ISSN 0074-4204

**Permanent International Association of Road Congresses**
43 Av. du President-Wilson, 75116 Paris, France.
- Association Internationale Permanente des Congres de la Route. Bulletin. 4 per yr. ISSN 0004-556X
- International Road Congresses. Proceedings. quadrennial since 1964; 1975, 15th, Mexico. ISSN 0074-7815

**Permanent International Committee on Canned Foods**
3 rue de Logelbach, 75017 Paris, France.
- International Congress on Canned Foods. Report. irreg., 6th, 1972, Paris. ISSN 0074-4034

**Editions G. M. Perrin**
108, Ave. Ledru-Rollin, 75011 Paris, France.
- Constructions Metalliques-Serrurerie. m.
- Installateur; amenagement de la cuisine et de la salle de bain. m(11 per yr.)
- Installateur; chauffage, plomberie, couverture, genie climatique. m. ISSN 0020-207X
- Officiel de l'Ameublement; Ameublement Informations. m. ISSN 0030-0446
- Quincailliers de France-l'Argus Menager. m.
- S D A I; syndicat de la distribution pour l'automobile et l'industrie. a. (Syndicat National de la Distribution pour l'Automobile et l'Industrie)
- Serrurerie Constructions Metalliques. m. ISSN 0037-2528
- Table et Cadeau. m. ISSN 0039-8780 (National China and Glass Federation of France)

**Petroleum Mirror**
50 rue Stanislas Torrent, 13 Marseille (6e), France.
- Petroleum Mirror; for the French oil and gas industry. m. ISSN 0031-6482

**Editions Peuples Amis**
13 rue Paul-Lelong, 75 Paris (2e), France.
- France-Pologne, Peuples Amis. q. ISSN 0015-9700

**Pharmacien de Reserve**
1 rue Desnovettes, Paris (15e), France.
- Pharmacien de Reserve. q. ISSN 0031-6946

**Pharmacien Rural**
67 Route de Chateau Thierry, Belleu, 02 Soissons, France.
- Pharmacien Rural. 5 per yr. Special no. ISSN 0031-6954

**Philaprint**
7 rue du Docteur-Belot, 76600 le Havre, France.
- Echangiste Universel. m.

**Editions A. et J. Picard**
82 rue Bonaparte, 75006 Paris, France.
- Archeocivilisation; etudes d'energologie culturelle. s-a. ISSN 0003-8156 (Ecole Pratique des Hautes Etudes. Centre d'Etudes Pre- et Protohistoriques)
- Etudes Picardes. irreg., 1969, no. 3. ISSN 0071-2140 (Societe d'Emulation Historique et Litteraire d'Abbeville)
- Recherches sur la Musique Francaise Classique. a. ISSN 0080-0139

- Vie Musicale en France Sous les Rois Bourbons.
  Serie 1: Etudes. irreg., 1975, vol. 23. ISSN 0083-6109
- Vie Musicale en France Sous les Rois Bourbons.
  Serie 2: Recherches sur la Musique Classique
  Francaise. a. ISSN 0083-6117

**Pinatel**
97 rue Saint Honore, 75001 Paris, France.
- Trait; revue dessinee. 5 per yr. ISSN 0041-0942

**Philippe Pinquier**
B.P. 246-08, Paris (8e), France.
- Observateur Europeen. m. ISSN 0048-1327

**Plaisir de France**
40 rue du Colisee, Paris (8e), France.
- Plaisir de France. m. ISSN 0032-048X

**Editions Plan et But**
8 rue de la Michodiere, 75002 Paris, France.
- Acheteurs; documentation technique sur les
  problemes d'approvisionnement dans l'industrie.
  m. ISSN 0001-4893
- France Graphique. m. ISSN 0015-9565
- Maintenance; revue d'etude des problemes de
  fiabilite, entretien et securite des equipements
  industriels. m. ISSN 0025-0880

**Plein Chant**
c/o Edmond Thomas, Ed., Bassac, 16120
Chateauneuf sur Charente, France.
- Plein Chant; cahiers poetiques, litteraires et
  champetres. q.

**Pneumatique**
94, rue Saint-Lazare, 75442 Paris Cedex 09, France.
- Pneumatique; publication d'education et de
  defense professionnelle. 5 per yr.

**Poesie**
184 Bd. Saint Germain, Paris (6e), France.
- Poesie; la poesie francaise de Belgique. m. ISSN
  0048-4555

**Point Veterinaire**
12, rue de Marseille, 94700 Maisons-Alfort, France.
- Point Veterinaire. 8 per yr.

**Points et Contrepoints**
19 rue Gerando, Paris (9e), France.
- Points et Contrepoints. q. ISSN 0032-2369

**Police**
8 rue Saint Martin, 75180 Paris, France.
- Police. m. ISSN 0048-8119

**Politique Hebdo**
14-16 rue Petits-Hotels, 75010 Paris, France.
- Politique Hebdo. w.

**Pollustop**
4 rue Leneveux, 75014 Paris, France.
- Pollustop. m. ISSN 0300-3574

**Pomme de Terre Francaise**
14 Rue Cardinal Mercier, 75009 Paris, France.
- Pomme de Terre Francaise. bi-m. ISSN 0032-4159

**Pompadour Notariat 2000**
19230 Pompadour, France.
- Pompadour Notariat 2000; revue independant
  d'animation et de promotion du notariat francais.
  m.

**Port Autonome du Havre**
Terre Plein de la Barre, 76067-le Havre, France
- Escale; revue de personnel du Port Autonome du
  Havre. m.
- Port of le Havre Flashes. m. (U.S. Orders to:
  Port of le Havre Authority, One World Trade
  Center, Suite 2551, New York, N.Y. 10048)

**Port of le Havre Authority**
*see* Port Autonome du Havre

**Portugal Liberation Front (FPL)**
Boite Postale 90, 75962 Paris, France.
- Portugal Libre; la voix libre du peuple portugais. 6
  per yr. ISSN 0032-5104

**Pour la Vie**
28 Place Saint-Georges, Paris (9e), France.
- Pour la Vie; revue d'etudes familiales. q. ISSN
  0032-583X

**Prefecture de Police de Paris**
9 Bd. du Palais, 75195 Paris, France.
- Liaisons; revue d'information et de relations
  publiques. m. ISSN 0024-1717

**Prefecture de Police de Paris. Laboratoire Central**
39 bis rue de Dantzig, 75015 Paris 15e, France.
- Etudes de Pollution Atmospherique a Paris et
  dans les Departments Peripheriques. a. ISSN
  0071-1942

**Julien Prelat**
17 rue du Petit-Pont, 75005 Paris, France.
- Academie de Chirurgie Dentaire. Bulletin. 1-2 per
  yr.
- Actualites Odonto-Stomatologiques. 4 per yr.
  ISSN 0001-7817
- Orthodontie Francaise. a. ISSN 0078-6608
- Revue d'Orthopedie Dento-Faciale. q. ISSN 0337-9736 (Association de la Revue d'Orthopedie
  Dento-Faciale)

**Premiere Imprimerie Ukrainienne en France**
3, rue du Sabot, 75006 Paris, France.
- A D U K. (Adresar Ukraintsiv u Vilnomu Sviti)
  irreg.
- Parole Ukrainienne. w.

**Prensa Latina, Agencia Informativa Latinoamericana**
10 rue Talma, 75766 Paris Cedex 16, France.
- Direct from Cuba. s-m. ISSN 0046-0338
- Latin American Roundup. s-w.
- P. E. L. (Panorama Economico Latinamericano)
  bi-m. ISSN 0030-7920

**Presence du Cinema**
25 Passage des Princes, Paris (2e), France.
- Presence du Cinema. m. ISSN 0032-7662

**Presence, S.A.R.L.**
Barberaz, 73 Chambery, France.
- Presence. bi-m. ISSN 0032-762X

**Presence Socialiste**
B.P. 331, 75626 Paris Cedex 13, France.
- Presence Socialiste. m.

**Presse Corporative Francaise**
5 rue d'Argout, Paris (2e), France.
- Boulanger-Patissier. m. ISSN 0006-8292
- Patisserie Francaise Illustree. m. ISSN 0031-3068
- Patissier de l'Ile-De-France. m. ISSN 0031-3076
  (Syndicat des Patissiers de la Region de Paris)

**Presse et Information**
140 rue de Rennes, 75006 Paris, France.
- Point. w.

**Presse Immobiliere**
11 Quai Anatole-France, 75007 Paris, France.
- Information Immobiliere. m. ISSN 0046-936X

**La Presse Libre**
217 rue du Faubourg St. Honore, 75008 Paris,
France.
- Pensee Russe. w.

**Presse Periodique Professionnelle**
14 Bd. Montmartre, 75 Paris (9e), France.
- Revue Generale de l'Hotellerie, de la Gastronomie
  et du Tourisme. m. ISSN 0035-3140

**Editions Presse Professionnelle**
3 Cite d'Hauteville, 75010 Paris, France.
- Bonne Cuisine; a la portee de tous. bi-m. ISSN
  0006-713X
- Market. m. ISSN 0025-3537

**Edition Presse Specialisee**
28 Rue de Richelieu, Paris (1er), France.
- Bridgeur. m. ISSN 0006-9914

**Editions Presselec**
5, rue Hamelin, 75116 Paris, France.
- Journal des Electriciens. m.

**Presses Continentales**
73 rue du Cherche-Midi, Paris 75006, France.
- Double Liaison; chimie des peintures. m. ISSN
  0012-5709 (Association Francaise des Techniciens
  des Peintures, Vernis, Encres d'Imprimerie, Colles
  et Adhesifs)

**Presses d'Europe**
6 rue de Trevise, 75009 Paris, France.
- Europe en Formation. m. ISSN 0014-2808
- Regions. irreg. ISSN 0080-0643

**Presses de l'Ecole Normale Superieure**
45, rue d'Ulm, 75230 Paris Cedex 05, France.
- Bulletin d'Information Proustienne. s-a. (Co-sponsors: Centre National de la Recherche
  Scientifique; Centre d'Histoire et d'Analyse des
  Manuscrits Moderne)

**Presses de la Fondation Nationale des Sciences
Politiques**
27 rue Saint-Guillaume, 75341 Paris Cedex 07,
France.
- Bibliographies Francaises de Sciences Sociales.
  (Fondation Nationale des Sciences Politiques)
- Bulletin Analytique de Documentation Politique,
  Economique et Sociale Contemporaine. m. ISSN
  0007-4071 (Fondation Nationale des Sciences
  Politiques)
- Fondation Nationale des Sciences Politiques.
  Cahiers. irreg., no. 175, 1969. (Fondation
  Nationale des Sciences Politiques)
- Fondation Nationale des Sciences Politiques.
  Textes et Documents de Sciences Sociales. irreg.
- Fondation Nationale des Sciences Politiques.
  Trauvaux et Recherches de Sciences
  Economiques. irreg., no. 17, 1971.
- Fondation Nationale des Sciences Politiques.
  Trauvaux et Recherches de Science Politique.
  irreg., no. 15, 1971.
- Guide Sommaire des Ouvrages de Reference en
  Sciences Sociales. irreg. ISSN 0072-8217
  (Fondation Nationale des Sciences Politiques)
- Revue Economique. bi-m. ISSN 0035-2764
- Revue Francaise de Science Politique. bi-m. ISSN
  0035-2950 (Fondation Nationale des Sciences
  Politiques) (Co-Sponsor: Association Francaise de
  Science Politique)

**Presses de la Tour Saint-Jacques**
9 rue Nicolas-Flamel, 75004 Paris, France.
- Unions Sexuelles; le premier magazine francais
  d'information sexuelle totale. m. ISSN 0397-0280

**Presses du Palais Royal**
49 Galerie Vivienne, Paris 2e, France.
- College de France. Annuaire. a. ISSN 0069-5580

**Presses du Temps Present**
18-20 Fg. du Temple, Paris (11e), France.
- Eurographie; les procedes de reproduction, leurs
  applications publicitaires et industrielles. bi-m.
  ISSN 0014-2417

**Presses Universitaires de France**
Service des Periodiques, 12 rue Jean- de- Beauvais,
75005 Paris, France.
- Annales Moreau de Tours. irreg. ISSN 0066-2186
- Annee Epigraphique; Revue des Publications
  Epigraphiques Relatives a l'Antiquite Romaine. a.
  ISSN 0066-2348 (Academie des Inscriptions et
  Belles-Lettres)
- Annee Psychologique. s-a. ISSN 0003-5033
- Annee Sociologique. a. ISSN 0066-2399
- Banque des Mots. irreg. ISSN 0067-3951
- Cahiers Internationaux de Sociologie. s-a. ISSN
  0008-0276
- Caracterologie. s-a. ISSN 0084-859X
- College de France. Institut des Hautes Etudes
  Chinoises. Memoirs. irreg.
- Colloque de Metallurgie. a. ISSN 0069-5807
- Demographie et Sciences Humaines. irreg. ISSN
  0070-3354 (France. Institut National d'Etudes
  Demographiques)
- Etudes Philosophiques. q. ISSN 0014-2166
- Institut des Etudes Occitanes. Publications. irreg.
  ISSN 0073-8263
- Institut des Hautes Etudes Scientifiques, Paris.
  Publications Mathematiques. a. ISSN 0073-8301
- International Conference on Shielding Around
  High Energy Accelerators. Papers. irreg. ISSN
  0534-8811
- Journal de Psychologie Normale et Pathologique.
  4 per yr. ISSN 0021-7956
- Linguistique. s-a. ISSN 0024-3957
- Litteratures Anciennes. irreg. ISSN 0069-5459
- Maison Franco-Japonaise. Bulletin. irreg. (approx.
  every 2-3 yrs.) ISSN 0495-7725
- Musee Guimet, Paris. Bibliotheque d'Etudes. irreg.
  ISSN 0078-9704
- Musee Guimet, Paris. Etude des Collections du
  Musee. irreg. ISSN 0078-9712
- Poetes et Prosateurs du Portugal. irreg. ISSN
  0079-2470 (Fondation Calouste Gulbenkian)

- Psychiatrie de l'Enfant. a.(in 2 issues) ISSN 0079-726X
- Recherches et Documents d'Art et d'Archeologie. irreg. ISSN 0080-0074 (Musee Guimet. Paris)
- Revue Archeologique. s-a. ISSN 0035-0737
- Revue d'Assyriologie et d'Archeologie Orientale. s-a.
- Revue d'Histoire de la Deuxieme Guerre Mondiale. q. ISSN 0035-2314
- Revue d'Histoire des Sciences et de Leurs Applications. q. ISSN 0048-7996 (Centre International de Synthese)
- Revue de l'Histoire des Religions. q. ISSN 0035-1423
- Revue Francaise de Psychanalyse. bi-m. ISSN 0035-2942 (Societe Psychanalytique de Paris)
- Revue Historique. q. ISSN 0035-3264
- Revue Philosophique de la France et de l'Etranger. q. ISSN 0035-3833
- Systemes-Decisions. Section II. Gestion Financiere et Comptabilite. irreg. ISSN 0082-1209
- Tiers Monde. q. ISSN 0040-7356 (Institut d'Etude du Developpement Economique et Social)
- Travail Humain. s-a. ISSN 0041-1868
- Universite de Dakar. Faculte des Lettres et Sciences Humaines. Annales. a.
- Universite de Paris. Faculte des Lettres et Sciences Humaines. Publications. Serie Acta. irreg. ISSN 0078-9887
- Universite de Paris. Faculte des Lettres et Sciences Humaines. Publications. Serie Recherches. irreg. ISSN 0078-9895

**Presses Universitaires de Grenoble**
Cite Gabriel Peri, Esc. 6, 93200 Saint Denis, France.
- Annuaire International des Dix-Huitiemistes. a. ISSN 0066-3247 (Societe Francaise d'Etude du Dix Huitieme Siecle)

**Pretres Diocesains**
179 rue de Tolbiac, 75013- Paris, France.
- Pretres Diocesains. m. ISSN 0032-7956

**Prevention Routiere dans l'Entreprise**
55 rue le Marois, 75016 Paris, France.
- Prevention Routiere dans l'Entreprise. bi-m. ISSN 0032-8030

**Editions Edouard Privat**
14 rue des Arts, 31-Toulouse 01, France.
- Annales du Midi; revue de la France Meridionale. q. ISSN 0003-4398
- Evolution Psychiatrique; cahiers de psychologie clinique et de psychopathologie generale. q. ISSN 0014-3855
- Information Psychiatrique.
- Revue de Medecine Psychosomatique. q. ISSN 0035-1547 (Societe Francaise de Medecine Psychosomatique)

**Procedes et Equipements Electroniques**
25 Rue Louis-Le-Grand, Paris (2e), France.
- Procedes et Equipements Electroniques. bi-m. ISSN 0032-955X

**Procure des Missions du Levant**
32 rue Boissonade, 75014 Paris, France.
- Missions. Messages. bi-m. ISSN 0026-6124

**Production et Gestion**
27-29 rue de Bassano, 75008 Paris, France.
- Production et Gestion. m.

**Professeurs de l'Ancienne Faculte de Medecine d'Alger**
- Antenne Medicale. (pub. by Societe C. R. E. N. A. F.)

**Profils Poetiques des Pays Latins**
c/o Henri Barbier, Ed., 86 Bd. de Cessole, Nice, France.
- Profils Poetiques des Pays Latins. q. ISSN 0033-0264

**Editions Programme**
20, rue Jean Bouton, 75012 Paris, France.
- Communist Program. q. (International Communist Party)
- Programme Communiste. q. ISSN 0033-037X (International Communist Party)
- Proletaire. fortn. ISSN 0033-0981 (International Communist Party)

**Progres Agricole et Viticole**
1, bis, R. de Verdun, 34-Montpellier, France.
- Progres Agricole et Viticole. bi-m.

**Progres Medical**
3 rue de Fleurus, 75006 Paris, France.
- Progres Medical. 10 per yr. ISSN 0033-0450

**Promapress**
28, rue Bayard, 75008 Paris, France.
- Circuits Culture. 10 per yr.
- Circuits Jardin. m.

**Promethee**
c/o Ed. Octave Prour, B. P. 166-10, 75463 Paris Cedex 10, France.
- Promethee; magazine bimestriel de creation et de recherches de la pensee. bi-m.

**Promodis**
18 rue Dauphine, 75006 Paris, France.
- Bulletin du Livre. 30 per yr. ISSN 0007-456X

**Promotion-Presse-Internationale (P.P.I.)**
7, Cour des Petites-Ecuries, Paris 75010, France.
- I.D. (Importation et Diffusion) 10 per yr.
- Promofluid. 10 per yr.

**Propagation de la Foi**
12 rue Sala, 69287 Lyon Cedex 1, France.
- Solidaires. q.

**Prospecta**
89 rue de Monceau, 75008 Paris, France.
- Ain Agricole. w. ISSN 0002-2136

**Prospective Medicale**
40, rue Paul-Valery, 75116 Paris, France.
- Annuaire National des Specialistes en Gynecologie-Obstetrique et des Competents Exlusifs en Gynecologie et Obstetrique. irreg. ISSN 0066-3395
- Annuaire National des Specialistes Qualifies en Chirurgie. irreg. ISSN 0066-3417
- Annuaire National des Specialistes Qualifies Exclusifs des Maladies de l'Appareil Digestif. a. ISSN 0066-3425
- Annuaire National des Specialistes Qualifies Exclusifs en Cardiologie. a. ISSN 0066-3441
- Annuaire National des Specialistes Qualifies Exclusifs en Dermatologie et Venereologie. a. ISSN 0066-345X
- Annuaire National des Specialistes Qualifies Exclusifs en Electroradiologie. irreg. ISSN 0066-3468
- Annuaire National des Specialistes Qualifies Exclusifs en Neuropsychiatrie. irreg. ISSN 0066-3476
- Annuaire National des Specialistes Qualifies Exclusifs en Ophtalmologie. irreg. ISSN 0066-3506
- Annuaire National des Specialistes Qualifies Exclusifs en Pediatrie. a. ISSN 0066-3514
- Annuaire National des Specialistes Qualifies Exclusifs en Pneumophtisiologie. irreg. ISSN 0066-3492
- Annuaire National des Specialistes Qualifies Exclusifs en Rhumatologie. a. ISSN 0066-3522

**Protection et Securite du Public**
12 Quai de Gesvres, Paris 4, France.
- Bulletin de la Protection Civile de la Prefecture de Police. q.

**Publi-Export**
9, rue de Chateaudun, Paris-(9e), France.
- Frantsia; panorama des industries francaises. m. ISSN 0085-0861

**Editions Publi-Guid**
195 Quai de la Gourdine, 77400 Lagny, France.
- Guide de la Parfumerie. biennial (approx.) 13th edition most recently issued. ISSN 0072-7989

**Publi-Inter**
75 rue Voltaire, 92300 Levallois, Paris.
- C R A; commerce reparation automobile. w.
- Inter Auto Ecoles de France/Inter Auto Route. m. ISSN 0020-5001

**Publi-Ric**
8 rue de Richelieu, 75001 Paris, France.
- Construction Neuve et Ancienne. m. ISSN 0335-2021

**Edition Publi-Team-Elysees**
34 Av. des Champs-Elysees, 75008 Paris, France.
- Annuaire des Avocats. a. ISSN 0396-2318

**Publicat**
17 Blvd. Poissonniere, 75002 Paris, France.
- Maxis; la route, les camions, les autocars, les engins speciaux. m.
- Perspectives Psychiatriques. 5 per yr. ISSN 0031-6032 (Groupe d'Etudes de Psychiatrie Psychologie et Sciences Sociales)

**Publications d'Art et d'Archeologie**
27 rue St.-Andre des Arts, Paris (6e), France.
- Archeologie Vivante. q. ISSN 0003-8229

**Publications de la Soudure Autogene**
32 Bd. de la Chapelle, 75018 Paris, France.
- Soudage et Techniques Connexes. bi-m. ISSN 0038-173X (Institut de Soudure)

**Publications de la Vie Catholique**
163 Bd. Malesherbes, Paris (27), France.
- Telerama. w. ISSN 0040-2699

**Publications des Cahiers Mode**
see P.C.M.

**Publications Enfantines**
3 rue la Rochefoucauld, 75009 Paris, France.
- Francs-Jeux. 20 per yr.

**Publications Fiduciaires**
54 rue de Chabrol, 75480 Paris Cedex 10, France.
- Legi-Social. m.

**Publications Periodiques Parisiennes**
78 rue Jouffroy, 75017 Paris, France.
- Golf Europeen. m. ISSN 0040-3458

**Publications Periodiques Specialisees**
11, rue d'Algerie, 69001 Lyon, France.
- Exister; cahiers du Centre Soeren Kierkegaard. q. (Centre Soeren Kierkegaard)
- Pomologie Francaise; revue d'arboriculture fruitiere. m. ISSN 0032-4175 (Societe Pomologique de France)
- Protection des Animaux. q. (Societe Protectrice des Animaux)
- Revue Alpine. q. (Club Alpin Francais. Section Rhone-Alpes)
- Revue Juridique de l'Environnement. q. (Societe Francaise pour le Droit de l'Environnement)
- Revue Medicale des Alpes Francaises. bi-m. (Societe Medico Chirurgicale des Hopitaux de Grenoble)
- Societe de Pharmacie de Lyon. Bulletin des Travaux. q. ISSN 0037-9107

**Publiclair**
38 rue des Mathurins, Paris (8e), France.
- Cahiers de Reeducation & de Readaptation Fonctionnelles. 8 per yr. ISSN 0007-9979 (Societe Nationale Francaise de Reeducation & de Readaptation Fonctionnelles)

**Publicness**
2, rue du Fg. Poissonniere, 75010 Paris, France.
- Zoom; le magazine de l'image. bi-m.

**Publijudo**
43, rue des Plantes, 75014 Paris, France.
- Judo. m. (Federation Francaise de Judo et Disciplines Associees)

**Editions Publiplast**
55 rue du Faubourg-Montmartre, Paris 9e, France.
- Appel Service; Repertoire d'Adresses Utiles pour le Commerce et l'Industrie. irreg. ISSN 0066-5398

**Publistyl**
47, Cours Gambetta, 69007 Lyon, France.
- Informateur des Chefs d'Entreprises Libres. m. ISSN 0046-9327 (Association des Chefs d'Entreprises Libres (A.C.E.L.))

**Pym Editeur**
27 rue Hermel, 75018 Paris, France.
- Cafetier Restaurateur Parisien. bi-m. (Syndicat des Cafetiers, Restaurateurs de Paris et Banlieues)
- Federation des Debitants de Tabac de l'Ile-de-France. Annuaire Officiel. a.

**Quatre Verites**
7 rue Mongolfier, 93116 Rosny-Sous-Bois, France.
- Quatre Verites. m. ISSN 0033-5878

**J. Quatreboeufs**
22 Merdrignac, Brittany, France.
- Bretagne Reelle; tribune libre-la voix du pays gallo. s-m. ISSN 0006-9647

- Keltia; organe de recherche d'un celtisme moderne. bi-m. ISSN 0022-9792

**Quercy Recherche**
B.P. 127, 46005 Cahors, France.
- Quercy Recherche. bi-m. ISSN 0335-3958

**Editions Quo Vadis**
2026 rue Caisserie, 13235 Marseille Cedex 1, France.
- Annuaire Medical du Dr. Porcheron et Prof. G. Beltrami. a.

**R.A.I.P.**
22, rue de la Saussiere, 92100 Boulogne, France.
- Ingenieurs de l'Automobile. m. ISSN 0020-1200 (Societe des Ingenieurs de l'Automobile)

**R.C.P. Edition**
6 Villa Emile Bergerat, 92200 Neuilly sur Seine, France
- Guide Kleber France. a. (Dist. by: French European Publications, 610 Fifth Ave., New York, NY 10020)

**R O C**
3 rue Pasteur, 78800 Houilles, France.
- R O C. (Reseau d'Organismes Culturels) w. ISSN 0033-703X

**Radical de Gauche**
c/o Francois Loncle, Ed., 11, rue de Grenelle, 750007 Paris, France.
- Radical de Gauche; journal de movement des radicals de gauche. m.

**Radiesthesie Magazine**
102 rue la Boetie, 75008 Paris, France.
- Radiesthesie Magazine. q.

**Rahla**
4 rue Coetlogon, 75006 Paris, France.
- Saharien. q. ISSN 0036-2646

**Rassemblement pour le Civisme, le Dialogue et le Renouveau**
23 rue Ballu, 75009 Paris, France.
- Citoyen; la voix de la majorite silencieuse. m. ISSN 0339-0934

**Realites 5-6**
12 rue Honore Chevalier, Paris (6e), France.
- Realites 5-6. m.

**Recherche et Architecture**
4, Avenue du Recteur Poincare, 75782 Paris, France.
- Recherche et Architecture. q. ISSN 0373-4285

**Recuperation**
41 rue d'Auteuil, Paris(16e), France.
- Recuperation. w. ISSN 0034-1924

**Reeducation**
25 rue des Ecoles, 75 Paris 5e, France.
- Reeducation; revue francaise de l'enfance delinquante, deficiente et socialement inadaptee. m. ISSN 0034-2211

**Reforme**
53-55 Avenue du Maine, 75014 Paris, France.
- Reforme. w.

**Regie Publicite Industrielle**
36 rue du Fer-a-Moulin, 75005 Paris, France.
- Agenda de la Quincaillerie; fers et metaux. a. ISSN 0065-4256
- Memento des Mines et Carrieres. a.

**Region Cynegetique du Sud-Ouest**
82, Quai des Chartrons, 33300 Bordeaux, France.
- Journal du Chasseur. m.

**Relations Exterieures et Diffusion**
45, rue Richer, 75009 Paris, France.
- Contact Rungis le Trait d'Union. m.

**Rencontres Sous le Signe de la Langue Francaise**
20 rue du Louvre, Paris (1er), France.
- Rencontres Sous le Signe de la Langue Francaise. m. ISSN 0034-4354

**Repertoire Analytique de Litterature Francaise**
Av. de Berlincan, Zone Industrielle, Saint-Medarden-Jalles, France.
- R A L F; Repertoire Analytique de Litterature Francaise. irreg. ISSN 0079-9297

**Repertoire des Voyages**
c/o Daniel V. Dedina, Ed., 78 Av. Champs-Elysees, F Paris 75008, France.
- Repertoire des Voyages/Travel Trade Repertory; international travel trade magazine. m. ISSN 0034-4575

**Repertoire du Marketing et du Management**
31 rue Francois-1er, Paris 8e, France.
- Repertoire du Marketing et du Management. a. ISSN 0080-1097

**Editions Replique**
9 rue Dupont-des-Loges, 75007 Paris, France.
- Psychanalyse a l'Universite. q. (Universite de Paris VII. Laboratoire de Psychanalyse et Psychopathologie)

**Reseau des Emetteurs Francais**
2 Square Trudaine, Paris 9, France.
- Radio R E F; la revue des ondes courtes. m. ISSN 0033-7994

**Resisters Inside the Army (RITA)**
10 Passage du Chantier, Paris (12e), France.
- Act. 4 per yr. ISSN 0001-5075

**Editions Retz**
114 Champs Elysees, 75008 Paris, France.
- Question de Spiritualite, Tradition, Litteratures. bi-m. (Centre d'Etudes Litteraires Traditionnelles)

**Reunion des Endocrinologistes de Langue France**
- Reunion des Endocrinologistes de Langue Francaise. Rapports/Association for French-Language Endocrinologists. Reports of Meetings. (pub. by Masson)

**Reunion Lyonnaise de Pediatrie**
Clinique Medicale Infantile, Hospital Debrousse, Lyon, France.
- Pediatrie. 8 per yr. ISSN 0031-4021 (Societe Francaise de Pediatrie)

**Reveil de l'Arrondissement de Fougeres**
c/o Monique Corvaisier, Ed., 53 bis rue Nationale, 35300 Fougerer, France.
- Reveil de l'Arrondissement de Fougeres. q.

**Revue Administrative**
Bureau 203, 2 rue de Viarmes, Paris (1er), France.
- Revue Administrative. bi-m. ISSN 0035-0672

**Revue Algologique**
12 rue Buffon, 75005 Paris, France.
- Revue Algologique. irreg. ISSN 0035-0702

**Revue Archeologique de l'Est et du Centre-Est**
c/o Danielle Garnier, 5 rue Docteur-Maret, Dijon (Cote-d'-or), France.
- Revue Archeologique de l'Est et du Centre-Est. q. ISSN 0035-0745

**Revue Archeologique du Centre de la France**
c/o Dr. Max Vauthey, Ed., 27 Bd. de Russie, 03200 Vichy, France.
- Revue Archeologique du Centre de la France. q. ISSN 0035-0753

**Revue Bryologique et Lichenologique**
12 rue Buffon, 75005 Paris, France.
- Revue Bryologique et Lichenologique. q.

**Revue d'Acoustique**
12 rue des Fosses St. Marcel, 75005 Paris, France.
- Revue d'Acoustique. q.

**Revue d'Economie et de Droit Immobilier**
11, Quai Anatole France, 75007 Paris, France.
- Revue d'Economie et de Droit Immobilier. bi-m.

**Revue d'Etudes Militaires, Aeriennes et Navales**
5 Bd. Beaumarchais, Paris (4e), France.
- Revue d'Etudes Militaires, Aeriennes et Navales. m. ISSN 0035-2306

**Revue d'Histoire de la Spiritualite**
c/o J. C. Guy, S. J., 15 rue Monsieur, 75 Paris (7e), France.
- Revue d'Histoire de la Spiritualite. q.

**Revue de Gerontologie d'Expression Francaise**
14 rue Alexandre Parodi, 75-Paris 10, France.
- Revue de Gerontologie d'Expression Francaise. 6 per yr.

**Revue de Jurisprudence Commerciale**
6 Rue de Mezieres, Paris(6e), France.
- Revue de Jurisprudence Commerciale; journal des agrees. m. ISSN 0048-7937

**Revue de l'Enseignement Superieur**
173 Bd. Saint-Germain, Paris (6e), France.
- Revue de l'Enseignement Superieur. q. ISSN 0035-1407

**Revue de Laryngologie**
114 Ave. d'Ares, 33000 Bordeaux, France.
- Revue de Laryngologie-Otologie-Rhinologie. bi-m. ISSN 0035-1334

**Revue de Metallurgie**
5, rue Paul Cezanne, 75008 Paris, France.
- Revue de Metallurgie. m. ISSN 0035-1563
- Revue de Metallurgie. Memoires Scientifiques. m. ISSN 0025-9128

**Revue de Mycologie**
12 rue Buffon, 75005 Paris, France.
- Revue de Mycologie. q. ISSN 0484-8578

**Revue des Finances Communales**
28 rue de Chateaudun, Paris (9e), France.
- Revue des Finances Communales. m. ISSN 0035-208X

**Revue des Hotesses**
41 Bd. des Capucines, 75 Paris 2e, France.
- Revue des Hotesses. q. ISSN 0035-2098

**Revue du Materiel d'Entreprise**
30 rue Tronchet, Paris (9e), France.
- Revue du Materiel d'Entreprise; travaux publics, batiment, mines et carrieres. m. ISSN 0048-8011

**Revue du Rouergue**
c/o M. Carrere, Ed., Place de la Cite, Rodez, France.
- Revue du Rouergue. q. ISSN 0035-2667

**Revue du Vivarais**
Planzolles, 07230 La Blachere, France.
- Revue du Vivarais. q. ISSN 0035-2748

**Revue Generale de l'Electricite**
48 rue de la Procession, 75724 Paris, France.
- Revue Generale de l'Electricite. 11 per yr. ISSN 0035-3116

**Revue Generale des Caoutchoucs et Plastiques**
42 rue Scheffer, Paris 75016, France.
- Revue Generale des Caoutchoucs et Plastiques. m. ISSN 0035-3175

**Revue Generale des Routes et des Aerodromes**
9 rue Magellan, 75008 Paris, France.
- Revue Generale des Routes et des Aerodromes. m. ISSN 0035-3191

**Revue Historique de Bordeaux et du Departement de la Gironde**
Hotel des Societes Savantes, 71, rue du Loup, 33000 Bordeaux, France.
- Revue Historique de Bordeaux et du Departement de la Gironde. 1-2 per yr.

**Revue Historique et Archeologique du Maine**
7 rue de la Reine Berengere 1, Le Mans, France.
- Revue Historique et Archeologique du Maine. irreg.

**Revue Internationale des Cadres**
30 rue de Gramont, Paris 2e, France.
- Revue Internationale des Cadres. a.

**Revue Internationale des Tabacs**
97 rue Saint-Lazare, Paris (9e), France.
- Revue Internationale des Tabacs. m. ISSN 0035-3477

**Revue Internationale du Droit d'Auteur**
10 rue Chaptal, 75441 Paris 9, France.
- Revue Internationale du Droit d'Auteur. q. ISSN 0035-3515

**Revue Mabillon**
86240 Liguge, France.
- Revue Mabillon. q. ISSN 0035-3620

**Revue Moderne**
14 rue de l'Armorique, 75015 Paris, France.
- Revue Moderne; des arts et de la vie. m. ISSN 0035-3698

**Revue Montalembert**
104 rue de Vaugirard, Paris (6e), France.
• Revue Montalembert. q. ISSN 0035-3701

**Revue Politique et Parlementaire**
88 bis rue Jouffroy, 75017 Paris, France.
• Revue Politique et Parlementaire; economie,
finance, urbanisme. bi-m. ISSN 0035-385X

**Revue Pratique de Droit Social**
33 rue Bouret, 75940 Paris Cedex 19, France.
• Revue Pratique de Droit Social. m.

**Revue Spiritus**
40 Rue La Fontaine, 75781 Paris, France.
• Spiritus; experience et recherche missionnaires. q.
ISSN 0038-7665 (Association Spiritus)

**Revue Stomato-Odontologique du Nord de la France**
Place de Verdun, 59 Lille, France.
• Revue Stomato-Odontologique du Nord de la
France. q. ISSN 0035-4147

**Revue 9 et 2**
21, Uue Gazan, 75014 Paris, France.
• Revue 9 et 2; architecture et mouvement. bi-m.

**SARL Revues Internationales**
97 rue Saint-Lazare, Paris (9e), France.
• Revue Internationale des Produits Tropicaux. m.
ISSN 0035-3450

**Rhone-Poulenc-Specia**
26 Av. de l'Observatoire, Paris (14e), France.
• Cahiers de Medecine Veterinaire. irreg. ISSN
0007-9944

**Editions Richelieu**
61 rue de Vaugirard, Paris 6e, France.
• Univers Politique; Relations Internationales. a.
ISSN 0083-3681

**Pierre Ricouard Syndic**
5, rue Racine, Rouen, France.
• Tout-Rouen; magazine bi-mensuel d'information
reflet de l'actualite economique; culturelle et
artistique de la vie rouennaise. fortn. ISSN 0040-
9839

**Editions Riegel**
45 Av. du Roule, 92200 Neuilly, France.
• Autocar et Cargo Routier; l'equipement
automobile. 11 per yr. ISSN 0005-0938
• Isolation et Revetements. 4 per yr. ISSN 0021-
1885

**Editions E. Robert**
28 rue du Bon Pasteur, B.P. 4384, 69241 Lyon
Cedex 1, France.
• Ecole et la Famille. m.

**Editions J. L. Roth S.A.**
1 Place du Theatre Francais, 75001 Paris (1e),
France.
• Caravaning; la revue gui defend les caravaniers.
m. (11 per yr.) ISSN 0008-6177
• Neptune Nautisme; le yacht et le motonautisme.
m. ISSN 0028-2782

**Editions Rouff**
36 rue du Vieux-Pont-De-Sevres, 92100 Boulogne
Billancourt, France.
• Blagues. s-m. ISSN 0006-4513
• Franc-Rire. s-m. ISSN 0015-9379
• Histoire pour Tous. m. ISSN 0018-2249

**Rougerie**
Mortemart, 87330 Mezieres-sur-Issoire, France.
• Poesie Presente. q. ISSN 0048-4563

**Imprimerie Rouille**
3 Ter, rue de la Gare, 28240-la Loupe, France.
• Association Francaise des Techniciens et
Ingenieurs de Securite et des Medecins du
Travail. Annuaire. a. ISSN 0066-927X

**Rudolf Steiner Nachlassverwaltung**
• Rudolf Steiner Publications. (pub. by Librairie
Fischbacher)

**Editions Ruedo Iberico**
6, rue de Latran, 75005 Paris, France.
• Cuadernos de Ruedo Iberico. bi-m. ISSN 0011-
2488

**S. A. D. E. P.**
48 rue de la Bienfaisance, Paris (8e), France.
• Officiel des Plastiques et du Caoutchouc. m(10
per yr.) ISSN 0030-0462

**S.A. des Editions de la Mode Chic de Paris**
14 rue Duphot, Paris (1e), France.
• Mode Chic de Paris. q. ISSN 0047-7621
• Officiel de la Couleur. q. ISSN 0030-039X

**S A F P**
68 Colmar-Ingersheim, France.
• Self. m (11 per yr) ISSN 0037-153X

**S A T R**
23 rue Etienne Pallu, Tours, France.
• Interet Europeen: Europe et Regions. q. ISSN
0020-5397

**S. D. M. S.**
• Archives Mediterraneennes de Medecine. (pub. by
Sud-Regie)

**S.E.B.A.M.**
42, rue de Louvre, Paris, France.
• Bricolage Maison Pratique. m.

**S. E D A.**
25, rue du General-Foy, 75008 Paris, France.
• Betteravier Francais. m. ISSN 0405-6701

**S.E.D.A.C. Editions**
46, Boulevard de Magenta, 75010 Paris, France.
• Chausser. w.

**S E D I P A**
3 rue Francois 1e, 75008 Paris, France.
• Nouveau Guide de l'Epicier Libre Service. m.
ISSN 0029-4667

**S. E. D. I. T**
48, rue de la Bienfaisance, 75008 Paris, France.
• Information Routiere et Touristique. m.

**S. E. F. A. G.**
12 Fue du Renard, 75004 Paris, France.
• Epicerie Francaise. w.

**S E G E D O**
12 rue du Quatre-Septembre, 75002 Paris, France.
• E S O P E. (Etudes Sociales-Politiques,
Economiques) m.
• Kouakou. 6 per m.

**S.E.I.D.**
54 rue de Paradis, 75010 Paris, France.
• Coiffeur de France. m. (Federation Nationale de
la Coiffure)
• Officiel de la Coiffure et de la Beaute. q.
• Voix de la Coiffure Francaise. q. (Federation
Nationale de la Coiffure)

**S E L I S la Quinzaine Litteraire**
43, rue du Temple, 75004 Paris 4, France.
• Quinzaine Litteraire. bi-w. ISSN 0048-6493

**S. E. M. A D**
*see* **Societe d'Editions Medicales et Alimentaires
Relatives au Diabete**

**S. E. M. I. S.**
49 rue de Maubeuge, Paris (9e), France.
• Auto-Volt; revue technique professionnelle de
l'electricite automobile. m. ISSN 0005-0881
• Poids Lourd; revue technique du vehicle
industriel. m. ISSN 0032-227X

**S.E.P.A.**
15 rue Jacques Bingen, 75 Paris 17e, France.
• Charcuterie de France. m.

**S. E. P. A. I C**
*see* **Societe d'Edition et de Publicite Agricoles,
Industrielles et Commerciales**

**S.E.P.E.**
*see* **Societe Europeenne de Presse et d'Edition**

**S E P Edition**
194-196 rue Marcadet, 75018 Paris, France.
• Annuaire National des Matieres Premieres de
Recuperation et du Materiel d'Occasion. a.
• Guide de la Chimie International. a?
• Sol et Murs Magazine. q. ISSN 0339-1507
• Toute la Boisson. International. a. ISSN 0082-
5484
• Usines d'Aujourd'hui. bi-m. ISSN 0042-1278

**S.E.R.A.**
2, rue Malus, 75005 Paris, France.
• Armes et Uniformes de l'Histoire. bi-m.

**S. E. T. I. C.**
54 rue Rene-Boulanger, Paris (10e), France.
• Technicuir. m. ISSN 0040-1072 (Centre
Technique du Cuir)

**S.I.E.**
10, Impasse Guemenee, 75004 Paris, France.
• Cahiers de la Quatrieme Internationale. irreg.
ISSN 0068-5038
• Cahiers Rouge. Nouvelle Serie Internationale.
irreg. ISSN 0068-5224

**S I E M**
40 rue Paul-Valery, 75116 Paris, France.
• Revue de Pediatrie. 10 per yr. ISSN 0035-1644

**S.I.P.E.**
22 Av. General de Gaulle, 74201 Thonon, France.
• Messager. w. ISSN 0026-024X

**S.I.R.P.E.**
8 rue du Colonel Moll, 75017 Paris, France.
• Materiaux et Techniques. m. ISSN 0032-6895

**S.L.E.E.S**
22 rue Constantine, 69281 Lyon, France.
• Bulletins et Documents. bi-m.

**Editions S.M.E.**
55 Montee de Choulans, 69323 Lyon, France.
• Bref Rhone Alpes; lettre hebdomadaire
d'informations economiques. w. ISSN 0006-9566
• Entreprises Rhone Alpes. m.

**S. N. E. M.**
11 Bd. de Bonne Nouvelle, Paris (2e), France.
• Plaisir de la Maison; revue mensuelle de
decoration. m. ISSN 0032-0498

**S.O.C.I.D.O.C.**
176 rue Montmartre, 75002 Paris, France.
• B I P. (Bulletin de l'Industrie Petroliere) d. ISSN
0300-4554
• Orient-Petrole. fortn.
• Techniques de l'Energie; revue mensuelle de
l'energie et de son equipement. m.

**S O C O T E L**
38-40 rue du General Leclerc, 92131 Issy les
Moulineaux, France.
• Commutation et Electronique. q. ISSN 0010-3926

**S.O.E. (Societe Occidentale d'Edition)**
7 Bd. de Sebastopol, 75001 Paris, France.
• Forces Nouvelles Info. m.
• Initiative National; journal des forces nouvelles.
m.
• Vaincre; journal du GUD, Front de la Jeunesse. 10
per yr. (Groupe, Union, Defense)

**S.O.F.I.A.C.**
13 rue du Four, 75006 Paris, France.
• Afrique et l'Asie Modernes; revue politique sociale
et economique. q.

**S. O. G. E. T. A. P.**
47, rue de la Victoire, 75009 Paris, France.
• Tribune du Monde Rural. m(11 per yr)

**S O P I C**
21, rue de la Nuee-Bleue, 67000 Strasbourg, France.
• Alsace Automobile. m. (Automobile-Club
d'Alsace)

**S O P P E P**
2 a 12, rue de Bellevue, Paris (19e), France.
• Moniteur Professionel de l'Electricite. m. ISSN
0026-9735

**S O P R A L**
16, Place Sainte-Claire, 38000 Grenoble, France.
• Sud-Est Industriel et Commercial. m.

**Editions S.O.S.**
106 rue du Bac, 75341 Paris, France.
• Grandes Figures de la Charite. irreg. ISSN 0072-
5404
• Messages du Secours Catholique. m. ISSN 0026-
0290

**S.O.S. Amitie France**
Boite Postale 21, Boulogne 92, France.
● Amitie S.O.S. Par Telephone. q. ISSN 0003-1887

**Editions S.O.S.P.**
59-61, Avenue de la Grande-Armee, 75782 Paris Cedex 16, France.
● Automarques; revue francaise du marche des automobiles neuves et d'occasion. bi-m.

**S.P.E.B.**
Rue du Chateau, 06640 Saint Jeannet, France.
● Artitudes International. q.

**S. P. E. K. (La Maison des Kinesitherapeutes)**
11 rue des Petits Hotels, 75010 Paris, France.
● Kinesitherapie Scientifique. 6 per yr. ISSN 0023-1576

**S.P.E.L.D.**
6, Rue Victor-Cousin, Paris (5e), France.
● S. P. E. L. D. Information; droit, politique, economie, sciences sociales, erudition. q. ISSN 0038-7282

**S. P. E. O. C.**
*see* Societe de Presse et d'Edition Ovine et Caprine (S.P.E.O.C.)

**S. P. E. R.**
21 rue du Fg St-Antoine, Paris (11e), France.
● Agri Sept; moniteur agricole. w. ISSN 0044-6750

**S.P.O.T. Publicite**
58, rue Saint-Lazare, 75009 Paris, France.
● Medecin de Paris. m (10 per yr.)

**S T E P E**
*see* Societe Technique d'Editions pour l'Entreprise (S T E P E)

**Sageret**
5 et 7 rue Plumet, 75015 Paris, France.
● Sageret; Annuaire General du Batiment et des Travaux Publics. a.

**Jacques Saillot, Ed. & Pub.**
34, rue du Petit Thouars, 49000 Angers, France.
● Cahiers de Saint-Louis. q.

**Saint Hubert Club de France**
10 Rue de Lisbonne, 75008 Paris, France.
● Saint Hubert. m. ISSN 0036-2867

**St. Joan's Alliance**
19 Avenue de la Porte Brunet, 75019 Paris, France.
● Catholic Citizen. bi-m. ISSN 0045-5989

**Editions Saint Paul**
184 Av. de Verdun, 92130 Issy-les-Moulineaux, France.
● Pirogue; revue Africaine realisee par des Africains. q. ISSN 0048-4229

**Salon International de la Confiserie Chocolaterie Biscuiterie**
● Confiserie. (pub. by Editions de la Confiserie)

**Salon International de la Machine Agricole**
95 rue Saint-Lazare, 75441 Paris, France.
● Guide-Annuaire de l'Equipement Agricole; catalogue officiel du Salon International de la Machine Agricole. a.

**Sante et Sport**
94 Blvd. Richard-Lenoir, Paris (11e), France.
● Sante et Sport. m. ISSN 0036-4576

**Sauvage**
12 rue du Mail, 75002 Paris, France.
● Sauvage; le nouvel observateur-ecologie. m.

**Editions J. Savaron**
6, Rond-Point-Winston-Churchill, 92200 Neuilly sur Seine, France.
● Evolution Medicale; revue medicale et medico-sociale. 6 per yr. ISSN 0014-3847

**Editions de Saxe**
52 Avenue Marechal-de-Saxe, 69006 Lyon, France.
● Ami des Jardins et de la Maison. m. ISSN 0044-8095
● Marielle. m.
● Natacha. m.
● Playa. m.
● Rebecca. m.
● Tricot-Selection. q.

**Science et Industrie**
6 Av. Pierre Premier de Serbie, 75116 Paris, France.
● Travaux. m. ISSN 0041-1906 (Federation Nationale des Travaux Publics)

**Science-Service**
10 rue Notre Dame de Lorette, Paris (9e), France.
● Futur; aux frontieres de l'inconnu. s-m. ISSN 0016-3244

**Sciences de l'Information**
9 rue de Hanovre, 75002 Paris, France.
● Sciences de l'Information. 10 per yr.

**Sciences et Avenir**
c/o Paul Ceuzin, Ed., 14-16 rue de la Baume, Paris 8e, France.
● Sciences et Avenir; revue de Grande Information scientifique. m. ISSN 0036-8636

**Scientific Ballooning and Radiations Monitoring Organization**
Observatoire de Parc Saint-Marie, 4 Avenue Neptune, 94 Saint-Maur des Fosses, France.
● S B A R M O. Bulletin. q.

**Scouts de France**
23, rue Ligner, 75020-Paris, France.
● Rangers Scout. 8 per yr. ISSN 0033-9237
● Scout Pionnier. 8 per yr. ISSN 0036-9470
● Scouts Louveteaux, Rangers, Pionniers. m(8 per yr.) (Association des Scouts de France)

**Securitas**
2 rue de Chateaudun, Paris (9e), France.
● Argus; journal international des assurances. w. ISSN 0004-1173
● Argus International. bi-m.
● Jurisprudence Automobile. m. ISSN 0022-6823

**Editions Sedom**
10 Av. Hoche, 75382 Paris Cedex 08, France.
● Industries Mecaniques. w. ISSN 0019-9370 (Federation des Industries Mecaniques et Transformatrices des Metaux)

**SARL Sedotourmovico**
4, rue Barye, 75017 Paris, France.
● Toutes les Nouvelles de l'Hotellerie et du Tourisme. m.

**Editions Seghers**
118, rue de Vaugirard, Paris 6e, France.
● Collection "Humor d'Aujourd'hui". irreg.

**Selection du Reader's Digest, S.A.**
216 Saint-Germain, 75349 Paris, France.
● Selection du Reader's Digest (French Edition) m. ISSN 0037-1386

**Selections Medicales et Scientifiques**
27 rue George-Sand, Paris 16e, France.
● Societe Medico-Chirurgicale des Hopitaux Libres de France. Annuaire. a. ISSN 0081-1149

**Semaine des Hopitaux**
15 rue Saint-Benoit, Paris (6e), France.
● Annales de Chirurgie. m. ISSN 0003-3944
● Annales de Chirurgie Plastique. 4 per yr. ISSN 0003-3960
● Annales de Genetique. q. ISSN 0003-3995 (Societe Francaise de Genetique)
● Annales de Pediatrie. 10 per yr. ISSN 0037-1769
● Annales de Radiologie; radiologie clinique, radiobiologie. 8 per yr. ISSN 0003-4185
● Archives d'Anatomie et de Cytologie Pathologiques. 6 per yr.
● Pathologie Biologie. 10 per yr. ISSN 0031-3009 (Societe de Pathologie Biologique)
● Therapeutique. 10 per yr. ISSN 0040-5922

**Sennacieca Asocio Tutmonda**
67 Av. Gambetta, Paris (20e), France.
● Kalejdoskopo. q.

**Sepreco S.A.R.L**
2, rue du Pont Neuf, 75001 Paris, France.
● Hors Cote. fortn. ISSN 0018-5132
● Previsions. w.

**Septieme Aurore**
Box 253, 75024 Paris, France.
● Antiquite Gauloise. q.
● Hesperide; renaissance celtique. q. ISSN 0018-0998

**SEPTIMA**
14, rue Falguiere, 75015 Paris, France.
● Ciments, Betons, Platres, Chaux; revue des materiaux. bi-m. (Centre d'Etudes et de Recherches de l'Industrie des Liants Hydrauliques)
● Industrie Ceramique. m.(except Aug) ISSN 0019-9044

**Patrick Sermadiras**
11, rue Arsene Houssaye, 75008 Paris, France.
● Annuaire de l'Art International. biennial.

**Service Biblique Evangile et Vie**
6, Avenue Vavin, 75006 Paris, France.
● Cahiers Bibliques Trimestriels Evangile. q. ISSN 0007-960X

**Service Central d'Organisation et Methodes**
20 rue N.D. des Victoires, Paris (2e), France.
● O. et M. Bulletin. (Organisation et Methodes); organisation, methodes et automatisation dans les services publics. q. ISSN 0007-4748

**Service d'Exploitation Industrielle des Tabacs et Allumettes**
53 Quai d'Orsay, 75340 Paris, France.
● Annales du Tabac. a.

**Service de Presse Economique des Industries Alimentaires**
1, rue du Mail, 75002 Paris, France.
● S P E C I A L; l'hebdomadaire economique et financier des industries alimentaires. w.

**Service de Presse, Edition, Information**
14 rue Drouot, 75009 Paris, France.
● Agressologie; revue internationale de physiobiologie et de pharmacologie appliquees aux effets de l'Agression. 10 per yr. ISSN 0002-1148 (Hopital Boucicaut-Paris. Laboratoire d'Eutonologie) (Subscriptions to: Masson Editeur, 120 Bd. Saint-Germain, 75280 Paris Cedex 06, France)
● Annales Medicales de Nancy. m. ISSN 0003-4460 (Societe de Medecine de Nancy)
● Armee et Defense; revue d'informations et de liaison. m. ISSN 0004-2242 (Union Nationale des Officiers de Reserve)
● Industrie Francaise du Coton et des Fibres Alliees. 6 per yr. ISSN 0019-9087 (Syndicat General de l'Industrie Cotonniere Francaise et Textiles Allies)
● Psychologie Medicale. 10 per yr. ISSN 0048-5756
● Revue Internationale des Services de Sante des Armees de Terre, de Mer et de l'Air/International Review of the Army, Navy and Air Force Medical Services. 10 per yr. ISSN 0035-3469 (International Committee of Military Medicine and Pharmacy)

**Service de Recherches Juridiques Comparatives**
● Annuaire de Legislation Francaise et Etrangere. (pub. by Centre National de la Recherche Scientifique)

**Service de Renseignements du Repertoire Industriel**
13 rue de Marivaux, Paris 2e, France.
● Repertoire Dictionnaire Industriel. a. ISSN 0080-1089

**Service des Instruments de Mesure**
102 rue de la Tour, 75016 Paris, France.
● Revue de Metrologie Pratique et Legale. m. ISSN 0035-158X

**Service des Relations Publiques de Houilleres du Nord et du Pas-de-Calais**
20 rue des Minimes, 59505 Douai, France.
● Relais; magazine mensuel de la region miniere. m.

**Service Social d'Aide aux Emigrants**
391 rue de Vaugirard, 75732 Paris, France.
● Accueillir. m.

**Service Technique pour l'Education**
19 Bld. Poissonniere, Paris 2e, France.
● Sir Moses Montefiore Collections des Juifs Celebres. irreg. ISSN 0075-4544

**Services Techniques et Commerciaux de la Reunion des Musees Nationaux**
10, rue de l'Abbaye, Paris 75006, France.
● Laboratoire de Recherche des Musees de France. Annales. a.

**Servir Mieux**
25 Bis, Boulevard du Lac, Enghien-Les-Bains (95), France.
- Servir Mieux. 10 per yr. ISSN 0037-2757

**Editions du Seuil**
27 rue Jacob, 75261 Paris Cedex 06, France.
- Communications. s-a. ISSN 0588-8018 (Ecole Pratique des Hautes Etudes. Centre d'Etudes des Communications de Masse)
- Economie et Societe. irreg. ISSN 0070-8801
- Etudes Teilhardiennes/Teilhardian Studies. irreg. ISSN 0082-2612
- Musique en Jeu. q.
- Poetique; revue de theorie et d'analyse litteraires. q. ISSN 0032-2024
- Points. Films. irreg. ISSN 0079-2535
- Sociologie du Travail. q. ISSN 0038-0296
- Tel Quel; litterature-philosophie-science-politique. q. ISSN 0040-2419
- Univers Historique. irreg. ISSN 0083-3673

**Sexpol Association**
B.P. 265, 75866 Paris Cedex 18, France.
- Revue Sexpol; sexologie politique. 10 per yr. ISSN 0336-9609

**Show-Business**
22 rue Huyghens, Paris (16e), France.
- Show-Business. w. ISSN 0037-430X

**Sideler**
219 Bd. Saint Germain, 75007 Paris, France.
- Experiences et Gestions Municipales; revue de promotion et de gestion comparee. q.

**Editions Revue Signature**
55, rue Pierre-Charron, 75008 Paris, France.
- Signature. m. (Diners Club de France)

**Editions les Signes des Temps**
60 Av. Emile Zola, 77190 Danmarie les Lys, France.
- Vie et Sante. m. ISSN 0042-5524

**Silex**
B.P. 554 R.P., 38013 Grenoble Cedex, France.
- Silex; la culture dans tous ses etats. q.

**Sillon Catholique**
4, Passage Olivier de Serres, 75015 Paris, France.
- Ame Populaire. m.

**Editions Andre Silvaire**
20 rue Domat, Paris (5e), France.
- Amis de Milosz. ISSN 0003-181X (Association des Amis de Milosz)
- Lettres; poesie, philosophie, litterature, arts, critique. q. ISSN 0024-1369

**M. I. Simansky, Pub.**
6 Ave. Paul Valery, 95 Sarcelles, France.
- Collection Denise Miege. irreg. ISSN 0084-8832

**Editions la Simarre**
11 rue de la Bourde, 37000 Tours, France.
- Cahiers d'Odonto-Stomatologie. irreg. ISSN 0068-5135 (Societe d'Odonto-Stomatologie de Touraine)
- Medecine et Nutrition. 6 per yr. (Societe d'Hygiene de Langue Francaise)

**SIMEP Editions**
47-49 rue du 4 Aout, B.P. 1214, 69611 Villeurbanne Cedex, France.
- Cahiers Medicaux; hebdomaire regional de formation continue. w. ISSN 0338-1439
- Journal Francais d'Oto-Rhino-Laryngologie et Chirurgie Maxillo-Faciale. 10 per yr. ISSN 0021-8332

**Editions Sirey**
22 rue Soufflot, 75005 Paris, France.
- Archives de Philosophie du Droit. a. ISSN 0066-6564
- Revue Critique de Droit International Prive. q. ISSN 0035-0958
- Revue d'Economie Politique. bi-m. ISSN 0035-1830
- Revue d'Histoire Economique et Sociale. q. ISSN 0035-239X
- Revue de Science Criminelle et de Droit Penal Compare. q. ISSN 0035-1733 (Universite de Paris II (Universite Droit, d'Economie et des Sciences Sociales). Institut de Droit Compare)
- Revue Francaise de Droit Aerien. q. ISSN 0035-287X (Association d'Etudes et de Documentation de Droit Aerien)

- Revue Historique de Droit Francais et Etranger. 4 per yr. ISSN 0035-3280
- Revue Trimestrielle de Droit Civil. q. ISSN 0397-9873
- Revue Trimestrielle de Droit Commercial. q. ISSN 0048-8208
- Revue Trimestrielle de Droit Europeen. q. ISSN 0035-4317
- Revue Trimestrielle de Droit Sanitaire et Social. q. ISSN 0035-4325

**Ski-Flash-Neige et Glace**
Ed. Jacqueline Saulnier, 38 Proveyzleux, France.
- Ski-Flash-Neige et Glace. 6 per yr. ISSN 0028-2545

**Skol Vreizh**
Run-Avel, 29210 Plourin-Morlaix, Bretagne, France.
- Skol Vreizh- l'Ecole Bretonne. q. ISSN 0037-6442 (Skolaerien Ha Kelennerien Ar Falz)

**Skolaerien Ha Kelennerien Ar Falz**
- Skol Vreizh- l'Ecole Bretonne. (pub. by Skol Vreizh)

**Editions Slog**
20 rue de Leningrad, Paris 8e, France.
- Chambre Syndicale des Commissionaires pour le Commerce Exterieur. Annuaire Officiel. a. ISSN 0071-8378
- Slog-Europa; European import export directory. a. ISSN 0081-0053

**Societe Academique d'Agen**
9 Bd. de la Republique, 47000 Agen, France.
- Revue de l'Agenais. q. ISSN 0035-1288

**Societe Academique des Arts Liberaux de Paris**
3, Avenue Chanzy, La Varenne-Saint Hilaire (Val-De-Marne), France.
- Societe Academique des Arts Liberaux de Paris. Anthologie. a. ISSN 0081-072X

**Societe Afrique Information**
93 rue Lafayette, Paris (10e), France.
- Interafrique Presse. w. ISSN 0020-5125

**Societe Amicale des Anciens Eleves de l'Ecole Polytechnique**
17 rue Descartes, 75230 Paris 5, France.
- Jaune et la Rouge. 10-11 per yr (plus special nos.) ISSN 0021-5554

**Societe Anonyme de Presse et de Publicite**
7 rue Dom Vaissette, 34 Montpellier (Hlt), France.
- Journee des Fruits & Legumes. d. ISSN 0022-5622
- Vignes & Raisins. m. ISSN 0042-6040

**Societe Anonyme des Publications de l'Indicateur Universel des P. T. T.**
6 rue le Goff, Paris (5e), France.
- Indicateur Universel des P. T. T. m. ISSN 0019-6908
- P T T Informations; revue d'informations generales des postes et des telecommunications. s-m. ISSN 0030-8374

**Societe Archeologique de Touraine**
- Societe Archeologique de Touraine. Memoires. (pub. by Musee de l'Hotel Gouin)

**Societe Archeologique, Historique et Artistique de Marly-le-Roi**
27 Grand rue, 78160 Marly-le-Roi, France.
- Vieux Marly. s-a.

**Societe Archeologique, Historique, Litteraire & Scientifique du Gers**
13 Place Saluste du-Bartas, Auch (Gers), France.
- Societe Archeologique, Historique, Litteraire & Scientifique du Gers. Bulletin. q. ISSN 0037-8895

**Societe Asiatique**
- Journal Asiatique. (pub. by Librairie Orientaliste Paul Geuthner)

**Societe Astronomique**
3 rue Beethoven, 75016 Paris, France.
- Astronomie. m. ISSN 0004-6302

**Societe Astronomique de Bordeaux**
Hotel des Societes Savantes, 71 rue du Loup, Bordeaux, France.
- Societe Astronomique de Bordeaux. Bulletin. a. ISSN 0081-0738

**Societe Automobiles M. Berliet**
69-Venissieux, France.
- Berliet-Informations. q. ISSN 0005-9218

**Societe Auxiliaire Technique de l'Automobile, du Motocycle et du Cycle**
157 rue Lecourbe, 75015 Paris, France.
- Union Technique de l'Automobile du Motocycle et du Cycle. Bulletin Mensuel de Documentation. m. ISSN 0041-705X

**Societe Bordelaise de Diffusion de Travaux des Lettres et Sciences Humaines**
Universite de Bordeaux, Batiment B, Domaine Universitaire, 33405 Talence, France.
- Etudes et Recherches Anglaises et Anglo-Americaines. irreg. ISSN 0071-2019

**Societe Botanique de France**
Rue J.B. Clement, 92290 Chatenay-Malabry, France.
- Societe Botanique de France. Bulletin. 7 per yr. ISSN 0037-8941

**Societe Bourbonnaise des Etudes Locales**
21 rue Leopold-Maupas A, Moulins, France.
- Notre Bourbonnais; revue de vulgarisation et d'action regionaliste. q. ISSN 0029-4489

**Societe Bureau de Presse et d'Informations**
14 rue de Berri, Paris (8e), France.
- Prestige de l'Hotellerie, de la Restauration et du Tourisme; equipement, gestion, formation. m. ISSN 0032-7921

**Societe C. R. E. N. A. F.**
J. M. Vidal, 24 rue Verdi, 06-Nice, France.
- Antenne Medicale. bi-m. ISSN 0003-5394 (Professeurs de l'Ancienne Faculte de Medecine d'Alger)

**Societe Calviniste de France**
10 rue de Villars, 78100 Saint-Germain-en-Laye, France.
- Societe Calviniste de France. Revue Reformee. q. ISSN 0035-3884

**Societe Centrale d'Agriculture, d'Horticulture et d'Acclimatation de Nice et des Alpes-Maritimes**
Palais de l'Agriculture, 113 Promenade des Anglais, Nice, France.
- Cote d'Azur Agricole et Horticole. m. ISSN 0010-9681

**Societe Centrale d'Aviculture de France**
34 Rue de Lille, Paris (7e), France.
- Revue Avicole. m. 11 per yr. ISSN 0048-7902

**Societe Centrale d'Education et d'Assistance pour les Sourds-Muets en France**
254 rue Saint-Jacques, Paris (5e), France.
- Societe Centrale d'Education et d'Assistance pour les Sourds-Muets en France. Bulletin d'Information. q. ISSN 0037-895X

**Societe Centrale des Architectes**
Hotel de Chaulnes, 9 Place des Vosges, Paris (4e), France.
- Academie d'Architecture. q. ISSN 0001-3994

**Societe Chateaubriand**
122 Bd. de Courcelles, Paris, France
(Subscr. to: Librairie Pierre Chretien, 178 Faubourg St. Honore, Paris 8e, France)
- Societe Chateaubriand. Bulletin. Nouvelle Series. a. ISSN 0081-0754

**Societe Chimique de France**
250, rue Saint Jacques, 75005 Paris, France.
- Actualite Chimique. m. (10 per yr.) (Co-Sponsor: Societe de Chimie Industrielle)
- Societe Chimique de France. Bulletin. (pub. by Masson)

**Societe Chronometrique de France**
- Annales Francaises de Chronometrie et de Micromecanique. (pub. by Observatoire de Besancon)

**Societe Civile du Repertoire du Notariat Defrenois**
83, Avenue Denfert-Rochereau, 75014 Paris, France.
- Repertoire du Notariat Defrenois. bi-m.

**Societe Cooperative d'Edition et de Librairie**
89 rue de la Boetie, 75008 Paris, France.
- Annuaire de la Cooperation F.N.C.C. biennial. ISSN 0071-4356 (Federation Nationale des Cooperatives de Consommation)
- Cooperation-Distribution-Consommation; idees, faits, techniques. m.

**Societe d'Agriculture, Sciences & Arts de Douai**
102 rue Gambetta, 59500 Douai, France.
- Societe d'Agriculture, Sciences et Arts de Douai. Memoires. irreg: approx. bienniel. ISSN 0037-8976

**Societe d'Anthropologie de Paris**
1 rue Rene Panhard, Paris (13e), France.
- Societe d'Anthropologie de Paris. Bulletin & Memoires. 4 times a year. ISSN 0037-8984

**Societe d'Archeologie, de Litterature, Sciences et Arts d'Avranches, Mortain et Granville**
26 rue d'Auditoire, Avranches (Manche), France.
- Revue de l'Avranchin et du Pays de Granville. q. ISSN 0035-1342

**Societe d'Archeologie et d'Histoire de la Charente-Maritime**
Musee Archeologique, 2, rue Gauthier, 17100 Saintes, France
(Subscr. to: Secretaire de la Societe, Bibliotheque Municipale, rue des Jacobins, 17100 Saintes, France)
- Societe d'Archeologie et d'Histoire de la Charente- Maritime. Recueil. a.

**Societe d'Archeologie et d'Histoire de la Manche**
B.P. 110, 50010 St-Lo Cedex, France.
- Societe d'Archeologie et d'Histoire de la Manche. Departement de la Manche. Revue. q. ISSN 0583-8193

**Societe d'Archeologie et d'Histoire du Berry**
8 Pl. des 4 Piliers, B.P. 69, 18002 Bourges Cedex, France.
- Cahiers d'Archeologie et d'Histoire du Berry. q. ISSN 0007-9693

**Societe d'Archeologie et de Statistique de la Drome**
2 rue Andre Lacroix, Valence-sur-Rhone, France.
- Bulletin d'Archeologie et de Statistique de la Drome. q. ISSN 0037-8992

**Societe d'Archeologie Lorraine**
Palais Ducal, Grande-Rue 64, Nancy, France.
- Pays Lorrain. q. ISSN 0031-3394 (Co-sponsor: Musee Historique Lorrain)

**Societe d'Art et d'Histoire**
Hotel-de-Ville, 61100 Flers, France.
- Pays Bas-Normand. q. ISSN 0031-3386

**Societe d'Astronomie Populaire de Toulouse**
9 rue Ozenne, 31000 Toulouse, France.
- Societe d'Astronomie Populaire de Toulouse. Bulletin Mensuel. m. ISSN 0037-900X

**Societe d'Ecologie**
- Bulletin d'Ecologie. (pub. by Masson)

**Societe d'Economie et de Science Sociales**
4, Place de Bretevil, 75015 Paris, France.
- Etudes Sociales. q. ISSN 0014-2204

**Societe d'Edition de Documentation Economique et Commerciale (S. E. D. E C)**
10 Av. d'Iena, 75783 Paris Cedex 16, France.
- M.O.C.I. (Moniteur de Commerce International) w. ISSN 0026-9719 (Centre Francais du Commerce Exterieur)

**Societe d'Edition de l'Expertise Automobile et Materiel Industriel**
19,rue des Filles du Calvaire, 75003 Paris, France.
- Expert Automobile. m.

**Societe d'Edition de la Brasserie Malterie**
1 Rue Grandville, B.P. 53, 54002 Nancy, France.
- Bios; brasserie malterie biotechnique. m.

**Societe d'Edition de la Revue des Loyers**
8 rue Ventadour, 75001 Paris, France.
- Revue des Loyers et des Fermages. m.

**Societe d'Edition de la Revue Francaise**
7 rue Lafayette, Paris (9e), France.
- Beautes de Mon Pays. fortn. ISSN 0005-7452
- Revue Francaise de l'Elite Europeenne. m. ISSN 0048-8054

- Spirales. m. ISSN 0038-7568

**Societe d'Edition de Publications Medicales**
80620 Domart-en-Ponthieu, France.
- Medecins de Groupe. m. ISSN 0025-6838

**Societe d'Edition du CONATEF**
5, rue Greffulhe, 75008 Paris, France.
- C. O. N. A. T. E. F. Bulletin d'Information. w.
- R. B. Region Parisienne Bassin Parisien. m.

**Societe d'Edition du Libre Service**
46 rue de Clichy, 75009 Paris, France.
- COCLICO. 21 per yr.
- L S A. (Libre Service Actualites); la vente de masse dans les magasins libre service, superettes, supermarches et hypermarches. w. ISSN 0024-2632
- Neo Restauration Hotellerie. m (11 per yr.)

**Societe d'Edition et d'Exploitation de Supports**
8, rue Milton, 75009 Paris, France.
- Aero-Club et le Pilote Prive; revue des loisirs de l'air. m.

**Societe d'Edition et d'Information**
9 Bd. des Italiens, Paris (2e), France.
- Nouvelle Revue Internationale; problemes de la paix et du socialisme. m. ISSN 0048-0975

**Societe d'Edition et d'Information Economique**
83 Av. de la Grande Armee, 75782 Paris Cedex 16, France.
- Union Agriculture. m. ISSN 0041-6819

**Societe d'Edition et de Documentation des Alliages Legers**
5 Rue Saint-Philippe-Du-Roule, Paris (8e), France.
- Revue de l'Aluminium. m. ISSN 0035-1318

**Societe d'Edition et de Presse**
106 Boulevard Malesherbes, 75828 Paris, France.
- Chauffage-Plomberie; techniques et informations. m. ISSN 0009-2037
- Droguerie Couleurs; menage. m.
- Equipment Architecture Interieure. 8 per yr.
- Quincaillesie Moderne. m.
- Special Bricolage. q.
- Special Commerce 2000. m.

**Societe d'Edition et de Presse T.G. Sarl**
8, Avenue du Maine, 75015 Paris, France.
- Tribune Gaulliste. m.

**Societe d'Edition et de Publication "las Talmeliers" (S O T A L)**
Avenue d'Eylau, 75782 Paris Cedex 16, France.
- Nouvelles de la Boulangerie. 2 per mo.

**Societe d'Edition et de Publicite**
see S. E. P Edition

**Societe d'Edition et de Publicite Agricoles, Industrielles et Commerciales (SEPAIC)**
42 rue du Louvre, 75001 Paris, France.
- Biscuits, Biscottes, Panification Industrielle, Produits Dietetiques Chocolat. Confiserie. m. ISSN 0006-3797
- Bricolage-Service-Bois Detail. m.
- Chocolaterie Confiserie de France. 11 per yr. ISSN 0009-4943 (Association pour le Perfectionnement et l'Expansion de la Chocolaterie et de la Confiserie de France)
- Embouteillage. 10 per yr.
- Industries de l'Alimentation Animale. bi-m. ISSN 0046-9300
- Meunerie Francaise. m. ISSN 0026-167X (Association Nationale de la Meunerie Francaise)
- Phytoma; defense des cultures. m. ISSN 0048-4091
- Revue de l'Embouteillage et des Industries du Conditionnement, Traitement, Distribution Transport. 10 per yr.
- Revue Technique et Economique de l'Industrie Alimentaire. m. ISSN 0035-4244
- Sucrerie Francaise; journal des fabricants de sucre. m. ISSN 0039-4491

**Societe d'Edition et de Publicite Techniques et Artistiques**
47 des Renaudes, 75017 Paris, France.
- Construction Moderne; revue d'architecture. bi-m. ISSN 0010-6852

**Societe d'Edition les Belles Lettres**
95 Bd. Raspail, 75006 Paris, France.
- Association Guillaume Bude. Bulletin. q. ISSN 0004-5527
- Confluents. irreg.
- Dialogues d'Histoire Ancienne. a. (Universite de Besancon. Centre de Recherches d'Histoire Ancienne)
- Etudes Celtiques. a. (Centre National de la Recherche Scientifique)
- Revue des Etudes Anciennes. a. ISSN 0035-2004 (Universite de Bordeaux III)
- Revue des Etudes Grecques. irreg. ISSN 0035-2039
- Revue des Etudes Latines. a. (Societe des Etudes Latines)
- Revue Numismatique. a. ISSN 0484-8942 (Societe Francaise de Numismatique)

**Societe d'Edition les Nouvelles Esthetiques**
7 Av. Stephane Mallarme, Paris (17e), France
- Nouvelles Esthetiques. m. ISSN 0029-490X (Orders for Spanish edition to: Beethoven 15, Barcelona 6; Italian edition to: via Archimede, 57 Milan 20129; Greek edition to: Technica International S.R.L., 4 rue Rethymnou, Musee National, Athens 147)

**Societe d'Edition Lyon-Sud-Est**
6, rue Mazard, Lyon (Rhone), France.
- Boulangerie Rhone-Alpes. bi-m.

**Societe d'Edition Medicale Europeenne**
20, Avenue de l'Opera, 75001 Paris, France.
- Cahiers de Chirurgie. 4 per yr. ISSN 0301-0791
- Cahiers de Stomatologie et de Chirurgie Maxillo-Faciale. 6 per yr.
- Femmes Chirugiens-Dentistes. q. (Syndicat des Femmes Chirugiens-Dentistes)
- Medicine Europeene/Europaeische Medizin/Medicina Europea; premiere revue de la communaute medicale europeenne/erste Zeitschrift der europaeischen Aerztegemeinschaft/prima revista della comunita medica europea. q. ISSN 0025-8016
- Ordre National des Medicins. Conseil Departemental des Hauts- de- Seine. Bulletin. bi-m.
- Psychiatries; revue francaise des psychiatres d'exercice prive. bi-m.

**Societe d'Edition pour Engins a Moteur**
"Jalna" Parc d'Ausnieres, 74500 Evian-les Bains, France.
- Special Motoculteurs et Tondeuses a Gazon. bi-m.
- Special Scies a Moteur et Accessoires. bi-m.

**Societe d'Edition pour la Mecanique et la Machine-Outil**
35 rue Grande Fontaine, 78100 St. Germain en Laye, France.
- Machine-Outil. m. ISSN 0024-9149
- Machines Francaises. q. ISSN 0024-9238

**Societe d'Edition Technique de l'Ennoblissement Textile**
12 rue d'Anjou, 12 Paris (8e), France.
- Teinture et Apprets. 6 per yr. ISSN 0040-2206 (Federation Nationale Teinture et Apprets)

**Societe d'Editions Afrique-Asie, Amerique Latine**
9 rue d'Aboukir, 75002 Paris, France
(U. S. Subscr. to: European Publishers, 36 W. 61st St., New York, NY 10023)
- Afrique-Asie. fortn.

**Societe d'Editions Commerciales et Techniques**
29 Bd. Henri IV, Paris (4e), France.
- Journal de la Navigation. w. ISSN 0047-2123

**Societe d'Editions de l'Habitation**
72 rue Saint-Charles, 75740 Paris Cedex 15, France.
- Habitation-Cahiers de l'UNIL/Logement C. I. L. m. ISSN 0017-6427 (Union Nationale Interprofessionnelle du Logement)

**Societe d'Editions de la Famille Educatrice**
277, rue Saint Jacques, 75005 Paris, France.
- Nouvelle Famille Educatrice. 8-9 per yr. ISSN 0029-4748 (Union Nationale des Associations de Parents d'Eleves de l'Enseignement Libre (UNAPEL))

**Societe d'Editions de la Siderurgie**
B.P. 707-08, 75367 Paris 8e, France.
- Chambre Syndicale de la Siderurgie Francaise. Bulletin. Serie Verte. m.

**Societe d'Editions de Periodiques d'Aviation Generale**
15 Allee Vendome, Box 26, 93 Livry-Gargan,
France.
- Aviasport; la revue du pilote. m. ISSN 0005-2094

**Societe d'Editions de Revues d'Armes**
- Gazette des Armes. (pub. by Argout Editions)

**Societe d'Editions des Ingenieurs Agricoles**
- Agriculture. (pub. by Agri-Scop)

**Societe d'Editions et d'Etudes de Transports**
43 rue de la Chaussee d'Antin, Paris (9e), France.
- Vie des Transports. w. ISSN 0042-5451

**Societe d'Editions et d'Etudes Techniques
(S.E.D.E.T.E.C.)**
12 rue Duguay-Trouin, 75006 Paris, France.
- Plaisirs de la Peche. bi-m. ISSN 0032-0501
- Plaisirs du Cinema. bi-m.

**Societe d'Editions et d'Information Viti-Vinicoles**
Rue de l'Ecole-des-Tambours, Macon, France.
- Journal de France des Appellations d'Origine;
  vignobles et vins. m. ISSN 0021-7735

**Societe d'Editions et de Documentation de l'Industrie
Hoteliere**
3 rue de la Ville l'Eveque, Paris (8e), France.
- Industrie Hoteliere. m.

**Societe d'Editions et de Periodiques Techniques**
79, Av. des Champs-Elysees, Paris (8e), France.
- L'Hotellerie. fortn.

**Societe d'Editions et de Publications Economiques et
Techniques de l'Alimentation (S.E.P.E.T.A.)**
57 rue Ampere, 75849 Paris, France.
- Boucherie Francaise. m. ISSN 0006-8284

**Societe d'Editions et de Publications Internationales
du Batiment et des Travaux Publics**
9 rue la Perouse, 75784 Paris 16, France.
- Entreprise Europeenne. q. ISSN 0014-9373
  (Federation Europeenne de la Construction)

**Societe d'Editions et de Publications l'Assurance
Francaise**
13 rue de Londres, Paris (9e), France.
- Assurance Francaise; revue internationale. m.
  ISSN 0004-6019

**Societe d'Editions et de Publicite Professionnelles et
Interprofessionnelles**
64 rue Caumartin, 75009 Paris, France.
- Glacier Francais; la revue des glaciers, artisans,
  semi-industriels, industriels. m. ISSN 0017-0704
  (Confederation Nationale des Syndicats de
  Fabricants de Glaces, Sorbets et Cremes Glacees)

**Societe d'Editions LANCRY**
45 rue de Lancry, 75010 Paris, France.
- Opticien-Lunetier; l'optique Francaise. m. ISSN
  0030-3984

**Societe d'Editions Medicales et Alimentaires
Relatives au Diabete**
25 rue Marechal-Joffre, 64000 Pau, France.
- Diabete et Nutrition. 4 per yr. ISSN 0012-1789

**Societe d'Editions Medico-Pharmaceutiques**
26, rue le Brun, 75013 Paris, France.
- Accessoirex. a; with quarterly supplements.
- Formulaire Thera. a. ISSN 0071-7622
- Parapharmex. a; with 16 supplements.
- Sempex Pharmaceutique. w. ISSN 0488-2644

**Societe d'Editions Modernes Parisiennes**
38 rue Jean Mermoz, 75008 Paris, France.
- Coiffure de Paris. 11 per yr. ISSN 0010-034X
- Votre Beaute; votre bonheur et twenty reunis. m.
  ISSN 0042-8965

**Societe d'Editions Parisiennes Associees**
49, Avenue Marceau, Paris 16, France.
- Crapouillot; magazine non conformiste. 5 per yr.
- Minute. w. ISSN 0026-573X

**Societe d'Editions Pharmaceutiques et Scientifiques
(S.E.P.E.S.)**
3 bis, rue de Montevideo, Paris 16(e), France.
- Sciences et Technique Pharmaceutiques. m.

**Societe d'Editions Radio-Phono**
65, rue du Faubourg Saint-Honore, 75008 Paris,
France.
- Guide du Show-Business; Guide Professionnel du
  Spectacle. a. ISSN 0072-8063

**Societe d'Editions Regionales**
38 rue des Martyrs, 75009 Paris, France.
- Paris Madame; mensuel pratique de la parisienne.
  m. ISSN 0398-0006

**Societe d'Editions Scientifiques**
4 Place de l'Odeon, 75 Paris (6e), France.
- Recherche. m. ISSN 0029-5671

**Societe d'Editons Modernes Parisiennes**
38, rue Jean-Mermoz, 75008 Paris, France.
- Suffrages. 8 per yr.

**Societe d'EEG et de Neurophysiologie Clinique de
Langue Francaise**
- Revue d'Electroencephalographie et de
  Neurophysiologie Clinique. (pub. by Masson)

**Societe d'Emulation de Montbeliard**
Musee Beurnier, 8, Place Saint-Martin, 25200
Montbeliard, France.
- Societe d'Emulation de Montbeliard. Memoires.
  irreg.

**Societe d'Emulation du Bourbonnais**
12, Avenue de la Republique, 03005 Moulins
Allier, France.
- Cahiers Bourbonnais et du Centre; arts, lettres,
  regionalisme. q. ISSN 0007-9618
- Societe d'Emulation du Bourbonnais. Bulletin;
  lettres, sciences et arts. q. ISSN 0037-9158

**Societe d'Emulation Historique et Litteraire
d'Abbeville**
Hotel de Ville, 80101 Abbeville, France.
- Etudes Picardes. (pub. by Editions A. et J. Picard)
- Societe d'Emulation Historique et Litteraire
  d'Abbeville. Bulletin. a. ISSN 0081-0819

**Societe d'Endocrinologie et Societe Belge
d'Endocrinologie**
- Annales d'Endocrinologie. (pub. by Masson)

**Societe d'Ergonomie de la Langue Francaise**
Centre d'Etudes Bioclimatiques, 21 rue Becquerel,
F-67087 Strasbourg.
- Journees de Physiologie Appliquee au Travail
  Humain. (pub. by N.E.B. Editions Scientifiques)
- Societe d'Ergonomie de Langue Francaise. Actes
  du Congres. irreg. ISSN 0081-0835

**Societe d'Ethnographie de Paris**
- Ethnographie. (pub. by Librairie Orientaliste Paul
  Geuthner)

**Societe d'Etude du Dix-Septieme Siecle**
24 Bd. Poissonniere, 75009 Paris, France.
- Dix-Septieme Siecle. q. ISSN 0012-4273

**Societe D'Etude du Vingtieme Siecle**
24 rue Emile Dubois, 75014 Paris, France.
- Cahiers du Vingtieme Siecle. (pub. by Editions
  Klincksieck)
- Societe d'Etude du Vingtieme Siecle. Bulletin.
  irreg. ISSN 0085-624X

**Societe d'Etude et d'Information Medicales**
- Mises a Jour d'Hepato-Gastro-Enterologie. (pub.
  by Editions Medicales D.H.R.)

**Societe d'Etude et de Vulgarisation de la Zoologie
Agricole**
Institut de Biologie Animale, Faculte des Sciences,
Avenue des Facultes, 33400 Talence, France.
- Revue de Zoologie Agricole et de Pathologie
  Vegetale. q. ISSN 0035-1806

**Societe d'Etudes Allemandes**
5, Quai Koch, F 67000 Strasbourg, France.
- Revue d'Allemagne et des Pays de Langue
  Allemande. q. (Centre d'Etudes Germaniques)

**Societe d'Etudes Ardennaises**
Charleville-Mezieres, Ardennes, France.
- Revue Historique Ardennaise. q. ISSN 0035-3272

**Societe d'Etudes de Brest et du Leon**
11 rue de Royan, Brest, France.
- Cahiers de l'Iroise. q. ISSN 0007-9898

**Societe d'Etudes de Chimie Therapeutique (S.E.C.T.)**
3, rue J. B. Clement, 92290 Chatenay-Malaby,
France.
- Chimica Therapeutica/Chimie Therapeutique. bi-
  m. ISSN 0009-4374 (Societe Francaise de Chimie
  Therapeutique)

**Societe d'Etudes et d'Informations Economiques**
55, rue de Chateaudun, 75009 Paris, France.
- Perspectives. w.

**Societe d'Etudes et de Diffusion des Industries
Thermiques et Aerauliques**
78 rue Boissiere, 75116 Paris, France.
- Promoclim A: Applications Thermiques et
  Aerauliques. q.
- Promoclim B: Bulletin du Genie Climatique. m.

**Societe d'Etudes et de Documentation Economiques,
Industrielles et Sociales**
44 rue Francois, 75008 Paris, France.
- Chroniques d'Actualite de la S.E.D.E.I.S. fortn.
  ISSN 0396-437X

**Societe d'Etudes et de Documentation Municipale**
50, rue de Rivoli, 75004 Paris, France.
- Communes de France. m. ISSN 0573-0910

**Societe d'Etudes et de Preparation aux Examens
Publics et Prives**
5 Bd Beaumarchais, Paris (4e), France.
- Informateur de la Quinzaine. s-m. ISSN 0019-
  9893
- Societe d'Etudes et de Preparation aux Examens
  Publics et Prives. Revue d'Etudes; revue
  mensuelle pour l'enseignement par
  correspondence. m. ISSN 0049-1063

**Societe d'Etudes et de Publications Artistiques**
13 rue Saint-Georges, Paris (9e), France.
- Connaissance des Arts. m. ISSN 0010-5988

**Societe d'Etudes et de Publications Economiques**
13 rue Saint-Georges, 75439 Paris, France
- Entreprise. w. ISSN 0013-9068
- Preuves; les idees qui changent le monde. q. ISSN
  0032-7980
- Realites. m. ISSN 0034-0944 (Dist. in U.S. by:
  Madame Juka, Box 86, Bronx, N.Y. 10471)

**Societe d'Etudes et de Realisations Publicitaires**
38, rue Marceau, 94-Ivry, France
- Phenix; revue internationale de la bande dessinee.
  4 per yr. ISSN 0300-3639 (Societe d'Etudes et de
  Recherches des Litteratures Dessinees)
  (Dist. in U.S., Graphic Story Bookshop, Box 2053,
  Culver City, CA. 90230)

**Societe d'Etudes et de Recherches des Litteratures
Dessinees**
- Phenix. (pub. by Societe d'Etudes et de
  Realisations Publicitaires)

**Societe d'Etudes Historiques des Relations
Internationales Contemporaines (S.E.H.R.I.C.)**
17, rue de la Sorbonne, 75230 Paris Cedex 05,
France.
- Relations Internationales. q. ISSN 0335-2013
  (Universite de Paris I (Pantheon-Sorbonne).
  Institut d'Histoire des Relations Internationales
  Contemporaines) (Co-Sponsor: Institut
  Universitaire de Hautes Etudes Internationales,
  Geneva)

**Societe d'Etudes Italiennes**
Grand Palais-Perron Alexander III, Cours la Reine,
Paris 8e, France.
- Revue des Etudes Italiennes. q. ISSN 0035-2047

**Societe d'Etudes Jauresiennes**
Secretariat: c/o M.J.P. Riouy, 25 rue Damremont,
75018 Paris, France
(Orders to Mme. A. Waingart, 131 rue de l'Abbe
Groult, 75015 Paris, France)
- Societe d'Etudes Jauresiennes. Bulletin. q.

**Societe d'Etudes Linguistiques et Anthropologiques de
France**
5 rue de Marseille, 75010 Paris, France.
- Societe d'Etudes Linguistiques et
  Anthropologiques de France. Numero Special.
  irreg.

**Societe d'Etudes Napoleoniennes**
Sorbonne, Ecole Pratique des Hautes Etudes,
Section IV, 45 rue des Ecoles, Paris (5e), France.
- Institut Napoleon. Revue. a. ISSN 0020-2371

**Societe d'Etudes Numismatiques et Archeologiques**
3 rue des Arts, 92100 Boulogne Billancourt, France.
- Cahiers Numismatiques. q. ISSN 0008-0373

**Societe d'Etudes Ornithologiques**
46 rue d'Ulm, 75230 Paris 5, France.
- Alauda; revue internationale d'ornithologie. q. ISSN 0002-4619

**Societe d'Etudes, Recherches, et Documentation Cinematographiques**
c/o Bernard Chardere, Ed., Boite Postale 3, 69396 Lyon 3, France.
- Premier Plan; hommes, oeuvres, problemes du cinema. q. ISSN 0032-7387

**Societe d'Expansion Technique et Economique S.A.**
5 rue Jules Lefebvre, 75009 Paris, France.
- Informations-Chimie. m. ISSN 0020-045X
- Parfums,Cosmetiques,Aromes. 8 per yr.

**Societe d'Exploitation de l'Officiel du Batiment et des Travaux Publics de Toulouse et de Midi-Pyrenees (SODOFI)**
11, Bd des Recollets, 31078 Toulouse Cedex, France.
- Officiel du Batiment et des Travaux Publics de Toulouse et de Midi-Pyrenees. m.

**Societe d'Exploitation du Courrier du Parlement**
7 rue d'Aboukir, Paris (2e) France.
- Courrier du Parlement. w.(40 per yr.) ISSN 0045-8899

**Societe d'Histoire d'Archeologie de la Lorraine**
Archives Prefecture, F. 57034 Metz, France.
- Societe d'Histoire et d'Archeologie de la Lorraine. Annuaire. a.

**Societe d'Histoire de France**
- Societe d'Histoire de France. Annuaire. (pub. by Editions Klincksieck)

**Societe d'Histoire de la Medecine Hebraique**
c/o Isidore Simon, Ed., 177 Bd. Malesherbes, Paris (17e), France.
- Revue d'Histoire de la Medecine Hebraique. q. ISSN 0035-2330

**Societe d'Histoire de la Pharmacie**
4 Av. de l'Observatoire, 75270 Paris Cedex 06, France.
- Revue d'Histoire de la Pharmacie. q. ISSN 0035-2349

**Societe d'Histoire des Communications dans le Midi de la France**
24, Allees des Demoiselles, 31400 - Toulouse, France.
- Histoire des Communications. q.

**Societe d'Histoire du Theatre**
98 Bd. Kellermann, 75013 Paris, France.
- Revue d'Histoire du Theatre. q. ISSN 0035-2373

**Societe d'Histoire Ecclesiastique de la France**
28,rue d'Assas, 75006 Paris, France.
- Revue d'Histoire de l'Eglise de France. s-a. ISSN 0048-7988

**Societe d'Histoire et d'Archeologie de Haguenau**
c/o A.M. Burg, Musee de Haguenau, F-67500 Haguenau, France.
- Etudes Haguenoviennes. triennial. ISSN 0085-0322

**Societe d'Histoire et d'Archeologie de la Goele**
Mairie, Dammartin-en-Goele 77230, France.
- Societe d'Histoire et d'Archeologie de la Goele. Bulletin d'Information. a. ISSN 0081-0967

**Societe d'Histoire et d'Archeologie de Vichy et des Environs**
1, Avenue Thermale, 03200 Vichy, France.
- Societe d'Histoire et d'Archeologie de Vichy et des Environs. Bulletin. s-a.

**Societe d'Histoire Litteraire de la France**
- Revue d'Histoire Litteraire de la France. (pub. by Librairie Armand Colin)

**Societe d'Histoire Moderne**
5 Villa Poirier, 75015 Paris, France.
- Societe d'Histoire Moderne. Annuaire. q. ISSN 0081-0975
- Societe d'Histoire Moderne. Bulletin. q.

**Societe d'Histoire Moderne et Contemporaine**
c/o M. J. Cointet, 4 Square Emile Zola, 75015 Paris, France.
- Revue d'Histoire Moderne et Contemporaine. q. ISSN 0048-8003

**Societe d'Horticulture et des Jardins Populaires de France**
95-107 Bd. Saly, 59308 Valenciennes (Nord), France.
- Pour Nos Jardins. bi-m.

**Societe d'Hygiene de Langue Francaise**
- Medecine et Nutrition. (pub. by Editions la Simarre)

**Societe d'Informations Agricoles et Commerciales**
51, rue Olivier Metra, 75020 Paris, France.
- Marches Agricoles-l'Echo des Halles. 5 per w. ISSN 0397-5754

**Societe d'Odonto-Stomatologie de Touraine**
- Cahiers d'Odonto-Stomatologie. (pub. by Editions la Simarre)

**Societe d'Organisatierciale**
21, rue de la Nuee-Bleue, 67000 Strasbourg, France.
- Presence de Strasbourg. q.

**Societe d'Organisation Professionnelle**
136, Cours Lafayette, 69-Lyon (3e), France.
- France Mecanographique. m.

**Societe de Biogeographie**
57 rue Cuvier, 75 231 Paris, France.
- Societe de Biogeographie, Compte Rendu. q. ISSN 0037-9018

**Societe de Biologie et de ses Filiales**
- Societe de Biologie et de ses Filiales. Comptes Rendus des Seances. (pub. by Masson)
- Societe de Pathologie Exotique et de ses Filiales. Bulletin. (pub. by Masson)

**Societe de Biometrie Humaine**
41 rue Gay-Lussac, Paris (5e), France.
- Biometrie Humaine. 2 per yr. ISSN 0006-3428

**Societe de Chimie Biologique**
- Biochimie. (pub. by Masson)

**Societe de Chimie Organique et Biologique**
Commentry (Allier), France.
- Amino Acides, Peptides, Proteines. Cahier. irreg. ISSN 0066-1244

**Societe de Chimie Physique**
Ecole de Physique et de Chemie, 10 rue Vauquelin, Paris 5e, France.
- Journal de Chimie Physique et de Physicochimie Biologique. m. ISSN 0021-7689 (U.S. Subscr. Address: Stechert Macmillan, Inc., 7250 Westfield Avenue Pennsauken, NJ 08110)
- Societe de Chimie Physique. Annuaire. a. ISSN 0081-0770

**Societe de Chirurgie de Lille**
- Lille Chirurgical. (pub. by Pierre Decoulx, Ed. & Pub.)

**Societe de Chirurgie de Lyon**
- Lyon Chirurgical. (pub. by Masson)

**Societe de Chirurgie Thoracique de Langue Francaise**
- Annales de Chirurgie Thoracique et Cardio-Vasculaire. (pub. by Expansion Scientifique)

**Societe de Controle et d'Exploitation de Transports Auxiliaires**
Centre de Documentation, 7 rue Pablo Neruda, 92300 Levallois Perret, France.
- S C E T A Documentation. w.

**Societe de Diffusion d'Informations Halieutiques**
B.P. 179, 8, rue du Chalutier-la Tanche, 56014 Lorient, France.
- France-Europeche et Marches du Poisson. 10 per yr.
- France Peche; la plus importante revue europeenne de peche professionnelle. m.(10 per yr) ISSN 0015-9689

**Societe de Diffusion Historique**
8 rue de Monttessuy, 75007 Paris, France (Orders to: Anthinea, B.P. 229, 75827 Paris Cedex 17, France)
- Anthinea; Revue d'Etudes Historiques. q.

**Societe de Documentation et d'Analyses Financieres (D.A.F.S.A.)**
125 rue Montmartre, 75002 Paris, France.
- Bourse de Paris. Statistiques Mensuelles. m. ISSN 0039-0623 (Chambre Syndicale des Agents de Change)

**Societe de Geographie**
184 Bd. Saint-Germain, Paris (6e), France.
- Acta Geographica. q. ISSN 0001-5687

**Societe de Geographie Commerciale de Paris**
8 rue Roquepine, Paris (8e), France.
- Revue Economique Francaise. q. ISSN 0035-2780

**Societe de Geographie de Lille**
116 rue de l'Hopital Militaire, Lille, France.
- Hommes et Terres du Nord. s-a. ISSN 0018-439X (Co-sponsor: Institut de Geographie de Lille)

**Societe de Geographie de Marseille**
Bibliotheque de la Faculte des Sciences, Place V. Hugo, Marseilles 3, France.
- Societe de Geographie de Marseille. Bulletin. biennial. ISSN 0081-0789

**Societe de Gestion des Participations de l' Enterprise de Recherches et d' Activities Petrolieres**
7 rue Nelation, Paris 75739 (15), France.
- Sogerap Lettre. m.

**Societe de Kinesitherapie**
- Annales de Kinesitherapie. (pub. by Masson)

**Societe de l'Histoire du Protestantisme Francais**
54 rue des Saints-Peres, 75016 Paris, France.
- Societe de l'Histoire du Protestantisme Francais. Bulletin. q. ISSN 0037-9050

**Societe de l'Industrie Minerale**
19 rue du Grand Moulin, 42029 St.-Etienne Cedex, France.
- Industrie Minerale. m. ISSN 0035-1431
- Industrie Minerale. Mine. 5 per yr.
- Societe de l'Industrie Minerale. Annuaire. a. ISSN 0081-0797

**Societe de la Revue des Deux Mondes**
15 rue de l'Universite, 75007 Paris, France.
- Nouvelle Revue des Deux Mondes. m.

**Societe de la Revue "Pollution Atmospherique"**
21 rue Murillo, 75008 Paris, France.
- Pollution Atmospherique. q. ISSN 0032-3632

**Societe de Laryngologie des Hopitaux de Paris**
- Annales d'Oto-Laryngologie et de Chirurgie Cervico Faciale. (pub. by Masson)

**Societe de Legislation Comparee**
31 rue Saint-Guillaume, Paris (7e), France.
- Revue Internationale de Droit Compare. q. ISSN 0035-3337

**Societe de Linguistique de Paris**
- Societe de Linguistique de Paris. Bulletin. (pub. by Editions Klincksieck)

**Societe de Linguistique Romane**
c/o Georges Straka, Universite des Sciences Humaines, 25 rue du Mal Juin, 67084 Strasbourg, France.
- Revue de Linguistique Romane. s-a. ISSN 0035-1458

**Societe de Medecine de Nancy**
- Annales Medicales de Nancy. (pub. by Service de Presse, Edition, Information)

**Societe de Medecine de Vittel**
44 Ave. Georges V, Paris 8, France.
- Rein et Foie; Maladies de la Nutrition. irreg., vol. 15, 1974. ISSN 0085-5464 (Co-sponsor: Societe des Eaux Minerales et Vittel)

**Societe de Mythologie Francaise**
Lycee Felix Faure, 60021 Beauvais, France.
- Societe de Mythologie Francaise Bulletin. q. ISSN 0037-9077

**Societe de Neuro-Chirurgie de Langue Francaise**
- Neuro-Chirurgie. (pub. by Masson)

**Societe de Neuro-Psychiatrie de l'Ouest**
Box 52, Rennes, France.
- Revue de Neuropsychiatrie de l'Ouest. q. ISSN 0035-161X

**Societe de Pathologie Biologique**
- Pathologie Biologie. (pub. by Semaine des Hopitaux)

**Societe de Pharmacie de Bordeaux**
c/o Faculte de Medecine et de Pharmacie, Rue Leyteire, Bordeaux, France.
● Societe de Pharmacie de Bordeaux. Bulletin. q. ISSN 0037-9093

**Societe de Pharmacie de Lyon**
● Societe de Pharmacie de Lyon. Bulletin des Travaux. (pub. by Publications Periodiques Specialisees)

**Societe de Pharmacie de Montpellier**
Montpellier, France.
● Societe de Pharmacie de Montpellier. Travaux. q. ISSN 0037-9115

**Societe de Pharmacie de Nancy**
B. P. 403, Nancy, France.
● Sciences Pharmaceutiques et Biologique de Lorraine. q. ISSN 0301-0635

**Societe de Pharmacie de Strasbourg**
● Societe de Pharmacie de Strasbourg. Bulletin. (pub. by Faculte de Pharmacie de Strasbourg)

**Societe de Physiologie et de Medecine Aeronautiques et Cosmonautiques**
● Revue de Medecine Aeronautique et Spatiale. (pub. by I.F.P.)

**Societe de Presse, d'Edition et de Diffusion d'Informations Sociales**
44 Rue Vieille-Du-Temple, 75-Paris (4e), France.
● Voix du Retraite. m. ISSN 0049-6707

**Societe de Presse, de Publicite et d'Edition de Landehen**
B.P. 540, 22010 Saint-Brieuc, France.
● Armor; magazine de la Bretagne. m. ISSN 0044-8966

**Societe de Presse et d'Edition de la Kinesitherapie**
see under S. P. E. K (La Maison des Kinesitherapeutes)

**Societe de Presse et d'Edition Ovine et Caprine (S.P.E.O.C.)**
149, rue de Bercy, 75579 Paris Cedex 12, France.
● Chevre; revue des eleveurs de chevres. 6 per yr. ISSN 0045-6608 (Institut Technique de l'Elevage Ovin et Caprin)
● Patre. m(10 per yr.) ISSN 0475-9141 (Institut Technique de l'Elevage Ovin et Caprin)

**Societe de Presse et d'Editions Saint-Honore-Vacances 365 Jours**
45 rue Saint-Honore, 75001 Paris, France.
● Paris Selection. m. (Office de Tourisme de Paris)

**Societe de Presse et de Diffusion d'Informations**
14 rue Armand Moisant, Paris (15e), France.
● Cooperation Agricole. m. ISSN 0010-8359

**Societe de Presse Jours de France**
7 Rond-Point des Champs-Elysees, 75008 Paris, France.
● Jours de France. w. ISSN 0022-5681

**Societe de Production Litteraire**
10, rue du Regard, 75006 Paris, France.
● Item: Revue d'Opinion Libre. m.

**Societe de Productions Documentaires**
80, Route de Saint-Cloud, 92500 Rueil-Malmaison, France.
● Chimie et Industrie. 22 per yr. ISSN 0009-4358
● Corrosion: Traitements, Protection, Finition. m(8 mos. per yr) ISSN 0010-9398
● Energie Nucleaire; revue de physique et de chimie nucleaires et de genie atomique. 6 per yr. ISSN 0013-7375
● Parfums, Cosmetiques, Savons de France. 11 per yr. ISSN 0031-1960
● Peintures, Pigments, Vernis. m. ISSN 0031-4102
● Produits et Problemes Pharmaceutiques; revue du pharmacien. 11 per yr. ISSN 0032-9959

**Societe de Publications Economiques et Feminines**
114 Av. des Champs-Elysees, Paris (8e), France.
● Marie-France. m. ISSN 0025-3057

**Societe de Publications Radio-Electriques et Scientifiques**
2 12, rue de Bellevue, 75019 Paris, France.
● Haut-Parleur. w.

**Societe de Sciences, Lettres et Arts de Pau**
13 Avenue Trespoey, Pau, France.
● Revue de Pau et du Bearn. a.

**Societe de Statistique de Paris**
29, rue de Rome, Paris 75008, France.
● Societe de Statistique de Paris. Journal; la revue internationale des statisticiens d'expression francaise. q. ISSN 0037-914X

**Societe de Stomatologie et de Chirurgie Maxillo-Faciale de France**
● Revue de Stomatologie et de Chirurgie Maxillo-Faciale. (pub. by Masson)

**Societe des Africanistes**
Musee de l'Homme, Place du Trocadero, 75116 Paris, France.
● Societe des Africanistes. Journal. s-a. ISSN 0037-9166

**Societe des Agreges**
1 rue Laplace, 75005 Paris, France.
● Agregation. 8 per yr. ISSN 0044-6742

**Societe des Americanistes de Paris**
Palais de Chaillot, Pl. du Trocadero, 75116 Paris, France.
● Bibliographie Americaniste. s-a. ISSN 0006-131X
● Societe des Americanistes. Journal. s-a. ISSN 0037-9174

**Societe des Amis de Charles du Bos**
24 Boulevard Victor Hugo, 92200 Neuilly-sur-Seine, France.
● Cahiers Charles du Bos. a. ISSN 0575-0415

**Societe des Amis de Felix d'Herelle**
11 Rue Boissiere, 75116 Paris, France.
● Nouvelles Archives Hospitalieres. q. ISSN 0029-4853

**Societe des Amis de Han Ryner**
3 Allee du Chateau, Pavillons-Sous-Bois 93320, France.
● Amis de Han Ryner. Cahiers. q. ISSN 0003-178X

**Societe des Amis de l'Orgue**
76 bis rue des Saints-Peres, 75007-Paris, France.
● Orgue; histoire-technique-esthetique. q. ISSN 0030-5170

**Societe des Amis de l'Universite de Clermont**
3 Av. Vercingetorix, 63000 Clermont- Ferrand, France.
● Revue d'Auvergne. q. ISSN 0035-1008

**Societe des Amis de la Romania**
19 Rue de la Sorbonne, Paris(5e), France.
● Romania; revue consacree a l'etude des langues et des literatures romanes. q. ISSN 0035-8029

**Societe des Amis de Montaigne**
6, Villa Chanez, 75016 Paris, France.
● Societe des Amis de Montaigne. Bulletin. irreg. ISSN 0037-9182

**Societe des Amis de Paul-Louis Courier**
17 rue Claude Debussy, Tours, France.
● Cahiers Paul-Louis Courier. s-a. ISSN 0084-8239

**Societe des Amis de Port-Royal**
23 Quai de Conti, 75006 Paris, France.
● Chroniques de Port-Royal. ISSN 0529-4975

**Societe des Amis de St-Jacques de Compostelle**
87 rue Vieille-Du-Temple, Paris (3e), France.
● Compostelle. q. ISSN 0010-4396 (Centre d'Etudes Compostellanes)

**Societe des Amis du Chateau de Pau**
Chateau de Pau, France.
● Amis du Chateau de Pau. Bulletin. q. ISSN 0003-1852

**Societe des Amis du Musee Carnavalet**
23 rue de Sevigne, 75003 Paris, France.
● Musee Carnavalet. Bulletin. s-a. ISSN 0027-3767

**Societe des Amis du Musee d'Ingres**
19, rue de l'Hotel de Ville, 82000 Montauban, France.
● Musee Ingres. Bulletin. s-a. ISSN 0027-3783

**Societe des Amis du Musee des Antiquites Nationales et du Chateau de Saint Germain en Laye**
2 Place de Mareil, 78100 Saint-Germain en Laye, France.
● Antiquites Nationales. a. ISSN 0066-4898

**Societe des Amis du Museum National d'Histoire Naturelle**
12 bis, Place Henri Bergson, Paris (8e), France.
● Science et Nature. bi-m. ISSN 0036-8342

**Societe des Anciens Eleves de l'Ecole Nationale Superieure d'Arts & Metiers**
9 bis, Av. d'Iena, Paris (16e), France.
● Arts et Metiers. m. ISSN 0004-4008

**Societe des Anciens Eleves de l'Ecole Nationale Superieure des Arts et Industries de Strasbourg**
56, Bd. d'Anvers, 67000 Strasbourg, France.
● Arts et Industries. q. ISSN 0004-3982

**Societe des Annales de Bourgogne**
8 rue Jeannin, Dijon, 21000, France.
● Annales de Bourgogne; revue historique trimestrielle. q. ISSN 0003-3901 (Co-sponsors: Association Bourguignonne des Societes Savantes; Centre d'Etudes Bourguignonnes; Centre National de la Recherche Scientifique)

**Societe des Antiquaires de l'Ouest**
Passage de l'Echevinage, 86000 Poitiers, France.
● Societe des Antiquaires de l'Ouest. Bulletin. q. ISSN 0037-9190

**Societe des Antiquaires de Picardie**
Musee de Picardie, Rue de la Republique, Amiens, France.
● Societe des Antiquaires de Picardie. Quarterly Bulletin. q. ISSN 0037-9204

**Societe des Architectes Diplomes Par le Gouvernement**
100 rue du Cherche-Midi, Paris (6e), France.
● A M C. (Architecture, Mouvement, Continuite) 4 per yr. ISSN 0336-1675

**Societe des Arts et Metiers**
3 Bd. Desaix, 63000 Clermont-Ferrand, France.
● Centre Auvergne Gadz'arts. Bulletin Trimestriel des Ingenieurs Arts et Metiers de la Region Auvergne. q. ISSN 0339-1116

**Societe des Auteurs, Compositeurs, Editeurs pour la Gerance des Droits de Reproduction Mecanique**
62 rue Blanche, Paris 9e, France.
● Societe des Auteurs, Compositeurs, Editeurs pour la Gerance des Droits de Reproduction Mecanique. (Bulletin) irreg. ISSN 0081-0843

**Societe des Bibliophiles de Guyenne**
c/o Bibliotheque Municipale, 3 rue Mably, 33075 Bordeaux, France.
● Revue Francaise d'Histoire du Livre. s-a. ISSN 0037-9212

**Societe des Editions Air et Cosmos**
6 rue Anatole de la Forge, Paris 75017, France.
● Air et Cosmos; hebdomadaire aerospatial et des techniques avancees. w. ISSN 0044-6971

**Societe des Editions de l'Imprimerie Nouvelle**
89 rue Barrault, 75013 Paris, France.
● Faconnage de l'Imprimerie. a.

**Societe des Editions du Genie Civil et de la Metallurgie**
● Genie Civil. (pub. by E. G. C. M.)
● Metallurgie et la Construction Mecanique. (pub. by E. G. C. M.)

**Societe des Editions du Tresor**
13 Quai Voltaire, Paris (7e), France.
● Revue du Tresor; organe d'etudes et d'informations professionnelles. m. ISSN 0035-2713

**Societe des Editions Electro Negoce**
13, rue Marivaux, 75002 Paris, France.
● Electro-Negoce. m (10 per yr.)

**Societe des Editions Flash**
3 rue de Palestro, 75 Paris (2e), France.
● Rail Miniature Flash. m. ISSN 0033-8737

**Societe des Editions Radio**
9 rue Jacob, 75006 Paris, France.
● Automatique et Informatique Industrielles. irreg.
● Electronique Actualites. w.

- Electronique et Applications Industrielles. 16 per yr.
- Electronique pour Vous International. 11 per yr.
- Nouvelle Revue du Son. 11 per yr.
- Toute l'Electronique; technique expliquee et appliquee. 11 per yr. ISSN 0040-9855

**Societe des Editions Regirex-France**
62 rue Ampere, 75017 Paris.
- Techniques et Architecture. bi-m.
- Urbanisme; revue francaise. bi-m. ISSN 0042-1014 (Societe Nouvelle de la Revue Urbanisme)

**Societe des Electriciens, Electroniciens et Radioelectriciens SEE**
- Onde Electrique. (pub. by Masson)

**Societe des Etudes des Hautes Alpes**
23 rue Carnot, Gap, France.
- Queyras. q. ISSN 0048-6450

**Societe des Etudes du Comminges**
2 rue Thiers, 31800 Saint Gaudens, France.
- Revue de Comminges. q. ISSN 0035-1059

**Societe des Etudes Juives**
17 rue Saint Georges, 75009 Paris, France.
- Revue des Etudes Juives. q. ISSN 0035-2055
- Societe des Etudes Juives. Memoires. (pub. by Mouton Publishers NE)

**Societe des Etudes Latines**
- Revue des Etudes Latines. (pub. by Societe d'Edition "les Belles-Lettres")

**Societe des Etudes Renaniennes**
16 rue Chaptal, Paris (9e), France.
- Etudes Renaniennes Bulletin. q. ISSN 0046-2659

**Societe des Etudes Robespierristes**
Universite de Paris I, Sorbonne, Paris (5e), France.
- Annales Historiques de la Revolution Francaise. q. ISSN 0003-4436

**Societe des Etudes Romantiques**
29, Boulevard Gergovia, 63037 Clermont-Ferrand Cedex, France.
- Romantisme; revue de la societe des Etudes Romantiques. 3 per yr. ISSN 0048-8593

**Societe des Explorateurs et des Voyageurs Francais**
9 bis Avenue de Montespan, 75116 Paris, France.
- Cahiers des Explorateurs. a. ISSN 0526-8133
- Societe des Explorateurs et des Voyageurs Francais. Annuaire General. irreg. ISSN 0081-086X

**Societe des Francs-Bibliophiles**
39 rue Raynouard, 75016 Paris, France.
- Societe des Francs-Bibliophiles. Annuaire. a. ISSN 0081-0878

**Societe des Gens de Lettres de France**
Hotel de Massa, 38 rue du Faubourg Saint- Jacques, 75014 Paris, France.
- Revue des Lettres. q. ISSN 0035-2128

**Societe des Ingenieurs Civils de France**
19 rue Blanche, 75009 Paris, France.
- Sciences et Techniques; revue de l'ingenieur. m. ISSN 0036-8652
- Societe des Ingenieurs Civils de France. Annuaire. irreg. ISSN 0081-0886

**Societe des Ingenieurs de l'Automobile**
- Ingenieurs de l'Automobile. (pub. by R.A.I.P.)

**Societe des Ingenieurs Diplomes E.T.P**
- Ingenieur-Constructeur. (pub. by Compagnie Francaise d'Editions)

**Societe des Mines et Transports**
3 rue de la Boetie, Paris (8e), France.
- Mineurs de France. m. ISSN 0026-5071

**Societe des Missionnaires d'Afrique (Peres Blancs)**
5, rue Roger-Verlomme, 75003 Paris, France.
- Voix d'Afrique; d'Alsace et de Lorraine. 6 per yr.

**Societe des Missions Africaines**
150 Cours Gambetta, 69361 Lyon, France.
- Appel de l'Afrique. q. (plus special annual no.)

**Societe des Oceanistes**
Musee de l'Homme, 75116 Paris, France.
- Societe des Oceanistes. Journal. q.
- Societe des Oceanistes. Publications. irreg. ISSN 0081-0894

**Societe des Poetes Francais**
Hotel de Massa, 38 rue du Faubourg Saint-Jacques, Paris 14e, France.
- Societe des Poetes Francais. Annuaire. a. ISSN 0081-0908
- Societe des Poetes Francais. Bulletin Trimestriel. 3 per yr.

**Societe des Presses Alpines**
16 Place Sainte-Claire, B.P. 656, 38015 Grenoble Cedex, France.
- Journal du Four Electrique et des Industries Electrochimiques. 10 per yr. ISSN 0021-8189
- Mines et Metallurgie; revue des industries minieres et metallurgiques. 6 per yr. ISSN 0026-5047
- Revue Technique du Feu. 10 per yr. ISSN 0048-8194

**Societe des Professeurs d'Histoire et de Geographie**
8 Rue Nicolas-Charlet, 75015 Paris, France.
- Historiens et Geographes. bi-m. ISSN 0046-757X

**Societe des Publications du Moniteur**
- Cahiers Techniques du Moniteur. (pub. by Usine Publications S.A.)

**Societe des Publications "Le Cuir"**
54 rue Rene-Boulanger, Paris, (10e), France.
- Cuir. 3 per wk. ISSN 0011-2690
- Revue Technique des Industries du Cuir. m. ISSN 0004-5462

**Societe des Publications Radio-Electriques et Scientifiques**
- Hifi Stereo. (pub. by Publications Georges Ventillard)

**Societe des Sciences Entomologiques des Alpes Maritimes et de la Corse**
3 rue Bergondi, 06 Nice, France.
- Entomops; revue trimestrielle des entomologistes des alpes maritimes et de la corse. q. ISSN 0013-8967

**Societe des Sciences Historiques et Naturelles de Semur en Auxois**
21140 Semur en Auxois, France.
- Tour de l'Orle d'Or. s-a.

**Societe des Sciences Medicales de la Moselle**
22, Avenue Foch, 57000 Metz, France.
- Societe des Sciences Medicales de la Moselle. Bulletin et Memoires. q.

**Societe des Sciences Naturelles de Dijon**
Faculte de Sciences, 6 Bd Gabriel, F 21000-Dijon, France
(Subscr. Address: Librairie de l'Universite, 17 rue de la Liberte, 21014 Dijon, France)
- Bulletin Scientifique de Bourgogne. a.

**Societe des Sciences Physiques et Naturelles de Bordeaux**
- Societe des Sciences Physiques et Naturelles de Bordeaux. Memoires. (pub. by Bibliotheque Interuniversitaire de Bordeaux)

**Societe Droit et Liberte**
120 rue Saint-Denis, 75002 Paris, France.
- Droit et Liberte. m. ISSN 0012-6411 (Mouvement contre le Racisme l'antisemitisme et pour la Paix)

**Societe du Journal Actuel**
2, Impasse Lebouis, 75014 Paris, France.
- Actuel. m.

**Societe du Journal des Usines a Gaz**
62 rue de Courcelles, Paris (8e), France.
- Gaz d'Aujourd'Hui; journal des Usines a Gaz. 11 per yr. ISSN 0016-5328 (Association Technique De' l'Industrie du Gaz en France)

**Societe du Moniteur des Scieries**
70 Blvd. Beaumarchais, 75011 Paris, France.
- Bois Hebdo; scierie-menuiserie-batiment. w.

**Societe du Souvenir et Etudes Cathares**
23 Av. Pres. J. Kennedy, 11100 Narbonne, Aude, France.
- Cahiers d'Etudes Cathares. q. ISSN 0008-0063

**Societe Edisem**
37, rue de Bassano, 75-Paris (8e), France.
- Actualite; mensuelle. m.

**Societe Editions Cinematographiques Francaises**
12 Avenue Georges V, 75008 Paris, France.
- Film Francais. w. ISSN 0397-8702

**Societe Entomologique de France**
45, rue Buffon, 75005 Paris, France.
- Societe Entomologique de France. Annales. q. ISSN 0037-9271
- Societe Entomologique de France. Bulletin. bi-m. ISSN 0037-928X

**Societe Entomologique de Mulhouse**
35 Place de la Reunion, 68100 Mulhouse, France.
- Societe Entomologique de Mulhouse. Bulletin. q. ISSN 0037-9298

**Societe Europeenne d'Etudes et de Relations Internationales**
C.C.P. Paris 7002-76, Paris, France.
- Annuaire International des Foires-Expositions et Salons Specialises. q.

**Societe Europeenne de Presse et d'Edition**
142 rue d'Aguesseau, 92100 Boulogne, France.
- Emballage Digest. m. ISSN 0013-6557

**Societe Europeenne de Presse Fiscale et Juridique**
54 rue de Chabrol, 75480 Paris Cedex 10, France.
- Interets Prives; revue pratique du chef de famille. m.
- Revue Fiduciaire. w.

**Societe Europeenne Editions Professionelles**
65 Ave. des Champs-Elysees, Paris (8e), France.
- Parlons Bas. bi-m. ISSN 0031-2304

**Societe Financiere du Camion (SOFINCAM)**
140, Avenue des Champs-Elysees, 75008 Paris, France
(Subscription address: 6, rue Nicolas Copernic, 78190 Trappes, France)
- Routes et Chantiers. 3 per yr.

**Societe Financiere Europeenne**
20 rue de la Paix, Paris 2, France.
- World Money Outlook. s-a.

**Societe Fleuriste de France**
33 rue du Pont Neuf, 75001 Paris, France.
- Fleuriste de France. m.

**Societe Francaise d'Allergie**
- Revue Francaise d'Allergologie et d'Immunologie. (pub. by Expansion Scientifique)

**Societe Francaise d'Anesthesie, d'Analgesie et de Reanimation**
- Anesthesie, Analgesie, Reanimation. (pub. by Masson)

**Societe Francaise d'Archeologie**
Musee National des Monuments Francais, Palais de Chaillot, 75016 Paris, France.
- Bulletin Monumental. q. ISSN 0007-473X
- Congres Archeologique de France (Publication.) a. ISSN 0069-8881

**Societe Francaise d'Economie Rurale**
Route de Saint-Cyr, 78000 Versailles, France.
- Economie Rurale. 6 per yr. ISSN 0013-0559

**Societe Francaise d'Editions Medicales**
24-26, rue de la Cerisaie, 75004 Paris, France.
- Medecine et Maladies Infectieuses; revue francaise d'epidemiologie, de pathologie infectieuse et parasitaire. m.

**Societe Francaise d'Editions Techniques**
22 rue de la Saussiere, 92100 Boulogne, France.
- Machines Production. w. ISSN 0047-536X

**Societe Francaise d'Editions Vinicoles**
6 Ave. du Coq, 75009 Paris, France.
- Cuisine et Vins de France. m. ISSN 0011-2704
- Revue du Vin de France; technical and topical information-defense of quality. 5 per yr. ISSN 0035-273X

**Societe Francaise d'Egyptologie**
College de France, 11 Place Marcelin Berthelot, Paris (5e), France.
- Societe Francaise d'Egyptologie. Bulletin. 3 per yr. ISSN 0037-9379

**Societe Francaise d'Electroradiologie Medicale et Filiales**
- Journal de Radiologie. d'Electrologie et de Medecine Nucleaire. (pub. by Masson)

**Societe Francaise d'Etude des Phenomenes Psychiques**
41 rue Claude Bernard, 75 Paris (5e), France.
● Tribune Psychique. q. ISSN 0049-4666

**Societe Francaise d'Etude du Dix-Huitieme Siecle**
1 rue Victor Cousin, Paris (5e), France.
● Annuaire International des Dix-Huitiemistes. (pub. by Presses Universitaires de Grenoble)
● Dix-Huitieme Siecle. (pub. by Editions Garnier Freres)
● Societe Francaise d'Etude du Dix-Huitieme Siecle. Bulletin. q.

**Societe Francaise d'Histoire d'Outre-Mer**
● Revue Francaise d'Histoire d'Outre-Mer. (pub. by Imprimerie F. Paillart)

**Societe Francaise d'Hydrologie et de Climatologie Medicales**
● Presse Thermale et Climatique. (pub. by Expansion Scientifique)

**Societe Francaise d'Immunologie**
● Annales d'Immunologie. (pub. by Masson)

**Societe Francaise d'Urologie**
● Journal d'Urologie et de Nephrologie. (pub. by Masson)

**Societe Francaise de Cardiologie**
● Societe Francaise de Cardiologie. Bulletin d'Informations. (pub. by Editions, Publicites, Recherches et Inventions)

**Societe Francaise de Ceramique**
23 rue de Cronstadt, 75015 Paris, France.
● Societe Francaise de Ceramique. Bulletin. q. ISSN 0037-931X
● Societe Francaise de Ceramique. Traductions Brevets. q.

**Societe Francaise de Chimie Therapeutique**
● Chimica Therapeutica/Chimie Therapeutique. (pub. by Societe d'Etudes de Chimie Therapeutique (S.E.C.T.))

**Societe Francaise de Chirurgie Infantile**
● Annales de Chirurgie Infantile. (pub. by Masson)

**Societe Francaise de Chirurgie Orthopedique et Traumatologique**
● Societe Francaise de Chirurgie Orthopedique et Traumatologique. Conferences d'Enseignement. (pub. by Expansion Scientifique)

**Societe Francaise de Dermatologie et de Syphiligraphie**
● Annales de Dermatologie et de Venereologie. (pub. by Masson)

**Societe Francaise de Genetique**
● Annales de Genetique. (pub. by Semaine des Hopitaux)

**Societe Francaise de Gynecologie**
● Gynecologie. (pub. by Editions Vigot Freres)

**Societe Francaise de Medecine Psychosomatique**
● Revue de Medecine Psychosomatique. (pub. by Editions Edouard Privat)

**Societe Francaise de Metallurgie**
47 rue Boissiere, 75116 Paris, France.
● Societe Francaise de Metallurgie. Annuaire. biennial. ISSN 0081-105X

**Societe Francaise de Microbiologie**
● Societe Francaise de Microbiologie. Annuaire. (pub. by Institut Pasteur)

**Societe Francaise de Microscopie Electronique**
67 rue Maurice Guensbourg, 24 rue Lhomond, France.
● Biologie Cellulaire. 9 per yr. ISSN 0399-0311 (Co-sponsor: Centre National de la Recherche Scientifique)
● Journal de Microscopie et de Spectroscopie Electroniques. 6 per yr. ISSN 0395-9279

**Societe Francaise de Mineralogie et de Cristallographie**
● Societe Francaise de Mineralogie et de Cristallographie. Bulletin. (pub. by Masson)

**Societe Francaise de Musicologie**
● Revue de Musicologie. (pub. by Heugel)

**Societe Francaise de Mycologie Medicale**
25 rue du Docteur Roux, Paris (15e), France.
● Societe Francaise de Mycologie Medicale. Bulletin. 2 per yr. ISSN 0037-9336

**Societe Francaise de Neurologie**
● Revue Neurologique. (pub. by Masson)

**Societe Francaise de Neuroradiologie**
● Journal de Neuroradiologie/Journal of Neuroradiology. (pub. by Masson)

**Societe Francaise de Numismatique**
58 rue de Richelieu, 75084 Paris, France.
● Revue Numismatique. (pub. by Societe d'Edition "les Belles Lettres")
● Societe Francaise de Numismatique. Bulletin. m. ISSN 0037-9344

**Societe Francaise de Pediatrie**
● Pediatrie. (pub. by Reunion Lyonnaise de Pediatrie)

**Societe Francaise de Philosophie**
● Societe Francaise de Philosophie. Bulletin. (pub. by Librairie Armand Colin)

**Societe Francaise de Phlebologie**
● Phlebologie. (pub. by Expansion Scientifique)

**Societe Francaise de Photogrammetrie**
2 Ave. Pasteur, 94160 Saint Mande, France.
● Societe Francaise de Photogrammetrie. Bulletin. q. ISSN 0049-108X

**Societe Francaise de Physiologie Vegetale**
● Physiologie Vegetale. (pub. by Centrale des Revues Dunod Gauthier Villars)

**Societe Francaise de Physique**
33 rue Croulebarbe, 75013 Paris, France
● Revue de Physique Appliquee. m. ISSN 0035-1687 (Subscriptions to: 87 bis, Avenue du General-Leclerc, 75014 Paris, France)
● Societe Francaise de Physique. Annuaire. triennial. ISSN 0081-1076
● Societe Francaise de Physique. Bulletin. q. ISSN 0037-9360

**Societe Francaise de Physique Biologique**
● Journal Francais de Biophysique et Medecine Nucleaire. (pub. by Centrale des Revues Dunod Gauthier-Villars)

**Societe Francaise de Phytiatrie et de Phytopharmacie**
● Phytiatrie-Phythopharmacie. (pub. by C. N. R. A.)

**Societe Francaise de Presse Illustree**
22, rue Bergere, 75009 Paris, France.
● Aglae et Sidonie. bi-m.
● Journal de Nounours. m.
● Pepin la Bulle. bi-m.
● Toutou-Journal. m. ISSN 0040-9863
● Zorro. m.

**Societe Francaise de Psychologie**
28 Rue Serpente, 75006 Paris, France.
● Psychologie Francaise. q. ISSN 0033-2984

**Societe Francaise de Psychoprophylaxie Obstetricale**
32, Av. General Leclere, Nimes, France.
● Societe Francaise de Psychoprophylaxie Obstetricale. Bulletin Officiel. q.

**Societe Francaise de Radioprotection**
● Radioprotection. (pub. by Centrale des Revues Dunod Gauthier- Villars)

**Societe Francaise de Reeducation Fonctionnelle de Readaptation et de Medecine Physique**
11, rue Jeanne-d'Arc, 59000 Lille, France.
● Annales de Medecine Physique. q. ISSN 0402-4621

**Societe Francaise de Rhumatologie**
● Revue du Rhumatisme et des Maladies Osteoarticulaires. (pub. by Expansion Scientifique)

**Societe Francaise de Therapeutique et de Pharmacodynamie**
● Therapie. (pub. by Doin Editeurs)

**Societe Francaise de Tuberculose**
● Revue Francaise des Maladies Respiratoires. (pub. by Masson)

**Societe Francaise des Roses**
Parc de la Tete d'Or, 69459 Lyon, France.
● Amis des Roses. q. ISSN 0003-1844

**Societe Francaise des Sciences et Techniques Pharmaceutiques**
● Fate of Drugs in the Organism; a Bibliographic Survey. (pub. by Marcel Dekker, Inc. US)

**Societe Francaise des Traducteurs**
1 rue de Courcelles, 75008 Paris, France.
● Traduire. q. ISSN 0395-773X

**Societe Francaise du Vide**
19 rue du Renard, 75004 Paris, France.
● Societe Francaise du Vide. Comptes Rendus des Travaux des Congres et Colloques. irreg.
● Vide; les couches minces. bi-m. ISSN 0042-5281

**Societe Francaise pour le Droit de l'Environnement**
● Revue Juridique de l'Environnement. (pub. by Publications Periodiques Specialisees)

**Societe G.E.C.E.**
23 rue de l'Esperance, 75013 Paris, France.
● Services-Marche Commun Europeen. q (with 4 supplements)

**Societe Galvano**
● Galvano-Organo. (pub. by S.A.R.L. Galvano)

**Societe Garon**
10 rue Bleue, Paris(9e), France.
● Officiel des Comites d'Entreprise et Services Sociaux. m. ISSN 0010-2458

**Societe Generale des Prisons et de Legislation Criminelle**
M. Dutheillet. Lamonthezie, Secy., 27 rue de Fleurus, 75006 Paris, France.
● Revue Penitentiaire et de Droit Penal. q. ISSN 0035-3825

**Societe Geographie**
● Annales de Geographie. (pub. by Librairie Armand Colin)

**Societe Geologique de France**
77 rue Claude Bernard, 75005 Paris, France.
● Societe Geologique de France. Bulletin. 6 per yr. ISSN 0037-9409
● Societe Geologique de France. Memoires. irreg (1-4 nos. per yr.)

**Societe Geologique de Normandie et des Amis du Museum du Havre**
Place du Vieux Marche, 76600 le Havre, France.
● Societe Geologique de Normandie et des Amis du Museum du Havre. Bulletin. a.

**Societe Historique de la Province du Maine**
26 Rue des Chanoines, 72000 Lemans, Sarthe, France.
● Province du Maine. q. ISSN 0033-1880

**Societe Historique du Bas-Limousin**
c/oRobert Joudoux, Ed., 13 Place Municipale, 19000 Tulle, France.
● Lemouzi; revue franco-limousine. q. ISSN 0024-0761

**Societe Historique du Quatorzieme Arrondissement de Paris**
Pl. Ferdinand Brunot, 75675 Paris Cedex 14, France.
● Revue d'Histoire du Quatorzieme Arrondissement de Paris. a. ISSN 0556-7335

**Societe Historique et Archeologique du Perigord**
18 rue du Plantier, Perigueux, France.
● Societe Historique et Archeologique du Perigord. Bulletin. q. ISSN 0037-9425

**Societe Hydrotechnique de France**
199 rue de Grenelle, 75007 Paris, France.
● Annuaire Hydrologique de la France. a.
● Houille Blanche. (pub. by Association pour la Diffusion de la Documentation Hydraulique)

**Societe Idiste Francaise**
c/o Georges Moureaux, Ed., 11 rue J. Donier, 01100 Oyonnax, France.
● Langue Internationale. a. ISSN 0085-2686

**Societe Industrielle de Lunetterie et d'Optique Rationnelle**
94100 Saint-Maur, France.
- Cahiers de l'Optique de Contact. 3 per yr. ISSN 0007-9901 (prep. by its Departement Optique de Contact)

**Societe Industrielle de Mulhouse**
10 Rue de la Bourse, 68056 Mulhouse, France.
- Societe Industrielle de Mulhouse. Bulletin. q. ISSN 0037-9441

**Societe Industrielle de Rouen**
- Normandie Industrielle. (pub. by Editions Lecerf)

**Societe Inform' Optique**
10, rue de Buci, 75006 Paris, France.
- Inform' Optique; revue de liaison bimestrielle entre les professionnels de l'optique. bi-m.

**Societe Internationale d'Ethnopsychologie Normale et Pathologique**
Ed. & Pub. Dr. Charles L. Pidoux, 96 rue Pierre Demours, Paris (17e), France.
- Revue Internationale d'Ethnopsychologie Normale et Pathologique. q. ISSN 0035-3485

**Societe Internationale de Bio-Mathematique**
- Revue de Bio-Mathematique/Biomathematics. (pub. by Editions Europeennes)

**Societe Internationale de Criminologie**
*see* International Society of Criminology

**Societe Internationale de Prophylaxie Criminelle**
16 Pierre Nicole, 75005 Paris, France
(Subcriptions to: 43 rue Chaudet, 91290 Saint-German-les-Arpajon, France.)
- Etudes Internationales de Psycho-Sociologie Criminelle. q. ISSN 0014-2131

**Societe Internationale de Psycho-Prophylaxie Obstetricale**
31 rue Saint-Guillaume, 75 Paris (7e), France.
- Societe Internationale de Psycho-Prophylaxie Obstetricale. Bulletin Officiel. 4 per yr. ISSN 0037-9468

**Societe J A M**
7 Square de Chatillon, Paris (14e), France.
- Butane Propane; la revue des gaz de petrole. q. ISSN 0007-7240

**Societe J.K. Huysmans**
12 rue Jacob, Paris 6, France.
- Societe J.K. Huysmans.Bulletin. irreg.

**Societe Jibena**
La Petite Motte, Senille, 86100 Chatellerault, France.
- Casse-Tete et Amusettes; mensuel des jeux d'esprit. m. ISSN 0008-7432
- Grilles de Poche. m. ISSN 0017-4262
- Mots Croises Amusants. s-m. ISSN 0027-240X
- Mots Croises de Poche. m. ISSN 0027-2418
- Mots Croises Detente. m. ISSN 0027-2426
- Mots Croises Express. s-m. ISSN 0027-2434
- Mots Croises Jeunesse. m. ISSN 0027-2442
- Mots Croises Recreatifs. m. ISSN 0027-2469
- Sport de l'Esprit; culture et loisirs. m.

**Societe Languedocienne de Geographie**
Universite P. Valery, B. P. 5043, 34032 Montpellier, France.
- Societe Languedocienne de Geographie. Bulletin. q.

**Societe le Mausolee**
26 rue du Moulin, B.P. 8, Givors, France.
- Mausolee; arts et techniques des roches de qualite. m. ISSN 0025-6072

**Societe les Techniques des Specialites du Batiment**
107 Bd. Raspail, Paris (6e), France.
- Revue Generale de l'Etancheite et de l'Isolation. q. ISSN 0035-3132

**Societe Litteraire des Amis d'Emile Zola**
- Cahiers Naturalistes. (pub. by Fasquelle Editeurs)

**Societe Litteraire des P.T.T.**
20 Avenue de Segur, 75700 Paris, France.
- Societe Litteraire des P.T.T. Bulletin. q.

**Societe Lyonnaise d'Editions Rhone-Alpes**
7, Avenue de Birmingham, 69004 Lyon, France.
- Batiment Rhone-Alpes. m.

**Societe Mathematique de France**
11, rue Pierre et Marie Curie, 75231 Paris Cedex 05, France.
- Asterisque. 10 per yr.
- Societe Mathematique de France. Bulletin. q. ISSN 0037-9484

**Societe Medicale d'Information Scientifique et Professionnelle**
40 rue Paul-Valery, 75116 Paris, France.
- Revue de Medecine. w.(45 per yr.) ISSN 0035-1512

**Societe Medicale de Biotherapie**
11, Avenue Carnot, Paris 17, France.
- Cahiers de Biotherapie. q. ISSN 0575-0563

**Societe Medicale des Hopitaux de Lyon**
- Lyon Medical. (pub. by Publicite Paul Chatelain)

**Societe Medicale des Hopitaux de Marseille**
Hopital Michel Levy, 84a Rue de Lodi, 13281 Marseille, France.
- Marseille Medical. m. ISSN 0025-4053

**Societe Medicale des Hopitaux de Paris**
- Annales de Medecine Interne. (pub. by Masson)

**Societe Medicale des Praticiens**
- Clinique. (pub. by Editions de Medecine Pratique)

**Societe Medico Chirurgicale des Hopitaux de Grenoble**
- Revue Medicale des Alpes Francaises. (pub. by Publications Periodiques Specialisees)

**Societe Medico-Chirurgicale des Hopitaux et Formations Sanitaires des Armees**
Val-De-Grace, 277 bis, rue Saint Jacques, Paris (5e), France.
- Societe Medico-Chirurgicale des Hopitaux et Formations Sanitaires des Armees. Bulletin. 10 per yr. ISSN 0037-9492

**Societe Medico-Psychologique**
- Annales Medico-Psychologiques. (pub. by Masson)

**Societe Meteorologique de France**
73-77 rue de Sevres, 92100 Boulogie-sur-Seine, France.
- Meteorologie. q. ISSN 0026-1181

**Societe Midi Pyreenenne de Presse**
30 Cheminement le Tintoret, 31300 Toulouse, France.
- T M P Magazine; Toulouse Midi Pyrenees. m.

**Societe Mixte pour le Developpement de la Technique des Transmissions dans le Domain des Telecommunications (SOTELEC)**
16 rue de la Baume, 75008 Paris, France.
- Cables & Transmission. q. ISSN 0007-9308

**Societe Mutualiste du Personnel des Caisses d'Epargne**
6 rue de la Grosse-Ecritoire, B.P. 2747, 51062 Reims Cedex, France.
- Revue des Caisses d'Epargne. m. ISSN 0035-1938

**Societe Mycologique de France**
- Odimy/Observations et Disputationes Mycologicae. (pub. by Marcel Locquin, Ed. & Pub.)

**Societe Nationale d'Etude et de Construction de Moteurs d'Aviation**
2 Bd. Victor, 75724 Paris Cedex 15, France.
- S N E C M A Informations; journal d'information du personnel. m.

**Societe Nationale d'Horticulture de France**
84 rue de Grenelle, Paris (7e), France.
- Jardins de France. 10 per yr. ISSN 0021-5481

**Societe Nationale de Protection de la Nature (S N P N)**
57 rue Cuvier, 75 Paris (5e), France.
- Courrier de la Nature, Homme et l'Oiseau. q. ISSN 0011-0477
- Terre et la Vie; revue d'ecologie appliquee. q. ISSN 0040-3865

**Societe Nationale de Transfusion**
- Revue Francaise de Transfusion et Immuno-Hematologie. (pub. by Librairie Arnette)

**Societe Nationale des Antiquaires de France.**
Pavillon Mollien, Palais du Louvre, Paris 75001, France
(Orders to: Editions Klincksieck, 11 rue de Lille, Paris 7E, France)
- Societe Nationale des Antiquaires de France. Bulletin. a. ISSN 0081-1181

**Societe Nationale des Chemins de Fer Francais**
- Revue Generale des Chemins de Fer. (pub. by Centrale des Revues Dunod Gauthier Villars)

**Societe Nationale ELF-Aquitaine**
7 rue Nelaton, 75739 Paris Cedex 15, France.
- E L F; bulletin mensuel d'informations. m. ISSN 0012-7701 (prep. by its Direction des Relations Exterieures)

**Societe Nationale ELF-Aquitaine (Production)**
Centre Micoulau, Avenue de President P. Angot, 6400 Paris, France.
- Bulletin des Centres de Recherches Exploration-Production ELF Aquitaine. s-a. ISSN 0396-2687

**Societe Nationale Francaise de Gastro-Enterologie**
- Gastro-Enterologie Clinique et Biologique. (pub. by Masson)

**Societe Nationale Francaise de Reeducation & de Readaptation Fonctionnelles**
- Cahiers de Reeducation & de Readaptation Fonctionnelles. (pub. by Publiclair)

**Societe Nationale Industrielle Aerospatiale**
37 Bld. de Montmorency, Paris 16e, France.
- Aerospatiale. m. ISSN 0065-3780

**Societe Nationale Mutualiste**
36 Rue de la Bienfaisance, Paris (8e), France.
- Medaille Militaire. q. ISSN 0047-6390

**Societe Nationale Presse Francaise**
17, rue des Petits-Champs, 75001 Paris, France.
- Arsenal. m.
- Royaliste; bi-mensuel de l'action royaliste. bi-m.

**Societe Nouvelle d'Edition de l'Est**
12/14 rue du Chanoine-Collin, 57000 Metz, France.
- Home, Maisons et Decors de l'Est. irreg. ISSN 0395-160X

**Societe Nouvelle d'Editions et de Presse (S N E P)**
7 rue de Lille, 75007 Paris, France.
- AUTOhebdo. w.

**Societe Nouvelle d'Editions Industrielles**
22 Avenue F.D. Roosevelt, 75008-Paris, France.
- Kompass Alimentation. a.
- Kompass Textile et Habillement. a.
- Qui Represente Qui. a. ISSN 0079-9262
- Repertoire General de la Production Francaise. a. ISSN 0337-5714 (Co-Sponsors: Centre Francais du Commerce Kompass International Ag,Zurich)

**Societe Nouvelle d'Editions Publicitaires**
16, Av. de Verdun, 75010 Paris, France.
- Annuaire Electro. a.

**Societe Nouvelle de la Revue Urbanisme**
- Urbanisme. (pub. by Societe des Editions Regirex-France)

**Societe Nouvelle de Publications Medicales et Dentaires (SNPMD)**
20 rue Godot-de-Mauroy, 75009 Paris, France.
- Journal de Biologie Buccale. q. ISSN 0301-3952

**Societe Nouvelle des Editions France Outre-Mer**
6 rue de Bassano, Paris (16e), France.
- Europe Outre-Mer. m.

**Societe Nouvelle des Publications M.R.A.**
12 rue Mulet, 69001 Lyon, France.
- Modele Reduit d'Avion. m. ISSN 0026-7406
- Modele Reduit de Bateau. bi-m. ISSN 0026-7414

**Societe Nouvelle du Journal de l'Amateur d'Art**
1 Cite Bergere, 6 rue de Faubourg Montmartre, Paris (9e), France.
- Journal de l'Amateur d'Art. fortn. ISSN 0021-7808

**Societe Odonto-Stomatologique de Lyon**
- Annales Odonto-Stomatologiques. (pub. by Union des Etudes et Recherches des Sciences Odontologiques)

**Societe Odonto-Stomatologique du Nord-Est**
9 rue Saint-Nicolas, 54000 Nancy, France.
● Societe Odonto-Stomatologique du Nord-Est.
Revue Annuelle. a. ISSN 0081-1203

**Societe Odontologique de Paris**
● Revue d'Odonto-Stomatologie. (pub. by Editions
Labo Pharma)

**Societe Ornithologique de France**
55 rue Bufton, 75005 Paris, France.
● Oiseau et la Revue Francaise d'Ornithologie. q.
ISSN 0030-1531

**Societe Parisienne d'Edition**
2-12 rue de Bellevue, 75019 Paris, France.
● T R I O. m.

**Societe Parisienne d'Editions et de Publications**
9 Passage des Marais, 75010 Paris, France.
● Ecrits de Paris; revue des questions actuelles. m.
ISSN 0013-0710 (Centre d'Etudes des Questions
Actuelles)

**Societe Parisienne d'Editions et de Publications
Immobilieres**
274 Bd. Saint-Germain, Paris (7e), France.
● Revue de l'Habitat Francais. m. ISSN 0048-7953

**Societe Parisienne d'Histoire et d' Archeologie**
8, rue de la Sorbonne, Paris 5e, France.
● Cahiers Leopold Delisle. q.

**Societe Paul Claudel**
● Societe Paul Claudel. Bulletin. (pub. by O. P. E.
R. A.)

**Societe Pegit**
12 rue de Chateaudun, 75009 Paris, France.
● Paris Post. w. ISSN 0339-0071

**Societe Philomatique Vosgienne**
Bibliotheque Municipale, Rue St.-Charles, 88100
Saint-die, France.
● Societe Philomatique Vosgienne. Bulletin. a.

**Societe Phycologique de France**
Laboratoire de Biologie Vegetale Marine, 7 Quai St.
Bernard, 75230 Paris 05, France.
● Societe Phycologique de France. Bulletin. a. ISSN
0081-122X

**Societe Pomologique de France**
● Pomologie Francaise. (pub. by Publications
Periodiques Specialisees)

**Societe pour l'Etude des Langues Africaines**
5, rue de Marseille, 75010 Paris, France.
● Bibliotheque de la S F L A F. irreg. ISSN 0081-
1238
● Langues et Litteratures de l'Afrique Noire. irreg.
ISSN 0075-7993

**Societe pour l'Etude et la Connaissance du Monde
Insulindien**
23290 Saint-Etienne de Fursac, France.
● Archipel. s-a. ISSN 0044-8613

**Societe Prehistorique Francaise**
16 rue Saint-Martin, 75004 Paris, France.
● Societe Prehistorique Francaise. Bulletin. m. ISSN
0037-9514

**Societe Presse et Publications Missionnaires**
● Lumiere du Monde. (pub. by Oeuvre de Saint
Pierre Apotre)

**Societe Protectrice des Animaux**
● Protection des Animaux. (pub. by Publications
Periodiques Specialisees)

**Societe Protestante Francaise d'Edition et de
Publication**
14, rue du Cherche-Midi, 75006 Paris, France.
● Tant Qu'il Fait Jour. m (10 per yr)

**Societe Psychanalytique de Paris**
● Revue Francaise de Psychanalyse. (pub. by
Presses Universitaires de France)

**Societe Racinienne**
52 rue Jacques- Dulud, 92200 Neuilly- sur- Seine,
France.
● Cahiers Raciniens. s-a. ISSN 0008-0454

**Societe S G A P**
59 rue de Billancourt, 92100 Boulogne, France.
● G A P. (Groupe Avant-Premiere) m.

**Societe S.L.O.C.A.M.**
59-61 Avenue de la Grande Armee, 75782 Paris
Cedex 16, France.
● Officiel de l'Automobile; la Premiere Revue de la
Profession. s-m. ISSN 0030-0454 (Federation
Nationale du Commerce et de l'Artisanat
Automobile)
● Officiel du Cycle, du Motocycle et de la
Motoculture; revue de la profession. fortn. ISSN
0030-0519 (Federation Nationale du Commerce
et de la Reparation du Cycle & Motocycle)

**Societe Savoisienne d'Histoire et d'Archeologie**
Square de Lannoy de Bissy, 73- Chambery, 73000
Chambery.
● Histoire en Savoie; revue de culture et
d'information historique. q. ISSN 0046-7510

**Societe Scientifique d'Hygiene Alimentaire**
39 bis, rue Henri Barbusse, 75005 Paris, France.
● Alimentation et la Vie. q. ISSN 0065-6267

**Societe Scientifique de Bretagne**
Faculte des Sciences, 35000 Rennes, France.
● Societe Scientifique de Bretagne. Bulletin. q. ISSN
0037-9581

**Societe Scientifique Sevcenko**
29, rue des Bauves, 95200 Sarcelles, France.
● Visiti Iz Sarseliu. irreg., no. 16, 1974. ISSN 0083-
6672

**Societe Sebastien Thomas**
● Dictionnaire des Parfums de France et des Lignes
pour Hommes. (pub. by Editions Sebastien
Thomas)
● Dictionnaire des Produits de Soins de Beaute.
(pub. by Editions Sebastien Thomas)

**Societe Secograins**
239, Bourse de Commerce, Paris (1er), France.
● Grains; revue francaise du commerce des grains-
oleagineux-caution mutuelle. m. ISSN 0046-6263

**Societe Speleologique et Prehistorique de Bordeaux**
Hotel des Societes Savantes, 71 rue du Loup,
Bordeaux, France.
● Societe Speleologique et Prehistorique de
Bordeaux. Memoire. irreg.

**Societe Tarif Media S. A.**
6 Avenue Matignon, 75008 Paris, France.
● Tarif Media. 5 per yr.

**Societe Technique d'Art et de Realisation**
11 rue de Chateaudun, 75009 Paris, France.
● Enfance et la Mode. q. ISSN 0046-1962

**Societe Technique d'Editions pour l'Entreprise (S T E
P E)**
54 rue de Monceau, 75384 Paris-Cedex 08, France.
● Index SVP; publication hebdomadaire
d'informations. w.

**Societe Theosophique de France**
4 Square Rapp, Paris(7e), France.
● Lotus Bleu; revue theosophique. m. ISSN 0024-
6670 (Federation Europeenne des Societes
Theosophiques)

**Societe Universitaire d'Editions et de Librairie**
20 rue Corvisart, 75640 Paris Cedex, France.
● Cahiers de l'Enfance Inadaptee; adaptation,
education speciale. 8 per yr. ISSN 0007-9863
(Syndicat National des Instituteurs)

**Societe Versaillaise des Sciences Naturelles**
E.N.S.H, 4 rue Hardy, 7800 Versailles, France.
● Societe Versaillaise des Sciences Naturelles.
Bulletin. q. ISSN 0336-8300

**Societe Zoologique de France**
195 rue Saint-Jacques, Paris (5e), France.
● Societe Zoologique de France. Bulletin. q. ISSN
0037-962X

**Societes de Medecine du Travail de France**
● Archives des Maladies Professionnelles de
Medecine du Travail et de Securite Sociale. (pub.
by Masson)

**Society for International Development**
49 rue de la Glaciere, 75013 Paris, France
(U.S. Address: 1346 Connecticut Ave. N.W.,
Washington, DC 20036)
● Actuel Developpement. (pub. by Groupement
d'Edition et d'Information Technique,
Economique et Culturelle)

● Apercu sur le Developpement International. bi-m.

**Socpresse-Auto-Journal**
43 Boulevard Barbes, 75880 Paris Cedex 18, France.
● Auto-Journal. s-m. ISSN 0005-0768

**Socpresse Bateaux**
71 rue Fondary, Paris (15e), France.
● Bateaux. m. ISSN 0005-6235

**Editions Sodel**
336 rue de St. Honore, 75001 Paris, France.
● Revue Francaise de l'Electricite. q. ISSN 0035-
2926

**Soldecor**
51, Avenue Aristide-Briand, 94110 Arcueil, France.
● Decor a Coeur. q.

**Soleil**
4 Bis rue Caillaux, Paris (13e), France.
● Soleil; journal de la droite nationale et populaire.
w. ISSN 0038-1012

**Solidarite des Refugies Israelites**
14 rue St. Lazare, 75009 Paris, France.
● Solidarite; bulletin d'information des refugies
victimes du nazisme. q.

**Editions Solin**
c/o M. Jean-Louis Saillant, 1, rue des Fosses Saint-
Jacques, 75005-Paris, France.
● Actes; cahiers d'action juridique. bi-m.
● Impascience. q.

**Editions Sols-Soils**
54 Av. de la Motte-Picquet, 75015 Paris, France.
● Sols-Soils; revue internationale de mecanique des
sols et travaux de fondations. q. ISSN 0038-1217

**Editions Sonedis**
18 rue de Cotte, 75012 Paris, France.
● Cuisine Collective; la revue professionnelle des
responsables de la restauration collective. m. ISSN
0045-9208
● Econome Catholique et le Moniteur des
Collectivites. bi-m.

**Sopusi**
10,rue du Faubourg Montmartre, 75009 Paris,
France
(Subscriptions to: 13,rue d'Enghien, 75010 Paris,
France)
● France Football. w. ISSN 0015-9557

**Souvenir Vendeer**
B. P. 204-44 rue du Paradis, 49306 Cholet, France.
● Souvenir Vendeer. bi-m.

**Spanish Socialist Labour Party (P.S.O.E.)**
73, rue Bayard, 31000 Toulouse, France.
● Nouveau Socialiste. w.

**Sport Bowling**
26 rue Vernet, 75008 Paris, France.
● Sport Bowling. 9 per yr. ISSN 0038-7843

**Station Biologique de Roscoff**
29211 Roscoff, France.
● Cahiers de Biologie Marine. q. ISSN 0007-9723

**Stendhal Club**
3 rue Maurice Gignoux, 38000 Grenoble, France.
● Stendhal Club. Quarterly. q. ISSN 0039-1158

**STEPE**
16 rue Vezelay, 75008 Paris, France.
● Chantiers de France. 10 per yr.

**Editions Stock**
6 rue Casimir-Delavigne, Paris 6e, France.
● Theatre Ouvert. irreg. ISSN 0082-383X

**Strategies**
5 rue d'Alger, 75001 Paris, France.
● Strategies; annonceurs/agences/media. fortn.

**Editions Subervie**
21, rue de l'Embergue, F-12 Rodez, France.
● Sentiers Poesie. irreg.

**Sud**
c/o Yves Broussard, 11, rue Peyssonnel, 13003
Marseille, France.
● Sud. q. ISSN 0049-2450

**Sud-Regie**
58 Ave. de la Marne, 92600 Asnieres, France.
- Archives Mediterraneennes de Medecine. 3 per mo. ISSN 0003-9845 (S. D. M. S.)
- Mediterranee Medicale. 3 per mo. (Faculte de Medecine de Marseille)

**Syndicat de la Librairie Ancienne et Moderne**
Hotel du Cercle de la Librairie, 117 Boulevard Saint-Germain, 75006 Paris, France.
- Guide du Livre Ancien et du Livre d'Occasion. a.

**Syndicat des Cadres et Agents de Maitrise de l'Imprimerie, des Arts Graphiques et du Cartonnage**
- Agenda Memento des Cadres et Maitrises de l'Imprimerie, de l'Edition et des Industries Graphiques. (pub. by France Lafayette)

**Syndicat des Cafetiers, Restaurateurs de Paris et Banlieues**
- Cafetier Restaurateur Parisien. (pub. by Pym Editeur)

**Syndicat des Constructeurs de Moteurs a Combustion Interne**
10 Av. Hoche, 75382 Paris, France.
- Industrie Francaise des Moteurs a Combustion Interne; repertoire alphabetique des constructeurs. biennial. ISSN 0073-7747

**Syndicat des Critiques Litteraires**
58 rue Claude Bernard, 75005 Paris, France.
- Syndicat des Critiques Litteraires. Bulletin. q. ISSN 0039-7776

**Syndicat des Femmes Chirugiens-Dentistes**
- Femmes Chirugiens-Dentistes. (pub. by Societe d'Edition Medicale Europeenne)

**Syndicat des Grades de la Police Nationale**
11 rue des Ursins, 75004 Paris, France.
- Defense des Grades de la Police Nationale. m.
- Police Nationale. m. ISSN 0048-4695

**Syndicat des Industries du Livres**
- Guide des Prix Litteraires. (pub. by Cercle de la Librairie)

**Syndicat des Journalistes et Ecrivains**
27 Villa des Lilas, Paris (19e), France.
- Revue Independante. bi-m. ISSN 0035-3310

**Syndicat des Journalistes Francais C.F.D.T.**
Paul Parisot, 26 rue Montholon, Paris 9e, France.
- Journalistes Francais. bi-m. ISSN 0047-293X

**Syndicat des Patissiers de la Region de Paris**
- Patissier de l'Ile-De-France. (pub. by Presse Corporative Francaise)

**Syndicat des Pisciculteurs-Salmoniculteurs de France**
28, Rue Milton, Paris (9e), France.
- Pisciculture Francaise; d'eau vive et d'etang saumatre et marine. q. ISSN 0048-4237

**Syndicat Federal des Industries Polygraphiques (SYFIP)**
7 rue du Printemps, 75017 Paris, France.
- Circulaire des Protes; arts et industries graphiques, papier, carton et industries annexes. 10 per yr.

**Syndicat General de l'Industrie Cotonniere Francaise et Textiles Allies**
3 Av. Ruysdael, 75367 Paris Cedex 08, France.
- Industrie Francaise du Coton et des Fibres Alliees. (pub. by Service de Presse, Edition, Information)
- Repertoire des Productions de l'Industrie Cotonniere Francaise. irreg. ISSN 0080-102X
- Syndicat General de l'Industrie Cotonniere Francaise. Annuaire. a. ISSN 0082-1047

**Syndicat General de l'Industrie du Jute**
33 rue de Miromesnil, 75008 Paris, France.
- Annuaire Statistique de l'Industrie Francaise du Jute. a. ISSN 0066-3697

**Syndicat General des Fondeurs de France et Industries Connexes**
2 rue de Bassano, 75783 Paris, France.
- Cahiers de la Fonderie; bulletin economique mensuel. m.

**Syndicat General du Caoutchouc et des Plastiques**
112 Bd. Haussmann, Paris (8e), France.
- Informations du Caoutchouc; Caoutchouc et Plastiques. m. ISSN 0020-0468

**Syndicat Medecins du Travail**
60 Bd. Latour-Maubourg, Paris (7e), France.
- Medecine et Travail. q. ISSN 0025-6757

**Syndicat National d'Apiculture**
- Abeille de France et l'Apiculteur. (pub. by Abeille de France, S.A.R.L.)

**Syndicat National de Cadres Hospitaliers**
Lisieux (Calvados) 14, France.
- Hospitalier. m.(10 per yr.) ISSN 0018-5922

**Syndicat National de l'Enseignement Superieur**
78 rue du Faubourg Saint-Denis, 75010 Paris, France.
- S N E S U P Bulletin. bi-w.

**Syndicat National de la Distribution pour l'Automobile et l'Industrie**
- S D A I. (pub. by Centre d'Editions Publicitaires Perrin)

**Syndicat National des Agences**
16 Av. l'Opera, Paris (1e), France.
- France-Theatre; la vie du spectacle. bi-m. ISSN 0015-9433

**Syndicat National des Anesthesiologistes-Reanimateurs Francais**
R. Deleuze, B. P. 26 Lyon- Montchat, 69394 Lyon Cedex 3, France.
- Anesthesiologie Mondiale. Annuaire. a. ISSN 0066-1740

**Syndicat National des Angeiologues**
- Actualites d'Angeiologie et de Pathologie Vasculaire. (pub. by Editions Medicales D.H.R.)

**Syndicat National des Antiquaires**
11 rue Jean-Mermoz, Paris (8e), France.
- Art et Curiosite. 6 per yr. ISSN 0004-315X

**Syndicat National des Chercheurs Scientifiques**
28 rue Monsieur le Prince, 75006 Paris, France.
- Vie de la Recherche Scientifique. m & q. ISSN 0042-5427

**Syndicat National des Constructeurs de Moules et Modeles**
- Moules et Modeles. (pub. by Centre de Productivite dans l'Industrie des Moules et Modeles)

**Syndicat National des Courtiers d'Assurances et de Reassurances**
31 rue d'Amsterdam, 75008 Paris, France.
- Assureur Conseil. m. ISSN 0004-6043

**Syndicat National des Createurs d'Architectures Interieures et de Modeles (C.A.I.M.)**
5 rue Casimir Pinel, 92200 Neuilly sur Seine, France.
- Repertoire C A I M. m.

**Syndicat National des Depositaires de Presse**
10 rue St. Marc, Paris (2e), France.
- Depositaire de France. m. ISSN 0011-8966

**Syndicat National des Employes Techniciens et Cadres de la Publicite C. G. T.**
10, rue des Messageries, 75010 Paris 10e, France.
- Spot; bulletin d'information du Syndicat National de la Publicite C. G. T. q.

**Syndicat National des Enseignements de Second Degre**
Rue de Courty, 75341 Paris, France.
- Universite Syndicaliste. w.

**Syndicat National des Entreprises du Froid et du Conditionnement de l'Air**
6 rue de Montenotte, Paris (17e), France.
- Froid et la Climatisation. 10 per yr. ISSN 0046-5151

**Syndicat National des Fabricants de Ciments et de Chaux**
41, Avenue de Friedland, 75008 Paris, France.
- Ciments et Chaux. m.

**Syndicat National des Instituteurs**
- Cahiers de l'Enfance Inadaptee. (pub. by Societe Universitaire d'Editions et de Librairie)

**Syndicat National des Lycees et Colleges**
5 rue las-Cases, 75007 Paris, France.
- Quinzaine Universitaire. s-m.

**Syndicat National des Officers de la Marine Marchande C.F.D.T.**
19 rue du Bastion, 76600 le Havre, France.
- Syndicat National des Officers de la Marine Marchande C.F.D.T. Bulletin de Liaison. q. ISSN 0039-7784

**Syndicat National des Pilotes de Ligne Francais**
Cedex No. A 213, 94396 Orly Aerogare, France.
- Icare; revue de l'aviation francaise. q. ISSN 0018-8786

**Syndicat National des Services Veterinaires**
- Informations Techniques des Directions des Services Veterinaires. (pub. by Informations Techniques des Services Veterinaires)

**Syndicat National des Techniciens Superieurs en Dietetique**
95, rue de la Loubiere, 13005 Marseille, France.
- Revue Francaise de Dietetique. q. ISSN 0556-7793

**Syndicat National Unifie des Douanes et Droits Indirects**
5 rue Geoffroy Marie, 75009 Paris, France.
- Guide National des Douanes et Droits Indirects. biennial. ISSN 0072-8187

**Syndicat Patronal des Cafes**
- Limonadier de Paris. (pub. by Excelsior Publications)

**Synthese Editeur**
51 rue Vivienne, Paris 2e, France.
- Guide Analytique du Pharmacien d'Officine. irreg. ISSN 0072-7954

**Editions Syrus**
9 rue Borromee, Paris(15e), France.
- Critique Socialiste. bi-m. ISSN 0045-9089 (Parti Socialiste Unifie)

**Societe T.E.S.T**
194 rue de Rivoli, 75001 Paris, France.
- Cahiers de Nutrition et de Dietetique. q. ISSN 0007-9960

**Table Ronde Francaise**
Raymond Aupetit, 5 rue de la Paroisse, Versailles, France.
- Table Ronde Francaise. Annuaire. a. ISSN 0082-1403

**Tal**
34, Fbg. de Pierre, Strasbourg 67000, France.
- Tal; journal Juif pour enfants. s-m.

**Librairie Jules Tallandier**
17 rue Remy-Dumoncel, 75680 Paris Cedex 14, France
(Orders to: 61, rue de la Tombe-Issoire-75680 Paris Cedex 14, France)
- Historia. m. ISSN 0018-2281
- Nef. q. ISSN 0028-2413

**Tchou Editeur**
6 rue du Mail, Paris 2e, France.
- Bibliotheque de la Mer. irreg. ISSN 0067-8260
- Profits. irreg. ISSN 0079-5984

**Technic Hebdo**
78 Av. Raymond Poincare, 75116 Paris, France.
- Technic Hebdo; produits, techniques, idees. w. ISSN 0395-367X

**Editions Technip**
27 rue Ginoux, 75737 Paris 15, France.
- Institut Francais du Petrole. Collection Colloques et Seminaires. irreg., 1976, no. 31. ISSN 0073-8360
- Institut Francais du Petrole. Revue. 6 per yr.
- Photo Interpretation. bi-m. ISSN 0031-8523

**Technique Laitiere**
8 rue de Port-Mahon, Paris (2e), France.
- Technique Laitiere. q. ISSN 0040-1242

**Techno-Loisirs**
3 rue Sivel, Paris (14e), France.
- Constructions Equipements pour les Loisirs. bi-m. ISSN 0010-6976
- International Reference Annual for Building and Equipment of Sports, Tourism, Recreation Installations. a. ISSN 0074-7645

**Editions Technorama**
31 Place Saint-Ferdinand, 75017 Paris, France.
- Art et Metiers du Livre. m.
- Cartonnages. m.
- Cartonnages et Complexes. m.
- Tech-Embal; annuaire des fournisseurs de l'emballage. a.

**Editions Teintex, S.A.R.L.**
60 rue de Richelieu, 75002 Paris, France.
- Teintex; revue generale des matieres colorantes. m. ISSN 0040-2192

**Tele Magazine**
5 rue de Chartres, 92522 Neuilly-sur-Seine Cedex, France.
- Tele Magazine. w. ISSN 0040-2443

**Telecine**
49 rue du Faubourg Poissonniere, 75009 Paris, France.
- Telecine. w. ISSN 0049-3287

**Telediffusion de France**
- Revue Radiodiffusion et Television. (pub. by Information-Promotion Francaises)

**Editions du Temoignage Chretien**
49 Faubourg Poissonniere, Paris (9e), France.
- Temoignage Chretien. w. ISSN 0040-2923

**Temps Modernes**
26 rue de Conde, Paris (6e), France.
- Temps Modernes. m. ISSN 0040-3075

**Tennis de France**
5 rue de Teheran, 75008 Paris, France.
- Tennis de France. m. ISSN 0040-344X

**Librairie "le Terrain Vogue"**
14-16 rue de Verneuil, Paris(7e), France.
- Midi-Minuit Fantastique. 10 per yr. ISSN 0047-7273

**Editions Tests**
41 rue de la Grange-aux-Belles, 75010 Paris, France.
- Informatique. irreg. ISSN 0073-7941
- Journal de l'Equipement Electrique et Electronique. m. ISSN 0021-7816

**Textilyon: Bulletin des Soies et Soieries**
4 rue Gentil, 69002 Lyon, France.
- Textilyon: Bulletin des Soies et Soieries; organe international de la soie des fibres chimiques et du textile Lyonnais. m.

**Editions Dany Thibaud**
52 rue Labrouste, 75015 Paris, France.
- Annuaire des Notables Regionaux.
- Annuaire International des Collectionneurs. a.
- Annuaire National de la Musique. a. ISSN 0066-331X
- Annuaire National des Beaux-Arts. a. ISSN 0066-3352
- Annuaire National des Lettres. a. ISSN 0066-3387

**Editions Sebastien Thomas**
95 Bd. Magenta, Paris 10e, France.
- Dictionnaire des Parfums de France et des Lignes pour Hommes. biennial. ISSN 0070-475X (Societe Sebastien Thomas)
- Dictionnaire des Produits de Soins de Beaute. biennial. (Societe Sebastien Thomas)
- Museum National d'Histoire Naturelle, Paris. Bulletin. bi-m. ISSN 0027-4070

**Thomson C S F**
23, rue de Courcelles, 75 Paris 8e, France
(Orders to: Masson & Cie, 120 Bd. Saint-Germain, 75280 Paris Cedex 06)
- Revue Technique Thomson-C S F. q. ISSN 0035-4279
- Telonde. 3 per yr. ISSN 0040-2834

**Touring Club de France**
65, Avenue de la Grande-Armee, 75782 Paris Cedex 16, France.
- Plein Air Touring. m.

**Tourisme**
21 rue Mademoiselle, 75015 Paris, France.
- Tourisme; courrier des affaires touristiques. 3 per month.

**Tout Lyon**
40, rue du President-Edouard-Herriot, 69282 Lyon Cedex 1, France.
- Tout Lyon; et le moniteur judiciaire reunis. s-w.

**Librarie Jean Touzot**
38 rue St. Sulpice, Paris 5, France.
- Fondation Nationale des Sciences Politiques, Paris. Catalogue General des Periodiques Recus. irreg. ISSN 0071-8114

**Traces**
c/o Michel-Francois Lavaur, Ed., Le Pallet, 44330 Vallet, France.
- Traces; cahiers trimestriels de lettres et d'arts. q. ISSN 0041-0276

**Tramontane**
c/o Charles Bauby, Ed.' 6 rue Jean - Baptiste Lulli, Berpicnan, France.
- Tramontane; revue du roussillon, lettres et arts. m. ISSN 0041-1000

**Transflor**
14 rue de Bretagne, Paris (3e), France.
- Revue Internationale des Fleuristes. q. ISSN 0035-3426

**Tribunal de Commerce de Paris**
1 Bld. du Palais, Paris, France.
- Tribunal de Commerce, Paris. Annuaire. a. ISSN 0071-9129

**Tribune des Nations**
150 Champs-Elysees, Paris (8e), France.
- Tribune des Nations. w. ISSN 0041-2848

**Tribune Medicale**
24, rue Clement Marot, 75 Paris (8e), France.
- Tribune Medicale. w.

**Tricots Chics**
23 rue d'Abbeville, 75009 Paris, France.
- Tricots Chics; layette, juniors, hommes, adults, super-layette. m.

**Editions des Tuileries**
9 Passage des Marais, 75010 Paris, France.
- Rivarol; hebdomadaire de l'opposition nationale. w. ISSN 0035-5666

**U. E. M**
B.P. 87-08, Paris (8e), France.
- Salut les Copains. 12 per yr. ISSN 0036-3650

**Editions U F A F**
Av. Vladimir Komarov, B.P. 36, 78190 Trappes, France.
- Memento General Tequi Quincaillerie. a. ISSN 0025-9055

**U.N.A.E.D.E.**
89 rue du Cherche Midi, 75006 Paris, France.
- Action Educative Specialisee. q.

**U. P. E. M**
see Union de Publications et d'Editions Modernes (U.P.E.M.)

**U P R A Maine Anjou**
36-38 rue de Razilly, B.P. 52, 53200 Chateau Gontier, France.
- Eleveur Maine Anjou. q. ISSN 0046-1822

**U.R.O.G**
1 Place Stes. Scarbes, 31073 Toulouse Cedex 01, France.
- Arc-Boutant; organe d'information des questions scolaires et familiales. m.

**Unesco**
For publications of this agency see section for UNITED NATIONS

**Unifrance Film**
77 Champs-Elysees, 75008 Paris, France.
- Cinema Francais. 11 per yr. ISSN 0041-6746

**Union Confederale des Ingenieurs & Cadres C F D T Francaise**
26 rue de Montholon, 75439 Paris 09, France.
- Cadres et Profession. bi-m. ISSN 0007-9472

**Union Culturelle et Technique de Langue Francaise**
47 Bd. Lannes, 75 Paris (16e), France.
- Lisez at Choisissez. ISSN 0024-4295

**Union de la Presse Europeenne**
48 Bd. des Batignolles, Paris 75017, France.
- Aviation Magazine International; l'air et l'espace, les ailes, air revue. s-m. ISSN 0005-2132

**Union de Publications et d'Editions Modernes (U.P.E.M.)**
51 rue Pierre Charron, 75380 Paris Cedex 08, France
- Histoire d'Aujourd'hui; revue de l'information audio-visuelle. m. (12 slides and text) ISSN 0046-7502 (Subscriptions to: Paris-Match, Service Diapositives, 35 rue Francois Premier, 75008 Paris, France)
- Parents. m. (U.S. and Canadian Subscr. to: 22 E. 67th St., New York, NY 10021)

**Union Departementale des Societes Mutualistes d'Indre-et-Loire**
6 rue Emile Zola, B.P. 97, 37017 Tours Cedex, Indre et Loire, France.
- Mutualiste de Touraine. q. ISSN 0027-5212

**Union Departmentale Mutaliste des Travailleurs**
19 rue St. Eloi, B.P. 117, 13363 Marseille, France.
- Vie Mutualiste. m. ISSN 0049-6286

**Union des Aveugles de Guerre**
49 rue Blanche 75009 Paris, France.
- Union des Aveugles de Guerre. Bulletin Mensuel. m. ISSN 0041-6843

**Union des Caisses Centrales de la Mutualite Agricole**
8 rue d'Astorg, 75008 Paris, France.
- Caisses Centrales de Mutualite Sociale Agricole. Statistiques. a.

**Union des Editeurs de Langue Francaise**
- Repertoire des Livres Disponibles. (pub. by France Expansion)

**Union des Editeurs Francais**
117 Bld. Saint-Germain, Paris 6e, France.
- Bulletin Bibliographique Thematique; informations bibliographiques,-philosophie, religion, sciences humaines. irreg. ISSN 0076-0137

**Union des Editions Modernes**
63, Avenue des Champs-Elysees, B. P. 87-08, 75360 Paris, France.
- Ski-Flash. m.

**Union des Etudes et Recherches des Sciences Odontologiques**
6 Place Deperet, 69- Lyon 7E, France.
- Annales Odonto-Stomatologiques. irreg. ISSN 0066-2194 (Societe Odonto-Stomatologique de Lyon)

**Union des Fabricants pour la Protection de la Propriete Industrielle et Artistique**
16 rue de la Faisanderie, 75017 Paris, France.
- Revue Internationale de la Propriete Industrielle et Artistique. q. ISSN 0035-337X

**Union des Federalistes Polonais**
20 rue Legendre, Paris 17, France.
- Polska w Europie; Pologne en Europe. m.

**Union des Jeunes Avocats a la Cour de Paris**
Palais de Justice, Paris, France.
- Jeunes Avocats. ISSN 0021-6151

**Union des Jeunes pour le Progres**
B.P. 132, 75663 Paris 14, France.
- Renaissance Deux-Mille. irreg. ISSN 0034-4311

**Union des Libraires d'Art et d'Essai**
61, rue Quincampoix, 75004 Paris, France.
- Livre d'Art et d'Essai; informations de l'union des libraires d'art et d'essai. m. ISSN 0339-1337

**Union des Oeuvres Catholiques de France**
- Christiane. (pub. by Fleurus-Presse International)
- Dans la Lumiere. (pub. by Fleurus-Presse International)
- Djin. (pub. by Fleurus-Presse International)
- Enjeu. (pub. by Fleurus-Presse International)
- Formule 1. (pub. by Fleurus-Presse International)
- Fripounet-Marisette. (pub. by Fleurus-Presse International)
- Perlin et Pinpin. (pub. by Fleurus-Presse International)

**Union des Organisations Agricoles du Sud-Est**
O.P.G.-114, Champs-Elysees, 75008 Paris, France.
- Agriculteur du Sud-Est. w. ISSN 0002-130X

**Union des Societes Bretonnes de l'Ile de France**
19 rue du Deport, 75014 Paris, France.
- Pays Breton. m.

**Union des Societes d'Education Physique et de Preparation Militaire**
23 rue de la Sourdiere, Paris-1, France.
- Formation Premilitaire et Physique. q. ISSN 0046-4627
- Union des Societes d'Education Physique et de Preparation Militaire. Bulletin. q.

**Union des Societes Francophones pour l'Investigation Psychique et l'Etude de la Survivance**
c/o Andre Dumas, Ed., Ave. des Sablons, 77230 Dammartin-en-Goele, France.
- Renaitre 2000; revue des investigations psychiques et des recherches theoriques et experimentales sur la survivance humaine. 5 per yr.

**Union des Superieures Majeures de France.**
10 rue Jean-Bart, 75006 Paris, France.
- Union des Superieures Majeures de France. Annuaire. a. ISSN 0396-2393

**Union des Syndicats de Medecins de Centres de Sante**
Centre de Sante, 3 rue de Stockholm, Paris (8e), France.
- Revue de Medecine Moderne. m.(10 per yr) ISSN 0035-1539

**Union des Syndicats Dentaires de Bourgogne-Franche-Comte**
20, rue Monge, 21000 Dijon, France.
- Accords. q.

**Union des Vieux de France**
80 Avenue Secretan, 75019 Paris, France.
- Echo des Vieux de France; organe de l'union des vieux de france. m. ISSN 0046-1083

**Union Eglises Evangeliques Libres de France**
c/o Pasteur Gauthier de Smidt, 338, rue Lavoisier, 30000 Nimes, France.
- Pour la Verite. m.

**Union Federale Francaise de Musique Sacree**
4 Avenue Vavin, 75006 Paris, France.
- Musique et Musiciens d'Eglise. q.

**Union Federaliste Mondiale**
8 bis rue Jouffroy, Paris (17e), France.
- Monde Uni. m.(bi-m.)(June-July; Aug-Sept) ISSN 0026-945X

**Union Feminine Civique et Sociale**
6 rue Beranger, Paris (3b), France.
- Dialoguer. bi-m. ISSN 0012-2297

**Union Francaise d'Annuaires Professionnels**
13 Avenue Vladimir Komarov, B.P. 36, 78190 Trappes, France.
- Annuaire de la Mecanique. a. (Federation des Industries Mecaniques et Transformatrices des Metaux)
- Annuaire Technique de la Sous - Traitance Mecanique. biennial. (Federation des Industries Mecaniques et Transformatrices des Metaux)
- Conseil National du Patronat Francais. Annuaire. a.
- Estampage, Forge, Extrusion et Techniques Connexes. triennial. (Federation des Industries Mecaniques et Transformatrices des Metaux. Syndicat National de l'Estampage et de la Forge)
- Guide-Annuaire Officiel de l'Artisanat et des Metiers. a. (Chambre de Metiers Departementale)
- Guide de l'Artisan; chambres de metiers de France. a. (Chambre de Metiers Departementale)
- Memento A.B.C. Construction. a.
- Repertoire Technique de la Sous-Traitance des Industries Plastiques. biennial. (Federation Francaise des Industries Transformatrices des Plastiques)
- Syndicat General de la Construction Electrique. Annuaire. a. (Federation des Industries Electriques et Electroniques. Syndicat General de la Construction Electrique)

**Union Francaise des Centres de Vacances**
54 rue du Theatre, 75 Paris 15e, France.
- M.A. m.
- U. F. C. V. m (10 per yr)

**Union Francaise des Oeuvres Laiques d'Education Physique**
3, R. Recamier, 75341 Paris, France.
- Informations U F O L E P-U S E P. m(10 per yr.)

**Union Francaise pour l'Esperanto**
4 bis, rue de la Cerisaie, 75004 Paris, France.
- Esperanto-Actualites. a.
- Franca Esperantisto. bi-m.

**Union Hospitaliere Privee**
87, rue d'Amsterdam, 75008 Paris, France.
- Hospitalisation Nouvelle. m (10 per yr)

**Union Interlinguiste de France**
Foyer Alizes Theureau, 81 rue Saint Fargeau, F-75020 Paris, France.
- Unir. q.

**Union Internationale des Architectes**
1 rue d'Ulm, 75005 Paris, France
(U.S. orders to: American Institute of Architects, Committee on International Relations, 1735 New York Ave. N.W., Washington, DC 20006)
- U I A Information. (Union Internationale des Architectes) m. ISSN 0041-6916

**Union Internationale d'Histoire des Sciences**
12 rue Colbert, 75- Paris 2e, France.
- Congres International d'Historie des Sciences. Actes. irreg., 11th, 1965, Warsaw; 13th, 1971, Moscow. ISSN 0074-9540

**Union Internationale des Maires**
Hotel de Ville, Paris 4e, France.
- France-Allemagne. irreg., approximately 3 per yr. ISSN 0071-8181

**Union Internationale des Producteurs et Distributeurs d'Energie Electrique**
see International Union of Producers and Distributors of Electrical Energy

**Union Intersyndicale des Medecins Cinesiologues: Sport et Reeducation**
45 Ave. de Sceaux, 78000 Versailles, France.
- Cinesiologie. q. ISSN 0009-7209

**Union Litteraire et Artistique de France**
35 rue Gayet, 42000 Saint-Etienne (Loire), France.
- Pensee Francaise. bi-m. ISSN 0031-479X (Co-sponsor: College des Bardes d'Oil)

**Union Nationale de l'Apiculture Francaise**
38 Bd. de Sebastopol, 75004 Paris, France.
- Revue Francaise d'Apiculture; l'abeille et le miel. m. ISSN 0035-2853

**Union Nationale de l'Enseignement Agricole Prive**
277 rue Saint-Jacques, 75005 Paris, France.
- Union Nationale de l'Enseignement Agricole Prive. Annuaire. a. ISSN 0082-7711

**Union Nationale des Associations de Parents d'Eleves de l'Enseignement Libre (UNAPEL)**
- Nouvelle Famille Educatrice. (pub. by Societe d'Editions de la Famille Educatrice)

**Union Nationale des Associations de Parents d'Enfants Inadaptes**
28 Place Saint- Georges, 75442 Paris Cedex 09, France.
- Epanouir. m.

**Union Nationale des Associations Familiales**
28 Place St. Georges, 75442 Paris Cedex 09, France.
- U N A F. Bulletin de Liaison. m. ISSN 0041-5219

**Union Nationale des Caisses d'Epargne de France**
5 Rue Masseran, Paris (8e), France.
- Journal des Caisses d'Epargne. m. ISSN 0047-2182

**Union Nationale des Chambres Syndicales de Couverture et de Plomberie de France**
9 rue de la Perouse, 75784 Paris, France.
- Informations Couverture Plomberie; technique et documentation. q.

**Union Nationale des Eleveurs de Porcs**
29, rue Fortuny, 75017 Paris, France.
- Porc. 11 per yr.

**Union Nationale des Federations d'Organismes d'Habitations a Loyer Modere**
2Rue Lord Byron, 75008 Paris, France.
- H; revue de l'habitat social. 11 per yr.
- Union Nationale des Federations d'Organismes d'Habitations a Loyer Modere. Guide Annuaire HLM. a.

**Union Nationale des Grandes Pharmacies**
57, rue Spontini, 75116 Paris, France.
- Evolution Pharmaceutique. m.

**Union Nationale des Industries de Carrieres et Materiaux de Construction**
3, rue Alfred-Roll, 75017 Paris, France.
- U.N.I.C.E.M. Annuaire Officiel. a.

**Union Nationale des Industries de la Manutention dans les Ports Francais**
76 Av. Marceau, Paris 8e, France.
- Industrie de la Manutention dans les Ports Francais. a. ISSN 0073-7720

**Union Nationale des Oenologues**
123 rue de Lille, Paris 75007, France.
- Union Nationale des Oenologues. Annuaire. a. ISSN 0082-7738

**Union Nationale des Officiers de Reserve**
- Armee et Defense. (pub. by Service de Presse, Edition, Information)

**Union Nationale Inter-Universitaire**
8, rue de Musset, 75016 Paris, France.
- Action Universitaire. m. ISSN 0065-177X

**Union Nationale Interfederale des Oeuvres Privees Sanitaires et Sociales**
103 Faubourg St.-Honore, Paris (8e), France.
- Union Sociale. m. ISSN 0041-7041

**Union Nationale Interprofessionnelle du Cheval**
51 rue Dumont d'Urville, 75116 Paris, France.
- Courses et Elevage. bi-m. ISSN 0300-5607
- Eperon. 8 per yr. ISSN 0300-5658

**Union Nationale Interprofessionnelle du Logement**
- Habitation-Cahiers de l'UNIL/Logement C. I. L. (pub. by Societe d'Editions de l'Habitation)

**Union Nationale pour l'Avenir de la Medecine**
- Assure Social. (pub. by Editions de l' Avenir)
- Profils Medico-Sociaux. (pub. by Editions de l' Avenir)

**Union of the Armenian Evangelical Churches in France**
151 A, rue F. de Pressense, 69100 Villeurbanne, France.
- Panpere. m. ISSN 0031-0972

**Union Pontificale Missionnaire**
5 rue Monsieur, 75007 Paris, France.
- Mission de l'Eglise. q. ISSN 0026-6035

**Union pour la Defense des Peuples Opprimes**
c/o Francois de Romainville, 7 Av. Leon-Heuzey, Paris (16e), France.
- Exil et Liberte; Organe de l'Internationale de la Liberte. m. ISSN 0014-4665

**Union Professionnelle des Professeurs Cadres et Techniciens du Secretariat et de la Comptabilite**
21 rue Croulebarbe, 75013 Paris, France.
- Revue du Secretariat et de la Comptabilite. q.
- Secretaires d'Aujourd'hui. m. ISSN 0397-6505

**Union Rationaliste**
- Cahiers Rationalistes. (pub. by Editions Rationalistes)

**Union Regionale des Sapeurs-Pompiers Professionnels et Volontaires d'Aquitaine**
56, rue d'Ornano, 33 Cestas, Bordeaux, France.
- Sauver. q.

**Union Regionale du Sud-Est pour la Sauvegarde de la Vie, de la Nature et de l'Environment**
Moulin des Serres, 83490 le Muy, France.
- S. O. S. - Vie - Nature. q.

**Union Syndicale des Artistes**
18, Avenue Carnot, 75017 Paris, France.
- Professionnel du Spectacle. q.

**Union Syndicale des Magistrats**
33 rue du Four, 75006 Paris, France.
- Nouveau Pouvoir Judiciaire. m. ISSN 0338-1552

**Union Syndicale Nationale des Enseignants de France (U. S. N. E. F.)**
30 rue de Gramont, 75 Paris 2e, France.
- Voix des Enseignants. m. ISSN 0042-837X

**Union Technique de l'Automobile du Motocycle et du Cycle**
- Union Technique de l'Automobile du Motocycle et du Cycle. Bulletin Mensuel de Documentation. (pub. by Societe Auxiliaire Technique de l'Automobile, du Motocycle et du Cycle)

**Uniono Por la Linguo Internaciona Ido (Reformed Esperanto)**
Ed. Roger Moureaux, F39320 Saint Julien-sur-Suran, Jura, France.
- Progreso. q. ISSN 0048-5489

**Unions des Federations de Fonctionnaires et Assimiles**
26 rue de Montholon, 75009 Paris, France.
- Fonction Publique. m.

**Unions Regionales de la C.N.T.F.**
Bourse du Travail, Place Saint-Sernin, 31000 Toulouse, France.
- Espoir. w. ISSN 0014-0724

**Unite**
41, Boulevard de Magenta, 75010 Paris, France.
- Unite; hebdomadaire socialiste. w.

**U. S. Information Service**
2, rue St. Florentin, Paris 75001, France.
- Informations & Documents. m. ISSN 0020-0417

**United Towns Organization**
13 rue Racine, 75006 Paris, France.
- Cites Unies. q. ISSN 0529-8016
- Repertoire Officiel des Relations Internationales des Communes du Monde/Official Index of the International Relations of the Towns of the World. a. ISSN 0066-3573

**Universite Catholique de l'Ouest**
- Impacts. (pub. by Association Saint-Yves)

**Universite Claude Bernard**
*see* Universite de Lyon I

**Universite d'Aix-Marseille I (Universite de Provence) Centre d'Etudes des Societes Mediterraneennes**
- Universite d'Aix-Marseille I. Centre d'Etudes des Societes Mediterraneennes. Cahiers. (pub. by Diffusion Ophrys)

**Universite d'Aix-Marseille I (Universite de Provence) Centre d'Etudes et de Recherches Helleniques**
- Universite d'Aix-Marseille I. Centre d'Etudes et de Recherches Helleniques. Publications. (pub. by Diffusion Ophrys)

**Universite d'Aix-Marseille I (Universite de Provence) Faculte des Lettres et Sciences Humaines**
- Universite d'Aix-Marseille I. Faculte des Lettres et Sciences Humaines. Annales. (pub. by Diffusion Ophrys)

**Universite d'Aix-Marseille I (Universite de Provence) Institut de Geographie**
29, Av. Robert Schuman, 13 Aix-en-Provence, France.
- Collection Etudes et Travaux de la Revue "Mediterranee". (pub. by Diffusion Ophrys)
- Mediterranee; revue geographique des pays mediterraneens. q. ISSN 0025-8296

**Universite d'Aix-Marseille I (Universite de Provence) Laboratoire d'Anthropologie et de Prehistoire des Pays de la Mediterrance Occidentale**
Place Victor Hugo, 13331 Marseille Cedex 1, France.
- Revue de l'Occident Musulman et de la Mediterranee. s-a. ISSN 0035-1474

**Universite d'Aix-Marseille II. Station Marine d'Endoume**
Rue de la Batterie des Lions, 13007 Marseille, France.
- Tethys. q. ISSN 0040-4012

**Universite d'Aix-Marseille III (Universite de Droit, d'Economie et des Sciences.) Centre des Hautes Etudes Touristiques**
18 rue de l'Opera, 13100 Aix-en-Provence, France.
- Cahiers du Tourisme. irreg., 1972, no. 85. ISSN 0068-5151

- Documentation Touristique: Bibliographie Analytique Internationale. q.
- Touristic Analysis Review. q.
- Universite d'Aix-Marseille III. Centre des Hautes Etudes Touristiques. Etudes et Memoires. irreg., no. 28, 1977. ISSN 0065-4965

**Universite d'Aix-Marseille III (Universite de Droit, d'Economie et des Sciences) Institut d'Histoire des Pays d'Outre- Mer**
3 Avenue Robert Schuman, 13621 Aix- en-Provence, France.
- Universite d'Aix-Marseille III. Institut d'Histoire des Pays d'Outre-Mer. Etudes et Documents. irreg. ISSN 0065-5007

**Universite de Besancon. Centre de Documentation et de Bibliographie Philosophiques**
95, Boulevard Raspail, Paris, France.
- Universite de Besancon. Centre de Documentation et de Bibliographie Philosophiques. Travaux. irreg.

**Universite de Besancon. Centre de Linguistique Appliquee**
- Etudes de Linguistique Appliquee. (pub. by Librairie Marcel Didier)

**Universite de Besancon. Centre de Recherches d'Histoire Ancienne**
- Dialogues d'Histoire Ancienne. (pub. by Societe d'Edition les Belles Lettres)

**Universite de Besancon. Laboratoire de Biologie et d'Ecologie Animales**
Faculte des Sciences, Besancon, France.
- Station Biologique de Bonnevaux (Doubs). Section de Biologie et d'Ecologie Animales. Publications. irreg. ISSN 0068-0087

**Universite de Bordeaux I. Faculte de Droit et des Sciences Economiques**
- Revue Economique du Sud-Ouest. (pub. by Editions Biere)

**Universite de Bordeaux I. Laboratoire de Botanique**
Avenue des Facultes, 33405 Talence, France.
- Botaniste. 6 per yr. ISSN 0045-2637

**Universite de Bordeaux II. Centre d'Etudes et de Recherches Ethnologiques**
20 Cours Pasteur, 33 Bordeaux, France.
- Universite de Bordeaux II. Centre d'Etudes et de Recherches Ethnologiques. Cahiers. a.

**Universite de Bordeaux III**
Domaine Universitaire, 33405 Talence, France.
- International Comparative Literature Association. Proceedings of the Congress. triennial, 1970, 6th, Bordeaux, France. ISSN 0074-2813
- Revue des Etudes Anciennes. (pub. by Societe d'Edition les Belles Lettres)

**Universite de Bordeaux III. Centre d'Etude d'Afrique Noire**
- Annee Africaine. (pub. by Editions A. Pedone)

**Universite de Bordeaux III. Centre d'Etudes de Geographie Tropicale**
Domaine Universitaire, 33405 Talence, France.
- Travaux et Documents de Geographie Tropicale. irreg.

**Universite de Bordeaux III. Institut de Geographie**
Domaine Universitaire, 33405 Talence, France.
- Cahiers d'Outre-Mer; revue de geographie. q. ISSN 0045-3765

**Universite de Bordeaux III. Societe Bordelaise de Diffusion de Travaux des Lettres et Sciences Humaines**
Domaine Universitaire, 33405 Talence, France.
- Universite de Bordeaux. Collection Sinologique. irreg; only one volume published. ISSN 0068-0273

**Universite de Bretagne Occidentale**
19 rue Jean Mace, 29200 Brest, France.
- Universite de Bretagne Occidentale. Guide de l'Etudiant. a.

**Universite de Clermont-Ferrand II**
Unite d'Enseignement et de Recherche de Sciences Exactes et Naturelles, B.P. 45, 63170 Aubiere, France.
- Universite de Clermont-Ferrand II. Annales Scientifiques. Serie Biologie Animale. irreg. ISSN 0069-4681

- Universite de Clermont-Ferrand II. Annales Scientifique. Serie Biologie Vegetale. irreg. ISSN 0069-469X
- Universite de Clermont-Ferrand II. Annales Scientifique. Serie Chemie. irreg. ISSN 0069-4703
- Universite de Clermont-Ferrand. Annales Scientifiques. Serie Geologie et Mineralogie. irreg. ISSN 0069-4711
- Universite de Clermont-Ferrand. Annales Scientifiques. Serie Mathematique. irreg. ISSN 0069-472X
- Universite de Clermont-Ferrand. Annales Scientifiques. Serie Physiologie Animale. irreg. ISSN 0069-4746
- Universite de Clermont-Ferrand II. Annales Scientifiques. Serie Physique. irreg. ISSN 0069-4738

**Universite de Clermont-Ferrand II. Institut et Observatoire de Physique du Globe du Puy de Dome**
12 Av. des Landais, 63001 Clermont-Ferrand Cedex, France.
- Journal de Recherches Atmospheriques. q. ISSN 0021-7972

**Universite de Clermont-Ferrand II. Laboratoire de Biologie Vegetale**
4, rue Ledru, F-63000 Clermont-Ferrand, France.
- Arvernia Biologica: Botanique; recueil des travaux des laboratoires de botanique de la Faculte des Sciences de Clermont-Ferrand et de la Station Biologique de Besse. irreg.(approx. a. since 1964) ISSN 0066-8184

**Universite de Droit, d'Economie et des Sciences**
*see* Universite d'Aix-Marseille III

**Universite de Droit, d'Economie et des Sciences Sociales**
*see* Universite de Paris II

**Universite de Droit et Sante de Lille**
*see* Universite de Lille II

**Universite de Grenoble**
- Universite de Grenoble. Institut Francais de Florence. Publication. Serie 1: Collection d'Etudes d'Histoire. (pub. by Casa Editrice G. C. Sansoni S.p.A. IT)
- Universite de Grenoble. Institut Francais de Florence. Publication. Serie 2: Collection d'Etudes Bibliographiques. (pub. by Casa Editrice G. C. Sansoni S.p.A. IT)

**Universite de Grenoble I (Universite Scientifique et Medicale de Grenoble) Institut des Sciences Nucleaires**
B.P. 257, 53, Avenue des Martyrs, Grenoble 38044, France.
- Universite Scientifique et Medicale de Grenoble. Institut des Sciences Nucleaires. Rapport Annuel. a.

**Universite de Grenoble I (Universite Scientifique et Medicale de Grenoble) Institut Fourier**
Boite Postale 116, 38402 Saint-Martin d'Heres, France.
- Universite Scientifique et Medicale de Grenoble. Institut Fourier. Annales. a. ISSN 0073-8328

**Universite de Grenoble I (Universite Scientifique et Medicale de Grenoble. Laboratoire de Biologie Vegetale**
Domaine Universitaire de Saint-Martin-d'Heres, B.P. 53 Centre de Tri, 38041 Grenoble Cedex, France.
- Documents de Cartographie Ecologique. s-a. ISSN 0335-5330

**Universite de Grenoble II (Universite des Sciences Sociales)**
- Universite des Sciences Sociales de Grenoble. Collection Generale. (pub. by Mouton Publishers NE)

**Universite de Grenoble II (Universite des Sciences Sociales) Centre de Recherche d'Histoire Economique, Sociale et Institutionnelle**
- Universite des Sciences Sociales de Grenoble. Centre de Recherche d'Histoire Economique, Sociale et Institutionnelle. Collection. Serie Histoire Institutionnelle. (pub. by Mouton Publishers NE)
- Universite des Sciences Sociales de Grenoble. Centre de Recherche d'Histoire Economique, Sociale et Institutionnelle. Collection. Serie Histoire Sociale. (pub. by Mouton Publishers NE)

**Universite de Grenoble II (Universite des Sciences Sociales) Centre de Recherche Economique et Sociale**
- Universite des Sciences Sociales de Grenoble. Centre de Recherche Economique et Sociale. Collection. Serie Agriculture et Devenir Social. (pub. by Mouton Publishers NE)
- Universite des Sciences Sociales de Grenoble. Centre de Recherche Economique et Sociale. Collection. Serie Economie du Developpement. (pub. by Mouton Publishers NE)
- Universite des Sciences Sociales de Grenoble. Centre de Recherche Economique et Sociale. Collection. Serie Etudes d'Economie de l'Energie. (pub. by Mouton Publishers NE)
- Universite des Sciences Sociales de Grenoble. Centre de Recherche Economique et Sociale. Collection. Serie Economie du Financement. (pub. by Mouton Publishers NE)

**Universite de Grenoble II (Universite des Sciences Sociales) Centre de Recherche Juridique**
- Universite des Sciences Sociales de Grenoble. Centre de Recherche Juridique. Collection. Serie Droit de la Propriete Industrielle. (pub. by Mouton Publishers NE)
- Universite des Sciences Sociales de Grenoble. Centre de Recherche Juridique. Collection. Serie Droit du Tourisme. (pub. by Mouton Publishers NE)
- Universite des Sciences Sociales de Grenoble. Centre de Recherche Juridique. Collection. Serie Droits Etrangers et Droit Compare. (pub. by Mouton Publishers NE)

**Universite de Grenoble II (Universite des Sciences Sociales) Institut d'Etudes Politiques**
- Universite des Sciences Sociales de Grenoble. Institut d'Etudes Politiques. Serie Essais et Travaux. (pub. by Mouton Publishers NE)
- Universite des Sciences Sociales de Grenoble. Institut d'Etudes Politiques. Serie Textes et Documents. (pub. by Mouton Publishers NE)

**Universite de Grenoble III (Universite des Langues et Lettres) Institut de Phonetique**
Domaine Universitaire de Saint-Martin-d'Heres, B.P. 25 Centre de Tri, 38040 Grenoble Cedex, France.
- Universite de Grenoble III. Institut de Phonetique. Bulletin. irreg.
- Universite de Grenoble III. Institut de Phonetique. Travaux de Recherche. Serie A: Manuals. a.
- Universite de Grenoble III. Institut de Phonetique. Travaux de Recherche. Serie B. irreg. ISSN 0085-1272

**Universite de Haute Bretagne**
*see* **Universite de Rennes II**

**Universite de Lille I (Universite des Sciences et Techniques de Lille)**
U.E.R. de Biologie (SN2), Box 36, F - 59650 Villeneuve d'Ascq, France.
- Societe de Botanique du Nord de la France. Bulletin. s-a. ISSN 0037-9034

**Universite de Lille II (Droit et Sante)**
Faculte de Medecine, 86, rue de Paris, 59000 Lille, France.
- Lille Medical. m. ISSN 0024-3507

**Universite de Lille III (Sciences Humaines, Lettres et Arts)**
S.P. 18, 59650 Villeneuve d'Ascq, France.
- Revue des Sciences Humaines. q. ISSN 0035-2195
- Revue du Nord. (pub. by D.U.L.J.V.A.)

**Universite de Lyon I. Departement de Mathematiques**
43, Boulevard du 11 November 1918, 69621 Villeurbanne, France.
- Universite Claude Bernard. Departement de Mathematiques. Publications. irreg., ISSN 0076-1656

**Universite de Lyon I. Departement Sciences de la Terre**
43, Bd. du 11 Novembre 1918, 69621 Villeurbanne, France.
- Geobios; paleontology, stratigraphy, paleoecology. bi-m. ISSN 0016-6995

**Universite de Lyon II. Centre d'Etudes Gidiennes**
69500 Bron, France.
- Amis d'Andre Gide. Bulletin. q. ISSN 0044-8133 (Association des Amis d'Andre Gide)

**Universite de Lyon III. Faculte de Droit**
- Universite de Lyon III. Faculte de Droit. Annales. (pub. by Librairie Generale de Droit et de Jurisprudence)

**Universite de Metz. Centre d'Analyse Syntaxique**
Metz, France
(Subscr. to: Librairie Klincksieck, 11 rue de Lille, 75007 Paris, France)
- Recherches Linquistiques. irreg.

**Universite de Metz. Centre de Recherches Relations Internationales**
Ile de Saulcy, 57000 Metz, France.
- Universite de Metz. Centre de Recherches Relations Internationales. Travaux et Recherches. irreg.

**Universite de Nancy II**
23 Bd. Albert, 54000 Nancy, France.
- Annales de l'Est. (pub. by Imprimerie et Librairie Berger-Levrault)
- Universite de Nancy II. Centre de Recherches et d'Applications Pedagogiques en Langues. Melanges. a. ISSN 0077-2712

**Universite de Nancy II. Centre Europeen Universitaire**
15, Place Carnot, 54 Nancy, France.
- Universite de Nancy II. Centre Europeen Universitaire. Publications. irreg. ISSN 0077-2720

**Universite de Nancy II. Faculte de Droit et des Sciences Economiques**
13 Place Carnot, Nancy, France.
- Universite de Nancy II. Faculte de Droit et des Sciences Economiques. Etudes et Travaux. Serie Droit International Public. irreg.
- Universite de Nancy II. Faculte de Droit et des Sciences Economiques. Etudes et Travaux. Serie Droit Prive. irreg.
- Universite de Nancy II. Faculte de Droit et des Sciences Economiques. Etudes et Travaux. Serie Economie Regionale. irreg.
- Universite de Nancy II. Faculte de Droit et des Sciences Economiques. Etudes et Travaux. Serie Science Politique. irreg.

**Universite de Nantes. Centre de Recherches sur l'Histoire de la France Atlantique**
Chemin de la Sensive du Tertre, Nantes (44), France.
- Universite de Nantes. Centre de Recherches sur l'Histoire de la France Atlantique. Enquetes et Documents. a.

**Universite de Nice. Centre du Vingtieme Siecle**
117, rue de France, 06000 Nice, France.
- Cahiers Paul Eluard. a.

**Universite de Paris (Pantheon-Sorbonne)**
*see* **Universite de Paris I**

**Universite de Paris (Paris-Nanterre)**
*see* **Universite de Paris X**

**Universite de Paris (Paris-Val-de-Marne)**
*see* **Universite de Paris XII**

**Universite de Paris (Pierre et Marie Curie)**
*see* **Universite de Paris VI**

**Universite de Paris (Rene Descartes)**
*see* **Universite de Paris V**

**Universite de Paris I (Pantheon-Sorbonne) Centre d'Etudes Archeologiques de la Mediterranee Occidentale**
- Karthago. (pub. by Editions Klincksieck)
- Karthago. Collection Epigraphique. (pub. by Editions Klincksieck)

**Universite de Paris I (Pantheon-Sorbonne) Institut d'Histoire des Relations Internationales Contemporaines**
- Relations Internationales. (pub. by Societe d'Etudes Historiques des Relations Internationales Contemporaines (S.E.H.R.I.C.))

**Universite de Paris I (Paris-Nanterre) Centre d'Etudes Theatrales**
2, rue de Rouen, 92001 Nanterre Cedex, France (Orders to: Librairie de Coupe-Papier, 19 rue de l'Odeon, 75006 Paris, France)
- Documentation Theatrale; fiches analytiques. a. (Co-sponsor: Centre de Recherches Historiques de l'Ecole des Hautes Etudes en Sciences Sociales)

**Universite de Paris II (Universite Droit, d'Economie et des Sciences Sociales) Institut de Droit Compare**
- Revue de Science Criminelle et de Droit Penal Compare. (pub. by Editions Sirey)

**Universite de Paris V (Rene Descartes)**
12 rue de l'Ecole de Medicine, 75270 Paris Cedex 06, France.
- Universite Rene Descartes. Bulletin. s-a.

**Universite de Paris VI (Pierre et Marie Curie) Institut de Statistique**
4 Place Jussieu, 75230 Paris Cedex 05, Paris, France.
- Revue de Statistique Appliquee. q. ISSN 0035-175X
- Universite de Paris VI (Pierre et Marie Curie). Institut de Statistique. Publications. s-a.

**Universite de Paris VI (Pierre et Marie Curie) Institut Henri Poincare**
Secretariat Mathematique, 11 rue Pierre et Marie Curie, Paris 5e, France.
- Institut Henri Poincare. Annales. Section A: Physique Theorique. (pub. by Centrale des Revues Dunod Gauthier- Villars)
- Institut Henri Poincare. Annales. Section B: Calcul des Probabilites et Statistiques. (pub. by Centrale des Revues Dunod Gauthier-Villars)
- Universite de Paris VI. Institut Henri Poincare. Seminair Lions. irreg. ISSN 0079-0036
- Universite de Paris VI. Institut Henri Poincare. Seminaire Choquet. Initiation a l'Analyse. a., in 1-2 fascicules. ISSN 0078-9909

**Universite de Paris VI (Pierre et Marie Curie) Laboratoire Arago de Biologie Marine**
- Vie et Milieu. (pub. by Masson)

**Universite de Paris VII. Groupe de Linguistique Japonaise**
2 Place Jussieu, 75005 Paris, France.
- Universite de Paris VII. Groupe de Linguistique Japonaise. Travaux. irreg. ISSN 0339-8811

**Universite de Paris VII. Laboratoire de Psychanalyse et Psychopathologie**
- Psychanalyse a l'Universite. (pub. by Editions Replique)

**Universite de Paris VIII (Paris-Vincennes) Departement de Linguistique**
- Lingvisticae Investigationes. (pub. by John Benjamins B.V. NE)

**Universite de Paris X (Paris-Nanterre) Centre d'Etudes Finno-Ougriennes**
- Etudes Finno-Ougriennes. (pub. by Editions Klincksieck)

**Universite de Paris X Laboratoire d'Ethnologie et de Sociologie Comparative**
Centre d'Etudes Mongoles, 92001 Nanterre, France.
- Etudes Mongoles. a.

**Universite de Paris XII (Paris-Val-de-Marne) Institut d'Urbanisme**
Avenue du General-de-Gaulle, 94010 Creteil, France.
- Vie Urbaine. q. ISSN 0042-563X

**Universite de Poitiers. Centre de Recherches Latino-Americaines**
95, Av. de Recteur-Pineau, 86022 Poitiers, France.
- Universite de Poitiers. Centre de Recherches Latino-Americaines. Publications. irreg. (approx. 1-2 per yr.)

**Universite de Poitiers. Centre d'Etudes Superieures de Civilisation Medievale**
24, rue de la Chaine, 86022 Poitiers, France.
- Cahiers de Civilisation Medievale. Supplement. irreg. ISSN 0068-5011
- Universite de Poitiers. Centre d'Etudes Superieures de Civilizattion Medievale. Publications. irreg. ISSN 0079-256X

**Universite de Poitiers. Departement d'Etudes Portugaises et Bresiliennes**
95 Avenue du Recteur Pineau, 86022 Poitiers, France.
- Sillages. a.

**Universite de Provence**
*see* **Universite d'Aix-Marseille I**

**Universite de Reims. Institut de Geographie**
57 rue Pierre Taittinger, 51100 Reims, France.
• Universite de Reims. Institut de Geographie.
Travaux. q. ISSN 0048-7163

**Universite de Rennes I. Institut de Geologie**
Av. du General Leclerc B.P. 25A, 35031 Rennes
Cedex, France.
• Societe Geologique et Mineralogique de Bretagne.
Bulletin, Serie C. s-a.

**Universite de Rennes II (Universite de Haute
Bretagne)**
6 Avenue Gaston Berger, 35043 Rennes, France.
• Annales de Bretagne. q. ISSN 0003-391X
• Classiques Bretons. irreg. ISSN 0045-7108
• Universite de Haute Bretagne. Centre d'Etudes
Hispaniques, Hispano-Americaines et Luso-
Bresiliennes. Travaux. a. ISSN 0080-0929

**Universite de Strasbourg I (Universite Louis Pasteur)
Institut de Geologie**
Bibliotheque, 1 rue Blessig, 67084 Strasbourg
Cedex, France.
• Sciences Geologiques. Bulletin. q.
• Sciences Geologiques - Memoires. irreg.

**Universite de Strasbourg II**
22 rue Descartes, 6700 Strasbourg, France.
• Recherches Anglaises et Americaines. a. ISSN
0557-6989 (Association Strasbourgeoise des
Periodiques de Sciences Humaines)
• Recherches Germaniques. a.

**Universite de Strasbourg II. Centre de Philologie et
de Litteratures Romanes**
25 rue du Marechal-Juin, F-67084 Strasbourg,
France
• Bibliotheque Francaise et Romane. Serie A:
Manuels et Etudes Linguistiques. (pub. by
Editions Klincksieck)
• Bibliotheque Francaise et Romane. Serie B:
Editions Critiques de Textes. (pub. by Editions
Klincksieck)
• Bibliotheque Francaise et Romane. Serie C:
Etudes Litteraires. (pub. by Editions Klincksieck)
• Bibliotheque Francaise et Romane. Serie D:
Initiation, Textes et Documents. (pub. by Editions
Klincksieck)
• Bibliotheque Francaise et Romane. Serie E:
Langue et Litterature Francaises au Canada. (pub.
by Editions Klincksieck)
• Etudes Gobiniennes. (pub. by Editions
Klincksieck)
• Travaux de Linguistique et de Litterature. (pub. by
Editions Klincksieck)
• Universite de Strasbourg II. Centre de Philologie
et Litteratures Romanes. Actes et Colloques.
irreg. ISSN 0081-5918

**Universite de Strasbourg II. Centre de Recherche et
de Documentation des Institutions Chretiennes**
9 Place de l'Universite, 67084 Strasbourg Cedex,
France.
• Hommes et Eglise; Annuaire du Cerdic. a.
• R I C. (Repertoire Bibliographique des Institutions
Chretiennes.) a., plus 8-10 supplements. ISSN
0079-9300
• Universite de Strasbourg. Centre de Recherche et
de Documentation des Institutions Chretiennes.
Bulletin du CERDIC. a. ISSN 0081-5926

**Universite de Strasbourg II. Faculte de Theologie
Catholique**
22 rue Rene Descartes, 67084 Strasbourg, France.
• Revue des Sciences Religieuses. q. ISSN 0035-
2217

**Universite de Strasbourg II. Groupe de Recherche
d'Histoire Romaine**
• Ktema. (pub. by A. E. C. R.)

**Universite de Strasbourg II. Institut de Phonetique**
25 rue du Soleil, Strasbourg, France.
• Universite de Strasbourg II. Institut de
Phonetique. Travaux. a. ISSN 0081-5934

**Universite de Strasbourg. Institut d'Etudes Latino-
Americaines**
25 rue du Soleil, 67 Strasbourg, France.
• Universite de Strasbourg, Institut d'Etudes Latino-
Americaines. Travaux. a.

**Universite de Toulouse I (Sciences Sociales)**
Place Anatole France, 31070 Toulouse, France.
• Universite des Sciences Sociales de Toulouse.
Annales. a. ISSN 0563-9727

**Universite de Toulouse I (Sciences Sociales) Institut
d'Etudes Internationaux et des Pays en Voie de
Developpement**
Place Anatole France, 31070 Toulouse Cedex,
France.
• Echanges Internationaux et Developpement. (Co-
Publisher: Association Echanges Internationaux et
Developpement)

**Universite de Toulouse II (le Mirail)**
109 bis, rue Vauquelin, 31081 Toulouse Cedex,
France.
• Caliban; etudes anglaises et nord-americaines. a.
ISSN 0575-2124 (prep. by its Institut d'Etudes
Anglaises et Nord-Americaines)
• Grammatica. irreg.
• Homo. a. ISSN 0563-9743
• Litteratures. ISSN 0563-9751 (prep. by its Faculte
des Lettres et Sciences Humaines)
• Pallas. q. ISSN 0031-0387
• Philosophie. a.
• Revue Geographique des Pyrenees et du Sud-
Ouest. q. ISSN 0035-3221 (Co-Sponsor: Institut
de Geographie des Universites de Toulouse,
Bordeaux et Pau)
• Universite de Toulouse II (le Mirail). Annales. q.
ISSN 0014-6749
• Universite de Toulouse II (le Mirail). Departement
de Mathematique. Cours et Seminars. irreg. ISSN
0082-5387
• Universite de Toulouse II. Institut d'Art
Prehistorique. Travaux. a. ISSN 0563-9794
• Universite de Toulouse II (le Mirail). Institut
d'Etudes Politiques. Bulletin de Documentation. a.
ISSN 0082-5425

**Universite de Toulouse II (le Mirail) Institut
d'Etudes Hispaniques, Hispanoamericaines**
109 bis, rue Vauquelin, 31081 Toulouse Cedex,
France.
• Cahiers du Monde Hispanique et Luso- Bresilien
(Caravelle) s-a. ISSN 0008-0152
• France-Iberie Recherche. Etudes et Documents.
irreg. ISSN 0082-5409

**Universite des Langues et Lettres de Grenoble**
*see* **Universite de Grenoble III**

**Universite des Sciences et Techniques de Lille**
*see* **Universite de Lille I**

**Universite des Sciences Humaines de Strasbourg**
*see* **Universite de Strasbourg II**

**Universite des Sciences Humaines, Lettres et Arts de
Lille**
*see* **Universite de Lille III**

**Universite des Sciences Sociales**
*see* **Universite de Grenoble III**

**Universite Francois Rabelais, Tours**
• Bref. (pub. by Larousse)

**Universite Jean Moulin**
*see* **Universite de Lyon III**

**Universite Louis Pasteur**
*see* **Universite de Strasbourg I (Universite Louis
Pasteur)**

**Universite Moderne**
43 Faubourg Saint-Honore, Paris (8e), France.
• Universite Moderne. bi-m. ISSN 0041-9222

**Universite Montpellier III (Universite Paul Valery)
Centre d'Etudes et de Recherches Elisabethaines**
B.P. 5043, 34032 Montpellier, France.
• Cahiers Elisabethains; etudes sur la pre-
renaissance et la renaissance anglaises. s-a.

**Universite Montpellier III (Universite Paul Valery)
Centre d'Etudes Occitanes**
B.P. 5043, 34032 Montpellier, France.
• Bibliographie Occitane. irreg.

• Obradors. q.
• Revue des Langues Romanes. s-a.

**Universite Paul Sabatier (Toulouse) Station
Biologique du Lac d'Oredon**
• Annales de Limnologie. (pub. by Masson)

**Universite Paul Valery**
*see* **Universite Montpellier III**

**Universite Scientifique et Medicale de Grenoble**
*see* **Universite de Grenoble I**

**Usine Moderne**
127 Champs-Elysees, Paris 8e, France.
• Usine Moderne au Service de l'Afrique Noire.
Annuaire. a. ISSN 0083-4815

**Usine Publications S.A.**
17 rue d'Uzes B. P. 47902, 75065 Paris Cedex 02,
France.
• Cahiers Techniques du Moniteur. 6 per yr.
(Societe des Publications du Moniteur)
• Moniteur des Travaux Publics et du Batiment. w.
ISSN 0026-9700

**Editions V.M.**
3 Place Malesherbes, 75017 Paris, France.
• Phot 'argus (Edition Generale); journal
professionnel des materiels et produits
photographiques. bi-m.
• Phot 'argus(Edition Professionnelle); pour
revendeurs et professionnels. bi-m.

**Vacances 2000**
18 Av. de l'Opera, Paris 75001, France.
• Periscope 2000. irreg. ISSN 0079-0885

**Nguyen Van Nghi, Ed. & Pub.**
27 Bd d'Athenes, 13001 Marseille, France.
• Mensuel du Medecin Acupuncteur. m. ISSN
0301-6366

**Edition et Publicite Jean Vanvert**
32 rue Yves-Toudic, Paris 10e, France.
• Annuaire National des Fournisseurs des
Administrations Francaises. a. ISSN 0066-3379

**Editions Varia**
3, rue de l'Abbe-Gregoire, 75006 Paris, France.
• Feuillets de Biologie; le repertoire medical
pratique. bi-m. ISSN 0428-2779 (Comite
Intersyndical des Biologistes Francais)

**Regitec, J. de Vaubernier et Cie**
12, Boulevard de la Madelaine, 75009 Paris, France.
• Annuaire Federal de l'Horticulture et des
Pepinieres. triennial. (Federation Nationale des
Producteurs de l'Horticulture et des Pepinieres.)

**Editions Vauclair S.A.R.L.**
8 rue d'Aboukir, 75002 Paris, France.
• L'Homme. q.

**R. Veillith Ed. and Pub.**
43400 le Chambon sur Lignon, France.
• Lumieres dans la Nuit; mysterieux objets celestes
et problemes connexes. 10 per yr.

**Vendre Aujourd'hui**
29, rue Violet, 75015 Paris, France.
• Vendre Aujourd'hui. s-m.

**Publications Georges Ventillard**
2 a 12 rue de Bellevue, C.C.P. 424-19, 75019 Paris,
France.
• Hifi Stereo; le journal de la haute fidelite, disques,
musique. m (11 per yr.) (Societe des Publications
Radio-Electriques et Scientifiques)
• Marius. w.
• Quinze Ans. m.
• Radio - Plans. m. ISSN 0033-7668
• Systeme D; la revue des bricoleurs. m. ISSN
0039-8012
• Systeme D. Cahiers. q.

**Vers la Vie Nouvelle**
73 rue Ste-Anne, Paris (2e), France.
• Vers la Vie Nouvelle. m. ISSN 0049-5980

**Editions H. Vial**
Rue des Moines, 91410 Dourdan, France.
• Nouveau Journal de Charpente-Menuiserie-
Parquets; revue technique du travail du bois. m.
ISSN 0029-4675

**Vie au Soleil**
13 rue Emile Lepeu, 75011 Paris, France.
- Vie au Soleil. bi-m.

**Editions de la Vie Catholique**
163 Bd. Malesherbes, Paris (17e), France.
- Informations Catholiques Internationales. s-m.
  ISSN 0020-0441
- Internationale Katholieke Informatie. m.

**Vie Collective**
26 Bd. Poissonniere, Paris 75009, France.
- Vie Collective. m. ISSN 0042-5370

**Vie Communale et Departementale**
35 Rue Marbeuf (Champs-Elysees), Paris (8e),
France.
- Vie Communale et Departementale. m. ISSN
  0042-5400

**Vie de la Douane**
74 Bd. Bourdon, 92202 Neuilly- sur-Seine, France.
- Vie de la Douane. q. ISSN 0042-5419

**Vie des Collectivites Ouvrieres**
33 rue Bouret, Paris (19e), France.
- Vie des Collectivites Ouvrieres; revue des comites
  d'entreprise et similaires. q. ISSN 0042-5389

**Vie et Travail**
219 rue St Denis, Paris (2e), France.
- Vie et Travail. w. ISSN 0042-5532

**Vie Judiciaire**
c/o Ed. Francois Bidou, 41 rue de Richelieu, Paris
(1), France.
- Vie Judiciaire; problemes judiciaires et juridiques.
  w. ISSN 0042-5567

**Editions de la Vie Medicale**
133 bis, rue de l'Universite, 75007 Paris, France.
- Questions Facultes. bi-m.
- Questions Internat. 24 per yr. ISSN 0033-636X
- Tele Medecine. w.
- Vie Medicale. 31 per yr. ISSN 0042-5583

**Vie Musicale**
27 rue Dareau, 75014 Paris, France.
- Scherzo. 10 per yr.

**Vie Publique**
140 rue de Rennes, 75006 Paris, France.
- Vie Publique; le journal des elus et des
  administrateurs locaux. m. ISSN 0049-6294

**Vie Theresienne**
c/o Ed. Georges Durand, 33 rue du Carmel, B.P.
205, 14102 Lisieux, France.
- Vie Theresienne. q. ISSN 0042-5621

**Viens et Vois**
9, rue Claude Boyet, 69007 Lyon, France.
- Assemblees de Dieu de France. Annuaire. a. ISSN
  0083-6184

**Editions Vigot Freres**
23 rue de l'Ecole de Medecine, 75006 Paris, France.
- Gynecologie; revue internationale de gynecologie.
  bi-m. ISSN 0301-2204 (Societe Francaise de
  Gynecologie) (Co-Sponsor: Federation
  Internationale de Gynecologie Infantile et
  Juvenile)
- Poumon & le Coeur. 6 per yr. ISSN 0032-5821
- Recueil de Medecine Veterinaire d'Alfort. 12 per
  yr. ISSN 0034-1843 (Ecole d'Alfort)
- Revue d'Elevage et de Medecine Veterinaire des
  Pays Tropicaux. q. ISSN 0035-1865

**Guy Vinatrel**
62 rue Nationale, Paris (13e), France.
- Lettres Mensuelles; Revue Philosophique et
  Sociale. m. ISSN 0047-4436

**Editions Charles Vincent, S. A.**
36 rue Debelleyme, 75003 Paris, France.
- Independant-Chaussures. m. ISSN 0019-3615
- Officiel des Metiers de la Chaussure. m.

**Visages de l'Ain**
Rte. de Jassans, Trevoux-0-1, France.
- Visages de l'Ain. bi-m. ISSN 0042-6865

**Editions Vitesse Speed**
5 Place Violet, 75015 Paris, France.
- Vitesse-Speed. m. ISSN 0042-7489

**Editions Vivienne**
36 rue Vivienne, Paris (9e), France.
- Revue Parlementaire; politique, diplomatique,
  economique, sociale, internationale. m. ISSN
  0002-077X

**Vivre en Harmonie**
5 rue Emile-Level, 75017 Paris, France.
- Vivre en Harmonie. m. ISSN 0042-7608

**Voie de la Paix**
B.P. 20, 14 Villers-S/Mer, France.
- Voie de la Paix; le journal du pacifiste integral. m.
  ISSN 0042-8329

**Voix Dentaire**
26 rue du Faubourg-Saint-Jacques, Paris (14e),
France.
- Voix Dentaire; revue de l'Association des
  Etudiants en Chirurgie Dentaire de Paris. 9 per
  yr. ISSN 0042-8353

**Volonte du Commerce et de l'Industrie et des
Prestataires de Services**
23 rue Declery, 75002 Paris, France.
- Volonte du Commerce et de l'Industrie. m. ISSN
  0042-8612

**Votre Opinion**
c/o Robert Allezaud, Ed., 2 rue Michel Ange,
75016 Paris, France.
- Votre Opinion; europinion. q.

**Editions Vrille-Copalic**
32 Boulevard Flandrin, Paris 16e, France.
- France en Poche. Total Guide. a. ISSN 0071-8734

**Librairie Philosophique J. Vrin**
6 Place de la Sorbonne, 75005 Paris, France.
- Archives d'Histoire Doctrinale et Litteraire du
  Moyen Age. a.
- Bibliographie de la Philosophie/Bibliography of
  Philosophy. q. ISSN 0006-1352 (International
  Institute of Philosophy)
- Revue des Sciences Philosophiques et
  Theologiques. q. ISSN 0035-2209 (Faculte de
  Philosophie et de Theologie)

**Librairie Vuibert**
63 Boulevard St Germain, 75005 Paris, France.
- Education Mathematique. s-m. ISSN 0046-1431
- Institut d'Etudes Politiques de Paris. Livret.
  biennial. ISSN 0078-995X
- Journal de Mathematiques Elementaires. 18 per
  yr. ISSN 0047-2158
- Revue de Mathematiques et de Sciences
  Physiques. m.
- Revue de Mathematiques Speciales. 10 per yr.
  ISSN 0035-1504

**Editions Publicitaires Waltz P.R. et M. Puget**
9 Bld. des Italiens, Paris 2e, France.
- Annuaire de la France Rurale dans le Marche
  Commun. irreg., 1968, 5th ed. ISSN 0066-2534
  (France. Ministere de l'Agriculture et du
  Developpement Rural)
- Syndicat General des Impots. Guide National de
  l'Enregistrement et des Domaines. a. ISSN 0082-
  1055

**Week End Publications**
37, rue du Louvre, 75002 Paris, France.
- Actualite Hippique. m.
- Week-End; le magazine du tierce et des loisirs. w.
  ISSN 0043-1761

**Editeur R. Weiss**
16, rue Etienne Marcel, 75002 Paris, France.
- Corderie Francaise. m. (Chambre Syndicale
  Generale de la Corderie)

**Western European Airport Association**
291, Bd. Raspail, 75014 Paris, France.
- Western European Airport Association.
  Statistiques de Trafic. irreg. (Co-Sponsor:
  International Civil Airport Association)

**Laboratoires Winthrop**
92-98 Bld. Victor-Hugo, Clichy, France.
- Uro-Nephro; Annuaire de l'Urologie et de la
  Nephrologie. irreg. ISSN 0083-4769

**Women's International Cultural Federation**
62 rue de Rome, 75006 Paris, France.
- Expression; revue culturelle feminine
  internationale. a. ISSN 0014-5327

**World Medical Association**
13 Chemin du Levant, F01210, Ferney-Voltaire,
France.
- World Conference on Medical Education.
  Proceedings. irreg.; 4th, Copenhagen, 1972. ISSN
  0084-1579

**World Underwater Federation**
34 rue du Colisee, Paris (8e), France.
- C M A S Bulletin d'Information. /C M A S
  Newsletter. q.   ISSN 0007-8603
- International Yearbook of the Underwater World/
  Annuaire International du Monde Sous-Marin.
  biennial. ISSN 0074-9648

**World Union for the Safeguard of Youth**
28 Place Saint-Georges, 75442 Paris, France.
- World Union for the Safeguard of Youth.Bulletin.
  q.
- World Union for the Safeguard of Youth.
  Conference Proceedings. triennial, 1972, 5th,
  Paris.

**Yaovank-Jeune Breton**
5 rue Francais Jammes, 29200 Brest, France.
- Yaovank-Jeune Breton; journal d'information
  critique et de formation. bi-m.

**Editions des 4 Seigneurs**
39, rue Marceau, 38000 Grenoble, France.
- Petit Perroquet. bi-m.

# FRENCH GUIANA

**Institut Pasteur de la Guyane Francaise**
B.P. 304. Cayenne, French Guiana.
- Institut Pasteur de la Guyane Francaise. Archives.
  31 per yr. ISSN 0020-2479

# GABON

**Agence Havas Gabon**
B.P. 213, Libreville, Gabon.
- Annuaire National Officiel de la Republique
  Gabonaise. a.

**Chambre de Commerce, d'Agriculture, d'Industrie, et
des Mines du Gabon**
Box 110, Libreville, Gabon.
- Chambre de Commerce, d'Agriculture, d'Industrie
  et des Mines du Gabon. Bulletin. m. ISSN 0045-
  6276

**Gabon. Direction de l'Enseignement du Premier
Degre**
B.P. 221, Libreville, Gabon.
- Message; bulletin de liaison des enseignants
  gabonais. irreg.

**Gabon. Direction de la Statistique et des Etudes
Economiques**
B.P. 2081, Libreville, Gabon.
- Gabon. Direction de la Statistique et des Etudes
  Economique. Bulletin Mensuel de Statistique. m.

**Gabon. Direction Generale des Finances et du Budget**
Ministere de l'Economie et des Finances, Libreville,
Gabon.
- Gabon. Direction Generale des Finances et du
  Budget. Projet du Budget General. irreg.

**Gabon. Institut Pedagogique National**
B.P. 813, Libreville, Gabon.
- Realites Gabonaises. bi-m. ISSN 0486-106X

**Gabon. Ministere de l'Education Nationale. Direction
de l'Administration Generale et de la Planification**
B.P. 334, Libreville, Gabon.
- Statistiques de l'Enseignement au Gabon. a.

**Gabonese Press and Publishing Co.**
B.P. 3849, Libreville, Gabon.
- Union; hebdomadaire Gabonais d'information. w.

# GAMBIA

**Central Bank of Gambia**
3-4 Buckle St., Banjul, Gambia.
- Central Bank of Gambia. Bulletin. q.

**Gambia. Central Statistics Division**
Banjul, Gambia.
- External Trade Statistics of Gambia. a.
- Gambia. Central Statistics Division. Directory of Establishments. a.
- Gambia. Central Statistics Division. Quarterly Survey of Employment and Earnings. q.
- Gambia. Central Statistics Division. Statistical Working Paper. irreg.
- Gambia. Central Statistics Division. Tourist Statistics. irreg.

**Gambia. Education Department**
Banjul, Gambia.
- Gambia. Education Department. Education Statistics. a.

**Gambia. Information Services**
Banjul, Gambia.
- Gambia News Bulletin. 3 per w. ISSN 0046-5380

**Gambia. Produce Marketing Board**
Box 284, Marina, Bathurst, Ghana.
- Gambia. Produce Marketing Board. Annual Report. a.

**Gambia Family Planning Association**
Box 325, Banjul, Gambia.
- What's On. q. (prep. by its Information & Education Section)

# GERMANY, EAST

**Akademie der Landwirtschaftswissenschaften der DDR**
- Archiv fuer Acker- und Pflanzenbau und Bodenkunde. (pub. by Akademie-Verlag)
- Archiv fuer Gartenbau. (pub. by Akademie-Verlag)
- Archiv fuer Naturschutz und Landschaftsforschung. (pub. by Akademie-Verlag)
- Archiv fuer Phytopathologie und Pflanzenschutz. (pub. by Akademie-Verlag)
- Archiv fuer Tierzucht. (pub. by Akademie-Verlag)
- Feldwirtschaft. (pub. by VEB Deutscher Landwirtschaftsverlag)

**Akademie der Landwirtschaftswissenschaften der DDR. Institut fuer Landwirtschaftliche Information und Dokumentation**
Krausenstr. 38-39, Postfach 1295, 1086 Berlin, E. Germany (D.D.R.)
- Bienen. 6 per yr. ISSN 0006-2138
- Industriemaessige Gemueseproduktion. bi-m.
- Industriemaessige Rinderproduktion. bi-m.
- Industriemaessige Schweineproduktion. bi-m.
- Landwirtschaftliches Zentralblatt. Abteilung 1: Landtechnik; an agricultural abstracting journal. 9 per yr. ISSN 0023-818X
- Landwirtschaftliches Zentralblatt. Abteilung 2: Pflanzliche Produktion; an agricultural abstracting journal. m. ISSN 0023-8198
- Landwirtschaftliches Zentralblatt. Abteilung 3: Tierzucht, Tierernaehrung, Fischerei; an agricultural abstracting journal. m. ISSN 0023-8201
- Landwirtschaftliches Zentralblatt. Abteilung 4: Veterinaermedizin; an agricultural abstracting journal. m. ISSN 0023-821X

**Akademie der Paedagogischen Wissenschaften der DDR**
- Erziehungs- und Schulgeschichte Jahrbuch. (pub. by Verlag Volk und Wissen)
- Vergleichende Paedagogik/Comparative Education. (pub. by Verlag Volk und Wissen)

**Akademie der Paedagogischen Wissenschaften der DDR. Zentralstelle fuer Paedagogische Information und Dokumentation**
- Bibliographie der Paedagogischen Veroeffentlichungen in der Deutschen Demokratischen Republik. (pub. by VEB Bibliographisches Institut)

**Akademie der Wissenschaften der DDR**
Otto- Nuschke- Str. 22-23, Berlin 108, E. Germany (D.D.R.)
- Akademie der Wissenschaften der DDR. Zentralinstitut fuer Wirtschaftswissenschaften. Schriften. (pub. by Akademie-Verlag)
- Corpus Medicorum Graecorum. (pub. by Akademie-Verlag)
- Deutsche Literaturzeitung. (pub. by Akademie-Verlag)
- Monumenta Paedagogica. (pub. by Verlag Volk und Wissen)
- Orientalistische Literaturzeitung. (pub. by Akademie-Verlag)
- Spektrum. m. ISSN 0049-1861

**Akademie der Wissenschaften der DDR. Geodaetisches Institut**
Potsdam, E. Germany (D.D.R.)
- Akademie der Wissenschaften der DDR. Geodaetisches Institut. Veroeffentlichungen. irreg. ISSN 0065-5015

**Akademie der Wissenschaften der DDR. Geographisches Institut**
- Werte Unserer Heimat. (pub. by Akademie-Verlag)

**Akademie der Wissenschaften der DDR. Institut fuer Griechisch-Roemische Altertumskunde**
- Corpus Medicorum Latinorum. (pub. by Akademie-Verlag)

**Akademie der Wissenschaften der DDR. Institut fuer Meereskunde, Warnemuende**
- Beitraege zur Meereskunde. (pub. by Akademie-Verlag)

**Akademie der Wissenschaften der DDR. Institut fuer Wirtschaftsgeschichte**
- Wirtschaftsgeschichte. Jahrbuch. (pub. by Akademie-Verlag)

**Akademie der Wissenschaften der DDR. Nationalkomitee fuer Geodaesie und Geophysik**
- Bibliographia Geodaetica/Bibliographie Geodesique Internationale Nouvelle Serie. (pub. by Akademie-Verlag)

**Akademie der Wissenschaften der DDR. Rat fuer Sprachwissenschaft**
- Zeitschrift fuer Phonetik, Sprachwissenschaft und Kommunikationsforschung. (pub. by Akademie-Verlag)

**Akademie der Wissenschaften der DDR. Zentralinstitut fuer Alte Geschichte und Archaeologie**
Leipziger Str. 3-4, E. Germany (D.D.R.)
- Altertum. (pub. by Akademie-Verlag)
- Altorientalische Forschungen. (pub. by Akademie-Verlag)
- Archaeologie. Zeitschrift. (pub. by VEB Deutscher Verlag der Wissenschaften)
- Ausgrabungen und Funde; archaeologische Berichte und Informationen. bi-m. ISSN 0004-8127
- Berliner Byzantinistische Arbeiten. (pub. by Akademie-Verlag)
- Klio: Beitraege zur Alten Geschichte. (pub. by Akademie-Verlag)
- Philologus. (pub. by Akademie-Verlag)
- Schriften und Quellen der Alten Welt. (pub. by Akademie-Verlag)
- Schriften zur Geschichte und Kultur des Alten Orient. (pub. by Akademie-Verlag)
- Schriften zur Ur- und Fruehgeschichte. (pub. by Akademie-Verlag)
- Texte und Untersuchungen zur Geschichte der Altchristlichen Literatur. (pub. by Akademie-Verlag)

**Akademie der Wissenschaften der DDR. Zentralinstitut fuer Ernaehrung**
- Ernaehrungsforschung. (pub. by Akademie-Verlag)
- Die Nahrung. (pub. by Akademie-Verlag)

**Akademie der Wissenschaften der DDR. Zentralinstitut fuer Genetik und Kulturpflanzenforschung Gatersleben**
- Kulturpflanze. (pub. by Akademie-Verlag)

**Akademie der Wissenschaften der DDR. Zentralinstitut fuer Geschichte**
- Akademie der Wissenschaften der DDR. Zentralinstitut fuer Geschichte. Schriften. (pub. by Akademie-Verlag)
- Demos. (pub. by Akademie-Verlag)

- Deutsche Geschichte. Jahresberichte. (pub. by Akademie-Verlag)
- Geschichte der Sozialistischen Laender Europas. Jahrbuch. (pub. by VEB Deutscher Verlag der Wissenschaften)
- Keilschrifturkunden aus Boghazkoei. (pub. by Akademie-Verlag)

**Akademie der Wissenschaften der DDR. Zentralinstitut fuer Isotopen- und Strahlenforschung**
Permoserstr. 15, 705 Leipzig, E. Germany (D.D.R.)
- Isotope Titles. m. ISSN 0047-1550

**Akademie der Wissenschaften der DDR. Zentralinstitut fuer Literaturgeschichte**
- Textausgaben zur Fruehen Sozialistischen Literatur in Deutschland. (pub. by Akademie-Verlag)
- Zeitschrift fuer Slawistik. (pub. by Akademie-Verlag)

**Akademie der Wissenschaften der DDR. Zentralinstitut fuer Mathematik und Mechanik**
- Biometrische Zeitschrift. (pub. by Akademie-Verlag)
- Mathematische Lehrbuecher und Monographien. Abteilung: Mathematische Monographien. (pub. by Akademie-Verlag)
- Mathematische Nachrichten. (pub. by Akademie-Verlag)
- Mathematische Operationsforschung und Statistik. (pub. by Akademie-Verlag)
- Zentralinstitut fuer Mathematik und Mechanik. Schriftenreihe. (pub. by Akademie-Verlag)

**Akademie der Wissenschaften der DDR. Zentralinstitut fuer Physik der Erde**
- Zentralinstitut fuer Physik der Erde. Seismologischer Dienst Jena. Seismologische Belletins. (pub. by Akademie-Verlag)

**Akademie der Wissenschaften der DDR. Zentralinstitut fuer Sprachwissenschaft**
- Bausteine zur Sprachgeschichte des Neuhochdeutschen. (pub. by Akademie Verlag GmbH.)
- Sprache und Gesellschaft. (pub. by Akademie-Verlag)
- Studia Grammatica. (pub. by Akademie-Verlag)

**Akademie der Wissenschaften der DDR. Zentralinstitut fuer Wirtschaftswissenschaften**
- Oekonomische Studientexte. (pub. by Akademie-Verlag)

**Akademie fuer Aerztliche Fortbildung der DDR**
Noeldnerstr. 34-36, 1134 Berlin, German Democratic Republic.
- Akademie fuer Aerztliche Fortbildung der DDR. Bibliographie. irreg. ISSN 0070-3915
- Zeitschrift fuer Aerztliche Fortbildung. (pub. by VEB Gustav Fischer Verlag)

**Akademie fuer Staats und Rechtswissenschaft der DDR**
- Staat und Recht. (pub. by Staatsverlag der DDR)

**Akademie fuer Staats und Rechtswissenschaft der DDR. Informationszentrum Staat und Recht**
August-Bebel-Str. 89, 1502 Potsdam-Babelsberg, E. Germany (D.D.R.)
- Bibliographie "Staat und Recht". s-m.
- Bibliographie Staat und Recht der Deutschen Demokratischen Republik (Vierteljahresbibliographie) q. ISSN 0006-1468
- Spezialbibliographien zu Fragen des Staates und des Rechts. irreg. ISSN 0081-3680

**Akademie-Verlag GmbH.**
Leipziger Str. 3-4, 108 Berlin, E. Germany (D.D.R.)
- Acta Biologica et Medica Germanica; Zeitschrift fuer funktionelle Biowissenschaften. m. ISSN 0001-5318
- Acta Hydrochimica et Hydrobiologica; Naturwissenschaftliche Grundlagen des Gewaesserschutzes und der Wasserbehandlung. bi-m. (Chemische Gesellschaft der DDR) (Co-Sponsor: Biologische Gesellschaft der DDR)
- Acta Hydrophysika. 1 vol. per yr. (4 nos. per vol.) ISSN 0065-1338
- Akademie der Wissenschaften der DDR. Abhandlungen. Abteilung Mathematik, Naturwissenschaften, Technik. irreg.
- Akademie der Wissenschaften der DDR. Jahrbuch. a. ISSN 0065-5066

- Akademie der Wissenschaften der DDR. Zentralinstitut fuer Geschichte. Schriften. irreg., vol. 52, 1977. ISSN 0065-5236
- Akademie der Wissenschaften der DDR. Zentralinstitut fuer Wirtschaftswissenschaften. Schriften. irreg.,no. 15,1976. ISSN 0065-5279
- Altertum. q. ISSN 0002-6646 (Akademie der Wissenschaften der DDR. Zentralinstitut fuer Alte Geschichte und Archaeologie)
- Altorientalische Forschungen. irreg. (Akademie der Wissenschaften der DDR. Zentralinstitut fuer Alte Geschichte und Archaeologie.)
- Archiv fuer Acker- und Pflanzenbau und Bodenkunde; Arbeiten aus den Gebieten Bodenkunde, Pflanzenernaehrung, Duengung, Acker- und Pflanzenbau. m. (Akademie der Landwirtschaftswissenschaften der DDR)
- Archiv fuer Gartenbau. 8 per yr. ISSN 0003-908X (Akademie der Landwirtschaftswissenschaften der DDR)
- Archiv fuer Naturschutz und Landschaftsforschung. 4 per yr. ISSN 0003-9306 (Akademie der Landwirtschaftswissenschaften der DDR)
- Archiv fuer Phytopathologie und Pflanzenschutz. 6 per yr. (Akademie der Landwirtschaftswissenschaften der DDR)
- Archiv fuer Tierernaehrung. m. ISSN 0003-942X
- Archiv fuer Tierzucht. 6 per yr. ISSN 0003-9438 (Akademie der Landwirtschaftswissenschaften der DDR)
- Bausteine zur Sprachgeschichte des Neuhochdeutschen. irreg. (Akademie der Wissenschaften der DDR. Zentralinstitut fuer Sprachwissenschaft)
- Beitraege aus der Plasmaphysik. bi-m. ISSN 0005-8025
- Beitraege zur Entomologie. s-a. ISSN 0005-805X (Institut fuer Pflanzenschutzforschung. Abteilung Taxonomie der Insekten) (Co-sponsor: Akademie der Landwirtschaftswissenschaften der DDR)
- Beitraege zur Geschichte des Religioesen und Wissenschaftlichen Denkens. irreg., vol. 9, 1971. ISSN 0067-5059
- Beitraege zur Inkunabelkunde. Dritte Folge. irreg., vol. 6, 1975. ISSN 0067-5091 (Deutsche Staatsbibliothek)
- Beitraege zur Meereskunde. irreg., no. 39, 1977. ISSN 0067-5148 (Akademie der Wissenschaften der DDR. Institut fuer Meereskunde, Warnemuende)
- Beitrage fuer Die Forstwirtschaft. q. (Institut fuer Forstwissenschaften)
- Berliner Byzantinistische Arbeiten. irreg., no. 47, 1976. ISSN 0067-6055 (Akademie der Wissenschaften der DDR. Zentralinstitut fuer Alte Geschichte und Archaelogie) (Co-sponsor: Martin-Luther-Universitaet, Halle/Wittenberg)
- Bestimmungsbuecher zur Bodenfauna Europas. irreg., vol. 10, 1977. ISSN 0067-6314
- Bibliographia Geodaetica/Bibliographie Geodesique Internationale Nouvelle Serie; internationale geodaetische dokumentation. m. ISSN 0006-1239 (Akademie der Wissenschaften der DDR. Nationalkomitee fuer Geodaesie und Geophysik)
- Biometrische Zeitschrift; Zeitschrift fuer mathematische Methoden in den Biowissenschaften. 8 per yr. ISSN 0006-3452 (Akademie der Wissenschaften der DDR. Zentralinstitut fuer Mathematik und Mechanik)
- Corpus Medicorum Graecorum. irreg., vol. 20, 1977. ISSN 0070-0347 (Akademie der Wissenschaften der DDR) (Co-sponsors: Koenigliche Daenische Akademie; Saechsische Akademie der Wissenschaften, Leipzig)
- Corpus Medicorum Latinorum. irreg. ISSN 0070-0355 (Akademie der Wissenschaften der DDR. Institut fuer Griechisch-Roemische Altertumskunde)
- Demos; Internationale ethnographische und folkloristische Informationen. 4 per yr. ISSN 0011-832X (Akademie der Wissenschaften der DDR. Zentralinstitut fuer Geschichte. Wissenschaftsbereich Kulturgeschichte / Volkskunde)
- Deutsch-Slawische Forschungen zur Namenkunde und Siedlungsgeschichte. irreg., vol. 31, 1972. ISSN 0070-3893 (Saechsische Akademie der Wissenschaften, Leipzig. Historische Kommission)
- Deutsche Entomologische Zeitschrift. 5 per yr. ISSN 0012-0073 (Humboldt-Universitaet zu Berlin. Museum fuer Naturkunde)
- Deutsche Geschichte. Jahresberichte. a. ISSN 0075-286X (Akademie der Wissenschaften der DDR. Zentralinstitut fuer Geschichte. Abteilung Information und Dokumentation)

- Deutsche Literaturzeitung; fuer Kritik der internationalen Wissenschaft. m. ISSN 0012-043X (Akademie der Wissenschaften der DDR)
- Deutsche Texte des Mittelalters. irreg., vol. 69, 1976. ISSN 0070-4334
- Elektronische Informationsverarbeitung und Kybernetik. 10 per yr. ISSN 0013-5712 (Mathematische Gesellschaft der DDR) (Co-sponsor: Zentralinstitut fuer Kybernetik und Informationsprozesse)
- Ernaehrungsforschung. bi-m. ISSN 0071-1179 (Akademie der Wissenschaften der DDR. Zentralinstitut fuer Ernaehrung)
- Faserforschung und Textiltechnik; zeitschrift fuer polymerforschung. m. ISSN 0014-8628
- Feddes Repertorium; Zeitschrift fuer botanische Taxonomie und Geobotanik. 10 per yr. ISSN 0014-8962
- Forschungen zur Mittelalterlichen Geschichte. irreg., vol. 23, 1975. ISSN 0071-7673
- Fortschritte der Physik. m. ISSN 0015-8208 (Physikalische Gesellschaft der DDR)
- Geophysik und Geologie; Geophsikalische Veroeffentlichungen der Karl-Marx-Universitaet Leipzig. Dritte Serie. irreg. (Karl-Marx-Universitaet)
- Germany (Democratic Republic, 1949- ) Meteorologischer Dienst. Abhandlungen. irreg., no. 118, 1976. ISSN 0072-1506
- Hirnforschung. Journal; internationales Journal fuer Neurobiologie. 6 per yr. ISSN 0021-8359
- Internationale Revue der gesamten Hydrobiologie. 6 per yr. ISSN 0020-9309
- Ionenaustauscher in Einzeldarstellungen. irreg., vol. 8, 1970. ISSN 0075-0336
- Isotopenpraxis; Zeitschrift fuer Anwendung, Kontrolle und Analyse radioaktiver und stabiler Isotope. m. ISSN 0021-1915
- Jahrbuch fuer Volkskunde und Kulturgeschichte. Neue Folge. a.
- Keilschrifturkunden aus Boghazkoei. irreg., vol. 13, 1977. ISSN 0075-532X (Akademie der Wissenschaften der DDR. Zentralinstitut fuer Geschichte)
- Kernenergie; Zeitschrift fuer Kernforschung und Kerntechnik. m. ISSN 0023-0642 (Ingenieurhochschule Zittau)
- Klio: Beitraege zur Alten Geschichte. bi-a. ISSN 0075-6334 (Akademie der Wissenschaften der DDR. Zentralinstitut fuer Alte Geschichte und Archaelogie)
- Kristall und Technik; Zeitschrift fuer experimentelle und technische Kristallographie. 12 per yr. ISSN 0023-4753
- Kulturpflanze. irreg., vol. 24, 1976. ISSN 0075-7209 (Akademie der Wissenschaften der DDR. Zentralinstitut fuer Genetik und Kulturpflanzenforschung Gatersleben)
- Limnologica. irreg., vol. 11, 1976. ISSN 0075-9511
- Mathematical Operations Research and Statistics. q. ISSN 0025-5599
- Mathematische Lehrbuecher und Monographien. Abteilung: Mathematische Monographien. irreg., vol. 41, 1977. ISSN 0076-5430 (Akademie der Wissenschaften der DDR. Zentralinstitut fuer Mathematik und Mechanik)
- Mathematische Nachrichten. 5 per yr. ISSN 0025-584X (Akademie der Wissenschaften der DDR. Zentralinstitut fuer Mathematik und Mechanik)
- Mathematische Operationsforschung und Statistik. 4 per yr. of each series. ISSN 0047-6277 (Akademie der Wissenschaften der DDR. Zentralinstitut fuer Mathematik und Mechanik)
- Museum fuer Voelkerkunde, Leipzig. Jahrbuch. irreg., vol. 30, 1975. ISSN 0075-8663
- Museum fuer Voelkerkunde, Leipzig. Veroeffentlichungen. irreg., vol. 30, 1976. ISSN 0075-8671
- Die Nahrung; Chemie, Biochemie, Mikrobiologie, Technologie, Ernaehrung. 10 per yr. ISSN 0027-769X (Akademie der Wissenschaften der DDR. Zentralinstitut fuer Ernaehrung)
- Oekonomische Studientexte. irreg. ISSN 0078-3404 (Akademie der Wissenschaften der DDR. Zentralinstitut fuer Wirtschaftswissenschaften)
- Orientalistische Literaturzeitung; Zeitschrift fuer die Wissenschaft vom ganzen Orient und seinen Beziehungen zu den angrenzenden Kulturkreisen. bi-m. ISSN 0030-5383 (Akademie der Wissenschaften der DDR)
- Paediatrie und Grenzgebiete. 6 per yr. ISSN 0030-932X
- Philologus; Zeitschrift fuer klassische Philologie. s-a.(double no) ISSN 0031-7985 (Akademie der Wissenschaften der DDR. Zentralinstitut fuer Alte Geschichte und Archaeologie)

- Philosophische Studientexte. irreg. ISSN 0079-1717
- Physica Status Solidi (A). Applied Research. 6 vols. per yr. (2 nos. per vol.) ISSN 0031-8965 (Co-publisher: Pergamon Press, London) (U.S. subscription to: Academic Press, Inc., 111 Fifth Ave., New York, NY 10003)
- Physica Status Solidi (B). Basic Research. 6 vols. per yr. (2 nos. per vol.) ISSN 0031-8957 (Co-publisher: Pergamon Press, London) (U.S. Subscr. to: Academic Press Inc., 111 Fifth Ave., New York 10003, N.Y.)
- Quellen und Studien zur Geschichte Osteuropas. irreg., vol. 18, 1977. ISSN 0079-9114
- Saechsische Akademie der Wissenschaften, Leipzig. Jahrbuch. irreg., vol. for 1973-74, 1976. ISSN 0080-5262
- Saechsische Akademie der Wissenschaften, Leipzig. Mathematisch-Naturwissenschaftliche Klasse. Abhandlungen. irreg., vol. 52, 1974. ISSN 0080-5289
- Saechsische Akademie der Wissenschaften, Leipzig. Mathematisch-Naturwissenschaftliche Klasse. Sitzungsberichte. irreg., vol. 112, 1977. ISSN 0080-5270
- Saechsische Akademie der Wissenschaften, Leipzig. Philologisch Historische Klasse. Abhandlungen. irreg., vol, 67, 1977. ISSN 0080-5297
- Saechsische Akademie der Wissenschaften, Leipzig. Philologisch-Historische Klasse. Sitzungsberichte. irreg., vol. 119, 1977. ISSN 0080-5300
- Schriften und Quellen der Alten Welt. irreg., vol. 36, 1977. ISSN 0080-696X (Akademie der Wissenschaften der DDR. Zentralinstitut fuer Alte Geschichte und Archaeologie)
- Schriften zur Geschichte und Kultur des Alten Orient. irreg., vol. 12, 1977. ISSN 0080-6994 (Akademie der Wissenschaften der DDR. Zentralinstitut fuer Alte Geschichte und Archaeologie)
- Schriften zur Ur- und Fruehgeschichte. irreg., vol. 29, 1976. (Akademie der Wissenschaften der DDR. Zentralinstitut fuer Alte Geschichte und Archaeologie)
- Signalaufzeichnungsmaterialien. Journal. bi-m. (VEB Filmfabrik Wolfen. Photochemisches Kombinat)
- Sprache und Gesellschaft. irreg., vol. 9, 1976. (Akademie der Wissenschaften der DDR. Zentralinstitut fuer Sprachwissenschaft)
- Staatliche Museen zu Berlin. Jahrbuch. Forschungen und Berichte. a. ISSN 0067-6004
- Studia Biophysica; internationale zeitschrift fuer ausgewaehlte gebiete der biophysik. irreg (every 4 weeks at least) ISSN 0081-6337 (Gesellschaft fuer Physikalische und Mathematische Biologie der DDR) (Co-Sponsor: Koordinierungszentrum fuer das RGW-Programm Biophysik)
- Studia Grammatica. irreg., vol. 14, 1977. ISSN 0081-6469 (Akademie der Wissenschaften der DDR. Zentralinstitut fuer Sprachwissenschaft)
- Studien ueber Asien, Afrika und Lateinamerika. irreg., vol. 22, 1976. (Zentraler Rat fuer Asien-, Afrika- und Lateinamerikawissenschaften in der DDR)
- Textausgaben zur Fruehen Sozialistischen Literatur in Deutschland. irreg., vol. 20, 1977. ISSN 0081-3257 (Akademie der Wissenschaften der DDR. Zentralinstitut fuer Literaturgeschichte)
- Texte und Untersuchungen zur Geschichte der Altchristlichen Literatur. irreg., vol. 119, 1976. ISSN 0082-3589 (Akademie der Wissenschaften der DDR. Zentralinstitut fuer Alte Geschichte und Archaeologie)
- Veroeffentlichungen zur Volkskunde und Kulturgeschichte. irreg., vol. 64, 1977.
- Werte Unserer Heimat; Ergebnisse der heimatkundlichen Bestandsaufnahme in der DDR. irreg., no. 30, 1977. ISSN 0083-8063 (Akademie der Wissenschaften der DDR. Geographisches Institut)
- Wirtschaftsgeschichte. Jahrbuch. a. ISSN 0075-2800 (Akademie der Wissenschaften der DDR. Institut fuer Wirtschaftsgeschichte)
- Wissenschaftliche Taschenbuecher. Reihe Biologie. irreg. ISSN 0084-0963
- Wissenschaftliche Taschenbuecher. Reihe Chemie. irreg. ISSN 0084-0971
- Wissenschaftliche Taschenbuecher. Reihe Mathematik, Physik. irreg. ISSN 0084-098X
- Zeitschrift fuer Aegyptische Sprache und Altertumskunde. 2 per yr. ISSN 0044-216X (Co-Publisher: J. C. Hinrichs Verlag, Leipzig)

- Zeitschrift fuer allgemeine Mikrobiologie; Morphologie, Physiologie, Genetik und Oekologie der Mikroorganismen. 8 per yr. ISSN 0044-2208
- Zeitschrift fuer Angewandte Geologie. m. ISSN 0044-2259 (Zentrales Geologisches Institut)
- Zeitschrift fuer Angewandte Mathematik und Mechanik; ingenieurwissenschaftliche Forschungsarbeiten. m. ISSN 0044-2267
- Zeitschrift fuer Meteorologie. 6 per yr. ISSN 0084-5361 (Meteorologische Gesellschaft der DDR)
- Zeitschrift fuer Phonetik, Sprachwissenschaft und Kommunikationsforschung. 6 per yr. ISSN 0044-331X (Akademie der Wissenschaften der DDR. Rat fuer Sprachwissenschaft)
- Zeitschrift fuer Slawistik. 6 per yr. ISSN 0044-3506 (Akademie der Wissenschaften der DDR. Zentralinstitut fuer Literaturgeschichte)
- Zentrales Geologisches Institut. Palaeontologische Abhandlungen. irreg., vol. 26, 1976. ISSN 0078-8600
- Zentralinstitut fuer Mathematik und Mechanik. Schriftenreihe. irreg. (Akademie der Wissenschaften der DDR. Zentralinstitut fuer Mathematik und Mechanik)
- Zentralinstitut fuer Physik der Erde. Seismologischer Dienst Jena. Seismologische Belletins. irreg. ISSN 0065-5023 (Akademie der Wissenschaften der DDR. Zentralinstitut fuer Physik der Erde. Seismologischer Dienst Jena)

**Anatomische Gesellschaft**
- Anatomische Gesellschaft. Verhandlungen. (pub. by VEB Gustav Fischer Verlag)

**Aufbau-Verlag Berlin und Weimar**
Franzoesische Str. 32, 108 Berlin, E. Germany.
- Marginalien; Zeitschrift fuer Buchkunst und Bibliophilie. q. ISSN 0025-2948 (Kulturbund der DDR. Pirckheimer-Gesellschaft)
- Neue deutsche Literatur/N D L. m. ISSN 0028-3150 (Schriftstellerverband der Deutschen Demokratischen Republik)
- Sonntag; kulturpolitische Wochenzeitung. w. ISSN 0038-1411 (Kulturbund der DDR)
- Weimarer Beitraege; Zeitschrift fuer Literaturwissenschaft, Aesthetik und Kultur. m. ISSN 0043-2199

**Johann Ambrosius Barth Verlag**
Salomonstr 18b, 701 Leipzig, E. Germany (D.D.R.)
- Abhandlungen Moderner Medizin. irreg., vol. 8, 1976. ISSN 0065-0315
- Acta Chirurgiae Maxillo-Facialis. irreg. (Internationale Gesellschaft fuer Kiefer-Gesichts-Chirurgie)
- Acta Historica Leopoldina. irreg., vol. 10, 1976. ISSN 0001-5857 (Deutsche Akademie der Naturforscher Leopoldina. Archiv fuer Geschichte der Naturforschung und Medizin)
- Aerztliche Jugendkunde. 5 per yr. ISSN 0001-9518
- Allergie und Immunologie. q. ISSN 0002-5755 (Gesellschaft fuer Klinische und Experimentelle Immunologie der DDR)
- Annalen der Physik. bi-m. ISSN 0003-3804
- Arbeitsmedizin; Abhandlungen ueber Berufskrankheiten und deren Verhuetung. irreg., no. 34, 1968. ISSN 0066-5843
- Beitraege zur Hygiene und Epidemiologie. irreg., no. 22, 1974. ISSN 0067-5083
- Beitraege zur Neurochirurgie. irreg., no. 16, 1970. ISSN 0067-5156
- Bibliothek fuer das Gesamtgebiet der Lungenkrankheiten. irreg., no. 104, 1972. ISSN 0067-8228
- Dermatologische Monatsschrift. m. ISSN 0011-9083 (Dermatologische Gesellschaft der DDR)
- Deutsche Zeitschrift fuer Verdauungs- und Stoffwechselkrankheiten. 6 per yr. ISSN 0012-1053 (Gesellschaft fuer Gastroenterologie der DDR)
- Endokrinologie. 2 vols.(3 nos.) per year. ISSN 0013-7251 (Gesellschaft fuer Endokrinologie und Stoffwechselkrankheiten)
- Hals-, Nasen- und Ohrenheilkunde. Zwangslose Schriftenreihe. irreg., no. 25, 1975. ISSN 0072-9418
- Journal fuer praktische Chemie. 6 per yr. ISSN 0021-8383 (Chemische Gesellschaft der DDR)
- Lebensdarstellungen Deutscher Naturforscher. irreg. ISSN 0075-8418 (Deutsche Akademie der Naturforscher Leopoldina)
- Nova Acta Leopoldina. irreg. (Deutsche Akademie der Naturforscher Leopoldina)

- Sammlung Meusser; Abhandlungen aus dem Gebiete der klinischen Zahnheilkunde. irreg., 1971, no. 43. ISSN 0080-584X
- Sportmedizinische Schriftenreihe. irreg., no. 14, 1977. ISSN 0075-8655 (Deutsche Hochschule fuer Koerperkultur Leipzig)
- Sterne; Zeitschrift fuer alle Gebiete der Himmelskunde. 4 per yr. ISSN 0039-1255
- Sudhoffs Klassiker der Medizin und der Naturwissenschaften. irreg., vol. 38, 1964. ISSN 0081-9069 (Deutsche Akademie der Naturforscher Leopoldina)
- Zahn- Mund- und Kieferheilkunde; mit Zentralblatt. 8 per yr. ISSN 0012-1010 (Deutsche Gesellschaft fuer Zahn-, Mund- und Kieferheilkunde)
- Zahnaerztliche Fortbildung. irreg., vol. 21, 1974. ISSN 0084-4462
- Zeitschrift fuer Anorganische und Allgemeine Chemie. 10 per yr. ISSN 0044-2313
- Zeitschrift fuer Erkrankungen der Atmungsorgane. 3 vols. per year, 3 issues each. ISSN 0044-2631 (Gesellschaft fuer Bronchopneumonologie und Tuberkulose der DDR) (Co-Sponsor: Internationale Gesellschaft fuer Aerosole in der Medizin)
- Zeitschrift fuer Psychologie. 4 per yr. ISSN 0044-3409
- Zentralblatt fuer Chirurgie. s-m. ISSN 0044-409X (Gesellschaft fuer Chirurgie der DDR)
- Zentralblatt fuer Gynaekologie. s-m. ISSN 0044-4197 (Gesellschaft fuer Gynaekologie und Geburtshilf der DDR)
- Zentralblatt fuer Neurochirurgie. 3 per yr. ISSN 0044-4251

**Bauakademie der DDR**
Wallstr. 27, 102 Berlin, E. Germany (D.D.R.)
- Architektur der DDR. (pub. by VEB Verlag fuer Bauwesen)
- Bauinformation Wissenschaft und Technik. bi-m.

**VEB Verlag fuer Bauwesen**
Franzoesische Str. 13/14, 108 Berlin, E. Germany (D.D.R.)
- Architektur der DDR. m. (Bauakademie der DDR) (Co-sponsor: Bund der Architekten der DDR)
- Bauplanung - Bautechnik; wissenschaftlich-technische Zeitschrift fuer ingenieurbauwesen. m. ISSN 0005-6758
- Baustoffindustrie. Ausgabe A. Primaerbaustoffe; Fachzeitschrift fuer Produktion, Technologie und Oekonomie der Baumaterialienindustrie. m.
- Baustoffindustrie. Ausgabe B. Bauelemente. m.
- Bauzeitung; Fachzeitschrift fuer komplexen Wohungsbau, kommunalen Tiefbau, laendliches Bauwesen. m. ISSN 0005-6871
- Farbe und Raum; Zeitschrift fuer Oberflaechengestaltung Anstrichtechnologie und Farbgebung. m. ISSN 0014-7702
- Magazin fuer Haus und Wohnung. m. ISSN 0024-9769
- Silikattechnik; Wissenschaftlich-technische Zeitschrift fuer Glas. Email. Keramik und Bindemittel. m. ISSN 0037-5233 (Kammer der Technik)
- Stadt- und Gebaeudetechnik; Fachzeitschrift fuer Heizung. Lueftung. Waerme. Sanitaertechnik. Rohrleitungsbau und Isoliertechnik. m. ISSN 0038-898X (Kombinat Technische Gebaeudeausruestung Institut)
- Vermessungstechnik; Zeitschrift fuer Geodaesie. Photogrammetrie und Kartographie der DDR. m. ISSN 0042-4102 (Kammer der Technik)
- Wasserwirtschaft-Wassertechnik (W W T); Wissenschaftliche Zeitschrift fuer Technik und Oekonomik der Wasserwirtschaft. m. ISSN 0043-0986 (Kammer der Technik)

**Verlag Begegnung**
Friedrichstr. 169-170, 108 Berlin, E. Germany (Subscr. to: Buchexport, Leninstr. 16, 701 Leipzig, E. Germany (D.D.R.))
- Begegnung; Zeitschrift progressiver Katholiken. m. ISSN 0005-7800

**Bergakademie Freiberg**
- Freiberger Forschungshefte. Montanwissenschaften: Reihe A. Geotechnik/ Ingenieurgeologie, Bergbautechnologie, Verfahrenstechnik, Energiewandlung. (pub. by VEB Deutscher Verlag fuer Grundstoffindustrie)
- Freiberger Forschungshefte. Montanwissenschaften: Reihe B. Metallurgie und Werbstofftechnik. (pub. by VEB Deutscher Verlag fuer Grundstoffindustrie)

- Freiberger Forschungshefte. Montanwissenschaften: Reihe C. Geowissenschaften. (pub. by VEB Deutscher Verlag fuer Grundstoffindustrie)

**Bergakademie Freiberg. Wissenschaftliches Informationszentrum**
Akademiestr. 6, 92 Freiberg, E. Germany (D.D.R.)
- Bergakademie Freiberg. Wissenschaftliches Informationszentrum. Veroeffentlichungen. irreg., no. 68, 1975.

**Berlin-Information**
108 Berlin, E. Germany (D.D.R.)
- Berlin; journal from the capital of the GDR. q. ISSN 0005-9226

**Berliner-Verlag**
Karl-Liebknecht-Str. 29, 1056 Berlin, E. Germany (D.D.R.)
- Horizont; sozialistische Wochenzeitung fuer internationale Politik und Wirtschaft. w. ISSN 0046-791X

**VEB Bibliographisches Institut**
Gerichtsweg 26, 701 Leipzig, E. Germany (D.D.R.)
- Bibliographie der Paedagogischen Veroeffentlichungen in der Deutschen Demokratischen Republik. a. ISSN 0067-6969 (Akademie der Paedagogischen Wissenschaften der DDR. Zentralstelle fuer Paedagogische Information und Dokumentation)
- Der Bibliothekar; Zeitschrift fuer das Bibliothekswesen. m. ISSN 0006-1964 (Zentralinstitut fuer Bibliothekswesen)
- Einfuehrung in die Information und Dokumentation. irreg., no. 13, 1976. ISSN 0070-9522
- Jahrbuch der Bibliotheken, Archive und Informationstellen der Deutschen Demokratischen Republik. biennial. ISSN 0075-2215 (Co-Sponsor: Bibliotheksverband der DDR)
- Literaturkunde. Beitraege; Bibliographie ausgewaehlter Zeitungs- und Zeitschriftenbeitraege. s-a. ISSN 0005-8092
- Sprachpflege; Zeitschrift fuer gutes Deutsch. m. ISSN 0049-2019
- Zentralblatt fuer Bibliothekswesen. m. ISSN 0044-4081

**Blinden- und Sehschwachen-Verband der DDR. Deutsche Zentralbuecherei fuer Blinde zu Leipzig**
Gustav-Adolf-Str. 7, 701 Leipzig, E. Germany (D.D.R.)
- Gegenwart. m. ISSN 0016-5859
- Wissenschaftliche Blaetter zu Problemen des Blinden- und Sehschwachenwesens. s-a.

**Hermann Boehlaus Nachfolger**
Meyer Str. 50a, 53 Weimar, E. Germany (D.D.R.)
- Abhandlungen zur Handels- und Sozialgeschichte. irreg., vol. 16, 1977. ISSN 0065-0358 (Historiker-Gesellschaft der DDR. Hansische Arbeitsgemeinschaft)
- Alt-Thueringen. a. ISSN 0065-6585 (Museum fuer Ur- und Fruehgeschichte Thueringens)
- Goethe-Jahrbuch. a. (Goethe-Gesellschaft, Weimar)
- Jahrbuch fuer Regionalgeschichte. irreg. ISSN 0085-2341 (Saechsische Akademie der Wissenschaften, Leipzig. Historische Kommission)
- Museum fuer Ur- und Fruehgeschichte Thueringens. Veroeffentlichungen. irreg., vol. 5, 1974. ISSN 0077-2291
- Shakespeare-Jahrbuch. a. ISSN 0080-9128 (Deutsche Shakespeare Gesellschaft)
- Zeitschrift der Savigny-Stiftung fuer Rechtsgeschichte. Germanistische, Romanistische und Kanonistische Abteilung. a. ISSN 0084-5264 (Savigny-Stiftung)

**Boersenverein der Deutschen Buchhaendler. Historische Kommission**
- Geschichte des Buchwesens. Beitraege. (pub. by VEB Fachbuchverlag)

**Brunnquell-Verlag**
Postfach 99, 7418 Metzingen, E. Germany (D.D.R.)
- Das Heilige Band; der Galiziendeutsche. m. ISSN 0017-9612 (Hilfskomitee der Galiziendeutschen)

**VEB Verlag fuer Buch- und Bibliothekswesen**
Gerichtsweg 26, 701 Leipzig, E. Germany (D.D.R.)
- Bibliographie der Bibliographien. m. (Deutsche Buecherei)
- Bibliographie der Uebersetzungen deutschsprachiger Werke. q. ISSN 0006-1409 (Deutsche Buecherei)
- Bibliographie Fremdsprache Germanica. q.
- Deutsche Nationalbibliographie. Reihe A: Neuerscheinungen des Buchhandels. w. ISSN 0012-0529
- Deutsche Nationalbibliographie. Reihe B: Neuerschinungen ausserhalb des Buchhandels. s-m. ISSN 0012-0537 (Deutsche Buecherei)
- Deutsche Nationalbibliographie. Reihe C: Dissertationen und Habilitationsschriften. m. ISSN 0012-0545
- Fremdsprachige Germanica. q.
- Jahresverzeichnis der Hochschulschriften der DDR, der BRD und Westberlins. irreg.
- Jahresverzeichnis der Verlagsschriften und Einer Auswahl der ausserhalb des Buchhandels Erschienenen Veroeffentlichungen der DDR, der BRD und Westberlins sowie der Deutschsprachigen Werke Anderer Laender. irreg., vol. 172 (for 1969), 1975.

**Buchexport**
Leninstr 16, 701 Leipzig, E. Germany (D.D.R.)
- Buch der Zeit; books and periodicals from the German Democratic Republic/Buecher und Zeitschriften aus der Deutschen Demokratischen Republik. m.' ISSN 0007-2761
- I P W Forschungshefte. q. (Institut fuer Internationale Politik und Wirtschaft)
- Nova; Vorankuendigungen-forthcoming books-livres en preparation. m. ISSN 0029-4993

**Buerger Deutscher Herkunft in Ausland**
Mauerstr. 52, 108 Berlin, D.D.R.
- Neue Heimat; journal aus der Deutschen Demokratischer Republic. bi-m. ISSN 0548-2801

**Bundesvorstand des FDGB**
- Die Arbeit. (pub. by Verlag Tribune)

**Chemische Gesellschaft der DDR**
- Acta Hydrochimica et Hydrobiologica. (pub. by Akademie-Verlag)
- Journal fuer praktische Chemie. (pub. by Johann Ambrosius Barth Verlag)

**Confederation of Free German Trade Unions**
- F D G B-Rundschau/F D G B-Review. (pub. by Verlag Tribune)

**D E E A Studio for Shortfilms**
Milastr. 2, 1058 Berlin, E. Germany (D.D.R.)
- D D R Film Information. irreg.

**Dermatologische Gesellschaft der DDR**
- Dermatologische Monatsschrift. (pub. by Johann Ambrosius Barth Verlag)

**Deutsche Akademie der Landwirtschaftswissenschaften**
Krausenstr. 38/39, 108 Berlin, E. Germany (D.D.R.)
- Deutsche Akademie der Landwirtschaftswissenschaften, Berlin. Jahrbuch. a. ISSN 0070-3907

**Deutsche Akademie der Naturforscher Leopoldina**
August-Bebel-Str. 50a, 01 Halle/S, E. Germany (D.D.R.)
- Lebensdarstellungen Deutscher Naturforscher. (pub. by Johann Ambrosius Barth Verlag)
- Leopoldina; Mitteilungen aus der Deutschen Akademie der Naturforscher Leopoldina, Reihe 3. a.
- Nova Acta Leopoldina. (pub. by Johann Ambrosius Barth Verlag)
- Sudhoffs Klassiker der Medizin und der Naturwissenschaften. (pub. by Johann Ambrosius Barth Verlag)

**Deutsche Akademie der Naturforscher Leopoldina. Archiv fuer Geschichte der Naturforschung und Medizin**
- Acta Historica Leopoldina. (pub. by Johann Ambrosius Barth Verlag)

**Deutsche Buecherei**
Deutscher Platz, 701 Leipzig, E. Germany (D.D.R.)
- Bibliographie der Bibliographien. (pub. by VEB Verlag fuer Buch- und Bibliothekswesen)

- Bibliographie der Uebersetzungen deutschsprachiger Werke. (pub. by VEB Verlag fuer Buch- und Bibliothekswesen)
- Deutsche Musikbibliographie. (pub. by VEB Friedrich Hofmeister Musikverlag)
- Deutsche Nationalbibliographie. Reihe B: Neuerschinungen ausserhalb des Buchhandels. (pub. by VEB Verlag fuer Buch- und Bibliothekswesen)
- Informationsdienst Bibliothekwesen. bi-m. ISSN 0044-1457 (Co-Sponsor: Zentralinstitut fuer Bibliothekswesen)

**Deutsche Gesellschaft fuer Zahn-, Mund- und Kieferheilkunde**
- Zahn- Mund- und Kieferheilkunde. (pub. by Johann Ambrosius Barth Verlag)

**Deutsche Hochschule fuer Koerperkultur Leipzig**
Friedrich Ludwig Jahn Allee 59, 701 Leipzig, E. Germany (D.D.R.)
- Deutsche Hochschule fuer Koerperkultur. Wissenschaftliche Zeitschrift. 2 per yr.
- Sportmedizinische Schriftenreihe. (pub. by Johann Ambrosius Barth Verlag)

**Deutsche Hochschule fuer Musik "Hanns Eisler". Leitstelle fuer Information und Dokumentation "Musik"**
Otto-Grotewohl-Strasse 19, 108 Berlin, E. Germany (D.D.R.)
- Musik-Information; bibliographische Titeluebersicht. m.

**Deutsche Shakespeare Gesellschaft**
- Shakespeare-Jahrbuch. (pub. by Hermann Boehlaus Nachfolger)

**Deutsche Staatsbibliothek**
- Beitraege zur Inkunabelkunde. Dritte Folge. (pub. by Akademie-Verlag)

**Deutsche Staatsbibliothek. Theodor Fontane Archiv**
Dortustr. 30/34, Potsdam, E. Germany (D.D.R.)
(Subscr. Address: Deutscher Buchexport, Leninstr. 16, Leipzig, E. Germany)
- Fontane-Blaetter. s-a. ISSN 0015-6175

**Deutscher Anglerverband der DDR**
- Deutscher Angelsport. (pub. by Sportverlag D D R)

**Deutscher Demokratischer Rundfunk. Staatliches Rundfunkkomitee**
Nalepastr. 18-50, 116 Berlin, E. Germany (D.D.R.)
- Rundfunkjournalistik in Theorie und Praxis. m. ISSN 0035-9882

**Deutscher Modelleisenbahn-Verband der DDR**
- Modelleisenbahner. (pub. by Transpress VEB Verlag fuer Verkehrswesen)

**Deutscher Radsport-Verband der DDR**
Storkower Strasse 118, 1055 Berlin, E. Germany (D.D.R.)
- Radsportler. w.

**Deutscher Schach-Verband**
- Schach. (pub. by Sportverlag D D R)

**Deutscher Turn- und Sportbund**
Storkower Str. 118, Berlin 1055, E. Germany (D.D.R.)
- D D R-Sport; Sportinformation aus der D D R. bi-m. ISSN 0011-4812

**Deutsches Mode Institut**
- Mode. (pub. by Verlag Fuer die Frau)

**Deutsches Paedagogisches Zentralinstitut, Berlin**
- Paedagogik. Ausgabe A. (pub. by Verlag Volk und Wissen)

**Dietz Verlag**
Wallstr. 76-79, Postfach 273, 102 Berlin, E. Germany (D.D.R.)
- Einheit; Zeitschrift fuer Theorie und Praxis des wissenschaftlichen Sozialismus. m. ISSN 0013-2659 (Sozialistische Einheitspartei Deutschlands. Zentralkomitee)
- Geschichte der Arbeiterbewegung. Beitraege. bi-m. ISSN 0005-8068 (Sozialistische Einheitspartei Deutschlands. Zentralkomitee. Institut fuer Marxismus-Leninismus)
- Neuer Weg. s-m. (Sozialistische Einheitspartei Deutschlands. Zentralkomitee)

- Probleme des Friedens und des Sozialismus; Zeitschrift der kommunistischen Arbeiterparteien fuer Theorie und Information. m. ISSN 0032-9258

**VEB Domowina Verlag**
Tuchmacherstr. 27, 86 Bautzen, E. Germany.
- Plomjo. bi-m. ISSN 0032-1605
- Pomhaj Boh. m. ISSN 0032-4132

**VEB Verlag Enzyklopaedie**
Gerichtsweg 26, 701 Leipzig, E. Germany (D.D.R.)
- Anglistik und Amerikanistik. Zeitschrift. 4 per yr. ISSN 0044-2305
- Fremdsprachen; Zeitschrift fuer Dolmetscher, Uebersetzer und Sprachkundige. q. ISSN 0016-0970 (Vereinigung der Sprachmittler der DDR Beim VDJ) (Co-Sponsor: Intertext, Fremdsprachendienst der DDR; Karl-Marxuniversitaet Leipzig, Sektion Theoretische und Angewardte Sprachwissenschaft)

**Erkenntnistheorie Philosophische Probleme der Methodologie und Logik**
Joh-Dieckmann-Str. 19-23, 108 Berlin, E. Germany (D.D.R.)
- Erkenntnistheorie Philosophische Probleme der Methodologie und Logik. 3 per yr. ISSN 0014-0198

**Ernst-Moritz-Arndt-Universitaet**
Domstr. 11, 22 Greifswald, E. Germany (D.D.R.)
- Greifswald. Universitaet. Wissenschaftliche Zeitschrift. Gesellschafts- und Sprachwissenschaftliche Reihe. m. ISSN 0072-7504
- Greifswald. Universitaet. Wissenschaftliche Zeitschrift. Mathematisch-Naturwissenschaftliche Reihe. m. ISSN 0072-7512

**Evangelisch-Lutherisches Landeskirchenamt Sachsens**
- Evangelisch-Lutherische Landeskirche Sachsens. Amtsblatt. (pub. by Union-Verlag)

**Evangelisch-Methodistische Kirche in der DDR**
Haydnstr. 18, 8019 Dresden, E. Germany (D.D.R.)
- Friedensglocke. s-m.

**Evangelische Verlagsanstalt GmbH**
Krautstr. 52, 1017 Berlin, E. Germany (D.D.R.)
- Bach-Jahrbuch. a. ISSN 0084-7682 (Neue Bachgesellschaft, Internationale Vereinigung)
- Christenlehre; Zeitschrift fuer das katethetische Amt. m. ISSN 0009-5192
- Evangelischer Nachrichtendienst in der DDR. w. ISSN 0014-3553
- Theologische Literaturzeitung; Monatsschrift fuer das gesamte Gebiet der Theologie und Religionswissenschaft. m. ISSN 0040-5671
- Zeichen der Zeit; Evangelische Monatsschrift fuer Mitarbeiter der Kirche. m. ISSN 0044-2038

**VEB Fachbuchverlag**
Karl-Heine-Str. 16, 7031 Leipzig, E. Germany (D.D.R.)
- Baecker und Konditor. m. ISSN 0005-383X
- Bekleidung und Maschenware; Protozoen - Algen - Pilze. 6 per yr. ISSN 0005-8270
- Boersenblatt fuer den Deutschen Buchhandel; Protozoen - Algen - Pilze. w. ISSN 0006-5641
- Bruehl. 6 per yr. ISSN 0007-2664
- Druck und Verarbeitung; Fachzeitschrift fuer Drucktechnik, buchbinderische Weiterverarbeitung und Papierverarbeitung. m. ISSN 0007-2788 (Kammer der Technik. Fachausgabe der Zeitschrift "Papier und Druck")
- Druckformenherstellung; Fachzeitschrift fuer Typografie und Reproduktionstechnik. m. ISSN 0012-6489
- Fleisch; Fachzeitschrift fuer die Fleischgewinnung und Verarbeitung. m. ISSN 0015-3575
- Frisur und Kosmetik. m.
- Geschichte des Buchwesens. Beitraege. irreg. ISSN 0067-5040 (Boersenverein der Deutschen Buchhaendler. Historische Kommission)
- Holzindustrie. m. ISSN 0018-3857
- Holztechnologie. q. ISSN 0018-3881 (Zentralinstitut fuer Holztechnologie Dresden)
- L S L (Leder, Schuhe, Lederwaren) m. ISSN 0024-0192
- Lebensmittelindustrie; Zeitschrift fuer Oekonomik und Technologie. m. ISSN 0024-0028
- Modische Linie (Ausgabe B) q. ISSN 0026-8771
- Moebel und Wohnraum. m. ISSN 0026-8844
- Papier und Druck; Fachzeitschrift fuer Typografie, polygrafische Technik und Papierverarbeitung. m. ISSN 0031-1375
- Spiegel Deutscher Buchkunst. a. ISSN 0081-3702

• Textilreinigung; Chemischreinigung, Kleiderfarberei, Waescherei. m. ISSN 0040-5302
• Textiltechnik. m.
• Verpackung. bi-m. ISSN 0011-0590
• Zellstoff und Papier. m. ISSN 0044-3867

**Fachverband Maschinenbau.**
• Schweisstechnik. (pub. by VEB Verlag Technik)

**VEB Filmfabrik Wolfen. Photochemisches Kombinat**
• Signalaufzeichnungsmaterialien. Journal. (pub. by Akademie-Verlag)

**VEB Gustav Fischer Verlag**
Villengang 2, Postfach 176, 69 Jena, E. Germany (D.D.R.)
• Acta Histochemica; Zeitschrift fuer Histologische Topochemie. irreg., 3-4 vols. per yr., 2 nos. per vol. ISSN 0065-1281
• Anatomische Gesellschaft. Verhandlungen. ISSN 0066-1562
• Anatomischer Anzeiger; Zentralblatt fuer die gesamte wissenschaftliche Anatomie. m.(2 vol.per yr.) ISSN 0003-2786
• Angewandte Parasitologie; Organ fuer die gesamte Parasitologie. 4 per yr. ISSN 0003-3162
• Archiv fuer Protistenkunde; Protozoen-Algen-Pilze. 4 per yr. ISSN 0003-9365
• B P P. (Biochemie und Physiologie der Pflanzen) 6 nos. per vol. (1-2 vols. per yr.) ISSN 0015-3796
• Biologische Rundschau; Zeitschrift fuer die gesamte Biologie und ihre Grenzgebiete. bi-m. ISSN 0006-3290
• Botanische Studien. a. ISSN 0068-0427
• Chemie der Erde; Zeitschrift fuer chemische Mineralogie, Petrographie, Bodenkunde, Geochemie und Meteoritenkunde. 4 per yr. ISSN 0009-2819
• Experimentelle Pathologie/Experimental Pathology. 6 per yr. ISSN 0014-4908
• Monatshefte fuer die Veterinaermedizin. s-m. ISSN 0026-9263 (Wissenschaftliche Gesellschaft fuer Veterinaermedizin der DDR)
• Pedobiologia. 6 per yr. ISSN 0031-4056
• Tierwelt Deutschlands. irreg, no. 63, 1977. ISSN 0082-4305
• Zeitschrift fuer Aerztliche Fortbildung. fortn. ISSN 0044-2178 (Akademie fuer Aerztliche Fortbildung der DDR)
• Zeitschrift fuer Versuchstierkunde/Journal of Experimental Animal Science. 6 per yr. ISSN 0044-3697
• Zentralblatt fuer Allgemeine Pathologie und Pathologische Anatomie/General Pathology, Pathological Anatomy. 6 per yr. ISSN 0044-4030 (Organ of: Gesellschaft fuer Allgemeine Pathologie und Pathologische Anatomie der DDR; Gesellschaft fuer Neuropathologie der DDR)
• Der Zoologische Garten; Zeitschrift fuer die gesamte Tiergaertnerei. bi-m. ISSN 0044-5169 (Organ of: Kommission fuer Tiergaerten der DDR; Verband Deutscher Zoodirektoren; Internationaler Verband von Direktoren Zoologischer Gaerten)
• Zoologische Jahrbuecher. Abteilung fuer Allgemeine Zoologie und Physiologie der Tiere. q. ISSN 0044-5185
• Zoologische Jahrbuecher. Abteilung fuer Anatomie und Ontogenie der Tiere. q. ISSN 0044-5177
• Zoologische Jahrbuecher. Abteilung fuer Systematik, Oekologie und Geographie der Tiere. q. ISSN 0044-5193
• Zoologischer Anzeiger. m. ISSN 0044-5231

**VEB Fotokinoverlag Leipzig**
Karl-Heine-Str. 16, 7031 Leipzig, E. Germany (D.D.R.)
• Bild und Ton; Zeitschrift fuer Film und Fototechnik. m. ISSN 0006-2383
• Fotografie; periodical for cultural, aesthetical and technical questions of photography. m. ISSN 0015-8836
• Fotokino-Magazin. m. ISSN 0015-8879

**Freiburger Studentenschaft**
• Freiburger Studentenzeitung. (pub. by Buchdruckerei Rudolf Goldschagg)

**Friedrich-Schiller-Universitaet Selbstverlag**
Jena, E. Germany (D.D.R.)
• Friedrich-Schiller-Universitaet Jena Mathematisch-Naturwissenschaftliche Reihe. Wissenschaftliche Zeitschrift. 6 per yr. ISSN 0043-6836

**Verlag Fuer die Frau**
Friedrich-Ebert-Str. 76-78, 701 Leipzig, E. Germany (D.D.R.)
• Boutique. a. ISSN 0068-0532

• Frauen der Ganzen Welt. q. ISSN 0016-0229 (Women's International Democratic Federation)
• Guter Rat. q. ISSN 0017-582X
• Handarbeit. q. ISSN 0017-7156
• Mode. s-a. ISSN 0026-7279 (Deutsches Mode Institut)
• Modische Maschen. q. ISSN 0026-878X
• Pramo. m. ISSN 0032-6852
• Saison. q. ISSN 0036-3294
• Sibylle. bi-m. ISSN 0037-4482
• Spezial. a. ISSN 0081-3672
• Uroda/Schoenheit. s-a
• Vollschlank. s-a. ISSN 0083-6893

**G D R Peace Council**
Schliessfach 210, 108 Berlin, E. Germany (D.D.R.)
• G. D. R. Peace Council. Information. m. ISSN 0016-3481

**Akademische Verlagsgesellschaft Geest und Portig K.G.**
Sternwartenstr. 8, 701 Leipzig, E. Germany (D.D.R.)
• Beitraege zur Vogelkunde. 6 per yr. ISSN 0005-8211
• Folia Haematologica; Internationales Magazin fuer klinische und morphologische Blutforschung. 6 per yr. ISSN 0015-556X
• Gegenbaurs Morphologisches Jahrbuch. 6 per yr. ISSN 0016-5840
• Gerlands Beitraege zur Geophysik. 6 per yr. ISSN 0016-8696
• Geschichte der Naturwissenschaften, Technik und Medizin. Schriftenreihe. a. ISSN 0036-6978
• Hercynia; fuer die Fachgebiete Botanik, Geographie, Geologie, Geophysik, Palaeontologie, Zoologie. 4 per yr. ISSN 0018-0637 (Martin-Luther-Universitaet Halle-Wittenberg. Mathematisch-Naturwissenschaftliche Fakultaet)
• I E T: Zeitschrift fuer Elektrische Informations-und Energietechnik. 6 per yr. ISSN 0046-8398
• Milu; Wissenschaftliche und Kulturelle Mitteilungen aus dem Tierpark Berlin. irreg., vol. 3, 1973. ISSN 0076-8839 (Tierpark Berlin)
• Monographien zur Terrestrischen, Solaren und Kosmischen Physik. irreg.
• Zeitschrift fuer Mikroskopisch-Anatomische Forschung. 6 per yr. ISSN 0044-3107

**Gehoerlosen- und Schwerhoerigenverband der DDR**
Poststr. 4-5, 102 Berlin, E. Germany (D.D.R.)
• Gemeinsam; Zeitschrift der Hoergeschaedigten. m.

**Geographische Gesellschaft der DDR**
• Geographische Berichte. (pub. by VEB Hermann Haack)
• Petermanns Geographische Mitteilungen. (pub. by VEB Hermann Haack)

**Germany, Democratic Republic. Amt fuer Erfindungs-und Patentwesen**
• Der Neuerer. (pub. by Verlag die Wirtschaft)
• Warenzeichen- und Musterblatt. (pub. by Verlag die Wirtschaft)

**Germany, Democratic Republic. Amt fuer Erfindungs-und Patentwesen der DDR. Abteilung Dokumentembereitstellung**
Christburger Str. 4, 1055 Berlin, E. Germany (D.D.R.)
• Germany (Democratic Republic). Amt fuer Erfindungs- und Patentwesen. Bekanntmachungen. s-m. ISSN 0005-8246 (Subscr. to; Buchexport, Leninstr. 16, 701 Leipzig, D.D.R.)

**Germany, Democratic Republic. Amt fuer Standardisierung, Messwesen und Warenpruefung**
• Standardisierung und Qualitaet. (pub. by Staatsverlag der DDR)

**Germany, Democratic Republic. Meteorologischer Dienst**
• Germany (Democratic Republic, 1949- ) Meteorologischer Dienst. Abhandlungen. (pub. by Akademie-Verlag)

**Germany, Democratic Republic. Ministerium fuer Auswaertige Angelegenheiten**
Postfach 101, 102 Berlin, E. Germany (D.D.R.)
• Aussenpolitische Korrespondenz. w.

**Germany, Democratic Republic. Ministerium fuer Auswaertige Angelegenheiten. Presseabteilung**
Marx-Engels-Platz 2, E. Germany (D.D.R.)
• Aussenpolitische Korrespondenz. (pub. by Staatsverlag der DDR)
• Foreign Affairs Bulletin. every 10 days. ISSN 0015-7139

**Germany, Democratic Republic. Ministerium fuer Gesundheitswesen**
• D D R-Medizin-Report. (pub. by VEB Verlag Volk und Gesundheit)

**Germany, Democratic Republic. Ministerium fuer Hoch- und Fachschulwesen. Beirat fuer das Wissenschaftliche Bibliothekswesen und die Wissenschaftliche Information**
Unter den Linden 8, Postfach 1312, 1086 Berlin, E. Germany (D.D.R.)
(Subscr. to: Deutsche Staatsbibliothek, Unter den Linden 8, 108 Berlin, E. Germany (D.D.R.))
• Mitteilungen aus dem Wissenschaftlichen Bibliothekswesen der DDR. m. ISSN 0043-6763

**Germany, Democratic Republic. Ministerium fuer Hoch- und Fachschulwesen**
Rechtsabteilung, Marx-Engels-Platz 2, Berlin 102, E. Germany (D.D.R.)
• Fachschule. (pub. by VEB Deutscher Verlag der Wissenschaften)
• Germany (Democratic Republic, 1949- ). Ministerium fuer Hoch- und Fachschulwesen. Verfuegungen und Mitteilungen. irreg.
• Hochschulwesen. (pub. by VEB Deutscher Verlag der Wissenschaften)

**Germany, Democratic Republic. Ministerium fuer Justiz**
Otto-Grotewohl-Str. 17, 108 Berlin, E. Germany (D.D.R.)
• Neue Justiz. (pub. by Staatsverlag der DDR)
• Schoeffe; Zeitschrift fuer Schoeffen und Schiedskommissionen. m. ISSN 0036-6250

**Germany, Democratic Republic. Ministerium fuer Kultur. Rat fuer Museumswesen**
• Neue Museumskunde. (pub. by Veb Deutscher Verlag der Wissenschaften)

**Germany, Democratic Republic. Ministerium fuer Land-, Forst- und Nahrungsgueterwirtschaft**
• Kooperation. (pub. by VEB Deutscher Landwirtschaftsverlag)
• Zeitschrift fuer die Binnenfischerei der DDR. (pub. by VEB Deutscher Landwirtschaftsverlag)

**Germany, Democratic Republic. Ministerium fuer Verkehrswesen**
• Fahrt Frei. (pub. by Transpress VEB Verlag fuer Verkehrswesen)

**Germany, Democratic Republic. Ministerium fuer Verkehrswesen. Hauptverwaltung der Zivilen Luftfahrt**
E. Germany (D.D.R.), 108 Berlin, E. Germany (D.D.R.)
• Nachrichten fuer Die Zivile Luftfahrt, Deutsche Demokratische Republik. m. ISSN 0027-7428

**Germany, Democratic Republic. Ministerium fuer Volksbildung**
• Astronomie in der Schule. (pub. by Verlag Volk und Wissen)
• Deutsche Lehrerzeitung. (pub. by Verlag Volk und Wissen)
• Kunsterziehung. (pub. by Verlag Volk und Wissen)

**Germany, Democratic Republic. Presseamt beim Vorsitzenden des Ministerrates der DDR**
• Presse der Sowjetunion. (pub. by Verlag Volk und Welt)

**Germany, Democratic Republic. Seehydrographischer Dienst**
Dierkower Damm 45, 25 Rostock 1, Deutsche Demokratische Republik
(Subscr. to: Buchexport, Leninstr. 16, Leipzig, E. Germany)
• Nautisches Jahrbuch. a.

**Germany, Democratic Republic. Staatliche Archivverwaltung**
• Archivmitteilungen. (pub. by Staatsverlag der DDR)

**Germany, Democratic Republic. Staatliche Zentralverwaltung fuer Statistik**
Berlin, Deutsche Demokratische Republik.
• Bevoelkerungsstatistisches Jahrbuch der Deutschen Demokratischen Republik. a.
• Statistical Yearbook of the GDR. (pub. by Staatsverlag der DDR)
• Statistische Praxis; Zeitschrift fuer Rechnungsfuehrung und Statistik. bi-m. ISSN 0039-064X

- Statistisches Jahrbuch der DDR. (pub. by Staatsverlag der DDR)

**Germany, Democratic Republic. Staatssekretariat fuer Arbeit und Loehne. Zentrales Forschunginstitut fuer Arbeit**
- Sozialistische Arbeitswissenschaft. (pub. by Verlag die Wirtschaft)

**Germany, Democratic Republic. Zentralinstitut fuer Berufsbildung**
Reinhold-Huhn-Str 5, 108 Berlin, E. Germany (D.D.R.)
- Forschung der Sozialistischen Berufsbildung. bi-m.

**Germany, Democratic Republic. Zentralinstitut fuer Bibliothekswesen**
Hermann-Matern-Str. 57, Berlin 104, E. Germany (D.D.R.)
- Entwicklung des Bibliothekswesens in der Deutschen Demokratischen Republik; Jahresbericht. Berlin. a.

**Gesellschaft der Augenaertzte der DDR**
- Folia Ophthalmologica. (pub. by VEB Georg Thieme)

**Gesellschaft fuer Anaesthesiologie und Reanimation der DDR**
- Anaesthesiologie und Reanimation. (pub. by VEB Verlag Volk und Gesundheit)

**Gesellschaft fuer Bronchopneumonologie und Tuberkulose der DDR**
- Zeitschrift fuer Erkrankungen der Atmungsorgane. (pub. by Johann Ambrosius Barth Verlag)

**Gesellschaft fuer Chirurgie der DDR**
- Zentralblatt fuer Chirurgie. (pub. by Johann Ambrosius Barth Verlag)

**Gesellschaft fuer Chirurgie der DDR. Sektion Experimentelle Chirurgie**
- Zeitschrift fuer experimentelle Chirurgie. (pub. by VEB Verlag Volk und Gesundheit)

**Gesellschaft fuer Deutsch-Sowjetische Freundschaft. Zentralvorstand**
- Kunst und Literatur. (pub. by Verlag Volk und Welt)
- Sowjetwissenschaft. (pub. by Verlag Volk und Welt)

**Gesellschaft fuer die gesamte Hygiene**
- Zeitschrift fuer die Gesamte Hygiene und ihre Grenzgebiete. (pub. by VEB Verlag Volk und Gesundheit)

**Gesellschaft fuer Endokrinologie und Stoffwechselkrankheiten**
- Endokrinologie. (pub. by Johann Ambrosius Barth Verlag)

**Gesellschaft fuer Gastroenterologie der DDR**
- Deutsche Zeitschrift fuer Verdauungs- und Stoffwechselkrankheiten. (pub. by Johann Ambrosius Barth Verlag)

**Gesellschaft fuer Gerontologie der DDR**
- Zeitschrift fuer Alternsforschung. (pub. by Verlag Theodor Steinkopff)

**Gesellschaft fuer Geschwulstbekaempfung der DDR**
- Archiv fuer Geschwulstforschung. (pub. by Verlag Theodor Steinkopff)

**Gesellschaft fuer Gynaekologie und Geburtshilf der DDR**
- Zentralblatt fuer Gynaekologie. (pub. by Johann Ambrosius Barth Verlag)

**Gesellschaft fuer Innere Medizin der DDR**
- Zeitschrift fuer die Gesamte Innere Medizin und ihre Grenzgebiete. (pub. by VEB Georg Thieme)

**Gesellschaft fuer Klinische Medizin der DDR**
- Das Deutsche Gesundheitswesen. (pub. by VEB Verlag Volk und Gesundheit)

**Gesellschaft fuer Klinische und Experimentelle Immunologie der DDR**
- Allergie und Immunologie. (pub. by Johann Ambrosius Barth Verlag)

**Gesellschaft fuer Orthopaedie der DDR**
- Beitraege zur Orthopaedie und Traumatologie. (pub. by VEB Verlag Volk und Gesundheit)

**Gesellschaft fuer Pediatrie der DDR**
- Kinderaerztliche Praxis. (pub. by VEB Georg Thieme)

**Gesellschaft fuer Physikalische und Mathematische Biologie der DDR**
- Studia Biophysica. (pub. by Akademie-Verlag)

**Gesellschaft fuer Physiotherapie der DDR**
- Zeitschrift fuer Physiotherapie. (pub. by VEB Georg Thieme)

**Gesellschaft fuer Psychiatrie und Neurologie**
- Psychiatrie, Neurologie und Medizinische Psychologie. (pub. by S. Hirzel Verlag)

**Gesellschaft fuer Psychologie der DDR**
- Probleme und Ergebnisse der Psychologie. (pub. by VEB Deutscher Verlag der Wissenschaften)

**Gesellschaft fuer Sport und Technik**
- Flieger-Revue. (pub. by Militaerverlag der Deutschen Demokratischen Republik)

**Gesellschaft fuer Sportmedizin der DDR**
- Medizin und Sport. (pub. by VEB Verlag Volk und Gesundheit)

**Gesellschaft fuer Stenografie und Maschinenschreiben der DDR**
- Der Stenopraktiker. (pub. by Verlag die Wirtschaft)

**Gesellschaft fuer Stomatologie der DDR**
- Stomatologie der DDR. (pub. by VEB Verlag Volk und Gesundheit)

**Gesellschaft fuer Urologie der DDR**
- Zeitschrift fuer Urologie und Nephrologie. (pub. by VEB Georg Thieme)

**Goethe-Gesellschaft, Weimar**
- Goethe-Jahrbuch. (pub. by Hermann Boehlaus Nachfolger)

**Buchdruckerei Rudolf Goldschagg**
Herrenstr 6, 78 Freiburg, E. Germany (D.D.R.)
- Freiburger Studentenzeitung. m. ISSN 0016-0709 (Freiburger Studentenschaft)

**VEB Deutscher Verlag fuer Grundstoffindustrie**
Karl-Heine-Str. 27, 7031 Leipzig, E. Germany (D.D.R.)
- Chemische Technik; Wissenschaftliche Zeitschrift fuer Technik und Oekonomie der Chemieindustrie. m. ISSN 0045-6519 (Kammer der Technik)
- Energieanwendung. m. ISSN 0013-7405 (Institut fuer Energetik. Zentralstelle fuer Rationelle Energieanwendung)
- Energietechnik; Technisch-wissenschaftliche Zeitschrift fuer Energieerzeugung. Energieuebertragung und -verteilung. m. ISSN 0013-7421 (Kammer der Technik)
- Freiberger Forschungshefte. Montanwissenschaften: Reihe A. Geotechnik/Ingenieurgeologie, Bergbautechnologie, Verfahrenstechnik, Energiewandlung. irreg. ISSN 0071-9390 (Bergakademie Freiberg)
- Freiberger Forschungshefte. Montanwissenschaften: Reihe B. Metallurgie und Werkstofftechnik. irreg. (Bergakademie Freiberg)
- Freiberger Forschungshefte. Montanwissenschaften: Reihe C. Geowissenschaften. irreg. ISSN 0071-9404 (Bergakademie Freiberg)
- Giessereitechnik; Technische Zeitschrift fuer das Giessereiwesen. m. ISSN 0016-9803 (Kammer der Technik. Montanwissenschaftliche Gesellschaft der DDR)
- Neue Bergbautechnik; wissenschaftliche Zeitschrift fuer Bergbau, Geowissenschaften und Aufbereitung. m. ISSN 0047-9403
- Neue Huette; Zeitschrift fuer Entwicklung, Gewinnung, Umformung und Pruefung Metallischer Werkstoffe. m. ISSN 0028-3207 (Kammer der Technik. Montanwissenschaftliche Gesellschaft der DDR)
- Plaste und Kautschuk; Zeitschrift fuer Wirtschaft, Wissenschaft und Technik der hochpolymeren Werkstoffe. m. ISSN 0048-4350
- Sicherheit Bergbau, Energiewirtschaft, Metallurgie. 6 per yr. ISSN 0037-4520
- Zeitschrift fuer Chemie; Wissenschaftliche Zeitschrift fuer Chemie und Grenzgebiete. m. ISSN 0044-2402

**VEB Hermann Haack**
Geographisch-Kartographische Anstalt Gotha-Leipzig, Justus-Perthes-Str. 3/9, 58 Gotha, E. Germany (D.D.R.)
- Geographische Berichte. 4 per yr. ISSN 0016-7452 (Geographische Gesellschaft der DDR)
- Geographisches Jahrbuch. a. ISSN 0072-095X
- Petermanns Geographische Mitteilungen. q. ISSN 0031-6229 (Geographische Gesellschaft der DDR)

**Henschelverlag Kunst und Gesellschaft**
Oranienburger Str. 67-68, 104 Berlin, E. Germany (D.D.R.)
- Filmspiegel. fortn. ISSN 0015-1734
- Melodie und Rhythmus; devoted to light music song and jazz. m. ISSN 0025-9004
- Musik und Gesellschaft. m. ISSN 0027-4755 (Verband der Komponisten und Musikwissenschaftler der DDR)
- Theater der Zeit. m. ISSN 0040-5418 (Verband der Theaterschaffenden der DDR)
- Unterhaltungskunst; Zeitschrift fuer Buhne, Podium und Manege. m. ISSN 0042-0565

**Hilfskomitee der Galiziendeutschen**
- Das Heilige Band. (pub. by Brunnquell-Verlag)

**Hinstorff Verlag**
Kroopeliner Str. 25, 25 Rostock, E. Germany (D.D.R.)
- Trajekt. s-a.

**S. Hirzel Verlag**
Postfach 506, 701 Leipzig, E. Germany (D.D.R.)
- Archiv fuer Experimentelle Veterinaermedizin. 6 per yr. ISSN 0003-9055
- Psychiatrie, Neurologie und Medizinische Psychologie; Zeitschrift fuer die gesamte Nervenheilkunde und Psychotherapie. m. ISSN 0033-2739 (Gesellschaft fuer Psychiatrie und Neurologie) (Co-Sponsor: Gesellschaft fuer Aerztliche Psychotherapie der DDR)

**Historiker-Gesellschaft der DDR. Hansische Arbeitsgemeinschaft**
- Abhandlungen zur Handels- und Sozialgeschichte. (pub. by Hermann Boehlaus Nachfolger)

**Hochschule fuer Film und Fernsehen der DDR**
Franzoesische Str. 47, 108 Berlin, E. Germany (D.D.R.)
- Filmo-Bibliografischer Jahresbericht. a. ISSN 0015-1750

**Hochschule fuer Oekonomie**
Berlin-Karlhorst, E. Germany (D.D.R.)
- Hochschule fuer Oekonomie, Berlin. Wissenschaftliche Zeitschrift. irreg. ISSN 0067-5954

**Hochschule fuer Verkehrswesen "Friedrich List"**
Friedrich-List-Platz 1, Dresden 801, E. Germany (D.D.R.)
- Hochschule fuer Verkehrswesen "Friedrich List". Wissenschaftliche Zeitschrift. 5 per yr. ISSN 0043-6844

**VEB Friedrich Hofmeister Musikverlag**
Karlstr. 10, 701 Leipzig, E. Germany (D.D.R.)
- Deutsche Musikbibliographie. m. ISSN 0012-0502 (Deutsche Buecherei)
- Jahresverzeichnis der Musikalien und Musikschriften; Veroeffentlichungen der DDR. der BRD und Westberlins sowie deutschsprachige Werke anderer Laender. a. ISSN 0075-2959

**Humboldt-Universitaet zu Berlin**
Mittel Str. 7-8, 108 Berlin, E. Germany (D.D.R.).
- Humboldt- Universitaet zu Berlin. Wissenschaftliche Zeitschrift. 6 per yr. ISSN 0043-6852

**Humboldt-Universitaet zu Berlin. Institut fuer Mathematische Logik**
- Mathematische Logik und Grundlagen der Mathematik. Zeitschrift. (pub. by VEB Deutscher Verlag der Wissenschaften)

**Humboldt-Universitaet zu Berlin. Museum fuer Naturkunde**
- Deutsche Entomologische Zeitschrift. (pub. by Akademie-Verlag)

**Ingenieurhochschule Zittau**
- Kernenergie. (pub. by Akademie-Verlag)

**Institut fuer Binnenfischerei**
Muggelseedamm 310, 1162 Berlin Friedrichskagen,
E. Germany
(Subscr. Address: Deutscher Landwirtschaftsverlag,
Reinhardtstr. 14, 104 Berlin, E. Germany)
● Zeitschrift fuer Binnenfischerei der DDR. q.

**Institut fuer Deutsche Militaergeschichte**
● Militaergeschichte. (pub. by Militaerverlag der
Deutschen Demokratischen Republik)

**Institut fuer Energetik. Zentralstelle fuer Rationelle
Energieanwendung**
● Energieanwendung. (pub. by Deutscher Verlag
fuer Grundstoffindustrie)

**Institut fuer Forstwissenschaften**
● Beitrage fuer Die Forstwirtschaft. (pub. by
Akademie-Verlag)

**Institut fuer Internationale Beziehungen der DDR**
● Deutsche Aussenpolitik. (pub. by VEB Deutscher
Verlag der Wissenschaften)

**Institut fuer Internationale Politik und Wirtschaft**
Breite Str. 11, 102 Berlin, E. Germany (D.D.R.)
● D D R-Publikationen zur Imperialismusforschung,
Auswahlbibliographie. a.
● I P W Berichte. m. ISSN 0046-970X
● I P W Forschungshefte. (pub. by Buchexport)

**Institut fuer Kommunalwirtschaft**
● Kommunale Dienstleistungen. (pub. by Verlag die
Wirtschaft)

**Institut fuer Leichtbau und Oekonomische
Verwendung von Werkstoffen**
Postschliessfach 44, 808 Dresden, E. Germany
(Subscr. To: Deutscher Buch-Export Und-Import
GmbH, Leninstr. 16, 701 Leipzig, E. Germany)
● I F L-Mitteilungen. m. ISSN 0018-9693

**Institut fuer Museumswesen der Deutschen
Demokratischen Republik**
Information-Dokumentation, Mucggelseedamm 200,
1162 Berlin, E. Germany (D.D.R.)
● Informationen fuer die Museen in der DDR. 5 per
yr.

**Institut fuer Pflanzenschutzforschung. Abteilung
Taxonomie der Insekten**
● Beitraege zur Entomologie. (pub. by Akademie-
Verlag)

**Institut fuer Schiffbau**
Wismarsche Str. 6/7, 25 Rostock, E. Germany
(D.D.R.)
● Schiffbauforschung; wissenschaftlich-technische
Mitteilungen. ISSN 0036-6056 (Co-Sponsor:
Universitaet Rostock, Sektion Schiffstechnik)

**Institut fuer Technologie Kultureller Einrichtungen**
Clara Zetkin- Str. 1205, DDR-108 Berlin, E.
Germany.
● Scena. q. ISSN 0036-5726

**Institut fuer Weiterbildung Mittlerer Medizinischer
Fachkraefte**
● Die Heilberufe. (pub. by VEB Verlag Volk und
Gesundheit)

**Institut und Museum fuer Geschichte der Stadt
Dresden**
Ernst-Thaelmann-Str. 2, 801 Dresden A 1, E.
Germany (D.D.R.)
● Jahrbuch zur Geschichte Dresdens. a.

**Internationale Gesellschaft fuer Kiefer-Gesichts-
Chirurgie**
● Acta Chirurgiae Maxillo-Facialis. (pub. by Johann
Ambrosius Barth Verlag)

**Jenoptik Jena GmbH**
Carl-Zeiss-Str. 1, 69 Jena, E. Germany (D.D.R.)
● Vermessungs-Informationen/Surveying News/
Informations Topografiques. irreg.

**Verlag Junge Welt**
Mauerstr. 39-40, 108 Berlin, E. Germany (D.D.R.)
● Die A B C-Zeitung. m. ISSN 0001-0375
● Forum; Zeitung fuer geistige Probleme der Jugend.
s-m. ISSN 0015-8313 (Zentralrat der Freien
Deutschen Jugend)
● Jugend & Technik; popular technical journal. m.
ISSN 0022-5878 (Zentralrat der Freien Deutschen
Jugend)
● Junge Generation. m. ISSN 0022-6297 (Zentralrat
der Freien Deutschen Jugend)

**Kammer der Technik**
● Chemische Technik. (pub. by VEB Deutscher
Verlag fuer Grundstoffindustrie)
● Elektrie. (pub. by VEB Verlag Technik)
● Energietechnik. (pub. by VEB Deutscher Verlag
fuer Grundstoffindustrie)
● K F T. (pub. by VEB Verlag Technik)
● Seewirtschaft. (pub. by VEB Verlag Technik)
● Silikattechnik. (pub. by VEB Verlag fuer
Bauwesen)
● Vermessungstechnik. (pub. by VEB Verlag fuer
Bauwesen)
● Wasserwirtschaft-Wassertechnik (W W T) (pub. by
VEB Verlag fuer Bauwesen)

**Kammer der Technik. Fachausgabe der Zeitschrift
"Papier und Druck"**
● Druck und Verarbeitung. (pub. by VEB
Fachbuchverlag)

**Kammer der Technik. Fachverband Elektrotechnik**
● Fernmeldetechnik. (pub. by VEB Verlag Technik)
● Nachrichtentechnik-Elektronik. (pub. by VEB
Verlag Technik)

**Kammer der Technik. Fachverband Fahrzeugbau und
Verkehr**
● D E T. (pub. by VEB Verlag Technik)

**Kammer der Technik. Fachverband Land-, Forst- und
Nahrungsguetertechnik**
● Agrartechnik. (pub. by VEB Verlag Technik)

**Kammer der Technik. Fachverband Maschinenbau**
● Fertigungstechnik und Betrieb. (pub. by VEB
Verlag Technik)
● Hebezeuge und Foerdermittel. (pub. by VEB
Verlag Technik)
● Maschinenbautechnik. (pub. by VEB Verlag
Technik)
● Metallverarbeitung. (pub. by VEB Verlag Technik)

**Kammer der Technik. Montanwissenschaftliche
Gesellschaft der DDR**
● Giessereitechnik. (pub. by VEB Deutscher Verlag
fuer Grundstoffindustrie)
● Neue Huette. (pub. by VEB Deutscher Verlag fuer
Grundstoffindustrie)

**Kammer der Technik. Praesidium**
● Schmierungstechnik. (pub. by VEB Verlag
Technik)

**Kammer der Technik. Wissenschaftlich-Technische
Gesellschaft fuer Mess- und
Automatisierungstechnik**
● Feingeraetetechnik. (pub. by VEB Verlag Technik)
● Messen-Steuern-Regeln. (pub. by VEB Verlag
Technik)

**Karl Marx Universitaet**
Goethestr 315, 701 Leipzig, E. Germany (D.D.R.),
E. Germany.
● Geophysik und Geologie. (pub. by Akademie-
Verlag)
● Karl Marx Universitaet Leipzig. Gesellschafts-und
Sprachwissenschaftliche Reihe. Wissenschaftliche
Zeitschrift. 6 per yr. ISSN 0043-6879
● Karl Marx Universitaet, Leipzig, Mathematisch
Naturwissenschaftliche Reihe. Wissenschaftliche
Zeitschrift. 6 per yr. ISSN 0043-6860
● Tropische Landwirtschaft und Veterinaermedizin.
Beitraege. q. ISSN 0301-567X (Subscr. to:
Buchexport Volkseigener Aussenhandelsbetrieb
der DDR, Leninstr. 16, 701 Leipzig, E. Germany
(D.D.R.))

**Karl-Marx-Universitaet. Herder-Institut**
Lumumbastr. 4, 7022 Leipzig, E. Germany (D.D.R.)
● Deutsch als Fremdsprache; Zeitschrift fuer
Theorie und Praxis des Deutschunterrichts fuer
Auslaender. bi-m. ISSN 0011-9741

**Karl-Marx-Universitaet. Universitaetsbibliothek**
Beethovenstr. 6, 701 Leipzig, E. Germany (D.D.R.)
● Bibliographie der Antiquariats-, Auktions- und
Kunstkataloge. irreg.

**Kombinat VEB Keramische Werke Hermsdorf**
Friedrich-Engels-Str. 79, Hermsdorf 653, East
Germany (D.D.R.)
(Subscriptions to: Deutscher Buch-Export und
Import GmbH, Leninstr. 16, Leipzig 701, E.
Germany)
● Zeitschriftenschau Keramik; Fachbibliographie fuer
die gesamte Sintertechnik. m.

**Kombinat Technische Gebaeudeausruestung Institut**
● Stadt- und Gebaeudetechnik. (pub. by VEB Verlag
fuer Bauwesen)

**Kulturbund der DDR**
● Sonntag. (pub. by Aufbau-Verlag Berlin und
Weimar)

**Kulturbund der DDR. Pirckheimer-Gesellschaft**
● Marginalien. (pub. by Aufbau-Verlag Berlin und
Weimar)

**Kulturbund der DDR. Zentraler Arbeitskreis
Esperanto**
Charlottenstr. 60, 108 Berlin, E. Germany (D.D.R.)
● Der Esperantist. bi-m. ISSN 0014-0619
● Paco; bulteno de la Mondpaca Esperantista
Movado, sercio de G D R. a. (U.S. Subscr. to: J.
M. Deer, 12946 N.E. Nancock, Portland, OR
97230)

**Verlag fuer Kunst und Wissenschaft**
Karlstr. 20, 701 Leipzig, E. Germany (D.D.R.)
● Weltstaedte der Kunst. Edition Leipzig/Great
Centers of Art. irreg. ISSN 0083-7954

**Landeskirchenrat der Evangelische-Lutherische Kirche
in Thueringen**
● Evangelische-Lutherische Kirche in Thueringen.
Amtsblatt. (pub. by Wartburg Verlag Max
Kessler)

**Landesmuseum fuer Vorgeschichte, Dresden**
● Landesmuseum fuer Vorgeschichte, Dresden.
Veroeffentlichungen. (pub. by VEB Deutscher
Verlag der Wissenschaften)

**Landesmuseum fuer Vorgeschichte, Halle**
● Landesmuseum fuer Vorgeschichte, Halle.
Veroeffentlichungen. (pub. by VEB Deutscher
Verlag der Wissenschaften)

**VEB Deutscher Landwirtschaftsverlag**
Reinhardstr. 14, 104 Berlin, E. Germany (D.D.R.)
● Feldwirtschaft. m. ISSN 0014-9799 (Akademie
der Landwirtschaftswissenschaften der DDR)
● Kooperation. m. ISSN 0023-3811 (Germany,
Democratic Republic. Ministerium fuer Land-,
Forst- und Nahrungsgueterwirtschaft)
● Sozialistische Forstwirtschaft. m. ISSN 0038-6154
● Zeitschrift fuer die Binnenfischerei der DDR. m.
(Germany, Democratic Republic. Ministerium
fuer Land-, Forst- und Nahrungsgueterwirtschaft)

**Lawyers Association of the G.D.R.**
Littenstr. 15-17, 102 Berlin, E. Germany (D.D.R.)
● Law and Legislation in the German Democratic
Republic. s-a.

**League of the German Democratic Republic for
Friendship Among the Peoples**
Thalmannplatz 8-9, 108 Berlin, E. Germany
(D.D.R.)
● Current Documents from the German Democratic
Republic. ISSN 0011-3433

**VEB Lied der Zeit Musikverlag**
Rosa-Luxemburg-Str. 41, 102 Berlin, E. Germany
(D.D.R.)
● Hallo-Beat. bi-m.
● Record-Serie. s-m.
● Schlager fuer Dich. q. ISSN 0036-6137

**VEB Magdeburger Armaturenwerke "Karl Marx"**
Liebknechtstr. 65-91, 301 Magdeburg, E. Germany
(D.D.R.)
● Technische Information Armaturen. 3 per yr.
ISSN 0040-1420

**Martin-Luther-Universitaet Halle-Wittenberg**
August-Bebel-Str. 13, 401 Halle, E. Germany.
● Martin- Luther- Universitaet Halle- Wittenberg.
Wissenschaftliche Zeitschrift. Gesellschafts-und
Sprachwissenschaftliche Reihe. bi-m.
● Martin-Luther-Universitaet Halle-Wittengerg.
Wissenschaftliche Zeitschrift. Mathematisch-
Natur-Wissenschaftliche Reihe. bi-m.

**Martin-Luther-Universitaet Halle-Wittenberg.
Mathematisch-Naturwissenschaftliche Fakultaet**
● Hercynia. b. pub. by Akademische
Verlagsgesellschaft Geest und Portig K.G.)

**Mathematische Gesellschaft der DDR**
● Elektronische Informationsverarbeitung und
Kybernetik. (pub. by Akademie-Verlag)

**Medizinische Akademie "Carl Gustav Carus".
Zentralbibliothek**
Fiedlerstr. 27, 8019 Dresden, E. Germany (D.D.R.)
- Medizinische Akademie "Carl Gustav Carus"
Dresden. Schriften. irreg., vol. 11, 1974. ISSN
0070-721X

**Meteorologische Gesellschaft der DDR**
- Zeitschrift fuer Meteorologie. (pub. by Akademie-
Verlag)

**Militaerverlag der Deutschen Demokratischen
Republik**
Storkower Str. 158, 1055 Berlin, E. Germany
(D.D.R.)
- Armee-Rundschau. m. ISSN 0004-2277
- Flieger-Revue. m. ISSN 0001-9445 (Gesellschaft
fuer Sport und Technik)
- Funk Amateur. m.
- Militaergeschichte. 6 per yr. (Institut fuer
Deutsche Militaergeschichte)
- Militaertechnik; Fachzeitschrift fuer technische
Fragen der Land-, Luft- und Seestreitkraefte. m.
ISSN 0047-7346
- Militaerwesen. ISSN 0026-3923
- Poseidon; Tauchsport Tauchertechnik
Unterwassertechnologie Unterwasserforschung
Meeresbiologie Unterwasserfotografie u.a.
Sachgebiete. m. ISSN 0032-5198
- Sport und Technik. m. ISSN 0038-7932

**Museen der Stadt Erfurt**
Erfurt, E. Germany (D.D.R.)
- Beitraege zur Geschichte Thueringens. irreg.

**Museum fuer Geschichte der Stadt Dresden**
Ernst--Thaelmann--Str. 2, 801 Dresden, E. Germany
(D.D.R.)
- Bildung im Geschichtsmuseum. a.

**Museum fuer Ur- und Fruehgeschichte, Potsdam**
- Museum fuer Ur- und Fruehgeschichte des
Bezirkes Potsdam, Frankfurt/Oder und Cottbus.
Veroeffentlichungen. (pub. by VEB Deutscher
Verlag der Wissenschaften)

**Museum fuer Ur- und Fruehgeschichte, Schwerin**
- Bodendenkmalpflege in Mecklenburg. (pub. by
VEB Deutscher Verlag der Wissenschaften)

**Museum fuer Ur- und Fruehgeschichte Thueringens**
Amalienstr., 53 Weimar, E. Germany (D.D.R.)
- Alt-Thueringen. (pub. by Hermann Boehlaus
Nachfolger)
- Bibliographie der Chemisch-Archaeologischen
Literatur. irreg. ISSN 0067-6950
- Museum fuer Ur- und Fruehgeschichte
Thueringens. Veroeffentlichungen. (pub. by
Hermann Boehlaus Nachfolger)

**Museum fuer Voelkerkunde, Leipzig**
- Museum fuer Voelkerkunde, Leipzig. Jahrbuch.
(pub. by Akademie-Verlag)
- Museum fuer Voelkerkunde, Leipzig.
Veroeffentlichungen. (pub. by Akademie-Verlag)

**VEB Deutscher Verlag fuer Musik**
Karlstr. 10, 701 Leipzig, E. Germany (D.D.R.)
- Europaeische Volksmusikinstrumente. Handbuch.
irreg. ISSN 0073-0025

**Zeitungsverlag National**
Prenzlauer Allee 36, 1055 Berlin, E. Germany
(D.D.R.)
- Der Nationale Demokrat. m. ISSN 0028-0437
(National-Demokratische Partei Deutschlands)

**National-Demokratische Partei Deutschlands**
- Der Nationale Demokrat. (pub. by Zeitungsverlag
National)

**Nationales Komitee fuer Gesundheitserziehung der
DDR**
- Deine Gesundheit. (pub. by VEB Verlag Volk und
Gesundheit)

**Naturkundliches Museum "Mauritianum"**
74 Altenburg, E. Germany (D.D.R.)
- Naturkundliches Museum "Mauritianum"
Altenburg. Abhandlungen und Berichte. biennial.
ISSN 0065-6631

**Neue Bachgesellschaft, Internationale Vereinigung**
- Bach-Jahrbuch. (pub. by Evangelische
Verlagsanstalt GmbH)

**Verlag Neue Musik**
Leipziger Str. 26, 108 Berlin, E. Germany (D.D.R.)
- Musikwissenschaft. Beitraege. q. ISSN 0005-8106
(Verband der Komponisten und
Musikwissenschaftler der DDR)
- Musikwissenschaftliche Arbeiten in der DDR.
Bericht. a. ISSN 0084-7798 (Zentralinstitut fuer
Musikforschung)

**Paedagogische Hochschule, Potsdam**
Dortusstr. 30, 15 Potsdam, E. Germany (D.D.R.)
- Potsdam. Paedagogische Hochschule.
Wissenschaftliche Zeitschrift. 5 per year. ISSN
0079-4384

**Panorama D.D.R. - Auslandspresseagentur**
Wilhelm Pieck Str. 49, 1054 Berlin, E. Germany
(D.D.R.)
- First Hand Information. irreg.
- Political Documents of the German Democratic
Republic. irreg.

**Peace Council of the German Democratic Republic**
Clara-Zetkin-Str. 103, 108 Berlin, E. Germany
(D.D.R.)
- Information from the Peace Movement of the
German Democratic Republic. m. ISSN 0020-
0085

**Pharmazeutische Gesellschaft der DDR**
- Die Pharmazie. (pub. by VEB Verlag Volk und
Gesundheit)

**Physikalische Gesellschaft der DDR**
- Fortschritte der Physik. (pub. by Akademie-
Verlag)

**Robotron-Elektronik Radeberg**
Wilhelm-Pick-Str. 70, 8142 Radeberg, E. Germany
(D.D.R.)
- Robotron Technische Mitteilungen. irreg.

**Verlag Ruetten und Loening**
Franzoesische Str. 32, 108 Berlin, E. Germany
(D.D.R.)
- Romanische Philologie. Beitraege. s-a. ISSN 0005-
8181
- Sinn und Form; Beitraege zur Literatur. bi-m.
ISSN 0037-5756

**Rundfunk-und Fernsehtechnisches Zentralamt**
Agastrasse, Berlin, E. Germany (D.D.R.)
- R F Z. Technische Mitteilungen. q. ISSN 0040-
1455

**Saechsische Akademie der Wissenschaften, Leipzig**
- Saechsische Akademie der Wissenschaften,
Leipzig. Jahrbuch. (pub. by Akademie-Verlag)

**Saechsische Akademie der Wissenschaften, Leipzig.
Historische Kommission**
- Deutsch-Slawische Forschungen zur Namenkunde
und Siedlungsgeschichte. (pub. by Akademie-
Verlag)
- Jahrbuch fuer Regionalgeschichte. (pub. by
Hermann Boehlaus Nachfolger)

**Saechsische Akademie der Wissenschaften, Leipzig.
Mathematisch-Naturwissenschaftliche Klasse**
- Saechsische Akademie der Wissenschaften,
Leipzig. Mathematisch-Naturwissenschaftliche
Klasse. Abhandlungen. (pub. by Akademie-Verlag)
- Saechsische Akademie der Wissenschaften,
Leipzig. Mathematisch-Naturwissenschaftliche
Klasse. Sitzungsberichte. (pub. by Akademie-
Verlag)

**Saechsische Akademie der Wissenschaften, Leipzig.
Philologisch-Historische Klasse**
- Saechsische Akademie der Wissenschaften,
Leipzig. Philologisch Historische Klasse.
Abhandlungen. (pub. by Akademie-Verlag)
- Saechsische Akademie der Wissenschaften,
Leipzig. Philologisch-Historische Klasse.
Sitzungsberichte. (pub. by Akademie-Verlag)

**Saechsische Landesbibliothek**
Marienallee 12, 806 Dresden, E. Germany (D.D.R.)
- Bibliographie Bildende Kunst. irreg.

**Savigny-Stiftung**
- Zeitschrift der Savigny-Stiftung fuer
Rechtsgeschichte. Germanistische, Romanistische
und Kanonistische Abteilung. (pub. by Hermann
Boehlaus Nachfolger)

**Kurt Schmidt Verlag**
Neuwerkstr. 9, Postschliessfach 248, 5010 Erfurt, E.
Germany (D.D.R.)
- Der Lustige Grillenfaenger; Denksportprobleme -
Geschicklichkeitsaufgaben - Froehliche Kurzweil.
q.
- Steckenpferd; das bunte Raetselbuechlein. q.

**Schriftstellerverband der Deutschen Demokratischen
Republik**
- Neue deutsche Literatur/N D L. (pub. by Aufbau-
Verlag Berlin und Weimar)

**Society for Anesthesiology and Resuscitation of the
GDR**
Karowerstr. 11, Berlin X1115, E. Germany (D.D.R.)
- Symposium Anaesthesiologiae Internationale.
Berichte. biennial; latest issue, 1975.

**Sozialistische Einheitspartei Deutschlands.
Zentralkomitee**
- Einheit. (pub. by Dietz Verlag)
- Geschichte der Arbeiterbewegung. Beitraege. (pub.
by Dietz Verlag)
- Neuer Weg. (pub. by Dietz Verlag)

**Sportverlag D D R**
Neustaedtische Kirchstr. 15, 108 Berlin, E.
Germany (D.D.R.)
- Deutscher Angelsport. m. (Deutscher
Anglerverband der DDR)
- Deutsches Sportecho. 5 per w.
- Fuwo. w.
- Illustrierter Motorsport. m. ISSN 0442-3054
- Schach. m. ISSN 0048-9328 (Deutscher Schach-
Verband)
- Theorie und Praxis der Koerperkultur. m. ISSN
0563-4458

**Staatliche Kunstsammlungen Dresden**
Albertinum, 801 Dresden, E. Germany (D.D.R.)
- Dresdner Kunstblaetter. bi-m.

**Staatliche Museen zu Berlin**
- Archiv fuer Papyrusforschung und Verwandte
Gebiete. (pub. by Teubner Verlagsgesellschaft)
- Staatliche Museen zu Berlin. Jahrbuch.
Forschungen und Berichte. (pub. by Akademie-
Verlag)

**Staatlicher Mathematisch-Physikalischer Salon,
Dresden**
- Staatlicher Mathematisch-Physikalischer Salon,
Dresden. Veroeffentlichungen. (pub. by VEB
Deutscher Verlag der Wissenschaften)

**Staatliches Filmarchiv der DDR. Filmtheater**
Kronenstr. 10, 108 Berlin, E. Germany (D.D.R.)
- Camera. q. ISSN 0008-2066

**Staatliches Museum fuer Mineralogie und Geologie,
Dresden**
- Staatliches Museum fuer Mineralogie und
Geologie, Dresden. Abhandlungen. (pub. by
Verlag Theodor Steinkopff)

**Staatliches Museum fuer Tierkunde in Dresden**
Augustusstr. 2, 801 Dresden, E. Germany (D.D.R.)
- Reichenbachia; Zeitschrift fuer entomologische
Taxonomie. irreg. ISSN 0070-7279
- Staatliches Museum fuer Tierkunde in Dresden.
Entomologische Abhandlungen. irreg. ISSN 0070-
7244
- Staatliches Museum fuer Tierkunde in Dresden.
Faunistische Abhandlungen. irreg. ISSN 0070-
7252
- Staatliches Museum fuer Tierkunde in Dresden.
Malakologische Abhandlungen. irreg. ISSN 0070-
7260
- Staatliches Museum fuer Tierkunde in Dresden.
Zoologische Abhandlungen. irreg. ISSN 0070-
7287

**Staatliches Museum fuer Voelkerkunde Dresden**
Leipziger Str. 3-4, Berlin, E. Germany (D.D.R.)
- Staatliches Museum fuer Voelkerkunde Dresden.
Abhandlungen und Berichte. irreg., vol. 34, 1975.
ISSN 0070-7295

**Staatsverlag der DDR**
Otto-Grotewohl-Str. 17, 108 Berlin, E. Germany
(D.D.R.)
- Archivmitteilungen; Zeitschrift fuer Theorie und
  Praxis des Archivwesens. bi-m. ISSN 0004-038X
  (Germany, Democratic Republic. Staatliche
  Archivverwaltung)
- Aussenpolitische Korrespondenz. w. ISSN 0004-
  8208 (Germany, Democratic Republic.
  Ministerium fuer Auswaertige Angelegenheiten.
  Presseabteilung)
- Neue Justiz; Zeitschrift fuer Recht und
  Rechtswissenschaft. s-m. ISSN 0028-3231
  (Germany, Democratic Republic. Ministerium
  fuer Justiz)
- Staat und Recht. m. ISSN 0038-8858 (Akademie
  fuer Staats und Rechtswissenschaft der DDR)
- Standardisierung und Qualitaet. m. (Germany,
  Democratic Republic. Amt fuer Standardisierung,
  Messwesen und Warenpruefung)
- Statistical Yearbook of the GDR. a. ISSN 0072-
  1514 (Germany, Democratic Republic. Staatliche
  Zentralverwaltung fuer Statistik)
- Statistisches Jahrbuch der DDR. a. (Germany,
  Democratic Republic. Staatliche
  Zentralverwaltung fuer Statistik)
- Wirtschaftsrecht; Zeitschrift fuer sozialistische
  Kooperation. q.

**Verlag Theodor Steinkopff**
Loschwitzer Str. 32, 8053 Dresden, E. Germany
(D.D.R.)
- Archiv fuer Geschwulstforschung. 8 per yr. ISSN
  0003-911X (Gesellschaft fuer
  Geschwulstbekaempfung der DDR)
- Krebsforschung. Beitraege. irreg., vol. 14, 1974.
  ISSN 0067-5113
- Staatliches Museum fuer Mineralogie und
  Geologie, Dresden. Abhandlungen. a. ISSN 0070-
  7228
- Technische Fortschrittsberichte; landtechnische
  Zeitschrift der dDR. irreg., vol. 63, 1974. ISSN
  0082-2566
- Waermelehre und Waermewirtschaft in
  Einzeldarstellungen. irreg., vol. 22, 1974. ISSN
  0083-6982
- Zeitschrift fuer Alternsforschung. 6 per yr. ISSN
  0044-2224 (Gesellschaft fuer Gerontologie der
  DDR)'
- Zeitschrift fuer Alternsforschung.
  Supplementbaende. irreg. ISSN 0084-5272

**VEB Verlag Technik**
Postfach 293, 102 Berlin, E. Germany (D.D.R.)
(Dist. in U.S. by Atlas for Action Books, Inc., 162
Fifth Ave., New York, N.Y. 10010)
- Agrartechnik; Landtechnische Zeitschrift der
  DDR. m. (Kammer der Technik. Fachverband
  Land-, Forst- und Nahrungsguetertechnik)
- Augenoptik; Fachzeitschrift fuer Augenoptiker
  und Ophthalmologen. bi-m. ISSN 0004-7910
- D E T. (Eisenbahntechnik); wissenschaftlich-
  technische Zeitschrift fuer Bau, Betrieb und
  Instandehaltung schienengebundener
  Verkehrseinrichtungen. m. ISSN 0012-0057
  (Kammer der Technik. Fachverband Fahrzeugbau
  und Verkehr)
- Elektrie; Ingenieurtechnische Fachzeitschrift fuer
  die Elektroindustrie-Starkstromtechnik. m. ISSN
  0013-5399 (Kammer der Technik)
- Der Elektro-Praktiker; Fachzeitschrift fuer den
  Praktiker der Starkstromtechnik in Industrie und
  Handwerk. m. ISSN 0013-5569
- Feingeraetetechnik; Wissenschaftlich-technische
  Zeitschrift fuer Entwicklung, Fertigung und
  Anwendung von Feingeraeten. m. ISSN 0014-
  9683 (Kammer der Technik. Wissenschaftlich-
  Technische Gesellschaft fuer Mess- und
  Automatisierungstechnik)
- Fernmeldetechnik; Fachzeitschrift fuer
  Fernschreib-Fernsprech-Fernwirk - und
  Funktechnik. bi-m. ISSN 0015-0126 (Kammer der
  Technik. Fachverband Elektrotechnik)
- Fertigungstechnik und Betrieb; Zeitschrift fuer
  Technik, Organisation und Oekonomie des
  Machinenbaus. m. ISSN 0015-024X (Kammer der
  Technik. Fachverband Maschinenbau)
- Hebezeuge und Foerdermittel; Zeitschrift fuer
  Konstruktion, Fertigung und Organisation auf den
  Gebieten der Foerdertechnik. m. ISSN 0017-9442
  (Kammer der Technik. Fachverband
  Maschinenbau)
- K F T. (Kraftfahrzeugtechnik); Technische
  Zeitschrift des Kraftfahrwesens. m. ISSN 0023-
  4419 (Kammer der Technik)
- Luft- und Kaeltetechnik; technisch-
  wissenschaftliche Zeitschrift fuer Forschung und
  Praxis. bi-m. ISSN 0024-7251

- Maschinenbautechnik; Wissenschaftlich-technische
  Zeitschrift fuer Forschung, Entwicklung und
  Konstruktion. m. ISSN 0025-4495 (Kammer der
  Technik. Fachverband Maschinenbau)
- Messen-Steuern-Regeln. m. ISSN 0026-0347
  (Kammer der Technik. Wissenschaftlich-
  Technische Gesellschaft fuer Mess- und
  Auomatisierungstechnik)
- Metallverarbeitung; Zeitschrift fuer alle Gebiete
  der Metallbe- und- verarbeitung. bi-m. ISSN
  0026-0908 (Kammer der Technik. Fachverband
  Maschinenbau)
- Monthly Technical Review; new technical
  developments of the gDR. m. ISSN 0027-061X
- Nachrichtentechnik-Elektronik; Technisch-
  wissenschaftliche Zeitschrift fuer die gesamte
  elektronische Nachrichtentechnik. m. (Kammer
  der Technik. Fachverband Elektrotechnik)
- Neue Technik im Buero; zeitschrift fuer
  informationsverarbeitung. bi-m.(3 nos.per yr. in
  Russian) ISSN 0028-3401
- Probleme der Festkoerperelektronik. a. ISSN
  0079-564X
- Radio Fernsehen Elektronik; Zeitschrift fuer
  Theorie und Praxis der Elektronik. fortn. ISSN
  0033-7900
- Schmierungstechnik. m. ISSN 0036-6226
  (Kammer der Technik. Praesidium. Kommission
  fuer Schmierungstechnik)
- Schweisstechnik; Zeitschrift fuer alle Gebiete der
  Schweiss-, Schneid-, Loet-, Kleb-, und
  Spritztechnik. m. ISSN 0036-7192 (Fachverband
  Machinenbau. Fachverband Maschinenbau)
- Seewirtschaft; Schiffbau, Schiffahrt,
  Hochseefischerei, Meerestechnik. m. ISSN 0037-
  0886 (Kammer der Technik)
- Die Technik; Technisch-wissenschaftliche
  Zeitschrift fuer Grundsatz- und
  Querschnittsfragen. m. ISSN 0040-1099
- Uhren und Schmuck; Fachzeitschrift fuer die
  Branchen Uhren und Schmuck. bi-m. ISSN 0041-
  5847 (Uhren und Maschinenkombinat Ruhla)
  (Co-sponsor: VEB Ostsee-Schmuck Ribnitz)

**Technische Hochschule Carl Schorlemmer Leuna-
Merseburg. Wissenschaftliche Zeitschrift.**
Geusaer Str., 42 Merseburg, E. Germany (D.D.R.)
- Technische Hochschule Carl Schorlemmer Leuna-
  Merseburg. Wissenschaftliche Zeitschrift. q. ISSN
  0043-6909 (Subscr. to: Deutsche Post, Str. der
  Pariser Kommune 3-4, 1004 Berlin, E. Germany,
  Str. der Pariser Kommune 3-4, 1004 Berlin)

**Technische Hochschule, Ilmenau**
Postfach 327, 63 Ilmenau, E. Germany (D.D.R.)
(Postschliessfach 327, Ilmenau, D.D.R.)
- Technische Hochschule Ilmenau.
  Wissenschaftliche Zeitschrift. 5 per yr. ISSN
  0043-6917

**Technische Hochschule Karl-Marx-Stadt. Bibliothek**
Postfach 964, 901 Karl-Marx-Stadt, E. Germany
(D.D.R.)
- Technische Hochschule Karl-Marx-Stadt.
  Wissenschaftliche Zeitschrift. a. ISSN 0040-1528

**Technische Hochschule Otto von Guericke**
Mozartstr. 1, 301 Magdeburg, E. Germany (D.D.R.)
- Technische Hochschule Otto von Guericke.
  Wissenschaftliche Zeitschrift. 8 per yr.

**Technische Universitaet Dresden**
Mommsenstr. 13, 8027 Dresden, E. Germany
(D.D.R.)
- Technische Universitaet Dresden.
  Wissenschaftliche Zeitschrift. bi-m. ISSN 0043-
  6925

**Teubner Verlagsgesellschaft**
Sternwartenstr. 8, 701 Leipzig, E. Germany
(D.D.R.)
- Archiv fuer Papyrusforschung und Verwandte
  Gebiete. irreg. ISSN 0066-6459 (Staatliche
  Museen zu Berlin)

**VEB Georg Thieme**
Hainstr. 17-19, 701 Leipzig, E. Germany.
- Biologisches Zentralblatt. bi-m. ISSN 0006-3304
- Folia Ophthalmologica. q. (Gesellschaft der
  Augenaertzte der DDR)
- H N O - Praxis. (Hals, Nase, Ohren); an
  international journal of cell biology, genetics,
  evolution and theoretical biology. q.
- Kinderaerztliche Praxis. m. ISSN 0023-1495
  (Gesellschaft fuer Pediatrie der DDR)

- Zeitschrift fuer die Gesamte Innere Medizin und
  ihre Grenzgebiete; Klinik, Pathologie, Experiment.
  s-m. ISSN 0044-2542 (Gesellschaft fuer Innere
  Medizin der DDR)
- Zeitschrift fuer Physiotherapie. bi-m. ISSN 0003-
  9357 (Gesellschaft fuer Physiotherapie der DDR)
- Zeitschrift fuer Urologie und Nephrologie. m.
  ISSN 0044-3611 (Gesellschaft fuer Urologie der
  DDR) (Co-sponsor: Gesselschaft fuer Nephrologie
  der DDR)

**Tierpark Berlin**
Am Tierpark 125, 1136 Berlin, E. Germany
(D.D.R.)
- Berliner Tierpark-Buch. irreg., no. 26, 1974. ISSN
  0067-6098
- Milu; Wissenschaftliche und Kulturelle
  Mitteilungen aus dem Tierpark Berlin. (pub. by
  Akademische Verlagsgesellschaft Geest und Portig
  K.G.)

**Transpress VEB Verlag fuer Verkehrswesen**
Franzoesische Str. 13/14, Postfach 1235, 108 Berlin,
E. Germany (D.D.R.)
- D D R-Verkehr; Zeitschrift fuer komplexe Fragen
  der Leitung und Plannung des Verkehrswesens. m.
  ISSN 0011-4820
- Der Deutsche Strassenverkehr; Zeitschrift fuer
  Verkehr und Wirtschaft. m. ISSN 0012-0804
- Eisenbahnpraxis. m. ISSN 0013-2780
- Fahrt Frei; Zeitung der Eisenbahner. fortn. ISSN
  0014-6846 (Germany, Democratic Republic.
  Ministerium fuer Verkehrswesen)
- Kraftverkehr; Zeitschrift fuer Theorie und Praxis
  des Kraftverkehrs, des Staedt. Verkehrs und der
  Instandehaltung. m. ISSN 0023-4443
- Modelleisenbahner; Zeitschrift fuer den
  Modelleisenbahnbau und alle Freunde der
  Eisenbahn. m. ISSN 0026-7422 (Deutscher
  Modelleisenbahn-Verband der DDR)
- Sammler Express; Fachzeitschrift fuer Philatelie
  und andere Sammelgebiete. s-m. ISSN 0036-3820
- Schienenfahrzeuge; Fachzeitschrift fuer den
  Einsatz, die Instandhaltung und den Bau von
  Schienenfahrzeugen. m. ISSN 0036-6021
- Signal und Schiene; Fachzeitschrift fuer den
  Eisenbahnbau sowie das Sicherungs- und
  Fernmeldewesen. m. ISSN 0037-5004
- Die Strasse; Zeitschrift fuer Forschung und Praxis
  des Strassenwesens. q. ISSN 0039-2146
- Verkehrsmedizin und ihre Grenzgebiete. m. ISSN
  0042-4021

**Verlag Tribune**
Am Treptower Park 28/30, 1193 Berlin, E.
Germany (D.D.R.)
- Die Arbeit; Zeitschrift fuer Theorie und Praxis der
  Gewerkschaften. m. ISSN 0003-7613
  (Bundesvorstand des FDGB)
- F D G B-Rundschau/F D G B-Review. m. ISSN
  0014-5769 (Confederation of Free German Trade
  Unions)
- Sozial Versicherung - Arbeitsschutz; Zeitschrift
  des FDGB fuer Fragen des Gesundheits-und
  Arbeitsschutzes und der Sozialversicherung. m.
  ISSN 0038-6200
- Die Weltgewerkschaftsbewegung. m. ISSN 0043-
  2601

**Uhren und Maschinenkombinat Ruhla**
- Uhren und Schmuck. (pub. by VEB Verlag
  Technik)

**VEB Kombinat Umformtechnik "Herbert Warnke"
Erfort. Forschungszentrum fuer Umformverfahren**
Scheringerstr. 1, 95 Zwickau, E. Germany (D.D.R.)
- Umformtechnik. bi-m. ISSN 0300-3167

**Union-Verlag**
Strasse der Befreiung 21, 806 Dresden, E. Germany
(D.D.R.)
- Evangelisch-Lutherische Landeskirche Sachsens.
  Amtsblatt. s-m. ISSN 0423-8346 (Evangelisch-
  Lutherisches Landeskirchenamt Sachsens)

**Universitaet Rostock**
Universitaetsplatz 1, 25 Rostock 1, E. Germany
(D.D.R.)
- Rostock Universitaet. Wissenschaftliche
  Zeitschrift. Mathematisch-Naturwissenschaftliche
  Reihe. 10 per yr.
- Rostock Universitaet, Wissenschaftliche
  Zeitschrift. Gesellschafts-und
  Sprachwissenschaftliche Reihe. 8 per yr. ISSN
  0043-6933.

**Universitaet Rostock. Instituto Latinoamericano**
Friedrich-Engels-Str. 104/107, Postfach 969,
701leipzig, E. Germany (D.D.R.)
• Lateinamerika. s-a.

**Universitaets- und Landesbibliothek Sachsen-Anhalt**
August-Bebelstr. 13/50, Halle, E. Germany
(D.D.R.)
• Universitaets- und Landesbibliothek Sachsen-
Anhalt. Arbeiten. irreg., vol. 17, 1975.

**Universitaetsbibliothek Berlin**
Clara-Zetkin-Str. 27, 108 Berlin, Deutsche
Demokratische Republik.
• Universitaetsbibliothek Berlin. Schriftenreihe.
irreg., no. 20, 1975.

**Urania-Verlag**
Salomonstr. 26, Postf. 969, DDR 701 Leipzig, E.
Germany.
• Urania; populaerwissenschaftliche Zeitschrift. m.
ISSN 0049-562X

**Verband Bildender Kuenstler der DDR**
Oranienburger Str. 67-68, 104 Berlin, E. Germany
(D.D.R.)
• Bildende Kunst. m. ISSN 0006-2391

**Verband der Journalisten der DDR**
Friedrichstr. 101, 108 Berlin, E. Germany (D.D.R.)
• Neue Deutsche Presse. s-m.

**Verband der Komponisten und Musikwissenschaftler der DDR**
• Musik und Gesellschaft. (pub. by Henschelverlag
Kunst und Gesellschaft)
• Musikwissenschaft. Beitraege. (pub. by Verlag
Neue Musik)

**Verband der Theaterschaffenden der DDR**
• Theater der Zeit. (pub. by Henschelverlag Kunst
und Gesellschaft)

**Vereinigung der Sprachmittler der DDR Beim VDJ**
• Fremdsprachen. (pub. by VEB Verlag
Enzyklopaedie)

**Visite**
Thalmannplatz 8-9, 103 Berlin, E.
Germany(D.D.R.)
• Visite. m. ISSN 0049-6529

**VEB Verlag Volk und Gesundheit**
Neue Gruenstr. 18, DDR 102 Berlin, E. Germany
(D. D. R.)
(Subscr. address: Buchexport, Leninstr. 16, DDR
701 Leipzig, E. Germany (D. D. R.))
• Anaesthesiologie und Reanimation; Zeitschrift fuer
Anesthesie, Intensivtherapie und dringliche
medizinische Hilfe. q. (Gesellschaft fuer
Anaesthesiologie und Reanimation der DDR)
• Beitraege zur Orthopaedie und Traumatologie. m.
ISSN 0005-8149 (Gesellschaft fuer Orthopaedie
der DDR)
• D D R-Medizin-Report. m. (Germany,
Democratic Republic. Ministerium fuer
Gesundheitswesen)
• Deine Gesundheit. m. ISSN 0415-1798
(Nationales Komitee fuer Gesundheitserziehung
der DDR)
• Das Deutsche Gesundheitswesen; Wochenschrift
fuer die gesamte Medizin. w. ISSN 0012-0219
(Gesellschaft fuer Klinische Medizin der DDR)
• Die Heilberufe; Zeitschrift fuer mittlere
medizinische Fachkraefte. m. ISSN 0017-9604
(Institut fuer Weiterbildung Mittlerer
Medizinischer Fachkraefte)
• Humanitas; Zeitung fuer Medizin und
Gesellschaft. fortn. ISSN 0018-7445
• Medizin und Sport. m. ISSN 0025-8415
(Gesellschaft fuer Sportmedizin der DDR)
• Die Pharmazie. m. ISSN 0031-7144
(Pharmazeutische Gesellschaft der DDR)
• Radiobiologia-Radiotherapia; Internationale
Zeitschrift fuer das Gebiet der Strahlentherapie,
Strahlenbiologie, Strahlenphysik und
Nuklearmedizin. 6 per yr. ISSN 0033-8184
• Radiologia Diagnostica; internationale Zeitschrift
fuer das Gebiet der Roentgendiagnostik und der
nuklearmedizinishcen Diagnostik. 6 per yr. ISSN
0033-8354
• Rheumatologie. Beitraege. irreg. ISSN 0067-5199
• Stomatologie der DDR. m. (Gesellschaft fuer
Stomatologie der DDR)
• Zahntechnik; Zeitschrift fuer Theorie und Praxis
der stomatologischen Technik. m. ISSN 0513-
7926 (Zahn Techniker-Meisterschule, Halle)

• Zeitschrift fuer die Gesamte Hygiene und ihre
Grenzgebiete. m. ISSN 0049-8610 (Gesellschaft
fuer die gesamte Hygiene)
• Zeitschrift fuer experimentelle Chirurgie. bi-m.
ISSN 0044-2704 (Gesellschaft fuer Chirurgie der
DDR. Sektion Experimentelle Chirurgie)
• Zeitschrift fuer medizinische
Laboratoriumsdiagnostik. bi-m.
• Zentralblatt fuer Pharmazie, Pharmakotherapie
und Laboratoriumsdiagnostik. m. ISSN 0049-8696

**Verlag Volk und Welt**
Glinkastr. 13, 108 Berlin, E. Germany (D.D.R.)
• Buecherkarren. 8 per yr.
• Kunst und Literatur; Zeitschrift fuer Fragen der
Aesthetik und Kunsttheorie. m. ISSN 0023-544X
(Gesellschaft fuer Deutsch-Sowjetische
Freundschaft. Zentralvorstand)
• Presse der Sowjetunion. w. ISSN 0032-7840
(Germany, Democratic Republic. Presseamt beim
Vorsitzenden des Ministerrates der DDR) (Co-
sponsor: Gesellschaft fuer Deutsch-Sowjetische
Freundschaft)
• Roman-Zeitung. m. ISSN 0035-7979
• Sowjetwissenschaft; gesellschaftswissenschaftliche
Beitraege. m. ISSN 0038-6006 (Gesellschaft fuer
Deutsch-Sowjetische Freundschaft.
Zentralvorstand)

**Verlag Volk und Wissen**
Lindenstr. 54a, 108 Berlin, E. Germany (D.D.R.)
• Alpha-Mathematische Schuelerzeitschrift. bi-m.
ISSN 0002-6395
• Astronomie in der Schule. bi-m. ISSN 0004-6310
(Germany, Democratic Republic. Ministerium
fuer Volksbildung)
• Berufsbildung; Zeitschrift fuer Theorie und Praxis
der beruflichen Bildung und Erziehung. m. ISSN
0005-9536
• Chemie in der Schule. m. ISSN 0009-2843
• Deutsche Lehrerzeitung. w. ISSN 0012-0421
(Germany, Democratic Republic. Ministerium
fuer Volksbildung)
• Deutschunterricht. m. ISSN 0012-1460
• Elternhaus und Schule; Ratgeber fuer Eltern. q.
ISSN 0036-6951
• Erziehungs- und Schulgeschichte Jahrbuch. a.
ISSN 0075-2622 (Akademie der Paedagogischen
Wissenschaften der DDR)
• Fremdsprachenunterricht/Around the World/A
Travers le Monde/Po Svetu. m.
• Geschichtsunterricht und Staatsburgerkunde. m.
ISSN 0016-9072
• Jugendhilfe. m. ISSN 0022-5940
• Kunsterziehung. m. ISSN 0451-0887 (Germany,
Democratic Republic. Ministerium fuer
Volksbildung)
• Mathematik in der Schule. 10 per yr. ISSN 0465-
3750
• Monumenta Paedagogica. irreg., 1965, vol. 2.
ISSN 0077-1481 (Akademie der Wissenschaften
der DDR)
• Musik in der Schule; Zeitschrift fuer Theorie und
Praxis des Musikunterrichts. m. ISSN 0027-4704
• Neue Erziehung im Kindergarten. m.
• Paedagogik. Ausgabe A. q. (Deutsches
Paedagogisches Zentralinstitut, Berlin)
• Physik in der Schule. m. ISSN 0031-9244
• Polytechnische Bildung und Erziehung. m. ISSN
0032-4116
• Sonderschule. bi-m. ISSN 0038-1357
• Unterstufe. m. ISSN 0042-0638
• Vergleichende Paedagogik/Comparative
Education. q. ISSN 0042-3920 (Akademie der
Paedagogischen Wissenschaften der DDR)
• Zeitschrift fuer den Erdkundeunterricht. m. ISSN
0044-2461

**Wartburg Verlag Max Kessler**
Inselplatz 11, Jena, E. Germany (D.D.R.)
• Evangelische-Lutherische Kirche in Thueringen.
Amtsblatt. 2 per m. ISSN 0014-326X
(Landeskirchenrat der Evangelische-Lutherische
Kirche in Thueringen)

**Verlag die Weltbuehne**
Karl-Liebknechstr. 29, 1056 Berlin, E. Germany
(D.D.R.)
• Die Weltbuehne; Wochenschrift fuer Politik -
Kunst - Wirtschaft. w. ISSN 0043-2598

**Weltgewerkschaftsbund**
Am Treptower Park 28-30, 1193 Berlin, E.
Germany (D.D.R.)
• Gewerkschafts Presse. s-m. ISSN 0016-9463

**Verlag Werbekreis Werbe und Anzeigen KG**
Am Friedrichshain 22, 705 Waiblingen, E. Germany
(D.D.R.)
• Waiblinger Anzeigenblatt. w. ISSN 0043-0005

**Verlag die Wirtschaft**
Am Friedrichshain 22, 1055 Berlin, E. Germany
(D.D.R.)
• Arbeit und Arbeitsrecht; Zeitschrift fuer
sozialistische Arbeit und Arbeitsrecht. s-m.
• Gastronomie; Fachzeitschrift fuer Gaststaetten,
Hotels und Gemeinschaftsverpflegung. 6 per yr.
• Der Handel; Zeitschrift fuer Theorie und Praxis
des Binnenhandels in der Deutschen
Demokratischen Republik. m. ISSN 0017-7229
• Handelswoche. fortn. ISSN 0017-7350
• Informatik; Theorie und Praxis der
wissenschaftlichtechnischen Information. 6 per yr.
ISSN 0019-9915 (Zentralinstitut fuer Information
und Dokumentation)
• Kommunale Dienstleistungen. 6 per yr. ISSN
0454-255X (Institut fuer Kommunalwirtschaft)
• Kultur im Heim. 6 per yr.
• Neue Werbung; Fachzeitschrift fuer Theorie und
Praxis der Sozialistischen Werbung. 6.yr. ISSN
0028-3452
• Der Neuerer; Zeitschrift fuer Erfindungs- und
Vorschlagswesen. m. ISSN 0028-3584 (Germany,
Democratic Republic. Amt fuer Erfindungs- und
Patentwesen)
• Das Neue Handwerk; Organ der
Handwerkskammern der Bezirke der DDR. bi-m.
ISSN 0028-3193
• Rechentechnik-Datenverarbeitung. m. (plus
quarterly supplement) ISSN 0300-3450
• Rechentechnik-Datenverarbeitung. Beiheft. q.
• Sozialistische Arbeitswissenschaft; theoretische
Zeitschrift fuer arbeitswissenschaftliche
Disziplinen. 8 per yr. ISSN 0038-6111 (Germany,
Democratic Republic. Staatssekretariat fuer Arbeit
und Loehne. Zentrales Forschunginstitut fuer
Arbeit)
• Sozialistische Finanzwirtschaft; Zeitschrift fuer das
Finanz- und Kreditwesen der DDR. m. ISSN
0012-0103
• Der Stenopraktiker; Zeitschrift der Gesellschaft
fuer Stenografie und Maschinenschreiben. m.
ISSN 0039-1174 (Gesellschaft fuer Stenografie
und Maschinenschreiben der DDR)
• Warenzeichen- und Musterblatt. m. (Germany,
Democratic Republic. Amt fuer Erfindungs- und
Patentwesen)
• Die Wirtschaft: Ausgabe A; Zeitung fuer Politik,
Wirtschaft und Technik. 26 per yr. ISSN 0043-
6119
• Die Wirtschaft: Ausgabe B; Zeitung fuer Politik,
Wirtschaft und Technik. 26 per yr. ISSN 0043-
6127
• Wirtschaftswissenschaft. m. ISSN 0043-633X

**VEB Deutscher Verlag der Wissenschaften**
Johannes-Dieckmann-Str. 10, Postfach 1216, 108
Berlin, E. Germany (D.D.R.)
• Archaeologie. Zeitschrift. s-a. ISSN 0044-233X
(Akademie der Wissenschaften der DDR.
Zentralinstitut fuer Alte Geschichte und
Archaelogie)
• Asien - Afrika - Lateinamerika. Jahrbuch. a.
(Zentraler Rat fuer Asien-, Afrika- und
Lateinamerikawissenschaften in der DDR)
• Bodenkmalpflege in Mecklenburg. a. ISSN
0067-9461 (Museum fuer Ur- und
Fruehgeschichte, Schwerin)
• Deutsche Aussenpolitik. m. ISSN 0011-9881
(Institut fuer Internationale Beziehungen der
DDR)
• Deutsche Zeitschrift fuer Philosophie. m. ISSN
0012-1045
• E A Z. (Ethnographisch-Archaeologische
Zeitschrift) q. ISSN 0012-7477 (Subscr. to:
Buchexport, Volkseigener Aussenhandelsbetrieb
der D.D.R., Leninstr. 16, 701 Leipzig, D.D.R.)
• Experimentelle Technik der Physik. bi-m. ISSN
0014-4924
• Fachschule; Zeitschrift fuer das Fachschulwesen
der DDR. m. ISSN 0014-6390 (Germany,
Democratic Republic. Ministerium fuer Hoch-
und Fachschulwesen)
• Geschichte der Sozialistischen Laender Europas.
Jahrbuch. s-a. ISSN 0075-2665 (Akademie der
Wissenschaften der DDR. Zentralinstitut fuer
Geschichte)
• Geschichtswissenschaft. Zeitschrift. m. ISSN
0044-2828
• Hochschulbuecher fuer Mathematik. irreg. ISSN
0073-2842
• Hochschulbuecher fuer Physik. irreg. ISSN 0073-
2850

- Hochschulwesen; wissenschaftspolitische Rundschau. m. ISSN 0018-2974 (Germany, Democratic Republic. Ministerium fuer Hoch- und Fachschulwesen)
- Kriminalistik und Forensische Wissenschaften. q. ISSN 0023-4702 (Subscr. to: Buchexport, Volkseigener Aussenhandelsbetrieb der D.D.R., Leninstr. 16, 701 Leipzig, D.D.R.)
- Landesmuseum fuer Vorgeschichte, Dresden. Veroeffentlichungen. irreg. ISSN 0070-7201
- Landesmuseum fuer Vorgeschichte, Halle. Veroeffentlichungen. irreg. ISSN 0072-940X (Landesmuseum fuer Vorgeschichte, Halle)
- Mathematische Logik und Grundlagen der Mathematik. Zeitschrift. bi-m. ISSN 0044-3050 (Humboldt-Universitaet zu Berlin. Institut fuer Mathematische Logik)
- Mathematische Schuelerbuecherei. irreg. ISSN 0076-5449
- Mitteldeutsche Vorgeschichte. Jahresschrift. a. ISSN 0075-2932
- Museum fuer Ur- und Fruehgeschichte des Bezirkes Potsdam, Frankfurt/Oder und Cottbus. Veroeffentlichungen. a. ISSN 0079-4376 (Museum fuer Ur- und Fruehgeschichte, Potsdam)
- Neue Museumskunde; Theorie und Praxis der Museumsarbeit. q. ISSN 0028-3282 (Germany, Democratic Republic. Ministerium fuer Kultur. Rat fuer Museumswesen)
- Physikalisch-Chemische Trenn- und Messmethoden. irreg. ISSN 0079-1997
- Probleme und Ergebnisse der Psychologie. q. ISSN 0048-5403 (Gesellschaft fuer Psychologie der DDR)
- Staatlicher Mathematisch-Physikalischer Salon, Dresden. Veroeffentlichungen. irreg. ISSN 0081-4113
- Studienbuecherei. irreg. ISSN 0081-7384
- Taschenbuchreihe Geschichte. irreg. ISSN 0082-1950

**Wissenschaftliche Gesellschaft fuer Veterinaermedizin der DDR**
- Monatshefte fuer die Veterinaermedizin. (pub. by VEB Gustav Fischer Verlag)

**Women's International Democratic Federation**
Unter den Linden 13, 108 Berlin, D.D.R.
- Frauen der Ganzen Welt. (pub. by Verlag Fuer die Frau)
- Women of the Whole World. q. ISSN 0043-7476 (U. S. and Canadian Subscr. to: Congress of Canadian Women, Box 188, Station e, Toronto, Ontario, Canada)

**Zahn Techniker-Meisterschule, Halle**
- Zahntechnik. (pub. by VEB Verlag Volk und Gesundheit)

**VEB Carl Zeiss**
Carl-Zeiss-Str. 1, Jena, E. Germany (D.D.R.)
- Jenaer Rundschau/Jena Review. bi-m. ISSN 0021-5864

**Verlag Zeit im Bild**
Julian T--Grimau--Allee, 8010 Dresden, E. Germany (D.D.R.)
- Documents on the Policy of the German Democratic Repubic. irreg.
- G D R Review/D D R-Revue. m. ISSN 0016-349X (Subscr. In. U.S.A. to: Universal Distributors Comp., 52-54 W 13th Str., New York, N.Y. 10011)

**Zentraler Rat fuer Asien-, Afrika- und Lateinamerikawissenschaften in der DDR**
- Asien - Afrika - Lateinamerika. Jahrbuch. (pub. by VEB Deutscher Verlag der Wissenschaften)
- Studien ueber Asien, Afrika und Lateinamerika. (pub. by Akademie-Verlag)

**Zentrales Geologisches Institut**
- Zeitschrift fuer Angewandte Geologie. (pub. by Akademie-Verlag)
- Zentrales Geologisches Institut. Palaeontologische Abhandlungen. (pub. by Akademie-Verlag)

**Zentralhaus fuer Kulturarbeit**
Dittrichring 4, Postfach 1051, 701 Leipzig, E. Germany (D.D.R.)
- Ich Schreibe; Zeitschrift fuer schreibende Arbeiter. m. ISSN 0445-1821
- Kultur und Freizeit. m.
- Musikforum. bi-m.
- Szene; Zeitschrift fuer das Laientheater und das Laienkabarett. m. ISSN 0039-811X

**Zentralinstitut fuer Bibliothekswesen**
- Der Bibliothekar. (pub. by VEB Bibliographisches Institut)

**Zentralinstitut fuer Bibliothekswesen. Zentralstelle fuer die Information und Dokumentation Bibliothekswesen**
Hermann-Matern-Str. 57, 104 Berlin, E. Germany (D.D.R.)
- Zentralinstitut fuer Bibliothekswesen. Mitteilungen und Materialien. bi-m. ISSN 0433-6933

**Zentralinstitut fuer Holztechnologie Dresden**
- Holztechnologie. (pub. by VEB Fachbuchverlag)

**Zentralinstitut fuer Information und Dokumentation**
Unter den Linden 8, 108 Berlin, E. Germany.
- Informatik. (pub. by Verlag die Wirtschaft)
- Informationsdienst Information/Dokumentation; annotierte titelliste. m. ISSN 0036-6242

**Zentralinstitut fuer Musikforschung**
- Musikwissenschaftliche Arbeiten in der DDR. Bericht. (pub. by Verlag Neue Musik)

**Zentralinstitut fuer Schweisstechnik der DDR**
Koethener Str. 33a, 403 Halle/Saale, E. Germany (D.D.R.)
- Z I S Mitteilungen. m. ISSN 0044-1465

**Zentralrat der Freien Deutschen Jugend**
- Forum. (pub. by Verlag Junge Welt)
- Jugend & Technik. (pub. by Verlag Junge Welt)
- Junge Generation. (pub. by Verlag Junge Welt)

**Zentralstelle fuer die Philosophische Information und Dokumentation**
J.-Dieckmann-Str. 19-23, 108 Berlin, E. Germany (D.D.R.)
- Aktuelle Probleme der Buergerlichen Philosophie. 3 per yr. ISSN 0002-3833
- Bibliographie Philosophie mit Autoren und Sach Register. q. ISSN 0034-2262
- Information ueber Aktuelle Probleme der Marxistisch-Leninistischen Philosophie in der U.D.S.S.R. bi-m. ISSN 0020-0301
- Informationen aus dem Philosophischen Leben in der DDR. 6 per yr. ISSN 0020-0328
- Philosophische Probleme der Naturwissenschaften. 3 per yr. ISSN 0031-8132
- Philosophische Probleme der Sozialistischen Bewusstseinsbildung und der Moral. 3 per yr. ISSN 0031-8124
- Philosophische Probleme des Sozialistischen Aufbaus und der Wissenschaftlich-Technischen Revolution. 3 per yr. ISSN 0031-8140

**Zentralstelle fuer Korrosionsschutz**
Karl-Marx-Str., Haus 228 Postfach 38, 808 Dresden, E. Germany (D.D.R.)
- Korrosion. bi-m. ISSN 0023-4133 (Subscr. to: Zeitungsvertriebsamt Berlin, Str. der Pariser Kommune 3-4, 1004 Berlin, E. Germany, Str. D. Pariser Komm. 3-4, DDR- 1004 Berlin)

**Zentralstelle fuer Soziologische Information und Dokumentation Am Institut fuer Gesellschaftswissenschaftenbeim ZK der SED**
Johannes-Dieckmann-Str. 19-23, 108 Berlin, E. Germany (D.D.R.)
- Soziologische Forschung in der DDR. Informationen. 6 per yr. ISSN 0020-0395

# GERMANY, WEST

**A B C der Deutschen Wirtschaft**
Berliner Allee 8, 6100 Darmstadt, W. Germany (B.R.D.)
- A B C der Deutschen Wirtschaft; Quellenwerk fuer Einkauf-Verkauf. a.

**A E G-Telefunken**
- A E G-Telefunken. Technische Mitteilungen. (pub. by Elitera-Verlag GmbH)
- A E G-Telefunken. Wissenschaftliche Berichte. (pub. by Elitera-Verlag GmbH)
- A E G - Telefunken al Dia. (pub. by Elitera-Verlag GmbH)
- A E G - Telefunken Progress. (pub. by Elitera-Verlag GmbH)
- Datenverarbeitung A E G-Telefunken. (pub. by Elitera-Verlag GmbH)
- Rassegna Tecnica A E G-Telefunken. (pub. by Elitera-Verlag GmbH)

**A F Z -Fischwaid Verlagsgesellschaft mbH**
Bahnhofstr. 37, 6050 Offenbach/Main, W. Germany (B.R.D.)
- Fischwirt; Zeitschrift fuer die Binnenfischerei. m.

**A.-G.-T.-Verlag Georg Thum**
Teinacher Str. 34, Postfach 109, 7140 Ludwigsburg, W. Germany (B.R.D.)
- A.G.T. Dokumentation; Antriebs. 2 per yr.
- Deutsche Hebe- und Foerdertechnik; German material handling magazine. m. ISSN 0012-0278
- H O B-Die Holzbearbeitung. 10 per yr. ISSN 0018-3822
- M F M-Moderne Fototechnik. m. ISSN 0024-8142 (Deutsches Institut fuer Normung e.V.. Fachnormenausschuss Photo Technik)
- Die Maschine; Antriebs-und Getriebetechnik, Pneumatik-und Hydraulik-Praxis, Zeitschrift fuer Fertigungstechnik und Konstruktion. m. ISSN 0025-4444

**A Q Verlag**
Beim Weisenstein 6, 6602 Saarbruecken-Dudweiler, W. Germany (B.R.D.)
- A Q. irreg.

**A T-Fachverlag GmbH**
Koenig-Karl-Str. 19, Postfach 500180, 7000 Stuttgart 50, W. Germany (B.R.D.)
- Der Elektroniker; mit Opto-Elektronik und Fachteil fuer technisches English. m. ISSN 0531-9218
- Laser und Elektro-Optik; erste deutschsprachige Fachzeitschrift fuer Laser, Elektro-Optik und Strahlentechnik. q.
- S I Information; sanitaer, heizung, klima. 9 per yr.

**A und O Handelsgesellschaft mbH und Co. KG**
- Der A und O Weg. (pub. by Curt Hafner Verlag)

**A v D Verlag GmbH**
Lyoner Str. 16, Postfach 710166, 6000 Frankfurt 71, W. Germany (B.R.D.)
- Motor Reise Revue. m. ISSN 0027-1950 (Automobilclub von Deutschland e.V.)
- Reisen mit dem Auto Durch Europa. s-a. (Automobilclub von Deutschland e.V.)

**Aachener Geschichtsverein**
Fischmarkt 3, 5100 Aachen, W. Germany (B.R.D.)
- Aachener Geschichtsverein. Zeitschrift. a. ISSN 0065-0137

**Abt-Herwegen-Institut fuer Liturgische und Monastische Forschung**
- Archiv fuer Liturgiewissenschaft. (pub. by Verlag Friedrich Pustet)

**Academie Internationale d'Histoire des Sciences**
- Academie Internationale d'Histoire des Sciences. Collection des Travaux. (pub. by Franz Steiner Verlag GmbH)

**Achalm-Verlag**
Burgstr. 1, Postfach 35, 7410reutlingen, W. Germany (B.R.D.)
- Der Fussballtrainer. m. ISSN 0016-3228

**ADAC Verlag GmbH**
Baumgartnerstr. 53, 8000 Munich 70, West Germany (B.R.D.)
- ADAC-Campingfuehrer. Band 1: Suedeuropa. a.
- ADAC-Campingfuehrer. Band 2: Deutschland, Mittel- und Nordeuropa. a.
- ADAC Motorwelt. m. ISSN 0007-2842 (Allgemeiner Deutscher Automobil-Club e.V.)
- ADAC-Schriftenreihe. irreg. ISSN 0065-6380 (Allgemeiner Deutscher Automobil-Club e.V.)
- ADAC-Schriftenreihe. Jugendverkehrserziehung. irreg. (Allgemeiner Deutscher Automobil-Club e.V.)
- ADAC-Schriftenreihe Strassenverkehr. irreg. (Allgemeiner Deutscher Automobil-Club e.V.)
- Alpenpaesse und Alpenstrassen; aDAC-Reisefuehrer. irreg. (Allgemeiner Deutscher Automobil-Club e.V.)
- D A R. (Deutsches Autorecht) m. ISSN 0012-1231 (Allgemeiner Deutscher Automobil-Club e.V.)
- Hotelfuehrer Deutschland. irreg. (Allgemeiner Deutscher Automobil-Club e.V.) (Co-sponsor: Oesterreichischer Automobil-, Motorrad- und Touring-Club)
- Strand Europa. irreg.
- Was kostet mein Auto? a.

**Adressbuch-Gesellschaft Berlin mgH**
Friedrichstr. 210, 1000 Berlin 61, W. Germany
(B.R.D.)
• Berliner Handelsregister Verzeichnis. a. ISSN
0067-6063

**Deutscher Adressbuch-Verlag**
Holzhofallee 38, Postfach 320, 6100 Darmstadt, W.
Germany (B.R.D.)
• Das Deutsche Firmen-Alphabet; Industrie,
Handel, Verkehr, organisationen. a. ISSN 0418-
8381
• Einkaufs 1x1 der Deutschen Industrie. a.

**Aegis-Verlag**
Breite Gasse 2, 7900 Ulm, W. Germany (B.R.D.)
• Deutsche Seiler-Zeitung. m. ISSN 0012-0758
(Bundesverband des Deutschen Seiler-, Segel-und
Netzmacherhandwerks e.V.) (Co-Sponsor:
Bundesverband Verschnuerungs- und
Verpackungsmittel e. V. Sitz Frankfurt)

**Deutscher Aerzte-Verlag GmbH**
Dieselstr. 2, Postfach 1440, 5023 Loevenich.
• Die Berliner Aerztekammer. m. ISSN 0568-0743
(Aerztekammer Berlin)
• Bonner Aerztliche Nachrichten. m.
• Deutsches Aerzteblatt; aerztliche Mitteilungen. w.
ISSN 0012-1207 (Bundesaerztekammer)
• Medizin Heute; das Gesundheitsmagazin. m.
• Rheinisches Aerzteblatt. s-m. ISSN 0035-4481
(Aerztekammer Nordrhein)
• Zahnaerztliche Mitteilungen. s-m. ISSN 0044-
1643 (Bundesverband der Deutschen Zahnaerzte
e.V.)

**Aerztekammer Berlin**
• Die Berliner Aerztekammer. (pub. by Deutscher
Aerzte-Verlag GmbH)

**Aerztekammer Bremen**
• Bremer Aerzteblatt. (pub. by Carl Schuenemann
Verlag)

**Aerztekammer Niedersachsen**
• Niedersaechsisches Aerzteblatt. (pub. by
Schluetersche Verlagsanstalt und Druckerei)

**Aerztekammer Nordrhein**
• Rheinisches Aerzteblatt. (pub. by Deutscher
Aerzte-Verlag GmbH)

**Aesthetik und Kommunikation Verlags-GmbH**
Bogotastr. 27, 1000 Berlin 37, W. Germany
(B.R.D.)
• Aesthetik und Kommunikation; Beitraege zur
politischen Erziehung. q. ISSN 0341-7212
(Institut fuer Kunst und Aesthetik)

**Afrika-Verlag**
Tuerltorstr. 14, Postfach 86, 8068 Pfaffenhofen, W.
Germany (B.R.D.)
• Afrika; review of German-African relations. m.
ISSN 0340-5796
• Afrika Spectrum; deutsche Zeitschrift fuer
moderne Afrikaforschung. 3 per yr. ISSN 0002-
0397 (Institut fuer Afrika-Kunde)
• Hamburger Beitraege zur Afrika-Kunde. irreg.
(Deutsches Institut fuer Afrika-Forschung)

**Agis Verlag GmbH**
Eberbachstr 7, Postfach 7, 7570 Baden-Baden 19,
W. Germany (B.R.D.)
• Gesundheit in Betrieb und Familie. bi-m. ISSN
0016-9269

**Agrarsoziale Gesellschaft e.V.**
Kurze Geismarstr. 23/25, 3400 Goettingen, W.
Germany (B.R.D.)
• Agrarsoziale Gesellschaft. Geschaefts- und
Arbeitsbericht. a. ISSN 0065-437X
• Agrarsoziale Gesellschaft. Rundbriefe. m. ISSN
0065-4388
• Schriftenreihe fuer Laendliche Sozialfragen. irreg.,
no. 76, 1975. ISSN 0080-7133

**Akademie der Wissenschaften, Goettingen**
• Akademie der Wissenschaften, Goettingen.
Jahrbuch. (pub. by Vandenhoeck und Ruprecht)
• Akademie der Wissenschaften, Goettingen.
Nachrichten 1. Philologisch-Historische Klasse.
(pub. by Vandenhoeck und Ruprecht)
• Akademie der Wissenschaften, Goettingen.
Nachrichten 2. Mathematisch-Physikalische
Klasse. (pub. by Vandenhoeck und Ruprecht)
• Goettingische Gelehrte Anzeigen. (pub. by
Vandenhoeck und Ruprecht)

**Akademie der Wissenschaften und der Literatur,
Mainz**
Geschwister-Scholl-Str. 2, 6500 Mainz, W. Germany
(B.R.D.)
• Akademie der Wissenschaften und der Literatur.
Geistes- und Sozialwissenschaftliche Klasse.
Abhandlungen. (pub. by Franz Steiner Verlag
GmbH)
• Akademie der Wissenschaften und der Literatur,
Mainz. Jahrbuch. (pub. by Franz Steiner Verlag
GmbH)
• Akademie der Wissenschaften und der Literatur,
Mainz. Klasse der Literatur. Abhandlungen. (pub.
by Franz Steiner Verlag GmbH)
• Altern und Entwicklung/Aging and Development.
(pub. by F. K. Schattauer Verlag)
• Mainzer Reihe. irreg. ISSN 0076-2784
• Musikalische Denkmaeler. irreg. ISSN 0077-2526
• Untersuchungen zur Sprach- und
Literaturgeschichte der Romanischen Voelker.
(pub. by Franz Steiner Verlag GmbH)

**Akademie der Wissenschaften und der Literatur,
Mainz. Kommission fuer Geschichte des Altertums**
• Forschungen zur Antiken Sklaverei. (pub. by
Franz Steiner Verlag GmbH)

**Akademie der Wissenschaften und der Literatur,
Mainz. Kommission fuer Geschichte der Medizin
und der Naturwissenschaften**
• Medizinhistorisches Journal. (pub. by Georg Olms
Verlag GmbH)

**Akademie der Wissenschaften und der Literatur,
Mainz. Mathematisch-Naturwissenschaftliche
Klasse**
• Akademie der Wissenschaften und der Literatur,
Mainz. Mathematisch-Naturwissenschaftliche
Klasse. Abhandlungen. (pub. by Franz Steiner
Verlag GmbH)
• Informationsaufnahme und
Informationsverarbeitung im Lebenden
Organismus. (pub. by Franz Steiner Verlag
GmbH)
• Karl-August-Forster-Lectures. (pub. by Franz
Steiner Verlag GmbH)
• Mikrofauna des Meeresbodens. (pub. by Franz
Steiner Verlag GmbH)
• Research in Molecular Biology. (pub. by Franz
Steiner Verlag GmbH)
• Tropische und Subtropische Pflanzenwelt. (pub. by
Franz Steiner Verlag GmbH)

**Akademie fuer Fuehrungskraefte der Wirtschaft**
• Akademie fuer Fuehrungskraefte der Wirtschaft.
Taschenbuecher zur Betriebspraxis. (pub. by
Verlag fuer Wissenschaft, Wirtschaft und Technik
GmbH und Co.)

**Akademie fuer Oeffentliches Gesundheitswesen**
Auf'm Hennekamp 70, 4000 Duesseldorf 1, W.
Germany (B.R.D.)
• Akademie fuer Oeffentliches Gesundheitswesen.
Schriftenreihe. irreg.

**Akademische Verlagsgesellschaft**
Bahnhofstr. 39, Postfach 1107, 6200 Wiesbaden, W.
Germany (B.R.D.)
• Archiv fuer Psychologie. q. ISSN 0066-6475
(Deutsche Gesellschaft fuer Psychologie)
• Radiochimica Acta. 8 per yr. ISSN 0033-8230
(U.S. subscr. to: Academic Press, 111 Fifth Ave.,
New York, N.Y. 10003)
• Systematische Politikwissenschaft. irreg.
• Zeitschrift fuer Kristallographie/Journal of
Cristallography; Kristallgeometrie, Kristallphysik,
Kristallchemie. 2 vols per year(6 nos. per vol.)
ISSN 0044-2968
• Zeitschrift fuer Physikalische Chemie/Journal of
Physical Chemistry. 5 vols per year. ISSN 0044-
3336

**Aktuell Verlagsgesellschaft mbH**
Hermann Str. 12, Postfach 1110, 5100 Aachen, W.
Germany (B.R.D.)
• Mission Aktuell. bi-m. (Internationales
Katholisches Missionswerk e.V.)

**Karl Alber GmbH**
Hermann- Herder- Str. 4, 7800 Freiburg, W.
Germany (B. R. D.)
• Dacoromania; Jahrbuch fuer oestliche Latinitaet.
a.
• Grenzfragen. irreg., vol. 4, 1974. (Goerres-
Gesellschaft)
• Historisches Jahrbuch. s-a. ISSN 0018-2621
(Goerres-Gesellschaft)

• Phaenomenologische Forschungen/
Phenomenological Studies. s-a. (Deutsche
Gesellschaft fuer Phaenomenologische Forschung)
• Philosophisches Jahrbuch. a. ISSN 0031-8183
(Goerres-Gesellschaft)
• Saeculum; Jahrbuch fuer Universalgeschichte. a.
ISSN 0080-5319
• Zeitschrift fuer Klinische Psychologie und
Psychotherapie. q. ISSN 0300-869X (Goerres-
Gesellschaft)

**Albrecht-Altdorfer-Gymnasium, Regensburg**
Minoritenweg 33, 8400 Regensburg, W. Germany
(B.R.D.)
• Extemporale. q. ISSN 0014-5386

**E. Albrecht-Verlags-KG**
Freihamer Str. 2, 8032 Graefelfing, W. Germany
(B.R.D.)
• Magazin der Hausfrau. w.
• Rundschau fuer den Deutschen Einzelhaendler. m.
ISSN 0035-9904
• Schuh-Service-Magazin. m.

**Alcan Aluminiumwerke GmbH**
Nopitschstr. 67, 8500 Nuernberg 1, W. Germany
(B.R.D.)
• Alcan Informiert. bi-m.

**Alektor-Verlag**
Kniebisstr. 29, 7000 Stuttgart 1, W. Germany
(B.R.D.)
• E S G - Nachrichten. 7-9 per yr. ISSN 0012-7981
(Evangelische Studentengemeinde in der
Bundesrepublik Deutschland und Berlin (West))

**Alexander von Humboldt-Stiftung**
Schillerstr. 12, 5300 Bonn-Bad Godesberg, W.
Germany (B.R.D.)
• Alexander von Humboldt-Stiftung. Mitteilungen.
s-a.
• Alexander von Humbolt-Stiftung. Jahresbericht. a.
ISSN 0065-6178

**Allgemeine Aerztliche Gesellschaft fuer
Psychotherapie**
• Psychotherapie und Medizinische Psychologie.
(pub. by Georg Thieme Verlag)

**Allgemeine Gesellschaft fuer Philosophie in
Deutschland e.V.**
• Allgemeine Zeitschrift fuer Philosophie. (pub. by
Friedrich Fromman Verlag Guenther Holzboog
KG)

**Allgemeine Ortskrankenkasse**
Mehringplatz 15, 1000 Berlin 61, W. Germany
(B.R..D)
(Subscr. Address: Zillestr. 10, 1 Berlin 10, W.
Germany (B.R.D.))
• A O K-Gesundheitsblatt. q. ISSN 0514-9886

**Allgemeine Waermetechnik**
Postfach 191, 6230 Hoechst, W. Germany (B.R.D.)
• Allgemeine Waermetechnik; Zeitschrift fuer
Waerme-Kaelte und Verfahrenstechnik. m. ISSN
0002-5976

**Allgemeiner Caecilien-Verband**
Koelnstr. 415, 5300 Bonn, W. Germany (B.R.D.)
• Kirchenmusikalisches Jahrbuch. a. ISSN 0075-
6199

**Allgemeiner Deutscher Automobil-Club e.V.**
• ADAC Motorwelt. (pub. by ADAC Verlag
GmbH)
• ADAC-Schriftenreihe. (pub. by ADAC Verlag
GmbH)
• ADAC-Schriftenreihe. Jugendverkehrserziehung.
(pub. by ADAC Verlag GmbH)
• ADAC-Schriftenreihe Strassenverkehr. (pub. by
ADAC Verlag GmbH)
• Alpenpaesse und Alpenstrassen. (pub. by ADAC
Verlag GmbH)
• D A R. (pub. by ADAC-Verlag GmbH)
• Hotelfuehrer Deutschland. (pub. by ADAC Verlag
GmbH)

**Allgemeiner Deutscher Tanzlehrer Verband**
Oberheidter Str. 34 B, 5600wuppertal 12, W.
Germany (B.R.D.)
• A D T V - Nachrichten. a. ISSN 0001-0979

**Allianz Versicherungs-AG**
Koeniginstr. 28, Postfach 24, 8000 Munich 44, W.
Germany (B.R.D.)
• Allianz Zeitung; Zeitschrift fuer den Aussen- und
Innendienst der Allianz-Gesellschaften. m.

- Der Maschinenschaden; Schadenforschung und Schadenverhuetung bei technischen Anlagen. bi-m. ISSN 0025-4517

**Almanach-Verlags-Gesellschaft**
Wilhelm-Leuschner-Str. 6, Postfach 4134, 6100 Darmstadt, W. Germany (B.R.D.)
- Polizeimagazin; Motor, Sport, Information. bi-m. ISSN 0032-3543

**Almwirtschaftlicher Verein Oberbayern**
- Der Almbauer. (pub. by B L V Verlagsgesellschaft mbH)

**Alpeninstitut fuer Umweltforschung und Entwicklungsplanung in der GFL**
- Alpeninstitut. Schriftenreihe. (pub. by Geographische Buchhandlung R. Michels)

**Alternative Verlag GmbH**
Postfach 150230, 1000 Berlin 15, W. Germany (B.R.D.)
- Alternative; zeitschrift fuer Literatur/Theorie. bi-m. ISSN 0002-6611

**Altherrenverband der Saengerschaft Franco-Palatia Bayreuth**
Richthofenhoehe 50, 8580 Bayreuth, W. Germany (B.R.D.)
- Bundesbruder Saengerschaft Franco-Palatia Bayreuth. 5 per yr.

**Aluminium-Verlag GmbH**
Koenigsallee 30, Postfach 1207, 4000 Duesseldorf, W. Germany (B.R.D.)
- Aluminium. m. ISSN 0002-6689 (Aluminium-Zentrale e.V.)
- Bauen mit Aluminium. a. (Aluminium-Zentrale e.V.)
- World Aluminum Abstracts; surveys current literature on the production, fabrication and uses of aluminium and its alloys and on related scientific and technical subjects. m. ISSN 0002-6697 (European Primary Aluminum Association) (Co-Sponsors: Aluminum Assn.: Japan Light Metal Assn.: Aluminum Development Council)

**Aluminium-Zentrale e.V.**
- Aluminium. (pub. by Aluminium-Verlag GmbH)
- Bauen mit Aluminium. (pub. by Aluminium-Verlag GmbH)

**Fachverlag Ernst Aly**
Jahnstr. 13, 8032 Graefelfing, W. Germany (B.R.D.)
- Element und Fertigbau; Fachzeitschrift fuer industrialisiertes Bauen. bi-m. ISSN 0013-5925

**Albert Amann Verlag**
Richterstr. 2, Postfach 1240, 8762 Amorbach, W. Germany (B.R.D.)
- Gesundheitspolitische Umschau. m. ISSN 0016-9307

**Amt fuer Fremdenverkehr und Kongresswesen**
- Frankfurter Wochenschau. (pub. by Verlag Bodet und Link)

**Anderson Advertisers**
Englerstr. 6, 6900 Heidelberg 1, W. Germany (B.R.D.)
- R & R Entertainment Digest - with Guide to TV. m.

**Angestelltenverband Deutscher Milchkontroll- und Tierzuchtangestellten**
- Unser Milchvieh. (pub. by Heinrichs Verlag KG)

**Verlag fuer Angewandte Psychologie**
Daimlerstr. 40, 7000 Stuttgart-Bad Cannstadt, W. Germany (B. R. D.)
- Psychologie und Praxis; Zeitschrift fuer die Anwedungsgebiete der Psychologie. q. ISSN 0033-2992

**Anthroposophische Gesellschaft in Deutschland**
- Die Drei. (pub. by Verlag Freies Geistesleben GmbH)

**Antibolschewistisches Block der Nationen**
Zeppelinstr. 67, 8000 Munich 80, W. Germany (B.R.D.)
- A B N Correspondence. bi-m. ISSN 0001-0545

**Apostolischer Visitator fuer Klerus und Glaeubige des Ermlandes**
Ermlandweg 22, 4400 Muenster, W. Germany (B.R.D.)
- Ermlandbriefe. q. ISSN 0014-0201

**Deutscher Apotheker-Verlag**
Birkenwaldstr. 44, Postfach 44, 7000 Stuttgart 1, W. Germany (B.R.D.)
- A. P. V. Informationsdienst. q. ISSN 0001-2254 (Arbeitsgemeinschaft fuer Pharmazeutische Verfahrenstechnik e. V.)
- Acta Pharmaceutica Technologica. q. ISSN 0340-3157 (Arbeitsgemeinschaft fuer Pharmazeutische Verfahrenstechnik e.V.)
- Acta Pharmaceutica Technologica. Supplementa. irreg. ISSN 0341-0854 (Arbeitsgemeinschaft fuer Pharmazeutische Verfahrenstechnik e. V.)
- Das Aktuelle Schaufenster. m. ISSN 0568-7632
- Die Apothekenhelferin. m. ISSN 0570-4723
- Apotheker und Kunst. s-a. ISSN 0341-0110
- Beitraege zur Geschichte der Pharmazie. 4 per yr. ISSN 0341-0099 (Internationale Gesellschaft fuer Geschichte der Pharmazie)
- Deutsche Apotheker-Zeitung. w. ISSN 0011-9857
- Die Krankenhaus-Apotheke. q. ISSN 0075-7071 (Arbeitsgemeinschaft Deutscher Krankenhausapotheker)
- Neue Arzneimittel und Spezialitaeten. m. ISSN 0548-2674
- P T A Heute. m. ISSN 0302-167X
- Pharmazie Heute. m. ISSN 0369-979X
- Technische Universitaet Braunschweig. Pharmaziegeschichtlichen Seminar. Veroeffentlichungen. irreg., vol. 16, 1976. ISSN 0068-0729

**Arabidopsis Information Service**
Siesmayerstr. 70, 3400 Goettingen, W. Germany (B.R.D.)
- Arabidopsis Information Service. Newsletter. a. ISSN 0066-5657

**Aral AG**
Wittener Str. 45, 4630 Bochum 1, W. Germany (B.R.D.)
- Aral-Journal. s-a.

**Verlag Arbeit und Beruf**
Viatisstr. 202, 8500 Nuernberg, W. Germany (B. R. D.)
- Arbeit und Beruf; Fachzeitschrift fuer die Aufgaben der Bundesanstalt fuer Arbeit. m.

**Arbeiterwohlfahrt Bundesverband E.V**
Ollenhauerstr. 3, 5300 Bonn, W. Germany (B.R.D.)
- Theorie und Praxis der Sozialen Arbeit. m.

**Arbeitsausschuss des Evangelischen Kirchenbautages und Dioezesan-Kunstvereins, Linz**
- Kunst und Kirche. (pub. by Guetersloher Verlagshaus Gerd Mohn)

**Arbeitsgemeinschaft Allensbach e.V.**
Kappeler-Berg-Str. 54, 7753 Allensbach, W. Germany (B.R.D.)
- Allensbacher Almanach.

**Arbeitsgemeinschaft Berliner Haus-, Grund-, und Ruinenbesitzervereine e. V.**
- Berliner Haus- und Grundbesitz. (pub. by Verlag Adalbert Bestgen)

**Arbeitsgemeinschaft der Berufsvertretungen Deutscher Apotheker**
- Neue Apotheken Illustrierte. (pub. by Pharmapress-Verlagsgesellschaft)
- Pharmazeutische Zeitung. (pub. by Govi-Verlag GmbH)

**Arbeitsgemeinschaft der Bitumen-Industrie E.V.**
Mittelweg 13, 2000 Hamburg 13, W. Germany (B.R.D.)
- Bitumen. bi-m. ISSN 0006-3916

**Arbeitsgemeinschaft der Familienkundlichen Gesellschaften in Hessen**
- Hessische Familienkunde. (pub. by Dr. Heinz F. Friederichs)

**Arbeitsgemeinschaft der Karpatendeutschen aus der Slowakei**
Schwabstr. 2, 7000 Stuttgart 7, W. Germany (B.R.D.)
- Die Karpatenpost. m. ISSN 0022-9105

**Arbeitsgemeinschaft der Oeffentlich-rechtlichen Rundfunkanstalten der Bundesrepublik Deutschland**
- Beitraege zum Rundfunkrecht. (pub. by Alfred Metzner Verlag GmbH)

**Arbeitsgemeinschaft der Parlaments- und Behoerdenbibliotheken**
Bibliothek des Deutschen Bundestages, Bundeshaus, 5300 Bonn, W. Germany (B.R.D.)
- Arbeitsgemeinschaft der Parlaments-und Behoerden Bibliotheken. Mitteilungen. s-a.
- Arbeitsgemeinschaft der Parlaments- und Behoerdenbibliotheken. Arbeitshefte. a. ISSN 0518-2220

**Arbeitsgemeinschaft der Verbaende der Technischen Haendler**
- Technischer Handel. (pub. by Curt R. Vincentz Verlag)

**Arbeitsgemeinschaft der Verbraucher E.V. (AGV)**
Provinzialstr. 89-93, 5300 Bonn-Lengsdorf, W. Germany (B.R.D.)
- Verbraucher-Politische Korrespondenz. w. ISSN 0042-3653
- Verbraucher Rundschau. m. ISSN 0042-3661

**Arbeitsgemeinschaft Deutscher Krankenhausapotheker**
- Die Krankenhaus-Apotheke. (pub. by Deutscher Apotheker-Verlag)

**Arbeitsgemeinschaft Deutscher Schweineerzeuger e.V.**
- Schweinezucht und Schweinemast. (pub. by Verlag M. und H. Schaper)

**Arbeitsgemeinschaft Deutscher Tierzuechter**
- Der Tierzuechter. (pub. by Verlag Mann und Bartels GmbH)

**Arbeitsgemeinschaft Deutscher Verkehrsflughaefen**
Flughafen, Stuttgart, W. Germany (B.R.D.)
- A D V-Informationsdienst. m. ISSN 0001-0987

**Arbeitsgemeinschaft die Moderne Kueche**
- Die Moderne Kueche. (pub. by Die Planung Verlagsgesellschaft mbH)

**Arbeitsgemeinschaft Ethnomedizin, Hamburg**
Curschmannstr. 23, 2000 Hamburg 20, W. Germany (B.R.D.)
- Ethnomedizin. a. ISSN 0071-1853

**Arbeitsgemeinschaft Europaeischer Kalibreure**
- Kalibreur/Calibreur. (pub. by Verlag Stahleisen mbH)

**Arbeitsgemeinschaft Fernwaerme e.V.**
- Fernwaerme International/District Heating/Chauffage Urbain. (pub. by Verlags- und Wirtschaftsgesellschaft der Elektrizitaetswerke mbH)

**Arbeitsgemeinschaft Frau und Mutter**
- Frau und Mutter. (pub. by Kreuz-Verlag)

**Arbeitsgemeinschaft fuer Berlin-Brandenburgische Kirchengeschichte**
- Jahrbuch fuer Berlin-Brandenburgische Kirchengeschichte. (pub. by Christlicher Zeitschriftenverlag)

**Arbeitsgemeinschaft fuer Betriebliche Altersversorgung e.V.**
Postfach 101108, 6900 Heidelberg 1, W. Germany (B. R. D.)
- Betriebliche Altersversorgung. bi-m. ISSN 0005-9951

**Arbeitsgemeinschaft fuer Evangelische Kinderpflege**
- Theorie und Praxis der Sozialpaedagogik. (pub. by Luther-Verlag)

**Arbeitsgemeinschaft fuer Jugendhilfe**
Haager Weg 44, 5300 Bonn 1, W. Germany (B.R.D.)
- Arbeitsgemeinschaft fuer Jugendhilfe. Mitteilungen. 4 per yr.

**Arbeitsgemeinschaft fuer Juristisches Bibliotheks- und Dokumentationswesen**
Wilhelmstr. 7, 7400 Tuebingen, W. Germany (B. R. D.)
- Arbeitsgemeinschaft fuer Juristisches Bibliotheks- und Dokumentationswesen. Mitteilungen. irreg. ISSN 0300-0990

**Arbeitsgemeinschaft fuer Kameradenwerke und Traditionsverbaende**
- Alte Kameraden. (pub. by Verlag G. Braun GmbH)

**Arbeitsgemeinschaft fuer Medizinisches Bibliothekswesen**
- Medizin Bibliothek Dokumentation. (pub. by Medizin Bibliothek Dokumentation-Verlag)

**Arbeitsgemeinschaft fuer Pharmazeutische Verfahrenstechnik e. V.**
- A. P. V. Informationsdienst. (pub. by Deutscher Apotheker-Verlag)
- Acta Pharmaceutica Technologica. (pub. by Deutscher Apotheker-Verlag)
- Acta Pharmaceutica Technologica. Supplementa. (pub. by Deutscher Apotheker-Verlag)

**Arbeitsgemeinschaft fuer Rheinische Musikgeschichte e. V.**
c/o Paedagogische Hochschule, Institut fuer Musikalische Volkskunde, 4040 Neuss, W. Germany (B.R.D.)
- Arbeitsgemeinschaft fuer Rheinische Musikgeschichte. Mitteilungen. q.

**Arbeitsgemeinschaft fuer Salesianische Studien**
- Jahrbuch fuer Salesianische Studien. (pub. by Franz-Sales-Verlag)

**Arbeitsgemeinschaft Getreideforschung**
- Getreide, Mehl und Brot. (pub. by Rheinisch-Westfaelischer Baecker-Verlag GmbH)

**Arbeitsgemeinschaft Industriebau e.V.**
- Zentralblatt fuer Industriebau. (pub. by Curt R. Vincentz Verlag)

**Arbeitsgemeinschaft Korrosion**
- Werkstoffe und Korrosion. (pub. by Verlag Chemie International, Inc. US)

**Arbeitsgemeinschaft Moebeltransport Bundesverband e.V.**
- Der Moebelspediteur. (pub. by Verlag der Moebelspediteur)

**Arbeitsgemeinschaft ostdeutscher Familienforscher, Herne**
Fasanenweg 21, 6057 Dietzenbach-Hesse, W. Germany (B.R.D.)
(Subscr. to: R. Schoenthuer, Eibenkamp 25, 433 Muelheim 73, W. Germany)
- Archiv Ostdeutscher Familienforscher. bi-m. ISSN 0003-9470

**Arbeitsgemeinschaft Sozialwissenschaftlicher Institute e.V.**
- Soziale Welt. (pub. by Verlag Otto Schwartz und Co)

**Arbeitsgemeinschaft Spekulative Thematik**
Weissenburger Str. 6, 2850 Bremerhaven 1, W. Germany (B.R.D.)
- Science Fiction Times. q. ISSN 0048-9654

**Arbeitsgemeinschaft Verstaerkte Kunstsoffe e. V.**
Niddastr. 44, 6000 Frankfurt 1, W. Germany (B.R.D.)
- Informationen ueber Verstaerkte Kunststoffe. irreg., approx. 4 per yr.

**Arbeitsgemeinschaft Waermebehandlung und Werkstoff-Technik e.V.**
- Haerterei-Technische Mitteilungen (HTM) (pub. by Carl Hanser Verlag)

**Arbeitsgemeinschaft zur Foerderung der Partnerschaft in der Wirtschaft e.V.**
Maarstr. 1, 5022 Cologne-Junkersdorf, W. Germany (B.R.D.)
- A G P -Mitteilungen. bi-m. ISSN 0001-1347

**Arbeitsgruppe fuer Empirische Bildungsforschung**
Zeppelinstr. 151, 6900 Heidelberg 1, W. Germany (B.R.D.)
- Arbeitsgruppe fuer Empirische Bildungsforschung. Uebersicht ueber die Bisherigen Arbeiten. irreg.

**Arbeitskammer des Saarlandes**
Sophienstr. 6-8, 6600 Saarbruecken, W. Germany (B.R.D.)
- Der Saarlaendische Arbeitnehmer. m. ISSN 0003-7737

**Arbeitskreis der Kampftruppen**
- Kampftruppen. (pub. by Verlag E. S. Mittler und Sohn GmbH)

**Arbeitskreis Deutscher Bildungsstaetten e.V.**
- Materialien zur Politischen Bildung. (pub. by Luchterhand Verlag)

**Arbeitskreis fuer Jugendliteratur**
- Arbeitskreis fuer Jugendliteratur. Jahrbuch. (pub. by Verlag Julius Klinkhardt)

**Arbeitskreis fuer Wehrforschung**
- Beitraege zur Wehrforschung. (pub. by Wehr und Wissen Verlagsgesellschaft GmbH)
- Marine-Rundschau. (pub. by Bernard und Graefe Verlag)
- Wehrwissenschaftliche Berichte. (pub. by Bernard und Graefe Verlag)
- Wehrwissenschaftliche Rundschau. (pub. by E. S. Mittler und Sohn GmbH)

**Arbeitskreis Progressive Kunst**
Josefplatz 3, 4200 Oberhausen, W. Germany (B.R.D.)
- Neue Volkskunst. q. ISSN 0012-0944

**Arbeitskreis Sozialwissenschaftliche Informationen**
- Sozialwissenschaftliche Informationen fuer Unterricht und Studium. (pub. by Ernst Klett Verlag)

**Arbeitsring fuer Paedagogische Elternhilfe E. V., Aachen**
- Leben und Erziehen. (pub. by Einhard-Verlag GmbH)

**Verlag Architektur und Baudetail GmbH**
Ainmillerstr. 34, Postfach 606, 8000 Munich 43, W. Germany (B. R. D.)
- Detail; Zeitschrift fuer Architektur & Baudetail & Einrichtung. bi-m. ISSN 0011-9571

**Archiv fuer Energiewirtschaft**
Angerburger Allee 53, 1000 Berlin 19, W. Germany (B.R.D.)
- Archiv fuer Energiewirtschaft; Zeitschrift fuer Energiewesen. m. ISSN 0003-9047

**Archiv fuer Psychiatrie und Nervenkrankheiten**
- Zentralblatt fuer Die Gesamte Neurologie und Psychiatrie/Neurology-Psychiatry. (pub. by Springer-Verlag US)

**Argument-Verlag GmbH**
Rheinstr. 122, Postfach 210730, 7500 Karlsruhe 21, W. Germany (B.R.D.)
- Das Argument; Zeitschrift fuer Philosophie und Sozialwissenschaften. bi-m. ISSN 0004-1157

**Argus-Verlag**
Luetzenkirchener Str. 83, 5670 Opladen, W. Germany (B.R.D.)
- Ruhrtangente; Nordrhein-Westfaelisches Jahrbuch fuer Literatur. irreg.

**Aristo-Werke Dennert und Pape KG**
Haferweg 46, 2000 Hamburg 50, W. Germany (B.R.D.)
- Aristo-Mitteilungen fuer die Schulpraxis. s-a.
- Aristo - Mitteilungen fuer Ingenieur- und Hochschulen. a. ISSN 0518-5378

**Arne-Verlag**
Wintergasse 4, 6203 Hochheim, W. Germany (B.R.D.)
- Arnes Journal fuer Guten Geschmack. 10 per yr. (Chaine des Rotisseurs)

**Verlag Ernst Arnold GmbH**
Siegburgstr. 5-7, 4600 Dortmund-Mengede, W. Germany (B.R.D.)
- Elektrowirtschaft. s-m. ISSN 0013-5887 (Bundesverband des Elektro-Grosshandels (VEG) e.V.)

**Art Adress Verlag Mueller KG**
Grosse Eschenheimer Str. 16, Postfach 2187, 6000 Frankfurt 1, W. Germany (B.R.D.)
(Dist. in U.S. and Canada by Editions Publisol, P.O.B. 339, 235 E. 85th St., New York, N.Y. 10028)
- International Directory of Arts. biennial. ISSN 0074-4565

**Arzneimittel-Informationsdienst GmbH (A.T.I.)**
Petzower Str. 6f, 1000 Berlin 39, W. Germany (B.R.D)
- Arznei-Telegramm. m. ISSN 0066-8192 (Unabhaengiger Arbeitskreis Arzneimittelpolitik)

**Verlag fuer Arztrecht**
Schinnrainstr.15, 7500 Karlsruhe 41, W. Germany (B.R.D.)
- Arztrecht. m.

**Aschendorffsche Verlagsbuchhandlung**
Soester Str. 13, 440 Muenster, W. Germany (B.R.D.)
- Acta Pacis Westphalicae. irreg. ISSN 0065-146X (Vereinigung zur Erforschung der Neueren Geschichte e.V.)
- Beitraege zur Geschichte der Philosophie und Theologie des Mittelalters Neue Folge. irreg. ISSN 0067-5024
- Beitraege zur Geschichte des Alten Moenchtums und des Benediktinerordens. irreg. ISSN 0067-5032
- Beitraege zur Westfaelischen Familienforschung. irreg. ISSN 0067-5261 (Westfaelische Gesellschaft fuer Genealogie und Familienforschung)
- Catholica; Vierteljahresschrift fuer oekumenische Theologie. 4 per yr. ISSN 0008-8501 (Johann Adam Moehler-Institut Paderborn)
- Corpus Catholicorum. irreg. ISSN 0070-0320
- Cusanus-Gesellschaft. Buchreihe. irreg. ISSN 0070-2234
- Fontes et Commentationes. irreg. ISSN 0077-1953 (Universitaet Muenster. Institut fuer Epigraphik)
- Forschungen zur Romanischen Philologie. irreg. ISSN 0071-7681
- Jahrbuch fuer Antike und Christentum. a. ISSN 0075-2541 (Universitaet Bonn. Franz Joseph Doelger-Institut)
- Katholisches Leben und Kirchenreform im Zeitalter der Glaubensspaltung. irreg. ISSN 0075-5273
- Landschaftsverband Westfalen-Lippe. Volkskundliche Kommission. Schriften. irreg. ISSN 0075-7942
- Liturgiewissenschaftliche Quellen und Forschungen. irreg. ISSN 0076-0048
- Liturgisches Jahrbuch. 4 per yr. ISSN 0024-5100 (Liturgisches Institut Trier)
- Maerchen der Europaeischen Voelker. irreg. ISSN 0076-2326 (Gesellschaft zur Pflege der Maerchengutes der Europaeischen Voelker)
- Missionswissenschaftliche Abhandlungen und Texte/Etudes et Documents Missionnaires/Mission Studies and Documents. irreg. ISSN 0076-941X (Internationales Institut fuer Missionswissenschaftliche Forschungen)
- Muenstersche Beitraege zur Deutschen Literaturwissenschaft. irreg. ISSN 0077-1996
- Neue Beitraege zur Englischen Philologie. irreg. ISSN 0077-7684
- Neue Muenstersche Beitraege zur Geschichtsforschung. irreg. ISSN 0077-7706
- Niederdeutsches Wort; Beitraege zur niederdeutschen Philologie. irreg. ISSN 0078-0545
- Orbis Antiquus. irreg. ISSN 0078-5555
- Portugiesische Forschungen der Goerresgesellschaft. Reihe 1: Aufsaetze zur Portugiesischen Kulturgeschichte. irreg. ISSN 0079-421X (Goerres-Gesellschaft)
- Portugiesische Forschungen der Goerresgesellschaft. Reihe 2: Monographien. irreg. ISSN 0079-4228 (Goerres-Gesellschaft)
- Provinzialinstitut fuer Westfaelische Landes- und Volksforschung. Veroeffentlichungen. irreg. ISSN 0079-709X
- Reformationsgeschichtliche Studien und Texte. irreg. ISSN 0080-0473
- Spanische Forschungen der Goerresgesellschaft. Reihe 1: Gesammelte Aufsaetze zur Kulturgeschichte Spaniens. irreg. ISSN 0081-3486 (Goerres-Gesellschaft)
- Spanische Forschungen der Goerresgesellschaft. Reihe 2: Monographien. irreg. ISSN 0081-3494 (Goerres-Gesellschaft)
- Theologische Revue. 6 per yr. ISSN 0040-568X (Universitaet Muenster. Katholisch-Theologische Fakultaet)
- Universitaet Muenster. Institut fuer Christliche Sozialwissenschaften. Schriften. irreg. ISSN 0077-1945
- Universitaet Muenster. Institut fuer Missionswissenschaft. Veroeffentlichungen. irreg. ISSN 0077-197X
- Vorreformationsgeschichtliche Forschungen. irreg. ISSN 0083-6923
- Westfaelische Forschungen. a. ISSN 0083-9027 (Provinzialinstitut fuer Westfaelische Landes- und Volksforschung)
- Westfalia Sacra; Quellen und Forschungen zur Kirchengeschichte Westfalens. irreg.
- Zeitschrift fuer Missionswissenschaft und Religionswissenschaft. 4 per yr. ISSN 0044-3123 (Internationales Institut fuer Missionswissenschaftliche Forschungen)

**Asgard-Verlag Dr. Werner Hippe KG**
Einsteinstr. 10, Postfach 3080, 5205 St. Sugustin 3,
W. Germany (B.R.D.)
- Fortbildung und Praxis. irreg. ISSN 0071-7835
- Wege zur Sozialversicherung. m. ISSN 0043-2059

**Asien Buecherei**
Laustr. 26, 3590 Bad Wilbungen, W. Germany
(B.R.D.)
- Bibliographia Asiatica. q. ISSN 0006-1220

**Aspekte Verlag GmbH**
Zeppelinallee 77, 6000 Frankfurt 1, W. Germany
(B.R.D.)
- Analysen; Zeitschrift zur Wissenschafts und
Berufspraxis. m.

**Association Internationale de Linguistique Appliquee**
Schloss-Str. 26, 7000 Stuttgart 1, W. Germany
(B.R.D.)
- A I L A Bulletin. q. ISSN 0044-9490

**Astronomisches Rechen-Institut**
- Astronomische Grundlagen fuer den Kalender.
(pub. by Verlag G. Braun GmbH)

**Athenaeum-Verlag GmbH**
Falkensteiner Str. 75-77, 6000 Frankfurt 18, W.
Germany (B.R.D.)
- Indices zur Deutschen Literatur. irreg., vol. 7.
ISSN 0073-7208
- Wirkung der Literatur. irreg., 1973, vol. 4. ISSN
0084-0467

**Athletik-Verlag**
Woertelstr. 8, 7554 Kuppenheim, W. Germany
(B.R.D.)
- Athletik; illustrierte Fachzeitschrift fuer
Schwerathletik. m. ISSN 0004-6698 (Deutscher
Ringer-Bund)

**Ludwig Auer Verlag**
Postfach 239, 885 Donauwoerth, W. Germany.
- Monika; Zeitschrift fuer die Frau. m. ISSN 0047-
7885

**Verlag fuer Aufbereitung**
Witteisbacherstr. 10, 6200 Wiesbaden, W. Germany
(B.R.D.)
- Aufbereitungs-Technik.

**Aufklaerungsdienst fuer Jugendschutz**
- Gib Acht. (pub. by Universum-Verlagsanstalt
GmbH KG)

**Augsburg. Amt fuer Statistik und Stadtforschung**
Von-Cobres-Str. 1, 8900 Augsburg 22, W. Germany
(B.R.D.)
- Augsburg in Zahlen. q. ISSN 0004-7953

**Augsburg. Kulturreferat**
Maximilianstr. 4, 8900 Augsburg, W. Germany
(B.R.D.)
- Augsburger Kulturnachrichten. m. ISSN 0004-
7961

**Augustinus-Verlag**
Grabenberg 2, 8700 Wuerzburg, W. Germany
(B.R.D.)
- Ostkirchliche Studien. q. ISSN 0030-6487
(Ostkirchliches Institut der Deutschen
Augustiner)

**Aulis-Verlag Deubner und Co. KG**
Antwerpener Str. 6/12, 5000 Cologne 1, W.
Germany (B.R.D.)
- Naturwissenschaften im Unterricht. Biologie. m.
- Naturwissenschaften im Unterricht. Physik/
Chemie. m.
- Praxis der Mathematik. m. ISSN 0032-7042
- Praxis der Naturwissenschaften. Biologie im
Unterricht der Schulen. m. ISSN 0032-7050
- Praxis der Naturwissenschaften. Chemie im
Unterricht der Schulen. m.
- Praxis der Naturwissenschaften. Physik im
Unterricht der Schulen. m.
- Sachunterricht und Mathematik in der
Grundschule. m.
- Steuer-Telex; Spezialdienst fuer den
Steuerfachmann. w.

**Aurich. Regierungspraesident**
Schlossplatz 3, 2960 Aurich /Ostfriesland 1, W.
Germany (B.R.D.)
- Amtsblatt fuer den Regierungsbezirk Aurich. s-m.
ISSN 0003-228X

**Ausstellungs- und Messe-Ausschuss der Deutschen Wirtschaft E.V.**
Lindenstr. 8, 5000 Cologne 5, W. Germany
(B.R.D.)
- Deutsche Messen und Ausstellungen - Ein
Zahlenspiegel. a. ISSN 0084-9766

**Austauschzentrale der Vogelliebhaber und Zuechter Deutschlands e V.**
- A Z-Nachrichten. (pub. by L. Keidel)

**Auto und Reise GmbH Verlag und Wirtschaftsdienst**
Oberntiefer Str. 20, Postfach 440, 8532 Bad
Windsheim, W. Germany (B.R.D.)
- Auto und Reise. m. ISSN 0045-1010

**Automobilclub von Deutschland e.V.**
- Motor Reise Revue. (pub. by A v D Verlag
GmbH)
- Reisen mit dem Auto Durch Europa. (pub. by A v
D Verlag GmbH)

**Axtmann-Verlag**
Wilhelmstr. 42, 6200 Wiesbaden 1, W. Germany
(B.R.D.)
- Film-Echo Filmwoche. Verleih-Katalog. a. ISSN
0071-4879

**B A I Verlag GmbH**
Haselnussweg 4, Postfach 1160, 6277 Camberg, W.
Germany (B.R.D.)
- Agraringenieur und Agrarmanager; Zeitschrift der
landwirtschaftlichen Fuehrungspraxis. m.
(Bundesverband der Agraringenieure (BAI) e.V.)

**B A S F Landwirtschaftliche Versuchsstation**
Carl-Bosch-Str. 64, 6703 Limburgerhof, W.
Germany (B.R.D.)
- Kurz und Buendig. m. ISSN 0023-5687

**B L V Verlagsgesellschaft mbH**
Lothstr. 29, 8000 Munich 40, W. Germany (B.R.D.)
(In Cooperation with Verlag E. Ulmer, Gerokstr. 19,
Postfach 1032, 7 Stuttgart O, W. Germany)
- Allgemeine Forstzeitschrift; illustrierte
Wochenzeitschrift fuer Waldwirtschaft und
Landschaftspflege. w. ISSN 0002-5860
- Der Almbauer; Mitteilungen fuer Alm-, Berg- und
Gruenlandbauern und ueber Forstrechte. m. ISSN
0002-6298 (Almwirtschaftlicher Verein
Oberbayern)
- Ausbildung und Beratung in Land- und
Hauswirtschaft; Monatsschrift fuer Lehr- und
Beratungskraefte. m. ISSN 0045-0049 (Land- und
Hauswirtschaftlicher Auswertungs- und
Informationsdienst)
- Bayerisches Landwirtschaftliches Jahrbuch. 8 per
yr. ISSN 0005-7150
- Bayerisches Landwirtschaftliches Wochenblatt. w.
ISSN 0005-7169 (Bayerischer Bauernverband)
- D L Z (Landtechnische Zeitschrift (die)) m. ISSN
0011-5010
- Fachberater fuer das Deutsche Kleingartenwesen.
q. ISSN 0014-6315 (Bundesverband Deutscher
Kleingaertner e.V.)
- Gemuese; Spezialblatt fuer den Feld- und
Intensivgemuesebau. m. ISSN 0016-6286 (Co-
publisher: Verlag Eugen Ulmer)
- Jagdgebrauchshund. m. ISSN 0021-3942
(Jagdgebrauchshundverband)
- Pirsch/Deutscher Jaeger; illustrierte
Jagdzeitschrift. fortn.
- Saenger-und Musikantenzeitung; Zweimonatschrift
fuer volksmusikpflege. bi-m. ISSN 0036-2328
- Saeugetierkundliche Mitteilungen. q. ISSN 0036-
2344
- Universitaet Freiburg in Bresgau.
Forstwissenschaftliche Fakultaet. Schriftenreihe.
irreg. ISSN 0429-646X
- V D L-Nachrichten. m. (Verband Deutscher
Akademiker fuer Landwirtschaft, Ernaehrung und
Landespflege e.V.)

**Verlag Bachem und Sohn**
Friedrich- Ebert- Str. 37, 4000 Duesseldorf 1, W.
Germany (B. R. D.)
- Der Deutsche Rundfunk- Einzelhandel. m. ISSN
0012-0634 (Deutscher Radio- und Fernseh-
Fachverband e.V.)

**J. P. Bachem Verlag GmbH**
Ursulaplatz 1, 5000 Cologne 1, W. Germany
(B.R.D.)
- S A E. (Sammlung Arbeitsrechtlicher
Entscheidungen) 8 per yr. ISSN 0048-9069
(Bundesvereinigung der Deutschen
Arbeitgeberverbaende e.V.)

**Baden-Wuerttemberg. Innenministerium**
Dorotheenstr. 6, Postfach 277, 7000 Stuttgart 1, W.
Germany (B.R.D.)
- Gemeinsames Amtsblatt des Landes Baden-
Wuerttemberg. irreg., a. 40 per yr. ISSN 0016-
6200

**Baden- Wuerttemberg. Kommission fuer Geschichtliche Landeskunde**
- Lebensbilder aus Schwaben und Franken. (pub. by
W. Kohlhammer GmbH (Stuttgart))

**Baden-Wuerttemberg. Landesdenkmalamt**
Eugenstr. 3, 7000 Stuttgart 1, W. Germany (B.R.D.)
- Denkmalpflege in Baden-Wuerttemberg. q.

**Baden-Wuerttemberg. Landesgewerbeamt**
Kanzleistr. 19, Postfach 831, 7000 Stuttgart 1, W.
Germany (B.R.D.)
- Betriebswirtschaftlicher Informationsdienst;
Kurzreferate aus Fachzeitschriften. 10 per yr.

**Baden-Wuerttemberg. Landeswohlfahrtswerk**
Falkerstr. 29, 7000 Stuttgart 1, W. Germany
(B.R.D.)
- Blaetter der Wohlfahrtspflege; Fachzeitschrift fuer
Sozialarbeit und Sozialpaedagogik in der
Bundesrepublik Deutschland. m.

**Baden-Wuerttemberg. Ministerium fuer Arbeit, Gesundheit und Sozialordnung**
- Arbeits- und Sozialrecht. (pub. by Neckar-Verlag)

**Baden-Wuerttemberg. Ministerium fuer Ernaehrung, Landwirtschaft und Umwelt**
Marienstr. 41, 7000 Stuttgart 1, W. Germany
(B.R.D.)
- Forstatistisches Jahrbuch. a. ISSN 0084-7690

**Baden-Wuerttembergischer Luftfahrtverband e.V.**
Kanzleistr. 19, Postfach 970, 7000 Stuttgart 1, W.
Germany (B.R.D.)
- Der Adler; Monatszeitschrift fuer Luftsport und
Luftfahrt. m. ISSN 0001-8279

**Badische Anilin- und Soda-Fabrik A.G.**
6700 Ludwigshafen, W. Germany (B.R.D.)
- B A S F Review. q. ISSN 0005-2655

**Badischer Landesverein fuer Naturkunde und Naturschutz e.V**
Albertstr. 5, 7800 Freiburg, W. Germany (B.R.D.)
- Badischer Landesverein fuer Naturkunde und
Naturschutz, Freiburg. Mitteilungen. Neue Folge.
a. ISSN 0067-2858

**Rheinisch-Westfaelischer Baecker-Verlag GmbH**
Berg-Str. 79, Postfach 2050, 4630 Bochum, W.
Germany (B.R.D.)
- Deutsche Baecker Zeitung. w. ISSN 0046-0117
- Getreide, Mehl und Brot. m. (Arbeitsgemeinschaft
Getreideforschung)

**Baeder und Kurverwaltung**
- Baden-Baden Program. (pub. by Pruefer-Werbung)

**Baeren-Druck**
Felsenstr. 23, Postfach 2120, 6200 Wiesbaken-
Dotzheim, W. Germany (B.R.D.)
- Burgkeller-Zeitung. bi-m. (Jenaische
Burschenschaft Arminia auf dem Burgkeller)

**Baerenreiter Verlag**
Henrich-Schuetz-Allee 31-37, 3500 Kassel-
Wilhelmshoehe, W. Germany (B.R.D.)
- Acta Musicologica. 2 per yr. (International
Musicological Society)
- Catalogus Musicus. irreg., no. 7, 1975. ISSN
0069-116X (International Association of Music
Libraries) (Co-sponsor: International
Musicological Society)
- Fontes Artis Musicae. 4 per yr. ISSN 0015-6191
(International Association of Music Librarians)
- Der Kirchenchor. bi-m. ISSN 0023-1800 (Verband
Evangelischer Kirchenchoere Deutschlands)
- Mozart-Jahrbuch. a. ISSN 0077-1805
(Internationale Stiftung Mozarteum AU)
- Musica; Zweimonatsschrift fuer alle Gebiete des
Musiklebens. bi-m. ISSN 0027-4518
- Musik und Kirche. bi-m. ISSN 0027-4771
- Die Musikforschung. q. ISSN 0027-4801
(Gesellschaft fuer Musikforschung)
- Oesterreichische Gesellschaft fuer Musik.
Beitraege. irreg. ISSN 0078-3471
- Saarbruecker Studien zur Musikwissenschaft. irreg.
ISSN 0080-519X (Universitaet des Saarlandes.
Musikwissenschaftliches Institut)

- Sagittarius; Beitraege zur Erforschung und Praxis alter und neuer Kirchenmusik. irreg., vol. 4, 1973. ISSN 0080-5408 (Internationale Heinrich Schuetz-Gesellschaft e.V.)

**August Bagel Verlag**
Grafenberger Allee 100, Postfach 1520, 4000 Duesseldorf, W. Germany (B.R.D.)
- Amtliches Schulblatt fuer den Regierungsbezirk Duesseldorf. m. ISSN 0003-2190

**Bahnsport Aktuell Verlag**
Vorm Hain 4, 6451 Rodenbach, W. Germany (B.R.D.)
- Bahnsport Aktuell; Sandtrack - Speedway - Motorcross. m.

**Alexander Baier-Presse**
Rheinstr. 33, 6500 Mainz, W. Germany (B.R.D.)
- Kunst Magazin. q.

**Balatroswerke H. Rost und Co.**
Goldtschmidtstr. 51, 2100 Hamburg 90, W. Germany (B.R.D.)
- Balatros Berichtet. q.

**Verlag Baltische Briefe Wolf J. von Kleist**
Deefkamp 13, 2070 Grosshansdorf, W. Germany (B.R.D.)
- Baltische Briefe. m. ISSN 0005-4526

**Baltische Gesellschaft in Deutschland e.V.**
Lessingstr. 5, 8000 Munich 2, W. Germany (B.R.D.)
- Mitteilungen aus Baltischem Leben. q. ISSN 0026-6833

**Verlag der Schillerbuchhandlung Hans Banger**
Alte Neusser Landstr. 302, 5000 Cologne 71, W. Germany (B. R. D.)
- Anschriften Deutscher Verlage und Auslaendischer Verlage mit Deutschen Auslieferungen. a. ISSN 0066-4596
- Deutschsprachige Zeitschriften Deutschland - Oesterreich - Schweiz. a.

**Bank fuer Gemeinwirtschaft Aktiengesellschaft**
Postfach 2244, 6000 Frankfurt, W. Germany (B.R.D.)
- Amerikanischer Wirtschaftsbrief. m. ISSN 0003-1623
- Aussenhandelsdienst. s-m. ISSN 0004-8178
- Commonweal Economy Series. irreg.
- Wirtschaftsblaetter. m. ISSN 0043-6208

**Bank Verlag GmbH**
Gereonstr. 58, 5000 Cologne 1, W. Germany (B.R.D.)
- Bank-Betrieb; Zeitschrift fuer Bankpolitik und Bankpraxis. m. ISSN 0005-5034 (Bundesverband Deutscher Banken e.V.)

**Barmer Ersatzkasse**
Untere Lichtenplatzer Str. 100, Postfach 200108, 5600 Wuppertal 2, W. Germany (B.R.D.)
- Die Barmer. q.
- Barmer Bruecke; Zeitschrift fuer die Vertrauensleute der Barmer Ersatzkasse. 7 per yr.

**Verlag Bartels und Wernitz KG**
Reinickendorfer Str. 113, 1000 Berlin 65, W. Germany (B.R.D)
- Jahrbuch der Leichtathletik. a. (Deutsches Leichtathletik-Verband)
- Leichtathletik. w. ISSN 0047-4355
- Polizeischau; Zeitschrift fuer die Berliner Polizei. 10 per yr. ISSN 0032-3551 (Berlin (West) Senator fuer Inneres)

**Verlag Dr. Albert Bartens**
Lueckhoffstr. 16, 1000 Berlin 38, W. Germany (B.R.D.)
- Zeitschrift fuer die Zuckerindustrie; internationales Fachblatt fuer Technik, Anbau und Wirtschaft. m. ISSN 0044-2623
- Zuckerwirtschaftliches Taschenbuch/Sugar Economy/Economie Sucriere. a. ISSN 0084-5736

**Erwin Barth Verlag KG**
Kiesstr. 11, Postfach 271, 6730 Neustadt, W. Germany (B.R.D.)
- B S R. (Bohren, Sprengen, Raeumen); im Bergbau, Steinbruch, Bauwesen, in der Erdolgewinnung und Landeskultur. m. ISSN 0005-3333
- Explosivstoffe. m. ISSN 0014-5068

**Bartsch Verlag KG**
Alte Landstr. 8-10, 8012 Ottobrunn B, Munich, W. Germany (B.R.D.)
- Autohaus; Fachzeitschrift fuer den modernen Kraftfahrzeugbetrieb. fortn ISSN 0005-0989 (Zentralverband des Kraftfahrzeughandels e.V.)
- Das Bayerische Kraftfahrzeughandwerk. m. ISSN 0005-7061 (Landesinnungsverband des Bayerischen Kraftfahrzeughandwerks Muenchen)

**A. Bast**
Huettmannstr. 52, 4300 Essen 1, W. Germany (B.R.D.)
- Aktion; Zeitung junger Arbeitnehmer. m. (Junge Christliche Arbeitnehmer)

**Bastei-Verlag Gustav H. Luebbe**
Scheidtbachstr. 25-31, 5070 Bergisch Gladbach, W. Germany (B.R.D.)
- Das Goldene Blatt. w. ISSN 0046-6093

**Henrich Bauer Fachzeitschriften Verlag KG**
Graeffstr. 5, 5000 Cologne 30, W. Germany (B.R.D.)
- Selbst mit 1000 Tips. m.

**Verlag Hermann Bauer KG**
Staudingerstr. 7, Postfach 167, 7800 Freiburg, W. Germany (B.R.D.)
- Esotera; Monatszeitschrift fuer geistiges Leben und alle Gebiete der Grenzwissenschaften. m. ISSN 0003-2921

**Heinrich Bauer Verlag**
Burchardstr. 11, 2000 Hamburg 1, W. Germany (B.R.D.)
- Auto Zeitung. s-m.
- Das Neue Blatt. w.
- Neue Mode. m.
- Neue Post. w. (Dm)
- Neue Revue. w.
- Praline. w. ISSN 0032-6828
- Wochenend. w.

**Heinrich Bauer Verlag Muenchen**
Augustenstr. 10, 8000 Munich 2, W. Germany (B.R.D.)
- Bravo. w.

**Bauernverband Wuerttemberg-Baden**
- Wuerttembergisches Wochenblatt fuer Landwirtschaft. (pub. by Verlag Eugen Ulmer)

**Verlag E. C. Baumann KG**
Oskar-von-Miller-Str. 5, Postfach 1149, 8650 Kulmbach, W. Germany (B.R.D.)
- Krankenhaus-Umschau; Fachzeitschrift fuer Wirtschaft und Technik im Krankenhaus. m. ISSN 0023-4508 (Fachvereinigung der Verwaltungsleiter Deutscher Krankenanstalten e.V.)

**Baumgartner-Verlag**
3135 Warpke, W. Germany (B.R.D.)
- Astrologischer Auskunftsbogen; Zeitschrift fuer Forschung, Fortbildung und Erfahrungsaustausch. m. ISSN 0004-6175

**Bausparkasse Wuestenrot**
Wuestenrot-Haus, 7140 Ludwigsburg, W. Germany (B.R.D.)
- Mein Eigenheim. bi-m. ISSN 0025-8792

**Bauverlag GmbH**
Wittelsbacherstr. 10, 6200 Wiesbaden, W. Germany (B.R.D.)
- Airport Forum; airport construction and operation. bi-m. ISSN 0002-2802
- Baumaschine und Bautechnik; building machinery and construction methods. m. ISSN 0005-6693
- Bauwirtschaft (B W); Wohnenmagazin fuer Fuehrungskraefte im Bauwesen. w. ISSN 0005-6863 (Hauptverband der Deutschen Bauindustrie) (Co-sponsor: Bundesverband Steine und Erden e.V.)
- Beton- und Fertigteil-Jahrbuch. a. ISSN 0067-6365
- Betonwerk und Fertigteil-Technik; Zeitschrift fuer Beton-und-Stahlbetonfertigteile,Betonwaren und Betonwerkstein. m. ISSN 0373-4331 (Bundesverband Deutscher Beton- und Fertigteil-Industrie)
- Bundesbaublatt; Zeitschrift fuer Raumordnung, Bauwesen, Staedtebau, Baurecht und Bauforschung. m. ISSN 0007-5884 (Germany, Federal Republic. Bundesministerium fuer Raumordnung, Bauwesen und Staedtebau)

- Z I International; journal for the brick and tile, structural ceramics, refractory and stoneware industries. m. ISSN 0341-0552 (Bundesverband der Deutschen Ziegelindustrie e.V.)
- Zement-Kalk-Gips. Edition A. m. ISSN 0340-5095
- Zement-Kalk-Gips. Edition B. m.
- Zement-Taschenbuch. biennial. ISSN 0514-2938 (Verein Deutscher Zementwerke e.V.)
- Ziegeleitechnisches Jahrbuch. a. ISSN 0084-5485

**Bauverlag GmbH. Zweigniederlassung Berlin**
Nikolsburger Str. 11, 1000 Berlin 31, W. Germany (B.R.D.)
- Berliner Bauwirtschaft. bi-w. ISSN 0045-1762

**Bayer AG**
5090 Leverkusen-Bayerwerk, W. Germany (B.R.D.)
- Bayer-Berichte/Bayer Reports. s-a. ISSN 0005-6960
- Bayer-Mitteilungen fuer die Gummi-Industrie. 3 per yr. ISSN 0005-6987
- Bayer-Symposien. (pub. by Springer-Verlag US)
- Correo Fitosanitario (International) irreg.
- Correo Fitosanitario (South America) irreg.
- Crop Protection Courier (International) irreg. ISSN 0590-1243
- Crop Protection Courier (South Africa) irreg.
- Informaciones Bayer para la Industria del Caucho. 3 per yr.
- Informations Bayer pour l'Industrie du Caoutchouc. 3 per yr.
- Pflanzenschutz-Kurier. 2-4 per yr. ISSN 0405-0738
- Pflanzenschutz-Nachrichten Bayer. 3 per yr. ISSN 0079-1342
- Technical Notes for the Rubber Industry. 3 per yr.

**Bayerische Akademie der Schoenen Kuenste**
- Ensemble. (pub. by Verlagsgruppe Langen-Mueller)

**Bayerische Akademie der Wissenschaften**
Marstallplatz 8, 8000 Munich 22, W. Germany (B.R.D.)
- Bayerische Akademie der Wissenschaften. Jahrbuch. (pub. by C. H. Beck'sche Verlagsbuchhandlung)
- Bayerische Akademie der Wissenschaften. Mathematisch-Naturwissenschaftliche Klasse. Abhandlungen. 2-3 per yr. ISSN 0005-6995
- Bayerische Akademie der Wissenschaften. Philosophisch Historische Klasse. Sitzungsberishte. Abhandlungen. 5-10 per yr. ISSN 0005-710X

**Bayerische Akademie der Wissenschaften. Institut fuer Volkskunde**
- Bayerisches Jahrbuch fuer Volkskunde. (pub. by Karl Hart)

**Bayerische Akademie der Wissenschaften. Kommission fuer Bayerische Landesgeschichte**
- Bayerische Vorgeschichtsblaetter. (pub. by C. H. Becksche Verlagsbuchhandlung)
- Zeitschrift fuer Bayerische Landesgeschichte. (pub. by C. H. Beck'sche Verlagsbuchhandlung)

**Bayerische Botanische Gesellschaft**
Menzinger Str. 67, 8000 Munich, W. Germany (B.R.D.)
- Bayerische Botanische Gesellschaft. Berichte. a. ISSN 0067-4680

**Bayerische Jungbauernschaft e.V.**
Lessingstr. 3, 8000 Munich 2, W. Germany (B.R.D. )
- Bayerische Landjugend. m.

**Bayerische Landesaerztekammer**
Muehlbaurstr. 16, 8000 Munich 80, W. Germany (B. R. D.)
- Bayerisches Aerzteblatt. m. ISSN 0005-7126

**Bayerische Landeszahnaerztekammer**
- B z B. (pub. by Karl Demeter Verlag)

**Bayerische Numismatische Gesellschaft**
- Jahrbuch fuer Numismatik und Geldgeschichte. (pub. by Verlag Michael Lassleben)

**Bayerische Staatliche Bibliotheken**
- Bibliotheksforum Bayern. (pub. by Verlag Dokumentation)

**Bayerische Staatsbibliothek**
Ludwigstr. 16, 8000 Munich 34, W. Germany
(B.R.D.)
- Bayerische Staatsbibliothek. Inhaltsverzeichnisse
  Slavistischer Zeitschriften aus den Bereichen
  Literaturwissenschaft und Volkskunde - ISZ. q.
- Bayerische Staatsbibliothek. Osteuropa-
  Neuerwerbungen. m (10 per yr)
- Bayerische Staatsbibliothek, Munich.
  Jahresbericht. a. ISSN 0342-0221

**Bayerische Staatssammlung fuer Palaeontologie und
Historische Geologie**
Richard-Wagner-Strasse 10, 8000 Munich 2, W.
Germany (B.R.D.)
- Bayerische Staatssammlung fuer Palaeontologie
  und Historische Geologie. Mitteilungen. a. ISSN
  0077-2070
- Zitteliana; Abhandlungen der Bayerischen
  Staatssammlung fuer Palaeontologie und
  Historische Geologie. irreg.

**Bayerischer Bauernverband**
- Bayerisches Landwirtschaftliches Wochenblatt.
  (pub. by B L V-Verlagsgesellschaft mbH)

**Bayerischer Beamtenbund**
- Bayerisches Beamten-Jahrbuch. (pub. by Walhalla-
  u. Praetoria-Verlag Georg Zwickenpflug)

**Bayerischer Landessportverband e.V.**
Briennerstrasse 50, 8000 Munich 2, W. Germany
(B.R.D.)
- Bayernsport. w.

**Bayerischer Landesverein fuer Familienkunde e.V.**
Winzererstr. 68, 8000 Munich 40, W. Germany
(B.R.D.)
- Bayerischer Landesverein fuer Familienkunde.
  Blaetter. 3 per yr. ISSN 0005-7118

**Bayerischer Lehrer- und Lehrerinnenverband**
- B L L V Bayerische Schule. (pub. by Verlag Alois
  Erdl KG)

**Bayerischer Lehrer- und Lehrerinnenverband.
Bezirksverbaende Niederbayern und Oberpfalz**
- Heimatliche Schule. (pub. by Wolf Verlag GmbH)

**Bayerischer Reallehrerverband e.V.**
- R L V die Bayerische Realschule. (pub. by Verlag
  Gebr. Geiselberger)

**Bayerischer Rundfunk**
Rundfunkplatz 1, 8000 Munich 2, W. Germany
(B.R.D.)
- Gehoert-Gelesen. (pub. by Verlag Lambert
  Mueller GmbH)
- Schulfernsehen. m. ISSN 0036-7125

**Bayerischer Schachbund e.V.**
- Deutsche Schachblaetter. (pub. by Verlag
  Deutsche Schachblaetter)

**Bayerischer Turnverband e.V.**
Brienner Str. 50, Haus des Sports, 8000 Munich 2,
W. Germany (B.R.D.)
- Bayernturner. s-m. ISSN 0005-7231

**Bayerisches Geologisches Landesamt**
Prinzregen Str. 28, 8000 Munich 22, W. Germany
(B.R.D.)
- Geologica Bavarica. irreg. ISSN 0016-755X

**Druckerei und Verlagsanstalt Bayerland (Anton
Steigenberger)**
Konrad- Adenauer- Str. 19, Postfach 1868, 8060
Dachau, W. Germany (B. R. D.)
- Amperland; Heimatkundliche Vierteljahresschrift
  fuer die Kreise Dachau, Freising und
  Fuerstenfeldbruck. q. ISSN 0003-1992

**Bayern. Generaldirektion der Bayerischen Staatlichen
Bibliotheken**
Ludwigstr. 16, Postfach 150, 8000 Munich 34, W.
Germany (B.R.D.)
- Die Neue Buecherei; Zeitschrift fuer die
  oeffentliche Buechereien in Bayern. q. ISSN
  0028-3126

**Bayern. Hauptstaatsarchiv**
- Archivalische Zeitschrift. (pub. by Boehlau Verlag)

**Bayern. Landesamt fuer Brand- und
Katastrophenschutz**
Willi-Gebhardt-Ufer 32, 8000 Munich 40, Postfach
400226, W. Germany (B.R.D.)
- Brandwacht. m. ISSN 0006-9116

**Bayern. Landesamt fuer Denkmalpflege**
- Jahresbericht der Bayerischen
  Bodendenkmalpflege. (pub. by Rudolf Habelt
  Verlag)

**Bayern. Landesamt fuer Wasserwirtschaft**
Lazarettstr. 67, 8000 Munich 19, W. Germany
(B.R.D.)
- Deutsches Gewaesserkundliches Jahrbuch.
  Donaugebiet. a.
- Deutsches Gewaesserkundliches Jahrbuch.
  Rheingebiet: Abschnitt Main. a.

**Bayern. Staatsministerium der Justiz**
Justizpalast, 8000 Munich 35, W. Germany (B.R.D.)
- Bayerisches Justizministerialblatt. m. ISSN 0005-
  7142 (Subscr. Address: J. Schweizer Sortiment,
  Marsstr. 4, 8 Munich 2, W. Germany)

**Bayern. Staatsministerium des Innern**
Odeonsplatz 3, 8000 Munich 22, W. Germany
(B.R.D.)
- Bayerisches Staatsministerium des Innern.
  Ministerialamtsblatt der bayerischen inneren
  Verwaltung. w. ISSN 0005-7185
- Wasser und Abwasser /Bau-Intern. (pub. by Nord-
  Sued Werbung GmbH und Co. KG)

**Bayern. Staatsministerium fuer Arbeit und
Sozialordnung**
Winzererstr. 9, Postfach 56, 8000 Munich 40, W.
Germany (B.R.D.)
- Arbeit und Soziales; statistische mitteilungen. m.
- Bayerisches Staatsministerium fuer Arbeit und
  Sozialordnung. Amtsblatt. s-m.

**Bayern. Staatsministerium fuer Unterricht und Kultus**
Salvatorstr.2, 8000 Munich 2, W. Germany (B.R.D.)
- Bayerisches Staatsministerium fuer Unterricht und
  Kultus. Amtsblatt. (pub. by Kommunalschriften-
  Verlag J. Jehle)
- Schule und Wir. bi-m.

**Bayern. Statistisches Landesamt**
- Bayern in Zahlen. (pub. by Karl Wenschow
  GmbH)

**Bayernbund e.V.**
Falkenstr. 4, 8000 Munich 90, W. Germany
(B.R.D.)
- Weiss-Blaue Rundschau; Bayerische Zeitschrift
  fuer Politik, Wirtschaft und kultur. m. ISSN 0043-
  2202

**Bayernpartei**
Landsberger Str. 4, 8000 Munich 2, W. Germany
(B.R.D.)
- Freies Bayern. m. ISSN 0016-0806

**Beacon-Verlag Koerber oHG**
Birkental 13, Postfach 1420, 6702 Bad Duerkheim,
W. Germany (B.R.D.)
- Beacon; the English student's own magazine. 11
  per yr. ISSN 0005-7347
- Beaconette; the beginner's English magazine. 11
  per yr. ISSN 0005-7363
- C P S Reporter. (Cultural-Political-Scientific) 11
  per yr. ISSN 0007-8921
- Il Faro; Eine Monatszeitschrift zur Weiterbildung
  im Italienischen. m. ISSN 0014-8555

**Beckman Instruments GmbH**
Frankfurter Ring 115, 8000 Munich 40, W.
Germany (B.R.D.)
- Beckman Report. q. ISSN 0005-755X

**Verlag Eduard F. Beckmann KG**
Haus Heideck, Postfach 1120, 3160 Lehrte, W.
Germany (B.R.D.)
- C C B. (Review for Chocolate, Confectionery and
  Bakery) q.
- Landtechnik; vereinigt mit Die Landarbeit. m.
  (Kuratorium fuer Technik und Bauwesen in der
  Landwirtschaft e.V.)
- Lohnunternehmen in Land- und Forstwirtschaft;
  Zeitschrift fuer mehrbetrieblichen
  Maschineneinsatz. m.
- Zucker- und Suesswaren Wirtschaft;
  Fachzeitschrift fuer alle Bereiche der Suesswaren-
  Industrie. m. ISSN 0373-0204

**C. H. Beck'sche Verlagsbuchhandlung**
Wilhelmstr. 9, 8000 Munich 40, W. Germany
(B.R.D.)
- Bayerische Akademie der Wissenschaften.
  Jahrbuch. a. ISSN 0084-6090

- Bayerische Vorgeschichtsblaetter. a. ISSN 0341-
  3918 (Bayerische Akademie der Wissenschaften.
  Kommission fuer Bayerische Landesgeschichte)
- Behring Institut. Mitteilungen. irreg. ISSN 0301-
  0457 (Behring-Werke, Marburg)
- Byzantinische Zeitschrift. s-a. ISSN 0007-7704
- Chiron. a. ISSN 0069-3715 (Deutsches
  Archaeologisches Institut. Kommission fuer Alte
  Geschichte und Epigraphik)
- D S W R. (Datenverarbeitung - Steuer,
  Wirtschaft, Recht) m. ISSN 0341-5449
- Deutsche Notar-Zeitschrift. m. ISSN 0340-8604
  (Bundesnotarkammer)
- Deutsches Steuerrecht; Zeitschrift fuer Praxis und
  Wissenschaft des Gesamten Steuerrechts. s-m.
  ISSN 0012-1347 (Bundessteuerberaterkammer)
- Europarecht. q. (Wissenschaftliche Gesellschaft
  fuer Europarecht)
- Fundheft fuer Arbeitsrecht. a. ISSN 0071-9900
- Fundheft fuer Oeffentliches Recht. a. ISSN 0071-
  9919
- Fundheft fuer Zivilrecht. a. ISSN 0071-9927
- Gnomon; Kritische Zeitschrift fuer die gesamte
  klassische Altertumswissenschaft. 8 per yr. ISSN
  0017-1417
- Jean-Paul-Gesellschaft. Jahrbuch. a. ISSN 0075-
  3580
- Juristische Schulung. m. ISSN 0022-6939
- Karlsruher Juristische Bibliographie. m. ISSN
  0453-3283
- Neue Juristische Wochenschrift. w. ISSN 0341-
  1915
- Nova Kepleriana. Neue Folge. irreg., no. 6, 1976.
  ISSN 0078-2246 (Kepler-Kommission)
- Recht der Arbeit. bi-m.
- Rechtsprechung zum Wiedergutmachungsrecht. bi-
  m.
- Verwaltungsrechtsprechung in Deutschland;
  Sammlung obergerichtlicher Entscheidungen aus
  dem Verfassungs und Verwaltungsrecht. 8 per yr.
- WISt. (Wirtschaftwissenschaftliches Studium);
  Zeitschrift fuer Ausbildung und
  Hochschulkontakt. m. ISSN 0340-1650
- Zeitschrift fuer Bayerische Landesgeschichte. 3
  per yr. ISSN 0044-2364 (Bayerische Akademie
  der Wissenschaften. Kommission fuer Bayerische
  Landesgeschichte) (Co-sponsor: Gesellschaft fuer
  Fraenkische Geschichte)
- Zeitschrift fuer Rechtspolitik. m. ISSN 0514-6496

**Behring-Werke, Marburg**
- Behring Institut. Mitteilungen. (pub. by C. H.
  Beck'sche Verlagsbuchhandlung)

**B. Behr's Verlag GmbH**
Averhoffstr. 10, 2000 Hamburg 76, W. Germany
(B.R.D.)
- Bauern und Gaertner; Obstbau - Landwirtschaft -
  Gemuesebau. w. ISSN 0005-657X
- Behoerden und Organisationen der Land- Forst-
  und Ernaehrungswirtschaft. approx. a. ISSN 0522-
  604X
- Die Brotindustrie. m. ISSN 0007-246X
  (Bundesverband der Deutschen Brot- und
  Backwarenindustrie e.V)
- Ernaehrungswirtschaft. m. ISSN 0014-0244
  (Bundesverband der Deutschen
  Ernaehrungsindustrie)
- Handbuch der Gemeinschaftsverpflegung. a. ISSN
  0073-0041
- Der Industriebackmeister; Mensch, Maschine und
  Backtechnik im Grossbackbetrieb. bi-m. ISSN
  0046-9297 (Vereinigung Deutscher
  Industriebackmeister e.V.)
- International Encyclopedia on Packaging
  Machines/Catalogue International des Machines
  d' Emballage/Catalogo Internazionale delle
  Macchine per l' Imballaggio/Internationaler
  Verpackungsmaschinen- Katalog fuer Die
  Abpackende Industrie. irreg. ISSN 0074-5766
- Lebensmitteltechnik. m. ISSN 0047-4290
- Suesswaren. s-m. ISSN 0039-4653
- Suesswaren Jahrbuch. a. ISSN 0081-9174
- Taschenbuch fuer Agrarjournalisten. a. ISSN
  0082-1845 (Verband der Agrarjournalisten)

**A. Beig Verlag**
Damm 11, Postfach 1220, 2080 Pinneberg, W.
Germany (B.R.D.)
- Jahrbuch fuer den Kreis Pinneberg. a. ISSN 0448-
  150X (Heimatverband fuer den Kreis Pinneberg)

**Verlag das Beispiel**
Karlheinz Roemer KG, Platz der Deutschen Einheit
2, 6100 Darmstadt 1, W. Germany (B. R. D.)
- Das Bauzentrum. bi-m. ISSN 0005-688X (Verein
  Deutsches Bauzentrum e.V.)

**Chr. Belser Verlag**
Augustenstr. 3-15, 7000 Stuttgart, W. Germany
(B.R.D.)
- Belser Kunstquartal; Vorschau auf
Kunstausstellungen des In- und Auslandes. q.

**Verlag Julius Beltz**
Am Hauptbahnhof 10, Postfach 1120, 6940
Weinheim, W. Germany (B.R.D.)
- Betrifft: Erziehung; Forum fuer Bildungspolitik
und Erziehungswissenschaft. m. ISSN 0045-1789
- Psychologie Heute. m.
- Studien und Dokumentationen zur Deutschen
Bildungsgeschichte. irreg. (Deutsches Institut fuer
Internationale Paedagogische Forschung)
- Vorgaenge; Zeitschrift fuer Gesellschaftspolitik. q.
- Zeitschrift fuer Paedagogik. q. ISSN 0044-3247

**Benediktinerabtei Braunau**
8421 Rohr, W. Germany (B.R.D.)
- Braunauer Rundbrief. bi-m.

**Benediktinerabtei Muensterschwarzach**
- Muensterschwarzacher Studien. (pub. by Vier-
Tuerme-Verlag)

**Benediktinerabtei Niederaltaich**
8351 Niederaltaich, W. Germany (B.R.D.)
- Die Beiden Tuerme; niederaltaicher Rundbrief. s-
a.

**Hans W. Bentz**
Ottilienstr. 9, Bad Homburg V.D.H., W. Germany
(B.R.D.)
- Chartotheca Translationum Alphabetica;
international bibliography of translations on index
cards, in 160 series. m, with annual cumulation.
ISSN 0009-1944

**Beratungsstelle fuer Autogentechnik GmbH**
- B E F A-Mitteilungen. (pub. by Deutscher Verlag
fuer Schweisstechnik GmbH)

**Beratungsstelle fuer Stahlverwendung**
- Stahl und Form. (pub. by Verlag Stahleisen mbH)

**Berg-Verlag GmbH**
Clemensstr. 17, Postfach 209, 4630 Bochum, W.
Germany (B.R.D.)
- Gewerkschaftliche Bildungspolitik;
Stellungnahmen - Analysen - Informationen. m.
(Deutscher Gewerkschaftsbund)

**Bergbau-Berufsgenossenschaft**
Hunscheidtstr. 18, 4630 Bochum, W. Germany
(B.R.D.)
- Bergbau-Berufsgenossenschaft. Geschaeftsbericht.
a.

**Bergischer Geschichtsverein e. V.**
Kolpingstrasse 8, 5600 Wuppertal-Elberfeld, W.
Germany (B.R.D.)
- Bergischer Geschichtsverein. Zeitschrift. irreg.
ISSN 0067-5792

**Verlag Siegfried Bergmann**
Werler Str. 271a, Postfach 784, 4700 Hamm, W.
Germany (B.R.D.)
- Natur- und Landschaftskunde in Westfalen. q.
- Westfaelischer Jaegerbote. m.

**Bergmann und Co.**
Eintrachtstr. 110, 5000 Cologne 1, W. Germany (B.
R. D.)
- Blick ins Fleischer-Fachgeschaeft. m. ISSN 0006-
4734

**Berlin (West) Senator fuer Inneres**
- Amtsblatt fuer Berlin. (pub. by Kulturbuch-Verlag
GmbH)
- Polizeischau. (pub. by Verlag Bartels und Wernitz
KG)

**Berlin (West) Senator fuer Wirtschaft**
Martin Luther Str. 105, 1000 Berlin 62, W.
Germany (B.R.D.)
- Berliner Wirtschaftsdaten. irreg.

**Berlin (West) Statistisches Landesamt**
- Berliner Statistik. (pub. by Kulturbuch-Verlag
GmbH)
- Statistisches Jahrbuch Berlin. (pub. by Kulturbuch-
Verlag GmbH)

**Berlin (West) Verkehrsamt**
- Berlin Programm. (pub. by Irene Eggert)

**Berlin Verlag**
Pacelliallee 5, 1000 Berlin 33, W. Germany (B.R.D.)
- Friedens-Warte. q.

**Berlin Wertpapierboerse**
Hardenbergstr. 16, 1000 Berlin 12, W. Germany
(B.R.D.)
- Berlin Wertpapierboerse. Amtliches Kursblatt. 5
per w. ISSN 0003-214X

**Berliner Bank Aktiengesellschaft**
Hardenbergstr. 32, 1000 Berlin 12, W. Germany
(B.R.D.)
- Berliner Bank. Boersenbrief. w.
- Berliner Bank. Wirtschaftsbericht. 3 per yr. ISSN
0005-9277
- Mitteilungen fuer den Aussenhandel. m. ISSN
0026-6930

**Berliner Flughafen-GmbH**
Zentralflughafen, 1000 Berlin 42, W. Germany
(B.R.D.)
- Berlin-Flugplan. m. ISSN 0005-9242

**Berliner Hausbesitz Verlag, Manfred Schoeneck**
Petkusser Str. 58, 1000 Berlin 49, W. Germany
(B.R.D.)
- Berliner Hausbesitz. s-m. (Schutzbund fuer
Hausbesitz)

**Berliner Historische Kommission**
- Berliner Historische Kommission.
Veroeffentlichungen. (pub. by Walter de Gruyter
und Co.)

**Berliner Kraft- und Licht-(Bewag) Aktiengesellschaft**
Stauffenberg-Str. 26, 1000 Berlin 30, W. Germany
(B.R.D.)
- Berliner Kraft- und Licht (Bewag)
Aktiengesellschaft. Gesellschaftsbericht. a. ISSN
0067-608X

**Berliner Missionswerk**
Handjery Str. 19, 1000 Berlin 41, W. Germany
(B.R.D.)
- Im Lande der Bibel; neue Folge der neuesten
Nachrichten aus dem Morgenland. 3 per yr. ISSN
0019-2597 (Jerusalemsverein)

**Berliner Turnerbund E.V.**
Vorarlberger Damm 39, 1000 Berlin 41, W.
Germany (B.R.D.)
- Berliner Turnzeitung. m. ISSN 0005-9358

**Berliner Wort Verlagsgesellschaft mbH.**
Bismarckplatz 1, 1000 Berlin 33, W. Germany
(B.R.D.)
- Berliner Liberale Zeitung. fortn. ISSN 0005-9307
(Freie Demokratische Partei. Landesverband
Berlin)

**Bernard und Graefe Verlag fuer Wehrwesen**
Agnes-Bernauer-Platz 8, 8000 Munich 21, W.
Germany (B.R.D.)
- Bibliothek fuer Zeitgeschichte, Stuttgart.
Jahresbibliographie; Neue Folge der Buecherschau
der Weltkriegsbuecherei. irreg., 1973, vol. 44.
ISSN 0081-8992 (Bibliothek fuer Zeitgeschichte,
Stuttgart)
- Bibliothek fuer Zeitgeschichte, Stuttgart. Schriften.
irreg., 1973, no. 13. ISSN 0081-900X
- Handbuch zur Deutschen Militaergeschichte.
irreg., vol. 6, 1970. (Militaergeschichtliches
Forschungsamt)
- Marine-Rundschau. m. ISSN 0025-3294
(Arbeitskreis fuer Wehrforschung)
- Wehrmedizinische Monatsschrift; Organ des
Sanitaets- und Gesundheitswesen der Bundeswehr.
m. ISSN 0043-2156 (Deutsche Gesellschaft fuer
Wehrmedizin und Wehrpharmazie)
- Wehrwissenschaftliche Berichte. irreg., no. 18,
1976. ISSN 0083-7822 (Arbeitskreis fuer
Wehrforschung)

**Verlag A. Bernecker**
Unter dem Schoeneberg 1, Postfach 140, 3508
Melsungen, W. Germany (B. R. D.)
- B G S. (Bundesgrenzschutz); Zeitschrift des
Bundesgrenzschutzes. m. (Germany, Federal
Republic. Bundesministerium des Innern)

**Bertelsmann-Fachverlag**
Carl-Bertelsmann-Str. 270, Postfach 5555, 4830
Guetersloh, W. Germany (B.R.D.)
- Baumarkt. w.
- D B Z. (Deutsche Bauzeitschrift); Architektur,
Entwurf, Detail. m. ISSN 0011-4782
- Tiefbau, Ingenieurbau, Strassenbau. m. ISSN
0040-7240

**Bertelsmann Fachzeitschriften GmbH**
Kreuzstr. 14-16, Postfach 200421, 8000 Munich 2,
W. Germany (B.R.D.)
- Adhaesion; Klebstoffe, Farben und Lacke,
Coating, Verfahrenstechnik. m. ISSN 0001-8198
- Bauwelt. w. ISSN 0005-6855
- Bauwelt Katalog. a. ISSN 0067-4664
- Betriebsausruestung; Kennziffer Zeitschrift fuer
Produktion Organisation. m. ISSN 0005-996X
- Betriebsverpflegung. 9 per yr.
- Bureauausruestung. 7 per yr.
- Notes from Europe/Cahiers Europeens/
Europaeische Hefte; European literature cultural
review. q.
- Oberflaeche. m. ISSN 0029-7488

**Verlagsgruppe Bertelsmann GmbH**
Carl-Bertelsmann-Str. 270, Postfach 5555, 4830
Guetersloh, W. Germany (B.R.D.)
- Bertelsmann Briefe; wissenschaftliche Zeitschrift
fuer Fragen der Lesekultur und der
Medienentwicklung. q. ISSN 0005-9455

**W. Bertelsmann Verlag KG**
Gadderbaumer Str. 21, 4800 Bielefeld, W. Germany
(B. R. D.)
- Der Ausbilder. m. ISSN 0004-8100

**Berufsgenossenschaft der Chemischen Industrie**
Gaisbergerstr. 11, 6900 Heidelberg, W. Germany
(B.R.D.)
- Sichere Chemiearbeit. m.

**Berufsgenossenschaft der Feinmechanik und
Elektrotechnik**
Oberlaender Ufer 130, 5000 Cologne 61, W.
Germany (B.R.D.)
- Impuls; Zeitung fuer Sicherheit im Betrieb.

**Berufsverband der Augenaerzte Deutschlands e.V.**
- Der Augenarzt. (pub. by M. C. Wolf Kg)

**Berufsverband der Deutschen Chirurgen, e-V.**
- Chirurg. (pub. by Springer-Verlag US)

**Berufsverband der Deutschen Urologen**
- Urologe-Ausgabe B. (pub. by Springer-Verlag US)

**Berufsverband der Frauenaerzte e. V.**
- Der Frauenarzt. (pub. by M. K. Wolf KG)

**Berufsverband der Heilpraktiker Nordrhein-Westfalen
e.V.**
Suppenheider Str. 7, Postfach 110170, 5650
Solingen 11, W. Germany (B. R. D.)
- Zeitschrift fuer Naturheilkunde. m. ISSN 0044-
3182

**Berufsverband der Kinderaerzte Deutschlands e.V.**
- Der Kinderarzt. (pub. by Hansisches
Verlagskontor H. Scheffler)

**Berufsverband Deutscher Internisten**
- Internist. (pub. by Springer-Verlag US)

**Berufsverband Deutscher Psychologen**
- Psychologische Rundschau. (pub. by Verlag fuer
Psychologie)
- Zeitschrift fuer Klinische Psychologie - Forschung
und Praxis. (pub. by Verlag fuer Psychologie)

**Fachverlag N. Besselich**
Heideweg 3, 2252 St. Peter-Ording, W. Germany
(B.R.D.)
- R A K - Riechstoffe, Aromen, Kosmetica. m.
ISSN 0341-440X

**Verlag das Beste GmbH**
Rotebuehlplatz 1, Postfach 178, 7000 Stuttgart 1,
W. Germany (B.R.D.)
- Das Beste aus Reader's Digest (German Edition);
Ein internationales Magazin. m. ISSN 0005-9668

**Verlag Adalbert Bestgen**
Spessartstr. 13, Abholfach, 1000 Berlin 33, W.
Germany (B.R.D.)
 • Berliner Haus- und Grundbesitz; Fachzeitschrift
   fuer Immobilienbesitz und Verwaltung in Berlin.
   m. (Arbeitsgemeinschaft Berliner Haus-, Grund-,
   und Ruinenbesitzervereine e. V.)

**Verlagsbuchhandlung Bethel - Dirk Dolman und Co.
KG Nachfolger**
Gluckstr. 53, 2000 Hamburg 76, W. Germany
(B.R.D.)
 • Botschafter des Kommenden Koenigs. m. ISSN
   0006-8276

**Beton-Verlag GmbH**
Duesseldorfer Str. 8, Postfach 450, 4000
Duesseldorf 11, W. Germany (B.R.D.)
 • Betontechnische Berichte. a. ISSN 0409-2740
   (Verein Deutscher Zementwerke e.V.)

**Betriebswirtschaftliche Beratungsstelle fuer den
Einzelhandel**
Sachsenring 89, 5000 Cologne 1, W. Germany
(B.R.D.)
 • B B E Chef-Telegramm; Betriebswirtschaftlicher
   Informations-und Auskunftsdienst fuer den
   Einzelhandel. s-m.
 • Einzelhandels Berater. m.

**Beuroner Kunstverlag GmbH**
7792 Beuron, W. Germany (B.R.D.)
 • Erbe und Auftrag; Benediktinische Monatsschrift.
   bi-m. ISSN 0013-9963

**Beuth Verlag GmbH**
Burggrafenstr. 4/7, 1000 Berlin 30, W. Germany
(B.R.D.)
 • D I N Mitteilungen. (Institut fuer Normung) m.
   ISSN 0011-4952 (Deutsches Institut fuer
   Normung e.V.)
 • D K-Mitteilungen. bi-m. ISSN 0011-4987
   (Deutsches Institut fuer Normung e.V.. Ausschuss
   fuer Klassifikation)
 • DIN-Taschenbuecher. irreg. ISSN 0070-4261
   (Deutsches Institut fuer Normung e.V.)
 • English Translations of German Standards. irreg.
   ISSN 0071-0660 (Deutsches Institut fuer
   Normung e.V.)
 • Handbuch der Klassifikation. irreg.' ISSN 0073-
   0106 (Deutsches Institut fuer Normung e.V.)

**Bibelbund**
Eggensteiner Str. 137, Postfach 24, 7513 Stutensee-
Blankenloch, W. Germany (B. R. D.)
 • Bibel und Gemeinde. q. ISSN 0006-0615

**Bibliographisches Institut AG**
Dudenstr. 6, Postfach 311, 6800 Mannheim 41, W.
Germany (B.R.D.)
 • Meyers Grosses Jahreslexikon. a. ISSN 0076-7670
 • Theoretische und experimentelle Methoden der
   Regelungstechnik. irreg., vol. 10, 1974.
 • Wissenschaftliche Redaktion. irreg. ISSN 0084-
   0955

**Bibliothek fuer Zeitgeschichte, Stuttgart**
 • Bibliothek fuer Zeitgeschichte, Stuttgart.
   Jahresbibliographie. (pub. by Bernard und Graefe
   Verlag fuer Wehrwesen)
 • Bibliothek fuer Zeitgeschichte, Stuttgart. Schriften.
   (pub. by Bernard und Graefe Verlag fuer
   Wehrwesen)

**Bibliothekar-Lehrinstitut des Landes Nordrhein-
Westfalen**
 • Bibliothekar-Lehrinstitut des Landes Nordrhein-
   Westfalen. Arbeiten aus dem B L I. (pub. by
   Greven Verlag Koeln)
 • Bibliothekar-Lehrinstitut des Landes Nordrhein-
   Westfalen. Bibliographische Hefte. (pub. by
   Greven Verlag Koeln)

**Bielefelder Verlagsanstalt KG**
Niederwall 53, Postfach 1140, 4800 Bielefeld, W.
Germany (B.R.D.)
 • Bielefelder Katalog. s-a. ISSN 0006-2103
 • D N Z International. (Die Naehmaschinen-
   Zeitung) ISSN 0011-507X
 • Dental-Dienst. m. ISSN 0011-8559 (Verband der
   Deutschen Dental-Industrie e.V.)
 • Deutsche Bibliographie. Schallplatten-Verzeichnis.
   q. (Deutsche Bibliothek. Abteilung Deutsches
   Musikarchiv)
 • Elektro Nachrichten; unabhaengige Fachzeitschrift
   fuer Geraete, Beleuchtung, Installation. fortn.
   ISSN 0013-5550

 • Fahrzeug und Karosserie; Fachzeitschrift fuer
   Konstruktion, Fertigung, Instandsetzung. m. ISSN
   0014-6862 (Zentralverband Karosserie und
   Fahrzeugtechnik e. V.) (Co-publisher: A. W.
   Gentner Verlag)
 • Fono Forum; Zeitschrift fuer Schallplatte, Musik,
   HiFi-Technik. m. ISSN 0015-6140
 • Gummibereifung; Fachzeitschrift fuer
   Vulkanisation, Runderneuerung, Reifenhandel und
   Zubehoer. m. ISSN 0017-5609 (Zentralverband
   des Deutschen Vulkaniseurhandwerks)
 • Kantinen Anzeiger. m.
 • Radmarkt; einzige deutsche Fachzeitschrift der
   Zweiradwirtschaft. m. ISSN 0033-8540
 • Uhren-Juwelen-Schmuck. s-m. (Zentralverband
   fuer Uhren, Schmuck und Zeitmesstechnik)
 • Uhrmacher-Jahrbuch fuer Handwerk und Handel.
   a. ISSN 0082-7290
 • Vulkaniseur-Jahrbuch. a. ISSN 0083-694X

**Verlag die Biene**
Am Urnenfeld 12, 6300 Giessen 2, W. Germany (B.
R. D.)
 • Die Biene. m. ISSN 0006-212X (Landesverband
   Hessischer Imker e.V.)

**Biermann KG**
Rathenaustr. 43, 5600 Wuppertal 1, W. Germany
(B.R.D.)
 • Polizeispiegel. m. (Polizeigewerkschaft im
   Deutschen Beamtenbund)

**Verlag Bildpost**
Alboinstr. 17-23, 1000 Berlin 42, W. Germany
(B.R.D.)
 • Raiffeisenbote. m. ISSN 0033-8710 (Deutscher
   Raiffeisenverband e.V.)

**Bildungspolitische Verlagsanstalt**
Philadelphiastr. 156-160, 4150 Krefeld, W. Germany
(B. R. D.)
 • In; das deutsche Bildungsmagazin. m. ISSN 0301-
   9004

**Billy Graham Evangelistic Association Deutschland
e.V.**
Bismarkstr. 4, Postfach 1147, 7303 Neuhausen/
Stuttgart, W. Germany (B.R.D.)
 • Entscheidung. bi-m. ISSN 0013-9092

**Zeitschriftenverlag Dr. Bilz und Dr. Fraund KG**
Abeggstr. 2, Postfach 6220, 6200 Wiesbaden, W.
Germany (B.R.D.)
 • Der Deutsche Weinbau; Fachzeitschrift fuer
   Weinbau, Kellerwirtschaft und Weinvermarktung.
   3 per mo. ISSN 0012-0979 (Deutscher
   Weinbauverband)

**Binnenschiffahrts-Verlag GmbH**
Dammstrasse 15-17, 4100 Duisburg 13, W.
Germany (B.R.D.)
 • Binnenschiffahrts-Nachrichten. every 10 days.
   ISSN 0006-2847 (Bundesverband der Deutschen
   Binnenschiffahrt E.V.)

**Biochemischer Bund Deutschlands e.V.**
 • Weg zur Gesundheit. (pub. by Verlag Weg zur
   Gesundheit)

**Biologie Verlag**
Postfach 1449, 6200 Wiesbaden, W. Germany
(B.R.D.)
 • Biologische Abhandlungen. 2-3 per yr. ISSN
   0006-3282
 • Leben und Umwelt; Internationale Zeitschrift fuer
   Biologie, Umwelt und Lebensschutz. bi-m.
 • Ornithologische Mitteilungen. m. ISSN 0030-5723

**Biologische Anstalt Helgoland**
Palmaille 9, 2000 Hamburg 50, W. Germany
(B.R.D.)
 • Helgolaender wissenschaftliche
   Meeresuntersuchungen; marine investigations/
   recherches maritimes. 4 per yr. ISSN 0017-9957

**Biologische Bundesanstalt fuer Land- und
Forstwirtschaft**
 • Nachrichtenblatt des Deutschen
   Pflanzenschutzdienstes. (pub. by Verlag Eugen
   Ulmer)

**Biologische Bundesanstalt fuer Land- und
Forstwirtschaft in Berlin- Dahlem**
 • Bibliographie der Pflanzenschutzliteratur/
   Bibliography of Plant Protection/Bibliographie de
   la Protection des Plantes. (pub. by Verlag Paul
   Parey (Berlin))

 • Biologische Bundesanstalt fuer Land- und
   Forstwirtschaft, Berlin-Dahlem. Mitteilungen.
   (pub. by Verlag Paul Parey (Berlin))

**Bionomica-Gemeinschaft e.V.**
 • Bionomica. (pub. by Bionomica-Verlag)

**Bionomica-Verlag**
Altriper Faehre, Postfach 106, 6800 Mannheim 24,
W. Germany (B.R.D.)
 • Bionomica. bi-m. ISSN 0006-3487 (Bionomica-
   Gemeinschaft e.V.)

**Bischoeflicher Stuhl, Passau**
Ed. Dr. Emil Janik, Domplatz 3, 8390 Passau, W.
Germany (B.R.D.)
 • Passauer Bistumsblatt; Kirchenzeitung der
   Dioezese des hl.Valentin. w. ISSN 0031-2681

**Bischoeflicher Stuhl Regensburg**
 • Regensburger Bistumsblatt. (pub. by Verlag
   Regensburger Bistumsblatt)

**Bischoefliches Generalvikariat, Essen**
Zwoelfling 16, Postfach 1428, 4300 Essen, W.
Germany (B.R.D.)
 • Kirchliches Amtsblatt fuer das Bistum Essen. s-m.
   ISSN 0023-1827

**Bit-Verlag**
Sofienstr. 28, 7570 Baden-Baden, W. Germany
(B.R.D.)
 • Bit; buero & informationstechnik. m. ISSN 0006-
   3843

**Blasmusikverlag**
Am Maerzengraben 6, 7801 Freiburg-Tiengen, W.
Germany (B.R.D.)
 • Die Blasmusik. m. (Bund Deutscher
   Blasmusikverbaende e.V.)

**Blaues Kreuz in Deutschland e.V.**
 • Rettung. (pub. by Blaukreuz-Verlag)

**Blaukreuz-Verlag**
Freiligrathstr. 27, 5600 Wuppertal 2, W. Germany
(B.R.D.)
 • Rettung. w. ISSN 0048-7430 (Blaues Kreuz in
   Deutschland e.V.)

**Blick und Bild Verlag S. Kappe KG**
Gruenstr. 10, Postfach 227, 5620 Velbert, W.
Germany (B.R.D.)
 • Blick und Bild; illustrierter Monatsspiegel. m.
   ISSN 0006-4718

**Verlag Bockau und Freese**
Postfach 345, 4630 Bochum, W. Germany (B.R.D.)
 • Muster und Farbe. bi-m.

**Verlag Bodet und Link**
Wilhelm-Leuschner-Str. 89, 6000 Frankfurt 1, W.
Germany (B.R.D.)
 • Frankfurter Gastronomie. m. ISSN 0015-9964
   (Hotel- und Gaststaetten-Vereinigung Frankfurt
   am Main e.V.)
 • Frankfurter Wochenschau. s-m. ISSN 0016-0024
   (Amt fuer Fremdenverkehr und Kongresswesen)
   (Co-sponsor: Frankfurter Verkehrsverein e. V.)

**Boehlau-Verlag**
Niehler Str. 272-274, 5000 Cologne 60, W.
Germany (B.R.D.)
 • Archiv fuer Diplomatik, Schriftgeschichte, Siegel-
   und Wappenkunde. a. ISSN 0066-6297
 • Archiv fuer Kulturgeschichte. 2 per yr. ISSN
   0003-9233
 • Archivalische Zeitschrift. a. ISSN 0003-9497
   (Bayern. Hauptstaatsarchiv)
 • Boehlau Philosophica. irreg.
 • Deutsches Archiv fuer Erforschung des
   Mittelalters. 2 vols. per year. ISSN 0012-1223
 • Hansische Geschichtsblaetter. a. ISSN 0073-0327
   (Hansischer Geschichtsverein)
 • Jahrbuch fuer Geschichte von Staat, Wirtschaft
   und Gesellschaft Lateinamerikas. a. ISSN 0075-
   2673

**Boersenverein des Deutschen Buchhandels**
Gr. Hirschgraben 17-21, 6000 Frankfurt, W.
Germany (B.R.D.)
 • Archiv fuer Geschichte des Buchwesens. (pub. by
   Buchhaendler-Vereinigung GmbH)
 • Boersenblatt fuer den Deutschen Buchhandel.
   Frankfurter Ausgabe. (pub. by Buchhaendler-
   Vereinigung GmbH)
 • Buch und Buchhandel in Zahlen. a. ISSN 0068-
   3051

● Buch und Leser. q.

**Boldt Verlag KG**
Postfach 110, 5407 Boppard, W. Germany (B.R.D.)
● Angewandte Forschung in der Bundesrepublik
Deutschland. irreg. ISSN 0066-1767 (Deutsche
Forschungsgemeinschaft)
● Deutsche Forschungsgemeinschaft. Denkschriften
zur Lage der Deutschen Wissenschaft. a. ISSN
0070-3974
● Deutsche Forschungsgemeinschaft.
Forschungsberichte. irreg. ISSN 0070-3982
● Deutsche Forschungsgemeinschaft. Kommissionen.
Mitteilungen. irreg. ISSN 0070-3990

**Verlag Aurel Bongers**
Hubertusstr. 13, Postfach 220, 4350 Recklinghausen,
W. Germany (B. R. D.)
● Beitraege zur Kunst des Christlichen Ostens. irreg.
ISSN 0067-5121
● Heilige in Bild und Legende. irreg., vol. 27, 1974.
ISSN 0440-6087
● Iconographia Ecclesiae Orientalis. irreg., vol. 12,
1974. ISSN 0341-8448
● Ikonenkalender. a.
● Kleine Ikonenbuecherci. irreg., vol. 8, 1974. ISSN
0445-2577
● Monographien zur Rheinisch- Westfaelischen
Kunst der Gegenwart. irreg., vol. 50, 1976. ISSN
0463-1935
● Muenstersche Studien zur Kunstgeschichte. irreg.,
vol. 5, 1973. ISSN 0580-1583

**Bonifacius-Druckerei**
Liboristr. 1, 4790 Paderborn, W. Germany (B.R.D.)
● Die Neue Ordnung in Kirche, Staat, Gesellschaft,
Kultur. 6 per yr. ISSN 0028-3304

**Bonifatiuswerk der Deutschen Katholiken e.V.**
Kamp 22, 4790 Paderborn, W. Germany (B.R.D.)
● Bonifatiusblatt. q. ISSN 0006-7113
● Lebendiges Zeugnis. q. ISSN 0023-9941
● Priesterjahrheft. a.

**Bonn. Verein fuer Niederdeutsche Sprachforschung**
● Verein fuer Niederdeutsche Sprachforschung.
Korrespondenzblatt. (pub. by Karl Wachholtz
Verlag)

**Bonn. Werbe und Verkehrsamt**
Kurfuerstenstr. 2, Postfach 864, 5300 Bonn, W.
Germany (B.R.D.)
● Bonn-Information; Veranstaltungskalender der
Bundeshauptstadt. s-m.

**Bonner Heimat- und Geschichtsverein**
Quantiusstr. 9, 5300 Bonn, W. Germany (B.R.D.)
● Bonner Geschichtsblaetter. a. ISSN 0068-0052
(Co-sponsor: Stadtarchiv Bonn)

**Richard Boorberg Verlag (Muenchen)**
Levelingstr. 8, Postfach 800340, 8000 Munich 80,
W. Germany (B.R.D.)
● Bayerische Verwaltungsblaetter; Zeitschrift fuer
oeffentliches Recht und oeffentliche Verwaltung.
s-m. ISSN 0522-5337
● Die Fundstelle; Erlaeuterungen zu allen wichtigen
Vorschriften fuer die Bayerische
Kommunalverwaltungen. s-m. ISSN 0016-2779
● Die Gemeindekasse; Fachzeitschrift fuer das
kommunale Finanzwesen. s-m. ISSN 0016-612X

**Richard Boorberg Verlag (Stuttgart)**
Scharrstr. 2, 7000 Stuttgart 80, W. Germany
(B.R.D.)
● Gemeindeverwaltung in Rheinland - Pfalz. s-m.
ISSN 0016-6170
● Neues Polizeiarchiv; ein Nachschlagewerk in
Monatsheften. m. ISSN 0028-3681
● Recht der Wirtschaft. s-m.

**Verlag fuer Bootswirtschaft**
Jungiusstr. Messehaus, 2000 Hamburg 36, W.
Germany (B. R. D.)
● Bootswirtschaft. m. ISSN 0006-7644 (Deutscher
Boots- und Schiffbauer-Verband)

**Verkehrsblattverlag Dr. Borgmann**
Hohe Str. 39, 4600 Dortmund 1, W. Germany
(B.R.D.)
● Verkehrsblatt; Amtsblatt des Bundesminister fuer
Verkehr der Bundesrepublik Deutschland. s-m.
ISSN 0042-4013 (Germany, Federal Republic.
Bundesministerium fuer Verkehr)
● Zeitschrift fuer Verkehrserziehung. 4 per yr. ISSN
0341-2334

**Verlag Born**
Frankfurter Str. 180, Postfach 420220, 3500 Kassel,
W. Germany (B. R. D.)
● Anruf. m. (Deutscher Verband der Jugenbuende
fuer Entschiedenes Christentum e.V.)
● Auftrag und Weg. bi-m. (Deutscher Verband der
Jugenbuende fuer Entschiedenes Christentum
e.V.)

**Gebrueder Borntraeger Verlagsbuchhandlung**
Johannesstr. 3 a, 7000 Stuttgart 1, W. Germany
(B.R.D.)
(and 175 Fifth Ave., New York, N.Y. 10010)
● Annales Universitatis Saraviensis. Reihe:
Mathematisch-Naturwissenschaftliche Fakultaet.
irreg., no. 12, 1975. ISSN 0080-5165
(Universitaet des Saarlandes)
● Materialkundlich-Technische Reihe. irreg.
● "Meteor" Forschungsergebnisse. Reihe A.
Allgemeines, Physik und Chemie des Meeres.
irreg., no. 16, 1975. (Deutsche
Forschungsgemeinschaft)
● "Meteor" Forschungsergebnisse. Reihe B.
Meteorologie und Aeronomie. irreg., no. 10, 1975.
(Deutsche Forschungsgemeinschaft)
● "Meteor" Forschungsergebnisse. Reihe C.
Geologie und Geophysik. irreg., no. 23, 1975.
(Deutsche Forschungsgemeinschaft)
● "Meteor" Forschungsergebnisse. Reihe D. Biologie.
irreg. (Deutsche Forschungsgemeinschaft)
● Meteorologische Rundschau. 6 per yr. ISSN 0026-
1211 (Deutsche Meteorologische Gesellschaft)
● Newsletters on Stratigraphy. irreg. ISSN 0078-
0421
● Zeitschrift fuer Geomorphologie/Annals of
Geomorphology/Annales de Geomorphologie. 4
per yr. ISSN 0044-2798

**Borromaeusverein**
Wittelsbacherring 9, 5300 Bonn, W. Germany (B. R.
D.)
● Das Neue Buch; Buchprofile fuer die Katholische
Buechereiarbeit. bi-m. ISSN 0028-3118

**Robert Bosch GmbH. Abteilung FSD**
Postfach 50, 7000 Stuttgart 1, W. Germany (B.R.D.)
● Bosch Technische Berichte. 3 per yr. ISSN 0006-
789X

**Robert Bosch GmbH. Geschaeftsbereich Elektronik**
Forckenbeckstr. 9-13, 1000 Berlin 33, W. Germany
(B.R.D.)
● Audio-Technik. irreg., no. 23, 1974. ISSN 0571-
8678

**Gustav Bosse Verlag**
Von-der-Tann-Str. 38, Postfach 417, 8400
Regensburg 1, W. Germany (B.R.D.)
● Neue Musikzeitung; musikalische Jugend -
Jeunesses musicales. bi-m. ISSN 0028-3290
(Musikalische Jugend Deutschlands) (Co-sponsor:
Verband Deutscher Musikschulen)
● Studien zur Musikgeschichte des Neunzehnten
Jahrhunderts. irreg. ISSN 0081-7341

**Botanische Staatssammlung Muenchen**
Menzinger Str. 67, 8000 Munich 19, W. Germany
(B.R.D.)
● Botanische Staatssammlung Muenchen.
Mitteilungen. 1-2 per yr. ISSN 0006-8179

**Bouvier Verlag Herbert Grundmann**
Am Hof 32, Postfach 1268, 5300 Bonn 1, W.
Germany (B.R.D.)
● Abhandlungen zur Kunst-, Musik- und
Literaturwissenschaft. irreg., vol. 134, 1974.
● Abhandlungen zur Philosophie, Psychologie und
Paedagogik. irreg., vol. 113, 1976. ISSN 0065-
0366
● Akademische Vortraege und Abhandlungen. irreg.,
no. 42, 1976. ISSN 0065-5538
● Archiv fuer Begriffsgeschichte; Bausteine zu einem
historischen Woerterbuch der Philosophie. 2 per
yr. ISSN 0003-8946
● Bonner Arbeiten zur Deutschen Literatur. irreg.
ISSN 0068-001X
● Bonner Beitraege zur Bibliotheks- und
Buecherkunde. irreg., vol. 24, 1973. ISSN 0068-
0028
● Hegel-Studien. irreg., vol. 11, 1976. ISSN 0073-
1587 (Deutsche Forschungsgemeinschaft. Hegel
Kommission)
● Internationale Vereinigung zur Foerderung des
Studiums der Hegelschen Philosophie.
Veroeffentlichung. irreg.
● Koelner Ethnologische Mitteilungen. irreg. ISSN
0075-6490

● Literatur und Wirklichkeit. irreg., vol. 17, 1976.
ISSN 0075-9937
● Mainzer Philosophische Forschungen. irreg., vol.
17, 1976. ISSN 0076-2776
● Schriften zur Rechtslehre und Politik. irreg., vol.
66, 1974. ISSN 0080-7060
● Studien zur Literatur der Moderne. irreg.
● Zeitschrift fuer Aesthetik und allgemeine
Kunstwissenschaft. s-a. ISSN 0044-2186

**Westholsteinische Verlagsanstalt Boyens und Co.**
Am Wulf- Isebrand-Platz, Postfach 1880, 2240
Heide, W. Germany (B.R.D.)
● Dithmarschen; Zeitschrift fuer Landeskunde und
Heimatpflege. q. ISSN 0012-4125 (Verein fuer
Dithmarscher Landeskunde)
● Hebbel- Jahrbuecher. a. ISSN 0073-1560 (Hebbel-
Gesellschaft)
● Klaus-Groth-Gesellschaft . Jahresgaben. a.
● Die Kueste; Archiv fuer Forschung und Technik
an der Nord- und Ostsee. irreg (1-2 per yr.)
(Kuestenausschuss Nord- und Ostsee, Kiel)
● Nordelbingen; Beitraege zur Kunst- und
Kulturgeschichte. a. ISSN 0078-1037
(Gesellschaft fuer Schleswig-Holsteinische
Geschichte)
● Theodor-Storm-Gesellschaft. Schriften. a. ISSN
0082-3880

**Brahms-Gesellschaft Hamburg**
Hamburg, W. Germany (B.R.D.)
● Brahms-Gesellschaft Hamburg. Jahresgabe. a.

**Druckerei H. Brandt**
Stedinger Str. 18, 2870 Delmenhorst, W. Germany
(B.R.D.)
● Astronautik; Mitteilungen, Tagungs- und
Forschungsberichte. bi-m. ISSN 0004-6221
(Hermann-Oberth-Gesellschaft)

**Verlag G. Braun GmbH**
Karl-Friedrich-Str. 14, Postfach 1709, 7500
Karlsruhe 1, W. Germany (B.R.D.)
● Aerztliche Kosmetologie; Fachzeitschrift fuer
kosmetische Dermatologie. bi-m.
● Alte Kameraden. m. (Arbeitsgemeinschaft fuer
Kameradenwerke und Traditionsverbaende)
● Astronomische Grundlagen fuer den Kalender. a.
ISSN 0067-0014 (Astronomisches Rechen-
Institut)
● Baden-Wuerttemberg. s-a.
● Der Deutsche Fall Schirmjaeger. bi-m. ISSN
0012-0081 (Bund Deutscher Fallschirmjaeger
e.V.)
● HiFi Stereophonie. m. ISSN 0018-1382
(Deutsches High-Fidelity Institut)
● Der Krankenhausarzt; Zeitschrift fuer klinische
wissenschaftliche Information. m. ISSN 0023-
4516
● Militaergeschichtliche Mitteilungen. s-a. ISSN
0026-3826 (Militaergeschichtliches
Forschungsamt)
● Therapiewoche. w. ISSN 0040-5973

**Braunschweigischer Geschichts Verein e.V.**
Staatsarchiv, Forstweg 2, 3340 Wolfenbuettel, W.
Germany (B.R.D.)
● Braunschweigisches Jahrbuch. a. ISSN 0068-0745

**Brede-Verlag**
3501 Habichtswald-Ehlen, W. Germany (B.R.D.)
● Blaue Feder; alle "Thema Null"-Beitraege. m.

**Verlag Friedl Brehm**
Poeckinger Weg 10, 8133 Feldafing, W. Germany
(B. R. D.)
● Schmankerl; literarische Blaetter fuer Bayerisch-
Oesterreichische Mundarten. 4-6 per yr. ISSN
0085-5952

**Breitkopf und Haertel**
Walkmuehlstr. 52, Postfach 1707, 6200 Wiesbaden,
W. Germany (B.R.D.)
● Max-Reger-Institut, Bonn. Mitteilungen. irreg.
ISSN 0076-5694
● Neue Musikgeschichtliche Forschungen. irreg.
ISSN 0077-7714

**Bremen. Senator fuer Bildung, Wissenschaft und
Kunst**
Rembertiring 8-12, 2800 Bremen, W. Germany
(B.R.D.)
● Bremer Schulblatt. irreg. ISSN 0006-9582

**Bremer Gesellschaft fuer Vorgeschichte**
● Bremer Archaeologische Blaetter. (pub. by Rudolf
Habelt Verlag)

**Bremische Evangelische Kirche**
- Bremer Kirchenzeitung. (pub. by Carl Schuenemann Verlag)

**Bremische Hafenvertretung e. V.**
- Weserlotse. (pub. by Weser-Kurier GmbH)

**Verlag Joh. Brendow und Sohn**
Gutenbergstr. 1, 4130 Moers 1, W. Germany (B.R.D.)
- Neues Leben; Zeitschrift fuer aktive Christen. m. ISSN 0028-3665 (Missionswerk Neues Leben e.V.)

**Breuberg-Bund**
Am Ziegelgraben 1, 6127 Breuberg, W. Germany (B. R. D.)
- Der Odenwald; Zeitschrift des Breuberg-Bundes. q. ISSN 0029-8360

**E. J. Brill GmbH**
Antwerpener Str. 6-12, 5000 Cologne 1, W. Germany (B.R.D.)
- Ethnologia. irreg., vol. 8, 1976. ISSN 0071-1845 (Gesellschaft fuer Voelkerkunde)
- Zeitschrift fuer Religions- und Geistesgeschichte. q. ISSN 0044-3441

**Verlag F.A. Brockhaus**
Leberberg 25, Postfach 261, 6200 Wiesbaden 1, W. Germany (B.R.D.)
- Brockhaus-Greif - Neue Berichte; eine Leserzeitschrift fuer die Freunde von F. A. Brockhaus.

**R. Brockhaus Verlag**
Champagne 7, 5600 Wuppertal 11, W. Germany (B.R.D.)
- Offene Tueren. bi-m. ISSN 0030-011X (Missionshaus Bibelschule Wiedenest)
- Theologische Beitraege. bi-m.

**Studienverlag Dr. N. Brockmeyer**
Querenburger Hoehe 281, 4630 Bochum, W. Germany (B. R. D.)
- Materialia Turcica. irreg.

**Broenner-Verlag**
Stuttgarter Str. 18, 6000 Frankfurt, W. Germany (B.R.D.)
- German Motor Tribune. a. ISSN 0072-145X

**Brown, Boveri & Cie. Aktiengesellschaft**
Kallstadter Str. 1, 6800 Mannheim, W. Germany (B.R.D.)
- B B C-Nachrichten. m. ISSN 0005-2825

**Verlag F. Bruckmann KG**
Nymphenburgerstr. 86, 8000 Munich 20, W. Germany (B.R.D.)
- Der Bergsteiger. m. ISSN 0005-8963
- Fikrun Wa Fann. s-a. ISSN 0015-0932
- Humboldt. q. ISSN 0018-7615
- Humboldt (Portuguese Edition); revista para o mondo Luso-Brasileiro. s-a. ISSN 0018-7623
- Novum Gebrauchsgraphik/International Advertising Art. m.
- Pantheon; internationale Zeitschrift fuer Kunst. q. ISSN 0031-0999

**Bruderverlag**
Bismarckstr. 21, Postfach 1748, 7500 Karlsruhe 1, W. Germany (B.R.D.)
- Bauen mit Holz. m. ISSN 0005-6545 (Bund Deutscher Zimmermeister)

**Verlag die Bruecke GmbH**
Adolf-Kolping Str. 9, 8000 Munich 2, W. Germany (B. R. D.)
- Die Bruecke. w. ISSN 0007-2613

**Bruecke-Museum**
Bussardsteig 9, 1000 Berlin 33, W. Germany (B.R.D.)
- Bruecke-Archiv. a. ISSN 0572-7146

**Brunnen-Verlag GmbH**
Pestalozzistr. 1, Postfach 5205, 6300 Giessen 1, W. Germany (B.R.D.)
- Theologie und Dienst. irreg. (Prediger- und Missionsseminar St. Chrischona)

**Bryologisch-Lichenologische Arbeitsgemeinschaft fuer Mittel-Europa**
- Herzogia. (pub. by J. Cramer)

**Zeit-Verlag Gerd Bucerius**
Speersort 1, Postfach 1101, 2000 Hamburg 1, W. Germany (B.R.D.)
(U. S. Subscr. to: German Language Publications, Inc., 75 Varick St., New York, NY 10013)
- Die Zeit; Wochenzeitung fuer Politik, Wirtschaft, Handel und Kultur. w. ISSN 0044-2070

**Buchhaendler-Vereinigung GmbH**
Grosser Hirschgraben 17-21, Postfach 2404, 6000 Frankfurt 1, W. Germany (B.R.D.)
- Adressbuch fuer den Deutschsprachigen Buchhandels. a. ISSN 0065-2032
- Archiv fuer Geschichte des Buchwesens. bi-m. ISSN 0066-6327 (Boersenverein des Deutschen Buchhandels)
- Archiv Ungedruckter Wissenschaftlicher Schriften. irreg. ISSN 0071-9188 (Deutsche Bibliothek)
- Boersenblatt fuer den Deutschen Buchhandel. Frankfurter Ausgabe. s-w. ISSN 0006-565X (Boersenverein des Deutschen Buchhandels)
- Deutsche Bibliographie. Das Deutsche Buch; Auswahl wichtiger Neuerscheinungen. bi-m. ISSN 0011-9954 (Deutsche Bibliothek)
- Deutsche Bibliographie. Fuenfjahres-Verzeichnis. irreg. (Deutsche Bibliothek)
- Deutsche Bibliographie. Halbjahres-Verzeichnis; Verzeichnis aller im Woechentlichen Verzeichnis, Reihe A, angezeigten Veroeffentlichungen, der eingesandten oesterreichischen und schweizerischen Verlagswerke sowie einer Auswahl von Erscheinungen ausserhalb des Verlagsbuchhandels. s-a. (Deutsche Bibliothek)
- Deutsche Bibliographie. Hochschulschriften-Verzeichnis. m. ISSN 0301-4665 (Deutsche Bibliothek)
- Deutsche Bibliographie. Verzeichnis Amtlicher Druckschriften; Veroeffentlichungen der Behoerden, Koerperschaften, Anstalten und Stiftungen des oeffentlichen Rechts sowie der wichtigsten halbamtlichen Institutionen in der Bundesrepublik Deutschland und West-Berlin. irreg. (Deutsche Bibliothek)
- Deutsche Bibliographie. Wochentliches Verzeichnis. Reine A: Erscheinungen des Verlagsbuchhandels; Amtsblatt der Deutschen Bibliothek. w. (Deutsche Bibliothek)
- Deutsche Bibliographie. Woechentliches Verzeichnis. Reihe B: Erscheinungen ausserhalb des Verlagsbuchhandels. fortn. (Deutsche Bibliothek)
- Deutsche Bibliographie. Woechentliches Verzeichnis. Reihe C: Karten. q. (Deutsche Bibliothek)
- Deutsche Bibliographie. Zeitschriften-Verzeichnis; in Deutschland erscheinende periodische Veroeffentlichungen sowie deutschsprachige Periodika Oesterreichs, der Schweiz und anderer Laender. irreg. (Deutsche Bibliothek)
- Verzeichnis Lieferbarer Buecher/German Books in Print. (pub. by Verlag Dokumentation)

**Buechergilde Gutenberg Verlagsgesellschaft mbH**
Untermainkai 66, Postfach 16220, 6000 Frankfurt/ Main 16, W. Germany (B.R.D.)
- Buechergilde. q. ISSN 0007-3032

**Verlag Buecherschiff Walter Reutin**
Rheinstr. 122, Postfach 210947, 7500 Karlsruhe 21, W. Germany (B.R.D.)
- Buecherschiff; die deutsche Buecherzeitung. 4 per yr. ISSN 0007-3059

**Buehnenschriften-Vertriebs-Gesellschaft**
Feldbrunnenstr. 74, 2000 Hamburg 13, W. Germany (B.R.D.)
- Die Buehnengenossenschaft. 10 per yr. ISSN 0007-3083 (Genossenschaft Deutscher Buehnenangehoeriger)
- Deutsches Buehnen-Jahrbuch; Theatergeschichtliches Jahr- und Adressbuch. a. ISSN 0070-4431 (Genossenschaft Deutscher Buehnenangehoeriger)

**Buero- und Organisationstechnik Verlagsgesellschaft Dr. H. Benad**
Spaldingstr. 64, 2000 Hamburg 1, W. Germany (B.R.D.)
- Buerotechnische Sammlung. m. ISSN 0007-3172

**Bulkowsky Verlag**
Zietenstr. 61, 4000 Duesseldorf, W. Germany (B.R.D.)
- Pro; ein schriftlicher Vorgang. a. ISSN 0032-9045

**Bund der Berliner und Freunde Berlins e.V. Kreisverband Muenchen**
Klenzestr. 30, 8000 Munich 5, W. Germany (B.R.D.)
- Der Berliner Baer. m. ISSN 0005-9269

**Bund der Blindenfreunde e.V.**
Aeussere Bayreuther Str. 45, 8500 Nuernberg, W. Germany (B.R.D.)
- Der Blindenhelfer. q.

**Bund der Deutschen Zollbeamten**
- Zollkalender. (pub. by Walhalla-u. Praetoria-Verlag Georg Zwickenpflug)

**Bund der Fliegergeschaedigten, Evakuierten, Waehrungsgeschaedigten**
Leuschnerstr. 17, Postfach 220, 7000 Stuttgart, W. Germany (B.R.D.)
- Selbsthilfe. m. ISSN 0037-1165

**Bund der Freien Waldorfschulen e.V.**
- Erziehungskunst. (pub. by Verlag Freies Geistesleben GmbH)

**Bund der Ingenieure des Gartenbaues**
- Der Gartenbauingenieur. (pub. by Verlag Eugen Ulmer)

**Bund der Kriegsblinden Deutschlands e. V.**
Alexandrastr 1, 6200 Wiesbaden, W. Germany (B.R.D.)
- Der Kriegsblinde; Zeitschrift fuer Verstaendnis und Verstaendigung. m. ISSN 0023-463X

**Bund der Mitteldeutschen**
- Mitteldeutscher Kurier. (pub. by Heimatliche Verlags- und Vertriebsgesellschaft MbH)

**Bund der Oeffentlich Bestellten Vermessungsingenieure e.V.**
Graf Gesslerstr. 5, 5000 Cologne-Deutz 21, W. Germany (B.R.D.)
- B D V I - Forum. m.

**Bund der Sozialversicherungs-Beamten und -Angestellten**
- Der Sozialversicherungs-Beamte und -Angestellte bsba. (pub. by G. Grote'sche Verlagsbuchhandlung KG)

**Bund der Theatergemeinden e.V.**
- Theater-Rundschau. (pub. by Theater-Rundschau-Verlag)

**Bund der Verfolgten des Naziregimes Berlin e.V.**
Mommsenstr. 27, 1000 Berlin 12, W. Germany (B.R.D.)
- Die Mahnung. m. ISSN 0025-0511

**Bund der Versorgungsbeamten**
- Der Versorgungsbeamte. (pub. by W. Kohlhammer GmbH (Koeln))

**Bund der Vertriebenen. Landesverband Niedersachsen e.V.**
Haus Deutscher Osten, Koenigsworther Str.2, 3000 Hannover, W. Germany (B.R.D.)
- Deutsche Umschau; Zeitung fuer Gesamtdeutsche und europaeische Politik, Wirtschaft und Kultur. m. ISSN 0012-0871

**Bund Deutscher Architekten**
- Der Architekt. (pub. by Forum-Verlag GmbH)

**Bund Deutscher Baumeister, Architekten und Ingenieure e.V.**
- Deutsche Bauzeitung. (pub. by Deutsche Verlagsanstalt GmbH)

**Bund Deutscher Blasmusikverbaende e.V.**
- Die Blasmusik. (pub. by Blasmusikverlag)

**Bund Deutscher Champignonzuechter e.V.**
Kurfuerstendamm 91, 1000 Berlin 31, W. Germany (B.R.D.)
- Champignon. m. ISSN 0009-1308

**Bund Deutscher Fallschirmjaeger e.V.**
- Der Deutsche Fall Schirmjaeger. (pub. by Verlag G. Braun GmbH)

**Bund Deutscher Forstmaenner**
- Der Deutsche Forstmann. (pub. by Vereinigte Verlagsanstalten GmbH)

**Bund Deutscher Forstmaenner. Landesverband Bayern e.V.**
- Bayerisches Forstdienst-Taschenbuch. (pub. by Walhalla-u. Praetoria-Verlag Georg Zwickenpflug)

**Bund Deutscher Hebammen**
- Deutsche Hebammen-Zeitschrift. (pub. by Elwin Staude Verlag GmbH)

**Bund Deutscher Kriminalbeamter**
- Der Kriminalist. (pub. by Muth-Verlag)

**Bund Deutscher Philatelisten e.V.**
Neue Mainzer Str. 60, 6000 Frankfurt, W. Germany (B.R.D.)
- Philatelie. q.

**Bund Deutscher Rassegefluegelzuechter e.V**
- Gefluegel-Boerse. (pub. by Verlag Juergens KG)

**Bund Deutscher Rechtspfleger**
Postfach, 8000 Munich 35, W. Germany (B. R. D.)
- Rechtspflegerblatt. 4 per yr. ISSN 0034-1363

**Bund Deutscher Steuerbeamten**
- Steuer-Gewerkschafts-Handbuch. (pub. by Walhalla- u. Praetoria-Verlag Georg Zwickenpflug)

**Bund Deutscher Taubstummenlehrer**
Gronewaldstr. 1, 5000 Cologne 41, W. Germany (B.R.D.)
- Das Bunte Blatt; Monatsschrift in einfacher Sprache. m. ISSN 0007-5965
- Hoergeschaedigten-Paedagogik. (pub. by Julius Groos Verlag)
- Statistische Nachrichten ueber Bildungs-und Sozialeinrichtungen fuer Hoergeschaedigte im Deutschsprachigen Raum. triennial.

**Bund Deutscher Zimmermeister**
- Bauen mit Holz. (pub. by Bruderverlag)

**Bund Evangelisch-Freikirchlicher Gemeinden**
- Die Gemeinde. (pub. by Verlag J.G. Oncken Nachf. GmbH)

**Bund Freireligioeser Gemeinden Deutschlands**
- Der Humanist. (pub. by Verlag Humanitas)

**Bund fuer Deutsche Schrift**
Rehbergstr. 5, 3000 Hannover-Sued, W. Germany (B.R.D.)
- Die Deutsche Schrift. s-a. ISSN 0012-0693

**Bund gegen Alkohol im Strassenverkehr e.V.**
- Blutalkohol. (pub. by Steintor-Verlag Hamburg GmbH)

**Bund Katholischer Religions Lehrervereinigungen**
- Religionsunterricht an hoeheren Schulen. (pub. by Patmos Verlag)

**Bund und Land**
- Deutsche Studien. (pub. by Otto Meissners Verlag)

**Bund und Landesverbaende der Wasser - und Kulturbauingenieure**
- Wasser und Boden. (pub. by Verlag Paul Parey (Hamburg))

**Bund-Verlag GmbH**
Deutz-Kalker Str. 46, Postfach 210140, 5000 Cologne 21, W. Germany (B.R.D.)
- A F A Informationen. 12 per yr. ISSN 0001-1126 (Deutscher Gewerkschaftsbund. Arbeitskreis fuer Arbeitsstudien)
- Arbeit und Recht; Zeitschrift fuer Arbeitsrechtspraxis. m. ISSN 0003-7648 (Deutscher Gewerkschaftsbund)
- Der Deutsche Beamte. m. ISSN 0011-9938 (Deutscher Gewerkschaftsbund)
- Gewerkschaftliche Monatshefte. m. ISSN 0016-9447 (Deutscher Gewerkschaftsbund)
- Laboratoriums-Praxis; Fachzeitschrift fuer Chemotechniker und Laboranten. m. ISSN 0023-6721 (Deutscher Gewerkschaftsbund)
- Die Quelle; Funktionaerzeitschrift des Deutschen Gewerkschaftsbundes. m. ISSN 0033-6246 (Deutscher Gewerkschaftsbund)
- Ran; ein politisches Jugendmagazin. m. ISSN 0004-7899 (Deutscher Gewerkschaftsbund)
- W S I Mitteilungen. m. (Deutscher Gewerkschaftsbund. Wirtschafts- und Sozialwissenschaftliches Institut)
- Welt der Arbeit. w. ISSN 0043-2482 (Deutscher Gewerkschaftsbund)

- Wirtschaft und Wissen. m. ISSN 0043-616X (Deutscher Gewerkschaftsbund)

**Bundes Arbeitsgemeinschaft der Mittel- und Grossbetriebe des Einzelhandels e.V.**
Lindenallee 70, 5000 Cologne 51, W. Germany (B.R.D.)
- B A G-Nachrichten. m. ISSN 0005-2639

**Bundesaerztekammer**
- Deutsches Aerzteblatt. (pub. by Deutscher Aerzte-Verlag GmbH)

**Bundesarbeitsgemeinschaft Hilfe fuer Behinderte**
- Das Behinderte Kind. (pub. by Rehabilitations-Verlag Gmbh)

**Bundesarchitektenkammer**
- Deutsches Architektenblatt. (pub. by Forum-Verlag GmbH)

**Bundesfachverband Fleischereibedarf- Grosshandel e.V., Wuppertal**
Rosenstrasse 13, 5600 Wuppertal-Barmen, W. Germany (B.R.D.)
- Fleischereibedarf. m. (Co-Sponsor: Zentralverband der Deutschen Importeure e.V.) (Subscriptions to: Fleischereibedarf, Saaselkoppel 4, 2000 Hamburg 65, W. Germany (B.R.D.))

**Bundesfachverband fuer Grosskuechen**
- Grosskuechen und GV. (pub. by Suedwestdeutsche Verlagsanstalt GmbH)

**Bundesforschungsanstalt fuer Fischerei**
Palmaille 9, 2000 Hamburg 50, W. Germany (B.R.D.)
- Informationen fuer die Fischwirtschaft. bi-m. ISSN 0020-0344

**Bundesgewerbeverband Imbissbetriebe E. V.**
- Snack. (pub. by F. L. Fischer-Werbung)

**Bundesgremium fuer Schulphotographie**
- Kamera und Schule. (pub. by Manz Verlag)

**Bundesgrosshandelsverband fuer Uhren- und Uhrentechnischen Bedarf e.V.**
- Uhrenjournal. (pub. by Fixdruck)

**Bundesinnungsverband des Gebaeudereiniger-Handwerks**
- Rationell Reinigen. (pub. by Lobrecht Verlag Max Rauscher KG)

**Bundesinnungsverband des Orthopaedieschuhmacherhandwerks**
- Der Orthopaedieschuhmachermeister. (pub. by Carl Maurersche Buchdruckerei)

**Bundesinstitut fuer Berufsbildungsforschung**
- Literaturinformationen zur Berufsbildungsforschung. (pub. by Verlag Dokumentation)

**Bundesinstitut fuer Ostwissenschaftliche und Internationale Studien**
Lindenborn Str. 22, 5000 Cologne, W. Germany (B.R.D.)
- Bundesinstitut fuer Ostwissenschaftliche und Internationale Studien. Berichte. irreg. ISSN 0435-7183

**Bundesinstitut fuer Sportwissenschaft**
Hertztrasse 1, 5023 Loevenich (Bez. Koeln), W. Germany (B.R.D.)
- Bundesinstitut fuer Sportwissenschaft. Berichte und Aspekte. irreg.

**Bundesnotarkammer**
- Deutsche Notar-Zeitschrift. (pub. by C. H. Beck'sche Verlagsbuchhandlung)

**Bundesstelle fuer Aussenhandelsinformation**
*see under* **Germany, Federal Republic**

**Bundessteuerberaterkammer**
- Deutsches Steuerrecht. (pub. by C. H. Beck'sche Verlagsbuchhandlung)

**Bundesverband der Agraringenieure (BAI) e.V.**
- Agraringenieur und Agrarmanager. (pub. by B A I Verlag GmbH)

**Bundesverband der Betriebskrankenkassen**
Kronprinzenstr. 6, Postfach 6909, 4300 Essen, W. Germany (B.R.D.)
- Betriebskrankenkasse. m. ISSN 0068-4228

**Bundesverband der Deutschen Binnenschiffahrt E.V.**
- Binnenschiffahrts-Nachrichten. (pub. by Binnenschiffahrts-Verlag GmbH)

**Bundesverband der Deutschen Brot- und Backwarenindustrie e.V**
- Die Brotindustrie. (pub. by B. Behr's Verlag Gmbh)

**Bundesverband der Deutschen Ernaehrungsindustrie**
- Ernaehrungswirtschaft. (pub. by B. Behr's Verlag GmbH)

**Bundesverband der Deutschen Feinkostindustrie e. V.**
- Die Feinkostwirtschaft. (pub. by SN-Werbe- und Verlagsgesellschaft Steinert und Co.)

**Bundesverband der Deutschen Fleischwarenindustrie e.V.**
- Die Fleischwirtschaft. (pub. by Verlagshaus Sponholz)

**Bundesverband der Deutschen Gas- und Wasserwirtschaft**
Th.-Heuss-Allee 90-98, 6000 Frankfurt, W. Germany (B.R.D.)
- B G W Gasstatistik. a.
- B G W Jahresbericht. a.
- B G W Wasserstatistik. a.
- B G W Zahlenspiegel. a.

**Bundesverband der Deutschen Industrie**
Oberlaender Ufer 84-88, 5000 Cologne 51, W. Germany (B.R.D.)
- B D I Deutschland Liefert/ B D I Germany Supplies. (pub. by Gemeinschaftsverlag GmbH)
- B D I-Mitteilungen. m. ISSN 0407-8985
- B D I-Organisationsplan. biennial.

**Bundesverband der Deutschen Schrottwirtschaft**
- Der Schrottbetrieb. (pub. by Handelsblatt GmbH)

**Bundesverband der Deutschen Standesbeamten e.V**
- Das Standesamt. (pub. by Verlag fuer Standesamtswesen GmbH und Co. KG)

**Bundesverband der Deutschen Zahnaerzte e.V.**
- Zahnaerztliche Mitteilungen. (pub. by Deutscher Aerzte-Verlag GmbH)

**Bundesverband der Deutschen Ziegelindustrie e.V.**
- Z I International. (pub. by Bauverlag GmbH)

**Bundesverband der Dolmetscher und Uebersetzer e. V.**
Wolfsgangstr. 148, 6000 Frankfurt 1, W. Germany (B.R.D.)
- Mitteilungsblatt fuer Dolmetscher und Uebersetzer. bi-m. ISSN 0026-6973

**Bundesverband der Innungskrankenkassen**
- Die Krankenversicherung. (pub. by Erich Schmidt Verlag (Bielefeld))

**Bundesverband der Lehrer an Beruflichen Schulen**
- Die Berufsbildende Schule. (pub. by Heckners Verlag)

**Bundesverband der Naturstein-Industrie**
- Die Naturstein- Industrie. (pub. by F. W. Wesel)

**Bundesverband der Ortskrankenkassen**
- Bleib Gesund. (pub. by Wirtschaftsdienst Verlag und Druckerei GmbH)
- Die Ortskrankenkasse. (pub. by Verlag der Ortskrankenkassen)

**Bundesverband der Soldaten der ehemaligen Waffen-SS e.V.**
- Der Freiwillige. (pub. by Munin-Verlag Gmbh)

**Bundesverband des Deutschen Farbengrosshandels**
- Der Farbenhaendler. (pub. by Rechtsverlag GmbH)

**Bundesverband des Deutschen Gueternah- und Gueterfernverkehrs**
- Der Gueterverkehr. (pub. by Kirschbaum Verlag)

**Bundesverband des Deutschen Gueterverkehrs e.V**
Haus des Strassenverkehrs, 6000 Frankfurt 93, W. Germany (B.R.D.)
- V W z. (Verkehrswirtschaftliche Zahlen) a. ISSN 0083-5021

**Bundesverband des Deutschen Personenverkehrsgewerbes**
• Der Personenverkehr. (pub. by Kirschbaum Verlag)

**Bundesverband des Deutschen Schuheinzelhandels**
• Schuhmarkt. (pub. by Umschau Verlag)

**Bundesverband des Deutschen Seiler-, Segel-und Netzmacherhandwerks e.V.**
• Deutsche Seiler-Zeitung. (pub. by Aegis-Verlag)

**Bundesverband des Deutschen Textileinzelhandels e.V.**
Sachsenring 89, 5000 Cologne 1, W. Germany (B.R.D.)
• B T E Marketing-Berater; fachzeitschrift fuer textile Absatzmittler. m.

**Bundesverband des Elektro-Grosshandels (VEG) e.V.**
• Elektrowirtschaft. (pub. by Verlag Ernst Arnold GmbH)

**Bundesverband des Schmuckwarengrosshandels**
• Goldscmiede Zeitung - European Jeweler und Deutsche Uhrmacherzeitschrift. (pub. by Ruehle-Diebener Verlag GmbH und Co. KG)

**Bundesverband des Werbenden Buch- und Zeitschriftenhandels E.V.**
Akazienstr. 10, 5000 Cologne 71, W. Germany (B.R.D.)
• Handbuch fuer den Werbenden Buch- und Zeitschriftenhandel. a. ISSN 0073-0165

**Bundesverband Deutschen Beton- und Fertigteil-Industrie**
• Betonwerk und Fertigteil-Technik. (pub. by Bauverlag Gmbh.)

**Bundesverband Deutscher Banken e.V.**
• Bank-Betrieb. (pub. by Bank Verlag GmbH)

**Bundesverband Deutscher Baustoffhaendler e.V.**
• Der Baustoffmarkt. (pub. by Gert Wohlfahrth KG Verlag Fachtechnik und Mercator-Verlag)

**Bundesverband Deutscher Kleingaertner e.V.**
• Fachberater fuer das Deutsche Kleingartenwesen. (pub. by B L V-Verlagsgesellschaft mbH)

**Bundesverband Deutscher Mittelstandsbrauereien e.V.**
• Brauerei Journal. (pub. by Dreistern Verlag)

**Bundesverband Deutscher Stahlhandel**
Westring 43, 4630 Bochum, W. Germany (B.R.D.)
• Lernen und Leisten. m. ISSN 0024-1059

**Bundesverband Deutscher Versicherungskaufleute (BVK)**
Kekulestr. 12, 5300 Bonn 1, W. Germany (B.R.D.)
• Versicherungsvermittlung; Zeitschrift selbstaendiger Versicherungskaufleute. m. ISSN 0049-6014

**Bundesverband Deutscher Volks- und Betriebswirte e.V.**
• Der Volks- und Betriebswirt. (pub. by Wilhelm Stollfuss Verlag)

**Bundesverband Deutscher Zeitungsverleger**
• Z V und Z V. (pub. by Zeitungs- und Zeitschriften-Verlag GmbH)

**Bundesverband Druck e.V.**
Postfach 1869, 6200 Wiesbaden, W. Germany (B.R.D.)
• Tiefdruck Jahrbuch. biennial.

**Bundesverband Freischaffender Architekten und Bauingenieure e.V.**
• Der Architekt und der Bauingenieur. (pub. by Isar-Post, Druck- und Verlagsgesellschaft mbH)

**Bundesverband fuer den Selbstschutz**
Eupener Str. 74, 5000 Cologne 41, W. Germany (B.R.D.)
• Z S Magazin; Zeitschrift fuer Zivilschutz, Katastrophenschutz und Selbstschutz. m.

**Bundesverband fuer Spastisch Gelaehmte und andere Koerperbehinderte e.V.**
Koelner Landstr. 375, Postfach 8132, 4000 Duesseldorf 1, W. Germany (B.R.D.)
• Das Band. bi-m.

**Bundesverband Materialwirtschaft und Einkauf e.V.**
• Beschaffung Aktuell. (pub. by Konradin-Verlag Robert Kohlhammer GmbH)

**Bundesverband Metall**
• Metall-Handwerk und Technik. (pub. by Charles Coleman, Buch- und Zeitschriften-Verlag KG)

**Bundesverband Oelfeuerungen und Gasfeuerungen E. V.**
• Feuerungstechnik - Gebaeudetechnik. (pub. by T.O.P. Verlag GmbH)

**Bundesverband Ring Deutscher Makler (RDM) E.V**
An der Alster 42, 2000 Hamburg 1, W. Germany (B.R.D.)
• A I Z. (Allgemeine Immobilien-Zeitung); Grund - Haus - Wohnen. m. ISSN 0001-1673

**Bundesvereinigung der Deutschen Arbeitgeberverbaende e.V.**
Oberlaender Ufer 72, 5000 Cologne, W. Germany (B.R.D.)
• Arbeitgeber. s-m.
• S A E. (pub. by J. P. Bachem Verlag GmbH)
• Soziale Selbstverwaltung. (pub. by Heider-Verlag)

**Bundesvereinigung Evangelischer Eltern und Erzieher E.V**
• Praxis Bilden und Erziehen. (pub. by Schriftenmissions-Verlag)

**Bundesvereinigung Lebenshilfe fuer Geistig Behinderte e.V**
Postfach 80, 3550 Marburg/Lahn 7, W. Germany (B.R.D.)
• Lebenshilfe; Vierteljahresschrift fuer die Probleme geistig Behinderter in Familie und Gesellschaft. q. ISSN 0023-995X

**Bundesversicherungsanstalt fuer Angestellte. Dezernat fuer Presse- und Oeffentlichkeitsarbeit**
Ruhrstr. 2, 1000 Berlin 31, W. Germany (B.R.D.)
• Die Angestelltenversicherung. m. ISSN 0003-312X

**Bundesvorstand des Sozialistischen Hochschulbundes**
Meckenheimer Allee 152, 5300 Bonn, W. Germany (B.R.D.)
• Frontal.

**Deutscher Bundeswehr-Verlag GmbH**
Suedstr. 123, Postfach 668, 5300 Bonn-Bad Godesberg 1, W. Germany (B.R.D.)
• Die Bundeswehr; groesste deutsche Soldatenzeitschrift-unabhaengig-ueberparteilich. m. ISSN 0007-5949 (Deutscher Bundeswehr-Verband e.V)

**Bundeszentrale fuer Politische Bildung**
Berliner Freiheit 7, Postfach 2000, 5300 Bonn 1, W. Germany (B.R.D.)
• Informationen zur Politischen Bildung/ Information for Civic Education. 6 per yr. ISSN 0046-9408

**Bunsengesellschaft fuer Physikalische Chemie**
• Bunsengesellschaft fuer Physikalische Chemie. Berichte. (pub. by Verlag Chemie International, Inc. US)

**Verlag Aenne Burda**
Am Kestendamm 2, Postfach 1160, 7600 Offenburg, W. Germany (B.R.D.)
• Burda Moden. m. ISSN 0007-6031

**Burda Verlag GmbH**
Hauptstr. 130, Postfach 1230, 7600 Offenburg, W. Germany.
• Bunte Illustrierte. w.
• Freizeit Revue. w.
• Freundin; Leben im jungen Stil. fortn. ISSN 0016-1187
• Mein Schoener Garten. m.

**Hans Burghagen Verlag**
Schroederstr. 35, 2000 Hamburg 76, W. Germany (B.R.D.)
• B T. (Bueromaschinen Technik) 13 per yr. (Gesamtverband Bueromaschinen-Technik B.V.)

**Verlag Helmut Buske**
Schlueterstr. 14, 2000 Hamburg 13, W. Germany (B.R.D.)
• Bibliotheca Russica. irreg.
• Finnisch-ugrische Mitteilungen. s-a. ISSN 0341-7816
• Finno-Ugrica. irreg. ISSN 0341-311X

• Forum Phoneticum. irreg. ISSN 0341-3144
• Hamburger Beitraege fuer Russischlehrer. irreg. ISSN 0072-9515
• Hamburger Beitraege zur Archaeologie. irreg., vol. 4, 1974. ISSN 0341-3152
• Hamburger Historische Studien. irreg. ISSN 0072-9558
• Hamburger Juristische Studien. irreg. ISSN 0341-3179
• Hamburger Philologische Studien. irreg., no. 43, 1976. ISSN 0072-9582
• Hamburger Phonetische Beitraege; Untersuchungen zur Phonetik und Linguistik. irreg. ISSN 0341-3187
• Hamburger Studien zur Philosophie. irreg. ISSN 0072-9604
• Papiere zur Textlinguistik/Papers in Textlinguistics. irreg., 1973, no. 12. ISSN 0341-3195 (Universitaet Bielefeld)
• Studien zur Altaegyptischen Kultur. irreg. ISSN 0340-2215
• Universitaet Bonn. Institut fuer Kommunikations Forschung und Phonetik. Forschungsberichte. irreg., vol. 64, 1977. ISSN 0067-9992
• Vereinigung von Afrikanisten in Deutschland. Schriften. irreg., vol. 8, 1976. ISSN 0341-275X

**Verlag Butzon und Bercker**
Neustr. 7, Postfach 215, 4178 Kevelaer, W. Germany (B.R.D.)
• Berckers Taschenkalender. a.
• Dienender Glaube; Zeitschrift fuer Ordensfrauen. m. ISSN 0012-2572
• Rheinisches Landesmuseum in Bonn. Bonner Jahrbuecher. a. ISSN 0067-9976

**C B-Verlag Carl Boldt**
Baseler Str. 80, 1000 Berlin 45, W. Germany (B.R.D.)
• Die Pelzwirtschaft; Internationale Fachzeitschrift fuer Pelz- und Lederbekleidung. m. ISSN 0048-3176

**C V J M Gesamtverband in Deutschland e.V. C V J M- Westbund**
Bundeshoehe 6, 5600 Wuppertal 2, W. Germany (B.R.D.)
• Baustein; Jugend unter dem Wort. m. ISSN 0005-6790

**Verlag Georg D.W. Callwey**
Streitfeldstr. 35, 8000 Munich 80, W. Germany (B.R.D.)
• Baumeister; Zeitschrift fuer Architektur, Planung, Umwelt. m. ISSN 0005-674X
• Garten und Landschaft. m. ISSN 0016-4720 (Deutsche Gesellschaft fuer Gartenkunst und Landschaftspflege)
• Maltechnik-Restauro. q. ISSN 0025-1445
• Die Mappe; Deutsche Maler- und Lackierer-Zeitschrift. m. ISSN 0025-2697
• Steinmetz und Bildhauer; Handwerk, Technik, Industrie. m. ISSN 0039-1034

**Calwer Verlag**
Hohe Str. 4, 7000 Stuttgart 1, W. Germany (B.R.D.)
• Arbeiten zur Paedagogik. irreg., vol. 19, 1975. ISSN 0066-569X
• Arbeiten zur Theologie. Reihe 1. irreg., vol. 61, 1975. ISSN 0066-5711
• Biblisches Seminar. irreg.
• Botschaft des Alten Testaments; Erlauterungen Alttestamentlicher Schriften. irreg. ISSN 0068-0443
• Calwer Predigthilfen. irreg., vol. 14, 1975. ISSN 0068-6557
• Calwer Theologische Monographien. Reihe A: Bibelwissenschaft. irreg., no. 4, 1974.
• Calwer Theologische Monographien. Reihe B: Systematische Theologie und Kirchengeschichte. irreg., no. 2, 1974.
• Quellen und Forschungen zur Wuerttembergischen Kirchengeschichte. irreg., vol. 6, 1975. ISSN 0079-9084

**Editio Cantor KG**
Postfach 10, 7960 Aulendorf, W. Germany (B.R.D.)
• Arzneimittel-Forschung/Drug Research. m. ISSN 0004-4172
• Berufs-Dermatosen. bi-m. ISSN 0005-9498
• Drugs Made in Germany. 4 per yr. ISSN 0012-6683
• Die Pharmazeutische Industrie. m. ISSN 0031-711X

**Buchhandlung Adalbert Carl**
Bahnhofstr. 53, 5928 Laasphe, W. Germany
(B.R.D.)
- Wittgenstein. q. ISSN 0043-7093 (Wittgensteiner
Heimatvereins e.V)

**Verlag Hans Carl KG**
Breite Gasse 58-60, Postfach 9110, 8500 Nuernberg
11, W. Germany (B. R. D.)
- Brautechnik Aktuell; Information, Fortbildung,
Erfahrungsaustausch. m. ISSN 0006-9310
- Brauwelt; allgemeine Brauer- und Hopfenzeitung.
w. ISSN 0006-9329
- Brauwissenschaft. m. ISSN 0006-9337 (Technische
Universitaet Muenchen)
- Kunstchronik; Monatsschrift fuer
Kunstwissenschaft, Museumswesen und
Denkmalpflege. m. ISSN 0023-5474
(Zentralinstitut fuer Kunstgeschichte in
Muenchen)

**Cassella-Riedel Pharma GmbH**
Hanauer Landstr. 521, 6000 Frankfurt 61, W.
Germany (B.R.D.)
- Cassella-Riedel Archiv. 4 per yr. ISSN 0008-7440

**Catholic Media Council**
Hermannstr. 12, 5100 Aachen, W. Germany
(B.R.D.)
- Catholic Media Council. Information Bulletin. s-a.

**Ceto-Verlag GmbH**
Goethestr. 34, Postfach 104029, 3500 Kassel, W.
Germany (B.R.D.)
- Brennstoffspiegel. m.

**Chaine des Rotisseurs**
- Arnes Journal fuer Guten Geschmack. (pub. by
Arne-Verlag)

**Chemie Gruenenthal GmbH**
Steinfeldstr. 2, 5190 Stolberg, W. Germany (B.R.D.)
- Die Waage; Zeitschrift der Chemie Gruenenthal.
bi-m. ISSN 0017-4874

**Verlag Chemie International, Inc.**
For publications of this company see section for
UNITED STATES

**Verlag fuer Chemische Industrie**
Beethovenstr. 16, 8900 Augsburg 1, W. Germany
(B. R. D.)
- Seifen, Oele, Fette, Wachse. 20 per yr. ISSN
0037-0983 (Vereinigung der Seifen-, Parfuem- und
Waschmittel- Fachleute e.V.) (Co-Sponsor:
Gesellschaft fuer Kosmetologie e.V.)

**Verlag Chmielorz GmbH und Co**
Wilhelmstr. 42, 6200 Wiesbaden, W. Germany.
- Journalisten-Handbuch. irreg.
- Sport und Mode. m. ISSN 0049-1926 (Verband
Deutscher Sportgeschaefte e.V.)
- Der Vermessungsingenieur. bi-m. ISSN 0042-4099
(Verband Deutscher Vermessungsingenieure e.V.)

**Verlagsverein der Christ im Zwanzigsten Jahrhundert**
Wasmannstr 15, 2000 Hamburg 60, W. Germany
(B.R.D.)
- Der Christ im Zwanzigsten Jahrhundert. q. ISSN
0009-5060

**A. Christ Zeitschriftenverlag GmbH und Co. KG**
Staedelstr. 19, 6000 Frankfurt 70, W. Germany
(B.R.D.)
- Deutsche Automobil Revue. m. ISSN 0011-989X
- Journal fuer Mehr Freude am Fahren. bi-m.

**Verlag Dr. Ing. Paul Christiani**
Hermann-Hesse-Weg 2, 7750. Konstanz, W.
Germany (B.R.D.)
- Ausbau; Illustrierte Monatshefte fuer technische
Berufe. m. ISSN 0004-8097

**Hans Christians Verlag**
Kl. Theaterstr. 9, 2000 Hamburg 36, W. Germany
(B.R.D.)
- Lichtwark-Stiftung. Veroeffentlichung. irreg.

**Christlich-Demokratische Union (CDU)**
**Frauenvereinigung**
- Frau und Politik. (pub. by Union-Betriebs-
Gesellschaft mbH)

**Christlich-Soziale Kollegenschaft**
Schumannstr. 14, 5300 Bonn 1, W. Germany
(B.R.D.)
- Gesellschaftspolitische Kommentare. s-m. ISSN
0016-9102

**Christliche Allianz**
- Gnade und Herrlichkeit. (pub. by Paulus-Verlag
Karl Geyer)

**Christliche Postvereinigung in Deutschland**
Kamerunweg 14, 3000 Hannover-Linden, W.
Germany (B.R.D.)
- Die Christus-Post. bi-m. ISSN 0009-5869

**Christliche Verlagsgesellschaft mbH**
Moltkestr. 1, Postfach 168, 6340 Dillenburg, W.
Germany (B.R.D.)
- Das Wort fuer Heute. s-m. ISSN 0043-9428

**Christlicher Zeitschriftenverlag**
Fregestr. 71, 1000 Berlin 41, W. Germany (B.R.D.)
- Jahrbuch fuer Berlin-Brandenburgische
Kirchengeschichte. a. ISSN 0075-2568
(Arbeitsgemeinschaft fuer Berlin-
Brandenburgische Kirchengeschichte)
- Mathilde-Zimmer-Stiftung. Blaetter. bi-m.
(Mathilde-Zimmer-Stiftung e.V.)

**Christliches Verlagshaus GmbH**
Senefelderstr. 109, 7000 Stuttgart 1, W. Germany
(B.R.D.)
- Fuer Heute. w. ISSN 0016-2442 (Evangelisch-
methodistische Kirche)
- Wort und Weg; Sonntagsblatt der Evangelisch-
Methodistischen Kirche. w. ISSN 0043-9444
(Evangelisch-methodistische Kirche)

**Christoffel Blindenmission e. V.**
Nibelungenstr. 124, 6140 Bensheim-Schoenberg, W.
Germany (B.R.D.)
- Christoffel-Blindenmission. Bericht. bi-m. ISSN
0009-580X

**Clemens-Sels-Museum**
Im Obertor, 4040 Neuss, W. Germany (B.R.D.)
- Neusser Jahrbuch fuer Kunst, Kulturgeschichte
und Heimatkunde. a. ISSN 0077-7862

**Club Politikon e.V.**
Kiesseestr. 93, 3400 Goettingen, W. Germany
(B.R.D.)
- Politikon; Goettinger Studentenzeitschrift. 5-6 per
yr. ISSN 0032-3403 (Subscriptions to: Spartakus-
Buchversand, Postfach 13 22 51, 2 Hamburg 13,
W. Germany)

**Coburger Landesstiftung**
Schloss Ehrenburg, 8630 Coburg, W. Germany
(B.R.D.)
- Coburger Landesstiftung. Jahrbuch. a. ISSN 0084-
8808

**Dietrich Coelde Verlag GmbH**
Steinergraben 53, 4760 Werl, W. Germany (B.R.D.)
- Franziskanische Studien. q. ISSN 0016-0067

**Charles Coleman, Buch- und Zeitschriften-Verlag KG**
Koenigstr. 1, Postfach 2134, 2400 Luebeck, W.
Germany (B.R.D.)
- Metall-Handwerk und Technik. m.
(Bundesverband Metall)

**Collegium Carolinum**
- Handbuch der Sudetendeutschen Kulturgeschichte.
(pub. by Verlag Robert Lerche)

**Colloquium Verlag**
Unter den Eichen 93, 1000 Berlin 45, W. Germany
(B.R.D.)
- Abhandlungen und Materialen zur Publizistik.
irreg. ISSN 0065-0323 (Freie Universitaet Berlin.
Institut fuer Publizistik)
- Berlin, Theater und Drama. irreg. ISSN 0067-
6047
- Bibliotheca Ibero-Americana. irreg. ISSN 0067-
8015 (Ibero-Amerikanisches Institut)
- Historische Kommission zu Berlin.
Einzelverdeffentlichungen. irreg. ISSN 0067-5857
- Ibero-Amerikanishes Archiv. q. ISSN 0340-3068
(Ibero-Amerikanisches Institut)
- R I A S-Funkuniversitaet, Berlin. Forschung und
Information. irreg. ISSN 0067-5997
- Studien zur Europaeischen Geschichte. irreg.
ISSN 0081-7252

**Cologne. Museen der Stadt Koeln**
An der Rechtschule, 5000 Cologne 1, W. Germany
(B.R.D.)
- Museen in Koeln. Bulletin. m. ISSN 0027-3813
(Co-sponsors: Walraf-Richartz-Museum; Museum
Ludwig)

**Cologne. Oberstadtdirektor**
Rathaus, 5000 Cologne 1, W. Germany (B.R.D.)
- Amtsblatt der Stadt Koeln. w.
- Der Feierabend. (pub. by Der Feierabend)

**Cologne. Statistisches Amt**
Johannisstr. 72-80, 5000 Cologne 1, W. Germany
(B.R.D.)
- Koelner Monatszahlen. q. ISSN 0023-2645
- Statistische Mitteilungen der Stadt Koeln. 3 per
yr.

**Cologne. Verkehrsamt**
Unter Fettenhennen 19, 5000 Cologne 1, W.
Germany (B. R. D.)
- Koeln. q. ISSN 0075-6482

**Comite Internacional de Andrologia**
- Andrologia. (pub. by Grosse Verlag GmbH)

**Commerzbank AG**
Neue Mainzer Str. 32, 6000 Frankfurt, W. Germany
(B.R.D.)
- Aussenhandelsblaetter. m.
- Commerzbank, Frankfurt. Business Notes. m.

**Commerzia-Verlag**
Luetzowstr. 60-61, 1000 Berlin 36, W. Germany
(B.R.D.)
- Industriespiegel; Internationales Messe- und
Ausstellungsorgan. m. ISSN 0019-9168

**Communio-Verlag**
Moselstrasse 34, 5038 Rodenkirchen, W. Germany
(B.R.D.)
- Internationale Katholische Zeitschrift.

**Gerhard Conrad**
Von-Stauffenberg-Str. 24, 5750 Menden 1, W.
Germany (B.R.D.)
- Jazzfreund; Mitteilungsblatt fuer Jazzfreunde in
Ost und West. q. ISSN 0021-5724

**Deutscher Consulting Verlag**
Pressehaus am Otto-Hausmann-Ring, 5600
Wuppertal 1, W. Germany (B.R.D.)
- Beratende Ingenieure; Zeitschrift des deutschen
Consulting. q. ISSN 0005-8866 (Verband
Beratender Ingenieure)

**Co-Op Verlag GmbH**
Adenauerallee 12, 2000 Hamburg 1, W. Germany
(B.R.D.)
- Pro Magazin. m. ISSN 0032-9037

**Cornelsen-Velhagen und Klasing GmbH und Co.**
Luetzowstr. 105, 1000 Berlin 30, W. Germany
(B.R.D.)
- Englisch; eine Zeitschrift fuer den
Englischerlehrer. q. ISSN 0013-8185
- Neusprachliche Mitteilungen aus Wissenschaft
und Praxis. q. ISSN 0028-3983

**Verlagsanstalt Courier GmbH**
Hauptvorstand, Kronprinzstr. 24, 7000 Stuttgart 1,
W. Germany (B.R.D.)
- Die Polizei im Lande Berlin. m. ISSN 0032-3527
(Gewerkschaft Oeffentliche Dienste, Transport
und Verkehr. Hauptabteilung Polizei)

**Technischer Verlag Herbert Cram**
Genthiner Str. 13, 1000 Berlin 30, W. Germany
(B.R.D.)
- Holzforschung; Mitteilungen zur Chemie, Physik,
Biologie und Technologie des Holzes. bi-m. ISSN
0018-3830

**J. Cramer**
Postfach 48, 3301 Lehre, W. Germany (B.R.D.)
(Dist. in U.S. by Stechert-Hafner Service Agency,
866 Third Ave., New York, N.Y. 10022)
- Bibliotheca Mycologica. irreg., 1973, vol. 37.
ISSN 0067-8066
- Bibliotheca Phycologica. irreg., 1973, vol. 16.
ISSN 0067-8112
- Diatomeenschalen im Elektronenmikroskopschen
Bild. a. ISSN 0070-4687
- Dissertationes Botanicae. irreg., 1973, vol. 20.
ISSN 0070-6728
- Flora et Vegetatio Mundi. irreg. ISSN 0071-576X
- Herzogia. s-a. ISSN 0018-0971 (Bryologisch-
Lichenologische Arbeitsgemeinschaft fuer Mittel-
Europa)
- Historiae Naturalis Classica. irreg., 1973, vol. 100.
ISSN 0073-2524
- Icones Fungorium Maris. irreg. ISSN 0073-439X
- Index Hepaticarum. irreg. ISSN 0073-5787

- Nova Hedwiga; journal of cryptogamic science. 2 vols. per yr. ISSN 0029-5035
- Nova Hedwiga, Beihefte. irreg., 1973, vol. 42. ISSN 0078-2238
- Phanerogamarum Monographiae. irreg., 1973, vol. 7. ISSN 0079-1369
- Plant Monograph: Reprints. irreg., 1973, vol. 8. ISSN 0079-2233

**Crash**
Bergstedter Chaussee 73, 2000 Hamburg 65, W. Germany (B.R.D.)
- Crash; Zeitung fuer junge Leute. m.

**Criticon Verlag GmbH**
Prannerstr. 15, 8000 Munich 2, W. Germany (B.R.D.)
- Criticon; konservative Zeitschrift. bi-m. ISSN 0011-1597

**Cusanus-Gesellschaft**
- Cusanus-Gesellschaft. Buchreihe. (pub. by Aschendorffsche Verlagsbuchhandlung)

**Verlag Ingrid Czwalina**
Reesenbuettler Redder 75, 2070 Ahrensburg, W. Germany (B.R.D.)
- Dokumente zum Hochschulsport. irreg.
- Schriftenreihe fuer Sportwissenschaft und Sportpraxis. irreg., vol. 25, 1974. ISSN 0080-7141
- Sportwissenschaftliche Dissertationen. irreg. ISSN 0340-0956
- Zeitschrift fuer Sportpaedagogik. q. ISSN 0340-9058

**D C C -Wirtschaftsdienst und -Verlag GmbH**
Mandlstr. 28, 8000 Munich 40, W. Germany (B.R.D.)
- D C C -Camping Fuehrer Europa. a. ISSN 0078-3943 (Deutscher Camping-Club e.V.)

**D D K-Verlag Ingeborg Weber**
Rotbuchenstr. 21, 8000munich 90, W. Germany (B.R.D.)
- Der Film und TV Kameramann. m.
- Jahrbuch des Kameramanns. a. ISSN 0075-2509

**D G Bank (Deutsche Genossenschaftsbank)**
Taunustor 3, 6000 Frankfurt, W. Germany (B.R.D.)
- D G K - Mitteilungen. (Deutsche Genossenschaftskasse) bi-m. ISSN 0340-7314
- Die Genossenschaften in der Bundesrepublik Deutschland. irreg.

**D L G Verlag**
see Deutsche Landwirtschafts-Gesellschaft-Verlags GmbH

**D L W Aktiengesellschaft**
Postfach 140, 7120 Bietigheim-Bissengen, W. Germany (B.R.D.)
- D L W Nachrichten; Zeitschrift fuer Architektur und Innenausbau. 2 per yr.

**D R W-Verlag Weinbrenner-KG**
Fasanenweg 18, 7022 Leidenfelden-Echterdingen 1, W. Germany (B.R.D.)
- Holz- und Kunststoffverarbeitung; Zeitschrift fuer Unternehmer und Fuehrungskraefte in der Moebelindustrie und sonstigen Zweigen der Holzindustrie. m. ISSN 0026-8615
- Holz-Zentralblatt; Unabhaengiges Organ fuer die Forst und Holzwirtschaft. 3 per wk. ISSN 0018-3792

**D S Z Druckschriften- und Zeitungs-Verlag GmbH**
Paosostr. 2a, 8000 Munich 60, W. Germany (B.R.D.)
- Deutsche National-Zeitung. w. ISSN 0012-0510

**D V G-Deutsche Verlagsgesellschaft mbH**
Brueckenstr. 1, Postfach 270, 8200 Rosenheim, W. Germany (B.R.D.)
- Deutsche Wochen-Zeitung. w. ISSN 0302-7503
- Deutscher Kurier. m.

**Daco-Verlag Guenter Blaese**
Richard Wagner Str. 10, 7000stuttgart 1, W. Germany (B.R.D.)
- Leistung. irreg. ISSN 0024-0702

**Damals-Verlag**
Marburger Str. 20, Postfach 5323, 6300 Giessen, W. Germany (B.R.D.)
- Damals; Zeitschrift fuer Geschichtliches Wissen. m. ISSN 0011-5908

**Damnitz Verlag**
Hohenzollernstr. 144, 8000 Munich 40, W. Germany (B.R.D.)
- Kuerbiskern; Zeitschrift--Literatur-Kritik Klassenkampf. q. ISSN 0023-5016

**Richard Danehl's Verlag**
Postfach 500344, 2000 Hamburg 50, W. Germany (B.R.D.)
- International Naturist Guide/Internationaler FKK-Reisefuehrer/Guide Naturiste Internationale. a. ISSN 0074-7122 (International Naturist Federation)

**Druck und Verlagshaus Hermann Daniel KG**
Friedrichstr. 10, 7460 Balingen, W. Germany (B.R.D.)
- I B N. (Internationale Bodensee & Boot Nachrichten); Zeitschrift fuer die Freunde des Bodensees. s-m. ISSN 0020-921X

**Data Verlag**
Postfach 165, Grill Parzerstr. 1, 8012 Ottobrunn / Munich, W. Germany (B.R.D.)
- Computer Adress. s-a. (Deutsches Computer Forum)
- Computer Magazin. m.

**R.v. Decker's Verlag, G. Schenk GmbH**
Akademiestr. 6, 6900 Heidelberg, W. Germany (B.R.D.)
- Goldammer's Archiv fuer Strafrecht. m. ISSN 0017-1956 (Germany, Federal Republic. Bundesministerium der Justiz)
- Handbuch der Justiz. a. ISSN 0073-0092 (Deutscher Richterbund)
- Unterrichtsblaetter fuer die Bundeswehrverwaltung; Zeitschrift fuer Ausbildung, Fortbildung und Verwaltungspraxis mit Unterstuetzung des Bundesministers der Verteidigung. m. ISSN 0042-0611 (Germany, Federal Republic. Bundesministerium der Verteidigung)

**Deere & Company**
Steubenstr. 36-42, Postfach 503, 6800 Mannheim 1, W. Germany (B.R.D.)
- Flur und Furche; Landwirtschaftsmagazin. bi-m. ISSN 0015-4733

**Verlag Degener und Co.**
Nuernberger Str. 27, Postfach 1340, 8530 Neustadt/Aisch, W. Germany (B.R.D.)
- Genealogie; Deutsche Zeitschrift fuer Familienkunde. m. ISSN 0016-6383
- Genealogisches Handbuch des Bayerischen Adels. biennial. ISSN 0085-0934 (Vereinigung des Adels in Bayern)
- Norddeutsche Familienkunde. q. (Familienkundliche Kommission fuer Niedersachsen und Bremen)

**Deike-Verlag**
Wollmatinger Str. 6, Postfach 178, 7750 Konstanz, W. Germany (B.R.D.)
- Deike-Gedenktage. m.
- Sport-Vorschau. every 4 wks.
- Vorschau Europa; internationaler Terminkalender. 4 per yr. ISSN 0042-8892
- Vorschau-Tabelle. q. ISSN 0042-8914

**Verlag Delius, Klasing und Co.**
Siekerwall 21, Postfach 4809, 4800 Bielefeld, W. Germany (B.R.D.)
- Der Blaue Peter; Zeitschrift fuer Segeln und Seefahrt. 6 per yr. ISSN 0006-4637 (Deutscher Hochseesportverband Hansa e.V.)
- Boote; magazin fuer Freizeit - Kapitaene. bi-m. ISSN 0006-7636
- Gute Fahrt; Zeitschrift fuer den Volkswagenfahrer. m. ISSN 0017-5765
- Klasings Bootsmarkt International; Yachten und Boote Zubehoer, Ausruestung, Motoren. a. ISSN 0075-627X
- Die Yacht; Deutschlands fahrende Yacht-Zeitschrift. fortn. ISSN 0043-9932

**Delta-Verlag Martin Buske**
Moltkestr. 41, Postfach 182, 5300 Bonn-Bad Godesberg, W. Germany (B.R.D.)
- Allgemeine Deutsche Imkerzeitung. m. ISSN 0002-5828

**Demag AG**
Wolfgang-Reuter-Platz, 4100 Duisburg, W. Germany (B.R.D.)
- Demag Kurier. 6-8 per yr. ISSN 0011-815X

**Karl Demeter Verlag**
Wuermstr. 13, 8032 Graefelfing, W. Germany (B.R.D.)
- B z B. (Bayerisches Zahnaerzteblatt) m. ISSN 0005-3473 (Bayerische Landeszahnaerztekammer)
- Deutsche Drogisten Zeitung. s-m. ISSN 0012-0049
- Zeitschrift fuer Gastroenterologie. m. ISSN 0044-2771 (Deutsche Gesellschaft fuer Verdauungs- und Stoffwechselkrankheiten) (Co-sponsor: Deutsche Gesellschaft fuer Gastroenterologische Endoskopie; Oesterreichische Gesellschaft fuer Gastroenterologie)

**Demokrit-Verlag**
Postfach 2707, 7400tuebingen, W. Germany.
- Zeitschrift fuer Markt-, Meinungs- und Zukunftsforschung. q. ISSN 0044-3042

**Verlag fuer Demoskopie**
7735 Allensbach, W. Germany (B. R. D.)
- Jahrbuch der Oeffentlichen Meinung. irreg. ISSN 0075-2347 (Institut fuer Demoskopie, Allensbach)

**Design International**
Kaufering 57, 5330 Koenigswinter, W. Germany (B.R.D.)
- Design International. q. ISSN 0011-9393

**Deutsch-Indische Gesellschaft**
- Indo-Asia. (pub. by Horst Erdmann Verlag)

**Deutsch-Russlaendische Gesellschaft E.V.**
- Russland und Wir. (pub. by Russland und Wir - Verlag und Handlung)

**Deutsche Akademie der Wissenschaften zu Berlin**
- Zentralblatt fuer Mathematik und ihre Grenzgebiete. (pub. by Springer-Verlag US)

**Deutsche Akademie fuer Psychoanalyse**
- Dynamische Psychiatrie/Dynamic Psychiatry. (pub. by Pinel-Publikationen)

**Deutsche Akademie fuer Sprache und Dichtung, Darmstadt**
- Deutsche Akademie fuer Sprache und Dichtung, Darmstadt. Jahrbuch. (pub. by Verlag Lambert Schneider)

**Deutsche Akademie fuer Staedtebau und Landesplanung**
Friedrichswall 4, 3000 Hannover, W. Germany (B.R.D.)
- Deutsche Akademie fuer Staedtebau und Landesplanung. Mitteilungen. s-a. ISSN 0011-9822

**Deutsche Angestellten-Gewerkschaft**
- Der Angestellte. (pub. by Waren Einkaufs- und Vertriebs-Gesellschaft mbH)
- Der Bankangestellte. (pub. by Walhalla- U. Praetoria-Verlag Georg Zwickenpflug)
- Jugendpost. (pub. by Waren Einkaufs - und Vertriebs - Gesellschaft MbH)
- Der Standpunkt. (pub. by Waren Einkaufs- und Vertriebs-Gesellschaft mbH)
- Taschenbuch fuer Ingenieure und Techniker im Oeffentlichen Dienst. (pub. by Walhalla-u. Praetoria-Verlag Georg Zwickenpflug)

**Verlag der Deutsche Apotheker**
Hans-Thoma-Str. 1, Postfach 350, 6370 Oberursel, W. Germany (B.R.D.)
- Der Deutsche Apotheker; die aktuelle Zeitschrift fuer pharmazeutische Berufe. m. ISSN 0011-9849

**Deutsche Arbeitsgemeinschaft Vakuum**
- Vakuum-Technik. (pub. by Rudolf A. Lang Verlag)

**Deutsche B P Aktiengesellschaft**
Veberseering 2, 2000 Hamburg 60, W. Germany (B.R.D.)
- B P Kurier. q.

**Deutsche Bausparkasse**
Heinrichstr. 2, 6100 Darmstadt, W. Germany (B.R.D.)
- Heim und Herd. q. ISSN 0017-968X

**Deutsche Bibliothek**
- Archiv Ungedruckter Wissenschaftlicher Schriften. (pub. by Buchhaendler-Vereinigung GmbH)
- Deutsche Bibliographie. Das Deutsche Buch. (pub. by Buchhaendler-Vereinigung GmbH)
- Deutsche Bibliographie. Fuenfjahres-Verzeichnis. (pub. by Buchhaendler-Vereinigung GmbH)

● Deutsche Bibliographie. Halbjahres-Verzeichnis.
(pub. by Buchhaendler-Vereinigung GmbH)
● Deutsche Bibliographie. Hochschulschriften-
Verzeichnis. (pub. by Buchhaendler-Vereinigung
GmbH)
● Deutsche Bibliographie. Verzeichnis Amtlicher
Druckschriften. (pub. by Buchhaendler-
Vereinigung GmbH)
● Deutsche Bibliographie. Wochentliches
Verzeichnis. Reine A: Erscheinungen des
Verlagsbuchandels. (pub. by Buchhaendler-
Vereinigung GmbH)
● Deutsche Bibliographie. Woechentliches
Verzeichnis. Reihe B: Erscheinungen ausserhalb
des Verlagsbuchhandels. (pub. by Buchhaendler-
Vereinigung GmbH)
● Deutsche Bibliographie. Woechentliches
Verzeichnis. Reihe C: Karten. (pub. by
Buchhaendler-Vereinigung GmbH)
● Deutsche Bibliographie. Zeitschriften-Verzeichnis.
(pub. by Buchhaendler-Vereinigung GmbH)

**Deutsche Bibliothek. Abteilung Deutsches
Musikarchiv**
● Deutsche Bibliographie. Schallplatten-Verzeichnis.
(pub. by Bielefelder Verlagsanstalt KG)

**Deutsche Blindenstudienanstalt**
Am Schlag 8, 3550 Marburg, W. Germany (B.R.D.)
● Marburger Umschau. m. ISSN 0025-2778

**Deutsche Bodenkundliche Gesellschaft**
● Zeitschrift fuer Pflanzenernaehrung und
Bodenkunde/Journal of Plant Nutrition and Soil
Science. (pub. by Verlag Chemie International,
Inc. US)

**Deutsche Botanische Gesellschaft**
● Deutsche Botanische Gesellschaft. Berichte. (pub.
by Gustav Fischer Verlag)

**Deutsche Buch-Gemeinschaft**
Berliner Allee 6, 6100 Darmstadt, W. Germany
(B.R.D.)
● Lesestunde mit dem Grossen Freizeit-Programm.
q. ISSN 0024-1083

**Deutsche Bundesbahn**
● Blickpunkt D B. (pub. by Redactor-Verlag GmbH)
● Die Bundesbahn. (pub. by Hestra Verlag)
● D B. (pub. by Eisenbahn-Fachverlag)
● D B-Pressedienst. (pub. by Druck- und
Verlagshaus Frankfurt am Main GmbH)
● D B Report. (pub. by Hestra-Verlag)
● Jahrbuch des Eisenbahnwesens. (pub. by Hestra-
Verlag)
● Kurzauszuege aus dem Schrifttum fuer das
Eisenbahnwesen. (pub. by Tetzlaff Verlag GmbH)

**Deutsche Bundesbahn. Werbe- und Auskunftsamt fuer
den Personen- und Gueterverkehr**
Gueterstr. 9, 6000 Frankfurt 1, W. Germany
(B.R.D.)
● D B - Kundenbrief. m. ISSN 0011-4758

**Deutsche Bundesbank**
Postfach 2633, 6000 Frankfurt 1, W. Germany
(B.R.D.)
● Auszuege aus Presseartikeln. s-w. ISSN 0005-0598
● Deutsche Bundesbank. Geschaeftsbericht. a. ISSN
0070-394X
● Deutsche Bundesbank. Monatsberichte. m. ISSN
0012-0006
● Die Waehrungen der Welt; Statistische Beihefte,
Reihe 5, zu den Monatsberichten der Deutschen
Bundesbank. q.

**Deutsche Bundespost**
● Z P F. (pub. by Josef Keller Verlag)

**Deutsche Burgenvereinigung e.V.**
Marksburg, 5423 Braubach, W. Germany (B.R.D.)
● Burgen und Schloesser. s-a. ISSN 0007-6201

**Deutsche Dendrologische Gesellschaft**
Hardtstr., Postfach 20, 5608 Radevormwald-
Dahlhausen, W. Germany (B.R.D.)
● Deutsche Dendrologische Gesellschaft. Jahrbuch.
a. ISSN 0070-3958

**Deutsche Dermatologische Gesellschaft**
● Archives for Dermatological Research/Archiv fuer
Dermatologische Forschung. (pub. by Springer-
Verlag US)
● Zentralblatt fuer Haut- und
Geschlechtskrankheiten Sowie Deren
Grenzgebiete/Dermatology. (pub. by Springer-
Verlag US)

**Deutsche Entomologische Gesellschaft**
● Entomologica Germanica. (pub. by Gustav Fischer
Verlag)

**Deutsche Evangelische Missionshilfe Verlag**
Mittelweg 143, 2000 Hamburg 13, W. Germany (B.
R. D.)
● Evangelische Mission Jahrbuch. a. ISSN 0531-
4798 (Verband Evangelischer
Missionskonferenzen)
● Das Wort in der Welt. bi-m. (Deutscher
Evangelischer Missionsrat) (Co-Sponsor:
Evangelische Arbeitsgemeinschaft fuer
Weltmission)

**Deutsche Exlibris-Gesellschaft e.V.**
Marienstr. 35, 3000 Hannover, W. Germany
(B.R.D.)
● Exlibriskunst und Gebrauchsgraphik. Jahrbuch. a.
ISSN 0075-2630

**Deutsche Forschungs- und Versuchsanstalt fuer Luft-
und Raumfahrt e.V.**
Linder Hoehe, Postfach 906058, 5000 Cologne 90,
W. Germany (B.R.D.)
● D F V L R Jahresbericht. a. ISSN 0070-3966
● D F V L R - Nachrichten. s-a. ISSN 0011-4901
● Deutsche Luft- und Raumfahrt.
Forschungsberichte/German Aeronautics and
Astronautics. Research Reports. irreg. ISSN 0070-
4245

**Deutsche Forschungsgemeinschaft**
● Angewandte Forschung in der Bundesrepublik
Deutschland. (pub. by Boldt Verlag KG)
● Bibliothek und Wissenschaft. (pub. by Verlag Otto
Harrassowitz)
● Deutsche Forschungsgemeinschaft. Denkschriften
zur Lage der Deutschen Wissenschaft. (pub. by
Boldt Verlag KG)
● Deutsche Forschungsgemeinschaft.
Forschungsberichte. (pub. by Boldt Verlag KG)
● Deutsche Forschungsgemeinschaft. Kommissionen.
Mitteilungen. (pub. by Boldt Verlag KG)
● Freiburger Geographische Arbeiten. (pub. by Hans
Ferdinand Schulz Verlag)
● I P E K/Annual Review of Prehistoric and
Ethnographical Art. (pub. by Walter de Gruyter
und Co.)
● "Meteor" Forschungsergebnisse. Reihe A.
Allgemeines, Physik und Chemie des Meeres.
(pub. by Gebrueder Borntraeger
Verlagsbuchhandlung)
● "Meteor" Forschungsergebnisse. Reihe B.
Meteorologie und Aeronomie. (pub. by Gebrueder
Borntraeger Verlagsbuchhandlung)
● "Meteor" Forschungsergebnisse. Reihe C.
Geologie und Geophysik. (pub. by Gebrueder
Borntraeger Verlagsbuchhandlung)
● "Meteor" Forschungsergebnisse. Reihe D. Biologie.
(pub. by Gebrueder Borntraeger
Verlagsbuchhandlung)
● Poetica. (pub. by B. R. Gruener B. V. NE)

**Deutsche Forschungsgemeinschaft. Hegel Kommission**
● Hegel-Studien. (pub. by Bouvier Verlag Herbert
Grundmann)

**Deutsche Forschungsgesellschaft fuer Druck- und
Reproduktionstechnik e.V. (FOGRA)**
Streitfeld Str. 19, 8000 Munich 80, W. Germany
(B.R.D.)
● Fogra-Literaturdienst. m. ISSN 0015-5322
● Fogra-Mitteilungen. q. ISSN 0015-5330

**Deutsche Friedensgesellschaft-Vereinigte
Kriegsdienstgegner (DFG-VK)**
Haserstr. 6, 5000 Cologne 21, W. Germany
(B.R.D.)
● Zivilcourage; Antimilitaristische Zeitschrift. m.

**Deutsche Gemmologische Gesellschaft e.V.**
Gewerbehalle, Postfach 2717, 6580 Idar-Oberstein
2, W. Germany (B.R.D.)
● Deutsche Gemmologische Gesellschaft. Zeitschrift.
q.

**Deutsche Geodaetische Kommission**
Marstallplatz 8, 8000 Munich 22, W. Germany
(B.R.D.)
● Deutsche Geodaetische Kommission.
Veroeffentlichungen: Reihe A. Theoretische
Geodaesie. irreg. ISSN 0065-5309
● Deutsche Geodaetische Kommission.
Veroeffentlichungen: Reihe B. Angewandte
Geodaesie. irreg. ISSN 0065-5317

● Deutsche Geodaetische Kommission.
Veroeffentlichungen: Reihe C. Dissertationen.
irreg. ISSN 0065-5325
● Deutsche Geodaetische Kommission.
Veroeffentlichungen: Reihe D. Tafelwerke. irreg.
ISSN 0065-5333
● Deutsche Geodaetische Kommission.
Veroeffentlichungen: Reihe E. Geschichte und
Entwicklung der Geodaesie. irreg. ISSN 0065-
5341

**Deutsche Gesellschaft fuer Agrarrecht**
● Agrarrecht. (pub. by Landwirtschaftsverlag
GmbH)

**Deutsche Gesellschaft fuer Amerikastudien**
Marburg, W. Germany (B.R.D.)
● Amerikastudien/American Studies. (pub. by J. B.
Metzlersche Verlagsbuchhandlung)
● Deutsche Gesellschaft fuer Amerikastudien.
Mitteilungsblatt. a.

**Deutsche Gesellschaft fuer Anaesthesie und
Wiederbelebung**
● Anaesthesist. (pub. by Springer-Verlag US)
● Praktische Anaesthesie, Wiederbelebung und
Intensivtherapie. (pub. by Georg Thieme Verlag)

**Deutsche Gesellschaft fuer Anaesthesie und
Wiederbelebung. Berufsverband Deutscher
Anaesthesisten**
● Anaesthesiologische Informationen. (pub. by Peri-
Med Verlag Dr. D. Straube)

**Deutsche Gesellschaft fuer Anthropologie**
● Homo. (pub. by Musterschmidt-Verlag)

**Deutsche Gesellschaft fuer Arbeitsschutz e.V.**
● Zentralblatt fuer Arbeitsmedizin, Arbeitsschutz
und Prophylaxe. (pub. by Verlag fuer Medizin Dr.
Ewald Fischer)

**Deutsche Gesellschaft fuer Auswaertige Politik e.V.**
● Europa-Archiv. (pub. by Verlag fuer Internationale
Politik GmbH)
● Ruestungsbeschraenkung und Sicherheit. (pub. by
Alfred Metzner Verlag GmbH)

**Deutsche Gesellschaft fuer Bewaesserungswirtschaft
E.V**
● Zeitschrift fuer Bewaesserungswirtschaft. (pub. by
Deutsche Landwirtschafts-Gesellschaft-Verlags
GmbH)

**Deutsche Gesellschaft fuer Biomedizinische Technik**
● Biomedizinische Technik/Biomedical Engineering.
(pub. by Fachverlag Schiele und Schoen GmbH)

**Deutsche Gesellschaft fuer Chemisches Apparatewesen
e.V. - DECHEMA**
● Dechema Monographien. (pub. by Verlag Chemie
International, Inc. US)

**Deutsche Gesellschaft fuer Chirurgie**
● Langenbecks Archiv fuer Chirurgie Vereinigt mit
Bruns Beitraege fuer Klinische Chirurgie. (pub. by
Springer-Verlag US)
● Zentralorgan fuer Die Gesamte Chirurgie und ihre
Grenzgebiete. (pub. by Springer-Verlag US)

**Deutsche Gesellschaft fuer Chronometrie e. V.**
Christophstr. 5, Postfach 590, 7000 Stuttgart 1, W.
Germany (B.R.D.)
● Deutsche Gesellschaft fuer Chronometrie.
Jahrbuch. a. ISSN 0070-4040

**Deutsche Gesellschaft fuer die Vereinten Nationen**
● Vereinte Nationen. (pub. by Moench
Verlagsgesellschaft mbH)

**Deutsche Gesellschaft fuer Dokumentation e.V.**
● D G D Schriftenreihe. (pub. by Verlag
Dokumentation)
● Nachrichten fuer Dokumentation. (pub. by Verlag
Dokumentation)

**Deutsche Gesellschaft fuer Dokumentation e.V.
Komitee fuer Terminologie und Sprachfragen**
Unterdorf 7, 5308 Rheinbach--Wormersdorf, W.
Germany (B.R.D.)
(Subscr. to: Westendplatz 29, 6000 Frankfurt, W.
Germany (B.R.D.))
● SPRACH--TER--OR; Mitteilungsblatt fuer
Sprachfragen, Terminologie und
Ordnungsprobleme in Information und
Dokumentation. irreg., appr. 4 per yr.

**Deutsche Gesellschaft fuer Elektronenmikroskopie e.V.**
- Methodensammlung der Elektronenmikroskopie. (pub. by Wissenschaftliche Verlagsgesellschaft mbH)
- Optik. (pub. by Wissenschaftliche Verlagsgesellschaft mbH)

**Deutsche Gesellschaft fuer Erd-und Grundbau**
Kronprinzenstr. 35a, 43 Essen, W. Germany.
- Geotechnical Abstracts. m. ISSN 0016-8491 (International Society for Soil Mechanics and Foundation Engineering)

**Deutsche Gesellschaft fuer Ernaehrung**
- Deutsche Gesellschaft fuer Ernaehrung. Wissenschaftliche Veroeffentlichungen. (pub. by Dr. Dietrich Steinkopff Verlag)
- Ernaehrungs-Umschau. (pub. by Umschau Verlag)

**Deutsche Gesellschaft fuer Fettwissenschaft e. V.**
- Fette - Seifen - Anstrichmittel. (pub. by Industrieverlag Von Hernhaussen KG)

**Deutsche Gesellschaft fuer Gartenkunst und Landschaftspflege**
- Garten und Landschaft. (pub. by Verlag Georg D. W. Callwey)

**Deutsche Gesellschaft fuer Gerontologie**
- Aktuelle Gerontologie. (pub. by Georg Thieme Verlag)
- Zeitschrift fuer Gerontologie. (pub. by Dr. Dietrich Steinkopff Verlag)

**Deutsche Gesellschaft fuer Geschichte der Medizin, Naturwissenschaft und Technik e.V.**
c/o Dr. C. Huenemoerder, Institut fuer Geschichte der Naturwissenschaften, Universitaet Hamburg, Bundesstr. 55, 2000 Hamburg, W. Germany (B.R.D.)
- Beitraege zur Geschichte der Wissenschaft und der Technik. (pub. by Franz Steiner Verlag GmbH)
- Deutsche Gesellschaft fuer Geschichte der Medizin, Naturwissenschaft und Technik. Nachrichtenblatt. s-a. ISSN 0027-7460

**Deutsche Gesellschaft fuer Gynaekologie**
- Archiv fuer Gynaekologie. (pub. by Springer-Verlag US)

**Deutsche Gesellschaft fuer Hals-, Nasen-, Ohrenheilkunde, Kopf- und Halschirurgie**
- Archives of Oto-Rhino-Laryngology. (pub. by Springer-Verlag US)
- Laryngologie, Rhinologie, Otologie und ihre Grenzgebiete - Vereinigt mit Monatsschrift fuer Ohrenheilkunde. (pub. by Georg Thieme Verlag)
- Zentralblatt fuer Hals-, Nasen- und Ohrenheilkunde- Plastische Chirurgie an Kopf und Hals. (pub. by Springer Verlag US)

**Deutsche Gesellschaft fuer Hauswirtschaft e.V.**
- Hauswirtschaft und Wissenschaft. (pub. by Verlag Karl M. Lipp)

**Deutsche Gesellschaft fuer Heereskunde e.V.**
Augustin-Wibbelt-Str. 8, 472 Beckum, W. Germany (B.R.D.)
- Zeitschrift fuer Heereskunde. bi-m. ISSN 0044-2852

**Deutsche Gesellschaft fuer Herpetologie und Terrarienkunde e.V.**
Senckenberganlage 25, 6000 Frankfurt, W. Germany (B.R.D.)
- Salamandra; Zeitschrift fuer Herpetologie und Terrarienkunde. 4 per yr. ISSN 0036-3375

**Deutsche Gesellschaft fuer Holzforschung**
- Holz als Roh- und Werkstoff. (pub. by Springer-Verlag US)

**Deutsche Gesellschaft fuer Hygiene und Mikrobiologie**
- Deutsche Gesellschaft fuer Hygiene und Mikrobiologie. Berichte ueber Tagungen. (pub. by Gustav Fischer Verlag)

**Deutsche Gesellschaft fuer Innere Medizin**
- Kongresszentralblatt fuer die Gesamte Innere Medizin. (pub. by Springer-Verlag US)

**Deutsche Gesellschaft fuer Kartographie e.V**
- Kartographische Nachrichten. (pub. by Kirschbaum Verlag)

**Deutsche Gesellschaft fuer Kieferorthopaedie**
- Fortschritte der Kieferorthopaedie. (pub. by Urban und Schwarzenberg)

**Deutsche Gesellschaft fuer Kinderheilkunde**
- Monatsschrift fuer Kinderheilkunde. (pub. by Springer-Verlag US)
- Zentralblatt fuer Die Gesamte Kinderheilkunde. (pub. by Springer-Verlag US)

**Deutsche Gesellschaft fuer Klinische Chemie**
- Zeitschrift fuer klinische Chemie und klinische Biochemie/Journal of Clinical Chemistry and Clinical Biochemistry. (pub. by Walter de Gruyter und Co.)

**Deutsche Gesellschaft fuer Kommunikationsforschung**
- Internationale Zeitschrift fuer Kommunikationsforschung. (pub. by Verlag Hans Richarz)

**Deutsche Gesellschaft fuer Kreislaufforschung**
- Deutsche Gesellschaft fuer Kreislaufforschung. Verhandlungen. (pub. by Dr. Dietrich Steinkopff Verlag)
- Zeitschrift fuer Kardiologie. (pub. by Dr. Dietrich Steinkopff Verlag)

**Deutsche Gesellschaft fuer Luft- und Raumfahrt e.V.**
Goethestr. 10, 5000 Cologne 51, W. Germany (B.R.D.)
- Deutsche Gesellschaft fuer Luft- und Raumfahrt. D.G.L.R. Jahrbuecher. a. ISSN 0070-4083
- Raumfahrtforschung/Space Flight Research. bi-m. ISSN 0034-0103

**Deutsche Gesellschaft fuer Lungen- und Atmungsforschung**
- Lung. (pub. by Springer-Verlag US)
- Lung. Supplement. (pub. by Springer-Verlag US)

**Deutsche Gesellschaft fuer Manuelle Medizin**
- Manuelle Medizin. (pub. by Verlag fuer Medizin Dr. Ewald Fischer)

**Deutsche Gesellschaft fuer Metallkunde**
- Zeitschrift fuer Metallkunde. (pub. by Dr. Riederer Verlag GmbH)
- Zeitschrift fuer Werkstofftechnik, Materials Technology and Testing. (pub. by Verlag Chemie International, Inc. US)

**Deutsche Gesellschaft fuer Mineraloelwissenschaft und Kohlechemie**
- Erdoel und Kohle, Erdgas, Petrochemie. (pub. by Industrieverlag Von Hernhaussen KG)

**Deutsche Gesellschaft fuer Musik des Orients**
Bruemmerstrasse 48, 1000 Berlin 53, W. Germany (B.R.D.)
- Deutsche Gesellschaft fuer Musik des Orients. Mitteilungen. irreg. ISSN 0417-2051

**Deutsche Gesellschaft fuer Neurologie**
- Journal of Neurology. (pub. by Springer-Verlag US)

**Deutsche Gesellschaft fuer Operations Research**
- Zeitschrift fuer Operations Research. (pub. by Physica-Verlag Rudolf Liebing GmbH und Co.)

**Deutsche Gesellschaft fuer Orthopaedie und Traumatologie**
- Zeitschrift fuer Orthopaedie und ihre Grenzgebiete. (pub. by Ferdinand Enke Verlag)

**Deutsche Gesellschaft fuer Ostasienkunde**
Rothenbaumchaussee 32, 2000 Hamburg 13, W. Germany (B.R.D.)
- Deutsche Gesellschaft fuer Ostasienkunde. Koordinierungsstelle fuer Gegenwartsbezogene Ostasienforschung. Mitteilungen. irreg. ISSN 0070-4105

**Deutsche Gesellschaft fuer Osteuropakunde**
- International Bulletin for Research on Law in Eastern Europe/Bulletin International de Recherches sur le Droit en Europe de l'Est/ Internationales Bulletin zur Ostrechtsforschung. (pub. by Deutsche Verlagsanstalt GmbH)
- Osteuropa. (pub. by Deutsche Verlagsanstalt GmbH)

- Osteuropa-Recht. (pub. by Deutsche Verlagsanstalt GmbH)
- Osteuropa-Wirtschaft. (pub. by Deutsche Verlagsanstalt GmbH)

**Deutsche Gesellschaft fuer Parasitologie**
- Zeitschrift fuer Parasitenkunde. (pub. by Springer-Verlag US)

**Deutsche Gesellschaft fuer Pathologie**
- Deutsche Gesellschaft fuer Pathologie. Verhandlungen. (pub. by Gustav Fischer Verlag)

**Deutsche Gesellschaft fuer Phaenomenologische Forschung**
- Phaenomenologische Forschungen/ Phenomenological Studies. (pub. by Karl Alber GmbH)

**Deutsche Gesellschaft fuer Photogrammetrie**
- Bildmessung und Luftbildwesen. (pub. by Herbert Wichmann Verlag)

**Deutsche Gesellschaft fuer Polarforschung**
c/o Institut fuer Geophysik, Gievenbecker Weg 61, 4400 Muenster, W. Germany (B.R.D.)
- Polarforschung. s-a. ISSN 0032-2490

**Deutsche Gesellschaft fuer Psychiatrie und Nervenheilkunde**
- Nervenarzt. (pub. by Springer-Verlag US)

**Deutsche Gesellschaft fuer Psychologie**
- Archiv fuer Psychologie. (pub. by Akademische Verlagsgesellschaft)
- Psychologische Beitraege. (pub. by Verlag Anton Hain KG)
- Zeitschrift fuer Experimentelle und Angewandte Psychologie. (pub. by Verlag fuer Psychologie)

**Deutsche Gesellschaft fuer Qualitaet**
- Qualitaet und Zuverlaessigkeit. (pub. by Carl Hanser Verlag)

**Deutsche Gesellschaft fuer Rechtsmedizin**
- Zeitschrift fuer Rechtsmedizin/Journal of Legal Medicine. (pub. by Springer Verlag US)
- Zentralblatt fuer Die Gesamte Rechtsmedizin und ihre Grenzgebiete/Legal Medicine. (pub. by Springer-Verlag US)

**Deutsche Gesellschaft fuer Rheumatologie**
- Deutsche Gesellschaft fuer Rheumatologie. Verhandlungen. (pub. by Dr. Dietrich Steinkopff Verlag)

**Deutsche Gesellschaft fuer Saeugetierkunde**
- Zeitschrift fuer Saeugetierkunde. (pub. by Verlag Paul Parey (Hamburg))

**Deutsche Gesellschaft fuer Schiffahrts-und Marinegeschichte e. V.**
- Schiff und Zeit. (pub. by Koehlers Verlagsgesellschaft mbH)

**Deutsche Gesellschaft fuer Sexualforschung**
- Beitraege zur Sexualforschung. (pub. by Ferdinand Enke Verlag)

**Deutsche Gesellschaft fuer Thorax-, Herz- und Gefaesschirurgie**
- Thoraxchirurgie - Vaskulaere Chirurgie. (pub. by Georg Thieme Verlag)

**Deutsche Gesellschaft fuer Unfallheilkunde, Versicherungs-, Versorgungs- und Verkehrsmedizin**
- Archiv fuer Orthopaedische und Unfall-Chirurgie. (pub. by Springer-Verlag US)
- Unfallheilkunde/Traumatology. (pub. by Springer-Verlag US)

**Deutsche Gesellschaft fuer Ur- und Fruehgeschichte**
- Archaeologische Informationen. Mitteilungen zur Ur- und Fruehgeschichte. (pub. by Rudolf Habelt Verlag)
- Mannus. (pub. by Mannus-Verlag Peter Wegener)

**Deutsche Gesellschaft fuer Verdauungs- und Stoffwechselkrankheiten**
- Zeitschrift fuer Gastroenterologie. (pub. by Karl Demeter Verlag)

**Deutsche Gesellschaft fuer Versicherungsmathematik**
Schneegloeckchenstr. 103, 800munich, W. Germany (B.R.D.)
- Deutsche Gesellschaft fuer Versicherungsmathematik. Blaetter. s-a. ISSN 0012-0200

**Deutsche Gesellschaft fuer Voelkerkunde**
- Zeitschrift fuer Ethnologie. (pub. by Albert Limbach Verlag)

**Deutsche Gesellschaft fuer Volkskunde e.V.**
Domplatz 23, 4400 Muenster, W. Germany (B.R.D.)
- Deutsche Gesellschaft fuer Volkskunde. D G V Informationen. irreg.
- Zeitschrift fuer Volkskunde. (pub. by W. Kohlhammer GmbH (Stuttgart))

**Deutsche Gesellschaft fuer Volkskunde e.V. Kommission fuer Ostdeutsche Volkskunde**
- Jahrbuch fuer Ostdeutsche Volkskunde. (pub. by N.G. Elwert Verlag)

**Deutsche Gesellschaft fuer Wehrmedizin und Wehrpharmazie**
- Wehrmedizinische Monatsschrift. (pub. by Bernard und Graefe Verlag)

**Deutsche Gesellschaft fuer Zahn-, Mund- und Kieferheilkunde**
- Deutsche Zahnaerztliche Zeitschrift. (pub. by Carl Hanser Verlag)

**Deutsche Gesellschaft fuer Zuechtungskunde e.V.**
- Zuechtungskunde. (pub. by Verlag Eugen Ulmer)

**Deutsche Gesellschaft zur Foerderung der Hoer-Sprach-Geschaedigten e.V.**
- Hoergeschaedigte Kinder. (pub. by Verlag Hoergeschaedigte Kinder)

**Deutsche Glastechnische Gesellschaft**
Bockenheimer Landstr. 126, 6000 Frankfurt, W. Germany (B.R.D.)
- Glastechnische Berichte; Zeitschrift fuer Glaskunde. m. ISSN 0017-1085 (Co-Sponsor: Huettentechnische Vereinigung der Deutschen Glasindustrie)

**Deutsche Gustav Freytag Gesellschaft**
Rheinstr. 55-57, G200 Wiesbaden, W. Germany (B.R.D.)
- Gustav-Freytag-Blaetter. s-a.

**Deutsche Heilpraktikerschaft e.V.**
- Naturheilpraxis. (pub. by Richard Pflaum Verlag KG)

**Deutsche Industriemeistervereinigung e.V**
- Industriemeister Nachrichten. (pub. by Verlag Neuer Merkur GmbH)

**Deutsche Kakteen Gesellschaft**
c/o Horst Bork, Marientalstr. 70-72, 4400 Muenster, W. Germany (B.R.D.)
- Kakteen. Gesamtdarstellung (Monographie) der Eingefuehrten Arten nebst Anzucht- und Pflege. 4 per yr. ISSN 0075-4676

**Deutsche Keramische Gesellschaft e.V.**
Menzenberger Str. 47, Postfach 1226, 5340 Bad Honnef 1, W. Germany (B.R.D.)
- Deutsche Keramische Gesellschaft. Berichte. m. ISSN 0365-9542
- Deutsche Keramische Gesellschaft. Fachausschussberichte. irreg., no. 19, 1974. ISSN 0070-4199

**Deutsche Kolpingsfamilie e.V.**
Kolpingplatz 9, 5000 Cologne 1, W. Germnay (B.R.D.)
- Kolpingblatt. ISSN 0023-2947

**Deutsche Krankenhausgesellschaft**
Tersteegenstr. 9, 4000 Duesseldorf 30, W. Germany (B.R.D.)
- Deutsche Krankenhausgesellschaft. Jahresbericht. biennial.

**Deutsche Krebsgesellschaft**
- Zeitschrift fuer Krebsforschung und Klinische Onkologie/Cancer Research and Clinical Oncology. (pub. by Springer Verlag US)

**Deutsche Kriminologische Gesellschaft**
- Kriminologische Schriftenreihe. (pub. by Verlag fuer Kriminalistische Fachliteratur)

**Deutsche Landwirtschafts-Gesellschaft e. V.**
- D L G - Mitteilungen. (pub. by Deutsche Landwirtschafts-Gesellschaft-Verlags-GmbH)
- Das Wirtschaftseigene Futter. (pub. by Deutsche Landwirtschafts-Gesellschaft-Verlags-GmbH)

**Deutsche Landwirtschafts-Gesellschaft-Verlags-GmbH**
Ruesterstr. 13, Postfach 2674, 6000 Frankfurt 1, W. Germany (B.R.D.)
- D L G - Mitteilungen. s-m. (Deutsche Landwirtschafts-Gesellschaft e. V.)
- Entwicklung und Laendlicher Raum. bi-m. (Deutsche Stiftung fuer Internationale Entwicklung. Zentralstelle fuer Ernaehrung und Landwirtschaft) (Co-sponsor: Deutsche Landwirtschafts-Gesellschaft e. V.)
- Das Wirtschaftseigene Futter; Erzeugung-Konservierung-Verwertung. q. ISSN 0049-7711 (Deutsche Landwirtschafts-Gesellschaft e. V.)
- Zeitschrift fuer Agrargeschichte und Agrarsoziologie. s-a. ISSN 0044-2194 (Gesellschaft fuer Agrargeschichte und Agrarsoziologie)
- Zeitschrift fuer Auslaendische Landwirtschaft/ Quarterly Journal of International Agriculture/ Journal Trimestriel d'Agriculture International. q. ISSN 0049-8599
- Zeitschrift fuer Bewaesserungswirtschaft. s-a. ISSN 0049-8602 (Deutsche Gesellschaft fuer Bewaesserungswirtschaft E.V)

**Deutsche Meteorologische Gesellschaft**
- Meteorologische Rundschau. (pub. by Gebrueder Borntraeger Verlagsbuchhandlung)

**Deutsche Mineralogische Gesellschaft**
- Fortschritte der Mineralogie. (pub. by E. Schweizerbart'sche Verlagsbuchhandlung)

**Deutsche Morgenlaendische Gesellschaft**
- Deutsche Morgenlaendische Gesellschaft. Zeitschrift. (pub. by Franz Steiner Verlag GmbH)
- Deutsche Morgenlaendische Gesellschaft. Zeitschrift. Supplementa. (pub. by Franz Steiner Verlag GmbH)

**Deutsche Mozart-Gesellschaft e.V.**
Halderstr. 12, 8900 Augsburg, W. Germany (B.R.D.)
- Acta Mozartiana. q. ISSN 0001-6233

**Deutsche Orchestervereinigung**
- Das Orchester. (pub. by B. Schott's Soehne)

**Deutsche Orient-Gesellschaft**
- Keilschrifttexte aus Boghazkoi. (pub. by Gebr. Mann Verlag)
- Uruk-Warka: Abhandlungen der Deutschen Orient-Gesellschaft. (pub. by Gebr. Mann Verlag)

**Deutsche Ornithologen-Gesellschaft e.V.**
Hardenberg Platz 8, 1000 Berlin 30, W. Germany (B.R.D.)
- Journal fuer Ornithologie. q. ISSN 0021-8375

**Deutsche Pestalozzi-Gesellschaft**
Lisztstr. 5, 5860 Luedenscheid, W. Germany (B.R.D.)
- Ost-West Paedagogik. irreg. ISSN 0078-6810

**Deutsche Pharmakologische Gesellschaft**
- Archives of Toxicology/Archiv fuer Toxikologie. (pub. by Springer-Verlag US)
- Naunyn-Schmiedeberg's Archives of Pharmacology. (pub. by Springer-Verlag US)

**Deutsche Pharmazeutische Gesellschaft**
- Archiv der Pharmazie. (pub. by Verlag Chemie International, Inc. US)
- Pharmazie in Unserer Zeit. (pub. by Verlag Chemie International, Inc. US)

**Deutsche Philatelisten-Jugend E.V.**
Rotkehlchenweg 35, 5881 Luedenscheid, W. Germany (B.R.D.)
- Junge Sammler; Zeitschrift fuer junge Briefmarkenfreunde. m. ISSN 0022-6343

**Deutsche Photo-und Kinohaendler-Bund**
- Inpho. (pub. by G F W-Verlag GmbH)

**Deutsche Physikalische Gesellschaft**
Gotenstr. 1-3, 5300 Bonn-Bad Godesberg, W. Germany (B.R.D.)
- Acustica. (pub. by S. Hirzel Verlag)
- Applied Physics. (pub. by Springer-Verlag US)
- Deutsche Physikalische Gesellschaft. Verhandlungen. 8-12 per yr. ISSN 0420-0195
- Zeitschrift fuer Physik. Section A: Atoms and Nuclei. (pub. by Springer-Verlag US)

**Verlagsanstalt Deutsche Polizei GmbH**
Forststr. 3a, 4010 Hilden, W. Germany (B.R.D.)
- Deutsche Polizei. m. ISSN 0012-057X (Gewerkschaft der Polizei)
- Taschenbuch fuer Kriminalisten. a. ISSN 0082-1934

**Deutsche Postgewerkschaft**
Rhonestr. 2, 6000 Frankfurt 71, W. Germany.
- Deutsche Post. s-m. ISSN 0012-0596
- Posthalter-Kurier. m. ISSN 0032-549X

**Deutsche Roentgengesellschaft**
- RoeFo. Fortschritte auf dem Gebiete der Roentgenstrahlen und der Nuklearmedizin. (pub. by George Thieme Verlag)
- Strahlentherapie. (pub. by Urban und Schwarzenberg)
- Zentralblatt fuer Die Gesamte Radiologie/ Radiology. (pub. by Springer-Verlag US)

**Verlag Deutsche Saengerzeitung GmbH**
Luepertzender Str. 157-163, 4050 Moenchengladbach, W. Germany (B. R. D.)
- Lied und Chor; Zeitschrift fuer das gesamte Chorwesen. m. ISSN 0024-290X (Deutscher Saengerbund e.V.)
- Saenger-Taschenkalender. a. (Deutscher Saengerbund e.V.)

**Deutsche Schiller-Gesellschaft**
- Deutsche Schiller-Gesellschaft. Jahrbuch. (pub. by Alfred Kroener Verlag)

**Der Deutsche Schreiner, Verlags-GmbH**
Neckar Str. 121, Postfach 209, 7000 Stuttgart 1, W. Germany (B. R. D.)
- Der Deutsche Schreiner. m. ISSN 0012-0685

**Deutsche Schuhfachschule Pirmasens**
- Schuh-Technik. (pub. by Dr. Alfred Huethig Verlag GmbH)

**Deutsche Schutzvereinigung fuer Wertpapierbesitz e.V.**
Humboldtstr. 9, 4000 Duesseldorf, W. Germany (B. R. D.)
- Wertpapier; Zeitschrift fuer Kapitalanlage. s-m. ISSN 0049-7169

**Deutsche Shakespeare-Gesellschaft West**
- Deutsche Shakespeare-Gesellschaft West. Jahrbuch. (pub. by Quelle und Meyer)

**Deutsche Statistische Gesellschaft**
- Allgemeines Statistisches Archiv. (pub. by Vandenhoeck und Ruprecht)

**Deutsche Stiftung fuer Internationale Entwicklung**
Simrockstr. 1, 5300 Bonn 1, W. Germany (B.R.D.)
- Entwicklung und Zusammenarbeit. m. (German edt.); 4 per yr (other edts.) ISSN 0013-9114

**Deutsche Stiftung fuer Internationale Entwicklung. Zentralstelle fuer Ernaehrung und Landwirtschaft**
- Entwicklung und Laendlicher Raum. (pub. by Deutsche Landwirtschafts-Gesellschaft-Verlags-GmbH)

**Deutsche Theatertechniker Gesellschaft**
- Buehnentechnische Rundschau. (pub. by Erhard Friedrich Verlag)

**Deutsche Tieraerzteschaft e.V.**
- Deutsches Tieraerzteblatt. (pub. by Schluetersche Verlagsanstalt und Druckerei)

**Deutsche Tropenmedizinische Gesellschaft**
- Tropenmedizin und Parasitologie. (pub. by Georg Thieme Verlag)

**Deutsche Ueberseeische Bank**
Ballindamm 7, 2000 Hamburg 1, W. Germany (B.R.D.)
- Lateinamerika: Wirtschaftliche Daten. a.
- Wirtschaftsbericht Lateinamerika. m.

**Deutsche UFO-Studiengesellschaft (DUIST e. V.)**
- UFO-Nachrichten. (pub. by Ventla-Verlag)

**Deutsche UNESCO-Kommission**
- Deutsche UNESCO-Kommission. Seminarbericht. (pub. by Verlag Dokumentation)

**Deutsche Vereinigung fuer die Rehabilitation Behinderter**
- Die Rehabilitation. (pub. by Georg Thieme Verlag)

**Deutsche Vereinigung fuer Gewerblichen Rechtsschutz und Urheberrecht**
- Gewerblicher Rechtsschutz und Urheberrecht. (pub. by Verlag Chemie International, Inc. US)

**Deutsche Vereinigung fuer Internationales Steuerrecht**
- Internationale Wirtschafts-Briefe. (pub. by Verlag Neue Wirtschafts-Briefe GmbH)

**Deutsche Vereinigung fuer Parlamentsfragen**
- Zeitschrift fuer Parlamentsfragen. (pub. by Westdeutscher Verlag GmbH)

**Deutsche Verkehrswissenschaftliche Gesellschaft**
Apostelnstr. 11, 5000 Cologne 1, W. Germany (B.R.D.)
- Deutsche Verkehrswissenschaftliche Gesellschaft. Schriftenreihe. Reihe A. Dokumentation. irreg.
- Internationales Verkehrswesen. (pub. by Tetzlaff Verlag GmbH)

**Deutsche Verlagsanstalt GmbH**
Neckarstr. 121, Postfach 209, 7000 Stuttgart 1, W. Germany (B.R.D.)
- Bild der Wissenschaft; Zeitschrift fuer Naturwissenschaft und Technik in unserer Zeit. m. ISSN 0006-2375
- Brennpunkte. bi-m. (Gottlieb Duttweiler Institute for Economic & Social Studies)
- Deutsche Bauzeitung; Fachzeitschrift fuer Architektur, Bautechnik und Ingenieurwesen. m. (Bund Deutscher Baumeister, Architekten und Ingenieure e.V.)
- Das Deutsche Malerblatt. m. ISSN 0012-0448 (Hauptverband des Deutschen Maler- und Lackiererhandwerks)
- Exakt; Wissenschaft und Technik in der Sowjetunion. m. (Akademiya Nauk S.S.S.R. UR)
- International Bulletin for Research on Law in Eastern Europe/Bulletin International de Recherches sur le Droit en Europe de l'Est/ Internationales Bulletin zur Ostrechtsforschung. s-a. (Deutsche Gesellschaft fuer Osteuropakunde)
- L W. (Lichtwerbung - Lichtinformation - Lichtarchitektur) bi-m. (Fachverband Lichtwerbung)
- Osteuropa; Zeitschrift fuer Gegenwartsfragen des Ostens. m. ISSN 0030-6428 (Deutsche Gesellschaft fuer Osteuropakunde)
- Osteuropa-Recht. q. ISSN 0030-6444 (Deutsche Gesellschaft fuer Osteuropakunde)
- Osteuropa-Wirtschaft. q. ISSN 0030-6460 (Deutsche Gesellschaft fuer Osteuropakunde)
- Vierteljahrshefte fuer Zeitgeschichte. q. ISSN 0042-5702 (Institut fuer Zeitgeschichte)

**Deutsche Viehhandelsgesellschaft MbH Fachverlag**
c/o Dr. Otto Plagge, Adenauerallee 176, 5300 Bonn, W. Germany (B. R. D.)
- Vieh und Fleisch. m. (Deutscher Vieh und Fleischhandelsbund)

**Deutsche Volksgesundheits-Bewegung E.V.**
- Das Gewissen. (pub. by Medizinalpolitischer Verlag)
- Naturgemaesser Land- und Gartenbau. (pub. by Medizinalpolitischer Verlag)
- U B N. (pub. by Medizinalpolitischer Verlag)

**Deutsche Volkswirtschaftliche Gesellschaft**
- Management Heute und Marktwirtschaft. (pub. by Verlag fuer Wissenschaft, Wirtschaft und Technik GmbH und Co.)

**Deutsche Wissenschaftliche Kommission fuer Meeresforschung**
- Meeresforschung/Reports on Marine Research. (pub. by Verlag Paul Parey (Hamburg))

**Verlag Deutsche Wohnungswirtschaft GmbH**
Cecilienallee 45, 4000 Duesseldorf 30, W. Germany (B. R. D.)
- Deutsche Wohnungswirtschaft. m. ISSN 0012-0995 (Zentralverband der Deutschen Haus, Wohnungs und Grundeigentuemer e.V.)

**Deutsche Zeitung Christ und Welt Verlag GmbH**
Martin-Luther-Platz 28, 4000 Duesseldorf 1, W. Germany (B.R.D.)
- Deutsche Zeitung Christ und Welt. w.

**Deutsche Zoologische Gesellschaft**
- Deutsche Zoologische Gesellschaft. Verhandlungen. (pub. by Gustav Fischer Verlag)
- Fortschritte der Zoologie. Neue Folge. (pub. by Gustav Fischer Verlag)

**Deutscher Adressbuch-Verlag**
Holzhofallee 38, Postfach 320, 6100 Darmstadt, W. Germany (B.R.D.)
- Deutsches Bundes-Adressbuch: Industrie, Gross- und Aussenhandel, Dienstleistungen, Organisationen. a.

**Deutscher Aero Club**
- Deutscher Aerokurier. (pub. by Verlag Dr. Neufang KG)

**Deutscher Agrarverlag GmbH**
Koelner Str. 142-148, 5300 Bonn-Bad Godesberg, W. Germany (B.R.D.)
- Deutsche Bauern-Korrespondenz. m. (Deutscher Bauernverband e V.)

**Deutscher Akademischer Austauschdienst (DAAD)**
Kennedyallee 50, 5300 Bonn- Bad Godesberg, W. Germany (B.R.D.)
- Mitteilungsblatt fuer Wissenschaffliche Lehrkraefte im Ausland. m.

**Deutscher Alpenverein**
Praterinsel 5, 8000 Munich 22, W. Germany (B.R.D.)
- Alpenvereins-Jahrbuch. a. ISSN 0065-6534 (Co-sponsor: Oesterreichischer Alpenverein)
- Deutscher Alpenverein; Mitteilungen-Jugend am Berg. bi-m. ISSN 0012-1088
- Wissenschaftliche Alpenvereinshefte. irreg. ISSN 0084-0912

**Deutscher Altphilologen-Verband**
- Deutscher Altphilologen-Verband. Mitteilungsblatt. (pub. by Carl Winter Universitaetsverlag)

**Deutscher Amateur-Radio-Club**
Lindenallee 6, 3507 Baunatal, W. Germany (B.R.D.)
- CQ DL. m.

**Deutscher Anwaltverein e.V.**
Sievekingplatz 1, Ziviljustizgebaeude Zimmer 811, 2000 Hamburg 36, W. Germany (B.R.D.)
- Anwaltsblatt; Nachrichten fuer die Mitglieder des Deutschen Anwaltvereins e.V. m.
- Anwaltsverzeichnis. (pub. by Juristischer Verlag W. Ellinghaus und Co. GmbH)

**Deutscher Apotheker-Verein**
- Apotheker-Jahrbuch. (pub. by Wissenschaftliche Verlagsgesellschaft mbH)

**Deutscher Arbeitsring fuer Laermbekaempfung e.V.**
- Kampf dem Laerm. (pub. by Springer- Verlag US)

**Deutscher Badminton Verband**
- Badminton. (pub. by Oskar Klokow, Verlag und Versandbuchhandlung)

**Deutscher Bauernverband e V.**
- Deutsche Bauern-Korrespondenz. (pub. by Deutscher Agrarverlag GmbH)

**Deutscher Beamtenbund**
Dreizehnmorgenweg 36, 5300 Bonn - Bad Godesberg, W. Germany (B.R.D.)
- Der Beamten-Bund. m. ISSN 0405-1033

**Deutscher Beamtenbund, Landesbund Bremen e.V.**
Am Wall 172, 2800 Bremen, W. Germany.
- Beamte im Lande Bremen. m. ISSN 0005-7401

**Deutscher Beamtenbund. Landesbund Rheinland-Pfalz**
Adam-Karrillon-Str. 62, Postfach 1706, 6500 Mainz 1, W. Germany (B.R.D.)
- Der Beamte in Rheinland-Pfalz; Zeitschrift fuer Angehoerige des oeffentlichen Dienstes. m. ISSN 0005-741X

**Deutscher Beamtenbund. Verband der Beamten der Obersten Bundesbehoerden**
- Die Bundesverwaltung. (pub. by Wilhelm Stollfuss Verlag)

**Deutscher Berufsverband fuer Krankenpflege**
Heinrich - Hoffmann - Str. 3, 6000 Frankfurt 71, W. Germany (B. R. D.)
- Krankenpflege. m. ISSN 0002-1008
- Sprachfuehrer fuer die Krankenpflege. irreg.

**Deutscher Bibliotheksverband e.V.**
Fehrbelliner Platz 3, 1000 Berlin 31, W. Germany (B.R.D.)
- Schulbibliothek Aktuell. q.

**Deutscher Bibliotheksverband e.V. Arbeitsstelle fuer das Bibliothekswesen**
Fehrbelliner Platz 3, 1000 Berlin 31, W. Germany (B.R.D.)
- A G B-Titeldienst. (Amerika-Gedenk-Bibliothek); Katalogaufnahmen neuerschiener deutschsprachiger Buecher. s-m.
- Bibliotheksdienst; Kurzinformationen zur bibliothekarischen Arbeit. m. ISSN 0006-1972
- Fachbibliographischer Dienst Bibliothekswesen. q. ISSN 0429-9655
- Handbuch der Oeffentlichen Bibliotheken. biennial.
- Inspel. q. ISSN 0019-0217 (International Federation of Library Associations. Special Libraries Section)
- M D. (Musikbibliographischer Dienst) bi-m.
- Musikbibliothek Aktuell. q. (International Association of Music Libraries)
- Statistik der Kommunalen Oeffentlichen Bibliotheken der Bundesrepublik. a. ISSN 0081-5241
- Z D. (Zeitschriftendienst); Nachweis von Aufsaetzen aus 200 deutschen Zeitschriften. m. (10 per yr)
- Zeitschriftendienst Musik. m. ISSN 0044-3824

**Deutscher Blindenverband e.V.**
Bismarckstr. 30, 5300 Bonn- Bad Godesberg, W. Germany (B.R.D.)
- Die Blindenselbsthilfe; Zeitschrift fuer alle Fragen des Blindenwesens. m.

**Deutscher Boots- und Schiffbauer-Verband**
- Bootswirtschaft. (pub. by Verlag fuer Bootswirtschaft)

**Deutscher Buehnenverein e.V.**
- Die Deutsche Buehne. (pub. by Verlag Rommerskirchen und Co.)

**Deutscher Bund fuer Naturgemasse Lebens- und Heilweise e.V.**
- Der Naturarzt. (pub. by Verlag der Naturarzt)

**Deutscher Bundeswehr-Verband e.V**
- Die Bundeswehr. (pub. by Deutscher Bundeswehr-Verlag GmbH)

**Deutscher Camping-Club e.V.**
- D C C -Camping Fuehrer Europa. (pub. by D C C -Wirtschaftsdienst und -Verlag GmbH)

**Deutscher Caritasverband**
Karlstr. 40, 7800 Freiburg, W. Germany (B.R.D.)
- Caritas. (pub. by Lambertus-Verlag GmbH)
- Caritas; Jahrbuch des Deutschen Caritasverbandes. a. ISSN 0069-0570
- Caritas-Kalender. (pub. by Lambertus-Verlag GmbH)
- Caritas-Korrespondenz. (pub. by Lambertus-Verlag GmbH)
- Jugendwohl. (pub. by Lambertus-Verlag GmbH)

**Deutscher Diabetikerbund e.V.**
- Diabetes-Journal. (pub. by Verlag Kirchheim und Co. GmbH)

**Deutscher Drucker Verlagsgesellschaft mbH und Co. KG**
Forststr. 60, Postfach 2650, 7000 Stuttgart 1, W. Germany (B.R.D.)
- Deutscher Drucker. w. ISSN 0012-1096

**Deutscher Edelkatzenzuechter-Verband e.V.**
Friedrichstr. 46/48, 6200 Wiesbaden, W. Germany (B.R.D.)
- Die Edelkatze; illustrierte Fachzeitschrift fuer Rassekatzenzucht. q. ISSN 0013-0826

**Deutscher Erfinderring e.V.**
Schlegelstr. 25, 8500 Nuernberg, W. Germany (B.R.D.)
- Erfinder und Neuheitendienst. m.

**Deutscher Evangelischer Missionsrat**
- Das Wort in der Welt. (pub. by Deutsche Evangelische Missionshilfe Verlag)

**Deutscher Fachverlag GmbH**
Schumannstr. 27, Postfach 2625, 6000 Frankfurt 1, W. Germany (B.R.D.)
- Chemiefasern /Textil-Industrie; Zeitschrift fuer die gesamte Textilindustrie. m.
- D F Z Magazin. (Deutsches Fachzeitschriften-Magazin); die Zeitschrift in der Fachzeitschrift. m.

- G V-Praxis mit Tiefkuehlpraxis; Zeitschrift fuer moderne Grossverpflegung. m.
- Herrenjournal. m. ISSN 0018-0874 (Verein zur Foerderung der Deutschen Herrenmode e.V.)
- Lebensmittel Zeitung. w. ISSN 0024-0001
- Moderner Markt mit Neue Laeden. m. ISSN 0580-6631
- Papier und Kunststoff Verarbeiter; die fachzeitschrift fuer druck, veredelung und weiterverarbeitung von papier, vollpappe, wellpape, zellglas, kunststoff und folien aller art. m. ISSN 0048-2897
- Taschenbuch des Textileinzelhandels. a. ISSN 0082-1837
- Textil-Wirtschaft. w. ISSN 0040-487X
- Z L R -Zeitschrift fuer das Gesamte Lebensmittelrecht. q.

**Deutscher Feuerwehrverband**
Hochkreuzallee 89, 5300 Bonn-Bad Godesberg, W. Germany (B.R.D.)
- Feuerwehr-Jahrbuch; ein Jahresbericht ueber das Feuerwehrwesen in der Bundesrepublik Deutschland. a. ISSN 0071-4674

**Deutscher Fleischerverband**
- Allgemeine Fleischer Zeitung. (pub. by Verlagshaus Sponholz)

**Deutscher Forschungsdienst**
Ahrstr. 45, 5300 Bonn-Bad Godesberg, W. Germany (B.R.D.)
- German Research Service. m. ISSN 0072-1476

**Deutscher Forstverein**
Josefstr. 10, 7710 Donaueschingen, W. Germany (B.R.D.)
- Deutscher Forstverein. Jahresbericht. a.

**Deutscher Frauenrat**
Augustastr. 42, 5300 Bonn-Bad Godesberg, W. Germany (B.R.D.)
- Informationen fuer Die Frau. m. ISSN 0020-0352

**Deutscher Fussball-Bund**
- Fussball-Jugend. (pub. by Sport- und Jugend-Verlag GmbH und Co. KG)

**Deutscher Genossenschafts-Verlag GmbH**
Postfach 1369, 5450 Neuwied, W. Germany (B.R.D.)
- Der Goldene Pfennig; Zeitschrift fuer junge Sparer. q. ISSN 0017-1646 (Deutscher Raiffeisenverband e.V.)

**Deutscher Germanisten-Verband**
- Deutsches Germanisten-Verband. Mitteilungen. (pub. by Verlag Moritz Diesterweg)

**Deutscher Gewerkschaftsbund**
Postfach 2601, 4000 Duesseldorf, W. Germany (B.R.D.)
- A F A Informationen. (pub. by Bund-Verlag GmbH)
- Arbeit und Recht. (pub. by Bund-Verlag GmbH)
- Der Deutsche Beamte. (pub. by Bund-Verlag GmbH)
- Gewerkschafter im Handwerk. m. ISSN 0016-9439
- Gewerkschaftliche Bildungspolitik. (pub. by Berg-Verlag GmbH)
- Gewerkschaftliche Monatshefte. (pub. by Bund-Verlag GmbH)
- Laboratoriums-Praxis. (pub. by Bund-Verlag GmbH)
- Die Quelle. (pub. by Bund-Verlag GmbH)
- Ran. (pub. by Bund-Verlag GmbH)
- Welt der Arbeit. (pub. by Bund-Verlag GmbH)
- Wirtschaft und Wissen. (pub. by Bund-Verlag GmbH)

**Deutscher Gewerkschaftsbund. Wirtschafts- und Sozialwissenschaftliches Institut**
- W S I Mitteilungen. (pub. by Bund-Verlag GmbH)

**Deutscher Handelsvereinigung Spar**
- Der Neue Weg. (pub. by Verlag fuer Wirtschaftspraxis GmbH)

**Deutscher Harmonikaverband e.V.**
Postfach 160, 7217 Trossingen, W. Germany (B.R.D.)
- Harmonika-Revue. bi-m.

**Deutscher Hochseesportverband Hansa e.V.**
- Der Blaue Peter. (pub. by Verlag Delius, Klasing und Co.)

**Deutscher Hotel- und Gaststaettenverband E.V. (DEHOGA)**
- Allgemeine Hotel-und Gaststaetten-Zeitung. (pub. by Matthaes Verlag GmbH)

**Deutscher Hugenotten-Verein e.V.**
Schoeneberger Str. 15, 3400 Goettingen, W. Germany (B.R.D.)
- Der Deutsche Hugenott. q. ISSN 0012-0294
- Deutscher Hugenotten-Verein E.V. Geschichtsblaetter. irreg.

**Deutscher Imkerbund e.V.**
Moltkestr. 41, 5300 Bonn-Bad Godesberg, W. Germany (B.R.D.)
- Apidologie. q. (Co-Sponsor: Arbeitsgemeinschaft der Institute fuer Bienenforschung e.V.)

**Deutscher Instituts-Verlag GmbH**
Oberlaender Ufer 84-88, Postfact 510670, 5000cologne 51, W. Germany (B.R.D.)
- Gesellschaftspolitische Bildungsmaterialien. irreg. (Stiftung Gesellschaft und Unternehmen)
- Informationen zur Beruflichen Bildung. s-m.
- Institut der Deutschen Wirtschaft. Gewerkschaftsreport. irreg. ISSN 0084-9782
- Wirtschafts- und Gesellschaftspolitische Grundinformationen. bi-m.

**Deutscher Journalisten-Verband e.V**
- Der Journalist. (pub. by Verlag Rommerskirchen und Co.)

**Deutscher Kanu-Verband e.V.**
Berta-Allee 8, 4100 Duisburg 1, W. Germany (B.R.D.)
- Kanu-Sport. m. ISSN 0022-8923

**Deutscher Kommunal-Verlag GmbH**
Roseggerstr. 5a, 4000 Duesseldorf, W. Germany (B.R.D.)
- Industrieabwaesser. a. ISSN 0073-7755
- Kommunalwirtschaft. m. (Verein fuer Kommunalwirtschaft)
- Luftverunreinigung. a. ISSN 0460-2374

**Deutscher Konditorenbund**
- Konditorei und Cafe. (pub. by Hugo Matthaes Verlag GmbH)

**Deutscher Koordinierungsrat der Gesellschaften fuer Christlichjuedische Zusammenarbeit**
- Emuna. (pub. by Verlag Israel-Forum Landesberger und Co.)

**Deutscher Landkreistag**
- Der Landkreis. (pub. by W. Kohlhammer GmbH (Koeln))

**Deutscher Lehrerverband**
Koelner Str. 93, 5300 Bonn- Bad Godesberg, W. Germany (B.R.D.)
- Bildung Konkret. m.

**Deutscher Medizinischer Informationsdienst e. V.**
- D M I-Nachrichten. (pub. by Verlag H. Hoffmann)

**Deutscher Mieterbund e.V.**
Spichernstr. 61, 5000 Cologne 1, W. Germany (B.R.D.)
- Mieterzeitung. m.

**Deutscher Motoryachtverband e.V.**
- Stander. (pub. by Westdeutsche Verlagsanstalt GmbH)

**Deutscher Musikrat**
Michaelstrasse 4a, 5300 Bonn-Bad Godesberg, W. Germany (B.R.D.)
- International Music Council. German Committee. Referate Informationen. 3 per yr. ISSN 0538-8791

**Deutscher Oekumenischer Ausschuss**
- Oekumenische Rundschau. (pub. by Lembeck-Verlag)

**Deutscher Paritaetischer Wohlfahrtsverband E.V.**
Heinrich-Hoffmann-Str. 3, 6000 Frankfurt, W. Germany (B.R.D.)
- D P W V - Nachrichten. m. ISSN 0011-510X

**Deutscher Radio- und Fernseh- Fachverband e.V.**
- Der Deutsche Rundfunk- Einzelhandel. (pub. by Verlag Bachem und Sohn)

**Deutscher Raiffeisenverband e.V.**
- Der Goldene Pfennig. (pub. by Deutscher Genossenschafts-Verlag GmbH)
- Raiffeisenbote. (pub. by Verlag Bildpost)

**Deutscher Rat der Europaeischen Bewegung e.V.**
- Informationsdienst des Deutschen Rates der Europaeischen Bewegung. (pub. by Europa Union Verlag GmbH)

**Deutscher Richterbund**
- Handbuch der Justiz. (pub. by R. v. Decker's Verlag, G. Schenk GmbH)

**Deutscher Ringer-Bund**
- Athletik. (pub. by Athletik-Verlag)

**Deutscher Saengerbund e.V.**
- Lied und Chor. (pub. by Verlag Deutsche Saengerzeitung GmbH)
- Saenger-Taschenkalender. (pub. by Verlag Deutsche Saengerzeitung GmbH)

**Deutscher Sauna-Bund e.V.**
- Sauna Nachrichten mit Sauna Archiv. (pub. by Sauna-Verlag Werner Thomas)

**Deutscher Schaedlingsbekaempfer-Verband**
- Der Praktische Schaedlingsbekaempfer. (pub. by Verlag der Praktische Schaedlingsbekaempfer)

**Deutscher Schuetzenbund**
Schiesssportschule, 6200 Wiesbaden-Klarenthal, W. Germany (B.R.D.)
- Deutsche Schuetzen Zeitung. m. ISSN 0012-0707

**Deutscher Sparkassen- und Giroverband e.V.**
- Betriebswirtschaftliche Blaetter fuer die Praxis der Sparkassen und Girozentralen. (pub. by Deutscher Sparkassenverlag GmbH)
- Deutsche Sparkassenzeitung. (pub. by Deutscher Sparkassenverlag GmbH)

**Deutscher Sparkassenverlag GmbH**
Kernerstr. 52, Postfach 733, 7000 Stuttgart 1, W. Germany (B.R.D.)
- Betriebswirtschaftliche Blaetter fuer die Praxis der Sparkassen und Girozentralen. bi-m. ISSN 0006-0011 (Deutscher Sparkassen- und Giroverband e.V.)
- Deutsche Sparkassenzeitung. s-w. ISSN 0012-0766 (Deutscher Sparkassen- und Giroverband e.V.)
- Sparkasse. m. ISSN 0038-6561

**Deutscher Sportlehrerverband e.V.**
- Sportunterricht. (pub. by Verlag Karl Hofmann)

**Deutscher Staedte- und Gemeindebund**
- Staedte- und Gemeindebund. (pub. by Verlag Otto Schwartz und Co.)

**Deutscher Stenografenbund e. V.**
- D S T Z-Deutsche Stenografenzeitung. (pub. by Heckners Verlag)

**Deutscher Studenten-Anzeiger**
Postfach 713, 8630 Coburg, W. Germany (B.R.D.)
- Deutscher Studenten-Anzeiger; unabhaengiges Forum deutscher Hochschueler. 4 per yr. ISSN 0012-1177

**Deutscher Supplement Verlag KG**
Luebener Str. 6, 8500 Nuernberg-Langwasser, W. Germany (B.R.D.)
- R T V; illustriertes Programm. w.

**Deutscher Teckelklub**
Prinzenstr. 38, 4100 Duisburg, W. Germany (B.R.D.)
- Dachshund. m. ISSN 0011-5231

**Deutscher Textilreinigungs-Verband e.V.**
- D T V -Intern. (pub. by Gebr. Giehrl)

**Deutscher Turnerbund**
- Deutscher Turner-Bund. Jahrbuch der Turnkunst. (pub. by Pohl Druckerei und Verlagsanstalt)

**Deutscher Verband der Jugenbuende fuer Entschiedenes Christentum e.V.**
- Anruf. (pub. by Verlag Born)
- Auftrag und Weg. (pub. by Verlag Born)

**Deutscher Verband Frau und Kultur e.V.**
Vennstr. 9, 4830 Guetersloh, W. Germany (B.R.D.)
- Frau und Kultur; Erleben & Gestalten. s-m'

**Deutscher Verband fuer Material Pruefung**
- Materialpruefung/Materials Testing/Materiaux, Essais et Recherches. (pub. by V D I-Verlag GmbH)

**Deutscher Verband fuer Schweisstechnik e.V.**
- Der Praktiker. (pub. by Deutscher Verlag fuer Schweisstechnik GmbH)
- Schweissen und Schneiden. (pub. by Deutscher Verlag fuer Schweisstechnik GmbH)

**Deutscher Verband fuer Wasserwirtschaft e.V.**
- Die Wasserwirtschaft. (pub. by Franckh'sche Verlagshandlung W. Keller und Co.)

**Deutscher Verband fuer Wohnungswesen, Staedtebau und Raumplanung e.V.**
Simrockstr. 4, 5300 Bonn 1, 5000 Cologne 80, W. Germany (B.R.D.)
- Stadtbau-Informationen. w. ISSN 0038-8998

**Deutscher Verein fuer Gesundheitspflege e. V.**
- Leben und Gesundheit. (pub. by Saatkorn-Verlag GmbH)

**Deutscher Verein fuer Kunstwissenschaft**
- Deutscher Verein fuer Kunstwissenschaft. Zeitschrift. (pub. by Deutscher Verlag fuer Kunstwissenschaft)
- Schrifttum zur Deutschen Kunst. (pub. by Deutscher Verlag fuer Kunstwissenschaft)

**Deutscher Verein fuer Oeffentliche und Private Fuersorge**
Beethovenstr. 61, 6000 Frankfurt, W. Germany (B.R.D.)
- Deutscher Verein fuer Oeffentliche und Private Fuersorge. Nachrichtendienst. m. ISSN 0012-1185

**Deutscher Verein fuer Vermessungswesen**
Nordbahnhofstr. 16, Postfach 147, 7000 Stuttgart 1, W. Germany (B. R. D.)
- Zeitschrift fuer Vermessungswesen. m. ISSN 0044-3689

**Deutscher Verein fuer Versicherungswissenschaft e.V.**
- Zeitschrift fuer die gesamte Versicherungswissenschaft. (pub. by Duncker und Humblot)

**Deutscher Vieh und Fleischhandelsbund**
- Vieh und Fleisch. (pub. by Deutsche Viehhandelsgesellschaft MbH Fachverlag)

**Deutscher Volkshochschulverband. Paedagogische Arbeitsstelle**
- Zielsprache Englisch. (pub. by Max Hueber Verlag)

**Deutscher Weinbauverband**
- Der Deutsche Weinbau. (pub. by Zeitschriftenverlag Dr. Bilz und Dr. Fraund KG)

**Deutscher Werkbund E.V.**
Alexandraweg 26, 6100 Darmstadt, W. Germany (B.R.D.)
- Werk und Zeit; Monatszeitung fuer Umweltgestaltung. m. ISSN 0049-7150

**Deutscher Wetterdienst**
Frankfurter Str. 135, Postfach 185, 6050 Offenbach (Main) 1, W. Germany (B.R.D.)
- Annalen der Meteorologie. Neue Folge. irreg., no. 9, 1974. ISSN 0072-4122
- Deutscher Wetterdienst. Berichte. irreg., no. 138, 1975. ISSN 0072-4130
- Deutscher Wetterdienst. Bibliographien. irreg., no. 30, 1975. ISSN 0072-4149
- Deutscher Wetterdienst. Monatlicher Witterungsbericht. m. ISSN 0016-8955
- Europaeischer Wetterbericht. d. ISSN 0341-2970
- Grosswetterlagen Europas. m. ISSN 0017-4645
- Promet: Meteorologische Fortbildung. q.

**Deutscher Wetterdienst. Seewetteramt**
Bernhard Nocht-Str. 76, Postfach 180, 2000 Hamburg 4, W. Germany (B.R.D.)
- Deutscher Wetterdienst. Seewetteramt. Einzelveroeffentlichungen. irreg., no. 91, 1977. ISSN 0072-1603
- Witterung in Uebersee. m. ISSN 0043-7085

**Deutscher Wissenschaftler Verband**
Hoehlenweg 31, 3380 Goslar 1, W. Germany (B.R.D.)
- D W V-Mitteilungen. q. ISSN 0011-5193

**Deutscher Zentralverein Homoeopatischer Aerzte e.V.**
- Allgemeine Homoeopathische Zeitung. (pub. by Karl F. Haug Verlag GmbH)

**Deutsches Afrika-Korps e.V.**
- Die Oase. (pub. by H. Poeppinghaus)

**Deutsches Archaeologisches Institut**
- Archaeologische Mitteilungen aus Iran. Neue Folge. (pub. by Dietrich Reimer Buchhandlung)
- Archaeologischer Anzeiger. (pub. by Walter de Gruyter und Co.)
- Samos. (pub. by Rudolf Habelt Verlag)
- Sylloge Nummorum Graecorum Deutschland. (pub. by Gebr. Mann Verlag)

**Deutsches Archaeologisches Institut. Kommission fuer Alte Geschichte und Epigraphik**
- Chiron. (pub. by C. H. Beck'sche Verlagsbuchhandlung)

**Deutsches Archaeologisches Institut. Roemisch-Germanische Kommission**
- Germania. (pub. by Walter de Gruyter und Co.)
- Materialien zur Roemisch-Germanischen Keramik. (pub. by Rudolf Habelt Verlag)

**Deutsches Atomforum e.V.**
Allianzplatz 10, 5300 Bonn, W. Germany (B.R.D.)
- Atom-Informationen. m. ISSN 0004-7031

**Deutsches Bucharchiv, Muenchen**
- Buchwissenschaftliche Beitraege. (pub. by Verlag Dokumentation)

**Deutsches Computer Forum**
Postfach 165, 8012 Ottobrunn, W. Germany (B.R.D.)
- Computer Adress. (pub. by Data Verlag)
- Minicomputer Annual. a.

**Deutsches Evangelisches Institut fuer Altertumswissenschaft des Heiligen Landes**
- Deutscher Palaestina-Verein. Zeitschrift. (pub. by Verlag Otto Harrassowitz)

**Deutsches High-Fidelity Institut**
- HiFi Stereophonie. (pub. by Verlag G. Braun GmbH)

**Deutsches Hydrographisches Institut**
Bernhard-Nocht-Str. 78, 2000 Hamburg 4, W. Germany (B.R.D.)
- Deutsche Hydrographische Zeitschrift. 6 per yr. ISSN 0012-0308
- Deutsche Hydrographische Zeitschrift. Ergaenzungsheft. Reihe A. irreg., no. 13, 1973. ISSN 0070-4164
- Deutsche Hydrographische Zeitschrift. Ergaenzungsheft. Reihe B. irreg., no. 14, 1973. ISSN 0070-4172
- Deutsches Hydrographisches Institut. Jahresbericht. a. ISSN 0070-4458
- Eisbericht. d.(during Winter & Spring seasons) ISSN 0013-2705
- Gezeitentafeln. a. ISSN 0084-9774
- Nachrichten fuer Seefahrer. w. ISSN 0027-7444
- Nautisches Jahrbuch, oder Ephemeriden und Tafeln. a. ISSN 0077-6211
- Der Seewart. (pub. by Kommissions-Verlag Eckardt und Messtorff)

**Deutsches Institut fuer Aerztliche Mission**
Paul-Lechler-Str. 24, 740 Tuebingen, W. Germany (B.R.D.)
- Nachrichten aus der Aerztlichen Mission. q. ISSN 0027-7398

**Deutsches Institut fuer Afrika-Forschung**
- Hamburger Beitraege zur Afrika-Kunde. (pub. by Afrika Verlag)

**Deutsches Institut fuer Betriebswirtschaft**
- Betriebliches Vorschlagswesen. (pub. by Erich Schmidt Verlag (Bielefeld))

**Deutsches Institut fuer Erforschung des Mittelalters**
- Schriften der Monumenta Germaniae Historica. (pub. by Anton Hiersemann Verlag)

**Deutsches Institut fuer Filmkunde**
Schloss, 6202 Wiesbaden- Biebrich, W. Germany (B.R.D.)
- Deutsches Institut fuer Filmkunde. Information. m.

**Deutsches Institut fuer Internationale Paedagogische Forschung**
- Studien und Dokumentationen zur Deutschen Bildungsgeschichte. (pub. by Verlag Julius Beltz)

**Deutsches Institut fuer Normung e.V.**
- D I N Mitteilungen. (pub. by Beuth Verlag GmbH)
- DIN-Taschenbuecher. (pub. by Beuth Verlag GmbH)
- English Translations of German Standards. (pub. by Beuth Verlag GmbH)
- Handbuch der Klassifikation. (pub. by Beuth Verlag GmbH)

**Deutsches Institut fuer Normung e.V. Ausschuss fuer Klassifikation**
- D K-Mitteilungen. (pub. by Beuth Verlag GmbH)

**Deutsches Institut fuer Normung e.V. Fachnormenausschuss Photo Technik**
- M F M-Moderne Fototechnik. (pub. by A. G. T.-Verlag Georg Thum)

**Deutsches Institut fuer Normung e.V. Normenausschuss Schiffbau**
Kirchenallee 57, 2000 Hamburg 1, W. Germany (B.R.D.)
- Schiffbau-Normung. 4-5 per yr. ISSN 0036-6048

**Deutsches Institut fuer Puppenspiel**
Bergstr. 115, 4630 Bochum, W. Germany (B.R.D.)
- Deutsches Institut fuer Puppenspiel. Forschung und Lehre. ISSN 0070-4490
- Meister des Puppenspiels. irreg. ISSN 0076-6216

**Deutsches Institut fuer Urbanistik**
- Archiv fuer Kommunalwissenschaften. (pub. by W. Kohlhammer GmbH (Stuttgart))

**Deutsches Institut fuer Vormundschaftswesen**
Zaehringerstr 10, 6900 Heidelberg, W. Germany (B.R.D.)
- Amtsvormund. m. ISSN 0003-2336

**Deutsches Institut fuer Wirtschaftsforschung**
- Deutsches Institut fuer Wirtschaftsforschung. Vierteljahrshefte zur Wirtschaftsforschung. (pub. by Duncker und Humblot)
- Deutsches Institut fuer Wirtschaftsforschung. Wochenbericht. (pub. by Duncker und Humblot)

**Deutsches Jugendherbergswerk**
Buelowstr. 26, 4930 Detmold 1, W. Germany (B.R.D.)
- Jugendherberge. bi-m. ISSN 0022-5932
- Jugendherbergs-Verzeichnis. a. ISSN 0075-4528
- Jugendherbergswerk. bi-m.

**Deutsches Jugendinstitut e.V.**
Saarstr. 7, 8000 Munich 40, W. Germany (B.R.D.)
- Bibliographie Sozialisation und Sozialpaedagogik. q. ISSN 0342-3964

**Deutsches Komitee fuer Elektrowaerme**
- Elektrowaerme International. (pub. by Vulkan-Verlag Dr. W. Classen)

**Deutsches Krebsforschungszentrum**
Im Neuenheimer Feld 280, 6900 Heidelberg 1, W. Germany (B.R.D.)
- Deutsches Krebsforschungszentrum. Veroeffentlichungen. irreg. ISSN 0070-4229

**Deutsches Kunststoff-Institut**
Schlossgartenstr. 6R, Darmstadt 61, W. Germany (B.R.D.)
- Literatur-Schnelldienst Kunststoffe Kautschuk Fasern. m.

**Deutsches Leichtathletik-Verband**
- Jahrbuch der Leichtathletik. (pub. by Verlag Bartels und Wernitz KG)

**Deutsches Museum**
- Deutsches Museum. Abhandlungen und Berichte. (pub. by R. Oldenbourg Verlag GmbH)

**Deutsches Orient-Institut**
- Orient. (pub. by Leske Verlag und Budrich GmbH)

**Deutsches Patentamt**
- Blatt fuer Patent-, Muster- und Zeichenwesen. (pub. by Carl Heymanns Verlag KG)
- Patentblatt. (pub. by Carl Heymanns Verlag KG)

- Wahrenzeichenblatt. Teil 2: Eingetragene Zeichen. (pub. by Wila Verlag fuer Wirtschaftswerbung Wilhelm Lampl)
- Warenzeichenblatt. Teil 1: Angemeldete Zeichen. (pub. by Wila Verlag fuer Wirtschaftswerbung Wilhelm Lampl)

**Deutsches Rotes Kreuz**
- Die Gute Tat. (pub. by Sueddeutscher Verlag GmbH)

**Deutsches Volksheimstaettenwerk e.V.**
Friesenplatz 16, 5000 Cologne, W. Germany (B.R.D.)
- Deutsches Volksheimstaettenwerk. Informationsdienst. s-m. ISSN 0012-1371

**Deutsches Volksliederarchiv**
- Jahrbuch fuer Volksliedforschung. (pub. by Erich Schmidt Verlag (Bielefeld))

**Deutsches Wirtschaftswissenschaftliches Institut fuer Fremdenverkehr**
Hermann-Sack-Str. 2, Postfach 264, 8000 Munich 33, W. Germany (B.R.D.)
- Jahrbuch fuer Fremdenverkehr. a. ISSN 0075-2649

**Deutsches Wissenschaftliches Steuerinstitut der Steuerberater und Steuerbevollmaechtigten e.V.**
5300 Bonn 1, W. Germany (B.R.D.)
- Handbuch der Steuerveranlagungen: Einkommensteuer, Koerperschaftsteuer, Gewerbesteuer, Umsatzsteuer. a.

**Deutsches Wollforschungsinstitut**
Technische Hochschule Aachen, Veltmanplatz 8, 5100 Aachen, W. Germany (B.R.D.)
- Deutsches Wollforschungsinstitut. Vortraege. irreg.

**Deutsches Zentralinstitut fuer soziale Fragen**
Miquelstr. 83, 1000 Berlin 33, W. Germany (B.R.D.)
- Soziale Arbeit; deutsche Zeitschrift fuer soziale und sozialverwandte Gebiete. m. ISSN 0490-1606

**Deutsches Zentralkommittee zur Bekaempfung der Tuberkulose**
- Praxis der Pneumologie. (pub. by Georg Thieme Verlag)

**Deutschland-Berichte**
Koenigstr. 17a, Bonn, W. Germany (B.R.D.)
- Deutschland-Berichte. m. ISSN 0012-1436

**Verlag Deutschland Magazin**
Koenigstr. 42, 8211 Breitbrunn, W. Germany (B.R.D.)
- Deutschland-Magazin. bi-m. ISSN 0012-141X (Deutschland Stiftung e.V.)

**Deutschland Stiftung e.V.**
- Deutschland-Magazin. (pub. by Verlag Deutschland Magazin)

**Deutschlandfunk**
Lindenallee 7, 5000 Cologne 51, W. Germany (B.R.D.)
- Deutschlandfunk. Jahrbuch. biennial. ISSN 0084-9790

**Deutschsprachige Arbeitsgemeinschaft fuer Handchirurgie**
- Handchirurgie. (pub. by V L E Verlags-GmbH)

**Diakoniewerk Kaiserswerth**
Alte Landstr. 121, 4000 Duesseldorf 31-Kaiserswerth, W. Germany (B.R.D.)
- Kaiserswerther Mitteilungen. m. ISSN 0022-779X

**Diakonisches Werk der Evangelischen Kirche im Rheinland**
Lenaustr. 4l, 4000 Duesseldorf 30, W. Germany (B.R.D.)
- Diakonie im Rheinland. 6 per yr. ISSN 0012-1975

**Diakonisches Werk in Hessen und Nassau**
Ederstr. 12, 6000 Frankfurt 90, W. Germany (B.R.D.)
- Weltweite Hilfe. 6 per yr. ISSN 0043-2644

**Didaktischer Dienst**
Brehmstr. 59, Postfach 1351, 3200 Hildesheim, W. Germany (B. R. D.)
- Chimica Didacta. q.
- Divice. m.
- Physica Didacta. q.

**Eugen Diederichs Verlag**
Bremer Str. 5, 5000 Cologne 1, W. Germany
- Nerthus; nordisch-deutsche Beitraege. irreg., 1972, vol. 3. ISSN 0077-6610

**Verlag Moritz Diesterweg**
Hochstr. 31, 6000 Frankfurt 1, W. Germany
- Blaetter fuer den Deutschlehrer. 4 per yr. ISSN 0006-4394
- Deutsches Germanisten-Verband. Mitteilungen. q. ISSN 0012-1061 (Deutscher Germanisten-Verband)
- Diskussion Deutsch; Zeitschrift fuer Deutschlehrer aller Schulformen in Ausbildung und Praxis. bi-m.
- Der Evangelische Erzieher; Zeitschrift fuer Paedagogik und Theologie. bi-m. ISSN 0014-3413
- Franzoesisch Heute; Informationsblaetter fuer Franzoesisch Lehrer in Schule und Hochschule. q. (Vereinigung der Franzoesischlehrer e.V.)
- Die Neueren Sprachen; Zeitschrift fuer Forschung und Unterricht. bi-m. ISSN 0028-3576
- Schule und Museum; Das Museum in Unterricht und Wissenschaft. 3 per yr.

**Felix Dietrich Verlag**
Jahnstr. 15, Postfach 1949, 4500 Osnabrueck, W. Germany (B.R.D.)
- I B R. (International Bibliographie der Rezensionen Wissenschaftlicher Literatur) 6 vols. per yr. ISSN 0020-918X
- Internationale Bibliographie der Zeitschriftenliteratur; aus allen Gebieten des Wissens. 12 vols per yr. ISSN 0020-9201

**Diskus-Verlag**
Juegelstr. 1, 6000 Frankfurt, W. Germany (B.R.D.)
- Diskus; Frankfurter Studentenzeitung. 8 per yr. ISSN 0012-3730 (Studentenschaft der Johann Wolfgang Goethe-Universitaet Frankfurt)

**Distribution-Verlag GmbH**
Lessingstr. 12a, Postfach 2760, 6500 Mainz, W. Germany (B.R.D.)
- Druckluft-Praxis; Unabhaengige Zeitschrift fuer die Anwendung der Druckluft im Betrieb. bi-m. ISSN 0012-6497
- Und-oder-nor und Steuerungstechnik; Elektronik und Fluidtechnik. 6 per yr.

**Gildeverlag Hans Gerhard Dobler GmbH**
Bruchhausstr. 57, Postfach 1450, 3220 Alfeld, W. Germany (B.R.D.)
- Archaeographie. w. ISSN 0005-3821
- Backjournal. m.
- Deutsches Handwerksblatt. s-m. ISSN 0012-1274 (Zentralverband des Deutschen Handwerks)
- Der Fass- und Weinkuefer. s-m. ISSN 0012-110X (Verband des Deutschen Fass- und Weinkuefer-Handwerks e.V.)
- Gesund Leben. m. ISSN 0016-9234
- Rallye Racing. m. ISSN 0033-9148

**Verlag Dokumentation**
Poessenbacherstr. 2, Postfach 711009, 8000 Munich 71, W. Germany (B.R.D.)
- Archaeograpttie. irreg., no. 5, 1975. ISSN 0587-3460
- Archivum. a. ISSN 0066-6793 (International Council on Archives FR)
- Beitraege zur Informations- und Dokumentationswissenschaft. irreg., vol. 8, 1976. (Freie Universitaet Berlin. Institut fuer Publizistik)
- Bibliographia Cartographica; international documentation of cartographical literature. a. ISSN 0340-0409 (Staatsbibliothek Preussischer Kulturbesitz) (Co-sponsor: Deutsche Gesellschaft fuer Kartographie e.V.)
- Bibliographie Paedagogik/Educational Bibliography. bi-m. ISSN 0523-2678 (Dokumentationsring Paedagogik)
- Bibliotheksforum Bayern. 3 per yr. ISSN 0340-000X (Bayerische Staatliche Bibliotheken)
- Bibliothekspraxis. irreg., vol. 20, 1971.
- Bibliotheksstudien. irreg, no. 2, 1974.
- Buch und Bibliothek. m. ISSN 0340-0301 (Verein der Bibliothekare an Oeffentlichen Buechereien e.V)
- Buch und Zeitschrift in Geistesgeschichte und Wissenschaft. irreg.
- Buchwissenschaftliche Beitraege. irreg., no. 3, 1971. ISSN 0407-5439 (Deutsches Bucharchiv, Muenchen)
- Bulletin of Reprints. q. ISSN 0303-4550
- D G D Schriftenreihe. irreg., no. 5, 1976. (Deutsche Gesellschaft fuer Dokumentation e.V.)
- Deutsche UNESCO-Kommission. Seminarbericht. irreg., no. 29, 1975.

- Dortmunder Beitraege zur Zeitungsforschung. irreg., no. 23, 1976. ISSN 0417-9994
- Fachliteratur zum Buch- und Bibliothekswesen/ International Bibliography of the Book Trade and Librarianship. irreg., 11th edition, 1976. ISSN 0071-3627 (Distr. throughout the world except Europe, by R. R. Bowker Co., P. O. Box 1807, Ann Arbor, Mich. 48106)
- Fernsehen und Bildung; internationale Zeitschrift fuer Medienpsychologie und Medienkunde. 3 per yr. ISSN 0015-0150 (Internationale Zentralinstitut fuer das Jugend-und Bildungsfernsehen)
- Freie Universitaet Berlin. Zentralinstitut. fuer Sozialwissenschaftliche Forschung. Berichte und Materialien. irreg., vol.4, 1976.
- H I S Briefe. irreg., no. 61, 1977. (Hochschul-Informations-System GmbH)
- Handbuch der Internationalen Dokumentation und Information. irreg., no. 14, 1976.
- Hochschulplanung. irreg., vol. 26, 1976. (Hochschul-Informations-System GmbH)
- I F L A Annuals; proceedings of the General Council Meetings. a. ISSN 0074-5987 (International Federation of Library Associations)
- I F L A Journal. q. ISSN 0340-0352 (International Federation of Library Associations)
- I F L A Publications. irreg., vol. 8, 1976. (International Federation of Library Associations)
- Informationssysteme. Grundlagen und Praxis der Informationswissenschaften. irreg., no. 7, 1973.
- Infoterm Series. irreg., no. 3, 1976. (International Information Centre for Terminology, Vienna AU)
- International Classification; journal of theory and practice of universal and special classification systems and thesauri. s-a. ISSN 0340-0050 (International Federation for Documentation. Classification Research Committee) (Co-sponsor: International Federation of Library Associations)
- International Journal of Law Libraries. 3 per yr. ISSN 0340-045X (International Association of Law Libraries)
- Internationale Bibliographie der Fachadressbuecher/International Bibliography of Directories. irreg., 6th ed. in preparation. ISSN 0074-9672 (Distr. throughout the world, except Europe, by R. R. Bowker Co., P. O. Box 1807, Ann Arbor, Mich. 48106)
- Internationale Bibliographie der Fachwoerterbuecher/International Bibliography of Dictionaries. irreg., 6th ed., 1977. ISSN 0074-9702 (Distr. throughout the world, except Europe, by R. R. Bowker Co., P. O. Box 1807, Ann Arbor, Mich. 48106)
- Internationaler betriebswirtschaftlicher Zeitschriften-Report. q. ISSN 0020-9414
- Internationaler Kongress fuer Reprographie und Information. Fachreferate und Plenarvortraege. irreg., 4th, 1975.
- Internationales Bibliotheks-Handbuch/World Guide to Libraries. irreg., 1974, 4th. ISSN 0000-0221 (Distr. throughout the world, except Europe, by R. R. Bowker Co., P. O. Box 1807, Ann Arbor, Mich. 48106)
- Internationales Verlagsadressbuch/Publishers' International Directory. irreg., 7th ed. in preparation. ISSN 0074-9877 (Distr. throughout the world, except Europe, by R. R. Bowker Co., P. O. Box 1807, Ann Arbor, Mich. 48106)
- Internationales Verzeichnis der Wirtschaftsverbaende/World Guide to Trade Associations. irreg., vol. 12, 1973. (Dist. in Western Hemisphere by R. R. Bowker Co., Box 1807, Ann Arbor MI 48106)
- Kommunikation und Politik. irreg., no. 9, 1976.
- Literaturinformationen zur Berufsbildungsforschung. bi-m. ISSN 0340-2614 (Bundesinstitut fuer Berufsbildungsforschung) (Co-sponsor: Technische Universitaet Berlin. Unversitaets Bibliothek)
- Museums of the World/Museen der Welt. irreg., no. 2, 1975.
- Nachrichten fuer Dokumentation; Zeitschrift fuer Information und Dokumentation. 6 per yr. ISSN 0027-7436 (Deutsche Gesellschaft fuer Dokumentation e.V.)
- P R D. (Publizistik Wissenschaftlicher Referate-Dienst) a. ISSN 0552-6981 (Freie Universitaet Berlin. Institut fuer Publizistik)
- Pol Dok. (Politische Dokumentation) m. ISSN 0032-3438 (Freie Universitaet Berlin. Leitstelle Politische Dokumentation)
- Politikwissenschaftliche Forschung. a. (Freie Universitaet Berlin. Leitstelle Politische Dokumentation)
- Publizistik-Historische Beitraege. irreg., no. 4, 1975.
- Studiengruppe fuer Systemsforschung e.V. Berichte. irreg., no. 114, 1974.

- Verband der Bibliotheken des Landes Nordrhein-Westfalen. Mitteilungsblatt. q. ISSN 0042-3629
- Verzeichnis Lieferbarer Buecher/German Books in Print. a. ISSN 0067-8899 (Buchhaendler-Vereinigung GmbH) (Distr. throughout the world, except Europe, by R. R. Bowker Co., P.O. Box 1807, Ann Arbor, Mich. 48106)
- Werkstatt des Buches. irreg.
- Who's Who at the Frankfurt Book Fair; an International Publishers' Guide. a. (Frankfurt Book Fair)
- Who's Who in der Politik/Who's Who in German Politics. irreg. ISSN 0000-0256 (Distr. throughout the world, except Europe, by R. R. Bowker Co., P. O. Box 1807, Ann Arbor, Mich. 48106)
- Zeitungs-Index; Verzeichnis wichtiger Aufsaetze aus deutschsprachigen Zeitungen. q.

**Dokumentationsring Paedagogik**
- Bibliographie Paedagogik/Educational Bibliography. (pub. by Verlag Dokumentation)

**Domus-Verlag GmbH**
Dottendorfer Str. 82, Postfach 37, 5300 Bonn 5, W. Germany (B.R.D.)
- Privates Bausparwesen. a. ISSN 0085-5154
- Zeitschrift fuer Eigenheimfreunde. q. ISSN 0049-8629

**Don-Verlag Henry Ferling**
Kleyer Str. 18, Postfach 4155, 6100 Darmstadt, W. Germany (B.R.D.)
- Don; das grosse deutsche Magazin fuer Maenner und ihre Freunde. m.

**Donau-Verlag**
Gutenbergstr. 13, Postfach 207, 8870 Guenzburg, W. Germany (B.R.D.)
- Blumen. m. (Verband des Deutschen Blumen-Gross- und Importhandels e.V.)
- Florist. s-m. ISSN 0015-4393 (Fachverband Deutscher Floristen e.V)
- Der Junge Florist. m. ISSN 0022-6262 (Fachverband Deutscher Floristen e.V.)

**Donauschwaebischer Heimatverlag**
Bahnhof Str. 65, Postfach 1680, 7080 Aalen, W. Germany (B.R.D.)
- Der Donauschwabe; Bundesorgan der Heimatvertriebenen aus Jugoslawien, Rumaenien und Ungarn. w. ISSN 0012-5423 (Heimatvertriebene aus Suedosteuropa)

**Dornier AG**
Postfach 2160, 8000 Munich 66, W. Germany (B.R.D.)
- Dornier-Post; a quarterly journal for friends of the Dornier Company. q. ISSN 0012-5563

**Draegerwerk AG**
Moislinger Allee 53, 2400 Luebeck 1, W. Germany (B.R.D.)
- Draegerheft/Draeger Review. q. ISSN 0012-5857

**Dreibrunnen-Verlag**
Friedhofstr. 11, Postfach 1124, 7000 Stuttgart 1, W. Germany (B.R.D.)
- Caravaning; illustrierte Wohnwagen-Spezialzeitschrift. m. ISSN 0008-6185

**Dreistern Verlag**
Claude-Lorrain-Str. 27, 8000 Munich 90, W. Germany (B.R.D.)
- Brauerei Journal. s-m. (Bundesverband Deutscher Mittelstandsbrauereien e.V.)

**Dresdner Bank A.G.**
Postfach 2601, 6000 Frankfurt 1, W. Germany (B.R.D.)
- Dresdner Bank. Economic Quarterly. q.
- Wirtschaftsberichte. q. ISSN 0043-6259

**Droste-Verlag GmbH**
Pressehaus Am Martin-Luther-Platz, 4000 Duesseldorf 1, W. Germany (B.R.D.)
- Artist. s-m. ISSN 0004-3885
- Braunkohle; Zeitschrift fuer Tagebautechnik und Energieversorgung. m.
- Technic International. ISSN 0033-0876

**Druckspiegel-Fachzeitschriftenverlags- Gesellschaft mbH und Co. KG**
Schottstr. 107, Postfach 23, 7000 Stuttgart 1, W. Germany (B.R.D.)
- Der Druckspiegel; Zeitschrift fuer deutsche und internationale Drucktechnik. m. ISSN 0012-6500

**Druffel-Verlag**
Assenbucher Str. 19, 8131 Berg-Leoni, W. Germany (B.R.D.)
- Deutsche Annalen. a.

**Duemmlers Verlag**
Kaiserstr. 31, 5300 Bonn 1, W. Germany (B.R.D.)
- Arbeiten zur Rheinischen Landeskunde. s-a. ISSN 0518-2131 (Universitaet Bonn. Geographisches Institut)
- Beiheft zur Kommunikativen Grammatik. irreg.
- Bonner Meteorologische Abhandlungen. 1-3 per yr. ISSN 0006-7156 (Universitaet Bonn. Meteorologisches Institut)
- Erdkunde; Archiv fuer wissenschaftliche Geographie. q. ISSN 0014-0015 (Universitaet Bonn. Geographisches Institut)
- Der Mathematische und Naturwissenschaftliche Unterricht. 8 per yr. ISSN 0025-5866
- Rheinisches Jahrbuch fuer Volkskunde. a. ISSN 0080-2697 (Rheinische Vereinigung fuer Volkskunde)
- Universitaetssternwarte zu Wien. Annalen. irreg. ISSN 0041-9028
- Vermessungswesen und Raumordnung (VR) 8 per yr. ISSN 0340-5141

**Verlag Duerrsche Buchhandlung**
Plittersdorfer Str. 91, 5300 Bonn - Bad Godesberg 1, W. Germany (B.R.D.)
- Sonderschuldienst. irreg., (approx. 3-4 per yr.)

**Duesseldorf. Amt fuer Fremdenverkehr und Wirtschaftsfoerderung**
- Duesseldorf. (pub. by Rheinisch-Bergische Druckerei- und Verlagsgesellschaft mbH)

**Duesseldorf. Amt fuer Statistik und Wahlen**
Postfach 1120, Duesseldorf, W. Germany (B.R.D.)
- Duesseldorf in Zahlen; Duesseldorf in Zahlen. q.

**Duesseldorf. Hauptstaatsarchiv**
- Der Archivar. (pub. by Verlag Franz Schmitt OHG)

**Duesseldorf. Presseamt**
Marktplatz 2, 4000 Duesseldorf, W. Germany (B.R.D.)
- Duesseldorfer Amtsblatt. w. ISSN 0012-7019

**Duncker und Humblot**
Dietrich-Schaefer-Weg 9, 1000 Berlin 41, W. Germany (B.R.D.)
(and Verlag Versicherungswirtschaft, Karlsruhe, W. Germany)
- Beitraege zur Biologie der Pflanzen. 3 per yr. ISSN 0005-8041
- Deutsches Institut fuer Wirtschaftsforschung. Vierteljahreshefte zur Wirtschaftsforschung. q. ISSN 0012-1290
- Deutsches Institut fuer Wirtschaftsforschung. Wochenbericht. w. ISSN 0012-1304
- F F H Mitteilungen. m. ISSN 0014-5831 (Forschungsstelle fuer den Handel, Berlin)
- Gesellschaft Naturforschender Freunde zu Berlin. Sitzungsberichte. Neue Folge. s-a. ISSN 0037-5942
- I F O Schnelldienst. 3 per mo. ISSN 0018-974X (I F O Institut fuer Wirtschaftsforschung)
- I F O Studien. s-a. ISSN 0018-9731 (I F O Institut fuer Wirtschaftsforschung)
- Internationales Gewerbearchiv; der Klein- und Mittelbetrieb in der modernen Wirtschaft. q. ISSN 0020-9481 (Schweizerisches Institut fuer Gewerbliche Wirtschaft SZ) (With: Hochschule St. Gallen fuer Wirtschafts-und Sozialwissenschaft)
- Jahrbuch der Absatz - und Verbrauchsforschung. q. ISSN 0021-3985 (Gesellschaft fuer Konsum-, Markt- und Absatzforschung)
- Jahrbuch fuer Internationales Recht. ISSN 0021-3993 (Universitaet Kiel. Institut fuer Internationales Recht)
- Konjunktur im Handwerk. a. ISSN 0341-0978 (Rheinisch-Westfaelisches Institut fuer Wirtschaftsforschung, Essen)
- Konjunkturberichte. q. ISSN 0023-3447 (Rheinisch-Westfaelisches Institut fuer Wirtschaftsforschung, Essen)
- Konjunkturpolitik; Zeitschrift fuer angewandte Konjunkturforschung. bi-m. ISSN 0023-3498
- Konjunkturpolitik. Beihefte. a.
- Kredit und Kapital. q. ISSN 0023-4591
- Literaturwissenschaftliches Jahrbuch. Neue Folge. a. ISSN 0075-997X (Goerres-Gesellschaft)
- Material und Organismen. 4 per yr. ISSN 0025-5270

- Mendelsohn Studien; Beitraege zur neueren deutschen Kultur- und Wirtschaftsgeschichte. irreg., vol. 2, 1975. ISSN 0340-8140 (Mendelsohn-Gesellschaft e. V.)
- Rechtstheorie; Zeitschrift fuer Logik, Methodenlehre, Kybernetik und Soziologie des Rechts. s-a. ISSN 0034-1398
- Rheinisch-Westfaelisches Institut fuer Wirtschaftsforschung. Mitteilungen. q. ISSN 0035-4465
- Sociologia Internationalis; internationale Zeitschrift fuer Soziologie und Sozialpsychologie. s-a. ISSN 0038-0164
- Sociologus; Zeitschrift fuer empirische Ethnosoziologie und Ethnopsychologie. s-a. ISSN 0038-0377
- Sozialer Fortschritt. m. ISSN 0038-609X (Gesellschaft fuer Sozialen Fortschritt E.V., Bonn)
- Der Staat; Zeitschrift fuer Staatslehre, Oeffentliches Recht und Verfassungsgeschichte. q. ISSN 0038-884X
- Universitaet Keil. Institut fuer Internationales Recht. Studien. irreg.
- Verfassung und Verfassungswirklichkeit. irreg., vol. 8, 1973. ISSN 0083-5676 (Universitaet zu Koeln. Forschungsinstitut fuer Politische Wissenschaften und Europaeische Fragen)
- Die Verwaltung; Zeitschrift fuer Verwaltungswissenschaft. q. ISSN 0042-4498
- Die Vogelwelt. bi-m. ISSN 0042-7993
- Wirtschaftskonjunktur. m. ISSN 0043-6283 (I F O Institut fuer Wirtschaftsforschung)
- Zeitschrift fuer Angewandte Zoologie. q. ISSN 0044-2291
- Zeitschrift fuer die gesamte Versicherungswissenschaft. 4 per yr. ISSN 0044-2585 (Deutscher Verein fuer Versicherungswissenschaft e.V.)
- Zeitschrift fuer Historische Forschung. q. ISSN 0340-0174
- Zeitschrift fuer Wirtschafts- und Sozialwissenschaften. q. (Gesellschaft fuer Wirtschafts- und Sozialwissenschaften)
- Zoologische Beitraege; Neue Folge. 3 per yr. ISSN 0044-5150

**Dustri-Verlag Dr. Karl Feistle**
Bahnhofstr. 5, 8024 Oberhaching-Deisenhofen, W. Germany (B.R.D.)
- Clinical Nephrology. m.
- Intensiv Behandlung. q.

**Dynamit Nobel AG. Sprengtechnischer Dienst**
Maerkische Str. 96, 4600 Dortmund, W. Germany (B.R.D.)
- Nobel Hefte; Sprengmittel in Forschung und Praxis. 3-6 per yr. ISSN 0029-0858 (Co-sponsor: Wasag-Chemie GmbH)

**E F B - Verlag**
Darmstaedter Landstr. 199, 6000 Frankfurt 70, W. Germany (B.R.D.)
- E F B. (Eisenhaendler Fachblatt); Hausrat, Werkzeuge, Beschlaege, Kunststoffe, Elektrogerate. m. ISSN 0046-0877

**E K S F-Zentralstelle**
Zuelpicher Str. 275, 5000 Cologne 41, W. Germany (B.R.D.)
- Elemente; Zeitschrift kath. Studenten an Fachhochschulen. s-a. ISSN 0013-600X

**E M N I D-Institut GmbH**
Bodelschwinghstr. 21-23, 4800 Bielefeld, W. Germany (B.R.D.)
- E M N I D-Informationen. m. ISSN 0012-7760

**E.T.A. Hoffmann-Gesellschaft**
Goennerstr. 2/II, 8600 Bamberg, W. Germany (B.R.D.)
- E.T.A. Hoffmann-Gesellschaft. Mitteilungen. irreg. ISSN 0073-2885

**Ebertin-Verlag**
Dieseltr. 17, Postfach 1223, 7080 Aalen, W. Germany (B.R.D.)
- Cosmobiology International. q. ISSN 0045-8694
- Kosmobiologie. q. ISSN 0023-4214

**Ebner Verlag GmbH und Co. KG**
Frauenstr. 77, 7900 Ulm, W. Germany (B.R.D.)
- Der Naturstein; fachzeitschrift fuer Steinmetzen, Steinindustrie, Architekten, Baubehoerden. m. ISSN 0028-1026

**Echter-Verlag**
Juliuspromenade 64, Postfach 1066, 8700
Wuerzberg 2, W. Germany (B.R.D.)
- Erdkreis. m. ISSN 0014-0007
- Geist und Leben. bi-m. ISSN 0016-5921
- Gottes Wort; im Kirchenjahr... 3 per yr. ISSN
  0017-2480
- Wuerzburg-Heute; Zeitschrift fuer Kultur und
  Wirtschaft. s-a. ISSN 0043-9614
  (Universitaetsbund Wuerzburg)

**Kommissions-Verlag Eckardt und Messtorff**
Roedingsmarkt 16, 2000 Hamburg 11, W. Germany
(B.R.D)
- Der Seewart; Nautische Zeitschrift fuer die
  deutsche Seeschiffahrt. 6 per yr. ISSN 0037-0878
  (Deutsches Hydrographisches Institut)

**Eckart-Verlag**
Richard-Wagner-Strasse 1, 4812 Brackwede, W.
Germany (B.R.D.)
- World Association for Christian Communication.
  Journal. q.

**Econ-Verlag GmbH**
Grupellostr. 28, Postfach 9229, 4000 Duesseldorf 1,
W. Germany (B.R.D.)
- Werbung in Deutschland. a. ISSN 0083-8012

**Edeka Verlag GmbH**
New York Ring 6, 2000 Hamburg 60, W. Germany
(B.R.D.)
- Die Kluge Hausfrau; Kundenzeitschrift des Edeka
  Kaufmanns. w. ISSN 0023-222X

**Edition Text und Kritik GmbH**
Levelingstr. 6a, 8000 Munich 80, W. Germany
(B.R.D.)
- Text und Kritik; Zeitschrift fuer Literatur. q. ISSN
  0040-5329

**Egerer Landtag e.V.**
- Egerer Zeitung. (pub. by Verlag Egerer Zeitung)

**Verlag Egerer Zeitung**
Herrnstr. 14, 8450 Amberg, W. Germany (B. R. D.)
- Egerer Zeitung; fuer die Heimatvertriebenen aus
  dem Stadt- und Landkreis Eger. m. ISSN 0013-
  2241 (Egerer Landtag e.V.)

**Hanns Eggen GmbH und Co. KG**
Postfach 1746, 3000 Hannover, W. Germany
(B.R.D.)
- Fachberater; Fachtechnische Beratungen und
  Anregungen fuer das Gesamtgebiet des
  Offsetdruckes. 4 per yr. ISSN 0014-6293

**Irene Eggert**
Am Fischtal 85, 1000 Berlin 37, W. Germany
(B.R.D.)
- Berlin Programm. every 10 days. ISSN 0005-9250
  (Berlin (West) Verkehrsamt)

**Ehapa-Verlag GmbH**
Im Riedenberg 54, Postfach 1215, 7000 Stuttgart 1,
W. Germany (B.R.D.)
- Hobby. fortn. ISSN 0018-2923

**Ehrenwirth Verlag GmbH**
Vilshofener Str. 8, 8000 Munich 86, W. Germany
(B.R.D.)
- Blaetter fuer Lehrerfortbildung; Zeitschrift fuer
  das Seminar. m.
- Ehrenwirth Grundschulmagazin; Zeitschrift fuer
  die Unterrichtspraxis.
- Der Imkerfreund; Bienenzeitung zur Wahrung und
  Foerderung der Interessen der Bienenzuechter. m.
  ISSN 0019-2732 (Landesverband Bayerischer
  Imker e.V.)
- Welt der Schule; Zeitschrift fuer das Kollegium.
  bi-m.

**Verlag Ehrlich und Sohn KG**
Dr.-Julius-Leber-Str. 3-7, Postfach 2139, 2400
Luebeck 1, W. Germany (B. R. D.)
- Delphin; Revue der Unterwasserwelt. m. ISSN
  0011-796X (Verband Deutscher Sporttaucher
  e.V.)
- Frau im Spiegel. w. ISSN 0046-497X

**Eichendorff-Gesellschaft**
Postfach 988, 8700 Wuerzburg, W. Germany
(B.R.D.)
- Aurora; Jahrbuch der Eichendorff-Gesellschaft. a.

**Eichholz-Verlag GmbH**
Argelanderstr. 173, Postfach 458, 5300 Bonn 1, W.
Germany (B.R.D.)
- Eichholzbrief. q. ISSN 0013-2497 (Konrad-
  Adenauer-Stiftung fuer Politische Bildung und
  Studienfoerderung e.V.. Politische Akademie
  Eichholz)
- Frau in der Offenen Gesellschaft; Materialien zur
  freiheitlich sozialen Politik. q. (Konrad-Adenauer-
  Stiftung fuer Politische Bildung und
  Studienfoerderung e.V.. Politische Akademie
  Eichholz)
- Die Politische Meinung; zwei-Monatszeitschrift
  fuer Fragen der Zeit. bi-m. ISSN 0032-3446

**Verlag der Eigenwohner GmbH**
Tangstedter Landstr. 83, 2000 Hamburg 62, W.
Germany.
- Wohnungseigentum. m. ISSN 0043-7166

**Eilers und Schuenemann Verlagsgesellschaft mbH**
Schuenemannhaus, 2800 Bremen 1, W. Germany
(B.R.D.)
- Unsere Zeitung. m.
- World and Press. fortn.

**Einhard-Verlag GmbH**
Klappergasse 2-4, 5100 Aachen 1, W. Germany
(B.R.D.)
- Leben und Erziehen. m. ISSN 0047-4274
  (Arbeitsring fuer Paedagogische Elternhilfe E. V.,
  Aachen)

**Eisenbahn-Fachverlag**
Am Linsenberg 16, 6500 Mainz, W. Germany
(B.R.D.)
- D B. (Deine Bahn); Zeitschrift fuer das
  Bildungswesen der deutschen Bundesbahn. m.
  (Deutsche Bundesbahn) (Organ of: Verband
  Deutscher Eisenbahn-Fachschulen)

**Eisenwaren- Zeitung GmbH**
Schadowstr. 11, 4000 Duesseldorf 1, W. Germany
(B. R. D.
- Eisenwaren-Zeitung. fortn. ISSN 0013-2861
  (Fachverband Deutscher Eisenwaren-und
  Hausrathaendler e.V)

**Verlag Karl-Heinz Eisert**
Kreis Schwab. Hall, Uhlandstr., 7161 Buehlertann,
W. Germany (B.R.D.)
- Gross Wartenberger Heimatblatt. m. ISSN 0017-
  4599

**Elbe-Wochenblatt Verlagsgesellschaft MbH**
Eissendorfer Pferdeweg 34, Postfach 298, 2100
Hamburg 90, W. Germany (B.R.D.)
- Elbe Wochenblatt. m.

**Verlags- und Wirtschafts- Gesellschaft der
Elektrizitaetswerke mbH**
Stresemannallee 23, 6000 Frankfurt 70, W.
Germany (B. R. D.)
- Atom und Strom. bi-m. ISSN 0004-7066
  (Vereinigung Deutscher Elektrizitaetswerke e.V.)
- Elektrizitaetswirtschaft. s-m. ISSN 0013-5496
  (Vereinigung Deutscher Elektrizitaetswerke e.V.)
- Fernwaerme International/District Heating/
  Chauffage Urbain. bi-m. ISSN 0340-3572
  (Arbeitsgemeinschaft Fernwaerme e.V.)
- Strom Praxis. bi-m. ISSN 0340-7519
  (Hauptberatungsstelle fuer
  Elektrizitaetsanwendung e.V)

**Elektro-Welt Verlag Dr. Huethig**
*see* Huethig Verlag GmbH

**Element-Verlag GmbH**
Zeppelinstr. 3, 7050 Waiblingen, W. Germany
(B.R.D.)
- F und I-Bau. (Fertigteilbau und Industrialisiertes
  Bauen) q. ISSN 0340-2967

**Elitera-Verlag GmbH**
Fritz-Wildung-Str. 22, 1000 Berlin 33, W. Germany
(B.R.D.)
- A E G-Telefunken. Technische Mitteilungen.
  (Allgemeine Elektrizitaets Gesellschaft) 7 per yr.
  ISSN 0040-1447 (A E G-Telefunken)
- A E G-Telefunken. Wissenschaftliche Berichte.
  (Allgemeine Elektrizitaets Gesellschaft) q. ISSN
  0043-6801 (A E G-Telefunken)
- A E G - Telefunken al Dia. (Allgemeine
  Elektrizitaets Gesellschaft) q. ISSN 0001-1061 (A
  E G-Telefunken)
- A E G - Telefunken Progress. (Allgemeine
  Elektrizitaets Gesellschaft) q. ISSN 0001-107X
  (A E G-Telefunken)

- Datenverarbeitung A E G-Telefunken.
  (Allgemeine Elektrizitaets Gesellschaft) 3 per yr.
  ISSN 0340-1553 (A E G-Telefunken)
- Rassegna Tecnica A E G-Telefunken. (Allgemeine
  Elektrizitaets Gesellschaft) q. (A E G-Telefunken)

**Ellenberg Publishers Ltd.**
5000 Cologne 1, Postfach 100705, W. Germany
(B.R.D.)
- Diplomatic Observer/Observateur Diplomatique/
  Diplomatisches Magazin. m. (Institute for
  International Sociological Research) (Co-sponsor:
  Akademie fuer Diplomatie und Internationale
  Beziehungen)

**Otto Elsner Verlagsgesellschaft**
Schoefferstr. 15, 6100 Darmstadt, W. Germany
(B.R.D.)
- Bauma-Trends. s-a. ISSN 0041-2368 (International
  Construction Machinery Fair, Munich (B A U M
  A))
- Elsners Handbuch fuer Staedtisches
  Ingenieurwesen. a.
- Elsners Handbuch fuer Strassenwesen. a.

**Werbegemeinschaft Elwert und Meurer**
Hauptstr. 101, 1000 Berlin 62, W. Germany
(B.R.D.)
- Jahresfachkatalog Recht-Wirtschaft-Steuern. a.
  ISSN 0075-2886
- Jahreskatalog Philosophie. a. ISSN 0075-2916
- Jahreskatalog Psychologie. a. ISSN 0075-2924
- Kybernetik Jahreskatalog; Datenverarbeitung,
  Automation, Bildungstechnologie, Grenzgebiete. a.
- Studienkatalog-Grundkatalog. Rechtswissenschaft.
  s-a.

**N.G. Elwert Verlag**
Reitgasse 719, Postfach 1128, 3550 Marburg, W.
Germany (B.R.D.)
- Geologica et Palaeontologica. a. ISSN 0072-1018
- Jahrbuch fuer Ostdeutsche Volkskunde. a. ISSN
  0075-2738 (Deutsche Gesellschaft fuer
  Volkskunde e.V.. Kommission fuer Ostdeutsche
  Volkskunde)
- Preussenland. q. ISSN 0032-7972 (Historische
  Kommission fuer Ost- und Westpreussische
  Landesforschung) (Co-Sponsor: Stiftung
  Preussischer Kulturbesitz)
- Veterinaer-Medizinische Nachrichten. 4 per yr.
  ISSN 0083-5862

**Elwi-Verlag**
Fuessener Str. 2, 8952 Marktoberdorf, W. Germany
(B.R.D.)
- Die Demokratische Schule. m. ISSN 0011-8311
  (Gewerkschaft Erziehung und Wissenschaft.
  Landesverband Bayern)

**Emha-Verlag**
Sendlinger-Tor-Platz 8, 8000 Munich 2, W.
Germany (B.R.D.)
- Muenchner Kammerspiele. m.

**Energiewirtschaft und Technik Verlagsgesellschaft
mbH**
Wendelsteinstr. 8, Postfach 1229, 8032 Graefelfing,
W. Germany (B.R.D.)
- Energiewirtschaftliche Tagesfragen; Zeitschrift fuer
  die Elektrizitaets-und Gasversorgung. m. ISSN
  0013-743X
- Musteranlagen der Energiewirtschaft. irreg. ISSN
  0580-3403

**Verlag N. P. Engel**
Postfach 1670, 7640 Kehl, W. Germany (B.R.D.)
- Grundrechte; Die Rechtsprechung in Europa. bi-
  m.

**Verlag der Engel des Herrn**
Baeckerweg 12, Postfach 3608, 6000 Frankfurt 1,
W. Germany (B.R.D.)
- Anzeiger des Reiches der Gerechtigkeit;
  Menschenfreundliche Zeitung fuer Jedermann. s-
  m. ISSN 0003-6285 (Menschenfreundliche
  Gesellschaft)

**Verlag Alfred Engelmann**
Untertalen 15, Postfach 242, 5427 Bad Ems, W.
Germany (B.R.D.)
- Butonia. m.

**Enka Glanzstoff AG**
Glanzstoff-Haus, Wuppertal-Elberfled, W. Germany
(B.R.D.)
- Enka Glanzstoff. Trend und Information. 5 per yr.

**Ferdinand Enke Verlag**
Herdweg 63, 7000 Stuttgart 1, W. Germany
(B.R.D.)
- Beitraege zur Sexualforschung. irreg., vol. 56,
1976. ISSN 0067-5210 (Deutsche Gesellschaft
fuer Sexualforschung)
- Bonner Beitraege zur Soziologie. irreg., no. 16,
1976. ISSN 0068-0044 (Rheinische Friedrich-
Wilhelms-Universitaet. Institut fuer Soziologie)
- Buecherei des Augenarztes. irreg., no. 70, 1976.
ISSN 0068-3361
- Buecherei des Frauenarztes. irreg., vol. 7, 1975.
ISSN 0068-337X
- Buecherei des Orthopaeden. irreg., no. 15, 1976.
ISSN 0068-3388
- Buecherei des Paediaters. irreg., no. 72, 1974.
- Chemische Analyse. irreg.
- Forum der Psychiatrie. irreg. ISSN 0071-8025
- Goettinger Abhandlungen zur Soziologie. irreg,
vol. 23, 1976. ISSN 0072-4874
- Handbuch der Stratigraphischen Geologie. irreg.
ISSN 0073-0130
- Klinische Monatsblaetter fuer Augenheilkunde
und fuer Augenarztliche Fortbildung. m. (2 vols.
per yr.) ISSN 0023-2165
- Klinische Paediatrie; Zeitschrift fuer Klinik und
Praxis. bi-m. ISSN 0300-8630
- Kriminalitaet und ihre Verwalter. irreg., no. 5,
1975.
- Kriminologie. Abhandlungen ueber abwegiges
Sozialverhalten. irreg., no. 12, 1974. ISSN 0075-
7144
- Kriminologische Gegenwartsfragen. irreg. , 1974,
no. 11. ISSN 0075-7136
- Kunst und Gesellschaft. irreg., no. 2, 1975.
- M M G. (Medizin-Mensch-Gesellschaft) q.
- Muenchener Universitaetsschriften. Abhandlungen
des Instituts fuer Europaeisches und
Internationales Wirtschaftsrecht. irreg., 1973, no.
9. ISSN 0077-1848
- Praktische Chirurgie. irreg., no. 90, 1976. ISSN
0079-4899
- Sammlung Chemischer und Chemisch-Technischer
Beitraege. Neue Folge. irreg. ISSN 0080-5793
- Sozialforschung und Gesellschaftspolitik. irreg.,
no. 3, 1974.
- Sozialisation und Kommunikation. irreg., no. 6,
1976. (Universitaet Erlangen-Nuernberg)
- Soziologische Gegenwartsfragen. Neue Folge.
irreg., no. 42, 1976. ISSN 0081-3265
- Zeitschrift fuer Geburtshilfe und Perinatologie. bi-
m. ISSN 0300-967X
- Zeitschrift fuer Orthopaedie und ihre
Grenzgebiete. bi-m. ISSN 0044-3220 (Deutsche
Gesellschaft fuer Orthopaedie und Traumatologie)
- Zeitschrift fuer Soziologie. q.
- Zeitschrift fuer vergleichende Rechtswissenschaft.
1-2 per yr. ISSN 0044-3638

**Ente pro Italia**
Speyererstr. 2, 6000 Frankfurt, W. Germany
(B.R.D.)
- Corriere d'Italia; settimanale d'informazione per
gli Italiani in Germania. w. ISSN 0010-924X

**Entwicklungspolitische Korrespondenz**
c/o Erfried Adam, Postfach 2846, 2000 Hamburg
19, W. Germany (B.R.D.)
- Entwicklungspolitische Korrespondenz. bi-m.

**Epitaph-Verlag**
Belgradstr. 24, 8000 Munich 40, W. Germany
(B.R.D.)
- Epitaph; Junge Zeitschrift fuer Literatur. 4 per yr.

**Verlag Alois Erdl KG**
Gabelsbergerstr. 4-6, 8223 Trostberg, W. Germany
(B.R.D.)
- B L L V Bayerische Schule. bi-w. (Bayerischer
Lehrer- und Lehrerinnenverband)

**Horst Erdmann Verlag**
Hartmeyerstr. 117, Postfach 1380, 7400 Tuebingen,
W. Germany (B.R.D.)
- Alte Abenteuerliche Reiseberichte. irreg.
- Bochumer Schriften zur Entwicklungsforschung
und Entwicklungspolitik. irreg. (Ruhr-Universitaet,
Bochum. Institut fuer Entwicklungsforschung und
Entwicklungspolitik)
- Deutsch-Auslaendische Beziehungen.
Schriftenreihe. irreg. ISSN 0080-7125 (Institut
fuer Auslandsbeziehungen, Stuttgart)
- Geistige Begegnung; Moderne Erzaehler der Welt.
irreg. ISSN 0072-0550 (Institut fuer
Auslandsbeziehungen, Stuttgart)
- Indo-Asia; fuer Politik, Kultur und Wirtschaft
Indiens. 4 per yr. ISSN 0019-719X (Deutsch-
Indische Gesellschaft)

- Institut fuer Iberoamerika-Kunde. Schriftenreihe.
irreg., no. 23, 1974. ISSN 0073-8948
- Institut fuer Ostrecht. Studien. irreg. ISSN 0073-
8492
- Jahrbuch fuer Ostrecht. annual in 2 pts. ISSN
0075-2746 (Institut fuer Ostrecht, Munich)
- Laendermonographien. irreg. (Institut fuer
Auslandsbeziehungen, Stuttgart)
- Zeitschrift fuer Kulturaustausch. q. ISSN 0044-
2976 (Institut fuer Auslandsbeziehungen,
Stuttgart)

**Ernst-Deutsch Theater**
Ulmenau 25, 2000 Hamburg 76, W. Germany
(B.R.D.)
- Ernst-Deutsch-Theater; das junge Theater;
Programmheft. m. ISSN 0022-6386

**Ernst-Mach Institut**
Eckerstr. 4, 7800 Freiburg, W. Germany (B.R.D.)
- Ernst-Mach Institut, Freiburg. Wissenschaftlicher
Bericht. irreg. ISSN 0071-1217
- International Shock Tube Symposium. (Papers)
biennial. ISSN 0579-6946

**Wilhelm Ernst und Sohn KG**
Hohenzollerndamm 170, 1000 Berlin 31, W.
Germany (B. R. D.)
- Bauingenieur-Praxis. irreg. ISSN 0522-4950
- Die Bautechnik. m.
- Die Bautechnik; ausgabe b. m.
- Beton-Kalender. a.
- Beton-und Stahlbetonbau. m. ISSN 0005-9900
- Schrifttenkartei Bauwesen. m. ISSN 0036-6994
(Fraunhofer Gesellschaft. Dokumentationsstelle
fuer Bautechnik)
- Schrifttenkartei Beton. m. ISSN 0036-7001
(Fraunhofer Gesellschaft. Dokumentationsstelle
fuer Bautechnik)
- Der Stahlbau. m. ISSN 0038-9145

**Erzbischoefliches Ordinariat Bamberg**
- Amtsblatt fuer die Erzdioezese Bamberg. (pub. by
St.-Otto-Verlag)

**Verlag Erziehung und Wissenschaft**
Rothenbaumchaussee 15, 2000 Hamburg 13, W.
Germany (B. R. D.)
- Hamburger Lehrerzeitung; Zeitschrift fuer Schul-
und Sozialpaedagogen. 16 per yr. ISSN 0017-6966
(Gewerkschaft Erziehung und Wissenschaft)

**R. Eschenburg**
Olshausenstr. 40/60, 2300 Kiel, W. Germany
(B.R.D.)
- Meyniana. irreg., vol. 25, 1974. ISSN 0076-7689
(Universitaet zu Koeln. Geologisch-
Palaeontologisches Institut)

**Essen. Stadtbibliothek**
Hindenburgstr. 25, Essen, W. Germany (B.R.D.)
- Essener Bibliographie. a. ISSN 0071-1462

**Essener Verlag fuer Sozialversicherung GmbH**
Postfach 467, 4300 Essen, W. Germany (B.R.D.)
- Der Ratgeber; Monatshefte fuer die Aus- und
Fortbildung der Krankenkassenangestellten. m.
ISSN 0033-9989

**J. Esslinger Druckerei und Verlag**
Poststr. 5, 7530 Pforzheim, W. Germany (B.R.D.)
- Fussball Club Pforzheim. Club-Nachrichten. m.
ISSN 0009-9600

**Europ Export Edition GmbH**
Berliner Allee 8, 6100 Darmstadt, W. Germany
(B.R.D.)
(Dist. by International Publications Service, 114 E.
32nd St., New York, N.Y. 10016)
- A B C Europ Production. a. ISSN 0065-003X

**Europa-Fachpresse-Verlag GmbH**
Leopoldstr. 175, 8000 Munich 40, W. Germany
(B.R.D.)
- Buero-Kompress. bi-m.
- Die Chemische Produktion.
- Elektronik Journal. m. ISSN 0013-5674
- Foerdermittel-Journal; Materialfluss, Lager,
Transport und Verpackung. m. ISSN 0015-5233
- Kunststoff-Journal. m. ISSN 0047-3766
- W & V. (Werben und Verkaufen) w. ISSN 0042-
9538
- Wirtschafts-Correspondent; Zeitschrift fuer
Transport u. Verkehr. m. ISSN 0043-6216

**Europa-Union Deutschland e.V.**
- Europa Union. (pub. by Europa Union Verlag
GmbH)

**Europa Union Verlag GmbH**
Stockenstr. 1-5, 5300 Bonn 1, W. Germany (B.R.D.)
- Europa Union. m. ISSN 0014-2611 (Europa-
Union Deutschland e.V.)
- Europaeische Schriften. irreg. ISSN 0071-2329
(Institut fuer Europaeische Politik, Bonn)
- Informationsdienst des Deutschen Rates der
Europaeischen Bewegung. m. ISSN 0020-0549

**Europa-Verlag**
Kirchenstr. 88, Postfach 800540, 8000 Munich 80,
W. Germany (B.R.D.)
- Europa; politics, economics, culture. m. ISSN
0014-2468

**Europaeisch-Festlaendische Brueder-Unitaet**
Zinzendorfplatz 3, 7744 Koenigsfeld (Schwarzwald),
W. Germany (B.R.D.)
- Der Bruederbote. m.

**Europaeische Union der Pianomacher-Fachverbaende**
- Euro Piano. (pub. by Verlag das Musikinstrument)

**Europaeische Vereinigung fuer Veterinaerchirurgie**
- Chirurgia Veterinaria. (pub. by Verlag Paul Parey
(Berlin))

**Europaeische Verlagsanstalt GmbH**
Deutz-Kalker-Str. 46, 5000 Cologne 21, W.
Germany (B.R.D.)
- Kritische Justiz. q. ISSN 0023-4834

**Verlag Europaeische Wehrkunde GmbH**
Herzog-Rudolph-Str.1, 8000 Munich 22, W.
Germany (B.R.D.)
- Europaeische Wehrkunde. m. (Gesellschaft fuer
Wehrkunde e.V.)

**Europaeisches Institut fuer Politische, Wirtschaftliche
und Soziale Fragen e.V.**
- Internationales Afrikaforum. (pub. by Weltforum
Verlags-Gesellschaft mbH)
- Internationales Asienforum. (pub. by Weltforum
Verlags-Gesellschaft mbH)

**European Association for Maxillofacial Surgery**
- Journal of Maxillofacial Surgery. (pub. by Georg
Thieme Verlag)

**European Cell Biology Organization**
- Cytobiologie. (pub. by Wissenschaftliche
Verlagsgesellschaft MbH)

**European Court of Human Rights**
- European Court of Human Rights. Publications.
Series A: Judgments and Decisions/Cour
Europeenne des Droits de l'Homme. Publications.
Serie a: Arrets et Decisions. (pub. by Carl
Heymanns Verlag KG)
- European Court of Human Rights. Publications.
Series B: Pleadings, Oral Arguments and
Documents/Cour Europeenne des Droits de
l'Homme. Publications. Serie B: Memoires,
Plaidoiries et Documents. (pub. by Carl
Heymanns Verlag KG)

**European Federation of Chemical Engineering**
c/o DECHEMA, Postfach 970146, 6000 Frankfurt
97, W. Germany (B.R.D.)
- European Federation of Chemical Engineering.
Annual Report. biennial.
- European Symposium on Chemical Reaction
Engineering. Proceedings. irreg., 6th, 1976,
heidelberg. ISSN 0071-3112

**European Foundation for Management Development
(EFMD)**
- Management International Review. (pub. by
Betriebswirthschaftlicher Verlag Dr. Th. Gabler
KG)

**European Primary Aluminum Association**
- World Aluminum Abstracts. (pub. by Aluminium-
Verlag GmbH)

**European Society of Linguistics**
c/o Peter Hartmann, Universitaet Konstanz, W.
Germany (B.R.D.)
- Folia Linguistica. a. ISSN 0430-862X

**European Southern Observatory**
Schleissheimerstr. 17, 8046 Garching, West
Germany (B.R.D.)
- Astronomy and Astrophysics. (pub. by Springer-
Verlag US)

- European Southern Observatory. Annual Report.
  a. ISSN 0531-4496

**Wirtschafts- und Forstverlag Euting KG**
Tannenstr. 1, 5451 Strassenhaus, W. Germany (B. R. D.)
- Arbeitstechnische Merkhefte der Waldarbeit. 3-4 per yr. ISSN 0003-7796
- Forstkalender. a.
- Forstpflanzen-Forstsamen. 4 per yr. ISSN 0015-7996
- Handbuch der Waldarbeit. a.
- Handbuch Holz. a. ISSN 0518-0147
- Die Waldarbeit; Forstbetrieb, Forsttechnik, Forstarbeit. m. ISSN 0043-0048

**Evangelisch-Lutherische Dreikoenigsgemeinde**
Oppenheimer Str. 5, 6000 Frankfurt 70, W. Germany (B.R.D.)
- Dreikoenigsbote. m. ISSN 0012-608X

**Evangelisch-Lutherischer Landeskirchenrat**
- Evangelisch-Lutherische Kirche in Bayern. Ausgabe Oberfranken. Sonntagsblatt. (pub. by Evangelischer Presseverband fuer Bayern e.V.)

**Evangelisch-methodistische Kirche**
- Fuer Heute. (pub. by Christliches Verlagshaus GmbH)
- Wort und Weg. (pub. by Christliches Verlagshaus GmbH)

**Evangelische Akademie Berlin**
Koenigstr. 64b, 1000 Berlin 39, W. Germany (B.R.D.)
- Kommunitaet. q. ISSN 0023-3137

**Evangelische Akademie Rheinland-Westfalen**
Haus Ortlohn, Baarstr. 59-63, 5860 Iserlohn, W. Germany (B.R.D.)
- Forum Haus Ortlohn. Freundesbrief. q. ISSN 0015-8534

**Evangelische Akademie Tutzing**
- Tutzinger Studien. (pub. by Evangelischer Presseverband fuer Bayern e.V.)

**Evangelische Akademie von Kurhessen-Waldeck**
Schloesschen Schoenburg, 3520 Hofgeismar, W. Germany (B.R.D.)
- Anstoesse; Berichte aus der Arbeit der Evangelischen Akademie Hofgeismar. bi-m. ISSN 0003-5270

**Evangelische Akademikerschaft in Deutschland**
- Radius. (pub. by Radius-Verlag GmbH)

**Evangelische Buchhilfe e.V.**
Alte Hauptstr. 14, Postfach 81, 3502 Vellmar 3, W. Germany (B.R.D.)
- Christ und Buch; eine Hilfe fuer die Auswertung und Andwendung des gedruckten Wortes. q. ISSN 0009-5087

**Evangelische Gemeinde Koeln-Kalk-Humboldt**
Zum Milchmaedchen 9, 5000 Cologne 91, W. Germany (B.R.D.)
- Humboldtglocke. m. ISSN 0018-7631

**Evangelische Gemeindepresse GmbH**
Furtbachstr. 12a, 7000 Stuttgart 1, W. Germany (B.R.D.)
- Evangelisches Gemeindeblatt fuer Wuerttemberg. w. ISSN 0014-360X

**Evangelische Gesellschaft fuer Deutschland e.V.**
Ottenbrucherstr. 38, 560 Wuppertal-Elberfeld, W. Germany (B.R.D.)
- Der feste Grund. m. ISSN 0015-0320
- Licht und Leben. (pub. by Schriftenmissions-Verlag)

**Evangelische Kirche in Deutschland**
Herrenhaeuser Str. 2A, 3000 Hannover-Herrenhausen, W. Germany (B. R. D.)
- Evangelische Kirche in Deutschland. Amtsblatt. m. ISSN 0014-343X

**Evangelische Kirche in Hessen und Nassau in Frankfurt. Amt fuer Kirchenmusik**
Miquelallee 7, 6000 Frankfurt 13, W. Germany (B.R.D.)
- Kirchenmusikalische Nachrichten. q.

**Evangelische Landjugend Bayern**
- Neues Dorf. (pub. by Evangelischer Presseverband fuer Bayern e. V.)

**Evangelische-Lutherische Kirchengemeinde Bayreuth**
Kanzleistr. 9, 8580 Bayreuth, W. Germany (B.R.D.)
- Bayreuther Gemeindeblatt. bi-w. ISSN 0005-7282

**Evangelische Studentengemeinde in der Bundesrepublik Deutschland und Berlin (West)**
- E S G - Nachrichten. (pub. by Alektor-Verlag)

**Evangelische Weibliche Jugend in Bayern e.V.**
Hummelsteiner Weg 100, 8500 Nuernberg, W. Germany (B.R.D.)
- Das Baugeruest; Mitarbeiterzeitschrift fuer ausserschul. Jugendbildung. 6 per yr. ISSN 0005-6618

**Evangelische Zentralstelle fuer Weltanschauungsfragen**
- Evangelische Zentralstelle fuer Weltanschauungsfragen. Materialdienst. (pub. by Quell Verlag)

**Verlag Evangelischer Gemeindeblatt Berlin**
Grazer Platz 4, 1000 Berlin 41, W. Germany (B.R.D.)
- Evangelisches Gemeindeblatt Berlin. m. ISSN 0014-3561

**Evangelischer Missionsverlag GmbH**
Mirander Str. 10, 7015 Korntal, W. Germany (B.R.D.)
- Zeitschrift fuer Mission. q.

**Evangelischer Oberkirchenrat**
- Fuer Arbeit und Besinnung. (pub. by Quell Verlag)

**Evangelischer Oberkirchenrat Karlsruhe**
Blumenstr. 1, 75 Karlsruhe 1, W. Germany.
- Beitraege zur Paedagogischen Arbeit. q. ISSN 0005-8157 (Gemeinschaft Evangelischer Erzieher in Baden)

**Evangelischer Oberkirchenrat Stuttgart**
Gaensheidestr. 4, Postfach 92, 7000 Stuttgart 1, W. Germany (B.R.D.)
- Evangelische Landeskirche in Wuerttemberg. Amtsblatt. s-m. ISSN 0014-3529

**Evangelischer Presseverband fuer Baden e.V.**
Blumenstr. 7, 7500 Karlsruhe, W. Germany (B.R.D.)
- Aufbruch; evangelische Kirchenzeitung fuer Baden. w. ISSN 0004-7848

**Evangelischer Presseverband fuer Bayern e.V.**
Birkerstr. 22, 8000 Munich 19, W. Germany (B.R.D.)
- Evangelisch-Lutherische Kirche in Bayern. Ausgabe Oberfranken. Sonntagsblatt. w. ISSN 0014-3391 (Evangelisch-Lutherischer Landeskirchenrat)
- Gottesdienst und Kirchenmusik. bi-m. ISSN 0017-2499
- Muenchner Gemeindeblatt. w.
- Neues Dorf; Jugend und Familie auf dem Land. bi-m. ISSN 0028-3614 (Evangelische Landjugend Bayern)
- Sonntagsblatt - Coburger Heimatglocken. w. ISSN 0010-0072
- Tutzinger Studien; Texte und Dokumente zur politischen Bildung. q. (Evangelische Akademie Tutzing)

**Gemeinschaftswerk der Evangelischer Publizistik**
Friedrichstr. 34, 6000 Frankfurt 1, Friedrichstr. 2-6.
- Medium; Zeitschrift fuer Hoerfunk, Fernsehen, Film, Bild, Ton. m. ISSN 0025-8350

**Evangelisches Bibliothekar-Lehrinstitut, Goettingen**
Groner-Tor-Str. 32a, 3400 Goettingen, W. Germany (B.R.D.)
- Evangelisches Bibliothekar-Lehrinstitut, Goettingen. Arbeiten. irreg.

**Evangelisches Verlagswerk GmbH**
Stafflenberg Str. 76, Postfach 476, 7000 Stuttgart 1, W. Germany (B.R.D.)
- Diakonie Report. s-m.

**Ex Libris-Verlag**
Postfach 410308, 5000 Cologne 41, W. Germany (B.R.D.)
- Ex Libris; Aktueller Buchdienst fuer Studenten und Dozenten der Rechts, Wirtschafts, und Sozialwissenschaften. s-a. ISSN 0014-391X

**Fachinstitut der Steuerberater**
- Steurberater-Jahrbuch. (pub. by Verlag Dr. Otto Schmidt KG)

**Fachschriften-Verlag GmbH**
Hoehenstr. 17, Postfach 1329, 7012 Fellbach, W. Germany (B.R.D.)
- Bauen und Fertighaus. bi-m. ISSN 0005-6510
- Der Fertighaus-Katalog. a. ISSN 0071-4585
- Der Grosse Gartenkatalog. a. ISSN 0072-7717
- Offsetpraxis; Europaeische Fachzeitschrift fuer Offset-, Kleinoffset-Druck, Reprofotographie und Fotosatz. m. (except August) ISSN 0030-0594
- Schwimmbad und Sauna; Zeitschrift fuer Planung und Bau von Schwimmbaedern und Saunas. bi-m.
- Wir Bauen Unser Haus Selbst. a.
- Wochenend-, Ferien- und Zweithaus-Katalog. every other year.

**Fachverband der Bayerischen Standesbeamten E.V.**
- Das Bayerische Standesamt. (pub. by Verlag fuer Standesamtswesen GmbH und Co. KG)

**Fachverband der Futtermittelindustrie e.V.**
- Kraftfutter. (pub. by Alfred Strothe Verlag)

**Fachverband der Reprografie e.V.**
Kaiser-Friedrich-Ring 1a, 4000 Duesseldorf 11, W. Germany (B.R.D.)
- Der Reprograf. m.

**Fachverband des Deutschen Fliesengewerbes**
- Fliesen und Platten. (pub. by Verlagsgesellschaft Rudolf Mueller)

**Fachverband des Deutschen Teppich- und Gardinenhandels e.V.**
- Heimtex. (pub. by Westdeutsche Verlagsanstalt GmbH)

**Fachverband Deutscher Eisenwaren-und Hausrathaendler e.V**
- Eisenwaren-Zeitung. (pub. by Eisenwaren- Zeitung GmbH)

**Fachverband Deutscher Floristen e.V**
- Florist. (pub. by Donau-Verlag)
- Der Junge Florist. (pub. by Donau-Verlag)

**Fachverband Lichtwerbung**
- L W. (pub. by Deutsche Verlagsanstalt GmbH)

**Fachverband Stickstoffindustrie**
Sternstr. 9-11, 4000 Duesseldorf 1, W. Germany (B.R.D.)
- Duengungsratschlaege fuer den Bauernhof. irreg.
- Der Stickstoff. irreg. ISSN 0081-5535

**Fachvereinigung der Verwaltungsleiter Deutscher Krankenanstalten e.V.**
Am Roemerhof 35, 6000 Frankfurt, W. Germany (B.R.D. )
- Battelle Information. 3 per yr.
- Krankenhaus-Umschau. (pub. by Verlag E. C. Baumann KG)

**Verlagsgesellschaft C. J. Fahle**
Neubrueckenstr. 8-11, 4400 Muenster, W. Germany (B.R.D.)
- Westpreussen-Jahrbuch. a. ISSN 0511-8484 (Landsmannschaft Westpreussen e.V.)

**Familienkundliche Kommission fuer Niedersachsen und Bremen**
- Norddeutsche Familienkunde. (pub. by Verlag Degener und Co.)

**Familienverband Avenarius e.V.**
Gesmolder Str. 16, 4520 Melle, W. Germany (B.R.D.)
- Familienverband Avenarius. Familienzeitschrift. irreg. ISSN 0014-7176

**Faust-Gesellschaft**
Rathaus, 7134 Knittlingen/Wurtt., W. Germany (B.R.D.)
- Faust Blaetter; Archiv-Nachrichten; halbjahres Zeitschrift der Faust-Gesellschaft. s-a.

**Der Feierabend**
Schaevenstr. 1b, 5000 Cologne 1, W. Germany (B.R.D.)
- Der Feierabend. m. (Cologne. Oberstadtdirektor)

**Fernseh-Funk-Verlag**
Neuchatellerstr. 16, 1000 Berlin 45, W. Germany
(B.R.D.)
- Allpress; FFA Korrespondenz. m. ISSN 0002-
6158

**Fernseh- und Kinotechnische Gesellschaft**
- Fernseh- und Kino-Technik. (pub. by Huethig und
Pflaum Verlag)

**Ferrovia Verlag GmbH**
Riehenstr. 107, 7851 Inzlingen, W. Germany
(B.R.D.)
- Welt der Eisenbahn.
- Welt der Modellbahn; Modellbau-Magazin. bi-m.

**Festland-Verlag**
Postfach 649, 5300 Bonn, W. Germany (B.R.D.)
- Taschenbuch des Oeffentlichen Lebens. a. ISSN
0082-1829

**Feuersozietaet Berlin**
Am Karlsbad 4-5, 1000 Berlin 30, W. Germany
(B.R.D.)
- Schadenprisma; Zeitschrift fuer
Schadenverhuetung und Schadenforschung der
oeffentlichen Versicherer. q.

**Filmbewertungsstelle Wiesbaden**
Schloss, 6200 Wiesbaden 12, W. Germany (B.R.D.)
- Besonders Wertvoll. Kurzfilme. a. ISSN 0067-
6209
- Besonders Wertvoll. Langfilme. a. ISSN 0067-
6217

**Filmkritiker Kooperative**
Kreittmayrstr. 3, 8000 Munich 2, W. Germany
(B.R.D.)
- Filmkritik. m. ISSN 0015-1572

**Finanz- und Korrespondenzverlag**
Taunusstr. 2, 1000 Berlin 33, W. Germany (B.R.D.)
- Handbuch der Direktoren und Aufsichtsraete. 2
per yr.

**Wilhelm Fink Verlag**
Nikolaistr. 2, 8000 Munich 40, W. Germany (B. R.
D.)
- Beitraege zur Romanischen Philologie des
Mittelalters. irreg. ISSN 0067-5202
- Kleine Deutsche Prosadenkmaeler des
Mittelalters; Erst und Neuausgaben der
Forschungsstelle fuer deutsche prosa des
Mittelalters. irreg. ISSN 0075-6318 (Universitaet
Wuerzburg. Seminar fuer Deutsche Philologie)
- Muenchner Germanistische Beitraege. irreg. ISSN
0077-1872

**J. Fink Verlag Gmbh**
Gebelsbergstr. 41, 7000 Stuttgart 1, W. Germany
(B.R.D.)
- Auslandsreisen. 20 per m. ISSN 0004-8135
(Industrie- und Handelskammer Mittlerer Necker)
- Europaeischer Fernwanderweg. irreg.

**Fischer-Bergst-Verlag**
Kreisstr. 16, 2000 Hamburg 52, W. Germany
(B.R.D.)
- Fleisch und Feinkost. m. ISSN 0015-3583

**Fischer Taschenbuch Verlag**
Geleitsstr. 25, 6000 Frankfurt, W. Germany
(B.R.D.)
- Arbeiterbewegung- Theorie und Geschichte.
Jahrbuecher. a.

**Gustav Fischer Verlag**
Wollgrasweg 49, Postfach 720143, 7000 Stuttgart
70, W. Germany (B.R.D.)
- Arbeiten aus dem Paul-Ehrlich-Institut, dem
Georg-Speyer-Haus und dem Ferdinand-Blum-
Institut. a. ISSN 0066-5665
- Beitraege zur Pathologie. 4 nos. to vol.(2 vols. per
yr.) ISSN 0005-8165
- Deutsche Botanische Gesellschaft. Berichte. 1 vol.
of 3 nos. per year. ISSN 0011-9970
- Deutsche Gesellschaft fuer Hygiene und
Mikrobiologie. Berichte ueber Tagungen. biennial.
ISSN 0084-9758
- Deutsche Gesellschaft fuer Pathologie.
Verhandlungen. a. ISSN 0070-4113
- Deutsche Zoologische Gesellschaft.
Verhandlungen. a. ISSN 0070-4342
- E D V in Medizin und Biologie. q. ISSN 0300-
8282

- Entomologica Germanica; Zeitschrift fuer das
Gesamtgebiet der wissenschaftlichen Entomologie.
irreg. (Deutsche Entomologische Gesellschaft)
- Excerpta Botanica. Sectio A: Taxonomica et
Chorologica. 14 per yr. ISSN 0014-4037
- Excerpta Botanica. Sectio B: Sociologica. 1 vol.
per yr.(4 nos. per vol.) ISSN 0014-4045
- Fortschritte der Zoologie. Neue Folge. irreg. ISSN
0071-7991 (Deutsche Zoologische Gesellschaft)
- Grundbegriffe der Modernen Biologie. irreg. ISSN
0085-1299
- Jahrbuecher fuer Nationaloekonomie und Statistik.
6 per yr. ISSN 0021-4027
- Literaturberichte ueber Wasser, Abwasser, Feste
Abfallstoffe und Luft. 1 vol. per yr. (6 nos. per
vol.) ISSN 0024-4732 (Verein fuer Wasser-,
Boden- und Lufthygiene)
- Ordo; Jahrbuch fuer die Ordnung von Wirtschaft
und Gesellschaft. a. ISSN 0048-2129
- Progress in Histochemistry and Cytochemistry.
irreg., vol. 9, 1976. ISSN 0079-6336
- Verein fuer Wasser-, Boden- und Lufthygiene.
Schriftenreihe. irreg., no. 39, 1972.
- Zeitschrift fuer Immunitaetsforschung,
Experimentelle und Klinische Immunologie. 2
vols. of 5 nos. per year. ISSN 0300-872X
- Zeitschrift fuer Pflanzenphysiologie. 1-2 vols. per
yr.(5 nos. per vol.) ISSN 0044-328X
- Zentralblatt fuer Bakteriologie, Parasitenkunde,
Infektionskrankheiten und Hygiene. Abteilung 1:
Referate. 4 vols. of 7 nos. per year. ISSN 0044-
4073
- Zentralblatt fuer Bakteriologie, Parasitenkunde,
Infektionskrankheiten und Hygiene. Originale
Reihe A: Medizinische Mikrobiologie und
Parasitologie. 16 per yr.
- Zentralblatt fuer Bakteriologie, Parasitenkunde,
Infektionskrankheiten und Hygiene. Originale
Reihe B: Hygiene - Praeventive Medizin. 6 per yr.

**S. Fischer Verlag GmbH (Frankfurt)**
Mainzer Landstr. 10-12, 6000 Frankfurt 1, W.
Germany (B.R.D.)
- Neue Rundschau. q. ISSN 0028-3347

**F. L. Fischer-Werbung**
Kreisstr. 16, 2000 Hamburg 52, W. Germany
(B.R.D.)
- Snack; Grill & Imbiss, Cafeteria, Kantinen, Kiosk,
Snack bars. m. ISSN 0037-7392
(Bundesgewerbeverband Imbissbetriebe E. V.)

**Fischwirtschaftliches Marketing-Institut**
- A F Z. (pub. by Verlag Carl Th. Goerg KG)

**Fixdruck**
Neue Rothofstr 5, 6000 Frankfurt 1, W. Germany
(B.R.D.)
- Uhrenjournal. m. ISSN 0041-5855
(Bundesgrosshandelsverband fuer Uhren- und
Uhrentechnischen Bedarf e.V.)

**Verlag Hermann Fleischhauer und Co.**
Am Ellenbogen 12, Postfach 110309, 4300 Essen
11, W. Germany (B.R.D.)
- Eisenbahn-Landwirt. m. ISSN 0013-2772
(Hauptverband der Bundesbahn-Landwirtschaft
e.V.)
- Der Freizeitgaertner; Fachzeitschrift fuer
Gartenfreunde und Siedler. m. ISSN 0016-0946

**Flemmings Verlag**
Leinpfad 75, 2000 Hamburg 39, W. Germany
(B.R.D.)
- Archaeologia Geographica. irreg. ISSN 0066-5908

**Flensburger Zeitungsverlag GmbH**
Nikolaistr. 7, 2390 Flensburg, W. Germany (B.R.D.)
- Nordfriesland; Chronik in Wort und Bild;
Handbuch fuer den Kreis Nordfriesland. a.

**Fleurop GmbH**
Lindenstr. 3-4, 1000 Berlin 45, W. Germany
(B.R.D.)
- Bunte Blumenwelt. m. ISSN 0007-5973

**Floristisch-Soziologische Arbeitsgemeinschaft**
Untere Karspuele 2, 3260 Todenmann ueber
Rinteln, W. Germany (B.R.D.)
- Floristisch-Soziologische Arbeitsgemeinschaft.
Mitteilungen. a. ISSN 0071-6219

**Von Flotow**
3451 Kirchbrak, W. Germany (B. R. D.)
- Deutsches Adelsblatt. m. ISSN 0012-1193
(Vereinigung der Deutschen Adelsverbaende)

**Verlag Fluessiges Obst GmbH**
Am Elisabethenbrunnen 1, Postfach 2324, 6380 Bad
Homburg, W. Germany (B. R. D.)
- Fluessiges Obst. m. ISSN 0015-4539 (Verband der
Deutschen Fruchtsaft-Industrie e.V.)

**Flughafen Hamburg GmbH**
- Hamburg Air. (pub. by Kuehn-Verlag)

**Foerderer Verein "Nemzetor"**
Ferchenbach Str. 88, 8000 Munich 50, W. Germany
(B.R.D.)
- Nemzetor. m (Hungarian); bi-m (others) ISSN
0028-2626

**Foerderungsgemeinschaft der Kartoffelwirtschaft E.V**
- Der Kartoffelbau. (pub. by Verlag Th. Mann)

**Ford-Werke AG**
Henry Ford Str. 1, 5000 Cologne-Niehl, W.
Germany (B.R.D.)
- Ford-Nachrichten; Zeitschrift fuer die Mitarbeiter
der Ford-Werke AG. m. ISSN 0015-7007

**Forkel Verlag GmbH**
Koenigstr. 2, Postfach 104, 7000 Stuttgart 70, W.
Germany (B.R.D.)
(or Postfach 2120, 6200 Wiesbaden, W. Germany
(B.R.D.)
- R W P. (Rechts- und Wirtschafts-Praxis) s-m.
ISSN 0034-1347

**Verlag Form GmbH**
Ernsthoefer Str. 12, 6101 Seeheim 3, W. Germany
(B. R. D.)
- Form; Zeitschrift fuer Gestaltung. q. ISSN 0015-
7678

**Forschinginstitut fuer Deutsche Sprache, Marburg**
- Germanistische Linguistik. (pub. by Georg Olms
Verlag GmbH)

**Forschinginstitut fuer Wirtschaftsverfassung und
Wettbewerb e.V.**
- F I W - Schriftenreihe. (pub. by Carl Heymanns
Verlag KG)

**Forschungsgesellschaft fuer das Strassenwesen e.V.**
Maastrichter Str. 45, 5000 Cologne 1, W. Germany
(B.R.D.)
- Dokumentation Strasse; Kurzauszuege aus dem
Schrifttum ueber das Strassenwesen. m. ISSN
0012-5148
- Forschung im Strassenwesen. irreg.
- Forschungsgesellschaft fuer das Strassenwesen.
Arbeitsgruppe Asphalt- und Teerstrassen.
Schriftenreihe. (pub. by Kirschbaum Verlag)
- Forschungsgesellschaft fuer das Strassenwesen.
Arbeitsgruppe Betonstrassen. Schriftenreihe. (pub.
by Kirschbaum Verlag)
- Strasse und Autobahn. (pub. by Kirschbaum
Verlag)
- Strassenverkehrstechnik. (pub. by Kirschbaum
Verlag)

**Forschungsgesellschaft fuer Genossenschaftswesen,
Muenster**
- Schriften zur Kooperationsforschung. Berichte.
(pub. by Verlag J.C.B. Mohr (Paul Siebeck))
- Schriften zur Kooperationsforschung. Studien.
(pub. by Verlag J.C.B. Mohr (Paul Siebeck))
- Schriften zur Kooperationsforschung. Vortraege.
(pub. by Verlag J.C.B. Mohr (Paul Siebeck))

**Forschungsring fuer Biologisch-Dynamische
Wirtschaftsweise**
Baumschulenweg 19, 6100 Darmstadt, W. Germany
(B.R.D.)
- Lebendige Erde. bi-m. ISSN 0023-9917

**Forschungsstelle fuer den Handel, Berlin**
- F F H Mitteilungen. (pub. by Duncker und
Humblot)

**Forschungsstelle fuer Jagdkunde und
Wildschadenverhuetung**
- Forschungsstelle fuer Jagdkunde und
Wildschadenverhuetung. Schriftenreihe. (pub. by
Verlag Paul Parey (Hamburg))

**Forschungsstelle fuer Juristische Dokumentation,
Frankfurt**
- Kybernetik - Datenverarbeitung - Recht. (pub. by
Alfred Metzner Verlag GmbH)

**Forschungsvereinigung Antriebstechnik e. V.**
- Antriebstechnik. (pub. by Krausskopf-Verlag fuer
Wirtschaft GmbH)

**Forstliche Forschungsanstalt Muenchen**
- Forstwissenschaftliche Forschungen. (pub. by Verlag Paul Parey (Hamburg))
- Forstwissenschaftliches Zentralblatt. (pub. by Verlag Paul Parey (Hamburg))

**Verlag Fortschritte der Medizin M B Schwappach und Co. - GmbH und Co.**
Wessobrunner Str. 4, Postfach 1220, 8035 Gauting, W. Germany (B. R. D.)
- Fortschritte der Medizin; Internationale Zeitschrift fuer die gesamte Heilkunde. 4 per month. ISSN 0015-8178

**Forum-Verlag GmbH**
Schrempfstr. 10, 7000 Stuttgart 70, W. Germany (B.R.D.)
- Der Architekt. m. ISSN 0003-875X (Bund Deutscher Architekten)
- Bibliographie Hochschulplanung. irreg. (Zentralarchiv fuer Hochschulbau)
- Deutsches Architektenblatt. fortn. ISSN 0012-1215 (Bundesarchitektenkammer)

**Fraenkische Geographische Gesellschaft**
Kochstr. 4, 8520 Erlangen, W. Germany (B.R.D.)
- Fraenkische Geographische Gesellschaft. Mitteilungen. a. ISSN 0071-8173

**Franckh'sche Verlagshandlung W. Keller und Co.**
Pfizerstr 5, Postfach 640, 7000 Stuttgart 1, W. Germany (B.R.D.)
- A T Z. (Automobiltechnische Zeitschrift); fuer Konstruktion, Entwicklung, Forschung und Fertigung. m. ISSN 0001-2785
- Aquarien Magazin; neue Monatshefte fuer Aquarien- und Vivarienkunde. m. ISSN 0003-7257
- Kosmos; Bild unserer Welt. m. ISSN 0023-4230 (Kosmos Gesellschaft der Naturfreunde)
- Kosmos Bibliothek. q. ISSN 0452-621X (Kosmos Gesellschaft der Naturfreunde)
- Lok Magazin; Eisenbahn gestern heute morgen. bi-m. ISSN 0458-1822
- M T Z. (Motortechnische Zeitschrift) m. ISSN 0024-8525
- Mikrokosmos; Zeitschrift fuer angewandte Mikroskopie, Mikrobiologie, Mikrochemie und mikroskopische Technik. m. ISSN 0026-3680
- Mineralien Magazin. bi-m.
- Die Schaltung; Zeitschrift fuer den Hobby-Elektroniker. bi-m.
- Strassenbahn Magazin. 9 per yr.
- Die Wasserwirtschaft; Zeitschrift fuer das gesamte Wasserwesen, insbesondere fuer Hydrologie, Hydromechanik und Wasserbau. m. ISSN 0043-0978 (Deutscher Verband fuer Wasserwirtschaft e.V.)

**Frankenbund - Vereinigung fuer Fraenkische Landeskunde und Kulturpflaege e.V.**
Hofstr. 3, 8700 Wuerzburg, W. Germany (B.R.D.)
- Frankenland; Zeitschrift fuer fraenkisch Landeskunde und Kulturpflege. m. ISSN 0015-9905

**Frankfurt am Main. Statistisches Amt und Wahlamt**
Kurt Schumacherstr. 41, 6000 Frankfurt, W. Germany (B.R.D.)
- Frankfurt am Main. Statistisches Amt und Wahlamt. Statistisches Jahrbuch. a. ISSN 0071-9218

**Druck- und Verlagshaus Frankfurt am Main GmbH**
Grosse Eschenheimer Str. 16-18, 6000 Frankfurt, W. Germany (B.R.D.)
(U. S. Subscr. to: German Federal Railroad, 11 W. 42nd St., New York, N.Y. 10036)
- D B-Pressedienst. w. ISSN 0011-4774 (Deutsche Bundesbahn)

**Frankfurt Book Fair**
- Who's Who at the Frankfurt Book Fair. (pub. by Verlag Dokumentation)

**Frankfurter Allgemeine Zeitung**
Hellerhofstr. 2-4, 6000 Frankfurt 1, W. Germany (B.R.D.)
- Ein Buechertagebuch; Buchbesprechungen aus der Frankfurter Allgemeinen Zeitung. a. ISSN 0068-3396

**Frankfurter Bund fuer Volksbildung GmbH**
Eschersheimer Landstr. 2, 6000 Frankfurt 1, W. Germany (B.R.D.)
- AKT. (Aktuelles Theater) m.

**Frankfurter Fachverlag**
Emil Sulzbach Str. 12, 6000 Frankfurt 97, W. Germany (B.R.D.)
- Das Junge Elektrohandwerk. m. ISSN 0022-6246
- Der Junge Metallhandwerker. m. ISSN 0022-6335

**Frankfurter Geographische Gesellschaft**
- Frankfurter Geographische Hefte. (pub. by Verlag Dr. Waldemar Kramer)

**Frankfurter Societaetsdruckerei GmbH**
Frankenallee 71-81, 6000 Frankfurt 1, W. Germany (B.R.D.)
- Scala International. m. ISSN 0036-5416

**Franz-Sales-Verlag**
Rosental 1, Abholfach, 8833 Eichstaett /Bay., W. Germany (B.R.D.)
- Jahrbuch fuer Salesianische Studien. a. ISSN 0075-2754 (Arbeitsgemeinschaft fuer Salesianische Studien)

**Franzis-Verlag**
Karlstr. 37, 8000 Munich 37, W. Germany (B.R.D.)
- Elektronik; Fachzeitschrift fuer angewandte Elektronik und Datentechnik. m. ISSN 0013-5658
- Funkschau; Fachzeitschrift fuer Radio- und Fernschtechnik, Hi-Fi und elektronik. s-m. ISSN 0016-2841

**Fraunhofer-Gesellschaft**
Leonzodstr. 54, 8000 Munich 19, W. Germany (B.R.D.)
- Fraunhofer-Gesellschaft. Mitteilungsblatt. q. ISSN 0016-0253

**Fraunhofer Gesellschaft. Dokumentationsstelle fuer Bautechnik**
- Schrifttumkartei Bauwesen. (pub. by Wilhelm Ernst und Sohn KG)
- Schrifttumkartei Beton. (pub. by Wilhelm Ernst und Sohn KG)

**Fraunhofer-Gesellschaft. Dokumentationszentrale Wasser**
- Dokumentation Wasser. (pub. by Erich Schmidt Verlag (Bielefeld))
- Dokumentationszentrale Wasser Schriftenreihe. (pub. by Erich Schmidt Verlag (Bielefeld))

**Freie Demokratische Partei. Landesverband Berlin**
- Berliner Liberale Zeitung. (pub. by Berliner Wort Verlagsgesellschaft mbH.)

**Freie Demokratische Partei Saar**
Eisenbahnstr. 70, 6600 Saarbruecken 1, W. Germany (B.R.D.)
- F D P Informationsdienst; Liberales Monatsblatt an der Saar. m. ISSN 0016-0792

**Freie Universitaet Berlin. Institut fuer Meteorologie**
- Meteorologische Abhandlungen. (pub. by Dietrich Reimer Buchhandlung)

**Freie Universitaet Berlin. Institut fuer Publizistik**
- Abhandlungen und Materialen zur Publizistik. (pub. by Colloquium Verlag)
- Beitraege zur Informations- und Dokumentationswissenschaft. (pub. by Verlag Dokumentation)
- P R D. (pub. by Verlag Dokumentation)

**Freie Universitaet Berlin. John F. Kennedy-Institut fuer Nordamerika-Studien**
Lansstr. 7-9, 1000 Berlin 33, W. Germany (B.R.D.)
- Freie Universitaet Berlin. John F. Kennedy-Institut fuer Nordamerika Studien. Materialien. irreg., no. 2, 1973.

**Freie Universitaet Berlin. Leitstelle Politische Dokumentation**
- Pol Dok. (pub. by Verlag Dokumentation)
- Politikwissenschaftliche Forschung. (pub. by Verlag Dokumentation)

**Freie Universitaet Berlin. Osteuropa-Institut**
Garystr. 55, 1000 Berlin 33 (Dahlem), W. Germany (B.R.D.)
- Freie Universitaet Berlin. Osteuropa-Institut. Berichte. irreg. ISSN 0067-5873
- Freie Universitaet Berlin. Osteuropa-Institut. Bibliographische Mitteilungen. irreg., no. 11, 1975. ISSN 0067-5881
- Freie Universitaet Berlin. Osteuropa-Institut. Erziehungswissenschaftliche Veroeffentlichungen. irreg. ISSN 0067-589X

**Freie Universitaet Berlin. Osteuropa-Institut. Historische Veroeffentlichungen. (pub. by Verlag Otto Harrassowitz)**
- Freie Universitaet Berlin. Osteuropa-Institut. Philosophische und Soziologische Veroeffentlichungen. irreg. ISSN 0067-5911
- Freie Universitaet Berlin. Osteuropa-Institut. Rechtswissenschaftliche Veroeffentlichungen. irreg.
- Freie Universitaet Berlin. Osteuropa-Institut. Slavistische Veroeffentlichungen. irreg. ISSN 0067-592X
- Freie Universitaet Berlin. Osteuropa-Institut. Wirtschaftswissenschaftliche Veroeffentlichungen. irreg. ISSN 0067-5938

**Freie Universitaet Berlin. Zentralinstitut fuer Sozialwissenschaftliche Forschung**
- Freie Universitaet Berlin. Zentralinstitut. fuer Sozialwissenschaftliche Forschung. Berichte und Materialien. (pub. by Verlag Dokumentation)

**Verlag der Freien Volksbuehne Berlin e.V.**
Ruhrstr. 6, 1000 Berlin 31, W. Germany (B.R.D.)
- Blaetter der freien Volksbuehne Berlin. bi-m. ISSN 0006-4378

**Freier Verband Deutscher Zahnaerzte e.V.**
- Der Freie Zahnarzt. (pub. by Druck und Verlag Kern und Birner)

**Freies Deutsches Hochstift**
- Freies Deutsches Hochstift, Frankfurt am Main. Jahrbuch. (pub. by Max Niemeyer Verlag)

**Verlag Freies Geistesleben GmbH**
Haussmannstr. 76, 7000 Stuttgart, W. Germany (B. R. D.)
- Denken, Schauen, Sinnen. irreg. ISSN 0070-3419
- Die Drei; Zeitschrift fuer Wissenschaft, Kunst und soziales Leben. m. ISSN 0012-6063 (Anthroposophische Gesellschaft in Deutschland)
- Erziehungskunst; Monatsschrift zur Paedagogik R. Steiners. m. ISSN 0014-0333 (Bund der Freien Waldorfschulen e.V.)

**Freireligioese Landesgemeinde Baden**
- Freie Religion. (pub. by Freireligioese Verlagsbuchhandlung)

**Freireligioese Verlagsbuchhandlung**
L 10, 4-6, 6800 Mannheim 1, W. Germany (B.R.D.)
- Freie Religion; Monatsschrift fuer religioese Selbstbestimmung. m. ISSN 0016-0776 (Freireligioese Landesgemeinde Baden)

**Freisoziale Union**
Feldstr. 46, 2000 Hamburg 6, W. Germany (B.R.D.)
- Der Dritte Weg. m. ISSN 0012-6268

**Fremdenverkehrszentrale Hamburg**
- Hamburger Vorschau. (pub. by Hanseatisches Werbekontor Heuser und Co.)

**Freunde des Wallraf-Richartz-Museums**
An der Rechtschule, 5000 Cologne 1, W. Germany (B.R.D.)
- Wallraf-Richartz-Jahrbuch; Westdeutsches Jahrbuch fuer Kunstgeschichte. a. ISSN 0083-7105

**Freunde Mainfraenkischer Kunst und Geschichte**
Friedensstr. 47, 8700 Wuerzburg, W. Germany (B.R.D.)
- Mainfraenkisches Jahrbuch fuer Geschichte und Kunst. a. ISSN 0076-2725

**Dr. Heinz F. Friederichs**
Dehnhardtstr. 32, 6000 Frankfurt 50, W. Germany (B.R.D.)
- Hessische Familienkunde. q. ISSN 0018-1064 (Arbeitsgemeinschaft der Familienkundlichen Gesellschaften in Hessen)

**Friedrich-Alexander-Universitaet, Nuernberg**
Findelgasse 7, Nuernberg, West Germany (B.R.D.)
- Nuernberger Wirtschafts-und Sozialgeographische Arbeiten. irreg., vol. 21, 1974.

**Friedrich-Ebert-Stiftung**
Koelner Str. 149, 5300 Bonn-Bad Godesberg, W. Germany (B.R.D.)
- African Biographies. irreg.
- Archiv fuer Sozialgeschichte. (pub. by Verlag Neue Gesellschaft GmbH)

**Friedrich-Ebert-Stiftung. Forschung Institut**
- Vierteljahresberichte - Probleme der Entwicklungslaender. (pub. by Verlag Neue Gesellschaft GmbH)

**Erhard Friedrich Verlag**
Im Brande 15, 3016 Seelze 6, 3W. Germany (B.R.D.)
- Buehnentechnische Rundschau; Zeitschrift fuer Theatertechnik, Buehnenbau und Buehnengestaltung. 6 per yr. ISSN 0007-3091 (Deutsche Theatertechniker Gesellschaft)
- Kunst und Unterricht. q. ISSN 0023-5466
- Opernwelt; die deutsche Opernzeitschrift. m. ISSN 0030-3690
- Theater Heute. m. ISSN 0040-5507

**Werner Fritsch Verlag**
Postfach 751, 8000 Munich 1, W. Germany (B. R. D.)
- Historiae Scientiarum Elementa. irreg., 1973, vol. 5. ISSN 0073-2532
- Neue Muenchner Beitraege zur Geschichte der Medizin und Naturwissenschaften. Medizinhistorische Serie. irreg., vol. 7, 1977.
- Neue Muenchner Beitraege zur Geschichte der Medizin und Naturwissenschaften. Naturwissenschaftshistorische Reihe. irreg., vol. 5, 1977.

**Frobenius-Institut**
- Paideuma. (pub. by Franz Steiner Verlag GmbH)

**Friedrich Fromman Verlag Guenther Holzboog KG**
Koenig-Karl-Str. 27, 7000 Stuttgart 50, W. Germany (B.R.D.)
- Allgemeine Zeitschrift fuer Philosophie. 3 per yr. (Allgemeine Gesellschaft fuer Philosophie in Deutschland e.V.)
- Kultur und Gesellschaft; Neue historische Forschungen. irreg.

**Verlag A. Fruehmorgen**
Schwindstr. 5, 8000 Munich 40, W. Germany (B. R. D.)
- Forum des Praktischen Arztes. m. ISSN 0015-850X (Vereinigung der Praktischen Aerzte Bayerns e.V.)

**H. H. Fuehring**
Auf der Erk 2, 5300 Bonn-Lessenich, W. Germany (B.R.D.)
- Alte und Neue Zinnfiguren; Monatsschrift fuer Sammler u. Liebhaber kulturhistorischer Figuren. bi-m. ISSN 0044-474X

**Fuldaer Geschichtsverein**
Stadtschloss, 6400 Fulda, W. Germany (B.R.D.)
- Fuldaer Geschichtsblaetter. bi-m. ISSN 0016-2612

**Furche-Verlag H. Rennebach KG**
Papenhuder Str. 2, 2000 Hamburg 76, W. Germany (B.R.D.)
- Theologia Practica; Zeitschrift fuer Praktische Theologie und Religionspaedagogik. q. ISSN 0049-3643

**Fussball Club Pforzheim**
- Fussball Club Pforzheim. Club-Nachrichten. (pub. by J. Esslinger Druckerei und Verlag)

**G F W Verlag GmbH**
Poststr. 21, Postfach 3533, 4000 Duesseldorf, W. Germany (B.R.D.)
- Fachkontakt; Journal fuer Foto, Film, Ton, Video. bi-m. (Zentralverband Deutscher Photographen)
- Inpho. s-m. ISSN 0019-0179 (Deutsche Photo-und Kinohaendler-Bund)

**G.I. Counselling Center**
Herbertstr. 6, 1000 Berlin 62, W. Germany (B.R.D.)
- Forward. m.

**G I T-Verlag Ernst Giebeler**
Schumannstr. 15, Postfach 572, 6100 Darmstadt, W. Germany (B.R.D.)
- G I T; Fachzeitschrift fuer das Laboratorium. m. ISSN 0016-3538
- Lab-Compact Service; direktinformation labortechnik. 5 per yr.

**Betriebswirtschaftlicher Verlag Dr. Th. Gabler KG**
Taunusstr. 54, Postfach 1546, 6200 Wiesbaden 1, W. Germany (B.R.D.)
- Der Aufstieg; Wissen, Bildung, Koennen. m. ISSN 0004-7864
- Der Aussenhandelskaufmann; Zeitschrift fuer Export-Import-Spedition. m. ISSN 0004-8186

- Der Bankkaufmann; Zeitschrift fuer bankpraktische Aus- und Fortbildung. m. ISSN 0005-5085
- Betriebswirtschafts-Magazin; Zeitschrift fuer Betriebswirtschaft, Steuer, Wirtschaftsrecht. s-m. ISSN 0005-9986
- Bilanz- und Buchhaltungs-Praxis; zeitschrift fuer Rechnungswesen und steuer. m. ISSN 0006-2359
- Gabriele; Sekretaerin und Chefassistentin. m. ISSN 0016-3708
- Kostenrechnungs-Praxis; Zeitschrift fuer Betriebsabrechnung, Kostenrechnung und Planung. bi-m. ISSN 0023-4265
- Management International Review. q. ISSN 0025-181X (European Foundation for Management Development (EFMD))
- Schriftenreihe Betriebswirtschaftliche Beitraege zur Organisation und Automation. irreg., vol. 23, 1976. ISSN 0067-6381
- Schriftenreihe Unternehmensfuehrung und Marketing. irreg., vol. 6, 1976.
- Schriftenreihe zur Theoretischen und Angewandten Betriebswirtschlaftslehre. irreg., no. 36, 1975. ISSN 0080-7087
- Technischer Ansporn; Zeitschrift fuer Vorwaertsstrebende. m. ISSN 0040-1536
- Der Versicherungskaufmann. m. ISSN 0049-6006
- Westfaelische Wilhelms-Universitaet Muenster. Institut fuer Kreditwesen. Schriftenreihe. irreg., vol. 18, 1975. ISSN 0077-2119
- Zeitschrift fuer Betriebswirtschaft. m. ISSN 0044-2372
- Zeitschrift fuer Organisation. 8 per yr. ISSN 0044-3212 (Gesellschaft fuer Organisation e.V.)

**Gaertnerische Verlagsgesellschaft**
Am Schlosspark 67, Postfach 9421, 6202 Wiesbaden-Biebrich, W. Germany (B.R.D.)
- Allgemeiner Samen- und Pflanzen Anzeiger; Fachzeitung fuer den deutschen Erwerbsgaertner. s-m. ISSN 0002-600X

**Galerie Nierendorf**
Hardenbergstr. 19, 1000 Berlin 12, W. Germany (B.R.D.)
- Galerie Nierendorf, Berlin. Kunstblaetter. irreg., no. 32, 1974. ISSN 0072-0089

**Gastgewerbe Verlag**
Pressehaus Am Martin-Luther-Platz, Postfach 1122, 4000 Duesseldorf 1, W. Germany (B.R.D.)
- D G das Hessische Gastgewerbe. w.
- D G Deutsche Gaststaette/Deutsche Hotel-Zeitung Gastwirt und Hotelier; Fachzeitschrift fuer das gesamte Hotel- und Gaststaettenwesen. w.

**Gaswaerme- Institut Essen**
- Gas Waerme International. (pub. by Vulkan-Verlag Dr. W. Classen)

**Gebetsapostolat**
Elsheimer Str. 9, 6000 Frankfurt 1, W. Germany (B. R. D.)
- Gebetsapostolat und Seelsorge. s-m. ISSN 0016-5735

**Geci Verlag**
Altkoenigstr. 34, 6231 Sulzbach, W. Germany (B.R.D.)
- Europa Vincet; Meinungen und Kommentare zu europaeischen Fragen. bi-m.

**Verlag Dr. Max Gehlen**
Daimlerstr. 12, Postfach 2247, 6380 Bad Homburg, W. Germany (B. R. D.)
- Arbeitsrecht in Stichworten; Arbeitsrechtliche Entscheidungssammlung. m. ISSN 0003-7761
- Bad Homburger Veranstaltungsspiegel Kurzeitung. m. ISSN 0005-3708 (Kurverwaltung Bad Homburg)
- Gesetz und Verordnungsblatt fuer das Land Hessen. ISSN 0016-9137 (Hessen. Staatskanzlei)
- Die Helferin des Arztes. m. ISSN 0017-9949
- Wirtschaft und Gesellschaft im Unterricht. bi-m.

**Industrie-Verlag Carlheinz Gehlsen**
Dechenstr. 7, Postfach 287, 5300 Bonn, W. Germany (B.R.D.)
- Handbuch der Rationalisierung. irreg. ISSN 0073-0122 (Rationalisierungskuratorium der Deutschen Wirtschaft)

**Verlag Gebr. Geiselberger**
Postfach 69, 8262 Altoetting, W. Germany (B.R.D.) (Subscriptions to: H. Pfitzner, Amselfeld 18, 8520 Erlangen, W. Germany (B.R.D.))
- R L V die Bayerische Realschule. (Real-Lehrer-Verband) m. (Bayerischer Reallehrerverband e.V.)

**Verlag W. Geissler-Werry**
In den Benden 13, 5160 Dueren, W. Germany (B.R.D.)
- Magische Welt; Zeitschrift fuer angewandte Tricktechnik und Wahrnehmungstaeuschung. bi-m. ISSN 0024-9912

**Gemeindejugendwerk**
- Jungscharhelfer. (pub. by Verlag J. G. Oncken Nachf. GmbH)

**Gemeinnuetzige Verwaltungsgesellschaft fuer Wissenschaftspflege MbH**
Brucker Holt 56, 4300 Essen, W. Germany (B.R.D.)
- Vademecum Deutscher Lehr- und Forschungsstaetten. irreg. ISSN 0083-5080 (Stifterverband fuer die Deutsche Wissenschaft)
- Wirtschaft und Wissenschaft; Nachrichten, Beitraege, Informationen. q. ISSN 0039-1409

**Gemeinschaft der Jagdflieger**
Frahmsallee 21, 2427 Malente-Gremsmuehlen, W. Germany (B.R.D.)
- Jaegerblatt; fuer Angehoerige ehemaliger Jagdfliegereinheiten. bi-m. ISSN 0021-3896

**Gemeinschaft Evangelischer Erzieher in Baden**
- Beitraege zur Paedagogischen Arbeit. (pub. by Evangelischer Oberkirchenrat Karlsruhe)

**Gemeinschaftsverlag GmbH**
Spreestr. 9, 6100 Darmstadt, W. Germany (B.R.D.)
- B D I Deutschland Liefert/B D I German Supplies; official export register of the Federation of German Industries. a. ISSN 0415-7508 (Bundesverband der Deutschen Industrie)

**Genealogische Gesellschaft, Sitz Hamburg e.V.**
Postfach 239, 2000 Hamburg 36, W. Germany (B.R.D.)
- Zeitschrift fuer Niederdeutsche Familienkunde. bi-m. ISSN 0044-3190

**Genossenschaft Deutscher Buehnenangehoeriger**
- Die Buehnengenossenschaft. (pub. by Buehnenschriften-Vertriebs-Gesellschaft)
- Deutsches Buehnen-Jahrbuch. (pub. by Buehnenschriften-Vertriebs-Gesellschaft)

**A. W. Gentner Verlag**
Forststr. 131, Postfach 688, 7000 Stuttgart 1, W. Germany (B.R.D.)
- Aerzteblatt Baden-Wuerttemberg. m. ISSN 0001-947X (Landesaerztekammer Baden-Wuerttemberg)
- Arbeitsmedizin, Sozialmedizin, Praeventivmedizin; Zeitschrift fuer Praxis, Klinik, Forschung, Begutachtung, Rehabilitation. m. ISSN 0300-581X
- Glaswelt/Deutsche Glaserzeitung; Fachzeitschrift fuer Handwerk, Handel und Industrie. m. ISSN 0017-1107
- Gummi, Asbest, Kunststoffe; Internationale unabhaengige Fachzeitschrift. m. ISSN 0017-5595
- K K - die Kaelte und Klimatechnik. m.
- Kuechenforum. bi-m.
- M B - Der Arzt in Krankenhaus und Gesundheitswesen. m. ISSN 0024-7979 (Marburger Bund)
- Der Medizinische Sachverstaendige. q. ISSN 0025-8490
- Medizinische Technik. bi-m. ISSN 0025-8504
- Oel- und Gasfeuerung; Fachzeitschrift fuer Heizung und Lufttechnik. m. ISSN 0029-8662
- S B Z - Sanitaer-, Heizungs- und Klimatechnik. s-m. (Zentralverband fuer Sanitaer-, Klima- und Heizungstechnik)
- Zahnaerzteblatt Baden-Wuerttemberg. m. (Landeszahnaerztekammer Baden-Wuerttemberg)

**Geo-Buch Verlag**
Rosental 6, 8000 Munich 2, W. Germany (B.R.D.)
- Muenchener Geographische Abhandlungen. 3-4 copies per year. (Universitaet Muenchen. Institut fuer Geographie)

- Universitaet Muenchen. Wirtschaftsgeographisches Institut. "W G I"-Berichte zur Regionalforschung. irreg., no. 14, 1974. ISSN 0077-2127

**Geo Center, International Map Center**
Honigwiesenstr. 25, Postfach 800830, 7000 Stuttgart 1, W. Germany (B.R.D.)
- Europa Camping und Caravaning. Internationaler Fuehrer. a. ISSN 0071-2272

**Geographische Gesellschaft e.V., Muenchen**
Heinrich Voglstr. 7, 8000 Munich 71, W. Germany (B.R.D.)
- Geographische Gesellschaft, Munich. Mitteilungen. a. ISSN 0072-0941

**Verlag Dr. Rudolf Georgi OHG**
Aureliusstr. 42, Postfach 407, 5100 Aachen, W. Germany (B.R.D.)
- Deutsche Baumschule. m. ISSN 0011-992X
- G B und G W - Gaertner Boerse und Gartenwelt. w. (Co-publisher: Paul Parey (Hamburg))

**Fachverlag Gerardi KG**
Heinrich-Heine-Ring 9, 7500 Karlsruhe 51, W. Germany (B.R.D.)
- Versandhausberater. w. ISSN 0049-5999

**Ernst Gerdes Verlag**
Wakendorfer Str. 61, Postfach 140, 2308 Preetz, W. Germany (B.R.D.)
- Blumenfreundin Blumenpost. m. ISSN 0006-5226
- Die Frau von Heute. m. ISSN 0016-0210

**German Congress of Scholars of English**
- English and American Studies in German. (pub. by Max Niemeyer Verlag)

**Germanisches Nationalmuseum Nuernberg**
- Bilder aus Deutscher Vergangenheit. (pub. by Prestel-Verlag)

**Germany, Federal Republic. Bundesanstalt fuer Arbeit**
Regensburger Strasse 104, 8500 Nuernberg, W. Germany (B.R.D.)
- Germany (Federal Republic, 1949- ) Bundesanstalt fuer Arbeit. Amtliche Nachrichten. m. ISSN 0007-585X
- Germany (Federal Republic, 1949- ) Bundesanstalt fuer Arbeit. Berufsberatung. Ergebnisse der Berufsberatungsstatistik. a.
- Germany (Federal Republic, 1949- ) Bundesanstalt fuer Arbeit. Foerderung der Beruflichen Bildung; Ergebnisse der Teilnehmerstatistik. irreg.

**Germany, Federal Republic. Bundesanstalt fuer Arbeit. Institut fuer Arbeitsmarkt- und Berufsforschung**
Regensburger Str. 104, 8500 Nuernberg, W. Germany (B.R.D.)
- Literaturdokumentation zur Arbeitsmarkt- und Berufsforschung. a.

**Germany, Federal Republic. Bundesanstalt fuer Bodenforschung**
- Geologisches Jahrbuch. Reihe A: Allgemeine und Regionale Geologie BR Deutschland und Nachbargebiete, Tektonik, Stratigraphie, Paleontologie. (pub. by E. Schweizerbart'sche Verlagsbuchhandlung)
- Geologisches Jahrbuch. Reihe B: Regionale Geologie Ausland. (pub. by E. Schweizerbart'sche Verlagsbuchhandlung)
- Geologisches Jahrbuch. Reihe C: Hydrogeologie. Ingenieurgeologie. (pub. by E. Schweizerbart'sche Verlagsbuchhandlung)
- Geologisches Jahrbuch. Reihe D: Mineralogie. Petrographie, Geochemie, Lagerstaettenkunde. (pub. by E. Schweizerbart'sche Verlagsbuchhandlung)
- Geologisches Jahrbuch. Reihe E: Geophysik. (pub. by E. Schweizerbart'sche Verlagsbuchhandlung.)
- Palaeontographica. Abt. A: Palaeozoologie - Stratigraphie. (pub. by E. Schweizerbart'sche Verlagsbuchhandlung)

**Germany, Federal Republic. Bundesanstalt fuer Gewaesserkunde**
Kaiserin-Augusta-Anlagen 15, 5400 Koblenz, W. Germany (B.R.D.)
- Deutsche Gewaesserkundliche Mitteilungen; Mitteilungsblatt der Gewaesserkundlichen Dienststellen des Bundes und der Laender. bi-m. ISSN 0012-0235
- Germany (Federal Republic, 1949- ). Bundesanstalt fuer Gewaesserkunde. Jahresbericht. a.

**Germany, Federal Republic. Bundesanstalt fuer Landeskunde**
- Freiburger Geographische Mitteilungen. (pub. by Dr. Tesdorpf Verlag)

**Germany, Federal Republic. Bundesanstalt fuer Materialpruefung**
Unter den Eichen 87, 1000 Berlin 45, W. Germany (B.R.D.)
- Dokumentation Rheologie/Documentation Rheology. a. ISSN 0340-8388 (Co-sponsor: Deutsche Rheologische Gesellschaft)
- Dokumentation Tribologie/Documentation Tribology. a. ISSN 0340-3475
- Germany (Federal Republic, 1949- ) Bundesanstalt fuer Materialpruefung. Jahresbericht. a. ISSN 0341-0528
- Referate Organ: Schweissen und Verwandte Verfahren/Bulletin of Abstracts: Welding and Allied Processes. bi-m. ISSN 0340-4749 (Co-sponsor: Deutscher Verband fuer Schweisstechnik (DVS))

**Germany, Federal Republic. Bundesanstalt fuer Milchforschung**
- Kieler Milchwirtschaftliche Forschungsberichte. (pub. by Verlag Th. Mann)

**Germany, Federal Republic. Bundesanstalt fuer Strassenwesen**
Bruehler Str. 1, 5000 Cologne 51, W. Germany (B.R.D.)
- Germany (Federal Republic, 1949- ) Bundesanstalt fuer Strassenwesen, Erfahrungsaustauch ueber Erdarbeiten im Strassenbau. a.

**Germany, Federal Republic. Bundesanstalt fuer Vegetationskunde, Naturschutz und Landschaftspflege**
- Dokumentation fuer Umweltschutz und Landespflege. (pub. by W. Kohlhammer GmbH (Stuttgart))
- Natur und Landschaft. (pub. by W. Kohlhammer GmbH (Stuttgart))
- Schriftenreihe fuer Vegetationskunde. (pub. by Landwirtschaftsverlag GmbH)

**Germany, Federal Republic. Bundesaufsichtsamt fuer das Versicherungswesen**
Ludwigkirchpkatz 3-4, Postfach 180, 1000 Berlin 15, W. Germany (B.R.D.)
- Germany (Federal Republic, 1949- ) Bundesaufsichtsamt fuer das Versicherungswesen. Geschaeftsbericht. a. ISSN 0525-1737

**Germany, Federal Republic. Bundesforschungsanstalt fuer Fischerei**
- Archiv fuer Fischereiwissenschaft. (pub. by H. Heenemann GmbH)

**Germany, Federal Republic. Bundesforschungsanstalt fuer Fischerei. Institut fuer Fangtechnik**
Palmaille 9, 2000 Hamburg 50, W. Germany (B.R.D.)
- Protokolle zur Fischereitechnik. 1-3 per yr. ISSN 0438-4555

**Germany, Federal Republic. Bundesforschungsanstalt fuer Forst- und Holzwirtschaft in Reinbeck**
- Bundesforschungsanstalt fuer Forst- und Holzwirtschaft in Reinbeck. Mitteilungen. (pub. by Kommissionverlag Max Wiedebusch)

**Germany, Federal Republic. Bundesforschungsanstalt fuer Landeskunde und Raumordnung**
Michaelstr. 8, Postfach 130, 5300 Bonn- Bad Godesberg, W. Germany (B.R.D.)
- Dokumentation zur Raumentwicklung/ Documentation of Regional Development. q. ISSN 0341-2431
- Informationen zur Raumentwicklung. m. ISSN 0303-2493
- Referatblatt fuer Raumentwicklung. q.

**Germany, Federal Republic. Bundesforschungsanstalt fuer Rebenzuechtung Geilweilerhof**
6741 Siebeldingen, W. Germany (B.R.D.)
- Vitis; Berichte ueber Rebenforschung mit Dokumentation der Weinbauforschung. q. ISSN 0042-7500

**Germany, Federal Republic. Bundesgesundheitsamt**
- Bundesgesundheitsblatt. (pub. by Carl Heymanns Verlag KG)
- Germany (Federal Republic, 1949- ) Bundesgesundheitsamt. Abhandlungen. (pub. by Springer-Verlag US)

**Germany, Federal Republic. Bundesgesundheitsamt. Kunststoff-Kommission**
- Kunststoffe im Lebensmittelverkehr. (pub. by Carl Heymanns Verlag KG)

**Germany, Federal Republic. Bundesminister fuer Innerdeutsche Beziehungen**
- Dokumente zur Deutschlandpolitik. (pub. by Alfred Metzner Verlag GmbH)

**Germany, Federal Republic. Bundesministerium der Finanzen**
- Deutsche Steuer-Zeitung: Ausgabe A. (pub. by Wilhelm Stollfuss Verlag)
- Deutsche Steuer-Zeitung: Ausgabe B. (pub. by Wilhelm Stollfuss Verlag)

**Germany, Federal Republic. Bundesministerium der Justiz**
- Goltdammer's Archiv fuer Strafrecht. (pub. by R.v. Decker's Verlag, G. Schenk GmbH)

**Germany, Federal Republic. Bundesministerium der Verteidigung**
Postfach 161, 5300 Bonn, W. Germany (B.R.D.)
- Luftwaffe. (pub. by Moench Verlagsgesellschaft mbH)
- Soldat und Technik. (pub. by Umschau Verlag)
- Der Sprachmittler; Informationshefte des Sprachendienstes der Bundeswehr. q. ISSN 0038-8505
- Truppenpraxis. (pub. by Verlag Offene Worte)
- Unterrichtsblaetter fuer die Bundeswehrverwaltung. (pub. by R.v. Decker's Verlag, G. Schenk GmbH)
- Wehrausbildung in Wort und Bild. (pub. by Verlag Offene Worte)
- Weissbuch zur Sicherheit der Bundesrepublik Deutschland und zur Lage der Bundeswehr. irreg.

**Germany, Federal Republic. Bundesministerium des Innern**
- B G S. (pub. by Verlag A. Bernecker)

**Germany, Federal Republic. Bundesministerium des Innern. Schutzkommission**
5300 Bonn, W. Germany (B.R.D.)
- Germany (Federal Republic, 1949- ) Bundesminister des Innern. Schutzkommission. Berichte der Fachausschuesse. a.

**Germany, Federal Republic. Bundesministerium fuer Arbeit und Sozialordnung**
5300 Bonn, W. Germany (B.R.D.)
- Bundesarbeitsblatt. (pub. by W. Kohlhammer GmbH (Koeln))
- Germany (Federal Republic, 1949-) Bundesministerium fuer Arbeit und Sozialordnung. Arbeits- und Sozialstatistik. m.
- Germany (Federal Republic,1949-) Bundesministerium fuer Arbeit und Sozialordnung. Hauptergebnisse der Arbeits-und Sozialstatistik. a. ISSN 0072-1557

**Germany, Federal Republic. Bundesministerium fuer Bildung und Wissenschaft**
Stresemannstr. 2, Postfach 120124, 5300 Bonn 12, W. Germany (B.R.D.)
- Bildung im Zahlenspiegel. (pub. by W. Kohlhammer-Verlag GmbH. Abt. Veroeffentlichungen des Statistischen Bundesamtes)
- Informationen - Bildung, Wissenschaft. m.

**Germany, Federal Republic. Bundesministerium fuer das Post - und Fernmeldewesen**
Adenauerallee 81, 5300 Bonn, W. Germany (B.R.D.)
- Archiv fuer das Post - und Fernmeldewesen. bi-m. (Subscr. to Verlagspostamt, 5000 Cologne 1, W. Germany (B.R.D.))
- Germany (Federal Republic, 1949- ) Bundesminister fuer das Post- und Fernmeldewesen. Amtsblatt. s-w. ISSN 0003-2263
- Germany (Federal Republic, 1949- ) Bundesministerium fuer das Post-und Fernmeldewesen. Jahresrechnung, Nachweisung ueber die Einnahmen und Ausgaben der Deutschen Bundespost. a. ISSN 0435-7329

**Germany, Federal Republic. Bundesministerium fuer Ernaehrung, Landwirtschaft und Forsten**
5300 Bonn, W. Germany (B.R.D.)
- Berichte ueber Landwirtschaft. (pub. by Verlag Paul Parey (Hamburg))

- Germany (Federal Republic,1949-)
  Bundesministerium fuer Ernaehrung,
  Landwirtschaft und Forsten. Agrarbericht der
  Bundesregierung. a. ISSN 0072-1565
- Germany (Federal Republic,1949-)
  Bundesministerium fuer Ernaehrung,
  Landwirtschaft und Forsten. Jahresbericht.
  Forschung in Geschaeftsbereich des
  Bundesministers. a. ISSN 0072-1573
- Informationen ueber die Fischwirtschaft des
  Auslandes. m. ISSN 0020-0379
- Jahresbericht ueber die Deutsche Fischwirtschaft.
  (pub. by Gebr. Mann Verlag)
- Statistisches Jahrbuch ueber Ernaehrung,
  Landwirtschaft und Forsten der Bundesrepublik
  Deutschland. a. ISSN 0072-1581

**Germany, Federal Republic. Bundesministerium fuer
Forschung und Technologie**
Stresemann Str. 2, 5300 Bonn-Bad Godesberg, W.
Germany (B.R.D.)
- Germany (Federal Republic,1949-)
  Bundesministerium fuer Forschung und
  Technologie. BMFT Foerderungskatalog. a.

**Germany, Federal Republic. Bundesministerium fuer
Raumordnung, Bauwesen und Staedtebau**
- Die Bauverwaltung. (pub. by Curt R. Vincentz
  Verlag)
- Bundesbaublatt. (pub. by Bauverlag GmbH)

**Germany, Federal Republic. Bundesministerium fuer
Unterricht**
- Internationale Universitaetswochen fuer
  Kernphysic der Karl-Franzenus-Universitaet Graz.
  Proceedings. (pub. by Springer-Verlag US)

**Germany, Federal Republic. Bundesministerium fuer
Verkehr**
5300 Bonn, W. Germany (B.R.D.)
- Forschung Stadtverkehr. (pub. by Kirschbaum
  Verlag)
- Forschung Stadtverkehr: Sonderreihe/Urban
  Transport Research: Special Series. (pub. by
  Kirschbaum Verlag)
- Germany (Federal Republic), Bundesministerium
  fuer Verkehr. Strassenbaubericht. irreg.
- Verkehrsblatt. (pub. by Verkehrsblattverlag Dr.
  Borgmann)

**Germany, Federal Republic. Bundesministerium fuer
Wirtschaft**
5300 Bonn, W. Germany (B.R.D.)
- Economic Situation in the Federal Republic of
  Germany. m.
- Reden zur Wirtschaftspolitik. irreg.

**Germany, Federal Republic. Bundesministerium fuer
Wirtschaftliche Zusammenarbeit**
Friedrich Ebert-Allee 116, Postfach 120322, 5300
Bonn 12, W. Germany (B.R.D.)
- B M Z-Materialen. bi-m.
- Weltblick. q. ISSN 0043-258X

**Germany, Federal Republic. Bundessortenamt**
- Blatt fuer Sortenwesen. (pub. by Alfred Strothe
  Verlag)

**Germany, Federal Republic. Bundesstelle fuer
Aussenhandelsinformation**
Blaubach 13, 5000 Cologne 1, W. Germany
(B.R.D.)
- Germany, Federal Republic. Bundesstelle fuer
  Aussenhandelsinformation. Publikations-Spiegel. a.
- Nachrichten fuer Aussenhandel. (pub. by
  Vereinigte Wirtschaftsdienste GmbH)
- Ostinformation. irreg.

**Germany, Federal Republic. Bundesversicherungsamt**
Reichpietschufer 72-76, 1000 Berlin 30, W.
Germany (B.R.D.)
- Germany (Federal Republic, 1949-).
  Bundesversicherungsamt. Taetigkeitsbericht. irreg.

**Germany, Federal Republic. Deutscher Bundestag.
Abteilung Wissenschaftliche Dokumentation**
Bundeshaus, 5300 Bonn, W. Germany (B.R.D.)
- Germany (Federal Republic, 1949-) Deutscher
  Bundestag. Wissenschaftliche Dienste. Aufsaetze
  aus Zeitschriften und Sammelwerken. 6 per yr.
- Germany (Federal Republic, 1949-) Deutscher
  Bundestag. Wissenschaftliche Dienste.
  Bibliographien. irreg. ISSN 0433-762X
- Germany (Federal Republic, 1949-) Deutscher
  Bundestag. Wissenschaftliche Dienste.
  Materilien. irreg. ISSN 0435-7590

**Germany, Federal Republic. Presse und
Informationsamt**
5300 Bonn, W. Germany (B.R.D.)
- Germany (Federal Republic, 1949-) Presse- und
  Informationsamt Bulletin Archive Supplement.
  irreg.
- Germany (Federal Republic, 1949-) Presse- und
  Informationsamt. Bulletin. w. ISSN 0032-7794

**Germany, Federal Republic. Sachverstaendigenrat zur
Begutachtung der Gesamtwirtschaftlichen
Entwicklung**
- Germany (Federal Republic, 1949-)
  Sachverstaendigenrat zur Begutachtung der
  Gesamtwirtschaftlichen Entwicklung.
  Jahresgutachten. (pub. by W. Kohlhammer Verlag
  GmbH. Abt. Veroeffentlichungen des Statistischen
  Bundesamtes)

**Germany, Federal Republic. Statistisches Bundesamt**
- Das Arbeitsgebiet der Bundesstatistik. (pub. by W.
  Kohlhammer-Verlag GmbH. Abt.
  Veroeffentlichungen des Statistischen
  Bundesamtes)
- Bevoelkerungsstruktur und Wirtschaftskraft der
  Bundeslaender. (pub. by W. Kohlhammer-Verlag
  GmbH. Abt. Veroeffentlichungen des Statistischen
  Bundesamtes)
- German (Federal Republic, 1949- ) Statistisches
  Bundesamt. Fachserie 7, Reihe 1:
  Zusammenfassende Uebersichten fuer den
  Aussenhandel. (pub. by W. Kohlhammer-Verlag
  GmbH. Abt. Veroeffentlichungen des Statistischen
  Bundesamtes)
- Germany (Federal Republic, 1949- ) Statistisches
  Bundesamt. Fachserie 17, Reihe 9: Preise fuer
  Verkehrsleistungen. (pub. by W. Kohlhammer-
  Verlag GmbH. Abt. Veroeffentlichungen des
  Statistischen Bundesamtes)
- Germany (Federal Republic, 1949- ) Statistisches
  Bundesamt. Alphabetisches Laenderverzeichnis
  fuer die Aussenhandelsstatistik. (pub. by W.
  Kohlhammer-Verlag GmbH. Abt.
  Veroeffentlichungen des Statistischen
  Bundesamtes)
- Germany (Federal Republic, 1949- ) Statistisches
  Bundesamt. Ausgewaehlte Zahlen fuer die
  Bauwirtschaft. (pub. by W. Kohlhammer-Verlag
  GmbH. Abt. Veroeffentlichungen des Statistischen
  Bundesamtes)
- Germany (Federal Republic, 1949- ) Statistisches
  Bundesamt. Auslandsstatistik Nr. 6370070:
  Special Trade According to the Classification for
  Statistics and Trade (CST) (pub. by W.
  Kohlhammer-Verlag GmbH. Abt.
  Veroeffentlichungen des Statistischen
  Bundesamtes)
- Germany (Federal Republic, 1949- ) Statistisches
  Bundesamt. Aussenhandel. Reihe 7:
  Sonderbeitraege. (pub. by W. Kohlhammer-Verlag
  GmbH. Abt. Veroeffentlichungen des Statistischen
  Bundesamtes)
- Germany (Federal Republic, 1949- ) Statistisches
  Bundesamt. Fachserie Auslandsstatistik, Reihe 2:
  Produzierende Gewerbe im Ausland. (pub. by W.
  Kohlhammer-Verlag GmbH. Abt.
  Veroeffentlichungen des Statistischen
  Bundesamtes)
- Germany (Federal Republic, 1949- ) Statistisches
  Bundesamt. Fachserie Auslandsstatistik, Reihe 4:
  Loehne und Gehaelter im Ausland. (pub. by W.
  Kohlhammer-Verlag GmbH. Abt.
  Veroeffentlichungen des Statistischen
  Bundesamtes)
- Germany (Federal Republic, 1949- ) Statistisches
  Bundesamt. Fachserie Auslandsstatistik, Reihe 5:
  Preise und Preisindizes im Ausland. (pub. by W.
  Kohlhammer-Verlag GmbH. Abt.
  Veroeffentlichungen des Statistischen
  Bundesamtes)
- Germany (Federal Republic, 1949- ) Statistisches
  Bundesamt. Fachserie 1, Reihe 1: Gebiet und
  Bevoelkerung. (pub. by W. Kohlhammer-Verlag
  GmbH. Abt. Veroeffentlichungen des Statistischen
  Bundesamtes)
- Germany (Federal Republic, 1949- ) Statistisches
  Bundesamt. Fachserie 1, Reihe 2:
  Bevoelkerungsbewegung. (pub. by W.
  Kohlhammer-Verlag GmbH. Abt.
  Veroeffentlichungen des Statistischen
  Bundesamtes)
- Germany (Federal Republic, 1949- ) Statistisches
  Bundesamt. Fachserie 1, Reihe 2.3: Wanderungen.
  (pub. by W. Kohlhammer-Verlag GmbH. Abt.
  Veroeffentlichungen des Statistischen
  Bundesamtes)

- Germany (Federal Republic, 1949- ) Statistisches
  Bundesamt. Fachserie 1, Reihe 3: Haushaelte und
  Familien. (pub. by W. Kohlhammer-Verlag
  GmbH. Abt. Veroeffentlichungen des Statistischen
  Bundesamtes)
- Germany (Federal Republic, 1949-) Statistisches
  Bundesamt. Fachserie 1, Reihe 4:
  Erwerbetaetigkeit. (pub. by W. Kohlhammer-
  Verlag GmbH. Abt. Veroeffentlichungen des
  Statistischen Bundesamtes)
- Germany (Federal Republic, 1949- ) Statistisches
  Bundesamt. Fachserie 2, Reihe 2: Abschluesse der
  Kapitalgesellschaften. (pub. by W. Kohlhammer-
  Verlag GmbH. Abt. Veroeffentlichungen des
  Statistischen Bundesamtes)
- Germany (Federal Republic, 1949- ) Statistisches
  Bundesamt. Fachserie 2, Reihe 3: Abschluesse der
  Oeffentlichen Versorgungs- und
  Verkehrsunternehmen. (pub. by W. Kohlhammer-
  Verlag GmbH. Abt. Veroeffentlichungen des
  Statistischen Bundesamtes)
- Germany (Federal Republic, 1949- ) Statistisches
  Bundesamt. Fachserie 2, 4:
  Zahlungsschwierigkeiten. (pub. by W.
  Kohlhammer-Verlag GmbH. Abt.
  Veroeffentlichungen des Statistischen
  Bundesamtes)
- Germany (Federal Republic, 1949- ) Statistisches
  Bundesamt. Fachserie 3, Reihe 2: Betriebs- ,
  Arbeits- und Einkommensverhaeltnisse. (pub. by
  W. Kohlhammer-Verlag GmbH. Abt.
  Veroeffentlichungen des Statistischen
  Bundesamtes)
- Germany (Federal Republic, 1949- ) Statistisches
  Bundesamt. Fachserie 3, Reihe 3: Gartenbau und
  Weinwirtschaft. (pub. by W. Kohlhammer-Verlag
  GmbH. Abt. Veroeffentlichungen des Statistischen
  Bundesamtes)
- Germany (Federal Republic, 1949- ) Statistisches
  Bundesamt. Fachserie 3, Reihe 4: Tierische
  Erzeugung. (pub. by W. Kohlhammer-Verlag
  GmbH. Abt. Veroeffentlichungen des Statistischen
  Bundesamtes)
- Germany (Federal Republic, 1949- ) Statistisches
  Bundesamt. Fachserie 3, Reihe 4.5: Fischerei.
  (pub. by W. Kohlhammer-Verlag GmbH. Abt.
  Veroeffentlichungen des Statistischen
  Bundesamtes)
- Germany (Federal Republic, 1949- ) Statistisches
  Bundesamt. Fachserie 4, Reihe S:
  Sonderbeitraege. (pub. by W. Kohlhammer-Verlag
  GmbH. Abt. Veroeffentlichungen des Statistischen
  Bundesamtes)
- Germany (Federal Republic, 1949- ) Statistisches
  Bundesamt. Fachserie 4, Reihe 1:
  Zusammenfassende Daten fuer das Produzierende
  Gewerbe. (pub. by W. Kohlhammer-Verlag
  GmbH. Abt. Veroeffentlichungen des Statistischen
  Bundesamtes)
- Germany (Federal Republic, 1949- ) Statistisches
  Bundesamt. Fachserie 4, Reihe 2: Indizes des
  Auftragseinangs und des Auftragsbestands in
  Ausgewaehlten Industriezwigen und im
  Bauhauptgewerbe. (pub. by W. Kohlhammer-
  Verlag GmbH. Abt. Veroeffentlichungen des
  Statistischen Bundesamtes)
- Germany (Federal Republic, 1949- ) Statistisches
  Bundesamt. Fachserie 4, Reihe 2: Indizes fuer das
  Produzierende Gewerbe. (pub. by W.
  Kohlhammer-Verlag GmbH. Abt.
  Veroeffentlichungen des Statistischen
  Bundesamtes)
- Germany (Federal Republic, 1949- ) Statistisches
  Bundesamt. Fachserie 4, Reihe 3: Produktion im
  Produzierenden Gewerbe. (pub. by W.
  Kohlhammer-Verlag GmbH. Abt.
  Veroeffentlichungen des Statistischen
  Bundesamtes)
- Germany (Federal Republic, 1949- ) Statistisches
  Bundesamt. Fachserie 4, Reihe 5: Beschaeftigung,
  Umsatz, Investitionen und Kosten Struktur im
  Baugewerbe. (pub. by W. Kohlhammer-Verlag
  GmbH. Abt. Veroeffentlichungen des Statistischen
  Bundesamtes)
- Germany (Federal Republic, 1949- ) Statistisches
  Bundesamt. Fachserie 4, Reihe 7: Handwerk.
  (pub. by W. Kohlhammer-Verlag GmbH. Abt.
  Veroeffentlichungen des Statistischen
  Bundesamtes)
- Germany (Federal Republic, 1949- ) Statistisches
  Bundesamt. Fachserie 5, Reihe 1: Bautaetigkeit.
  (pub. by W. Kohlhammer-Verlag GmbH. Abt.
  Veroeffentlichungen des Statistischen
  Bundesamtes)

- Germany (Federal Republic, 1949- ) Statistisches Bundesamt. Fachserie 5, Reine 2: Bewilligungen im Sozialen. (pub. by W. Kohlhammer-Verlag GmbH. Abt. Veroeffentlichungen des Statistischen Bundesamtes)
- Germany (Federal Republic, 1949- ) Statistisches Bundesamt. Fachserie 5, Reihe 3: Bestand an Wohnungen. (pub. by W. Kohlhammer-Verlag GmbH. Abt. Veroeffentlichungen des Statistischen Bundesamtes)
- Germany (Federal Republic, 1949- ) Statistisches Bundesamt. Fachserie 6, Reihe 1: Grosshandel. (pub. by W. Kohlhammer-Verlag GmbH. Abt. Veroeffentlichungen des Statistischen Bundesamtes)
- Germany (Federal Republic, 1949- ) Statistisches Bundesamt. Fachserie 6, Reihe 3: Einzelhandel. (pub. by W. Kohlhammer-Verlag GmbH. Abt. Veroeffentlichungen des Statistischen Bundesamtes)
- Germany (Federal Republic, 1949- ) Statistisches Bundesamt. Fachserie 6, Reihe 5: Wahrenverkehr mit Berlin (West) (pub. by W. Kohlhammer-Verlag GmbH. Abt. Veroeffentlichungen des Statistischen Bundesamtes)
- Germany (Federal Republic, 1949- ) Statistisches Bundesamt. Fachserie 6, Reihe 6: Wahrenverkehr mit der Deutschen Demokratischen Republik und Berlin (Ost) (pub. by W. Kohlhammer-Verlag GmbH. Abt. Veroeffentlichungen des Statistischen Bundesamtes)
- Germany (Federal Republic, 1949- ) Statistisches Bundesamt. Fachserie 6, Reihe 7: Reiseverkehr. (pub. by W. Kohlhammer-Verlag GmbH. Abt. Veroeffentlichungen des Statistischen Bundesamtes)
- Germany (Federal Republic, 1949- ) Statistisches Bundesamt. Fachserie 7, Reihe 2: Aussenhandel nach Waren und Laendern (Spezialhandel) (pub. by W. Kohlhammer-Verlag GmbH. Abt. Veroeffentlichungen des Statistischen Bundesamtes)
- Germany (Federal Republic, 1949- ) Statistisches Bundesamt. Fachserie 7, Reihe 3: Aussenhandel Nach Laendern und Warengruppen (Spezialhandel) (pub. by W. Kohlhammer-Verlag GmbH. Abt. Veroeffentlichungen des Statistischen Bundesamtes)
- Germany (Federal Republic, 1949- ) Statistisches Bundesamt. Fachserie 7, Reihe 4. Aussenhandel mit Ausgewaehlten Waren. (pub. by W. Kohlhammer-Verlag GmbH. Abt. Veroeffentlichungen des Statistischen Bundesamtes)
- Germany (Federal Republic, 1949- ) Statistisches Bundesamt. Fachserie 7, Reihe 6: Durchfuhr im Seeverkehr und Seeumschlag. (pub. by W. Kohlhammer-Verlag GmbH. Abt. Veroeffentlichungen des Statistischen Bundesamtes)
- Germany (Federal Republic, 1949- ) Statistisches Bundesamt. Fachserie 8, Reihe 1: Gueterverkehr der Verkehrszweige. (pub. by W. Kohlhammer-Verlag GmbH. Abt. Veroeffentlichungen des Statistischen Bundesamtes)
- Germany (Federal Republic, 1949- ) Statistisches Bundesamt. Fachserie 8, Reihe 2: Eisenbahnverkehr. (pub. by W. Kohlhammer-Verlag GmbH. Abt. Veroeffentlichungen des Statistischen Bundesamtes)
- Germany (Federal Republic, 1949- ) Statistisches Bundesamt. Fachserie 8, Reihe 3: Strassenverkehr. (pub. by W. Kohlhammer-Verlag GmbH. Abt. Veroeffentlichungen des Statistischen Bundesamtes)
- Germany (Federal Republic, 1949- ) Statistisches Bundesamt. Fachserie 8, Reihe 4: Binneschiffahrt. (pub. by W. Kohlhammer-Verlag GmbH. Abt. Veroeffentlichungen des Statistischen Bundesamtes)
- Germany (Federal Republic, 1949- ) Statistisches Bundesamt. Fachserie 8, Reihe 5: Seeschiffahrt. (pub. by W. Kohlhammer-Verlag GmbH. Abt. Veroeffentlichungen des Statistischen Bundesamtes)
- Germany (Federal Republic, 1949- ) Statistisches Bundesamt. Fachserie 8, Reihe 6: Luftverkehr. (pub. by W. Kohlhammer-Verlag GmbH. Abt. Veroeffentlichungen des Statistischen Bundesamtes)
- Germany (Federal Republic, 1949- ) Statistisches Bundesamt. Fachserie 8, Reihe 33: Strassenverkehrsunfaelle. (pub. by W. Kohlhammer-Verlag GmbH. Abt. Veroeffentlichungen des Statistischen Bundesamtes)

- Germany (Federal Republic, 1949- ) Statistisches Bundesamt. Fachserie 9, Reihe 1: Boden- und Kommunalkreditinstitute. (pub. by W. Kohlhammer-Verlag GmbH. Abt. Veroeffentlichungen des Statistischen Bundesamtes)
- Germany (Federal Republic, 1949- ) Statistisches Bundesamt. Fachserie 9, Reihe 2: Aktienmaerkte. (pub. by W. Kohlhammer-Verlag GmbH. Abt. Veroeffentlichungen des Statistischen Bundesamtes)
- Germany (Federal Republic, 1949- ) Statistisches Bundesamt. Fachserie 10. Rechtspflege. (pub. by W. Kohlhammer-Verlag GmbH. Abt. Veroeffentlichungen des Statistischen Bundesamtes)
- Germany (Federal Republic, 1949- ) Statistisches Bundesamt. Fachserie 11: Bildung und Kultur. (pub. by W. Kohlhammer-Verlag GmbH. Abt. Veroeffentlichungen des Statistischen Bundesamtes)
- Germany (Federal Republic, 1949- ) Statistisches Bundesamt. Fachserie 12, Reihe 1: Ausgewaehlte Zahlen fuer das Gesundheitswesen. (pub. by W. Kohlhammer-Verlag GmbH. Abt. Veroeffentlichungen des Statistischen Bundesamtes)
- Germany (Federal Republic, 1949- ) Statistisches Bundesamt. Fachserie 13, Reihe 2-3: Sozialhilfe; Kriegsopferfuersorge. (pub. by W. Kohlhammer-Verlag GmbH. Abt. Veroeffentlichungen des Statistischen Bundesamtes)
- Germany (Federal Republic, 1949- ) Statistisches Bundesamt. Fachserie 13, Reihe 6: Oeffentliche Jugendhilfe. (pub. by W. Kohlhammer-Verlag GmbH. Abt. Veroeffentlichungen des Statistischen Bundesamtes)
- Germany (Federal Republic, 1949- ) Statistisches Bundesamt. Fachserie 14: Finanzen und Steuern. (pub. by W. Kohlhammer-Verlag GmbH. Abt. Veroeffentlichungen des Statistischen Bundesamtes)
- Germany (Federal Republic, 1949- ) Statistisches Bundesamt. Fachserie 15, Reihe 1: Wirtschaftsrechnungen. (pub. by W. Kohlhammer-Verlag GmbH. Abt. Veroeffentlichungen des Statistischen Bundesamtes)
- Germany (Federal Republic, 1949- ) Statistisches Bundesamt. Fachserie 16, Reihe 2: Arbeitnehmerverdienste in Industrie und Handel. (pub. by W. Kohlhammer-Verlag GmbH. Abt. Veroeffentlichungen des Statistischen Bundesamtes)
- Germany (Federal Republic, 1949- ) Statistisches Bundesamt. Fachserie 16, Reihe 3: Arbeiterverdienste im Handwerk. (pub. by W. Kohlhammer-Verlag GmbH. Abt. Veroeffentlichungen des Statistischen Bundesamtes)
- Germany (Federal Republic, 1949- ) Statistisches Bundesamt. Fachserie 16, Reihe 4: Tarifloehne und Tarifgehaelter. (pub. by W. Kohlhammer-Verlag GmbH. Abt. Veroeffentlichungen des Statistischen Bundesamtes)
- Germany (Federal Republic, 1949- ) Statistisches Bundesamt. Fachserie 17, Reihe 1: Preise und Preisindizes fuer die Land- und Forstwirtschaft. (pub. by W. Kohlhammer-Verlag GmbH. Abt. Veroeffentlichungen des Statistischen Bundesamtes)
- Germany (Federal Republic, 1949- ) Statistisches Bundesamt. Fachserie 17, Reihe 2: Preise und Preisindizes fuer Industrielle Produkte. Erzeugerpreise. (pub. by W. Kohlhammer-Verlag GmbH. Abt. Veroeffentlichungen des Statistischen Bundesamtes)
- Germany (Federal Republic, 1949- ) Statistisches Bundesamt. Fachserie 17, Reuhe 3: Index der Grundstoffpreise. (pub. by W. Kohlhammer-Verlag GmbH. Abt. Veroeffentlichungen des Statistischen Bundesamtes)
- Germany (Federal Republic, 1949- ) Statistisches Bundesamt. Fachserie 17, Reihe 4: Messzahlen fuer Bauleistungspreise und Preisindizes fuer Bauwerke. (pub. by W. Kohlhammer-Verlag GmbH. Abt. Veroeffentlichungen des Statistischen Bundesamtes)
- Germany (Federal Republic, 1949- ) Statistisches Bundesamt. Fachserie 17, Reihe 7: Preise und Preisindizes der Lebenserhaltung. (pub. by W. Kohlhammer-Verlag GmbH. Abt. Veroeffentlichungen des Statistischen Bundesamtes)

- Germany (Federal Republic, 1949- ) Statistisches Bundesamt. Fachserie 17, Reihe 8: Preise und Preisindizes fuer den Ein- und Ausfuhr. (pub. by W. Kohlhammer-Verlag GmbH. Abt. Veroeffentlichungen des Statistischen Bundesamtes)
- Germany (Federal Republic, 1949- ) Statistisches Bundesamt. Fachserie 17, Reihe 10: . Internationaler Vergleich der Preise fuer die Lebenserhaltung. (pub. by W. Kohlhammer-Verlag GmbH. Abt. Veroeffentlichungen des Statistischen Bundesamtes)
- Germany (Federal Republic, 1949- ) Statistisches Bundesamt. Fachserie 18, Reihe 1: Konten und Standardtabellen. (pub. by W. Kohlhammer-Verlag GmbH. Abt. Veroeffentlichungen des Statistischen Bundesamtes)
- Germany (Federal Republic, 1949-) Statistisches Bundesamt Fachserie 19, Reihe 2: Wasserversorgung und Abwasserbeseitigung. (pub. by W. Kohlhammer-Verlag GmbH. Abt. Veroeffentlichungen des Statistischen Bundesamtes)
- Germany (Federal Republic, 1949- ) Statistisches Bundesamt. Laenderberichte. (pub. by W. Kohlhammer-Verlag GmbH. Abt. Veroeffentlichungen des Statistischen Bundesamtes)
- Germany (Federal Republic, 1949- ) Statistisches Bundesamt. Laenderkurzberichte. (pub. by W. Kohlhammer-Verlag GmbH. Abt. Veroeffentlichungen des Statistischen Bundesamtes)
- Germany (Federal Republic, 1949- ) Statistisches Bundesamt. Preise, Loehne, Wirtschaftsrechnungen. Reihe 5: Preise und Preisindices fuer Bauwerke und Bauland. (pub. by W. Kohlhammer-Verlag GmbH. Abt. Veroeffentlichungen des Statistischen Bundesamtes)
- Germany (Federal Republic,1949- ) Statistisches Bundesamt. Preise, Loehne, Wirtschaftsrechnungen. Reihe 14: Arbeiterverdienste in der Landwirtschaft. (pub. by W. Kohlhammer-Verlag GmbH. Abt. Veroeffentlichungen des Statistischen Bundesamtes)
- Germany (Federal Republic, 1949- ) Statistisches Bundesamt. Warenverzeichnis fuer die Aussenhandelsstatistik. (pub. by W. Kohlhammer-Verlag GmbH. Abt. Veroeffentlichungen des Statistischen Bundesamtes)
- Germany (Federal Republic, 1949- ) Statistisches Bundesamt. Zahlenkompass/Statistical Compass/ Boussole des Chiffres/Compas de Cifras. (pub. by W. Kohlhammer-Verlag GmbH. Abt. Veroeffentlichungen des Statistischen Bundesamtes)
- Internationale Monatszahlen. (pub. by W. Kohlhammer-Verlag GmbH. Abt. Veroeffentlichungen des Statistischen Bundesamtes)
- Statistischer Wochendienst. (pub. by W. Kohlhammer-Verlag GmbH. Abt. Veroeffentlichungen des Statistischen Bundesamtes)
- Statistisches Jahrbuch fuer die Bundesrepublik Deutschland. (pub. by W. Kohlhammer-Verlag GmbH. Abt. Veroeffentlichungen des Statistischen Bundesamtes)
- Studies on Statistics. (pub. by W. Kohlhammer-Verlag GmbH. Abt. Veroeffentlichungen des Statistischen Bundesamtes)
- Survey of German Federal Statistics/Apercu de la Statistique Federale Allemande. (pub. by W. Kohlhammer-Verlag GmbH. Abt. Veroeffentlichungen des Statistischen Bundesamtes)
- Wirtschaft und Statistik. (pub. by W. Kohlhammer-Verlag GmbH. Abt. Veroeffentlichungen des Statistischen Bundesamtes)
- Wirtschaftskalender. (pub. by W. Kohlhammer-Verlag GmbH. Abt. Veroeffentlichungen des Statistischen Bundesamtes)

**Gerold und Appel Verlagsgesellschaft**
Neumann-Reichardt-Str. 29-33, 2000 Hamburg 70, W. Germany (B.R.D.)
- Hamburger Abhandlungen. irreg., no. 63, 1974. ISSN 0072-9507 (Universitaet Hamburg. Seminar fuer Oeffentliches Recht und Staatslehre)

**Verlag Dr. H. A. Gerstenberg**
Rathausstr. 18, Postfach 390, 3200 Hildesheim, W. Germany (B. R. D.)
- Studia Irenica. irreg., 1971, no. 19. ISSN 0081-6663

**Gesamtdeutsches Institut**
Bundesallee 216-218, 1000 Berlin 15, W. Germany
(B.R.D.)
- Pressespiegel aus Zeitungen und Zeitschriften der
DDR. fortn.

**Gesamtverband Bueromaschinen-Technik B.V.**
- B T. (pub. by Hans Burghagen Verlag)

**Gesamtverband der Christlichen Gewerkschaften
Deutschlands**
Rheinweg 97, 5300 Bonn, W. Germany (B.R.D.)
- C G D Betriebsraete-Mitteilungen. bi-m. ISSN
0007-8352

**Gesamtverband der Deutschen Geschichts- und
Altertumsvereine**
Nikolausberger Weg 9c, 3400 Goettingen, W.
Germany (B.R.D.)
- Blaetter fuer Deutsche Landesgeschichte; neue
Folge des Korrespondenzblattes. a. ISSN 0006-
4408

**Gesamtverband der Evangelischen Kirchengemeinden
in Marburg**
Bienenweg 27, Marbach b. Marburg, W. Germany
(B.R.D.)
- Kirche in Marburg; Mitteilungen der
Evangelischen und Katholischen Gemeinden. m.
(Co-Sponsor: Katholische Pfarrgemeinden in
Marburg-Stadt)

**Gesamtverband der Kraftfahrzeug- Vermieter
Deutschlands e.V.**
- Der Kraftfahrzeugvermieter. (pub. by Verlag
Heinrich Vogel)

**Gesamtverband der Nichtsesshaftenhilfe**
Postfach, 4800 Bielefeld, W. Germany (B. R. D.)
- Gefaehrdetenhilfe. q. ISSN 0016-5794

**Gesamtverband Deutscher Musikfachgeschaefte e.V.**
- Musikhandel. (pub. by Musikhandel
Verlagsgesellschaft mbH)

**Gesamtverband Deutscher Nervenaerzte**
- Archiv fuer Psychiatrie und Nervenkrankheiten.
(pub. by Springer-Verlag US)

**Gesamtverband Deutscher Realschullehrer**
- Die Realschule. (pub. by Hermann Schroedel
Verlag (Hannover))

**Gesamtverband Kunststoffverarbeitende Industrie e.V.**
Niddastr. 44, 6000 Frankfurt, W. Germany (B.R.D.)
- K-Mitteilungen. m. ISSN 0451-1646

**Gesamtverband Neuzeitliche Textilpflege- Betriebe
Deutschlands e.V.**
- Waescherei- und Reinigungs- Praxis. (pub. by
Westdeutsche Verlagsanstalt GmbH)

**Geschichtsverein fuer Goettingen und Umgebung**
- Goettinger Jahrbuch. (pub. by Reise Verlag)

**Gesellschaft Boden und Gesundheit**
7183 Langenburg, W. Germany (B.R.D.)
- Boden und Gesundheit; Schriftenfolge fuer
angewandte Oekologie. q. ISSN 0006-5455

**Gesellschaft der Bibliophilen**
Merckstr. 32, 6100 Darmstadt, W. Germany
(B.R.D.)
- Imprimatur; Jahrbuch fuer Buecherfreunde. Neue
Folge. a. ISSN 0073-5620

**Gesellschaft der Circusfreunde in Deutschland e.V.**
Klosterhof 10, 2308 Preetz, W. Germany (B.R.D.)
- Die Circuszeitung/Circus Magazine. m.

**Gesellschaft der Orgelfreunde e.V.**
- Acta Organologica. (pub. by Verlag Merseburger
Berlin GmbH)
- Ars Organi. (pub. by Verlag Merseburger Berlin
GmbH)

**Gesellschaft der Staudenfreunde e.V.**
Justinus-Kerner-Str. 11, 7250 Leonberg, W.
Germany (B.R.D.)
- Staudengarten. q.

**Gesellschaft Deutscher Chemiker**
- Angewandte Chemie. (pub. by Verlag Chemie
International, Inc. US)
- Chemie in Unserer Zeit. (pub. by Verlag Chemie
International, Inc. US)
- Chemie-Ingenieur-Technik. (pub. by Verlag
Chemie International, Inc. US)
- Chemische Berichte. (pub. by Verlag Chemie
International, Inc. US)
- Chemischer Informationsdienst. (pub. by Verlag
Chemie International, Inc. US)
- Farbe und Lack. (pub. by Curt R. Vincentz
Verlag)
- Nachrichten aus Chemie, Technik und
Laboratorium. (pub. by Verlag Chemie
International, Inc. US)
- Tenside - Detergents. (pub. by Carl Hanser
Verlag)

**Gesellschaft Deutscher Chemiker. Fachgruppe
Analytische Chemie**
- Fresenius' Zeitschrift fuer Analytische Chemie.
(pub. by Springer-Verlag US)

**Gesellschaft Deutscher Chemiker. Fachgruppe
Wasserchemie**
- Vom Wasser. (pub. by Verlag Chemie
International, Inc. US)
- Zeitschrift fuer Wasser- und Abwasserforschung.
(pub. by Wasser- und Abwasser-Forschung
Verlagsgesellschaft MbH und Co.)

**Gesellschaft Deutscher Metallhuetten und Bergleute
e.V.**
- Erzmetall. (pub. by Dr. Riederer Verlag GmbH)

**Gesellschaft Deutscher Naturforscher und Aerzte**
- Klinische Wochenschrift. (pub. by Springer-Verlag
US)

**Gesellschaft fuer Agrargeschichte und Agrarsoziologie**
- Zeitschrift fuer Agrargeschichte und
Agrarsoziologie. (pub. by Deutsche
Landwirtschafts-Gesellschaft-Verlags-GmbH)

**Gesellschaft fuer angewandte Mathematik und
Mechanik**
- Ingenieur-Archiv. (pub. by Springer-Verlag US)

**Gesellschaft fuer Angewandtes Marketing mbH**
Parkallee 21, 2000 Hamburg 13, W. Germany
(B.R.D.)
- Marketing Journal. bi-m. ISSN 0025-3774

**Gesellschaft fuer Arbeitswissenschaft e. V.**
- Zeitschrift fuer Arbeitswissenschaft. (pub. by
Verlag Dr. Otto Schmidt KG)

**Gesellschaft fuer Bedrohte Voelker**
Parkallee 18, 2000 Hamburg 13, W. Germany
(B.R.D.)
- Pogrom. m.

**Gesellschaft fuer Bibliothekswesen und
Dokumentation des Landbaues**
Paracelsusstrasse 2, 7000 Stuttgart 70, W. Germany
(B.R.D.)
- Gesellschaft fuer Bibliothekswesen und
Dokumentation des Landbaues. Mitteilungen. 2-3
per yr. ISSN 0433-860X

**Gesellschaft fuer Deutsch-Sowjetische Freundschaft
Westberlin**
Kurfuerstendamm 72, 1000 Berlin 31, W. Germany
(B.R.D.)
- D S F-Journal. q. ISSN 0011-5142

**Gesellschaft fuer deutsche Postgeschichte**
Schaumainkai 53, 6000 Frankfurt, W. Germany
(B.R.D.)
- Archiv fuer deutsche Postgeschichte. s-a. ISSN
0003-8989

**Gesellschaft fuer Deutsche Sprache**
Postfach 2669, 6200 Wiesbaden 1, W. Germany
(B.R.D.)
- Muttersprache; Zeitschrift zur Pflege und
Erforschung der deutschen Sprache. irreg. ISSN
0027-514X
- Sprachdienst. m. ISSN 0038-8459

**Gesellschaft fuer die Gesamte Kriminologie**
- Monatsschrift fuer Kriminologie und
Strafrechtsreform. (pub. by Carl Heymanns Verlag
KG)

**Gesellschaft fuer die Geschichte und Bibliographie des
Brauwesens**
Seestr. 13, 1000 Berlin 65, W. Germany (B.R.D.)
- Gesellschaft fuer die Geschichte und Bibliographie
des Brauwesens. Jahrbuch. a. ISSN 0072-422X

**Gesellschaft fuer Dokumentation Bodenmechanik und
Grundbau e.V.**
Kronprinzenstr. 35a, 4300 Essen, W. Germany
(B.R.D.)
- Dokumentation fuer Bodenmechanik - Grundbau -
Felsmechanik - Ingenieurgeologie. m. ISSN 0012-
5105

**Gesellschaft fuer Erdkunde zu Berlin**
Arno-Holz-Str. 14, 1000 Berlin 41, W. Germany
(B.R.D.)
- Die Erde. 4 per yr. ISSN 0013-9998

**Gesellschaft fuer Familienkunde in Franken e.V.**
Archivstr. 17, 8500 Nuernberg, W. Germany
(B.R.D.)
- Blaetter fuer Fraenkische Familienkunde. 2 per yr.
ISSN 0006-4424

**Gesellschaft fuer Historische Waffen- und
Kostuemkunde**
- Waffen- und Kostumkunde. (pub. by Deutscher
Kunstverlag GmbH)

**Gesellschaft fuer Internationale Geldgeschichte**
Postfach 501177, 6000 Frankfurt 50, W. Germany
(B.R.D.)
- Geldgeschichtliche Nachrichten. s-m. ISSN 0435-
1835

**Gesellschaft fuer Internationale Sprache e.V.**
Schaumanns Kamp 126, 2057 Reinbek, W.
Germany (B.R.D.)
- Interlinguistika Informa Servo. q. ISSN 0020-5540

**Gesellschaft fuer Kernforschung mbH**
Weberstr. 5, Postfach 3640, 7500 Karlsruhe, W.
Germany (B.R.D.)
- Gesellschaft fuer Kernforschung. Bericht ueber
Forschungs- und Entwicklungsarbeiten. irreg.

**Gesellschaft fuer Konservative Publizistik e.V.**
- Konservativ Heute. (pub. by Verlag fuer
Konservative Publizistik)

**Gesellschaft fuer Konsum-, Markt- und
Absatzforschung**
- Jahrbuch der Absatz - und Verbrauchsforschung.
(pub. by Duncker und Humblot)

**Gesellschaft fuer Laender- und Voelkerkunde**
- Die Karawane. (pub. by Karawane Verlag)

**Gesellschaft fuer Mittelrheinische Kirchengeschichte**
Jesuitenstr. 13, 5500 Trier, W. Germany (B.R.D.
- Archiv fuer Mittelrheinische Kirchengeschichte. a.
ISSN 0066-6432

**Gesellschaft fuer Musikforschung**
- Die Musikforschung. (pub. by Baerenreiter-Verlag)

**Gesellschaft fuer Naturkunde in Wuerttemberg**
Schloss Rosenstein, 7000 Stuttgart 1, W. Germany
(B.R.D.)
- Gesellschaft fuer Naturkunde in Wuerttemberg.
Jahreshefte. a. ISSN 0084-3059

**Gesellschaft fuer Nuclear-Medizin**
- Nuclear-Medizin/Nuclear Medicine/Medecine
Nucleaire. (pub. by F. K. Schattauer Verlag)

**Gesellschaft fuer Oeffentliche Wirtschaft und
Gemeinwirtschaft e.V.**
Bleibtreustr. 24, 1000 Berlin 15, W. Germany
(B.R.D.)
- Oeffentliche Wirtschaft und Gemeinwirtschaft. q.

**Gesellschaft fuer Organisation e.V.**
- Zeitschrift fuer Organisation. (pub. by
Betriebswirtschaftlicher Verlag Dr. Th. Gabler
KG)

**Gesellschaft fuer Pommersche Geschichte,
Altertumskunde und Kunst**
- Baltische Studien. (pub. by Christoph von der
Ropp)

**Gesellschaft fuer Praktische Psychologie e.V**
Haus Heidberg, 2073 Luetjensee, W. Germany (B.R.D)
- Praktische Psychologie; Berufsbegleitende Studienhefte fuer Leistungssteigerung, Menschenkunde und Persoenlichkeitsbildung. bi-m. ISSN 0032-6798

**Gesellschaft fuer Rechtsvergleichung**
- Arbeiten zur Rechtsvergleichung. (pub. by Alfred Metzner Verlag GmbH)
- Auslaendische Aktiengesetze. (pub. by Alfred Metzner Verlag GmbH)

**Gesellschaft fuer Regionalforschung**
Spanische Allee 95E, 1000 Berlin 38, W. Germany (B.R.D.)
- Gesellschaft fuer Regionalforschung. Seminarberichte. irreg., no.10,1974.

**Gesellschaft fuer Schleswig-Holsteinische Geschichte**
- Gesellschaft fuer Schleswig-Holsteinische Geschichte. Zeitschrift. (pub. by Karl Wachholtz Verlag)
- Nordelbingen. (pub. by Westholsteinische Verlagsanstalt Boyens und Co.)

**Gesellschaft fuer Sozialen Fortschritt E.V., Bonn**
- Sozialer Fortschritt. (pub. by Duncker und Humblot)

**Gesellschaft fuer Tribologie und Schmierungstechnik**
- Schmiertechnik und Tribologie. (pub. by Curt R. Vincentz Verlag)

**Gesellschaft fuer Uebernationale Zusammenarbeit e.V.**
Hohenstaufenring 11, 5000 Cologne, W. Germany (B.R.D.)
- Dokumente; Zeitschrift fuer uebernationale Zusammenarbeit. s-a. ISSN 0012-5172

**Gesellschaft fuer Unternehmungsgeschichte**
- Zeitschrift fuer Unternehmungsgeschichte. (pub. by Franz Steiner Verlag GmbH)

**Gesellschaft fuer Voelkerkunde**
- Ethnologia. (pub. by E. J. Brill GmbH)

**Gesellschaft fuer Wehrkunde e.V.**
- Europaeische Wehrkunde. (pub. by Verlag Europaeische Wehrkunde GmbH)

**Gesellschaft fuer Wirtschafts- und Sozialwissenschaften**
- German Economic Review. (pub. by Wissenschaftliche Verlagsgesellschaft mbH)
- Zeitschrift fuer Wirtschafts- und Sozialwissenschaften. (pub. by Duncker und Humblot)

**Gesellschaft fuer Wissenschaftliche Symbolforschung**
- Symbolon. (pub. by Wienand Verlag KG)

**Gesellschaft fuer Zukunftsfragen e.V.**
Giesebrechtstr. 15, 1000 Berlin 12, W. Germany (B. R. D.)
- Analysen und Prognosen ueber die Welt von Morgen. bi-m. ISSN 0044-8192

**Gesellschaft Naturforschender Freunde zu Berlin**
- Gesellschaft Naturforschender Freunde zu Berlin. Sitzungsberichte. Neue Folge. (pub. by Duncker und Humblot)

**Gesellschaft zur Foerderung der Inneren Kolonisation (GFK)**
- K O - Innere Kolonisation - Land und Gemeinde. (pub. by Landschriften-Verlag GmbH)

**Gesellschaft zur Foerderung des New Orleans Jazz**
Hochst 2a, 6230 Frankfurt, W. Germany (B.R.D.)
- Hot Jazz. bi-m.

**Gesellschaft zur Foerderung Tiefenpsychologischer und Psychotherapeutischer Forschung und Weiterbildung**
- Gesellschaft zur Foerderung Tiefenpsychologischer und Psychotherapeutischer Forschung und Weiterbildung, Munich. Beitraege und Berichte. (pub. by Vandenhoeck und Ruprecht)

**Gesellschaft zur Pflege der Maerchengutes der Europaeischen Voelker**
- Maerchen der Europaeischen Voelker. (pub. by Aschendorffsche Verlagsbuchhandlung)

**Gewerkschaft der Eisenbahner Deutschlands**
Beethovenstr. 16-18, 6000 Frankfurt, W. Germany (B.R.D.)
- Eisenbahn-technische Praxis. q. ISSN 0013-2837

**Gewerkschaft der Polizei**
- Deutsche Polizei. (pub. by Verlagsanstalt Deutsche Polizei GmbH)

**Gewerkschaft Erziehung und Wissenschaft**
- Die Deutsch Schule. (pub. by Hermann Schroedel Verlag KG (Darmstadt))
- Erziehung und Wissenschaft. (pub. by Stamm-Verlag GmbH)
- Hamburger Lehrerzeitung. (pub. by Verlag Erziehung und Wissenschaft)
- Informationen Jugendliteratur und Medien. (pub. by Hermann Schroedel Verlag KG (Hannover))

**Gewerkschaft Erziehung und Wissenschaft. Landesverband Bayern**
- Die Demokratische Schule. (pub. by Elwi-Verlag)

**Gewerkschaft Erziehung und Wissenschaft. Landesverband Nordrhein-Westfalen**
- Neue Deutsche Schule. (pub. by Neue Deutsche Schule Verlagsgesellschaft MbH)

**Gewerkschaft Gartenbau, Land- und Forstwirtschaft**
- Forstliche Mitteilungen. (pub. by Saemann Verlagsgesellschaft mbH)

**Gewerkschaft Handel, Banken und Versicherungen**
Tersteegenstr. 30, 4000 Duesseldorf 30, W. Germany (B.R.D.)
- Ausblick. m. ISSN 0004-8119

**Gewerkschaft Holz und Kunststoff**
Sonnenstr. 14, 4000 Duesseldorf, W. Germany (B.R.D.)
- Holzarbeiter-Zeitung. m. ISSN 0018-3806

**Gewerkschaft Leder**
Kanzleistr. 20, 7000 Stuttgart 1, W. Germany (B.R.D.)
- Leder Echo. m. ISSN 0024-0184

**Gewerkschaft Oeffentliche Dienste, Transport und Verkehr. Hauptabteilung Polizei**
- Die Polizei im Lande Berlin. (pub. by Verlagsanstalt Courier GmbH)

**Neuer Deutscher Gewerkschafts-Verlag GmbH**
Gaensemarkt 29-31, Postfach 288, 4300 Essen 1, W. Germany (B.R.D.)
- D G Z. (Deutsche Gewerkschafts-Zeitung) m. ISSN 0011-4928

**Gebr. Giehrl**
Ingoldstaedter Str. 63, 8000 Munich 46, W. Germany (B.R.D.)
- D T V -Intern. m. (Deutscher Textilreinigungs-Verband e.V.)

**Wolfgang Gielow Verlag**
Theatinerstr. 35, 8000 Munich 2, W. Germany (B. R. D.)
- Information G. bi-m. ISSN 0046-9343

**Gieseking-Verlag**
Deckerstr. 2, Postfach 42, 4813 Bielefeld-Bethel, W. Germany (B.R.D.)
- Industriegesellschaft und Recht. irreg., vol. 5, 1975.
- Rechtspflege Jahrbuch. a. ISSN 0080-018X
- Zeitschrift fuer das gesamte Familienrecht; Ehe und Familie im privaten und oeffentlichen Recht. m. ISSN 0044-2410

**Fachverlag Giesserei-Erfahrungsaustausch**
Kleiststr. 10, 6805 Heddesheim, W. Germany (B.R.D.)
- Giesserei-Erfahrungsaustausch. m. ISSN 0016-9773

**Giesserei-Verlag GmbH**
Breite Str. 27, Postfach 3503, 4000 Duesseldorf 1, W. Germany (B.R.D.)
- Giesserei; Zeitschrift fuer das gesamte Giessereiwesen. s-m. ISSN 0016-9765 (Verein Deutscher Giessereifachleute e.V.)
- Giessereiforschung. q. ISSN 0046-5933 (Verein Deutscher Giessereifachleute e.V.)
- Gisserei-Literaturschau. s-m.

**Verlag W. Girardet**
Girardetstr. 2, Postfach 9, 4300 Essen, W. Germany (B. R. D.)
- Cooperation Ost-West. 6 per yr.
- Elektro-Anzeiger; Zeitschrift fuer Elektrotechnik und Elektronik. 24 per yr. ISSN 0013-5518
- Elektronik-Anzeiger. m. ISSN 0013-5666
- Feld und Wald. w. ISSN 0014-9748
- Haustechnik. 14 per yr.
- Industrie-Anzeiger; Eisen- und Metallverarbeitung, Anzeiger fuer Maschinenwesen, Kunststofftechnologie, Zeitschrift fuer die europaeische technische Industrie. s-w. ISSN 0019-9036 (Wirtschaftsverband Eisen, Blech und Metall Verarbeitende Industrie)

**Verlag Dieter Gitzel**
Groetzinger Str. 61, 7500 Karlsruhe 41, W. Germany (B.R.D.)
- Format; Zeitschrift fuer verbale und visuelle Kommunikation. bi-m. ISSN 0015-7759

**Globus-Verlagsanstalt**
Ellerstr. 157, 4000 Duesseldorf, W. Germany (B.R.D.)
- Polizei und Verkehrsjournal; Zeitschrift fuer Verkehrsproblematik und Verkehrssicherheit. m. ISSN 0048-4776

**Glock und Lutz Verlag**
Feldgasse 38, 8500 Nuernberg, W. Germany (B.R.D.)
- Die Besinnung. q.

**Verlag Glueckauf GmbH**
Frillendorfer Str. 351, Postfach 1794, 4300 Essen 1, W. Germany (B.R.D.)
- Glueckauf; Zeitschrift fuer Technik und Wirtschaft des Bergbaus. fortn. ISSN 0017-1379
- Glueckauf-Forschungshefte; Zeitschrift zur Verbreitung von Forschungsergebnissen im Bergbau. 6 per yr. ISSN 0017-1387
- Grubensicherheit; Zeitschrift fuer Unfallverhuetung und Grubensicherheitswesen. m. ISSN 0017-4858 (Nordrhein-Westfalen. Landesoberbergamt)
- Jahrbuch fuer Bergbau, Energie, Mineraloel und Chemie. a. ISSN 0075-255X

**Dr. Klaus Goebel**
Kiebitzweg 22, 8013 Harr, W. Germany (B.R.D.)
- Christophorus. bi-m. ISSN 0009-5818

**Verlag Goecke und Evers**
Duererstr. 13, 4150 Krefeld, W. Germany (B.R.D.)
- Entomologische Blaetter fuer Biologie und Systematik der Kaefer. 3 per yr. ISSN 0013-8835

**Goeller-Verlag**
Hauptstr. 4, Postfach 240, 7570 Baden-Baden, W. Germany (B.R.D.)
- Buerotechnik Automation und Organisation. m.
- Fachzeitung fuer den Buerofachhandel ueber Papier, Buerobedarf, Schreibwaren. s-m. (Verband Papier, Buerobedarf, Schreibwaren)

**Verlag Carl Th. Goerg KG**
Am Sorgfeld 110, 2000 Hamburg 55, W. Germany (B. R. D.)
- A F Z. (Allgemeine Fischwirtschaftszeitung) fortn. ISSN 0001-1258 (Fischwirtschaftliches Marketing-Institut)

**Goerres-Gesellschaft**
- Grenzfragen. (pub. by Karl Alber GmbH)
- Historisches Jahrbuch. (pub. by Karl Alber GmbH)
- Literaturwissenschaftliches Jahrbuch. Neue Folge. (pub. by Duncker und Humblot)
- Philosophisches Jahrbuch. (pub. by Karl Alber GmbH)
- Portugiesische Forschungen der Goerresgesellschaft. Reihe 1: Aufsaetze zur Portugiesischen Kulturgeschichte. (pub. by Aschendorffsche Verlagsbuchhandlung)
- Portugiesische Forschungen der Goerresgesellschaft. Reihe 2: Monographien. (pub. by Aschendorffsche Verlagsbuchhandlung)
- Spanische Forschungen der Goerresgesellschaft. Reihe 1: Gesammelte Aufsaetze zur Kulturgeschichte Spaniens. (pub. by Aschendorffsche Verlagsbuchhandlung)
- Spanische Forschungen der Goerresgesellschaft. Reihe 2: Monographien. (pub. by Aschendorffsche Verlagsbuchhandlung)
- Zeitschrift fuer Klinische Psychologie und Psychotherapie. (pub. by Karl Alber GmbH)

**Goethe-Institut, Munich**
- Zielsprache Deutsch. (pub. by Max Hueber Verlag)

**Goethe-Institut zur Pflege Deutscher Sprache und Kultur im Ausland**
Lenbachplatz 3, 8000 Munich 2, W. Germany (B.R.D.)
- Goethe-Institut zur Pflege Deutscher Sprache und Kultur im Ausland. Jahrbuch. a. ISSN 0072-4858

**Goettinger Arbeitskreis e.V.**
Calswostr. 54, 3400 Goettingen, W. Germany (B.R.D.)
- Archiv. w. ISSN 0003-8857
- Expellee Press Service; news items & comments on the problems of the uprooted millions & their home countries behind the Iron Curtain. w. ISSN 0014-4746

**Goettinger Druckerei- und Verlagsgesellschaft mbH**
Maschmuehlenweg 8-10, Postfach 206, 3400 Goettingen, W. Germany (B.R.D.)
- Briefmarken - Spiegel; internationale Filatelie. m. ISSN 0007-0041
- Briefmarken-Spiegel. m. ISSN 0007-005X

**Wilhelm Goldmann Verlag GmbH**
Neumarkterstr. 22, 8000 Munich 80, W. Germany (B.R.D.)
- Goldmanns Mitteilungen fuer den Buchhandel. m. ISSN 0017-1670

**Verlag Erich Goltze KG**
Stresemannstr. 28, 3400 Goettingen, W. Germany (B.R.D.)
- Goettinger Geographische Abhandlungen. 2 per yr. (Universitaet Goettingen. Geographisches Institut)

**Gong Verlag**
Luitpoldstr. 5, 8500 Nuernberg, W. Germany (B.R.D.)
- Gong; die Fernsehzeitschrift fuer die schoenen Stunden daheim. w. ISSN 0017-1999 (Verband der Rundfunkhoerer und Fernsehteilnehmer in Bayern e.V.)

**Verlag Gordian-Max Rieck GmbH**
Sandtorkai 4, 2000 Hamburg 11, W. Germany (B.R.D.)
- Kaffee und Tee Markt. s-m. ISSN 0022-7609

**Gottfried-Wilhelm-Leibniz Gesellschaft e.V.**
- Studia Leibnitiana. (pub. by Franz Steiner Verlag GmbH)

**Gottlieb Duttweiler Institute for Economic & Social Studies**
- Brennpunkte. (pub. by Deutsche Verlagsanstalt GmbH)

**Verlag Max Gottschalk**
Bergedorfer Str. 118, 2050 Hamburg 80, W. Germany (B.R.D.)
- Bille-Anzeigen-Rundschau. w. ISSN 0006-2529

**Govi-Verlag GmbH**
Beethovenplatz 1-3, Postfach 970108, 6000 Frankfurt 97, W. Germany (B. R. D.)
- Pharmazeutische Zeitung. w. ISSN 0031-7136 (Arbeitsgemeinschaft der Berufsvertretungen Deutscher Apotheker)

**Grabert-Verlag**
Am Apfelberg 18, 7400 Tuebingen, W. Germany (B. R. D.)
- Deutschland in Geschichte und Gegenwart. q. (Institut fuer Deutsche Nachkriegsgeschichte)

**Grafenwerther Musen Werk- und Foerderkreis fuer Literatur, Kunst und Wissenschaft e.V.**
- Jonas. (pub. by Peter Hanstein Verlag GmbH)

**Verlag G. Grandpierre**
Obergasse 16, Postfach 1360, 6270 Idstein, W. Germany (B.R.D.)
- Unser Pferd; Fachzeitschrift fuer Pferdesport und Pferdezucht in Hessen. m.

**Graphikum**
Allgaeuerstr. 27, 8000 Munich 71, W. Germany (B.R.D.)
- Dichter und Zeichner. irreg., no. 13, 1974. ISSN 0070-4695

**Willi Gressner Verlag**
Deglerstr. 1a, Postfach 1427, 7570 Baden- Baden, W. Germany (B. R. D.)
- Der Fachberater; Monatszeitschrift fuer den Papier-Buerobedarfs und Schreibwaren-Einzelhandel. m. ISSN 0014-6307

**Greven Verlag Koeln**
Neue Weyerstr. 1-3, 5000 Cologne 1, W. Germany (B.R.D.)
- Bibliothekar-Lehrinstitut des Landes Nordrhein-Westfalen. Arbeiten aus dem B L I. irreg. ISSN 0069-5858
- Bibliothekar-Lehrinstitut des Landes Nordrhein-Westfalen. Bibliographische Hefte. irreg. ISSN 0069-5866

**Julius Groos Verlag**
Hertzstr. 6, Postfach 102423, 6900 Heidelberg 1, W. Germany (B. R. D.)
- Deutsch Lernen. q. ISSN 0341-3675 (Sprachverband Deutsch fuer Auslaendische Arbeitnehmer e.V.)
- Hoergeschaedigten-Paedagogik. q. (Bund Deutscher Taubstummenlehrer)
- I R A L. (International Review of Applied Linguistics in Language Teaching.) q. ISSN 0019-042X
- Journal of Literary Semantics. s-a.

**Verlag Grossbild - Technik GmbH**
Rupert- Mayer- Str. 45, 8000 Munich 70, W. Germany (B. R. D.)
- International Photo Technik. q. ISSN 0020-8280

**Grosse Verlag GmbH**
Kurfuerstendamm 152, 1000 Berlin 31, W. Germany (B.R.D.)
- Andrologia. q. ISSN 0303-4569 (Comite Internacional de Andrologia)
- Mykosen. m. ISSN 0027-5557
- Der Sozialversicherungs-Beamte und -Angestellte. s-m. ISSN 0301-0481 (Vereinigung Suedwestdeutscher Dermatologen)

**G. Grote'sche Verlagsbuchhandlung KG**
Luxemburger Str. 72, 5000 Cologne 1, W. Germany (B.R.D.)
- Der Sozialversicherungs-Beamte und -Angestellte bsba. m. (Bund der Sozialversicherungs-Beamten und -Angestellten)

**G. Grote'sche Verlagsbuchhandlung KG (Stuttgart)**
Urbanstr. 12-16, Postfach 747, 7000 Stuttgart 1, W. Germany (B.R.D.)
- Stiftung Preussische Kulturbesitz. Jahrbuch. a. ISSN 0081-5578

**Verlag Dr. Carl Grueb**
Eggstr. 11, 7800 Freiburg, W. Germany (B.R.D.)
- Nachrichtenblatt fuer die Buersten- und Pinselindustrie. bi-m. ISSN 0027-7487

**Matthias Gruenewald Verlag**
Bischofsplatz 6, 6500 Mainz, W. Germany (B.R.D.)
- Diakonia; internationale Zeitschrift fuer praktische Theologie. bi-m. ISSN 0012-1967

**Grundig AG**
Fuerth (Bayern), W. Germany (B.R.D.)
- Grundig Technische Informationen; Zeitschrift fuer Elektronic, Radio-, Fernseh- und Tonbandtechnik. bi-m. ISSN 0017-4912

**Gruner und Jahr GmbH und Co.**
Warburgstr. 50, 2000 Hamburg 36, W. Germany (B.R.D.)
- Capital; das deutsche Wirtschaftsmagazin. m. ISSN 0008-5847
- Eltern mit Schule. m.
- Essen und Trinken. w.
- Schoener Wohnen. m.
- Sesamstrasse. m.
- Stern. w. ISSN 0039-1239

**Gruppe Internationaler Marxisten. Deutsche Sektion der IV. Internationale**
- Was Tun. (pub. by Internationale Sozialistische Publikationen GmbH)

**Walter de Gruyter und Co.**
Genthiner Str. 13, 1000 Berlin 30, W. Germany (B.R.D.)
   (162 Fifth Ave., New York, N.Y. 10010)
- Antike und Abendland; Beitraege zum Verstaendnis der Griechen und Roemer und ihres Nachlebens. 1 vol. of 2 nos. per year. ISSN 0003-5696
- Arcadia; Zeitschrift fuer vergleichende Literaturwissenschaft. 3 per yr. ISSN 0003-7982
- Archaeologische Bibliographie. irreg.
- Archaeologischer Anzeiger. q. ISSN 0003-8105 (Deutsches Archaeologisches Institut)
- Archiv fuer Geschichte der Philosophie. 3 per yr. ISSN 0003-9101
- Berliner Historische Kommission. Veroeffentlichungen. irreg., vol. 47, 1976. ISSN 0067-6071
- Botanica Marina; internationale Zeitschrift zur Erforschung und Auswertung von Meeresalgen. 8 per yr. ISSN 0006-8055
- Fabula; Zeitschrift fuer Erzaehlforschung/Journal of Folktale Studies/Revue des Etudes sur le Conte Populaire. 2 per yr. ISSN 0014-6242
- Fruehmittelalterliche Studien; Jahrbuch. a. ISSN 0071-9706 (Universitaet Muenster. Institut fuer Fruehmittelalterforschung)
- Germania. a. ISSN 0016-8874 (Deutsches Archaeologisches Institut. Roemisch-Germanische Kommission)
- Hoppe-Seyler's Zeitschrift fuer Physiologische Chemie. m. ISSN 0018-4888
- I P E K. (Jahrbuch fuer Praehistorische und Ethnographische Kunst)/Annual Review of Prehistoric and Ethnographical Art. irreg., vol. 24, 1976. ISSN 0075-0468 (Deutsche Forschungsgemeinschaft)
- Indogermanische Forschungen; Zeitschrift fuer Indogermanistik und allgemeine Sprachwissenschaft. irreg., vol. 81, 1976. ISSN 0019-7262
- Internationales Jahrbuch der Erwachsenenbildung/International Yearbook of Adult Education. a. ISSN 0074-9818
- Internationales Jahrbuch fuer die Nietzsche-Forschung. irreg. vol. 5, 1976.
- Journal fuer die Reine und Angewandte Mathematik. irreg., vol. 289, 1977. ISSN 0075-4102
- Der Islam; Zeitschrift fuer Geschichte und Kultur des islamischen Orients. 2 per yr. ISSN 0021-1818
- Journal of Non-Equilibrium Thermodynamics. 4 per yr.
- Journal of Perinatal Medicine. 6 per yr. ISSN 0300-5577
- Juristische Rundschau. m. ISSN 0022-6920
- Kadmos; Zeitschrift fuer vor- und fruehgriechische Epigraphik. 2 per yr. ISSN 0022-7498
- Kant-Studien. 4 per yr. ISSN 0022-8877 (Kant-Gesellschaft)
- Minerva; Internationales Verzeichnis Wissenschaftlicher Institutionen. irreg.
- Miscellanea Mediaevalia. irreg, vol. 10, 1976. (Universitaet zu Koeln. Thomas-Institut)
- Neue Zeitschrift fuer Systematische Theologie und Religionsphilosophie. 3 per yr. ISSN 0028-3517
- Praehistorische Zeitschrift. 2 per yr. ISSN 0079-4848
- Romanistisches Jahrbuch. irreg., vol. 26, 1976. ISSN 0080-3898 (Universitaet Hamburg. Ibero-Amerikanisches Forschungsinstitut)
- Saalburg-Jahrbuch. a. ISSN 0080-5157 (Saalburg-Museum)
- Theoretical Linguistics. 3 per yr. ISSN 0301-4428
- Tierreich; eine Zusammenstellung und Kennzeichnung der rezenten Tierformen. irreg. ISSN 0040-7305
- Zeitschrift fuer Assyriologie und Vorderasiatische Archaeologie. 2 per yr., ISSN 0084-5299
- Zeitschrift fuer die alttestamentliche Wissenschaft. 3 per yr. ISSN 0044-2526
- Zeitschrift fuer die Alttestamentliche Wissenschaft. Beihefte. irreg., no. 147, 1976.
- Zeitschrift fuer die gesamte Strafrechtswissenschaft. 4 per yr. ISSN 0084-5310
- Zeitschrift fuer die neutestamentliche Wissenschaft und die Kunde der Aelteren Kirche. 2 per yr. ISSN 0044-2615
- Zeitschrift fuer germanistische Linguistik. 3 per yr.
- Zeitschrift fuer klinische Chemie und klinische Biochemie/Journal of Clinical Chemistry and Clinical Biochemistry. m. ISSN 0044-2933 (Deutsche Gesellschaft fuer Klinische Chemie)
- Zeitschrift fuer Unternehmens- und Gesellschaftsrecht. 4 per yr.

**Guentter-Staib Verlag**
Bismarckring 49, Postfach 180, 7950 Biberach, W. Germany (B.R.D.)
- Wochenblatt fuer Papierfabrikation; Fachzeitschrift fuer die Papier-, Pappen- und Zellstoff-industrie. s-m. ISSN 0043-7131 (Co-sponsors: Akademischer Papieringenieur-Verein e.V.; Vereinigter Papierfachverband Munchen e.V.; Papiermacher-Berufsgenossenschaft Mainz)

**Guetersloher Verlagshaus Gerd Mohn**
Koenigstr. 23, Postfach 2368, 4830 Guetersloh, W.
Germany (B.R.D.)
- Archiv fuer Reformationsgeschichte/Archive for
  Reformation History; Internatonale Zeitschrift zur
  Erforschung der Reformation und ihrer
  Weltwirkungen. s-a. ISSN 0003-9381 (Verein fuer
  Reformations Geschichte) (Co-Sponsor: American
  Society for Reformation Research)
- Geschichte der Ethik. irreg. ISSN 0072-4173
- Kirchliches Jahrbuch fuer die Evangelische Kirche
  in Deutschland. a. ISSN 0075-6210
- Kunst und Kirche; Oekumenische Zeitschrift fuer
  Architektur und Kunst. q. ISSN 0023-5431
  (Arbeitsausschuss des Evangelischen
  Kirchenbautages und Dioezesan-Kunstvereins,
  Linz)
- Missionswissenschaftliche Forschungen. irreg.
  ISSN 0076-9428
- Sozialpaedagogik. bi-m. ISSN 0038-6189
- Studien zu Religion, Geschichte und
  Geisteswissenschaften. irreg. ISSN 0081-718X
- Studien zur Evangelischen Ethik. irreg. ISSN
  0081-7260
- Texte zur Kirchen- und Theologiegeschichte. irreg.
  ISSN 0082-3597
- Zeitschrift fuer Evangelische Ethik. bi-m. ISSN
  0044-2674
- Zeitwende; wissenschaft - theologie - literatur. bi-
  m.

**Gustav-Adolph-Werk**
Olgastr. 8, 3500 Kassel 1, W. Germany (B.R.D.)
- Gustav-Adolf-Blatt. 1-4 per yr. ISSN 0017-5730

**Gustav Werner Stiftung**
Ringelbachstr. 277, 7410 Reutlingen, W. Germany
(B.R.D.)
- Bruderhaus. s-a.

**Gutenberg-Gesellschaft**
Liebfrauenplatz 5, 6500 Mainz, W. Germany
(B.R.D.)
- Gutenberg-Jahrbuch. a. ISSN 0072-9094

**H W W A - Institut fuer Wirtschaftsforschung,
Hamburg**
- Bibliographie der Wirtschaftspresse. (pub. by
  Verlag Weltarchiv GmbH)
- Intereconomics. (pub. by Verlag Weltarchiv
  GmbH)
- Konjunktur von Morgen. (pub. by Verlag
  Weltarchiv GmbH)
- Wirtschaftsdienst. (pub. by Verlag Weltarchiv
  GmbH)

**Verlag Otto Haase**
Blankenseer Str. 11, Postfach 2006, 2400 Luebeck
1, W. Germany (B.R.D.)
- Physiotherapie. m. ISSN 0031-9392 (Verband
  Deutscher Badebetriebe e.V.)

**Helmut Haase-Verlag**
Turnerstr. 20, 6900 Heidelberg 1, W. Germany
(B.R.D.)
- Dental Echo. every 6 weeks. ISSN 0011-8575
  (Verband der Deutschen Dental-Industrie e.V)

**Haasenstein'scher Verlag KG**
Steinplatz 1, 1000 Berlin 12, W. Germany (B.R.D.)
- Berliner Aerzteblatt. s-m.

**Verlag Josef Habbel**
Gutenbergstr. 17, 8400 Regensburg, W. Germany
(B. R. D.)
- Der Bayerische Krippenfreund. q. ISSN 0005-
  707X (Verein Bayerischer Krippenfreunde)
- Der Katholische Gedanke. 4 per yr. ISSN 0022-
  9385 (Katholischer Akademikerverband
  Deutschland)

**Rudolf Habelt Verlag**
Am Buchenhang 1, 5300 Bonn 5, W. Germany
(B.R.D.)
- Acta Rei Cretariae Romanae Fautorum.
  Supplementa. irreg.
- Altes Handwerk. irreg., no. 40, 1976. (Gesellschaft
  fuer Volkskunde, Basel. Abteilung Film SZ)
- Anthropologie. irreg., vol. 11, 1973. ISSN 0066-
  4685 (Moravske Museum, Brno CS)
- Anthropos; studie z oboru anthropologie,
  paleoethnologie a kvarterni geologie. irreg. ISSN
  0066-4723 (Moravske Museum, Brno CS)
- Antiquitas. Reihe 1. Abhandlungen zur Alten
  Geschichte. irreg., no. 28, 1977. ISSN 0066-4839
- Antiquitas. Reihe 2. Abhandlungen aus dem
  Gebiete der Vor- und Fruehgeschichte. irreg., no.
  11, 1977. ISSN 0066-4847

- Antiquitas. Reihe 3. Abhandlungen zur Vor- und
  Fruehgeschichte, zur Klassischen und Provinzial-
  Roemischen Archaeologie und zur Geschichte des
  Altertums. irreg., no. 20, 1977. ISSN 0066-4855
- Antiquitas. Reihe 4. Beitraege zur Historia-
  Augusta-Forschung. irreg., no. 12, 1976. ISSN
  0066-4863
- Archaeologica Slovaca. Catalogi. irreg. ISSN
  0066-5932 (Instituti Archaeologici Nitriensis
  Academiae Scientiarum Slovacae CS)
- Archaeologica Slovaca. Fontes. irreg., no. 11,
  1972. ISSN 0066-5940 (Instituti Archaeologici
  Nitriensis Academiae Scientiarum Slovacae CS)
- Archaeologische Informationen. Mitteilungen zur
  Ur- und Fruehgeschichte. irreg. (Deutsche
  Gesellschaft fuer Ur- und Fruehgeschichte)
- Aus Forschung und Kunst. irreg., no. 21, 1975.
  ISSN 0067-0642 (Geschichtsverein fuer Kaernten,
  Klagenfurt AU)
- Bauernhaeuser der Schweiz. irreg., no. 4, 1976.
  ISSN 0067-4591
- Beitraege zur Ur- und Fruehgeschichtlichen
  Archaeologie des Mittelmeerkulturraumes. irreg.,
  no. 18, 1977. ISSN 0067-5245
- Bremer Archaeologische Blaetter. irreg., no. 7,
  1977. ISSN 0068-0907 (Bremer Gesellschaft fuer
  Vorgeschichte) (Co-sponsor: Focke-Musuem;
  Vaeterkunde-Museum)
- Ethnographica. irreg., no. 5 per 6, 1966. ISSN
  0071-1837 (Moravske Museum, Brno CS)
- Fundberichte aus Hessen. irreg., no. 14, 1974.
  ISSN 0071-9889
- Habelts Dissertationsdrucke. Reihe Alte
  Geschichte. irreg., no. 10, 1970. ISSN 0072-9175
- Habelts Dissertationsdrucke. Reihe Germanistik.
  irreg.
- Habelts Dissertationsdrucke. Reihe Klassische
  Archaeologie. irreg., no. 9, 1976. ISSN 0072-9183
- Habelts Dissertationsdrucke. Reihe Klassische
  Philologie. irreg., no. 26, 1977. ISSN 0072-9191
- Habelts Dissertationsdrucke. Reihe
  Kunstgeschichte. irreg. ISSN 0072-9205
- Habelts Dissertationsdrucke. Reihe
  Mittelalterliche Geschichte. irreg., no. 2, 1977.
  ISSN 0072-9213
- Informationsblaetter zu Nachbarwissenschaften
  der Ur- und Fruehgeschichte. a.
- Inschriften Griechischer Staedte aus Kleinasien.
  irreg., no. 3, 1975. (Oesterreichische Akademie
  der Wissenschaften. Kommission fuer die
  Archaeologische Erforschung AU)
- Internationale Volkskundliche Bibliographie/
  International Folklore Bibliography/Bibliographie
  Internationale des Arts et Traditions Populaires.
  irreg., 1977, covering 1973-74. ISSN 0074-9737
- Inventaria Archaeologica Belgique. irreg. ISSN
  0075-0034 (International Congress of Prehistoric
  and Protohistoric Sciences)
- Inventaria Archaeologica Ceskoslovensko. irreg.,
  1967, no. 4. ISSN 0075-0042 (International
  Congress of Prehistoric and Protohistoric
  Sciences)
- Inventaria Archaeologica Denmark. irreg., 1971,
  no. 8. ISSN 0075-0050 (International Congress of
  Prehistoric and Protohistoric Sciences)
- Inventaria Archaeologica Deutschland. irreg.,
  1977, no. 18. ISSN 0075-0069 (International
  Congress of Prehistoric and Protohistoric
  Sciences)
- Inventaria Archaeologica Espana. irreg., 1967, no.
  7. ISSN 0075-0077 (International Congress of
  Prehistoric and Protohistoric Sciences)
- Inventaria Archaeologica France. irreg., no. 4,
  1975. ISSN 0075-0085 (International Congress of
  Prehistoric and Protohistoric Sciences)
- Inventaria Archaeologica Great Britain. irreg.,
  1968, no. 9. ISSN 0075-0093 (International
  Congress of Prehistoric and Protohistoric
  Sciences)
- Inventaria Archaeologica Italia. irreg., 1967, no. 4.
  ISSN 0075-0107 (International Congress of
  Prehistoric and Protohistoric Sciences)
- Inventaria Archaeologica Jugoslavija. irreg., no.
  17, 1973. ISSN 0075-0115 (International
  Congress of Prehistoric and Protohistoric
  Sciences)
- Inventaria Archaeologica Norway. irreg. ISSN
  0075-0123 (International Congress of Prehistoric
  and Protohistoric Sciences)
- Inventaria Archaeologica Oesterreich. irreg. ISSN
  0075-0131 (International Congress of Prehistoric
  and Protohistoric Sciences)
- Inventaria Archaeologica Pologne. irreg., no. 36,
  1976. ISSN 0075-014X (International Congress of
  Prehistoric and Protohistoric Sciences)
- Inventaria Archaeologica Ungarn. irreg., 1971, no.
  3. ISSN 0075-0158 (International Congress of
  Prehistoric and Protohistoric Sciences)

- Jahresbericht der Bayerischen
  Bodendenkmalpflege. a. ISSN 0075-2835 (Bayern.
  Landesamt fuer Denkmalpflege)
- Materialien zur Roemisch-Germanischen Keramik.
  irreg., 1972, no. 9. ISSN 0076-5171 (Deutsches
  Archaeologisches Institut. Roemisch-Germanische
  Kommission)
- Papyrologische Texte und Abhandlungen. irreg.,
  no. 23, 1977.
- Quellenschriften zur Westdeutschen Vor- und
  Fruehgeschichte. irreg., no. 9, 1974. ISSN 0079-
  9149
- Roemisch-Germanisches Zentralmuseum, Mainz.
  Ausstellungskataloge. irreg., no. 4, 1970. ISSN
  0076-2733
- Roemisch-Germanisches Zentralmuseum, Mainz.
  Jahrbuch. a. ISSN 0076-2741
- Roemisch-Germanisches Zentralmuseum, Mainz.
  Kataloge Vor- und Fruehgeschichtlicher
  Altertuemer. irreg., 1970, no. 18. ISSN 0076-
  275X
- Saarbruecker Beitraege zur Altertumskunde. irreg.,
  no. 22, 1977. ISSN 0080-5181
- Samos. irreg. ISSN 0080-5866 (Deutsches
  Archaeologisches Institut)
- Schweizerische Gesellschaft fuer Volkskunde.
  Schriften. irreg., no. 60, 1976. ISSN 0080-732X
- Studia Archaeologica. irreg., no. 33, 1974.
  (Universidad, Santiago de Compostela. Seminario
  de Arqueologia SP) (Co-sponsor: Universidad de
  Valladolid. Departamento de Prehistoria y
  Arqueologia)
- Technische Beitraege zur Archaeologie. irreg.
  ISSN 0067-4974 (Roemisch-Germanisches
  Zentralmuseum, Mainz)
- Tuebinger Aegyptologische Beitraege. irreg., no. 2,
  1976.
- Universitaet Bonn. Seminar fuer Orientalische
  Kunstgeschichte. Veroeffentlichungen. Reihe A.
  Nimruz. irreg.
- Vetus Testamentum Coptice. irreg.
- Volkstum der Schweiz. irreg., 1968, no. 11. ISSN
  0083-6877
- Wege Vor- und Fruehgeschichtlicher Forschung.
  irreg.
- Zeitschrift fuer Papyrologie und Epigraphik. irreg.
  ISSN 0084-5388

**Dr. Curt Haefner Verlag**
Bachstr. 14, 6900 Heidelberg 1, W. Germany
(B.R.D.)
- Der A und O Weg. m. (A und O
  Handelsgesellschaft mbH und Co. KG)
- Blaetter fuer Vorgesetzte. m.
- Informationsbrief fuer Fuehrungskraefte in der
  Chemischen Industrie. m.
- Mutter und Kind. q. ISSN 0047-8482
- Der Papiermacher. 13 per yr. ISSN 0031-1405
  (Vereinigung der Arbeitgeberverbaende der
  Deutschen Papierindustrie e.V.)
- Sicherheitsbeauftragter; Zeitschrift fuer
  Unfallverhuetung und Arbeitssicherheit. m. ISSN
  0300-3337
- Sicherheitsingenieur; Zeitschrift fuer
  Arbeitssicherheit. m. ISSN 0300-3329
- Verhuetet Unfaelle. 13 per yr. ISSN 0042-3939
  (Papiermacher Berufsgenossenschaft)

**Haenssler-Verlag**
Postfach 1220, Bismarckstrasse 4, 7303 Neuhausen-
Stuttgart, Germany (B.R.D.)
- American Institute of Musicology. Miscellanea.
  irreg. ISSN 0065-8855 (American Institute of
  Musicology US)
- Corpus Mensurabilis Musicae. irreg. ISSN 0070-
  0363 (American Institute of Musicology US)
- Corpus Scriptorum de Musica. irreg. ISSN 0070-
  0460 (American Institute of Musicology US)
- Musica Disciplina; yearbook of the history of
  music, Medieval and Renaissance. a. ISSN 0077-
  2461 (American Institute of Musicology US)
- Musicological Studies and Documents. irreg. ISSN
  0077-2496 (American Institute of Musicology US)
- Renaissance Manuscript Studies. irreg., vol 1 in
  prep. (American Institute of Musicology US)

**Hafenbautechnische Gesellschaft**
- Hafenbautechnische Gesellschaft. Jahrbuch. (pub.
  by Springer-Verlag US)

**Hahn-Meitner-Institut fuer Kernforschung Berlin**
Glienicker St. 100, 1000 Berlin 39, W. Germany
(B.R.D.)
- Hahn-Meitner-Institut fuer Kernforschung Berlin.
  Bericht. irreg. ISSN 0072-9280

**Verlag Hahnsche Buchhandlung**
Leinstr. 32, 3000 Hannover 1, W. Germany
(B.R.D.)
- Hannoversche Geschichtsblaetter. 4 per yr.
- Schulverwaltungsblatt fuer Niedersachsen. m.
  ISSN 0048-9484 (Niedersachsen.
  Kultusministerium)

**Verlag Anton Hain KG**
Muehlgasse 3, Postfach 180, 6554 Meisenheim, W.
Germany (B.R.D.)
- Beitraege zur Datenverarbeitung und
  Unternehmensforschung. irreg., vol. 11, 1975.
- Die Dritte Welt. q.
- Hegel-Jahrbuch. a. ISSN 0073-1579 (Hegel-
  Gesellschaft)
- Mathematical Systems in Economics. irreg., vol.
  20, 1975.
- Operations Research-Verfahren / Methods of
  Operations Research. irreg., vol. 21, 1974. ISSN
  0078-5318
- Philosophia Naturalis; Archiv fuer
  Naturphilosophie und die philosophischen
  Grenzgebiete der exakten Wissenschaften und
  Wissenschaftsgeschichte. q. ISSN 0031-8027
- Philosophischer Literaturanzeiger. 6 per yr. ISSN
  0031-8175
- Psychologische Beitraege; Vierteljahresschrift fuer
  alle Gebiete der Psychologie. q. ISSN 0033-3018
  (Deutsche Gesellschaft fuer Psychologie)
- Studien zur Wissenschaftstheorie im Neunzehnten
  Jahrhundert. irreg., vol. 9, 1975. ISSN 0081-7376
- Zeitschrift fuer philosophische Forschung. 4 per
  yr. ISSN 0044-3301

**Josef Hall KG**
Frauentorstr. 5, 8900 Augsburg 1, W. Germany
(B.R.D.)
- Frau im Leben. m. ISSN 0016-0148

**Verlag Alfred Halscheidt**
Verdistr. 19, Postfach 1406, 7920 Heidenheim, W.
Germany (B.R.D.)
- Fernkurs Textiltechnik. m. ISSN 0015-0088
- Der Junge Elektro-Techniker. m. ISSN 0022-6238
- Der Junge Metall-Techniker. m. ISSN 0022-6327

**Hamburg. Statistisches Landesamt**
Steckelhoern 12, 2000 Hamburg 11, W. Germany
(B.R.D.)
- Hamburg in Zahlen. m. ISSN 0017-6877
- Handel und Schiffahrt des Hafens Hamburg. a.
  ISSN 0073-0203

**Hamburger Arzte-Verlag GmbH**
Humboldtstr. 56, 2000 Hamburg 76, W. Germany
(B.R.D.)
- Hamburger Aerzteblatt. m. ISSN 0017-6915

**Hamburger Gesellschaft fuer Voelkerrecht und
Auswaertige Politik**
Rothenbaumchaussee 21-23, 2000 Hamburg 13, W.
Germany (B.R.D.)
- Verfassung und Recht in Uebersee; a quarterly on
  law and modernization. q. ISSN 0506-7286 (Co-
  sponsor: Universitaet Hamburg. Institut fuer
  Internationale Angelegenheiten)

**Hamburger Hochbahn Aktiengesellschaft**
Steinstr. 20, 2000 Hamburg 1, W. Germany
(B.R.D.)
- Fahr mit Uns; Hamburger illustrierte
  Nahverkehrszeitschrift. q. ISSN 0014-6803

**Hamburger Kunsthalle**
- Jahrbuch der Hamburger Kunstsammlungen. (pub.
  by Dr. Ernst Hauswedell und Co., Verlag)

**Hamburger Museumsverein**
Holstenwall 24, 2000 Hamburg 36, W. Germany
(B.R.D.)
- Hamburger Beitraege zur Numismatik. a. ISSN
  0072-9523

**Hamburger Sport-Verein e.V.**
Rothenbaumchaussee 115, 2000 Hamburg 13, W.
Germany (B.R.D.)
- H S V - Post. s-m. ISSN 0017-6257

**Hamburger Sportbund e.V.**
- Hamburger Sport-Mitteilungen. (pub. by Sport-
  und Jugend-Verlag GmbH und Co. KG)

**Hamburgisches Museum fuer Voelkerkunde**
Binderstr. 14, 2000 Hamburg 13, W. Germany
(B.R.D.)
- Beitraege zur Mittelamerikanischen Voelkerkunde.
  (pub. by Klaus Renner Verlag)
- Hamburgisches Museum fuer Voelkerkunde.
  Mitteilungen. a. ISSN 0072-9469

**Hamburgisches Zoologisches Museum und Institut**
Papendamm 3, 2000 Hamburg 13, W. Germany
(B.R.D.)
- Hamburgisches Zoologisches Museum und
  Institut. Mitteilungen. a. ISSN 0072-9612

**Verlag Handels- und Werbepraxis GmbH**
Hermannstr. 40, Postfach 1920, 5450 Neuwied, W.
Germany (B.R.D.)
- Lebensmittel Praxis; Fachmagazin fuer
  Unternehmensfuehrung, Werbung und Verkauf im
  Lebensmittelhandel. m. ISSN 0023-9992

**Neuer Handels-Verlag GmbH und Co. KG**
Zugspitzstr. 17, Postfach 407, 8939 Bad
Woerishofen, W. Germany (B.R.D.)
- Cash and Carry; Fachzeitschrift fuer den gesamten
  Selbstbedienungs-Grosshandel. 12 per yr.
  (Verband fuer Cash and Carry Grosshandel e.V.)
- S B - Warenhaus. (Selbstbedienung); Fachblatt
  fuer Verbrauchmaerkte, Discount und SB-
  Warenhaeuser. m.
- Service Manager; internationales magazin fuer
  Hotellerie und Gastronomie. 12 per yr.

**Handelsblatt GmbH**
Kreuzstr. 21, Postfach 1102, 4000 Duesseldorf 1, W.
Germany (B.R.D.)
- A T W News of the Month; nuclear information
  from the Federal Republic of Germany. m.
- Absatzwirtschaft; Zeitschrift fuer Marketing. m.
  ISSN 0001-3374
- Atomwirtschaft - Atomtechnik. m.
- Der Betrieb; Wochenzeitschrift fuer
  Betriebswirtschaft, Steuerrecht, Wirtschaftsrecht,
  Arbeitsrecht. w. ISSN 0005-9935
- Chemische Industrie. m. ISSN 0009-2959
  (Verband der Chemischen Industrie)
- Chemische Industrie International. q. ISSN 0009-
  2967 (Verband der Chemischen Industrie)
- Europa Chemie; Aktueller Nachrichtendienst der
  Zeitschrift Chemische Industrie. s-m. ISSN 0014-
  2484
- Handelsblatt; Deutsche Wirtschaftszeitung. 5 per
  w. ISSN 0017-7296
- Ost-Wirtschaftsreport. fortn.
- Ozean und Technik; Informationsdienst fuer
  Meerestechnik und Meereswirtschaft. s-m.
- Packung und Transport in der Chemischen
  Industrie. m.
- Der Schrottbetrieb. m. (Bundesverband der
  Deutschen Schrottwirtschaft)
- Technischer Fortschritt; Handelsblatt-
  Informationsdienst fuer die Fuehrungskraefte der
  Wirtschaft. -m. ISSN 0040-1544
- Wirtschaft und Wettbewerb; Zeitschrift fuer
  Kartellrecht, Wettbewerbsrecht und
  Marktorganisation. m. ISSN 0043-6151
- Wirtschaftswoche; das Nachrichtenmagazin fuer
  die Wirtschaft. w.

**Handelskammer Bremen**
- Der Schluessel. (pub. by Carl Schuenemann
  Verlag)

**Handelskammer Hamburg**
Borse, 2000 Hamburg 11, W. Germany (B.R.D.)
- Handelskammer Hamburg. Mitteilungen. m. ISSN
  0017-730X

**Verlag fuer Handwerk und Gewerbe GmbH**
Hessbruehlstr. 69, Postfach 800430, 7000 Stuttgart
80, W. Germany (B.R.D.)
- Handwerks- und Gewerbezeitung fuer Baden-
  Wuerttemberg. every 3 wks. (Handwerkskammer
  Stuttgart)

**Handwerkskammer Stuttgart**
- Handwerks- und Gewerbezeitung fuer Baden-
  Wuerttemberg. (pub. by Verlag fuer Handwerk
  und Gewerbe GmbH)

**Hanns-Seidel-Stiftung e.V.**
- Politische Studien. (pub. by Guenter Olzog
  Verlag)

**Hans-Bredow-Institut**
Heimhuder Str. 21, 2000 Hamburg 13, W. Germany
(B.R.D.)
- A R D - Jahrbuch. a. ISSN 0066-5746
- Internationales Handbuch fuer Rundfunk und
  Fernsehen. biennial. ISSN 0535-4358
- Rundfunk und Fernsehen. q. ISSN 0035-9874

**Hans-Pfitzner-Gesellschaft e.V.**
Forsthausstr. 26, 6384 Schmitten 1, W. Germany
(B.R.D.)
- Hans-Pfitzner-Gesellschaft. Mitteilungen. s-a.
  ISSN 0440-2863

**Carl Hanser Verlag**
Kolberger Str. 22, Postfach 860420, 8000 Munich
80, W. Germany (B.R.D.)
- Akzente; Zeitschrift fuer Literatur. bi-m. ISSN
  0002-3957
- Die Arbeitsvorbereitung. bi-m. ISSN 0003-780X
- Computer Monographien. irreg., vol. 12, 1976.
- Deutsche Zahnaerztliche Zeitschrift. m. ISSN
  0012-1029 (Deutsche Gesellschaft fuer Zahn-,
  Mund- und Kieferheilkunde)
- Deutscher Zahnaerztekalender. a.
- F und M, Feinwerktechnik und Messtechnik. 8
  per yr. ISSN 0340-1952
- Haerterei-Technische Mitteilungen (HTM) 6 per
  yr. ISSN 0017-6583 (Arbeitsgemeinschaft
  Waermebehandlung und Werkstoff-Technik e.V.)
- Kunststoffe; Organ deutscher Kunststoff-
  Fachverbaende. m. ISSN 0023-5563
- Kunststoffe - German Plastics. m.
- Plasticonstruction / Bauen mit Kunststoffen / Plastics
  in Building / Plastiques et Construction. bi-m.
  ISSN 0032-1117
- Plastics Universales. 6 per yr.
- Qualitaet und Zuverlaessigkeit. m. ISSN 0033-
  5126 (Deutsche Gesellschaft fuer Qualitaet)
- Rationalisierung. m. ISSN 0034-0057
  (Rationalisierungskuratorium der Deutschen
  Wirtschaft)
- Tenside - Detergents; journal for theory,
  technology & application of surfactants. bi-m.
  ISSN 0040-3490 (Gesellschaft Deutscher
  Chemiker)
- Werkstatt und Betrieb; Zeitschrift fuer
  Maschinenbau, Konstruktion und Fertigung. m.
  ISSN 0043-2792
- Zeitschrift fuer Wirtschaftliche Fertigung. m. ISSN
  0044-3743

**Hansischer Geschichtsverein**
- Hansische Geschichtsblaetter. (pub. by Boehlau
  Verlag)

**Hansischer Gildenverlag**
Theodorstr. 41c, 2000 Hamburg 50, W. Germany
(B.R.D.)
- W G O - Monatshefte fuer Osteuropaeisches
  Recht. m. ISSN 0042-9678 (Universitaet
  Hamburg. Abteilung fuer Ostrechtforschung)

**Peter Hanstein Verlag GmbH**
Speestr. 12, Postfach 420624, 5000 Cologne 41, W.
Germany (B.R.D.)
- Jonas; Werkbuecher Literatur, Kunst und
  Wissenschaft. q. (Grafenwerther Musen Werk-
  und Foerderkreis fuer Literatur, Kunst und
  Wissenschaft e.V.)

**Industrie- und Handelswerbung A. Hanuschik**
Ungererstr. 19/VI (Fuchsbau), 8000 Munich 40, W.
Germany (B.R.D.)
- Oper und Konzert. m. ISSN 0030-3518
- Zahnaerztlicher Anzeiger. fortn. ISSN 0027-3198
  (Zahnaerztlicher Bezirksverband Muenchen Stadt
  und Land)

**Verlag Otto Harrassowitz**
Taunusstr. 6, Postfach 2929, 6200 Wiesbaden, W.
Germany (B.R.D.)
- Bibliothek und Wissenschaft. a. ISSN 0067-8236
  (Deutsche Forschungsgemeinschaft)
- Central Asiatic Journal; international periodical
  for the languages, literature, history and
  archaeology of Central Asia. 4 per yr. ISSN 0008-
  9192
- Deutscher Palaestina-Verein. Zeitschrift. 2 per yr.
  ISSN 0012-1169 (Deutsches Evangelisches
  Institut fuer Altertumwissenschaft des Heiligen
  Landes)
- Enchoria; Zeitschrift fuer Demotistik und
  Koptologie. a. ISSN 0340-627X

- Freie Universitaet Berlin. Osteuropa-Institut. Historische Veroeffentlichungen; Forschungen zur Osteuropaeischen Geschichte. irreg, vol. 24, 1977. ISSN 0067-5903
- Jahrbuch der Deutschen Bibliotheken. biennial. ISSN 0075-2223 (Verein Deutscher Bibliothekare)
- Journal of Asian History. 2 per yr. ISSN 0021-910X
- Muenchner Indologische Studien. irreg. ISSN 0077-1880
- Oriens Christianus; Hefte fuer die Kunde des christlichen Orients. a. ISSN 0340-6407
- Oriens Extremus; Zeitschrift fuer Sprache, Kunst und Kultur der Laender des fernen Ostens. 2 per yr. ISSN 0030-5197
- Osteuropa Institut, Munich. Veroeffentlichungen. Reihe Geschichte. irreg, vol. 45, 1977. ISSN 0078-687X
- Die Sprache; Zeitschrift fuer Sprachwissenschaft. 2 per yr. ISSN 0038-8467
- Ural-Altaische Jahrbuecher. s-a. ISSN 0042-0786 (Universitaet Hamburg. Finnisch-Ugrisches Seminar)
- Zentralasiatische Studien. a. ISSN 0514-857X

**Karl Hart**
8712 Volkach, W. Germany (B.R.D)
- Bayerisches Jahrbuch fuer Volkskunde. a. ISSN 0067-4729 (Bayerische Akademie der Wissenschaften. Institut fuer Volkskunde)

**Richard F. Hartmann**
Wilhelmstr. 10, 6300 Giessen, W. Germany (B.R.D.)
- Boom. q.

**Hartmannbund - Verband der Aertzte Deutschlands e.V.**
- Der Duetsche Arzt. (pub. by Verlag Kirchheim und Co. GmbH)

**Hartung und Karl**
Karolinenplatz 5a, 8000 Munich 2, W. Germany (B.R.D.)
- Hartung und Karl. Auktion. irreg.

**Harzverein fuer Geschichte und Altertumskunde**
Zehnstr. 24, 3380 Goslar /Hartz, W. Germany (B.R.D.)
- Harz-Zeitschrift. a. ISSN 0073-0882

**V. Hase und Koehler Verlag**
Bahnhofstr. 3, Postfach 2269, 6500 Mainz, W. Germany (B.R.D.)
- Ungarn-Jahrbuch; Zeitschrift fuer die Kunde Ungarns und Verwandte Gebiete. a. ISSN 0082-755X (Ungarisches Institut, Muenchen)

**Haude und Spenersche Verlagsbuchhandlung GmbH**
Moltkestr. 1, 1000 Berlin 45, W. Germany (B.R.D.) (Subscr. to: Gemeinsame Verlagsauslieferung Melanchthon-Versandbuchhandlung GmbH, Postfach 1180, 2919 Struecklingen, W. Germany (B.R.D.))
- Berlinische Reminiszenzen. irreg., no. 48, 1975. ISSN 0067-611X

**Haueisen Verlag KG**
Oraniendamm 45, 1000 Berlin 28, W. Germany (B.R.D.)
- Der Deutsche Tischlermeister. m. ISSN 0012-0855
- Malerzeitung Drei Schilde. m. ISSN 0025-1372

**Karl F. Haug Verlag GmbH**
Blumenthalstr. 38, 6900 Heidelberg 1, W. Germany (B.R.D.)
- Acta Homoeopathica; organum Ligae Medicorum Homoeopathicae Internationalis. a. ISSN 0001-5881 (International Homoeopathic League)
- Allgemeine Homoeopathische Zeitung. bi-m. ISSN 0002-5887 (Deutscher Zentralverein Homoeopatischer Aerzte e.V.)
- Erfahrungsheilkunde; Zeitschrift fuer die aerztiche Praxis. m. ISSN 0014-0082

**Verlag B. Haugg KG**
Postfach 190207, Postfach 207, 8000 Munich 19, W. Germany (B.R.D.)
- Bayerisches Sonntagsblatt fuer die Katholische Familie. w. ISSN 0005-7177

**Hauptberatungsstelle fuer Elektrizitaetsanwendung e.V**
- Strom Praxis. (pub. by Verlags- und Wirtschaftsgesellschaft der Elektrizitaetswerke mbH)

**Hauptverband der Bundesbahn-Landwirtschaft e.V.**
- Eisenbahn-Landwirt. (pub. by Verlag Hermann Fleischhauer und Co.)

**Hauptverband der Deutschen Bauindustrie**
Abraham-Lincoln-Str. 30, Postach 2966, 6200 Wiesbaden, W. Germany (B.R.D.)
- Baustatistisches Jahrbuch. a. ISSN 0084-7739
- Bauwirtschaft (B W) (pub. by Bauverlag GmbH)

**Hauptverband der Deutschen Filmtheater e.V.**
- Film-Echo/Filmwoche. (pub. by Kommanditgesellschaft Verlag Horst Axtmann GmbH und Co.)

**Hauptverband der Gewerblichen Berufsgenossenschaften e.V.**
- Die Berufsgenossenschaft. (pub. by Erich Schmidt Verlag (Bielefeld))

**Hauptverband des Deutschen Maler- und Lackiererhandwerks**
- Das Deutsche Malerblatt. (pub. by Deutsche Verlagsanstalt GmbH)

**Haus der Technik e.V., Essen**
- Technische Mitteilungen. (pub. by Vulkan-Verlag Dr. W. Classen)

**Verlag Haus und Grund GmbH**
Luetticher Str. 1-3, 5000 Cologne 1, W. Germany (B.R.D.)
- Haus und Grund. m. ISSN 0017-8403

**Dr. Ernst Hauswedell und Co., Verlag**
Poeseldorfer Weg 1, 2000 Hamburg 13, W. Germany (B.R.D.)
- Jahrbuch der Auktionspreise; fuer Buecher, Handschriften und Autographen. a. ISSN 0075-2193
- Jahrbuch der Hamburger Kunstsammlungen. a. ISSN 0075-2274 (Hamburger Kunsthalle) (Co-sponsor: Museum fuer Kunst und Gewerbe, Hamburg)
- Philobiblon. q. ISSN 0031-7969 (Maximilian-Gesellschaft e.V.)
- Wolfenbuetteler Barock-Nachrichten. q. ISSN 0340-6318
- Wolfenbuetteler Notizen zur Buchgeschichte. 3 per yr. ISSN 0341-2253 (Wolfenbuetteler Arbeitskreis fuer Geschichte des Buchwesens)

**Verlag A. W. Hayn's Erben**
Sonnenallee 61, 1000 Berlin 44, W. Germany (B.R.D.)
- Recht in Ost und West; Zeitschrift fuer Rechtsvergleichung und innerdeutsche Rechtsprobleme. bi-m.

**Hebauf Travel Press**
Hafenstr 59, 6000 Frankfurt 1, W. Germany (B.R.D.)
- Deutsche Reisebuero-Zeitung. w. ISSN 0034-3668
- Tagung und Kongress; Magazin fuer Geschaeftsreisen. bi-m. (International Congress Union)

**Hebbel-Gesellschaft**
- Hebbel- Jahrbuecher. (pub. by Westholsteinische Verlagsanstalt Boyens und Co.)

**Heckners Verlag**
Postfach 260, 3340 Wolfenbuettel, W. Germany (B.R.D.)
- Die Berufsbildende Schule. m. ISSN 0005-951X (Bundesverband der Lehrer an Beruflichen Schulen)
- D S T Z-Deutsche Stenografenzeitung. m. ISSN 0011-5169 (Deutscher Stenografenbund e. V.)

**H. Heenemann GmbH**
Bessemerstr. 83, 1000 Berlin 42, W. Germany (B.R.D.)
- Archiv fuer Fischereiwissenschaft. irreg., vol. 26, 1975. ISSN 0003-9063 (Germany, Federal Republic. Bundesforschungsanstalt fuer Fischerei)

**Heering Verlag GmbH**
Ortlerstr. 8, 8000 Munich 70, W. Germany (B.R.D.)
- Alpinismus. m. ISSN 0002-6484
- Film und Ton-Magazin. m. ISSN 0015-1114
- Foto-Magazin. m. ISSN 0015-8712
- Die Fotowirtschaft; Unabhaengiges Wirtschaftsmagazin der Fotobranche fuer Industrie, Handel, Handwerk. s-m.
- Submarin; Magazin der Unterwasserwelt. m. ISSN 0340-6679

- Suedkurs; Magazin fuer Wassersport, Segler, Windsurfer, Motorbootfahrer. m. ISSN 0340-9929

**Hegel-Gesellschaft**
- Hegel-Jahrbuch. (pub. by Verlag Anton Hain KG)

**Verlag Dr. Heger**
Goethestrasse 54, 53 Bonn-Bad Godesberg, W. Germany (B.R.D.)
- Germany (Federal Republic, 1949- ). Bundesministerium fuer Bildung and Wissenschaft. Forschungsbericht der Bundesregierung. irreg.

**Verlag fuer Wissenschaft und Leben Georg Heidecker**
Kuelsheimer Str. 11, 8532 Bad Windsheim, W. Germany (B.R.D.)
- Der Fernmelde-Ingenieur; Zeitschrift fuer Ausbildung und Fortbildung. m. ISSN 0015-010X
- Jahrbuch des Elektrischen Fernmeldewesens. a. ISSN 0075-2487

**Heider-Verlag**
Paffrather Str. 102, Postfach 190, 5070 Bergisch Gladbach, W. Germany (B.R.D.)
- Soziale Selbstverwaltung; fuer die Mitglieder der Selbstverwaltung in der Sozialversicherung. m. ISSN 0038-6057 (Bundesvereinigung der Deutschen Arbeitgeberverbaende E.V)

**Verlag Dr. H. Heilmaier**
Altheimer Eck 13, Postfach 444, 800 Munich 2, W. Germany (B.R.D.)
- Friseurhandwerk Friseurspiegel. fortm. ISSN 0016-1454
- Der Fuss. m. (Zentralverband der Fusspfleger Deutschlands e.V.)
- Madame; Internationale Gesellschafts-Zeitschrift. m. ISSN 0024-936X

**Heilsarmee GmbH**
Salierring 27, 5000 Cologne 1, W. Germany (B.R.D.)
- Der Junge Soldat; Kinderzeitschrift der heilsarmee. w. ISSN 0022-6351

**Zeitungs- und Zeitschriften-Verlag Heim und Welt**
Am Jungfernplan 3, 3000 Hannover 1, W. Germany (B.R.D.)
- Heim und Welt. w.

**Verlag fuer Heimat und Werk**
Hohenzollerndamm 89, 1000 Berlin 33, W. Germany (B. R. D.)
- Das Betten-Magazin; Fachzeitschrift fuer gesunde Schlafkultur fuer Bettenfachhandel und Bettwaren-Industrie. bi-m. ISSN 0005-9285

**Heimatbund Allgaeu**
Rathausplatz 5 (Stadtarchiv), 8960 Kempten, W. Germany (B.R.D.)
- Allgaeuer Geschichtsfreund. a.

**Heimatkreis Roemerstadt-Altxater e.V.**
Koenigsberger Str. 26, 6451 Bruchkoebel, W. Germany.
- Heimat-Zeitung Roemerstaedter Laendchen; und angrenzende Gemeinden. bi-m. ISSN 0017-9752

**Heimatliche Verlags- und Vertriebsgesellschaft MbH**
Kaiser-Wilhelm-Ring 11, Postfach 4112, 6500 Mainz 1, W. Germany (B.R.D.)
- Mitteldeutscher Kurier. m. ISSN 0015-4520 (Bund der Mitteldeutschen)

**Heimatverband fuer den Kreis Pinneberg**
- Jahrbuch fuer den Kreis Pinneberg. (pub. by A. Beig Verlag)

**Heimatverein des Kreises Segeberg**
Klosterkamp 9, 2360 Bad Segeberg, W. Germany (B.R.D.)
- Heimatkundliches Jahrbuch fuer den Kreis Segeberg. a.

**Heimatverein Porz e.V.**
Aachener Str. 27, 5000 Cologne 90, W. Germany (B.R.D.)
- Rechtsrheinisches Koeln; Jahrbuch fuer Geschichte und Volkskunde. a.

**Heimatvertriebene aus Suedosteuropa**
- Der Donauschwabe. (pub. by Donauschwaebischer Heimatverlag)

**Verlag die Heimstatt**
Zeughausstr. 13, 5000 Cologne, W. Germany
(B.R.D.)
- Die Heimstatt; Werkheft Jugendsozialarbeit und
Jugendpflege in Heim und Gruppe. s-a. ISSN
0017-9868 (Katholische
Landesarbeitsgemeinschaft fuer
Jugendsozialarbeit)

**Heinrich-Heine-Institut, Duesseldorf**
- Heine-Jahrbuch. (pub. by Hoffmann und Campe
Verlag)

**Fachzeitschriftenverlag Heinrichs**
Brueggekamp 1, 3013 Barsinghausen 4, W.
Germany (B.R.D.)
- Baugeschaeft und Bauunternehmer. q. ISSN 0005-
6626
- Baumaschinen- und Baugeraete-Handel. q. ISSN
0005-6715
- Baustoff- und Baubedarfs-Grosshandel. q. ISSN
0005-6804
- Deutscher Lebensmittelgrosshandel; Der
Supermarkt, der Cash- und Carry-Grosshandel. q.
ISSN 0012-1134
- Deutscher Lebensmittelhandel. q. ISSN 0012-1142
- EWG-Warenhandel. q. ISSN 0014-3871
- Gastwirt. q. ISSN 0016-5158
- Gemischtwarenhandel; der Feinkost- und
Delikatessenhandel. q. ISSN 0016-6243
- Getraenkehandel. q. ISSN 0016-9331
- Hotelier. q. ISSN 0018-6287
- Kaufhaus und Warenhaus. q. ISSN 0022-9474
- Spiritudsen- und Weinhandel. q. ISSN 0038-7657

**Heinrichs Verlag KG**
POB 271, Postfach 8851, 3200 Hildesheim 1, W.
Germany (B.R.D.)
- Eier-Wild-Gefluegel-Markt; Fett-Kaese-Butter
boerse. 3 per w. ISSN 0013-2500
- Milch-Fettwaren-Eier-Handel. 3 per w. ISSN
0026-3761
- Molkerei-Zeitung Welt der Milch. w. ISSN 0043-
2512
- Unser Milchvieh. m. (Angestelltenverband
Deutscher Milchkontroll- und
Tierzuchtangestellten)

**Heinrichshofen's Verlag**
Liebigstr. 16, 2940 Wilhelmshaven, W. Germany
(B.R.D.)
(Dist. in U.S. by C.F. Peters Corp., 373 Park Ave.,
S., New York, N.Y. 10016)
- Musikpaedagogische Bibliothek. irreg., vol. 15,
1977.
- Quellenkataloge zur Musikgeschichte. irreg., vol.
11, 1977. ISSN 0079-905X
- Taschenbuecher zur Musikwissenschaft. irreg., vol.
45, 1977. ISSN 0082-1969

**Heinze Verlag GmbH und Co.**
Bremer Weg 184, Postfach 505, 3100 Celle, W.
Germany (B.R.D.)
- Handbuch des Bauherrn; Neubau - Umbau -
Modernisierung. a. ISSN 0017-7202

**Helfer-Verlag E. Schwabe**
Kisseleffstr. 10, 6380 Bad Homburg, W. Germany
(B.R.D.)
- Atem; Zeitschrift fuer Atempflege - Massage -
Entspannung - moderne Gymnastik. q. ISSN
0004-6477
- Volksgesundheit; Monatzeitschrift fuer Gesundes
Leben und Naturgemaesse Heilverfahren. m.
ISSN 0042-8493

**A. Hellendoorn Verlag**
Stettiner Str. 1, Postfach 78, 4442 Bentheim 1, W.
Germany (B.R.D.)
- Zeitschrift fuer Verkehrswissenschaft. q. ISSN
0044-3670

**Verlag Marie Hemmerle**
Pullacher Str. 1, 8000 Munich 70, W. Germany
(B.R.D.)
- Bau-Buch-Berater. q.
- Literarische Umschau. q.

**Henkel GmbH**
Postfach 1100, 4000 Duesseldorf 1, W. Germany
(B.R.D.)
- Henkel GmbH Duesseldorf. Schriften des
Werksarchivs. irreg., no. 5 per 6, 1973.

**G. Henle Verlag**
Schongauerstrasse 24, 8000 Munich 70, W.
Germany (B.R.D.)
- Haydn-Studien. irreg., 1-2 per yr. ISSN 0440-5323
(Joseph-Haydn-Institut e.V.)

**Aloys Henn Verlag KG**
Bahnhofstr. 17, Postfach 1180, 5448 Kastellaun, W.
Germany (B.R.D.)
- Die Gestalt; Vierteljahreszeitschrift fuer
bildnerische Erziehung. m.
- Mittellateinisches Jahrbuch. a. ISSN 0076-9762
- Paedagogische Rundschau. m. ISSN 0030-9273
- Schriftenreihe zur Geschichte und Politischen
Bildung. irreg., 1971, vol. 7. ISSN 0080-7168
- Zeitschrift fuer Kunstpaedagogik. bi-m.

**Gisbert Hennessen Verlag**
Kasernenstr. 49, 4000 Duesseldorf, W. Germany
(B.R.D.)
- Der Herr; Internationales Fachorgan fuer
Herrenmode und -Marketing. m. ISSN 0018-0858

**Henriettenstiftung Hannover**
Marienstr. 80, 3000 Hannover 1, W. Germany
(B.R.D.)
- Blaetter aus dem Henriettenstift. s-a.

**Georg Herde**
Mauerweg 20, 6000 Frankfurt, W. Germany
(B.R.D.)
- Neue Kommentare. m. ISSN 0028-3258

**Verlag Herder KG**
Hermann-Herder-Str. 4, 7800 Freiburg, W.
Germany (B.R.D.)
- Herder-Korrespondenz; Monatshefte fuer
Gesellschaft und Religion. m. ISSN 0018-0645
- K M - Die Katholischen Missionen; Zeitschrift
des Internationalen Katholischen Missionwerkes
(MISSIO) 6 per yr.
- Kontraste Impuls. q. ISSN 0023-3749
- Roemische Quartalschrift fuer Christliche
Altertumskunde und Kirchengeschichte. s-a. ISSN
0035-7812
- Stimmen der Zeit; Monatsschrift fuer das
Geistesleben der Gegenwart. m. ISSN 0039-1492
- Theologie und Philosophie. q. ISSN 0040-5655
- Die Welt der Buecher. 2 per yr. ISSN 0043-2490

**Herforder Verein fuer Heimatkunde**
- Herforder Jahrbuch; Beitraege zur Geschichte der
Stadt und des Stiftes Herford. (pub. by
Maximilian Verlag)

**Verlag Klaus Edgar Herfurth**
Boehmerstr. 18, Postfach 2588, 6000 Frankfurt 1,
W. Germany (B.R.D.)
- Dresdner Monats-Blaetter; Zeitschrift der Freunde
Dresdens. m. ISSN 0012-6101

**Hermann-Oberth-Gesellschaft**
- Astronautik. (pub. by Druckerei H. Brandt)

**Hermes Verlags- und Werbe-Gesellschaft mbH**
Cheruskerweg 39, 6230frankfurt 80, W. Germany
(B.R.D.)
- Der Block. m. ISSN 0006-4904
- Frankfurter Blaetter fuer Heimatvertriebene. m.
ISSN 0015-993X

**Industrieverlag von Hernhaussen KG**
Postfach 1380, 7022 Leinfelden-Echterdingen 1, W.
Germany (B.R.D.)
- T Z fuer Praktische Metallbearbeitung. m. ISSN
0039-8667

**Verlag des Herold Herbert Sexauer KG**
Lisztstr. 27, 8000 Munich 80, W. Germany (B.R.D.)
- Herold; Fachblatt fuer Pferdezucht und -Sport.
ISSN 0018-0807

**Herold-Verlag Dr. Franz Wetzel und Co. KG**
Kirchbachweg 16, 8000 Munich 71, W. Germany
(B.R.D.)
- Zeitschrift fuer Radiaesthesie. q. ISSN 0044-3425
(Verband fuer Ruten- und Pendelkunde
(Radiaesthesie))

**Rudolf Herzfeldt Verlag**
Sonnenberger Str. 19a, 6200 Wiesbaden, W.
Germany (B.R.D.)
- Modellhut und Accessoires. m.

**Herzog-August-Bibliothek, Wolfenbuettel**
- Wolfenbuetteler Beitraege. (pub. by Vittorio
Klostermann)

**Verlag Guenther Heske**
Kloster, 7417 Pfullingen, W. Germany (B.R.D.)
- Opuscula - aus Wissenschaft und Dichtung. irreg.
ISSN 0078-5539

**Hessen. Hessisches Landesamt fuer Geschichtliche
Landeskunde**
Krummbogen 28c, 3550 Marburg, W. Germany
(B.R.D.)
- Hessisches Jahrbuch fuer Landesgeschichte. a.
ISSN 0073-2001

**Hessen. Kultusministerium**
Luisenplatz 10, 6200 Wiesbaden, W. Germany
(B.R.D.)
- Hessischer Kultusminister. Bildungspolitische
Informationen. irreg.

**Hessen. Landeszentrale fuer Politische Bildung**
Mainzer Str. 19, 6200 Wiesbaden, 62 Wiesbaden,
W. Germany (B.R.D.)
- Zum Nachdenken. 6 per yr.(approx) ISSN 0044-
5487

**Hessen. Minister der Justiz**
Luisenstr. 13, 6200 Wiesbaden, W. Germany
(B.R.D.)
- Justiz-Ministerial-Blatt fuer Hessen. s-m. ISSN
0022-7064

**Hessen. Ministerium fuer Landwirtschaft und Umwelt**
6200 Wiesbaden, W. Germany (B.R.D.)
- Hesse. Ministerium fuer Landwirtschaft und
Umwelt. Ernten, Maerkte, Preise. Jahresbericht. a.

**Hessen. Staatskanzlei**
- Gesetz und Verordnungsblatt fuer das Land
Hessen. (pub. by Verlag Dr. Max Gehlen)

**Hessen. Statistisches Landesamt**
Rheinstr. 35/37, 6200 Wiesbaden, W. Germany
(B.R.D.)
- Hessische Kreiszahlen. s-a.
- Staat und Wirtschaft in Hessen. m.

**Hessischer Jugendring**
Albrechtstr. 15, 6200 Wiesbaden, W. Germany
(B.R.D.)
- Hessische Jugend. 6 per yr. ISSN 0018-1099

**Hessischer Volkshochschulverband**
Winterbachstr.38, 6000 Frankfurt 1, W. Germany
(B.R.D.)
- Hessische Blaetter fuer Volksbildung. q. ISSN
0018-103X

**Hestra-Verlag**
Holzhofallee 33, Postfach 4244, 6100 Darmstadt 1,
W. Germany (B.R.D.)
- Archiv fuer Eisenbahntechnik. irreg. ISSN 0066-
6300
- Die Bundesbahn. fortn. ISSN 0007-5876
(Deutsche Bundesbahn)
- Buss Handbuch Europaeischer Produktenboersen.
triennial. ISSN 0525-2989
- D B Report. a. ISSN 0072-1549 (Deutsche
Bundesbahn)
- Eisenbahntechnische Rundschau; Zeitschrift fuer
die gesamte Eisenbahntechnik. m. ISSN 0013-
2845
- Jahrbuch des Eisenbahnwesens. a. ISSN 0075-
2479 (Deutsche Bundesbahn)
- Railway Technical Review. a. ISSN 0079-9548
- Transportieren Umschlagen Lagern. a. ISSN 0082-
5964

**Hanseatisches Werbekontor Heuser und Co.**
Stubbenhuk 10, 2000 Hamburg 11, W. Germany
(B.R.D.)
- Die Freie Wohnungswirtschaft. m. ISSN 0016-
0784 (Verband Freier Wohnungsunternehmen
e.V.)
- Hamburger Vorschau; Offizielles
Veranstaltungsprogramm der Freien und
Hansestadt Hamburg. s-m. ISSN 0017-6990
(Fremdenverkehrszentrale Hamburg)

**Carl Heymanns Verlag KG**
Gereonstr. 18-32, 5000 Cologne 1, W.Germany
(B.R.D.)
- Blatt fuer Patent-, Muster- und Zeichenwesen. m.
ISSN 0006-4602 (Deutsches Patentamt)
- Bundesgesundheitsblatt. fortn. ISSN 0007-5914
(Germany, Federal Republic.
Bundesgesundheitsamt)

- Demokratische Existenz Heute. irreg., vol. 20, 1973. ISSN 0070-3389 (Universitaet zu Koeln. Forschungsinstitut fuer Politische Wissenschaften und Europaeische Fragen)
- Deutsches Verwaltungsblatt. s-m. ISSN 0012-1363
- European Court of Human Rights. Publications. Series A: Judgments and Decisions/Cour Europeenne des Droits de l'Homme. Publications. Serie a: Arrets et Decisions. irreg., vol. 16, 1973. ISSN 0073-3903
- European Court of Human Rights. Publications. Series B: Pleadings, Oral Arguments and Documents/Cour Europeenne des Droits de l'Homme. Publications. Serie B: Memoires, Plaidoiries et Documents. irreg., vol. 14, 1973. ISSN 0073-3911
- F I W - Schriftenreihe. irreg., vol. 68, 1974. ISSN 0071-769X (Forschunginstitut fuer Wirtschaftsverfassung und Wettbewerb e.V.)
- Konkurs-, Treuhand- und Schiedsgerichtswesen; Zeitschrift fuer alle Fragen des Konkurs-, Vergleichs- und Treuhandwesens sowie der Zwangsversteigerung und -verwaltung. q. ISSN 0023-3552
- Kunststoffe im Lebensmittelverkehr. irreg., no. 22, 1975. ISSN 0075-7292 (Germany, Federal Republic. Bundesgesundheitsamt. Kunststoff-Kommission)
- Mitteilungen der Deutschen Patentanwaelte. m. ISSN 0026-6884 (Patentanwaltskammer)
- Monatsschrift fuer Kriminologie und Strafrechtsreform. bi-m. ISSN 0026-9301 (Gesellschaft fuer die Gesate Kriminologie)
- Patentblatt. w. ISSN 0031-2894 (Deutsches Patentamt)
- Die Polizei; Zentralorgan fuer das Sicherheits- und Ordnungswesen. m. ISSN 0032-3519
- Raumforschung und Raumordnung. bi-m. ISSN 0034-0111 (Institut fuer Raumordnung) (C0-Sponsor: Akademie fuer Raumforschung und Landesplanung)
- Sammlung Lebensmittelrechtlicher Entscheidungen. irreg., vol. 9, 1975. ISSN 0080-5831
- Verwaltungsarchiv; Zeitschrift fuer Verwaltungslehre, Verwaltungsrecht und Verwaltungspolitik. q. ISSN 0042-4501
- Z F A. (Zeitschrift fuer Arbeitsrecht) q.
- Zeitschrift fuer Luft- und Weltraumrecht. q. (Universitaet zu Koeln. Institut fuer Luft- und Weltraumrecht)
- Zeitschrift fuer Politik. q. ISSN 0044-3360 (Hochschule fuer Politik)
- Zeitschrift fuer Wasserrecht. 3 per yr (plus 1 special no.) ISSN 0044-3735

**Anton Hiersemann Verlag**
Rosenbergstr. 113, Postfach 723, 7000 Stuttgart 1, W. Germany (B.R.D.)
- Deutsches Mittelalter, Kritische Studientexte der Monumenta Germaniae Historica. irreg. ISSN 0340-8396
- Monographien zur Geschichte des Mittelalters. 2 per yr. ISSN 0026-9832
- Monumenta Germaniae Historica. Staatsschriften des Spaeteren Mittelalters. irreg. ISSN 0340-8035
- Paepste und Papsttum. 3 per yr. ISSN 0340-7993
- Romanfuehrer; der Inhalt der Romane und Novellen der Weltliteratur. irreg., vol. 16, 1977. ISSN 0557-2614
- Schauspielfuehrer. triennial. (Universitaet Wien. Institut fuer Theaterwissenschaft AU)
- Schriften der Monumenta Germaniae Historica. irreg., no. 26, 1977. ISSN 0080-6951 (Deutsches Institut fuer Erforschung des Mittelalters)

**Hippokrates-Verlag GmbH**
Neckarstr. 121, Postfach 593, 7000 Stuttgart 1, W. Germany (B.R.D.)
- Hippokrates; Informationen aus der Medizinischen Wissenschaft und Praxis. q. ISSN 0018-2001
- Neuropaediatrie; journal of pediatric neurobiology, neurology and neurosurgery. 4-6 vols. per year. ISSN 0028-3797
- Planta Medica; Zeitschrift fuer Arzneipflanzenforschung. 2 vols per yr.(8 nos.) ISSN 0032-0943
- Zeitschrift fuer Allgemeinmedizin. 3 per m. ISSN 0300-8673
- Zeitschrift fuer Kinderchirurgie und Grenzgebiete. m. ISSN 0044-2909

**Harro V. Hirschheydt**
Postfach 281769, 3000 Hannover-Doehren, W. Germany (B.R.D.)
- Baltische Hefte. a. ISSN 0005-4534

**S. Hirzel Verlag**
Birkenwaldstr. 44, Postfach 347, 7000 Stuttgart 1, W. Germany (B.R.D.)
- A E Ue. (Archiv fuer Elektronik und Uebertragungstechnik); electronics and communication. m. ISSN 0001-1096
- Acustica; international journal on acoustics. m. ISSN 0001-7884 (Deutsche Physikalische Gesellschaft) (Co-sponsor: Groupement des Acousticiens de Langue Francaise)
- Microscopica Acta; Zeitschrift fuer wissenschaftliche Mikroskopie und mikroskopische Technik. bi-m. ISSN 0044-376X
- Roentgenpraxis; Zeitschrift fuer Radiologische Technik. m. ISSN 0035-7820

**Historiographisches Institut GmbH (Solothurn)**
- Geschichte. (pub. by Stamm-Werbung GmbH und Co.)

**Historische Kommission fuer Niedersachsen und Bremen**
- Niedersaechsisches Jahrbuch fuer Landesgeschichte. (pub. by Verlag August Lax)

**Historische Kommission fuer Ost- und Westpreussische Landesforschung**
- Preussenland. (pub. by N. G. Elwert Verlag)

**Historische Kommission Zu Berlin**
Kirchweg 33, 1000 Berlin 38, W. Germany (B.R.D.)
- Historische Kommission zu Berlin. Einzelverdeffentlichungen. (pub. by Colloquium Verlag)
- I. W. K. (Internationale Wissenschaftliche Korrespondenz Zur Geschichte der Deutschen Arbeiterbewegung) 4 per yr. ISSN 0046-8428

**Historischer Verein der Pfalz**
Gr. Pfaffengasse 7, 6720 Speyer, W. Germany (B.R.D.)
- Historischer Verein der Pfalz. Mitteilungen. a. ISSN 0073-2680

**Historischer Verein Dillingen an der Donau**
Oertelstr. 10, 8880 Dillingen, W. Germany (B.R.D)
- Historischer Verein Dillingen an der Donau. Jahrbuch. a. ISSN 0073-2699

**Historischer Verein fuer Hessen**
C/O Dr. A. Eckhardt, Schloss, Staatsarchiv, 6100 Darmstadt, W. Germany (B.R.D.)
- Archiv fuer Hessische Geschichte und Altertumskunde. a. ISSN 0066-636X

**Historischer Verein fuer Oberfranken**
Ludwigstr. 21, Neues Schloss, 8580 Bayreuth, W. Germany (B.R.D.)
- Archiv fuer Geschichte von Oberfranken. a. ISSN 0066-6335

**Historischer Verein fuer Wuerttembergisch Franken**
Dr. G. Wunder, Postfach 664, 7170 Schwaebisch Hall, W. Germany (B.R.D.)
- Wuerttembergisch Franken. a. ISSN 0084-3067

**Hochschul-Informations-System GmbH**
- H I S Briefe. (pub. by Verlag Dokumentation)
- Hochschulplanung. (pub. by Verlag Dokumentation)

**Hochschule fuer Politik**
- Zeitschrift fuer Politik. (pub. by Carl Heymanns Verlag KG)

**Hochschule fuer Wirtschaft und Politik, Hamburg**
- Analysen. (pub. by Leske Verlag und Budrich GmbH)

**Hochschullehrerbund**
- Die Neue Hochschule. (pub. by Technischer Verlag Resch KG)

**Hoechst AG**
Postfach 800320, 6230 Frankfurt 80, W. Germany (B.R.D.)
- Remedia Hoechst. irreg. ISSN 0080-0899

**Hoefling Verlag Dr. V. Mayer**
Postfach 1421, 6940 Weinheim, W. Germany (B.R.D.)
- In Sachen Spiel und Feier. s-m.

**Verlag Hoergeschaedigte Kinder**
Bernadottestr. 126, 2000 Hamburg 52, W. Germany (B.R.D.)
- Hoergeschaedigte Kinder. q. ISSN 0018-3121 (Deutsche Gesellschaft zur Foerderung der Hoer-Sprach-Geschaedigten e.V.)

**Verlag K. Hoerning GmbH**
Weberstr. 1, 6900 Heidelberg, W. Germany (B.R.D.)
- Gastronomie-Rundschau. m. ISSN 0016-5123

**Verlag H. Hoffmann**
Bergengruenstr. 26b, Postfach 140, 1000 Berlin 38, W. Germany (B.R.D.)
- D M I-Nachrichten; Modernes Gesundheitswesen. m. ISSN 0011-5053 (Deutscher Medizinischer Informationsdienst e. V.)

**Verlag Dieter Hoffmann (Mainz)**
Senefelder Str. 25, 6500 Mainz 41, W. Germany (B.R.D.)
- Jagd und Jaeger in Rheinland-Pfalz. m. ISSN 0021-3926 (Landesjagdverband Rheinland-Pfalz)

**Verlag Dr. Hoffmann KG**
Tullastr. 18, Postfach 2545, 6800 Mannheim, W. Germany (B.R.D.)
- Kohle und Heizoel; Fachblatt fuer den Handel. m. ISSN 0023-2742

**Hoffmann und Campe Verlag**
Harvestehuder Weg 45, 2000 Hamburg 13, W. Germany (B.R.D.)
- Heine-Jahrbuch. a. ISSN 0073-1692 (Heinrich-Heine-Institut, Duesseldorf)
- Merian; Monatsheft der Staedte und Landschaften. m. ISSN 0026-0029

**Otto Hoffmanns Verlag**
Havelstr. 16, 61 Darmstadt, W. Germany.
- D D F - das Drogisten Fachblatt. s-m. ISSN 0011-4804

**Verlag Karl Hofmann**
Steinwasenstr. 6, Postfach 1360, 7060 Schorndorf, W. Germany (B.R.D.)
(Subscr. Address: ICHPER, 1201 16th St. NW, Washington, DC 20036)
- Deutscher Glaserkalender; Ratgeber und Helfer fuer Glaser und Fensterbauer. a.
- Glas und Rahmen. s-m.
- Glasforum; Zeitschrift fuer Architektur, Raumgestaltung, Kunst. 6 per yr. ISSN 0017-0852
- International Journal of Physical Education/ Internationale Zeitschrift fuer Sportpaedagogik. q. (International Council on Health, Physical Education and Recreation)
- Sportunterricht. m. (Deutscher Sportlehrerverband e.V.)
- Sportwissenschaft. q.

**Rudolf Hofmann Verlag**
Buchwaldstr. 22a, Postfach 600368, 6000 Frankfurt 60, W. Germany (B.R.D.)
- Freies Leben. m. ISSN 0016-0814
- Naturist und Welt; Internationales Magazin fuer Freikoerperkultur und Volksgesundheit. m. ISSN 0028-0976

**Hohenzollerischer Geschichtsverein**
Karlstr. 32, 7480 Sigmaringen, W. Germany (B.R.D.)
- Hohenzollerische Heimat. ISSN 0018-3253

**Holz-Verlag GmbH**
Postfach 1110, 8905 Mering, W. Germany (B.R.D.)
- A K Holz. 50 per yr.
- Bildlexikon der Nutzhoelzer. m. ISSN 0006-2413
- Holz-Kunststoff. m. ISSN 0018-375X
- Werkstoffe und Technik. m.

**Ferdinand Holzmann Verlag**
Neue Rabenstr. 28, 2000 Hamburg 36, W. Germany (B.R.D.)
- Moebel-Kultur; Fachzeitschrift fuer die Moebelwirtschaft. m. ISSN 0047-7796
- Moebel Wirtschaft; Fachmagazin fuer Handel, Industrie und Innenausbau. m.

**Hans Holzmann Verlag KG**
Gewerbe.Str. 2, Postfach 460, 8939 Bad Woerishofen, W. Germany (B.R.D.)
- Beruf und Bildung. m.
- Die Fleischerei; Internationale Fachzeitschrift fuer Fleischverarbeiter in Handwerk und Industrie. m. ISSN 0015-3613
- Messen und Pruefen. m. ISSN 0026-0339

**Holzner-Verlag**
Neubaustr. 22, Postfach 130, 8700 Wuerzburg 1, W.
Germany (B.R.D.)
• Wuerzburger Wehrwissenschaftliche
Abhandlungen. irreg., vol. 5, 1975. ISSN 0084-
3083 (Universitaet Wuerzburg. Institut fuer
Wehrrecht)

**Hopfenverlag**
Kellerstr. 1, Postfach 229, 8069 Wolnzach, W.
Germany (B.R.D.)
• Hopfen-Rundschau. s-m. ISSN 0018-4845
(Verband Deutscher Hopfenpflanzer e.V.)

**Verlag Hoppenstedt und Co.**
Havelstr. 9, Postfach 4006, 6100 Darmstadt, W.
Germany (B.R.D.)
• Brauereien und Maelzereien in Europa. a. ISSN
0068-0710
• Handbuch der Grossunternehmen. a. ISSN 0073-
0068
• Hoppenstedt-Kurstabellen - Kursanalysen. m.
• Hoppenstedt Vademecum der Investmentfonds.
irreg. ISSN 0073-3342
• Hoppenstedt Versicherungs-Jahrbuch. a. ISSN
0073-3350
• Labo; Kennziffer-Zeitschrift fuer Labortechnik. 14
per yr.
• Leitende Maenner der Wirtschaft. a. ISSN 0075-
871X
• Saling Aktienfuehrer. a. ISSN 0080-5572
• Scope-Journal; Kennziffer-Zeitschrift fuer den
Betrieb. m. ISSN 0084-9735
• Verbaende, Behoerden, Organisationen der
Wirtschaft. a. ISSN 0085-7661
• Wer Baut Maschinen/Who Makes Machinery. a.
ISSN 0083-9299 (Verein Deutscher
Maschinenbau-Anstalten e.V.)

**Hortus-Verlag GmbH**
Rheinalee 4b, 5300bonn-Bad Godesberg 1, W.
Germany (B.R.D.)
• Bunte Tierwelt; Ratgeber fuer Tierfreunde. m.
ISSN 0007-599X

**Hotel- und Gaststaetten-Vereinigung Frankfurt am
Main e.V.**
• Frankfurter Gastronomie. (pub. by Verlag Bodet
und Link)

**Hottinger Baldwin Messtechnik GmbH**
Im Tiefen See 45, 6100 Darmstadt, W. Germany
(B.R.D.)
• Messtechnische Briefe fuer Elektrisches Messen
Mechanischer Groessen. 3 per yr. ISSN 0026-
0428

**Hermann Huebener Verlag KG**
Clausbruchstr. 14, Postfach 2080, 3380 Goslar, W.
Germany (B.R.D.)
• Tonindustrie-Zeitung und Keramische Rundschau;
Zentralblatt fuer das Gesamtgebiet der Steine und
Erden. s-m. ISSN 0040-9200

**Max Hueber Verlag**
Krausstr. 30, 8045 Ismaning, W. Germany (B.R.D.)
• Bibliographie Moderner Fremdsprachenunterricht.
q. (Informationszentrum fuer
Fremdsprachenforschung)
• Der Deutsche Lehrer im Ausland. m. ISSN 0418-
8802
• Heutiges Deutsch. Reihe I: Linguistische
Grundlagen. irreg., vol. 6, 1975. ISSN 0073-201X
(Institut fuer Deutsche Sprache) (Co-sponsor:
Goethe-Institut, Munich)
• Hueber Hochschulreihe. irreg., vol. 35, 1975.
ISSN 0073-3792
• Lessing Yearbook. a. ISSN 0075-8833 (Lessing
Society)
• Linguistische Reihe. irreg., vol. 22, 1975. ISSN
0075-9686
• Mainzer Amerikanistische Beitraege. irreg., 1970,
vol. 11. ISSN 0076-2768
• Russisch; Zeitschrift fuer eine Weltsprache. q.
ISSN 0036-035X
• Theologische Fragen Heute. irreg., 1970, vol. 14.
ISSN 0082-3910
• Zielsprache Deutsch; Zeitschrift fuer
Unterrichtesmethodik und angewandte
Sprachwissenschaft. 4 per yr. ISSN 0012-1479
(Goethe-Institut, Munich)
• Zielsprache Englisch; Zeitschrift fuer den
Englischunterricht in der Weiterbildung. 4 per yr.
(Deutscher Volkshochschulverband.
Paedagogische Arbeitsstelle)
• Zielsprache Franzoesisch; Zeitschrift fuer den
Franzoesischunterricht in der Weiterbildung. 4 per
yr.

• Zielsprache Spanisch; Zeitschrift fuer den
Spanischunterricht in der Weiterbildung. 2 per yr.
• Zweisprachige Reihe. irreg. ISSN 0084-5817

**Hadayatullah Huebsch**
Wickerer Str. 12, 6000 Frankfurt 1, W. Germany
(B.R.D.)
• Wudd; dedicated to the cause of Islam. a. ISSN
0040-8646

**Chemische Werke Huels AG**
4370 Marl Kr. Recklinghausen, W. Germany.
• Blick vom Hochhaus. m. ISSN 0006-4750
• Lichtbogen; Hauszeitschrift der Huels-
Gesellschaften. q. ISSN 0024-2845

**Huethig und Pflaum Verlag**
Lazarettstr. 4, 8000 Munich 19, W. Germany
(B.R.D.)
• D E - der Elektromeister und Deutsches
Elektrohandwerk. s-m. (Zentralverband des
Deutschen Elektrohandwerks)
• E M A - Elektrische Maschinen. m. ISSN 0013-
5445 (Zentralverband des Deutschen
Elektrohandwerks. Bundesfachgruppe
Elektromaschinenbau)
• Fernseh- und Kino-Technik. m. ISSN 0015-0142
(Fernseh- und Kinotechnische Gesellschaft)
• Funk-Technik; fachzeitschrift fuer die gesamte
Unterhaltungselectronic. s-m. ISSN 0016-2825
(Zentralverband des Deutschen Elektrohandwerks.
Bundesfachgruppe Radio- und Fernsehtechnik)
• Lichttechnik. m. ISSN 0024-2861
(Lichttechnische Gesellschaft e.V.)

**Dr. Alfred Huethig Verlag GmbH**
Wilckensstr. 3, Postfach 102869, 6900 Heidelberg 1,
W. Germany (B.R.D.)
• Aerosol Report. m. ISSN 0001-9313
• Chemie-Technik. m.
• Chemiker-Zeitung; mit Chemieboerse. s-m. ISSN
0009-2894
• E H - Elektro Handel. m. ISSN 0013-5542
• E I. (Elektronik Industrie) m.
• I E A - Industrie, Elektrik und Elecktronik. s-m.
ISSN 0019-9079
• Kautschuk und Gummi. Kunststoffe. m. ISSN
0022-9520 (Verband der Deutschen
Kautschukgesellschaften)
• Der Kunsthandel; Zeitschrift fuer Bild und
Rahmen. m. ISSN 0023-5504
• Nachrichten-Elektronik. m.
• Parfuemerie und Kosmetik. m. ISSN 0031-1952
• Schuh-Technik; Fachzeitschrift fuer die
Schuhindustrie. m. ISSN 0036-7052 (Deutsche
Schuhfachschule Pirmasens)
• Z W R. s-m. ISSN 0044-166X

**Hugo-Obermaier-Gesellschaft**
• Quartaer. (pub. by Verlag Ludwig Roehrscheid
GmbH)

**Hugo von Hofmannstahl-Gesellschaft**
Postfach 900511, 6000 Frankfurt, W. Germany
(B.R.D.)
• Hofmannsthal-Blaetter. 2 per yr. ISSN 0441-6813

**Humanistische Union e.V.**
Braeuhausstr. 2, 8000 Munich 2, W. Germany
(B.R.D.)
• Humanistische Union. Mitteilungen. q. ISSN
0046-824X

**Verlag Humanitas**
Woerthstr. 6a, 6700 Ludwigshafen, W. Germany
(B.R.D.)
• Der Humanist. m. (Bund Freireligioeser
Gemeinden Deutschlands)

**Annelies Huter Verlag**
Lipowskystr. 10, 8000 Munich 70, W. Germany
(B.R.D.)
• Z Das Neue Zeitalter. w. ISSN 0028-3487

**Neuer Hygiene Verlag in der Medizinisch-Literarische
Verlagsgesellschaft mbH**
Ringstr. 4, Postfach 120/140, 3110 Uelzen, W.
Germany (B.R.D.), W. Germany.
• Hospital-Hygiene. m. ISSN 0340-997X

**I B M Deutschland GmbH**
Pascalstr. 100, 7000 Stuttgart 80, W. Germany
(B.R.D.)
• I B M Nachrichten. 5 per yr. ISSN 0018-8662

**I D W Verlag GmbH**
Cecilienallee 36, Postfach 320580, 4000 Duesseldorf
30, W. Germany (B.R.D.)
• U E C Journal. q. ISSN 0041-5030 (Union
Europeenne des Experts Comptables
Economiques et Financiers)
• Die Wirtschaftspruefung. s-m. ISSN 0043-6313
(Institut der Wirtschaftspruefer in Deutschland
e.V.)

**I F O Institut fuer Wirtschaftsforschung**
Poschingerstr. 5, 8000 Munich 80, W. Germany
• Arbeitskreis der Deutschen Afrika-Forschungs-
und Dokumentationsstellen. Rundbrief. irreg.
• I F O Institut fuer Wirtschaftsforschung. Studien
zu Handelsfragen. irreg., no. 20, 1976. ISSN
0073-4268
• I F O Mitteilungen: Entwicklungslaender - Afrika
Studienstelle. q.
• I F O Schnelldienst. (pub. by Duncker und
Humblot)
• I F O Studien. (pub. by Duncker und Humblot)
• Spiegel der Wirtschaft; Struktur und Konjunktur
in Bild und Zahl. s-a.
• Studien zur Agrarwirtschaft. irreg., no. 14, 1976.
ISSN 0081-7198
• Studien zur Finanzpolitik. irreg., no. 22, 1976.
ISSN 0081-7279
• Wirtschaftskonjunktur. (pub. by Duncker und
Humblot)

**I N C A-F I E J Research Association (IFRA)**
Washingtonplatz 1, 6100 Darmstadt, W. Germany
• Newspaper Techniques. m.

**Ibero-Amerikanisches Institut**
• Bibliotheca Ibero-Americana. (pub. by Colloquium
Verlag)
• Ibero-Amerikanishes Archiv. (pub. by Colloquium-
Verlag)

**Ibero-Amerikanisches Institut Preussischer
Kulturbesitz Berlin**
• Indiana. (pub. by Gebr. Mann Verlag)
• Monumenta Americana. (pub. by Gebr. Mann
Verlag)
• Quellenwerke zur Alten Geschichte Amerikas.
(pub. by Gebr. Mann Verlag)
• Stimmen Indianischer Voelker. (pub. by Gebr.
Mann Verlag)

**Ichthys-Verlag**
Frauenkopfstr. 34, Postfach 834, 7000 Stuttgart 1,
W. Germany (B.R.D.)
• Z F M T H. (Zeitschrift fuer Musiktheorie) s-a.

**Karl Ihl und Co. KG**
Postfach 683, 8630 Coburg, W. Germany (B.R.D.)
• A M Z. (Auto Motor und Zubehoer);
Fachzeitschrift fuer das gesamte
Kraftfahrzeugwesen. m. ISSN 0001-1983
• Chefbuero.
• Eisenwaren-Boerse. fortn. ISSN 0013-2853
• Elektro Boerse; Fach-Zeitschrift fuer Handel und
Handwerk. m.
• Maschine und Werkzeug; Fachblatt fuer
Neukonstruktionen Betriebstechnik, Fabrik- u.
Werkstatt-Bedarf. fortn. ISSN 0025-4452
• Sammler-Dienst; Fachblatt fuer die gesamte
Philatelie und Numismatik. fortn.
• World Trade Information. m.

**Immunbiologische Informationen e.V.**
• Die Gelben Hefte. (pub. by Medizinische
Verlagsgesellschaft mbH)

**Indische Botschaft in Deutschland**
Adenauerallee 262-264, 5300 Bonn, W. Germany
(B.R.D.)
• Indien. q. ISSN 0046-9149

**Industerieschau-Verlagsgesellschaft**
Berliner Allee 8, 6100 Darmstadt, W. Germany
(B.R.D.)
• Textil-Industrie und ihre Helfer. a. ISSN 0082-
3627

**Industrie- und Handelskammer Frankfurt Am Main.**
Borsenstr. 8-10, Frankfurt Am Main, W. Germany
(B.R.D.)
• Industrie- und Handelskammer Frankfurt am
Main.Mitteilungen. s-m. ISSN 0019-8986

**Industrie- und Handelskammer fuer Augsburg und
Schwaben**
Stettenstr. 1-3, 8900 Augsburg, W. Germany
(B.R.D.)
• Bayerisch-Schwaebische Wirtschaft. m.

**Industrie- und Handelskammer fuer Oberfranken**
Bahnhofstr. 25/27, 8580 Bayreuth, W. Germany
(B.R.D.)
- Oberfraenkische Wirtschaft. m. ISSN 0029-7496

**Industrie- und Handelskammer fuer Rheinhessen**
Schillerplatz 7, 6500 Mainz 1, W. Germany
(B.R.D.)
- Rheinhessische Wirtschaft. m. ISSN 0035-4449

**Industrie- und Handelskammer Hannover-Hildesheim**
Berliner Allee 25, 3000 Hannover, W. Germany
(B.R.D.)
- Industrie- und Handelskammer Hannover-
Hildesheim. Information - Kommentaire. a.

**Industrie- und Handelskammer Mittlerer Necker**
- Auslandsreisen. (pub. by J. Fink Verlag Gmbh)

**Industrie- und Handelskammer Mittlerer Oberrhein**
- Industrie und Handel. (pub. by Verlag C. F.
Mueller GmbH (Karlsruhe))

**Industrie- und Handelskammer Ostwuerttemberg**
Paulinenstr. 8, Postfach 1460, 7920 Heidenheim, W.
Germany (B.R.D.)
- Wirtschaft in Ostwuerttemberg. m.

**Industrie- und Handelskammer Reutlingen**
Hindenburgstr. 54, Postfach 118, 7410 Reutlingen,
W. Germany (B.R.D.)
- Industrie- und Handelkammer Reutlingen.
Mitteilungen. s-m. ISSN 0026-6892

**Industrie- und Handelskammer Wuppertal**
Islandufer 21, Wuppertal-Elberfeld, W. Germany
(B.R.D.)
- I H K Wuppertal. Wirtschaftliche Mitteilungen. s-
m. ISSN 0018-9839

**Industrie- und Handelskammer zu Duesseldorf**
- Industrie- und Handelskammer zu Duesseldorf.
Schnelldienst. (pub. by Bergische
Verlagsgesellschaft Menzel KG)
- Unsere Wirtschaft. (pub. by Neuer Vorwaerts
Verlag)

**Industrie und Handelskammer Zu Luebeck**
Breite Strasse 6-8, 2400 Luebeck, W. Germany
(B.R.D.)
- Wirtschaft im Ostseeraum. a. ISSN 0084-0483

**Industrie- und Handelskammern zu Kiel und zu Flensburg**
Lorentzendamm 24, 2300 Kiel 1, W. Germany
(B.R.D.)
- Wirtschaft zwischen Nord- und Ostsee. m. ISSN
0049-7703

**Industriegewerkschaft Druck und Papier**
Friedrichstr. 15, Postfach 1282, 7000 Stuttgart 1, W.
Germany (B.R.D.)
- Druck und Papier. fortn. ISSN 0012-6470
- Die Feder. (pub. by Presseverlag)
- Industriegewerkschaft Druck und Papier.
Schriftenreihe fuer Betriebsrate. irreg.

**Industriemagazin Verlagsgesellschaft**
Ehrenbreitsteiner Str. 36, Postfach 500461, 8000
Munich 50, W. Germany (B.R.D.)
- Industriemagazin; Management, Marketing,
Technologie. m. ISSN 0019-929X

**Industrieschau-Verlagsgesellschaft**
Berliner Allee 8, 6100 Darmstadt, W. Germany
(B.R.D.)
- Elektro-Industrie; Elektronik und Ihre Helfer. a.
- Kunststoff-Industrie und ihre Helfer. a. ISSN
0075-7276
- Moebel-Industrie und Ihre Helfer. a. ISSN 0077-
0205

**Industrieverband Deutscher Bandweber und Flechter e.V**
- Band- und Flechtindustrie/Narrow Fabric and
Braiding Industry. (pub. by Melliand
Textilberichte KG)

**INFO-Verlag H. G. Thal**
Macherscheider Str. 130, 4040 Neuss, W. Germany
(B.R.D.)
- Deutscher Werbekalender. a.

**Informationszentrum fuer Fremdsprachenforschung**
- Bibliographie Moderner Fremdsprachenunterricht.
(pub. by Max Hueber Verlag)

**Ingenieur Digest Verlagsgesellschaft mbH**
Mainzer Landstr. 160, 6000 Frankfurt 1, W.
Germany (B.R.D.)
- A S R. (Antrieb mit Steuerung und Regelung) 10
per yr.
- Ingenieur Digest; internationaler Fortschritt in
Konstruktion, Betrieb, angewandter Forschung. m.
ISSN 0579-6407
- Pneumatik Digest. bi-m. ISSN 0048-4504
- Verbindungtechnik; Kennziffer-Fachzeitschrift
fuer thermisches und mechanisches Verbinden-
Handhaben-Montieren. m. ISSN 0049-5921

**Insel-Verlag**
Lindenstr. 29, 6000 Frankfurt, W. Germany
(B.R.D.)
- Insel-Almanach. a. ISSN 0443-2460

**Institut der Deutschen Wirtschaft**
- Institut der Deutschen Wirtschaft.
Gewerkschaftsreport. (pub. by Deutscher Instituts-
Verlag GmbH)

**Institut der Wirtschaftspruefer in Deutschland e.V.**
- Die Wirtschaftspruefung. (pub. by I D W-Verlag
GmbH)

**Institut "Finanzen und Steuern." e.V.**
Markt 10, Postfach 1808, 5300 Bonn, W. Germany
(B.R.D.)
- Institut "Finanzen und Steuern." Gruene Briefe.
irreg., no. 159, 1976. ISSN 0067-9941
- Institut "Finanzen und Steuern." Schriftenreihe.
irreg., no. 112, 1976. ISSN 0067-995X

**Institut fuer Afrika-Kunde**
- Afrika Spectrum. (pub. by Afrika Verlag)

**Institut fuer Allgemeine Botanik und Botanischer Garten**
Jungiusstr. 6, 2000 Hamburg 36, W. Germany
(B.R.D.)
- Institut fuer Allgemeine Botanik und Botanischer
Garten. Mitteilungen. irreg., vol. 15, 1975.

**Institut fuer Angewandte Geodaesie**
Richard-Strauss-Allee 11, 6000 Frankfurt 70, W.
Germany (B.R.D.)
- Institut fuer Angewandte Geodaesie. Mitteilungen.
irreg. ISSN 0071-9196
- Nachrichten aus dem Karten- und
Vermessungswesen. irreg. ISSN 0071-920X

**Institut fuer Asienkunde**
Rothenbaumchaussee 32, 2000 Hamburg 13, W.
Germany (B.R.D.)
- Institut fuer Asienkunde. Schriften. irreg., no. 43,
1976. ISSN 0073-8387
- North Korea Quarterly. q.

**Institut fuer Auslandsbeziehungen, Stuttgart**
- Deutsch-Auslaendische Beziehungen.
Schriftenreihe. (pub. by Horst Erdmann Verlag)
- Geistige Begegnung. (pub. by Horst Erdmann
Verlag)
- Laendermonographien. (pub. by Horst Erdmann
Verlag)
- Zeitschrift fuer Kulturaustausch. (pub. by Horst
Erdmann Verlag)

**Institut fuer Demoskopie, Allensbach**
- Jahrbuch der Oeffentlichen Meinung. (pub. by
Verlag fuer Demoskopie)

**Institut fuer den Wissenschaftlichen Film**
Nonnenstieg 72, 3400 Goettingen, W. Germany
(B.R.D.)
- Institut fuer den Wissenschaftlichen Film.
Publikationen zu Wissenschaftlichen Filmen.
Sektion Biologie. irreg., series 10, 1977. ISSN
0073-8417
- Institut fuer den Wissenschaftlichen Film.
Publikationen zu Wissenschaftlichen Filmen.
Sektion Ethnologie. irreg., ser. 7, 1977. ISSN
0341-5910
- Institut fuer den Wissenschaftlichen Film.
Publikationen zu Wissenschaftlichen Filmen.
Sektion Geschichte, Publizistik. irreg., ser. 4,
1977. ISSN 0341-5937
- Institut fuer den Wissenschaftlichen Film.
Publikationen zu Wissenschaftlichen Filmen.
Sektion Medizin. irreg., ser. 4, 1977. ISSN 0341-
5929
- Institut fuer den Wissenschaftlichen Film.
Publikationen zu Wissenschaftlichen Filmen.
Sektion Technische Wissenschaften,
Naturwissenschaften. irreg., ser. 3, 1977. ISSN
0073-8433

- Research Film/Film de Recherche/
Forschungsfilm. s-a. ISSN 0034-5202 (Co-
sponsor: International Scientific Film Association)

**Institut fuer Deutsche Nachkriegsgeschichte**
- Deutschland in Geschichte und Gegenwart. (pub.
by Grabert-Verlag)

**Institut fuer Deutsche Sprache**
- Deutsche Sprache. (pub. by Erich Schmidt Verlag
(Berlin))
- Heutiges Deutsch. Reihe I: Linguistische
Grundlagen. (pub. by Max Hueber Verlag)

**Institut fuer Dokumentation und Information ueber Sozialmedizin und Oeffentliches Gesundheitswesen**
Westerfeldstr. 15, Postfach 5408, 4800 Bielefeld 1,
W. Germany (B.R.D.)
- Dokumentation Arbeitsmedizin. 10 per yr.
- Dokumentation Drogengefaehrdung und
Alkoholmissbrauch. bi-m.
- Dokumentation Impfschaeden-Impferfolge. a.
- Dokumentation Medizin im Umweltschutz. q.
- Dokumentation Sozialmedizin, Oeffentlicher
Gesundheitsdienst, Arbeitsmedizin. m. ISSN
0012-513X

**Institut fuer Dokumentationswesen**
- Verzeichnis Deutscher Informations- und
Dokumentationsstellen. (pub. by Dr. Ludwig
Reichert Verlag)

**Institut fuer Europaeische Politik, Bonn**
- Europaeische Schriften. (pub. by Europa Union
Verlag GmbH)

**Institut fuer Europaeisches und Internationales Wirtschaftsrecht**
- Muenchener Universitaetsschriften. Abhandlungen
des Instituts fuer Europaeisches und
Internationales Wirtschaftsrecht. (pub. by
Ferdinand Enke Verlag)

**Institut fuer Festkoerperforschung. Kernforschungsanlage Juelich**
Postfach 365, Juelich, W. Germany (B.R.D.)
- I F F Bulletin. irreg.

**Institut fuer Film- und Fernsehrecht**
Amalienstr. 10/I, 8000 Munich 2, W. Germany
(B.R.D.)
- Film und Recht. m. ISSN 0015-1440

**Institut fuer Iberoamerika-Kunde**
Neuer Jungfernstieg 21, 2000 Hamburg 36, W.
Germany (B.R.D.)
- Dokumentationsdienst Lateinamerika/
Documentacion Latinoamerica. 4 per yr. ISSN
0300-4899
- Institut fuer Iberoamerika-Kunde. Schriftenreihe.
(pub. by Horst Erdmann Verlag)

**Institut fuer Internationale Schulbuchforschung**
Rebenring 53, 3300 Braunschweig, W. Germany
(B.R.D.)
- Internationales Jahrbuch fuer Geschichts und
Geographieunterricht. a. ISSN 0074-9834

**Institut fuer Interne Revision**
- Zeitschrift Interne Revision. (pub. by Erich
Schmidt Verlag (Bielefeld))

**Institut fuer Konstruktiven Ingenieurbau**
- Konstruktiver Ingenieurbau Berichte. (pub. by
Vulkan-Verlag Dr. W. Classen)

**Institut fuer Kunst und Aesthetik**
- Aesthetik und Kommunikation. (pub. by Aesthetik
und Kommunikation Verlags-GmbH)

**Institut fuer Landwirtschaftliche Marktforschung Braunschweig**
- Agrarwirtschaft. (pub. by Alfred Strothe Verlag)

**Institut fuer Meeres Forschung, Bremerhaven**
Am Handelshafen 12, Bremerhaven, W. Germany
(B.R.D.)
- Institut fuer Meeresforschung, Bremerhaven.
Veroeffentlichungen. irreg., vol. 14, 1974. ISSN
0068-0915

**Institut fuer Menschen- und Menschheitskunde**
- Institut fuer Menschen- und Menschheitskunde,
Rengsdorf. Studien und Materialien. (pub. by
Anthropological Publications NE)

**Institut fuer Musikalische Volkskunde**
Humboldtstr. 2, 4040 Neuss, W. Germany (B.R.D.)
- Ad Marginem; Randbemerkungen zur musikalischen Volkskunde. 3 per yr. ISSN 0001-7965

**Institut fuer Ostdeutsche Kirchen- und Kulturgeschichte**
- Archiv fuer Schlesische Kirchengeschichte. (pub. by Verlag August Lax)

**Institut fuer Ostrecht, Munich**
- Institut fuer Ostrecht. Studien. (pub. by Horst Erdmann Verlag)
- Jahrbuch fuer Ostrecht. (pub. by Horst Erdmann Verlag)

**Institut fuer Paedogogik**
For publications of this agency see section for
UNITED NATIONS

**Institut fuer Raumordnung**
- Raumforschung und Raumordnung. (pub. by Carl Heymanns Verlag KG)

**Institut fuer Reaktorsicherheit der Technischen Ueberwachungs-Vereine**
Glockengasse 2, 5000 Cologne 1, W. Germany (B.R.D.)
- Institut fuer Reaktorsicherheit der Technischen Ueberwachungs-Vereine. Taetigkeitsbericht. irreg.

**Institut fuer Rundfunktechnik GmbH**
Floriansmuehlstr. 60, 8000 Munich 45, W. Germany (B.R.D.)
- Rundfunktechnische Mitteilungen. bi-m. ISSN 0035-9890

**Institut fuer Seeverkehrswirtschaft Bremen**
Hollerallee 32, 2800 Bremen 1, West Germany (B.R.D.)
- Institut fuer Seeverkehrswirtschaft Bremen. Statistik der Schiffahrt/Shipping Statistics. m.

**Institut fuer Staedtebau, Raumplanung und Raumordnung**
- Institut fuer Staedtebau, Raumplanung und Raumordnung. Schriftenreihe. (pub. by Springer-Verlag US)

**Institut fuer Weltwirtschaft, Kiel**
- Die Weltwirtschaft. (pub. by Verlag J.C.B. Mohr (Paul Siebeck))
- Weltwirtschaftliches Archiv/Review of World Economics. (pub. by Verlag J.C.B. Mohr (Paul Siebeck))

**Institut fuer Wissenschaftliche Information aus der Sowjetunion**
Postfach 721, 5100 Aachen, W. Germany (B.R.D.)
- Maschinenbau und Fertigungstechnik der U d S S R. m. ISSN 0025-4487

**Institut fuer Wissenschaftliche Zusammenarbeit**
Landhausstr. 18, 7400 Tuebingen, W. Germany (B.R.D.)
- Literature, Music, Fine Arts; a review of German-language research contributions on literature, music, and fine arts. s-a. ISSN 0024-4775
- Modern Law and Society; a review of German-language research contributions on law, political science, and sociology. s-a. ISSN 0026-7953
- Philosophy and History; a review of German-language research contributions on philosophy, history and cultural developments. s-a. ISSN 0016-884X

**Institut fuer Zeitgeschichte**
- Vierteljahrshefte fuer Zeitgeschichte. (pub. by Deutsche Verlagsanstalt GmbH)

**Institut Jugend Film Fernsehen e.V.**
Waltherstr. 23, 8000 Munich 2, W. Germany (B.R.D.)
- Medien und Erziehung; vierteljahresschrift fuer audiovisuelle kommunikation. q. (Dist. by: Leske Verlag und Budrich GmbH, 5090 Leverkusen 3, W. Germany (B.R.D.)
- Spielfilmliste. a. ISSN 0071-4933

**Institute for Education**
For publications of this agency see section for
UNITED NATIONS

**Institute for International Sociological Research**
- Diplomatic Observer/Observateur Diplomatique/ Diplomatisches Magazin. (pub. by Ellenberg Publishers Ltd.)

**Institute for Scientific Co-Operation**
- Mundus. (pub. by Wissenschaftliche Verlagsgesellschaft mbH)

**Institute for the Study of the USSR**
Mannhardtstr. 6, 8000 Munich, W. Germany (B.R.D.)
- Studies on the Soviet Union. irreg.

**Institutum Balticum**
Haus der Begegnung, Bischof-Kaller-Str. 3, 6240 Koenigstein, W. Germany (B.R.D.)
- Acta Baltica. a. ISSN 0567-7289

**Institutum Iudaicum, Tuebingen**
- Arbeiten zur Geschichte des Antiken Judentums und des Urchristentums. (pub. by E. J. Brill NE)

**Institutum Liturgicum Ratisbonense**
- Textus Patristici et Liturgici. (pub. by Verlag Friedrich Pustet)

**Inter Nationes**
Kennedy-Allee 91, 5300 Bonn-Bad Godesberg, W. Germany (B.R.D.)
- Bildung und Wissenschaft. m.
- Kulturbrief - A German Review. m.

**Interessengemeinschaft deutschsprachiger Autoren**
Vossplatz 2, 2420 Eutin, W. Germany (B.R.D.)
- Das Literarische Wort. q.

**International Amateur Basketball Federation**
Rugendas Str. 19, Munich/Solln., W. Germany (B.R.D.)
- International Amateur Basketball Federation. Official Report of the World Congress. irreg., 1976, 20th, Montreal. ISSN 0534-6622

**International Association for Educational and Vocational Guidance**
104 Regensbuerger Str., D-8500 Nuremberg, W. Germany (B.R.D.)
- A I O S P Bulletin. s-a. ISSN 0044-9504

**International Association of Engineering Geology**
c/o Geologisches Landesamt NW, Dr.-Grieff-Str. 195, Postfach 1080, 4150 Krefeld, W. Germany (B.R.D.)
- International Association of Engineering Geology. Bulletin. s-a. ISSN 0074-1612

**International Association of Law Libraries**
Universitaetstr. 6, 3550 Marburg, W. Germany (B.R.D.)
- I A L L Newsletter. bi-m.
- International Association of Law Libraries. Directory. irreg.
- International Journal of Law Libraries. (pub. by Verlag Dokumentation)

**International Association of Music Libraries**
- Catalogus Musicus. (pub. by Baerenreiter Verlag)
- Fontes Artis Musicae. (pub. by Baerenreiter-Verlag)
- Musikbibliothek Aktuell. (pub. by Deutscher Bibliotheksverband e.V. Arbeitsstelle fuer das Bibliothekswesen)

**International Cartographic Association**
- Internationales Jahrbuch fuer Kartographie. (pub. by Kirschbaum Verlag)

**International College of Dentists. European Section**
Vohwinkelallee 3, 4000 Duesseldorf, W. Germany (B.R.D.)
- International College of Dentists. European Section. Newsletter. a.

**International Commission for the Protection of the Rhine Against Pollution**
Kaiserin-Augusta-Anlagen 15, Postfach 309, 5400 Koblenz, W. Germany (B.R.D.)
- Zahlentafeln der Physikalisch-Chemischen Untersuchungen des Rheins sowie der Mosel/ Tableaux Numeriques des Analyses Physico-Chimiques des Eaux du Rhin Ainsi Que de la Moselle. a. ISSN 0539-1539

**International Congress of Prehistoric and Protohistoric Sciences**
- Inventaria Archaeologica Belgique. (pub. by Rudolf Habelt Verlag)
- Inventaria Archaeologica Ceskoslovensko. (pub. by Rudolf Habelt Verlag)
- Inventaria Archaeologica Denmark. (pub. by Rudolf Habelt Verlag)
- Inventaria Archaeologica Deutschland. (pub. by Rudolf Habelt Verlag)
- Inventaria Archaeologica Espana. (pub. by Rudolf Habelt Verlag)
- Inventaria Archaeologica France. (pub. by Rudolf Habelt Verlag)
- Inventaria Archaeologica Great Britain. (pub. by Rudolf Habelt Verlag)
- Inventaria Archaeologica Italia. (pub. by Rudolf Habelt Verlag)
- Inventaria Archaeologica Jugoslavija. (pub. by Rudolf Habelt Verlag)
- Inventaria Archaeologica Norway. (pub. by Rudolf Habelt Verlag)
- Inventaria Archaeologica Oesterreich. (pub. by Rudolf Habelt Verlag)
- Inventaria Archaeologica Pologne. (pub. by Rudolf Habelt Verlag)
- Inventaria Archaeologica Ungarn. (pub. by Rudolf Habelt Verlag)

**International Construction Machinery Fair, Munich (B A U M A)**
- Bauma-Trends. (pub. by Otto Elsner Verlagsgesellschaft)

**International Copyright Society**
Herzog-Wilhelm-Str. 28, 8000 Munich 2, W. Germany (B.R.D.)
- Internationale Gesellschaft fuer Urheberrecht. Yearbook. a. ISSN 0539-1512

**International Council on Environmental Law**
214 Adenauerallee, 5300 Bonn, W. Germany (B. R. D.)
- I C E L References; to publications concerning legal, administrative and policy aspects of environmental conservation. 17-20 per yr.

**International Council on Health, Physical Education and Recreation**
- International Journal of Physical Education/ Internationale Zeitschrift fuer Sportpaedagogik. (pub. by Verlag Karl Hofmann)

**International Federation for Documentation. Classification Research Committee**
- International Classification. (pub. by Verlag Dokumentation)

**International Federation of Air Traffic Controllers' Associations**
- Controller. (pub. by Verlag Dr. Waldemar Kramer)

**International Federation of Automatic Control**
c/o M. A. Kaaz, Graf-Recke Str. 84, Postfach 1139, 4000 Duesseldorf 1, W. Germany (B.R.D.)
- International Congress of Automatic Control. Proceedings. triennial, 1975, 6th, Boston. ISSN 0074-3526

**International Federation of Library Associations**
- I F L A Annuals. (pub. by Verlag Dokumentation)
- I F L A Journal. (pub. by Verlag Dokumentation)
- I F L A Publications. (pub. by Verlag Dokumentation)

**International Federation of Library Associations. Special Libraries Section**
- Inspel. (pub. by Deutscher Bibliotheksverband E.V. Arbeitsstelle fuer das Bibliothekswesen)

**International Geographical Union**
- Orbis Geographicus. (pub. by Franz Steiner Verlag GmbH)

**International Homoeopathic League**
- Acta Homoeopathica. (pub. by Karl F. Haug Verlag GmbH)

**International Hotel Association. Deutsche Sektion**
- Hotel Restaurant. (pub. by Matthaes Verlag GmbH)

**International Institute of Public Finance**
Universitaet, 6600 Saarbruecken 11, W. Germany (B.R.D.)
- International Institute of Public Finance. Papers and Proceedings. a. ISSN 0074-6533

**International Musicological Society**
- Acta Musicologica. (pub. by Baerenreiter Verlag)

**International Naturist Federation**
- International Naturist Guide/Internationaler FKK-Reisefuehrer/Guide Naturiste Internationale. (pub. by Richard Danehl's Verlag)

**International Project in the Field of Food Irradiation**
Postfach 3640, 7500 Karlsruhe, W. Germany (B.R.D.)
- Food Irradiation Information/Informations sur l'Irradiation des Denrees. 2 per yr. ISSN 0301-049X

**International Shooting Union**
Webergasse 7, 6200 Wiesbaden, W. Germany (B.R.D.)
- Shooting Sport/Tir Sportif/Tiro Deportivo/Schiess-Sport. 6 per yr. ISSN 0037-4156

**International Society for Music Education**
- I S M E Yearbook. (pub. by B. Schott's Soehne)

**International Society for Soil Mechanics and Foundation Engineering**
- Geotechnical Abstracts. (pub. by Deutsche Gesellschaft fuer Erd-und Grundbau)

**International Society of Lymphology**
- Lymphology. (pub. by Georg Thieme Verlag)

**International Society of Organbuilders**
Postfach 234, 7128 Lauffen, W. Germany (B.R.D.)
- I S O Information. irreg. ISSN 0579-5613

**International Society on Thrombosis and Haemostasis**
- Thrombosis et Diathesis Haemorrhagica. (pub. by F. K. Schattauer Verlag)

**International Telephone and Telegraph Corporation**
Hellmuth-Hirth-Str. 42, 7000 Stuttgart 40, W. Germany (B.R.D.)
- I T T Elektrisches Nachrichtenwesen. q. ISSN 0013-5453

**International Union for Applied Ornithology. Institut fuer Biologie, Umwelt und Lebensschutz**
Weiberallee 29, 6229 Schlangenbad-Georgenborn, W. Germany (B.R.D.)
- Angewandte Ornithologie. 1-2 per yr. ISSN 0003-3154

**International Union of Anthropological and Ethnological Sciences**
c/o Prof. Lawrence Krader, Secretary General, Institut fuer Ethnologie, Freie Universitat Berlin, Thielallee 43, 1 Berlin 33, W. Germany (B.R.D.)
- International Congress of Anthropological and Ethnological Sciences. Proceedings. irreg., 1971, 8th, Copenhagen. ISSN 0074-3496

**Internationale Arbeitsgemeinschaft fuer Hymnologie**
- Jahrbuch fuer Liturgik und Hymnologie. (pub. by Johannes Stauda Verlag GmbH)

**Internationale Brecht-Gesellschaft**
- Brecht Heute/Brecht Today. (pub. by Suhrkamp Verlag)

**Internationale Buergermeister-Union**
Im Geiger 64, 7000 Stuttgart-Bad Cannstatt, W. Germany (B.R.D.)
- Deutschland - Frankreich; Beitraege zur europaeischen Einigung. 2 per yr. ISSN 0012-1401

**Internationale Congress Union**
- Tagung und Kongress. (pub. by Hebauf Travel Press)

**Internationale Gesellschaft fuer Geschichte der Pharmazie**
- Beitraege zur Geschichte der Pharmazie. (pub. by Deutscher Apotheker-Verlag)

- Internationale Gesellschaft fuer Geschichte der Pharmazie. Veroeffentlichungen. Neue Folge. (pub. by Wissenschaftliche Verlagsgesellschaft mbH)

**Internationale Gesellschaft fuer Religionspsychologie**
- Archiv fuer Religionspsychologie. (pub. by Vandenhoeck und Ruprecht)

**Internationale Heinrich Schuetz-Gesellschaft e.V.**
Heinrich-Schuetz-Allee 35, 3500 Kassel-Wilhelmshoehe, W. Germany (B.R.D.)
- Acta Sagittariana. a. ISSN 0001-6942
- Sagittarius. (pub. by Baerenreiter Verlag)

**Verlag fuer Internationale Politik GmbH**
Stockenstr. 1-5, Postfach 1529, 5300 Bonn, W. Germany (B.R.D.)
- Europa-Archiv; Zeitschrift fuer internationale Politik. s-m. ISSN 0014-2476 (Deutsche Gesellschaft fuer Auswaertige Politik e.V.)

**Internationale Sozialistische Publikationen GmbH**
Speicherstr. 5, 6000 Frankfurt 1, W. Germany (B.R.D.)
- Was Tun. w. (Gruppe Internationaler Marxisten. Deutsche Sektion der IV. Internationale)

**Internationale Vereinigung fuer Rechts- und Sozialphilosophie**
- A R S P. Beihefte. Neue Folge. (pub. by Franz Steiner Verlag GmbH)
- A R S P - Archiv fuer Rechts- und Sozial Philosophie/Archives de Philosophie du Droit et de Philosophie Sociale/Archives for Philosophy of Law and Social Philosophy. (pub. by Franz Steiner Verlag GmbH)

**Internationale Vereinigung fuer theoretische und angewandte Limnologie**
- Archiv fuer Hydrobiologie. (pub. by E. Schweizerbart'sche Verlagsbuchhandlung)
- Ergebnisse der Limnologie. (pub. by E. Schweizerbart'sche Verlagsbuchhandlung)

**Internationale Zentralinstitut fuer das Jugend-und Bildungsfernsehen**
- Fernsehen und Bildung. (pub. by Verlag Dokumentation)

**Internationaler Bodensee Verkehrsverein**
- Bodensee Hefte. (pub. by Dr. Neinhaus Verlag GmbH)

**Internationales Entomologisches Verein**
- Entomologische Zeitschrift. (pub. by Alfred Kernen Verlag)

**Internationales Institut fuer Missionswissenschaftliche Forschungen**
- Missionswissenschaftliche Abhandlungen und Texte/Etudes et Documents Missionnaires/Mission Studies and Documents. (pub. by Aschendorffsche Verlagsbuchhandlung)
- Zeitschrift fuer Missionswissenschaft und Religionswissenschaft. (pub. by Aschendorffsche Verlagsbuchhandlung)

**Internationales Katholisches Missionswerk e.V.**
- Mission Aktuell. (pub. by Aktuell Verlagsgesellschaft mbH)

**Irus-Verlag**
Silberburgstr. 72, Postfach 29, 7000 Stuttgart 1, W. Germany (B.R.D.)
- Landmaschinen-Rundschau; Agrartechnik Report. bi-m. ISSN 0047-3995

**Isar-Post, Druck- und Verlagsgesellschaft mbH**
Nikolausstr. 49, Postfach 426, 8300 Landshut 2, W. Germany (B.R.D.)
- Der Architekt und der Bauingenieur. q. ISSN 0003-8768 (Bundesverband Freischaffender Architekten und Bauingenieure e.V.)

**Verlag Israel-Forum Landesberger und Co.**
Postfach 69, 8803 Rothenburg, W. Germany (B.R.D.)
- Emuna; Horizonte zur Diskussion ueber Israel und das Judentum. bi-m. ISSN 0013-6913 (Deutscher Koordinierungsrat der Gesellschaften fuer Christlichjuedische Zusammenarbeit (Co-Sponsor: Deutsch-Israelische Gesellschaft)

**J.-G.-Herder-Institut**
Gisonenweg 7, 3550 Marburg, W. Germany (B.R.D.)
- Dokumentation Ostmitteleuropa. bi-m. ISSN 0340-3297
- Zeitschrift fuer Ostforschung; Laender und Voelker im oestlichen Mitteleuropa. 4 per yr. ISSN 0044-3239

**Jaeger-Verlag GmbH**
Holzhofallee 38a, Postfach 110320, 6100 Darmstadt, W. Germany (B.R.D.)
- Der Fremdenverkehr und das Reisebuero. m.
- Jaeger's Intertravel; world guide to travel agencies, countries and hotels. a. ISSN 0075-2150
- Reisen in Deutschland; Deutsches Handbuch fuer Fremdenverkehr. a (3 volumes) ISSN 0080-0805
- Touristik Aktuell; Die deutsche Fremdenverkehrszeitung. w. ISSN 0049-4283

**Jagdgebrauchshundverband**
- Jagdgebrauchshund. (pub. by B L V Verlagsgesellschaft mbH)

**Jagdspaniel-Klub**
Trainsjochstr. 6, 8000 Munich 82, W. Germany (B.R.D.)
- Der Jagdspaniel. 6 per yr. ISSN 0021-3950

**John Jahr Verlag KG**
Burchardstr. 14, 2000 Hamburg 1, W. Germany (B.R.D.)
- Dritte Reich. bi-m.
- Jaeger; Zeitschrift fuer das Jagdrevier, Deutsche Jaeger-Zeitung. fortn.
- Where to Golf in Europe. a. ISSN 0083-9213

**Verlag Jahrbuch der Lehrer der Hoeheren Schulen**
Richard Wagner Str. 1, 5000 Cologne 10, W. Germany (B.R.D.)
- Philologen-Jahrbuch. a. ISSN 0079-1598

**Jahrbuch-Verlag**
Schwabstr. 20, Postfach 1180, 7102 Weinsberg, W. Germany (B.R.D.)
- Rebe und Wein. m. ISSN 0034-1118

**Jahreszeiten-Verlag GmbH**
Possmoorweg 1, 2000 Hamburg 39, W. Germany (B.R.D.)
- Architektur und Wohnen. s-a.
- Fuer Sie. fortn. ISSN 0016-2450
- Petra. m. ISSN 0031-630X
- Vital Gesundheit, Freizeit, Lebensfreude. m.
- Zuhause; Wohnung, Haus und Garten. m.

**Jal-Verlag**
Postfach 1136, 8700 Wuerzburg 2, W. Germany (B.R.D.)
- Quellen und Studien zur Geschichte der Pharmazie. irreg., vol. 14, 1975. ISSN 0085-5367

**Jean-Paul Gesellschaft**
- Jean-Paul-Gesellschaft. Jahrbuch. (pub. by C. H. Beck'sche Verlagsbuchhandlung)

**Kommunalschriften-Verlag J. Jehle**
Barer Str. 32, 8000 Munich 34, W. Germany (B.R.D.)
- Bayerisches Staatsministerium fuer Unterricht und Kultus. Amtsblatt. irreg. ISSN 0005-7207 (Bayern. Staatsministerium fuer Unterricht und Kultus)

**Jenaische Burschenschaft Arminia auf dem Burgkeller**
- Burgkeller-Zeitung. (pub. by Baeren-Druck)

**Jerusalemsverein**
- Im Lande der Bibel. (pub. by Berliner Missionswerk)

**Johann Adam Moehler-Institut Paderborn**
- Catholica. (pub. by Aschendorffsche Verlagsbuchhandlung)

**Johannes Wagner Schriftgiesserei und Messinglinienfabrik**
Theodor-Heuss-Strasse 49, Postfach 227, 8070 Ingolstadt, W. Germany (B.R.D.)
- Handsatzletter; Monografien der modernen Typographie. irreg., no. 17, 1974.

**Joseph Haas-Gesellschaft**
Fichtenstr. 16, 8031 Puchheim, W. Germany (B.R.D.)
- Joseph Haas-Gesellschaft. Mitteilungsblatt. a. ISSN 0446-9577

**Joseph-Haydn-Institut e.V.**
- Haydn-Studien. (pub. by G. Henle Verlag)

**Journal Verlagsgesellschaft mbH**
Im Sachsenlager 17, 6000 Frankfurt, W. Germany (B.R.D.)
- Confructa; international journal for technology of fruit and vegetable processing. bi-m. ISSN 0016-2213
- Hessische Gaertner; Mitteilungsblatt fuer den hessischen Gemuese-, Obst- und Erwerbsgartenbau. m. ISSN 0018-1072

**Juedische Presse GmbH**
Zietenstr. 50, 4000 Duesseldorf 30, W. Germany (B.R.D.)
- Allgemeine juedische Wochenzeitung. w.

**Verlag Juergens KG**
Kurwenalstr. 7, 8000 Munich 40, W. Germany (B.R.D.)
- Gefluegel-Boerse; westdeutsche Ausgabe. s-m. ISSN 0016-5824 (Bund Deutscher Rassegefluegelzuechter e.V)

**Jugendhaus Duesseldorf E.V.**
Carl-Mosterts-Platz 1, 4000 Duesseldorf, W. Germany (B.R.D.)
- Bund der Deutschen Katholischen Jugend. Informationsdienst. s-m. ISSN 0007-5833

**Junge Christliche Arbeitnehmer**
- Aktion. (pub. by A. Bast)

**Verlag Junge Kirche**
Mathildenstr. 86, 2800 Bremen 1, W. Germany (B.R.D.)
- Junge Kirche; eine Zeitschrift Europaeischer Christen. m. ISSN 0022-6319

**Jurid Werke GmbH**
Postfach 1249, 2057 Reinbek, W. Germany (B.R.D.)
- Jurid-Tip. 3 per yr.

**Juristischer Verlag W. Ellinghaus und Co. GmbH**
Bocholder Str. 259, 4300 Essen 11, W. Germany (B.R.D.)
- Anwaltsverzeichnis. biennial. ISSN 0402-6802 (Deutscher Anwaltverein e.V.)

**Juventa Verlag**
Tizianstr. 115, 8000 Munich 19, W. Germany (B.R.D.)
- Deutsche Jugend; Zeitschrift fuer Jugendfragen und Jugendarbeit. m. ISSN 0012-0332

**K V D A Verlag**
Johanna-Melber-Weg 8, 6000 Frankfurt 70, W. Germany (B.R.D.)
- Arzt und Auto; der kraftfahrende Arzt. m. ISSN 0341-4434

**Christian Kaiser Verlag**
Isabellastr. 20, 8000 Munich 40, W. Germany (B.R.D.)
- Abhandlungen zum Christlich-Juedischen Dialog. ISSN 0065-0331
- Evangelische Theologie. bi-m. ISSN 0014-3502
- Theologische Stimmen aus Asien, Afrika und Lateinamerika. ISSN 0082-3929

**Georg Kallmeyer Verlag**
Grosser Zimmerhof 20, Postfach 347, 334 Wolfenbuettel, W. Germany (B.R.D.)
- Zeichenwerk. irreg. ISSN 0084-523X

**Verlag Ferdinand Kamp**
Wildumestr. 6, 4630 Bochum, W. Germany (B.R.D.)
- Hellenika; Zeitschrift fuer deutsch-griechische kulturelle und wirtschaftliche Zusammenarbeit. a. ISSN 0018-0084 (Vereinigung der Deutsch-Griechischen Gesellschaften)

**Kant-Gesellschaft**
- Kant-Studien. (pub. by Walter de Gruyter und Co.)

**Karawane Verlag**
Marbacherstr. 96, 7140 Ludwigsburg, W. Germany (B.R.D.)
- Die Karawane. q. ISSN 0047-3227 (Gesellschaft fuer Laender- und Voelkerkunde)

**Karl-May-Gesellschaft**
Erdkampsweg 33, Postfach 630225, 2000 Hamburg 63, W. Germany (B.R.D.)
- Karl-May-Gesellschaft. Jahrbuch. a.

**Deutscher Kartei-Verlag**
7971 Aitrach, (Wuertt.), W. Germany (B.R.D.)
- Kartei der Praktischen Medizin; unabhaengige Referatenzeitschrift des in- und auslaendischen Fachschrifttums. s-m. ISSN 0022-9113

**Kartellverband Katholischer Deutscher Studentenvereine**
Postfach 1505, 4720 Beckum, W. Germany (B.R.D.)
- Akademische Monatsblaetter. m. ISSN 0002-3000

**Katholische Bundesarbeitsgemeinschaft Land**
Lothstr. 29, 8000 Munich 40, W. Germany (B.R.D.)
- Land Aktuell. s-m.

**Katholische Landesarbeitsgemeinschaft fuer Jugendsozialarbeit**
- Die Heimstatt. (pub. by Verlag die Heimstatt)

**Katholischer Akademikerverband Deutschland**
- Der Katholische Gedanke. (pub. by Verlag Josef Habbel)

**Katholischer Deutscher Frauenbund**
Kaesenstr. 18, 5000 Cologne 1, W. Germany (B.R.D.)
- Die Christliche Frau. 4 per yr. ISSN 0009-5788

**Katholischer Krankenhausverband Deutschlands e.V.**
- Krankendienst. (pub. by Lambertus-Verlag GmbH)

**Katholischer Siedlungsdienst e.V.**
Georgstr. 20, 5000 Cologne 1, W. Germany (B.R.D.)
- Bauen und Siedeln. q. ISSN 0005-6553

**Katholisches Bibelwerk e.V.**
Silberburgstr. 121, 7000 Stuttgart 1, W. Germany (B.R.D.)
- Bibel heute. q. ISSN 0006-0593
- Bibel und Kirche. q. ISSN 0006-0623

**Katholisches Bistum der Alt-Katholiken in Deutschland**
Gregor-Mendel-Str. 28, 5300 Bonn 1, W. Germany (B.R.D.)
- Alt-Katholische Kirchenzeitung. m. ISSN 0002-6522
- Alt-Katholisches Jahrbuch. a.

**Katholisches Militaerbischofsamt**
Adenauerallee 115, 5300 Bonn, W. Germany (B.R.D.)
- Militaerseelsorge. q. ISSN 0047-7362

**Kauka-Verlag**
Gabriel-von-Seidl-Str. 41, 8022 Gruenwald, W. Germany (B.R.D.)
- Bussi-Baer; Zeithschrift fuer unser Kind. m. ISSN 0007-7208

**L. Keidel**
Eduard-Spranger-Str. 45, 8000 Munich 45, W. Germany (B.R.D.)
- A Z-Nachrichten. m. (Austauschzentrale der Vogelliebhaber und Zuechter Deutschlands e V.)

**Josef Keller Verlag**
Postfach 1440, 8130 Starnberg, W. Germany (B.R.D.)
- Der Ingenieur der Deutschen Bundespost. bi-m. ISSN 0020-1170 (Verband Deutscher Postingenieure)
- Der Musikmarkt. s-m. ISSN 0047-8474
- RadioFernseh-Haendler. m. ISSN 0048-6590
- Z P F. (Zeitschrift fuer das Post- und Fernmeldewesen) m. (Deutsche Bundespost)

**Kempter Verlag**
Olgastr. 129a, 7900 Ulm, W. Germany (B.R.D.)
- Schmuck und Uhren. fortn.

**Kepler-Kommission**
- Nova Kepleriana. Neue Folge. (pub. by C. H. Beck'sche Verlagsbuchhandlung)

**P. Keppler Verlag KG**
Industriestr. 2, 6056 Heusenstamm, W. Germany (B.R.D.)
- A P R. (Allgemeine Papier-Rundschau) w. ISSN 0002-5917
- A V R. (Allgemeiner Vliesstoff-Report) m.
- Deutsche Papierwirtschaft. q. ISSN 0070-4296
- Druck - Print. m. ISSN 0012-6462
- Verpackungs Berater. m. ISSN 0042-4293
- Verpackungs-Rundschau. m. ISSN 0042-4307

**Druck und Verlag Kern und Birner**
Werrastr. 4, 6000 Frankfurt 90, W. Germany (B.R.D.)
- Der Freie Zahnarzt. m. (Freier Verband Deutscher Zahnaerzte e.V.)

**Alfred Kernen Verlag**
Schlossstr. 80, 7000stuttgart 1, W. Germany (B.R.D.)
- Die Aquarien-und Terrarien-Zeitschrift. m. ISSN 0003-7265 (Verband Deutscher Vereine fuer Aquarien- und Terrarienkunde)
- Entomologische Zeitschrift. fortn. ISSN 0013-8843 (Internationales Entomologisches Verein)

**Friedrich Kiehl Verlag GmbH**
Pfaustr. 13, 6700 Ludwigshafen, W. Germany (B.R.D.)
- Aktuelle Sammlung; Steuerrecht, Verfuegungen, Erlasse, Rechtsprechung. s-m. ISSN 0002-3841
- Briefe fuer junge Steuerfachleute; Zeitschrift der Gehilfen und Lehrlinge in den steuerberatenden Berufen. m. ISSN 0007-0009

**Kiel. Wasser-und Schiffahrtsdirektion Nord**
Hindenburgufer 247, 2300 Kiel, W. Germany (B.R.D.)
- Nord-Ostsee-Kanal. q. ISSN 0029-1218

**Kinder- und Jugenddorf Klinge e.V.**
6966 Seckach, W. Germany (B.R.D.)
- Klinge. q.

**Verlag Kirchheim und Co. GmbH**
Kaiserstr. 41, Postfach 2524, 6500 Mainz, W. Germany (B.R.D.)
- Aerzteblatt Rheinland-Pfalz. m. ISSN 0001-9488 (Landesaerztekammer Rheinland-Pfalz)
- Archiv fuer Katholisches Kirchenrecht. s-a. ISSN 0003-9160
- Der Duetsche Arzt. 22 per yr. ISSN 0011-9873 (Hartmannbund - Verband der Aertzte Deutschlands e.V.)
- Diabetes-Journal. m. (Deutscher Diabetikerbund e.V.)

**Kirschbaum Verlag**
Siegfriedstr. 28, Postfach 9109, 5300 Bonn-Bad Godesberg 10, W. Germany (B.R.D.)
- Forschung Stadtverkehr. irreg., no. 10, 1975. ISSN 0534-0217 (Germany, Federal Republic. Bundesministerium fuer Verkehr)
- Forschung Stadtverkehr: Sonderreihe/Urban Transport Research: Special Series. irreg., no. 7, 1974. (Germany, Federal Republic. Bundesministerium fuer Verkehr)
- Forschungsgesellschaft fuer das Strassenwesen. Arbeitsgruppe Asphalt- und Teerstrassen. Schriftenreihe. irreg. ISSN 0426-9918 (Forschungsgesellschaft fuer das Strassenwesen e.V.)
- Forschungsgesellschaft fuer das Strassenwesen. Arbeitsgruppe Betonstrassen. Schriftenreihe. irreg. ISSN 0429-1816 (Forschungsgesellschaft fuer das Strassenwesen e.V.)
- Der Gueterverkehr; Lastkraftwagen, Zugmaschinen, Lieferwagen. m. ISSN 0017-5137 (Bundesverband des Deutschen Gueternah- und Gueterfernverkehrs)
- Internationales Jahrbuch fuer Kartographie. a. ISSN 0074-9842 (International Cartographic Association)
- Kartographische Nachrichten. bi-m. ISSN 0022-9164 (Deutsche Gesellschaft fuer Kartographie e.V)
- Kraftfahrt-Bundesamt. Statistische Mitteilungen. m.
- Der Personenverkehr; Privater Omnibus-Taxi-Mietwagen. m. ISSN 0031-5672 (Bundesverband des Deutschen Personenverkehrsgewerbes)
- Strasse und Autobahn; Zeitschrift fuer Strassen- und Brueckenbau, Strassenplanung und Strassenverwaltung. m. ISSN 0039-2162 (Forschungsgesellschaft fuer das Strassenwesen e.V.)
- Strassenverkehrstechnik. bi-m. ISSN 0039-2219 (Forschungsgesellschaft fuer das Strassenwesen e.V.)
- Transport und Lager; Zeitschrift fuer Betriebsleitung, Einkauf und Lagerverwaltung. m. ISSN 0041-1566

**R. Kitzinger**
Schellingstr. 25, 8000 Munich 13, W. Germany (B.R.D.)
- Muenchener Studien zur Sprachwissenschaft. irreg., no. 31, 1973. ISSN 0077-1910

**Kjellberg-ESAB GmbH**
Postfach 100763, 5650 Solingen, W. Germany
(B.R.D.)
- Svetsaren; Schweisstechnische Erfahrungsberichte.
irreg.

**Verlag W.W. Ed. Klambt KG**
Wormser Landstr., Postfach 803A, 6720 Speyer, W.
Germany (B.R.D.)
- Sieben Tage. w. ISSN 0037-461X

**Klaus-Groth-Gesellschaft**
- Klaus-Groth-Gesellschaft . Jahresgaben. (pub. by
Westholsteinische Verlagsanstalt Boyens und Co.)

**Ernst Klett Verlag**
Rotebuehlstr. 77, Postfach 809, 7000 Stuttgart 1, W.
Germany (B.R.D.)
- Der Altsprachliche Unterricht; Arbeitshefte zu
seiner wissenschaftlichen Begruendung und
praktischen Gestalt. 5 per yr. ISSN 0002-6670
- Die Arbeitslehre; Zeitschrift fuer die Didaktik der
technisch-oekonomisch-politischen Aufgabe der
Schule. q.
- Der Biologieunterricht; Beitraege zu seiner
Gestaltung. q. ISSN 0006-3274
- Der Chemieunterricht. 3 per yr.
- Der Deutschunterricht; Beitraege zu seiner Praxis
und wissenschaftlichen Grundlegung. 6 per yr.
ISSN 0340-2258
- Der Erdkundeunterricht; Beitraege zu seiner
wissenschaftlichen und methodischen Gestaltung.
s-a. ISSN 0014-0023
- Familiendynamik; Interdisziplinaere Zeitschrift
fuer Praxis und Forschung. q.
- Der Fremdsprachliche Unterricht;
Wissenschaftliche Grundlegung - methodische
Gestaltung. q. ISSN 0340-2207
- Geschichte in Wissenschaft und Unterricht. m.
ISSN 0016-9056 (Verband der Geschichtslehrer
Deutschlands)
- Gruppendynamik; Forschung und Praxis. bi-m.
- Der Mathematikunterricht; Beitraege zu seiner
wissenschaftlichen und methodischen Gestaltung. 6
per yr. ISSN 0025-5807
- Merkur; Deutsche Zeitschrift fuer europaeisches
Denken. m. ISSN 0026-0096
- Der Physikunterricht; Beitraege zu seinen
fachlichen, methodischen und didaktischen
Problemen. 4 per yr. ISSN 0031-9295
- Politische Bildung; Beitraege zur
wissenschaftlichen Grundlegung. 3 per yr. ISSN
0554-5455
- Psyche; Zeitschrift fuer Psychoanalyse und ihre
Anwendungen. m. ISSN 0033-2623
- Scheidewege; Vierteljahresschrift fuer skeptisches
Denken. q. ISSN 0048-9336
- Sozialwissenschaftliche Informationen fuer
Unterricht und Studium. q. (Arbeitskreis
Sozialwissenschaftliche Informationen)
- Suedwestdeutsche Schulblaetter. 2 per yr.
(Philologenverband Baden-Wuerttemberg)
- Zentralblatt fuer Didaktik der Mathematik. 4 per
yr. ISSN 0044-4103 (Universitaet Karlsruhe.
Zentrum fuer Didaktik der Mathematik) (Co-
sponsor: International Mathematische
Unterrichtskommission)

**Verlag Julius Klinkhardt**
Ramsauer Weg 5, 8173 Bad Heilbrunn, W.
Germany (B.R.D.)
- Arbeitskreis fuer Jugendliteratur. Jahrbuch. a.

**Oskar Klokow, Verlag und Versandbuchhandlung**
Kalandstr. 19, 2400 Luebeck, W. Germany (B.R.D.)
- Badminton. a. (Deutscher Badminton Verband)

**Vittorio Klostermann**
Frauenlobstr. 22, Postfach 900601, 6000 Frankfurt
90, W. Germany (B.R.D.)
- Das Abendland; Forschung zur Geschichte
europaeischen Geisteslebens. Neue Folge. irreg.,
vol. 6, 1974.
- Analecta Romanica. irreg., vol. 38, 1977. ISSN
0569-986X
- Bibliographie der Deutschen Sprach- und
Literaturwissenschaft. a. ISSN 0523-2449
- Bibliographie der Franzoesischen
Literaturwissenschaft. a. ISSN 0523-2465
- Bibliographische Berichte/Bibliographical Bulletin.
2 per yr. ISSN 0006-1506 (Staatsbibliothek
Preussischer Kulturbesitz)
- Juristische Abhandlungen. irreg., vol. 14, 1976.
ISSN 0449-4342
- Philosophische Abhandlungen. irreg., vol. 47,
1977.
- Romanische Forschungen. 4 per yr. ISSN 0035-
8126

- Studien zur Philosophie und Literatur des
Neunzehnten Jahrhunderts. irreg, vol. 34, 1977.
ISSN 0081-735X
- Wissenschaft und Gegenwart.
Geisteswissenschaftliche Reihe. irreg., no. 60.
1976.
- Wissenschaft und Gegenwart. Juristische Reihe.
irreg., no. 6, 1973.
- Wolfenbuetteler Beitraege. irreg. ISSN 0300-2012
(Herzog-August-Bibliothek, Wolfenbuettel)
- Zeitschrift fuer Bibliothekswesen und
Bibliographie. bi-m. ISSN 0044-2380 (Verein
Deutscher Bibliothekare)

**Verlag Wilhelm Kluge**
Saalmannstr. 9, 1000 Berlin 52, W. Germany
(B.R.D.)
- Sicher ist Sicher; Zeitschrift fuer Arbeitsschutz. m.
ISSN 0037-4504 (Verein Deutscher
Sicherheitsingenieure e.V.)

**Fritz Knapp Verlag GmbH**
Neue Mainzer Str. 60, 6000 Frankfurt 1, W.
Germany (B.R.D.)
- Bank und Markt; Zeitschrift fuer
Unternehmensfeuierung und Market. bi-m. ISSN
0341-3667
- Bankhistorisches Archiv; Zeitschrift fuer
Bankgeschichte. s-a. ISSN 0341-6208
- Monatsblaetter fuer Freiheitliche
Wirtschaftspolitik. bi-m. ISSN 0026-9239
- Tradition; Zeitschrift fuer Firmengeschichte und
Unternehmerbiographie. 2 per yr. ISSN 0041-
0616
- Zeitschrift fuer das Gesamte Kreditwesen. s-m.
ISSN 0044-2445

**Kneipp-Verlag GmbH**
Jaudesring 16, 8939 Bad Woerishofen, W. Germany
(B.R.D.)
- Kneipp Blaetter. m. ISSN 0023-2254

**Verlag Harald Kobold**
Brenscheder Str. 7, Postfach 1404, 4630 Bochum,
W. Germany (B.R.D.)
- Der Praeparator. s-a. ISSN 0032-6542

**Verlagsanstalt Alexander Koch GmbH**
Postfach 3081, 7000 Stuttgart 1, W. Germany
(B.R.D.)
- Architektur und Wohnwelt. 6 per yr. ISSN 0003-
4126
- Tapetenzeitung Tapete und Bodenbelag. 2 per m.
ISSN 0039-9566

**Kodak Ag**
Hedelfinger Str. 54, 7000 Stuttgart-Wangen, W.
Germany (B.R.D.)
- Medizinische Radiographie und Photographie.
irreg. ISSN 0076-6178

**Kodex-Verlag GmbH**
Eugenstr. 16, 7000 Stuttgart 1, W. Germany
(B.R.D.)
- Blick hinter die Fassade; Aspekte moderner
Sozialarbeit. a. ISSN 0067-9178

**Hein Koehler**
Vogelsbergstr. 21, 6451 Maintal 3, Gelnhausen 646,
W. Germany (B.R.D.)
- Rochade; Schachzeitung und Pressespiegel. m.

**Koehler und Foltmer**
Ostlandstr. 14, 2900 Oldenburg, W. Germany
(B.R.D.)
- Memeler Dampfboot; die Heimat-Zeitung der
Memellaender. fortn. ISSN 0025-9047

**Koehlers Verlagsgesellschaft mbH**
Steintorwall 17, Postfach 371, 4900 Herford, W.
Germany (B.R.D.)
- Koehlers Flottenkalender. Jahrbuch fuer Schiffahrt
und Haefen. a. ISSN 0075-6474
- Schiff und Zeit. irreg., vol. 6, 1977. (Deutsche
Gesellschaft fuer Schiffahrts-und
Marinegeschichte e. V.)
- Schiffahrt International mit Seekiste und Nautilus.
m.

**Koelner Vortraege zur Sozial- und
Wirtschaftsgeschichte**
Unter Sachsenhausen 10-26, 5000 Cologne 1, W.
Germany (B.R.D.)
- Koelner Vortraege zur Sozial- und
Wirtschaftsgeschichte. a.

**Otto Koeltz Antiquariat**
Postfach 1360, Koenisgspein, W. Germany (B.R.D.)
- Kurtziana. irreg., approx. 1 issue per year. ISSN
0075-7314

**Verlag Valentin Koerner**
Yburgstr. 36, Postfach 304, 7570 Baden-Baden, W.
Germany (B.R.D.)
- Bibliographie zur Symbolik, Ikonographie und
Mythologie. a. ISSN 0067-706X
- Bibliotheca Bibliographica Aureliana. irreg., vol.
69, 1977. ISSN 0067-7884
- Repertoire Bibliographique des Libres Imprimes en
France au Seizieme Siecle. irreg., vol. 26, 1977.
ISSN 0085-5499
- Sammlung Musikwissenschaftlicher
Abhandlungen/Collection d'Etudes
Musicologiques. irreg., no. 61, 1977. ISSN 0085-
588X
- Studien zur Deutschen Kunstgeschichte. irreg.,
vol. 335, 1975. ISSN 0081-7228

**Koerner GmbH**
Bildstr. 4, Postfach 9, 7016 Gerlingen, W. Germany
(B.R.D.)
- Deutsche Schaefereizeitung. w. ISSN 0012-0677
(Union of German Sheep-Breeders, Bonn)
- Hobbyfunk C.B.-Radio; Fachmagazin fuer den
Citizens-Band-Funk. m.
- QRV Amateur Radio; Unabhaengiges Amateur-
Radio-Magazin. m.

**Verlag Carl Kohler**
Kaiser-Wilhelm-Str. 31, Postfach 210827, 6700
Ludwigshafen 1, W. Germany (B.R.D.)
- Der Buechsenmacher. m. ISSN 0007-3067
- Messer und Schere. m. ISSN 0026-0398 (Verband
deutscher Stahlwaren-Fachhandler e.V)

**W. Kohlhammer GmbH (Koeln)**
Luxemburger Str. 72, 5000 Cologne 1, W. Germany
(B.R.D.)
- Bundesarbeitsblatt. m. ISSN 0007-5868 (Germany,
Federal Republic. Bundesministerium fuer Arbeit
und Sozialordnung)
- Der Landkreis. m. (Deutscher Landkreistag)
- Der Versorgungsbeamte; Fach-Zeitschrift fuer die
Kriegs- und Wehrdienstopferversorgung sowie die
angrenzenden Fachgebiete. m. (Bund der
Versorgungsbeamten)
- Volkshochschule im Westen. bi-m. ISSN 0042-
8515 (Landesverband der Volkshochschulen von
Nordrhein-Westfalen)
- Zeitschrift fuer Beamtenrecht. m. ISSN 0514-2571

**W. Kohlhammer GmbH (Stuttgart)**
Urbanstr. 12, Postfach 747, 7000 Stuttgart 1, W.
Germany (B.R.D.)
- Archiv fuer Kommunalwissenschaften. s-a. ISSN
0003-9209 (Deutsches Institut fuer Urbanistik)
- Archiv fuer Mathematische Logik und
Grundlagenforschung. s-a. ISSN 0003-9268
- Baden-Wuerttembergische Verwaltungspraxis;
Fachzeitschrift fuer die Ausbildung und
Fortbildung in der oeffentlichen Verwaltung. m.
- Buerger im Staat. q. ISSN 0007-3121
(Landeszentrale fuer Politische Bildung)
- Deutsche Krankenpflege-Zeitschrift. m. ISSN
0012-074X
- Dokumentation fuer Umweltschutz und
Landespflege. q. ISSN 0026-6957 (Germany,
Federal Republic. Bundesanstalt fuer
Vegetationskunde, Naturschutz und
Landschaftspflege)
- Der Gemeindetag; Zeitschrift fuer die
gemeindliche Selbstverwaltung Hessen. m.
- Das Kunstwerk; eine Zeitschrift ueber alle Gebiete
der bildenden Kunst. bi-m. ISSN 0023-561X
- Landesversicherungsanstalt Wuerttemberg.
Mitteilungen. bi-m.
- Lebensbilder aus Schwaben und Franken. irreg.
(Baden- Wuerttemberg. Kommission fuer
Geschichtliche Landeskunde)
- Natur und Landschaft. m. ISSN 0028-0615
(Germany, Federal Republic. Bundesanstalt fuer
Vegetationskunde, Naturschutz und
Landschaftspflege)
- Die Oeffentliche Verwaltung; Zeitschrift fuer
Verwaltungsrecht und Verwaltungspolitik. s-m.
ISSN 0029-859X
- Polizeiblatt fuer das Land Baden-Wuerttemberg.
m. ISSN 0048-4768
- Sprache im Technischen Zeitalter. q. ISSN 0038-
8475

- Der Staedtetag; Zeitschrift fuer Praxis und Wissenschaft der kommunalen Verwaltung. m. ISSN 0038-9048 (Verband Kommunaler Stadtreinigungsbetriebe)
- V F D B Zeitschrift. q. ISSN 0042-1804 (Vereinigung zur Foerderung des Deutschen Brandschutzes e.V.)
- Zeitschrift fuer Auslaendisches Oeffentliches Recht und Voelkerrecht. 4 per yr. ISSN 0044-2348 (Max- Planck- Institut fuer Voelkerrecht)
- Zeitschrift fuer Kirchengeschichte. 3 per yr. ISSN 0044-2925
- Zeitschrift fuer Stadtgeschichte, Stadtsoziologie und Denkmalpflege. s-a.
- Zeitschrift fuer Volkskunde. s-a. ISSN 0044-3700 (Deutsche Gesellschaft fuer Volkskunde e.V.)

**W. Kohlhammer-Verlag GmbH. Abt. Veroeffentlichungen des Statistischen Bundesamtes**
Philipp-Reis-Str. 3, Postfach 421120, 6500 Mainz 42, W. Germany (B.R.D.)
- Das Arbeitsgebiet der Bundesstatistik. irreg. ISSN 0072-162X (Germany, Federal Republic. Statistisches Bundesamt.
- Bevoelkerungsstruktur und Wirtschaftskraft der Bundeslaender. a. ISSN 0072-1867 (Germany, Federal Republic. Statistisches Bundesamt)
- Bildung im Zahlenspiegel. a. (Germany, Federal Republic. Bundesministerium fuer Bildung und Wissenschaft) (Co-sponsor: Statistisches Bundesamt)
- Germany (Federal Republic, 1949- ) Sachverstaendigenrat zur Begutachtung der Gesamtwirtschaftlichen Entwicklung. Jahresgutachten. a. ISSN 0072-159X (Germany, Federal Republic. Sachverstaendigenrat zur Begutachtung der Gesamtwirtschaftlichen Entwicklung)
- Germany (Federal Republic, 1949- ) Statistisches Bundesamt. Alphabetisches Laenderverzeichnis fuer die Aussenhandelsstatistik. irreg. ISSN 0072-1638
- Germany (Federal Republic, 1949- ) Statistisches Bundesamt. Ausgewaehlte Zahlen fuer die Bauwirtschaft. m. ISSN 0072-1719
- Germany (Federal Republic, 1949- ) Statistisches Bundesamt. Auslandsstatistik Nr. 6370070: Special Trade According to the Classification for Statistics and Trade (CST) q. with a. cumulation. ISSN 0072-1689
- Germany (Federal Republic, 1949- ) Statistisches Bundesamt. Aussenhandel. Reihe 7: Sonderbeitraege. irreg. ISSN 0072-1700
- Germany (Federal Republic, 1949- ) Statistisches Bundesamt. Fachserie Auslandsstatistik, Reihe 2: Produzierende Gewerbe im Ausland. irreg.
- Germany (Federal Republic, 1949- ) Statistisches Bundesamt. Fachserie Auslandsstatistik, Reihe 4: Loehne und Gehaelter im Ausland. a.
- Germany (Federal Republic, 1949- ) Statistisches Bundesamt. Fachserie Auslandsstatistik, Reihe 5: Preise und Preisindizes im Ausland. m. ISSN 0072-3940
- Germany (Federal Republic, 1949- ) Statistisches Bundesamt. Fachserie 1, Reihe 1: Gebiet und Bevoelkerung. a. ISSN 0072-1786
- Germany (Federal Republic, 1949- ) Statistisches Bundesamt. Fachserie 1, Reihe 2: Bevoelkerungsbewegung. a. ISSN 0072-1794
- Germany (Federal Republic, 1949- ) Statistisches Bundesamt. Fachserie 1, Reihe 2.3: Wanderungen. a. ISSN 0072-1808
- Germany (Federal Republic, 1949- ) Statistisches Bundesamt. Fachserie 1, Reihe 3: Haushaelte und Familien. irreg.
- Germany (Federal Republic, 1949-) Statistisches Bundesamt. Fachserie 1, Reihe 4: Erwerbetaetigkeit. irreg. ISSN 0072-1832
- Germany (Federal Republic, 1949- ) Statistisches Bundesamt. Fachserie 2, Reihe 2: Abschluesse der Kapitalgesellschaften. a.
- Germany (Federal Republic, 1949- ) Statistisches Bundesamt. Fachserie 2, Reihe 3: Abschluesse der Oeffentlichen Versorgungs- und Verkehrsunternehmen. a.
- Germany (Federal Republic, 1949- ) Statistisches Bundesamt. Fachserie 2, 4: Zahlungsschwierigkeiten. q. ISSN 0072-2030
- Germany (Federal Republic, 1949- ) Statistisches Bundesamt. Fachserie 3, Reihe 2: Betriebs-, Arbeits- und Einkommensverhaeltnisse. irreg. ISSN 0072-3681
- Germany (Federal Republic, 1949- ) Statistisches Bundesamt. Fachserie 3, Reihe 3: Gartenbau und Weinwirtschaft. a.

- Germany (Federal Republic, 1949- ) Statistisches Bundesamt. Fachserie 3, Reihe 4: Tierische Erzeugung. m, s-a, a.
- Germany (Federal Republic, 1949- ) Statistisches Bundesamt. Fachserie 3, Reihe 4.5: Fischerei. m, a. ISSN 0072-3673
- Germany (Federal Republic, 1949- ) Statistisches Bundesamt. Fachserie 4, Reihe S: Sonderbeitraege. irreg. ISSN 0072-2073
- Germany (Federal Republic, 1949- ) Statistisches Bundesamt. Fachserie 4, Reihe 1: Zusammenfassende Daten fuer das Produzierende Gewerbe. irreg.
- Germany (Federal Republic, 1949- ) Statistisches Bundesamt. Fachserie 4, Reihe 2: Indizes des Auftragseinangs und des Auftragsbestands in Ausgewaehlten Industriezweigen und im Bauhauptgewerbe. m. ISSN 0072-209X
- Germany (Federal Republic, 1949- ) Statistisches Bundesamt. Fachserie 4, Reihe 2: Indizes fuer das Produzierende Gewerbe. m.
- Germany (Federal Republic, 1949- ) Statistisches Bundesamt. Fachserie 4, Reihe 3: Produktion im Produzierenden Gewerbe. q.
- Germany (Federal Republic, 1949- ) Statistisches Bundesamt. Fachserie 4, Reihe 5: Beschaeftigung, Umsatz, Investitionen und Kosten Struktur im Baugewerbe. a. ISSN 0072-1727
- Germany (Federal Republic, 1949- ) Statistisches Bundesamt. Fachserie 4, Reihe 7: Handwerk. irreg. ISSN 0072-2103
- Germany (Federal Republic, 1949- ) Statistisches Bundesamt. Fachserie 5, Reihe 1: Bautaetigkeit. a. ISSN 0072-1735
- Germany (Federal Republic, 1949- ) Statistisches Bundesamt. Fachserie 5, Reine 2: Bewilligungen im Sozialen. a. ISSN 0072-1743
- Germany (Federal Republic, 1949- ) Statistisches Bundesamt. Fachserie 5, Reihe 3: Bestand an Wohnungen. a. ISSN 0072-1751
- Germany (Federal Republic, 1949- ) Statistisches Bundesamt. Fachserie 6, Reihe 1: Grosshandel. a. ISSN 0072-1964
- Germany (Federal Republic, 1949- ) Statistisches Bundesamt. Fachserie 6, Reihe 2: Einzelhandel. a. ISSN 0072-1972
- Germany (Federal Republic, 1949- ) Statistisches Bundesamt. Fachserie 6, Reihe 5: Wahrenverkehr mit Berlin (West) m.
- Germany (Federal Republic, 1949- ) Statistisches Bundesamt. Fachserie 6, Reihe 6: Wahrenverkehr mit der Deutschen Demokratischen Republik und Berlin (Ost) m. ISSN 0072-1980
- Germany (Federal Republic, 1949- ) Statistisches Bundesamt. Fachserie 6, Reihe 7: Reiseverkehr. irreg. ISSN 0072-1999
- German (Federal Republic, 1949- ) Statistisches Bundesamt. Fachserie 7, Reihe 1: Zusammenfassende Uebersichten fuer den Aussenhandel. m. ISSN 0072-1646
- Germany (Federal Republic, 1949- ) Statistisches Bundesamt. Fachserie 7, Reihe 2: Aussenhandel nach Waren und Laendern (Spezialhandel) m. with a. cumulation. ISSN 0072-1654
- Germany (Federal Republic, 1949- ) Statistisches Bundesamt. Fachserie 7, Reihe 3: Aussenhandel Nach Laendern und Warengruppen (Spezialhandel) q. with a. cumulation. ISSN 0072-1662
- Germany (Federal Republic, 1949- ) Statistisches Bundesamt. Fachserie 7, Reihe 4. Aussenhandel mit Ausgewaehlten Waren. m. with a. cumulation.
- Germany (Federal Republic, 1949- ) Statistisches Bundesamt. Fachserie 7, Reihe 6: Durchfuhr im Seeverkehr und Seeumschlag. a. ISSN 0072-1697
- Germany (Federal Republic, 1949- ) Statistisches Bundesamt. Fachserie 8, Reihe 1: Gueterverkehr der Verkehrszweige. q. ISSN 0072-4092
- Germany (Federal Republic, 1949- ) Statistisches Bundesamt. Fachserie 8, Reihe 2: Eisenbahnverkehr. m. ISSN 0072-4041
- Germany (Federal Republic, 1949- ) Statistisches Bundesamt. Fachserie 8, Reihe 3: Strassenverkehr. irreg. ISSN 0072-405X
- Germany (Federal Republic, 1949- ) Statistisches Bundesamt. Fachserie 8, Reihe 4: Binnenschiffahrt. m. ISSN 0072-4017
- Germany (Federal Republic, 1949- ) Statistisches Bundesamt. Fachserie 8, Reihe 5: Seeschiffahrt. m. ISSN 0072-4025
- Germany (Federal Republic, 1949- ) Statistisches Bundesamt. Fachserie 8, Reihe 6: Luftverkehr. m. ISSN 0072-4033
- Germany (Federal Republic, 1949- ) Statistisches Bundesamt. Fachserie 8, Reihe 33: Strassen verkehrsunfaelle. m and a. ISSN 0072- 4068

- Germany (Federal Republic, 1949- ) Statistisches Bundesamt. Fachserie 9, Reihe 1: Boden- und Kommunalkreditinstitute. a; supplements monthly numbers. ISSN 0072-2014
- Germany (Federal Republic, 1949- ) Statistisches Bundesamt. Fachserie 9, Reihe 2: Aktienmaerkte. m.
- Germany (Federal Republic, 1949- ) Statistisches Bundesamt. Fachserie 10. Rechtspflege. a. ISSN 0072-1859
- Germany (Federal Republic, 1949- ) Statistisches Bundesamt. Fachserie 11: Bildung und Kultur. a. ISSN 0072-1778
- Germany (Federal Republic, 1949- ) Statistisches Bundesamt. Fachserie 12, Reihe 1: Ausgewaehlte Zahlen fuer das Gesundheitswesen. a. ISSN 0072-1840
- Germany (Federal Republic, 1949- ) Statistisches Bundesamt. Fachserie 13, Reihe 2-3: Sozialhilfe; Kriegsopferfuersorge. a. ISSN 0072-3754
- Germany (Federal Republic, 1949- ) Statistisches Bundesamt. Fachserie 13, Reihe 6: Oeffentliche Jugendhilfe. a. ISSN 0072-3762
- Germany (Federal Republic, 1949- ) Statistisches Bundesamt. Fachserie 14: Finanzen und Steuern. irreg.
- Germany (Federal Republic, 1949- ) Statistisches Bundesamt. Fachserie 15, Reihe 1: Wirtschaftsrechnungen. m. ISSN 0072-386X
- Germany (Federal Republic, 1949- ) Statistisches Bundesamt. Fachserie 16, Reihe 2: Arbeitnehmerverdienste in Industrie und Handel. q. ISSN 0072-3789
- Germany (Federal Republic, 1949- ) Statistisches Bundesamt. Fachserie 16, Reihe 3: Arbeiterverdienste im Handwerk. s-a. ISSN 0072-3797
- Germany (Federal Republic, 1949- ) Statistisches Bundesamt. Fachserie 16, Reihe 4: Tarifloehne und Tarifgehaelter. s-a. ISSN 0072-3843
- Germany (Federal Republic, 1949- ) Statistisches Bundesamt. Fachserie 17, Reihe 1: Preise und Preisindizes fuer die Land- und Forstwirtschaft. m. ISSN 0072-3894
- Germany (Federal Republic, 1949- ) Statistisches Bundesamt. Fachserie 17, Reihe 2: Preise und Preisindizes fuer Industrielle Produkte. Erzeugerpreise. m. ISSN 0072-3886
- Germany (Federal Republic, 1949- ) Statistisches Bundesamt. Fachserie 17, Reihe 3: Index der Grundstoffpreise. m. ISSN 0072-3878
- Germany (Federal Republic, 1949- ) Statistisches Bundesamt. Fachserie 17, Reihe 4: Messzahlen fuer Bauleistungspreise und Preisindizes fuer Bauwerke. m.
- Germany (Federal Republic, 1949- ) Statistisches Bundesamt. Fachserie 17, Reihe 7: Preise und Preisindizes der Lebenserhaltung. m. ISSN 0072-3916
- Germany (Federal Republic, 1949- ) Statistisches Bundesamt. Fachserie 17, Reihe 8: Preise und Preisindizes fuer den Ein- und Ausfuhr. m.
- Germany (Federal Republic, 1949- ) Statistisches Bundesamt. Fachserie 17, Reihe 10: Internationaler Vergleich der Preise fuer die Lebenserhaltung. m. ISSN 0072-3827
- Germany (Federal Republic, 1949- ) Statistiches Bundesamt. Fachserie 17, Reihe 9: Preise fuer Verkehrsleistungen. q. ISSN 0072-3924
- Germany (Federal Republic, 1949- ) Statistisches Bundesamt. Fachserie 18, Reihe 1: Konten und Standardtabellen. a. ISSN 0072-4009
- Germany (Federal Republic, 1949- ) Statistisches Bundesamt Fachserie 19, Reihe 2: Wasserversorgung und Abwasserbeseitigung. irreg.
- Germany (Federal Republic, 1949- ) Statistisches Bundesamt. Laenderberichte. irreg.
- Germany (Federal Republic, 1949- ) Statistisches Bundesamt. Laenderkurzberichte. 4 per mo.
- Germany (Federal Republic, 1949- ) Statistisches Bundesamt. Preise, Loehne, Wirtschaftsrechnungen. Reihe 5: Preise und Preisindices fuer Bauwerke und Bauland. q. ISSN 0072-3908
- Germany (Federal Republic,1949- ) Statistisches Bundesamt. Preise, Loehne, Wirtschaftsrechnungen. Reihe 14: Arbeiterverdienste in der Landwirtschaft. a. (Germany, Federal Republic. Statistisches Bundesamt)
- Germany (Federal Republic, 1949- ) Statistisches Bundesamt. Warenverzeichnis fuer die Aussenhandelsstatistik. a. ISSN 0072-4106
- Germany (Federal Republic, 1949- ) Statistisches Bundesamt. Zahlenkompass/Statistical Compass/ Boussole des Chiffres/Compas de Cifras. a. ISSN 0072-4114

- Internationale Monatszahlen. m. (Germany, Federal Republic. Statistisches Bundesamt)
- Statistischer Wochendienst. w. (Germany, Federal Republic. Statistisches Bundesamt)
- Statistisches Jahrbuch fuer die Bundesrepublik Deutschland. a. ISSN 0081-5357 (Germany, Federal Republic. Statistisches Bundesamt)
- Studies on Statistics. irreg. ISSN 0072-3967 (Germany, Federal Republic. Statistisches Bundesamt)
- Survey of German Federal Statistics/Apercu de la Statistique Federale Allemande. irreg. (Germany, Federal Republic. Statistisches Bundesamt)
- Wirtschaft und Statistik. m. ISSN 0043-6143 (Germany, Federal Republic. Statistisches Bundesamt)
- Wirtschaftskalender. q and a. (Germany, Federal Republic. Statistisches Bundesamt)

**Peter Kolbe Verlag**
Kurfuerstenstr. 2, Postfach 84, 8034 Germering, W. Germany (B.R.D.)
- Bauanalysis. q.

**Verlag H. Kolbenstetter**
Kibbelstr. 37, 4300 Essen, W. Germany (B.R.D.)
- Der Augenspiegel; Forum der Augenaerzte. m. ISSN 0004-7937

**Kolloid- Gesellschaft**
- Kolloid-Gesellschaft. Verhandlungsberichte. (pub. by Dr. Dietrich Steinkopff Verlag)

**Kommanditgesellschaft Verlag Horst Axtmann GmbH und Co.**
Wilhelmstr. 42, 6200 Wiesbaden, W. Germany (B.R.D.)
- Fernseh und Film Technikum. m. ISSN 0015-1424
- Film-Echo/Filmwoche. s-w. ISSN 0015-1149 (Hauptverband der Deutschen Filmtheater e.V.)
- Filmtheater-Praxis - Werbung Heute. m.

**Verlag die Kommenden GmbH**
Rosastr. 21, 7800 Freiburg im Breisgau, W. Germany (B.R.D.)
- Der Elternbrief; Ratschlaege und Hilfen fuer die Erziehungspraxis. m. ISSN 0013-645X
- Die Kommenden; eine unabhaengige Zeitschrift fuer geistige und soziale Erneuerung. s-m. ISSN 0023-3005
- Wege zur Pflege eines Meditativen Lebens und zu einem Vertieften Christusverstaendniss. bi-m.
- Das Wesentliche im Zeitgeschehen.

**Kommission fuer Geschichtliche Landeskunde in Baden-Wuerttemberg**
Konrad-Adenauer-Str. 4, 7000 Stuttgart 1, W. Germany (B.R.D.)
- Kommission fuer Geschichtliche Landeskunde in Baden-Wuerttemberg. Veroeffentlichungen. Reihe A. Quellen. irreg. ISSN 0067-2831
- Kommission fuer Geschichtliche Landeskunde in Baden-Wuerttemberg. Veroeffentlichungen. Reihe B: Forschungen. irreg. ISSN 0521-9884
- Zeitschrift fuer Wuerttembergische Landesgeschichte. s-a. ISSN 0044-3786

**Kommunistischer Arbeiterbund Deutschlands (KABD)**
- Rote Fahne. (pub. by Verlag Neuer Weg GmbH)

**Kommunistischer Bund fuer den Proletarischen Internationalismus**
- Internationale. (pub. by Arbeiterkampf-Verlag J. Reents)

**Kommunistischer Bund Westdeutschland**
- Kommunismus und Klassenkampf. (pub. by Kuehl KG)
- Kommunistische Volkszeitung. (pub. by Kuehl KG)

**Konditorei, Verlagsgesellschaft mbH**
Krefelder Str. 645, Postfach 581, 4050 Moenchengladbach, W. Germany (B.R.D.)
- Der Konditormeister; Fachzeitschrift des Konditorenhandwerks. w. ISSN 0023-3250 (Landesinnungsverband des Bayerischen Konditorenhandwerkes)

**Kongressgesellschaft fuer Aerztliche Fortbildung e.V.**
- Das Aerztliche Laboratorium. (pub. by Medicus Verlag GmbH)

**Konkordanter-Verlag**
Buechenbronner Str. 16, 7530 Pforzheim, W. Germany (B.R.D.)
- Unausforschlicher Reichtum; Zweimonatsschrift fuer Gott und sein Wort. bi-m. ISSN 0041-6444

**Konrad-Adenauer-Stiftung fuer Politische Bildung und Studienfoerderung e.V. Politische Akademie Eichholz**
- Eichholzbrief. (pub. by Eichholz-Verlag GmbH)
- Frau in der Offenen Gesellschaft. (pub. by Eichholz-Verlag GmbH)

**Konradin-Verlag Robert Kohlhammer GmbH**
Postfach 1380, 7022 Leinfelden, W. Germany (B.R.D.)
- Bau- und Moebelschreiner. m. ISSN 0005-6464 (Verband des deutschen Tischlerhandwerks)
- Baupraxis. m. ISSN 0005-6766
- Beschaffung Aktuell; Zeitschrift fuer industrielle Beschaffungswesen. 11 per yr. (Bundesverband Materialwirtschaft und Einkauf e.V.)
- Betrieb und Meister. m.
- Chemie-Anlagen und Verfahren; Zeitschrift fuer die Praxis in der Chemie-Technik. m. ISSN 0009-2800
- Die Computer Zeitung. fortn.
- E Z. (Elektronik-Zeitung) fortn. ISSN 0012-8074
- Gold und Silber - Uhren und Schmuck. m. ISSN 0017-1573 (Verband der Taschen- und Armbanduhren Industrie e.V.)
- Loyal; das kritische Wehrmagazin. m. (Verband der Deutschen Bundeswehr e.V.)
- M A V. (Maschinen - Anlagen - Verfahren) m.
- M D. m.
- Raum und Textil. m.
- Textil Praxis International. m. ISSN 0040-4853 (Verein Deutscher Faerber e.V.)

**Verlag fuer Konservative Publizistik**
Goerresplatz 5, 5400 Koblenz, W. Germany (B.R.D.)
- Konservativ Heute. bi-m. (Gesellschaft fuer Konservative Publizistik e.V.)

**Universitaetsverlag Konstanz GmbH**
Bahnhofstr. 8, Postfach 632, 7750 Konstanz, W. Germany (B.R.D.)
- Publizistik. q. ISSN 0033-4006

**Kopfklinik**
Wasserturmstr. 8, 8520 Erlangen, W. Germany (B.R.D.)
- Kopfklinik; Zeitschrift fuer die Fachgebiete im Bereich des Kopfes. q. ISSN 0341-0609

**Kosmos Gesellschaft der Naturfreunde**
- Kosmos. (pub. by Franckh'sche Verlagshandlung W. Keller und Co.)
- Kosmos Bibliothek. (pub. by Franckh'sche Verlagshandlung W. Keller und Co.)

**Karl Kraemer Verlag**
Schulze-Delitzsch-Str. 15, 7000 Stuttgart 80, W. Germany (B.R.D.)
- Architektur Wettbewerbe. q. ISSN 0003-8806
- G A. (Gas und Architektur); internationale Zeitschrift ueber Verwendungsmoeglichkeiten von Gas im Bauwesen. 6 per yr. ISSN 0016-3406

**Kraftfahrt-Bundesamt**
- Kraftfahrt-Bundesamt. Statistische Mitteilungen. (pub. by Kirschbaum Verlag)

**Verlag Dr. Waldemar Kramer**
Bornheimer Landwehr 57a, 6000 Frankfurt 60, W. Germany (B.R.D.)
- Controller; journal of air traffic control. q. ISSN 0010-8073 (International Federation of Air Traffic Controllers' Associations) (The Federation's Address: P.O.B. 196, 1215 Geneva 15, Airport, Switzerland)
- Frankfurter Geographische Hefte. irreg. ISSN 0071-9234 (Frankfurter Geographische Gesellschaft)
- Rhein-Mainische Forschungen. irreg. ISSN 0080-2662 (Universitaet Frankfurt. Geographisches Institut)
- Schopenhauer-Jahrbuch. a. ISSN 0080-6935 (Schopenhauer Gesellschaft e.V.)
- Senckenbergiana Maritima. Zeitschrift fuer Meeresgeologie und Meeresbiologie. a. ISSN 0080-889X (Senckenbergische Naturforschende Gesellschaft)

**Verlag A. Krammer und Co.**
Hermannstr. 3, 4000 Duesseldorf, W. Germany (B.R.D.)
- R A S. (Rohr-Armatur-Sanitaer-Heizung) m. ISSN 0033-6769
- Sanitaer und Heizungs Report. bi-m.
- Sanitaer- und Heizungstechnik. m. ISSN 0036-4401
- Sport- und Baederbauten; internationale Fachzeitschrift fuer Planung, Bau, Einrichtung, Betrieb und Forschung. 6 per yr. ISSN 0038-7924

**Krausskopf-Verlag fuer Wirtschaft GmbH**
Lessingstr. 12a, 6500 Mainz 1, W. Germany (B.R.D.)
- Antriebstechnik. m. ISSN 0003-6099 (Forschungsvereinigung Antriebstechnik e. V.)
- Foerdern und Heben; independent periodical for rationalisation and automation in mechanical handling and storing. 22 per yr. ISSN 0015-5241
- Oelhydraulik und Pneumatik; unabhaengige Zeitschrift fuer Kraftuebertragung, Regelung und Steuerung. m. ISSN 0029-8697
- Verfahrenstechnik. m. ISSN 0049-5948

**Kreisgemeinschaft Osterode Ostpreussen**
Schuetzenwall 13, 3330 Helmstedt, W. Germany (B.R.D.)
- Osteroder Zeitung. s-a. ISSN 0030-638X

**Kreuz-Verlag**
Breitwiesenstr. 30, Postfach 800669, 7000 Stuttgart 80, W. Germany (B.R.D.)
- Evangelische Kommentare; Monatsschrift zum Zeitgeschehen in Kirche und Gesellschaft. m. ISSN 0300-4236
- Frau und Mutter. every 4 weeks. ISSN 0016-0180 (Arbeitsgemeinschaft Frau und Mutter)
- Fuer Alle. every 4 weeks. ISSN 0016-2426
- Pastoralblaetter. m. ISSN 0031-2800
- Predigtstudien. s-a. ISSN 0079-4961

**Verlag fuer Kriminalistische Fachliteratur**
Hochallee 32, 2000 Hamburg 13, W. Germany (B.R.D.)
- Kriminalistik; Zeitschrift fuer die gesamte kriminalistische Wissenschaft und Praxis. m. ISSN 0023-4699
- Kriminologische Aktualitaet. a.
- Kriminologische Schriftenreihe. irreg. (Deutsche Kriminologische Gesellschaft)

**Dr. F. Krins**
Fritz-Thomee-Str. 75, 5990 Altena, W. Germany (B.R.D.)
- Der Maerker; Heimatblatt fuer die ehemalige Grafschaft Mark und den maerkischen Kreis. bi-m. ISSN 0024-9661 (Maerkischer Kreis)

**Kroegers Buch- und Verlagsdruckerei**
Blankeneser Bahnhofstr. 17, Postf. 550270, 2000 Hamburg 55, W. Germany (B.R.D.)
- Deutscher Kuesten-Almanach; ein Nachschlagewerk fuer die Berufs- und Sportschiffahrt in Nord- und Ostsee und auf den deutschen Seeschiffahrts-strassen. a. ISSN 0070-4377

**Alfred Kroener Verlag**
Reuchlinstr. 4, 7000 Stuttgart 1, W. Germany (B.R.D.)
- Deutsche Schiller-Gesellschaft. Jahrbuch. a. ISSN 0070-4318

**Verlag Dr. Krueger KG**
Wetzlarer Str., Postfach 70, 6349 Sinn, W. Germany (B.R.D.)
- Die Auslese; Zeitschrift fuer Offerten auserlesener Firmen des kirchlichen Bedarfs. 4 per yr.

**Krueger-Verlag**
Westenhellweg 9, Postfach 227, 4600 Dortmund 1, W. Germany (B.R.D.)
- Handbuch fuer Berufskraftfahrer. irreg. ISSN 0073-0157

**Krupp GmbH**
Postfach 10, 4300 Essen 1, W. Germany (B.R.D.)
- Krupp Technische Mitteilungen. Forschungsberichte und Werksberichte. 2-4 per yr. ISSN 0040-1463

**Kuehl KG**
Sandhofer Str. 29, 6800 Mannheim 31, W. Germany (B.R.D.)
- Kommunismus und Klassenkampf. (Kommunistischer Bund Westdeutschland)

- Kommunistische Volkszeitung. w.
  (Kommunistischer Bund Westdeutschland)

**Verlag Werner Kuehn**
Postfach 309, Roemerstr. 47, 5427 Bad Ems, W.
Germany (B.R.D.)
- D B Z. (Deutsche Zeitung fuer Briefmarkenkunde)
  s-m. ISSN 0011-4790

**Kuehn-Verlag**
Mittelweg 14, Postfach 132222, 2000 Hamburg 13,
W. Germany (B.R.D.)
- Hamburg Air. q. ISSN 0017-6869 (Flughafen
  Hamburg GmbH)

**Kuestenausschuss Nord- und Ostsee, Kiel**
- Die Kueste. (pub. by Westholsteinische
  Verlagsanstalt Boyens und Co.)

**Kugelfischer Georg Schaefer & Co.**
1260, 8720 Schweinfurt 2, W. Germany (B.R.D.)
- Ball and Roller Bearing Engineering. 2-3 per yr.
  ISSN 0522-0629
- Technique du Roulement. 2-3 per yr.
- Tecnica de los Rodamientos. 2-3 per yr.
- Waelzlagertechnik. 2-3 per yr. ISSN 0511-0653

**G. Kuhlmann**
Admiralstr. 149, 2800 Bremen, W. Germany (B. R.
D.)
- Arbeiterpolitik. m.

**Buch- und Zeitschriften-Verlag Kultur und Wissen
GmbH und Co. KG**
Wilhelmstr. 42, Postfach 1329, 6200 Wiesbaden, W.
Germany (B.R.D.)
- Hilton in Deutschland. bi-m. ISSN 0046-743X
- Wiesbadener Leben. m. ISSN 0049-7622

**Kulturbuch-Verlag GmbH**
Passauer Str. 4, 1000 Berlin 30, W. Germany
(B.R.D.)
- Amtsblatt fuer Berlin. w. (Berlin (West) Senator
  fuer Inneres)
- Berliner Statistik. m. ISSN 0005-9331 (Berlin.
  Statistisches Landesamt)
- Statistisches Jahrbuch Berlin. a. ISSN 0081-5322
  (Berlin (West) Statistisches Landesamt)

**Kulturplatz Dammweg e.V.**
Dammweg 15, 2800 Bremen, W. Germany (B.R.D.)
- Kulturplatz. 2 per yr.

**Kulturwerk Schlesien e.V.**
- Schlesien. (pub. by Verlag Nuernberger Presse)

**Kunst und Technik Verlagsgesellschaft mbH**
Lipowskystr. 8, 8000 Munich 70, W. Germany
(B.R.D.)
- Weltkunst; the world art review. s-m. ISSN 0043-
  261X

**Kunststoff-Verlag**
Auf der Heide 20, Postfach 10, 3001 Isernhagen, W.
Germany (B.R.D.)
- K I B. (Kunststoffe im Bau); Themenhefte ueber
  moderne Baustoffe und Konstruktionen. bi-m.
  ISSN 0023-5571
- Kunstoffberater, -rundschau, -technik. m. ISSN
  0340-8442
- Leitende Angestellte. m. ISSN 0024-0737 (Union
  der Leitenden Angestellten)

**Deutscher Kunstverlag GmbH**
Vohburger Str. 1, 8000 Munich 21, W. Germany
(B.R.D.)
- Architectura; Zeitschrift fuer Geschichte der
  Baukunst. s-a. ISSN 0044-863X
- Deutsche Kunst und Denkmalpflege. s-a. ISSN
  0012-0375 (Vereinigung der
  Landesdenkmalpfleger in der Bundesrepublik
  Deutschland)
- Niederdeutsche Beitraege zur Kunstgeschichte. a.
  ISSN 0078-0537 (Niedersaechsisches
  Landesmuseum, Hannover)
- Staatliche Kunstsammlungen in Baden-
  Wuerttemberg. Jahrbuch. a. ISSN 0067-284X
- Waffen- und Kostumkunde. s-a. ISSN 0042-9945
  (Gesellschaft fuer Historische Waffen- und
  Kostuemkunde)
- Zeitschrift fuer Kunstgeschichte. 5 per yr. ISSN
  0044-2992

**Deutscher Verlag fuer Kunstwissenschaft**
Lindenstr. 76, 1000 Berlin 61, W. Germany
(B.R.D.)
- Deutscher Verein fuer Kunstwissenschaft.
  Zeitschrift. s-a. ISSN 0044-2135 (Deutscher
  Verein fuer Kunstwissenschaft)
- Schrifttum zur Deutschen Kunst. irreg., vol. 31,
  1975. ISSN 0080-7176 (Deutscher Verein fuer
  Kunstwissenschaft)

**Kupijai und Prochnow, Verlag und Druckerei**
Bluecherstr. 22, 1000 Berlin 61, W. Germany (B. R.
D.)
- Handbuch fuer die Druckindustrie Berlin. a. ISSN
  0073-0173

**Kuratorium fuer Technik und Bauwesen in der
Landwirtschaft e.V.**
- Landtechnik. (pub. by Verlag Eduard F.
  Beckmann KG)

**Kursbuch Verlag**
Potsdamer Str. 98, 1000 Berlin 31, W. Germany
(B.R.D.)
- Kursbuch. 4 per yr. ISSN 0023-5652

**Kurverwaltung Bad Homburg**
- Bad Homburger Veranstaltungsspiegel Kurzeitung.
  (pub. by Verlag Dr. Max Gehlen)

**Laboratorium fuer Sediment Forschung**
Postfach 104040, 6900 Heidelberg, W. Germany
(B.R.D.)
- International Sedimentological Congress.
  Guidebook. quadrennial, 1971, 8th, Heidelberg.
  ISSN 0074-7904

**Lack und Chemie Verlag Elvira Moeller GmbH**
Karl Benz Str. 11, Postfach 1168, W. Germany
(B.R.D.), W. Germany (B. R. D.)
- Defazet. (Deutsche Farben- Zeitschrift) m.

**Laetare-Verlag Stein**
Herzbachweg 2, 6460 Gelnhausen, W. Germany
(B.R.D.)
- Getroster Tag/Hopeful Day. 3 per yr. ISSN 0016-
  934X
- Schriftenreihe fuer Die Evangelische Frau. 6 per
  yr. ISSN 0036-696X
- Stichwoerter zur Entwicklungspolitik.

**Lambertus-Verlag GmbH**
Sternwaldstr. 4, Postfach 1026, 7800 Freiburg, W.
Germany (B.R.D.)
- Caritas; Zeitschrift fuer Caritasarbeit und
  Caritaswissenschaft. bi-m. ISSN 0008-6614
  (Deutscher Caritasverband)
- Caritas-Kalender. a. (Deutscher Caritasverband)
- Caritas-Korrespondenz; Informationsblaetter fuer
  die Caritaspraxis. m. ISSN 0008-6622 (Deutscher
  Caritasverband)
- Jugendwohl; Zeitschrift fuer Kinder- und
  Jugendhilfe. m. ISSN 0022-5975 (Deutscher
  Caritasverband)
- Krankendienst; Zeitschrift fuer kath.
  Krankenhaeuser, Sozialstationen und
  Pflegekraefte. m. ISSN 0023-4486 (Katholischer
  Krankenhausverband Deutschlands e.V.)

**Land- und Hauswirtschaftlicher Auswertungs- und
Informationsdienst**
- Ausbildung und Beratung in Land- und
  Hauswirtschaft. (pub. by B L V
  Verlagsgesellschaft mbH)
- Rinderproduktion. Zucht, Leistungspruefungen,
  Besamung in der Bundesrepublik Deutschland.
  (pub. by Landwirtschaftsverlag GmbH)

**Landbuch-Verlag GmbH**
Kabelkamp 6, Postfach 160, 3000 Hannover 1, W.
Germany (B.R.D.)
- Das Landvolk. s-m. ISSN 0023-8104 (Verband der
  Niedersaechsischen Landvolkes e.V.)
- Niedersaechsischer Jaeger. s-m. ISSN 0048-0339
  (Landesjagdverband Niedersachsen)

**Landesaerztekammer Baden-Wuerttemberg**
- Aerzteblatt Baden-Wuerttemberg. (pub. by A. W.
  Gentner Verlag)

**Landesaerztekammer Rheinland-Pfalz**
- Aerzteblatt Rheinland-Pfalz. (pub. by Verlag
  Kirchheim und Co. GmbH)

**Landesdenkmalamt Baden-Wuerttemberg**
- Fundberichte aus Baden-Wuerttemberg. (pub. by
  E. Schweizerbart'sche Verlagsbuchhandlung)

**Landesfeuerwehrverband Baden-Wuerttemberg**
- Die Brandhilfe. (pub. by Neckar-Verlag)

**Landesfischereiverband Schleswig Holstein**
Holstenstr. 108, 2300 Kiel, W. Germany (B.R.D.)
- Fischerblatt; Mitteilungsblatt fuer die Kutter- und
  Kuesten-fischerei. m. ISSN 0015-2854

**Landesgewerbeanstalt Bayern**
Postfach 305, 8500 Nuernberg 1, W. Germany
(B.R.D.)
- L G A-Rundschau. q. ISSN 0023-6268

**Landesinnungsverbaende des Bayerischen Maler- und
Lackiererhandwerks und des Maler- und
Lackiererhandwerks Baden-Wuerttemberg**
- Der Maler und Lackierermeister. (pub. by Verlag
  W. Sachon)

**Landesinnungsverband des Bayerischen
Konditorenhandwerkes**
- Der Konditormeister. (pub. by Konditorei,
  Verlagsgesellschaft mbH)

**Landesinnungsverband des Bayerischen
Kraftfahrzeughandwerks Muenchen**
- Das Bayerische Kraftfahrzeughandwerk. (pub. by
  Bartsch Verlag KG)

**Landesjagdverband Niedersachsen**
- Niedersaechsischer Jaeger. (pub. by Landbuch-
  Verlag GmbH)

**Landesjagdverband Rheinland-Pfalz**
- Jagd und Jaeger in Rheinland-Pfalz. (pub. by
  Verlag Dieter Hoffmann (Mainz))

**Landesjugendring Berlin**
Muenchener Str. 24, 1000 Berlin 30, W. Germany
(B.R.D.)
- Blickpunkt; Zeitschrift fuer junge Menschen. 8 per
  yr. ISSN 0006-4769

**Landesmuseum fuer Naturkunde zu Muenster in
Westfalen**
Himmelreichallee 50, 4400 Muenster, W. Germany
(B.R.D.)
- Landesmuseum fuer Naturkunde zu Muenster in
  Westfalen. Abhandlungen. 2-4 per yr. ISSN 0023-
  7906
- Natur und Heimat. 4 per yr. ISSN 0028-0593

**Landessammlungen fuer Naturkunde**
Erbprinzenstr. 13, 7500 Karlsruhe 1, W. Germany
(B.R.D.)
- Beitraege zur Naturkundlichen Forschung in
  Suedwestdeutschland. a. ISSN 0005-8122

**Landessternwarte Heidelberg-Koenigstuhl**
- Sterne und Weltraum. (pub. by Verlag Sterne und
  Weltraum Dr. Vehrenberg)

**Landesverband Bayerischer Imker e.V.**
- Der Imkerfreund. (pub. by Ehrenwirth Verlag
  GmbH)

**Landesverband der Tonkuenstler und Musiklehrer**
Husumer Str. 31, 2000 Hamburg 20, W. Germany
(B.R.D.)
- Landesverband der Tonkuenstler und Musiklehrer.
  Mitteilungsblatt. q. ISSN 0047-3979

**Landesverband der Volkshochschulen von Nordrhein-
Westfalen**
- Volkshochschule im Westen. (pub. by W.
  Kohlhammer GmbH (Koeln))

**Landesverband des Gross- und Aussenhandels fuer
Hessen e.V.**
Telemannstr. 12, 6000 Frankfurt, W. Germany
(B.R.D.)
- Grosshandel-Aussenhandel. m.

**Landesverband fuer Obstbau, Garten und Landschaft
Baden-Wuerttemberg e. V.**
- Obst und Garten. (pub. by Verlag Eugen Ulmer)

**Landesverband Hessischer Imker e.V.**
- Die Biene. (pub. by Verlag die Biene)

**Landesverband Schleswig-Holsteinischer Imker**
Burgfeldstr. 41, 2360 Bad Segeberg, W. Germany
(B.R.D.)
- Neue Bienenzucht. m.

**Landesversicherungsanstalt Hessen**
Staedelstr. 28, 6000 Frankfurt 70, W. Germany (B.R.D.)
- Landesversicherungsanstalt Hessen. Nachrichten. 26 per yr. ISSN 0023-7922

**Landeszahnaerztekammer Baden-Wuerttemberg**
- Zahnaerzteblatt Baden-Wuerttemberg. (pub. by A. W. Gentner Verlag)

**Landeszentrale fuer Politische Bildung**
- Buerger im Staat. (pub. by W. Kohlhammer GmbH (Stuttgart))

**Landschaftsverband Rheinland**
- Rheinische Ausgrabungen. (pub. by Rheinland-Verlag)

**Landschaftsverband Rheinland. Archivberatungsstelle**
- Inventare Nichtstaatlicher Archive. (pub. by Rheinland-Verlag)

**Landschaftsverband Rheinland. Referat Landschaftspflege**
- Beitraege zur Landesentwicklung. (pub. by Rheinland-Verlag)

**Landschaftsverband Westfalen-Lippe**
- Landschaftsverband Westfalen-Lippe. Volkskundliche Kommission. Schriften. (pub. by Aschendorffsche Verlagsbuchhandlung)

**Landschriften-Verlag GmbH**
Kurfuerstenstr. 53, 5300 Bonn, W. Germany (B.R.D.)
- K O - Innere Kolonisation - Land und Gemeinde; Zeitschrift fuer Agrar-und Bodenordnung, Infrastruktur, Siedlung und Staedtebau, Umweltgestaltung. bi-m. ISSN 0341-1869 (Gesellschaft zur Foerderung der Inneren Kolonisation (GFK))

**Landsmannschaft Berlin-Mark Brandenburg. Landesverband Berlin**
Stresemannstr. 90, 1 Berlin 61, W. Germany (B.R.D.)
- Maerkische Zeitung. m. ISSN 0024-967X

**Landsmannschaft der Deutschen aus Litauen**
c/o Alfred Franzkeit and Edith Kunfert, Eds. & Pubs., 2839 Freistatt, W. Germany (B.R.D.)
- Heimatgruss. a. ISSN 0440-6230

**Landsmannschaft der Deutschen aus Russland e.V.**
Stafflenbergstr. 66, 7000 Stuttgart, W. Germany (B.R.D.)
- Volk auf dem Weg. m. ISSN 0042-8337

**Landsmannschaft der Donauschwaben**
Charlottenplatz 17, 7000 Stuttgart 1, W. Germany (B.R.D.)
- Donauschwaebisches Schrifttum. irreg. ISSN 0070-7074

**Landsmannschaft Westpreussen E.V.**
Warendorfer Str. 21, 4400 Muenster, W. Germany (B.R.D.)
- Westpreusse. s-m. ISSN 0043-4418
- Westpreussen-Jahrbuch. (pub. by Verlagsgesellschaft C. J. Fahle)

**Landwirtschaftskammer Hannover**
- Hannoversche Land- und Forstwirtschaftliche Zeitung. (pub. by Verlagsgruppe Langen-Mueller)

**Landwirtschaftskammer Weser-Ems GmbH**
- Landwirtschaftsblatt Weser-Ems. (pub. by Landwirtschaftsverlag Weser-Ems GmbH)

**Landwirtschaftsverlag GmbH**
Marktallee 89, Postfach 480210, 4400 Muenster-Hiltrup, W. Germany (B.R.D.)
- Agrarrecht. m. ISSN 0340-840X (Deutsche Gesellschaft fuer Agrarrecht)
- Rinderproduktion. Zucht, Leistungspruefungen, Besamung in der Bundesrepublik Deutschland. irreg. (Land- und Hauswirtschaftlicher Auswertungs- und Informationsdienst)
- Schriftenreihe fuer Vegetationskunde. irreg., no. 9, 1975. ISSN 0085-5960 (Germany, Federal Republic. Bundesanstalt fuer Vegetationskunde, Naturschutz und Landschaftspflege)
- Taschenbuch des Pflanzenarztes. a. ISSN 0082-1799

**Landwirtschaftsverlag Weser-Ems GmbH**
Hindenburgstr. 29, Postfach 689, 2900 Oldenburg, W. Germany (B.R.D.)
- Landwirtschaftsblatt Weser-Ems. w. ISSN 0047-4029 (Landwirtschaftskammer Weser-Ems GmbH)

**Rudolf A. Lang Verlag**
Auf der Au 2, Postfach 1228, 6270 Idstein, W. Germany (B.R.D.)
- Vakuum-Technik. 8 per yr. ISSN 0042-2266 (Deutsche Arbeitsgemeinschaft Vakuum)

**Verlagsgruppe Langen- Mueller**
Hubertusstr. 4, 8000 Munich 19, W. Germany (B.R.D.)
- Ensemble; international literary yearbook. a. (Bayerische Akademie der Schoenen Kuenste)
- Hannoversche Land- und Forstwirtschaftliche Zeitung. w. ISSN 0017-7466 (Landwirtschaftskammer Hannover)

**Verlag Langenscheidt KG**
Crellestr. 29, 1000 Berlin 62, W. Germany (B.R.D.)
- Langenscheidt's Sprach-Illustrierte; a German language journal. 4 per yr. ISSN 0023-8252
- Lebende Sprachen; Zeitschrift fuer fremde Sprachen in Wissenschaft und Praxis. q. ISSN 0023-9909

**Verlag Heinrich Lapp**
Luepertzender Str. 157/163, Postfach 345, 4050 Moenchengladbach, W. Germany (B.R.D.)
- Bekleidung und Waesche. s-m. ISSN 0005-8289
- Kakao und Zucker; Technische Fachzeitschrift fuer die gesamte Suesswarenindustrie. m. ISSN 0022-7838
- Reiter Revue International. m. ISSN 0034-3692

**Verlag Michael Lassleben**
Lange Gasse 19, Postfach 20, 8411 Kallmuenz, W. Germany (B.R.D.)
- Beitraege zur Oberpfalzforschung. irreg. ISSN 0067-5164
- Frankfurter Althistorische Studien. irreg., no. 7, 1973. (Universitaet Frankfurt. Seminar fuer Alte Geschichte)
- Jahrbuch fuer Numismatik und Geldgeschichte. a. ISSN 0075-2711 (Bayerische Numismatische Gesellschaft)
- Muenchner Studien zur Sozial- und Wirtschaftsgeographie. irreg., vol. 10, 1974. ISSN 0077-1902 (Universitaet Muenchen. Wirtschaftsgeographisches Institut)

**Verlag Latvija**
Ferd. Toennies Str. 11, Postfach 107, 2420 Eutin, W. Germany (B.R.D.)
- Latvija; Latvian newspaper. 4 per m. ISSN 0023-8899

**C.J. Laumanns**
Kolpingstr. 5, Postfach 584, 4780 Lippstadt, W. Germany (B.R.D.)
- Sagan-Sprottauer Heimatbriefe; offizielles Organ und Monatschrift fuer den Kreis Sprottau. m. ISSN 0036-2573

**Verlag August Lax**
3200 Hildesheim, W. Germany (B.R.D.)
- Alt-Hildesheim; Zeitschrift fuer Stadt und Stift Hildesheim. a. (Stadtarchiv Hildesheim)
- Archiv fuer Schlesische Kirchengeschichte. a. ISSN 0066-6491 (Institut fuer Ostdeutsche Kirchen- und Kulturgeschichte)
- Muenstersche Beitraege zur Vor- und Fruehgeschichte. irreg., 1971, vol. 6. ISSN 0077-2003 (Universitaet Muenster)
- Niedersaechsisches Jahrbuch fuer Landesgeschichte. a. ISSN 0078-0561 (Historische Kommission fuer Niedersachsen und Bremen)

**J. F. Lehmanns Verlag**
Agnes-Bernauer-Platz 8, Postfach 210140, 8000 Munich 21, W. Germany (B.R.D.)
- Almanach fuer die Aerztliche Fortbildung. irreg.
- Weyers Flottentaschenbuch. a. ISSN 0083-9078

**Lehrervereinigung Duesseldorf**
- Paedagogik und Schule in Ost und West. (pub. by Ferdinand Schoeningh)

**Lembeck-Verlag**
Leerbachstr. 42, 6000 Frankfurt 1, W. Germany (B.R.D.)
- Oekumenische Rundschau. q. ISSN 0029-8654 (Deutscher Oekumenischer Ausschuss)

**Gebr. Lensing, Verlagsanstalt KG**
Kampstr. 42, Postfach 875, 4600 Dortmund 1, W. Germany (B. R. D.)
- Praxis des Neusprachlichen Unterrichts. q. ISSN 0032-7085

**Verlag Robert Lerche**
Waltherstr. 27, 8000 Munich 15, W. Germany (B.R.D.)
- Handbuch der Sudetendeutschen Kulturgeschichte. irreg., vol. 6, 1973. ISSN 0073-0149 (Collegium Carolinum)

**Verlag Robert Lerche. Abt. Praeger Nachrichten**
Abt. Praeger Nachrichten, Pullacherstr. 1, 8000 Munich 70, W. Germany (B.R.D.)
- Prager Nachrichten. m.

**Lesen Verlag GmbH**
Eulenhof, 2351 Hardebek, W. Germany (B.R.D.)
- Bulletin Jugend und Literatur. m. ISSN 0045-351X
- Imprint; Literaturjournal. bi-m.
- Spektrum des Geistes; Literaturkalender. a. ISSN 0085-6584

**Leserinitiative Publik e.V.**
Postfach 700771, 6000 Frankfurt 70, W. Germany (B.R.D.)
- Publik-Forum. s-m.

**Leske Verlag und Budrich GmbH**
Rennbaumstr. 25, Postfach 300406, 5090 Leverkusen 3, W. Germany (B.R.D.)
- Analysen. irreg. ISSN 0072-9426 (Hochschule fuer Wirtschaft und Politik, Hamburg)
- Gegenwartskunde; Gesellschaft, staat, erziehung. q. ISSN 0016-5875
- Medien und Erziehung; Vierteljahresschrift fuer audiovisuelle Kommunikation. q.
- Orient; Deutsche Zeitschrift fuer Wirtschaft und Politik des Orients. q. ISSN 0030-5227 (Deutsches Orient-Institut)

**Lessing Society**
- Lessing Yearbook. (pub. by Max Hueber Verlag)

**Leybold-Heraeus GmbH und Co. KG**
Bonner Str. 504, Postfach 510760, 5000 Cologne 51, W. Germany (B.R.D.)
- Contact. 3 per yr.

**F. O. Licht KG**
Am Muehlengraben 22, 2418 Ratzeburg, W. Germany (B.R.D.)
- F. O. Licht's Europaeisches Zuckerjournal. ISSN 0014-6048
- F. O. Lichts's International Molasses Report. s-m. ISSN 0014-6056

**Lichttechnische Gesellschaft e.V.**
- Lichttechnik. (pub. by Huethig und Pflaum Verlag)

**Lichtwark-Stiftung**
- Lichtwark-Stiftung. Veroeffentlichung. (pub. by Hans Christians Verlag)

**Albert Limbach Verlag**
Hutfiltern 8, Postfach 3363, 3300 Braunschweig, W. Germany (B.R.D.)
- Zeitschrift fuer Ethnologie. s-a. ISSN 0044-2666 (Deutsche Gesellschaft fuer Voelkerkunde)

**Linden-Museum fuer Voelkerkunde**
Hegelplatz 1, 7000 Stuttgart 1, W. Germany (B.R.D.)
- Tribus. a. ISSN 0082-6413

**Carl Ling Presse GmbH**
Kolpingstr. 10, Postfach 160, 8640 Kronach, W. Germany (B.R.D.)
- Bayerische Gemeindezeitung. s-m. ISSN 0005-7045

**Verlag Linguistica Biblica**
Kirchweg 15, 5300 Bonn-Roettgen 1, W. Germany (B.R.D.)
- Linguistica Biblica; Interdisziplinaere Zeitschrift fuer Theologie und Linguistik. 3 per yr. ISSN 0342-0884

**V.D. Linnepe Verlagsgesellschaft KG**
Bahnhofstr. 28, Postfach 2260, 5800 Hagen, W. Germany (B. R. D.)
- Suedwestfaelische Wirtschaft. m. ISSN 0039-4637 (Suedwestfaelische Industrie- und Handelskammer zu Hagen)

**Verlag Karl M. Lipp**
Lautensackstr. 2, 8000 Munich 21, W. Germany (B. R. D.)
- Hauswirtschaft und Wissenschaft. 6 per yr. ISSN 0017-8454 (Deutsche Gesellschaft fuer Hauswirtschaft e.V.)
- Muenchner Woche/Munich Weekly. w. ISSN 0027-2981

**Lippischer Heimatbund**
Bismarckstr. 8, 4930 Detmold, W. Germany (B.R.D.)
- Heimatland Lippe. bi-m. ISSN 0017-9787

**Lipsius & Tischer**
Holstenstr. 80, 2300 Kiel, W. Germany (B.R.D.)
- Naturwissenschaftlicher Verein fuer Schleswig-Holstein. Schriften. irreg. ISSN 0077-6165

**Literarische Union e.V.**
Schulstr. 8, 6645 Beckingen 1, W. Germany (B.R.D.)
- Bunte Blaetter. m.

**Verlag der Literat**
Konrad- Brosswitz- Str. 10, Postfach 4386, 6000 Frankfurt 1, W. Germany (B. R. D.)
- Der Literat; Zeitschrift fuer Literatur und Kunst. m. ISSN 0024-4627

**Liturgisches Institut Trier**
- Liturgisches Jahrbuch. (pub. by Aschendorffsche Verlagsbuchhandlung)

**Lobrecht Verlag Max Rauscher KG**
Postfach 250, 8939 Bad Woerishofen, W. Germany (B.R.D.)
- Boden, Wand, Decke. m. ISSN 0006-5463
- Rationell Reinigen; das fach magazin der gebaeudereinigung. m. (Bundesinnungsverband des Gebaeudereiniger-Handwerks)

**Luchterhand Verlag**
Heddesdorfer Str. 31, Postfach 1780, 5450 Neuwied, W. Germany (B.R.D.)
- Blaetter fuer Grundstuecks-, Bau- und Wohnungsrecht. m. ISSN 0006-4440
- Blaetter fuer Steuerrecht, Sozial Versicherung und Arbeitsrecht. s-m. ISSN 0006-4475
- Materialien zur Politischen Bildung; Analysen - Berichte - Dokumente. q. (Arbeitskreis Deutscher Bildungsstaetten e.V.)
- Neue Praxis; kritische Zeitschrift fuer Sozialarbeit und Sozialpaedagogik. q.
- Politik-Aktuell fuer den Unterricht. m.
- Recht der Jugend und des Bildungswesens. m. ISSN 0034-1312
- Recht im Amt; Zeitschrift fuer Behoerden, Verwaltungen und oeffentliche Betriebe. m. ISSN 0034-1339

**Luebecker Nachrichten GmbH**
Koenigstr 51, 2400 Luebeck, W. Germany (B.R.D.)
- Amtliches Kreisblatt fuer den Kreis Herzogtum Lauenburg. m. ISSN 0003-2131

**Dr. Ernst Lueddemann und Sohn**
Laerchenweg 6, Postfach 350, 3388 Bad Harzburg, W. Germany (B.R.D.)
- News on Russian Medicine and Biochemistry. m. ISSN 0028-9310

**Luftfahrt-Verlag Walter Zuerl**
Amselweg 6, 8031 Woerthsee-Steinebach, W. Germany (B.R.D.)
- Der Flieger. m. ISSN 0015-3680
- Zuerl's Adressbuch der Deutschen Luft- und Raumfahrt. a. ISSN 0065-2024

**Luftwaffen-Ring e.V.**
Postfach 7025, 2800 Bremen 34, W. Germany (B.R.D.)
- Luftwaffen Revue. q.

**Horst Lummert**
Norderstr. 145, Postfach 518, 2390 Flensburg, W. Germany (B.R.D.)
- Kuckuck; Knust, Literatur, kritik. q.

**Luther-Gesellschaft**
- Luther. (pub. by Vandenhoeck und Ruprecht)

**Luther-Verlag**
Cansteinstr. 1, 4800 Bielefeld, W. Germany (B.R.D.)
- Theorie und Praxis der Sozialpaedagogik. bi-m. (Arbeitsgemeinschaft fuer Evangelische Kinderpflege)

**Lutherisches Verlagshaus GmbH**
Mittelweg 111, 2000 Hamburg 13, W. Germany (B.R.D.)
- Lutherische Monatshefte. m. ISSN 0024-7618
- Vereinigte Evangelisch-Lutherische Kirche Deutschlands. Amtsblatt. irreg. ISSN 0083-5633

**Made in Europe Marketing Organization GmbH & Co. KG**
Unterlindau 21-29, 6000 Frankfurt 1, W. Germany (B.R.D.)
(U.S. subs. to: Made in Europe, 150 Green St., Brooklyn, N.Y. 11222)
- Made in Europe; your business guide and continuous trade fair in print. m. ISSN 0024-9378
- Made in Europe. Technical Equipment Catalog. m. ISSN 0047-5424
- Made in Europe Buyers' Guide. a. ISSN 0085-2937

**Maerkischer Kreis**
- Der Maerker. (pub. by Dr. F. Krins)

**Otto Maier Verlag**
Marktstr. 22, 7980 Ravensburg, W. Germany (B.R.D.)
- Buch der Jugend. a. ISSN 0068-3043

**Mainzer Altertumsverein**
Rheinallee 3b, 6500 Mainz, W. Germany (B.R.D.)
- Mainzer Zeitschrift; Mittelrheinisches Jahrbuch fuer Archaeologie, Geschichte und Kunst. a. ISSN 0076-2792

**Mainzer Verlagsanstalt und Druckerei Will und Rothe KG**
Grosse Bleiche 44-50, 6500 Mainz, W. Germany (B.R.D.)
- Tabak Journal International. bi-m. ISSN 0039-8748
- Die Tabak Zeitung; Fachorgan der Tabakwirtschaft. w. ISSN 0049-2825

**Malaysian Rubber Bureau**
Eschersheimer Landstrasse 2-5, 6000 Frankfurt 1, W. Germany (B.R.D.)
- Naturkautschuk; Fortschritte und Entwicklungen. q. ISSN 0028-0984

**Walter Mallin Verlag**
Hermann-Loens-Weg 6, 3340 Wolfenbuettel, W. Germany (B.R.D.)
- Amusement-Industrie; Fachrevue fuer Freizeittechnologie. q.

**Manager Magazin Verlagsgesellschaft mbH**
Brandstwiete 19, 2000 Hamburg 11, W. Germany (B.R.D.)
- Manager Magazin. m. ISSN 0047-5726

**Fr. Mangold'sche Buchhandlung**
Karlstr. 6, 7902 Blaubeueren, W. Germany (B.R.D.)
- Jahreshefte fuer Karst- und Hoehlenkunde. a. ISSN 0075-2894 (Verband Deutscher Hoehlen- und Karstforscher e.V.)

**Verlag Th. Mann**
Nordring 10, 4660 Gelsk-Buer, W. Germany (B.R.D.)
- Deutsche Milchwirtschaft. w. ISSN 0012-0480 (Zentralverband Deutscher Molkereifachleute und Milchwirtschaftler)
- Der Futterberater; Fachzeitschrift fuer alle baeuerlichen Veredlungsbetriebe. m.
- Der Kartoffelbau. m. ISSN 0022-9156 (Foerderungsgemeinschaft der Kartoffelwirtschaft E.V)
- Kieler Milchwirtschaftliche Forschungsberichte. 4 per yr. ISSN 0023-1347 (Germany, Federal Republic. Bundesanstalt fuer Milchforschung)
- Die Milcherzeugung; das Mitteilungsblatt fuer Milchlieferanten. m.
- Die Milchpraxis und Rindermast. q.

**Verlag Mann und Bartels GmbH**
Michaelistr. 53/56, 3200 Hildesheim, W. Germany (B.R.D.)
- Der Tierzuechter. m. ISSN 0040-7364 (Arbeitsgemeinschaft Deutscher Tierzuechter)

**Gebr. Mann Verlag**
Lindenstr. 76, Postfach 110303, 1000 Berlin 61, W. Germany (B.R.D.)
- Indiana; contributions to ethnology and linguistics, archaeology and physical anthropology of Indian America. irreg. (Ibero-Amerikanisches Institut Preussischer Kulturbesitz Berlin)
- Jahrbuch der Berliner Museen. a. ISSN 0075-2207 (Staatliche Museen Preussischer Kulturbesitz Berlin)
- Jahresbericht ueber die Deutsche Fischwirtschaft. a. ISSN 0075-2851 (Germany, Federal Republic. Bundesministerium fuer Ernaehrung, Landwirtschaft und Forsten)
- Keilschrifttexte aus Boghazkoi. irreg., vol. 23, 1975. ISSN 0075-5338 (Deutsche Orient-Gesellschaft)
- Koelner Jahrbuch fuer Vor- und Fruehgeschichte. irreg., vol. 13, 1975. ISSN 0075-6512 (Roemisch-Germanisches Museum) (Co-sponsor: Archaeologische Gesellschaft, Cologne)
- Monumenta Americana. irreg., vol. 9, 1972. ISSN 0077-1384 (Ibero-Amerikanisches Institut Preussischer Kulturbesitz Berlin)
- Monumenta Artis Romanae. irreg. ISSN 0077-1406
- Quellenwerke zur Alten Geschichte Amerikas. irreg., vol. 11, 1975. ISSN 0079-9157 (Ibero-Amerikanisches Institut Preussischer Kulturbesitz Berlin)
- Stimmen Indianischer Voelker. irreg., vol. 2, 1976. ISSN 0081-5608 (Ibero-Amerikanisches Institut Preussischer Kulturbesitz Berlin)
- Sylloge Nummorum Graecorum Deutschland. irreg. ISSN 0082-061X (Deutsches Archaeologisches Institut)
- Uruk-Warka: Abhandlungen der Deutschen Orient-Gesellschaft. irreg., no. 18, 1975. ISSN 0083-4793 (Deutsche Orient-Gesellschaft) (Co-sponsor: Deutsches Archaeologisches Institut)

**Mannus-Verlag Peter Wegener**
Postfach 2513, 5300 Bonn 1, W. Germanny (B.R.D.)
- Mannus; Deutsche Zeitschrift fuer Vor- und Fruehgeschichte. 4 per yr. ISSN 0025-2360 (Deutsche Gesellschaft fuer Ur- und Fruehgeschichte)

**Manz Verlag**
Anzinger Str. 1, 8000 Munich 80, W. Germany (B.R.D.)
- Kamera und Schule. q. ISSN 0022-8109 (Bundesgremium fuer Schulphotographie)

**Marburger Bund**
- M B - Der Arzt in Krankenhaus und Gesundheitswesen. (pub. by A. W. Gentner Verlag)

**Carl Marhold Verlagsbuchhandlung**
Hessenallee 12, Postfach 409, 1000 Berlin 19, W. Germany (B.R.D.)
- Bad WC Hausarbeitsraum. bi-m.
- Haustechnische Rundschau; Zeitschrift fuer Versorgungstechnik: Heizung, Lueftung, Sanitaertechnik, Gas- und Oelfeurungstechnik. m. ISSN 0017-8438
- Heilpaedagogische Forschung; Zeitschrift fuer Erziehung und Unterricht behinderter Kinder und Jugendlicher. 3 per yr. ISSN 0017-9647
- Sonderpaedagogik. q.

**Markus Verlagsgesellschaft mbH**
Hohenzollernring 85-87, 5000 Cologne 1, W. Germany (B.R.D.)
- Beitraege zur Konfliktforschung; psycho-politische Aspekte. q. ISSN 0045-169X

**Hans Marseille Verlag**
Buerkleinstr. 12, 8000 Munich 22, W. Germany (B.R.D.)
- Anasthesiologische Praxis. a. ISSN 0044-8214
- Chirurgische Praxis; taegliche Praxis der gesamten Chirurgie. bi-m. ISSN 0009-4846
- Internistische Praxis; taegliche Praxis der gesamten Inneren Medizin. q. ISSN 0020-9570
- Paediatrische Praxis; Zeitschrift fuer den Kinderarzt. bi-m. ISSN 0030-9346

**Marxistische Blaetter GmbH**
Heddersheimer Landstr. 78a, 6000 Frankfurt 50, W. Germany (B.R.D.)
- Marxistische Blaetter; fuer Probleme der Gesellschaft, Wirtschaft und Politik. bi-m. ISSN 0542-7770

**Maschinenfabrik Augsburg-Nuernberg AG**
8900 Augsburg, W. Germany (B.R.D.)
- M.A.N. Forschen, Planen, Bauen. a.

**Maschinenfabrik Fahr AG**
7702 Gottmadingen, W. Germany (B.R.D.)
- Fahr Betriebsleben. bi-m. ISSN 0014-6811

**Verlag der Massstaebe**
Hafenstr. 6, Postfach 143, 2890 Nordenham, W. Germany (B.R.D.)
- Massstaebe. irreg.

**Mathilde-Zimmer-Stiftung e.V.**
- Mathilde-Zimmer-Stiftung. Blaetter. (pub. by Christlicher Zeitschriftenverlag)

**Matthaes Verlag GmbH**
Olgastr. 87, 7000 Stuttgart 1, W. Germany (B.R.D.)
- Allgemeine Hotel-und Gaststaetten-Zeitung; Deutsche Hotel-Nachrichten. w. ISSN 0002-5895 (Deutscher Hotel- und Gaststaettenverband E.V. (DEHOGA))
- Hotel Restaurant. m. ISSN 0018-621X (International Hotel Association. Deutsche Sektion)
- Konditorei und Cafe; die Konditorei, der Konditormeister. w. ISSN 0023-3234 (Deutscher Konditorenbund)

**Matus-Cernak-Institut**
Kulturelles Zentrum der Slowaken in Deutschland, Postfach 100924, 5000 Cologne 1, W. Germany (B.R.D.)
- Cernakov Odkaz/Cernak's Legacy; newspaper of the Slovaks abroad. bi-m. ISSN 0009-0395
- Slowakei; kulturpolitische Revue. a. ISSN 0037-7058

**Carl Maurersche Buchdruckerei**
Schubartstr. 21, Postfach 34, 7340 Geislingen, W. Germany (B.R.D.)
- Das Deutsche Schuhmacherhandwerk. m. ISSN 0012-0723
- Der Orthopaedieschuhmachermeister. m. ISSN 0030-5871 (Bundesinnungsverband des Orthopaedieschuhmacherhandwerks)

**Max-Planck-Gesellschaft zur Foerderung der Wissenschaften**
Residenzstr. 1a, 8000 Munich 2, W. Germany (B.R.D.)
- M P G Spiegel. bi-m.
- Max-Planck-Gesellschaft zur Foerderung der Wissenschaften. Jahrbuch. a. ISSN 0076-5635
- Max-Planck-Gesellschaft zur Foerderung der Wissenschaften Berichte und Mitteilungen. irreg.
- Naturwissenschaften. (pub. by Springer-Verlag US)

**Max-Planck-Institut fuer Auslaendisches Oeffentliches Recht und Voelkerrecht**
Berliner Str. 48, 6900 Heidelberg, W. Germany (B.R.D.)
- Max-Planck-Institut fuer Auslaendisches Oeffentliches Recht und Voelkerrecht. Fontes. irreg. ISSN 0076-5651
- Zeitschrift fuer Auslaendisches Oeffentliches Recht und Voelkerrecht. (pub. by W. Kohlhammer GmbH (Stuttgart))

**Max-Planck-Institut fuer Auslaendisches und Internationales Privatrecht**
- Rabels Zeitschrift fuer auslaendisches und internationales Privatrecht. (pub. by Verlag J.C.B. Mohr (Paul Siebeck))

**Max-Planck-Institut fuer Bildungsforschung**
Blissestr. 2, 1000 Berlin 31, W. Germany (B.R.D.)
- Max-Planck-Institut fuer Bildungsforschung, Berlin. Studien und Berichte. irreg., 1973, vol. 28. ISSN 0076-5627

**Max-Planck-Institut fuer Kohlenforschung. Institut fuer Strahlenchemie**
Stiftstr. 34-36, 4330 Muelheim, W. Germany (B.R.D.)
- Match; informal communications in mathematical chemistry. q.

**Max-Planck-Institut fuer Landarbeit und Landtechnik**
- Landarbeit und Technik. (pub. by Verlag Paul Parey (Hamburg))

**Max-Planck-Institut fuer Stroemungsforschung**
Bunsenstr. 10, 3400 Goettingen, W. Germany (B.R.D.)
- Mitteilungen aus dem Max-Planck-Institut fuer Stroemungsforschung und der Aerodynamischen Versuchsanstalt. irreg., no. 60, 1974. ISSN 0076-5678 (Co-sponsor: Forschungszentrum Aerodynamische Versuchsanstalt)

**Max-Planck-Institute for Foreign and International Patent, Copyright and Competitition Law, Munich**
- I I C. (pub. by Verlag Chemie International, Inc. US)

**Max-Reger-Institut**
- Max-Reger-Institut, Bonn. Mitteilungen. (pub. by Breitkopf und Haertel)

**Maximilian-Gesellschaft e.V.**
- Philobiblon. (pub. by Dr. Ernst Hauswedell und Co., Verlag)

**Maximilian-Verlag**
Steintorwall 17, Postfach 371, 4900 Herford, W. Germany (B.R.D.)
- Chef. s-w.
- Deutsche Verwaltungspraxis. m. ISSN 0012-0928
- Herforder Jahrbuch; Beitraege zur Geschichte der Stadt und des Stiftes Herford. a. ISSN 0073-196X (Herforder Verein fuer Heimatkunde)

**Karl Mayer GmbH**
Postfach 109, 6053 Obertshausen, W. Germany (B.R.D.)
- Kettenwirk-Praxis. q. ISSN 0047-3405

**F. C. Mayer Verlag**
Kunigundenstr. 79, 8000 Munich 40, W. Germany (B.R.D.)
- Der Deutsche Pelztierzuechter. m. ISSN 0012-0553

**Median Verlag**
Hauptstr. 64, 6900 Heidelberg 1, W. Germany (B.R.D.)
- Optometrie; Zeitschrift fuer Augenoptik und Optometrie. bi-m. ISSN 0030-4123 (Wissenschaftliche Vereinigung fuer Augenoptik und Optometrie E.V.)
- Wissenschaftliche Vereinigung fuer Augenoptik und Optometrie. Fachvortraege des WVAO - Jahreskongresses. a.
- Zeitschrift fuer Hoergeraete Akustik/Journal of Audiological Technique. bi-m. ISSN 0044-2860

**Medicus Mundi Internationalis**
Mozartstr. 9, 5100 Aachen, W. Germany (B.R.D.)
- International Organization for Medical Cooperation. General Assembly. Report. a. ISSN 0579-3912

**Medicus Verlag GmbH**
Klingsorstr. 21, 1000 Berlin 41, W. Germany (B.R.D.)
- Das Aerztliche Laboratorium; Zeitschrift fuer den Laboratoriumsarzt und die aerztliche Praxis. m. ISSN 0001-9526 (Kongressgesellschaft fuer Aerztliche Fortbildung e.V.)

**Medizin Bibliothek Dokumentation-Verlag**
Loheide 35, 4800 Bielefeld 1, W. Germany (B.R.D.)
- Medizin Bibliothek Dokumentation. q. (Arbeitsgemeinschaft fuer Medizinisches Bibliothekswesen)

**Verlag fuer Medizin Dr. Ewald Fischer**
Blumenthalstr. 38, 6900 Heidelberg, W. Germany (B.R.D.)
- Cardiologisches Bulletin. a. ISSN 0084-8603
- Manuelle Medizin; Interdisziplinaere Zeitschrift fuer Arthrologie, Kinesiologie und Chirotherapie. 6 per yr. ISSN 0025-2514 (Deutsche Gesellschaft fuer Manuelle Medizin)
- Technik in der Medizin; Arzt/Technik. bi-m.
- Zentralblatt fuer Arbeitsmedizin, Arbeitsschutz und Prophylaxe. m. ISSN 0340-7047 (Deutsche Gesellschaft fuer Arbeitsschutz e.V.)

**Medizinalpolitischer Verlag**
In der Herrenwiese 7, Postfach 1160, 5912 Hilchenbach, W. Germany (B.R.D.)
- Gesundes Leben; Medizinalpolitische Rundschau, Zeitschrift fuer natuerliche Lebensordnung. m. ISSN 0016-9250
- Das Gewissen; Zeitschrift fuer Lebensschutz. m. ISSN 0016-9471 (Deutsche Volksgesundheits-Bewegung E.V.)
- Naturgemaesser Land- und Gartenbau. 6 per yr. ISSN 0028-0933 (Deutsche Volksgesundheits-Bewegung E.V.)
- U B N. (Unabhaengiger Biologischer Nachrichtendienst) m. ISSN 0041-5006 (Deutsche Volksgesundheits-Bewegung E.V)

**Medizinisch-Literarische Verlagsgesellschaft mbH**
Ringstr. 4, Postfach 120, 3110 Uelzen, W. Germany (B.R.D.)
- Orthopaedische Praxis; mit Traumatologie, Rheumatologie, physikalischer, physiotherapeutischer und balneologischer Therapie des Bewegungsapparates. m. ISSN 0030-588X (Vereinigung Sueddeutscher Orthopaeden e.V.)
- Physikalische Medizin und Rehabilitation; Diaetetik, Pharmakologie, Ordnungs- und Umstimmungsbehandlung in Klinik und Praxis. m. ISSN 0031-9287 (Zentralverband der Aerzte fuer Naturheilverfahren e.V.)

**Medizinische Verlagsgesellschaft mbH**
Reitgasse, Postfach 1504, 3550 Marburg, W. Germany (B.R.D.)
- Die Gelben Hefte. q. ISSN 0016-6006 (Immunbiologische Informationen e.V.)

**Verlag von Meier's Adressbuch der Exporteure Rudolf Dudy KG**
Feldweg 9, 6394 Graevenwiesbach 5, W. Germany (B.R.D.)
(Dist. by Intl. Publications Service, 114 E. 32nd St., New York, N.Y. 10016)
- Meier-Dudy/Meier's Directory of Exporters and Importers; Meier's Addressbuch der Exporteure und Importeure. a. ISSN 0076-6208

**Mein Standpunkt**
Breslauer Str. 88 B, Postfach 1211, 2910 Westerstede, W. Germany (B.R.D.)
- Mein Standpunkt; Gedanken zur Zeit. m. ISSN 0025-8814

**Verlag D. Meininger**
Maximilianstr. 11-17, 6730 Neustadt an der Weinstrasse, W. Germany (B.R.D.)
- Pfalz am Rhein; Pfaelzische Verkehrs- und Heimatzeitschrift. q. ISSN 0031-6695

**Meisenbach KG**
Hainstr. 18, 8600 Bamberg 2, W. Germany (B.R.D.)
- Baby & Junior; international trade magazine for children's fashions and supplies. m. ISSN 0005-3554
- Eurosport und Freizeitmode. m. ISSN 0340-739X
- Present; Fachblatt fuer Kunsthandwerk, Kunstgewerbe, Geschenkartikel und Einrichtungen. m. ISSN 0032-7697 (Verband der Korbwaren-, Korbmoebel- und Kinderwagenindustrie e.V.)
- Die Schaulade; independent international trade magazine for china, ceramics, glass, giftware and household articles. m. ISSN 0036-5947

**Otto Meissners Verlag**
Schlossstr. 10, Postfach 106, 3142 Bleckede, W. Germany (B.R.D.)
- Deutsche Studien. q. ISSN 0012-0812 (Bund und Land)
- Recht der Schiffahrt/Maritime Law Review; a card index periodical of the international shipping law. bi-m. ISSN 0034-1320

**Melliand Textilberichte KG**
Rohrbacher Str. 76, 6900 Heidelberg, W. Germany (B.R.D.)
- Band- und Flechtindustrie/Narrow Fabric and Braiding Industry. q. ISSN 0005-4925 (Industrieverband Deutscher Bandweber und Flechter e.V)
- Melliand Textilberichte /International Textile Reports. m. ISSN 0341-0781 (Verein der Textilchemiker und Coloristen e.V.)

**Mendelssohn-Gesellschaft e. V.**
- Mendelssohn Studien. (pub. by Duncker und Humblot)

**Verlag Mensch und Arbeit**
Vogelweideplatz 10, 8000 Munich 80, W. Germany (B.R.D.)
- Personal; Mensch und Arbeit im Betrieb. 8 times a year. ISSN 0031-5605

**Menschenfreundliche Gesellschaft**
- Anzeiger des Reiches der Gerechtigkeit. (pub. by Verlag der Engel des Herrn)

**Bergische Verlagsgesellschaft Menzel KG**
Islandufer 21, 5600 Wuppertal, W. Germany (B.R.D.)
- Industrie- und Handelskammer zu Duesseldorf. Schnelldienst. w.

**Universitaetsbuchhandlung Rudolf Merkel**
Untere Karlstr. 9-11, 8520 Erlangen, W. Germany
(B.R.D.)
- Das Neue Erlangen; Zeitschrift fuer Wissenschaft,
Wirtschaft und kulturelles Leben. q. ISSN 0028-
3169

**Verlag Merseburger Berlin GmbH**
Motz Str. 13, 3500 Kassel, W. Germany (B.R.D.)
- Acta Organologica. a. ISSN 0567-7874
(Gesellschaft der Orgelfreunde e.V.)
- Ars Organi; Zeitschrift fuer das Orgelwesen. ISSN
0004-2919 (Gesellschaft der Orgelfreunde e.V.)
- Der Kirchenmusiker. bi-m. ISSN 0023-1819
(Verband Evangelischer Kirchenmusiker
Deutschlands)

**Messerschmitt-Boelkow-Blohm GmbH**
Postfach 801109, 8000 Munich 80, W. Germany
(B.R.D.)
- M B B Aktuell; Zeitung fuer die Mitarbeiter und
Freunde der Messerschmitt-Boelkow-Blohm
GmbH. m.

**Metall-Verlag GmbH**
Hubertusallee 18, 1000 Berlin 33, W. Germany
(B.R.D.)
- Jahrbuch Oberflaechentechnik. a. ISSN 0075-2819
- Metall; Internationale Zeitschrift fuer Technik und
Wirtschaft. m. ISSN 0026-0746

**Metallgesellschaft AG**
Reuterweg 14, 6000 Frankfurt 1, W. Germany
(B.R.D.)
- Metallgesellschaft Aktiengesellschaft. Review of
the Activities. a. ISSN 0026-0770

**J. B. Metzlersche Verlagsbuchhandlung**
Kernerstr. 43, 7000 Stuttgart 1, W. Germany
(B.R.D.)
- Amerikastudien/American Studies. s-a. (Deutsche
Gesellschaft fuer Amerikastudien)
- Deutsche Vierteljahrsschrift fuer
Literaturwissenschaft und Geistesgeschichte. 4 per
yr. ISSN 0012-0936
- Zur Praxis des Politischen Unterrichts. irreg., no.
2, 1973.

**Alfred Metzner Verlag GmbH**
Zeppelinallee 43, Postfach 970148, 6000 Frankfurt
97, W. Germany (B.R.D.)
- Arbeiten zur Rechtsvergleichung. irreg., vol. 86,
1977. ISSN 0066-5703 (Gesellschaft fuer
Rechtsvergleichung)
- Auslaendische Aktiengesetze. irreg., 1973, vol. 15.
ISSN 0067-0669 (Gesellschaft fuer
Rechtsvergleichung)
- Beitraege zum Rundfunkrecht. irreg., vol. 16,
1977. ISSN 0067-4966 (Arbeitsgemeinschaft der
Oeffentlich-rechtlichen Rundfunkanstalten der
Bundesrepublik Deutschland)
- Dokumente zur Deutschlandpolitik. irreg., reihe 4,
no. 7, 1976. ISSN 0070-7031 (Germany, Federal
Republic. Bundesminister fuer Innerdeutsche
Beziehungen)
- Das Geltende Seekriegsrecht in
Einzeldarstellungen. irreg., vol. 9, 1974. ISSN
0435-1924 (Universitaet Hamburg. Institut fuer
Internationale Angelegenheiten)
- Hamburger Oeffentlich-Rechtliche Nebenstunden.
irreg., vol 29, 1975. ISSN 0072-9574 (Universitaet
Hamburg. Institut fuer Internationale
Angelegenheiten)
- Kybernetik - Datenverarbeitung - Recht. irreg.,
vol. 6, 1977. (Forschungsstelle fuer Juristische
Dokumentation, Frankfurt)
- Planungsstudien. irreg., vol. 14, 1977. ISSN 0079-
2284
- Ruestungsbeschraenkung und Sicherheit. irreg.,
vol. 13, 1977. ISSN 0080-4800 (Deutsche
Gesellschaft fuer Auswaertige Politik e.V.)
- Sammlung Geltender Staatsangehoerigkeitsgesetze.
irreg., vol. 35, 1975. ISSN 0080-5823
(Universitaet Hamburg. Institut fuer Internationale
Angelegenheiten)
- Universitaet Hamburg. Institut fuer Internationale
Angelegenheiten. Veroeffentlichungen. irreg., vol.
4, 1976.
- Universitaet Hamburg. Institut fuer Internationale
Angelegenheiten. Werkhefte. irreg., vol. 30, 1976.
ISSN 0341-3241 (Co-Sponsor: Deutscher Verein
fuer Internationales Seerecht)

**Miba-Verlag**
Spittlertorgraben 39-41, 8500 Nuernberg, W.
Germany (B.R.D.)
- Miniaturbahnen. m. (plus special toy fair issue)
ISSN 0047-7478

**Geographische Buchhandlung R. Michels**
Rosental 6, 8000 Munich 2, W. Germany (B.R.D.)
- Alpeninstitut. Schriftenreihe. irreg. (Alpeninstitut
fuer Umweltforschung und Entwicklungsplanung
in der GFL)

**Verlag Ista Mielke und Co.**
Langenberg 23, Postfach 200803, 2100 Hamburg 90,
W. Germany (B.R.D.)
- Oil World; the information service for statistical
analysis of the world markets of oilseeds,
oilmeals, vegetable, animal and marine oils and
fats. w. (with 5 special issues) ISSN 0029-8700

**Militaergeschichtliches Forschungsamt**
Kaiser-Joseph-Str. 262, Freiburg 1, W. Germany
(B.R.D.)
- Handbuch zur Deutschen Militaergeschichte. (pub.
by Bernard und Graefe Verlag fuer Wehrwesen)
- Militaergeschichtliche Mitteilungen. (pub. by
Verlag G. Braun GmbH)
- War and Society Newsletter. s-a. (Dist. by: G.
Baun-Verlag, Karl-Friedrich-Strasse 14-18, D-75
Karlsruhe, W. Germany (B.R.D.))

**Mineraloelwirtschafts Verband e.V.**
Steindamm 71, 2000 Hamburg 1, W. Germany
(B.R.D.)
- M W V /A E V Jahresbericht.
(Arbeitsgemeinschaft Erdoel-Gewinnung und-
Verarbeitung) a. ISSN 0076-891X

**Minerva-Verlag**
Rosmarinstr. 24, 4040 Neuss, W. Germany (B.R.D.)
- Die Hundewelt. m. ISSN 0018-7682

**Minerva-Verlag Thinnes und Nolte**
Futterstr. 25, 6600 Saarbruecken, W. Germany
(B.R.D.)
- Saarbruecker Hefte. s-a. ISSN 0036-2115
(Saarbruecken. Kulturamt)

**Missionsanstalt der Pallottiner**
- Pallottis Werk. (pub. by Pallottiner Druck und
Lahn-Verlag)

**Missionsbund zur Ausbreitung des Evangeliums**
Kullen Str. 1, Postfach 1340, 7015 Korntal-
Muenchingen 1, W. Germany (B.R.D.)
- Dein Reich Komme. bi-m. ISSN 0011-7692

**Missionshaus Bibelschule Wiedenest**
- Offene Tueren. (pub. by R. Brockhaus Verlag)

**Missionwerk Neues Leben e.V.**
- Neues Leben. (pub. by Verlag Joh. Brendow und
Sohn)

**Mitteldeutscher Saengerbund e.V.**
Ulmenstr. 16, 3500 Kassel, W. Germany (B.R.D.)
- Chorsaenger. q.

**Verlag E. S. Mittler und Sohn GmbH**
Postfach 371, 4900 Herford, W. Germany (B.R.D.)
- Kampftruppen. bi-m. ISSN 0022-8257
(Arbeitskreis der Kampftruppen)
- Wehrwissenschaftliche Rundschau. q. (Arbeitskreis
fuer Wehrforschung)

**Modellbahnen-Welt Verlags-GmbH**
Stuttgarter Str. 57, Postfach 940, 7320 Goeppingen,
W. Germany (B.R.D.)
- Maerklin-Magazin; Zeitschrift fuer grosse und
kleine Modell-Eisenbahner. q. ISSN 0024-9688

**Moderne Industrie Publikationsgesellschaft**
Ehrenbreitsteiner Str. 36, Postfach 500461, 8000
Munich 50, W. Germany (B.R.D.)
- Betriebsreinigung. bi-m.
- Buero und EDV; Zeitschrift fuer Organisation,
Rationalisierung, Automation. m.
- Bueromarkt; Magazin der Buerowirtschaft. m.
ISSN 0007-3148
- Fluid; Zeitschrift fuer Hydraulik und penumatik.
m. ISSN 0015-461X
- Instandhaltung; Zeitschrift fuer Wartung,
Inspektion, Instandsetzung. bi-m.
- J O T. (Journal fuer Oberflaechentechnik);
Lackieren, Galvanisieren, Emaillieren. m. ISSN
0021-3756
- Materialfluss; Zeitschrift fuer Transport, Lager
und Verpackung. m.
- Moderne Fertigung; Zeitschrift fuer Bearbeitung,
Montage, Kontrolle. 10 per yr.
- Produktion; Zeitschrift fuer Konstruktion und
Betrieb. m. ISSN 0032-9967

**Moderner Verlag**
Herzogstr. 64, 8000 Munich 40, W. Germany
(B.R.D.)
- Sport. m.

**Verlag der Moebelspediteur**
Frauenhofstr. 28, 6000 Frankfurt 73, W. Germany
(B.R.D.)
- Der Moebelspediteur. fortn. ISSN 0047-780X
(Arbeitsgemeinschaft Moebeltransport
Bundesverband e.V.)

**Heinrich Moeller Soehne GmbH**
Bahnhofstr. 12-16, 2370 Rendsburg, W. Germany
(B.R.D.)
- Schleswig-Holsteinischer Heimatkalender. irreg.
(Schleswig-Holsteinischer Heimatbund)

**Heinz Moeller-Verlag**
Provinzialstr. 89, 5300 Bonn-Lengsdorf, W.
Germany (B.R.D.)
- Esprit; the German society magazine. m.
- German International. m. ISSN 0016-8769

**Moench Verlagsgesellschaft mbH**
Heilsbachstr., 5300 Bonn-Duisdorf, W. Germany
(B.R.D.)
- Aerospace International. bi-m. ISSN 0001-9372
(U.S. Air Force Association US)
- Luftwaffe. m. ISSN 0015-3699 (Germany,
Federal Republic. Bundesministerium der
Verteidigung)
- Vereinte Nationen. bi-m. ISSN 0042-384X
(Deutsche Gesellschaft fuer die Vereinten
Nationen)

**Verlag J.C.B. Mohr (Paul Siebeck)**
Wilhelmstr. 18, Postfach 2040, 7400 Tuebingen, W.
Germany (B.R.D.)
- Archiv des Oeffentlichen Rechts. 4 per yr. ISSN
0003-8911
- Archiv des Voelkerrechts. q. ISSN 0003-892X
- Archiv fuer die Civilistische Praxis. 6 per yr.
ISSN 0003-8997
- Finanzarchiv. 3 per yr. ISSN 0015-2218
- Hamburger Jahrbuch fuer Wirtschafts- und
Gesellschaftspolitik. a. ISSN 0072-9566
- Jahrbuch des Oeffentlichen Rechts der Gegenwart.
a. ISSN 0075-2517
- Juristenzeitung. s-m. ISSN 0022-6882
- Philosophische Rundschau. 4 per yr. ISSN 0031-
8159
- Rabels Zeitschrift fuer auslaendisches und
internationales Privatrecht. 4 per yr. ISSN 0033-
7250 (Max-Planck-Institut fuer Auslaendisches
und Internationales Privatrecht)
- Schriften zur Kooperationsforschung. Berichte.
irreg. ISSN 0080-7028 (Forschungsgesellschaft
fuer Genossenschaftswesen, Muenster)
- Schriften zur Kooperationsforschung. Studien.
irreg. ISSN 0080-7036 (Forschungsgesellschaft
fuer Genossenschaftswesen, Muenster)
- Schriften zur Kooperationsforschung. Vortraege.
irreg. ISSN 0080-7044 (Forschungsgesellschaft
fuer Genossenschaftswesen, Muenster)
- Soziale Forschung und Praxis. irreg. ISSN 0081-
3230 (Universitaet Muenster.
Sozialforschungsstelle)
- Theologische Rundschau. 4 per yr. ISSN 0040-
5698
- Tuebinger Rechtswissenschaftliche Abhandlungen.
irreg. ISSN 0082-6731 (Universitaet Tuebingen.
Rechts- und Wirtschaftswissenschaftliche
Fakultaet)
- Die Weltwirtschaft. s-a. ISSN 0043-2652 (Institut
fuer Weltwirtschaft, Kiel)
- Weltwirtschaftliches Archiv/Review of World
Economics. 4 per yr. ISSN 0043-2636 (Institut
fuer Weltwirtschaft Kiel)
- Wirtschaftswissenschaftliche und
Wirtschaftsrechtliche Untersuchungen. irreg., no.
10, 1974. ISSN 0083-7113 (Walter Eucken
Institut)
- Wissenschaftsrecht. Wissenschaftsverwaltung.
Wissenschaftsfoerderung; Zeitschrift fuer Recht
und Verwaltung der wissenschaftlichen
Hochschulen und der wissenschaftpflegenden
und-foerdernden Organisationen und Stiftungen. 3
per yr. ISSN 0043-6976
- Zeitschrift fuer die Gesamte Staatswissenschaft. 4
per yr. ISSN 0044-2550
- Zeitschrift fuer Evangelisches Kirchenrecht. 4 per
yr. ISSN 0044-2690
- Zeitschrift fuer Theologie und Kirche. 4 per yr.
ISSN 0044-3549

**Monitor-Verlag**
Oststr. 154, Postfach 5707, 4000 Duesseldorf 1, W.
Germany (B.R.D.)
• Deutsche Volkszeitung. w.

**Montan- und Wirtschaftsverlag GmbH**
Lange Str. 13, 6000 Frankfurt, W. Germany
(B.R.D.)
• Continentaler Stahlmarkt; Informationen ueber
Erzeugnisse aus Stahl und anderen Werkstoffen.
m. ISSN 0010-7743

**Monumenta Serica Institute**
Arnold-Janssen-Str. 26, 5205 St. Augustin, W.
Germany (B.R.D.)
• Monumenta Serica; Journal of Oriental Studies. a.
ISSN 0077-149X

**Vereinigte Motor-Verlage GmbH und Co. KG**
Leuschnerstr. 1, Postfach 1042, 7000 Stuttgart 1, W.
Germany (B. R. D.)
• Auto-Katalog. a.
• Flug Revue; vereinigt mit Flugwelt International
mit Flugkoerper. m. ISSN 0015-4547
• Lastauto Omnibus. m. ISSN 0023-866X
• Das Motorrad. fortn. ISSN 0027-237X
• Sport Auto. m.

**Verlag Walter G. Muehlau**
Holtenauer Str. 116, 2300 Kiel, W. Germany (B. R.
D.)
• Amazoniana; Limnologia et Oecologia Regionalis
Systemae Fluminis Amazonas. irreg (4 issues per
vol.) ISSN 0065-6755
• Beitraege zur Sozial- und Wirtschaftsgeschichte. a.
• Kieler Meeresforschungen. a. ISSN 0023-1339
(Universitaet Kiel. Institut fuer Meereskunde)

**Verlagsgesellschaft Rudolf Mueller**
Stolberger Str. 84, Postfach 410949, 5000 Cologne
41, W. Germany (B.R.D.)
• A D L Nachrichten - Online; Journal fuer
Informationsverarbeitung mit OeVD /
Oeffentliche Verwaltung und Datenverarbeitung.
10 per yr.
• B B R. (Brunnenbau, Bau von Wasserwerken,
Rohrleitungsbau) m. ISSN 0006-5765
• Baugewerbe; mit Sonderteil Strassenbautechnik. s-
m. ISSN 0005-6634 (Zentralverband des
Deutschen Baugewerbes e.V.) (Co-sponsors:
Strassen- und Tiefbaugewerbe im Zdb;
Baugewerbliche Landesverbaende)
• Das Dachdecker-Handwerk; Zeitschrift fuer
Wand-, Dach- und Abdichtungs-Technik. 23 per
yr. (Zentralverband des Dachdeckerhandwerks
e.V)
• Fliesen und Platten. s-m. (Fachverband des
Deutschen Fliesengewerbes) (Co-sponsor: Bund
Deutscher Fliesengeschaefte e.V.)

**Verlag Lambert Mueller GmbH**
Hofmannstr. 7, 8000 Munich 70, W. Germany (B.
R. D.)
• Gehoert-Gelesen; Manuskriptauslese der
interessantesten Sendungen des Bayerischen
Rundfunks. m. ISSN 0016-5883 (Bayerischer
Rundfunk)
• Jugend in Schule und Beruf. (Verband Bayerischer
Berufsschullehrer)

**Verlag C. F. Mueller GmbH (Karlsruhe)**
Rheinstr. 122, Postfach 210729, 7500 Karlsruhe 21,
W. Germany (B.R.D.)
• Beitraege zur Strafvollzugswissenschaft. irreg., no.
15, 1976. ISSN 0067-5237
• Industrie und Handel. m. ISSN 0019-9192
(Industrie- und Handelskammer Mittlerer
Oberrhein)
• K I. (Klima und Kaelteingenieur); Informations-
System fuer Klima-, Kaelte- und Umwelttechnik.
m.
• Oberrheinische Geologische Abhandlungen. a.
ISSN 0078-2939
• Rechtsstaat in der Bewaehrung. irreg.

**Muenchen. Amt fuer Statistik und Datenanalyse**
Tal 30, 8000 Munich 2, W. Germany (B.R.D.)
• Statistisches Jahrbuch Muenchen. a. ISSN 0077-
2062

**Muenchner Entomologische Gesellschaft**
Maria-Ward-Str. 1b, 8000 Munich 19, W. Germany
(B.R.D.)
• Muenchner Entomologische Gesellschaft.
Mitteilungen. a. ISSN 0077-1864
• Nachrichtenblatt der Bayerischen Entomologen.
bi-m. ISSN 0027-7452

**Muenchner Handelsverein**
Lenbachplatz 2, Munich 2, W. Germany.
• Bayerische Boerse in Muenchen. Amtliches
Kursblatt. 5 per w. ISSN 0005-7029

**Muenchner Kammerspiele**
• Muenchner Kammerspiele. (pub. by Emha-Verlag)

**Kommissions-Verlag Muenstermann**
Postfach 4227, 3000 Hannover, W. Germany
(B.R.D.)
• Voelkerkundliche Abhandlungen. irreg., vol. 6,
1974. ISSN 0073-0270 (Niedersaechsisches
Landesmuseum, Hannover)

**Munich Roundup**
Herzogspitalstr. 5, 8000 Munich 2, W. Germany
(B.R.D.)
• Munich Roundup. m.

**Munin-Verlag Gmbh**
Postfach 3023, 4500 Osnabrueck, W. Germany
(B.R.D.)
• Der Freiwillige. m. ISSN 0016-092X
(Bundesverband der Soldaten der ehemaligen
Waffen-SS e.V.)

**Munzinger-Archiv**
Hans-Zuericher-Weg. 7, 7980 Ravensburg, W.
Germany (B.R.D.)
• Internationales Biographisches Archiv. w. ISSN
0020-9457
• Internationales Handbuch. w. ISSN 0020-949X
• Zeit- und Kulturarchiv; Chronik-Dokumente-
Uebersichten. w. ISSN 0044-2097

**Museum fuer Voelkerkunde - Berlin**
Arnimallee 23/27, 1000 Berlin 33, W. Germany
(B.R.D.)
• Baessler Archiv. (pub. by Dietrich Reimer
Buchhandlung)
• Museum fuer Voelkerkunde, Berlin.
Veroeffentlichungen. Neue Folge. Abteilung:
Afrika. irreg., vol. 8, 1972. ISSN 0067-5962
• Museum fuer Voelkerkunde, Berlin.
Veroeffentlichungen. Neue Folge. Abteilung:
Amerikanische Naturvoelker. irreg., vol. 4, 1974.
• Museum fuer Voelkerkunde, Berlin.
Veroeffentlichungen. Neue Folge. Abteilung:
Suedsee. irreg., vol. 10, 1973. ISSN 0067-5989

**Museum fuer Voelkerkunde und Vorgeschichte**
Binderstr. 14, 2000 Hamburg, W. Germany (B.R.D.)
• Museum fuer Voelkerkunde in Hamburg.
Mitteilungen. a.

**Museum G. Frey. Entomologisches Institut**
8132 Tutzing, W. Germany (B.R.D.)
• Entomologische Arbeiten aus dem Museum G.
Frey, Tutzing-Bei Muenchen. a. ISSN 0013-8819

**Musikalische Jugend Deutschlands**
• Neue Musikzeitung. (pub. by Gustav Bosse
Verlag)

**Musikhandel Verlagsgesellschaft mbH**
Friedrich-Wilhelm-Str. 31, 5300 Bonn, W. Germany
(B.R.D.)
• Musikhandel. 8 per yr. ISSN 0027-481X
(Gesamtverband Deutscher Musikfachgeschaefte
e.V.) (Co-Sponsor: Deutscher Musikverleger
Verband E.V.)

**Verlag das Musikinstrument**
Klueberstr. 9, 6000 Frankfurt 1, W. Germany
(B.R.D.)
• Euro Piano; information & service. q. ISSN 0014-
2387 (Europaeische Union der Pianomacher-
Fachverbaende)
• Das Musikinstrument. m. ISSN 0027-4828

**Musterschmidt-Verlag**
Turmstr. 7, Postfach 421, 3400 Goettingen, W.
Germany (B.R.D.)
• Die Farbe; Zeitschrift fuer alle Zweige der
Farbenlehre und ihre Anwendung. 6 per yr. ISSN
0014-7680
• Goettinger Studien zur Rechtsgeschichte. irreg.
• Das Historisch-Politische Buch; Ein Wegweiser
durch das Schrifttum. m. ISSN 0018-2605

• Homo; Zeitschrift fuer die vergleichende
Forschung am Menschen. 4 per yr. ISSN 0018-
442X (Deutsche Gesellschaft fuer Anthropologie)

**Mut-Verlag**
Bahnhofstr 1, Postfach 20, 3091 Asendorf, W.
Germany (B.R.D.)
• Mut; Das Nationaleuropaeische Magazin. m. ISSN
0027-5093

**Muth-Verlag**
Kaiser-Friedrich-Ring 9, 4000 Duesseldorf 11, W.
Germany (B.R.D.)
• Der Kriminalist. m. (Bund Deutscher
Kriminalbeamter)

**Nachrichten-Verlags-Gesellschaft mbH**
Glauburgstr. 66, 6000 Frankfurt 1, W. Germany
(B.R.D.)
• Nachrichten zur Wirtschafts- und Sozialpolitik;
Informationen und Kommentare. m. ISSN 0047-
8598

**Nachrichtentechnische Gesellschaft im VDE (NTG)**
• Elektronische Rechenanlagen mit Computer-
Praxis. (pub. by R. Oldenbourg Verlag GmbH)

**Nahrungs- und Genussmittel-Fachverlag A.Gordian
GmbH & Co. KG**
Bellevue 24, 2000 Hamburg 60, W. Germany
(B.R.D.)
• Gordian; Internationale Zeitschrift fuer
Lebensmittel und Lebensmittel-technologie. m.
ISSN 0017-2243

**Namos Verlagsgesellschaft**
Postfach 610, 7570 Baden-Baden, W. Germany
(B.R.D.)
• Schriften zur Oeffentlichen Verwaltung und
Oeffentlichen Wirtschaft. irreg.

**Nation Europa Verlag GmbH**
Bahnhofstr. 25, Postfach 670, 8630 Coburg, W.
Germany (B.R.D.)
• Nation Europa; Monatsschrift im Dienst der
europaeischen Erneuerung. m. ISSN 0027-8408

**Verlag der Naturarzt**
Wielandstr. 4, 6200 Wiesbaden, W. Germany
(B.R.D.)
• Der Naturarzt; Zeitschrift fuer naturgemaesse
Lebens- und Heilweise. m. ISSN 0028-081X
(Deutscher Bund fuer Naturgemasse Lebens- und
Heilweise e.V.)

**Naturforschende Gesellschaft Freiburg**
Hebelstr. 40, 7800 Freiburg, W. Germany (B.R.D.)
• Naturforschende Gesellschaft zu Freiburg.
Berichte. s-a. ISSN 0028-0917

**Naturhistorische Gesellschaft Nuernberg**
Gewerbemuseumsplatz 4, Luitpoldhaus, 8500
Nuernberg, W. Germany (B.R.D)
• Natur und Mensch; Jahresmitteilungen der
Naturhistorischen Gesellschaft Nuernberg. a.
ISSN 0077-6025
• Naturhistorische Gesellschaft Nuernberg.
Abhandlungen. irreg. ISSN 0077-6149

**Naturhistorisches Museum zu Luebeck**
Muehlendamm 1, 2400 Luebeck, W. Germany
(B.R.D.)
• Berichte des Vereins Natur und Heimat und des
Naturhistorischen Museums zu Luebeck. a. ISSN
0067-5806

**Naturwissenschaftlicher Verein fuer Schleswig-
Holstein**
• Naturwissenschaftlicher Verein fuer Schleswig-
Holstein. Schriften. (pub. by Lipsius & Tischer)

**Naturwissenschaftlicher Verein Hamburg**
• Naturwissenschaftlicher Verein in Hamburg.
Abhandlungen und Verhandlungen. (pub. by
Verlag Paul Parey (Hamburg)

**Naturwissenschaftlicher Verein Osnabrueck**
Heger-Tor-Wall 27, 4500 Osnabrueck, W. Germany
(B.R.D.)
• Osnabruecker Naturwissenschaftliche
Mitteilungen. a. (Co-sponsor:
Naturwissentschaftliches Museum Osnabrueck)

**Neckar-Verlag**
Klosterring 1, Postfach 1820, 7730 Villingen-Schwenningen, W. Germany (B.R.D.)
- Arbeits- und Sozialrecht. m. ISSN 0003-7664 (Baden-Wuerttemberg. Ministerium fuer Arbeit, Gesundheit und Sozialordnung)
- Die Brandhilfe. m. ISSN 0006-906X (Landesfeuerwehrverband Baden-Wuerttemberg)
- Weltgeschehen. q. ISSN 0049-7134

**Dr. Neinhaus Verlag GmbH**
St. Stephans-Platz 33, Postfach 1188, 7750 Konstanz, W. Germany (B.R.D.)
- Artis. m. ISSN 0004-3842
- Bodensee Hefte; das aktuelle Monatsmagazin. m. ISSN 0006-548X (Internationaler Bodensee Verkehrsverein)
- Die Landpost; das Fach-und Familienblatt fuer das sueddeutsche Land. w. ISSN 0023-8007

**Verlag Neue Deutsche Hefte**
Kindelbergweg 7, 1000 Berlin 46, W. Germany (B.R.D.)
- Neue Deutsche Hefte. q. ISSN 0028-3142

**Neue Deutsche Schule Verlagsgesellschaft MbH**
Schuetzenbahn 11-13, 4300 Essen 1, W. Germany (B.R.D.)
- Neue Deutsche Schule. s-m. (Gewerkschaft Erziehung und Wissenschaft. Landesverband Nordrhein-Westfalen)

**Verlag Neue Gesellschaft GmbH**
Koelnerstr. 143, 5300 Bonn-Bad Godesberg, W. Germany (B.R.D.)
- Archiv fuer Sozialgeschichte. a. ISSN 0066-6505 (Friedrich-Ebert Stiftung) (Co-sponsor: Institut fuer Sozialgeschichte)
- Bildung und Politik. m.
- Die Neue Gesellschaft. m. ISSN 0028-3177
- Vierteljahresberichte - Probleme der Entwicklungslaender. q. ISSN 0015-7910 (Friedrich-Ebert-Stiftung. Forschung Institut)

**Verlag fuer Neue Werbung GmbH**
Postfach 101110, 2850 Bremerhaven, W. Germany (B. R. D.)
- Die Horen; Zeitschrift fuer Literatur, Grafik und Kritik. q. ISSN 0018-4942

**Verlag Neue Wirtschafts-Briefe GmbH**
Eschstr. 22, Postfach 1620, 4690 Herne 1, W. Germany (B. R. D.)
- Betriebswirtschaftliche Forschung und Praxis. 6 per yr. ISSN 0006-002X
- Internationale Wirtschafts-Briefe; Zeitschrift fuer internationales Steuer- und Wirtschaftsrecht, Euratom, OECD, Steuern und Zoelle im gemeinsamen Markt. fortn. ISSN 0020-9368 (Deutsche Vereinigung fuer Internationales Steuerrecht)
- Neue Wirtschafts-Briefe; Zeitschrift fuer Steuer- und Wirtschaftsrecht. w. ISSN 0028-3460

**Neuer Konkret Verlag**
Grosse Reichenstr. 25, 2000 Hamburg 11, W. Germany (B.R.D.)
- Konkret. m.

**Verlag Neuer Merkur GmbH**
Ingolstaedter Str. 63a, 8000 Munich 46, W. Germany (B.R.D.)
- Dental Labor. m. ISSN 0011-8656 (Verband Deutscher Zahntechnikerinnungen e.V.)
- Eisenwaren Allgemeine. m. ISSN 0024-6603
- Fahrzeug- und Metall-Lackierer. m. ISSN 0014-6854
- Funk Fachhaendler. m. ISSN 0016-2817
- Industriemeister Nachrichten. m. ISSN 0019-9303 (Deutsche Industriemeistervereinigung e.V)
- Radio Mentor Electronic; Internationale Fach-Zeitschrift fuer Bauelemente, Messtechnik und Geraete der Unterhaltungselectronic. m. ISSN 0033-7935
- Rationelle Hauswirtschaft; die Hauswirtschaftsmeisterin. m.
- Reiniger und Waescher; Fachblatt fuer die gesamte Textilpflege. m. ISSN 0034-3625 (Textilreinigungsverband e.V.)
- Rundfunk - Fernseh - Wirtschaft. m. (Verband Deutscher Rundfunk- und Fernseh-Fachgrosshaendler e.V.)

**Neuer Vorwaerts Verlag**
Islandufer 21, 5600 Wuppertal, W. Germany (B.R.D.)
- Unsere Wirtschaft. m. ISSN 0042-0549 (Industrie- und Handelskammer zu Duesseldorf)

**Neuer Vorwaerts-Verlag Nau und Co.**
Koelner Str. 108-112, Postfach 910, Bonn-Bad Godesberg, W. Germany (B. R. D.)
- Die Demokratische Gemeinde; Monatsschrift fuer Kommunalpolitik in Stadt und Land. m. ISSN 0011-8303
- Vorwaerts; sozialdemokratische Wochenzeitung fuer Politik, Wirtschaft und Kultur. w. ISSN 0042-8949

**Verlag Neuer Weg GmbH**
Postfach 3080, 7000 Stuttgart 1, W. Germany (B.R.D.)
- Rote Fahne. fortn. (Kommunistischer Arbeiterbund Deutschlands (KABD))

**Neues Optikerjournal Verlag**
Schlossberg 15-17, 7530 Pforzheim, W. Germany (B.R.D.)
- Neues Optikerjournal. m. ISSN 0028-3673

**Verlag Dr. Neufang KG**
Nordring 10, 4660 Gelsenkirchen-Buer, W. Germany (B.R.D.)
- Deutscher Aerokurier. m. ISSN 0012-107X (Deutscher Aero Club)

**Neuland-Verlagsgesellschaft mbH**
Adenauerallee 48, 2000 Hamburg 1, W. Germany (B.R.D.)
- Jahrbuch zur Frage der Suchtgefahren. a.

**Neuwerk-Gemeinschaft e.V.**
Otto- Roehm- Str. 69, 6100 Darmstadt, W. Germany (B.R.D.)
- Ans Werk. bi-m. ISSN 0003-522X

**Niederrheinische Industrie- und Handelskammer Duisburg-Wesel-Kleve zu Duisburg**
Mercatorstr. 22, Postfach 101123, 4100 Duisburg 1, W. Germany (B.R.D.)
- Niederrheinische Industrie- und Handelskammer Duisburg-Wesel zu Duisburg. Wirtschaftliche Mitteilungen. s-m. ISSN 0028-9752

**Niedersachsen. Kultusministerium**
- Schulverwaltungsblatt fuer Niedersachsen. (pub. by Verlag Hahnsche Buchhandlung)

**Niedersachsen. Ministerium der Justiz**
- Niedersaechsischer Staatsanzeiger. (pub. by Schluetersche Verlagsanstalt und Druckerei)

**Niedersachsen. Niedersaechsischer Gemeindetag**
Seelhorststr. 18, 3000 Hannover, W. Germany (B.R.D.)
- Niedersaechsische Gemeinde; Monatsschrift fuer kommunale Selbstverwaltung. m. ISSN 0028-9779

**Niedersaechsische Staats- und Universitaetsbibliothek**
Prinzenstr.1, 3400 Goettingen, W. Germany (B.R.D.)
- Niedersaechsische Staats- und Universitaetsbibliothek, Goettingen. Arbeiten. irreg. ISSN 0072-4866

**Niedersaechsisches Landesmuseum, Hannover**
- Niederdeutsche Beitraege zur Kunstgeschichte. (pub. by Deutscher Kunstverlag GmbH)
- Voelkerkundliche Abhandlungen. (pub. by Kommissions-Verlag Muenstermann)

**Max Niemeyer Verlag**
Pfrondorfer Str. 4, 7400 Tuebingen, W. Germany (B.R.D.)
- Altdeutsche Textbibliothek. Ergaenzungsreihe. irreg. ISSN 0065-6607
- Anglia; Zeitschrift fuer englische Philologie. s-a. ISSN 0003-3251
- Beitraege zur Geschichte der deutschen Sprache und Literatur. 3 per yr. ISSN 0005-8076
- English and American Studies in German; summaries of theses and monographs. a. ISSN 0071-0490 (German Congress of Scholars of English)
- Forschungsprobleme der Vergleichenden Literaturgeschichte. irreg., no. 5, 1976. ISSN 0071-7703
- Freies Deutsches Hochstift, Frankfurt am Main. Jahrbuch. a. ISSN 0071-9463
- Germanistik; internationales Referatenorgan mit bibliographischen Hinweisen. q. ISSN 0016-8912
- Internationales Archiv fuer Sozialgeschichte der Deutschen Literatur. a.

- Neudrucke Deutscher Literaturwerke. irreg. ISSN 0077-7668
- Neudrucke Deutscher Literaturwerke. Sonderreihe. irreg. ISSN 0077-7676
- Nuntiaturberichte aus Deutschland nebst Ebgaenzenden Aktenstuecken. irreg. ISSN 0078-2742 (Deutsches Historisches Institut in Rom IT)
- Quellen und Forschungen aus Italienischen Archiven und Bibliotheken. a. ISSN 0079-9068 (Deutsches Historisches Institut in Rom IT)
- Romanische Bibliographie/Bibliographie Romane/Romance Bibliography. irreg. ISSN 0080-388X
- Studien zur Deutschen Literatur. irreg., no. 50, 1976. ISSN 0081-7236
- Studien zur Englischen Philologie, Neue Folge. irreg., no. 18, 1975. ISSN 0081-7244
- Untersuchungen zur Deutschen Literatur-Geschichte. irreg., no. 16, 1977. ISSN 0083-4564
- Zeitschrift fuer Celtische Philologie. a. ISSN 0084-5302
- Zeitschrift fuer Romanische Philologie. 3 per yr. ISSN 0049-8661
- Zeitschrift fuer Romanische Philologie. Beihefte. irreg., no. 159, 1977. ISSN 0084-5396

**Nomos Verlagsgesellschaft mbH und Co. KG**
Waldseestr. 3-5, Postfach 610, 7570 Baden-Baden, W. Germany (B.R.D.)
- Arbeit und Sozialpolitik. m.
- Stifterverband fuer die Deutsche Wissenschaft. Schriftenreihe zum Stiftungswesen. irreg., vol. 9, 1973. ISSN 0081-556X

**Nord-Sued Werbung GmbH und Co. KG**
Menzingerstr. 37, 8000 Munich 19, W. Germany (B.R.D.)
- Wasser und Abwasser /Bau-Intern. m. (Bayern. Staatsministerium des Innern)

**Norddeutsche Missions-Gesellschaft**
Vahrer Str. 243, 2800 Bremen, W. Germany (B.R.D.)
- Bremer Missionsschiff. bi-m. ISSN 0006-9574

**Norddeutscher Wirtschaftsverlag**
Haart 224, 2350 Neumuenster, W. Germany (B.R.D.)
- B I. (Bauwirtschaftliche Informationen) d. ISSN 0341-3896

**Nordelbisches Zentrum fuer Weltmission und Kirchlichen Weltdienst**
2257 Breklum, W. Germany (B.R.D.)
- Nordelbische Mission; Breklumer Sonntagsblat fuers Haus. m.

**Nordfriisk Instituut**
Osterstr. 63, 2257 Bredstedt, W. Germany (B.R.D.)
- Nordfriesisches Jahrbuch. a. ISSN 0078-1045
- Nordfriesland; Kultur, Politik, Wirtschaft. q. ISSN 0029-1196

**Nordhaeuser Heimatfreunde e.V.**
Koenigstr. 7, 3000 Hannover, W. Germany (B.R.D.)
- Nordhaeuser Nachrichten. q. ISSN 0029-1269

**Nordland-Druck**
Am Sande 18, Postfach 2343, 3140 Lueneburg, W. Germany (B.R.D.)
- Jahrbuch des Baltischen Deutschtums. a. ISSN 0075-2436

**Nordmark-Werke Hamburg**
Postfach 44, 2082 Uetersen 1, W. Germany (B.R.D.)
- Materia Medica Nordmark. m. ISSN 0025-5238

**Nordostdeutsches Kulturwerk e.V.**
Herderstr. 1-11, 3140 Lueneburg, W. Germany (B.R.D.)
- Nordost-Archiv; Zeitschrift fuer Sammler und Landeshistoriker. q. ISSN 0029-1595

**Nordrhein-Westfalen. Geologisches Landesamt**
De Greiff-Str. 195, 4150 Krefeld, W. Germany (B.R.D.)
- Fortschritte in der Geologie von Rheinland und Westfalen. irreg., vol. 24, 1974. ISSN 0071-8009

**Nordrhein-Westfalen. Landesoberbergamt**
- Grubensicherheit. (pub. by Verlag Glueckauf GmbH)

**Nordwestverlag**
Guentherstr. 21, 3000 Hannover 26, W. Germany
(B.R.D.)
- D F W Dokumentation-Information.
(Dokumentation - Fachbibliothek -
Werksbuecherei); Zeitschrift fuer technische
Archive, Betriebs- u. Volksbuechereien. bi-m plus
special nos. ISSN 0012-5059

**Nortwestdeutsche Gesellschaft fuer Innere Medizin**
- Nordwestdeutsche Gesellschaft fuer Innere
Medizin. Kongressbericht. (pub. by Hansisches
Verlagskontor H. Scheffler)

**Nova Press**
Friedrichstr. 60, 6000 Frankfurt, W. Germany
(B.R.D.)
- Gasolin 23. irreg, no. 4, 1976.

**Nuernberg. Stadtbibliothek**
Egidien-Platz 23, 8500 Nuernberg 2, W. Germany
(B.R.D.)
- Beitraege zur Geschichte und Kultur der Stadt
Nuernberg. irreg. ISSN 0078-2785
- Stadtbibliothek Nuernberg. Ausstellungskatalog.
irreg., vol. 87, 1976. ISSN 0078-2777

**Nuernberg. Stadtverwaltung**
- Nuernberg Heute. (pub. by Sebald Druck und
Verlag)

**Verlag Nuernberger Presse**
Marienplatz 1, 8500 Nuernberg 1, W. Germany
(B.R.D.)
- Schlesien; arts, science, folklore. q. ISSN 0036-
6153 (Kulturwerk Schlesien e.V.)

**Numismatische Gesellschaft e.V.**
Postfach 202, 6720 Speyer, W. Germany (B.R.D.)
- Numismatisches Nachrichtenblatt. m. ISSN 0029-
6082

**Numismatische Gesellschaft zu Berlin**
Warnemunder Str. 2, 1000 Berlin 33, W. Germany
(B.R.D.)
- Berliner Numismatische Zeitschrift. irreg., no. 36,
1974.

**Nymphenburger Verlagshandlung**
Romanstr. 16, 8000 Munich 19, W. Germany
(B.R.D.)
- Nymphenburger Texte zur Wissenschaft. irreg.
- Sammlung Dialog. irreg. ISSN 0080-5815

**OARCA - Freie Akademie zur Koordinierung von
Esoterik und Wissenschaft e.V.**
Donnersbergerstr. 11, 8000 Munich 19, W.
Germany (B.R.D.)
- Esoterik und Wissenschaft. q.

**Oberflaechenbearbeitung Metallischer und
Nichtmetallischer Werkstoffe**
Kolbergerstr. 22, Postfach 860420, 8000 Munich 80,
W. Germany (B.R.D.)
- Metalloberflaeche. m. ISSN 0026-0797

**Oberhessische Gesellschaft fuer Natur- und
Heilkunde, Giessen**
- Oberhessische Gesellschaft fuer Natur- und
Heilkunde, Giessen. Berichte. (pub. by Wilhelm
Schmitz Verlag)

**Oberrheinischer Geologischer Verein**
- Oberrheinischer Geologischer Verein.
Jahresberichte und Mitteilungen. (pub. by E.
Schweizerbart'sche Verlagsbuchhandlung)

**Oel Verlag GmbH**
Alsterkamp 20, 2000 Hamburg 13, W. Germany
(B.R.D.)
- Oel; Zeitschrift fuer die Mineraloelwirtschaft. m.
ISSN 0029-8689

**Dr. H. Oelke**
Kastanienallee 13, 3150 Peine, W. Germany
(B.R.D.)
(Subscr. to: W. Hansen, Muschelweg 8, 3000
Hanover-Limmer)
- Beitraege zur Naturkunde Niedersachsens. q.
ISSN 0340-4277

**Oerlikon Elektrodenfabrik Eisenberg GmbH**
6719 Eisenberg/Pfalz, W. Germany (B.R.D.)
- Oerlikon Schweissmitteilungen. irreg, no. 73,
1975. ISSN 0078-3420 (Co-sponsor:
Schweissindustrie Oerlikon Buehrle AG, Zurich)

**Off Duty**
Eschersheimer Landstr. 69, 6000 Frankfurt 1, West
Germany (B. R. D.)
- Off Duty. m.

**Verlag Offene Worte**
Bonngasse 3, 5300 Bonn, W. Germany (B.R.D.)
- Truppenpraxis. m. ISSN 0041-3666 (Germany,
Federal Republic. Bundesministerium der
Verteidigung)
- Wehrausbildung in Wort und Bild. m. ISSN 0043-
2121 (Germany, Federal Republic.
Bundesministerium der Verteidigung)

**Verlag Arthur Ohm**
Wilschenbrucher Weg 92, 3140 Lueneburg, W.
Germany (B.R.D.)
- Heimatblatt fuer Deutsche Volksgemeinschaft. m.

**KG Oil-Telegram GmbH und Co.**
Carl-Petersen-Str. 70/76, Postfach 260443,
2000hamburg 26, W. Germany (B.R.D.)
- Europe Oil-Telegram. 2 per w. ISSN 0014-2824

**R. Oldenbourg Verlag GmbH**
Rosenheimer Str. 145, 8000 Munich 80, W.
Germany (B.R.D.)
- Ausruestung in Luft- und Raumfahrt. irreg. ISSN
0067-0685
- Beitraege zur Linguistic und
Informationsverarbeitung. s-a.
- Deutsches Museum. Abhandlungen und Berichte.
3 per yr. ISSN 0012-1339
- Elektrische Bahnen; Zeitschrift fuer
Elektrotechnik und Elektronik im
Eisenbahnwesen. m. ISSN 0013-5437
- Elektronische Rechenanlagen mit Computer-
Praxis; Theorie, Technik und Anwendung der
Computer. bi-m. ISSN 0013-5720
(Nachrichtentechnische Gesellschaft im VDE
(NTG))
- G W F. (Das Gas- und Wasserfach) m. ISSN
0016-3651
- Gesundheits-Ingenieur; Zeitschrift fuer Hygiene,
Gesundheitstechnik, Bauphysik, mit den
Fachgebieten Heizungs- und Klimatechnik,
Haustechnik, Wasser, Abwasser, Umwaltschutz.
m. ISSN 0016-9277
- Historische Zeitschrift. bi-m. ISSN 0018-2613
- Impulstechniken. irreg., vol. 6, 1976.
- Rationalisierung der Datenverarbeitung. irreg.
- Regelungstechnik; Zeitschrift fuer Steuerung,
Regelung und Prozessdatenverarbeitung. m. ISSN
0034-3226
- Regelungstechnische Praxis; Zeitschrift fuer
Steuerung, Regelung und
Prozessdatenverarbeitung im Betrieb. m. ISSN
0034-3234
- Der Sanitaerinstallateur und Heizungsbauer. bi-m.
ISSN 0036-441X
- Studien zur Geschichte des Neunzehnten
Jahrhunderts. irreg. ISSN 0081-7309
- Suedostdeutsche Historische Kommission.
Buchreihe. irreg.
- Suedostdeutsches Archiv. a. ISSN 0081-9085
(Suedostdeutsche Historische Kommission)
- Suedosteuropaeische Arbeiten. irreg. (Suedost-
Institut)
- Technisches Messen - A T M. (Archiv fuer
Technisches Messen) m. ISSN 0340-837X
- Untersuchungen zur Gegenwartskunde
Suedosteuropas. irreg. (Suedost-Institut)

**Oldenburgische Gesellschaft fuer Familienkunde**
Lerigauweg 14, 2900 Oldenburg, W. Germany
(B.R.D.)
- Oldenburgische Familienkunde. q. ISSN 0030-
2074

**Olle und Wolter GmbH und Co.**
Postfach 4310, 1000 Berlin 30, W. Germany
(B.R.D.)
- Kritik der Politischen Oekonomie; Beitraege des
internationalen Marxismus. q.

**Georg Olms Verlag GmbH**
Hagentorwall 7, 3200 Hildesheim, W. Germany
(B.R.D.)
(Dist. by Adler's Foreign Books, Inc., 162 Fifth
Ave., New York, N.Y. 10010)
- Germanistische Linguistik. irreg., no. 3 per 4,
1976. ISSN 0072-1492 (Forschunginstitut fuer
Deutsche Sprache, Marburg)
- Medizinhistorisches Journal. irreg. (previously
quarterly), vol. 12, 1977. ISSN 0025-8431
(Akademie der Wissenschaften und der Literatur,
Mainz. Kommission fuer Geschichte der Medizin
und der Naturwissenschaften)

**Olympia-Verlag GmbH**
Badstr. 4-6, 8500 Nuernberg, W. Germany (B.R.D.)
- Kicker-Sportmagazin; Deutschlands groesste
Sportzeitung. 2 per wk. ISSN 0023-1290

**Guenter Olzog Verlag**
Thierschstr. 11, 8000 Munich 22, W. Germany
(B.R.D.)
- Gegenwartsfragen der Ost-Wirtschaft. irreg. ISSN
0072-0534 (Osteuropa-Institut, Munich)
- Jahrbuch der Wirtschaft Osteuropas/Yearbook of
East-European Economics. a. ISSN 0449-5225
(Osteuropa-Institut, Munich)
- Politische Studien. bi-m. ISSN 0032-3462 (Hanns-
Seidel-Stiftung e.V.)
- Sozialwissenschaftliches Jahrbuch fuer Politik. a.

**Verlag J.G. Oncken Nachf. GmbH**
Langenbeckstr. 28/30, 3500 Kassel 1, W. Germany
(B.R.D.)
- Die Gemeinde; Wochenschrift fuer Gemeinde und
Haus. w. ISSN 0016-6073 (Bund Evangelisch-
Freikirchlicher Gemeinden)
- Jungscharhelfer; Mitarbeiterhilfe fuer Jungen- und
Maedchenarbeit. bi-m. ISSN 0022-6467
(Gemeindejugendwerk)
- Sonntagschulmitarbeiter; religionspaedagogisches
Monatsblatt. bi-m. ISSN 0012-2580

**Theodor Oppermann Verlag**
Ostfeldstr. 46, Postfach 710140, 3000 Hannover 71,
W. Germany (B.R.D.)
- Chemie Neuerscheinungen; Buch und
Zeitschriften-Erscheinungen. bi-m.
- Juristische Neuerscheinungen. bi-m.
- Medizinische Neuerscheinungen; Buch- und
Zeitschriften-Erscheinungen. bi-m. ISSN 0025-
8482

**Orbis-Verlag**
Adenauerallee 2, 2000 Hamburg 1, W. Germany
(B.R.D.)
- Blumen und Garten. w.
- Handarbeiten. bi-w.
- Selbermachen. bi-w.

**Organisation of European Aluminium Smelters**
Graf-Adolf-Str. 18, 4100 Duesseldorf, W. Germany
(B.R.D.)
- Aluminium Smelters, Europe, U S A. a.

**Ornithologische Gesellschaft in Bayern**
Zoologische Staatssammlung, Maria-Ward-Str. 1b,
(Schloss Nymphenburg), 8000 Munich 19, W.
Germany (B.R.D.)
- Ornithologische Gesellschaft in Bayern. Anzeiger.
2 per yr. ISSN 0030-5715

**Verlag der Ortskrankenkassen**
Euskirchener Str. 60, Postfach, 1120 Bonn-Duisdorf,
W. Germany (B. R. D.)
- Die Ortskrankenkasse. s-m. ISSN 0030-5995
(Bundesverband der Ortskrankenkassen)

**Osang Verlag**
In der Lache 1, Postfach 1669, 5465 Erpel/Rhein,
W. Germany (B.R.D.)
- Zivilverteidigung; Forschung-Technik-
Organisation-Recht. q. ISSN 0044-4839

**Osram-Gesellschaft**
- Osram-Gesellschaft. Technisch-Wissenschaftliche
Abhandlungen. (pub. by Springer-Verlag US)

**Ost-West-Kontakte Verlags- und Werbegesellschaft
mbH**
Findelgasse 10, Postfach, 8500 Nuernberg 1, W.
Germany (B.R.D.)
- Ost-West Commerz; Europaeisches
Handelsmagazin. m.

**Osteuropa-Institut, Munich**
- Gegenwartsfragen der Ost-Wirtschaft. (pub. by
Guenter Olzog Verlag)
- Jahrbuch der Wirtschaft Osteuropas/Yearbook of
East-European Economics. (pub. by Guenter
Olzog Verlag)
- Osteuropa Institut, Munich. Veroeffentlichungen.
Reihe Geschichte. (pub. by Verlag Otto
Harrassowitz)

**Ostfriesische Landschaft**
- Ostfriesland. (pub. by Verlag Gerhard Rautenberg)

**Ostkirchliches Institut der Deutschen Augustiner**
- Ostkirchliche Studien. (pub. by Augustinus-Verlag)

**Ostseegesellschaft e.V.**
Johnsallee 18, 2000 Hamburg 13, W. Germany
(B.R.D.)
- Mare Balticum. irreg. ISSN 0542-6758

**P C Moderner Verlag**
Herzogstr. 64, 8000 Munich 40, W. Germany (B. R.
D.)
- Stereo; das deutsche Hi-Fi- und Musikmagazin. m.

**Pahl-Rugenstein Verlag**
Gottesweg 54, 5000 Cologne 51, W. Germany
(B.R.D.)
- Blaetter fuer deutsche und internationale Politik.
m. ISSN 0006-4416
- Demokratie und Recht. q.
- Demokratische Erziehung. bi-m.

**Paleontologische Gesellschaft e.V.**
- Palaeontologische Zeitschrift. (pub. by E.
Schweizerbart'sche Verlagsbuchhandlung)

**Pallottiner Druck und Lahn-Verlag**
Wiesbadener Str. 1, Postfach 140, 6250 Limburg, W.
Germany (B.R.D.)
- Pallottis Werk. q. ISSN 0031-0395
(Missionsanstalt der Pallottiner)

**Papiermacher Berufsgenossenschaft**
- Verhuetet Unfaelle. (pub. by Dr. Curt Haefner
Verlag)

**Pardon Verlagsgesellschaft mbH**
Oeder Weg 157, 6000 Frankfurt 1, W. Germany
(B.R.D.)
- Pardon; die Deutsche satirische Monatsschrift. m.
ISSN 0031-1855

**Verlag Paul Parey (Berlin)**
Lindenstr. 44-47, 1000 Berlin 61, W. Germany
(B.R.D.)
- Acta Phytomedica; Beihefte zur
Phytopathologischen Zeitschrift. irreg. ISSN 0065-
1567
- Anatomia, Histologia, Embryologia; Zentralblatt
fuer Veterinaermedizin, Reihe C. q. ISSN 0340-
2096 (World Association of Veterinary
Anatomists)
- Angewandte Botanik. 6 per yr. ISSN 0066-1759
- Anzeiger fuer Schaedlingskunde, Pflanzen- und
Umweltschutz. m. ISSN 0340-7322
- Berliner und Muenchener Tieraerztliche
Wochenschrift. s-m. ISSN 0005-9366
- Betriebs- und Marktwirtschaft im Gartenbau.
irreg. ISSN 0303-1241
- Bibliographie der Pflanzenschutzliteratur/
Bibliography of Plant Protection/Bibliographie de
la Protection des Plantes; Neue Folge. 4 per yr.
ISSN 0006-1387 (Biologische Bundesanstalt fuer
Land- und Forstwirtschaft in Berlin- Dahlem)
- Biologische Bundesanstalt fuer Land- und
Forstwirtschaft, Berlin-Dahlem. Mitteilungen.
irreg., no. 174, 1977. ISSN 0067-5849
(Biologische Bundesanstalt fuer Land- und
Forstwirtschaft in Berlin-Dahlem)
- Chirurgia Veterinaria; Referate-Abstracts.
Chirurgia, Ophthalmologia, Radiologia. q. ISSN
0009-482X (Europaeische Vereinigung fuer
Veterinaerchirurgie)
- Der Erwerbsobstbau. m. ISSN 0014-0309
- Fortschritte der Pflanzenzuechtung/Advances in
Plant Breeding. irreg., no. 5, 1975. ISSN 0301-
2727
- Fortschritte der Verhaltensforschung/Advances in
Ethology. irreg., no. 19, 1977. ISSN 0301-2808
- Fortschritte der Veterinaermedizin/Advances in
Veterinary Medicine. irreg., no. 27, 1977. ISSN
0301-2794
- Fortschritte im Acker- und Pflanzenbau/Advances
in Agronomy and Crop Science. irreg., no. 3,
1974. ISSN 0301-2735
- Gaertnerische Berufspraxis. irreg., no. 48, 1976.
ISSN 0301-2719
- Grundlagen und Fortschritte der
Lebensmitteluntersuchung. irreg., no. 15, 1973.
ISSN 0432-7454
- Phytopathologische Zeitschrift/Journal of
Phytopathology. 12 per yr. ISSN 0031-9481
- Schriftenreihe Versuchstierkunde. irreg. ISSN
0300-1016
- Zeitschrift fuer Acker- und Pflanzenbau/Journal of
Agronomy and Crop Science. 8 per yr. ISSN
0044-2151
- Zeitschrift fuer Kulturtechnik und Flurbereinigung.
bi-m. ISSN 0044-2984
- Zeitschrift fuer Pflanzenzuechtung/Journal of
Plant Breeding. 8 per yr. ISSN 0044-3298

- Zeitschrift fuer Tierpsychologie/Journal of
Comparative Ethology. 12 per yr (in 3 vols.)
ISSN 0044-3573
- Zentralblatt fuer Veterinaermedizin. 10 per yr
(series A & B); 4 per yr (series C) ISSN 0044-
4294
- Zuchthygiene; Zeitschrift fuer Biologie und
Pathologie der Fortpflanzung sowie Besamung der
Haustiere. q. ISSN 0044-5371

**Verlag Paul Parey (Hamburg)**
Spitalerstr. 12, 2000 Hamburg 1, W. Germany
(B.R.D.)
- Agrarmarkt-Studien. irreg., no. 23, 1976. ISSN
0065-4345 (Universitaet Kiel. Institut fuer
Agrarpolitik und Marktlehre)
- Agrarpolitik und Marktwesen. irreg., no. 14, 1974.
ISSN 0065-4353
- Aktuelle Fragen des Landbaues. irreg., no. 8,
1971. ISSN 0568-7594
- Berichte ueber Landwirtschaft. q. ISSN 0005-9080
(Germany, Federal Republic. Bundesministerium
fuer Ernaehrung, Landwirtschaft und Forsten)
- Berichte ueber Landwirtschaft. Sonderhefte. irreg.,
no. 193, 1976. ISSN 0301-2689
- Betriebs- und Arbeitswirtschaft in der Praxis; Eine
Schriftenreihe fuer die landwirtschaft. irreg., no.
21, 1976. ISSN 0405-6485
- European Journal of Forest Pathology/Journal
Europeen de Pathologie Forestiere/Europaeische
Zeitschrift fuer Forstpathologie. bi-m. ISSN 0300-
1237
- Fisch und Fang; Zeitschrift fuer Angler und alle
Freunde des Fischwassers. m. ISSN 0015-2838
- Forschungsstelle fuer Jagdkunde und
Wildschadenverhuetung. Schriftenreihe. irreg., no.
7, 1972. ISSN 0071-7711
- Forstliche Umschau; Referate ueber das forst- und
holzwirtschaftliche schrifttum. q. ISSN 0015-7988
- Forstwissenschaftliche Forschungen; Beihefte zum
Forstwissenschaftlichen Centralblatt. irreg., no.
36, 1976. ISSN 0071-772X (Forstliche
Forschungsanstalt Muenchen)
- Forstwissenschaftliches Zentralblatt; Vereinigt mit
Tharandter Forstliches Jahrbuch. bi-m. ISSN
0015-8003 (Forstliche Forschungsanstalt
Muenchen)
- Fortschritte in der Tierphysiologie und
Tierernaehrung/Advances in Animal Physiology
and Animal Nutrition. irreg., no. 8, 1977. ISSN
0301-2743
- Giessener Schriftenreihe Tierzucht und
Haustiergenetik. irreg., vol. 37, 1976. ISSN 0434-
0035
- Landarbeit und Technik. irreg., no. 35, 1968.
ISSN 0455-2342 (Max-Planck-Institut fuer
Landarbeit und Landtechnik)
- Mammalia Depicta. irreg., no. 10, 1976. ISSN
0301-2778
- Meeresforschung/Reports on Marine Research;
berichte der Wissenschaftlichen Kommission fuer
Meeresforschung. 4 per yr.
- Monographien zur Angewandten Entomologie;
Beihefte zur Zeitschrift fuer angewandte
Entomologie. irreg. ISSN 0077-0698
- Monumenta Venatoria; Faksimile-Drucke seltener
Jagdbuecher des 15. bis 18. Jahrhunderts. irreg.,
no. 4, 1973. ISSN 0301-276X
- Naturwissenschaftlicher Verein in Hamburg.
Abhandlungen und Verhandlungen. a. ISSN 0301-
2697
- Universitaet Kiel. Agrarwissenschaftliche
Fakultaet. Schriftenreihe. irreg., no. 55, 1976.
- Wasser und Boden. m. ISSN 0043-0951 (Bund
und Landesverbaende der Wasser - und
Kulturbauingenieure) (Co-Sponsor: Kuratorium
fuer Wasser und Kulturbauwesen e.V. (K W K))
- Zeitschrift fuer Angewandte Entomologie/Journal
of Applied Entomology. 12 per yr. ISSN 0044-
2240
- Zeitschrift fuer Jagdwissenschaft. q. ISSN 0044-
2887
- Zeitschrift fuer Saeugetierkunde. 6 per yr. ISSN
0044-3468 (Deutsche Gesellschaft fuer
Saeugetierkunde)
- Zeitschrift fuer Tierphysiologie, Tierernaehrung
und Futtermittelkunde/Journal of Animal
Physiology and Animal Nutrition. m. ISSN 0044-
3565
- Zeitschrift fuer Tierzuechtung und
Zuechtungsbiologie/Journal of Animal Breeding
and Genetics. 5-6 per yr. ISSN 0044-3581
- Zeitschrift fuer Zoologische Systematik und
Evolutionsforschung. q. ISSN 0044-3808

**Verlag Parzeller und Co.**
Peterstor 18, Postfach 409, 6400 Fulda, W.
Germany (B.R.D.)
- Beitraege zur Naturkunde in Osthessen. a. (Verein
fuer Naturkunde in Osthessen e.V.)

**Verlag Passavia**
Vornholzstr. 40, 8390 Passau, W. Germany (B.R.D.)
- Das Schaufenster; illustrierte Monatshefte fuer
moderne Werbung. m. ISSN 0036-5939

**Patentanwaltskammer**
- Mitteilungen der Deutschen Patentanwaelte. (pub.
by Carl Heymanns Verlag KG)

**Patmos Verlag**
Am Wehrhahn 100, Postfach 6213, 4000
Duesseldorf 1, W. Germany (B.R.D.)
- Religionsunterricht an hoeheren Schulen. bi-m.
ISSN 0034-4028 (Bund Katholischer Religions
Lehrervereinigungen)

**Patzer-Verlag GmbH und Co. KG**
Alter Flughafen 15, 3000 Hannover 1, W. Germany
(B.R.D.)
- Allgemeine Bauzeitung. w. ISSN 0002-5801
- Gaertnerischer Fachhandel. m. ISSN 0016-3902
- Das Gartenamt. m. ISSN 0016-4739

**Hauke (Hank) Paul**
Einsteinstr. 3A, 2800 Bremen 44, W. Germany
(B.R.D.)
- Country Corner; Country Music Zeitschrift. 5 per
yr.

**Paul-Ehrlich-Gesellschaft**
- Infection. (pub. by Verlagsgesellschaft Otto Spatz
oHG)

**Paul-Ehrlich-Institut**
- Arbeiten aus dem Paul-Ehrlich-Institut, dem
Georg-Speyer-Haus und dem Ferdinand-Blum-
Institut. (pub. by Gustav Fischer Verlag)

**Paul-Ernst-Gesellschaft**
Postfach 279, 4680 Wanne-Eickel, W. Germany
(B.R.D.)
- Wille zur Form. s-a. ISSN 0043-5570

**Paul-Hindemith-Institut**
- Hindemith-Jahrbuch/Annales Hindemith. (pub. by
B. Schott's Soehne)

**Paulinus-Verlag**
Fleischstr. 61-65, 5500 Trier, W. Germany (B.R.D.)
- Trierer Theologische Zeitschrift. q. ISSN 0041-
2945 (Theologische Fakultaet Trier)

**Paulus-Verlag Karl Geyer**
Goethestr. 38, 7100 Heilbronn, W. Germany
(B.R.D.)
- Gnade und Herrlichkeit. bi-m. ISSN 0017-1409
(Christliche Allianz)

**Publizistisches Archiv Karl R. Pawlas**
Hasstr. 21, 8500 Nuernberg 122, W. Germany
(B.R.D.)
- Luftfahrt International. bi-m.

**Dr. Pelzer Verlag**
Grimmstr. 20, 4000 Duesseldorf, W. Germany
(B.R.D.)
- Zentralblatt fuer Sozialversicherung, Sozialhelfe
und Versorgung; Zeitschrift fuer das Recht der
Sozialen Sicherheit. m. ISSN 0044-4278

**Peri-Med Verlag Dr. D. Straube**
Vogelherd 35, Postfach 3740, 8520 Erlangen, W.
Germany (B.R.D.)
- Anaesthesiologische Informationen. m. (Deutsche
Gesellschaft fuer Anaesthesie und
Wiederbelebung. Berufsverband Deutscher
Anaesthesisten)
- Der Klinikarzt; Medizin im Krankenhaus. m.
ISSN 0341-2350
- Medizin; Zeitschrift fuer Diagnose und Therapie.
s-m. ISSN 0341-2911
- Der Medizinstudent. m. ISSN 0461-6529
- Notfallmedizin. m. ISSN 0340-7845
- Psycho; Neurologie und Psychiatrie fuer die
Praxis. bi-m. ISSN 0341-2903
- Zeitschrift fuer Praeklinische Geriatrie; Medizin
des Alternden. m. ISSN 0341-034X

**Pestalozzi-Froebel-Verband**
- Sozialpaedagogische Blaetter. (pub. by Quelle und
Meyer)

**Pestalozzi Kinder- und Jugenddorf Wahlwies**
7768 Stockach 14, W. Germany (B.R.D.)
- Ballon Kurier. a. ISSN 0005-4364
- Brief aus Wahlwies; Mitteilungen aus dem Pestalozzi Kinder- und Jugenddorf. q. ISSN 0006-9949

**Verlag C. F. Peters**
Kennedyallee 101, Postfach 700906, 6000 Frankfurt 70, W. Germany (B. R. D.)
- Deutsches Jahrbuch der Musikwissenschaft. a. ISSN 0070-4504 (Distr. by: C. F. Peters Corp., 373 Park Avenue South, New York, NY 10016)

**Pfadfinderinnenschaft St. Georg**
Kleinheiderweg, 5090 Leverkusen 3, W. Germany (B.R.D.)
- Dienen und Fuehren. q. ISSN 0012-2564
- Unser Kleeblatt. bi-m. ISSN 0049-5581

**Pfaelzer Bauernverlag GmbH**
Hauptstr. 61, Postfach 43, 6757 Waldfischbach-Burgalben, W. Germany (B.R.D.)
- Pfaelzer Bauer; Wochenblatt fuer Landwirtschaft und Weinbau. w. ISSN 0031-6660 (Pfaelzische Bauern- und Winzerschaft e.V.)

**Pfaelzer Saenger**
Hauptstr. 80, Postfach 31, 6757 Waldfischbach-Burgalben, W. Germany (B.R.D.)
- Pfaelzer Saenger. m. ISSN 0031-6687 (Pfaelzischer Saengerbund)

**Pfaelzische Bauern- und Winzerschaft e.V.**
- Pfaelzer Bauer. (pub. by Pfaelzer Bauernverlag GmbH)

**Pfaelzische Gesellschaft zur Foerderung der Wissenschaften in Speyer**
Gr. Pfaffengasse 7, 6720 Speyer, W. Germany (B.R.D.)
- Pfaelzer Heimat; Zeitschrift fuer pfaelzische Landeskunde, zugleich Mitteilungsblatt fuer Archivpflege, Bibliotheks-und Museumswesen in der Pfalz. q. ISSN 0031-6679

**Pfaelzischer Saengerbund**
- Pfaelzer Saenger. (pub. by Pfaelzer Saenger)

**Ph. Pfeiffer's Buchdruckereien und Verlage**
Glockenstr. 85, Postfach 3050, 6750 Kaiserslautern, W. Germany (B.R.D.)
- Der Deutsche Tabakbau. s-m. ISSN 0012-0820

**Richard Pflaum Verlag KG**
Lazarettstr. 4, Postfach 201920, 8000 Munich 19, W. Germany (B.R.D.)
- Die Baeckerjugend; apprentices' edition of Baeckermeister. m.
- Der Baeckermeister. w.
- Die Fleischerjugend. m. ISSN 0015-3621
- Krankengymnastik; Zeitschrift fuer Bewegungstherapie Massage und physikalisch-therapeutische Verfahren. m. ISSN 0023-4494 (Zentralverband Krankengymnastik e.V.)
- Medizinal-Markt Acta Medicotechnica; Zentralorgan fuer die medizinisch angewandte Technik, Biotechnik und praktische Orthopaedie. m. ISSN 0025-8423
- Der Metzgermeister. w. ISSN 0005-7088
- Naturheilpraxis. m. ISSN 0028-0941 (Deutsche Heilpraktikerschaft e.V.)

**Udo Pfriemer Verlag GmbH**
Landwehrstr. 68, 8000 Munich 2, W. Germany (B.R.D.)
- Abwassertechnik. 6 per yr. ISSN 0001-3706

**Pharmapress-Verlagsgesellschaft**
Beethovenplatz 1-3, 6000 Frankfurt 97, W. Germany (B.R.D.)
- Neue Apotheken Illustrierte. m. ISSN 0047-9381 (Arbeitsgemeinschaft der Berufsvertretungen Deutscher Apotheker)

**Pharmazeutischer Verlag**
Spaldingstr. 152, 2000 Hamburg 1, W. Germany (B.R.D.)
- Pharmazeutische Rundschau. m. ISSN 0031-7128 (Zweckverband Deutscher Apotheker)

**Philips GmbH**
Moenckebergstr. 7, Postfach 101420, 2000 Hamburg 1, W. Germany (B.R.D.)
- Kontakte; Information fuer Fachhandel, Werkstaetten und Techniker. irreg., approx 4 per yr.

**Phillumenists Worldring**
Jupiterstr. 20, 1000 Berlin 44, W. Germany (B.R.D.)
- Allround-Collector Address-List. m. ISSN 0002-6166

**Philologenverband Baden-Wuerttemberg**
- Suedwestdeutsche Schulblaetter. (pub. by Ernst Klett Verlag)

**Philosophisch-Theologische Hochschule, Passau. Institut fuer Ostbairische Heimatforschung**
Michaelisgasse 13, 8390 Passau, W. Germany (B.R.D.)
- Ostbairische Grenzmarken; Passauer Jahrbuch fuer Geschichte, kunst und Volkskunde. a. ISSN 0078-6845

**Physica-Verlag Rudolf Liebing GmbH und Co.**
Werner-von-Siemens-Str. 5, Postfach 5840, 8700 Wuerzburg 1, W. Germany (B.R.D.)
- Arbeiten zur Angewandten Statistik. irreg., no. 18, 1976. ISSN 0066-5673
- Bankwirtschaftliche Studien. irreg., no. 8, 1975. ISSN 0067-3838
- Empirical Economics. q.
- International Journal of Game Theory. 4 per yr. ISSN 0020-7276 (Institute for Advanced Studies, Vienna AU)
- Universitaet Wien. Institut fuer Statistik. Schriftenreihe. Neue Folge. irreg., 1972, no. 7. ISSN 0083-6168
- Unternehmensforschung fuer die Wirtschaftspraxis. irreg. ISSN 0083-453X
- Zeitschrift fuer Operations Research. 6 per yr. (Deutsche Gesellschaft fuer Operations Research)

**Physikalisch-Medizinische Sozietaet Erlangen**
Krankenhausstr. 12, 8520 Erlangen, W. Germany (B.R.D.)
- Physikalisch-Medizinische Sozietaet Erlangen. Sitzungsberichte. a. ISSN 0079-2004

**Physikalisch-Technische Bundesanstalt**
- P T B Mitteilungen Forschen und Pruefen. (pub. by Friedr. Vieweg und Sohn Verlagsgesellschaft mbH)

**Pick-Verlag**
Postfach 2723, 5800 Hagen, W. Germany (B.R.D.)
- Zeitschrift fuer Wirtschaftsgeographie. 8 per yr. ISSN 0044-3751

**Ed. Piepersche Buchdruckerei und Verlagsanstalt**
Osteroeder Str. 3, Postfach 10, 3392 Clausthal-Zellerfeld, W. Germany (B.R.D.)
- Statistische Mitteilungen der Bergbehoerden der Bundesrepublik. a.

**Ellen Pilger**
Berlinerstr. 125, 3392 Clausthal 2, W. Germany (b.R.D.)
- Clausthaler Geologische Abhandlungen. q. ISSN 0009-8523

**Pinel-Publikationen**
Wielandstr. 27-28, 1000 Berlin 15, W. Germany (B.R.D.)
- Dynamische Psychiatrie/Dynamic Psychiatry; international Zeitschrift fuer Psychiatrie und Psychoanalyse. bi-m. ISSN 0012-740X (Deutsche Akademie fuer Psychoanalyse)

**Die Planung Verlagsgesellschaft mbH**
Holzhofallee 25-31, 6100 Darmstadt, W. Germany (B.R.D.)
- Die Moderne Kueche. bi-m. ISSN 0026-864X (Arbeitsgemeinschaft die Moderne Kueche)

**H. Poeppinghaus**
Alte Bahnhofstr. 148a, 4630 Bochum-Langendreer, W. Germany (B. R. D.)
- Die Oase. m. ISSN 0029-7402 (Deutsches Afrika-Korps e.V.)

**Carl Ernst Poeschel Verlag**
Kernerstr. 43, 7000 Stuttgart 1, W. Germany (B.R.D.)
- Die Betriebswirtschaft. q.

**Pohl Druckerei und Verlagsanstalt**
Herzog-Ernst-Ring 1, Postfach 103, 3100 Celle, W. Germany (B.R.D.)
- Deutscher Turner-Bund. Jahrbuch der Turnkunst. a. ISSN 0075-2401
- TuS-Turnen und Sport. m.

**Polizei Technik Verkehr, Verlagsgesellschaft mbH und Co. KG**
Juliusstr. 2, Postfach 19, 6200 Wiesbaden 1, W. Germany (B.R.D.)
- Polizei Technik Verkehr. m. ISSN 0032-3535

**Polizeigewerkschaft im Deutschen Beamtenbund**
- Polizeispiegel. (pub. by Biermann KG)

**Polygraph-Verlag GmbH**
Schaumainkai 85, 6000 Frankfurt 70, W. Germany (B.R.D.)
- Export Polygraph International; export review for the printing industry. 6 per yr. ISSN 0014-5173
- Der Polygraph. s-m. ISSN 0032-3845

**Pommerscher Zentralverband e.V.**
Johnsallee 18, 2000 Hamburg 13, W. Germany (B.R.D.)
- Pommern; Kunst - Geschichte - Volkstum. q. ISSN 0032-4167

**Dr. Kurt Port Verlag GmbH**
Dulkweg 9, 7300 Esslingen-Wiflingshausen, W. Germany (B.R.D.)
- Die Pforte; Zeitschrift fuer Philosophie und Kultur. a. ISSN 0031-6784

**Portfolio Verlagsgesellschaft mbH**
Postfach 245, 8939 Bad Woerishofen, W. Germany (B.R.D.)
- Wirtschaft und Investment. m. ISSN 0043-6194

**Possev-Verlag**
Flurscheideweg 15, 6230 Frankfurt 80, W. Germany (B.R.D.)
- Grani; zhurnal literatury, iskusstva, nauki i obshchestvenno-politicheskoy mysli. q. ISSN 0017-3185
- Possev; obchshestvenno-politicheskii zhurnal. m. ISSN 0032-5201
- Vol'noe Slovo; samizdat. izbrannoe. q.

**Verlag der Praktische Schaedlingsbekaempfer**
Steinbrecherstr. 13, 3300 Braunschweig, W. Germany (B.R.D.)
- Der Praktische Schaedlingsbekaempfer. m. ISSN 0032-6801 (Deutscher Schaedlingsbekaempfer-Verband)

**Prediger- und Missionsseminar St. Chrischona**
- Theologie und Dienst. (pub. by Brunnen-Verlag GmbH)

**Presse und Bildung GmbH**
Fischerfeldstr. 7, 6000 Frankfurt, W. Germany (B.R.D.)
- Der Sozialdemokrat. m. ISSN 0038-6030 (Sozialdemokratische Partei Deutschlands)

**Presse und Sport**
Rhoenstr. 9, 6380 Bad Homburg 6, W. Germany (B.R.D.)
- Der Sportjournalist. bi-m. ISSN 0014-6145 (Verband Deutsche Sportpresse E.V)

**Presseverlag**
Grosse Str. 37, 2130 Rotenburg, W. Germnay (B.R.D.)
- Die Feder. m. ISSN 0014-8970 (Industriegewerkschaft Druck und Papier)

**Prestel-Verlag**
Mandlstr. 26, 8000 Munich 40, W. Germany (B.R.D.)
- Bilder aus Deutscher Vergangenheit. irreg. ISSN 0067-821X (Germanisches Nationalmuseum Nuernberg)
- Muenchner Jahrbuch der Bildenden Kunst. a. ISSN 0077-1899 (Staatliche Kunstsammlungen Bayerns) (Co-sponsor: Zentralinstitut fuer Kunstgeschichte, Munich)
- Studien zur Kunst des Neunzehnten Jahrhunderts. irreg. ISSN 0081-7325

**Promotor Verlags- und Forderungsgesellschaft mbH**
Hardstr. 26, Postfach 210148, 7500 Karlsruhe 21, W. Germany (B.R.D.)
- Clima Commerce International. m. ISSN 0009-8914

**Prost und Meiner-Verlag**
Uferstr. 11, Postfach 691, 8630 Coburg, W. Germany (B.R.D.)
- Alambre; revista tecnica sobre la fabricacion elaboracion y el empleo de alambres. bi-m. ISSN 0002-4406

- Blech - Rohre - Profile; Fachzeitschrift fuer die Band, Blech, Rohr und Profiltechnik. m. ISSN 0006-4688
- Draht; Fachzeitschrift fuer das gesamte Gebiet der Drahtherstellung, Drahtbearbeitung, Drahtverarbeitung. m. ISSN 0012-5911
- Il Filo Metallico. q.
- S T S - Sheet Metal - Tubes - Sections. bi-m.
- Le Trefile. bi-m.
- Wire; the technical journal for the wire industry. bi-m. ISSN 0043-5996
- Wirkerei- und Strickerei-Technik. m. ISSN 0043-6097

**Provinzialinstitut fuer Westfaelische Landes- und Volksforschung**
- Provinzialinstitut fuer Westfaelische Landes- und Volksforschung. Veroeffentlichungen. (pub. by Aschendorffsche Verlagsbuchhandlung)
- Westfaelische Forschungen. (pub. by Aschendorffsche Verlagsbuchhandlung)

**Pruefer-Werbung**
Lange Str. 71, Postfach 1262, 7570 Baden-Baden, W. Germany (B.R.D.)
- Baden-Baden Program. fortn. (Baeder und Kurverwaltung)

**Verlag fuer Psychologie**
Rohnsweg 25, Postfach 414, 3400 Goettingen, W. Germany (B.R.D.)
- Diagnostica; Zeitschrift fuer Psychologische Diagnostik, zugleich Informationsorgan ueber psychologische Tests und Untersuchungsmethoden. 4 per yr. ISSN 0012-1924
- Fortschritte der Psychoanalyse; internationales Jahrbuch zur Weiterentwicklung der Psychoanalyse. a. ISSN 0071-7940
- Praxis der Klinischen Psychologie. irreg., 1971, no. 2. ISSN 0079-4945
- Psychologische Rundschau; Ueberblick ueber die Fortschritte der Psychologie in Deutschland, Oesterreich und der Schweiz. q. ISSN 0033-3042 (Berufsverband Deutscher Psychologen) (Co-Sponsor: Deutsche Gesellschaft fuer Psychologie)
- Zeitschrift fuer Entwicklungspsychologie und Paedagogische Psychologie. ISSN 0049-8637
- Zeitschrift fuer Experimentelle und Angewandte Psychologie. 4 per yr. ISSN 0044-2712 (Deutsche Gesellschaft fuer Psychologie)
- Zeitschrift fuer Klinische Psychologie - Forschung und Praxis. q. ISSN 0084-5345 (Berufsverband Deutscher Psychologen)

**Psychophysikalische Gesellschaft e.V. (P.P.G.)**
Wolfratshauserstr. 26, 8000 Munich 70, W. Germany (B.R.D.)
- Erfahrungswissenschaftliche Blaetter (EWB) q. ISSN 0014-0090

**Public Finance Verlag**
Duesternbrooker Weg 120, 2300 Kiel, W. Germany (B.R.D.)
- Public Finance/Finances Publiques/Openbare Financien; international quarterly journal devoted to the study of fiscal theory and policy and related problems. 3 per yr. ISSN 0033-3476

**Verlag fuer Publizitaet**
Auf der Heide 20, Postfach 10, 3001 Isernhagen HB, W. Germany (B.R.D.)
- Bau-Zentralblatt; die Fachzeitschrift fuer Bauunternehmer im Hoch-, Tief- und Strassenbau. m.
- Motorboote und Yachten. s-a. ISSN 0077-166X
- Strassen- und Tiefbau Vereinigt mit Strasse-Bruecke-Tunnel, Bitumen-Teere-Asphalts-Peche. m.

**Verlag Friedrich Pustet**
Gutenbergstr. 8, 8400 Regensburg 1, W. Germany (B.R.D.)
- Archiv fuer Liturgiewissenschaft. a. ISSN 0066-6386 (Abt-Herwegen-Institut fuer Liturgische und Monastische Forschung)
- Biblische Untersuchungen. irreg. ISSN 0523-5154
- Renovatio; Zeitschrift fuer das interdisziplinaere Gespraech. q. (St. Albertus Magnus Apothekergilde e.V.) (Co-Sponsor: Katholische Aerztearbeit Deutschlands)
- Studien zur Geschichte der Katholischen Moraltheologie. irreg., 1973, vol. 20. ISSN 0081-7295
- Taschenbuch fuer Liturgie und Kirchenmusik. a. ISSN 0082-187X
- Textus Patristici et Liturgici. irreg. ISSN 0082-3775 (Institutum Liturgicum Ratisbonense)

**Quell Verlag**
Furtbachstr. 12A, Postfach 897, 7000 Stuttgart 1, W. Germany (B.R.D.)
- Evangelische Zentralstelle fuer Weltanschauungsfragen. Materialdienst. s-m. ISSN 0085-0357
- Fuer Arbeit und Besinnung. s-m. ISSN 0016-2434 (Evangelischer Oberkirchenrat)

**Quelle und Meyer**
Schloss-Wolfsbrunnen-Weg 29, Postfach 104480, 6900 Heidelberg 1, W. Germany (B.R.D.)
- Deutsche Shakespeare-Gesellschaft West. Jahrbuch. a. ISSN 0070-4326
- Die Mitarbeit; Zeitschrift zur Gesellschafts und Kulturpolitik. bi-m.
- Sozialpaedagogische Blaetter. bi-m. (Pestalozzi-Froebel-Verband)

**Buch- und Zeitschriften-Verlag die Quintessenz W. Haase**
Ifenpfad 2-4, 1000 Berlin 42, W. Germany (B.R.D.)
- Quintessence International. m. ISSN 0033-6572
- Quintessenz Journal; Zeitschrift fuer die Zahnarzthelferin. m. ISSN 0033-6599

**R I A S - Funkuniversitaet**
- R I A S-Funkuniversitaet, Berlin. Forschung und Information. (pub. by Colloquium Verlag)

**Verlag Dr. Josef Raabe**
Langer Grabenweg 1B, 5300 Bonn, W. Germany (B.R.D.)
- Akademischer Dienst; kultur- und bildungspolitische Informationen. w. ISSN 0002-3019
- Deutsche Universitaetszeitung; vereinigt mit Hochschuldienst. s-m. ISSN 0012-088X
- Deutscher Hochschulfuehrer. a. ISSN 0070-4385

**Raabe-Gesellschaft**
- Raabe-Gesellschaft. Jahrbuch. (pub. by Verlag Otto Wagner KG)
- Raabe- Gesellschaft. Jahrbuch. (pub. by Waisenhaus Buchdruckerei und Verlag)

**Radius-Verlag GmbH**
Kniebisstr. 29, 7000 Stuttgart 1, W. Germany (B.R.D.)
- Radius. q. ISSN 0033-8532 (Evangelische Akademikerschaft in Deutschland)

**Raith Verlag**
Herzog Heinrich Str. 21, 8000 Munich 2, W. Germany (B.R.D.)
- Literarische Hefte. irreg.

**Rat fuer Formgebung**
Eugen-Bracht-Weg 6, 6100 Darmstadt, W. Germany (B.R.D.)
- Design-Report. m.
- Rat fuer Formgebung. Literaturhinweise. q. ISSN 0024-4805

**Rationalisierungskuratorium der Deutschen Wirtschaft**
- Handbuch der Rationalisierung. (pub. by Industrie-Verlag Carlheinz Gehlsen)
- Rationalisierung. (pub. by Carl Hanser Verlag)

**Verlag Gerhard Rautenberg**
Blinke 8, Postfach 909, 2950 Leer, W. Germany (B.R.D.)
- Ostfriesland; Zeitschrift fuer Kultur, Wirtschaft und Verkehr. q. ISSN 0030-6479 (Ostfriesische Landschaft)

**Verlagsgesellschaft Recht und Wirtschaft mbH**
Haeusserstr. 14, Postfach 105960, 6900 Heidelberg 1, W. Germany (B.R.D.)
- Abhandlungen aus dem Gesamten Buergerlichen Recht, Handelsrecht und Wirtschaftsrecht. irreg., 1973, no. 45. ISSN 0065-0307
- Betriebs-Berater; Zeitschrift fuer Recht und Wirtschaft. 3 per mo. ISSN 0340-7918
- Recht der Internationalen Wirtschaft; Aussenwirtschaftsdienst des Betriebs-Berater. m. ISSN 0340-7926
- Der Steuerberater. m. ISSN 0049-223X
- Zeitschrift fuer das gesamte Handelsrecht und Wirtschaftsrecht. bi-m. ISSN 0044-2437

**Deutsche Rechtsprechung, Verlags-Gesellschaft mbH und Co. KG**
Eschstr. 22, Postfach 1620, 4690 Herne 1, W. Germany (B.R.D.)
- Deutsche Rechtsprechung. 18 per yr. ISSN 0012-060X

**Rechtsverlag GmbH**
Oststr. 119, 4000 Duesseldorf, W. Germany (B.R.D.)
- Der Farbenhaendler. m. ISSN 0046-3280 (Bundesverband des Deutschen Farbengrosshandels)

**Redactor-Verlag GmbH**
Moerikestr. 14, 6000 Frankfurt, W. Germany (B.R.D.)
- Blickpunkt D B. m. (Deutsche Bundesbahn)

**Arbeiterkampf-Verlag J. Reents**
Lerchenstr.75, 2000 Hamburg 50, W. Germany (B.R.D.)
- Arbeiterkampf.
- Internationale. every 6 weeks. (Kommunistischer Bund fuer den Proletarischen Internationalismus)

**Verlag Regensberg**
Daimlerweg 58, Postfach 6748/6749, 4400 Muenster, W. Germany (B.R.D.)
- Jahrbuch fuer Christliche Sozialwissenschaften. a. ISSN 0075-2584 (Universitaet Muenster. Institut fuer Christliche Sozialwissenschaften)
- Westfaelische Zeitschrift. a. ISSN 0083-9043 (Verein fuer Geschichte und Altertumskunde Westfalens)

**Verlag Regensburger Bistumsblatt**
Koenigsstr. 2, 8400 Regensburg 2, W. Germany (B.R.D.)
- Regensburger Bistumsblatt. w. ISSN 0034-3250 (Bischoeflicher Stuhl Regensburg)

**Rehabilitations-Verlag Gmbh**
Kronprinzenstr. 67, 5300 Bonn-Bad Godesberg, W. Germany (B.R.D.)
- Das Behinderte Kind. bi-m. ISSN 0005-7991 (Bundesarbeitsgemeinschaft Hilfe fuer Behinderte)

**Dr. Ludwig Reichert Verlag**
Reissstr. 10, 6200 Wiesbaden-Dotzheim, W. Germany (B.R.D.)
- Kratylos; kritisches Berichts- und Rezensionsorgan fuer indogermanische und allgemeine Sprachwissenschaft. s-a. ISSN 0023-4567
- Verzeichnis Deutscher Informations- und Dokumentationsstellen. irreg. (Institut fuer Dokumentationswesen)

**Dietrich Reimer Buchhandlung**
Unter den Eichen 57, 1000 Berlin 45, W. Germany (B.R.D.)
- Afrika und Uebersee; Sprachen, Kulturen. 4 per yr. ISSN 0002-0427 (Universitaet Hamburg)
- Archaeologische Mitteilungen aus Iran. Neue Folge. a. ISSN 0066-6033 (Deutsches Archaeologisches Institut)
- Baessler Archiv; Beitraege zur Voelkerkunde. s-a. ISSN 0005-3856 (Museum fuer Voelkerkunde, Berlin)
- Meteorologische Abhandlungen. ISSN 0026-1203 (Freie Universitaet Berlin. Institut fuer Meteorologie)

**Reinecke-Verlag GmbH**
Schoene Aussicht 23, 2000 Hamburg 76, W. Germany (B.R.D.)
- German Tribune; a weekly review of the German press. w. (Portuguese edition, monthly) ISSN 0016-8858
- He Atid.

**Ernst Reinhardt Verlag**
Kemnatenstr. 46, 8000 Munich 19, W. Germany (B.R.D.)
- Beitraege zur Kinderpsychotherapie. irreg., vol. 25, 1976. ISSN 0067-5105
- Erziehung und Psychologie. irreg., no. 73, 1976. ISSN 0071-1241
- Jahrbuch der Psychohygiene. irreg., vol. 2, 1974.
- Monographien und Studien zur Konfliktpsychologie. irreg. ISSN 0077-068X
- Psychologie in Erziehung und Unterricht. 6 per yr.
- Psychologie und Person. irreg., no. 19, 1977. ISSN 0079-7405
- Rehabilitation der Entwicklungsgehemmten. irreg., no. 8, 1975. ISSN 0080-0708
- Studienhefte Psychologie in Erziehung und Unterricht. irreg. ISSN 0081-7392
- Zeitschrift fuer Individualpsychologie. s-a.

**Reise Verlag**
Hanssenstr. 24, Postfach 359, 3400 Goettingen, W.
Germany (B.R.D.)
- Goettinger Jahrbuch. a. ISSN 0072-4882
(Geschichtsverein fuer Goettingen und
Umgebung)

**Religioese Bildungsarbeit Stuttgart GmbH**
Moehringer Str. 87 B, 7000 Stuttgart 1, W.
Germany (B.R.D.)
- Dienst am Wort - Gedanken zur Sonntagspredigt.
8 per yr. ISSN 0016-576X

**Religionsgemeinschaft Deutsche Unitarier e.V.**
Goethestr. 27, 2300 Kiel 1, W. Germany (B.R.D.)
- Glaube und Tat; deutsch-unitarische Blaetter. m.
ISSN 0017-1123

**Klaus Renner Verlag**
Konrad Celtis-Str. 33, 8000 Munich 25, W.
Germany (B.R.D.)
- Beitraege zur Mittelamerikanischen Voelkerkunde.
irreg., no. 12, 1973. ISSN 0408-8514
(Hamburgisches Museum fuer Voelkerkunde)

**Technischer Verlag Resch KG**
Irminfriedstr. 22, Postfach 1129, Graefelfing, W.
Germany (B.R.D.)
- Betriebstechnik; Zeitschrift fuer Betriebsleiter und
-ingenieure. m. ISSN 0409-2791 (Verband der
Energieabnehmer e.V.)
- Energie; Zeitschrift fuer praktische
Energietechnik. m. ISSN 0013-7359
- Die Neue Hochschule; Zeitschrift fuer
anwendungsbezogene Studiengaenge. bi-m.
(Hochschullehrerbund)
- Waerme; Zeitschrift fuer Forschung und Praxis
der Waerme, Kaelte- und Verfahrenstechnik. bi-m.

**Rheinisch-Bergische Druckerei- und
Verlagsgesellschaft mbH**
Presshaus am Martin-Luther-Platz, 4000
Duesseldorf 1, W. Germany (B.R.D.)
- Duesseldorf; Magazin der Landeshauptstadt. q.
ISSN 0046-0796 (Duesseldorf. Amt fuer
Fremdenverkehr und Wirtschaftsfoerderung)

**Rheinisch-Westfaelische Akademie der Wissenschaften**
- Papyrologica Coloniensia. (pub. by Westdeutscher
Verlag GmbH)
- Rheinisch-Westfaelische Akademie der
Wissenschaften. Veroeffentlichungen. (pub. by
Westdeutscher Verlag)

**Rheinisch-Westfaelische Boerse zu Duesseldorf.**
Berliner Allee 10, 4000 Duesseldorf, W. Germany
(B.R.D.)
- Rheinisch-Westfaelische Boerse zu Duesseldorf.
Amtliches Kursblatt. d (Monday-Friday) ISSN
0035-4457

**Rheinisch-Westfaelisches Institut fuer
Wirtschaftsforschung, Essen**
- Konjunktur im Handwerk. (pub. by Duncker und
Humblot)
- Konjunkturberichte. (pub. by Duncker und
Humblot)
- Rheinisch-Westfaelisches Institut fuer
Wirtschaftsforschung. Mitteilungen. (pub. by
Duncker und Humblot)

**Rheinische Friedrich-Wilhelms-Universitaet. Institut
fuer Soziologie**
- Bonner Beitraege zur Soziologie. (pub. by
Ferdinand Enke Verlag)

**Rheinische Vereinigung fuer Volkskunde**
- Rheinisches Jahrbuch fuer Volkskunde. (pub. by
Ferdinand Duemmlers Verlag)

**Rheinischer Landwirtschaftsverlag GmbH**
Bonner Str. 108, 5300 Bonn-Duisdorf, W. Germany
(B.R.D.)
- Landwirtschaftliche Zeitschrift Rheinland. w.
ISSN 0023-8163

**Rheinischer Verband fuer Schwarzbundt-Rinderzucht**
Endenicher Allee 60, 5300 Bonn, W. Germany
(B.R.D.)
- Mitteilungen aus der Rheinischen Rinderzucht. 3
per yr. ISSN 0026-6868

**Rheinisches Landesmuseum, Bonn**
- Rheinisches Landesmuseum, Bonn. Schriften.
(pub. by Rheinland-Verlag)
- Rheinisches Landesmuseum in Bonn. Bonner
Jahrbuecher. (pub. by Verlag Butzon und Bercker)

**Rheinisches Landesmuseum, Trier**
- Trierer Grabungen und Forschungen. (pub. by
Philipp Von Zabern)

**Rheinland-Pfalz. Landesarchivverwaltung**
Karmeliterstr. 1/3, 5400 Koblenz, W. Germany
(B.R.D.)
- Jahrbuch fuer Westdeutsche Landesgeschichte. a.

**Rheinland Verlag**
Kennedy-Ufer 2, 5 Cologne, B.R.D.
(Distr. by: Rudolf Habelt Erlag, Am Buchenhang 1,
5300 Bonn, W. Germany (B.R.D.))
- Archaeo-Physika. irreg., vol. 6, 1976. ISSN 0066-
5886
- Archaeologische Funde und Denkmaeler des
Rheinlandes. irreg, vol 4, 1977. ISSN 0066-6009
- Beihefte der Bonner Jahrbuecher. irreg., no. 37,
1977. ISSN 0067-4893
- Beitraege zur Landesentwicklung. irreg., no. 35,
1976. ISSN 0525-4736 (Landschaftsverband
Rheinland. Referat Landschaftspflege)
- Bonner Beitraege zur Kunstwissenschaft. irreg.,
1971, no. 11. ISSN 0068-0036
- Epigraphische Studien. irreg., vol. 11, 1976. ISSN
0071-0989
- Inventare Nichtstaatlicher Archive. irreg., no. 21,
1977. ISSN 0535-5079 (Landschaftsverband
Rheinland. Archivberatungsstelle)
- Kleine Museumshefte. irreg. ISSN 0075-6326
- Kunst und Altertum am Rhein. irreg., vol. 47,
1975. ISSN 0075-725X
- Landeskonservator Rheinland. Arbeitsheft. irreg.,
no. 21, 1977.
- Rheinische Ausgrabungen. irreg., no. 18, 1977.
ISSN 0557-7853 (Landschaftsverband Rheinland)
- Rheinische Lebensbilder. irreg., vol. 7, 1977. ISSN
0080-2670
- Rheinische Schriften. irreg. ISSN 0080-2689
- Rheinisches Landesmuseum, Bonn. Schriften.
irreg. ISSN 0067-9968
- Werken und Wohnen. irreg., vol. 11, 1977. ISSN
0083-8047
- Zeitschrift fuer Archaeologie des Mittelalters. a.

**Rhenania Fachverlag GmbH**
Goerresplatz 5, Postfach 2260, 5400 Koblenz, W.
Germany (B.R.D.)
- Kueche; Zeitung der Koeche. m. (Verband der
Koeche Deutschlands e.V.)
- Rund um den Pelz International; Fachzeitschrift
fuer das Kuerschnerhandwerk und die
Rauchwarenwirtschaft. m. ISSN 0048-8755
(Zentralverband des Kuerschnerhandwerks)

**Verlag Hans Richarz**
Postfach 6053, 5205 St. Augustin 1, W. Germany
(B.R.D.)
- Internationale Zeitschrift fuer
Kommunikationsforschung. 3 per yr. (Deutsche
Gesellschaft fuer Kommunikationsforschung)

**Dr. Riederer Verlag GmbH**
Johannesstr. 60, 7000 Stuttgart 1, W. Germany
(B.R.D.)
- Erzmetall; Zeitschrift fuer Erzbergbau und
Metallhuettenwesen. m. ISSN 0044-2658
(Gesellschaft Deutscher Metallhuetten und
Bergleute e.V.)
- Praktische Metallographie. m. ISSN 0032-678X
- Zeitschrift fuer Metallkunde. m. ISSN 0044-3093
(Deutsche Gesellschaft fuer Metallkunde e. V.)

**Rinderzuchtzentrale Angeln**
Postfach 60, 2347 Suederbrarup/Angelnhalle, W.
Germany (B.R.D.)
- Angler Rinderzucht. s-a. (Verband Deutscher
Rotviehzuechter) (Co-Sponsor: Verband der
Zuechter des Angler Rindes e.V.)

**Verlag Matthias Ritthammer KG**
Burgschmiet Str. 25, Postfach 2229, 8500
Nuernberg 1, W. Germany (B.R.D.)
- Moebelmarkt. m.

**Rochus Verlag GmbH**
Rochusstr. 43, 4000 Duesseldorf 30, W. Germany
(B.R.D.)
- Begegnung mit Polen; Zeitschrift fuer deutsch-
polnische Verstaendigung. q. ISSN 0005-7819

**Roehl Verlagsgesellschaft mbH**
Ferdinandshoeh 10, 2000 Hamburg 20, W. Germany
(B.R.D.)
- Das da; Monatsmagazin fuer Kultur und Politik.
m.

**Verlag Ludwig Roehrscheid GmbH**
Am Hof 28, Postfach 2227, 5300 Bonn, W.
Germany (B.R.D.)
- Quartaer; Jahrbuch fuer Erforschung des
Eiszeitalters und der Steinzeit. a. ISSN 0375-7471
(Hugo-Obermaier-Gesellschaft)
- Rheinische Vierteljahrsblaetter. q. ISSN 0035-
4473 (Universitaet Bonn. Institut fuer
Geschichtliche Landeskunde der Rheinlande)

**Roemisch-Germanisches Museum**
Columbastr. 5, 5000 Cologne 1, W. Germany (B. R.
D.)
- Koelner Jahrbuch fuer Vor- und Fruehgeschichte.
(pub. by Gebr. Mann Verlag)
- Koelner Roemer-Illustrierte. irreg.

**Roemisch-Germanisches Zentralmuseum, Mainz**
- Arbeitsblaetter fuer Restauratoren. (pub. by
Philipp Von Zabern)
- Archaeologisches Korrespondenzblatt. (pub. by
Philipp Von Zabern)
- Fuehrer zu Vor- und Fruegeschichtlichen
Denkmaelern. (pub. by Philipp Von Zabern)
- Roemisch-Germanisches Zentralmuseum, Mainz.
Ausstellungskataloge. (pub. by Rudolf Habelt
Verlag)
- Roemisch-Germanisches Zentralmuseum, Mainz.
Jahrbuch. (pub. by Rudolf Habelt Verlag)
- Roemisch-Germanisches Zentralmuseum, Mainz.
Kataloge Vor- und Fruehgeschichtlicher
Altertuemer. (pub. by Rudolf Habelt Verlag)
- Technische Beitraege zur Archaeologie. (pub. by
Rudolf Habelt Verlag)

**Alfred Roeper**
Schlueterstr. 56, 2000 Hamburg 13, W. Germany
(B.R.D.)
- Internationales Zucker-Jahrbuch. a. ISSN 0074-
9907

**Marita Roeser-Bley**
Beuttenmuellerstr. 11, 7570 Baden-Baden, W.
Germany (B.R.D.)
- Kultur und Leben. m.

**Eduard Roether Verlag**
Berliner Allee 56, 6100 Darmstadt, W. Germany
(B.R.D.)
- Auszuege aus der Literatur der Zellstoff- und
Papier-Erzeugung und Celluloseverarbeitung. a.
(Verein der Zellstoff- und Papier-Chemiker und
Ingenieure)
- Das Leder; Fachzeitschrift fuer die Chemie und
Technologie der Lederherstellung. m. ISSN 0024-
0176 (Verein fuer Gerberei-Chemie und Technik
e.V.)
- Das Papier; Zeitschrift fuer die Erzeugung von
Holzstoff, Zellstoff, Papier und Pappe, Chemische
Technologie der Cellulose. m. ISSN 0031-1340

**Verlag Roever**
Muehlenweg 67, 2820 Leuchtenburg, W. Germany
(B.R.D.)
- Jahrbuch der Wittheit zu Bremen. a. ISSN 0447-
2624

**Rohde und Schwarz**
Muehldorfstr. 15, 8000 Munich 80, W. Germany
(B.R.D.)
- Neues von Rohde und Schwarz. q. ISSN 0548-
3093

**Rohrleitungsverband e.V.**
- 3 R-International. (pub. by Vulkan-Verlag Dr. W.
Classen)

**Verlag Rombach und Co. GmbH**
Loerracher Str. 3, Postfach 1349, 7800 Freiburg, W.
Germany (B.R.D.)
- Buecherkommentare; Zeitung fuer Buchkritik. bi-
m. ISSN 0007-3016
- Freiburger Universitaetsblaetter. q. ISSN 0016-
0717 (Universitaet Freiburg)
- Wissenschaftlicher Literaturanzeiger. bi-m. ISSN
0043-6968

**Verlag Rommerskirchen und Co.**
Bonner Str 47, 5486 Remagen-Rolandseck, W.
Germany (B.R.D.)
- Die Deutsche Buehne. m. ISSN 0011-975X
(Deutscher Buehnenverein e.V.)
- Frankfurter Hefte; Zeitschrift fuer Kultur und
Politik. m. ISSN 0015-9999
- Der Journalist. m. ISSN 0022-5576 (Deutscher
Journalisten-Verband e.V)
- P R; erste Zeitschrift fuer public relations. bi-m.

**Christoph von der Ropp**
Wulfsdorfer Weg 17, 2000 Hamburg 67, W.
Germany (B.R.D.)
- Baltische Studien. a. ISSN 0067-3099
(Gesellschaft fuer Pommersche Geschichte,
Altertumskunde und Kunst)

**St. Pauli Verlag Helmut Rosenberg GmbH und Co.
KG**
Hein-Hoyer Str. 12, Postfach 248, 2000 Hamburg 4,
W. Germany (B.R.D.)
- Him; das Magazin mit dem Mann. m. ISSN 0046-
7448

**Ross-Verlag OHG**
Spichernstr. 12, 5000 Cologne 1, W. Germany
(B.R.D.)
- Chic. m. ISSN 0009-3483
- D F Z. (Deutsche Friseur-Zeitung); Europe Haute
Coiffure. s-m. ISSN 0011-491X

**Rot-Gelb-Gruen Verlag**
Theodor-Heuss-Str., Postfach 4544, 3300
Braunschweig, W. Germany (B.R.D.)
- Lehrer-Briefe zur Verkehrserziehung. 10 per yr.
ISSN 0075-8612

**Verlag Dr. Hans Werner Rothe**
Kasselerstr. 53, 6368 Bad Vilbel, W. Germany (B.
R. D.)
- Beitraege zur Geologie von Thueringen. irreg.
ISSN 0067-5008 (Thueringer Geologischer Verein
e.V.)

**Bergverlag Rudolf Rother**
Landshuter Allee 49, Postfach 67, 8000 Munich 19,
W. Germany (B.R.D.)
- Bergwelt; Winter-Bergkamerad. m.

**Ruehle-Diebener Verlag GmbH und Co. KG**
Wolfschlugener Str. 5a, Postfach 250, 7000 Stuttgart
70, W. Germany (B.R.D.)
- Diebeners Goldschmiede- und Uhrmacher-
Jahrbuch. a. ISSN 0070-4814
- Goldschmiede Zeitung - European Jeweler und
Deutsche Uhrmacherzeitschrift. m. ISSN 0017-
1689 (Bundesverband des
Schmuckwarengrosshandels)
- Graveur Flexograf; Fachzeitung fuer Formenbauer,
Formgestalter und Fertigungstechniker, Graveure,
Gurtler. m. ISSN 0015-7775

**Ruhr-Universitaet, Bochum. Institut fuer
Entwicklungsforschung und Entwicklungspolitik**
- Bochumer Schriften zur Entwicklungsforschung
und Entwicklungspolitik. (pub. by Horst Erdmann
Verlag)

**Ruhrlaendische Verlags-Gesellschaft mbH**
Lazarettstr. 15, 4300 Essen 1, W. Germany (B.R.D.)
- Magazin fuer Fortschrittliche Haustechnik und
Wohnkultur. bi-m. ISSN 0024-9750

**Rundschau-Verlag, Otto G. Koeniger GmbH und Co**
Ohmstr. 15, Postfach 401568, 8000 Munich 40, W.
Germany (B.R.D.)
- DOB und Haka Praxis; Internationale
Fachzeitschrift fuer die gesamte
Bekleidungsindustrie. m.
- Europaeische Mode nach Mass. s-a. ISSN 0014-
2670
- Rundschau fuer Internationale Damenmode;
Fachzeitschrift fuer Damenbekleidung. m. ISSN
0035-9912
- Rundschau fuer Internationale Herrenmode;
Fachzeitschrift fuer Die gesamte
Herrenbekleidung. m.

**Russland und Wir - Verlag und Handlung**
Sindlinger Weg 1, 6380 Bad Homburg, W. Germany
(B.R.D.)
- Russland und Wir; ein Forum. q. ISSN 0036-0414
(Deutsch-Russlaendische Gesellschaft E.V.)

**S B 67 Verlagsgesellschaft mbH**
Bleriotstr. 6, Postfach 320340, 5000 Cologne 30, W.
Germany (B.R.D.)
- S B. (Sportstaettenbau und Baederanlagen) bi-m.
ISSN 0036-102X

**Saalburg-Museum**
- Saalburg-Jahrbuch. (pub. by Walter de Gruyter
und Co.)

**Saarbruecken. Kulturamt**
- Saarbruecker Hefte. (pub. by Minerva-Verlag
Thinnes und Nolte)

**Saatkorn-Verlag GmbH**
Grindelberg 13-17, 2000 Hamburg 13, W. Germany
(B.R.D.)
- Leben und Gesundheit. bi-m. ISSN 0023-9895
(Deutscher Verein fuer Gesundheitspflege e. V.)

**Verlag W. Sachon**
Schloss Mindelburg, Postfach 325, 8948
Mindelheim, W. Germany (B.R.D.)
- Brauindustrie. s-m.
- Getraenke-Industrie. m. ISSN 0016-9323
- Der Maler und Lackierermeister. m.
(Landesinnungsverbaende des Bayerischen Maler-
und Lackiererhandwerks und des Maler- und
Lackiererhandwerks Baden-Wuerttemberg)

**Saemann Verlagsgesellschaft mbH**
Druselstalstr. 51, 3500 Kassel-Wilhelmshoehe 1, W.
Germany (B.R.D.)
- Forstliche Mitteilungen. s-m. ISSN 0015-797X
(Gewerkschaft Gartenbau, Land- und
Forstwirtschaft)

**Johann Michael Sailer Verlag GmbH**
Aeusserer Laufer Platz 22, 8500 Nuernberg, W.
Germany (B.R.D.)
- Neue Stafette. m. ISSN 0028-3363

**St. Albertus Magnus Apothekergilde e.V.**
- Renovatio. (pub. by Verlag Friedrich Pustet)

**St.-Otto-Verlag**
Domplatz 3, Postfach 4034, 8600 Bamberg, W.
Germany (B.R.D.)
- Amtsblatt fuer die Erzdioezese Bamberg. s-m.
ISSN 0003-2328 (Erzbischoefliches Ordinariat
Bamberg)

**Satire-Verlag**
Fuldaer Wende 24, 3000 Hannover, W. Germany
(B.R.D.)
- Hannover Extra. bi-m.

**J.D. Sauerlaender's Verlag**
Finkenhofstr. 21, 6000 Frankfurt, W. Germany
(B.R.D.)
- Allgemeine Forst- und Jagdzeitung. m. ISSN
0002-5852
- Landwirtschaftliche Forschung. q. ISSN 0023-
8147
- Rheinisches Museum fuer Philologie. q. ISSN
0035-449X
- Silvae Genetica; Zeitschrift fuer Forstgenetik und
Forstpflanzenzuechtung. 6 per yr. ISSN 0037-
5349

**Sauna-Verlag Werner Thomas**
Neuser Weg 17, 8631 Weidach, W. Germany
(B.R.D.)
- Sauna Nachrichten mit Sauna Archiv. q. ISSN
0036-5033 (Deutscher Sauna-Bund e.V.)

**Verlag Deutsche Schachblaetter**
Wodanstr. 78, 8500 Nuernberg, W. Germany
(B.R.D.)
- Deutsche Schachblaetter. m. ISSN 0012-0650
(Bayerischer Schachbund e.V.)

**Schacht Verlag GmbH**
Neustr. 5, 4630 Bochum, W. Germany (B.R.D.)
- B I Z. (Bochumer Illustrierte Zeitung) w.

**Schachverlag Gerhard Katzer**
Wiesbadener Str. 26, Am Bruchrain 8, 6395 Weilrod
3, W. Germany (B.R.D.)
- Schach-Echo; die Zeitschrift fuer jeden
Schachfreund. s-m. ISSN 0036-5831

**Verlag Moritz Schaefer**
Paulinstr. 43, Postfach 450, 4930 Detmold 1, W.
Germany (B. R. D.)
- Die Muehle und Mischfuttertechnik. w. ISSN
0027-2949

**Hans Schaefer, Ed. & Pub.**
Frauenschuhstr. 3, 8000 Munich 50, W. Germany
(B.R.D.)
- Fernseh-Informationen. s-m. ISSN 0015-0134

**L. Schaffrath**
Hartstr. 4, 4170 Geldern, W. Germany (B.R.D.)
- Der Grosshandelskaufmann. m. ISSN 0046-6441
(Wirtschaftsvereinigung Gross- und
Aussenhandel)

**Verlag M. und H. Schaper**
Grazer Str. 20, 3000 Hannover 81, W. Germany
(B.R.D.)
- Archiv fuer Lebensmittelhygiene, insbesondere
fuer Fleisch-, Fisch- und Milchhygiene. bi-m.
ISSN 0003-925X
- D T W - Deutsche Tieraerztliche Wochenschrift.
m. ISSN 0341-6593
- Der Forst- und Holzwirt. s-m. ISSN 0015-7961
- Forstarchiv. m. ISSN 0300-4112
- Kleintier-Praxis; Archiv fuer kleine Haus-und
Nutztiere sowie Laboratoriums- und Zoo-Tiere. 8
per yr. ISSN 0023-2076 (World Small Animal
Veterinary Association. Deutsche Gruppe)
- Rundschau fuer Fleischuntersuchung und
Lebensmittelueberwachung. m. ISSN 0341-0668
- Schweinezucht und Schweinemast. m. ISSN 0036-
7176 (Arbeitsgemeinschaft Deutscher
Schweineerzeuger e.V.)
- Die Zuckerruebe. bi-m. ISSN 0044-5398

**Scharnhorst-Buchkameradschaft GmbH**
Postfach 220, 6903 Neckargemuend, W. Germany
(B.R.D.)
- Scharnhorst Auslese. q. ISSN 0036-5920

**F. K. Schattauer Verlag**
Lenzhalde 3, Postfach 2945, 7000 Stuttgart 1, W.
Germany (B.R.D.)
- Altern und Entwicklung/Aging and Development.
irreg; vol. 4, 1972. ISSN 0084-6252 (Akademie
der Wissenschaften und der Literatur, Mainz)
- Biomineralisation Forschungsberichte. irreg; vol.
5, 1972.
- Medizinische Welt. w. ISSN 0025-8512
- Methods of Information in Medicine/Methodik
der Information in der Medizin. q. ISSN 0026-
1270
- Nuclear-Medizin/Nuclear Medicine/Medecine
Nucleaire; isotopes in medicine and biology. q.
ISSN 0029-5566 (Gesellschaft fuer Nuclear-
Medizin)
- Thrombosis et Diathesis Haemorrhagica. bi-m.
ISSN 0040-6597 (International Society on
Thrombosis and Haemostasis)
- Zeitschrift fuer Angewandte Baeder- und
Klimaheilkunde. bi-m. ISSN 0084-5280 (Verband
Deutscher Badeaerzte) (Co-sponsor: Verband
Oesterreichischer Kuraerzte)

**Hansisches Verlagskontor H. Scheffler**
Friedrich-Wilhelm-Pl. 3, Postfach 3045, 2400
Luebeck 111, W. Germany (B.R.D.)
- Der Kinderarzt. bi-m. ISSN 0023-1487
(Berufsverband der Kinderaerzte Deutschlands
e.V.)
- Nordwestdeutsche Gesellschaft fuer Innere
Medizin. Kongressbericht. s-a. ISSN 0029-1609

**Fachverlag Schiele und Schoen GmbH**
Markgrafen Str. 11, 1000 Berlin 61, W. Germany
(B.R.D.)
- Biomedizinische Technik/Biomedical Engineering.
6 per yr. ISSN 0013-5585 (Deutsche Gesellschaft
fuer Biomedizinische Technik)
- Fernmelde Praxis. s-m. ISSN 0015-0118
- Frequenz; Zeitschrift fuer Schwingungs- und
Schwachstromtechnik. m. ISSN 0016-1136
- Giesserei-Praxis. s-m. ISSN 0016-9781
- Jahrbuch fuer Optik und Feinmechanik. a. ISSN
0075-272X
- Schmalfilm; die richtige Zeitschrift fuer den
Schmalfilmamateur. m. ISSN 0036-620X
- Taschenbuch der Fernmelde-Praxis. a. ISSN 0082-
1764
- Taschenbuch der Giesserei-Praxis. a. ISSN 0082-
1772
- Taschenbuch der Post- und Fernmelde-
Verwaltung. a. ISSN 0082-190X
- Taschenbuch der Werkzeugmaschinen und
Werkzeuge. a. ISSN 0082-1810
- Taschenbuch fuer die Bekleidungs-Industrie. a.
- Taschenbuch fuer die Textil-Industrie. a. ISSN
0082-1896

**Schiffahrtmedizinisches Institut der Marine**
Kopperpahler Allee 120, 2300 Kiel-Kronshagen, W.
Germany (B.R.D.)
- Schiffahrtmedizinisches Institut der Marine, Kiel.
Veroeffentlichungen. irreg. ISSN 0080-679X

**Schiffahrts-Verlag Hansa C. Schroedter und Co.**
Stubbenhuk 10, 2000 Hamburg 11, W. Germany
(B.R.D.)
- Hansa; Zeitschrift fuer Schiffahrt, Schiffbau,
Hafen. fortn. ISSN 0017-7504
- Schiffstechnik; Forschungshefte fuer Schiffbau und
Schiffsmaschinenbau. 4 per yr. ISSN 0036-6064

• Transport-Dienst. w. ISSN 0041-1426

**Schiffahrts-Verlag Rheinschiffahrt**
Haus Oberrhein, 6800 Mannheim 23, W. Germany
(B.R.D.)
• Die Rheinschiffahrt. s-m.

**Schiffbautechnische Gesellschaft e.V.**
• Schiff und Hafen /Kommandobruecke. (pub. by
Seehafen-Verlag Erik Blumenfeld)
• Schiffbautechnische Gesellschaft. Jahrbuch. (pub.
by Springer-Verlag US)

**Schild-Verlag GmbH**
Federseestr. 1, 8000 Munich 60, W. Germany
(B.R.D.)
• Deutsches Soldatenjahrbuch. a. ISSN 0417-3635

**Schillerschule**
Ebellstr. 15, 3000 Hannover 61, W. Germany
(B.R.D.)
• Glocke; Schuelerzeitung der Schillerschule. 4 per
yr. ISSN 0017-1247

**Max Schimmel Verlag OHG**
Robert-Koch-Str. 34-36, 8700 Wuerzburg, W.
Germany (B.R.D.)
• Der Industrie-und Handelsvertreter; Unabhaengige
Fach-und Wirtschaftszeitschrift fuer die Handels-
und Versicherungsvertreter-Berufe. s-m. ISSN
0019-9214
• Zentralmarkt; Unabhaengige Zeitschrift fuer
Politik und Wirtschaft. w.

**Schimmelpfeng GmbH**
Schimmelpfenghaus, Am Hauptbahnhof 6, Postfach
16720, 6000 Frankfurt 1, W. Germany (B.R.D.)
• Schimmelpfeng Review. s-a.

**G. Schindele Verlag GmbH**
Alte Rheinstr. 13a, 7501 Neuburgweier, W.
Germany (B.R.D.)
• Horus; Marburger Beitraege zum Blind-Sehen. s-a.
(Verein der Blinden Geistesarbeiter Deutschlands
e.V.)

**Schlach Peremohy**
Zeppelinstr. 67, 8000 Munich 80, W. Germany
(B.R.D.)
• Schlach Peremohy/Way to Victory. w.

**Schleswig-Holstein. Innenministerium**
Duerstenbrocker Weg 70, 2300 Kiel 1, W. Germany
(B.R.D.)
• Gesetz- und Verordnungsblatt fuer Schleswig-
Holstein. 27 per yr. ISSN 0016-9129

**Schleswig-Holstein. Kultusministerium**
Duesternbrooker Weg 64-68, 2300 Kiel, W.
Germany (B.R.D.)
• Schleswig- Holstein Kultusminister.
Nachrichtenblatt; als besondere Ausgabe des
Amtsblatts fuer Schleswig-Holstein. s-m. ISSN
0023-7868

**Schleswig-Holstein. Landesamt fuer Wasserhaushalt
und Kuesten**
Saarbrueckenstr. 38, 2300 Kiel 1, W. Germany
(B.R.D.)
• Deutsches Gewaesserkundliches Jahrbuch.
Kuestengebiet der Nort- und Ostsee. a.

**Schleswig- Holsteinischer Heimatbund**
• Schleswig-Holstein. (pub. by Karl Wachholtz
Verlag)
• Schleswig-Holsteinischer Heimatkalender. (pub. by
Heinrich Moeller Soehne GmbH)

**Willy Schleunung GmbH und Co. KG**
Kirchenstr. 88, 8000 Munich 80, W. Germany
(B.R.D.)
• Katholischer Digest; Zeitschrift fuer die Familie.
m. ISSN 0047-3294

**Schluetersche Verlagsanstalt und Druckerei**
Georgswall 4, Postfach 5440, 3000 Hannover 1, W.
Germany (B.R.D.)
• Allgemeiner Anzeiger fuer Buchbindereien;
Internationale Fachzeitschrift fuer Buchherstellung
und Druckverarbeitung. m. ISSN 0002-5984
• Deutsches Tieraerzteblatt. m. ISSN 0012-1355
(Deutsche Tieraerzteschaft e.V.)
• Druckwelt; Journal der Unternehmer und
Fuehrungskrafte. bi-m. ISSN 0012-6519
• Niedersaechsische Wirtschaft. s-m. ISSN 0028-
9760

• Niedersaechsischer Staatsanzeiger. w. ISSN 0028-
9787 (Niedersachsen. Ministerium der Justiz)
• Niedersaechsisches Aerzteblatt. s-m. ISSN 0028-
9795 (Aerztekammer Niedersachsen)
• Nordwestdeutsches Handwerk. s-m. ISSN 0029-
1617
• Der Praktische Tierarzt. m. ISSN 0032-681X

**Schmalenbach-Gesellschaft**
• Schmalenbachs Zeitschrift fuer
Betriebswirtschaftliche Forschung. (pub. by
Westdeutscher Verlag GmbH)

**Verlag Schmid GmbH (Freiburg)**
Kaiser-Josef-Str. 217, Postfach 1722, 7800 Freiburg,
W. Germany (B.R.D.)
• Interceram; International Ceramic Review. q.
ISSN 0020-5214
• Keramische Zeitschrift; Technik - Wissenschaft -
Kunst. m. ISSN 0023-0561
• Powder Metallurgy International; metals-
composite materials-special ceramics-application.
q. ISSN 0048-5012

**Verlag Dr. Otto Schmidt KG**
Ulmenallee 96-98, 5000 Cologne 51, W. Germany
(B.R.D.)
• Die Aktiengesellschaft; Zeitschrift fuer das
gesamte Aktienwesen. m. ISSN 0002-3752
• Finanz-Rundschau; deutsches Steuerblatt. s-m.
ISSN 0015-2196
• GmbH-Rundschau. m. ISSN 0016-3570 (Zentrale
fuer GmbH Dr. O. Schmidt)
• Monatsschrift fuer Deutsches Recht. m. ISSN
0340-1812
• Steuer und Wirtschaft; Zeitschrift fuer die
gesamten Steuerwissenschaften. q.
• Steurberater-Jahrbuch; zugleich Bericht ueber den
jaehrlich stattfindenden Fachkongress der
Steuerberater der B R D. a. ISSN 0081-5519
(Fachinstitut der Steuerberater)
• Umsatzsteuer-Rundschau. m.
• Zeitschrift fuer Arbeitswissenschaft; Zentralblatt
fuer Arbeitswissenschaft und soziale
Betriebspraxis. q. (Gesellschaft fuer
Arbeitswissenschaft e. V.)

**Max Schmidt-Roemhild Verlag**
Mengstr. 16, 2400 Luebeck 1, W. Germany
(B.R.D.)
• Archiv fuer Kriminologie; unter besonderer
Beruecksichtigung der gerichtlichen Physik,
Chemie und Medizin. 3 double nos. per
vol.(2vols. per yr.) ISSN 0003-9225
• Verein fuer Luebeckische Geschichte und
Altertumskunde. Zeitschrift. a. ISSN 0083-5609

**Erich Schmidt Verlag (Berlin)**
Genthiner Str. 30g, 1000 Berlin 30, W. Germany
(B.R.D.)
• Beitraege zur Umweltgestaltung. irreg.
• Deutsche Sprache; Zeitschrift fuer Theorie, Praxis
und Dokumentation. q. (Institut fuer Deutsche
Sprache)
• Grundlagen und Praxis des Bank- und
Boersenwesens. irreg.
• Muell und Abfall; Fachzeitschrift fuer Behandlung
und Beseitigung von Abfaellen. 8 per yr. ISSN
0027-2957
• Redaktions-Archiv; Zahlenbilder aus Politik,
Wirtschaft und Kultur. m. ISSN 0034-2092
• Wasser-Kalender; Jahrbuch fuer das gesamte
Wasserfach. a. ISSN 0511-3520
• Wasser und Abwasser in Forschung und Praxis.
irreg., vol. 14, 1977. ISSN 0512-5030
• Wasserrecht und Wasserwirtschaft. irreg., vol. 17,
1977. ISSN 0508-1254
• Zeitschrift fuer Deutsche Philologie. q. ISSN
0044-2496

**Erich Schmidt Verlag (Bielefeld)**
Herforder Str. 10, Postfach 7330, 4800 Bielefeld 1,
W. Germany (B.R.D.)
• Arbeitsrecht der Gegenwart. a. ISSN 0066-586X
• Die Berufsgenossenschaft. m. ISSN 0005-9544
(Hauptverband der Gewerblichen
Berufsgenossenschaften e.V.)
• Betriebliches Vorschlagswesen; Fachzeitschrift fuer
die Praxis in Wirtschaft und Verwaltung. q.
(Deutsches Institut fuer Betriebswirtschaft)
• Dokumentation Wasser. m. ISSN 0012-5156
(Fraunhofer-Gesellschaft. Dokumentationszentrale
Wasser)
• Dokumentationszentrale Wasser Schriftenreihe. 3-
4 per yr.(approx) ISSN 0012-0030 (Fraunhofer-
Gesellschaft. Dokumentationszentrale Wasser)

• Handbuch Oeffentlicher Verkehrsbetriebe. a. ISSN
0073-019X (Verband Oeffentlicher
Verkehrsbetriebe)
• Jahrbuch fuer Volksliedforschung. a. ISSN 0075-
2789 (Deutsches Volksliederarchiv)
• Die Krankenversicherung. m. ISSN 0301-4835
(Bundesverband der Innungskrankenkassen)
• Marktforscher; vereint mit GFM-Mitteilungen zur
Markt- und Absatzforschung. bi-m. ISSN 0465-
0166
• Verkehr und Technik; Zeitschrift fuer
Verkehrstechnik, Verkehrspolitik,
Verkehrswissenschaft. m. ISSN 0042-4005
(Verband Oeffentlicher Verkehrsbetriebe) (Co-
sponsor: Bundesverband Deutscher Eisenbahnen
e.V.)
• Zeitschrift Interne Revision; Fachzeitschrift fuer
Wissenschaft und Praxis. q. ISSN 0044-3816
(Institut fuer Interne Revision)

**Verlag Franz Schmitt OHG**
Kaiserstr. 99-101, 5200 Siegburg, W. Germany
(B.R.D.)
• Der Archivar; Mitteilungsblatt fuer deutsches
Archivwesen. q. ISSN 0003-9500 (Duesseldorf.
Hauptstaatsarchiv)
• Instrumentenbau-Zeitschrift. m. ISSN 0020-4390

**Wilhelm Schmitz Verlag**
Pestalozzistr. 1, 6300 Giessen, W. Germany (B. R.
D.)
• Oberhessische Gesellschaft fuer Natur- und
Heilkunde, Giessen. Berichte. a. ISSN 0078-2920

**P.-A. Schmueking**
Kastanienallee 2a, 3300 Braunschweig, W. Germany
(B.R.D.)
• Der Spielplan. m. ISSN 0038-7517

**Verlag Lambert Schneider**
Hausackerweg 16, 6900 Heidelberg 1, W. Germany
(B. R. D.)
• Deutsche Akademie fuer Sprache und Dichtung,
Darmstadt. Jahrbuch. a. ISSN 0070-3923

**Verlag Schnell und Steiner**
Von-der-Pfordten-Str. 15, 8000 Munich 21, W.
Germany (B.R.D.)
• Das Muenster; Zeitschrift fuer Christliche Kunst
und Kunstwissenschaft. bi-m. ISSN 0027-299X

**Ferdinand Schoeningh**
Juehenplatz 1, 4790 Paderborn, W. Germany
(B.R.D.)
• Annuarium Historiae Conciliorum; Internationale
Zeitschrift fuer Konziliengeschichtsforschung. s-a.
ISSN 0003-5157
• Beitraege zur Oekumenischen Theologie. irreg.,
no. 10, 1974. ISSN 0067-5172
• Biblische Zeitschrift. s-a. ISSN 0006-2014
• Communicatio Socialis; Zeitschrift fuer Publizistik
in Kirche und Welt. q. ISSN 0010-3497
• Paedagogik und Schule in Ost und West. bi-m.
ISSN 0030-9265 (Lehrervereinigung Duesseldorf)
• Theologie und Glaube. m. ISSN 0049-366X

**Schopenhauer Gesellschaft e.V.**
• Schopenhauer-Jahrbuch. (pub. by Verlag Dr.
Waldemar Kramer)

**B. Schott's Soehne**
Weihergarten 2-9, 3640, 6500 Mainz 1, W Germany
(B.R.D.)
• Der Chordirigent; Nachrichtenblatt fuer
Chorleiter. a. ISSN 0009-5036
• Hindemith-Jahrbuch/Annales Hindemith. a. (Paul-
Hindemith-Institut)
• I S M E Yearbook. a. (International Society for
Music Education)
• Melos; Neue Zeitschrift fuer Musik. bi-m. ISSN
0025-9020
• Musik und Bildung; Zeitschrift fuer Theorie und
Praxis der Musikerziehung. m. ISSN 0027-4747
(Verband Deutscher Schulmusikerzieher)
• Das Orchester; Zeitschrift fuer deutsche
Orchesterkultur und Rundfunk-Chorwesen. m.
ISSN 0030-4468 (Deutsche Orchestervereinigung)
• Schott Aktuell. m.

**Schrader und Partner**
Menterschwaigstr. 9, 8000 Munich 90, W. Germany
(B.R.D.)
• Automobil- und Motorrad-Chronik. m.

**Verlag Willy Schrickel (Duesseldorf)**
Klever Str. 33, 4000 Duesseldorf 30, W. Germany
(B. R. D.)
• Der Augenoptiker. m. ISSN 0004-7929

- Die Contactlinse. 6 per yr. ISSN 0010-7336 (Vereinigung Deutscher Contactlinsen-Spezialisten e.V.)

**Schriftenmissions-Verlag**
Goethestr. 79, Postfach 548, 4390 Gladbeck/Westf., W. Germany (B.R.D.)
- Der Evangelische Religionslehrer an Beruflichen Schulen. bi-m. ISSN 0014-3480
- Licht und Leben. m. ISSN 0047-4584 (Evangelische Gesellschaft fuer Deutschland e.V.)
- Praxis Bilden und Erziehen. bi-m. (Bundesvereinigung Evangelischer Eltern und Erzieher E.V)

**Hermann Schroedel Verlag (Hannover)**
Zeisstr. 10, Postfach 810620, 3000 Hannover 81, W. Germany (B.R.D.)
- Grundlagenstudien aus Kybernetik und Geisteswissenschaft. 4 nos. per yr. ISSN 0017-4939
- Informationen Jugendliteratur und Medien; Jugendschriften-Warte. bi-m. (Gewerkschaft Erziehung und Wissenschaft)
- Die Realschule; Zeitschrift fuer das gesamte mittlere Schulwesen. m. (Gesamtverband Deutscher Realschullehrer) (Co-Publisher: Ernst Klett Verlag)
- Steinbruch und Sandgrube; unabhaengige Fach-Zeitschrift fuer Steinbrueche, Kies- und Sandgruben, Betonsteinwerke. m. ISSN 0039-1018

**Hermann Schroedel Verlag KG (Darmstadt)**
Am Kavalleriesand 47, Postfach 1026, 6100 Darmstadt, W. Germany (B.R.D.)
- Die Deutsch Schule; Zeitschrift fuer Erziehungswissenschaft und Gestaltung der Schulwirklichkeit. m. ISSN 0012-0731 (Gewerkschaft Erziehung und Wissenschaft)

**Horst Schroeder Verlag**
Darmstaedterstr. 11, Postfach, 6101 Bickenbach, W. Germany (B.R.D.)
- Humana; Nudisten-Magazin. m. ISSN 0018-7321

**Anton Schroll und Co.**
Boosstr. 15, Postfach 348, 8000 Munich 95, W. Germany (B.R.D.)
(and Spengergasse 39, 1051 Vienna, Austria)
- Linzer Jahrbuch fuer Kunstgeschichte. a. ISSN 0075-9732

**Carl Schuenemann Verlag**
Zweite Schlachtpforte 7, Postfach 1109, 2800 Bremen 1, W. Germany (B.R.D.)
- Bremer Aerzteblatt. m. (Aerztekammer Bremen)
- Bremer Kirchenzeitung. bi-w. (Bremische Evangelische Kirche)
- Fuehrer durch die Quellen zur Geschichte der Nationen. Reihe A. Lateinamerika. irreg. (Staatsarchiv Bremen)
- Jahrbuch der Deutschen Marine Vereint mit Prochnow, die Deutsche Marine. a.
- Marine/Atlantische Welt. m. ISSN 0004-6914
- Der Schluessel; Zeitschrift fuer Wirtschaft und Kultur. q. ISSN 0036-6188 (Handelskammer Bremen)

**Bayerischer Schulbuch-Verlag**
Hubertusstr. 4, Postfach 87, 8000 Munich 19, W. Germany (B.R.D.)
- Linguistik und Didaktik. q. ISSN 0047-472X

**Verlagsgesellschaft Schulfernsehen**
Aachener Str. 456, 5000 Cologne 41, W. Germany (B.R.D.)
- Jahrbuch fuer Wissenschaft, Ausbildung, Schule, W. A. S. a.

**Krafthand Verlag Walter Schulz**
St.-Anna-Str. 26, Postfach 160, 8939 Bad Woerishofen, W. Germany (B.R.D.)
- B D fuer Baustoffe und Baumaschinen. m.
- Baumaschinendienst. m ISSN 0005-6723
- Kraftfahrzeug-Gewerbe Suedbaden. s-m.
- Krafthand. bi-w. ISSN 0023-4435
- Taschenfachbuch der Kraftfahrzeugbetriebe. a.

**Hans Ferdinand Schulz Verlag**
Friedrichring 13, 7800 Freiburg, W. Germany (B.R.D.)
- Freiburger Geographische Arbeiten. irreg., 1972, no. 4. ISSN 0071-9439 (Deutsche Forschungsgemeinschaft)

**Schutzbund fuer Hausbesitz**
- Berliner Hausbesitz. (pub. by Berliner Hausbesitz Verlag, Manfred Schoeneck)

**Heinrich Schwab Verlag**
Hebelstr. 32, 7860 Schopfheim, W. Germany (B.R.D.)
- Lebensweiser; Zeitschrift fuer gesunde Lebensfuehrung - rundschau der praktischen Lebenskunst. m. ISSN 0024-0052
- Organische Land -und Gartenkultur; Monatsschrift fuer naturgemaesse Feldwirtschaft - Rundschau fuer biologischen Obst- und Gemuesebau. bi-m. ISSN 0030-5006

**Schwalbe, Deutsche Vereinigung fuer Problemschach**
Lisenkamp 4, 4700 Hamm 1, W. Germany (B.R.D.)
- Die Schwalbe. bi-m. ISSN 0048-9506

**Schwaneberger Verlag GmbH**
Muthmannstr. 4, 8000 Munich 45, W. Germany (B.R.D.)
- Michel-Briefmarken-Kataloge. a and irreg. ISSN 0076-7727
- Michel-Rundschau. 12 per yr. ISSN 0026-198X

**Paedagogischer Verlag Schwann Gmbh**
Postfach 7640, 4 Duesseldorf, W.Germany.
- Bildung und Erziehung. bi-m. ISSN 0006-2456
- Wirkendes Wort; deutsche Sprache in Forschung und Lehre. bi-m. ISSN 0043-6089

**Verlag Otto Schwartz und Co.**
Annastr. 7, 3400 Goettingen, W. Germany (B.R.D.)
- Archiv fuer Oeffentliche und Freigemeinnuetzige Unternehmen; Zeitschrift fuer Strukturlehre der Einzelwirtschaften und fuer Einzelwirtschaftspolitik. 4 per yr. ISSN 0003-9314 (Universitaet zu Koeln. Forschungsinstitut fuer Sozialpolitik)
- Die Mitarbeit; Zeitschrift zur Gesellschafts- und Kulturpolitik. q. ISSN 0026-6779
- Schriften zur Handelsforschung. irreg., no. 53, 1975. ISSN 0080-7001 (Universitaet zu Koeln. Institut fuer Handelsforschung)
- Soziale Welt; Zeitschrift fuer sozialwissenschaftliche Forschung und Praxis. q. ISSN 0038-6073 (Arbeitsgemeinschaft Sozialwissenschaftlicher Institute e.V.)
- Staedte- und Gemeindebund. m. (Deutscher Staedte- und Gemeindebund)
- Zeitschrift fuer den Lastenausgleich. m. ISSN 0044-247X

**Verlag Adalbert Schweiger**
Monschauer Str. 24, Postfach 227, 5160 Dueren, W. Germany (B.R.D.)
- Das Eigene Haus. 4 per yr.

**Deutscher Verlag fuer Schweisstechnik GmbH**
Aachener Str. 172, Postfach 2725, 4000 Duesseldorf, W. Germany (B.R.D.)
- B E F A-Mitteilungen. m. ISSN 0005-3031 (Beratungsstelle fuer Autogentechnik GmbH)
- Der Praktiker; Schweissen und Schneiden. m. (Deutscher Verband fuer Schweisstechnik e. V.)
- Schweissen und Schneiden. m. ISSN 0036-7184 (Deutscher Verband fuer Schweisstechnik e. V.)

**J. Schweitzer Verlag**
Genthiner Str. 13, 1000 Berlin 30, W. Germany (B.R.D.)
- Datenverarbeitung im Recht. q. ISSN 0301-2980
- Juristische Arbeitsblaetter; fuer Ausbildung und Examen. 12 per yr. ISSN 0022-6904
- Neue Zeitschrift fuer Wehrrecht. 6 per yr. ISSN 0028-3525
- U F I T A. (Archiv fuer Urheber-, Film-, Funk- und Theaterrecht) 4 per yr. ISSN 0003-9454
- Vierteljahrsschrift fuer Sozialrecht. q. ISSN 0301-2999

**E. Schweizerbart'sche Verlagsbuchhandlung**
Johannesstr. 3a, 7000 Stuttgart 1, W. Germany (B.R.D.)
- Anthropologischer Anzeiger. q. ISSN 0003-5548
- Archiv fuer Hydrobiologie. 4 nos. per vol. (1-2 vols. per yr.) ISSN 0003-9136 (Internationale Vereinigung fuer theoretische und angewandte Limnologie)
- Bibliotheca Botanica; Originalabhandlungen aus dem Gesamtgebiet der Botanik. irreg., 1970, Heft 130. ISSN 0067-7892
- Die Binnengewaesser; Einzeldarstellungen aus der Limnologie und ihren Grenzgebieten. irreg., vol. 27, 1976. ISSN 0067-8643

- Botanische Jahrbuecher fuer Systematik, Pflanzengeschichte und Pflanzengeographie. 4 nos. per vol.(1-2 vols.per yr.) ISSN 0006-8152
- Ergebnisse der Limnologie. irreg., no. 7, 1973. ISSN 0071-1128 (Internationale Vereinigung fuer Theoretische und Angewandte Limnologie)
- Fortschritte der Mineralogie. 1 vol.per yr.(2 nos.per vol) ISSN 0015-8186 (Deutsche Mineralogische Gesellschaft)
- Fundberichte aus Baden-Wuerttemberg. a. (Landesdenkmalamt Baden-Wuerttemberg)
- Geologisches Jahrbuch. Reihe A: Allgemeine und Regionale Geologie BR Deutschland und Nachbargebiete, Tektonik, Stratigraphie, Paleontologie. irreg. (Germany, Federal Republic. Bundesanstalt fuer Bodenforschung)
- Geologisches Jahrbuch. Reihe B: Regionale Geologie Ausland. irreg. (Germany, Federal Republic. Bundesanstalt fuer Bodenforschung)
- Geologisches Jahrbuch. Reihe C: Hydrogeologie. Ingenieurgeologie. irreg. (Germany, Federal Republic. Bundesanstalt fuer Bodenforschung)
- Geologisches Jahrbuch. Reihe D: Mineralogie. Petrographie, Geochemie, Lagerstaettenkunde. irreg. (Germany, Federal Republic. Bundesanstalt fuer Bodenforschung)
- Geologisches Jahrbuch. Reihe E: Geophysik. irreg. (Germany, Federal Republic. Bundesanstalt fuer Bodenforschung)
- Geotektonische Forschungen. irreg., no. 47, 1973. ISSN 0016-8548
- Neues Jahrbuch fuer Geologie und Palaeontologie. Abhandlungen. a. about 1-2 Bd.(1 Bd. of 3 Hefte) ISSN 0077-7749
- Neues Jahrbuch fuer Geologie und Palaeontologie, Monatshefte. m. ISSN 0028-3630
- Neues Jahrbuch fuer Mineralogie. Abhandlungen. a. about 1-2 Bd. (1 Bd. of 3 Hefte) ISSN 0077-7757
- Neues Jahrbuch fuer Mineralogie. Monatshefte. m. ISSN 0028-3649
- Oberrheinischer Geologischer Verein. Jahresberichte und Mitteilungen. a. ISSN 0078-2947
- Palaeontographica. Abt. A: Palaeozoologie - Stratigraphie. irreg. (Germany, Federal Republic. Bundesanstalt fuer Bodenforschung)
- Palaeontographica. Abt. B: Palaeophytologie. 1-2 vols per yr.
- Palaeontographica. Supplementbaende. irreg., vol. 12, 1967. ISSN 0085-4611
- Palaeontologische Zeitschrift. q. ISSN 0031-0220 (Paleontologische Gesellschaft e.V.)
- Zentralblatt fuer Geologie und Palaeontologie. Teil 1: Allgemeine, Angewandte, Regionale und Historische Geologie. 13 per yr. ISSN 0044-4170
- Zentralblatt fuer Geologie und Palaeontologie. Teil 2: Palaeontologie. 7 per yr. ISSN 0044-4189
- Zentralblatt fuer Mineralogie. Teil 1: Kristallographie, Mineralogie. q.
- Zentralblatt fuer Mineralogie. Teil 2: Petrographie, Technische Mineralogie, Geochemie und Lagerstaettenkunde. 7 per yr.

**Journal-Verlag Schwend GmbH**
In der Herrenaeckern 5, Postfach 340, 7170 Schwaebisch Hall, W. Germany (B.R.D.)
- Deutsches Waffen-Journal. m. ISSN 0012-138X

**Die Schwesternrevue GmbH**
Am Schwarzenberg 28, 8700 Wuerzburg, W. Germany (B.R.D.)
- Schwestern Revue; das Journal fuer die Krankenpflege. m. ISSN 0048-9549

**Scientia Verlag**
Haldenweg 9, Postfach 1660, 7080 Aalen, W. Germany (B.R.D.)
- Bibliotheca Rerum Historicarum. Studia. irreg.
- Untersuchungen zur Deutschen Staats- und Rechtsgeschichte. Neue Folge. irreg, vol. 21, 1977. ISSN 0083-4572

**Scripta Mercaturae Verlag**
Kurparkstr. 37, 8000 Munich 70, W. Germany (B.R.D.)
- Scripta Mercaturae; half-yearly publication on the history of world economic relations. s-a. ISSN 0036-973X

**Sebald Druck und Verlag**
Aus. Laufer Platz 22, 8500 Nuernberg, W. Germany (B.R.D.)
- Nuernberg Heute. s-a. (Nuernberg. Stadtverwaltung)

**Seehafen-Verlag Erik Blumenfeld**
Celsiusweg 15, Postfach 1347, 2000 Hamburg 50,
W. Germany (B.R.D.)
- Die Deutsche Handelsflotte. irreg. ISSN 0070-
4148
- Hamburger Hafen-Nachrichten. w.
- New Ships/Neubauten. m. ISSN 0028-6702
- Schiff und Hafen /Kommandobruecke. m.
(Schiffbautechnische Gesellschaft e.V.)
- Taeglicher Hafenbericht. d.

**Verlag Seiler und Co.**
Roemerstr. 47, Postfach 207, 5427 Bad Ems, W.
Germany (B.R.D.)
- ABC der Schuhfabrikation. m. ISSN 0001-0405

**Selecta-Verlag**
Pasinger Str. 8, 8033 Planegg, W Germany (B.R.D.)
- P K. (Praxis-Kurier); prophylaxe - diagnostik -
therapie. w. ISSN 0030-8056

**Seminar fuer Freiheitliche Ordnung**
Boslerweg 11, 7325 Boll-Eckwaelden, W. Germany
(B.R.D.)
- Fragen der Freiheit; Schriftenreihe fuer
Ordnungsfragen der Wirtschaft des Staates und
des kulturellen Lebens. bi-m. ISSN 0015-928X

**Senckenbergische Naturforschende Gesellschaft**
Senckenberganlage 25, 6000 Frankfurt 1, W.
Germany (B.R.D.)
- Archiv fuer Molluskenkunde. 3 per yr. ISSN
0003-9284
- Natur und Museum. m. ISSN 0028-1301
- Senckenbergiana biologica. 3 per yr. ISSN 0037-
2102
- Senckenbergiana Lethaea. 6 per yr. ISSN 0037-
2110
- Senckenbergiana Maritima. Zeitschrift fuer
Meeresgeologie und Meeresbiologie. (pub. by
Verlag Dr. Waldemar Kramer)

**Horst Siebert Verlag**
Laufamholzstr. 349, Postfach 170309, 8500
Nuernberg 17, W. Germany (B.R.D.)
- Europaeer; Unternehmer-Magazin. s-a. ISSN
0022-6254

**Siegel-Verlag Otto Mueller**
Grosse Eschenheimer Str. 16, 6000 Frankfurt 1, W.
Germany (B.R.D.)
- Der Handelsvertreter und Handelsmakler. s-m.
ISSN 0046-6808 (Zentralvereinigung Deutscher
Handelsvertreter- und Handelsmaklerverbaende
e.V.)

**Siegler und Co. Verlag fuer Zeitarchive GmbH**
Kronprinzenstr. 26, 5300 Bonn-Bad Godesberg, W.
Germany (B.R.D.)
- Archiv der Gegenwart; die weltweite
Dokumentation fuer Politik und Wirtschaft. w.
ISSN 0003-8865

**Siemens Aktiengesellschaft**
Postfach 3240, 8520 Erlangen 2, W. Germany
(B.R.D.)
- Components Report. 5 per yr (English edition); 4
per yr (French edition)
- Data Report; Informationen ueber Datentechnik /
a review of data processing applications. 6 per yr
(German); 4 per yr (English)
- Electromedica. 5 per yr.
- Elektrodienst. 8 per yr (German); 4 per yr
(English) ISSN 0037-4687
- Revista Siemens. 8 per yr.
- Revue Siemens. 8 per yr.
- Rivista Siemens. 4 per yr.
- Siemens Forschungs- und Entwicklungsberichte/
Siemens Research and Development Report. (pub.
by Springer-Verlag US)
- Siemens-Mitteilungen. m. ISSN 0080-9500
- Siemens-News. q.
- Siemens Review. m.
- Siemens-Zeitschrift. 12 per yr. ISSN 0037-4709
- Telefon Report. 4 per yr (German and English
editions); 2 per yr (Spanish edition)

**Sigert-Verlag GmbH**
Ekbertstr. 14, 3300 Braunschweig, W. Germany
(B.R.D.)
- Automaten-Markt. m. ISSN 0005-1039
- Musik-Informationen. m. ISSN 0027-4712

**Egon Siller Verlag**
Ost Str.65, Postfach 7024, Duesseldorf, W.
Germany (B.R.D.)
- P K V Informationdienst. (Private
Krankenversicherung) w.

**SIN-Staedtebauinstitut**
Koenigstr. 40, 8500 Nuernberg 1, W. Germany
(B.R.D.)
- SIN-Staedtebauinstitut. Schriftenreihe. irreg. ISSN
0078-2807
- SIN-Staedtebauinstitut. Studienhefte. irreg. ISSN
0078-2815
- SIN-Staedtebauinstitut. Werkberichte. irreg. ISSN
0078-2823
- Die Stadt. irreg.

**Skiklub Duesseldorf**
c/o Hanns Schmal, Lindenstr. 257, 4000
Duesseldorf, W. Germany (B.R.D.)
- Ski. bi-m. ISSN 0037-6167 (Co-Sponsor;
Ortsverband Duesseldorfer Sportvereine)

**Societaets-Verlag**
Frankenallee 71, Postfach 3429, 6000 Frankfurt 1,
W. Germany (B.R.D.)
- Boersen- und Wirtschaftshandbuch. a. ISSN 0067-
9496

**Hamburger Fachverlag Gerhard Sondermann**
Michaelisstr. 4, 2000 Hamburg 11, W. Germany
(B.R.D.)
- D N V. (Der Neue Vertrieb) m. ISSN 0028-355X
- Edit; Magazin fuer das Pressemanagement. bi-m.
- Presse Report (PR); Magazin fuer den
Presseeinzelhandel. m.

**Sounds Verlag**
Hellwigstr. 33, 2000 Hamburg 20, W. Germany
(B.R.D.)
- Musik Express. m.
- Popfoto. m.

**Sozialdemokratische Partei Deutschlands**
- Der Sozialdemokrat. (pub. by Presse und Bildung
GmbH)

**Verlag Sozialistische Politik**
Businstr. 17, 1000 Berlin 41, W. Germany (B.R.D.)
- Sozialistische Politik. bi-m. ISSN 0005-9374

**Sozialistischer Hochschulbund**
Rosental 11, 5300 Bonn, W. Germany (B.R.D.)
- Sozialistische Hochschulblaetter. irreg.

**Sozialistisches Buero**
- Links. (pub. by Verlag 2000 GmbH)

**Sozialpaedagogischer Verlag**
2105 Seevetal 11, W. Germany (B.R.D.)
- Archiv fuer Angewandte Sozialpaedagogik. bi-m.
ISSN 0341-8332

**Verlagsgesellschaft Otto Spatz oHG**
Blumenstr. 48, 8000 Munich 2, W. Germany
(B.R.D.)
- Infection; journal for the clinical study and
treatment of infections /Zeitschrift fuer Klinik
und Therapie der Infektionen. q. ISSN 0300-8126
(Paul-Ehrlich-Gesellschaft)
- Monatskurse fuer Die Aerztliche Fortbildung. m.
ISSN 0026-928X
- Muenchener Medizinische Wochenschrift. w.
ISSN 0027-2973

**Spiegel-Verlag**
Brandstwiete 19, 2000 Hamburg 11, W. Germany
(B.R.D.)
- Der Spiegel. w. ISSN 0038-7452

**Spitzenorganisation der Filmwirtschaft E.V.**
Langenbeckstr. 9, 6200 Wiesbaden, W. Germany
(B.R.D.)
- Filmstatistisches Taschenbuch. a. ISSN 0071-4941

**Verlagshaus Sponholz**
Grosser Hasenpfad 42-48, 6000 Frankfurt 70, W.
Germany (B.R.D.)
- Allgemeine Fleischer Zeitung. 3 per w. ISSN
0002-5844 (Deutscher Fleischerverband)
- Feinkost-Revue; Deutsche Milchhandels- und
Feinkost-Zeitung. a. ISSN 0014-9691
- Fleisch-Lebensmittel-Markt. m.
- Die Fleischwirtschaft. m. ISSN 0015-363X
(Bundesverband der Deutschen
Fleischwarenindustrie e.V.)
- N. G. Z; Fachillustrierte fuer Gastronomie und
Hotellerie. bi-m. ISSN 0027-6529
- Schuh im Bild. s-a. ISSN 0036-7036
- Schuhwirtschaft. w. ISSN 0036-7087

**Sport- und Jugend-Verlag GmbH und Co. KG**
Laemmersieth 21, Postfach 600609, 2000 Hamburg
60, W. Germany (B.R.D.)
- Fussball-Jugend. m. ISSN 0016-321X (Deutscher
Fussball-Bund)
- Hamburger Sport-Mitteilungen. w. ISSN 0017-
6982 (Hamburger Sportbund e.V.)

**Sprachverband Deutsch fuer Auslaendische
Arbeitnehmer e.V.**
- Deutsch Lernen. (pub. by Julius Groos Verlag)

**Sprechsaal-Verlag**
Mauer 2, Postfach 401, 8630 Coburg, W. Germany
(B.R.D.)
- Oberflaechentechnik; Bearbeitung, Veredelung,
Schutz. m.
- Sprechsaal fuer Keramik, Glas, Baustoffe,
Rohstoffe, Aufbereitung, Produktion. m.

**Springer-Verlag**
For publications of this company see section for
UNITED STATES

**Axel Springer Verlag AG**
Kaiser-Wilhelm-Str. 6, 2000 Hamburg 36, W.
Germany (B.R.D.)
- Hoer zu. w. ISSN 0018-3113

**Staatliche Kunsthalle Karlsruhe**
Hans-Thoma-Str. 2, 7500 Karlsruhe, W. Germany
(B.R.D.)
- Staatliche Kunsthalle Karlsruhe. Bildhefte. irreg.
ISSN 0075-5133
- Staatliche Kunsthalle Karlsruhe. Graphik-
Schriftenreihe. irreg. ISSN 0075-5141

**Staatliche Kunstsammlungen Bayerns**
- Muenchner Jahrbuch der Bildenden Kunst. (pub.
by Prestel-Verlag)

**Staatliche Kunstsammlungen in Baden-Wuerttemberg**
- Staatliche Kunstsammlungen in Baden-
Wuerttemberg. Jahrbuch. (pub. by Deutscher
Kunstverlag GmbH)

**Staatliche Museen Preussischer Kulturbesitz Berlin**
- Jahrbuch der Berliner Museen. (pub. by Gebr.
Mann Verlag)

**Staatliches Institut fuer Musikforschung**
14 Stauffenbergstr., 1000 Berlin 30, W. Germany
(B.R.D.)
- Jahrbuch fuer Musikalische Volks- und
Voelkerkunde. a.

**Staatsarchiv Bremen**
Praesident-Kennedy-Platz 2, 2800 Bremen, W.
Germany (B.R.D.)
- Bremisches Jahrbuch. a. (Co-sponsor: Historische
Gesellschaft Bremen)
- Fuehrer durch die Quellen zur Geschichte der
Nationen. Reihe A. Lateinamerika. (pub. by Carl
Schuenemann Verlag)

**Staatsbibliothek Preussischer Kulturbesitz**
Potsdamer Str. 33, Postfach 1407, 1000 Berlin 30,
W. Germany (B.R.D.)
- Bibliographia Cartographica. (pub. by Verlag
Dokumentation)
- Bibliographische Berichte/Bibliographical Bulletin.
(pub. by Vittorio Klostermann)
- Gesamtverzeichnis der Zeitschriften und Serien in
Bibliotheken der Bundesrepublik Deutschland
Einschliesslich Berlin (West)/Union List of Serials
in Libraries of the Federal Republic of Germany
Including Berlin (West) irreg.
- Staatsbibliothek Preussischer Kulturbesitz.
Ausstellungskataloge. irreg.
- Staatsbibliothek Preussischer Kulturbesitz.
Mitteilungen. q. ISSN 0038-8866

**Staatsbibliothek Preussischer Kulturbesitz.
Arbeitsstelle fuer Bibliothekstechnik**
Potsdamer Str. 33, 1000 Berlin 30, W. Germany
(B.R.D.)
- A B T Informationen. irreg., no. 23, 1977. ISSN
0340-3440

**Stadtarchiv Hildesheim**
- Alt-Hildesheim. (pub. by Verlag August Lax)

**Staedtisches Gymnasium, Wuppertal**
Bayreuther Str. 35, 5600 Wuppertal 1, W. Germany
(B.R.D.)
- Bayreuther Pauke; Schuelerzeitung des
Gymnasiums, Bayreutherstr. q.

**Verlag Stahleisen mbH**
Breite Str. 27, Postfach 8229, 4000 Deusseldorf 1,
W. Germany (B.R.D.)
- Archiv fuer das Eisenhuettenwesen. m. ISSN
0003-8962 (Verein Deutscher Eisenhuettenleute)
(Co-sponsor: Max-Planck-Institut fuer
Eisenforschung)
- Kalibreur/Calibreur. s-a. ISSN 0022-796X
(Arbeitsgemeinschaft Europaeischer Kalibreure)
- Stahl und Eisen; Zeitschrift fuer Technik und
Wissenschaft der Herstellung und Verarbeitung
von Eisen und Stahl. s-m. ISSN 0038-9137
(Verein Deutscher Eisenhuettenleute) (Co-
sponsor: Wirtschaftsvereinigung Eisen- und
Stahlindustrie)
- Stahl und Form. irreg. ISSN 0081-4172
(Beratungsstelle fuer Stahlverwendung)
- Stahleisen Kalender. a. ISSN 0081-4180 (Verein
Deutscher Eisenhuettenleute)
- Statistisches Jahrbuch der Eisen- und
Stahlindustrie. a. ISSN 0081-5365
(Wirtschaftsvereinigung Eisen- und Stahlindustrie)

**Stamm-Verlag GmbH**
Goldammerweg 16, 4300 Essen 1, W. Germany
(B.R.D.)
- Erziehung und Wissenschaft; Allgemeine Deutsche
Lehrer-Zeitung. m. (Gewerkschaft Erziehung und
Wissenschaft)
- Stamm Leitfaden Durch Presse und Werbung/
Annual Directory of Press and Advertising. a.
ISSN 0075-8728

**Stamm-Werbung GmbH und Co.**
Dinnendahlstr. 16, 4300 Essen 1, W. Germany
(B.R.D.)
- Geschichte; historisches Magazin. 6 per yr.
(Historiographisches Institut GmbH (Solothurn))

**Verlag fuer Standesamtswesen GmbH und Co. KG**
Hebelstr. 17, 6000 Frankfurt 1, W. Germany
(B.R.D.)
- Das Bayerische Standesamt. m. ISSN 0005-7096
(Fachverband der Bayerischen Standesbeamten
E.V.)
- Handakten fuer die Standesamtliche Arbeit. irreg.,
1973, vol. 14. ISSN 0438-5004
- Kleine Fachbibliothek des Standesbeamten. irreg.,
1972, vol. 17.
- Das Standesamt. m. (Bundesverband der
Deutschen Standesbeamten e.V)
- Wissenschaftliche Gesellschaft fuer
Personenstandswesen und Verwandte Gebiete.
Schriftenreihe. Neue Folge. irreg., 1971, vol. 9.
ISSN 0084-0939

**C.-A. Starke Verlag**
Frankfurter Str. 51, Postfach 310, 6250 Limburg, W.
Germany (B.R.D.)
- Archiv fuer Sippenforschung; und alle verwandten
Gebiete. q. ISSN 0003-9403

**Johannes Stauda Verlag GmbH**
Heinrich-Schuetz-Allee 33, 3500 Kassel-
Wilhelmshoehe, W. Germany (B.R.D.)
- Jahrbuch fuer Liturgik und Hymnologie. a. ISSN
0075-2681 (Internationale Arbeitsgemeinschaft
fuer Hymnologie)

**Elwin Staude Verlag GmbH**
Walderseestr 14, 3000 Hannover 1, W. Germany
(B.R.D.)
- Deutsche Hebammen-Zeitschrift; Fachblatt zur
Foerderung des Hebammenwesens. m. ISSN
0012-026X (Bund Deutscher Hebammen)

**Franz Steiner Verlag GmbH**
Friedrichstr. 24, Postfach 5529, 6200 Wiesbaden,
W. Germany (B.R.D.)
- A R S P. Beihefte. Neue Folge. (Archiv fuer
Rechts- und Sozialphilosophie) irreg. ISSN 0341-
079X (Internationale Vereinigung fuer Rechts-
und Sozialphilosophie)
- A R S P - Archiv fuer Rechts- und Sozial
Philosophie/Archives de Philosophie du Droit et
de Philosophie Sociale/Archives for Philosophy of
Law and Social Philosophy. q. ISSN 0001-2343
(Internationale Vereinigung fuer Rechts- und
Sozialphilosophie)
- Academie Internationale d'Histoire des Sciences.
Collection des Travaux. irreg.

- Akademie der Wissenschaften und der Literatur.
Geistes- und Sozialwissenschaftliche Klasse.
Abhandlungen. irreg. ISSN 0002-2977
- Akademie der Wissenschaften und der Literatur,
Mainz. Jahrbuch. a. ISSN 0084-6104
- Akademie der Wissenschaften und der Literatur,
Mainz. Klasse der Literatur. Abhandlungen. irreg.
ISSN 0002-2985
- Akademie der Wissenschaften und der Literatur,
Mainz. Mathematisch-Naturwissenschaftliche
Klasse. Abhandlungen. irreg. ISSN 0002-2993
- Archiv fuer Musikwissenschaft. q. ISSN 0003-
9292
- Archiv fuer Musikwissenschaft. Beihefte. irreg.
ISSN 0570-6769
- Archives Internationales d'Histoire des Sciences. 2
per yr. ISSN 0003-9810
- Beiruter Texte und Studien. irreg. ISSN 0067-
4931 (Deutsche Morgenlaendische Gesellschaft
Beirut. Orient-Institut LE)
- Beitraege zur Geschichte der Wissenschaft und
der Technik. irreg. (Deutsche Gesellschaft fuer
Geschichte der Medizin, Naturwissenschaft und
Technik e.V.)
- Beitraege zur Suedasien Forschung. irreg., vol. 24,
1976. (Universitaet Heidelberg. Suedasien-Institut)
- Boethius; Texte und Abhandlungen zur
Geschichte der exacten Wissenschaften. irreg.
- Die Deutsche Berufs- und Fachschule; Zeitschrift
fuer Berufs- und Wirtschaftspaedagogik. m. ISSN
0011-9946
- Deutsche Morgenlaendische Gesellschaft.
Zeitschrift. s-a. ISSN 0012-0499
- Deutsche Morgenlaendische Gesellschaft.
Zeitschrift. Supplementa. irreg. ISSN 0341-0803
- Erasmus; Speculum Scientiarum. International
bulletin of contemporary scholarship. m. ISSN
0013-9955
- Erdkundliches Wissen; Schriftenfolge fuer
Forschung und Praxis. irreg. ISSN 0425-1741
- Forschungen zur Antiken Sklaverei. irreg., vol. 7,
1976. ISSN 0071-7665 (Akademie der
Wissenschaften und der Literatur, Mainz.
Kommission fuer Geschichte des Altertums)
- Geographische Zeitschrift. q. ISSN 0016-7479
- Geographisches Taschenbuch. irreg. ISSN 0072-
0968
- Geschichtliche Landeskunde. irreg., vol. 16, 1976.
ISSN 0072-4203 (Universitaet Mainz. Institut fuer
Geschichtliche Landeskunde)
- Hermes; Zeitschrift fuer klassische Philologie. q.
ISSN 0018-0777
- Hermes-Einzelschriften. irreg. ISSN 0341-0064
- Historia; Zeitschrift fuer Alte Geschichte. q. ISSN
0018-2311
- Historia-Einzelschriften. irreg. ISSN 0341-0056
- Informationsaufnahme und
Informationsverarbeitung im Lebenden
Organismus. irreg., vol. 3, 1975. (Akademie der
Wissenschaften und der Literatur, Mainz.
Mathematisch-Naturwissenschaftliche Klasse)
- Jahrbuecher fuer Geschichte Osteuropas. q. ISSN
0021-4019
- Karl-August-Forster-Lectures;
Informationsgesteuerte Synthese / information-
directed synthesis. irreg. (Akademie der
Wissenschaften und der Literatur, Mainz.
Mathematisch-Naturwissenschaftliche Klasse)
- Kunst des Orients/Art of the Orient. s-a. ISSN
0023-5393
- Mikrofauna des Meeresbodens. irreg., no. 63,
1977. (Akademie der Wissenschaften und der
Literatur, Mainz. Mathematisch-
Naturwissenschaftliche Klasse)
- Neue Politische Literatur; Berichte ueber das
internationale Schrifttum. q. ISSN 0028-3320
- Orbis Geographicus; world directory of geography.
irreg., pt. II of vol. for 1968 per 74 in 1974. ISSN
0030-4395 (International Geographical Union)
- Paideuma; Mitteilungen zur Kulturkunde. a. ISSN
0078-7809 (Frobenius-Institut)
- Research in Molecular Biology. irreg., vol. 7,
1977. (Akademie der Wissenschaften und der
Literatur, Mainz. Mathematisch-
Naturwissenschaftliche Klasse)
- Studia Leibnitiana; Zeitschrift fuer Geschichte der
Philosophie und der Wissenschaften vom 16 bis
18 Jahrhundert. s-a. ISSN 0039-3185 (Gottfried-
Wilhelm-Leibniz Gesellschaft e.V.)
- Sudhoffs Archiv; Zeitschrift fuer
Wissenschaftsgeschichte. 4 per yr. ISSN 0039-
4564
- Sudhoffs Archiv. Beihefte. irreg. ISSN 0341-0773
- Tropische und Subtropische Pflanzenwelt. irreg.,
no. 18, 1976. ISSN 0302-9417 (Akademie der
Wissenschaften und der Literatur, Mainz.
Mathematisch-Naturwissenschaftliche Klasse)

- Universitaet Frankfurt. Wissenschaftliche
Gesellschaft. Sitzungsberichte. irreg, vol. 13, 1976.
- Untersuchungen zur Sprach- und
Literaturgeschichte der Romanischen Voelker.
irreg., vol. 9, 1976. ISSN 0083-4580 (Akademie
der Wissenschaften und der Literatur, Mainz.
Kommission fuer Romanische Philologie)
- Verhandlungen des Deutschen Geographentages.
biennial. ISSN 0083-5684 (Zentralverband der
Deutschen Geographen)
- Vierteljahrschrift fuer Sozial- und
Wirtschaftsgeschichte. 4 per yr. ISSN 0340-8728
- Vierteljahrschrift fuer Sozial-und
Wirtschaftsgeschichte. Beihefte. irreg. ISSN 0341-
0846
- Zeitschrift fuer Allgemeine Wissenschaftstheorie/
Journal for General Philosophy of Science. s-a.
ISSN 0044-2216
- Zeitschrift fuer Deutsches Altertum und Deutsche
Literatur. 4 per yr. ISSN 0044-2518
- Zeitschrift fuer Dialektologie und Linguistik. 3 per
yr. ISSN 0044-1449
- Zeitschrift fuer Dialektologie und Linguistik.
Beihefte. irreg. ISSN 0341-0838
- Zeitschrift fuer Franzoesische Sprache und
Literatur. 4 per yr. ISSN 0044-2747
- Zeitschrift fuer Franzoesische Sprache und
Literatur. Beihefte. irreg. ISSN 0341-0811
- Zeitschrift fuer Unternehmungsgeschichte. 3 per
yr. (Gesellschaft fuer Unternehmungsgeschichte)

**SN-Werbe- und Verlagsgesellschaft Steinert und Co.**
Schulstr. 4, Postfach 84, 8873 Ichenhausen, W.
Germany (B.R.D.)
- Die Feinkostwirtschaft. m. ISSN 0014-9705
(Bundesverband der Deutschen Feinkostindustrie
e. V.)
- Fussboden-Zeitung. m. ISSN 0016-3236

**Dr. Dietrich Steinkopff Verlag**
Saalbaustr. 12, Postfach 1008, 6100 Darmstadt, W.
Germany (B.R.D.)
- Aktuelle Probleme der Intensivmedizin/Current
Topics in Intensive Care Medicine. irreg.
- Aktuelle Probleme der Polymer-Physik. a.
- Basic Research in Cardiology/Archiv fuer
Kreislaufforschung. bi-m. ISSN 0003-9217
- Beitraege zur Kardiologie und Angiologie. irreg.
ISSN 0075-7101
- C.I.I.A. Symposia. (Commission Internationale des
Industries Agricole et Alimentaires) irreg.
- Colloid and Polymer Science/Kolloid-Zeitschrift
und Zeitschrift fuer Polymere. m. ISSN 0023-
2904
- Current Topics in Nutritional Sciences/Beitraege
zur Ernaehrungswissenschaft. irreg., vol. 7, 1974.
ISSN 0067-4982
- D T I. Diagnostische und Therapeutische
Informationen. irreg. ISSN 0300-8096
- Deutsche Gesellschaft fuer Ernaehrung.
Wissenschaftliche Veroeffentlichungen. s-a. ISSN
0043-6828
- Deutsche Gesellschaft fuer Kreislaufforschung.
Verhandlungen. a. ISSN 0070-4075
- Deutsche Gesellschaft fuer Rheumatologie.
Verhandlungen. irreg., vol. 4, 1975. ISSN 0070-
4121
- Fortschritte der Physikalischen Chemie/Current
Topics in Physical Chemistry. irreg., vol. 10,
1975. ISSN 0071-7924
- Fortschritte der Urologie und Nephrologie. irreg.,
vol. 6, 1975. ISSN 0071-7975
- Fortschritte im Integrierten Pflanzenschutz. irreg.
- Immunology Reports and Reviews/Fortschritte
der Immunitaetsforschung. irreg., vol. 7, 1975.
ISSN 0071-7908
- Intensivmedizin. bi-m.
- Kolloid-Gesellschaft. Verhandlungsberichte.
biennial. ISSN 0075-6555
- Medizinische Praxis; Sammlung fuer aerztliche
Fortbildung. irreg., vol. 48, 1974. ISSN 0076-
616X
- Nauheimer Fortbildungs-Lehrgaenge. a. ISSN
0077-6173
- Progress in Colloid and Polymer Science/
Fortschrittsberichte ueber Kolloide und Polymere.
irreg., vol. 57, 1975. ISSN 0071-8017
- Rheologica Acta. m. ISSN 0035-4511
- Rheumatismus. irreg., vol. 42, 1974. ISSN 0080-
2719
- Spezielle Anorganische Chemie. irreg.
- Wissenschaftliche Forschungsberichte. Reihe 1.
Grundlagenforschung und Grundlegende
Methodik. Abt. A. Chemie und Physic/Current
Topics in Science. Reihe 1. Basic Research. Abt.
A. Chemistry and Physics. irreg.

- Wissenschaftliche Forschungsberichte. Reihe 1. Grundlagenforschung und Grundlegende Methodik. Abt. B. Biologie und Medizin/Current Topics in Science. Reihe 1. Basic Research. Abt. B. Biology and Medicine. irreg.
- Zeitschrift fuer Ernaehrungswissenschaft/Journal of Nutritional Sciences/Journal des Sciences de la Nutrition. 4 vols. per yr.(4 nos. per vol.) ISSN 0044-264X
- Zeitschrift fuer Ernaehrungswissenschaft. Supplementa. irreg., no. 18, 1975. ISSN 0084-5337
- Zeitschrift fuer Gerontologie. bi-m. ISSN 0044-281X (Deutsche Gesellschaft fuer Gerontologie) (Co-Sponsor: Oesterreichische Gesellschaft fuer Geriatrie)
- Zeitschrift fuer Kardiologie. m. ISSN 0300-5860 (Deutsche Gesellschaft fuer Kreislaufforschung)
- Zeitschrift fuer Rheumatologie. bi-m. ISSN 0301-6382 (Co-sponsors: Deutsche Gesellschaft fuer Rheumatologie; Oesterreichische Liga zur Bekaempfung des Rheumatismus; Schweizerische Gesellschaft fuer Physikalische Medizin und Rheumatologie; Berufsverband Deutscher Rheumatologen)

**Steintor-Verlag Hamburg GmbH**
Hammerbrookstr. 93, 2000 Hamburg 1, W. Germany (B.R.D.)
- Blutalkohol; wissenschaftliche Zeitschrift fuer die medizinische und juristische Praxis. q. ISSN 0006-5250 (Bund gegen Alkohol im Strassenverkehr e.V.)
- Grundlagen der Kriminalistik. s-a. ISSN 0072-7822

**Stephanus-Gemeinde**
Gartenstr. 2, 6000 Frankfurt, W. Germany (B.R.D.)
- Die Bruecke. bi-m. ISSN 0007-2575

**Stephenson Verlag**
Gutenbergstr. 12, 2390 Flensburg, W. Germany (B.R.D.)
- Sex Magazin. bi-m.

**Verlag Sterne und Weltraum Dr. Vehrenberg**
Schillerstr. 17, Postfach 140365, 4000 Duesseldorf 14, W. Germany (B.R.D.)
- Sterne und Weltraum. m. ISSN 0039-1263 (Landessternwarte Heidelberg-Koenigstuhl)

**Verlag Otto Sternefeld GmbH**
Karlstr. 104, 4000 Duesseldorf, W. Germany (B.R.D.)
- Lederwaren-Report. m. ISSN 0024-0214
- Schuh-Kurier. w. ISSN 0036-7044

**Steyler Missionswissenschafliches Institut**
5205 St. Augustin 1, W. Germany (B.R.D.)
- Steyler Missionschronik. s-a.

**Stifterverband fuer die Deutsche Wissenschaft**
Brucker Holt 56, 4300 Essen, W. Germany (B.R.D.)
- Stifterverband fuer die Deutsche Wissenschaft. Schriftenreihe zum Stiftungswesen. (pub. by Nomos Verlagsgesellschaft mbH und Co. Kg.)
- Stifterverband fuer die Deutsche Wissenschaft. Taetigkeitsbericht. a.
- Vademecum Deutscher Lehr- und Forschungsstaetten. (pub. by Gemeinnuetzige Verwaltungsgesellschaft fuer Wissenschaftspflege MbH)

**Stiftung Gesellschaft und Unternehmen**
- Gesellschaftspolitische Bildungsmaterialien. (pub. by Deutscher Instituts-Verlag GmbH)

**Verlag der Stiftung Gralsbotschaft**
Lenzhalde 15, 7000 Stuttgart 1, W. Germany (B. R. D.)
- Gralswelt; Zeitschrift fuer Wahrenaufbau durch neues Wissen. bi-m. ISSN 0017-3088 (Stiftung Gralsbotschaft)

**Stiftung Preussische Kulturbesitz**
- Stiftung Preussische Kulturbesitz. Jahrbuch. (pub. by G. Grote'sche Verlagsbuchhandlung KG (Stuttgart))

**Stiftung Warentest**
Luetzowpl. 11-13, Postfach 4141, 1000 Berlin 30, W. Germany (B.R.D.)
- Test; die Zeitschrift fuer den Verbraucher. m. ISSN 0040-3946

**Verlag Werner Stock**
Koessener Str. 11, 4800 Bielefeld 14, W. Germany (B.R.D.)
- Der Stadtverkehr. m. ISSN 0038-9013

**Wilhelm Stollfuss Verlag**
Dechenstr 7-11, Postfach 2428, 5300 Bonn 1, W. Germany (B.R.D.)
- Die Bundesverwaltung. m. ISSN 0007-5930 (Deutscher Beamtenbund. Verband der Beamten der Obersten Bundesbehoerden)
- Deutsche Steuer-Zeitung: Ausgabe A. s-m. ISSN 0012-0774 (Germany, Federal Republic. Bundesministerium der Finanzen)
- Deutsche Steuer-Zeitung: Ausgabe B. w. ISSN 0012-0782 (Germany, Federal Republic. Bundesministerium der Finanzen)
- Hoechstrichterliche Finanzrechtsprechung. m. ISSN 0018-3059
- Intertax; Europaeische Steuer-Zeitung. 10 per yr. (Co-publisher: Uitgeverij Kluwer B.V. Deventer, Netherlands)
- Der Volks- und Betriebswirt. m. (Bundesverband Deutscher Volks- und Betriebswirte e.V.)

**Gebr. Storck GmbH**
Bebelstr. 102, 4200 Oberhausen, W. Germany (B.R.D.)
- Ratgeber aus der Apotheke. s-m.

**K. O. Storck und Co., Verlag und Druckerei GmbH**
Stahltwiete 7, 2000 Hamburg 50, W. Germany (B.R.D.)
- Jahrbuch der Export- und Versandtleiter. a. ISSN 0075-224X

**Dr. N. Stoytscheff**
Adelungstr. 53, Postfach 1069, 6100 Darmstadt, W. Germany (B.R.D.)
- Der Junge Textilverkaeufer. m. ISSN 0022-6378

**Verlag A. Strobel KG**
Zur Feldmuehle 9-11, 5760 Arnsberg 2, W. Germany (B.R.D.)
- I K Z; Fachzeitschrift fuer Sanitaer-, Heizung-, Klimatechnik. s-m. ISSN 0018-9936 (Zentralverband fuer Sanitaer-, Klima- und Heizungtechnik)

**Alfred Strothe Verlag**
Osterstr. 32, Postfach 5847, 3000 Hannover 1, W. Germany (B.R.D.)
- Agrarwirtschaft; Zeitschrift fuer Betriebswirtschaft und Marktforschung. m. ISSN 0002-1121 (Institut fuer Landwirtschaftliche Marktforschung Braunschweig)
- Blatt fuer Sortenwesen. m. ISSN 0300-4627 (Germany, Federal Republic. Bundessortenamt)
- Ernaehrungsdienst; deutsche Getreidezeitung; Boersen- u. Handelsblatt fuer Getreide u. Landesprodukte. 3 per wk. ISSN 0014-0228
- Kraftfutter; Monatszeitschrift fuer die Futtermittel-Wirtschaft. m. ISSN 0023-4427 (Fachverband der Futtermittelindustrie e.V.)

**Structur-Verlag**
Haidaer Str. 1, 5308 Rheinbach, W. Germany.
- Structur; Zeitschrift fuer Planung, Entwicklung und Umwelt. m.

**Studentenschaft der Johann Wolfgang Goethe-Universitaet Frankfurt**
- Diskus. (pub. by Diskus-Verlag)

**Studiengesellschaft fuer Fragen Mittel - und Osteuropaeischer Partnerschaft**
- East Europe Monographs. (pub. by Park College US)

**Studiengesellschaft fuer Holzschwellenoberbau e.V.**
Waldstr. 11, 5300 Bonn-Ippendorf, W. Germany (B.R.D.)
- Die Holzschwelle. 3 per yr. ISSN 0018-3865

**Studiengesellschaft zur Foerderung der Kernenergieverwertung in Schiffbau und Schiffahrt e.V.**
- Atomkernenergie. (pub. by Verlag Karl Thiemig)
- Kerntechnik. (pub. by Verlag Karl Thiemig)

**Studiengruppe fuer Systemsforschung e.V., Heidelberg**
- Studiengruppe fuer Systemsforschung e.V. Berichte. (pub. by Verlag Dokumentation)

**Studienstiftung**
Koblenzer Str. 77, 5300 Bonn 1, W. Germany (B.R.D.)
- Studienstiftung. Jahresbericht. a.

**Verlag fuer das Studium der Arbeiterbewegung**
Erkelenzdamm 7, Postfach 307, 1000 Berlin 36, W. Germany (B. R. D.)
- Arch Plus; Studienhefte fuer Planungspraxis und Planungstheorie. q. ISSN 0587-3452 (Verein zur Erforschung der Fragen der Produktion und Planung Gebauter Umwelt in Zusammenhang Sozialistischer Politik)

**Verlag Herbert Stuenings**
Ballindamm 38, 2000 Hamburg 1, W. Germany (B.R.D.)
- Hamburger Export-Woche. w. ISSN 0017-6931

**Verlag Willi Stuenings GmbH**
Luisenstr. 102, Postfach 2980, 4150 Krefeld 1, W. Germany (B.R.D.)
- Bus-Fahrt; internationale Fachzeitschrift fuer Omnibusverkehr. m. ISSN 0007-6368
- K F Z Anzeiger. (Kraftfahrzeug); die Deutsche Fachzeitschrift fuer Transport, Nutzfahrzeug und Werkstatt. s-m.
- Mot-Bau; Fachzeitschrift fuer Strassenbau und Verkehr. m. ISSN 0027-1470

**Suchasnist**
Karlsplatz 8-III, 8000 Munich, W. Germany (B.R.D.)
- Digest of the Soviet Ukrainian Press. m. ISSN 0012-2815

**Verlag Sueddeutsche Bauwirtschaft**
Wilhelm-Hertz-Str. 14, 7000 Stuttgart, W. Germany (B.R.D.)
- Sueddeutsche Bauwirtschaft.

**Sueddeutscher Verlag GmbH**
Sendlinger Str. 80, Postfach 202220, 8000 Munich 2, W. Germany (B.R.D.)
- Die Gute Tat. q. ISSN 0017-5803 (Deutsches Rotes Kreuz)

**Suedost-Institut**
Guellstr. 7, 8000 Munich 2, W. Germany (B.R.D.)
- Suedost-Forschungen; Internationale Zeitschrift fuer Geschichte, Kultur und Landeskunde Suedosteuropas. a. ISSN 0081-9077
- Suedosteuropa-Bibliographie. irreg. ISSN 0081-9131
- Suedosteuropaeische Arbeiten. (pub. by R. Oldenbourg Verlag GmbH)
- Untersuchungen zur Gegenwartskunde Suedosteuropas. (pub. by R. Oldenbourg Verlag GmbH)
- Wissenschaftlicher Dienst Suedosteuropa; Quellen und Berichte ueber Staat, Verwaltung, Recht, Bevoelkerung, Wirtschaft, Wissenschaft und Veroeffentlichngen in Suedosteuropa. m. ISSN 0043-695X

**Suedostdeutsche Historische Kommission**
- Suedostdeutsche Historische Kommission. Buchreihe. (pub. by R. Oldenbourg Verlag GmbH)
- Suedostdeutsches Archiv. (pub. by R. Oldenbourg Verlag GmbH)

**Suedostdeutsches Kulturwerk**
Guellstr. 7, 8000 Munich 2, W. Germany (B.R.D.)
- Suedostdeutsches Kulturwerk, Munich. Kleine Suedostreihe. irreg. ISSN 0081-9093
- Suedostdeutsches Kulturwerk, Munich. Schriftenreihe. Reihe A. Kultur und Dichtung. irreg. ISSN 0081-9107
- Suedostdeutsches Kulturwerk, Munich. Schriftenreihen. Reihe B. Wissenschaftliche Arbeiten. irreg. ISSN 0081-9115
- Suedostdeutsches Kulturwerk, Munich. Schriftenreihen. Reihe C. Erinnerungen und Quellen. irreg. ISSN 0081-9123

**Suedosteuropa Gesellschaft e.V.**
Widenmayerstr. 49, 8000 Munich 22, W. Germany (B.R.D.)
- Suedosteuropa-Jahrbuch. irreg., 1973, vol. 10. ISSN 0081-914X
- Suedosteuropa-Mitteilungen. q.
- Suedosteuropa-Schriften. irreg., 1968, vol. 9. ISSN 0081-9158
- Suedosteuropa-Studien. irreg., no. 24, 1976. ISSN 0081-9166

**Suedwestdeutsche Verlagsanstalt GmbH**
Am Marktplatz, Postfach 5760, 6800 Mannheim 1,
W. Germany (B.R.D.)
- Grosskuechen und GV; Magazin fuer Technik,
Organisation, Ernaehrung and Management. m.
(Bundesfachverband fuer Grosskuechen)
- Reuss Jahrbuch der Luft- und Raumfahrt. a.

**Suedwestfaelische Industrie- und Handelskammer zu Hagen**
- Suedwestfaelische Wirtschaft. (pub. by V.D.
Linnepe Verlagsgesellschaft KG)

**Suhrkamp Verlag**
Lindenstr. 29-35, 6000 Frankfurt 1, W. Germany
(B.R.D.)
(Subscr. to: John Fuegi, University of Wisconsin,
Department of Comparative Literature, Milwaukee,
WI 53201)
- Basis: Jahrbuch fuer Deutsche
Gegenwartsliteratur. a. ISSN 0067-446X
- Brecht Heute/Brecht Today. a. (Internationale
Brecht-Gesellschaft)

**T.O.P. Verlag GmbH**
Heusteigstr. 86a, Postfach 424, 7000 Stuttgart 1, W.
Germany (B.R.D.)
- Feuerungstechnik - Gebaeudetechnik;
Internationale Fachzeitschrift fuer Oelfeuerung
und Gasfeuerung. m. ISSN 0015-0401
(Bundesverband Oelfeuerungen und
Gasfeuerungen E. V.)

**Verlag das Tanzarchiv**
Stadion, Aachener Str., 5000 Cologne 41, W.
Germany (B.R.D.)
- Das Tanzarchiv; Deutsche Zeitschrift fuer
Tanzkunst und Folklore. m. ISSN 0039-9515

**Taylorix-Fach-Verlag**
Rotebuehlstr. 72, Postfach 829, 7000 Stuttgart 1, W.
Germany (B.R.D.)
- Jahrbuch fuer Praktiker des Rechnungswesens. a.

**Team Verlag GmbH und Fachzeitschriften KG**
Auwanne 19, 8752 Dettingen, W. Germany
(B.R.D.)
- Alkohol-Industrie; deutsche Spirituosen-Zeitung
und Brennerei-Zeitung. s-m. ISSN 0002-5496
- Europa Handbuch der Werbegesellschaften. a.
ISSN 0085-0349
- Marken-Handbuch der Werbung und
Etatbetreuung. a. ISSN 0085-3119

**Verlag fuer Technik und Handwerk**
Iburgstr. 38, 7570 Baden-Baden, W. Germany
(B.R.D.)
- Flug und Modell-Technik. m. ISSN 0015-458X

**Verlag fuer Technik und Wirtschaft Meynen KG**
Kaiser-Friedrich-Ring 49, Postfach 5769, 6200
Wiesbaden, W. Germany (B.R.D.)
- Bauelemente der Elektrotechnik; Fachzeitschrift
fuer Entwicklung und Konstruktion. m.
- Betriebs-Management Service. m.

**Technische Akademie Wuppertal**
- Technische Akademie Wuppertal. Berichte. (pub.
by Vulkan-Verlag Dr. W. Classen)

**Technische Universitaet Berlin. Institut fuer
Sozialoekonomie der Agrarentwicklung**
Podbielskiallee 64-66, 1000 Berlin 33 (Dahlem), W.
Germany (B.R.D.)
- Technische Universitaet Berlin. Institut fuer
Sozialoekonomie der Agrarentwicklung. Annual
Report (Abridged Version) a.
- Technische Universitaet Berlin. Institut fuer
Sozialoekonomie der Agrarentwicklung.
Taetigkeitsbericht. a. ISSN 0067-6039

**Technische Universitaet Berlin.
Universitaetsbibliothek**
Str. des 17. Juni 135, 1000 Berlin 12
(Charlottenburg), W. Germany (B.R.D.)
- Aktuelle Literaturinformation aus dem Obstbau.
m.

**Technische Universitaet Braunschweig**
Pockelsstr. 14, Postfach 3329, 3300 Braunschweig,
W. Germany (B.R.D.)
- Technische Universitaet Braunschweig.
Berichtsband. Forschung. every 5 years.
- Technische Universitaet Braunschweig.
Mitteilungen. q.

- Technische Universitaet Braunschweig.
Pharmaziegeschichtlichen Seminar.
Veroeffentlichungen. (pub. by Deutscher
Apotheker-Verlag)

**Technische Universitaet Clausthal**
Adolf-Roemer-Str. 2a, 3392 Clausthal-Zellerfeld, W.
Germany (B. R. D.)
- Technische Universitaet Clausthal.
Mitteilungsblatt. s-a. ISSN 0040-1501

**Technische Universitaet Hannover**
Welfengarten 1, 3000 Hannover 1, W. Germany
(B.R.D.)
- Deutsche Forschungsberichte. q. (prep. by its
Universitaetsbibliothek)
- T U Hannover. s-a.
- Technische Universitaet Hannover. Lehrstuhl fuer
Stahlbau. Schriftenreihe. irreg. ISSN 0073-0289
(prep. by its Lehrstuhl fuer Stahlbau)

**Technische Universitaet Hannover. Franzius-Institut
fuer Wasserbau und Kuesteningenieurwesen**
Nienburger Str. 4, 3000 Hannover 1, W. Germany
(B.R.D.)
- Technische Universitaet Hannover. Franzius-
Institut fuer Wasserbau und
Kuesteningenieurwesen. Mitteilungen. irreg., no.
41, 1974. ISSN 0340-0077

**Technische Universitaet Hannover. Institut fuer
Siedlungswasserwirtschaft**
Welfengarten 1, 3000 Hannover, W. Germany
(B.R.D.)
- Technische Universitaet Hannover. Institut fuer
Siedlungswasserwirtschaft. Veroeffentlichungen.
irreg., no. 39, 1974. ISSN 0073-0319

**Technische Universitaet Hannover. Institut fuer
Statik**
Callinstr. 15, II, 3000 Hannover 1, W. Germany
(B.R.D.)
- Technische Universitaet Hannover. Institut fuer
Statik. Mitteilungen. irreg., no. 21, 1974. ISSN
0073-0300

**Technische Universitaet Hannover. Institut fuer
Theoretische Geodaesie**
Nienburger Str. 5, 3000 Hannover 1, W. Germany
(B.R.D.)
- Technische Universitaet Hannover. Astronomische
Station. (Veroeffentlichungen) irreg

**Technische Universitaet Muenchen**
Arcisstr. 21, 8000 Munich 2, W. Germany (B.R.D.)
- Asta-Press. irreg. ISSN 0076-1745 (prep. by its
Studentenvertretung)
- Brauwissenschaft. (pub. by Verlag Hans Carl KG)

**Technische Universitaet Muenchen. Institut fuer
Wirtschaftslehre des Gartenbaues**
Weihenstephan, 8000 Munich, W. Germany
(B.R.D.)
- Technische Universitaet Muenchen. Institut fuer
Wirtschaftslehre des Gartenbaues.
Forschungsberichte zur Oekonomie in Gartenbau.
irreg.

**Technische Vereinigung der Grosskraftwerksbetreiber
e.V.**
Klinkestr. 29, Postfach 1791, 4300 Essen, W.
Germany (B. R. D.)
- V G B Kraftwerkstechnik. m. ISSN 0372-5715

**Technischer Verlag Resch KG**
*see* Resch KG

**Tele-Afrika-Verlagsgesellschaft mbH**
Robert-Bosch-Str. 4, 7000 Stuttgart, W. Germany
(B.R.D.)
- Tele-Africa Revue/Revue Tele-Africa. s-a.

**Telex-Verlag Jaeger und Waldmann oHG**
Holzhofallee 38, Postfach 1060, 6100 Darmstadt 2,
W. Germany (B.R.D.)
- Jaeger and Waldmann World Telex Directory. a.
(Distr. by: International Publications Service, 114
E. 32nd St., New York, NY 10016)

**Alf Teloeken-Verlag KG**
Roemerstr. 9, 4000 Duesseldorf 30, W. Germany
(B.R.D.)
- Bus und Bahn. m. (Verband Oeffentlicher
Verkehrsbetriebe)

**Terra-Verlag**
Neuhauser Str. 21, Postfach 1222, 7750 Konstanz,
W. Germany (B.R.D.)
- Friseurwelt; die grosse Fachillustrierte. m. ISSN
0016-1470
- Hochzeit; die Zeitschrift fuer Brautpaare. 4 per yr.
ISSN 0046-7685
- Kamm und Schere; Zeitschrift fuer den jungen
Friseur. m. ISSN 0022-8176
- Kosmetik Journal; internationale Fachzeitschrift
fuer Kosmetik in Theorie und Praxis. m.
- Lady International. m.
- Tieraerztliche Umschau; Zeitschrift fuer alle
Gebiete der Veterinaermedizin. m. ISSN 0049-
3864
- Die Veterinaermedizin; Gesammelte Referate aus
allen Gebieten der Tierheilkunde. bi-m. ISSN
0049-6057

**Dr. Tesdorpf Verlag**
Uferstrasse 22, 7070 Schwaebisch-Gmuend, W.
Germany (B.R.D.)
- Freiburger Geographische Mitteilungen. 2 per yr.
(Germany, Federal Republic. Bundesanstalt fuer
Landeskunde)

**Tessner-Verlag**
Sofienstr. 3, Postfach 510, 7570 Baden-Baden, W.
Germany.
- Kosmetik International. m.

**Tetra Werke**
c/o Dr. Ulrich Baensch, Ed., Herrenteich 70,
Postfach 1580, 4520 Melle, W. Germany (B.R.D.)
- Aquarium Digest International. q.

**Tetzlaff Verlag GmbH**
Havelstr. 9, Postfach 4006, 6100 Darmstadt 1, W.
Germany (B.R.D.)
- Der Eisenbahningenieur; Fachzeitschrift fuer
Eisenbahntechnik. m. ISSN 0013-2810 (Verband
Deutscher Eisenbahningenieure)
- Elsners Taschenbuch der Eisenbahntechnik. a.
ISSN 0071-0075
- Internationales Verkehrswesen; Zeitschrift fuer
Verkehrspolitik, Verkehrswirtschaft, Verkehrsrecht
und Verkehrstechnik, mit Beilage
Verkehrswissenschaftliche Nachrichten. bi-m.
ISSN 0020-9511 (Deutsche
Verkehrswissenschaftliche Gesellschaft)
- Kurzauszuege aus dem Schrifttum fuer das
Eisenbahnwesen. m. ISSN 0023-5695 (Deutsche
Bundesbahn)
- Signal und Draht; Zeitschrift fuer Informatik im
Eisenbahnwesen. m. ISSN 0037-4997
- Zeitschrift fuer Verkehrssicherheit. q. ISSN 0044-
3654

**Otto Teubel Verlag**
Heinrich-Stamme-Str. 6, 3000 Hannover, W.
Germany (B.R.D.)
- Einkaufsfuehrer durch die Pelz- und Ledermode.
a. ISSN 0070-9530

**Textilreinigungsverband e.V.**
- Reiniger und Waescher. (pub. by Verlag Neuer
Merkur GmbH)

**Theater-Rundschau-Verlag**
Bonner Talweg 10, 5300 Bonn 1, W. Germany
(B.R.D.)
- Theater-Rundschau; Blaetter fuer Buehne, Film,
Musik und Literatur. m. ISSN 0040-5442 (Bund
der Theatergemeinden e.V.)

**Deutscher Theaterverlag GmbH**
Koenigsberger Str. 18-22, Postfach 1227, 6940
Weinheim, W. Germany (B.R.D.)
- Spiel und Theater; Zeitschrift fuer
Amateurtheater, Darstellendes Kinderspiel, Schul-
und Jugendtheater, Theatererziehung und
Medienkunde. q. ISSN 0038-7509

**Themis-Verlag**
Postfach 1622, 7800 Freiburg, W. Germany
(B.R.D.)
- Zeitschrift fuer Staatssoziologie; Politik,
Wirtschaft, Kultur, Erziehung. q. ISSN 0044-3530

**Theodor-Storm-Gesellschaft**
- Theodor-Storm-Gesellschaft. Schriften. (pub. by
Westholsteinische Verlagsanstalt Boyens und Co.)

**Theologische Fakultaet Trier**
- Trierer Theologische Zeitschrift. (pub. by
Paulinus-Verlag)

**Thesen-Verlag, Vowinckel und Co**
Dreibrunnenstr. 3, 6100 Darmstadt, W. Germany (B.R.D.)
- Kritikon Litterarum; international book review for American, English, Romance and Slavic studies and for linguistics. q. ISSN 0340-9767

**Verlag Thiele und Schwarz**
Wilhelmshoeher Allee 254, Postfach 160, 3500 Kassel-Wilhelmshoehe, W. Germany (B.R.D.)
- Kasseler Sonntagsblatt; christliches Volksblatt fuer Deutschland. w. ISSN 0022-9245

**Georg Thieme Verlag**
Herdweg 63, Postfach 732, 7000 Stuttgart 1, W. Germany (B.R.D.)
- Acta Hepato-Gastroenterologica. bi-m. ISSN 0300-970X
- Aktuelle Chirurgie; Zeitschrift und Kartei fuer praktische Chirurgie. bi-m. ISSN 0001-785X
- Aktuelle Ernaehrungsmedizin; in Klinik und Praxis. m.
- Aktuelle Gerontologie. m. ISSN 0300-5704 (Deutsche Gesellschaft fuer Gerontologie) (Co-sponsors: Schweizerische Gesellschaft fuer Gerontologie; Oesterreichische Gesellschaft fuer Geriatrie)
- Aktuelle Neurologie. q. ISSN 0302-4350
- Aktuelle Oto-Rhino-Laryngologie. irreg., no. 5, 1972. ISSN 0065-5570
- Aktuelle Rheumatologie. m.
- Aktuelle Traumatologie. bi-m. ISSN 0044-6173
- Aktuelle Urologie; Zeitschrift und Kartei. bi-m. ISSN 0001-7868
- Deutsche Medizinische Wochenschrift. w. ISSN 0012-0472
- E E G-E M G; Zeitschrift fuer Elektroenzephalographie, Elektromyographie und verwandte Gebiete. q. ISSN 0012-7590
- Endoscopy; journal for clinical use, biospy and techique/Zeitschrift fuer klinische Anwendung, Biopsie und Technik. q. ISSN 0013-726X
- Environmental Quality and Safety: Chemistry, Toxicology and Technology. ISSN 0300-824X
- Fortschritte der Kiefer- und Gesichts-Chirurgie. irreg., vol. 18, 1974. ISSN 0071-7916
- Fortschritte der Neurologie, Psychiatrie und ihrer Grenzgebiete. m. ISSN 0015-8194
- Geburtshilfe und Frauenheilkunde; Ergebnisse der Forschung fuer die Praxis. m. ISSN 0016-5751
- Hormone and Metabolic Research. bi-m. ISSN 0018-5043
- Journal of Maxillofacial Surgery. q. ISSN 0301-0503 (European Association for Maxillofacial Surgery)
- Laryngologie, Rhinologie, Otologie und ihre Grenzgebiete - Vereinigt mit Monatsschrift fuer Ohrenheilkunde. m. ISSN 0340-1588 (Deutsche Gesellschaft fuer Hals-, Nasen-, Ohrheilkunde, Kopf- und Halschirurgie) (Co-Sponsor: Oesterreichische Gesellschaft fuer Hals-Nasen-Ohrenheilkunde, Kopf und Halschirurgie)
- Lymphology. q. ISSN 0024-7766 (International Society of Lymphology)
- Neurochirurgia; Advances/Fortschritte/Progres. bi-m. ISSN 0028-3819
- Das Oeffentliche Gesundheitswesen; Monatsschrift fuer Praeventivmedizin und Rehabilitation, fuer Sozialhygiene und oeffentlichen Gesundheitsdienst. m. ISSN 0029-8573
- Pharmakopsychiatrie - Neuro-Psychopharmakologie; Advances in Theoretical and Clinical Research. Fortschritte in Theorie, Klinik und Praxis. bi-m. ISSN 0031-7098
- Praktische Anaesthesie, Wiederbelebung und Intensivtherapie. bi-m. ISSN 0302-7600 (Deutsche Gesellschaft fuer Anaesthesie und Wiederbelebung)
- Praxis der Pneumologie. m. ISSN 0032-7069 (Deutsches Zentralkommittee zur Bekaempfung der Tuberkulose) (Co-Sponsor: Deutsche Gesellschaft fuer Lungenkrankheiten und Tuberkulose)
- Psychiatrische Praxis. q. ISSN 0303-4259
- Psychotherapie und Medizinische Psychologie. bi-m. ISSN 0302-8984 (Allgemeine Aerztliche Gesellschaft fuer Psychotherapie) (Co-Sponsor: Oesterreichische Aerzte-Gesellschaft fuer Psychotherapie)
- Die Rehabilitation; Zeitschrift fuer alle Fragen der medizinischen, schulisch-beruflichen und sozialen Eingliederung. q. ISSN 0034-3536 (Deutsche Vereinigung fuer die Rehabilitation Behinderter)
- RoeFo. Fortschritte auf dem Gebiete der Roentgenstrahlen und der Nuklearmedizin. m. ISSN 0340-1618 (Deutsche Roentgengesellschaft) (Co-sponsor: Oesterreichische Roentgengesellschaft)

- Sprache - Stimme - Gehoer; Zeitschrift fuer Kommunikationsstoerungen. q. ISSN 0342-0477
- Synthesis; international journal of methods in synthetic organic chemistry. m. ISSN 0039-7881 (U.S. Subscr. to: Academic Press, 111 Fifth Ave., New York, Ny 10003)
- Thoraxchirurgie - Vaskulaere Chirurgie. bi-m. ISSN 0040-6384 (Deutsche Gesellschaft fuer Thorax-, Herz- und Gefaesschirurgie)
- Tropenmedizin und Parasitologie. q. ISSN 0303-4208 (Deutsche Tropenmedizinische Gesellschaft)

**Verlag Karl Thiemig**
Pilgersheimer Str. 38, 8000 Munich 90, W. Germany (B.R.D.)
- Atomkernenergie. irreg. ISSN 0004-7147 (Studiengesellschaft zur Foerderung der Kernenergieverwertung in Schiffbau und Schiffahrt e.V.)
- Graphik; Magazin fuer Visuelles Marketing. m.
- Kerntechnik; journal for nuclear engineers and scientists. m. ISSN 0004-7198 (Studiengesellschaft zur Foerderung der Kernenergieverwertung in Schiffbau und Schiffahrt e.V.)
- Die Kunst und das Schoene Heim; Monatsschrift fuer Malerei, Plastik, Graphik, Architektur, Wohnkultur. m. ISSN 0023-5423
- Motor im Bild; Technik, Unterhaltung, Reise und Kultur. m. ISSN 0027-1896

**Thueringer Geologischer Verein e.V.**
- Beitraege zur Geologie von Thueringen. (pub. by Verlag Dr. Hans Werner Rothe)

**Thyssen Edelstahlwerke AG**
Postfach 730, 4150 Krefeld, W. Germany (B.R.D.)
- Thyssen Edelstahl Technische Berichte. 4 per yr.

**August Thyssen-Huette Ag**
Zentrale Forschung der Thyssen-Gruppe, Postfach 67, 4100 Duisburg-Hamborn, W. Germany (B.R.D.)
- Thyssen Technische Berichte. irreg.

**Transpatent GmbH.**
Postfach 8005, 4000 Duesseldorf, W. Germany (B.R.D.)
- Transpatent. 18 per yr. ISSN 0041-1310

**Tribuene-Verlag**
Habsburgerallee 72, 6000 Frankfurt, W. Germany (B.R.D.)
- Tribuene; Zeitschrift zum Verstaendnis d. Judentums. q. ISSN 0041-2716

**Trier. Bezirks-Regierung. Schulabteilung**
5500 Trier 1, W. Germany (B.R.D.)
- Amtliches Schulblatt fuer die Volks-, Real- und Berufsschulen fuer den Bezirksregierung Trier. m. ISSN 0003-2204

**Michael Triltsch Verlag**
Jahnstr. 36, 4000 Duesseldorf, W. Germany (B. R. D.
- Buchhaendler Heute. m. ISSN 0007-2796
- Duesseldorfer Hefte. s-m. ISSN 0012-7027
- Universitaet Duesseldorf. Jahrbuch. a. ISSN 0070-7457

**Dr Rudolf Trofenik Verlag**
Elisabethstr. 18, 8000 Munich 40, W. Germany (B.R.D.)
- Zeitschrift fuer Balkanologie. s-a. ISSN 0044-2356

**Tuduv-Verlagsgesellschaft**
Gabelsbergerstr. 15, 8000 Munich 2, W. Germany (B.R.D.)
- Tuduv-Studien. Reihe Sozialwissenschaften. irreg.

**Tuermer-Verlag**
Lenbachstr. 4, 8032 Graefelfing-Lochham, W. Germany (B.R.D.)
- Klueter Blaetter; deutsche Sammlung. m. ISSN 0023-2211

**Uebersee-Museum, Bremen**
Bahnhofsplatz 13, 2800 Bremen, W. Germany (B.R.D.)
- Uebersee-Museum, Bremen. Veroeffentlichungen. Reihe A: Naturwissenschaften. irreg. ISSN 0068-0885
- Uebersee-Museum, Bremen. Veroeffentlichungen. Reihe B: Voelkerkunde. irreg. ISSN 0068-0893

**Uebersee-Post Verlag Dr. Harnisch GmbH und Co. KG**
Findelgasse 10, 8500 Nuernberg 1, W. Germany (B.R.D.)
- Industrie-Post. bi-m. ISSN 0019-9141

- Uebersee-Post - Europa-Post/Overseas- Post Trade Journal. m. ISSN 0030-7475

**Uebersee-Verlag GmbH**
Schoene Aussicht 23, 2000 Hamburg 76, W. Germany (B.R.D.)
- Aussenpolitik; Zeitschrift fuer internationale Fragen. q(English edt.); m. (German edt.) ISSN 0004-8194
- Trade Contacts; special service for export-import industry. bi-m.
- Uebersee Rundschau. m. ISSN 0041-5707

**Verlag Eugen Ulmer**
Gerokstr. 19, Postfach 1032, 7000 Stuttgart 1, W. Germany (B.R.D.)
- Archiv fuer Gefluegelkunde/Archives of Poultry Science/Archives de Science Avicole. bi-m. ISSN 0003-9098
- Blumen Einzelhandel. m.
- D G S. (Deutsche Gefluegelwirtschaft und Schweineproduktion) w. (Zentralverband der Deutschen Gefluegelwirtschaft)
- Der Gartenbauingenieur; Zeitschrift fuer Fuehrungskraefte im Gartenbau. 6 per yr. ISSN 0016-4763 (Bund der Ingenieure des Gartenbaues)
- Gartenbauwissenschaft. 6 per yr. ISSN 0016-478X
- Gartenpraxis. m.
- Hohenheimer Arbeiten. irreg., no. 77, 1975. (Universitaet Hohenheim)
- Jahrbuch der Gefluegelwirtschaft. a. ISSN 0447-2713 (Zentralverband der Deutschen Gefluegelwirtschaft)
- Die Kleinbrennerei. m.
- Landschaft und Stadt. q. ISSN 0023-8058
- Nachrichtenblatt des Deutschen Pflanzenschutzdienstes. m. ISSN 0027-7479 (Biologische Bundesanstalt fuer Land- und Forstwirtschaft)
- Obst und Garten. m. ISSN 0029-7798 (Landesverband fuer Obstbau, Garten und Landschaft Baden-Wuerttemberg e. V.)
- Wuerttembergisches Wochenblatt fuer Landwirtschaft. w. ISSN 0043-9606 (Bauernverband Wuerttemberg-Baden)
- Zeitschrift fuer Pflanzenkrankheiten und Pflanzenschutz. m. ISSN 0044-3271
- Zuechtungskunde. 6 per yr. ISSN 0044-5401 (Deutsche Gesellschaft fuer Zuechtungskunde e.V.)

**Umschau Verlag**
Stuttgarterstr. 18-24, 6000 Frankfurt, W. Germany (B.R.D.)
- Chemie fuer Labor und Betrieb. m. ISSN 0009-2835
- Ernaehrungs-Umschau; Zeitschrift ueber die Ernaehrung des Gesunden und Kranken. m. ISSN 0014-021X (Deutsche Gesellschaft fuer Ernaehrung)
- Lederwaren-Zeitung. m. ISSN 0047-4312
- Leica-Fotografie; Zeitschrift der Kleinbildfotografie. bi-m. ISSN 0024-0621
- Schuhmarkt. w. ISSN 0036-7079 (Bundesverband des Deutschen Schuheinzelhandels)
- Soldat und Technik. m. ISSN 0038-0989 (Germany, Federal Republic. Bundesministerium der Verteidigung)
- Umschau in Wissenschaft und Technik. s-m. ISSN 0041-6347

**Unabhaengiger Arbeitskreis Arzneimittelpolitik**
- Arznei-Telegramm. (pub. by Arzneimittel-Informationsdienst GmbH (A.T.I.))

**Unesco. Institut fuer Paedogogik**
For publications of this agency see section for UNITED NATIONS

**Ungarisches Institut, Muenchen**
- Ungarn-Jahrbuch. (pub. by V. Hase und Koehler Verlag)

**Union-Betriebs-Gesellschaft mbH**
Argelanderstr. 173, 5300 Bonn, W. Germany (B.R.D.)
- Frau und Politik. m. ISSN 0016-0202 (Christlich-Demokratische Union (CDU). Frauenvereinigung)

**Union der Leitenden Angestellten**
- Leitende Angestellte. (pub. by Kunststoff-Verlag)

**Union Europeenne des Experts Comptables Economiques et Financiers**
- U E C Journal. (pub. by I D W Verlag GmbH)

**Union of German Sheep-Breeders, Bonn**
- Deutsche Schaefereizeitung. (pub. by Koerner GmbH)

**United Bible Societies**
Bible House, Hauptstaetterstr. 51, Postfach 755, 7000 Stuttgart 1, W. Germany (B.R.D.)
- United Bible Societies. Bulletin. q. ISSN 0041-719X

**Uniti Bundesverband Mittelstaendischer Mineraloelunternehmen e.V.**
Buchstr. 10, 2000 Hamburg 76, W. Germany (B.R.D.)
- Mineraloelrundschau; Zeitschrift fuer die Deutsche Mineraloelwirtschaft. m.

**Universitaet Bielefeld**
- Papiere zur Textlinguistik/Papers in Textlinguistics. (pub. by Verlag Helmut Buske)

**Universitaet Bonn**
- Universitaet Bonn. Institut fuer Kommunikations Forschung und Phonetik. Forschungsberichte. (pub. by Verlag Helmut Buske)

**Universitaet Bonn. Forschungstelle fuer Orientalische Kunstgeschichte**
- Universitaet Bonn. Seminar fuer Orientalische Kunstgeschichte. Veroeffentlichungen. Reihe A. Nimruz. (pub. by Rudolf Habelt Verlag)

**Universitaet Bonn. Franz Joseph Doelger-Institut**
- Jahrbuch fuer Antike und Christentum. (pub. by Aschendorffsche Verlagsbuchhandlung)

**Universitaet Bonn. Geographisches Institut**
- Arbeiten zur Rheinischen Landeskunde. (pub. by Duemmlers Verlag)
- Erdkunde. (pub. by Duemmlers Verlag)

**Universitaet Bonn. Institut fuer Geschichtliche Landeskunde der Rheinlande**
- Rheinische Vierteljahrsblaetter. (pub. by Verlag Ludwig Roehrscheid GmbH)

**Universitaet Bonn. Institut fuer Oekonometrie und Operations Research**
Nassestr. 2, 5300 Bonn, W. Germany (B.R.D.)
- Universitaet Bonn. Institut fuer Oekonometrie und Operations Research. Neuanschaffungslisten. q.

**Universitaet Bonn. Mathematisches Institut**
Wegeler Str. 10, 5300 Bonn, W. Germany (B.R.D.)
- Bonner Mathematische Schriften. irreg. ISSN 0524-045X

**Universitaet Bonn. Meteorologisches Institut**
- Bonner Meteorologische Abhandlungen. (pub. by Duemmlers Verlag)

**Universitaet Bremen**
Postfach, 2800 Bremen 33, W. Germany (B.R.D.)
- Bremer-Univeristaets-Zeitung; Nachrichten, Kommentare, Diskussionen. bi-m.
- Materialien zur Hochschulpolitik. irreg.

**Universitaet des Saarlandes**
6600 Saarbruecken 11, W. Germany (B.R.D.)
- Annales Universitatis Saraviensis. Reihe: Mathematisch-Naturwissenschaftliche Fakultaet. (pub. by Gebrueder Borntraeger Verlagsbuchhandlung)
- Annales Universitatis Saraviensis. Reihe Medizin. 4 per yr. ISSN 0003-4533

**Universitaet des Saarlandes. Geographisches Institut**
6600 Saarbruecken 11, W. Germany (B.R.D.)
- Universitaet des Saarlandes. Geographisches Institut. Arbeiten. irreg., vol. 19, 1974. ISSN 0563-1491

**Universitaet des Saarlandes. Musikwissenschaftliches Institut**
- Saarbruecker Studien zur Musikwissenschaft. (pub. by Baerenreiter Verlag)

**Universitaet des Saarlandes. Universitaetsbibliothek**
6600 Saarbruecken 11, W. Germany (B.R.D.)
- Universitaet des Saarlandes. Jahresbibliographie. a. ISSN 0080-5173

**Universitaet Duesseldorf**
- Universitaet Duesseldorf. Jahrbuch. (pub. by Michael Triltsch Verlag)

**Universitaet Erlangen. Geologisches Institut**
Schlossgarten 5, 8520 Erlangen, W. Germany (B.R.D.)
- Erlanger Geologische Abhandlungen. irreg., no. 102, 1975. ISSN 0071-1160
- Geologische Blaetter fuer Nordost-Bayern und Angrenzende Gebiete. q. ISSN 0016-7797

**Universitaet Erlangen-Nuernberg**
- Sozialisation und Kommunikation. (pub. by Ferdinand Enke Verlag)

**Universitaet Frankfurt**
- Frankfurter Althistorische Studien. (pub. by Verlag Michael Lassleben)

**Universitaet Frankfurt. Geographisches Institut**
- Rhein-Mainische Forschungen. (pub. by Verlag Dr. Waldemar Kramer)

**Universitaet Frankfurt. Seminar fuer Sprach- und Kulturwissenschaft Zentralasiens**
- Zentralasiatische Studien. (pub. by Verlag Otto Harrassowitz)

**Universitaet Frankfurt. Wissenschaftliche Gesellschaft**
- Universitaet Frankfurt. Wissenschaftliche Gesellschaft. Sitzungsberichte. (pub. by Franz Steiner Verlag GmbH)

**Universitaet Freiburg**
- Freiburger Universitaetsblaetter. (pub. by Verlag Rombach und Co. GmbH)

**Universitaet Freiburg. Geographisches Institut**
Werderring 4, 7800 Freiburg, W. Germany (B.R.D.)
- Freiburger Geographische Hefte. irreg., 1972, vol. 12. ISSN 0071-9447
- I G U Bulletin/Bulletin de l'UGI. s-a. ISSN 0018-9804

**Universitaet Giessen**
Landgraf-Philipp-Platz 4, 6300 Giessen, W. Germany (B.R.D.)
- Universitaet Giessen. Ergebnisse Landwirtschaftlicher Forschung. irreg. ISSN 0075-4609

**Universitaet Giessen. Bibliothek**
Bismarckstr. 37, 6300 Giessen, W. Germany (B. R. D.)
- Universitaet Giessen. Bibliothek. Berichte und Arbeiten. irreg. ISSN 0072-4483
- Universitaet Giessen. Bibliothek. Kurzberichte aus den Papyrus-Sammlungen. irreg., no. 35, 1975. ISSN 0072-4491

**Universitaet Giessen. Matematisches Institut**
Arndt Str. 2, 6300 Giessen, W. Germany (B.R.D.)
- Universitaet Giessen. Matematisches Institut. Vorlesungen. irreg.

**Universitaet Giessen. Zentrum fuer Kontinentale Agrar- und Wirtschaftsforschung**
Otto Behaghel-Str. 10, 6300 Giessen, W. Germany (B.R.D.)
- Osteuropastudien der Hochschulen des Landes Hessen. Reihe 1. Giessener Abhandlungen zur Agrar- und Wirtschaftsforschung des Europaeischen Ostens. irreg. ISSN 0078-6888

**Universitaet Goettingen**
Wilhelmsplatz 1, 3400 Goettingen, W. Germany (B.R.D.)
- Georgia Augusta. (pub. by Vandenhoeck und Ruprecht)
- Universitaet Goettingen. Jahresbericht. irreg. ISSN 0436-1202

**Universitaet Goettingen. Geographisches Institut**
- Goettinger Geographische Abhandlungen. (pub. by Verlag Erich Goltze KG)

**Universitaet Goettingen. Niedersaechsisches Institut fuer Landeskunde und Landesentwicklung**
Gosslerstr. 15a, 3400 Goettingen, W. Germany (B.R.D.)
- Neues Archiv fuer Niedersachsen. bi-m.

**Universitaet Hamburg**
- Afrika und Uebersee. (pub. by Dietrich Reimer Buchhandlung)
- W G O - Monatshefte fuer Osteuropaeisches Recht. (pub. by Hansischer Gildenverlag)

**Universitaet Hamburg. Finnisch-Ugrisches Seminar**
- Ural-Altaische Jahrbuecher. (pub. by Verlag Otto Harrassowitz)

**Universitaet Hamburg. Geologisch-Palaeontologisches Institut**
Von Melle Park 11, 2000 Hamburg 13, W. Germany (B.R.D.)
- Universitaet Hamburg. Geologisch-Palaeontologisches Institut. Mitteilungen. a. ISSN 0072-1115

**Universitaet Hamburg. Ibero-Amerikanisches Forschungsinstitut**
- Romanistisches Jahrbuch. (pub. by Walter de Gruyter und Co.)

**Universitaet Hamburg. Institut fuer Internationale Angelegenheiten**
Edmund-Siemers-Allee 1, 2000 Hamburg 13, W. Germany (B.R.D.)
- Das Geltende Seekriegsrecht in Einzeldarstellungen. (pub. by Alfred Metzner Verlag GmbH)
- Hamburger Oeffentlich-Rechtliche Nebenstunden. (pub. by Alfred Metzner Verlag GmbH)
- Sammlung Geltender Staatsangehoerigkeitsgesetze. (pub. by Alfred Metzner Verlag GmbH)
- Universitaet Hamburg. Institut fuer Internationale Angelegenheiten. Veroeffentlichungen. irreg.
- Universitaet Hamburg. Institut fuer Internationale Angelegenheiten. Werkhefte. (pub. by Alfred Metzner Verlag GmbH)

**Universitaet Hamburg. Mathematisches Seminar**
- Universitaet Hamburg. Mathematisches Seminar. Abhandlungen. (pub. by Vandenhoeck und Ruprecht)

**Universitaet Hamburg. Seminar fuer Oeffentliches Recht und Staatslehre**
- Hamburger Abhandlungen. (pub. by Gerold und Appel Verlagsgesellschaft)

**Universitaet Hamburg. Seminar fuer Sprache und Kultur Japans**
Von Melle Park 6/7, 2000 Hamburg 13, W. Germany.
- Gesellschaft fuer Natur- und Voelkerkunde Ostasiens; Zeitschrift fuer Kultur und Geschichte Ostasiens. s-a. ISSN 0016-9080

**Universitaet Heidelberg**
Grabengasse 1, 6900 Heidelberg, W. Germany (B.R.D.)
- Unispiegel. irreg. (approx. 20-25 per yr)

**Universitaet Heidelberg. Institut fuer Soziologie und Ethnologie**
- Heidelberger Sociologica. (pub. by Verlag J.C.B. Mohr (Paul Siebeck))

**Universitaet Heidelberg. Juristische Fakultaet**
- Heidelberger Rechtswissenschaftliche Abhandlungen. Neue Folge. (pub. by Carl Winter Universitaetsverlag)

**Universitaet Heidelberg. Suedasien-Institut**
Im Neuenheimer Feld 330, 6900 Heidelberg 1, W. Germany (B.R.D.)
- Beitraege zur Suedasien Forschung. (pub. by Franz Steiner Verlag GmbH)
- Universitaet Heidelberg. Suedasien-Institut. Sonderdrucke der Mitglieder. irreg., no. 160, 1974. ISSN 0073-1617

**Universitaet Hohenheim**
- Hohenheimer Arbeiten. (pub. by Verlag Eugen Ulmer)

**Universitaet Hohenheim. Informations- und Pressestelle**
Paracelsusstr. 2, Postfach 106, 7000 Stuttgart 70, W. Germany (B.R.D.)
- Daten und Dokumente Zum Umweltschutz/Data and Documents About Environment Protection. irreg., no. 13, 1974.

**Universitaet Hohenheim. Institut fuer Sozialwissenschaften**
Postfach 106, 7000 Stuttgart 70, W. Germany (B.R.D.)
- Fachdokumentation Agrargeschichte. 3 per yr (200 abstracts each) (prep. by its Abteilung Wirtschafts-, Sozial- und Agrargeschichte)

**Universitaet Karlsruhe. Zentrum fuer Didaktik der Mathematik**
- Zentralblatt fuer Didaktik der Mathematik. (pub. by Ernst Klett Verlag)

**Universitaet Kiel. Agrarwissenschaftliche Fakultaet**
- Universitaet Kiel. Agrarwissenschaftliche Fakultaet. Schriftenreihe. (pub. by Verlag Paul Parey (Hamburg))

**Universitaet Kiel. Englisches Seminar**
- Literatur in Wissenschaft und Unterricht. (pub. by Karl Wachholtz Verlag)

**Universitaet Kiel. Geographisches Institut**
Neue Universitaet, Olshausenstr. 40-60, 2300 Kiel, W. Germany (B.R.D.)
- Universitaet Kiel. Geogrpahisches Institut. Schriften. irreg.

**Universitaet Kiel. Institut fuer Agrarpolitik und Marktlehre**
- Agrarmarkt-Studien. (pub. by Verlag Paul Parey (Hamburg))

**Universitaet Kiel. Institut fuer Internationales Recht**
- Jahrbuch fuer Internationales Recht. (pub. by Duncker und Humblot)
- Universitaet Keil. Institut fuer Internationales Recht. Studien. (pub. by Duncker und Humblot)

**Universitaet Kiel. Institut fuer Meereskunde**
- Kieler Meeresforschungen. (pub. by Verlag Walter G. Muehlau)

**Universitaet Mainz. Institut fuer Geschichtliche Landeskunde**
- Geschichtliche Landeskunde. (pub. by Franz Steiner Verlag GmbH)

**Universitaet Marburg**
Am Krummbogen 28, 3550 Marburg, W. Germany (B.R.D.)
- Africana Marburgensia. s-a. ISSN 0002-0311

**Universitaet Marburg. Institut fuer Medizinisch-biologische Statistik**
Coelber Str. 1, 3550 Marburg 1, W. Germany (B.R.D.)
- I M B I S; Information fuer medizinisch-biologische Statistik und deren Grenzgebiete. irreg.

**Universitaet Muenchen. Geophysikalisches Observatorium**
Ludwigshoehe 8, 8080 Fuerstenfeldbruck, W. Germany (B.R.D.)
- Universitaet Muenchen. Geophysikalisches Observatorium, Fuerstenfeldbruck. Veroeffentlichungen. Serie A. a.
- Universitaet Muenchen. Geophysikalisches Observatorium, Fuerstenfeldbruck. Veroeffentlichungen. Serie B. irreg., no. 5, 1974. ISSN 0077-2100

**Universitaet Muenchen. Institut fuer Byzantinistik und Neugriechische Philologie**
Geschwister Scholl Platz 1, 8000 Munich 22, W. Germany (B.R.D.)
- Miscellanea Byzantina Monacensia. irreg., no. 19, 1975. ISSN 0076-9347

**Universitaet Muenchen. Institut fuer Geographie**
- Muenchener Geographische Abhandlungen. (pub. by Geo-Buch Verlag)

**Universitaet Muenchen. Wirtschaftsgeographisches Institut**
- Muenchner Studien zur Sozial- und Wirtschaftsgeographie. (pub. by Verlag Michael Lassleben)
- Universitaet Muenchen. Wirtschaftsgeographisches Institut. "W G I"-Berichte zur Regionalforschung. (pub. by Geo-Buch Verlag)

**Universitaet Muenster**
- Muenstersche Beitraege zur Vor- und Fruehgeschichte. (pub. by Verlag August Lax)
- Universitaet Muenster. Institut fuer Missionswissenschaft. Veroeffentlichungen. (pub. by Aschendorffsche Verlagsbuchhandlung)

**Universitaet Muenster. Astronomisches Institut**
Steinfurterstr. 107, 4400 Muenster, W. Germany (B.R.D.)
- Universitaet Muenster. Astronomisches Institut. Mitteilungen. irreg. ISSN 0077-1929
- Universitaet Muenster. Astronomisches Institut. Sonderdrucke. irreg. ISSN 0077-1937

**Universitaet Muenster. Forschungsstelle fuer Allgemeine und Textile Marktwirtschaft**
- Zeitschrift fuer allgemeine und textile Marktwirtschaft. (pub. by Vandenhoeck und Ruprecht)

**Universitaet Muenster. Institut fuer Christliche Sozialwissenschaften**
- Jahrbuch fuer Christliche Sozialwissenschaften. (pub. by Verlag Regensberg)
- Universitaet Muenster. Institut fuer Christliche Sozialwissenschaften. Schriften. (pub. by Aschendorffsche Verlagsbuchhandlung)

**Universitaet Muenster. Institut fuer Epigraphik**
- Fontes et Commentationes. (pub. by Aschendorffsche Verlagsbuchhandlung)

**Universitaet Muenster. Institut fuer Fruehmittelalterforschung**
- Fruehmittelalterliche Studien. (pub. by Walter de Gruyter und Co.)

**Universitaet Muenster. Institut fuer Kreditwesen**
- Westfaelische Wilhelms-Universitaet Muenster. Institut fuer Kreditwesen. Schriftenreihe. (pub. by Betriebswirtschaftlicher Verlag Dr. Tr. Gebler KG)

**Universitaet Muenster. Katholisch-Theologische Fakultaet**
- Theologische Revue. (pub. by Aschendorffsche Verlagsbuchhandlung)

**Universitaet Muenster. Sozialforschungsstelle**
- Soziale Forschung und Praxis. (pub. by Verlag J.C.B. Mohr (Paul Siebeck))

**Universitaet Stuttgart**
- Universitaet Stuttgart. Institut fuer Steuerungstechnik der Werkzeugmaschinen und Fertigungseinrichtungen. I S W Berichte. (pub. by Springer-Verlag US)

**Universitaet Stuttgart. Geographisches Institut**
Silcherstr. 9, 7000 Stuttgart 1, W. Germany (B.R.D.)
- Stuttgarter Geographische Studien. 2-3 per yr.

**Universitaet Stuttgart. Institut fuer Geologie und Palaeontologie**
Boeblinger Str. 72, 7000 Stuttgart 1, W. Germany (B.R.D.)
- Universitaet Stuttgart. Institut fuer Geologie und Palaeontologie Arbeiten Neue Folge. irreg., no. 70, 1973. ISSN 0585-7856

**Universitaet Tuebingen. Geographisches Institut**
Schloss, 7400 Tuebingen, W. Germany (B.R.D.)
- Tuebinger Geographische Studien. irreg. (approx. 5 per yr) ISSN 0564-4232

**Universitaet Tuebingen. Rechts- und Wirtschaftswissenschaftliche Fakultaet**
- Tuebinger Rechtswissenschaftliche Abhandlungen. (pub. by Verlag J.C.B. Mohr (Paul Siebeck))

**Universitaet Ulm**
Oberer Eselsberg, Postfach 4066, 7900 Ulm, W. Germany (B.R.D.)
- Uni Ulm Intern; Mitteilungen des Rektors der Universitaet Ulm. m. (approx.)

**Universitaet Wuerzburg. Geographisches Institut**
Am Hubland, 8700 Wuerzburg, W. Germany (B.R.D.)
- Wuerzburger Geographische Arbeiten. irreg., (approx. 3-4 per yr.) ISSN 0510-9833

**Universitaet Wuerzburg. Institut fuer Wehrrecht**
- Wuerzburger Wehrwissenschaftliche Abhandlungen. (pub. by Holzner-Verlag)

**Universitaet Wuerzburg. Seminar fuer Deutsche Philologie**
- Kleine Deutsche Prosadenkmaeler des Mittelalters. (pub. by Wilhelm Fink Verlag)

**Universitaet zu Koeln**
- Universitaet Zu Koeln. Jahrbuch. (pub. by Universitaets Buchhandlung Dr. J.C. Witsch)

**Universitaet zu Koeln. Forschungsinstitut fuer Politische Wissenschaften und Europaeische Fragen**
- Demokratische Existenz Heute. (pub. by Carl Heymanns Verlag KG)
- Koelner Schriften zur Politischen Wissenschaft. (pub. by Westdeutscher Verlag GmbH)
- Verfassung und Verfassungswirklichkeit. (pub. by Duncker und Humblot)

**Universitaet zu Koeln. Forschungsinstitut fuer Sozialpolitik**
- Archiv fuer Oeffentliche und Freigemeinnuetzige Unternehmen. (pub. by Verlag Otto Schwartz und Co.)

**Universitaet zu Koeln. Geologisch-Palaeontologisches Institut**
- Meyniana. (pub. by R. Eschenburg)

**Universitaet zu Koeln. Geologisches Institut**
Zuelpicher Str. 49, 5000 Cologne 41, W. Germany (B.R.D.)
- Universitaet zu Koeln. Geologiches Institut. Sonderveroeffentlichungen. irreg., 1973, no. 22. ISSN 0069-5874

**Universitaet zu Koeln. Institut fuer Geophysik und Meteorologie**
Albertus Magnus Platz, 5000 Cologne, W. Germany (B.R.D.)
- Universitaet zu Koeln. Institut fuer Geophysik und Meteorologie. Mitteilungen. irreg., no. 22, 1975. ISSN 0069-5882

**Universitaet zu Koeln. Institut fuer Handelsforschung**
Sackinger Str. 5, 5000 Cologne-Lindenthal, W. Germany (B.R.D.)
- Schriften zur Handelsforschung. (pub. by Verlag Otto Schwartz und Co.)
- Universitaet zu Koeln. Institut fuer Handelsforschung. Mitteilungen. m.

**Universitaet zu Koeln. Institut fuer Luft- und Weltraumrecht**
- Zeitschrift fuer Luft- und Weltraumrecht. (pub. by Carl Heymanns Verlag KG)

**Universitaet zu Koeln. Institut fuer Massenkommunikation**
Berrenrather Str. 138, 5000 Cologne 41, W. Germany (B.R.D.)
- International Journal of Communication Research. 3 per yr.

**Universitaet zu Koeln. Institut fuer Verkehrswissenschaft**
Universitaetsstr.22, 5000 Cologne 41, W. Germany (B.R.D.)
- Dokumentation der Deutschen Binnenschiffahrt. m. ISSN 0012-5067

**Universitaet zu Koeln. Institut fuer Wirtschaftspolitik**
Lindenburger Allee 32, 5000 Cologne 41, W. Germany (B.R.D.)
- Wirtschaftspolitische Chronik. 3 per yr. ISSN 0043-6305

**Universitaet zu Koeln. Romanisches Seminar**
- Koelner Romanistische Arbeiten. (pub. by Librarie Droz SZ)

**Universitaet zu Koeln. Thomas-Institut**
- Miscellanea Mediaevalia. (pub. by Walter de Gruyter und Co.)

**Universitaetsbund Wuerzburg**
- Wuerzburg-Heute. (pub. by Echter-Verlag)

**Universum-Verlagsanstalt GmbH KG**
Roesslerstr. 7, 6200 Wiesbaden, W. Germany (B.R.D.)
- Gib Acht; illustrierte Jugend-Zeitschrift mit Beitraegen zur Verkehrserziehung fuer den Unterricht und fuer den Schuelerlotsen. m. ISSN 0016-9668 (Aufklaerungsdienst fuer Jugendschutz)

**Verlag Unser Weg**
Meesenring 15, 2400 Luebeck 1, W. Germany (B.R.D.)
- Jahrbuch fuer Schlesische Kirchengeschichte. a. ISSN 0075-2762 (Verein fuer Schlesische Kirchengeschichte e.V.)

**Unternehmerwirtschaft Verlags GmbH**
Mainzer Str. 238, Postfach 842, 5300 Bonn-Bad
Godesberg 1, W. Germany (B.R.D.)
- Junge Wirtschaft; Zeitschrift fuer fortschrittliches
Unternehmertum. m. ISSN 0022-6416

**Verlag Urachhaus**
Urachstr. 41, 7000 Stuttgart 1, W. Germany
(B.R.D.)
- Die Christengemeinschaft; Monatsschrift zur
religioesen Erneuerung. m. ISSN 0009-5184

**Urban und Schwarzenberg**
Pettenkoferstr. 18, Postfach 145, 8000 Munich 2,
W. Germany (B.R.D.)
- European Journal of Behavioural Analysis and
Modification. s-a. ISSN 0340-6695
- Fortschritte der Kieferorthopaedie. q. ISSN 0015-
816X (Deutsche Gesellschaft fuer
Kieferorthopaedie)
- Herz. q.
- International Journal of Clinical Pharmacology
and Biopharmacy. m. ISSN 0340-0026
- Medizinische Klinik; Wochenschrift fuer Klinik
und Praxis. w. ISSN 0025-8458
- Progress in Pediatric Surgery. a. ISSN 0079-6654
(Dist. in U.S. and Canada by: University Park
Press, Chamber of Commerce Bldg., Baltimore,
MD 21202)
- Strahlentherapie; Archiv fuer klinische und
experimentelle Radiologie. 12 per yr. ISSN 0039-
2073 (Deutsche Roentgengesellschaft)
- Therapie der Gegenwart; Monatsschrift fuer
praktishe Medizin. m. ISSN 0040-5965

**Urban-Verlag GmbH**
Alfredstr. 1, 2000 Hamburg 76, W. Germany
(B.R.D.)
- Erdoel-Erdgas Zeitschrift; Bohr- und
Foerdertechnik, Aufbereitung, Transport. m. (Co-
Sponsors: German Association of Petroleum
Geologists and Petroleum Engineers (DVGI);
Austrian Society of Petroleum Sciences
(OEGEW))
- The European Oil and Gas Magazine;
international edition of Erdoel-Erdgas Zeitschrift.
2 per yr.

**V D A - Gesellschaft fuer Deutsche
Kulturbeziehungen im Ausland**
Braeuhausstr. 10, 8000 Munich 2, W. Germany
(B.R.D.)
- Globus. q.

**V D E-Verlag GmbH**
Bismarckstr. 33, 1000 Berlin 12, W. Germany
(B.R.D.)
- Deutscher Fachhochschulfuehrer. irreg.
- Elektrotechnische Zeitschrift. Ausgabe A;
Zeitschrift fuer Elektrische Energietechnik. m.
(Verband Deutscher Elektrotechniker e.V.)
- Elektrotechnische Zeitschrift. Ausgabe B. s-m.
ISSN 0012-8631 (Verband Deutscher
Elektrotechniker e.V.)
- N T Z Nachrichtentechnische Zeitschrift. m.
ISSN 0027-707X (Verein Deutscher
Elektrotechniker e.V.)

**V D I-Verlag GmbH**
Graf-Recke-Str. 84, Postfach 1139, 4000
Duesseldorf 1, W. Germany (B.R.D.)
- B W K (Brennstoff-Waerme-Kraft); Zeitschrift
fuer Energietechnik und Energiewirtschaft. m.
ISSN 0006-9612 (Verein Deutscher Ingenieure)
- Deutsche Kraftfahrtforschung und
Strassenverkehrstechnik. irreg. ISSN 0070-4210
(Verein Deutscher Ingenieure)
- Dokumentation Regelungstechnik. m. ISSN 0340-
3955 (Verein Deutscher Ingenieure. Gesellschaft
fuer Mess- und Regelungstechnik)
- Forschung im Ingenieurwesen. bi-m. ISSN 0015-
7899 (Verein Deutscher Ingenieure)
- Grundlagen der Landtechnik; Verfahren -
Konstruktion - Wirtschaft. bi-m. ISSN 0017-4920
(Verein Deutscher Ingenieure)
- H L H, Zeitschrift fuer Heizung, Lueftung,
Klimatechnik, Haustechnik. m. ISSN 0017-9906
(Verein Deutscher Ingenieure. Gesellschaft
Technische Gebaeudeausruestung)
- M T. (Meerestechnik/Marine Technology) bi-m.
ISSN 0025-8644 (Verein Deutscher Ingenieure.
Deutsches Komitee fuer Meeresforschung und
Meerestechnik)
- Materialpruefung/Materials Testing/Materiaux,
Essais et Recherches. m. ISSN 0025-5300
(Deutscher Verband fuer Material Pruefung)

- Staub Reinhaltung der Luft. m. ISSN 0039-0771
(Verein Deutscher Ingenieure. Kommission
Reinhaltung der Luft)
- T U - Sicherheit und Zuverlaessigkeit in
Wirtschaft, Betrieb, Verkehr. (Technische
Ueberwachung) m. (Vereinigung der Technischen
Ueberwachungsvereine e.V.)
- Technikgeschichte. q. ISSN 0040-117X (Verein
Deutscher Ingenieure)
- Technikgeschichte in Einzeldarstellungen. irreg.
ISSN 0082-2361 (Verein Deutscher Ingenieure)
- Umwelt; Forschung - Gestaltung - Schutz. bi-m.
ISSN 0041-6355 (Verein Deutscher Ingenieure.
Aktionszentrum Technik und Umwelt)
- V D I-Berichte. 10-20 per yr. ISSN 0083-5560
(Verein Deutscher Ingenieure)
- V D I - Forschungshefte. 6 per yr. ISSN 0042-
174X (Verein Deutscher Ingenieure)
- V D I-Nachrichten; Wochenzeitung fuer Technik
Wirtschaft-Wissenschaft. w. ISSN 0042-1758
(Verein Deutscher Ingenieure)
- V D I-Z; Zeitschrift fuer Entwicklung,
Konstruktion, Produktion. 24 per yr. ISSN 0042-
1766 (Verein Deutscher Ingenieure)

**V F V Verbands- und Fachschriftenverlag**
Wiesbadener Str. 63, 6503 Mainz-Kastel, W.
Germany (B.R.D.)
- Die Gefiederte Welt; Fachzeitschrift fuer
Vogelliebhaber und Vogelzuechter. m. ISSN 0016-
5816
- Zoologischer Zentral-Anzeiger. fortn. ISSN 0044-
524X (Zentralverband Zoologischer
Fachgeschaefte Deutschlands e.V.)

**V-Illustriert**
Koelner Str. 108-112, 5300 Bonn-Bad Godesberg,
W. Germany.
- V-Illustriert. s-a. ISSN 0042-1871

**V L E Verlags-GmbH**
Wasserturmstr. 8, 8520 Erlangen, W. Germany (B.
R. D.)
- Handchirurgie. q. ISSN 0046-6794
(Deutschsprache Arbeitsgemeinschaft fuer
Handchirurgie)
- Unfallchirurgie. q.

**Vandenhoeck und Ruprecht**
Theaterstr. 13, Postfach 77, 3400 Goettingen, W.
Germany (B. R. D.)
- Akademie der Wissenschaften, Goettingen.
Jahrbuch. a. ISSN 0084-6082
- Akademie der Wissenschaften, Goettingen.
Nachrichten 1. Philologisch-Historische Klasse.
irreg. ISSN 0065-5287
- Akademie der Wissenschaften, Goettingen.
Nachrichten 2. Mathematisch-Physikalische
Klasse. irreg. ISSN 0065-5295
- Allgemeines Statistisches Archiv. q. ISSN 0002-
6018 (Deutsche Statistische Gesellschaft)
- Archiv fuer Religionspsychologie. irreg., 1970, vol.
10. ISSN 0084-6724 (Internationale Gesellschaft
fuer Religionspsychologie)
- Frohe Botschaft; Predigten fuer jeden Sonntag des
Jahres. bi-m.
- Georgia Augusta. s-a. ISSN 0016-8157
(Universitaet Goettingen)
- Geschichte und Gesellschaft; Zeitschrift fuer
historische Sozialwissenschaft.
- Gesellschaft zur Foerderung Tiefenpsychologischer
und Psychotherapeutischer Forschung und
Weiterbildung, Munich. Beitraege und Berichte.
irreg. ISSN 0085-106X
- Glotta; Zeitschrift fuer griechische und lateinische
Sprache. 2 double nos. per year. ISSN 0017-1298
- Goettinger Predigtmeditationen. q. ISSN 0017-
1530
- Goettinger Quellenhefte. irreg., no. 8, 1973.
- Goettinger Universitaetsreden. irreg. ISSN 0085-
1108
- Goettingische Gelehrte Anzeigen. s-a. ISSN 0017-
1549 (Akademie der Wissenschaften, Goettingen)
- Gruppenpsychotherapie und Gruppendynamik. 3
per yr. ISSN 0017-4947
- Gruppenpsychotherapie und Gruppendynamik.
Beihefte. irreg. ISSN 0085-1302
- Homiletische Monatshefte. m. ISSN 0018-4276
- Hypomnemata; Untersuchungen zur Antike und
zu ihrem Nachleben. irreg., no. 43, 1975. ISSN
0085-1671
- Jahrbuch fuer Sozialwissenschaft; Zeitschrift fuer
Wirtschaftswissenschaft. 3 per yr. ISSN 0075-
2770
- Kerygma und Dogma; Zeitschrift fuer theologische
Forschung und kirchliche Lehre. q. ISSN 0023-
0707

- Kritische Studien zur Geschichtswissenschaft.
irreg.
- LiLi. (Zeitschrift fuer Literaturwissenschaft und
Linguistik) q. ISSN 0049-8653
- Lustrum; Internationale Forschungsberichte aus
dem Bereich des Klassischen Altertums. irreg.
ISSN 0024-7421
- Luther. 3 per yr. (Luther-Gesellschaft)
- Materialien zur Psychoanalyse und analytisch
orientierten Psychotherapie. irreg.
- Mathematisch-Physikalische Semesterberichte; zur
Pflege des Zusammenhangs von Schule und
Universitaet. s-a. ISSN 0025-5823
- Medizinische Psychologie. s-a.
- Neue Hefte fuer Philosophie. irreg., no. 8, 1975.
ISSN 0085-3917
- Neue Sammlung; Goettinger Zeitschrift fuer
Erziehung und Gesellschaft. bi-m. ISSN 0028-
3355
- Opera Slavica. irreg., 1965, no.5. ISSN 0085-4514
- Paedagogica; Daten - Meinungen - Analysen.
irreg., 1971, vol. 10. ISSN 0085-4603
- Praxis der Kinderpsychologie und
Kinderpsychiatrie. 8 per yr. ISSN 0032-7034
- Praxis der Kinderpsychologie und
Kinderpsychiatrie. Beihefte. irreg., 1972, no. 12.
ISSN 0085-5073
- Studien zur Medizingeschichte des Neunzehnten
Jahrunderts. irreg. ISSN 0081-7333
- Universitaet Hamburg. Mathematisches Seminar.
Abhandlungen. 1 vol. per yr. in 2 double nos.
ISSN 0025-5858
- Wege zum Menschen; Monatsschrift fuer Arzt
und Seelsorger, Erzieher, Psychologen und soziale
Berufe. 8 per yr. ISSN 0043-2040
- Wissenschaft und Praxis in Kirche und
Gesellschaft. m. ISSN 0031-2827
- Zeitschrift fuer allgemeine und textile
Marktwirtschaft. q. (Universitaet Muenster.
Forschungsstelle fuer Allgemeine und Textile
Marktwirtschaft)
- Zeitschrift fuer das Gesamte
Genossenschaftswesen. 4 per yr. ISSN 0044-2429
- Zeitschrift fuer Psychosomatische Medizin und
Psychoanalyse. q.
- Zeitschrift fuer Psychosomatische Medizin und
Psychoanalyse. Beihefte. irreg., 1971, no. 3. ISSN
0085-8412
- Zeitschrift fuer Vergleichende Sprachforschung/
Journal of Comparative Linguistic Research into
Indo-European Philology; auf dem Gebiet der
indogermanischen Sprachen. s-a. ISSN 0044-3646

**Redaktion VARTA-Fuehrer**
Schoene Aussicht 6, Postfach 2307, 6380 Bad
Homburg, W. Germany (B.R.D.)
- VARTA Fuehrer durch Deutschland, Westlicher
Teil und Berlin. irreg. ISSN 0083-5250

**Ventla-Verlag**
Postfach 130185, 6200 Wiesbaden 13, W. Germany
(B.R.D.)
- UFO-Nachrichten. bi-m. ISSN 0041-5081
(Deutsche UFO-Studiengesellschaft (DUIST e. V.)

**Verband Bayerischer Berufsschullehrer**
- Jugend in Schule und Beruf. (pub. by Verlag
Lambert Mueller GmbH)

**Verband Beratender Ingenieure**
- Beratende Ingenieure. (pub. by Deutscher
Consulting Verlag)

**Verband der Agrarjournalisten**
- Taschenbuch fuer Agrarjournalisten. (pub. by B.
Behr's Verlag GmbH)

**Verband der Angestellten-Krankenkassen e.V.**
Frankfurter Str. 84, Postfach 241, 5200 Siegburg, W.
Germany (B.R.D.)
- Die Ersatzkasse. m. ISSN 0014-0279

**Verband der Automobilindustrie**
Westendstr. 61, Postfach 174249, 6000 Frankfurt
17, W. Germany (B.R.D.)
- Tatsachen und Zahlen aus der
Kraftverkehrswirtschaft. a. ISSN 0083-548X
- Verband der Automobilindustrie. Jahresbericht. a.

**Verband der Beamten der Bundesanstalt fuer Arbeit**
Dientzenhofer Str. 9a, 8500 Nuernberg, W.
Germany (B.R.D.)
- Der Beamte in der Bundesanstalt fuer Arbeit. bi-
m.

**Verband der Bibliotheken des Landes Nordrhein-Westfalen**
- Verband der Bibliotheken des Landes Nordrhein-Westfalen. Mitteilungsblatt. (pub. by Verlag Dokumentation)

**Verband der Caritas-Konferenzen Deutschlands**
Lorenz-Werthmann-Haus, Postfach 420, 7800 Freiburg i. Br., W. Germany (B.R.D.)
- Begegnen und Helfen. bi-m. (Co-Sponsor: Gemeinschaft der Vinzenzkonferenzen Deutschlands)

**Verband der Chemischen Industrie**
- Chemische Industrie. (pub. by Handelsblatt GmbH)
- Chemische Industrie International. (pub. by Handelsblatt GmbH)

**Verband der Cigarettenindustrie**
Harvestehuder Weg 88, 2000 Hamburg 13, W. Germany (B.R.D.)
- Beitraege zur Tabakforschung. 4 per yr. ISSN 0005-819X

**Verband der Deutschen Bundeswehr e.V.**
- Loyal. (pub. by Konradin-Verlag Robert Kohlhammer GmbH)

**Verband der Deutschen Dental-Industrie e.V.**
- Dental-Dienst. (pub. by Bielefelder Verlagsanstalt KG)
- Dental Echo. (pub. by Helmut Haase-Verlag)

**Verband der Deutschen Fruchtsaft-Industrie e.V.**
- Fluessiges Obst. (pub. by Verlag Fluessiges Obst GmbH)

**Verband der Deutschen Kautschukgesellschaften**
- Kautschuk und Gummi. Kunststoffe. (pub. by Dr. Alfred Huethig Verlag GmbH)

**Verband der Deutschen Schiffbauindustrie e.V.**
An der Alster 1, 2000 Hamburg 1, W. Germany (B.R.D.)
- Deutscher Schiffbau. a.

**Verband der Energieabnehmer e.V.**
- Betriebstechnik. (pub. by Technischer Verlag Resch KG)

**Verband der Freien Presse e.V.**
Postfach 208, 8000 Munich 40, W. Germany (B.R.D.)
- Freie Presse-Korrespondenz. m. ISSN 0016-0768

**Verband der Geschichtslehrer Deutschlands**
- Geschichte in Wissenschaft und Unterricht. (pub. by Ernst Klett Verlag)

**Verband der Haftpflicht-, Unfall- und Kraftverkehrsversicherer e.V.**
Glockengiesserwall 1, 2000 Hamburg 1, W. Germany (B.R.D.)
- Gesamtstatistik der Kraftfahrtversicherung. a. ISSN 0435-7442

**Verband der Koeche Deutschlands e.V.**
- Kueche. (pub. by Rhenania Fachverlag GmbH)

**Verband der Korbwaren-, Korbmoebel- und Kinderwagenindustrie e.V.**
- Present. (pub. by Meisenbach Kg)

**Verband der Kraftfahrzeugteile- und Zweirad-Grosshaendler**
Oberstr. 36-42, 4030 Ratingen, W. Germany (B.R.D.)
- V K G Jahrbuch; Mitgliederverzeichnis. a.

**Verband der Kriegs- und Wehrdienstopfer, Behinderten und Sozialrentner Deutschlands e.V.**
Wurzerstr. 2, 5300 Bonn-Bad Godesberg, W. Germany (B.R.D.)
- Die Fackel. m. ISSN 0014-6447
- V d K-Mitteilungen. m. ISSN 0042-1774

**Verband der Lebensversicherungsunternehmen e.V.**
- Die Deutsche Lebensversicherung. (pub. by Verlag Versicherungswirtschaft e.V.)
- Lebensversicherungs-Medizin. (pub. by Verlag Versicherungswirtschaft e.V.)

**Verband der Niedersaechsischen Landvolkes e.V.**
- Das Landvolk. (pub. by Landbuch-Verlag GmbH)

**Verband der Parlaments- und Verhandlungsstenographen**
Bundeshaus, 5300 Bonn, W. Germany (B.R.D.)
- Neue Stenographische Praxis. q. ISSN 0028-3371

**Verband der Privaten Krankenversicherung e.V.**
- Die Private Krankenversicherung. (pub. by Verlag Versicherungswirtschaft e.V.)

**Verband der Rundfunkhoerer und Fernsehteilnehmer in Bayern e.V.**
- Gong. (pub. by Gong Verlag)

**Verband der Taschen- und Armbanduhren Industrie e.V.**
- Gold und Silber - Uhren und Schmuck. (pub. by Konradin- Verlag Robert Kohlhammer GmbH)

**Verband der Teer- und Asphaltmischwerke e.V.**
- Das Stationaere Mischwerk. (pub. by F.W. Wesel)

**Verband der Tropenlandwirte aus Witzenhausen e.V.**
Stein Str. 19, 3430 Witzenhausen, W. Germany (B.R.D.)
- Tropenlandwirt; Zeitschrift fuer die Landwirtschaft in den Tropen und Subtropen. s-a. ISSN 0041-3186

**Verband der Weiblichen Angestellten e.V.**
Koenigstr. 21, 3000 Hannover, W. Germany (B.R.D.)
- Frau im Beruf. bi-m. ISSN 0016-013X

**Verband der Zuechter des Holsteiner Pferdes**
- Pferde. (pub. by Verlag Wartenberg und Soehne)

**Verband der Zuechter des Oldenburger Pferdes**
Johannisstr. 1, 2900 Oldenburg, W. Germany (B.R.D.)
- Das Oldenburger Sportpferd. 4 per yr. ISSN 0030-2066

**Verband des Deutschen Blumen-Gross- und Importhandels e.V.**
- Blumen. (pub. by Donau-Verlag)

**Verband des Deutschen Fass- und Weinkuefer-Handwerks e.V.**
- Der Fass- und Weinkuefer. (pub. by Gildeverlag Hans-Gerhard Dobler GmbH)

**Verband der Deutschen Gas- und Wasserwerke**
- Allgemeine Gastarife in der Bundesrepublik Deutschland. (pub. by ZfGW-Verlag GmbH)

**Verband des deutschen Tischlerhandwerks**
- Bau- und Moebelschreiner. (pub. by Konradin-Verlag Robert Kohlhammer GmbH)

**Verband Deutsche Sportpresse E.V**
- Der Sportjournalist. (pub. by Presse und Sport)

**Verband Deutscher Akademiker fuer Landwirtschaft, Ernaehrung und Landespflege e.V.**
- V D L-Nachrichten. (pub. by B L V Verlagsgesellschaft MbH)

**Verband Deutscher Badeaerzte**
- Zeitschrift fuer Angewandte Baeder- und Klimaheilkunde. (pub. by F. K. Schattauer Verlag)

**Verband Deutscher Badebetriebe e.V.**
- Physiotherapie. (pub. by Verlag Otto Haase)

**Verband Deutscher Eisenbahningenieure**
- Der Eisenbahningenieur. (pub. by Tetzlaff Verlag GmbH)

**Verband Deutscher Elektrotechniker e.V.**
- Archiv fuer Elektrotechnik. (pub. by Springer-Verlag US)
- Elektrotechnische Zeitschrift. Ausgabe A. (pub. by V D E-Verlag GmbH)
- Elektrotechnische Zeitschrift. Ausgabe B. (pub. by V D E-Verlag Gmbh)

**Verband Deutscher Flugleiter e.V.**
Muehlenweg 41, 3012 Langenhagen, W. Germany (B.R.D.)
- Der Flugleiter. q. ISSN 0015-4563

**Verband Deutscher Hoehlen- und Karstfoerscher e.V.**
- Jahreshefte fuer Karst- und Hoehlenkunde. (pub. by Fr. Mangold'sche Buchhandlung)

**Verband Deutscher Hopfenpflanzer e.V.**
- Hopfen-Rundschau. (pub. by Hopfenverlag)

**Verband Deutscher Mineralbrunnen e.V.**
Kennedyallee 28, 5300 Bonn- Bad Godesberg 6, W. Germany (B.R.B.)
- Der Mineralbrunnen. m.

**Verband Deutscher Postingenieure**
- Der Ingenieur der Deutschen Bundespost. (pub. by Josef Keller Verlag)

**Verband Deutscher Rentenversicherungstraeger**
- Deutsche Rentenversicherung. (pub. by Wirtschaftsdienst Verlag und Druckerei GmbH)

**Verband Deutscher Rotviehzuechter**
- Angler Rinderzucht. (pub. by Rinderzuchtzentrale Angeln)

**Verband Deutscher Rundfunk- und Fernseh-Fachgrosshaendler e.V.**
- Rundfunk - Fernseh - Wirtschaft. (pub. by Verlag Neuer Merkur GmbH)

**Verband Deutscher Schiffswerften e.V.**
An der Alster 1, 2000 Hamburg 1, W. Germany (B.R.D.)
- Werft-Informationen. irreg. (approx. 4 per yr.)

**Verband Deutscher Schulmusikerzieher**
- Musik und Bildung. (pub. by B. Schott's Soehne)

**Verband Deutscher Soldaten e.V.**
Nettelbeckstr. 5, 4000 Duesseldorf 30, W. Germany (B.R.D.)
- Soldat im Volk. ISSN 0038-0970

**Verband Deutscher Sportgeschaefte e.V.**
- Sport und Mode. (pub. by Verlag Chmielorz GmbH und Co)

**Verband Deutscher Sporttaucher e.V.**
- Delphin. (pub. by Verlag Ehrlich und Sohn KG)

**Verband deutscher Stahlwaren-Fachhandler e.V**
- Messer und Schere. (pub. by Verlag Carl Kohler)

**Verband Deutscher Vereine fuer Aquarien- und Terrarienkunde**
- Die Aquarien-und Terrarien-Zeitschrift. (pub. by Alfred Kernen Verlag)

**Verband Deutscher Vermessungsingenieure e.V.**
- Der Vermessungsingenieur. (pub. by Verlag Chmielorz GmbH und Co.)

**Verband Deutscher Zahntechnikerinnungen e.V.**
- Dental Labor. (pub. by Verlag Neuer Merkur GmbH)

**Verband Evangelischer Kirchenchoere Deutschlands**
- Der Kirchenchor. (pub. by Baerenreiter Verlag)

**Verband Evangelischer Kirchenmusiker Deutschlands**
- Der Kirchenmusiker. (pub. by Verlag Merseburger Berlin GmbH)

**Verband Evangelischer Missionskonferenzen**
- Evangelische Mission Jahrbuch. (pub. by Deutsche Evangelische Missionshilfe Verlag)

**Verband Freier Wohnungsunternehmen e.V.**
- Die Freie Wohnungswirtschaft. (pub. by Hanseatisches Werbekontor Heuser und Co.)

**Verband fuer Arbeitsstudien**
Wittichstr. 2, 6100 Darmstadt, W. Germany (B.R.D.)
- Fortschrittliche Betriebsfuehrung and Industrial Engineering. bi-m.
- Refa Nachrichten. bi-m. ISSN 0033-6874

**Verband fuer Cash and Carry Grosshandel e.V.**
- Cash and Carry. (pub. by Neuer Handels-Verlag GmbH und Co. KG)

**Verband fuer Ruten- und Pendelkunde (Radiaesthesie)**
- Zeitschrift fuer Radiaesthesie. (pub. by Herold-Verlag Dr. Franz Wetzel und Co. KG)

**Verband Hannoverscher Warmblutzuechter e.V.**
Johannssenstr. 10, 3000 Hannover, W. Germany (B.R.D.)
- Hannoversches Pferd. bi-m. ISSN 0017-7474

**Verband Kommunaler Stadtreinigungsbetriebe**
- Der Staedtetag. (pub. by W. Kohlhammer GmbH (Stuttgart))

**Verband Oeffentlicher Verkehrsbetriebe**
- Bus und Bahn. (pub. by Alf Teloeken-Verlag KG)
- Handbuch Oeffentlicher Verkehrsbetriebe. (pub. by Erich Schmidt Verlag (Bielefeld))
- Verkehr und Technik. (pub. by Erich Schmidt Verlag (Bielefeld))

**Verband Papier, Buerobedarf, Schreibwaren**
- Fachzeitung fuer den Buerofachhandel ueber Papier, Buerobedarf, Schreibwaren. (pub. by Goeller Verlag)

**Verein Bayerischer Krippenfreunde**
- Der Bayerische Krippenfreund. (pub. by Verlag Josef Habbel)

**Verein Beethoven-Haus Bonn**
Postfach 73, 5300 Bonn 1, W. Germany (B.R.D.)
- Beethoven-Jahrbuch. biennial. ISSN 0522-5949

**Verein der Bibliothekare an Oeffentlichen Buechereien e.V**
- Buch und Bibliothek. (pub. by Verlag Dokumentation)

**Verein der Blinden Geistesarbeiter Deutschlands e.V.**
- Horus. (pub. by G. Schindele Verlag GmbH)

**Verein der Schiffsingenieure in Bremen e.V.**
Brahmsstr. 17, 2863 Ritterhude, W. Germany (B.R.D.)
- Antrieb; Fachzeitschrift fuer Schiffs- und Schiffsbetriebstechnik. bi-m.

**Verein der Textilchemiker und Coloristen e.V.**
- Melliand Textilberichte /International Textile Reports. (pub. by Melliand Textilberichte KG)

**Verein der Zellstoff- und Papier-Chemiker und Ingenieure**
- Auszuege aus der Literatur der Zellstoff- und Papier-Erzeugung und Celluloseverarbeitung. (pub. by Eduard Roether Verlag)

**Verein Deutscher Bibliothekare**
- Jahrbuch der Deutschen Bibliotheken. (pub. by Verlag Otto Harrassowitz)
- Zeitschrift fuer Bibliothekswesen und Bibliographie. (pub. by Vittorio Klostermann)

**Verein Deutscher Eisenhuettenleute**
- Archiv fuer das Eisenhuettenwesen. (pub. by Verlag Stahleisen mbH)
- Stahl und Eisen. (pub. by Verlag Stahleisen mbH)
- Stahleisen Kalender. (pub. by Verlag Stahleisen mbH)

**Verein Deutscher Elektrotechniker e.V.**
- N T Z Nachrichtentechnische Zeitschrift. (pub. by V D E-Verlag GmbH)

**Verein Deutscher Faerber e.V.**
- Textil Praxis International. (pub. by Konradin-Verlag Robert Kohlhammer GmbH)

**Verein Deutscher Giessereifachleute e.V.**
- Giesserei. (pub. by Giesserei-Verlag GmbH)
- Giessereiforschung. (pub. by Giesserei-Verlag GmbH)

**Verein Deutscher Ingenieure**
- B W K. (pub. by V D I-Verlag GmbH)
- Deutsche Kraftfahrtforschung und Strassenverkehrstechnik. (pub. by V D I-Verlag GmbH)
- Forschung im Ingenieurwesen. (pub. by V D I-Verlag GmbH)
- Grundlagen der Landtechnik. (pub. by V D I-Verlag GmbH)
- Technikgeschichte. (pub. by V D I-Verlag GmbH)
- Technikgeschichte in Einzeldarstellungen. (pub. by V D I-Verlag GmbH)
- V D I-Berichte. (pub. by V D I-Verlag GmbH)
- V D I - Forschungshefte. (pub. by V D I-Verlag GmbH)
- V D I-Nachrichten. (pub. by V D I Verlag GmbH)
- V D I-Z. (pub. by V. D. I.-Verlag GmbH)

**Verein Deutscher Ingenieure. Aktionszentrum Technik und Umwelt**
- Umwelt. (pub. by V D I-Verlag GmbH)

**Verein Deutscher Ingenieure. Deutsches Komitee fuer Meeresforschung und Meerestechnik**
- M T. (pub. by V D I-Verlag Gmbh)

**Verein Deutscher Ingenieure. Fachgruppe Betriebstechnik**
- Werkstattstechnik. (pub. by Springer-Verlag US)

**Verein Deutscher Ingenieure. Fachgruppe Textiltechnik**
- Textilbetrieb. (pub. by Vogel- Verlag KG)

**Verein Deutscher Ingenieure. Gesellschaft fuer Mess- und Regelungstechnik**
- Dokumentation Regelungstechnik. (pub. by V D I-Verlag GmbH)

**Verein Deutscher Ingenieure. Gesellschaft Konstruktion und Entwicklung**
- Konstruktion im Maschinen-, Apparate-und Geraetebau. (pub. by Springer-Verlag US)

**Verein Deutscher Ingenieure. Gesellschaft Technische Gebaeudeausruestung**
- H L H, Zeitschrift fuer Heizung, Lueftung, Klimatechnik, Haustechnik. (pub. by V D I-Verlag Gmbh)

**Verein Deutscher Ingenieure. Kommission Reinhaltung der Luft**
- Staub Reinhaltung der Luft. (pub. by V D I-Verlag GmbH)

**Verein Deutscher Maschinenbau Anstalten e.V.**
Lyoner Str. 18, Postfach 710109, 6000 Frankfurt 71, W. Germany (B.R.D.)
- V D M A-Wirtschaftsbild. 5-6 per yr. ISSN 0042-1782
- Wer Baut Maschinen/Who Makes Machinery. (pub. by Verlag Hoppenstedt und Co.)

**Verein Deutscher Sicherheitsingenieure e.V.**
- Sicher ist Sicher. (pub. by Verlag Wilhelm Kluge)

**Verein Deutscher Zementwerke e.V.**
Tannenstr. 2, 4000 Duesseldorf 30, W. Germany (B.R.D.)
- Betontechnische Berichte. (pub. by Beton-Verlag GmbH)
- Verein Deutscher Zementwerke. Forschungsinstitut der Zementindustrie. Taetigkeitsbericht. triennial. ISSN 0507-6714
- Zement-Taschenbuch. (pub. by Bauverlag GmbH)

**Verein Deutsches Bauzentrum e.V.**
- Das Bauzentrum. (pub. by Verlag das Beispiel)

**Verein Freunde und Foerderer der Deutschen Studentenschaft e.V.**
Untere Hausbreite 11, 8000 Munich 45, W. Germany (B.R.D.)
- Durch Stipendien Studieren. a. ISSN 0070-7767
- Numerus Clausus - Alternativen. a.
- Der Studienbeginn. a.
- Der Untermieter. irreg.
- Zulassungsarbeit. irreg.

**Verein fuer die Geschichte Berlins**
Haendelallee 61, 1000 Berlin 21, W. Germany (B.R.D.)
- Verein fuer die Geschichte Berlins. Mitteilungen. w.

**Verein fuer Dithmarscher Landeskunde**
- Dithmarschen. (pub. by Westholsteinische Verlagsanstalt Boyens und Co.)

**Verein fuer Gerberei-Chemie und Technik e.V.**
- Das Leder. (pub. by Eduard Roether Verlag)

**Verein fuer Geschichte der Stadt Nuernberg**
Egidienplatz 23, 8500 Nuernberg, W. Germany (B.R.D.)
- Nuernberger Forschungen. irreg. ISSN 0078-2653
- Verein fuer Geschichte der Stadt Nuernberg. Mitteilungen. a. ISSN 0083-5579

**Verein fuer Geschichte und Altertumskunde Westfalens**
- Westfaelische Zeitschrift. (pub. by Verlag Regensberg)

**Verein fuer Geschichte und Heimatpflege Soest**
Stadtarchiv, 4770 Soest, W. Germany (B.R.D.)
- Soester Beitraege. irreg.
- Soester Zeitschrift. a.

**Verein fuer Hamburgische Geschichte**
ABC-Str. 19, 2000 Hamburg 36, W. Germany (B.R.D.)
- Hamburgische Geschichts- und Heimatblaetter. s-a.
- Verein fuer Hamburgische Geschichte. Zeitschrift. a. ISSN 0083-5587

**Verein fuer Heimatkunde Schwelm**
Haynauer Str. 3, 5830 Schwelm, W. Germany (B.R.D.)
- Beitraege zur Heimatkunde der Stadt Schwelm und ihrer Umgebung. a.

**Verein fuer Heraldik, Genealogie und Verwandte Wissenschaften**
Archivstr. 12-14, 1000 Berlin 33, W. Germany (B.R.D.)
- Herold. q. ISSN 0018-0793

**Verein fuer Kommunalwirtschaft**
- Kommunalwirtschaft. (pub. by Deutscher Kommunal-Verlag GmbH)

**Verein fuer Luebeckische Geschichte und Altertumkunde**
- Verein fuer Luebeckische Geschichte und Altertumskunde. Zeitschrift. (pub. by Max Schmidt-Roemhild Verlag)

**Verein fuer Nassauische Altertumskunde und Geschichtsforschung**
Mainzer Str. 80, 6200 Wiesbaden, W. Germany (B.R.D.)
- Nassauische Annalen. a. ISSN 0077-2887

**Verein fuer Naturkunde in Osthessen e.V.**
- Beitraege zur Naturkunde in Osthessen. (pub. by Verlag Parzeller und Co.)

**Verein fuer Naturwissenschaftliche Heimatforschung zu Hamburg**
Museumstr. 23, Postfach 125, 2000 Hamburg 50, W. Germany (B.R.D.)
- Bombus; Faunistische Mitteilungen aus Nordwestdeutschland. s-a.

**Verein fuer Niedersaechsisches Volkstum e.V.**
Am Wall 187, 2800 Bremen 1, W. Germany (B.R.D.)
- Heimat und Volkstum; Bremer Beitraege zur Niederdeutschen Volkskund. irreg. ISSN 0017-9744

**Verein fuer Reformations Geschichte**
- Archiv fuer Reformationsgeschichte/Archive for Reformation History. (pub. by Guetersloher Verlagshaus Gerd Mohn)

**Verein fuer Schlesische Kirchengeschichte e.V.**
- Jahrbuch fuer Schlesische Kirchengeschichte. (pub. by Verlag Unser Weg)

**Verein fuer Wasser-, Boden- und Lufthygiene**
- Literaturberichte ueber Wasser, Abwasser, Feste Abfallstoffe und Luft. (pub. by Gustav Fischer Verlag)
- Verein fuer Wasser-, Boden- und Lufthygiene. Schriftenreihe. (pub. by Gustav Fischer Verlag)

**Verein fuer Wuerttembergische Kirchengeschichte**
Gaensheidestr. 4, 7000 Stuttgart 1, W. Germany (B.R.D.)
- Blaetter fuer Wuerttembergische Kirchengeschichte. a.

**Verein Naturschutzpark e.V.**
Pfizerstr. 5-7, Postfach 640, 7000 Stuttgart 1, W. Germany (B. R. D.)
- Naturschutz- und Naturparke. q. ISSN 0028-1018

**Verein Trierisch e.V.**
Loewenbrueckener Str. 23, 5500 Trier, W. Germany (B.R.D.)
- Neues Trierisches Jahrbuch fuer Heimatpflege und Heimatgeschichte. a.

**Verein zum Schutze der Alpenpflanzen und -Tiere**
Praterinsel 5, 8000 Munich 22, W. Germany.
- Verein zum Schutze der Alpenpflanzen und -tiere. Jahrbuch. a. ISSN 0083-5625

**Verein zur Erforschung der Fragen der Produktion und Planung Gebauter Umwelt in Zusammenhang Sozialistischer Politik**
- Arch Plus. (pub. by Verlag fuer das Studium der Arbeiterbewegung)

**Verein zur Foerderung der Blindenbildung e.V.**
Bleekstr. 26, 3000 Hannover, W. Germany (B.R.D.)
• Zeitschrift fuer das Blinden- und
  Sehbehindertenbildungswesen. bi-m. ISSN 0006-
  4858

**Verein zur Foerderung der Deutschen Herrenmode
e.V.**
• Herrenjournal. (pub. by Deutscher Fachverlag
  GmbH)

**Verein zur Foerderung Studentischer Sozialarbeit und
Sozialpolitik**
Mollwitzstr. 5, 1000 Berlin 19, W. Germany
(B.R.D.)
• Sozialkompress. s-a.

**Verein zur Pflege der Natur- und Landeskunde in
Schleswig-Holstein und Hamburg**
• Die Heimat. (pub. by Karl Wachholtz Verlag)

**Vereinigte Evangelisch-Lutherische Kirche
Deutschlands**
• Vereinigte Evangelisch-Lutherische Kirche
  Deutschlands. Amtsblatt. (pub. by Lutherisches
  Verlagshaus GmbH)

**Vereinigte Verlagsanstalten GmbH**
Hoeherweg 278, Postfach 8227, 4000 Duesseldorf,
W. Germany (B.R.D.)
• Der Deutsche Forstmann. m. ISSN 0012-012X
  (Bund Deutscher Forstmaenner)

**Vereinigte Wirtschaftsdienste GmbH**
Niederurseler Allee 8-10, Postfach 6105, 6236
Eschborn 1, W. Germany (B.R.D.)
• Aussenhandelsdienst der Industrie- und
  Handelskammern und Wirtschaftsverbaende. w.
  ISSN 0001-1401
• Nachrichten fuer Aussenhandel. d(6 per wk.)
  ISSN 0027-741X (Germany, Federal Republic.
  Bundesstelle fuer Aussenhandelsinformation)
• V W D - Kaffee-Spezialdienst. d. ISSN 0042-1960
• V W D-Kaffee Uebersee Sonderdienst. d. ISSN
  0042-1979
• V W D-Kakao-Spezialdienst. d. ISSN 0042-1987
• V W D - Landwirtschaft und Ernaehrung. 6 per
  w. ISSN 0023-8120

**Vereinigung der Arbeitgeberverbaende der Deutschen
Papierindustrie e.V.**
• Der Papiermacher. (pub. by Dr. Curt Haefner
  Verlag)

**Vereinigung der Deutsch-Griechischen Gesellschaften**
• Hellenika. (pub. by Verlag Ferdinand Kamp)

**Vereinigung der Deutschen Adelsverbaende**
• Deutsches Adelsblatt. (pub. by Von Flotow)

**Vereinigung der Franzoesischlehrer e.V.**
• Franzoesisch Heute. (pub. by Verlag Moritz
  Diesterweg)

**Vereinigung der Freunde der Studentenschaft der
Universitaet Heidelberg e.V.**
Universitaets- Archiv, 6900 Heidelberg 1, W.
Germany (B.R.D.)
• Ruperto-Carola. s-a. ISSN 0035-998X

**Vereinigung der Haus-, Grund- und
Wohnungseigentuemer Frankfurt am Main e.V.**
Niedenau 61, 6000 Frankfurt 1, W. Germany
(B.R.D.)
• Privates Eigentum. m.

**Vereinigung der Landesdenkmalpfleger in der
Bundesrepublik Deutschland**
• Deutsche Kunst und Denkmalpflege. (pub. by
  Deutscher Kunstverlag GmbH)

**Vereinigung der Opfer des Stalinismus e.V.**
Lennestr. 8, 5300 Bonn, W. Germany (B.R.D.)
• Die Freiheitsglocke/Bell of Freedom. 11 per yr.
  ISSN 0016-0911

**Vereinigung der Praktischen Aerzte Bayerns e.V.**
• Forum des Praktischen Arztes. (pub. by Verlag A.
  Fruehmorgen)

**Vereinigung der Seifen-, Parfuem- und Waschmittel-
Fachleute e.V.**
• Seifen, Oele, Fette, Wachse. (pub. by Verlag fuer
  Chemische Industrie)

**Vereinigung der Technischen Ueberwachungsvereine
e.V.**
• T U - Sicherheit und Zuverlaessigkeit in
  Wirtschaft, Betrieb, Verkehr. (pub. by V D I-
  Verlag Gmbh)

**Vereinigung der Verfolgten des Naziregimes**
Rossertstr. 4, 6000 Frankfurt, W. Germany (B.R.D.)
• V V N -Statistik ueber NZ Prozesse. m.

**Vereinigung des Adels in Bayern**
• Genealogisches Handbuch des Bayerischen Adels.
  (pub. by Verlag Degener und Co.)

**Vereinigung Deutscher Contactlinsen-Spezialisten e.V.**
• Die Contactlinse. (pub. by Verlag Willy Schrickel
  (Duesseldorf))

**Vereinigung Deutscher Eisenbahneresperantisten im
Bundesbahn-Sozialwerk**
6000 Frankfurt 1, W. Germany (B.R.D.)
• Germana Esperanta Fervojista Asocio. Bulteno. bi-
  m. ISSN 0016-8866

**Vereinigung Deutscher Elektrizitaetswerke e.V.**
Stresemannallee 23, 6000 Frankfurt, W. Germany
(B.R.D.)
• Atom und Strom. (pub. by Verlags- und
  Wirtschafts- Gesellschaft der Elektrizitaetswerke
  mbH)
• Elektrizitaetswirtschaft. (pub. by Verlags- und
  Wirtschafts- Gesellschaft der Elektrizitaetswerke
  mbH)
• V D E W Arbeitsbericht. a.

**Vereinigung Deutscher Industriebackmeister e.V.**
• Der Industriebackmeister. (pub. by B. Behr's
  Verlag GmbH)

**Vereinigung Freunde der Universitaet Mainz**
Ludwigstr. 8-10, 6500 Mainz, W. Germany (B.R.D.)
• Vereinigung Freunde der Universitaet Mainz.
  Jahrbuch. a. ISSN 0083-565X

**Vereinigung Quickborn e.V.**
Schlueterstr. 50, 2000 Hamburg 13, W. Germany
(B.R.D.)
• Quickborn; Zeitschrift fuer Plattdeutsche Sprache
  und Dichtung. q.

**Vereinigung Sueddeutscher Orthopaeden e.V.**
• Orthopaedische Praxis. (pub. by Medizinisch-
  Literarische Verlagsgesellschaft mbH)

**Vereinigung Suedwestdeutscher Dermatologen**
• Der Sozialversicherungs-Beamte und -Angestellte.
  (pub. by Grosse Verlag GmbH)

**Vereinigung von Afrikanisten in Deutschland**
• Vereinigung von Afrikanisten in Deutschland.
  Schriften. (pub. by Verlag Helmut Buske)

**Vereinigung zur Erforschung der Neueren Geschichte
e.V.**
• Acta Pacis Westphalicae. (pub. by
  Aschendorffsche Verlagsbuchhandlung)

**Vereinigung zur Foerderung des Deutschen
Brandschutzes e.V.**
• V F D B Zeitschrift. (pub. by W. Kohlhammer
  GmbH (Stuttgart))

**Deutscher Verkehrs-Verlag GmbH**
Nordkanalstr. 36, 2000 Hamburg 1, W. Germany
(B.R.D.)
• D V Z. (Deutsche Verkehrs-Zeitung) 3 per wk.
  ISSN 0012-0901
• T I-Touristik Information. bi-m.

**Verkehrs-Verlag J. Fischer**
Paulusstr. 1, Postfach 140175, 4000 Duesseldorf 4,
W. Germany (B.R.D.)
• Fischers Tarif Nachrichten fuer Eisenbahn und
  Kraftwagen; Informationen fuer den
  Gueterverkehr. m. ISSN 0015-2862

**Verlag und Vertriebsgesellschaft mbH**
Breite Str. 69, Postfach 8232, 4000 Duesseldorf 1,
W. Germany (B.R.D.)
• Betriebliche Ausbildungspraxis; Merkblaetter fuer
  Ausbilder in der Eisen- und Metallindustrie. bi-m.
  (Wirtschafts vereinigung Eisen- und Stahlindustrie)
  (Co-sponsors: Arbeitgeberverband Eisen- und
  Stahlindustrie e.V.; Verband Metallindustrieller
  Arbeitgeberverbaende Nordrhein-Westfalen e.V.)

**Verlag 2000 GmbH**
Hohe Str. 28, Postfach 591, 6050 Offenbach 4, W.
Germany (B.R.D.)
• Links; Sozialistische Zeitung. m. ISSN 0024-404X
  (Sozialistisches Buero)
• Theorie und Organisation. irreg.

**Verlag Versicherungswirtschaft e.V.**
Klosestr. 22, 7500 Karlsruhe, W. Germany (B.R.D.)
• Die Deutsche Lebensversicherung. a. ISSN 0070-
  4237 (Verband der
  Lebensversicherungsunternehmen e.V.)
• Lebensversicherungs-Medizin; Zeitschrift fuer
  Diagnose und Prognose. bi-m. ISSN 0024-0044
  (Verband der Lebensversicherungsunternehmen
  e.V.)
• Neumanns Jahrbuch der Deutschen
  Versicherungswirtschaft. Teil 1:
  Personenversicherung (Lebens- und
  Krankenversicherung) a. ISSN 0077-7773
• Neumanns Jahrbuch der Deutschen
  Versicherungswirtschaft. Teil 2: Schaden- und
  Rueckversicherung. a. ISSN 0077-7781
• Neumanns Jahrbuch der Deutschen
  Versicherungswirtschaft. Teil 3: Institutionen,
  Uebersichten und Anschriften. a. ISSN 0077-
  779X
• Die Private Krankenversicherung. bi-m. (Verband
  der Privaten Krankenversicherung e.V.)
• Versicherungswirtschaft. s-m. ISSN 0042-4358

**Versoehnungsbund e.V.**
Jochen-Klepper-Str., 2082 Uetersen, W. Germany
(B.R.D.)
• Gewaltfreie Aktion; Vierteljahreshefte fuer
  Frieden und Gerechtigkeit. q. ISSN 0016-9390

**Verlag Versorgungswirtschaft**
Isoldenstr. 2, 8000 Munich 40, W. Germany
(B.R.D.)
• Versorgungswirtschaft. m. ISSN 0042-4382

**Versuchs- und Lehranstalt fuer Brauerei in Berlin**
Seestr. 13, 1000 Berlin 65, W. Germany (B.R.D.)
• Monatsschrift fuer Brauerei; Fachzeitschrift fuer
  Brauereien, Maelzereien und die
  Getraenkeindustrie. m.
• Tageszeitung fuer Brauerei; Fachzeitung fuer
  Brauereien, Maelzereien und d.
  Getraenkeindustrie. bi-w. ISSN 0039-8942

**Versuchs- und Lehranstalt fuer Spiritusfabrikation
und Fermentationstechnologie**
Seestr. 13, 1000 Berlin 65, W. Germany (B.R.D.)
• Die Branntweinwirtschaft; Zeitschrift fuer
  Spiritusindustrie. s-m. ISSN 0006-9159
• Spirituosen-Jahrbuch. a. ISSN 0081-3729

**Vier-Tuerme-Verlag**
8711 Muensterschwarzach, W. Germany (B.R.D.)
• Muensterschwarzacher Studien. irreg. ISSN 0077-
  2011 (Benediktinerabtei Muensterschwarzach)

**Verlag und Werbung Otto Vieth**
Alfredstr. 1, 2000 Hamburg 76, W. Germany
(B.R.D.)
• ANEP-Europen Petroleum Yearbook/Jahrbuch
  der Europaeischen Erdoelindustrie/Annuaire
  Europeen du Petrole. a. ISSN 0066-1716

**Friedr. Vieweg und Sohn Verlagsgesellschaft mbH**
Gustav-Stresemann-Ring 12-16, 6200 Wiesbaden,
W. Germany (B.R.D.)
• Angewandte Informatik/Applied Informatics. m.
  ISSN 0013-5704
• Beitraege zur Physik der Atmosphaere/
  Contributions to Atmospheric Physics. q. ISSN
  0005-8173
• Linguistische Berichte. bi-m. ISSN 0024-3930
• P T B Mitteilungen Forschen und Pruefen. bi-m.
  (Physikalisch-Technische Bundesanstalt)
• Zeitschrift fuer Flugwissenschaften. m. ISSN
  0044-2739 (Wissenschaftliche Gesellschaft fuer
  Luft- und Raumfahrt e.V GW)

**Curt R. Vincentz Verlag**
Am Schiffsgraben 43, Postfach 6247, 3000
Hannover, W. Germany (B.R.D.)
- Das Altenheim; Organ der gemeinnuetzigen und
  privaten Alten- und Altenpflegeheime. m. ISSN
  0002-6573
- Altenpflege; Organ der Fachkraefte in Altenpflege
  und Altenhilfe. m.
- Die Bauverwaltung. m. (Germany, Federal
  Republic. Bundesministerium fuer Raumordnung,
  Bauwesen und Staedtebau)
- Farbe und Lack. m. ISSN 0014-7699 (Gesellschaft
  Deutscher Chemiker)
- Industrie Lackierbetrieb. m. ISSN 0019-9109
- Schmiertechnik und Tribologie. bi-m. ISSN 0036-
  6218 (Gesellschaft fuer Tribologie und
  Schmierungstechnik)
- Technischer Handel; Zentralblatt fuer technische
  Bedarfsartikel aller Art. m. ISSN 0040-1552
  (Arbeitsgemeinschaft der Verbaende der
  Technischen Haendler)
- Zentralblatt fuer Industriebau. m. ISSN 0044-4227
  (Arbeitsgemeinschaft Industriebau e.V.)

**Verlag Curt Visel**
Schelhornstr. 17, 8940 Memmingen, W. Germany
(B.R.D.)
- Graphische Kunst. s-a.
- Illustration 63. 3 per yr. ISSN 0019-2457

**Verlag Heinrich Vogel**
Kreuzstr. 14, 8000 Munich 2, W. Germany (B.R.D.)
- Fahrschule; Zeitschrift fuer die Kraftfahrlehrer. m.
  ISSN 0014-6838
- Der Kraftfahrzeugvermieter. q. ISSN 0023-4400
  (Gesamtverband der Kraftfahrzeug- Vermieter
  Deutschlands e.V.)
- Nutzfahrzeug; Transport und Technik. m. ISSN
  0029-6686
- Omnibus-Revue. m. ISSN 0030-2279

**Vogel-Verlag KG**
Max-Planck-Str. 7, Postfach 800, 8700 Wuerzburg,
W. Germany (B. R. D.)
- Agrartechnik International. 4 per yr.
- Autofachmann. m. (Zentralverband des
  Kraftfahrzeughandwerks)
- Automobil-Industrie; Fachjournal fuer Forschung,
  Konstruktion und Fertigung in der gesamten
  Automobilwirtschaft. 4 per yr. ISSN 0005-1306
- Consulting; Fachmagazin fuer beratende
  Ingenieure und ihre Auftraggeber. m. ISSN 0045-
  821X
- Elektrische Ausruestung fuer Maschine und
  Betrieb. bi-m. ISSN 0013-5429 (U.S. Subscr. to:
  Ernest L. Weinbert, 424 Madison Ave., New
  York, NY 10017)
- Elektro-Jahr; eine Neuheiten-Dokumentation der
  Elektro-Industrie. a. ISSN 0070-9956
- Elektro Markt. m. ISSN 0013-5577
- Elektronikpraxis. 10 per yr. ISSN 0013-5682
- Elektrotechnik. s-m. ISSN 0013-581X
- Europa Industrie Revue. Maschinenmarkt. q.
- Export-Berater. 6 per yr. ISSN 0014-5114
- Export-Markt. 2 per wk. ISSN 0046-2942
- K F Z-Betrieb und Automarkt. (Kraftfahrzeug) bi-
  w. ISSN 0047-3049 (Zentralverband des
  Kraftfahrzeughandwerks)
- Management Wissen. m.
- Management Wissen Jahrbuch. a.
- Maschinenmarkt. s-w. ISSN 0025-4509
- Radio Fernseh Phono Praxis. m. ISSN 0033-7897
- Textilbetrieb. m. (Verein Deutscher Ingenieure.
  Fachgruppe Textiltechnik)
- Werbeartikel-Berater; adviser for the use of
  business gifts. q.

**Vogel-Verlag. Zweigniederlassung Duesseldorf**
Talstr. 32A, Postfach 8311, 4000 Duesseldorf 1, W.
Germany (B.R.D.)
- Baender, Bleche, Rohre; Fachzeitschrift fuer
  Walzwerkstechnik, Blechbearbeitung, gezogene
  und geschweisste Rohre. m. ISSN 0005-3848
- Draht-Welt; Fachorgan fuer die Erzeugung,
  Bearbeitung und Verarbeitung von Draehten und
  Stangen. m. ISSN 0012-592X
- Wire World International. bi-m. ISSN 0043-6046

**Vogelkundliche Beobachtungsstation Untermain**
Steinauer Str. 44, 6000 Frankfurt, W. Germany
(B.R.D.)
- Luscinia; vogelkundliche Zeitschrift fuer Hessen.
  s-a. ISSN 0024-7391

**Vogelzug-Verlag**
Moeggingen, W. Germany (B.R.D.)
- Vogelwarte. 2 per yr. ISSN 0049-6650

**Arno Volk Verlag Hans Gerig KG**
Drususgasse 7-11, 5000 Cologne 1, W. Germany
(B.R.D.)
- Analecta Musicologia. irreg., vol. 14, 1975. ISSN
  0569-9827 (Deutsches Historisches Institut in
  Rom IT. Musikgeschichtliche Abteilung)
- Concentus Musicus. irreg., vol. 3, 1974.
  (Deutsches Historisches Institut in Rom IT.
  Musikgeschichtliche Abteilung)

**Volksbund Deutsche Kriegsgraeberfuersorge E.V.**
Werner- Hilpert- Str. 2, 3500 Kassel 1, W. Germany
(B.R.D.)
- Kriegsgraeberfuersorge. q. ISSN 0023-4648
- Stimme und Weg; Zeitschrift fuer junge
  Menschen. q. ISSN 0039-1484

**Volkswirtschaftlicher Verlag GmbH**
Sandstr. 17, Postfach 1120, 8960 Kempten 1, W.
Germany (B.R.D.)
- Milchwissenschaft; Zeitschrift fuer
  Ernaehrungsforschung und
  Lebensmittelwissenschaften. m. ISSN 0026-3788

**Industrieverlag Von Hernhaussen KG**
Ernst-Mey-Str. 8, Postfach 1380, 7022 Leinfelden,
W. Germany (B.R.D.)
- Erdoel und Kohle, Erdgas, Petrochemie. m. ISSN
  0014-0058 (Deutsche Gesellschaft fuer
  Mineraloelwissenschaft und Kohlechemie)
- Die Ernaehrungsindustrie. bi-m. ISSN 0014-0236
- Fette - Seifen - Anstrichmittel. m. ISSN 0015-
  038X (Deutsche Gesellschaft fuer
  Fettwissenschaft e. V.)

**Philipp Von Zabern**
Welschnonnengasse 11, Postfach 4065, 6500 Mainz,
W. Germany (B.R.D.)
- Arbeitsblaetter fuer Restauratoren. 2 per yr. ISSN
  0066-5738 (Roemisch-Germanisches
  Zentralmuseum, Mainz)
- Archaeologisches Korrespondenzblatt. irreg.
  (Roemisch-Germanisches Zentralmuseum, Mainz)
- Fuehrer zu Vor- und Fruegeschichtlichen
  Denkmaelern. irreg., vol. 32, 1977. ISSN 0071-
  9757 (Roemisch-Germanisches Zentralmuseum,
  Mainz)
- Kolloquium ueber Spaetantike und
  Fruehmittelalterliche Skulptur. biennial. ISSN
  0075-6563
- Roemische Bronzen aus Deutschland. irreg. ISSN
  0080-3782
- Tiryns. irreg., 1971, vol. 5. ISSN 0082-450X
  (Deutsches Archaeologisches Institut, Athens GR)
- Trierer Grabungen und Forschungen. irreg, vol.
  10, 1977. ISSN 0082-643X (Rheinisches
  Landesmuseum, Trier)

**Vulkan-Verlag Dr. W. Classen**
Hollestr. 1G, Postfach 7049, 4300 Essen, W.
Germany (B.R.D.)
- Elektrowaerme International. m. ISSN 0020-9147
  (Deutsches Komitee fuer Elektrowaerme)
- Gas Waerme International. m. ISSN 0020-9384
  (Gaswaerme- Institut Essen)
- Jahrbuch der Schleiff-, Iton-, Laepp- und
  Poliertechnik. a. ISSN 0075-2398
- Konstruktiver Ingenieurbau Berichte. 3 per yr.
  ISSN 0023-3633 (Institut fuer Konstruktiven
  Ingenieurbau)
- Technische Akademie Wuppertal. Berichte. irreg.
  ISSN 0084-3091
- Technische Mitteilungen. m. ISSN 0040-1439
  (Haus der Technik e.V., Essen)
- 3 R-International. m. (Rohrleitungsverband e.V.)

**Karl Wachholtz Verlag**
Gaensemarkt 1, Postfach 255, 2350 Neumuenster,
W. Germany (B.R.D.)
- Gesellschaft fuer Schleswig-Holsteinische
  Geschichte. Zeitschrift. irreg. ISSN 0072-4254
- Die Heimat. m. ISSN 0017-9701 (Verein zur
  Pflege der Natur- und Landeskunde in Schleswig-
  Holstein und Hamburg)
- Literatur in Wissenschaft und Unterricht. q. ISSN
  0024-4643 (Universitaet Kiel. Englisches Seminar)
- Offa-Jahrbuch; Vor- und Fruehgeschichte. a. ISSN
  0078-3714
- Schleswig-Holstein. m. ISSN 0036-6161
  (Schleswig- Holsteinischer Heimatbund)
- Verein fuer Niederdeutsche Sprachforschung.
  Korrespondenzblatt. q.

**Karl Dieter Wagner (Hamburg)**
Rothenbaumchaussee 1, 2000 Hamburg 13, W.
Germany (B.R.D.)
- Hamburger Jahrbuch fuer Musikwissenschaft. a.

**Waisenhaus Buchdruckerei und Verlag**
Waisenhausdamm 13, 3300 Braunschweig, W.
Germany (B. R. D.)
- Raabe- Gesellschaft. Jahrbuch. a. ISSN 0075-2371

**Walhalla- U. Praetoria-Verlag Georg Zwickenpflug**
Dolomitenstr. 1, Postfach 340, 8400 Regensburg 2,
W. Germany (B.R.D.)
- Der Bankangestellte. a. ISSN 0067-3781
  (Deutsche Angestellten-Gewerkschaft)
- Bayerisches Beamten-Jahrbuch. a. ISSN 0067-
  4702 (Bayerischer Beamtenbund)
- Bayerisches Forstdienst-Taschenbuch. a. ISSN
  0067-4710 (Bund Deutscher Forstmaenner.
  Landesverband Bayern e.V.)
- Deutscher Arbeitsamtskalender. a. ISSN 0415-
  6552
- Deutscher Justiz-Kalender. a.
- Deutscher Sozialversicherungs- Kalender. a. ISSN
  0417-3228
- Deutsches Beamten-Jahrbuch; Bundesausgabe. a.
  ISSN 0070-4423
- Jahrbuch fuer Bundesbahnbeamte. a. ISSN 0075-
  2576
- Steuer-Gewerkschafts-Handbuch. a. (Bund
  Deutscher Steuerbeamten) (Co-sponsor: Deutsche
  Steuer-Gewerkschaft)
- Taschenbuch fuer den Oeffentlichen Dienst. a.
  ISSN 0082-1888
- Taschenbuch fuer Ingenieure und Techniker im
  Oeffentlichen Dienst. a. ISSN 0082-1926
  (Deutsche Angestellten-Gewerkschaft)
- Taschenbuch fuer Ingenieure und Techniker in
  Industrie und Wirtschaft. a. ISSN 0082-1918
- Zollkalender. a. (Bund der Deutschen
  Zollbeamten)

**Walter Eucken Institut**
- Wirtschaftswissenschaftliche und
  Wirtschaftsrechtliche Untersuchungen. (pub. by
  Verlag J.C.B. Mohr (Paul Siebeck))

**Walter-Verlag GmbH**
Erwinstr. 58, Postfach 1708, 7800 Freiburg, W.
Germany (B.R.D.)
- Zeitschrift fuer Parapsychologie und Grenzgebiete
  der Psychologie. q. ISSN 0028-3479

**Waren Einkaufs- und Vertriebs-Gesellschaft mbH**
Karl-Muck-Platz 1, 2000 Hamburg 36, W. Germany
(B.R.D.)
- Der Angestellte. 8 per yr. ISSN 0028-307X
  (Deutsche Angestellten-Gewerkschaft)
- Jugendpost; Zeitschrift der D A G- Jugend. 8 per
  yr. ISSN 0022-5959 (Deutsche Angestellten-
  Gewerkschaft)
- Der Standpunkt. 8 per yr. ISSN 0038-9722
  (Deutsche Angestellten-Gewerkschaft)

**Verlag Wartenberg und Soehne**
Theodorstr. 41, 2000 Hamburg 50, W. Germany
(B.R.D.)
- Pferde; Zucht und Sport in Schleswig-Holstein
  und Hamburg. m. (Verband der Zuechter des
  Holsteiner Pferdes)

**Wasser- und Abwasser-Forschung Verlagsgesellschaft
MbH und Co.**
Ainmillerstr. 34, 8000 Munich 40, W. Germany
(B.R.D.)
- Zeitschrift fuer Wasser- und Abwasserforschung.
  (Journal for Water and Waste Water Research) bi-
  m. ISSN 0044-3727 (Gesellschaft Deutscher
  Chemiker. Fachgruppe Wasserchemie)

**Webe Mit**
Post Winterbach, 7065 Manolzweiler, W. Germany
(B.R.D.)
- Webe Mit; Zeitschrift fuer das Handweben. 4 per
  yr. ISSN 0043-1699

**Gerd-Volker Weege**
Bruening Str. 35, 2150 buxtehude, W. Germany
(B.R.D.)
- Konditor-Zeitung; Blaetter fuer die
  Suesswarenindustrie. m. ISSN 0023-2432

**Verlag Weg zur Gesundheit**
Fallersleber- Tor- Wall 21, 3300 Braunschweig, W.
Germany (B.R.D.)
- Weg zur Gesundheit; Zeitschrift fuer naturliche
  Gesundheitspflege. bi-m. ISSN 0043-2032
  (Biochemischer Bund Deutschlands e.V.)

**Wehr und Wissen Verlagsgesellschaft GmbH**
Heilsbachstr., Postfach 87, 5300 Bonn-Duisdorf, W.
Germany (B.R.D.)
- Beitraege zur Wehrforschung. irreg. ISSN 0067-
  5253 (Arbeitskreis fuer Wehrforschung)
- Jahrbuch der Luftwaffe. a. ISSN 0075-2320
- Jahrbuch der Wehrmedizin. biennial. ISSN 0075-
  241X
- Jahrbuch der Wehrtechnik. a. ISSN 0075-2428
- Jahrbuch des Heeres. biennial. ISSN 0075-2282
- Taschenbuch fuer den Fernmeldedienst. a. ISSN
  0082-1861
- Taschenbuch fuer Logistik. a. ISSN 0082-1942
- Wehrtechnik, Vereinigt mit Wehr und Wirtschaft;
  Monatsschrift fuer Wirtschaftliche Fragen der
  Verteidigung, Luftfahrt und Industrie. m.

**Wehrpolitische Information**
Spichernstr. 34a, Postfach 190302, 5000 Cologne 1,
W. Germany (B.R.D.)
- Wehrpolitische Information. w. ISSN 0043-2164

**Fr. Weidemann's Buchhandlung (H.Witt)**
Georgstr. 11, Postfach 6406, 3000 Hannover, W.
Germany (B.R.D.)
- Fuehrer durch die Technische Literatur; Katalog
  technischer Werke fuer Studium und Praxis. a.
  ISSN 0071-9749

**Weinberg und Keller Verlag**
Poststr. 7, Postfach 260, 5580 Traben-Trarbach, W.
Germany (B.R.D.)
- Weinberg und Keller. m.

**Deutscher Weinwirtschaftsverlag Diemer und
Meininger KG**
Uferstr. 23, Postfach 1680, 6500 Mainz, W.
Germany (B.R.D.)
- Die Weinwirtschaft; Fachzeitschrift fuer Technik
  und Marketing. w.

**Ch. Wellmann**
Wielandstr. 32, 6000 Frankfurt 1, W. Germany
(B.R.D.)
- Antilmilitarismus Information. m. (Subscr. to: c/o
  Brigitta Gruending, Noerdliche Auffahrtsallee 20/
  I, D-8000 Munich 19, W. Germany (B.R.D.))

**Welt Am Sonnabend GmbH**
Adlerstr. 22, Postfach 8509, 4000 Duesseldorf 1, W.
Germany (B.R.D.)
- Frau. w.
- Neue Welt. w.

**Verlag Weltarchiv GmbH**
Neuer Jungfernstieg 21, 2000 Hamburg 36, W.
Germany (B.R.D.)
- Bibliographie der Wirtschaftspresse. m. ISSN
  0006-1417 (H W W A - Institut fuer
  Wirtschaftsforschung, Hamburg)
- Intereconomics; review of international trade and
  development. bi-m. ISSN 0020-5346 (H W W A -
  Institut fuer Wirtschaftsforschung, Hamburg)
- Konjunktur von Morgen. bi-w. ISSN 0023-3439
  (H W W A - Institut fuer Wirtschaftsforschung,
  Hamburg)
- Wirtschaftsdienst. m. ISSN 0043-6275 (H W W A
  - Institut fuer Wirtschaftsforschung, Hamburg)

**Weltfernschachbund (I J C F)**
Ottersbekallee 21, 2000 Hamburg 19, W. Germany
(B.R.D.)
- Fernschach. bi-m.

**Weltforum Verlags-Gesellschaft mbH**
Tintorettostr. 1, 8000 Munich 19, W. Germany
(B.R.D.)
- Internationales Afrikaforum. q. ISSN 0020-9430
  (Europaeisches Institut fuer Politische,
  Wirtschaftliche und Soziale Fragen e.V.)
- Internationales Asienforum. q. ISSN 0020-9449
  (Europaeisches Institut fuer Politische,
  Wirtschaftliche und Soziale Fragen e.V.)

**Karl Wenschow GmbH**
(Subsidiary of: Sueddeutschr Verlag GmbH)
Wartburgplatz 9, 8000 Munich 40, W. Germany
(B.R.D.)
- Bayern in Zahlen. m. ISSN 0005-7215 (Bayern.
  Statistisches Landesamt)

**Werk-Verlag Dr. Edmund Banaschewski**
Hans-Cornelius-Str.4, 8032 Munich-Graelfelfing, W.
Germany (B.R.D.)
- Aerztliche Praxis; Die Zeitung des Arztes in
  Klinik und Praxis. s-w. ISSN 0001-9534
- Euromed; Das europaeisch-medizinische Magazin.
  s-m. ISSN 0014-2425
- Pro Medico. m. ISSN 0032-907X
- Rohstoff-Rundschau; Fachblatt des gesamten
  Handels mit Alt-und Abfallstoffen. s-m. ISSN
  0035-7863
- Zahnaerztliche Praxis. fortn. ISSN 0044-1651

**Werkschriften- Verlag GmbH**
Bachstr. 4, 6900 Heidelberg 1, W. Germany
(B.R.D.)
- Magazin fuer Mitarbeiter - Werk und Leben.
  fortn.

**Werner-Verlag GmbH**
Berliner Allee 11a, Postfach 8529, 4000 Duesseldorf
1, W. Germany (B.R.D.)
- Baurecht. bi-m. ISSN 0340-7489
- Rechtsprechung der Bau-Ausfuehrung. m. ISSN
  0034-1371
- Das Wirtschaftsstudium- WISU; Zeitschrift fuer
  Studium und Examen. m.
- Zeitschrift fuer Miet- und Raumrecht. m. ISSN
  0340-7497

**Wertpapierboerse in Stuttgart**
Hospitalstr. 12, Postfach 390, 7000 Stuttgart 1, W.
Germany (B.R.D.)
- Wertpapierboerse in Stuttgart. Amtliches
  Kursblatt. d.(5 per w.) ISSN 0003-2158

**F. W. Wesel**
Rheinstr. 219, Postfach 1110, 7570 Baden-Baden,
W. Germany (B.R.D.)
- Die Naturstein- Industrie. m. ISSN 0028-1034
  (Bundesverband der Naturstein-Industrie)
- Das Stationaere Mischwerk. q. (Verband der Teer-
  und Asphaltmischwerke e.V.)

**Weser-Kurier GmbH**
Martinistr. 43, Postfach 38, 2800 Bremen 1, W.
Germany (B.R.D.)
- Weserlotse; Bremer Wirtschafts- und Hafendienst.
  m. ISSN 0043-2857 (Bremische Hafenvertretung
  e. V.)

**Weserbund e. V.**
Am Wall 187, Postfach 1861, 2800 Bremen 1, W.
Germany (B.R.D.)
- Die Weser; Organ fuer Angelegenheiten des
  Wesergebietes, insbesondere des Verkehrs, der
  Wirtschaft, der Landeskultur und
  Wasserwirtschaft. m. ISSN 0043-2849

**Westdeutsche Verlagsanstalt GmbH**
Bruederstr. 30, Postfach 335, 4900 Herford, W.
Germany (B. R. D.)
- Aussteuer Bett und Couch. m. ISSN 0004-8259
- Caravan Camping-Journal; Zeitschrift fuer
  Camper, Caravaner, Touristen. m.
- Heimtex; trade journal for interior decoration. m.
  ISSN 0017-9876 (Fachverband des Deutschen
  Teppich- und Gardinenhandels e.V.)
- Stander. m. ISSN 0038-9706 (Deutscher
  Motoryachtverband e.V.)
- Waescherei- und Reinigungs- Praxis. m. ISSN
  0042-9937 (Gesamtverband Neuzeitliche
  Textilpflege- Betriebe Deutschlands e.V.)

**Westdeutscher Rundfunk**
Wallrafplatz 5, 5000 Cologne, W. Germany (B.R.D.)
- Hoerspiele im Westdeutschen Rundfunk. s-a.
  ISSN 0018-313X

**Westdeutscher Verlag**
Openhovener Str. 1, Postfach 1620, 5670 Opladen,
W. Germany (B.R.D.)
- Rheinisch-Westfaelische Akademie der
  Wissenschaften. Veroeffentlichungen. irreg. ISSN
  0066-5754
- Zeitschrift fuer Handelswissenschaftliche
  Forschung. m.

**Westdeutscher Verlag GmbH**
Gustav-Stresemann-Ring 12, 6200 Wiesbaden, W.
Germany (B.R.D.)
- Internationales Jahrbuch fuer Religionssoziologie.
  a. ISSN 0074-9850
- Koelner Schriften zur Politischen Wissenschaft.
  irreg. ISSN 0075-6539 (Universitaet zu Koeln.
  Forschungsinstitut fuer Politische Wissenschaft
  und Europaeische Fragen)

- Koelner Zeitschrift fuer Soziologie und
  Sozialpsychologie. 4 per yr. ISSN 0023-2653
- Leviathan; Zeitschrift fuer Sozialwissenschaft. q.
- Papyrologica Coloniensia. ISSN 0078-9410
  (Rheinisch-Westfaelische Akademie der
  Wissenschaften)
- Schmalenbachs Zeitschrift fuer
  Betriebswirtschaftliche Forschung. m. ISSN 0036-
  6196 (Schmalenbach-Gesellschaft)
- Statistische Hefte/Cahiers Statistiques/Statistical
  Papers. q. ISSN 0039-0631
- Zeitschrift fuer Parlamentsfragen. q. (Deutsche
  Vereinigung fuer Parlamentsfragen)

**Georg Westermann Verlag**
Georg-Westermann-Allee 66, Postfach 3320, 3300
Braunschweig, W. Germany (B.R.D.)
- Archiv fuer das Studium der neueren Sprachen
  und Literaturen. 2 per yr. ISSN 0003-8970
- Geographische Rundschau. m. ISSN 0016-7460
- Geographische Rundschau. Beiheft. bi-m.
- Geolit. s-a until 1978, q. thereafter.
- Die Grundschule. m. ISSN 0533-3431
- Lehrmittel Aktuell; Informationen fuer die
  Unterrichtspraxis. bi-m.
- Museum. m.
- Paedagogica Europaea. 3 per yr. ISSN 0078-7787
  (European Cultural Foundation. Council for
  Cultural Co-Operation FR)
- Schul-Management. bi-m.
- Schulleiter Handbuch. q.
- Unterricht. s-a until 1978, q. thereafter.
- Westermanns Monatshefte; welt - kunst -kultur.
  m. ISSN 0043-3438
- Westermanns Paedagogische Beitraege. m. ISSN
  0043-3446

**Westfaelische Gesellschaft fuer Genealogie und
Familienforschung**
- Beitraege zur Westfaelischen Familienforschung.
  (pub. by Aschendorffsche Verlagsbuchhandlung)

**Westfaelische Verlagsgesellschaft MbH**
Ostenhellweg 42, 4600 Dortmund, W. Germany
(B.R.D.)
- Bilanz; magazine for economics and politics. bi-m.

**Westkreuz Druckerei und Verlag**
Rehagener Str. 30, 1000 Berlin 49, W. Germany
(B.R.D.)
- Der Arzneimittelbrief; unabhaengiges
  Informationsblatt fuer den Arzt. m.

**Erich Wewel Verlag**
Anzinger Str. 1, 8000 Munich 80, W. Germany
(B.R.D.)
- Der Prediger und Katechet. 6 per yr. ISSN 0032-
  7212

**A.u.I. Wezler Verlag**
Langenhege 62b, 2057 Reinbeck, W. Germany
(B.R.D.)
- Studien zur Indologie und Iranistik. irreg.

**Herbert Wichmann Verlag**
Rheinstr. 122, Postfach 210729, 7500 Karlsruhe 21,
W. Germany (B.R.D.)
- Allgemeine Vermessungs-Nachrichten; Zeitschrift
  fuer alle Zweige des Vermessungs,- Karten-und
  Liegenschaftswesens sowie fuer Landesplanung
  und die Ermittlung von Grundstueckswerten. m.
  ISSN 0002-5968
- Bildmessung und Luftbildwesen; Zeitschrift fuer
  Photogrammetrie und Fernerkundung. q. ISSN
  0006-2421 (Deutsche Gesellschaft fuer
  Photogrammetrie)

**Kommissionverlag Max Wiedebusch**
Dammtorstr. 20, 2000 Hamburg 6, W. Germany
(B.R.D.)
- Bundesforschungsanstalt fuer Forst- und
  Holzwirtschaft in Reinbeck. Mitteilungen. ISSN
  0007-5892 (Germany, Federal Republic.
  Bundesforschungsanstalt fuer Forst- und
  Holzwirtschaft in Reinbeck)

**Wienand Verlag KG**
Postfach 410948, 5000 Cologne 41, W. Germany
(B.R.D.)
- Symbolon; Jahrbuch fuer Symbolforschung. irreg.,
  vol. 9 (n.f. 2), 1975. ISSN 0082-0660
  (Gesellschaft fuer Wissenschaftliche
  Symbolforschung)

**Wienerwald GmbH**
Elsenheimerstr. 61, 8000 Munich 21, W. Germany
(B. R. D.)
- W Wintern; Zeitschrift fuer alle Mitarbeiter des
  Wienerwaldes. bi-m.
- Wienerwald; Zeitung fuer alle Gaeste. bi-m.

**Wila Verlag fuer Wirtschaftswerbung Wilhelm Lampl**
Landsberger Str. 191a, 8000 Munich 21, W.
Germany (B.R.D.)
- Auszuege aus den Auslegeschriften. w.
- Auszuege aus den Gebrauchsmustern. w. ISSN
  0005-0571
- Auszuege aus den Offenlegungsschriften. Teil 1.
  Grund- und Rohstoffindustrie, Chemie und
  Huettenwesen, Bauwesen, Bergbau. w.
- Auszuege aus den Offenlegungsschriften. Teil 2.
  Elektrotechnik, Physik, Feinmechanik und Optik,
  Akustik. w.
- Auszuege aus den Offenlegungsschriften. Teil 3.
  Uebrige Verarbeitungsindustrie und
  Arbeitsverfahren, Maschinen- und Fahrzeugbau,
  Ernaehrung, Landwirtschaft. w.
- Warenzeichenblatt. Teil 1: Angemeldete Zeichen.
  s-m. ISSN 0043-0331 (Deutsches Patentamt)
- Wahrenzeichenblatt. Teil 2: Eingetragene Zeichen.
  s-m. ISSN 0043-034X (Deutsches Patentamt)

**Wilhelm- Forster- Sternwarte e.V**
Munsterdamm 90, 1000 Berlin 41, W. Germany
(B.R.D.)
- Gruppe Berliner Mondbeobachter. Protokoll der
  Sitzung. m. (prep. by its Gruppe Berliner
  Mondbeobachter)

**Winfried-Werk GmbH**
Frauenorstr. 5, Postfach 100085, 8900 Augsburg 1,
W. Germany (B.R.D.)
- Weltbild; das Magazin fuer kritische Leser. fortn.
  ISSN 0049-7126

**Carl Winter Universitaetsverlag**
Lutherstr. 59, 6900 Heidelberg, W. Germany
(B.R.D.)
- Beitraege zur Namenforschung. 4 per yr. ISSN
  0005-8114
- Bibliothek der Klassischen
  Altertumswissenschaften. Neue Folge. irreg. ISSN
  0067-8201
- Deutscher Altphilologen-Verband.
  Mitteilungsblatt. q. ISSN 0011-9830
- Euphorion; Zeitschrift fuer Literaturgeschichte. 4
  per yr. ISSN 0014-2328
- Frankfurter Beitraege zur Germanistik. irreg., vol.
  15, 1977. ISSN 0071-9226
- Germanisch-Romanische Monatsschrift. 4 per yr.
  ISSN 0016-8904
- Gymnasium; Zeitschrift fuer Kultur der Antike
  und Humanistische Bildung. 6 per yr. ISSN 0017-
  5943
- Heidelberger Rechtsvergleichende und
  Wirtschaftsrechliche Studien. a.
- Heidelberger Rechtswissenschaftliche
  Abhandlungen. Neue Folge. irreg. ISSN 0073-
  165X (Universitaet Heidelberg. Juristische
  Fakultaet)
- Sprachwissenschaft. q.
- Zeitschrift fuer slavische Philologie. s-a. ISSN
  0044-3492

**J. H. Wipper**
B.-v.-Senestrey-Str. 13, 8400 Regensburg, W.
Germany (B.R.D.)
- Bibliographische Zeitschrift fuer Aesthetik. q.
  ISSN 0006-1514

**Wirtschaftsdienst Verlag und Druckerei GmbH**
Lange Str. 13, 6000 Frankfurt, W. Germany
(B.R.D.)
- Bleib Gesund. bi-m. (Bundesverband der
  Ortskrankenkassen)
- Deutsche Rentenversicherung. bi-m. ISSN 0012-
  0618 (Verband Deutscher
  Rentenversicherungstraeger)
- Gesichertes Leben. bi-m. ISSN 0016-9153
- J O. (Junge Ortskrankenkasse) q.
- Tag. q.

**Wirtschaftshilfe des Bayerischen Einzelhandels**
Brienner Str. 45, 8000 Munich 2, W. Germany
(B.R.D.)
- Bayerischer Einzelhandel. m.

**Verlag fuer Wirtschaftspraxis GmbH**
Schumannstr. 27, Postfach 2625, 6000 Frankfurt 1,
W. Germany (B.R.D.)
- Der Neue Weg. m. (Deutscher
  Handelsvereinigung Spar)

**Wirtschaftsverband Eisen, Blech und Metall
Verarbeitende Industrie**
- Industrie-Anzeiger. (pub. by Verlag W. Girardet)

**Wirtschaftsverband Eisen, Maschinen und
Apparatebau**
Karolingerplatz 10-11, 1000 Berlin 19, W. Germany
(B.R.D.)
- W E M A Bezugsquellenverzeichnis; suppliers'
  register of the iron and metal processing industry
  in West Berlin. irreg.

**Wirtschaftsvereinigung Eisen- und Stahlindustrie**
- Betriebliche Ausbildungspraxis. (pub. by Verlag
  und Vertriebsgesellschaft mbH)
- Statistisches Jahrbuch der Eisen- und
  Stahlindustrie. (pub. by Verlag Stahleisen mbH)

**Wirtschaftsvereinigung Gross- und Aussenhandel**
Gotenstr. 21, 2000 Hamburg 1, W. Germany
(B.R.D.)
- Der Grosshandelskaufmann. (pub. by L.
  Schaffrath)
- W G A Geschaeftsbericht. a. ISSN 0042-966X

**Verlag Wissenschaft und Politik Berend von Nottbeck**
Salierring 14, 5000 Cologne 1, W. Germany
(B.R.D.)
- Deutschland Archiv; Zeitschrift fuer Fragen der
  DDR und der Deutschlandpolitik. m. ISSN 0012-
  1428
- Internationales Recht und Diplomatie. irreg. ISSN
  0020-9503

**Wissenschaft und Werbung**
Freiburger Str. 23, 7844 Neuenburg, W. Germany
(B.R.D.)
- Probatum Est; Informationen fuer den Arzt. 10
  per yr.

**Verlag fuer Wissenschaft, Wirtschaft und Technik
GmbH und Co.**
An den Weiden 15, Postfach 242, 3388 Bad
Harzburg, W. Germany (B.R.D.)
- Akademie fuer Fuehrungskraefte der Wirtschaft.
  Taschenbuecher zur Betriebspraxis. irreg. ISSN
  0065-5384
- Management Heute und Marktwirtschaft. m. ISSN
  0302-668X (Deutsche Volkswirtschaftliche
  Gesellschaft)

**Wissenschaftliche Gesellschaft fuer Europarecht**
- Europarecht. (pub. by C. H. Beck'sche
  Verlagsbuchhandlung)

**Wissenschaftliche Gesellschaft fuer Luft- und
Raumfahrt e.V**
- Zeitschrift fuer Flugwissenschaften. (pub. by
  Friedrich Vieweg und Sohn Verlagsgesellschaft
  mbH GW)

**Wissenschaftliche Gesellschaft fuer
Personenstandswesen und Verwandte Gebiete**
- Wissenschaftliche Gesellschaft fuer
  Personenstandswesen und Verwandte Gebiete.
  Schriftenreihe. Neue Folge. (pub. by Verlag fuer
  Standesamtswesen GmbH und Co. KG)

**Wissenschaftliche Vereinigung fuer Augenoptik und
Optometrie E.V.**
- Optometrie. (pub. by Median Verlag)
- Wissenschaftliche Vereinigung fuer Augenoptik
  und Optometrie. Fachvortraege des WVAO -
  Jahreskongresses. (pub. by Median-Verlag)

**Wissenschaftliche Verlagsgesellschaft mbH**
Birkenwaldstr. 44, Postfach 40, 7000 Stuttgart 1, W.
Germany (B.R.D.)
- Apotheker-Jahrbuch. a. ISSN 0066-5347
  (Deutscher Apotheker-Verein)
- Cytobiologie; European journal of cell biology. bi-
  m. ISSN 0070-2463 (European Cell Biology
  Organization) (Co-sponsors: Deutsche
  Gesellschaft fuer Elektronenmikroskpie e.V.;
  Deutsche Gesellschaft fuer Zellbiologie e.V.)
- Deutsche Lebensmittel-Rundschau; Zeitschrift fuer
  Lebensmittelkunde und Lebensmittelrecht. m.
  ISSN 0012-0413
- German Economic Review. q. ISSN 0016-8734
  (Gesellschaft fuer Wirtschafts- und
  Sozialwissenschaften)
- Grosse Naturforscher. irreg., vol. 39, 1976. ISSN
  0072-7741
- Internationale Gesellschaft fuer Geschichte der
  Pharmazie. Veroeffentlichungen. Neue Folge.
  irreg., vol. 40, 1976. ISSN 0074-9729

- Medizinische Monatsschrift; Zeitschrift fuer
  allgemeine Medizin und Therapie. m. ISSN 0025-
  8474
- Methodensammlung der Elektronenmikroskopie.
  irreg., no. 8, 1975. ISSN 0076-6771 (Deutsche
  Gesellschaft fuer Elektronenmikroskopie e.V.)
- Mundus; a quarterly review of German research
  contributions on Asia, Africa and Latin America -
  arts and science. q. ISSN 0027-3392 (Institute for
  Scientific Co-Operation)
- Naturwissenschaftliche Rundschau. m. ISSN 0028-
  1050
- Naturwissenschaftliche Rundschau. Buecher der
  Zeitschrift. irreg. ISSN 0077-6157
- Optik; Zeitschrift fuer Licht- und Elektronenoptik.
  m. ISSN 0030-4026 (Deutsche Gesellschaft fuer
  Elektronenmikroskopie e.V.) (Co-sponsor:
  Deutsche Gesellschaft fuer angewandte Optik
  e.V.)
- Universitas; Zeitschrift fuer Wissenschaft, Kunst
  und Literatur. m(German edt.); q(English and
  Spanish edts.) ISSN 0041-9079

**Universitaets Buchhandlung Dr. J.C. Witsch**
Universitaetsstr. 18, 5000 Cologne, W. Germany
(B.R.D.)
- Universitaet Zu Koeln. Jahrbuch. a. ISSN 0069-
  5890

**Wittgensteiner Heimatvereins e.V**
- Wittgenstein. (pub. by Buchhandlung Adalbert
  Carl)

**Dr. Heinrich Wittmann Verlag**
Menzelstr. 3, Postfach 860844, 8000 Munich 86, W.
Germany (B. R. D.)
- Der Deutschland- Sammler; Mitteilungsblatt fuer
  den Spezialsammler von Deutschland. 6-8 per yr.
  ISSN 0012-1452

**Verlag Gerhard Witzstrock**
Bismarckstr. 5, Postfach 509, 7570 Baden-Baden,
W. Germany (B.R.D.)
- Herz Kreislauf; Zeitschrift fuer Kardiologie und
  Angiologie in Klinik und Praxis. 16 per yr. ISSN
  0046-7324
- Immunitaet und Infektion; zeitschrift fuer
  klinische Immunologie und Infektionskrankheiten.
  bi-m. ISSN 0340-1162
- Innere Medizin. 8 per yr. ISSN 0303-4305
- Leber Magen Darm. bi-m. ISSN 0300-8622

**Wochenschau-Verlag**
Adolf-Damschke-Str. 105, 6231 Schwalbach, W.
Germany (B.R.D.)
- Arbeitshefte zur Gemeinschaftskunde. irreg. ISSN
  0066-5827

**Gert Wohlfarth KG Verlag Fachtechnik und
Mercator-Verlag**
Pressehaus, Koehnenstr. 5-11, 4100 Duisburg 1, W.
Germany (B.R.D.)
- Bau und Baustoff. m. ISSN 0005-643X
- Baubeschlag Magazin. m.
- Baubeschlag-Taschenbuch. a. ISSN 0067-4583
- Baukeramik; Information des Fachhandels ueber
  fein- und grobkeramische Erzeugnisse. q.
- Der Baustoffmarkt. m. ISSN 0005-6448
  (Bundesverband Deutscher Baustoffhaendler e.V.)
- Heim und Hobby; Kundenfachzeitschrift fuer
  Heimwerker in Haus. Hof und Garten. m.
- Informationsdienst fuer den Kfz-Zubehoer
  Fachhandel und -Ersatzteile. m.
- Werkzeug-Information; Kundenfachzeitschrift des
  Werkzeug- und Werkzeugmaschinenhandels. m.

**Verlag Juergen Wohlrabe**
Schloss-Str. 67a, 1000 Berlin 19, W. Germany (B.
R. D.)
- Berliner Studentenzeitung. q. ISSN 0005-934X

**M. C. Wolf Kg**
Herzogstr./Eickeler Str.2, Postfach 546, 4690 Herne
2, W. Germany (B.R.D.)
- Der Augenarzt. bi-m. ISSN 0004-7902
  (Berufsverband der Augenaerzte Deutschlands
  e.V.)
- Der Frauenarzt. bi-m. ISSN 0016-0237
  (Berufsverband der Frauenaerzte e. V.)

**Wolf Verlag GmbH**
Haidplatz 2, Postfach 112, 8400 Regensburg, W.
Germany (B.R.D.)
- Heimatliche Schule. m. ISSN 0017-9795
(Bayerischer Lehrer- und Lehrerinnenverband.
Bezirksverbaende Niederbayern und Oberpfalz)

**Wolfenbuetteler Arbeitskreis fuer Geschichte des Buchwesens**
- Wolfenbuetteler Notizen zur Buchgeschichte.
(pub. by Dr. Ernst Hauswedell und Co., Verlag)

**World Association for Buiatrics**
Bischofsholer Damm 15 (Rinderklinik), 3000
Hannover, W. Germany (B.R.D.)
- International Meeting on Cattle Diseases. Reports.
biennial, 9th, paris, 1976. ISSN 0074-6975

**World Association for Christian Communication**
- World Association for Christian Communication.
Journal. (pub. by Eckart-Verlag)

**World Association of Veterinary Anatomists**
- Anatomia, Histologia, Embryologia. (pub. by
Verlag Paul Parey (Berlin))

**World Small Animal Veterinary Association.
Deutsche Gruppe**
- Kleintier-Praxis. (pub. by Verlag M. und H.
Schaper)

**Worms. Stadtbibliothek**
Marktplatz 10, 6520 Worms, W. Germany (B.R.D.)
- Der Wormsgau; Zeitschrift der Kulturinstitute der
Stadt Worms und des Altertumsvereins Worms. a.
ISSN 0084-2613

**Verlag Wort und Bild Rolf Becker**
Konradshoehe, 8021 Baierbrunn, W. Germany
(B.R.D.)
- Aerztlicher Ratgeber fuer Werdende und Junge
Muetter; die Schwangerschaft und das wichtige 1.
Lebensjahr des Kindes. 3 per yr.
- Drogerie-Journal. m. ISSN 0012-6322

**Verlag Wort und Werk GmbH**
Arnold-Janssen-Str. 20, 5205 St. Augustin 1, W.
Germany (B.R.D.)
- Die Anregung; Seelsorglicher Dienst in der Welt
von heute. m. ISSN 0003-519X

**Wudd Verlag**
Wickererstr. 12, 6000 Frankfurt 1, W. Germany
(B.R.D.)
- Sadid; Zeitschrift der Worte des neuen Menschen.
2 per yr.

**Wuerttemberg. Landesversicherungsanstalt**
- Landesversicherungsanstalt Wuerttemberg.
Mitteilungen. (pub. by W. Kohlhammer GmbH
(Stuttgart))

**Wuerttembergische Bau-Berufsgenossenschaft**
Werastr. 23, Postfach 547, 7000 Stuttgart 1, W.
Germany (B.R.D.)
- Wuerttembergische Bau-Berufsgenossenschaft.
Mitteilungen. q.

**Wuerzburger Dioezesangeschichtsverein**
Domerschulstrasse, 8700 Wuerzburg 1, W. Germany
(B.R.D.)
- Wuerzburger Dioezesangeschichtsblaetter. a.

**Verlag Zahnaerztlich-Medizinisches Schrifttum**
Insterburger Str. 2, Postfach 810509, 8000 Munich
81, W. Germany (B.R.D.)
- Informationen aus Orthodontie und
Kieferorthopaedie. q. ISSN 0020-0336
- Der Zahnarzt; colloquium med. dent. bi-m. ISSN
0044-1678

**Zahnaerztlicher Bezirksverband Muenchen Stadt und
Land**
- Zahnaerztlicher Anzeiger. (pub. by Industrie- und
Handelswerbung A. Hanuschik)

**Zauberkreis Verlag**
Karlsruher Str. 22, Postfach 2300, 7550 Rastatt, W.
Germany (B.R.D.)
- Butler Parker. m.

**Zechner und Huethig Verlag GmbH**
Daimlerstr. 9, Postfach 68, 6720 Speyer, W.
Germany (B.R.D.)
- Plastverarbeiter; Kunststofftechnik-
Kunststoffmarkt-Plastic Revue. m. ISSN 0032-
1338

**Verlag Zeichentechnik**
Schulstr. 4-6, 6277 Camberg, W. Germany (B.R.D.)
- Zeichnen in Technik, Architektur, Vermessung. bi-
m. ISSN 0044-2046

**Zeil-Verlag GmbH**
Frankfurter Landstr. 6a, 6370 Oberursel, W.
Germany (B.R.D.)
- Der Akademiker in Wirtschaft und Verwaltung;
Wegweiser fuer den Fuehrungsnachwuchs aus
Universitaeten, Hochschulen und
Fachhochschulen in Industrie, Handel und
Behoerden. a. ISSN 0568-7276

**Carl Zeiss**
Postfach 1369/1380, 7082 Oberkochen, W.
Germany (B.R.D.)
- Zeiss Informationen. irreg. ISSN 0044-2054

**Verlag der Zeitschrift fuer Naturforschung**
Postfach 2645, 7400 Tuebingen, W. Germany
(B.R.D.)
- Zeitschrift fuer Naturforschung. Section A:
Physics, Physical Chemistry, Cosmic Physics. m.
ISSN 0340-4811
- Zeitschrift fuer Naturforschung. Section B:
Inorganic and Organic Chemistry. m. ISSN 0340-
5087
- Zeitschrift fuer Naturforschung. Section C:
Biosciences. m. ISSN 0341-0382

**Zeitungs- und Zeitschriften-Verlag GmbH**
Wurzerstr. 46, 5300 Bonn- Bad Godesberg, W.
Germany (B.R.D.)
- Z V und Z V; Zeitschrift fuer Presse und
Werbung. w. ISSN 0044-1511 (Bundesverband
Deutscher Zeitungsverleger) (Co-sponsor:
Verband Deutscher Zeitschriftenverleger e.V.)

**Fachverlag Erwin P. H. Zellmer**
Huegelstr. 74, Postfach 4694, 6000 Frankfurt 50, W.
Germany (B.R.D.)
- Handels-Magazin FSB und Fachblatt fuer
Selbstbedienung. m.

**Zentralarchiv fuer Hochschulbau**
- Bibliographie Hochschulplanung. (pub. by Forum-
Verlag GmbH)

**Zentralausschuss fuer Deutsche Landeskunde**
Postfach 130, 5300 Bonn-Bad Godesberg, W.
Germany (B.R.D.)
- Berichte zur deutschen Landeskunde. q. ISSN
0005-9099

**Zentrale der Caritas-Schwesternschaft e.V.**
Maria Theresiastr. 10, 78 Freiburg, W. Germany
(B.R.D.)
- Caritasschwester. bi-m.

**Zentrale fuer Gasverwendung e.V.**
- Gas-Beispiele. (pub. by ZfGW Verlag GmbH)
- Gasverwendung. (pub. by ZfGW Verlag GmbH)

**Zentrale fuer GmbH Dr. O. Schmidt**
- GmbH-Rundschau. (pub. by Verlag Dr. Otto
Schmidt KG)

**Zentralgenossenschaft fuer Viehverwertung e.V.**
Adenaueralle 18, 3000 Hannover, W. Germany
(B.R.D.)
- C G-Kurier. q. (Co-Sponsor: Landwirtschaftliche
Fleischzentrale GmbH)

**Zentralinstitut fuer Kunstgeschichte in Muenchen**
- Kunstchronik. (pub. by Verlag Hans Carl KG)

**Zentralkomitee der Deutschen Katholiken**
Hochkreuzallee 246, 5300 Bonn-Bad Godesberg, W.
Germany (B.R.D.)
- Zentralkomitee der Deutschen Katholiken.
Mitteilungen. m.

**Zentralstelle fuer Atomkernenergie-Dokumentation.
Kernforschungszentrum**
7514 Eggenstein-Leopoldshafen, W. Germany
(B.R.D.)
- High Energy Physics Index/Hochenergiephysik-
Index. fortn. ISSN 0018-1447
- Informationen zur Kernforschung und
Kerntechnik. m. ISSN 0020-0387
- Surface and Vacuum Physics Index/Index zur
Oberflaechen- und Vakuumphysik. m. ISSN 0340-
2924
- Technology Index for Plasma Physics Research
and Fusion Reactors/Technik-Index ueber
Plasmaphysikalische Forschung und
Fusionsreaktoren. m. ISSN 0340-2975

**Zentralverband Demokratischer Widerstandskaempfer
und Verfolgtenorganisationen e.V.**
Hauptstr. 216, 5300 Bonn-Oberkassel, W. Germany
(B. R. D.)
- Freiheit und Recht; die Stimme der
Widerstandskaempfer fuer ein freies Europa. m.

**Zentralverband der Aerzte fuer Naturheilverfahren
e.V.**
- Physikalische Medizin und Rehabilitation. (pub.
by Medizinisch-Literarische Verlagsgesellschaft
MbH)

**Zentralverband der Deutschen Gefluegelwirtschaft**
- D G S. (pub. by Verlag Eugen Ulmer)
- Jahrbuch der Gefluegelwirtschaft. (pub. by Verlag
Eugen Ulmer)

**Zentralverband der Deutschen Geographen**
- Verhandlungen des Deutschen Geographentages.
(pub. by Franz Steiner Verlag GmbH)

**Zentralverband der Deutschen Haus, Wohnungs und
Grundeigentuemer e.V.**
- Deutsche Wohnungswirtschaft. (pub. by Verlag
Deutsche Wohnungswirtschaft GmbH)

**Zentralverband der Fusspfleger Deutschlands e.V.**
- Der Fuss. (pub. by Verlag Dr. H. Heilmaier)

**Zentralverband des Dachdeckerhandwerks e.V**
- Das Dachdecker-Handwerk. (pub. by
Verlagsgesellschaft Rudolf Mueller)

**Zentralverband des Deutschen Baugewerbes e.V.**
- Baugewerbe. (pub. by Verlagsgesellschaft Rudolf
Mueller)

**Zentralverband des Deutschen Elektrohandwerks**
- D E - der Elektromeister und Deutsches
Elektrohandwerk. (pub. by Huethig und Pflaum
Verlag)

**Zentralverband des Deutschen Elektrohandwerks.
Bundesfachgruppe Elektromaschinenbau**
- E M A - Elektrische Maschinen. (pub. by Huethig
und Pflaum Verlag)

**Zentralverband des Deutschen Elektrohandwerks.
Bundesfachgruppe Radio- und Fernsehtechnik**
- Funk-Technik. (pub. by Huethig und Pflaum
Verlag)

**Zentralverband des Deutschen Handwerks**
- Deutsches Handwerksblatt. (pub. by Gildeverlag
Hans-Gerhard Dobler GmbH)

**Zentralverband des Deutschen Vulkaniseurhandwerks**
- Gummibereifung. (pub. by Bielefelder
Verlagsanstalt KG)

**Zentralverband des Kraftfahrzeughandels e.V.**
- Autohaus. (pub. by Bartsch Verlag KG)

**Zentralverband des Kraftfahrzeughandwerks**
- Autofachmann. (pub. by Vogel- Verlag KG)
- K F Z-Betrieb und Automarkt. (pub. by Vogel-
Verlag KG)

**Zentralverband des Kuerschnerhandwerks**
- Rund um den Pelz International. (pub. by
Rhenania-Fachverlag GmbH)

**Zentralverband Deutscher Molkereifachleute und
Milchwirtschaftler**
- Deutsche Milchwirtschaft. (pub. by Verlag Th.
Mann)

**Zentralverband Deutscher Photographen**
- Fachkontakt. (pub. by G F W Verlag GmbH)

**Zentralverband fuer Sanitaer-, Klima- und
Heizungstechnik**
- I K Z. (pub. by Verlag A. Strobel KG)
- S B Z - Sanitaer-, Heizungs- und Klimatechnik.
(pub. by A. W. Gentner Verlag)

**Zentralverband fuer Uhren, Schmuck und
Zeitmesstechnik**
- Uhren-Juwelen-Schmuck. (pub. by Bielefelder
Verlagsanstalt KG)

**Zentralverband Karosserie und Fahrzeugtechnik e. V.**
- Fahrzeug und Karosserie. (pub. by Bielefelder
Verlagsanstalt KG)

**Zentralverband Krankengymnastik e.V.**
- Krankengymnastik. (pub. by Richard Pflaum Verlag KG)

**Zentralverband Zoologischer Fachgeschaefte Deutschlands e.V.**
- Zoologischer Zentral-Anzeiger. (pub. by V F V Verbands- und Fachschriftenverlag)

**Zentralvereinigung Deutscher Handelsvertreter- und Handelsmaklerverbaende e.V.**
- Der Handelsvertreter und Handelsmakler. (pub. by Siegel-Verlag Otto Mueller)

**ZfGW-Verlag GmbH**
Voltastr. 79, 6000 Frankfurt 90, W. Germany (B.R.D.)
- Allgemeine Gastarife in der Bundesrepublik Deutschland. a. (Verband des Deutschen Gas- und Wasserwerke)
- Gas-Beispiele; Sammlung von Beispielen zweckmaessiger Gasverwendung fuer Architekten und Bauschaffende. q. ISSN 0016-5034 (Zentrale fuer Gasverwendung e.V.)
- Gasverwendung; Zeitschrift fuer neuzeitliche Energieverwendung. m. ISSN 0016-5182 (Zentrale fuer Gasverwendung e.V.)

**Verlag Dieter Zimmerle**
Vogelsangstr. 32, 7000 Stuttgart 1, W. Germany (B.R.D.)
- Jazz Podium. m. ISSN 0021-5686

**Zimmermann-Verlag**
Haus Nr. 4, Postfach 252, 3430 Witzenhausen, W. Germany (B.R.D.)
- Nemuno Krastas; the country on the Njemen-River. bi-m. ISSN 0028-260X

**Zoologische Staatssammlung Muenchen**
Maria-Ward-Str. 1b, 8000 Munich 19, W. Germany (B.R.D.)
- Opuscula Zoologica. irreg. ISSN 0030-4158
- Zoologische Staatssammlung, Muenchen. Veroeffentlichungen. irreg. ISSN 0077-2135

**Zoologisches Forschungsinstitut und Museum A. Koenig**
Adenauerallee 150-164, 5300 Bonn 1, W. Germany (B.R.D.)
- Bonner Zoologische Beitraege. q. ISSN 0006-7172 (Co-Sponsor: Museum Alexander Koenig)

**Zoologisches Museum Hamburg**
Martin-Luther-King-Platz 3, 2000 Hamburg 13, W. Germany (B.R.D.)
- Zoologisches Museum Hamburg. Entomologische Mitteilungen. 4 per yr. ISSN 0044-5223

**Hubert Zuerl**
Sendlinger Str. 53, 8000 Munich 2, W. Germany (B.R.D.)
- Aero; unabhaengige Monatsschrift fuer die gesamte Luft- und Raumfahrt. -m. ISSN 0001-9100

**Werbeagenturen Zuhlke und Scholz KG**
Schinkestr. 12/13, 1000 Berlin 44, W. Germany (B.R.D.)
- Berlin Today, what to do - to see - where to go - to eat - to stay. m.

**Zweckverband Deutscher Apotheker**
- Pharmazeutische Rundschau. (pub. by Pharmazeutischer Verlag)

# GHANA

**Archdiocese of Cape Coast**
- Catholic Voice. (pub. by Catholic Mission Press)

**Association of African Universities**
P.O. Box 5744, Accra, Ghana.
- Association of African Universities. Bulletin. s-a.

**Bank of Ghana**
Accra, Ghana.
- Bank of Ghana. Quarterly Economic Bulletin. q. ISSN 0005-5182

**Bartels Publications Ltd**
P.O. Box 4446, Accra, Ghana.
- Who's Who in Ghana. biennial.

**Catholic Mission Press**
Box 60, Cape Coast, Ghana.
- Catholic Voice. m. ISSN 0008-8412 (Archdiocese of Cape Coast)
- Standard; national Catholic weekly. w. ISSN 0038-9374 (Ghana Catholic Hierarchy)

**Cocoa Research Institute**
Box 8, Tafo, Ghana.
- Cocoa Research Institute. Annual Report. a.

**Council for Law Reporting**
Box M-165, Accra, Ghana.
- Ghana Law Reports. q. ISSN 0072-436X
- Review of Ghana Law. 3 per yr. ISSN 0034-6578

**Council for Scientific and Industrial Research**
Box M-32, Accra, Ghana.
- C S I R Annual Report. a.
- C S I R Handbook. a.
- Ghana Journal of Agricultural Science. s-a.
- Ghana Journal of Science. q. ISSN 0016-9544 (Co-sponsor: Ghana Science Association)
- Ghana Science Abstracts. q.

**Council for Scientific and Industrial Research, Ghana. Forest Products Research Institute**
University P. O. Box 63, Kumasi, Ghana.
- Council for Scientific and Industrial Research, Ghana. Forest Products Research Institute. Annual Report. a. ISSN 0586-8440

**Economic Society of Ghana**
Box 22, Legon, Accra, Ghana.
- Economic Bulletin of Ghana. q. ISSN 0013-0044

**Editorial and Publishing Services**
Box 5743, Accra, Ghana.
- Ghana Economic Review. a.

**Encyclopaedia Africana Project**
Box 2797, Accra, Ghana.
- Encyclopaedia Africana. Information Report. irreg., no. 15, 1976. ISSN 0013-712X

**Forest Products Research Institute**
see under Council for Scientific and Industrial Research

**Ghana. Central Bureau of Statistics**
Accra, Ghana.
- Ghana. Central Bureau of Statistics. Economic Survey. a. ISSN 0072-4335

**Ghana. Cocoa Marketing Board**
Box 933, Accra, Ghana.
- C. M. B. Newsletter. q. ISSN 0007-8611

**Ghana. Information Services Department**
Box 745, Accra, Ghana.
- Ghana. irreg.
- Ghana Digest. m.
- Ghana Review. m. ISSN 0016-9587
- Kakyevole. m. ISSN 0022-7862
- New Ghana. m.
- Official Handbook of Ghana. a. ISSN 0072-9825
- Statistical Handbook of the Republic of Ghana. a.

**Ghana. Meteorological Services Department**
Box 87, Legon, Accra, Ghana.
- Ghana. Meteorological Services Department. Agro-Meteorological Bulletin. m.
- Ghana. Meteorological Services Department. Annual Summary of Observations. a. ISSN 0431-8293

**Ghana. Ministry of Education**
Box M 45, Accra, Ghana.
- Ghana. Ministry of Education. Educational Statistics. a.
- Ghana Journal of Education. q.

**Ghana. Ministry of Social Welfare and Community Development**
Box 778, Accra, Ghana.
- Advance. q. ISSN 0515-4510

**Ghana. National Council for Higher Education**
Accra, Ghana.
- Ghana. National Council for Higher Education. Annual Report. a.

**Ghana. National Redemption Council**
Ministry of Finance, Accra, Ghana.
- Ghana. National Redemption Council. Budget Proposals. a.

**Ghana. Railway and Ports Administration**
P.O. Box 251, Takoradi, Ghana.
- Ghana. Railway and Ports Administration. Report. a. ISSN 0072-4408

**Ghana Broadcasting Corporation**
Box 1633, Accra, Ghana.
- G B C Radio and T V Times. w.

**Ghana Catholic Hierarchy**
- Standard. (pub. by Catholic Mission Press)

**Ghana Commercial Bank**
Box 134, Accra, Ghana.
- Ghana Commercial Bank. Monthly Economic Bulletin. m. (prep. by its Economic Intelligence Department)

**Ghana Geographical Association**
University of Ghana, Department of Geography, Legon, Accra, Ghana.
- Ghana Geographical Association. Bulletin. a. ISSN 0016-9536

**Ghana Home Scientist Association**
Box M.192, Accra, Ghana.
- Home Scientist. s-a.

**Ghana Institute of Management and Public Administration**
Box 50, Achimoto, Ghana.
- Administrator. q. ISSN 0044-6319

**Ghana Institution of Engineers**
Tema, Ghana.
- Ghana Engineer.

**Ghana Library Association**
Box 60, Legon, Ghana.
- Ghana Library Journal. s-a. ISSN 0016-9552

**Ghana Medical Association**
Korle Bu Post Office, Accra, Ghana.
- Ghana Medical Journal. q. ISSN 0016-9560

**Ghana Publishing Corporation**
Box 4348, Accra, Ghana.
- Ghana Social Science Journal. s-a. ISSN 0046-5925 (University of Ghana. Faculty of Social Studies)

**Ghana Sociological Association**
c/o Department of Sociology, University of Ghana, Legon, Ghana.
- Ghana Journal of Sociology. s-a. ISSN 0435-9380

**Ghana Water & Sewerage Corporation**
Box M194, Accra, Ghana.
- Water News. bi-m. ISSN 0043-1265

**Graphic Corporation**
Box 742, Accra, Ghana.
- Ghana Year Book. a. ISSN 0433-969X

**Historical Society of Ghana**
P.O. Box 12, Legon, Ghana.
- Historical Society of Ghana. Transactions. s-a. ISSN 0073-2648

**Nananom Publishers**
Box 5446, Accra, Ghana.
- Insight Publication; quarterly for current African thinking. q.
- New Era. m. ISSN 0028-4998

**National Investment Bank**
Liberty Avenue, P.O. Box 3726, Accra, Ghana.
- N I B Annual Report. a; latest issue, 1973.

**One World Spotlight**
Box 983, Accra, Ghana.
- International Week End Spotlight. w.

**Pictorial Publications**
Box 3460, Accra, Ghana.
- Voice of the People. fortn. ISSN 0042-8221

**Planned Parenthood Association of Ghana**
Box 5756, Accra, Ghana.
- P P A G Newsletter. q.

**Presbyterian Book Depot**
Box 3075, Accra, Ghana.
- Christian Messenger. m. ISSN 0009-5478

**Research Library on African Affairs**
P.O. Box 2970, Accra, Ghana.
- Ghana: a Current Bibliography. bi-m.

• Ghana National Bibliography. a. ISSN 0072-4378

**Spark Publications Ltd.**
Box 346, Accra, Ghana.
• Spark; a weekly of the African revolution. w. ISSN 0038-6553

**Statesman Publications**
Box 3876, Accra, Ghana.
• Statesman. m. ISSN 0039-0305

**Teiba Publications Ltd.**
Box 5737, Accra, Ghana.
• Ideal Woman/Obaa Sima. m.

**Trades Union Congress of Ghana**
Hall of Trade Union, Box 701, Accra, Ghana.
• T U C Newsletter. m.

**Trinity College, Legon**
Box 48, Legon, Ghana.
• Ghana Bulletin of Theology. s-a. ISSN 0046-5909 (Co-sponsor: University of Ghana, Department for the Study of Religions)

**University of Cape Coast**
Cape Coast, Ghana.
• Asemka s-a.

**University of Ghana. Department of Library Studies**
Legon, Ghana
• Education for Librarianship in Ghana. irreg. (Dist. by University Bookshop, Legon, Ghana)

**University of Ghana. Department of Philosophy**
P.O. Box 69, Legon, Ghana.
• Universitas. s-a. ISSN 0049-5530

**University of Ghana. Department of Sociology**
Legon, Ghana.
• University of Ghana. Department of Sociology. Current Research Report Series. irreg.

**University of Ghana. Faculty of Law**
Legon, Ghana.
• University of Ghana Law Journal. s-a. ISSN 0041-9605

**University of Ghana. Faculty of Social Studies**
• Ghana Social Science Journal. (pub. by Ghana Publishing Corporation)

**University of Ghana. Institute of African Studies**
Box 73, Legon, Ghana.
• Legon Family Research Papers. irreg. no. 2, 1975.
• Odawuru in Series. a.
• Okyeame; Ghana's literary magazine. irreg. ISSN 0048-1629
• University of Ghana. Institute of African Studies. Collected Language Notes. irreg.
• University of Ghana. Institute of African Studies. Local Studies Series. irreg. ISSN 0533-8646
• University of Ghana. Institute of African Studies. Research Review. 3 per yr. ISSN 0020-2703

**University of Ghana. Institute of Statistical, Social and Economic Research**
Legon, Ghana.
• University of Ghana. Institute of Statistical, Social and Economic Research. Technical Publication Series. irreg.; no. 35, 1975.

**University of Ghana. School of Administration**
Box 78, Achimota, Legon, Ghana.
• Journal of Management Studies. s-a. ISSN 0022-2399

**University of Science and Technology**
Kumasi, Ghana.
• University of Science and Technology. Journal. irreg., approx. a. ISSN 0075-7225

**University of Science and Technology. Students' Representative Council**
Kumasi, Ghana.
• Focus. bi-m. ISSN 0046-4260

# GREECE

**A. M. G. International**
28 Emm. Benaki St., Athens 142, Greece.
• Phoni Tou Evangeliou/Voice of the Gospel. m. ISSN 0031-8396

**Agriculturist Association of Macedonia-Thrace**
29 Pavlou Mela Str., Thessaloniki, Greece.
• Gheoponica. bi-m. ISSN 0016-9625

**Aiolika Grammata**
Hodos Nireos 41, Palaion Phaliron, Athens, Greece.
• Aiolika Grammata. irreg.

**Alieia**
Stadiou St. 51, Athens 121, Greece.
• Alieia/Fishing. m. ISSN 0002-5399

**American-Hellenic Chamber of Commerce**
17 Valaoritou St., Athens 134, Greece.
• American-Hellenic Chamber of Commerce. Business Directory. Special Issue. biennial. ISSN 0065-8537
• Greek-American Trade. m. ISSN 0046-6379

**George Anastasopoulos, Ed. & Pub.**
Aristotelion Panepistimion. Thessalonikis, Box 200, Salonica, Greece.
• Acta Neurologica et Psychiatrica Hellenica. q. ISSN 0001-6292

**Anthropologike Hetaireia Tes Hellados**
Daphnomili 5, T.T. 706, Athens, Greece.
• Anthropos. irreg.

**Army Pension Share Hospital**
Athens, Greece.
• Iatrika Pepragmena. s-a. ISSN 0019-0942

**Nicholas Aspiotis, Ed. & Pub.**
Morgenthau 1, Thessaloniki, Greece.
• Ellenike Kteniatrike/Hellenic Veterinary Medicine/Medecine Veterinaire Hellenique. q. ISSN 0018-0068

**Association Internationale des Etudes Byzantines**
*see* **International Association for Byzantine Studies**

**Athens Center of Ekistics**
24, Strat. Syndesmou St., Box 471, Athens 136, Greece.
• Ancient Greek Cities Report. irreg, no. 23, 1973.
• Athens Center of Ekistics. Research Report. irreg., no. 13, 1973. ISSN 0067-0073
• Ekistic Index; a quarterly index of periodical articles on human settlements. q. ISSN 0013-2934
• Ekistics; reviews on the problems and science of human settlements. m. ISSN 0013-2942

**Athens Chamber of Commerce and Industry**
8 Amerikis St., Athens 134, Greece.
• Athens Chamber of Commerce and Industry. Monthly Bulletin. m. ISSN 0004-6612
• Trade with Greece; quarterly journal. q. ISSN 0041-0543

**Athens College**
P.O. Box 5, Psychico - Athens, Greece.
• Athens College Bulletin. s-a.

**Athens Cultural Center**
A.Baharian, Xenofontos 7, Athens 118, Greece.
• Chroniko; the cultural events of the year.

**Athens Technological Organization. Athens Center of Ekistics**
*see* **Athens Center of Ekistics**

**Azinlik Postasi**
Ioanninon 24, Komotini, Greece.
• Birlik. m. ISSN 0006-3681 (Turkish Teachers' Union of Western Thrace)

**Bank of Greece**
Box 105, Athens, Greece.
• Bank of Greece. Monthly Statistical Bulletin. m. ISSN 0005-5190

**Boukoumanis Publications**
57, Acadimias St., T.T. 143, Athens, Greece.
• Katathese. irreg.

**Central Bureau for Satellite Geodesy**
*see under* **International Association of Geodesy**

**Centre des Sciences Sociales d'Athenes**
• Centre des Sciences Sociales d'Athenes. Publications/Social Sciences Center, Athens. Publications. (pub. by Mouton Publishers NE)

**Chambre Technique de Grece**
*see* **Technical Chamber of Greece**

**George Chilaris, Ed. & Pub.**
14 Navarinou St., Athens 144, Greece.
• Ofthalmologika Chronika/Annals of Ophthalmology. q. ISSN 0030-0683

**Commercial Bank of Greece**
11, Sofokleous St., Athens 122, Greece.
• Commercial Bank of Greece. Economic Bulletin. q. ISSN 0013-0028
• Commercial Bank of Greece. Report of the Chairman of the Board of Directors. a. ISSN 0424-9402
• Notes on Foreign Trade. m. ISSN 0029-4063 (prep. by its Economic Research Department)

**Committee of Greek Agronomists**
• Nea Agrotiki Epitheorisis. (pub. by Spiros Spirou & Son Co.)

**Deutsches Archaeologisches Institut, Athens**
• Tiryns. (pub. by Philipp Von Zabern GW)

**Dikegorikos Syllogos Athenon**
Solonos 73 Kai Hippokratous, T.T. 143, Athens, Greece.
• Kodix Nomikou Vematos. s-m.
• Nomikon Vema. m.

**Orestis B. Doumanis, Ed. & Pub.**
5 Kleomenous-Loukianou Str., P.O. Box 545, Athens 139, Greece
(Dist. in the U.S. by Wittenborn and Co., 1018 Madison Ave., New York, N.Y. 10021)
• Architecture in Greece/Architectonika Themata. a. ISSN 0066-6262
• Design in Greece/Themata Chorou & Technon. a. ISSN 0074-1191

**Doxiadis Associates International Co., Ltd.**
24 Strat. Syndesmou St., Athens 136, Greece.
• D A Review. q. ISSN 0011-4723

**N. Drikakes, Ed. & Pub.**
G. Staurou 6, T.T. 121, Athens, Greece.
• Ekpaideutike Nomothesia. m.

**Ecole Francaise d'Athenes**
• Bulletin de Correspondance Hellenique. (pub. by Diffusion de Boccard FR)

**Ekdosis Panelleniou Henoseos Ephoriakon Hypallelon**
Akadimias 76, Athens, Greece.
• Phorologike Epitheorisis. m.

**Eleftherotypia**
Socratous 59 St., Athens, Greece.
• Eleftherotypia. m. ISSN 0013-5348

**G.C. Eleftheroudakis S.A.**
4 Nikis St., Athens 126, Greece.
• Nea Hestia. bi-m. ISSN 0028-1735

**Ellinikos Organismos Tourismou**
*see* **National Tourist Organisation of Greece**

**Emporike Trapeza Tes Hellados**
*see* **Commercial Bank of Greece**

**Epitheoresis Synkoinoniakou Dikaiou**
c/o O. Onouphriades, Metamorphoseos 3, Kalamaki, Attikis, Athens, Greece.
• Epitheoresis Synkoinoniakou Dikaiou. m.

**Erevna**
Dompoli 26, Athens 502, Greece.
• Erevna; political and economical. m. ISSN 0014-0074

**Ethnike Trapeza Tes Hellados**
*see* **National Bank of Greece**

**Ethnikon Idrimatos "Vassilefs Pavlos"**
*see* **National Foundation "King Paul"**

**Editions Europe Sud-Est**
18 Anagnostopoulou, Athens 136, Greece.
• Europe Sud-Est; la revue d'Athenes. q.

**Federation of Greek Industries**
5 Xenophontos Str., Athens 118, Greece.
• State of Greek Industry in (Year) a. ISSN 0072-7458

**Free Evangelical Churches of Greece**
3 Alkiviadou, Athens, Greece.
• Salpisma. m. ISSN 0036-357X

**Goulandris Natural History Museum**
13, Levidou Str., Kifissia Attikis, Hellas, Greece.
- Annales Musei Goulandris; contributiones ad historiam naturalem graeciae et regionis mediterraneae. a.

**Greece. Department of Antiquities and Archaeological Restoration**
*see* Greece. General Direction of Antiquities and Restoration

**Greece. General Direction of Antiquities and Restoration**
T A P Service, 17, Philellinon St., Athens 118, Greece
(Dist. by: Wasmuth K. G., Hardenbergstr. 9A, 1 Berlin, W. Germany (B.R.D.))
- Athens Annals of Archaeology. 3 per yr. ISSN 0004-6604

**Greece. Hypourgeion Koinonikon Hyperesion**
*see* Greece. Ministry of Social Services

**Greece. Ministry of Social Services**
17 Aristotelous St., Athens, Greece.
- Archives of Hygiene. s-a. ISSN 0003-9918
- Koinonike Epitheoresis. m. ISSN 0302-1173

**Greece. National Statistical Service**
Publications and Information Division, 14-16 Lycourgou St., Athens, Greece.
- Agricultural Statistics of Greece. a; latest 1973. ISSN 0065-4574
- Commerce Exterieur de la Grece. a, latest 1971.
- Concise Statistical Yearbook of Greece. a, 74. ISSN 0069-8245
- Greece. National Statistical Service. Annual Industrial Survey. a, latest 1973. ISSN 0072-7393
- Greece. National Statistical Service. Annual Statistical Survey of Mines, Quarries and Salterns. a, latest 1974. ISSN 0072-7415
- Greece. National Statistical Service. Bulletin de Statistique de Commerce Exterieur. q.
- Greece. National Statistical Service. Education Statistics. a,
- Greece. National Statistical Service. Public Finance Statistics. a; latest 1974.
- Greece. National Statistical Service. Shipping Statistics. a, latest 1974. ISSN 0072-7423
- Greece. National Statistical Service. Statistical Bulletin of Public Finance. q.
- Mouvement Naturel de la Population de la Grece. a, latest 1972. ISSN 0077-6114
- Star. m.
- Statistical Yearbook of Greece. a. ISSN 0081-5071

**Greece. Office National de Statistique**
*see* Greece. National Statistical Service

**Greece. Secretariat General of Press and Information**
Zalokosta 1, Athens, Greece.
- Yearbook of Greek Press. a.

**Greek Institute for Foreign and International Law**
*see* Hellenic Institute of International and Foreign Law

**Greek Mathematical Society**
34, Panepistimiou Street, Athens 143, Greece.
- Greek Mathematical Society. Bulletin/Hellenike Mathematike Hetaireia. Deltion. a. ISSN 0072-7466

**Greek National Committee for Astronomy**
Academy of Athens, 14 Anagnostopolou St., Athens 136, Greece.
- Greek National Committee for Astronomy. Annual Reports of the Astronomical Institutes of Greece. a. ISSN 0072-7385

**Greek National Tourist Organization**
*see* National Tourist Organisation of Greece

**Greek Pharmaceutical Society**
Emm. Benakis 30, Athens 142, Greece.
- Archeia Tes Pharmakeutikes (Athens) bi-m. ISSN 0003-8148

**Greek Speleological Society**
11 Mantzarou Str., Athens 135, Greece.
- Greek Speleological Society. Deltion/Societe Speleogique de Grece. Bulletin Trimestriel. q. ISSN 0011-8117

**K. Hartofylakadis, Ed. & Pub.**
Fotiou Patriarchou 21, Athens 706, Greece.
- Nisaki Mas i Kea; periodikon tou syndesmou ton Kion. q. ISSN 0040-8255

**Hellenews Ltd.**
39 Amaroussiou-Halandriou Rd., Amaroussion, Athens, Greece.
- Tourism in Greece. a. ISSN 0082-545X
- Travel in Greece. a.

**Hellenic Dental Association**
38 Themistocleous St, Athens 142, Greece.
- Hellenic Stomatological Annals. bi-m.

**Hellenic Industrial Development Bank**
18 El. Venizelos St., Athens 135, Greece.
- Greece Investment Guide; the land to invest. irreg., 2nd edt. 1972. ISSN 0072-7377

**Hellenic Institute of International and Foreign Law**
73 Solonos St., Athens, Greece.
- Revue Hellenique de Droit International. q. ISSN 0035-3256

**Hellenic Junior Red Cross**
1 Lycavittoy Str., Athens 135, Greece.
- Hellenicos Erythros Stavros Neotitos. 8 per yr. ISSN 0018-0076

**Hellenic Numismatic Society**
Box 736, Athens, Greece.
- Nomismatika Chronica. a.

**Hellenic Olympic Committee**
4 Kapsali St., Athens 138, Greece.
- International Olympic Academy. Report of the Sessions. a; 13th, Olympia, Greece, 1973. ISSN 0074-7181

**Hellenic Philotelic Federation**
57 Akadimias St., Athens, Greece.
- Philotelia; revue philotelique publiee tous les deux mois. bi-m. ISSN 0031-8264

**Hellenic Society for Aesthetics**
Vassilissis Sophias 79, Athens 140, Greece.
- Annales d'Esthetique/Chronika Aisthetikes. a. ISSN 0066-2119

**Hellenic Society for Philosophical Studies**
40 Hypsilantou St., Athens 140, Greece.
- Diotima; epitheoresis philosophikes ereunes/revue de recherche philosophique/review of philosophical research. irreg.

**Hellenic Society of Marine Molecular Biology**
- Folia Biochimica et Biologica Graeca. (pub. by Institute of Marine Molecular Biology)

**Hellenike Mathematike Hetaireia**
*see* Greek Mathematical Society

**Hellenike Nomismatike Hetaireia**
*see* Hellenic Numismatic Society

**Hellenike Spelaiologike Hetaria**
*see* Greek Speleological Society

**Hellenike Trapeza Biomechanikes Anaptyxeos**
*see* Hellenic Industrial Development Bank

**Hellinicos Erythros Stavros**
*see* Hellenic Junior Red Cross

**Hetaireia Makedonikon Spoudon**
*see* Society for Macedonian Studies

**Holy Synod of the Church of Greece**
14 Ioannou Gennadiou St., Athens 140, Greece.
- Theologia. q. ISSN 0049-3635

**Imera Publishing Co.**
4 Vissarionos St., Athens 135, Greece.
- Dimossiotis. m. ISSN 0012-2920

**Institut Hellenique de Droit International et Etranger**
*see* Hellenic Institute of International and Foreign Law

**Institut Pasteur Hellenique**
127 Av. Vassilissis Sofias, Athens 602, Greece.
- Institut Pasteur Hellenique. Archives. a. ISSN 0004-6620

**Institute for Balkan Studies**
45 Tsimiski St., Thessaloniki, Greece
(Dist. in U.S. by Stecher and Hafner, Inc., 31 E. 10 St., New York, NY 10003)
- Balkan Studies. s-a. ISSN 0005-4313 (Co-sponsor: Society for Macedonian Studies)
- Institute for Balkan Studies. Publications/Idryma Meleton Chersonesou Aimou. Ekthoseis. irreg., 1973, no. 130. ISSN 0073-862X

**Institute of Marine Molecular Biology**
2 Lampsaku St., Athens 611, Greece.
- Folia Biochimica et Biologica Graeca. 3-4 per yr. ISSN 0015-5489 (Hellenic Society of Marine Molecular Biology)

**International Association for Byzantine Studies**
c/o D. A. Zakythinos, Pres., Rue Sissini 31, Athens 612, Greece.
- International Association for Byzantine Studies. Bulletin d'Information et de Coordination. irreg. ISSN 0571-5857
- International Congress for Byzantine Studies. Acts/Congres International des Etudes Byzantines. Actes. irreg., 1971, 14th, Bucharest. ISSN 0074-3542

**International Association of Geodesy. Central Bureau for Satellite Geodesy**
National Technical University, K. Zographou 9, Athens 624, Greece.
- International Association of Geodesy. Central Bureau for Satellite Geodesy. Bibliography. irreg., no. 10, 1975.
- International Association of Geodesy. Central Bureau for Satellite Geodesy. Information Bulletin. irreg., no. 12, 1975. ISSN 0081-0312

**International Commission on Irrigation and Drainage. Greek National Committee**
13 Tsakona St., Psychico, Athens, Greece.
- Bulletin G C I D. s-a.

**International Congresses on Tropical Medicine and Malaria**
c/o Prof. J. Papa Vassilious, University of Athens, Athens, Greece.
- International Congresses on Tropical Medicine and Malaria. (Proceedings) quinquennial; 9th Athens. ISSN 0074-4212

**International Contacts Office**
Box 1381, Omonia, Athens, Greece.
- Greek Agricultural Directory. a.
- I.C.O. bi-m.

**International Olympic Academy**
- International Olympic Academy. Report of the Sessions. (pub. by Hellenic Olympic Committee)

**Ipirotiki Estia**
Smirnis 11, Ioannina, Greece.
- Ipirotiki Estia. m. ISSN 0021-0765

**Jesuit Fathers**
Apostleship of Prayer, 28 Michael Voda Str., Athens 109, Greece.
- Angeliaforos. m. ISSN 0003-3073

**H. Kambouridis, Ed. &. Pub.**
Box 19, Thessaloniki, Greece.
- Kodikas/Code; papers in semiotics. irreg (approx. 2 per yr.)

**Kentron Erevnis tes Hellenikes Philosophias**
14 Anagnostopoulou St., T.T. 136, Athens, Greece.
- Philosophia. a.

**Helen Panopalis Kotsonis, Ed. & Pub.**
Alopekis 20, Kolonaki, Athens 139, Greece.
- Athenian; Greece's English language monthly. m.

**Lambrakis Press S.A.**
3 Christou Lada Str., Athens 124, Greece.
- Economicos Tachydromos; weekly economic and financial review. w. ISSN 0013-0443
- Tachydromos. w. ISSN 0039-8888

**Lettres Eoliennes**
Nireos 41, P. Faliron, Athens, Greece.
- Lettres Eoliennes; revue bimensuelle d'art lesbien. bi-m.

**Naftika Chronika Ltd.**
Notara St., Piraeus 77, Greece.
- Naftika Chronika. s-m. ISSN 0047-861X

**National Bank of Greece**
86 Eolou St., Athens 121, Greece.
- National Bank of Greece. Annual Report/Ethnike Trapeza Tes Hellados. Apologismos. a. ISSN 0077-3514
- National Bank of Greece. Economic and Statistical Bulletin/Banque Nationale de Grece. Bulletin Economique et Statistique/Ethnike Trapeza Tes Hellados. Deltion Ikonomikon Ke Statistikon. b-m.

**National Centre of Social Research**
1 Sophocleous Str., Athens 122, Greece.
- Greek Review of Social Research/Epitheorisis Koinonikon Erevnon. 3 per yr. ISSN 0013-9696

**National Foundation "King Paul"**
9 Philellinon St., Athens 118, Greece.
- Protovoulia/Initiative. q.

**National Tourist Organisation of Greece**
General Direction of Promotion, Odos Amerikis 2, Athens, Greece.
- Greece. a. ISSN 0432-6105

**Neo Aftokinito**
1,Polytechniou Street, Athens 103, Greece.
- Neo Aftokinito. m. ISSN 0028-2642

**Nomikon Periodikon Dikaiosyne**
Hodos Euolpidos 10, T.T. 111, Athens, Greece.
- Nomikon Periodikon Dikaiosyne. m.

**Organisation for the Prevention of Accidents**
28 Sygrou Avenue, Athens 403, Greece.
- Prolipsis Ton Atychimaton. m. ISSN 0033-099X

**Pandecte Neon Noman Kediataghmaton**
11 Efozionos, Athens, Greece.
- Pandecte Neon Noman Kediataghmaton. m. ISSN 0031-0697

**Panhellenic Confederation of Agricultural Cooperatives**
56, El. Venizelou Str., Athens 142, Greece.
- Voice of the Cooperatives. m.

**Panhellenic Pharmaceutical Association**
1 Chalcocondyli St., Athens 1, Greece.
- Pharmakeftikon Deltion. m.(regular edt.); 4 per yr.(scientific edt.) ISSN 0031-708X

**C. Papagheorghiou**
209 Leoforos Alexandras, Athens, Greece.
- Ios. 3-12 per yr. ISSN 0021-0404

**John Papamichalakis, Ed. & Pub.**
26 Rigillis Str., Athens 138, Greece.
- Deltion Diikiseos Epichiriseon/Business Administration Bulletin; monthly review. m. ISSN 0011-8087

**Panagiotis Pavlouros, Ed. & Pub.**
Theras 113, Athens 220, Greece.
- Vivliothiki Ghoneon. 8 per yr. ISSN 0042-7594

**Philologikos Syllogos Parnassos**
Plateia Hag. Georgiou Karytsi 8, Athens, Greece.
- Parnassos; philologikon periodikon. q. ISSN 0048-301X

**Piraiki-Patraiki Cotton Manufacturing Co. Inc.**
Dragatsaniou St. 8, Athens 122, Greece.
- Piraiki-Patraiki. bi-m. ISSN 0032-0234

**Port of Piraeus Authority**
Akti Miaouli II, Merarchias Corner, Piraeus, Greece.
- Port of Piraeus Authority. Statistical Bulletin. a. ISSN 0079-399X

**Psychic Society of Athens**
32 Tsiller St, Athens, Greece.
- Kosmos Tis Psychis/World of Soul. m. ISSN 0023-4257

**S.H.Y.**
c/o Ann Rivers, Ed., Poste Restante, Hydra, Greece.
- S.H.Y; a literate quarterly. q.

**I. N. Serges**
Zoodochou Peges, 3, T.T. 142, Athens, Greece.
- Epitheoresis Nautiliakou Dikaiou. m.

**Societe Speleogique de Grece**
see Greek Speleological Society

**Society for Macedonian Studies**
Vass, Sofias 4, Thessaloniki, Greece.
- Ellinika; philological, historical and folkloric review. s-a. ISSN 0013-6336
- Makedonika. a. ISSN 0076-289X

**Society for Medical Studies**
Gr. Parisianos. Solonos Str. 69, Athens 609, Greece.
- Iatriki. m. ISSN 0019-0950

**Society of Odontostomatological Research**
70 Micras Asias St., Athens 609, Greece.
- Odontostomatological Progress. bi-m. ISSN 0029-8506

**Soma Hellinon Proscopon**
1 Ptolemeon St., Athens 516, Greece.
- Krikos Ton Vathmoforon. m. ISSN 0023-4664
- Proscopos. m. ISSN 0033-1465

**Spiros Spirou & Son Co.**
1 Deligiorgi Str., Athens 107, Greece.
- Nea Agrotiki Epitheorisis; monthly agricultural and farming review. m. ISSN 0028-1727 (Committee of Greek Agronomists)

**Stomatological Society of Greece**
26 Skoufa Str., Athens 136, Greece.
- Stomatologia. bi-m. ISSN 0039-1700

**Svenska Institutet i Athen**
9 Mitseon St., Athens 402, Greece
(Dist. by: Paul Aastroems Foerlag, Soedra Vaegen 61, S-412 54 Gothenburg, Sweden)
- Opuscula Atheniensia. irreg., no. 11, 1975. ISSN 0078-5520
- Svenska Institutet i Athen. Skrifter. irreg., no. 23, 1974. ISSN 0081-9921

**Technical Chamber of Greece**
Rue Karageorgi Servias 4, Athens 125, Greece.
- Technika Chronika/Annales Techniques. m. ISSN 0040-4764

**Basil Thassitis, Ed. & Pub.**
Fokylidou 8, Athens 136, Greece.
- Tobacco Review/Kapniki Epitheorissis. m. ISSN 0049-3953

**Trapeza Tes Hellados**
see Bank of Greece

**Travel International Associates Ltd.**
Dora d'Istria No. 1, Athens 140, Greece.
- African and Oriental Holiday; handbook of international travel and tourism. a. ISSN 0084-5981

**Turkish Teachers' Union of Western Thrace**
- Birlik. (pub. by Azinlik Postasi)

**Union Agricultural Cooperative of Syra**
Platia Iroon, Ermoypolis, Syra, Greece.
- Union Agricultural Cooperative of Syra. Bulletin. m. ISSN 0041-6800

**Viomichaniki Epitheorissis**
4 Zalokosta Str., Athens 134, Greece.
- Viomichaniki Epitheorissis/Industrial Review. m. ISSN 0042-6415

**Vivliographike Hetaireia Tes Hellados**
3, Vamva St., T. T. 138, Athens, Greece.
- Vivliographika.

**Zoological Laboratory and Museum, Athens**
Panepistimiopolis (Kouponia), Athens 621, Greece.
- Acta Biologica Hellenica. a. ISSN 0065-1095 (Co-sponsor: University of Salonica, Department of Biological Sciences)

# GRENADA

**Grenada. Government Printing Office**
St. George's, Grenada, West Indies.
- Grenada. Government Gazette. w.

# GUADELOUPE

**Caribbean Archives Association**
Boite Postale 74, Basse-Terre, Guadeloupe.
- Caribbean Archives/Archives Antillaises/Archivos del Caribe. s-a. ISSN 0396-2679

**Societe d'Histoire de la Guadeloupe. Archives Departementales**
Box 74, Basse-Terre, Guadeloupe
- Societe d'Histoire de la Guadeloupe. Bulletin. q. ISSN 0085-6258

# GUAM

**Guam. Department of Commerce**
Agana, GU 96910.
- Facts About Doing Business in Guam U.S.A. irreg., latest issue 1973.
- Guam. Department of Commerce. Annual Economic Report. a. (prep. by its Economic Research Center)
- Guam. Department of Commerce. Occasional Paper. irreg., latest issue 1976.
- Guam. Department of Commerce. Personal Income Study. a.
- Guam. Department of Commerce. Proceedings from Economic Conference. a.
- Guam. Department of Commerce. Quarterly Report on the Guam Consumer Price Index. q.
- Guam. Department of Commerce. Statistical Abstract. a. (prep. by its Economic Research Center)
- Guam Business Directory. irreg. ISSN 0072-7865 (prep. by its Economic Research Center)
- Guam Economic Annual Review. a.

**Guam. Department of Public Health and Social Services**
Office of Vital Statistics, P.O. Box 2816, Agana, Guam.
- Guam Statistical Annual Report. a. ISSN 0085-1310

**Guam. Department of Revenue and Taxation**
P.O. Box 2796, Agana, GU 96910.
- Guam. Department of Revenue and Taxation. Report. a. ISSN 0072-7873

**Micronesian Area Research Center**
see under University of Guam

**University of Guam. Micronesian Area Research Center**
Box E.K., Agana, GU 96910.
- Guam Recorder. q. ISSN 0046-6522
- Micronesica; devoted to the natural sciences of Micronesia. s-a. ISSN 0026-279X

# GUATEMALA

**Asociacion Filatelica de Guatemala**
Apartado Postal 39, Guatemala, Guatemala.
- Guatemala Filatelica. a. ISSN 0046-6549

**Asociacion General de Agricultores**
- A G A. (pub. by Publicidad Nacional)

**Asociacion Latino Americana de Facultades de Odontologia**
9A Calle 1-42, Zona 1, Guatemala, Guatemala.
- A L A F O. Revista. s-a. ISSN 0001-1703

**Asociacion Nacional del Cafe. Departamento de Asuntos Agricolas**
Edificio Etisa, Plazuela Espana, Zona 9, Guatemala, Guatemala.
- Asociacion Nacional del Cafe. Departamento de Asuntos Agricolas. Informe Anual. a. ISSN 0066-8567

**Asociacion Pediatrica de Guatemala**
- Guatemala Pediatrica. (pub. by Imprenta Fray Payo)

**Banco de Guatemala**
7A. Av. 22-01, Zona 1, Guatemala City, Guatemala.
- Banco de Guatemala. Boletin Estadistico. 4 per yr. ISSN 0005-481X

- Banco de Guatemala. Estudio Economico y
  Memoria de Labores. a.
- Banco de Guatemala. Informe Economico. q.
  ISSN 0045-1401
- Carta Semanal de Cafe. w.

**Camara de Industria de Guatemala**
Ruta 6, 9-21, Zona 4, Guatemala City, Guatemala.
- Industria. m. ISSN 0019-7408

**Central America Report**
Calle 3-19, Zone 1, Guatemala City, Guatemala.
- Central America Report. s-a.

**Centro de Estudios Militares**
Zona 17, Guatemala, Guatemala.
- Revista Militar de Guatemala. s-a. ISSN 0035-0133

**General Treaty on Central American Economic
Integration. Permanent Secretariat**
4 Avenida No. 10-25, Zona 14, Guatemala City,
Guatemala.
- Anuario Estadistico Centroamericano de
  Comercio Exterior. a. ISSN 0570-426X
- Compendio Estadistico Centroamericano. a. ISSN
  0588-912X
- Convenios Centroamericanos de Integration
  Economica. irreg. ISSN 0553-6863
- Directorio Industrial, Centroamerica- Panama.
  irreg.
- General Treaty for Central American Economic
  Integration. Permanent Secretariat Carta
  Informativa. irreg. ISSN 0553-6855
- General Treaty for Central American Economic
  Integration. Permanent Secretariat. Newsletter.
  irreg. ISSN 0553-6898
- Indicadores Economicos Centroamericanos. q.

**Guatemala. Direccion General de Estadistica**
Ministerio de Economia, 10a. Calle 7-69, Zona 1,
Guatemala, Guatelala.
- Estadisticas de Vehiculos en Circulacion en
  Guatemala. a.
- Guatemala. Direccion General de Estadistica.
  Anuario Estadistico. a.
- Guatemala. Direccion General de Estadistica
  Boletin Estadistico. a. ISSN 0017-5048
- Guatemala. Direccion General de Estadistica.
  Directoria Nacional de Establecimientos
  Industriales. a.

**Guatemala. Ministerio de Educacion. Instituto
Indigenista Nacional**
6A Ave. 1-22, Zona 1, Ciudad de Guatemala,
Guatemala.
- Guatemala Indigena. q. ISSN 0017-5056
- Instituto Indigenista Nacional. Boletin. 4 per yr.

**Guatemala. Observatorio Nacional de Guatemala**
Digesa Direccion de Recursos Naturales
Renovables, Guatemala, Guatemala.
- Observatorio Nacional de Guatemala. Boletin. m.

**Guatemala. Oficina de Planeamiento Integral de la
Educacion**
4A. Avenida 8-56, Zona 1, Guatemala Guatemala.
- Educacion y Planeamiento. irreg.

**Guayacan**
c/o Jose Guillermo Pacheco, Ed., 8 A. Calle 6-69,
Zone 4, Apartado 1352, Guatemala, Guatemala.
- Guayacan; revista de agricultura y ganaderia. m.
  ISSN 0046-6557

**Historia Natural y pro Natura**
c/o Jorge a Ibarra, Apdo Postal 987, Guatemala,
Guatemala.
- Historia Natural y pro Natura. q. ISSN 0018-2346

**Institute of Nutrition of Central America and Panama**
For publications of this agency see section for
UNITED NATIONS

**Instituto Centro Americano de Investigacion y
Tecnologia Industrial**
Avenida la Reforma 4-47, Zona 10, Apto. Postal
1552, Guatemala, Guatemala.
- I C A I T I. Boletin Informativo. bi-m.
- Instituto Centro Americano de Investigacion y
  Tecnologia Industrial. Publicaciones Geologicas.
  irreg.; no. 5, 1977. ISSN 0073-9936
- Technological Monographs. a.

**Instituto Centroamericano de Mercadotecnia de
Alimentos**
Apdo Postal 752, Guatemala, Guatemala.
- Mercadotecnia. m. ISSN 0025-9772

**Instituto de Antropologia e Historia**
Edificio No. 5, La Aurora, Guatemala City 13,
Guatemala.
- Antropologia e Historia de Guatemala (IDAEH)
  biennial. ISSN 0003-6102

**Instituto Interamericano de Ciencias Agricolas de la
O E A**
*see also* country section for COSTA RICA -
Instituto Interamericano de Ciencias Agricolas de
la O E A

**Instituto Interamericano de Ciencias Agricolas de la
O E A**
Apartado 1815, Guatemala, Guatemala.
- La Zona Norte. Informa. q.

**Empresa Editorial Luz, S. A.**
16 Calle No. 12-49, Zona 1, Guatemala City,
Guatemala.
- Alerta. d. ISSN 0002-5178

**Imprenta Fray Payo**
Ciudad 7, Guatemala , Guatemala.
- Guatemala Pediatrica. q. ISSN 0017-5064
  (Asociacion Pediatrica de Guatemala)

**Programa de Desarrollo de la Comunidad**
Presidencia de la Republica, Guatemala City,
Guatemala.
- Accion Conjunta. m. ISSN 0001-4613

**Publicidad Nacional**
4 Av. 8-66, Guatemala City 1, Guatemala.
- A G A. m. ISSN 0001-1274 (Asociacion General
  de Agricultores)

**Universidad de San Carlos de Guatemala**
Extension Universitaria Universidad de San Carlos,
Ciudad Universitaria, Zona 12 Guatemala,
Guatemala.
- Alero. bi-m.
- Humanidades. 2-3 per yr. ISSN 0018-7356
- Universidad de San Carlos Anual. a.

**Universidad de San Carlos de Guatemala. Escuela
Regional de Ingenieria Sanitaria**
Faculty de Ingeneria, Ciudad Universitaria, Zona
12, Guatemala, Guatemala.
- Brujula. irreg., 1972, vol. 4.

**Universidad de San Carlos de Guatemala. Facultad de
Humanidades**
Departamento de Publicaciones, 9a Avenida 13-39,
Zona 1, Guatemala City, Guatemala.
- Cuadernos de Antropologia. q.

**Universidad de San Carlos de Guatemala. Facultad de
Medicina Veterinaria y Zootecnia**
Ciudad Universitaria, Zona 12, Guatemala, Guatemala
- Universidad de San Carlos de Guatemala.
  Facultad de Medicina Veterinaria y Zootecnia
  Revista. irreg.

**Universidad de San Carlos de Guatemala. Instituto de
Investigaciones Economicas y Sociales**
Avenida de la Reforma No. 0-63, Zona 10,
Guatemala City, Guatemala.
- Economia. bi-m. ISSN 0046-113X

**Universidad de San Carlos. Facultad de Odontologia**
Aptdo. Postal 183, Guatemala City, Guatemala.
- Revista Guatemalteca de Estomatologia. 3 per yr.
  (prep. by its Colegio Estomatologico de
  Guatemala) (Co-sponsor: Sociedad Dental de
  Guatemala)

## GUINEA

**Patrice Lumumba Printing Office**
P.O. Box 156, Conakry, Guinea.
- Journal Officiel de Guinee. fortn. ISSN 0533-5701

## GUINEA-BISSAU

**Centro de Estudos da Guine Portuguesa**
Museu da Guine Portuguesa, Caixa Postal 37,
Bissau, Guinea-Bissau.
- Boletim Cultural da Guine Portuguesa. q; vol. 28,
  1973. ISSN 0006-5854

## GUYANA

**Georgetown Chamber of Commerce**
Box 189, 156 Waterloo St., Georgetown, Guyana
- Guyana Business. q. ISSN 0017-5854 (Subsc. to:
  Yusuf Ali, Box 190,
  Georgetown, Guyana)

**Guyana. Central Agricultural Station. Research
Division**
Mon Repos, E.C. Demerara, Guyana.
- Agricultural Research Guyana. a. ISSN 0065-4523

**Guyana. Geological Survey Department**
P.O. Box 1028, Georgetown, Guyana.
- Guyana. Geological Survey Department. Annual
  Reports. a. ISSN 0072-9108
- Guyana. Geological Survey Department. Mineral
  Resources Pamphlet. irreg., 1971, no. 14. ISSN
  0072-9124
- Inter-Guiana Geological Conference. Proceedings.
  irreg., 1969, 8th, Guyana. ISSN 0074-1027

**Guyana. Hydrometeorological Serivce**
Georgetown, Guyana.
- Guyana. Hydrometeorological Service. Annual
  Climatological Data Summary. a.

**Guyana. Ministry of Agriculture**
Georgetown, Guyana.
- Guyana. Ministry of Natural Development and
  Agriculture. Annual Report. a.

**Guyana. Ministry of External Affairs**
Carmichael St., Georgetown, Guyana.
- Guyana Journal. q. ISSN 0046-6654

**Guyana. Ministry of Information and Culture**
18 Brickdam, Georgetown, Guyana.
- News from Guyana. w. ISSN 0028-9078
- Official Gazette of Guyana. w. ISSN 0030-0314

**Guyana. National Library**
Box 110, Georgetown, Guyana.
- Guyanese National Bibliography. q.

**Guyana. Office of the Ombudsman**
18/20 Croal St. Stabroek, Georgetown, Guyana.
- Guyana. Ombudsman. Report. a.

**Guyana Association of Professional Engineers**
Georgetown, Guyana.
- G.A.P.E. irreg.

**Guyana Institute for Social Research and Action**
P.O. Box 528, Georgetown, Guyana.
- G I S R A. q.

**Guyana Library Association**
c/o National Library, Box 110, Georgetown,
Guyana.
- Guyana Library Association Bulletin. q.

**Guyana Rice Producers Association**
- Rice Review. (pub. by New Guyana Co. Ltd.)

**New Guyana Co. Ltd.**
Lot 9, Government Industrial Estate, East Bank,
Demerara, Guyana.
- Rice Review. q. ISSN 0035-497X (Guyana Rice
  Producers Association)

**New World Associates**
215 King St., Georgetown, Guyana.
- New World. fortn. ISSN 0028-7008

**People's Progressive Party**
Freedom House, 41 Robb St., Georgetown, Guyana.
- Guyana Information Bulletin. m. ISSN 0017-5862
- Thunder. q. ISSN 0040-6635

**U.S. Embassy**
31 Main St., Cummingsburg, Georgetown, Guyana.
- Commercial Newsletter - U.S. Embassy. m.

**University of Guyana**
Box 841, Georgetown, Guyana.
- University of Guyana. Department of Geography. Occasional Papers. irreg.
- University of Guyana Language Forum; review of literary, linguistic and educational studies. s-a.

# HAITI

**Centre Haitien d'Investigation en Science Sociales**
Rue Bonne Foi 23, B. P. 1294, Port-au-Prince, Haiti.
- C H I S S Cahiers. s-a (with supplements) ISSN 0045-6098

**College Saint Pierre**
Rue Capois (Champs de Mars), Port-au-Prince, Haiti.
- Haiti Tim'tim. q.

**Haiti. Administration Generale des Douanes**
Port-au-Prince, Haiti.
- Annuaire du Commerce Exterieur d'Haiti: Importations, Exportations. a.

**Haiti. Bureau d'Ethnologie**
Port-au-Prince, Haiti.
- Bureau d'Ethnologie. Bulletin. q.

**Haiti. Departement du Travail et du Bien-Etre Social**
Port-au-Prince, Haiti.
- Revue du Travail. a. ISSN 0482-8062

**Haiti. Institut Haitien de Statistique. Departement des Finances et des Affaires Economique**
Cite de l'Exposition, Blvd. Harry Truman, Port-au-Prince, Haiti.
- Haiti. Institut Haitien de Statistique. Bulletin Trimestriel de Statistique. q. ISSN 0017-6788

**Haiti. Office d'Assurance Accidents du Travail, Maladie et Maternite**
Port-Au-Prince, Haiti.
- Prevention. s-a. ISSN 0048-5241

**Haiti-Culture**
Boite Postale T, Port-au-Prince, Haiti.
- Haiti-Culture. irreg.

# HONDURAS

**Academia Hondurena de la Lengua**
Apartado Postal 38, Tegucigalpa, Honduras.
- Academia Hondurena de la Lengua. Boletin. a. ISSN 0065-0471

**Ariel**
3 Calle 1084, Apdo. 61, Tegucigalpa, Honduras.
- Ariel. m. ISSN 0034-7051

**Asociacion de Prensa Hondurena**
Tegucigalpa, D.C., Honduras.
- Revista A P H. m. ISSN 0034-6926

**Asociacion Pediatrica Hondurena**
c/o Dr. Rodolfo Valenzuela, Box 105-C, Tegucigalpa D.C., Honduras.
- Honduras Pediatrica. q. ISSN 0018-4535

**Banco Central de Honduras. Departamento de Estudios Economicos**
Tegucigalpa D.C., Honduras.
- Banco Central de Honduras. Departamento de Estudios Economicos. Boletin Estadistico. bi-m.
- Banco Central de Honduras. Informe Economico. irreg.
- Banco Central de Honduras. Memoria. a. ISSN 0067-3218
- Honduras en Cifras. irreg.

**Banco Centroamericano de Integracion Economica**
Apdo Postal 772, Tegucigalpa,D.C., Honduras.
- Banco Centroamericano de Integracion Economica. Carta Informativa. m.

**Banco National de Fomento**
Tegucigalpa, Honduras.
- Banco Nacional de Fomento, Tegucigalpa. Memoria Anual. irreg.; latest issue, 1973. ISSN 0067-3390

**Camara de Comercio e Industrias de Tegucigalpa**
- Comercio. (pub. by Honduras Industrial, S. A.)

**Clubes Rotarios de la Republica**
Aptdo Postal 38, Tegucigalpa, Honduras.
- Honduras Rotaria. m.

**Colegio de Abogados de Honduras**
Tegucigalpa, D.C. Honduras.
- Ley. q. ISSN 0024-1644

**Colegio Hondureno Economistas**
Tegucigalpa, D.C., Honduras.
- Pensamiento Economico. q.

**Comite Regional de Recursos Hidraulicos**
Apartado 718, Tegucigalpa, Honduras.
- Proyecto Hidrometeorologico Centroamericano. Boletin Informativo. bi-m. ISSN 0033-1953

**Cultural Comercial**
Apdo. Postal 239, Tegucigalpa, Honduras.
- Cultural Comercial. m. ISSN 0011-2836

**Escuela Agricola Panamericana**
Apartado 93, Tegucigalpa, Honduras.
- Ceiba. s-a. ISSN 0008-8692

**Hibueras**
Grupo 12, Bloque 27, No. 15 Colonia Presidente Kennedy, Tegucigalpa, Honduras.
- Hibueras; revista de informacion y divulgacion general. q. ISSN 0046-7359

**Honduras. Corte Suprema de Justicia**
Tegucigalpa D.C., Honduras.
- Honduras. Corte Suprema de Justicia. Gaceta Judicial. bi-m. ISSN 0016-3791

**Honduras. Empresa Nacional de Energia Electrica. Departamento de Planificacion Economica**
Tegucigalpa, Honduras.
- Empresa Nacional de Energia Electrica. Datos Estadisticos. a.

**Honduras. Instituto Hondureno de Seguridad Social. Departamento de Estadistica y Actuarial**
Apartado 555, Tegucigalpa, D.C., Honduras.
- Instituto Hondureno de Seguridad Social. Departamento de Estadistica y Procesamiento de Datos. Anuario Estadistico. a (with supplements) ISSN 0074-0233

**Honduras Industrial, S. A.**
Apto. Postal No. 17-G, Tegucigalpa, D. C., Honduras.
- Comercio. m. ISSN 0010-2245 (Camara de Comercio e Industrias de Tegucigalpa)

**Ideas**
Tegucigalpa, Honduras.
- Ideas; revista de letras femeninas. bi-m.

**Instituto Hondureno de Antropologia e Historia**
Apartado 1518, Tegucigalpa, Honduras.
- Yaxkin. q.

**Instituto Hondureno de Cultura Interamericana**
Avda. 2 No. 511, Comayaguela, D.C., Apdo 201, Tegucigalpa, Honduras.
- Sol. m. ISSN 0049-1276

**Partido Liberal. Consejo Central Ejecutivo**
Tegucigalpa, Honduras.
- Consejo Central Ejecutivo del Partido Liberal de Honduras. Memoria. irreg.

**Proyecto Hidrometeorologico Centroamericano**
- Proyecto Hidrometeorologico Centroamericano. Boletin Informativo. (pub. by Comite Regional de Recursos Hidraulicos)

**Sociedad de Abogados**
Tegucigulpa, D.C., Honduras.
- Foro Hondureno. 12 per yr (some issues quadruple)

**Universidad Nacional Autonoma de Honduras. Facultad de Ciencias Juridicas y Sociales**
Bloque de Aulas, 2, Ciudad Universitaria, Tegucigalpa, D.C., Honduras.
- Revista de Derecho. a.

**Universidad Nacional Autonoma de Honduras. Instituto de Investigaciones Economicas y Sociales**
Ciudad Universitaria, Tegucigalpa, Honduras.
- Economia Politica. irreg.; no. 6, 1973. ISSN 0424-2483

- Universidad Nacional Autonoma de Honduras. Instituto de Investigaciones Economicas y Sociales. Boletin. m.

# HONG KONG

**A.V.A. Promotions Ltd.**
907 Takshing House, Des Voeux Rd, Hong Kong, Hong Kong.
- Hi-Fi Musical Life/Yin Yueh Sheng Huo. m. (Chung Kuang Yu Hsien Kung Ssu)

**Action Committee Against Narcotics**
c/o Security Branch, Colonial Secretariat, International Bldg., 24th Floor, Des Voeux Rd, Hong Kong, Hong Kong.
- Action Committee Against Narcotics. Annual Report. irreg.

**Artists Associates**
G.P.O. Box 1623, Hong Kong, Hong Kong.
- A.A.'s Far East Businessman's Directory. a. ISSN 0532-9175

**Arts of Asia Publications**
Metropole Bldg., 57 Peking Rd., Kowloon, Hong Kong.
- Arts of Asia. 6 per yr. ISSN 0004-4083

**Asia Letter Ltd**
Box 3477, Sheungwan Post Office, Hong Kong, Hong Kong
(U.S. Address: Box 54149, Los Angeles, CA 90054)
- Asia Letter; a weekly newsletter containing an authoritative analysis of Asian Affairs. w. ISSN 0004-4466
- China Letter. m.
- Indonesia Letter. m. ISSN 0019-7297
- Japan Letter. s-m.

**Asia Trade Journals Ltd.**
10th Floor, Tung Hing Building, 57-59 Lockhart Road, Hong Kong, Hong Kong.
- Asian Money Manager. bi-m.
- Hong Kong Engineer. m.

**Asian Finance Publications Ltd.**
Suite D, 9th Floor, Hyde Centre, 223 Gloucester Rd., Hong Kong, Hong Kong.
- Asian Finance. m.

**Asian Research Service**
Box 2232, G. P. U., Hong Kong, Hong Kong.
- Asian Profile. bi-m.

**Business International Asia-Pacific**
301 Asian House, No. 1 Hennessy Rd., Hong Kong, Hong Kong.
- Business Asia; weekly report to managers of Asia/ Pacific operations. w. ISSN 0572-7545
- Business China. m.

**Business Press Ltd.**
Tak Yan Commercial Building, 11/F., 30-32 d'Aguilar St., Hong Kong, Hong Kong.
- Textile Asia. m. ISSN 0049-3554

**Business Publications Ltd.**
28th Floor, Connaught Centre, Connaught Road, Hong Kong, Hong Kong.
- Asian Forum. m.

**C.N.A.**
Box 3225, Hong Kong, Hong Kong.
- China News Analysis. w. ISSN 0009-4404

**Catholic Truth Society**
Grand Bldg, P.O. Box 2984, Hong Kong, Hong Kong.
- Hong Kong Catholic Directory and Year Book/ Hsiang-Kang T'ien Chu Chiao Shou T'se. a. ISSN 0073-3210

**Chi Luen Press**
B1, Carnarvon Mansion, 10th Fl., 12, Carnarvon Rd., Kowloon, Hong Kong.
- Look Fortnightly. bi-m ISSN 0024-6387

**Chinese University of Hong Kong**
Shatin N.T., Hong Kong, Hong Kong.
- Chinese University of Hong Kong. Journal. a.

**Chinese University of Hong Kong. Chung Chi College**
Shatin N.T., Hong Kong.
- Chinese University of Hong Kong. Chung Chi College. Music Department. Holdings of the Chinese Music Archives. a.
- Chung Chi Bulletin. 2-3 per yr. ISSN 0009-6261
- Chung Chi Journal. s-a. ISSN 0009-627X

**Chinese University of Hong Kong. Economic Research Centre**
Shatin, N.T., Hong Kong.
- Chinese University of Hong Kong. Economic Research Centre. Hong Kong Series. Occasional Paper. irreg.
- Chinese University of Hong Kong. Economic Research Centre. Industrial Country Series. Occasional Paper. irreg.
- Chinese University of Hong Kong. Economic Research Centre. Mainland China Series. Occasional Paper. irreg.

**Chinese University of Hong Kong. Institute of Chinese Studies**
677 Nathan Road., 12th Floor, Kowtoon, Hong Kong.
- Chinese University of Hong Kong. Institute of Chinese Studies. Journal. a.

**Chinese University of Hong Kong. Translation Centre**
Shatin N.T., Hong Kong.
- Renditions; a Chinese-English translation magazine. s-a.

**Ching Hsin Chih Tso Kung Ssu Chu Pan Pu**
*see* Fresh Productions

**Christian Study Centre on Chinese Religion and Culture**
P.O. Box 33, Shatin N.T., Hong Kong.
- Ching Feng; quarterly notes on Christianity and Chinese religion and culture. q. ISSN 0009-4668

**Chung Kuang Yu Hsien Kung Ssu**
- Hi-Fi Musical Life/Yin Yueh Sheng Huo. (pub. by A.V.A. Promotions Ltd.)

**Continental Research Institute**
199/203 Hennessy Rd., Hong Kong, Hong Kong.
- Continental Research Series. irreg. ISSN 0069-9535
- Peking Informers. s-m. ISSN 0031-4110

**Cosmorama Cultural Enterprise Co. Ltd.**
12 Tsing Fung St., 3-F North Point, Hong Kong, Hong Kong.
- Cosmorama Pictorial. m. ISSN 0010-9568

**Eastern Horizon Press**
472 Hennessy Rd. 3rd. Floor, Hong Kong, Hong Kong.
- Eastern Horizon; a cultural magazine. m. ISSN 0012-8813

**Economic Information & Agency**
342 Hennessy Rd., 11th Floor, Hong Kong, Hong Kong.
- Economic Reporter. q. ISSN 0013-0265

**Engineering Society of Hong Kong**
- Hong Kong Engineer. (pub. by Asia Trade Journals, Ltd.)

**Far East Trade Press Ltd.**
1908 Prince's Building, Des Voeux Rd., Hong Kong, Hong Kong.
- Asian Building & Construction. m.
- Asian Business and Industry. m.
- Asian Product News.
- Hong Kong Builder Directory. irreg.
- Modern Medicine of Asia. m.
- Travelnews Asia. bi-m.

**Far Eastern Economic Review Ltd.**
Box 47, Hong Kong, Hong Kong
(Dist. in U.S. by Chas. E. Tuttle Co., 28 So. Main St., Rutland, Vt. 05701)
- All-Asia Guide. a. ISSN 0072-4939
- Asia Yearbook. a.
- China Trade Report. m. ISSN 0009-448X
- Far Eastern Economic Review. w. ISSN 0014-7591
- Far Eastern Economic Review. Yearbook. a. ISSN 0071-3821

**Fei Yi-Ming**
342 Hennessy Rd., Hong Kong, Hong Kong.
- Ta Kung Pao. w. ISSN 0039-8675

**Fresh Productions**
Room 11a, 11th Floor, 30-32 Queen's Rd. East, Hong Kong, Hong Kong.
- Fresh/Ching Hsin. m.

**Hong Kong. Census and Statistics Department**
Kai Tak Commercial Bldg., Des Voeux Rd., Central, Hong Kong, Hong Kong
(Subscr. to: Government Information Services, Beaconsfield House, Queen's Rd., Central, Victoria, Hong Kong)
- Hong Kong. Census and Statistics Department. Estimates of Gross Domestic Product. a.
- Hong Kong. Census and Statistics Department. The Budget: Economic Background. a.
- Hong Kong Economic Trends and Indexes. m.
- Hong Kong Monthly Digest of Statistics. m. ISSN 0300-418X
- Hong Kong Social and Economic Trends. biennial.
- Hong Kong Trade Statistics. m.

**Hong Kong. Education Department**
- Geography Bulletin. (pub. by Hong Kong Government Information Services)

**Hong Kong. Fisheries Research Station**
100A Shek Pai Wan Rd., Aberdeen, Hong Kong.
- Hong Kong. Fisheries Research Station. Bulletin. irreg., latest issue, 1973. ISSN 0065-0269

**Hong Kong. Government Information Services**
Beaconsfield House, Queen's Rd., Central, Victoria, Hong Kong, Hong Kong.
- Agriculture Hong Kong. a.
- Astronomical Tables and Star Charts for Hong Kong. irreg.
- Geography Bulletin. a. (Hong Kong. Education Department)
- Hong Kong. Broadcasting Department. Annual Departmental Report by the Director of Broadcasting. a.
- Hong Kong. Department of Commerce and Industry. Annual Statistical Review. a.
- Hong Kong. Legal Aid Department. Annual Departmental Report by the Director of Legal Aid. a.
- Hong Kong. Prison Department. Drug Addiction Research Programme. biennial.
- Hong Kong. Supreme Court. Annual Judicial Statistics. a.
- Hong Kong. Transport Department. Hong Kong Departmental Report by the Commissioner for Transport. irreg.
- Hong Kong. Urban Services Department. Annual Departmental Report. a.
- Hong Kong Annual Report. a.

**Hong Kong. Government Publications Centre**
Star Ferry Concourse, Hong Kong, Hong Kong.
- Hong Kong Government Gazette. w.
- Scientific Directory of Hong Kong. irreg. ISSN 0586-5751

**Hong Kong. Royal Observatory**
Nathan Road, Kowloon, Hong Kong, Hong Kong.
- Hong Kong. Royal Observatory. Climatological Note. a.
- Hong Kong. Royal Observatory. Monthly Weather Summary. m.

**Hong Kong Economic Association**
Box 14004, Hong Kong, Hong Kong.
- Hong Kong Economic Papers. a. ISSN 0018-4578

**Hong Kong General Chamber of Commerce**
Box 852, Union House, Hong Kong, Hong Kong.
- Hong Kong News. q.

**Hong Kong Geographical Association**
c/o Poon Chung-Shing, Secretary, Dept of Geography and Geology, Hong Kong University, Hong Kong, Hong Kong.
- Hong Kong Geographical Association. Bulletin. a.

**Hong Kong Junior Chamber**
23. Ice House St., Hong Kong, Hong Kong.
- Hong Kong Junior Chamber. Annual Review. a.

**Hong Kong Library Association**
c/o Univ. of Hong Kong Library, Pokfulum Rd., Hong Kong, Hong Kong.
- Hong Kong Library Association. Journal. irreg. ISSN 0073-3237

**Hong Kong Management Association**
Management House, 26 Canal Road West, Happy Valley, Hong Kong, Hong Kong.
- Hong Kong Manager. m. ISSN 0018-4594

**Hong Kong Medical Association**
Duke of Windsor Building, 15 Hennessy Road, 5th Floor, Hong Kong, Hong Kong.
- Hong Kong Medical Association. Bulletin. a.

**Hong Kong Nurses Association**
Hong Kong, Hong Kong.
- Hong Kong Nursing Journal/Hsiang-Kang Hu Li Tsa Chih. s-a. ISSN 0073-3253

**Hong Kong Tourist Association**
Box 2597, Hong Kong, Hong Kong.
- Hong Kong Travel Bulletin. m. ISSN 0018-4616
- Statistical Review of Tourism in Hong Kong. a.

**Hong Kong Trade Development Council**
Connaught Centre, Connought Rd., Hong Kong, Hong Kong.
- Apparel. s-a.
- Hong Kong Enterprise. m. ISSN 0018-4586
- Industrial Investment Hong Kong. a.

**Hong Kong University Press**
Hong Kong, Hong Kong.
- Contemporary China/Tang-Tai Chung-Kuo. a. (University of Hong Kong. Department of Economics and Political Science)
- Journal of Oriental Studies. s-a. ISSN 0022-331X (University of Hong Kong. Centre of Asian Studies)

**Hsiang-kang Chi-tu Chiao Kung Yeh Wei Yuan Hui**
57, Peking Road, 4th Floor, Chiu-Lung, Hong Kong, Hong Kong.
- Hong Kong Journal of Trade Unions/Hsiang-Kang Kung Hui. m.

**Hsiang-Kang Kung i Chih Pin Chang Fa Chan Hsieh Hui.**
Handicrafts Manufacturers Development Association, P.O. Box: K-880, Chiu-Lung, Kowloon, Hong Kong.
- Hong Kong Industrial Products Directory/Hsiang-Kang Kung Yeh Chih Pin Nien Chien. irreg.

**Hsing-Tao Pao Yeh Yu Hsien Kung Ssu**
News Building 8th Floor, 635 King's Road, Hong Kong, Hong Kong.
- Sing Tao Tour Magazine. m.

**Hsinhua News Agency**
Hong Kong Branch, 5 Sharp St., W. Hong Kong, Hong Kong.
- Hsinhua; selected news items. ISSN 0018-6945

**Interasia Publications**
257 Gloucester Rd., Fifth Floor, Hong Kong, Hong Kong.
- Asia Travel Trade. m.

**Johnston International Publishing Corp**
P. O. Box 9765, Hong Kong, Hong Kong.
- Modern Asia. 10 per yr. ISSN 0026-7481

**Kompass Hong Kong**
c/o Commerce and Industry Dept., 46 Connaught Rd., Hong Kong, Hong Kong.
- Kompass Hong Kong; register of HongKong industry and commerce. a. ISSN 0075-6679

**Letters from Asia**
P.O. 13225, Hong Kong, Hong Kong.
- Letters from Asia. m.

**Louise Bao**
G.P.O. Box 13154, Hong Kong, Hong Kong.
- Mercury Magazine/Shui Hsing Cha Chi. m. ISSN 0037-4415

**Lutheran Church-Missouri Synod, Hong Kong Mission**
c/o Rev. Philip Ho, 68 Begonia Road, Yau Yat Chen, Kowloon, Hong Kong.
- Morning Bell. q.

**Media Publishers Ltd.**
Room 603, Kayamally Bldg., Queens Road Central, Hong Kong, Hong Kong.
- Media. m.

**New Asia College. Institute of Advanced Chinese Studies and Research**
Chinese University of Hong Kong, 6 Farm Rd., Kowloon, Hong Kong.
- Hsin-Ya Hsueh Pao. a. ISSN 0073-375X

**Ocean Literary Press**
No.3. on Ning Lane, Sai Ying Pun, Hong Kong, Hong Kong.
- Ocean Literature. m.

**Oriental Publicity Service**
P.O. Box 4366, N.P., Hong Kong, Hong Kong.
- Hong Kong Manufacturers and Exporters Register. irreg., 1975, 8th edt. ISSN 0073-3245

**Pacific Magazines Ltd.**
S/F, 257 Gloucester Road, Hong Kong, Hong Kong.
- Insight. bi-m.
- Insight for Decision Makers in Asia. m.

**R. V. Pandit, Ed. & Pub.**
31 Queen's Rd. Central, Hong Kong, Hong Kong (U.S. Address: 122 E. 42nd St., New York, NY 10017)
- Asia Magazine. fortn. ISSN 0004-4474

**People to People**
20 Carnavon Rd., 2nd Fl., Kowloon, Hong Kong.
- People to People/Jen Jen Tsa Chih. m.

**Radiotronics Publishers**
1 A, Min St., 9/F, Kowloon, Hong Kong.
- Wu Hsien Tien Yueh Kan/Radiotronics.

**Reader's Digest Association Far East Ltd.**
22 Westlands Rd., Toppan Bldg., 7th Floor, Quarry Bay, Hong Kong, Hong Kong.
- Reader's Digest (Asian Edition) m. ISSN 0034-0383
- Tu Cher Wen Cher Reader's Digest(Chinese Edition) m. ISSN 0041-3836

**Royal Asiatic Society**
Hong Kong Branch, Box 13864, Hong Kong, Hong Kong.
- Royal Asiatic Society. Hong Kong Branch. Journal. a. ISSN 0085-5774

**South China Morning Post Ltd.**
Box 47, Hong Kong, Hong Kong.
- Around Hong Kong. w.
- Asian Golf Digest. m.

**South East Wind Monthly**
Flat "T", Hung Lee Bldg., 21/F., Ngoi Man St., Shaukeiwan, Hong Kong, Hong Kong.
- South East Wind Monthly/Tung Nan Feng. m.

**Ssu Hai Chu Pan Shih Yeh Yu Hsien Kung Ssu**
122b, Argyle St., Kowloon 1/F, Hong Kong, Hong Kong.
- Golden Movie News/Chia Ho Tien Ying. m.

**Teens' Magazine Publishing Co.**
No. 1 on Ning Lane, Sai Ying Pun, Hong Kong, Hong Kong.
- Nien Ching Jen/Teens. m.

**Time Press**
17-F Flat B7, Canal Road, Hong Kong, Hong Kong.
- Chinese Learning/Chung Wen Hsueh Hsi. m.

**Trade Media Ltd.**
Box K-1786, Kowloon Central Post Office, Kowloon, Hong Kong.
- Asian Sources Hardwares. m.

**Trade Press Media Ltd.**
P.O. Box K-1786, Kowloon, Hong Kong.
- Asian Sources. m.

**Transpacific Magazines Ltd.**
77 New Henry House, Hong Kong, Hong Kong.
- Daring Confessions. bi-m. ISSN 0011-6645
- Intimate Confessions. bi-m. ISSN 0020-9805
- My Personal Love Secrets. bi-m.
- Real Life Confessions. bi-m. ISSN 0034-0839
- Revealing Confession. bi-m. ISSN 0034-625X
- Secret Confessions. bi-m. ISSN 0037-0592
- True Confidential Confessions. bi-m. ISSN 0041-3496
- True Life Secrets. bi-m. ISSN 0041-3534

- True Modern Romances. bi-m. ISSN 0041-3569

**Union Cultural Organization Ltd.**
No. 9 College Road, Kowloon, Hong Kong.
- Communist China Problem Research Series. irreg. ISSN 0069-7788
- Communist China Yearbook Series. irreg. ISSN 0069-7796
- Index to Titles of English News Releases of Hsinhua News Agency. irreg. ISSN 0082-7789
- Who's Who in Communist China. irreg., 1969, 2nd ed. vols. 1 & 2. ISSN 0083-9477

**United States Information Service**
26 Garden Rd., Hong Kong, Hong Kong.
- Current Scene; developments in the People's Republic of China. m. ISSN 0011-3883

**University of Hong Kong. Centre of Asian Studies**
Pokfulam Road, Hong Kong, Hong Kong.
- Journal of Oriental Studies. (pub. by Hong Kong University Press)
- University of Hong Kong. Centre of Asian Studies. Bibliographies and Research Guides. irreg. ISSN 0441-1900
- University of Hong Kong. Centre of Asian Studies. Occasional Papers and Monographs. irreg.

**University of Hong Kong. Department of Economics and Political Science**
- Contemporary China/Tang-Tai Chung-Kuo. (pub. by Hong Kong University Press)

**Univ. of Hong Kong. English Society**
Hong Kong, Hong Kong.
- Chimes. a. ISSN 0069-3642

**Western Pacific Orthopaedic Association**
Orthopaedic Dept., Queen Elizabeth Hospital, Kowloon, Hong Kong.
- Western Pacific Orthopaedic Association. Journal. s-a. ISSN 0043-4019

**Wide Angle Press**
186, Johnston Road, Hong Kong, Hong Kong.
- Wide Angle/Kuang Chiao Ching. m.

# HUNGARY

**Actio Catholica**
Kossuth Lajos u. 1, 1053 Budapest 5, Hungary (Subscr. to: Kultura, Box 149, H-1389 Budapest, Hungary)
- Vigilia. m. ISSN 0042-6024

**Akademiai Kiado, Publishing House of the Hungarian Academy of Sciences**
P.O. Box 24, H-1363 Budapest, Hungary
- Absorption Spectra in the Ultraviolet and Visible Region. irreg. ISSN 0065-0412 (Magyar Tudomanyos Akademia) (Distr. in U.S. by Robert E. Krieger Publishing Co. Inc., 645 New York Ave., Huntington, N.Y. 11743)
- Acta Agronomica. 4 per yr. ISSN 0001-513X (Magyar Tudomanyos Akademia)
- Acta Alimentaria. q. ISSN 0302-7368 (Magyar Tudomanyos Akademia)
- Acta Antiqua. q. ISSN 0044-5975 (Magyar Tudomanyos Akademia)
- Acta Archaeologica. q. ISSN 0001-5210 (Magyar Tudomanyos Akademia)
- Acta Biochimica et Biophysica. q. ISSN 0001-5253 (Magyar Tudomanyos Akademia)
- Acta Biologica. q. ISSN 0001-5288 (Magyar Tudomanyos Akademia)
- Acta Botanica. q. ISSN 0001-5350 (Magyar Tudomanyos Akademia)
- Acta Chimica. m.(4 nos.to a vol.) ISSN 0001-5407 (Magyar Tudomanyos Akademia)
- Acta Chirurgica. q. ISSN 0001-5431 (Magyar Tudomanyos Akademia)
- Acta Ethnographica. q. ISSN 0001-5628 (Magyar Tudomanyos Akademia)
- Acta Geodaetica, Geophysica et Montanistica. q. ISSN 0001-5679 (Magyar Tudomanyos Akademia)
- Acta Geologica. q. ISSN 0001-5695 (Magyar Tudomanyos Akademia)
- Acta Historiae Artium. q. ISSN 0001-5830 (Magyar Tudomanyos Akademia)
- Acta Historica. q. ISSN 0001-5849 (Magyar Tudomanyos Akademia)
- Acta Juridica. q. ISSN 0001-592X (Magyar Tudomanyos Akademia)

- Acta Linguistica. q. ISSN 0001-5946 (Magyar Tudomanyos Akademia)
- Acta Litteraria. q. ISSN 0567-7661 (Magyar Tudomanyos Akademia)
- Acta Mathematica. 2 vols. in 4 issues per yr. ISSN 0001-5954 (Magyar Tudomanyos Akademia)
- Acta Medica. q. ISSN 0001-5989 (Magyar Tudomanyos Akademia)
- Acta Microbiologica. q. ISSN 0001-6187 (Magyar Tudomanyos Akademia)
- Acta Morphologica. q. ISSN 0001-6217 (Magyar Tudomanyos Akademia)
- Acta Oeconomica. 2 vols. per yr.(4 nos. per vol.) ISSN 0001-6373 (Magyar Tudomanyos Akademia)
- Acta Orientalia. 3 nos. to a vol. ISSN 0001-6446 (Magyar Tudomanyos Akademia)
- Acta Paediatrica. q. ISSN 0001-6527 (Magyar Tudomanyos Akademia)
- Acta Physica. 2 vols. per yr.(4 nos. per vol.) ISSN 0001-6705 (Magyar Tudomanyos Akademia)
- Acta Physiologica. 2 vols. per yr.(4 nos per vol.) ISSN 0001-6756 (Magyar Tudomanyos Akademia)
- Acta Phytopathologica. q. ISSN 0001-6780 (Magyar Tudomanyos Akademia)
- Acta Technica. q. ISSN 0001-7035 (Magyar Tudomanyos Akademia)
- Acta Veterinaria. q. ISSN 0001-7205 (Magyar Tudomanyos Akademia)
- Acta Zoologica. q. ISSN 0001-7264 (Magyar Tudomanyos Akademia)
- Agrartorteneti Szemle/Agricultural History Review. q. ISSN 0002-1105 (Magyar Tudomanyos Akademia)
- Agrartudomanyi Kozlemenyek. q. (Magyar Tudomanyos Akademia)
- Agrokemia es Talajtan. q. ISSN 0002-1873 (Magyar Tudomanyos Akademia. Agrokemiai Kutato Intezet)
- Alkalmazott Matematikai Lapok. q. (Magyar Tudomanyos Akademia. Matematikai es Fizikai Tudomanyok Osztalya)
- Allam- es Jogtudomany/Political Science and Jurisprudence. q. ISSN 0002-564X (Magyar Tudomanyos Akademia. Allam-es Jogtudomanyi Intezet)
- Allattani Kozlemenyek/Zoological Proceedings. q. ISSN 0002-5658 (Magyar Tudomanyos Akademia)
- Analysis Mathematica. q. (Magyar Tudomanyos Akademia) (Co-sponsor: Akademiya Nauk S.S.S.R.)
- Antik Tanulmanyok; Studia Antiqua. s-a. ISSN 0003-567X (Magyar Tudomanyos Akademia)
- Archaeologia Hungarica. Series Nova. irreg. ISSN 0066-5916 (Magyar Tudomanyos Akademia. Regeszeti Intezet)
- Archaeologiai Ertesito/Archaeological Bulletin. s-a. ISSN 0003-8032 (Magyar Tudomanyos Akademia)
- Architectura. irreg. ISSN 0066-6270 (Magyar Tudomanyos Akademia) (Co-sponsor: Magyar Epitomuveszek Szovetsege)
- Bibliotheca Hungarica Antiqua. irreg. ISSN 0067-8007 (Magyar Tudomanyos Akademia)
- Bibliotheca Orientalis Hungarica. irreg. ISSN 0067-8104 (Magyar Tudomanyos Akademia)
- Biologia. s-a. (Magyar Tudomanyos Akademia)
- Botanikai Kozlemenyek/Botanical Proceedings. q. ISSN 0006-8144 (Magyar Tudomanyos Akademia)
- Budapest Varostorteneti Monografiai. imeg. ISSN 0068-3337 (Magyar Tudomanyos Akademia)
- Diplomaciai Iratok Magyarorszag Kulpolitikajahoz. irreg. ISSN 0070-492X (Magyar Tudomanyos Akademia)
- Disquisitiones Mathematicae Hungariae. irreg. ISSN 0070-671X (Magyar Tudomanyos Akademia)
- Epites es Epiteszettudomany/Building and Architectural Science. q. ISSN 0013-9661 (Magyar Tudomanyos Akademia)
- Ertekezesek a Torteneti Tudomanyok Korebol. Uj Sorozat. irreg. ISSN 0071-1233 (Magyar Tudomanyos Akademia)
- Etudes Historiques. quinquennial. ISSN 0071-2108 (Magyar Tudomanyos Akademia)
- Filologiai Kozlony/Philological Review. q. ISSN 0015-1785 (Magyar Tudomanyos Akademia)
- Filozofiai Irok Tara. irreg. ISSN 0071-4984 (Magyar Tudomanyos Akademia)
- Filozofiai Tanulmanyok. irreg. ISSN 0071-4992 (Magyar Tudomanyos Akademia)
- Foldrajzi Ertesito. q. ISSN 0015-5403 (Magyar Tudomanyos Akademia. Foldrajztudomanyi Kutato Intezet)

- Foldrajzi Kozlemenyek. q. ISSN 0015-5411 (Magyar Foldrajzi Tarsasag)
- Foldrajzi Monografiak. irreg. ISSN 0071-6642 (Magyar Tudomanyos Akademia)
- Foldrajzi Tanulmanyok. irreg. ISSN 0071-6650 (Magyar Tudomanyos Akademia)
- Foldtani Kozlony. q. ISSN 0015-542X (Magyarhoni Foldtani Tarsulat)
- Gazdasag es Jogtudomany. q. (Magyar Tudomanyos Akademia)
- Gazdasagtorteneti Ertekezesek. irreg. ISSN 0072-033X (Magyar Tudomanyos Akademia)
- Geography of World Agriculture. irreg. (Magyar Tudomanyos Akademia)
- Geonomia es Banyaszat. q. (Magyar Tudomanyos Akademia)
- Gorog es Latin Irok Tara/Scriptores Graeci et Latini. irreg. ISSN 0072-5021 (Magyar Tudomanyos Akademia)
- Haematologia; international quarterly of haematology. q. ISSN 0017-6559 (Magyar Tudomanyos Akademia)
- Helikon Vilagirodalmi Figyelo/Helikon Review of World Literature. q. ISSN 0017-999X (Magyar Tudomanyos Akademia. Irodalomtudomanyi Intezet)
- Indices Verborum Linguae Mongoliae Monumentis Traditorum. irreg. ISSN 0073-7194 (Magyar Tudomanyos Akademia)
- International Urology and Nephrology. q. ISSN 0301-1623 (Magyar Tudomanyos Akademia)
- Irodalom - Szocializmus. irreg. ISSN 0075-0824 (Magyar Tudomanyos Akademia)
- Irodalomelmelet Klasszikusai. irreg. ISSN 0075-0832 (Magyar Tudomanyos Akademia)
- Irodalomtortenet/Literary History. q. ISSN 0021-1478 (Magyar Irodalomtorteneti Tarsasag)
- Irodalomtorteneti Fuzetek. irreg. ISSN 0075-0840 (Magyar Tudomanyos Akademia)
- Irodalomtorteneti Konyvtar. irreg. ISSN 0075-0859 (Magyar Tudomanyos Akademia)
- Irodalomtorteneti Kozlemenyek/Literary History Communications. bi-m. ISSN 0021-1486 (Magyar Tudomanyos Akademia. Irodalomtudomanyi Intezet)
- Kemia Ujabb Eredmenyei. irreg. ISSN 0075-5397 (Magyar Tudomanyos Akademia)
- Kemiai Kozlemenyek. 2 vols.per yr.(4 nos.to vol) (Magyar Tudomanyos Akademia. Kemiai Tudomanyok Osztalya)
- Koranyi Sandor Tarsasag. Tudomanyos Ulesek. irreg. ISSN 0075-6792
- Korosi Csoma Kiskonyvtar. irreg. ISSN 0075-6911 (Magyar Tudomanyos Akademia)
- Korunk Tudomanya. irreg. ISSN 0075-6946 (Magyar Tudomanyos Akademia)
- Koszen es Koolaj Anyagismereti Monografiak. irreg. ISSN 0075-6962 (Magyar Tudomanyos Akademia)
- Kozgazdasagi Ertekezesek. irreg. ISSN 0075-6989 (Magyar Tudomanyos Akademia)
- Kozgazdasagi Szemle/Economic Review. m. ISSN 0023-4346 (Magyar Tudomanyos Akademia. Kozgazdasagtudomanyi Intezet)
- Leveltari Kozlemenyek/Archival Communications. s-a. ISSN 0024-1512 (Magyar Orszagos Leveltar)
- Literatura. q. (Magyar Tudomanyos Akademia. Irodalomtudomanyi Intezet)
- Magyar Filozofiai Szemle/Hungarian Philosophical Review. bi-m. ISSN 0025-0090 (Magyar Tudomanyos Akademia. Filozofiai Bizottsag)
- Magyar Fizikai Folyoirat/Hungarian Journal of Physics. bi-m. ISSN 0025-0104 (Magyar Tudomanyos Akademia)
- Magyar Irodalomtortenetiras Forrasai; Fontes Ad Historiam Litterariam Hungariae Spectantes. irreg. ISSN 0076-2385 (Magyar Tudomanyos Akademia)
- Magyar Konyvszemle; review of bookhistory, bibliography and documentation. q. ISSN 0025-0171 (Magyar Tudomanyos Akademia)
- Magyar Nyelv/Hungarian Language. q. ISSN 0025-0228 (Magyar Tudomanyos Akademia. Nyelvtudomanyi Intezet)
- Magyar Nyelvor/Hungarian Purist. q. ISSN 0025-0236 (Magyar Tudomanyos Akademia. Nyelvtudomanyi Intezet)
- Magyar Pedagogia/Hungarian Pedagogy. q. ISSN 0025-0260 (Magyar Tudomanyos Akademia)
- Magyar Pszichologiai Szemle/Hungarian Psychological Review. q. ISSN 0025-0279 (Magyar Tudomanyos Akademia) (Co-sponsor: Magyar Pszichologiai Tarsasag)
- Magyar Tudomany/Hungarian Science. m. ISSN 0025-0325 (Magyar Tudomanyos Akademia)
- Magyar Tudomanyos Akademia. Agrartudomanyok Osztalya. Monografiasorozat. irreg. ISSN 0076-2423

- Magyar Tudomanyos Akademia. Biologiai Tudomanyok Osztalya. Kozlemenyek. q. ISSN 0025-0333
- Magyar Tudomanyos Akademia. Filozofiai es Tortenettudomanyi Osztaly. Kozlemenyek. 3 per yr. ISSN 0025-0376
- Magyar Tudomanyos Akademia. Mikrobiologiai Kutato Intezet. Proceedings/Hungarian Academy of Sciences. Research Institute for Microbiology. Proceedings. irreg. ISSN 0076-2431
- Magyar Tudomanyos Akademia. Nyelv- es Irodalomtudomanyi Osztaly. Kozlemenyek. 4 per yr. ISSN 0025-0368
- Magyarorszag Allatvilaga/Fauna Hungariae. irreg. ISSN 0076-2474 (Magyar Tudomanyos Akademia)
- Magyarorszag Kulturfloraja. irreg., no. 5 per 20, 1974. ISSN 0076-2482 (Magyar Tudomanyos Akademia)
- Magyarorszag Muemleki Topografiaja. irreg. ISSN 0076-2490 (Magyar Tudomanyos Akademia)
- Magyarorszag Regeszeti Topografiaja. irreg. ISSN 0076-2504 (Magyar Tudomanyos Akademia)
- Magyarorszag Tajfoldrajza. irreg. ISSN 0076-2512 (Magyar Tudomanyos Akademia)
- Matematikai Lapok/Mathematical Papers. q. ISSN 0025-519X (Bolyai Janos Matematikai Tarsulat)
- Modern Filologiai Fuzetek. irreg. ISSN 0076-9967 (Magyar Tudomanyos Akademia)
- Monographie der Flaumeichen-Buschwaelder. irreg. ISSN 0077-0663 (Magyar Tudomanyos Akademia)
- Monumenta Antiquitatis Extra Fines Hungariae Reperta Que in Museo Artium Hungarico Aliisque Museis et Collectionibus Hungaricis Conservatur. irreg. ISSN 0077-1392 (Magyar Tudomanyos Akademia)
- Monumenta Historica Budapestinensia. irreg. ISSN 0077-1430 (Magyar Tudomanyos Akademia)
- Monumenta Linguae Mongolicae Collecta. irreg. (Magyar Tudomanyos Akademia)
- Musicologica Hungarica. Neue Folge. irreg. ISSN 0077-2488 (Magyar Tudomanyos Akademia)
- Muszaki Tudomany. 2 vols. (4 parts each) ISSN 0027-5085 (Magyar Tudomanyos Akademia. Muszaki Tudomanyok Osztalya) (Subscr. to: John Benjamins B.V., Amsteldijk 44, Amsterdam, Netherlands)
- Muveszettorteneti Ertesito; journal for history of art. q. ISSN 0027-5247 (Magyar Tudomanyos Akademia)
- Nagyuzemi Gazdalkodas Kerdesei. irreg. ISSN 0077-2658 (Magyar Tudomanyos Akademia)
- Neohelicon; Acta Comparationis Litterarum Universarum. q. (International Comparative Literature Association) (Subscr. to: Mouton et Cie, Subscr. to John Benjamins B.V., Amsteldijk 44, Amsterdam, Netherlands)
- Nepi Kultura-Nepi Tarsadalom. irreg. (Magyar Tudomanyos Akademia. Neprajzi Kutato Csoport)
- Neprajzi Tanulmanyok. irreg. ISSN 0077-6602 (Magyar Tudomanyos Akademia. Neprajzi Kutato Csoport)
- Nyelveszeti Tanulmanyok. irreg. ISSN 0078-2858 (Magyar Tudomanyos Akademia)
- Nyelvtudomanyi Ertekezesek. irreg. ISSN 0078-2866 (Magyar Tudomanyos Akademia. Nyelvtudomanyi Intezet)
- Nyelvtudomanyi Kozlemenyek/Linguistic Studies. s-a. ISSN 0029-6791 (Magyar Tudomanyos Akademia. Nyelvtudomanyi Intezet)
- Orszagos Muemleki Felugyeloseg. Kiadvanyok. irreg., no. 9, 1970. ISSN 0073-4063 (Hungary. Orszagos Muemlekvedelmi Bizottsag)
- Orvostudomany. q. ISSN 0030-6045 (Magyar Tudomanyos Akademia. Orvosi Tudomanyok Osztalya)
- Periodica Mathematica Hungarica. q. ISSN 0031-5303 (Bolyai Janos Matematikai Tarsulat)
- Periodica Polytechnica. Architecture. q. ISSN 0031-5346 (Budapesti Muszaki Egyetem)
- Periodica Polytechnica. Chemical Engineering. q. ISSN 0031-5311 (Budapesti Muszaki Egyetem)
- Periodica Polytechnica. Civil Engineering. q. (Budapesti Muszaki Egyetem)
- Periodica Polytechnica. Electrical Engineering. q. ISSN 0031-532X (Budapesti Muszaki Egyetem)
- Periodica Polytechnica. Mechanical Engineering. q. ISSN 0031-5338 (Budapesti Muszaki Egyetem)
- Problems of Control and Information Theory/ Problemy Upravleniya i Teorii Informatsii. 6 per yr. ISSN 0370-2529 (Magyar Tudomanyos Akademia) (Co-sponsor: Akademiya Nauk S.S.S.R.)
- Pszichologia a Gyakorlatban. irreg. ISSN 0079-7456 (Magyar Tudomanyos Akademia)
- Pszichologiai Tanulmanyok. irreg. ISSN 0079-7464 (Magyar Tudomanyos Akademia)

- Recent Developments in the Chemistry of Natural Carbon Compounds. irreg. ISSN 0079-9947 (Magyar Tudomanyos Akademia)
- Recent Developments of Neurobiology in Hungary. irreg. ISSN 0079-9955 (Magyar Tudomanyos Akademia)
- Regi Magyar Dallamok Tara/Corpus Musicae Popularis Hungaricae. irreg. ISSN 0080-0562 (Magyar Tudomanyos Akademia. Nepzenekutato Csoport)
- Regi Magyar Prozai Emlekek. irreg. ISSN 0080-0570 (Magyar Tudomanyos Akademia)
- Studia Archaeologica. irreg. ISSN 0081-6280 (Magyar Tudomanyos Akademia. Regeszeti Intezet)
- Studia Biologica Academiae Scientiarum Hungaricae. irreg. ISSN 0076-244X (Magyar Tudomanyos Akademia)
- Studia Historica Academiae Scientiarum Hungaricae. irreg. ISSN 0076-2458 (Magyar Tudomanyos Akademia)
- Studia Musicologica. q. ISSN 0039-3266 (Magyar Tudomanyos Akademia)
- Studia Philosophica Academiae Scientiarum Hungaricae. irreg. ISSN 0076-2466 (Magyar Tudomanyos Akademia)
- Studia Scientiarum Mathematicarum. a. ISSN 0081-6906 (Magyar Tudomanyos Akademia)
- Studia Slavica. q. ISSN 0039-3363 (Magyar Tudomanyos Akademia)
- Studies in Geography in Hungary. irreg. ISSN 0081-7961 (Magyar Tudomanyos Akademia)
- Symposia Biologica Hungarica. irreg. ISSN 0082-0695 (Magyar Tudomanyos Akademia)
- Szazadok/Centuries. bi-m. ISSN 0039-8098 (Magyar Tortenelmi Tarsulat)
- Szigma; mathematics in economical science. q. ISSN 0039-8128 (Magyar Kozgazdasagi Tarsasag)
- Szilikatkemiai Monografiak. irreg. ISSN 0082-1306 (Magyar Tudomanyos Akademia)
- Szociologiai Tanulmanyok. irreg. ISSN 0082-1322 (Magyar Tudomanyos Akademia)
- Tanulmanyok a Nevelestudomany Korebol. irreg. ISSN 0082-1632 (Magyar Tudomanyos Akademia)
- Tarsadalomtudomanyi Kismonografiak. irreg. ISSN 0082-1748 (Magyar Tudomanyos Akademia)
- Tortenelmi Szemle/Historical Review. q. ISSN 0040-9634 (Magyar Tudomanyos Akademia. Tortenettudomanyi Intezet)
- Tudomanyszervezesi Fuzetek. irreg. ISSN 0082-6707 (Magyar Tudomanyos Akademia)
- Tudomanyszervezesi Tajekoztato/Bulletin of Science Organization; periodical of international literature on the planning, management and organization of scientific research. bi-m. ISSN 0040-862X (Magyar Tudomanyos Akademia. Konyvtar)
- Tudomanytorteneti Tanulmanyok. irreg. ISSN 0082-6715 (Magyar Tudomanyos Akademia)
- Uj Magyar Nepkoltesi Gyujtemeny. irreg. ISSN 0082-7312 (Magyar Tudomanyos Akademia)
- Vaskohaszati Enciklopedia. irreg. ISSN 0083-5277 (Magyar Tudomanyos Akademia)
- Vegetation Ungarischer Landschaften. irreg. ISSN 0083-5323 (Magyar Tudomanyos Akademia)

**Bolyai Janos Matematikai Tarsulat**
- Matematikai Lapok/Mathematical Papers. (pub. by Akademiai Kiado, Publishing House of the Hungarian Academy of Sciences)
- Periodica Mathematica Hungarica. (pub. by Akademiai Kiado, Publishing House of the Hungarian Academy of Sciences)

**Bor- es Cipoipari Tarsasag**
- Bor- es Cipotechnika. (pub. by Lapkiado Vallalat)

**Borsod Megyei Lapkiado Vallalat**
Bajcsy-Zsilinszky u. 15, 3527 Miskolc, Hungary (Subscr. to: Kultura, Box 149, H-1389 Budapest, Hungary)
- Napjaink. m. ISSN 0027-7819

**Budapesti Izraelita Hitkozseg**
Sip u. 12, 1075 Budapest, Hungary.
- Uj Elet; magyar izraelitak lapja. fortn.

**Budapesti Muszaki Egyetem**
Muegyetem rakpart 3, 1521 Budapest 21, Hungary.
- Periodica Polytechnica. Architecture. (pub. by Akademiai Kiado, Publishing House of the Hungarian Academy of Sciences)
- Periodica Polytechnica. Chemical Engineering. (pub. by Akademiai Kiado, Publishing House of the Hungarian Academy of Sciences)

- Periodica Polytechnica. Civil Engineering. (pub. by Akademiai Kiado, Publishing House of the Hungarian Academy of Sciences)
- Periodica Polytechnica. Electrical Engineering. (pub. by Akademiai Kiado, Publishing House of the Hungarian Academy of Sciences)
- Periodica Polytechnica. Mechanical Engineering. (pub. by Akademiai Kiado, Publishing House of the Hungarian Academy of Sciences)
- Telepulestudomanyi Kozlemenyek. a. ISSN 0040-2680

**Budapesti Muszaki Egyetem. Kozponti Konyvtar**
Budafoki ut 4-6, 1111 Budapest 11, Hungary.
- Muszaki Egyetemi Konyvtaros. s-a. ISSN 0027-3015

**BUDAVOX Telecommunication Foreign Trading Company Ltd.**
- Budavox Telecommunication Review. (pub. by Lapkiado Vallalat)

**Cartographia**
P.O.B. 76, 1367 Budapest, Hungary
(Subscr. to: Kultura, Box 149, H-1389 Budapest, Hungary)
- Cartactual; topical map service. bi-m. ISSN 0008-7009
- Geodezia es Kartografia/Geodesy and Cartography. 6 per yr. ISSN 0016-7118

**Debreceni Orvostudomanyi Egyetem**
Nagyerdei korut 98, 4012 Debrecen, Hungary.
- Debreceni Orvostudomanyi Egyetem. Evkonyv. a.

**Energiagazdalkodasi Tudomanyos Egyesulet**
- Energia es Atomtechnika. (pub. by Lapkiado Vallalat)
- Energiagazdalkodas. (pub. by Lapkiado Vallalat)

**Eotvos Lorand Fizikai Tarsulat**
Anker koz 1, 1061 Budapest, Hungary
(Subscr. to: Kultura, Box 149, H-1389 Budapest, Hungary)
- Fizikai Szemle/Physical Review. m. ISSN 0015-3257

**Epitesugyi Tajekoztatasi Kozpont**
Harsfa u. 21, 1074 Budapest 7, Hungary.
- Hungarian Building Bulletin. q. ISSN 0018-7720
- Hungarian Building Marketing. s-a.

**Epitoipari Tudomanyos Egyesulet**
- Epuletgepeszet. (pub. by Lapkiado Vallalat)
- Magyar Epitoipar/Hungarian Building Industry. (pub. by Lapkiado Vallalat)

**Faipari Tudomanyos Egyesulet**
- Faipar. (pub. by Lapkiado Vallalat)

**Fovarosi Szabo Ervin Konyvtar**
Szabo Ervin ter 1, Budapest VIII, Hungary.
- Szociologiai Informacio; a magyarnyelvu szakirodalom valogatott bibliografiaja. q.

**Gepipari Tudomanyos Egyesulet**
- Gep. (pub. by Lapkiado Vallalat)
- Gepgyartastechnologia. (pub. by Lapkiado Vallalat)
- Jarmuvek, Mezogazdasagi Gepek. (pub. by Lapkiado Vallalat)
- Muanyag es Gumi/Plastics and Rubber. (pub. by Lapkiado Vallalat)

**Gyogynoveny Kutato Intezet**
P.O.B. 11, 2011 Budakalasz, Hungary
(Subscr. to: Kultura, Box 149, H-1389 Budapest, Hungary)
- Herba Hungarica. 3 per yr. ISSN 0018-0580

**Hadtortenelmi Intezet**
Toth Arpad setany 40, Budapest 1, Hungary
(Subscr. to: Kultura, Box 149, H-1389 Budapest, Hungary)
- Hadtortenelmi Kozlemenyek. q. ISSN 0017-6540

**Hiradastechnikai Tudomanyos Egyesulet**
- Hiradastechnika. (pub. by Lapkiado Vallalat)

**Hirlapkiado Vallalat**
Blaha Lujza ter 3, 1959 Budapest 8, Hungary
(Subscr. to: Kultura, Box 149, H-1389 Budapest, Hungary)
- Buvar. m. ISSN 0007-7356 (Hungary. Orszagos Termeszetvedelmi Hivatal)
- Elet es Tudomany. w. ISSN 0013-6077 (Tudomanyos Ismeretterjeszto Tarsulat)

- Figyelo; gazdasagpolitikai hetilap. w. ISSN 0015-086X
- Fold es Eg. bi-m. ISSN 0015-539X (Tudomanyos Ismeretterjeszto Tarsulat)
- Fules. w. ISSN 0016-240X
- Hungarian Economy; a quarterly economic and business review. q.
- Ludas Matyi Evkonyve. a.
- Magyar Allatorvosok Lapja. m. ISSN 0025-004X (Hungary. Mezogazdasagi es Elelmezesugyi Miniszterium)
- Magyar Mezogazdasag/Hungarian Agriculture. w. ISSN 0025-018X (Hungary. Mezogazdasagi es Elelmezesugyi Miniszterium)
- Mezogazdasagi Technika. m. ISSN 0026-1890 (Hungary. Mezogazdasagi es Elelmezesugyi Miniszterium)
- Nok Lapja. w. ISSN 0029-0963
- Termeszet Vilaga. m. ISSN 0040-3717 (Tudomanyos Ismeretterjeszto Tarsulat)

**Hungara Esperanto Asocio**
Kenyermezo u. 6, Budapest 8, Hungary
(Subscr. to: Kultura, Box 149, H-1389 Budapest, Hungary)
- Hungara Vivo. q. ISSN 0018-7704

**Hungarian Central Technical Library and Documentation Centre-Technoinform**
Reviczky u. 6, 1428 Budapest, P.O.B. 12, Hungary
(Subscr. to: Kultura, Box 149, H-1389 Budapest, Hungary)
- Audiovizualis Technikai es Modszertani Kozlemenyek. bi-m.
- Hungarian Technical Abstracts/Zentralblatt der Ungarischen Technik. q. ISSN 0018-7771
- Modszertani Kiadvanyok. irreg., no. 41, 1974.
- Muszaki-Gazdasagi Tajekoztato/Technical and Economical Information; a digest of foreign literature. m. ISSN 0027-4933
- Muszaki Lapszemle. Anyagmozgatas, Csomagolas/ Technical Abstracts. Materials Handling, Packaging. m. ISSN 0027-3023
- Muszaki Lapszemle. Banyaszat/Technical Abstracts. Mining. m. ISSN 0027-495X
- Muszaki Lapszemle. Elektrotechnika/Technical Abstracts. Electrical Engineering. m.
- Muszaki Lapszemle. Elelmiszeripar/Technical Abstracts. Food Industry. m. ISSN 0027-4976
- Muszaki Lapszemle. Energia/Technical Abstracts. Energy. m. ISSN 0027-4984
- Muszaki Lapszemle. Faipar, Papir-es Nyomdaipar/ Technical Abstracts. Woodworking Industry, Paper and Printing Industry. m. ISSN 0027-4992
- Muszaki Lapszemle. Fizika, Meres- es Muszertechnika/Technical Abstracts. Physics, Measurement and Instrument Technology. m. ISSN 0027-500X
- Muszaki Lapszemle. Gepeszet/Technical Abstracts. Machinery. m. ISSN 0027-5018
- Muszaki Lapszemle. Gepgyartastechnologia. m.
- Muszaki Lapszemle. Hiradastechnika. m.
- Muszaki Lapszemle.Kemia. Vegyipar/Technical Abstracts. Chemistry, Chemical Industry. m. ISSN 0027-5026
- Muszaki Lapszemle. Kohaszat, Onteszet/ Technical Abstracts. Metallurgy, Foundry. m. ISSN 0027-5034
- Muszaki Lapszemle. Kozlekedes/Technical Abstracts. Transport. m. ISSN 0027-5042
- Muszaki Lapszemle. Melyepites, Vizepites, Kozmuvek/Technical Abstracts. Civil and Hydraulic Engineering. m. ISSN 0027-5050
- Muszaki Lapszemle. Textilipar, Bor- es Borfeldolgozoipar/Technical Abstracts. Textile Industry, Leather and Leatherprocessing Industry. m. ISSN 0027-5069
- Muszaki Lapszemle. Uzemszervezes, Ipargazdasag/Technical Abstracts. Plant Organisation, Industrial Economy. m. ISSN 0027-4941
- Technical Film Cards/International Selections. q.
- Technika. (pub. by Nepszava Lapkiado Vallalat)
- Tudomanyos es Muszaki Tajekoztatas. m. ISSN 0041-3917

**Hungarian P.E.N. Club**
Vorosmarty ter 1, 1051 Budapest, Hungary.
- Hungarian P.E.N/P.E.N. Hongrois. irreg. ISSN 0439-9080

**Hungarofilm**
Bathory u. 1C, Budapest 5, Hungary.
- Hungarofilm Bulletin. 5 per yr. ISSN 0018-7798

**Hungary. Belkereskedelmi Miniszterium**
- Lakaskultura. (pub. by Lapkiado Vallalat)

**Hungary. Egeszsegugyi Miniszterium**
- Egeszsegugyi Gazdasagi Szemle. (pub. by Kultura (Distributor))

**Hungary. Epitesugyi es Varosfejlesztesi Miniszterium**
- Epitesugyi Ertesito. (pub. by Lapkiado Vallalat)
- Epitesugyi Szemle. (pub. by Lapkiado Vallalat)
- Muszaki Tervezes. (pub. by Lapkiado Vallalat)

**Hungary. Koho- es Gepipari Miniszterium. Ipargazdasagi, Szervezesi es Szamitastechnikai Intezet**
- Ergonomia. (pub. by Lapkiado Vallalat)

**Hungary. Koho- es Gepipari Miniszterium. Tudomanyos-Muszaki Tajekoztato Intezet**
Arany Janos u. 24, 1372 Budapest, Hungary
(Subscr. to: Kultura, Box 149, H-1389 Budapest, Hungary)
- Minoseg es Megbizhatosag. bi-m. ISSN 0580-4485

**Hungary. Kozponti Statisztikai Hivatal**
- Hungary. Kozponti Statisztikai Hivatal. Belkereskedelmi es Idegenforgalmi Adatok. (pub. by Statisztikai Kiado Vallalat)
- Hungary. Kozponti Statisztikai Hivatal. Demografiai Evkonyv. (pub. by Statisztikai Kiado Vallalat)
- Hungary. Kozponti Statisztikai Hivatal. Epitoipari Arak Alakulasa. (pub. by Statisztikai Kiado Vallalat)
- Hungary. Kozponti Statisztikai Hivatal. Kepzettseg-Kereset. (pub. by Statisztikai Kiado Vallalat)
- Hungary. Kozponti Statisztikai Hivatal. Kulkereskedelmi Statisztikai Evkonyv. (pub. by Statisztikai Kiado Vallalat)
- Hungary. Kozponti Statisztikai Hivatal. Maganautok Teljesitmenyei es Uzemeltetesi Korulmenyei. (pub. by Statisztikai Kiado Vallalat)
- Hungary. Kozponti Statisztikai Hivatal. Mezogazdasagi Adatok. (pub. by Statisztikai Kiado Vallalat)
- Hungary. Kozponti Statisztikai Hivatal, Nepgazdasagi Merlegek. (pub. by Statisztikai Kiado Vallalat)
- Informacio - Elektronika. (pub. by Statisztikai Kiado Vallalat)
- Ipari es Epitoipari Statisztikai Ertesito. (pub. by Statisztikai Kiado Vallalat)
- Statisztikai Evkonyv/Statistical Yearbook. (pub. by Statisztikai Kiado Vallalat)
- Statisztikai Havi Kozlemenyek. (pub. by Statisztikai Kiado Vallalat)
- Statisztikai Szemle. (pub. by Statisztikai Kiado Vallalat)
- Teruleti Statisztika. (pub. by Statisztikai Kiado Vallalat)
- Vas Megye Statisztikai Evkonyve. (pub. by Statisztikai Kiado Vallalat)

**Hungary. Kulugymininiszterium**
Steindl u., Budapest 5, Hungary.
- Magyar Kulpolitikai Evkonyv. a. ISSN 0541-9220

**Hungary. Mezogazdasagi es Elelmezesugyi Miniszterium**
Kossuth Lajos ter 6-8, Budapest 5, Hungary
(Subscr. to: Kultura, Box 149, H-1389 Budapest, Hungary)
- Gazdalkodas; journal for farm economics and management. m. ISSN 0046-5518 (Co-sponsor: Magyar Agrartudomanyi Egyesulet)
- Kerteszet es Szoleszet. w. ISSN 0023-0677
- Magyar Allatorvosok Lapja. (pub. by Hirlapkiado Vallalat)
- Magyar Mezogazdasag/Hungarian Agriculture. (pub. by Hirlapkiado Vallalat)
- Mezogazdasagi Technika. (pub. by Hirlapkiado Vallalat)

**Hungary. Mezogazdasagi es Elelmezesugyi Miniszterium. Informacios Kozpont**
Attila u. 93, 1253 Budapest 13, Hungary
(Subscr. to: Kultura, Box 149, H-1389 Budapest, Hungary)
- Agrarirodalmi Szemle. m. ISSN 0002-1067
- Hungarian Agricultural Review/Ungarische Agrarrundschau/Vestnik Vengerskoi Sel'skokhozyaistvennoi Literatury. q. ISSN 0018-7712
- Magyar Mezogazdasagi Bibliografia. q. ISSN 0025-0198

• Mezogazdasagi Vilagirodalom. bi-m. ISSN 0026-1904

**Hungary. Minisztertanacs**
• Allam es Igazgatas. (pub. by Lapkiado Vallalat)
• Magyar Kozlony. (pub. by Kultura (Distributor))

**Hungary. Orszagos Idegenforgalmi Hivatal**
• Hungarian Travel Magazine. (pub. by Lapkiado Vallalat)

**Hungary. Orszagos Meresugyi Hivatal**
• Meresugyi Kozlemenyek. (pub. by Lapkiado Vallalat)

**Hungary. Orszagos Muemlekvedelmi Bizottsag**
• Orszagos Muemleki Felugyeloseg. Kiadvanyok. (pub. by Akademiai Kiado, Publishing House of the Hungarian Academy of Sciences)

**Hungary. Orszagos Szabadalmi Hivatal**
• Szabadalmi Kozlony es Vedjegyertesito/Patent and Trade Mark Review. (pub. by Lapkiado Vallalat)

**Hungary. Orszagos Termeszetvedelmi Hivatal**
• Buvar. (pub. by Hirlapkiado Vallalat)

**Hungary. Orszagos Vizugyi Foigazgatosag**
Kazinczy u. 37B, Budapest 7, Hungary.
• Vizgazdalkodas es Kornyezetvedelem. irreg.

**Hungary. Penzugyminiszterium**
• Penzugyi Szemle. (pub. by Lapkiado Vallalat)
• Szamvitel - Ugyviteltechnika. (pub. by Lapkiado Vallalat)

**Hungary. Vizgazdalkodasi Tudomanyos Kutato Intezet**
Fo u. 44-50, Budapest, Hungary
(Subscr. to: Kultura, Box 149, H-1389 Budapest, Hungary)
• Vizgazdalkodas. bi-m.

**Ifjusagi Lapkiado Vallalat**
Revai u 16, 1065 Budapest 6, Hungary
(Subscr. to: Kultura, Box 149, H-1389 Budapest, Hungary)
• Delta; magazine on natural sciences and technics. m. ISSN 0011-7994 (Magyar Kommunista Ifjusagi Szovetseg)
• Fogorvosi Szemle. m. ISSN 0015-5314 (Magyar Fogorvosok Egyesulete)
• Ful-, Orr-, Gegegyogyaszat. q. ISSN 0016-237X
• Gyermekgyogyaszat. q. ISSN 0017-5900
• Gyogyszereszet. m. ISSN 0017-6036 (Magyar Gyogyszereszeti Tarsasag)
• Ideggyogyaszati Szemle. 12 per yr. ISSN 0019-1442 (Magyar Neurologiai es Pszichiatriai Tarsasag)
• Magyar Belorvosi Archivum. bi-m. ISSN 0025-0066
• Magyar Noorvosok Lapja. bi-m. ISSN 0025-021X
• Magyar Onkologia. q. ISSN 0025-0244 (Magyar Rakkutatok Tarsasaga)
• Magyar Radiologia. 6 per yr. ISSN 0025-0287 (Magyar Radiologiai Tarsasag)
• Magyar Sebeszet. 6 per yr. ISSN 0025-0295
• Magyar Traumatologia, Orthopedia es Helyreallito-Sebeszet/Hungarian Traumatology, Orthopaedy and Restorative Surgery. q. ISSN 0025-0317
• Orvosi Hetilap. w. ISSN 0030-6002 (Orvos- es Egeszsegugyi Dolgozok Szakszervezete)
• Orvoskepzes. 6 per yr. ISSN 0030-6037
• Pajtas. w. ISSN 0030-9583 (Magyar Uttorok Szovetseg)
• Rheumatologia, Balneologia, Allergologia. q. ISSN 0035-4554 (Reumatologiai Tarsasag)
• Szemeszet/Ophthalmologica Hungarica. q. ISSN 0039-8101 (Orvos- es Egeszsegugyi Dolgozok Szakszervezete)
• Tuberkulozis es Tudobetegsegek. m. ISSN 0041-3887

**International Comparative Literature Association**
• Neohelicon. (pub. by Akademiai Kiado, Publishing House of the Hungarian Academy of Sciences)

**International Measurement Confederation. IMEKO Secretariat**
P.O.B. 457, 1371 Budapest, Hungary
(Dist. in U.S. by Plenum Press, 227 W. 17 St., New York, N.Y. 10011)
• International Measurement Congress. Proceedings. Acta IMEKO. triennial; 6th, 1973. (Co-publisher: North-Holland Publishing Co.)

**International Organization of Journalists. Graphic Club**
• Interpressgrafik. (pub. by Interpress Publishing Co.)

**International Union of Physiological Sciences**
c/o A. Kovach, Experimental Research Department, Semmelweis Medical University, Ulloi ut 78/A, 1082 Budapest, Hungary.
• International Union of Physiological Sciences. Newsletter. irreg. ISSN 0539-1113

**Interpress Publishing Co.**
Budapest, Hungary
(Subscr. to: Kultura, Box 149, H-1389 Budapest, Hungary)
• Interpressgrafik; international quarterly of graphic design. q. ISSN 0020-9619 (International Organization of Journalists. Graphic Club)

**Iparmuveszeti Muzeum**
Ulloi ut 33, 1091 Budapest 9, Hungary.
• Ars Decorativa; annuaire du Musee des Arts Decoratifs et du Musee d'Art d'Extreme Orient Ferenc Hopp. a.

**Istvan Kiraly Muzeum**
Szekesfehervar, Hungary.
• Nepmuveszet Evszazadai/Jahrhunderte der Volkskunst. irreg.

**Jozsef Attila Tudomanyegyetem**
Dugonics ter 13, Szeged, Hungary
(Subscr. to: Kultura, Box 149, H-1389 Budapest, Hungary)
• Acta Scientiarum Mathematicarum. q. ISSN 0001-6969
• Acta Universitatis Szegediensis de Attila Jozsef Nominatae. Acta Bibliothecaria. 1-4 per yr. ISSN 0001-7175 (prep. by its Kozponti Konyvtar)
• Acta Universitatis Szegediensis de Attila Jozsef Nominatae. Acta Geographica. a. ISSN 0567-7467 (prep. by its Foldrajzi Tanszek)
• Acta Universitatis Szegediensis de Attila Jozsef Nominatae. Acta Physica et Chemica. q. ISSN 0001-6721

**Kereskedelmi Munka- es Uzemszervezesi Intezet (KERORG)**
• Kereskedelmi Szervezes/Commercial Organization. (pub. by Kultura (Distributor))

**Kisipari Szovetkezetek Orszagos Szovetsege (OKISZ)**
Pesti Barnabas u. 6, 1052 Budapest 5, Hungary.
• Szovetkezeti Ipar. m.

**Koranyi Sandor Tarsasag**
• Koranyi Sandor Tarsasag. Tudomanyos Ulesek. (pub. by Akademiai Kiado, Publishing House of the Hungarian Academy of Sciences)

**Kossuth Konyvkiado**
Steindl Imre u. 6, Budapest 5, Hungary
(Subscr. to: Kultura, Box 149, H-1389 Budapest, Hungary)
• Nemzetkozi Szemle. m. ISSN 0028-2618
• Tarsadalomtudomanyi Kozlemenyek. q. (Magyar Szocialista Munkaspart (MSZMP). Tarsadalomtudomanyi Intezet)

**Kossuth Lajos Tudomanyegyetem**
Nagyerdei korut, Debrecen 10, Hungary
(Subscr. to: Kultura, Box 149, H-1389 Budapest, Hungary)
• Angol Filologiai Tanulmanyok/Hungarian Studies in English. irreg., vol. 9, 1975. ISSN 0570-0973 (prep. by its Angol Tanszek)
• Publicationes Mathematicae Debrecen. s-a. ISSN 0033-3883 (prep. by its Matematikai Intezet)

**Kozlekedestudomanyi Egyesulet**
• Kozlekedestudomanyi Szemle. (pub. by Lapkiado Vallalat)
• Melyepitestudomanyi Szemle. (pub. by Lapkiado Vallalat)

**Kozponti Kolorisztikai Kutato Laboratorium**
• Kolorisztikai Ertesito/Coloristical Review. (pub. by Nepszava Lapkiado Vallalat)

**Kultura (Distributor)**
Box 149, H-1389 Budapest, Hungary.
• Egeszsegugyi Gazdasagi Szemle. q. ISSN 0013-2276 (Hungary. Egeszsegugyi Miniszterium) (Co-sponsor: Orvos-Egeszsegugyi Dolgozok Szakszervezete)
• Kereskedelmi Szervezes/Commercial Organization. q. ISSN 0023-057X (Kereskedelmi Munka- es Uzemszervezesi Intezet (KERORG))
• Magyar Kozlony; official gazette. irreg. ISSN 0076-2407 (Hungary. Minisztertanacs)

**Lapkiado Vallalat**
Lenin korut 9-11, 1073 Budapest 7, Hungary
(Subscr. to: Kultura, Box 149, H-1389 Budapest, Hungary)
• Allam es Igazgatas. m. (Hungary. Minisztertanacs)
• Anyagmozgatas-Csomagolas. m. ISSN 0003-6242 (Muszaki es Termeszettudomanyi Egyesuletek Szovetsege) (Co-sponsor: Anyagmozgatasi es Csomagolasi Intezet)
• Auto-Motor. s-m. ISSN 0005-0792
• Banyaszati es Kohaszati Lapok - Kohaszat. m. ISSN 0005-5670 (Orszagos Magyar Banyaszati es Kohaszati Egyesulet)
• Banyaszati es Kohaszati Lapok - Ontode. m. (Orszagos Magyar Banyaszati es Kohaszati Egyesulet)
• Baromfiipar. bi-m. ISSN 0005-6049 (Magyar Elelmezesipari Tudomanyos Egyesulet)
• Bor- es Cipotechnika. bi-m. ISSN 0006-7652 (Bor- es Cipoipari Tarsasag)
• Borgazdasag. q. ISSN 0006-7741 (Magyar Elelmezesipari Tudomanyos Egyesulet)
• Borgyogyaszati es Venerologiai Szemle. bi-m. ISSN 0006-7768
• Budapest. m. ISSN 0007-2885
• Budapester Rundschau. w. ISSN 0007-2893
• Budavox Telecommunication Review. q. ISSN 0007-2907 (BUDAVOX Telecommunication Foreign Trading Company Ltd.)
• Cukoripar. bi-m. ISSN 0011-2720 (Magyar Elelmezesipari Tudomanyos Egyesulet)
• Dohanyipar. bi-m. ISSN 0012-4931 (Magyar Elelmezesipari Tudomanyos Egyesulet)
• Edesipar. bi-m. ISSN 0013-0842 (Magyar Elelmezesipari Tudomanyos Egyesulet)
• Egeszsegtudomany. q. ISSN 0013-2268
• Elektrotechnika. m. ISSN 0013-6271 (Magyar Elektrotechnikai Egyesulet)
• Elelmezesi Ipar. m. ISSN 0013-5909 (Magyar Elelmezesipari Tudomanyos Egyesulet)
• Energia es Atomtechnika. m. ISSN 0013-7316 (Energiagazdalkodasi Tudomanyos Egyesulet)
• Energiagazdalkodas. m. (Energiagazdalkodasi Tudomanyos Egyesulet)
• Epitesugyi Ertesito. w. (Hungary. Epitesugyi es Varosfejlesztesi Miniszterium)
• Epitesugyi Szemle. m. ISSN 0013-967X (Hungary. Epitesugyi es Varosfejlesztesi Miniszterium)
• Epitoanyag/Building Materials. m. ISSN 0013-970X (Szilikatipari Tudomanyos Egyesulet)
• Epuletgepeszet. bi-m. ISSN 0013-9742 (Epitoipari Tudomanyos Egyesulet)
• Erdogazdasag es Faipar. m. ISSN 0014-0066 (Magyar Elelmezesipari Tudomanyos Egyesulet)
• Ergonomia; munkalettan, munkalelektan, munkaszociologia. q. ISSN 0014-0120 (Hungary. Koho- es Gepipari Miniszterium. Ipargazdasagi, Szervezesi es Szamitastechnikai Intezet)
• Ez a Divat. m.
• Faipar. m. ISSN 0014-6897 (Faipari Tudomanyos Egyesulet)
• Film, Szinhaz, Muzsika. w. ISSN 0015-1416
• Filmkultura. m. ISSN 0015-1580 (Magyar Filmtudomanyi Intezet)
• Finommechanika-Mikrotechnika. m. (Optikai, Akusztikai es Filmtechnikai Egyesulet)
• Foto. m. ISSN 0427-0576
• Fotomuveszet. q. ISSN 0532-3010 (Magyar Fotomuveszet Szovetsege)
• Gabonaipar. bi-m. (Magyar Elelmezesipari Tudomanyos Egyesulet)
• Gazdasag/Economy. q. ISSN 0016-5360 (Magyar Kozgazdasagi Tarsasag)
• Gep. m. ISSN 0016-8572 (Gepipari Tudomanyos Egyesulet)
• Gepgyartastechnologia. m. ISSN 0016-8580 (Gepipari Tudomanyos Egyesulet)
• Hiradastechnika. m. ISSN 0018-2028 (Hiradastechnikai Tudomanyos Egyesulet)
• Hungarian Journal of Industrial Chemistry. 3-4 per yr. (Veszpremi Vegyipari Egyetem)
• Hungarian Review. m. ISSN 0018-7763

- Hungarian Travel Magazine. q. ISSN 0438-2013 (Hungary. Orszagos Idegenforgalmi Hivatal)
- Husipar. bi-m. ISSN 0018-800X (Magyar Elelmezesipari Tudomanyos Egyesulet) (Co-sponsor: Allatforgalmi es Husipari Troszt)
- Hutoipar. q. ISSN 0018-8085 (Magyar Elelmezesipari Tudomanyos Egyesulet)
- Ipargazdasag. m. ISSN 0021-0749 (Muszaki es Termeszettudomanyi Egyesuletek Szovetsege)
- Jarmuvek, Mezogazdasagi Gepek; motorok, vasuti jarmuvek, kozuti jarmuvek, hajok, mezogazdasagi gepek, epitoipari gepek, repulogepek. m. ISSN 0021-5511 (Gepipari Tudomanyos Egyesulet)
- Kep- es Hangtechnika. bi-m. ISSN 0023-0480 (Optikai, Akusztikai es Filmtechnikai Egyesulet)
- Kortars. m. ISSN 0023-415X (Magyar Irok Szovetsege)
- Kozlekedestudomanyi Szemle. m. ISSN 0023-4362 (Kozlekedestudomanyi Egyesulet)
- Kritika. m. ISSN 0023-4818 (Magyar Tudomanyos Akademia. Irodalomtudomanyi Intezet)
- Kulpolitika/Foreign Affairs. q. (Magyar Kulugyi Intezet)
- Lakaskultura. q. ISSN 0047-391X (Hungary. Belkereskedelmi Miniszterium)
- Magyar Aluminium/Hungarian Aluminum. m. ISSN 0025-0058
- Magyar Epitoipar/Hungarian Building Industry. m. ISSN 0025-0074 (Epitoipari Tudomanyos Egyesulet)
- Magyar Epitomuveszet. 6 per yr. ISSN 0025-0082 (Magyar Epitomuveszek Szovetsege)
- Magyar Kemiai Folyoirat/Hungarian Journal of Chemistry. m. ISSN 0025-0155 (Magyar Kemikusok Egyesulete)
- Magyar Kemikusok Lapja. m. ISSN 0025-0163 (Magyar Kemikusok Egyesulete)
- Magyar Textiltechnika. m. ISSN 0025-0309 (Textilipari Muszaki es Tudomanyos Egyesulet)
- Magyar Zene. q. ISSN 0025-0384 (Magyar Zenemuveszek Szovetsege)
- Marketing in Hungary. q. ISSN 0025-3731 (Magyar Kereskedelmi Kamara) (Co-sponsor: Orszagos Piackutato Intezet)
- Melyepitestudomanyi Szemle. m. ISSN 0025-9039 (Kozlekedestudomanyi Egyesulet)
- Meres es Automatika. m. ISSN 0025-9993 (Merestechnikai es Automatizalasi Tudomanyos Egyesulet)
- Meresugyi Kozlemenyek. q. ISSN 0026-0002 (Hungary. Orszagos Meresugyi Hivatal)
- Muanyag es Gumi/Plastics and Rubber. m. ISSN 0027-2914 (Gepipari Tudomanyos Egyesulet) (Co-sponsor: Magyar Kemikusok Egyesulete)
- Muszaki Tervezes. m. (Hungary. Epitesugyi es Varosfejlesztesi Miniszterium)
- Muzsika. m. ISSN 0027-5336
- New Hungarian Quarterly. q. ISSN 0028-5390
- Pedagogiai Szemle/Pedagogical Review. m. ISSN 0031-3785 (Magyar Pedagogiai Tarsasag) (Co-sponsor: Orszagos Pedagogiai Intezet)
- Penzugyi Szemle. m. ISSN 0031-496X (Hungary. Penzugyminiszterium)
- Szabadalmi Kozlony es Vedjegyertesito/Patent and Trade Mark Review. m. ISSN 0039-8071 (Hungary. Orszagos Szabadalmi Hivatal)
- Szamvitel - Ugyviteltechnika. m. ISSN 0039-808X (Hungary. Penzugyminiszterium)
- Szinhaz. m. ISSN 0039-8136 (Szinhazmuveszeti Szovetseg)
- SZOVOSZ Tajekoztato. m. (Szovetkezetek Orszagos Szovetsege)
- Uj Iras. m. ISSN 0041-5952 (Magyar Irok Szovetsege)
- Villamossag. m. ISSN 0042-6210 (Magyar Elektrotechnikai Egyesulet)

**Magveto Kiado**
Vorosmarty ter 1, Budapest V, Hungary.
- Szep Versek. a. ISSN 0586-3783

**Magyar Allami Eotvos Lorand Geofizikai Intezet**
Columbus u. 17-23, 1145 Budapest 14, Hungary
(Subscr. to: Kultura, Box 149, H-1389 Budapest, Hungary)
- Geofizikai Kozlemenyek/Geophysical Transactions. a. ISSN 0016-7177

**Magyar Elektrotechnikai Egyesulet**
- Elektrotechnika. (pub. by Lapkiado Vallalat)
- Villamossag. (pub. by Lapkiado Vallalat)

**Magyar Elelmezesipari Tudomanyos Egyesulet**
- Baromfiipar. (pub. by Lapkiado Vallalat)
- Borgazdasag. (pub. by Lapkiado Vallalat)
- Cukoripar. (pub. by Lapkiado Vallalat)
- Dohanyipar. (pub. by Lapkiado Vallalat)
- Edesipar. (pub. by Lapkiado Vallalat)

- Elelmezesi Ipar. (pub. by Lapkiado Vallalat)
- Erdogazdasag es Faipar. (pub. by Lapkiado Vallalat)
- Gabonaipar. (pub. by Lapkiado Vallalat)
- Husipar. (pub. by Lapkiado Vallalat)
- Hutoipar. (pub. by Lapkiado Vallalat)

**Magyar Elettani Tarsasag**
Puskin u. 9, Budapest 8, Hungary
(Subscr. to: Kultura, Box 149, H-1389 Budapest, Hungary)
- Kiserletes Orvostudomany. bi-m. ISSN 0023-1878

**Magyar Epitomuveszek Szovetsege**
- Magyar Epitomuveszet. (pub. by Lapkiado Vallalat)

**Magyar Eszperanto Szovetseg**
see Hungara Esperanto Asocio

**Magyar Filmtudomanyi Intezet**
- Filmkultura. (pub. by Lapkiado Vallalat)

**Magyar Fogorvosok Egyesulete**
- Fogorvosi Szemle. (pub. by Ifjusagi Lapkiado Vallalat)

**Magyar Foldrajzi Tarsasag**
Nepkoztarsasag utja 62, Budapest, Hungary
(Subscr. to: Kultura, Box 149, H-1389 Budapest, Hungary)
- Foldrajzi Kozlemenyek. (pub. by Akademiai Kiado, Publishing House of the Hungarian Academy of Sciences)
- Geographia Medica. a. (approx.) ISSN 0435-3730

**Magyar Fotomuveszek Szovetsege**
- Fotomuveszet. (pub. by Lapkiado Vallalat)

**Magyar Geofizikusok Egyesulete**
P.O.B. 240, 1368 Budapest, Hungary
(Subscr. to: Kultura, Box 149, H-1389 Budapest, Hungary)
- Magyar Geofizika. bi-m. ISSN 0025-0120

**Magyar Gyogyszereszeti Tarsasag**
Visegradi u 19, 1132 Budapest, Hungary
(Subscr. to: Kultura, Box 149, H-1389 Budapest, Hungary)
- Acta Pharmaceutica Hungarica. bi-m. ISSN 0001-6659
- Gyogyszereszet. (pub. by Ifjusagi Lapkiado Vallalat)

**Magyar Hidrologiai Tarsasag**
Kossuth Lajos ter 6-8, 1372 Budapest 5, Hungary
(Subscr. to: Kultura, Box 149, H-1389 Budapest, Hungary)
- Hidrologiai Kozlony. m. ISSN 0018-1323

**Magyar Irodalomtorteneti Tarsasag**
- Irodalomtortenet/Literary History. (pub. by Akademiai Kiado, Publishing House of the Hungarian Academy of Sciences)

**Magyar Irok Szovetsege**
- Kortars. (pub. by Lapkiado Vallalat)
- Uj Iras. (pub. by Lapkiado Vallalat)

**Magyar Jogasz Szovetseg**
Szemere u. 10, Budapest 5, Hungary
(Subscr. to: Kultura, Box 149, H-1389 Budapest, Hungary)
- Hungarian Law Review. a.
- Jogtudomanyi Kozlony/Law Gazette. m. ISSN 0021-7166
- Magyar Jog es Kulfoldi Jogi Szemle. m. ISSN 0034-6829
- Revue de Droit Hongrois. 2 per yr.

**Magyar Kemikusok Egyesulete**
- Magyar Kemiai Folyoirat/Hungarian Journal of Chemistry. (pub. by Lapkiado Vallalat)
- Magyar Kemikusok Lapja. (pub. by Lapkiado Vallalat)

**Magyar Kereskedelmi Kamara**
Kossuth Lajos ter 6-8, 1055 Budapest 5, Hungary
(Subscr. to: Kultura, Box 149, H-1389 Budapest, Hungary)
- Hungarian Exporter. m. ISSN 0018-7739
- Hungarian Foreign Trade. q. ISSN 0018-7747
- Hungarian Heavy Industries. q. ISSN 0018-7755
- Kulgazdasag. m. (Co-sponsor: Konjunktura es Piackutato Intezet)
- Marketing in Hungary. (pub. by Lapkiado Vallalat)
- New Hungarian Exporter. m.

**Magyar Kommunista Ifjusagi Szovetseg**
- Delta. (pub. by Ifjusagi Lapkiado Vallalat)

**Magyar Konyvkiadok es Konyvterjesztok Egyesulese**
Vorosmarty ter 1, 1051 Budapest 5, Hungary
(Subscr. to: Kultura, Box 149, H-1389 Budapest, Hungary)
- Hungarian Book Review. q.
- Magyar Konyv. irreg. ISSN 0076-2393

**Magyar Korhazszovetseg**
Budapest, Hungary.
- Magyar Korhazak es Klinikak Evkonyve.

**Magyar Kozgazdasagi Tarsasag**
- Gazdasag/Economy. (pub. by Lapkiado Vallalat)
- Szigma. (pub. by Akademiai Kiado, Publishing House of the Hungarian Academy of Sciences)

**Magyar Kulugyi Intezet**
- Kulpolitika/Foreign Affairs. (pub. by Lapkiado Vallalat)

**Magyar Munkasmozgalmi Muzeum**
- Magyar Munkasmozgalmi Muzeum. Evkonyv. (pub. by Nepmuvelesi Propaganda Iroda)

**Magyar Nemzeti Muzeum**
Muzeum-krt. 14-16, Budapest VIII, Hungary.
- Folia Historica. a.

**Magyar Neprajzi Tarsasag**
Konyves Kalman korut 40, 1087 Budapest, Hungary
(Subscr. to: Kultura, Box 149, H-1389 Budapest, Hungary)
- Ethnographia. q. ISSN 0014-1798

**Magyar Neurologiai es Pszichiatriai Tarsasag**
- Ideggyogyaszati Szemle. (pub. by Ifjusagi Lapkiado Vallalat)

**Magyar Orszagos Leveltar**
- Leveltari Kozlemenyek/Archival Communications. (pub. by Akademiai Kiado, Publishing House of the Hungarian Academy of Sciences)

**Magyar Pedagogiai Tarsasag**
- Pedagogiai Szemle/Pedagogical Review. (pub. by Lapkiado Vallalat)

**Magyar Radiologiai Tarsasag**
- Magyar Radiologia. (pub. by Ifjusagi Lapkiado Vallalat)

**Magyar Rakkutatok Tarsasaga**
- Magyar Onkologia. (pub. by Ifjusagi Lapkiado Vallalat)

**Magyar Szocialista Munkaspart (MSZMP) Kozponti Bizottsag**
Szechenyi rakpart 19, Budapest 5, Hungary
(Subscr. to: Kultura, Box 149, H-1389 Budapest, Hungary)
- Tarsadalmi Szemle. m. ISSN 0039-971X

**Magyar Szocialista Munkaspart (MSZMP) Tarsadalomtudomanyi Intezet**
- Tarsadalomtudomanyi Kozlemenyek. (pub. by Kossuth Konyvkiado)

**Magyar Tavirati Iroda**
P.O.B. 3, 1426 Budapest, Hungary
(Subscr. to: Kultura, Box 149, H-1389 Budapest, Hungary)
- Weekly Bulletin. w. ISSN 0024-8495

**Magyar Termeszettudomanyi Muzeum**
Baross u. 13, 1088 Budapest, Hungary.
- Anthropologia Hungarica. a.

**Magyar Testnevelesi Foiskola**
Alkotas u.44, Budapest 12, Hungary.
- Magyar Testnevelesi Foiskola. Tudomanyos Kozlemenyek. irreg.

**Magyar Tortenelmi Tarsulat**
- Szazadok/Centuries. (pub. by Akademiai Kiado, Publishing House of the Hungarian Academy of Sciences)

**Magyar Tudomanyos Akademia**
Akademia u. 2, P.O.B. 7, 1054 Budapest V, Hungary.
- Absorption Spectra in the Ultraviolet and Visible Region. (pub. by Akademiai Kiado, Publishing House of the Hungarian Academy of Sciences)

- Acta Agronomica. (pub. by Akademiai Kiado, Publishing House of the Hungarian Academy of Sciences)
- Acta Alimentaria. (pub. by Akademiai Kiado, Publishing House of the Hungarian Academy of Sciences)
- Acta Antiqua. (pub. by Akademiai Kiado, Publishing House of the Hungarian Academy of Sciences)
- Acta Archaeologica. (pub. by Akademiai Kiado, Publishing House of the Hungarian Academy of Sciences)
- Acta Biochimica et Biophysica. (pub. by Akademiai Kiado, Publishing House of the Hungarian Academy of Sciences)
- Acta Biologica. (pub. by Akademiai Kiado, Publishing House of the Hungarian Academy of Sciences)
- Acta Botanica. (pub. by Akademiai Kiado, Publishing House of the Hungarian Academy of Sciences)
- Acta Chimica. (pub. by Akademiai Kiado, Publishing House of the Hungarian Academy of Sciences)
- Acta Chirurgica. (pub. by Akademiai Kiado, Publishing House of the Hungarian Academy of Sciences)
- Acta Ethnographica. (pub. by Akademiai Kiado, Publishing House of the Hungarian Academy of Sciences)
- Acta Geodaetica, Geophysica et Montanistica. (pub. by Akademiai Kiado, Publishing House of the Hungarian Academy of Sciences)
- Acta Geologica. (pub. by Akademiai Kiado, Publishing House of the Hungarian Academy of Sciences)
- Acta Historiae Artium. (pub. by Akademiai Kiado, Publishing House of the Hungarian Academy of Sciences)
- Acta Historica. (pub. by Akademiai Kiado, Publishing House of the Hungarian Academy of Sciences)
- Acta Juridica. (pub. by Akademiai Kiado, Publishing House of the Hungarian Academy of Sciences)
- Acta Linguistica. (pub. by Akademiai Kiado, Publishing House of the Hungarian Academy of Sciences)
- Acta Litteraria. (pub. by Akademiai Kiado, Publishing House of the Hungarian Academy of Sciences)
- Acta Mathematica. (pub. by Akademiai Kiado, Publishing House of the Hungarian Academy of Sciences)
- Acta Medica. (pub. by Akademiai Kiado, Publishing House of the Hungarian Academy of Sciences)
- Acta Microbiologica. (pub. by Akademiai Kiado, Publishing House of the Hungarian Academy of Sciences)
- Acta Morphologica. (pub. by Akademiai Kiado, Publishing House of the Hungarian Academy of Sciences)
- Acta Oeconomica. (pub. by Akademiai Kiado, Publishing House of the Hungarian Academy of Sciences)
- Acta Orientalia. (pub. by Akademiai Kiado, Publishing House of the Hungarian Academy of Sciences)
- Acta Paediatrica. (pub. by Akademiai Kiado, Publishing House of the Hungarian Academy of Sciences)
- Acta Physica. (pub. by Akademiai Kiado, Publishing House of the Hungarian Academy of Sciences)
- Acta Physiologica. (pub. by Akademiai Kiado, Publishing House of the Hungarian Academy of Sciences)
- Acta Phytopathologica. (pub. by Akademiai Kiado, Publishing House of the Hungarian Academy of Sciences)
- Acta Technica. (pub. by Akademiai Kiado, Publishing House of the Hungarian Academy of Sciences)
- Acta Veterinaria. (pub. by Akademiai Kiado, Publishing House of the Hungarian Academy of Sciences)
- Acta Zoologica. (pub. by Akademiai Kiado, Publishing House of the Hungarian Academy of Sciences)
- Agrartorteneti Szemle/Agricultural History Review. (pub. by Akademiai Kiado, Publishing House of the Hungarian Academy of Sciences)
- Agrartudomanyi Kozlemenyek. (pub. by Akademiai Kiado, Publishing House of the Hungarian Academy of Sciences)

- Alkalmazott Matematikai Lapok. (pub. by Akademiai Kiado, Publishing House of the Hungarian Academy of Sciences)
- Allattani Kozlemenyek/Zoological Proceedings. (pub. by Akademiai Kiado, Publishing House of the Hungarian Academy of Sciences)
- Analecta Linguistica. (pub. by John Benjamins B. V. NE)
- Analysis Mathematica. (pub. by Akademiai Kiado, Publishing House of the Hungarian Academy of Sciences)
- Antik Tanulmanyok. (pub. by Akademiai Kiado, Publishing House of the Hungarian Academy of Sciences)
- Archaeologiai Ertesito/Archaeological Bulletin. (pub. by Akademiai Kiado, Publishing House of the Hungarian Academy of Sciences)
- Architectura. (pub. by Akademiai Kiado, Publishing House of the Hungarian Academy of Sciences)
- Bibliotheca Hungarica Antiqua. (pub. by Akademiai Kiado, Publishing House of the Hungarian Academy of Sciences)
- Bibliotheca Orientalis Hungarica. (pub. by Akademiai Kiado, Publishing House of the Hungarian Academy of Sciences)
- Biologia. (pub. by Akademiai Kiado, Publishing House of the Hungarian Academy of Sciences)
- Botanikai Kozlemenyek/Botanical Proceedings. (pub. by Akademiai Kiado, Publishing House of the Hungarian Academy of Sciences)
- Budapest Varostorteneti Monografiai. (pub. by Akademiai Kiado, Publishing House of the Hungarian Academy of Sciences)
- Demografia. (pub. by Statisztikai Kiado Vallalat)
- Diplomaciai Iratok Magyarorszag Kulpolitikajahoz. (pub. by Akademiai Kiado, Publishing House of the Hungarian Academy of Sciences)
- Disquisitiones Mathematicae Hungariae. (pub. by Akademiai Kiado, Publishing House of the Hungarian Academy of Sciences)
- Epites es Epiteszettudomany/Building and Architectural Science. (pub. by Akademiai Kiado, Publishing House of the Hungarian Academy of Sciences)
- Ertekezesek a Torteneti Tudomanyok Korebol. Uj Sorozat. (pub. by Akademiai Kiado, Publishing House of the Hungarian Academy of Sciences)
- Etudes Historiques. (pub. by Akademiai Kiado, Publishing House of the Hungarian Academy of Sciences)
- Filologiai Kozlony/Philological Review. (pub. by Akademiai Kiado, Publishing House of the Hungarian Academy of Sciences)
- Filozofiai Irok Tara. (pub. by Akademiai Kiado, Publishing House of the Hungarian Academy of Sciences)
- Filozofiai Tanulmanyok. (pub. by Akademiai Kiado, Publishing House of the Hungarian Academy of Sciences)
- Foldrajzi Monografiak. (pub. by Akademiai Kiado, Publishing House of the Hungarian Academy of Sciences)
- Foldrajzi Tanulmanyok. (pub. by Akademiai Kiado, Publishing House of the Hungarian Academy of Sciences)
- Gazdasag es Jogtudomany. (pub. by Akademiai Kiado, Publishing House of the Hungarian Academy of Sciences)
- Gazdasagtorteneti Ertekezesek. (pub. by Akademiai Kiado, Publishing House of the Hungarian Academy of Sciences)
- Geography of World Agriculture. (pub. by Akademiai Kiado, Publishing House of the Hungarian Academy of Sciences)
- Geonomia es Banyaszat. (pub. by Akademiai Kiado, Publishing House of the Hungarian Academy of Sciences)
- Gorog es Latin Irok Tara/Scriptores Graeci et Latini. (pub. by Akademiai Kiado, Publishing House of the Hungarian Academy of Sciences)
- Haematologia. (pub. by Akademiai Kiado, Publishing House of the Hungarian Academy of Sciences)
- Indices Verborum Linguae Mongoliae Monumentis Traditorum. (pub. by Akademiai Kiado, Publishing House of the Hungarian Academy of Sciences)
- International Urology and Nephrology. (pub. by Akademiai Kiado, Publishing House of the Hungarian Academy of Sciences)
- Irodalom - Szocializmus. (pub. by Akademiai Kiado, Publishing House of the Hungarian Academy of Sciences)
- Irodalomelmelet Klasszikusai. (pub. by Akademiai Kiado, Publishing House of the Hungarian Academy of Sciences)

- Irodalomtorteneti Fuzetek. (pub. by Akademiai Kiado, Publishing House of the Hungarian Academy of Sciences)
- Irodalomtorteneti Konyvtar. (pub. by Akademiai Kiado, Publishing House of the Hungarian Academy of Sciences)
- Kemia Ujabb Eredmenyei. (pub. by Akademiai Kiado, Publishing House of the Hungarian Academy of Sciences)
- Kemiai Kozlemenyek. (pub. by Akademiai Kiado, Publishing House of the Hungarian Academy of Sciences)
- Korosi Csoma Kiskonyvtar. (pub. by Akademiai Kiado, Publishing House of the Hungarian Academy of Sciences)
- Korunk Tudomanya. (pub. by Akademiai Kiado, Publishing House of the Hungarian Academy of Sciences)
- Koszen es Koolaj Anyagismereti Monografiak. (pub. by Akademiai Kiado, Publishing House of the Hungarian Academy of Sciences)
- Kozgazdasagi Ertekezesek. (pub. by Akademiai Kiado, Publishing House of the Hungarian Academy of Sciences)
- Magyar Filozofiai Szemle/Hungarian Philosophical Review. (pub. by Akademiai Kiado, Publishing House of the Hungarian Academy of Sciences)
- Magyar Fizikai Folyoirat/Hungarian Journal of Physics. (pub. by Akademiai Kiado, Publishing House of the Hungarian Academy of Sciences)
- Magyar Irodalomtortenetiras Forrasai; Fontes Ad Historiam Litterariam Hungariae Spectantes. (pub. by Akademiai Kiado, Publishing House of the Hungarian Academy of Sciences)
- Magyar Konyvszemle. (pub. by Akademiai Kiado, Publishing House of the Hungarian Academy of Sciences)
- Magyar Pedagogia/Hungarian Pedagogy. (pub. by Akademiai Kiado, Publishing House of the Hungarian Academy of Sciences)
- Magyar Pszichologiai Szemle/Hungarian Psychological Review. (pub. by Akademiai Kiado, Publishing House of the Hungarian Academy of Sciences)
- Magyar Tudomany/Hungarian Science. (pub. by Akademiai Kiado, Publishing House of the Hungarian Academy of Sciences)
- Magyar Tudomanyos Akademia. Agrartudomanyok Osztalya. Monografiasorozat. (pub. by Akademiai Kiado, Publishing House of the Hungarian Academy of Sciences)
- Magyar Tudomanyos Akademia. Biologiai Tudomanyok Osztalya. Kozlemenyek. (pub. by Akademiai Kiado, Publishing House of the Hungarian Academy of Sciences)
- Magyar Tudomanyos Akademia. Filozofiai es Tortenettudomanyi Osztaly. Kozlemenyek. (pub. by Akademiai Kiado, Publishing House of the Hungarian Academy of Sciences)
- Magyar Tudomanyos Akademia. Konvytar. Kiadvanyok. 4-6 per yr. ISSN 0025-0341 (prep. by its Konyvtar)
- Magyar Tudomanyos Akademia. Nyelv- es Irodalomtudomanyi Osztaly. Kozlemenyek. (pub. by Akademiai Kiado, Publishing House of the Hungarian Academy of Sciences)
- Magyarorszag Allatvilaga/Fauna Hungariae. (pub. by Akademiai Kiado, Publishing House of the Hungarian Academy of Sciences)
- Magyarorszag Kulturfloraja. (pub. by Akademiai Kiado, Publishing House of the Hungarian Academy of Sciences)
- Magyarorszag Muemleki Topografiaja. (pub. by Akademiai Kiado, Publishing House of the Hungarian Academy of Sciences)
- Magyarorszag Regeszeti Topografiaja. (pub. by Akademiai Kiado, Publishing House of the Hungarian Academy of Sciences)
- Magyarorszag Tajfoldrajza. (pub. by Akademiai Kiado, Publishing House of the Hungarian Academy of Sciences)
- Modern Filologiai Fuzetek. (pub. by Akademiai Kiado, Publishing House of the Hungarian Academy of Sciences)
- Monographie der Flaumeichen-Buschwaelder. (pub. by Akademiai Kiado, Publishing House of the Hungarian Academy of Sciences)
- Monumenta Antiquitatis Extra Fines Hungariae Reperta Que in Museo Artium Hungarico Aliisque Museis et Collectionibus Hungaricis Conservatur. (pub. by Akademiai Kiado, Publishing House of the Hungarian Academy of Sciences)
- Monumenta Historica Budapestinensia. (pub. by Akademiai Kiado, Publishing House of the Hungarian Academy of Sciences)

- Monumenta Linguae Mongolicae Collecta. (pub. by Akademiai Kiado, Publishing House of the Hungarian Academy of Sciences)
- Musicologica Hungarica. Neue Folge. (pub. by Akademiai Kiado, Publishing House of the Hungarian Academy of Sciences)
- Muszaki Tudomany. (pub. by Akademiai Kiado, Publishing House of the Hungarian Academy of Sciences)
- Muveszettorteneti Ertesito. (pub. by Akademiai Kiado, Publishing House of the Hungarian Academy of Sciences)
- Nagyuzemi Gazdalkodas Kerdesei. (pub. by Akademiai Kiado, Publishing House of the Hungarian Academy of Sciences)
- Nyelveszeti Tanulmanyok. (pub. by Akademiai Kiado, Publishing House of the Hungarian Academy of Sciences)
- Orvostudomany. (pub. by Akademiai Kiado, Publishing House of the Hungarian Academy of Sciences)
- Problems of Control and Information Theory/Problemy Upravleniya i Teorii Informatsii. (pub. by Akademiai Kiado, Publishing House of the Hungarian Academy of Sciences)
- Pszichologia a Gyakorlatban. (pub. by Akademiai Kiado, Publishing House of the Hungarian Academy of Sciences)
- Pszichologiai Tanulmanyok. (pub. by Akademiai Kiado, Publishing House of the Hungarian Academy of Sciences)
- Recent Developments in the Chemistry of Natural Carbon Compounds. (pub. by Akademiai Kiado, Publishing House of the Hungarian Academy of Sciences)
- Recent Developments of Neurobiology in Hungary. (pub. by Akademiai Kiado, Publishing House of the Hungarian Academy of Sciences)
- Regi Magyar Prozai Emlekek. (pub. by Akademiai Kiado, Publishing House of the Hungarian Academy of Sciences)
- Studia Biologica Academiae Scientiarum Hungaricae. (pub. by Akademiai Kiado, Publishing House of the Hungarian Academy of Sciences)
- Studia Historica Academiae Scientiarum Hungaricae. (pub. by Akademiai Kiado, Publishing House of the Hungarian Academy of Sciences)
- Studia Musicologica. (pub. by Akademiai Kiado, Publishing House of the Hungarian Academy of Sciences)
- Studia Philosophica Academiae Scientiarum Hungaricae. (pub. by Akademiai Kiado, Publishing House of the Hungarian Academy of Sciences)
- Studia Scientiarum Mathematicarum. (pub. by Akademiai Kiado, Publishing House of the Hungarian Academy of Sciences)
- Studia Slavica. (pub. by Akademiai Kiado, Publishing House of the Hungarian Academy of Sciences)
- Studies in Geography in Hungary. (pub. by Akademiai Kiado, Publishing House of the Hungarian Academy of Sciences)
- Symposia Biologica Hungarica. (pub. by Akademiai Kiado, Publishing House of the Hungarian Academy of Sciences)
- Szilikatkemiai Monografiak. (pub. by Akademiai Kiado, Publishing House of the Hungarian Academy of Sciences)
- Szociologiai Tanulmanyok. (pub. by Akademiai Kiado, Publishing House of the Hungarian Academy of Sciences)
- Tanulmanyok a Nevelestudomany Korebol. (pub. by Akademiai Kiado, Publishing House of the Hungarian Academy of Sciences)
- Tarsadalomtudomanyi Kismonografiak. (pub. by Akademiai Kiado, Publishing House of the Hungarian Academy of Sciences)
- Tudomanyszervezesi Fuzetek. (pub. by Akademiai Kiado, Publishing House of the Hungarian Academy of Sciences)
- Tudomanyszervezesi Tajekoztato/Bulletin of Science Organization. (pub. by Akademiai Kiado, Publishing House of the Hungarian Academy of Sciences)
- Tudomanytorteneti Tanulmanyok. (pub. by Akademiai Kiado, Publishing House of the Hungarian Academy of Sciences)
- Uj Magyar Nepkoltesi Gyujtemeny. (pub. by Akademiai Kiado, Publishing House of the Hungarian Academy of Sciences)
- Vaskohaszati Enciklopedia. (pub. by Akademiai Kiado, Publishing House of the Hungarian Academy of Sciences)
- Vegetation Ungarischer Landschaften. (pub. by Akademiai Kiado, Publishing House of the Hungarian Academy of Sciences)

**Magyar Tudomanyos Akademia. Agrargazdasagi Kutato Intezet**
Zsil u. 3, P.O.B. 5, 1355 Budapest, Hungary.
- Hungarian Academy of Sciences. Research Institute for Agricultural Economics. Bulletin. s-a.

**Magyar Tudomanyos Akademia. Agrokemiai Kutato Intezet**
- Agrokemia es Talajtan. (pub. by Akademiai Kiado, Publishing House of the Hungarian Academy of Sciences)

**Magyar Tudomanyos Akademia. Allam-es Jogtudomanyi Intezet**
- Allam- es Jogtudomany/Political Science and Jurisprudence. (pub. by Akademiai Kiado, Publishing House of the Hungarian Academy of Sciences)

**Magyar Tudomanyos Akademia. Atommag Kutato Intezet**
Bem ter 18, 4001 Debrecen, Hungary.
- ATOMKI Kozlemenyek. q. ISSN 0004-7155

**Magyar Tudomanyos Akademia. Foldrajztudomanyi Kutato Intezet**
- Foldrajzi Ertesito. (pub. by Akademiai Kiado, Publishing House of the Hungarian Academy of Sciences)

**Magyar Tudomanyos Akademia. Ipargazdasagtani Kutatocsoport**
Szecheny rakpart 3, 1054 Budapest 5, Hungary.
- Ipargazdasagi Szemle. q.

**Magyar Tudomanyos Akademia. Irodalomtudomanyi Intezet**
- Helikon Vilagirodalmi Figyelo/Helikon Review of World Literature. (pub. by Akademiai Kiado, Publishing House of the Hungarian Academy of Sciences)
- Irodalomtorteneti Kozlemenyek/Literary History Communications. (pub. by Akademiai Kiado, Publishing House of the Hungarian Academy of Sciences)
- Kritika. (pub. by Lapkiado Vallalat)
- Literatura. (pub. by Akademiai Kiado, Publishing House of the Hungarian Academy of Sciences)

**Magyar Tudomanyos Akademia. Izotop Intezet**
P.O.B. 77, 1525 Budapest, Hungary
(Subscr. to: Kultura, Box 149, H-1389 Budapest, Hungary)
- Izotoptechnika/Isotope Technics. m. ISSN 0004-7201

**Magyar Tudomanyos Akademia. Kozgazdasagtudomanyi Intezet**
- Kozgazdasagi Szemle/Economic Review. (pub. by Akademiai Kiado, Publishing House of the Hungarian Academy of Sciences)

**Magyar Tudomanyos Akademia. Kozponti Fizikai Kutato Intezet**
P.O.B. 49, 1525 Budapest, Hungary.
- Magyar Tudomanyos Akademia. Kozponti Fizikai Kutato Intezet. Evkonyv. a.

**Magyar Tudomanyos Akademia. Mikrobiologiai Kutato Intezet**
- Magyar Tudomanyos Akademia. Mikrobiologiai Kutato Intezet. Proceedings/Hungarian Academy of Sciences. Research Institute for Microbiology. Proceedings. (pub. by Akademiai Kiado, Publishing House of the Hungarian Academy of Sciences)

**Magyar Tudomanyos Akademia. Neprajzi Kutato Csoport**
- Nepi Kultura-Nepi Tarsadalom. (pub. by Akademiai Kiado, Publishing House of the Hungarian Academy of Sciences)
- Neprajzi Tanulmanyok. (pub. by Akademiai Kiado, Publishing House of the Hungarian Academy of Sciences)

**Magyar Tudomanyos Akademia. Nepzenekutato Csoport**
- Regi Magyar Dallamok Tara/Corpus Musicae Popularis Hungaricae. (pub. by Akademiai Kiado, Publishing House of the Hungarian Academy of Sciences)

**Magyar Tudomanyos Akademia. Nyelvtudomanyi Intezet**
- Magyar Nyelv/Hungarian Language. (pub. by Akademiai Kiado, Publishing House of the Hungarian Academy of Sciences)

- Magyar Nyelvor/Hungarian Purist. (pub. by Akademiai Kiado, Publishing House of the Hungarian Academy of Sciences)
- Nyelvtudomanyi Ertekezesek. (pub. by Akademiai Kiado, Publishing House of the Hungarian Academy of Sciences)
- Nyelvtudomanyi Kozlemenyek/Linguistic Studies. (pub. by Akademiai Kiado, Publishing House of the Hungarian Academy of Sciences)

**Magyar Tudomanyos Akademia. Regeszeti Intezet**
Uri utca 49, 1250 Budapest, Hungary.
- Archaeologia Hungarica. Series Nova. (pub. by Akademiai Kiado, Publishing House of the Hungarian Academy of Sciences)
- Studia Archaeologica. (pub. by Akademiai Kiado, Publishing House of the Hungarian Academy of Sciences)
- Ungarische Akademie der Wissenschaften. Archaelogisches Institut. Mitteilungen. a.

**Magyar Tudomanyos Akademia. Szociologiai Intezet**
Uri u. 62, 1014 Budapest 1, Hungary.
- Szociologia. q.

**Magyar Tudomanyos Akademia. Tortenettudomanyi Intezet**
Uri utca 53, 1014 Budapest, Hungary
(Subscr. to: Kultura, Box 149, H-1389 Budapest, Hungary)
- Tortenelmi Szemle/Historical Review. (pub. by Akademiai Kiado, Publishing House of the Hungarian Academy of Sciences)
- Vilagtortenet. q. ISSN 0083-6265

**Magyar Uttorok Szovetsege**
- Pajtas. (pub. by Ifjusagi Lapkiado Vallalat)

**Magyar Zenemuveszek Szovetsege**
- Magyar Zene. (pub. by Lapkiado Vallalat)

**Magyarhoni Foldtani Tarsulat**
- Foldtani Kozlony. (pub. by Akademiai Kiado, Publishing House of the Hungarian Academy of Sciences)

**Marx Karoly Kozgazdasagtudomanyi Egyetem**
Dimitrov ter 8, Budapest 9, Hungary.
- Tajekoztato a Kulfoldi Kozgazdasagi Irodalomrol/Information on the Foreign Economic Literature. m. ISSN 0020-0166

**Medicina Kiado**
Beloiannisz u. 8, 1054 Budapest, Hungary.
- Egeszsegneveles Szakkonyvtara. irreg. ISSN 0073-4012
- Therapia Hungarica/Hungarian Medical Journal. 4 per yr. ISSN 0040-5949

**Merestechnikai es Automatizalasi Tudomanyos Egyesulet**
- Meres es Automatika. (pub. by Lapkiado Vallalat)

**Mora Ferenc Konyvkiado**
Lenin korut 9-11, Budapest 7, Hungary.
- Kincskeresok. irreg.

**Muszaki es Termeszettudomanyi Egyesuletek Szovetsege**
- Anyagmozgatas-Csomagolas. (pub. by Lapkiado Vallalat)
- Ipargazdasag. (pub. by Lapkiado Vallalat)

**Muszaki es Termeszettudomanyi Egyesuletek Szovetsege. Baranya Megyei Szervezet**
Janus Pannonius u. 11, Pecs, Hungary.
- Pecsi Muszaki Szemle. q. ISSN 0031-3750

**Muszaki Konyvkiado**
Bajcsy-Zsilinszky ut 22, 1374 Budapest, Hungary.
- Muszaki Konyv Hirado. q.

**Nemzetkozi Zenei Versenyek es Fesztivalok Irodaja**
Vorosmarty ter 1, P.O.B. 80, 1366 Budapest 5, Hungary.
- Hungarian Music News. bi-m. ISSN 0441-5973
- Hungarian Musical Guide. a. ISSN 0441-4446

**Nepmuvelesi Propaganda Iroda**
Gorkij fasor 45, Budapest VII, Hungary.
- Konyvtartudomanyi Tanulmanyok. irreg. ISSN 0075-6784 (Orszagos Konyvtarugyi es Dokumentacios Tanacs)
- Magyar Konyvtari Szakirodalom Bibliografiaja/Hungarian Library Literature. q. (Orszagos Szechenyi Konyvtar. Konyvtartudomanyi es Modszertani Kozpont)

- Magyar Munkasmozgalmi Muzeum. Evkonyv. biennial. ISSN 0076-2415

**Neprajzi Muzeum**
Kossuth Lajos ter 12, 1055 Budapest, Hungary.
- Neprajzi Ertesito/Ethnographic Review. a. ISSN 0077-6599
- Neprajzi Kozlemenyek. a. ISSN 0028-2774

**Nepszava Lapkiado Vallalat**
Rakoczi ut 54, 1964 Budapest 7, Hungary
(Subscr. to: Kultura, Box 149, H-1389 Budapest, Hungary)
- Kolorisztikai Ertesito/Coloristical Review. bi-m. ISSN 0023-2939 (Kozponti Kolorisztikai Kutato Laboratorium) (Co-sponsor: Magyar Szinbizottsag)
- Munkavedelem/Labor Safety. q. ISSN 0027-3619 (Szakszervezetek Orszagos Tanacsa. Munkavedelmi Tudomanyos Kutatointezet) (Co-sponsor: Orszagos Munkaegeszsegugyi Intezet)
- Technika. m. ISSN 0040-1110 (Hungarian Central Technical Library and Documentation Centre - Technoinform)

**Optikai, Akusztikai es Filmtechnikai Egyesulet**
- Finommechanika-Mikrotechnika. (pub. by Lapkiado Vallalat)
- Kep- es Hangtechnika. (pub. by Lapkiado Vallalat)

**Orszagos Erdeszeti Egyesulet**
Anker koz 1, 1061 Budapest 6, Hungary
(Subscr. to: Kultura, Box 149, H-1389 Budapest, Hungary)
- Erdo. m. ISSN 0014-0031

**Orszagos Filharmonia**
Box 46, 1364 Budapest, Hungary
(Subscr. to: Kultura, Box 149, H-1389 Budapest, Hungary)
- Ifju Zenebarat. 5 per yr. ISSN 0019-1558

**Orszagos Konyvtarugyi es Dokumentacios Tanacs**
- Konyvtartudomanyi Tanulmanyok. (pub. by Nepmuvelesi Propaganda Iroda)

**Orszagos Magyar Banyaszati es Kohaszati Egyesulet**
- Banyaszati es Kohaszati Lapok - Kohaszat. (pub. by Lapkiado Vallalat)
- Banyaszati es Kohaszati Lapok - Ontode. (pub. by Lapkiado Vallalat)

**Orszagos Muszaki Konyvtar es Dokumentacios Kozpont**
*see* **Hungarian Central Technical Library and Documentation Centre - Technoinform**

**Orszagos Orvostudomanyi Konyvtar es Dokumentacios Kozpont**
Szentkiralyi u. 21, 1372 Budapest 5, P.O.B. 452, Hungary
(Subscr. to: Kultura, Box 149, H-1389 Budapest, Hungary)
- Gyogyszereszeti es Gyogyszerterapias Dokumentacios Szemle. q. ISSN 0017-6044
- Hungarian Medical Bibliography. Abstracts. s-a.
- Magyar Orvosi Bibliografia; Bibliographia Medica Hungarica. bi-m. ISSN 0025-0252
- Orvosi Konyvtaros/Medical Librarian. q. ISSN 0030-6010
- Tuberkulozis es Tudogyogyaszat Referalo Szemle. q. ISSN 0041-3895

**Orszagos Szechenyi Konyvtar**
Muzeum korut 14-16, Budapest 8, Hungary.
- M N B Idoszaki Kiadvanyok Repertoriuma. fortn. (prep. by its Magyar Nemzeti Bibliografia Szerkesztosege)

**Orszagos Szechenyi Konyvtar. Konyvtartudomanyi es Modszertani Kozpont**
Muzeum v. 3, 1827 Budapest, Hungary
(Subscr. to: Kultura, Box 149, H-1389 Budapest, Hungary)
- Hungarian Library and Information Science Abstracts. s-a. ISSN 0046-8304
- Konyvtari es Dokumentacios Szakirodalom; referalo lap. q.
- Konyvtari Figyelo. bi-m. ISSN 0023-3773
- Magyar Konyvtari Szakirodalom Bibliografiaja/Hungarian Library Literature. (pub. by Nepmuvelesi Propaganda Iroda)
- Uj Konyvek. s-m. ISSN 0049-5069

**Orszagos Szovetkezeti Tanacs**
Szabadsag ter 14, Budapest 5, Hungary.
- Hungarian Co-operation. s-a. ISSN 0046-8290

**Orvos- es Egeszsegugyi Dolgozok Szakszervezete**
- Orvosi Hetilap. (pub. by Ifjusagi Lapkiado Vallalat)
- Szemeszet/Ophthalmologica Hungarica. (pub. by Ifjusagi Lapkiado Vallalat)

**Papir- es Nyomdaipari Muszaki Egyesulet**
Kossuth Lajos ter 6-8, 1055 Budapest 5, Hungary
(Subscr. to: Kultura, Box 149, H-1389 Budapest, Hungary)
- Magyar Grafika/Hungarian Graphic Arts. bi-m. ISSN 0025-0139
- Papiripar. bi-m. ISSN 0031-1448

**Pecsi Tudomanyegyetem**
48-as ter 1, Pecs, Hungary.
- Studia Iuridica. irreg., vol. 83, 1975. (prep. by its Allam- es Jogtudomanyi Kar)

**Pest Megyei Muzeumok Igazgatosaga**
Szentendre, Hungary.
- Studia Comitatensia. a.

**Reumatologiai Tarsasag**
- Rheumatologia, Balneologia, Allergologia. (pub. by Ifjusagi Lapkiado Vallalat)

**Semmelweis Orvostorteneti Muzeum**
Torok u. 12, 1023 Budapest, Hungary
(Subscr. to: Kultura, Box 149, H-1389 Budapest, Hungary)
- Communicationes de Historia Artis Medicinae/Orvostorteneti Kozlemenyek. q. ISSN 0010-3551

**Statisztikai Kiado Vallalat**
Keleti Karoly u. 18 B, P.O.B. 34, 1525 Budapest 2, Hungary
- Demografia; review of population sciences. q. ISSN 0011-8249 (Magyar Tudomanyos Akademia. Demografiai Bizottsag) (Co-sponsor: Hungary. Kozponti Statisztikai Hivatal) (Subscr. to: Kultura, Box 149, H-1389 Budapest, Hungary)
- Hungary. Kozponti Statisztikai Hivatal. Belkereskedelmi es Idegenforgalmi Adatok. q.
- Hungary. Kozponti Statisztikai Hivatal. Demografiai Evkonyv. a. ISSN 0073-4020
- Hungary. Kozponti Statisztikai Hivatal. Epitoipari Arak Alakulasa. irreg.
- Hungary. Kozponti Statisztikai Hivatal. Kepzettseg-Kereset. irreg.
- Hungary. Kozponti Statisztikai Hivatal. Kulkereskedelmi Statisztikai Evkonyv. irreg. (Hungary. Kozponti Statisztikai Hivatal)
- Hungary. Kozponti Statisztikai Hivatal. Maganautok Teljesitmenyei es Uzemeltetesi Korulmenyei. irreg.
- Hungary. Kozponti Statisztikai Hivatal. Mezogazdasagi Adatok. q. ISSN 0441-4675
- Hungary. Kozponti Statisztikai Hivatal, Nepgazdasagi Merlegek. irreg.
- Informacio - Elektronika. q. ISSN 0019-9753 (Hungary. Kozponti Statisztikai Hivatal) (Subscr. to: Kultura, Box 149, H-1389 Budapest, Hungary)
- Ipari es Epitoipari Statisztikai Ertesito. m. ISSN 0018-7801 (Hungary. Kozponti Statisztikai Hivatal)
- Statisztikai Evkonyv/Statistical Yearbook. a. ISSN 0073-4039 (Hungary. Kozponti Statisztikai Hivatal)
- Statisztikai Havi Kozlemenyek. m. ISSN 0018-781X (Hungary. Kozponti Statisztikai Hivatal)
- Statisztikai Szemle. m. ISSN 0039-0690 (Hungary. Kozponti Statisztikai Hivatal)
- Teruleti Statisztika. bi-m. ISSN 0018-7828 (Hungary. Kozponti Statisztikai Hivatal)
- Vas Megye Statisztikai Evkonyve. a. (Hungary. Kozponti Statisztikai Hivatal)

**Szakszervezetek Orszagos Tanacsa**
Dozsa Gyorgy ut 84B, Budapest 6, Hungary.
- Hungarian Trade Union News. m. ISSN 0018-778X
- Munka. m. ISSN 0027-3600 (Subscr. to: Kultura, Box 149, H-1389 Budapest, Hungary)
- Szakszervezeti Szemle. (pub. by Tancsics Konyvkiado)

**Szakszervezetek Orszagos Tanacsa. Munkavedelmi Tudomanyos Kutatointezet**
- Munkavedelem/Labor Safety. (pub. by Nepszava Lapkiado Vallalat)

**Szilikatipari Tudomanyos Egyesulet**
- Epitoanyag/Building Materials. (pub. by Lapkiado Vallalat)

**Szinhazmuveszeti Szovetseg**
- Szinhaz. (pub. by Lapkiado Vallalat)

**Szovetkezetek Orszagos Szovetsege**
- SZOVOSZ Tajekoztato. (pub. by Lapkiado Vallalat)

**Tancsics Konyvkiado**
Dozsa Gyorgy ut 84B, Budapest VI, Hungary.
- Szakszervezeti Szemle. q. (Szakszervezetek Orszagos Tanacsa)

**Tavkozlesi Kutato Intezet**
Budapest, Hungary.
- Tavkozlesi Kutato Intezet. Annual. a.

**Technoinform**
*see* **Hungarian Central Technical Library and Documentation Centre - Technoinform**

**Textilipari Muszaki es Tudomanyos Egyesulet**
- Magyar Textiltechnika. (pub. by Lapkiado Vallalat)

**Trade Unions International of Chemical, Oil and Allied Workers**
Dozsa Gyorgy ut 84B, 1415 Budapest, Hungary.
- World Conference of Trade Unions International of Chemical, Oil and Allied Workers. Report. irreg., 1971, 6th, Leuna, D.D.R. ISSN 0084-1544

**Tudomanyos Ismeretterjeszto Tarsulat**
- Elet es Tudomany. (pub. by Hirlapkiado Vallalat)
- Fold es Eg. (pub. by Hirlapkiado Vallalat)
- Termeszet Vilaga. (pub. by Hirlapkiado Vallalat)

**United Incandescent Lamp and Electrical Co. Ltd.**
Vaci ut 77, 1340 Budapest, Hungary.
- Tungsram Technische Mitteilungen. 4 per yr. ISSN 0041-4107

**Veszpremi Vegyipari Egyetem**
- Hungarian Journal of Industrial Chemistry. (pub. by Lapkiado Vallalat)

**Vilaggazdasagi Tudomanyos Tanacs**
Kallo esperes u. 15, P.O.B. 36, 1531 Budapest 12, Hungary
(Subscr. to: Kultura, Box 149, H-1389 Budapest, Hungary)
- Abstracts of Hungarian Economic Literature. bi-m. ISSN 0044-5800
- Trends in World Economy. irreg (4-6 per yr)

**Vizgazdalkodasi Tudomanyos Kutato Kozpont**
Kvassay J.ut 1, 1095 Budapest 9, Hungary
(Subscr. to: Kultura, Box 149, H-1389 Budapest, Hungary)
- Vizminosegi es Viztechnologiai Kutatasi Eredmenyek/Research in Water Quality and Water Technology. irreg.
- Vizugyi Kozlemenyek. q. ISSN 0042-7616

**World Federation of Democratic Youth**
Ady Endre u. 19, Budapest 2, Hungary
(Subscr. to: Kultura, Box 149, H-1389 Budapest, Hungary)
- W F D Y News. m. ISSN 0049-8076
- World Youth/Jeunesse du Monde/Juventud del Mundo; international youth magazine. bi-m. ISSN 0043-9274

**Zrinyi Katonai Kiado**
Dozsa Gyorgy ut 49, 1134 Budapest 13, Hungary
(Subscr. to: Kultura, Box 149, H-1389 Budapest, Hungary)
- Radiotechnika. m. ISSN 0033-8478

# ICELAND

**Agricultural Society of Iceland**
*see* **Bunadarfelag Islands**

**Atlantica & Iceland Review**
Storagerdi 27, Box 93, Reykjavik, Iceland.
- Atlantica & Iceland Review. q. ISSN 0304-1263
- News from Iceland. m.

**Bioradii Publications**
Box 722, Reykjavik, Iceland.
- Interstellar Communication. 3-4 per yr. ISSN 0020-9740 (Felag Nyalssinna)

**Bokaforlag Odds Bjoernssonar**
88 Hafnarstraeti, Akureyri, Iceland.
- Heima Er Bezt. m. ISSN 0017-9698

**Bokautgafa Menningarsjod**
Skalholtsstig 7, Reykjavik, Iceland.
- Acta Botanica Islandica; Timarit Um Islenzka
Grasafraedi. a. (Menningarsjodur)

**Bunadarfelag Islands**
Box 7080, Reykjavik, Iceland.
- Bunadarrit. s-a.
- Freyr. fortn. ISSN 0016-1209

**Central Bank of Iceland**
see Sedlabanki Islands

**Eimreidin**
Box 437, Reykjavik, Iceland.
- Eimreidin/Progress. q. ISSN 0013-2624

**Federation of Icelandic Master-Craftsmen**
see Landssamband Idnadarmanna

**Felag Islenzkra Storkaupmanna**
Tjarnargata 14, Box 476, Reykjavik, Iceland.
- F I S Frettabref. irreg. (approx. 8-10 per yr)

**Felag Nyalssinna**
- Interstellar Communication. (pub. by Bioradii
Publications)

**Fisheries Association of Iceland**
see Fiskifelag Islands

**Fiskifelag Islands**
Box 20, Reykjavik, Iceland.
- Aegir/Sea. s-m. ISSN 0001-9038

**Hilmir H.F.**
Sioumula 12, Reykjavik, Iceland.
- Urval. m. ISSN 0042-1197
- Vikan. w. ISSN 0042-6105

**Hjukrunarfelags Islands**
Skrifstofa, Thingholtsstraeti 30, Reykjavik, Iceland.
- Hjukrunarfelags Islands. Timarit. 4 per yr. ISSN
0046-7634

**Iceland. Hagstofa Islands**
Reykjavik, Iceland.
- Hagtidindi. m. ISSN 0019-1078
- Iceland. Statistical Bureau. Statistical Bulletin. q.
ISSN 0019-1086 (Co-sponsor: Sedlabanki Islands)
- Statistical Abstract of Iceland. irreg., latest 1974.
ISSN 0081-4652

**Iceland. Statistical Bureau**
see Iceland. Hagstofa Islands

**Icelandic Natural History Society**
see Islenzka Natturufraedifelag

**Icelandic Nurses' Association**
see Hjukrunarfelags Islands

**Icelandic Scientific Society**
see Visindafelag Islendinga

**Islenzka Natturufraedifelag**
Box 846, Reykjavik, Iceland.
- Natturufraedingurinn. 2-4 per yr. ISSN 0028-0550

**Olafs Jenssonar Loeknir**
Laugarasvegi 3, Reykjavik, Iceland.
- Laeknabladid. bi-m. ISSN 0023-7213

**Kvenfelagasamband Islands**
Hallveigarstoeoum, Tungotu 14, Reykjavik, Iceland.
- Husfreyjan. q. ISSN 0018-7984

**Landssamband Idnadarmanna**
Hallveigarstig 1, Reykjavik, Iceland.
- Timarit Idnadarmanna. q.

**Menningarsjodur**
- Acta Botanica Islandica; Timarit Um Islenzka
Grasafraedi. (pub. by Bokautgafa Menningarsjod)

**Rjettur**
Sidumula 6, Reykjavik, Iceland.
- Rjettur. q. ISSN 0034-6195

**Sedlabanki Islands**
Austurstraeti 11, Reykjavik, Iceland.
- Fjarmalatidindi/Financial Times Icelandic. q.
ISSN 0015-3346

**Union of Women's Societies**
see Kvenfelagasamband Islands

**Visindafelag Islendinga**
Haskoli Islands, Reykjavik, Iceland.
- Scientia Islandica/Science in Iceland. irreg.

# INDIA

**A & P Publications**
3 Krishnier St., Nungambakkam, Madras 34, India.
- Adam and Eve. m. ISSN 0044-6181

**A I R**
see India. All India Radio

**A.N. Sinha Institute of Social Studies**
see Sinha Institute of Social Studies

**A V A R D**
see Association of Voluntary Agencies for Rural
Development

**Aavesh**
62-3 Rajendra Nagar, New Delhi 5, India.
- Aavesh; a rejoinder of writings by Indian youth
biased to liberated thinking. s-a. ISSN 0001-3064

**Z. Abedin, Ed. & Pub.**
41/87 Wodehouse Rd., Bombay 400005, India.
- Children's Digest. m. ISSN 0009-4080

**Abhayaduta**
High Court Rd., Jodhpur, India.
- Abhayaduta. w.

**Academic Journals of India**
E-30 South Extension (Part II), New Delhi 49,
India.
- Indian Journal of Sociology. s-a. ISSN 0019-5642
(Indian Academy of Social Sciences)

**Academy of Comparative Philosophy and Religion,
Belgaum**
Tilakwadi East, Belgaum 590011, India.
- Pathway to God. q.

**Academy of Fine Arts**
14-2 Old China Bazar St., Calcutta 1, India.
- Art and the Artist. q.

**Academy of Tamil Culture**
13/11 Jeremiah Rd., Vepery, Madras 7, India.
- Tamil Culture. q. ISSN 0039-9299

**Academy of Zoology**
Khandari Rd., Agra 2, Uttar Pradesh, India.
- Annals of Zoology. q. ISSN 0003-5009

**Adarsh Seva Sangha**
Ishwardas Mansions, Nana Chowk, Bombay 7,
India.
- Rural India. m. ISSN 0036-0058

**P. Adimoolam, Ed. & Pub.**
140 Gaudiamath Rd., Madras 600014, India.
- Poyyamozhi; astrological Tamil monthly. m.

**Administrative Change**
B. Mehta at C-13 Bal Marg, Tilak Nagar, Jaipur 4,
India.
- Administrative Change. s-a. ISSN 0302-2986

**Administrative Staff College of India**
Bella Vista, Hyderabad 4, India.
- A S C I Journal of Management. s-a.
- Current Management Literature. m.
- National Bibliography of Cases in Business
Administration. a. ISSN 0550-7448

**Advaita Ashrama**
5 Dehi Entally Rd., Calcutta 700014, India.
- Prabuddha Bharata/Awakened India. m. ISSN
0032-6178 (Ramakrishna Order)

**Advancing Frontiers of Plant Sciences**
c/o Ed. Prof. Dr. Lokesh Chandra, J. 22 Hauz Khas
Enclave, New Delhi 16, India.
- Advancing Frontiers of Plant Sciences. irreg., vol.
30, 1975. ISSN 0065-3543

**Adyar Library and Research Centre**
Adyar, Madras 600020, India.
- Brahmavidya. irreg. (1-2 yr.) ISSN 0001-902X

**Aeronautical Publications of India Private Limited**
Santacruz Airport, Bombay 400029, India
(U.S. Subscr. Address: INTA Advertising, Inc.,
1560 Broadway, New York, NY 10036)
- Skyways; aviation magazine of Asia. m.

**Aeronautical Society of India**
13-B Indraprastha Estate, New Delhi 110002, India.
- Aeronautical Society of India. Journal. q. ISSN
0001-9267

**Africa Publications (India)**
F-15 Bhagat Singh Market, Box 702, New Delhi 1,
India.
- Africa Diary. w. ISSN 0001-978X
- Indian Economic Diary. w. ISSN 0019-4654
- Indo-African Trade Journal; publication aiming at
larger trade between India and Africa. q. ISSN
0019-7181
- West Asia Diary. w.

**Agra Geographical Society**
Raja Balwant Singh College, Department of
Geography, Agra 2, India.
- Geographical View Point. s-a. ISSN 0046-5712

**Agra University**
Agra 282004, Uttar Pradesh, India.
- Agra University. Bulletin. q. ISSN 0044-6734
- Agra University Journal of Research (Science) 3
per yr. ISSN 0002-1032

**Agra University. Institute of Social Sciences**
Agra 282004, Uttar Pradesh, India.
- Journal of Social Sciences. s-a. ISSN 0449-3168

**Agri Horticultural Society of India**
1 Alipore Rd., Calcutta 27, India.
- Agri Horticultural Society of India. Horticultural
Bulletin. q.

**Agricultural Economist**
10 North St., Ganapathi Nagar, Thanjavur, Madras,
India.
- Agricultural Economist. m. ISSN 0002-1431

**Agricultural Engineering Society**
c/o M. K. Diwan, Ed., 3-A St. George Terrace,
Hasting, Calcutta 22, India.
- Harvester; agricultural engineering journal. q.
ISSN 0017-8225

**Agricultural Finance Corporation Ltd.**
Dhanraj Mahal, First Floor, Chhatrapati Shivaji
Maharaj Marg, Bombay, India.
- Financing Agriculture. q. ISSN 0015-2110

**Agricultural Research Communication Centre**
Sadar, Karnal 132001, Haryana, India.
- Bhartiya Krishi Anusandhan Patrika; half-yearly
research journal of plant and animal sciences. s-a.
- Indian Journal of Agricultural Research; quarterly
journal of plant and soil science. q.
- Indian Journal of Animal Research; half-yearly
research journal of animal, food and zoological
sciences. s-a.

**Agricultural Society of India**
- Indian Agriculturist. (pub. by Calcutta University
Press)

**Agriculture Digest**
4-5 B Asaf Ali Rd., New Delhi, India.
- Agriculture Digest; magazine for progressive
farmers. m.

**Agro-Service**
3491 Gali Bajrangbali, Chawri Bazar, Delhi 6, India.
- Crops in India. q. ISSN 0011-1872

**Ahmedabad Textile Industry's Research Association**
Polytechnic P.O., Ahmedabad 380015, India.
- A T I R A Technical Digest. q.
- Ahmedabad Textile Industry's Research
Association. Joint Technological Conferences.
Proceedings. a. ISSN 0075-4005
- Ahmedabad Textile Industry's Research
Association. Proceedings of the Management
Conference. a. ISSN 0065-4779

**Ajoy Bhavan**
Kutla Road, New Delhi, India.
- Hayat. w.

**Akashvani Group of Journals**
PTI Building, Parliament St., New Delhi 1, India.
- Akashvani. w. (India. All India Radio)

**Akhil Mithila Maithili Pracharak Sangh**
No. 81/2-1 Road No. 6, Adityapor, Jamshedpur,
Bihar, India.
- Tatka. m. ISSN 0039-9892

**Akhila Bharatiya Sanskrit Parishad**
c/o Gopal Chandra Sinha, Sec'y, Mahatma Gandhi
Marg, Hazratganj, Lucknow, Uttar Pradesh, India.
- Rtam. s-a. ISSN 0035-9424

**Alakendu Bodh Niketan**
1/7-A Ramakrishna das Lane, Calcutta 700009,
India.
- Retarded. q. ISSN 0034-6152

**Aligarh Muslim University**
Aligarh, Uttar Pradesh, India.
- General Education Reading Material Series. irreg.
ISSN 0072-0720

**Aligarh Muslim University. Center for Advanced Study**
- Medieval India; a Miscellany. (pub. by Asia
Publishing House, Inc. US)

**Aligarh Muslim University. Department of History**
- Aligarh Muslim University, Aligarh, India.
Department of History. Publication. (pub. by Asia
Publishing House, Inc. US)

**Aligarh Muslim University. Department of Political Science**
Aligarh, Uttar Pradesh, India.
- Indian Journal of Politics. 3 per yr.

**Aligarh Muslim University. Geographical Society**
Aligarh, Uttar Pradesh, India.
- Geographer. a. ISSN 0072-0909

**S. M. Alimuddin, Ed. & Pub.**
No. 23 Zakeria St., Calcutta 1, West Bengal, India.
- Homoeopathic Science Quarterly. q. ISSN 0018-4454

**All Bengal Teachers' Association**
15 Bankim Chatterjee St., Calcutta 12, India.
- Siksha - O - Sahitya; teachers' journal. m. ISSN
0037-5160

**All India Administrative Offices Employees Union**
9 Pusa Rd., New Delhi 5, India.
- Bullet. m. ISSN 0045-348X

**All India Air Conditioning and Refrigeration Association**
c/o S. Sajjan Singh, 7/17 Kirti Nagar, New Delhi
110015, India.
- Climate Control; serving the air conditioning and
refrigeration industry. bi-m. ISSN 0009-8930

**All India Anglo-Indian Association**
Bombay Life Bldg., Connaught Circus, New Delhi,
India.
- All-India Anglo-Indian Association. Review. m.
ISSN 0002-5585

**All India Association for Christian Higher Education**
4 Raj Niwas Marg, Delhi 110054, India.
- New Frontiers in Education. q. ISSN 0047-9705

**All India Association of Mental Retardation**
c/o Dr. K. G. Agrawal, Ed., National Labour
Institute, AB-6 Safdarjang Enclave, New Delhi
110016, India.
- Indian Journal of Mental Retardation. s-a. ISSN
0019-5375

**All-India Automobile and Ancillary Industries Association**
80 Dr. Annie Besant Rd, Worli, Bombay 400018,
India.
- Automotive and Ancillary Industry. a.

**All India Bank Employees Federation**
c/o V. N. Sekhri, 26-104 Birhana Rd., Kanpur
208001, India.
- Bank Karamchari. m. ISSN 0005-5077

**All India Basic Education Council**
Sevagram, Wardha, Maharashtra, India.
- Nayi Talim/Basic Education. bi-m.

**All-India Bee Keepers Association**
817 Sadashiv Peth, Poona 411030, India.
- Indian Bee Journal. q. ISSN 0019-4425

**All India Catholic University Federation**
Sterling Rd., Madras 34, India.
- Rally. m. ISSN 0048-668X

**All India Central Land Development Banks Cooperative Union Ltd.**
Barkatpura, Hyderabad 27, India.
- All India Central Land Development Banks
Cooperative Union. Journal. q. ISSN 0569-0196

**All India Coffee Workers Cooperative Societies Federation Ltd.**
10 U.B. Bungalow Rd., Jawahar Nagar, Delhi 7,
India.
- Coffee Mazdoor Sahakari. q. ISSN 0010-0250

**All India Commercial Association**
Daryaganj, Delhi 6, India.
- Commercial Journal. m. ISSN 0010-3039

**All India Congress Committee**
Publications Department, 5 Dr. Rajendra Prasad
Rd., New Delhi 110001, India.
- All India Congress Committee. Congress Bulletin.
m.
- Congress Marches Ahead. irreg.
- Socialist India. w. ISSN 0037-8208

**All India Congress Committee. Women's Department**
Dept. 7, Jautar Mantar Rd., New Delhi 1, India.
- Women on the March. m.

**All India Council of Mayors**
48-B Municipal Colony, Azad Pur, Delhi 33, India.
- Mayors' Newsletter. m.

**All India Crime Prevention Society**
Pragati Ashram, Balaganj, Lucknow, India.
- All India Crime Prevention Society. Annual
Report and Audited Statement of Accounts. a.
ISSN 0065-6283

**All India Federation of Education Associations**
Jha Seshadri Khattry Bhawan, Box 52, Kanpur 1,
Uttar Pradesh, India.
- Bhartiya Shikcha. m.
- Indian Education. m. ISSN 0019-4689

**All India Federation of Master Printers**
- All India Federation of Master Printers. (pub. by
Bolton Fine Art Litho Works)

**All India Federation of University and College Teachers Organisations**
4-37 Roop Nagar, Delhi 110007, India.
- University Affairs; all India journal of education
and allied matters. m.

**All-India Fine Arts and Crafts Society**
Rafi Marg, New Delhi 1, India.
- Roopa-Lekha; an illustrated journal of Indian arts
and crafts. s-a. ISSN 0035-8215

**All India Food Preservers' Association**
- Indian Food Packer. (pub. by Kissan Products
Ltd.)

**All India Handloom Exporters Guide**
c/o S. Narayanan, 11-B Ramachandra Iyer St.,
Madras 600017, India.
- All India Handloom Exporters Guide. irreg.

**All India Homeopathic Association**
4457 Pahari Dhiraj Sadar Bazar, Delhi 6, India.
- Homeopathic Sandesh. m. ISSN 0018-4446

**All India Indo-Korean Friendship Association**
F60 Bhagat Singh Market, New Delhi 1, India.
- Indo-Korean Friendship. m.

**All India Institute of Homeopathy**
- Journal of Dynamic Medicine. (pub. by Swaran
Publishing House)

**All India Institute of Local Self Government**
11 Horniman Circle, Fort, Bombay, India.
- All India Institute of Local Self Government.
Quarterly Journal. q. ISSN 0024-5623

**All India Institute of Medical Sciences**
New Delhi 110016, India.
- All India Institute of Medical Sciences. Journal. q.

**All India Institute of Medical Sciences. Department of Orthopaedic Surgery**
New Delhi 110016, India.
- Indian Journal of Orthopaedics. s-a. ISSN 0019-5413 (Indian Orthopaedic Association)

**All India Instrument Manufacturers and Dealers Association**
A-32 Navyug Niwas, Laminton Rd., Opp. Minerva
Cinema, Bombay 7, India.
- Instruments India. bi-m. ISSN 0047-0376

**All India Iron and Steel Stockholders Federation**
4635 Ajmeri Gate, Delhi, India.
- Steel Trade. m. ISSN 0039-0968

**All India Kasiraja Trust**
Puruna Department, Varanasi, India.
- Puranam. s-a. ISSN 0555-7860

**All India Magic Circle**
276-1 Rash Behary Ave., Ballyganj, Calcutta
700019, India.
- All India Magic Circle Bulletin. q. (Indian Magic
Expansion Board)

**All India Management Association**
Deepak, 13 Nehru Place, Flats 51-53, New Delhi
110024, India.
- Management Abstracts. q.

**All-India Manufacturers' Organization**
- Industrial India. (pub. by Chary Publications)

**All India Non-Edible Oil Association**
c/o Mrs. Savitri Madan, Asson Taru Sneha, 1153
Shivaji Nagar, Ganeshkind Rd., Poona 16, India.
- Sneha Sandesh. bi-m. ISSN 0037-7449

**All India Occupational Therapists' Association**
c/o BM Institute of Mental Health, Nr. Nehru
Bridge, Navrangpura, Ahmedabad 380009, India.
- Indian Journal of Occupational Therapy. q. ISSN
0445-7706

**All India Ophthalmological Society**
Sarojini Sadan, Congress House, V. Patel Rd.,
Bombay 400004, India
(Subscr. to: S. R. K. Malik, Ed., 44 Kotla Rd., New
Delhi 110001, India)
- Indian Journal of Ophthalmology. q. ISSN 0301-4738

**All India Organisation of Employers**
Federation House, New Delhi 110001, India.
- A I O E Labour News. fortn. ISSN 0001-1630

**All India Panchayat Parishad**
A-23 Kailash Colony, New Delhi 110048, India.
- Panchayat Aur Insan. m. ISSN 0031-0670

**All India Radio**
see India. All India Radio

**All India Reporter Ltd.**
Box 209, Nagpur 440012, India.
- All India Reporter; full reports of all reportable
(civil, criminal and revenue) cases of the High
Courts and Supreme Court in India. m. ISSN
0002-5593
- Criminal Law Journal; full reports of all reportable
criminal cases of the High Courts and the
Supreme Court of india. m. ISSN 0011-1325
- Labour and Industrial Cases. m.
- Taxation Law Reports. m.

**All India Sai Samaj**
Madras 4, Tamil Nadu, India.
- Sai Suddha. m.

**All India State Cooperative Banks Federation**
Garment House, 2nd Floor, Dr. Annie Besant Rd.,
Worli, Bombay 18, India.
- Cooperative Banker. q.

**All India Trade Union Congress**
Rani Jhansi Rd., New Delhi 55, India.
- Trade Union Record. s-m. ISSN 0041-0535

**All India Youth Federation**
4/7 Asaf Ali Rd., New Delhi 110001, India.
- Youth Life. bi-w.

**All Kerala Homeopathic Physicians Association**
Kanjikuzhy, Kottayam 4, Kerala, India.
- Kerala Homoeo Journal. q. ISSN 0300-3957 (Co-sponsor: Indian Homoeo Chemists Association)

**Allahabad Geographical Society**
University of Allahabad, Department of Geography,
Allahabad 211002, Uttar Pradesh, India.
- National Geographer. a. ISSN 0470-0929

**Allahabad Law Journal Co., Ltd.**
5 Prayag St., Allahabad, India.
- Allahabad Law Journal. w.
- Bihar Law Journal Reports. w.

**Allahabad Mathematical Society**
Lakshmi Niwas, Georgetown, Allahabad 211002, India.
- Indian Journal of Mathematics. 3 per yr. ISSN 0019-5324

**Allahabad University**
*see* University of Allahabad

**Allied Publishers Private Ltd.**
13-14 Asaf Ali Rd., New Delhi 110001, India.
- Alternatives. q.

**Allied Trades Association**
7-32 Daryaganj, Delhi 6, India.
- Allied Trades Association. Commercial News. m. ISSN 0010-3071

**Aloka Bharati**
K-15 Green Park, New Delhi 16, India.
- Aloka Bharati. a.

**Aloy Steel Producers Association of India**
332 Hind Rajasthan Bldg., D. S. Phalka Rd., Dadar, Bombay 400014, India.
- Tool and Alloy Steels. bi-m.

**Amalgamated Press**
Narang House, 41 Ambalal Doshi Marg, Bombay 400023, India.
- Beverage and Food World. q.
- Export Gazette. m.
- World Register of Chambers of Commerce/Associations & Trades. biennial.

**Amateur Radio Society of India**
Treasurer, 5-E Connaught Place, New Delhi 1, India.
- Indian Radio Amateur. 3 per yr. ISSN 0019-624X

**P. R. Ambike, Ed. & Pub.**
1398 Sadashiv Peth, Poona, India.
- Maharashtra. fortn. ISSN 0025-0392

**American Institute of Indian Studies**
D-176 Defence Colony, New Delhi 110024, India.
- A I I S Quarterly Newsletter. q. ISSN 0304-6214

**American Studies Research Centre**
Hyderabad 500007, India.
- American Studies Research Centre. Newsletter. irreg. ISSN 0066-0795
- Indian Journal of American Studies. s-a. ISSN 0019-5030

**Anaesthesiology and Resuscitation Research Forum**
Department of Anaesthesiology and Resuscitation, Goa Medical College, Panaji 403001, Goa, India (Distr. by: Prints India, 11 Darya Ganj, New Delhi 110002, India)
- Asian Archives of Anaesthesiology and Resuscitation. s-a.

**Anatomical Society of India**
Motilal Nehru Medical College, Department of Anatomy, Allahabad, Uttar Pradesh, India.
- Anatomical Society of India. Journal. 3 per yr. ISSN 0003-2778

**Andhra Agricultural Union**
Agricultural College Campus Bapatla, Guntur, A.P., India.
- Andhra Agricultural Journal. bi-m. ISSN 0003-2956

**Andhra Pradesh. Department of Archaeology and Museums**
Hyderabad 500001, Andhra Pradesh, India
(Or: Publications Bureau, Directorate of Government Printing, Chanchalguda, Hyderabad, India)
- Andhra Historical Research Society. Journal. a.
- Andhra Pradesh, India. Department of Archaeology and Museums. Archaeology, History and Culture Series. irreg., no. 47, 1975-1976.
- Andhra Pradesh, India. Department of Archaeology and Museums. Art and Architecture Series. irreg.
- Andhra Pradesh, India. Department of Archaeology and Museums. Epigraphy Series. irreg., no. 11, 1975-76.

- Andhra Pradesh, India. Department of Archaeology and Museums. Museum Objects and Numismatics Series. irreg., no. 18, 1975-76.

**Andhra Pradesh. Department of Information and Public Relations**
Hyderabad 500001, Andhra Pradesh, India.
- Andhra Pradesh. m. ISSN 0570-0655

**Andhra Pradesh. Director of State Archives**
Hyderabad, Andhra Pradesh, India.
- Itihas; journal of the Andhra Pradesh archives. s-a.

**Andhra Pradesh. Directorate of Marketing**
Hyderabad, Andhra Pradesh, India.
- Report on the Marketing of Tobacco in Andhra Pradesh. a.

**Andhra Pradesh. Office of the Comptroller and Auditor-General**
Director of Printing and Stationery, Hyderabad, Andhra Pradesh, India.
- Government of Andhra Pradesh. Report. a.

**Andhra Pradesh. State Council of Educational Research and Training**
Dept. of Public Instruction, Hyderabad, Andhra Pradesh, India.
- S C E R T Journal. s-a.

**Andhra Pradesh Productivity Council**
Box No. 21(10-1-200, A. C. Guards), Hyderabad 500004, Andhra Pradesh, India.
- Andhra Pradesh Productivity Council Journal. s-a. ISSN 0003-2964

**Andhra Pradesh State Financial Corporation**
5-9-194 Chirag Ali Lane, Hyderabad 500001, India.
- Andhra Pradesh State Financial Corporation. Report and Accounts. a.

**Andhra University**
- Andhra University Memoirs in Oceanography. (pub. by Andhra University Press and Publications)
- Indian Psychology. (pub. by Andhra University Press and Publications)

**Andhra University Press and Publications**
Waltair, Visakhapatnam 530003, Andhra Pradesh, India.
- Andhra University Memoirs in Oceanography. irreg. ISSN 0066-1686
- Indian Psychology. s-a. (Andhra University)

**R.N.S. Anil, Ed. & Pub.**
B-146 East of Kailash, New Delhi 110024, India.
- International Post. q.

**Anjuman Taraggi Urdu (Hind)**
Sultan Jahan Manzil, Aligarh, Uttar Pradesh, India.
- Urdu Adab. q. ISSN 0042-1057

**Annamalai University. Department of Economics**
Annamalainagar P.O., Tamil Nadu, India.
- Southern Economic Review. q.

**Anthropological Society of Bombay**
136 Apollo St., Fort, Bombay, India.
- Anthropological Society of Bombay. Journal. s-a.

**Anthropological Survey of India**
Indian Museum, 27 Jawaharlal Nehru Marg, Calcutta 13, India.
- Anthropological Survey of India. Bulletin. s-a. ISSN 0003-5513

**Antiseptic**
323 Thambu Chetty St., Madras 600001, India.
- Antiseptic; monthly journal of medicine and surgery. m. ISSN 0003-5998

**Appointments Market Weekly**
C-7 Chaupatian Colony, Lucknow 5, India.
- Appointments Market Weekly. w.

**Arab Republic of Egypt Embassy**
*see* Embassy of the Arab Republic of Egypt

**Architects Publishing Corp. of India**
51 Sujata, Quarry Rd. Crossing, Malad East, Bombay 400064, India.
- Architects Trade Journal. bi-m.
- Indian Institute of Architects. Journal. q. ISSN 0019-4913

**Architecture and Building Industry**
87-88 New Market, Begam Bridge, Meerut, Uttar Pradesh, India.
- Architecture and Building Industry. m. ISSN 0003-8652

**Archives of Child Health**
144 Ashutosh Mukherji Rd., Calcutta 25, India.
- Archives of Child Health. bi-m. ISSN 0044-8710

**Arid Zone Research Association of India**
Jodhpur 342001, Rajasthan, India.
- Annals of Arid Zone. q.

**Art Study Centre**
B 20-185 Bhelupura, Varanasi 1, India.
- Art and Life. a. ISSN 0004-3044

**Arthika Cetana**
X-45 Green Park, New Delhi 16, India.
- Arthika Cetana. m.

**Artillery Association**
School of Artillery, Deolali, India.
- Artillery Journal. a. ISSN 0004-3826

**Arun Group of Publications**
Box 27, Civil Lines, Moradabad, India.
- Arun. m.

**Arut Perum Jothi**
Arumbakkam, Madras 29, India.
- Arut Perum Jothi. m.

**Ashok Prakashan Mandir**
28/11 Shaktinagar, Delhi 7, India.
- Sampada. m. ISSN 0036-3871

**Asia Publishing House**
Calicut St., Ballard Estate, Bombay 400038, India (and 440 Park Ave. S., New York NY 10016)
- Asia Monograph Series. irreg., no. 26, 1975. ISSN 0066-8265

**Asian Studies Press**
23-354 Azadnagar, Jaiprakash Rd., Andheri, Bombay 400058, India.
- Asian Economic and Social Review; techno-economic quarterly of Asian co-operation. q. (Indian Institute of Asian Studies)

**Asiatic Society, Bombay**
Town Hall, Bombay 1, India
(Subscr. to: Arthur Probsthain, 41 Great Russell St., London, W.C. 1, England)
- Asiatic Society, Bombay. Journal. a. ISSN 0004-4709

**Asiatic Society, Calcutta**
1 Park St., Calcutta 16, India.
- Asiatic Society, Calcutta. Journal. a. ISSN 0571-3161

**Assam. Directorate of Information and Public Relations**
Silpukhuri, Gauhati 3, Assam, India.
- Assam Information. m. ISSN 0004-4989

**Assam Review Publishing Co.**
29 Waterloo St., Calcutta 700069, India.
- Assam Review and Tea News. m. ISSN 0004-4997

**Assam State Social Welfare Advisory Board**
Uzanbazar, Gauhati 1, Assam, India.
- Pariyal Kalyan. m. ISSN 0031-2096
- Samaj Kalyan. m. ISSN 0036-3693

**Associated Management Consultants (P) Ltd.**
Y-21 Hauz Khas, New Delhi 110016, India.
- Indian Journal of Marketing; journal of marketing, advertisement and sales management. m. ISSN 0019-5316

**Association for Commonwealth Literature and Language Studies**
Department of English, University of Mysore, Manasagangotri, Mysore 570006, India.
- Association for Commonwealth Literature and Language Studies. Bulletin. s-a. ISSN 0066-9083 (prep. by its Indian Branch)
- Commonwealth Newsletter. (prep. by its Indian Branch)
- Moko. (prep. by its Indian Branch)

**Association for the Promotion of Science Education**
95-A R. K. Mutt Rd., Tiruvengadum St., Madras 600028, India.
- Junior Scientist. s-m.

**Association for the Study of Oriental Insects**
Department of Zoology, University of Delhi, Delhi 110007, India.
- Oriental Insects; a journal of systematic entomology, ecology & zoogeography of South & South-East Asia. q. ISSN 0030-5316

**Association of Engineers, India**
24 Netaji Subhas Rd., Calcutta 700001, India.
- Association of Engineers, India. Journal. q. ISSN 0044-9598

**Association of Engineers, Kerala State**
Chief Engineer's Office, Public Works Department, Trivandrum 1, Kerala State, India.
- Association of Engineers, Kerala State. Journal. q. ISSN 0004-5713

**Association of Food Scientists and Technologists (India)**
Central Food Technological Research Institute, Mysore 570013, India.
- Journal of Food Science and Technology. b-m. ISSN 0022-1155

**Association of Geography Teachers of India**
110-A Kodambakkam High Rd., Madras 600034, India.
- Geography Teacher. bi-m. ISSN 0016-7517

**Association of Indian Engineering Industry**
Secretary, 172 Jorbaugh, New Delhi 110003, India.
- Association of Indian Engineering Industry. Handbook of Statistics. a.
- Engineering & Metals Review. w.
- Engineering News. m.

**Association of Indian Pharmaceutical Manufacturers**
2 Jawaharlal Nehru Rd., Calcutta 13, India.
- Journal of Indian Pharmaceutical Manufacturers/J I P M A. m. ISSN 0022-1783

**Association of Man-Made Fibre Industry**
Resham Bhavan, 78 Veer Nariman Rd., Bombay 400020, India.
- Modern Fibres. q.

**Association of Medical Technologists**
55 Harish Mukherjee, Calcutta 25, India.
- A M T Chronicle. q.

**Association of Medical Women in India**
IMA Bldg., 16 Haji Ali Park, Keshavrao Khudye Marg, Bombay 34, India.
- Association of Medical Women in India. Journal. 3 per yr.

**Association of Microbiologists of India**
c/o Antibiotics Research Centre, Pimpri, Poona 411018, India.
- Indian Journal of Microbiology. q. ISSN 0046-8991

**Association of Otolaryngologists of India**
61 Lenin Saranee, Calcutta 13, India.
- Indian Journal of Otolaryngology. q. ISSN 0019-5421

**Association of Pharmaceutical Teachers of India**
c/o College of Pharmacy, Manipal 576119, India.
- Indian Journal of Pharmaceutical Education. q. ISSN 0019-5464

**Association of Physicians of India**
Laud Mansion, 3rd Floor, 21 M. Karve Rd., Bombay 400004, India.
- Association of Physicians of India. Journal. m. ISSN 0004-5772

**Association of Physiologists and Pharmacologists of India**
30 Lady Hardinge Rd., New Delhi 1, India.
- Indian Journal of Physiology and Pharmacology. q. ISSN 0019-5499

**Association of Scientific Workers of India**
Box 137, New Delhi 1, India.
- Vijnan Karmee. 9 per yr. ISSN 0042-6091

**Association of State Road Transport Undertakings**
Poona Nasik Rd., Poona 411026, India.
- Association of State Road Transport Undertakings. State Transport News. m. ISSN 0039-016X

**Association of Surgeons of India**
Madurai Medical College, Madurai, India.
- Association of Surgeons of India. Plastic Surgery Section. Journal. s-a.
- Indian Journal of Surgery. (pub. by Popular Prakashan)

**Association of Voluntary Agencies for Rural Development (AVARD)**
A-1 Kailash Colony, New Delhi 48, India.
- Voluntary Action. m. ISSN 0042-8647

**Astrology and Athrishta**
c/o K.S. Krishnamurti, 2 Brahmin St., Saidapet, Madras 600015, India.
- Astrology and Athrishta. m. ISSN 0044-9792

**Astronomical Society of India**
c/o Department of Astronomy, Osmania University, Hyderabad 500007, India.
- Astronomical Society of India. Bulletin. q.

**Auto Dealers' & Fleet Operators' Associations**
- Motorindia. (pub. by Gopali Printers)

**Autospark**
Vijay Colony, C. D. Barfiwala Marg (Juhu Lane), Andheri (West), Bombay 400058, India.
- Autospark. m. ISSN 0005-0695

**Avatar Meher Baba Mission**
1-8-7 Sriramanagar, Kakinada 3, Andhra Pradesh, India.
- Divya Vani/Divine Voice. m. ISSN 0012-4265

**Avion**
16-Park Area, New Delhi 5, India.
- Avion; a monthly on aviation. m.

**Ayurveda Bijnan Parishad**
see **Institute of Ayurvedic Studies and Research**

**Bahri Publications Ltd.**
57 Santnagar, New Delhi, India.
- Indian Journal of Applied Linguistics. s-a.

**Maya Bajapeyi, Ed. & Pub.**
A-12 Jivantarang, Bombay 77, India.
- Asiryada. s-a. ISSN 0304-8683

**Banaras Hindu University**
Varanasi 221005, Uttar Pradesh, India.
- Prajna. q. ISSN 0554-9884

**Banaras Hindu University. Institute of Medical Sciences**
Varanasi 221005, Uttar Pradesh, India.
- Indian Journal of Preventive and Social Medicine. q. ISSN 0301-1216 (prep. by its Department of Preventive and Social Medicine)
- Journal of Research in Indian Medicine. q. ISSN 0022-4286 (Central Council for Research in Indian Medicine & Homoeopathy)
- Quarterly Journal of Surgical Sciences. q. ISSN 0033-5657 (prep. by its Surgical Research Laboratory)

**Banasthali-Vidyapith**
Rajasthan, India.
- Banasthali Patrika. q.

**Siba Prosad Banerjee, Ed. & Pub.**
P-36 India Exchange Place, 2nd Floor, Room No. 40, Calcutta 700001, India.
- Economic Age. m.

**Nilratan Banerji, Ed. & Pub.**
39-B Mahim Halder St., Calcutta 700026, India.
- Surchhanda. m.

**Bangalore Printing & Publishing Co. Ltd.**
Box 1807, 88 Mysore Rd., Bangalore 560018, India.
- Mallige; the BAPCO family magazine. m. ISSN 0025-1399

**Bangladesh High Commission**
56 Ring Rd., New Delhi, India.
- Bangladesh News. s-m.

**Bank of India**
Express Towers, Nariman Point, Bombay 400021, India.
- Bank of India. Bulletin. m. ISSN 0005-5212

**Bar Association of India**
Chamber No. 93, Supreme Court Building, Tilak Marg, New Delhi 110001, India.
- Indian Advocate. q. ISSN 0019-4301

**Bar Council of Maharashtra**
High Court Extension, Bombay 400032, India.
- Maharashtra Bar Council Journal. q.

**Baroda. Oil & Natural Gas Commission**
Makarpura Road, Baroda 390009, India.
- Gasoil. m.

**Baroda University**
see **Maharaja Sayajirao University of Baroda**

**Basanti Library**
22/1 Bidhan Sarani, Calcutta, India.
- Transition. q. ISSN 0041-1205

**Basic Chemicals, Pharmaceuticals & Cosmetics Export Promotion Council**
Jhansi Castle, 7 Cooperage Rd., Bombay 400039, India.
- Chemexcil Export Bulletin. m. ISSN 0009-2207

**Behavioural Sciences Centre**
32 Netaji Subhash Marg, Delhi 110006, India.
- I B S A. (Indian Behavioural Sciences Abstracts) q. ISSN 0018-8727

**Bela Abela Publications**
Block P-701A/1, New Alipore, Calcutta 700053, West Bengal, India.
- Bela Abela; poetry quarterly. q. ISSN 0005-8300

**Bengal Engineering College**
Howrah 711103, West Bengal, India.
- Journal of Technology. 2 per yr. ISSN 0047-2824

**Bengal Library Association**
P134 C.I.T. Scheme No., Calcutta 14, India (Subscr. Address: Calcutta University, Central Library, Calcutta 12, India)
- Granthagar. m. ISSN 0017-324X

**Bengali International**
107-2 Raja Rammohan Sarani, Calcutta 9, India.
- Bengali International. bi-m.

**Bengali Literature**
53 Bidhan Palli, Jadavpur, Calcutta 32, India.
- Bengali Literature. q. ISSN 0005-8815

**Bennett, Coleman & Co., Ltd. Times of India**
7 Bahadur Shah Zaffar Marg, New Delhi 110002, India
(U.S. Subscr. Address: India Publications, Ltd., 307 Fifth Ave., New York, NY 10016)
- Dharmayug. w. ISSN 0417-3937
- Dinaman; weekly Hindi news magazine. w. ISSN 0012-3005
- Economic Times. d. ISSN 0013-0389
- Economic Times Annual. a.
- Femina. fortn. ISSN 0430-2990
- Filmfare. fortn. ISSN 0015-1548
- Illustrated Weekly of India. w. ISSN 0019-2430
- Madhuri. fortn. ISSN 0024-9432
- Navbharat Times; daily Hindi newspaper. d. ISSN 0028-1506
- Parag. m. ISSN 0031-1642
- Sarika. m. ISSN 0036-4797
- Science Today. m. ISSN 0036-858X
- Times of India Annual. ISSN 0082-4437
- Times of India Directory and Yearbook Including Who's Who. a. ISSN 0082-4445
- Youth Times. fortn.

**Bennett, Coleman & Co., Ltd. Times of India, Bombay**
Microfilm and Index Service, Reference Department, Bombay, India.
- Times of India. Index. 3 per yr. ISSN 0304-162X

**Navin Berry, Ed. & Pub.**
188 Golf Links, New Delhi 110003, India.
- Cross Section. bi-m.

**Besant Cultural Centre. Kalakshetra (International Arts Centre)**
Tiruvanmiyur, Madras 600014, India
(U.S. Suscr. Address: Ruth Doak, Box 943, Ojai, CA 93023)
- Kalakshetra. q. ISSN 0047-3111

**Best Books Private Ltd.**
Komal, First Floor, Plot 86, Road No. 2, P.B. 7205, Chembur P.O., Bombay 400071, India.
- Current Engineering Practice. q. ISSN 0045-9291

**Better Life Movement**
Better Life Center, Aloor, Kollettumkara, Kerala, India.
- Kerala Sabha. m. ISSN 0047-3367

**Bhabha Atomic Research Centre**
Trombay, Bombay 400085, India.
- Bhabha Atomic Research Centre. Nuclear Physics Division. Annual Report. a.

**Bhagalpur University**
Bhagalpur 7, India.
- Bhagalpur University Journal. q.

**Bhagyavati Library**
Sagolband Road, Meino Lane, Manipur State, Imphal 795001, India.
- Bhagyavati Panchanga. a.

**S. K. Bhanot, Ed. & Pub.**
640 Double Storey, New Rajinder Nagar, New Delhi 5, India.
- Indian Steel Age; a journal on iron, steel and engineering. m. ISSN 0019-641X

**Bharari**
6 Hanuman Bldg., Kiln Lane, Bombay, India.
- Bharari. m.

**Bharat Krishak Samaj**
A-1 Nizamuddin West, New Delhi 110003, India.
- Bharat Krishak Samaj. Year Book. a. ISSN 0067-6454
- Krishak Samachar. m. ISSN 0023-4710

**Bharat Sevak**
House No. 600, Sector 16-D, Chandigarh 17, India.
- Bharat Sevak. m. ISSN 0006-0488

**Bharat Sevashram Sangha**
Hyderabad 500029, India.
- Hindu Regeneration. m. (prep. by its Hyderabad Branch)

**Bharata Ganita Parisad**
University of Lucknow, Department of Mathematics and Astronomy, Lucknow, Uttar Pradesh, India.
- Ganita. s-a. ISSN 0046-5402

**Bharata Manisha**
c/o J. D. Bhattacharya, Ed., D28/171 Panda Haveli, Varanasi 221001, India.
- Bharata Manisha Quarterly; journal of Indological and Oriental studies. q.

**Bharathan Publications Private Ltd.**
20 Dr. Guruswamy Mudaliar Rd., Chetput, Madras 31, India.
- Swarajya. w. ISSN 0039-7199

**Bharatiya Adimjati Sevak Sangh**
New Link Rd. (Dr. Ambedkar Road), Jhandewalan, New Delhi 55, India.
- Vanyajati. q. ISSN 0042-2622

**Bharatiya Janasangh Kerala Pradesh**
M.G. Road, Cochin 11, India.
- Jana Sangh Patrika. s-m. ISSN 0021-4205

**Bharatiya Natya Sangh**
34 New Central Market, New Delhi, India.
- Natya. q. ISSN 0028-1115

**Bharatiya Vidya Bhavan**
Kulapati K.M. Munshi Marg, Bombay 400007, India.
- Bhavan's Journal. fortn. ISSN 0006-0518
- Word. q. ISSN 0043-7948

**T. E. Bhaskaran, Ed. & Pub.**
Lakshmi Vihar, Dooraswamy Iyer Rd., Ernakulam, Cochin 11, S. India.
- Film; cine monthly. m. ISSN 0015-1041

**Sant Ram Bhatia, Ed. & Pub.**
233 Model Town, Jullundur City 3, India.
- Indian Librarian. q. ISSN 0019-5774

**Brojendra K. Bhattacharya, Ed. & Pub.**
12/1 Sarsuna Main Rd., Calcutta 61, India.
- Pratishruti; literary-cultural weekly. w. ISSN 0032-6917

**Bhavan's College of Mass Communication**
Bharatiya Vidya Bhavan, Kulapati K. M. Munshi Marg, Bombay 400007, India.
- Alpha Communications Monthly. m.
- Alpha News. fortn.

**Bhopal University Research Council**
Bhopal University, Bhopal, Madhya Pradesh, India.
- Bhopal University Research Journal. a.

**Bhubaneswar Review**
Type Va, 10-4 Asoka Nagar, Bhubaneswar 1, India.
- Bhubaneswar Review; half-yearly journal on literature, art and culture. s-a. ISSN 0006-0534

**Bihar. Directorate of Industries**
Department of Industries and Technical Education, Patna, Bihar, India.
- Bihar Industries; quarterly bulletin for small industries. q. ISSN 0006-2219

**Bihar Research Institute of Prakit, Jainology, and Ahimsa**
Vaishali, India.
- Prakit Jain Institute Research Publication Series. irreg. ISSN 0554-9906

**Bihar Research Society**
Patna, India.
- Bihar Research Society. Journal. a.

**Bihar State Digamber Jain Youth Association**
- Jain Jagran. (pub. by Randi Printers)

**Binay Bhusan Bhattacharya**
National Council, Silchar, Assam, India.
- Prasna. m. ISSN 0032-6879

**Biological Photographic Association**
10-D Medical Enclave, Patiala, Punjab, India.
- Indian Journal of Medical Photography. q. (prep. by its Indian Chapter)

**Birbal Sahni Institute of Palaeobotany**
53 University Rd., Lucknow 7, India.
- Palaeobotanist. 3 per yr. ISSN 0031-0174

**Birla Institute of Art and Music**
Prachya Niketan, Birla Museum, Laxminarayan Giri, Bhopal, India.
- Prachya Pratibha. s-a.

**Blitz Publications Private Ltd.**
17-17 H Cowasji Patel St., Fort, Bombay 1, India.
- Blitz. w. ISSN 0006-4882

**Board of Management**
c/o Working Plan Officer, Western Circle, Ranchi 2, India.
- Kanan. q.

**Bolton Fine Art Litho Works**
274 Javi Dadaji Marg, Bombay 400007, India.
- All India Federation of Master Printers. m. ISSN 0401-3956

**Bombay Art Society**
Jehangir Art Gallery, 16-B Mahatma Gandhi Rd, Bombay 1, India.
- Bombay Art Society's Art Journal. q.

**Bombay Biological Association**
c/o Biology Dept., R. J. College, Ghatkopar, Bombay 400086, India.
- Journal of Biological Sciences. s-a. ISSN 0021-9282

**Bombay Chartered Accountants' Society**
69-71 Don-bin-Shir, Ghoga St., Bombay 400001, India.
- Bombay Chartered Accountant Journal. m.

**Bombay Hospital Trust**
19 Marine Lines, Bombay 400020, India.
- Bombay Hospital Journal. q. ISSN 0524-0182 (prep. by its Medical Research Centre)

**Bombay Labour Institute**
Dadabhai Chamarbaugwala Rd., Parel, Bombay 12, India.
- Bombay Labour Journal. a. ISSN 0067-9917

**Bombay Law Reporter Pvt. Ltd.**
Krishna Mahal 63, Marine Dr., Bombay 20, India.
- Bombay Law Reporter. m.

**Bombay Market**
505 Arun Chambers, Tardeo Rd., Bombay 34, India.
- Bombay Market. fortn. ISSN 0006-6974

**Bombay Natural History Society**
Hornbill House, Shahid Bhagat Singh Rd., Bombay 400023, India.
- Bombay Natural History Society. Journal. 3 per yr. ISSN 0006-6982

**Bombay Oilseeds & Oils Exchange Ltd.**
Jenabai Bldg., Yusuf Meherali Road, Bombay 400003, India.
- Oils and Oilseeds Journal. q. ISSN 0030-1507

**Bombay University**
*see* University of Bombay

**Bombay Zionist Association**
41 Hamam St., Bombay 1, India.
- Indo-Israel. bi-m.

**Book Review**
A-1/45 Safdarjung Enclave, New Delhi 110016, India.
- Book Review. q.

**Books & Journals Private Ltd.**
6-2 Madan St., Calcutta 700072, India.
- Indian Journal of Power and River Valley Development. m. ISSN 0019-5537
- Journal of Mines, Metals and Fuels. m. ISSN 0022-2755

**Bose Institute**
93/1 Acharya Prafulla Chandra Rd., Calcutta 700009, India.
- Bose Institute. Transactions. q. ISSN 0006-7903

**Botanical Society of Bengal**
35 Ballygunge Circular Rd., Calcutta 19, India.
- Botanical Society of Bengal. Bulletin. s-a. ISSN 0006-811X

**Brahmana-Gaurava**
Moti Katra, Agra 3, India.
- Brahmana-Gaurava. m. ISSN 0304-9272

**Builders Association of India**
c/o R. S. Desai, Ed., G-1/G-20 Commerce Centre, J. Dadajee Rd., Bombay 400034, India.
- Builders Association of India. Bulletin. m.

**Builders Publications of India (P) Ltd.**
11 Amrita Shergill Marg, New Delhi 110003, India.
- Design. m. ISSN 0011-9261

**Bureau of Educational and Psychological Research**
25-3 Ballygunge Circular Rd., Calcutta 19, India.
- Bureau of Educational and Psychological Research. Bulletin.

**Business Press Private Ltd.**
Surya Mahal, 5 Burjorji Bharucha Marg, Bombay 400023, India.
- Imprint. m. ISSN 0019-3046
- Indian Textile Journal. m. ISSN 0019-6436
- Industrial Products Finder. m.
- Preprint. m.
- Products from India. bi-m.

**Business Publications International**
United India Life Building, Box 548, F-Block, Connaught Place, New Delhi 1, India.
- Asia-Africa World Trade Register. irreg. ISSN 0066-8230
- Bankers' Who's Who. irreg. ISSN 0067-3803
- World Commerce Annual. a. ISSN 0084-1501

**Businessman**
12-1-9 Old Mallapally, Box 239, Hyderabad, India.
- Businessman. m. ISSN 0007-7151

**Byomkes Chakrabarti**
Kapgari, Midnapore, West Bengal, India.
- Seva-Bharati. fortn. ISSN 0037-2951

**C M R**
D 1/24, Rajouri Garden, New Delhi, India.
- C M R. (Civil and Military Review) m. ISSN 0007-8670

**C. S. I. R.**
see **India. Council of Scientific and Industrial Research**

**Cactus Publications**
12 Congress Exhibition Rd., Calcutta 17, India.
- Industrial Enterprise. m. ISSN 0019-8269

**Calcutta. Superintendent of Printing**
5 Surendranath Banerjee Rd., Calcutta, India.
- Calcutta Municipal Gazette. w. ISSN 0008-0675

**Calcutta Historical Society**
33/1 Amherst St., Calcutta 9, India.
- Bengal: Past and Present. 3 per yr. ISSN 0005-8807

**Calcutta Management Association**
1 Shakespeare Sarani, Calcutta 16, India.
- Calcutta Management Association. Annual Report. a. ISSN 0068-5356

**Calcutta Mathematical Society**
92 Acharya Prafulla Chandra Rd., Calcutta 700009, India.
- Calcutta Mathematical Society. Bulletin. q. ISSN 0008-0659

**Calcutta Medical Club**
91-B Chittaranjan Ave., Calcutta 12, India.
- Calcutta Medical Journal. m. ISSN 0008-0667

**Calcutta Motor Dealers' Association**
c/o Amalendu Syam, Ed., 60 Lake Place, Suite No 9, Calcutta 29, India.
- Auto Age. bi-m. ISSN 0005-0709

**Calcutta Press (P) Ltd.**
1 Raja Subodh Mullick Sq., Calcutta 13, India.
- Chartered Accountant. m. ISSN 0009-188X (Institute of Chartered Accountants of India)

**Calcutta Retail Dealer's Samity**
- Banijya Barta. (pub. by Kamalalaya Stores Pvt. Ltd.)

**Calcutta Statistical Association**
Calcutta University, New Science Bldg., 35 B.C. Rd., Calcutta 19, India.
- Calcutta Statistical Association. Bulletin. q. ISSN 0008-0683

**Calcutta University**
see **University of Calcutta**

**Calcutta University Press**
see also **University of Calcutta**

**Calcutta University Press**
Sri Sibendra Nath Kanjilal, 48 Hazra Rd., Calcutta 19, West Bengal, India.
- Calcutta Review. q. ISSN 0045-3846 (University of Calcutta)
- Indian Agriculturist. q. ISSN 0019-4336 (Agricultural Society of India)
- University of Calcutta. Department of English. Bulletin. s-a. ISSN 0008-0691
- University of Calcutta. University College of Medicine. Bulletin. s-a. ISSN 0008-0705

**Calico Museum of Textiles**
Calico Mills Premises, Outside Jamalpur Gate, Ahmedabad, India.
- Historic Textiles of India. irreg., vol. 2, 1973.

**Calicut University**
see **University of Calicut**

**Cardamom Board**
see **India. Cardamom Board**

**Cardiological Society of India**
Bombay Mutual Terrace, 534 Sandhurst Bridge, Bombay 400007, India.
- Indian Heart Journal. q. ISSN 0019-4832

**Caritas India**
C.B.C.I. Centre, Ashok Pl., New Delhi 110001, India.
- Seva Vani. bi-m.

**Cartoons International**
4 Lal Bagh, Lucknow 226001, India.
- Cartoons International. m.

**Cashew Export Promotion Council**
Chittoor Rd., Cochin 682016, India.
- Cashew Bulletin. m. ISSN 0008-7300
- Indian Cashew Journal. q. ISSN 0019-4484

**Catholic Hospital Association of India**
C.B.C.I. Centre, Ashok Place, New Delhi 110001, India.
- Medical Service. bi-m. ISSN 0008-8102

**Cecidological Society of India**
14 Park Rd., Allahabad 211002, India.
- Cecidologia Indica. 3 per yr. ISSN 0008-8676

**Cement Manufacturers' Association**
Express Bldg., Bombay, India.
- Cement. q. ISSN 0008-8803

**Cement Research Institute of India**
M-10 South Extension II, Ring Road, New Delhi 110049, India.
- C R I Abstracts; digest of developments & research in cement and concrete. q. ISSN 0576-9922
- C R I Current Contents; a documentation list of current literature on cement and concrete. bi-m.
- Cement Research Institute of India. Annual Report. a.

**Cencus Publications**
C-7 Main Market, Vasant Vihar, New Delhi 110057, India.
- C E N C U S: Central Excise and Customs Journal. m.

**Central Board for Workers Education**
1400 West High Court, Gokulpeth, Nagpur 440010, India.
- Workers Education. q.

**Central Building Research Institute**
see **India. Central Building Research Institute**

**Central Coffee Research Institute**
Coffee Board Research Department, C. R. Station 577117, Chikmagalur District, Karnataka, India.
- Journal of Coffee Research. q.

**Central Council for Research in Indian Medicine and Homoeopathy**
OMC Bldgs., Residency, Hyderabad 500001, India.
- Institute of History of Medicine. Bulletin. q.
- Journal of Research in Indian Medicine. (pub. by Banaras Hindu University. Institute of Medical Sciences)

**Central Electrochemical Research Institute**
see **India. Central Electrochemical Research Institute**

**Central Food Technological Research Institute**
see **India. Central Food Technological Research Institute**

**Central Glass and Ceramic Research Institute**
see **India. Central Glass and Ceramic Research Institute**

**Central Health Education Bureau**
see **India. Central Health Education Bureau**

**Central Homoeopathic and Biochemic Association**
Vivekanand Marg, Lashkar, Gwalior 1, India.
- Homoeopathic Vikas. q. ISSN 0018-4462

**Central Inland Fisheries Research Institute**
P.O. Barrackpore, West Bengal, India.
- Bibliography of Indian Fisheries. q. ISSN 0006-1557
- Central Inland Fisheries Research Institute. Bulletin. irreg. ISSN 0008-9427
- Central Inland Fisheries Research Institute. Technical Progress Report. a.

**Central Institute of Education**
c/o D. B. Batra, Delhi, India.
- C. I. E. Newsletter. 3-4 per yr. ISSN 0007-8425

**Central Institute of Education. Alumni Association**
Delhi, India.
- Educational Forum. q. ISSN 0013-1733

**Central Institute of Research and Training in Public Cooperation**
New Delhi, India
(Dist. by: International Publications Service, 114 E. 32nd St., New York, NY 10016)
- Central Institute of Research and Training in Public Cooperation, New Delhi. Publications. irreg., 1967, no. 4. ISSN 0069-1631

**Central Leather Research Institute**
see **India. Central Leather Research Institute**

**Central Marine Fisheries Research Institute**
Marine Fisheries P.O., Mandapam Camp, Tamil Nadu, India.
- Central Marine Fisheries Research Institute. Bulletin. irreg., no. 25, 1973. ISSN 0577-084X
- Indian Journal of Fisheries. a. ISSN 0537-2003
- Marine Biological Association of India. Journal. s-a. ISSN 0025-3146

**Central Mechanical Engineering Research Institute**
see **India. Central Mechanical Engineering Research Institute**

**Central Mining Research Station**
see **India. Central Mining Research Station**

**Central Road Research Institute**
see **India. Central Road Research Institute**

**Central Salt and Marine Chemicals Research Institute**
see **India. Central Salt and Marine Chemicals Research Institute**

**Central Scientific Instruments Organization**
see **India. Central Scientific Instruments Organization**

**Central Silk Board**
see **India. Central Silk Board**

**Central Social Welfare Board**
Jeevan Deep, Parliament St., New Delhi 1, India.
- Samaj Kalyan. m. ISSN 0036-3707
- Social Welfare. m. ISSN 0037-8038

**Central Soil and Water Conservation Research and Training Institute**
218 Kaulagarh Rd., Dehradun 248195, India.
- Soil Conservation Digest. s-a. (Co-sponsor: Association of Soil and Water Conservationists and Trainees)

**Central Tobacco Research Institute**
Rajahmundry 1, India.
- Central Tobacco Research Institute and its Regional Research Stations. Annual Report. a.

**Centre for Asian Dokumentation**
Box 11215, Calcutta 700014, India.
- Index Asia Series in Humanities. irreg.
- Index Indo-Asiaticus. q. ISSN 0019-3852
- Indian Biography. q.
- Indian Science Index (Calcutta). m.

**Centre for the Study of Developing Societies**
Bombay, India
(Dist. in U.S. by Paragon Book Gallery, 14 E. 38th St., New York, N.Y. 10016)
- Centre for the Study of Developing Societies. Occasional Papers. irreg. ISSN 0069-195X

**Centre for Urban Studies**
- Nagarlok. (pub. by Indian Institute of Public Administration)

**Centre of Advanced Study in Ancient Indian History and Culture**
see under **University of Calcutta**

**Centre of Advanced Study in Philosophy**
Visva-Bharati, Santiniketan, West Bengal, India.
- Visva-Bharati Journal of Philosophy. s-a. ISSN 0042-7187

**Centre of Indian Trade Unions**
172 Lenin Sarani, Calcutta 700013, India.
- Working Class. m.

**Chanakya Publishing House**
3 Thornhill Rd., Allahabad 1, India.
- Chanakya Defence Annual. a. ISSN 0069-2654

**Charanjit Chanana**
E-71 Greater Kailish 1, New Delhi 110048, India.
- South Asian Survey. m.

**S. Chand & Co. Ltd.**
Ravindra Mansion, Ram Nagar, New Delhi 5, India.
- Publishers' Monthly. m.

**Kalyan Chanda, Pub.**
311 Ganguli Bagan Lane, Calcutta 47, India.
- Sahitya Chinta. s-a.

**Chandigarh Post**
H. No. 2017 Sector 15-C, Chandigarh 160017, India.
- Chandigarh Post. w.

**Chandita Prakasani**
- Uthon/Platform. (pub. by Raja Rammohan Sarani)

**Chandrabhaga**
Ed. Ramanath Sinha, P.O. Suri., Dist. Birbhum, West Bengal, India.
- Chandrabhaga. w. ISSN 0009-1359

**Chandrakant Chimanlal Vora**
57-2 Gandhi Rd., Box 163, Ahmedabad 380001, Gujarat, India.
- Gujarat Law Reporter; reportable judgements of the Supreme Court and the Gujarat High Court. m. ISSN 0017-551X
- Gujarat Law Times; law journal publishing short-notes on the cases decided by the High Court of Gujarat (India) as well as those of Supreme Court of India. fortn. ISSN 0017-5528
- Gujarat Revenue Tribunal Law Reporter; judgements of the Gujarat Revenue Tribunal. m. ISSN 0017-5536

**Chariot**
Cuttack 2, Orissa, India.
- Chariot. q.

**Chary Publications**
14 Sidh Prasad, Ghatkopar Mahul Rd., Tilak Nagar, Bombay 400089, India.
- Agriculture and Agro-Industries Journal. m. ISSN 0002-1725
- Chemicals and Petro-Chemicals Journal. m.
- Electrical India. fortn. ISSN 0013-435X (Indian Electrical Manufacturers' Association)
- Indian Drugs and Pharmaceuticals Industry. bi-m. ISSN 0019-4638
- Industrial Engineering and Management. q. ISSN 0019-8242 (Indian Institution of Industrial Engineering)
- Industrial India. m. ISSN 0019-8412 (All-India Manufacturers' Organization)
- M B I's Indian Industries Annual. a. ISSN 0541-5357
- Machine Building Industry. m. ISSN 0541-6388 (Indian Machine Tool Manufacturers' Association)
- Textile Machinery; accessories & stores. bi-m. ISSN 0040-5035

**R. N. Chatterjee, Pub.**
15 India Exchange Pl., 3rd Floor, Calcutta 700017, India.
- Indian Pulp and Paper; India's leading journal on paper, printing and packaging. bi-m. ISSN 0019-6231

**K. Chatterji**
122-A Ballygunge Gardens, Calcutta 19, India.
- Patranu; world's first mini magazine. m. ISSN 0031-3122

**Amala Chaudhuri, Ed. & Pub.**
Valley View, Landour Cantt., Mussoorie 248179, Uttar Pradesh, India.
- Indian Journal of Pediatrics. m. ISSN 0019-5456

**Manjari Chaudhuri**
188/78. Prince Anwar Shah Rd., Calcutta 45, India.
- Industrial Situation in India. q.

**S. B. Chaudhuri, Ed. & Pub.**
59 Ballygunge Gardens, Calcutta 19, India.
- National Diary; a weekly record of Indian events with index. w. ISSN 0027-9145

**Chaukhambha Orientalia**
Gokul Bhawan, K 37/39 Gwaldas Shah Lane, Varanasi 221001, India.
- Chaukhambha Oriental Research Studies. irreg.
- Gokuldas Sanskrit Series. irreg.

**Chavhata Weekly**
Dhebarbhai Road, Ramdaspeth, Nagpur 1, India.
- Chavhata Weekly. w. ISSN 0009-2061

**Chemical India Annual**
c/o S. K. Bhanot, 640 Double Storey, New Rajinder Nagar, New Delhi, India.
- Chemical India Annual. a.

**Chemical Process Industries of India**
- Chemical Age of India. (pub. by Technical Press Publications)

**Chemical Take-Off**
G-77 Himalaya House, Curzon Road, New Delhi, India.
- Chemical Take-Off; monthly journal of chemical and chemical-based industries. m. ISSN 0045-6497

**Chemicals & Allied Products Export Promotion Council**
World Trade Centre, 14/1B Ezra St., Calcutta 700001, India.
- Chemicals & Allied Products Export News. q. ISSN 0009-2738

**Cherravuru Nagabhushanacharyulu**
V.B. Bhavan, Narasaraopet, P.O. Guntur. Dist., Andhra Pradesh, India.
- Viswasilpi. m. ISSN 0042-7217

**Chhandita**
B-59 Rabindra Nagar, Calcutta 18, India.
- Chhandita. m . (10-12 per yr.) ISSN 0009-3432

**Chief Engineers & Chief Mechanical Engineers of the Major Ports of India**
3 Mangoe Lane, Calcutta 700001, India.
- Port and Harbour Engineer; technical magazine of major ports of India. q.

**Child Guidance School Society**
32 Rajindra Park, Shankar Rd., New Delhi 110060, India.
- Growing Minds. bi-m. ISSN 0046-6484

**Children's Book Trust**
Nehru House, New Delhi 110002, India.
- Children's World. m. ISSN 0009-420X

**S. S. Chimanlal, Ed. & Pub.**
Evergreen Industrial Estate, Block No. 47, Mahalaxmi, Bombay 11, India.
- Navalkatha. m. ISSN 0028-1492
- Savita. m. ISSN 0036-5149
- Seema. m. ISSN 0037-2005

**China Study Centre**
29 Rajpur Rd., Delhi 6, India.
- China Report. bi-m. ISSN 0009-4455

**Chitralekha Karyalaya**
62 Karwar St., Bombay 1, India.
- Chitralekha. w.

**Chittaranjan Publishers**
Bharat House, 104 Apollo St., Bombay 1, India.
- Forum. m. ISSN 0015-8364

**Ramesh Chopra, Ed. & Pub.**
E-9 Green Park, New Delhi 110016, India.
- Electronics for You. m. ISSN 0013-516X

**P.S. Chowdary, Ed. & Pub.**
8-106 G.R. Compound, Anantapur 515001, India.
- Sudarsanam. w.

**Christ Church College**
Kanpur, India.
- Endeavour. m. ISSN 0013-7170

**Christavashram Press**
Manganam P.O., Kottayam 686018, Kerala, India.
- Arunodayam. bi-m. ISSN 0004-413X (Society of St. Thomas) (Co-sponsor: International Fellowship of Reconciliation)

**Christian Institute for the Study of Religion and Society**
Box 4600, 17 Miller's Rd., Bangalore 560046, India.
- Religion and Society. q. ISSN 0034-3951

**Christian Institutes of Islamic Studies**
Box 153, Hyderabad 500001, Andhra Pradesh, India.
- Al-Basheer; English quarterly. q. (Co-sponsor: Henry Martyn Institute of Islamic Studies)

**Christian Medical Association of India**
- Christian Medical Association of India. Journal. (pub. by Wesley Press)

**Christian Medical Association of India. Christian Nurses League**
- Christian Nurse. (pub. by Wesley Press)

**Christian Medical College Hospital**
Vellore 632004, Tamil Nadu, India.
- Christian Medical College Alumni Journal. q. ISSN 0009-5451

**Church History Association of India**
c/o R. W. Bryan, 224 Lower Circular Rd., Calcutta 17, India.
- Indian Church History Review. s-a. ISSN 0019-4530

**Church of North India**
I.S.P.C.K., Box 1585, Kashmiri Gate, Delhi 110006, India.
- North India Churchman. m.

**Church of South India**
c/o Christian Literature Society, Box 501, Park Town, Madras 600003, India.
- South India Churchman. m. ISSN 0038-3465

**Cine Advance**
74 Lenin Saranee, Calcutta 13, India.
- Cine Advance. w.

**Cine Central**
2 Chowringhee Rd., Calcutta 700013, India.
- Citrabikshana/Chitra-Bikshan. m.

**Cine Technicians' Association of South India**
34 Usman Rd., Madras 17, India.
- C.T.A. Journal. m.

**Cinmay Smrti Pathagara**
26-8A Mahatma Gandhi Rd., Calcutta 9, India.
- Cinmay Smrti Pathagara. a.

**Citizen Publications**
Box 188, Bhargova Estate, Kanpur 1, India.
- Civic Affairs. m. ISSN 0009-7772

**Citizens Gazette**
31 Theatre Communication Bldg., Connaught Place, New Delhi 1, India.
- Citizens Gazette. s-m.

**Coal Consumers Association of India**
India Exchange, 7th Floor, Calcutta 1, India.
- C. C. A. I. Monthly News Letter. m.

**Cochin Port Trust**
Willingdon Island, Cochin 682003, India.
- Cochin Port News. m.

**Cochin University**
*see* **University of Cochin**

**College of Engineering**
Trivandrum 16, Kerala, India.
- College of Engineering, Trivandrum. Magazine. a.

**College of Engineering Technology**
Edepalli, Machilipatam, India.
- Auto-Writing; human electricity and experiments on soul. m. ISSN 0005-089X

**College of Textile Technology, Serampore**
Students Union, Serampore, West Bengal, India.
- C.T.T.S. Annual. a. ISSN 0084-8859

**Colour Publications Pvt. Ltd.**
126-A Dhurunadi, Off Dr. Nariman Rd., Bombay 400025, India.
- Chemical Industry Developments. m. ISSN 0302-7678
- Chemical Times. w.
- Colourage. fortn. ISSN 0010-1826
- Oil Technologists Association of India. Journal. q. ISSN 0030-1485
- Paintindia. m. ISSN 0030-9540
- Pesticides. m. ISSN 0031-6148
- Pesticides Annual. a.
- Popular Plastics. fortn. ISSN 0032-4604

**Colour Society**
c/o S. P. Potnis, Department of Chemical Technology, Matunga, Bombay 400019, India.
- Colour Society. Journal. q. ISSN 0588-5094

**Commerce (1935) Limited**
Manek Mahal, 90 Veer Nariman Rd., Churchgate,
Bombay 400020, India.
- Commerce; a weekly review of Indian financial,
  commercial and industrial progress. w. ISSN
  0010-275X
- Commerce Pamphlet Series. m.
- Commerce Yearbook of Ports, Shipping and
  Shipbuilding. a.
- Commerce Yearbook of Public Sector. a. ISSN
  0591-1710
- Commerce Yearbook of Road Transport. a.
- Directory of Wool, Hosiery & Fabrics. a.
- Worrall's Textile & Engineering Directory. a.

**Commercial & Technical Publications**
133 Vithal Bhai Patel Rd., Bombay 4 BR, India.
- Air Conditioning & Refrigeration in India. q.
  ISSN 0002-2268
- Radio & Electronics. m. ISSN 0033-7730

**Commercial Herald**
Ed. Sudarshan Paul Bahri, 75-C Saheed
Udhamsingh Nagar, Civil Lines, Ludhiana, India.
- Commercial Herald. s-m. ISSN 0010-3012

**Commercial Products Ltd.**
1 India Exchange Place, Calcutta 1, India.
- Indian Print & Paper; a journal for printers,
  papermakers and the allied industries. q. ISSN
  0019-6185

**Commercial Publications Bureau**
Post Box No. 3005, New Delhi, India.
- India at a Glance. a.

**Commission Internationale des Irrigations et du
Drainage**
see **International Commission on Irrigation and
Drainage**

**Committee of Communist Revolutionaries**
129-A Circular Garden Reach Rd., Calcutta 23,
India.
- New Democracy. m.

**Committee of Concerned Indian Philosophers for
Social Action**
Institute of Socio-Political Dynamics, M-120
Greater Kailish, New Delhi 110048, India.
- Philosophy and Social Action. q.

**Communist Party of India**
35 Ferozeshah Rd., New Delhi 110001, India.
- New Age. w. ISSN 0047-9500
- Party Life. (pub. by People's Publishing House
  Private Ltd.)

**Community Mental Health Center**
Indira Health Home, 8-2-547/2 Road No. 7,
Banjara Hills, Hyderabad 500034, Andra Pradesh,
India.
- Child Psychiatry Quarterly; a journal devoted to
  the mental health of child and adolescent. q.
  ISSN 0009-3998

**Company Law Institute of India Pvt. Ltd.**
21 Thayagaraja Rd., Madras 600017, India.
- Company Law Institute of India. Reports of
  Company Cases. fortn. ISSN 0045-7787
- Income Tax Reports; a journal of the law of
  income tax, wealth tax, gift tax and estate duty.
  w. ISSN 0019-3453

**Competition Master**
126 Industrial Area, Chandigarh 160002, India.
- Competition Master. m.

**Computer Society of India**
Computer Group, Tata Institute of Fundamental
Research, Homi Baba Rd., Bombay 400005, India
(Available from: INSDOC, Hillside Rd. New Delhi
110012, India)
- C S I Newsletter. m.
- Computer Society of India. Journal. s-a. ISSN
  0045-7892

**Concrete Association of India**
Cement House, 121 M. Karve Rd., Bombay 400020,
India.
- Indian Concrete Journal. m. ISSN 0019-4565

**Confederation of Indian Industrial Editors**
2. E-6 New Link Rd., New Delhi 5, India.
- Industrial Editor. q. ISSN 0019-8196

**Consumers Guidance Society**
Hutment J. Mahapalika Marg, Bombay 400001,
India.
- Keemat. m.

**Cosme Matias Menezes Pvt. Ltd.**
Rua de Ourem, Box 12, Panjim-Goa, India.
- Clinician; monthly journal of medical science and
  news. m. ISSN 0009-9341

**Cosmopolitan Institute of Public Affairs**
c/o Shiv Prasad "Muflis", 1-17 South T. T. Nagar,
Bhopal 462003, India.
- Impulse. q. ISSN 0027-4690

**Cotton Corporation of India**
Air India Building, P.B. No. 1350, Bombay 400021,
India.
- Cotton News. m.

**Cotton Textiles Export Promotion Council.**
Engineering Centre 9, 4 Mathew Rd., Bombay,
India.
- Handbook of the Indian Cotton Textile Industry.
  a.

**Council for Political Studies**
34 Panditra Terrace, Calcutta 29, India.
- Socialist Perspective; a quarterly journal of social
  services. q.

**Council for Social Development**
Sangha Rachana, New Delhi 110003, India.
- Social Change. q. ISSN 0049-0857

**Council of Behavioral Research**
Maharani Rd., Gaya 823002, Bihar, India.
- Behaviorometric. s-a.

**Council of Scientific and Industrial Research**
see **India. Council of Scientific and Industrial
Research**

**A. Cour, Ed. & Pub.**
M-109 Greater Kailash, New Delhi 48, India.
- Rupee Trade. m.

**Criminalistics Research Institute**
c/o Pyani Bhavan, 3A Lake View Rd., Calcutta 29,
India.
- Araksha. bi-m. ISSN 0003-7540

**Cultural Research Institute**
New Secretariat Bldgs., 1st Floor, Block A, 1 Kiron
Sankar Roy Rd., Calcutta 700001, India.
- Cultural Research Institute. Bulletin. q. ISSN
  0011-2895

**Current Events**
15 Rajpur Rd., Dehra Dun, Uttar Pradesh, India.
- Current Events; India's journal on world affairs.
  m. ISSN 0011-3484

**Current Indian Statutes**
36, Sector 9-A, Chandigarh 11, India.
- Current Indian Statutes. m. ISSN 0011-3573

**Current Law Publishers**
Box 1268 G.P.O., Delhi 6, India.
- Current Income Tax Law. m.
- Digest of Current Industrial and Labour Law. m.
  ISSN 0419-1293

**Current Publications Private Ltd.**
Meher House, 15 Cawasji Patel St., P. B. 1862,
Bombay 400001, India.
- Current. w. ISSN 0011-3123

**Current Science Association**
Raman Research Institute, S. R. S. Sastry, Bangalore
560006, India.
- Current Science. fortn. ISSN 0011-3891

**Current Tax Reporter (Supreme Court)**
861 Sardarpura, Chopasani Rd., Jodhpur, Rajasthan,
India.
- Current Tax Reporter (Supreme Court) m.

**Current Technical Literature Co. Pvt. Ltd.**
India House, Box 1374, Bombay 1, India.
- Current Medical Practice. m. ISSN 0011-3700

**D.A.V. College. Post-Graduate Department of
Political Science**
Jullundur, Punjab, India.
- Journal of Political Studies. s-a. ISSN 0047-2700

**Damn You**
37 Balrampur House, Allahabad 2, India.
- Damn You; a magazine of the arts. m. ISSN
  0011-5940

**Darshana International**
Moradabad, India.
- Darshana International; an international quarterly
  of philosophy, psychology, sociology, religion,
  mysticism, and physical research. q. ISSN 0011-
  6734

**Tapan Kumar Das, Ed. & Pub.**
12B 4 Indra Roy Rd., Calcutta 25, India.
- Flame and Flavour. m. ISSN 0046-4031

**Ranadhir Dasgupta**
10 Bondel Rd., Calcutta 700019, India.
- Problems of National Liberation. irreg.

**Datta Waman Kale**
D-188 Kantichandra Rd., Jaipur 302006, India.
- G N P; monthly devoted to industry and trade. m.

**De Indiana Overseas Publications**
1424 Chandni Chowk, Delhi 6, India.
- Seminar Reporteur; journal of science and
  technology. m.

**Ranajit Deb, Ed. & Pub.**
Tribritta Prakashan, 1 Tribritta, Sarani, Cooch
Behar, India.
- Tribritta; news & literary monthly. m. ISSN 0041-
  2708

**Debonair Publications Private Ltd.**
Bombay, India.
- Debonair; Diwana parody. m.

**Deccan College Research Institute. Postgraduate &
Research Institute**
Poona 6, India.
- Deccan College Research Institute. Bulletin. q.
  ISSN 0045-9801

**Deccan Geographical Society**
Mohd. Inamullah, 120/A Nehru Nagar East,
Secunderabad 500026, Andhra Pradesh, India.
- Deccan Geographer. s-a. ISSN 0011-7269 (Co-
  sponsor: Indian Institute of Geography)

**Deepsadhana Publications**
J-18 Rajori Garden, New Delhi 110027, India.
- Traviana; monthly of tourism, aviation and
  adventure. m.

**Defence Employees Welfare Council, New Delhi**
D-1/24, Rajouri Garden, New Delhi 27, India.
- Civil & Military Law Journal. q. ISSN 0045-7043

**Delhi. Labour Commissioner**
15 Rajpur Rd., Delhi, India.
- Shram Patrika. q.

**Delhi Law Times**
36 Sector 9-A, Chandigarh 11, India.
- Delhi Law Times. fortn. ISSN 0011-7846

**Delhi Library Association**
Box 1270, c/o Hardinge Public Library, Queen's
Garden, Delhi 6, India.
- Indian Book Review Supplement. q. ISSN 0019-
  4441
- Indian Press Index. m. ISSN 0019-6177
- Library Herald. q. ISSN 0024-2292

**Delhi Medical Association**
House Daryaganj, Delhi 6, India.
- Delhi Medical Journal. s-a. ISSN 0011-7854

**Delhi Press Samachar Patra**
Delhi Press Bldg., E-3 Jhandewala Estate, New
Delhi 110055, India.
- Bhoo Bharati. m.
- Caravan. fortn. ISSN 0008-6150
- Champak. fortn. ISSN 0009-1332
- Mukta. fortn. ISSN 0027-3104
- Sarita. fortn.
- Woman's Era. fortn.

**Delhi Sangita Samaj**
7A/13 W.E. Area, New Delhi 110005, India.
- Indian Music Journal; devoted to general reader
  and student. s-a. ISSN 0019-5995

**Delhi Surgical Society**
- Surgical Journal of Delhi. (pub. by Goldwater
  Publications)

**Delhi University**
*see* **University of Delhi**

**Delhi University Botanical Society**
Department of Botany, University of Delhi, Delhi
110007, India.
- Botanica. s-a. ISSN 0045-2629

**Delhi Writers Club**
- Lore. (pub. by Rami Press)

**Democratic Forum**
19 Dharmatala St., Calcutta 13, India.
- Democratic Forum. m.

**Democratic Research Service**
Maneckjee Wadia Bldg., 4th Floor, Mahatma
Gandhi Rd., Bombay 1, India.
- Freedom First; journal of liberal ideas. m. ISSN
0016-0547

**Demographic Research Centre, Baroda**
Maharajah Sayajirao University of Baroda, Faculty
of Science, Baroda 2, India.
- Baroda Reporter. a.

**V. Lakshmi Devi**
11 Barracks St., Seven Wells, Madras 1, India.
- My Magazine of India. m. ISSN 0027-5433

**Dey Biswas Enterprises**
7-2 Amherst St., Calcutta 9, India.
- Team. ISSN 0040-0696

**Dhanvantari Karyalaya**
Aligarha, India.
- Sudhanidhi. m.

**Dharmaram College**
Bangalore 560029, India
(Dist. in U.S. by Paragon Book Gallery, 14 E. 38th
St., New York, N.Y. 10016)
- Dharmaram Publications. irreg., no. 16, 1973.

**Dharmaram College. Centre for the Study of World
Religions**
Bangalore 560029, India
(U.S. Subscr. Address: c/o Frank Podgorski, Seton
Hall University, South Orange, NJ 07079)
- Journal of Dharma; an international quarterly of
world religions. q.

**Ramasarana Dhaundiyala**
G-375 Nayi Dilli, Srinivaspur 110024, India.
- Alakananda. m.

**Pankaj Dhawan, Pub.**
12 Malka Ganj, Delhi 110007, India.
- Accidents Claims Journal. m. ISSN 0001-4583

**Diabetic Association of India**
Maneckji Wadia Bldg., Bell Lane, 127 Mahatma
Gandhi Rd., Bombay 400001, India.
- Diabetic Association of India. Journal. q.

**Dialogue Publications**
5 Pearl Rd., Calcutta 17, India.
- Dialogue India; Indian poetry review. 6 per yr.

**Dibrugarh University. Centre for Sociological Study
of Frontier Region**
Dept. of Sociology, Rajabheta, Dibrugarh, Assam,
India.
- Dibrugarh University. Centre for Sociological
Study of the Frontier Region. North Eastern
Research Bulletin. a.

**Divine Life Society**
Sivananda Nagar, Tehri-Garhwal 249192, Uttar
Pradesh, India.
- Divine Life. m. ISSN 0012-4206

**Diwanchand Institute of National Affairs**
Arya Bhawan, Jor Bagh, New Delhi 3, India.
- Indian Recorder & Digest. m. ISSN 0019-6290

**Drift Publications**
P-1 Hide Lane, Calcutta 12, India.
- Drift. w. ISSN 0012-6217

**Dungadhiwasa**
823 Shivaji Nagar, Poona 4, India.
- Artha. s-m. ISSN 0004-3540

**Dev Dutt, Ed. & Pub.**
2C/36 Rohtak Rd., New Delhi 5, India.
- Point of View; anti-news weekly colloquim. w.
ISSN 0032-230X

**East India Hotels Ltd.**
7 Alipur Road, Delhi 110054, India.
- Soma; magazine for Oberoi hotels. q.

**Eastern Centre of International Studies**
22 Ritherdon Rd., Vepery, Madras 7, India.
- Eastern Journal of International Law. q. ISSN
0012-8821

**Eastern Economist Ltd.**
UCO Bank Bldg., Box 34, Parliament St., New
Delhi 110001, India.
- Eastern Economist. w. ISSN 0012-8767
- Records and Statistics; quarterly bulletin of the
Eastern Economist. q. ISSN 0034-1703

**Eastern Pharmacist**
E-38, Hauz Khas, New Delhi 16, India.
- Eastern Pharmacist. m. ISSN 0012-8872

**Eastern Press Services (India)**
c/o T. V. R. Chandran, Ed., 3-49 East, Sion,
Bombay 22, India.
- Textile India. m. ISSN 0040-4977

**Eastern Railway Magazine**
14-16 Govt. Place East, Calcutta 1, India.
- Eastern Railway Magazine. m. ISSN 0012-8880

**Eastern Regional Organisation for Planning and
Housing**
4-A Ring Rd., Indraprastha Estate, New Delhi
110001, India.
- E A R O P H News and Notes. m. ISSN 0012-
7450

**Eastern Trade Press Co.**
43 Sunder Mahal, Church Gate, Bombay 400020,
India.
- S S I. (Small Scale Industries) m.

**Eastland Publications Private Ltd.**
44 Chittaranjan Ave., Calcutta 12, India.
- Textile Trends. m. ISSN 0040-5205

**Economic and Scientific Research Foundation**
c/o P. Chentsal Rao, SAPRU House, New Delhi
110001, India.
- Economic and Scientific Research Foundation,
New Delhi. Annual Report. a. ISSN 0070-8437
- Natural Resources and Industrial Development.
irreg. ISSN 0077-6076

**Economic Cooperation Study Group**
c/o Raj Virmani, Ed., 32-33 Nehru Place, Flat 408,
New Delhi 110024, India.
- Public Enterprise Recorder. w. ISSN 0033-3468
- Public Undertakings. q. ISSN 0033-3794

**Economic Studies & Journals Publishing Co.**
Box 10838, Calcutta 9, India.
- Economic Studies. m. ISSN 0013-0362

**Educational India**
Vidya Bhavan, Jagannath Puram, Masulipatnam,
Andhra Pradesh, India.
- Educational India. m. ISSN 0013-1768

**Educational Journalists Forum**
159 Golf Links, New Delhi 110003, India.
- Educational Reporter. m. ISSN 0046-1539

**Educational Review**
16 Sunkuwar St., Triplicane, Madras 5, India.
- Educational Review. m. ISSN 0013-192X

**Efficiency Aids Private Ltd.**
17 Ghulam Mohammed Mohideen St., Madras 6,
India.
- Journal of Efficiency. bi-m.

**Ek Bacharer Srestha Kabita**
c/o Mrs. Bhaswati Sinha, 36 Ballygunge Place,
Calcutta 19, India.
- Ek Bacharer Srestha Kabita. a.

**Electric Component Industries Association**
C-40 South Extension, New Delhi 110049, India.
- Indian Electronics Directory. biennial.

**Electrochemical Society of India**
c/o Indian Institute of Science, Bangalore 560012,
India.
- Electrochemical Society of India. Journal. q. ISSN
0013-466X

**Electronics Commission**
C-4/41 Safdarjung Development Area, New Delhi
110016, India.
- Electronics Information and Planning; techno-
economics of electronics industry in developing
countries. m. (prep. by its Information, Planning
and Analysis Group)

**Embassy of the Arab Republic of Egypt**
Press Bureau, 55-57 Sunder Nagar, New Delhi 3,
India.
- Cairo/Egyptian Monthly. m.

**Embassy of the Federal Republic of Germany**
Press and Information Office, No. 6 Shanti Path,
Chanakyapuri, New Delhi, India.
- German News. fortn. ISSN 0016-8793

**Embassy of the Republic of Iraq**
Press Section, 33 Golf Links, New Delhi, India.
- Iraq News Bulletin. q. ISSN 0047-1429

**Embassy of the U. S. S. R. in India**
*see* **U. S. S. R. Embassy in India**

**Empire of India Philatelic Society**
17 Souter St., Bombay 8, India.
- India's Stamp Journal. m. ISSN 0019-6851

**Encee Technical Publications Corporation**
1-E-22 Jhandewalan Extension, New Delhi, India.
- Chemicals-International. m. ISSN 0009-2746

**Engineering Export Promotion Council**
World Trade Centre, 3rd Floor, 14/1B Ezra St.,
Calcutta 700001, India.
- Directory of Indian Engineering Exporters. irreg.
ISSN 0417-5964
- Indian Engineering Exporter. q. ISSN 0019-4719

**Engineering Research Institute**
Gujaret State, Baroda, India.
- Navnirman. q. ISSN 0028-162X

**Engineering Times Publications Pvt. Ltd.**
Wachel Molla Mansion, 8 Lenin Sarani, Calcutta
700013, India.
- Engineering Times. w. ISSN 0013-8134
- Engineering Times Annual Directory. a.

**Engineering World**
505 Arun Chambers, Tardeo Rd., Bombay 34, India.
- Engineering World. m.

**Engineers Club, India**
- Professional Engineer. (pub. by India-International
News Service)

**Enquiry Association**
- Enquiry. (pub. by New Age Press)

**Entente Pvt. Ltd.**
137 Chandni Chouk, Delhi 6, India.
- S I M. (Small Industries Magazine) m.

**Entomological Society of India**
Division of Entomology, Indian Agricultural
Research Institute, Delhi 12, India.
- Entomological Society of India. Bulletin of
Entomology. s-a. ISSN 0013-8762

**Epigraphical Society of India**
- Studies in Indian Epigraphy/Bharatiya
Purabhilekha Patrika. (pub. by Geetha Book
House)

**Equals One**
Pondicherry 605002, India.
- Equals One. q. ISSN 0013-9815

**Essential Oil Association of India**
c/o Regional Research Laboratory, Jammu-Tawi
180001, India.
- Indian Perfumer. q. ISSN 0019-607X

**Ethnographic & Folk Culture Society**
c/o Department of Anthropology, Lucknow
University, Lucknow, India.
- Eastern Anthropologist. q. ISSN 0012-8686

**Evangelical Fellowship of India**
M96 Greater Kailash I, New Delhi 110048, India.
- Aim. m.

**Eve's Weekly Ltd.**
c/o J. C. Jain, Peraj Bldg., Bombay Samachar Marg,
Bombay, India.
- Eve's Weekly. w. ISSN 0014-3812

- Industrial Times. fortn. ISSN 0019-8803
- Mirror. m. ISSN 0026-5845
- Star & Style. fortn. ISSN 0038-9862

**Explosion Hunger-1975**
Seema Apts., Bullock Rd., Banra Bandstand, Bombay, India.
- Explosion Hunger-1975. q. ISSN 0014-5041

**Exporters-Importers Club**
- Export-Import News. (pub. by India-International News Service)

**Fact Technical Society**
Udyogamandal, Kerala, India.
- Plant Maintenance. q.

**Facts and Figures**
18 Ananddham Society, Nava Vadaj, Ahmedabad 13, India.
- Facts and Figures; monthly bulletin of basic data of economic significance. m.

**Family Planning Association of India**
1 Jeevan Udyog, Dadabhai Naoroji Rd., Bombay 400001, India.
- Family Planning Association of India. Report. a.
- Journal of Family Welfare; personal, marital and sociological. q. ISSN 0022-1074
- Planned Parenthood. m.

**Farmers' Forum, India**
see **Bharat Krishak Samaj**

**Farmers' Parliamentary Forum**
16 South Ave., New Delhi 11, India.
- Farmer & Parliament. m. ISSN 0014-8369

**Fazal Printing Bureau**
Fort, Cochin 1, India.
- Janashakti News Weekly. w.

**Federal Republic of Germany Embassy**
see **Embassy of the Federal Republic of Germany**

**Federation of Evangelical Lutheran Churches in India**
Diocesan Press, 10 Church Rd., Vepery, Madras, India.
- Gospel Witness. m. ISSN 0017-2391

**Federation of Hotel and Restaurant Associations of India**
15-A Nizamuddin West, New Delhi 13, India.
- Indian Hotelier and Caterer. m. ISSN 0019-4883

**Federation of Indian Chambers of Commerce and Industry**
Federation House, Tansen Marg, New Delhi 110001, India.
- Economic Trends. fortn.

**Federation of Insurance Institutes**
Universal Insurance Bldg., 6th Floor, Sir Pherozshah Mehta Rd., Bombay 400001, India.
- Federation of Insurance Institutes. Bulletin. q.

**Federation of Karnataka Chambers of Commerce & Industry**
Post Box 39, Bangalore 560009, India.
- Mysore Commerce. s-m. ISSN 0027-559X

**Federation of Obstetric & Gynaecological Societies of India**
Purandare Griha, 31/C, Dr. N. A. Purandare Marg, Bombay 400007, India.
- Journal of Obstetrics and Gynaecology of India. bi-m. ISSN 0022-3190

**Federation of Publishers & Booksellers Associations in India**
4833/24 Govind Lane, Ansari Rd., Delhi 110006, India.
- Indian Publisher and Bookseller. (pub. by Popular Book Depot)
- Recent Indian Books. q. (Co-sponsor: Federation of Indian Publishers)

**Fertiliser Association of India**
Near Jawaharlal Nehru University, New Delhi 110057, India.
- F. A. I. Abstract Service. m. ISSN 0014-5564
- Fertiliser Marketing News. m.
- Fertiliser News. m. ISSN 0015-0266
- Khad Patrika. m. ISSN 0023-1010

**Fertilizer Corporation of India Ltd.**
F-43 South Extension Area, Part 1, Ring Road, New Delhi 110049, India.
- Fertilizer Digest. bi-m.

**Fertilizer Corporation of India Ltd. Planning & Development Division**
Sindri, Dhanbad 828122, Bihar, India.
- Fertilizer Technology. q.

**Film World International Publications Private Ltd.**
A-15 Anand Nager, Juhu Tara Rd., Bombay 400054, India.
- Film World. m. ISSN 0015-1475

**Filmfare**
Times of India Bldg., Dr. Dadabhai Naoroji Rd., Bombay 400001, India.
- Filmfare. fortn.

**Food Corporation of India**
No. 1 Bahadurshah Zafar Marg, New Delhi 1, India.
- Foodcorp Quarterly. ISSN 0046-4422

**Food Farming and Agriculture**
Ed. L. K. Pandeya, Block F, 105C New Alipore, Calcutta 53, India.
- Food Farming and Agriculture. m. ISSN 0015-6396

**Foodgrain Technologists' Research Association of India**
Hapur, Uttar Pradesh, India.
- Bulletin of Grain Technology. 3 per yr. ISSN 0007-4896

**Forest Research Institute & Colleges**
P.O. New Forest, Dehra Dun, India.
- Indian Forester; a monthly journal of forestry, agriculture and travel. m. ISSN 0019-4816

**Forum for Interdisciplinary Mathematics**
F-9/12 Model Town, Delhi 110009, India.
- Journal of Combinatorics, Information & System Sciences. q.

**Forum for Sociologists**
c/o N. L. Ainapur, Secy., Dhanvantri Bldg., T. C. Rd., Dharwar, India.
- Indian Journal of Comparative Sociology. s-a.

**Forum of Industrial Technologists**
1233-A Apte Rd., Poona 411004, India.
- F I T News. m.

**Foundation for Management Education**
see **University of Cochin. Foundation for Management Education**

**Foundry News**
c/o Bibhash Gupta, 6B Olai Chandi Rd., Calcutta 37, India.
- Foundry News. m. ISSN 0046-4821

**Free News & Feature Service Publishers**
G-74 Sujan, Singh Park, New Delhi 3, India.
- Free News & Feature Service. w. ISSN 0016-0393

**Friends of the Trees**
Army and Navy Bldg., 148 Mahatma Gandhi Rd, Bombay, India.
- Vanashoba. q.

**Al-Furqan**
Kutchery Road, Lucknow, India.
- Al-Furqan. m.

**G. B. Pant University of Agriculture and Technology**
Pantnagar (Nainital), Uttar Pradesh, India.
- Indian Agricultural Index. m. ISSN 0579-4757

**Gandhi Peace Foundation**
221/223 Deen Dayal Upadhyaya Marg, New Delhi 110002, India.
- Gandhi Marg (English Edition) q. ISSN 0016-4437
- Gandhi Marg (Hindi Edition) m.
- Gandhi Peace Foundation Lectures. (pub. by Radakrishna Indraprastha Estate)

**Gandhian Institute of Studies**
Box 116, Rajghat, Varanasi 1, India.
- Dakshinesia. s-a. (prep. by its Department of Political Science)
- Interdiscipline. q. ISSN 0020-5338

**Gandhian Thought**
27-C Irwin Rd., New Delhi, India.
- Gandhian Thought. m. ISSN 0016-4445

**Ganganatha Jha Kendriya Sanskrit Vidyapeetha**
Motilal Nehru Park, Allahabad 2, Uttar Pradesh, India.
- Ganganatha Jha Kendriya Sanskrit Vidyapeetha. Journal. q.

**Gita Ganguli**
78-2 Bir Roy Rd. West, Calcutta 61, India.
- Sattara Dasaka. q.

**Garg Publishing Co.**
775 Nicholson Rd., Delhi 6, India.
- Automobile India. m. ISSN 0005-1403
- Two Wheeler. m. ISSN 0041-4697

**Gauhati University. Department of Anthropology**
Gauhati 14, Assam, India.
- Gauhati University. Department of Anthropology. Bulletin. a.

**Gaveshana**
c/o J. P. Atreya, Moradabad 19, India.
- Gaveshana; Hindi quarterly of philosophy, psychology, sociology, mysticism, and parapsychology. q. ISSN 0016-5263

**Geetha Book House**
New Statue Circle, Mysore, India.
- Studies in Indian Epigraphy/Bharatiya Purabhilekha Patrika. a. (Epigraphical Society of India)

**Gem and Jewellery Information Centre of India**
A-95 Journal House, Janta Colony, Jaipur 302004, India.
- Diamond World. bi-m.
- Gem & Jewellery Yearbook. a.
- Journal of Gem Industry. bi-m. ISSN 0022-1244

**Geochemical Society of India**
Patna 5, India.
- Geochemical Society of India. Journal. a.

**Geographical Research Centre**
- Indian Geographical Studies. (pub. by Kailash Mahto)

**Geographical Society of India**
c/o Calcutta University, Geography Department, 39 Ballygunge Circular Rd., Calcutta 19, India.
- Geographical Review of India. q. ISSN 0046-5690

**Geological, Mining and Metallurgical Society of India**
Geology Department, University of Calcutta, 35 B.C. Rd., Calcutta 19, India.
- Geological, Mining and Metallurgical Society of India. Bulletin. q. ISSN 0016-7576
- Geological, Mining and Metallurgical Society of India. Quarterly Journal. q. ISSN 0016-7584

**Geological Society of India**
16 Ali Asker Road, Bangalore 560052, India.
- Geological Society of India. Journal. m. ISSN 0016-7622

**Germinal Publications (P) Ltd.**
61 Mott Lane, Calcutta 13, India.
- Frontier. w. ISSN 0016-2094

**P. Ghosh**
5 Dhakuria Kalibari Lane, Calcutta 31, India.
- Indranil. m. ISSN 0300-4007

**Amal Ghosh-hajra, Ed. & Pub.**
240 Diamond Harbour Rd., Behala, Calcutta 700060, West Bengal, India.
- Chikitsak Barta. fortn.
- Chikitsak Samaj. m. ISSN 0009-3858
- Medical Express; newspaper of the medical profession. fortn.

**Gidwaney's Publishing Co.**
401 Arun Chambers, Tardeo Rd., Bombay 400034, India.
- Automobile News. m. ISSN 0005-142X
- Automobile News Annual. a. ISSN 0067-2548
- Cycling & Motorcycling; the magazine of the cycle, motorcycle & scooter industry. m. ISSN 0011-4324
- Motorist. m. ISSN 0027-2299

**Gita Press**
Sri Moti Lalji Jalan, Gorakhpur, India.
- Kalyan. m. ISSN 0022-8028

**Gita Publishing House**
10 Sadhu Vaswani Rd., Mira Nagar, Poona 1, India.
● East and West Series; an interpreter of the life of the spirit. m. ISSN 0012-8384

**Gnananada Ashram**
P.O. Pallur, Via Cheruthuruthi, Trichur District, Kerala State, India.
● Atmanirvrithi. m. ISSN 0004-6965

**Goa, Daman, and Diu. Bureau of Economics, Statistics, and Evaluation**
Panaji, Goa, India.
● Goa, Daman, and Diu. Bureau of Economics, Statistics, and Evaluation. Evaluation Report. irreg., no. 9, 1974.

**Goa, Daman, and Diu. Department of Information and Tourism**
Panaji, Goa, India.
● Nave Parva. m.

**Goa Publications**
Dr. Gomes Pereira Road, Box 9, Panjim, Goa, India.
● Goa Today. m. ISSN 0017-1484

**M. N. Gogate, Ed. & Pub.**
Tardeo Airconditioned Market, 4th Floor, Bombay 400034, India.
● Building Practice. a. ISSN 0007-3571

**Gokhale Institute of Politics and Economics**
c/o V. M. Dandekar, Ed., Poona 411004, India.
● Artha Vijnana. q. ISSN 0004-3559
● Gokhale Institute of Politics and Economics. Studies. irreg., 1969, no. 55. ISSN 0072-4912 (Dist. by: Orient Longman Ltd., Nicol Rd., Ballard Estate, Bombay 400038, India)

**Gokhale Institute of Public Affairs**
N. R. Colony, Bangalore 560019, India.
● Public Affairs. m. ISSN 0048-5802

**Goldwater Publications**
A-23 Nizamuddin East, New Delhi 110013, India.
● Surgical Journal of Delhi. q. ISSN 0039-6117 (Delhi Surgical Society)

**Gopali Printers**
5A-147 Mount Rd., Madras 600006, India.
● Motorindia. m. ISSN 0027-223X (Auto Dealers' & Fleet Operators' Associations)
● Textile Magazine. m. ISSN 0040-5078 (Textile Mills and Manufacturing Association)

**Government Dental College and Hospital**
D'Mello Rd., Bombay 1, India.
● Indian Academy of Dentistry. Journal. s-a. ISSN 0019-4255

**Gramophone Company of India**
Calcutta, India.
● Indian Records. irreg. ISSN 0302-6744

**Gray Book**
Box 39, Cuttack 1, Orissa, India.
● Gray Book. s-a.

**Greater Bombay and Thana District Cooperative Housing Federation Ltd.**
19 Bell Bldg., Sir P. Mehta Rd. Fort, Bombay 1, India.
● Housing Times. m.

**Guide Publications**
60-20 Prabhat Rd., New Delhi 110005, India
(Dist. in U.S. by International Publications Service, 114 E. 32 St., New York, N.Y 10016)
● Military Year Book. a. ISSN 0076-8782

**Gujarat. Bureau of Economics and Statistics**
Sector No. 18, Gandhinagar, India.
● Locations of Industries in Gujarat State. irreg. ISSN 0076-0269
● State Government Undertakings in Gujarat. a. ISSN 0081-4504

**Gujarat. Directorate of Geology and Mining**
New Mental Hospital Bldg., Aswara, Ahmedabad 16, India.
● Mineral Wealth. s-a. ISSN 0026-4571

**Gujarat. Directorate of Manpower, Employment and Training**
Ahmedabad 15, Gujarat, India.
● Gujarat. Directorate of Manpower, Employment and Training. Report on Shortage Occupations. q.

**Gujarat. Office of the Commissioner of Labour**
Ahmedabad, India.
● Gujarat Labour Gazette. m. ISSN 0017-5501

**Gujarat Ayurveda University**
Jamnagar, Box 511, Gujarat, India.
● Ayu. q. ISSN 0005-2469

**Gujarat Industrial Development Corporation**
Ashram Rd., Ahmedabad 9, India.
● Gujarat Industrial Development Corporation. Annual Report. a.

**Gujarat Pustakalaya Sahayak Sahakari Mandal Ltd.**
Raopura, Box 10, Baroda, Gujarat, India.
● Pustakalaya. m. ISSN 0033-4693

**Gujarat Research Society**
Samsodhana Sadan, South Ave., Khar, Bombay 52, India.
● Gujarat Research Society. Journal. q.

**Gujarat State Financial Corporation**
Jaladarshan Bldg., Ashram Rd., Navrangpura, Box 4030, Ahmedabad 380009, India.
● Gujarat State Financial Corporation. Annual Report. a. ISSN 0533-649X

**Gujarat University**
Navrangpura, Ahmedabad 380009, Gujarat, India.
● Vidya; Gujarat University journal. s-a. ISSN 0505-4753

**S. R. Gunjal, Ed. & Pub.**
Granthalaya Vijnana Prakashana, Saptapur, Dharwar, Karnatak State, India.
● Karnatak Granthalaya. q. ISSN 0022-9083

**Bibash Gupta, Ed. & Pub.**
5-B Olai Chandi Rd., Calcutta 37, India.
● Stamp Digest. m. ISSN 0014-5467

**G. S. Balarma Gupta, Ed. & Pub.**
Dept. of English, Post-Graduate Centre, Gulbarga 585105, India.
● Journal of Indian Writing in English. s-a.

**J. C. Gupta, Ed. & Pub.**
157-E Kamla Nagar, Delhi 7, India.
● Lottery Gazette. w. ISSN 0024-6654

**Gura Sandesha**
Yamuna Nagar, Santpura, India.
● Gura Sandesha/Gur-Sandesh. m.

**Guru Nanak Dev University. Department of Guru Nanak Studies**
Amritsar, India.
● Journal of Sikh Studies. s-a.

**Gurukul Kangri University**
Hardwar, Uttar Pradesh, India.
● Gurukul Kangri Vishwavidyalaya/Journal of Scientific Research. s-a. ISSN 0017-5706

**N. Gurulingam, Ed. & Pub.**
9/4 Krishnapuram, Choolai Medu, Kodambakkam, Madras, India.
● Yogasana Alaya Vijayam. m.

**H.C.M. State Institute of Public Administration**
Jaipur, India.
● Prashasnika. q.

**M. W. Hague, Ed. & Pub.**
17-1A Ratu Sarkar Lane, Calcutta 1, India.
● Struggle; English weekly. w. ISSN 0039-2588

**Hahnemann Homoeopathic Pharmacy**
Parangot Malekal, Kodimatha, Kottayam, India.
● Fifty Millesimal; the journal of pure homoeopathy. q. ISSN 0015-0827

**Hardy & Ally**
8-44 Regal Bldg., Box 184, New Delhi 1, India.
● All India Government Travellers Bungalows Annual Recorder. triennial. ISSN 0065-6291
● Hardy's Encyclopaedia Guide to Agra, Jaipur, Delhi, Varanasi. a. ISSN 0073-0378
● Hardy's Encyclopaedia Hotels of India and Nepal. a. ISSN 0073-0386

**P. Haridas, Ed. & Pub.**
Vakayar P.O., Kouni, Kerala, India.
● Jnanadhara. m. ISSN 0021-700X

**Shukla Hariprasad, Ed. & Pub.**
Halvad 363330, Gujarat, India.
● Red Light. bi-w.

**Harishchandra Mathur State Institute of Public Administration**
Jaipur 302004, India.
● H C M State Institute of Public Administration. s-a.

**Haryana**
*see also* Punjab

**Haryana. Department of Education**
650 Sector 16-2, Chandigarh 17, India.
● Haryana Journal of Education. q. ISSN 0017-825X

**Haryana. Department of Labour**
Haryana, Chandigarh, India.
● Haryana Labour Journal. q. ISSN 0046-6921

**Haryana. Director of Public Relations**
Chandigarh, India.
● Facts About Haryana. irreg.

**Haryana. State Health Education Bureau**
Directorate of Health Services, 36 Madhaya Marg, Sector 7-C, Chandigarh, Haryana, India.
● Haryana Health Journal. q. ISSN 0017-8241

**Haryana Agricultural University**
Hissar, Haryana, India.
● Thesis Abstracts. q.

**Haryana Agricultural University. College of Veterinary Medicine**
Hissar, Haryana, India.
● Haryana Veterinarian. s-a. ISSN 0033-4359

**Haryana Agricultural University. Directorate of Research**
Hissar, Haryana, India.
● Haryana Agricultural University. Journal of Research. q.

**Haryana Cooperative Union Ltd.**
No. 96, Sector 18-A, Chandigarh, India.
● Haryana Cooperation. q. ISSN 0017-8233

**Haryana State Electricity Board**
Office Sector 17-D, Chandigarh, India.
● Haryana Electricity. q. ISSN 0046-6913

**Health**
323 Thambu Chetty St., Madras 600001, India.
● Health; devoted to healthful living. m. ISSN 0017-8861

**Heavy Engineering Corporation**
● H E C Technical Journal. (pub. by L. K. Sharma)

**Heenayana**
c/o Mr. Biplab Bhusan Bose, 33-D, Sreemohon Lane, Calcutta 700026, India.
● Heenayana; literary and cultural quarterly. q.

**Helicon**
10-3C Nepal Bhattacharya St., Calcutta 26, India.
● Helicon. m.

**Helminthological Society of India**
14 Mahatma Gandhi Rd., Dilkusha, Lucknow 2, India
(Address inquiries and subscriptions to: Prints India, 11 Darya Ganj, New Delhi 110002, India)
● Indian Journal of Helminthology. s-a. ISSN 0019-5227

**Hem Publishers Private Ltd.**
C-123 Greater Kailish I, New Delhi 110048, India.
● Indian Journal of Communication Arts. m.

**Heras Institute of Indian History and Culture**
St. Xavier's College, Bombay 400001, India.
● Indica. s-a. ISSN 0019-686X

**Heritage Publishers**
M-116 Connaught Circus, New Delhi 11001, India.
● Intellectuals' Rendezvous. m.

**Highlights**
c/o E. H. Tippoo, Ed., Wachel Molla Mansion, 8 Lenin Sarani, Calcutta 13, India.
● Highlights. w. ISSN 0018-1625

**Himachal Pradesh. Department of Agriculture**
c/o G. S. Agarval, Agricultural Information Officer,
Simla, Himachal Pradesh, India.
- Himachal Agricultural Newsletter. q. ISSN 0018-1889

**Himachal Pradesh. Department of Education**
Solan PIN 173212, Simla 1, Himachal Pradesh,
India.
- Himshiksha. q.

**Himachal Pradesh. Directorate of Economics and Statistics**
Simla, Himachal Pradesh, India.
- State Income of Himachal Pradesh. a.

**Himachal Pradesh. State Museum, Simla**
Department of Languages and Cultural Affairs,
Simla, Himachal Pradesh, India.
- Arts of Himachal. irreg.

**Himalayan Club**
- Himalayan Journal. (pub. by Oxford University Press)

**Himalayan Federation**
63E Mohanirban Rd., Calcutta 700029, India.
- Himavanta; India's only mountaineering monthly. m. ISSN 0018-1897

**Himalayan Observer Press**
9th Mile, Kalimpong, India.
- Himalayan Observer. w. ISSN 0046-7456

**Himmat Publications Trust**
501 Arun Chambers, Tardeo Road, Bombay 400034,
India.
- Himmat/Courage; Asia's new voice. w. ISSN 0018-1900

**Hind Kusht Nivaran Sangh**
see Indian Leprosy Association

**Hind Mazdoor Sabha**
Nagindas Chambers, 167 P. d'Mello Rd., Bombay
400001, India.
- Hind Mazdoor Sabha. Report of the Annual Convention. a. ISSN 0073-2273

**Hindustan Antibiotics Ltd.**
Pimpri, Poona 411018, India.
- Hindustan Antibiotics Bulletin. q. ISSN 0018-1935

**Hindustan Chamber of Commerce**
8 Kondi Chetty St., Madras 1, India.
- Hindustan Chamber Review. m. ISSN 0018-1943

**Hindustan Machine Tools Ltd.**
Bangalore 560031, India.
- Machine Tool Engineer. q. ISSN 0541-6434

**Hindustan Publishing Corp.**
6-U.B. Jawahar Nagar, Delhi 110007, India.
- International Monographs on Advanced Biology and Biophysics. irreg. ISSN 0074-7033
- International Monographs on Advanced Chemistry. irreg. ISSN 0074-7041
- International Monographs on Advanced Mathematics and Physics. irreg., 1973, no. 44. ISSN 0074-705X
- International Monographs on Studies in Indian Economics. irreg., 1970, no. 2. ISSN 0074-7068

**Hindustan Shipyard Ltd.**
Visakhapatnam 5, India.
- Shipyard Review. q. ISSN 0037-3958

**Hindustan Steel Limited**
Ranchi 834002, India.
- Statistics for Iron and Steel Industry in India. irreg., 1973, 4th ed. ISSN 0081-511X

**Hindustan Steel Limited. Bhilai Steel Plant**
Bhilai 1, Madhya Pradesh, India.
- B S P Magazine. q. ISSN 0005-3325
- Steel Bulletin. w.

**Hindustan Thompson Associates**
Express Towers, Express Towers, Nariman Point,
Bombay 400001, India.
- Thompson Rural Market Index. irreg.
- Thompson Urban Market Index. irreg.

**Hindustan Times**
18-20 Kasturba, New Delhi 110001, India
(London office: c/o London International Press
Centre, Shoe Lane, London EC4, England)
- Overseas Hindustan Times. w. ISSN 0048-2536

**Home Science Association of India**
Sri Avinashilingam Home Science College for
Women, Coimbatore 641011, India.
- Indian Journal of Home Science. q.

**Homeopathic Herald**
73 Netaji Subhas Rd., Calcutta 700001, India.
- Homeopathic Herald. m.

**Homoeopathic Education Society**
Near Irla Naka, Vile Parle (West), Bombay 400056,
India.
- Indian Journal of Homoeopathic Medicine. q. ISSN 0019-5243

**Horticultural Society of India**
255 Upper Palace Orchards, Bangalore 566006,
India.
- Indian Journal of Horticulture. q. ISSN 0019-5251

**Hosiery and Textile Journal**
195/B-11 Kucha Mangat Rai, Ludhiana, India.
- Hosiery and Textile Journal; monthly review for manufacturers and merchants. m. ISSN 0018-5388

**I. A. C. P.**
see Indian Association of Clinical Psychologists

**I A S L I C**
see Indian Association of Special Libraries and
Information Centres

**I C F T U**
see International Condeferation of Free Trade
Unions

**I C I D**
see International Commission on Irrigation and
Drainage

**I I F T**
see Indian Institute of Foreign Trade

**I I T C**
see Indian International Trade Center

**I N F A Publications**
Jeevan Deep Bldg., New Delhi 110001, India.
- I N F A Press and Advertisers Year Book. a. ISSN 0073-4284 (India News and Feature Alliance)
- India Who's Who. a. ISSN 0073-6244 (India News and Feature Alliance)

**I N S D O C**
see Indian National Scientific Documentation
Centre

**I O L**
see Institute of Librarians

**I P A G**
see Electronics Commission (Information, Planning
and Analysis Group)

**I P S S**
see Institute of Political and Social Studies

**I. R. C.**
see Indian Roads Congress

**I S P T Journal of Research**
110 Karanpur, Dehradun, India.
- I S P T Journal of Research. s-a.

**Idara-I-Farogh-I-Urdu**
37 Aminabad Park, Lucknow 1, India.
- Farogh-I-Urdu. m. ISSN 0014-8571

**Impact Publications Pvt. Ltd.**
3-7 Nizamuddin East, New Delhi 3, India.
- Citizen and Week End Review. s-m. ISSN 0009-7551

**Impex India**
2/18 Ansari Rd., Daryaganj, Delhi 110006, India.
- Comparative Physiology and Ecology. q.
- Indian Journal of Textile Research. q.

**India. All India Radio**
Akashvani Bhawan, Eden Gardens, Calcutta
700001, India.
- Akashi. fortn. ISSN 0002-3620
- Akashvani. (pub. by Akashvani Group of Journals)
- Betar Jagat. fortn. ISSN 0005-9773
- India Calling; Overseas programme journal of All India Radio. m. ISSN 0019-4158

**India. Archaeological Survey of India**
Janpath, New Delhi 110011, India
(Order from: Controller of Publications,
Government of India, Civil Lines, Delhi 110054,
India)
- Epigraphia Indica. irreg. ISSN 0013-9564

**India. Armed Forces Medical Services**
Director General, Ministry of Defence, "M" Block,
New Delhi 110001, India.
- Medical Journal Armed Forces, India. q.

**India. Botanical Survey of India**
P.O. Botanic Garden, Howrah 71103, India.
- Botanical Survey of India. Bulletin. q. ISSN 0006-8128

**India. Bureau of Public Enterprises**
see also India. Ministry of Finance

**India. Bureau of Public Enterprises**
F Wing, Nirman Bhavan, New Delhi 110011, India.
- Lok Udyog/Public Enterprise. m. ISSN 0024-5925

**India. Cardamom Board**
Banerji Rd., Cochin 682018, India.
- Cardamom. bi-m.
- Cardamom Statistics. irreg.
- Directory of Cardamom Planters. irreg.
- India. Cardamom Board. Annual Report. a.

**India. Central Board of Irrigation and Power**
Kasturba Gandhi Marg, New Delhi 110001, India.
- Irrigation and Power. q. ISSN 0021-1664
- Irrigation and Power Abstracts. bi-m. ISSN 0021-1672

**India. Central Board of Revenue**
Ministry of Finance, New Delhi, India.
- India. Central Board of Revenue. Central Excise Manual. a. ISSN 0073-6120

**India. Central Building Research Institute**
Roorkee, Uttar Pradesh, India.
- C. B. R. I. Abstracts. q. ISSN 0007-7968
- Central Building Research Institute. Building Digests. irreg. ISSN 0557-319X
- Central Building Research Institute. List of Publications. irreg. ISSN 0557-322X
- Central Building Research Institute. Technical Notes. irreg.

**India. Central Bureau of Investigation**
Ministry of Home Affairs, New Delhi, India.
- C B I Bulletin. m.

**India. Central Electrochemical Research Institute**
Kairikudi 623003, Tamil Nadu, India.
- Seminar on Electrochemistry. a. ISSN 0080-8822

**India. Central Food Technological Research Institute**
Mysore 570013, India.
- Khadya Vigyan. q. ISSN 0023-1037

**India. Central Glass and Ceramic Research Institute**
P.O. Jadavpur University, Calcutta 700032, India.
- Central Glass and Ceramic Research Institute. Bulletin. q. ISSN 0008-9397
- Indian Ceramic Society. Transactions. bi-m.

**India. Central Health Education Bureau**
Kotla Rd., Temple Lane, New Delhi 110001, India.
- Swasth Hind. m.

**India. Central Leather Research Institute**
Adyar, Madras 600020, India.
- Current Leather Literature. m. ISSN 0011-3638
- Leather Science. m. ISSN 0023-9771

**India. Central Mechanical Engineering Research Institute**
Duragapur 9, West Bengal, India.
- West Bengal. Central Mechanical Engineering Research Institute. Mechanical Engineering Bulletin. q. ISSN 0049-7207

**India. Central Mining Research Station**
Barwa Rd., Dhanbad 826001, Bihar, India.
- C M R S Bulletin. bi-m.
- Central Mining Research Station, Dhanbad. Progress Report. a. ISSN 0070-4628

**India. Central Road Research Institute**
P.O. Central Road Research Institute, New Delhi 110020, India.
- C R R I Road Abstracts. s-a. ISSN 0045-6055
- Central Road Research Institute, New Delhi. Road Research Paper. irreg., 1969, no. 108. ISSN 0069-1690

**India. Central Salt and Marine Chemicals Research Institute**
Waghawadi Rd., Bhavnagar 364002, Gujarat, India.
- C S M C R I Documentation List Monthly Bulletin. m.
- Salt Research & Industry. s-a. ISSN 0581-3999

**India. Central Scientific Instruments Organization**
Sector 30, Chandigarh 160020, India.
- C S I O Communications. q.

**India. Central Silk Board**
Meghdoot, 95-B Marine Drive, Bombay 400002, India.
- Indian Journal of Sericulture. a.
- Indian Silk. m. ISSN 0019-6355

**India. Central Statistical Organization**
Sardar Patel Bhavan, Parliament St., New Delhi 1, India.
- India. Central Statistical Organization. Annual Survey of Industries/Udyogom Ka Varshika Sarvekshana. a. ISSN 0073-6139
- India. Central Statistical Organization. Estimates of National Income. a. ISSN 0073-6147
- India. Central Statistical Organization. Monthly Abstract of Statistics. m. ISSN 0019-4174
- India. Central Statistical Organization. Sample Surveys of Current Interest in India; Report. biennial. ISSN 0073-6163
- India. Central Statistical Organization. Statistical Abstract. irreg. ISSN 0073-6155
- Statistical Pocket Book: India. irreg. ISSN 0081-5012

**India. Central Vigilance Commission**
3 Dr. Rajendra Prasad Rd., New Delhi, India.
- India. Central Vigilance Commission. Report. a. ISSN 0073-6171

**India. Coffee Board**
Box 5366, Bangalore 560001, India.
- Indian Coffee. m. ISSN 0019-4549

**India. Coir Board**
c/o T. Devidas, Ed., Cochin 682016, India.
- Coir. q. ISSN 0530-0495
- India's Production, Exports, and Internal Consumption of Coir. a.

**India. Committee on Science and Technology**
Cabinet Secretariat, Department of Cabinet Affairs, New Delhi, India.
- India. Committee on Science and Technology. Annual Report. a. ISSN 0085-1779

**India. Council of Scientific and Industrial Research**
Publications and Information Directorate, Hillside Rd., New Delhi 110012, India.
- Current Literature on Science of Sciences. m.
- Indian Journal of Biochemistry and Biophysics. q. ISSN 0301-1208 (Co-sponsor: Society of Biological Chemists)
- Indian Journal of Chemistry. Section A: Inorganic, Physical, Theoretical and Analyltical Chemistry. m.
- Indian Journal of Chemistry. Section B: Organic and Medicinal Chemistry. m. (Co-sponsor: Indian National Science Academy)
- Indian Journal of Experimental Biology. m. ISSN 0019-5189
- Indian Journal of Marine Sciences. s-a. (Co-sponsor: Indian National Science Academy)
- Indian Journal of Pure & Applied Physics. m. ISSN 0019-5596 (Co-sponsor: Indian National Science Academy)
- Indian Journal of Radio & Space Physics. q. (Co-sponsor: Indian National Science Academy)
- Indian Journal of Technology. m. ISSN 0019-5669
- Indian Journal of Textile Research (CSIR) q.
- Journal of Scientific and Industrial Research. m. ISSN 0022-4456
- Research and Industry. q. ISSN 0034-513X
- Vigyan Pragati. m. ISSN 0042-6075

**India. Department of Atomic Energy**
Publications Officer, Chhatrapati Shivaji Maharaj Marg, Bombay 400039, India.
- India. Department of Atomic Energy. Annual Report. a. ISSN 0073-618X
- Nuclear India. m. ISSN 0029-5523

**India. Department of Commercial Intelligence and Statistics**
1 Council House St., Calcutta 700001, India
(Order from: Controller of Publications, Civil Lines, New Delhi 110054, India)
- Directory of Indian Exporters. triennial.
- Indian Trade Journal. w. ISSN 0019-6444
- Monthly Statistics of Foreign Trade of India. m. ISSN 0027-0547

**India. Department of Company Affairs**
*see also* **India. Ministry of Industrial Development**

**India. Department of Company Affairs**
Shastri Bhawan, Dr. Rajendraprasad Rd., New Delhi, India
(Order from: Controller of Publications, Civil Lines, Delhi 110054, India)
- Company News and Notes. m. ISSN 0010-4027
- Quarterly Blue Book on Joint Stock Companies in India. q. ISSN 0033-5312 (prep. by its Research and Statistics Division)

**India. Department of Culture**
- India, Department of Culture. Demands for Grants/Samskriti Vibhaga Ki Anudanom Ki Mangem. (pub. by India. Government of India Press)

**India. Department of Economic Affairs**
Office of the Controller of Capital Issues, New Delhi, India
(Order from: Controller of Publications, Civil Lines, New Delhi 110054, India)
- India. Department of Economic Affairs. Quarterly Statistics on the Working of Capital Issues Control. q. ISSN 0536-8014

**India. Department of Family Planning**
Ministry of Health and Family Planning and Works, Nirman Bhaven, New Delhi, India.
- Centre Calling. m.
- Family Planning Quarterly. q. ISSN 0014-7362
- Pathways in Population Planning. m.

**India. Department of Labour and Employment**
*see* **India. Ministry of Labour**

**India. Department of Personnel and Administrative Reforms**
Sardar Patel Bhawan, Parliament St., New Delhi 110001, India.
- Management in Government. q. ISSN 0047-570X

**India. Department of Power**
Ministry of Energy, New Delhi, India.
- India. Department of Power. Report. a.

**India. Department of Publication**
Controller of Publications, Civil Lines, Delhi 110054, India.
- India. Department of Publication. Publications. m.

**India. Department of Science and Technology**
Technology Bhavan, New Mehrauli Rd., New Delhi 110029, India.
- India. Department of Science and Technology. Report. a.

**India. Department of Science and Technology. Botanical Survey of India**
*see* **India. Botanical Survey of India**

**India. Department of Science and Technology. Khadi and Village Industries Commission**
*see* **India. Khadi and Village Industries Commission**

**India. Department of Space**
Cauvery Bhavan, District Office Road, Bangalore 560009, India.
- India. Department of Space. Annual Report. a.

**India. Director of Military Training**
General Staff Branch MT4, Army Headquarters, DHQ P.O., New Delhi, India.
- Military Digest. q. ISSN 0462-4874

**India. Directorate General of Factory Advice and Labour Institutes**
Central Labour Institute Bldg., Sion, Bombay 22, India
(Order from: Controller of Publications, Government o· India, Civil Lines, Delhi 110054, India)
- Industrial Safety & Health Bulletin. q. ISSN 0019-8765

**India. Directorate General of Health Services. Central Health Education Bureau**
*see* **India. Central Health Education Bureau**

**India. Directorate General of Mines Safety**
Dhanbad, India.
- Bulletin for Metalliferous Mines in India. q. ISSN 0536-9657

**India. Directorate of Arecanut and Spices Development**
1/500 Cannanore Rd., Calicut 673005, Kerala, India.
- Arecanut and Spices Bulletin. q. ISSN 0044-8796

**India. Directorate of Cashew Nut Development**
New Dehli 110001, India.
- Cashew News Teller. q. ISSN 0045-5911

**India. Directorate of Coconut Development**
Ernakulam, Cochin 11, India.
- Coconut Bulletin. ISSN 0010-0145

**India. Directorate of Cotton Development**
Box 1002, Bombay 400001, India.
- Indian Cotton Journal. q.

**India. Directorate of Extension**
Shastri Bhavan, New Delhi, India.
- Intensive Agriculture. m. ISSN 0020-4919 (prep. by its Farm Information Unit)

**India. Directorate of Inspection**
Publications and Public Relations Wing, Income Tax Dept., Mayur Bhavan, New Delhi, India
(Order from: Controller of Publications, Government of India, Civil Lines, Delhi 110054, India)
- Direct Taxes Bulletin. q.

**India. Directorate of Jute Development**
c/o Dr. P. Sanyal, Nizam Palace Campus, 234/4 Acharyya Jagadish Bose Rd., Calcutta 20, India.
- India. Directorate of Jute Development. Jute Bulletin. m. ISSN 0046-8940

**India. Directorate of Marketing and Inspection**
Nagpur, India.
- Agricultural Marketing; devoted to the problems of agricultural marketing in India. q. ISSN 0002-1555

**India. Directorate of Oilseeds Development**
Telhan Bhavan, Himayatnagar, Hyderabad 500029, India.
- Telhan Patrika/Oilseeds Journal. q. ISSN 0040-2818

**India. Directorate of Sugarcane Development**
No. 1 Shyam Enclave, Giani Border, P.O. Sahibabad, Distt. Ghaziabad, Uttar Pradesh, India.
- Indian Sugar Crops Journal. q.

**India. Directorate of Tobacco Development**
3-A Eldams Rd., Madras 600018, India.
- Indian Tobacco Bulletin. q.

**India. Finance Department**
New Delhi, India.
- India. Finance Department. Budget of the Central Government. a.

**India. Forest Research Institute & Colleges**
P.O. New Forest, Dehra Dun, India.
- Forest Research in India. a. ISSN 0071-7533
- Forest Research Institute and Colleges, Dehra Dun. Quarterly News Letter. q. ISSN 0015-7481
- Indian Forest Bulletin (New Series) irreg.,No. 271,1975. ISSN 0073-635X
- Indian Forest Leaflets (New Series) irreg., no. 195, 1974. ISSN 0073-6368
- Indian Forest Records (New Series) Botany. irreg., 1964, vol. 5, no. 3. ISSN 0073-6376
- Indian Forest Records (New Series) Composite Wood. irreg., 1964, vol. 1, no. 2. ISSN 0073-6384
- Indian Forest Records (New Series) Entomology. irreg. vol. 11, no. 2, 1973. ISSN 0073-6392

- Indian Forest Records (New Series) Forest Pathology. irreg., vol. 2, no. 11, 1973. ISSN 0073-6406
- Indian Forest Records (New Series) Logging. irreg., 1972, vol. 1, no. 3. ISSN 0073-6414
- Indian Forest Records (New Series) Silviculture. irreg., vol. 13, no. 1, 1974. ISSN 0073-6422
- Indian Forest Records (New Series) Statistical. irreg., 1970, vol. 1, no. 3. ISSN 0073-6430
- Indian Forest Records (New Series) Timber Mechanics. irreg., 1972, vol. 2, no. 2. ISSN 0073-6449

**India. Forward Markets Commission**
Government of India, 100 Marine Drive, Bombay, India.
- Forward Markets Bulletin. q. ISSN 0015-864X

**India. Geological Survey of India**
29 Jawaharlal Nehru Rd., Calcutta 700016, India.
- Geological Survey of India. News. bi-m.
- Indian Minerals. q. ISSN 0019-5936

**India. Government of India Press**
General Manager, Minto Rd., New Delhi, India.
- India, Department of Culture. Demands for Grants/Samskriti Vibhaga Ki Anudanom Ki Mangem. a.

**India. Indian Bureau of Mines**
New Secretariat Building, Nagpur 440001, India.
- Indian Bureau of Mines. Documentation Notes. 3 per yr. (prep. by its Mineral Economics Division)
- Indian Bureau of Mines. Monthly Bulletin of Mineral Statistics and Information. m. ISSN 0027-0261 (Order from: Controller of Publications, Civil Lines, Delhi 110054, India)
- Indian Minerals Year Book. irreg., latest issue, 1970. ISSN 0445-7897 (Order from: Controller of Publications, Civil Lines, Delhi 110054, India)

**India. Khadi and Village Industries Commission**
Gramodaya, Irla Rd., Vile Parle (West), Bombay 400056, India.
- Jagriti; fortnightly news magazine on rural reconstruction. fortn. ISSN 0447-2500
- K V I C Annual Report. a.
- Khadi Gramodyog; journal of rural economy. m. ISSN 0023-1029

**India. Labour Bureau**
see also India. Ministry of Labour

**India. Labour Bureau**
Simla 171004, India
(Order from: Controller of Publications, Government of India, Civil Lines, Delhi 110054, India)
- India. Labour Bureau. Pocket Book of Labour Statistics. a.
- Indian Labour Journal. m. ISSN 0019-5723

**India. Meteorological Department**
Lodi Rd., New Delhi 110003, India
- Air Almanac. s-a. (Order from: Controller of Publications, Government of India, Civil Lines, Delhi 110054, India)
- India. Meteorological Department. Memoirs. irreg. (Order from: Controller of Publications, Government of India, Civil Lines, Delhi 110054, India)
- Indian Journal of Meteorology, Hydrology and Geophysics. q. (Order from: Controller of Publications, Government of India, Civil Lines, Delhi 110054, India)
- National Report for India: Meteorology and Atmospheric Analysis. triennial.
- National Report for India: Seismology and Physics of the Earth's Interior. triennial.

**India. Ministry of Agriculture**
- Kurukshetra. (pub. by India. Ministry of Information and Broadcasting)

**India. Ministry of Agriculture and Irrigation. Department of Agriculture. Directorate of Arecanut and Spices Development**
see India. Directorate of Arecanut and Spices Development

**India. Ministry of Agriculture and Irrigation. Department of Agriculture. Directorate of Oilseeds Development**
see India. Directorate of Oilseeds Development

**India. Ministry of Agriculture and Irrigation. Department of Agriculture. Directorate of Tobacco Development**
see India. Directorate of Tobacco Development

**India. Ministry of Agriculture and Irrigation. Department of Agriculture**
Directorate of Economics and Statistics, A-2E/3 Kasturba Gandhi Marg Barracks, New Delhi 110001, India
(Order from: Controller of Publications, Civil Lines, Delhi 110054, India)
- Agricultural Situation in India. m. ISSN 0002-1679
- Agricultural Wages in India. a. ISSN 0084-6066
- Economic Survey of Indian Agriculture. a. ISSN 0085-0160
- Estimates of Area and Production of Principal Crops in India. Summary Tables. a. ISSN 0085-0314
- Indian Agriculture in Brief. irreg. ISSN 0084-781X
- Studies in the Economics of Poultry Farming in Punjab. a.

**India. Ministry of Agriculture and Irrigation. National Sugar Institute**
see India. National Sugar Institute

**India. Ministry of Agriculture. Directorate of Coconut Development**
see India. Directorate of Coconut Development

**India. Ministry of Agriculture. Directorate of Extension**
see India. Directorate of Extension

**India. Ministry of Agriculture. Directorate of Marketing and Inspection**
see India. Directorate of Marketing and Inspection

**India. Ministry of Agriculture. Directorate of Tobacco Development**
see India. Directorate of Tobacco Development

**India. Ministry of Commerce**
New Delhi, India
(Order from: Controller of Publications, Government of India, Civil Lines, Delhi 110054, India)
- Import Trade Control: Handbook of Rules and Procedures. a. ISSN 0536-9983
- Import Trade Control Policy. a. ISSN 0536-9061

**India. Ministry of Commerce and Industry. Department of Commercial Intelligence and Statistics**
see India. Department of Commercial Intelligence and Statistics

**India. Ministry of Commerce. Cardamom Board**
see India. Cardamom Board

**India. Ministry of Commerce. Department of Textiles. Central Silk Board.**
see India. Central Silk Board

**India. Ministry of Commerce. Exhibitions and Commercial Publicity**
Udyog Bhavan, New Delhi, India.
- Economic and Commercial News. w.
- Journal of Industry and Trade. m. ISSN 0022-1880

**India. Ministry of Commerce. Textiles Committee**
see India. Textiles Committee

**India. Ministry of Defence**
Scientific Information & Documentation Centre, Metcalfe House, Delhi 110054, India.
- Defence Science Journal. q. ISSN 0011-748X
- Popular Science and Technology. s-a. ISSN 0032-4639

**India. Ministry of Defence. Directorate of Public Relations**
AFO Mess, Dr. Rajendera Prasad Rd., New Delhi 1, India.
- Sainik Samachar. w. ISSN 0036-2743

**India. Ministry of Defense. Armed Forces Medical Services**
see India. Armed Forces Medical Services

**India. Ministry of Education and Social Welfare. Department of Education**
Shastri Bhavan, New Delhi 110001, India
- Education Quarterly. q. ISSN 0013-1482 (Orders to: Controller of Publications, Government of India, Civil Lines, Delhi 110054, India)
- India. Ministry of Education and Social Welfare. Department of Education. Report. a. ISSN 0073-6201 (Available from: Assistant Educational Adviser (Publications), Ministry of Education, Room No. 503, "C" Wing, Shastri Bhavan, New Delhi 110001)
- India. Ministry of Education and Social Welfare. Provisional Statistics of Education in the States. a. ISSN 0579-6105 (Available from: Assistant Educational Adviser (Publications), Ministry of Education, Room No. 503, "C" Wing, Shastri Bhavan, New Delhi 110001, India)
- Indian Education Abstracts. q. ISSN 0019-4697 (Orders to: Controller of Publications, Government of India, Civil Lines, Delhi 110054, India)

**India. Ministry of Education and Social Welfare. Department of Social Welfare**
Shastri Bhavan, New Delhi 110001, India.
- India. Ministry of Education and Social Welfare. Department of Social Welfare. Documentation Service Bulletin. a.

**India. Ministry of Energy. Department of Power**
see India. Department of Power

**India. Ministry of External Affairs**
Publicity Division, New Delhi, India.
- Foreign Affairs Record. m.

**India. Ministry of Finance**
see also India. Bureau of Public Enterprises

**India. Ministry of Finance**
New Delhi, India.
- India. Ministry of Finance. Quarterly Statistics on the Working of Capital Issues Control. q. (prep. by its Office of the Controller of Capital Issues)

**India. Ministry of Finance. Central Board of Revenue**
see India. Central Board of Revenue

**India. Ministry of Finance. Department of Banking. State Bank of India**
see India. State Bank of India

**India. Ministry of Finance. Finance Library**
Central Secretariat, New Delhi, India.
- India. Ministry of Finance. Finance Library. Weekly Bulletin. w. ISSN 0019-4204

**India. Ministry of Food, Agriculture, Community Development and Co-Operation. Department of Agriculture. Directorate of Cotton Development**
see India. Directorate of Cotton Development

**India. Ministry of Food and Agriculture. National Sugar Institute**
see India. National Sugar Institute

**India. Ministry of Foreign Trade**
Directorate of Commercial Publicity, Udyog Bhawan, New Delhi, India.
- Indian Export Service Bulletin. m.

**India. Ministry of Health and Family Planning and Works. Department of Family Planning**
see India. Department of Family Planning

**India. Ministry of Health, Family Planning, Works, Housing and Urban Development. Town and Country Planning Organization. Documentation Centre**
see India. Town and Country Planning Organization. Documentation Centre

**India. Ministry of Heavy Industry**
New Delhi, India.
- India. Ministry of Heavy Industry. Report. irreg.

**India. Ministry of Home Affairs**
Registrar General, West Block No. 1, R. K. Puram, New Delhi 110022, India.
- India. Ministry of Home Affairs. Vital Statistics Division. Sample Registration Bulletin. q.

**India. Ministry of Home Affairs. Central Bureau of Investigation**
see India. Central Bureau of Investigation

**India. Ministry of Home Affairs. Intelligence Bureau**
25 Akbar Rd., New Delhi 110011, India.
• Indian Police Journal. q. ISSN 0537-2429

**India. Ministry of Industrial Development**
*see also* **India. Coir Board**

**India. Ministry of Industrial Development**
*see also* **India. Department of Company Affairs**

**India. Ministry of Industrial Development**
*see also* **India. Labour Bureau**

**India. Ministry of Industrial Development**
Development Commissioner-Small Scale Industries,
Internal Trade and Company Affairs, New Delhi,
India.
• Small Industries Guide. irreg.; 1969, no. 2.

**India. Ministry of Industrial Development.
Department of Science and Technology. Council of
Scientific and Industrial Research**
*see* **India. Council of Scientific and Industrial
Research**

**India. Ministry of Information & Broadcasting**
Publications Division, Patiala House, Tilak Marg,
New Delhi 110001, India
(U.S. Subscr. Address: M/S Inter Culture
Associates, Thompson, CT 06277)
• Bal Bharati. m. ISSN 0005-4194
• Bhagirath; irrigation and power quarterly. q. ISSN
0006-0461 (India. Ministry of Irrigation & Power.
Central Water Commission)
• Gazeteer of India. irreg. ISSN 0072-0348
• India; A Reference Annual. a. ISSN 0073-6090
(prep. by its Research and Reference Division)
• Indian & Foreign Review. fortn. ISSN 0019-4379
• Kurukshetra; journal of community development
and village democracy. fortn. ISSN 0023-5660
(India. Ministry of Agriculture)
• Yojana. fortn. ISSN 0044-0515 (India. Planning
Commission)

**India. Ministry of Information and Broadcasting.
Registrar of Newspapers for India**
Shastri Bhawan, New Delhi, India
(Order from: Controller of Publications,
Government of India, Civil Lines, Delhi 110054,
India)
• Press in India. a. ISSN 0445-6653

**India. Ministry of Irrigation & Power. Central Water
Commission**
• Bhagirath. (pub. by India. Ministry of Information
and Broadcasting)

**India. Ministry of Labour**
*see also* **India. Labour Bureau**

**India. Ministry of Labour**
New Delhi, India
(Order from: Controller of Publications,
Government of India, Civil Lines, Delhi 110054,
India)
• India. Ministry of Labour. Annual Report. a.
• Labour in the Public Sector Undertakings: Basic
Information. irreg. (prep. by its Implementation
and Evaluation Division)

**India. Ministry of Labour and Employment.
Directorate General of Mines Safety**
*see* **India. Directorate General of Mines Safety**

**India. Ministry of Labour. Library**
Sharam Shakti Bhavan, Rafi Marg, New Delhi,
India.
• Labour Bulletin of Current Awareness.
• Labour Literature: A Bibliography. a. ISSN 0075-
756X

**India. Ministry of Petroleum and Chemicals**
Economics and Statistics Division, New Delhi,
India.
• Indian Chemicals and Pharmaceuticals Statistics.
a.
• Indian Fertilizer Statistics. a.
• Indian Petroleum and Chemicals Statistics. s-a.
• Indian Petroleum and Petrochemicals Statistics. a.

**India. Ministry of Railways. Railway Board**
*see* **India. Railway Board**

**India. Ministry of Shipping and Transport**
Transport Research Division, I D A Bldg., Jamnagar
House, Shahjahan Rd, New Delhi 110011, India
(Orders to: Controller of Publications, Civil Lines,
Delhi 110006, India)
• Basic Road Statistics of India. a; latest editions in
print: 1971-72 (Engilsh edt.) 1970-71 (Hindi edt.)
ISSN 0067-6462
• Pocket Book of Transport Statistics of India. a;
latest edition in print: 1970-1971. ISSN 0079-
2381
• Port Transport Statistics of India. a.; latest edition
in print 1972-1973. ISSN 0079-4015
• Road Facts India. quinquennial. ISSN 0080-3286
• Water Transport Statistics of India. a.

**India. Ministry of Works and Housing. National
Buildings Organisation**
*see* **India. National Buildings Organisation**

**India. National Aeronautical Laboratory**
Box 1779, Kodihalli, Bangalore 560017, India.
• N A L Technical Translation. irreg. ISSN 0077-
2968
• National Aeronautical Laboratory. Annual Report.
a. ISSN 0077-2976
• National Aeronautical Laboratory. Technical
Note. irreg., latest issue, 1975. ISSN 0077-300X

**India. National Archives of India**
Janpath, New Delhi 110001, India.
• Indian Archives. s-a. ISSN 0046-8975

**India. National Botanic Gardens**
Lucknow 226001, India.
• National Botanic Gardens. Lucknow. Bulletin.
irreg. ISSN 0076-1419
• National Botanic Gardens, Lucknow. Annual
Report. a. ISSN 0076-1400

**India. National Buildings Organisation**
G Wing, Nirman Bhavan, Maulana Azad Rd., New
Delhi 11, India.
• N B O Abstracts. m. ISSN 0027-6138
• National Buildings Organisation. Journal. s-a.
ISSN 0027-8815

**India. National Environmental Engineering Research
Institute**
Documentation and Library Services, Nehru Marg,
Nagpur 440020, India.
• Guide to Current Literature in Environmental
Health Engineering and Science. fortn.
• Indian Journal of Environmental Health. q.
• Indian Literature in Environmental Engineering;
annual bibliography. a.

**India. National Geophysical Research Institute**
Uppal Rd., Hyderabad 500007, India.
• Geophysical Research Bulletin. q.
• National Geophysical Research Institute,
Hyderabad. Publications. 1974, vol. 10. ISSN
0073-4144
• Progress in Geophysics; annual report on the
geophysical activities in the Republic of India. a.
ISSN 0079-628X

**India. National Institute of Oceanography**
P.O. NIO, Dona Paula, Panaji-Goa 403004, India.
• Mahasagar. q.

**India. National Library**
Central Reference Library, Belvedere, Calcutta
700027, India.
• Indian National Bibliography. m. (q. before 1964);
annual cumulations. ISSN 0019-6002

**India. National Medical Library**
Directorate General of Health Services, Ansari
Nagar, New Delhi, India.
• Index to Indian Medical Periodicals. s-a. ISSN
0019-4042

**India. National Metallurgical Laboratory**
P.O. Burmamines, Jamshedpur 7, India.
• Documented Survey on Metallurgical
Developments. m.
• N M L Technical Journal. q. ISSN 0027-6839

**India. National Physical Laboratory**
Hillside Rd., New Delhi 110012, India.
• N P L Technical Bulletin. q. ISSN 0027-6898

**India. National Research Development Corporation of
India**
20 Ring Rd., New Delhi 110024, India.
• Awishkar. m.
• Invention Intelligence. m. ISSN 0020-9902

**India. National Sugar Institute**
Kalyanpur, Kanpur 17, Uttar Pradesh, India.
• Sharkara. q. ISSN 0037-332X

**India. National Tuberculosis Institute**
No. 8 Bellary Rd., Bangalore 560003, India.
• N T I Newsletter. q. ISSN 0047-9136

**India. North Arcot Police Department. Police
Training College**
Vellore, North Arcot District, Tamil Nadu, India.
• Tamil Nadu Police Journal. q. ISSN 0039-9329

**India. Office of the Comptroller and Auditor-General**
Controller of Publications, Civil Lines, Delhi
110054, India.
• India. Office of the Comptroller and Auditor-
General. Report: Union Government (Posts and
Telegraphs) a. ISSN 0536-7506

**India. Planning Commission**
• Yojana. (pub. by India. Ministry of Information
and Broadcasting)

**India. Posts and Telegraphs Department**
Parliament St., New Delhi 110001, India.
• Dak Tar. m. ISSN 0011-5762
• Telecommunications. s-a. ISSN 0497-1388

**India. Railway Board**
Joint Director, Public Relations, New Delhi 110001,
India.
• Indian Railways; devoted to railway affairs in
India and abroad. m. ISSN 0019-6274
• Indian Railways Yearbook. a. (prep. by its
Directorate of Statistics and Economics)
• Monthly Railway Statistics. (Relave Ke Masika
Sankhyikiya Vivarana) m. ISSN 0027-0504
• Review of Accidents on Indian Government
Railways. a. ISSN 0080-1933 (prep. by its
Directorate of Safety)

**India. Research Designs and Standards Organization**
Alambagh, Lucknow 5, India.
• Indian Railway Technical Bulletin. q. ISSN 0019-
6266

**India. Reserve Bank of India**
Box 1036, Bombay 400001, India.
• Cooperative News Digest. m. ISSN 0525-6402
(prep. by its Agricultural Credit Department)
• Reserve Bank of India. Annual Report. a. ISSN
0080-1801
• Reserve Bank of India. Bulletin. m. ISSN 0034-
5512
• Reserve Bank of India. Bulletin. Weekly Statistical
Supplement. w.

**India. Rubber Board**
Kottayam 686009, Kerala, India.
• Indian Rubber Statistics. irreg. (vol. 13, 1975 in
prep.) ISSN 0073-6651
• Rubber Board Bulletin. q.

**India. State Bank of India**
New Administrative Building, Backbay Reclamation,
Box 12, Bombay 400021, India.
• State Bank of India. Monthly Review. m. ISSN
0039-0003 (prep. by its Economic and Statistical
Research Department)
• State Bank of India. Report of the Central Board
of Directors. (pub. by International Book House,
Ltd.)

**India. Supreme Court, Jodhpur**
High Court Rd., Jodhpur, Rajasthan, India.
• India. Supreme Court. Unreported Judgments. s-
m.

**India. Supreme Court, New Delhi**
D-8 Nizamuddin East, New Delhi 13, India.
• Supreme Court Notes. fortn. ISSN 0039-596X

**India. Textile Commissioner**
Bombay 20, India
(Order from: Controller of Publications,
Government of India, Civil Lines, Delhi 110054,
India)
• Indian Textile Bulletin. m.

**India. Textiles Committee**
406 Kakad Chambers, 132 Dr. Annie Besant Rd.,
Worli, Bombay 400018, India.
• India. Textiles Committee. Consumer Purchases of
Textiles. m.

**India. Town and Country Planning Organization. Documentation Centre**
Ministry of Health, Family Planning, Works, Housing and Urban Development, New Delhi, India.
- Quarterly Bulletin of Documentation in Urban and Regional Planning. q.

**India. Union Public Service Commission**
Minto Rd., New Delhi, India.
- India. Union Public Service Commission Report. a. ISSN 0073-6236

**India. University Grants Commission**
Publication Officer, 35 Ferozeshah Rd., New Delhi 110001, India.
- Directory of Scientific Research in Indian Universities. (pub. by Indian National Scientific Documentation Centre)
- Journal of Higher Education. 3 per yr.

**India. Zoological Survey of India**
34 Chittaranjan Ave., Calcutta 12, India.
- India. Zoological Survey. Annual Report. a. ISSN 0537-0744
- India. Zoological Survey. Newsletter. irreg.
- India. Zoological Survey. Records. q.

**India and the World**
Kakinada 1, Andhra Pradesh, India.
- India and the World. s-m.

**India Committee for Studies on Economic Development in India and Japan**
Yojana Rhauan, Parliament St., New Delhi, India.
- Japan Quarterly. q.

**India International Centre**
40 Lodi Estate, New Delhi 110003, India.
- India International Centre. Quarterly. q.

**India-International News Service**
12 India Exchange Place, Calcutta 700001, India.
- Director; India's top management journal. q. ISSN 0012-3250 (Institute of Directors, India)
- Export-Import News; a fortnightly journal about export-import trade. fortn. ISSN 0014-5149 (Exporters-Importers Club)
- Professional Engineer. q. ISSN 0033-0078 (Engineers Club, India)
- What's on in Calcutta; city's entertainment guide. fortn. ISSN 0043-4647

**India News and Feature Alliance**
- I N F A Press and Advertisers Year Book. (pub. by I N F A Publications)
- India Who's Who. (pub. by I N F A Publications)

**India Publications Co.**
Denabank House, 2nd Floor, 31 Hamam St., Bombay 1, India.
- Chemist & Drugstore News. m. ISSN 0009-3041
- Drug News. m. ISSN 0026-8194
- Purchasing. m. ISSN 0014-6544

**India Society of Engineers**
12B Netaji Subhas Rd., Calcutta 1, India.
- Science and Engineering. m. ISSN 0036-8164

**India Tourism Development Corporation**
Himalaya House, 6th Floor, 23 Kasturba Gandhi Marg, New Delhi 110001, India.
- Yatri; a monthly newsletter of Indian tourism. m. ISSN 0049-8289

**Indian Academy of Applied Psychology**
Madras 5, India.
- Indian Academy of Applied Psychology. Journal. 3 per yr. ISSN 0019-4247

**Indian Academy of Geoscience**
Osmania University, Department of Geology, Hyderabad 500007, Andhra Pradesh, India.
- Indian Academy of Geoscience. Journal. a.

**Indian Academy of Medical Sciences**
C-II/16, Ansari Nagar, New Delhi 16, India.
- Indian Academy of Medical Sciences, Annals. q. ISSN 0019-4263

**Indian Academy of Pediatrics**
c/o Dr. O. P. Ghei, Editor, All-India Institute of Medical Sciences, Department of Pediatrics, New Delhi 110016, India.
- Indian Pediatrics. m. ISSN 0019-6061

**Indian Academy of Philosophy**
Belgachia-Villa, Block F, Flat 8, Calcutta 37, India.
- Indian Academy of Philosophy. Journal. s-a. ISSN 0019-4271

**Indian Academy of Sciences**
Hebbal, Bangalore 560006, India.
- Indian Academy of Sciences. Proceedings. m. ISSN 0019-428X
- Pramana; a journal of physics. m. ISSN 0304-4289

**Indian Academy of Social Sciences**
- Indian Journal of Sociology. (pub. by Academic Journals of India)

**Indian Academy of Wood Science**
- Indian Academy of Wood Science. Journal. (pub. by Indian Plywood Industries Research Institute)

**Indian Adult Education Association**
17-B Indraprastha Marg, New Delhi 1, India.
- Indian Journal of Adult Education. m. ISSN 0019-5006

**Indian & Eastern Engineer Co .Ltd.**
Piramal Mansion, 235 Dr. D. Naoroji Rd., Bombay 400001, India.
- Indian and Eastern Engineer. m. ISSN 0019-4352

**Indian and Eastern Newspaper Society**
I. E. N. S. Bldgs., Rafi Marg, New Delhi 110001, India.
- Indian & Eastern Newspaper Society Press Handbook. irreg.
- Indian Press. m. ISSN 0445-801X

**Indian Anthropological Association**
Department of Anthropology, University of Delhi, Delhi 110007, India.
- Indian Anthropologist. s-a.

**Indian Anthropological Society**
27 Jawaharlal Nehru Marg, Calcutta 700013, India.
- Indian Anthropological Society. Journal. 3 per yr. ISSN 0019-4387

**Indian Association for Animal Production**
E.6, N.D. S.E. Part 2, New Delhi, India.
- Indian Journal of Animal Production. q.

**Indian Association for English Studies**
- Indian Journal of English Studies. (pub. by Orient Longman Ltd.)

**Indian Association for Quality and Reliability**
c/o SQC Unit, ISI, 4 Richmond Rd., Bangalore 560025, India.
- Q R Journal. (Quality - Reliability) 3 per yr.

**Indian Association for the Advancement of Medical Education**
- Indian Journal of Medical Education. (pub. by Orient Longman Ltd.)

**Indian Association for the Cultivation of Science**
2-3 Raja Subodh Mallick Rd., Jadavpur, Calcutta 700032, India.
- Indian Journal of Physics and Proceedings of the Indian Association for the Cultivation of Science. m. ISSN 0019-5480

**Indian Association for the Study of Conservation of Cultural Property**
c/o National Archives of India, Janpath, New Dehli, India.
- Conservation of Cultural Property in India. a.

**Indian Association for the Study of Population**
Institute of Economic Growth, University Enclave, Delhi 7, India.
- Demography India. s-a.

**Indian Association of Biological Sciences**
c/o Life Science Centre, University of Calcutta, 35 Ballygunge Circular Rd., Calcutta 19, India.
- Indian Biologist. s-a. ISSN 0302-7554

**Indian Association of Clinical Psychologists**
Postgraduate Institute of Medical Education and Research, Department of Psychiatry, Chandigarh 160011, India.
- Indian Journal of Clinical Psychology. s-a.

**Indian Association of Dermatologists, Venereologists and Leprologists**
C.M.C. Hospital, Vellore 632004, India.
- Indian Journal of Dermatology, Venereology and Leprology. bi-m.

**Indian Association of Lawyers**
29-B Maharani Bagh, New Delhi, India.
- Law and Progress. q.

**Indian Association of Occupational Health**
82/B Shakespeare Sarani, Calcutta 700017, India.
- Indian Journal of Industrial Medicine. q. ISSN 0019-5278

**Indian Association of Pathologists and Microbiologists**
Department of Pathology, Chandigarh, India.
- Indian Journal of Pathology & Microbiology. q.

**Indian Association of Radiological Technologists**
Postgraduate Institute of Medical Education and Research, Dept. of Radiology, Chandigarh, India.
- Roentgen Technology. s-a. ISSN 0303-2590

**Indian Association of Special Libraries and Information Centres**
P-291 C.I.T. Scheme No. 6M, Kankurgachi, Calcutta 700054, India.
- I A S L I C Bulletin. q. ISSN 0018-8441
- I A S L I C Newsletter. m. ISSN 0018-845X
- I A S L I C Special Publication; working papers of seminars and conferences. a. ISSN 0073-6279
- I A S L I C Technical Pamphlets. irreg. ISSN 0073-6260
- Indian Library Science Abstracts. q. ISSN 0019-5790

**Indian Association of Sports Medicine**
- Sports Medicine. (pub. by Netaji Subhas National Institute of Sports)

**Indian Association of Teacher Educators**
33 Chatra Marg, Delhi 7, India.
- Teacher Education. q.

**Indian Association of the History of Medicine**
497 Poonamalee, Madras 7, India.
- Indian Journal of the History of Medicine. s-a. ISSN 0019-5677

**Indian Association of Trained Social Workers**
3 University Rd., Delhi 110007, India.
- Social Work Forum. q. ISSN 0583-7065

**Indian Bibliographic Centre**
- Indian Books; Bibliography of Indian Books Published or Reprinted in the English Language. (pub. by Today and Tomorrow's Printers and Publishers)

**Indian Brain Research Association**
Dept. of Biochemistry, 35 Ballygunge Circular Rd., Calcutta 19, India.
- Brain News. s-a. ISSN 0006-8985

**Indian Cancer Society**
Hospital Ave., Parel, Bombay 400012, India.
- Indian Journal of Cancer. q. ISSN 0019-509X

**Indian Ceramics**
17 Sourin Roy Rd., Behala, Calcutta 700034, India.
- Indian Ceramics. m. ISSN 0019-4492

**Indian Chamber of Commerce, Calcutta. World Trade Department**
India Exchange Place, Calcutta 700001, India.
- Survey of India's Exports. a. ISSN 0537-1120

**Indian Chemical Manufacturers Association**
Bombay Regional Office, Sir Vithaldas Chambers, 16 Bombay Samachar Marg, Bombay 400023, India.
- Chemical Industry News. m. ISSN 0009-2576

**Indian Chemical Society**
92 Acharya Prafulla Chandra Rd., Calcutta 700009, India.
- Indian Chemical Society. Journal. m. ISSN 0019-4522

**Indian College of Allergy and Applied Immunology**
- Aspects of Allergy and Applied Immunology. (pub. by Rainbow Book Co. Educational Publishers)

**Indian Commerce Association**
B.Y.K. College of Commerce, Nasik 5, Maharashtra, India.
- Indian Journal of Commerce. q. ISSN 0019-512X

**Indian Congress of American History**
c/o Dwijendra Tripathi, Indian Institute of Management, Vastrapur, Ahmedabad 380015, India.
- Indian Congress of American History. Papers. a.

**Indian Construction News**
Box 934, 24 Brabourne Rd., Calcutta 1, India.
- Indian Construction News. m. ISSN 0019-4573

**Indian Cotton Mills Federation**
Textile Centre, 34 P. d'Mello Rd., Box 1449, Bombay 1, India.
- Indian Cotton Mills Federation. Journal. m. ISSN 0019-459X

**Indian Council for Africa**
Library, 5 Balvantray Mehta Lane, New Delhi, India.
- Indian Council for Africa. Library. Monthly Index of Important Articles and Editorials on Africa. m. ISSN 0537-1198

**Indian Council for Child Welfare**
4 Deen Dayal Upadhayaya Marg, New Delhi 110002, India.
- I.C.C.W. News Bulletin. m. ISSN 0018-8867

**Indian Council for Cultural Relations**
Azad Bhavan, Indraprastha Estate, New Delhi 110001, India.
- Africa: a Documentation List. m. ISSN 0012-4664
- Africa Quarterly; a journal of African affairs. q. ISSN 0001-9828 (prep. by its Indian Centre for Africa)
- Cultural News from India. q. ISSN 0011-2887
- Indian Horizons. q.

**Indian Council of Agricultural Research**
Krishi Bhavan, Dr. Rajendra Prased Rd., New Delhi 110001, India.
- Indian Farming. m. ISSN 0019-4786
- Indian Horticulture. q. ISSN 0019-4875
- Indian Journal of Agricultural Science. m. ISSN 0019-5022
- Indian Journal of Agronomy. q. ISSN 0537-197X
- Indian Journal of Animal Sciences. m.
- Kheti. m. ISSN 0023-1088

**Indian Council of Basic Education**
c/o Gandhi Shikshan Bhavan, Opposite Iris Park, Juhu, Bombay 54, India.
- Quest in Education. q. ISSN 0048-6434

**Indian Council of Foreign Trade**
Co-operative Insurance Bldg., P. M. Rd., Bombay, India.
- I C O F T News Review. m. ISSN 0018-8980
- International Trade Review. (pub. by United Asia Publications Pvt. Ltd.)

**Indian Council of Historical Research**
35 Ferozeshah Rd., New Delhi 110001, India.
- I C H R Newsletter. q.
- Indian Council of Historical Research. Annual Report. a. ISSN 0304-7032
- Indian Historical Review. (pub. by Vikas Publishing House Pvt. Ltd.)
- Role of State Legislatures in the Freedom Struggle. irreg. (Distributed by: People's Publishing House Ltd., Rani Jhansi Rd., New Delhi 110005, India)

**Indian Council of Medical Research**
Box 4508, Ansari Nagar, New Delhi 110016, India.
- Indian Council of Medical Research. Report of the Advisory Committees. irreg. ISSN 0073-6317
- Indian Council of Medical Research. Special Report Series. ISSN 0073-6325
- Indian Journal of Medical Research. m. ISSN 0019-5340

**Indian Council of Social Science Research**
IPA Hostel Bldg., Indraprastha Estate, New Delhi 110001, India.
- Directory of Social Science Research Institutions in India. irreg.
- Gandhi Bibliography Series. (pub. by Orient Longman Ltd.)
- I C S S R Journal of Abstracts and Reviews. s-a. ISSN 0302-7546
- I C S S R Newsletter. q. ISSN 0018-9049
- I C S S R Research Abstracts Quarterly. q.
- Indian Dissertation Abstracts. (pub. by Popular Prakashan)
- Indian Psychological Abstracts. q. (Co-sponsor Indian Psychological Association)

**Indian Council of World Affairs**
Sapru House, Barakhamba Rd., New Delhi 110001, India.
- Foreign Affairs Reports. m. ISSN 0015-7155
- India Quarterly. q. ISSN 0019-4220

**Indian Cryogenics Council**
Jadavpur University, Calcutta 700032, India.
- Indian Journal of Cryogenics. q.

**Indian Dairy Science Association**
W-III-A Greater Kalish, P.O. Karnal. 132001 Haryana, India.
- Indian Dairyman. m. ISSN 0019-4603
- Indian Journal of Dairy Science. q. ISSN 0019-5146

**Indian Dental Association**
Bhart Bldgs., 1-18 Mount Rd., Madras 600002, India.
- Indian Dental Association, Journal. m. ISSN 0019-4611

**Indian Documentation Service**
Nai Subzi Mandi, Gurgaon 122001, Haryana, India.
- Guide to Indian Periodical Literature. q.(annual cumulation) ISSN 0017-5285
- Index to Indian Periodical Literature. a.

**Indian Drug Manufacturers Association**
332 Hind Rajastan Bldg., D.S. Phalke Rd., Dadar, Bombay 400014, India.
- Indian Drugs. m. ISSN 0019-462X

**Indian Ecological Society**
Punjab Agricultural University, Ludhiana 141004, Punjab, India.
- Indian Journal of Ecology. s-a. ISSN 0304-5250

**Indian Economic Association**
University of Bombay, Dept. of Economics, Bombay 400032, India.
- Indian Economic Journal. q. ISSN 0019-4662

**Indian Electrical Manufacturers' Association**
- Electrical India. (pub. by Chary Publications)

**Indian Express Newspapers (Bombay) Pvt. Ltd.**
Express Towers, Nariman Point, Bombay 400021, India.
- Financial Express. d. ISSN 0015-2005
- Screen. w. ISSN 0036-9551

**Indian Farm Mechanization**
C-62 Soami Nagar, New Delhi 11017, India.
- Indian Farm Mechanization. m. ISSN 0019-4778

**Indian Films**
c/o B. V. Dharap, Alaka Talkies, Poona 30, India.
- Indian Films. a.

**Indian Financial Journals Private Ltd.**
6-2 Moira St., Calcutta 17, India.
- Indian Finance. w. ISSN 0019-4794

**Indian Folklore Society**
- Folklore. (pub. by Indian Publications)

**Indian Foreign Affairs Association**
1 Jiwandal Bldg., Janpath, New Delhi, India.
- Indian Foreign Affairs. m. ISSN 0537-166X

**Indian Geographical Society**
University Centenary Bldgs., Chepauk, Madras 600005, India.
- Indian Geographical Journal. q. ISSN 0019-4824

**Indian Geologists' Association**
c/o Department of Geology, Panjab University, Chandigarh 160014, India.
- Indian Geologists' Association. Bi-Annual Bulletin. s-a.

**Indian Geophysical Union**
Hyderabad 7, India.
- Indian Geophysical Union Bulletin. a.
- Indian Geophysical Union Journal. q.

**Indian Geotechnical Society**
Institution of Engineers (India), Delhi Centre, Bahadur Shah Zafar Marg, New Delhi 110001, India.
- Indian Geotechnical Journal. q. ISSN 0046-8983

**Indian Gerontological Association**
C-207 Arvind Marg, Tilaknagar, Jaipur, India.
- Indian Journal of Gerontology. q. ISSN 0019-5219

**Indian Hospital Association**
c/o Dr. P. N. Ghei, Directorate General of Health Services, Nirman Bhavan, New Delhi 110001, India.
- Hospital Administration. q. ISSN 0018-5531

**Indian Hospital Pharmacists' Association**
R-566 New Rajinder Nagar, New Delhi 110060, India.
- Indian Journal of Hospital Pharmacy. bi-m. ISSN 0019-526X

**Indian Hotels Company Ltd.**
Taj Mahal Hotel, Apollo Bunder, Bombay, India.
- Taj. q.

**Indian Humanist Union**
4 Windsor Place, Lucknow, Uttar Pradesh, India.
- Humanist Outlook. q. ISSN 0018-7429

**Indian Industrial Directory**
29A Chandra Nath Chatterjee St., Calcutta 25, India.
- Calcutta Market. ISSN 0008-0640

**Indian Institute for National Integration**
Tulsipur, Cuttack 8, Orissa, India.
- Bharata Varsha. q.

**Indian Institute for Population Studies**
Gandhinagar, Madras 20, India.
- Population Review. s-a. ISSN 0032-471X

**Indian Institute of Advanced Study**
Rashtrapati Nivas, Summer Hill, Simla 171005, India.
- I I A S Newsletter. s-a.
- I I A S Occasional Papers. irreg.
- Indian Institute of Advanced Study. Transactions and Monographs. irreg. ISSN 0073-6465

**Indian Institute of Architects**
- Indian Institute of Architects. Journal. (pub. by Architects Publishing Corp. of India)

**Indian Institute of Asian Studies**
- Asian Economic and Social Review. (pub. by Asian Studies Press)

**Indian Institute of Bankers**
State Bank of India Bldg., Apollo St., Bombay 1, India.
- Indian Institute of Bankers. Journal. q. ISSN 0019-4921

**Indian Institute of Chemical Engineers**
Jadavpur University, c/o Dept of Chemical Engineering, Calcutta 700032, India.
- Indian Chemical Engineer. q. ISSN 0019-4506

**Indian Institute of Economics**
Himayatnagar, Hyderabad 500029, India.
- Asian Economic Review. q. ISSN 0004-4555

**Indian Institute of Foreign Trade**
Ashok Bhawan, 93 Nehru Pl., New Delhi 110024, India.
- Foreign Trade Bulletin. m. ISSN 0015-7317
- Foreign Trade Review. q. ISSN 0015-7325
- Indian Institute of Foreign Trade. Report. a. ISSN 0073-6473

**Indian Institute of Geography**
120/A Nehru Nagar East, Secunderabad 500026, Andhra Pradesh, India.
- Social Sciences Research Series. irreg.

**Indian Institute of History of Medicine**
Osmania Medical College Bldgs., Residency, Hyderabad 500001, Andhra Pradesh, India.
- Indian Institute of History of Medicine. Bulletin. q. (Co-sponsor: Central Council for Research in Indian Medicine and Homeopathy)

**Indian Institute of Homoeopaths**
c/o Dr. R. J. Murty, Murty Gardens, Srinagar Colony, Kumbakonam, India.
- Homoeopathy; for health and life. m. ISSN 0046-7820

**Indian Institute of Islamic Studies**
Panchkuin Rd., New Delhi 1, India.
- Studies in Islam. q. ISSN 0039-3711

**Indian Institute of Legal History**
- Legal History. (pub. by K. K. Roy (Private) Ltd.)

**Indian Institute of Management**
56-A B.T. Rd., Calcutta, India.
- Decision. s-a.

**Indian Institute of Metals**
2 Sambhunath Pandit St., Calcutta 700020, India.
- Indian Institute of Metals. Transactions. bi-m. ISSN 0019-493X

**Indian Institute of Packaging**
E-2 Marol Industrial Estate, MIDC, Andheri East, Bombay 400093, India.
- Packaging Digest. q.
- Packaging/India. q. ISSN 0030-9125

**Indian Institute of Personnel Management**
Park Hotel (Annexe), 17 Park St., Calcutta 700016, India.
- Industrial Relations. bi-m. ISSN 0019-8684

**Indian Institute of Public Administration**
Indraprastha Estate, Ring Rd., New Delhi 110002, India.
- Book Reviews in Public Administration. s-a.
- Documentation in Public Administration. q.
- F M U Occasional Lectures. irreg. ISSN 0085-1795 (prep. by its Financial Management Unit) (Order from: UBS Publishers Distributors Ltd., 5 Daryagang, Ansari Rd., Box 7015, New Delhi 110002, India)
- I P P A Newsletter. m.
- Indian Journal of Public Administration. q. ISSN 0019-5561
- Nagarlok; urban affairs quarterly. q. ISSN 0027-7584 (Centre for Urban Studies)

**Indian Institute of Public Opinion Private Ltd.**
2-A National Insurance Bldg., Parliament St., Box 288, New Delhi 110001, India.
- Indian Institute of Public Opinion. Monthly Public Opinion Surveys. m.
- Indian Institute of Public Opinion. Quarterly Economic Report. q. ISSN 0019-4948
- Monthly Commentary on Indian Economic Conditions. m. ISSN 0027-030X

**Indian Institute of Road Transport**
BEST House, Box 192, Fort, Bombay 1, India.
- Indian Institute of Road Transport. Monthly Bulletin. m. ISSN 0019-4956

**Indian Institute of Romani Studies**
- Roma. (pub. by Roma Publications)

**Indian Institute of Science**
Bangalore 560012, India.
- Indian Institute of Science. Journal. m. ISSN 0019-4964

**Indian Institute of Social Welfare and Business Management**
College Square West, Calcutta 7, India.
- Survey; a quarterly journal. q.

**Indian Institute of Sugarcane Research**
Indian Council of Agricultural Research, Lucknow 2, Uttar Pradesh, India.
- Indian Institute of Sugarcane Research, Lucknow. Annual Report. a. ISSN 0073-649X

**Indian Institute of Technology, Bombay**
Powai, Bombay, India.
- Indian Institute of Technology, Bombay. Series. irreg., 1971, no. 3. ISSN 0073-6503
- Metallurgical Engineer. a. (prep. by its Department of Metallurgical Engineering)

**Indian Institute of Technology, Calcutta**
5 Esplanade East, Calcutta 1, India.
- Journal of Science and Engineering Research. s-a. ISSN 0022-4413

**Indian Institute of Technology, Kanpur**
Computer Centre, Kanpur 20816, India.
- Indian Institute of Technology, Kanpur. Computer Centre. Quarterly Bulletin. q.

**Indian Institute of Technology, Kharagpur**
Kharagpur 721302, West Bengal, India.
- Indian Journal of Regional Science. s-a. ISSN 0046-9017 (Regional Science Association, India)

**Indian Institute of Technology, Madras**
The Registrar, Madras 36, India.
- Indian Institute of Technology, Madras. Annual Report. a. ISSN 0073-6511
- Indian Institute of Technology, Madras. Technical Communications. a. ISSN 0073-652X
- Journal of Mathematical and Physical Sciences. bi-m. ISSN 0047-2557

**Indian Institute of Tropical Meteorology**
Ramdurg House, University Rd., Poona 411005, India.
- Indian Institute of Tropical Meteorology. Annual Report. a.

**Indian Institute of Welding**
48-1 Diamond Harbour Rd., Calcutta 27, India.
- Indian Welding Journal. 3 per yr. ISSN 0046-9092

**Indian Institute of World Culture**
6 Shri B.P. Wadia Rd., Box 402, Basavangudi, Bangalore 4, India.
- Indian Institute of World Culture. Transactions. ISSN 0019-4972

**Indian Institution of Industrial Engineering**
- Industrial Engineering and Management. (pub. by Chary Publications)

**Indian International Trade Center**
59 Jolly Maker Chambers I, Nariman Point, Bombay 400021, India.
- I I T C Bulletin. s-m. ISSN 0019-4980
- I I T C Directory. a. ISSN 0073-6546

**Indian Investment Centre**
Jeevan Vihar Bldg., Parliament St., New Delhi 110001, India.
- Indian Investment Centre. Monthly Newsletter. m. ISSN 0019-4999

**Indian Journal of Animal Health**
61-4 Belgachia Rd., Calcutta 700037, India.
- Indian Journal of Animal Health. s-a. ISSN 0019-5057

**Indian Journal of Engineers**
21-B Lansdowne Terrace, Calcutta 26, India.
- Indian Journal of Engineers. q.

**Indian Journal of Medical Sciences Trust**
c/o J. C. Patel, Back Bay View, New Queen's Rd., Bombay 4, India.
- Indian Journal of Medical Sciences. m. ISSN 0019-5359

**Indian Journal of Photography**
612-A Band Stand Area, Delhi 110009, India.
- Indian Journal of Photography. m.

**Indian Journal of Theology**
c/o Bishops's College, 224 Lower Circular Rd., Calcutta 700017, India.
- Indian Journal of Theology. q. ISSN 0019-5685

**Indian Jute Mills Association**
Royal Exchange, 26 Netaji Subhas Rd., Calcutta 1, India.
- Indian Jute Mills Association. Annual Summary of Jute and Gunny Statistics. a. ISSN 0073-6562
- Indian Jute Mills Association. Loom and Spindle Statistics. biennial. ISSN 0073-6570
- Jute Chronicle. bi-m. ISSN 0022-7110
- Monthly Summary of Jute and Gunny Statistics. m. ISSN 0027-0598

**Indian Law Institute**
Bhagwandas Rd., New Delhi 110001, India.
- Annual Survey of Indian Law. a. ISSN 0570-2666
- Index to Indian Legal Periodicals. s-a. ISSN 0019-4034
- Indian Law Institute. Journal. q. ISSN 0019-5731

**Indian Leather Technologists' Association**
Mercantile Bldgs., Lalbazar St., Calcutta 700001, India.
- Indian Leather Technologists' Association. Journal. m. ISSN 0019-5758

**Indian Leprosy Association**
A-2/50 Safdarjung Enclave, New Delhi 110016, India.
- Leprosy in India. q. ISSN 0024-1024

**Indian Library Association**
Delhi Public Library, S.P. Mukerji Marg, Delhi 110006, India.
- Indian Library Association. Bulletin. q. ISSN 0019-5782

**Indian Library Movement**
148 Allenby Lines, Ambala Cantt, India.
- Indian Library Movement. q.

**Indian Machine Tool Manufacturers' Association**
- Machine Building Industry. (pub. by Chary Publications)

**Indian Machine Tools Journal**
75 New Stock Exchange Building, Apollo Street, Fort, Bombay 400001, India.
- Indian Machine Tools Journal. m. ISSN 0445-7854

**Indian Magic Expansion Board**
- All India Magic Circle Bulletin. (pub. by All India Magic Circle)

**Indian Mathematical Society**
Tata Institute of Fundamental Research, Homi Bhabha Rd., Bombay 400005, India.
- Indian Mathematical Society. Journal. a. ISSN 0019-5839
- Mathematics Student. q. ISSN 0025-5742

**Indian Medical Association**
I.M.A. House, Indraprastha Marg, New Delhi 110001, India
- Apka Swasthya. m. ISSN 0003-6498 (Subscr. Address: Apka Swasthya, I.M.A. Building, C. 7/31 Chet Ganj, Varanasi 1, India)
- Indian Medical Association. Journal. s-m. ISSN 0019-5847

**Indian Medical Association, Bengal State Branch**
67 Dharmatola St., Calcutta 13, India.
- Bengal Medical Journal. m. ISSN 0005-8793

**Indian Medical Association, Bihar State Branch**
Medical Association Bldg., Patna 800004, India.
- Patna Journal of Medicine. m. ISSN 0031-3084 (Co-sponsor: Patna Medical Association)

**Indian Medical Association, Karnataka State Branch**
IMA House, Alur Venkata Rao Rd., Bangalore 560018, India.
- Karnataka Medical Journal. q.

**Indian Medical Association, Kerala State Branch**
Sreedevi Clinic, Palghat 1, India.
- Kerala Medical Journal. q.

**Indian Merchants' Chamber**
Indian Merchants' Chamber Bldg., 76 Veer Nariman Rd., Fort, Bombay, India.
- Indian Merchants' Chamber. Journal. m. ISSN 0019-5901

**Indian Meteorological Society**
The Observatory, Lodi Rd., New Delhi 3, India.
- Vayu Mandal; science journal on the human environment. q.

**Indian Military Academy**
Calcutta, India.
- Indian Military Academy Journal. ISSN 0019-591X

**Indian Museum, Calcutta**
27 Jawaharlal Nehru Rd., Calcutta 13, India.
- Indian Museum Bulletin. s-a. ISSN 0019-5987

**Indian Musicological Society**
Jambu Bet, Dandia Bazar, Baroda, India.
- Indian Musicological Society. Journal. q.

**Indian National Congress. All India Congress Committee**
*see* All India Congress Committee

**Indian National Science Academy**
Bahadur Shah Zafar Marg, New Delhi 110001, India.
- Indian Journal of History of Science. s-a. ISSN 0019-5235
- Indian Journal of Pure and Applied Mathematics. m. ISSN 0019-5588
- Indian National Science Academy. Biographical Memoirs of Fellows. irreg.
- Indian National Science Academy. Bulletin. irreg.
- Indian National Science Academy. Mathematical Tables. irreg.
- Indian National Science Academy. Monographs. irreg.
- Indian National Science Academy. Proceedings. parts A and B published in alternate months. ISSN 0073-6600
- Indian National Science Academy. Transactions. irreg.
- Indian National Science Academy. Year Book. a. ISSN 0073-6619
- Progress of Science in India. irreg. ISSN 0556-1906
- Source Materials on the History of Science in India. irreg.

**Indian National Scientific Documentation Centre**
Hillside Rd., New Delhi 110012, India.
- Annals of Library Science and Documentation. q. ISSN 0003-4835
- Contents List of Soviet Scientific Periodicals. m.
- Directory of Scientific Research in Indian Universities. a. (India. University Grants Commission) (Co-sponsor: Council of Scientific and Industrial Research)
- I N S D O C. Russian Scientific and Technical Publications. Accessions List. bi-m.
- I N S D O C Union Catalogue Series. irreg., 1973, no. 13. ISSN 0073-6627
- Indian Science Abstracts. m. ISSN 0019-6339

**Indian National Shipowners' Association**
Scindia House, Ballard Estate, Bombay 400038, India.
- Indian Shipping. m.

**Indian National Trade Union Congress**
17 Janpath, New Delhi 1, India.
- I N T U C Session: Brief Review. a.
- Indian Worker; English weekly journal of labour movement in India led by INTUC. w.

**Indian Oil Corporation Ltd.**
Indianoil Bhawan, Janpath, New Delhi, India.
- Oil Stream. m. (prep. by its Refineries and Pipelines Division)

**Indian Optometric Association**
- Optometry Today. (pub. by Professional Publications)

**Indian Orthopaedic Association**
- Indian Journal of Orthopaedics. (pub. by All India Institute of Medical Sciences. Department of Orthopaedic Surgery)

**Indian Parliamentary and Scientific Committee**
2 Telegraph Lane, New Delhi 1, India.
- Science in Parliament. q. ISSN 0036-8407

**Indian Pharmaceutical Association**
Kalina Santacruz East, Bombay 400029, India.
- Indian Journal of Pharmacy. bi-m. ISSN 0019-5472
- Pharma Times. m. ISSN 0031-6849

**Indian Philosophical Association, Amravati**
- Philosophical Association. Journal. (pub. by Popular Prakashan)

**Indian Physical Society**
2-3 Raja Subodh Mallik Rd., Calcutta 700032, India.
- Physics Teacher. q.

**Indian Physics Association**
I. I. T., Powai, Bombay 400076, India (Subscr. Address: Editor, Physics News, Tata Institute of Fundamental Research, Homi Bhabha Rd., Bombay 400005, India)
- Physics News. q.

**Indian Phytopathological Society**
Indian Agricultural Research Institute, Division of Mycology, New Delhi 110012, India.
- Indian Phytopathology. q.

**Indian Plywood Industries Research Institute**
Box 2273, Tumkur Rd., Bangalore 560022, India.
- I P I R I Journal. s-a. ISSN 0046-9033
- Indian Academy of Wood Science. Journal. s-a.

**Indian Political Science Association**
38/18 Probyn Rd., Delhi 110007, India.
- Indian Journal of Political Science. q. ISSN 0019-5510

**Indian Poultry Club**
Indian Veterinary Research Institute, Izatnagar, Uttar Pradesh, India.
- Indian Poultry Gazette. q. ISSN 0019-6142

**Indian Poultry Lovers Association**
14/1-A Beltala Rd., Calcutta 26, India.
- Indian Poultry Review. fortn. ISSN 0019-6150

**Indian Poultry Science Association**
Krishi Bhavan, New Delhi 1, India.
- Indian Journal of Poultry Science. q. ISSN 0019-5529

**Indian Psychiatric Society**
c/o S. C. S. Master, 322 M. Gandhi Rd., Poona, India.
- Indian Journal of Psychiatry. q. ISSN 0019-5545

**Indian Psychoanalytical Society**
14 Parsibagan Lane, Calcutta 700009, India.
- Samiksa. q.

**Indian Psychological Association**
I.I.P.A. Hostel Building, Indraprastha Estate, Ring Rd., New Delhi 110001, India.
- Indian Journal of Psychology. q. ISSN 0019-5553

**Indian Psychometric and Educational Research Association**
University of Patna, Dept. of Education, Patna 4, India.
- Indian Journal of Psychometry and Education. s-a. ISSN 0046-9009

**Indian Public Health Association**
110 Chittaranjan Ave., Calcutta 700012, India.
- Indian Journal of Public Health. q. ISSN 0019-557X

**Indian Publications**
3 British Indian St., Calcutta 700069, India.
- Folklore; devoted to folk literature, folk arts & crafts, folk music & dance, tribal studies and related social science objects. m. ISSN 0015-5896 (Indian Folklore Society)
- Human Events; devoted to human culture, literature and civilization. m. ISSN 0018-7186 (Monograph Association of India)

**Indian Radiological Association**
13 Bheemanna Mudali Garden St., Madras 600018, India.
- Indian Journal of Radiology. q. ISSN 0019-560X

**Indian Reading Association**
J-15 Haus Khas Enclave, Mehrauli Road, New Delhi 16, India.
- Reading Journal. a.

**Indian Roads Congress**
Jamnagar House, Shahjahan Rd., New Delhi 110011, India.
- General Report on Road Research Work Done in India. a. (prep. by its Highway Research Board)
- I R C Special Publication. irreg.
- Indian Highways. m.
- Indian Roads Congress. Highway Research Board Bulletin. s-a.
- Indian Roads Congress. Journal. 4 per yr (approx.) ISSN 0046-905X

**Indian Rubber Industries Association**
Navjivan Society, Bldg. No. 3, 8th Fl., Lamington Road, Bombay 400008, India.
- Rubber India. m. ISSN 0035-9491

**Indian School of Mines**
Dhanbad 826004, Bihar, India.
- Indian School of Mines. Annual Report. a. ISSN 0304-1158

**Indian School of Social Sciences**
Trivandrum 695001, Kerala, India.
- Social Scientist. m.

**Indian Science Congress Association**
14 Dr. Biresh Guha St., Calcutta 700017, India.
- Everyman's Science. bi-m. ISSN 0531-495X
- Indian Science Congress Association. Proceedings. a. in 4 pts. ISSN 0085-1817

**Indian Science News Association**
92 Acharya Prafullachandra Rd., Calcutta 9, India.
- Science and Culture; a monthly journal of natural and cultural sciences. m. ISSN 0036-8156

**Indian Scientific Translators Association**
c/o Indian National Scientific Documentation Centre, Hillside Rd., New Delhi 110012, India.
- J I S T A. (Journal of the Indian Scientific Translators Association) q.

**Indian Secular Society**
4 Joothica, 22 Naushir Bharucha Rd., Bombay 7, India.
- Secularist. m. ISSN 0049-0008

**Indian Social Institute**
Lodi Rd., New Delhi 110003, India.
- Social Action. 4 per yr. ISSN 0037-7627

**Indian Society for Information Science**
c/o Library, Indian Institute of Science, Bangalore 560012, India.
- I S I S Bulletin. q.

**Indian Society for Malaria and Other Communicable Diseases**
22 Alipur Rd., Delhi 110006, India.
- Journal of Communicable Diseases. q.

**Indian Society for Nuclear Techniques**
Nuclear Research Laboratory, Indian Agricultural Research Institute, New Delhi 110012, India.
- Journal of Nuclear Agriculture and Biology. q.

**Indian Society for Plant Physiology**
Division of Plant Physiology & Phytotron, Indian Agricultural Research Institute, New Delhi 110012, India.
- Indian Journal of Plant Physiology. s-a. ISSN 0019-5502

**Indian Society for Plantation Crops**
Kasaragod, India.
- Journal of Plantation Crops. s-a. ISSN 0304-5242

**Indian Society for Training and Development**
- I S T D Review. (pub. by Subhas Chandra Roy)

**Indian Society of Agricultural Chemists**
c/o Department of Chemistry, University of Allahabad, Allahabad 211002, India.
- Indian Journal of Agricultural Chemistry. s-a.

**Indian Society of Agricultural Economics**
46-48 Esplanade Mansions, Mahatma Gandhi Rd., Fort, Bombay 400023, India.
- Indian Journal of Agricultural Economics. q. ISSN 0019-5014

**Indian Society of Agricultural Engineers**
G. B. Pant University of Agriculture and Technology, Dept. of Agricultural Engineering, Pannagar 263145, India.
- Journal of Agricultural Engineering. q.

**Indian Society of Agricultural Statistics**
Box 310, New Delhi, India.
- Indian Journal of Agricultural Statistics. Journal. s-a. ISSN 0019-6363

**Indian Society of Anaesthetists**
c/o Dr. N. K. Misra, Secretary, IMA Bldg., Medical Association Rd., Patna 800004, India.
- Indian Journal of Anaesthesia. q. ISSN 0019-5049

**Indian Society of Criminology**
University of Madras, Madras 600005, India.
- Indian Journal of Criminology. s-a.

**Indian Society of Earth Sciences**
Department of Geology, Presidency College, Calcutta 700073, India.
- Indian Journal of Earth Sciences. s-a.

**Indian Society of Earth Scientists**
c/o Dept. of Geology, Poona University, Poona 7, India.
- Bulletin of Earth Sciences. a.

**Indian Society of Earthquake Technology**
Secretary, Roorkee, Uttar Pradesh, India.
- Indian Society of Earthquake Technology. Bulletin; journal of international earthquake engineering. q. ISSN 0019-6371

**Indian Society of Extension Education**
Indian Agricultural Research Institute, Delhi 110012, India.
- Indian Journal of Extension Education. q. ISSN 0537-1996 (prep. by its Division of Agricultural Extension)

**Indian Society of Gandhian Studies**
University of Allahabad, Gandhi Bhawan, Allahabad, India.
- Journal of Gandhian Studies. q.

**Indian Society of Genetics and Plant Breeding**
c/o Indian Agricultural Research Institute, New Delhi 1100, India.
- Indian Journal of Genetics and Plant Breeding. 3 per yr. ISSN 0019-5200 (prep. by its Division of Genetics)

**Indian Society of International Law**
7-8 Scindia House, New Delhi 110001, India.
- Indian Journal of International Law. q. ISSN 0019-5294
- Indian Society of International Law. Publications. irreg. ISSN 0073-6678

**Indian Society of Psychiatric Social Work**
Hospital for Mental Diseases, Kanke, Ranchi 6, India.
- Indian Journal of Psychiatric Social Work. a. ISSN 0302-1610

**Indian Society of Soil Science**
Indian Agricultural Research Institute, Division of Soil Science and Agricultural Chemistry, New Delhi 110012, India.
- Indian Society of Soil Science. Journal. q. ISSN 0019-638X

**Indian Sociological Society**
Centre for the Study of Social Systems, Jawaharlal Nehru University, New Delhi 110057, India.
- Sociological Bulletin. s-a. ISSN 0038-0229

**Indian Standards Institution**
Manak Bhavan, 9 Bahadur Shah Zafar Marg, New Delhi 110002, India.
- I S I Bulletin. m. ISSN 0019-0632
- Standards: Monthly Additions. m. ISSN 0038-9684

**Indian Statistical Institute**
203 Barrackpore Trunk Rd., Calcutta 700035, India.
- Indian Statistical Institute. Annual Report. (pub. by Statistical Publishing Society)
- Indian Statistical Institute. Econometric and Social Sciences Series. Research Monographs. (pub. by Statistical Publishing Society)
- Indian Statistical Institute. Research and Training School. Publications. (pub. by Statistical Publishing Society)
- Indian Statistical Institute. Statistics and Probability Series. Research Monographs. (pub. by Statistical Publishing Society)
- Indian Statistical Series. irreg, 1970, nos. 24, 25. ISSN 0073-6724
- Samvadadhvam. (pub. by Statistical Publishing Society)
- Sankhya. (pub. by Statistical Publishing Society)

**Indian Statistical Institute. Documentation Research and Training Centre**
112 Cross Rd., Malleswaram, Bangalore 3, India.
- Indian Statistical Institute. Documentation Research and Training Centre. Annual Seminar. a. ISSN 0067-3439

**Indian Statistical Institute. Library**
Asutosh Bldg., Calcutta 12, India.
- Indian Statistical Institute. Library. Bibliographic Series. irreg. ISSN 0073-6708

**Indian Study Group of International Affairs**
University of Madras, Chepauk, Triplicane P.O., Madras 600005, Tamil Nadu, India.
- Indian Yearbook of International Affairs. a. ISSN 0537-2704

**Indian Sugar Mills Association**
India Exchange, India Exchange Place, Calcutta 1, India.
- Indian Sugar. m. ISSN 0019-6428

**Indian Technical Education Society**
394 Lamington Rd., Bombay 400004, India.
- Radio Services; India's oldest magazine of radio, electronics, TV. m. ISSN 0033-8044

**Indian Tourist**
45 Bipin Behari Ganguly St., Calcutta 12, India.
- Indian Tourist. m. ISSN 0046-9068

**Indian Town and Country Planning Association**
11 Horniman Circle, Fort, Bombay, India.
- Town and Country Planning Association Quarterly Journal. q.

**Indian Vacuum Society**
c/o Technical Physics Division, Bhabha Atomic Research Centre, Bombay 400085, India.
- V A C News. q.

**Indian Vegetarian Congress**
The Grove, No. 1, Eldams Rd., Madras 18, India.
- Indian Vegetarian Congress Quarterly. q. ISSN 0019-6460

**Indian Verse**
9-3 Tamer Lane, Calcutta 9, India.
- Indian Verse; voice of the Indian poets. q.

**Indian Veterinary Association**
10 Ave. Rd., Madras 34, India.
- Indian Veterinary Journal; a monthly record of veterinary science. m. ISSN 0019-6479

**Indian Veterinary Research Institute**
Mukteswar-Kumaon, Izatnagar, Uttar Pradesh, India.
- Indian Veterinary Research Institute. Annual Report. a. ISSN 0304-7067

**Indian Woollen Mills' Federation**
Churchgate Chambers, 7th Floor, 5 New Marine Lines, Bombay 400020, India.
- Wool and Woolens of India. q. ISSN 0043-7808

**Indian Youth Congress**
16-C Ferozeshah Rd., New Delhi 110001, India.
- Young March. m.

**India's Stamp Journal**
17 Scouter St., Byculla, Bombay 400008, India.
- India's Stamp Journal. m.

**Indo-American Chamber of Commerce**
Vulcan Insurance Bldg., Veer Nariman Rd., Churchgate, Bombay 20, India.
- Indo-American Chamber of Commerce Newsletter. m.

**Indo-American Society**
2B, Mona Lisa, 17 Camac St., Calcuta 700017, India.
- Calcuttan. s-a. ISSN 0045-3862

**Indo-British Historical Society**
4 Rajaram Mehta Ave., Madras 29, India.
- Indo-British Review. q. ISSN 0019-7211

**Indo-Burma Petroleum Company**
Gillander House, Netaji Subhas Rd., Calcutta 1, India.
- Indo-Burma Petroleum Company. Annual Report. a.

**Indo Foreign Publications**
127 Mahatma Gandhi Rd., Bombay 1, India.
- Indo-German Review. m. ISSN 0019-7238

**Indo-Iran Society**
Tilak Marg, New Delhi 110001, India.
- Indo-Iran Journal. q. ISSN 0042-9740

**Indo-Soviet Cultural Society**
6 Jamuna Bhavan, Asaf Ali Rd., New Delhi 1, India.
- Amity. m.

**Indore Sambagh Pustakalaya Sangh**
11 Khatipura Marg, Indore 2, India.
- Pustakalaya Sandesh. q. ISSN 0033-4707

**Indore University**
see University of Indore

**Industrial Development Bank of India**
Jolly Maker Chambers No. 1, 227 Backbay Reclamation Scheme, Bombay 400021, India.
- Industrial Development Bank of India. Annual Report. a. ISSN 0073-7372

**Industrial Economist**
1/124 Lloyds Rd., Madras 600086, India.
- Industrial Economist; a fortnightly on industry and finance. fortn. ISSN 0019-8188

**Industrial Expansion**
K.S. South Extension, Part 1, New Delhi, India.
- Industrial Expansion. q.

**Industrial Links Ltd.**
F-4 Kailash Colony, New Delhi 48, India.
- National Debate. m.

**Industrial Publications**
Taj Building, 3rd Floor, 210 Dr. D. N. Rd., Bombay 400001, India.
- Chemical Engineering World; India's foremost technical journal. m. ISSN 0009-2517
- Electrical and Electronics World. bi-m.

**Industrial Vista**
BI-23A Hauz Khas, New Delhi 110016, India.
- Industrial Vista. m.

**Industrocom International**
10 Mangal Baugh, Pushpa Park, Malad, Bombay 400064, India.
- Buy from India; Indian exporters directory. a.

**Industry & Finance**
G Block, Ambewadi, Girgaum, Bombay 4, India.
- Industry & Finance. m. ISSN 0019-9443

**Infantry School**
Mhow, India.
- Infantry Journal. s-a. ISSN 0019-9540

**Information Research Academy**
Ground Floor, Flat No. 9, 37 Syed Amir Ali Ave., Calcutta 700019, India.
- Bibliography of Publications from Economic Research Centres in India. irreg., latest edition, 1974.
- Directory of Economic Research Centres in India. irreg., 2nd edition, 1975.
- Index to Indian Economic Journals. m. ISSN 0019-4026
- Indian Management Abstracts. q. ISSN 0019-5820
- Indiana. q. ISSN 0019-6509

**Inquilab Publications**
245 Ripon Rd., Bombay 400034, India.
- Sports Week. w.

**Institut Francais d'Indologie**
Pondicherry, India.
- Institut Francais d'Indologie. Publications. irreg., 1973, no. 50. ISSN 0073-8352

**Institut Francais de Pondichery**
Box 33, Pondichery 605001, India.
- Institut Francais de Pondichery. Section Scientifique et Technique. Travaux. irreg., no. 12, 1973. ISSN 0073-8336
- Institut Francais de Pondichery. Section Scientifique et Technique. Travaux. Hors Serie. irreg. 1973, vol.12. ISSN 0073-8344

**Institute for Defence Studies and Analyses**
Sapru House, Barakhamba Rd., New Delhi 110001, India.
- Institute for Defence Studies and Analyses. Journal. q. ISSN 0020-2606
- Institute for Defence Studies and Analyses. Strategic Digest. m.
- News Review on China, Mongolia and the Koreas. m.
- News Review on Japan, South East Asia, and Australasia. m.
- News Review on North America & Europe. m.
- News Review on West Asia. m.

**Institute for Electoral Studies**
CA-33, Tagore Garden, New Delhi 110027, India.
- Election Archives. q. ISSN 0046-1644

**Institute for Financial Management and Research, Madras**
Madras 600034, India
- I F M R Publications. irreg. (Dist. by: Vora & Co., Publishers, 3 Round Bldg., Kalbadevi, Bombay 400002, India)

**Institute of Afro-Asian and World Affairs**
14 Theatre Communication Bldg., Connaught Circus, New Delhi 1, India.
- Afro-Asian and World Affairs. q. ISSN 0002-0605

**Institute of Applied Manpower Research**
Indrapastha Estate, Ring Rd., New Delhi 110001, India.
- I.A.M.R. Reports. irreg. (3-4 per year) ISSN 0418-5633
- Manpower Documentation. q. ISSN 0047-5793
- Manpower Journal. q. ISSN 0542-5808

**Institute of Ayurvedic Studies and Research**
52 Mahatma Gandhi Rd., Calcutta 700009, India.
- Ayurveda-Bharati; a multilingual quarterly journal of Ayurveda & Indian culture. q. ISSN 0005-2485

**Institute of Chartered Accountants of India**
- Chartered Accountant. (pub. by Calcutta Press (P) Ltd.)

**Institute of Community Psychiatry and Mental Health**
Department of Psychiatry, J. J. Group of Hospitals, Byculla, Bombay 400008, India.
- Community Psychiatry Journal.

**Institute of Company Secretaries of India.**
1 Rani Jhansi Rd., New Delhi 110055, India.
- Chartered Secretary. m.

**Institute of Constitutional and Parliamentary Studies**
18-21 Vithalbhai Patel House, Rafi Marg, New
Delhi 110001, India.
- Conparlist. m. ISSN 0010-6313
- Journal of Constitutional & Parliamentary Studies.
  q. ISSN 0022-0043
- Law and Society Quarterly. q. (prep. by its Centre
  for the Study of Law and Society)
- Loktantra Samiksha. q. ISSN 0024-595X

**Institute of Consulting Engineers**
9 Hastings St., Calcutta 1, India.
- Institute of Consulting Engineers. Journal. q.
  ISSN 0020-2800

**Institute of Cost and Works Accountants of India**
12 Sudder St., Calcutta 700016, India.
- Management Accountant. m. ISSN 0025-1674

**Institute of Defence Management**
Bolarum P.O., Secunderabad 500010, India.
- Defence Management. s-a.

**Institute of Directors, India**
- Director. (pub. by India-International News
  Service)

**Institute of Economic Geography**
4/1 Ashton Rd., Calcutta 20, India.
- Institute of Economic Geography, India. Journal.
  s-a.

**Institute of Economic Growth, Delhi**
Delhi, India.
- Asian Social Science Bibliography with
  Annotations and Abstracts. (pub. by Vikas
  Publishing House Pvt. Ltd.)
- Contributions to Indian Sociology. (pub. by Vikas
  Publishing House Pvt. Ltd.)
- Institute of Economic Growth, Delhi. Census
  Studies. irreg., 1969, no. 1. ISSN 0070-3311
- Studies in Economic Growth. (pub. by Vikas
  Publishing House Pvt. Ltd.)

**Institute of Economic Research**
Deputy Director, Vidyagiri, Dharwar 580004,
Karnataka, India.
- Hukerikar Memorial Lecture Series. irreg. ISSN
  0419-0432
- Institute of Economic Research. Journal. s-a.
  ISSN 0020-2851 (prep. by its Demographic
  Research Centre)
- Institute of Economic Research. Publications on
  Demography. irreg.
- Institute of Economic Research. Publications on
  Economics. irreg.
- Institute of Economic Research. Publications on
  Family Planning. irreg.

**Institute of Hematology**
4 Pusa Road, New Delhi 5, India.
- Blood Therapy Journal. bi-m. ISSN 0006-5005

**Institute of Historical Studies**
35 Theatre Rd., Calcutta 17, India.
- Quarterly Review of Historical Studies. q. ISSN
  0033-5800

**Institute of History of Medicine**
- Institute of History of Medicine. Bulletin. (pub. by
  Central Council for Research in Indian Medicine
  and Homoeopathy)

**Institute of Human Study**
Hyderabad 7, India.
- New Race. q. ISSN 0028-6532

**Institute of Indian Foundrymen**
Allenby Court, 1/2 Allenby Road, Calcutta 700020,
W. Bengal, India.
- Indian Foundry Journal. m.

**Institute of Librarians (I.O.L.)**
c/o Sanskrit College, 1 Bankim Chatterjee St.,
Calcutta 700073, India.
- Indian Journal of Library Science. q.

**Institute of Marketing and Management**
Box 120, New Delhi, India.
- Marketing & Management Digest. m.

**Institute of Mathematical Sciences**
Adyar, Madras 20, India.
- Symposia on Theoretical Physics and
  Mathematics. irreg., 1970, vol. 10. ISSN 0082-
  075X

**Institute of Medical Sciences**
*see under* **Banaras Hindu University**

**Institute of Office Management (India)**
N-34 Jangpura Extension, New Delhi 110014,
India.
- Office Management. bi-m.

**Institute of Political and Social Studies**
357-1C Prince Anwar Shah Rd., Calcutta 31, India.
- I P S S Bulletin. ISSN 0019-0403

**Institute of Psychology and Graphology**
c/o P. N. Gupta, Ed., 32 Tilak Rd., Dehra Dun,
India.
- Practical Psychology. m. ISSN 0032-6453

**Institute of Public Enterprises**
University Campus, Hyderabad, India.
- I. P. E. News Letter. q.

**Institute of Rail Transport**
Room No. 264, Rail Bhavan, New Delhi, India.
- Institute of Rail Transport. Journal. q. ISSN 0020-
  3114

**Institute of Secretariat Training and Management**
Ramakrishnapuram, New Delhi 110022, India.
- Institute of Secretariat Training and Management.
  Annual Report. a. ISSN 0304-7083

**Institute of Social Sciences**
*see under* **Agra University**

**Institute of Social Studies**
179 Bipin Behari Ganguly St., Calcutta 12, India.
- Society and Culture. s-a. ISSN 0037-9662

**Institute of Socialist Education**
4 Rajendra Prasad Rd., New Delhi, India.
- Peoples Sector.

**Institute of Theoretical Physics**
Bignan Kutir, 4-1 Mohan Bagan Lane, Calcutta
700004, India.
- Indian Journal of Theoretical Physics. q. ISSN
  0019-5693

**Institute of Town Planners, India**
4-A Ring Rd., Indraprastha Estate, New Delhi,
India.
- Institute of Town Planners, India. Journal. q.
  ISSN 0537-9679
- Institute of Town Planners, India. Newsletter. m.

**Institute of Traditional Cultures, Madras**
University of Madras, Madras 600005, India.
- Institute of Traditional Cultures, Madras. Bulletin.
  s-a.

**Institute of Workers Education**
2A Prospect Chambers, Dr. D.N. Rd., Bombay
400001, India.
- Labour Chronicle. m.

**Institution of Chemists (India)**
Chemical Dept., Medical College, Calcutta 73,
India.
- Institution of Chemists (India). Journal. bi-m.
  ISSN 0020-3254
- Institution of Chemists (India). Proceedings. q.

**Institution of Electrical Engineers-Institution of
Electronic and Radio Engineers**
54 Nandidurg Rd., Bangalore 560046, India.
- I. E. E. - I. E. R. E. Proceedings - India. bi-m.
  ISSN 0018-9146

**Institution of Electronics and Telecommunication
Engineers**
Plot No. 2, Institutional Area, Lodi Rd., New Delhi
110003, India.
- Institution of Electronics and Telecommunication
  Engineers. Journal. m.
- Institution of Electronics and Telecommunication
  Engineers. Students' Journal. q.

**Institution of Engineers (India)**
8 Gokdale Rd., Calcutta 700020, India.
- Institution of Engineers (India). Bulletin. m. ISSN
  0020-3343

- Institution of Engineers (India). Chemical
  Engineering Division. Journal. 3 per yr. ISSN
  0020-3351
- Institution of Engineers (India). Civil Engineering
  Division. Journal. bi-m. ISSN 0020-336X
- Institution of Engineers (India). Directory.
  quadrennial. ISSN 0073-9782
- Institution of Engineers (India). Electrical
  Engineering Division. Journal. bi-m. ISSN 0020-
  3386
- Institution of Engineers (India). Electronics and
  Telecommunication Engineering Division. Journal.
  3 per yr. ISSN 0020-3378
- Institution of Engineers (India). Environmental
  Engineering Division. Journal. 3 per yr.
- Institution of Engineers (India). General
  Engineering Division. Journal. 3 per yr.
- Institution of Engineers (India). Hindi Section.
  Journal. 3 per yr.
- Institution of Engineers (India). Industrial
  Development and General Engineering Division.
  Journal. 3 per yr.
- Institution of Engineers (India). Mechanical
  Engineering Division. Journal. bi-m. ISSN 0020-
  3408
- Institution of Engineers (India). Mining and
  Metallurgy Division. Journal. 3 per yr. ISSN
  0020-3394
- Institution of Engineers (India). Students' Journal.
  q.

**Institution of Engineers (India) National Design and
Research Forum**
No. 3 Vidhana Vee Dhi, Bangalore 1, India.
- Engineering Design. q.

**Institution of Marine Technologists**
c/o Ericson & Richards, 32 Nicol Rd., Ballard
Estate, Bombay 400038, India.
- Institution of Marine Technologists. Journal. s-a.
  ISSN 0020-3475

**Institution of Surveyors**
c/o Chief Engineer, Delhi Zone, Delhi Cantt 10,
India.
- Indian Surveyor. s-a.

**Integrated Management**
51 11th Main Rd., Malleswaram, Bangalore 560066,
India.
- Integrated Management; the manager's magazine
  of India. m. ISSN 0020-4870

**International Academy of Indian Culture**
J-22 Hauz Khas Enclave, New Delhi 16, India.
- International Academy of Indian Culture. Report.
  a. ISSN 0074-123X

**International Agency for Research in Library History**
- Library History Review. (pub. by K. K. Roy
  (Private) Ltd.)

**International Aryan League**
- Vedic Light. (pub. by Sarvadeshik Arya Pratinidhi
  Sabha)

**International Association for the History of
Agriculture**
- History of Agriculture. (pub. by K. K. Roy
  (Private) Ltd.)

**International Book House, Ltd.**
9 Ash Lane, Mahatma Gandhi Rd., Bombay 1,
India.
- State Bank of India. Report of the Central Board
  of Directors. a. ISSN 0585-0991

**International Centre for Kathakali**
1-84 Rajendra Nagar, New Delhi 5, India.
- Kathakali. q. ISSN 0022-9326

**International Co-Operative Alliance. Regional Office
and Education Centre for South-East Asia**
Box 3312, 43 Friends Colony, New Delhi 110014,
India
(Publications of regional offices can also be ordered
from: International Cooperative Alliance, World
Headquarters, 11 Upper Grosvenor St., London
WIX 9PA, England)
- Annotated Bibliography of Literature on
  Cooperative Movements in South-East Asia. s-a.
- Cooperative News Service. m. ISSN 0443-899X
- Cooperative Press in South-East Asia. irreg.
- Cooperative Trade Directory for Southeast Asia.
  irreg., 1970, 3rd ed. supplement. ISSN 0069-9837
- Directory of Cooperative Organisations in South-
  East Asia. irreg. ISSN 0419-2443
- Documentation Bulletin for South-East Asia. q.

• I C A Regional Bulletin. q.
• I C A Trade News. m.
• International Cooperative Alliance. Cooperative Series. irreg. ISSN 0074-4255

**International Commission on Irrigation and Drainage**
48 Nyaya Marg, Chanakyapuri, New Delhi 110021, India.
• Bibliography on Irrigation, Drainage, River Training and Flood Control/Bibliographie Relative aux Irrigations, au Drainage, a la Regularisation des Cours d'Eau et la Matrise des Crues. a.; no. 20, 1975. ISSN 0523-302X
• I C I D Bulletin. s-a. ISSN 0579-5427
• International Commission on Irrigation and Drainage. Congress Reports. triennial since 1969; 1975, 9th, Moscow. ISSN 0074-2732
• International Commission on Irrigation and Drainage. Report. a.; latest issue, 1976. ISSN 0538-5768

**International Confederation of Free Trade Unions (ICFTU) Asian Regional Organization**
P-20, Green Park Extension, Delhi 110016, India.
• Asian Labour. m. ISSN 0004-4601

**International Council on Social Welfare**
Regional Office for Asia and Western Pacific, 175 Dadabhai Naorji Rd., Bombay 400001, India.
• International Council on Social Welfare. Regional Office for Asia and Western Pacific. Newsletter. q.
• International Social Work. q. ISSN 0020-8728 (Co-sponsors: International Association of Schools of Social Work; International Federation of Social Workers) (U.S. Subscr. Address: Room 1016, 345 E. 46th St., New York, NY 10017)

**International Institute for Population Studies**
Govandi Station Rd., Deonar, Bombay 400088, India.
• International Institute for Population Studies. Director's Report. a.
• International Institute for Population Studies. Newsletter. q. ISSN 0047-0716

**International Institute of Tamil Studies**
Adyar, Madras 600020, Tamil Nadu, India.
• Journal of Tamil Studies. s-a. ISSN 0022-4855

**International Journal of Sexology**
Whiteaway Bldg., Hornby Rd., Bombay 1, India.
• International Journal of Sexology. q.

**International Law Book Co.**
Nijhawan Bldg., 1562 Church Rd., Kashmere Gate, Delhi 6, India.
• Municipalities and Corporation Cases; a monthly law reporter. m.
• Prevention of Food Adulteration Cases. m.
• Rent Cases; a monthly law reporter. m.
• Services Law Cases; monthly law reporter dealing with law relating to promotion, discharge, dismissals, etc. containing recent judgments of all the high courts in the country and Supreme Court of India. m.

**International Penpals Pool**
Sundar Mahal, R.No.43, Subhash Rd., Marine Drive, Bombay 20, India.
• Friend International. ISSN 0046-5100

**International Press Cutting Service**
Box 63, Allahabad 211001, India.
• Automobile & Tractor (Ancillary & Agri Equipment) w. ISSN 0045-1053
• International Press Cutting Service: Ceramics - Porcelain - Refractory - Cement - Glass. w. ISSN 0047-0902
• International Press Cutting Service: Chemical Process Engineering. Drugs - Pharmaceuticals. w. ISSN 0047-0910
• International Press Cutting Service: Computer World--Data Processing--Accounting. w.
• International Press Cutting Service: Dyestuff Industry and Chemicals. w. ISSN 0047-0929
• International Press Cutting Service: Electronics and Electricals Industry. w. ISSN 0047-0937
• International Press Cutting Service: Export Opportunities-New Addresses-Handlooms. w.
• International Press Cutting Service: Fermented Wines, Liquers, Brandy, Gin, Rum, Whisky, Beer and Alcoholic Drinks. w. ISSN 0047-0945
• International Press Cutting Service: Import-Export-Licenses; New Materials for Industry. w. ISSN 0047-0953
• International Press Cutting Service: Jute - Gunny - Hessian-Burlap -Coir. w. ISSN 0047-0961

• International Press Cutting Service: Labour Welfare - Industrial Legislation and Personnel Management. w. ISSN 0047-097X
• International Press Cutting Service: Leather - Hides - Skin - Footwear. w. ISSN 0047-0988
• International Press Cutting Service: List of Industrial Licences Issued. 3-4 times a month.
• International Press Cutting Service: Machine Tool and Iron Steel Industry. w. ISSN 0047-0996
• International Press Cutting Service: Mines & Minerals (Coal/Ores) w. ISSN 0047-1003
• International Press Cutting Service: Modern Plastics and Engineering. w. ISSN 0047-0899
• International Press Cutting Service: Non-Ferrous Metals - Aluminium. w. ISSN 0047-1011
• International Press Cutting Service: Oils (Vegetable) Fats - Soap - Animalfeed. w. ISSN 0047-102X
• International Press Cutting Service: Paint-Colour-Varnish-Inks. w.
• International Press Cutting Service: Paper - Pulp - Board/Straw. w. ISSN 0047-1038
• International Press Cutting Service: Petroleum - Petrochemicals - Fertilisers - Agricultural Chemistry. w. ISSN 0047-1046
• International Press Cutting Service: Plywood-Timber-Particle Board. w. ISSN 0047-1054
• International Press Cutting Service: Processed Food Products/Spices. w. ISSN 0047-1151
• International Press Cutting Service: Rubber and Rubber Technology. w. ISSN 0047-1062
• International Press Cutting Service: Scientific Instruments, Laboratory Equipment & Chemicals. w. ISSN 0047-1070
• International Press Cutting Service. Sugar-Gur-Khandasari. w. ISSN 0047-1089
• International Press Cutting Service: Taxation - Finance - Company Law. w. ISSN 0047-1097
• International Press Cutting Service: Tea and Coffee News. w. ISSN 0047-1100
• International Press Cutting Service: Tender Notifications (Indian & Global) fortn. ISSN 0047-1127
• International Press Cutting Service: Textile News. w. ISSN 0047-1119
• International Press Cutting Service: Tobacco News; cigarettes - cigars - bidis. w. ISSN 0047-1135
• International Press Cutting Service: Weekly Energy-Ecology-Pollution Report. w.
• International Press Cutting Service: Wheat & Wheat Products (Rice/Food Grains) w. ISSN 0047-1143

**International Scientific Publications**
386 Street 2, Raja Park, Jaipur 302004, India.
• International Journal of Ecology and Environmental Sciences. 3 per yr.

**International Society for Tropical Ecology**
Dept. of Botany, Banaras Hindu University, Varanasi 221005, India.
• Tropical Ecology. s-a. ISSN 0564-3295

**International Society of Ichthyology and Hydrobiology**
Box 64, Srinagar, Kashmir, India.
• Ichthyologica; an international journal of ichthyology & hydrobiology. s-a. ISSN 0019-1108

**International Society of Plant Morphologists**
University of Delhi, Department of Botany, Delhi 110007, India.
• International Society of Plant Morphologists. Yearbook. a; 1974-1975 not published. ISSN 0539-0346
• Phytomorphology; an international journal of plant morphology. q. ISSN 0031-9449

**International Telugu Institute**
Barkatpura, Hyderabad 500027, Andhra Pradesh.
• Telugu Vaani/Voice of Telugus. 3 per yr.

**International Trade Fair Association**
• World Fairs Guide. (pub. by Trade Digest Publications)

**International Understanding**
G-38, Connaught Circus, Box 618, New Delhi 110001, India.
• International Understanding. m.

**Intlaw Publishers Corporation**
Box 3528, New Delhi 110024, India.
• International Law Reporter. m. ISSN 0300-4058

**Iran Society**
12 Dr. M. Ishaque Rd., Calcutta 16, India.
• Indo-Iranica. q.

**Islam and the Modern Age Society**
Jamia Nagar, New Delhi 110025, India.
• Islam and the Modern Age. q. ISSN 0021-1826

**Islamic Culture Board**
Box 171, Hyderabad 7, India.
• Islamic Culture. q. ISSN 0021-1834

**J.J. Group of Hospitals**
c/o Dr. J. G. Parekh, Dept. of Medicine, Byculla, Bombay 400008, India.
• Journal of J. J. Group of Hospitals and Grant Medical College. q. ISSN 0022-2054

**J.K. Publications**
16 Park Area, Delhi 5, India.
• Industries Directory, Capitals. irreg. ISSN 0073-7763
• Industries Directory, Delhi. irreg. ISSN 0073-7771
• Industries Directory, Metropolises: Bombay, Calcutta, Delhi and Madras. irreg. ISSN 0073-778X
• Industries Directory, Northern India. irreg. ISSN 0073-7798

**Jadavpur University. Department of Comparative Literature**
Calcutta 32, India.
• Jadavpur Journal of Comparative Literature. a. ISSN 0448-1143

**Jai Hind**
Jai Hind Bldg., Sharda Baug, Rajkot, India.
• Niranjan. w. ISSN 0029-0688

**Jaideva Bros.**
Atmaram Marg, Baroda 1, India.
• Bookseller Pustak Vikreta Baroda; sahitya - pracharak Baroda. m. ISSN 0006-7555

**Jain Bhawan**
P-25 Kalakar St., Calcutta 700007, India.
• Jain Journal. q. ISSN 0021-4043

**S. C. Jain, Ed. & Pub.**
192 Kotwali, Jabalpur, India.
• Jagawani. w. ISSN 0021-3918

**N. Jaiswal, Ed. & Pub.**
Gonda City, Uttar Pradesh, India.
• Jantantra. w. ISSN 0021-423X

**Jammu and Kashmir. Directorate of Economics and Statistics**
Planning and Development Department, Jammu and Kashmir, India.
• Jammu and Kashmir. Directorate of Economics and Statistics. Digest of Statistics. q.

**Jammu and Kashmir. High Court**
Srinagar, Jammu, India.
• Jammu and Kashmir Law Reporter. m.

**Jammu and Kashmir. Legislative Council. Comittee on Privileges**
Srinagar, Jammu and Kashmir, India.
• Jammu and Kashmir. Legislative Council. Committee on Privileges. Report. irreg. ISSN 0448-2433

**Jammu and Kashmir Academy of Art Culture and Languages**
Canal Road, Jammu 180001, India.
• Shiraza. s-a.

**Jammu and Kashmir Cooperative Union**
Vir Marg, Jammu, India.
• Cooperator's Bulletin. m. ISSN 0045-8503

**Jammu University**
see University of Jammu

**Janmabhoomi Group of Newspapers**
Janmabhoomi Bhaven, Ghoga St., Fort, Box 62, Bombay 400001, India.
• Kavita. bi-m. ISSN 0022-9547
• Sudha. w.
• Vyapar. s-w. ISSN 0042-9325

**Javaharicam**
Jnanamalar Padippagam, 88 Varadamuttiyappar St., Madras 600001, India.
• Javaharicam. w.

**Jawaharlal Nehru Agricultural University**
see **Jawaharlal Nehru Krishi Vishwa Vidyalala**

**Jawaharlal Nehru Krishi Vishwa Vidyalaya**
c/o Information and Public Relations Office,
Jabalpur 482004, India.
- J N K V V News. q. ISSN 0021-3713
- J N K V V Research Journal. q. ISSN 0021-3721

**Jawaharlal Nehru Technological University. Regional Engineering College**
Department of English, Warrangal, Andhra Pradesh,
India.
- Kakatiya University. s-a.

**Jawaharlal Nehru University Literary Society**
New Mehrauli Rd., New Delhi 110057, India.
- Prayasa. q.

**Jawaharlal Nehru University. School of International Studies**
New Mehrauli Rd., New Delhi 110057, India.
- India and World Affairs: an Annual Bibliography. a.
- International Studies. (pub. by Vikas Publishing House Pvt. Ltd.)
- Jawaharlal Nehru University, New Delhi, India. School of International Studies Series. q. ISSN 0075-3548

**Jawaharlal Nehru University. School of Languages**
New Mehrauli Rd., New Delhi 110057, India.
- Jawaharal Nehru University. School of Languages. Journal. s-a.

**Jeevak Anshathlya**
Sahitya Marg, Barnalla, India.
- Jeevak. q.

**Jiwaji University**
Vidhya Vihar, Gwalior 2, Madhya Pradesh, India.
- Jiwaji University. Journal: Science, Technology & Medicine. a.

**Jnana Sadhak Publishing Company**
Babupara-Mishralodge, Jalpaiguri 735101, West Bengal, India.
- Universalist. 2-4 per yr. ISSN 0041-8218 (World Jnana Sadhak Society)

**Jodhpur University**
see **University of Jodhpur**

**V. J. Joseph, Ed. & Pub.**
3 Radhe Nivas, 36th Rd., Bandra, Bombay 400050,
India.
- India Today and Tomorrow. q. ISSN 0019-4239
- Shipping and Marine Industries Journal; devoted to shipping and shipbuilding industries, fisheries and oceanography. q.

**Joshi Foundation**
N-3 Panchsheel Park, New Delhi 110017, India.
- Vagartha; critical quarterly of Indian literature. q.

**Joshi Hospital**
778 Shivajinagar, Poona 411004, Maharashtra,
India.
- Medical News, Medicine and Law. m. ISSN 0047-6536

**Journal of Genetics**
c/o Helen Haldane, Habshiguda 16, Hyderabad 7,
India.
- Journal of Genetics. irreg. ISSN 0022-1333

**Journal Publications**
Road No. 12, Dhantoli, Nagpur 1, India.
- Madhya Pradesh Law Journal. m. ISSN 0024-9459
- Maharashtra Law Journal. m. ISSN 0025-0465

**Joy Dev Ray**
123-2 Acharya Prafulla Chandra Rd., Calcutta 6,
India.
- Velki; quarterly English magic magazine. q. ISSN 0042-3238

**Junior Statesman**
Statesman House, 4 Chowringhee Square, Calcutta
700001, India.
- Junior Statesman. w.

**K. M. Manju Joshi Memorial Society**
Jain School, Mathur House, Sikar, Rajasthan, India.
- Rajasthan Journal of English Studies. s-a.

**V. S. Kain, Ed. & Pub.**
977 Sadashi Peth Laxmi Rd., Poona 30,
Maharashtra, India.
- Panchayat Monthly. m. ISSN 0031-0689

**Kaivalyadhama Institution**
Lonavla, District Poona, India.
- Yoga-Mimamsa. q. ISSN 0044-0507

**Kalakeli**
Gandhi Nagar, Kakinada, Andhra Pradesh, India.
- Kalakeli; modern literary monthly. 6 per yr. ISSN 0022-7889

**Kalapatra**
F-14/22 Krishnanagar, Delhi 110051, India.
- Kalapatra. m.

**Kamal Kumar Lahiri**
17/1-D Surjya Sen St., Calcutta 12, India.
- Galpakabita. m. ISSN 0016-4216

**Kamalalaya Stores Pvt. Ltd.**
156 A Dharamtola St., Calcutta, India.
- Banijya Barta. m. ISSN 0005-500X (Calcutta Retail Dealer's Samity)

**Kanara Chamber of Commerce & Industry**
Box 116, Bunder, Mangalore 575001, India.
- Kanara Chamber of Commerce & Industry Journal. m. ISSN 0300-4074

**Kanci**
86 Thirukkach Nambi St., Kanchipuram 3, India.
- Kanci. w.

**G. L. Kapoor, Ed. & Pub.**
3474 Nicholson Rd., Delhi 6, India.
- N I F Weekly. (National Investment & Finance) w. ISSN 0027-6642

**K. C. Kapoor, Ed. & Pub.**
Main Rd., Banga, Punjab, India.
- Indian Journal of Medicine & Surgery. m. ISSN 0019-5367

**P. K. Kar, Ed. & Pub.**
P.O. Navapalli 743203, Via Barasat, Parganas 24,
West Bengal, India.
- Satya Prakash. w. ISSN 0036-4991

**Karnatak Law Journal**
c/o Sri K. P. Rao, Ed., No. 4 Fourth Cross,
Shankarapura, Bangalore 4, India.
- Karnatak Law Journal. m. ISSN 0022-9091

**Karnatak University**
S. S. Wodeyar, Registrar, Dharwar 580003,
Karnataka, India.
- Karnatak University, Dharwar, India. Bulletin. m. ISSN 0047-326X
- Karnatak University, Dharwar, India. Journal. Humanities. a. ISSN 0075-515X
- Karnatak University, Dharwar, India. Journal. Science. a. ISSN 0075-5168
- Karnatak University, Dharwar, India. Journal. Social Sciences. a. ISSN 0075-5176
- Library of Social Work and Social Work Education. irreg.

**Karnatak University. College of Education**
Dharwar 580003, Karnataka, India.
- Journal of the College of Education. s-a. ISSN 0022-4979

**Karnatak University. Department of Social Anthropology**
Dharwar 580003, Karnataka, India.
- International Journal of Comparative Sociology. s-a. ISSN 0538-8082

**Karnatak University Library Association**
Karnatak University, Dharwar 580003, Karnataka,
India.
- Timeless Fellowship; annual journal of comparative librarianship. a. ISSN 0563-5489

**Karnataka**
see also **Mysore**

**Karnataka. Commissioner of Labour**
Manickyavelu Mansion, Palace Road, Bangalore
560052, India.
- Karnataka Labour Journal. m.

**Karnataka. Department of Agriculture. Farm Advisory and Extension Services**
see **Karnataka. Farm Advisory and Extension Services**

**Karnataka. Department of Information and Tourism**
5 Infantry Rd., Bangalore, India.
- Karnataka. Department of Tourism. Annual Report. a.
- March of Karnataka. m.

**Karnataka. Farm Advisory and Extension Services**
Bangalore, Karnataka, India.
- Farm Front. m.

**Karnataka. Finance Department**
Bangalore, Karnataka, India.
- Karnataka. Finance Department. Annual Report. a.

**Karnataka. Mysore Minerals Ltd.**
Bangalore, Karnataka, India.
- Annual Report of the Working and Affairs of Mysore Minerals Limited. a.

**Karnataka. Mysore Sales International Limited**
Bangalore, India.
- Annual Report on the Working and Affairs of Mysore Sales International Limited. a.

**Karnataka Patrika Private Limited**
Koppikar Rd., Hubli, Karnataka, India.
- Kasturi; Kannada digest. m. ISSN 0022-9261

**Karnataka Small Industries Development Corporation Ltd.**
Industrial Estate, Rajajinagar, Bangalore 560004,
India.
- Mysore Industrial Diary. q. ISSN 0027-5611

**Karnataka State Education Federation**
2 Main Rd., 4th Block, Rajajinagar, Bangalore 10,
India.
- Karnataka State Education Federation Journal. m.

**Karyalaya Natya Kala Kendram Institute**
Ed. Ammini S. Menon, 30-A Paddapukur Rd.,
Calcutta 20, India.
- Kalakalpam. s-a. ISSN 0047-3103

**Kashmir Affairs**
Karan Nagar, Jammu, India.
- Kashmir Affairs. bi-m. ISSN 0022-9210

**Kashmir University**
see **University of Kashmir**

**Kerala. Department of Industries and Commerce**
Trivandrum 1, India.
- Kerala Commerce and Industry. m. ISSN 0023-0499

**Kerala. Directorate of Archives**
State Archives Dept., Trivandrum, Kerala, India.
- Kerala Archives Newsletter. q.

**Kerala. Kerala Legislature**
Secretariat, Research and Reference Section,
Trivandrum, India.
- Focus; fortnightly digest for the law maker. fortn.

**Kerala. Kerala State Planning Board**
Trivandrum, India.
- Kerala; an Economic Review. irreg. ISSN 0453-7440

**Kerala. Labour and Industrial Bureau**
Trivandrum 1, Kerala, India.
- Kerala Labour & Industries Review. q. ISSN 0023-0502

**Kerala. State Co-Operative Union**
Box 35, Trivandrum 695001, Kerala, India.
- Kerala Co-Operative Journal. m.

**Kerala Academy of Biology**
Trivandrum, India.
- Kerala Academy of Biology. Journal. s-a.

**Kerala Agricultural University. College of Agriculture**
Vellayani 695522, Kerala, India.
- Agricultural Research Journal of Kerala. ISSN 0002-1628

**Kerala Aided Primary Teachers' Union**
Karshaka Rd., Cochin 682016, Kerala, India.
- K A P T Union Patrika. m.

**Kerala Arya Prathinidhi Sabha**
- Arshanadam. (pub. by Vaidic Sahitya Parishad)

**Kerala Industry**
Box 108, Trivandrum 695001, India.
- Kerala Industry. m. ISSN 0047-3359

**Kerala Institute of Marxist Studies**
Trivandrum 14, India.
- Marxist Veekshanam; theoretical discussion forum. m. ISSN 0025-4134

**Kerala Law Times**
High Court Rd., Ernakulam, Cochin 11, Kerala, India.
- Kerala Law Times. w. ISSN 0023-0529

**Kerala State Productivity Council**
Kalamassery, Kerala, India.
- Kerala Productivity Journal. q.

**Kerala University**
*see* University of Kerala

**Kesari-Mahratta Trust Publication**
The Kesari and the Mahratta Office, 568 Narayan, Poona 2, India.
- Mahratta. a. ISSN 0076-2571

**Khatoon-e-Mashriq**
4162 Urdu Bazar, Jama Masjid, Delhi 6, India.
- Khatoon-e-Mashriq. m. ISSN 0023-107X

**M. S. R. Khemchand, Ed. & Pub.**
C-2 Gulmohar Park, Box 595, New Delhi 110049, India.
- African Recorder; fortnightly digest of events in Africa with index. fortn. ISSN 0002-0133
- Asian Recorder; weekly record of Asian events with index. w. ISSN 0004-4644

**Khosla Publishing Co.**
3 Netaji Subhash Marg, Karyaganj, Post Box 1389, Delhi, India.
- Khosla's Industrial and Commercial Directory of India, Afghanistan, Burma, Ceylon, Japan and Foreign. irreg. ISSN 0075-6016

**Kick to Corruption**
Red Road, Hoshiarpur, India.
- Kick to Corruption. m. ISSN 0023-1282

**Kirloskar Press**
Veer Savarkar Marg, Poona 411009, India.
- Manohara. w.

**Nawal Kishore, Ed. & Pub.**
Paras Kothi Nayatola, Patna 4, India.
- Bomsel; fortnightly of Bihar. fortn.

**Kissan Products Ltd.**
Old Madras Rd., Bangalore 560016, India.
- Indian Food Packer. bi-m. ISSN 0019-4808 (All India Food Preservers' Association)

**Komal Patra**
153 Sarat Chandra Chatterjee Rd., Shibpur, Howrah 2, India.
- Komal Patra. q. ISSN 0023-2963

**Kontakt**
c/o Surender Sachdev, Ed., Box 337, Kanpur 208001, India.
- Kontakt. q.

**P. J. Koshy, Ed. & Pub.**
35/217-A NDS, Lajpat Nagar 4, New Delhi 110024, India.
- Path. m.

**M. V. Kotak, Ed. & Pub.**
62 Karwar St., Mint Rd., Bombay 1, India.
- Beej. m.

**Kothari & Sons**
20 Naugambakkam Rd., Madras 34, India.
- Kothari's Economic and Industrial Guide of India. a.

**Kothari Publications**
12 India Exchange Place, Calcutta 700001, India.
- Directory of Company Secretaries. irreg.; latest 1969. ISSN 0070-5322
- Directory of Directors. irreg.; latest 1975. ISSN 0070-542X
- Kothari's World of Reference Works. irreg.; latest 1963. ISSN 0075-6970

- Professional and Trade Organisations in India. irreg., latest 1977. ISSN 0079-5925
- Who's Who in Indian Engineering and Industry. irreg.; latest 1962. ISSN 0083-9558
- Who's Who in Indian Science. irreg., 1969, 2nd ed. ISSN 0083-9566

**G. P. Koushal, Ed. & Pub.**
Tripti Bhavan, Station Rd., Jusalai, Jamshedpur 831006, India.
- Azad Mazdur; Hindi weekly. w. ISSN 0005-2515

**K. S. Kowshik**
c/o Bharatha Darshan, First Main Rd., Thyagarajanagar, Bangalore 28, India.
- Bharatha Darshan. m. ISSN 0006-0496

**Kranti Parishad**
8B College Row, Calcutta 9, India.
- Kranti. q. ISSN 0023-4532

**Krishnamurti Foundation**
111 Golf Links, New Delhi 110003, India.
- Krishnamurti Foundation. Bulletin. q. ISSN 0047-3693

**K. Kumar, Ed. & Pub.**
D-34 South Extension Part 1, New Delhi 49, India.
- Fortnightly Journal of Industry & Commerce; oil and coal news. fortn. ISSN 0015-8127

**Kumar Karyalaya Ltd.**
1454 Raipur, Ahmedabad 1, India.
- Kumar. m. ISSN 0023-5342

**Shiva Kumar, Ed. & Pub.**
P.M.V. Keshighat, Vrindaban, Uttar Pradesh, India.
- World Federation. m. ISSN 0043-8448

**Kuppuswami Sastri Research Institute**
66 Royapettah High Rd., Madras 4, India.
- Journal of Oriental Research. a. ISSN 0022-3301

**Kurinji Quarterly**
536 Raja Basantha Roy Rd., Calcutta, India.
- Kurinji Quarterly. q.

**Labour Law Journal**
No.1/174 Royapettah High Rd., Madras 600014, India.
- Labour Law Journal. m. ISSN 0023-6977

**Labour World Publications**
36-4 Ganya Ram Hospital, New Delhi 5, India.
- Labour World. m. ISSN 0023-7035

**N. K. Lahiri, Ed. & Pub.**
45-9 Choudhurypara Lane, Calcutta 711104, India.
- Industrial Courier. q. ISSN 0019-8099

**B. Bhushan Lal, Ed. & Pub.**
738 Mammaran St., Jagadhri, Haryana, India.
- Bhushan's World Trade Enquiries. bi-m. ISSN 0006-0542

**Madan Lal, Ed. & Pub.**
D-21, Malviya Nagar Extn., (DDA Flats), New Delhi 110012, India.
- Indian Promenade. q. ISSN 0019-6207

**Lal Bahadur Shastri National Academy of Administration**
Mussoorie 248179, India.
- Administrator. q.

**Lalbhai Dalpatbhai Institute of Indology**
Near Gujarat University, P.O. Navarangpura, Ahmedabad 380009, India.
- Sambodhi. q.

**Lalit Kala Akademi**
*see* National Academy of Art

**Latin America Recorder**
4 Lala Lajpatrai Marg, Jangpura Extension, New Delhi 110014, India.
- Latin America Recorder. fortn.

**Lava Publications**
26/53 W.E.A., New Delhi 110005, India.
- Lava. irreg.

**Law Academy**
1-9-322 Vidyanagar, Hyderabad 500044, India.
- Constitutional Law Journal. q.

**Law Book Co.**
Sardar Patel Marg, Box 4, Allahabad 1, India.
- Lawyers' Recreation. m. ISSN 0023-9488
- Yearly All India Criminal Digest. a.

**Law Journal Publication**
Jayendraganj, Gwalior 1, India.
- Jabalpur Law Journal. m.

**Law Referencer**
35 Lawyers' Chambers, Supreme Court, New Delhi 110001, India.
- Law Referencer. m.

**Law Reporters**
The Repose, Gurudwara Rd., Karol Bagh, New Delhi 5, India.
- Delhi High Court Notes. s-m. ISSN 0011-7838

**Law Review Ltd.**
51 Jhamapooker Lane, Calcutta 19, India.
- Indian Law Review. q.

**Laws of India Private Ltd.**
18 Crescent Park St., Thyagarayanagar, Madras 600017, India.
- Indian Factories Journal. s-m. ISSN 0019-476X

**League of Arab States Mission**
62 Golf Links, New Delhi, India.
- New Arab. m.

**Leather Export Promotion Council**
Marble Hall, 3-38 Vepery High Road, Madras 600003, India.
- Leathers. m. ISSN 0023-9828

**Legislator**
D-32 Kirti Nagar, New Delhi 15, India.
- Legislator. m. ISSN 0024-0508

**Leonard Theological College**
Jabalpur 482001, Madhya Pradesh, India.
- India Cultures Quarterly. q. ISSN 0019-4166 (prep. by its School of Research)

**Liberation**
c/o Nimai Ghose, 60A Keshab Chandra Seu St., Calcutta 9, India.
- Liberation. m. ISSN 0024-1881

**Liberation War**
23 Lansdowne Place, Calcutta 29, India.
- Liberation War. m. ISSN 0047-4495

**Library**
13/417 Ravishankar Sukla Chowk, Nayapara, Raipur 492001, India.
- Library; a journal dedicated to the library profession. s-a.

**Library Literature House**
Chandigarh, India.
- Library Literature in India Series. irreg.

**Library of Tibetan Works and Archives**
Dist. Kangra, H.P., Dharamsala, India.
- Tibet Journal. q.

**Light of Life Society of India**
21 Club Back Rd., Bombay 400008, India.
- Light of Life; all India magazine of Christian witness. m.

**Linge Gowda Detective & Security Chambers**
J. C. Road, Bangalore 560002, India.
- Administration. m.

**Linguistic Society of India**
c/o Deccan College Postgraduate and Research Institute, Poona 411006, India.
- All-India Conference of Linguists. Proceedings. a.
- All-India Conference of Linguists. Souvenir. irreg.
- Indian Linguistics; journal of the Linguistic Society of India. q.
- Indian Linguistics Monograph Series. irreg. ISSN 0073-6589
- Linguistic Society of India. Bulletin. irreg., 1970, no. 3. ISSN 0075-9627

**Lipika Foundation**
F-20 Nizamuddin West, New Delhi 110013, India.
- Lipika; journal of the performing arts. q.

**Literary Press**
Mysore 12, India.
- Literary Half-Yearly. s-a. ISSN 0024-4554 (University of Mysore. Department of Post-Graduate Studies in English) (Co-Sponsor: Centre for Commonwealth Literature and Research)

**Literary Studies**
Razdan House, Sirhindi Darwaza, Patiala, Panjab, India.
- Literary Studies; a quarterly review of literature and criticism from the Panjab. q. ISSN 0024-4600

**Little-Flower Press**
146 Bepin Behari Ganguly Street, Calcutta, India.
- Indian Modeller. bi-m. ISSN 0019-5952 (Society of Medical Aeronautical Engineers of India)

**Local Self-Government**
Sohanganj St., Delhi 7, India.
- Local Self-Government. m. ISSN 0024-5615

**Lok-Milap Trust**
P.O. 23, Bhavnagar 364001, India.
- Bulletin of Indian Books. 3 per yr.

**Lord International**
2/6 Canal Rd., Vijay Nagar, Delhi 110009, India.
- American Books: a quarterly book trade journal. q.
- Directory of Institutions of Oriental Studies in Overseas Countries. irreg.

**Low Income Family Emancipation Society**
B-3/40 Safdarjang Enclave, New Delhi 110016, India.
- Uplift. q.

**Lucknow Publishing House**
37 Cantonment Rd., Lucknow, Uttar Pradesh, India.
- International Review of Modern Sociology. s-a.

**Lucknow University**
*see* University of Lucknow

**M. G. Textile School**
Parel, Bombay 12, India.
- National Institute of Labour Management. Journal. q.

**M M C School of Management**
3 E-1 Court Chambers, New Marine Lines, Bombay 400020, India.
- Management Ideas. m. ISSN 0025-1771

**M M L Centre for Rheumatic Diseases**
17 Pusa Rd., New Delhi 5, India.
- Rheumatism. q. ISSN 0035-4546

**M. S. University of Baroda**
*see* Maharaja Sayajirao University of Baroda

**Madan Printers**
40 Mir Dard Road Market, New Delhi 100001, India.
- See India. q. ISSN 0037-0762

**Madhya Pradesh. Directorate of Tribal Welfare**
- Tribal Research and Development Institute. Bulletin. (pub. by Tribal Research and Development Institute)

**Madhya Pradesh. Planning and Development Department**
Bhopal, Madhya Pradesh, India.
- Annual Development Plan of Madhya Pradesh. a. ISSN 0066-3891

**Madhya Pradesh Varshiki**
c/o Kamla Kundra, E-32, 45 Bungalows, Bhopal, India.
- Madhya Pradesh Varshiki. a.

**Madras**
*see also* Tamil Nadu

**Madras Institute of Development Studies**
74 Second Main Rd., Gandhinagar, Adyar, Madras 600020, India.
- Madras Development Seminar Series. m.

**Madras Institute of Technology**
- Madras Institute of Neurology. Proceedings. (pub. by Wardha Press)

**Madras Law Journal Office**
Box 604, Mylapore, Madras 4, India.
- Andhra Weekly Reporter. w.

- Central Acts. m.
- Central and Andhra Acts. m.
- Central and Madras Acts. m.
- Central, Madras and Andhra Acts. m.
- Income-Tax Journal. fortn. ISSN 0019-3437
- Madras Law Journal. w.
- Madras Law Journal (Criminal) fortn.
- Supreme Court Journal. fortn.
- Yearly Digest. m.
- Yearly Digest of Criminal Cases. m. ISSN 0513-2088

**Madras Psychology Society**
University of Madras, Department of Psychology, Madras 600005, India.
- Journal of Psychological Researches. 3 per yr. ISSN 0022-3972

**Madras Reporters Guild**
Government Estate, Madras 2, India.
- Newsman. m. ISSN 0028-9531

**Madras University**
*see* University of Madras

**Magadh University**
Registrar, Bodh Gaya, Camp Gaya, Bihar, India.
- Magadh University Journal. s-a. ISSN 0024-9726

**Maha Bodhi Society of India**
4A Bankim Chatterjee St., Calcutta 12, India.
- Maha Bodhi; international Buddhist monthly. m. ISSN 0025-0406

**Mahajan Brothers**
Super Market Basement, Ashram Rd., Ahmedabad 380009, Gujarat, India.
- Textile Association (India). Journal. q.
- Textile Highlights. s-a.

**Maharaja Sayajirao University of Baroda**
Baroda 390002, Gujarat, India.
- Maharaja Sayajirao University of Baroda. Journal. 1 vol.per year in 3 parts: humanities, social science, science. ISSN 0025-0422

**Maharaja Sayajirao University of Baroda. Centre for Advanced Study in Education**
Faculty of Education and Psychology, Baroda 390002, Gujarat, India.
- Advances in Education. q. ISSN 0001-8694

**Maharaja Sayajirao University of Baroda. Department of Archaeology and Ancient History**
Baroda 390002, Gujarat, India.
- Maharaja Sayajirao University of Baroda. Department of Archaeology and Ancient History. Archaeology Series. irreg.(approx. 1 issue per year) ISSN 0076-2520

**Maharaja Sayajirao University of Baroda. Department of History**
Baroda 390002, Gujarat, India.
- Maharaja Sayajirao University of Baroda. Department of History Series. irreg. ISSN 0464-5030

**Maharaja Sayajirao University of Baroda. Department of Museology**
Sayaji Park, Baroda 390002, Gujarat, India.
- Studies in Museology. a. ISSN 0081-8259

**Maharaja Sayajirao University of Baroda. Faculty of Education and Psychology**
Baroda 390002, Gujarat, India.
- Education and Psychology Review. q. ISSN 0046-1385

**Maharashtra. Bureau of Economics and Statistics**
D.D. Bldg, Old Custom House, Bombay 400023, India.
- Handbook of Basic Statistics of Maharashtra State. a. ISSN 0072-9728
- Maharashtra: An Economic Review. a. ISSN 0076-2539
- Maharashtra Quarterly Bulletin of Economics and Statistics. q. ISSN 0025-0481 (Order from: Government Printing and Stationery, Charni Rd. Gardens, Bombay 400004, India)
- Maharashtra State Budget in Brief. a. ISSN 0076-2555
- Statistical Abstract of Maharashtra State. a. ISSN 0081-4709

**Maharashtra. Commissioner of Labour and Director of Employment**
Commerce Centre, Tardeo, Bombay 400034, India.
- Industrial Court Reporter. m. ISSN 0019-8102

- Labour Gazette. m. ISSN 0023-6934

**Maharashtra. Department of Agriculture**
Poona 1, India.
- Shetkari. m. ISSN 0037-3648

**Maharashtra. Department of Archives**
Governmental Printing and Stationery, Charni Road Gardens, Bombay 400004, Maharashtra, India.
- Maharashtra Archives Bulletin. irreg. ISSN 0076-2547

**Maharashtra. Directorate of Geology, Mining, and Groundwater Development**
Old Secretariat Building, Nagpur, Maharashtra, India.
- Mineral Research. s-a.

**Maharashtra. Directorate of Information and Public Relations**
Sachivalaya, Bombay 400032, India.
- Lok Rajya. s-m. ISSN 0024-5917

**Maharashtra. Maharashtra Information Centre**
A-8 State Emporia Bldg., Baba Khadak Singh Rd., New Delhi 1, India.
- Maharashtra Parichaya. q. ISSN 0025-0473

**Maharashtra. Maharashtra State Institute of Education**
Poona 411030, India.
- Maharashtra State Institute of Education. Research Bulletin. q.

**Maharashtra Economic Development Council**
106 Nagindas Master Rd., Bombay 400001, India.
- Maharashtra Economic Development Council. Monthly Economic Digest for Business Economics. m.

**Maharashtra Rajya Sahakari Sangh**
*see* Maharashtra State Co-Operative Union

**Maharashtra Small Scale Industries Association**
c/o Samuel Valiaparampil, Ed., 0-10 Bhavana Prabbadevi, Bombay 25, India.
- Small Scale Industries Envoy. m.

**Maharashtra State Co-Operative Union**
5 B. J. Rd., Pune 411001, India.
- Maharashtra Co-Operative Quarterly. q. ISSN 0025-0430

**Maharashtra State Financial Corporation**
New Excelsior Building, 7, 8 & 9th Floors, Amrit Keshav Nayak Marg, Fort, Bombay 400001, India.
- Maharashtra State Financial Corporation. Annual Report. a. ISSN 0076-2563

**Mahatma Gandhi Memorial Research Centre**
Netaje Subhash Rd., Bombay 400002, India.
- Hindustani Zaban. q.

**Mahenjodaro**
5514 Natabar Pal Rd., Howrah, West Bengal, India.
- Mahenjodaro. q. ISSN 0025-049X

**Kailash Mahto**
c/o Department of Geography, Patna University, Patna 800005, India.
- Indian Geographical Studies. s-a. (Geographical Research Centre)

**Malim Dulta**
18 Surja Sen St., Calcutta, West Bengal, India.
- Krishanu. q. ISSN 0023-4737

**Mamane International Academy**
265-I-N Block, Rajajinagar, Bangalore 10, India.
- Mamane. m.

**Man in India**
18 Church Rd., Ranchi, Bihar, India.
- Man in India. q. ISSN 0025-1569

**Management Development Centre**
1 Shakespeare Sarani, Calcutta 16, India.
- Manager's Digest. m.

**Manasayan**
32 Netaji Subhash Marg, Delhi 110006, India.
- Manas; a journal of scientific psychology. s-a. ISSN 0025-1984

**Manohar Book Service**
2 Daryaganj, Ansari Rd., Panna Bhawan, Delhi 110006, India.
● Studies in Electoral Politics in the Indian States. irreg.

**Maranatha Revival Crusade**
94-E Sarajini Devi Rd., Secunderabad 500003, India.
● Message of Life. m. ISSN 0047-6803

**Marathwada University**
Shri V. K. Dhamankar, Registrar, Aurangabad, Maharashtra, India.
● Marathwada University Journal. 3 per yr. (alternating social sciences, languages and natural sciences nos.) ISSN 0025-2751

**D. L. Marayana, Ed. & Pub.**
Dubagunta Nivas, Vijayawada 2, India.
● Indian Medicine/Indiyan Medisin. m.

**Marg Publications**
(Subsidiary of: Tata Sons Pvt. Ltd.)
148 M. G. Road, Fort, Bombay 400001, India.
● Marg. q. ISSN 0025-2913

**Marine Products Export Development Authority**
World Trade Centre, M. G. Rd., P.B. 1708, Cochin 682016, India.
● Indian Seafoods. q. ISSN 0019-6347

**Maritime Union of India**
204 Dr. D. Naoroji Rd., Bombay 400001, India.
● Oceanite; the maritime magazine of India. q. ISSN 0029-8123

**Marketing & Economic Research Bureau**
E-71 Greater Kailash, New Delhi 48, India.
● Journal of Marketing and Economic Research. q. ISSN 0047-2549

**Martin & Harris Private Ltd.**
Savory Chambers, Wallace St., Bombay 400001, India.
● Indian Medical Gazette. m. ISSN 0019-5863

**Maruee**
Rajni Hamsraj Panjabi, F-19 Kubernagar, Ahmedabad, India.
● Maruee. m. ISSN 0025-4096

**Masihi Avaza**
277 Angrahpuri, Gaya, Bihar, India.
● Masihi Avaza. m.

**Materials Management Journal of India**
D-409 Defence Colony, New Delhi 110003, India.
● Materials Management Journal of India. m. ISSN 0543-0313

**Mathematical Association of India**
Indian Institute of Technology, Mathematics Department, Kanpur, India.
● Mathematical Association of India. Bulletin. q. ISSN 0025-5556

**Mathematical Society**
Central College, Bangalore 1, India.
● Mathematics Newsletter. every 6 weeks.

**Mathematics Education**
Station Rd., Siwan, Bihar, India.
● Mathematics Education. q. ISSN 0047-6269

**Mathematika Sciences Society**
M.S. College, Department of Mathematics, Saharanpur, India.
● Pure and Applied Mathematika Sciences. s-a.

**Mathrubhumi Press**
c/o Mr. C.P.M. Sundaram, T. D. Road, "Menons", Cochin 682011, Kerala, India.
● Kerala Law Journal. w. ISSN 0023-0510

**Maya Deb**
22 Bonfield Lane, Calcutta 1, India.
● Anukta. q. ISSN 0003-620X

**Mechanical Engineering Research and Development Organisation**
c/o Central Mechanical Engineering Research Institute, Duragapur 9, West Bengal, India.
● M E R A D O News. q.

**Mechanical Engineers' Association**
Janmabhoomi Chambers, 3rd Fl., 29 Walchand, Hirachand Marg, Bombay 400001, India.
● Engineer & M. E. A. News. q.

**Med-House**
Chowghat, S. India.
● Indian Homoeopathic Gazette. q. ISSN 0019-4867

**Medical College and Hospital**
88 College St., Calcutta 12, India.
● Medical College and Hospital, Calcutta. Bulletin. ISSN 0025-7133 (prep. by its Department of Medicine)

**Medical Digest**
1 Nagindas Mansion, Girgaum Rd., Bombay 4, India.
● Medical Digest. m. ISSN 0025-7184

**Medical Publications**
6 Owners Court, Near Strand Cinema, Colaba, Bombay 400005, India.
● Medical Book News; a guide to new books. bi-m. ISSN 0025-7060

**T. D. Meenakchisundaram, Ed. & Pub.**
c/o Sakuntala, C-28 Eleventh Cross, Thillainagar, Trichy 18, India.
● Light of Pandrimalai. q.

**Meerut College Geographical Society**
c/o Department of Geography, Meerut College, Meerut, Uttar Pradesh, India.
● Geographical Observer. a. ISSN 0072-0925

**Meerut University Economics Association**
3-1 Professor's Lodge, Modinagar, India.
● Journal of Economics. s-a.

**Meerut University. Meerut College**
Meerut, Cantt, Uttar Pradesh, India.
● Research Journal of Philosophy and Social Sciences. s-a.

**Meghalaya. Directorate of Information and Public Relations**
Shillong, India.
● Meghalaya Chronicle. q.

**S. S. Mehan, Ed. & Pub.**
2778 Jorawar Singh Marg, Galli Muglan, Delhi 6, India.
● Hosiery Report. 3 per m. ISSN 0018-5418

**Methodist Church in Southern Asia**
25 Lodi Rd., New Delhi 110003, India
(U.S. Subscr. Address: c/o 1st United Methodist Church, 1589 W. Maple, Birmingham, MI 48010)
● Indian Witness. s-m. ISSN 0019-6487

**Midland Publications**
14 Sultanja Rd., Bhopal, India.
● Midland Weekly. w.

**Milan Law Publishers**
Box 4591, 15-2 Navjivan, Bombay 8, India.
● Journal of Shipping, Customs, and Transport Law. m.

**Minaret**
Ahmadiyya Building, West Silk St., Calcutta, India.
● Minaret. q.

**Mineralogical Society of India**
Manasagangotri, Mysore 6, India.
● Indian Mineralogist. s-a. ISSN 0019-5928

**Minerals and Metals Trading Corp. of India Ltd.**
9 - 10 Bahadur Shah Zafar Marg, New Delhi, India.
● M M T C News. q.

**Minimax**
K-5/8 Model Town, Delhi 110009, India.
● Minimax; quarterly of creative and critical writing in English. q.

**Mining and Allied Machinery Corporation**
Durgapur, India.
● Mining and Allied Machinery Corporation. Annual Report. a.

**Mining Engineers Association**
Esperanca Ground Floor, Colaba Causeway, Bombay 1, India.
● I M E Directory: Mines, Minerals, Equipment. (Indian Mining and Engineering) a. ISSN 0073-6597

● Indian Mining & Engineering Journal. m. ISSN 0019-5944

**Mining, Geological & Metallurgical Institute of India**
200 Chowringhee Rd., Calcutta 700016, India.
● Mining, Geological and Metallurgical Institute of India. Transactions. s-a.

**Minority Forum**
E-1 Lawrence Terrace, Hazratganj, Lucknow 1, India.
● Minority Forum. m.

**Mira**
10 Sadhu Vaswani Rd., Poona 1, India.
● Mira; a monthly journal of Indian culture. m. (10 per yr.) ISSN 0026-5780

**Mirchandi & Co. Pvt. Ltd.**
29 Worli House Rd., Bombay 1, India.
● Executive Reading. m. ISSN 0014-4584
● India Book House News. m. ISSN 0019-414X

**Basudeo Misra, Ed. & Pub.**
At 4 Post Khetasarai District, Janpur, Uttar Pradesh, India.
● Ganmitram. w. ISSN 0016-4496

**Mithila Research Institute**
Darbhanga, India.
● Mithila Institute of Post Graduate Studies and Research in Sanskrit Learning. Bulletin. s-a. ISSN 0026-6787

**Dhiren Mitra, Ed. & Pub.**
45 Raja Rammohan Sarani, Calcutta 700009, India.
● Advertlink; a newspaper on advertising and marketing. fortn. ISSN 0001-8988

**Mitra & Ghosh Publishers Pvt. Ltd.**
10 Shama Charan De St., Calcutta 12, India.
● Katha-Sahitya. m. ISSN 0022-9318

**S. S. Mohan**
31/13 East Patel Nagar, New Delhi 110008, India.
● Economic & Business Review. q. ISSN 0012-995X

**Monograph Association of India**
● Human Events. (pub. by Indian Publications)

**S. C. Mookerjee**
14 Purand Chand Nahar Ave., Calcutta 13, India.
● Indian Medical Record. m. ISSN 0019-5898

**Mukherjee Library**
1 Gopi Mohan Dutta Lane, Calcutta 700003, India.
● Dhandha. m. ISSN 0300-4309
● Indian Books. m. ISSN 0019-445X
● Journal of Indexing & Reference Work. m.

**Municipal Corporation of Greater Bombay**
Public Relations Dept., Municipal Extension Bldg., Mahapalika Marg, Bombay 1, India.
● Bombay Civic Journal. m. ISSN 0524-0166

**Music Academy**
115-E Mowbray's Rd., Royapettah, Madras 14, India.
● Music Academy. Conference Souvenir. irreg.
● Music Academy. Journal. q.

**Muslim Review**
Madrasat-Ul-Waizeen, 16 Canning St., Lucknow, India.
● Muslim Review. q. ISSN 0027-4895

**Philip Myaboo**
Sangeet A-3, Delisle Rd., Byculla, Bombay 27, India.
● Tourist Trade of India. q.

**Mysore**
*see also* **Karnataka**

**Mysore Economic Review**
Saraswathi Bldgs., 34 Sri Narasimharaja Rd., India.
● Mysore Economic Review. m. ISSN 0027-5603

**Mysore Horticultural Society**
Lalbaugh, Bangalore 560004, India.
● Lal-Baugh. q. ISSN 0023-7388

**Mysore University**
*see* **University of Mysore**

**Mythic Society**
Nrupatunga Rd., Bangalore 2, India.
- Mythic Society Quarterly Journal. q. ISSN 0047-8555

**Nabya Bangla Natya Parishad**
9-3 Tamar Lane, Calcutta 9, India.
- Darshak; a Bengali fortnightly on art news & views. fortn. ISSN 0045-9658

**Nagaland. Cultural Research and State Museum**
Kohima, Nagaland, India.
- Highlander. s-a.

**Nagaland. Director of Information, Publicity & Tourism**
Kohima, Nagaland, India.
- Warrior. m.

**Nagaland. Directorate of Education**
Kohima, Nagaland, India.
- Nagaland Education Bulletin. irreg.

**Nagaland Nationalist Cooperative Society Ltd.**
Box 12, Dimapur, Nagaland, India.
- Nagaland Times. w.

**M. L. Nahar, Ed. & Pub.**
20/1 Maharashi Debendra Rd., Calcutta 7, India.
- Sales Tax Advices. m. ISSN 0036-3472

**Natabar Naik, Ed. & Pub.**
Tilottame Homoeo House, P.O. Jagatsinghpur, Cuttack, Orissa, India.
- Orissa Homoeopathic Bulletin. m. ISSN 0048-2242

**S. K. Nair, Ed. & Pub.**
New India Printers, Quilon 13, India.
- Malayalanadu. w.
- Malayalanadu Film Fortnightly. fortn.

**A. K. Krishna Nambiar, Ed. & Pub.**
1615 Madarsa Road, Kashmere Gate, Delhi 110006, India.
- Spiritual India; a quarterly newsmagazine of spiritual life and thought. q.

**R. N. Nandy**
2 Bazarpara Main Rd., Halisahar, Parganas 24, West Bengal, India.
- Adhuna Sahitya. q. ISSN 0001-8228

**C. P. Narang, Ed. & Pub.**
20 Tyag Raj Nagar Market, Prem Nag, New Delhi 3, India.
- Poultry Guide. m. ISSN 0032-5740

**Chitra Narayann, Ed. & Pub.**
A-1/45 Safdarjung Enclave, New Delhi 110016, India.
- Book Review. q.

**Narula Dwakhana**
Maisewan, Amritsar, India.
- Sukh Datta. m. ISSN 0039-4882

**Nasim Book Depot**
25 Latouche Rd., Lucknow 226001, India.
- Kaliyan. m. ISSN 0022-7986

**Manian Natesan**
2-A Cathedral Rd., Madras 86, India.
- Indian Review; devoted to the discussion of all topics of interest. m. ISSN 0019-6304

**Nation Trust**
54 Ganesh Chandra Ave., Calcutta 13, India.
- Now. w. ISSN 0029-5345

**National Academy of Art**
Rabindra Bhavan, New Delhi 110001, India.
- Lalit Kala Contemporary. s-a. ISSN 0023-7396

**National Academy of Letters**
Rabindra Bhavan, New Delhi 110001, India.
- Indian Literature. bi-m. ISSN 0019-5804
- Sahitya Akademi, New Delhi. Report. a. ISSN 0080-5416

**National Academy of Music, Dance and Drama**
Rabindra Bhavan, Ferozeshah Rd., New Delhi 110001, India.
- Sangeet Natak; journal on the performing arts. q. ISSN 0036-4339

**National Academy of Sciences**
5 Lajpatra Rd., Allahabad 2, Uttar Pradesh, India.
- National Academy of Sciences, India. Proceedings. Section A. Physical Sciences. q.
- National Academy of Sciences, India. Proceedings. Section B. Biological Sciences. q.

**National Aeronautical Laboratory**
*see* India. National Aeronautical Laboratory

**National Agricultural Marketing Federation of India Limited**
Sapna Theatre Bldg., 54 East of Kailash, New Delhi 110024, India.
- N A F E D Marketing Review. m.

**National Alliance of Young Entrepreneurs**
Alliance House, C-20-B Green Park Extension, New Delhi 16, India.
- Young Alliance; the journal of entrepreneurs of India. m. ISSN 0049-836X

**National Archives**
*see* India. National Archives of India

**National Association for the Blind**
Jehangir Wadia Bldg., 51 Mahatma Gandhi Rd., Bombay 400023, India.
- Blind Welfare. 3 per yr. ISSN 0006-4823

**National Association of Materials Management**
Cecil Court, 5th Floor, Lansdowne Rd., Apollo Bunder, Bombay 400001, India.
- National Association of Materials Management. Journal. m.

**National Botanic Gardens**
*see* India. National Botanic Gardens

**National Buildings Organisation**
*see* India. National Buildings Organisation

**National Centre for the Performing Arts**
Nariman Point, Bombay 400021, India.
- National Centre for the Performing Arts. Quarterly Journal. q.

**National College of Astrology**
c/o S. Pakala, Ed., 314 Pycrofts Rd., Madras 14, India.
- Fortune. m. ISSN 0015-8240

**National Cooperative Consumers' Federation**
25 Ring Rd., Lajpat Nagar IV, New Delhi 110024, India.
- Indian Consumer Cooperator. m.

**National Cooperative Development Corporation**
C-56 South Extension, Part 2, New Delhi 110049, India.
- N. C. D. C. Bulletin. q. ISSN 0027-6278

**National Cooperative Union of India**
Eros Apartments, Building No. 56 (6th Floor), Nehru Place, New Delhi 110024, India.
- Cooperator. fortn. ISSN 0010-8464
- Indian Cooperative Review. q. ISSN 0019-4581

**National Cooperative Union of India. Committee for Cooperative Training**
34 S. Patel Nagar, New Delhi 8, India.
- Cooperative Law Journal. q.

**National Council for Science Education**
c/o Indian Institute of Science, Department of Mechanical Engineering, Bangalore 560012, India.
- Indian Journal of Technical Education. 3 per yr.

**National Council of Applied Economic Research**
Parisila Bhawan, 11 Indraprastha Estate, New Delhi 1, India
(Dist. by: International Publications Service, 303 Park Ave. South, New York, NY 10010)
- Margin. q. ISSN 0025-2921
- N C A E R Occasional Papers. irreg. ISSN 0077-4065

**National Council of Educational Research and Training**
Publication Department, Sri Aurbindo Marg, New Delhi 110016, India
(Dist. by: International Publications Service, 303 Park Ave. South, New York, NY 10010)
- Indian Educational Review. q. ISSN 0019-4700
- Journal of Indian Education. bi-m.
- N C E R T Newsletter. q. ISSN 0302-508X

- School Science; quarterly journal for secondary schools. q. ISSN 0036-679X (prep. by its Department of Education in Science and Mathematics)

**National Council of Educational Research and Training. Regional College of Education**
Ajmer, India.
- Educational Trends. s-a. (prep. by its Alumni Association)
- Journal of Commerce Education. q. (prep. by its Department of Commerce Education)

**National Council of Women in India**
- N. C. W. I. Bulletin. (pub. by Standard Press)

**National Council of YMCA's of India**
Box No. 14, Jai Singh Road, New Delhi 110001, India.
- Yuvak. bi-m. ISSN 0044-1414

**National Environmental Engineering Research Institute**
*see* India. National Environmental Engineering Research Institute

**National Federation of Co-operative Sugar Factories Ltd.**
L-8 South Extension, Part II, New Delhi 110049, India.
- Co-operative Sugar. m.

**National Federation of Petroleum Workers & Indian National Chemical Workers' Federation**
c/o Raja Kulkarni, Ed., Tel-Rasayan Bhavan, Tilak Rd., Dadar, Bombay 14, India.
- Oil & Chemical Worker. m. ISSN 0030-1329

**National Forum of Public Enterprises**
C-40 South Extension II, New Delhi 49, India.
- Directory of Public Enterprises in India. a.

**National Geographical Society of India**
Banaras Hindu University, Department of Geography, Varanasi 221005, Uttar Pradesh, India.
- National Geographical Journal of India. q. ISSN 0027-9374

**National Geophysical Research Institute**
*see* India. National Geophysical Research Institute

**National Institute of Community Development**
Box 164, Rajendra Nagar, Hyderabad 500030, India.
- Behavioural Sciences and Community Development. s-a. ISSN 0005-7843
- Community Development and Panchayati Raj Digest. q.

**National Institute of Design**
Paldi, Ahmedabad 7, India.
- National Institute of Design, Ahmedabad. Documentation. irreg. ISSN 0077-4901

**National Institute of Family Planning**
L-17 Green Park, New Delhi 110016, India.
- Journal of Population Research. bi-m.
- N I F P General Series. irreg., 1970, no. 22. ISSN 0077-4944
- N I F P Manual Series. irreg. ISSN 0077-4952
- N I F P Monograph Series. irreg., 1973, no. 19. ISSN 0077-4960
- N I F P Report Series. irreg., 1973, no. 12. ISSN 0077-4979
- N I F P Technical Paper Series. irreg., 1973, no. 17. ISSN 0077-4987
- New Books on Family Planning. bi-m. ISSN 0028-4327

**National Institute of Health Administration and Education**
R-55 Greater Kailish 1, New Delhi 110048, India.
- N I H A E Bulletin; a journal of health administration. q.

**National Institute of Labour Management**
- National Institute of Labour Management. Journal. (pub. by M. G. Textile School)

**National Institute of Nutrition**
c/o Indian Council of Medical Research, Jamia-Osmania, Hyderabad 7, India.
- National Institute of Nutrition. Report. a.

**National Institute of Oceanography**
*see* India. National Institute of Oceanography

**National Institute of Sciences of India**
*see* **Indian National Science Academy**

**National Institute of Social Defence**
Dept. of Social Welfare, Block 1 Wing 7,
Ramakrishnapuram, New Delhi 22, India.
• Social Defence; a quarterly review of policies and
practices in the field of prevention of crime and
treatment of offenders. q. ISSN 0037-7716

**National Integrated Medical Association**
307 Erangere Ashoka Rd., Mysore 1, India.
• National Integrated Medical Association Journal.
q.

**National Library**
*see* **India. National Library**

**National Medical Library**
*see* **India. National Medical Library**

**National Physical Laboratory**
*see* **India. National Physical Laboratory**

**National Productivity Council**
Lodi Rd., New Delhi 110003, India.
• Productivity. q. ISSN 0032-9924
• Productivity News. m.

**National Research Development Corporation of India**
*see* **India. National Research Development
Corporation of India**

**National Safety Council**
Central Labour Institute Bldg., Sion, Bombay 22,
India.
• Industrial Safety Chronicle. q. ISSN 0301-4746
• National Conference on Safety. Proceedings. a.

**National Sugar Institute**
*see* **India. National Sugar Institute**

**National Tonnage Club of Farmers**
Tonnage Club Farm, F-2 South Extension, Part 1,
New Delhi 49, India.
• Tonnage Club Farm News. m. ISSN 0049-4089

**National Union of Journalists (India)**
7 Jantar Mantar Rd., New Delhi 110001, India.
• Inkworld. m.

**Natun Thikana**
71-4 Dr. Nilmani Sarkar St., Calcutta 50, India.
• Natun Thikana. q. ISSN 0300-3809

**Nature Cure Hospital**
Begumpet, Hyderabad, India.
• Prakriti. m.

**Nature Cure Research Hospital**
51 Gwynne Rd., Lucknow 1, India.
• Prakriti-Vani/Voice of Nature. m.

**Nava Niketan**
39B Dent Mission Rd., Calcutta 23, India.
• Pragati. m. ISSN 0032-6550

**Naveenandhra Printing and Agricultural Co.**
Vijayawada 4, India.
• Pragathi Illustrated Weekly. w.

**K.G.P. Nayar**
Herald House, Box 133, Trivandrum, Kerala, India.
• Business Herald; management magazine. m. ISSN
0007-6783

**Ned-Sannyas International**
• Sannyas. (pub. by Rajneesh Publications)

**Neighbourhood Publications Cooperative Society Ltd.**
19A Theatre Communications Bldg., Connaught
Place, New Delhi 110001, India.
• Dateline Delhi. m. ISSN 0011-698X

**Nematological Society of India**
New Delhi 1, India.
• Indian Journal of Nematology. s-a.

**Netaji Subhas National Institute of Sports**
Patiala 147001, India.
• Sports Medicine. s-a. (Indian Association of
Sports Medicine)

**Neurological Society of India**
534 Sandhurst Bridge, Bombay 7, India.
• Neurology India. q. ISSN 0028-3886

**New Age Press**
15C University Rd., Delhi 7, India.
• Enquiry. 3 per yr. ISSN 0013-8517 (Enquiry
Association)

**New Prima Press**
11 Raja Subodh Mullick Square, Calcutta 700013,
India
(U.S. Distr.: South Asia Books, Colombia, MO
65201)
• Social Science Review; journal on books and book
reviews. bi-m.

**New Wave Society**
c/o Ganesh Shukla, Rohit House, Tolstoy Marg,
New Delhi 110001, India.
• New Wave; India's national newsweekly. w. ISSN
0047-9969

**W. Newman and Co.**
3 Old Court House St., Calcutta 700001, India.
• Indian Bradshaw. m. .

**Newsletter for Birdwatchers**
C. D. Barfiwala Marg, Andheri West, Bombay
400058, India.
• Newsletter for Birdwatchers. m. ISSN 0028-9426

**Nilkant Industries Pvt. Ltd.**
24 Gola Market, Netaji Subash Marg, New Delhi 6,
India.
• Tourism and Wildlife. q.

**Nimbkar Rehabilitation Trust**
Amerind, 15th Rd., Bombay 400052, India.
• Journal of Rehabilitation in Asia. q. ISSN 0022-
4162

**Nirmala Sadanand Publishers**
35 C Tardeo Rd., Bombay 400034, India.
• Asian Book Trade Directory. irreg., 1967, 2nd ed.
ISSN 0066-8362

**Nirmok**
27 Biswas Nursery Lane, Calcutta 10, India.
• Nirmok. m. ISSN 0029-0696

**Swami Nirvananda, Ed. & Pub.**
Santi Ashram P.O., Totapalli Hills, (via)
Sankhavaram, E. Godavari Dist., Andhra Pradesh,
India.
• Peace; monthly journal devoted to peace and
illumination. m. ISSN 0031-3467
• Santi. m.

**Nizami Press**
Badaun, Uttar Pradesh, India.
• Zulqarnain. w. ISSN 0044-5479

**Norm**
18/18 Ballygunge Place East, Calcutta 19, India.
• Norm; journal of comparison and change. q.

**North East India Geographical Society**
c/o Department of Geography, Gauhati University,
Gauhati 781014, Assam, India.
• North East India Geographical Society. Journal. s-
a.

**North East Industrial Cooperative Society Ltd**
Maukhar, Shillong 79301, India.
• Implanter. w.

**North-Eastern Affairs**
c/o S. Sarin, Ed., Jowai Rd., Shillong 3, India.
• North-Eastern Affairs. q.

**Northern Railway**
Public Relations Office Bldg., State Entry Rd., New
Delhi, India.
• Northern Railway Newsletter. m. ISSN 0029-3210

**Nowhere Press**
Govind Niwas, Sarojini Rd., Vile Parle (W),
Bombay 56, India.
• Tornado. ISSN 0040-9499

**Numismatic Society of India**
Banaras Hindu University, Varanasi 221005, India.
• Numismatic Society of India. Journal. s-a. ISSN
0029-6066

**Nazir Ahmad Nuri**
Mahmood Manzil Gwynne Rd., Lakhnau, India.
• Subh-i-Adab. m.

**Oil & Natural Gas Commission, Dehradun**
Institute of Petroleum Exploration, Kaulagarh,
Dehradun, India.
• Bibliography on Petroleum & Allied Literature. s-
a.

**Oil Technologists Association of India**
• Oil Technologists Association of India. Journal.
(pub. by Colour Publications Pvt. Ltd.)

**Om Rama - Yoga Sangam**
D.D.A. Flat No. 4, 7 Bhagwandas Rd., New Delhi
1, India.
• Udgeeth; devoted to spiritual enlightenment. q.

**Onlooker Publications Pvt. Ltd.**
20-G Sleater Rd., Bombay 7, India.
• World Trade. s-a. ISSN 0043-9142

**Operational Research Society of India**
Defence Science Laboratory, 7/3 Maudeville
Garden, Calcutta 700019, India.
• Opsearch. q. ISSN 0030-3887

**Operational Research Society of India, Calcutta
Branch**
Ed. P. K. Ghosh, Research and Development Mgr.,
Macneill & Barry Ltd., 2 Fairlie Place, Calcutta 1,
India.
• C O R S I Bulletin. a. ISSN 0078-5261

**Optical Society of India**
c/o Dept. of Applied Physics, University of
Calcutta, 92 Acharya Prafulla Chandra Rd.,
Calcutta 700009, India.
• Journal of Optics. q.

**Orbit Weekly**
3 Sadhana Enclave, New Delhi 17, India.
• Orbit Weekly. w. ISSN 0048-2110

**Orient Longman Ltd.**
3-5 Asaf Ali Rd., New Delhi 110002, India.
• Gandhi Bibliography Series. a. (Indian Council of
Social Science Research)
• Indian Journal of English Studies. a. ISSN 0537-
1988 (Indian Association for English Studies)
• Indian Journal of Medical Education. q. ISSN
0019-5332 (Indian Association for the
Advancement of Medical Education)

**Oriental Institute**
Maharaja Sayajirao University of Baroda, Baroda
390002, Gujarat, India.
• Oriental Institute. Journal. q. ISSN 0030-5324

**Oriental Medical Publications**
2350 Rajguru Rd., Raharganj, New Delhi, India.
• Eastern Archives of Ophthalmology. bi-m. ISSN
0301-469X

**Oriental Research Institute**
University of Mysore, P.O.B. 14, Mysore 5,
Karnataka, India.
• Indian Antiquary. (pub. by Popular Prakashan)
• Mysore Orientalist. a. ISSN 0580-4396

**Oriental Watchman Publishing House**
V. Raju, Box 35, Poona 411001, India.
• Herald of Health. m. ISSN 0018-0491 (Seventh-
Day Adventists)

**Orissa. Director of Public Instruction**
Publicity Officer, Orissa, Bhubaneswar, India.
• Orissa Education. q. ISSN 0030-5588

**Orissa. Finance Department**
• Orissa, India. Finance Department. White Paper
on the Economic Conditions and the
Developmental Activities in Orissa. (pub. by
Orissa Government Press)

**Orissa. State Family Planning Bureau**
Director of Family Planning, Orissa, Bhubaneswar,
India.
• Orissa Family Planning Bulletin. m.

**Orissa Government Press**
Cuttack, Orissa, India.
• Orissa, India. Finance Department. White Paper
on the Economic Conditions and the
Developmental Activities in Orissa. a. (Orissa.
Finance Department)

**Orissa State Auroville Committee**
39 Udyan Marg, Bhubaneswar, Orissa, India.
• Oriya-Aurovilian. q.

**Osmania University. Centre of Exploration Geophysics**
Hyderabad 500007, Andhra Pradesh, India.
- C. E. G. Bulletin. irreg.

**Osmania University. Department of Commerce**
Hyderabad 500007, Andhra Pradesh, India.
- Applied Economic Papers. s-a. ISSN 0570-4839

**Osmania University. Department of Linguistics**
Hyderabad 500007, Andhra Pradesh, India.
- Osmania Papers in Linguistics. s-a.

**Osmania University. Department of Psychology**
Hyderabad 500007, Andhra Pradesh, India.
- Osmania University. Department of Psychology. Research Bulletin. irreg.

**Oxford & IBH Publishing Co.**
17 Park St., Calcutta 700016, India.
- India in Industries. q. ISSN 0019-4182

**Oxford University Press**
Oxford House, Apollo Bunder, Bombay 400001, India.
- Himalayan Journal. a. (Himalayan Club)

**P.E.N. All-India Centre**
Theosophy Hall, 40 New Marine Lines, Bombay 400020, India.
- Indian P.E.N. bi-m. ISSN 0019-6053

**P. K. Endowment for Library and Information Science**
C-1 Banaras Hindu University, Varanasi 221005, India.
- Granthalaya Vijnana. s-a.
- Herald of Library Science. q. ISSN 0018-0521

**P. R. Publications**
16-199 Lane No 7 Joshi Rd., Karol Bagh, New Delhi 5, India.
- Public Relations Journal of India. bi-m. ISSN 0033-3689

**P. S. G. & Sons Charities**
Peelamedu, Coimbatore 641004, India.
- Kalaikathir. m. ISSN 0022-7870

**Pahala**
763 Agrawal Colony, Jabalpur, India.
- Pahala. q.

**Palaeobotanical Society**
53 University Rd., Lucknow 7, India.
- Geophytology; a journal of palaeobotany and allied sciences. s-a.

**Palynological Society of India**
- Journal of Palynology. (pub. by Today and Tomorrow's Printers & Publishers)
- New Botanist. (pub. by Today and Tomorrow's Printers & Publishers)

**Pamposh Publications**
E-38 Hauz Khas, New Delhi 110016, India.
- Indian Pharmaceutical Guide. a. ISSN 0073-6635

**L. K. Pandey, Ed. & Pub.**
105-C Block F, New Alipore, Calcutta 700053, India.
- Concrete Construction and Architecture. m. ISSN 0010-5341
- Electricity and Electronics. m. ISSN 0013-4538
- Indian & Eastern Pharmacy. m. ISSN 0019-4360
- Machine and Machinery. m. ISSN 0024-9092
- Metals and Minerals Review. m. ISSN 0026-0959
- Textile News. m. ISSN 0040-5124

**O. N. Pandeya, Ed. & Pub.**
105-C Block F, New Alipore, Calcutta 700053, India.
- Chemical Era. m. ISSN 0009-2533
- Nagarjun. m. ISSN 0027-7576
- Transport and Communications. m. ISSN 0041-1388
- Vishwakarma. m. ISSN 0042-6881

**C. M. Pandit & Co.**
Sayajiganj, Baroda 390005, India.
- Construction Industries and Trade Journal. a. ISSN 0010-6828

- Glass, Potteries and Ceramic Journal. a. ISSN 0017-1042
- Mining Industry & Trade Journal. a. ISSN 0026-5217

**Pandulipi Club**
5/1 D. T. N. Chatterji St., Calcutta 50, India.
- Pandulipi. q.

**Panjab University**
Publication Bureau, Chandigarh 160014, Union Territory, India.
- Panjab University News. q.
- Panjab University Research Bulletin (Arts) s-a.
- Parkh. s-a.

**Panjab University. Extension Library**
Publication Bureau, Chandigarh 160014, Union Territory, India.
- Panjab University Doctoral Dissertations. irreg. ISSN 0079-8053

**Panjabi University**
see **Punjabi University**

**Parabas**
21-B, Quarter-6D, Chittaranjan, West Bengal, India.
- Parabas. m. ISSN 0031-1553

**Parichiti Cultural Association**
Gorerhat, Via-Baruipur, 24 Parganas, West Bengal, India.
- Parichiti; only literary magazine for the new writers. m. ISSN 0031-1979

**Paschim Maharashtra Pradeshik Sahakari Mandal, Ltd.**
10 Zilla Parishad Bldg., Poona 11, India.
- Sahakari Jagat. m. ISSN 0036-2611

**J. R. Patel, Ed. & Pub.**
Box 892 G.P.O., Bombay 400001, India.
- Parsiana. m. ISSN 0048-3036

**L. M. Patel, Ed. & Pub.**
Wadi, Vayada Pole, Baroda 1, India.
- Baljivan. m. ISSN 0005-4291

**Pathikrit Association**
88-B Bipin Behari Ganguli St., Calcutta 12, India.
- Trend. q.

**G. V. Patil**
White Hall, Congress Nagar, Nagpur, India.
- Botanique. q.

**Patna University**
Deputy Registrar, Patna 5, India.
- Patna University Journal. q. ISSN 0031-3092

**Paul's Press**
B-258 Naraina, Industrial Area Phase I, New Delhi 110028, India.
- Enact; monthly theatre magazine. m. ISSN 0013-6980

**Pavlov Institute**
132-1A Bidhan Sarani, Calcutta 4, India.
- Manab Mon; a journal depicting the modern trends in psychology, biology & sociology. q. ISSN 0025-1615

**Pediatric Clinics of India**
LTMG Hospital, Sion, Bombay 400022, India.
- Pediatric Clinics of India. q. ISSN 0048-3133

**People's Party of India**
c/o Vishan das Veer, 24 Vithalbhai Patel Bhawan, New Delhi, India.
- About Us. fortn. ISSN 0044-5754

**People's Publishing House Private Ltd.**
Rani Jhansi Road, New Delhi 110055, India.
- Party Life; fortnightly journal of the Communist Party of India. s-m.

**Perspective Publications Pvt. Ltd.**
F-24 Bhagat Singh Market, New Delhi 110001, India.
- Mainstream. w. ISSN 0542-1462

**A. Peters, Pub.**
231 Dadabhoy Naoroji Rd., Box 376, Bombay 1, India.
- Indian Practitioner; a monthly journal of medicine, surgery & public health. m. ISSN 0019-6169

**Petroleum Information Service**
Sethi Bhawan, 7 Rajindra Pl., New Delhi 110008, India.
- Oil Commentary. fortn.
- Oil Statistics. q. ISSN 0030-1477 (prep. by its Statistics Division)

**Pharos**
J5-79 Rajouri Garden, New Delhi, India.
- Pharos. bi-m.

**Philips India Ltd.-ELCOMA (Electronic Components and Materials)**
(Subsidiary of: Philips India Ltd.)
Band Box House, Box 9143, 254-D Dr. Annie Besant Rd., Prabhadevi, Bombay 400025, India.
- Electronic Application News. bi-m. ISSN 0013-4813

**Shashi Phukan, Ed. & Pub.**
Bismoi Prakash, Maligaon, Gauhati 11, Assam, India.
- Bismoi. bi-m. ISSN 0006-3827

**Physical Research Laboratory**
Ahmedabad, India.
- Physical Research Laboratory, Ahmedabad: Annual Report. a.

**Physicians' Association of Madras**
c/o M. Viswanthan, 53 Main Rd., Royapuram, Madras 13, India.
- Physicians' Association of Madras. Journal. q. ISSN 0031-9031

**A. Sivasubramonia Pillai, Ed. & Pub.**
7/578 Meiyagam Vadivee Swaran, Nagercoil 2, Kanyakumari District, Tamil Nadu, India.
- Kaviamuthu. m. ISSN 0022-9539

**Plant Biochemical Society**
c/o Y. P. Arbol, Nuclear Research Laboratory, Indian Argicultural Research Institute, New Delhi 110012, India.
- Plant Biochemical Journal. s-a.

**S. K. Poddar, Ed. & Pub.**
50-8A Gouri Bari Lane, Calcutta 4, India.
- Annrinya. m. ISSN 0003-5203

**K. R. Polavarapu, Ed. & Pub.**
C-1/26 Safdarjang Development Area, New Delhi 110016, India.
- Consumeraids; compendium of consumer information. m.

**Polymer Publications**
59 Alli Chambers, Tamarind Lane, Bombay 1, India.
- Rubber News. m. ISSN 0035-9513

**Pondicherry. Home (Plan Publicity and Tourism) Department**
Pondicherry, India.
- News from Pondy. q. ISSN 0028-9094

**Poona Agricultural College**
Poona 411005, India.
- Journal of Maharashtra Agricultural Universities. bi-m. (Co-sponsors: Mahatma Phule Krishi Vidyapeeth, Rahuri; Marathwada Krishi Vidyapeeth Parbhani; Konkan Krishi Vidyapeeth, Dapoli; Punjabrao Krishi Vidyapeeth, Akola)
- Poona Agricultural College Magazine. ISSN 0032-4299

**Poona University**
see **University of Poona**

**Popular Book Depot**
Dr. Bhadkamkar Marg, Bombay 400007, India.
- Indian Publisher and Bookseller. m. ISSN 0019-6223 (Federation of Publishers and Booksellers Associations in India)

**Popular Prakashan**
35-C Tardeo Rd., Bombay 400034, India.
- Indian Antiquary. q. ISSN 0019-4395 (Oriental Research Institute)
- Indian Dissertation Abstracts. q. (Indian Council of Social Science Research) (Co-Sponsor: Inter-University Board of India)
- Indian Journal of Surgery. bi-m. ISSN 0019-5650 (Association of Surgeons of India)
- Literary Criterion. s-a.(4 nos. to vol) ISSN 0024-452X
- Philosophical Association. Journal. s-a. ISSN 0031-8043 (Indian Philosophical Association, Amravati)

**Ports Consultative Organization**
N. S. Ghosh, Administrative Officer, 11-B Rajinder Park, New Delhi 60, India.
- Indian Ports. q. ISSN 0019-6134

**Postgraduate Institute of Medical Education and Research**
Chandigarh, India.
- Postgraduate Institute of Medical Education and Research. Bulletin. q.

**Poultry Patrika**
Box 4804, New Delhi 110023, India.
- Poultry Patrika. m.

**Prabasi Press Private Ltd.**
77-2-1 Dharamtala St., Calcutta 13, India.
- Modern Review. m. ISSN 0026-8380

**Practical Tax Publishers**
Bagla Buildings, Nahar Shahadat Khan, Delhi 6, India.
- Sales Tax Affairs. s-m.

**Praga Publications**
43 Sundar Mahal, Churchgate, Bombay 400020, India.
- Heart Care. q. ISSN 0046-7111 (Society for the Prevention of Heart Disease and Rehabilitation)

**Pragati Prakashan**
Box 62, Meerut, India.
- Acta Ciencia Indica. q. (Society for the Progress of Science)

**Praja Socialist Party**
c/o G.G. Parikh, National House, 6 Tulloch Rd., Bombay 1, India.
- Janata. w. ISSN 0021-4221

**Prajamata Illustrated Weekly**
c/o G.V. Anji, Bangalore 4, India.
- Prajamata Illustrated Weekly. w.

**P. V. Griha Prakashan**
1786 Sadashiv Peth, Poona 30, India.
- Progress of Education; a journal devoted to the discussion of problems relating to the theory, practice & administration of education. 55 per yr. ISSN 0033-0663

**Ram Prasad & Sons**
Hospital Rd., Agra 3, India.
- Indian Journal of Engineering Mathematics. s-a.

**Sarju Prasad**
10-A Himalaya, 41-A Sahar Rd., Andheri (East), Bombay 400069, India.
- Orient. q.

**Praveen Corp.**
Sayajiganj, Baroda 390005, India.
- Engineering Industries & Trade Journal. m. ISSN 0013-7987
- Food Agriculture and Plantation Journal. bi-m. ISSN 0015-6213
- Indian Export Trade Journal. m. ISSN 0019-4735
- Journal of Chemicals and Allied Industries. bi-m. ISSN 0021-9622
- Medicine & Surgery. m. ISSN 0025-8008
- Plastics, Rubber and Leather Industries Journal. bi-m. ISSN 0032-1249
- Selection. bi-m.
- Textile Industry & Trade Journal. bi-m. ISSN 0040-4993
- Transport Industry and Trade Journal. bi-m. ISSN 0041-1477

**Preet Lari Publishers**
c/o S. Darshan Singh, Preet Nagar, Amritsar, Punjab, India.
- Bal Sandesh. m. ISSN 0005-4208
- Preet Lari. m. ISSN 0032-7239

**Press and Public Relations Association**
17 Fire Brigade Lane, New Delhi 1, India.
- Press and Public Relations; for decision-makers and publicists. m. ISSN 0032-7808

**Press and Publications Agency**
5703 Nai Sarak, Delhi 6, India.
- Industrial Informika. s-m. ISSN 0046-9203

**Press Council of India**
10 Janpath, New Delhi 110001, India.
- P.C.I. Review. q.

**Press Institute of India**
Sapru House Annexe, Barakhamba Rd., New Delhi 110001, India.
- Data India. w.
- Vidura. bi-m. ISSN 0042-5303

**Prestige Journals of India**
Indu House, Ground Floor, Narottam Moraijee Marg, Ballard Estate, Bombay 1, India.
- International Markets Directory. biennial.
- Modern Agriculture. bi-m. ISSN 0047-7656
- Modern Agriculture Buyers Guide and Directory. biennial.
- Physicians Guide. biennial.
- Plastics Progress Directory. biennial.

**Prestige Publications**
461-1 Sadashiv Peth, Tilak Rd., Poona 411030, Maharashtra, India.
- Birbal. m. ISSN 0006-3614
- Kridangan. m. ISSN 0023-4621

**Print Craft Publishers**
Rakesh Marg, Pili Kothi, G. T. Rd., Ghaziabad, Uttar Pradesh, India
- International Journal of Contemporary Sociology. q. ISSN 0019-6398 (Editorial Office: c/o Raj P. Mohan, Dept. of Sociology and Anthropology, Auburn University, Auburn, Alabama 36830)

**Processed Foods Exports Promotion Council**
c/o Shri P. S. Srinivasan, Ed., 105 New Delhi House, Barakhamba Rd., New Delhi 110001, India.
- Profodcil Bulletin. q. ISSN 0030-8242

**Processlabs Private Ltd.**
S.V. Road, Dahisar, Bombay 68, India.
- Motion Pictures Technical Bulletin. q. ISSN 0027-1632

**Prodyut Kumar Som**
19 Nagar Bagan, Haltu, Parganas 24, West Bengal, India.
- Krishnachura. s-a. ISSN 0023-4745

**Professional Publications**
Box 2812, New Delhi 110060, India.
- Optometry Today. q. ISSN 0048-203X (Indian Optometric Association)

**Proletarian Path**
25-1 Jyotish Roy Rd., Calcutta 53, India.
- Proletarian Path. bi-m.

**Psycholinguistic Association of India**
c/o Dept. of Psychology, Ravishankar University, Raipur, India
- Psycho-Lingua; a bi-annual research journal devoted to communicative behavior. s-a. (Distr. by: National Psychological Corporation, 4/230 Kacheri Ghat, Agra 282004, India)

**Publicity Society of India**
c/o Mrs. F. N. Kanga, 20 G. Sleater Rd., Bombay 7, India.
- Onlooker. s-m. ISSN 0030-2619

**Pulse of Youth**
c/o Kamlendra Kanwar, 86 Hindu College Hostel, New Delhi, India.
- Pulse of Youth. q. ISSN 0033-4227

**Punjab**
see also **Haryana**

**Punjab. Economic and Statistical Organisation**
Chandigarh, Punjab, India.
- Socio-Economic Review of Punjab. a.

**Punjab Agricultural University**
Ludhiana 141004, Punjab, India.
- Punjab Agricultural University. Journal of Research. q. ISSN 0048-6019

**Punjab Law Reporter**
36 Sector 9-A, Chandigarh 11, India.
- Punjab Law Reporter. fortn. ISSN 0033-4332

**Punjab Medical Journal**
Partap Nagar, Jullundur 1, India.
- Punjab Medical Journal. m. ISSN 0033-4340

**Punjab National Bank, Ltd.**
5 Parliament St., New Delhi 10001, India.
- Punjab National Bank. Annual Report. a. ISSN 0304-8101

**Punjab Pharmacists' Federation; All India Medical Practitioners' Association; All India Homoepathic League**
- Pharmacy News. (pub. by Rajesh Publications)

**Punjab State Cooperative Fruit Development Federation Ltd**
Baradari Gardens, Patiala, India.
- Punjab Horticultural Journal. q. ISSN 0033-4324

**Punjab State Industrial Development Corporation**
United Commercial Bank Bldg., 3rd Floor, Sector 17-B, Chandigarh, India.
- Punjab State Industrial Development Corporation. Annual Report. a.

**Punjab University**
see **Panjab University**

**Punjabi University**
Patiala 4, Punjab, India.
- Bharati Te Videshi Sahita. s-a. ISSN 0006-050X
- Nanak Prakash Patrika. m. ISSN 0027-7770
- Panjab Past and Present. s-a. ISSN 0031-0786

**Punjabi University. Department of Linguistics**
Patiala 4, Punjab, India.
- Pakha Sanjam. s-a.

**Punjabi University. Department of Religious Studies**
Patiala 4, Punjab, India.
- Journal of Religious Studies. s-a. ISSN 0047-2735

**Purabi Publishers**
85 Bepin Behari Ganguly St., Calcutta 12, India.
- Jeevan Jauban. m. ISSN 0021-5813

**Qaumi Ekta Trust**
19-A Theatre Communications Bldg., Connaught Circus, New Delhi 110001, India.
- Secular Democracy; a journal of national integration. s-m. ISSN 0582-3730

**Rabindra Bharati University**
6/4 Dwarkanath Tagore Lane, Calcutta 700007, India.
- Rabindra Bharati Journal. irreg., latest issue, 1973.

**Radakrishna Indraprastha Estate**
Nehru House, 221/3 Deen Royal Upadhyaya Marg, New Delhi 110002, India.
- Gandhi Peace Foundation Lectures. irreg.

**Radio-Transistronic Constructor**
132-3612 Pantnagar, Bombay 75, India.
- Radio-Transistronic Constructor; radio, television audio electronics. m.

**P. Raghavan, Ed. & Pub.**
Kartar Bhuvan, Flat No. 11, First Floor, Behind Fariyas Hotel, Colaba, Bombay 400005, India.
- Indian Chemical Manufacturer. m.

**Rainbow Book Co. Educational Publishers**
Nai Sarak, Delhi 110006, India.
- Aspects of Allergy and Applied Immunology. irreg; vols 1-3 consist of convention proceedings. ISSN 0066-8664 (Indian College of Allergy and Applied Immunology)

**Baldev Raj, Ed. & Pub.**
M-48A Malviyanagar, New Delhi 17, India.
- International Reporter. w. ISSN 0020-8493

**Raja Rammohan Sarani**
Dipok Dey, 107-2 Amherst St., Calcutta 9, India.
- Uthon/Platform. 6 per yr. ISSN 0042-157X (Chandita Prakasani)

**S. Raja**
No. 7 Jer Mansion, Bandra, Bombay 50, India.
- Tanner. m. ISSN 0039-9442

**Rajasthan. Board of Secondary Education**
Rajasthan, Ajmer, India.
- Rajasthan Board Journal of Education. q. ISSN 0033-9083

**Rajasthan. Directorate of Economics and Statistics**
Krishi Bhawan, Jaipur, Rajasthan, India.
- Industrial Structure of Rajasthan. a. ISSN 0073-7666
- Rajasthan, India. Directorate of Economics and Statistics. Basic Statistics. a. ISSN 0079-9564
- Rajasthan, India. Directorate of Economics and Statistics. Budget Study. a. ISSN 0079-9556
- Statistical Abstract of Rajasthan. a. ISSN 0081-4717

**Rajasthan. Directorate of Medical, Health, and Family Planning Services**
Jaipur, Rajasthan, India.
• Rajasthan Medical Journal. q. ISSN 0485-9561

**Rajasthan. Forest Department**
Jaipur, Rajasthan, India.
• Rajasthan Forest Statistics. irreg.

**Rajasthan. State Institute of Education**
Udaipur, Rajasthan, India.
• State Institute of Education, Rajasthan. Annual Report. a.

**Rajasthan Agricultural Research Workers Association**
Government Agricultural Research Sta., Durgapur, Jaipur, India.
• Rajasthan Journal of Agricultural Sciences. s-a.

**Rajasthan Ayurvedic Research Laboratories**
Ayurveddoot Karyalaya 4, Dhamani Market, Sawai Mansingh Highway, Jaipur 3, India.
• Ayurveda Doot. w. ISSN 0005-2493

**Rajasthan Library Association**
D-191 Moti Marg Bapu Nagar, Jaipur 302004, India.
• R L A Quarterly Journal/Rajasthana Pustakalaya Sangha Patrika. q.

**Rajasthan State Warehousing Corporation**
Govind Bhavan, Subhash Marg, C-Scheme, Jaipur 1, India.
• Rajasthan State Warehousing Corporation. Annual Report and Accounts. a.

**Rajasthan University Library**
Gandhi Nagar, Jaipur 302004, India.
• Index India; a quarterly documentation list of selected articles, editorials, notes, and letters, etc., from periodicals and newspapers published in the English language all over the world. q. ISSN 0019-3844

**Rajesh Publications**
Pindi St., Ludhiana, Punjab, India.
• Pharmacy News. m. ISSN 0031-7063 (Punjab Pharmacists' Federation; All India Medical Practitioners' Association; All India Homoepathic League)

**Rajneesh Publications**
Selprint 249, A-Z Industrial Estate, Fergusson Rd., Bombay 400013, India.
• Sannyas. bi-m. (Ned-Sannyas International)

**K. N. Ramachandran, Ed. & Pub.**
Kottayam 686001, Kerala, India.
• Mass Line; Indian revolutionary movement. m.

**C. Ramakrishna, Ed. & Pub.**
Strand Hotel, 25 Strand Rd., Apollo Bunder, Bombay 1, India.
• Hyphen. m. ISSN 0018-8336

**Ramakrishna Mission Institute of Culture**
Gol Park, Calcutta 700029, India.
• Ramakrishna Mission Institute of Culture. Bulletin. m. ISSN 0033-9156

**Ramakrishna Order**
• Prabuddha Bharata/Awakened India. (pub. by Advaita Ashrama)

**Raman Publications**
"Sri Rajeswari", 115/1 New Extension, Seshadripuram, Bangalore 560020, India.
• Astrological Magazine. m. ISSN 0004-6140

**Ramanath Publications Private Ltd.**
65/5 Arcot Rd., Kodambakkam, Madras 600024, India.
• Cinema Rangam. m. ISSN 0009-7144
• Pesum Padam. m. ISSN 0031-6164

**Rami Press**
48 Mandirwali Gali, Yusof Sarai, New Delhi, India.
• Lore; magazine of new writing. m. (Delhi Writers Club)

**Ranchi University**
Ranchi 1, Bihar, India.
• Research Journal of Philosophy. s-a. ISSN 0048-7325

**Ranchi University. Department of Anthropology**
Ranchi 1, Bihar, India.
• Journal of Social Research. s-a. (Co-sponsor: Council of Social and Cultural Research)

**Ranchi University. Department of History**
Ranchi 1, Bihar, India.
• Journal of Historical Research. s-a. ISSN 0022-1562 (Co-sponsor: Historical and Archaeological Society)

**Ranchi University. Department of Mathematics**
Ranchi 1, Bihar, India.
• Ranchi University Mathematical Journal. a. ISSN 0079-9602

**Ranchi University. Department of Political Science**
Ranchi 1, Bihar, India.
• Political Scientist. s-a. ISSN 0032-3209

**Randi Printers**
Hind Piri, 23rd St., Ranchi, Bihar, India.
• Jain Jagran. m. ISSN 0021-4035 (Bihar State Digamber Jain Youth Association)

**Rani Suhasini Roy**
Tamluk Raj House, Tamluk, Midnapore, West Bengal, India.
• Beduin. a. ISSN 0005-769X

**C. M. Rao, Ed. & Pub.**
Varregudem, Machilipattanamu, Andhra Pradesh.
• Pasidibala. m. ISSN 0031-2622

**Nageswara Rao Estates Private Ltd.**
72 Thambu Chetty St., Madras 600001, India.
• Andhrasacitra Varapatrika. w.

**T. S. K. Rao, Ed. & Pub.**
2235 Bhutgoswami Vattaram, Manojiappa St., Thanjavur 613001, India.
• Journal of Plant and Machinery. s-a. ISSN 0449-5721

**T.S.N. Rao, Ed. & Pub.**
West View, 309 Ghodbunder Rd., Santacruz West, Bombay 54, India.
• Journal of Industrial Engineering. q. ISSN 0022-183X

**Raptakos, Brett & Co., Ltd**
47 Dr. Annie Besant Rd., Worli, Bombay 400025, India.
• Quarterly Medical Review. q. ISSN 0481-2158

**Rasi Palam**
12 Ranganathan St., Adaikkalam St., Chepauk, Madras 5, India.
• Rasi Palam. m.

**Ratna Dhar Jha**
C-19 Model Town, Delhi 9, India.
• New Tones. m.

**Ravikrupa Trust**
1760 Gandhi Rd., Ahmedabad 1, India.
• Journal of Library Service. m.

**Reader's Digest Association Private Ltd.**
Orient House, 2nd Floor, Mangalore St., Bombay 400038, India.
• Reader's Digest (Indian Edition) m. ISSN 0034-0421

**Regional Engineering College**
*see* **Jawaharlal Nehru Technological University. Regional Engineering College**

**Regional Science Association, India**
• Indian Journal of Regional Science. (pub. by Indian Institute of Technology, Kharagpur)

**Rehabilitation Industries Corporation Ltd.**
25 Free School St., Calcutta 16, India.
• Rehabilitation Industries Corporation. Annual Report. a. ISSN 0080-0724

**Republic Forge Company**
Maula Ali, Hyderabad 40, India.
• Republic Forge Company. Annual Report. a.

**Republic of Iraq Embassy**
*see* **Embassy of the Republic of Iraq**

**Reserve Bank of India**
*see* **India. Reserve Bank of India**

**Retailer**
c/o Mohinder Manocha, D49 South Extension, Part 1, New Delhi 110049, India.
• Retailer; national socio-economic journal for retailer and consumer. m.

**Review Publications**
Rastogi St., Subhash Bazar, Meerut 2, India.
• International Review of History and Political Science. q. ISSN 0020-8574

**Revolutionary Socialist Party**
780 Ballimaran, Delhi 6, India.
• Call. m. ISSN 0008-1728

**Rhythm**
21-2C Harish Mukherji Rd., Calcutta 25, India.
• Rhythm. q. ISSN 0035-4937

**Risalat**
5 Abdul Khaliq Chishti, Ajmer, India.
• Risalat; Islamic journal in English. m.

**Rising Sun**
52-A Kodam Bakkam, High Road, Madras 600034, India.
• Rising Sun. w.

**Roller Flour Millers' Federation of India**
6 Todar Mal Lane, Bengali Market, New Delhi, India.
• Indian Miller. bi-m.

**Roma Publications**
3290/15-D Chandigarh, India.
• Roma; journal of life, language and culture. s-a. (Indian Institute of Romani Studies) (Co-sponsor: Institute of Contemporary Romani Research and Documentation)

**Roorkee University**
*see* **University of Roorkee**

**Rosy Penfriends Service**
Keonijhar Garh, Orissa, India.
• Ruby. s-a. ISSN 0035-9580

**Round Table Publications**
F-15 Bhagat Singh Market, New Delhi 110001, India.
• Weekly Round Table; free forum on current affairs. w.

**Aditi Nath Roy, Ed. & Pub.**
49-11-A Hindustan Park, Calcutta 700029, India.
• Oh Calcutta. q.

**Himansu Roy, Ed. & Pub.**
10 Galiff St., Block 5, Suite 64, Calcutta 3, India.
• Economic Affairs; a monthly journal of economics. m.

**K. K. Roy (Private) Ltd.**
55 Gariahat Rd., Box 10210, Calcutta 700019, India.
• Africa Letter. w. ISSN 0044-6491
• African Books Newsletter. m. ISSN 0001-9941
• Agriculture Checklist. bi-m. ISSN 0002-1733
• Asian Books Newsletter. m. ISSN 0004-4547
• Asian Journal of European Studies. 3 per yr.
• Bibliographia Africana. m. ISSN 0006-1190
• Bibliographia Asiatica. m. ISSN 0006-1212
• Creative Book Selection Index. m.
• History of Agriculture. q. (International Association for the History of Agriculture)
• International Journal of Arbitration. 3 per yr. ISSN 0020-7098
• Latin American Books Newsletter. m. ISSN 0023-8740
• Legal History. q. (Indian Institute of Legal History)
• Library History Review. q. (International Agency for Research in Library History)
• Medical Checklist. bi-m. ISSN 0025-7109
• Religious Book Review Index. bi-m. ISSN 0034-4060
• Research in Tourism. q.
• World Report on Technical Advancement. m. ISSN 0043-8944

**Subhas Chandra Roy**
143 Jodhpur Park, Calcutta 700068, India.
• I S T D Review. bi-m. (Indian Society for Training and Development)

**Rubber and Plastics Digest**
640 Double Storey, New Rajinder Nagar, New Delhi 60, India.
- Rubber and Plastics Digest. q.

**Rupambara**
22B Pratapaditya Rd., Calcutta 26, India.
- Rupambara. q. ISSN 0035-9963

**Rural Electrification Corporation**
D-5 N. D. S. E. Part II, Ring Rd., New Delhi 110049, India.
- R E C Bulletin. m.
- Rural Electrification Corporation. Annual Report and Statement of Accounts. a.

**S A S M I R A**
see Silk and Art Silk Mills' Research Association

**S E N D O C (Small Enterprises National Documentation Center)**
see Small Industry Extension Training Institute

**Sadhana Publications**
Vincent Rd., Cochin 18, India.
- Partisan. w. ISSN 0048-3044

**Sadhna Prakashan**
Rastogi St., Subhash Bazar, Meerut 2, India.
- International Behavioural Scientist. q. ISSN 0020-613X

**Sahitya Akademi**
see National Academy of Letters

**Saifia College. Department of Zoology**
Bhopal, India.
- Indian Journal of Zoology. q. ISSN 0302-7562

**Saiva Siddhanta Mahasamajam**
12 E. Mada St., Mylapore, Madras 600004, India.
- Saiva Siddhanta. q. ISSN 0036-3316

**Sajit Print**
2 F Dilkusha St., Calcutta 17, India.
- Sajit Monthly. m.

**Saket Economic Survey**
Kalyan Rd., Dombivli 421201, Maharashtra, India.
- Saket Economic Survey. bi-m.

**Sakthi Sugars Ltd.**
6 Poes Garden, Madras 600086, India.
- Kisan World. m.

**Salar Jung Museum**
Hyderabad 500002, Andhra Pradesh, India.
- Salar Jung Museum. Annual Report. a.
- Salar Jung Museum Bi-Annual Research Journal. s-a.

**Sales Tax Practitioners' Association**
Mohatta Market, Palton Rd., Bombay 1, India.
- Sales Tax Review. m.

**Samatat Prakashan**
5-1B Deshapriya Park E., Calcutta 29, India.
- Samatat Prakashan. q. ISSN 0036-374X

**Samriddhi Publications**
C-5 Bapunagar, Jaipur 4, India.
- Rajasthan Year Book and Who's Who. a. ISSN 0079-9572

**Sangeet Natak Akademi**
see National Academy of Music, Dance and Drama

**S. Sankaran, Ed. & Pub.**
25 Sivaraman St., Triplicane, Madras 600005, India.
- Indian Leather. m. ISSN 0019-574X

**Sanskrit College. Department of Postgraduate Training and Research**
1 Bankim Chatterjee St., Calcutta 12, India.
- Our Heritage. s-a. ISSN 0474-9030

**Sant Sipahi**
Lal Haveli, Gate Mahan Singh, Amritsar 24, India.
- Sant Sipahi. m.

**Sarada Ranganathan Endowment for Library Science, Bangalore**
DRTC 112, Cross Rd. 11, Malleswaram, Bangalore 560003, India.
- Library Science with a Slant to Documentation. q. ISSN 0024-2543

**Sarasvat**
206 Bidhan Sarani, Calcutta 6, India.
- Sarasvat; literary and cultural. q. ISSN 0036-4754

**Sarathi Karyalaya**
Box 276, Rajkot, India.
- Sarathi Gujarati Weekly. w.

**Sardar Patel Institute of Economics and Social Research**
Box 4062, Navarangpura, Ahmedabad, India.
- Anvesak. s-a.

**Sardar Patel University**
Vallabh Vidyanagar, Gujarat, India.
- Journal of Education and Psychology. q. ISSN 0022-0590

**Sardar Patel University. Department of Economics**
Vallabh Vidyanagar, Gujarat, India.
- Artha-Vikas; a journal of economic development. s-a. ISSN 0004-3567

**Sarvadeshik Arya Pratinidhi Sabha**
Dayanand Bhavan, Ramila Ground, New Delhi 1, India.
- Vedic Light. 10 per yr. (International Aryan League)

**Sarvodaya Prachuralayam**
Punkunnam, Trichur 2, Pin 680002, Kerala, India.
- Sarvodaya. m. ISSN 0036-4835

**Sarvotkrushta Marathi Katha**
c/o Mrs. Chhaya Kolarkar, Ed., 43/348 Sant Tukaram Nagar, Pimpri, Poona 411018, India.
- Sarvotkrushta Marathi Katha. a.

**Sastu Sahitya Mudranalaya Trust**
Swami Akhandanand Marg, Bhadra, Box 50, Ahmedabad 380001, India.
- Akhand Anand. m. ISSN 0002-3639

**Saugar University**
see University of Saugar

**School of Planning and Architecture**
Indraprastha Estate, New Delhi 1, India.
- Urban and Rural Planning Thought. q. ISSN 0042-0824

**School of Tropical Medicine, Calcutta**
- School of Tropical Medicine, Calcutta. Bulletin. (pub. by Scientific Instrument Co. Ltd.)

**Scientific Instrument Co. Ltd.**
6 Tej Bahadur Sapru Rd., Allahabad, India.
- School of Tropical Medicine, Calcutta. Bulletin. q. ISSN 0068-5372

**Scientific Research Committee, Uttar Pradesh**
Chhattar Manzil Palace, Lucknow, Uttar Pradesh, India.
- Uttar Pradesh, India. Scientific Research Committee Monograph Series. irreg. ISSN 0083-5013

**Seafood Exporters Association of India**
VII/389 Kochangadi, Cochin 682002, India.
- Seafood Export Journal. m. ISSN 0037-010X

**Narender K. Sehgal, Ed. & Pub.**
465-R Model Town, Jullundur 144003, Punjab, India.
- Scientific Opinion. q.

**SENDOC (Small Enterprises National Documentation Centre)**
see Small Industry Extension Training Institute

**Servants of the People Society**
Lajpat Bhawan, Lajpat Nagar, New Delhi 110024, India.
- Lajpat Bhawan Bulletin. m.

**Seth G.S. Medical College and K.E.M. Hospital. Staff Society**
c/o Dr. S.M. Bhatnagar, Bombay 12, India.
- Journal of Postgraduate Medicine. q. ISSN 0022-3859

**Mrs. Padma Seth, Ed. & Pub.**
A-3 Pandara Rd., New Delhi 11, India.
- Indian Administrative & Management Review; a journal of advanced learning in administration and management. q. ISSN 0019-4298
- Indian Review of Public and Co-operative Economy. bi-m.

**Sarabjeet Seth, Ed. & Pub.**
R-867 New Rajinder Nagar, New Delhi 110060, India.
- Soliloquy; magazine of prose and poetry. q.

**Sevak Publications**
B-26 Royal Industrial Estate, Naigaum Cross Rd., Wadala, Bombay 400031, India.
- Chemical Weekly. w. ISSN 0045-6500
- Indian Chemical Journal. m. ISSN 0019-4514
- Polymer India. w. ISSN 0048-4806
- Textile Dyer and Printer. m. ISSN 0040-4926

**Swami Bholananda Sevamandal**
1 Mahesh Choudhury Lane, Calcutta 25, India.
- Sivam. m. ISSN 0037-5950

**Seventh-Day Adventists**
- Herald of Health. (pub. by Oriental Watchman Publishing House)

**Navalchad T. Shah & Co.**
15 Union Bank Bldg., 4th Floor, Dalal St., Bombay 1, India.
- Investors' Guide. m. ISSN 0021-020X

**P. M. Shah, Ed. & Pub.**
12 Fort Chambers, Haman St., Bombay 1, India.
- Indian Exporter and Importer. m. ISSN 0019-4743

**Shahpar**
848 Daryabad, Allahabad 3, India.
- Shahpar. m. ISSN 0037-3184

**Shama Magazine**
13/14 Asaf Ali Rd., New Delhi 110001, India.
- Bano. m. ISSN 0005-5573
- Khilauna. m. ISSN 0023-1096
- Shabistan Urdu Digest. m. ISSN 0037-3125
- Shama. m. ISSN 0037-3273
- Sushama. m. ISSN 0039-6370

**Shantarani Sons & Co.**
7-104 Nariman Passage, Prabhadevi, Bombay 400025, India.
- Paperprintpack India. m. ISSN 0048-2862

**L. K. Sharma**
Ranchi, India.
- H E C Technical Journal. a. (Heavy Engineering Corporation)

**S. K. Sharma, Pub.**
5-A Daryaganj, Ansari Rd., Delhi 6, India.
- Machinery & Machine Tool Journal. m. ISSN 0047-5351

**Sudhir Sharma, Ed. & Pub.**
2165 Sector 21-C, Chandigarh, India.
- Inquisitor; a student's magazine. m. ISSN 0046-9599

**Shellac Export Promotion Council**
14/1-B Ezra St., Calcutta 1, India.
- Shellac Export Promotion Council. Annual Report. a.

**Shikshak Publishing House**
61 Ballygunge Place, Calcutta 19, India.
- Shikshak. m. ISSN 0008-9710

**Shipping and Port Review**
Wachel Molla Mansion, 8 Lenin Sarani, Calcutta 13, India.
- Shipping and Port Review. bi-m. ISSN 0037-3885

**Shot Publications**
3-B Madan St., Calcutta 700013, India.
- Indian Motion Picture Almanac. a.

**Shree Gurudev Ashram**
P.O. Ganeshpuri District, Thana 401206, India.
- Shree Gurudev Ashram Newsletter. m.

**Shree Jiwaji Observatory**
Ujain, Madhya Pradesh, India.
- Astronomical Ephemeris of Geocentric Places of Planets. a. ISSN 0066-9970

**Shri Chhatrapati Shivaji University**
Kolhapur, India.
- Shri Chhatrapati Shivaji University. Report. a. ISSN 0080-9322

**Shri Ram Centre for Industrial Relations & Human Resources**
5 Pusa Rd., New Delhi 5, India.
- Indian Journal of Industrial Relations. q. ISSN 0019-5286

**Shri Ram College of Commerce**
Delhi 7, India.
- Business Analyst. 3 per yr. ISSN 0007-6430

**Shugoofa**
27 Bachelor's Quarters, Moazamjahi Market, Hyderabad 500001, India.
- Shugoofa. bi-m.

**U. Shukla, Ed. & Pub.**
107 Gopalganj, Sagar, Madhya Pradesh, India.
- Janaman; a spokesman for democratic socialism. w. ISSN 0021-4213

**Satyendra Shyam, Ed. & Pub.**
92 Daryaganj, Delhi, India.
- Lalita. m. ISSN 0023-740X
- Nav-Chitrapat. m. ISSN 0042-2444

**Sidarth Publications**
A-27 Shalimar Industrial Estate, Matunga, Bombay 19, India.
- Dye-Chem Sphere. w.

**Siddha Yoga Dham**
32/A Nizamiddin East, New Delhi, India.
- Siddha Vani. a.

**Sikh Cultural Centre**
113/1A C.R. Ave., Calcutta, India.
- Sikh Review. m. ISSN 0037-5128

**Silk and Art Silk Mills' Research Association**
Sasmira Marg, Worli, Bombay 400025, India.
- Man-Made Textiles in India. m.

**Silk and Rayon Textiles Export Promotion Council**
Resham Bhawan, 18 Veer Nariman Rd., Bombay 400020, India.
- Indian Silk and Rayon. q. ISSN 0442-736X

**G. Singh, Ed. & Pub.**
A-148 Defence Colony, New Delhi 24, India.
- East European Trade. m. ISSN 0012-8457

**M. Gulab Singh & Sons (P). Ltd.**
6 Bahadur Shah Zafar Marg, New Delhi 1, India.
- Democratic World. w. ISSN 0301-9047

**Pritam Singh**
Pleasure Garden Market, Chadni Chowk, Delhi 6, India.
- Roopvati.

**Sardar Amar Singh & Sons**
Union Bank Bldg., Ajmal Khan Rd., Karol Baugh, New Delhi 5, India.
- Punjabi Digest. m. (Sri Guru Singh Sabha)

**Singhal House**
Shivaji Marg, Meerut, Uttar Pradesh, India.
- Indian Journal of Social Research. 3 per yr. ISSN 0019-5626

**A. N. Sinha Institute of Social Studies**
Patna 800001, Bihar, India.
- Journal of Social and Economic Studies. s-a.

**Sinha Publishing House**
39 S. R. Das Rd., Calcutta 700026, India.
- Review of Indian Spiritualism. m.

**V. M. Sinkar, Ed. & Pub.**
"Prabhat", 47-A Gophale Rd. (North), Dadar, Bombay 28, India.
- Ideal Education. m. ISSN 0019-1353

**Giani Balwant Singh Sant Sipahi , Ed. & Pub.**
M-90 Raghuvir Nagar, Najaf Garh Rd., New Delhi 110027, India.
- Gurmat Sagar. m.

**Skylark**
Skylark Building, 284 Frere Rd., Bombay 400001, India.
- Economic and Political Weekly; a journal of current economic and political affairs. w. ISSN 0012-9976

**Small Industry Extension Training Institute**
Yousufguda, Hyderabad 500045, India.
- Appropriate Technology Documentation Bulletin. q.
- S E D M E. (Small Enterprises Development, Management and Extension) 4 per yr.

**F. K. Soans, Ed. & Pub.**
Zita Villa, 129-C Kalina, Santa Cruz E., Bombay 29, India.
- Industrial Welder. m.

**Social Life**
1184 Bahadur Garh Rd., Delhi 6, India.
- Social Life. m.

**Socialist Digest**
174 D.N. Rd., Bombay 1, India.
- Socialist Digest; quarterly anthology of socialist literature. q. ISSN 0037-8186

**Socialist World**
4126 Urdu Bazar, Delhi, India.
- Socialist World. s-m.

**Society & Commerce Publications (Pvt) Ltd.**
2 Waterloo St., Calcutta 700069, India.
- Society and Commerce; for balanced social change. m.

**Society for Advancement of Electrochemical Science and Technology**
Karaikudi 623006, Tamil Nadu, India.
- Current Titles in Electrochemistry. m. ISSN 0037-9689
- S A E S T Transactions. q. ISSN 0036-0678

**Society for Geographical Studies, Kanpur**
7-125 Swarup Nagar, Kanpur 2, India.
- Geographical Knowledge. s-a. ISSN 0016-7401

**Society for the Advancement of Botany**
Department of Botany, Meerut College, Meerut 250001, India.
- Acta Botanica Indica. s-a.

**Society for the Prevention of Heart Disease and Rehabilitation**
- Heart Care. (pub. by Praga Publications)

**Society for the Progress of Science**
- Acta Ciencia Indica. (pub. by Pragati Prakashan)

**Society for the Study of Industrial Medicine**
8 Tala Park Ave., Calcutta 700002, India.
- Asian Conference on Occupational Health. Proceedings. irreg.; latest issue, 1974. ISSN 0518-8857

**Society for the Study of Industrial Medicine, Bombay Branch**
c/o Dr. S. V. Bhatt, 243 Khetwadi, Main Rd., Bombay 4, India.
- Indian Journal of Occupational Health. m. ISSN 0019-5391

**Society for the Study of Social Sciences**
c/o Treasurer, Dept. of Sociology, Osmania University, Hyderabad 7, India.
- Indian Journal of Social Sciences. 3 per yr.

**Society for the Study of State Governments**
Kopparti Pl., Karaundi, Varanasi 221005, Uttar Pradesh, India.
- Society for the Study of State Governments. Journal. q. ISSN 0037-9786

**Society of Animal Morphologists & Physiologists**
c/o Maharaja Sayajirao University of Baroda, Dept. of Zoology, Faculty of Science, Baroda 390002, India.
- Journal of Animal Morphology and Physiology. s-a. ISSN 0021-8804
- Pavo; the Indian Journal of Ornithology. s-a. ISSN 0031-3297

**Society of Biological Chemists**
Dept. of Biochemistry, Indian Institute of Science, Bangalore 560012, India.
- Biochemical Reviews. a.
- S B C Newsletter. 3 per yr.

**Society of Electronic Engineers**
Box 108, High Grounds, Bangalore 1, India.
- Electro-Technology. q. ISSN 0013-4643

**Society of Fisheries Technologists (India)**
c/o Central Institute of Fisheries Technology, Box 1039, Chittoor Rd., Ernakulam, Cochin 682011, India.
- Fishery Technology. s-a. ISSN 0015-3001

**Society of Management Science and Applied Cybernetics**
c/o CSIR, Rafi Marg, New Delhi 110001, India.
- Scima. s-a.

**Society of Medical Aeronautical Engineers of India**
- Indian Modeller. (pub. by Little-Flower Press)

**Society of Mycology and Plant Pathology**
Rajasthan College of Agriculture, Udaipur, India.
- Indian Journal of Mycology and Plant Pathology. s-a.

**Society of St. Thomas**
- Arunodayam. (pub. by Christavashram Press)

**Society of Servants of God**
Yashwant Place, Satya Marg, Chanakyapuri, New Delhi 110021, India.
- Discourse. fortn.

**Soil Conservation Society of India**
DVC Campus, Hazaribagh, Bihar, India.
- Journal of Soil and Water Conservation in India. a. ISSN 0022-457X

**South Asian Studies Center**
*see* **University of Rajasthan. South Asian Studies Center**

**South India Teachers' Union**
Rajah Annamalaipuram, Madras 28, India.
- South Indian Teacher. m. ISSN 0038-3481

**South India Textile Research Association**
Coimbatore 641014, India.
- Conference on Human Relations in Industry. Proceedings. a. ISSN 0069-8555

**South Indian Horticultural Association**
Lawley Rd. (Post), Coimbatore 3, India.
- South Indian Horticulture. q. ISSN 0038-3473

**South Indian Steam & Fuel Users' Association**
Stephenson Rd., Perambur Barracks, Madras 12, India.
- Steam & Fuel Users' Journal. q. ISSN 0039-0828

**Southern Economist Private Ltd.**
106-108 Infantry Rd., Bangalore 560001, India.
- Southern Economist. fortn. ISSN 0038-4046

**Southern Plastic Industries Association**
5A/147 Mount Rd., Madras 6, India.
- Industrial Herald. w. (Co-sponsor: Industrial & Scientific Research Association)

**Southern Publishers**
12 Third Main Rd., Kasturbanagar, Madras 20, India.
- Facts File; economic and sociological monthly. m. ISSN 0046-3132

**Southern Railways**
c/o T. S. Rao, 2235 Bhut Gosami Vattaram, Manojiappa St., Tanjore S., India.
- Southern Railways. m. ISSN 0038-450X

**Space Age Publishers**
237 Netaji Subhas Rd., Calcutta 47, India.
- Current Dynamics. m.

**Speedwriter**
2-58 Ramesh Nagar, New Delhi 110015, India.
- Speedwriter. m.

**Spices Export Promotion Council**
World Trade Centre, Mahatma Gandhi Rd., Ernakulam, Cochin 682016, India.
- Indian Spices. q. ISSN 0019-6401
- Spices Newsletter. m.

**Sri Aurobindo Ashram Trust**
Pondicherry 605002, India.
- Advent. q.
- Mother India; review of culture. m. ISSN 0027-1543
- Sri Aurobindo International Center of Education. Bulletin. q.

**Sri Aurobindo International Center of Education**
- Sri Aurobindo International Center of Education. Bulletin. (pub. by Sri Aurobindo Ashram Trust)

**Sri Avinashilingam Home Science College for Women**
c/o R. P. Devadas, Ed., Coimbatore 641011, India.
- Indian Journal of Nutrition and Dietetics. m. ISSN 0022-3174

**Sri Baktha Samaj**
6-A Station Rd., West Mambalam, Madras 33, India.
- Kamakoti Vani; voice of Kamakoti. m. ISSN 0022-8052

**Sri Birendra Nath Ghosh**
Off Exhibition Rd., Patna 1, India.
- Aatma Katha. w.

**Sri Guru Singh Sabha**
- Punjabi Digest. (pub. by Sardar Amar Singh & Sons)

**Sri Ramakrishna Math**
Mylapore, Madras 4, India.
- Vedanta Kesari. m. ISSN 0042-2983

**Sri Ramakrishna Mission Vidyalaya Teachers College**
Sri Ramakrishna Vidyalaya P.O. Coimbatore Dt., Tamil Nadu, India.
- Journal of Educational Research and Extension. q. ISSN 0022-068X

**Sri Ramanasramam**
Tiruvannamalai 606603, India.
- Mountain Path. q. ISSN 0027-2574

**Sri Venkateswara University. Department of Sanskrit**
Tirupati, Andhra Pradesh, India.
- Sri Venkateswara University. Department of Sanskrit. Symposium. irreg., 1967, no. 4. ISSN 0081-3915

**Sri Venkateswara University. Oriental Research Institute**
Tirupati 517502, District Chittoor, India.
- Sri Venkateswara University. Oriental Journal. a.(issued in 2 pts.) ISSN 0081-3907

**K. Srinivas, Ed. & Pub.**
16 Dandapani St., Madras 17, India.
- Indian Industries. m. ISSN 0019-4891

**Standard Press**
263 Kamla Market, New Delhi, India.
- N. C. W. I. Bulletin. s-a. (National Council of Women in India)

**State Bank of India**
see India. State Bank of India

**State Institute of Education, Maharashtra**
see Maharashtra. Maharashtra State Institute of Education

**State Institute of Education, Rajasthan**
see Rajasthan. State Institute of Education

**State Supplies**
552 Bapa Nagar, Military Rd., Anand Parbat, New Delhi 5, India.
- State Supplies. m. ISSN 0049-2159

**Statesman Ltd.**
4 Chowringhee Sq., Calcutta 700001, India.
- Statesman Weekly; news and comments from "The Statesman" of New Delhi and Calcutta. w. ISSN 0039-0321

**Statistical Publishing Society**
204/1 Barrackpore Trunk Rd., Calcutta 700035, India.
- Indian Statistical Institute. Annual Report. a. ISSN 0073-6686
- Indian Statistical Institute. Econometric and Social Sciences Series. Research Monographs. irreg. ISSN 0073-6694
- Indian Statistical Institute. Research and Training School. Publications. irreg.
- Indian Statistical Institute. Statistics and Probability Series. Research Monographs. irreg. ISSN 0073-6716
- Samvadadhvam. irreg. ISSN 0581-4790 (Indian Statistical Institute)
- Sankhya; Indian journal of statistics. q. (Indian Statistical Institute)

**Sterling Publishers Pvt. Ltd.**
AB/9 Safdarjang Enclave, New Delhi 110016, India.
- Indian Book Industry. m. ISSN 0019-4433

**Stir**
A-422 Defence Colony, New Delhi 24, India.
- Stir. w.

**Stock Exchange Foundation**
Dalal St., Fort, Bombay 1, India.
- Stock Exchange Official Directory. w.

**Stride**
49 Milan Park, Garia, Calcutta 32, India.
- Stride. m. ISSN 0039-2340

**Structural Engineering Research Centre**
Roorkee 247667, Uttar Pradesh, India.
- Journal of Structural Engineering. q.

**Students' Information Centre**
A-147 Defence Colony, New Delhi 3, India.
- Youth Chronicle. m. ISSN 0044-1201

**V. Subramanian Ed. & Pub.**
337 Thambu Chetty St., Madras 600001, India.
- Digest of Labour Cases. m. ISSN 0012-2750

**Suganitam Trust**
Department of Mathematics, Gujarat University, Ahmedabad 380009, India.
- Suganitam. bi-m.

**Sulekha Press**
Arambagh, Hooghly, W. Bengal, India.
- Mahajanmer Lagna. w. ISSN 0025-0414

**Sundar Homoeo Sadan**
113 Netaji Subhas Rd., Calcutta 1, India.
- Homoeopathic World. m. ISSN 0046-7812

**Sunshine Foundation**
6 Parvati Villa Rd., Poona 1, Maharashtra, India.
- Sunshine. m. ISSN 0039-5420

**Super Power Publications**
331/333 Thambu Chetty St., 1st Floor, Madras 600001, India.
- Super Power Publications. m. ISSN 0039-5668

**Swami Nirmalananda. Bharat Sevasram Sangha**
211 Rash Behari Ave., Calcutta 1, India.
- Pronab. m. ISSN 0033-1201

**Swaran Publishing House**
C6-23-2 Safdarjang Development Area, New Delhi 16, India.
- Journal of Dynamic Medicine. q. ISSN 0301-4789 (All India Institute of Homeopathy)

**Rama Swarup, Ed. & Pub.**
G-74 Sujan Singh Park, New Delhi 110003, India.
- Free News and Feature Service; weekly bulletin for small and medium newspapers. w.

**Swati Prakashan**
Purvalaya Building, 14-15 Ramkrishna Nagar, Rajkot 360002, India.
- Tax-Planning. m.
- Tax-Vyapar; periodical devoted to problems of commerce and taxes. m.

**Tagore Institute of Creative Writing, International**
Diparun, 7th Ave., Besant Nagar, Madras 600090, India.
- Ocarina; a bi-monthly journal of poetry and aesthetics. bi-m.

**Tagore Research Institute**
c/o Ms. Pronoti Mukerji, 4 Elgin Rd., Calcutta 20, India.
- Tagore Studies. a. ISSN 0082-1454

**Taj Mahal Hotel**
- Taj. (pub. by Indian Hotels Company Ltd.)

**Tamil Nadu**
see also Madras

**Tamil Nadu. Commissioner of Labour**
Chepauk, Madras 5, India.
- Tamil Nadu Labour Journal. m.

**Tamil Nadu. Department of Archaeology**
Madras, Tamil Nadu, India.
- Damilica. irreg.

**Tamil Nadu. Director of Employment and Training**
Madras, India.
- Review of Employment in Tamil Nadu. q.

**Tamil Nadu. Director of Information and Public Relations**
Government Estate, Madras 600002, India.
- Tamil Arasu. m.(English edition), fortn.(Tamil edition) ISSN 0039-9280

**Tamil Nadu. Director of Information and Publicity**
Fort St. George, Madras 9, India.
- Tamil Nadu Information. m. ISSN 0039-9310

**Tamil Nadu. Director of Statistics**
Madras 600006, India
(Subscription to: Government Publication Depot, 166 Anna Road, Madras 600002, India)
- Abstract of Statistics for Tamil Nadu. q.
- Tamil Nadu. Department of Statistics. Annual Statistical Abstract. a. ISSN 0082-1578
- Tamil Nadu. Department of Statistics. Season and Crop Report. a. ISSN 0082-1586

**Tamil Nadu. Government Museum, Madras**
Director of Museums, Pantheon Road, Egmore, Madras, India.
- Madras. Government Museum. Bulletin. New Series. irreg. ISSN 0085-2945

**Tamil Nadu. Government Oriental Manuscripts Library**
Curator, University Library Buildings, Chepauk, Madras 600005, India.
- Government Oriental Manuscripts Library. Bulletin. a.

**Tamil Nadu. Legislative Council**
Fort St. George, Madras 600009, India.
- Tamil Nadu. Legislative Council. Quinquennial Review. quinquennial. ISSN 0082-1594
- Who Is Who. biennial.

**Tamil Nadu Agricultural University**
Coimbatore 641003, India.
- Madras Agricultural Journal. m. ISSN 0024-9602

**Tamil Nadu Co-operative Union**
TNCU Bldg., Near Walajah Bridge, Madras 600009, India.
- Tamil Nadu Journal of Co-operation. m.

**Tamil Nadu Industrial Development Corporation**
Local Library Authority Building, 3rd Floor, 150-A Anna Salai, Madras, India.
- Tamil Nadu Industrial Development Corporation. Annual Report. a.

**Tamil Nadu P. W. D. Workers' Union**
Sankarankoul, Tirunnelveli, Madras 627756, India.
- Tozhil Uravu. m.

**Tamil Nadu Tourism Development Corporation**
V. S. T. Motors Bldgs., 34 Mount Rd., Madras, India.
- Tamil Nadu Tourism Development Corporation. Annual Report. a.

**Ram Ballabh Tapuriah, Pub.**
Naya Shaher, Sikar, Rajasthan, India.
- Jiwan Dhara. 8 per yr. ISSN 0021-6976

**Tara Cultural Trust**
10 Harrington Rd., Madras 600031, Tamil Nadu, India.
- Tapovan Prasad. m.

**W. H. Targett and Co. Ltd.**
Box 14, 19 R. N. Mookerjee Rd., Calcutta 700001, India.
- Capital; India's oldest financial weekly dealing with economics, industry and public affairs. w. ISSN 0008-5839

**Tata Economic Consultancy Services**
Orient House, Mangalore Estate, Ballard Estate, Bombay 400038, India.
- Business Environment. w.
- Economic Scene. m.

**Tata Institute of Fundamental Research. Bombay**
- Studies in Mathematics. (pub. by Oxford University Press US)

**Tata Institute of Social Sciences**
Sion-Trombay Rd., Deonar, Bombay 400088, India.
- Indian Journal of Social Work. q. ISSN 0019-5634

**Tata Iron and Steel Co. Ltd.**
Jamshedpur 831001, Bihar, India.
- T I S C O Technical Journal. q. ISSN 0039-8411

**Tax Affairs**
Bagla Bldgs., Nahar Shahadat Khan, Delhi 6, India.
- Tax Affairs. m. ISSN 0039-9965

**Tax Times Trust**
Sarafa, Jhansi, Uttar Pradesh, India.
- Tax Times. w. ISSN 0040-0122

**Taxation**
174 Jorbagh, New Delhi 110003, India.
- Taxation. m.

**Taxes and Planning**
11 E. Kalpana, Tilaknagar, Sardar Patel Rd.,
Bombay 4, India.
- Taxes and Planning. m.

**Tea Board**
14 Brabourne Rd., Calcutta 1, India.
- Tea Directory. irreg., latest issue, 1970.

**Tea Research Association**
Tocklai Experimental Station, Jorhat 785008,
Assam, India.
- Tea Research Association. Advisory Bulletin. 4
per yr.
- Tea Research Association. Memorandum. irreg.
- Tea Research Association. Occasional Scientific
Papers. irreg., 1970, no. 9.
- Tea Research Association. Scientific Annual
Report. a. ISSN 0564-6723
- Two and a Bud. s-a.

**Teachers' Cooperative Education Journals and
Publications Ltd.**
Kanyakubija College, 10 Staff Colony, Lucknow,
Uttar Pradesh, India.
- Education. m. ISSN 0013-1180

**Technical and General Press. Engineers' Bureau**
c/o Jyotsnmay Guha Thakurta, 21B Lansdowne
Terrace, Calcutta 26, India.
- Indian Journal of Engineers. Annual Foundry
Number. a. ISSN 0073-6554

**Technical Press Publications**
5 Convent St., Colaba, Bombay 1, India.
- Chemical Age of India. m. ISSN 0009-2320
(Chemical Process Industries of India)
- Guide to Indian Chemical Plants and Equipment.
irreg.
- Indian Chemical Directory. 11th edt., 1975. ISSN
0073-6295

**Technical Teachers' Training Institute**
7 Mayurbhanj Rd., Calcutta 700023, India.
- Prajnan. 2-3 per yr. ISSN 0032-6690

**Technological Association**
University of Bombay, Department of Chemical
Technology, Matunga, Bombay 19, India.
- Bombay Technologist. a. ISSN 0067-9925

**Aravind Teki, Ed. & Pub.**
R-289A Greater Kailash One, New Delhi 110048,
India.
- Indian Art Direction; magazine of graphic
communication. q.

**Telugu Akademi**
Hyderabad 500029, India.
- Telugu Akademi Language Monograph Series.
irreg.

**Telugu Bhasha Samiti**
71 University Buildings, Madras 600005, India.
- Vijnana Pragati. m.

**Textile Association (India)**
- Textile Association (India). Journal. (pub. by
Mahajan Brothers)

**Textile Mills and Manufacturing Association**
- Textile Magazine. (pub. by Gopali Printers)

**Thapas Yogi**
111-112 Kodambakkam High Rd., Madras 34, India.
- Thapas Yogi. q.

**Theosophical Publishing House**
Adyar, Madras 600020, India.
- Theosophist. m. ISSN 0040-5892 (Theosophical
Society)

**Theosophical Society**
- Theosophist. (pub. by Theosophical Publishing
House)

**Theosophy Company (India) Private Ltd.**
40 New Marine Lines, Bombay 400020, India.
- Aryan Path. bi-m. ISSN 0004-4156 (United Lodge
of Theosophists)
- Theosophical Movement. m. ISSN 0040-5884
(United Lodge of Theosophists)

**Thilaga Medical Publications**
28 Melaponnagaram, 8th St., Madurai 10, India.
- Helan Medical Magazine. m. ISSN 0017-9922

**Thomson Living Media India Ltd.**
9 K Block Connaught Circus, New Delhi 110001,
India.
- India Today. s-m. ISSN 0537-0922
- Journal of Applied Medicine. m.

**Thornes (Private) Ltd.**
12 Ezra Mansions, Box 2361, Calcutta 1, India.
- Indian Aviation; India's premier aviation journal.
m. ISSN 0019-4417
- Indian Medical Forum; devoted to the
advancement of medical science. m. ISSN 0019-
5855
- Indian Railway Gazette; India's premier railway
journal. m. ISSN 0019-6258
- Planters Journal and Agriculturist; devoted to
planting, agriculture, commerce & social news. m.
ISSN 0032-0986

**Tibetan Review**
Box 3314, New Delhi 110014, India.
- Tibetan Review. m. ISSN 0040-6708

**Timber Development Association of India**
P.O. New Forest, Dehra Dun, Uttar Pradesh, India.
- Timber Development Association of India.
Journal. q. ISSN 0040-7755

**Time and Tide Publications**
1 Ansari Rd., Daryaganj, New Delhi 110002, India.
- Time & Tide; Indian journal of international films.
m. ISSN 0040-7836

**Tobacco Export Promotion Council**
World Trade Centre, 123-C Mount Rd., Madras
600006, India.
- Indian Tobacco; directory of exporters and
statistical handbook. a. ISSN 0445-8192
- Tobacco Export Promotion Council. Annual
Report and Accounts. a.

**Today and Tomorrow's Printers and Publishers**
24-B5 Original Rd., Karol Baugh, New Delhi
110005, India
- Indian Books; Bibliography of Indian Books
Published or Reprinted in the English Language.
a. ISSN 0073-6287 (Indian Bibliographic Centre)
(Dist. in U.S. by Stechert-Hafner Inc., P.O. Box
900, Riverside, NJ 08075)
- Journal of Palynology. s-a. ISSN 0022-3379
(Palynological Society of India)
- New Botanist. q. (Palynological Society of India)

**Topic Publications Pvt. Ltd.**
Bombay Mutual Bldg., 3rd Floor, Tilak Rd.,
Ahmedabad 1, India.
- Topic News Weekly. w. ISSN 0040-9316

**Trade & Investment Publications**
No. 74 Greater Kailish 1, New Delhi 110048, India.
- Export Times. m.

**Trade Development Authority**
16 Parliament St., New Delhi 110001, India.
- Market Information Series. irreg., latest issue,
1974.

**Trade Digest Publications**
A-222 Defence Colony, New Delhi 24, India.
- American Market.
- World Fairs Guide; devoted to industrial
expansion, export, and travel trade. q.
(International Trade Fair Association)

**Trado Publications Pvt. Ltd.**
1-24 Asaf Ali Rd., New Delhi 1, India
(Dist. by International Publications Service, 114 E.
32nd St., New York, N.Y. 10016)
- Trado; Asian-African Directory of Exporters,
Importers and Manufacturers. a. ISSN 0082-5824

**Trained Nurses Association of India**
c/o Mrs. N. Nagpal, Ed., L-16 Green Park, New
Delhi 16, India.
- Nursing Journal of India. m. ISSN 0029-6503

**Translators' Association of India**
916 Kucha Patiram, Delhi 6, India.
- Anuvad/Translation; a quarterly on the theoretical
and practical aspects of translation. q. ISSN 0003-
6218

**Transport and Tourism Journal**
1969 Gali Mearkhan, Daryaganj, Delhi 6, India.
- Transport and Tourism Journal. q. ISSN 0300-
449X

**Transport Publications**
20 Noble Chambers, S.A. Brelvi Rd., Bombay
400001, India.
- Transport; automobile, aviation, railways, shipping,
tourism. bi-m. ISSN 0041-137X

**Travancore-Cochin Chemicals Ltd.**
Udyogamandal 683501, Alwaye, Kerala, India.
- Caustic. q. ISSN 0008-8579

**Tribal Research and Development Institute**
35 Simla Rd., Bhopal 2, Madhya Pradesh, India.
- Tribal Research and Development Institute.
Bulletin. s-a. ISSN 0564-2159 (Madhya Pradesh.
Directorate of Tribal Welfare)

**Trimurti Prakashan**
19 Lansdowne Rd., Apollo Bunder, Bombay 1,
India.
- Samarambh. m.

**Tripura. Department of Agriculture**
- Krishan. (pub. by Tripura Government Press)

**Tripura Government Press**
Agartala, Tripura, India.
- Krishan. q. ISSN 0023-4729 (Tripura. Department
of Agriculture)

**Triveni Press**
Machilipatnam, India.
- Triveni; a journal of Indian renaissance. q. ISSN
0041-3135

**Tuberculosis Association of India**
c/o B. M. Cariappa, 3 Red Cross Rd., New Delhi 1,
India.
- Indian Journal of Tuberculosis. q. ISSN 0019-5707

**Tulika Prakashan-Quill**
5C-14 New Rohtak Road, New Delhi, India.
- Quill. m.

**U. P. Irrigation Research Institute**
Roorkee, Uttar Pradesh, India.
- U. P. Irrigation Research Institute. General
Annual Report. a. ISSN 0080-4045
- U.P. Irrigation Research Institute. Technical
Memorandum. irreg. ISSN 0080-4053

**U.S.S.R. Embassy in India**
Information Department, 25 Barakhamba Rd., New
Delhi 110001, India.
- Russian for Everbody. m.
- Russian Language Monthly. m. ISSN 0036-0260
- Soviet Land/S. L. E. s-m. ISSN 0038-5522
- Soviet Panorama/S. P. w. ISSN 0038-5611
- Soviet Review. s-w. ISSN 0038-5786
- Sputnik Junior. m. ISSN 0038-8726
- Youth Review. w. ISSN 0044-1260

**Udbodhan**
P-94 New Delhi South Extension, Part 2, New
Delhi 49, India.
- Udbodhan. m.

**M. Umapathi, Pub.**
27 Thanikachalam Chetty Rd., T'nagar, Madras
600017, India.
- Mediscope; journal of medicine and surgery. m.
ISSN 0025-8253

**Unifier**
c/o E. C. Sastry, Ed., 41 Sardar Sankar Rd.,
Calcutta 29, India.
- Unifier. m. ISSN 0049-5239

**Union of Evangelical Students of India**
Box 1030, 5-C Millers Rd., Madras 600010, India.
- Our Link. q.

**United Asia Publications Pvt. Ltd.**
12 Rampart Row, Bombay 1, India.
- International Trade Review. m. ISSN 0020-8981 (Indian Council of Foreign Trade)
- Journal of the Indian Medical Profession. m. ISSN 0022-507X
- United Asia; international magazine of Afro-Asian affairs. bi-m. ISSN 0041-7173

**United Lodge of Theosophists**
- Aryan Path. (pub. by Theosophy Company (India) Private Ltd.)
- Theosophical Movement. (pub. by Theosophy Company (India) Private Ltd.)

**United Planters' Association of Southern India**
Box 11, Glenview, Coonoor 1, Nilgiris, Tamil Nadu, India.
- Planters' Chronicle. m. ISSN 0032-0978 (Co-sponsor: Indian Tea Association)

**United Schools Organisation of India**
1715 Arya Samaj Rd., New Delhi 5, India.
- United Schools Organisation of India. Annual Report. a.
- World Informo; current events of national and international importance and matters connected with the United Nations and its specialized agencies. m. ISSN 0043-857X

**United Service Institution of India**
Kashmir House, King George's Ave., New Delhi 110011, India.
- U. S. I. Journal. q. ISSN 0041-770X

**United States Educational Foundation in India**
Fulbright House, 12 Hailey Rd., New Delhi 110001, India.
- Directory of Fulbright Alumni. triennial. ISSN 0084-9936
- Fulbright Newsletter. q. ISSN 0046-5259

**Unity Compound**
Juhu, Bombay 54, India.
- People's Power. m.

**University Book House**
15 W. B. Bungalow Rd., Tawehar Nagar, Delhi 7, India.
- Law Thesaurus. m. (8-12 per yr.) ISSN 0023-9399

**University College of Medicine**
*see* University of Calcutta. University College of Medicine

**University of Agra**
*see* Agra University

**University of Agricultural Sciences, Bangalore**
Communication Centre, Hebbal, Bangalore 560024, Karnataka, India.
- Mysore Journal of Agricultural Sciences. q. ISSN 0047-8539
- U A S Extension Series. irreg., 1971, no. 3. ISSN 0067-3471
- U A S Miscellaneous Series. irreg., no. 26, 1975. ISSN 0067-348X
- University of Agricultural Sciences, Bangalore. Annual Report. a. ISSN 0067-3455
- University of Agricultural Sciences, Bangalore. Research Series. irreg., no. 15, 1973. ISSN 0067-3463

**University of Allahabad. Department of Economics and Commerce**
Allahabad 211002, Uttar Pradesh, India.
- Indian Journal of Economics. q. ISSN 0019-5170

**University of Allahabad. Education Department**
Allahabad 211002, Uttar Pradesh, India.
- University of Allahabad. Education Department. Researches and Studies. a. ISSN 0084-621X

**University of Annamalai**
*see* Annamalai University

**University of Baroda**
*see* Maharaja Sayajirao University of Baroda

**University of Bombay**
Fort, Bombay 400032, India.
- University of Bombay. Journal. issued in two parts: Arts, Oct.; Science, Nov.

**University of Bombay. Department of Law**
Fort, Bombay 400032, India.
- Asian Legal Aid and Defender Association Newsletter.

**University of Calcutta**
*see also* Calcutta University Press

**University of Calcutta**
- Calcutta Review. (pub. by Calcutta University Press)

**University of Calcutta. Centre of Advanced Study in Ancient Indian History and Culture**
51-2 Hazra Rd., Calcutta 19, India.
- Journal of Ancient Indian History. a. ISSN 0075-4110
- University of Calcutta. Centre of Advanced Study in Ancient Indian History and Culture. Lectures. irreg., 1969, no. 3. ISSN 0068-5380
- University of Calcutta. Centre of Advanced Study in Ancient Indian History and Culture. Proceedings of Seminars. irreg., 1973, vol. 11. ISSN 0068-5399

**University of Calcutta. Department of Botany**
35 Ballygunj Circular Rd., Calcutta 19, West Bengal, India.
- Nucleus; international journal of cytology and allied topics. 3 per yr. ISSN 0029-568X (prep. by its Cytogenetics Laboratory)

**University of Calcutta. Department of Economics**
56-A Barrackapore Trunk Rd., Calcutta 700050, India.
- Arthaniti. s-a. ISSN 0004-3575

**University of Calcutta. Department of English**
- University of Calcutta. Department of English. Bulletin. (pub. by Calcutta University Press)

**University of Calcutta. University College of Medicine**
- University of Calcutta.University College of Medicine. Bulletin. (pub. by Calcutta University Press)

**University of Calicut**
Calicut, Kerala, India.
- Calicut University News. q.

**University of Cochin. Department of Marine Sciences**
Foreshore Rd., Ernakulam, Cochin 16, Kerala, India.
- University of Cochin. Department of Marine Sciences. Bulletin. irreg.

**University of Cochin. Foundation for Management Education**
School of Management, Cochin 22, Kerala, India.
- Indian Manager. q. ISSN 0046-9025
- Management Information Service. 10 per yr. ISSN 0300-2667

**University of Delhi. Department of African Studies**
Delhi 110007, India.
- Journal of African and Asian Studies. s-a. ISSN 0449-2145

**University of Delhi. Department of Anthropology**
Delhi 110007, India.
- Anthropologist. s-a. ISSN 0003-5556

**University of Delhi. Department of Library Science**
Delhi 110007, India.
- Journal of Library and Information Science. s-a.

**University of Delhi. Department of Political Science**
Delhi 110007, India.
- Indian Political Science Review. s-a. ISSN 0019-6126

**University of Delhi. Department of Sanskrit**
Delhi 110007, India.
- Indological Studies. s-a.

**University of Delhi. Faculty of Law**
Delhi 110007, India.
- Delhi Law Review. q.

**University of Delhi. Library**
Delhi 6, India.
- University of Delhi. Library. Documentation List: Africa. q. ISSN 0418-582X

**University of Delhi. School of Economics**
Delhi 110007, India.
- Indian Economic Review. s-a. ISSN 0019-4670
- Review of Commerce Studies. a. (prep. by its Department of Commerce)

**University of Gauhati**
*see* Gauhati University

**University of Gujarat**
*see* Gujarat University

**University of Haryana**
*see* Haryana Agricultural University

**University of Indore**
University House, Indore 452001, Madhya Pradesh, India.
- Research Journal: Humanities and Social Sciences. irreg.
- Research Journal: Science. q.

**University of Jadavpur**
*see* Jadavpur University

**University of Jammu**
Canal Rd., Jammu (Tawi), India.
- University Review. q.

**University of Jodhpur. Botany Department**
Box 14, Jodhpur 342001, Rajasthan, India.
- Geobios; an international journal of life sciences on earth. bi-m. (prep. by its Ecology Laboratory)

**University of Jodhpur. Faculty of Commerce**
Jodhpur 342001, Rajasthan, India.
- Jodhpur Management Journal. a.

**University of Karnataka**
*see* Karnatak University

**University of Kashmir**
Hazratbal, Srinagar 6, India.
- University of Kashmir. Annual Report. a.

**University of Kerala. Department of History**
Trivandrum, Kerala, India.
- Journal of Indian History. 3 per yr. ISSN 0022-1775
- Journal of Kerala Studies. q.

**University of Kerala. Department of Linguistics**
Trivandrum, Kerala, India.
- I J D L. (International Journal of Dravidian Linguistics) s-a.

**University of Kerala. Department of Tamil**
Trivandrum, Kerala, India.
- University of Kerala. Department of Tamil. Journal. a.

**University of Lucknow. Anthropology Research Association**
Department of Anthropology, Badshaw Bagh, Lucknow, Uttar Pradesh, India.
- Anthropology Research Association. Research Bulletin. q.

**University of Lucknow. Demographic Research Centre**
Department of Economics, Lucknow, Uttar Pradesh, India.
- Demography and Development Digest. s-a. ISSN 0011-8281

**University of Lucknow. Department of Mathematics and Astronomy**
Lucknow, Uttar Pradesh, India.
- Hindu Astronomical and Mathematical Text Series. irreg. ISSN 0073-2281

**University of Lucknow. Indian Society of Labour Economics**
Badshaw Bagh, Lucknow, Uttar Pradesh, India.
- Indian Journal of Labour Economics. q. ISSN 0019-5308

**University of Madras**
Chepauk, Triplicane, Madras 600005, Tamil Nadu, India.
- Annals of Oriental Research. s-a.
- University of Madras. Archaeological Series. irreg. ISSN 0076-2202
- University of Madras. Endowment Lectures. a. ISSN 0076-2210
- University of Madras. Historical Series. irreg. ISSN 0076-2229
- University of Madras. Kannada Series. irreg. ISSN 0076-2237
- University of Madras. Malayalam Series. irreg. ISSN 0076-2245
- University of Madras. Philosophical Series. irreg. ISSN 0076-2253
- University of Madras. Sanskrit Series. irreg. ISSN 0076-2261

- University of Madras. Tamil Series. irreg. ISSN 0076-227X
- University of Madras. Telugu Series. irreg. ISSN 0076-2288
- University of Madras. Urdu Series. irreg. ISSN 0076-2296

**University of Madras. Alagappa Chettiar College of Technology**
Chepauk, Triplicane P.O., Madras 600005, Tamil Nadu, India.
- Altech. a. ISSN 0065-6623

**University of Madras. Centre for Advanced Study in Philosophy**
Chepauk, Triplicane P.O., Madras 600005, Tamil Nadu, India.
- Indian Philosophical Annual. a.

**University of Madras. Department of Psychology**
Chepauk, Triplicane P.O., Madras 600005, Tamil Nadu, India.
- Indian Journal of Applied Psychology. s-a. ISSN 0019-5073

**University of Meerut**
see **Meerut University**

**University of Mysore. Department of Post-Graduate Studies in English**
- Literary Half-Yearly. (pub. by Literary Press)

**University of Mysore. Post-Graduate Department of Psychology**
c/o B. Krishnan, Ed., Mysore 2, India.
- Psychological Studies. s-a. ISSN 0033-2968

**University of Nagpur**
Nagpur 1, Maharashtra, India.
- University of Nagpur. Journal: Science. a.

**University of Poona. Centre of Advanced Study in Sanskrit**
Ganeshkhind, Poona 411007, India.
- University of Poona. Centre of Advanced Study in Sanskrit. Publications. irreg. ISSN 0079-3809

**University of Poona. Department of Journalism**
Laxman Narayan Gokhale, Director, Ranade Institute, Poona 4, India.
- Vritta Vidya; experimental journal. bi-m.

**University of Poona. Department of Philosophy**
Ganeshkhind, Poona 411007, India.
- Indian Philosophical Quarterly. q. (Co-sponsor: Pratap Centre of Philosophy, Amalner)

**University of Rajasthan**
Gandhi Nagar, Jaipur 302004, India.
- Rajasthan University Studies in English. a. ISSN 0448-1690
- Studies in Sociology. a.
- University of Rajasthan. Studies in Engineering and Technology. irreg.

**University of Rajasthan. Department of Adult Education**
Gandhi Nagar, Jaipur 302004, India.
- Prasar; journal devoted to theory, research and field practices in adult continuing education. q.

**University of Rajasthan. Department of History and Indian Culture**
Gandhi Nagar, Jaipur 302004, India.
- Jijnasa; journal of the history of ideas and culture. q.

**University of Rajasthan. Department of Parapsychology**
Gandhi Nagar, Jaipur 302004, India.
- Parapsychology; Indian journal of parapsychological research. q. ISSN 0031-1782

**University of Rajasthan. Department of Political Science**
Gandhi Nagar, Jaipur 302004, India.
- Political Science Review. s-a. ISSN 0554-5196

**University of Rajasthan. Department of Public Administration**
Gandhi Nagar, Jaipur 302004, India.
- University of Rajasthan. Studies in Public Administration. irreg.

**University of Rajasthan. Departments of Sanskrit and Hindi**
Gandhi Nagar, Jaipur 302004, India.
- University of Rajasthan. Studies in Sanskrit and Hindi. irreg. ISSN 0448-1712

**University of Rajasthan Library**
see **Rajasthan University Library**

**University of Rajasthan. School of Commerce**
Gandhi Nagar, Jaipur 302004, India.
- Commercium. s-a. ISSN 0010-3160

**University of Rajasthan. South Asian Studies Centre**
Department of Political Science, Gandhi Nagar, Jaipur 302004, India.
- South Asian Studies. s-a. ISSN 0038-285X
- University of Rajasthan. South Asian Studies Centre. Annual Report. irreg., latest issue, 1973.

**University of Ranchi**
see **Ranchi University**

**University of Roorkee**
Roorkee, Uttar Pradesh, India.
- University of Roorkee Research Journal. s-a. ISSN 0557-3254

**University of Saugar. Botanical Society**
Department of Botany, Gour Nagar, Sagar 470003, Madhya Pradesh, India.
- University of Saugar. Botanical Society. Bulletin. s-a.

**Utama Kheti Bari**
B 1/23-A Hauz Khas, New Delhi 16, India.
- Utama Kheti Bari. m.

**Uttar Bharat Parishad**
c/o V. K. Shrivastava, Secy., University of Gorakhpur, Daudpur, Gorakhpur, India.
- Uttar Bharat Bhoogol Patrika. s-a. ISSN 0042-1618

**Uttar Pradesh. Directorate of Animal Husbandry**
Badshahbagh, Lucknow, Uttar Pradesh, India.
- U.P. Veterinary Journal. (Uttar Pradesh) q.

**Uttar Pradesh. Directorate of Fruit Utilization**
18-B Outram Road, Lucknow, Uttar Pradesh, India.
- Progressive Horticulture. q. (prep. by its Hill Horticulture Development Board)

**Uttar Pradesh. Information and Public Relations Department**
Lucknow, Uttar Pradesh, India.
- Uttar Pradesh. m.

**Uttar Pradesh. Labour Department**
Box 220, Kanpur, Uttar Pradesh, India.
- Labour Bulletin. m.

**Uttar Pradesh. State Planning Institute**
Directorate of Economic Intelligence and Statistics, Lucknow, Uttar Pradesh, India.
- Uttar Pradesh. State Planning Institute. Quarterly Bulletin of Statistics. q. ISSN 0042-1626

**Uttar Pradesh Library Association, Lucknow Branch**
Lucknow University, Tagore Library, Lucknow, Uttar Pradesh, India.
- Lucknow Librarian. q. ISSN 0024-7219

**Uttar Pradesh Management Association**
P.O. Sahjanwa Dist., Gorakhpur U.P., India.
- Management in Enterprises and Management Education in Business. q.
- Management in Enterprises and Management Education in Universities. q.

**Uttarakhanda Sevanidhi**
2 Badri Niwas, Nainitala, India.
- Uttarakhanda Bharati. q.

**V. M. Book Co.**
c/o A. J. Prabhu, Ed., 1334 Shukrawar Peth, Poona 2, India.
- Ekalabya. m. ISSN 0013-2926

**Vaidic Sahitya Parishad**
Chengannur 689121, Kerala, India.
- Arshanadam; Vedic monthly. m. (Kerala Arya Prathinidhi Sabha)

**Vaikunth Mehta National Institute of Cooperative Management**
Reserve Bank of India Bldg., Ganeshkind Rd., Poona 411016, India.
- Cooperative Perspective. q.
- Vaikunth Mehta National Institute of Cooperative Management. Publications. irreg. ISSN 0083-5102

**Vaikunthbhai Mehta Smarak Trust. Centre for Studies in Decentralised Industries**
NKM International House, 5th Floor, 178 Backbay Reclamation, Churchgate, Bombay 400020, India.
- Vaikunthbhai Mehta Smarak Trust. Centre for Studies in Decentralised Industries. Documentation Bulletin. q.

**Vallabhbhai Patel Chest Institute**
University of Delhi, Box 2101, Delhi 110007, India.
- Indian Journal of Chest Diseases and Allied Sciences. q. (Co-sponsor: Indian Association for Chest Diseases)

**N. Vanamalai, Ed. & Pub.**
258 Tiruchendur Rd., Palayamkottai, Tirunelveli 2, India.
- Aaraaichi. q. ISSN 0001-303X

**Vanambadi**
5 East Maada St., Mylapore, Madras 600004, India.
- Kavithamandalam. m.

**Vasantha Vilas**
No. 3 South Mada St., Mylapore, Madras 600004, India.
- Law Weekly. w.

**K. Venkataraman, Ed. & Pub.**
7-9 State Bank St., First Lane, Mount Road, Madras 600002, India.
- Motor. m. ISSN 0027-1713

**S. Venkatraman, Ed. & Pub.**
331/333 Thambu Chetty St., 1st Floor, Madras 600001, Tamil Nadu, India.
- Printindia. m. ISSN 0032-857X

**O.P. Verma**
A-165 Defence Colony, New Delhi, India.
- Indian Left Review. m.

**Vidarbha Industries Association**
Bank of Maharashtra Bldg., 2nd Floor, Sitabuldi, Nagpur 1, Maharashtra, India.
- Enterprise. m. ISSN 0013-8673

**Vikas Publishing House Pvt. Ltd.**
5 Ansari Rd., New Delhi 110002, India
- Asian Social Science Bibliography with Annotations and Abstracts. a. ISSN 0066-8478 (Institute of Economic Growth, Delhi)
- Contributions to Indian Sociology. a. ISSN 0069-9659 (Institute of Economic Growth, Delhi. Asian Research Centre)
- Indian Economic and Social History Review. q. ISSN 0019-4646
- Indian Historical Review. s-a. (Indian Council of Historical Research)
- International Journal of Sociology of the Family. s-a.
- International Review of Modern Sociology. s-a.
- International Studies. q. ISSN 0020-8817 (Jawaharlal Nehru University. School of International Studies)
- Studies in Economic Growth. irreg., 1969, no. 11. ISSN 0081-7848 (Institute of Economic Growth, Delhi)

**Vikram University**
Registrar, Ujain, Madhya Pradesh, India.
- Vikram. 4 per yr.(Nos. 1 & 3 devoted to Physical and Biological Sciences, Agriculture, Medicine, etc., Nos. 2 & 4 devoted to Arts & Indology, etc.) ISSN 0042-6121

**Vikram University. Maharaja Jiwajirao Library**
P.O. 12, Ujjain, Madhya Pradesh, India.
- Vikram Research Guide. q.

**Vikrant Publications**
1 Todarmal Rd., Bengali Market, New Delhi 110001, India.
- Vayuyan; air journal of the East. m.
- Vikrant; Asia's defence journal. m. ISSN 0042-613X
- Vikrant's Defence Diary. w.

**Vimal Prasad Jain**
D-426 Defence Colony, New Delhi 110024, India.
- Radical Humanist; English monthly devoted to dispassionate and scientific study of sociological, philosophical and cultural problems of our time in the spirit of humanism. m. ISSN 0033-7625

**Virendra Prasad Jain**
*see* World Jain Mission

**Vishva Hindu Parishad**
16-10 Arya Samaj Marg, Karol Bagh, New Delhi, India.
- Hindu Vishva. m.

**Vishveshvaranand Vedic Research Institute**
P. O. Sadhu Ashram, Hoshiarpur 146021, Punjab, India.
- Nityanand Universal Series. irreg., 1970, no. 6. ISSN 0078-0855
- Santakuti Vedic Research Series. irreg,, 1965, no. 22. ISSN 0080-6137
- Sarvadanand Universal Series. irreg., 1973, no. 62. ISSN 0080-6471
- Vishvshvaranand Indological Journal. s-a. ISSN 0507-1410
- Vishveshvaranand Indological Paper Series. irreg., 1969, no. 242. ISSN 0083-6613
- Vishveshvaranand Indological Series. irreg., 1969, no. 46. ISSN 0083-6621
- Woolner Indological Series. irreg., 1969, no. 15. ISSN 0084-1242

**Vishwa Hindu Dharma Sammelan**
B. 21/81 Kamachha, Varanasi 221001, India.
- Hindutva. m.

**Visva-Bharati**
P.O. Santiniketan District, Birbhum, West Bengal, India.
- Visva-Bharati Quarterly. q. ISSN 0042-7195

**Visva - Bharati University**
Publishing Department, 10 Pretoria St., Calcutta 700071, India.
- Visva - Bharati Patrika. q. ISSN 0042-7179

**Viswa Sahiti**
208 New Bhoiguda, Secunderabad 3, India.
- Unilit. q. ISSN 0041-6762
- Viswa Rachana. fortn. ISSN 0042-7209

**Vivek Trust**
G-11 Hauz Khas Market, New Delhi 110016, India.
- Indian Book Chronicle; news and reviews. fortn.

**Vivekananda Rock Memorial Committee**
36 Singarachari St., Triplicane, Madras 600005, India.
- Brahmavadin. q. ISSN 0006-8721 (Co-sponsor: Swami Vivekananda Centenary Celebration)
- Vivekananda Kendra Patrika; distinctive cultural magazine of India. s-a. (Co-sponsor: Swami Vivekananda Centenary Celebration)
- Yuva Bharati; voice of youth. q. (Co-sponsor: Swami Vivekananda Centenary Celebration)

**Vrishchik**
B-2 Shirali Apartments, Fateh Gunj, Baroda 2, Gujarat, India.
- Vrishchik. q. ISSN 0042-9198

**Vyapari-Mitra**
106-9 Parashram Kuti Erandawana J, Poona 4, India.
- Vyapari-Mitra. m.

**Wadhera Publications**
General Assurance Bldg., Dr. D. N. Rd., Bombay 1, India.
- Indian Rubber & Plastics Age. m. ISSN 0019-6312
- Iron & Steel Journal of India. m. ISSN 0021-1613

**M. A. Walli**
78 Lenin Saranee, Calcutta 700013, India.
- Indian Journal of Dermatology. q. ISSN 0019-5154

**Wardha Press**
541 Swami Naichen St., Madras 600002, India.
- Madras Institute of Neurology. Proceedings. 3 per yr.

**Water and Power Development Consultancy Services (India) Ltd.**
Kailash, 26 K. G. Marg, New Delhi 110001, India.
- Water and Power Development Consultancy Services. Annual Report and Statement of Accounts. a.

**Weekly Notes Printing Works, Pvt. Ltd.**
34 Ballygunge Circular Road, Calcutta 700019, India.
- Calcutta Weekly Notes; a journal of law notes of the Calcutta high court. w. ISSN 0045-3854

**Wesley Press**
Box 37, Mysore 570001, India.
- Christian Medical Association of India. Journal. m. ISSN 0009-5443
- Christian Nurse. bi-m. ISSN 0009-5540 (Christian Medical Association of India. Christian Nurses League)

**West Bengal. Bureau of Applied Economics and Statistics**
Calcutta, West Bengal, India.
- West Bengal. Bureau of Applied Economics and Statistics. Statistical Handbook. a. ISSN 0511-5493

**West Bengal. Commerce & Industries Department**
- Calcutta Gazette. (pub. by West Bengal Government Press)

**West Bengal. Department of Information and Public Relations** .
Writers' Buildings, Calcutta 700001, India.
- Maghrebi Bengal. fortn.
- Pachim Bangla. fortn.
- Panchayati Raj. m.
- Paschim Banga. w.
- Sramik Barta. fortn.
- West Bengal. fortn. ISSN 0049-7193

**West Bengal. Department of Labour**
- West Bengal Labour Gazette. (pub. by West Bengal Government Press)

**West Bengal Government Press**
Publication Branch, 38 Gopal Nagar Rd., Alipore, Calcutta 27, India.
- Calcutta Gazette. w. ISSN 0045-3838 (West Bengal. Commerce & Industries Department)
- West Bengal Labour Gazette. m. ISSN 0043-3071 (West Bengal. Department of Labour)

**West Coast Publicity Service**
M.G. Rd., Cochin 11, India.
- Sree Sabarimala Sastha Souvenir. a.

**Western India Automobile Association**
76 Veer Nariman Rd., Churchgate, Bombay 20, India.
- Motoring. m. ISSN 0027-2248

**Western Publicity Service**
Ayurved Vikas Dept., 171-H Rash-Behari Ave., Calcutta 19, India.
- Ayurved Vikas. m. ISSN 0005-2477

**Wild Life Camp**
A-268 Defence Colony, New Delhi 3, India.
- Jungle; a journal for promotion of tourism and nature study. bi-m. ISSN 0047-2999

**Wool & Woollens Export Promotion Council**
Churchgate Chambers, 5 New Marine Lines, Bombay 20, India.
- Wool News. m. ISSN 0043-7824
- Woollens & Worsteds of India. q. ISSN 0043-7883

**World Jain Mission**
Jain Bhawan, Aliganj, Etah, Uttar Pradesh, India.
- Voice of Ahinsa; magazine of the non-violence Ahinsa cult. m. ISSN 0042-8086

**World Jnana Sadhak Society**
- Universalist. (pub. by Jnana Sadhak Publishing Company)

**World Poetry Society Intercontinental**
c/o Krishna Srinivas, Ed., 20-A Venkatesan St., Madras 17, India.
- Poet. m. ISSN 0032-194X

**World Union International Centre**
Pondicherry 605002, India
(U.S. Subscr. Address: World Goodwill, 886 United Nations Plaza, Suite 569-7, New York, NY 10017; or Sri Aurobindo's Action Center, Box 1977, Boulder, CO 80306)
- World Union. m. ISSN 0043-9185

**Writers Foundation Favorable Trust**
Barrack No. 3/2-3, Adarsh Nagar, Prabhadevi, Bombay 400025, India.
- Clarity; newsman's newsweekly. w.

**Writers Workshop**
162-92 Lake Gardens, Calcutta 700045, India.
- Miscellany. bi-m. ISSN 0026-5896
- Writers Workshop Literary Reader. a.

**Yoga Institute**
Santa Cruz East, Bombay 400055, India.
- Yoga Institute. Journal. m. ISSN 0044-0493

**Young Age**
3968 Rasta M. S. B., Jaipur 302003, India.
- Young Age; social and cultural fortnightly. s-m. ISSN 0049-8351

**Young Farmers' Association, India**
A-68 N.D.S.E. Part 2, New Delhi 3, India.
- Rural Youth. m. ISSN 0036-0120

**Young India**
7 Darya Ganj, Delhi 6, India.
- Young India. ISSN 0044-0795

**Yukranda**
790 Right Town, Jabalpur, India.
- Yukranda. m.

**Yura Bhasati Trust**
9-B Theatre Communication Bldg., Connaught Pl., New Delhi 1, India.
- Young Indian. w. ISSN 0049-8378

**Z**
8-B (2) Land's End, Dongersey Rd., Bombay 400006, India.
- Z. m.

**Zoological Society, Calcutta**
35 Ballygunge Circular Rd., Calcutta 700019, India.
- Zoological Society, Calcutta. Proceedings. s-a.

**Zoological Society of India**
34 Chittaranjan Ave., Calcutta 12, India.
- Zoological Society of India. Journal. s-a. ISSN 0049-8769

# INDONESIA

**Afro-Asian Journalist Association**
Press House, Jakarta, Indonesia.
- Afro-Asian Journalist. m. ISSN 0002-0621

**Akedemi Gizi**
Hang Djebat 3, P.O. Box 8 K.B.P. Kebajoran Baru, Jakarta, Indonesia.
- Gizi Indonesia. b-m. ISSN 0436-0265 (Indonesian Nutrition Association)

**Badan Penerbit Almanak Jakarta**
Jl. Gajahmada No. 25, Jakarta, Indonesia.
- Almanak Jakarta. irreg.

**Balai Penelitian Perkebunan Bogor**
*see* Research Institute for Estate Crops

**Balai Penyelidikan Purusahaan Perkebunan Gula**
*see* Experimental Station of the Sugar Industry

**Bank Indonesia**
2 Jalan M. H. Thamrin, Jakarta, Indonesia.
- Bank Indonesia. Data Kredit Perbankan. m. ISSN 0302-2013
- Statistik Ekonomi-Keuangan Indonesia/Indonesian Financial Statistics. m. (prep. by its Urusan Ekonomi dan Statistik)

**Bank Pembangunan Indonesia**
Box 140, Jakarta, Indonesia.
- Bank Pembangunan Indonesia. Annual Report. a.
  ISSN 0408-4632
- Bank Pembangunan Indonesia Newsletter. q. ISSN
  0045-1495

**Yayasan Adan Penerbit Basis**
Abu Bakar Ali 1, Trompolpos 20, Yogyakarta,
Indonesia.
- Basis; madjalah bulanan kebudajaan umum/
  monthly for culture in general. m. ISSN 0005-
  6138

**Bibliotheca Bogoriensis**
Jalan Ir. Haji Juanda 2, Bogor, Indonesia.
- Index of Biology, Agriculture and Agro Economy.
  bi-m.

**Bogor Zoological Museum**
see Museum Zoologicum Bogoriense

**Cellulose Research Institute**
Jl. Tamansari 126, Bandung, Indonesia.
- Berita Selulosa. 4 per yr. ISSN 0005-9145

**Central Library for Biological Sciences and
Agriculture**
see Bibliotheca Bogoriensis

**Centre for Strategic and International Studies**
Jalan Tanah Abang III/27, Jakarta, Indonesia.
- Indonesian Quarterly. 3 per m.

**Council of Churches in Indonesia**
Jalan Selemba Raya 10, Jakarta, Indonesia.
- Ecumenical News. m.

**P.T. Data Search Indonesia**
Box 2729, Jakarta, Indonesia.
- Indonesian Commercial Newsletter. s-m.

**Development Bank of Indonesia**
see Bank Pembangunan Indonesia

**Dinas Intelijen Medan dan Geografi Jawatan
Topografi T.N.I.-A.D.**
Jalan Dr. Wahidin I/II, Jakarta, Indonesia.
- Berita Topografi. q.

**Dunia Usaha**
Jalan Kembang Jepun 25-27, Surabaya, Indonesia.
- Dunia Usaha. m.

**Experimental Station of the Sugar Industry**
Jalan Pahlawan 25, Pasuruan, Indonesia.
- Balai Penyelidikan Perusahaan Perkebunan Gula.
  Warta Bulanan. m. ISSN 0043-0382

**Forest Research Institute**
Box 66, Bogor, Indonesia.
- Rimba Indonesia; Indonesian journal of forestry.
  q. ISSN 0035-5372

**Garuda Indonesian Airways**
Marketing Department, Jalan Ir. H. Juanda 15,
Jakarta, Indonesia.
- Garuda Indonesian Airways Magazine. q. ISSN
  0046-5453

**GINSI**
Wisma Nusantara Building, Jalan Mojopahit No. 1,
Jakarta.
- Business Guide Book to Jakarta. a.

**P.T. Gunung Agung**
Jalan Kwitang 6, Jakarta, Indonesia
- Berita Idayu Bibliografi; Indonesian book news. m.
  (Yayasan Idayu)

**Handjuawg**
Jl. Balonggede 43, Bandung, Indonesia.
- Handjuawg. s-m. ISSN 0440-2278

**Herbarium Bogoriense**
Jalan Ir. H. Juanda 22-24, Bogor, Indonesia.
- Reinwardtia; a journal on taxonomic botany, plant
  sociology and ecology. irreg. ISSN 0034-365X

**Ikatan Akuntan Indonesia**
Jalan Tosari 26, Jakarta, Indonesia.
- Akuntansi & Administrasi; Indonesian journal of
  accountancy. m. ISSN 0002-3892

**Ikatan Hakim Indonesia. Tjabang Semarang**
Jalan Siliwangi 151, Semarang, Indonesia.
- Sangkakala Peradilan. ISSN 0303-321X

**Inbavan Tanah Air**
Membangun. D.J.L. Melawai 12, No. 191 Blok N.
Kebajoran, Baru-Jakarta, Indonesia.
- Inbavan Tanah Air. m. ISSN 0046-8797

**Indonesia. Armed Forces**
Jakarta, Indonesia.
- Yudhagama; madjallah resmi kementerian
  pertananan republik indonesia. m. ISSN 0044-
  1325

**Indonesia. Badan Tenaga Atom Nasional**
see Indonesia. National Atomic Energy Agency

**Indonesia. Departemen Pendidikan dan Kebudayaan**
see Indonesia. Department of Education and
Culture

**Indonesia. Departemen Tenaga Kerja, Transmigrasi
dan Koperasi**
see Indonesia. Department of Manpower,
Transmigration and Cooperatives

**Indonesia. Department of Education and Culture.
Proyek Pengembangan Perpustakaan**
Medan Merdeka Selatan No. 11, Jakarta, Indonesia.
- Bibliografi Nasional Indonesia. q. ISSN 0523-1639

**Indonesia. Department of Information**
Jakarta, Indonesia.
- Indonesia Today. m.

**Indonesia. Department of Manpower, Transmigration
and Cooperatives**
Djakarta, Jakarta.
- Edisi Chusus Bulletin Koperasi. irreg.

**Indonesia. Directorate General of Oil and Gas**
Merdeka Selatan 18, Jakarta, Indonesia.
- Monthly Bulletin of the Petroleum and Natural
  Gas Industry of Indonesia. m.

**Indonesia. Directorate General of Sea Communication**
Jl. Merdeka Timur 5, Jakarta, Indonesia.
- Dunia Maritim. m.

**Indonesia. Directorate of Agriculture Extension**
Jalan Ragunan, Jakarta, Indonesia.
- Madjalah Pertanian. 4-12 per yr. ISSN 0024-9556

**Indonesia. Direktorat Bina Sarana Usaha Kehutanan**
Jl. Salemba Raya 16, Jakarta, Indonesia.
- Forest Products Trade Statistics of Indonesia. a.

**Indonesia. Direktorat Jenderal dan Gas Bumi**
see Indonesia. Directorate General of Oil and Gas

**Indonesia. Direktorat Penyaluhan Pertanian**
see Indonesia. Directorate of Agriculture Extension

**Indonesia. Direktorat Perumahan Rakjat**
Jalan Wijaya I/68, Kebayoran Baru, Jakarta,
Indonesia.
- Indonesia. Direktorat Perumahan Rakjat. Laporan
  Kerdja. a.

**Indonesia. Lembaga Oseanologi Nasional**
see Indonesia. National Institute of Oceanography

**Indonesia. Lembaga Pertahanan Nasional**
Jalan Kebon Sirih 28, Jakarta, Indonesia.
- Indonesia. Lembaga Pertahanan Nasional.
  Ketahanan Nasional. q.

**Indonesia. Marine Corps**
Jalan Prapatan No. 40, Jakarta, Indonesia.
- Mari Jo. q.

**Indonesia. National Atomic Energy Agency**
Jl. Palatehan I/26, Kebayoran Baru, Indonesia.
- Indonesia. Badan Tenaga Atom Nasional.
  Majalah.

**Indonesia. National Institute of Oceanography**
Djakarta, Pasar Ikan, Box 580, Jakarta Barat,
Indonesia.
- Marine Research in Indonesia. irreg. ISSN 0079-
  0435

**Indonesia. Pusat Nuklir Biologi Dan Kimia.**
Jakarta, Indonesia.
- Almanak Nuklir Biologi dan Kimia. irreg.

**Indonesian Dental Association**
Jalan Prapatan 14, Jakarta, Indonesia.
- Madjalah Persatuan Dokter Gigi Indonesia. 4 per
  yr. ISSN 0024-9548

**Indonesian Institute of International Affairs**
82 Jalan Tjikini Raya, Jakarta 4, Indonesia.
- Indonesian Review of International Affairs. q.
  ISSN 0046-9173

**Indonesian Institute of Sciences**
Jalan Teuku Tjhik Ditiro 43, Jakarta, Indonesia.
- Berita L.I.P.I. q. ISSN 0005-9137
- Index of Indonesian Learned Periodicals. a. ISSN
  0019-3607
- Indonesian Abstracts. q. ISSN 0019-7319

**Indonesian Institute of Sciences. National Scientific
Documentation Centre**
see National Scientific Documentation Centre

**Indonesian Journal of Public Health**
Pegangsaan Timur 16, Jakarta, Indonesia.
- Indonesian Journal of Public Health/Majalah
  Ilmukesehatan Masyarakat Indonesia. q.

**Indonesian Nutrition Association**
- Gizi Indonesia. (pub. by Akedemi Gizi)

**Indonesian Pediatric Association**
c/o Department of Child Health, University of
Indonesia Medical School, 6 Salemba, Jakarta,
Indonesia.
- Paediatrica Indonesiana. bi-m. ISSN 0030-9311

**P.T. Inscore Indonesia**
Jalan Thamrin 57, Box 2702, Jakarta, Indonesia.
- Mobil & Motor. m. ISSN 0047-7591

**Institut Keguruan dan Ilmu Pendidikan**
Kampus I.K.I.P. Karangmalang, Yogyakarta,
Indonesia.
- Forum Pendidikan Science d an Matematika. q.

**Institut Teknologi Bandung. Ikatan Mahasiswa
Arsitektur "Gunadharma"**
Jl. Dipati Ukur 9, Bandung, Indonesia.
- Pola.

**Institute for Economic and Social Research,
Education and Information**
Jalan Jambu 2, Box 493, Jakarta, Indonesia.
- Prisma; Indonesian journal for social and
  economic affairs. s-a; English ed. quarterly.

**Kamar Dagang dan Industri Jakarta**
Jalan W. Jakarta Fair, Tromol Post 3077, Jakarta,
Indonesia.
- Jakarta Business Directory. irreg.

**Kamar Dagang dan Industri Jawa-Barat**
Suniaraja 3, Bandung, West Java, Indonesia.
- Dinamika. q.

**Lembaga Administrasi Negara**
Jl. Veteran 10, Jakarta, Indonesia.
- Administrasi Negara; Indonesian journal of public
  administration. m.

**Lembaga Biologi Nasional. Herbarium Bogoriense**
see Herbarium Bogoriense

**Lembaga Biologi Nasional. Museum Zoologicum
Bogoriense**
see Museum Zoologicum Bogoriense

**Lembaga Biologi Nasional. Pusat Pewelitian Botani**
see Treub Laboratory

**Lembaga Biologi Nasional. Treub Laboratory**
see Treub Laboratory

**Lembaga Ilmu Pengetahuan Indonesia**
see Indonesian Institute of Sciences

**Lembaga Ilmu Pengetahuan Indonesia. Pusat
Dokumentasi Ilmiah Nasional**
see National Scientific Documentation Centre

**Lembaga Meteorological dan Geofisika**
see Meteorological and Geophysical Institute

**Lembaga Oseanologi Nasional**
see Indonesia. National Institute of Oceanography

**Lembaga Penelitian, Pendidikan dan Penerangan Ekonomi dan Sosial**
*see* Institute for Economic and Social Research, Education and Information

**Lembaga Penelitian Selulose**
*see* Cellulose Research Institute

**Mario Press**
Jalan Kramat Raya 146, Jakarta, Indonesia.
● Indonesian Shipping Directory. a.

**Maritime Press Foundation**
Jalan Raya Pelabuhan No. 7, Tandjung Priok, Jakarta, Indonesia.
● Indonesian Maritime and Economic News/Warta Ekonomi Maritim Review. m.

**Meteorological and Geophysical Institute**
Jalan Arif Rachman Hakim 3, Jakarta, Indonesia.
● Climatological Data for Jakarta Observatory. m. ISSN 0009-8957

**Metru**
Jalan Pluit 200, Jakarta, Indonesia.
● Metru. bi-m.

**Museum Zoologicum Bogoriense**
Jalan Ir. H. Juanda 3, Bogor, Indonesia.
● Treubia; a journal of zoology and hydrobiology of the indo-australian archipelago. irreg., vol. 28, 1975. ISSN 0082-6340

**National Archaeological Institute of Indonesia. Department of Prehistory**
Jalan Kimia 12, P.O. Box 2533, Jakarta, Indonesia.
● Bulletin of Prehistory/Berita Prasejarah. irreg.

**National Biological Institute. Bogor Zoological Museum**
*see* Museum Zoologicum Bogoriense

**National Biological Institute. Herbarium Bogoriense**
*see* Herbarium Bogoriense

**National Biological Institute. Treub Laboratory**
*see* Treub Laboratory

**National Importers Association of Indonesia**
*see* GINSI

**National Institute of Oceanography**
*see* Indonesia. National Institute of Oceanography

**National Scientific Documentation Centre**
Jalan Jendral Gatot Subroto, Box 3065/Jkt., Jakarta, Indonesia.
● Baca/Read; brief communication for information workers and information users in science and technology. bi-m.
● Directory of Special Libraries in Indonesia. irreg., latest issue, 1970 (1975 issue in prep.)

**Pacific Area Travel Association. Indonesia Chapter**
Jalan Kramat Raya 81, Jakarta, Indonesia.
● P.A.T.A. Indonesia. bi-m. ISSN 0048-2625

**Pertamina**
Jalan Perwira 2-4, Box 12, Jakarta, Indonesia.
● Bulletin Yaperna. bi-m. (Yayasan Perpustakaan Nasional)

**Pusat Dokumentasi Ilmiah Nasional**
*see* National Scientific Documentation Centre

**Pusat Penelitian Botani**
*see* Treub Laboratory

**Research Institute for Estate Crops**
Jl. Taman Kencana 1, Box 81, Bogor, Indonesia.
● Balai Penelitian Perkebunan Bogor. Statistik Coklat/Research Institute for Estate Crops, Bogor, Indonesia. Cocoa Statistics. a.
● Balai Penelitian Perkebunan Bogor. Statistik Karet/Research Institute for Estate Crops, Bogor. Rubber Statistics. a.
● Balai Penelitian Perkebunan Bogor. Statistik Kopi/ Research Institute for Estate Crops, Bogor. Coffee Statistics. a.
● Menara Perkebunan. bi-m.
● Research Institute for Estate Crops. Bogor. Communications. irreg.

**Sekretariat Pemerintah Daerah**
Propinsi Djawa Tengah, Lamporan, Indonesia.
● Lembaga Keluarga Berentjana Nasional. a.

**Selection Sketsmasa**
Jl. Kawung 2, Surabaya, Indonesia.
● Selection Sketsmasa. irreg.

**P. T. Septenarius**
Jalan Duri 1-5, Tilpun, Jakarta, Indonesia.
● Mimbar. s-m.

**Tempo**
Jalan Senen Raya 83, Jakarta 4, Indonesia.
● Tempo. w.

**Treub Laboratory**
Bogor, Indonesia.
● Annales Bogorienses; journal of tropical general botany. irreg., vol. 6, no. 3, 1977. ISSN 0517-8452

**Udayana State University**
Box 105, Jalan Jendral Sudirman, Denpasar, Indonesia.
● Udayana State University Bulletin. irreg.

**United Nations Regional Housing Centre**
c/o Ministry, 84 Taman Sari (Tromol Pos 15), Bandung, Indonesia.
● Masalah Bangunan/Housing, Planning & Building Problems; technology, planning, architecture and housing. q. ISSN 0025-4436

**Universitas Airlangga. Fakultas Kedokteran**
Jalan Dharmahusada No. 47, Surabaya, Indonesia.
● Majalah Kedokteran Surabaya. q. ISSN 0303-7932

**Universitas Browijaya. Fakultas Ketatanegaraan dan Ketataniagaan**
Jalan Mayor Jendral Haryono 163, Malang, Indonesia.
● Administrator. m.

**Universitas Gadjah Mada. College of Medicine**
Yogyakarta, Indonesia.
● Journal of the Medical Sciences/Berkala Ilmu Kedokteran. q. (prep. by its Department of Physiology)

**Universitas Gadjah Mada. Faculty of Geography**
Yogyakarta, Indonesia.
● Indonesian Journal of Geography/Majalah Geografi Indonesia. s-a. ISSN 0024-9521

**Universitas Indonesia**
*see* University of Indonesia

**Universitas Lambung Mangkurat. Fakultas Keguruan**
Jl. Veteran No. 268, Banjarmasin, Indonesia.
● Vidya Karya. bi-m.

**Universitas Udayana**
*see* Udayana State University

**University of Indonesia. Department of Anthropology**
● Berita Antropologi. (pub. by Yayasan Perpustakaan Nasional)

**University of Indonesia. Lembaga Demografi**
Jalan Salemba 4, Jakarta, Indonesia.
● Journal of Indonesian Demography/Majalah Demografi Indonesia. s-a.
● Warta Demografi. m.

**West Java Chamber of Commerce and Industry**
*see* Kamar Dagang dan Industri Jawa-Barat

**Yayasan Foto Indonesia**
Jalan Pandu 32A, Bandung, Indonesia.
● Foto Indonesia. bi-m.

**Yayasan Harapan Kita**
Jakarta, Indonesia.
● Indonesia. m.

**Yayasan Idayu**
● Berita Idayu Bibliografi. (pub. by P.T. Gunung Agung)

**Yayasan Komunikasi**
Matramanx Raya 10 A, Jakarta, Indonesia.
● Komunikasi; demokrasi, persatuan dan pembangunan berdasarkan pantjasila. 2 per mo. ISSN 0023-3188

**Yayasan Media Pembangunan**
Jalan Mojophahit 1, Jakarta, Indonesia.
● Ekonomis. m.

**Yayasan Perpustakaan Nasional**
P.O. Box 001/Jng., Rawamangun, Jakarta, Indonesia.
● Berita Antropologi. bi-m. (Univerity of Indonesia. Department of Anthropology)
● Bulletin Yaperna. (pub. by Pertamina)

# IRAN

**Iraj Afshar, Ed. & Pub.**
Box 66-1642 Niyavaran, Teheran, Iran.
● Farhang-e Iran Zamin. q. ISSN 0014-7788

**Ancient Iranian Cultural Society**
Nadri Ave., Kuche-Ye Shahrowkh, Box 14-1262, Teheran, Iran.
● Ancient Iranian Cultural Society. Publication/ Ansoman-e Farhang-e Iran-e Bastan. Nashrijeh. irreg. ISSN 0517-8045

**Arak College of Science**
Shahpur Ave., Arak, Iran.
● Majalle-Ye Danesh-e Ruz. q.

**Art & Architecture**
Av. Shahreza No. 256, Teheran, Iran.
● Art & Architecture/Honar Va Meemari. 6 per yr. ISSN 0018-4519

**Arya Mehr University of Technology**
Ayzenhover Ave., Teheran, Iran.
● Computer Science/Olum-e Kampiuter. 3 per yr.

**Asian Institute**
*see under* Pahlavi University

**Association of Notaries**
53 Sepah Ave. Near Pahlavi intersection, Teheran, Iran.
● Association of Notaries. Journal/Kanun-e Sardaftaran. Majalleh. m.

**Bank Markazi Iran**
Ave. Ferdowsi, Teheran, Iran.
● Bank Markazi Iran Bulletin. q. ISSN 0005-5093 (prep. by its Economic Research Department)
● Survey of Construction Activities of the Private Sector in Urban Areas of Iran. a. (prep. by its Economic Statistics Department)

**Bank Melli Iran**
Ferdowsi Ave., Teheran, Iran.
● Bank Melli Iran. Bulletin/Bank Melli Iran. Nashrieh Dakheli. m. ISSN 0045-1444 (prep. by its Research and Public Relations Department)

**Book Society of Persia**
Box 1936, Teheran, Iran.
● Rahnema-Ye Ketab. q. ISSN 0033-8699

**Cardio-Vascular Bulletin**
272 Shah Ave., Teheran, Iran.
● Cardio-Vascular Bulletin/Qalb Va 'oruq. bi-m.

**Central Bank of Iran**
*see* Bank Markazi Iran

**Centre for Iranian Anthropology**
*see under* Iran. Ministry of Culture and Arts

**Centre Francais d'Information Technique et Industrielle**
62 Forsat Ave., Shahreza Ave., Box 11-1555, Teheran, Iran.
● Informations et Nouveautes Techniques/Ettela'at Va Tazeha-Ye Fanni. m.

**College of Agriculture and Animal Husbandry**
Reza'iyeh, Iran.
● College of Agriculture and Animal Husbandry, Reza'iyeh. Journal of Science and Research/ Daneshkade-Ye Keshavarzi va Damparvari-Ye Reza'iyeh. Majalle-Ye 'elmi va Tahqiqi. irreg.

**Dehqan-e Ruz**
112 Sasan Ave, Ayzenhover Ave., Teheran, Iran.
● Dehqan-e Ruz. m.

**Dentists Association of Iran**
82 Hafez Ave., Teheran, Iran.
● Dentists Association of Iran. Journal/Jame'e-Ye Dandanpezeshkan-e Iran. Majalleh. bi-m.

**Echo of Iran**
4 Kuche Khalkhali, Hafez Ave., P.O. Box 2008, Teheran, Iran.
- Iran Almanac and Book of Facts. a. ISSN 0075-0476
- Iran Trade and Industry. m. ISSN 0021-0803

**English Language Teachers Association**
Box 33-59, Tajrish, Teheran, Iran.
- English Language Teachers Association. Review/ Anjoman-e Dabiran-e Zabanha-Ye Khareji. Nashriyeh. irreg.

**Faculte des Lettres et Sciences Humaines, Meched**
Meched, Iran.
- Faculte des Lettres et Sciences Humaines, Meched. Revue. q.

**Food and Nutrition Institute of Iran**
462 Pahlavi Ave., Opposite Hilton Hotel, Box 3234, Teheran, Iran.
- Taghziyeh. q.

**Gilan Business College**
Box 132, Lahijan, Iran.
- Baran. s-a.

**Imperial Iran Academy of Philosophy**
Avenue France Kucheh Nezami 6, P.O. 14-1699, Teheran, Iran
- Sophia Perennis. s-a. (Western subscr. to: Kraus-Thomson Ltd., FL-9491 Nandeln, Liechtenstein)

**Institut International pour les Methodes d'Alphabetisation des Adultes**
see International Institute for Adult Literacy Methods

**Institute for Protection of Mothers and New Born**
Bagh-e Ferdows, Mowlavi Ave., Teheran, Iran.
- Institute for Protection of Mothers and New Born. Publication/Bongah-e Hemayat-e Madaran Va Nowzadan. Nashriyeh. q.

**Institute for Research and Planning in Science and Education. Iranian Documentation Centre**
46 Shahreza Ave., Kakh Intersection, Box 11-1387, Teheran, Iran.
- Contents Pages of Iranian Science and Social Science Journals. m. ISSN 0010-7611

**Institute for Research and Planning in Science and Education. Tehran Book Processing Centre**
46 Shahreza Ave., Kakh Cross Rd., Box 11-1126, Teheran, Iran.
- Books Cataloged by Tehran Book Processing Center. q. with a. cum.
- Directory of Iranian Periodicals. a. ISSN 0084-9960
- Union List of Library and Information Science Periodicals in the Libraries of Iran. biennial.

**Institute for the Intellectual Development of Children and Young Adults**
31 Jam Ave., Teheran, Iran.
- Puyeh. q.

**Institute of Standards and Industrial Research of Iran**
Box 2937, Teheran, Iran.
- Standard. m.

**International Chamber of Commerce. Iranian Committee**
254 Takht-e Jamshid Ave., Teheran, Iran.
- International Chamber of Commerce. Iranian Committee. Publication/Komite-Ye Irani-Ye Otaq-e Bazargani-Ye Beynolmelali. Nashriyeh. irreg.

**International Institute for Adult Literacy Methods**
Box 1555, Teheran, Iran.
- Literacy Discussion. q. ISSN 0024-4503
- Literacy Documentation; an international bulletin for libraries and information centre. 3 per yr. ISSN 0047-4789
- Literacy in Development; a series of training monographs. irreg.
- Literacy Work. q.

**Interpub Co. Ltd.**
140 Abbasabad Ave., Passage Parvin (4th Floor), Teheran, Iran.
- Royal Tehran Hilton. q. ISSN 0035-9262 (Royal Tehran Hilton)

**Iran. Geological Survey**
Box 1555, Teheran, Iran.
- Iran. Geological Survey. Report. irreg., no. 24, 1972. ISSN 0075-0484

**Iran. Ministry of Culture and Arts. Centre for Iranian Anthropology**
Bldg. No.3, Bandar Pahlavi St., Takht-e Jamshid Ave., Teheran, Iran.
- Mardom Senasi Va Farhang-e Amme-e Iran/ Ethnologie et Traditions Populaires de l'Iran. irreg.

**Iran. Ministry of Culture and Arts. General Department of Cultural and Artistic Cooperations**
31 South Iranshahr St., Teheran, Iran.
- Rudaki/Mahname-Ye Farhangi-Honari. m.

**Iran. Ministry of Finance and Economic Affairs**
Naser Khosrow Ave., Teheran, Iran.
- Foreign Trade Statistics of Iran/Amar-e Bazargani-Ye Khareji-Ye Iran. q.
- Foreign Trade Statistics of Iran. Yearbook. a. ISSN 0075-0492

**Iran. Ministry of Health. Family Planning Division**
Takhte Jamshid Ave. & Kuche Jahan, Teheran, Iran.
- Iran Family Planning Bulletin/Behdasht Va Tanzim e Khanevadeh Bultan. m. (Persian edt.); q. (English edt.) ISSN 0047-1410

**Iran. Ministry of Industries and Mines**
Arg Square, Teheran, Iran.
- Iran. Ministry of Industries and Mines. Trends in Industrial and Commercial Statistics. q.

**Iran. Ministry of Information and Tourism**
174 Elizabeth II Boulevard, Teheran, Iran.
- Iran Travel News. m.

**Iran. National Library**
Ghavamossalteneh St., Teheran, Iran.
- Iranian National Bibliography. q. ISSN 0075-0522

**Iran. State Civil Defence Organization**
69 Kakh Shomali, Teheran, Iran.
- Iran. State Civil Defence Authority. Journal/ Sazman-e Defa'-e Gheyr-e Nezami-Ye Keshvar. Majalleh. m.

**Iran. Statistical Centre**
Iran Novin Ave, Teheran, Iran.
- Statistical Yearbook of Iran. a. (Farsi edt.) biennial (English edt.)

**Iran. Supreme Commander's Staff**
Arg Square, Teheran, Iran.
- Barrasiha-Ye Tarikhi. bi-m (Persian edt.) s-a (English & French edts.)

**Iran Marketing Co.**
P.O. Box 12-1499, Nadershah 140, Teheran, Iran.
- Trade Index of Iran. a. ISSN 0082-5751

**Iran Press Organization**
17 Kuche-Ye Bidi, Pahlavi Ave., Teheran, Iran.
- Majalle-Ye Danash-e Pezeshki. bi-m.

**Iranian Association for the United Nations**
440 Ferdowsi Ave., Teheran, Iran.
- Masa'el-e Jahan. m.

**Iranian Association of Obstetricians and Gynecologists**
c/o Dr. A. Mahdavi, Jam Clinic, Takhi-e Tavuv Ave., Teheran, Iran.
- Iranian Association of Obstetricians and Gynecologists. Journal. q.

**Iranian Bankers' Association**
41 Daryaye Noor St., Takht Tavous Ave., Teheran, Iran.
- Iran Banking Almanac. a.

**Iranian Chamber of Commerce and Industry and Mines**
254 Takht-e Jamshid Ave., Teheran, Iran.
- Iranian Chamber of Commerce and Industry and Mines. Journal/Otaq-e Bazargani Va Sanaye'Va Ma'aden-e Iran. Majalleh. m.
- Iranian Chamber of Commerce and Industry and Mines. Weekly Letter/Otaq-e Bazargani Va Sanaye' Va Ma'aden-e Iran. Haftenameh. w.

**Iranian Documentation Centre**
see under Institute for Research and Planning in Science

**Iranian Library Association**
Box 11-1391, Teheran, Iran.
- Iranian Library Association Bulletin/Anjoman-e Ketabdaran-e Iran. Nameh. q. ISSN 0021-0846
- Iranian Library Association Monthly News/ Anjoman-e Ketabdaran-e Iran. Akhbar-e Mahaneh. m.

**Iranian Mathematical Society**
Box 14-1248, Teheran, Iran.
- Iranian Mathematical Society. Bulletin/Anjoman-e Riyazi-Ye Iran. Bultan. s-a.

**Iranian Orthopaedic Association**
54 Takht-e Jamshid-e Gharbi Ave., Teheran, Iran.
- Iranian Journal of Orthopedic Surgery/Majalle-Ye Jarrahi-Ye Ortopedi-Ye Iran. 3 per yr.

**Iranian Petroleum Institute**
315 Takht-e-Tavoos Ave., Box 2232, Teheran, Iran.
- Iranian Petroleum Institute. Bulletin. q. ISSN 0021-0854 (prep. by its Publications and Lectures Committee)

**Iranian Public Health Association**
21 Azar Ave., P.O.B. 1310, Teheran, Iran.
- Iranian Journal of Public Health/Majalle-Ye Behdasht-e Iran. q. ISSN 0304-4556
- Majalle-Ye Behdasht-e Jahan. q.

**Jundi Shapur University. College of Education**
Box 223, Ahvaz, Iran.
- Jundi Shapur Educational Journal. s-a.

**Jundi Shapur University. Faculty of Medicine**
Ahvaz, Iran.
- Jundi Shapur University. Faculty of Medicine. Journal/Daneshgah-e Jondishapur. Daneshkade-Ye Pezeshki. Majalleh. q.
- Jundi Shapur University. Faculty of Medicine. Library Bulletin/Daneshgah-e Jondishapur. Daneshkade-Ye Pezesaki. Bultan-e Ketabkhaneh. q.

**Kayhan Group of Newspapers**
Ferdowsi Ave., Teheran, Iran.
- Kayhan-E-Bacheha. w. ISSN 0022-9563

**Majalle-Ye Tarikh-e Eslam**
94 Ansari Ave., Amiriyeh Ave., Teheran, Iran.
- Majalle-Ye Tarikh-e Eslam. 3 per yr.

**Medical Council of Iran**
40 Shirin Ave., Hafez Ave., Box 3474, Teheran, Iran.
- Medical Council of Iran. Journal/Nezam Pezeshki-Ye Iran. Majalleh. bi-m.
- Medical Council of Iran. Publication/Nezam Pezeshki-Ye Iran. Nashriyeh. irreg.

**National Iranian Oil Company**
c/o Miss Y. Mostofian, Takhte Jamshid Ave., Box 1863, Teheran, Iran.
- Iran Oil Journal/Iran Petrole/Nameh Sanaat-E-Naft. m. ISSN 0021-079X
- Oil News. fortn. ISSN 0030-1450

**National University of Iran. Dental School**
Evin, Teheran, Iran.
- National University of Iran. Dental School. Journal. q. ISSN 0011-8745

**Pahlavi University. Asian Institute**
Zand Ave., P.O.B. 494, Shiraz, Iran.
- Pahlavi University. Asian Institute. Bulletin. q.

**Pahlavi University. Faculty of Agriculture**
- Iranian Journal of Agricultural Research. (pub. by Pergamon Press, Inc. US)

**Pahlavi University. Faculty of Engineering**
- Iranian Journal of Science and Technology. (pub. by Pergamon Press, Inc. US)

**Pahlavi University Publications**
Shiraz, Iran.
- Pahlavi Medical Journal. q. ISSN 0030-9427 (Pahlavi University. School of Medicine)

**Pahlavi University. School of Medicine**
- Pahlavi Medical Journal. (pub. by Pahlavi University Publications)

**Plant Pests and Diseases Research Institute**
Box 3178, Evin, Teheran, Iran.
- Entomologie et Phytopathologie Appliquees. irreg. ISSN 0013-8800

- Iranian Journal of Plant Pathology/Bimarihaye Guiahi. q. ISSN 0006-2774

**Regional Cultural Institute**
5 Los Angeles Ave., North of Elizabeth II Blvd., Teheran, Iran.
- Regional Cultural Institute. Journal. q. ISSN 0034-3358

**Rose Advertising Co.**
6 Yasaman Ave., Teheran, Iran.
- This Week in Tehran. w.

**Royal Tehran Hilton**
- Royal Tehran Hilton. (pub. by Interpub Co. Ltd.)

**Society of Engineers of Iran**
Kanun Ave., Near Vanak Square, Pahlavi Ave., Teheran, Iran.
- Society of Engineers of Iran. Journal/Kanun-e Mohandesin-e Iran. Nashriyeh. q.

**Statistical Centre of Iran**
see **Iran. Statistical Centre**

**Shamseddin Tavakoli, Ed. & Pub.**
Box 14-1145, Teheran, Iran.
- Iran News; oil bulletin. 5 per wk. ISSN 0021-0781

**Teacher Training College, Teheran. Educational Research Institute**
6 Sorayya Ave., P.O.B. 3071, Teheran, Iran.
- Nama-Ye Tarbiyat. q.

**Teachers Training College, Shiraz**
Sibuyeh Ave., Shiraz, Iran.
- Dena. bi-m.

**TEBROC**
see **Institute for Research and Planning in Science and Education. Tehran Book Processing Centre**

**Tehran Book Processing Centre**
see under **Institute for Research and Planning in Science and Education**

**Tehran Economist**
99 Sevvom-e Esfand Ave., Teheran, Iran.
- Tehran Economist. w. ISSN 0494-9870

**Tehran Poultry Syndicate**
49 Kenedi Ave., Teheran, Iran.
- Name-Ye Morghdaran. m. (Co-sponsor: Co-Operative Poultry Society)

**U.S. Information Service**
Saba-Ye Shomali Ave., Teheran, Iran.
- Marzha-Ye Now. m.

**University of Azarabadegan. Faculty of Letters and Humanities**
Tabriz, Iran.
- University of Azarabadegan. Faculty of Letters and Humanities. Publication/Daneshgah-e Azarabadegan. Daneshkade-Ye Adabiyat va 'olume Ensani. Nashriyeh. q.

**University of Azarabadegan. Medical Faculty**
Tabriz, Iran.
- University of Azarabadegan. Medical Faculty. Journal/Daneshkaden Pezeshki Azarabadegan. Majallah. q.

**University of Esfahan. Faculty of Medicine**
Esfahan, Iran.
- University of Esfahan. Faculty of Medicine. Library Bulletin/Daneshgah-e Esfahan. Daneshkade-Ye Pezeshki. Nashriye-Ye Ketabkhaneh. q.

**University of Ferdowsi. Faculty of Letters and Humanities**
Mashhad, Iran.
- University of Ferdowsi. Faculty of Letters and Humanities. Journal/Daneshgah-e Ferdowsi. Daneshkade-Ye Adabiyat va 'olume-e Ensani. Majalleh. q.

**University of Ferdowsi. Faculty of Medicine**
Ta'lifat Va Entesharat, Mashhad, Iran.
- University of Ferdowsi. Faculty of Medicine. Letters/Daneshgah-e Ferdowsi. Daneshkade-Ye Pazeshki. Nameh. bi-m.

**University of Ferdowsi. Faculty of Theology and Islamic Studies**
Mashhad, Iran.
- University of Ferdowsi. Faculty of Theology and Islamic Studies. Publication/Daneshgah-e Ferdowsi. Daneshkade-Ye Elahiyat Va Ma'aref-e Eslami. Nashriyeh. q.

**University of Teheran**
Shahreza Ave., Teheran, Iran.
- Name-Ye 'olum-e Ejtema'i. q.
- University of Teheran. Scientific Review/Daneshgah-e Tehran. Nashriye-Ye Akhbar-e 'elmi. s-a.

**University of Teheran. Center for International Studies**
43, Avenue Anatole France, Teheran, Iran.
- Iranian Review of International Relations/Revue Iranienne de Relations Internationales. q.

**University of Teheran. Central Library**
Shahreza Ave., Teheran, Iran.
- University of Teheran. Central Library. Library Bulletin/Daneshgah-e Tehran. Ketabkhane-Ye Markazi. Nashriye-Ye Ketabkhaneh. irreg. ISSN 0497-1000

**University of Teheran. Children's Medical Center**
62 Bayat Ave., Ayzenhover Ave., Teheran, Iran.
- Childrens' Medical Center. Publication/Markaz-e Tebbi-Ye Kudakan. Nashriyeh. q.

**University of Teheran. College of Education**
Building No.2, Kenedi Square, Teheran, Iran.
- Kelk. q.

**University of Teheran. Faculty of Agriculture**
Karaj, Iran.
- University of Teheran. Faculty of Agronomy. Publication/Daneshgah-e Tehran. Daneshkade-Ye Keshavarzi. Nashriyeh. q.

**University of Teheran. Faculty of Education**
7/35 Kenedi Ave., Teheran, Iran.
- University of Teheran. Faculty of Education. Journal/Daneshgah-e Tehran. Daneshkade-Ye'olum-e Tarbiyati. Nashriyeh. q.
- University of Teheran. Faculty of Education. Library Bulletin/Daneshgah-e Tehran. Daneshkade-Ye 'olum-e Tarbiyati. Nashriye-Ye Ketabkhaneh. q.

**University of Teheran. Faculty of Engineering**
Shahreza Ave., Teheran, Iran.
- University of Teheran. Faculty of Engineering. Memoirs/Daneshgah-e Tehran. Daneshkade-Ye Fanni. Nashriyeh. 3 per yr.

**University of Teheran. Faculty of Health**
P.O.B. 1310, Teheran 5, Iran.
- University of Teheran. Faculty of Health. Institute of Research. List of Publications Received in the Library/Daneshgah-e Tehran. Daneshkade-Ye Bedasht Va Anstitu Tahqiqat-e Behdashti. Akhbar-e Ketabkhaneh Va Surat-e Nashriyat-e Resideh. m.

**University of Teheran. Faculty of Law and Political Science**
Shahreza Ave., Teheran, Iran.
- University of Teheran. Faculty of Law and Political Science. Law Review/Daneshgah-e Tehran. Daneshkade-Ye Hoquq va'olum-Siyasi. Majalleh. q.

**Univ. of Teheran. Faculty of Letters and Humanities**
Shahreza Ave., Teheran, Iran.
- Universite de Tehran. Faculte des Lettres et des Sciences Humaines. Revue. bi-m. ISSN 0041-9192
- University of Teheran. Faculty of Letters and Humanities. Bulletin of Iranian Studies/Daneshgah-e Tehran. Daneshkade-Ye Adabiyat va 'olum-e Ensani. Majalle-Ye Iranshenasi. irreg.

**University of Teheran. Faculty of Medicine**
Shahreza Ave., Teheran, Iran.
- Acta Medica Iranica. q. ISSN 0044-6025
- University of Teheran. Faculty of Medicine. Journal/Daneshgah-e Tehran. Daneshkade-Ye Pezeshki. Majalleh. 10 per yr.
- University of Teheran. Faculty of Medicine. Library Bulletin/Daneshgah-e Tehran. Daneshkade-Ye Pezeshki. Nashriye-Ye Ketabkhaneh. s-a.

**University of Teheran. Faculty of Pharmacy**
Shahreza Ave., Teheran, Iran.
- University of Teheran. School of Pharmacy. Journal/Daneshgah-e Teheran. Daneshkade-Ye Darusazi. Majalleh. s-a.

**University of Teheran. Faculty of Science**
Shahreza Ave., Teheran, Iran.
- University of Teheran. Faculty of Science. Quarterly Bulletin. q. ISSN 0042-0131

**University of Teheran. Faculty of Veterinary Medicine**
Box 3262, Teheran, Iran.
- University of Teheran. Faculty of Veterinary Medicine. Journal. q. ISSN 0042-0123
- University of Teheran. Faculty of Veterinary Medicine. Library Bulletin/Daneshgah-e Tehran. Daneshkade-Ye Dam'ezeshki. Nashriye-Ye Ketabkhaneh. q.

**University of Teheran. Institute for Economic Research**
P.O.B. 14-1322, Teheran, Iran.
- Journal of Economic Research. q.
- Tahqiqat e Eqtesadi; quarterly journal of economic research. q. ISSN 0039-8969

**University of Teheran. Institute of Geophysics**
Amirabad-e Shomali Ave., Teheran, Iran.
- Journal of the Earth and Space Physics. s-a.

**University of Teheran. Institute of Psychology**
21 Daneshkadeh Ave., Baharestan Square, Teheran, Iran.
- Bibliography of Psychology/Ketabname-Ye Ravanshenasi. irreg.

**University of Teheran. School of Dental Medicine**
Shahreza Avenue, Teheran, Iran.
- University of Teheran. School of Dental Medicine. Journal. q.

**Veterinary Medicine Association of Iran**
596 Shah Ave., Golshan Intersection, Teheran, Iran.
- Veterinary Medicine Association of Iran. Journal/Jame'e-Ye Dampezeshkan-e Iran. Majalleh. m.

**Wealth of Nations**
Ed. M. H. Yazdanfar, 52 Berlin St., P.O. Box 700, Teheran, Iran.
- Wealth of Nations/Sarvate Melal. m. ISSN 0049-7045

**Womens' Organization of Iran**
Qavamossaltaneh Ave., Box 3297, Teheran, Iran.
- Womens' Organization of Iran. Weekly Bulletin/Sazman-e Zanan-e Iran. Bulan-e Haftegi. w.

# IRAQ

**Baghdad Chamber of Commerce**
Mustansir St., Baghdad, Iraq.
- Baghdad Chamber of Commerce. Weekly Bulletin. w. ISSN 0005-3899 (prep. by its Research and Publishing Department)
- Commerce. q. ISSN 0010-2768 (prep. by its Research and Publishing Department)

**Basrah Natural History Museum**
University of Basrah, Basrah, Iraq.
- Basrah Natural History Museum. Bulletin. irreg?

**Central Bank of Iraq**
Box 64, Baghdad, Iraq.
- Central Bank of Iraq. Quarterly Bulletin. q. and monthly statement of accounts. ISSN 0008-9257 (prep. by its Statistics and Research Department)
- Central Bank of Iraq, Baghdad. Report. a. ISSN 0069-1534 (prep. by its Statistics and Research Department)

**College of Medicine, Mosul**
Mosul, Iraq.
- College of Medicine, Mosul. Annals. q. ISSN 0027-1446

**Folklore Centre**
Ministry of Information, Baghdad, Iraq.
- Al-Turath Al-Sha'bi; folklore monthly magazine. m. ISSN 0002-4082

**Geological Society of Iraq**
P.O. Box 547, Baghdad, Iraq.
- Geological Society of Iraq. Journal. a. ISSN 0533-8301

**Ghurfat al-Tijarah Wa-al-Sinaah Bi-al-Jazair**
Al-Jazair, Iraq.
- Al-Anba al-Iqtisadiyah. m.

**Institute of Endemic Diseases**
Baghdad, Iraq.
- Bulletin of Endemic Diseases. s-a. ISSN 0007-4845

**Iraq. Al-Jihaz al-Markazi Lil-Ihsa**
*see* Iraq. Central Statistical Organization

**Iraq. Central Statistical Organization**
Publication and Public Relations Department, Baghdad, Iraq.
- Iraq. al-Jihaz al-Markazi Lil-Ihsa. Annual Abstract of Statistics. a.

**Iraq. Central Statistical Organization. Department of Foreign Trade Statistics**
Baghdad, Iraq.
- Iraq. Department of Foreign Trade Statistics. Monthly Bulletin of Foreign Trade Statistics. m. ISSN 0027-0245
- Iraq. Department of Foreign Trade Statistics. Summary of Foreign Trade. m. ISSN 0021-0900

**Iraq. Central Statistical Organization. Industrial Statistics Department**
Baghdad, Iraq.
- Iraq. Industrial Statistics Department. Results of the Industrial Survey. Large Establishments. a.

**Iraq. Department of Tourism Services**
Baghdad, Iraq.
- Mesopotamia. m.

**Iraq. Directorate General of Antiquities**
Jamal Abdul Nasr St., Baghdad, Iraq.
- Al-Maskukat. a. ISSN 0002-4058
- Sumer; journal of archaeology in Iraq. a. ISSN 0081-9271

**Iraq. Ministry of Culture and Information**
Baghdad, Iraq.
- Al-Aqlam Journal/Pen. m. ISSN 0570-507X
- Iraq Government Gazette. w. (English edt.) irreg. (Arabic edt.)

**Iraq. Ministry of Education**
Baghdad, Iraq.
- Iraq. Ministry of Education. al-Mu'allem al-Jadid. q.

**Iraq. Ministry of Health. Institute of Endemic Diseases**
*see* Institute of Endemic Diseases

**Iraq. Ministry of Justice. Legal Drafting Department**
Baghdad, Iraq.
- Adala. q.

**Iraq National History Museum**
Waziriya, Baghdad, Iraq.
- Iraq Natural History Museum. Bulletin. irreg. ISSN 0021-0897

**Iraq Natural History Research Centre**
Baba-Moadham, Baghdad, Iraq.
- Iraq Natural History Research Centre. Publication. irreg.(approx. a.) ISSN 0085-2260

**Iraqi Federation of Industries**
Iraqi Federation of Industries Building, Al-Khullani Sq, Baghdad, Iraq.
- Industrialist/Sinai. q. ISSN 0046-9270

**Iraqi Medical Professions' Association**
Republican Hospital, Baghdad, Iraq.
- Iraqi Medical Professions' Association. Journal. 3 per yr. ISSN 0021-0927

**Al-Jamaheer Press House**
Box 257, Baghdad, Iraq.
- Baghdad Observer. d. ISSN 0005-3902

**Nation**
Mid-East House, Shahrah, Iraq.
- Nation. m.

**University of Baghdad. Biological Research Centre**
Baghdad, Iraq.
- University of Baghdad. Biological Research Centre. Bulletin. a. ISSN 0067-2890

**University of Baghdad. College of Agriculture**
Abu-Ghraid, Baghdad, Iraq.
- Iraqi Journal of Agricultural Science. a. ISSN 0075-0530

**University of Baghdad. College of Medicine**
Baghdad, Iraq.
- University of Baghdad. Faculty of Medicine. Journal. q. ISSN 0041-9419

**University of Baghdad. College of Science**
Adhamiah, Baghdad, Iraq.
- University of Bagdad. College of Science. Bulletin. a. ISSN 0067-2904

# IRELAND

**Aer Lingus**
Staff Development Dept., Box 180, Dublin Airport, Dublin, Ireland.
- Aesceala; staff magazine of Aer Lingus. every 3 weeks. ISSN 0001-9550
- Cara; staff magazine of Aer Lingus. q. ISSN 0008-6088

**Agricultural Trust**
Irish Farm Centre, Bluebell, Dublin 12, Ireland.
- Irish Farmers' Journal. w. ISSN 0021-1168

**Aiseiri**
c/o Gearold O. Cuinneagain, Ed., 11 Paire Blarna, Ath Cliath, Dublin 12, Ireland.
- Aiseiri. bi-m. ISSN 0002-290X

**An Cosantoir Army Headquarters**
Parkgate, Dublin 7, Ireland.
- An Cosantoir; Irish defence journal. m.

**An Foras Taluntais**
19 Sandymount Ave., Dublin 4, Ireland.
- Farm and Food Research. bi-m. ISSN 0046-3302
- Irish Journal of Agricultural Economics and Rural Sociology. s-a. ISSN 0021-1249

**John Arigho & Sons (1974) Ltd.**
17b Palmerston Park, Dublin, 6, Ireland.
- Genuine Irish Old Moore's Almanac. a. ISSN 0072-0887

**Association of Ophthalmic Opticians**
11 Harrington St., Dublin 8, Ireland.
- Radharc. bi-m. ISSN 0048-654X

**Association of Veterinary Students of Great Britain and Ireland**
Veterinary College of Ireland, Ballsbridge, Dublin, 4, Ireland.
- A. V. S. Journal. a. ISSN 0066-9768

**John Balding (Publishing & Publicity) Ltd.**
61 Northumberland Rd., Dublin 4, Ireland.
- Showcase; journal of the Irish entertainment industry. q. ISSN 0037-4350
- Zone; journal of environmental engineering in Ireland. ISSN 0044-5010

**Belenes Publications Ltd.**
93 Lr. Baggot St., Dublin 2, Ireland.
- Build. m. ISSN 0007-3229
- Business and Finance. w. ISSN 0007-6473

**Books Ireland**
Kingston House, Ballinteer, Dublin, Ireland.
- Books Ireland. 10 per yr. ISSN 0376-6039

**Bord Failte**
Baggot St. Bridge, Dublin 2, Ireland.
- Ireland of the Welcomes. bi-m. ISSN 0021-0943

**Bord na Mona**
Scientific Office, Droichead Nua, Co. Kildare, Ireland.
- Peat Abstracts. q. ISSN 0031-367X

**Breandan Breathnach, Ed. & Pub.**
47 Frascati Park, Blackrock, Dublin, Ireland.
- Ceol; a journal of Irish music. irreg. ISSN 0009-0174

**Breifne Historical Society**
St. Patrick's College, Cavan, Co.Cavan, Ireland.
- Breifne; journal of Cumann Seanchais Bhreifne. a. ISSN 0068-0877

**Capuchin Publications**
Church St, Dublin 7, Ireland
(U.S. Address: Capuchin Fathers, St. Francis of Assisi, 494 Laba Rd., Bend, OR 97701)
- Capuchin Annual. a. ISSN 0069-0244

**Catholic Boy Scouts of Ireland**
19 Herbert Pl., Dublin 2, Ireland.
- Scout Leader. m. ISSN 0048-9816

**Catholic Record Society of Ireland**
c/o St. Patrick's College, Maynooth, Co. Kildare, Ireland.
- Archivium Hibernicum; Irish historical records. a. ISSN 0044-8745

**Celtic League**
9 Bothar Cnoc Sion, Ath Cliath 9, Ireland.
- Carn. q.

**Central Bank of Ireland**
Fitzwilton House, Dublin 2, Ireland.
- Central Bank of Ireland. Quarterly Bulletin. q.
- Central Bank of Ireland, Dublin. Report. a. ISSN 0069-1542

**Christian Brothers**
274 N. Circular Rd., Dublin 7, Ireland.
- Our Boys. m. (10 per yr.) ISSN 0030-6797

**Christus Rex Society**
c/o Department of Sociology, St. Patrick's College, Maynooth, County Kildare, Ireland.
- Social Studies; Irish journal of sociology. q.

**Comhaltas Ceoltoiri Eireann**
6 Sraid Fhearchair, Dublin 2, Ireland.
- Treoir. s-m.

**Comhar**
37 Sraid na Bhfinini, Dublin, Ireland.
- Comhar. m. ISSN 0010-2369

**Confederation of Irish Industry**
Confederation House, Kildare St., Dublin 2, Ireland.
- C I I/E S R I Business Forecast. m.
- C. I. I. Newsletter. w.
- Confederation of Irish Industry. Economic Review. q.

**Conradh na Gaeilge**
6 Harcourt St., Dublin 2, Ireland.
- Feasta. m. ISSN 0014-8946
- R O S C. m. ISSN 0033-7048

**Construction and Property News**
175 N. Strand Rd., Dublin 1, Ireland.
- Construction and Property News. w.

**Construction Industry Federation of Ireland**
9 Leeson Park, Dublin 6, Ireland.
- Construction. m.

**Consumers Association of Ireland Ltd.**
35 Wicklow, Dublin 2, Ireland.
- Inform. m.

**Coras Trachtala**
Merrion Hall, Strand Road, Sandymount, Dublin 4, Ireland.
- Export. 4 per yr. ISSN 0014-5092

**Cork Historical and Archaeological Society**
c/o Univ. College, Cork, Ireland.
- Cork Historical and Archaeological Society. Journal. s-a. ISSN 0010-8731

**Cork University Press**
Cork, Ireland.
- U. C. C. Record. a. (University College, Cork)

**County Kildare Archaeological Society, Tullig**
Dublin Road Naas, County Kildare, Ireland.
- County Kildare Archaeological Society. Journal. a.

**Covas Iompair Eircann**
- C. I. E. Travel Express. (pub. by Marine and General Publicity Ltd.)

**Creation Group Ltd.**
Botanic Road, Glasnevin, Dublin 9, Ireland.
- Irish Householder and Gardener. m.
- Man Alive. m.
- Woman's Way Weekly; Ireland's leading women's magazine. w. ISSN 0043-7409

**Thomas Crosbie & Co. Ltd.**
95 Patrick St., Cork, Ireland.
● Cork Weekly Examiner & Weekly Herald. w.
ISSN 0010-874X

**Cumann Leabharlannaithe Scoile**
75 Mobhi Rd., Glasnevin, Dublin 9, Dublin, Ireland.
● Cumann Leabharlannaithe Scoile. C L S Bulletin.
a. ISSN 0007-8565

**Deirdre**
c/o Gearold O. Cuinneagain, Ed., 11 Pairc Blarna,
Ath Cliath, Dublin 12, Ireland.
● Deirdre. bi-m. ISSN 0011-7706

**Development and Progress**
c/o Gearoid Ocuinneagain, Ed., 11 Pairc Blarna,
Ath Cliath 12, Ireland.
● Development and Progress. 10 per yr. ISSN 0012-
1568

**Discalced Carmelite Fathers**
St. Mary's, Morehampton Rd., Dublin 4, Ireland.
● Carmel. bi-m. ISSN 0008-6665

**Dolmen Press**
North Richmond Industrial Estate, North Richmond
St, Dublin 1, Ireland.
● New Yeats Papers. irreg.

**Donegal Democrat**
Ballyshannon, Co. Donegal, Ireland.
● Biblical Theology. s-a. ISSN 0006-0917

**Dublin Chamber of Commerce**
● Dublin Chamber of Commerce Journal. (pub. by
Libra House Ltd.)

**Dublin Institute for Advanced Studies**
10 Burlington Rd., Dublin, 4, Ireland.
● Celtica. irreg., vol. 10, 1974. ISSN 0069-1399
● Dublin Institute for Advanced Studies.
Communications. Series A. irreg., no. 23, 1975.
ISSN 0070-7414
● Dublin Institute for Advanced Studies. School of
Cosmic Physics. Geophysical Bulletin. irreg., no.
33, 1975. ISSN 0070-7422
● Dunsink Observatory. Publications;
communications of the Dublin Institute for
Advanced Studies, Series C. irreg., vol. 1, no. 7,
1975. ISSN 0070-7643

**Dublin University**
200 Pearse St., Dublin 2, Ireland.
● Dublin University Law Journal. s-a.

**Dublin University Press Ltd.**
Trinity College, Dublin 2, Ireland.
● Irish Historical Studies. s-a. ISSN 0021-1214
(Irish Historical Society) (Co-sponsor: Ulster
Society for Irish Historical Studies)

**James Duffy & Co. Ltd.**
21 Shaw St, Dublin 2, Ireland.
● Irish Catholic Directory. a. ISSN 0075-0735
(Roman Catholic Church in All Ireland)

**Dun & Bradstreet - Stubbs Ltd.**
Holbrook House, Holles St., Dublin, Ireland.
● Guide to Irish Manufacturers. s-a.

**Dundalgan Press (W. Tempest) Ltd.**
Dundalk, Ireland.
● County Louth Archaeological and Historical
Journal. a. ISSN 0070-1327

**Eason & Son, Ltd.**
57 Merrion Sq., Dublin 2, Ireland.
● Dental Register of Ireland. a. ISSN 0084-9723

**Economic and Social Research Institute**
4 Burlington Rd., Dublin 4, Ireland.
● Economic and Social Research Institute.
Publications Series. Paper. irreg. ISSN 0070-8755

**Economic and Social Review**
4 Burlington Rd., Dublin 4, Ireland.
● Economic and Social Review. q. ISSN 0012-9984

**Elsevier-North Holland Scientific Publishers Co., Ltd.**
Box 85, Limerick, Ireland.
● Atherosclerosis; international journal for research
and investigation on atherosclerosis and related
diseases. bi-m. ISSN 0021-9150
● Biosystems. q.
● Cancer Letters; journal covering all aspects of
cancer research. bi-m.

● Cell Differentiation; an international journal for
the rapid publication of original research papers
on the aspects of cellular differentiation in
eukaryotes. bi-m. ISSN 0045-6039
● Chemico-Biological Interactions; an international
journal devoted to the mechanisms by which
exogenous chemicals produce changes in
biological systems. 12 per yr (2 vols.) ISSN 0009-
2797
● Chemistry and Physics of Lipids. 8 per yr. (4 nos.
per vol.) ISSN 0009-3084
● Electroencephalography and Clinical
Neurophysiology; the E E G journal. m. ISSN
0013-4694 (International Federation of Societies
for Electroencephalography and Clinical
Neurophysiology)
● Journal of Molecular Medicine. bi-m.
● Molecular and Cellular Endocrinologie. bi-m.
● Neuroscience Letters; international
multidisciplinary journal devoted to the rapid
publication of basic research in the brain sciences.
bi-m.
● Plant Science Letters; an international journal of
experimental plant biology. m.
● Toxicology; an international journal concerned
with the effects of chemicals on living systems. bi-
m. ISSN 0300-483X

**Ergon Press**
45 South Mall, Cork, Ireland.
● Manpower and Applied Psychology. s-a. ISSN
0025-2409

**European Association of Teachers. Irish Section**
● European Teacher. (pub. by Wicklow Press)

**Federation of Irish Beekeeping Associations**
Mon Chalet, Boston Park, Cork, Ireland.
● Irish Bee-Keeper; an beacaire. m. ISSN 0021-1079

**Folk Music Society of Ireland**
c/o Hugh Shields, Ed., 3 Syderham Road,
Dundrum, Dublin 14, Ireland.
● Irish Folk Music Studies. a.

**Furrow Trust**
Maynooth, Co. Kildare, Ireland.
● Furrow. m. ISSN 0016-3120

**Garda Review Ltd.**
Floor 5, Philsboro Tower, Philsboro, Dublin 7,
Ireland.
● Garda Review. m.

**Geographical Society of Ireland**
Department of Geography, Trinity College, Dublin
2, Ireland.
● Irish Geography; bulletin of the Geographical
Society of Ireland. a. ISSN 0075-0778

**Geological Survey of Ireland**
Department of Industry and Commerce, 14, Hume
Street, Dublin 2, Ireland.
● Geological Survey of Ireland. Bulletin. irreg., vol.
2, pt. 2, 1976. ISSN 0085-0985
● Geological Survey of Ireland. Information
Circulars. irreg. ISSN 0085-0993
● Geological Survey of Ireland. Memoirs. irreg.
ISSN 0085-1000
● Geological Survey of Ireland. Special Papers.
irreg. ISSN 0085-1019

**Glun na Buaidhe**
29 Lower O'Connell St., Dublin, Ireland.
● Inniu. w. ISSN 0020-1596

**Greyhound & Sporting Press Ltd.**
Davis Rd., Clonmel County, Tipperary, Ireland.
● Sporting Press. w. ISSN 0049-1942

**Grille**
14 Kinvara Rd., Dublin 7, Ireland.
● Grille; Irish Christian left. bi-m. ISSN 0017-4254

**Guy & Co.**
Blackrock Road, Cork, Ireland.
● S M A-the African Missionary. bi-m. (S M A
Fathers)

**Haymarket Publishing Ltd.**
24, Merchants Quay, Dublin 8, Ireland.
● Irish Medical Times. w. ISSN 0047-147X

**Hibernia National Review Ltd.**
206 Pearse St., Dublin 2, Ireland.
● Hibernia; fortnightly review. fortn. ISSN 0018-
1277

**Hodges Figgis & Co. Ltd.**
Stephen Court 2, Dublin 2, Ireland
(and Academic Press Inc. (London) Ltd., 24-28
Oval Rd., London NW1 7DX, England)
● Hermathena; a Dublin University Review. s-a.
ISSN 0018-0750 (Trinity College)

**Holyrood Publications Ltd.**
80 Upper Drumconda Road, Dublin 9, Ireland.
● Gaelic Sport. m.

**Independent Newspapers Ltd.**
90 Middle Abbey St., Dublin 1, Ireland.
● Irish Independent. d. ISSN 0021-1222
● Sunday Independent. w. ISSN 0039-5218

**Institute for Industrial Research and Standards**
Ballymun Road, Dublin 9, Ireland.
● Building Progress. bi-m.
● Engineering Progress. bi-m.
● Food Progress. bi-m.
● Technology Ireland. m. ISSN 0040-1676

**Institute of Bankers in Ireland**
Nassau House, Nassau St., Dublin 2, Ireland.
● Institute of Bankers in Ireland. Journal. q. ISSN
0020-272X
● Irish Banking Review. q. ISSN 0021-1060 (prep.
by its Irish Banks' Standing Committee)

**Institute of Chartered Accountants in Ireland**
7 Fitzwilliam Place, Dublin 2, Ireland.
● Accountancy Ireland. bi-m. ISSN 0001-4699

**Institute of Public Administration**
57-61 Lansdowne Rd., Dublin 4, Ireland.
● Administration. q. ISSN 0001-8325
● Institute of Public Administration, Dublin.
Administration Yearbook and Diary. a. ISSN
0073-9596
● Institute of Public Administration, Dublin. Annual
Report. a. ISSN 0073-9588
● Ireland: A Directory and Yearbook. a.
● Young Citizen; a civics and social education
magazine. m.(during school) ISSN 0044-0736

**Institution of Engineers of Ireland**
● Institution of Engineers of Ireland. Register of
Chartered Engineers and Members. (pub. by Irish
Engineering Publications Ltd.)
● Institution of Engineers of Ireland. Transactions.
(pub. by Irish Engineering Publications Ltd.)

**International Federation of Societies for
Electroencephalography and Clinical
Neurophysiology**
● Electroencephalography and Clinical
Neurophysiology. (pub. by Elsevier-North
Holland Scientific Publishers Co., Ltd.)

**Iona Print Ltd.**
33 Botanic Rd., Glasnevin, Dublin 9, Ireland.
● Irish Law Times and Solicitors' Journal. w. ISSN
0021-1281

**Ireland. Central Statistics Office**
Earlsfort Terrace, Dublin 2, Ireland.
● Ireland. Central Statistics Office. Distribution of
Cattle and Pigs by Size of Herd. biennial.
● Ireland. Central Statistics Office. Pig
Enumeration. a.
● Ireland (Eire) Central Statistics Office. Crops and
Pasture and Numbers of Livestock. a.
● Ireland (Eire) Central Statistics Office. Estimated
Gross and Net Agricultural Output. a.
● Ireland (Eire) Central Statistics Office. Hire-
Purchase and Credit Sales. a. ISSN 0075-0573
● Ireland (Eire) Central Statistics Office. Inquiry
into Advertising Agencies Activities. a. ISSN
0075-0581
● Ireland (Eire) Central Statistics Office. Livestock
Numbers. a. ISSN 0075-059X
● Ireland (Eire) Central Statistics Office. National
Income and Expenditure. a. ISSN 0075-0603
● Ireland (Eire) Central Statistics Office. Trend of
Employment and Unemployment. a. ISSN 0075-
0638
● Ireland (Eire) Central Statistics Office. Tuarascail
Ar Staidreamh Beatha. Report on Vital Statistics.
a. ISSN 0075-062X
● Irish Statistical Bulletin. q. ISSN 0021-1370
● Statistical Abstract of Ireland. a. ISSN 0081-4660
● Trade Statistics of Ireland. m.

**Ireland. Department of Agriculture and Fisheries**
Dublin, Ireland.
- Ireland (Eire) Department of Agriculture and Fisheries. an Roinn Talmhaiochta Agus Iascaigh. Farm Bulletin. m.

**Ireland. Department of Education**
Marlboro St., Dublin 1, Ireland
(Avail. from H.M.S.O., c/o Liaison Officer, Atlantic House, Holborn Viaduct, London EC1P 1BN, England)
- Dublin. National Library of Ireland. Council of Trustees Report. a.

**Ireland. Department of External Affairs. Information Section**
- Ireland Today. (pub. by Netherlands - Ireland Institute NE)

**Ireland. Department of Finance**
Dublin, Ireland.
- Ireland (Eire) Department of Finance. Financial Statement of the Minister for Finance. a. ISSN 0075-0670

**Ireland. Department of Industry and Commerce**
Kildare St., Dublin 2, Ireland
(Avail. from H.M.S.O., c/o Liaison Officer. Atlantic House, Holborn Viaduct, London EC1P 1BN, England)
- Ireland (Eire). Merchandise Marks Commission. Report. irreg.

**Ireland. Government Publications Sales Office**
G.P.O. Arcade, Dublin 1, Ireland.
- Developments in the European Communities. Report. s-a.
- Ireland (Eire) Department of Agriculture and Fisheries. Annual Report. a. ISSN 0075-0646
- Ireland (Eire) Department of Agriculture and Fisheries. Journal. a. ISSN 0075-0654
- Ireland (Eire) Department of Education. Liosta de Iar-Bhunscoileanna Aitheanta. List of Recognised Post-Primary Schools. a. ISSN 0075-0662
- Ireland. Public Service Advisory Council. Report. a.
- National Science Council (Ireland). Progress Report. irreg., latest 1969-71.
- National Science Council (Ireland). Register of Scientific Research Personnel. irreg. ISSN 0085-3836
- Official Journal of Industrial and Commercial Property. fortn. ISSN 0030-0349
- Research and Development in Ireland. irreg. ISSN 0085-5545

**Irish Agricultural Organization Society Ltd.**
Plunkett House, 84 Merrion Square, Dublin, Ireland.
- Irish Agricultural Organization Society. Annual Report. a. ISSN 0075-0719

**Irish Ancestor**
c/o Rosemary Ffolliott, Ed., Pirton House, Sydenham Villas, Dundrum, Dublin 14, Ireland.
- Irish Ancestor. s-a. ISSN 0047-1437

**Irish Association for the Blind**
8 North Great George's St., Dublin 1, Ireland.
- Blind Citizen. m. ISSN 0006-4815

**Irish Congress of Trade Unions Research Service**
19 Raglan Rd., Ballsbridge, Dublin 4, Ireland.
- Trade Union Information. m. ISSN 0041-0500

**Irish Contracts Weekly**
5 Lower Mount St., Dublin 2, Ireland.
- Irish Contracts Weekly. w. ISSN 0021-1117

**Irish Countrywomens Association**
58 Merrion Rd, Ballsbridge, Dublin 4, Ireland.
- Irish Countrywoman. 10 per yr.
- Irish Countrywomen's Association. an Grianan Programme. a.

**Irish Creamery Managers Association**
33 Kildare St., Dublin 2, Ireland.
- Irish Agricultural and Creamery Review. m. ISSN 0021-1036
- Irish Creamery Managers' Association. Creamery Directory and Diary. a.

**Irish Creamery Milk Suppliers Association**
John Feely House, 15 Upper Mallow St., Limerick, Ireland.
- Irish Farming News. q. ISSN 0021-1176

**Irish Dairy Board**
Dublin, Ireland.
- Kerrygold International. irreg. ISSN 0303-7002

**Irish Dental Association**
29 Kenilworth Sq., Dublin 6, Ireland.
- Irish Dental Association. Journal. bi-m. ISSN 0021-1133

**Irish Dominican Fathers**
St. Saviour's, Dublin 1, Ireland.
- Doctrine and Life. m. ISSN 0012-446X

**Irish Engineering Publications Ltd.**
22 Clyde Road, Ballsbridge, Dublin, 4, Ireland.
- Institution of Engineers of Ireland. Register of Chartered Engineers and Members. a.
- Institution of Engineers of Ireland. Transactions. a. ISSN 0073-9790
- Irish Engineers. m. ISSN 0021-115X

**Irish Federation of Women's Clubs**
- Women's Clubs Magazine. (pub. by Maxwell Publicity)

**Irish Georgian Society**
Castletown, Celbridge, Co. Kildare, Ireland.
- Irish Georgian Society. Quarterly Bulletin. q. ISSN 0021-1206

**Irish Guild of Catholic Nurses**
91 Lower Baggot St., Dublin 2, Ireland.
- Irish Nursing Newsletter. q.

**Irish Hardware and Allied Trader Ltd.**
21 Camden Row, Dublin 8, Ireland.
- Irish Hardware and Allied Trader. m. ISSN 0047-1461

**Irish Historical Society**
- Irish Historical Studies. (pub. by Dublin University Press Ltd.)

**Irish Hotel and Catering Institute**
- Irish Catering Review. (pub. by National Publishing Group Ltd.)

**Irish Management Institute**
Sandyford Rd., Dublin 14, Ireland.
- Management. m. ISSN 0025-164X

**Irish Medical Association**
P M A House, 10 Fitzwilliam Place, Dublin 2, Ireland.
- I M J Appointments. w.
- Irish Medical Journal. m.

**Irish Messenger Publications**
37 Lower Leeson St., Dublin 2, Ireland.
- Sacred Heart Messenger. m. (Jesuit Fathers)

**Irish Nurses' Organization**
- World of Irish Nursing. (pub. by Maxwell Publicity)

**Irish Pigs & Bacon Commission**
Ferry House, Lr. Mount Street, Dublin 2, Ireland.
- Irish Bacon News. q. ISSN 0047-1445

**Irish Province of the Society of Jesus**
- Jesuit Year Book. (pub. by Leinster Leader)

**Irish Publication Surveys Ltd.**
Creation House, Botanic Rd., Glasnevin, Dublin 9, Ireland.
- New Spotlight; Ireland's national music/ entertainment magazine. w. ISSN 0028-6834

**Irish Publishing Co. Ltd.**
44 Lower Leeson St., Dublin 2, Ireland.
- Building & Contract Journal. fortn. ISSN 0007-3350

**Irish Republican Movement**
30 Gardiner Pl., Dublin 1, Ireland.
- Eolas; international newsletter. m.

**Irish Road Transport Association**
- Transport. (pub. by Transport Press Ltd.)

**Irish Sea Fisheries Board**
Box 275 Hume House, Ballsbridge, Dublin 4, Ireland.
- Bord Iascaigh Mhara. Tuarascail Agus Cuntaisi/ Irish Sea Fisheries Board. Annual Report. a. ISSN 0068-0265

**Irish Sisters of Charity**
Seville Place, Dublin 1, Ireland.
- Little Flower Monthly; Irish magazine of St. Therese. m. ISSN 0047-4819

**Irish Society for Archives**
82 St. Stephen's Green, Dublin 2, Ireland.
- Irish Archives Bulletin. a.

**Irish Sugar Co.**
St. Stephen's Green Hse., Dublin 2, Ireland.
- Biatas-the Tillage Farmer. m.

**Irish Tatler & Sketch Ltd.**
34 High St., Kilkenny, Ireland.
- Irish Tatler & Sketch. m. ISSN 0021-1397

**Irish Times Ltd.**
13 d' Olier St., Dublin 2, Ireland.
- Irish Field. w. ISSN 0021-1184

**Irish Trade and Technical Publications Ltd.**
5-7 Main St., Blackrock, Co. Dublin, Ireland.
- Futura. m. ISSN 0016-3252
- Irish Electrical Industries Review. m. ISSN 0021-1141
- Irish H & V News. m.
- Irish Travel Trade News. ISSN 0021-1419

**Irish Transport & General Workers' Union**
Liberty Hall, Dublin 1, Ireland.
- Liberty. m. ISSN 0024-2063

**Irish University Review**
University College, Room J210, Belfield, Dublin 4, Ireland.
- Irish University Review. s-a. ISSN 0021-1427

**Irish Wildbird Conservancy**
Dublin, Ireland.
- Irish Bird Report. a.

**Jemma Publications Ltd.**
22 Brookfield Avenue, Blackrock, Co. Dublin, Ireland.
- Irish Hotel and Catering Review. m.
- Irish Motor Industry. m. (Society of the Irish Motor Industry)
- Irish Printer. m.
- Licensing World. m.

**Jesuit Fathers**
- Sacred Heart Messenger. (pub. by Irish Messenger Publications)

**Jurist Publishing Co.**
University College, Dublin 4, Ireland.
- Irish Jurist. s-a. ISSN 0021-1273

**Kenlis Publications Ltd.**
18 Mary's Abbey, Dublin 7, Ireland.
- Irish Builder and Engineer; architecture, engineering and the arts and handicrafts of building. m. ISSN 0021-1087
- Irish Pharmacy Journal. m.

**Kerry Archaeological and Historical Society**
County Library, Tralee, Co Kerry, Ireland.
- Kerry Archaeological and Historical Society. Journal. a. ISSN 0085-2503

**Kilbrittain Newspapers Ltd.**
58 Haddington Rd., Dublin 4, Ireland.
- Special Office Brief. bi-m.

**Lay Theology in Ireland**
Black Abbey, Ireland.
- Lantern. m. ISSN 0023-8406

**Leinster Leader**
Naas, Ireland.
- Jesuit Year Book. a. ISSN 0075-370X (Irish Province of the Society of Jesus)

**Libra House Ltd.**
7 Clare St., Dublin 2, Ireland.
- Dublin Chamber of Commerce Journal. m. ISSN 0009-1138
- Farm Holidays in Ireland. a.

**Licensed Vintners' Associations**
Anglesea Road, Ballsbridge, Dublin 4, Ireland.
- Vintner. m.

**Marathon Publications**
High St., Ballinamore, Co. Leitrim, Ireland.
- Marathon; Ireland's international athletics magazine. m. ISSN 0047-5874

**Marine and General Publicity Ltd.**
127 Lower Baggot St., Dublin 2, Ireland.
● C. I. E. Travel Express. m. (Covas Iompair
Eircann)

**Maxwell Publicity**
49 Wainsfort Park, Dublin 6, Ireland.
● Women's Clubs Magazine. q. (Irish Federation of
Women's Clubs)
● World of Irish Nursing. m. (Irish Nurses'
Organization)

**Medical Research Council of Ireland**
9 Clyde Rd., Dublin 4, Ireland.
● Medical Research Council (Ireland). Report. a.
ISSN 0076-5996

**Military History Society of Ireland**
c/o Newman House, St. Stephen's Green, Dublin 2,
Ireland.
● Irish Sword. s-a. ISSN 0021-1389

**Mount Salus Press**
Tritonville Road, Sandymount, Dublin 4, Ireland.
● Communications Directory & Yearbook. a.

**Music Association of Ireland**
11 Suffolk St., Dublin 2, Ireland.
● Music Association of Ireland. Annual Report. a.

**National Publishing Group Ltd.**
22 Brookfield Ave., Blackrock, Co. Dublin, Ireland.
● Irish Catering Review. m. ISSN 0021-1095 (Irish
Hotel and Catering Institute)

**National University of Ireland**
49 Merrion Square, Dublin 2, Ireland.
● Eigse; a journal of Irish studies. s-a. ISSN 0013-
2608

**Nationalist Newspaper Co. Ltd.**
Market St., Clonmel Co., Tipperary, Ireland.
● Tipperary Star. w. ISSN 0040-8034

**Neptune's Kingdom**
c/o Martin Gleeson, Ed., 5 Victoria Terrace, Kilkee,
Co. Clare, Ireland.
● Neptune's Kingdom; poetry review. irreg.

**New Square Publications Ltd.**
Elstow, Knapton Rd., Dun Laoghaire, Dublin,
Ireland.
● Dublin Magazine. q. ISSN 0012-687X

**Nicholson and Bass Ltd**
3 Clarence St. W., Belfast BT2 7GP, Ireland.
● Royal Society of Ulster Architects. Year Book. a.
ISSN 0080-472X

**Old Athlone Society**
Scotch Parade, Athlone, Ireland.
● Old Athlone Society Journal. biennial (approx)
ISSN 0475-1388

**Old Dublin Society**
City Assembly House, 58 S. William St., Dublin 2,
Ireland.
● Dublin Historical Record. q. ISSN 0012-6861

**Open Press**
20 Vernon Grove, Dublin 6, Ireland.
● Open Press. m.

**Organisation Mondiale pour l'Education Prescolaire**
c/o University College, Dept. of Psychology,
Belfield, Dublin 4, Ireland.
● International Journal of Early Childhood. 2 per
yr. ISSN 0020-7187

**Pacemaker Publications**
Irish Farm Centre, Dublin 12, Ireland.
● Pacemaker and the Horseman. m.

**Passionist Fathers**
Mount Argus, Dublin 6, Ireland.
● Cross. m. ISSN 0011-1899

**People Newspapers Ltd.**
Wexford, Dublin 1, Ireland.
● Ireland's Own. w. ISSN 0021-0951

**Pharmaceutical Society of Ireland**
● Chemist and Druggist. (pub. by Benn Brothers
Ltd. UK)

**Photographic Society of Ireland**
38-39 Parnell Sq., Dublin, Ireland.
● Lens. bi-m.

**Pioneer Total Abstinence Association**
27 Upper Sherrard St., Dublin 1, Ireland.
● Pioneer. m. ISSN 0031-997X

**Post Office Workers Union**
52 Parnell Sq., Dublin 1, Ireland.
● Postal Worker. m. ISSN 0032-5392

**Private Motorist Protection Association**
Wolfe Tone St., Dublin 1, Ireland.
● Motoring Life. m. ISSN 0027-2256

**Provincial Newspapers Association**
24 Dawe St., Dublin, 2, Ireland.
● Ireland's Press and Print. bi-m. ISSN 0021-096X
(Co-Sponsor: Irish Master Printers Association)

**Psychological Society of Ireland**
Woodlands, Renmore, Galway, Ireland.
● Irish Journal of Psychology. 2 per yr per

**Radio Telefis Eireann**
Hawkins House, Hawkins St., Dublin 2, Ireland.
● R T E Guide. w. ISSN 0033-7145

**Redemptorist Publications**
75 Orwell Rd., Dublin 6, Ireland.
● Reality. m. ISSN 0034-0960

**Regional & Technical Publications**
36 Morehampton Rd., Dublin 4, Ireland.
● Education Environment. irreg.
● Irish Construction Materials Review Series. irreg.

**Repsol Publications**
30 Gardiner Pl., Dublin 1, Ireland.
● Irish People. w. (Sinn Fein the Workers' Party)
● Teoiric. q. (Sinn Fein the Workers' Party)

**Republican Educational Department**
30 Gardiner Place, Dublin 1, Ireland.
● Repsol Pamphlets. irreg.

**Retail Grocery Dairy and Allied Trade Association**
24 Earlsfort Terrace, Dublin 2, Ireland.
● Grocery Review. s-m. ISSN 0017-4440

**Roman Catholic Church in All Ireland**
● Irish Catholic Directory. (pub. by James Duffy &
Co. Ltd.)

**Royal College of Surgeons**
St.Stephens Green, Dublin 2, Ireland.
● Irish Colleges of Physicians and Surgeons. Journal.
q. (Co-Sponsor: Royal College of Physicans)

**Royal Dublin Society**
Ballsbridge, Dublin 4, Ireland.
● Royal Dublin Society. Scientific Proceedings
Series A. irreg. ISSN 0080-4339
● Royal Dublin Society. Scientific Proceedings.
Series B. irreg. ISSN 0080-4347

**Royal Institute of the Architects of Ireland**
8 Merrion Sq., Dublin 2, Ireland.
● Royal Institute of the Architects of Ireland.
Yearbook. a. ISSN 0080-4444

**Royal Irish Academy**
19 Dawson St., Dublin 2, Ireland.
● Royal Irish Academy. Proceedings. Section A:
Mathematical, Astronomical and Physical Science.
irreg.
● Royal Irish Academy. Proceedings. Section B:
Biological, Geological and Chemical Sciences.
irreg. ISSN 0035-8983

**Royal Irish Academy of Music**
36/38 Westland Row, Dublin, 2, Ireland.
● Royal Irish Academy of Music. Prospectus. a.

**Royal Society of Antiquaries of Ireland**
63 Merrion Square, Dublin 2, Ireland.
● Royal Society of Antiquaries of Ireland. Journal.
s-a. ISSN 0035-9106

**Royal Society of Ulster Architects**
● Royal Society of Ulster Architects. Year Book.
(pub. by Nicholson and Bass Ltd)

**S M A Fathers**
● S M A-the African Missionary. (pub. by Guy &
Co.)

**St. Patrick's College. Editorial Committee**
Dublin 9, Ireland.
● Studia Hibernica. a. ISSN 0081-6477

**St. Patrick's College. Educational Research Centre**
Dublin 9, Ireland.
● Irish Journal of Education/Iris Eireannach an
Oideachais. s-a. ISSN 0021-1257

**Sinn Fein the Workers' Party**
● Irish People. (pub. by Repsol Publications)
● Teoiric. (pub. by Repsol Publications)

**Society of Irish Foresters**
Royal Dublin Society, Ballsbridge, Dublin 4,
Ireland.
● Irish Forestry. s-a. ISSN 0021-1192

**Society of the Irish Motor Industry**
● Irish Motor Industry. (pub. by Jemma Publications
Ltd.)

**Stagecast Publications**
15 Eaton Square, Monkstown, Dublin, Ireland.
● Irish Numismatics. bi-m. ISSN 0021-132X
● Stagecast-Irish Stage and Screen Directory.
biennial.

**Standard (1938) Ltd.**
11 Talbot St., Dublin 1, Ireland.
● Catholic Standard. w. ISSN 0008-8366

**Statistical and Social Inquiry Society of Ireland**
c/o Economic and Social Research Institute, 4
Burlington Road, Dublin 4, Ireland.
● Statistical and Social Inquiry Society of Ireland.
Journal. a. ISSN 0081-4776

**Talbot Press Ltd.**
20 Talbot St., Dublin 1, Ireland.
● Studies; an Irish quarterly review of letters,
philosophy and science. q. ISSN 0039-3495

**Thom's Directories**
38 Merrion Square, Dublin 2, Ireland.
● Thom's Commercial Directory. a. ISSN 0082-
4224

**Transport Press Ltd.**
Transport Centre, 34 Upper O'Connell St., Dublin
1, Ireland.
● Transport; Irish and international transport news.
m. ISSN 0049-4461 (Irish Road Transport
Association) (Co-Sponsor: Road Transport
Organisation)

**Trinity College**
Dublin, Ireland.
● Hermathena. (pub. by Hodges Figgis & Co. Ltd.)
● Trinity News. w.(during school term) ISSN 0041-
3062

**Trinity College. Friends of the Library**
Friends of the Library, Dublin 2, Ireland.
● Long Room. s-a. ISSN 0024-631X

**United Irishman**
30 Gardiner Place, Dublin-1, Ireland.
● United Irishman. m.

**University College**
Dublin 2, Ireland.
● University College, Dublin. Faculty of Commerce.
Department of Business Administration. Business
Research Report. irreg., no. 3, 1971.

**University College, Cork**
● U. C. C. Record. (pub. by Cork University Press)

**University of Dublin. Trinity College**
Dublin, Ireland.
● Icarus. irreg. ISSN 0019-1027

**Wicklow Press**
South Quay, Wicklow, Ireland.
● European Teacher. 3 per yr. ISSN 0014-3146
(European Association of Teachers. Irish Section)

# ISRAEL

**A. G. Publications Ltd.**
Box 8100, 91080 Jerusalem, Israel.
● Innovation; monthly report on industrial R & D
and science based industry in Israel. m.
● Israel Business and Investors' Report. m.

**Academy of the Hebrew Language**
P.O.B.3449, Jerusalem, Israel.
● Academy of the Hebrew Language. Specialized
Dictionaries. irreg. ISSN 0065-0692

● Academy of the Hebrew Language. Texts &
Studies. irreg.
● Leshonenu La'am. 10 per yr. ISSN 0024-1091

**Achiever Publishing House**
22 Ha-Histadrut St., Jerusalem, Israel.
● Guide to Israel. a. ISSN 0072-8543

**Adult Education Association of Israel**
P.O.B. 2378, Jerusalem, Israel.
● Hinukh Mevugarim Be-Yisrael. bi-m.

**Agricultural Research Organization**
P.O. Box 6, Bet Dagan, Israel.
● Agricultural Research Organization. Pamphlet.
irreg., 1976, no. 162.
● Agricultural Research Organization. Preliminary
Reports. 3-4 per yr.
● Agricultural Research Organization. Special
Publications. 12-14 per yr.
● Phytoparasitica: Israel Journal of Plant Protection
Science. s-a. (Co-sponsors: Phytopathological
Society of Israel; Weed Science Society of Israel)

**Agricultural Workers' Organization of Israel**
25 Lilienblum St., Box 4, Tel Aviv, Israel.
● Hassadeh; a monthly review of agriculture. m.
ISSN 0017-8314

**Akim-Israel Association for Rehabilitation of the
Mentally Handicapped**
116 Allenby St., Tel Aviv, Israel.
● Tidings. a.

**Am Oved Ltd. Publishers**
22 Mazah St., Box 470, Tel-Aviv, Israel.
● Arav ve-Yisrael. bi-m.
● Ofakim. 8 per yr. ISSN 0017-8926
● Sifriya Laam. m. ISSN 0037-4792

**Arabic Publishing House**
17a Hagra S.T, Box 28049, Tel-Aviv, Israel.
● Sindbad. m. (Histadrut)

**Armenian Patriarchate**
Old City, Jerusalem, Israel.
● Sion. bi-m. ISSN 0037-5810

**Ashuach**
HaGedud Ha'Ivri 28, Tel Aviv, Israel.
● Problemen. (Fash, New York US)

**Association for Peace**
5 Ahuzat Bayit St., P.O.B. 17197, Tel Aviv, Israel.
● Middle East Essential. 5-6 per yr.

**Association of Americans and Canadians in Israel
(Jerusalem Region)**
9 Alkalai St., Jerusalem, Israel.
● A. A. C. I. Jerusalem Voice. m.

**Association of Engineers and Architects in Israel**
200 Dizengoff Rd., P.O.B. 3082, Tel Aviv, Israel.
● A-A/Architecture in Israel. q.
● Handasa W'adrikhalut. 10-12 per yr. ISSN 0017-
7164
● I T C C Review. (International Technical
Cooperation Centre) q. ISSN 0047-1216
● Technical Progress in Israel. m. ISSN 0040-098X

**Association of Secondary School Teachers of English
in Israel**
19 Blvd. Ben Gurion, 63454 Tel Aviv, Israel.
● Association of Secondary School Teachers of
English in Israel. Notes and Papers. a.

**Association of the Deaf and Mute in Israel. Helen
Keller Home**
P.O. Box 9001, Tel Aviv, Israel.
● Demama. q. ISSN 0011-8176

**Aurora**
c/o Arieh Avidor, Ed., Box 18066, Tel Aviv, Israel.
● Aurora; semanario Israeli de actualidad. w.

**Baha'i World Centre**
Box 155, Haifa 31-000, Israel.
● Baha'i World. irreg., 1973, vol. 14. ISSN 0045-
1320

**Bamah Association**
P.O.B. 4069, Jerusalem 91040, Israel.
● Bamah; educational theatre review. q. ISSN 0045-
138X

**Bank Leumi Le-Israel**
24-32 Yehuda Halevi St., Tel-Aviv, Israel.
● Bank Leumi Economic Review. q. ISSN 0034-
6519
● Weekly Report on the Tel-Aviv Stock Exchange.
(pub. by International Consultants
(ICCONSULT) Ltd.)

**Bank of Israel**
Mizpeh Building, 29 Jaffa Rd., Box 780, Jerusalem,
Israel.
● Bank of Israel. Economic Review. q. (prep. by its
Research Department)
● Bank of Israel. Main Points of the Annual Report.
a. ISSN 0067-3641
● Bank of Israel. Recent Economic Developments.
q. (prep. by its Research Department)
● Bank of Israel. Report. a. ISSN 0067-365X
● Banking Statistics. m. ISSN 0039-0607 (prep. by
its Research Department)

**Baptist Convention in Israel**
● Hayahad Digest/Together. (pub. by Dugith
Publishers)

**Bar-Ilan University**
Ramat-Gan, Israel.
● Bar-Ilan: Annual of Bar-Ilan University. a. ISSN
0067-4109
● Contrast. a. ISSN 0010-7948 (prep. by its English
Department)
● Criticism and Interpretation; journal for literature,
linguistics. history and aesthetics. irreg. ISSN
0084-9456
● Hebrew Computational Linguistics. 1-2 per yr.
(prep. by its Department of Hebrew and Semitic
Languages)
● Philosophia; philosophical quarterly of Israel. q.
ISSN 0048-3893 (prep. by its Department of
Philosophy)

**Ben-Gurion University of the Negev**
Box 2053, Beersheva, Israel.
● Beer-Sheva. a.
● Ben-Gurion University of the Negev. Research
and Development Authority. Scientific Activities.
a.

**Bet Midrash Lerabanim**
P.O. Box 642, Jerusalem, Israel.
● Bet Ha-Talmud. ISSN 0005-9749

**Verlag Bitaon Ltd.**
15 Rambam St., P.O. Box 1480, Tel-Aviv, Israel.
● Leo Baeck Institut. Bulletin. ISSN 0024-0915
● M B. (Mitteilungsblatt) w. (Irgun Oley Merkaz
Europa)

**B'minhal Hachinuch**
Box 4659, Haifa, Israel.
● B'minhal Hachinuch/Policy, Planning and
Administration in Education. 3 per yr.

**Yehuda Borovik**
P.O. Box 16368, Tel-Aviv 61160, Israel.
● BIAF-Israel Aviation and Space Magazine. bi-m.

**Brith Hasmoll**
Box 26115, 8-12 HaNegev St., Tel-Aviv 66186,
Israel.
● Turay Smoll. m.

**Bronfman & Cohen, Publishers Ltd.**
Box 1109, Tel Aviv, Israel.
● Who's Who in Israel. biennial. ISSN 0083-9590

**Building Centre of Israel**
P. O.Box 7102, Hakiryah, Tel-Aviv, Israel.
● Building Centre of Israel Quarterly. q.

**Cenaclul Literar "Menora"**
Box 763, Jerusalem, Israel.
● Caiet Pentru Literatura si Istoriografie. q. ISSN
0008-0527
● Note Stiri de Cenaclu. m. ISSN 0029-392X

**Center for Agricultural Economic Research**
Box 12, Rehovot, Israel.
● Center for Agricultural Economic Research,
Rehovot. Working Papers. irreg.

**Center for Arabic and Afro-Asian Studies**
Giv'at Haviva, Israel.
● Arab and Afro-Asian Monograph Series. irreg.,
no. 12, 1973. ISSN 0066-5622

**Center for Public Libraries**
Box 242, Jerusalem, Israel.
● Yad la-Kore/Reader's Aid; Israel journal for
libraries and archives. q. ISSN 0334-200X

**Central Archives for the History of the Jewish People**
Hebrew University Campus, Sprinzak Bldg., P.O.
Box 1149, Jerusalem, Israel.
● Central Archives for the History of the Jewish
People Newsletter/Ha-Arkhiyon Ha-Merkazi le-
Toldot Ha-Am Ha-Yehudi. Yediot. irreg.

**Central Union of Industrial Transport & Services Co-
Operative Societies in Israel**
24 Haarbaa St., Box 7151, (Hakirya), Tel-Aviv,
Israel.
● Shituf/Cooperation. bi-m. ISSN 0037-4008

**Committee for Jewish Culture**
228 Bne Efraim Maoz Aviv, Tel Aviv, Israel
(Subscr. to: P.O. Box 1217, Tel Aviv, Israel)
● Folk Un Medene.

**Communist Party of Israel**
P.O. Box 26205, Tel Aviv, Israel.
● Arakhim/Values; a magazine of problems of peace
and socialism. bi-m.
● Der Veg. w.
● Zo Haderekh. w.

**Continuation Committee of International Conference
on Science in the Advancement of New States**
P.O. Box 150, Rehovot, Israel.
● Rehovot Conference on Science in the
Advancement of New States. (Proceedings)
biennial. ISSN 0080-0759

**Council of the Sephardi Community**
Box 10, 12A Havatzelet St., Jerusalem, Israel.
● Bama'arakha. m. ISSN 0005-4542
● Israel's Oriental Problem. irreg. ISSN 0021-2350

**Dapei Zeev Ltd.**
66 Harakevet St., P.O.B. 33389, Tel Aviv, Israel.
● Best of Israel's Press. w.

**Dead Sea Bromine Company Ltd.**
Box 180, Beersheva, Israel.
● Bromides in Agriculture. irreg. ISSN 0007-2192

**Dead Sea Works, Ltd.**
Beersheba, Israel.
● Dead Sea Works, Beersheba, Israel. Report of the
Directors. a. ISSN 0070-3095

**Delek, Israel Fuel Corporation**
6 Ahuzat Bayit St, Tel Aviv, Israel.
● Delek. Annual Report. a.

**Dugith Publishers**
43 Frishman, Tel Aviv, Israel.
● Hayahad Digest/Together. q. ISSN 0017-8675
(Baptist Convention in Israel)

**Ecumenical Theological Research Fraternity in Israel**
Box 249, Jerusalem, Israel.
● Immanuel; religious thought and research in Israel.
2 per yr. ISSN 0302-8127

**Aba Elhanani, Ed. and Publ.**
27, Shlomo Hamelech St., Tel-Aviv, Israel.
● Tvai; periodical for architecture, town planning,
industrial design & the plastic arts. 2 per yr. ISSN
0041-4549

**Entomological Society of Israel**
Box 6, Beth Dagan, Israel.
● Israel Journal of Entomology. a. ISSN 0075-1243

**Estudiantes y Egresados de Cursos en Israel**
Box 13006, Jerusalem, Israel.
● Shalom. s-a.

**N.A. Etrogy Publishing Company**
Tel Aviv, Israel
(Dist. by International Publications Service, 303
Park Ave. S., New York, N.Y. 10010)
● Directory of Israeli Merchants and Manufacturers;
commercial and industrial directory. a. ISSN
0070-5705

**Etzb'omi Publishing House**
9 Eiger St., Tel-Aviv, Israel.
● Tom Thumb; a magazine for the young Jewish
child. m. ISSN 0040-912X

**European Conference on Electron Microscopy**
Inquire: Prof. D. Danon, Weizmann Institute of
Science, Rehovot, Israel.
- European Conference on Electron Microscopy.
  Proceedings. quadrennial; 6th, Jerusalem, 1976.
  ISSN 0071-2647

**Federation of Kibbutz Movements**
Box 303, Tel Aviv 61-000, Israel.
- The Kibbutz; interdisciplinary research review. a.

**Franciscan Printing Press**
Box 14064, Jerusalem 91140, Israel.
- Holy Places of Palestine. irreg.
- Quaderni de "la Terra Santa". irreg.
- Studium Biblicum Franciscanum. Analecta. irreg.,
  no. 11, 1975. ISSN 0081-8909
- Studium Biblicum Franciscanum. Collectio Major.
  irreg., no. 23, 1976. ISSN 0081-8917
- Studium Biblicum Franciscanum. Collectio Minor.
  irreg., no. 17, 1976. ISSN 0081-8925
- Studium Biblicum Franciscanum. Liber Annuus. a.
  ISSN 0081-8933
- Terra Santa. m. ISSN 0040-3784

**Freund Publishing House Ltd.**
Box 35010, Tel Aviv, Israel.
- Analytical Chemistry. Reviews. q. ISSN 0048-
  752X
- Coatings and Corrosion. Reviews. q. ISSN 0048-
  7538
- Deformation Behavior of Materials. Reviews. q.
  ISSN 0048-7589
- Drug Interactions. Reviews. q. ISSN 0048-7546
- Environmental Health. Reviews. q. ISSN 0048-
  7554
- High Temperature Materials. Reviews; a quarterly
  review of progress in high-temperature materials.
  q.
- Reactive Species in Chemical Reactions. Reviews.
  q. ISSN 0048-7562
- Silicon, Germanium, Tin and Lead Compounds.
  Reviews. q. ISSN 0048-7570

**Friends of the Midrashia, Israel**
A25 Lilienblum Str., Tel Aviv, Israel.
- Niv Hamidrashia. a. ISSN 0048-0460

**Hadassah Medical Organization**
Jerusalem, Israel.
- Hadassah Medical Organization. Report. irreg.,
  ISSN 0072-923X

**Hadassah Vocational Guidance Institute**
P.O. Box 1406, Jerusalem, Israel.
- Hadassah Vocational Guidance Institute. Report.
  a. ISSN 0072-9248 (Co-sponsor: Hadassah
  Women Zionist Organization of America)

**Haifa Music Museum and Amli Library**
P.O. Box 5111, Haifa, Israel.
- AMLI Studies in Music Bibliography. irreg. ISSN
  0066-1260
- Tatzlil/Chord; forum for music research and
  bibliography. a. ISSN 0082-2132

**Haifa University**
Mount Carmel, Haifa, Israel.
- Iyunim Bi-Hinukh. q. (prep. by its School of
  Education)
- Social Research Review/Riv'on Le-Mehkar
  Hevrati. q.

**Hakibbutz Hameuchad Publishing House Ltd.**
P.O. Box 16040, Tel Aviv, Israel.
- Mibifnim/From Within. q. ISSN 0046-5178

**Haolam Hazeh Ltd.**
3 Gordon St., Tel Aviv, Israel.
- Haolam Hazeh; the leading Israeli news magazine.
  w. ISSN 0017-7555

**Hebrew University of Jerusalem**
Jerusalem, Israel.
- Hebrew University of Jerusalem. Authority for
  Research and Development. Research Report.
  Vol. 1: Science and Agriculture. biennial. ISSN
  0075-3653
- Hebrew University of Jerusalem. Authority for
  Research and Development. Research Report. Vol
  2: Medicine, Pharmacy. Dental Medicine.
  triennial. ISSN 0075-3637
- Hebrew University of Jerusalem. Authority for
  Research and Development. Research Report.
  Vol. 3: Humanities, Social Sciences, Law,
  Education, Social Work, Library. biennial. ISSN
  0075-3645

- Hebrew University of Jerusalem. Bi-weekly/
  Dushavuon. bi-w.
- Hebrew University of Jerusalem. Department of
  Atmospheric Sciences. List of Contributions. a.
  (prep. by its Department of Atmospheric
  Sciences)
- Hebrew University of Jerusalem. Folklore
  Research Center. Studies. (pub. by Magnes Press)
- Hebrew University of Jerusalem. Lionel Cohen
  Lectures. (pub. by Magnes Press)
- Image; English literary magazine. q. ISSN 0019-
  2619
- Misifrut Ha-Hinukh: Educational Issues;
  translations from the educational literature.
  irreg.(approx.3 per yr.) (prep. by its School of
  Education)
- Papers in Sociology. a. (prep. by its Department
  of Sociology) (Subscr. to: Jerusalem Academic
  Press, Box 2390, Jerusalem, Israel)
- Scopus. s-a. ISSN 0036-9020
- Scripta Hierosolymitana. (pub. by Magnes Press)
- Textus. (pub. by Magnes Press)

**Hebrew University of Jerusalem. Alumni Association**
University Campus, Jerusalem, Israel.
- Expression/Maba. m. ISSN 0046-2977

**Hebrew University of Jerusalem. Graduate Library
School**
Jerusalem, Israel.
- Sefarim ve-Korim. a.

**Hebrew University of Jerusalem. H.S. Truman
Research Institute**
- Harry S. Truman Research Institute, Jerusalem.
  Annual Report. (pub. by Jerusalem Academic
  Press)
- Harry S. Truman Research Institute, Jerusalem.
  Publications. (pub. by Jerusalem Academic Press)
- Jerusalem Studies on Asia. (pub. by Jerusalem
  Academic Press)

**Hebrew University of Jerusalem. Hadassah Medical
School**
Division of the History of Medicine, Box 1172,
Jerusalem, Israel.
- Jerusalem Historical Medical Publications. irreg.
  ISSN 0449-4881

**Hebrew University of Jerusalem. Institute of
Archaeology**
Jerusalem, Israel.
- Kedem. irreg.

**Hebrew University of Jerusalem. Institute of
Criminology**
Jerusalem, Israel.
- Hebrew University of Jerusalem. Institute of
  Criminology. Publication. irreg.(approx. 2 issues
  per year) 1969, no. 16. ISSN 0075-3688

**Hebrew University of Jerusalem. Institute of
Languages and Literatures**
- H S L. (pub. by Jerusalem Academic Press)

**Hebrew University of Jerusalem. Institute of Urban
& Regional Studies**
Jerusalem, Israel.
- Jerusalem Urban Studies. irreg.

**Hebrew University of Jerusalem. Leonard Davis
Institute of International Relations**
Givat-Ram, Jerusalem, Israel.
- Jerusalem Journal of International Relations. q.
  ISSN 0363-2865

**Hebrew University of Jerusalem. Students' Union**
Givat Ram, Jerusalem, Israel.
- Lillit. 10 per yr. ISSN 0047-4665

**Hebrew Writers Association in Israel**
Box 7098, Tel Aviv, Israel.
- Moznayim. m. ISSN 0027-2892

**Hechal Shlomo**
Box 7440, Jerusalem, Israel.
- Hadashot Me Hachaim Hadatiyim Be Israel. bi-m.
  ISSN 0017-6508

**Henrietta Szold Institute**
9 Colombia St., Kiryat Menachem, Jerusalem,
Israel.
- Be'ad Ve- Neged/Pro and Con. 5 per yr. ISSN
  0005-7371
- Henrietta Szold Institute. Report on Activities.
  biennial. ISSN 0073-1846
- Leket Misifrut Ha-Chinuch Ba-Olam/Survey of
  World Literature in Education. q.

- Megamot; behavioural sciences quarterly. q. ISSN
  0025-8679

**Histadrut**
93 Arlozoroff St., Tel Aviv, Israel.
- Gimlaoth/Review on Pension Problems. q. ISSN
  0017-0003 (prep. by its Department of Labor)
- Die Goldene Keit. q. ISSN 0017-1638
- Hadshot Hahistadrut. fortn. ISSN 0005-3996
- Kalimat Al-Mar'ah. bi-m. ISSN 0022-7978 (prep.
  by its Council of Women Workers)
- Kupat-Holim Yearbook. a.
- Labour in Israel. 3 per yr. ISSN 0023-6969
- Naamat; magazine for women-in work, society &
  family   m. (prep. by its Council of Women
  Workers)
- Sindbad. (pub. by Arabic Publishing House)
- Al-Ta'awun; cooperation, economics and social
  welfare. q. ISSN 0002-4074 (prep. by its Arab
  Workers' Department)
- Urim La-Orim; educational magazine for parents.
  m. ISSN 0042-1073 (prep. by its Department for
  Culture and Education)

**Histadrut. Union of Clerical, Administrative and
Public Service Employees**
93 Arlosorof St., Tel Aviv, Israel.
- Shorooth. m. ISSN 0037-413X

**Historical Society of Israel**
Box 1062, Jerusalem, Israel.
- Zion; a quarterly for research in Jewish history. q.
  ISSN 0044-4758

**Hitahdut Oley Britannia**
53a Hayarkon St., Box 26072, Tel-Aviv 63902,
Israel.
- Oley Britannia. s-m.

**Hitahdut Oley Bukovina**
Box 1356, Tel Aviv, Israel.
- Stimme; kol haole. m.

**I.L.T.A.M. Corporation for Planning and Research**
18 Keren Hayesod, Box 7170, Jerusalem, Israel.
- I L T A M Newsletter for Information
  Technology in Israel. bi-m. ISSN 0019-2546

**Ichud Habonim**
Hayarkon 111, Box 3214, Tel Aviv, Israel.
- Yesodot. q. ISSN 0044-0361

**Ichud Ha'kvutzot Ve'hakibbutzim. Youth Division**
10 Dubnov St., Tel Aviv, Israel.
- Shdemot; literary digest of the kibbutz movement.
  s-a.

**Industrial Development Bank of Israel Limited**
27/29 Yehuda Halevi St., Tel-Aviv, Israel.
- Business Review and Economic News from Israel.
  q. ISSN 0007-7038
- Industrial Development Bank of Israel Limited.
  Report. a. ISSN 0073-7380

**Information Processing Association of Israel**
Box 13009, Jerusalem, Israel.
- Information Processing Association of Israel.
  National Conference on Data Processing.
  Proceedings. a. ISSN 0073-7879
- Ma'aseh Choshev. bi-m.

**Institute for International Sociological Research**
Box 7025, Tel Aviv, Israel.
- Mediterranean Diplomatic Observer; a publication
  of the Mediterranean Observer Group. m. ISSN
  0025-827X

**Institute for Petroleum Research and Geophysics**
Box 1717, Holon, Israel.
- Institute for Petroleum Research and Geophysics,
  Holon, Israel. Report. irreg. ISSN 0073-8832

**Institute for the Translation of Hebrew Literature**
8 Modigliani St., Tel Aviv, Israel.
- Modern Hebrew Literature; incorporating Hebrew
  Book Review. q.

**Institute of Agricultural Engineering**
Bet Dagan, Israel.
- Institute of Agricultural Engineering, Bet Dagan.
  Scientific Activities. irreg.

**Institute of Certified Public Accountants in Israel**
P. O. Box 29281, 1 Montefiore St., Tel Aviv, Israel.
- The Israel C P A. irreg., no.3, 1975.
- Jerusalem Conference on Accountancy. triennial.
- Roeh Hacheshbon. m. ISSN 0035-7790

**Institute of Farm Income Research**
6 Hachashmonaim Blvd., Tel Aviv, Israel.
- Profitability of Cotton Growing in Israel/Ha-Rivhiyut Shel Gidul Ha-Kutnah. a. ISSN 0079-595X
- Profitability of Poultry Farming in Israel/Ha-Rivhiyut Shel 'anaf Ha-Lul. irreg. ISSN 0079-5968
- Profitability of Sugarbeet Growing in Israel/Ha-Rivhiyut Shel Gidul Selek Ha-Sukar. a. ISSN 0079-5976

**Institute of Field and Garden Crops**
Bet Dagan, Israel.
- Institute of Field and Garden Crops. Scientific Activities. irreg.

**Institute of Management**
93 Arlozoroff St., Tel Aviv, Israel.
- Israel Review of Business Economics. q.

**Integration**
Box 3330, Tel Aviv, Israel.
- Integration; review for Western immigrants, residents and tourists. m. ISSN 0047-0392

**Intergovernmental Council for Automatic Data Processing**
c/o A. Gertz, Secretary-General, P. O. Box 7170, Jerusalem, Israel.
- Intergovernmental Council for Automatic Data Processing. Proceedings of Conference. irreg.; 1972, 6th West Germany. ISSN 0085-1981

**International Centre of Research and Information on Public and Cooperative Economy. Israeli Section.**
- Review of Public and Co-Operative Economy in Israel. (pub. by Jerusalem Academic Press.)

**International Consultants (ICCONSULT) Ltd.**
11 Hibat Zion St., Ramat Gan, Israel.
- Weekly Report on the Tel-Aviv Stock Exchange. w. (Bank Leumi le-Israel)

**International Council of the Aeronautical Sciences**
- I C A S Proceedings. (pub. by Weizmann Science Press of Israel)

**International Federation of Municipal Engineers**
23 Sderoth Yelin, Beersheva, Israel.
- International Federation of Municipal Engineers. Questionnaires and General Reports on Themes of the Congress/Questionnaires et Rapports Generaux sur les Themes du Congress. irreg., 1973, 5th, Jerusalem. ISSN 0538-7434

**International Free-Lancers' Organization**
c/o Uri Paz, Ed., 45 Palmach St., Rishon-le-Zion, Israel
(Subscr. to: Box 26424, Tel Aviv, Israel)
- A B C Magazine International. m.

**International Research Center on Rural Cooperative Communities**
24 Ha'arba'a St., P. O. B. 7020, Tel-Aviv, Israel
- Journal of Rural Cooperation. s-a. (Subscriptions to: Jerusalem Academic Press, P. O. Box 2390, Jerusalem, Israel)

**Irgun Hagananim B'israel**
Box 40035, Tel-Aviv, Israel.
- Gan Vanof/Garden and Landscape. m. ISSN 0016-4402

**Irgun Hayatsivim**
111 Allenby St., Tel-Aviv, Israel.
- Hayatsiv; organ of permanent workers in Solel-Boneh. bi-m. ISSN 0017-8691

**Ha-Irgun le-Milhamah ve-Tipul Be-Hatsalat Rekhush Yehudi**
Rehov Ha-Shoftim 10, P.O.B. 14110, Tel-Aviv, Israel.
- Ha-Tovea Ha-Yehudi.

**Irgun Oley Merkaz Europa**
- M B. (pub. by Verlag Bitaon Ltd.)

**Israel. Air Force**
Doar Zwai 2704, Zahal, Israel.
- Bitaon Heyl Ha'avir/Air Force Magazine. q. ISSN 0006-3878

**Israel. Atomic Energy Commission**
P.O. Box 17120, Tel Aviv, Israel.
- Israel. Atomic Energy Commission. IA-Reports. irreg., latest issue, 1974. ISSN 0075-0980

- Israel. Atomic Energy Commission. Technical Information Department. Literature Surveys. irreg. (prep. by its Technical Information Department)

**Israel. Central Bureau of Statistics**
P.O.B. 13015, Jerusalem, Israel.
- Israel. Central Bureau of Statistics. Annual Foreign Trade Statistics. a.
- Israel. Central Bureau of Statistics. Causes of Death. a. ISSN 0075-0999
- Israel. Central Bureau of Statistics. Construction in Israel/Ha-Binui Be-Yisrael. a. ISSN 0069-9195
- Israel. Central Bureau of Statistics. Criminal Statistics. irreg., latest issue, no. 417, 1970. ISSN 0075-1006
- Israel. Central Bureau of Statistics. Diagnostic Statistics of Hospitalized Patients. a. ISSN 0075-1014
- Israel. Central Bureau of Statistics Ha-Yarhon Ha-Statisti le-Yisrael. Musaf.
- Israel. Central Bureau of Statistics. Immigration Statistics. m. and q.
- Israel. Central Bureau of Statistics. Inputs in Research and Development in Academic Institutions. irreg.
- Israel. Central Bureau of Statistics. Insurance in Israel/Iske Ha-Bituah Be-Yisrael. a. ISSN 0074-0705
- Israel. Central Bureau of Statistics. Israel's Foreign Trade/Sehar Huts Shel Yisrael. irreg., latest issue, no. 463, 1973. ISSN 0075-1421
- Israel. Central Bureau of Statistics. Judicial Statistics. irreg., latest issue, no. 475, 1973. ISSN 0075-1030
- Israel. Central Bureau of Statistics. Juvenile Delinquency. irreg., latest issue, no. 408, 1970. ISSN 0075-1022
- Israel. Central Bureau of Statistics. Kupot Gemel Be-Yisrael. irreg.
- Israel. Central Bureau of Statistics. Labour Force Surveys. irreg., latest issue, no. 451, 1972. ISSN 0075-1049
- Israel. Central Bureau of Statistics. Monthly Bulletin of Statistics. m. ISSN 0021-1982
- Israel. Central Bureau of Statistics. Monthly Price Statistics. m. ISSN 0021-2008
- Israel. Central Bureau of Statistics. Motor Vehicles. irreg., latest issue, no. 462, 1973. ISSN 0075-1057
- Israel. Central Bureau of Statistics. New Statistical Projects and Publications in Israel. q.
- Israel. Central Bureau of Statistics. Quarterly Statistics of the Administered Territories. q.
- Israel. Central Bureau of Statistics. Road Accidents with Casualties. irreg.
- Israel. Central Bureau of Statistics. Schools and Kindergartens. irreg. ISSN 0075-1065
- Israel. Central Bureau of Statistics. Statistical Abstract of Israel/Shenaton Statisti le-Yisrael. irreg., latest issue, no. 25, 1974. ISSN 0081-4679
- Israel. Central Bureau of Statistics. Strikes and Lock-Outs. irreg., latest issue, no. 257, 1967. ISSN 0075-1073
- Israel. Central Bureau of Statistics. Students in Academic Institutions. a. ISSN 0075-1081
- Israel. Central Bureau of Statistics. Suicides and Attempted Suicides. irreg., latest issue, 1971.
- Israel. Central Bureau of Statistics. Survey of Housing Conditions. irreg., latest issue, no. 405, 1971. ISSN 0075-109X
- Israel. Central Bureau of Statistics. Trade Survey. a ISSN 0075-1103
- Israel. Central Bureau of Statistics. Traveling Habits Survey. irreg.
- Israel. Central Bureau of Statistics. Vital Statistics. irreg., latest issue, no. 466, 1972. ISSN 0075-1111
- Israel Tourist Statistics/Ha-Tayarut Be-Yisrael. irreg., latest edition, 1973. ISSN 0075-1405

**Israel. Commissioner for Complaints from the Public**
66 Rashi St., Jerusalem, Israel.
- Israel. Commissioner for Complaints from the Public (Ombudsman) Annual Report. a.

**Israel. Department of Customs and Excise**
32 Agron St., Box 302, Jerusalem 91000, Israel.
- Israel. Department of Customs and Excise. Journal. irreg. ISSN 0578-8250

**Israel. Department of Surveys**
P. O. B. 14171, Tel Aviv 61140, Israel.
- Israel. Department of Surveys. Geodetic Papers. irreg. ISSN 0075-1138

**Israel. Environmental Protection Agency**
Jerusalem, Israel.
- Israel. Environmental Protection Agency. Ekhut Ha-Sevivah Be-Yisrael. Eduah Shenti. irreg.

**Israel. Geological Survey**
30 Malkhe Israel St., Jerusalem, Israel.
- Israel. Geological Survey. Bulletin. irreg., 1973, no. 58. ISSN 0075-1200
- Israel. Geological Survey. Current Bibliography of Middle East Geology. m.
- Israel. Geological Survey. Current Research. a.

**Israel. Government Press Office**
Agron House, 37 Hillel St., Jerusalem, Israel.
- Israel. Goverment Press Office. Newspapers and Periodicals Appearing in Israel. a. ISSN 0078-0448
- Israel. Government Press Office. Weekly News Bulletin. w.
- Israel Government Press Office. d.

**Israel. Hydrological Service**
Box 6381, Jerusalem, Israel.
- Hydrological Yearbook of Israel/Shenaton Hidrologi Le-Yisrael. a. ISSN 0073-4217
- Israel. Hydrological Service. Hydrological Paper. irreg. ISSN 0075-1219

**Israel. Knesset**
Jerusalem, Israel.
- Israel. Knesset. Divrei Haknesset. w. ISSN 0012-4249
- Israel. Knesset. Hava'ada Leinyanei Bikoret Hamedina. Sikumeha ve-Hatsa 'oteha Shel Hava'ada Leinyanei Bikoret Hamedina le-Din ve-Hesbon Shel Mevaker Ha-Medina. a. (prep. by its State Control Committee)
- Israel. Knesset. Netunim 'al 'avodat ha-Knesset/Data on the Activities of the Knesset. quadrennial.
- Israel. Knesset. Va'adat Ha-Kesafim Misparim al Va'adat Ha-Kesafim/Israel. Knesset. Finance Committee. Data on Activities. a. (prep. by its Finance Committee)

**Israel. Meteorological Service**
Box 25, Bet Dagan, Israel.
- Israel. Meteorological Service. Annual Rainfall Summary. Series B (Observational Data) a. ISSN 0075-126X
- Israel. Meteorological Service. Annual Weather Report. Series B (Observational Data) a. ISSN 0075-1286
- Israel. Meteorological Service. Meteorologia Be-Israel. q. ISSN 0026-1122
- Israel. Meteorological Service. Monthly Agroclimatical Report. m.
- Israel. Meteorological Service. Monthly Weather Report. Series B (Observational Data) m. ISSN 0021-2261
- Israel. Meteorological Service. Series A (Meteorological Notes) irreg. ISSN 0075-1278
- Israel. Meteorological Service. Series C (Miscellaneous Papers) irreg. ISSN 0444-6801
- Israel. Meteorological Service. Solar Radiation and Radiation Balance at Bet Dagan, Israel. Series B (Observational Data) a.

**Israel. Ministry for Foreign Affairs**
Jerusalem, Israel
(Dist. in U. S. by Israel Office of Information, 11 East 70 Street, New York, N.Y. 10021)
- Arab View. irreg. (prep. by its Research Division)
- Ariel. (pub. by Jerusalem Publishing House, Ltd.)
- Facts About Israel. a. ISSN 0071-3635

**Israel. Ministry of Agriculture. Agriculture and Settlement Planning and Development Center**
Tel Aviv, Israel.
- Agricultural and Settlement Planning and Development Center. Agricultural and Rural Development Report. a.

**Israel. Ministry of Agriculture. Dept. of Fisheries**
Box 21170, Tel Aviv 62263, Israel.
- Israel. Ministry of Agriculture. Department of Fisheries. Bamidgeh; bulletin of fish culture in Israel. q. ISSN 0005-4577 (Co-Sponsor: Fish Breeders Association)
- Israel. Ministry of Agriculture. Department of Fisheries. Dayig u-Midgeh be-Yisrael/Fisheries and Fishbreeding in Israel. q. ISSN 0011-7110 (Co-Sponsors: Fish Breeders' Associations; Fishermen's Union in Israel)
- Israel. Ministry of Agriculture. Department of Fisheries. Israel Fisheries in Figures/Ha-Dayig Be-Yisrael Be-Misparim. a. ISSN 0075-1189

**Israel. Ministry of Commerce and Industry**
Jerusalem, Israel.
- Israel. Ministry of Commerce and Industry. Surveys and Development Plans of Industry in Israel/Ha-Ta'Asiyah Ha-Yisre'Elit. a. ISSN 0081-9743
- Israel Export Directory. (pub. by Israel Publications Corp. Ltd.)

**Israel. Ministry of Commerce and Industry. Foreign Trade Division**
Jerusalem, Israel.
- Israel Export Annual. a.

**Israel. Ministry of Communications**
Jaffa Rd. 23, Jerusalem, Israel.
- Israel. Ministry of Communications. Statistics/Israel. Misrad Ha-Do'ar. Statistikah. a. ISSN 0075-1308

**Israel. Ministry of Education and Culture**
Jerusalem, Israel.
- Hed Ha-Ulpan. q. (prep. by its Department of Adult Education)
- Israel. Ministry of Education and Culture. Department of Antiquities and Museums. Atiqot (English Series) irreg., 1976, vol. 11. ISSN 0066-488X (prep. by its Department of Antiquities and Museums)
- Israel. Ministry of Education and Culture. Department of Antiquities and Museums. Atiqot (Hebrew Series) irreg., vol. 7, 1974. ISSN 0067-0138 (prep. by its Department of Antiquities and Museums)
- Israel. Ministry of Education and Culture. Department of Antiquities and Museums. Archaeological News/Hadashot Arkhiologiyot. q. ISSN 0047-1569 (prep. by its Department of Antiquities and Museums)
- Israel. Ministry of Education and Culture. Department of Educational Technology. Bulletin/Alon le-Technologyah Be-Khinukh. irreg. (prep. by its Department of Educational Technology)
- Israel. Ministry of Education and Culture. English Teachers' Journal. s-a. (prep. by its Pedagogical Secretariat)
- Israel. Ministry of Education and Culture. Rural Education Division. English Teaching Guidance. q. (prep. by its Rural Education Division)
- Lada'at. (pub. by Weizmann Science Press of Israel)

**Israel. Ministry of Health**
20 King David St., Jerusalem, Israel.
- Briuth Hatzibbur/Public Health. q. ISSN 0007-1986
- Israel. Ministry of Health. Division of Epidemiology. Infectious Diseases Surveillance. s-a. (prep. by its Division of Epidemiology)
- Israel. Ministry of Health. Division of Epidemiology. Monthly Epidemiological Record of Infectious Diseases Not Included in the Weekly Records. m. (prep. by its Division of Epidemiology)
- Israel. Ministry of Health. Division of Epidemiology. Weekly Epidemiological Record. w. (prep. by its Division of Epidemiology)
- Israel Medical Bibliography. biennial. ISSN 0075-1251

**Israel. Ministry of Justice. Patent Office**
P.O. Box 717, Jerusalem, Israel
(Subscr. to: Distribution Service of Government Publications, 29-B St., Hakirya, Tel-Aviv, Israel)
- Israel. Ministry of Justice. Patent Office. Patents and Designs Journal. m. ISSN 0021-2326

**Israel. Ministry of Labour**
Jerusalem, Israel.
- Avoda Ubituach le-Umi/Labour & National Insurance. m. ISSN 0005-2299
- Israel. Ministry of Labour. Registrar of Cooperative Societies. Report on the Cooperative Movement in Israel. a. ISSN 0080-1313 (prep. by its Registrar of Cooperative Societies)

**Israel. Ministry of Religious Affairs**
Box 1167, 30 Jaffa St., Jerusalem, Israel.
- Christian News from Israel. q. ISSN 0009-5532

**Israel. Ministry of Social Welfare**
8 King David St., Jerusalem, Israel.
- Israel. Ministry of Social Welfare. Department of International Relations. Sa'ad; bi-monthly for social welfare. bi-m. (prep. by its Department of International Relations)

- Israel. Ministry of Social Welfare. Department of International Relations. the Press on Welfare; a selection of articles on welfare from the Israeli press. s-a. (prep. by its Department of International Relations)

**Israel. Ministry of the Interior**
Jerusalem, Israel.
- Israel. Ministry of the Interior. City and Region/Ir ve Ezor. q. ISSN 0302-8267

**Israel. Ministry of Tourism**
P.O. Box 1018, Jerusalem, Israel.
- Israel. Ministry of Tourism. Tourist Promotion Department. Information Letter. m. (prep. by its Information Unit)

**Israel. National Council for Research and Development**
Jerusalem, Israel.
- Israel. National Council for Research and Development. Scientific Research in Israel. irreg., 1971, 3rd ed. ISSN 0080-7753

**Israel. National Council for Research and Development. Center of Scientific and Technological Information**
84 Hachashmonaim St., Box 20125, Tel Aviv, Israel.
- Artificial Rainfall Newsletter. q. ISSN 0044-9105
- Calendar of Forthcoming Scientific and Technological Meetings to Be Held in Israel. s-a. ISSN 0008-0764
- Current Research and Development Projects in Israel: Natural Sciences and Technology. irreg.
- Desalination Abstracts. q. ISSN 0011-9172
- Directory of Scientific and Technical Associations and Institutes in Israel. irreg. ISSN 0070-6264
- Directory of Serials in Pure and Applied Science and Economics Published in Israel. irreg., 1968, 2nd ed. ISSN 0070-6302
- Directory of Special Libraries in Israel. irreg., 4th edt., 1976. ISSN 0070-637X

**Israel. State Revenue Administration**
Custom Square, 32 Agron St., Jerusalem, Israel.
- Ha'Rivon Ha'Israeli Le'Misim/Israel Tax Review. q.

**Israel Academy of Sciences and Humanities**
Box 4040, Jerusalem 91040, Israel.
- Israel Academy of Sciences and Humanities. Section of Sciences. Proceedings. irreg. ISSN 0075-0956
- Jerusalem Symposia on Quantum Chemistry and Biochemistry. (pub. by D. Reidel Publishing Co. NE)

**Israel Association for International Cooperation**
Box 13006, Jerusalem, Israel.
- Courses in Israel. a.

**Israel Bar Association**
Box 14152, Tel-Aviv, Israel.
- Hapraklit. q. ISSN 0017-7571

**Israel Business Books Ltd.**
Ed. Gabriel Alon, Box 1313, Haifa, Israel.
- Gold, Money, Commodities. s-m.
- Israel Business Diary. m.
- Zrak'or. m. ISSN 0007-6643

**Israel Chess Federation**
Box 21143, Tel Aviv, Israel.
- Shahmat. m.

**Israel Clinical Pediatric Society**
Meretz, P.O.B. 344, Tel Aviv, Israel.
- Child Health in Israel/Beri'ut Ha-Yeled Be-Yisrael. a. ISSN 0069-3413

**Israel Consumers' Association**
35 King George St., Tel Aviv, Israel.
- Bamat Hatzarkhan/Consumer's Tribune. s-a. ISSN 0005-4569

**Israel Dental Association**
49 Bar-Kochba St., Tel Aviv, Israel.
- Refuat Hape Vehashinaim/Israel Journal of Dental Medicine. q. ISSN 0034-3161

**Israel Diamond Institute**
3 Jabotinsky Rd., P.O.B. 3237, Ramat Gan, Israel.
- Israel Diamonds. q. ISSN 0021-2016

**Israel Discount Bank, Ltd.**
27-29 Yehuda Halevy St., Tel Aviv, Israel.
- Israel Discount Bank. Report. a. ISSN 0075-1146

**Israel Exploration Society**
P.O. Box 7041, Jerusalem, Israel.
- Eretz-Israel Volumes. Archaeological, Historical and Geographical Studies. biennial. ISSN 0071-108X
- Israel Exploration Journal. q. ISSN 0021-2059
- Judean Desert Studies. irreg. ISSN 0075-4501
- Qadmoniot; quarterly for the Antiquities of Eretz-Israel and Biblical lands. q. ISSN 0033-4839
- Studies in the Geography of Israel/Mehkarim Be-Ge'ografyah Shel Erets-Yisrael. irreg., vol. 9 in prep., 1975. ISSN 0081-8585 (prep. by its Geographical Department)

**Israel Export Institute**
- Israel Export and Trade Journal. (pub. by Israel Periodicals Company Ltd.)

**Israel Export Institute. Book and Printing Center**
47 Nahlat Benyamin St., Box 29732, Tel-Aviv, Israel.
- Books from Israel. a.
- Israel Book Trades Directory: a Select List. biennial.
- Israel Book World. q. ISSN 0021-1974

**Israel Feminist Movement**
P. O. Box 4667, Haifa, Israel.
- Nilham. q.

**Israel Film Centre**
Box 299, Jerusalem, Israel.
- Filmmaking in Israel. a.
- Israel Film Centre. Information Bulletin. q.
- Israel Films. a. ISSN 0075-1170

**Israel Forestry Association**
Ilanot, Doar na Lev Hasharon, Israel.
- La-Yaaran. q. ISSN 0023-6446

**Israel Gerontological Society**
Box 11243, Tel Aviv, Israel.
- Gerontology. q.
- Israel Gerontological Society. Information Bulletin/Ha'Agudah Ha'Israelit Le'Gerontologyah. Yedion. q. ISSN 0047-1577

**Israel Hotel Association**
Box 11586, Tel Aviv, Israel.
- Hamlonai/Hotelier. m. ISSN 0017-7091

**Israel Industry and Commerce and Export News**
21 Hasharon St., Tel Aviv, Israel.
- Israel Industry and Commerce and Export News. bi-m.

**Israel Institute for Biological Research**
Box 19, Ness-Ziona, Israel.
- Israel Institute for Biological Research. OHOLO Biological Conference. Proceedings. a.

**Israel Institute of Applied Social Research**
19 Washington St., Jerusalem, Israel.
- Israel Institute of Applied Social Research. Research Report. biennial. ISSN 0075-1227

**Israel Institute of Energy and Petroleum**
26 University St., Ramat Aviv, Tel-Aviv, Israel.
- Israel Oil News. s-a. ISSN 0047-1585
- Kiyum.
- Ostracodologist. irreg. ISSN 0085-4573

**Israel Institute of International Affairs**
P. O. B. 17027, Tel Aviv 61170, Israel.
- International Problems. 2-4 per yr. ISSN 0020-840X

**Israel Institute of Productivity**
4 Henrietta Szold St., P.O.B. 33010, Tel-Aviv, Israel.
- Hamifal/Enterprise. m. ISSN 0017-7059
- Israel Institute of Productivity. Report of Activities/Ha-Makhon Le-Firyon Ha-'avodah Veha-Yitsur. Din Veheshbon. irreg, ISSN 0075-1235

**Israel Institute of Public Administration**
P.O. Box 1077, Jerusalem, Israel.
- Public Administration in Israel and Abroad. a. ISSN 0079-7499

**Israel Journal of Physiotherapy**
93 Arlozorov St., Tel-Aviv, Israel.
- Israel Journal of Physiotherapy. 3-4 per yr. ISSN 0021-2199

**Israel Law Review Association**
c/o Hebrew University, Faculty of Law, P.O.B.
24100, Mount Scopus, Jerusalem, Israel.
- Israel Law Review. q. ISSN 0021-2237

**Israel Malacological Society**
Netzer Sereni, 70-395, Israel.
- Argamon; Israel journal of malacology. irreg. (Co-
sponsor: Nahariya Municipal Malacological
Museum)

**Israel Medical Association**
39 King Saul Blvd., Tel Aviv, Israel.
- Harefuah. fortn. ISSN 0017-7768
- Israel Journal of Medical Sciences. m. ISSN 0021-
2180 (Co-Sponsor: National Council for Research
and Development)
- Israel Medical Association. Quarterly Review;
devoted to the promotion of cultural and
professional relations between the physicians of
Israel and other colleagues abroad. q. ISSN 0021-
2253
- Mikhtav Lehaver. fortn. ISSN 0026-363X

**Israel Museum**
Jerusalem, Israel.
- Israel Museum News. a. ISSN 0021-227X

**Israel Numismatic Society**
Box 750, Jerusalem, Israel.
- Israel Numismatic Journal. ISSN 0021-2288

**Israel Oceanographic and Limnological Research**
120 Haatzmaut St., Haifa, Israel.
- Israel Oceanographic and Limnological Research.
Annual Report. a.

**Israel Oriental Society**
Hebrew University, Jerusalem, Israel.
- Asian and African Studies. (pub. by Jerusalem
Academic Press)
- Hamizrah Hehadash/New East. q. ISSN 0017-
7083
- Oriental Notes and Studies. irreg. ISSN 0078-
6543

**Israel Overseas Publications Ltd.**
13 Montefiore St., Box 2032, Tel Aviv, Israel.
- Israel Financial Review. m. ISSN 0021-2075

**Israel Painters and Sculptors Association**
9 Alharizi St., Tel-Aviv, Israel.
- Tsiyur u-Fisul. q.

**Israel Periodicals Company Ltd.**
14 Chissin St., Tel Aviv, Israel.
- Israel Export and Trade Journal. m. ISSN 0021-
2067 (Israel Export Institute) (Co-sponsor: Israel
Company for Fairs and Exhibitions)
- Israels Aussenhandel. m. ISSN 0578-9427
(Israelisch-Deutsche Industrie-und
Handelskammer) (Co-Sponsor: Deutsch-
Israelische Wirtschaftsvereinigung E.V.)

**Israel Plastics Society**
c/o Center for Industrial Research, P.O.B. 311,
Haifa, Israel.
- Polimerim ve-Homarim Plastiyim/Polymers and
Plastic Materials. 3-4 per yr.

**Israel Ports Authority**
Box 20121, Tel-Aviv, Israel.
- Ha-Nemalim Be-Israel. Berashut. m.
- Yearbook of Israel Ports Statistics/Shenaton
Statisti: Le Nemlei Israel. a. ISSN 0084-3830

**Israel Program for Scientific Translations**
Box 7145, Jerusalem, Israel
- Fauna of Russia and Adjacent Countries. irreg.
(U.S. Distributor: International Scholarly Book
Services, Inc., 10300 S. W. Allen Blvd.,
Beaverton, OR 97005)
- Fauna of the U.S.S.R. irreg. (U.S. Distributor:
International Scholarly Book Services, Inc., 10300
S.W. Allen Blvd., Beaverton, OR 97005)
- Flora of the U.S.S.R. irreg. (U.S. Distributor:
International Scholarly Book Services, Inc., 10300
S.W. Allen Blvd., Beaverton, OR 97005)
- International Clay Conference. Proceedings.
triennial, 1969, 3rd, Tokyo. ISSN 0074-2597

**Israel Public Council for Soviet Jewry. Scientists'
Committee**
4A Chissin St., Entrance B, 4th Floor, Tel-Aviv,
Israel.
- Israel Public Council for Soviet Jewry. Scientists'
Committee. News Bulletin. s-m.

**Israel Publications Corp. Ltd.**
P.O.B. 11587, Tel Aviv, Israel.
- Israel Export Directory. a. ISSN 0075-1154
(Israel. Ministry of Commerce and Industry)
- Melaha Vetaassiva/Israel Industry. m. (Union of
Artisans and Manufacturers)

**Israel Shipping Research Institute**
Box 1860, Haifa, Israel.
- Israel Shipping Research Institute. Information
Paper. m. (prep. by its Freight Research Division)
- Sapanut. 3 per yr.

**Israel Society for Biblical Research**
Box 7024, Jerusalem, Israel.
- Beth Mikra. q. ISSN 0005-979X
- Dor le-Dor. q.

**Israel Society for Rehabilitation of the Disabled**
10 Ibn Gvirol St., Tel Aviv, Israel.
- Israel Society for Rehabilitation of the Disabled.
Annual. a. ISSN 0075-1383

**Israel Society for the Promotion of Classical Studies**
- Scripta Classica Israelica. (pub. by Jerusalem
Academic Press)

**Israel Society of Special Libraries and Information
Centers**
Box 20125, Tel-Aviv, Israel.
- Contributions to Information Science. irreg.
- I S L I C Bulletin. 3 per yr. ISSN 0021-2318

**Israel Society of the History of Medicine and Science**
Maon Harofe, 37 Gedaljahu St., Nave Shaanan,
Haifa, Israel.
- Koroth; a journal devoted to the history of
medicine and science. q. ISSN 0023-4109 (Co-
sponsor: Israel Institute of Medical History)

**Israel Teachers Union**
8 Ben Sarouk St., Tel Aviv, Israel.
- Hahinukh; journal for educational thought. q.
ISSN 0017-646X
- Hed Hahinukh. w. ISSN 0017-9493

**Israel Veterinary Medical Association**
Box 18, Bet Dagan, Israel.
- Refuah Veterinarith. q. ISSN 0034-3153

**Israel Yearbook Publications**
Tel Aviv, Israel
(Dist. in U.S. by International Publications Service,
303 Park Ave. So., New York, N.Y. 10010)
- Israel Yearbook. a. ISSN 0075-1413

**Israelisch-Deutsche Industrie-und Handelskammer**
- Israels Aussenhandel. (pub. by Israel Periodicals
Company Ltd.)

**Jerusalem Academic Press**
Box 2390, Jerusalem, Israel.
- Asian and African Studies. 3 per yr. ISSN 0066-
8281 (Israel Oriental Society)
- H S L. (Hebrew University Studies in Literature)
s-a. (Hebrew University of Jerusalem. Institute of
Languages and Literatures)
- Harry S. Truman Research Institute, Jerusalem.
Annual Report. a. (Hebrew University of
Jerusalem. H.S. Truman Research Institute)
- Harry S. Truman Research Institute, Jerusalem.
Publications. irreg. ISSN 0073-0424 (Hebrew
University of Jerusalem. H.S. Truman Research
Institute)
- International Civil Engineering Monthly. q. ISSN
0020-6377
- Israel Annals of Psychiatry and Related
Disciplines. q. ISSN 0021-1958
- Jerusalem Studies on Asia. irreg. (Hebrew
University of Jerusalem. H. S. Truman Research
Institute. Asia Research Unit)
- Review of Public and Co-Operative Economy in
Israel. irreg. (International Centre of Research
and Information on Public and Cooperative
Economy. Israeli Section.)
- Scripta Classica Israelica. a. (Israel Society for the
Promotion of Classical Studies)

**Jerusalem International Book Fair**
22 Jaffa Road, Jerusalem 91000, Israel.
- Jerfair News; the Jerusaleum International Book
Fair newsletter. q.

**Jerusalem Philosophical Society**
Hebrew University Campus, Jerusalem, Israel.
- Iyyun; a Hebrew philosophical quarterly. q. ISSN
0021-3306 (Co-sponsor: Hebrew University of
Jerusalem. S.H. Bergman Centre for Philosophical
Studies)

**Jerusalem Post Publications, Ltd.**
Romena Industrial Quarter, P.O.B. 81, Jerusalem,
Israel
- Contact; Jerusalem youth magazine. bi-w. (And
Board of Jewish Education, Inc., 426 W. 58st.,
N.Y., N.Y. 10019)
- Jerusalem Post. d. & w. ISSN 0021-597X

**Jerusalem Publishing House, Ltd.**
39 Tchernechovsky St., P.O.B. 7147, Jerusalem,
Israel.
- Ariel; a quarterly review of arts and letters in
Israel. q. ISSN 0004-1343 (Israel. Ministry for
Foreign Affairs. Cultural and Scientific Relations
Division)

**Jewish Agency for Israel**
Box 92, Jerusalem, Israel.
- Jewish Agency for Israel. Office for Economic and
Social Research. Annual. a. (prep. by its Office
for Economic and Social Research)

**Jewish Demographic Society**
7 Solomon St., Box 28086, Tel Aviv, Israel.
- Ephrath. q.

**Jewish Music Research Centre**
- Yuval. (pub. by Magnes Press)

**Jewish National and University Library**
P.O. Box 503, Jerusalem, Israel.
- Index of Articles on Jewish Studies/Reshimat
Ma'amarim Be-Mada'e Ha-Yahadut. a. ISSN
0073-5817
- Kirjath Sepher; bibliographical quarterly. q. ISSN
0023-1851
- New Reference Books. s-a.
- Union List of Serials in Israel Libraries. irreg., 4th
edt., 1975. ISSN 0082-7665

**Jewish National Fund**
Box 283, Jerusalem, Israel.
- J N F Illustrated/Karnenu. q. ISSN 0021-3705

**Keren Hayesod**
P.O. Box 583, Jerusalem, Israel.
- Our World. 4-5 per yr. ISSN 0030-6983

**Keter Publishing House Ltd.**
Givat Shaul Industrial Area, P.O.B. 7145,
Jerusalem, Israel.
- Encyclopaedia Judaica Year Book. a.
- Middle East Record. irreg., vol. 4, 1968 (vols. 5-6,
1969-1970, published at end of 1975) ISSN 0076-
8529 (Tel-Aviv University. Shiloah Center for
Middle Eastern and African Studies) (U.S. Orders
to: Halsted Press-John Wiley & Sons, Inc., 605
Third Avenue, New York 10016 NY)

**Kibbutz Artzi Hashomer Hatzair**
Leonardo de Vinci 13, Box 40009, Tel-Aviv, Israel.
- Kibbutz Artzi Hashomer Hatzair. Ha- Shavua. w.

**Kollek and Sons**
16 King George Ave., Box 7052, Jerusalem, Israel.
- Israel Economist. m. ISSN 0021-2040

**Komitet far Yidisher Kultur in Yisroel**
228 Bnei Ephraim St., Tel Aviv, Israel.
- Bay Zikh. ISSN 0302-8178
- Folk, Velt un Medine/Am, Olam u-Medinah. m.
(Co-sponsor: World Jewish Congress)

**David Kraft Publishing Company**
26 Ficus St., P. O. B. 28117, Tel Aviv, Israel.
- Israel Petroleum and Energy Year Book. a. ISSN
0075-1367

**Kupat Holim Health Insurance Institution**
148 Arlosoroff St., Box 16250, Tel Aviv, Israel.
- Family Physician. q.
- Kupat-Holim. Information Series; "Meida" on
Medical Sociology and Health. q.

**Land Use Research Institute**
King George St. 43, P.O.B. 7816, Jerusalem, Israel.
- Karka/Land; journal of the land use research
institute. q.

**Leo Baeck Institut**
• Leo Baeck Institut. Bulletin. (pub. by Verlag Bitaon Ltd.)

**Maccabi World Union**
Kfar Hamaccabiah, Israel.
• Maccabi World Union. Newsletter. m.

**Magnes Press**
Hebrew University of Jerusalem, Jerusalem, Israel.
• Hebrew University of Jerusalem. Folklore Research Center. Studies. irreg., 1973, vol. 3. ISSN 0075-3661
• Hebrew University of Jerusalem. Lionel Cohen Lectures. irreg. ISSN 0075-9740
• Scripta Hierosolymitana. irreg. ISSN 0080-8369 (Hebrew University of Jerusalem)
• Textus. approx. a. ISSN 0082-3767 (Hebrew University of Jerusalem. Bible Project)
• University of London. Institute of Jewish Studies. Papers. irreg. ISSN 0076-0838
• Yuval. irreg. ISSN 0084-439X (Jewish Music Research Centre)

**Makhteshim Agan**
P.O. Box 60, Beersheva, Israel.
• Plant Protection Abstracts. q. ISSN 0032-0897
• Plant Protection Abstracts. Supplement. irreg., latest issue, 1969. ISSN 0079-225X

**Maritime Bank of Israel, Ltd**
P.O. Box 1529, Tel Aviv 61000, Israel.
• Maritime Bank of Israel. Annual Report/Bank Ha-Sapanut le-Yisrael. Annual Report. a. ISSN 0076-4515

**Maurice Falk Institute for Economic Research in Israel**
17 Keren Hayesod St., Jerusalem, Israel.
• Maurice Falk Institute for Economic Research in Israel. Report. triennial. ISSN 0076-5473

**Ha-Merkaz Ha-Artsi Shel Irgune Ha-Kablanim Veha-Bonim Be-Yisrael**
Rehov Mikveh Yisrael 18, Tel-Aviv, Israel.
• Ha-Kablan Veha-Boneh. bi-m.

**Middle East Information Media Ltd.**
8 Mendele St., Tel Aviv, Israel.
• Brief: Middle East Highlights. fortn.
• Middle East Intelligence Survey. s-m.

**Mitzion Tetzeh Torah, Ltd.**
P.O.B. 29435, 9 Derech Haifa Rd., Tel-Aviv, Israel.
• Mitzion Tetzeh Torah. M.T.T. irreg.; (approx. 2 per yr.) ISSN 0541-5632

**Museum Haaretz**
Ramat Aviv, P.O.B. 17068, Tel Aviv, Israel.
• Museum Haaretz, Tel-Aviv. Shenaton. Yearbook. a. ISSN 0077-2305

**Museum of Antiquites of Tel-Aviv-Yafo**
Box 8406, Tel Aviv-Jaffa, Israel.
• Museum of Antiquities of Tel-Aviv-Yafo. Publications. irreg. ISSN 0082-2620

**National Association of Nurses in Israel**
Box 303, Tel-Aviv, Israel.
• Nurse in Israel. 4 per yr. ISSN 0048-1165

**National Insurance Institute**
Weizmann Ave., Jerusalem, Israel.
• Israeli Life Table. irreg. ISSN 0077-5037
• National Insurance Institute, Jerusalem. Full Actuarial Report. triennial. ISSN 0075-1324
• National Insurance Institute, Jerusalem. Statistical Abstract. s-a. ISSN 0075-1340

**National Maritime Museum**
198 Allenby Road, Haifa, Israel.
• Sefunim. a. ISSN 0077-5193

**Peres Blancs de Sainte-Anne de Jerusalem**
B.P. 19079, Jerusalem, Israel.
• Proche-Orient Chretien. q. ISSN 0032-9622

**Peylim-Yad l'Achim**
4 Jona St., P.O.B. 5195, Jerusalem, Israel.
• Yad l'Achim Wall Calendar. bi-m.

**Pharmaceutical Association of Israel**
6 Rothschild Blvd., Tel Aviv, Israel.
• Israel Pharmaceutical Journal/Harokeach Haivri. bi-m. ISSN 0017-7865

**Settlement Study Center, Rehovot**
Box 555, Rehovot, Israel.
• Settlement Study Center, Rehovot. Publications on Problems of Regional Development. irreg.

**Shaare Zedek Hospital. Falk Schlesinger Institute for Medical Halachic Research**
Jaffa Road, Jerusalem, Israel.
• Assia. irreg.

**SIACH (Israeli New Left)**
P.O.B.9013, Jerusalem, Israel.
• ISRALEFT Bi-Weekly News Service. fortn.

**Jacob Slonim Publishing Ltd.**
Box 35, Tel-Aviv, Israel.
• International Journal of Radiation Engineering. m. ISSN 0047-0759

**Society for International Development. Israel Chapter**
3 Moshe Wallach St., P.O.B. 13130, Jerusalem 94385, Israel.
• Kidma; Israel journal of development. 3 per yr. (Co-sponsor: Israel Association for International Cooperation)

**Society for the Protection of Nature in Israel**
Rehov Hashfela 4, Tel Aviv, Israel.
• Israel-Land and Nature. q.
• Teva Vaaretz. bi-m. ISSN 0563-2153

**Standards Institution of Israel**
Unversity St., Ramat-Aviv, Tel-Aviv, Israel.
• Mati. q. ISSN 0025-5912

**Swedish Theological Institute**
P.O. Box 37, Jerusalem, Israel.
(and E. J. Brill, Leiden, Netherlands)
• Swedish Theological Institute, Jerusalem. Annual. a. ISSN 0082-0423

**Tanne Advertising Ltd.**
19 Gruzenberg St., P.O.B. 29322, Tel Aviv, Israel.
• We Represent in Israel and Abroad. irreg.

**Tazpiot, Ltd.**
8 Rehov Karl Netter, Tel Aviv, Israel.
• New Outlook; Middle East monthly. m. ISSN 0028-6427

**Bezalel Tcherikover, Pubs., Ltd.**
12 Ha'sharon St., Tel Aviv, Israel.
• Israel Studies in Criminology. irreg. ISSN 0075-1391 (Tel Aviv University. Institute of Criminology and Criminal Law)

**Technion-Israel Institute of Technology**
Haifa, Israel.
• Israel Annual Conference on Aviation and Astronautics. Proceedings. a. ISSN 0075-0972 (prep. by its Department of Aeronautical Engineering)
• Israel Institute of Technology. President's Report and Reports of Other Officers. a. ISSN 0072-9329
• M E D Report. irreg. ISSN 0072-9310 (prep. by its Department of Material Engineering)
• T. A. E. Report. irreg. ISSN 0072-9302 (prep. by its Department of Aeronautical Engineering)
• Technion. bi-m. ISSN 0040-1188
• Technion-Israel Institute of Technology. Braverman Memorial Lecture. irreg. ISSN 0068-0761 (prep. by its Department of Food Engineering and Biotechnology)
• Technion-Israel Institute of Technology. Faculty of Agricultural Engineering. Publications. irreg. (prep. by its Faculty of Agricultural Engineering)

**Technosdar, Ltd.-International Scientific Publications**
12 Hahashmal St., P.O.B. 31684, Tel Aviv, Israel.
• Public Health Reviews; an international quarterly. q. ISSN 0301-0422

**Tel-Aviv University**
Ramat Aviv, Tel-Aviv, Israel.
• Aleph-Tav Quarterly; Tel-Aviv University Review. q.
• Dine Israel; an annual of Jewish and Israeli family law. a. ISSN 0070-4903 (prep. by its Faculty of Law)
• Israel Oriental Studies. a. (prep. by its Department of Arabic Studies)
• Israel Yearbook on Human Rights. a. (prep. by its Faculty of Law)
• Merhavim; collection of geographical research about Israel and the Middle East. irreg. (prep. by its Department of Geography)

• Ha-Sifrut/Literature; theory, poetics, Hebrew and comparative literature. q. ISSN 0017-8284
• Tel Aviv University. Law Review/Iyunei Mishpat. q. (prep. by its Faculty of Law)
• Tel-Aviv University. Ph.D. Degrees and Abstracts. irreg.

**Tel-Aviv University. David Horowitz Institute for the Research of Developing Countries**
Tel-Aviv, Israel.
• Tel-Aviv University. David Horowitz Institute for the Research of Developing Countries. Research Reports and Papers. irreg.

**Tel-Aviv University. Diaspora Research Institute**
Sales Division, Gilman Bldg., Rms. 464-5, Tel Aviv, Israel.
• Michael; on the history of the Jews in the Diaspora. irreg., 1976, vol. 4.
• Shvut; Jewish problems in the USSR and Eastern Europe. a.

**Tel-Aviv University. Institute for German History**
Tel-Aviv, Ramat-Aviv, Israel.
• Tel Aviv University. Institut fuer Deutsche Geschichte. Jahrbuch. a.

**Tel Aviv University. Institute for Zionist Research**
Tel Aviv, Israel.
• Zionism; Studies in the History of the Zionist Movement and of the Jews in Palestine/Ha-Tsiyonut. a. ISSN 0084-5523

**Tel Aviv University. Institute of Criminology and Criminal Law**
• Israel Studies in Criminology. (pub. by Bezalel Tcherikover, Pubs., Ltd.)

**Tel-Aviv University. Shiloah Center for Middle Eastern and African Studies**
• Middle East Record. (pub. by Keter Publishing House Ltd.)

**Tel Aviv-Yafo. Department of Research and Statistics**
Tel Aviv, Israel.
• Tel Aviv-Yafo. Department of Research and Statistics. Yearbook. a.
• Tel Aviv-Yafo. Research and Statistical Department. Special Surveys/Tel Aviv. Ha-Mahlakah Le-Mehkar Veli-Statistikah. Sedarim Meyuhadim. irreg. ISSN 0082-2639

**Tel-Aviv Zoological Garden Society**
93 Ben Gurion Blvd., Tel-Aviv, Israel.
• Bevar/Zoo. s-a. ISSN 0006-033X

**Union of Artisans and Manufacturers**
• Melaha Vetaassiva/Israel Industry. (pub. by Israel Publications Corp. Ltd)

**Union of Israel Seamen's Federation**
3 Bankim Str., Haifa, Israel.
• Israel Seaman. m. ISSN 0021-230X

**United States - Israel Binational Science Foundation**
Jerusalem, Israel.
• United States - Israel Binational Science Foundation. Annual Report. a.

**University Publishing Projects Ltd.**
28 Hanatziv St., Tel Aviv, Israel.
• D I A. (Decisions, Issues, and Alternatives) m.

**Weizmann Institute of Science**
Rehovot, Israel.
• Rehovot. a. ISSN 0034-3609
• Weizmann Institute of Science, Rehovot, Israel. Scientific Activities. a. ISSN 0083-7849

**Weizmann Science Press of Israel**
P.O. Box 801, Jerusalem 91000, Israel.
• I C A S Proceedings. irreg. (International Council of the Aeronautical Sciences)
• Israel Journal of Botany. q. ISSN 0021-213X
• Israel Journal of Chemistry. q. ISSN 0021-2148
• Israel Journal of Earth Sciences. q. ISSN 0021-2164
• Israel Journal of Mathematics. 3 vols. per yr. (4 nos. per vol.) ISSN 0021-2172
• Israel Journal of Technology. 6 per yr. ISSN 0021-2202
• Israel Journal of Zoology. q. ISSN 0021-2210
• Journal d'Analyse Mathematique. s-a. ISSN 0021-7670
• Lada'at; science for youth. m.(10 per yr) ISSN 0023-7094 (Israel. Ministry of Education and Culture. Science Teaching Center)

● Mada; Hebrew bimonthly of popular science. bi-m.
ISSN 0024-9335

**Women's International Zionist Organization**
Rebecca Sieff Wizo Centre, 38 Sderot David
Hamelekh, Tel Aviv, Israel.
● W I Z O Review. bi-m. ISSN 0042-9732

**World Federation of Diamond Bourses**
P.O. Box 1381, Tel Aviv, Israel.
● Diamond World Review. m.

**World Federation of Jewish Journalists**
Jerusalem, Israel.
● Zshurnalist. irreg. (Co-sponsor: World Zionist
Organization. Information Department)

**World Jewish Congress**
20 Gaza St., Jerusalem, Israel.
● Jewish Cultural News. q. (prep. by its Cultural
Department)

**World Union of Mapam**
4 Itamar Ben Avi St., Tel Aviv, Israel.
● Brit Mapam. q.

**World Zionist Organization**
Box 92, Jerusalem, Israel.
● Forum; a quarterly on the Jewish people, Zionism
and Israel. q. (prep. by its Organization and
Information Department)
● Israel Digest. fortn. (prep. by its Organization and
Information Department) (U.S. address: Israel
Digest, 515 Park Ave., New York, N.Y. 10022)
● Leket. irreg.
● Ma'yanot. irreg; latest issue, no. 4. ISSN 0543-
1786
● Sources of Contemporary Jewish Thought/
Mekevot. irreg., 1969, no. 4. ISSN 0082-4585
(prep. by its Department for Torah Education and
Culture in the Diaspora) (Subscr. to: Jewish
Agency, Publication Service, 515 Park Ave., New
York, N.Y. 10022)
● Torah Education. q. (prep. by its Department for
Torah Education and Culture in the Diaspora)
● Volunteer. s-m. ISSN 0042-8671 (prep. by its
Youth and Hechalutz Department)
● Word and Deed. irreg. (prep. by its Youth and
Hechalutz Department)
● World Zionist Organization. General Council.
Addresses, Debates, Resolutions. a. ISSN 0084-
2516
● World Zionist Organization. Zionist Congress.
Kongres Ha-Tsiyoni. Hahlatot. irreg.
● World Zionist Organziation Press Service. 15 per
m.
● Zionist Literature. bi-m. ISSN 0044-4774 (prep.
by its Central Zionist Archives)

**Yad Maimon Research Institute**
Jerusalem, Israel.
● Menorah. q.

**Yad Vashem Martyr's and Heroes Remembrance
Authority**
P.O.B. 3477, Jerusalem, Israel.
● Yad Vashem Studies on the European Jewish
Catastrophe and Resistance. irreg., 1976, vol. 11.
ISSN 0084-3296

**Yedon le-Tekhnologyah Shel Meda u-Mahshevim**
Rehov Keren Hayesod 18, P.O.B. 7170, Jerusalem,
Israel.
● Yedon le-Tekhnologyah Shel Meda u-Mahshevim.

**Yeshivat Ohr Somayach College of Judaic Studies.
Joseph and Faye Tanenbaum Centre**
P.O.B. 15014, 76 Shmuel Hanavi-3 Tidhar Sts.,
Jerusalem, Israel.
● Shma Yisrael; a magazine of Jewish thought and
culture. q.

**Yidishe Shrayber Grupe in Yerusholaim.**
Shederot Eshkol 12/6, Jerusalem, Israel.
● Yerusholaymer Almanakh. a.

# ITALY

**Editrice A**
Box 3240, 20100 Milan, Italy.
● A - Rivista Anarchica. m. ISSN 0044-5592

**A.G.E.**
Via Alberico 2, No. 10, 00193 Rome, Italy.
● Strade e Motori. m.

**A.N.I.C.A.**
Viale Regina Margherita 286, 00198 Rome, Italy.
● Cinema d'Oggi. w.

**A. N. S. I. Societa A. R. L.**
Galleria Umberto I 83, 80132 Naples, Italy.
● Corriere Mercantile Politico d'Informazioni;
settimanale economico di informazioni marittimo
industriale-turistico. s-m. ISSN 0025-9780

**Editrice A R C O**
Via Filippo Tommaso Marinetti 3, 20127 Milan,
Italy.
● Casa, Arredamento, Giardino. m. ISSN 0576-8519
● Scienza e Tecnica Lattiero-Casearia. bi-m. ISSN
0036-889X (Associazione Italiana Tecnici del
Latte)

**A.R.T.E.**
Viale Gramsci 19, 56100 Pisa, Italy.
● Tecnica e Metodologia Economale. bi-m. ISSN
0494-9501 (Federazioni Associazioni Regionali
Economi)

**A. T. S. I. L**
Viale IV Novembre 21, 20075 Lodi, Milan, Italy.
● Lodigiano Sudmilano; mensile di informazione
economico finanziario amministrativo. m. ISSN
0024-5763

**Editrice A.V.E**
Via Aurelia 481, 00165 Rome, Italy.
● Orientamenti Sociali. bi-m. ISSN 0030-5405
(Istituto Cattolico di Attivita Sociale)
● Rassegna di Teologia; per un aggiornamento
cristiano teorico e pratico. bi-m. ISSN 0033-9644

**Editoriale A. Z**
Via Kolbe 8, 20137 Milan, Italy.
● Compratore. bi-m.
● Poligrafico Italiano. m. ISSN 0032-2709
● Serigrafia. bi-m.

**Abbaco**
Via Gen. Magliocco 19, Palermo, Italy.
● Universita di Palermo. Facolta di Economia e
Commercio. Annali. s-a.

**Edizioni Abete**
Corso Vitt. Emanuele 39, 00186 Rome, Italy.
● Proteus; revista di filosofia. q. ISSN 0033-1791

**Accademia Anatomico-Chirurgica di Perugia**
● Universita degli Studi di Perugia. Facolta di
Medicina e Chirurgia. Annali. (pub. by Universita
degli Studi di Perugia. Facolta di Medicina e
Chirurgia)

**Accademia dei Cinquecento per le Arti, Lettere,
Scienze e Cultura**
Via Trebio Littore, 11, 00152 Rome, Italy.
● Accademia dei Cinquecento per le Arti, Lettere,
Scienze e Cultura. Anali. irreg.

**Accademia dei Fisiocritici, Siena. Sezione Medico-
Fisica**
Via S. Bandini 49, Siena, Italy.
● Accademia dei Fisiocritici, Siena. Sezione Medico-
Fisica. irreg. ISSN 0065-0722

**Accademia del Corpo delle Guardie di P.S.**
Via Pier della Francesca 3, 00196 Rome, Italy.
● Polizia Moderna; periodico mensile illustrato. m.
ISSN 0032-356X

**Accademia delle Scienze di Torino**
Via Maria Vittoria 3, 10123 Turin, Italy
● Accademia delle Scienze di Torino. Classe di
Scienze Fisiche. Matematiche e Naturali. Atti.
Part I. 4-6 per yr. ISSN 0001-4419 (Subscr. to:
Mario Destefanis, Reparto Estero, Via Donati 27,
10121 Turin, Italy)

**Accademia Dialettale Siciliana Giovanni Meli**
Viale delle Sirene 15, 90149 Palermo, Sicily, Italy.
● Poty Cuntu; e chiddus cun ti piaci ti lu canci. s-m.
ISSN 0032-5686

**Accademia Etrusca di Cortona**
● Accademia Etrusca di Cortona. Annuario. (pub.
by Casa Editrice Leo S. Olschki)

**Accademia Italiana di Stenografia**
c/o Giuseppe Aliprandi, Ed., Via Soncin 17, 35100
Padua, Italy.
● Studi Grafici. bi-m. ISSN 0039-2960 (Co-Sponsor:
Primo Centro Italliano di Studi Dattilografici)

**Accademia Ligure di Scienze e Lettere**
Via Balbi 10, Palazzo Reale, 16126 Genoa, Italy.
● Accademia Ligure di Scienze e Lettere. Atti. a.

**Accademia Lucchese di Scienze, Lettere ed Arti**
● Accademia Lucchese di Scienze, Lettere ed Arti.
Atti. Nuova Serie. (pub. by Casa Editrice Felice
le Monnier)

**Accademia Medica Lombarda**
Ospedale Policlinico "Paciglione Beretta Est", Via F.
Sforza 35, 20122 Milan, Italy.
● Accademia Medica Lombarda. Atti. q. ISSN
0001-4427

**Accademia Medica Pistoiese "Filippo Pacini"**
Via della Rosa, Pistoia, Italy.
● Accademia Medica Pistoiese "Filippo Pacini".
Bolletino. a.

**Accademia Musicale Chigiana, Siena**
● Accademia Musicale Chigiana. Quaderni. (pub. by
Casa Editrice Leo S. Olschki)
● Chigiana. (pub. by Casa Editrice Leo S. Olschki)

**Accademia Nazionale dei Lincei**
Via della Lungara 10, Rome, Italy.
● Accademia Nazionale dei Lincei. Classe di
Scienze Fisiche Matematiche e Naturali.
Rendiconti. 2 vols. per yr. ISSN 0001-4435

**Accademia Nazionale di Agricoltura**
Via Farini 14, 40124 Bologna, Italy.
● Accademia Nazionale di Agricoltura. Annali. q.
ISSN 0001-4443

**Accademia Nazionale di Ragionera**
● Accademia Nazionale di Ragionera Papers on
Business Administration. (pub. by Casa Editrice
Dott. A. Giuffre)

**Accademia Nazionale di San Luca**
Rome, Italy.
● Accademia Nazionale di San Luca. Annuario. a.

**Accademia Nazionale Italiana di Entomologia**
Bologna, Italy.
● Accademia Nazionale Italiana di Entomologia.
Rendiconti. a. ISSN 0065-0757

**Accademia Patavina di Scienze Lettere ed Arti**
Via Accademia 13, 35100 Padua, Italy.
● Accademia Patavina di Scienze Lettere ed Arti.
Collana Accademica. irreg., 1967, no. 3. ISSN
0065-0765

**Accademia Santa Cecilia di Roma**
● Studi Musicali. (pub. by Casa Editrice Leo S.
Olschki)

**Accademia Toscana di Scienze e Lettere La
Colombaria**
● Accademia Toscana di Scienze e Lettere La
Colombaria. Studi. (pub. by Casa Editrice Leo S.
Olschki)

**Acta Anaesthesiologica**
Via Montona 4, 235100 Padua, Italy.
● Acta Anaesthesiologica; rivista di anestesia e cure
pre e post-operatiorie. bi-m. ISSN 0001-5156

**Acta Embryologiae Experimentalis**
Via Archirafi 18, 90123 Palermo, Italy.
● Acta Embryologiae Experimentalis. 3 per yr.
● Acta Embryologiae Experimentalis. a. ISSN 0065-
1184

**Actio Catholica Hungarorum in Exteris**
Via Conciliazione 44, 00153 Rome, Italy.
● Katolikus Szemle. q. ISSN 0022-9431

**Adriatico**
Via Cesare Beccaria N.4, Trieste, Italy.
● Adriatico. 5-6 per yr. ISSN 0001-8465

**Adriatrica Editrice**
Bari, Italy.
● Universita di Bari. Facolta di Scienza. Atti del
Seminario di Studi Biologici. biennial. ISSN 0067-
4192

**Aemmepi Editrice**
Corso Magenta 27, 20123 Milan, Italy.
● Arte Mercato; mensile internazionale d'arte
contemporanea. m.

**Aeronautica Macchi S.P.A.**
Via Silvestro Sanvito 80, Varese, Italy.
- Aermacchi Informazioni. q. ISSN 0001-9089

**Aeronews**
Aeroporto Fiumicino, Rome, Italy.
- Avia. m. ISSN 0005-2027

**African Association of St. Augustine**
Via Urbano VIII, 16, Rome, Italy.
- Lux. s-a.

**Editrice Age**
Via S. Filippo 14b, 42100 Reggio Emilia, Italy.
- Acta Paediatrica Latina. 6 per yr. ISSN 0001-6551 (Universita di Padova. Clinica Pediatrica)

**Agenzia d'Informazione dell'Unione Sovietica**
Via di Villa Ricotti 26, Rome, Italy.
- Ecotass; economic-Commercial bulletin. 3 per w. ISSN 0013-0702

**Agenzia d'Informazioni E. R. P**
Via Maurolico 18, 00146 Rome, Italy.
- Interstampa della Capitale. every 3 wks. ISSN 0020-9724

**Agenzia d'Informazioni per la Stampa**
Via Savoia 78, Rome 00198, Italy.
- Pesca Italiana. w. ISSN 0031-6075 (Federazione Nazionale delle Imprese di Pesca)

**Agenzia di Viaggi**
Via Quattro Fontane 147, 00184 Rome, Italy.
- Agenzia di Viaggi; settimanale di notizie di interesse professionale. w. ISSN 0002-0869

**Agenzia Economica Finanziaria**
Via delle Coppelle No. 16, 00186 Rome, Italy.
- Agenzia Economica Finanziaria; giornale politico-finanziario. 3 per wk. ISSN 0002-0877

**Agenzia Europea d'Informazioni Giornalistiche**
Via Quattro Fontane 22, 00197 Rome, Italy.
- Europa Nazione. 3-4 per yr. ISSN 0014-2581

**Agenzia Gestione Periodici**
Via M. Gioia 66, 20125 Milan, Italy.
- Alimentarista. m.
- Casa Stile. bi-m.
- Droghiere. w.

**Agenzia Internazionale Letteraria Artistica**
- A. I. L. A. (pub. by Francesco Boneschi, Ed. & Pub.)

**Aggiornamenti di Terapia Oftalmologica**
Via Dietro la Corte 7R, Pisa, Italy.
- Aggiornamenti di Terapia Oftalmologica. bi-m. ISSN 0002-0915

**Aggiornamento Pediatrico**
Viale Gorizia 24-A, 00198 Rome, Italy.
- Aggiornamento Pediatrico; rivista mensile di pediatria. m. ISSN 0002-0958

**Agnesotti S.a.S.**
Piazza M. Fani 2, 01100 Viterbo, 80134 Naples, Italy.
- Monitor Ecclesiasticus; commentarius de re cannoica et pastorali post Vaticanum II. q. ISSN 0026-976X

**Vittorio d' Agostino, Ed. & Pub.**
Via S. Pio V 16, 10125 Turin, Italy.
- Rivista di Studi Classici. 3 per yr. ISSN 0035-6581

**Editoriale Agricola**
Piazza Indipendenza 11/B, 00185 Rome, Italy.
- Tuttociclismo. w.

**Agricoltore Ferrarese**
Viale Cavour 34, Ferrara, Italy.
- Agricoltore Ferrarese. m. ISSN 0002-1210

**Alanno**
Via E. L. Pellegrino 23, Messina, Italy.
- Controvento; rivista di lettere-arti-scienze. m. ISSN 0010-8103

**Alessandria. Amministrazione Provinciale di Alessandria**
Alessandria, Italy.
- Alessandria, Italy (Province) Centro Documentazione e Richerche Economico-Sociali. Quaderno. irreg., no. 82, 1974. ISSN 0065-6151

**ALFA Edizioni**
Via Santo Stefano 13, I-40125 Bologna, Italy.
- Fonti e Studi per la Storia di Bologna e delle Province Emiliane e Romagnole. irreg.; 1975, no. 5.
- Storia, Costumi e Tradizioni. irreg.; no. 12, 1976. ISSN 0081-5837

**Alla Bottega**
Via Plinio 38, Milan, Italy.
- Alla Bottega; rivista di cultura ed arte. bi-m. ISSN 0002-5631

**Editrice Alluminio**
Via Sansovino 33, 20133 Milan, Italy.
- Alluminio. m. ISSN 0002-6212

**G. Alparone, Ed. & Pub.**
Viale Cavalleggeri Aosta, 77, 80124 Naples, Italy.
- Rassegna d'Arte.

**Edizioni Alpe**
Via Piolti De' Bianchi 4, 20129 Milan, Italy.
- Cucciolo. m. ISSN 0011-264X
- Gran Tiramolla. m. ISSN 0017-3126
- Picchiarello. m. ISSN 0031-9589
- Selezione di Picchiarello. 2 per yr. ISSN 0037-1491
- Tiramolla. fortn. ISSN 0040-8077
- Tutto Cucciolo. m. ISSN 0041-4417

**Altra Italia**
Via del Corso 52, Rome 00186, Italy.
- Altra Italia. s-m. ISSN 0002-6662

**Altrafrica**
Via Ferruccio, 44, 00185 Rome, Italy.
- Altrafrica; Africa dell'est. 3 per yr.

**Altri Termini**
Via Edificio Scolastico 33, Marano di Napoli, Italy.
- Altri Termini. 3 per yr.

**Casa Editrice Ambrosiana**
Via G. Frua 6, 20146 Milano, Italy.
- Tumori. bi-m. ISSN 0041-4352 (Istituto Nazionale per Lo Studio e la Cura dei Tumori)

**American Academy in Rome**
Library, Via Angelo Masina, 5, Rome, 00153, Italy.
- American Academy in Rome. Memoirs. irreg. ISSN 0065-6801
- American Academy in Rome. Papers and Monographs. irreg. ISSN 0065-681X

**American Chamber of Commerce in Italy**
Via Agnello 12, 20121 Milan, Italy.
- American Chamber of Commerce in Italy. Directory. a. ISSN 0569-3667
- Italian American Business. m. ISSN 0021-2873

**Amici del Museo del Risorgimento**
Via Borgonuovo 23, 20121 Milan, Italy.
- Risorgimento. 3 per yr. ISSN 0035-5607

**Amicizia**
c/o Ufficio Centrale Studenti Esteri in Italia, Via Tagliamento 25, 00198 Rome, Italy.
- Amicizia; rivista mensile per studenti esteri. m. ISSN 0003-1720

**Amicizia Ebraico-Cristiana di Firenze**
Casella Postale282, 50100 Firenze, Italy.
- Amicizia Ebraico-Cristiana di Firenze. q. ISSN 0003-1739

**Amministrazione per le Attivita Assistenziale Italiane e Internazionali**
Via Giovanni Lanza 194-200, Rome, Italy.
- Promozione Sociale. m.

**Amministrazione Provinciale di Cremona**
Corso V. Emanuele 17, 26100 Cremona, Italy.
- Provincia Nuova. bi-m.

**Amministrazione Socialista**
Via dei Crociferi N. 44, Rome, Italy.
- Amministrazione Socialista. m. ISSN 0003-1917

**Ammonitore**
Via Verga 3, Milan, Italy.
- Ammonitore. w. ISSN 0003-1925

**Editrice Ancora**
Via G.B. Niccolini 8, 20154 Milan, Italy.
- Vita Consacrata; rivista mensile di studio e informazione per Istituti Religiosi e Secolari. m. ISSN 0042-7330

**Andar per Ceramiche**
Via C. Cavour 24, 42013 Casalgrande, Reggio Emilia, Italy.
- Andar per Ceramiche. a. ISSN 0003-2891

**Angeletti Editore**
Via Ripamonti 115, 20141 Milan, Italy.
- Elettrodomestica. m. ISSN 0013-6107
- Giornale della Radio Industria e dell'Elettrodomestica. m.
- Listino della Radio Industria e dell'Elettrodomestica. s-a. ISSN 0024-4422
- Radio Industria. m. ISSN 0033-7919

**Franco Angeli Editore**
Viale Monza 106, Casella Postale 4294, 20127 Milan, Italy.
- Affari Sociali Internazionali. q.
- Annuario del Commercio Estero. a. ISSN 0304-0364
- Annuario Sindacale. a.
- Collana di Studi Urbani e Regionali. irreg.
- Direzione Aziendale. m. ISSN 0012-3331
- Dirigente Amministrativo; mensile per dirigenti e funzionari di aziende private e pubbliche. m. ISSN 0012-334X
- Distribuzione Moderna. m. ISSN 0012-3978
- Economia delle Fonti di Energia. 5 per yr. (Universita Commerciale Luigi Bocconi. Istituto di Economia delle Fonti di Energia)
- Idee di Vendita; mensile de tecnica organizzazione e psicologia della vendita. m.
- M & P; rivista di direzione commerciale. m.
- Management e Informatica. m.
- Produrre; rivista d'organizzazione e tecnica della produzione. m. ISSN 0032-9983
- Rassegna di Meccanica. m.
- Rassegna Internazionale di Meccanica; rivista di tecnica e organizzazione dell' industria meccanica. m. ISSN 0033-9709
- Repertorio del Film Industriale. irreg., latest issue, 1973. (Confederazione Generale dell'Industria Italiana)
- Ricerca Operativa. q. (Associazione Italiana de Ricerca Operativa)
- Studi e Ricerche Sociologiche. irreg.
- Studi Economici. m. ISSN 0039-2928
- Tecniche Dell Imballaggio. m. (Istituto Italiano Imballaggio)

**Angelicum**
Largo Angelicum 1, Rome, Italy.
- Angelicum; periodicum trimestre pontificae studiorum. q. ISSN 0003-3081

**Angelicum-Convento di S.Angelo**
- In Famiglia. (pub. by Stamperia Editrice Commerciale)

**Casa Editrice Giacomo d' Anna**
Via della Robbia 26, 50132 Florence, Italy.
- Generazione Zero; istanze e verifiche nella societa in movimento. bi-m. ISSN 0046-5615

**Annali di Medicina Navale**
Lungo Tevere delle Navi, 00100 Rome, Italy.
- Annali di Medicina Navale. 3 per mo. ISSN 0003-4630

**Editrice Antenore**
Via G. Rusca 15, 35100 Padua, Italy.
- Studia Aristotelica. irreg.; 1977, no. 8. ISSN 0081-6310 (Universita di Padova)
- Universita di Padova. Centro per la Storia della Tradizione Artistotelica nel Veneto. Saggi e Testi. irreg.; no. 14, 1977. ISSN 0078-771X
- Universita di Padova. Istituto per la Storia. Contributi. irreg.; no. 8, 1976. ISSN 0078-7752
- Universita di Padova. Istituto per la Storia. Quaderni. irreg.; no. 8, 1975. ISSN 0078-7760

**Antiauto Sport**
Via Germanico 216, 00192 Rome, Italy.
- Antiauto Sport. m.

**Periodici Aracne Nuova Editrice**
Via Solferino 32, 20121 Milan, Italy.
- Lineamaglia. q. ISSN 0024-3787

**Casa Editrice Araldo della Verite**
Via Chiantigiana 30, Falcianci, 1-50023 Impruneta,
Florence, Italy.
- Segni dei Tempi; mensile per un cristianesimo
  attuale e attivo. bi-m.

**Arbiter**
Largo Toscanini 1, 20122 Milan, Italy.
- Arbiter; rivista internazionale di moda maschile. 3
  per yr. ISSN 0003-7869

**Archivio-Biblioteca-Museo Civico**
Palazzo degli Studi, Altamura, Italy.
- Altamura. a. ISSN 0569-1346

**Archivio Botanico e Biogeografico Italiano**
Corso Diaz 182, 47100-Forli, Italy.
- Archivio Botanico e Biogeografico Italiano. q.
  ISSN 0004-0053

**Archivio di Studi Urbani e Regionali**
Box 4296, Milan, Italy.
- Archivio di Studi Urbani e Regionali. 3 per yr.
  ISSN 0004-0177

**Archivio Storico per la Calabria e la Lucania**
Palazzo Taverna, Monte Giordano 36, Rome, Italy.
- Archivio Storico per la Calabria e la Lucania. q.
  ISSN 0004-0355

**Archivio Trimestrale**
Via Nazionale 46, 00184 Rome, Italy.
- Archivio Trimestrale; rassegna storica di studi sul
  movimento republicano. q.

**Arcispedale S. Anna di Ferrara**
Ferrara, Italy.
- Arcispedale S. Anna di Ferrara. bi-m. ISSN 0004-
  0819

**Aretusa Editrice srl.**
Piazzetta Municipio 8, 37100 Verona, Italy.
- Giornale degli Allevatori. m. ISSN 0017-0135

**Armando Argalia Editore**
Via N. Sauro, 1, Urbino, Italy.
- Studi Urbinati. Serie B: Letteratura, Storia,
  Filosofia. s-a. ISSN 0039-3088

**Argileto Editore**
Casella Postale 1-28973, Rome, Italy.
- Rapporti. q.

**Edizioni Ariminum**
Via Negroli 51, 20133 Milan, Italy.
- Fercasa International. bi-m.
- Industria della Vernice; rivista tecnica sulla
  fabbricazione e l'impiego di vernici pitture, smalti,
  cere, inchiostri, adesivi e loro materie prime. m.
  ISSN 0019-7564
- Ingegneria Chimica. bi-m. ISSN 0020-093X
- Laboratorio. bi-m. ISSN 0456-9814
- Tinctoria. m.
- Tintoria, Lavanderia e Pulitura a Secco. m.
  (Unione Nazionale Autonoma Tintorie, Puliture a
  Secco, Lavanderie)
- Vedere CONTACT International. bi-m.
- Vedere-International; international journal on
  optics frame industry and optical instruments. bi-
  m. ISSN 0302-6256

**Casa Editrice Armando Armando**
Via della Gensola 60-61, Rome, Italy.
- Servizio Informazioni Avio; periodico di vita
  scolastica e amministrativa. m. ISSN 0037-279X

**Arrivi e Partenze**
c/o Pericle Staderini, Ed., Via Pasquale Baffi 26,
00149 Rome, Italy.
- Arrivi e Partenze. bi-m.

**Ars Sutoria S.A.S.**
Via I. Nievo 33, 20145 Milan, Italy.
- Arpel. q.
- Ars Sutoria; quarterly cultural review of italian
  clothes and footwear fashion. q. ISSN 0004-265X

**Ars-Uomo**
Via F. Bocco Ortu 120, 0139 Rome, Italy.
- Ars-Uomo; mensile di vita artistica e culturale. m.

**Art Directors Club Milano**
1 Piazza de Mozzi, Florence 50125, Italy.
- Art Directors Club Milano. a. ISSN 0066-7943

**Arte**
Via Passo Pordoi 21, 20139 Milan, Italy.
- Arte; nuova edizione. q. ISSN 0004-3362

**Edizioni d' Arte Alfieri**
San Marco 1991, Venice, Italy
(Dist. by George Wittenborn, Inc., 1018 Madison
Ave., New York, N.Y. 10021)
- Metro. s-a. ISSN 0026-1343

**Edizioni Arte Lombarda**
Via Lovanio 4, Milan, Italy.
- Arte Lombarda; rivista di storia dell'arte. s-a.
  ISSN 0004-3443

**Arte Nuova**
Corso Matteotti 11, 60035 Jesi, Italy.
- Arte Nuova. m.

**Arti Grafiche Friulane**
Via Treppo 1, 33100 Udine, Italy.
- Arc; periodico dell regioni: dell'Arco Alpino. q.

**Asbestos Cement Service Co. Ltd.**
Via Bianze No 24, Turin 10143, Italy.
- A C M; magazine devoted to the industry of
  asbestos-cement. bi-m. ISSN 0001-0758

**Asmeccanica**
Piazzale Rodolfo Morandi 2, 20121 Milan, Italy.
- Meccanica Italiana. m.

**Assessorato Alla Gioventu, Cultura, Pubbliche
Relazioni e Stampa**
Palazzo Vecchio, Florence, Italy.
- Firenze. irreg., latest issue, 1974.

**Assistenza Sindicale per Gli Autotrasportatori
Professionali**
Via Ovidio 32, 00186 Rome, Italy.
- Camion; la voce degli autotrasportatori
  professional. m. ISSN 0008-2252

**Association pour l'Etude des Problemes de l'Europe**
c/o P. Sampieri, Ed., Viale Platone 47, 00136
Rome, Italy.
- Problemes de l'Europe. q. ISSN 0552-1734

**Associazione Alpinistica "Giovane Montagna"**
- Giovane Montagna. (pub. by Rosso Pio Camillo,
  Ed. & Pub.)

**Associazione Amici di Castel San Angelo**
- Museo Nazionale di Castel San Angelo. Quaderni.
  (pub. by De Luca Editore)

**Associazione Antiquari d'Italia**
Lungarno Soderini 5, 50124 Florence, Italy.
- Gazzetta Antiquaria. 8 per yr. ISSN 0016-559X

**Associazione ARES**
Via A. Stradivari 7, Milan, Italy.
- Studi Cattolici; mensile di studi ed attualita. m.
  ISSN 0039-2901

**Associazione Artiglieri d'Italia**
Via Aureliana 25, 00187 Rome, Italy.
- Artigliere; La voce di tutti gli artiglieri. m. ISSN
  0004-3745

**Associazione Bancaria Italiana**
- Bancaria. (pub. by Bancaria Editrice S.p.A.)

**Associazione Biblica Italiana**
- Rivista Biblica. (pub. by Paideia Editrice)

**Associazione Cenacolo**
Via Madama Cristina 90, Turin, Italy.
- Cenacolo; arte e letteratura. a. ISSN 0008-8935

**Associazione Commercianti di Reggio Emilia**
Via Roma 13, 42100 Reggio Emilia, Italy.
- Commerciante. m.

**Associazione Cotoniera Italiana**
Via Borgonuovo 11, 20121 Milan, Italy.
- European Cotton Industry Statistics. a. ISSN
  0423-7269
- Industria Cotoniera. bi-m. ISSN 0019-7491

**Associazione Cultural della Provincia di Rieti**
Via Roma, 36, Rieti, Italy.
- Rieti. bi-m.

**Associazione Culturale Progresso Grafico**
Viale Mattioli 39, Castello del Valentino, 10125
Turin, Italy.
- Graphicus. m (9 per yr) ISSN 0017-3436 (Turin,
  Italy. Comitato Provinciale di Educacione
  Grafica)

**Associazione degli Africanisti Italiani**
Via G. Rovelli, 32, 22100 Como, Italy.
- Associazione degli Africanisti Italiani. Bollettino.
  q. ISSN 0004-590X

**Associazione degli Industriali di Arezzo**
Via Roma 2, C.P. 214, 52100 Arezzo, Italy.
- Notiziario. m. ISSN 0004-5918

**Associazione degli Industriali di Siena**
Banchi di Sopra 58, Siena, Italy.
- Notizie per Gli Industriali della Provincia di
  Siena; industria toscana. w. ISSN 0029-4446

**Associazione dei Medici Provinciali Italiani**
Via Stamira 7, 00162 Rome, Italy.
- Igiene e Sanita Pubblica. m. ISSN 0019-1639

**Associazione dei Medici Scrittori Italiani**
Via Filippo Maria Pirelli 19, 00165 Rome, Italy.
- Serpe; rivista letteraria. q. ISSN 0037-2498

**Associazione del Mercato Alimentari Coloniali Oli
Grassi e Prodotti Chimici Industriali**
Via S. Vittore al Teatro 14, Milan, Italy.
- Rassegna del Mercato; settimanale tecnico di
  informazioni economiche e commerciali. w. ISSN
  0033-9407

**Associazione di Storia Ecclesiastica Novarese**
Presso Archivio Storico Diocesano, Palazzo
Vescovile, I-28100 Novara, Italy.
- Novarien. irreg. ISSN 0078-253X

**Associazione Elettrotecnica ed Elettronica Italiana**
Viale Monza 259, 20126 Milan, Italy.
- Alta Frequenza; rivista di studi e ricerca applicata
  in elettrotecnica ed elettronica. 6 per yr. ISSN
  0002-6557
- Associazione Elettrotecnica Ed Elettronica
  Italiana. Rendiconti della Riunione Annuale. a.
  ISSN 0066-9822
- Elettrotecnica; rivista generale di elettrotecnica ed
  elettronica. m. ISSN 0013-6131

**Associazione Emilia Romagna Contro la Tubercolosi e
la Malatie Polmonari**
c/o. Clelia Constantini Soglia, Via Marconi 49,
Bologna, Italy.
- Revista di Patologia e Clinica della Tubercolosi e
  di Pneumologia. bi-m.

**Associazione Enotecnici Italiani**
Viale Murillo 17, 20149 Milan, Italy.
- Enotecnico. m.

**Associazione Ex Allievi Istituto Sperimentale di
Caseificio**
Via Carlo Besana 8, 20075 Lodi, Italy.
- Rivista del Latte. q.

**Associazione fra i Costruttori in Acciaio Italiani**
Via Filippo Turati 38, 20121 Milan, Italy.
- Costruzioni Metalliche; rivista dei tecnici
  dell'acciaio. bi-m. ISSN 0010-9673

**Associazione fra Industrie Chimico-Farmaceutiche**
Via Romagnosi 18/A, 00196 Rome, Italy.
- Segnalazioni Assofarma; problemi ed informazioni
  dell'industria farmaceutica. m. ISSN 0582-3978

**Associazione fra le Cassa di Risparmio Italiana**
Viale di Villa Grazioli, 23, 00198 Rome, Italy.
- Risparmio. (pub. by Casa Editrice Dott. A.
  Giuffre)
- Via Migliore. m. ISSN 0042-4994

**Associazione fra le Societa Italiana per Azioni**
Piazza Venezia 11, Rome, Italy.
- Italian Economic Survey. bi-m. ISSN 0021-2911
- Massimario Tributario. (pub. by Casa Editrice
  Dott. A. Giuffre)
- Rassegna della Stampa; problemi fiscali. m. ISSN
  0033-9458

**Associazione Frigorifera Italiana**
- Freddo. (pub. by Propaganda Editoriale Grafica
  S.p.A.)

**Associazione Friulana Donatori di Sangue**
Ospedale Civile, Udine, Italy.
- Dono. 3 per yr. ISSN 0012-544X

**Associazione Generale delle Cooperative Italiane**
Via Parma 22, 00184 Rome, Italy.
- Libera Cooperazione. bi-w. ISSN 0024-1768

**Associazione Generale Italiana dello Spettacolo**
Via di Villa Patrizi 10, Rome, Italy.
- Automat; rivista italiana dell'automatico. m. ISSN 0005-1012
- Giornale dello Spettacolo. w. ISSN 0017-0232

**Associazione Genetica Italiana**
c/o Laboratorio di Mutagenesi e Differenzianento CNR, Via Cisanello 147/B, 56100 - Pisa, Italy.
- Associazione Genetica Italiana. Atti. a. ISSN 0066-9830

**Associazione Genitori**
Casella Postale 622, Bologna, Italy.
- Genitori; incontri mensili tra scuola e famiglia. m. ISSN 0016-6871
- Nostri Ragazzi; incontri tra scuola elementare e famiglia. 7 per yr. ISSN 0029-3792

**Associazione Geofisica Italiana.**
Box 3145, 16100 Genoa, Italy.
- Revista Italiana di Geofisica. a.

**Associazione Geotecnica Italiana**
- Geotecnica. (pub. by Istituto Propaganda Internazionale)

**Associazione Grossisti Ortofrutticoli**
Via Lombroso 54, Milan, Italy.
- Eurofrutta. m.

**Associazione Gruppi Archeologici d'Italia**
41 via Tacito, 00192 Rome, Italy.
- Archeologia. bi-m. ISSN 0003-8164

**Associazione Industriale Lombarda**
Via Pantano 9, 20122 Milan, Italy.
- Comparazione dei Salari e del Costo del Lavoro in Europa. irreg., latest issue, 1969. ISSN 0069-794X
- Industria Lombarda. w. ISSN 0019-7661

**Associazione Industriali**
Via Valfonda 9, 50123 Florence, Italy.
- Industria Toscana. w. ISSN 0019-7769
- Ingegneri E Costruttori. m.

**Associazione Industrie Siderurgiche Italiane**
Piazza Velasca 8, 20122 Milan, Italy.
- Repertorio delle Industrie Siderurgiche Italiane. every 5 years. ISSN 0080-1216
- Siderurgia Italiana in Cifre. irreg.

**Associazione Ingegneri della Provincia di Bologna**
Strada Maggiore 13, Bologna, Italy.
- Ingegneri Architetti Construttori. m.

**Associazione Insegnanti Ebrei d'Italia**
Via Canova 7A, Milan, Italy.
- Eco dell'Educazione Ebraica. q. ISSN 0012-9518 (Histadruth Ha-Morim)

**Associazione Internazionale della Stampa Medica**
58 via Mauro Macchi, 20124 Milan, Italy.
- Associazione Internazionale della Stampa Medica. Bollettino Bibliografico. irreg. ISSN 0066-9857

**Associazione Internazionale di Poesia**
Via Poliziano 69, 00184 Rome, Italy.
- Giornale dei Poeti. bi-m.

**Associazione Irrigazione Est Sesia**
Via Negroni 7, Novara, Italy.
- Est Sesia. q. ISSN 0014-1100

**Associazione Italiana Allevatori**
Via Tomassetti 9, 00161 Rome, Italy.
- Allevatore. w.

**Associazione Italiana Assistenza Spastici**
Via Cipro 4/H, 00136 Rome, Italy.
- Associazione Italiana Assistenza Spastici. Notiziaro; sotto l'alto patronato del Presidenta della Repubblica. q.

**Associazione Italiana Barmen e Sostenitori**
- Barman. (pub. by Editoriale Lariana S.p. A.)
- I B A Gazette. (pub. by Editoriale Lariana S.p.A.)

**Associazione Italiana Biblioteche**
c/o Instituto di Patologia del Libro, Instituto di Patologia del Libro, 00184 Rome, Italy.
- Associazione Italiana Biblioteche. Bollettino d'Informazioni. q. ISSN 0004-5934
- Associazione Italiana Biblioteche. Quaderni del Bollettino d'Informazioni. irreg. ISSN 0519-2048

**Associazione Italiana Condizionamento dell 'Aria, Riscaldamento Refrigerazione**
- Condizionamento dell'Aria. (pub. by Propaganda Editoriale Grafica S. p. A.)

**Associazione Italiana Culturale Aeronautica**
Via Varese 5, 00185 Rome, Italy.
- Volare Necesse Est. m. ISSN 0049-6715

**Associazione Italiana de Ricerca Operativa**
- Ricerca Operativa. (pub. by Franco Angeli Editore)

**Associazione Italiana dei Centri Trasfusionali**
- Trasfusione del Sangue. (pub. by Pensiero Scientifico)

**Associazione Italiana dei Pubblici Istitute di Credito Su Pegno**
- Credito Pignoratizio. (pub. by Casa Editore Dott. A. Giuffre)

**Associazione Italiana del Vuoto**
- Vuoto, Scienza e Tecnologia. (pub. by Masson Italia Editori S.p.A.)

**Associazione Italiana di Aeronautica e Astronautica**
- Aerotecnica, Missili e Spazio. (pub. by Tamburini Editore S.p.A.)

**Associazione Italiana di Cartografia**
c/o Instituto di Geografia dell'Universita, Largo San Marcellino 10, 80138 Naples, Italy.
- Associazione Italiana di Cartografia. A I C Bolletino. q. ISSN 0044-9733

**Associazione Italiana di Cultura Classica**
- Atene e Roma. (pub. by Casa Editrice Felice le Monnier)

**Associazione Italiana di Genio Rurale**
- Rivista di Ingegneria Agraria. (pub. by Gruppo Giornalistico Edagricole)

**Associazione Italiana di Idroclimatologia, Talassologia e Terapia Fisica**
- Clinica Termale. (pub. by Societa Editrice Universo)

**Associazione Italiana di Illuminazione**
Via Revere 14, 20123 Milan, Italy.
- Luce. bi-m. ISSN 0024-7189

**Associazione Italiana di Metallurgia**
Piazzale Rodolfo Morandi 2, 20121 Milan, Italy.
- Fonderia Italiana. m. ISSN 0015-6086
- Metallurgia Italiana. m. ISSN 0026-0843

**Associazione Italiana Editori**
Foro Buonoparte 24, 20121 Milan, Italy.
- Editori Librai Cartolibrai e Biblioteche d'Italia. a. ISSN 0070-9093
- Elenco dei Quotidiani e Periodici Italiani. a. ISSN 0013-6042
- Giornale della Libreria. m. ISSN 0017-0216

**Associazione Italiana Filatelia Religiosa "San Gabriele"**
Casella Postale 175, Venice 30100, Italy.
- Informatore Filatelico; per il tema religioso. bi-m. ISSN 0020-0727

**Associazione Italiana Giuristi Democratici**
- Democrazia e Diritto. (pub. by Editori Riuniti)

**Associazione Italiana Industriali Tintori, Stampatori e Finitori Tessili**
Via della Moscova, 33 Milan, Italy.
- Associazione Italiana Industriali Tintori Stampatori e Finitori Tessili. Notiziario. s-m. ISSN 0004-5950
- Tintoria; i progressi delle industrie tintorie e tessili. m. ISSN 0040-7984

**Associazione Italiana Laringectomizzati**
Piazza Bertarelli, 4, Milan, Italy.
- Associazione Italiana Laringectomizzati. Atti (Del) Convegno Nazionale. a. ISSN 0066-9865

**Associazione Italiana Maestri Cattolici**
Clivo Monte del Gallo 50, Rome, Italy.
- Maestro. s-m. ISSN 0024-9696

**Associazione Italiana Manufatturieri Pelli-Cuoio e Succedanei**
- M I P E L. (pub. by Aurelio Canevari Editore)

**Associazione Italiana Ottici**
Corso Venezia, 8, 20121 Milan, Italy.
- Ottico. bi-m.

**Associazione Italiana per gli Studi di Marketing**
Via Olmetto 3, 20123 Milan, Italy.
- Giornale di Marketing. q.

**Associazione Italiana per gli Studi di Politica Estera**
24 via Monte Zebio, 00195 Rome, Italy.
- Affari Esteri. q. ISSN 0001-964X

**Associazione Italiana per i Rapporti Culturali Con l'Unione Sovietica**
Piazza di Campitelli 2, 00186 Rome, Italy.
- Associazione Italiana per i Rapporti Culturali Con l'Unione Sovietica. Rassegna Sovietica; rivista bimestrale di cultura. bi-m. ISSN 0033-9857
- Realta Sovietica. m. ISSN 0034-1029

**Associazione Italiana per il Calcolo Automatico**
c/o Fast, Piazza Morandi, 2, 20121 Milan, Italy.
- Rivista di Informatica. q.

**Associazione Italiana per Il Consiglio dei Comuni d'Europa**
- Comuni d'Europa. (pub. by Umberto Serafini)

**Associazione Italiana per Il Controllo della Qualita**
Piazza Diaz 2, Milan, Italy.
- Qualita. q.

**Associazione Italiana per Il Progresso dell'Industria del Latte**
Corso Mazzini 67, 20075 Lodi, Milan, Italy.
- Industria del Latte. q. ISSN 0019-7513

**Associazione Italiana per l'Arbitrato**
Via XX Settembre 5, 00187 Rome, Italy.
- Rassegna dell' Arbitrato. q. ISSN 0033-9415

**Associazione Italiana Prefabbricazione per l'Edilizia Industrializzata**
Galleria Passarella 1, 20122 Milan, Italy.
- Prefabbricare. bi-m. ISSN 0032-7247

**Associazione Italiana Santa Cecilia**
Via della Scrofa 70, 00186 Rome, Italy.
- Bollettino Ceciliano; rivista di musica sacra. m. (10 per yr.) ISSN 0006-663X

**Associazione Italiana Scientifica di Metapsichica**
Via Mazzini 9, 20123 Milan, Italy.
- Metapsichica. q. ISSN 0026-1076 (Co-sponsor: Centro Studi Parapsicologici)

**Associazione Italiana Societa Concessionarie Autostrade e Trafori**
Via Sardegna 40, 00187 Rome, Italy.
- A I S C A T Informazioni. q.

**Associazione Italiana Strumentisti**
- Tecniche dell'Automazione. (pub. by Etas Kompass Periodici Tecnici S.p.A.)

**Associazione Italiana Studi Americanistici**
Piazzale Kennedy, 16129 Genova, Italy.
- Terra Ameriga. q. ISSN 0040-375X

**Associazione Italiana Studi del Paranormale**
Via Puggia 47, 16131 Genoa, Italy.
- Dimensione Psi; rivista internazaionale di parapsicologia. s-a.

**Associazione Italiana Tecnici del Latte**
- Scienza e Tecnica Lattiero-Casearia. (pub. by A.R.C.O.)

**Associazione Italiana Tecnico Economica del Cemento**
Via di S. Teresa 23, Rome, Italy.
- Industria Italiana del Cemento. m. ISSN 0019-7637

**Associazione Libraio Italiani**
Piazza G. G. Belli 2, Rome, Italy.
- Libreria. fortn. ISSN 0024-2640

**Associazione Linguistica Salentina**
Villa Sebaste, Via per Campi, 73051, Novoli (Lecce)
, Italy.
- Studi Linguistici Salentini.

**Associazione Lombarda Dirigenti Aziende Industriali**
Via Larga 31, 20122 Milan, Italy.
- Dirigenti Industria. m.

**Associazione Mazziniana Italiana**
Associazione Mazziniana Italiana, Via S. Francesco
da Paola 10 Bis, 10123 Turin, Italy.
- Pensiero Mazziniano. m. ISSN 0031-482X

**Associazione Medica Chirurgica di Tivoli e della Val
d'Aniene**
Tivoli, Italy.
- Associazione Medica Chirurgica di Tivoli e della
Val d'Aniene. Atti e Memorie. biennial. ISSN
0066-9873

**Associazione Medici Dentisti Italiani**
Via Savoia 78, Rome, Italy.
- A M D I Bollettino. m. ISSN 0001-1908
- Rivista Italiana di Stomatologia. (pub. by Gruppo
Editoriale Cadmos)

**Associazione Mineraria Italiana**
- Industria Mineraria. (pub. by Servizio Italiana
Pubblicazioni Internazionali s.r.l.)

**Associazione Nationale fra le Industrie
Automobilistche**
Corso G. Ferraris 61, 10128 Turin, Italy.
- A.N.F.I.A. Notiziario di Informazioni. m. ISSN
0001-2025

**Associazione Nazionale Allevatori Bovini di Razza
Piemontese**
Via Valeggio 22, 10128 Turin, Italy.
- Razza Bovina Piemontese. m. ISSN 0300-3477

**Associazione Nazionale Alpini**
Via Marsala 9, 20121 Milan, Italy.
- Alpino. m. ISSN 0002-6492

**Associazione Nazionale Armieri Affini**
C.So Venezia 47, 20121 Milan, Italy.
- Armieri. m. ISSN 0004-2412

**Associazione Nazionale Autoriparatori e
Autoricambisti**
- Garage & Officina. (pub. by Edistampa s.r.l.)

**Associazione Nazionale Bieticoltori**
Via d'Azeglio 48, 40123 Bologna, Italy.
- Giornale del Bieticoltore. 9 per yr. ISSN 0017-
0143

**Associazione Nazionale Ciclo, Motociclo e Accessori**
Via M. Macchi 32, Milan, Italy.
- Industria Italiana del Ciclo e del Motociclo.
Annuario. biennial. ISSN 0073-7291

**Associazione Nazionale Combattenti e Reduci
Federazione Provinciale di Milano**
Via Bagutta 12, Milan, Italy.
- Nuova Tradotta. m. ISSN 0048-1122

**Associazione Nazionale Costruttori Edili**
- Corriere dei Costruttori. (pub. by Edilstampa)
- Industria delle Costruzioni. (pub. by Edilstampa)

**Associazione Nazionale degli Industriali dei Laterizi**
Via Cavour 71, Rome, Italy.
- Industria Italiana dei Laterizi. bi-m. ISSN 0019-
7610

**Associazione Nazionale dei Musei Italiani**
- Musei e Gallerie d'Italia. (pub. by De Luca
Editore)

**Associazione Nazionale dei Procuratori e
Patrocinatori Legali**
- Arringa. (pub. by Emilio Ponticello, Ed. & Pub.)

**Associazione Nazionale del Libero Pensiero "Giordano
Bruno"**
Via Torre Argentina 18, Rome 00186, Italy.
- Ragione/Reason. bi-m. ISSN 0033-8656

**Associazione Nazionale dell'Industria Chimica**
Via Fatebenefratelli 10, Milan 20121, Italy.
- Industria Chimica. bi-m.

**Associazione Nazionale dell'Industria della Saponeria
della Detergenza e dei Prodotti d'Igiene**
Via Tomacelli, 132, 00186 Rome, Italy.
- Olearia; rivista delle materie grasse. bi-m. ISSN
0030-2090

**Associazione Nazionale delle Bonifiche, delle
Irrigazioni e dei Miglioramenti Fondiari**
- Bonifica e l'Assetto Territoriale. (pub. by Editrice
San Marco)

**Associazione Nazionale di Ingegneria Sanitaria**
Piazza Sallustio 24, Rome, Italy.
- Ingegneria Sanitaria; rivista tecnica bimestrale. bi-
m. ISSN 0020-0980

**Associazione Nazionale di Vernicatura Decorazione e
Stuccatura**
Piazza Colombo 3-12, 16121 Genoa, Italy.
- Vernicature e Decorazioni e Applicazioni
Protettive. m.

**Associazione Nazionale Esercenti Spettacoli Vaggianti**
Via di Villa Patrizi 10, 00161 Rome, Italy.
- Spettacolo Viaggiante. bi-m.

**Associazione Nazionale Ex Internati**
Via 20 Settembre 27-B, Rome 00187, Italy.
- Associazione Nazionale Ex Internati. Bollettino
Ufficiale. bi-m. ISSN 0004-5985

**Associazione Nazionale Fabbricanti Giocattoli**
Via Bianca di Savoia 6, 20122 Milan, Italy.
- Giocattoli. 12 per yr. ISSN 0017-0054

**Associazione Nazionale fra le Imprese Assicuratrici**
Via della Frezza, 70, 00186 Rome, Italy.
- Annuario Italiano delle Imprese Assicuratrici. a.
ISSN 0084-6635

**Associazione Nazionale Fra le Industrie
Automobilistche**
Corso G. Ferraris 61, 10128 Turin, Italy.
- A.N.F.I.A. Notiziario Statistico. m. ISSN 0001-
2033 (Co-sponsor: Unione Italiana Costruttori
Autoveicoli)

**Associazione Nazionale fra le Industrie della Gomma**
- Annuario dell' Industria Italiana della Gomma/
Yearbook of the Italian Rubber Industry. (pub. by
N I G Editrice)

**Associazione Nazionale fra le Industrie della Gomma
Cavi Elettrici ed Affini**
- Industria della Gomma. (pub. by N I G Editrice)

**Associazione Nazionale Giovani Agricoltori**
Corso Vittorio Emanuele 101, Rome, Italy.
- Agricoltura Nuova. m.

**Associazione Nazionale Industriali Laterizi**
Via Cavour 71, 00184 Rome, Italy.
- Costruire Laterizi; rivista di architettura e tecnica.
bi-m. ISSN 0010-9649

**Associazione Nazionale Industrie Elettrotechiche ed
Elettroniche**
- Industria Italiana Elettrotecnica Ed Elettronica.
(pub. by Edizioni Techniche S.A.S.)

**Associazione Nazionale Industrie Metalli Non Ferrosi**
Via Leopardi, 18, Milan, Italy.
- Metalli Non Ferrosi in Italia: Statistiche. a.

**Associazione Nazionale Ingegneri e Architetti Italiani**
- Ingegnere. (pub. by Edizioni Pi-Erre)

**Associazione Nazionale Instituti Autonomi e Case
Consorzi Popolari**
Viale Romagna 26, 20133 Milan, Italy.
- Edilizia Popolare. bi-m.

**Associazione Nazionale Invalidi Esiti Poliomielite**
Via Coltelli 7/D, 40124 Bologna, Italy.
- Orizzonti Aperti; la voce dei poliomielitici. 3-5
per yr. ISSN 0030-5618

**Associazione Nazionale Italia Albania**
Via Torino 122, 00184 Rome, Italy.
- Albania Oggi. bi-m. ISSN 0002-4643
- Albania Socialista. 3 per yr.
- Notizie dall'Albania. m. ISSN 0048-0916

**Associazione Nazionale Italiana Grossisti Orologiai**
Piazza G. G. Belli 2, 00153 Rome, Italy.
- Clessidra. m. ISSN 0009-8752

**Associazione Nazionale Italiana Industrie Grafiche
Cartotecniche e Trasformatrici**
Piazza Conciliazione 1, 20123 Milano, Italy.
- Italia Grafica. m.

**Associazione Nazionale Italiana per l'Automazione**
- Automazione e Strumentazione. (pub. by Dr.
Antonio Barbieri-Editore)

**Associazione Nazionale "L.Luzzatti"**
Fra le Banche Popolari, Via Donizetti 14, 00198
Rome, Italy.
- Credito Popolare. bi-m. ISSN 0011-1090

**Associazione Nazionale Laureati in Scienze
Biologiche**
- Biologia Contemporanea. (pub. by Edizioni
Minerva Medica)

**Associazione Nazionale Lavoratori Anziani di Azienda**
- Esperienza. (pub. by Editoriale Esperienza)

**Associazione Nazionale Medici Direttori di Ospedali**
Ospedale Maurifiano, Corso Turati 46, 10128 Turin,
Italy.
- Ospedale. m. ISSN 0030-6231

**Associazione Nazionale Mutilati e Invalidi di Guerra**
Sezione di Roma, Lungotevere Castello N.2, 00193
Rome, Italy.
- Associazione Nazionale Mutilati e Invalidi di
Guerra. Sezione di Roma. Notiziario. m. ISSN
0004-5993

**Associazione Nazionale Partigiani d'Italia**
Via degli Scipioni 271, 00192 Rome, Italy.
- Patria Indipendente; Quindicinale della Resistenza
e degli ex combattenti. fortn. ISSN 0031-3130

**Associazione Nazionale per Aquileia**
Casa Bertoli, 33051 Aquileia, Italy.
- Aquileia Nostra. a.

**Associazione Nazionale per Il Controllo della
Combustione**
Via Urbana 167, 00184 Rome, Italy.
- Calore. m. ISSN 0008-1760

**Associazione Nazionale per Il Progresso della Scuola
Italiana**
Piazza SS, Apostoli N. 80, Rome, Italy.
- Politica della Scuola. s-a.

**Associazione Nazionale per la Tutela del Patrimonio
Storico Artistico e Naturale della Nazione**
Corso Vittorio Emanuele N.287, 00186 Rome, Italy.
- Italia Nostra. m. ISSN 0021-2822

**Associazione Nazionale Reduci Dalla Prigionia**
Via Umberto I 9/2, 20038 Seregno, Milan, Italy.
- Vedetta. 2 per yr. ISSN 0042-3009

**Associazione Nazionale Sottufficiali Marina Fuori
Servizio**
Viale Giulio Cesare 54-A, 00192 Rome, Italy.
- Gran Pavese. m. ISSN 0017-3118

**Associazione Nazionale Tecnici Zucchero ed Alcole**
Via Tito Speri, 5, Ferrara, Italy.
- Industria Saccarifera Italiana. bi-m. ISSN 0019-
7734

**Associazione Nazionale Termotecnici e Aerotecnici**
- Progettista. (pub. by Paleari Edizioni Milano)

**Associazione Nazionale Uccelatori ed Uccellinai**
Via Verdi 14, 24100 Bergamo, Italy.
- Uccellagione e Piccola Caccia. bi-m.

**Associazione Nazionale Ufficiali Aeronautica**
Viale Giulio Cesare 54/A, 00192 Rome, Italy.
- Corriere dell'Aviatore. m. ISSN 0010-9223

**Associazione Nazionale Ufficiali Sanitari Medici
Igienisti**
G. Marconi 45, 40122 Bologna, Italy.
- Tecnica Sanitaria. bi-m. ISSN 0040-1897

**Associazione Orafo Valenzano**
Piazza Don Minzoni 1, 15048 - Valenza Po, Italy.
- Orafo Valenzano. bi-m. ISSN 0030-4190

**Associazione Ottica Italiana**
Largo Enrico Fermi 6, 50125 Florence, Italy.
- Luce e Immagini. bi-m. ISSN 0024-7197

**Associazione Piccole e Medie Industrie**
Via Manzoni 2, 40121 Bologna, Italy.
- Orizzonti Industriali. m.

**Associazione Piemontese Orafi Orologiai**
Via Bogino N. 1, 10123 Turin, Italy.
- Orafo Orologiaio. bi-m. ISSN 0030-4182

**Associazione Piscicultori Italiani**
Via Indipendenza 5, 31100 Treviso, Italy.
- Rivista Italiana di Piscicultura e Ittiopatologia. q. ISSN 0557-1413

**Associazione pro Padova**
Via S. Francesco 36, Padua 35100, Italy.
- Padova e la sua Provincia. m. ISSN 0030-9192

**Associazione Problemistica Italiana**
Via Grottin 53, 16012 Busalla (Genova), Italy.
- Sinfonie Scacchistiche. q. ISSN 0037-5608

**Associazione Professionale Autonoma Cineoperatori**
- A P A C Inform. (pub. by Mariso Varagnolo, Ed. & Pub.)

**Associazione Profumieri Milano**
Corso Venezia 47, 20122 Milan, Italy.
- Nuove Armonie; listino ufficiale dei prezzi dei prodotti della profumeria in Italia. q.

**Associazione Provinciale Agricoltori**
Piazza Martiri Belfiore 7, 46100 Mantova, Italy.
- Agricoltura Mantovana. w.

**Associazione Radiotecnica Italiana**
- Radio Rivista. (pub. by Faenza Editrice S.p.A.)

**Associazione Relazioni Culturali Spagna, Portogallo e America Latina**
Palazzo dell' Universita, Via Po 19, Turin, Italy.
- Quaderni Ibero-Americani; attualita culturale nella penisola Iberica e America Latina. s-a. ISSN 0033-4960

**Associazione Relazioni Sociali**
Via S. Michele del Carso, 16, 20144 Milan, Italy.
- Relazioni Sociali; rivista di critica politica, economia e cultura. m. ISSN 0034-3862

**Associazione Romana di Entomologia**
c/o Museo Civico di Zoologia, Via Ulisse Aldrovandi, 18, 00197 Rome, Italy.
- Associazione Romana di Entomologia. Bollettino. q. ISSN 0004-6000

**Associazione Scientifica di Produzione Animale**
- Zootechnica e Nutrizione Animale. (pub. by Gruppo Giornalistico Edagricole)

**Associazione Scout Cattolici Italiani**
Via Olona 25, 20123 Milan, Italy.
- Servire; rivista rover per giovani. bi-m. ISSN 0037-2765

**Associazione Siciliana contro la Tubercolosi**
- Rivista Siciliana della Tubercolosi e delle Malattie Respiratorie. (pub. by Universita degli Studi di Palermo. Clinica Tisiologica)

**Associazione Tecnica dell' Automobile**
Via Carlo Allerto 61, 10123 Turin, Italy.
- A. T. A. Associazione Tecnica dell'Automobile. m. ISSN 0001-2661

**Associazione Termotecnica Italiana**
- Termotecnica. (pub. by Dr. Antonio Barbieri-Editore)

**Associazione Turistica pro Empoli**
Piazza Farinata 9, Empoli, Florence, Italy.
- Bullettino Storico Empolese. s-a. ISSN 0007-5795

**Associazioni Dottori in Scienze Agrarie di Bari**
Via Japigia, 70126 Bari, Italy.
- Scienza e Tecnica Agraria; rivista mensile di agricoltura meridionale. m. ISSN 0036-8881

**Associazioni Italiana Societa Concessionaire Autostrade e Trafori**
Via Campania 47, 00187 Rome, Italy.
- Associazioni Italiana Societa Concessionaire Autostrade e Trafori. A I S C A T Informazioni. q. ISSN 0044-975X

**Assofermet**
Corso Venezia 47-49, 20121 Milan, Italy.
- Mercato Metalsiderurgico. s-m. ISSN 0025-9829

**Assogiocattoli**
- Giornale dei Giocattoli. (pub. by Pubbliemme)

**Astral S.C.L.**
Salita Viale 1-21, Via 20 Settembre, 16128 Genoa, Italy.
- Corriere dei Trasporti; settimanale indipendente di informazioni. w. ISSN 0010-9193

**Astrolabio**
Via di Torre Argentina 18, 00186 Rome, Italy.
- Astrolabio. fortn. ISSN 0004-6132

**Atena S. p. A.**
Via di Val Tellina, 47-00151 Rome, Italy.
- Sport Equestri. bi-m.

**Edizioni dell' Ateneo**
Via Ruggero Bonghi 11 B, 00184 Rome, Italy
(Subsc. to: Box 7216, 00100 Rome Italy)
- Bianco e Nero. bi-m. ISSN 0006-0577
- Biblioteca di Classici Greci e Latini. irreg., 1964, no. 2. ISSN 0067-7426
- Bibliotheca Athena. irreg., no. 15, 1975. ISSN 0067-7868 (Universita di Rome. Scuola di Filologia Classica)
- Civilta del Mondo Antico. irreg., 1969, no. 3. ISSN 0069-4320
- Collana di Cultura. irreg., 1969, no. 24. ISSN 0069-5165
- Filologia e Critica. irreg., no. 15, 1975. ISSN 0071-4968
- Flos Latinitatis. irreg., 1968, no. 5. ISSN 0071-6227
- Incunabula Graeca. irreg., no. 60, 1975. ISSN 0073-5752
- Lessico Intellettuale Europeo. irreg., no. 9, 1975. ISSN 0075-8825
- Libro e la Scuola. irreg., 1967, no. 3. ISSN 0075-9171
- Lyricorum Graecorum Quae Exstant. irreg., 1969, no. 4. ISSN 0076-1702
- Nuovi Saggi. irreg., no. 63, 1975. ISSN 0078-2769
- Officina Romanica. irreg., 1969, no. 20. ISSN 0078-3935
- Poeti e Prosatori Francesi. irreg., 1966, no. 6. ISSN 0079-2489
- Poeti e Prosatori Italiani. irreg., 1969, no. 5. ISSN 0079-2497
- Poeti e Prosatori Tedeschi. irreg., 1969, no. 5. ISSN 0079-2500
- Quaderni Athena. irreg., 1968, no. 7. ISSN 0079-8231
- Quaderni di Bibliografia. irreg. ISSN 0079-8266
- Quaderni Urbinati di Cultura Classica. 3 per yr. ISSN 0033-4987
- Ricerche di Storia della Lingua Latina. irreg., no. 12, 1975. ISSN 0080-293X
- Rivista di Cultura Classica e Medioevale. 3 per yr. ISSN 0035-6085
- Rivista di Cultura Classica e Medioevale. Quaderni. irreg., no. 15, 1975. ISSN 0080-3251
- Scriptores Latini; Collana di Scrittori Latini ad Uso Accademico. irreg., no. 14, 1975. ISSN 0080-8393
- Studi di Metrica Classica. irreg., 1968, no. 5. ISSN 0081-6159
- Studi di Pedagogia. irreg., 1965, no. 2. ISSN 0081-6167
- Studi e Materiali di Storia delle Religioni. Quaderni. irreg., no. 9, 1975. ISSN 0081-6175 (Universita di Roma. Scuola di Studi Storico - Religiosi)
- Studi Germanici. 3 per yr. ISSN 0039-2952 (Istituto Italiano di Studi Germanici-Roma)
- Testi Universitari di Linguistica. irreg., 1963, no. 3. ISSN 0082-2914
- Universita di Roma. Istituto di Economia Politica. Collana di Studi. irreg., 1969, no. 5. ISSN 0080-4010
- Universita di Trieste. Istituto di Storia dell'Arte (Pubblicazioni) irreg. ISSN 0564-2477

**Ateneo Bruzio**
Via Nicola Serra 52, 87100 Cosenza, Italy.
- Ateneo Bruzio. m (9 per yr)

**Ateneo Veneto**
Campo S. Fantin 1897, Venice, Italy.
- Ateneo Veneto; revista di science, lettere ed arti. s-a. ISSN 0004-6558

**Athena Mediterranea**
Piazza Municipio 22, 81031 Aversa, Italy.
- Athena Mediterranea; periodico trimestrale di lettere, storia, arte e cultura varia. q.

**Verlagsanstalt Athesia**
Museumstrasse 42, I-39100 Bozen, Italy.
- Jugendwacht; monatszeitschrift der jugend sudtirols. m. ISSN 0022-5967
- Schlern; illustrierte monatshefte fuer heimat und volkskunde. m. ISSN 0036-6145

**Atlas Copco Italia**
Casella Postale 3287, Milan, Italy.
- Aria Compressa. q. ISSN 0004-1300

**Edizioni Atomo e Industria s.r.l.**
Via Paisiello 26/28, 00198 Rome, Italy.
- Atomo e Industria; journal of international nuclear information. s-m. ISSN 0004-7171 (Forum Italiano dell'Energia Nucleare)

**Atomo Petrolio Elettricita**
Piazza Borghese, 3, Rome, Italy.
- Atomo Petrolio Elettricita. bi-m. ISSN 0004-718X

**Atterraggio Forzato**
Viale Guilio Cesare 54A, Rome, Italy.
- Atterraggio Forzato; voce libera dei sottufficiali dell'aeronautica. m. ISSN 0004-7279

**Audiovisione**
Viale degli Ammiragli 71, 00136 Rome, Italy.
- Audiovisione. m.

**Audiovisivi**
Via Taranto 21, 00182 Rome, Italy.
- Audiovisivi. m. ISSN 0004-7627

**Aula Magna Universita di Roma. Istituzione Universitarie dei Concerti**
Casella Postale 7181, Rome, Italy.
- Musica Universita; periodico quindicinale di cultura e informazioni musicali. fortn. ISSN 0027-4550

**Aulo Gaggi**
Via S. Stefano, 130, 40125 Bologna, Italy.
- Archivio Putti di Chirurgia degli Organi di Movimento. a. ISSN 0066-670X
- Italian Journal of Orthopaedics and Traumatology. 3 per yr. plus supplement.

**Aurea Parma**
Vicolo Leon d'Oro 8, Parma, Italy.
- Aurea Parma; rivista di lettere, arte e storia. q. ISSN 0004-8062

**M. d' Auria Editore Pontificio**
Calata Trinita Maggiore 52, 80134 Naples, Italy.
- Asprenas. q. ISSN 0004-4970 (Pontificia Facolta Teologica dell'Italia Meridionale-Sezione di Capodimonte)

**Auto Service Editrice**
Via Tolstoi 70, 20146 Milan, Italy.
- Auto Service. 8 per yr. (Unione Italiana Autoriparatori) (Co-sponsor: Federazione Italiana Rettificatori di Motori)

**Auto 70**
Via G. Verdi 53, 10124 Turin, Italy.
- Auto 70. m.

**Autoaccessorio**
Via G.B. Pirelli 5, 20124 Milan, Italy.
- Autoaccessorio. bi-m. ISSN 0005-0903

**Automobile Club d'Italia**
Via Marsala 8, Rome, Italy.
- A. C. I. Informazioni. m. ISSN 0001-0715
- Automobile. (pub. by Editrice Dell Automobile S.p.A.)
- Automobilismo e Automobilismo Industriale; revue de la federation internationale de l'automobile (F.I.A.) bi-m. ISSN 0005-1454
- H P Energia Trasporti. (pub. by Editrice Dell Automobile S.p.A.)
- Rivista Giuridica della Circolazione e dei Trasporti. (pub. by Editrice Dell Automobile S.p.A.)
- World Cars. (pub. by Herald Books US)

**Automobile Club di Milano**
Corso Venezia 43, 20121 Milan, Italy.
- Autoclub & Via. m. ISSN 0005-0962
- Automobile Club di Milano. Notiziario Economico. m. ISSN 0005-1373

**Editrice Dell Automobile S.p.A.**
Viale Regina Margherita 279, Rome 00198, Italy.
- Automobile. m. ISSN 0005-1349 (Automobile Club d'Italia)

- H P Energia Trasporti. bi-m. (Automobile Club d'Italia)
- Rivista Giuridica della Circolazione e dei Trasporti. bi-m. ISSN 0035-6700 (Automobile Club d'Italia)

**Automotoclub Storico Italiano**
- Manovella. (pub. by Editrice la Manovella s.r.l.)

**Autonomi**
Piazza Carignano 8, 10123 Turin, Italy.
- Autonomi. q. ISSN 0045-1118

**Autorama s.r.l.**
Via Manzoni 38, 20121 Milan, Italy.
- Autorama; panoramica mensile delle attivita motoristiche. m. ISSN 0005-1683

**Autostrade Concessioni e Costruzioni Autostrade S.p. A.**
Via Antonio Nibby 10, 00161 Rome, Italy.
- Autostrade; rivista di tecnica e di informazioni autostradali. m. ISSN 0005-1756

**Avesta S.p. A. Acciai Inossidabili**
Via Lancetti 36, Milan, Italy.
- Acciaio Inossidabile. q. ISSN 0001-4567

**Azienda Autonoma di Turismo - Prato**
Via Luigi Muzzi 51, Prato, Italy.
- Prato - Storia e Arte. q. ISSN 0032-6925

**Azienda Cataloghi Italiani**
Piazzale Lugano 8, 20158 Milan, Italy.
- Catalogo Motoristico. a.
- Notiziario Motoristico. fortn.

**Azimut**
Via Pozzi 11, 21052 Bustro Arsizio, Italy.
- Azimut. m. ISSN 0005-254X

**Azione Cattolica Giovanile**
Via S. Antonio 5, 20122 Milan, Italy.
- Giovani in Dialogo. s-m. ISSN 0017-1336

**Azione Cattolica Italiana**
Via della Conciliazione 1, Rome, Italy.
- Presenza Pastorale. 10 per yr. ISSN 0032-7727 (Collegio Assistenti)

**B. F. B**
Via Dogana 3, Milan, Italy.
- Apparecchi Elettrodomestici Nella Casa Moderna. m. ISSN 0003-6668
- Radiotecnica TV; hi-fi elettronica professionale. m. ISSN 0481-6781

**B.S.C.**
Via G. Servais 126, 10146 Turin, Italy.
- Zooespresso. m.

**Badia Greca di Grottaferrata**
Grottaferrata, Rome, Italy.
- Badia greca di Grottaferrata, Bollettino. s-a. ISSN 0005-3783 (Monastero esarchico di Grottaferrata)

**Edizioni Alessandro Baltadori**
Casella Postale 197, Perugia, Italy.
- Ecologia Agraria. 4 per yr. ISSN 0012-9607

**Banca d'Italia**
Via Nazionale, 91, Rome, Italy.
- Banca d'Italia. Assemblea Generale Ordinaria dei Partecipanti. a. ISSN 0067-3161
- Banca d'Italia. Bollettino. q. ISSN 0005-4593

**Banca Nazionale del Lavoro**
Via Vittorio Veneto 119, 00187 Rome, Italy.
- Banca Nazionale del Lavoro Quarterly Review. q. ISSN 0005-4607
- Italian Stock Market. m. ISSN 0021-2989
- Italian Trends. m. ISSN 0021-3004
- Moneta e Credito. q. ISSN 0026-9611

**Banca Nazionale dell'Agricoltura**
Via Lovanio 16, Rome, Italy.
- Rassegna Quindicinale dell'Agricoltura. s-m. ISSN 0033-9830

**Paolo F. Bancale Ed. & Pub.**
Via Tagliamento 29/2, 00198 Rome, Italy.
- Aviazione. s-w.
- Aviazione di Linea Difesa e Spazio. m (except Jan.-Aug.) ISSN 0005-2205

**Bancaria Editrice S.p.A.**
Piazza del Gesu 49, 00186 Rome, Italy.
- Bancaria. m. ISSN 0005-4623 (Associazione Bancaria Italiana)

**Banco di Napoli**
- Revue Internationale d'Histoire de la Banque. (pub. by Librarie Droz SZ)

**Banco di Napoli. Direzione Generale**
Servizio Segretaria, Ufficio Studi, Via Roma 177-178, 80100 Naples, Italy.
- Rassegna Economica. bi-m.

**Banco di Roma**
Direzione Centrale, Via del Corso 307, 00186 Rome, Italy.
- Journal of European Economic History. 3 per yr.
- Review of the Economic Conditions in Italy. bi-m. ISSN 0034-6799
- Villaggio; rivista per il personale del Banco di Roma. m.

**Banco di Sardegna**
Viale Umberto, 36, 07100 Sassari, Italy.
- Quaderni dell'Economia Sarda. q.

**Banco di Sicilia**
Via del Corso 271, 00186 Rome, Italy.
- Banco di Sicilia. Informazioni Sulla Congiuntura. m. ISSN 0005-4860

**Dr. Antonio Barbieri-Editore**
Viale Premuda 2, 20129 Milan, Italy.
- Automazione e Strumentazione. m. ISSN 0005-1284 (Associazione Nazionale Italiana per l'Automazione)
- Termotecnica. m. ISSN 0040-3725 (Associazione Termotecnica Italiana)

**Societa Tipografica Barbieri, Noccioli & C.**
Casella Postale 155, 50053 Empoli, Italy.
- Amministrazione Italiana. m.

**Silvio Basile**
Lungobisagno Istria 34, Genoa, Italy.
- Marina Mercantile. m. ISSN 0025-3103

**Basilica di S. Francesco**
Santuario delle Ss. Particole, Siena, Italy.
- Tesoro Eucaristico. bi-m. ISSN 0040-3938

**Basilica di San Antonio**
- Messaggero di S. Antonio. (pub. by Edizioni Messaggero)

**Editrice Basilicata**
Via Ridola 20, Casella Postale 70, Matera 75100, Italy.
- Basilicata; mensile di politica e attualita. m. ISSN 0005-6111

**Bayer Italia S. p A.**
Viale Certosa 126, Milan, Italy.
- Corriere Fitopatologico. s-a. ISSN 0010-9258

**Felice del Beccaro, Ed. & Pub.**
Via Sercambi, 9, 55100 Lucca, Italy.
- Rassegna Lucchese; periodico di cultura. q. ISSN 0033-975X

**A. Bellinvia, Ed. & Pub.**
Via Grez 24, 38066 Riva del Garda (Trento), Italy.
- Magnifici delle 7 Note. q.

**Berben Editore**
Via Redipuglia 65, 60100 Ancona, Italy.
- Strumenti & Musica. m. ISSN 0039-260X

**Francesco Berlingieri, Ed. & Pub.**
Via Roma 10/2, Genoa, Italy.
- Diritto Marittimo; rivista trimestrale di dottrina guirisprudenza Legislazione Italiana e Straniera. q. ISSN 0012-348X

**Vito Bianco, Ed. & Pub.**
Via in Arcione 71, 00187 Rome, Italy.
- Giornale del Mezzogiorno; economico-politico. w. ISSN 0017-0186
- Italia Sul Mare; mensile internazionale di nautica e di turismo marinaro. m. ISSN 0021-2857 (Salone Nautico Internazionale di Genoa)

**Bibbia e Oriente**
Colegio Emiliani, 16167, Italy.
- Bibbia e Oriente; rivista per la conoscenza della Bibbia. bi-m. ISSN 0006-0585

**Biblical Institute Press**
Piazza della Pilotta 35, I-00187 Rome, Italy.
- Analecta Biblica. Investigationes Scientificae in Res Biblicas. irreg. ISSN 0066-135X
- Biblica. q. ISSN 0006-0887 (Pontificio Istituto Biblico)
- Studia Papyrologica. s-a. ISSN 0039-3290 (Pontifical Biblical Institute)

**Editrice Bibliografica s.r.l.**
Viale Vittorio Veneto 12, 20124 Milan, Italy (Dist. in U.S., Canada and Latin America by R. R. Bowker Co., P.O. Box 1807, Ann Arbor, Mich. 48106)
- Catalogo dei Libri Italiani in Commercio/Italian Books in Print. a. ISSN 0069-1054

**Biblioteca Forteguerriana**
Via della Sapienza 12, Pistoia, Italy.
- Bullettino Storico Pistoiese. s-a. ISSN 0007-5809 (Societa Pistoiese di Storia Patria)

**Biblioteca Francescana**
Conto Corrente Postale 15/27009, Falconara M. 60015, Italy.
- Picenum Seraphicum. irreg.

**Biblioteca Labronica Notiziario**
Piazza Matteotti 6, 57100 Livorno, Italy.
- Biblioteca Labronica Notiziario. bi-m. ISSN 0006-1700

**Biblioteca Malatestiana**
47023 Cesena, Italy.
- Societa di Studi Romagnoli. Guide. irreg., 1973, no. 3. ISSN 0081-0681
- Studi Romagnoli. a. ISSN 0081-6205 (Societa di Studi Romagnoli)
- Studi Romagnoli. Estratti di Sezione. irreg., 1971, no. 12. ISSN 0081-6213 (Societa di Studi Romagnoli)
- Studi Romagnoli. Quaderni. irreg., 1973, no. 8. ISSN 0081-6221 (Societa di Studi Romagnoli)

**Biblioteca Marsilio**
Marsilio, Padua, Italy.
- Biblioteca Marsilio: Architettura e Urbanistica. irreg.

**Biblioteca Nazionale Centrale di Firenze**
- Bibliografia Nazionale Italiana. (pub. by Istituto Centrale per Il Catalogo Unico delle Biblioteche Italiane e per le Informazioni Bibliografiche)

**Biblioteca Statale e Libreria Civica, Cremona**
Via Ugolani Dati 4, Cremona, Italy.
- Biblioteca Statale e Libreria Civica, Cremona. Annali. irreg., approx. 2 per yr.

**Biblioteca Statale Isontina di Gorizia**
Via Mameli 12, Gorizia, Itlay.
- Studi Goriziani. s-a.

**Biosophia**
Piazza del Navigatori 8, Rome, Italy.
- Biosophia; mensile di cultura universale e rigenerazione ideale, scienza e filosofia della vita, indirizzi di pensiero. m. ISSN 0006-3576

**Edizione Bizzari**
11B via Ruggero Bonghi, 00184 Rome, Italy.
- Economia e Storia. irreg. ISSN 0070-8402

**Aldo Blanc, Ed. & Pub**
Via Carducci 32, Milan, Italy.
- Mobile; quindicinale indipendente di economia e informazione. s-m. ISSN 0026-7112

**Aguet Blanc Redaz, Ed. & Pub.**
Via Giulio Caccini No. 1, 00198 Rome, Italy.
- Quaternaria. a. ISSN 0085-5235

**Bolaffi e Mondadori**
Via Cavour 17F, 10123 Turin, Italy.
- BolaffiArte. m. ISSN 0045-236X
- Bolaffi's Catalogues of Art and Architecture. a. ISSN 0067-9569 (U.S. Distrib: Speedimpex U.S.A. Inc., 123-16 40 Ave., Long Island City, N.Y. 11101)
- Catalogo Internazionale Bolaffi d'Arte Antica e di Antiquariato. irreg.
- Weekend; la rivista del tempo libero. 5 per yr.

**Casa Editrice Bolletino Metallografico**
Via Speronari 7, Milan, Italy.
- Bollettino-Metallografico e di Odonto-Stoma-Tologia. 4 per yr. ISSN 0006-6826

**Bollettino Bibliografico Sardo e Archivio Tradizioni Popolari**
Casella Postale 118, Cagliari, Sardegna, Italy.
- Bollettino Bibliografico Sardo e Archivio Tradizioni Popolari. bi-m. ISSN 0045-2432

**Bollettino dei Prezzi All'ingrosso**
Via Modonella, 41, Modena, Italy.
- Bollettino dei Prezzi All'ingrosso. w. ISSN 0006-6672

**Bollettino di Collegamento**
c/o Tony Sansone, Via delle Cascine 22, 50144 Florence, Italy.
- Bollettino di Collegamento; fra comunita cristiane in Italia. m. ISSN 0300-4589

**Bollettino Tributario d'Informazioni**
Via T. Salvini,N.1, Milan 20122, Italy.
- Bollettino Tributario d'Informazioni; quindicinale di legislazione giurisprudenza consulenza. s-m. ISSN 0006-6893

**Francesco Boneschi, Ed. & Pub.**
Via Giolitti 202, Rome, Italy.
- A. I. L. A. w. ISSN 0001-1584 (Agenzia Internazionale Letteraria Artistica)

**Edizioni Bora S.N.C. di P. Prandin & C.**
Via Jacopo di Paolo, 42, Bologna, Italy.
- Terzo Occhio. 3 per yr. ISSN 0390-0355

**Borghese**
Largo Toniolo 6, Rome, Italy.
- Borghese. w. ISSN 0006-775X

**Editoriale Il Borgo**
Via dell'Industria 6, San Lazzaro di Savena, Bologna, Italy.
- Autosprint. w. ISSN 0005-1748

**Borsa Valori di Torino**
- Listino Ufficiale della Borsa Valori di Torino. (pub. by Camera di Commercio Industria Artigianato e Agricoltura di Torino)

**Boxe Ring s.r.l.**
Via G.B. Vico 1, 00196 Rome, Italy.
- Boxe Ring. fortn. ISSN 0006-8497

**Gianni Baget Bozzo, Ed. & Pub.**
Via 12 Ottobre 14, Genoa, Italy.
- Renovatio. q. ISSN 0034-4486

**Breve, Il Gruppo, la Cultura, l'Idee**
Traversa Merbellina 24, Naples, Italy.
- Breve, Il Gruppo, la Cultura, l'Idee. m. ISSN 0006-968X

**Edizioni Bucalo**
Via Bixio 8, 04100 Latina, Italy.
- Dialectica; rassegna bimestrale di giustizia. bi-m.
- Rivista del Cancelliere; rassegna di dottrina, giurisprudenza, legislazione, circolari. bi-m.

**Bulzoni Editore**
Via dei Liburni 14, 00185 Rome, Italy.
- Archivio Penale. bi-m. ISSN 0004-0304
- Biblioteca Teatrale; rivista di studi e ricerche sullo spettacolo. q. ISSN 0045-1959
- D W F. (Donna/Woman/Femme); rivista internazionale di studi antropologici storici. q.
- Educazione e Quartiere. q.
- Micromegas. 3 per yr. (Universita di Roma. Istituto di Studi Francesi) (Co-sponsor: Services Culturels dell' Ambasciata di Francia)
- Neuropsichiatria Infantile. m. ISSN 0028-3924 (Societa Italiana di Neuropsichiatria Infantile)
- Nuovi Studi Politici.
- Quadrangolo. q. (Centro Studi Psicologici "Lo Spazio") (Co-sponsor: Societa Italiana di Psicoterapia di Gruppo)
- Rassegna Italiana di Linguistica Applicata. 3 per yr. ISSN 0033-9725 (Italian Center for Applied Linguistics)
- Rivista Italiana de Drammaturgia. q. (Istituto del Dramma Italiano)
- Scrittura Scenica. q.
- Sessualita/Sexuality; review of international studies of sexuality and sexual education. q.

**Edizioni C A M**
Strada Provinciale Cassanese, 20060 Vignate-Milano, Italy.
- Tecnica dell'Aria Compressa. q. ISSN 0040-1757 (Ingersoll-Rand Italiana)

**Edizioni C D**
Via C. Boldrini 22, Bologna 40121, Italy.
- C Q Elettronica. m. ISSN 0007-8948

**Edizioni C.E.D.A.M.**
*see* **Casa Editrice Dott. Antonio /Milani**

**C E S E S**
Corso Magenta 42, Milan, Italy.
- Controcorrente; quaderni trimestrali di studi e ricerche su temi e problemi delle scienze umane. q. ISSN 0010-8014
- Documentazione Sui Paesi dell'Est. m. ISSN 0012-4710
- Est; rivista trimestrale di studi sui paesi dell'est. q. ISSN 0014-1089

**Edizioni C E S I**
14 via Revere, 20123 Milan, Italy.
- Energia Elettrica. m. ISSN 0013-7308
- Rassegna Tecnica di Problemi dell'Energia Elettrica. bi-m. (Ente Nazionale per l'Energia Elettrica)

**C E S P E T R O L**
Via Pompeo Magno 4, 00192 Rome, Italy.
- Rassegna Petrolifera. w. ISSN 0033-9822

**C.I.R.**
Via G. Pisanelli 2, 00196 Rome, Italy.
- Tipo. m.

**C.I.S.E. S.p.A.**
Casella Postale 3986, 20100 Milan, Italy.
- Energia Nucleare. m. ISSN 0013-7332

**C I S I A**
*see* **Centro Italiano Sviluppo Impeighi Acciaio**

**C.I.S.L.**
25 via Castiglione, Bologna, Italy.
- Corriere Sindacale; periodico della unione provinciale C.I.S.L. di Bologna. m. ISSN 0010-9282

**Editrice C.I.S.P.E.L.**
Piazza Cola di Rienzo 80, 900192 Rome, Italy.
- C I S P E L Notizie. s-m. (Confederazione Italiana dei Servizi Pubblici degli Enti Locali)
- Confederazione Italiana dei Servizi Pubblici degli Enti Locali. Annuario. a.
- Impresa Pubblica; municipalizzazione. bi-m (with monthly supplements) ISSN 0019-3003 (Confederazione Italiana Servizi Pubblici degli Enti Locali)
- Notizario Interfederale. m. (Confederazione Italiana dei Servizi Pubblici degli Enti Locali)

**C S S R**
Via Altinate 16, Padova, Italy.
- Sociologia Religiosa; rivista di storia e sociologia delle religioni. s-a. ISSN 0038-0180

**Cacciatore Siciliano**
Viale S. Martino 146, Messina, Sicily, Italy.
- Cacciatore Siciliano. m. ISSN 0007-9359

**Gruppo Editoriale Cadmos**
Via L.da Viadana 9, 20122 Milano, Italy.
- Dental Cadmos; Revista mensile di odontoiatria e tecnica dentaria. m. ISSN 0011-8524
- Dental Press. bi-m.
- Mondo Odontostomatologico. bi-m. ISSN 0026-9565
- Mondo Ortodontico. bi-m.
- Prevenzione Stomatologica. bi-m.
- Rivista Italiana di Stomatologia. m. ISSN 0035-6905 (Associazione Medici Dentisti Italiani) (Editorial Address, Via Greppi 4, 20135 Milan, Italy)

**Caffe**
Via della Croce 67, Rome, Italy.
- Caffe; letterario e satirico. m. ISSN 0007-9553

**Michele Calabrese, Ed. & Pub.**
Via Margutta 53/B, Rome 00187, Italy.
- Poliedro; rassegna mensile d'Arte. m.

**Calabria - Domani**
Via Roma, 74, Casella Postale 399, 81100 Cosenza, Italy.
- Calabria - Domani. w.

**Calabria Letteraria**
4 Piazzo Nicola Presta, Longobardi, Italy.
- Calabria Letteraria. bi-m. ISSN 0008-0551

**Alberto Calcagno, Ed. & Pub.**
Viale Somalia 5, Rome, Italy.
- Agenzia Nazionale Informazioni Turistiche. w. ISSN 0002-0893

**Colletivo Editoriale Calusca**
Corso Porto Ticinese, 106, 20131 Milan, Italy.
- Primo Maggio; saggi e documenti per una storia di classe. 3 per yr.

**Camara Oficial de Comercio de Espana en Italia**
Via Rugabella 1, 20122 Milan, Italy.
- A G I E S. (Agenzia Informazioni Economiche Spagnole) m. ISSN 0001-1339

**Camera di Comercio Industria, Artigianato e Agricoltura di Reggio Emilia**
Piazza della Vittoria, Palazzo degli Affari, Reggio Emilia, Italy.
- Filugello. q (with 2 monthly supplements)

**Camera di Commercio di Asti**
Piazza Medici No.8, 14100 Asti, Italy.
- Asti Informazioni Economiche. m. ISSN 0004-6078

**Camera di Commercio Industria, Artigianato e Agricoltura Ancona**
1 Piazza 24 Maggio, Ancona, Italy.
- Bollettino Economico. m. ISSN 0006-6796

**Camera di Commercio, Industria, Artigianato e Agricoltura della Spezia**
Via Veneto 28, 19100 la Spezia, Italy.
- SpeziaOggi. m.

**Camera di Commercio Industria Artigianato e Agricoltura di Arezzo**
Viale Giotto 4, Arezzo, Italy.
- Economia Aretina. m. ISSN 0012-9747

**Camera di Commercio Industria Artigianato e Agricoltura di Belluno**
32100 Belluno, Piazza S. Stefano 19, Italy.
- Camera di Commercio Industria Artigianato Ed Agricoltura di Belluno. Rassegna Economica. bi-m. ISSN 0008-2147

**Camera di Commercio, Industria, Artigianato e Agricoltura di Brindisi**
Via Congragazione, Brindisi, Italy.
- Economia Brindisina. bi-m.

**Camera di Commercio Industria Artigianato e Agricoltura di Cuneo**
Via Emanuele Filiberto 3, Cuneo, Italy.
- Camera di Commercio Industria Artigianato e Agricoltura di Cuneo. Notiziario Economico. m.

**Camera di Commercio, Industria, Artigianato e Agricoltura di Ferrara**
Via Borgoleoni 11, 44100 Ferrara, Italy.
- Pianura. q (with m supplements) ISSN 0031-9570
- Prezzi dei Materiali e delle Opere Edili in Ferrara. q. ISSN 0300-3566

**Camera di Commercio Industria Artigianato e Agricoltura di Forli**
Piazza Saffi 36, 47100 Forli, Italy.
- Camera di Commercio, Industria Artigianato e Agricoltura. Bollettino Mensile. m.
- Provincia di Forli in Cifre. bi-m. ISSN 0033-1902

**Camera di Commercio Industria Artigianato e Agricoltura di Livorno**
Piazza del Municipio 48, 57100 Livorno, Italy.
- Porto di Livorno. m. ISSN 0032-4949

**Camera di Commercio Industria Artigianato e Agricoltura di Milano**
Via Meravigli 11, 20123 Milan, Italy.
- Milan, Italy. Camera di Commercio Industria Artigianato e Agricoltura. Notiziario Commerciale. s-m. ISSN 0026-3729
- Realta Economica. bi-m.

**Camera di Commercio, Industria, Artigianato e Agricoltura di Padova**
Via E. Filiberto, 34 Padua, Italy.
- Padova Economica. m. ISSN 0030-9206
- Provincia di Padova in Cifre. bi-m. ISSN 0033-1910

**Camera di Commercio Industria Artigianato e Agricoltura di Palermo**
Via Emerico Amari, 11, Palermo 90139, Italy.
- Mediterraneo; meusile di economia e cultura. m. ISSN 0047-6609

**Camera di Commercio Industria Artigianato e Agricoltura di Pavia**
Via Mentana 27, 27100 Pavia, Italy.
- Pavia Economica. q.

**Camera di Commercio Industria, Artigianato e Agricoltura di Perugia**
1 Piazza Italia, Perugia, Italy.
- Nuova Economia. m. ISSN 0029-6171

**Camera di Commercio, Industria, Artigianato e Agricoltura di Pesaro**
Pesaro, Italy.
- Convegno Nazionale dei Commercianti de Mobili. Atti e Relazioni. a. ISSN 0069-9764
- Economia Pesarese. m.
- Gazzetta Commerciale; rassegna economica camera di commercio. m. ISSN 0016-5611

**Camera di Commercio Industria Artigianato e Agricoltura di Roma**
Via De'Burro 147, 00186 Rome, Italy.
- Roma e Provincia Attraverso la Statistica; dati mensili e annuali. a. ISSN 0035-7960

**Camera di Commercio Industria Artigianato e Agricoltura di Teramo**
Piazza Martiri della Liberta, 64100 Teramo, Italy.
- Notizie dell'Economia Teramana. m.

**Camera di Commercio Industria Artigianato e Agricoltura di Torino**
Via. S. Francesco da Paola 24, Turin, Italy.
- Camera di Commercio Industria Artigianato e Agricoltura. Dati e Notizie. q. ISSN 0008-2139
- Cronache Economiche. m. ISSN 0011-1775
- Elenco Ufficiale dei Protesti Cambiari Levati Nella Provincia di Torino. fortn. ISSN 0013-6050
- Listino Ufficiale della Borsa Valori di Torino. d. ISSN 0024-4430 (Borsa Valori di Torino)

**Camera di Commercio Industria Artigianato e Agricoltura di Trento**
Via Calepina 13, 38100 Trento, Italy.
- Economia Trentina. q. ISSN 0012-9879

**Camera di Commercio Industria Artigianato e Agricoltura di Treviso**
Piazza della Borsa, 31100 Treviso, Italy.
- Economia della Marca Trevigiana. w.

**Camera di Commercio Industria Artigianato e Agricoltura di Venezia**
Via 22 Marzo 2032, Venice, Italy.
- Giornale Economico. bi-m. ISSN 0017-0429

**Camera di Commercio Industria Artigianato e Agricoltura, Modena**
Via Ganaceto 134, 41100 Modena, Italy.
- Modena Economica. m.

**Camera di Commercio Industria e Agricoltura di Cagliari**
Cagliari, Italy.
- Sardegna Economica. m. ISSN 0036-4770

**Camera di Commercio Industria e Agricoltura di Firenze**
Industria Artigianato e Agricoltura di Firenze, Piazza dei Giudici, 3 Florence, Italy.
- Arti e Mercature. bi-m. ISSN 0004-363X

**Camera di Commercio Industria e Agricoltura di Mantova**
Via P.F. Calvi 28, Mantua, Italy.
- Mantova. bi-m. ISSN 0025-2506

**Camera di Commercio Industria e Agricoltura di Reggio Emilia**
Piazza Liberta, 42100 Reggio Emilia, Italy.
- Materiali da Costruzione Ed Opere Edili Prezzi Indicativi. m.

**Camera Francese di Commercio ed Industria in Italia**
Via Meravigli 12, 20123 Milan, Italy.
- Contacts Franco Italiens. bi-m.

**Rosso Pio Camillo, Ed. & Pub.**
Via Bligny 8, Turin 10122, Italy.
- Giovane Montagna; rivista di vita alpina. q. ISSN 0017-0534 (Associazione Alpinistica "Giovane Montagna")

**Cammino**
Viale Piave 2, Milan 20129, Italy.
- Cammino; annali Francescani. m. ISSN 0008-2260

**Cammino Economico**
Via G. Verdi 13, Benevento, Italy.
- Cammino Economico; information bollettin. m. ISSN 0008-2279

**Campi & C. S.p.A.**
Via Virgilio 8, 00193 Rome, Italy.
- Sorrisi e Canzoni T V. w. ISSN 0041-4522

**Editrice Il Campo**
Via G. Amendola 11, 40121 Bologna, Italy.
- Piscine Oggi. q.

**Candido**
Via Bellarimino 19, Milan 20141, Italy.
- Candido; settimanale del sabato. w. ISSN 0045-5636

**Aurelio Canevari Editore**
Via Aleardo Aleardi 12, 20154 Milan, Italy.
- Confezione Italiana; moda e costume. 4 per yr. ISSN 0010-5619
- M I P E L. (Mercato Italiano della Pelletteria) q. ISSN 0026-5772 (Associazione Italiana Manufatturieri Pelli-Cuoio e Succedanei)
- Tecnica Delia Confezione. bi-m. ISSN 0040-1749

**Libreria Editrice Canova**
Via Panciera 3/B, 31100 Treviso, Italy.
- Urologia. bi-m. ISSN 0042-112X (Italian Society of Urology)

**Luigi Cantone, Ed. & Pub.**
Via Lucia 10, Benevento, Italy.
- Sannio Elegante. q. ISSN 0036-4460

**Casa Editrice Licinio Cappelli**
Via Marsili 9, 40124 Bologna, Italy.
- Acta Geneticae Medicae et Gemellologiae; international quarterly of medical genetics and twin research. q. ISSN 0001-5660 (Gregor Mendel Institute for Medical Genetics and Twin Studies. Permanent Committee) (Co-sponsors: International Congress of Human Genetics; International Society for Twin Studies)
- Annali di Radiologia Diagnostica. bi-m. ISSN 0003-4673 (Federazione Italiana della Stampa Radiologica)
- Annali di Radiologia Diagnostica. 6 per yr.
- Annali Italiani di Chirurgia. 6 per yr. ISSN 0003-469X
- Archivio di Scienze Biologiche. q. ISSN 0004-0169 (Societa Italiana di Biologia Sperimentale)
- Archivio Italiano delle Malattie dell'Apparato Digerente. q. ISSN 0004-0215
- Archivio Italiano di Anatomia e Istologia Patologica. bi-m. ISSN 0004-0231
- Archivio Italiano di Chirurgia. q. ISSN 0004-024X (Societa Lombarda di Chirurgia)
- Archivio Italiano di Urologia e Nefrologia. 6 per yr. ISSN 0004-0290
- Archivio Italiano di Dermatologia, Venereologia e Sessuologia. 6 per yr. ISSN 0004-0460
- Bollettino d'Oculistica. 12 per yr. ISSN 0006-677X
- Chirurgia degli Organi di Movimento. bi-m. ISSN 0009-4749
- Maia; rivista di letterature classiche. 3 per yr. ISSN 0025-0538
- Metroeconomica; international review of economics. 3 per yr. ISSN 0026-1386
- Oto-Rino-Laringologia Italiana. bi-m. ISSN 0030-6630
- Rivista Italiana di Ginecologia. 6 per yr. ISSN 0035-6840

**Capuchin-Franciscan Order**
- Laurentianum. (pub. by Collegio Internazionale S. Lorenzo da Brindisi)

**Giuseppe Caraciolo, Ed. & Pub.**
Via Cimarosa 180-A, 80127 Naples, Italy.
- Ospedali Italiani-Pediatria; e specialita chirurgiche. bi-m. ISSN 0030-6274

**Mario Cardinali, Ed. & Pub.**
Piazza Grande 64, Livorno, Italy.
- Livornocronaca; periodico indipendente. m. ISSN 0024-5321

**Caritas Internationalis**
Piazza San Calisto 16, 00153 Rome, Italy.
- Caritas Internationalis. International Yearbooks. a. ISSN 0069-0554

- Caritas Internationalis. Reports of General Assemblies. irreg., 1972, 9th. ISSN 0069-0562

**Edizioni Carrara**
Casella Postale 158, 24100 Bergamo, Italy.
- Organista. bi-m.

**Editoriale del Carriere della Sera**
Via Solferino 28, 201200 Milan, Italy.
- Carriere dei Ragazzi. w.

**Cartabianca**
Via Susani 2, Mantova, Italy.
- Cartabianca. q. ISSN 0008-6991

**Edizioni Carte Segrete**
Piazza d'Aracoeli 6, 00186 Rome, Italy.
- Carte Segrete; rivista-libro di letteratura ed arte. q. ISSN 0008-7025

**Beniamino Carucci Editore**
Casella Postale 12014, 00100 Rome, Italy.
- Cannocchiale; rivista trimestrale di cultura. q. ISSN 0008-5618

**Casa Cardinale Maffi**
Via Aurelia Nord 9, Cecina (Livorno), Italy.
- Casa Nostra. bi-m.

**Casa Dello Scugnizzo**
Piazza S. Gennaro a Materdei 3, Naples, Italy.
- Scugnizzo. q. ISSN 0036-9802 (Materdei Community Centre)

**Casa di Dante in Roma**
- Lectura Dantis Romana. (pub. by Casa Editrice Felice le Monnier)

**Casalini Libri**
50014 Fiesole, Italy.
- Diogenes; an international review of philosophy and humanistic studies. 4 per yr. ISSN 0012-3048 (International Council for Philosophy and Humanistic Studies)
- Yearbook of Italian Studies. irreg. (Italian Cultural Institute CN)

**Caselli Giovanni**
Via Tripoli 24, Biella, Italy.
- Eco dell'Industria Tessile. s-w. ISSN 0012-9526

**Gino Caserta, Ed. & Pub.**
Via Baiamonti, 10, Rome, Italy.
- Cinematografia Ita. m. ISSN 0009-7187

**Edizioni Casimiri**
Via S. Caterina da Siena 61, Rome, Italy.
- Psalterium; rivista internazionale di musica sacra. bi-m. ISSN 0033-2550

**Casino di Campione d' Italia**
Via Francesco, Redi 6, Milan, Italy.
- Rendez Vous. bi-m. ISSN 0034-4389

**Cassa Centrale di Risparmio V.E.**
Palermo, Italy.
- Economia e Credito. q. ISSN 0012-9771

**Cassa di Risparmio delle Provincie Lombarde**
Via Monte di Pieta 8, 20121 Milan, Italy.
- Cassa di Risparmio delle Provincie Lombarde Quarterly; bulletin on the Italian economy. q. ISSN 0008-7408
- Congiuntura Economica Lombarda. m. ISSN 0045-8082

**Cassa di Risparmio di Genova e Imperia**
15 via Cassa di Risparmio, I 16123 Genoa, Italy.
- Casana. q. ISSN 0008-719X

**Cassa di Soccorso e Malattia per i Dipendenti dell'Azienda Trasporti Municipali di Milano**
Via. P. Lomazzo 27, 20154 Milan, Italy.
- Cassa di Soccorso e Malattia per i Dipendenti dell'Azienda Trasporti Municipali di Milano. Bollettino d'Informazione. bi-m. ISSN 0008-7416

**Dott. Ottorimo Catani, Ed. & Pub.**
Riviera di Chiaia 127, Naples, Italy.
- Medico Italiano. w. ISSN 0025-8156 (Sindacato Unitario Medici d'Italia)

**Giacomo A. Caula, Ed. & Pub.**
Corso Fiume 16, Turin, Italy.
- Convegno Musicale; rivista di storia della musica. 3 per yr. ISSN 0010-8111

- Studia et Documenta Historiae Musicae: Bibliotheca. irreg. ISSN 0081-6388

**Cavalletto e Tavolozza**
Via Pomponazzi 6b, Milan, Italy.
- Cavalletto e Tavolozza. m. ISSN 0045-5997

**Giorgio Cavicchioli, Ed. & Pub.**
Via Andrea Doria 15, 10123 Turin, Italy.
- Eco degli Spettacoli; cinema, arte, sport. 40 per yr. ISSN 0012-9461
- Informazione Arte; critica, quotazioni, notizie; rassegna di attualita culturale ed artistica. m.

**Cenacolo di Cultura "Publius Ovidius Naso"**
- Circolo Letterario. (pub. by Ovidius)

**Edizioni del Centro**
Centro Camuno di Studi Preistorici, Capo di Ponte 25044, Italy.
- Centro Camuno di Studi Preistorici. Publicazioni. a. ISSN 0577-2176

**Centro Acustico Nazionale**
Belvedere Golfo Paradiso 21, 16036 Recco, Genoa, Italy.
- Audiotecnica; il problema del rumore. bi-m. ISSN 0004-7619

**Centro Archivistico di Ricerca e Documentazione Giornalistica**
Via Giano Parrasio 24, Rome, Italy.
- Centro Archivistico di Ricerca e Documentazione Giornalistica. Bolletino. m.

**Centro Auxologico Italiano di Piancavallo**
Via Ariosto, 20145 Milan, Italy.
- Acta Medica Auxologica. 3 per yr. ISSN 0001-6004

**Centro Campano Studi Francescani**
- Studi e Ricerche Francescane. (pub. by Edizioni Dehoniane)

**Centro Camuno di Studi Preistorico**
25044 Capo di Ponte, Brescia, Italy.
- Centro Camuno di Studi Preistorici. Bollettino. a. ISSN 0577-2168

**Centro Catechistico Salesiano**
- Armonia di Voci. (pub. by Edtrice Libreria Dottrina Cristiana)
- Note di Pastorale Giovanile. (pub. by Editrice Libreria Dottrina Cristiana)
- Parole di Vita. (pub. by Editrice Libreria Dottrina Cristiana)
- Rivista Liturgica. (pub. by Editrice Libreria Dottrina Cristiana)

**Centro Culturale degli Istituti Penali di Parma**
Piazzale S. Francesco 3, 43100 Parma, Italy.
- Vero Dialogo. bi-m. ISSN 0042-420X

**Centro Culturale San Fedele**
Via Ulrico Hoepli 3-5, Milan 20121, Italy.
- Rassegna San Fedele. a.

**Centro della Statistica Aziendale**
Via A. Baldesi 20, Florence, Italy.
- Centro della Statistica Aziendale. Lettere d'Affari. m.

**Centro di Cultura dell'Alto Adige**
Via Napoli 1, 39100 Bolzano, Italy.
- Cristallo; rassegna di varia umanita. 3 per yr. ISSN 0011-1449

**Centro di Documentazione Alpina**
Corso Moncalieri 23d, Turin 10131, Italy.
- Rivista della Montagna. q.

**Centro di Documentazione e Valorizzazione dell'Operosita Italiana**
Galleria del Corso 4, Milan, Italy.
- Ripresa Nazionale; rassegna economico-sociale. m. ISSN 0035-5534

**Centro di Documentazione Sul Movimento dei Disciplinati**
Casella Postale 130, Perugia 06100, Italy.
- Centro di Documentazione Sul Movimento dei Disciplinati. Quaderni. s-a. ISSN 0009-0026

**Centro di Educazione Professionale per Assistenti Sociali**
Piazza Cavalieri di Malta 2, Rome, Italy.
- International Review of Community Development. a. ISSN 0020-854X

**Centro di Orientamento Pastorale**
- Orientamenti Pastorali. (pub. by Edizioni Pastorali)

**Centro di Ricerca e Documentazione Luigi Einaudi**
Corso Appio Claudio, 7, Turin 10143, Italy.
- Biblioteca della Liberta. q. ISSN 0006-1654

**Centro di Ricerca per le Scienze Morali e Sociali**
- Homine. (pub. by Casa Editrice G. C. Sansoni S.p.A.)

**Centro di Studi e Ricerche "Mario Pannunzio"**
Via Barbaroux 2, 10122 Turin, Italy.
- Pannunzio. bi-m.

**Centro di Studi Salentini**
Palazzo Adorni, Via Umberto 132, 7300 Lecce, Italy.
- Studi Salentini. q. ISSN 0039-3002

**Centro di Studi Storici Toscani**
- Quaderni di Studi Storici Toscani. (pub. by Libreria L. de Re)

**Centro di Studi Sull'Antico Cristianesimo**
Universita di Catania, Piazzo Universita, Catania, Italy.
- Nuovo Didaskaleion; studi di letteratura e storia cristiana antica. s-a. ISSN 0029-635X

**Centro di Studie Tassiani, Bergamo**
24100 Bergamo, Via Pignolo 103, Italy.
- Studi Tassiani. a. ISSN 0081-6256

**Centro Didattico Nazionale di Studi e Documentazione di Firenze. Sezione di Letteratura Giovanile**
Via Scipione Ammirato 37, Florence, Italy.
- Schedario. bi-m. ISSN 0036-5955 (Co-Sponsors: Unions Internazionale per la Letteratura Giovanile; Foyer International du Livre de Jeunesse)

**Centro Didattico Nazionale per la Scuola Elementare**
Corso Vitt. Emanuele 21, 00186 Rome, Italy.
- Scuola di Base. 4-5 per yr. ISSN 0036-9837

**Centro Documentazione Anarchica**
Guido Reni 96, 10136 Turin, Italy.
- Centro Documentazione Anarcha. bi-m.

**Centro Economico Scambi Italo Nipponici**
Via Stimigliano 28, 00199 Rome, Italy.
- C E S I N News; relazioni economiche Italo-Nipponiche. m. ISSN 0007-8336

**Centro Editoriale Pubblicitario Italiano**
Via G. B. Martini 6, Rome, Italy.
- Metabolismo. bi-m. ISSN 0026-0509 (Societa Italiana per la Studio del Metabolismo Normale e Patologico)
- Rassegna di Medicina del Traffico. bi-m. ISSN 0048-6744 (Societa Italiana di Medicina del Traffico)
- Settimana Medica. s-m. ISSN 0037-2927

**Centro G. Zambon**
Universita di Milan, Via Venezian 1, Milan 20133, Italy.
- Applicazioni Biomediche del Calcolo Elettronico. q.

**Centro Internazionale di Giustizia Sociale**
Via Dego 4, 00168 Rome, Italy.
- Vera Giustizia Sociale. q. ISSN 0042-3599

**Centro Internazionale di Studi e di Relazioni Culturali**
Via Panisperna 261, 00184 Rome, Italy.
- Incontri Culturali. q. ISSN 0019-347X

**Centro Internazionale di Studi Rosminiani**
- Rivista Rosminiana di Filosofia e di Cultura. (pub. by Libreria Editoriale Sodalitas)

**Centro Internazionale Studi sull'Irrigazione**
- Irrigazione. (pub. by Gruppo Giornalistico Edagricole)

**Centro Internazionale Viabilita Invernale e Ingegneria Montana**
Corso Massimo d'Azeglio 13, 10126 Turin, Italy.
- Neve International. q. ISSN 0028-4114

**Centro Italiano Contro le Intossicazioni**
- Rivista di Tossicologia Sperimentale e Clinica. (pub. by Societa Editrice Universo)

**Centro Italiano di Gastroenterologia**
- Rassegna Italiana di Gastroenterologia. (pub. by Societa Editrice Universo)

**Centro Italiano di Parapsicologia**
Via Belvedere 87, 80127 Naples, Italy.
- Informazioni di Parapsicologia. 2 per yr. ISSN 0046-9491

**Centro Italiano di Ricerche e Informazione Sull'Economia delle Imprese Pubbliche e di Pubblico Interesse**
Via Fratelli Gabba 6, 20121 Milan, Italy.
- Economia Pubblica. m.

**Centro Italiano di Studi Amministrativi**
- Consiglio di Stato. (pub. by Casa Editrice Italedi)

**Centro Italiano Moda**
Casella Postale 19, San Remo, Italy.
- C. I. M. Notiziario; ente per l'incremento e la valorizzazione della moda italiana. s-a. ISSN 0007-8468

**Centro Italiano per lo Studio delle Relazioni Economiche Estere e Mercati**
Via. G. A. Guattani 8, Rome, Italy.
- Mondo Aperto; rivista di politica economica internazionale. bi-m. ISSN 0026-9492

**Centro Italiano Relazioni Umane**
Corso Vittorio Emanuele II, 287, Rome, Italy.
- ERREu. (Relazioni Umane) bi-m. ISSN 0014-0260

**Centro Italiano Studi per la Pesca**
Via Cassia 6, 00131 Rome, Italy.
- Rivista di Diritto Economia e Tecnica della Pesca. q. ISSN 0035-6115

**Centro Italiano Sviluppo Impeighi Acciaio**
Piazza Velasca 8, 20122 Milan, Italy.
- Acciaio. m. ISSN 0001-4559

**Centro Italiano Tessili-Abbigliamento-Alta Moda**
- Linea Italiana. (pub. by Arnoldo Mondadori Editore)

**Centro Ligure di Storia Sociale**
Piazza Campetto 8A, 16123 Genoa, Italy.
- Movimento Operaio e Socialista; rivista trimestrale di storia e bibliografia. q. ISSN 0027-2817

**Centro Nazional Associazione Mariana**
Via Francesco Albergotti 75, 00167 Rome, Italy.
- Maria Nostra Luce. m.
- Verso l'Azzurro. m. ISSN 0042-4374

**Centro Nazionale di Prevenzione e Difesa Sociale. Commissione Permanente di Sociologia del Diritto**
- Sociologia del Diritto. (pub. by Casa Editrice Dott. A. Giuffre)

**Centro Nazionale di Studi Napoleonici e di Storia dell'Elba**
- Rivista Italiana di Studi Napoleonici. (pub. by Casa Editrice Leo S. Olschki)

**Centro Nazionale Economi di Comunita**
- Annuario Cattolico d'Italia. (pub. by Editoriale Italiana)
- Insieme. (pub. by Editoriale Italiana)

**Centro Nazionale per l'Edilizie e la Tecnica Ospedaliera**
- Tecnica Ospedaliera. (pub. by Tecniche Nuove s. r. l.)

**Centro Nazionale Strade e Motorizzazione**
Belvedere Golfo Paradiso 49, 16036 Recco Sodea, Genoa, Italy.
- Tecnica e Circolazione Autostradale; il giornale della strada. fortn. ISSN 0040-1773

**Centro Orientamento Immigrati del Mezzogiorno**
Via E. de Gennaro 67, 86043 Cascaleda, Italy.
- Risveglio del Molise e del Mezzogiorno; rassegna di attualita e di problemi meridionali. m. ISSN 0035-5623

**Centro per la Cinematografia Scientifica**
Universita di Padova, 35100 Padua, Italy.
- Rassegna Internazionale del Film Scientifico - Didattico. biennial. ISSN 0079-9726

**Centro per la Statistica Aziendale**
Via A. Baldesi 20, 50131 Florence, Italy.
- Italy. Centro per la Statistica Aziendale. Index. m. ISSN 0021-3101
- Lettere d'Affari. ISSN 0024-1326
- Previsioni a Breve Termine. m.

**Centro per le Antichita e la Storia dell'Arte del Vicino Oriente**
Via Caroncini 27, Rome, Italy.
- Oriens Antiquus. q. ISSN 0030-5189 (Istituto per l'Oriente)

**Centro per le Relazioni Italo-Arabe**
Via Caroncini 19, Rome, Italy.
- Levante. 9 per yr. ISSN 0024-1504

**Centro per lo Sviluppo dei Trasporti Aerei**
Via Sardegna 38, 00187 Rome, Italy.
- Aviazione Civile. fortn.
- Trasporti Aerei; rivista, economia e politica dei trasporti. s-m. ISSN 0041-1795

**Centro Piombinese di Studi Storici**
- Ricerche Storiche. (pub. by Casa Editrice Leo S. Olschki)

**Centro Regionale di Programmazione**
Via Mameli, 106, Cagliari, Italy.
- Programmazione in Sardegna.

**Centro Ricerche e Studi Amplifon**
Via Ripamonti, 129, 20141 Milan, Italy.
- Notiziario Bibliografico di Audiologia. s-a.

**Centro Salesiano Dello Spettacolo**
Via M. Ausiliatrice 32, 10121 Turin, Italy.
- Cineschedario - Letture Drammatiche. m. ISSN 0024-1458

**Centro Sperimentale di Avicoltura**
Via Giosue Borsi 21, Florence, Italy.
- Selezione per l'Avicoltore; settimanale della pollicoltura italiana. w. ISSN 0037-1505

**Centro Sportivo Italiano**
Via delle Conciliazione 3, 00193 Rome, Italy.
- Stadium; problemi dello sport. s-m.

**Centro Studi Architettura OUROBOROS**
Piazza San Lorenzo 5, 50129 Florence, Italy.
- Psicon. irreg.

**Centro Studi Comunita Europee**
Corso Vittorio Emanuele 193, 70122 Bari, Italy.
- Eurosud. w. ISSN 0014-3235
- Eurosud - Il Mezzogiorno e le Comunita' Europee; rivista di politica economica sociale e finanziaria. bi-m. ISSN 0026-1912

**Centro Studi del Presbiterio Diocesano**
Via Covignano, 238, 47037 Rimini, Italy.
- Rivista Diocesana Rimini. bi-m. ISSN 0035-6662

**Centro Studi Dialogic dell' Istituto Euromediterraneo di Scienze Umane della Citta- Studio di Urbino**
- Dialogo. (pub. by A. Testa, Ed. & Pub.)

**Centro Studi e Pubblicazioni della Federazione Italiana dei Consorzi Agrari**
Via Yser 14, 00198 Rome, Italy.
- Notiziario Agricolo. d. ISSN 0029-4314

**Centro Studi e Pubbliche Relazioni Petrolifere**
see C E S P E T R O L

**Centro Studi Emigrazione**
Via Calandrelli M, 00153 Rome, Italy.
- Dossier Europa-Emigrazione. m.
- Studi Emigrazione/Etudes Migrations. 4 per yr. ISSN 0039-2936

**Centro Studi G. Toniolo**
Piazza Toniolo 2, Pisa, Italy.
- Studi Economici i Sociali. q.

**Centro Studi Investimenti Sociali**
Piazza di Novella, 2-00, 00186 Rome, Italy.
- C E N S I S Quindicinale di Note e Commenti. s-m. ISSN 0007-8271

**Centro Studi Metodologici**
2, via della Signora, 20122 Milan, Italy.
- Nuovo 75. a.

**Centro Studi per la Magna Grecia**
Istituto di Archeologia, Via Giovanni Palladino, 39, 80138 Naples, Italy.
- Centro Studi per la Magna Grecia, Naples. Pubblicazioni Proprie. irreg., 1969, no. 6. ISSN 0069-2204
- Convegno di Studi Sulla Magna Grecia. Atti. a. ISSN 0069-9748

**Centro Studi per le Fonti della Storia della Chiesa nel Veneto**
- Ricerche di Storia Sociale e Religiosa. (pub. by Edizioni di Storia e Letteratura)

**Centro Studi Politici Economici e Sociali Sen. A. Rizzati**
Corso Italia 9, 34170 Gorizia, Italy.
- Iniziativa Isontina. 3 per yr. ISSN 0020-1359

**Centro Studi Psicologici "Lo Spazio"**
- Quadrangolo. (pub. by Bulzoni Editore)

**Centro Studi Russia Cristiana**
Via Martinengo 16, Milan, Italy.
- Russia Cristiana. bi-m. ISSN 0036-018X

**Centro Studi Sociali**
Piazza S. Fedele 4, 20121 Milan, Italy.
- Aggiornamenti Sociali. m. ISSN 0002-094X

**Centro Studi Terzo Mondo**
Via G. B. Morgagni 39, 20129 Milan, Italy.
- Corso di Sociologia. m.
- Quaderni Terzo Mondo. q.
- Terzo Mondo/Third World; rivista trimestrale di studi, ricerche e documentazione sui paesi afro-asiatici e latino-americani. q. ISSN 0040-392X

**Centro Studi U S M I**
Via Zanardelli 32, 00186 Rome, Italy.
- F. I. R. O. Quaderni. q. ISSN 0014-5912
- Religiose nell' Apostolato Diretto. q. ISSN 0034-4036

**Centro Teatrale Internazionale di Documentazione e di Collaborazione Tra Teatri di Ricerca e Universitari**
Via Fabiola 1, 00152 Rome, Italy.
- Theatron; revista quindicinale di cultura, documentazione e informazione teatrale. fortn. ISSN 0040-5604

**Centro Universitario Sportivo Italiana**
Via Angelo Brofferio 7, 00195 Rome, Italy.
- Sport Universitario. q. ISSN 0490-5113

**Ceramurgica S.p.A.**
Casella Postale 174, 48018 Faenza, Italy.
- Ceramurgia; tecnologia ceramica. q. ISSN 0045-6152

**Cerastico Editore**
Via Brisa 7, Milan, Italy.
- Investimenti e Prospettive. m. ISSN 0021-0021

**Gianni Cerutti, Ed. & Pub.**
Via Giulietti 6, 28100 Novara, Italy.
- Nord; settimanale indipendente d'informazione. w.

**Chambre de Commerce Francaise et d'Industrie en Italie**
Via Meravigli, 12, I-20123-Milan, Italy.
- Annuaire du Commerce Franco-Italien. a. ISSN 0069-6625

**Chiesa Santa Rosalia**
Cagliari 09100, Italy.
- San Salvatore da Horta. m. ISSN 0036-424X

**Chiesa Universale Giuris-Davidica**
Via Tevere 21, 00198 Rome, Italy.
- Torre Davidica. 3-4 per yr. ISSN 0040-960X

**Chiriotti Editori**
Box 66, Pinerolo 10064, Italy.
- Industrie Alimentari. m. ISSN 0019-901X
- Industrie delle Bevande. bi-m.
- Tecnica Molitoria. m. ISSN 0040-1862

**Chirurgia Triveneta**
Divisione Chirurgica, Ospedale Civile Maggiore, Piazzale Stefanil, 37100 Verona, Italy.
- Chirurgia Triveneta. q. ISSN 0009-4811

**Christian Democratic World Union**
107 via del Plebiscito, Rome 00186, Italy.
- Cahiers d'Etudes. irreg.

- Christian Democratic World Union. Information Bulletin. irreg.
- Panorama Democrate Chretien. irreg.

**Ciceroniana**
Piazza dei Cavalieri di Malta 2, Rome, Italy.
- Ciceroniana; rivista di studi Ciceroniani. s-a. ISSN 0009-6687

**Ciclismo d'Italia**
Via Ponte Vetero 22, Milan, Italy.
- Ciclismo d'Italia. w. ISSN 0009-6695 (Federazione Ciclistica Italiana)

**Cidue Edizioni s.r.l.**
Via Manzoni 21, 50121 Florence, Italy.
- Cinquemattoni; informazione e promozione immobiliare. m.

**Cimone**
Via della Balduina 67, 00136 Rome, Italy.
- Cimone. q. ISSN 0009-6865

**Cinecorriere**
c/o Alberto Crucilla, Ed., Circonvallazione Clodia 80, 00195 Rome, Italy.
- Cinecorriere. m.

**Cinemasud**
Via degli Imbinibo, Palazzo Lazzerini, Avellino, Italy.
- Cinemasud; rivista neorealista di avanguardia. m. ISSN 0009-7160

**Edizione Cinemeccanica**
Viale Campania 23, Milan, Italy.
- Rivista Tecnica di Cinematografia; elettroacustica, televisione. s-a. ISSN 0035-7081

**Editrice Ciranna Latina**
Viale di Villa Pamphili 199, Rome 00152, Italy.
- Biologia Culturale. q. ISSN 0006-310X

**Circolo Artistico di Bologna**
Via Clavature 8, Bologna, Italy.
- Iterarte. bi-m.

**Circolo Cooperazione Concordia**
Casella Postale 1432, 16100 Genova, Italy.
- Concordia; voce periodica internationale. s-a. ISSN 0010-5252 (Co-Sponsor: Accademia Universale Marinara "Cristoforo Colombo")

**Circolo Culturale A.F. Formiggini**
Piazza Giuseppe Mazzini, 25, Modena, Italy.
- Quaderni Modenesi. q.

**Circolo Culturale G. Faldella**
Saluggia - (Vercelli) 13040, Italy.
- Fischietto di Saluggia. m. ISSN 0015-2870

**Circolo del Cinema di Rovigo**
Via All'ara 8, Rovigo, Italy.
- Cinecronache. m. ISSN 0009-7020

**Circolo Speleologico Romano**
Via Ulisse Aldrovandi 18, I 00197 Rome, Italy.
- Circolo Speleologico Romano. Notiziario. s-a. ISSN 0009-7268

**Circulo Culturale Costa Rossa**
Via Roma 55, Cuneo, Italy.
- Costarossa; rivista subalpinia di studi politici e sociali. q.

**Cisalpino-Goliardica**
Via Bassini 17-2, 20133 Milan, Italy.
- Giornale degli Economisti e Annali di Economia. bi-m. ISSN 0017-0097 (Universita Commerciale Luigi Bocconi)
- Si e No. 3 per yr.

**Edizioni Cisterciensi**
Piazza Tempio di Diana 14, I-00153 Rome, Italy.
- Analecta Cisterciensia. s-a. ISSN 0003-2476

**Citta di Vita**
Piazza S. Croce 16, 50122 Florence, Italy.
- Citta di Vita; bimestrale di religione arte e scienza. bi-m. ISSN 0009-7632

**Citta e Societa**
Piazza S. Ambrogio 15, Milan, Italy.
- Citta e Societa; studi e analisi sui problemi delle comunita urbane. bi-m. ISSN 0009-7640

**Edizioni Citta Eterna**
Piazza Cola di Rienzo, 6919, 00192 Roma, Italy.
● Rivista del Cinematografo; e della
comunicazione sociale. m. ISSN 0035-5879

**Citta Futura**
Via Rocca Simbalda 10, 00199 Rome, Italy.
● Citta Futura. m. ISSN 0045-6977

**Citta Nuova**
Via degli Scipioni 265, 00192 Rome, Italy.
● Citta Nuova. fortn.

**Civica Biblioteca A. Maj**
Piazza Vecchia 15, Bergamo, Italy.
● Bergomun; studi di letteratura, storia e arte. q.
ISSN 0005-8955

**Civica Stazione Idrobiologica di Milano**
Viale Gadio, 2, 20121 Milan, Italy.
● Civica Stazione Idrobiologica di Milano.
Quaderni. irreg.

**Civilta Cattolica**
Via di Porta Pinciana 1, 00187 Rome, Italy.
● Civilta Cattolica. s-m. ISSN 0009-8167

**Civilta Italica**
Piazza del Gesu, 49, Rome, Italy.
● Civilta Italica; mensile di studi politici economici
sociali. m. ISSN 0412-6963

**Edizioni Civitas**
Via Tirso 92, Rome, Italy.
● Civitas; rivista di studi politici. m. ISSN 0009-
8191

**Claretian Juridical Institute in Rome**
● Commentarium pro Religiosis et Missionariis.
(pub. by Editrice Commentarium pro Religiosis)

**Clinica Chirurgica dell'Universita**
Policlinico Borgo Roma, Verona, Italy.
● Chirurgia Italiana. bi-m. ISSN 0009-4773

**Clinica della Malattie Nervose e Mentali**
Via Re Morgani-Policlinico, Florence, Italy.
● Rivista di Patologia Nervosa e Mentale. bi-m.
ISSN 0035-6433

**Edizioni Clinica Europea**
Via Concordia 20, Rome, Italy.
● Clinica Europea; attualita' di medicina. bi-m.
ISSN 0009-9007

**Clinica Oculistica**
Policlinico S. Orsola, Bologna, Italy.
● Rivista Oto-Neuro-Oftalmologica. ISSN 0048-
8410

**Clinica Ostetrica e Ginecologica**
Universita di Genova, Genoa, Italy.
● Monitore Ostetrico-Ginecologico di
Endocrinologia e del Metabolismo. bi-m. ISSN
0026-9778 (Societa Italiana per gli Studi Sulla
Sterilita)

**Clinica Ostetricia e Ginecologia "L. Mangiagalli"**
Via Commenda 12, Milan, Italy.
● Anali di Ostetricia Ginecologia Medicina
Perinatale. bi-m. ISSN 0300-0087

**Clinica Pediatrica**
Via Massarenti 11, Bologna, Italy.
● Clinica Pediatrica. m. ISSN 0009-9058

**Club Alpino Italiano**
Via Barbaroux 1, Turin, Italy.
● Club Alpino Italiano. Rivista Mensile. m. ISSN
0009-9511

**Club Alpino Italiano Sezioni Trivenete**
D.D. 1737-a, Venice, Italy.
● Alpi Venete. s-a. ISSN 0002-6468

**Club de Commone**
c/o Ed. Lorenzo Janni, Via Cavour 38, 20094
Corsico (Milan), Italy.
● Automoto Giornale. m.

**Libreria Cocco**
Piazza Jenne 31, Cagliari, Italy.
● Cagliari. Universita. Faculta di Scienze. Seminario.
Rendiconti. q. ISSN 0041-8951

**Collegio Alberoni**
● Divus Thomas. (pub. by Editrice Divus Thomas)

**Collegio Alla Querce**
Via della Piazzola 44, Florence 50133, Italy.
● Querce; rivista giovanile di cultura e
d'informazione. q. ISSN 0033-6262

**Collegio Araldico**
Via S. Maria dell'Anima 16, Rome, Italy.
● Rivista Araldica. m. ISSN 0035-5771

**Collegio Assistenti**
● Presenza Pastorale. (pub. by Azione Cattolica
Italiana)

**Collegio dei Geometri di Torino e Provincia e
dell'Union Regionale Collegi Geometri del
Piemonte e della Valle d'Aosta**
Corso Re Umberto 57, Turin, Italy.
● Geometra. q. ISSN 0016-7959

**Collegio Ingegneri Ferroviari Italiani**
Via Giolitti 34, Rome, Italy.
● Ingegneria Ferroviaria; rivista di tecnica ed
economia dei trasporti. m. ISSN 0020-0956
● Tecnica Professionale. m.

**Collegio Internazionale S. Lorenzo da Brindisi**
G.R.A. Km. 68,800, 00163 Rome, Italy.
● Laurentianum. q. ISSN 0023-902X (Capuchin-
Franciscan Order)

**Collegio San Bonaventura. Commissione Storica**
Colle S. Antonio, 00046 Grottaferrata (Roma),
Italy.
● Archivum Franciscanum Historicum. q. ISSN
0004-0665

**Collegium Internationale Chirugiae Digestivae**
● Surgical Gastroenterology. (pub. by Piccin
Editore)

**Editrice Collins**
Via della Commenda 41, 20122 Milan, Italy.
● Ferramenta e Casalinghi. m.

**Colloqui Cremonese**
Via Monteverdi 2, Cremona 26100, Italy.
● Colloqui Cremonese. q. ISSN 0010-132X

**Comando General dell'Arma dei Carabinieri**
Viale Romania 45, 00196 Rome, Italy.
● Carabiniere. m. ISSN 0008-610X

**Comando Scuola di Guerra**
00053 Civitavecchia, Italy.
● Alere Flammam; bollettino d'informazione della
Scuola di Guerra. s-a.

**Combattente della Liberta**
Via Quattro Fontane 25, 00184 Rome, Italy.
● Combattente della Liberta. m. ISSN 0010-2148

**Combustione e Combustibili**
Via Burchielli, 1, Casella Postale 45, 26100
Cremona, Italy.
● Combustione e Combustibili. a. ISSN 0069-6390

**Comitato Civico Nazionale**
Via del Corso 300, 00186 Rome, Italy.
● Azione. m. ISSN 0005-2558

**Comitato di Esperti Statistici per Il Settore
Petrolifero**
Ministero dell'Industria e del Commercio, Rome,
Italy.
● Industria del Petrolio in Italia. a. ISSN 0073-7275

**Comitato Glaciologico Italiano**
Via Academia delle Scienze N. 5, I-10123 Turin,
Italy.
● Comitato Glaciologico Italiano. Bollettino. a.
ISSN 0084-8948

**Comitato Italiano per Lo Studio dei Problemi della
Popolazione**
Via Nomentana 41, Rome, Italy.
● Genus. w. ISSN 0016-6987

**Comitato Nazionale per Il Turismo**
Piazza Venezia N.11, 00187 Rome, Italy.
● Informatore Turistico; agenzia settimanale di
notizie. w. ISSN 0020-076X

**Comitato Nazionale per l'Energia Nucleare**
Redazione Notiziario, Viale Regina Margherita, 125
- Rome 00198, Italy.
● C. N. E. N. Notiziario. m. ISSN 0007-8751

**Comitato Nazionale per l'Organizzazione Scientifica**
Viale dell'Astronomia 30, 00144 Rome, Italy.
● Organizzazione Scientifica. m.

**Comitato Nazionale Serre**
● Informatore di Ortoflorofrutticoltura. (pub. by
Gruppo Giornalistico Edagricole)

**Comitato Olimpico Nazionale Italiano**
● Rivista di Diritto Sportivo. (pub. by Casa Editrice
Dott. A. Giuffre)

**Comitato per le Scienze Politche e Sociali**
● Scienze Sociali. (pub. by Societa Editrice Il
Mulino)

**Comitato Regionale della Democrazia Cristiana**
Piazza S. Giovanni 5, 34122 Trieste, Italy.
● Popolo del Friuli-Venezia Giulia. 10 per yr. ISSN
0032-437X

**Editrice Commentarium pro Religiosis**
Via Giacomo Medici 5, 00153 Rome, Italy.
● Commentarium pro Religiosis et Missionariis. q.
ISSN 0010-2598 (Claretian Juridical Institute in
Rome)

**Commercianti Italiani Filatelici**
Piazza Paleocapa 1, 10121 Turin, Italy.
● Cronaca Filatelica; rivista informativa del catalogo
unificato. m.

**Commercio del Colore**
Via Palmaria 4, 20161 Milan, Italy.
● Commercio del Colore. bi-m.

**Commercio del Popolo**
c/o E. Schiavello, Ed., Via Ponte Severso 19, Milan,
Italy.
● Commercio del Popolo. m.

**Commercio Italiana per la Gran Bretagna e il
Commonwealth**
Lungotevere Mellini 39, 00193 Rome, Italy.
● British Italian Trade Review. m. ISSN 0007-0858
● Segnalazioni della Camera di Commercio Italiana
per la Gran Bretagna e Il Commonwealth. (pub.
by Tipografia della Pace)

**Commissariato Nazionale per Il Terz' Ordine
Francescano**
Via delle Mura Aurelie 9, 00165 Rome, Italy.
● Fiamma Nova. m.

**Commissione delle Comunita Europee**
Via Poli 29, 00187 Rome, Italy.
● Comunita Europee; di divulgazione ed
orientamento. m. ISSN 0010-5058

**Compagnia Balestrieri Lucca. Commissione Storica**
Casermetta S. Donato, Casella Postale 314, 100
Lucca, Italy.
● Actum Luce; rivista de Studi Lucchesi. s-a.

**Compagnia Italiana Turismo**
Piazza della Repubblica 68, Rome, Italy.
● Cosmorama; viaggi e turismo. q. ISSN 0045-8716

**Editrice Compositori s.r.l.**
Viale 12 Giugno 1, 40124 Bologna, Italy.
● Giornale di Fisica. q. ISSN 0017-0283 (Societa
Italiana di Fisica)
● Lettere al Nuovo Cimento. 3 per yr. ISSN 0024-
1318 (Societa Italiana di Fisica)
● Rivista del Nuovo Cimento. q. ISSN 0035-5917
(Societa Italiana di Fisica)
● Societa Italiana di Fisica. Bollettino. irreg. ISSN
0037-8801
● Societa Italiana di Fisica. Nuovo Cimento A. s-m.
● Societa Italiana di Fisica. Nuovo Cimento B. m.

**Comune**
Vicolo del Cinque 22, Rome 00153, Italy.
● Comune. q. ISSN 0010-4922

**Comune di Bologna. Direzione dei Servizi
d'Informazione**
Palazzo d'Accursio, Piazza Maggiore 6, Bologna,
Italy.
● Bologna; notizie del comune quindicinale. w.

**Comune di Genova**
Via Garibaldi 9, Genoa, Italy.
● Genova. m. ISSN 0016-6901
● L. G. Argomenti. (Letteratura Giovanile
Argomenti) q.

**Comune di Lodi. Biblioteca Comunale Laudense**
Corso Umberto 63, 20075 Lodi, Milan, Italy.
- Archivio Storico Lodigiano. s-a. ISSN 0004-0347

**Comune di Padova**
Ufficio Stampa, Gabinetto del Sindaco, Padua, Italy.
- Patavium. bi-m. ISSN 0009-7624

**Comune di Roma. Officio di Statistica e Censimento**
Via della Greca 5, 00186 Rome, Italy.
- Rome. Ufficio di Statistica e Censimento.
  Bollettino Statistico. irreg; latest 1968, no. 8.
  ISSN 0010-4957

**Comune di Trieste**
Piazza Unita d'Italia, Trieste, Italy.
- Revista della Citta di Trieste. m. ISSN 0035-6972

**Edizioni di Comunita**
Via Manzoni 12, 20121 Milan, Italy.
- Comunita; rivista quadrimestrale di informazione
  culturale. 3 per yr. ISSN 0010-504X
- Italia Nella Politica Internazionale. a. (Istituto
  Affari Internazionali)

**Comunita Europea dei Giornalisti**
Via Venti Settembre 26, 00187 Rome, Italy.
- Giornalismo Europeo. m. ISSN 0017-0518

**Comunita Gnostica**
- Conoscenza. (pub. by Carlesi Loris, Ed. & Pub.)

**Comunita Israelitica di Milano**
Via Guastalla 19, 20122 Milan, Italy.
- Comunita Israelitica di Milano. Bollettino. m.
  ISSN 0010-5074

**Comunita Israelitica di Roma**
Lungotevere Cenci, 00186 Rome, Italy.
- Shalom. m. ISSN 0037-3265

**Comunita Mediterranea**
Lungotevere Flaminio 34, 00196 Rome, Italy.
- Comunita Mediterranea; rivista di diritto e
  relazioni internazionali, politica economica e
  finanziari. q. ISSN 0045-7981

**Conciliatore**
Corso di Porta Vittoria 32, 20122 Milan, Italy.
- Conciliatore. q. ISSN 0010-5228

**Edizioni Conde Nast S.p.A.**
Piazza Castello 27, 20121 Milan, Italy.
- Casa Vogue. m. ISSN 0008-7173
- Lei. m.
- Uomo Mare. bi-m.
- Uomo Vogue. m.
- Vogue (Italy) 13 per yr. ISSN 0042-8027
- Vogue Bambini. q.

**Confederazione Cooperativa Italiana**
- Italia Cooperativa. (pub. by Editoriale Cooperativa
  Borge)

**Confederazione delle Libere Associazioni Artigane Italiane**
Piazzetta Pattari 4, Milan, Italy.
- Previdenza Sociale nell'Artigianato. bi-m. ISSN
  0032-809X

**Confederazione Generale Agricoltura Italiana**
- Mondo Agricolo. (pub. by Societa Editrice
  Periodici Enotria)

**Confederazione Generale dell' Industria Italiana**
Promotion Office, Piazza Venezia 11, 00187 Rome,
Italy.
- Italian Business. m. ISSN 0021-289X
- Repertorio del Film Industriale. (pub. by Franco
  Angeli Editore)

**Confederazione Generale Italiana del Commercio e del Turismo**
Piazza Gioacchino Belli N.2, Rome, Italy
(Subscriptions to: via Boschetti 1, Milan, Italy)
- Commercio Turismo. w. ISSN 0017-0151

**Confederazione Italiana d'Azienda**
- Realta. (pub. by Publindex s.r.l.)

**Confederazione Italiana dei Servizi Pubblici degli Enti Locali**
- C I S P E L Notizie. (pub. by Editrice
  C.I.S.P.E.L.)
- Confederazione Italiana dei Servizi Pubblici degli
  Enti Locali. Annuario. (pub. by Editrice
  C.I.S.P.E.L)

- Impresa Pubblica. (pub. by Editrice C.I.S.P.E.L.)
- Notizario Interfederale. (pub. by Editrice
  C.I.S.P.E.L.)

**Confederazione Italiana Sindacati Lavoratori**
- Conquiste del Lavoro. (pub. by Editrice
  Finlavoro)

**Confederazione Nazionale Coltivatori Diretti**
Via 24 Maggio, 43, 00187 Rome, Italy.
- Coltivatore. m.

**Congregazione dei Missionari di S. Carlo**
Via Scalabrini 3, 36061 Bassano del Grappa
(Vicenza), Italy.
- Emigrato Italiano. m. ISSN 0013-6697

**Congregazione di S. Giuseppe (Giuseppini del Murialdo)**
Via della Fanella 39, 00148 Rome, Italy.
- Vita Giuseppina. m. ISSN 0042-7276

**Congregazione Universale della Santa Casa**
60025 Loreto, (Ancona), Italy.
- Santa Casa di Loreto. Messaggio. m; English edt.
  bi-m. ISSN 0036-116X

**Consiglio della Gioventu Evangelica Italiana**
Via Monte Grappa 62b, 20092 Cinisello, Milan,
Italy.
- Gioventu Evangelica. bi-m. ISSN 0017-0542

**Consiglio Nazionale degli Ingegneri**
- Ingegnere Italiano. (pub. by Propaganda Editoriale
  Grafica S. p. A.)

**Consiglio Nazionale delle Ricerche**
Ufficio Pubblicazioni, Piazzale delle Scienze 7,
Rome, Italy.
- Ricerca Scientifica; rendiconti dell'attivita del
  Consiglio Nazionale delle Richerche. bi-m. ISSN
  0035-5011
- Ricerche di Automatica. (pub. by Edizioni
  Scientifiche Inglesi Americane)
- Ricerche Sulle Dimore Rurali in Italia. (pub. by
  Casa Editrice Leo S. Olschki)
- Tecnica Italiana; rivista di ingegneria. m. ISSN
  0040-1846

**Consiglio Nazionale delle Ricerche. Istituto di Elaborazione della Informazione**
c/o Angela Cocchella, Admin. Secretary, Via S.
Maria 44, 56100 Pisa, Italy.
- Calcolo. q. ISSN 0008-0624

**Consiglio Nazionale per la Professione; Federazione Nazionale dei Periti Industriali**
- Perito Industriale. (pub. by S A G S A S.p.A.)

**Consiglio Regionale delle Miniere**
- Rivista Mineraria Siciliana. (pub. by S. F.
  Flaccovio Editore)

**Consorzio Agrario Provinciale**
Piazzale Barezzi, 3 Parma, Italy.
- Avvenire Agricolo. m. ISSN 0005-2361

**Consorzio Agrario Provinciale di Forli**
Via Pedriali 1, Forli, Italy.
- Agricoltura Romagnola. s-m. ISSN 0002-1296

**Consorzio Nazionale Cooperativa Pescatori ed Affini**
Via Tirso 90, 00198 Rome, Italy.
- Corriere della Pesca. m.

**Consorzio Nazionale Dettaglianti**
Via Michelino 59, 40127 Bologna, Italy.
- Conad. m.

**Consorzio Provinciale Istruzione Tecnica**
Piazza Solferino 7, Turin 10121, Italy.
- Istruzione Tecnica e Realizzazioni. q. ISSN 0021-
  2687

**Consorzio Provinciale per la Pubblica Lettura**
Strada Maggiore 71, 40100 Bologna, Italy.
- Consorzio Provinciale per la Pubblica Lettura.
  Informazione Bibliografica. q.

**Consulente Immobiliare**
Via Vittor Pisani 16, 20124 Milan, Italy.
- Consulente Immobiliare. m. ISSN 0010-7050

**Consulta Agricoltura e Foreste delle Venezie**
S. Croce 270/B, Piazzale Roma, 30125 Venice,
Italy.
- Agricoltura delle Venezie. m. ISSN 0002-1261

**Controborghese**
Via Vignali 5, Frosinone, Italy.
- Controborghese. m. ISSN 0010-8006

**Convento Cappuccini**
C.P. Ferrovia, 42100 Reggio Emilia, Italy.
- Frate Francesco. m. ISSN 0016-0091

**Convento S. Antonio al Monte**
Rieti, Italy.
- Valle Santa di Rieti; periodico di cultura e
  propaganda Francescana. q. ISSN 0042-2304
  (Santuari Francescani Valle di Rieti)

**Coop Italia**
Viale Famagosta 75, 20142 Milan, Italy.
- Coop Italia. bi-m.

**Editrice Cooperativa**
Via Tagliamento 25, 00198 Rome, Italy.
- Cooperazione e Societa. q. ISSN 0010-8499 (Lega
  Nazionale delle Cooperative e Mutue)
- Cooperazione Italiana. m. ISSN 0010-8510 (Lega
  Nazionale delle Cooperative e Mutue)

**Editoriale Cooperativa Borge**
Santo Spitito 78, 00193 Roma, Italy.
- Italia Cooperativa. w. (Confederazione
  Cooperativa Italiana)

**Cooperativa E F F E**
Piazza Campo Marzio F, 00186 Rome, Italy.
- Effe. m.

**Cooperativa Editrice Nuova Cultura**
Via Broseta 2, Bergamo, Italy.
- Passato e Presente; rivista di lotta ideologica e
  politica per la rifondazione del movimento
  marxista-leninista. q.

**Editrice Cooperativa Letteratura Arte**
50123 Florence, Italy.
- F D L; rivista trimestrale di letteratura, arte,
  cultura. q.

**Cooperativa Libera Stampa**
Via della Trinita dei Pellegrini 12, 00186 Rome,
Italy.
- Noi Donne. w. ISSN 0029-0920 (Unione Donne
  Italiane)

**Cooperativa Libraria Universitaria**
Piazza Verdi 2a, Bologna, Italy.
- Statistica. q. ISSN 0039-0380

**Cooperativa Vie Nuove s.r.l.**
Via Zuretti, 34, 20125 Milan, Italy.
- Giorni. w. ISSN 0046-5984

**Editrice "Cor Unum" Figlie della Chiesa**
Viale Vaticano 62, 00165 Rome, Italy.
- Mater Ecclesiae. 3 per yr. ISSN 0025-522X

**Cordani Editore**
36 via Donatello, 20131 Milan, Italy.
- Shop. bi-m.

**Corpo Nazionale Giovani Esploratori Italiani. Clan Nazionale Seniores**
P. Liberta 10, 00192 Rome, Italy.
- Scautismo; rivista di divulgazione del metodo
  educativo scout. q. ISSN 0036-5696

**Corriere del Teatro**
Corso Vittorio Emanuele 1, 20122 Milan, Italy.
- Corriere del Teatro. bi-m. ISSN 0010-9215

**Editoriale del Corriere della Sera**
Via Solferino 28, 20100 Milan, Italy.
- Amica. w.
- Brava. w.
- Corrierboy. w.
- Corriere dei Piccoli. w. ISSN 0010-9185
- Domenica del Corriere. w. ISSN 0012-5296
- Mondo. w.

**Corriere Internazionale del Teatro**
Via Goldoni 32, Milan, Italy.
- Corriere Internazionale del Teatro. bi-m. ISSN
  0010-9266

**Corriere Internazionale della Musica**
20123, via Carducci, Milan 8, Italy.
- Chie - Dove; Annuario dell'Industria Fonografica e dell'Editoria Musicale in Italia. a.
- Musica e Dischi. m. ISSN 0027-4526

**Corriere Nuova Europa**
Via Filippo Casini 8-7, 00153 Rome, Italy.
- Corriere Nuova Europa; periodico culturale collaborazione Europea. bi-m. ISSN 0574-1602

**Corrispondenza Socialista**
Via Milano 42, Rome, Italy.
- Corrispondenza Socialista. m. ISSN 0010-9304

**Corso Andrea Podesta**
5A-20 Genoa, Italy.
- Marina Italiana; Rassegna delle Industrie del Mare. m. ISSN 0025-309X

**Cortex**
Via Tonale 49, Varese, Italy.
- Cortex; journal devoted to study of the nervous system and behavior. q. ISSN 0010-9452

**Costituente di Destra**
Via del Corso 75, Rome, Italy.
- Democrazia Nazionale; mensile internazionale di cultura e politica. m.

**Goffredo Cozzi, Ed. & Pub.**
Via Santa Prisca 15, Rome, Italy
(Subscr. Address: Casella Postale 5027, Rome, Italy)
- Rivista Italiana del Petrolio; e delle altre fonti di energia. m. ISSN 0035-6778

**Crisan**
Via Monte Leone 2, Milan, Italy.
- Ricerca Sociale; quadrimestrale di sociologia urbana, rurale e cooperazione. 3 per yr. (Universita degli Studi di Bologna. Centro Studi Sui Problemi della Citta e del Territorio)

**Crisis**
Via Famagosta 8, Rome, Italy.
- Crisis; polemiche e problemi di psicologia della societa. q. ISSN 0011-1414

**Cristiani nel Mondo**
Via Serchio 7, Rome, Italy.
- Cristiani nel Mondo. m. ISSN 0045-9054

**Critica Umbra**
Piazza Fanti, 1, Citta di Castello (Pg), Italy.
- Critica Umbra. m.

**Cronac Viva**
Via Toschi 25, Reggio Emilia, Italy.
- Cronac Viva. m.

**Cronache d'Altri Tempi**
Via Montecatini 11, Rome, Italy.
- Cronache d'Altri Tempi. m. ISSN 0011-1740

**Cucina Italiana**
Via S. Antonio Zaccaria 3, 20122 Milan, Italy.
- Cucina Italiana. m.

**Edizioni di Cultura Contemporanea**
Via Piolti da Bianchi 29, 20129 Milan Italy.
- B't; arte oggi in Italia. m. ISSN 0007-2753
- Da-a /U dela; a magazine of arts & literature. s-a. ISSN 0011-5207

**Cultura nel Mondo**
Via Gramsci, 16, 00197 Rome, Italy.
- Cultura nel Mondo. bi-m. ISSN 0011-2798

**Edizioni Curci s.r.l.**
Galleria del Corso 4, 20122 Milan, Italy.
- Rassegna Musicale Curci; cultural and musical actuality periodical. q. ISSN 0033-9806

**Curia Arcivescovile di Ferrara**
- Voce di Ferrara. (pub. by I.P.A.G.)

**Curia Arcivescovile di Monreale**
Palermo, Italy.
- Archidiocesi di Monreale. Bollettino Ecclesiastico. m. ISSN 0003-8296

**Curia Episcopalis Bauzanensis-Brixinensis**
39100 Bolzano, Italy.
- Folium Diocesanum Bauzanense-Brixinense. m. ISSN 0015-5802

**Curia Metropolitana di Reggio Calabria**
Via T. Campanella 63, Reggio Calabria, Italy.
- Bollettino Ecclesiastico. bi-m. ISSN 0006-6788

**Curia Patriarcale di Venezia**
S. Marco 320a, 30124 Venezia, Italy.
- Rivista Diocesana del Patriarcato di Venezia. 10 per yr. ISSN 0035-6654

**Curia Vescovile di Verona**
Via Pieta Vecchia 2, Verona 37100, Italy.
- Verona Fedele; settimanale cattolico della diocesi. w. ISSN 0042-4242

**D. de Giorgio, Ed. & Pub.**
Via Domenico Muratori 25, Reggio Calabria, Italy.
- Historica; rivista trimestrale di cultura. q. ISSN 0018-2427

**D O X A**
6 Galleria San Carlo, 20122 Milan, Italy.
- D O X A. Bollettino. s-m. ISSN 0006-6656 (Istituto per le Ricerche Statistiche e l'Analisi dell'Opinione Pubblica)

**D'Urso**
Via della Mercede 11, 00187 Rome, Italy.
- Filatelia Italiana. fortn. ISSN 0015-0940

**Casa Editrice G. Dainese**
Via Aldrovandi, 5, 20129 Milan, Italy.
- Stati Uniti d'Europa; rivista internazionale indipendente economica, sociale, culturale, tecnica, scientifica, industriale, turistica. bi-m. ISSN 0039-0348

**Societa Editrice Dante Alighieri**
Via Timavo. 3/5, 00195 Rome, Italy.
- Nuova Rivista Storica. q. ISSN 0029-6236

**Data Arte**
52 Foro Buonaparte, 20121 Milan, Italy
- Data; practice and theory of art. bi-m. ISSN 0045-9666 (U.S. Distrib.: Eastern News Distributors, 111 Eighth Ave., New York, N.Y. 10011)

**De Luca Editore**
Via S. Anna 11, 00186 Rome, Italy.
- Arte e Poesia. q. ISSN 0004-3419
- Musei e Gallerie d'Italia. s-a. ISSN 0027-3872 (Associazione Nazionale dei Musei Italiani)
- Museo Nazionale di Castel San Angelo. Quaderni. a. (Associazione Amici di Castel San Angelo)
- Nuova Critica; studi e rivista di filosofia delle scienze. q' ISSN 0029-6163
- Rivista Trimestrale di Scienza Politica e Dell Amministrazione. q. ISSN 0035-7111

**Pasquale De Orsi, Ed. & Pub.**
Via Alessandro Longo 11, 80127-Naples, Italy.
- Valori Umani; bimestrale di educazione letteraria scientifica, artistica e di costume. bi-m. ISSN 0300-3175

**Edizioni Dedalo**
Casella Postale 362, 70100 Bari, Italy.
- Classe. s-a.
- Controspazio/Counterspace; architettura e urbanistica. bi-m. ISSN 0010-809X
- Inchiesta; ricerca e practica sociale. bi-m. ISSN 0046-8819
- Istituto di Storia Greca e Romana. Quaderni di Storia. s-a.
- Lavoro Critico. q.
- Magistra Democratica. bi-m.
- Monthly Review. m.
- Saggi di Storia Contemporanea. irreg. (Istituto per gli Studi di Politica Internazionale)
- Sapere. m. ISSN 0036-4681

**Edizioni Dehoniane**
Via Marechiaro 46, 80123 Naples, Italy
(Subscr. to: Centro Campano Studi Francescani, Corso Vittorio Emmanuele 730, 80122 Naples, Italy)
- Studi e Ricerche Francescane. q. (Centro Campano Studi Francescani)

**Centro Editoriale Dehoniano**
Via Nosadella 6, 40123 Bologna, Italy.
- Regno; attualita e documentazione cattolica. s-m. ISSN 0034-3498
- Regno-Documenti. m. ISSN 0009-000X

**Editoriale Delfino**
Via Simone d'Orsenigo 27, 20135 Milan, Italy.
- Elettrificazione. m. ISSN 0013-6093

**Democrazia Cristiana**
Via Quattro Novembre 149, 00184 Rome, Italy.
- Discussione. w. ISSN 0416-0371
- Torre Civica. m. ISSN 0040-9596

**Casa Editrice Denaro**
Via Maqueda 177, Palermo, Italy.
- Collage; rivista internazionale di nuova musica e arti visiva contemporanee. 2 per yr. ISSN 0010-0706

**Deputazione di Storia Patria Florence**
- Archivio Storico Italiano. (pub. by Casa Editrice Leo S. Olschki)
- Fonti Sui Comuni Rurali Toscani. (pub. by Casa Editrice Leo S. Olschki)
- Fonti Sulle Corporazioni Medioevali. (pub. by Casa Editrice Leo S. Olschki)

**Deputazione di Storia Patria per l'Umbria**
Palazzo dei Priori, C.P. 130, 06100 Perugia, Italy.
- Deputazione di Storia Patria per l'Umbria. Bollettino. s-a. ISSN 0300-4422

**Derby Societa Editrice**
Corso DiPorta Nuova 46, Milan, Italy.
- Esquire & Derby. m.(10 per yr)
- European Racing Manual. a.

**Design**
c/o Elio Cenci, Ed., Via Tremana 1, 24100 Bergamo, Italy.
- Design; strumento per migliorare la qualita della vita. q.

**Deutsches Historisches Institut in Rom**
- Analecta Musicologia. (pub. by Arno Volk Verlag Hans Gerig KG GW)
- Concentus Musicus. (pub. by Arno Volk Verlag Hans Gerig KG GW)
- Nuntiaturberichte aus Deutschland nebst Ebgaenzenden Aktenstuecken. (pub. by Max Niemeyer Verlag GW)
- Quellen und Forschungen aus Italienischen Archiven und Bibliotheken. (pub. by Max Niemeyer Verlag GW)

**Di Baio Editore**
Via F. Casati i/A, 20124 Milan, Italy.
- Milanocasa. m.

**Di Modica**
Via 20 Settembre, 69, Palermo, Italy.
- Quaderni Siciliani. irreg. (Partito Comunista Italiano)

**Dialetti d'Italia**
Via Venti Settembre 26, 00187 Rome, Italy.
- Dialetti d'Italia. m. ISSN 0012-2025

**Dialoghi**
Via Acciaioli 7, Rome, Italy.
- Dialoghi; rivista bimestrale di letteratura arti scienze. bi-m. ISSN 0012-205X

**Dialogos**
Casella Postale 30098, Rome 47, Italy.
- Dialogos; problemi dell'istruzione e della ricerca scientifica. q. ISSN 0012-2106

**Diana**
Via Raffaele Musone 175, 81025-Marcianise (Caserta), Italy.
- Diana; rassegna di politica e di cultura. bi-m. ISSN 0012-2335

**Dimensioni**
Via N. Fabrizi 32, Pescara, Italy.
- Dimensioni; rivista abruzzese di cultura e d'arte. bi-m. ISSN 0012-2904

**Dio e Popolo**
Piazzale Prenestino 53, Rome, Italy.
- Dio e Popolo; peridico mazziniano aderente al partito naziona ""La Giovine Italia" w. ISSN 0046-0303

**Diocesi Cattolica, Comacchio**
Via Menegazzi 3, Comacchio, Italy.
- Croce. w. ISSN 0011-1651

**Diocesi di Cremona**
Piazza S.A.M. Zaccaria 6, 26100 Cremona, Italy.
- Vita Cattolica. w. ISSN 0042-7233

**Direzione Belle Arti del Comune di Venezia**
San Marco 52, Venice, Italy.
- Musei Civici Veneziani. Bollettino. q. ISSN 0027-3864 (Direzione Civici Musei)

**Direzione Civici Musei**
- Musei Civici Veneziani. Bollettino. (pub. by Direzione Belle Arti del Comune di Venezia)

**Diritti della Scuola**
Cicerone, 44, Rome, Italy.
- Diritti della Scuola; rassegna decadale dell'istruzione primaria. fortn. ISSN 0012-3382

**Casa Editrice Discoteca s.r.l.**
Via Martignoni 1, 20144 Milan, Italy.
- Discoteca Alta Fedelta; revista di dischi e musica e alta fedelta. m. ISSN 0012-3560

**Divine World Missionaries**
Via dei Verbiti 1, C.P. 5080, I-00153 Rome, Italy.
- Verbum. q. ISSN 0042-3696

**Editrice Divus Thomas**
29100 Piacenza, Italy.
- Divus Thomas; commentarium de philosophia et theologia. q. ISSN 0012-4257 (Collegio Alberoni)

**Documentation Center of Architecture and Urban and Regional Planning**
Largo V Alpini 12, 20145 Milan, Italy.
- Centro di Documentazione d'Ingegneria Civile, Architetturae Pianificazione Territoriale. Schede. m.
- Centro di Documentazione d'Ingegneria Civile Architetturae Pianificazione Territoriale Documenti. 3 per yr.

**Documenti di Attualita Politica**
Via Tevere 9, Rome, Italy.
- D A P. w. ISSN 0011-4715

**Documenti Sul Comunismo**
29 Piazza Rondanini, 00186 Rome, Italy.
- Documenti Sul Comunismo. m. ISSN 0012-4745

**Domani**
Strada dell'Alpo 114, 37062 Verona, Italy.
- Domani; rivista di cultura e arte. m. ISSN 0046-0524

**Societa Editrice Domani S.p.A.**
Corso Magenta 42, 20123 Milan, Italy.
- Europa Domani. m.

**Domenico Del Bianco**
Via Spilimbergo 18, Udine, Italy.
- Mio Lavora; rivista di formazione professionale. m. ISSN 0026-5764

**Dominican Fathers**
Vicoletto S. Pietro A Maiella 4, 80134 Napoli, Italy.
- Sapienza; rivista internazionale di filosofia e di teologia. q. ISSN 0036-4711

**Editoriale Domus**
Viale del Ghisallo, 20, 20151 Milan, Italy.
- Domus; architettura arredamento arte. m. ISSN 0012-5377
- Quattroruote. m. ISSN 0033-5916

**Donato Editore**
Lungomare N. Sauro 25, 70121 Bari, Italy.
- Rivista della Proprieta' Industriale e della Concorrenza. q. ISSN 0035-5976

**Donna di Casa**
44 via Benedetto Marcello, Milan, Italy.
- Donna di Casa; mensile femminile. m. ISSN 0046-0591

**Dopolavoro Ferroviario**
Via A. Doria 13, 16126 Genoa, Italy.
- Superba. m. ISSN 0039-5706

**Edizioni E C O**
64048 S. Gabriele (Teramo), Italy.
- Gioventu Passionista/Passionist Youth; rivista di formazione e d'informazione passionista. irreg., 1960, no. 3. ISSN 0072-4548

**Edizioni E.C.R.A.**
Via Adige 26, 00198 Rome, Italy.
- Cooperazione di Credito; rivista del movimento delle casse rurali ed artiqiane. bi-m. ISSN 0010-8480 (Ente Nazionale Casse Rurali Agrarie Ed Enti Ausiliari)

**E D A**
Via Avogadro, 22, Turin, Italy.
- Vin Valdotain, Piemonteis, Ligure. q.

**Casa Editrice E D A M**
Piazza Pitti, 12 Florence, Italy.
- Antichita Viva; rassegna d'arte. bi-m. ISSN 0003-5645

**E.P.T.**
Via Lombruschini 27, 20158 Milan, Italy.
- Chimica e Petrolchimica. m.

**E R I Edizioni**
Via Arsenale 41, 10121 Turin, Italy.
- Approdo Letterario; rivista trimestrale di lettere e arti. q. ISSN 0570-5029
- Diritto delle Radiodiffusioni e delle Telecomunicazioni. 3 per yr. ISSN 0012-3412
- Elettronica e Telecomunicazioni. bi-m. ISSN 0013-6123
- Nuova Rivista Musicale Italiana; trimestrale di cultura e informazione musicale. q. ISSN 0029-6228
- Radiocorriere-TV. w. ISSN 0033-8257

**E R I S S.p.A.**
Piazza della Republica 26, 20124 Milan, Italy.
- Design e Habitat. bi-m.
- Market-Espresso; rivista del commercio. fortn.
- Plast; rivista delle materie plastiche. m.

**E.S.A.V.**
Via Cavour 50, 10123 Turin, Italy.
- Estetica. bi-m.

**E.S.T. Editrice**
Via Rialdoli 136, 50018 Scandicci (Florence), Italy.
- Prodotto Chimico e Aerosol Selezione; rivista mensile dei prodotti chimici e parachimici. m. ISSN 0032-9673

**E.T.A.**
Via Goldoni 19, 20129 Milan, Italy.
- Cosmesi. m.

**Eco del Chisone**
c/o Vittorio Morero, Ed., Via Tenlada 52, 00195 Rome, Italy.
- Eco del Chisone; settimanale di penerolo. w.

**Eco Motori**
Piazza Roma 33-a, 70122 Bari, Italy.
- Eco Motori. m. ISSN 0422-2628

**Economia Sociale Contrattuale**
Via Poliziano 8, Milan, Italy.
- Economia Nuova per Un Mondo Nuovo. s-a. ISSN 0012-9852

**Gruppo Giornalistico Edagricole**
Via Emilia Levante 31, 40139 Bologna, Italy (Subscr. to: Pergamon Press, Inc., Maxwell House, Fairview Pk, Elmsford, NY 10523)
- Avicoltura. m. ISSN 0005-2213 (Italian Committee)
- Colture Protete; rivista professionale dell'Ortofloro frutticoltura intensiva. m.
- Coniglicoltura. m. ISSN 0010-5929 (National Association of Rabbit Breeders)
- Frutticoltura. m. ISSN 0016-2310
- Genio Rurale. m. ISSN 0016-6863
- Giardino Fiorito. m. ISSN 0016-965X (Societa Italiana Amici dei Fiori)
- I M A Trattorista; informatore de meccanica agraria. m. ISSN 0041-1841
- Informatore di Ortoflorofrutticoltura. m. ISSN 0020-0719 (Comitato Nazionale Serre)
- Informatore Fitopatologico. m. ISSN 0020-0735
- Informatore Zootecnico. fortn. ISSN 0020-0778
- Irrigazione. bi-m. ISSN 0021-1680 (Centro Internazionale Studi sull'Irrigazione)
- M & M A-Macchine e Motori Agricoli; rivista mensile de meccanica agraria. m. ISSN 0024-8967
- Micologia Italiana. q. (Unione Micologica Italiana)
- Montanaro d'Italia-Monti e Boschi. bi-m. (Unione Nazionale Comuni, Comunita ed Enti Montani)
- Monti e Boschi; ecologia e tecnica applicate alle foreste e alla protezione della natura. bi-m. ISSN 0027-0660
- Rivista di Agronomia. q. ISSN 0035-6034 (Societa Italiana di Agronomia)
- Rivista di Ingegneria Agraria. q. ISSN 0034-916X (Associazione Italiana di Genio Rurale)
- Rivista di Politica Agraria. q. ISSN 0035-645X

- S & T A-Scienza e Tecnologia degli Alimenti. bi-m. ISSN 0036-1933 (Societa Italiana Progresso Industrie Agrarie Alimentari) (Co-Sponsor: Societa Italiana de Nutrizione Umana)
- Sementi Elette. bi-m. ISSN 0037-1890 (National Seed Advisory Council)
- Suinicoltura; rivista tecnico-economica per gli allevatori di suini. m. ISSN 0035-662X
- Terra e Vita. w. ISSN 0040-3776
- VigneVini; rivista italiana di viticoltura e di enologia. m.
- Zootechnica e Nutrizione Animale; bi-monthly for the breeders and producers of feeding stuffs. q. (Associazione Scientifica di Produzione Animale)

**Edilstampa**
Via Guattani 20, 00161 Rome, Italy.
- Corriere dei Costruttori. w. (Associazione Nazionale Costruttori Edili)
- Industria delle Costruzioni. m. (Associazione Nazionale Costruttori Edili)

**Casa Editrice Edimark**
Via Anfossi 36, 20135 Milan, Italy.
- Eco-Cuoio. bi-m.
- Eco-Cuoio delle Industrie e dei Commerci del Cuoio e delle Calzature. fortn. ISSN 0012-9437
- Tecnica Calzaturiera. bi-m.

**Edimoda**
Via C. Goldoni 32, 20129 Milan, Italy.
- Corriere della Moda e Calzatura. m.

**Edisette s.r.l.**
Via San Marino 36, 00198 Rome, Italy.
- Forza-Sette. m. ISSN 0015-8666

**Edisport S.P.A.**
Via Boccaccio 47, 20123 Milan, Italy.
- Motociclismo. m. ISSN 0027-1691
- Vela e Motore. m. ISSN 0042-3181

**Edistampa s.r.l.**
Via Privata Maria Teresa 4, 20123 Milan, Italy.
- Autogiornale. m.
- Garage & Officina. m. ISSN 0016-4542 (Associazione Nazionale Autoriparatori e Autoricambisti)

**Editalia**
Via di Pallacorda 7, Rome, Italy.
- Qui Arte Contemporanea. q. ISSN 0004-3397

**Editecnica Italiana s.r.l.**
Via Turati 29, 20121 Milan, Italy.
- Foto Shoe 15. m.
- Foto Shoe 30. m.
- Nuovo Corriere della Calzatura. fortn.

**Editgraf**
Piazza Tirana 24/4, 20147 Milan, Italy.
- Ortopedici e Sanitari. m. ISSN 0030-5979

**Casa Editrice Edithema**
Piazza della Republica 32, 20124 Milan, Italy.
- Direttore Commerciale; rivista di marketing per lo sviluppo delle vendite. m (11 per yr) ISSN 0012-3323
- Self Magazine. m.

**Editip**
Corso Sebastopoli 233a, 10137 Turin, Italy.
- Rivista di Scienze dell'Educazione. 3 per yr. (Instituto Figlie di Maria Ausiliatrice Salesiane di Don Bosco)

**Editphoto**
Via degli Imbriani, 20158 Milan, Italy.
- Diaframma Fotografia Italiana. m.

**Editoriale Effe**
Via Lipari 8, 00141 Rome, Italy.
- Almanacco di Fotografare. q.

**Edizioni Effe Emme**
Viale.E. Caldara 8, 20122 Milan, Italy.
- Uomini e Libri. bi-m. ISSN 0042-0654

**Casa Editrice Einaudi**
Via Biancamano 1, Turin 10129, Italy.
- Rivista di Filosofia. q. ISSN 0035-6239
- Strumenti Critici. 3 per yr. ISSN 0039-2618

**Gruppo Editoriale Electa S.p.A.**
Via Goldoni 1, 20129 Milan, Italy.
- Arredamento Interni. m.
- Casabella; rivista di urbanistica, architettura e disegno industriale. m. ISSN 0008-7181

- Lotus International. q.
- Storia della Citta; rivista internazionale di storia urbana e territoriale. q.
- Ville-Giardini. m. ISSN 0042-6237

**Editrice Elia**
Viale dell'Universita 27-23, 00185 Rome, Italy.
- Giornale Italiano di Filologia; rivista di cultura. 3 per yr. ISSN 0017-0461

**Eloquenza**
Viale Giulio Cesare 14, 00192 Rome, Italy.
- Eloquenza; antologia, critica-cronaca. bi-m. ISSN 0013-6352

**Embassy of the Republic of South Africa**
c/o Information Counsellor, Piazza Monte Grappa 4, 00195 Rome, Italy.
- Sud Africa - Ieri, Oggi, Domani; rivista di informazione economica, culturale, politica e scientifica. m. ISSN 0039-4505

**Editoriale Emme Elle s.r.l.**
Via Reno, 30, Rome, Italy.
- Agenda del Dirigente di Azienda. a. ISSN 0065-4264

**Edizioni Encia**
Via S. Osvaldo, 49, 33100 Udine, Italy.
- Giornale degli Uccelli; rivista di ornitologia. m. ISSN 0017-0100

**Engineers Union of Milan**
- Giornale dell' Ingegnere. (pub. by Propaganda Editoriale Grafica S.p.A.)

**Societa Editrice Periodici Enotria**
Corso Vittorio Emanuele 101, 00186 Rome, Italy.
- Mondo Agricolo; settimanale di tecnica, economia e politica agraria. w. ISSN 0026-9484 (Confederazione Generale Agricoltura Italiana)

**Ente Autonomo del Porto di Savona**
Via Gramsci 14, 17100 Savona, Italy.
- Porto di Savona. m. ISSN 0032-4957

**Ente Dello Spettacolo**
Via della Conciliazione, 00193 2/C Rome, Italy.
- Guida Allo Spettacolo. w. ISSN 0017-5188
- Segnalazioni Cinematografiche. s-m. ISSN 0037-0932

**Ente Internazionale per la Stampa**
Via Gesu 6, 20121 Milan, Italy.
- Ruota Diorama; avvenimenti aerospaziali. q. ISSN 0035-9955

**Ente Italiano de Servicio Sociale**
Via Colossi 50, 00146 Rome, Italy.
- Rassegna di Servizio Sociale. q. ISSN 0033-9601

**Ente Italiano per Lo Sviluppo dell' Esportazione**
- Buyers' Guide. (pub. by Istituto Pubblicazioni Internazionali)
- E I S E Notizie. (pub. by Istituto Pubblicazioni Internazionali)
- Esportazione. (pub. by Istituto Pubblicazioni Internazionali)

**Ente Nazionale A C L I Istruzione Professionale**
Via Giuseppe Marcora 18/20, 00153-Rome, Italy.
- Formazione e Lavoro. bi-m. ISSN 0015-7767

**Ente Nazionale Artigianato e Piccole Industrie**
Via Vittoria Colonna 39, Rome, Italy.
- E N A P I. bi-m. ISSN 0012-7809

**Ente Nazionale Assistenza Lavoratori**
Via Caltagirone 6, 00182 Rome, Italy.
- Tempo Libero. m.

**Ente Nazionale Casse Rurali Agrarie Ed Enti Ausiliari**
- Cooperazione di Credito. (pub. by Edizioni E.C.R.A.)

**Ente Nazionale della Cinofilia Italiana**
Viale Premuda 21, Milan, Italy.
- Nostri Cani. m. ISSN 0029-3784

**Ente Nazionale di Previdenza e di Assistenza per gli Impiegati dell' Agricoltura**
Viale Beethoven N.48, 00144 Rome, Italy.
- Previdenza Agricola. m. ISSN 0032-8057

**Ente Nazionale di Previdenza e di Assistenza per i Dipendenti Statali**
55 via Santa Croce in Gerusalemme, Rome, Italy.
- E N P A S; bimestral review of the national welfare and assistance fund for state employees. bi-m. ISSN 0012-7817

**Ente Nazionale Italiano per Il Turismo**
Via S. Martino della Battaglia, 4, Rome 00185, Italy.
- Italia. m. ISSN 0021-2741
- Statistica del Turismo. q. ISSN 0039-0399

**Ente Nazionale per l'Energia Elettrica**
Via Dalmazia 15, Rome, Italy.
- Bibliografia Elettrotecnica. m. ISSN 0006-1018
- Rassegna Tecnica di Problemi dell'Energia Elettrica. (pub. by Edizioni C E S I)

**Ente Nazionale per la Cellulosa e per la Carta**
Viale Regina Margherita 262, Rome, Italy.
- Cellulosa e Carta. m. ISSN 0008-8765
- Indicatore Cartotecnico. m. ISSN 0019-6959
- Indicatore Grafico; rassegna bibliografica mensile. m. ISSN 0019-6967

**Ente Nazionale per la Prevenzione degli Infortuni**
Via Alessandria 200-E, Rome, Italy.
- Educazione Alla Sicurezza. q. ISSN 0013-2071
- Securitas; rivista di studi e documentazione sulla sicurezza nel lavoro. m. ISSN 0037-0657

**Ente Nazionale per le Biblioteche Popolari e Scholastiche**
Via Michele Mercati 4, 00153 Rome, Italy.
- Cultura e Scuola. q. ISSN 0011-2771
- Leonardo; almanacco di educazione popolare. a. ISSN 0075-8760
- Parola e Il Libro; the word and the book. m. ISSN 0031-2371

**Ente Nazionale Risi**
Piazza Pio XI 1, Milan, Italy.
- Risicoltore. m.

**Ente Nazionale Serico**
Via Moscova 44-1, 20121 Milan, Italy.
- Bollettino di Informazioni Seriche. w. ISSN 0006-6737

**Ente Nazionale Sordomuti**
120 via Gregorio VII, 00165 Rome, Italy.
- Settimana del Sordomuto. w. ISSN 0037-2919

**Ente Provinciale per Il Turismo di Bologna**
Via Foscherari 2, Bologna, Italy.
- Bologna Incontri. m.

**Ente Provinciale per Il Turismo di Nuoro**
Nuoro 08100, Italy.
- Ente Provinciale per Il Turismo di Nuoro. Notiziario. 5 per yr. ISSN 0013-8622

**Ente Provinciale per Il Turismo di Salerno**
Via Velia, 15, 84100 Salerno, Italy.
- Civilta della Campania. bi-m.

**Ente Provinciale per Il Turismo di Teramo**
Teramo, Italy.
- Teramo; le notizie del turismo. m. ISSN 0040-3652

**Ente Provinciale per Il Turismo di Trapani**
Corso Italia, 91100 Trapani, Sicily, Italy.
- Sicilia Archeologica. 3 per yr. ISSN 0037-4571

**Episteme Editrice S.R.L.**
Via XXV Aprile, 24058 Romano L, Italy.
- Episteme; rivista critica di storia della medicina e della biologia. q. ISSN 0013-9637

**Era**
Via A. Volta 27, 56025 Pontedera (Pisa), Italy.
- Era; bimestrale di lettere ed arti. bi-m. ISSN 0046-2403

**Carlo Erba S.p.A.**
Via Imbonati 24, 20159 Milan, Italy.
- Gazzetta Sanitaria. m. ISSN 0016-5697
- Rilancio; agricoltural veterinary zootechnical magazine. m (9-12 per yr) ISSN 0016-5700

**Ercole Gloria s.r.l.**
Piazza Pio XI, No. 1, 20123 Milan, Italy.
- Gazzetta Filatelica. m. ISSN 0016-5654

**Ercole Marelli**
Via Borgonuovo 24, 120100 Milan, Italy.
- Marelli. q. ISSN 0047-5904

**Eredi Vieri**
Via Oriuolo 3, 50100 Florence, Italy.
- Terra. fortn.

**Eremo Italico**
84085-Mercato S. Severino, Salerno, Italy.
- Fiorisce Un Cenacolo. m. ISSN 0015-2536

**Eris-Friedman**
see E R I S

**Erma di "Bretschneider"**
Via Cassiodoro, 19, Rome, Italy.
- Archeologia Classica. a. ISSN 0003-8172 (Universita di Roma. Istituti di Archeologia e Storia dell'Arte Greca e Romana e di Etruscologia e Anchichita Italiche)
- Corpus Vasorum Antiquorum. Italia. irreg., no. 55, 1974. ISSN 0070-0479
- Monografie di Archeologia Libica. irreg., no. 12, 1974. ISSN 0077-0493
- Museo dell'Impero Romano. Studi e Materiali. irreg., no. 8, 1974. ISSN 0080-3936
- Problemi e Ricerche de Storia Antica. irreg., 1964, no. 3. ISSN 0079-5682
- Quaderni di Archeologia della Libia. irreg; no. 9, 1977. ISSN 0079-8258
- Quaderni e Guide di Archeologia. irreg., no. 3, 1972. ISSN 0079-8282
- Scavi di Luni. irreg., latest issue, 1970-1971.
- Studi d'Architettura Antica. irreg., no. 5, 1974. ISSN 0081-6140
- Studi Miscellanei. irreg., 1964, no. 8. ISSN 0081-6191
- Studia Archaeologica. irreg; latest, 1976. ISSN 0081-6299
- Studia Historica. irreg; no. 123, 1976. ISSN 0081-6507
- Studia Juridica. irreg; vol. 82, 1976. ISSN 0081-6698
- Studia Philologica. irreg; vol. 19, 1976. ISSN 0081-6817
- Universita di Padova. Istituto di Storia Antica. Pubblicazioni. irreg; no. 12, 1975. ISSN 0078-7744

**Tolomelli Ermanno & C. S.N.C.**
97 via Mazzini, 40137-Bologna, Italy.
- Notiziario di Caccia e Pesca-Tiro a Volo. w. ISSN 0029-4365

**Errepi Editrice s.a.s.**
Via Console Marcello 8, Milan, Italy.
- Legno. s-m. ISSN 0024-0532 (Federazione Nazionale Commercianti Legno)
- Macchine del Legno. m.

**Casa Editrice ESEDRA**
Via Parigi 11, 00185 Rome, Italy.
- Fiorino; quotidiano del mattino e finanza e economia e actualita. d.

**Editoriale Esperienza**
Via del Teatro Valle 20, 00186 Rome, Italy.
- Esperienza; mensile di elevazione sociale. m. ISSN 0014-0678 (Associazione Nazionale Lavoratori Anziani di Azienda) (Co-Sponsor: Federazione Maestri del Lavoro d'Italia)

**Edizioni ESSE**
Via Zara 9, 00198 Rome, Italy.
- Oltre il Cielo; missili e razzi. s-m. ISSN 0030-2147

**Esso Italiana**
Servizio Publicita, Piazzale dell' Industria 46, Rome 00144, Italy.
- Esso Agricola. bi-m. ISSN 0014-097X
- Esso Rivista. q. ISSN 0014-1038

**Estetica Ambrosiana**
Via Lambro 15, Milan, Italy.
- Estetica Ambrosiana. q. ISSN 0014-1275

**Etas Kompass Periodici Tecnici S.p.A.**
Via Mantegna 6, 20154 Milan, Italy.
- Annuario Finanziario Europeo. a.
- Annunciatore Poligrafico; periodico mensile d'informazione tecnica per i settori poligrafico cartotecnico e legatoria. m. ISSN 0003-5165

- Apparecchiature Idrauliche e Pneumatiche; olio e
  aria sotto pressione lubrificazione. m. ISSN 0003-
  6676
- Carte d'Acquisto. m.
- From Italy; Italian production review. m. ISSN
  0016-1586
- I.M.E. bi-m.
- Imballaggio. m. ISSN 0019-2708
- Ingegneria Meccanica. m. ISSN 0020-0964
- Inquinamento; Rivista tecnica del trattamento
  delle acque. m. ISSN 0001-4982
- Kompass Italia; repertorio generale dell'economia
  Italiana. a. ISSN 0075-6687 (Dist. by: Iliffe NTP
  Inc., 300 E. 42 St., New York, N.Y. 10017)
- Nuovo Cantiere. m. ISSN 0029-6325
- Poliplasti e Materiali: Rinforzati. m.
- Repertorio dell' Imballaggio. a.
- Rivista di Meccanica. m. ISSN 0035-6301
- Tecniche dell'Automazione; elettronica-meccanica-
  strumenti-impianti. m (10 per yr) ISSN 0040-1927
  (Associazione Italiana Strumentisti)
- Trasporti Industriali. m. ISSN 0041-1809

**Etas Periodici del Tempo Libri S.p.A.**
Via C. Alberto 65, Turin, Italy.
- Alata Internazionale. m. ISSN 0002-4600
- Architettura; cronache e storia. m. ISSN 0003-
  8830
- Clic Fotografiamo. m. ISSN 0009-8906

**Etnologia-Antropologia Culturale**
Corso Vitt. Emanuele 110, Naples, Italy.
- Etnologia-Antropologia Culturale. a.

**Eura Press, Edizioni Italiane**
Via Lazzaro Papi, 15, Milan 20135, Italy.
- Poeti a Gradara. biennial.

**Eurograph-Bernardoni**
Via M. Melloni 17, 20129 Milan, Italy.
- Rassegna Grafica. fortn. ISSN 0033-9687

**Eurographik**
Casella Postale 204, 38100 Trento, Italy.
- Punto e a Capo; revista per giovani. m. ISSN
  0033-4383

**Europa Illustrata e l'Italia Illustrata**
Via Rossini N.22, 376568 Naples, Italy.
- Europa Illustrata e l'Italia Illustrata; lettere, arti,
  scienze, turismo e cultura varia. m. ISSN 0014-
  2506

**Europa Libera**
Via Emilia 47, 00187 Rome, Italy.
- Europa Libera; periodico di discussione
  democratica. fortn. ISSN 0014-2530

**Edizioni Europa s.r.l.**
Via degli Scipioni 268-A, 00192 Rome, Italy.
- Civilta. bi-m.
- Corrispondenza Europea. w.

**European Association for Animal Production**
Corso Trieste 67, 00198 Rome, Italy.
- European Association for Animal Production.
  Publications. irreg., 1976 no. 18. ISSN 0071-2477
- European Association for Animal Production.
  Symposia on Energy Metabolism. triennial; 6th,
  Stuttgart, 1973. ISSN 0071-2485 (Publisher Varies
  with Each Meeting, 6Th Publ. by Juris-Verlag,
  Darmstadt, W. Germany)

**European Association of Scientific Information
Dissemination Centers**
c/o ESRIN - SDS, C.P. 64, 0044 Frascati, Italy.
- NEWSIDIC; information bulletin. q.

**European Christian Democratic Union**
107 via del Plebiscito, 00186 Rome, Italy.
- Panorama Democrate Chretien/Panorama
  Democrata Cristiano/Christlich Demokratisches
  Panorama. q. ISSN 0031-0913

**European Federation of Physical and Rehabilitation
Medicine**
- Europa Medicophysica. (pub. by Edizioni Minerva
  Medica)

**Europlast**
Via Bianca di Savoia 6, 20122 Milan, Italy.
- Europlast. bi-m.

**Editoriale l' Expresso S.p. A.**
Via Po 12, 00198 Rome, Italy.
- Espresso. w. ISSN 0423-4243

**F L M**
Corso Trieste, 36, 00198 Roma, Italy.
- Consigli. m.

**Fratelli Fabbri Editori**
Via Mecenate 91, 20138 Milan, Italy.
- Educatore Italiano. fortn.

**Redazione Fabbrica e Stato**
Via della Consulta 50, 00184 Rome, Italy.
- Fabbrica e Stato. q. ISSN 0046-3027

**Facolta Biblica**
Via del Bollo 5, 20123 Milan, Italy.
- Ricerche Bibliche e Religiose. q. ISSN 0035-502X

**Facolta di Medicina Veterinaria**
Via Veterinaria 1, 80137 Naples, Italy.
- Acta Medica Veterinaria. bi-m. ISSN 0001-6136

**Faenza Editrice S.p.A.**
Casella Postale 68, 48018 Faenza, Italy.
- Analisi e Documenti. q.
- Bagno e Accessori; casa, albergo, comunita, terme.
  bi-m.
- Ceramica Informacion; revista mensual tecnica
  informativa. m.
- Ceramica Informazione; periodico tecnico
  specializzato. m. ISSN 0009-0271 (Societa
  Italiana per la Ceramica)
- Ceramica Italiana nell'Edilizia; pavimenti,
  revistimenti, sanitari. bi-m. ISSN 0009-028X
- Ceramica y Hogar; revista internacional de
  ceramica. bi-m.
- Parametro; international review of architecture
  and town planning. 10 per yr. ISSN 0031-1731
- Radio Rivista. m. ISSN 0033-8036 (Associazione
  Radiotecnica Italiana)
- Refrattari e Laterizi. m.

**Societa Editrice la Famiglia**
Viale Stazione 63, 25100 Brescia, Italy.
- Madre. m.

**Fante di Quadri**
Via Raffaello Sanzio 4, 20149 Milan, Italy.
- Fante di Quadri. bi-m. ISSN 0014-7524

**Societa Editoriale Farmaceutica**
Via Ausonio, 12, 20123 Milan, Italy.
- Bollettino Chimico Farmaceutico. m. ISSN 0006-
  6648
- Notiziario Chimico e Farmaceutico. bi-m. ISSN
  0550-1156

**Farmacia Nueva**
Via Sabaudia 23, Turin, Italy.
- Farmacia Nueva; bollettino dei farmacisti
  Piemontesi. m. ISSN 0014-8245

**Farmacisti d'Italia**
- Farmacista Sociale. (pub. by Dr. Franco Ricciardi,
  Ed. & Pub.)

**Editoriale Il Farmaco**
Corso Strada Nuova 86, 27100 Pavia, Italy.
- Farmaco. m. ISSN 0014-827X (Societa Italiana
  Scienze Farmaceutiche)

**Farmunione-Associazione Nazionale dell'Industria
Farmaceutica Italiana**
Via Nievo 61, Rome, Italy.
- Industria dei Farmaci. m. ISSN 0446-0243

**Fatebenefratelli**
Via S. Vittore 12, 20123 Milan, Italy.
- Res Medicae. bi-m. ISSN 0014-8784 (Ordine
  Ospedaliero di S. Giovanni di Dio)

**Fauno Editore**
Borgo Tegolaio 5, 50125 Florence, Italy.
- Fauno; mensile indipendente di cultura. m.

**Federaliste**
Corso Cavour 16, Pavia, Italy.
- Federaliste; revue de politique. q.

**Federazione Automobilistica Italiana**
- Autoriparatore. (pub. by Edizioni Pubbli Re)
- 3A, Autoricambi, Accessori, Attrezzature. (pub.
  by Edizioni Pubbli Re)

**Federazione Bowling Italiana**
Via Marco d'Agrate No. 23, 20139 Milan, Italy.
- Bowling Notizie; mensile dello sport del bowling.
  m. ISSN 0006-8438

**Federazione Ciclistica Italiana**
- Ciclismo d'Italia. (pub. by Ciclismo d'Italia)

**Federazione Circoli Giovanili**
Via S. Antonio 5, Milan 20122, Italy.
- Nuove Prospettive. m. ISSN 0033-1570

**Federazione delle Associazioni Italiane Alberghi e
Tourismo**
Via Toscana 1, 00100 Rome, Italy.
- Ospitalita e Alberghi. bi-m.

**Federazione Fra le Associazioni Piccole e Medie
Industrie, Regione Piemontese**
- A. P. I/Piccola e Media Industria. (pub. by S E I
  T S.N.C.)

**Federazione Ginnastica d'Italia**
Palazzo delle Federazioni Sportive, Viale Tiziano
70, Rome, Italy.
- Ginnasta. m. ISSN 0017-0046

**Federazione Impiegati Operai Metallurgici**
Via del Viminale 43, Rome 00184, Italy.
- Sindacato Moderno. m. ISSN 0037-5543

**Federazione Istituti di Attivita Educative**
Via della Pigna 13/A, Rome, Italy.
- Docete. m.

**Federazione Italian Tabaccai**
Via Leopoldo Serra 32, 00153 Rome, Italy.
- Voce del Tabaccaio. m. ISSN 0042-7829

**Federazione Italiana Amministratori Enti Locali**
- Esperienze Amministrative. (pub. by Paleari
  Edizioni Milano)

**Federazione Italiana Associazioni Regionali
Ospedaliere**
Via Napoleona 60, 22100 Como-Camerlata, Italy.
- Ospedali d'Italia. m. ISSN 0030-6258

**Federazione Italiana Biliardo Sportivo**
Via Caltagirone 6, 00182 Rome, Italy.
- Biliardo. m. ISSN 0006-2472

**Federazione Italiana Bridge**
3 Largo Augusto, 20122 Milan, Italy.
- Bridge d'Italia. m. ISSN 0006-985X

**Federazione Italiana Contro la Tubercolosi e le
Malattie Polmonari Sociali**
Via Ezio 24, 00192 Rome, Italy.
- Lotta Contro la Tubercolosi e le Malattie
  Polmonari Sociali. q.

**Federazione Italiana dei Cineforum**
Casella Postale 414, 30100 Venice, Italy.
- Cineforum; rivista di cultura cinematografica. m
  (10 per yr) ISSN 0009-7039

**Federazione Italiana del Campeggio e del
Caravanning**
Casella Postale 649, 50100 Florence, Italy.
- Campeggiare in Europa. biennial.
- Campeggio Italiano. m. ISSN 0008-2325
- Guida Camping d'Italia. a. ISSN 0072-792X

**Federazione Italiana della Stampa Radiologica**
- Annali di Radiologia Diagnostica. (pub. by Casa
  Editrice Licinio Cappelli)

**Federazione Italiana Dipendenti Enti Locali**
Casella Postale N.35, Piazza Caduti 26/5, 31021
Mogliano Veneto (Treviso), Italy.
- Nostra Voce. m (11 per yr) ISSN 0029-3768

**Federazione Italiana Escursionismo**
Via Cibrario 33, 10143 Turin, Italy.
- Escursionismo. q. ISSN 0014-0449

**Federazione Italiana Giuoco Calcio**
Via Gregorio Allegri 14, 00198 Rome, Italy.
- Arbitro. m. ISSN 0003-7907

**Federazione Italiana Hockey e Pattinaggio**
Palazzo Federazioni, Viale Tiziano 70, Rome, Italy.
- Hockey e Pattinaggio. m. ISSN 0018-2990

**Federazione Italiana Lotta Contro la Tubercolosi.
Sezione Toscana**
- Rassegna di Patologia dell' Apparato Respiratorio.
  (pub. by Sanatorio di Collinaia)

**Federazione Italiana Medici Igienisti**
ViaC. Battisti 15, Perugia, Italy.
- Federazione Italiana Medici Igienisti. Bolletino d'Informazioni Agli Iscritti. m. ISSN 0014-9497

**Federazione Italiana Sport Invernali**
Via Cerva 30, 20122 Milan, Italy.
- Guida Dello Sciatore. (pub. by Milano Sole Editore)
- Sport Invernali. m (Oct-Apr)

**Federazione Lombarda Proprieta Edilizia**
Via Meravigli 3, 20121 Milan, Italy.
- Proprieta Edilizia Lombarda. m. ISSN 0033-1422

**Federazione Nazionale Arditi d'Italia**
Via Quattro Fontane 25, 00184 Rome, Italy.
- Primalinea. s-m.

**Federazione Nazionale Casse Mutue Esercenti Attivita Commerciali**
- Mutualita' Democratica. (pub. by Nova Agep)

**Federazione Nazionale Commercianti Legno**
- Legno. (pub. by Errepi Editrice s.a.s.)

**Federazione Nazionale degli Istituti di Polizia Privata**
Via Vittoria Colonna 40, Rome, Italy
(Subscr. to Ernesto Manzini, via Accademia Albertina 40, 10123 Turin, Italy)
- Federazione Nazionale degli Istituti di Polizia Privata. Giornale Tecnico Professionale dell'Investigazione e dell'Informazione. s-m.
- Federpol; rivista di polizia privata. bi-m.

**Federazione Nazionale dei Cavalieri del Lavoro**
Palazzo della Civilta del Lavoro, Quadrato della Concordia 9, 00144 Rome, Italy.
- Convegno Nazionale per la Civilta del Lavoro. Atti. a. ISSN 0069-9772

**Federazione Nazionale dei Collegi delle Ostetriche**
Via Tarquinia 5-D, 00183 Rome, Italy.
- Lucina. m.

**Federazione Nazionale delle Imprese di Pesca**
- Pesca Italiana. (pub. by Agenzia d'Informazioni per la Stampa)

**Federazione Nazionale di Atletica Leggera**
Viale Tiziano 70, 00100 Rome, Italy.
- Atletica. m.

**Federazione Nazionale Dottori in Scienze Agrarie**
Via Livenza, 6, 00198 Rome, Italy.
- Dottore in Scienze Agrarie. m. ISSN 0012-5687

**Federazione Nazionale Insegnanti Scuole Medie**
4 via Ponza, 10121 Turin, Italy.
- Eco della Scuola Nuova. m. ISSN 0012-9496

**Federazione Nazionale Macellai**
Piazza G.G. Belli 2, 00153 Rome, Italy.
- Macelleria Italiana. s-m. ISSN 0024-9017

**Federazione Nazionale Orafi Gioiellieri Argentieri Orologiai d'Italia**
Studio Manca, Via Nervesa 2, 20139 Milan, Italy.
- Orafo Italiano. m. ISSN 0471-7376

**Federazione Nazionale Ordini Medici**
Piazza Cola di Rienzo 80/A, 00192 Rome, Italy.
- Federazione Medica. m. ISSN 0014-9500
- Medico d'Italia. w. ISSN 0025-8148

**Federazione Nazionale Profumieri Italian**
- Imagine. (pub. by Edizioni Pi-Erre)

**Federazione Nazionale Stampa Italiana**
Corso Vittorio Emanuele 2, No. 349, Rome 00186, Italy.
- Stampa Italiana. m.

**Federazione Oratori Milanesi**
5 via S. Antonio, 20122 Milan, Italy.
- Eco degli Oratori e dei Circoli Giovanili. m. ISSN 0012-9453 (Co-sponsor: Federazione Circoli Giovanili)

**Federazione Ordini Farmacisti Italiani**
Via Palestro 75, 00185 Rome, Italy.
- Farmacista. q.

**Federazione Provinciale Autoferrotranvieri di Milano**
Corso Porta Vittoria 43, Milan, Italy.
- Autoferrotranviere. m.

**Federazione Provinciale Coltivatori Diretti di Cuneo**
12100 Cuneo, Italy.
- Coltivatori Cuneese. m.

**Federazione Provinciale Coltivatori Diretti di Reggio Emilia**
Via Guidelli 10, 42100 Reggio Emilia, Italy.
- Coltivatore Reggiano. 3 per mo.

**Federazioni Associazioni Regionali Economi**
- Tecnica e Metodologia Economale. (pub. by A.R.T.E.)

**Fegato**
Via Crescenzio 48, 00193 Rome, Italy.
- Fegato. q. ISSN 0014-9659

**Editoriale Fenarete**
Via Beruto 7, 20131 Milan, Italy.
- Fenarete-Letture d'Italia; Italian cultural and literary periodical. bi-m. ISSN 0014-9969
- Italy's Contribution to the Promotion of World Wide Prosperity. q.
- Opera; a magazine dedicated to the International Lyric Theatre. q. ISSN 0030-3542
- Risveglio Ostetrico. s-m.

**Giovanni Fenaroli, Ed. & Pub.**
Viale Papiniano, 2, 20123 Milan, Italy.
- Rivista Italiana Essenze Profumi, Piante officinali, Aromi, Saponi, Cosmetici, Aerosol. m. ISSN 0035-6948

**Fermenti**
Via Campomorone 65, 00168 Rome, Italy.
- Fermenti; rivista di critica del costume e della cultura. m. ISSN 0046-3671

**Ferraro**
Via S. Sebastiano 14, Naples, Italy
(and University of Illinois, Dept. of Comparative Learning, 401 Lincoln Hall, Urbana, Ill. 61801)
- Umanesimo; quarterly of Italian and American culture. q. ISSN 0041-6290

**Franco Ferrarotti, Ed. & Pub.**
Via Appennini 42, Rome 00198, Italy.
- Critica Sociologica. q. ISSN 0011-1546

**Casa Editrice la Fiaccola**
Via Ravizza 62, 20149 Milan, Italy.
- Costruzioni; tecnica ed organizzazione dei cantieri. m. ISSN 0010-9665
- Edilizia alle Fiere; rassegna periodica tecnica di documentazione e informazione. 4 per yr. ISSN 0013-0877
- Rivista della Strada; rassegna di tecnica stradale trasporti e viabilita. m (10 per yr) ISSN 0035-5992

**Edizioni la Fiaccola**
Casella Postale 61, 95100 Catania, Italy.
- Anarchismo. bi-m.

**Fiat Grandi Motori**
Via Cuneo 20, Turin 10152, Italy.
- Fiat Grandi Motori. Technical Bulletin. q. ISSN 0015-0487

**Fiere e Mostre**
Via Mascheroni 5, 20123 Milan, Italy.
- Fiere e Mostre; saloni - congressi e convegni. m. ISSN 0015-0797

**Filmcritica**
Piazza del Grillo 5, Rome, Italy.
- Filmcritica. m. ISSN 0015-1513

**Filmstudio 70**
Via Orti d'Alibert, 1c, Rome, Italy.
- Filmstudio Settanta. m.

**Editrice Finlavoro**
23 via Po 23, 00198 Rome, Italy.
- Conquiste del Lavoro. w. ISSN 0010-6348 (Confederazione Italiana Sindacati Lavoratori)

**Libreria Editrice Fiorentina**
Via Ricasole, 105-107, Casella Postale 5/11965, Florence, Italy.
- Urbanisticaipotesi. q.

**F. Fiorentini & C.**
Via Tiburtina 772, Rome, Italy.
- Cantiere; rivista mensile per impianti meccanici da cantiere. m. ISSN 0008-5715

**Firenze Agricola**
Piazza della Repubbluca 6, Florence, Italy.
- Firenze Agricola; Rivista mensile di Tecnica e Propaganda Agraria. m. ISSN 0015-2706

**S. F. Flaccovio Editore**
Via Caltanissetta 2, 90141 Palermo, Italy.
- Rivista Mineraria Siciliana. bi-m. ISSN 0035-7006 (Consiglio Regionale delle Miniere)
- Sicilia. q. ISSN 0037-4563

**Florence. Ufficio della Provincia**
Florence, Italy.
- Collana di Studi Su Problemi Urbanistici Fiorentino. irreg.

**Casa Editrice Foglio**
Via Spalato 119, Macerata, Italy.
- Litografia Oggi. bi-m. ISSN 0024-4961

**Fondazione Cini**
Isola di Giorgio Maggiore, Venice, Italy.
- Jucunda Laudatio. q. ISSN 0022-5711

**Fondazione "Claudio Monteverdi"**
Corso Garibaldi 178, 26100 Cremona, Italy.
- Instituta/Monumenta. irreg., issued in 2 series: Monumenta (vol. 7, 1974); Instituta (vol. 3) ISSN 0073-8611 (Universita di Pavia. Scuola Universitaria di Paleografia e Filologia Musicale)

**Fondazione Diritto del Lavoro**
14 via Gramsci, Rome, Italy.
- Diritto del Lavoro; rivista di dottrina e di giurisprudenza. bi-m. ISSN 0012-3404

**Fondazione Giangiacomo Feltrinelli**
Via Andegari 6, 20121 Milan, Italy.
- Fondazione Giangiacomo Feltrinelli. Annali. a. ISSN 0544-1374

**Fondazione Giorgio Cini**
- Archivio Linguistico Veneto. Quaderni. (pub. by Casa Editrice Leo S. Olschki)
- Civilta Asiatiche. (pub. by Casa Editrice Leo S. Olschki)
- Civilta Veneziana. Dizionari Dialettali e Studi Linguistici. (pub. by Casa Editrice Leo S. Olschki)
- Civilta Veneziana. Fonti e Testi. Serie Prima: Fonti e Testi per la Storia dell'Arte Veneta. (pub. by Casa Editrice Leo S. Olschki)
- Civilta Veneziana. Fonti e Testi. Serie Terza. (pub. by Casa Editrice Leo S. Olschki)
- Civilta Veneziana. Saggi. (pub. by Casa Editrice Leo S. Olschki)
- Civilta Veneziana. Studi. (pub. by Casa Editrice Leo S. Olschki)
- Quaderni dei Padri Benedettini di San Giorgio Maggiore. (pub. by Casa Editrice Leo S. Olschki)
- Saggi e Memorie di Storia dell'Arte. (pub. by Casa Editrice Leo S. Olschki)
- Studi Veneziani. (pub. by Casa Editrice Leo S. Olschki)

**Fondazione Lerici Prospezioni Archeologiche**
Via V. Veneto 108, I-00187 Rome, Italy.
- Prospezioni Archeologiche/Archeological Prospection. a. ISSN 0079-7022

**Fondazione Ugo Bordoni**
Viale di Trastevere 108, 00153 Rome, Italy.
- Poste e Telecomunicazioni; rassegna mensile di studi e documentazione. m. ISSN 0032-5406

**Food and Agriculture Organization of the United Nations**
For publications of this agency see section for UNITED NATIONS

**Formaluce**
Corso Matteotti 8, 20121 Milan, Italy.
- Formaluce. bi-m.

**Formez**
Mostra d'Oltremare, Palazzo dei Congressi, 80125 Naples, Italy.
- Problemi di Gestione; selezione da riviste straniere. 9 per yr. ISSN 0032-9363

**Foro Padano**
Via Mercanti 2, 20121 Milan, Italy.
- Foro Padano; rivista mensile di giurisprudenza Italiana e di dottrina. m. ISSN 0015-7856

**Fortuna Italiana**
Via Ulpiano 47, 00193 Rome, Italy.
- Fortuna Italiana. m. ISSN 0015-8232

**Editrice Forum**
Via Bruni 15, 47100 Forli, Italy.
- Quinta Generazione: Rivista de Poesia. bi-m.

**Forum Italiano dell'Energia Nucleare**
- Atomo e Industria. (pub. by Edizioni Atomo e Industria s.r.l.)

**G. Fossataro, Ed. & Pub.**
Largo Carlo Felice 2, Cagliari, Italy.
- Convegno; rassegna mensile illustrata di cultura e di attualita. m. ISSN 0010-812X

**Fourth International - Posadist. International Secretariat**
C.P. 5059, 00153 Rome, Italy.
- Marxista Europea. s-a (with fortn. supplements)

**Ennio Francia Ed. & Pub.**
Via di S. Marco1, Rome, Italy.
- Notiziario d'Arte. bi-m. ISSN 0029-4322

**Fratelli Jovane**
Via Lungomare 162, Salerno, Italy.
- Serafico Vessillo; bollettino fer il Terz'Ordine e fer le Vocazioni. m. ISSN 0037-2439 (Terz'ordine e le Vocazioni Cappuccine Salernitane)

**Fratelli Lega Editori**
Corso Mazzini, 33, 48018 Faenza, Italy.
- Epigraphica; rivista italiana di epigrafia. a. ISSN 0013-9572

**Frati Minori Cappuccini della Provincia Consentina**
Covento del SS. Crocifisso, 87100 Cosenza, Italy.
- Beato Angelo. m. ISSN 0005-7436

**Fratini Missionari di Recco. Collegio Serafico**
Via S. Francesco 3, 16036 Recco, Genoa, Italy.
- Squilla. bi-m. ISSN 0038-8750

**Attilio Fregoli, Ed. & Pub.**
Via Lanino II, 20142 Milan, Italy.
- Zeffiro. m. (10 per yr.)

**Dr. Filippo Fretto, Ed. & Pub.**
Corso Vinzaglio 25, 10121 Turin, Italy.
- Rassegna della Letteratura Odontoiatrica. s-a. ISSN 0033-9431

**Fronte del Lavoro**
Via Germanico 54, 00192 Rome, Italy.
- Fronte del Lavoro. s-w. ISSN 0016-206X

**Fronte Italiano di Liberazione Femminile**
Piazza Ss. Apostoli 49, 00187 Rome, Italy.
- Quarto Mondo. m. ISSN 0048-6205

**Edizioni Il Fuoco**
Via Giacinto Carini 28, 00152 Rome, Italy.
- Fuoco; rassegna di cultura e d'arte. bi-m. ISSN 0016-2876 (Studium Christi)

**Edizioni G E P**
Via Tevere 15, 00198 Rome, Italy.
- Airfreight. bi-m.

**Gabriel Italiana**
Casella Postale 7090, 00100 Rome, Italy.
- Gabriel; informatore filatelico. bi-m. ISSN 0016-3694

**Gala International**
Via Turati 3, 20121 Milan, Italy.
- Gala International; rivista bimestrale di informazione visiva. 6 per yr.

**Editoriale Galfa**
Viale Monza 128, 20127 Milan, Italy.
- Tex Home. q.

**Galleria del Cavallino**
San Marco 1725, Venice, Italy.
- Galleria del Cavallino. Mostre. irreg.

**Galleria la Medusa**
- Medusa. (pub. by Medusa Editions)

**Gallo**
Casella Postale 1242, 16100 Genoa, Italy.
- Gallo. m. ISSN 0016-416X

**Galvanotecnica**
Via Campigli 16, Varese, Italy.
- Galvanotecnica. m. ISSN 0016-4240

**Editrice Gan**
Via Nicola Martelli 3, 00197 Rome, Italy.
- Tennis Club. m.

**Giacomo Gandolfi S.p.A.**
Corso Mombello 54, 18038 Sanremo, Italy.
- Eco della Riviera. s-w. ISSN 0012-9488

**Aldo Garzanti Editore**
Via Senato 25, 20121 Milan, Italy.
- Nuovi Argomenti. q. ISSN 0029-6295

**Gazzetta delle Arti**
S. Marco 2950, 30124 Venice, Italy.
- Gazzetta delle Arti. m. ISSN 0016-5638

**Gazzetta Farmaceutica**
Piazza S. Nazaro 15, 20122 Milan, Italy.
- Gazzetta Farmaceutica. m. ISSN 0016-5646

**Gazzettino del Jonio**
Via E. de Riso 2, 88100 Catanzaro, Italy.
- Gazzettino del Jonio. fortn.

**Gazzettino della Scuola**
Facolta di Magistero, Palazzo dei Capitani, 35100 Padova, Italy.
- Gazzettino della Scuola; quindicinale di problemi didattico-pedagogici e d'informazione scolastica. s-m. ISSN 0016-5719

**Gazzettino Numismatico**
Via G. Parini 23, 04100 Latina, Italy.
- Gazzettino Numismatico. bi-m.

**Edizioni Geiger**
Via Luisa del Carretto 44, 10131 Turin, Italy.
- Tam Tam. q.

**Gelatiere Italiano**
Via Cellini 6, 20129 Milan, Italy.
- Gelatiere Italiano; revista tecnico-professionale dei gelatieri Italiani. bi-m. ISSN 0016-5999

**Geloso S.p. A.**
Via Brenta 29, 20139 Milan, Italy.
- Bollettino Tecnico Geloso; pubblicazione trimestrale di radiofonia, televisione e scienze affini. q. ISSN 0006-6877

**Genova. Ripartizione Censimenti e Statistica**
Piazza della Vittoria 15-21, Genova, Italy.
- Notiziario Statistico Mensile. m.

**Gesualdi Editore Roma**
Via IV Novembre 152, 00187 Rome, Italy.
- Agricoltura d'Italia. m. 11 per yr. ISSN 0002-127X (Istituto di Studi Nucleari per l'Agricoltura)
- Corriere di Roma. s-m.

**Gesuiti di Sicilia**
Missioni Rettoria Casa Professa, 90134 Palermo, Italy.
- Ai Nostri Amici. m. ISSN 0002-4066

**G. Giappichelli Editore**
Via Po, 21, Turin, Italy.
- Mesopotamia; rivista di archeologia. a. ISSN 0076-6615 (Universita di Torino) (Co-sponsor: Centro Ricerche Archeologiche e Scavi di Torino per Il Medio Oriente e l'Asia)

**Giardini Editori e Stampatori in Pisa**
Via Santa Bibbiana 28, 56100 Pisa, Italy.
- Studi Classici e Orientali. irreg., vols. 1-22 published and avail. for sale. ISSN 0081-6124

**Editoriale Giganti del Basket s. r. l.**
Corso Venezia 16, 20121 Milan, Italy.
- Giganti del Basket. m(11 per yr.)

**Armando Giordano, Ed. & Pub.**
Piazza d'Aosta 37, 80047 San Giuseppe Vesuviano, Naples, Italy.
- Corriere del Farmacista. m. ISSN 0010-9207

**Alfonso Giordano, Ed. & Pub. (Milan)**
Via Francesco Sforza 38, 20122 Milan, Italy.
- Folia Hereditaria et Pathologica. q. ISSN 0015-5578
- Morgagni; rivista di morfologia clinica/journal of morbid anatomy. q. ISSN 0027-1071

**Gruppo Editoriale Il Giornale d'Italie S.p.A.**
Via Appia Nuova 692, 00179 Rome, Italy.
- Giornale d'Italia Agricolo. w. ISSN 0017-0410

**Giornale di Clinica Medica**
Via Gualandi 1, 40136 Bologna, Italy.
- Giornale di Clinica Medica. m. ISSN 0017-0275

**Giornale di Geologia**
Via Zamboni, 63, 40127 Bologna, Italy.
- Giornale di Geologia; annali del museo geologico di bologna. irreg. ISSN 0017-0291

**Giornale di Medicina e Pneumologia**
Via Cervignano 32, 95129 Catania, Italy.
- Giornale di Medicina e Pneumologia. bi-m.

**Giornale Italiano delle Malattie del Torace**
Via Luca Comerio 5, 20145 Milan, Italy.
- Giornale Italiano delle Malattie del Torace. bi-m. ISSN 0017-0437

**Giornale Italiano di Chirurgia**
Via Mezzo Cannone 69, 80121 Naples, Italy.
- Giornale Italiano di Chirurgia. bi-m. ISSN 0017-0453

**Giornalista Mario Borretti**
Via G.de Rada 10, Cosenza 87100, Italy.
- Calabria Nobilissima. s-a. ISSN 0008-056X

**Giovane Critica**
Via F. Scocilea 119, Catania, Italy.
- Giovane Critica. 5-6 per yr. ISSN 0017-0526

**Casa Editrice Dott. A. Giuffre**
Via Statuto 2, 20121 Milan, Italy (L.7000)
- Accademia Nazionale di Ragionera Papers on Business Administration. irreg.
- Amministrare. q. ISSN 0044-8141 (Istituto per la Scienza dell'Amministrazione Pubblica)
- Banca Borsa e Titoli di Credito. q.
- Cassazione Penale; massimario annotato. m. ISSN 0008-7424
- Credito Pignoratizio. s-a. (Associazione Italiana dei Pubblici Istitute di Credito Su Pegno)
- Daunia Giudiziaria; rivista di diritto, giurisprudenza e notiziario. q. ISSN 0011-7021
- Diritto di Autore. q. ISSN 0012-3420
- Diritto di Famiglia e delle Persone. q.
- Diritto Ecclesiastico. q. ISSN 0012-3455
- Economia e Storia; rivista italiana di storia economica e sociale. q. ISSN 0012-9798
- Foro Amministrativo e delle Acque Pubbliche. m.
- Giurisprudenza Annotata di Diritto Industriale. a.
- Giurisprudenza Commerciale-Societa e Fallimento. bi-m.
- Giurisprudenza Costituzionale. bi-m.
- Giurisprudenza delle Imposte. q.
- Giurisprudenza di Merito. bi-m.
- Giustizia Civile; rivista mensile di giurisprudenza. m. ISSN 0017-0631
- Istituto di Diritto Internazionale-D. Anzilotti. Pubblicazioni. irreg.
- Istituto di Diritto Romano. Bullettino. a.
- Ius Romanum Medii Aevi. irreg. ISSN 0075-2037
- Iustitia. q. ISSN 0021-3268 (Unione Giuristi Cattolici Italiani)
- Lavoro e Previdenza Oggi. m.
- Legislazione Italiana. w. ISSN 0024-0524
- Massimario Tributario. m. ISSN 0025-4967 (Associazione fra le Societa Italiana per Azioni)
- Monitore dei Tribunali. m.
- Politico; rivista italiana di scienze politiche. q. ISSN 0032-325X (Universita di Pavia. Istituto di Scienze Politiche)
- Processo Legislativo nel Parlamento Italiano. irreg. (Universita degli Studi di Firenze. Faculta di Scienze Politiche)
- Quaderni di Scienze Sociali. 3 per yr. ISSN 0033-4944 (Istituto di Scienze Sociali di Genova)
- Quaderni Fiorentini per la Storia del Pensiero Giuridico Moderno. a.
- Rassegna dei Magistrati. m. (Unione dei Magistrati Italiani)
- Regioni; rivista di documentazione e giurisprudenza. bi-m.
- Responsabilita Civile e Previdenza. bi-m.
- Risparmio. m. ISSN 0035-5615 (Associazione fra le Cassa di Risparmio Italiana)
- Rivista dei Dottori Commercialisti. bi-m. (Ordine del Dottori Commercialisti di Milano)
- Rivista del Notariato. bi-m.
- Rivista delle Societa. bi-m. ISSN 0035-6018
- Rivista di Diritto Agrario. q. (Istituto di Diritto Agratio Internazionale e Comparato)
- Rivista di Diritto del Lavoro. q. ISSN 0035-6107

- Rivista di Diritto Finanziario e Scienza delle Finanze. q. ISSN 0035-6131
- Rivista di Diritto Industriale. q. ISSN 0035-614X
- Rivista di Diritto Internazionale. q. ISSN 0035-6158
- Rivista di Diritto Sportivo. q. ISSN 0048-8372 (Comitato Olimpico Nazionale Italiano)
- Rivista Giuridica dell' Edilizia. bi-m. ISSN 0485-2435
- Rivista Giuridica della Scuola. bi-m.
- Rivista Internazionale di Filosofia del Diritto. q. ISSN 0035-6727 (Societa Italiana di Filosofia Giuridica e Politica) (Co-sponsor Istituto di Filosofia del Diritto dell'Universita di Roma)
- Rivista Italiana di Diritto e Procedura Penale. q. ISSN 0557-1391
- Rivista Italiana di Previdenza Sociale; dottrina, giurisprudenza, legislazione, bibliografia. bi-m. ISSN 0035-6891
- Rivista Trimestrale di Diritto e Procedura Civile. bi-m.
- Rivista Trimestrale di Diritto Pubblico. q. ISSN 0557-1464
- Rivista Trimestrale di Scienza della Amministrazione. q.
- Rolandino; monitore del notariato. m. ISSN 0035-7871
- Schedario Tributario. m. ISSN 0036-5963
- Sociologia del Diritto. s-a. (Centro Nazionale di Prevenzione e Difesa Sociale. Commissione Permanente di Sociologia del Diritto)
- Storia e Politica. q. ISSN 0039-1905
- Studi Sassaresi. a. ISSN 0081-623X (Universita di Sassari. Societa Sassarese per le Scienze Giuridiche)
- Studio Legale. m.
- Temi Romana. m. ISSN 0495-0658
- Universita di Trieste. Facolta di Scienze Politiche. Pubblicazioni. irreg.

**Giunta Centrale per gli Studi Storici**
E U R Palazzo delle Scienze, Rome, Italy.
- Giunta Centrale per gli Studi Storici, Rome. Bibliografia Storica Nazionale. a. ISSN 0085-2317

**Giunta Diocesana di A.C.**
Via Trento, 33170 Pordenone, Italy
(Subscriptions to: Il Popolo, Casella Postale 103, Pordenone, Italy)
- Popolo. w.

**Giunti-Barbera**
Via Vincenzo Gioberti 34, 50121 Florence, Italy.
- Rivista di Psicologia. q. ISSN 0035-6506 (Societa Italiana di Psicologia)
- Vita Scolastica; rassegna quindicinale della istruzione primaria. s-m. ISSN 0042-7349

**Giustizia e Costituzione**
Corso Vittorio Emanuele 142, 00186 Rome, Italy.
- Giustizia e Costituzione. bi-m.

**Edizioni Giustizia Nuova**
Via Bozzi 47-A, Bari, Italy.
- Giustizia Nuova. m. ISSN 0017-064X

**Giustizia Penale**
Via Giovanni Nicotera 10, Rome, Italy.
- Giustizia Penale. m. ISSN 0017-0658

**Editoriale Globo**
Via Boccaccio 24, 20123 Milan, Italy.
- Marmi Graniti Pietre; rivista specializzata del settore marmifero. bi-m. ISSN 0047-603X

**Gorlich Editore S.p.A.**
Via Privata Goerlich 1, 20037 Paderno Dugnano, Italy.
- Arredare la Casa. q. ISSN 0004-2846
- Interni; la rivista dell'arredamento. m. ISSN 0020-9538
- Tuttoville. q. ISSN 0041-445X

**Zalozba (Casa Editrice) Gospodarstvo**
Via Valdirivo 40, 34132 Trieste, Italy.
- Gospodarstvo. w. ISSN 0017-2456

**Grafica Toscana**
Via Mannelli 29R, 50132 Florence, Italy.
- Archivio de Vecchi; per l'anatomia patologica e la medicina clinica. 1-2 vols. per yr. (3 nos. per vol.) ISSN 0004-0061

**Giuseppe Grassi, Ed. & Pub.**
Cesare Correnti 6, 00179 Rome, Italy.
- Chirurgia Gastroenterologica (English Edition) q.
- Chirurgia Gastroenterologica (Italian Edition); rassegna trimestrale di chirurgia dell'apparato digerente e degli organi addominali. q. ISSN 0009-4765

**Gregor Mendel Institute for Medical Genetics and Twin Studies. Permanent Committee**
- Acta Geneticae Medicae et Gemellologiae. (pub. by Casa Editrice Licinio Cappelli)

**Gregorian University Press**
Piazza della Pilotta 4, 00187 Rome, Italy.
- Acta Nuntiaturae Gallicae. irreg. ISSN 0065-1443 (Pontificia Universita Gregoriana. Facolta di Storia Ecclesiastica) (Co-sponsor Ecole Francaise de Rome)
- Analecta Gregoriana. irreg. ISSN 0066-1376 (Pontificia Universita Gregoriana)
- Archivum Historiae Pontificae. a. ISSN 0066-6785 (Pontificia Universita Gregoriana. Facolta di Storia Ecclesiastica)
- Gregorianum; Periodicum trimestre a Pont. Univ. Gregoriana editum. q. ISSN 0017-4114 (Pontificia Universita Gregoriana)
- Periodica de Re Morali Canonica Liturgica. q. ISSN 0031-529X (Pontificia Universita Gregoriana)
- Pontificia Universita Gregoriana. Miscellanea Historiae Pontificiae. irreg. ISSN 0080-3979
- Pontificia Universita Gregoriana. Studia Missionalia. a. ISSN 0080-3987

**Libreria Gregoriana Editrice**
Via Roma 13, 35100 Padua, Italy.
- Studia Patavina; rivista di scienze religiose. 3 per yr. ISSN 0039-3304

**Grotta della Vipera**
Corso Vittorio Emanuele, 366, 09100 Cagliari, Italy.
- Grotta della Vipera; rivista trimestrale di cultura. q.

**Gruppi Grotte Italiani**
- Rassegna Speleologica Italiana. (pub. by Salvatore dell' Oca, Ed. & Pub.)

**Gruppo Agrochimica**
Via S. Michele degli Scalzi 2, Pisa, Italy.
- Agrochimica. 6 per yr. ISSN 0002-1857 (Istituto di Chimica Agraria)

**Gruppo di Studio Sul Societa e Istituzioni**
C. P. 6199, 00100 Rome, Italy.
- Queste Istituzioni; cronache del sistema politica. q.

**Gruppo Finanziario Tessile**
Corso Giulio Cesare 31, Turin, Italy.
- Vestire; rivista di alta moda maschile, di tessuti, di abbigliamento. s-a. ISSN 0042-4579

**Gruppo Otologi Ospedalieri Italiani**
- Annali di Laringologia, Otologia, Rinologia, Faringologia. (pub. by Vita Farmaceutici)

**Gruppo Savoia**
Via Bergognone 65, 20156 Milan, Italy.
- Savoia. bi-m. ISSN 0036-5157

**Antonio Guarasci, Ed. & Pub.**
Via Idria 26, 87100 Cosenza, Italy.
- Cronache Calabresi; mensile di politica e cultura. m. ISSN 0011-1732

**Guardia di Finanza**
Ufficio Stampa e Pubbliche Relazioni, Via Sicilia 178, 00187 Rome, Italy.
- Finanziere. fortn. ISSN 0015-2242
- Rivista della Guardia di Finanza. bi-m. ISSN 0035-595X

**Libreria Internazionale Guida**
Via Port'alba 19, 80134 Naples, Italy.
- Bollettino di Libri Antichi e Moderni di Varia Cultura Esauriti e Rari. s-a. ISSN 0006-6745
- E S. 3 per yr.
- Sigma. 3 per yr.

**Guida Monaci**
Via Francesco Crispi 10, 00187 Rome, Italy.
- Annuario Amministrativo Italiano. a. ISSN 0084-6619
- Annuario Generale Italiano. a. ISSN 0084-6627

**Augusto Guzzo, Ed. & Pub.**
Piazza Statuto 26, 10144 Turin, Italy.
- Filosofia. q. ISSN 0015-1823
- International Studies in Philosophy. s-a.

**Edizioni Hennessen Italia**
Via Baracchini 1, 20123 Milan, Italy.
- G T-Giornale Tessile. w.

**Herder Editrice e Libreria s.r.l.**
Piazza Montecitorio 120, 00186 Rome, Italy.
- Aquinas; Ephemerides Thomisticae. 3 per yr. ISSN 0003-7362 (Pontificia Universita Lateranense)
- Blue Guitar; rivista annuale di letteratura inglese e americana. a. (Universita degli Studi di Messina. Facolta di Magistero)
- Cina. irreg; vol. 12, 1975. ISSN 0529-7451 (Istituto Italiano per Il Medio ed Estremo Oriente)
- Giappone. a. (Japanese Institute of Culture)
- Istituto Orientale di Napoli. Annali. Sezione Orientale. q.
- Istituto Universitario Orientale Naples. Annali. Sezione Germanica. a. ISSN 0077-2763
- Istituto Universitario Orientale, Naples. Annali. Sezione Slava. a. ISSN 0077-2771
- Rivista di Storia della Chiesa in Italia. s-a. ISSN 0035-6557
- Romanobarbarica. a. (Universita di Roma. Istituto di Lingua e Letteratura Latina)

**Herder Editrice s.r.l.**
Via Merulana 248, Rome, Italy.
- East and West. q. ISSN 0012-8376 (Istituto Italiano per il Medio ed Estremo Oriente)

**Histadruth Ha-Morim**
- Eco dell'Educazione Ebraica. (pub. by Associazione Insegnanti Ebrei d'Italia)

**Editore Ulrico Hoepli**
Via Smareglia 9, Milan, Italy.
- Ingegneria; rivista di scienza e tecnica. m. ISSN 0035-6263

**I A C I C O**
Via Giovanni Lanza 130, Rome, Italy.
- Terra e Sole; agricoltura pratica e meccanica agraria. m. ISSN 0040-3768

**Edizioni I.C.I.**
Via Capecelatro 37, 20148 Milan, Italy.
- Giornale del Legno. m. ISSN 0017-0178 (Unione Italiana Sviluppo Tecnico Economico Industriale del Legno)

**I N A S**
Viale Aventino 45, Rome, Italy.
- Rivista Italiana di Diritto Sociale; dottrina giurisprudenza, legislazione, tutela del lavoro. q. ISSN 0035-6824

**I.P.A.G.**
Via Oberdan 6, 45100 Rovigo, Italy.
- Voce di Ferrara. w. ISSN 0042-7853 (Curia Arcivescovile di Ferrara)

**I T A - Uffici Informazioni Specializzati**
Via Milazzo 10, Milan, Italy.
- Eco-Tessili. w. ISSN 0012-9542

**I T E C Editrice**
Via dell'Uomo, 7, 20129 Milan, Italy.
- Prefabbricazione. m. ISSN 0032-7255

**Idea Centro Studi Roma**
Largo Angelicum 1-A, Rome, Italy.
- Idea; mensile di cultura e di critica sociale. m. ISSN 0019-1280

**Casa Editrice Idelson**
Via A. de Gasperi 55, 80133 Naples, Italy.
- Archivio di Ostetricia e Ginecologia. bi-m. ISSN 0004-0126
- Rassegna di Medicina Sperimentale. bi-m. ISSN 0033-9555
- Societa Italiana di Biologia Sperimentale. Bollettino. bi-m. ISSN 0037-8771

**Illustrazione Pubblicitaria**
Via Bernabei 39, Parma, Italy.
- Illustrazione Pubblicitaria; rivista mensile di attualita e informazione. m. ISSN 0019-2473

**Impegno Settanta**
Corso Umberto 22, 91026 Mazara del Vallo (Trapani), Italy.
- Impegno Settanta; rassegna di politica, cultura e attualita. q. ISSN 0046-8711

**Imprendinvest Italiana s.r.l.**
Via L. Manara 15, 20122 Milan, Italy.
- Automondo; mensile automobilistico di politica attualita e cultura. 11 per yr.

**L' Impresa Edizioni s.r.l.**
Corso Fiume 11, 10131 Turin, Italy.
- Impresa; rivista di scienze e tecniche manageriali. bi-m. ISSN 0035-6816 (Institution of Production Engineers) (Co-sponsors: American Institute of Industrial Engineers; Society of Manufacturing Engineers)

**Impresa Generale Pubblicita**
Piazza Cavour 1, 20121 Milan, Italy.
- Publitransport. 3 per yr. ISSN 0033-3999

**Incidenza**
Via Giordano Bruno, 30, Catania, Italy.
- Incidenza; rivista bimestrale di cultura e ricerche. bi-m. ISSN 0019-3410

**Incontri**
Via Carracci 7, 40121 Bologna, Italy.
- Incontri. s-m (20 per yr)

**Incontro**
Via Consolata N. 11, 10122 Torino, Italy.
- Incontro; pacifist periodical independent. m. ISSN 0019-3496

**Editrice l' Industria**
Piazzale Cadorna 5, 20123 Milan, Italy.
- Quattro Stagioni; periodico mensile di agricoltura. m.

**Industria del Mobile s.r.l.**
Via Giambalogna, Milan, Italy.
- Arredorama. m. (9 per yr.) ISSN 0004-2854
- Industria del Mobile. m. ISSN 0019-753X

**Industria della Carta s.r.l.**
Corso Italia N. 6, 20122 Milan, Italy.
- Industria della Carta. m.(11 per yr.) ISSN 0019-7548

**Industria Pubblicazioni Audiovisivi**
Piazzale Cardona 5, Milan, Italy.
- Industria; rivista di economia e problemi industriali. bi-m. ISSN 0019-7416
- Materie Plastiche Ed Elastomeri. m. ISSN 0025-5459

**Edizioni per Industria Specializzata**
*see* E R I S

**Editrice Periodici Industriali s.r.l.**
Corso Italia 13, 20122 Milan, Italy.
- Approvvigionamenti. m. (except Aug.)

**Industrie Grafiche Cino del Duca S.p.A.**
Via Borgogna 5, 20122 Milan, Italy.
- Historia. m.
- Intimita della Famiglia. w.
- Stop. w.

**Industrie Grafiche del Bianco**
Trieste, Italy.
- Consorzio Universitario. Pubblicazioni. Sezione Miscellanea. irreg. (Universita di Udine. Biblioteca Centrale)

**Industrie Grafiche Editoriali**
Divisione Periodiche, Via Carlo Goldoni 1, Milan, Italy.
- Lotus; a Review of Contemporary Architecture. 4 per yr. ISSN 0076-101X

**Inforav**
*see* Istituto per lo Sviluppo e la Gestione Avanzata dell'Informazione

**Ingersoll-Rand Italiana**
- Tecnica dell'Aria Compressa. (pub. by Edizioni C A M)

**Institut Suisse de Rome**
- Bibliotheca Helvetica Romana. (pub. by Librarie Droz SZ)

**Institute for Futures Research and Education**
- Social and Human Forecasting Documentation. (pub. by Edizioni Previsionali)

**Institute of Microbiology**
Opedale Maggiore, 43100 Parma, Italy.
- Synthesis Microbiologica; microbiological current literature. m. ISSN 0039-7903

**Institution of Production Engineers**
- Impresa. (pub. by L' Impresa Edizioni s.r.l.)

**Instituto Figlie di Maria Ausiliatrice Salesiane di Don Bosco**
- Rivista di Scienze dell'Educazione. (pub. by Editip)

**Instituto "la Casa"**
Via Lattuada 14, 20135 Milan, Italy.
- Riflessi. q. (prep. by its Consultorio Prematrimoniale e Matrimoniale)

**Instituto Nazionale della Previdenza Sociale**
Via Ciro Il Grande 21, 00144 Rome, Italy.
- Istituto Nazionale della Previdenza Sociale. Atti Ufficiali. m. ISSN 0021-2520

**Institutum Carmelitanum**
Via Sforza Pallavicini 10, 00193 Rome, Italy.
- Carmelus; Commentarii ab Instituto Carmelitano Editi. s-a. ISSN 0008-6673

**Institutum Historicum Polonicum Romae**
284 via degli Scipioni, 00192 Rome, Italy.
- Antemurale; annual periodical devoted to the history of Central and Eastern Europe. a. ISSN 0066-4642
- Elementa Ad Fontium Editiones; unpublished sources to mediaeval and modern European history, 14th-17th centuries. irreg; vol. 42, 1977. ISSN 0070-9972

**Institutum Historicum Societatis Iesu**
Via dei Penitenzieri 20, 00193 Rome, Italy.
- Archivum Historicum Societatis Iesu. s-a. ISSN 0037-8887

**Institutum Patristicum Augustinianum**
Via del S. Uffizio 25, 00193, Rome, Italy.
- Augustinianum. 3 per yr. ISSN 0004-8011
- Studia Ephemeridis Augustinianum. irreg.

**Intergovernmental Bureau for Informatics**
P. O. Box 10253, Viale Civilta del Lavoro 23, 00144 Rome, Italy.
- I B I Newsletter. q.

**Internacia Asocio de Bibliistoj Kaj Orientalistoj**
Piazza Duomo 4, 48100 Ravenna, Italy.
- Biblia Revuo. q. ISSN 0006-0879

**International Academy of Legal Medicine and Social Medicine**
c/o Prof. Ferdinando Antoniotti, Viale Regina, Elena 336, 00161 Rome, Italy.
- International Academy of Legal Medicine and of Social Medicine. (Congress Reports) triennial, 1973, 9th, Rome. ISSN 0074-1248

**International Association for Classical Archaeology**
49 Piazza San Marco, 00186 Rome, Italy.
- International Association for Classical Archaeology. Proceedings of Congress. irreg., 1973, 10th, Ankara and Izmir. ISSN 0074-1469

**International Association for Water Law**
Via Montevideo 5, 00197 Rome, Italy.
- International Conference on Water Law and Administration. Background Paper. irreg.

**International Association of Volcanology and Chemistry of the Earth's Interior**
c/o Dr. F. Esu Cugusi, Ed., Instituto di Geologia Applicata, Via Eudossiana 18, 00184 Rome, Italy.
- Bulletin Volcanologique. q. (approx)
- International Association of Volcanology and Chemistry of the Earth's Interior. Newsletter. irreg. ISSN 0579-5362

**International Atomic Energy Agency. International Centre for Theoretical Physics**
For publications of this agency see section for UNITED NATIONS

**International Cardiovascular Society**
- Journal of Cardiovascular Surgery. (pub. by Edizioni Minerva Medica)

**International Catholic Rural Association**
Piazza S. Calisto 16, 00153 Rome, Italy.
- Information Bulletin for Catholic Rural Organizations. s-a.

**International Council for Philosophy and Humanistic Studies**
- Diogenes. (pub. by Casalini Libri)

**International Documentation and Communication Center**
Via S. Maria dell'Anima 30, 00186 Rome, Italy.
- I D O C Documentation Service. m.

**International Federation for Hygiene, Preventive Medicine and Social Medicine**
Via Cola di Rienzo, 11, 00197 Rome, Italy.
- International Congress on Hygiene and Preventive Medicine. Proceedings. irreg. 7th, venice 1974.
- International Federation for Hygiene, Preventive and Social Medicine. News. bi-m.
- News of I.F.H.P.S.M. irreg.

**International Federation of Sportive Medicine**
- Journal of Sports Medicine and Physical Fitness. (pub. by Edizioni Minerva Medica)

**International Film and Television Council**
Via Santa Susanna, 17, 00187 Rome, Italy.
- World Screen Bulletin and Calendar/Ecrans du Monde Bulletin et Calendrier. a.

**International Institute for Geothermal Research, Pisa, Italy**
- Geothermics. (pub. by Pergamon Press, Inc. US)

**International Institute for the Unification of Private Law**
28 via Panisperna, 00184 Rome, Italy.
- International Institute for the Unification of Private Law. Rapport sur l'Activite de l'Institute. a. ISSN 0579-7918

**International Journal of Transport Economics**
Via G.A. Guattani 8, 00161 Rome, Italy.
- International Journal of Transport Economics/ Rivista Internazionale di Economica dei Trasporti. 3 per yr.

**International Music Council. International Institute for Comparative Music Studies and Documentation**
- World of Music. (pub. by B. Schott's Soehne)

**International Publishing Enterprises**
Via G.G. Belli 36, 00193 Rome, Italy.
- World Review of Animal Production. q. ISSN 0043-8979

**International Railway Union**
Via Marsala 9, Rome, Italy.
- Through Europe by Train. irreg. ISSN 0579-8256

**International Society for Chronobiology**
- Chronobiologia. (pub. by Casa Editrice Il Ponte)

**International Society of Cybernetic Medicine**
348 via Roma, 80134 Naples, Italy.
- Cybernetic Medicine. q. ISSN 0011-4219
- International Congress of Cybernetic Medicine. Proceedings. biennial. ISSN 0074-3615

**International Society of Medical Hydrology and Climatology**
Via Rovereto 11, 00198 Rome, Italy.
- Archives of Medical Hydrology. 3-4 per yr. ISSN 0003-9934

**International Society of Soil Science**
c/o FAO, Via delle Terme di Caracalla, 00153 Rome, Italy.
- International Society of Soil Science. Bulletin. s-a. ISSN 0020-8760

**International Society of Sports Psychology**
- International Journal of Sport Psychology. (pub. by Edizioni Luigi Pozzi)

**International Year & Hand-Books S.r.l.**
Via Montenapoleone 18, 20121 Milan, Italy.
- Pubblicita e Organizzazione Oggi. irreg.

**Societa Editrice Internazionale**
Corso R. Margherita 176, 10152 Torino, Italy.
- Orientamenti Pedagogici; rivista internazionale di scienze dell'educazione. bi-m. ISSN 0030-5391 (Universita Salesiana di Roma. Facolta di Scienze dell'Educazione)
- Scuola Viva; mensile per educatori. m. ISSN 0036-9926
- Studi Francesi; rivista dedicata alla cultura e alla civilta letteraria della Francia. 3 per yr. ISSN 0039-2944 (Universita degli Studi di Torino. Facolta di Lettere e Filosofia. Istituto di Lingua e Literatura Francese) (Co-Sponsor: Universita di Lione I I, U.E.R. d'Etudes Francaises)

**Compagnia Edizione Internazionali**
Via Luciano Manara 15, 20122 Milan, Italy.
- Italy Exports. q. (Italy. Ministero del Commercio Con l'Estero)

**Edizioni Interrogations**
Via G. Reni 96/6, 10136turin, Italy.
- Interrogations; revue internationale de recherche anarchiste. q.

**P. Introzzi, Ed. & Pub.**
Pavia, Italy.
- Rivista di Emoterapia e Immunoematologia. bi-m. ISSN 0035-6204 (Universita di Pavia. Policlinico)

**Ispettorato Provinciale dell'Agricoltura**
Via Zelasco 3, Bergamo, Italy.
- Agricoltura Bergamasca; pubblicazione mensile di tecnica e propaganda agraria Bergamo. m. ISSN 0002-1253
- Sentinella Agricola; periodico cremonese de tecnica e propaganda agraria fondato nel 1896. m. ISSN 0037-234X
- Umbria Agricola. bi-m. ISSN 0041-6312

**Ispettorato Provinciale dell' Agricoltura Pesaro**
Via Giusti 5, 61100 Pesaro, Italy.
- Agricoltura Nostra. m. ISSN 0002-1288

**Istituti Clinici di Perfezionamento**
Via S. Barnaba 8, Milan, Italy.
- Medicina del Lavoro. bi-m. ISSN 0025-7818

**Istituti de Pena Fiorentini**
Via della Mattonaia 6, 50121 Florence, Italy.
- Noi, gli Altri. q.

**Istituti di Archeologia e Storia dell'Arte**
Universita Catania, Catania, Italy.
- Cronache di Archeologia e di Storia dell'Arte. s-a. ISSN 0011-1767

**Istituti Ospedalieri Neuropsichiatrici di San Lazzaro**
Via Amendola 2, 42100-Reggio Emilia, Italy.
- Rivista Sperimentale di Freniatria; medicina legale delle alienazioni mentali. bi-m. ISSN 0035-7057

**Istituti Ospitalieri Verona**
Via Bassini 1, Verona, Italy.
- Fracastoro. 3 per yr. ISSN 0015-9271

**Istituto Affari Internazionali**
Viale Mazzini 88, 00195 Rome, Italy.
- Istituto Affari Internazionali. Quaderni. (pub. by Societa Editrice Il Mulino)
- Istituto Affari Internazionali, Rome. I A I Informa. m. ISSN 0047-1631
- Italia Nella Politica Internazionale. (pub. by Edizioni di Comunita)
- Spettatore Internazionale. (pub. by Societa Editrice Il Mulino)

**Istituto Agostino Gemelli**
Corso Concordia, 7, 20129 Milan, Italy.
- Ikon; cinema - television - iconographie. q. ISSN 0019-1744
- Istituto Agostino Gemelli. Collana di Studi Sull' Informazione Visiva. (pub. by Societa Editrice Il Mulino)

**Istituto Agronomico per l'Oltremare**
Via Antonio Cocchi 4, Florence 50131, Italy.
- Rivista di Agricoltura Subtropicale e Tropicale. q. ISSN 0035-6026

**Istituto Biochimico Sperimentale. Sezione Scientifica**
Viale Machiavelli 31, Florence 50125, Italy.
- Attualita Mediche. fortn. ISSN 0004-7325

**Istituto Botanico di Torino**
Universita di Torino, Viale Mattioli 25, 10125 Turin, Italy.
- Allionia. a. ISSN 0065-6429

**Istituto Cattolico di Attivita Sociale**
- Orientamenti Sociali. (pub. by Editrice A.V.E)

**Istituto Centrale per Il Catalogo Unico delle Biblioteche Italiane e per le Informazioni Bibliografiche**
Viale del Castro Pretorio, Via Osoppo, Rome, Italy.
- Bibliografia Nazionale Italiana. m (with supplement) ISSN 0006-1077 (Biblioteca Nazionale Centrale di Firenze)

**Istituto Clinicodi Odontostomatologia**
Viale Benedetto 15, Genoa, Italy.
- Stomatologica. q. ISSN 0039-1727

**Istituto Culturale per Pubblicazioni e Studi Rotariani**
Corso Venezia 16, 20121 Milan, Italy.
- Realta Nuova. m.
- Rotary. m.

**Istituto Dattilografico Italiano**
Via Ricasoli 9, Florence, Italy.
- Specializzazione; Trimestrale dell'istituto I D I E di tecniche aziendali. q. ISSN 0038-6863

**Istituto de Studi Sul Lavoro**
- Rivista del Lavoro. (pub. by Edizioni del Lavoro)

**Istituto del Dramma Italiano**
- Rivista Italiana de Drammaturgia. (pub. by Bulzoni Editore)

**Istituto della Enciclopedia Italiana**
Piazza Paganica 4, 00186 Rome, Italy.
- Istituto della Enciclopedia Italiana. Annuario. a.
- Istituto della Enciclopedia Italiana. Bibliotheca Biographica. irreg.

**Istituto della Produzione Animale**
Facolta di Agraria, 80055 Portici, Naples, Italy.
- Produzione Animale. q. ISSN 0033-0000

**Istituto Dermopatico dell'Immacolata**
Via Monti di Creta 104, 00167 Rome, Italy.
- Chronica Dermatologica; rassegna dell' istituto dermopatico, immacolata. bi-m. ISSN 0011-1759

**Istituto di Anatomia e Istologia Patologica**
Universita di Napoli, Naples, Italy.
- Rivista di Anatomia Patologica e di Oncologia. m. ISSN 0048-8364

**Istituto di Antichita Ravennati e Bizantine**
Via S. Vitale 28, Ravenna 48100, Italy.
- Felix Ravenna; Rivista di Antichita Ravennati, Cristiane e Bizantine. a. ISSN 0085-0500

**Istituto di Biologia del Mare**
Riva 7 Martiri, 1364 A, Venice, Italy.
- Archivio di Oceanografia e Limnologia. irreg., 1969, vol. 15, no. 2. ISSN 0066-667X

**Istituto di Chimica Agraria**
- Agrochimica. (pub. by Gruppo Agrochimica)

**Istituto di Clinica Dermatologica Dell Universita**
Via del Vespro 131, Palermo, Italy.
- Annali Italiani di Dermatologia Clinica e Sperimentale. q. ISSN 0003-4703

**Istituto di Diritto Agratio Internazionale e Comparato**
- Rivista di Diritto Agrario. (pub. by Casa Editrice Dott. A. Giuffre)

**Istituto di Diritto Romano**
- Istituto di Diritto Romano. Bullettino. (pub. by Casa Editrice Dott. A. Giuffre)

**Istituto di Economia Internazionale**
Via Garibaldi 4, Genoa, Italy.
- Bollettino Emerografico di Economia Internazionale. q. ISSN 0006-680X
- Economia Internazionale. q. ISSN 0012-981X

**Istituto di Entomologia Agraria**
Viale delle Scienze, 90128 Palermo, Italy.
- Universita di Palermo. Istituto di Entomologia Agraria. Bollettino. biennial. ISSN 0078-8619

**Istituto di Farmacologia della Universita Milano**
Via Vanvitelli 32, Milan, Italy.
- Archivio Italiano di Patologia e Clinica dei Tumori. q. ISSN 0004-0266

**Istituto di Filologia Romanza**
- Cultura Neolatina. (pub. by Societa Tipografia Editrice Modenese)

**Istituto di Filosofia della Universita di Roma**
Rome, Italy.
- Bollettino Bibliografico per le Scienze Morali e Sociale. q. ISSN 0006-6621

**Istituto di Fisica dell'Atmosfera**
Piazzale Luigi Sturzo 31, 00144 Rome, Italy.
- Istituto di Fisica dell'Atmosfera, Rome. Bibliografia Generale. irreg. ISSN 0075-1901
- Istituto di Fisica dell'Atmosfera, Rome. Contributi Scientifici: Pubblicazioni di Fisica dell'Atmosfera e di Metteorologia. irreg. ISSN 0075-191X
- Istituto di Fisica dell'Atmosfera, Rome. Pubblicazioni Didattiche. irreg. ISSN 0075-1928
- Istituto di Fisica dell'Atmosfera, Rome. Pubblicazioni Scientifiche. irreg. ISSN 0075-1936
- Istituto di Fisica dell'Atmosfera, Rome. Pubblicazioni Varie. irreg. ISSN 0075-1944
- Istituto di Fisica dell'Atmosfera, Rome. Rapporti Interni Provvisori Adiffusione Limitata. irreg. ISSN 0075-1952
- Istituto di Fisica dell'Atmosfera, Rome. Rapporti Scientifici. irreg. ISSN 0075-1960
- Istituto di Fisica dell'Atmosfera, Rome. Rapporti Tecnici. irreg. ISSN 0075-1979

**Istituto di Geografia Alpina**
10134 Turin, Italy.
- Istituto di Geografia Alpina, Turin. Pubblicazioni/ Alpine Geographic Institute. Publications. irreg. (approx. 2 per yr.) ISSN 0579-5788

**Istituto di Glottologia**
Via S. Maria 36, Pisa, Italy.
- Italia Dialettale; Rivista di Dialettologia Italiana. a. ISSN 0085-2295

**Istituto di Indagini Psicologiche**
Corso XXII Marzo 57, 20129 Milan, Italy.
- Rivista Internazionale di Psicologia e Ipnosi. q. ISSN 0035-6743 (Societa Internazionale di Psicologia della Scrittura and Centro Internazionale di Ipnosi Medica e Psicologica)

**Istituto di Microscopia Elettronica Clinica Policlinico S. Orsola**
- Journal of Submicroscopic Cytology. (pub. by S. Karger AG SZ)

**Istituto di Norvegia in Roma**
Viale 30 Aprile 33, 00153 Rome, Italy.
- Acta ad Archaeologiam et Artium Historiam Pertinentia. irreg., vol. 5, 1974. ISSN 0065-0900

**Istituto di Oncologia**
Via Cavour 31, 10123 Turin, Italy.
- Cancro. bi-m. ISSN 0008-5480

**Istituto di Parassitologia**
Via Cesare Battisti 48, 98100 Messina, Italy.
- Rivista di Parassitologia. 3 per yr. ISSN 0035-6387

**Istituto di Patologia del Libro "Alfonso Gallo"**
Via Milano 76, 00184 Rome, Italy.
- Istituto di Patologia del Libro "Alfonso Gallo". Bollettino. s-a. ISSN 0020-403X

**Istituto di Patronato per l'Assistenza Sociale**
Via Colossi 50, 00146 Rome, Italy.
- Proposte Sociali; studi giurisprudenza e informazione critica sulla sicurezza sociale. bi-m.

**Istituto di Propaganda Libraria**
Via Mercalli 23, Milan, Italy.
- Ragguaglio Librario; rassegna mensile bibliografica culturale. m. ISSN 0033-8648

**Istituto di Puericultura**
Via Ospedale 119, Cagliari, Italy.
- Annali Italiani di Pediatria. bi-m. ISSN 0003-4711

**Istituto di Ricerca e Documentazione Sui Trasporti**
Piazza Cimone, 2 Rome 00141, Italy.
- Politica dei Trasporti. q. ISSN 0477-244X

**Istituto di Scienze Sociali di Genova**
- Quaderni di Scienze Sociali. (pub. by Casa Editrice Dott. A. Giuffre)

**Istituto di Storia Greca e Romana**
- Istituto di Storia Greca e Romana. Quaderni di Storia. (pub. by Edizioni Dedalo)

**Istituto di Studi e Documentazione sull' Est Europeo**
Corso Italia, 27, 34122 Trieste, Italy.
- Est-Ovest; quadrimestrale di studi sull'Est Europeo. 3 per yr. ISSN 0046-256X
- Istituto di Studi e Documentazioni sull'Est Europeo. Serie Giuridica. irreg; latest issue, no. 5.

**Istituto di Studi e Richerche Carlo Cattaneo**
- Istituto di Studi e Ricerche Carlo Cattaneo. Quaderni. (pub. by Societa Editrice Il Mulino)

**Istituto di Studi Etruschi, Florence**
- Biblioteca di Studi Etruschi. (pub. by Casa Editrice Leo S. Olschki)

**Istituto di Studi Legislativi**
Palazzo de Ginnasi, Via dell'Arco De'ginnasi, Rome, Italy.
- I S L E. Rassegna Parlamentare - Schedario Legislativo. bi-m. ISSN 0033-9814

**Istituto di Studi Nucleari per l'Agricoltura**
- Agricoltura d'Italia. (pub. by Gesualdi Editore Roma)

**Istituto di Studi Pirandelliani e Sul Teatro Contemporaneo**
- Istituto di Studi Pirandelliani e Sul Teatro Contemporaneo. (pub. by Casa Editrice Felice le Monnier)

**Istituto di Studi Psicologici e Psichiatrici Villa S. Rita**
Piazze delle Murge 1, Rome, Italy.
- Clinica Psichiatrica; rivista di psichiatria e scienze affini. s-a. ISSN 0009-9066

**Istituto di Studi Romani**
Piazza dei Cavalieri di Malta 2, 00153 Rome, Italy.
- Istituto di Studi Romani. Rassegna d'Informazioni. fortn. ISSN 0021-2474
- Studi Romani. q. ISSN 0039-2995

**Istituto di Studi Sul Lavoro**
Palazzo della Civilta del Lavoro, Quadrato della Concordia, Rome, Italy.
- Corriere dei Congressi; mensile di informazione e documentazione. m. ISSN 0010-9177
- Studi Sul Lavoro. q. ISSN 0039-3053

**Istituto di Studi sull'Europa e Sui Paesi in via di Sviluppo**
Piazza Augusto Imperatore 32, 00186 Rome, Italy.
- Sinistra Europea. m.

**Istituto di Studi Verdiani**
Strada della Repubblica 57, 43100 Parma, Italy.
- International Congress of Verdi Studies. Proceedings. triennial.
- Verdi. 3 per yr. ISSN 0042-3734

**Istituto di Tecnica e Propaganda Agraria**
Via Caio Mario 27, Rome, Italy.
- Agricoltura; attualita italiane e straniere. m. ISSN 0002-1237
- Storia dell'Agricoltura. q. ISSN 0039-1883

**Istituto di Terapia Fisica e Riabilitazioni**
- Riabilitazione. (pub. by Masson Italia Editori S.p.A.)

**Istituto di Zoologia**
Universita di Pavia, Pavia, Italy.
- Genetica Agraria. q. ISSN 0016-6685

**Istituto e Museo di Storia della Scienza**
- Istituto e Museo di Storia della Scienza. Biblioteca. (pub. by Casa Editrice Leo S. Olschki)

**Istituto e Orto Botanico**
Via Foria 223, 80139 Naples, Italy.
- Delpinoa. a (biennial from 1964-1965) ISSN 0416-928X

**Istituto Editoriale Cisalpino**
Largo Richini 8, Milan, Italy.
- Criminologia. q. (Societa Lombarda di Criminologia)
- Pensiero e Linguaggio in Operazioni/Thought and Language in Operations. q. (Universita degli Studi di Milano. Centro di Cibernetica e di Attivita Linguistiche)

**Istituto Editoriale del Merrogiorno**
Rione Sirignane 10, Naples 80100, Italy.
- Ricerca; revista di matematiche pure e applicate. q. ISSN 0048-8283

**Istituto Editoriale Pubblicazioni Internazionali**
Piazza Ruggero di Sicilia 1, 00162 Rome, Italy.
- Guida Nazionale del Commercio Con l'Estero; annuario di consultazione per importatori ed exportatori. a. ISSN 0432-9120
- Inchieste di Urbanistica e Architettura; rivista di studi e informazioni. q. ISSN 0019-3399

**Istituto Elettrotecnico Nazionale Galileo Ferraris**
Corso Massimo d'Azeglio 42, Turin, Italy.
- I. E. N. Pubblicazioni. 50 per yr. ISSN 0018-957X

**Istituto Ellenico di Studi Bizantini e Post-Bizantini**
Castello, 3412 Venezia, Italy.
- Istituto Ellenico di Studi Bizantini e Postbizantini, Venice. Biblioteca. irreg., 1968, no. 3. ISSN 0075-1502
- Thesaurismata. a. ISSN 0082-4097

**Istituto Farmacobiologico Malesci di Firenze**
- Cardiologia Pratica. (pub. by Edizioni Mediche Italiane)

**Istituto Ganassini di Ricerche Biochimiche**
Via Gaggia 16, Milan, Italy.
- Relazioni Clinico Scientifiche. bi-m. ISSN 0048-7198

**Istituto Geografico de Agostini**
Corso della Vittoria 91, Novara, Italy.
- Atlante. m. ISSN 0004-6736

**Istituto Geografico Militare**
Via C. Battisti 10, I 50100, Florence, Italy.
- Bollettino di Geodesia e Scienze Affini. q. ISSN 0006-6710
- Universo. bi-m. ISSN 0042-0409

**Istituto Geografico Polare**
62010 Civitanova Marche (Macerata), Italy.
- Polo. q. ISSN 0032-3667

**Istituto Giapponese di Cultura in Roma**
Via Antonio Gramsci 74, 00197 Roma, Italy.
- Istituto Giapponese di Cultura, Rome. Annuario. a. ISSN 0080-391X (Kokusai Koryu Kikin)
- Istituto Giapponese di Cultura, Rome. Notiziario. a. ISSN 0080-3928 (Kokusai Koryu Kikin)

**Istituto Grafico Tiberino**
00185 Roma, Piazza G. Verdi 10, Rome, Italy.
- Palladio; rivista di storia dell'architectura. s-a. ISSN 0031-0379

**Istituto Gramsci Roma**
- Studi Storici. (pub. by Editori Riuniti)

**Istituto Gualandi per Sordomuti e Sordomute**
Via Nosadella 49, Bologna, Italy.
- Effeta; pubblicazione mensile dell'opera Gualandi. m. ISSN 0013-2195

**Istituto Internazionale di Studi Liguri**
Museo Bicknell, 39 bis via Romana, 18012 Bordighera, Italy.
- Cahiers Ligures de Prehistoire et d'Archeologie. irreg. ISSN 0575-108X
- Giornale Storico della Lunigiana e del Territorio Lucense. q. ISSN 0017-050X
- Istituto Internazionale di Studi Liguri. Collezione di Monografie Preistoriche Ed Archeologiche. a; latest issue, 1974. ISSN 0530-9867
- Rivista di Studi Liguri. q. ISSN 0035-6603
- Studi Genuensi. a. ISSN 0585-4911

**Istituto Italiano degli Attuari**
Via del Corea 3, 00186 Rome, Italy.
- Istituto Italiano degli Attuari. Giornale. s-a. ISSN 0021-2482

**Istituto Italiano della Saldatura**
Viale Sauli 39-5, I 16121 Genoa, Italy.
- Rivista Italiana della Saldatura. bi-m. ISSN 0035-6794

**Istituto Italiano di Antropologia**
Citta Universitaria, Rome, Italy.
- Rivista di Antropologia. a. ISSN 0085-5723

**Istituto Italiano di Etnoiatria**
Viale Tamagno 24, Varese, Italy.
- Etnoiatria; rivista di etnomedicina. s-a. ISSN 0425-4708

**Istituto Italiano di Idrobiologia**
Verbania Pallanza, Novara, Italy.
- Istituto Italiano di Idrobiologia. Memorie. a. ISSN 0075-1510

**Istituto Italiano di Medicina Sociale**
Via Pasquale Stanislao Mancini 28, Rome, Italy.
- Difesa Sociale. q. ISSN 0012-2653
- Informatore Medico-Sociale. m. ISSN 0020-0743

**Istituto Italiano di Navigazione**
Piazza Cavour, 25, Rome 00193, Italy.
- Instituto Italiano di Navigazione. Atti. q.

**Istituto Italiano di Preistoria e Protostoria. Atti della Riunione Scientifica**
Florence, Italy.
- Istituto Italiano di Preistoria e Protostoria. Atti della Riunione Scientifica. a.

**Istituto Italiano di Studi Germanici-Roma**
- Studi Germanici. (pub. by Edizioni dell' Ateneo)

**Istituto Italiano di Studi Legislativi**
Via Bertoloni 8, 00197 Rome, Italy.
- Annuario di Diritto Comparato e di Studi Legislativi. bi-m. ISSN 0003-5149

**Istituto Italiano Edizioni Atlas**
Via Crescenzi 88, 24100, Bergamo, Italy.
- Didattica Scientifica. 3 per yr.

**Istituto Italiano Imballaggio**
- Tecniche Dell Imballaggio. (pub. by Franco Angeli Editore)

**Istituto Italiano per Il Medio ed Estremo Oriente**
- Cina. (pub. by Herder Editrice e Libreria S.r.L.)
- East and West. (pub. by Herder e Libreria Editrice s.r.l.)

**Istituto Italiano per la Storia dei Movimenti Sociali e delle Structure Sociali**
Via G.B. Ruoppolo 69, Naples, Italy
(and Librairie Droz, rue Massot 11, Geneva, Switzerland)
- Quaderni Internazionali di Storia Economica e Sociale/International Journal of Economic and Social History/Cahiers Internationaux d'Histoire Economique et Sociale. a. ISSN 0066-2283

**Istituto Italo-Africano**
Via Aldrovandi 16, 00197 Rome, Italy.
- Africa; rivista trimestrale di studi e documentazione. q. ISSN 0001-9747
- Voce dell'Africa. m. ISSN 0049-6626

**Istituto "la Casa"**
Via Lattuada 14, 20135 Milan, Italy.
- Casa; rivista della famiglia - studi, esperienze, documentazioni e pagine varie per la famiglia e la casa. m. ISSN 0008-7122

**Istituto Lombardo Accademia di Scienze e Lettere**
Via Borgonuovo 25, Milan, Italy.
- Istituto Lombardo Accademia di Scienze e Lettere. Rendiconti. A. q. ISSN 0021-2504

**Istituto Luigi Sturzo**
Via delle Coppelle 35, 00186 Rome, Italy.
- Politica Popolare; rassegna di ispirazione sturziana. s-m.
- Sociologia; rivista di studi sociali. 3 per yr. ISSN 0038-0156

**Istituto Maria Ausiliatrice**
Via Laura Vicuna 1, 20092 Cinisello Balsamo, Milan, Italy.
- Primavera; la revista degli anni verdi. s-m. ISSN 0032-8340

**Istituto Mathematico G. Castlenuovo**
- Rendiconti di Matematica. (pub. by Edizioni Scientifiche Inglesi Americane)

**Istituto Medicamenta S.A. Milano**
Via Adelaide B. Cairoli 18, Milan, Italy.
- Acta Gerontologica. q. ISSN 0001-5741

**Istituto Microbiologia**
Via L. Mangiagalli 31, 20133 Milan, Italy.
- Giornale di Microbiologia. q. ISSN 0017-0380

**Istituto Mobiliare Italiano**
25 Viale dell' Arte, 00144 Rome, Italy.
- Istituto Mobiliare Italiano. Annual Report. a. ISSN 0075-1529
- Istituto Mobiliare Italiano. Quarterly Economic Review. q. ISSN 0021-2512 (prep. by its Research Department)

**Istituto Musicale F. Canneti**
Villa Cordellina-Lombardi, Montecchio Maggiore,
Vincenza, Italy.
- Seminario di Studi e Ricerche Sul Linguaggio
  Musicale. Atti. a.

**Istituto Nazionale dell' Informazione**
Via Calamatta 16, 00193 Rome, Italy.
- Rivista dell' Informazione/Information Review. bi-
  m. ISSN 0034-9135

**Istituto Nazionale della Previdenza Sociale**
Via Ciro Il Grande 21, Rome, Italy.
- Previdenza Sociale. bi-m. ISSN 0032-8065

**Istituto Nazionale delle Assicurazioni**
Via Sallustiana 51, Rome, Italy.
- Assicurazioni; rivista di diritto, economia e
  finanza delle assicurazioni private. bi-m. ISSN
  0004-511X
- I N A Cronache. m. ISSN 0019-0098

**Istituto Nazionale di Economia Agraria**
- Annuario dell'Agricoltura Italiana. (pub. by
  Societa Editrice Il Mulino)
- Rivista di Economia Agraria. (pub. by Societa
  Editrice Il Mulino)

**Istituto Nazionale di Entomologia**
Via Catone 34, 00192 Rome, Italy.
- Fragmenta Entomologica. irreg. ISSN 0429-288X

**Istituto Nazionale di Geofisica**
Via Ruggero Bonghi, 11/B, 00184 Rome, Italy.
- Istituto Nazionale de Geofisica. Anali di
  Geofisica. a.

**Istituto Nazionale di Urbanistica**
V. Lamarmora 41, 10128 Turin, Italy.
- Urbanistica. q. ISSN 0042-1022

**Istituto Nazionale Informazione**
- Doc; Documentazione. (pub. by Editoriale
  Italiana)

**Istituto Nazionale per Il Commercio Estero**
Via Liszt 21, Rome, Italy.
- Informazioni per Il Commercio Estero. w. ISSN
  0020-0808
- Notiziario Orto Frutticolo dei Prodotti Agricolo-
  Alimentari. m. ISSN 0029-4403

**Istituto Nazionale per l'Assicurazione Contro gli
Infortuni Sul Lavoro**
Via 4 Novembre 144, 00187 Rome, Italy.
- I N A I L Notiziario Statistico. q. ISSN 0021-
  2539
- Rivista degli Infortuni e delle Malattie
  Professionali. bi-m. ISSN 0035-5836

**Istituto Nazionale per l'Assicurazione Contro le
Malattie**
Via C. Colombo 210, Rome, Italy.
- Archivio di Medicina Mutualistica. q. ISSN 0004-
  041X
- Informazioni I N A M. m.
- Istituto Nazionale per l'Assicurazione Contro le
  Malattie, Rome. Bilancio Consuntivo. a. ISSN
  0075-1537
- Problemi della Sicurezza Sociale. bi-m. ISSN
  0032-9355

**Istituto Nazionale per l'Incremento della Produttivita**
Piazza Indipendenza 11-B, 00185 Rome, Italy.
- Produttivita. m. ISSN 0032-9991

**Istituto Nazionale per la Storia del Movimento di
Liberazione in Italia**
Piazza del Duomo 14, 20121 Milan, Italy.
- Italia Contemporanea; nuova serie de' il
  movimento di liberazione in italia. q.

**Istituto Nazionale per Lo Studio e la Cura dei Tumori**
- Tumori. (pub. by Casa Editrice Ambrosiana)

**Istituto Orientale di Napoli**
- Istituto Orientale di Napoli. Annali. Sezione
  Orientale. (pub. by Herder Editrice e Libreria
  s.r.l.)

**Istituto Ortopedico "G. Pini"**
Piazza C. Ferrari 1, Milan, Italy.
- Archivio di Ortopedia e Reumatologia. q.

**Istituto per gli Studi di Politica Internazionale**
Via Clerici 5, Milan, Italy.
- I.S.P.I. Economia. m.

- Manuali di Politica Internazionale. irreg.
- Relazioni Internazionali; settimanale di politica
  estera. w. ISSN 0034-3846
- Saggi di Storia Contemporanea. (pub. by Edizioni
  Dedalo)

**Istituto per gli Studi Sui Servizi Sociali**
Via Arno 2, Rome, Italy.
- Rivista di Servizio Sociale. q. ISSN 0035-6522

**Istituto per l'Oriente**
Via A. Caroncini 19, 00197 Rome, Italy.
- Oriens Antiquus. (pub. by Centro per le Antichita
  e la Storia dell'Arte del Vicino Oriente)
- Oriente Moderno. m. ISSN 0030-5472

**Istituto per la Cooperazione Universitaria**
Viale Rossini 26, 00198 Rome, Italy.
- Cooperation in Education. q.
- I.C.U. Papers. irreg.

**Istituto per la Documentazione e gli Studi Legislativi**
Via dell'Arco de Ginnasi, 00186 Roma, Italy.
- Rassegna Parlamentare. q. ISSN 0486-0373

**Istituto per la Documentazione Giuridica**
- Informatica e Diritto. (pub. by Casa Editrice
  Felice le Monnier)

**Istituto per la Scienza dell'Amministrazione Pubblica**
- Amministrare. (pub. by Casa Editrice Dott. A.
  Giuffre)

**Istituto per la Storia del Risorgimento Italiano**
Vittoriano, Rome 00186, Italy.
- Rassegna Storica del Risorgimento. q. ISSN 0033-
  9873

**Istituto per la Storia della Resistenza Reggio Emilia**
Piazza S. Giovanni 4, Reggio Emilia, Italy.
- Ricerche Storiche; rivista di storia della Resistenza
  reggiana. 3 per yr. ISSN 0035-5070

**Istituto per le Diffusione di Opere Scientifiche**
Via Farini 40, Milan, Italy.
- Nuovo Archivio Italiano di Otologia, Rinologia e
  Laringologia. q.

**Istituto per le Ricerche di Economia Applicata.
Gruppo Futuribili Italia**
- Futuribili. (pub. by Tumminelli)

**Istituto per le Ricerche Statistiche e l'Analisi
dell'Opinione Pubblica**
- D O X A. Bollettino. (pub. by D O X A)

**Istituto per Lo Sviluppo e la Gestione Avanzata
dell'Informazione**
Piazza della Liberta 10, Rome 00192, Italy.
- Informatica & Documentazione. q,(with s-a
  supplements) ISSN 0390-2439

**Istituto Professionale di Stato per l'Industria e
l'Artigianato "E. Ascione" Palermo**
Via Leonardo da Vinci 364, 90143 Palermo, Italy.
- Orizzonti Professionali; rivista bimestrale di
  tecnica, cultura ed informazioni. bi-m. ISSN 0030-
  5634

**Istituto Propaganda Internazionale**
Via Friuli 32, Milan, Italy
- Collegio degli Ingegneri di Milano. Atti. bi-m.
  ISSN 0010-1257 (Subscr. to: Collegio degli
  Ingegneri di Milano, Corso Venezia 16, Milan,
  Italy)
- Geotecnica; geologia tecnica, fondazioni,
  costruzioni di terra. bi-m. ISSN 0016-8513
  (Associazione Geotecnica Italiana)
- Ingegneria Nucleare; rassegna di tecnologia
  elettronica e nucleare. bi-m. ISSN 0020-0972

**Istituto Psichiatrico**
Via G. Maggio 6, 16147 Genoa, Italy.
- Neuropsichiatria. q. ISSN 0028-3916

**Istituto Pubblicazioni Internazionali**
Piazzale Giotto 8, Perugia, Italy
- Buyers' Guide. m. ISSN 0007-7380 (Ente Italiano
  per Lo Sviluppo dell' Esportazione)
- Cosmetici Profumi Saponi. ISSN 0010-9487
- E I S E Notizie. m. ISSN 0013-2721 (Ente
  Italiano per Lo Sviluppo Dell 'esportazione)
- Esportazione; mensile per gli esportatori. 11 per
  yr. ISSN 0014-0740 (Ente Italiano per lo
  Sviluppo dell' Esportazione)
- Italy-U. S. A. Trade Review; rassegna degli scambi
  commerciali italo-statunitensi. m. ISSN 0021-3179

**Istituto Publiaci**
Corso Vittorio Emanuele 326, 00186 Rome.
- Annali d'Italia. m.
- Rivista della Donna. q.

**Istituto Regina Apostalorum**
Via Mole 3, 00040 Castelgandolfo, Italy.
- Se Vuoi. bi-m. ISSN 0036-9950

**Istituto Siciliano di Studi Bizantini e Neoellenici**
Via Noto, 34, 90141 Palermo, Italy.
- Istituto Siciliano di Studi Bizantini e Neoellenici.
  Quaderni. irreg., no. 9, 1974. ISSN 0075-1545
- Istituto Siciliano di Studi Bizantini e Neoellenici.
  Testi e Monumenti. Testi. irreg., 1976, no. 12.
  ISSN 0075-1553
- Quaderni di Poesia Neogreca. irreg., no. 4, 1976.
  ISSN 0079-8274
- Universita di Palermo. Istituto di Filologia Greca.
  Quaderni. irreg., 1974, no. 6. ISSN 0078-8627

**Istituto Sieroterapico Milanese**
Via Darwin 20, Milan, Italy.
- Clinica Veterinaria. m. ISSN 0009-9082
- Istituto Sieroterapico Milanese. Bollettino;
  Archivo di Microbiologia ed Immunologia. bi-m.
  ISSN 0021-2547

**Istituto Sieroterapico Vaccinogeno Toscano Sclavo**
Via Fiorentina 1, 53100 Siena, Italy.
- Annali Sclavo; rivista di microbiologia e di
  immunologia. bi-m. ISSN 0003-472X
- Quaderni Sclavo di Diagnostica Clinica e di
  Laboratorio. m. ISSN 0033-4979

**Istituto Sociale Ambrosiano**
Via della Signora 3, Milan, Italy.
- Realta Sociale d'Oggi; rivista mensile di sintesi e
  documentazione sociale. m.

**Istituto Sperimentale Agronomico**
Via Celso Ulpiani 1, Bari, Italy.
- Osservazioni di Meteorologia Agraria della Puglia
  e Basilicata; dati meteorologici della Puglia e
  Lucania. q.

**Istituto Sperimentale per l'Enologia**
Via P. Micca 35, 14100 Asti, Italy.
- Istituto Sperimentale per l'Enologia Asti. Annali.
  a. ISSN 0374-5791

**Istituto Sperimentale per la Cerealicoltura. Sezione di
Bergamo**
Casella Postale 164, 24100-Bergamo, Italy.
- Maydica; rivista di tecnica e divulgazione
  maidicola. q. ISSN 0025-6153

**Istituto Sperimentale Talassografico**
Viale R. Gessi, 2, 34123 Trieste, Italy.
- Instituto Sperimentale Talassografico, Trieste.
  Pubblicazione. irreg.; no. 528, 1976. ISSN 0082-
  6456
- Istituto Sperimentale Talassografico, Trieste.
  Annuario. a. ISSN 0082-6448

**Istituto Stomatiologico Italiano**
Via Pace 21, 20122 Milan, Italy.
- Rassegna Trimestrale di Odontoiatria. q. ISSN
  0033-9911

**Istituto Storico Artistico Orvietano**
Piazza Febei N.1, Orvieto 05018, Italy.
- Istituto Storico Artistico Orvietano. Bollettino. a.
  ISSN 0085-2287

**Istituto Storico dei Cappuccini**
Casella Postale 9091, 00163 Rome, Italy.
- Bibliographia Franciscana. a.
- Bibliotheca Seraphico-Capuccina. irreg.; 1976, no.
  26. ISSN 0067-8163
- Collectanea Franciscana. s-a. ISSN 0010-0749
- Monumenta Historica Ordinis Minorum
  Capuccinorum. irreg., 1971, no. 14. ISSN 0077-
  1449
- Subsidia Scientifica Franciscalia. irreg; 1975, no.
  5. ISSN 0562-4649

**Istituto Storico della Resistenza**
Via. C. Battisti, 12, 41100 Modena, Italy.
- Istituto Storico della Resistenza in Modena e
  Provincia. Quaderni. irreg., 1969, no. 7. ISSN
  0075-1561

**Istituto Storico e di Cultura dell'Arma del Genio**
Lungotevere della Vittoria 31, 00195 Rome, Italy.
- Istituto Storico e di Cultura dell'Arma del Genio.
  Bollettino. q. ISSN 0021-2555

**Istituto Storico Ordine dei Servi di Maria**
Viale Trenta Aprile, 6, 00153 Rome, Italy.
- Studi Storici dell'Ordine dei Servi di Maria. s-a. ISSN 0039-3045

**Istituto Superiore de Sanita**
- Bioelectrochemistry and Bio-Energetics. (pub. by Birkhaeuser Verlag SZ)

**Istituto Superiore di Guerra**
Turin, Italy.
- Istituto Superiore di Guerra. Italy. Bollettino d'Informazione. ISSN 0021-2563

**Istituto Superiore di Sanita**
Viale Regina Elena 299, Rome, Italy.
- Istituto Superiore di Sanita. Annali. q. ISSN 0021-2571

**Istituto Superiore Europeo di Studi Politici**
- Istituto Superiore Europeo di Studi Politici. Collana di Studi. (pub. by Editori Meridionali Riuniti)

**Istituto Tecnico**
Casella Postale 4, Lanciano, Italy.
- Istituto Tecnico; rassegna trimestrale di cultura. s-a. ISSN 0021-258X

**Istituto Universitario Navale**
Via Acton 38, Naples 80100, Italy.
- Istituto Universitario Navale, Naples. Annali. a. ISSN 0075-1588

**Istituto Universitario Orientale, Naples**
- Istituto Universitario Orientale Naples. Annali. Sezione Germanica. (pub. by Herder Editrice e Libreria s.r.l.)
- Istituto Universitario Orientale, Naples. Annali. Sezione Slava. (pub. by Herder Editrice e Libreria, S.R.L.)

**Istituto Utriusque Iuris. Facolta di Diritto Civile**
Piazza Montecitorio 120, 00186 Rome, Italy.
- Studia et Documenta Historiae et Iuris. a.

**Istituto Vaccinogeno Antitubercolare**
Via Clericetti 45, 20133 Milan, Italy.
- Istituto Vaccinogeno e dei Consorzi Provinciali Antitubercolari. Rivista. q. ISSN 0021-2598

**Istituto Vendite Giudiziarie di Roma**
Via della Cava Aurelia 98, Rome, Italy.
- Aste Giudiziarie. w. ISSN 0004-606X

**Istituto Zooprofilattico Sperimentale della Lombardia e dell' Emilie**
Via Cremona N. 282, 25100 Brescia, Italy.
- Selezione Veterinaria. m. ISSN 0037-1521

**Istituzione di Cardio-Chirurgia**
- Istituzione di Cardio-Chirurgia. Giornale. (pub. by Edizioni Minerva Medica)

**Casa Editrice Italedi**
Piazza Cavour 19, 00193 Rome, Italy.
- Commissione Tributaria Centrale. m. (10 per yr.)
- Consiglio di Stato; rassegna di giurisprudenza e dottrina. m. ISSN 0010-6569 (Centro Italiano di Studi Amministrativi)
- Settimana Giuridica. w.

**Italia che Scrive**
Via dei Banchi Vecchi 61, Rome, Italy.
- Italia che Scrive; rassegna per coloro che leggono. m. ISSN 0021-2768

**Italia Editoriale**
Via Andrea Doria 3, 20124 Milan, Italy.
- Petrolieri International. m.

**Italia Forestale e Montana**
Piazzale delle Cascine N. 32, 50144 Florence, Italy.
- Italia Forestale e Montana. bi-m. ISSN 0021-2776

**Italia Numismatica**
Musei e Biblioteche, Mantova, Italy.
- Italia Numismatica. bi-m. ISSN 0021-2830

**Italia Scacchistica**
Via Passeroni 6, 20135, Milan, Italy.
- Italia Scacchistica. m. ISSN 0021-2849

**Italia Vinicola ed Agraria**
Via di Priscilla 31, 00199 Rome, Italy.
- Italia Vinicola ed Agraria. m. ISSN 0021-2865

**Italian Association of Biology and Nuclear Medicine**
- Minerva Mediconucleare/Journal of Nuclear Biology and Medicine. (pub. by Edizioni Minerva Medica)

**Italian Association of Health Physics**
- Minerva Fisiconucleare. (pub. by Edizioni Minerva Medica)

**Italian Association of Knitwear Producers**
- Annuario dell'Industria Italiana della Maglieria e della Calzetteria. (pub. by N I G Editrice)
- Maglie Calze Industria. (pub. by N I G Editrice)

**Italian Books and Periodicals**
Via Boncompagni 15, Rome, Italy.
- Italian Books and Periodicals; monthly book review. m. ISSN 0021-2881

**Italian Center for Applied Linguistics**
- Rassegna Italiana di Linguistica Applicata. (pub. by Bulzoni Editore)

**Italian Chamber of Commerce for the U K and the Commonwealth**
*see* **Commercio Italiana per la Gran Bretagna e il Commonwealth**

**Italian Committee**
- Avicoltura. (pub. by Gruppo Giornalistico Edagricole)

**Italian Institute for Foreign Trade**
*see* **Istituto Nazionale per Il Commercio Estero**

**Italian Medical Association**
- Panminerva Medica. (pub. by Edizioni Minerva Medica)

**Italian National Institute of Higher Mathematics Conventions**
- Symposia Mathematica. (pub. by Academic Press Inc. US)

**Italian National Olympic Committee**
C.O.N.I., Foro Italico, 00100 Rome, Italy.
- Quaderni Dello Sport. m. ISSN 0033-4898

**Italian Socialist Democratic Party**
- Umanita. (pub. by Edizioni Popolari)

**Italian Society for the Prevention and Diagnosis of Tumors**
- Acta Oncologia. (pub. by Piccin Editore)

**Italian Society for the Study of Sterility and Fertility**
- Acta Europaea Fertilitatis. (pub. by Piccin Editore)

**Italian Society of Anesthesiology**
- Minerva Anestesiologica. (pub. by Edizioni Minerva Medica)

**Italian Society of Biochemistry**
- Italian Journal of Biochemistry. (pub. by Pensiero Scientifico)

**Italian Society of Gastroenterology**
- Rendiconti di Gastroenterologia. (pub. by Edizioni Luigi Pozzi)

**Italian Society of Immunology and Immunopathology**
- Italian Journal of Immunology and Immunopathology. (pub. by Piccin Editore)

**Italian Society of Neurosurgery**
- Minerva Neurochirurgica/Journal of Neurological Sciences. (pub. by Edizioni Minerva Medica)

**Italian Society of Urology**
- Urologia. (pub. by Libreria Editrice Canova)

**Italian Sulfur Corporation**
*see* **Ente Zolfi Italian**

**Editoriale Italiana**
Via Vigliena 10, Rome, Italy.
- Annuario Cattolico d'Italia. a. ISSN 0066-4464 (Centro Nazionale Economi di Comunita)
- Doc; Documentazione. a. (Istituto Nazionale Informazione)
- Insieme; rassegna dell'economo di comunita. m. ISSN 0020-1871 (Centro Nazionale Economi di Comunita)

**Compagnia Editoriale Italiana**
Via Varese 2, Genova, Italy.
- Assicurazione. m. ISSN 0004-5098

**Italiani nel Mondo**
Via Condotti, 00187 Rome, Italy.
- Italiani nel Mondo; rivista dell'emigrazione e del lavoro Italiano all'estero. s-m. ISSN 0021-3012

**Italo Di Castri**
Box 107, Taranto, Italy.
- Cittadino; settimanale di attualita, politica e sport. w. ISSN 0009-7659

**Italy. Aeronautica Militare Italiana. Ispettorato Telecomunicazione e Assistenza al Volo**
Servizio Meteorologico Aeronautica, Palazzo della Civilta de Lavoro, Quadrato della Concordia 7, 00144 Rome, Italy.
- Rivista di Meteorologia Aeronautica. q. ISSN 0035-6328

**Italy. Consiglio dell'Ordine dei Medici di Torino. Bollettino Ordine dei Medici**
Via Caboto 35, Turin, Italy.
- Italy. Consiglio dell'Ordine dei Medici di Torino. Bollettino Ordine dei Medici. m. ISSN 0006-6842

**Italy. Ente Nazionale Idrocarburi**
Piazzale Enrico Mattei 1, 00144 Rome, Italy.
- Ente Nazionale Idrocarburi. Report and Statement of Accounts. a. ISSN 0071-0687

**Italy. Istituto Centrale di Statistica**
Via C. Balbo, 16, 00100 Rome, Italy.
- Annuario Statistico dell'Istruzione Italiana. irreg., latest issue, 1973. ISSN 0066-4537
- Annuario Statistico Italiano. a. ISSN 0066-4545
- Compendio Statistico Italiano. a. ISSN 0069-7958
- I S T A T. Notiziario. m. ISSN 0029-4381
- Italy. Instituto Centrale di Statistica. Indicatori Mensili. m.
- Italy. Istituto Centrale di Statistica. Annali di Statistica. Serie 8. irreg. ISSN 0075-1766
- Italy. Istituto Centrale di Statistica. Annuario delle Statistiche Culturali. irreg., latest issue, 1973. ISSN 0075-1677
- Italy. Istituto Centrale di Statistica. Annuario delle Statistiche Guidiziarie. a. ISSN 0075-1715
- Italy. Istituto Centrale di Statistica. Annuario di Statistica Agraria. a. ISSN 0075-1669
- Italy. Istituto Centrale di Statistica. Annuario di Statistica Forestale. a. ISSN 0075-1707
- Italy. Istituto Centrale di Statistica. Annuario di Statistiche del Lavoro. a. ISSN 0075-1693
- Italy. Istituto Centrale di Statistica. Annuario di Statistiche Demografiche. a. ISSN 0075-1685
- Italy. Istituto Centrale di Statistica. Annuario di Statistiche Industriali. a. ISSN 0075-1723
- Italy. Istituto Centrale di Statistica. Annuario di Statistiche Meteorologiche. irreg., latest issue, 1973. ISSN 0075-1731
- Italy. Istituto Centrale di Statistica. Annuario di Statistiche Provinciali. a. ISSN 0075-174X
- Italy. Istituto Centrale di Statistica. Annuario di Statistiche Sanitarie. a. ISSN 0075-1758
- Italy. Istituto Centrale di Statistica. Annuario di Statistiche Zootecniche. a. ISSN 0075-1774
- Italy. Istituto Centrale di Statistica. Annuario Statistico del Commercio Interno. irreg., latest issue, 1973. ISSN 0075-1782
- Italy. Istituto Centrale di Statistica. Annuario Statistico dell'Assistenza e della Previdenza Sociale. irreg., latest issue, 1970-71. ISSN 0075-1790
- Italy. Istituto Centrale di Statistica. Annuario Statistico dell'Attivita Edilizia e delle Opere Pubbliche. irreg., latest issue, 1973. ISSN 0075-1804
- Italy. Istituto Centrale di Statistica. Annuario Statistico della Navigazione Marittima. irreg., latest issue, 1973. ISSN 0075-1898
- Italy. Istituto Centrale di Statistica. Annuario Statistico della Pesca e della Caccia. a. ISSN 0075-1812
- Italy. Istituto Centrale di Statistica. Bilanci delle Amministrazioni Regionali, Provinciali e Comunali. irreg., latest issue, 1971. ISSN 0075-1820
- Italy. Istituto Centrale di Statistica. Bollettino Mensile di Statistica. m. ISSN 0021-3136
- Italy. Istituto Centrale di Statistica. Metodi e Norme. Serie A. Relazioni Metodologiche. irreg. ISSN 0075-1839
- Italy. Istituto Centrale di Statistica. Metodi e Norme. Serie B. Istruzioni per Gli Organi di Rilevazione. irreg. ISSN 0075-1847
- Italy. Istituto Centrale di Statistica. Metodi e Norme. Serie C. Classificazioni Statistiche. irreg. ISSN 0075-1855

- Italy. Istituto Centrale di Statistica. Popolazione e Movimento Anagrafico dei Comuni. a. ISSN 0075-1863
- Italy. Istituto Centrale di Statistica. Statistica Annuale del Commercio Con l'Estero. a. ISSN 0075-1871
- Italy. Istituto Centrale di Statistica. Statistica degli Incidenti Stradali. a. ISSN 0075-188X
- Italy. Istituto Centrale di Statistica. Statistica Mensile del Commercio Con l'Estero. m. ISSN 0535-9821

**Italy. Istituto Nazionale per Lo Studio della Congiuntura**
Via Palermo 20, 00184 Rome, Italy.
- Congiuntura Estera. m. ISSN 0010-5740
- Congiuntura Italiana. m. ISSN 0010-5759
- Italy. Istituto Nazionale per Lo Studio della Congiuntura. Quaderni Analitici. irreg. ISSN 0075-1987
- Rassegna della Letteratura Sui Cicli Economici. q. ISSN 0033-944X

**Italy. Istituto Poligrafico dello Stato**
Via Boncampagni 15, Piazza Verdi 10, 00100 Rome, Italy.
- Bollettino dei Brevetti per Invenzioni, Modelli e Marchi. s-m. ISSN 0006-6664 (Italy. Ministero dell'Industria, del Commercio e dell'Artigianato)
- Italy. Laboratorio di Idrobiologia. Bollettino di Pesca Piscicoltura e Idrobiologia. s-a. ISSN 0006-6753
- Italy, Ministero dell'Interno. Rassegna degli Archivi di Stato. 3 per yr. ISSN 0037-2781
- Italy. Officio della Proprieta Letteraria, Artistica e Scientifica. Bollettino. m.
- Libri e Riviste d'Italia/Italian Books and Periodicals; rassegna bibliografica mensile. m. (Italian edt.); q. (Int'l. edt.) ISSN 0024-2683
- Mongrafie della Scuola Archeologica di Atene e delle Missioni Italiane in Oriente. irreg., vol. 49, no. 33, N.S., 1971. ISSN 0067-009X (Scuola Archeologica di Atene)
- Rassegna Del Lavoro. m. ISSN 0033-9385

**Italy. Laboratorio di Studi Sulla Ricerca e Sulla Documentazione**
Via Cesare do Lollis 12, 00185 Rome, Italy.
- Laboratorio di Studi Sulla Ricerca e Sulla Documentaziene. Note di Bibliografiz e di Documentazione Scientifica. Italy. irreg. ISSN 0085-2309

**Italy. Ministera della Pubblica Istruzione**
- Italy. Ministero della Pubblica Istruzione. Annali della Pubblica Istruzione. (pub. by Casa Editrice Felice le Monnier)

**Italy. Ministero dei Lavori Pubblici-Consiglio Superiore**
Via Nomentana 2, Rome, Italy.
- Giornale del Genio Civile. m. ISSN 0017-016X

**Italy. Ministero dei Trasporti e dell'Aviazione Civile**
Rome, Italy.
- Trasporti Pubblici. m. ISSN 0041-1817

**Italy. Ministero dei Trasporti e dell' Aviazione Civile. Azienda Autona Dellle Ferrovie dello Stato**
Servizio Affari Generale, SEZ 7a, 00100 Rome, Italy.
- Bollettino di Documentazione. m. ISSN 0006-6702
- Bollettino Ufficiale delle Ferrovie Dello Stato. Parte Prima e Seconda. bi-w.
- Bollettino Ufficiale delle Ferrovie Dello Stato. Parte Terza. m.
- Italy. Ministero dei Trasporti e dell' Aviazione Civile. Azienda Autonoma delle Ferrovie dello Stato. Bollettino Statistico Mensile. (pub. by Edizioni Richerche)

**Italy. Ministero del Bilancio**
Rome, Italy.
- Italy. Ministero del Bilancio e della Programmazione Economica. Relazione Generale Sulla Situazione Economica del Paese. a. ISSN 0075-1995

**Italy. Ministero del Commercio Con l'Estero**
- Italy Exports. (pub. by Compagnia Edizione Internazionali)

**Italy. Ministero del Lavoro e della Previdenza Sociale**
Rome, Italy.
- Italy. Ministero del Lavoro e della Previdenza Sociale. Notiziario Mensile. Statistiche del Lavoro. m.

**Italy. Ministero dell'Industria del Commercio e dell'Artigianato**
Direzione Generale delle Fonti di Energia, Rome, Italy.
- Bollettino dei Brevetti per Invenzioni, Modelli e Marchi. (pub. by Italy. Istituto Poligrafico dello Stato)
- Italy. Direzione Generale delle Fonti di Energia e delle Industrie di Base. Bilanci Energetici. a. ISSN 0075-1650

**Italy. Ministero dell'Interno**
- Italy, Ministero dell'Interno. Rassegna degli Archivi di Stato. (pub. by Italy. Istituto Polifraco dello Stato)

**Italy. Ministero della Difesa-Aeronautico**
Rome, Italy.
- Notiziario di Aviazione. m. ISSN 0029-4357

**Italy. Ministero della Difesa-Esercito**
Rome, Italy.
- Giornale di Medicina Militare. bi-m. ISSN 0017-0364

**Italy. Ministero della Difesa. Servizio dei Informazione Pubblica**
Via XX Settembre 8, Rome, Italy.
- Amministrazione della Difesa. q. ISSN 0569-9460

**Italy. Ministero della Pubblica Istruzione**
Direzione Generale delle Antichita e Belle Arti, Libreria Dello Stato, Piazza Verdi 10, Rome, Italy.
- Bollettino d'Arte. s-a.

**Italy. Ministero della Sanita**
Piazzale dell' Industria, Rome, Italy.
- Annali della Sanita Pubblica. m. ISSN 0021-3071

**Italy. Ministero delle Finanze**
Largo Leopardi No. 5, Rome, Italy.
- Rivista del Catasto e dei Servizi Tecnici Erariari. bi-m. ISSN 0035-5860

**Italy. Ministero delle Poste e delle Telecomunicazioni**
Direzione Centrale Movimento e Trasporti, Via G. Massaia 31, 00100 Rome, Italy.
- Italy. Ministero delle Poste e delle Telecomunicazioni. Comunicazioni Postali Con l'Estero. Bollettino Mensile. m. ISSN 0021-3152

**Italy. Ministero di Grazia e Guistizia. Centro Studi Penitenziaria**
Rome, Italy.
- Quaderni di Criminologia Clinica. q. ISSN 0033-4928
- Rassegna di Studi Penitenziari. bi-m. ISSN 0033-9628

**Italy. Ministero per i Beni Culturali e Ambientali**
- Accademie e Biblioteche d'Italia. (pub. by Fratelli Palombi Editori)

**Italy. Officio della Proprieta Letteraria**
- Italy. Officio della Proprieta Letteraria, Artistica e Scientifica. Bollettino. (pub. by Italy. Istituto Poligrafico dello Stato)

**Italy. Presidenza del Consiglio dei Ministri**
Via Po 14, 00198 Rome, Italy.
- Italdoc; bulletin of information for the press. fortn. ISSN 0021-2733
- Vida Italiana; Documentos e Informaciones. bi-m. ISSN 0042-7292

**Italy. Presidenza del Consiglio dei Ministri. Servizio Informazioni**
Via Boncampagni 15, 00187 Rome, Italy.
- Italy - Documents and Notes. bi-m. ISSN 0021-3063

**Italy. Stato Maggiore Aeronautica**
Via dell' Universita 4, 0100 Rome, Italy.
- Rivista Aeronautica. bi-m.

**J.C.E.**
Via Pelizza da Volpedo 1, 20092 Cinisello B. (Milan), Italy.
- Elettronica Oggi. m.
- Sperimentale. m.

**Japadre Editore**
Corso Federico II, 49, 67100 l'Aquila, Italy.
- Pensiero. 3 per yr. ISSN 0031-4811

**Japan Foundation**
see **Kokusai Koryu Kikin**

**Japanese Institute of Culture**
- Giappone. (pub. by Herder Editrice e Libreria s.r.l.)

**Casa Editrice Dott. Eugenio Jovene**
Via Mezzocannone, 109, Naples 80134, Italy.
- Biblioteca di Labeo. irreg. ISSN 0067-7434
- Diritto e Giurisprudenza; rassegna bimestrale di dottrina e di giurisprudenza civile della corte di Napoli e delle corti meridionali. bi-m. ISSN 0012-3439
- Iura; rivista internazionale di diritto romano e antico. irreg. ISSN 0021-3241
- Labeo; rassegna quadrimestrale di diritto romano. 3 per yr. ISSN 0023-6462

**Judo Regionale**
c/o Cesare Violino, Ed., Via Mentana 5, 33100 Udine, Italy.
- Judo Regionale. m.

**Jus Gentium**
Corso Vittorio Emanuele 142, Rome, Italy.
- Jus Gentium; diritto delle relazioni internazionali. 3 per yr. ISSN 0022-6963

**Juventus F.C. S.p.A.**
Galleria San Federico 54, 10121 Turin, Italy.
- Hurra Juventus. m. ISSN 0018-7933

**Koh-i-Noor Hardtmuth S.p.A.**
Via Ugo Bassi 21, 20159 Milan, Italy.
- Immagini/Technika. q.

**Kokusai Koryu Kikin**
- Istituto Giapponese di Cultura, Rome. Annuario. (pub. by Istituto Giapponese di Cultura in Roma)
- Istituto Giapponese di Cultura, Rome. Notiziario. (pub. by Istituto Giapponese di Cultura in Roma)

**Kristall Editrice**
Via Zuretti 34, 20125 Milan, Italy.
- Coppia Moderna. w.
- Pop. w.

**Kunsthistorisches Institut in Florenz**
Via Giusti 44, I-50121 Florence, Italy.
- Kunsthistorisches Institut in Florenz. Mitteilungen. a.

**Edizioni L.E.T.I**
Via Boezio 2, 00192 Rome, Italy.
- Short. m.

**L. Loffredo Editore**
Via S. Biagio dei Librai 2, 80138 Naples, Italy.
- Critica Letteraria. q.

**Labor**
Via Tunisi 4, 98138 Palermo, Italy.
- Labor. q. ISSN 0023-6489

**Laboratorio Centrale di Idrobiologia**
Via A. Brisse 27, 00149 Rome, Italy.
- Bolletino di Pesca, Piscicoltura e Idrobiologia. s-a.

**Laboratorio di Nematologia Agraria**
Via G. Amendola, 165/A, 70126 Bari, Italy.
- Nematologia Mediterranea. s-a.

**Laboratorio di Tecnologia della Pesca**
Molo Mandracchio, 60100 Ancona, Italy.
- Laboratorio di Tecnologia della Pesca. Quaderni. irreg.

**Laboratorio di Zoologia Applicata Alla Caccia**
Via Malaguti 1, Bologna 40126, Italy.
- Ricerche di Biologia della Selvaggina. irreg., approx. 4 per yr.
- Richerche di Biologia della Selvaggina. 3 per yr.

**Lambert S.p.A.**
Via Manzoni 41, Milan, Italy.
- Budget. bi-m. ISSN 0007-294X

**Lana Moda**
Via San Martino 7, Milan, Italy.
- Italiana Stil Maglia. 6 per yr. ISSN 0021-2970
- Lana Moda; maglieria a macchina. 3 per yr. ISSN 0023-7450

**Lancio**
Via Tiburtina KM 11550, 00131 Rome, Italy.
- Darling; mensile de fotoromanzi - attualita. m.

**Editoriale Laniera S.p.A.**
Via Mure P. Castello 9, 36100 Vicenza, Italy.
- Commerciale Bollettino della Laniera. Supplemento. w.
- Laniera. m.

**Editoriale Lariana S.p. A.**
Via Baldissera 2, 20129 Milan, Italy.
- Barman. m. (Associazione Italiana Barmen e Sostenitori)
- Civilta del Bere. m.
- I B A Gazette. m. (Associazione Italiana Barmen e Sostenitori)

**Andrea Latorre Editore**
Viale Caterina da Forli 28, Italy.
- Eurotransports Illustrato-Container in Italia e nel Mondo; rassegna internazionale di automobilismo, trasporti e containerizzazione. m.

**Lattante**
Via S. Chiara6, Parma, Italy.
- Lattante. m. ISSN 0023-8864

**Edizioni del Lavoro**
Largo do Villa Massimo, Rome, Italy.
- Rivista del Lavoro. m. ISSN 0483-142X (Istituto de Studi Sul Lavoro)

**Lazio**
Via dei Frentani 4, Rome, Italy.
- Lazio. q. ISSN 0023-9526

**Lazio Ieri e Oggi**
Via Taranto 178, 00182 Rome, Italy.
- Lazio Ieri e Oggi; rivista mensile di cultura arte turismo. m. ISSN 0047-4231

**Leader**
Piazza Borromeo 1, 20/23 Milan, Italy.
- Leader; mensile di attualita economica e politica. m. ISSN 0023-9607

**Libreria Ledi**
P. Cadorna 9, 20123 Milan, Italy.
- Bibliografia Internazionale di Scienze ed Arti. w. ISSN 0006-1034

**Lega degli Stati Arabi a Roma**
Piazzale delle Belle Arti 6, Rome, Italy.
- Rassegna del Mondo Arabo. m.

**Lega dei Comuni**
Via Cesare Balbo 43, 00184 Rome, Italy.
- Comune Democratico; rivista delle autonomie locali. bi-m. ISSN 0010-4930

**Lega Italiana Contro Fumi e Rumori**
Belvedere Golfo Paradiso 21, 16036 Recco, Genoa, Italy.
- Smog; il problema dell'inquinamento. 3 per yr. ISSN 0037-735X

**Lega Italiana di Igiene e Profilassi Mentale**
Ospedale Psichiatrico Provinciale di Trapani, C.C. Postale N.7-7760, Trapani, Italy.
- Igiene Mentale. q. ISSN 0019-1647

**Lega Missionaria Studenti**
Via degli Astalli, 16, 00186 Rome, Italy.
- Gentes. m. ISSN 0016-6960

**Lega Navale Italiania**
Via 24 Maggio 11, Rome, Italy.
- Lega Navale. m. ISSN 0024-032X

**Lega Nazionale delle Cooperative e Mutue**
- Cooperazione e Societa. (pub. by Editrice Cooperativa)
- Cooperazione Italiana. (pub. by Editrice Cooperativa)

**Lega per le Autonomie e i Poteri Locali**
Via Cesare Balbo 43, 00184 Rome, Italy.
- Potere Locale. s-m.

**F. Legrand, Ed. & Pub.**
31 via G. Nicotera, 00195 Rome, Italy.
- Christ to the World/Cristo al Mondo; international review of Apostolic experiences. bi-m. ISSN 0011-1465

**Lem Editrice**
c/o San Gottardo 22, 20136 Milan, Italy.
- Human Design. bi-m. ISSN 0046-8150

**Leonardo Edizioni Scientifiche**
Via G. Baglivi 5, 00161 Rome, Italy.
- Parassitologia. q. ISSN 0048-2951 (Societa Italiana di Parassitologia)

**Gruppo Lepetit S.p.A.**
Via Roberto Lepetit 8, 20124 Milan, Italy.
- Acta Vitaminologica et Enzymologica; rivista internazionale di vitaminologia e di enzimologia. bi-m. ISSN 0300-8924
- Rassegna Medica e Culturale. bi-m. ISSN 0033-9768

**Letture**
Piazza San Fedele 4, 20121 Milan, Italy.
- Letture; libro e spettacolo, mensile di studi e rassegne. 10 per yr. ISSN 0024-144X

**Carlo de Leva, Ed. & Pub.**
Via Spallitta 14, 90145 Palermo, Italy.
- Informazione Mediterranea. w. ISSN 0020-0794

**Libera Universita Internazionale degli Studi Sociali pro Deo. Istituto di Sociologia**
Viale Pola 12, Rome, Italy.
- Rivista di Sociologia. q. ISSN 0035-6530

**Libero Artigianato e Piccole Aziende Modenesi**
Via Emilia Ouest 101, 41100 Modena, Italy.
- Artigiano Modenese. m. ISSN 0004-3737

**Editrice Libraria Tuscolana**
Viale Vittorio Veneto 5, 00044 Frascati (Rome), Italy.
- Imposte Dirette Erariali e l'Iva. m.

**Edtrice Libreria Dottrina Cristiana**
10096 Leumann (Turin), Italy.
- Armonia di Voci. bi-m. (Centro Catechistico Salesiano)
- Note di Pastorale Giovanile. m. ISSN 0029-3903 (Centro Catechistico Salesiano)
- Parole di Vita. bi-m. ISSN 0031-2398 (Centro Catechistico Salesiano)
- Rivista Liturgica. bi-m. ISSN 0035-6956 (Centro Catechistico Salesiano)

**Libreria Internazionale Guida**
Via Port'alba 20-21-24, Naples, Italy.
- Remainders' Book Italiano; il servizio internazionale per l'acqisto del libro a meta del prezzo di copertina. q. ISSN 0034-4176

**Licosa S.p.A.**
Via A. Lamarmora 45, 50121 Florence, Italy.
- Incontri Linguistici. a. (Universita di Trieste)

**Licosa-Sansoni S.p.A.**
Viale Mazzine 46, Florence 50100, Italy.
- Studia Historica et Philogica: 2 Sectio Romanica. irreg.

**Guiseppe Liguori, Ed. & Pub.**
S. Brigida 39, Naples, Italy.
- Riviera; politico di interessi regionali. s-m. ISSN 0035-5712

**Liguria-Sabatelli Editori**
Via Cairoli 8, 16124 Genova, Italy.
- Liguria. m(11 per yr)

**Lineastruttura**
Via Ferdinando Russo 29, Naples 80123, Italy.
- Lineastruttura. q. ISSN 0024-3817

**Lions International**
Strada del Nobile 21, 10131 Turin, Italy.
- Lion. m(9 per yr)

**Lirica nel Mondo**
Casella Postale 7246, 00100 Rome, Italy.
- Lirica nel Mondo. m.

**Edizioni Liturgiche e Vincenziane**
Via Pompeo Magno 21, Rome, Italy.
- Annali della Carita. m. ISSN 0003-4568 (Vincentian Fathers)

- Bollettino Vincenziano. bi-m. ISSN 0006-6907 (Preti della Missione della Provincia di Roma)
- Ephemerides Liturgicae; commentarium bimestre de re liturgica. 5 per yr. ISSN 0013-9505 (Pontificia Accademia Liturgica) (Co-Sponsor: Vincentian Fathers)

**Liviana Editrice**
Via Altinate 47, 35100 Padua, Italy.
- Studi Italiani di Linguistica Teorica ed Applicata. 3 per yr. (Universita degli Studi di Bologna. Centro Interfacolta de Linguistica Teorica e Applicata)

**Editore Loescher**
Via Vittorio Amedeo II, 18, Turin, Italy.
- Giornale Storico della Letteratura Italiana. q. ISSN 0017-0496
- Rivista di Filologia e di Istruzione Classica. q. ISSN 0035-6220
- Rivista di Storia Contemporanea. q.

**Luigi Loffredo, Ed. & Pub.**
Via S. Biagio dei Librai 2, Naples, Italy.
- Critica Letteraria. q.

**Editoriale Lombarda S.p.A.**
Piazza Cavour 1, 20121 Milan, Italy.
- Lombardo. Settimanale Politico e di Attualita. w.
- Speciale. w.

**Angelo Longo Editore**
Via Diaz 39, 48100 Ravenna, Italy.
- Lettore di Provincia; testi - ricerche - critica. q. ISSN 0024-1350

**Longonesi e Co.**
Sezione Redi, Via Borghetto 5, 20122 Milan, Italy.
- Reumatismo. bi-m. ISSN 0048-7449 (Societa Italiana per le Studio del Reumatismo e per la Lotta Contro le Malattie Reumatiche)

**Carlesi Loris, Ed. & Pub.**
Via San Zanobi 89, Florence, Italy.
- Conoscenza. bi-m. ISSN 0010-6305 (Comunita Gnostica)

**Lubranopublicitas**
Via Roma, 139 T, Ischia, Italy.
- Ischia Mondo. fortn.

**Luce Luongo, Ed. & Pub.**
Via Ormisda 10, Rome, Italy.
- Arcoscenico; giornale degli spettacoli. m. ISSN 0004-0835

**Editrice M E M A s.r.l.**
Via C. Menotti 28, 20129 Milan, Italy.
- Onda Quadra. m.

**Casa Editrice Maccari**
Via Fra Salimbene 6, 43100 Parma, Italy.
- Annali di Ottamologia e Clinica Oculista. m. ISSN 0003-4665
- Archivio di Medicina Interna. 4 per yr. ISSN 0004-010X
- Giornale Italiano di Patologia e Scienze Affini. q. ISSN 0017-047X
- Quaderni di Clinica Ostetrica e Ginecologica. bi-m. ISSN 0033-491X
- Rassegna di Urologia e Nefrologia. q. ISSN 0033-992X
- Rivista di Gastro-Enterologia. biennial. ISSN 0035-6255
- Rivista di Neuropsichiatria e Scienze Affini. q. ISSN 0035-6352
- Rivista di Patologia e Clinica. 6 per yr. ISSN 0035-6417
- Rivista Generale Italiana di Chirurgia. q. ISSN 0035-6689
- Stagione Delle Arti, Del Libro, E Del Turismo. m. ISSN 0049-2035

**A. Mario Macchi**
Piazza Trinita dei Pellegrini 36, 00186 Rome, Italy.
- Quid; rivista mensile di politica arte. m. ISSN 0033-6432

**Gaetano Macchiaroli Editore**
Via Carducci 59, Naples 80121, Italy.
- Cronache Ercolanesi. a.
- Cronache Meridionali. m. ISSN 0590-1111
- Cronache Pompeiane. a.
- Medioevo Romanzo. 3 per yr.
- Parola del Passato; rivista di studi antichi. bi-m. ISSN 0031-2355

**Madonna di Castelmonte**
33040 Castelmonte (UD), Italy.
- Madonna di Castelmonte. m. ISSN 0024-9599

**Magistratura Democratica**
Via B. d'Alviano 25, 20146 Milan, Italy.
- Bollettino di Magistratura Democratica. bi-m.
ISSN 0045-2424

**Editoriale Magna Graecia**
Viale della Repubblica 293/C, 87100 Cosenza, Italy.
- Magna Graecia; rassegna di archeologia storia arte
attualita. bi-m. ISSN 0024-9955

**Casa Editrice Maia**
Via di Malizia 38, Siena, Italy.
- Ausonia; rivista di lettere arti. bi-m. ISSN 0004-
8143

**Libreria Maiolo**
Via Tommaso Caravita No. 30, 80100 Naples, Italy.
- Aspetti Letterari; quaderni lucani. bi-m. ISSN
0004-4946 (Societa di Cultura per la Lucania)

**Malfasi Editore**
Via Mantova 21, Milan, Italy.
- Rivista Italiana di Scienze Commerciali. bi-m.
(Universita Commerciale Luigi Bocconi)

**Mamme e Bimbi**
Pinamonte da Vimercate 2, Milan, Italy.
- Mamme e Bimbi. ISSN 0025-147X

**Giovanni Mammucari, Ed. & Pub.**
Casella Postal 306, 00100 Rome, Italy.
- Nuova Dirigenza; richerche esperienze e
commenti sulla funzione pubblica. irreg., 1969, no.
11. ISSN 0078-2750

**Giuseppe Manassero, Ed. & Pub.**
Via Locana 14/A, 10143 Turin, Italy.
- Junior Dental; rivista d'informazione dentale. q.
ISSN 0022-6556

**Mario Mancini Editore**
Via San Simpliciano 4, 20121 Milan, Italy.
- Hotel-Restaurant. bi-m.
- Meeting & Congressi. bi-m.

**Editrice la Manovella s.r.l.**
Via Marmorata 169, Rome 00153, Italy.
- Manovella. bi-m. ISSN 0025-2387 (Automotoclub
Storico Italiano)

**Manzi Pietro**
Via Castellino Ola Castello 10, Milan, Italy.
- Stil Novo. 3 per yr. ISSN 0039-1433

**Marcolli Editore**
Via Vitruvio 43, Milan, Italy.
- Sciare. s-m.

**Marebesi Salvatore**
Viale della Liberta 198, Catania, 95129 Sicily, Italy.
- Questa Sicilia; periodico independente a
divulgasione. 24 per yr. ISSN 0033-6335

**Margutta**
Via Pietro della Valle, 2 Rome 00193, Italy.
- Margutta; periodico d'arte contemporanea. bi-m.
ISSN 0025-2964

**Giovanna Mariotti, Ed. & Pub.**
32043 Cortina d'Ampezzo, Italy.
- Cortina. s-a.

**Editrice Maro**
Via Altichiero 11, 37100 Verona, Italy.
- Industrie Agrarie; rivista di scienza e technologia
dei prodotti alimentari. m. ISSN 0019-9001
(Societa Italiana per Il Progresso delle Industrie
Agrarie Alimentari)

**Marsilio Editori S.p.A.**
Fondamenta Santa Chiara, Santa Croce 518-A,
30125 Venice, Italy.
- Cinema e Cinema. q.
- Rinnovamento Veneto.
- Rivista di Psicologia Analitica. s-a.
- Semiotica & Psicanalisi. irreg.
- Studi Novecenteschi. 3 per yr.
- Vel. 2 per yr.

**Martinella di Milano**
Via Fratelli Bronzetti 8, Milan, Italy.
- Martinella di Milano; rassegna di vita Italiana. bi-
m. ISSN 0025-407X

**Maria Martini Editore**
Via delle Loggeta 5, Fiuggi, Italy.
- Fiuggi. m.

**Gianni Marussi Ed. & Pub.**
Piazza Bertarelli 4, Milan, Italy.
- Arti. m(10 per yr plus monographic supplements)
ISSN 0024-3621

**Casa Editrice Bemporad Marzocco**
Via Scipione Ammirato 35, Florence, Italy.
- Vita dell'Infanzia. m. ISSN 0042-7241

**Marzorati Editore**
Via P. Martinetti 6, 20147 Milano, Italy.
- Italianistica. 3 per yr.

**Masson Italia Editori S.p.A.**
Via Giovanni Pascoli 55, Milan, Italy.
- Riabilitazione. q. ISSN 0557-9430 (Istituto di
Terapia Fisica e Riabilitazioni)
- Vuoto, Scienza e Tecnologia. q. (Associazione
Italiana del Vuoto)

**Luigi Massoni, Ed. & Pub.**
Via G. Cermenate 37, 22072 Cermenate, Italy.
- Forme. bi-m.

**Editoriale Match-Ball S.p.A.**
Viale Pietramellara 33, Casella Postale 1707 A.D.,
40100 Bologna, Italy.
- Match-Ball; la rivista del tennis giovane. fortn.

**Materdei Community Centre**
- Scugnizzo. (pub. by Casa Dello Scugnizzo)

**Achille Mauri Editore**
Via Martignoni 1, 20124 Milan, Italy.
- V S; quaderni di studi semiotici. 3 per yr.

**Mediaspazio**
Via M. Melloni 17, 20129 Milano, Italy.
- Fotonotiziario. 11 per yr.

**Edizioni Mediche e Scientifiche**
Largo A.Ravizza 17, Rome, Italy.
- Gazzetta Internazionale di Medicina e Chirurgia.
s-m. ISSN 0016-5662

**Edizioni Mediche Italiane**
Via Cavour 18, Florence, Italy.
- Cardiologia Pratica. bi-m. ISSN 0008-6339
(Istituto Farmacobiologico Malesci di Firenze)

**Edizioni Mediche S.A.**
Discesa Trinita Maggiore 53, 80134 Naples, Italy.
- Riforma Medica. w. ISSN 0035-5259

**Organizzazione Editoriale Medico-Farmaceutica**
Via Edolo 42, 20125 Milano, Italy.
- Farmacologia Veterinaria. a.
- Guida di Veterinaria e Zootecnia. a.
- Informatore Farmaceutico; Annuario Italiano dei
Medicamenti e dei Laboratori. a. ISSN 0073-7984
- Notiziario Medico Farmaceutico. bi-m. ISSN
0029-439X

**Medusa Editions**
Via Babuino 124, 00187 Rome, Italy.
- Medusa. 9 per yr. ISSN 0025-8571 (Galleria la
Medusa)

**Meglio**
Viale Giuseppe di Vittorio, 205/C, 71100 Foggia,
Italy.
- Meglio. bi-m. ISSN 0025-8717

**Mendel Institute for Medical Genetics and Twin
Studies**
*see* **Gregor Mendel Institute for Medical Genetics
and Twin Studies**

**Mercato dei Fiori di Pescia**
51017 Pescia, Italy.
- Floricoltura Pesciatina. m. ISSN 0015-3834

**Meridiano Dodici**
Piazza Maria Ausiliatrice 9, 10152 Turin, Italy.
- Meridiano Dodici. s-m. ISSN 0024-8533

**Editori Meridionali Riuniti**
Reggio Calabria, Italy.
- Istituto Superiore Europeo di Studi Politici.
Collana di Studi. irreg.
- Studi e Documenti. irreg. (Universita degli Studi
della Calabria. Dipartimento di Storia)

**Edizioni Messagero**
Basilica del Santo, 35100 Padua, Italy.
- Messaggero dei Ragazzi. s-m. ISSN 0026-0304

**Messaggerie Italiane S.p.A.**
Via G. Carcano 32, 20141 Milan, Italy.
- Repertorio Analitico della Stampa Italiana.
Quotidiani e Periodici. a. ISSN 0034-4591
- Sele Arte; rivista di cultura selezione informazione
artistica internazionale. bi-m. ISSN 0037-1173

**Messaggerie Musicali**
Via Quintiliano 40, 20138 Milan, Italy.
- Musica Jazz. m. ISSN 0027-4542

**Edizioni Messaggero**
Basilica del Santo, 35100 Padua, Italy.
- Messaggero di S. Antonio. m. ISSN 0026-0312
(Basilica di San Antonio)
- Specchio del Libro per Ragazzi; bimestrale di
studio e d'informazione per gli educatori. bi-m.
ISSN 0038-6685 (Subscr. to: via Orto Botanico 9,
35100 Padua, Italy)

**Guido Miano Editore**
Viale Caldara, 13, Milan, Italy.
- Documenti di Architettura; quaderni di
architettura e arti applicate. m. ISSN 0012-4729

**S. Migliarino**
Via Canonico Rotolo, 90143 Palermo, Italy.
- Osservatore Legale; periodico di informazione
giuridico-forense. s-m. ISSN 0030-6290

**Milan. Federazione Provinciale Cooperative e Mutue**
Via Ampere 87, 20131 Milan, Italy.
- Azione Cooperativa. m. ISSN 0005-2566

**Casa Editrice Dott. Antonio Milani**
Via Jappelli 5, 35100 Padua, Italy.
- Archivio di Filosofia. q. ISSN 0004-0088
(Universita di Roma. Istituto di Studi Filosofici)
- C E D A M Notiziario Bibliografico. q. ISSN
0007-8158
- Comunita Internazionale. q. ISSN 0010-5066
(Societa Italiana per l'Organizzazione
Internazionale)
- Diritto e Pratica Tributaria. bi-m. ISSN 0012-3447
- Diritto Fallimentare e delle Societa Commerciali.
bi-m.
- Economia e Lavoro. q. ISSN 0012-978X
- Indice Penale. 3 per yr. ISSN 0019-7084
- Quaderni di Radiologia. bi-m. ISSN 0048-6086
- Rivista di Diritto Civile. bi-m. ISSN 0035-6093
- Rivista di Diritto Internazionale e Comparato del
Lavoro. 3 per yr. ISSN 0035-6166
- Rivista di Diritto Internazionale Privato e
Processuale. ISSN 0035-6174
- Rivista di Diritto Processuale. q. ISSN 0035-6182
- Rivista Internazionale di Scienze Economiche e
Commerciali. m. ISSN 0035-6751
- Trasporti; diritto, economia, politica. 3 per yr.
- Universita di Padova. Scuola di Perfezionamento
in Filosofia. Pubblicazioni. irreg. ISSN 0078-7779
- Universita di Padova. Seminario Matematico.
Rendiconti. s-a. ISSN 0041-8994

**Milano Sole Editore**
Via Denti 2, 20133 Milan, Italy.
- Guida Dello Sciatore. a; 1969 per 70 no. 12.
(Federazione Italiana Sport Invernali)

**Mimar**
Piazza Santa Francesca Romana 1, 20129 Milan,
Italy.
- Arterama. 10 per yr. ISSN 0004-3451

**Edizioni Minerva Medica**
Corso Bramante 83-85, Turin, Italy.
- Aggiornamenti in Ostretricia e Ginecologia. bi-m.
ISSN 0002-0931
- Annali di Freniatria e Scienze Affini. q. ISSN
0003-4606
- Archivio per le Scienze Mediche. q.
- Audio Minerva. 10 per yr.
- Biologia Contemporanea. q. (Associazione
Nazionale Laureati in Scienze Biologiche)
- Dermofarmacia. 3 per yr.
- Europa Medica. w. ISSN 0014-2557
- Europa Medicophysica. q. ISSN 0014-2573
(European Federation of Physical and
Rehabilitation Medicine) (Co-sponsor: Italian
Society of Physical and Rehabilitation Medicine)
- Gazzetta Medica Italiana-Aggiornamenti
Clinicoterapeutici; monthly review of therapy. m.
- Giornale dei Congressi Medici. m.

- Giornale di Fisica Sanitaria e Protezione Contro le Radiazioni-Minerva Fisiconucleare. q. ISSN 0544-2648
- Giornale Italiano di Chemioterapia. s-a. ISSN 0017-0445 (Societa Italiana di Chemioterapia)
- Informazione e Attualita Mondiali. w.
- Istituzione di Cardio-Chirurgia. Giornale. q.
- Italia Medica. m. ISSN 0021-2792
- Italian Journal of Prevention, Diagnosis and Therapy of Tumors. bi-m.
- Journal of Cardiovascular Surgery. bi-m. ISSN 0021-9509 (International Cardiovascular Society) (Dist. in U.S. by: J. B. Lippincott Company, E. Washington Square, Philadelphia, PA 19105)
- Journal of Sports Medicine and Physical Fitness. q. ISSN 0022-4707 (International Federation of Sportive Medicine) (Dist. in U.S. by: J. B. Lippincott Company, E. Washington Square, Philadelphia, PA 19105)
- Medicina Dello Sport. m. ISSN 0025-7826
- Medicina Sociale; informative review of social medicine. q. ISSN 0025-7915
- Medicina Tedesca. q. ISSN 0025-7923
- Minerva Aerospaziale. q. ISSN 0026-4709
- Minerva Anestesiologica. m. ISSN 0026-4717 (Italian Society of Anesthesiology)
- Minerva Angiologica. s-a.
- Minerva Cardioangiologica. m. ISSN 0026-4725
- Minerva Chirurgica-Chirurgia. s-m.
- Minerva Dermatologica; review of dermatology and venereal diseases. m. ISSN 0026-4741
- Minerva Dietologica. q. ISSN 0026-475X
- Minerva Ecologica e Idroclimatologica. q. ISSN 0301-3863
- Minerva Endocrinologica. q.
- Minerva Fisiconucleare. q. ISSN 0026-4768 (Italian Association of Health Physics)
- Minerva Gastroenterologica. q. ISSN 0026-4776
- Minerva Ginecologica. m. ISSN 0026-4784
- Minerva Medica; gazette for the practitioner. w. (64 per yr) ISSN 0026-4806
- Minerva Medica Giuliana. w. ISSN 0026-4814
- Minerva Medica Siciliana. w. ISSN 0026-4822
- Minerva Medicobibliografica. q. ISSN 0026-4830
- Minerva Medicolegale; Archivio di Antropologia Criminale, Psichiatria e Medicina legale. bi-m. ISSN 0026-4849
- Minerva Mediconucleare/Journal of Nuclear Biology and Medicine. q. ISSN 0026-4857 (Italian Association of Biology and Nuclear Medicine)
- Minerva Medicopsicologica; review of psychiatrics, psycology, pedagogics, criminology and sociology. q. ISSN 0026-4865 (Services and Centres of Mental Hygiene)
- Minerva Nefrologica. bi-m. ISSN 0026-4873
- Minerva Neurochirurgica/Journal of Neurological Sciences. q. ISSN 0026-4881 (Italian Society of Neurosurgery)
- Minerva Nipiologica. q. ISSN 0026-489X
- Minerva Oftalmologica. q. ISSN 0026-4903
- Minerva Oncologica; the journal of prevention, diagnosis and therapy of tumors. m.
- Minerva Ortopedica. m. ISSN 0026-4911
- Minerva Ospedaliera. la Settimana degli Ospedali. le Medico Ospedaliero. m. ISSN 0026-492X
- Minerva Otorinolaringologica. q. ISSN 0026-4938
- Minerva Pediatrica; review of pediatrics, child psychology and puericulture. w. ISSN 0026-4946
- Minerva Pneumologica. q. ISSN 0026-4954
- Minerva Psichiatrica. q.
- Minerva Stomatologica. q. ISSN 0026-4970
- Minerva Urologica; review of medical-surgical urology. bi-m. ISSN 0026-4989
- Panminerva Medica; monthly review of Italian medicine. m. ISSN 0031-0808 (Italian Medical Association) (Dist. in U.S. by: J. B. Lippincott Company, E. Washington Square, Philadelphia, PA 19105)
- Pre-Medico. q. ISSN 0004-6523
- Professioni Infermieristiche. q. ISSN 0033-0205
- Quotidiano Minerva Medica. w. ISSN 0480-8207 (Riunioni Medico-Chirurgiche Internazionali)
- Radiologia Medica. m. ISSN 0033-8362
- Rassegna di Ipnosi e Medicina Psicosomatica. q. ISSN 0033-9539
- Sessuologia. q. ISSN 0037-2838
- Societa Italiana di Farmacia Ospedaliera. Bollettino. bi-m. ISSN 0037-8798
- Societa Italiana di Pediatria. Notiziario. bi-m. ISSN 0037-8836
- Terapia; information review for the practitioner. bi-m. ISSN 0040-3687
- Vitalita. m. ISSN 0042-7446

**Casa Editrice Miscellanea Francescana**
Via del Serafico 1, 00142 Rome, Italy.
- Miscellanea Francescana; rivista trimestrale di scienze teologiche e di studi francescani. q. ISSN 0026-587X (Pontificia Facolta Teologica S. Bonaventura)

**Missionari Comboniani**
Via di San Pancrazio 17, 00152 Rome, Italy.
- Nigrizia; fatti e problemi del mondo nero. m. ISSN 0029-0173
- Piccolo Missionario. s-m. ISSN 0031-9600

**Missionari del Preziosissimo Sangue**
Via Narni 29, 00187 Rome, Italy.
- Sangue della Redenzione. q. ISSN 0036-4363

**Missioni della Compagnia di Gesu**
Piazza S. Fedele 4, 20121 Milan, Italy.
- Popoli e Missioni. 10 per yr.

**Societa Tipografia Editrice Modenese**
Via Tabboni 4, Modena, Italy
(Distr. by: Cartolibri Mucchi, Cassella Postale 64 Centro, 41100 Modena, Italy)
- Archivio Giuridico. s-a.
- Cultura Neolatina. irreg. (Istituto di Filologia Romanza)

**Edizioni Moderne Internazionali**
Via Burlamacchi 11, 20135 Milan, Italy.
- Cherie Moda/Cherie Mode. q. ISSN 0009-3203
- Gomitolo. 5 per yr. ISSN 0017-1964
- Mio Bebe. s-a. ISSN 0026-5756
- Moda dei Bimbi. s-a. ISSN 0026-7252
- Sposa. s-a. ISSN 0038-8319

**Moditalia**
Via del Cappuccio 70, 50125 Florence, Italy.
- Moditalia. q.

**Edgardo Moltoni, Ed. & Pub.**
Museo Civico di Storia Naturale, Corso Venezia 55, Milan, Italy.
- Rivista Italiana di Ornitologia. q. ISSN 0035-6875

**Momento**
Via Duccio di Boninsegna 25, Milan, Italy.
- Momento; rivista di testimonianze e di dialogo. bi-m. ISSN 0544-7526

**Monastero esarchico di Grottaferrata**
- Badia greca di Grottaferrata, Bollettino. (pub. by Badia Greca di Grottaferrata)

**Monastero S. Benedetto**
Via Bellotti 10, 20129 Milan, Italy.
- Ora et Labora; rivista di spiritualita. q. ISSN 0030-4174

**Arnoldo Mondadori Editore**
20090 Segrate (Milan), Italy.
- Casaviva. m.
- Classici del Giallo. fortn. ISSN 0009-8426
- Confidenze. w.
- Duepiu; noi due piu i nostri figli. m. ISSN 0012-6977
- Epoca. w. ISSN 0013-9718
- Espansione. m. ISSN 0014-0554
- Grazia. w.
- Linea Italiana. m (10 per yr) ISSN 0024-3752 (Centro Italiano Tessili-Abbigliamento-Alta Moda) (U.S. Subscr. to:, 437 Madison Ave., New York, N.Y. 10022)
- Panorama. w.
- Storia Illustrata; mensile di storia, geografia archeologia. m. ISSN 0039-1913
- Topolino. w.

**Mondo Afro-Asiatico**
Via Marianna Dionigi 17, Rome, Italy.
- Mondo Afro-Asiatico. m. ISSN 0026-9476

**Mondo Bancario**
Via G. B. Falda, 12, Rome 00152, Italy.
- Mondo Bancario. bi-m. ISSN 0026-9506

**Mondo Cinese**
Via Carducci, 18, Milano, 20135, Italy.
- Mondo Cinese. q.

**Societa Editoriale Mondo Economico**
Via Mercanti 2, 20121 Milan, Italy.
- Mondo Economico; Settimanale di informazione e di politica economica. w. ISSN 0026-9522

**Mondo Occulto**
Corso Garibaldi 118, Naples, Italy.
- Mondo Occulto. m. ISSN 0047-7869

**Monete e Medaglie**
Via dei Bottai, Asti 14100, Italy.
- Monete e Medaglie; bimestrale di numismatica. bi-m. ISSN 0047-7877

**Casa Editrice Felice le Monnier**
Via Scipione Ammirato 100, C.P. 455, 50136 Florence, Italy.
- Accademia Lucchese di Scienze, Lettere ed Arti. Atti. Nuova Serie. irreg. ISSN 0065-0749
- Archimede; rivista per gli insegnanti e i cultori di matematiche pure e applicate. q. ISSN 0003-8369
- Archimede. Quaderni. irreg. ISSN 0066-6106
- Archivio Glottologico Italiano. s-a. ISSN 0004-0207
- Atene e Roma. q. ISSN 0004-6493 (Associazione Italiana di Cultura Classica)
- Classici Greci e Latini. irreg. ISSN 0069-4479
- Collana "Insegnare". irreg. ISSN 0069-5246
- Informatica e Diritto. q. (Istituto per la Documentazione Giuridica)
- Istituto di Studi Pirandelliani e Sul Teatro Contemporaneo. irreg. ISSN 0075-1480
- Italy. Ministero della Pubblica Istruzione. Annali della Pubblica Istruzione. bi-m. ISSN 0003-4584
- Lectura Dantis Romana. a. ISSN 0075-8426 (Casa di Dante in Roma)
- Museo Egizio, Turin. Catalogo. Serie Prima: Monumenti e Testi. irreg. ISSN 0082-6863
- Papiri Greci e Latini. irreg. ISSN 0078-9240 (Societa Italiana per la Ricerca dei Papiri Greci e Latini)
- Rassegna dell'Istruzione Secondaria; note di legislazione e di vita scolastica. bi-m. ISSN 0033-9466
- Rivista di Studi Politici Internazionali. q. ISSN 0035-6611
- Scienze, la Matematica e Il Loro Insegnamento. bi-m.
- Studi e Testi di Papirologia. irreg. ISSN 0081-6183 (Universita degli Studi di Firenze. Istituto Papirologico "G. Vitelli")
- Studi Italiani di Filologia Classica. s-a. ISSN 0039-2987
- Universita di Messina. Istituto di Filologia Moderna. Biblioteca Letteraria. irreg. ISSN 0076-6623
- Universita di Messina. Istituto di Storia Medievale e Moderna. Pubblicazioni. irreg. ISSN 0076-6631
- Universita di Trieste. Istituto di Pedagogia. Quaderni. irreg. ISSN 0082-6480 (Universita degli Studi di Trieste. Istituto di Pedagogia)

**Monte dei Paschi di Siena**
Piazza Salimbeni 3, 53100 Siena, Italy.
- Economic Notes. 3 per yr.
- Note Economiche. bi-m.

**Editrice Morcelliana**
S.P.a, Via Gabriele Rosa 71, Brescia, Italy.
- Humanitas; rivista di cultura. m. ISSN 0018-7461

**Motor Italia**
Via Viotti 8a, Turin, Italy.
- Motor Italia. q. ISSN 0027-1926

**Movimento Adulti Scouts e Guide Cattolici Italiani**
Via Gualtiero Castellini 24, Rome 00197, Italy.
- Strade Aperte. bi-m. ISSN 0039-2057

**Movimento Circoli della Didattica**
Via Crescenzio 25, Rome 00193, Italy.
- Ricerche Didattiche. m. ISSN 0035-5046

**Movimento Gaetano Salvemini**
Via di Torre Argentina 18, 00186 Rome, Italy.
- Quaderni del Salvemini. irreg.

**Movimento Laureati di Azione Cattolica**
Via della Conciliazione 1, 00193 Rome, Italy.
- Coscienza. m.

**Movimento Politico dei Lavoratori**
- Quaderni di Alternativa. (pub. by Nuove Edizioni Operaie s.r.l.)

**Movimento Universale de Ordine Integrale**
Piazzale Anteo N.2, 00042 Anzio, Rome, Italy.
- Ordinismo; periodico etico sociale e di cultura. q. ISSN 0030-4549

**Societa Editrice Il Mulino**
Via S. Stefano 6, 40125 Bologna, Italy.
- Annuario dell'Agricoltura Italiana. a. ISSN 0066-4502 (Istituto Nazionale di Economia Agraria)
- Bollettino delle Ricerche Sociali. bi-m. ISSN 0520-4895
- Collezione di Testi e di Studi Storiografia. irreg. ISSN 0069-5785
- Giornale Italiano di Psicologia/Italian Journal of Psychology. 3 per yr.
- Istituto Affari Internazionali. Quaderni. irreg., 1970, no. 12. ISSN 0075-1448
- Istituto Agostino Gemelli. Collana di Studi Sull' Informazione Visiva. irreg., 1972, no. 9. ISSN 0075-1456
- Istituto di Studi e Ricerche Carlo Cattaneo. Quaderni. irreg., 1968, no. 2. ISSN 0075-1464
- Lingua e Stile. q. ISSN 0024-385X (Universita degli Studi di Bologna. Istituto di Glottologia)
- Materiali per Una Storia della Cultura Giuridica. a. ISSN 0076-5163 (Universita di Genova. Istituto de Filosofia del Diritto)
- Mulino; rivista bimestrale di cultura e di politica. bi-m. ISSN 0027-3120
- Osservatorio di Economia Agraria per l'Europa. Studi e Ricerche. irreg., 1971, no. 5. ISSN 0078-6802
- Politica del Diritto. bi-m. ISSN 0032-3063
- Questione Criminale. 3 per yr.
- Rassegna Italiana di Sociologia. Quaderni. irreg., 1972, no. 5. ISSN 0079-9734
- Rivista di Economia Agraria. q. ISSN 0035-6190 (Istituto Nazionale di Economia Agraria) (Co-sponsor: Societa Italiana d'Economia Agraria)
- Rivista Italiana di Scienza Politica. 3 per yr. ISSN 0048-8402
- Scienze Sociali; bolletino d'informazione sull' organizzazione della ricerca e dell' insegnamento, a cura del COSPOS. q. (Comitato per le Scienze Politche e Sociali)
- Spettatore Internazionale. q. ISSN 0038-7398 (Istituto Affari Internazionali)
- Storia Contemporanea. q. ISSN 0039-1875

**Mundus**
Casella Postale 2236, Rome, Italy.
- Mundus. m. ISSN 0027-3384

**Egidio Muraglia, Ed. & Pub.**
Via Libeccio 13, 09100 Cagliari, Italy.
- Diafora; rivista di filosofia e varia scienza. s-a. ISSN 0012-1878

**Mursia Editore**
Via Tadino 29, Milan, Italy.
- Quaderni di Scacchi: i Grandi Giocatori. irreg.

**Museo Bodoniano**
Biblioteca Palatina, Palazzo della Pilotta, 43100 Parma, Italy.
- Museo Bodoniano. Bolletino. irreg.

**Museo Civici Veneziani**
Venice, Italy.
- Museo Civici Veneziani. Bollettino. q. ISSN 0083-5447

**Museo Civico di Storia Naturale "G. Doria"**
Via Brigata Liguria 9, 16121 Genova, Italy.
- Museo Civico di Storia Naturale "Giacomo Doria," Genoa. Annali. irreg.

**Museo Civico di Storia Naturale, Verona**
Lungadige Porta Vittoria Nr. 9, 37100 Verona, Italy.
- Museo Civica di Storia Naturale, Verona. Memorie. a. ISSN 0085-767X

**Museo dell'Impero Romano**
- Museo dell'Impero Romano. Studi e Materiali. (pub. by Erma di "Bretschneider")

**Museo Egizio, Turin**
- Museo Egizio, Turin. Catalogo. Serie Prima: Monumenti e Testi. (pub. by Casa Editrice Felice le Monnier)

**Museo Internazionale delle Ceramiche**
Via Campidori 2, 48018 Faenza, Italy.
- Faenza; rivista di studi di storia e di tecnica dell'arte ceramica. bi-m. ISSN 0014-679X

**Museo Nazionale d'Arte Orientale**
Via Merulana 248, Rome 00185, Italy.
- Arte Orientale in Italia. irreg.

**Museo Nazionale del Cinema**
Piazza San Giovanni 2, 10122 Turin, Italy.
- Museo Nazionale del Cinema. Notiziario. 3 per yr. ISSN 0027-3953

**Museo Nazionale della Scienza e della Tecnica Leonarda da Vinci**
Via San Vittore 21, 20100 Milan, Italy.
- Museoscienza. bi-m.

**Museo Trentino del Risorgimento e della Lotta per la Liberta**
Trento Castello Buon Consiglio, Trentino, Italy.
- Museo Trentino del Risorgimento e della Lotta per la Liberta. Bollettino. 3 per yr. ISSN 0027-3961

**Musicalbrande**
Corso Palermo 11, 10152 Turin, Italy.
- Musicalbrande; arvista Piemonteisa. q. ISSN 0027-4674

**Casa Editrice Musicale Carrara**
Casella Postale 158, 24100 Bergamo, Italy.
- Celebriamo; rivista mensile di musica per la liturgia. m. ISSN 0008-8706

**T. Musolini Editore**
Via Pianeza, 14, 10149 Turin, Italy.
- Critica del Diritto. 3 per yr.

**N I G Editrice**
Via C. Battisti, 21, 20122 Milan, Italy.
- Annuario dell' Industria Italiana della Gomma/ Yearbook of the Italian Rubber Industry. a. ISSN 0066-4499 (Associazione Nazionale fra le Industrie della Gomma)
- Annuario dell'Industria Italiana della Maglieria e della Calzetteria. a. (Italian Association of Knitwear Producers)
- Industria della Gomma. m. ISSN 0019-7556 (Associazione Nazionale fra le Industrie della Gomma Cavi Elettrici ed Affini)
- Maglie Calze Industria. bi-m. ISSN 0024-9947 (Italian Association of Knitwear Producers)
- Strade e Traffico. m. ISSN 0039-2065

**Franco Nacci**
Via Gerolamo Fracastoro 2, Roma 00161, Italy.
- Italiamondo. q (with 2 annual supplements)

**G. R. Namias, Ed. & Pub.**
Viale Piceno, 14, 20129 Milan, Italy.
- Progresso Fotografico; periodico culturale illustrato di fotografia. m. ISSN 0033-0868
- Tutti Fotografi; mensile Italiano di fotografia e cinematografia. m. ISSN 0041-4395

**Naples, Italy. Consorzio Autonomo del Porto**
Molo Pisacane, 80133 Naples, Italy.
- Rivista del Porto di Napoli. bi-m. ISSN 0035-5925

**Napoleone Editore**
Via Antonio Chinotto 16, 00195 Rome, Italy.
- Qualesocieta; rivista bimestrale di dialogo. bi-m.

**Societa Editrice Napoletana s.r.l.**
Corso Umberto I 34, 80138 Naples, Italy.
- Bollettino di Studi Latini. q. ISSN 0006-6583
- Foro Napoletano; rivista di dottrina e di giurisprudenza. q. ISSN 0015-7848
- Nuove Prospettive Letterarie. q.
- Sociologia. irreg.

**Compagnia Editrice Napoletano**
Via Chiatamone 65, 80121 Naples, Italy.
- Sport del Mezzogiorno. w.
- Sport Sud. w.

**Narciso**
Via Foligno 44, 10149 Turin, Italy.
- Narciso; rassegna internationale d'arte e cultura. m. ISSN 0027-7851

**National Association of Rabbit Breeders**
- Coniglicoltura. (pub. by Gruppo Giornalistico Edagricole)

**National Installation Contractors Association**
- Installatore Italiano. (pub. by Propaganda Editoriale Grafica S. p. A.)

**National Seed Advisory Council**
- Sementi Elette. (pub. by Gruppo Giornalistico Edagricole)

**Nautica Editrice**
Via Tevere 44, Rome, Italy.
- Mare. q.
- Nautica. m.

**Nazionale Istituzione Exallievi Don Bosco**
Viale dei Salesiani 9, 00175 Rome, Italy.
- Voci Fraterne. m. ISSN 0042-7888

**Nevesole**
Via Augusto Pierantoni 12, 00139 Rome, Italy.
- Nevesole. m(7 per yr)

**New Morality**
Via della Penna 51, Rome, Italy.
- New Morality; concerned with new literature, art and criticism. q. ISSN 0028-6354

**Giuseppe Niccolai, Ed. and Pub.**
Via S. Cecilia 27, Italy.
- Machiavelli. m. ISSN 0024-9084

**Nistri-Lischi Editori**
P. Castelletto 7, Pisa, Italy.
- Rivista Italiana d'Igiene. bi-m. ISSN 0035-6921

**Editrice le Nostre Scuole**
Piazza Victorio Veneto 13, Turin, Italy.
- Nostre Scuole. s-a. ISSN 0029-3776

**Nostro Tempo**
1A Trav. Mariano Semmola 48, 80131 Naples, Italy.
- Nostro Tempo; cultura arte vita. bi-m. ISSN 0029-3814

**Notiziario Famiglie Numerose**
Via Belenzani 37, 38100 Trento, Italy.
- Notiziario Famiglie Numerose; mensile d'informazione per le famiglie numerose. m. ISSN 0029-4373

**Nova Agep**
Via dei Giustiniani 15, Rome, Italy.
- Mutualita' Democratica. q. ISSN 0027-5220 (Federazione Nazionale Casse Mutue Esercenti Attivita Commerciali)

**Editrice Nuova Alba**
Via Antonio 10, 20122 Milan, Italy.
- Alba; settimanale femminile di attualita, narrativa, cultura e moda. w. ISSN 0002-4627

**Nuova Antologia**
Via Veneto 7, 00187 Rome, Italy.
- Nuova Antologia. m. ISSN 0029-6147

**Nuova Corrente**
Via Lattuada 26, Milan, Italy.
- Nuova Corrente; rivista di letteratura. q. ISSN 0029-6155

**Nuova Editrice s.r.l.**
Via L. Alberti 34-3, 40137 Bologna, Italy.
- Cronaca Politica. bi-m. ISSN 0011-1724

**Nuova Era**
Piazza Gherbiana 14, Mondovi Breo (Cuneo), Italy.
- Nuova Era. m. ISSN 0029-618X

**Nuova Fotografia**
Via Manzoni 214, 80123 Naples, Italy.
- Nuova Fotografia. m.

**Nuova Italia Editrice**
8 via Antonio Giacomini, 50132 Florence, Italy.
- Aut Aut; rivista di filosofia e di cultura. bi-m. ISSN 0005-0601
- Castoro. m. ISSN 0008-753X
- Castoro Cinema. m.
- Cooperazione Educativa. m. ISSN 0010-8502
- Giornale dei Genitori; mensile per l'educazione dei figli. m. ISSN 0017-0127
- Ideologie; quaderni di storia contemporanea. q. ISSN 0019-1477
- Infanzia. bi-m.
- Politica e Mezzogiorno. q. ISSN 0032-3071
- Politica Internazionale. 6 per yr. ISSN 0032-3101
- Ponte; rivista di politica e letteratura. m. ISSN 0032-423X
- Quale Giustizia. bi-m.

- Rivista Critica di Storia della Filosofia. q. ISSN 0035-581X
- Rivista Geografica Italiana. q. ISSN 0035-6697 (Societa di Studi Geografici di Firenze)
- Scuola e Citta; rivista de problemi educativi e di politica scolastica. m. ISSN 0036-9853
- Storia dell'Arte. irreg. ISSN 0587-1131
- Universita di Firenze. Istituto di Studi Americani. Pubblicazioni. irreg., 1969, no. 2. ISSN 0071-5921

**Nuova Mercurio S.p.A.**
Via S. Paolo 15, 20121 Milan, Italy.
- Sicurta. m.

**Nuova Rivista Pedagogica**
Via della Camilluccia 177, 00135 Rome, Italy.
- Nuova Rivista Pedagogica. bi-m. ISSN 0469-2454

**Nuova Rivista Tributaria**
Via Asmara 26, 00199 Rome, Italy.
- Nuova Rivista Tributaria. m. ISSN 0029-6244

**Editrice Nuova Societa S.p.A.**
Via Bocaccio 35, 20123 Milan, Italy.
- Prima. m. (11 per yr.)

**Nuova Vallecchi Editore S.p.A.**
Via G. Capponi 26, 50121 Florence, Italy.
- Critica d'Arte. 6 per yr. ISSN 0011-1511
- Vallecchi Informa. 12 per yr.(approx) ISSN 0042-2312

**Societa Editoriale Nuove Cronache Italiane**
Via Brenta 13, 00198 Rome, Italy.
- Adesso. m. ISSN 0400-5104

**Nuove Edizioni Operaie s.r.l.**
Via Crescenzio 58, 00193 Rome, Italy.
- Quaderni di Alternativa. irreg. (Movimento Politico dei Lavoratori)
- Quaderni di Rassegna Comunista. irreg.

**Nuove Iniziative Editoriali S.p.A.**
Via Leopardi 18, 20123 Milan, Italy.
- Pubblicita Domani. w. (42 per yr.)

**Editrice Nuovi Orientamenti**
C.C.P. No. 1/3133, Rome, Italy.
- Nuovi Orientamenti. m (10 per yr)

**Nuovo Agora Omaggio**
Villa Benia Rapallo, Genova, Italy.
- Nuovo Agora Omaggio. q. ISSN 0029-6309

**Nuovo Bollettino Bibliografico Sardo**
Via S. Giovanni 402, Cagliari, Italy.
- Nuovo Bollettino Bibliografico Sardo; archivio tradizioni popolari. bi-m. ISSN 0029-6317

**Nuovo Chirone**
Via M. Iannicelli 7, Salerno, Italy.
- Nuovo Chirone; rivista di cultura pedagogica. bi-m. ISSN 0029-6333

**Nuovo Diritto**
Via Asmara 16, Rome, Italy.
- Nuovo Diritto; giurisprudenza e dottrina. m. ISSN 0029-6368

**Nuovo Impegno**
Via Riminaldi 2, 56100 Pisa, Italy.
- Nuovo Impegno. q. ISSN 0048-1149

**Edizioni Nuovo Mezzogiorno**
Corso Vittorio Emanuele 154, Rome, Italy.
- Nuovo Mezzogiorno. m. ISSN 0029-6376

**Nuovo Osservatore**
Piazza di Pietra 31, 00186 Rome, Italy.
- Nuovo Osservatore. m. ISSN 0029-6384

**Nuovo Pensiero Militare**
Via dei Servi 25, 50122 Florence, Italy.
- Nuovo Pensiero Militare. s-m. ISSN 0029-6392

**O.G.E.T.**
Via Teulada 52, 00195 Rome, Italy.
- Eco del Turismo e del Commercio. m.

**O. P. B. International S.p.A.**
Via Antonio Banfi 3, 20122 Milan, Italy.
- Societa Italiana di Scienza dell' Alimentazione. Rivista. m.

**Edizioni O.R.G.A**
Via Amedeo d'Aosta 3, 20129 Milan, Italy.
- Organizzarsi. q. ISSN 0474-635X

**Salvatore dell' Oca, Ed. & Pub.**
Via Mentana 22, Como, Italy.
- Rassegna Speleologica Italiana. q. ISSN 0033-9865 (Gruppi Grotte Italiani)

**Editrice Ocean**
Vico Sanserverino 45, Naples 80138, Italy.
- Scuola dell'Adulto. 12 per yr. ISSN 0036-9829

**Oesterreichisches Kulturinstitut, Rom**
- Oesterreichisches Kulturinstitut, Rom. Abteilung fuer Historische Studien. Publikationen I. Abteilung: Abhandlungen. (pub. by Verlag der Oesterreichischen Akademie der Wissenschaften AU)
- Oesterreichisches Kulturinstitut, Rom. Abteilung fuer Historische Studien. Publikationen Ii. Abteilung: Quellen. (pub. by Verlag der Oesterreichischen Akademie der Wissenschaften AU)
- Roemische Historische Mitteilungen. (pub. by Verlag der Oesterreichischen Akademie der Wissenschaften AU)

**Officium Libri Catholic**
Catholic Book Agency, 00187 Rome, Italy.
- Ephemerides Iuris Canonici. q. ISSN 0013-9491

**Oikoumenikon**
Via Taddeide 24, 0060 Riana (Rome), Italy.
- Oikoumenikon; rassegna mensile sull'ecumenismo. m. ISSN 0030-1302

**Editoriale Olimpia**
Viale Milton 7, 50 129 Florence, Italy.
- Diana; rivista del cacciatore. fortn. ISSN 0012-2343
- Diana Armi. m. ISSN 0012-2351
- Pescare; la rivista dei pescatori. m. ISSN 0031-6091

**C. Olivetti & Co., S.p.A.**
77 via G. Jervis, Ivrea, Italy.
- Notizie Olivetti. m. ISSN 0029-4438

**Casa Editrice Leo S. Olschki**
Viuzzo del Pozetto (Viale Europa), 50126 Florence, Italy
(and Casella Postale 66, 50100 Florence, Italy)
- Accademia Etrusca di Cortona. Annuario. irreg., 1967, no. 13. ISSN 0065-0730
- Accademia Musicale Chigiana. Quaderni. irreg. ISSN 0065-0714
- Accademia Toscana di Scienze e Lettere La Colombaria. Studi. irreg., no. 42, 1975. ISSN 0065-0781
- Archivio Linguistico Veneto. Quaderni. irreg., 1969, no. 5. ISSN 0066-6696 (Fondazione Giorgio Cini)
- Archivio Storico Italiano. q. ISSN 0004-0339 (Deputazione di Storia Patria Florence)
- Archivio Storico Italiano. Biblioteca. irreg., no. 19, 1974. ISSN 0066-6718
- Archivum Romanicum. Biblioteca. Serie 1: Storia Letteratura-Paleografia. irreg., no. 124, 1975. ISSN 0066-6807
- Archivum Romanicum. Biblioteca. Serie 2: Linguistica. irreg., no. 35, 1975. ISSN 0066-6815
- Belfagor; rassegna di varia umanita. bi-m. ISSN 0005-8351
- Bibliofilia; rivista di storia del libro e di bibliografia. 3 per yr. ISSN 0006-0941
- Biblioteca di Bibliografia Italiana. irreg., no. 79, 1975. ISSN 0067-7418
- Biblioteca di Storia Toscana Moderna e Contemporanea Studi e Documenti. irreg., no. 11, 1975. ISSN 0067-7442 (Unione Regionale delle Provincie Toscane, Florence)
- Biblioteca di Studi Etruschi. irreg., 1971, no. 5. ISSN 0067-7450 (Istituto di Studi Etruschi, Florence)
- Biblioteca Storica Toscana. Serie I. irreg., no. 17, 1975.
- Biblioteca Storica Toscana. Serie II.
- Biblioteconomia e Bibliografia. Saggi e Studi. irreg., 1973, no. 9. ISSN 0067-7531
- Bolletino dell'Atlante Linguistico Mediterraneo/ Bulletin of the Linguistic Atlas of Mediterranean. irreg., vol. 15, 1976. ISSN 0067-9879 (Universita di Torino. Istituto dell' Atlante Linguistico Italiano)
- Chigiana. a. ISSN 0069-3391 (Accademia Musicale Chigiana, Siena)
- Civilta Asiatiche. irreg., 1963, no.5. ISSN 0069-4312 (Fondazione Giorgio Cini. Centro di Cultura e Civilta)

- Civilta Veneziana. Dizionari Dialettali e Studi Linguistici. irreg., 1969, no. 4. ISSN 0069-4339 (Fondazione Giorgio Cini)
- Civilta Veneziana. Fonti e Testi. Serie Prima: Fonti e Testi per la Storia dell'Arte Veneta. irreg., 1972, no. 8. ISSN 0069-4355 (Fondazione Giorgio Cini)
- Civilta Veneziana. Fonti e Testi. Serie Terza. irreg., no. 3, 1973. ISSN 0069-4347 (Fondazione Giorgio Cini)
- Civilta Veneziana. Saggi. irreg., no. 22, 1975. ISSN 0069-4371 (Fondazione Giorgio Cini)
- Civilta Veneziana. Studi. irreg., no. 30, 1974. ISSN 0069-438X (Fondazione Giorgio Cini)
- Collana di Monografie delle Biblioteche d'Italia. irreg., 1964, no. 7. ISSN 0069-5181
- Collana di Monografie Sui Palazzi Storici Italiani. irreg. ISSN 0069-519X
- Collana Ricciana. Fonti. irreg., 1973, no. 6. ISSN 0069-5254
- Collectanea Historiae Musicae. irreg., 1966, vol. 4. ISSN 0069-5270
- Fonti Sui Comuni Rurali Toscani. irreg., 1970, no. 7. ISSN 0071-6901 (Deputazione di Storia Patria, Florence)
- Fonti Sulle Corporazioni Medioevali. irreg., 1961, no. 9. ISSN 0071-691X (Deputazione di Storia Patria, Florence)
- Gabinetto Disegni e Stampe degli Uffizi. Cataloghi. irreg., no. 41, 1974. ISSN 0072-0070
- Historiae Musicae Cultores Biblioteca. irreg., no. 29, 1975. ISSN 0073-2516
- Inventari dei Manoscritti delle Biblioteche d'Italia. irreg., no. 89, 1974. ISSN 0075-0026
- Istituto e Museo di Storia della Scienza. Biblioteca. irreg., 1970, no. 8. ISSN 0075-1499
- Istituzioni e Monumenti dell' Arte Musicale Italiana Nuova Serie. irreg., 1964, no. 3. ISSN 0075-1596
- Lares. s-a. ISSN 0023-8503 (Societa di Etnografia Italiana)
- Lares. Biblioteca. irreg., no. 43, 1974. ISSN 0075-8019
- Lettere Italiane. q. ISSN 0024-1334
- Lettere Italiane. Biblioteca. irreg., no. 17, 1975. ISSN 0075-8892
- Pensiero Politico; revista di storia delle idee politiche e sociali. q. ISSN 0031-4846
- Physis; rivista di storia della scienza. q. ISSN 0031-9414
- Pocket Library of Studies of Art. irreg., 1973, no. 23. ISSN 0079-242X
- Quaderni dei Padri Benedettini di San Giorgio Maggiore. irreg., 1964, no. 3. ISSN 0079-824X (Fondazione Giorgio Cini)
- Rassegna Storica Toscana. s-a. ISSN 0033-9881 (Societa Toscana per la Storia del Risorgimento)
- Ricerche Storiche. s-a. (Centro Piombinese di Studi Storici)
- Ricerche Sulle Dimore Rurali in Italia. irreg., no. 30, 1973. ISSN 0080-2964 (Consiglio Nazionale delle Ricerche)
- Rivista di Storia e Letteratura Religiosa. 3 per yr. ISSN 0035-6573
- Rivista Italiana di Musicologia. s-a. ISSN 0035-6867 (Societa Italiana di Musicologia)
- Rivista Italiana di Studi Napoleonici. 3 per yr. ISSN 0035-6913 (Centro Nazionale di Studi Napoleonici e di Storia dell'Elba)
- Saggi e Memorie di Storia dell'Arte. irreg., 1973, no. 8. ISSN 0080-5394 (Fondazione Giorgio Cini)
- Storia della Miniatura. Studi e Documenti. irreg., no. 4, 1971. ISSN 0081-5845
- Studi Albanesi. Studi e Testi. irreg., 1972, no. 5. ISSN 0081-6116 (Universita di Roma. Istituto Studi Albanesi)
- Studi di Letteratura Francese. irreg., vol. 4, 1975. ISSN 0585-4768 (Universita di Padova. Istituto di Letterature Straniere)
- Studi Musicali. s-a. (Accademia Santa Cecilia di Roma)
- Studi Secenteschi. a. ISSN 0081-6248
- Studi Veneziani. a. ISSN 0081-6264 (Fondazione Giorgio Cini)
- Universita di Catania. Istituto di Storia delle Tradizioni Popolari. Studi e Testi. irreg., 1964, no. 2. ISSN 0069-1186
- Universita di Padova. Facolta di Lettere e Filosofia. Opuscoli Accademici. irreg. ISSN 0078-7728
- Universita di Padova. Facolta di Lettere e Filosofia. Pubblicazioni. irreg., no. 7, 1976. ISSN 0078-7736

**Edizioni Omnia Medica**
Via S. Michele, 56100 Pisa, Italy.
- Omnia Medica et Therapeutica. q. ISSN 0030-2260

**Op Cit**
Via Vincenzo Padula, 2, Naples 80123, Italy.
- Op Cit. 3 per yr. ISSN 0030-3305

**Opera Aperta**
Via Sabotino 45, Rome, Italy.
- Opera Aperta; periodico di cultura. bi-m. ISSN 0030-3569

**Opera Buona Stampa**
- Domenica del Popolo. (pub. by Editrice Orobica)

**Opera della Regalita' di N.S.G.C.**
Via L. Necchi 2, 20123 Milan, Italy.
- Adveniat. m. ISSN 0001-8740

**Opera di Santa Rita di Roccaporena di Cascia**
Via Stazione di S. Pietro 6, 00165 Rome, Italy.
- Dallo Scoglio di Santa Rita. m.

**Opera Madonna delle Grazie**
Via Andria, Corato, Bari 70033, Italy.
- Voce della Madonna delle Grazie. w. ISSN 0042-7845

**Opera Nazionale: Maternita e Infanzia**
Lungotevere Ripa 1, 00153 Rome, Italy.
- Maternita e Infanzia. m.

**Opinion Europeenne**
Via Glov. Bettolo 14, 00195 Rome, Italy.
- Opinion Europeenne. s-m. ISSN 0030-381X

**Opinione Repubblicana**
T. Tasso 109, 24100 Bergamo, Italy.
- Opinione Repubblicana. bi-m.

**Orario Nuovo Grippaudo**
c/o G. Grippaudo, Ed., Piazza Luigi di Savoia 2, 20124 Milan, Italy.
- Orario Nuovo Grippaudo. s-a.

**Order of Saint Augustine. Curia Generalizia**
Via S. Uffizio 25, 00193 Rome, Italy.
- Acta Ordinis Sancti Augustini; commentarium officiale. a. ISSN 0001-642X

**Order of St. Francis. Curia Generalis**
Via S. Maria Mediatrice 25, I-00165 Rome, Italy.
- Acta Ordinis Fratrum Minorum. bi-m. ISSN 0001-6411

**Ordine degli Ingegneri della Provincia di Catania**
Via Giuffrida 202, 95128 Catania, Sicily, Italy.
- Tecnica e Ricostruzione. bi-m. ISSN 0040-1803

**Ordine dei Medici della Provincia di Parma**
Borgo al Collegio Maria Luigia 17, Parma, Italy.
- Parmamedica; bollettino dell'ordine dei medici. m. ISSN 0031-2312

**Ordine dei Medici di Torino e Provincia**
Via Caboto 35, 10129 Turin, Italy.
- Ordine dei Medici. Bollettino. m. ISSN 0471-7708

**Ordine del Combattentismo Attivo**
Via Gallicciolli 5, Bergamo, Italy.
- Combattentismo. bi-m. ISSN 0045-7485

**Ordine del Dottori Commercialisti di Milano**
- Rivista dei Dottori Commercialisti. (pub. by Casa Editrice Dott. A. Giuffre)

**Ordine Ospedaliero di S. Giovanni di Dio**
- Res Medicae. (pub. by Fatebenefratelli)

**Ordre Souveraia Militaire Hospitalier de St. Jean de Jerusalem de Rhodes et de Malte**
Palazzo Malta, 68 via Condotti, Rome, Italy.
- Ordre Souveraia Militaire Hospitalier de St. Jean de Jerusalem de Rhodes et de Malte. Revue Internationale. 3 per yr.

**Orfanotrofio Antoniano dei PP. Rogazionisti**
25015 Desenzano del Garda, Brescia, Italy.
- Araldo di S. Antonio; incontri con Papa Giovani. w. ISSN 0003-7559

**Organizzazione Editoriale Medico Farmaceutica**
Via Edolo 42, 20125 Milan, Italy.
- Repertorio Terapeutico. irreg.

**Organizzazione "X"**
Via G. Pascoli, 28, 70123 Bari, Italy.
- Stadio Club; periodico di sport e attualita. fortn. ISSN 0038-8912
- Voce della Fiera; bisettimanale di economia e problemi di mercato. s-w. ISSN 0042-7837

**Organizzazione Zeppieri**
VialeCastro Preto Rio 82, Rome, Italy.
- Linea Z; quindicinale d'attualita e politica dei trasporti. fortn. ISSN 0024-3779

**Organizzazione Speciali**
Via Franchi 5, Florence, Italy.
- Bollettino di Psicologia Applicata. bi-m. ISSN 0006-6761

**Editrice Orobica**
Viale Papa Giovanni XXIII, 118, Bergamo, Italy.
- Domenica del Popolo. w. (Opera Buona Stampa)

**Orsa Maggiore Editrice**
Via Carlo Fea 9, Rome, Italy.
- Moebius; architettura urbanistica arte. bi-m.

**Tipografico Editrice dell' Orso**
Via dell'Orso 28, Rome, Italy.
- Molini d'Italia; rassegna mensile per lo studio dei problemi tecnico economici dei cereali, della macinazione e della pastificazione. m. ISSN 0026-9018

**Ospedale al Mare**
Lido di Venezia, Italy.
- Ospedale al Mare. Archivo. q. ISSN 0030-624X

**Ospedale Maria Vittoria**
Via Cibrario 72, 10144 Turin, Italy.
- Giornale di Batteriologia, Virologia Ed Immunologia Ed Annali dell'Ospedale Maria Vittoria di Torino. Parte 1. Microbiologia. s-a. ISSN 0301-1453
- Giornale di Batteriologia Virologia Ed Immunologia Ed Annali dell'Ospedale Maria Vittoria di Torino. Part 2. Scezione Clinica. s-a. ISSN 0301-1445

**Ospedale Neuropsichiatrico Provinciale**
Arezzo, Italy.
- Rivista di Neurobiologia. q. ISSN 0035-6336

**Ospedale Psichiatrico Provinciale**
Calata Capodichino 232, 80141 Naples, Italy.
- Ospedale Psichiatrico. q. ISSN 0048-2285

**Ospirio S. Famiglia**
20090 Cesano Boscone, Milan, Italy.
- Super Omnia Charitas. q. ISSN 0039-565X

**Osservatore Politico Letterario**
Via Solferino 32, Milan, Italy.
- Osservatore Politico Letterario. m. ISSN 0030-6304

**Osservatore Tributario e Rassegna Tributaria**
Via Celimontana 38, 00184 Rome, Italy.
- Osservatore Tributario e Rassegna Tributaria; rivista delle imposte di consumo. m. ISSN 0030-6320

**Osservatorio Astronomico di Roma**
Via del Parco Mellini 84, 00136 Rome, Italy.
- Photographic Journal of the Sun. m. ISSN 0048-4008

**Osservatorio Astronomico di Torino**
10025 Pino Torinese (Turin), Italy.
- Time Service. q.

**Osservatorio di Economia Agraria per l'Europa**
- Osservatorio di Economia Agraria per l'Europa. Studi e Ricerche. (pub. by Societa Editrice Il Mulino)

**Osservatorio Geofisico Sperimentale**
34123 Trieste, Italy.
- Bollettino di Geofisica, Teorica ed Applicata. q. ISSN 0006-6729

**Osservatorio Regionale per le Malattie della Vite**
Palermo, Italy.
- Osservatorio Regionale per le Malattie della Vite. Osservazioni di Meteorologia, Fenologia e Patologia della Vite. irreg. ISSN 0552-9506

**Ostomercato S. p.A.**
Via Cesare Lombroso 54, 20137 Milan, Italy.
- Ortonotizie. m (10 per yr)

**Editrice Ottavi s.r.l.**
Via Mameli 63, 15033 Casale Monferrato (Alessandria), Italy.
- Coltivatore e Giornale Vinicolo Italiano. m. ISSN 0010-1850

**Ovidius**
Via Mazara 12, Sulmona, Italy.
- Circolo Letterario; rivista di cultura e attualita. q. ISSN 0009-7241 (Cenacolo di Cultura "Publius Ovidius Naso")

**P.A.N. Editrice**
Via Solferino, 32, 20121 Milan, Italy.
- Linea Snia; quarterly for textile and clothing trade. q. (Snia Viscosa)
- Pitture e Vernici. m. ISSN 0048-4245
- Textilia. m. ISSN 0033-9067
- Vetrina. q.

**Tipografia della Pace**
Via della Pace, 35 Rome, Italy.
- Segnalazioni della Camera di Commercio Italiana per la Gran Bretagna e Il Commonwealth. w. ISSN 0037-0940 (Commercio Italiana per la Gran Bretagna e Il Commonwealth)

**Pacini Editore**
Via della Faggiola, 17, 56100 Pisa, Italy (Editorial Address: via Mordini 79, 55100 Lucca, Italy)
- Bollettino delle Malattie dell'Orrecchio, della Gola, del Naso. bi-m. ISSN 0006-6567
- Prassi e Teoria; rivista di filosofia della cultura. 3 per yr.

**Edizioni dei Padri Carmelitani Scalzi**
Corso d'Italia 38, 00198 Rome, Italy (and Piazza S. Pancrazio 5-a, 00152 Rome, Italy)
- Archivum Bibliographicum Carmelitanum. a. ISSN 0570-7242
- Bibliographia Internationalis Spiritualitatis. a. ISSN 0084-7836 (Pontificio Istituto di Spiritualita)
- Ephemerides Carmeliticae. s-a. (Theological Faculty of Saint Teresa and Saint John of the Cross)
- Rivista di Vita Spirituale. bi-m. ISSN 0035-6638 (Pontificio Istituto di Spiritualita)

**Paideia Editrice**
Via Corsica 58/M, Brescia, Italy.
- Antichita Classica e Cristiana. irreg., latest issue no. 16. ISSN 0066-4766
- Paideia; rivista letteraria di informazione bibliografica. bi-m. ISSN 0030-9435
- Rivista Biblica. bi-m. ISSN 0035-5798 (Associazione Biblica Italiana)
- Studi Biblici; pubblicazione bimestrale di argomento biblico. bi-m. ISSN 0039-2898

**Palaestra**
Casella Postale 16, C.C. 6-6626, Maddaloni 81024, Italy.
- Palaestra. bi-m. ISSN 0031-0255

**Edizioni Palatino in Roma**
Via Lazio 9, Rome, Italy.
- Palatino. q. ISSN 0031-028X

**Aldo Palazzi Editore**
Via Zuretti 34, Milan, Italy.
- Bellezza. m. ISSN 0005-8637

**Palazzi Editrice S.p.A.**
Via del Corso 184, Rome, Italy.
- Tempo; settimanale di politica e cultura. w.

**Palazzo Marino**
Piazza della Scala, Milan, Italy.
- Citta di Milano; rassegna del Comune e bollettino di statistica. m. ISSN 0009-7616

**Casa Editrice Palazzo Vecchio**
Via Vittorio Emanuele, 155, 50134 Florence, Italy.
- Annuario Ceramica. a. ISSN 0066-4472
- Ceramica. bi-m.

**Paleari Edizioni Milano**
Viale Fulvio Testi 117, 20092 Cinisello B. (Milan), Italy.
- Efficienza. bi-m.
- Esperienze Amministrative. bi-m. ISSN 0014-0686 (Federazione Italiana Amministratori Enti Locali)
- Progettista. m. (Associazione Nazionale Termotecnici e Aerotecnici)
- Tecnica del Trasporto. m.

**Paleari Industria Grafica s.r.l.**
Via S. Gottardo 74, 20032 Milan, Italy.
- Lipe. m(11 per yr)

**Ugo Palmisano, Ed. & Pub.**
Corso Gastaldi 11, Genoa 16131, Italy.
- Borsa dei Noli; settimanale dei traffici marittimi, aerei e terrestri. w. ISSN 0006-7849

**Fratelli Palombi Editori**
Via dei Gracchi 181-185, Rome, Italy.
- Accademie e Biblioteche d'Italia. bi-m. ISSN 0001-4451 (Italy. Ministero per i Beni Culturali e Ambientali)
- Istruzione Tecnica e Professionale. q. ISSN 0535-899X
- Urbe; rivista romana di storia, arte, lettere, costumanze. bi-m. ISSN 0042-1030

**Nino Palumbo, Ed. & Pub.**
Via Ai Castagneti 4, San Michele di Pagana (Rapallo), Italy.
- Prove di Letteratura. bi-m. ISSN 0033-1848

**Edizioni Palutan Grafica**
Quinto Romano 66, 20153 Milan, Italy.
- C. M. Mobilmarket. (Commercio Mobili) m.
- Sedia e Il Mobile. m. ISSN 0037-0711

**Pammatone**
Ospedali Civil, 16132 Genoa, Italy.
- Pammatone. m. ISSN 0031-0549

**Panorama Publicita Marketing**
Piazza della Repubblica 32, 2014 Milan, Italy.
- Panorama Publicita Marketing. q.

**Mario Pantaleo, Ed. & Pub**
Via dei Gracchi 181-185, Rome, Italy.
- Homo Faber; rassegna internazionale de lavoro e dell'istruzione. m. ISSN 0439-4291

**Edizioni Paoline**
Corso Regina Margherita 1, Turin, Italy.
- Pagine Aperte; selezione bibliografica edizioni paoline. m.

**Parallelo Trentotto**
Via Garibaldi 629, Reggio di Calabria 89100, Italy.
- Parallelo Trentotto; rivista per l'Unita Europea. m. ISSN 0031-1715

**L. Pardi, Ed. & Pub.**
Via Romana 17, 50125 Florence, Italy.
- Monitore Zoologico Italiano/Italian Journal of Zoology. q. ISSN 0026-9786 (Universita degli Studi di Firenze)

**Alfredo Parente, Ed. & Pub.**
Via Luca Giordano 7, Naples, Italy.
- Rivista di Studi Crociani; dedicated to work of Benedetto Croce. q. ISSN 0035-659X

**Parlameto**
Casella Postale 282, Rome, Italy.
- Parlameto. m. ISSN 0031-2266

**Edizioni Luigi Parma**
Via Collamarini 23, 40138 Bologna, Italy.
- Il Carrobbio; rivista di studi Bolognasi. a.

**Parole e le Idee**
Casella Postale 246, Naples, Italy.
- Parole e le Idee; Rivista internazionale de varia cultura e di informazione bibliografica. q. ISSN 0031-2401

**Parrocchia**
Vicolo Divino Amore 12, 00186 Rome, Italy.
- Parrocchia. m. ISSN 0031-2428

**Parrocchia S. Gerardo**
Piedimonte Etneo 95017, Sicily, Italy.
- Squilla di S. Gerardo. bi-m. ISSN 0038-8769

**Partito Comunista d'Italia. Comitato Centrale**
- Partito. (pub. by Unita S.p.A.)

**Partito Comunista Italiano**
- Critica Marxista. (pub. by Editori Riuniti)
- Nuova Rivista Internazionale. (pub. by Editori Riuniti)
- Quaderni Siciliani. (pub. by Di Modica)
- Unita. (pub. by Unita S.p.A.)

**Partito Comunista Rivoluzionario**
Sezione Italiana della 4 Internazionale (Posadista), C.P. 5059, 00153 Rome, Italy.
- Lotta Operaia. fortn. ISSN 0024-6646

**Partito Liberale Italiano**
Corso V. Emanuele 21, 20075, Italy.
- Corriere dell'Adda. bi-w.

**Partito Popolare Italiano**
Piazzetta Matilde Serao 7, 80132 Naples, Italy.
- Popolo e Liberta. w.

**Partito Socialista Italiano**
Via dei Pontefici 3, 00186 Rome, Italy.
- Mondo Operaio. m.

**Pass Editrice**
Via Padova 35, 20127 Milan, Italy.
- Sci; rivista degli sport invernali. 8 per yr. ISSN 0036-8040

**Passionist Fathers**
Rome, Italy.
- Fonti Vive; rivista della passione. bi-m. ISSN 0015-6205

**Passionisti**
15074 Molare, Alessandria, Italy.
- Santuario della Madonna delle Rocche. bi-m. ISSN 0036-4622

**Edizioni Pastorali**
Via Paisiello 6, 00198 Rome, Italy.
- Orientamenti Pastorali. 10 per yr. ISSN 0472-0784 (Centro di Orientamento Pastorale)

**Casa Editrice Patron**
Via Badini, 40127 Bologna, Italy.
- Organo; rivista di cultura organaria e organistica. s-a. ISSN 0474-6376
- Rivista Storica dell'Antichita. s-a. ISSN 0300-340X

**Patronato ACLI**
Via Ergisto Bezzi 23-25, 00153 Rome, Italy.
- Emigrazione; informazioni sociali. bi-m. ISSN 0013-6700
- Informazioni Sociali. q. ISSN 0020-0816
- Sicurezza Sociale; dottrina, giurisprudenza, informazioni. bi-m. ISSN 0037-4598

**Patronato Genovese pro Natura "A. Anfossi"**
c/o Museo di Storia Naturale, Via Brigata Liguria 9, Genoa 16121, Italy
(Subscr. to: l'Ambiente, Piazza Fontane Marose 6-5, 16123 Genoa, Italy)
- Ambiente Naturale e Urbano. q. (Co-sponsors: Italia Nostra; W.W.F.-Fondo Mondiale per la Natura)
- Patronato Genovese Pronatura "A. Anfossi." Notiziario. s-m. ISSN 0031-3173

**Ennio Pedrini**
Goffredo Casalis 13, 10143 Turin, Italy.
- Monitore Valdostano; le moniteur valdotain. w.

**Editrice Pellegrini**
Via Roma 74, Casella Postale 158, 87100 Cosenza, Italy.
- Contenuti; bimestrale di lettere e arti. bi-m. ISSN 0010-762X
- Incontri Meridionali; rassegna di politica, economia, cultura, attualita. m. ISSN 0019-3488
- Letterato; di varia cultura. m. ISSN 0024-130X
- Nuova Gazzetta di Calabria; settimanale d'informazione. w. ISSN 0029-6198
- Nuova Rassegna; periodico di attualita-lettere-arti-cinema-teatro. bi-m. ISSN 0029-6201
- Poeti della Nuova Italia; antologia semestrale. s-a. ISSN 0032-1982

**B. Pellerano & S. del Gaudia**
Via Mezzocannone 39/41, Naples, Italy.
- Giornale di Mathematiche di Battaglini. s-a. ISSN 0017-033X

**F. P. Pellicano, Ed. & Pub.**
Via Toscana 30, 00187 Rome, Italy.
- This Week in Rome/Settimana a Roma. w. ISSN 0040-6295

**Tipografia A. Pelligrini (Udine)**
Via della Vigne 26, 33100 Udine, Italy.
- Friuli Medico. m. ISSN 0016-1535 (Societa Medica del Friuli)

**Pelosi Alexandre**
41 Viale G. Mazzini, 00195 Rome, Italy.
- Rassegna dei Gas di Petrolio Liquefatti; del gas naturale e degli idrocarburi in genere. m. ISSN 0033-9369

**Penombra**
Viale Giulio Cesare 109, 00192 Rome, Italy.
- Penombra; rivista enimmistica mensile. m.

**Pensiero Nazionale**
Via Velletri 35, Rome 00198, Italy.
- Pensiero Nazionale. s-m. ISSN 0031-4838

**Pensiero Scientifico**
Via Panama 48, Rome, Italy
(U.S. Subscr. to: Grune & Stratton, Inc., 757 Third Ave., New York, N.Y. 10017)
- Aggiornamenti in Ematologia. q. ISSN 0002-0923
- Aggiornamenti in Oncologia Clinica. q.
- Bronchi. bi-m. ISSN 0007-2230
- Clinica e Laboratorio. q.
- Ematologia Clinica. 3 per yr.
- Endocrinologia Clinica e Metabolismo. 3 per yr.
- Gastroenterologia Clinica. 3 per yr.
- Haematologica. bi-m. ISSN 0017-6567
- Italian Journal of Biochemistry. bi-m. ISSN 0021-2938 (Italian Society of Biochemistry)
- Medicina Illustrata. q.
- Ortopedia Clinica. q.
- Ostetrica e Ginecologia Clinica. 3 per yr.
- Progressi in Patologia Cardiovascolare. bi-m. ISSN 0033-0701
- Progressi in Radiologia. q. ISSN 0033-071X
- Recenti Progressi in Medicina. m. ISSN 0034-1193
- Rivista degli Ospedali. bi-m. ISSN 0035-5844
- Rivista di Neurologia. q. ISSN 0035-6344
- Rivista di Psichiatria. bi-m. ISSN 0035-6484
- Rivista di Psicoanalisi. 3 per yr. ISSN 0035-6492 (Societa Psicoanalitica Italiana)
- Surgery in Italy. q.
- Terapia Moderna. bi-m. ISSN 0040-3695
- Trasfusione del Sangue. q. ISSN 0041-1787 (Associazione Italiana dei Centri Trasfusionali)
- Urologia Clinica. 3 per yr.

**Pentagramma**
Via Bolzano 32, Rome, Italy.
- Pentagramma. m. ISSN 0031-4889

**Edizioni Pergamena**
Viale Ezio 7, 20149 Milan, Italy.
- Idea Liberale. bi-m.
- Sistematica; rivista di filosofia. q. ISSN 0037-5888

**Perna Editore**
Via Mario Pagano 41, 20145 Milan, Italy.
- Pedale d'Oro. w. ISSN 0031-3866

**Alberto Peruzzo**
Tito Speri 8, Milan, Italy.
- Settimana T V. w.

**Publicazioni Petrolifere S.p.A.**
Piazza della Lega 14, Alessandria, Italy.
- Petrolio; economia e tecnica degli idrocarburi. m.(11 per yr) ISSN 0031-6571

**Petronio**
Via G. Fara 39, I 20124 Milan, Italy.
- Petronio; rivista di moda maschile. m. ISSN 0031-658X

**Philips S.p.A.**
Piazza IV Novembre 3, 20124 Milan, Italy.
- Cronache; per il personale de Gruppo Philips. m.

**Edizioni Pi-Erre**
Piazza Sallustio 24, 00187 Rome, Italy
(Subscr. to: Edizioni Pi/Erre, Viale Filopanti 4c, 40126 Bologna, Italy)
- Imagine. 1975. (Federazione Nazionale Profumieri Italian)
- Ingegnere; rivista tecnica mensile. m. ISSN 0020-0905 (Associazione Nazionale Ingegneri e Architetti Italiani)

**Pia Societa San Paolo**
Piazzo S. Paolo 14, 12051 Alba (Cuneo), Italy
(And: via Alessandro Severo 56, 00145 Rome, Italy)
- Bollettino Bibliografico Internazionale per l'Apostolato delle Edizioni. bi-m. ISSN 0006-6613
- Famiglia Cristiana. w. ISSN 0014-7095
- Giornalino; settimanale dei ragazzi. w.
- Vita Pastorale. m. (10 per yr.)

**Compagnia Editoriale Pianeta s.r.l.**
Via C. Capelli 93, 10146 Turin, Italy.
- Pianeta. bi-m. ISSN 0031-9538

**Piccin Editore**
Via Porciglia 10, 35100 Padua, Italy.
- Acta Europaea Fertilitatis. q. ISSN 0587-2421
(Italian Society for the Study of Sterility and
Fertility)
- Acta Oncologia. q. (Italian Society for the
Prevention and Diagnosis of Tumors) (Co-
sponsor: Italian Society for the Treatment of
Tumors)
- Biochimica e Biologia Sperimentale/Biochemistry
and Experimental Biology. q. ISSN 0006-2995
(Universita degli Studi di Milano)
- Giornale Italiano di Chimica Clinica. q. (Societa
Italiana de Biochimica Clinica)
- Italian Journal of Immunology and
Immunopathology. s-a. (Italian Society of
Immunology and Immunopathology)
- Quaderni di Anatomia Practica. q.
- Quintessenza; rivista mensile di
odontostomatologia pratica. m.
- Rivista di Patologia Clinica e Sperimentale. q.
ISSN 0035-6409
- Surgical Gastroenterology. q. (Collegium
Internationale Chirugiae Digestivae)

**Rachetto Piero, Ed. & Pub.**
Via Po 3, 10124 Turin, Italy.
- Voci Nuove. Quaderni di Poesia Contemporanea.
s-a. ISSN 0042-7896

**Guido Pietroni, Ed. & Pub.**
Via Bergamo 12a, 20135 Milan, Italy.
- Nevesport Illustrato. w (Oct.-Mar.), m (Apr.-Sep.)
ISSN 0028-4122

**Wilson Pignagnoli**
Piazza Scapinelli 2, 42100 Reggio Emilia, Italy.
- Liberta; settimanale cattolico reggiano. w. ISSN
0024-1997

**Fratelli Pini Editori S.p.A.**
Via Alberti 10, 20149 Milan, Italy.
- Tempo Economico; rivista mensile d'informazione
manageriale. m. (10 yr.) ISSN 0040-3040

**Pipe World Est.**
Via Pacini 2, Milan, Italy.
- Pipe World; international magazine for pipe
smokers and clubs. q. ISSN 0032-017X

**Industrie Pirelli S. p. A.**
Piazza Duca d'Aosta 3, 20124 Milan, Italy.
- Fatti E Notizie. m. ISSN 0014-8873

**Pitra Editoriale**
Via Plutarco 15, 20145 Milan, Italy.
- Illumino-Tecnica. m. ISSN 0019-2384

**Guiseppe Poidomani, Pub.**
Corso Umberto 174, Modica, Italy.
- Discretio. irreg. ISSN 0012-3668

**Pola Editrice s.r.l.**
Via Borromei, 9, 20133 Milan, Italy.
- Strategia. fortn.

**Franco Poli, Ed. & Pub.**
Via Bigli 2, 20121 Milan, Italy.
- Arte Illustrata; rivista d'arte antica e moderna. bi-
m. ISSN 0004-3435

**Poliedrica Editrice**
Plaza Bologna 1 bis, Rome, Italy.
- Guida Sardegna d'Oggi. ISSN 0487-3750
- Sardegna Informazioni; sardinform. w. ISSN 0036-
4789

**Edizioni Il Polifilo**
Via Borgonuovo 2, 20121 Milan, Italy.
- Archivio del Teatro Italiano. irreg; latest issue,
1976. ISSN 0066-6661
- Documenti Sulle Arti del Libro. irreg; latest issue,
1975. ISSN 0070-6906
- Trattati di Architettura. irreg. ISSN 0082-6006

**Giancarlo Politi Editore**
Via Donatello 36, 20137 Milan, Italy.
- Flash Art-Heute Kunst. bi-m.

**Politica Estera**
Via Bartolomeo Gosio 85, Rome, Italy.
- Politica Estera; Rassegna di commenti, studi,
notizie, documenti. m. ISSN 0032-308X

**Casa Editrice Il Ponte**
Via M.U. Triano 18, 20149 Milan, Italy.
- Acta Diabetologica Latina. bi-m. ISSN 0001-5563

- Chronobiologia. q. ISSN 0390-0037 (International
Society for Chronobiology)
- Folia Veterinaria Latina. q. ISSN 0301-0724
- Ricerca in Clinica e in Laboratorio. q (with
supplements) ISSN 0390-5748

**Emilio Ponticello, Ed. & Pub.**
Via Sampiero di Bastelica 93, 00176 Rome, Italy.
- Arringa. fortn. (Associazione Nazionale dei
Procuratori e Patrocinatori Legali)

**Pontifical Biblical Institute**
Piazza Pilotta 35, Rome I-00187, Italy.
- Orientalia. q. ISSN 0030-5367
- Studia Papyrologica. (pub. by Biblical Institute
Press)

**Pontificia Accademia Liturgica**
- Ephemerides Liturgicae. (pub. by Edizioni
Liturgiche e Vincenziane)

**Pontificia Facolta Teologica dell'Italia Meridionale-
Sezione di Capodimonte**
- Asprenas. (pub. by M. d' Auria Editore Pontificio)

**Pontificia Facolta Teologica Marianum**
Viale Trenta Aprile 6, 00153 Rome, Italy.
- Marianum. q.

**Pontificia Facolta Teologica S. Bonaventura**
- Miscellanea Francescana. (pub. by Casa Editrice
Miscellanea Francescana)

**Pontificia Unione Missionaria del Clero**
Via di Propaganda 1-C, 00187 Rome, Italy.
- Mondo e Missione. m. ISSN 0026-9514

**Pontificia Universita Gregoriana**
- Analecta Gregoriana. (pub. by Gregorian
University Press)
- Gregorianum. (pub. by Gregorian University
Press)
- Periodica de Re Morali Canonica Liturgica. (pub.
by Gregorian University Press)
- Pontificia Universita Gregoriana. Miscellanea
Historiae Pontificiae. (pub. by Gregorian
University Press)
- Pontificia Universita Gregoriana. Studia
Missionalia. (pub. by Gregorian University Press)

**Pontificia Universita Gregoriana. Facolta di Storia
Ecclesiastica**
- Acta Nuntiaturae Gallicae. (pub. by Gregorian
University Press)
- Archivum Historiae Pontificae. (pub. by Gregorian
University Press)

**Pontificia Universita Gregoriana. School of
Missiology**
Piazza della Pilotta 4, 00187 Rome, Italy.
- Documenta Missionalia. irreg.

**Pontificia Universita Gregoriana. School of Social
Sciences**
Piazza della Pilotta 4, 00187 Rome, Italy.
- Pontificia Universita Gregoriana. Istituto di
Scienze Sociali Studia Socialia. irreg. ISSN 0080-
3960

**Pontificia Universita Lateranense**
- Aquinas. (pub. by Herder Editrice e Libreria s.r.l.)

**Pontificia Universita Lateranense. Pontificio Instituto
Utriusque Iuris**
Piazza S. Giovanni in Laterano, 00184 Rome, Italy.
- Studia et Documenta Historiae et Iuris. a.

**Pontificia Universitas Lateranensis. Institutum
Theologiae Vitae Religiosae**
Via Aurelia 617, 00165 Rome, Italy.
- Claretianum; commentaria theologica opera et
studio. ISSN 0578-4182

**Pontificio Ateneo Antonianum**
Via Merulana 124, 00185 Rome, Italy.
- Antonianum. q. ISSN 0003-6064

**Pontificio Collegio Armeno**
Salita S. Nicola da Tolentino 17, 00187 Rome, Italy.
- Hromkla. 5 per yr. ISSN 0018-6899

**Pontificio Istituto Biblico**
- Biblica. (pub. by Biblical Institute Press)

**Pontificio Istituto di Archeologia Christiana**
Pontificia Commissione di Archeologia Sacra, Via
Napoleone III N 1, 00185 Rome, Italy.
- Rivista di Archeologia Cristiana. s-a. ISSN 0035-
6042

**Pontificio Istituto di Spiritualita**
- Bibliographia Internationalis Spiritualitatis. (pub.
by Edizioni dei Padri Carmelitani Scalzi)
- Rivista di Vita Spirituale. (pub. by Edizioni Padri
Carmelitani Scalzi)

**Edizioni Pontificio Istituto Missioni Estere**
Via Mose Bianchi 94, 20149 Milan, Italy.
- Italia Missionaria. s-m. ISSN 0021-2806
- Missionari del P.I.M.E. m(11 per yr)
- Mondo e Missione. m(11 per yr) ISSN 0026-6094
- Venga Il Tuo Regno. m. (11 per yr.) (Subscr. to:
Giuseppe Buono, Ed., Viale Colli Aminei 36)

**Pontificio Istituto Orientale**
Piazza S. Maria Maggiore 7, 00185 Rome, Italy.
- Orientalia Christiana Analecta. irreg.
- Orientalia Christiana Periodica; commentarii de re
orientali aetatis christianae sacra et profana. s-a.
ISSN 0030-5375

**Pontificio Santuario di Pompei**
Naples 80045, Italy.
- Rosario e la Nuova Pompei. bi-m. ISSN 0035-
8282

**Edizioni Popolari**
Via S. Nicolo da Tolentino, 18, 00187 Rome, Italy.
- Umanita. w. (Italian Socialist Democratic Party)

**Edizioni Luigi Pozzi**
Via Panama 68, 00198 Rome, Italy.
- Attualita in Chirurgia. 3 per yr.
- Giornale Italiano di Cardiologia. m. ISSN 0046-
5968
- International Journal of Sport Psychology. 3 per
yr. ISSN 0047-0767 (International Society of
Sports Psychology)
- Patologia e Clinica Ostetrica e Ginecologica;
rivista bimestrale per i medici practici. bi-m. ISSN
0304-0313
- Policlinico. Sezione Chirurgica. bi-m. ISSN 0032-
2636 (Societa di Ricerche in Chirurgia)
- Policlinico. Sezione Medica. bi-m. ISSN 0048-
4717
- Policlinico. Sezione Pratica. fortn. ISSN 0032-
2644
- Rendiconti di Gastroenterologia. 3 per yr. ISSN
0300-0877 (Italian Society of Gastroenterology)
- Valsalva. bi-m. ISSN 0042-2371

**Premio**
Via Val d'Ossola 75, 00141 Rome, Italy.
- Premio; periodico culturale. q. ISSN 0032-7409

**Presso Galleria S. Giorgio**
Via Casavorgnan 12, Mestre, Italy.
- Nuova Venezia; bimestrale di attualita culturale.
bi-m. ISSN 0029-6260

**Preti della Missione della Provincia di Roma**
- Bollettino Vincenziano. (pub. by Edizioni
Liturgiche e Vincenziane)

**Previdenza Sociale nell'Agricoltura**
Via Barberini 95, Rome, Italy.
- Previdenza Sociale nell'Agricoltura. bi-m. ISSN
0478-1805

**Edizioni Previsionali**
Via G. Paisiello 4, Rome, Italy.
- Social and Human Forecasting Documentation. a.
(Institute for Futures Research and Education)

**Primalinea**
Via Quattro Fontane 25, 00184 Rome, Italy.
- Primalinea. m. ISSN 0032-8251

**Editore Privitera**
Via Tiburtina 150, 00185 Rome, Italy.
- Rivista Di Anatomia Artistica; Periodico Di
Scienze E Arte. q. ISSN 0048-8356

**Pro Civitate Christiana**
Via Ancaiani 3, 06081 Assisi, Italy.
- Rocca. s-m.

**Pro Padova**
Via S. Francesco 16/A, 35100 Padova, Italy.
- Padova. m. ISSN 0479-1290

**Problemi**
Via Ricasoli 59, 90139 Palermo, Italy.
- Problemi; periodico trimestrale di cultura. 3 per yr. ISSN 0032-9339

**Problemi della Pedagogia**
Via Corsini N.12, Rome, Italy.
- Problemi della Pedagogia. bi-m. ISSN 0032-9347

**Prodotto Alimentare Italiano**
Via Burcelli 1, Casella Postale 45, 26100 Cremona, Italy.
- Prodotto Alimentare Italiano; annuario generale dell'industria alimentare italiana per il Mercato Nazionale e mEC. a.

**Progetto 80**
Via Guicciardini 4, 20129 Milan, Italy.
- Progetto 80; agenzia di stampa. fortn.

**Promark S.p.A.**
Corso Traiano 84, 10135 Turin, Italy.
- Abbigliamento. fortn.

**Propaganda Editoriale Grafica S.p. A.**
Via Fratelli Bressan 2, 20126 Milan, Italy.
- Bagno: Oggi e Domani/Bain: Aujourd'hui et Demain/Bathroom: Today and Tomorrow/Bad: Heute und Morgen. bi-m.
- Condizionamento dell'Aria. m. ISSN 0010-5406 (Associazione Italiana Condizionamento Dell 'aria, Riscaldamento Refrigerazione)
- Freddo. bi-m. ISSN 0016-0296 (Associazione Frigorifera Italiana)
- Giornale dell' Ingegnere. fortn. (Engineers Union of Milan)
- Ingegnere Italiano. m. ISSN 0020-0913 (Consiglio Nazionale degli Ingegneri)
- Ingegnere Libero Professionista. m. ISSN 0020-0921 (Sindacato Nazionale Ingegneri Liberi Professionisti Italiani)
- Installatore Italiano. m. ISSN 0020-2118 (National Installation Contractors Association)

**Proprieta Fondiaria Agricola**
Via Ravizza 4, 28100 Novara, Italy.
- Proprieta Fondiaria. m.

**Prospetti**
Casella Postale 732, 00100 Rome, Italy.
- Prospetti. q. ISSN 0033-1562

**Prospettive Regionali**
Via S. Francesco 11, Trieste, Italy.
- Prospettive Regionali; osservatorio del friuli venezia giulia. m. ISSN 0033-1589

**Edizioni di Protezione Civile s.r.l.**
Via Flavia 72, 00187 Rome, Italy.
- Antifurto; rivista mensile di studio dei problemi antifurto e antirapina. m.
- Antincendio e Protezione Civile. m.

**Provincia di Genova dei Frati Minori Cappuccini**
Piazza Cappuccini 1, 16122 Genoa, Italy.
- Padre Santo; periodico dei Cappuccini liguri. m. ISSN 0030-9214

**Provincia Iblea**
c/o Giovanni Gurrieri, Viale N. Colaianni 41, 97100 Ragusta, Italy.
- Provincia Iblea. s-m.

**Provincia Religiosa dei Frati Minori Conventuali di Puglia**
- Santo dei Voli. (pub. by Santuario S. Giuseppe da Copertino)

**Provincia Romana dei Frati Predicatori**
Piazza S. Domenico 1, 51100 Pistoia, Italy.
- Memorie Domenicane. (pub. by Edizioni di Vita Sociale)
- Vita Sociale. bi-m. ISSN 0042-7365

**Provo Radicale**
Via Baccina 90, 00184 Rome, Italy.
- Provo Radicale. q.

**Provveditorato al Porto di Venezia**
Zattere N. 1401, C.P. 30123, Venice, Italy.
- Porto di Venezia. m. ISSN 0032-4965

**Psicologia Contemporanea**
Via Gioberti, 34, Florence, Italy.
- Psicologia Contemporanea. bi-m.

**Edizioni Pubbli Re**
Via S. Lattuada 26, 20135 Milan, Italy.
- Automobilista. m.
- Autoriparatore; mensile d'informazione tecnico-economico. m. (Federazione Automobilistica Italiana)
- Carrozziere Italiano. m. ISSN 0008-6959
- Gommista. m.
- Pilota Moto. fortn.
- 3A, Autoricambi, Accessori, Attrezzature. q. (Federazione Automobilistica Italiana)

**Pubblicista**
Via Dandolo 8, Rome, Italy.
- Pubblicista; periodico di informazione dei giornalisti-pubblicisti. m. ISSN 0033-3247

**Pubblicita e Vendita**
Galleria Unione 3, 20122 Milan, Italy.
- Pubblicita e Vendita. bi-m. ISSN 0033-3255

**Pubblicita Editoriale Italiana**
Viale Mentana 92, 43100 Parma, Italy.
- Frantoio. m.

**Societa Editrice Pubblicitaria**
Corso Vittorio Emanuele 15, 20122 Milan, Italy.
- Italia Produce. m.
- Made in Italy; rivista del Comercio Estero. m.

**Pubbliemme**
Via Giotto 3, 20145 Milan, Italy.
- Arteregalo; selezione bimestrale della cristalleria, ceramica, articoli da regalo ed articoli di qualita per la casa. bi-m. ISSN 0004-3478
- Articoli Casalinghi. m. ISSN 0004-3672
- Giornale dei Giocattoli. m. (Assogiocattoli)

**Pubbliturist**
Via Natale Battaglia 27, 20127 Milan, Italy.
- Annuario Generale delle Imprese di Viaggio e Turismo. a.
- Via Vai. m.

**Publiepi**
Via Giotto 36, 20145 Milan, Italy.
- Millimetro; periodico di informazione pubbliciatria. q.

**Publigraf**
Via E. Nicolardi 40, 80131 Naples, Italy.
- Noi Giovani. m. ISSN 0029-0939

**Publimedia Editrice**
Corso Venezia 18, 20121 Milan, Italy.
- Calze & Maglia; rassegna della produzione nazionale ed estera. s-m.
- Civilta del Profumo. m. (10 per yr.)
- Civilta Farmaceutica. bi-m.

**Publindex s.r.l.**
Via Tagliamento 25, Rome, Italy.
- Realta. w. ISSN 0034-0995 (Confederazione Italiana d'Azienda)

**Publisicula S.N.C.**
Via Mariano Stabile 150, 90139 Palermo, Italy.
- Sicilia Tempo. m.

**Publiturist**
Via Natale Battaglia 27, 20127 Milan, Italy.
- Operatore Turistico. s-m.

**Publitype**
Via Filippino Lippi 16, 20131 Milano, Italy.
- Linea Intima. q.
- Ortopedico. bi-m.

**Pungolo del Sud**
Via F.9(Piazza Leoni), Palermo, Italy.
- Pungolo del Sud; periodico di cronache mediterranee. m. ISSN 0033-4286

**Pungolo Verde**
Via F. 9 No. 3, 86100 Campobasso, Italy.
- Pungolo Verde; arti-science e lettere. m. ISSN 0033-4294

**Puzz**
C. P. 395, 20100 Milan, Italy.
- Puzz. q.

**Quaderni di Critica**
V. Cicerone 28, 00193 Rome, Italy.
- Quaderni di Critica. 3 per yr.

**Quaderni di Dibattito Politico**
Via Mozart 21, 20122 Milan, Italy.
- Quaderni di Dibattito Politico. q. ISSN 0033-4936

**Quaderni Piacentini**
Via Poggiali 41, 29100 Piacenza, Italy.
- Quaderni Piacentini. bi-m. ISSN 0048-6094

**Quarto Potere**
Via Bartolomeo Gosio 59, 00191 Rome, Italy.
- Quarto Potere; rassegna di storia, tecnica ed esperienze del giornalismo. q. ISSN 0302-5063

**Quasi**
Via G. Modena 20, 50121 Florence, Italy.
- Quasi; testi poetici e altre approssimzaioni. 3 per yr. ISSN 0048-6213

**Editrice Queriniana**
Via Piamarta 6, 25100 Brescia, Italy.
- Rivista di Pastorale Liturgica. bi-m. ISSN 0035-6395
- Servizio della Parola. m. ISSN 0037-2773

**Questitalia**
S. Croce 598, Venice, Italy.
- Questitalia. m. ISSN 0033-6378

**Quintaparete**
Piazza Carignano, 10123 Turin, Italy.
- Quintaparete; rivista d'arte contemporanea. q. ISSN 0048-6485

**Ragioni Critiche**
Corso Italia 23, 951 29 Catania, Italy.
- Ragioni Critiche. q.

**Maria Ragno**
Via Crescenzio 42, Rome, Italy.
- Rassegna Chimica. bi-m. ISSN 0033-9334 (Unione Nazionale Chimici Italiani)

**RAI-Radiotelevisione Italiana**
Viale Mazzini 14, 00195 Rome, Italy.
- Informazione Radio TV; studi documenti e notizie. m. ISSN 0300-3973

**Ramo Editoriale degli Agricoltori**
Via Yser N. 14, Rome, Italy.
- Italia Agricola. m. ISSN 0021-275X

**Rassegna Alpina**
Via M. Melloni 17, 20124 Milan, Italy.
- Rassegna Alpina; rivista internazionale della montagna. bi-m. ISSN 0048-6736

**Rassegna dei Lavori Pubblici**
Corso Trieste 128, 00198 Rome, Italy.
- Rassegna dei Lavori Pubblici; rivista mensile di informazione tecnica e giuridica. m. ISSN 0033-9377

**Rassegna di Cultura e Vita Scolastica**
Via Giosue Borsi 3, 00197 Rome, Italy.
- Rassegna di Cultura e Vita Scolastica. m. ISSN 0033-9482

**Rassegna di Diritto Cinematografico, Teatrale e della Radiotelevisione**
Viale E. Quirino Visconti 99, 00193 Rome, Italy.
- Rassegna di Diritto Cinematografico, Teatrale e della Radiotelevisione. q. ISSN 0033-9504

**Rassegna di Diritto e Tecnica dell' Alimentazione**
c/o Franco Angeli, Ed., Via Monza 106, 20127 Milan, Italy.
- Rassegna di Diritto e Technica dell' Alimentazione. m.

**Rassegna di Diritto e Tecnica Doganale e delle Imposte di Fabbricazione**
c/o Guido Pastena, Ed., Via Montevideo 4, 00198 Rome, Italy.
- Rassegna di Diritto e Tecnica Doganale e delle Imposte di Fabbricazione. m. ISSN 0483-9722

**Rassegna di Politica e di Storia**
Largo S. Alfonso 5, 00185 Rome, Italy.
- Rassegna di Politica e di Storia. m. ISSN 0033-958X

**Rassegna di Studi Psichiatrici**
Ospedale Psichiatrico, Siena, Italy.
- Rassegna di Studi Psichiatrici. bi-m. ISSN 0033-9636

**Rassegna Europea**
13 via Mazzini, 33100 Udine, Italy.
- Rassegna Europea; revista per la Federazione Europea. bi-m. ISSN 0033-9660

**Rassegna Giuridica Ed Economica sui Danni di Guerra**
Via di S. Agnese N.16, 00198 Rome, Italy.
- Rassegna Giuridica Ed Economica sui Danni di Guerra. m. ISSN 0033-9679

**Rassegna Grafica Editrice**
V. M. Melloni, 17, 20129 Milan, Italy.
- Foto Notiziario; cine notiziario - notiziario ottica e occhialeria. q. ISSN 0015-8720

**Rassegna Internazionale di Logica**
Ed. Franco Spisani, Via Belmeloro, N. 3, 40126 Bologna, Italy.
- Rassegna Internazionale di Logica/International Logic Review. 2 per yr. ISSN 0048-6779

**Rassegna Melodrammatica**
Corso Porta Romana 80, 20122 Milan, Italy.
- Rassegna Melodrammatica; corriere de musica. s-m. ISSN 0033-9784

**Rassegna Mensile della Imposte Dirette**
c/o Antonino La Mattina, Ed., Via Fregene N. 14, 00183 Rome, Italy.
- Rassegna Mensile della Imposte Dirette. m.

**Rassegna Modi di Abitare Oggi**
c/o Manlio Arinellini, Ed., Via Aurelio Saffi 34, 20123 Milan, Italy.
- Rassegna Modi di Abitare Oggi. q.

**Libreria L. de Re**
Via dei Pucci 45 R., Florence, Italy.
- Quaderni di Studi Storici Toscani. irreg.; 3-4 per yr. (Centro di Studi Storici Toscani)

**Regione Calabrese**
Via dei Cardatori 14, Casella Postale 214, 23489 Catanzaro, Italy.
- Regione Calabrese; rivista trimestrale di studi e ricerche. q.

**Regione e Potere Locale**
Piazza S. Ambrogio 15, Milan, Italy.
- Regione e Potere Locale. m. ISSN 0034-3412

**Regione Toscana**
Via dei Servi 51, Florence, Italy.
- Regione Toscana; notizario della giunta. m. ISSN 0048-7090

**Relations Latines**
27 Galleria Umberto 1, 80132 Naples, Italy.
- Relations Latines. bi-m. ISSN 0034-3803

**Relazioni**
Piazza Navona 93, Rome, Italy.
- Relazioni; rivista di fatti e analisi. m. ISSN 0034-3838

**Relazioni Pubbliche Informazioni s.r.l.**
Via Isonzo 25, 00198 Rome, Italy.
- ETOCOM. m.

**Rendiconti**
Via Castiglione 35, Bologna, Italy.
- Rendiconti; rivista di letteratura e scienza. bi-m. ISSN 0034-4419

**Reportage**
Via Belvedere 7, Lamezia Terme, (Catanzaro) 88046, Italy.
- Reportage; politico-turistico-musicale-agricolo. m. ISSN 0034-4745

**Resistenza**
Casella Postale 100, Turin, Italy.
- Resistenza. m. ISSN 0034-5598

**Dr. Franco Ricciardi, Ed. & Pub.**
Trav. D. Fontana 53-57, Naples, Italy.
- Farmacista Sociale; periodico indipendente dei farmacisti d'Italia. m. ISSN 0014-8253 (Farmacisti d'Italia)

**Edizioni Richerche**
Viale Ippocrate 85, Rome, Italy.
- Italy. Ministero dei Trasporti e dell' Aviazione Civile. Azienda Autonoma delle Ferrovie dello Stato. Bollettino Statistico Mensile. m. ISSN 0021-3144

**Societa Editrice Il Rinnovamento**
Via dei Taurini 19, Rome 00185, Italy.
- Libri Paese Sera. w. ISSN 0024-2691

**Risveglio**
Via Garibaldi 1, 10073-Cirie, Italy.
- Risveglio; settimanale indipendente del Canavese e delle valli di Lanzo. w.

**Riunioni Medico-Chirurgiche Internazionali**
- Quotidiano Minerva Medica. (pub. by Edizioni Minerva Medica)

**Editori Riuniti**
Via IV Novembre 114, 00187 Rome, Italy.
- Cinema Sessanta. bi-m.
- Critica Marxista. bi-m. ISSN 0011-152X (Partito Comunista Italiano)
- Democrazia e Diritto. q. ISSN 0416-9565 (Associazione Italiana Giuristi Democratici)
- Donne e Politica. bi-m.
- Nuova Rivista Internazionale; le vie del socialismo. m. ISSN 0029-621X (Partito Comunista Italiano)
- Politica ed Economia. m.
- Riforma Agraria; rivista di economia e politica agraria. m. ISSN 0483-0474
- Riforma della Scuola. m. ISSN 0035-5240
- Studi Storici. q. ISSN 0039-3037 (Istituto Gramsci Roma)

**Riviera Eco**
Viale dei Mille 14, Riccione, Italy.
- Riviera Eco. w.

**Rivista Abruzzese**
Via F. di Cavallo 94, Lanciano 66034, Chieti, Italy.
- Rivista Abruzzese; rassegna trimestrale di culture. q. ISSN 0035-5739

**Rivista Amministrativa della Repubblica Italiana**
Via Enrico Petrella 4, Rome, Italy.
- Rivista Amministrativa della Repubblica Italiana. m. ISSN 0035-5763

**Rivista dei Lavori Pubblici**
Largo Brancaccio 82, 00184 Rome, Italy.
- Rivista dei Lavori Pubblici. m.

**Rivista del Colore**
Via degli Imbriani 10, 20158 Milan, Italy.
- Rivista del Colore; verniciatura industriale. m. ISSN 0048-8348

**Rivista di Estetica**
Via S. Rosa 20, Padua, Italy.
- Rivista di Estetica. 3 per yr. ISSN 0035-6212

**Rivista di Etnografia**
Via Alfrado Rocco No. 98, Naples, Italy.
- Rivista di Etnografia. a. ISSN 0085-5731

**Rivista di Patologia Vegetale**
Casella Postale 99, 27100 Pavia, Italy.
- Rivista di Patologia Vegetale. q. ISSN 0035-6441

**Rivista di Polizia**
Via Mazzocchi 175, Santa Maria Capua Vetere (Caserta), Italy.
- Rivista di Polizia; rassegna di dottrina tecnica e legislazione. m. ISSN 0035-6476

**Rivista di Scienze Preistoriche**
Via S. Egidio 21, 50122 Florence, Italy.
- Rivista di Scienze Preistoriche. s-a. ISSN 0035-6514

**Rivista di Suinicoltura**
Via Emilia Levante 31/2, 40139 Bologna, Italy.
- Rivista di Suinicoltura. m. ISSN 0035-662X

**Rivista Internazionale di Economia dei Trasporti**
Via G.A. Guattani 8, 00161 Rome, Italy.
- Rivista Internazionale di Economia dei Trasporti/International Journal of Transport Economics. 3 per yr.

**Rivista Italiana di Paleontologia e Stratigrafia**
Piazzale Gorini 15, 20133 Milano, Italy.
- Rivista Italiana di Paleontologia e Stratigrafia. q. ISSN 0035-6883

**Edizioni Rivista Mediche**
Via Masaccio 173, Florence, Italy.
- Ospedali d'Italia-Chirurgia. m. ISSN 0030-6266

**Rivista Tributaria**
Via Tronto 20, 00198 Rome, Italy.
- Rivista Tributaria; rassegna bimestrale di dottrina giurisprudenza e legislazione. bi-m. ISSN 0035-709X

**Rizzoli Editore**
Via Civitavecchia 102, 20132 Milan, Italy (U.S. Distributor: Rizzoli Bookstore, 712, Fifth Ave., New York, N.Y. 10019)
- Annabella. w. ISSN 0003-3766
- Bella; settimanale di attualita e moda. w. ISSN 0005-8602
- Buona Tavola. m.
- Europeo; settimanale politico di attualita. w. ISSN 0014-3189
- Linus. m.
- Milleidee. m.
- Novella 2000. w.
- Oggi. w. ISSN 0030-0705
- Playboy. m.
- Sorrisi E Canzoni T.V. w. ISSN 0038-156X

**Elena Rizzotti, Ed. & Pub.**
Largo Caldera II, Verona 37100, Italy.
- Informatore Agrario. w. ISSN 0020-0689

**Edizioni della Rocchetta**
Via Borgognona 47, Rome, Italy.
- Tribuna. w.

**Italo Rocco, Ed. & Pub.**
Box No.50, Battipaglia, Salerno, Italy.
- Silarus; rassegna bimestrale di cultura. bi-m. ISSN 0037-5179

**Roman Province of the Dominican Fathers**
Convento S. Domenico, 52100 - Arezzo, Italy.
- Missioni Domenicane. m.(10 per yr.) ISSN 0026-6108

**Romana Teatri s.r.l.**
Piazza Campo Marzio, 00186 Rome, Italy.
- Dramma. m. ISSN 0012-6012

**Romans d'Isonzo**
Gorizia, Italy.
- Arcobaleno; rivista periodica scolastica. q. ISSN 0004-0827

**Rome, Italy. Amministrazione Provinciale**
Piazza S. Maria della Pieta 5, 00135 Rome, Italy.
- Lavoro Neuropsichiatrico. bi-m. ISSN 0023-9097

**Rome, Italy. Comune di Roma. Ufficio di Statistica e Censimento**
Via della Greca 5, 00186 Rome, Italy.
- Rome. Ufficio de Statistica e Censimento. Notiziario Statistico Mensile. m. ISSN 0010-4965

**Fondazione Giorgio Ronchi**
Largo Enrico Fermi 6, 50125 Florence, Italy.
- Fondazione Giorgio Ronchi. Atti. bi-m. ISSN 0015-606X

**Massimo Panvini Rosati, Ed. & Pub.**
Piazza Adriana No.20, Rome 00193, Italy.
- Notaro; periodico quindicinale di libera discussione, organo della classe notarile. s-m. ISSN 0029-3857

**Giulo Rosel**
Via S.Andrea delle Dame 6, 80138 Naples, Italy.
- Archivio Stomatologico. q. ISSN 0004-0320

**Bruno Buonomo la Rossa, Ed. & Pub.**
Piazza S. Domenico Maggiore 9, 80134 Naples, Italy.
- Rassegna Internazionale di Clinica e Terapia. bi-m. ISSN 0033-9695

**Editrice Il Rostro**
Via Monte Generoso 6/A, Milan, Italy.
- Antenna; rassegna mensile di tecnica elettronica. m. ISSN 0003-5386
- Informazione Elettronica. m.

**Round Table International Academy**
Via Zante 21, C.C.P. 3/4190, 20138 Milan, Italy.
- Tavola Rotonda; mensile di scienze, arte e cultura. m. ISSN 0300-3132

**Ruggieri S. Ed C. Editori**
Via Castelfidardo 11, 20121 Milan, Italy.
- Elettrauto. m.

**Rusconi Editore S.p.A.**
Via Vitruvio 43, Milan, Italy.
- Eva Express. w. ISSN 0014-3308
- Gente. w. ISSN 0016-6944
- Gente Motori. m.
- Gioia. w. ISSN 0017-0062
- Gioielli di Rakam. m.
- Rakam; mensile d'moda e lavori femminili. m. ISSN 0033-9113
- Settimanale; settimanale di politica, economia, cultura. w.

**S A G S A S.p.A.**
Viale Lun'ingiana 16, 20125 Milan, Italy.
- Perito Industriale. bi-m. ISSN 0031-5435 (Consiglio Nazionale per la Professione; Federazione Nazionale dei Periti Industriali)

**Edizioni S A S I P**
Via S. Vittore al Teatro 1, 20123milan, Italy.
- Taccuino dell'Azionista. a. ISSN 0082-1446

**S E C T I**
Via Lipari 8, 00141 Roma, Italy.
- Fotografare Novita. m.

**S E I T S.N.C.**
Corso Orbassano 402/15, Turin, Italy.
- A. P. I/Piccola e Media Industria; notiziario mensile di informazione. m. ISSN 0031-9597 (Federazione Fra le Associazioni Piccole e Medie Industrie, Regione Piemontese)

**S.E.P.A.**
Via Gaetano Callani 20, 43100 Parma, Italy.
- Arboricoltura da Legno; pioppicoltura. m.
- Economia Montana. m. ISSN 0012-9836

**Editrice S.E.P.I.**
Piazzetta Matilde Serao, N.7, Naples, Italy.
- Stampa Sud. w. ISSN 0049-2051

**S.E.T.A. s.r.l.**
*see* Societa Edizioni Techniche Arredamento

**Editore S.I.P.I.**
*see* Servicio Italiana Pubblicazioni Internazionali s.r.l.

**Edizioni S T E M- MUCCHI**
*see* Societa Tipografica Editrice Modenese

**Edizioni E S S E**
Via Zara 9, 00198 Rome, Italy.
- Ali Nuove. fortn. ISSN 0002-5380

**Sabatelli Editori**
Piazza Diaz 11, 17100 Savona, Italy.
- Odontoiatria Pratica. q.
- Proposte di Poesia Narrativa Teatro Arte Critica. bi-m. ISSN 0033-1406

**Saggiatore S.p.A.**
Via San Senatore 10, 20122 Milan, Italy.
- Dialoghi di Archeologia. 3 per yr.

**Armando Saitta, Ed. & Pub.**
Via Port'Alba 19, 80134 Naples, Italy.
- Critica Storica. bi-m. ISSN 0011-1554

**Salamon e Agustoni Editori**
Via Montenapoleone 3, 20121 Milan, Italy.
- Conoscitore di Stampe-Print Collector; rivista bimestrale storica e d'attualita della stampa. 5 per yr.

**Editrice Salentina - Galatina**
Via R. Visconti 6, 73100 Lecce, Italy.
- Societa Jonico-Salentina di Medicina e Chirurgia. Bollettino. s-a.
- Voce del Sud. w.

**Salone Nautico Internazionale di Genoa**
- Italia Sul Mare. (pub. by Vito Bianco, Ed. & Pub.)

**Salotto Culturale**
Via M. Mirenghi 41, Bari, Italy.
- Salotto Culturale; giornale di storia, folklore lettere ed arte. q. ISSN 0036-3561

**Gaetano Salveti, Ed. & Pub.**
Via Bv. Meliana 12, 00195 Rome, Italy.
- Crisi e Letteratura; periodico di lettere filosofia arti. q. ISSN 0011-1406

**Salvo Imprevisti**
c/o M. Bettarini, Ed., Borgo SS, Apostoli 4, 50123 Florence, Italy.
- Salvo Imprevisti. 3 per yr.

**Editrice San Marco**
24069 Trescore Balneario, Italy.
- Bonifica e l'Assetto Territoriale. q. (Associazione Nazionale delle Bonifiche, delle Irrigazioni e dei Miglioramenti Fondiari)

**Sanatorio di Collinaia**
Livorno, Italy.
- Rassegna di Patologia dell' Apparato Respiratorio. q. ISSN 0033-9563 (Federazione Italiana Lotta Contro la Tubercolosi. Sezione Toscana)

**Casa Editrice G. C. Sansoni S.p.A.**
Viale Mazzine 46, Florence 50100, Italy
(Subscription Address: Licosa  via Lamarmora 45, Florence, Italy)
- Archivio di Chirurgia Toracica e Cardiovascolare. q. ISSN 0004-007X
- Archivio Italiano di Anatomia e di Embriologia. q. ISSN 0004-0223
- Cinema Nuovo. bi-m. ISSN 0009-711X (And via Santa Giulia 67, 10124 Turin, Italy)
- Diritto e Societa. q.
- Giornale Critico della Filosofia Italiana. q. ISSN 0017-0089
- Homine. irreg., latest issue, no. 38-40. ISSN 0018-4292 (Centro di Ricerca per le Scienze Morali e Sociali)
- Lingua Nostra. q. ISSN 0024-3868
- Paragone; rivista mensile di arte figurativa e letteratura. m. ISSN 0031-1650
- Problemi di Ulisse. q. ISSN 0048-5411
- Rassegna della Letteratura Italiana. q. ISSN 0033-9423
- Rinascimento. a. ISSN 0080-3073
- Rivista di Letterature Moderne e Comparate. q.
- Studi Danteschi. a.
- Universite de Grenoble. Institut Francais de Florence. Publication. Serie 1: Collection d'Etudes d'Histoire. irreg., 1968, no. 31. ISSN 0072-7652 (Universite de Grenoble FR) (Co-sponsor: Institut Francais de Florence)
- Universite de Grenoble. Institut Francais de Florence. Publication. Serie 2: Collection d'Etudes Bibliographiques. irreg., 1969, no. 10. ISSN 0072-7660 (Universite de Grenoble FR) (Co-sponsor: Institut Francais de Florence)

**Santuari Francescani Valle di Rieti**
- Valle Santa di Rieti. (pub. by Convento S. Antonio al Monte)

**Santuario della Madonna del Perpetuo Soccorso**
37012 Bussolengo, Verona, Italy.
- Soccorso Perpetuo di Maria. m. ISSN 0037-7562

**Santuario di Nettuno**
00048 Nettuno (Rome), Italy.
- Santuario di N.S.D. Grazie e di S. Maria Goretti. m. ISSN 0036-4630

**Santuario Madonna di Barbana**
Isola di Barbana, 34073 Grado (Go), Italy.
- Madonna di Barbana; peridico mensile del santuario. m. ISSN 0024-9580

**Santuario S. Giuseppe da Copertino**
Via Piave 2, Copertino, Italy.
- Santo dei Voli. m. ISSN 0036-4606 (Provincia Religiosa dei Frati Minori Conventuali di Puglia)

**Editrice Sarda Fossataro Cagliari**
Via Col della Porretta 14, Rome, Italy.
- Frontiera; rivista mensile illustrata della Sardegna. m. ISSN 0016-2132

**Sartotecnica S.p.A.**
Via Y.B. Vico 18, Milan, Italy.
- Moda Maschile. bi-m. ISSN 0026-7260

**Scena Illustrata**
Via Cernaia 43, Rome, Italy.
- Scena Illustrata; politica, turismo, attualita, arte, cultura. m. ISSN 0036-5742

**Scherma**
Via I. Pettinengo 39, Rome, Italy.
- Scherma. m. ISSN 0036-6005

**B. Schott's Soehne**
Via del Babuino, 96, 1-00187 Rome, Italy
(Subscr. to: Banco di Sicilia, Agenzia 2, Piazza Barberini, Rome, Italy)
- World of Music. q. ISSN 0043-8774 (International Music Council. International Institute for Comparative Music Studies and Documentation)

**Luigi Scialpi Editore**
Via Ugo de Carolis 31, 00136 Rome, Italy.
- Giornale dei Distillatori; Alcoli-Acqueviti-Liquori. m. ISSN 0017-0119
- Succhi di Frutta e Bevande Gassate. q. ISSN 0039-4459
- Vini d'Italia; rivista tecnica di enologia. bi-m. ISSN 0042-630X

**Salvatore Sciascia**
Corso Umberto 1, Caltanissetta, Italy.
- Galleria. bi-m. ISSN 0016-4097

**Scientia**
Via Guastalla 9, 20122 Milan, Italy.
- Scientia; international review of scientific synthesis. 3 per yr. ISSN 0036-8687

**Editrice Scientifica (Milan)**
Via Ariberto 20, Milan, Italy.
- Antroposofia. m. ISSN 0003-6145

**Editoriale Scientifica (Naples)**
Via Carducci 37, 80121 Naples, Italy
(Subscr. to: Oceana Publications, Inc., Dobbs Ferry, N.Y. 10522)
- Italian Yearbook of International Law. a.

**Libreria Scientifica Editrice**
Corso Umberto I 38-40, Naples, Italy.
- Foro Penale. q. ISSN 0015-7864
- Logos; rivista si filosofia. 3 per yr. ISSN 0024-5887
- Rassegna di Diritto Pubblico. q. ISSN 0033-9512
- Rassegna di Scienze Filosofiche. q. ISSN 0033-9598

**Edizioni Scientifiche Inglesi Americane**
Via Sommacampagna 11-13, 00185 Rome, Italy.
- Rendiconti di Matematica. q. ISSN 0034-4427 (Istituto Mathematico G. Castlenuovo) (Co-Sponsor: Istituto di Alta Mathematica; Istituto Mathematica Applicata)
- Ricerche di Automatica. 3 per yr. ISSN 0048-8291 (Consiglio Nazionale delle Ricerche) (Co-Sponsor: Associazione Italiane per Il Calcolo Automatico)

**Edizioni Scientifiche Italiane S.p.A.**
Via Carducci 29, Naples, Italy.
- Dermatologia; rassegna di terapia delle malattie cutanee e veneree. bi-m. ISSN 0011-9032
- Nord e Sud. m. ISSN 0029-1188
- Quaderni Camerti di Studi Romanistici. Index/ International Survey of Roman Law. Index. a.
- Rivista Storica Italiana. q. ISSN 0035-7073
- Sovietica. q. ISSN 0038-5921
- Universita di Turino. Istituto di Storia. Collana. irreg. ISSN 0082-688X

**Edizioni Scientifiche Techniche Europee**
Via Sauli 3, 20127 Milan, Italy.
- E D P Notizie. fortn.
- Rivista di Statistica Applicata. q. ISSN 0035-6549
- Sistemi e Automazione. m. ISSN 0037-5896
- Sviluppo e Organizzazione. bi-m.

**Scienza dell'Alimentazione**
Via G. Uberti 24, Milan, Italy.
- Scienza dell'Alimentazione. bi-m. ISSN 0036-8865

**Scienza e Tecnica**
Via Cornelio Celso, 7, Rome, Italy.
- Scienza e Tecnica. bi-m.

**Scienze S.p.A.**
Via Victor Hugo 2, 20123 Milan, Italy.
- Scienze. m. ISSN 0036-8083

**Scuola Archeologica di Atene**
- Mongrafie della Scuola Archeologica di Atene e delle Missioni Italiane in Oriente. (pub. by Italy. Istituto Poligrafico dello Stato)

**Scuola Artigiana del Libro- Pubblico Passeggio**
c/o Vittorio Fermi, 29012 Caorso (Piacenza), Italy.
- Bollettino Storico Piacentino. 2 per yr. ISSN 0006-6591

**Scuola Beato Angelico**
19 Viale S. Gimignano, 20146 Milan, Italy.
- Amico dell'Arte Cristiana. q. ISSN 0003-1747
- Arte Cristiana; rivista mensile illustrata d'arte liturgica. m. ISSN 0004-3400

**Scuola di Guerra, Biblioteca**
Civitavecchia, Italy.
- Scuola di Guerra. Biblioteca. Italy. Bollettino. bi-m. ISSN 0036-9845

**Scuola Normale Superiore di Pisa**
Piazza dei Cavalieri 7, 56100-Pisa, Italy.
- Scuola Normale Superiore di Pisa. Annali. Classe di Scienze. q.
- Scuola Normale Superiore di Pisa. Annali. Lettere e Filosofia. q.

**Editrice la Scuola S.p.A.**
Via Cadorna N.11, 25100 Brescia, Italy.
- Pedagogia e Vita. bi-m. ISSN 0031-3777
- Scuola e Didattica. fortn. ISSN 0036-9861
- Scuola Italiana Moderna. fortn. ISSN 0036-9888
- Scuola Materna. fortn.

**Editrice Segesta S.p.A.**
Via Guerrazzi 1, Milan, Italy.
- Abitare. 10 per yr. ISSN 0001-3218

**Editrice Segisa**
A.E. Mottei 4, 20144 Rome, Italy.
- Mercurio. m.

**Segretariato Diocesano Malati**
Via Longhin, 7, Treviso 31100 (Veneto), Italy.
- Ti Saluto Fratello. m. ISSN 0040-6686

**Selepress S.p. A.**
Corso Plebisciti, 1, 20129 Milan, Italy.
- Gazzetta Motoristica. m(9 per yr)
- Gourmet Club; mensile della buona tavola e del bere bene. m. ISSN 0017-2561
- Staff. m.
- Tuttobar. q. ISSN 0041-4425

**Selezione Dal Reader's Digest S.p.A.**
Via Alserio 10, 20159 Milan, Italy.
- Selezione Dal Reader's Digest(Italian Edition) m. ISSN 0037-1483

**Seminario Arcivescovile di Milano**
Venegono Inferiore, Varese, Italy.
- Scuola Cattolica. bi-m. ISSN 0036-9810

**Seminario Francescano di Giaccherino**
51030 Pontelungo, Italy.
- Fiori di S. Antonio. s-m. ISSN 0015-2528

**SEPeM s.r.l.**
Piazza de Angeli 9, 20146 Milan, Italy.
- Beauty-Line. m.

**Umberto Serafini**
Piazza di Trevi 86, 00187 Rome, Italy.
- Comuni d'Europa. m. ISSN 0010-4973 (Associazione Italiana per Il Consiglio dei Comuni d'Europa)

**Bruno Sereni, Ed. & Pub.**
Casella Postale No. 33, Lucca 55051, Italy.
- Giornale di Barga; voce indipendente di unita ideale con i barghigiani all'estero. m. ISSN 0017-0259

**Services and Centres of Mental Hygiene**
- Minerva Medicopsicologica. (pub. by Edizioni Minerva Medica)

**Servizio di Sanita Aeronautica**
Via P. Gobetti 2, Rome, Italy.
- Rivista di Medicina Aeronautica e Spaziale. q. ISSN 0035-631X

**Servizio Italiana Pubblicazioni Internazionali s.r.l.**
Viale dell'Astronomia, 30, 00144-Rome, Italy.
- Collana di Studi e Documentazione. irreg.
- Confederazione Generale dell'Industria Italiana. Servizio Studi e Rilevazioni. la Spesa dell'Industria Privata per la Ricerca Scientifica. irreg.
- Gazzetta della Piccola Industria. m.
- Industria Mineraria; miniere e cave, metallurgia, geologia applicata, fonti di energia. bi-m. ISSN 0019-7696 (Associazione Mineraria Italiana)
- Massimario di Giurisprudenza del Lavoro. bi-m. ISSN 0025-4959
- Quale Impresa. m.

- Rassegna di Statistiche del Lavoro. bi-m. ISSN 0033-961X
- Rivista di Politica Economica. m. ISSN 0035-6468

**Settanta Anni di Calcio**
c/o Totoguida, Casella Postale 295, 00100 Rome, Italy.
- Settanta Anni di Calcio. 15 per yr. ISSN 0037-2897

**Editrice Sfera**
Via Aurelio Saffi 26, 20123 Milan, Italy.
- Gas Liquefatti - le Apparecchiature. bi-m. ISSN 0016-495X

**Shejzat**
Piazza della Balduina 59, 00136 Rome, Italy.
- Shejzat/Pleiadi. bi-m. ISSN 0037-3478

**Sicilia del Lunedi**
Avv. Domenico Sanfilippo, Via Pietra dell'Ova 51, Catania, Italy.
- Sicilia. w. ISSN 0037-4555

**Oscar Signorini, Ed. & Pub.**
Via S. Agnese 3, 20123 Milan, Italy.
- D'Ars; periodico d'arte contemporanea. 3 per yr. ISSN 0011-6726

**Simes S.p.A.**
Casella Postale 3888, 20100 Milan, Italy.
- Cardiologia nel Mondo; recensioni delle riviste di cardiologia di tutto il mondo. m. ISSN 0008-6320

**Simmenthal S.p.A.**
Via Borgazzi 87, Monza, Milan, Italy.
- Simmenthal Club; rassegna degli alimentaristi. q. ISSN 0037-542X

**Sindacato di Mogliano**
Piazza Caduti 1, 31021 Magliano Veneto, Treviso, Italy.
- Documenti di Vita Comunale. 3 per yr (approx) ISSN 0012-4737

**Sindacato Direttivi delle Ferrovie Dello Stato**
13 Via Nomentana, Rome, Italy.
- Organizzazione Ferroviaria. m. ISSN 0030-509X

**Sindacato Italiano Lavoratori Bonifica Irrigazione**
Via Corso d'Este 4, 44100 Ferrara, Italy.
- S I L B I Bollettino. m. ISSN 0036-1542

**Sindacato Italiano Postelgrafonico**
Largo Argentina, N. 11, 00186 Rome, Italy.
- Battaglie Postelegrafoniche. m. ISSN 0005-6340

**Sindacato Nazionale Autonomo della Scuola Elementare**
Via del Tritone 46, 00139 Rome, Italy.
- Scuola Nostra. m.

**Sindacato Nazionale Estetisi Diplomati**
Via Gustavo Modena 16, 20129 Milano, Italy.
- Linea Estetica. bi-m.

**Sindacato Nazionale Ingegneri Liberi Professionisti Italiani**
- Ingegnere Libero Professionista. (pub. by Propaganda Editoriale Grafica S. p. A.)

**Sindacato Nazionale Odontotecnici**
Via Sassetti 36, 20124 Milan, Italy.
- Odontoprotesti. m. ISSN 0029-8492
- Rassegna Odontotecnica. bi-m. ISSN 0048-6787

**Sindacato Nazionale Presidi e Professori di Ruolo**
Via Filippo Casini 6, 00153 Rome, Italy.
- Corriere della Scuola. fortn.

**Sindacato Nazionale Scuola Media**
Via Lucullo 6, 00187 Rome, Italy.
- Rinnovamento della Scuola. w.

**Sindacato Unitario Medici d'Italia**
- Medico Italiano. (pub. by Dott. Ottorimo Catani, Ed. & Pub.)

**Editrice Sindicale Italia s.r.l.**
Corso d'Italia 25, Rome, Italy.
- Rassegna Sindacale. w. ISSN 0033-9849

**Sipario Editrice S.R.L.**
Via Flaminia 167, 00196 Rome, Italy.
- Sipario. m.

**Sisters Disciples of the Divine Master**
739 via Portuense, 00148 Rome, Italy.
- Vita in Cristo e Nella Chiesa; rivista liturgica per i fedeli. m. ISSN 0042-7284

**Skema s.r.l.**
Via Marzabotto 10/3, 40133 Bologna, Italy.
- Skema. m.

**Sloveni in Italia**
Via dei Montecchi, 6, Trieste 34137, Italy.
- Sloveni in Italia. s-m.

**Snia Viscosa**
- Linea Snia. (pub. by P.A.N. Editrice)

**Societa Accademica Romana**
Foro Traiano 1a, 00187 Rome, Italy.
- Acta Historica. irreg. ISSN 0065-1303
- Acta Philologica. irreg. ISSN 0065-1516
- Acta Philosophica et Theologica. irreg. ISSN 0065-1540
- Acta Scientiarum Socialium. irreg. ISSN 0065-1656
- Collana di Studi e Saggi. irreg. ISSN 0069-5203
- Revista Scriitorilor Romani. a. ISSN 0080-2441

**Societa Archeologica Comense**
Piazza Medaglie d'Oro 1, 22100 Como, Italy.
- Rivista Archeologica dell'Antica Provincia e Diocesi di Como; periodico di antichita ed arte. a. ISSN 0080-3235

**Societa Astronomica Italiana**
Ed. Dir. Prof. Guglielmo Righini, Via Brera 28, Milan, Italy.
- Societa Astronomica Italiana. Memorie. q. ISSN 0037-8720

**Societa Botanica Italiana**
Via Lamarmora N. 4, 50121 Florence, Italy.
- Giornale Botanico Italiano. bi-m. ISSN 0017-0070
- Informatore Botanico Italiano. w. ISSN 0020-0697

**Societa Chimica Italiana**
Viale Liegi, 48, Rome, Italy.
- Annali di Chimica. m. ISSN 0003-4592
- Chimica e l'Industria; giornale di chimica industriale ed applicata. m. ISSN 0009-4315
- Gazzetta Chimica Italiana. m. ISSN 0016-5603

**Societa Culturale Opere Tipografiche**
Via M. Vittoria 1, Turin 10123, Italy.
- Collezionista-Italia Filatelica. fortn. ISSN 0010-1265

**Societa degli Ingegneri e degli Architetti in Torino**
Via Giolitti 1, 10123 Turin, Italy.
- Societa delgi Ingegneri e degli Architetti in Torino. Atti e Rassegna Tecnica. m. ISSN 0004-7287
- Studentravel Magazine; the trade publication in the student travel industry. m.(8 per yr.) ISSN 0039-2855

**Societa di Cultura per Il Friuli Occidentale**
Via Montello 99, 33170 Pordenone, Italy.
- Noncello; rivista d'arte e di cultura. s-a. ISSN 0029-1080

**Societa di Cultura per la Lucania**
- Aspetti Letterari. (pub. by Libreria Maiolo)

**Societa di Etnografia Italiana**
- Lares. (pub. by Casa Editrice Leo S. Olschki)

**Societa di Medicina e Scienze Naturali di Parma**
Via Gramsci 14, 43100 Parma, Italy.
- Ateneo Parmense. Sezione 1: Acta Bio-Medica. bi-m. ISSN 0004-6531
- Ateneo Parmense. Sezione 2: Acta Naturalia. q. ISSN 0004-654X

**Societa di Ricerche in Chirurgia**
- Policlinico. Sezione Chirurgica. (pub. by Edizioni Luigi Pozzi)

**Societa di San Vincenzo de Paoli. Consiglio Superiore Italiano**
Piazza Duomo 16, 20122 Milan, Italy.
- Samaritano. m. ISSN 0036-3723

**Societa di Storia Patria per la Sicilia Orientale**
Piazza Stesicoro 29, 95124 Catania, Italy.
- Archivio Storico per la Sicilia Orientale. q. ISSN 0004-0363

**Societa di Studi Geografici di Firenze**
- Rivista Geografica Italiana. (pub. by Nuova Italia Editrice)

**Societa di Studi Romagnoli**
- Societa di Studi Romagnoli. Guide. (pub. by Biblioteca Malatestiana)
- Studi Romagnoli. (pub. by Biblioteca Malatestiana)
- Studi Romagnoli. Estratti di Sezione. (pub. by Biblioteca Malatestiana)
- Studi Romagnoli. Quaderni. (pub. by Biblioteca Malatestiana)

**Societa di Studi Valdesi**
Conto Corrente Postale 2/4428, 10066 Torre Pellice, Italy.
- Societa di Studi Valdesi. Bollettino. biennial. ISSN 0037-8739

**Societa Elettronica Lombarda**
Via G. di Vittorio 307-28, 20099 Sesto San Giovanni, Milan, Italy.
- Corriere Nucleare. bi-m. ISSN 0010-9150

**Societa Entomologica Italiana**
Via Brigata Liguria 9, 16121 Genoa, Italy.
- Societa Entomologica Italiana. Bollettino e Memorie. 10 per yr. ISSN 0037-8747

**Societa Farmaceutici Italia**
Viale Bezzi 24, 20146 Milan, Italy.
- Rivista di Zootecnia e Veterinaria; rassegna di informazione e.aggiornamento. bi-m.

**Societa Filologica Friulana**
Via Manin 18, Udine, Italy.
- Sot la Nape; filologje, literature, folclor. q. ISSN 0038-1659

**Societa Filosofica Calabrese**
Via R. Pereira, No. 8, Rome, Italy.
- Ricerche Filosofiche. s-a. ISSN 0035-5062

**Societa Generale di Telefonia ed Elettronica**
Via Davanzati 14, Milan, Italy.
- Ronzatore. q. ISSN 0035-8185

**Societa Geografica Italiana**
Via della Navicella 12, Rome, Italy.
- Societa Geografica Italiana. Bollettino. m. ISSN 0037-8755

**Societa Industrie Riunite Editorial: Siciliane**
Via Archirafi 34, 90123-Palermo, Italy.
- Circolo Matematico di Palermo. Rendiconti. q. ISSN 0009-725X

**Societa Internazionale di Psicologia della Scrittura and Centro Internazionale di Ipnosi Medica e Psicologica**
- Rivista Internazionale di Psicologia e Ipnosi. (pub. by Istituto di Indagini Psicologiche)

**Societa Italiana Amici dei Fiori**
- Giardino Fiorito. (pub. by Gruppo Giornalistico Edagricole)

**Societa Italiana Autori Drammatici**
Via Monte della Farina 42, 00186 Rome, Italy.
- Ridotto; rassegna mensile di teatro. m. ISSN 0035-5186

**Societa Italiana de Biochimica Clinica**
- Giornale Italiano di Chimica Clinica. (pub. by Piccin Editore)

**Societa Italiana degli Autori Ed Editori**
Viale della Letteratura 30, Rome, Italy.
- Spettacolo; rassegna economica e sociale degli spettacoli e delle attivita artistiche e culturali. q. ISSN 0038-738X

**Societa Italiana di Agopuntura**
Ospedale Maria Adelaide, Corso Firenze 87, 10152 Turin, Italy.
- Rivista Italiana di Agopuntura. 3 per yr.

**Societa Italiana di Agronomia**
- Rivista di Agronomia. (pub. by Gruppo Giornalistico Edagricole)

**Societa Italiana di Biologia Sperimentale**
- Archivio di Scienze Biologiche. (pub. by Casa Editrice Licinio Cappelli)

**Societa Italiana di Cardiologia**
Corso Francia 197, 00191 Rome, Italy.
- Societa Italiana di Cardiologia. Bollettino. m. ISSN 0037-878X

**Societa Italiana di Chemioterapia**
- Giornale Italiano di Chemioterapia. (pub. by Edizioni Minerva Medica)

**Societa Italiana di Economia Demografia e Statistica**
Via Boncompagni, 16, 00187 Rome, Italy.
- Rivista Italiana di Economia Demografia E Statistica. 4 per yr. ISSN 0035-6832

**Societa Italiana di Filosofia Giuridica e Politica**
- Rivista Internazionale di Filosofia del Diritto. (pub. by Casa Editrice Dott. A. Giuffre)

**Societa Italiana di Fisica**
- Giornale di Fisica. (pub. by Editrice Compositori s.r.l.)
- International School of Physics "Enrico Fermi." Proceedings. (pub. by Academic Press, Inc. US)
- Lettere al Nuovo Cimento. (pub. by Editrice Compositori s.r.l.)
- Rivista del Nuovo Cimento. (pub. by Editrice Compositori s.r.l.)
- Societa Italiana di Fisica. Bollettino. (pub. by Editrice Compositori s.r.l.)
- Societa Italiana di Fisica. Nuovo Cimento A. (pub. by Editrice Compositori s.r.l.)
- Societa Italiana di Fisica. Nuovo Cimento B. (pub. by Editrice Compositori s.r.l.)

**Societa Italiana di Fisiologia**
Viale Margagni 65, Florence, Italy.
- Archivio di Fisiologia. q. ISSN 0004-0096

**Societa Italiana di Fotogrammetria e Topografia**
Piazzale R. Morandi 2, 20121 Milan, Italy.
- Societa Italiana di Fotogrammetria e Topografia. Bollettino. q. ISSN 0037-881X

**Societa Italiana di Geofisica e Meteorologia**
26 via Medici, 10143 Turin, Italy.
- Rivista Italiana di Geofisica e Scienze Affini. bi-m.

**Societa Italiana di Gerontologia e Geriatria**
Via Malcontenti 12, Florence, Italy.
- Giornale di Gerontologia. m. ISSN 0017-0305

**Societa Italiana di Medicina del Traffico**
- Rassegna di Medicina del Traffico. (pub. by Centro Editoriale Pubblicitario Italiano)

**Societa Italiana di Medicina e Igiene della Scuola**
Corso Vercelli 2, Italy.
- Rivista Italiana di Medicina e Igiene della Scuola. q. ISSN 0035-6859

**Societa Italiana di Mineralogia e Petrologia**
Museo Storia Naturale, Corso Venezia 55, Milan 20121, Italy.
- Societa Italiana di Mineralogia e Petrologia. Rendiconti. s-a. ISSN 0037-8828

**Societa Italiana di Musicologia**
- Rivista Italiana di Musicologia. (pub. by Casa Editrice Leo S. Olschki)

**Societa Italiana di Neuropsichiatria Infantile**
- Neuropsichiatria Infantile. (pub. by Bulzoni Editore)

**Societa Italiana di Parapsicologia**
Via dei Montecatini 7, 00186 Rome, Italy.
- Rassegna Italiana di Ricerca Psichica. q. ISSN 0033-9733

**Societa Italiana di Parassitologia**
- Parassitologia. (pub. by Leonardo Edizioni Scientifiche)

**Societa Italiana di Psicologia**
- Rivista di Psicologia. (pub. by Giunti-Barbera, Eds. & Pub.)

**Societa Italiana di Scienza dell' Alimentazione**
- Societa Italiana di Scienza dell' Alimentazione. Rivista. (pub. by O. P. B. International S.p.A.)

**Societa Italiana di Scienze Farmaceutiche**
Via Giorgio Jan 18, 20129 Milan, Italy.
- Cronache Farmaceutiche. bi-m. ISSN 0011-1783
- S.I.S.F. Documenti. irreg. ISSN 0081-0703

**Societa Italiana di Scienze Naturali**
Corso Venezia, 55, 20121 Milan, Italy.
- Natura; rivista di scienze naturali. q. (Co-Sponsor: Museo Civico di Storia Naturale di Milano)
- Societa Italiana di Scienze Naturali e del Museo Civico di Storia Naturale. Atti. q. ISSN 0037-8844 (Co-sponsor: Museo Civico di Storia Naturale)

**Societa Italiana di Storia della Medicina**
- Rivista di Storia della Medicina. (pub. by Societa Editrice Universo)

**Societa Italiana per gli Studi Sulla Sterilita**
- Monitore Ostetrico-Ginecologico di Endocrinologia e del Metabolismo. (pub. by Clinica Ostetrica e Ginecologica)

**Societa Italiana per Il Progresso delle Industrie Agrarie Alimentari**
- Industrie Agrarie. (pub. by Editrice Maro)

**Societa Italiana per l'Organizzazione Internazionale**
- Comunita Internazionale. (pub. by Casa Editrice Dott. Antonio Milani)

**Societa Italiana per la Ceramica**
- Ceramica Informazione. (pub. by Faenza Editrice S.p.A.)

**Societa Italiana per la Ricerca dei Papiri Greci e Latini**
- Papiri Greci e Latini. (pub. by Casa Editrice Felice le Monnier)

**Societa Italiana per la Studio del Metabolismo Normale e Patologico**
- Metabolismo. (pub. by Centro Editoriale Pubblicitario Italiano)

**Societa Italiana per le Studio del Reumatismo e per la Lotta Contro le Malattie Reumatiche**
- Reumatismo. (pub. by Longonesi e Co.)

**Societa Italiana per Lo Studio delle Malattie Infettive e Parassitarie**
Via Appiani 5, 20121 Milan, Italy.
- Giornale di Malattie Infettive e Parassitarie. m. ISSN 0017-0321

**Societa Italiana Progresso Industrie Agrarie Alimentari**
- S & T A-Scienza e Tecnologia degli Alimenti. (pub. by Gruppo Giornalistico Edagricole)

**Societa Italiana Scienze Farmaceutiche**
- Farmaco. (pub. by Editoriale Il Farmaco)

**Societa Jonico-Salentina di Medicina e Chirurgia**
- Societa Jonico-Salentina di Medicina e Chirurgia. Bollettino. (pub. by Editrice Salentina - Galatina)

**Societa l'Arte Tipografica**
Via S. Biagio dei Librai 39, Naples, Italy.
- Napoli Nobilissima; rivista di arti figurative, archeologia e urbanistica. bi-m. ISSN 0027-7835

**Societa Ligura di Storia Patria**
Viale Villa Gloria 1-12, Genoa, Italy.
- Bollettino Ligustico per la Storia e la Cultura Regionale. q.

**Societa Ligure di Chirurgia**
Ospedali Civili, Genoa, Italy.
- Rassegna Ed Archivio di Chirurgia. 3 per mo. ISSN 0033-9652

**Societa Lombarda di Chirurgia**
- Archivio Italiano di Chirurgia. (pub. by Casa Editrice Licinio Cappelli)

**Societa Lombarda di Criminologia**
- Criminologia. (pub. by Istituto Editoriale Cisalpino)

**Societa Medica Chirurgica di Bologna-Archiginnasio**
Piazza Halvani 1, 40100 Bologna, Italy.
- Bullettino delle Scienze Mediche. 4 per yr. ISSN 0007-5787

**Societa Medica del Friuli**
- Friuli Medico. (pub. by Tipografia A. Pelligrini (Udine))

**Societa Medico Chirurgica, Cremona**
Via Alle Tramvie N. 5, Cremona, Italy.
- Societa Medico Chirurgica, Cremona. Bollettino. q. ISSN 0037-8852

**Societa Nazionale Cogne**
Via San Quintino 28, Turin, Italy.
- Giornale della Cogne. m. ISSN 0017-0208

**Societa per la Cremazione**
Via Saluzzo 22, 10125 Turin, Italy.
- Ara. q. ISSN 0003-7370

**Societa Pistoiese di Storia Patria**
- Bullettino Storico Pistoiese. (pub. by Biblioteca Forteguerriana)

**Societa Psicoanalitica Italiana**
- Rivista di Psicoanalisi. (pub. by Pensiero Scientifico)

**Societa Renardet Sauti Consulting Engineers**
Via Mascagni 160, Rome, Italy.
- Ingegneria Civile. q. ISSN 0020-0948

**Societa Sarten**
Via Macchi 42, 20124 Milan, Italy.
- Tennis Italiano. m.

**Societa Siracusana di Storia Patria**
Via G. M. Capodieci 16, c/o Museo Nazionale di Palazzo Bellomo, 96100 Siracusa, Italy.
- Archivio Storico Siracusano. a. ISSN 0044-8737

**Societa Storica della Valdelsa**
Via Tilli 27, 50051 - Castelfiorentino (Firenze), Italy.
- Miscellanea Storica della Valdelsa. q. ISSN 0026-5888

**Societa Storica di Terra d'Otranto**
Palazzo Adorni, Via Umberto 132, 73100 Lecce, Italy.
- Rivista Storica del Mezzogiorno. q. ISSN 0035-7065

**Societa Storica Valtellinese**
c/o Renzo Sertoli Salis, Via Gorizia 29, Sondrio, Italy.
- Societa Storica Valtellinese. Bollettino. a. ISSN 0085-6231

**Societa Toscana per la Storia del Risorgimento**
- Rassegna Storica Toscana. (pub. by Casa Editrice Leo S. Olschki)

**Societa Trentina di Scienze Umane**
Casella Postale 269, Trento, Italy.
- Verifiche. q.

**Societa Umanitaria**
Via F. Davario 7, Milan, Italy.
- Cultura Popolare. bi-m. ISSN 0011-2801 (Unione Italiana della Cultura Popolare)

**Societe Europeenne de Culture**
Piazza S. Marco 52, Venice, Italy.
- Comprendre; revue de politique de la culture. s-a. ISSN 0010-4418

**Libreria Editoriale Sodalitas**
28049 Stresa (Novara), Italy.
- Rivista Rosminiana di Filosofia e di Cultura. q. ISSN 0035-7030 (Centro Internazionale di Studi Rosminiani)

**Sodalizio Internazionale di Spiritualita Alpina. Ordine del Cardo**
Eremo San Salvatore, Casorezzo, 20010 Milan, Italy.
- Spiritualita; rassegna di cultura varia. q. ISSN 0038-7649

**Franco Soin Editore**
Lungarno Acciaioli 4, 50123 Florence, Italy.
- E'moda. q.

**Societa Editrice Sole s.r.l.**
Piazza Sallustio 3, 00187 Rome, Italy.
- Fiera Letteraria; settimanale d'informazione culturale. w.

**Soprintendenza Alle Gallerie**
Via Belle Arti 56, Bologna, Italy.
- Soprintendenza Alle Gallerie di Bologna. Rapporti. irreg.

**Sorpasso -CB**
Via Zara 8, 16145 Genoa, Italy.
- Sorpasso -CB. m.

**Ettore Sottsass, Ed. & Pub.**
14 via Manzoni, Milan 20121, Italy.
- Pianeta Fresco. a. ISSN 0079-2055

**Aldo Spallicci, Ed. & Pub.**
Via Flavio Biondo 17, Forli, Italy.
- Pie/Piada; rassegna d'illustrazione Romangnola. bi-m. ISSN 0031-9708

**Saverio Spaziani, Ed. & Pub.**
Viale Sabotino 21-A, Milan, Italy.
- Associazione Italiana Veterinari per Piccoli Animali.Bollettino. q. ISSN 0004-5977

**Edizioni Specializzate**
Via Cavalcanti 8, 20127 Milan, Italy.
- Promozione. bi-m.

**Speleologia Emiliana**
Cassero di Porta Lame, Piazza VII Novembre 1944, 40122 Bologna, Italy.
- Speleologia Emiliana. bi-m. ISSN 0038-7290 (Unione Speleologica Bolognese)

**Spettatore Musicale**
Via Nizza 45, 00198 Rome, Italy.
- Spettatore Musicale. bi-m. ISSN 0038-7401

**Sport Italia**
Largo Toscanini 1, Milano, Italy.
- Sport Italia. w. ISSN 0038-7916

**Societa Editrice Sportiva**
Via Villar 2, 10147 Torino, Italy.
- Tuttosport. d. ISSN 0041-4441

**Federico Stame, Ed. & Pub.**
Via Dante 28, 401925 Bologna, Italy.
- Classe e Stato. s-a. ISSN 0009-8299

**Stammer S.p.A.**
Centro Commerciale Milano San Felice, 20090 Segrate-Milan, Italy.
- Albergo Moderno. m.
- Commercio Elettrico. m.
- Giornale degli Apparecchi Domestici. q.
- Gommone. q.
- Tecnologie Elettriche; industria italiana elettrotecnica ed elettronica. m.
- Tecnologie Meccaniche. m.

**Societa Editrice Stampa Europea**
Via del Parlamento 9, Rome, Italy.
- Rivista di Diritto Europeo. q. ISSN 0035-6123

**Stampa Medica**
Via Postumia 6, 00198 Rome, Italy.
- Stampa Medica. m. ISSN 0038-9323

**Editrice la Stampa S.p.A.**
Via Marenco 32, 10100 Turin, Italy.
- Tuttolibri. w.

**Stamperia Editrice Commerciale**
Via G.B. Morono N. 206, 24100 Bergamo, Italy (Subscr. to: Angelicum, Piazza S. Angelo, 2-Milan, Italy)
- In Famiglia; rassegna mensile delle attivita spirituali, culturali e artistiche dell'angelicum-chiesa di s.angelo. m. ISSN 0019-3186 (Angelicum-Convento di S.Angelo)

**Stato Maggiore della Marina**
Via Romeo Romei 5, 00136 Rome, Italy.
- Rivista Marittima. m. ISSN 0035-6964

**Stato Maggiore Esercito**
Via di San Marco 8, Rome, Italy.
- Rivista Militare. m. ISSN 0035-6980

**Stazione Sperimentale del Vetro**
Via Briati 10, 30121 Murano (Venice), Italy.
- Stazione Sperimentale del Vetro. Rivista. bi-m.

**Stazione Sperimentale Oli e Grassi**
Via Giuseppe Colombo 79, Milan 20133, Italy.
- Rivista Italiana delle Sostanze Grasse. m. ISSN 0035-6808

**Stazione Sperimentale per i Combustibili**
Viale A. de Gasperi 3, 20097 S. Donato Milanese (Milan), Italy.
- Rivista dei Combustibili. m. ISSN 0035-5852

**Stazione Sperimentale per l'Industria delle Conserve Alimentari**
Viale F. Tanara 33, 43100 Parma, Italy.
- Industria Conserve. q. ISSN 0019-7483

**Stazione Sperimentale per l'Industria delle Essenze e dei Derivati Agrumari**
Corso Vittorio Emanuele 131, Reggio Calabria-89100, Italy.
- Essenze-Derivati Agrumari. q. ISSN 0014-0902

**Stazione Sperimentale per l'Industria delle Pelli e delle Materie Concianti**
Via Poggioreale 39, 80143 Naples, Italy.
- Cuoio Pelli Materie Concianti. bi-m. ISSN 0011-3034

**Stazione Zoologica di Napoli**
Villa Comunale, 80121 Naples, Italy.
- Stazione Zoologica di Napoli. Pubblicazioni. 2-3 per yr. ISSN 0039-081X

**Edizioni di Storia e Letteratura**
Via Lancellotti 18, Rome, Italy.
- Archivio Italiano per la Storia della Pieta. irreg., 1970, no. 6. ISSN 0066-6688
- English Miscellany; a symposium of history, literature and the arts. a. ISSN 0425-0575
- Ricerche di Storia Sociale e Religiosa. s-a. (Centro Studi per le Fonti della Storia della Chiesa nel Veneto) (Co-Sponsor: Centro Studi di Storia Sociale e Religiosa nel Mezzogiorno)
- Studi Americani. a. ISSN 0085-6819

**Storia e Nobilta**
Via Paola Falconieri 47, 00152 Rome, Italy.
- Storia e Nobilta; Rassegna di studi e ricerche storiche. m. ISSN 0039-1891

**Strada**
Via Antonio Bianchi 36, Casella Postale 118, Brescia, Italy.
- Strada; mensile de lettere, scienze, arti. m. ISSN 0049-2302

**Editrice le Strade**
Via Manin 37, 20121 Milan, Italy.
- Strade. bi-m. (Touring Club Italiano)

**Studi e Problemi di Critica Testuale**
Via Castiglione 8, 40124 Bologna, Italy.
- Studi e Problemi di Critica Testuale. s-a. ISSN 0049-2361

**Casa Editrice Studi Meridionali**
Via Emanuele Filiberto 106, 00185 Rome, Italy.
- Studi Meridionali. q.

**Studi Urbinati. Serie A: Diritto**
Via Pozzo Nuovo 16, 61029 Urbino (Pesaro), Italy.
- Studi Urbinati. Serie A: Diritto. s-a. ISSN 0039-307X

**Studio di Psicologia del Lavoro**
Via Andrea Doria 20, Milan, Italy.
- Psicologia e Lavoro. bi-m. ISSN 0048-5691

**Studio di Restauro Strini**
c/o Alessandro Strini, Rome, Italy.
- Studio di Restauro Strini. Bollettino. m. ISSN 0006-6699

**Studio Domenicano**
Piazza S. Domenico 13, 40124 Bologna, Italy.
- Sacra Doctrina; revista trimestrale di scienze religiose. q. ISSN 0036-2190

**Studio Edizioni**
Via F. Denti 2, 20133 Milan, Italy.
- Prodotti di Marca. bi-m. ISSN 0032-9665

**Studio Manca**
Via Nervesa 2, 20139 Milan, Italy.
- Orafo Italiano. m. ISSN 0471-7376 (Unione Italiana delle Federazioni Nazionali di Categoria Orafi, Argentieri, Orologiai, Metalli, Preziosi, Pietre Preziose)
- Orafo Italiano nel Mundo/Italian Goldsmith in the World. bi-m. ISSN 0473-1174

**Studio Strini**
Piazza della Liberta, 10 Rome, Italy.
- Tecnica dell'Arte; collana di monografie di studi tecnico-pittorici metodi conservativi e perizie techniche e artistiche di dipinti, stampe, documenti, carte valori. q. ISSN 0040-1765

**Studium Christi**
- Fuoco. (pub. by Edizioni Il Fuoco)

**Style Auto Editrice**
Corso Adriatico 26, 10129 Turin, Italy.
- Style Auto; architettura della carrozzeria. q. ISSN 0039-4254

**Vittorio Subilia, Ed. & Pub.**
Facolta Valdese di Teologia, Via Pietro Cossa 42, 00193 Rome, Italy.
- Protestantesimo. q. ISSN 0033-1767

**Suedtiroler Haupt Verband GmbH**
Bolzano, Italy.
- Landwirt; Fachblatt der Suedtiroler Bauern und Genossenschaften. s-m. ISSN 0023-8112

**Sumarie**
Piazza S. Domenico 11, Acireale, Italy.
- Sumarie; rassegna di letteratura-arte-folklore e attualita. m.

**Edizioni Suono**
Via del Casaletto 380, 00151 Rome, Italy.
- Stereoguida. 6 per yr.
- Stereoplay. m.
- Suono Stereo Hi-Fi. m.

**Suore Sacra Famiglia**
Via Filitteria 25, Spoleto, Italy.
- Nazareth. bi-m. ISSN 0028-1700

**Svenska Institutet i Rom**
Via Omero 14, 00197 Rome, Italy
(Dist. by: Paul Aastroems Foerlag, Soedra Vaegen 61, S-412 54 Gothenburg, Sweden)
- Svenska Institutet i Rom. Skrifter. Acta Series Prima. irreg., no. 35, 1976. ISSN 0081-993X

**Tabor**
Via Conciliazione 15, Rome, Italy.
- Tabor; rivista di vita spirituale per laici. bi-m. ISSN 0039-8861

**Tamburini Editore S.p.A.**
Via Pascole 55, 20133 Milan, Italy.
- Aerotecnica, Missili e Spazio. bi-m. (Associazione Italiana di Aeronautica e Astronautica)

**Tartarino**
Via Generale Berardi 1, 83100 Avellino, Italy.
- Tartarino; serio-semiserio-umoristico-pupazzettato. fortn. ISSN 0039-9728

**Tattilo Editrice S.p.A.**
Via del Casale Piombino N. 30, 00135 Rome, Italy.
- Playmen; mensile di cultura, attualita, politica e costume. m. ISSN 0032-1532

**Casa Editrice Taylor**
Corso Stati Uniti, 53, 10129 Torino, Italy.
- Collezione di Filosofia. irreg. ISSN 0069-5777
- Quaderni di Sociologia. q. ISSN 0033-4952

**Edizioni Techniche Moderne**
Via Fabio Filzi 22, 20124 Milan, Italy.
- Vado e Torno; magazine for lorry-drivers. bi-m. ISSN 0042-2096

**Edizioni Techniche S.A.S.**
Via Podgora 15, 20122 Milan, Italy.
- Industria Italiana Elettrotecnica Ed Elettronica. m. ISSN 0019-7645 (Associazione Nazionale Industrie Elettrotecniche ed Elettroniche)

**Tecnica della Scuola**
Corso delle Province 34/A, 95127 Catania, Italy.
- Tecnica della Scuola. 21 per yr.

**Tecnica e Uomo**
Via Conciliazione 3, 00193 Rome, Italy.
- Tecnica e Uomo. w. ISSN 0040-1811

**Editoriale Tecnica Macchine**
Via Uberti 13, 20129 Milan, Italy.
- Fonderia. m. ISSN 0015-6078
- Giornale dell'Officina. m. ISSN 0017-0240
- Macchine; rassegna tecnica dell'industria meccanica. m. ISSN 0024-8959
- Tranciatura Stampaggio; rivista tecnica delle lavorazioni meccaniche per deformazione. m. ISSN 0041-1027
- Trattamenti e Finitura. m. ISSN 0041-1833

**Societa Edizioni Tecniche**
Via Vincenzo Monti 25, Milan, Italy.
- Boutique. q.

**Societa Edizioni Tecniche Arredamento**
Corso Magenta 96, 20123 Milan, Italy.
- Industria del Legnoe Mobile. m. ISSN 0019-7521

**Edizioni Tecniche Publiedi**
Via San Siro 27, 20149 Milan, Italy.
- Arredo Tessile. 3 per yr.
- Selezione Tessile; periodico mensile di filatura, tessitura, tintoria, finissaggio, maglieria e calzetteria. m. ISSN 0037-1513

**Tecniche Nuove s.r.l.**
Via Moscova 46-9, 20121 Milan, Italy.
- Alam al Mugiauharat. 3 per yr.
- Controlli Numerici Macchine a C N Robot Industriali. bi-m.
- Lamiera. 11 per yr.
- Latte. m (11 per yr) ISSN 0023-8880
- Magazzini & Trasporti; rivista tecnica mensile. m. ISSN 0024-9874
- Mahsulate Italia. w.
- Oleodinamica-Pneumatica-Lubrificazione; rivista tecnica mensile di applicazioni fluidodinamiche. m.
- Organi di Trasmissione; rivista tecnica mensile. m. ISSN 0030-4905
- R.C.I. (Riscaldamento Condizionamento Idrosanitaria) m(with annual supplement)
- Sinaat Italiyah. q.
- Tecnica Ospedaliera. m. (Centro Nazionale per l'Edilizie e la Tecnica Ospedaliera)

**Edizioni Tecniche SIGMA 2**
Via Pietro da Cemmo, 20155 Milan, Italy.
- Evoluzione Agricola; mensile di attualita e tecnica zoo-agricola. m. ISSN 0014-3863

**Telespazio**
Via della Bufalotta 174, C.A.P., 00139 Rome, Italy.
- Telespazio. m. ISSN 0040-2737

**Societa Editrice Temi**
Piazza della Liberta 13, Rome, Italy.
- Rivista Penale. m. ISSN 0035-7022

**Adelberto Tempesta, Ed. & Pub**
Piazza della Liberta 4, Rome 00192, Italy.
- Diritto Aereo; rivista di dottrina, giurisprudenza e legislazione aeronautica. q. ISSN 0012-3390

**Redazione Tempi Moderni**
Via Nomentana 107, 00187 Rome, Italy.
- Tempi Moderni; dell'economia, della politica, della cultura. q. ISSN 0040-294X

**Tempo Medico s.r.l.**
Via Lanino 5, 20144 Milan, Italy.
- Tempo Medico. m. ISSN 0492-6749

**Termomeccanica Italiana S.p.A.**
Via del Molo, I19100 la Spezia, Italy.
- Bollettino Termomeccanica. m. ISSN 0006-6885

**Dott. G. Terzano & Co. S.p.A.**
Via Darwin 19-21, Milan, Italy.
- Attualita di Laboratorio. irreg. ISSN 0004-7309

**Terz'ordine e le Vocazioni Cappuccine Salernitane**
- Serafico Vessillo. (pub. by Fratelli Jovane)

**A. Testa, Ed. & Pub.**
Via S. Isaia 67, Bologna, Italy.
- Dialogo; quaderni europei di dialogica. ISSN 0012-2084 (Centro Studi Dialogic dell' Istituto Euromediterraneo di Scienze Umane della Citta-Studio di Urbino)

**Testimonianze**
Via Gino Capponi 36, 50121 Florence, Italy.
- Testimonianze. m. ISSN 0040-3989

**Theological Faculty of Saint Teresa and Saint John of the Cross**
- Ephemerides Carmeliticae. (pub. by Edizioni dei Padri Carmelitani Scalzi)

**Tipografia Gatti-Parma**
Casella Postale 94, 43100 Parma, Italy.
- Lottoroscopo. m. ISSN 0024-6662

**Toga Calabrese**
Corso Mazzini 291, 88100 Catanzaro, Italy.
- Toga Calabrese; periodico giuridico forense. m. ISSN 0040-8654

**Unione Tipografico Editrice Torinese**
Corso Raffaello 28, 10125 Turin, Italy.
- Giurisprudenza Italiana. m. ISSN 0017-0623
- Lex; Legislazione Italiana. q. ISSN 0024-1598
- Massimario della Giurisprudenza Italiana. m. ISSN 0025-4940

**Torino Motori**
Corso Galileo Ferraris 155, 10134 Turin, Italy.
- Torino Motori. bi-m. ISSN 0493-5306

**Torre**
Via Colombo 24, 92024 Canicatti, Italy.
- Torre. fortn.

**Michele Tosco**
Viale Shakespeare 57, 00144 Rome, Italy.
- Tribuna Postale e delle Telecomunicazioni. bi-m.

**Casa Editrice la Toscografica**
Via Pontorme 20, Empoli, Italy.
- Empoli; rassegna di vita cittadina e bollettino di statistica. s-a. ISSN 0013-6891

**Touring Club Italiano**
Corso Italia 10, 20122 Milan, Italy.
- Europa Facile. irreg.
- Qui Touring. m. ISSN 0042-546X
- Strade. (pub. by Editrice le Strade)

**Cino Traina Ed. & Pub.**
Via Antonio Meucci 9, Palermo, Italy.
- Eloquenza Siciliana; rassegna letteraria, culturale, giuridica. bi-m. ISSN 0013-6360

**Trapani Nuova**
Viale Regina Margherita 21, 91100 Tranpani, Sicily, Italy.
- Trapani Nuova. w. ISSN 0041-1779

**Trasumenus**
Corso Vannucci 66, 06062 Citta della Pieve (Perugia), Italy.
- Trasumenus. m.

**Trattamenti dei Metalli**
26010 Bagnolo Cremasco, Italy.
- Trattamenti dei Metalli; rivista tecnica bimestrale. q. ISSN 0041-1825

**Giorgio Trentin, Ed. & Pub.**
Via Monte Cervialto 102, 00139 Rome, Italy.
- Cinema Societa. irreg. ISSN 0009-7152

**Trevi Editore**
Via Germanico 109, 00192 Rome, Italy.
- Vantaggio; nelle lettere e nelle arti. 4 per yr. ISSN 0042-2614

**Tri I - Informatore Immobiliare Italiano**
Via Montenapoleone 21, 20121 Milan, Italy.
- Tri I - Informatore Immobiliare Italiano. bi-m.

**Tribuna Politica**
Via IV Novembre 24, 80052 Bellavista (Naples), Italy.
- Tribuna Politica; e cultura. m. ISSN 0041-2783

**Tributi Sugli Affari**
Via Tripoli 52, Rome, Italy.
- Tributi Sugli Affari; rivista mensile di dottrina, giurisprudenza e legislazione. m. ISSN 0041-2899

**Societa Editrice Trieste**
Via delle Zudecche 1-C, 34131 Trieste, Italy.
- Trieste; political review. q. ISSN 0041-2961

**Tringale Editore**
Corso Italia 23, 95129 Catania, Italy.
- Leragoni Critiche. q. ISSN 0047-4401

**Editrice Trotto Italiano**
Piazza Cavour 2, 20121 Milan, Italy.
- Trotto Sportsman. 3 per wk.

**Tu Sei Me**
Platone 29, 00136 Rome, Italy.
- Tu Sei Me; filosofia dell' unicita. q. ISSN 0041-3844

**Tumminelli**
Viale dell' Universita 38, 00185 Rome, Italy.
- Futuribili; rivista trimestrale di esplorazione e studio dei futuri possibili. q. ISSN 0016-3309 (Istituto per le Ricerche di Economia Applicata. Gruppo Futuribili Italia)

**Turin, Italy. Comitato Provinciale di Educacione Grafica**
- Graphicus. (pub. by Associazione Culturale Progresso Grafico)

**Edizioni Turistampa**
Via Confienza 19, 10101 Turin, Italy.
- Viaggi Vacanze. m. (10 per yr.)

**Ubezzi & Dones, S.p.A.**
Via Mecenate 79, 20138 Milan, Italy.
- Borsa Marmi; Periodico Mensile per lo sviluppo delle vendite nell'ambito del M.E.C. m. ISSN 0006-7857

**Ufficio Centrale per l'Emigrazione Italiana**
Circonvallazione Aurelia, 50, 00165 Roma, Italy.
- Servizio Migranti. m. ISSN 0037-2803

**Ufficio Moderno**
Via V. Foppa 7, 20144 Milan, Italy.
- Film Special. m. ISSN 0532-9841
- Linea Grafica. bi-m. ISSN 0024-3744
- Pubblicita in Italia; suggestione pubblicitaria. a. ISSN 0079-7472 (Dist. in U.S. by Speedimpex U.S.A. Inc.)
- Ufficio Moderno - Pubblicita. m. ISSN 0041-5731

**Ugo Ragozzino, Ed. & Pub.**
P.O. Box 701, 00100 Rome, Italy.
- Gazzetta del Mattino. w.
- Gazzetta della Domenica; settimanale politico, economico sociale della capitale. w. ISSN 0016-562X

**Unione Cattolica Infermieri**
Via Gregorio 7 N. 111, 00165 Rome, Italy.
- Rivista degli Infermieri. m. ISSN 0031-9961

**Unione Cattolica Italiana Insegnanti Medi**
Via Crescenio 25, 00193 Rome, Italy.
- Scuola e l'Uomo. m. ISSN 0036-987X

**Unione Comunale P S I di Faenza**
Via 20 Settembre 29, Faenza, Italy.
- Socialista. s-m. ISSN 0037-8275

**Unione Costruttori Romani**
Largo G. Tartini 3/4, 00198 Rome, Italy.
- Costruttori Romani. ISSN 0010-9657

**Unione degli Industriali della Provincia di Imperia**
Via Matteotti 32, Imperia, Italy.
- Unione degli Industriali della Provincia di Imperia. Notiziario. s-m. ISSN 0041-7076

**Unione degli Istriani**
Via Pellico 2, Trieste, Italy.
- Unione degli Istriani. bi-m.

**Unione dei Magistrati Italiani**
- Rassegna dei Magistrati. (pub. by Casa Editrice Dott. A. Giuffre)

**Unione delle Comunita Israelitiche Italiane**
Lungotevere Sanzio 9, Rome, Italy.
- Rassegna Mensile di Israel. m. ISSN 0033-9792

**Unione Donne Italiane**
- Noi Donne. (pub. by Cooperativa Libera Stampa)

**Unione Giuristi Cattolici Italiani**
- Iustitia. (pub. by Casa Editrice Dott. A. Giuffre)

**Unione Industriale di Torino**
Via Fanti 17, Turin, Italy.
- Informazione Industriale. s-m. ISSN 0020-0786

**Unione Italiana Autoriparatori**
- Auto Service. (pub. by Auto Service Editrice)

**Unione Italiana Chimici Igienisti dei Laboratori Provinciali**
Casella Postale 2-10620, Turin, Italy.
- Unione Italiana Chimici Igienisti dei Laboratori Provinciali. Bolletino. m.

**Unione Italiana dei Ciechi**
Via Borgognona 38, Rome, Italy.
- Corriere dei Ciechi. m. ISSN 0010-9169

**Unione Italiana del Lavoro**
Via Lucullo No. 6, 00187 Rome, Italy.
- Lavoro Italiano. fortn. ISSN 0023-9089

**Unione Italiana della Cultura Popolare**
- Cultura Popolare. (pub. by Societa Umanitaria)

**Unione Italiana delle Camara di Commercio, Industria, Artigianato e Agricoltura**
Piazza Sallustio 21, Rome, Italy.
- Sintesi Economica. m. ISSN 0037-5780

**Unione Italiana delle Federazioni Nazionali di Categoria Orafi, Argentieri, Orologiai, Metalli, Preziosi, Pietre Preziose**
- Orafo Italiano. (pub. by Studio Manca)

**Unione Italiana di Assistenza all'infanzia**
Via Ulpiano 47, Rome, Italy.
- Problemi Minorili. bi-m.

**Unione Italiana Lotta alla Distrofia Muscolare**
Via P.P. Vergerio 17, 35100 Padua, Italy.
- Distrofia Muscolare. q. ISSN 0012-4087

**Unione Italiana Sviluppo Tecnico Economico Industriale del Legno**
- Giornale del Legno. (pub. by Edizioni I.C.I.)

**Unione Italiana Vini**
Via S. Vittore al Teatro 3, Milan, Italy.
- Corriere Vinicolo; commercio vinicolo. w.
- Enotria. q.

**Unione Micologica Italiana**
- Micologia Italiana. (pub. by Gruppo Giornalistico Edagricole)

**Unione Nazionale Associazioni Filateliche Numiamatiche**
Corso Vittorio Emanuele 73, 10128 Turin, Italy.
- F E N. bi-m.

**Unione Nazionale Autonoma Tintorie, Puliture a Secco, Lavanderie**
- Tintoria, Lavanderia e Pulitura a Secco. (pub. by Edizioni Ariminum)

**Unione Nazionale Chimici Italiani**
- Rassegna Chimica. (pub. by Maria Ragno)

**Unione Nazionale Comuni, Comunita ed Enti Montani**
- Montanaro d'Italia-Monti e Boschi. (pub. by Gruppo Giornalistico Edagricole)

**Unione Nazionale Consumatori**
Via Andrea Doria 48, Rome 00192, Italy.
- U.N.C.-Notizie. m.

**Unione Nazionale dell'Avicoltura**
Via Pasubio, 4, 00195 Rome, Italy.
- U N A Notizie di Avicoltura. m.

**Unione Nazionale Ufficiali in Congedo**
Via Nomentana 313, 00162 Rome, Italy.
- U N U C I. 5 per yr. ISSN 0041-5375

**Unione Operaia Escursionisti Italiani. Sezione di Udine**
Via Grazzano N. 7, 33100 Udine, Italy.
- Stelutis Alpinis. m. ISSN 0039-1131

**Unione Provinciale Agricoltori di Arezzo**
Corso Italia 205, Arezzo, Italy.
- Agricoltura Aretina. m. ISSN 0002-1245

**Unione Provinciale Agricoltori di Bologna**
Via d'Azeglio 15, Bologna, Italy.
- Bologna Agricola. fortn.

**Unione Provinciale Agricoltori di Brescia**
Via Malta - Traversa 4a, 72, 25100 Brescia, Italy.
- Agricoltore Bresciano. w. ISSN 0515-6912

**Unione Provinciale Agricoltori di Parma**
Piazzale A. Barezzi 3, 43100 Parma, Italy.
- Gazzettino Agricolo (Parma) w.

**Unione Provinciale Agricoltori di Perugia**
Via Bonazzi 61, 06100 Perugia, Italy.
- Agricoltore; periodico degli agricoltori umbri. m. ISSN 0002-1202

**Unione Provinciale Agricoltori di Torino**
Via Meucci 2, 10121 Turin, Italy.
- Cronache dell'Agricoltura. m.

**Unione Provinciale Agricoltori di Treviso**
Viale Cadorna 10, Treviso 31100, Italy.
- Agricoltore Trevisano. s-m. ISSN 0002-1229

**Unione Provinciale del Lavoro CISNAL di Napoli**
Via Agostino Depretis N. 62, Naples, Italy.
- Lavoro Sud. m. ISSN 0023-9119

**Unione Regionale delle Provincie Toscane, Florence**
- Biblioteca di Storia Toscana Moderna e Contemporanea Studi e Documenti. (pub. by Casa Editrice Leo S. Olschki)

**Unione Sindacale Provinciale**
G. Paglia 16, Bergamo, Italy.
- Vita Sindacale Bergamasca. fortn. ISSN 0042-7357

**Unione Speleologica Bolognese**
- Speleologia Emiliana. (pub. by Speleologia Emiliana)

**Unione Stampa Periodica Italiana**
Via po 102, Rome, Italy.
- Guida della Stampa Periodica Italiana. irreg., 1974, v. 3.

**Unione Stenografica Italiana**
Via Balbis 1, 10144 Torino, Italy.
- Corriere Stenografico. q. ISSN 0010-9290

**Unione Stenografica Napoletana**
Via L. Settembrini 9, 80138 Naples, Italy.
- Lettura Stenografica. bi-m. ISSN 0024-1431

**Unione Superiore Maggiori d'Italia**
Via Zanardelli 32, Rome 00186, Italy.
- Consacrazione e Servizio; rivista delle religiose. m. ISSN 0035-600X

**Unione Zoologica Italiana**
Via Loredan 10, 35100 Padua, Italy.
- Bollettino di Zoologia. q.

**Unita Operaia**
Piazza Sallustio 24, 00187 Rome, Italy.
- Unita Operaia; mensile dei metalmeccanici. m. ISSN 0041-7114

**Unita Proletaria**
Via Tomacelli 146, 00186 Rome, Italy.
- Unita Proletaria. m.

**Unita S.p.A.**
Via d'Aracoeli 13, Firenze, Italy.
- Partito. w. ISSN 0031-2541 (Partito Comunista d'Italia. Comitato Centrale)
- Rinascita; rassegna politica di attualita, economia, e cultura. w. ISSN 0035-5380
- Unita. d. (Partito Comunista Italiano)

**Unitalia Film**
Via Luciani, 1, Rome, Italy.
- Italian Production. 2 per yr. ISSN 0021-2946

**United Nations Social Defense Research Institute**
For publications of this agency see section for UNITED NATIONS

**United States Information Service**
Via Boncompagni 2, Rome, Italy.
- Americana. bi-m.

**Unites s.r.l.**
12 via Silvio Pellico, 20121 Milan, Italy.
- Annuario Politecnico Italiano. a. ISSN 0066-4510

**Universita Cattolica del Sacro Cuore**
- Aegyptus. (pub. by Vita e Pensiero)
- Aevum. (pub. by Vita e Pensiero)
- Annali della Facolta di Agraria. (pub. by Vita e Pensiero)
- Jus. (pub. by Vita e Pensiero)
- Medicina e Morale. (pub. by Vita e Pensiero)
- Presenza. (pub. by Vita e Pensiero)
- Rivista del Clero Italiano. (pub. by Vita e Pensiero)
- Rivista di Filosofia Neoscolastica. (pub. by Vita e Pensiero)
- Scienze Pedagogiche. (pub. by Vita e Pensiero)
- Vita e Pensiero. (pub. by Vita e Pensiero)

**Universita Cattolica del Sacro Cuore. Clinica Chirurgica**
Universita Cattolica S. Cuore, Via della Pineta Sacchetti N. 526, 00168 Rome, Italy.
- Chirurgia e Patologia Sperimentale. m. ISSN 0009-4757

**Universita Cattolica del Sacro Cuore. Facolta di Medicina e Chirurgia**
V. Pineta Sacchetti 644, 00168 Rome, Italy.
- Acta Medica Romana. (pub. by Vita e Pensiero)
- Igiene Moderna. bi-m. ISSN 0019-1655 (prep. by its Istituto de Microbiologia)

**Universita Cattolica del Sacro Cuore. Istituto di Economia**
- Rivista Internazionale di Scienze Sociali. (pub. by Vita e Pensiero)

**Universita Cattolica del Sacro Cuore. Istituto di Psicologia**
- Archivio di Psicologia, Neurologia e Psichiatria. (pub. by Vita e Pensiero)

**Universita Cattolica del Sacro Cuore. Istituto di Sociologia**
- Studi di Sociologia. (pub. by Vita e Pensiero)

**Universita Commerciale Luigi Bocconi**
- Giornale degli Economisti e Annali di Economia. (pub. by Cisalpino-Goliardica)
- Rivista Italiana di Scienze Commerciali. (pub. by Malfasi Editore)

**Universita Commerciale Luigi Bocconi. Istituto di Economia delle Fonti di Energia**
- Economia delle Fonti di Energia. (pub. by Franco Angeli Editore)

**Universita degli Studi de Torino. Facolta di Lettere e Filosofia**
- Studi Francesi. (pub. by Societa Editrice Internazionale)

**Universita degli Studi della Calabria. Dipartimento di Storia**
- Studi e Documenti. (pub. by Editori Meridionali Riuniti)

**Universita degli Studi di Bologna. Centro Interfacolta de Linguistica Teorica e Applicata**
- Studi Italiani di Linguistica Teorica ed Applicata. (pub. by Liviana Editrice)

**Universita degli Studi di Bologna. Centro Studi Sui Problemi della Citta e del Territorio**
- Ricerca Sociale. (pub. by Crisan)

**Universita degli Studi di Bologna. Istituto di Glottologia**
- Lingua e Stile. (pub. by Societa Editrice Il Mulino)

**Universita degli Studi di Bologna. Osservatorio Astronomico**
Casella Post 596, 40100 Bologna, Italy.
- Coelum. bi-m.
- Universita di Bologna. Osservatorio Astronomico. Notizie e Rassegne. irreg. ISSN 0067-9887
- Universita di Bologna. Osservatorio Astronomico. Pubblicazioni. irreg., 1970, vol. 10, no. 7. ISSN 0067-9895

**Universita degli Studi di Firenze**
- Monitore Zoologico Italiano/Italian Journal of Zoology. (pub. by L. Pardi, Ed. & Pub.)

**Universita degli Studi di Firenze. Clinica Dermatologica**
Via Alfani 31, Florence, Italy.
- Italian General Review of Dermatology. bi-m. ISSN 0021-292X

**Universita degli Studi di Firenze. Faculta di Scienze Politiche**
- Processo Legislativo nel Parlamento Italiano. (pub. by Casa Editrice Dott. A. Giuffre)

**Universita degli Studi di Firenze. Instituto di Coltivazioni**
Piazzale delle Cascine 18, 50144 Florence, Italy.
- Rivista della Ortoflorofrutticoltura Italiana. bi-m. ISSN 0035-5968

**Universita degli Studi di Firenze. Istituto Botanico**
Via Lamarmora 4, 50121 Florence, Italy.
- Caryologia; giornale internazionale di citologia, citosistematica e citogenetica. 4 per yr. ISSN 0008-7114
- Webbia; Raccolta di Scritti Botanici. a(in 2 pts) ISSN 0083-7792

**Universita degli Studi di Firenze. Istituto di Composizione Architettonica**
Florence, Italy.
- Studi e Documenti di Architettura. q.

**Universita degli Studi di Firenze. Istituto di Microbiologia dell' Universita**
Piazza San Marco 4, Florence, Italy.
- Sperimentale; archivio di biologia normale e patologica. bi-m.(4 nos.to vol) ISSN 0038-7355

**Universita degli Studi di Firenze. Istituto di Statistica**
Via Curtatone N.1, Florence, Italy.
- Universita di Firenze. Istituto di Statistica. Documentazione; Ricerca sul problema delle abitazioni in Italia. 3-4 per yr. ISSN 0041-896X (Co-sponsor: Consiglio Nazionale delle Ricerche)

**Universita degli Studi di Firenze. Istituto Papirologico "G. Vitelli"**
- Studi e Testi di Papirologia. (pub. by Casa Editrice Felice le Monnier)

**Universita degli Studi di Messina**
Messina, Italy.
- Helikon; revista di tradizione e cultura classica. q' ISSN 0017-9981
- Societa Peloritana di Scienze Fisiche, Matematiche e Naturali. Atti. q. ISSN 0037-8860

**Universita degli Studi di Messina. Facolta di Magistero**
- Blue Guitar. (pub. by Herder Editrice e Libreria S.R.L.)

**Universita degli Studi di Messina. Istituto di Filogia Moderna**
- Universita di Messina. Istituto di Filologia Moderna. Biblioteca Letteraria. (pub. by Casa Editrice Felice le Monnier)

**Universita degli Studi di Messina. Istituto di Storia Medievale e Moderna**
- Universita di Messina. Istituto di Storia Medievale e Moderna. Pubblicazioni. (pub. by Casa Editrice Felice le Monnier)

**Universita degli Studi di Messina. Istituto di Zoologia**
Messina, Italy.
- Memorie di Biologia Marina e di Oceanografia. bi-m. (prep. by its Stazione di Biologia Marina)

**Universita degli Studi di Milano**
Via Festa del Perdono 7, Milan, Italy.
- Acme; annali della facolta di lettere e filosofia. q. ISSN 0001-494X
- Annali di Microbiologia Ed Enzimologia. q. ISSN 0003-4649
- Biochimica e Biologia Sperimentale/Biochemistry and Experimental Biology. (pub. by Piccin Editore)
- Universita di Milano. Annuario. a.

**Universita degli Studi di Milano. Centro di Cibernetica e di Attivita Linguistiche**
- Pensiero e Linguaggio in Operazioni/Thought and Language in Operations. (pub. by Istituto Editoriale Cisalpino)

**Universita degli Studi di Milano. Centro di Ricerche de Bioclimatologia Medica**
Via Vanvitelli 32, 20129 Milan, 20131 Milan, Italy.
- Medicina Termale e Climatologia. q. ISSN 0580-9320

**Universita degli Studi di Milano. Facolta di Veterinaria**
Via Celoria 10, 20133 Milan, Italy.
- Archivo Veterinario Italiano. 3 per yr. ISSN 0004-0479
- Rassegna di Diritto Legislazione e Medicina Legale Veterinaria. q. ISSN 0300-3485 (prep. by its Istituto di Medicina Legale Veterinaria)

**Universita degli Studi di Napoli. Clinica della Malattie Tropicali e Sub-Tropicali**
Via S. Lucia 15, Naples, Italy.
- Acta Medica Italica di Medicina Tropicale e Subtropicale e di Gastroenterologia. m. ISSN 0001-6039

**Universita degli Studi di Napoli. Clinica Pediatrica**
S. Andrea delle Dame 4, Naples, Italy.
- Pediatria; revista d'igiene, medicina e chirurgia dell'infanzia. q. ISSN 0031-3890

**Universita degli Studi di Napoli. Clinica Tisiologica**
Ospedale via Monaldi, Naples, Italy.
- Archivio Monaldi per la Tisiologia e le Malattie dell'Apparato Respiratorio. m. ISSN 0004-0185

**Universita degli Studi di Napoli. Facolta di Medicina e Chirurgia**
Nuova Policlinico, Cappella dei Cangiani, 80100 Naples, Italy.
- Acta Neurologica. bi-m. ISSN 0001-6276 (prep. by its Clinica Malattie Nervose e Mentali)

**Universita degli Studi di Napoli. Istituto di Geologia Applicata**
Naples, Italy.
- Universita di Napoli. Istituto di Geologia Applicata. Memorie e Note. irreg.

**Universita degli Studi di Napoli. Istituto di Matematica**
Via Mezzocannone 8, Naples, Italy.
- Ricerche di Matematica. s-a. ISSN 0035-5038

**Universita degli Studi di Palermo. Clinica Tisiologica**
Via Trabucco 180, Palermo 90146, Italy.
- Rivista Siciliana della Tubercolosi e delle Malattie Respiratorie. bi-m. ISSN 0035-7049 (Associazione Siciliana contro la Tubercolosi)

**Universita degli Studi di Perugia**
Casella Postale 317, Perugia, Italy.
- Rivista di Biologia. q. ISSN 0035-6050

**Universita degli Studi di Perugia. Division of Cancer Research**
P.O.Box 327, 06100 Perugia, Monteluce, Italy.
- Perugia Quadrennial International Conferences on Cancer. Proceedings. quadrennial. ISSN 0069-8520

**Universita degli Studi di Perugia. Facolta di Medicina e Chirurgia**
Perugia, Italy.
- Universita degli Studi di Perugia. Facolta di Medicina e Chirurgia. Annali. q. ISSN 0014-648X (Accademia Anatomico-Chirurgica di Perugia)

**Universita degli Studi di Perugia. Istituto di Anatomia e Istologia Patologica**
Casella Postale 327, Monteluce, Perugia 06100, Italy.
- Universita degli Studi Perugia. Istituto di Anatomia e Istologia. Lavori. 3 per yr. ISSN 0041-8943

**Universita degli Studi di Perugia. Istituto di Idrobiologia**
Via Elce di Sotto, Perugia, Italy.
- Rivista di Idrobiologia. q. ISSN 0048-8399

**Universita degli Studi di Perugia. Istituto di Igene**
Box 226, Perugia, Italy.
- Educazione Sanitaria. q. ISSN 0013-2098 (prep. by its Centro Sperimentale per l'Educazione Sanitaria)

**Universita degli Studi di Pisa. Istituto di Glottologia**
Via S. Maria 36, Pisa, Italy.
- Studi e Saggi Linguistici; supplemento alla rivista l'Italia Dialettale. a. ISSN 0085-6827

**Universita degli Studi di Pisa. Rettorato**
Lungarno A. Pacinotti 43, Pisa, Italy.
- Archives Italiennes de Biologie. q. ISSN 0003-9829

**Universita degli Studi di Sicilia**
Via Urbano 2, 84100 Salerno, Sicily, Italy.
- Rivista di Studi Salernitani. s-a. ISSN 0557-8019

**Universita degli Studi di Trieste**
Piazzale Europa 1, Trieste, Italy.
- Trieste. Universita. Istituto di Matematica. Rendiconti. s-a. ISSN 0049-4704 (prep. by its Istituto di Matematica)

**Universita degli Studi di Trieste. Facolta di Scienze Politiche**
- Universita di Trieste. Facolta di Scienze Politiche. Pubblicazioni. (pub. by Casa Editrice Dott. A. Giuffre)

**Universita degli Studi di Trieste. Istituto di Chimica Farmaceutica**
34700 Trieste, Italy.
- Universita di Trieste. Istituto di Chimica Farmaceutica. Pubblicazioni. irreg., 1969, no. 11. ISSN 0082-6472

**Universita degli Studi di Trieste. Istituto di Pedagogia**
- Universita di Trieste. Istituto di Pedagogia. Quaderni. (pub. by Casa Editrice Felice le Monnier)

**Universita degli Studi di Trieste. Istituto di Ricerche Economico-Agrarie**
Trieste, Italy.
- Universita degli Studi di Trieste. Istituto di Ricerche Economico Agrarie. Pubblicazione. irreg.

**Universita degli Studi di Trieste. Istituto di Storia dell'Arte**
- Universita di Trieste. Istituto di Storia dell'Arte (Pubblicazioni) (pub. by Edizioni dell' Ateneo)

**Universita degli Studi di Urbino. Istituto di Storia dell'Arte**
Argalia, Urbino, Italy.
- Notizie da Palazzo Albani. 3 per yr.

**Universita degli Studi di Venezia. Laboratorio di Economia Politica e Servizio Studi Economici "A. de Pietri-Tonelli"**
30100 Venice, Italy.
- Ricerche Economiche. q. ISSN 0035-5054

**Universita di Bari. Facolta di Scienza**
- Universita di Bari. Facolta di Scienza. Atti del Seminario di Studi Biologici. (pub. by Adriatrica Editrice)

**Universita di Cagliari**
Cattedra di Storia delle Tradizioni Popolari, Cagliari, Italy
(Distributed by: Libreria Cocco, Largo Carlo Felice 76, i-O 9100 Cagliari, Italy)
- B R A D S. (Bollettino del Repertorio e dell'Atlante Demologico Sardo) irreg; no. 7, 1976. ISSN 0067-9860
- Universita di Cagliari. Facolta de Lettere-Filosofia e Magistero. Annali. irreg; latest 1975.

**Universita di Cagliari. Facolta di Magistero**
09100 Cagliari, Italy.
- Archivo Sardo del Movimento Operaio Contadino e Autonomistico. q. (prep. by its Istituto di Studi Storici)

**Universita di Cagliari. Facolta di Medicina Chirurgia**
Casella Postale 170, 09100 Cagliari, Italy.
- Rassegna Medica Sarda. bi-m. ISSN 0033-9776

**Universita di Cagliari. Faculta di Scienze**
- Cagliari. Universita. Faculta di Scienze. Seminario. Rendiconti. (pub. by Libreria Cocco)

**Universita di Cagliari. Istituto di Storia Medioevale**
Cagliari, Italy.
- Universita di Cagliari: Istituto di Storia Medioevale. Pubblicazioni. irreg., 1973, no. 18. ISSN 0068-4805

**Universita di Cagliari. Istituto Economico-Statistico**
Libr. Fossataro, Via Gallura, 21, 09100 Cagliari, Italy.
- Cagliari. Universita. Istituto Economico Statistico. Studi di Economia. 3 per yr.

**Universita di Catania. Facolta di Lettere e Filosofia**
c/o Prof. E. Rapisarda, Catania, Sicily.
- Orpheus; rivista di umanita classica e cristiana. q. ISSN 0030-5790
- Siculorum Gymnasium. s-a. ISSN 0037-458X
- Teoresi; rivista di cultura filosofica. q. ISSN 0040-3563

**Universita di Catania. Istituto di Storia delle Tradizioni Popolari**
- Universita di Catania. Istituto di Storia delle Tradizioni Popolari. Studi e Testi. (pub. by Casa Editrice Leo S. Olschki)

**Universita di Catania. Istituto di Storia Economica**
Corso Italia N.55, 95129 Catania, Italy.
- Annali del Mezzogiorno. a. ISSN 0066-2259

**Universita di Ferrara**
Via de Pisis 24, 44100 Ferrara, Italy.
- Universita di Ferrara. Annali. Sezione 14. Fisica Sperimentale e Teorica. irreg. ISSN 0533-0386

**Universita di Ferrara. Istituto di Geologia, Paleontologia e Paleontologia Umana**
C.So Ercole 1 d'Este 32, Ferrara, Italy.
- Universita di Ferrara. Istituto di Geologia, Paleontologia e Paleontologia Umana. Annali. Sezione 9. Scienze Geologiche. irreg.; vol. 5, no. 11, 1976. ISSN 0071-4550
- Universita di Ferrara. Istituto di Geologia, Paleontologia e Paleontologia Umana. Annali. Sezione 15. Paleontologia Umana e Palentologia. irreg.; vol. 2, no. 12, 1976. ISSN 0071-4542
- Universita di Ferrara. Istituto di Geologia, Paleontologia e Paleontologia Umana. Memorie Geopaleontologiche. irreg., vol. 3, no. 1, 1971-1974. ISSN 0071-4569

**Universita di Ferrara. Istituto di Geologia, Paleontologia e Paleontologia Umana. Pubblicazioni.** a. ISSN 0071-4577

**Universita di Ferrara. Istituto di Mineralogia**
Ferrara, Italy.
- Universita di Ferrara. Annali. Nuova Serie. Sezione 17: Scienze Mineralogiche e Petrografiche. irreg.

**Universita di Genova. Instituto di Geologia**
Via Balbi 5, Genoa, Italy.
- Universita di Genova. Istituto di Geologia. Atti. 2 per yr. ISSN 0041-8978

**Universita di Genova. Istituto de Filosofia del Diritto**
- Materiali per Una Storia della Cultura Giuridica. (pub. by Societa Editrice Il Mulino)

**Universita di Genova. Istituto di Filologia Classica e Medievale**
Via Balbi 4, 16126 Genoa, Italy.
- Universita di Genova. Istituto di Filologia Classica e Medievale. Pubblicazioni. irreg. ISSN 0072-0852

**Universita di Genova. Istituto di Igiene**
Via A. Pastore 1, Genoa, Italy.
- Giornale di Igiene e Medicina Preventiva. q. ISSN 0017-0313

**Universita di Genova. Istituto di Paleografia e Storia Medievale**
Via Cairoli, 18, 16124 Genoa, Italy.
- Universita di Genova. Istituto di Paleografiz et Storia Medievale. Collana. Storica di Fonti e Studi. irreg. ISSN 0072-0860

**Universita di Genova. Istituto di Progettazione Architettonica**
Via Opera Pia Cousa 11, Genoa 16145, Italy.
- Universita di Genova. Istituto di Progettazione Architettonica. Quaderno. irreg.

**Universita di Genova. Istituto di Zoologia**
Via Balbi 5, Genoa, Italy.
- Universita di Genova. Bolletino dei Musei et degli Istituti Biologici. a. ISSN 0085-0950

**Universita di Genova. Istituto Scientifico di Medicina Interna**
16132 Genoa, Italy.
- Archivio E.Maragliano di Patologia e Clinica. bi-m. ISSN 0004-0193

**Universita di Macerata. Facolta di Lettere e Filosofie**
Macerata, Italy.
- Universita di Macerata. Facolta di Lettere e Filosofie. Annali. a. ISSN 0076-1818

**Universita di Modena. Seminario Matematico e Fisico**
Corso Canalgrande 45, 41100 Modena, Italy.
- Universita de Modena. Seminario Matematico e Fisico. Atti. s-a. ISSN 0041-8986

**Universita di Napoli. Istituto di Medicina del Lavoro**
Policlinico Piazza Miraglia, Naples, Italy.
- Folia Medica; rivista di medicina del lavoro e di medicina legale e delle assicurazioni sociali. m. ISSN 0015-5608

**Universita di Padova**
Istituto di Patologia Speciale Chirurgica e Propedeutica Clinica, Padua, Italy.
- Acta Chirurgica Italica. bi-m. ISSN 0001-5466
- Studia Aristotelica. (pub. by Editrice Antenore)
- Universita di Padova. Centro per la Storia della Tradizione Artistotelica nel Veneto. Saggi e Testi. (pub. by Editrice Antenore)
- Universita di Padova. Istituto per la Storia. Contributi. (pub. by Editrice Antenore)
- Universita di Padova. Istituto per la Storia. Quaderni. (pub. by Editrice Antenore)

**Universita di Padova. Clinica Ortopedica**
Padua, Italy.
- Clinica Ortopedica. q. ISSN 0009-9023

**Universita di Padova. Clinica Pediatrica**
- Acta Paediatrica Latina. (pub. by Editrice Age)

**Universita di Padova. Facolta di Lettere e Filosofia**
- Universita di Padova. Facolta di Lettere e Filosofia. Opuscoli Accademici. (pub. by Casa Editrice Leo S. Olschki)
- Universita di Padova. Facolta di Lettere e Filosofia. Publicazioni. (pub. by Casa Editrice Leo S. Olschki)

**Universita di Padova. Facolta di Medicina e Chirurgia**
- Attualiti di Ostetricia e Ginecologia. (pub. by Societa Editrice Universo)

**Universita di Padova. Istituto di Idraulica**
Padua, Italy.
- Bibliografia Italiana di Idraulica. q. ISSN 0006-1042 (prep. by its Centro di Documentazione Idraulica)

**Universita di Padova. Istituto di Letterature Straniere**
- Studi di Letteratura Francese. (pub. by Casa Editrice Leo S. Olschki)

**Universita di Padova. Istituto di Pedagogia**
Padua, Italy.
- Rassegna di Pedagogia. q. ISSN 0033-9571

**Universita di Padova. Istituto di Storia Antica**
- Universita di Padova. Istituto di Storia Antica. Pubblicazioni. (pub. by Erma di "Bretschneider")

**Universita di Padova. Istituto di Storia della Medicina**
Via Fallopia 50, 35100 Padua, Italy.
- Acta Medicae Historiae Patavina. a. ISSN 0065-1389

**Universita di Padova. Scuola di Perfezionamento in Filosofia**
- Universita di Padova. Scuola di Perfezionamento in Filosofia. Pubblicazioni. (pub. by Casa Editrice Dott. Antonio Milani)

**Universita di Palermo. Facolta di Economia e Commercio**
- Universita di Palermo. Facolta di Economia e Commercio. Annali. (pub. by Abbaco)

**Universita di Palermo. Facolta di Lettere e Filosofia**
Via delle Scienze, Palermo, Sicily, Italy.
- Nuova Stoa; rivista quadrimestrale di studi filosofici. 3 per yr. (prep. by its Istituto di Storia della Filosofia)

**Universita di Palermo. Istituto di Filologia Greca**
- Universita di Palermo. Istituto di Filologia Greca. Quaderni. (pub. by Istituto Siciliano di Studi Bizantini e Neoellenici)

**Universita di Parma**
Parma, Italy.
- Universita di Parma. Centro Studi e Archivio della Comunicazione. Istutito di Storia dell'Arte. Cataloghi. irreg., latest issue, 1976.

**Universita di Parma. Istituto di Chimica Generale**
Via M. d'Azeglio 85, 43100 Parma, Italy.
- Crystal Structure Communications. q.

**Universita di Parma. Istituto di Matematica**
Via Universita 12, 43100 Parma, Italy.
- Universita di Parma. Rivista di Matematica. a. ISSN 0035-6298

**Universita di Pavia. Facolta di Lettere**
Pavia, Italy.
- Athenaeum; studi periodici di letteratura e storia dell' antichita. s-a. ISSN 0004-6574

**Universita di Pavia. Istituto Botanico**
27100 Pavia, Italy.
- Universita di Pavia. Istituto Botanico. Atti. a. ISSN 0079-0265

**Universita di Pavia. Istituto di Scienze Politiche**
- Politico. (pub. by Casa Editrice Dott. A. Giuffre)

**Universita di Pavia. Policlinico**
- Rivista di Emoterapia e Immunoematologia. (pub. by P. Introzzi, Ed. & Pub.)

**Universita di Pavia. Scuola Universitaria di Paleografia e Filologia Musicale**
- Instituta/Monumenta. (pub. by Fondazione "Claudio Monteverdi")

**Universita di Roma**
Medicina Nei Secoli, Viale dell'Universita 34/A, Rome, Italy.
- Medicina Nei Secoli; rivista storico medica. q. ISSN 0025-7877
- Societa Geologica Italiana. Bollettino and Memorie. 4 per yr. ISSN 0037-8763

**Universita di Roma. Clinica Malattie Infettive**
Dirett. Prof, Germano Ricci, Policlinico, Rome
00161, Italy.
- Aggiornamenti Su Malattie Infettive Ed
Immunologia. bi-m. ISSN 0515-6610

**Universita di Roma. Facolta di Ingegneria**
Via Eudossiana 18, Rome, Italy.
- Istituto di Architettura e Urbanistica. Rassegna. q.
ISSN 0021-2458 (Co-sponsor: Istituto di
Architetura di Edilzie e di Tecnica Urbanistica)

**Universita di Roma. Facolta di Scienze Statistiche
Demografiche Ed Attuariali**
Istituto di Statistica e Ricerca Sociale C. Gini, Citta
Universitaria, 00100 Rome, Italy.
- Metron; rivista internazionale di statistica. irreg.
ISSN 0026-1424

**Universita di Roma. Istituti di Archeologia e Storia
dell'Arte Greca e Romana e di Etruscologia e
Anchichita Italiche**
- Archeologia Classica. (pub. by Erma di
"Bretschneider")

**Universita di Roma. Istituto Botanico**
Citta Universitaria, 00100 Rome, Italy.
- Universita di Roma. Istituto Botanico. Annali di
Botanica. a.

**Universita di Roma. Istituto di Automatica**
Via Eudossiana 18, 00184 Rome, Italy.
- Universita di Roma. Istituto di Automatica.
Notiziario. 3 per yr.

**Universita di Roma. Istituto di Clinica Pediatrica**
- Pediatria Internazionale. (pub. by Societa Editrice
Universo)

**Universita di Roma. Istituto di Economia Politica**
- Universita di Roma. Istituto di Economia Politica.
Collana di Studi. (pub. by Edizioni dell' Ateneo)

**Universita di Roma. Istituto di Lingua e Letteratura
Latina**
- Romanobarbarica. (pub. by Herder Editrice e
Libreria s.r.l.)

**Universita di Roma. Istituto di Medicina Legale**
Viale Regina Elena 336, 00161 Rome, Italy.
- Zacchia; archivio di medicina legale, sociale e
criminologica. q. ISSN 0044-1570

**Universita di Roma. Istituto di Microbiologia**
Citta Universitaria, 00100 Rome, Italy.
- Antibiotica; revista di studi sperimentali. q. ISSN
0003-5629

**Universita di Roma. Istituto di Studi Filosofici**
- Archivio di Filosofia. (pub. by Casa Editrice Dott.
Antonio Milani)

**Universita di Roma. Istituto di Studi Francesi**
- Micromegas. (pub. by Bulzoni Editore)

**Universita di Roma. Istituto Studi Albanesi**
- Studi Albanesi. Studi e Testi. (pub. by Casa
Editrice Leo S. Olschki)

**Universita di Roma. Scuola di Filologia Moderna**
11-B via Ruggero Bonghi, 00184 Rome, Italy.
- Universita di Roma. Scuola di Filologia Moderna.
Pubblicazioni. irreg., 1967, no. 12. ISSN 0080-
4029

**Universita di Roma. Scuola di Studi Storico -
Religiosi**
- Studi e Materiali di Storia delle Religioni.
Quaderni. (pub. by Edizioni dell' Ateneo)

**Universita di Roma. Scuola Orientale**
Rome, Italy.
- Rivista degli Studi Orientali. s-a.

**Universita di Rome. Clinica Odontoiatrica**
Viale Regina Elena 287a, Rome, Italy.
- Annali di Stomatologia; rivista mensile di scienze
odontostomatologiche. 4-6 per yr. ISSN 0003-
4681

**Universita di Rome. Scuola di Filologia Classica**
- Bibliotheca Athena. (pub. by Edizioni dell'
Ateneo)

**Universita di Sassari. Societa Sassarese per le
Scienze Giuridiche**
- Studi Sassaresi. (pub. by Casa Editrice Dott. A.
Giuffre)

**Universita di Siena**
Siena, Italy.
- Studi Senesi. q. ISSN 0039-3010 (prep. by its
Circolo Giuridico)

**Universita di Sienna. Istituto di Storia Dell Arte**
50125 Florence, Italy.
- Prospettiva; rivista di storia dell'arte antica e
moderna. q.

**Universita di Torino**
- Mesopotamia. (pub. by G. Giappichelli Editore)

**Universita di Torino. Clinica Oculista**
Via Juvara 19, Turin, Italy.
- Archivio e Rassegna Italiana di Ottalmologia. m.
ISSN 0300-0109

**Universita di Torino. Facolta di Scienze Agrarie**
Via P. Giuria 15, 10126 Turin, Italy.
- Universita di Torino. Facolta di Scienze Agrarie.
Annali. a. ISSN 0082-6871

**Universita di Torino. Istituto dell' Atlante Linguistico
Italiano**
- Bolletino dell'Atlante Linguistico Mediterraneo/
Bulletin of the Linguistic Atlas of Mediterranean.
(pub. by Casa Editrice Leo S. Olschki)

**Universita di Torino. Istituto di Storia**
- Universita di Torino. Istituto di Storia. Collana.
(pub. by Edizioni Scientifiche Italiane S.p.A.)

**Universita di Trieste**
- Incontri Linguistici. (pub. by Licosa S.p.A.)

**Universita di Udine. Biblioteca Centrale**
- Consorzio Universitario. Pubblicazioni. Sezione
Miscellanea. (pub. by Industrie Grafiche del
Bianco)

**Universita Internazionale dell'Arte. Centro di Studi
per la Museologia**
Via Incontri, 3, Florence, Itlay.
- Museologia. a.

**Universita' Ospedale Garibaldi. Otorinolaringoiatrica**
Catania, Italy.
- Clinica Otorinolaringoiatrica. bi-m. ISSN 0009-
904X

**Universita Pontificia Salesiana**
Piazza Ateneo Salesiano 1, 00139 Rome, Italy.
- Salesianum. q. ISSN 0036-3502

**Universita Salesiana di Roma. Facolta di Scienze
dell'Educazione**
- Orientamenti Pedagogici. (pub. by Societa Editrice
Internazionale)

**Casa Editrice Universo**
Via Strea 22, 20125 Milan, Italy.
- Cineromanzo. m. ISSN 0412-5568

**Societa Editrice Universo**
Via G.B. Morgagni 1, 00161 Rome, Italy.
- Attualiti di Ostetricia e Ginecologia. bi-m. ISSN
0004-7317 (Universita di Padova. Facolta di
Medicina e Chirurgia)
- Chirugia Generale. bi-m. ISSN 0412-2658
- Clinica Dietologica. q.
- Clinica Terapeutica. fortn. ISSN 0009-9074
- Clinica Termale. bi-m. (Associazione Italiana di
Idroclimatologia, Talassologia e Terapia Fisica)
- Epatologia. bi-m. ISSN 0013-9475
- Medicina Psicosomatica; rivista di medicina
psicosomatica, psicologia clinica e psicoterapia. q.
ISSN 0025-7893
- Nuntius Radiologicus. m.
- Nuovi Annali di Igiene e Microbiologia. bi-m.
ISSN 0029-6287
- Pediatria Internazionale. q. ISSN 0476-0069
(Universita di Roma. Istituto di Clinica
Pediatrica)
- Rassegna di Psicopedagogia Clinica. 3 per yr.
- Rassegna Italiana di Gastroenterologia. m. (Centro
Italiano di Gastroenterologia)
- Rivista di Radiologia. q.
- Rivista di Storia della Medicina. s-a. ISSN 0035-
6565 (Societa Italiana di Storia della Medicina)
- Rivista di Tossicologia Sperimentale e Clinica. bi-
m. (Centro Italiano Contro le Intossicazioni)

**Utensili**
Via Friuli 32, Milan, Italy.
- Utensili; attrezzi e strumenti di misura. bi-m.
ISSN 0042-1561

**V E R T s.r.l.**
Piazza Crispi 8, 31100 Treviso, Italy.
- Sentiamo. bi-m.

**Editrice V I P**
Via del Babuino 181, 00187 Rome, Italy.
- Almanacco della Canzone e del Cinema. m.

**Casa Editrice Dott. Francesco Vallardi**
Via Cesare da Sesto 15, Milan, Italy.
- Rivista del Diritto Commerciale E del Diritto
Generale delle Obbligazioni. bi-m. ISSN 0035-
5887

**Valmartina Editore**
Viale Gramsci 42, 50132-Florence, Italy.
- Lingue del Mondo; unica rivista Italiana di cultura
linguistica. bi-m. ISSN 0024-3876

**Mariso Varagnolo, Ed. & Pub.**
Via Inverigo, 10 Milan, Italy.
- A P A C Inform. 6 per yr. ISSN 0044-9741
(Associazione Professionale Autonoma
Cineoperatori)

**Vega**
Via le 17 Olimpiade 126, Rome 00196, Italy.
- Vega. fortn. ISSN 0042-305X

**Veltro Editrice**
Via S. Nicola De'cesarini, 3, 00185 Rome, Italy.
- Veltro; rivista della civilta italiana. bi-m. ISSN
0042-3254

**Editrice le Venezie e l'Italia**
Casella Postale 1139, Via Cappelli 28, 35100 Padua,
Italy.
- Italia Turistica; rivista di cultura e turismo delle
regioni Italiane. bi-m.

**Vernice**
San Marco 2407, Venice, Italy.
- Vernice. bi-m. ISSN 0049-5972

**Casa Editrice Luigi Veronelli**
Via degli Alerami 5, Milan, Italy.
- Gastronomo; rivista gastronomica. q. ISSN 0016-
514X

**Via Femminile**
Via T. Tasso 109, 24100 Bergano, Italy.
- Via Femminile. q.

**Via Libera**
Via Volturno 33, Milan, Italy.
- Via Libera. m. ISSN 0042-4986

**Vianelli Eleganza**
Via Verdi 10/1, Venice, Italy.
- Eleganza; rivista di alta moda. q. ISSN 0013-5364

**Vichiana**
Via San Biagio dei Librai, 2, 80138 Napoli, Italy.
- Vichiana. q. ISSN 0042-5079

**Vidya**
Via Sappusi 12, 91025 Marsala, Italy.
- Vidya; rivista trimestrale di cultura. q. ISSN 0042-
5311

**Vilmy Ricerche**
Via C. Cavour 24, 42013 Casalgrande, Italy.
- Bollettino delle Accessioni di Periodici e Libri. s-
a. ISSN 0006-6680

**Vincentian Fathers**
- Annali della Carita. (pub. by Edizioni Liturgiche e
Vincenziane)

**Leonardo da Vinci**
Lungomare N. Sauro 25, Bari, Italy.
- Confronto; mensile di politica e cultura. 6 per yr.
ISSN 0010-5732

**M'litograph di Virna Antoni & C.**
Via Arcangelo Corelli 83, 50127 Florence, Italy.
- Brivido Sportivo. w.

**Vita e Pensiero**
Largo Gemelli 1, 20123 Milan, Italy.
- Acta Medica Romana. bi-m. ISSN 0001-6098 (Universita Cattolica del Sacro Cuore. Facolta di Medicina e Chirurgia)
- Aegyptus; rivista Italiana di Egittologia e di Papirologia. q. ISSN 0001-9046 (Universita Cattolica del Sacro Cuore)
- Aevum; rassegna di scienze storiche, linguistiche e filologiche. bi-m. ISSN 0001-9593 (Universita Cattolica del Sacro Cuore)
- Annali della Facolta di Agraria. 3 per yr. ISSN 0003-4576 (Universita Cattolica del Sacro Cuore)
- Archivio di Psicologia, Neurologia e Psichiatria. q. ISSN 0004-0150 (Universita Cattolica del Sacro Cuore. Istituto di Psicologia)
- Jus; rivista di scienze giuridiche. q. ISSN 0022-6955 (Universita Cattolica del Sacro Cuore)
- Medicina e Morale. 3 per yr. ISSN 0025-7834 (Universita Cattolica del Sacro Cuore)
- Presenza. m. ISSN 0478-1376 (Universita Cattolica del Sacro Cuore)
- Rivista del Clero Italiano. m. ISSN 0042-7586 (Universita Cattolica del Sacro Cuore)
- Rivista di Filosofia Neoscolastica. q. ISSN 0035-6247 (Universita Cattolica del Sacro Cuore)
- Rivista Internazionale di Scienze Sociali. bi-m. ISSN 0035-676X (Universita Cattolica del Sacro Cuore. Istituto di Economia)
- Scienze Pedagogiche. irreg. (Universita Cattolica del Sacro Cuore)
- Studi di Sociologia. q. ISSN 0039-291X (Universita Cattolica del Sacro Cuore. Istituto di Sociologia)
- Vita e Pensiero; rassegna italiana di cultura. bi-m. ISSN 0042-725X (Universita Cattolica del Sacro Cuore)

**Luigi Vita, Ed. & Pub.**
Via Garibaldi N.132, 98100 Messina, Italy.
- Battaglia Letteraria; bimestrale di letteratura e attualita. bi-m. ISSN 0005-6332

**Vita Farmaceutici**
Via Cernaia 20, Turin, Italy.
- Annali di Laringologia, Otologia, Rinologia, Faringologia. irreg. ISSN 0066-2267 (Gruppo Otologi Ospedalieri Italiani)

**Vita Nova S.p.A.**
Via Crescenzio 63, 00193 Rome, Italy.
- Informazioni Librarie. q.
- Studium; rivista bimestrale di cultura. bi-m. ISSN 0039-4130

**Edizioni di Vita Sociale**
Piazza S. Domenico 1, 51100 Pistoia, Italy.
- Memorie Domenicane. a. (Provincia Romana dei Frati Predicatori)

**Dr. Carlo Alberto Viterbo**
Largo Don G. Morosini No. 1, 00195 Rome, Italy.
- Israel; settimanale ebraico. w.

**Viviamo**
Via S. Cipriano 1, Rome, Italy.
- Viviamo. bi-m. ISSN 0042-7551

**Voce**
06012 Citta di Castello, Italy.
- Voce; settimanale religioso sociale. w. ISSN 0042-7780

**Voce Bruzia**
Ed. Ruggiero Magliocchi, Via Nicola Serra 80, Cosenza, Italy.
- Voce Bruzia; indipendente politico letterario. m.(14 per yr) ISSN 0042-7802

**Voce di Siracusa**
Via S. Paolo 16, 96100 Syracuse, Italy.
- Voce di Siracusa. s-m. ISSN 0042-7861

**Voce Editrice s.r.l.**
Via G. Gentile 53-C, 70126 Bari, Italy.
- Voce della Regione. fortn.

**Edizioni della Voce s.r.l.**
Via Tomacelli 146, 00186 Rome, Italy.
- Almanacco Repubblicano. a.

**Voci del Nostro Tempo**
Via S. Anna 223, 97100 Ragusa, Italy.
- Voci del Nostro Tempo. bi-m.

**Volpe Editore**
Via Valvassori Peroni 43, 20133 Milan, Italy.
- Elevatori. bi-m.

- Intervento. q.

**Warrior**
G.T. Invrea 3/1, 16129 Genoa, Italy.
- Warrior; rivista del modellismo militare. bi-m.

**World Federation of Christian Life Communities**
Central Secretariat, Borgo Santo Spirito 8, Casella Postale 9048, 00100 Rome, Italy.
- Progressio. 8 per yr. ISSN 0033-0728

**World Federation of Parasitologists**
Prof. A. Mantovani, Secty., c/o Ist. di Malattie Infective, Profilassi e Polizia Veterinaria, 41026 Bologna, Italy.
- International Congress of Parasitology. Proceedings. irreg.; 3rd, Munich, Germany, 1970. ISSN 0074-3860

**World Federation of the Deaf**
120 via Gregoria VII, Rome 00165, Italy.
- Voix du Silence/Voice of Silence. q. ISSN 0042-8388
- World Congress of the Deaf. Lectures and Papers. quadrennial, 1971, 6th, Paris. ISSN 0084-1625
- World Congress of the Deaf. Proceedings. irreg. ISSN 0510-8292

**Worthington S.p.A.**
Via Pirelli 19, Milan, Italy.
- Notiziario Tecnico Worthington. q. ISSN 0029-442X

**Yachting Italiano-Altomare**
Box 7053, 16148 Genoa Quarto, Italy.
- Yachting Italiano-Altomare; mensile nazionale di navigazione sportiva. m. ISSN 0043-9975

**Zagaglia**
56 Via Duca d'Aosta, Box 38, 73100 Lecce, Italy.
- Zagaglia; rassegna di scienze, lettere ed arti. q. ISSN 0044-1627

**Nicola Zanichelli Editore**
Via Irnerio 34, Bologna 40126, Italy.
- Annali di Matematica; pura ed applicata. q. ISSN 0003-4622
- Foro Italiano. m. ISSN 0015-783X
- Leggi. 3 per m. ISSN 0024-0400
- Massimario di Il Foro Italiano. m. ISSN 0025-4932
- Repertorio del Foro Italiano. a.
- Unione Matamatica Italiana. Bolletino. Sezione a. bi-m. ISSN 0041-7084

**Edizioni Suvini Zerboni**
Via M. F. Quintiliano, 40, 20138 Milan, Italy.
- Fronimo; rivista trimestrale di chitarra e liuto. q.

**Giorgio Zusi Editore**
Via del Minatore 5-B, Verona, Italy.
- Informatore del Marmista. m. ISSN 0020-0700

**Editrice 18 Karati s.r.l.**
Viale Stefini 3, 20125 Milan, Italy.
- 18 Karati. bi-m.

# IVORY COAST

**African Development Bank**
B.P. No. 1387, Abidjan, Ivory Coast.
- African Development Bank. Report by the Board of Directors. irreg. ISSN 0568-1308

**African Institute for Economic and Social Development**
see Institut Africain pour le Developpement Economique et Social

**Association des Ingenieurs et Techniciens Africains de Cote d'Ivoire**
Autoroute de Port-Bouet, Boite Postale 794, Abidjan, Ivory Coast.
- Association des Ingenieurs et Techniciens Africains de Cote d'Ivoire. Annuaire. a.

**Awoura**
B. P. 2273, Abidjan, Ivory Coast.
- Awoura; la revue de la femme ivoirienne. m.

**C I R E S**
B.P. 20901, Abidjan, Ivory Coast.
- C I R E S. (Cahiers Ivoiriens de Recherche Economique et Sociale) irreg. (approx. 1-2 per yr.)

**Centre d'Edition et de Diffusion Africaines**
B.P. 4541, Abidjan, Ivory Coast.
- Revue Ivoirienne de Droit. a. ISSN 0048-816X

**Centre de Publications Evangeliques**
B.P. 8900, Abidjan, Ivory Coast.
- Champion. q. ISSN 0045-6314

**Centre de Recherches Oceanographiques d'Abidjan**
B.P. V 18, Abidjan, Ivory Coast.
- Centre de Recherches Oceanographiques d'Abidjan. Documents Scientifiques. q.

**Chambre d'Industrie de Cote d'Ivoire**
B.P. 1758, Abidjan, Ivory Coast.
- Principales Industries Ivoiriennes. irreg.

**Chastrusse et Co.**
Rue Andre-Devaud, Brive, Ivory Coast.
- Ivory Coast. Annuaire International/International Directory. biennial.

**Djassin'foue**
Cite Sogeliha 100a, B.P. 8042, Abidjan, Ivory Coast.
- Djassin'foue; le messager culturel. m. ISSN 0046-0443

**Institut Africain pour le Developpement Economique et Social**
15 Ave. Jean Mermoz, B.P. 8008, Abidjan, Ivory Coast.
- Fichier-Afrique/Africa Card-Index. bi-m.
- I.N.A.D.E.S. Documentation; liste des livres enregistres a la bibliotheque. 6 per yr.

**Institut Fondamental d'Afrique Noire. Centre de Cote-d'Ivoire**
Direction de la Recherche Scientifique, Ministere de l'Education Nationale, Abidjan, Ivory Coast.
- Etudes Eburneennes. a. ISSN 0423-5673

**Inter Afrique Presse**
Box 20991, Abidjan, Ivory Coast.
- Entente Africaine. q. ISSN 0013-8630
- Ivoire Dimanche. w. ISSN 0047-1674 (Societe de Presse et d'Edition de Cote d'Ivoire)

**S.A.R.L. Inter-Continents Promotion**
B.P. 20991, Abidjan, Ivory Coast.
- Decennie 2; magazine illustre de l'Afrique moderne. m.

**Ivory Coast. Bibliotheque Nationale**
B. P. 20915, Abidjan, Ivory Coast.
- Bibliographie de la Cote d'Ivoire. a. ISSN 0084-7860

**Ivory Coast. Bureau de Developpement Industriel**
B.P. 4196, Abidjan, Ivory Coast.
- Ivory Coast. Bureau de Developpement Industriel. Couts des Facteurs en Cote d'Ivoire. irreg.
- Ivory Coast. Bureau de Developpement Industriel. Programme d'Activite. irreg.
- Ivory Coast. Bureau de Developpement Industriel. Programme Triennial des Activites. triennial.
- Ivory Coast. Bureau de Developpement Industriel. Rapport d'Activites. irreg.
- Ivory Coast. Bureau du Developpement Industriel. Situation de l'Industrie Ivoirienne. irreg.
- Ivory Coast. Bureau du Developpement Industriel. Usine Ivoirienne. m.

**Ivory Coast. Bureau National d'Etudes Techniques de Developpement**
Abidjan, Ivory Coast.
- Ivory Coast. Bureau National d'Etudes Techiques de Developpement. Rapport d'Activite. irreg.

**Ivory Coast. Direction des Affaires Economiques et des Relations Economiques Exterieures**
Abidjan, Ivory Coast.
- Commerce Exterieur de la Cote d'Ivoire: Resultats et Evolution. irreg.

**Ivory Coast. Direction des Mines et de la Geologie**
B.P. 1368, Abidjan, Ivory Coast.
- Ivory Coast. Direction des Mines et de la Geologie. Rapport Provisoire sur les Activities du Secteur. irreg.

**Ivory Coast. Direction du Budget Special d'Investissement et d'Equipment**
Abidjan, Ivory Coast.
- Ivory Coast. Direction du Budget Special d'Investissement et d'Equipment. Rapport de Presentation du Budget Special d'Investissement et d'Equipment. irreg.

**Ivory Coast. Ministere de l'Agriculture**
Abidjan, Ivory Coast.
- Ivory Coast. Ministere de l'Agriculture.
Statistiques Agricoles. a.

**Ivory Coast. Ministere de l'Economie et des Finances**
B. P. 125, Abidjan, Ivory Coast.
- Ivory Coast. Ministere de l'Economie et des
Finances. Etudes Economiques et Financieres. q.

**Ivory Coast. Ministere du Plan**
B. P. 5-65, Abidjan, Ivory Coast.
- Ivory Coast. Ministere du Plan. Comptes de la
Nation. a.

**Ivory Coast. Ministry of Information**
11 Ave. Bir Hakeim, Abidjan, Ivory Coast.
- Eburnea. m. ISSN 0046-1024

**Ivory Coast. Service de la Statistique**
B.P. 222, Abidjan, Ivory Coast.
- Situation Economique de Cote d'Ivoire. irreg.
ISSN 0080-9829
- Statistique du Commerce Exterieur de Cote
d'Ivoire. irreg. ISSN 0081-5276

**Service Commercial. Division Relations Publiques Commerciales**
B.P. 1345, Abidjan, Ivory Coast.
- Circuits; revue periodique de l'energie electrique
de la Cote d'Ivoire. irreg.

**Societe de Presse et d'Edition de Cote d'Ivoire**
- Ivoire Dimanche. (pub. by Inter Afrique Presse)

**Societe pour le Developpement Minier de la Cote d'Ivoire**
B.P. 2816, Abidjan, Ivory Coast.
- Societe pour le Developpement Minier de la Cote
d'Ivoire. Rapport Annuel. a.

**Syndicat des Exportateurs et Negociants en Bois de Cote d'Ivoire**
B.P. 1979, Abidjan, Ivory Coast.
- Syndicat des Exportateurs et Negociants en Bois
de Cote d'Ivoire. Bulletin de Liaison et
d'Information. q.

**Syndicat des Industriels de la Cote d'Ivoire**
B.P. 1340, Abidjan, Ivory Coast.
- Industriel de Cote d'Ivoire. m. ISSN 0019-9230

**Universite d'Abidjan**
B.P. 8109, Abidjan, Ivory Coast.
- Enseignement Superieur en Cote-d'Ivoire. a.
- Universite d'Abidjan. Annales. Serie F:
Ethnosociologie. irreg, vol. 5, 1973. (prep. by its
Institut d'Ethnosociologie)
- Universite d'Abidjan. Annales. Serie G:
Geographie. irreg, vol. 6, 1974. (prep. by its
Tropical Geography Institute)

**Vaillante Afrique**
Centre National CV-AV, B.P. 1287, Abidjan, Ivory
Coast.
- Vaillante Afrique. bi-m.

# JAMAICA

**African Studies Association of the West Indies**
Box 222, Kingston 7, Jamaica.
- African Studies Association of the West Indies.
Bulletin. 2 per yr. ISSN 0044-6610

**Arawak Press Ltd.**
46 East St., Kingston, Jamaica.
- Jamaica and West Indian Review; the magazine of
the Caribbean. q. ISSN 0021-4086
- Jamaica Annual. a. ISSN 0447-3280

**Bank of Jamaica**
Research Dept., Box 621, Kingston, Jamaica.
- Balance of Payments of Jamaica. irreg.
- Bank of Jamaica. Bulletin. q. ISSN 0005-5239
- Bank of Jamaica. Monthly Review. m.
- Bank of Jamaica. Report and Statement of
Accounts. a. ISSN 0067-3668
- Bank of Jamaica. Statistical Digest. irreg. ISSN
0572-5968

**Beacon Publications Ltd.**
7 Strand St., Box 1258, Montego Bay, Jamaica, W.
Indies.
- Focus on Jamaica. s-a. ISSN 0015-5160 (Jamaica
Tourist Board) (Co-sponsor: Jamaica in-Bond
Merchants Association)

**Christian Literature Crusade Inc.**
Box 186, 55 Church St., Kingston, Jamaica, W.
Indies.
- Caribbean Challenge. m. ISSN 0008-6436

**Commonwealth Library Association**
2A Ruthven Rd., P.O. Box 534, Kingston 10,
Jamaica.
- C O M L A Newsletter. q.

**Diocese of Jamaica**
Anglican Church Office, Kingston 5, Jamaica, W.
Indies.
- Jamaica Churchman. m. ISSN 0047-1720

**Geological Society of Jamaica**
University of the West Indies, Geology Department,
Mona, Kingston 7, Jamaica.
- Geological Society of Jamaica Journal. a. ISSN
0435-401X

**Gleaner Company Ltd.**
7 North St., Kingston, Jamaica, W. Indies.
- Children's Own. w.(during school term) ISSN
0009-4153
- Daily Gleaner-Farmers Weekly. w. ISSN 0011-
541X (Subscr. to: Eppok Co., 19-25 W. 44th St.,
New York, NY 10036)
- Daily Gleaner-Food Supplement. w. ISSN 0011-
5428 (Subscr. to: Eppok Co., 19-25 W. 44th St.,
New York, NY 10036)
- Jamaican Weekly Gleaner. w. ISSN 0021-4159
- Sunday Gleaner. w. ISSN 0039-520X
- Weekend Star. w.

**Institute of Jamaica**
12-16 East St., Kingston, Jamaica, W. Indies.
- Jamaica Journal. q. ISSN 0021-4124
- Jamaican National Bibliography. q. ISSN 0075-
2991

**Institution of Engineers, Jamaica**
Box 122, Kingston 10, Jamaica, West Indies.
- Institution of Engineers, Jamaica. Journal. s-a.
ISSN 0046-9882

**Inter-School & Inter-Varsity Christian Fellowship Ltd.**
Box 281, Kingston 10, Jamaica, West Indies.
- Inter-School & Inter-Varsity Christian Fellowship;
for prayer and praise. m. ISSN 0020-5087

**Jamaica. Department of Statistics**
9 Swallowfield Rd., Kingston 5, Jamaica.
- Consumer Price Indices. m.
- Jamaica. Department of Statistics. Annual
Abstract of Statistics. a. (published 9 months after
year to which it relates) ISSN 0075-2983
- Jamaica. Department of Statistics. Consumer Price
Indices. m. ISSN 0302-9336
- Jamaica. Department of Statistics. Demographic
Statistics. a; latest issue, 1973.
- Jamaica. Department of Statistics. External Trade.
q.
- Jamaica. Department of Statistics. External Trade
Annual Review. a.
- Jamaica. Department of Statistics. External Trade
Summary Tables. m.
- Jamaica. Department of Statistics. National
Income and Product. a.
- Monetary Statistics Bulletin. a. ISSN 0026-9638
- Statistical Yearbook of Jamaica. a.

**Jamaica. Ministry of Health and Environmental Control. Bureau of Health Education**
Box 478, Kingston, Jamaica, W. Indies.
- Jamaica Public Health. q. ISSN 0021-4132

**Jamaica. Ministry of Pensions and Social Secuirty**
14 National Heroes Circle, Box 10, Kingston 5,
Jamaica.
- National Insurance Scheme, Jamaica. Annual
Report. a. ISSN 0077-5053

**Jamaica Agricultural Society**
North Parade, Kingston, Jamaica, W. Indies.
- Farmer. bi-m. ISSN 0014-8350

**Jamaica Chamber of Commerce**
Box 172, 7-8 East Parade, Kingston, Jamaica, W.
Indies.
- Jamaica Chamber of Commerce Journal. q. ISSN
0021-4094

**Jamaica Geographical Society**
Geography Dept., U. W. I., Kingston 7, Jamaica.
- Jamaica Geographical Society Newsletter. 3 per
yr.

**Jamaica Industrial Development Corp.**
Box 505, Kingston, Jamaica.
- News Review. m. ISSN 0021-4116

**Jamaica Tourist Board**
- Focus on Jamaica. (pub. by Beacon Publications
Ltd.)

**Jamaican Historical Society**
c/o Institute of Jamaica, 12-16 East St., Kingston,
Jamica.
- Jamaican Historical Review. a; 1973, vol. 10.
- Jamaican Historical Society. Bulletin. q.

**Nurses Association of Jamaica**
72 Arnold Rd., Kingston 5, Jamaica, W. Indies.
- Jamaican Nurse. 3 per yr. ISSN 0021-4140

**St. George's College**
Winchester Park, North St., Kingston, Jamaica, W.
Indies.
- Blue and White. ISSN 0006-5048

**Savacou**
Box 170, Mona, Kingston 7, Jamaica, W. Indies.
- Savacou; a journal of the Caribbean artists
movement. irreg; 1-2 per yr. ISSN 0036-5068

**Scientific Research Council**
Box 350, Kingston 6, Jamaica, W. Indies.
- Scientific Research Council of Jamaica. Journal. s-
a. ISSN 0036-8822

**University of the West Indies**
Mona, Kingston 7, Jamaica.
- West Indian Medical Journal. q. ISSN 0043-3144

**University of the West Indies. Caribbean Food & Nutrition Institute**
Box 140, Kingston 7, Jamaica.
- Cajanus. bi-m.

**University of the West Indies. Department of Extra-Mural Studies**
Box 42, Kingston 7, Jamaica.
- Caribbean Quarterly. q. ISSN 0008-6495

**University of the West Indies. Department of Geography**
Mona, Kingston 7, Jamaica.
- Caribbean Geographer. a.
- University of the West Indies, Jamaica.
Department of Geography. Occasional
Publications Series. irreg., 1972, no. 9. ISSN
0077-0264
- University of the West Indies, Jamaica.
Department of Geography. Research Notes
Series. irreg., 1971, no. 5. ISSN 0077-0272

**University of the West Indies. Faculty of Agriculture**
Box 174, Kingston 7, Jamaica, W. Indies.
- Caribbean Farming. q. ISSN 0045-5806

**University of the West Indies. Institute of Social and Economic Research**
Mona, Kingston 7, Jamaica.
- Social and Economic Studies. 4 per yr. ISSN
0037-7651
- University of the West Indies. Institute of Social
and Economic Research. Working Papers. irreg.

**University of the West Indies. School of Education**
Mona, St. Andrew, Jamaica.
- Caribbean Journal of Education. triennial.

**Urban Development Corporation**
Kingston, Jamaica.
- Urban Development Corporation. Annual Report.
a.

**Voice of Jamaica**
94 Maxfield Ave., P.O. Box 68, Kingston 13,
Jamaica.
- Voice of Jamaica. w. ISSN 0042-8140

**West Indian Sportsman**
c/o Alva P. Ramsay, 75 Church St., Kingston,
Jamaica.
- West Indian Sportsman. m. ISSN 0049-7231

# JAPAN

**A & U Publishing Co., Ltd.**
2-30-8 Yushima, Bunkyo-ku, Tokyo 113, Japan.
- A & U. (Architecture and Urbanism) m.

**A.D.A. Edita Tokyo Co., Ltd**
3-12-14 Sendagaya, Shibuya-ku, Tokyo, Japan.
- G A/Global Architecture. irreg.
- G I/Global Interior. irreg.

**A I G A**
see International Association of Geomagnetism and
Aeronomy

**Abayuma Seismological Observatory**
see under Kyoto University

**Academia Music Co., Ltd.**
2-26-11 Hongo, Bunkyo-ku, Tokyo 113, Japan.
- Nihon Ongaku Bunken Yoshi Mokuroku. a.

**Academic Press of Japan**
4-5-7 Konan, Minato-ku, Tokyo, Japan.
- Biogeographical Society of Japan. Bulletin.
irreg.(approx. 12 issues per year) ISSN 0067-8716

**Adhesion Society of Japan**
c/o Osaka-furitsu Kogyo Gijutsu Kenkyusho,
Enokojima, Nishi-ku, Osaka 550, Japan.
- Adhesion Society of Japan. Journal/Nihon
Setchaku Kyokaishi. 6-8 per yr. ISSN 0001-8201

**Aerosol Industry Association of Japan**
c/o No. 319, Maru Bldg., 2-4-1 Marunouchi,
Chiyoda-ku, Tokyo 100, Japan.
- Aerosol. q.

**Afurika Kenkyu Gakkai**
see Japan Association of Africanists

**Afurika Ruijin'en Gakujutsu Chosatai**
see Kyoto University. Committee of the Kyoto
University Africa Primatological Expedition

**Agricultural Chemical Society of Japan**
2-4-16 Yayoi, Bunkyo-ku, Tokyo 113, Japan.
- Agricultural and Biological Chemistry Journal. m.
ISSN 0002-1369
- Agricultural Chemical Society of Japan. Journal/
Nippon Nogei Kaggakai-shi. m. ISSN 0002-1407

**Agricultural Economic Society of Japan**
- Journal of Agricultural Economics/Nogyo Keizai
Kenkyu. (pub. by Iwanami Shoten Publishers)

**Agriculture and Forestry Market Research Institute**
3-6-6 Iidabashi, Chiyoda-ku, Tokyo 102, Japan.
- Farming Japan. bi-m.

**Aichi-Gakuin Society of Dental Science**
School of Dentistry, Aichi-Gakuin University, 2-11
Suemori-dori, Chikusa-ku, Nagoya 464, Japan.
- Aichi-Gakuin Journal of Dental Science/Aichi-
Gakuin Daigaku Ronso. q. ISSN 0044-6912

**Aichi Library Association**
1-12-1 Higashisakura, Higashi-ku, Nagoya, Aichi,
Japan.
- Aichi-ken Kyodo Shiryo Sogo Mokuroku. irreg.,
latest issue, 1973.

**Ajia Keizai Kenkyusho**
see Institute of Developing Economies

**Ajia Seikei Gakkai**
see Society for Asian Political and Economic
Studies

**Akita Association of Rural Medicine**
c/o Akita-ken Kosei Nogyo Kyodo Kumiai
Rengokai, 3 Omachi, Akita-shi 010, Japan.
- Akita Journal of Rural Medicine/Akita-ken Noson
Igakkai Zasshi. irreg. ISSN 0002-368X

**Akita-ken Noson Igakkai**
see Akita Association of Rural Medicine

**Akiyoshi-dai Science Museum**
Akiyoshi-dai, Akiyoshi-cho Miya-gun, Yamaguchi
754-05, Japan.
- Akiyoshi-dai Science Museum. Bulletin. irreg.,
1969, no. 6. ISSN 0065-5554

**Amakusa Marine Biological Laboratory**
see under Kyushu University

**Amakusa Rinkai Jikkensho**
see Kyushu University. Amakusa Marine Biological
Laboratory

**American Chamber of Commerce in Japan**
701 Tosho Bldg., 2-2 Marunouchi 3-chome,
Chiyoda-ku, Tokyo 100, Japan.
- American Chamber of Commerce in Japan.
Journal. m. ISSN 0002-7847

**Anglica Society**
Kansai University, 3-3-35 Yamate-cho, Suita-shi,
Osaka, Japan.
- Anglica; journal of English philology. s-a. ISSN
0003-326X

**Anritsu Electric Co., Ltd.**
4-12-20 Minamiazabu, Minato-ku, Tokyo 106,
Japan.
- Anritsu Technical Bulletin/Anritsu Tekunikaru. s-
a. ISSN 0003-5211

**Anthropological Society of Japan**
c/o Dept. of Anthropology, Faculty of Science,
University of Tokyo, 7-3-1 Hongo, Bunkyo-ku,
Tokyo 113, Japan.
- Anthropological Society of Japan. Journal/
Jinruigaku Zasshi. q. ISSN 0003-5505

**Aoki Shoten**
60 Kanda Jimbocho, Chiyoda-ku, Tokyo, Japan.
- Gendai to Shiso. q.

**Aomori Local Meteorological Observatory**
155-4 Tsukuda, Matsumori, Aomori 030, Japan.
- Aomori-ken Nogyo Kisho Junpo. every 10 days.
ISSN 0003-6323
- Aomori Prefecture. Monthly Report of
Meteorology/Aomori-ken Kisho Geppo. m. ISSN
0029-7399

**Aomori Prefecture Agricultural Improvement**
**Association**
c/o Aomori Kencho Norin-bu Nomu-ka, 1
Nagashima, Aomori 030, Japan.
- Agriculture in Aomori/Aomori Nogyo. m. ISSN
0003-6331

**Aoyama-Gakuin University**
4-4-25 Shibuya, Shibuya-ku, Tokyo 150, Japan.
- Aoyama Journal of Social Sciences/Aoyama
Shakai Kagaku Kiyo.

**Arachnological Society of East Asia**
Biological Laboratory, Ohtemon-Gakuin University,
230 Ai, Ibaraki 567, Osaka, Japan.
- Acta Arachnologica/Kumogaku Zasshi. s-a. ISSN
0001-5202

**Archaeological Society of Japan**
c/o Tokyo National Museum, 13-9 Ueno Park,
Daito-ku, Tokyo 110, Japan.
- Archaeological Society of Japan. Journal/
Kokogaku Zasshi. q. ISSN 0003-8075

**Architectural Institute of Japan**
3-2-19 Ginza, Chuo-ku, Tokyo 104, Japan.
- Architectural Institute of Japan. Transactions/
Nihon Kenchiku Gakkai Ronbun Hokokushu. m.
ISSN 0003-8555

**Art Directors Club of Tokyo**
- Annual of Advertising Art in Japan/Nenkan Koku
Bijutsu. (pub. by Bijutsu Shuppan-sha)

**Asahi Evening News**
Box 555, Tokyo, Japan.
- Asahi Evening News International. 4 per yr. ISSN
0025-2816

**Asahi Glass Co., Ltd.**
1150 Matsubara, Hazawa-cho, Kanagawa-ku,
Yokohama 221, Japan.
- Asahi Glass Company. Research Laboratory.
Reports/Asahi Garasu Kenkyu Hokoku. s-a. ISSN
0004-4210

**Asahi Shimbun**
2-6-1 Yuraku-cho, Chiyoda-ku, Tokyo 100, Japan
(Orders for export to: Japan Publications Trading
Co., Ltd., Box 5030, Tokyo International, Tokyo,
Japan)
- Asahi Camera. m. ISSN 0044-9148
- Japan Quarterly. q. ISSN 0021-4590

**Asakumo Shimbunsha**
9 Shiba Sakaecho, Minato-ku, Tokyo 105, Japan.
- Journal of National Defense/Shin Boei Ronsho. 4
per yr. (Boei Gakkai)

**Asia Electronics United**
- A E U. (pub. by Dempa Publications Inc.)

**Asian Cultural Centre for Unesco**
No.6 Fukuro-machi, Shinjuku-ku, Tokyo 162, Japan.
- Asian Cultural Centre for Unesco. Organization
and Activities. a.
- Asian Cultural Centre for Unesco/Tokyo Book
Development Centre. Newsletter. q. (Co-sponsor:
Tokyo Book Development Centre)
- Asian Culture. 3-4 per yr.

**Asian Pacific Dental Student Association**
c/o Nihon University School of Dentistry, 1-8
Surugadai, Chiyoda-ku, Tokyo 101, Japan.
- A.P.D.S.A. Journal. irreg. ISSN 0571-2912

**Asian Parliamentarians' Union**
TBR Bldg., Room 807, 2-10-2 Nagata-cho, Chiyoda-
ku, Tokyo, Japan.
- Asian Parliamentarians' Union. Central
Secretariat. Report on Meeting of APU
Secretaries-General in Tokyo. a.

**Asian Productivity Organization**
Aoyama Dai-Ichi Mansions, 8-4-14 Akasaka,
Minato-ku, Tokyo 107, Japan.
- A P O Annual Report. a. ISSN 0066-846X
- Asian Productivity Organization. A P O News. m.
ISSN 0044-9229
- Asian Productivity Organization. Review of
Activities of National Productivity. irreg. ISSN
0571-3005

**Assistance Association for Okinawa, Ogasawa and**
**Northern Islands**
Gloria Bldg., 3-6-15 Kasumigaseki, Chiyoda-ku,
Tokyo, Japan.
- North and South/Minami to Kita. q. (magazine
format); 3 per m. (newspaper format) ISSN 0026-
4407

**Associacao Japonesa de Estudos Luso-Brasileiros**
Brazilian Center, 7 Kioicho, Chiyoda-ku, Tokyo
102, Japan.
- Coloquio de Estudos Luso Brasileiros. Anais. a.
ISSN 0069-598X

**Associated General Contractors of Japan Inc.**
2-5-1 Hatcho-bori, Chuo-ku, Tokyo 104, Japan.
- Zenken Journal/Zenken Janaru. m. ISSN 0044-
4006

**Association for Documentation in Economics**
- Quarterly Bibliography of Economics/Keizaigaku-
Bunken-Kiho. (pub. by Kobe University. Research
Institute for Economics and Business
Administration)

**Association for Economic Development**
3-3 Kozimati, Chiyoda-ku, Tokyo, Japan.
- Analyst. m. ISSN 0003-2662

**Association for Studies in Economic Behavior**
2-9 Hatagaya, Shibuya-ku, Tokyo, Japan.
- Journal of Economic Behavior. s-a. ISSN 0447-
922X

**Association for the Care of the Child**
c/o Hokkaido University School of Medicine, Kita-
14-jo, Nishi-5-chome, Kita-ku, Sapporo 060, Japan.
- Journal of Clinical Pediatrics/Rinsho Shoni Igaku.
bi-m. ISSN 0035-550X

**Association for the Study of Law and Politics**
see under Keio University

**Association of Economic Geographers**
c/o Graduate School, Meiji University, 1-1 Kanda
Surugadai, Chiyoda-ku, Tokyo, Japan.
- Association of Economic Geographers. Annals. s-
a. ISSN 0004-5683

**Association of International Law**
Faculty of Law, University of Tokyo, 7-3-1 Hongo,
Bunkyo-ku, Tokyo 113, Japan.
- Journal of International Law and Diplomacy/
Kokusaiho Gaiko Zasshi. bi-m. ISSN 0023-2866

**Association of Japanese Geographers**
c/o Japan Academic Societies Centre, 2-4-16 Yayoi,
Bunkyo-ku, Tokyo 113, Japan.
- Association of Japanese Geographers. Special
Publication. irreg., 1971, no. 2. ISSN 0066-958X
- Geographical Review of Japan/Chirigaku Hyoron.
m. ISSN 0016-7444

**Association of Law and Political Science**
see under **Tohoku University**

**Association of Mining Labor Accident Prevention**
5-35-1 Shiba, Minato-ku, Tokyo 108, Japan.
• Report of Coal Mine Safety/Tanko Hoan Joho. m.
ISSN 0039-9434

**Association of Political and Social Science**
2-17 Jinbocho, Kanda, Chiyoda-ku, Tokyo, Japan.
• Association of Political and Social Science.
Journal/Kokka Gakkai Zasshi. bi-m. ISSN 0023-
2793

**Association of the Research Institutes**
see under **Tohoku University**

**Association of the Research Institutes for
Tuberculosis of National Universities in Japan**
• Japanese Journal of Tuberculosis and Chest
Diseases/Nippon Kekkaku Kyobushikka Zasshi.
(pub. by University of Tokyo. Institute of Medical
Science)

**Astronomical Society of Japan**
c/o Tokyo Astronomical Observatory, 2-21-1
Osawa, Mitaka-shi, Tokyo 181, Japan.
• Astronomical Society of Japan. Publications/
Nihon Tenmon Gakkai Obun Kenkyu Hokoku. q.
ISSN 0004-6264

**Atomic Bomb Casualty Commission**
see **Radiation Effects Research Foundation**

**Atomic Energy Commission, Japan**
see **Japan. Japan Atomic Energy Commission**

**Atomic Energy Research Institute**
see **Japan Atomic Energy Research Institute**

**Atomic Energy Society of Japan**
c/o Japan Atomic Energy Research Institute, 1-1-13
Shinbashi, Minato-ku, Tokyo 105, Japan.
• Atomic Energy Society of Japan. Journal/Nihon
Genshiryoku Gakkai Shi. m. ISSN 0004-7120
• Journal of Nuclear Science and Technology/
Nihon Genshiryoku Gakkai Obun Ronbushi. m.
ISSN 0022-3131

**Balneological Society of Japan**
c/o Tokyo-toritsu Daigaku Rigakubu Kagaku
Kyoshitsu, 2-1 Fukazawa, Setagaya-ku, Tokyo 158,
Japan.
• Science of Hot Springs/Onsen Kagaku. 3-4 per yr.
ISSN 0030-2821

**Bank of Japan**
C. P. O. Box 203, Tokyo 100-91, Japan
• Balance of Payments Monthly/Kokusai Shushi
Tokei Geppo. m. ISSN 0549-317X (prep. by its
Foreign Department) (Order from: Japan
Publications Trading Co., Ltd., Box 5030, Tokyo
International, Tokyo, Japan; or 1255 Howard St.,
San Francisco, CA 94103)
• Balance of Payments of Japan. a. ISSN 0067-
298X (prep. by its Foreign Exchange Control
Department) (Available from: Credit Information
Company of Japan, Ltd., 1-2-8 Uchikanda,
Chiyoda-ku, Tokyo, Japan)
• Bank of Japan. Annual Report of the Policy
Board. a. ISSN 0067-3676 (prep. by its Foreign
Department)
• Bank of Japan. Business Report. s-a. ISSN 0067-
3684 (prep. by its Foreign Department)
• Bank of Japan. Economic Research Department. B
O J Special Paper. irreg. ISSN 0067-3692
• Manual of Foreign Exchange Control in Japan.
irreg.
• Manual of Foreign Investment in Japan. irreg.
(prep. by its Foreign Department)

**Bank of Japan. Statistics Department**
2-2-1 Hongok-cho, Nihonbashi, Chuo-ku, Toyko
103, Japan
• Bank of Japan. Economic Statistics Annual. a.
ISSN 0070-8666 (Order from: Japan Publications
Trading Co., Ltd., Box 5030, Tokyo International,
Tokyo, Japan; or 1255 Howard St., San Francisco,
CA 94103)
• Bank of Japan. Economic Statistics Monthly. m.
ISSN 0005-5247 (Order from: Japan Publications
Trading Co., Ltd., Box 5030, Tokyo International,
Tokyo, Japan; or 1255 Howard St., San Francisco,
CA 94103)

• Bank of Japan. Price Indexes Annual. a. (Order
from: Japan Publications Trading Co., Ltd., Box
5030, Tokyo International, Tokyo, Japan; or 1255
Howard St., San Francisco, CA 94103)
• Short-Term Economic Survey of Principal
Enterprises in Japan; records and forecasts. q.
ISSN 0037-4253

**Bank of Tokyo Ltd.**
2-1-1 Nihombachi Muromachi, Chuo-ku, Tokyo
103, Japan.
• Bank of Tokyo Semiannual Report. s-a. ISSN
0005-5360
• Bank of Tokyo Weekly Review. w. ISSN 0005-
5379

**Behaviormetric Society of Japan**
• Behaviormetrika. (pub. by Japan Publications
Trading Co., Ltd.)

**Rene de Berval, Ed. & Pub.**
2-17-40 Koishikawa, Bunkyo-ku, Tokyo, Japan.
• France-Asie/Asia; bilingual review of Asian
culture and problems. q. ISSN 0015-9492

**Better Farming Association**
c/o Mainichi Shinbunsha, Dojima, Kita-ku, Osaka
530, Japan.
• Agriculture and Better Farming/Nogyo Fumin. m.
ISSN 0029-0882
• Agriculture and Economy/Nogyo to Keizai. m.
ISSN 0029-0912

**Bijutsu-shi Gakkai**
see **Japan Art History Society**

**Bijutsu Shuppan-sha**
15 Ichigaya, Honmura-cho, Shinjuku-ku, Tokyo 162,
Japan.
• Annual of Advertising Art in Japan/Nenkan Koku
Bijutsu. a. ISSN 0548-1643 (Art Directors Club
of Tokyo)
• Design. bi-m. ISSN 0011-927X
• Museum. m. ISSN 0027-4003 (Tokyo National
Museum)

**Biogeographical Society of Japan**
• Biogeographical Society of Japan. Bulletin. (pub.
by Academic Press of Japan)

**Biophysical Society of Japan**
• Advances in Biophysics. (pub. by University of
Tokyo Press)

**Biseibutsubyo Kenkyusho**
see **Osaka University. Research Institute for
Microbial Diseases**

**Boei-cho Koku Igaku Jikkentai**
see **Japan Air Self Defense Force. Aeromedical
Laboratory**

**Boei Daigakko**
see **National Defense Academy**

**Boei Gakkai**
• Journal of National Defense/Shin Boei Ronsho.
(pub. by Asakumo Shimbunsha)

**Bosai Kenkyusho**
see **Kyoto University. Disaster Prevention
Research Institute**

**Botanical Society of Japan**
c/o Oriental Library, 2-28-21 Honkomagome,
Bunkyo-ku, Tokyo 113, Japan.
• Botanical Magazine/Shokubutsugaku Zasshi. q.
ISSN 0006-808X

**Brazilian Center**
see under **Sophia University**

**Brewing Science Research Institute**
1-4-1 Mita, Meguro-ku, Tokyo 153, Japan.
• Bulletin of Brewing Science. a. ISSN 0521-7237

**Bridgestone Tire Co.**
c/o Kansen Bldg., 4-12-4 Hatcho Bori, Chuo-ku,
Tokyo 104, Japan.
• Marine and Industry News. bi-m.

**Building Research Institute**
see **Japan. Building Research Institute**

**Bunrin-do Co. Ltd.**
1-55 Kanda Jinbo-cho, Chiyoda-ku, Tokyo 101,
Japan.
• Aero-Fan/Koku-Fan. m.

**Business Intercommunication, Inc.**
Murakami Bldg., 3-2-1 Kita-Aoyama, Minato-ku,
Tokyo 107, Japan.
• White Paper on Japanese Economy. a.

**Bussei Kenkyusho**
see **University of Tokyo. Institute for Solid State
Physics**

**C B A International**
Box 12, Naka, Yokohama 232, Japan.
• U F O News. q. (International U F O Observer
Corps.)

**C Q Publishing Co.**
1-14-2 Sugamo, Toshima, Tokyo 170, Japan.
• Audio & Electronics/Toranjisuta Gijutsu. m. ISSN
0040-9413
• C Q Ham Radio. m. ISSN 0007-8964
• Ham Journal. q.
• Interface. bi-m.

**CamerArt, Inc.**
C.P.O. Box 620, Tokyo, Japan.
• CamerArt/Kamera Ato; all the news about
cameras and photography. m. ISSN 0008-2082
• CamerArt Photo Trade Directory. a. ISSN 0008-
2082

**Cancer Institute**
1-37-1 Kami-Ikebukuro, Toshima-ku, Tokyo 170,
Japan.
• Cancer Institute Scientific Report. a.

**Cancer Research Institute**
see under **Sapporo Medical College**

**Casting Research Laboratory**
see under **Waseda University**

**Cement Association of Japan**
c/o Hattori Bldg., 1-1 Kyobashi, Chuo-ku, Tokyo
104, Japan.
• Cement Association of Japan. Review of the
General Meeting. a.
• Cement Association of Japan. Review of the
General Meeting. Technical Session. a.

**Center for Adult Diseases, Osaka**
1-3-3 Nakamichi, Higashinari-ku, Osaka 537, Japan.
• Center for Adult Diseases, Osaka. Annual Report.
a. ISSN 0078-6632

**Center for Japanese Social & Political Studies**
659-13 Koadachi, Komae-Shi, Tokyo 182, Japan.
• Japan Interpreter. q. ISSN 0021-4450 (Co-
sponsor: Japan Center for International Exchange)

**Central Union of Agricultural Co-operatives**
1-8-3 Chiyoda-ku, Ohtemachi, Tokyo, Japan.
• Japan Agricultural Coop News. q. ISSN 0447-
5240

**Centre for East Asian Cultural Studies**
Toyo Bunko (Oriental Library), 2-28-21
Honkomagome, Bunkyo-ku, Tokyo 113, Japan.
• East Asian Cultural Studies. q. ISSN 0012-8414

**Ceramic Society of Japan**
2-22-17 Hyakunin-cho, Shinjuku-ku, Tokyo 160,
Japan.
• Ceramic Society of Japan. Journal/Yogyo Kyokai
Shi. m. ISSN 0009-0255
• Ceramics Japan/Seramikkusu. m. ISSN 0009-
031X

**Chemical Daily Co., Ltd.**
3-19-16 Shibaura, Minato-ku, Tokyo 108, Japan.
• Agricultural Chemicals Monthly/Kongetsu no
Noyaku. m. ISSN 0023-334X
• Japan Chemical Annual. a. ISSN 0075-319X
• Japan Chemical Directory. a. ISSN 0075-3203
• Japan Chemical Review. a. ISSN 0448-858X
• Japan Chemical Week. w. ISSN 0047-1755
• P E T. (Plant Engineering & Technology) a.

**Chemical Economy Research Institute**
1-13-7 Uchikanda, Chiyoda-ku, Tokyo 101, Japan.
• Chemical Economy and Engineering Review. m.
ISSN 0009-2436

**Chemical Society of Japan**
5 1-chome Kanda-Surugadai, Chiyoda-ku, Tokyo
101, Japan.
• Chemical Society of Japan. Bulletin. m. ISSN
0009-2673

- Chemical Society of Japan. Chemistry and Industrial Chemistry. Journal/Nippon Kagaku Keishi. m.
- Chemistry and Chemical Industry/Kagaku to Kogyo. m. ISSN 0022-7684
- Chemistry Letters. m.

**Chest Disease Research Institute**
*see under* **Kyoto University**

**Chiba Daigaku**
*see* **Chiba University**

**Chiba Igakkai**
*see* **Chiba Medical Society**

**Chiba Medical Society**
c/o Chiba University, Faculty of Medicine, 1-8-1 Inohama, Chiba-shi 280, Japan.
- Chiba Medical Society. Journal/Chiba Igakkai Zasshi. bi-m. ISSN 0009-3459

**Chiba University. Faculty of Engineering**
1-33 Yayoicho, Chiba 280, Japan.
- Chiba University. Faculty of Engineering. Journal/ Chiba Daigaku Kogakubu Kenkyu Hokoku. s-a.

**Chiba University. Faculty of Horticulture**
648 Tojo, Matsudo-shi, Chiba 271, Japan.
- Chiba University. Faculty of Horticulture. Technical Bulletin/Chiba Daigaku Engeigakubu Gakujutsu Hokoku. a. ISSN 0069-3227
- Chiba University. Faculty of Horticulture. Transactions/Chiba Daigaku Engeigakubu Tokubetsu Hokoku. a. ISSN 0069-3219

**Chiba University. Faculty of Humanities and Social Sciences**
1-33 Yayoicho, Chiba 280, Japan.
- Journal of Cultural Sciences/Bunka Kagaku Kiyo. a. ISSN 0521-7903

**Chigaku Kyoshitsu**
*see* **Kyoto University. Institute of Earth Science**

**Chikusan Shikenjo**
*see* **Japan. National Institute of Animal Industry**

**Chikyu Butsurigaku Kyoshitsu**
*see* **Kyoto University. Geophysical Institute**

**China Rebuilding Federation**
- Oriental Tide. (pub. by Oriental Tide Society)

**Chizu Kyokai**
*see* **Map Society**

**Choshi Local Meteorological Observatory**
31 Minami-cho, Chosi-shi 288, Chiba, Japan
- Monthly Report of Meteorology, Chiba Prefecture/Chiba-ken Kisho Geppo. m. ISSN 0009-3467 (Order from: Japan Weather Association, 3-21 Kanda Nishiki-cho, Chiyoda-ku, Tokyo, Japan)

**Christian Conference of Asia**
- Church Labor Letter. (pub. by Doshisha University. School of Theology)

**Chubu Institute of Technology**
1200-B Matsumoto-cho, Kasugai 487, Japan.
- Chubu Institute of Technology. Memoirs/Chubu Kogyo Daigaku. Kiyo. 1-2 per yr. ISSN 0009-6202

**Chugoku Electric Power Co., Inc.**
4-4-32 Osu, Hiroshima 730, Japan.
- Chugoku Electric Power Co. Technical Laboratory Report/Chugoku Denryoku K.K. Gikken Jiho. m. ISSN 0009-6237

**Chuo Daigaku Keizai Shogakkai**
*see* **Chuo University. Economic and Commercial Society**

**Chuo University. Economic and Commercial Society**
3 Kanda Surugadai, Chiyoda-ku, Tokyo, Japan.
- Economic Journal/Keizaigaku Ronsan. bi-m. ISSN 0453-4778

**Chuo University. Faculty of Law**
3-9 Kanda-Surugadai, Chiyoda-ku, Tokyo, Japan.
- Chuo Law Review/Hogaku Shimpo. m. ISSN 0009-6296

**Chuo University. Faculty of Science and Engineering**
1-13-27 Kasuga, Bunkyo-ku, Tokyo 112, Japan.
- Chuo University. Faculty of Science and Engineering. Bulletin/Chuo Daigaku Rikogakubu Kiyo. a. ISSN 0578-2228

**Chuo University. Institute of Comparative Law in Japan**
3-9 Kanda-Surugadai, Chiyoda-ku, Tokyo, Japan.
- Comparative Law Review/Hikakuho Zasshi. s-a. ISSN 0010-4116

**Chusho Kigyo Joho Senta**
*see* **Small Business Information Centre**

**Chuto Chosakai**
*see* **Middle East Institute of Japan**

**City Planning Association of Japan**
2-16-14 Hirakawa-cho, Chiyoda-ku, Tokyo 102, Japan.
- New Cities/Shin Toshi. m. ISSN 0037-3761

**Clay Science Society of Japan**
c/o Department of Mineral Industry, School of Science and Engineering, Waseda University, 4-170 Nishi Okubo, Shinjuku-ku, Tokyo 160, Japan.
- Clay Science. s-a. ISSN 0009-8574

**Clinical Electron Microscopy Society of Japan**
- Journal of Clinical Electron Microscopy/Nippon Rinsho Denshi Kenbikyo Gakkaishi. (pub. by Kissei Pharmaceutical Co., Ltd.)

**College of Dairy Agriculture**
82 Nishinopporo, Ebetsu-Shi 069-02, Hokkaido, Japan.
- College of Dairy Agriculture, Hokkaido. Journal/ Rakuno Gakuen Daigaku Kiyo. a. ISSN 0069-570X

**Collegium Ad Studium Historiae Medicae**
- Studies on History of Medicine/Igakushi Kenkyu. (pub. by Osaka University Medical School. Department of Hygiene)

**Committee of the Kyoto University Africa Primatological Expedition**
*see under* **Kyoto University**

**Communication Industries Association of Japan**
Sankei Kaikan Bldg., 1-7-2 Ote-machi, Chiyoda-ku, Tokyo 100, Japan.
- Communication Industries/Tsushin Kogyo. m. ISSN 0041-381X

**Communist Party of Japan**
Sendagaya 4-26-7, Shibuya-ku, Tokyo, Japan.
- Communist Party of Japan. Central Committee. Bulletin: Information for Abroad. irreg. ISSN 0007-4683

**Computer Age Co., Ltd.**
Kasumigaseki Bldg., 30th Floor, 3-2-5 Kasumigaseki, Chiyoda-ku, Tokyo 100, Japan.
- Computopia/Gekkan Konpyutopia. m. ISSN 0010-4906

**Congenital Anomalies Research Association of Japan**
Faculty of Medicine, Kyoto University, Kyoto 606, Japan.
- Congenital Anomalies/Senten Ijo. q. ISSN 0037-2285

**Corona Publishing Co., Ltd.**
4-46-10 Sengoku, Bunkyo-ku, Tokyo 112, Japan.
- Japanese Journal of Medical Electronics and Biological Engineering/Iyo Denshi to Seito Kogaku (Nihon M-E Gakkai Zasshi) bi-m. ISSN 0021-3675 (Japan Society of Medical Electronics and Biological Engineering)

**Cosmic-Ray Research Laboratory**
*see under* **Nagoya University**

**Criminal Law Society of Japan**
c/o Faculty of Law, University of Tokyo, Motofuji-cho, Bunkyo-ku, Tokyo, Japan.
- Journal of Criminal Law/Keiho Zasshi. q. ISSN 0022-0191

**Crop Science Society of Japan**
c/o Faculty of Agriculture, University of Tokyo, 7-3-1 Hongo, Bunkyo-ku, Tokyo 113, Japan.
- Crop Science Society of Japan. Proceedings/ Nippon Sakumotsu Gakkai Kiji. q. ISSN 0011-1848

**Daido Gakkan Shuppan-bu**
Kyushu University Medical School, 3576 Hako Zaki, Higashi-ku, Fukuoka 812, Japan.
- Japanese Journal of Clinical and Experimental Medicine/Rinsho to Kenkyu. m. ISSN 0021-4965

**Daiichi Kangyo Bank Ltd.**
1-6-2 Marunouchi, Chiyoda-ku, Tokyo 100, Japan.
- D K B Economic Report. m.

**Daiichi Kogyo Seiyaku Co. Ltd.**
55 Higashi Kubo-cho, Nishi-7-jo, Shimogyo-ku, Kyota 600, Japan.
- Daiichi Kogyo Seiyaku Review/Daiich Kogyo Seiyaku Shaho. bi-m. ISSN 0011-5355

**Daiichi Seiyaku Co., Ltd.**
3-4-10 Nihonbashi, Chuo-ku, Tokyo 103, Japan.
- Medical Pharmacy. m. ISSN 0025-7427

**Daiichi Shuppan K. K.**
1-39 Kanda Jinbo-cho, Chiyoda-ku, Tokyo 101, Japan.
- Japanese Journal of Nutrition/Eiyogaku Zasshi. bi-m. ISSN 0021-5147 (National Nutrition Society)

**Daiichi Shuppan Senta**
- Illustration in Japan. (pub. by Kodansha International Ltd)

**Daily Automotive News Co., Ltd.**
2-1-25 Kaigan, Minato-ku, Tokyo 105, Japan.
- Japan Automotive News. m. ISSN 0021-4329

**Dainichi-Nippon Cables Ltd.**
Umeda Bldg, 7-3 Umeda, Kita-ku, Osaka 530, Japan.
- Dainichi-Nippon Cables Review. 3 per yr. ISSN 0011-5541

**Dainihon Suisankai**
*see* **Japan Fisheries Association**

**Dempa Publications Inc.**
1-11-15 Higashi Gotanda, Shinagawa-ku, Tokyo 141, Japan
(U.S. Address: 380 Madison Ave., New York, NY 10017)
- A E U. s-a. (Asia Electronics United)
- Audiovideo International. m.
- E B G. (Electronics Buyers Guide) a.
- J E E. (Japan Electronic Engineering) m. ISSN 0021-3608
- J E I. (Japan Electronic Industry) m. ISSN 0021-3616
- O E P. (Office Equipment and Products) q.

**Denki Kagaku Kyokai**
*see* **Electrochemical Society of Japan**

**Denki Seiko Kenkyukai**
*see* **Electric Furnace Steel Research Association**

**Denki Tsushin Daigaku**
*see* **University of Electro-Communications**

**Denki Tsushin Kyokai**
*see* **Telecommunications Association**

**Denkisha Kenkyukai**
*see* **Institute of Electric Rolling Stock**

**Denpa Koho Kenkyukai**
*see* **Japanese Committee for Radio Aids to Navigation**

**Denshi Shashin Gakkai**
*see* **Society of Electro Photography of Japan**

**Denshi Tsushin Gakkai**
*see* **Institute of Electronics and Communication Engineers of Japan**

**Dentsu Advertising Ltd.**
1-11-10 Tsukiji, Chuo-ku, Tokyo 104, Japan.
- Dentsu's Japan Marketing/Advertising. s-a.

**Diamond Lead Co.**
4-2 Kasumigaseki 1-chome, Chiyoda-ku, Tokyo 100, Japan.
- Diamond's Who's Who in Japanese Business. irreg.

**Disaster Prevention Research Institute**
*see under* **Kyoto University**

**Doboku Gakkai**
*see* **Japan Society of Civil Engineers**

**Dojindo Laboratories**
2861 Murazoe Kengunmachi, Kumamoto 862,
Japan.
● Dojin News/Dojin Nuusu. q.

**Dojo Hiryo Gakkai**
*see* **Japanese Society of Soil and Manure**

**Doshisha Daigaku**
*see* **Doshisha University**

**Doshisha University. Economic Society**
Karasuma Imadegawa, Kamikyo-ku, Kyoto 602,
Japan.
● Doshisha University Economic Review/Doshisha
Daigaku Keizaigaku Ronso. bi-m.

**Doshisha University. English Literary Society**
Karasuma Imadegawa, Kamikyo-ku, Kyoto 602,
Japan.
● Doshisha Literature; journal of English literature
and philology. s-a. ISSN 0046-063X

**Doshisha University. Gaikoku Bungakukai**
Karasuma Imadegawa, Kamikyo-ku, Kyoto 602,
Japan.
● Doshisha Studies in Foreign Literature. irreg.

**Doshisha University. School of Theology**
Karasuma Imadegawa, Kamikyo-ku, Kyoto 602,
Japan.
● Church Labor Letter. 3 per yr. ISSN 0009-6415
(Christian Conference of Asia)

**Doshisha University. Science and Engineering
Research Institute**
Karasuma Imadegawa, Kamikyo-ku, Kyoto 606,
Japan.
● Doshisha University. Science and Engineering
Review/Doshisha Daigaku Rikogaku Kenkyu
Hokoku. q. ISSN 0036-8172

**Earthquake Research Institute**
*see under* **University of Tokyo**

**East Asia Publishing Co. Ltd.**
3-60-2 Sendagaya, Shibuya-ku, Tokyo, Japan.
● Importer. m. ISSN 0019-2988

**East Asia Travel Association**
c/o Japan National Tourist Organization, 2-13
Yurakucho, Tokyo, Japan.
● East Asia Travel Association. Proceedings of the
General Meeting. irreg. ISSN 0424-0944

**East Publications, Inc.**
10-5 Roppongi 3, Minato-ku, Tokyo 106, Japan.
● East. 6 per yr. ISSN 0012-8295
● Traditions. 4 per yr.

**Eastern Buddhist Society**
Otani University, 22 Kamifusa-cho Koyama, Kita-
ku, Kyoto, Japan
(U.S. Subscr. Address: Scholars Press, Member
Services Secretary, University of Montana,
Missoula, MT 59801)
● Eastern Buddhist. s-a. ISSN 0012-8708

**Ecological Society of Japan**
c/o Dept. of Biology, School of Education, Waseda
University, Nishiwaseda 1, Shinjuku-ku, Tokyo 160,
Japan.
● Japanese Journal of Ecology/Nippon Seitai
Gakkaishi. q. ISSN 0021-5007

**Eiken Chemical Co. Ltd.**
1-33-8 Hongo, Bunkyo-ku, Tokyo 113, Japan.
● Modern Media/Modan Media. m. ISSN 0026-
8054

**Electric Furnace Steel Research Association**
2-30 Daido-cho, Minami-ku, Nagoya 457, Japan.
● Electric Furnace Steel/Denki Seiko. q. ISSN
0011-8389

**Electrochemical Society of Japan**
1-12-1 Yurakucho, Chiyoda-ku, Tokyo 100, Japan.
● Electrochemistry and Industrial Physical
Chemistry/Denki Kagaku Oyobi Kogyo Butsuri
Kagaku. m.

**Electronics Association of Japan**
1 Toden Kyukan 1-chome, Shinbashi, Minato-ku,
Tokyo 105, Japan.
● Electronics in Japan. a. ISSN 0070-9913

**Embassy of the United States in Japan**
1-10-5 Akasaka, Minato-ku, Tokyo, Japan.
● Daily Summary of the Japanese Press. d.
● Economic Trends: Japan. s-a.

**Engei Gakkai**
*see* **Japanese Society for Horticultural Science**

**Engineering Research Institute**
*see under* **Kyoto University**

**English Literary Society of Japan**
18 Nakamachi, Shinjukuku, Tokyo 162, Japan.
● Studies in English Literature/Eibungaku Kenkyu.
s-a. ISSN 0039-3649

**Entomological Society of Japan**
c/o National Institute of Health, 2-10-35 Kamiosaki,
Shinagawa-ku, Tokyo, Japan.
● Entomology/Konchu. q. ISSN 0013-8770

**Entomological Society of Shinshu**
c/o Laboratory of Biology, Faculty of Textile
Science & Technology, Shinshu University, Ueda,
Nagano 386, Japan.
● New Entomologist/Nyu Entomorojisuto. q. ISSN
0028-4955

**Environmental Sanitation Research Association**
3-3 Kanda Jinbo-cho, Chiyoda-ku, Tokyo 101,
Japan.
● Environmental Sanitation/Kankyo Eisei. m. ISSN
0022-8389

**Esso Standard Oil Co.**
Public Affairs Dept., TBS Bldg., 5-3-3 Akasaka,
Minatoku, Tokyo 107, Japan.
● Energy. 3 per yr. ISSN 0013-7464

**Europe and Asia Association**
No. 11 Shiba Nishikubo-Sakuragawacho, Minatoku,
Tokyo 105, Tokyo, Japan.
● Japan Association on Communist States in Europe
and Asia. Review. q. ISSN 0047-1747

**Export-Import Bank of Japan**
1-9-1 Otemachi, Chiyoda-ku, Tokyo, Japan.
● Export-Import Bank of Japan. Report. a. ISSN
0071-3503

**Far East Reporters, Inc.**
1-4-28 Moto Azabu, Minato-ku, Tokyo, Japan.
● Far East Traveler. 10 per yr.

**Farm Machinery Industrial Research Corp.**
● A M A. (pub. by Shin-Norinsha Co., Ltd.)
● Product File for Agricultural Machinery and
Related Material. (pub. by Shin-Norinsha Co.,
Ltd.)

**Federation of Japan Confectionary Associations**
1-19-26 Ebisu, Shibuya-ku, Tokyo 150, Japan.
● Gateaux/Gatou. m.

**Fellowship of Christian Missionaries**
● Japan Christian Quarterly. (pub. by Japan
Publications Trading Co.Ltd.)

**Fermentation Research Institute**
*see* **Japan. Fermentation Research Institute**

**First Atomic Power Industry Group**
Nissho-Iwai Bldg., 6th Floor, 2-4-5 Akasaka,
Minato-ku, Tokyo, Japan.
● F A P I G. q. ISSN 0014-5645

**Food Hygienic Society of Japan**
● Food Hygienic Society of Japan. Journal/
Shokuhin Eiseigaku Zasshi. (pub. by National
Institute of Hygienic Sciences)

**Food Science Co., Ltd.**
Kamata Bldg., 35 Tomita-cho, Kita-ku, Osaka 530,
Japan.
● Food Science/Shokuhin to Kagaku. m. ISSN
0037-4105

**Foreign Affairs Association of Japan**
Togyo Kaikan, 1-7 Yuraku-cho, Chiyoda-ku, Tokyo,
Japan
(Overseas Distributor: Japan Publications Trading
Co., Ltd., Box 5030, Tokyo International, Tokyo
100-31, Japan; or 1255 Howard St., San Francisco,
CA 94103)
● Contemporary Japan. q.

**Foundation of Clinical Oncology**
c/o National Cancer Center, 5-1-1 Tsukiji, Chuo-ku,
Tokyo 104, Japan.
● Japanese Journal of Clinical Oncology. s-a.

**Free Asia Association**
Rm. 323, Yaesu Bldg., 2-6 Marunouchi, Chiyoda-ku,
Tokyo, Japan.
● Free World/Jiyu Sekai; liberty & responsibility. m.
ISSN 0021-6984

**Freshwater Fisheries Research Laboratory**
*see* **Japan. Freshwater Fisheries Research
Laboratory**

**Fuji Bank Ltd.**
1-5-5 Otemachi, Chiyoda-ku, Tokyo, Japan.
● Fuji Bank Bulletin. m. ISSN 0016-2493 (prep. by
its Research Division)

**Fuji Electric Manufacturing Co., Ltd.**
Shin-Yuraku Bldg., 1-11 Yuraku-cho, Chiyoda-ku,
Tokyo 100, Japan.
● Fuji Electric Review. bi-m. ISSN 0429-8284

**Fuji Marketing Research Co., Ltd.**
3-F Kohri Bldg., 6-11-17 Roppongi, Minato-ku,
Tokyo 106, Japan.
● Technocrat; a monthly survey on Japanese
technology and industry. m. ISSN 0040-1609

**Fujikura Cable Works Co., Ltd.**
3-2-5 Kasumigaseki, Chiyoda-ku, Tokyo 100, Japan.
● Fujikura Technical Review. a.

**Fujisawa Pharmaceutical Co. Ltd.**
● Fountain/Izumi. (pub. by Izumi and Co., Ltd.)

**Fujitsu Limited**
1015 Kamikodanaka, Nakahara-ku, Kawasaki 211,
Kanagawa-ken, Japan.
● Fujitsu. bi-m. ISSN 0016-2515
● Fujitsu Scientific & Technical Journal. q. ISSN
0016-2523 (Co-sponsor: Fujitsu Laboratories Ltd.)

**Fukui Daigaku**
*see* **Fukui University**

**Fukui University. Faculty of Education**
3-9-1 Bunkyo, Fukui-shi 910, Japan.
● Fukui University. Faculty of Education. Memoirs.
Series 2: Natural Science. irreg. ISSN 0071-9781
● Fukui University. Faculty of Education. Memoirs.
Series 5: Applied Science and Agricultural
Science. a.
● Fukui University. Faculty of Education. Memoirs.
Series 5: Applied Science and Home Economics.
a.
● Fukui University. Faculty of Education. Memoirs.
Series 5: Applied Science and Technology. a.
● Fukui University. Faculty of Education. Memoirs.
Series 6: Physical Education. a.

**Fukuoka Daigaku**
*see* **Fukuoka University**

**Fukuoka District Meteorological Observatory**
1-2-36 Ohori, Chuo-ku, Fukuoka 810, Japan.
● Fukuoka District Meteorological Observatory.
Technical Times/Fukuoka Kanku Kishodai
Gijutsu Tsushin. m. ISSN 0016-2566
● Fukuoka District Meteorological Observatory.
Unusual Meteorological Report/Fukuoka Kanku
Kishodai Ijo Kisho Hokoku. q. ISSN 0016-2558
● Fukuoka Prefecture. Monthly Report of
Meteorology/Fukuoka-ken Kisho Geppo. m. ISSN
0016-2574

**Fukuoka Entomological Society**
c/o Kyushu University, Faculty of Agriculture,
Entomological Laboratory, Fukuoka 812, Japan.
● Insects/Mushi. irreg.; approx. 1 vol. per year.
ISSN 0077-2356

**Fukuoka Kanku Kishodai**
*see* **Fukuoka District Meteorological Observatory**

**Fukuoka Medical Society**
Medical Library, Faculty of Medicine, Kyushu
University, Maidashi 3-1, Fukuoka 812, Japan.
● Fukuoka Acta Medica/Fukuoka Igaku Zasshi. m.
ISSN 0016-254X

**Fukuoka University. Faculty of Literature**
11 Nanakuma, Fukuoka City, Japan.
● Studies in Philosophy. irreg. ISSN 0081-8380

**Fukushima Medical Society**
Fukushima Medical College Library, 5-75
Sugitsuma-cho, Fukushima 960, Japan.
- Fukushima Journal of Medical Science. q. ISSN
0016-2590
- Fukushima Medical Journal/Fukushima Igaku
Zasshi. bi-m. ISSN 0016-2582

**Fumin Kyokai Shuppan-bu**
see Better Farming Association

**G.I. Movement-Yokosuka**
Box 26, Yokosuka, Japan.
- Yokosuka David. m.

**Gaimusho Joho Bunkakyoku**
Tokyo, Japan.
- Kokusai Mondai Shiryo. m.

**Gakki Shohosha**
c/o Gakki-Kaikan Bldg., 2-18-21 Soto Kanda,
Chiyoda-ku, Tokyo 101, Japan.
- Musical Instruments News/Gakki Shoho. m. ISSN
0016-3945

**Gakushuin Daigaku**
see Gakushuin University

**Gakushuin University. Department of Economics**
1-5-1 Mejiro, Toshima-ku, Tokyo, Japan.
- Gakushuin Economic Papers/Gakushuin Daigaku
Keizai Ronshu. 3-4 per yr. ISSN 0016-3953

**Gan Kenkyusho**
see Sapporo Medical College. Cancer Research
Institute

**Geirui Kenkyusho**
see Whales Research Institute

**Gekkan Gasorin Sutandosha**
3-2-3 Shinbashi, Minato-ku, Tokyo 105, Japan.
- Monthly Gasoline Stand/Gekkan Gasorin
Sutando. ISSN 0016-5069

**Genbaku Hoshano Kenkyusho**
see Hiroshima University. Research Institute for
Nuclear Medicine and Biology

**Genbaku Shogai Chosa Iinkai**
see Radiation Effects Research Foundation

**Gendaisha Publishing Co. Ltd.**
601 Mezon Sankou Bldg., 537 Waseda Tsurumaki-
cho, Shinjukuku, Tokyo 162, Japan.
- Sogo Kango; comprehensive nursing quarterly. q.
ISSN 0038-0660

**Genetics Society of Japan**
c/o National Institute of Genetics, 1111 Yata,
Mishima 411, Japan.
- Japanese Journal of Genetics/Idengaku Zasshi. bi-
m. ISSN 0021-504X

**Genkenku Shisetsu**
see Osaka University. Institute for Cancer
Research

**Genshi Enerugi Kenkyusho**
see Kyoto University. Institute of Atomic Energy

**Genshikaku Kenkyusho**
see University of Tokyo. Institute for Nuclear
Study

**Genshiryoku Anzen Kenkyu Kyokai**
see Nuclear Safety Research Association

**Genshiryoku Iinkai**
see Japan. Japan Atomic Energy Commission

**Genyosha Publications, Inc.**
3-18-2 Shibuya, Shibuya-ku, Tokyo 150, Japan.
- A M J Newsletter. m.
- Japan Camera Trade News; monthly information
on cameras, optical instruments and accessories.
m. ISSN 0021-4345
- M E J. (Medical Equipment Journal of Japan);
monthly information on medical, surgical,
scientific and dental instruments and drugs. m.
ISSN 0025-8830

**Geochemical Society of Japan**
c/o Business Center for Academic Societies Japan,
2-4-16 Yayoi, Bunkyo-ku, Tokyo 113, Japan.
- Geochemical Journal/Nihon Chikyu Kagakkaishi.
q. ISSN 0016-7002

**Geodetic Society of Japan**
c/o Geographical Survey Institute, 3-24-13
Higashiyama, Meguro-ku, Tokyo 153, Japan.
- Geodetic Society of Japan. Journal/Sokuchi
Gakkaishi. q. ISSN 0038-0830

**Geographical Survey Institute**
see Japan. Geographical Survey Institute

**Geological Society of Japan**
Faculty of Science, University of Tokyo, 7-3-1
Hongo, Bunkyo-ku, Tokyo 113, Japan.
- Geological Society of Japan. Journal/
Chishitsugaku Zasshi. m. ISSN 0016-7630

**Geological Survey of Japan**
see Japan. Geological Survey of Japan

**Geophysical Institute**
see under Kyoto University

**Gifu Daigaku**
see Gifu University

**Gifu University. Faculty of Agriculture**
3-1 Naka Monzen-cho, Kagamihara, Gifu 504,
Japan.
- Gifu University. Faculty of Agriculture. Research
Bulletin/Gifu Daigaku Nogakiu Kenkyu
Hokoku. irreg. 1969, no. 28. ISSN 0072-4513

**Gifu University. School of Medicine**
40 Tsukasa-machi, Gifu 500, Japan.
- Gifu University. School of Medicine. Archives/
Gifu Daigaku Igakubu Kiyo. bi-m. ISSN 0072-
4521

**Government Forest Experiment Station**
see Japan. Government Forest Experiment Station

**Government Industrial Development Laboratory,
Hokkaido**
see Japan. Government Industrial Development
Laboratory, Hokkaido

**Government Industrial Research Institute, Kyushu**
see Japan. Government Industrial Research
Institute, Kyushu

**Government Publications Service Center**
1-2-1 Kasumigaseki, Chiyoda-ku, Tokyo 100, Japan.
- Japan. Ministry of Agriculture and Forestry.
Annual Report/Norin-sho Nenpo. a. ISSN 0446-
5458

**Group of Japanese Pedologists**
c/o National Institute of Agricultural Sciences, 2-1-
7 Nishigahara, Kita-ku, Tokyo 114, Japan.
- Pedologist/Pedorojisuto. s-a. ISSN 0031-4064

**Gumma Daigaku**
see Gumma University

**Gumma University. Faculty of Education**
Gumma University Library, 1375 Aramaki-cho,
Maebashi, Gumma 371, Japan.
- Gumma University. Faculty of Education. Annual
Report: Art and Technology Series. a. ISSN 0072-
9051
- Gumma University. Faculty of Education. Science
Reports. ISSN 0017-5668

**Gumma University. Institute of Endocrinology**
39-15 Showa-machi, Maebashi, Gumma 371, Japan.
- Gumma Symposia on Endocrinology. a. ISSN
0533-6724

**Gumma University. School of Medicine**
39-22 Showa-machi, Maebashi, Gumma 371, Japan.
- Gumma Reports on Medical Sciences/Gumma
Repoto. s-a.

**Gunma University**
see Gumma University

**Gurafikkusha**
Box 102, 1-9-12 Kudan Kita, Chiyoda-ku, Tokyo,
Japan
(Overseas Distributor: Orion Books, Export Dept.,
1-58 Kanda Jimbocho, Chiyoda-ku, Tokyo 101,
Japan)
- Japan Typography Annual/Nihon Taipogurafi
Nenkan. a. (Japan Typography Association)

**Hakko Kenkyusho**
see Institute for Fermentation

**Hakodate Technical College**
226 Tokura-cho, 2 Hakodate 042, Japan.
- Hakodate Technical College. Research Reports/
Hakodate Kogyo Koto Senmon Gakko Kiyo. a.

**Handicapped Persons Association of Japan National
Railways**
5-1 Koji-machi, Chiyoda-ku, Tokyo 102, Japan.
- Rehabilitation/Rihabiriteshon. 10 per yr. ISSN
0035-5305

**Hattori Botanical Laboratory**
Obi, Nichinan-shi, Miyazaki-ken 889-25, Japan.
- Hattori Botanical Laboratory. Journal/Hattori
Shokubutsu Kenkyusho Hokoku; devoted to
byrology and lichenology. irreg.; approx. 1 per yr.
ISSN 0073-0912
- Miscellanea Bryologica et Lichenologica/Sentai
Chii Zeppo. 3 per yr. ISSN 0037-2277

**Health Science Research Association**
- Health Care/Hoken No Kagaku. (pub. by Kyorin
Shoin)

**Heavy & Chemical Industries News Agency**
Daiichi-Fuji Bldg., 15, 2-chome, Kanda-Jimbocho,
Chiyoda-ku, Tokyo 101, Japan.
- Foreign Investment News. m. ISSN 0046-4554
- Japan Trade and Industry News. 2 per wk.

**Heibonsha Ltd.**
4 Yombancho, Chiyoda-ku, Tokyo 102, Japan.
- Sun, Monthly Deluxe. m.

**Hekisuto Japan K. K.**
see Hoechst Japan, Ltd.

**High Polymer Publishing Association**
Chiekoin-Sagaru, Marutamachi, Kamikyoku, Kyoto
602, Japan.
- Adhesion and Adhesives/Setchaku. m. ISSN
0037-0495
- Polymer Application/Kobunshi Kako. m. ISSN
0023-2564

**Hikosan Biological Laboratory**
Kyushu University, Department of Agriculture,
Eihikosan, Soeda-cho, Tagawa-gun, Fukuoka 824-07,
Japan.
- Esakia; occasional papers of the Hikosan
Biological Laboratory in entomology. irreg. ISSN
0071-1268

**Hirosaki Daigaku**
see Hirosaki University

**Hirosaki University. Faculty of Agriculture**
3 Bunkyo-cho, Hirosaki 036, Japan.
- Hirosaki University. Faculty of Agriculture.
Bulletin/Hirosaki Daigaku Nogakubu Gakujutsu
Hokoku. a. ISSN 0073-229X

**Hirosaki University. Faculty of Science**
3 Bunkyo-cho, Hirosaki 036, Japan.
- Hirosaki University. Faculty of Science. Science
Reports. s-a. ISSN 0367-6439

**Hiroshima Botanical Club**
- Hikobia. (pub. by Hiroshima University. Botanical
Institute)

**Hiroshima Daigaku**
see Hiroshima University

**Hiroshima Daigaku Genbaku Hoshano Kenkyusho**
see Hiroshima University. Research Institute for
Nuclear Medicine and Biology

**Hiroshima Medical Association**
1-1-1 Kannonhon-machi, Hiroshima 733, Japan.
- Hiroshima Medical Association. Journal/
Hiroshima Igaku. m. ISSN 0018-2044

**Hiroshima Shinagakkai**
see Sinological Society of Hiroshima

**Hiroshima University. Botanical Institute**
Higashisenda-cho, Hiroshima 730, Japan.
- Hikobia. s-a. ISSN 0046-7413 (Hiroshima
Botanical Club)
- Hiroshima University. Journal of Science. Series
B. Division 2. Botany/Hiroshima Daigaku Rika
Kiyo, Shokubutsu. approx. a. ISSN 0075-4366

**Hiroshima University. Department of Geology and Mineralogy**
1-89 1-chome Higashisenda-cho, Hiroshima 730, Japan.
- Hiroshima University. Department of Geology. Geological Report. irreg., no. 19, 1974. ISSN 0073-2303
- Hiroshima University. Journal of Science. Series C. Geology and Mineralogy. irreg., vol. 7, no. 2, 1974. ISSN 0075-4374

**Hiroshima University. Department of Mathematics**
Faculty of Science, Senda-machi, Hiroshima 730, Japan.
- Hiroshima Mathematical Journal. 3 per yr. ISSN 0018-2079

**Hiroshima University. Faculty of Engineering**
Senda-machi 3, Hiroshima 730, Japan.
- Hiroshima University. Faculty of Engineering. Bulletin/Hiroshima Daigaku Kogakubu Kenkyu Hokoku. s-a. ISSN 0018-2060
- Hiroshima University. Faculty of Engineering. Memoirs. a. ISSN 0073-2311

**Hiroshima University. Faculty of General Education**
1-89 1-chome Higashisenda, Hiroshima 730, Japan.
- Hiroshima University. Faculty of General Education. Memoirs: Studies in Humanities and Social Sciences. a.
- Hiroshima University. Faculty of General Education. Memoirs: Studies in Natural Sciences. a.

**Hiroshima University. Faculty of Science**
Higashisenda-cho, Hiroshima 730, Japan.
- Hiroshima University. Journal of Science. Series B. Division 1: Zoology/Hiroshima Daigaku Rika Kiyo, Dobutsugaku. a.

**Hiroshima University. Laboratory for Amphibian Biology**
1-89 1-chome Higashisenda-cho, Hiroshima 730, Japan.
- Hiroshima University. Laboratory for Amphibian Biology. Scientific Report. a.

**Hiroshima University. Research Institute for Nuclear Medicine and Biology**
Kasumi, Hiroshima 734, Japan.
- Hiroshima University. Research Institute for Nuclear Medicine and Biology. Proceedings/Hiroshima Daigaku Genbaku Hoshano Igaku Kenkyusho Nenpo. a. ISSN 0073-232X

**Hiroshima University. Research Institute for Theoretical Physics**
Takehara-cho, Takehara-shi 725, Japan.
- Hiroshima University. Research Institute for Theoretical Physics. Scientific Reports. irreg. ISSN 0440-873X

**Hiroshima University. School of Medicine**
1-2-3 Kasumi, Hiroshima 734, Japan.
- Hiroshima Journal of Medical Sciences/Hiroshima Daigaku Igaku Zasshi. q. ISSN 0018-2052

**Hiroshima University Dental Society**
Hiroshima University, 1-2-3 Kasumi, Hiroshima 734, Japan.
- Hiroshima University Dental Society. Journal/Hiroshima Daigaku Shigaku Zasshi. s-a. ISSN 0046-7472

**Hissu Aminosan Kenkyu Iinkai**
*see* **Research Committee on Essential Amino Acids**

**Historical Society of Japan**
University of Tokyo, 7-3-1 Hongo, Bunkyo-ku, Tokyo 113, Japan.
- Historical Journal of Japan/Shigaku Zasshi. m. ISSN 0018-2478

**History of Science Society of Japan**
c/o Tokyo Institute of Technology, O-okayama, Meguro-ku, Tokyo 152, Japan.
- Japanese Studies in the History of Science. a. ISSN 0090-0176
- Journal of History of Science/Kagakushi Kenkyu. q. ISSN 0022-7692

**Hitachi, Ltd.**
Advertising Dept., 6-2 Ohtemachi, 2-chome, Chiyoda-ku, Tokyo, Japan.
- Age of Tomorrow. 4 per yr. ISSN 0002-0753
- Hitachi Review. m. ISSN 0018-277X

**Hitachi Zosen Technical Research Institute**
1-3-22 Sakurajima, Konohana-ku, Osaka 554, Japan.
- Hitachi Zosen Technical Review/Hitachi Zosen Giho. q. ISSN 0018-2788

**Hitotsubashi Academy**
- Hitotsubashi Review/Hitotsubashi Ronso. (pub. by Nippon Hyoronsha)

**Hitotsubashi Daigaku**
*see* **Hitotsubashi University**

**Hitotsubashi University**
2-1 Naka, Kunitachi, Tokyo 186, Japan.
- Hitotsubashi Journal of Arts and Sciences. a. ISSN 0073-2788
- Hitotsubashi Journal of Commerce and Management. irreg.; latest issue, 1976. ISSN 0018-2796
- Hitotsubashi Journal of Economics. s-a. ISSN 0018-280X
- Hitotsubashi Journal of Law and Politics. irreg. ISSN 0073-2796
- Hitotsubashi Journal of Social Studies. irreg. ISSN 0073-280X

**Hitotsubashi University. Institute of Economic Research**
- Economic Review/Keizai Kenkyu. (pub. by Iwanami Shoten Publishers)

**Hoechst Japan, Ltd.**
4-10-33 Akasaka, Minato-ku, Tokyo 107, Japan.
- Nova Angiologicae/Nova Angioroji. bi-m. (Japanese College of Angiology)

**Hogakkai**
*see* **Tohoku University. Association of Law and Political Science**

**Hogaku Kenkyukai**
*see* **Keio University. Association for the Study of Law and Politics**

**Hogaku Kyokai**
*see* **Jurisprudence Association**

**Hohasen Igaku Sogo Kenkyusho**
*see* **National Institute of Radiological Sciences**

**Hokekyo Bunka Kenkyujo**
*see* **Rissho University. Institute for the Comprehensive Study of Lotus Sutra**

**Hoken Kagaku Kenkyukai**
*see* **Kyorin-Shoin (Health Science Research Association)**

**Hokkaido Artificial Insemination Technician Association**
c/o Hokunoren, Nishi-1-chome, Kita-4-jo, Sapporo 060, Japan.
- Animal Reproduction Techniques/Hanshoku Gijutsu. q. ISSN 0017-7520

**Hokkaido Central Fisheries Experimental Station**
238 Hamanaka-cho, Yoichi-machi, Yoichi-gun, Hokkaido 046, Japan.
- Hokkaido Central Fisheries Experiment Station. Monthly Report/Hokusuishi Geppo. m. ISSN 0018-3504

**Hokkaido Daigaku**
*see* **Hokkaido University**

**Hokkaido Daigaku Oyo Denki Kenkyusho**
*see* **Hokkaido University. Research Institute of Applied Electricity**

**Hokkaido Daigaku Shokubai Kenkyusho Kiyo**
*see* **Hokkaido University. Research Institute for Catalysis**

**Hokkaido Dental Association**
7-2 Odori Nishi, Chuo-ku, Sapporo 060, Japan.
- Hokkaido Dental Association. Journal/Hokkaido Shika Ishikaishi, Doshikai Tsushin. a. ISSN 0073-2915

**Hokkaido Juishikai**
*see* **Hokkaido Veterinary Medical Association**

**Hokkaido Kachiku Jinko Juseishi Kyokai**
*see* **Hokkaido Artificial Insemination Technician Association**

**Hokkaido Kogai Boshi Kenkyujo**
*see* **Hokkaido Research Institute for Environmental Pollution**

**Hokkaido Kogyo Kaihatsu Shikenjo**
*see* **Japan. Government Industrial Development Laboratory, Hokkaido**

**Hokkaido Kyoiku Daigaku**
*see* **Hokkaido University of Education**

**Hokkaido Librarians Study Circle**
c/o Sapporo Ika Daigaku Fuzoku Toshokan, Nishi-17-chome, Minami 1-jo, Sapporo, Japan.
- Hokkaido Librarians Study Circle. Bulletin/Hokkaido Toshokan Kenkyukai. Kaiho. a. ISSN 0018-3431

**Hokkaido National Agricultural Experiment Station**
*see* **Japan. Hokkaido National Agricultural Experiment Station**

**Hokkaido Orthopedic and Traumatic Surgery Society**
c/o Hokkaido Daigaku Igakubu Seikei Geka Kyoshitsu, Nishi-5-chome, Kita-14-jo, Kita-ku, Sapporo 060, Japan.
- Hokkaido Journal of Orthopedic & Traumatic Surgery/Hokkaido Seikei Saigai Geka Zasshi. s-a. ISSN 0018-3377

**Hokkaido Research Institute for Environmental Pollution**
Nishi 12-chome, Kita 19-Jo, Kita-ku, Sapporo 060, Japan.
- Hokkaido Research Institute for Environmental Pollution. Report/Hokkaido Kogai Boshi Kenkyujo Ho. irreg.

**Hokkaido Seikei Saigai Geka Gakkai**
*see* **Hokkaido Orthopedic and Traumatic Surgery Society**

**Hokkaido Shika Ishikai**
*see* **Hokkaido Dental Association**

**Hokkaido Toshokan Kenkyukai**
*see* **Hokkaido Librarians Study Circle**

**Hokkaido University**
North 8, West 5, Kita-ku, Sapporo 060, Japan.
- Essays in Foreign Languages and Literatures/Gaikokugo Gaikoku Bungaku Kenkyu. irreg.

**Hokkaido University. Faculty of Agriculture**
Nishi-9-chome, Kita 9-jo, Kita-ku, Sapporo 060, Japan.
- Hokkaido University. Faculty of Agriculture. Journal. s-a. ISSN 0018-344X
- Insecta Matsumurana. irreg. ISSN 0020-1804 (prep. by its Entomological Institute)

**Hokkaido University. Faculty of Economics and Business Administration**
North 9, West 7, Kitaku, Sapporo 060, Japan.
- Hokkaido Economic Papers. irreg.

**Hokkaido University. Faculty of Engineering**
Nishi-8-chome, Kita-13-jo, Kita-ku, Sapporo 060, Japan.
- Hokkaido University. Faculty of Engineering. Memoirs. a.

**Hokkaido University. Faculty of Fisheries**
3-1-1 Minato-machi, Hakodate, Hokkaido 040, Japan.
- Hokkaido University. Faculty of Fisheries. Bulletin. q. ISSN 0018-3458
- Hokkaido University. Faculty of Fisheries. Data Record of Oceanographic Observations and Exploratory Fishing/Kaiyo Chosa Gyogyo Shiken Yoho. a. ISSN 0439-3511
- Hokkaido University. Faculty of Fisheries. Memoirs. s-a. ISSN 0018-3466

**Hokkaido University. Faculty of Science**
Nishi-8-chome, Kita-10-jo, Kita-ku, Sapporo 060, Japan.
- Hokkaido Mathematical Journal/Hokkaido Sugaku Zasshi. s-a.
- Hokkaido University. Faculty of Science. Journal. Series 4: Geology and Mineralogy. q. ISSN 0018-3474
- Hokkaido University. Faculty of Science. Journal. Series 5: Botany. irreg.
- Hokkaido University. Faculty of Science. Journal. Series 7: Geophysics. irreg. ISSN 0441-067X

**Institute of Atomic Energy**
see under **Kyoto University**

**Institute of Comparative Law in Japan**
see under **Chuo University**

**Institute of Constitutional Medicine**
see under **Kumamoto University**

**Institute of Developing Economies**
42 Ichigaya-Hommuracho, Shinjuku-ku, Tokyo 162, Japan.
- Asian Economies/Ajia Keizai. m. ISSN 0002-2942
- Catalogue of Statistical Materials of Developing Countries. m.
- Developing Economies. q. ISSN 0012-1533
- I. D. E. Occasional Papers Series. irreg. ISSN 0537-9202
- Institute of Developing Economies. Library Bulletin/Ajia Keizai Shiryo-Geppo. m. ISSN 0020-2827

**Institute of Earth Science**
see under **Kyoto University**

**Institute of Eastern Culture**
2-4-1 Nishi Kanda, Chiyoda-ku, Tokyo 101, Japan.
- Acta Asiatica. s-a. ISSN 0567-7254

**Institute of Electric Rolling Stock**
c/o Shin Kokusai Bldg, 3-4-1 Marunouchi, Chiyoda-ku, Tokyo 100, Japan.
- Denkisha No Kagaku/Railway Electric Rolling Stocks. m. ISSN 0011-8397

**Institute of Electrical Engineers of Japan**
1-11 Yuraku-cho, Chiyoda-ku, Tokyo 100, Japan.
- Electrical Engineering in Japan. (pub. by Scripta Publishing Co. US)
- Railway Electric Rolling Stocks/Denkisha No Kagaku. m. ISSN 0020-2878

**Institute of Electronics and Communication Engineers of Japan**
c/o Kikai Shinko Kaikan, 3-5-8 Shiba Koen, Minato-ku, Tokyo 105, Japan.
- Electronics and Communications in Japan. (pub. by Scripta Publishing Co. US)
- Institute of Electronics and Communication Engineers of Japan. Journal/Denshi Tsushin Gakkai Zasshi. m.
- Institute of Electronics and Communication Engineers of Japan. Transactions/Denshi Tsushin Gakkai Ronbunshi. m.

**Institute of Energy Economics**
No. 12 Mori Bldg., 28 Shiba-Nishikubo, Sakuragawa-cho, Minato-ku, Tokyo, Japan.
- Energy in Japan Quarterly Report. q.

**Institute of Geology and Paleontology**
see under **Tohoku University**

**Institute of Industrial and Commercial Research**
see under **Tokyo College of Economics**

**Institute of Industrial Health**
Sumitomo Hospital, 5-15 Nakanoshima, Kita-ku, Osaka 530, Japan.
- Sumitomo Bulletin of Industrial Health/Sumitomo Sangyo Eisei. a. ISSN 0081-928X

**Institute of Industrial Science**
see under **University of Tokyo**

**Institute of Insurance Research Co. Ltd.**
17-3 1-chome Honmachi, Shibuya-ku, Tokyo, Japan.
- Insurance Life/Non-Life Annual Statistics. a. ISSN 0085-1930

**Institute of Law and Politics**
see under **Kyushu University**

**Institute of Mathematics**
see under **Rikkyo University**

**Institute of Medical Science**
see under **University of Tokyo**

**Institute of Physical and Chemical Research**
2-1 Hirosawa, Wako 351, Japan.
- I P C R Cyclotron Progress Report. a.
- I P C R Cyclotron Report. irreg.
- I P C R Cyclotron Technical Report. irreg.
- Institute of Physical and Chemical Research. Reports/Rigagaku Kenkyusho Hokoku. bi-m. ISSN 0020-3084

- Institute of Physical and Chemical Research. Scientific Papers. q. ISSN 0020-3092

**Institute of Plasma Physics**
see under **Nagoya University**

**Institute of Polymer Industry, Inc.**
C.P.O. Box 1176, Tokyo, Japan.
- Plastics Industry News, Japan. m. ISSN 0032-1206
- Vinyls and Polymers/Enbi to Porima. m. ISSN 0013-8460

**Institute of Population Problems**
see **Japan. Institute of Population Problems**

**Institute of Public Health**
see **Japan. Institute of Public Health**

**Institute of Radiation Breeding**
see **Japan. Institute of Radiation Breeding**

**Institute of Research in Tokyo Municipal Problems**
Hibiya-Koen, Uchisaiwai-cho, Chiyoda-ku, Tokyo, Japan.
- Municipal Problems/Toshi Mondai. m.

**Institute of Scientific and Industrial Research**
see under **Osaka University**

**Institute of Social Science**
see under **University of Tokyo**

**Institute of Space and Aeronautical Science**
see under **University of Tokyo**

**Institute of Statistical Mathematics**
see **Japan. Institute of Statistical Mathematics**

**Institute of Transportation Economics**
2-5-6 Izumicho Kokubunji, Tokyo, Japan.
- Problems of Transportation in Japan. irreg.

**Intercontinental Marketing Corp.**
Box 5056, Tokyo International, Tokyo 100-31, Japan.
- Japan Publications Guide. m.

**Interia Shuppan**
5-2-4 Roppongi, Minato-ku, Tokyo 106, Japan.
- Nob/Nobu. q.

**Interia Shuppan K. K.**
1-22 Yotsuya, Shinjuku-ku, Tokyo 160, Japan.
- Japan Interior Design/Interia. m. ISSN 0021-4442

**International Association of Cytology**
c/o Oriental Library, 2-28-21 Hongomagome, Bunkyo-ku, Tokyo 113, Japan.
- Cytologia/Kitorogia. q.

**International Association of Geomagnetism and Aeronomy**
c/o Prof. Fukushima, Secretary, Geophysical Institute, University of Tokyo, Bunkyo-ku, Tokyo 113, Japan.
- I A G A News. irreg. ISSN 0536-1095

**International Association of Physical Education and Sports for Girls and Women**
- International Association of Physical Education and Sports for Girls and Women. Proceedings of the International Congress. (pub. by Japan Association of Physical Education for Women and Girls)

**International Association of Ports and Harbors**
1 Shiba Kotahira-cho, Minato-ku, Tokyo 105, Japan.
- Ports and Harbors. m. ISSN 0554-7555

**International Christian University**
3-10-2 Osawa, Mitaka, Tokyo, Japan.
- Summer Institute in Linguistics. Descriptive and Applied Linguistics. irreg., latest issue, 1974.

**International Christian University. Institute for the Study of Christianity and Culture**
3-10-2 Osawa, Mitaka, Tokyo, Japan.
- Humanities, Christianity and Culture. approx. a. ISSN 0073-3938

**International Council on Social Welfare. Japanese National Committee**
3-3-4 Kasumigaseki, Chiyoda-ku, Tokyo, Japan.
- Japanese Report to the International Council on Social Welfare. a.
- Social Welfare Services in Japan. a.

**International Federation of Automobile Engineers' and Technicians' Associations**
c/o Society of Automotive Engineers of Japan, Inc., 16-15 Takanawa 1-chome, Minato-ku, Tokyo 108, Japan.
- International Federation of Automobile Engineers and Technicians Associations. Reports of Congress/Federation Internationale des Societes d'Ingenieurs des Techniques de l'Automobile. Congres. Report. biennial, 16th, 1976. ISSN 0074-5901

**International Institute for the Study of Religions, Inc.**
1-15-1 Wada, Suginami-ku, Tokyo 166, Japan.
- Japanese Journal of Religious Studies. q.

**International Institute of Seismology and Earthquake Engineering**
see **Japan. International Institute of Seismology and Earthquake Engineering**

**International Legal Sciences Association**
2-12 Marunouchi, Chiyoda-ku, Tokyo, Japan.
- Japanese Annual of International Law. a. ISSN 0448-8806 (prep. by its Japanese Branch)

**International Management Association of Japan**
28 Shiba-Nishikuho-Sakuragawa-cho, Minato-ku, Tokyo, Japan
- International Council for Scientific Management. Proceedings of World Congress. triennial since 1951; 1969, 15th, Tokyo. ISSN 0085-2120 (Inquire: World Council of Management, Box 20, 1211 Geneva 20, Switzerland)
- Management Japan; IMAJ management review. s-a. ISSN 0025-1828

**International Medical Society of Japan**
40 Marunouchi Nomura Bldg., 1-1 2-chome Otemachi, Chiyoda-ku, Tokyo 100, Japan.
- International Medical News. m. ISSN 0535-1405

**International Polar Motion Service. Central Bureau**
International Latitude Observatory, Mizusawa 023, Japan.
- International Polar Motion Service. Annual Report/Kokusai Kyoku-Undo Kansoku Jigyo Nenpo. a. ISSN 0074-7432
- International Polar Motion Service. Monthly Notes/Kokusai Kyoku-Undo Kansoku Jigyo Geppo. m. ISSN 0020-8337

**International Society for Educational Information, Inc.**
Kikuei Bldg., 2-7-8 Shintomi, Chuo-ku, Tokyo, Japan.
- Changing Japan. irreg.
- Understanding Japan. s-a. ISSN 0041-6576

**International U F O Observer Corps.**
- U F O News. (pub. by C B A International)

**Iron and Steel Institute of Japan**
Keidanren Kaikan (3rd Floor), 1-9-4 Otemachi, Chiyoda-ku, Tokyo 100, Japan.
- Iron and Steel Institute of Japan. Journal/Tetsu to Hagane. m. ISSN 0021-1575
- Iron and Steel Institute of Japan. Transactions. m. ISSN 0021-1583

**Iryo Dokokai**
see **Medical Treatment Association**

**Ishikawajima-Harima Heavy Industries Co., Ltd.**
3-2-16 Toyosu, Kotoku, Tokyo 135, Japan.
- I H I Engineering Review. 3 per yr. ISSN 0018-9820

**Ishiyaku Publishers, Inc.**
7-10 Honkomagome 1-chome, Bunkyo-ku, Tokyo 113, Japan.
- Dental Outlook/Shikai Tenbo. m. ISSN 0011-8702
- Medical Technology/Rinsho Kensagaku Zasshi. m.
- Practice in Prosthodontics/Hotetsu Rinsho. q. ISSN 0018-6341
- Strides of Medicine/Igaku No Ayumi. w. ISSN 0039-2359

**Itsuu Laboratory**
2-28-10 Tamagawa, Setagaya-ku, Tokyo 173, Japan.
- Itsuu Laboratory, Tokyo. Annual Report/Itsuu Kenkyusho Nenpo. irreg.(a. or biennial) ISSN 0075-2010

**Iwanami Shoten Publishers**
2-5-5 Hitotsubashi, Chiyoda-ku, Tokyo 101, Japan (Overseas Distributor: Japan Publications Trading Co., Ltd., Box 5030, Tokyo International, Tokyo 100-31, Japan; or 1255 Howard St., San Francisco, CA 94103)
- Biological Science/Seibutsu Kagaku. q. ISSN 0045-2033 (Japanese Society of Biological Scientists)
- Economic Review/Keizai Kenkyu. q. ISSN 0022-9733 (Hitotsubashi University. Institute of Economic Research)
- Journal of Agricultural Economics/Nogyo Keizai Kenkyu. q. (Agricultural Economic Society of Japan)
- Mathematics/Sugaku. q. ISSN 0039-470X (Mathematical Society of Japan)
- Science/Kagaku. m. ISSN 0022-7625
- Thought/Shiso. m.

**Iwate Daigaku**
see Iwate University

**Iwate Igakkai**
see Iwate Medical Association

**Iwate Medical Association**
c/o Iwate Medical University, 19-1 Uchimaru, Morioka 020, Iwate, Japan.
- Iwate Medical Association. Journal/Iwate Igaku Zasshi. bi-m. ISSN 0021-3284

**Iwate University. Faculty of Engineering**
4-3-5 Ueda, Morioka 020, Iwate, Japan.
- Iwate University. Faculty of Engineering. Technology Reports/Iwate Daigaku Kogakubu Kenkyu Hokoku. irreg. ISSN 0085-2325

**Iwate University. Mountains Land Use Research Station**
3-18-8 Ueda, Morioka 020, Iwate, Japan.
- Iwate University. Mountains Land Use Research Laboratory. Bulletin. irreg.

**Iyo Kizai Kenkyusho**
see Tokyo Medical and Dental University. Institute for Medical and Dental Engineering

**Izumi and Co., Ltd.**
3-25-1 Imabashi, Higasha-ku, Osaka 541, Japan.
- Fountain/Izumi. m. ISSN 0021-339X (Fujisawa Pharmaceutical Co. Ltd.)

**J A E C**
see Japan. Japan Atomic Energy Commission

**J A E R I**
see Japan Atomic Energy Research Institute

**J A P I C**
see Japan Pharmaceutical Information Centre

**J A S D F**
see Japan Air Self Defense Force

**J E O L Ltd.**
1418 Nakagami-cho, Akishima-shi, Tokyo 196, Japan.
- J E O L News: Analytical Instruments/ Application. 2 per yr. ISSN 0385-4418 (prep. by its International Marketing Division)
- J E O L News: Electron Optics Instruments/ Application. 3 per yr. ISSN 0385-4426 (prep. by its International Marketing Division)

**J E R C**
see Japan Economic Research Center

**J E T R O**
see Japan External Trade Organization

**J I C A**
see Japan International Cooperation Agency

**J I C S T**
see Japan Information Center of Science and Technology

**J. N. R.**
see Japanese National Railways

**J. S. C.**
see Science Council of Japan

**Japan**
see also Japanese

**Japan. Atomic Energy Research Institute**
see Japan Atomic Energy Research Institute

**Japan. Building Research Institute**
Ministry of Construction, 8-28 3-chome Hyakunin-cho, Shinjuku-ku, Tokyo 160, Japan.
- B R I Research Papers/Kenchiku Kenkyusho Chosa Shiken Kenkyu Gaiyo Hokoku. irreg.

**Japan. Bureau of Statistics**
Office of the Prime Minister, 95 Wakamatsu-cho, Shinjuku-ku, Tokyo 162, Japan
(Subscr. to Government Publications Service Center, 1-2-1 Kasumigaseki, Chiyoda-ku, Tokyo 100, Japan)
- Japan. Bureau of Statistics. Annual Report on Family Income and Expenditures. a. ISSN 0075-3173
- Japan. Bureau of Statistics. Employment Status Survey/Japan. Sorifu. Tokeikyoku. Shugyokozo Kihon Chosa. triennial. ISSN 0075-3181
- Japan. Bureau of Statistics. News Bulletin. q. ISSN 0449-5314
- Japan Statistical Yearbook. a. ISSN 0075-3335
- Monthly Statistics of Japan. m. ISSN 0027-0555
- Statistical Handbook of Japan. a. ISSN 0081-4792

**Japan. Director of Statistical Standards**
Administrative Management Agency, 3-1-1 Kasumigaseki, Chiyoda-ku, Tokyo, Japan.
- Statistical Notes of Japan. irreg. ISSN 0561-922X

**Japan. Economic Planning Agency**
3-1-1 Kasumigaseki, Chiyoda-ku, Tokyo, Japan.
- Economic Survey of Japan. (pub. by Japan Times, Ltd.)
- Japanese Economic Indicators/Nihon Keizai Shihyo. m. ISSN 0029-0262

**Japan. Economic Planning Agency. Economic Research Institute**
see Japan. Economic Research Institute

**Japan. Economic Research Institute**
3-1-1 Kasumigaseki, Chiyoda-ku, Tokyo, Japan.
- Economic Research Institute. Economic Bulletin. q. ISSN 0422-2954

**Japan. Fermentation Research Institute**
Agency of Industrial Science and Technology, 5-8-1 Inage Higashi, Chiba 281, Japan.
- Fermentation Research Institute. Report/Kogyo Gijutsuin Biseibutsu Kogyo Gijutsu Kenkyusho. Kenkyu Hokoku. s-a. ISSN 0015-0061

**Japan. Fisheries Agency. Freshwater Fisheries Research Laboratory**
see Japan. Freshwater Fisheries Research Laboratory

**Japan. Fisheries Agency. Japan Sea Regional Fisheries Research Laboratory**
see Japan. Japan Sea Regional Fisheries Research Laboratory

**Japan. Fisheries Agency. Tohoku Regional Fisheries Research Laboratory**
see Japan. Tohoku Regional Fisheries Research Laboratory

**Japan. Fisheries Agency. Tokai Regional Fisheries Research Laboratory**
see Japan. Tokai Regional Fisheries Research Laboratory

**Japan. Forestry Agency**
- Forest Protection/Shinrin Boeki. (pub. by Zenkoku Shinrin Byochu Jugai Bojo Kyokai)

**Japan. Forestry Agency. Government Forest Experiment Station**
see Japan. Government Forest Experiment Station

**Japan. Freshwater Fisheries Research Laboratory**
399 Miya, Hino-shi, Tokyo 191, Japan.
- Freshwater Fisheries Research Laboratory, Tokyo. Bulletin/Tansui-ku Suisan Kenkyusho Kenkyu Hokoku. s-a. ISSN 0049-4054

**Japan. Geographical Survey Institute**
3-24-13 Higashiyama, Meguro-ku, Tokyo 153, Japan.
- Geographical Survey Institute, Tokyo. Bulletin/ Kokudo Chiri-in Hokoku. s-a.

**Japan. Geological Survey of Japan**
135 Hisamato, Takatsu-ku, Kawasaki 213, Japan.
- Geological Survey of Japan. Bulletin/Chishitsu Chosasho Geppo. m. ISSN 0016-7665
- Geology and Mineral Resources of Japan/Nihon Chishitsu Kosanshi. irreg.
- Japan. Geological Survey. Cruise Report. irreg.
- Monthly Review of Geology/Chishitsu Nyusu. m. ISSN 0009-4854

**Japan. Government Forest Experiment Station. Kyushu Branch**
4-11-16 Kurokami, Kumamoto 860, Japan.
- Japan. Government Forest Experiment Station. Kyushu Branch. Annual Report/Ringyo Shikenjo Kyushu Shijo Nenpo. a. ISSN 0557-0395

**Japan. Government Forest Experiment Station, Tokyo**
5-37-21 Shimomeguro, Meguro-ku, Tokyo 153, Japan.
- Abstracts of Japanese Literature in Forest Genetics and Related Fields. Part A. (pub. by Noorin Syuppan Co. Ltd.)
- Abstracts of Japanese Literature in Forest Genetics and Related Fields. Part B. (pub. by Noorin Syuppan Co. Ltd.)
- Japan. Government Forest Experiment Station, Tokyo. Annual Report/Norinsho Ringyo Shikenjo Nenpo. a. ISSN 0557-0352
- Japan. Government Forest Experiment Station, Tokyo. Bulletin. irreg; 8-10 per yr.

**Japan. Government Industrial Development Laboratory, Hokkaido**
41-2 Higashi-tsukisamu, Toyohira-ku, Sapporo 061-01, Hokkaido, Japan.
- Government Industrial Development Laboratory, Hokkaido. Annual Report/Hokkaido Kogyo Kaihatsu Shikenjo Nempo. a.
- Hokkaishi News. bi-m.

**Japan. Government Industrial Research Institute, Kyushu**
807-1 Shukumachi, Tosu 841, Japan.
- Government Industrial Research Institute, Kyushu. Annual Report/Kyushu Kogyo Gijutsu Shikenjo Nempo. a.

**Japan. Government Industrial Research Institute, Nagoya**
1 Hirate-machi, Kita-ku, Nagoya, Japan.
- Japan. Government Industrial Research Institute, Nagoya. Technical News. m. ISSN 0027-7614

**Japan. Government Mechanical Laboratory of Japan**
12-1 Igusa, 4-chome, Suginami-ku, Tokyo, Japan.
- Government Mechanical Laboratory of Japan. Journal. s-a. ISSN 0022-2550

**Japan. Hokkaido National Agricultural Experiment Station**
1 Hitsujigaoka, Toyohiro-ku, Sapporo 061-01, Japan (Dist. in U.S. by: New York Agricultural Experiment Station, Geneva, NY 14456)
- Hokkaido National Agricultural Experiment Station. Research Bulletin/Hokkaido Nogyo Shikenjo Kenkyu Hokoku. 2-3 per yr. ISSN 0018-3415
- Hokkaido National Agricultural Experiment Station. Soil Survey Report/Hokkaido Nogyo Shikenjo Dosei Chosa Hokoku. irreg. ISSN 0073-2923

**Japan. Institute of Population Problems**
Ministry of Health and Welfare, 1-2-2 Kasumigaseki, Chiyoda-ku, Tokyo 100, Japan.
- Journal of Population Problems/Jinko Mondai Kenkyu. q.

**Japan. Institute of Public Health**
4-6-1 Shiroganedai, Minato-ku, Tokyo 108, Japan.
- Japan. Institute of Public Health. Annual Report/ Kokuritsu Koshu Eisei-in Nenpo. a.
- Japan. Institute of Public Health. Bulletin/ Kokuritsu Koshu Eisei-in Kenkyu Hokoku. q. ISSN 0020-3106

**Japan. Institute of Radiation Breeding**
Omiya-cho, Naka-gun, Ibaraki 319-22, Japan.
- Acta Radiobotanika et Genetika/Hoshasen
  Ikushujo Kenkyu Hokoku; bulletin of the Institute
  of Radiation Breeding. irreg., no. 2, 1971. ISSN
  0065-1621
- Gamma Field Symposia. a. ISSN 0435-1096

**Japan. Institute of Statistical Mathematics**
4-6-7 Minami Azabu, Minato-ku, Tokyo 106, Japan.
- Institute of Statistical Mathematics. Annals. 3 per
  yr. ISSN 0020-3157
- Institute of Statistical Mathematics. Annual
  Report/Tokei Suri Kenkyusho Nenpo. a.

**Japan. Institute of Transportation Economics**
see Institute of Transportation Economics

**Japan. International Institute of Seismology and
Earthquake Engineering**
3-28-8 Hyakunincho, Shinjuku-ku, Tokyo 160,
Japan.
- International Institute of Seismology and
  Earthquake Engineering. Bulletin. a. ISSN 0074-
  655X
- International Institute of Seismology and
  Earthquake Engineering. Earthquake Report.
  irreg. ISSN 0074-6568
- International Institute of Seismology and
  Earthquake Engineering. Lecture Note. irreg;
  latest issue, 1972. ISSN 0074-6584
- International Institute of Seismology and
  Earthquake Engineering. Progress Report. irreg.
  ISSN 0074-6592
- International Institute of Seismology and
  Earthquake Engineering. Report of Individual
  Study by Participants to I I S E E. a. ISSN 0074-
  6606
- International Institute of Seismology and
  Earthquake Engineering. Year Book. a. ISSN
  0074-6614
- World Conference on Earthquake Engineering.
  Proceedings. irreg. ISSN 0084-1560

**Japan. Japan Atomic Energy Commission**
2-2-1 Kasumigaseki, Chiyoda-ku, Tokyo 100, Japan.
- Japan Atomic Energy Commission. Annual
  Report/Genshiryoku Nenpo. a. ISSN 0449-4830

**Japan. Japan Sea Regional Fisheries Research
Laboratory**
5939-22 Hamaura, Nishifunami-cho, Nigata 951,
Japan.
- Japan Sea Regional Fisheries Research
  Laboratory. Bulletin/Nihonkai-ku Suisan
  Kenkyusho Kenkyu Hokoku. 2 per yr.(approx.)
  ISSN 0021-4620

**Japan. Kaijo Hoancho**
see Japan. Maritime Safety Agency

**Japan. Kaijo Hoancho Suirobu**
see Japan. Maritime Safety Agency. Hydrographic
Division

**Japan. Kinki Agricultural Administration Bureau**
102 Shimochoja-machi Saguru, Nishinotoin-dori,
Kamigyo-ku, Kyoto 602, Japan.
- Annual Review of Agriculture, Kinkei District/
  Kinki Nogyo Josei Hokoku. a.

**Japan. Kobe Plant Protection Station**
3 Shinko-cho, Ikuta-ku, Kobe 650, Japan.
- Kobe Plant Protection and Plant Quarantine
  Information/Kobe Shokubutsu Boeki Joho. m.
  ISSN 0023-2521

**Japan. Kokudo Keikaku Kyokai**
21 Kotohiracho, Minato-ku, Tokyo 105, Japan.
- People and National Land Policy/Hito to Kokudo.
  irreg.

**Japan. Maritime Safety Agency**
2-1-3 Kasumigaseki, Chiyoda-ku, Tokyo 100, Japan.
- Annual Statistics of Maritime Safety. a. ISSN
  0448-3294

**Japan. Maritime Safety Agency. Hydrographic
Department**
5-3-1 Tsukiji, Chuo-ku, Tokyo 104, Japan.
- Japan. Maritime Safety Agency. Hydrographic
  Department. Hydrographic Bulletin/Suiryo Yoho.
  3 per yr. ISSN 0021-4485
- Japan. Maritime Safety Agency. Hydrographic
  Department. Notices to Mariners/Suiro Tsuho. w.
  ISSN 0447-3728

**Japan. Metal Mining Agency**
6-3 Shiba Nishikubo Sakuragawa-cho, Shiba,
Minato-ku, Tokyo 105, Japan.
- Close Examination Report: Jozankei Valley
  Region/Seimitsu Chosa Hokokusho: Jozankei
  Chiiki. s-a.
- Report of Overseas Mining Investigation: India,
  Pakistan, Bangladesh/Kaigai Kogyo Jijo Chosa
  Hokokusho: Indo, Pakisutan, Banguradisshu. irreg.
  (prep. by its Data Center)
- Report of Overseas Mining Investigation:
  Madagascar, Swaziland/Kaigai Kogyo Jijo Chosa
  Hokokusho: Madagasukaru, Suwajirando. irreg.
  (prep. by its Data Center)

**Japan. Meteorological Agency**
for publications of this agency, see Japan Weather
Association

**Japan. Ministry of Agriculture and Forestry**
- Japan. Ministry of Agriculture and Forestry.
  Annual Report/Norin-sho Nenpo. (pub. by
  Government Publications Service Center)

**Japan. Ministry of Agriculture and Forestry.
Agriculture and Forestry Economic Bureau**
1-2-1 Kasumigaseki, Chiyoda-ku, Tokyo 100, Japan.
- Fisheries Statistics of Japan. a. ISSN 0071-5581
  (prep. by its Statistics and Information Division)

**Japan. Ministry of Agriculture and Forestry. Forestry
Agency. Government Forest Experiment Station**
see Japan. Government Forest Experiment Station

**Japan. Ministry of Agriculture and Forestry.
Hokkaido National Agricultural Experiment
Station**
see Japan. Hokkaido National Agricultural
Experiment Station

**Japan. Ministry of Agriculture and Forestry. Institute
of Radiation Breeding**
see Japan. Institute of Radiation Breeding

**Japan. Ministry of Agriculture and Forestry. Kinki
Agricultural Administration Bureau**
see Japan. Kinki Agricultural Administration
Bureau

**Japan. Ministry of Agriculture and Forestry. National
Grassland Research Institute**
see Japan. National Grassland Research Institute

**Japan. Ministry of Agriculture and Forestry. National
Institute of Animal Health**
see Japan. National Institute of Animal Health

**Japan. Ministry of Agriculture and Forestry. National
Institute of Animal Industry**
see Japan. National Institute of Animal Industry

**Japan. Ministry of Agriculture and Forestry. National
Institute of Agricultural Sciences**
see Japan. National Institute of Agricultural
Sciences

**Japan. Ministry of Agriculture and Forestry. National
Institute of Fisheries. Tohoku Regional Fisheries
Research Laboratory**
see Japan. Tohoku Regional Fisheries Research
Laboratory

**Japan. Ministry of Agriculture and Forestry. National
Research Institute of Agriculture**
see Japan. National Research Institute of
Agriculture

**Japan. Ministry of Agriculture and Forestry.
Sericultural Experiment Station**
see Japan. Sericultural Experiment Station

**Japan. Ministry of Agriculture and Forestry. Shikoku
Agricultural Experiment Station**
see Japan. Shikoku Agricultural Experiment
Station

**Japan. Ministry of Agriculture and Forestry.
Statistics Bureau**
2-11-14 Meguro-ku, Tokyo 153, Japan
(Overseas Distributor: Japan Publications Trading
Co., Ltd., Box 5030, Tokyo International, Tokyo
100-31, Japan; or 1255 Howard St., San Francisco,
CA 94103)
- Monthly Statistics on Agriculture, Forestry and
  Fisheries/Norin Shusan Tokei Geppo. m. ISSN
  0029-1757
- Norin Tosho Shiryo Geppo. m. ISSN 0029-1773

**Japan. Ministry of Agriculture and Forestry. Tropical
Agriculture Research Center**
see Japan. Tropical Agriculture Research Center

**Japan. Ministry of Agriculture and Forestry.
Yokohama Plant Protection Station**
see Japan. Yokohama Plant Protection Station

**Japan. Ministry of Agriculture. Kobe Plant Protection
Station**
see Japan. Kobe Plant Protection Station

**Japan. Ministry of Construction. Building Research
Institute**
see Japan. Building Research Institute

**Japan. Ministry of Construction. Geographical Survey
Institute**
see Japan. Geographical Survey Institute

**Japan. Ministry of Construction. International
Institute of Seismology and Earthquake
Engineering**
see Japan. International Institute of Seismology
and Earthquake Engineering

**Japan. Ministry of Construction. Public Works
Research Institute**
see Japan. Public Works Research Institute

**Japan. Ministry of Education**
3-2-2 Kasumigaseki, Chiyoda-ku, Tokyo 100, Japan
- Education in Japan; A Graphic Presentation.
  irreg., 1971, 8th ed. ISSN 0070-9220 (Subscr. to
  Government Publications Service Center, 1-2-1
  Kasumigaseki, Chiyoda-ku, Tokyo 100, Japan)
- Educational Standards in Japan. irreg.

**Japan. Ministry of Education. Institute of Statistical
Mathematics**
see Japan. Institute of Statistical Mathematics

**Japan. Ministry of Education. National Institute of
Genetics**
see Japan. National Institute of Genetics

**Japan. Ministry of Finance**
Minister's Secretariat, 3-1-1 Kasumigaseki, Chiyoda-
ku, Tokyo 100, Japan.
- Finance/Fainansu. m. ISSN 0448-6072
- Monthly Finance Review. m. (prep. by its
  Research and Planning Division)

**Japan. Ministry of Finance. Economic Planning
Agency**
see Japan. Economic Planning Agency

**Japan. Ministry of Finance. National Tax Agency**
see Japan. National Tax Agency

**Japan. Ministry of Foreign Affairs**
Minister's Secretariat, Tokyo, Japan.
- Statistical Survey of Economy of Japan. a. ISSN
  0081-5047

**Japan. Ministry of Health and Welfare**
42 Honmura-cho, Ichigaya, Shinjuku-ku, Tokyo,
Japan.
- Japan. Ministry of Health and Welfare. Vital
  Statistics. a. (in 2 vols.) ISSN 0075-3270 (prep.
  by its Statistics Department)

**Japan. Ministry of Health and Welfare. Institute of
Population Problems**
see Japan. Institute of Population Problems

**Japan. Ministry of Health and Welfare. Institute of
Public Health**
see Japan. Institute of Public Health

**Japan. Ministry of Health and Welfare. National
Cancer Center**
see Japan. National Cancer Center

**Japan. Ministry of Health and Welfare. National
Institue for Leprosy Research**
see Japan. National Institute for Leprosy Research

**Japan. Ministry of Health and Welfare. National
Institute of Health**
see Japan. National Institute of Health

**Japan. Ministry of Health and Welfare. National
Institute of Nutrition**
see Japan. National Institute of Nutrition

**Japan. Ministry of International Trade and Industry**
Minister's Secretariat, 6-15-1 Ginza, Chuo-ku,
Tokyo 104, Japan.
- Foreign-Affiliated Enterprises in Japan. (pub. by
  Marunouchi Research Center Co., Ltd.)
- Japan Census of Manufactures: Report by
  Commodities. a. ISSN 0075-3289 (prep. by its
  Research and Statistics Division)
- Mining Yearbook of Japan/Honpo Kogyo No
  Susei. a. (prep. by its Research and Statistics
  Division)
- Monthly Statistics of Paper Distribution/Kami
  Ryutsu Tokei Geppo. (pub. by Japan Industry and
  Trade Research Association)
- Paper & Pulp Statistical Monthly/Kami Parupu
  Tokei Geppo. (pub. by Research Institute of
  International Trade and Industry (Tsusho Sangiyo
  Chosakai))
- Statistics on Japanese Industries. a. ISSN 0081-
  5209 (prep. by its Research and Statistics
  Division)
- Yearbook of Pulp and Paper Statistics/Kami
  Parupu Tokei Nenpo. (pub. by Research Institute
  of International Trade and Industry (Tsusho
  Sangiyo Chosakai))

**Japan. Ministry of International Trade and Industry.
Agency of Industrial Science and Technology.
Fermentation Research Institute**
see **Japan. Fermentation Research Institute**

**Japan. Ministry of International Trade and Industry.
Agency of Industrial Science and Technology.
Government Industrial Development Laboratory,
Hokkaido**
see **Japan. Government Industrial Development
Laboratory, Hokkaido**

**Japan. Ministry of International Trade and Industry.
Agency of Industrial Science and Technology.
Government Industrial Research Institute, Kyushu**
see **Japan. Government Industrial Research
Institute, Kyushu**

**Japan. Ministry of International Trade and Industry.
Agency of Industrial Science and Technology.
Geological Survey of Japan**
see **Japan. Geological Survey of Japan**

**Japan. Ministry of International Trade and Industry.
Agency of Industrial Science and Technology.
National Chemical Laboratory for Industry**
see **Japan. National Chemical Laboratory for
Industry**

**Japan. Ministry of International Trade and Industry.
Agency of Industrial Science and Technology.
National Research Institute for Pollution and
Resources**
see **Japan. National Research Institute for
Pollution and Resources**

**Japan. Ministry of International Trade and Industry.
Agency of Industrial Science and Technology.
National Research Laboratory of Metrology**
see **Japan. National Research Laboratory of
Metrology**

**Japan. Ministry of Labour**
Minister's Secretariat, Tokyo 100, Japan.
- Japan. Ministry of Labour. Yearbook of Labour
  Statistics. a. (prep. by its Statistics and
  Information Department)

**Japan. Ministry of Labour. National Institute of
Industrial Health**
see **Japan. National Institute of Industrial Health**

**Japan. Ministry of Posts and Telecommunications.
Radio Research Laboratories**
2-1 4-chome Nukui Kita-machi, Kaganei-shi, Tokyo
184, Japan.
- Ionospheric Data at Syowa Base (Antarctica) s-a.
- Ionospheric Data in Japan/Denriso Geppo. m.
  ISSN 0021-0382
- Radio Research Laboratories. Journal/Denpa
  Kenkyusho Eibun Ronbunshu. bi-m. ISSN 0033-
  8001
- Radio Research Laboratories. Review/Denpa
  Kenkyusho Kiho. bi-m. ISSN 0033-801X
- Standard Frequency and Time Service Bulletin. m.

**Japan. Ministry of Transport**
Minister's Secretariat, 2-1-3 Kasumigaseki, Chiyoda-
ku, Tokyo 100, Japan.
- Monthly Statistics of Actual Production of
  Railway Cars/Tetsudo Sharyoto Seisan Dotai
  Tokei Geppo. m. ISSN 0040-4055 (prep. by its
  Data Processing Division)

**Japan. Ministry of Transport. Port and Harbour
Technical Research Institute**
see **Japan. Port and Harbour Technical Research
Institute**

**Japan. Ministry of Transport. Ship Research Institute**
see **Japan. Ship Research Institute**

**Japan. National Aerospace Laboratory**
1880 Jindaiji-machi, Chofu, Tokyo 182, Japan.
- N A L News/Kogiken Nyusu. m. ISSN 0023-
  2726

**Japan. National Cancer Center**
5-1-1 Tsukiji, Chuo-ku, Tokyo 104, Japan.
- National Cancer Center. Annual Report/
  Kokuritsu Gan Senta Nenpo. a.
- National Cancer Center. Collected Papers/
  Kokuritsu Gan Senta, Tokyo. Collected Papers. a.
  ISSN 0077-3662

**Japan. National Chemical Laboratory for Industry**
1-1-5 Hon-machi, Shibuya-ku, Tokyo 150, Japan.
- Japan. National Chemical Laboratory for Industry.
  Journal/Tokyo Kogyo Shikensho Hokoku. m.

**Japan. National Diet Library**
see **National Diet Library**

**Japan. National Grassland Research Institute**
768 Nishinasuno-cho, Nasu-gun, Tochigi 329-27,
Japan.
- Sochi Gakkaishi. q. ISSN 0037-7570 (Co-sponsor:
  Japanese Society of Grassland Science)

**Japan. National Institute for Leprosy Research**
4-1455 Aoba-cho, Higashimurayama, Tokyo 189,
Japan.
- National Institute for Leprosy Research. Annual
  Report/Kokuritsu Tama Kenkyusho Nenpo. a.
  ISSN 0454-2029

**Japan. National Institute of Agricultural Sciences**
2-7-1 Nishihara, Kita-ku, Tokyo 114, Japan.
- National Institute of Agricultural Sciences, Tokyo.
  Bulletin. Series A (Physics and Statistics) irreg.,
  no. 24, 1977. ISSN 0077-4820
- National Institute of Agricultural Sciences, Tokyo.
  Bulletin. Series B (Soils and Fertilizers) irreg., no.
  29, 1977. ISSN 0077-4839
- National Institute of Agricultural Sciences, Tokyo.
  Bulletin. Series C (Plant Pathology and
  Entomology) irreg., no. 31, 1977. ISSN 0077-
  4847
- National Institute of Agricultural Sciences, Tokyo.
  Bulletin. Series D (Physiology and Genetics)
  irreg., no. 28, 1977. ISSN 0077-4855
- National Institute of Agricultural Sciences, Tokyo.
  Bulletin. Series H (Farm Management, Land
  Utilization, Rural Life) irreg., no. 49, 1977. ISSN
  0077-4863
- National Institute of Agricultural Sciences, Tokyo.
  Miscellaneous Publication. irreg. ISSN 0077-4871

**Japan. National Institute of Animal Health**
Extension and Information Service, 1500 Josuihon-
cho, Kodaira, Tokyo 187, Japan.
- Japan. National Institute of Animal Health.
  Annual Report/Norin-sho Kachiku Eisei Shikenjo
  Nenpo. a. ISSN 0453-0535
- Japan. National Institute of Animal Health.
  Bulletin/Norin-sho Kachiku Eisei Shikenjo
  Kenkyu Hokoku. s-a.
- Japan. National Institute of Animal Health
  Quarterly. q. ISSN 0027-951X

**Japan. National Institute of Animal Industry**
Chiba 280, Japan.
- National Institute of Animal Industry, Chiba,
  Japan. Annual Report. a.
- National Institute of Animal Industry, Chiba,
  Japan. Bulletin/Chikusan Shikenjo, Chiba, Japan.
  Chikusan Shikenjo Kenkyu Hokoku. irreg. ISSN
  0077-488X
- National Institute of Animal Industry, Chiba,
  Japan. Bulletin Summaries. irreg., no. 28, 1974.
  ISSN 0077-4898

**Japan. National Institute of Genetics**
1111 Yata, Mishima 411, Japan.
- National Institute of Genetics, Mishima, Japan.
  Annual Report/Kokuritsu Idengaku Kenkyusho,
  Mishima, Japan. Nenpo. a. ISSN 0077-4995

**Japan. National Institute of Health**
2-10-35 Kamiosaki, Shinagawaku, Tokyo 141, Japan.
- Japanese Journal of Medical Science and Biology/
  Nihon Igaku Seibutsugaku Zasshi. bi-m. ISSN
  0021-5112

**Japan. National Institute of Industrial Health**
2051 Kizuki Sumiyoshi-cho, Kawasaki 211, Japan.
- Industrial Health. q. ISSN 0019-8366

**Japan. National Institute of Nutrition**
1 Toyama-cho, Shinjuku-ku, Tokyo 162, Japan.
- National Institute of Nutrition. Annual Report/
  Kokuritsu Eiyo Kenkyusho Hokoku. a.

**Japan. National Police Agency. National Research
Institute of Police Science**
see **Japan. National Research Institute of Police
Science**

**Japan. National Research Institute for Pollution and
Resources**
188 Kotobuki-cho, Kawaguchi 332, Saitama, Japan.
- National Research Institute for Pollution and
  Resources. Annual Report/Kogai Shigen
  Kenkyusho Nenpo. a.
- National Research Institute for Pollution and
  Resources. Bulletin/Kogai Shigen Kenkyusho Iho.
  q.
- National Research Institute for Pollution and
  Resources. News/Kogai Shigenken Nyusu. m.
- National Research Institute for Pollution and
  Resources. Science Report/Kogai Shigen
  Kenkyusho Hokoku. irreg.

**Japan. National Research Institute of Agriculture**
2-2-1 Nishigahara, Kita-ku, Tokyo 114, Japan.
- Journal of Agricultural Economics/Nogyo Sogo
  Kenkyu. q.
- National Research Institute of Agriculture. Annual
  Report/Nogyo Sogo Kenkyusho Nenpo. a.

**Japan. National Research Institute of Police Science**
6 Sanban-cho, Chiyoda-ku, Tokyo 102, Japan.
- National Research Institute of Police Science.
  Annual Report/Kagaku Keisatsu Kenkyusho
  Nenpo. a. ISSN 0453-0667
- National Research Institute of Police Science.
  Data/Kagaku Keisatsu Kenkyusho Shiryo. irreg.
  ISSN 0453-0675
- National Research Institute of Police Science.
  Report/Kagaku Keisatsu Kenkyusho Hokoku. q.
  ISSN 0451-1980

**Japan. National Research Laboratory of Metrology**
1-10-4 Kaga, Itabashi, Tokyo 173, Japan.
- National Research Laboratory of Metrology.
  Bulletin. s-a. ISSN 0451-6109

**Japan. National Tax Agency**
3-1-1 Kasumigaseki, Chiyoda-ku, Tokyo 100, Japan.
- Outline of Japanese Tax. a. ISSN 0078-7094
- Zeimu Tokei Kara Mita Hojin Kigyo No Jittai. a.
  (prep. by its Income Tax Section)

**Japan. Office of the Prime Minister. Bureau of
Statistics**
see **Japan. Bureau of Statistics**

**Japan. Okurasho**
see **Japan. Ministry of Finance**

**Japan. Oriental Library**
see **Oriental Library**

**Japan. Port and Harbour Technical Research
Institute**
3-1-1 Nagase, Yokosuka 239, Kanagawa, Japan.
- Port and Harbour Technical Research Institute.
  Guide/Kowan Gijutsu Kenkyusho. Guide. irreg.

**Japan. Public Works Research Institute**
Ministry of Construction, 2-28-32 Honkomagome,
Bunkyo-Ku, Tokyo 113, Japan.
- Japan. Public Works Research Institute. Journal of
  Research/Doboku Kenkyusho Hokoku. irreg.

**Japan. Radiation Effects Research Foundation**
see **Radiation Effects Research Foundation**

**Japan. Rodosho**
*see* Japan. Ministry of Labour

**Japan. Science and Technology Agency**
2-2-1 Kasumigaseki, Chiyoda-ku, Tokyo 100, Japan.
● Scientific and Technical Information in Foreign
Countries/Kaigaki Kagaku Gijutsu Joho Shiryo.
irreg. (prep. by its Planning Bureau)
● Space in Japan. irreg.

**Japan. Science and Technology Agency. National
Aerospace Laboratory**
*see* Japan. National Aerospace Laboratory

**Japan. Sericultural Experiment Station**
3-55-30 Wada, Suginami-ku, Tokyo 166, Japan.
● Acta Sericologica/Sanshi Kenkyu. q. ISSN 0036-
4495
● Sericultural Experiment Station. Annual Report/
Sanshi Shikenjo, Tokyo. Nempo. a. ISSN 0581-
5908

**Japan. Shikoku National Agricultural Experiment
Station**
3 Zentsuji-cho, Kagawa 765, Japan.
● Shikoku National Agricultural Experiment
Station/Shikoku Nogyo Shikenjo Hokoku. s-a.
ISSN 0037-3702

**Japan. Ship Research Institute**
Ministry of Transport, 6-38-1 Shinkawa, Mitaka-shi,
Tokyo 181, Japan.
● Japan. Ship Research Institute. Papers/Senpaku
Gijutsu Kenkyusho Obun Hokoku. irreg.

**Japan. Sorifu. Tokeikyoku**
*see* Japan. Bureau of Statistics

**Japan. Tohoku Regional Fisheries Research
Laboratory**
27-5 Shinhama-cho, Shiogama 985, Miyagi-ken,
Japan.
● Tohoku Regional Fisheries Research Laboratory.
Bulletin/Tohoku-ku Suisan Kenkyusho Kenkyu
Hokoku. s-a. ISSN 0049-402X

**Japan. Tokai-Kinki National Agricultural Experiment
Station**
Ishinden-Ogoso, Tsu-City, Japan.
● Tokai-Kinki National Agricultural Experiment
Station, Tsu, Japan. Bulletin. a. ISSN 0082-4674

**Japan. Tokai Regional Fisheries Research Laboratory**
5-5-1 Kachidoki, Chuo-ku, Tokyo 104, Japan.
● Tokai Regional Fisheries Research Laboratory/
Tokaiku Suisan Kenkyusho Kenkyu Hokoku. q.
ISSN 0040-8859

**Japan. Tokeikyoku**
*see* Japan. Bureau of Statistics

**Japan. Tropical Agriculture Research Center**
Kitanakazuma, Yatabe, Tsukuba, Ibaraki 300-21,
Japan.
● Japan Agricultural Research Quarterly. q. ISSN
0021-3551

**Japan. Yokohama Plant Protection Station**
5-57 Kita-Naka-dori, Naka-ku, Yokohama 231,
Japan.
● Yokohama Plant Protection News/Yokohama
Shokubutsu Boeki Nyusu. s-m. ISSN 0049-8335

**Japan Academy**
Ueno Park, Taito-ku, Tokyo 110, Japan
(Order from: Maruzen Co., Ltd., 2-3-10 Nihon
Bashi, Chuo-ku, Tokyo 103, Japan; or Import and
Export Department, Box 5050, Tokyo International,
Tokyo 100-31, Japan)
● Japan Academy. Proceedings/Nippon Gakushiin
Kiyo. m. ISSN 0021-4280

**Japan Aeronautical Engineers' Association**
Saruta Bldg., 1-4-10 Akasaka, Minato-ku, Tokyo
107, Japan.
● Aircraft Engineering/Koku Gijutsu. m. ISSN
0023-284X

**Japan Agricultural Standards Association**
25 Shiba Nishikubo Akefune-cho, Minato-ku, Tokyo
105, Japan.
● J A S News/J A S Nyusu. m.

**Japan Air Cleaning Association**
Shirogane Bldg., 6-7-5 Soto Kanda, Chiyoda-ku,
Tokyo 101, Japan.
● Air Cleaning/Kuki Seijo. 8 per yr. ISSN 0023-
5032

**Japan Air Self Defense Force. Aeromedical
Laboratory**
1-2-10 Sakae-cho, Tachikawa-shi, Tokyo, Japan.
● Japan Air Self Defense Force. Aeromedical
Laboratory. Reports/Koku Igaku Jikkentai
Hokoku. q. ISSN 0023-2858

**Japan Anti-Tuberculosis Association**
1-3-12 Misaki-cho, Chiyoda-ku, Tokyo 101, Japan.
● Abstracts of the Current Literature on TB and
Other Respiratory Diseases/Kekkaku Oyobi
Kokyuki Shikkan Bunken No Shoroku Sokuho. m.
ISSN 0001-3668
● Japan Anti-Tuberculosis Association. Reports on
Medical Research Problems/Kekkaku Yobokai
Kenkyu Gyoseki. a. ISSN 0075-3165
● Red Double-Barred Cross/Fukijuji. bi-m. ISSN
0016-2531
● Review of Tuberculosis for Public Health Nurse/
Hokenfu No Kekkaku Tembo. s-a. ISSN 0018-
3369

**Japan Antibiotics Research Association**
2-20-8 Kamiosaki, Shinagawa-ku, Tokyo 141, Japan.
● Japanese Journal of Antibiotics. bi-m. ISSN 0021-
4906
● Journal of Antibiotics; an international journal
devoted to research on antibiotics and other
microbial products. m. ISSN 0021-8820

**Japan Architect Co., Ltd.**
2-31-2 Yushima, Bunkyo-ku, Tokyo 113, Japan.
● Japan Architect. m. ISSN 0021-4302

**Japan Architecture Association. Kansai Branch**
c/o Kensetsu Hosho Bldg., 5 Uemachi, Higashi-ku,
Osaka 540, Japan.
● Works of Architects. irreg.

**Japan Art History Society**
c/o Tokyo National Research Institute of Cultural
Properties, Ueno Park, Tokyo, Japan.
● Journal of Art History/Bijutsu Shi. q. ISSN 0021-
907X

**Japan Association for International Chemical
Information**
c/o Nihon Kagakukai, 1-5 Kanda Surugadai,
Chiyoda-ku, Tokyo 101, Japan
(Overseas Distributor: Japan Publications Trading
Co., Ltd., Box 5030, Tokyo International, Tokyo
100-31, Japan; or 1255 Howard St., San Francisco,
CA 94103)
● Chemical Abstracts/Kagaku Shoho. s-m.

**Japan Association for Philosophy of Science**
c/o Institute of Statistical Mathematics, 4-6-7
Minami Azabu, Minato-ku, Tokyo 106, Japan.
● Japan Association for Philosophy of Science.
Annals. a. ISSN 0453-0691
● Japan Association for Philosophy of Science.
Journal/Kagaku Kisoron Kenkyu. s-a. ISSN 0022-
7668

**Japan Association for Technical Information**
4-7-107 Yamazakicho, Machida, Tokyo 194-01,
Japan.
● Japan Shipbuilding & Marine Engineering. q. ISSN
0021-4647

**Japan Association of Africanists**
c/o University of Tokyo, Dept. of Geography,
Hongo, Bunkyo-ku, Tokyo 113, Japan.
● Journal of African Studies/Afurika Kenkyu. irreg.
ISSN 0065-4140

**Japan Association of Agricultural Librarians and
Documentalists**
29-31 Sakuragaoka, Shibuya-ku, Tokyo 150, Japan.
● Japanese Agricultural Science Index/Nihon
Nogaku Bunken Kiji Sakuin. m. (plus semi-annual
cumulative nos.)

**Japan Association of Automatic Control Engineers**
1 Yamabana, Itchoda-cho, Sakyo-ku, Kyoto 606,
Japan.
● Systems and Controls/Shisutemu to Seigyo. m.

**Japan Association of Civil Procedure**
● Journal of Civil Procedure/Minji Sosho Zasshi.
(pub. by Horitsu Bunka Sha)

**Japan Association of Industrial Health**
Public Health Bldg., 1-29-8 Shinjuku, Shinjuku-ku,
Tokyo 160, Japan.
● Japanese Journal of Industrial Health/Sangyo
Igaku. bi-m. ISSN 0047-1879

**Japan Association of Physical Education for Women
and Girls**
6-102 O.M.Y.C., 3-1 Jinen-cho Yoyogi, Shibuya-ku,
Tokyo, Japan.
● International Association of Physical Education
and Sports for Girls and Women. Proceedings of
the International Congress. irreg., 1969, 6th,
Tokyo. ISSN 0074-1728

**Japan Association of Rehabilitation Medicine**
● Japanese Journal of Rehabilitation Medicine/
Rihabiriteshon Igaku. (pub. by Igaku Shoin Ltd.)

**Japan Atomic Energy Commission**
*see* Japan. Japan Atomic Energy Commission

**Japan Atomic Energy Research Institute. Tokai
Research Establishment**
Tokai-mura, Naka-gun, Ibaraki 319-11, Japan.
● J A E R I Reports Abstracts/Genken Kenkyu
Seika Shorokusyu. m. ISSN 0385-6437
● Nuclear Science Information of Japan. bi-m. ISSN
0029-5620

**Japan Atomic Energy Society**
*see* Atomic Energy Society of Japan

**Japan Atomic Industrial Forum, Inc.**
1-1-13 Shinbashi, Minato-ku, Toykyo 105, Japan.
● Atomic Industry News/Genshiryoku Sangyo
Shinbun. w.
● Atoms in Japan. m. ISSN 0403-9319

**Japan Audio-Visual Education Association**
1-17-1 Toranomon, Minato-ku, Tokyo 105, Japan.
● A V E in Japan. a. ISSN 0065-0102
● Audio-Visual Education/Shichokaku Kyoiku. m.
ISSN 0037-3664

**Japan Audiological Society**
c/o Tokyo Daigaku Igakubu Jibika, 7-3-1 Hongo,
Bunkyo-ku, Tokyo 113, Japan.
● Audiology Japan. bi-m. ISSN 0303-8106

**Japan Automobile Federation**
3-5-8 Shibakoen, Minato-ku, Tokyo, Japan.
● J A F News Letter. m. ISSN 0021-3500

**Japan Automobile Manufacturers Association**
Ote-machi Bldg., 1-6-1 Ote-machi, Chiyoda-ku,
Tokyo 100, Japan.
● Motor Vehicle Statistics of Japan. a. ISSN 0463-
6635

**Japan Bicycle Industry Association**
1-9-15 Akasaka, Minato-ku, Tokyo 107, Japan.
● Japan's Bicycle Guide. a. ISSN 0446-6667

**Japan Broadcast Publishing Co., Ltd.(Nippon Hoso
Shuppan Kyokai)**
41-1 Udagawa-cho, Shibuyu-ku, Tokyo 150, Japan.
● N H K Technical Journal. (Nippon Hoso Kyokai)
/N H K Gijutsu Kenkyu. q. ISSN 0027-6553
(Japan Broadcasting Corp.)
● N H K Technical Report. (Nippon Hoso Kyokai)/
N H K Giken Geppo. m. ISSN 0027-6561 (Japan
Broadcasting Corp.)

**Japan Broadcasting Corp.**
2-2 Uchisaiwa-cho, Chiyoda-ku, Tokyo 100, Japan.
● N H K Technical Journal/N H K Gijutsu Kenkyu.
(pub. by Japan Broadcast Publishing Co.,
Ltd.(Nippon Hoso Shuppan Kyokai))
● N H K Technical Report/N H K Giken Geppo.
(pub. by Japan Broadcast Publishing Co.,
Ltd.(Nippon Hoso Shuppan Kyokai))
● Radio Japan News. m.(Japanese edition); bi-m
(other language editions) ISSN 0033-7927

**Japan Broadcasting Corp. Radio & TV Culture
Research Institute**
1-10 Atago-cho, Shiba, Minato-ku, Tokyo, Japan.
● Studies of Broadcasting; an international annual of
broadcasting science. a. (prep. by its Theoretical
Research Center)

**Japan Broadcasting Corp. Technical Research
Laboratories**
Research and Information Services Division, 1-10-
11 Kinuta, Setagaya-ku, Tokyo 157, Japan.
● N H K Laboratories Note. (Nippon Hoso Kyokai)
10 per yr. ISSN 0027-657X
● N H K Technical Monograph. (Nippon Hoso
Kyokai)/N H K Gijutsu Kenkyojo. irreg. ISSN
0077-2631

**Japan Broncho- Esophagological Society**
c/o Keio University Medical School, 35
Shinanomachi, Shinju-ku, Tokyo 160, Japan.
- Japan Broncho-Esophagological Society. Journal/
Nihon Kikan Shokudoka Gakkai Kaiho. bi-m.
ISSN 0029-0645

**Japan Cartographers Association**
c/o Japan Map Center, 2-10-12 Dogenzaka,
Shibuya-ku, Tokyo 150, Japan.
- Map/Chizu. q. ISSN 0009-4897

**Japan Center for Area Development Research**
Iino Bldg., 2-1-1 Uchisaiwaicho, Chiyoda-ku, Tokyo
100, Japan.
- Area Development in Japan. s-a.
- International Symposium on Regional
Development. Papers and Proceedings. irreg.,
1974, 4th. ISSN 0074-8897

**Japan Chamber of Commerce and Industry**
Room 505, World Trade Center Bldg., 2-4-1
Hamamatsu-cho, Minato-ku, Tokyo 105, Japan.
- Standard Trade Index of Japan. a. ISSN 0585-
0444

**Japan Chemical Fibres Association**
No. 3 Nihonbashi-Muromachi 3-chome, Chuo-ku,
Tokyo, Japan.
- Man-Made Fibers of Japan. irreg. (Co-sponsor:
Japan Silk and Synthetic Textiles Exporters'
Association)

**Japan Chemical Industry Association**
3-2-6 Kasumigaseki, Chiyoda-ku, Tokyo 100, Japan.
- Japan Chemical Industry Association Monthly/
Nikkakyo Geppo. m. ISSN 0029-0483

**Japan Christian Medical Association**
1-551-23 Totsuka, Shinjuku-ku, Tokyo 160, Japan.
- Medicine and Gospel/Igaku to Fukuin. m. ISSN
0019-1582

**Japan Concrete Institute**
c/o Shiba-Park Hotel, 1-5-10 Shiba Koen, Minato-
ku, Tokyo 105, Japan.
- Konkuriito Kogaku. m.

**Japan Cotton Traders' Association**
Box Osaka Central 951, 1-8-2 Utsubu-Honmachi,
Nishiku, Osaka, Japan.
- Cotton Statistics Monthly/Menka Tokei Geppo.
m. ISSN 0574-2374

**Japan Dental Association**
4-1-20 Kudan Kita, Chiyoda-ku, Tokyo 102, Japan.
- Dentistry in Japan/Nihon no Shika Iryo. irreg.,
no. 14, 1974. ISSN 0070-3737 (Japanese
Association for Dental Science)
- Japan Dental Association. Journal/Nihon Shika
Ishikai Zasshi. m. ISSN 0047-1763

**Japan Development Bank**
1-9-1- Otemachi, Chiyoda-ku, Tokyo, Japan.
- Nihon Kaihatsu Ginko. Chosabu. Chosa Geppo.
irreg.

**Japan Diabetic Society**
c/o Toyo Bunko, 28-21, 2-chome, Honkomagome,
Bunkyo-ku, Tokyo 113, Japan.
- Japan Diabetic Society. Journal/Tonyobyo. bi-m.
ISSN 0021-437X

**Japan Documentation Society**
Sasaki Bldg., 2-5-7 Koishikawa, Bunkyo-ku, Tokyo,
Japan.
- Bibliography of Agricultural Sciences in Japan.
irreg.
- Documentation Study/Dokumenteshon Kenkyu.
m. ISSN 0012-5180

**Japan Echo Inc.**
c/o Japan Publications Trading Co., Ltd., Box 5030,
Tokyo International, Tokyo 100-31, Japan
(or 1255 Howard St., San Francisco, CA 94103)
- Japan Echo. q.

**Japan Economic Journal**
1-9-5 Otemachi, Chiyoda-ku, Tokyo 100, Japan.
- Contemporary Economics/Gendai Keizai. q.
- Industrial Review of Japan; an annual in-depth
report on the state of the Japanese economy. a.
ISSN 0537-5452
- Japan Economic Journal/Nihon Keizai Shimbun.
w. ISSN 0021-4388

**Japan Economic Research Center**
1-9-5 Otemachi, Chiyoda-ku, Tokyo 100, Japan.
- Five Year Economic Forecast/Gokanen Keizai
Yosoku. a. (prep. by its Publications Department)
- Japan Economic Research Center. Bulletin/Nihon
Keizai Kenkyu Senta. Kaiho. s-m. (prep. by its
Publications Department)
- Quarterly Forecast of Japan's Economy; by the S.
A. method. 3 per yr. (prep. by its Publications
Department)

**Japan Economic Review**
c/o Kyodo Bunka Jigyosha, Kyodo Tsushin Bldg., 2
Akasaka, Aoicho, Minato-ku, Tokyo, Japan.
- Japan Economic Review. m. ISSN 0449-4636

**Japan Electric Power Survey Committee**
c/o Towden Kyukan, 1-1-13 Shinbashi, Minato-ku,
Tokyo 105, Japan.
- Electric Power Survey/Nihon Denryoku Chosa
Hokokusho. s-a.

**Japan Emergency Christian Conference on Korean
Problems**
c/o National Christian Council of Japan, Japan
Christian Center, Rm. 24, 2-3-18 Nishiwaseda,
Shinjuku-ku, Tokyo 160, Japan.
- Korea Communique. m.

**Japan Endocrine Society**
c/o Seirenkaikan Kouginbashi Nishizume, Kamigyo-
ku, Kyoto 602, Japan.
- Folia Endocrinologica Japonica/Nihon Naibunpi
Gakkai Zasshi. m. ISSN 0029-0300

**Japan Endocrine Society. Eastern Branch**
c/o Jikei University School of Medicine, Dept. of
Anatomy, 25-8, 3-chome, Nishishinbashi, Minato-
ku, Tokyo 105, Japan
(Overseas Distributor: Japan Publications Trading
Co., Ltd., Box 5030, Tokyo International, Tokyo
100-31, Japan; or 1255 Howard St., San Francisco,
CA 94103)
- Endocrinologia Japonica/Nihon Naibunpi Gakkai
Tobu Bukashi. bi-m. ISSN 0013-7219

**Japan Engineering News, Inc.**
Tomisu Bldg., 2nd Floor, 2-23-9 Higeshi-Ikebukuro,
Toshima-ku, Tokyo, Japan.
- Patents and Licensing. bi-m.

**Japan Environmental Sanitation Center**
10-6 Yotsuya Kami-cho, Kawasaki-ku, Kawasaki
210, Japan.
- Life and Environment/Seikatsu to Kankyo. m.
ISSN 0037-1025

**Japan Evangelical Missionary Association**
2-1 Kanda Surugadai, Chiyoda-ku, Tokyo 101,
Japan.
- Japan Harvest. q. ISSN 0021-440X

**Japan Experimental Animal Research Association**
c/o the Institute of Medical Science, University of
Tokyo, 4-6-1 Shiroganedai, Minato-ku, Tokyo 108,
Japan.
- Experimental Animals/Jikken Dobutsu. q. ISSN
0007-5124

**Japan External Trade Organization**
2 Akasaka Aoicho, Tokyo 107, Japan.
- Focus Japan. m.
- J I T Directory. (Japan International Trade) a.
ISSN 0075-3262
- Now in Japan. irreg.
- White Paper on International Trade: Japan. a.

**Japan F A O Association**
Bajichikusan Kaikan Bldg., 1-2 Kanda Surugadai,
Chiyoda-ku, Tokyo 101, Japan.
- World Agriculture, Forestry and Fisheries/Sekai
No Norinsuisan. m.

**Japan Federation of Composers**
Shinanomachi Bldg., 602 33-Shinanomachi,
Shinjuku-ku, Tokyo 160, Japan.
- Japan Federation of Composers. Catalogue of
Publications. a.

**Japan Federation of Economic Organizations**
1-9-4 Otemachi, Chiyoda-ku, Tokyo 100, Japan.
- Economic Picture of Japan. a. ISSN 0070-8593
- Keidanren Geppo. m. ISSN 0453-4484
- Keidanren Review. bi-m. ISSN 0022-9695

**Japan Feed Trade Association**
c/o Koizumi Bldg., 4-3-13 Ginza, Chuo-ku, Tokyo
104, Japan.
- Feed Trade. m. ISSN 0014-9586

**Japan Fisheries Association**
1-9-13 Akasaka, Minato-ku, Tokyo 107, Japan.
- Fisheries World/Suisan Kai. m. ISSN 0039-4866

**Japan Foundation**
Daito Building, 3-7-1 Kasumigaseki, Chiyoda-ku,
Tokyo 100, Japan.
- Japan Foundation Newsletter. bi-m.

**Japan Foundation for Shipbuilding Advancement**
Library, 35 Shiba-Kotohiracho, Minato-ku, Tokyo
105, Japan.
- J A F S A Library News. bi-m. ISSN 0385-1176
- Japan Shipbuilding Information Notes. s-a.

**Japan Foundrymen's Society**
8-12-13 Ginza, Chuo-ku, Tokyo 104, Japan.
- Japan Foundrymen's Society. Journal/Imono. m.
ISSN 0021-4396

**Japan Gas Association**
38 Shiba Kotohira-cho, Minato-ku, Tokyo 105,
Japan.
- Japan Gas Association. Journal/Nihon Gasu
Kyokaishi. m. ISSN 0029-0211

**Japan General Foundry Center Foundation**
Tokyo, Japan.
- Foundry Statistics of Japan. a.

**Japan Heat Management Association**
1-22, 3-chome, Shibakoen, Minato-ku, Tokyo,
Japan.
- Heat Management and Pollution Control/Netsu
Kanri to Kogai. m.

**Japan Hematological Society**
Department of Internal Medicine, Faculty of
Medicine, Kyoto University, 53 Shogoin-
Kawaramachi, Sakyo-ku, Kyoto 606, Japan.
- Acta Haematologica Japonica/Nihon Ketsueki
Gakkai Zasshi. bi-m. ISSN 0001-5806

**Japan Hospital Equipment Association**
c/o Byoin Kanri Kenkyusho, 1 Toyama-cho,
Shinjuku-ku, Tokyo 162, Japan.
- Hospital Equipment/Byoin Setsubi. bi-m. ISSN
0007-764X

**Japan Industrial & Vocational Training Association**
6th Floor, Minamizuka Bldg., 2-17-3 Shibuya,
Shibuya-ku, Tokyo 150, Japan.
- Industrial Training/Sangyo Kunren. m. ISSN
0036-438X

**Japan Industrial Location Center**
2-1 Shiba-Kotohiramachi, Minato-ku, Tokyo, Japan.
- Industrial Location Handbook/Kogyo Ritchi
Handobukku. triennial.

**Japan Industrial Safety Association**
35-4 Shiba, 5-chome, Minato-ku, Tokyo 108, Japan.
- International Congress on Occupational Health.
Proceedings. triennial, 1969, 16th, Tokyo. ISSN
0074-4131 (Permanent Commission and
International Association on Occupational Health)

**Japan Industrial Vehicles Association**
1-5-26 Moto-Akasaka, Minato-ku, Tokyo 107,
Japan.
- Industrial Vehicles/Sangyo Sharyo. m. ISSN 0036-
4398

**Japan Industry and Trade Research Association**
Kami-Parupu Kaikan Bldg., 3-9-11 Ginza, Chuo-ku,
Tokyo 104, Japan
- Monthly Statistics of Paper Distribution/Kami
Ryutsu Tokei Geppo. m. ISSN 0044-0663 (Japan.
Ministry of International Trade and Industry)
(Order from: Government Publications Service
Center, 1-2-1 Kasumigaseki, Chiyoda-ku, Tokyo
100, Japan)

**Japan Information Center of Science and Technology**
2-5-2 Nagata-cho, Chiyoda-ku, Tokyo 100, Japan.
- Current Bibliography on Science and Technology:
Chemistry and Chemical Engineering (Foreign)/
Kagaku Gijutsu Bunken Sokuho, Kagaku, Kagaku
Kogyo- Hen (Gaikoku- Hen) 3 per m.
- Current Bibliography on Science and Technology:
Chemistry and Chemical Engineering (Japanese)/
Kagaku Gijutsu Bunken Sokuho Kagaku, Kagaku
Kogyo-Hen (Kokunai-Hen) m.

- Current Bibliography on Science and Technology: Civil Engineering and Architecture/Kagaku Gijutsu Bunken Sokuho, Doboku, Kenchiku Kogaku-Hen. s-m.
- Current Bibliography on Science and Technology: Earth Science, Mining and Metallurgy/Kagaku Gijutsu Bunken Sokuho, Kinzoku Kogaku, Kozan Kogaku, Chikyu No Kagaku-Hen. s-m. ISSN 0011-3301
- Current Bibliography on Science and Technology: Electronics and Electrical Engineering/Kagaku Gijutsu Bunken Sokuho, Denshigaku to Denki Kogaku-Hen. s-m.
- Current Bibliography on Science and Technology: Environmental Pollution. m.
- Current Bibliography on Science and Technology: Management Science and Systems Engineering/ Kagaku Gijutsu Bunken Sokuho, Kanri Shisutemu-Hen. m.
- Current Bibliography on Science and Technology: Mechanical Engineering/Kagaku Gijutsu Bunken Sokuho, Kikai Kogaku-Hen. s-m.
- Current Bibliography on Science and Technology: Nuclear Engineering/Kagaku Gijutsu Bunken Sokuho, Genshiryoku Kogaku-Hen. m.
- Current Bibliography on Science and Technology: Pure and Applied Physics/Kagaku Gijutsu Bunken Sokuho, Butsuri, Oyobutsuri-Hen. s-m.
- Foreign Patent News/Gaikoku Tokkyo Sokuho, Kagaku-Hen. w.
- Information and Documentation/Joho Kanri. m. ISSN 0021-7298
- Technical Highlights/Kaigai Gijutsu Hairaito. m.
- Technical Information for Small Industries/Chuso Kigyo Kaigai Gijutsu Joho. bi-m.

**Japan Institute for Biological Science**
*see* Nippon Institute for Biological Science

**Japan Institute for International Study**
Second Ashike Bldg., 3-40 Andojibashi-Dori, Minami-ku, Osaka, Japan.
- Rikai; towards better understanding. q.

**Japan Institute of Industrial Engineering**
c/o San'yo Kokusaku Bldg., 1-7-8 Shibuya, Shibuya-ku, Tokyo 150, Japan.
- I E Review. (Industrial Engineering) bi-m. ISSN 0018-9596

**Japan Institute of Labour**
Chutaikin Bldg., 1-7-6 Shibakoen, Minato-ku, Tokyo, Japan.
- Japan Institute of Labour. Journal/Nihon Rodo Kyokai Zasshi. m. ISSN 0029-0378
- Japan Labour Bulletin. m. ISSN 0021-4469
- Nihon no Roshi Kankei. a.

**Japan Institute of Metals**
Aoba Aramaki, Sendai 980, Japan.
- Japan Institute of Metals. Bulletin/Nihon Kinzoku Gakkai Kaiho. m. ISSN 0021-4426
- Japan Institute of Metals. Journal/Nippon Kinzoku Gakkaishi. m. ISSN 0021-4876
- Japan Institute of Metals. Transactions. m. ISSN 0021-4434

**Japan Institution for Library Science**
Toshokangaku Kenkyushitsu, Tenri University, 1050 Somanouchi-cho, Tenri, Nara, Japan.
- Library World/Toshokan-Kai. bi-m. ISSN 0040-9669

**Japan International Cooperation Agency**
Box 216, Mitsui Bldg., Shinjuku-ku, Tokyo 160, Japan.
- International Cooperation/Kokusai Kyoryoku. m.

**Japan Investors Ltd.**
2-12-8 Kitaaoyama, Minato-ku, Tokyo 107, Japan.
- Japan Port Information. a.

**Japan Iron and Steel Exporter's Association**
c/o Tekko Kaikan, 3-16 Nihonbashi Kayaba-cho, Chuo-ku, Tokyo 103, Japan.
- Steel Today and Tomorrow. bi-m.

**Japan Iron & Steel Federation**
Keidanren Kaikan, 1-9-4 Otemachi, Chiyoda-ku, Tokyo 100, Japan.
- Journal of Labor Hygiene in Iron and Steel Industry/Tekko Rodo Eisei. q. ISSN 0040-2273

**Japan Journal, Inc.**
Box 702, Tokyo 100-91, Japan.
- Japan Stock Journal; Japan's financial and business news weekly. w. ISSN 0021-4736

**Japan Knitwear Designer's Association**
c/o Tokyo Bldg., 1-3-3 Yanagibashi, Taito-ku, Tokyo 111, Japan.
- Knit Design. m.

**Japan Lead Zinc Development Association**
New Hibiya Bldg., 1-3-6 Uchisaiwai-cho, Chiyoda-ku, Tokyo 100, Japan.
- Lead and Zinc/Namari to Aen. bi-m. ISSN 0027-772X

**Japan Library Association**
1-1-10 Taishido, Setagaya-ku, Tokyo 154, Japan.
- Catalogue of Books Recommended for Libraries/ Sentei Tosho Somokuroku. a.
- Contemporary Library Trends/Gendai no Toshokan. q. ISSN 0016-6332
- Library Journal/Toshokan Zasshi. m.

**Japan Light Metal Association**
c/o Nihonbashi Asahi Seimeikan, 2-1-3 Nihonbashi, Chuo-ku, Tokyo 102, Japan.
- Light Metal Statistics in Japan/Keikinzoku Kogyo Tokei Nenpo. irreg. ISSN 0451-6001

**Japan Lumber Journal, Inc.**
C.P.O. Box 1945, Tokyo 100-91, Japan.
- Japan Lumber Journal. s-m. ISSN 0021-4477
- White Paper on Japan's Forest Industries. decennial. ISSN 0083-9272

**Japan Machinery Federation**
Kikai Shinko Bldg., 8-5-3 Shiba Koen, Minato-ku, Tokyo 105, Japan.
- Selected Economic Indicators Related to Japan's Engineering Industries. s-a.

**Japan Management Science Institute**
4-28-26 Minami-Aoyama, Minato-ku, Tokyo 107, Japan.
- Computer Report/Konpyuta Repoto. m.

**Japan Map Center**
4-8-8 Kudanminami, Chiyoda-ku, Tokyo 102, Japan.
- Japan Map Center News/Chizu Senta Nyusu. m. ISSN 0302-0231

**Japan Medical Association (Nihon Ishikai)**
2-5 Kanda Surugadai, Chiyoda-ku, Tokyo 101, Japan.
- Asian Medical Journal. (pub. by Japan Medical Publishers, Inc. (Nihon Gakujutsu Shuppansha))
- Japan Medical Association. Journal/Nihon Ishikai Zasshi. s-m. ISSN 0021-4493

**Japan Medical Association (Nippon Igaku Kyokai)**
7-2-8 Hongo, Bunkyo-ku, Tokyo 113, Japan.
- Medical Science and Medical Care/Gekkan Igaku to Iryo. m. ISSN 0019-1590

**Japan Medical Library Association**
c/o Business Center for Academic Societies, 2-4-16 Yayoi, Bunkyo-ku, Tokyo 113, Japan.
- Medical Libraries/Igaku Toshokan. q. ISSN 0445-2429

**Japan Medical Publishers, Inc. (Nihon Gakujutsu Shuppansha)**
Zenkyoren Bldg., 7-9, 2-chome, Hirakawa-cho, Chiyoda-ku, Tokyo 102, Japan
- Asian Medical Journal. m. ISSN 0004-461X (Japan Medical Association (Nihon Ishikai)) (U.S. Subscr. Address: Maruzen Company, Ltd., 11251 Avenue of the Americas, New York, NY 10020)

**Japan Mental Health Society**
91 Bentencho, Shinjuku-ku, Tokyo 162, Japan.
- Mind and Society/Kokoro to Shakai. q. ISSN 0023-2807

**Japan Meteorological Agency**
*for publications of this agency, see* Japan Weather Association

**Japan Microphotography Association**
Kudo Bldg., 3-5 Kandakajicho, Chiyodaku, Tokyo 101, Japan.
- Journal of Microphotography/Maikuro Shashin. bi-m. ISSN 0026-2811

**Japan Monkey Centre**
26 Inuyama Kanrin, Aichi 484, Japan.
- Monkey/Monki. bi-m. ISSN 0026-9794
- Primates; journal of primatology. q. ISSN 0032-8332

**Japan National Tourist Organization**
- New Official Guide: Japan. (pub. by Japan Travel Bureau, Inc.)

**Japan Neurosurgical Society**
Department of Neurosurgery, Faculty of Medicine, University of Tokyo, 7-3-1 Hongo, Bunkyo-ku, Tokyo 113, Japan.
- Neurologia Medico-Chirurgica. a. ISSN 0470-8105
- Neurological Surgery/Noshinkei Geka. m.

**Japan Orthodontic Society**
c/o Department of Orthodontics, School of Dentistry, Tokyo Medical and Dental University, 1-5-45 Yushima, Bunkyo-ku, Tokyo 113, Japan.
- Japan Orthodontic Society. Journal/Nihon Kyosei Shika Gakkai Zasshi. q. ISSN 0021-454X

**Japan Patent Center, Inc.**
Box 192, Kanda, Tokyo 101-91, Japan (Distributor for North and South America: Japan Information Center, Los Angeles World Trade Center, 333 S. Flower St., Suite 505, Los Angeles, CA 90017)
- Japan Patent Report. d.

**Japan Pediatric Society**
Nippon-Koshu-Eisei Kyokai Bldg., 1-29-8 Shinjuku, Shinjuku-ku, Tokyo 160, Japan.
- Acta Paediatrica Japonica. s-a. ISSN 0001-6543

**Japan Petroleum Consultants, Ltd.**
Box 1185, Tokyo Central, Tokyo 100-91, Japan.
- Japan Petroleum Weekly. w. ISSN 0021-4566

**Japan Petroleum Institute**
c/o Nisseki Bldg., 3-4-2 Marunouchi, Chiyoda-ku, Tokyo 100, Japan.
- Japan Petroleum Institute. Bulletin. s-a. ISSN 0582-4656

**Japan Pharmaceutical Information Centre**
2-12-15 Shibuya, Shibuya-ku, Tokyo 150, Japan.
- Contents. w.

**Japan Pharmaceutical Library Association**
7-3-1 Hongo, Bunkyo-ku, Tokyo 113, Japan.
- Pharmaceutical Library Bulletin/Yakugaku Toshokan. q.

**Japan Pharmaceutical, Medical & Dental Supply Exporter's Association**
4-3-6 Nihonbashi Honcho, Chuo-ku, Tokyo 103, Japan.
- Japan Medical News. bi-m. ISSN 0021-4515

**Japan Pharmaceutical Traders' Association**
- J A P T A List: Japanese Drug Directory. (pub. by Yakuji Nippo Ltd.)

**Japan Phonograph Record Association**
8-9 Tsukiji, Chuo-ku, Tokyo, Japan.
- Japanese Phonograph Records of Folk Songs, Classical and Popular Music. a. ISSN 0075-3459

**Japan Plant Protection Association**
1-43-11 Komagome, Toshima-ku, Tokyo 170, Japan
- Japan Pesticide Information. bi-m. (Dist. by: Society of Agricultural Chemistry, Nihonbashi Club Bldg., 8-1 Nihonbashi-Muromachi, Chuo-ku, Tokyo, Japan)
- Plant Protection/Shokubutsu Boeki. m. ISSN 0037-4091

**Japan Plastics Industry Federation**
- Japan Plastics. (pub. by Japan Press & Service International Co., Ltd.)

**Japan Plastics Journal Ltd.**
Kimura Bldg., 38 Minamisumiya-cho, Minami-ku, Osaka 552, Japan.
- Japan Plastics Journal/Nihon Purasuchikkusu Shinpo. fortn. ISSN 0029-0351

**Japan Polar Research Association**
3-4-2 Kasumigaseki, Chiyoda-ku, Tokyo 100, Japan.
- Polar News/Kyokuchi. s-a. ISSN 0023-6004

**Japan Press & Service International Co., Ltd.**
Sankyo Bldg., Room 401, 1-43 Kanda Jimbo-cho, Chiyoda-ku, Tokyo 101, Japan.
- Japan Plastics. 8 per yr. ISSN 0021-4574 (Japan Plastics Industry Federation)

**Japan Press, Ltd.**
C.P.O. Box 6, Tokyo, Japan
(or 2-12-8 Kita Aoyama, Minato-ku, Tokyo 107, Japan)
- Japan Directory. a. ISSN 0075-322X
- Shipping Gazette; weekly digest of shipping schedules and news. w. ISSN 0037-3915

**Japan Printers' Association**
Publicity Bureau, 1-16-8 Shintomi, Chuo-ku, Tokyo, Japan.
- Graphic Arts Japan. a. ISSN 0072-548X

**Japan Printing News Publishing Co.**
1-16-18 Sintomi, Chuo-ku, Tokyo, Japan
(U.S. Subscr. to: North American Publishing Co., 134 N. 13th St., Philadelphia, PA 19107)
- Printing World/Insatsukai. m. ISSN 0020-1766

**Japan Public Law Association**
- Public Law Review/Koho Kenkyu. (pub. by Yuhikaku Publishing Co. Ltd.)

**Japan Publications Trading Co. Ltd.**
Box 5030, Tokyo International, Tokyo 100-31, Japan
(or 1255 Howard St., San Francisco, CA 94103)
- Ars Buddhica/Bukkyo Geijutsu. bi-m. ISSN 0004-2889
- Behaviormetrika. a. (Behaviormetric Society of Japan)
- Japan Christian Quarterly. q. ISSN 0021-4361 (Fellowship of Christian Missionaries)
- Journal of Art Studies/Bijutsu Kenkyu. bi-m. ISSN 0021-9088
- Keio Business Review. a. ISSN 0453-4557 (Keio University Society of Business and Commerce)
- Keio Monographs of Business and Commerce. irreg., 1971, no. 3. ISSN 0075-5346 (Keio University Society of Business and Commerce)
- Kokka. m. ISSN 0023-2785
- Psychiatria et Neurologia Japonica/Seishin Shinkeigaku Zasshi. m. ISSN 0033-2658
- Socio-Economic History/Shakai Keizai Shigaku. bi-m. ISSN 0038-0113
- Studies on Oriental Music/Toyo Ongaku Kenkyu. ISSN 0039-3851

**Japan Publishing House**
1966 Kamikawai-cho, Asahi-ku, Yokohama 241, Japan.
- Adventist Life. m.
- Signs of the Times/Jicho. m. ISSN 0037-5055

**Japan Radiation Research Society**
4-9-1 Anagawa, Chiba 280, Japan.
- Japan Radiation Research Society. Journal. q.

**Japan Radioisotope Association**
2-28-45 Honkomagome, Bunkyo-ku, Tokyo 113, Japan.
- Isotope News. m.
- Radioisotopes. m. ISSN 0033-8303

**Japan Radiological Society**
see Nippon Societas Radiologica

**Japan Railway Civil Engineering Association**
1-18-7 Higashiueno, Taito-ku, Tokyo 110, Japan.
- Permanent Way/Tetsudo Senro. q. ISSN 0031-5516

**Japan Railway Cybernetics Association**
2-4 Ote-machi, Chiyoda-ku, Tokyo 100, Japan.
- Symposium on the Use of Cybernetics on the Railway. a.

**Japan Railway Engineer's Association**
2-5-18 Ote-machi, Chiyoda-ku, Tokyo 100, Japan.
- Japanese Railway Engineering. q. ISSN 0448-8938

**Japan Real Estate Institute**
Kangin-Fujiya Bldg., No. 1 Kotohira-cho, Shiba, Minato-ku, Tokyo, Japan.
- Indices of Urban Land Prices and Construction Cost of Wooden Houses in Japan. a. ISSN 0073-7186

**Japan Refrigeration and Air Conditioning Press**
2-11-7 Tsukiji, Chuo-ku, Tokyo 104, Japan.
- Japan Refrigeration and Air Conditioning News/Nihon Reito Reibo Shinbun. w. ISSN 0029-036X

**Japan Research Association for Textile End-Uses**
Shin-Ohgibashi Bldg., 19 Suehiro-cho, Kita-ku, Osaka 530, Japan.
- Japan Research Association for Textile End-Uses. Journal/Sen'i Seihin Shohi Kagaku. m. ISSN 0037-2072

**Japan Road Association**
Shoyukaikan, 3-3-3 Kasumigaseki, Chiyoda-ku, Tokyo 100, Japan.
- Japan Road Association. Annual Report of Roads. a. ISSN 0075-3319
- Road/Doro. m. ISSN 0012-5571

**Japan Science Foundation**
2-1 Kitanomaru-Koen, Chiyoda-ku, Tokyo 102, Japan.
- Japan Science and Technology/Nihon No Kagaku to Gijutsu. m. ISSN 0029-0327

**Japan Science Society**
Senpaku Shinko Bldg., 1-15-16 Toranomon, Minato-ku, Tokyo 105, Japan.
- Collecting and Breeding/Saishu to Shiku. m. ISSN 0036-3286

**Japan Scientists' Association**
1-9-16 Yushima, Bunkyo-ku, Tokyo 113, Japan.
- Journal of Japanese Scientists/Nihon No Kagaku. m. ISSN 0029-0335

**Japan Sea Regional Fisheries Research Laboratory**
see Japan. Japan Sea Regional Fisheries Research Laboratory

**Japan Securities Research Institute**
Shokenkaikan, 1-14 Nihonbashi, Kabaya-cho, Chuo-ku, Tokyo, Japan.
- Securities Market in Japan. irreg.

**Japan Sewage Works Association**
c/o Kojimachi Kaikan, 2-3-4 Hirakawa-cho, Chiyoda-ku, Tokyo 102, Japan.
- Japan Sewage Works Association. Journal/Gesuido Kyokaishi. m. ISSN 0021-4639

**Japan Shipping Exchange, Inc.**
6 Mitsui Bldg., Nihonbashi Muromachi, Chuo-ku, Tokyo 103, Japan.
- Shipping/Kaiun. m. ISSN 0022-7803

**Japan Snake Institute**
Yabusuka Hon-cho, Nitta-gun, Gunma 379-23, Japan.
- Snake. s-a.

**Japan Society for Aeronautical and Space Sciences**
Saruta Bldg., 1-4-10 Akasaka, Minato-ku, Tokyo, Japan.
- Japan Society for Aeronautical and Space Sciences. Journal/Nihon Koku Uchu Gakkaishi. m. ISSN 0021-4663
- Japan Society for Aeronautical and Space Sciences. Transactions. q. ISSN 0549-3811

**Japan Society for Cancer Therapy**
Kyoto University Medical School, Second Surgical Division, 53 Shogoin-Kawaracho, Sakyo-ku, Kyoto 606, Japan.
- Japan Society for Cancer Therapy. Journal. q. ISSN 0021-4671
- Japan Society for Cancer Therapy. Proceedings of the Congress. a. ISSN 0075-3327

**Japan Society for Cell Biology**
Okayama, Japan.
- Cell Structure and Function. q.

**Japan Society for Technology of Plasticity**
Torikatsu Bldg., 5-2-5 Roppongi, Minato-ku, Tokyo 106, Japan.
- Japan Society for Technology of Plasticity. Journal/Sosei to Kako. m. ISSN 0038-1586

**Japan Society for the Promotion of Science**
2-1-2 Hitotsubashi, Chiyoda-ku, Tokyo 101, Japan.
- Corrosion Engineering/Boshoku Gijutsu. m. ISSN 0010-9355 (prep. by its Committee for Corrosion Prevention)
- Japan Science Review: Economic Sciences. a. ISSN 0448-8709 (Japan Union of Associations of Economic Sciences)

**Japan Society of Air Pollution**
4-6-1 Shiroganedai, Minato-ku, Tokyo 108, Japan.
- Air Pollution News/Taiki Osen Nyusu. bi-m. ISSN 0039-9019
- Japan Society of Air Pollution. Journal/Taiki Osen Kenkyu. bi-m. ISSN 0039-9000

**Japan Society of Bakery Technology**
4-24-14 Sendagaya, Shibuya-ku, Tokyo 151, Japan.
- Pain/Bread. m. ISSN 0030-9451

**Japan Society of Chemotherapy**
2-20-8 Kamiosaki, Shinagawa-ku, Tokyo 141, Japan.
- Chemotherapy/Nihon Kagaku Ryoho Gakkai Zasshi. bi-m. ISSN 0009-3165

**Japan Society of Civil Engineers**
1-chome, Yotsuya, Shinjuku-ku, Tokyo 160, Japan.
- Coastal Engineering in Japan. a. ISSN 0578-5634
- Japan Society of Civil Engineers. Journal/Doboku Gakkaishi. m. ISSN 0021-468X
- Japan Society of Civil Engineers. Transactions. a. ISSN 0047-1798

**Japan Society of Clinical Pathology**
c/o Rinsho Byori Kanko-kai, Kuramata Bldg., 4-5-4 Yushima, Bunkyo-ku, Tokyo 113, Japan.
- Japanese Journal of Clinical Pathology/Rinsho Byori. m. ISSN 0047-1860

**Japan Society of Colour Materials**
Saito Bldg., 2-2-13 Nishikando, Chiyoda-ku, Tokyo 101, Japan.
- Colour Materials/Shikizai Kyokaishi. m. ISSN 0010-180X

**Japan Society of Earth Science Education**
c/o Tokyo Gakugei University, Chigaku Kyoshitsu, Nukuita-machi, Koganei-shi, Tokyo 184, Japan.
- Education of Earth Science/Chigaku Kyoiku. bi-m. ISSN 0009-3831

**Japan Society of Histochemistry and Cytochemistry**
Department of Pathology, Faculty of Medicine, Kyoto University, Konoe-cho, Yoshida, Sakyo-ku, Kyoto 606, Japan
(Overseas Distributor: Japan Publications Trading Co., Ltd., Box 5030, Tokyo International, Tokyo 100-31, Japan; or 1255 Howard St., San Francisco, CA 94103)
- Acta Histochemica et Cytochemica/Nihon Soshiki Saibo Kagakkai Gakkaishi. q. ISSN 0044-5991

**Japan Society of Histological Documentation (Societatis Histochemicae Japonicae)**
c/o Department of Anatomy, Niigata University School of Medicine, Asahimachi, Niigata, Japan.
- Archivum Histologicum Japonicum/Nihon Soshikigaku Kiroku. 5 per yr. ISSN 0004-0681

**Japan Society of Human Genetics**
- Japanese Journal of Human Genetics/Jinrui Idengaku. (pub. by Tokyo Medical and Dental University. Department of Human Genetics)

**Japan Society of International Economics**
c/o Sekai Keizai Chosakai, 2-8 Otemachi, Chiyoda-ku, Tokyo, Japan.
- International Economy/Kokusai Keizai. irreg.

**Japan Society of Library Science**
c/o National College of Library Science, 1-4-1 Shimouma, Setagaya-ku, Tokyo, Japan.
- Japan Society of Library Science. Annals/Toshokan Gakkai Nempo. s-a. (approx.) ISSN 0040-9650

**Japan Society of Logopedics and Phoniatrics**
c/o Research Institute of Logopedics and Phoniatrics, Faculty of Medicine, University of Tokyo, 7-3-1 Hongo, Bunkyo-ku, Tokyo 113, Japan.
- Japan Journal of Logopedics and Phoniatrics/Onsei Gengo Igaku. 3 per yr. ISSN 0030-2813

**Japan Society of Lubrication Engineers**
No. 407-2 Kikai Shinko Bldg., 3-5-8 Shiba Koen, Minato-ku, Tokyo 105, Japan.
- Japan Society of Lubrication Engineers. Journal/Junkatsu. m.

**Japan Society of Materials Science**
1-101 Yoshida Izumidono-cho, Sakyo-ku, Kyoto 606, Japan.
- Japan Congress on Materials Research. Proceedings/Zairyo Kenkyu Rengo Koenkai Ronbunshu. a. ISSN 0514-5171

**Japan Society of Mathematical Education**
c/o Tokyo University of Education, 2-1-3
Zoshigaya, Toshima-ku, Tokyo 191, Japan.
- Japan Society of Mathematical Education. Journal.
m. ISSN 0021-471X

**Japan Society of Mechanical Engineers**
Sanshin Hokusei Bldg., 2-4-9 Yoyogi, Shibuya-ku,
Tokyo 151, Japan.
- J. S. M. E. Bulletin. m. ISSN 0021-3764
- Japan Society of Mechanical Engineers. Journal/
Nihon Kikai Gakkaishi. m. ISSN 0021-4728
- Japan Society of Mechanical Engineers.
Transactions/Nihon Kikai Gakkai Ronbunshu. m.
ISSN 0029-0270

**Japan Society of Medical Electronics and Biological Engineering**
- Japanese Journal of Medical Electronics and
Biological Engineering/Iyo Denshi to Seito
Kogaku (Nihon M-E Gakkai Zasshi) (pub. by
Corona Publishing Co., Ltd.)

**Japan Society of Neonatology**
c/o Nihon University, School of Medicine,
Department of Pediatrics, 30-1 Oyaguchi-Kami-
machi, Itabashi-ku, Tokyo 173, Japan.
- Acta Neonatological Japonica/Nihon Shinseiji
Gakkai Zasshi. q. ISSN 0029-0386

**Japan Society of Precision Engineering**
Ceramics Bldg., 2-22-17 Hyakunin-cho, Shinjuku-ku,
Tokyo 160, Japan.
- Japan Society of Precision Engineering. Bulletin.
q. ISSN 0582-4206

**Japan Society of Smooth Muscle Research**
Nara Medical University, 840 Shijo-cho, Kashihara-
shi 634, Nara, Japan.
- Japanese Journal of Smooth Muscle Research/
Nihon Heikatsukin Gakkai Zasshi. q. ISSN 0029-
0238

**Japan Society of Tropical Medicine**
c/o Tokyo Daigaku Ikagaku Kenkyusho,
Shiroganedai, Minato-ku, Tokyo 108, Japan.
- Japanese Journal of Tropical Medicine. s-a.

**Japan Steel & Tube Corporation**
1-1-2 Marunouchi, Chiyoda-ku, Tokyo 100, Japan.
- Seihin News/Seihin Nyusu. bi-m. ISSN 0037-0991

**Japan Steel Works, Ltd.**
1-12 Yuraku-cho, Chiyoda-ku, Tokyo 100, Japan.
- Japan Steel Works Technical News. irreg.
- Japan Steel Works Technical Review/Nihon
Seikosho Giho. s-a. ISSN 0546-126X

**Japan Storage Battery Association**
Kikai Shinko Bldg., 5-8, 3-chome, Shibakoen,
Minato-ku, Tokyo 105, Japan.
- Storage Battery/Chikudenchi. m. ISSN 0009-3866

**Japan Sugar Refiners' Association**
5-7 Sanbancho, Chiyoda-ku, Tokyo 102, Japan.
- Quarterly Information of Sugar Industry/Kikan
Togyo Shiho. q. ISSN 0023-138X
- World Sugar News/Kaigai Sato Joho. bi-m. ISSN
0049-8149

**Japan Surgical Society**
Japan Medical Association, 2-5 Kanda Surugadai,
Chiyoda-ku, Tokyo 101, Japan.
- Japanese Journal of Surgery/Nihon Geka Gakkai
Zasshi. q. ISSN 0047-1909

**Japan Tariff Association**
c/o Jibiki Daini Bldg., 4-7-8 Kojimachi, Chiyoda-ku,
Tokyo, Japan.
- Commodity Classification for Foreign Trade
Statistics: Japan. irreg. ISSN 0546-0786

**Japan Teachers' Union**
Kyoiku-Kaikan, 2-6-2 Hitotsubashi, Kanda,
Chiyoda-ku, Tokyo, Japan.
- Educational Review/Kyoiku Hyoron. 3 per yr.
ISSN 0023-5997
- Nikkyoso Kyoiku Shimbun. w. ISSN 0029-0505

**Japan Telegraph and Telephone Public Corporation**
- Japan Telecommunications Review. (pub. by
Telecommunications Association (Denki Tsushin
Kyokai))

**Japan Textiles and Fibers Research Institute**
c/o Toko Bldg., 1 Edobori, Nishi-ku, Osaka 550,
Japan.
- Textile Magazine/Sen'i Kai. m. ISSN 0037-2056

**Japan Times, Ltd.**
4-5-4 Shibaura, Minato-ku, Tokyo 108, Japan.
- Economic Survey of Japan. a. ISSN 0021-4833
(Japan. Economic Planning Agency)
- Japan Illustrated. q. ISSN 0021-4418
- Japan Times Directory. a.

**Japan Tourist Association**
1 Marunouchi, Chuo-ku, Tokyo, Japan.
- Japan Hotel Guide. irreg. ISSN 0446-6217

**Japan Trade Publications Ltd.**
2-1 Yotsuya, Shinjuku-ku, Tokyo 160, Japan.
- Volt; electrical trade monthly. m. ISSN 0042-8620

**Japan Travel Bureau, Inc.**
2-1 Yotsuya, Shinjuku-ku, Tokyo 160, Japan.
- New Official Guide: Japan. irreg. ISSN 0077-8591
(Japan National Tourist Organization)

**Japan Typography Association**
- Japan Typography Annual/Nihon Taipogurafi
Nenkan. (pub. by Gurafikkusha)

**Japan Ukiyo-e Society**
1-18 Kanda Jimbo-cho, Chiyoda-ku, Tokyo, Japan.
- Ukiyo-e Art/Ukiyoe Geijutsu. q. ISSN 0041-5979

**Japan Union of Associations of Economic Sciences**
- Japan Science Review: Economic Sciences. (pub.
by Japan Society for the Promotion of Science)

**Japan Water Works Association**
Osaka Godo Bldg., 33 Taiyuji-cho, Kita-ku, Osaka,
Japan.
- Water Japan/Suido Sangyo Shimbun; Japan's
waterworks yearbook. irreg.

**Japan Weather Association**
c/o Japan Meteorological Agency, 1-3-4 Otemachi,
Chiyoda-ku, Tokyo 101, Japan.
- Aerological Data of Japan/Jo-Koso Geppo. m.
ISSN 0001-9216
- Japan. Meteorological Agency. Annual Report/
Kisho-cho Nenpo Zenkoku Kishohyo. a. ISSN
0448-3758
- Japan. Meteorological Agency. Geophysical
Magazine/Kisho-cho Obun Iho. s-a. ISSN 0016-
8017
- Japan. Meteorological Agency. Mean Maps. Long
Range Weather Forecasting. m.
- Japan. Meteorological Agency. Monthly Report/
Kisho-Cho Geppo Zenkoku Kishohyo. m.
- Japan. Meteorological Agency. Oceanographical
Magazine/Kischo-cho Obun Kaiyo Hokoku. s-a.
- Japan. Meteorological Agency. Seismological
Bulletin/Jishin Geppo. m. ISSN 0446-5059
- Japan. Meteorological Agency. Volcanological
Bulletin/Kazan Hokoku. q. ISSN 0447-3892

**Japan Weather Association. Hokkaido Branch**
Nishi-18-chome, Kita-2-jo, Chuo-ku, Sapporo 060,
Japan.
- Meteorological Data of Hokkaido/Hokkaido No
Kisho. m.(plus special issue) ISSN 0018-3423

**Japan Weather Association. Kagoshima Local
Meteorological Observatory**
24-13, 1-chome, Arata, Kagoshima-shi 890, Japan.
- Monthly Report of Agricultural Meteorology,
Kagoshima Prefecture/Kagoshima-ken Nogyo
Kisho Geppo. m. ISSN 0022-7706

**Japan Welding Society**
1-11 Kanda Sakumo-cho, Chiyoda-ku, Tokyo 101,
Japan.
- Japan Welding Society. Journal/Yosetsu
Gakkaishi. m. ISSN 0021-4787
- Japan Welding Society. Transactions. s-a.

**Japan Wood Research Society**
c/o Japan Academic Societies Centre, 2-4-16 Yayoi,
Bunkyo-ku, Tokyo 113, Japan.
- Japan Wood Research Society. Journal/Mokuzai
Gakkaishi. m. ISSN 0021-4795

**Japana Esperanto Instituto**
2-2-14 Hongo, Bunkyo-ku, Tokyo 113, Japan.
- Revuo Orienta. m. ISSN 0035-4406

**Japanese**
see also Japan

**Japanese Aerospace Directory**
5-4-18 Ginza, Chuo-ku, Tokyo, Japan.
- Japanese Aerospace Directory. a.

**Japanese Anatomical Association**
c/o Dept. of Anatomy, Faculty of Medicine,
University of Tokyo, 7-3-1 Hongo, Bunkyo-ku,
Tokyo 113, Japan.
- Acta Anatomica Nipponica/Kaibogaku Zasshi. bi-
m. ISSN 0022-7722

**Japanese Archaeologists Association**
c/o Waseda Daigaku Kokogaku Kenkyushitsu, 647
Totsukamachi 1-chome, Shinjuku-ku, Tokyo 160,
Japan.
- Archaeologia Japonica. irreg. ISSN 0402-852X

**Japanese Association for Dental Science**
- Dentistry in Japan/Nihon no Shika Iryo. (pub. by
Japan Dental Association)

**Japanese Association for Infectious Diseases**
3-20-12 Komagome, Toshima-ku, Tokyo 170, Japan.
- Japanese Association for Infectious Diseases.
Journal/Kansenshogaku Zasshi. m. ISSN 0021-
4817

**Japanese Association for the Prevention of Venereal
Diseases and Treponematoses**
3-14-10 Hongo, Bunkyo-ku, Tokyo 113, Japan.
- V D; Japanese Journal of Veneral Diseases. q.

**Japanese Association of American Studies**
- American Review. (pub. by University of Tokyo.
Center for American Studies)

**Japanese Association of Criminal Psychology**
2-11-7 Hikawadai, Nerima-ku, Tokyo, Japan.
- Japanese Journal of Criminal Psychology/Hanzai
Shinrigaku Kenkyu. 3 per yr. ISSN 0017-7547

**Japanese Association of Educational Psychology**
c/o Faculty of Education, University of Tokyo, 7-3-
1 Hongo, Bunkyo-ku, Tokyo 113, Japan.
- Annual Report of Educational Psychology in
Japan/Kyoiku Shinrigaku Nempo. a. ISSN 0452-
9650
- Japanese Journal of Educational Psychology. q.
ISSN 0021-5015

**Japanese Association of Groundwater Hydrology**
c/o Water Resources Section, Geological Survey of
Japan, 135 Hisamoto, Takatasu-ku, Kawasaki 213,
Japan.
- Japanese Association of Groundwater Hydrology.
Journal/Nippon Chikasui Gakkai Kaishi. 3 per yr.
ISSN 0029-0602

**Japanese Association of Indian and Buddhist Studies**
c/o Dept. of Indian Philosophy and Sanskrit
Philology, Faculty of Letters, University of Tokyo,
7-3-1 Hongo, Bunkyo-ku, Tokyo 113, Japan.
- Journal of Indian and Buddhist Studies/Indogaku
Bunkkyogaku Kenkyu. s-a. ISSN 0019-4344

**Japanese Association of Leather Technology**
c/o Leather Research Institute, Tokyo Noko
University, 3-5-8 Saiwa-cho, Fuchu, Tokyo 183,
Japan.
- Leather Chemistry/Hikaku Kagaku. q. ISSN
0018-1811
- Leather Technology/Hikaku Gijutsu. s-a. ISSN
0018-1803

**Japanese Association of Marine Standardization**
Sumitomo Toranomon Bldg., 7 Shiba Kotohira-cho,
Minato-ku, Tokyo 105, Japan.
- Marine Standardization/Fune to Hyojunka. a.

**Japanese Association of Mineralogists, Petrologists
and Economic Geologists**
c/o Tohoku University Faculty of Science,
Aobayama, Sendai-shi 980, Japan.
- Japanese Association of Mineralogists, Petrologists
and Economic Geologists. Journal/Ganseki
Kobutsu Kosho Gakkaishi. m. ISSN 0021-4825

**Japanese Association of Museums**
c/o Uragami Tenshudo Daiichi Bldg., 1-10-1
Nihonbashi Kayabacho, Chuo-ku, Tokyo 103, Japan.
- Museum News/Hakubutsukan Nyusu. m.
- Museum Studies/Hakubutsukan Kenkyu. m.

**Japanese Association of Physical Medicine,
Balneology and Climatology**
c/o Japan Health and Research Institute, 1-5-20
Ishizuka Yaesu Bldg., Yaesu, Chuo-ku, Tokyo,
Japan.
- Japanese Association of Physical Medicine,
Balneology and Climatology. Journal/Nihon
Onsen Kiko Butsuri Igakkai Zasshi. s-a. ISSN
0029-0343

**Japanese Association of Refrigeration**
8 San'ei-cho, Shinjuku-ku, Tokyo 160, Japan.
- Refrigeration/Reito. m. ISSN 0034-3714
- Techniques of Refrigeration and Air Conditioning/Reito Kucho Gijutsu. m.

**Japanese Association of Theoretical Economics**
- Economic Studies Quarterly. (pub. by Oriental Economist)

**Japanese Association of Transportation Medicine**
c/o Chuo Tesudo Byoin, 2-1-3 Yoyogi, Shibuya-ku, Tokyo 151, Japan.
- Journal of Transportation Medicine/Kyushu Tetsudo Igakkaishi. bi-m. ISSN 0022-5274

**Japanese Biochemical Society**
c/o Japan Academic Societies Centre, 2-4-16 Yayoi, Bunkyo-ku, Tokyo 113, Japan.
- International Congress of Biochemistry. Proceedings. triennial, 1967, 7th, Tokyo. ISSN 0074-3534
- Japanese Biochemical Society. Journal/Seikagaku. m. ISSN 0037-1017
- Journal of Biochemistry. m. ISSN 0021-924X

**Japanese Cancer Association**
c/o Cancer Institute, 1-37-1 Kami-Ikebukuro, Toshima-ku, Tokyo 170, Japan.
- GANN Journal/Gan (Cancer); the Japanese journal of cancer research. bi-m. ISSN 0016-450X

**Japanese Circulation Society**
Kyoto University Hospital, Shogoin Kawara-cho, Sakyoku, Kyoto 606, Japan.
- Japanese Circulation Journal/Nihon Junkankigakushi. m. ISSN 0047-1828

**Japanese Climatological Seminar**
- Japanese Progress in Climatology/Nippon no Kikogaku no Shinpo. (pub. by Tokyo University of Education. Laboratory of Climatology)

**Japanese College of Angiology**
- Nova Angiologicae/Nova Angioroji. (pub. by Hoechst Japan, Ltd.)

**Japanese Committee for Radio Aids to Navigation**
c/o Kaijo Hoan-cho Todai-bu, 2-1-3 Kasumigaseki, Chiyoda-ku, Tokyo 100, Japan.
- Electronic Navigation Review/Denpa Koho. m.

**Japanese Commune Movement**
2083 Sakae-cho, Imaichi-shi, Tochigi-ken 321-12, Japan.
- Commumanity; transnational journal of the communes building man's future. bi-m.
- Cooperative Life/Gekkan Kyodatai. m.

**Japanese Dermatological Association**
Taisei Bldg., 3-14-10 Hongo, Bunkyo-ku, Tokyo 113, Japan.
- Japanese Journal of Dermatology: Series A & B/ Nihon Hifuka Gakkai Zasshi. m.(series A); q.(series B) ISSN 0021-499X

**Japanese Forestry Society**
c/o Ringyo Shikenjo, 5-37-21 Shimomeguro, Meguro-ku, Tokyo 153, Japan.
- Japanese Forestry Society. Journal/Nihon Ringakkaishi. m. ISSN 0021-485X

**Japanese Foundation for Cancer Research**
see Cancer Institute

**Japanese Journal of Applied Physics**
Second Toyo Kaiji Bldg., Daini Toyokaiiji Bldg., 4-24-8 Shinbashi, Minato-ku, Tokyo 105, Japan.
- Japanese Journal of Applied Physics. m. ISSN 0021-4922

**Japanese Labour Law Association**
Keio University, Shiba Mita, Minato-ku, Tokyo 108, Japan.
- Labour Law/Rodo Ho. s-a.

**Japanese Leprosy Association**
National Institute for Leprosy Research, 1455, 4-chome, Abacho, Higashimurayama-shi, Tokyo 189, Japan.
- Lepro/Repura. q. ISSN 0024-1008

**Japanese Literature Association**
2-17-10 Minami-otsuka, Toshima-ku, Tokyo, Japan.
- Japanese Literature/Nihon Bungaku. m.

**Japanese Medical Society of Alcohol Studies**
Dept. of Legal Medicine, Kyoto Prefectural University of Medicine, Kawaramachi, Hirokoji, Kamikyoku, Kyoto 602, Japan.
- Japanese Journal of Studies on Alcohol/Arukoru Kenkyu. q. ISSN 0021-5244

**Japanese Musicological Society**
Tokyo National University of Fine Arts and Music, Department of Musicology, Ueno Park, Taito-ku, Tokyo 110, Japan
(Order from: Maruzen Co., Ltd., 2-3-10 Nihonbashi, Chuo-ku, Tokyo 103, Japan: or their Import and Export Department, Box 5050, Tokyo International, Tokyo 100-31, Japan)
- Musicologica/Ongakugaku. q. ISSN 0030-2597

**Japanese National Committee on Large Dams**
Toden-Kyukan Bldg., 1-1-13 Shinbashi, Minato-ku, Tokyo 105, Japan.
- Large Dams/Dai Damu. q. ISSN 0011-5347

**Japanese National Railways**
International Dept., 1-6-5 Marunouchi, Chiyoda-ku, Tokyo 100, Japan.
- Japanese National Railways. Facts and Figures. a. ISSN 0546-093X
- Japanese National Railways. Quarterly Bulletin. q. ISSN 0047-1925

**Japanese National Railways. Railway Technical Research Institute**
- Railway Technical Research Institute (J N R). Quarterly Reports. (pub. by Ken-yusha, Inc.)

**Japanese Neurochemical Society**
c/o Dept. of Physiology, Keio University School of Medicine, Shinanomachi, Shinjuku-ku, Tokyo 160, Japan.
- Nerve Chemistry/Shinkei Kagaku. a. ISSN 0037-3796

**Japanese Nursing Association**
5-8-2 Jingumae, Shibuya-ku, Tokyo 150, Japan.
- Nursing/Kango. m. ISSN 0022-8362

**Japanese Ophthalmological Society**
2-5 Kanda Surugadai, Chiyoda-ku, Tokyo 101, Japan.
- Acta Societatis Ophthalmologicae Japonicae/ Nihon Ganka Gakkai Zasshi. m. ISSN 0029-0203

**Japanese Orthopaedic Assocation**
c/o Oriental Library, 2-28-21 Honkomagome, Bunkyo-ku, Tokyo 113, Japan.
- Japanese Orthopaedic Association. Journal/ Nippon Seikei Geka Gakkai Zasshi. m. ISSN 0021-5325

**Japanese Pathological Society**
c/o Department of Pathology, Faculty of Medicine, University of Tokyo, 7-3-1 Hongo, Bunkyo-ku, Tokyo 113, Japan
(Overseas Distributor: Japan Publications Trading Co., Ltd., Box 5030, Tokyo International, Tokyo 100-31, Japan; or 1255 Howard St., San Francisco, CA 94103)
- Acta Pathologica Japonica. bi-m. ISSN 0001-6632

**Japanese Pharmacological Society**
Dept. of Pharmacology, Faculty of Medicine, Kyoto University, Yoshida Konoe-cho, Sakyo-ku, Kyoto 606, Japan.
- Folia Pharmacologica Japonica/Nihon Yakurigaku Zasshi. 8 per yr. ISSN 0015-5691
- Japanese Journal of Pharmacology. bi-m. ISSN 0021-5198

**Japanese Physical Fitness Society**
Jikei University School of Medicine, 3-25-8 Nishi-Shimbashi, Minato-ku, Tokyo 105, Japan.
- Japanese Journal of Physical Fitness/Tairyoku Kagaku. q. ISSN 0039-906X

**Japanese Political Science Association**
c/o Faculty of Law, University of Tokyo, 7-3-1 Hongo, Bunkyo-ku, Tokyo 113, Japan.
- Japanese Political Science Association. Yearbook/ Nihon Seiji Gakkai Nenpo: Seijigaku. a. ISSN 0549-4192
- Publications on Political Science in Japan. a.

**Japanese Poultry Science Association**
c/o National Institute for Animal Industry, Aoba-cho, Chiba 280, Japan.
- Japanese Poultry Science/Nihon Kakin Gakkaishi. bi-m. ISSN 0029-0254

**Japanese Psychological Association**
802 Bunkyo Senta Bldg., 4-37-13 Hongo, Bunkyo-ku, Tokyo 113, Japan.
- Japanese Journal of Psychology/Shinrigaku Kenkyu. bi-m. ISSN 0021-5236
- Japanese Psychological Research. q. ISSN 0021-5368

**Japanese Red Cross Society**
Junior Red Cross Section, 5 Shiha Park, 3Minato-ku, Tokyo, Japan.
- Japanese Junior Red Cross/Seishone Sekijuji. 6 per yr. ISSN 0037-1092

**Japanese Rocket Society**
c/o Yomiuri Shinbunsha, 1-7-1 Ote-machi, Chiyoda-ku, Tokyo 100, Japan.
- Rocket News. irreg. ISSN 0485-2877

**Japanese Shipowners' Association**
c/o Kaiun Bldg., 2-6-4 Hirakawacho, Chiyoda-ku, Tokyo 102, Japan.
- Nihon Shosen Sempuku Tokei. a. (prep. by its Research Division)

**Japanese Social Labour College**
3 Hara-juku, Shibuya-ku, Tokyo, Japan.
- Studies in the Field of Social Labour/Shakai Jigyo No Shomondai. a. ISSN 0546-1324

**Japanese Society for Bacteriology**
c/o Japan Academic Societies Center, 2-4-16 Yayoi, Bunkyo-ku, Tokyo 113, Japan.
- Japanese Journal of Bacteriology/Nippon Saikingaku Zasshi. bi-m. ISSN 0021-4930
- Microbiology and Immunology. (pub. by Igaku Shoin Ltd.)

**Japanese Society for Crippled Children**
3-13-15 Higashi Ikebukuro, Toshima-ku, Tokyo 170, Japan.
- Crippled Children/Teashi No Fujiyuna Kodomotachi. m. ISSN 0040-0734
- Encouragement/Hagemi; a journal for the guidance of the parents with crippled children. bi-m. ISSN 0017-6605
- Japanese Journal of Education of the Handicapped/Shitai Fujiyu Kyoiku. q. ISSN 0037-3990
- Rehabilitation/Ryoiku. a. ISSN 0036-0538

**Japanese Society for Dental Health**
- Journal of Dental Health/Koku Eisei Gakkai Zasshi. (pub. by Tokyo Medical and Dental University. School of Dentistry)

**Japanese Society for Horticultural Science**
Faculty of Agriculture, University of Tokyo, 1-1-1 Yayoi, Bunkyo-ku, Tokyo 113, Japan.
- Japanese Society for Horticultural Science. Journal/Engei Gakkai Zasshi. q. ISSN 0013-7626

**Japanese Society for Hygiene**
c/o Kyoto University, Faculty of Medicine, Department of Hygiene, Kyoto 606, Japan.
- Japanese Journal of Hygiene/Nihon Eiseigaku Zasshi. bi-m. ISSN 0021-5082

**Japanese Society for Psychiatry and Neurology**
c/o Toyo Bunko, 2-28-21 Honkomagome, Bunkyo-ku, Tokyo 113, Japan.
- Folia Psychiatrica et Neurologica Japonica. q. ISSN 0015-5721

**Japanese Society for Public Administration**
c/o Faculty of Law, University of Tokyo, Motofuji-cho, Bunkyo-ku, Tokyo 113, Japan.
- Japanese Society for Public Administration. Annals/Nippon Gyosei Kenkyu Nenpo. a.

**Japanese Society for Tuberculosis**
c/o Research Institute of Tuberculosis, Matsuyama 3-chome, Kiyose-shi, Tokyo 180-04, Japan.
- Tuberculosis/Kekkaku. m. ISSN 0022-9776

**Japanese Society of Allergology**
c/o Dept. of Microbiology and Immunology, Nippon Medical School, 1-1-5 Sendagi, Bunkyo-ku, Tokyo 113, Japan.
- Japanese Journal of Allergology/Arerugi. m. ISSN 0021-4884

**Japanese Society of Applied Entomology and Zoology**
c/o Japan Plant Protection Association, 1-43-11 Komagome, Toshima-ku, Tokyo 170, Japan.
- Applied Entomology and Zoology. q. ISSN 0003-6862

- Japanese Journal of Applied Entomology and Zoology/Nihon Oyo Dobutsu Konchu Gakkaishi. q. ISSN 0021-4914
- Review of Plant Protection Research. a. ISSN 0557-7527

**Japanese Society of Biological Scientists**
- Biological Science/Seibutsu Kagaku. (pub. by Iwanami Shoten Publishers)

**Japanese Society of Child Health**
1-2 Ichigaya Satohara-cho, Shinjuku-ku, Tokyo 162, Japan.
- Journal of Child Health/Shoni Hoken Kenkyu. bi-m. ISSN 0037-4113

**Japanese Society of Comparative Law**
- Comparative Law Journal/Hikaku Ho Kenkyo. (pub. by Yuhikaku Publishing Co. Ltd.)

**Japanese Society of Criminology**
c/o Department of Forensic Medicine, Tokyo Medical and Dental University, 1-5-45 Yushima, Bunkyo-ku, Tokyo 113, Japan.
- Acta Criminologiae et Medicae Legalis Japonica/Hanzai Gaku Zasshi. bi-m.

**Japanese Society of Developmental Biologists**
c/o Biological Institute, Faculty of Science, Nagoya University, Furo-cho, Chikusa-ku, Nagoya 464, Japan.
- Development, Growth and Differentiation/Hassei, Seicho, Bunka. q. ISSN 0012-1592

**Japanese Society of Electron Microscopy**
c/o Japan Academic Societies Center, 2-4-16 Yayoi, Bunkyo-ku, Tokyo 113, Japan.
- Journal of Electron Microscopy. q. ISSN 0022-0744

**Japanese Society of Ethnology**
3-1-17 Higashi-cho, Hoya-shi, Tokyo 188, Japan.
- Japanese Journal of Ethnology/Minzokugaku-Kenkyu. q. ISSN 0021-5023

**Japanese Society of Fertility and Sterility**
7-5-22 Omorinishi, Ota-ku, Tokyo 143, Japan.
- Japanese Journal of Fertility and Sterility/Nippon Funin Gakkai Zasshi. q. ISSN 0029-0629

**Japanese Society of Fisheries Oceanography**
c/o Tokyo University of Fisheries, 4-5-7 Konan, Minato-ku, Tokyo 108, Japan.
- Advances in Fisheries Oceanography. irreg.

**Japanese Society of Food and Nutrition**
c/o Japan Academic Societies Center, 2-4-16 Yayoi, Bunkyo-ku, Tokyo 113, Japan.
- Food and Nutrition/Eiyo to Shokuryo. 9 per yr. ISSN 0021-5376

**Japanese Society of Food Science and Technology**
c/o National Food Research Institute, 1-4-12 Shiohama, Kota-ku, Tokyo 135, Japan.
- Journal of Food Science and Technology/Nippon Shokuhin Kogyo Gakkaishi. m. ISSN 0029-0394

**Japanese Society of Gastroenterology**
7-4-12 Ginza, Chuo-ku, Tokyo 104, Japan.
- Gastroenterologia Japonica. q. ISSN 0435-1339

**Japanese Society of Internal Medicine**
3-42-6 Hongo, Bunkyo-ku, Tokyo 113, Japan.
- Japanese Journal of Medicine. q. ISSN 0021-5120
- Japanese Society of Internal Medicine. Journal/Nihon Naika Gakkai Zasshi. m. ISSN 0021-5384

**Japanese Society of Limnology**
c/o Otsu Hydrobiological Station, Shimosakamoto, Otsu-shi, Shiga-ken 520-01, Japan.
- Japanese Journal of Limnology/Rikusui Gaku Zasshi. q. ISSN 0021-5104

**Japanese Society of Neurology**
Akamon Building, 5-26-4 Hongo, Bunkyo-ku, Tokyo 113, Japan.
- Clinical Neurology/Rinsho Shinkeigaku. m. ISSN 0009-918X

**Japanese Society of Neurology and Psychiatry**
c/o Oriental Library, 2-28-21 Honkomagome, Bunkyo-ku, Tokyo 113, Japan.
- Psychiatria et Neurologia Japonica/Kikan Horitsugaku. ISSN 0033-5673

**Japanese Society of Nuclear Medicine**
c/o Japan Radioisotope Association, 2-28-45 Honkomagome, Bunkyo-ku, Tokyo 113, Japan.
- Japanese Journal of Nuclear Medicine/Kaku Igaku (Nihon Kaku Igakkai Kikanshi) bi-m. ISSN 0022-7854

**Japanese Society of Oral Surgeons**
c/o Tokyo Ika Daigaku Koku Gekagaku Kyoshitsu, 7-1, 6-chome, Nishishinju, Shinjuku-ku, Tokyo 160, Japan.
- Japanese Journal of Oral Surgery/Nippon Koku Geka Gakkai Zasshi. bi-m. ISSN 0021-5163

**Japanese Society of Parasitology**
Dept. of Parasitology, School of Medicine, Chiba University, Chiba 280, Japan.
- Japanese Journal of Parasitology/Kiseichugaku Zasshi. bi-m. ISSN 0021-5171

**Japanese Society of Pediatric Neurology**
- Brain and Development/No to Hattatsu. (pub. by Shindan to Chiryosha Co.)

**Japanese Society of Pharmacognosy**
c/o Faculty of Pharmaceutical Sciences, Kyoto University, Kyoto 606, Japan.
- Japanese Journal of Pharmocognosy/Shoyakugaku Zasshi. s-a. ISSN 0037-4377

**Japanese Society of Phycology**
c/o Department of Botany, Tokyo University of Education, 3-29-1 Otsuka, Bunkyo-ku, Tokyo, Japan.
- Japanese Society of Phycology. Bulletin/Sorui. q. ISSN 0038-1578

**Japanese Society of Physical Education**
Kyorin Shoin, 4-2-1 Yushima, Bunkyo-ku, Tokyo 113, Japan.
- Journal of Health, Physical Education and Recreation/Taiiku No Kagaku. m.

**Japanese Society of Plant Physiologists**
Shimotachiuri Ogawa Higashi, Kamikyoku, Kyoto 602, Japan.
- Plant and Cell Physiology. bi-m. ISSN 0032-0781

**Japanese Society of Public Economy**
1-3 Yuraku-cho, Chiyoda-ku, Tokyo, Japan.
- Public Economy Journal/Koeki Jigyo Kenkyu. q.

**Japanese Society of Scientific Fisheries**
c/o Tokyo University of Fisheries, 4-5-7 Konan, Minato-ku, Tokyo 108, Japan.
- Japanese Society of Scientific Fisheries. Bulletin/Nihon Suisan Gakkaishi. m. ISSN 0021-5392

**Japanese Society of Sericultural Science**
c/o Sericultural Experiment Station, 3-55-30 Wada, Suginami-ku, Tokyo 166, Japan.
- Journal of Sericultural Science of Japan/Nippon Sanshigaku Zasshi. bi-m. ISSN 0037-2455

**Japanese Society of Soil Mechanics and Foundation Engineering**
1-13-5 Nishi Shinbashi, Minato-ku, Tokyo 105, Japan.
- Japanese Society of Soil Mechanics and Foundation Engineering. Journal/Doshitsu Kogakkai Ronbun Hokokushu. q.
- Soil Mechanics and Foundation Engineering/Tsuchi to Kiso. m. ISSN 0041-3798
- Soils & Foundations. q. ISSN 0038-0806

**Japanese Society of Starch Science**
c/o National Food Research Institute, 4-12, 1-chome, Shiohama, Koto-ku, Tokyo, Japan.
- Japanese Society of Starch Science. Journal/Denpun Kagaku. q. ISSN 0021-5406

**Japanese Society of Veterinary Science**
c/o Faculty of Agriculture, University of Tokyo, 1-1-1 Yayoi, Bunkyo-ku, Tokyo 113, Japan.
- Japanese Journal of Veterinary Science/Nihon Juigaku Zasshi. 7 per yr. ISSN 0021-5295

**Japanese Society of Zootechnical Science**
201 Nagatani Corporas, Ikenohata 2-9-4, Taito-ku, Tokyo 110, Japan.
- Japanese Journal of Zootechnical Science/Nihon Chikusan Gakkaiho. m. ISSN 0021-5309

**Japanese Sociological Society**
Dept. of Sociology, Faculty of Letters, University of Tokyo, 7-3-1 Hongo, Bunkyo-ku, Tokyo 113, Japan.
- Japanese Sociological Review/Shakaigaku Hyoron. q. ISSN 0021-5414

**Japanese Stomatological Society**
Department of Oral Surgery, School of Medicine, University of Tokyo, 7-3-1 Hongo, Bunkyo-ku, Tokyo 113, Japan.
- Japanese Stomatological Society. Journal/Nihon Kokuka Gakkai Zasshi. q. ISSN 0029-0297

**Japanese Technical Association of the Pulp and Paper Industry**
c/o Kami Parupu Kaikan, 3-9-11 Ginza, Chuo-ku, Tokyo 104, Japan.
- Japan T A P P I/Kami Pa Gikyoshi. m. ISSN 0022-815X

**Japanese Tissue Culture Association**
c/o Tokyo Daigaku Igakubu Kaibogaku Kyoshito, 7-3-1 Hongo, Bunkyo-ku, Tokyo 113, Japan.
- Tissue Culture Studies in Japan: The Annual Bibliography/Nihon Soshiki Baiyo Kenkyu Nenpo. a. ISSN 0082-4518

**Japanese Urological Association**
c/o Department of Urology, Faculty of Medicine, University of Tokyo, 7-3-1 Bunkyo-ku, Tokyo 113, Japan.
- Japanese Journal of Urology/Nihon Hinyokika Gakkai Zasshi. m. ISSN 0021-5287

**Japanese Urological Association. Nishi Nihon Section**
c/o Dept. of Urology, Faculty of Medicine, Kyushu University, 1276 Katakasu, Higashi-ku, Fukuoka 812, Japan.
- Nishi Nihon Journal of Urology/Nishi Nihon Hinyokika. bi-m. ISSN 0029-0726

**Japanese Weekly on Pharmacy and Chemistry**
1-13-12 Kikawa Nishino-cho, Higoshi Yodogawaku, Osaka, Japan.
- Japanese Weekly on Pharmacy and Chemistry/Yakugyo Shimbun. w. ISSN 0021-5201

**Jiji Press, Ltd.**
TBR Bldg., 2-10-2 Nagata-cho, Chiyoda-ku, Tokyo 100, Japan.
- Pacific Community; an Asian quarterly review. q. ISSN 0030-8633
- Pacific Friend. m.
- Photo. s-m. ISSN 0031-8442

**Jikei University School of Medicine**
3-25-8 Nishi Shinbashi, Minato-ku, Tokyo 105, Japan.
- Jikeikai Medical Journal. 3-4 per yr. ISSN 0021-6968

**Jimbun Kagaku Kenkyujo**
*see* Kyoto University. Research Institute for Humanistic Studies

**Jinbun Chiri Gakkai**
*see* Human Geography Society of Japan

**Jinbun Gakkai**
*see* Tokyo Metropolitan University. Institute for Social Sciences and Humanity

**Jinko Mondai Kenkyusho**
*see* Japan. Institute of Population Problems

**Jinrui Dotaigaku Kenkyukai**
*see* Human Ergology Research Association

**Jinsen Igaku Committee**
2-7 Daigakucho, Takatsuki-shi, Osaka-fu, Japan.
- Journal of Jinsen Medical Sciences/Jinsen Igaku. ISSN 0022-2100

**Jishin Gakkai**
*see* Seismological Society of Japan

**Jishin Kenkyusho**
*see* University of Tokyo. Earthquake Research Institute

**Jochi University**
*see* Sophia University

**Joho Shori Gakkai**
*see* Information Processing Society of Japan

**Jozo Kagaku Kenkyusho**
*see* Brewing Science Research Institute

**Juigaku Kenkyusho**
*see* Nihon University. Research Institute for Veterinary Science

**Juntendo Medical Society**
2-1-1 Hongo, Bunkyo-ku, Tokyo 113, Japan.
- Juntendo Medical Journal/Juntendo Igaku. q. ISSN 0022-6769

**Juntendo University. School of Medicine**
Medical Ultrasonics Research Center, 2-1-2 Hongo, Bunkyo-ku, Tokyo 113, Japan.
- Juntendo University, Tokyo. Medical Ultrasonics Research Center. Annual Report. a. ISSN 0075-4579

**Jurisprudence Association**
c/o Faculty of Law, University of Tokyo, Hongo, Bunkyo-ku, Tokyo 113, Japan.
- Jurisprudence Association. Journal/Hogaku Kyokai Zasshi. m. ISSN 0022-6815

**Juzen Medical Society of Kanazawa University**
School of Medicine, Kanazawa University, 13-1 Takara-machi, Kanazawa-shi 920, Japan.
- Juzen Medical Society. Journal/Juzen Igakkai Zasshi. 6 per yr. ISSN 0022-7226

**KEIDANREN**
see Japan Federation of Economic Organizations

**Kachiku Eisei Shikenjo**
see Japan. National Institute of Animal Health

**Kagaku Gijutsu Bunken Riyo Shinkokai**
see Society for Science and Technical Documents Utilization Promotion

**Kagaku Gijutsu-cho Kinzoku Zairyo Gijutsu Kenkyusho**
see National Research Institute for Metals

**Kagaku Gijutsu-cho Koku Uchu Gijutsu Kenkyusho**
see Japan. National Aerospace Laboratory

**Kagaku Gijutsucho**
see Japan. Science and Technology Agency

**Kagaku Keisatsu Kenkyusho**
see Japan. National Research Institute ∽f Police Science

**Kagaku Keisoku Kenkyusho**
see Tohoku University. Research Institute for Scientific Measurements

**Kagaku Keizai Kenkyusho**
see Chemical Economy Research Institute

**Kagaku Kenkyusho**
see Kyoto University. Institute for Chemical Research

**Kagaku Kisoron Gakkai**
see Japan Association for Philosophy of Science

**Kagaku Kogyo Nipposha**
see Chemical Daily Co., Ltd.

**Kagoshima Chiho Kishodai**
see Japan Weather Association. Kagoshima Local Meteorological Observatory

**Kagoshima Daigaku**
see Kagoshima University

**Kagoshima University**
Uerata-cho; Korimoto 1-chome, Kagoshima 890, Japan.
- Kagoshima University. Historical Science Reports. a.

**Kagoshima University. Faculty of Agriculture**
1946 Kamiarata-machi, Kagoshima 892, Japan.
- Kagoshima University. Faculty of Agriculture. Memoirs/Kagoshima Daigaku Nogakubu Kiyo. s-a.

**Kagoshima University. Faculty of Medicine**
7-82 Shiroyama-cho, Kagoshima 892, Japan.
- Acta Medica Universitatis Kagoshimaensis. s-a. ISSN 0001-611X

**Kaigai Denroyoku Chosakai**
see Overseas Electrical Industry Survey Institute

**Kaijo Hooncho**
see Japan. Maritime Safety Agency

**Kaijo Hooncho Suirobu**
see Japan. Maritime Safety Agency. Hydrographic Department

**Kaimen-kagaku Kenkyu Shisetsu**
see Okayama University. Research Laboratory for Surface Science

**Kaiyo Kenkyusho**
see University of Tokyo. Ocean Research Institute

**Kaiyo Sangyo Kenkyu Kai**
see Research Institute for Ocean Economics

**Kamakura-Shobo Publishing Co., Ltd.**
21 Ichigaya-Sanaicho Shinjuku, Shinjuku-ku, Tokyo 162, Japan.
- Children's Styles. q. ISSN 0009-417X
- Dressmaking. m. and. q. editions. ISSN 0012-611X
- Madam. m. & q. ISSN 0024-9343

**Kami Parupu Gijutsu Kyokai**
see Japanese Technical Association of the Pulp and Paper Industry

**Kanagawa Daigaku**
see Kanagawa University

**Kanagawa University. Institute of Humanities**
3-chome Rokkaku-bashi, Kanagawa-ku, Yokahama, Japan.
- Kanagawa University. Institute of Humanities. Bulletin. a.

**Kanazawa Daigaku**
see Kanazawa University

**Kanazawa Daigaku Juzen Igakkai**
see Juzen Medical Society of Kanazawa University

**Kanazawa University. College of Liberal Arts**
Kanazawa 920, Japan.
- Kanazawa University. College of Liberal Arts. Annals of Science/Kanazawa Daigaku Kyoyobu Ronshu, Shizenkagaku- Hen. a.

**Kanazawa University. Faculty of Education**
1-1 Marunouchi, Kanazawa 920, Japan.
- Kanazawa University. Faculty of Education. Bulletin: Humanities, Social and Educational Sciences. irreg.
- Kanazawa University. Faculty of Education. Bulletin: Natural Science/Kanazawa Daigaku Kyoikugakubu Kiyo, Shizenkagaku- Hen. irreg.
- Kyoka Kyoiku Kenkyu. a.

**Kanazawa University. Faculty of Law and Literature**
1-1 Marunouchi, Kanazawa 920, Japan.
- Kanazawa University. Faculty of Law and Literature. Studies and Essays. a. ISSN 0453-1981

**Kanazawa University. Faculty of Science**
1-1 Marunouchi, Kanazawa 920, Japan.
- Kanazawa University. Science Reports/Kanazawa Daigaku Rika Hokoku. s-a. ISSN 0022-8338

**Kanazawa University. Faculty of Technology**
2-40-20 Kodatsuno, Kanazawa 920, Japan.
- Kanazawa University. Faculty of Technology. Memoirs/Kanazawa Daigaku Kogakubu Kiyo. s-a. ISSN 0022-832X

**Kanazawa University. School of Medicine**
13-1 Takara-machi, Kanazawa 920, Ishikawa, Japan.
- Journal of Radiology and Physical Therapy/ Kanazawa Irigaku Sosho. 2-3 per yr. ISSN 0022-8311 (prep. by its Department of Radiology)

**Kanehara & Co., Ltd.**
2-31-14 Yushima, Bunkyoku, Tokyo 113-91, Japan.
- Clinical Dermatology/Hifuka No Rinsho. m. ISSN 0018-1404
- Clinical Pediatrics/Shonika. m. ISSN 0037-4121
- Clinical Radiology/Rinsho Hoshasen. m. ISSN 0009-9252
- Ikai Jiho. 3 per mo. ISSN 0019-1728
- Journal of Accidental Medicine/Saigai Igaku. m. ISSN 0036-2689
- Operation/Shujutsu. m. ISSN 0037-4423
- Ophthalmology/Ganka. m. ISSN 0016-4488

**Kankyo Eisei Kenkyukai**
see Environmental Sanitation Research Association

**Kankyo Igaku Kenkyusho**
see Nagoya University. Research Institute of Environmental Medicine

**Kansai Daigaku**
see Kansai University

**Kansai Daigaku Keizai Gakkai**
see Kansai University. Economic Society

**Kansai Ika Daigaku**
see Kansai Medical University

**Kansai Medical University**
1 Fumizono-cho, Moriguchi 570, Japan.
- Kansai Medical University. Journal/Kansai Ika Daigaku. Zasshi. q.

**Kansai University**
- Review of Economics and Business. (pub. by Kansai University Press)

**Kansai University. Economic Society**
Senriyama, Suita, Osaka, Japan.
- Kansai University Economic Review/Kansai Daigaku Keizai Ronshu. bi-m. ISSN 0449-7554

**Kansai University. Faculty of Engineering**
3-3-35 Yamate-cho, Suita 564, Osaka, Japan.
- Kansai University. Technology Reports of the Kansai University/Kansai Daigaku Kogaku Kenkyu Hokoku. a. ISSN 0453-2198

**Kansai University. Intercultural Research Institute**
333 Ogura, Hirakata City, Osaka, Japan.
- Journal of Intercultural Studies. a.

**Kansai University Press**
3-3-35 Yamate-cho, Suita 564, Osaka, Japan.
- Review of Economics and Business. (Kansai University)

**Kantosha Co. Ltd.**
601 Kojun Bldg., 8-7, 6-chome, Ginza, Chuo-ku, Tokyo 104, Japan.
- Aireview/Koku Joho. m.

**Yuzuru Katagiri, Ed. & Pub.**
Syoin College, Tarumi-ku, Kobe, Japan.
- Japanese Poetry in English. 1-2 per yr. ISSN 0021-535X

**Kawai Pharmaceutical Co., Ltd.**
2-51-8 Arai, Nakano-ku, Tokyo 165, Japan.
- Public Health Education/Kenko Kyoiku. q. ISSN 0022-9938

**Kawata Publicity Inc.**
Central P.O. Box 1157, Tokyo 100-91, Japan.
- Japan's Iron and Steel Industry. a. ISSN 0075-3475
- World Money Guide. irreg. ISSN 0084-2028

**KEIDANREN**
see Japan Federation of Economic Organizations

**Keie Kindaika Kenkyusho**
see Management Science Research Institute

**Keikinzoku Kyokai**
see Japan Light Metal Association

**Keio Daigaku**
see Keio University

**Keio Economic Society**
see under Keio University

**Keio Gijuku Daigaku Igaku Joho Senta**
see Keio University. Medical Library and Information Center

**Keio Gijuku Hogaku Kenkyukai**
see Keio University. Asssociation for the Study of Law and Politics

**Keio University. Association for the Study of Law and Politics**
2-2 Mita, Minato-ku, Tokyo 108, Japan.
- Journal of Law, Politics and Sociology/Hogaku Kenkyu. m.

**Keio University. Faculty of Engineering**
Matsushita Memorial Library, 832 Hiyoshi-cho, Kohoku-ku, Yokohama 223, Japan.
- Keio Engineering Reports. irreg.

**Keio University. Institute of Management and Labor Studies**
Mita, Minato-ku, Tokyo 108, Japan.
- Management and Labor Studies. English Series. irreg., 1970, no. 20. ISSN 0076-3586

**Keio University. Keio Economic Society**
Mita, Minato-ku, Tokyo 108, Japan.
- Keio Economic Studies. s-a. ISSN 0022-9709
- Mita Journal of Economics/Mita Gakkai Zasshi. m. ISSN 0026-6760

**Keio University. Medical Library and Information Center**
35 Shinamo-machi, Shinjuku-ku, Tokyo 160, Japan.
- Library System/Raiburari Shisutemu. q. ISSN 0024-2578

**Keio University. School of Medicine**
35 Shinanomachi, Shinjuku-ku, Tokyo 160, Japan.
- Keio Journal of Medicine. q. ISSN 0022-9717

**Keio University Society of Business and Commerce**
- Keio Business Review. (pub. by Japan Publications Trading Co., Ltd.)
- Keio Monographs of Business and Commerce. (pub. by Japan Publications Trading Co. Ltd.)

**Keisatsu-cho Kagaku Keisatsu Kenkyusho**
*see* **Japan. National Research Institute of Police Science**

**Keizai Chiri Gakkai**
*see* **Association of Economic Geographers**

**Keizai Dantai Rengokai**
*see* **Japan Federation of Economic Organizations**

**Keizai Hatten Kyokai**
*see* **Association for Economic Development**

**Keizai Kikakucho**
*see* **Japan. Economic Planning Agency**

**Keizai Riron Gakkai**
*see* **Society of Political Economy**

**Kekkaku Kyobu Shikkan Kenkyusho**
*see* **Kyoto University. Chest Disease Research Institute**

**Kekkaku Yobokai**
*see* **Japan Anti-Tuberculosis Association**

**Ken-yusha, Inc.**
1-45-6 Hikaricho, Kokubunji, Tokyo, Japan.
- Railway Technical Research Institute (J N R). Quarterly Reports. q. ISSN 0033-9008 (Japanese National Railways. Railway Technical Research Institute)

**Kenchiku Gijutsusha**
1-17-5 Hyakunincho, Shinjuku-ku, Tokyo 160, Japan.
- Building Engineering/Kenchiku Gijutsu. m. ISSN 0022-9911

**Kenko na Kurashi No Kai**
1-2, 5-chome, Hongo, Bunkyo-ku, Tokyo 113, Japan.
- Longer and Healthier Life/Kenko na Kurashi. m. ISSN 0022-9946

**Kenkyusho Rengokai**
*see* **Tohoku University. Association of the Research Institutes**

**Kensetsu-cho Kenchiku Kenkyusho Kokusai Jishin Kogakubu**
*see* **Japan. International Institute of Seismology and Earthquake Engineering**

**Kensetsu-sho Doboku Kenkyusho**
*see* **Japan. Public Works Research Institute**

**Kensetsu-sho Kokudo Chiri-in**
*see* **Japan. Geographical Survey Institute**

**Kigyo Horonsha**
Room No. 601, Toyo Bldg., 1-9-7 Kyomachibori, Nishi-ku, Osaka, Japan.
- Kigyoho Kenkyu. m. ISSN 0023-1355

**Kihara Institute for Biological Research**
3-122-23 Mutsugawa, Minami-ku, Yokohama 233, Japan.
- Kihara Institute for Biological Research. Report/Kihara Seibutsugaku Kenkyusho. Seiken Ziho. a. ISSN 0080-8539
- Kihara Institute for Biological Research. Wheat Information Service. irreg.

**Kikogaku Danwakai**
*see* **Tokyo University of Education. Laboratory of Climatology**

**Kindai-Eiga Corp.**
6-8-3 Ginza, Chuo-ku, Tokyo, Japan.
- Kindai Eiga. m. ISSN 0023-1460

**Kindai Kagaku Ltd.**
2-10 Ichigaya Tamachi, Shinjuku, Tokyo 162, Japan.
- Radio, TV, HiFi & Electronics/Denpa Gijutsu. m. ISSN 0011-8435

**Kindaikenchiku-sha Ltd. Co.**
2-22-11 Nishikata, Bunkyo-ku, Tokyo, Japan.
- Contemporary Architecture/Kindai Kenchiku. m. ISSN 0023-1479

**Kinki Agricultural Administration Bureau**
*see* **Japan. Kinki Agricultural Administration Bureau**

**Kinki Chugoku Agricultural Research Association**
c/o Chugoku National Agricultural Experiment Station, Higashi Fukatsu-machi, Fukuyama-shi 720, Japan.
- Chugoku Agricultural Research/Chugoku Nogyo Kenkyu. s-a. ISSN 0009-6229

**Kinki University. Faculty of Pharmaceutical Sciences**
321 Kowakae, Higashiosaka, Osaka, Japan.
- Kinki University. Bulletin of Pharmacy/Kinki Daigaku Yakugakubu Kiyo. irreg. ISSN 0023-1657

**Kinzoku Hyomen Gijutsu Kyokai**
*see* **Metal Finishing Society of Japan**

**Kinzoku Kogyo Jigyodan**
*see* **Japan. Metal Mining Agency**

**Kirin Brewery Co. Ltd.**
3 Miyahara-cho, Takasaki 370-12, Japan.
- Kirin Brewery Company, Tokyo. Research Laboratory. Report/Kirin Biru K. K. Sogo Kenkyusho Kenkyu Hokoku. a. ISSN 0075-6229

**Kisho-cho (Japan Meteorological Agency)**
*for publications of this agency, see* **Japan Weather Association**

**Kisho-cho Kisho Kenkyusho**
*see* **Meteorological Research Institute**

**Kiso Butsurigaku Kenkyusho Riron Butsurigaku Kankokai**
*see* **Kyoto University. Research Institute for Fundamental Physics**

**Kissei Pharmaceutical Co., Ltd.**
2-5 Nihonbashi Hon-cho, Chuo-ku, Tokyo 103, Japan.
- Journal of Clinical Electron Microscopy/Nippon Rinsho Denshi Kenbikyo Gakkaishi. q. (Clinical Electron Microscopy Society of Japan)

**Kita Nihon Byogaichu Kenkyukai**
*see* **Society of Plant Protection of North Japan**

**Kitakanto Medical Society**
c/o Gumma Daigaku Igakubu, 3-39-22 Showa-machi, Maebashi-shi 371, Japan.
- Kitikanto Medical Journal/Kitikanto Igaku. bi-m. ISSN 0023-1908

**Kitano Hospital**
*see* **Tazuke Kofukai Medical Research Institute**

**Kitazato Institute for Infectious Diseases**
c/o Kitazato Kenkyusho, 5-9-1 Shirogane, Minato-ku, Tokyo 108, Japan.
- Kitazato Archives of Experimental Medicine/Kitazato Jikken Igaku. q. ISSN 0023-1924

**Kobe Daigaku**
*see* **Kobe University**

**Kobe-shi Shokubutsu Boekisho**
*see* **Japan. Kobe Plant Protection Station**

**Kobe University. Faculty of Economics**
Rokkodai-cho, Nadu-ku, Kobe, Japan.
- Kobe University Economic Review. a. ISSN 0454-1111

**Kobe University Law Review Association**
Faculty of Law, Kobe University, Rokkodai-cho, Nadu-ku, Kobe, Japan.
- Kobe University Law Review. International Edition. irreg.; vol. 9, 1973. ISSN 0075-6423

**Kobe University Medical Society**
- Kobe University Medical Journal/Kobe Daigaku Igakubu Kiyu. (pub. by Kobe University. School of Medicine)

**Kobe University. Research Institute for Economics and Business Administration**
Rokkaido-cho, Nada-ku, Kobe, Japan.
- Kobe Economic and Business Research Series. irreg. ISSN 0075-6415
- Kobe Economic and Business Review. a. ISSN 0075-6407
- Quarterly Bibliography of Economics/Keizaigaku-Bunken-Kiho. q. ISSN 0033-5304 (Association for Documentation in Economics)

**Kobe University. School of Business Administration**
Rokkodai-cho, Nada-ku, Kobe, Japan.
- Kobe University. School of Business Administration. Annals. a. ISSN 0085-2570

**Kobe University. School of Medicine**
7-1-12 Kusonoki-cho, Ikuta-ku, Kobe 650, Japan.
- Kobe Journal of Medical Science. q. ISSN 0023-2513
- Kobe University Medical Journal/Kobe Daigaku Igakubu Kiyu. a. ISSN 0075-6431 (Kobe University Medical Society)

**Kobundo**
1-7-13 Kanda Surugadai, Chiyoda-ku, Tokyo, Japan.
- Shakai-jinruigaku Nenpo. a. (Tokyo Metropolitan University. Shakai-jinruigakkai)

**Kobunshi Gakkai**
*see* **Society of Polymer Science**

**Kobunshi Kankokai**
*see* **High Polymer Publishing Association**

**Kochi Daigaku**
*see* **Kochi University**

**Kochi University. Earthquake Observatory**
Asakura, Kochi 780, Japan.
- Kochi University. Earthquake Observatory. Seismological Bulletin. q.

**Kodansha International Ltd**
2-12-21 Otowa, Bunkyo-ku, Tokyo 112, Japan
(U. S. Subscr. Address: c/o Harper & Row, 10 E. 53rd St., New York, NY 10022)
- Illustration in Japan. a. (Daiichi Shuppan Senta)
- Masterworks of Ukiyo-e. irreg., 1970, no. 11. ISSN 0076-5120

**Kodansha Ltd.**
2-12-21 Otowa, Bunkyo-ku, Tokyo 112, Japan.
- Imototachi No Kagaribi. a.

**Kogaku Kenkyujo**
*see* **Kyoto University. Engineering Research Institute**

**Kogaku Kenkyusho**
*see* **Tokyo Kyoiku University. Institute for Optical Research**

**Kogyo Gijutsuin Biseibutsu Kogyo Gijutsu Kenkyusho**
*see* **Japan. Fermentation Research Institute**

**Kogyo Keizai Kenkyusho**
*see* **Industrial Chemical Consultants, Inc.**

**Kogyo Rodo Saigai Boshi Kyokai**
*see* **Association of Mining Labor Accident Prevention**

**Kojunsha**
2-9 Kitakarasuyama, Setagaya-ku, Tokyo, Japan.
- Nihon Hakushiroku. irreg.

**Kokugakuin University. Faculty of Economics**
4-10-28 Higashi, Shibuya-ku, Tokyo, Japan.
- Kokugakuin University Economic Review/
  Kokugakuin Keizaigaku. q.

**Kokugakuin University. Faculty of Law and Politics**
4-10-28 Higashi, Shibuya-ku, Tokyo, Japan.
- Kokugakuin University. Faculty of Law and
  Politics. Journal/Kokugakuin Hogaku. ISSN 0454-
  1723

**Kokuritsu Bosai Kagaku Gijutsu Senta**
*see* National Research Center for Disaster
Prevention

**Kokuritsu Eisei Shikenjo**
*see* National Institute of Hygienic Sciences

**Kokuritsu Gan Senta**
*see* Japan. National Cancer Center

**Kokuritsu Idengaku Kenkyusho**
*see* Japan. National Institute of Genetics

**Kokuritsu Kagaku Hakubutsukan**
*see* National Science Museum

**Kokuritsu Kokkai Toshokan**
*see* National Diet Library

**Kokuritsu Kokugo Kenkyusho**
*see* National Language Research Institute

**Kokuritsu Koshu Eisei-in**
*see* Japan. Institute of Public Health

**Kokuritsu Kyokuchi Kenkyujyo**
*see* National Institute of Polar Research

**Kokuritsu Tama Kenkyusho**
*see* Japan. National Institute for Leprosy Research

**Kokuritsu Tokushu Kyoiku Sogo Kenkyujo**
*see* National Institute for Special Education

**Kokusai Christian University**
Mitaka, Japan.
- Asian Cultural Studies. irreg. ISSN 0454-2150

**Kokusai Keizai Gakkai**
*see* Japan Society of International Economics

**Kokusai Kowan Kyokai**
*see* International Association of Ports and Harbors

**Kokusai Kyoku-Undo Kansoku Jigyo Chuo-Kyoku**
*see* International Polar Motion Service

**Kokusai Nogyo-Sha K.K.**
3-20-8 Ueno, Taito-ku, Tokyo 110, Japan.
- Agricultural Machinery News/Noson Kiki Nyusu.
  w.

**Kokusai Saibo Gakkai**
*see* International Association of Cytology

**Kokusai Shokuryo Nogyo Kyokai**
*see* Japan F A O Association

**Kokusaiho Gakkai**
*see* Association of International Law

**Kokusaiho Kyokai Nihon- Shibu**
*see* International Legal Sciences Association

**Kokuseido Publishing Co., Ltd.**
3-23-5 Hongo, Bunkyo-ku, Tokyo 113, Japan.
- Japanese Journal of Plastic & Reconstructive
  Surgery/Keisei Geka. q. ISSN 0021-5228

**Kokushikan Daigaku Kyoyo Gakkai**
*see* Kokushikan University. Society of Liberal Arts

**Kokushikan University. Society of Liberal Arts**
4-28-1 Setagaya, Setagaya-ku, Tokyo 154, Japan.
- Review on Liberal Arts/Kyoyo Ronshu. irreg.

**Kokuzeicho**
*see* Japan. National Tax Agency

**Konpyuta Eijisha**
*see* Computer Age Co., Ltd.

**Koronasha**
*see* Corona Publishing Co., Ltd.

**Kosei-cho Kokuritsu Eiyo Kenkyusho**
*see* Japan. National Institute of Health

**Kosei-sho Jinko Mondai Kenkyusho**
*see* Japan. Institute of Population Problems

**Kosei-sho Kokuritsu Tama Kenkyusho**
*see* Japan. National Institute for Leprosy Research

**Kotaigun Seitaigakkai**
*see* Society of Population Ecology

**Kowan Gijutsu Kenkyusho**
*see* Japan. Port and Harbour Technical Research
Institute

**Kuden Kenkyusho**
*see* Nagoya University. Research Institute of
Atmospherics

**Kuki Chowa Eisei Kogakkai**
*see* Society of Heating, Air Conditioning, and
Sanitary Engineers of Japan

**Kumamoto Daigaku**
*see* Kumamoto University

**Kumamoto Igakkai**
*see* Kumamoto Medical Society

**Kumamoto Medical Society**
c/o Kumamoto University Medical School, 2-2-1
Honjo, Kumamoto 860, Japan.
- Kumamoto Medical Society. Journal/Kumamoto
  Igakkai Zasshi. m.

**Kumamoto University. Faculty of Engineering**
2-39-1 Kurokami, Kumamoto 860, Japan.
- Kumamoto University. Faculty of Engineering.
  Memoirs/Kumamoto Daigaku Kogakubu Kiyo. 1-
  3 per yr. ISSN 0023-5334
- Kumamoto University. Faculty of Engineering.
  Technical Reports/Kumamoto Daigaku Kogakubu
  Kenkyu Hokoku. 3 per yr. ISSN 0023-5296

**Kumamoto University. Faculty of Science**
2-39-1 Kurokami, Kumamoto 860, Japan.
- Kumamoto Journal of Science. Mathematics. s-a.
  (prep. by its Department of Mathematics)
- Kumamoto University. Department of Geology.
  Journal. irreg.
- Kumamoto University. Department of Physics.
  Physics Reports. a.

**Kumamoto University. Institute of Constitutional
Medicine**
4-24-1 Kuhonzi, Kumamoto 862, Japan.
- Kumamoto University. Institute of Constitutional
  Medicine. Bulletin/Kumamoto Daigaku Taisitsu
  Igaku Kenkyusho Hokoku. q. ISSN 0023-530X
- Kumamoto University. Institute of Constitutional
  Medicine. Bulletin. Supplement. a. ISSN 0075-
  7217
- Kumamoto University. Institute of Constitutional
  Medicine. Report/Kumamoto Daigaku Taishitsu
  Igaku Kenkyusho Hokoku. q.

**Kumamoto University Medical School**
2-2-1 Honjo, Kumamoto 860, Japan.
- Kumamoto Medical Journal. q. ISSN 0023-5326

**Kurume Daigaku**
*see* Kurume University

**Kurume Medical Association**
c/o Kurume University School of Medicine, 67
Asahi-machi, Kurume 830, Japan.
- Kurume Medical Association. Journal/Kurume
  Igakkai Zasshi. m.

**Kurume University School of Medicine**
c/o Dept. of Microbiology, 67 Asahi-machi,
Kurume 830, Japan.
- Kurume Medical Journal. q. ISSN 0023-5679

**Kyorin Shoin**
4-2-1 Yushima, Tokyo 113, Japan.
- Health Care/Hoken No Kagaku. m. ISSN 0018-
  3342 (Health Science Research Association)

**Kyoritsu Shuppan Co., Ltd.**
4-6-19 Kohinata, Bunkyo-ku, Tokyo 112, Japan.
- Protein, Nucleic Acid, Enzyme/Tanpakushitsu
  Kakusan Koso. m. ISSN 0039-9450

**Kyoto Association for International Culture and
Tourism**
Room 307, Kyoto Grand Hotel, Horikawa, Shioni-
Koji, Shimogyo-ku, Kyoto 600, Japan.
- Monthly Guide Kyoto. m.

**Kyoto Daigaku**
*see* Kyoto University

**Kyoto Daigaku Afurika Ruijin'en Gakujutsu Chosatai**
*see* Kyoto University. Committee of the Kyoto
University Africa Primatological Expedition

**Kyoto Daigaku Bosai Kenkyusho**
*see* Kyoto University. Disaster Prevention
Research Institute

**Kyoto Daigaku Genshi Enerugi Kenkyusho**
*see* Kyoto University. Institute of Atomic Energy

**Kyoto Daigaku Jimbun Kagaku Kenkyujo**
*see* Kyoto University. Research Institute for
Humanistic Studies

**Kyoto Daigaku Kagaku Kenkyusho**
*see* Kyoto University. Institute for Chemical
Research

**Kyoto Daigaku Kekkaku Kyobu Shikkan Kenkyusho**
*see* Kyoto University. Chest Disease Research
Institute

**Kyoto Daigaku Kogaku Kenkyujo**
*see* Kyoto University. Engineering Research
Institute

**Kyoto Daigaku Rigakubu Chikyu Butsurigaku
Kyoshitsu**
*see* Kyoto University. Geophysical Institute

**Kyoto Daigaku Rigakubu Fuzoku Otsu Rinko
Jikkensho**
*see* Kyoto University. Otsu Hydrobiological Station

**Kyoto Daigaku Rigakubu Fuzoku Seto Rinkai
Jikkensho**
*see* Kyoto University. Seto Marine Biological
Laboratory

**Kyoto Daigaku Shokuryo Kogaku Kenkyusho**
*see* Kyoto University. Research Institute for Food
Science

**Kyoto Daigaku Suri Kaiseki Kenkyusho**
*see* Kyoto University. Research Institute for
Mathematical Sciences

**Kyoto Daigaku Uirusu Kenkyusho**
*see* Kyoto University. Institute for Virus Research

**Kyoto Daigaku Zinbum Kagata Kenkynsyo**
*see* Kyoto University. Institute for Humanistic
Studies

**Kyoto Fire Prevention Association**
c/o Kyoto-shi Shobo Gakko, Fukakusa Echigo
Yashiki-cho, Fushima-ku, Kyoto 612, Japan.
- Fire Prevention/Kyoto Shobo. m. ISSN 0023-
  6020

**Kyoto-furitsu Daigaku**
*see* Kyoto Prefectural University

**Kyoto-furitsu Ika Diagaku**
*see* Kyoto Prefectural University of Medicine

**Kyoto Kogei Sen'i Daigaku**
*see* Kyoto Technical University

**Kyoto Kyoiku Daigaku**
*see* Kyoto University of Education

**Kyoto Prefectural University**
Shimogamo Hangi-cho, Sakyo-ku, Kyoto 606, Japan.
- Kyoto Prefectural University. Scientific Reports:
  Agriculture/Kyoto-furitsu Daigaku Gakujutsu
  Hokoku Nagaku. irreg., no. 28, 1976. ISSN 0075-
  7373
- Kyoto Prefectural University. Scientific Reports:
  Humanities/Kyoto-furitsu Daigaku Gakujutsu
  Hokoku Jimbun. irreg., no. 28, 1976. ISSN 0075-
  7381
- Kyoto Prefectural University. Scientific Reports:
  Natural Science and Living Science/Kyoto-furitsu
  Daigaku Gakujutsu Hokoku Rigaku
  Seikatsukagaku. irreg., no. 27, 1976.

**Kyoto Prefectural University of Medicine**
Hirokoji, Kawara-machi, Kamigyo-ku, Kyoto 602, Japan.
- Kyoto Prefectural University of Medicine. Journal/Kyoto-furitsu Ika Daigaku Zasshi. m. ISSN 0023-6012

**Kyoto Shobo Henshu Iinkai**
see Kyoto Fire Prevention Association

**Kyoto Technical University. Faculty of Industrial Arts**
Matsugasaki, Sakyoku, Kyoto 606, Japan.
- Kyoto Technical University. Faculty of Industrial Arts. Memoirs: Science and Technology/Kyoto Kogei Sen'i Daigaku Kogeigakubu Kiyo Riko-hen. a. ISSN 0453-0047

**Kyoto University. Abuyama Seismological Observatory**
Nasahara, Takatsuki 569, Japan.
- Kyoto University. Abuyama Seismological Observatory. Seismological Bulletin/Kyoto Daigaku Abuyama Jishin Kansoku Hokoku. s-a. ISSN 0454-7659

**Kyoto University. Chest Disease Research Institute**
c/o Kyoto University, 53 Shogoin, Sakyo-ku, Kyoto 606, Japan.
- Kyoto University. Chest Disease Research Institute. Bulletin/Kyoto Daigaku Kekkaku Kyobu Shikkan Kenkyusho Kiyo. s-a. ISSN 0009-3378

**Kyoto University. College of Agriculture**
Kitashirakawa Oiwake-cho, Sakyo-ku, Kyoto 606, Japan.
- Kyoto University. College of Agriculture. Memoirs/Kyoto Daigaku Nogakubu Kyo. s-a.

**Kyoto University. Committee of the Kyoto University Africa Primatological Expedition**
Research Institute for Humanistic Studies, 47 Higashiogura-cho, Kitashirakawa, Sakyo-ku, Kyoto 606, Japan.
- Kyoto University African Studies/Kyoto Daigaku Afurika Kenkyu. a. ISSN 0454-7985

**Kyoto University. Data Processing Center**
Yoshida Hon-cho, Sakyo-ku, Kyoto-shi 606, Japan.
- Kyoto University. Data Processing Center. Report/Kyoto Daigaku Ogata Keisanki Senta Eibun Repoto. irreg.

**Kyoto University. Department of Architecture**
Yoshida Hon-cho, Sakyo-ku, Kyoto 606, Japan.
- Spaciology. q.

**Kyoto University. Department of Civil Engineering**
Sakyo-ku, Kyoto 606, Japan.
- Kyoto University. Research Activities in Civil Engineering and Related Fields. triennial. ISSN 0075-7365

**Kyoto University. Disaster Prevention Research Insitute**
Gokasho, Uji 611, Japan.
- Kyoto University. Disaster Prevention Research Institute. Bulletin/Kyoto Daigaku Bosai Kenkyusho Kiyo. q. ISSN 0454-7675

**Kyoto University. Economic Society**
Sakyo-ku, Kyoto 606, Japan.
- Economic Review/Keizai Ronso. m. ISSN 0013-0273

**Kyoto University. Engineering Research Institute**
Sakyo-ku, Kyoto 606, Japan.
- Kyoto University. Engineering Research Institute. Research Activities. a. ISSN 0454-7713

**Kyoto University. Faculty of Engineering**
Yoshida Hon-machi, Sakyo-ku, Kyoto 606, Japan.
- Kyoto University. Faculty of Engineering. Memoirs/Kyoto Daigaku Kogakubu Kiyo. q. ISSN 0023-6063

**Kyoto University. Faculty of Medicine**
53 Shogoin Kawara-machi, Sakyo-ku, Kyoto 606, Japan.
- Acta Dermatologica/Hifuka Kiyo. s-a. ISSN 0065-1176 (prep. by its Department of Dermatology)
- Acta Urologica Japonica/Hinyokika Kiyo. m. ISSN 0001-7191 (prep. by its Department of Urology)
- Annales Paediatrici Japonici/Shonika Kiyo. bi-m. ISSN 0003-4495 (prep. by its Department of Pediatrics)

- Archiv fuer Japanische Chirurgie/Nihon Geka Hokan. bi-m. ISSN 0003-9152 (prep. by its Department of Surgery)
- Central Japan Journal of Orthopaedic & Traumatic Surgery/Chubu Nippon Seikei Geka Saigai Geka Gakkai Zasshi. bi-m. ISSN 0008-9443 (prep. by its Department of Orthopaedic Surgery) (Co-sponsor: Central Japan Association of Orthopaedic and Traumatic Surgery)
- Kyoto University. Bulletin of Stomatology/Kyoto Daigaku Kokukagaku Kiyo. q. ISSN 0023-6039 (prep. by its Department of Stomatology)
- Practica Otologica Kyoto/Jibi Inkoka Rinsho. m. ISSN 0032-6313 (prep. by its Department of Otolaryngology)

**Kyoto University. Faculty of Science**
Kitashirakawa Oiwake-cho, Sakyo-ku, Kyoto 606, Japan.
- Kyoto University. Faculty of Science. Memoirs. Series of Biology. a. ISSN 0454-7802
- Kyoto University. Faculty of Science. Memoirs. Series of Geology and Mineralogy. s-a. ISSN 0454-7810
- Kyoto University. Faculty of Science. Memoirs. Series of Physics, Astrophysics, Geophysics and Chemistry. s-a.
- Kyoto University. Journal of Mathematics/Kyoto Daigaku Rigakubu Sugaku Kiyo. 3 per yr. ISSN 0023-608X (prep. by its Department of Mathematics) (Distributor: Kinokuniya Bookstore Co. Ltd, 3-17-7 Shinjuku, Shinjuku-ku, Tokyo 160, Japan)

**Kyoto University. Geophysical Institute**
Kitashirakawa Oiwake-cho, Sakyo-ku, Kyoto 606, Japan.
- Kyoto University. Geophysical Institute. Contributions/Kyoto Daigaku Rigakubu Chikyu Butsurigaku Kyoshitsu Obun Hokoku. a.

**Kyoto University. Institute for Chemical Research**
Gokasho, Uji Kyoto-fu, Japan.
- Kyoto University. Institute for Chemical Research. Bulletin/Kyoto Daigaku Kagaku Kenkyusho Hokoku. bi-m. ISSN 0023-6071

**Kyoto University. Institute for Virus Research**
Shogoin Kawahara-machi, Sakyo-ku, Kyoto 606, Japan.
- Kyoto University. Institute for Virus Research. Annual Report/Kyoto Daigaku Uirusu Kenkyusho Nenkan Kiyo. a. ISSN 0075-7357

**Kyoto University. Institute of Atomic Energy**
Gokasho, Uji 611, Japan.
- Kyoto University. Institute of Atomic Energy. Bulletin/Kyoto Daigaku Genshi Enerugi Kenkyusho Iho. s-a.
- Kyoto University. Institute of Atomic Energy. Research Activities. a.
- Kyoto University. Institute of Atomic Energy. Technical Reports/Kyoto Daigaku Genshi Enerugi Kenkyusho Kenkyu Hokoku. irreg.

**Kyoto University. Institute of Earth Science**
College of General Education, Yoshida-Honmachi, Sakyo-ku, Kyota 606, Japan.
- Tsukumo Earth Science/Tsukumo Chigaku. s-a. ISSN 0041-3801

**Kyoto University. Misaki Marine Biological Institute**
Misaki-Koen, Sennangun, Osaka-fu, Japan.
- Kyoto University. Misaki Marine Biological Institute. Bulletin. irreg. (approx. 2 per yr.) ISSN 0023-6098

**Kyoto University. Otsu Hydrobiological Station**
Shimosaka Hon-machi, Otsu 520-01, Japan.
- Kyoto University. Otsu Hydrobiological Station. Contributions/Kyoto Daigaku Rigakubu Fuzoku Otsu Rinko Jukkensho Obun Gyoseki. irreg.

**Kyoto University. Research Institute for Food Science**
Gokasho, Uji 611, Japan.
- Kyoto University. Research Institute for Food Science. Memoirs/Shokuryo Kagaku Kenkyusho Kiyo. irreg. ISSN 0452-9995

**Kyoto University. Research Institute for Fundamental Physics**
Publication Office, Kitashirakawa Owaike-cho, Sakyo-ku, Kyoto 606, Japan.
- Progress of Theoretical Physics/Riron Butsurigaku no Shinpo. m. ISSN 0033-068X

**Kyoto University. Research Institute for Humanistic Studies**
50 Kitashirakawa Oiwake-cho, Sakyo-ku, Kyoto 606, Japan.
- Jimbun. irreg., 1974, no. 13. ISSN 0084-5515
- Oriental Studies/Toho Gakuho. a.

**Kyoto University. Research Institute for Mathematical Sciences**
Kitashirakawa Oiwake-cho, Sakyo-ku, Kyoto 606, Japan.
- Research Institute for Mathematical Sciences. Publications. 3 per yr. ISSN 0034-5318

**Kyoto University. Seto Marine Biological Laboratory**
Shirahama-cho, Nishimuro-gun, Wakayama 649-22, Japan.
- Seto Marine Biological Laboratory. Contributions. irreg. ISSN 0080-908X
- Seto Marine Biological Laboratory. Publications/Seto Rinkai Jikkensho Kiyo. bi-m. ISSN 0037-2870
- Seto Marine Biological Laboratory. Special Publications. Series 2. irreg. ISSN 0080-9098

**Kyoto University of Education**
1 Fukakusa Fujinomori-cho, Fushimi-ku, Kyoto 612, Japan.
- Kyoto University of Education. Bulletin. Series B: Mathematics and Natural Science/Kyoto Kyoiku Daigaku Kiyo, B, Shizenkagaku. s-a. ISSN 0023-6101

**Kyoyo Gakkai**
see Kokushikan University. Society of Liberal Arts

**Kyushu American Literature Society**
- Kyushu American Literature Studies. (pub. by Kyushu University. College of General Education)

**Kyushu Association of Neuro-Psychiatry**
c/o Department of Neuro-Psychiatry, Faculty of Medicine, Kyushu University, Maidashi, Higashi-ku, Fukuoka 812, Japan.
- Kyushu Neuro-Psychiatry/Kyushu Shinkei Seishin Igaku. q. ISSN 0023-6144

**Kyushu Daigaku**
see Kyushu University

**Kyushu Daigaku Hosei Gakkai**
see Kyushu University. Institute of Law and Politics

**Kyushu Daigaku Oyo Rikigaku Kenkyusho**
see Kyushu University. Research Institute for Applied Mechanics

**Kyushu Daigaku Rigakubu Fuzoku Amakusa Rinkai Jikkensho**
see Kyushu University. Amakusa Marine Biological Laboratory

**Kyushu Daigaku Tokei Kagaku Kenkyukai**
see Kyushu University. Research Association of Statistical Sciences

**Kyushu Institute of Technology**
1-1 Sensui-cho, Tobata, Kitakyushu 804, Japan.
- Kyushu Institute of Technology. Bulletin: Humanities, Social Sciences/Kyushu Kogyo Daigaku Kenkyu Hokoku, Jinbun-Shakai-Kagaku. a. ISSN 0453-0349
- Kyushu Institute of Technology. Bulletin: Mathematics, Natural Science/Kyushu Kogyo Daigaku Kenkyu Hokoku, Shizenkagaku. a. ISSN 0454-8221
- Kyushu Institute of Technology. Memoirs: Engineering. a.

**Kyushu Kogyo Daigaku**
see Kyushu Institute of Technology

**Kyushu Kogyo Gijutsu Shikenjo**
see Japan. Government Industrial Research Institute, Kyushu

**Kyushu Sangyo University**
2-327 Shokadai, Higashi-ku, Tokyo, Japan.
- Journal of Industry and Management/Sangyo Keiei Kenkyushoho. irreg.

**Kyushu Shinkei Seishin Gakkai**
see Kyushu Association of Neuro-Psychiatry

**Kyushu University. Amakusa Marine Biological Laboratory**
2231 Tomioka, Reihoku-cho, Amakusa-gun, Kumamoto 863-25, Japan.
- Amakusa Marine Biological Laboratory. Contributions. biennial. ISSN 0065-6674
- Amakusa Marine Biological Laboratory. Publications. a. ISSN 0065-6682

**Kyushu University. College of General Education**
4-2-1 Ropponmatsu, Chuo-ku, Fukuoka 810, Japan.
- Kyushu American Literature Studies. a. ISSN 0454-8132 (Kyushu American Literature Society)
- Sieboldia Acta Biologica/Shiborudia. irreg. ISSN 0559-9822 (prep. by its Biological Laboratory)

**Kyushu University. Department of Fisheries**
3575-1 Hakozaki, Higashi-ku, Fukuoka 812, Japan.
- Kyushu University. Contributions from the Department of Fisheries and the Fishery Research Laboratory/Kyushu Daigaku Nogakubu Suisangakka Gyosekishu. a. ISSN 0453-0314

**Kyushu University. Faculty of Agriculture**
3575-1 Hakozaki, Higashi-ku, Fukuoka 812, Japan.
- Kyushu University. Faculty of Agriculture. Journal/Kyushu Daigaku Nogakubu Kiyo. q. ISSN 0023-6152

**Kyushu University. Faculty of Engineering**
3576 Hakozaki, Higashi-ku, Fukuoka 812, Japan.
- Kyushu University. Faculty of Engineering. Memoirs/Kyushu Daigaku Kogakubu Kiyo. q. ISSN 0023-6160
- Kyushu University. Faculty of Engineering. Technology Reports/Kyushu Daigaku Kogakubu Shuho. bi-m. ISSN 0023-2718

**Kyushu University. Faculty of Medicine**
Department of Dermatology, 1276 Katakasu, Fukuoka 812, Japan.
- Nishi Nihon Journal of Dermatology/Nishi Nihon Hifuka. bi-m.

**Kyushu University. Faculty of Science**
6-10-1 Hakozaki, Higashi-ku, Fukuoka 812, Japan.
- Kyushu University. Faculty of Science. Memoirs. Series A: Mathematics/Kyushu Daigaku Rigakubu Kiyo, A, Sugaku. s-a. ISSN 0373-6385 (prep. by its Department of Mathematics)
- Kyushu University. Faculty of Science. Memoirs Series B: Physics/Kyushu Daigaku Rigakubu Kiyo, B, Butsurigaku. a. ISSN 0085-2627 (prep. by its Department of Physics)
- Kyushu University. Faculty of Science. Memoirs. Series C: Chemistry/Kyushu Daigaku Rigakubu Kiyo, C. Kagaku. a. ISSN 0085-2635 (prep. by its Department of Chemistry)
- Kyushu University. Faculty of Science. Memoirs. Series D: Geology/Kyushu Daigaku Rigakubu Kiyo, D, Chishitsugaku. a. ISSN 0023-6179 (prep. by its Department of Geology)

**Kyushu University. Institute of Law and Politics**
c/o Faculty of Law, Kyushu University, Hakozaki, Higashi-ku, Fukuoka 812, Japan.
- Journal of Law and Politics/Ho-sei Kenkyu. m.

**Kyushu University. Research Association of Statistical Sciences**
Hakozaki-cho, Higashi-ku, Fukuoka 812, Japan.
- Bulletin of Mathematical Statistics. q. ISSN 0007-4993

**Kyushu University. Research Institute for Applied Mechanics**
87 Hakozaki Machi, Higashi-ku, Fukuoka 812, Japan.
- Research Institute for Applied Mechanics. Bulletin/Oyo Rikigaku Kenkyusho Shoho. s-a. ISSN 0030-7734
- Research Institute for Applied Mechanics. Reports /Oyo Rikigaku Kenkyusho Obun Hokoku. 4 per yr. ISSN 0023-6195

**Laboratory of Climatology**
see under Tokyo University of Education

**Lawyer's Association**
1-1 Kasumigaseki, Chiyoda-ku, Tokyo, Japan.
- Lawyer's Association. Journal/Hoso Jiho. m. ISSN 0023-9453

**Lepidopterological Society of Japan**
c/o Ogata Hospital, 3-18 Imabashi, Higashi-ku, Osaka 541, Japan.
- Lepidopterological Society of Japan. Transactions/ Cho to Ga. q. ISSN 0024-0974

**Life Science Co., Ltd.**
c/o Ito Bldg., 42-14 Udagawa-cho, Shibuya-ku, Tokyo 150, Japan.
- Geriatric Medicine/Ronen Igaku. m.

**Linguistic Society of Japan**
Taishukan Bldg., 3-26 Kandanishiki-cho, Chiyoda-ku, Tokyo 101, Japan.
- Linguistic Society of Japan. Journal/Gengo Kenkyu. s-a. ISSN 0024-3914

**Local Autonomy College**
4-6-2 Minami Azabu, Minato-ku, Tokyo, Japan.
- Local Government Review. a. ISSN 0449-0193

**Long Term Credit Bank of Japan Ltd.**
Economic Research Division, 1-2-4 Otemachi, Chiyoda-ku, Tokyo, Japan.
- L T C B Research; review of Japanese industry. q.

**M. H. Information Center**
Samariya Bldg., 3-26 Nishi-Okubo, Shinjuku-ku, Tokyo 160, Japan.
- Modern Material Handling/Seisan to Unpan. m. ISSN 0037-1068

**Mainichi Daily News**
- Industries of Japan. (pub. by Mainichi Newspapers)
- Japan Almanach. (pub. by Mainichi Newspapers)

**Mainichi Newspapers**
1-1-1 Hitotsubashi, Chiyoda-ku, Tokyo 100, Japan.
- Camera Mainichi. m. ISSN 0008-2155
- Economist. w. ISSN 0013-0621 (Order from: Oversea Courier Service Inc., Osaka Branch Office, 3-28 Nozatonishi, Nishiyodogawa-Ku, Osaka 541, Japan)
- Industries of Japan. a. ISSN 0446-1266 (Mainichi Daily News)
- Japan Almanach. a. (Mainichi Daily News)
- Mainichi Graphic. w. ISSN 0025-0813 (Order from: Oversea Courier Service Inc., Osaka Branch Office, 3-28 Nozatonishi, Nishiyodogawa-Ku, Osaka 541, Japan)
- Sunday Mainichi. w. ISSN 0039-5234 (Order from: Oversea Courier Service Inc., Osaka Branch Office, 3-28 Nozatonishi, Nishiyodogawa-Ku, Osaka 541, Japan)

**Mainichi Newspapers, Osaka. Braille Mainichi Section**
2-36 Dojima, Kita-ku, Osaka, Japan.
- Braille Mainichi Weekly. w.

**Malacological Society of Japan**
c/o National Science Museum, 3-23-1 Hyakunin-cho, Shinjuku-ku, Tokyo 160, Japan.
- Venus: Japanese Journal of Malacology/ Kairuigaku Zasshi. q. ISSN 0042-3580

**Management Science Research Institute**
c/o Rakuen, No. 101, 13-1, Shibuya-ku, Tokyo 150, Japan.
- Computer News. w.

**Map Society**
Shinsen Bldg., 8-2 Shinsen-cho, Shibuya, Tokyo 150, Japan.
- Map's Companion/Chizu no Tomo. m. ISSN 0009-4900

**Marine Park Research Station**
see Sabiura Marine Park Research Station

**Maritime Safety Agency**
see Japan. Maritime Safety Agency

**Marunouchi Research Center Co., Ltd.**
Nippon Bldg., 2-6-2 Ohtemachi, Chiyoda-ku, Tokyo 100, Japan.
- Foreign-Affiliated Enterprises in Japan. a. (Japan. Ministry of International Trade and Industry)
- M R C Consultant Monthly. m.

**Mathematical Society of Japan**
c/o University of Tokyo, Faculty of Science, 7-3-1 Hongo, Bunkyo-ku, Tokyo 113, Japan.
- Mathematical Society of Japan. Journal. q.
- Mathematical Society of Japan. Publications. irreg. ISSN 0549-4540
- Mathematics/Sugaku. (pub. by Iwanami Shoten Publishers)

**Matsushita Electric Industrial Co., Ltd.**
3-15 Yakumonakamachi Moriguchi, Osaka 571, Japan.
- National Technical Report. bi-m. ISSN 0028-0291

**Medical Association of Okayama**
c/o Okayama University Medical School, 2-5-1 Shikata-cho, Okayama 700, Japan.
- Medical Association of Okayama. Journal/ Okayama Igakkai Zasshi. m. ISSN 0030-1558

**Medical Friend Co., Ltd**
4-1-32 Kudankita, Chiyoda-ku, Tokyo 102, Japan.
- Japanese Journal of Nursing Art/Kango Gijutsu. m.

**Medical Instrument Society of Japan**
3-39-15 Hongo, Bunkyo-ku, Tokyo 113, Japan.
- Journal of Medical Instruments/Ikakikai Gaku Zasshi. m. ISSN 0019-1736

**Medical Library and Information Center, Keio University**
see under Keio University

**Medico-Legal Society of Japan**
Faculty of Medicine, University of Tokyo, 7-3-1 Hongo, Bunkyo-ku, Tokyo 113, Japan.
- Japanese Journal of Legal Medicine/Nippon Hoigaku Zasshi. bi-m. ISSN 0047-1887

**Meguro Parasitological Museum**
3-557 Shimomeguro, Meguro-ku, Tokyo 153, Japan.
- Progress of Medical Parasitology in Japan. a. ISSN 0555-4349

**Meidensha Electric Mfg. Co., Ltd.**
New Ohtemachi Bldg., 2-2-1 Ohtemachi, Chiyoda-ku, Tokyo, Japan.
- Meiden Review. 3 per yr.

**Menka Keizai Kenkyusho**
see Japan Cotton Traders' Association

**Metal Finishing Society of Japan**
New Otemachi Bldg., 2 Kanda-Iwamoto-cho, Chiyoda-ku, Tokyo 100, Japan.
- Meidensha Review/Kinzoku Hyomen Gijutsu. s-a. ISSN 0026-0614

**Metal Mining Agency**
see Japan. Metal Mining Agency

**Meteorological Research Institute**
4-35-8 Koenji-kita, Suginami, Tokyo 166, Japan.
- Papers in Meteorology and Geophysics/Kisho Kenkyusho Kenkyu Hokoku. q. ISSN 0031-126X

**Meteorological Society of Japan**
c/o Japan Meteorological Agency, 1-3-4 Ote-machi, Chiyoda-ku, Tokyo 100, Japan.
- Meteorological Society of Japan. Journal/Kisho Shushi. bi-m. ISSN 0026-1165

**Metropolitan Technical College**
6-6 Asahigaoka Hino, Tokyo 191, Japan.
- Metropolitan College of Technology, Tokyo. Memoirs/Tokyo-toritsu Koka Tanki Daigaku Kenkyu Hokoku. a.

**Microbiology Research Foundation**
Japan Academic Societies Center Bldg., 2-4-16 Yayoi, Bunkyo-ku, Tokyo 113, Japan.
- Journal of General and Applied Microbiology. bi-m. ISSN 0022-1260

**Middle East Institute of Japan**
10-21 Akasaka, Minato-ku, Tokyo, Japan.
- Middle East News/Chuto Tsuho. m.

**Midori-Shobo Co., Ltd.**
c/o Fuji Bldg., 4-6-5 Idabashi, Tokyo, Japan.
- Fish Culture/Yoshoku. m. ISSN 0044-0671

**Mie Daigaku**
see Mie University

**Mie-kenritsu Daigaku**
see Mie Prefectural University

**Mie Prefectural University. Faculty of Fisheries**
2-158 Edobashi, Tsu-shi 514, Japan.
- Mie Prefectural University. Faculty of Fisheries. Bulletin/Mie-kenritsu Daigaku Suisan Gakubu Kiyo. a. ISSN 0539-998X

**Mie Prefecture. Environmental Science Institute**
8-ban 12-jo Shinjo 4-chome, Yokkaichi, Japan.
- Mie Prefecture. Environmental Science Institute. Annual Report. a.

**Mie University. School of Medicine**
2-174 Edobashi, Tsu 514, Mie-ken, Japan.
- Mie Medical Journal. 3 per yr. ISSN 0026-3532

**Mineralogical Society of Japan**
c/o Osaka Daigaku Kyoyobu, 1-1 Machikaneyama-cho, Toyanaka 560, Japan
(Editorial Address: c/o K. Nagasawa, Ed., Department of Earth Sciences, Faculty of Science, Nagoya University, Chikusa-Ku, Nagoya 464, Japan)
- Mineralogical Journal. q. ISSN 0544-2540

**Misaki Marine Biological Station**
see under **University of Tokyo**

**Mita Society for Library and Information Science**
c/o Keio University, 2-15-15 Mita, Minato-ku, Tokyo 108, Japan.
- Library and Information Science. a.

**Mitsubishi Bank**
2-7-1 Marunouchi, Chiyoda-ku, Tokyo, Japan.
- Mitsubishi Bank Review. m. ISSN 0300-3914
(prep. by its Economic Research Department)

**Mitsubishi Economic Research Institute**
3-3-1 Marunouchi, Chiyoda-ku, Tokyo, Japan.
- M E R I's Monthly Circular. Survey of Economic Conditions in Japan. m. ISSN 0026-6809

**Mitsubishi Electric Corporation**
2-2-3 Marunouchi, Chiyoda-ku, Tokyo 100, Japan.
- Mitsubishi Electric Engineer. q. ISSN 0544-5779

**Mitsubishi Electric Corporation. Central Research Laboratory**
80 Nakano, Minami Shimizu, Amagasaki 661, Japan.
- Mitsubishi Denki Laboratory Reports/Mitsubishi Denki Kenkyusho Hokoku. q. ISSN 0026-6795

**Mitsubishi Heavy Industries Ltd.**
2-5-1 Marunouchi, Chiyoda-ku, Tokyo 100, Japan.
- Mitsubishi Heavy Industries Technical Review/ Mitsui Juko Giho. 3 per yr. ISSN 0026-6817 (prep. by its Technical Administration Department)
- Mitsubishi Technical Bulletin. irreg. ISSN 0540-469X

**Mitsui & Co., Ltd.**
1-2-9 Nishi Shimbashi, Minato-ku, Tokyo, Japan.
- Japan Sugar Yearbook. a.

**Mitsui Engineering & Shipbuilding Co., Ltd.**
5-6-4 Tsukiji, Chuo-ku, Tokyo 104, Japan.
- Mitsui Technical Review/Mitsui Zosen Giho. q. ISSN 0026-6825 (prep. by its Technical Division)

**Miyazaki University. Faculty of Engineering**
118 Nishimaruyama-cho, Miyazaki 880, Japan.
- Miyazaki University. Faculty of Engineering. Memoirs/Miyazaki Daigaku Kogakubu Kiyo. irreg. ISSN 0540-4924

**Mokuzai Kenkyusho**
see **Wood Research Institute**

**Monbu-sho Kokuritsu Idengaku Kenkyusho**
see **Japan. National Institute of Genetics**

**Mountains Land Use Research Laboratory**
see under **Iwate University**

**Movie-TV Marketing**
Box 30, Central Post Office, Tokyo 100-91, Japan.
- Annual Worldwide TV Survey. a.
- Communications. decennial. ISSN 0084-9081
- Movie/TV Marketing. m. ISSN 0047-8288
- Movie/TV Marketing Global Motion Picture Year Book. a. ISSN 0085-3577

**Musashino Art University**
1-736 Ogawamachi, Kodaira 187, Japan.
- Musashino Art University. Bulletin. a.

**Musen Jujisha Kyoiku Kyokai**
1-7-18 Shimomeguro, Meguroku, Tokyo, Japan.
- Radio Waves and Examination/Dempa to Juken. m. ISSN 0011-8346

**Musica Iberoamericana Co.**
1-21-6 Ebisu, Shibuya-ku, Tokyo, Japan.
- Musica Iberoamericana/Chunambei Ongaku. m. ISSN 0027-4534

**Mycological Society of Japan**
c/o National Science Museum, 7-20 Ueno Park, Daito-ku, Tokyo 110, Japan.
(Overseas Distributor: Japan Publications Trading Co., Ltd., Box 5030, Tokyo International, Tokyo 100-31, Japan; or 1255 Howard St., San Francisco, CA 94103)
- Mycological Society of Japan. Transactions/Nihon Kin Gakkai Kaiho. q. ISSN 0029-0289

**N D L**
see **National Diet Library**

**N H K**
see **Japan Broadcasting Corp.**

**N I K K I R E N**
see **Japan Machinery Federation**

**N I K K Y O S O**
see **Japan Teachers' Union**

**N T V**
see **Nippon Television Network Corp.**

**Nagano Medical Society**
- Shinshu Medical Journal/Shinshu Igaku Zasshi. (pub. by Shinshu University. Faculty of Medicine)

**Nagaoka Technical College**
888 Nishikatakai-machi, Nagaoka 940, Niigata-ken, Japan.
- Nagaoka Technical College. Research Reports/ Nagaoka Kogyo Koto Senmon Gakko Kenkyu Kiyo. q. ISSN 0027-7568

**Nagasaki Daigaku**
see **Nagasaki University**

**Nagasaki Daigaku Netti Igaku Kenkyusho**
see **Nagasaki University. Institute for Tropical Medicine**

**Nagasaki University. Institute for Tropical Medicine**
2-4 Sakamoto-machi, Nagasaki 852, Japan.
- Tropical Medicine/Nettai Igaku. q. ISSN 0041-3267

**Nagasaki University. School of Medicine**
12-4 Sakamoto-machi, Nagasaki 852, Japan.
- Acta Medica Nagasakiensia. q. ISSN 0001-6055

**Nagoya. Environmental Pollution Research Institute**
Nagoya, Japan.
- Nagoya. Environmental Pollution Research Institute. Annual Report. a.

**Nagoya City University. Medical Association**
Kawasumi, Mizuho-cho, Mizuho-ku, Nagoya 467, Japan.
- Nagoya City University. Medical Association. Journal/Nagoya-shiritsu Daigaku Igakkai Zasshi. q. ISSN 0027-7606

**Nagoya City University. Medical School**
Kawasumi, Mizuho-cho, Mizuho-ku, Nagoya 467, Japan.
- Nagoya Medical Journal. q. ISSN 0027-7649

**Nagoya Daigaku**
see **Nagoya University**

**Nagoya Daigaku Kankyo Igaku Kenkyusho**
see **Nagoya University. Research Institute of Environmental Medicine**

**Nagoya Daigaku Kuden Kenkyusho**
see **Nagoya University. Research Institute of Atmospherics**

**Nagoya Daigaku Purazuma Kenkyusho**
see **Nagoya University. Institute of Plasma Physics**

**Nagoya Daigaku Rigakubu Uchusen Boenkyo**
see **Nagoya University. Cosmic Ray Research Laboratory**

**Nagoya Daigaku Suishitsu Kagaku Kenky Shisetsu**
see **Nagoya University. Water Research Institute**

**Nagoya Port Authority**
1-8-21 Irifune, Minato-ku, Nagoya 455, Japan.
- Nagoya Port Statistics Annual/Nagoyako Tokei Nenpo. a. ISSN 0469-4783
- Nagoya Port Statistics Monthly/Nagoyako Tokei Geppo. m. ISSN 0027-7592

**Nagoya-shiritsu Daigaku**
see **Nagoya City University**

**Nagoya University. Cosmic-Ray Research Laboratory**
Department of Physics, Furo-cho, Chikusa-ku, Nagoya 464, Japan.
- Nagoya University. Cosmic-Ray Research Laboratory. Proceedings/Meidai Uchusen Kenkyushitsu Kiji. 1-2 per yr. ISSN 0025-8733

**Nagoya University. Department of Earth Sciences**
Faculty of Science, Chikusa-ku, Nagoya 464, Japan.
- Collected Papers on Earth Sciences. a.
- Journal of Earth Sciences. a. ISSN 0022-0442

**Nagoya University. Department of Economics**
Furo-cho, Chikusa-ku, Nagoya 464, Japan.
- Economic Science/Keizai Kagaku. q. ISSN 0022-9725

**Nagoya University. Department of Mathematics**
Faculty of Science, Furo-cho, Chikusa-ku, Nagoya 464, Japan
- Nagoya Mathematical Journal/Nagoya Sugaku Zasshi. q. ISSN 0027-7630 (Subscr. to: Kinokuniya Book Stores of America Co., Ltd., West Bldg., Japanese Cultural and Trade Center, 1581 Webster St., San Francisco, CA 94115)

**Nagoya University. Faculty of Engineering**
Furo-cho, Chikusa-ku, Nagoya 464, Japan.
- Nagoya University. Faculty of Engineering. Automatic Control Laboratory. Research Reports/Nagoya Daigaku Kogakubu Jido Seigyo. a.
- Nagoya University. Faculty of Engineering. Memoirs/Nagoya Daigaku Kogakubu Kiyo. s-a. ISSN 0027-7657

**Nagoya University. Institute of Plasma Physics**
Furo-cho, Chikusa-ku, Nagoya-shi 464, Japan.
- Nagoya University. Institute of Plasma Physics. Annual Review/Nagoya Daigaku Purazuma Kenkyusho Nenpo. a. ISSN 0547-1567
- Nagoya University. Institute of Plasma Physics. Technical Reports. irreg.

**Nagoya University. Research Institute of Atmospherics**
3-13 Honohara, Toyokawa 442, Aichi-ken, Japan.
- Nagoya University. Research Institute of Atmospherics. Proceedings/Nagoya Daigaku Kuden Kenkyusho Hokoku. a. ISSN 0077-264X

**Nagoya University. Research Institute of Environmental Medicine**
Furo-cho, Chikusa-ku, Nagoya 464, Japan.
- Nagoya University. Research Institute of Environmental Medicine. Annual Report/Nagoya Daigaku Kankyo Igaku Kenkyusho Nenpo. a.

**Nagoya University. School of Medicine**
65 Tsurimai, Showa-ku, Nagoya 466, Japan.
- Nagoya Journal of Medical Science. q. ISSN 0027-7622

**Nagoya University. Water Research Institute**
Furo-cho, Chikusa-ku, Nagoya 464, Japan.
- Collected Papers on Sciences of Atmosphere and Hydrosphere. a. ISSN 0547-1435
- Nagoya University. Water Research Institute. Annual Report/Suiken Kagaku Kenkyujo Nenpo. a.

**Nagoyako Kanri Kumai**
see **Nagoya Port Authority**

**Naikahoken Kankokai**
c/o Kyoto University, Medical Faculty, Dept. of Internal Medicine, 53 Shogoin Kawara-cho, Kyoto 606, Japan.
- Japanese Archives of Internal Medicine/ Naikahoken. m. ISSN 0021-4809

**Nankodo Co., Ltd.**
3-42-6 Hongo, Bunkyo-ku, Tokyo 113, Japan.
- Internal Medicine/Naika. m.
- Japanese Journal of Thoracic Surgery/Kyobu Geka. m. ISSN 0021-5252
- Journal of Japanese Chemistry/Kagaku No Ryoiki. m. ISSN 0022-2070
- Orthopedic Surgery/Seikei Geka. m. ISSN 0030-5901
- Surgery/Geka. m. ISSN 0016-593X

**Nanzando Co., Ltd.**
4-1-11 Yushima, Bunkyoku, Tokyo 113-91, Japan.
- Journal of Therapy/Chiryo. m. ISSN 0022-5207

- Practical Pharmacy/Yakkyoku. m. ISSN 0044-0035

**Nara Medical Association**
Nara Medical University, Kasihara 634, Nara, Japan.
- Nara Medical Association. Journal/Nara Igaku Zasshi. bi-m.

**National Aerospace Laboratory**
*see* Japan. National Aerospace Laboratory

**National Cancer Center**
*see* Japan. National Cancer Center

**National Chemical Laboratory for Industry**
*see* Japan. National Chemical Laboratory for Industry

**National Christian Council of Japan**
Japan Christian Center, Rm. 24, 2-13-18 Nishi Waseda, Shinju-ku, Tokyo 160, Japan.
- Japan Christian Activity News. s-m. ISSN 0021-4353

**National Christian Council of Japan. N C C Center for the Study of Japanese Religions**
c/o Kyoto Diocese of Japan Episcopal Church, Karasuma-Shimotachiuri, Kamikyo-ku, Kyoto 602, Japan.
- Japanese Religions. s-a. ISSN 0448-8954

**National Council of Social Welfare**
3-3-4 Kasumigaseki, Chiyoda-ku, Tokyo, Japan.
- Hoiku No Tomo. m. ISSN 0018-327X
- Shakai Fukushi No Doko. a.

**National Defense Academy**
1-10-20 Hashirimuzu, Yokosuka, Kanagawa-ken 239, Japan.
- Defense Academy. Memoirs/Boei Daigakko Kiyo Rikogaku-hen; mathematics, physics, electrical engineering, mechanical engineering, civil engineering, chemistry, applied physics, aeronautical engineering. 4 per yr. ISSN 0025-9136

**National Defense Medical Society**
c/o Boei-cho, Eisei-kyoku, Eisei-ka, 9-7-45 Akasaka, Minato-ku, Tokyo 107, Japan.
- National Defense Medical Journal/Boei Eisei. m. ISSN 0006-5528

**National Diet Library**
1-10-1 Nagata-cho, Chiyoda-ku, Tokyo 100, Japan.
- Biblos/Biburosu; Shibutoshokan Senmontoshokan Renrakushi; monthly report of special libraries. m. ISSN 0006-2030
- Current Publications: Serials/Chikuji Kankobutsu Mokuroku. w. ISSN 0529-1607
- Directory of Japanese Scientific Periodicals. irreg., latest 1974.
- Foreign Aero-Space Literature/Gaikoku Koku Uchu Bunken Mokuroku. a. ISSN 0454-191X
- Japanese National Bibliography. a.
- Japanese Periodical Index. Humanities and Social Science Section/Zasshi Kiji Sakuin, Jinbun Shakai-Hen. m.; s-a. in 1975; annual cumulations, 1976. ISSN 0021-5341
- Japanese Periodicals Index, Science and Technology Section/Zasshi Kiji Sakuin Kagaku Gijutsu-hen. m.; s-a in 1975; annual cumulations, 1976.
- List of Ad Reports Kept in the National Diet Library/Kokuritsu Kokkai Toshokan Ad Ripoto Shozo Mokuroku.
- List of Japanese Newspapers on Microfilm in Japan (1970- ) irreg.
- Materials on Asia and Africa-Accession List and Review/Ajia Afurika Shiryo Tsuho. m. ISSN 0025-536X
- Monthly List of Selected Atomic Energy Publications/Genshiryoku Shiryo Geppo. m.
- National Diet Library. Annual Report/Kokuritsu Kokkai Toshokan Nenpo. a.
- National Diet Library. Monthly Bulletin/Kokuritsu Kokkai Toshokan Geppo. m. ISSN 0027-9153
- National Diet Library. Monthly List of Foreign Scientific and Technical Publications/Kaigai Kagaku Gijutsu Shiryo Geppo. m.
- National Diet Library. Newsletter. q. ISSN 0027-9161
- National Diet Library. Reference/Refarensu. m. ISSN 0034-2912
- Science and Technology Information Service/Kagaku Gijutsu Bunken Sabisu. q. ISSN 0022-7633

**National Federation of Health Insurance Societies**
1-24-4 Minami-Aoyama, Minato-ku, Tokyo, Japan.
- Kempo Nyusu. q. ISSN 0022-989X
- Kenko Hoken Shimbun. s-m. ISSN 0022-992X

**National Grassland Research Institute**
*see* Japan. National Grassland Research Institute

**National Institute for Educational Research**
Planning Section, 6-5-22 Shimomeguro, Meguro-ku, Tokyo 153, Japan.
- National Institute for Educational Research. Research Bulletin. irreg. ISSN 0085-378X

**National Institute for Leprosy Research**
*see* Japan. National Institute for Leprosy Research

**National Institute for Special Education**
Yokosuka, Japan.
- National Institute for Special Education. Bulletin/Kokuritsu Tokushu Kyoiku Sogo Kenkyujo Kenkyu Kiyo.

**National Institute of Agricultural Sciences**
*see* Japan. National Institute of Agricultural Sciences

**National Institute of Animal Health**
*see* Japan. National Institute of Animal Health

**National Institute of Animal Industry**
*see* Japan. National Institute of Animal Industry

**National Institute of Genetics**
*see* Japan. National Institute of Genetics

**National Institute of Health**
*see* Japan. National Institute of Health

**National Institute of Hygienic Sciences**
1-18-1 Kamiyoga, Setagaya-ku, Tokyo 158, Japan.
- Food Hygienic Society of Japan. Journal/Shokuhin Eiseigaku Zasshi. bi-m. ISSN 0015-6426
- National Institute of Hygienic Sciences. Bulletin/Eisei Shikenjo Hokoku. a. ISSN 0077-5002
- National Institute of Hygienic Sciences. Monthly Report/Kokuritsu Eisei Shikenjo Chosa Geppo. bi-m.

**National Institute of Industrial Health**
*see* Japan. National Institute of Industrial Health

**National Institute of Nutrition**
*see* Japan. National Institute of Nutrition

**National Institute of Polar Research**
1-9-10 Kaga, Itabashi-ku, Tokyo 173, Japan.
- Japanese Antarctic Research Expedition, 1956-1962. Data Reports. irreg., No. 35, 1976. ISSN 0075-3343
- National Institute of Polar Research. Memoirs. Series A: Aeronomy. irreg. No. 14, 1976.
- National Institute of Polar Research. Memoirs. Series B: Meteorology. irreg., No. 2, 1974.
- National Institute of Polar Research. Memoirs. Series C: Earth Sciences. irreg., No. 10, 1976.
- National Institute of Polar Research . Memoirs. Series D: Oceanography. irreg., 1964, no. 1.
- National Institute of Polar Research. Memoirs. Series E. Biology and Medical Science. irreg., No. 32, 1976.
- National Institute of Polar Research. Memoirs. Series F: Logistics. irreg., No. 2, 1976.
- Tokyo. Polar Research Center. Antarctic Record. 3 per yr. ISSN 0085-7289

**National Institute of Radiological Sciences**
4-9-1 Anagawa, Chiba 280, Japan.
- Radioactivity Survey Data in Japan. a. ISSN 0441-2516

**National Language Research Institute**
3-9-14 Nisigaoka, Kita-ku, Tokyo 115, Japan.
- National Language Research Institute. Annual Report/Kokuritsu Kokugo Kenkyusho Nenpo. a.

**National Library**
*see* National Diet Library

**National Museum of Modern Art, Tokyo**
3 Kitanomarukoen, Chiyoda-ku, Tokyo, Japan.
- Gendai no Me. m. ISSN 0435-219X
- International Biennial Exhibition of Prints in Tokyo. biennial. ISSN 0074-2066

**National Nutrition Society**
- Japanese Journal of Nutrition/Eiyogaku Zasshi. (pub. by Daiichi Shuppan K. K.)

**National Research Center for Disaster Prevention**
6-15-1 Ginza, Chuo-ku, Tokyo 104, Japan.
- National Research Center for Disaster Prevention. Seismological Bulletin. irreg.
- Strong-Motion Earthquake Records in Japan/Kyoshin Kiroku. s-a. ISSN 0563-7902

**National Research Institute for Metals**
2-3-12 Nakameguro, Meguro-ku, Tokyo 153, Japan.
- National Research Institute for Metals. Transactions/Kinzoku Zairyo Gijutsu Kenkyusho Obun Kenkyu Hokoku. bi-m. ISSN 0453-9222

**National Research Institute for Pollution and Resources**
*see* Japan. National Research Institute for Pollution and Resources

**National Research Institute of Police Science**
*see* Japan. National Research Institute of Police Science

**National Research Laboratory of Metrology**
*see* Japan. National Research Laboratory of Metrology

**National Science Museum**
7-20 Ueno Park, Daito-ku, Tokyo 110, Japan.
- National Science Museum. Bulletin. Series A: Zoology/Kokuritsu Kagaku Hakubutsukan Kenkyu Hokoku. A-rui: Dobutsugaku. s-a.
- National Science Museum. Bulletin. Series B: Botany/Kokuritsu Kagaku Hakubutsukan Kenkyu Hokoku. B-rui: Shokubutsugaku. s-a.
- National Science Museum. Bulletin. Series C: Geology/Kokuritsu Kagaku Hakubutsukan Kenkyu Hokoku. C-rui: Chishitsugaku. s-a.
- National Science Museum. Memoirs. irreg., no. 7, 1974. ISSN 0082-4755

**National Tax Agency**
*see* Japan. National Tax Agency

**Nettai Nogyo Gakkai**
*see* Tropical Agriculture Research Association of Japan

**New Japan Casting and Forging Society**
31 Korai Hashizume-cho, Higashi-ku, Osaka 541, Japan.
- Casting & Forging/Chutzano. m. ISSN 0009-6652

**New Japanese Doctors' Association**
Hidaka Bldg., 1-10-2 Nishi Ikebukuro, Toshima-ku, Tokyo 171, Japan.
- Japana Medicina Revuo/Igaku Hyoron. s-a. ISSN 0019-1574

**New Nippon Electric Company Ltd.**
2-9-1 Seiran, Otsu 520, Shiga, Japan.
- New Nippon Electric Technical Review/Shin Nippon Denki Giho. a. ISSN 0037-3745

**Nichifutsu Ikakai**
*see* Societe Franco-Japonaise de Medecine

**Nichifutsu Kogyo Gijutsukai**
*see* Societe Franco-Japonaise des Techniques Industrielles

**Nihon**
*see also* Nippon

**Nihon Allergy Gakkai**
*see* Japanese Society of Allergology

**Nihon Arukoru Igakkai**
*see* Japanese Medical Society of Alcohol Studies

**Nihon Boeki Shuppansha**
*see* Japan Trade Publications Ltd.

**Nihon Bungaku Kyokai**
*see* Japanese Literature Association

**Nihon Bunko Gakkai**
*see* Spectroscopical Society of Japan

**Nihon Butsuri Gakkai**
*see* Physical Society of Japan

**Nihon Butsuri Kagaku Kenkyukai**
*see* Physico-Chemical Society of Japan

**Nihon Byoin Setsubi Kyokai**
*see* Japan Hospital Equipment Association

Nihon Byori Gakkai
    see Japanese Pathological Society

Nihon Cast Iron Foundry Association
    501 Kikai Shinko Kaikan, 3-5-8 Shiba Koen,
    Minato-ku, Tokyo 105, Japan.
    ● Casting Digest/Imono Daijesuto. m. ISSN 0019-
    2813

Nihon Chigaku Kyoiku Gakkai
    see Japan Society of Earth Science Education

Nihon Chiiki Kaihatsu Senta
    see Japan Center for Area Development Research

Nihon Chikudenchi Kogyokai
    see Japan Storage Battery Association

Nihon Chikusan Gakkai
    see Japanese Society of Zootechnical Science

Nihon Chikyu Denki Jiki Gakkai
    see Society of Terrestrial Magnetism and
    Electricity of Japan

Nihon Chikyu Kagakkai
    see Geochemical Society of Japan

Nihon Chishitsu Gakkai
    see Geological Society of Japan

Nihon Chizu Senta
    see Japan Map Center

Nihon Cho Gakkai
    see Ornithological Society of Japan

Nihon Dai Damu Kaigi
    see Japanese National Committee on Large Dams

Nihon Daigaku
    see Nihon University

Nihon Daigaku Igakkai
    see Nihon University Medical Association

Nihon Daigaku Juigaku Kenkyusho
    see Nihon University. Research Institute for
    Veterinary Science

Nihon Daigaku Keizaigaku Shogaku Kenkyu-kai
    see Nihon University. Economic and Commercial
    Research Society

Nihon Daigaku Rikogaku Kenkyusho
    see Nihon University. Research Institute of Science
    and Technology

Nihon Denki Gakkai
    see Institute of Electrical Engineers of Japan

Nihon Denki Seiki K. K.
    see Nippon Electric Industry Co., Ltd.

Nihon Denpun Gakkai
    see Japanese Society of Starch Science

Nihon Denryoku Chosa Iinkai
    see Japan Electric Power Survey Committee

Nihon Densenbyo Gakkai
    see Japanese Association for Infectious Diseases

Nihon Denshi K. K.
    see J E O L Ltd.

Nihon Denshi Kenbikyo Gakkai
    see Japanese Society of Electron Microscopy

Nihon Dobutsu Gakkai
    see Zoological Society of Japan

Nihon Dokumenteshon Kyokai
    see Japan Documentation Society

Nihon Doro Kyokai
    see Japan Road Association

Nihon Eibungakkai
    see English Literary Society of Japan

Nihon Eisei Gakkai
    see Japanese Society for Hygiene

Nihon Eiyo to Shokuryo Gakkai
    see Japanese Society of Food and Nutrition

Nihon Funin Gakkai Zasshi
    see Japanese Society of Fertility and Sterility

Nihon Gakujutsu Kaigi
    see Science Council of Japan

Nihon Gan Chiryo Gakkai
    see Japan Society for Cancer Therapy

Nihon Gan Gakkai
    see Cancer Institute

Nihon Ganka Gakkai
    see Japanese Ophthalmological Society

Nihon Ganseki Kobutsu Kosho Gakkai
    see Japanese Association of Minerologists,
    Petrologists and Economic Geologists

Nihon Gas Kyokai
    see Japan Gas Association

Nihon Geka Gakkai
    see Japan Surgical Society

Nihon Gengogakkai
    see Linguistic Society of Japan

Nihon Genshiroku Gakkai
    see Atomic Energy Society of Japan

Nihon Genshiryoku Kenkyusho
    see Japan Atomic Energy Research Institute

Nihon Genshiryoku Sangyo Kaigi
    see Japan Atomic Industrial Forum, Inc.

Nihon Gesuido Kyokai
    see Japan Sewage Works Association

Nihon Gijutsu Koho Kyokai
    see Japan Association for Technical Information

Nihon Ginko
    see Bank of Japan

Nihon Gomu Kyokai
    see Society of Rubber Industry

Nihon Gyorui Gakkai
    see Ichthyological Society of Japan

Nihon Hakubutsuken Kyokai
    see Japanese Association of Museums

Nihon Hanzai Gakkai
    see Japanese Society of Criminology

Nihon Hassei Seibutsu Gakkai
    see Japanese Society of Developmental Biologists

Nihon Hebizoku Gakujutsu Kenkyusho
    see Japan Snake Institute

Nihon Heikatsukin Gakkai
    see Japan Society of Smooth Muscle Research

Nihon Hifuka Gakkai
    see Japanese Dermatological Association

Nihon Hifukagakkai Osaka Chihokai
    see Osaka Dermatological Association

Nihon Hikaku Gijutsu Kyokai
    see Japanese Association of Leather Technology

Nihon Hikakuho Kenkyusho
    see Chuo University. Institute of Comparative Law
    in Japan

Nihon Hinyokika Gakkai
    see Japanese Urological Association

Nihon Hinyokika Gakkai Nishi Nihon Rengo
    see Japanese Urological Association. Nishi Nihon
    Section

Nihon Hoi Gakkai
    see Medico-Legal Society of Japan

Nihon Hoshasei Doigenso Kyokai
    see Japan Radioisotope Association

Nihon Hoso Times Co. Ltd.
    4-4-5 Iidabashi, Chiyoda-ku, Toyko 102, Japan.
    ● New Packaging/Atarashii. m. ISSN 0004-6469

Nihon Igaku Toshokan Kyokai
    see Japan Medical Library Association

Nihon Ikakikai Gakkai
    see Medical Instrument Society of Japan

Nihon Imono Kogyokai
    see Nihon Cast Iron Foundry Association

Nihon Indasutoriaru Enjiniaringu Kyokai
    see Japan Institute of Industrial Engineering

Nihon Indogaku- Bukkyogakukai
    see Japanese Association of Indian and Buddhist
    Studies

Nihon Insatsu Gakkai
    see Technical Association of Graphic Arts of Japan

Nihon Insatsu Shinbunsha
    see Japan Printing News Publishing Co.

Nihon Ishikai
    see Japan Medical Association

Nihon Iyaku Joho Senta
    see Japan Pharmaceutical Information Centre

Nihon Iyakuhin Yushutsu Kumiai
    see Japan Pharmaceutical, Medical and Dental
    Supply Exporter's Association

Nihon Jibi Inkoka Gakkai
    see Oto-Rhino-Laryngological Society of Japan

Nihon Jido Seigyo Kyokai
    see Japan Association of Automatic Control
    Engineers

Nihon Jidosha Kogyokai
    see Japan Automobile Manufacturers Association

Nihon Jikken Dobutsu Kenkyukai
    see Japan Experimental Animal Research
    Association

Nihon Jinrui Iden Gakkai
    see Tokyo Medical and Dental University.
    Department of Human Genetics

Nihon Jinruigaku Gakkai
    see Anthropological Society of Japan

Nihon Juigakkai
    see Japanese Society of Veterinary Science

Nihon Junkanki Gakkai
    see Japanese Circulation Society

Nihon Junkatsu Gakkai
    see Japan Society of Lubrication Engineers

Nihon Kagaku Gijutsu Joho Senta
    see Japan Information Center of Science and
    Technology

Nihon Kagaku Gijutsu Renmei
    see Union of Japanese Scientists and Engineers

Nihon Kagaku Gijutsu Shinko Zaidan
    see Japan Science Foundation

Nihon Kagaku Kogyo Kyokai
    see Japan Chemical Industry Association

Nihon Kagaku Ryoho Gakkai
    see Japan Society of Chemotherapy

Nihon Kagakusha Kaigi
    see Japan Scientists' Association

Nihon Kaibo Gakkai
    see Japanese Anatomical Association

Nihon Kaihatsu Ginko
    see Japan Development Bank

Nihon Kairui Gakkai
    see Malacological Society of Japan

Nihon Kaiun Shukaijo
    see Japan Shipping Exchange, Inc.

Nihon Kaiyo Gakkai
    see Oceanographical Society of Japan

Nihon Kakin Gakkai
  see Japanese Poultry Science Association

Nihon Kaku Igakkai
  see Japanese Society of Nuclear Medicine

Nihon Kango Kyokai
  see Japanese Nursing Association

Nihon Kankyo Eisei Senta
  see Japan Environmental Sanitation Center

Nihon Katei Seikatsu Mondai Kenkyu Kyokai
  c/o Shin Toranomon Jitsugyo Kaikan, Room 902, 5
  Shiba Toranomon, Minato-ku, Tokyo, Japan.
  ● Katei Seikatsu. q.

Nihon Kazan Gakkai
  see Volcanological Society of Japan

Nihon Keiei Kagaku Kenkyusho
  see Japan Management Science Institute

Nihon Keieisha Dantai Remmei Kohobu
  1-2-1 Marunouchi, Chiyoda-ku, Tokyo, Japan.
  ● Keiei Romu No Shishin. a.

Nihon Keiho Gakkai
  see Criminal Law Society of Japan

Nihon Keizai Kenkyu Senta
  see Japan Economic Research Center

Nihon Keizai Shinbunsha
  see Japan Economic Journal

Nihon Kekkaku Yobokai
  see Japan Anti-Tuberculosis Association

Nihon Kekkakubyo Gakkai
  see Japan Society for Tuberculosis

Nihon Kenchiku Gakkai
  see Architectural Institute of Japan

Nihon Ketsueki Gakkai
  see Japan Hematological Society

Nihon Kikai Gakkai
  see Japan Society of Mechanical Engineers

Nihon Kikon Shokudoka Gakkai
  see Japan Broncho-Esophagological Society

Nihon Kinzoku Gakkai
  see Japan Institute of Metals

Nihon Kirisutosha Ika Renmei
  see Japan Christian Medical Association

Nihon Kiseichu Gakkai
  see Japanese Society of Parasitology

Nihon Kisho Gakkai
  see Meteorological Society of Japan

Nihon Kisho Kyokai
  see Japan Weather Association

Nihon Kobutsu Gakkai
  see Mineralogical Society of Japan

Nihon Kogyo Keiei Gakkai
  see Japan Industrial Management Association

Nihon Kogyo Ritchi Senta
  see Japan Industrial Location Center

Nihon Kogyo Shimbun
  Sankei Bldg., 1-7-2 Otemachi, Chiyoda-ku, Tokyo
  100, Japan.
  ● Business Japan. m. ISSN 0300-4341 (prep. by its
  International Division)

Nihon Koko Gakkai
  see Archaeological Society of Japan

Nihon Koku Gakkai
  see Japan Society for Aeronautical and Space
  Sciences

Nihon Koku Seibi Kyokai
  see Japan Aeronautical Engineers' Association

Nihon Koku Uchu Gakkai
  see Japan Society for Aeronautical and Space
  Sciences

Nihon Kokuka Gakkai
  see Japanese Stomatological Society

Nihon Kokusai Chizu Gakkai
  see Japan Cartographers Association

Nihon Kokusai Igaku Kyokai
  see International Medical Society of Japan

Nihon Kokuyu Tetsudo
  see Japanese National Railways

Nihon Konkuriito Kogaku Kyokai
  see Japan Concrete Institute

Nihon Kosei Busshitsu Gakujutsu Kyogikai
  see Japan Antibiotics Research Association

Nihon Koseibutsu Gakkai
  see Palaeontological Society of Japan

Nihon Kotsu Igakkai Kyushu Chihokai
  see Japanese Association of Transportation
  Medicine

Nihon Kozan Chishitsu Gakkai
  see Society of Mining Geologists of Japan

Nihon Kuki Seijo Kyokai
  see Japan Air Cleaning Association

Nihon Kyoiku-shinri Gakkai
  see Japanese Association of Educational
  Psychology

Nihon Kyoikuho Gakkai
  ● Nihon Kyoikuho Gakkai Nempo. (pub. by
  Yuhikaku Publishing Co. Ltd.)

Nihon Kyosei Shika Gakkai
  see Japan Orthodontic Society

Nihon M-E Gakkai
  see Japan Society of Medical Electronics and
  Biological Engineering

Nihon Maikuro Shashin Kyokai
  see Japan Microphotography Association

Nihon Menka Kyokai
  see Japan Cotton Traders' Association

Nihon Minkan Kyoiku Kenkyu Dantai Renrakukai
  ● Nihon No Minken Kyoiku. (pub. by Yuri
  Shuppan)

Nihon Minzoku Gakkai
  see Japanese Society of Ethnology

Nihon Mokuzai Gakkai
  see Japan Wood Research Society

Nihon Mokuzai Kako Gijutsu Kyokai
  see Wood Technological Association of Japan

Nihon Monki Senta
  see Japan Monkey Centre

Nihon Myakkan Gakkai
  see Japanese College of Angiology

Nihon Naibunpi Gakkai Tobu-Bukai
  see Japan Endocrine Society. Eastern Branch

Nihon Naika Gakkai
  see Japanese Society of Internal Medicine

Nihon Namari Aen Juyo Kenkyukai
  see Japan Lead Zinc Development Association

Nihon Netsu Enerugi Gijutsu Kyokai
  see Japan Heat Management Association

Nihon Nettai Igakkai
  see Nissan Diesel Motor Co., Ltd.

Nihon Nissan Jizeru Kogyo K. K.
  see Japan Nissan Diesel Motor Co., Ltd.

Nihon Nitto Uea Dezain Kyokai
  see Japan Knitwear Designers Association

Nihon Nogaku Toshokan Kyogikai
  see Japan Association of Agricultural Librarians
  and Documentalists

Nihon Nogyo Keizai Gakkai
  see Agricultural Economic Society of Japan

Nihon Norin Kikaku Kyokai
  see Japan Agricultural Standards Association

Nihon Noshinkei Geka Gakkai
  see Japan Neurosurgical Society

Nihon Ojioroji Gakkai
  see Japan Audiological Society

Nihon Onsei Gengo Igakkai
  see Japan Society of Logopedics and Phoniatrics

Nihon Onsen Kiko Butsuri Igakkai
  see Japanese Association of Physical Medicine,
  Balneology and Climatology

Nihon Opereshonzu Risachi Gakkai
  see Operations Research Society of Japan

Nihon Oyo Dobutsu Konchu Gakkai
  see Japanese Society of Applied Entomology and
  Zoology

Nihon Oyo Igakkai
  see Society of Applied Medicine

Nihon Pan Gijutsusha Kyokai
  see Japan Society of Bakery Technology

Nihon Porarografu Gakkai
  see Polarographic Society of Japan

Nihon Purasuchikkusu Shinposa
  see Japan Plastics Journal Ltd.

Nihon Rai Gakkai
  see Japanese Leprosy Association

Nihon Reito Kyokai
  see Japanese Association of Refrigeration

Nihon Reito Reibo Shinbunsha
  see Japan Refrigeration and Air Conditioning Press

Nihon Rikusui Gakkai
  see Japanese Society of Limnology

Nihon Ringyo Kyokai
  see Japanese Forestry Society

Nihon Rodo Kyokai
  see Japan Institute of Labour

Nihon Rodosho
  see Japan. Ministry of Labour

Nihon Roketto Kyokai
  see Japanese Rocket Society

Nihon Sakumotsu Gakkai Kiji
  see Crop Science Society of Japan

Nihon Sangyo Eisei Gakkai
  see Japan Association of Industrial Health

Nihon Sangyo Kunren Kyokai
  see Japan Industrial and Vocational Training
  Association

Nihon Sangyo Sharyo Kyokai
  see Japan Industrial Vehicles Association

Nihon Sanshi Gakkai
  see Japanese Society of Sericultural Science

Nihon Seibutsu Kagakusha
  see Japanese Society of Biological Scientists

Nihon Seibyo Yobo Kyokai
  see Japanese Association for Prevention of
  Venereal Diseases and Treponematoses

Nihon Seiji Gakkai
  see Japanese Political Science Association

Nihon Seikagakkai
  see Japanese Biochemical Society

Nihon Seikosho
  see Japan Steel Works, Ltd.

Nihon Seiri Gakkai
  see Physiological Society of Japan

Nihon Seishin Eiseikai
   see Japan Mental Health Society

Nihon Seito Kogyokai
   see Japan Sugar Refiners Association

Nihon Sekiyu Konsarutanto K. K.
   see Japan Petroleum Consultants, Ltd.

Nihon Sen'i Kikai Gakkai
   see Textile Machinery Society of Japan

Nihon Sen'i Seihin Shohi Kagakkai
   see Japan Research Association for Textile End-
   Uses

Nihon Sen'i Shinbun Co., Ltd.
   3-9 Hongo, Nihonbashi, Chuo-ku, Tokyo 103,
   Japan.
   • Textile Japan/Tekisutairu Japan. a. ISSN 0082-
   366X

Nihon Senpaku Hyojun Kyokai
   see Japanese Association of Marine
   Standardization

Nihon Senshu Kyokai
   see Japanese Shipowners' Association

Nihon Senten Ijo Gakkai
   see Congenital Anomalies Research Association of
   Japan

Nihon Setchaku Kyokai
   see Adhesion Society of Japan

Nihon Shakai-jigyo Daigaku
   see Japanese Social Labour College

Nihon Shakaito
   see Socialist Party of Japan

Nihon Shashin Gakkai
   see Society of Photographic Science and
   Technology of Japan

Nihon Shashin Kyokai
   see Photographic Society of Japan

Nihon Shika Daigaku
   see Nippon Dental College

Nihon Shika Daigaku Shigakkai
   see Society of Nippon Dental College

Nihon Shika Ishikai
   see Japan Dental Association

Nihon Shinkei Gakkai
   see Japanese Society of Neurology

Nihon Shinri Gakkai
   see Japanese Psychological Association

Nihon Shiseniji Gakkai
   see Japan Society of Neonatology

Nihon Shitai Fujiyuji Kyokai
   see Japanese Society for Crippled Children

Nihon Shizai Kanrishi Kyokai
   see Japan Materials Management Association

Nihon Shokakibyo Gakkai
   see Japanese Society of Gastroenterology

Nihon Shokubutsu Boeki Kyokai
   see Japan Plant Protection Association

Nihon Shokubutsu Byori Gakkai
   see Phytopathological Society of Japan

Nihon Shokubutsu Gakkai
   see Botanical Society of Japan

Nihon Shokubutsu Seiri Gakkai
   see Japanese Society of Plant Physiologists

Nihon Shoni Hoken Kyokai
   see Japanese Society of Child Health

Nihon Shoni Shinkeigaku Kenkyukai
   see Japanese Society of Pediatric Neurology

Nihon Shonika Gakkai
   see Japan Pediatric Society

Nihon Shoyaku Gakkai
   see Japanese Society of Pharmacognosy

Nihon Sosei Kako Gakkai
   see Japan Society for Technology of Plasticity

Nihon Soshiki Baiyo Gakkai
   see Japanese Tissue Culture Association

Nihon Soshiki Kagakkai
   see Japan Society of Histological Documentation

Nihon Soshiki Saibo Kagakkai
   see Japan Society of Histochemistry and
   Cytochemistry

Nihon Sugakkai
   see Mathematical Society of Japan

Nihon Suisan Gakkai
   see Japanese Society of Scientific Fisheries

Nihon Taiiku Gakkai
   see Japanese Society of Physical Education

Nihon Tairyoku Igakkai
   see Japanese Physical Fitness Society

Nihon Tekko Kyokai
   see Iron and Steel Institute of Japan

Nihon Tekko Renmei
   see Japan Iron and Steel Federation

Nihon Tekko Yushutsu Kumiai
   see Japan Iron and Steel Exporters Association

Nihon Tenmon Gakkai
   see Astronomical Society of Japan

Nihon Tetsudo Gijutsu Kyokai
   see Japan Railway Engineer's Association

Nihon Tetsudo Saibanetikkusu Kyogikai
   see Japan Railway Cybernetics Association

Nihon Tonyobyo Gakkai
   see Japan Diabetic Society

Nihon Toshokan Kyokai
   see Japan Library Association

Nihon Uirusu Gakkai
   see Society of Japanese Virologists

Nihon University. Atomic Energy Research Institute
   1-8 Kanda Surugadai, Chiyoda-ku, Tokyo 101,
   Japan.
   • Nihon University. Atomic Energy Institute.
   Annual Report. a.

Nihon University. Economic and Commercial
Research Society
   1-2 Kanda Misakicho, Chiyoda-ku, Tokyo, Japan.
   • Studies in Economic Science/Keizai Shushi. bi-m.

Nihon University Medical Association
   30 Oyaguchi Kami-cho, Itabashi-ku, Tokyo 173,
   Japan.
   • Nihon University Journal of Medicine/Nichidai
   Igaku Zasshi. m. ISSN 0029-0424 (Co-sponsor:
   Nihon University School of Medicine)

Nihon University. Research Institute for Veterinary
Science
   Shimouma, Setagaya-ku, Tokyo 154, Japan.
   • Acta Veterinaria Japonica. q. ISSN 0001-7221

Nihon University. Research Institute of Science and
Technology
   1-8 Kanda Surugadai, Chiyoda-ku, Tokyo 101,
   Japan.
   • Nihon University. Research Institute of Science
   and Technology. Journal/Nihon Daigaku
   Rikogaku Kenkyusho Shoho. s-a.
   • Nihon University. Research Institute of Science
   and Technology. Report. s-a. ISSN 0549-2998

Nihon University. School of Dentistry
   1-8-13 Kanda Surugadai, Chiyoda-ku, Tokyo 101,
   Japan.
   • Nihon University. School of Dentistry. Journal/
   Nihon Daigaku Shigakubu Obun Zasshi. q. ISSN
   0029-0432

Nihon Wakkusuman Zaidan
   see Waksman Foundation of Japan

Nihon Yakugakkai
   see Pharmaceutical Society of Japan

Nihon Yakugaku Toshokan Kyogikai
   see Japan Pharmaceutical Library Association

Nihon Yakuri Gakkai
   see Japanese Pharmacological Society

Nihon Yogashi Kyokai Rengokai
   see Federation of Japan Confectionary Associations

Nihon Zairyo Gakkai
   see Japan Society of Materials Science

Nihon Zosen Shinko Zaidan
   see Japan Foundation for Shipbuilding
   Advancement

Niigata Airglow Observatory
   • Niigata Airglow Observatory. Bulletin. (pub. by
   Niigata University. Faculty of Science)

Niigata Daigaku Rigakubu Fuzoku Sado Rinko
Jikkenjo Kenkyu
   see Niigata University. Sado Marine Biological
   Station

Niigata Igakkai
   see Niigata Medical Society

Niigata Medical Society
   c/o Niigata University, School of Medicine,
   Asahimachi Library, Asahimachi 1, Niigata 951,
   Japan.
   • Niigata Medical Journal/Niigata Igakkai Zasshi.
   m. ISSN 0029-0440

Niigata University. Faculty of Agriculture
   106 Kogane-cho, Niigata-shi, Japan.
   • Niigata University. Faculty of Agriculture.
   Memoirs/Niigata Daigaku Nogakubu Kiyo. a.
   ISSN 0549-4826

Niigata University. Faculty of Science
   8050 Igarashi Nino-cho, Niigata-shi 950-21, Japan.
   • Niigata Airglow Observatory. Bulletin. a. (Niigata
   Airglow Observatory)
   • Niigata University. Faculty of Science. Science
   Reports. Series A: Mathematics. a.
   • Niigata University. Faculty of Science. Science
   Reports. Series B: Physics. irreg.
   • Niigata University. Faculty of Science. Science
   Reports. Series C: Chemistry. irreg.
   • Niigata University. Faculty of Science. Science
   Reports. Series D: Biology. a.
   • Niigata University. Faculty of Science. Science
   Reports. Series E: Geology and Mineralogy. a.

Niigata University. Sado Marine Biological Station
   2-8050 Igarashi, Niigata 950-21, Japan.
   • Sado Marine Biological Station. Annual Report/
   Niigata Daigaku Rigakubu Fuzoku Sado Rinkai
   Jikkenjo Kenkyu Nenpo. a.

Niigata University. School of Medicine
   Ichiban-cho, Asahicho-dori, Niigata 951, Japan.
   • Acta Medica et Biologica/Igaku Seibutsugaku
   Kenkyu Kiyo. q. ISSN 0567-7734

Nikkan Jidosha Shimbun-sha
   see Daily Automotive News Co., Ltd.

Nikkan Kogyo Shimbunsha
   see Industrial Daily News Ltd.

Nikkei Mc-Graw Hill Inc.
   c/o Nikkei Bekkan, 2-1-2 Uchikanda, Chiyoda-ku,
   Tokyo 101, Japan.
   • Nikkei Business. fortn. ISSN 0029-0491

Nikkyoso
   see Japan Teachers' Union

Ningen Igakusha
   5-16-23 Senrioka, Settsu-shi 564, Japan.
   • Human Medicine/Ningen Igaku. m. ISSN 0029-
   0572

Nippon
   see also Nihon

Nippon Bitamin Gakkai
   see Japan Vitamin Society

**Nippon Chikasui Gakkai**
*see* **Japanese Association of Groundwater Hydrology**

**Nippon Chiri Gakkai**
*see* **Association of Japanese Geographers**

**Nippon Denki Garasu**
*see* **Nippon Electric Glass Co. Ltd.**

**Nippon Denki K. K.**
*see* **Nippon Electric Co. Ltd.**

**Nippon Dental College**
1-9-20 Fujimi, Chiyoda-ku, Tokyo 102, Japan.
• Odontology/Shigaku. q. ISSN 0029-8484

**Nippon Dojo Hiryo Gakkai**
*see* **Japanese Society of Soil and Manure**

**Nippon Electric Co. Ltd.**
NEC Bldg., 5-33-1 Shiba, Minato-ku, Tokyo 108, Japan.
• N E C News. bi-m. ISSN 0027-6421
• N E C Research and Development. q. ISSN 0547-051X

**Nippon Electric Glass Co. Ltd.**
Higashihankyu Bldg., 16 Takagaki-cho, Kita-ku, Osaka 530, Japan.
• Glass Block and Brick. s-a.

**Nippon Electric Industry Co., Ltd.**
1-19-18 Tsutsumi-dori, Sumida-ku, Tokyo 131, Japan.
• Densei Technical Journal/Densei. q. ISSN 0011-8451

**Nippon Export Times**
2-28-5 Hongo, Bunkyo-ku, Tokyo, Japan.
• N E T. m.

**Nippon Gakushiin**
*see* **Japan Academy**

**Nippon Ginko**
*see* **Bank of Japan**

**Nippon Gyosei Gakkai**
*see* **Japanese Society for Public Administration**

**Nippon Hoso Kyokai**
*see* **Japan Broadcasting Corp.**

**Nippon Hoso Shuppan Kyokai**
*see* **Japan Broadcast Publishing Co., Ltd.**

**Nippon Hyoronsha**
14 Suga-machi, Shinjuku-ku, Tokyo, Japan.
• Hitotsubashi Review/Hitotsubashi Ronso. m. ISSN 0018-2818 (Hitotsubashi Academy)

**Nippon Igaku Hoshasen Gakkai**
*see* **Nippon Societas Radiologica**

**Nippon Igaku Kyokai**
*see* **Japan Medical Association**

**Nippon Ika Daigaku**
*see* **Nippon Medical School**

**Nippon Institute for Biological Science**
3-28-19 Akebono-cho, Tachikawa, Tokyo 190, Japan.
• N I B S Bulletin of Biological Research/Nihon Seibutsu Kagaku Kenkyusho Kenkyu Hokoku. a. ISSN 0078-0847
• Nippon Institute for Biological Science. Journal/Nisseiken Tayori. m. ISSN 0029-0750

**Nippon Jui Chikusan Daigaku Kiyo**
*see* **Nippon Veterinary and Zootechnical College**

**Nippon Kagakkai**
*see* **Chemical Society of Japan**

**Nippon Kagaku Gijutsu Renmei**
*see* **Union of Japanese Scientists and Engineers**

**Nippon Kagaku Kyokai**
*see* **Japan Science Society**

**Nippon Kagakushi Gakkai**
*see* **History of Science Society of Japan**

**Nippon Kikai-Kogyo Rengokai (NIKKIREN)**
*see* **Japan Machinery Federation**

**Nippon Kikinzoku Tokei Shimbunsha**
Tokyo Kikokaikan Bldg., 2-19-16 Negishi, Taito-ku, Tokyo 110, Japan.
• Japan Precious Metals and Watch News/Nippon Kikinzoku Tokei Shimbun. every 10 days. ISSN 0029-0653

**Nippon Kin Gakkai**
*see* **Mycological Society of Japan**

**Nippon Kisho Kyokai**
*see* **Japan Weather Association**

**Nippon Kogyo Ginko**
*see* **Industrial Bank of Japan**

**Nippon Kokan Kabushiki Kaishi**
*see* **Japan Steel & Tube Corporation**

**Nippon Kokogaku Kyokai**
*see* **Japanese Archaeologists Association**

**Nippon Koku Geka Gakkai**
*see* **Japanese Society of Oral Surgeons**

**Nippon Kontyu Gakkai**
*see* **Entomological Society of Japan**

**Nippon Life Insurance Social Welfare Foundation**
Social Services Department, 4-11 Itachibori, Minamidori, Nishi-ku, Osaka, Japan.
• Chiiki Fukushi. m. ISSN 0009-384X

**Nippon Medical School**
Medical Association of Nippon Medical School, 1-1-5 Sendagi, Bunkyo-ku, Tokyo 113, Japan.
• Nippon Medical School. Journal/Nippon Ika Daigaku Zasshi. 6 per yr. ISSN 0048-0444

**Nippon Nendo Gakkai**
*see* **Clay Science Society of Japan**

**Nippon Nogei Kagaku Kai**
*see* **Agricultural Chemical Society of Japan**

**Nippon Onsen Kagakkai**
*see* **Balneological Society of Japan**

**Nippon Orient Gakkai**
*see* **Society for Near Eastern Studies in Japan**

**Nippon Rihabiriteshon Igakkai**
*see* **Japan Association of Rehabilitation Medicine**

**Nippon Rinshi Gakkai**
*see* **Lepidopterological Society of Japan**

**Nippon Rinsho Byori Gakkai**
*see* **Japan Society of Clinical Pathology**

**Nippon Rinsho Co., Inc.**
3-1 Dosho-machi, Higashi-ku, Osaka 541, Japan.
• Japanese Journal of Clinical Medicine/Nippon Rinsho. m. ISSN 0047-1852

**Nippon Rinsho Denshi Kenbikyo Gakkai**
*see* **Clinical Electron Microscopy Society of Japan**

**Nippon Seibutsu Kagaku Kenkyusho**
*see* **Nippon Institute for Biological Science**

**Nippon Seibutsuchiri Gakkai**
*see* **Biogeographical Society of Japan**

**Nippon Seikei Geka Gakkai**
*see* **Japanese Orthopaedic Association**

**Nippon Seishin Shinkei Gakkai**
*see* **Japanese Society for Psychiatry and Neurology**

**Nippon Seitai Gakkai**
*see* **Ecological Society of Japan**

**Nippon Sen'i Kenkyukai**
*see* **Japan Textiles and Fibers Research Institute**

**Nippon Shakai Gakkai**
*see* **Japanese Sociological Society**

**Nippon Shashin Kogyo Tsushinsha**
2-7-13 Fujimi, Chiyoda-ku, Tokyo, Japan.
• Photo Trade of Japan. bi-m. ISSN 0031-8604

**Nippon Shokuhin Kogyo Gakkai**
*see* **Japanese Society of Food Science and Technology**

**Nippon Shoni Iji Shuppansha Co.**
Wakoda Bldg., 2-16 Kanda Kaji-cho, Chiyoda-ku, Tokyo 101, Japan.
• Japanese Journal of Pediatrics/Shonika Rinsho. m. ISSN 0021-518X

**Nippon Shuppan Boeki Kaishi, Ltd.**
*see* **Japan Publications Trading Co., Ltd.**

**Nippon Societas Radiologica**
Rm. 301 Akamon Habitation, 5-29-13 Hongo, Bunkyo-ku, Tokyo 113, Japan.
• Nippon Acta Radiologica/Nippon Igaku Hoshasen Gakkai Zasshi. m. ISSN 0048-0428

**Nippon Soda Co. Ltd.**
New Otemachi Bldg., 2-1-2 Otemachi, Chiyoda-ku, Tokyo 100, Japan.
• Ag-Chem Age/Noyaku Jidai. bi-m. ISSN 0029-5426

**Nippon Sokuchi Gakkai**
*see* **Geodetic Society of Japan**

**Nippon Sorui Gakkai**
*see* **Japanese Society of Phycology**

**Nippon Steel Corporation**
2-6-3 Otemachi, Chiyoda-ku, Tokyo 100, Japan (U.S. Address: 345 Park Ave., 41st Floor, New York, NY 10022)
• Nippon Steel News. m. ISSN 0048-0452
• Nippon Steel Report. a.
• Nippon Steel Technical Report. Overseas. s-a.

**Nippon Sugaku Kyoiku Gakkai**
*see* **Japan Society of Mathematical Education**

**Nippon Telegraph and Telephone Public Corp. Musashino Electrical Communication Laboratory**
3-9-11 Midori-machi, Musashino, Tokyo 180, Japan.
• Musashino Electrical Communication Laboratory. Review of the Electrical Communication Laboratories/Denki Tsushin Kenkyusho Eibun Geppo. bi-m. ISSN 0029-067X

**Nippon Televi Hoso**
*see* **Nippon Television Network Corp.**

**Nippon Television Network Corp.**
14 Niban-cho, Chiyoda-ku, Tokyo, Japan.
• Japanese Television/Nihon Terebi. q. ISSN 0029-0408

**Nippon Tetsudo Shisetsu Kyokai**
*see* **Japan Railway Civil Engineering Association**

**Nippon Toshokan Gakkai**
*see* **Japan Society of Library Science**

**Nippon Toshokan Kenkyukai**
*see* **Japan Institution for Library Science**

**Nippon Tungsten Co., Ltd.**
460 Sanno, Shiobaru, Minami-ku, Fukuoka-shi 815, Japan.
• Nippon Tungsten Review. a.

**Nippon Veterinary and Zootechnical College**
1-7-1 Sakaiminami-cho, Musashino, Tokyo 180, Japan.
• Nippon Veterinary and Zootechnical College. Bulletin/Nippon Jui Chikusan Daigaku Kiyo. a. ISSN 0078-0839

**Nishi Nihon Seikei Saigai Geka Gakkai**
*see* **West-Japanese Society of Orthopedics and Traumatology**

**Nishimura Publishing Co.**
1 Kami-machi, Kochi, Japan.
• Kusunoki Noho. m. ISSN 0023-5725

**Nissan Diesel Motor Co. Ltd.**
Saitama-ken, Ageo 362, Japan.
• Nissan Diesel Review/Nissan Diesel Giho. s-a. ISSN 0029-0734

**Nissan Motor Co. Ltd.**
Advertising Department, 1-17-6 Ginza, Tokyo 104, Japan.
• Nissan Graphic/Nissan Gurafu. m. ISSN 0029-0742

**Niwatori no Kenkyusha**
*see* **Poultry Research Publishing Co.**

**Noda Institute for Scientific Research**
399 Noda, Noda-shi 278, Japan.
- Noda Institute for Scientific Research. Report/
Noda Sangyo Kagaku Kenkyusho Kenkyu
Hokoku. a. ISSN 0078-0944

**Noorin Syuppan Co. Ltd.**
5-33-2 Sinbasi, Minato-ku, Tokyo 105, Japan.
- Abstracts of Japanese Literature in Forest
Genetics and Related Fields. Part A. irreg.
(Japan. Government Forest Experiment Station,
Tokyo)
- Abstracts of Japanese Literature in Forest
Genetics and Related Fields. Part B. irreg. (Japan.
Government Forest Experiment Station, Tokyo)

**Norin Shijo Kenkyujo, Ltd.**
see Agriculture and Forestry Market Research
Institute

**Norin-sho Daijin Kanbo**
see Japan. Ministry of Agriculture and Forestry

**Norin-sho Hokkaido Nogyo Shikenjo**
see Japan. Hokkaido National Agricultural
Experiment Station

**Norin-sho Hoshasen Ikushujo**
see Japan. Institute of Radiation Breeding

**Norin-sho Kachiku Eisei Shikenjo**
see Japan. National Institute of Animal Health

**Norin-sho Kinki Nosei-kyoku**
see Japan. Kinki Agricultural Administration
Bureau

**Norin-sho Nogyo Gijutsu Kenkyusho**
see Japan. National Institute of Agricultural
Sciences

**Norin-sho Nogyo Gijutsu Kenkyusho Hoshasen**
see Japan. Institute of Radiation Breeding

**Norin-sho Nogyo Sogo Kenkyusho**
see Japan. National Research Institute of
Agriculture

**Norin-sho Ringyo Shikenjo Kyusha Shijo**
see Japan. Government Forest Experiment Station.
Kyushu Branch

**Norin-sho Sanshi Shikenjo**
see Japan. Sericultural Experiment Station

**Norin-sho Shikoku Nogyo Shikenjo**
see Japan. Shikoku Agricultural Experiment
Station

**Norin-sho Sochi Shikenjo**
see Japan. National Grassland Research Institute

**Norin-sho Yokohama Shokubutsu Boekisho**
see Japan. Yokohama Plant Protection Station

**Northeast Asia Association of Theological Schools**
c/o Japan Lutheran Theological Seminary, 3-10-20
Osawa, Mitaka, Tokyo 181, Japan.
- Northeast Asia Journal of Theology. s-a. ISSN
0549-8899

**Nuclear Safety Research Association**
1-2-2 Uchisaiwai-cho, Chiyoda-ku, Tokyo 100,
Japan.
- N S R A Memo. irreg.

**Nukada Institute for Medical and Biological Research**
5-18 Inage-cho, Chiba-shi 280, Japan.
- Nukada Institute for Medical and Biological
Research. Reports. irreg. ISSN 0469-2071

**O A Kyokai**
see Europe and Asia Association

**Obihiro Zootechnical University. School of
Veterinary Science**
Inada-cho, Obihiro-shi 080, Japan.
- Obihiro Zootechnical University. School of
Veterinary Science. Contribution/Obihiro
Chikusan Daigaku Jui Ronbunshu. a.

**Ocean Age**
c/o Dai-1 Toei Bldg., 11-2 Kanda Mitushiro-cho,
Chiyoda-ku, Tokyo 101, Japan.
- Ocean Age/Oshan Ejisha. m.

**Ocean Research Institute**
see under University of Tokyo

**Oceanographical Society of Japan**
c/o Ocean Research Institute, University of Tokyo,
1-15-1 Minamidai, Nakano-ku, Tokyo 164, Japan.
- Oceanographical Society of Japan. Journal/Nihon
Kaiyo Gakkaishi. bi-m. ISSN 0029-8131

**Ochanomizu Women's University**
2-1-1 Otsuka, Bunkyo-ku, Tokyo 112, Japan.
- Ochanomizu Women's University. Natural Science
Report/Ochanomizu Joshi Daigaku Shizenkagaku
Hokoku. s-a. ISSN 0029-8190

**Ogata Institute for Medical and Chemical Research**
- Medicine and Biology/Igaku to Seibutsugaku.
(pub. by Society for Rapid Publication of Medical
and Biological Papers)

**Ohara Institute for Agricultural Biology**
see Okayama University. Ohara Institute fuer
Landwirtschaftliche Biologie

**Ohara Institute fuer Landwirtschaftliche Biologie**
see under Okayama University

**Oita Daigaku**
see Oita University

**Oita University. Economic Research Society**
Oita, Japan.
- Oita University Economic Review/Oita Daigaku
Keizai Ronshu. s-a. ISSN 0474-0157

**Oita University. Research Institute of Economics**
Oita, Japan.
- Oita University. Research Institute of Economics.
Bulletin. a.

**Okajima's Folia Anatomica Japonica**
c/o Department of Anatomy, School of Medicine,
Keio University, 35 Shinanomachi, Shinjuku-ku,
Tokyo 160, Japan.
- Okajima's Folia Anatomica Japonica/Okajima
Foria Anatomika Yaponika. bi-m. ISSN 0030-
154X

**Okayama Daigaku**
see Okayama University

**Okayama Daigaku Nogyo Seibutsu Kenkyusho**
see Okayama University. Ohara Institute fuer
Landwirtschaftliche Biologie

**Okayama Daigaku Rigakubu Kaimen-kagaku Kenkyu
Shisetsu**
see Okayama University. Research Laboratory for
Surface Science

**Okayama University. Ohara Institute for Agricultural
Biology**
see Okayama University. Ohara Institute fuer
Landwirtschaftliche Biologie

**Okayama University. Department of Biology**
Faculty of Science, Tsushima, Okayama 700, Japan.
- Biological Journal of Okayama University/
Okayama Daigaku Rigakubu Seibutsugaku Kiyo.
irreg. ISSN 0520-1810

**Okayama University. Department of Mathematics**
Faculty of Science, Tsushima, Okayama 700, Japan.
- Mathematical Journal of Okayama University. s-a.
ISSN 0030-1566

**Okayama University. Ohara Institute fuer
Landwirtschaftliche Biologie**
2-20-1 Chuo, Kurashiki 710, Japan.
- Okayama University. Ohara Institute fuer
Landwirtschaftliche Biologie. Berichte. irreg.

**Okayama University. Research Laboratory for
Surface Science**
Faculty of Science, Tsushima, Okayama 700, Japan.
- Okayama University. Research Laboratory for
Surface Science. Reports. irreg. ISSN 0078-429X

**Okayama University. School of Engineering**
Tsushima, Okayama 700, Japan.
- Okayama University. School of Engineering.
Memoirs. s-a. ISSN 0475-0071

**Okayama University. School of Medicine**
2-5-1 Shikata-cho, Okayama 700, Japan.
- Acta Medica Okayama. bi-m.

- Journal of Karyopathology/Saibokaku Byorigaku
Zasshi; tumor and tumor virus. irreg. ISSN 0022-
2119 (prep. by its Department of Pathology)

**Okinawa. Statistics Department**
1-2-14 Senzaki, Naha 900, Okinawa, Japan.
- Okinawa. Census of Agriculture/Okinawa Nogyo
Sensasu Hokokusho. irreg.

**Okinawa-ken Tokeika**
see Okinawa. Statistics Department

**Okinawa Library Association**
c/o Okinawa Prefectural Library, 312 Aza
Yorimiya, Naha, Okinawa.
- Okinawa Library Association. Annals/Okinawa
Toshokan Kyokai Shi.

**Okinawa Toshokan Kyokai**
see Okinawa Library Association

**Ongaku Gakkai**
see Japanese Musicological Society

**Ongaku No Tomo Sha Corp.**
Kagurazaka 6-30, Shinjuku-ku, Tokyo, Japan.
- Art of Music/Ongaku Geijutsu. m. ISSN 0030-
2600
- Band Journal. m. ISSN 0005-4933

**Oomoto and Universal Love and Brotherhood
Association**
Kameoka, Kyoto-fu 621, Japan.
- Oomoto. bi-m. ISSN 0030-3259

**Operations Research Society of Japan**
c/o Japan Academic Societies Centre, 2-4-16 Yayoi,
Bunkyo-ku, Tokyo 113, Japan.
- Operations Research/Opereisyonzu Risaachi. m.
- Operations Research as a Management Science/
Opereshionzu Risachi. m. ISSN 0030-3674
- Operations Research Society of Japan. Journal. q.

**Oriens Institute for Religious Research**
2-28-5 Matsubara, Setagaya-ku, Tokyo 156, Japan.
- Japan Missionary Bulletin. m. ISSN 0021-4531

**Oriental Economist**
1-4 Hongokucho, Nihonbashi, Chuo-ku, Tokyo 103,
Japan.
- Economic Studies Quarterly. irreg. (Japanese
Association of Theoretical Economics)
- Japan Company Handbook. s-a. (Dist. by: Japan
Publications Trading Co., Ltd., Box 5030, Tokyo
International, Tokyo 100-31, Japan)
- Japan Economic Year Book. a. ISSN 0075-3246
- Oriental Economist. m. ISSN 0030-5294

**Oriental Library**
2-28-21 Honkomagome, Bunkyo-ku, Tokyo 113,
Japan.
- Oriental Library. Research Department. Memoirs.
a. ISSN 0082-562X

**Oriental Tide Society**
Box 36, Omori Ota-ku, Tokyo, Japan.
- Oriental Tide. m. ISSN 0030-5359 (China
Rebuilding Federation)

**Orijin Denki K. K.**
1-18-1 Takada, Toshima-ku, Tokyo 171, Japan.
- Origin Technical Journal/Orijin. q. ISSN 0030-
5510

**Ornithological Society of Japan**
c/o National Science Museum, Department of
Zoology, 3-23-1 Hyakunin-cho, Shinjuku-ku, Tokyo
160, Japan.
- Bird/Tori. q. ISSN 0040-9480

**Osaka (City) Port and Harbour Bureau**
2-8-24 Chikko, Minato-ku, Osaka 552, Japan.
- Port of Osaka/Osakako. a.

**Osaka (Prefecture) Osaka District Meteorological
Observatory**
6-25 Hoenzakacho, Higashi-ku, Osaka 540, Japan.
- Osaka District Meteorological Observatory.
Monthly Report/Osaka-fu Kisho Geppo. m. ISSN
0030-6088

**Osaka (Prefecture) Radiaton Center**
704 Shinke-cho, Sakai 593, Japan.
- Osaka (Prefecture). Radiation Center, Annual
Report/Osaka-furitsu Hoshasen Chuo Kenkyusho
Nenpo. a.

**Osaka City Medical Center**
1-4-54 Asahimachi, Abenoku, Osaka 545, Japan.
- Osaka City Medical Journal. 1-2 per yr. ISSN 0030-6096

**Osaka City University. Department of Geosciences**
Faculty of Sciences, 459 Sugimoto-cho, Sumiyoshi-ku, Osaka 558, Japan.
- Journal of Geosciences/Osaka-shiritsu Daigaku Rigakubu Chigaku Kiyo. a. ISSN 0449-2560

**Osaka City University. Faculty of Economics**
459 Sugimoto-cho, Sumiyoshi-ku, Osaka 558, Japan.
- Osaka City University Economic Review. a. ISSN 0078-6640

**Osaka City University. Faculty of Engineering**
459 Sugimoto-cho, Sumiyoshi-ku, Osaka 558, Japan.
- Osaka City University. Faculty of Engineering. Memoirs/Osaka-shiritsu Daigaku Kogakubu Obun Kiyo. a. ISSN 0078-6659

**Osaka College of Music**
1-1-18 Shonai-Saiwaimachi, Toyonaka, Osaka, Japan.
- Data of Music in Kansai District/Kansai Ongaku Bunka Shiryo. a.

**Osaka Daigaku**
see Osaka University

**Osaka Daigaku Biseibutsubyo Kenkyusho**
see Osaka University. Research Institute for Microbial Diseases

**Osaka Daigaku Igakubu**
see Osaka University Medical School

**Osaka Daigaku Igakubu Fuzoku Genkenku Shisetsu**
see Osaka University. Institute for Cancer Research

**Osaka Daigaku Sangyo Kagaku Kenkyusho**
see Osaka University. Institute of Scientific and Industrial Research

**Osaka Daigaku Shigakkai**
see Osaka University Dental Society

**Osaka Daigaku Tanpakushitsu Kenkyusho**
see Osaka University. Institute for Protein Research

**Osaka Dental University**
1-47 Kyobashi, Higashi-ku, Osaka 540, Japan.
- Osaka Dental University. Journal. s-a. ISSN 0475-2058

**Osaka Dermatological Association**
c/o Osaka University School of Medicine, Dept. of Dermatology, 1-3 Dojima Hamadori, Fukushima-ku, Osaka 553, Japan.
- Skin Research/Hifu. q. ISSN 0018-1390

**Osaka-furitsu Daigaku**
see University of Osaka Prefecture

**Osaka-furitsu Hohasen Chuo Kenkyusho**
see Osaka (Prefecture). Radiation Center

**Osaka Ika Daigaku**
see Osaka Medical College

**Osaka Institute of Technology**
5-16-1 Omiya, Asahi-ku, Osaka 535, Japan.
- Osaka Institute of Technology. Memoirs. Series A: Science and Technology/Osaka Kogyo Daigaku Kiyo. Riko-hen. 3 per yr.
- Osaka Institute of Technology. Memoirs. Series B: Liberal Arts/Osaka Kogyo Daigaku Kiyo. Jimbun-hen. 3 per yr. ISSN 0030-6134

**Osaka Kanku Kishodai**
see Osaka (Prefecture). Osaka District Meteorological Observatory

**Osaka Kogyo Daigaku**
see Osaka Institute of Technology

**Osaka Medical College**
2-7 Daigaku-machi, Takatsuki, Osaka 569, Japan.
- Osaka Medical College. Bulletin. s-a. ISSN 0030-6142
- Osaka Medical College. Journal/Osaka Ika Daigaku Zasshi. q. ISSN 0030-6118

**Osaka Museum of Natural History**
Nagai Park, Higashinagai-cho, Higashisumiyoshi-ku, Osaka 546, Japan.
- Osaka Museum of Natural History. Bulletin/Osaka-shiritsu Shizenkagaku Hakubutsukan Kenkyu Hokoku. a. ISSN 0078-6675
- Osaka Museum of Natural History. Occasional Papers/Shizenshi Kenkyu. irreg.(1-3 per year) ISSN 0078-6683

**Osaka Odontological Society**
1-47 Kyobashi Higashiku, Osaka 540, Japan.
- Osaka Odontological Society. Journal/Shika Igaku. bi-m. ISSN 0030-6150

**Osaka Ongaku Daigaku**
see Osaka College of Music

**Osaka Prefectural University**
see University of Osaka Prefecture

**Osaka Science and Technology Center**
1-118 Utsubo, Nishi-ku, Osaka 550, Japan.
- Technology and Industries/Gijutsu to Kigyo. m. ISSN 0016-9935

**Osaka Senken Ltd.**
3-14 Kawaramachi, Higashi-ku, Osaka, Japan.
- J T N Weekly. (Japan Textile News) w.
- Japan Textile News. m. ISSN 0021-4752

**Osaka-shi Igakkai**
see Osaka City Medical Center

**Osaka Shika Daigaku**
see Osaka Dental University

**Osaka Shika Gakkai**
see Osaka Odontological Society

**Osaka-shiritsu Daigaku**
see Osaka City University

**Osaka-shiritsu Shizenkagaku Hakubutsukan**
see Osaka Museum of Natural History

**Osaka University. College of General Education**
1-1 Machikaneyama-cho, Toyonaka, Osaka 560, Japan.
- Osaka University. College of General Education. Science Reports. s-a. ISSN 0474-781X

**Osaka University. Department of Economics**
36 Joan-cho, Kita-ku, Osaka 530, Japan.
- Osaka Daigaku Keizaigaku-Osaka Economic Papers/Economic Review of Osaka University-Osaka Economic Papers. s-a.

**Osaka University. Department of Mathematics**
1-1 Machikaneyama-cho, Toyonaka, Osaka 560, Japan
- Osaka Journal of Mathematics. 3 per yr. ISSN 0030-6126 (Co-sponsor: Osaka City University, Department of Mathematics) (Subscr. to: Kinokuniya Book Store Co. Ltd., 17-7 Shinjuku 3-chome, Shinjuku-ku, Tokyo 160-91, Japan)

**Osaka University. Faculty of Engineering**
Yamadakami, Suita, Osaka 565, Japan.
- Osaka University. Faculty of Engineering. Technology Reports/Osaka Daigaku Kogaku Hokoku. s-a. ISSN 0030-6177

**Osaka University. Faculty of Pharmaceutical Sciences**
6-1-1 Toneyama, Toyonaka, Osaka 560, Japan.
- Osaka University. Faculty of Pharmaceutical Sciences. Memoirs/Osaka Daigaku Yakugakubu Kiyo. a.

**Osaka University. Institute for Cancer Research**
3-12 Dojimahama-dori, Fukushima-ku, Osaka-shi 553, Japan.
- Osaka University. Institute for Cancer Research. Annual Report. irreg.

**Osaka University. Institute for Protein Research**
5311 Yamadakami, Suita, Osaka 565, Japan.
- Osaka University. Institute for Protein Research. Memoirs. a. ISSN 0078-6705

**Osaka University. Institute of Scientific and Industrial Research**
Yamadakami, Suita, Osaka 565, Japan.
- Osaka University. Institute of Scientific and Industrial Research. Memoirs/Osaka Daigaku Sangyo Kagaku Kenkyusho Kiyo. a.

**Osaka University. Laboratory of Nuclear Study**
1-1 Machikanayama-cho, Toyonaka, Osaka 560, Japan.
- Osaka University. Laboratory of Nuclear Study. Report. irreg. ISSN 0473-4580

**Osaka University Dental Society**
33 Joan-cho, Kita-ku, Osaka 530, Japan.
- Osaka University Dental Society. Journal/Osaka Daigaku Shigaku Zasshi. s-a. ISSN 0078-6691

**Osaka University Medical School**
33 Joan-cho, Kita-ku, Osaka 530, Japan.
- Osaka University. Medical Journal/Osaka Daigaku Obun Igaku Zasshi. q. ISSN 0030-6169

**Osaka University Medical School. Department of Hygiene**
33 Joan-cho, Kita-ku, Osaka 530, Japan.
- Studies on History of Medicine/Igakushi Kenkyu. q. ISSN 0019-1612 (Collegium Ad Studium Historiae Medicae)

**Osaka University Medical School. Department of Ophthalmology**
1-1-5 Fukushima, Fukushima-ku, Osaka 553, Japan.
- Folia Ophthalmologica Japonica/Nihon Ganka Kiyokai. m. ISSN 0015-5667

**Osaka University. Research Institute for Microbial Diseases**
Yamada-kami, Oaza, Suita, Osaka 565, Japan.
- Biken Journal. q. ISSN 0006-2324

**Oto-Rhino-Laryngological Society of Japan**
3-23-14 Takanawa, Minato-ku, Tokyo 108, Japan.
- Oto-Rhino-Laryngological Society of Japan. Journal/Nihon Jibi Inkoka Gakkai Kaiho. m.

**Otsu Hydrobiological Station**
see under Kyoto University

**Otsu Rinko Jikkensho**
see Kyoto University. Otsu Hydrobiological Station

**Otsuka Pharmaceutical Factory**
115 Tateiwa, Muya-cho, Naruto 772, Tokushima, Japan.
- Otsuka Pharmaceutical Factory. Journal/Otsuka Yakuho. 11 per yr. ISSN 0030-669X

**Overseas Economic Cooperation Fund**
Ilino Bldg., 2-1-1 Uchisaiwai-cho, Chiyoda-ku, Tokyo, Japan.
- Overseas Economic Cooperation Fund. Annual Report/Kagai Keizai Kyoryoku Kikin Nenpo. a.

**Overseas Electrical Industry Survey Institute**
1-1-13 Shinbashi, Minato-ku, Tokyo 105, Japan.
- Electric Power Industry in Japan/Nihon no Denki Jigyo. a. ISSN 0420-9397

**Oyo Biseibutsu Kenkyusho**
see University of Tokyo. Institute of Applied Microbiology

**Oyo Biseibutsugaku Kenkyu Shoreikai**
see Microbiology Research Foundation

**Oyo Denki Kenkyusho**
see Hokkaido University. Research Institute of Applied Electricity

**Oyo Rikigaku Kenkyusho**
see Kyushu University. Research Institute for Applied Mechanics

**P A R C**
see Pacific-Asia Resources Center

**P H P Institute, Inc.**
Roi Roppongi Bldg., Suite 903, 5-5-1 Roppongi, Minato-ku, Tokyo 106, Japan
(U.S. Subscr. to P H P Inst., Box 4210 Grand Central Station, New York, NY 10017)
- P H P. (Peace, Happiness, Prosperity for All) m. ISSN 0030-798X

**Pacific-Asia Resources Center**
Box 5250 Tokyo International, Tokyo, Japan
(U.S. Subscr. Address: Multinational Media, c/o Angus McDonald, 114 Bedford St., S.E., Minneapolis, MN 55414)
- Ampo; Japan-Asia quarterly review. q. ISSN 0003-2026
- New Asia News. w.

**Palaeological Association of Japan, Inc.**
Takakura, Sanjyo, Nakagyo-ku, Kyoto, Japan.
- Cultura Antiqua/Kodai Bunka. m. ISSN 0045-9232

**Palaeontological Society of Japan**
c/o Business Center for Academic Societies, 2-4-16 Yayoi, Bunkyo-ku, Tokyo 113, Japan.
- Fossils/Kaseki. s-a. ISSN 0022-9202
- Palaeontological Society of Japan. Transactions and Proceedings/Nihon Koseibutsu Gakkai Hokoku Kiji. q. ISSN 0031-0204

**Pedolojisto Kondankai**
see Group of Japanese Pedologists

**Permanent Commission and International Association on Occupational Health**
- International Congress on Occupational Health. Proceedings. (pub. by Japan Industrial Safety Association)

**Pharmaceutical Research Association**
- Pharmaceutical Monthly/Gekkan Yakuji. (pub. by Yakugyo Jiho Co. Ltd.)

**Pharmaceutical Research Institute**
c/o Osaka Medical College, 2-7 Daigaku-cho, Takatsuki, Osaka 569, Japan.
- Pharmaceutical Research Institute. Bulletin/Yakugaku Kenkyusho Kiyo. bi-m. ISSN 0031-689X

**Pharmaceutical Society of Japan**
2-12-15 Shibuya, Shibuya-ku, Tokyo 150, Japan.
- Chemical & Pharmaceutical Bulletin. m. ISSN 0009-2363
- Journal of Hygienic Chemistry/Eisei Kagaku. bi-m. ISSN 0013-273X
- Pharmaceutical Society of Japan. Journal/Yakugaku Zasshi. m. ISSN 0031-6903
- Pharmacy/Farumashia. m. ISSN 0014-8601

**Photographic Society of Japan**
c/o Kyodo Bldg., 2-2 Kanda Nishiki-cho, Chiyoda-ku, Tokyo 101, Japan.
- Photography in Japan. m.

**Physical Society of Japan**
Kikai Shinko Bldg., 3-5-8 Shiba Koen, Minato-ku, Tokyo 105, Japan.
- Physical Society of Japan. Journal/Nihon Butsuri Gakkai Oji Hokoku. m. ISSN 0031-9015
- Physics/Butsuri. m.

**Physico-Chemical Society of Japan**
c/o Kyoto University, Faculty of Science, Kitashirakawa Oiwake-cho, Kyoto 606, Japan.
- International Conference on High Pressure. Proceedings. irreg.
- Review of Physical Chemistry of Japan/Butsuri Kagaku no Shinpo. s-a. ISSN 0034-6675

**Physiological Society of Japan**
c/o Oriental Library, 2-28-21 Honkomagome, Bunkyo-ku, Tokyo 113, Japan.
- Japanese Journal of Physiology. bi-m. ISSN 0021-521X
- Physiological Society of Japan. Journal/Nihon Seirigaku Zasshi. m. ISSN 0031-9341

**Phytogeographical Society**
c/o Dept. of Botany, Faculty of Science, Kyoto University, Kitashirakawa Oiwake-cho, Sakyo-ku, Kyoto 606, Japan.
- Acta Phytotaxonomica et Geobotanica/Shokubutsu Bunrui Chiri. 3 per yr. ISSN 0001-6799

**Phytopathological Society of Japan**
c/o Japan Plant Protection Association, 1-11-43 Komagome, Toshima-ku, Tokyo 170, Japan.
- Phytopathological Society of Japan. Annals/Nihon Shokubutsu Byori Gakkaiho. 5 per yr. ISSN 0031-9473

**Plastics Age Co. Ltd.**
2-5-14 Kaji-cho, Chiyoda-ku, Tokyo 101, Japan.
- Japan Plastics Age. m. ISSN 0021-4582
- Plastics Age/Purasuchikkusu Eji. m. ISSN 0551-0503

**Poetry Nippon Press**
5-11 Nagaike-cho, Showa-ku, Nagoya 466, Japan.
- Poetry Nippon. q. ISSN 0032-2105 (Poetry Society of Japan)

**Poetry Society of Japan**
- Poetry Nippon. (pub. by Poetry Nippon Press)

**Polarographic Society of Japan**
Department of Agricultural Chemistry, Kyoto University, Kyoto 606, Japan
(Order from: Japan Publications Trading Co., Ltd., Box 5030, Tokyo International, Tokyo 100-31, Japan; or 1255 Howard St., San Francisco, CA 94103)
- Review of Polarography/Porarogurafi. bi-m. ISSN 0034-6691

**Porima Kogyo Kenkyusho**
see Institute of Polymer Industry, Inc.

**Port and Harbour Technical Research Institute**
see Japan. Port and Harbour Technical Research Institute

**Poultry Research Publishing Co.**
623 Marunouchi Bldg., 2-4-1 Marunouchi, Chiyoda-ku, Tokyo 100, Japan.
- Poultry Researches/Niwatori no Kenkyu. m. ISSN 0029-0785

**Psychologia Society**
Dept. of Educational Psychology, Faculty of Education, Kyoto University, Yoshida Honcho, Sakyo-ku, Kyoto 606, Japan.
- Psychologia/Pushikorogia; Toyo Kokusai Shinrigaku-shi; an international journal of psychology in the Orient. q. ISSN 0033-2852

**Public Works Research Institute**
see Japan. Public Works Research Institute

**Publishers Association for Cultural Exchange**
1-2-1 Sarugaku-cho, Chiyoda-ku, Tokyo 101, Japan.
- Guide to Publishers and Related Industries in Japan. biennial.

**Publishing Research Associates**
c/o Kyowa Book Co., Kanda Box 173, Tokyo, Japan.
- Japan Book News. m. ISSN 0021-4337

**Purazuma Kenkyusho**
see Nagoya University. Institute of Plasma Physics

**Pushikorogia-kai**
see Psychologia Society

**Radiation Effects Research Foundation**
5-2 Hijiyama-Koen, Hiroshima 730, Japan
(Dist. in U.S. by National Technical Information Service, Springfield, Va. 22151)
- Bibliography of Published Papers of the Radiation Effects Research Foundation/Hoshasen Eikyo Kenkyusho Happyo Rombun Mokuroku. a. ISSN 0067-7221
- Radiation Effects Research Foundation. Annual Report/Hoshasen Eikyo Kenkyusho Nenpo. a.

**Radio Research Laboratories**
see Japan. Ministry of Posts and Telecommunications. Radio Research Laboratories

**Raifu Saiensu**
see Life Science Co., Ltd.

**Railway Technical Research Institute**
see under Japanese National Railways

**Rakuno Gakuen Daigaku**
see College of Dairy Agriculture

**Reader's Digest of Japan, Ltd.**
1-1-1 Hitotsubashi, Chiyoda-ku, Tokyo 100, Japan.
- Reader's Digest (Japanese Edition) m. ISSN 0034-043X

**Research Association of Powder Technology, Japan**
2-7 Shibunkaku-Kaikan, Tanakasekiden-cho, Sakyo-ku, Kyoto 606, Japan.
- Research Association of Powder Technology, Japan. Journal/Funtai Kogaku Kenkyukai-Shi. m. ISSN 0034-5156

**Research Association of Statistical Sciences**
see under Kyushu University

**Research Committee on Essential Amino Acids**
c/o Department of Nutrition and Biochemistry, Institute of Public Health, 4-6-1 Shiroganedai Minato-ku, Tokyo 108, Japan.
- Research Committee of Essential Amino Acids. Reports/Hissu Aminosan Kenkyu. bi-m.

**Research Institute for Applied Mechanics**
see under Kyushu University

**Research Institute for Humanistic Studies**
see under Kyoto University

**Research Institute for Mathematical Sciences**
see under Kyoto University

**Research Institute for Microbial Diseases**
see under Osaka University

**Research Institute for Nuclear Medicine and Biology**
see under Hiroshima University

**Research Institute for Ocean Economics**
c/o Murufuji Bldg., 3-1-10 Shimbashi, Minato-ku, Tokyo 105, Japan.
- Japan Oceanology Directory/Kaiyo Sangyo Jimmeiroku. irreg.

**Research Institute for Scientific Measurements**
see under Tohoku University

**Research Institute for Strength and Fracture of Materials**
see under Tohoku University

**Research Institute for Tuberculosis, Leprosy and Cancer**
see under Tohoku University

**Research Institute for Veterinary Science**
see under Nihon University

**Research Institute of Applied Electricity**
see under Hokkaido University

**Research Institute of Atmospherics**
see under Nagoya University

**Research Institute of Economics**
see under Oita University

**Research Institute of Electrical Communication**
see under Tohoku University

**Research Institute of Environmental Medicine**
see under Nagoya University

**Research Institute of International Trade and Industry (Tsusho Sangiyo Chosakai)**
Kobikikan Bekkan, 6-15-2 Ginza, Chuo-ku, Tokyo 104, Japan.
- Paper & Pulp Statistical Monthly/Kami Parupu Tokei Geppo. m. ISSN 0022-8168 (Japan. Ministry of International Trade and Industry. Research and Statistics Division)
- Yearbook of Pulp and Paper Statistics/Kami Parupu Tokei Nenpo. a. ISSN 0453-1515 (Japan. Ministry of International Trade and Industry. Research and Statistics Division)

**Research Institute of Logopedics and Phoniatrics**
see under University of Tokyo

**Research Institute of Mineral Dressing and Metallurgy**
see under Tohoku University

**Research Institute of Science and Technology**
see under Nihon University

**Research Laboratory for Surface Science**
see under Okayama University

**Resources Exploitation Institute**
Shibuya Paru Homu, 29-25 Sakuragaoka-cho, Shibuya-ku, Tokyo 150, Japan.
- Resources Exploitation Institute. Bulletin/Shigen Sogo Kaihatsu Kenkyusho Obun Hokoku. irreg.

**Rikagaku Kenkyusho Saikurotoron Kenkyushitsu**
see Institute of Physical and Chemical Research

**Rikkyo Daigaku Rigakubu Sugaku Kyoshitsu**
see Rikkyo University. Institute of Mathematics

**Rikkyo University**
Nishi-Ikebukuro, Toshima-ku, Tokyo 171, Japan.
- St. Paul's Economic Review/Rikkyo Keizaigaku Kenkyu. q. ISSN 0035-5356 (St. Paul's Economic Society)

**Rikkyo University. Institute for Atomic Energy**
10 Matsukoshi, Sajima, Yokosuka-shi 240-01, Japan.
- Rikkyo University. Institute for Atomic Energy. Report. irreg.

**Rikogaku Kenkyusho**
*see* Nihon University. Research Institute of Science and Technology

**Rikogaku Kenkyusho**
*see* Waseda University. Science and Engineering Research Laboratory

**Rikuyosha**
127 Banshu-cho, Shinju-ku, Tokyo, Japan.
- Annual of Ad Production in Japan. a.

**Ringyo Shikenjo**
*see* Japan. Government Forest Experiment Station

**Rinkai Jikkensho**
*see* University of Tokyo. Misaki Marine Biological Station

**Rinsho-Shikasha**
375 Sakaimachi Higashi Takoyakushi, Nakogyo-ku, Kyoto 604, Japan.
- Folia Odontologica Practica/Rinso Shika (Clinical Dentistry) q. ISSN 0035-5488

**Rin'ya-cho**
*see* Japan. Forestry Agency

**Rissho Daigaku Hokekyo Bunka Kenkyujo**
*see* Rissho University. Institute for the Comprehensive Study of Lotus Sutra

**Rissho University. Institute for the Comprehensive Study of Lotus Sutra**
4-2-16 Osaki, Shinagawa-ku, Tokyo 141, Japan.
- Institute for the Comprehensive Study of Lotus Sutra. Journal/Hokke Bunka Kenkyu. a.

**Ritsumeikan University. Economic Society**
Higashi-iru Tera-machi, Hirokoji, Kamigyo-ku, Kyoto, Japan.
- Ritsumeikan Economic Review/Ritsumeikan Keizaigaku. bi-m.

**Ro Zai Ho**
Chosun Shinbosa, 5 Tsukudo, Hachiman-cho, Shinjuku-ku, Tokyo, Japan.
- People's Korea. w. ISSN 0031-5036

**Rock Magnetism and Paleogeophysics Research Group in Japan**
c/o University of Tokyo, Faculty of Science, Geophysical Institute, 7-3-1 Hongo, Bunkyo-ku, Tokyo 113, Japan.
- Rock Magnetism and Paleogeophysics. a.

**Rodo Kagaku Kenkyusho**
*see* Institute for Science of Labour

**Rodo-sho Rodo Eisei Kenkyusho**
*see* Japan. National Institute of Industrial Health

**Ryukei Shosha**
4-22-15 Sengoku, Bunkyo-ku, Tokyo, Japan.
- Ryukei. q.

**SENTOKYO**
*see* Special Libraries Association, Japan

**Sabiura Marine Park Research Station**
1157 Kushimotocho Arita, Nishi-Muro-Gun, Kushimoto, Wakayama, Japan.
- Marine Park Research Station. Bulletin/Kaichu Koen Kenkyujo Kenkyu Hokoku. s-a.

**Sacred Heart University**
*see* University of the Sacred Heart

**Kase Sadako, Ed. & Pub.**
3-12-9 Taito, Taito-ku, Tokyo 110, Japan.
- Obelisk. a.

**Sado Marine Biological Station**
*see under* Niigata University

**Sado Rinko Jikkenjo Kenkyu**
*see* Niigata University. Sado Marine Biological Station

**St. Paul's Economic Society**
- St. Paul's Economic Review/Rikkyo Keizaigaku Kenkyu. (pub. by Rikkyo University)

**St. Paul's University**
*see* Rikkyo University

**Saitama University**
255 Shimookubo, Urawa-Shi 338, Japan.
- Saitama University. Science Reports. Series A: Mathematics, Physics and Chemistry. a. ISSN 0558-2431
- Saitama University. Science Reports. Series B: Biology and Earth Sciences. a. ISSN 0558-244X

**Saiwai Shoho**
1-5-2 Soto Kanda, Chiyoda-ku, Tokyo 101, Japan.
- Petroleum and Petrochemicals/Sekiyu to Sekiyu Kagaku. m.

**Sangyo Boeki Kenkyusho**
*see* Tokyo College of Economics. Institute of Industrial and Commercial Research

**Sangyo Kagaku Kenkyusho**
*see* Osaka University. Institute of Scientific and Industrial Research

**Sangyo Press Ltd.**
Toei Bldg., 4-2 Muromachi, Nihonbashi, Chuo-ku, Tokyo, Japan.
- Japan Metal Bulletin. 3 per wk. ISSN 0021-4523

**Sankyo Co. Ltd.**
2-7-12 Ginza, Chuo-ku, Tokyo 104, Japan.
- Stethoscope. m.

**Sankyo Co., Ltd. Central Research Laboratories**
1-2-58 Hiro-machi, Shinagawa-ku, Tokyo 140, Japan.
- Sankyo Research Laboratories. Annual Report. a. ISSN 0080-6064

**Sankyo K. K. Chuo Kenkyusho**
*see* Sankyo Co., Ltd., Research Laboratories

**Sanpo Inc.**
1-10-17 Hamamatsu-cho, Minato-ku, Tokyo 105, Japan.
- Japan Welding News. q. ISSN 0021-4779
- Liquefied Petroleum Gas/L P Gasu. m. ISSN 0024-709X

**Sanshi Shikenjo**
*see* Japan. Sericultural Experiment Station

**Sanyo Chemical Industries Ltd.**
11-1 Ikkyo Nomoto-cho, Higashiyama-ku, Kyoto 605, Japan.
- Sanyo Kasei News. bi-m. ISSN 0036-4649

**Sapporo Ika Daigaku**
*see* Sapporo Medical College

**Sapporo Ika Daigaku Fuzoka Gan Kenkyusho**
*see* Sapporo Medical College. Cancer Research Institute

**Sapporo Medical College**
Nishi-17-chome, Minami-1-jo, Chuo-ku, Sapporo 060, Japan.
- Sapporo Medical Journal/Sapporo Igaku Zasshi. bi-m. ISSN 0036-472X

**Sapporo Medical College. Cancer Research Institute**
Nishi-17-chome, Minami-1-jo, Chuo-ku, Sapporo 060, Japan.
- Tumor Research: Experimental and Clinical/Gan Kenkyu, Jikken to Rinsho. s-a. ISSN 0041-4093

**Science and Engineering Research Laboratory**
*see under* Waseda University

**Science Council of Japan**
7-22-34 Roppongi, Minato-ku, Tokyo 106, Japan.
- Japan Annual of Law and Politics. a. ISSN 0075-3157
- Report of Ionosphere and Space Research in Japan/Denriso Chokoso Taiki Kenkyu Hokokushi. irreg. (3-4 per yr.) ISSN 0034-4672 (prep. by its Ionosphere Research Committee)
- Science Council of Japan. Annual Report. a.
- Science Council of Japan. Monthly Report/Nihon Gakujutsu Kaigi Geppo. m. ISSN 0029-019X

**Seibundo Shinkosha Publishing Co., Ltd.**
5-1 Kanda Nishiki-cho, Chiyoda-ku, Tokyo 101, Japan.
- Idea; international advertising art. bi-m. ISSN 0019-1299

**Seido Language Institute**
12-6 Funado-cho, Ashiya, Hyogo 659, Japan.
- Modern English Journal/Eigo Kyoiku Jaanaru. a.

**Seiki Gakkai**
*see* Japan Society of Precision Engineering

**Seisan Gijutsu Kenkyusho**
*see* University of Tokyo. Institute of Industrial Science

**Seishin Igaku Institute of Psychiatry**
4-11-11 Komone, Itabashi-ku, Tokyo 174, Japan.
- Seishin-Igaku Institute of Psychiatry, Tokyo. Bulletin/Seishin Igaku Kenkyusho, Tokyo. Gyoseki Shu. a. ISSN 0080-8547

**Seismological Society of Japan**
Japan Academic Societies Centre, 2-4-16 Yayoi, Bunkyo-ku, Tokyo 113, Japan.
- Journal of Physics of the Earth. q. ISSN 0022-3743 (Co-sponsor: Volcanological Society of Japan)
- Seismological Society of Japan. Journal/Zisin. (pub. by University of Tokyo. Earthquake Research Institute)

**Sekai Sekiyu Kaigi Nihon Kokunai Iinkai**
*see* World Petroleum Congress. Japanese National Committee

**Sekiyu Gakkai**
*see* Japan Petroleum Institute

**Sekiyu Kogyo Jihyo-sha**
2-16-5 Misaki-cho, Chiyoda-ku, Tokyo 101, Japan.
- Petroleum Monthly/Gekkan Sekiyu. m. ISSN 0016-5972

**Semmon Toshokan Kyogikai**
*see* Special Libraries Association, Japan

**Sendai Fukusokan Kagaku Kenkyusho**
*see* Sendai Institute of Heterocyclic Chemistry

**Sendai Institute of Heterocyclic Chemistry**
c/o Prof. Tetsuji Kametami, Ed., Pharmaceutical Institute, Tohoku University, Aobayama, Sendai 980, Japan.
- Heterocycles; international journal for reviews and communications in heterocyclic chemistry. m.

**Sen'i Gakkai**
*see* Society of Fiber Science and Technology

**Sen'i Kenkyusha Co.**
No.6 Konyacho, Kanda, Chiyoda-ku, Tokyo 101, Japan.
- Dyeing & Finishing/Sen'i Kako. m. ISSN 0037-217X

**Senmon Toshokan Kyogikai**
*see* Special Libraries Association, Japan

**Sericultural Experiment Station**
*see* Japan. Sericultural Experiment Station

**Seto Marine Biological Laboratory**
*see under* Kyoto University

**Seto Rinkai Jikkensho**
*see* Kyoto University. Seto Marine Biological Laboratory

**Shakai Hosho Kenkyusho**
*see* Social Development Research Institute

**Shakai-jinruigakkai**
*see under* Tokyo Metropolitan University

**Shakai Kagaku Kenkyusho**
*see* University of Tokyo. Institute of Social Science

**Shakespeare Society of Japan**
18 Naka-machi, Shinjuku-ku, Tokyo 162, Japan.
- Shakespeare Studies. a. ISSN 0582-9402

**Shiga University. Institute for Economic Research**
1-1-1 Bamba, Hikone-shi, Shiga-ken, Japan.
- Hikone Ronso. bi-m. ISSN 0018-182X

**Shigaku-kai**
*see* Historical Society of Japan

**Shigen Sogo Kaihatsu Kenkyusho**
*see* Resources Exploitation Institute

**Shikizai Kyokai**
*see* Japan Society of Colour Materials

**Shikoku Agricultural Experiment Station**
see **Japan. Shikoku Agricultural Experiment Station**

**Shikoku Entomological Society**
c/o Eime University, College of Agriculture, Entomological Laboratory, 3-5-7 Tarumi, Matsuyama 790, Japan.
- Shikoku Entomological Society. Transactions/ Shikoku Konchu Gakkai Kaiho. ISSN 0037-3680

**Shikoku Konchu Gakkai**
see **Shikoku Entomological Society**

**Shimizu Construction Co. Ltd**
2-1-1 Takaracho, Chuo-ku, Tokyo 104, Japan.
- Monthly Report of Price and Wage in Construction Engineering/Kensetsu Kogyo Bukka Chingin Geppo. m. ISSN 0022-9997

**Shin Gijutsu-sha**
see **M. H. Information Center**

**Shin Nihon Chutanzo Kyokai**
see **New Japan Casting and Forging Society**

**Shin Nihon Ishi Kyokai**
see **New Japanese Doctors' Association**

**Shin-Norinsha Co., Ltd.**
2-7 Kanda Nishikicho, Chiyoda-ku, Tokyo 101, Japan.
- A M A. (Agricultural Mechanization in Asia) q. ISSN 0084-5841 (Farm Machinery Industrial Research Corp.)
- Agricultural Machinery News/Noki Shimbun. w. ISSN 0029-0971
- Farm Machinery Yearbook/Nogyo Kikai Nenkan. a. ISSN 0071-3937
- Farming Mechanization/Kikaika Nogyo. m. ISSN 0023-1371
- Product File for Agricultural Machinery and Related Material. a. (Farm Machinery Industrial Research Corp.)

**Shindan to Chiryosha Co.**
Marounichi Bldg., 4th Floor, Marounichi, Chiyoda-ku, Tokyo 100.
- Brain and Development/No to Hattatsu. bi-m. ISSN 0029-0831 (Japanese Society of Pediatric Neurology)

**Shinohara Publishers, Inc.**
Taniguchi Bldg., 2-11-7 Hongo, Bunkyo-ku, Tokyo, Japan.
- Japanese Journal of Cancer Clinics/Gan No Rinsho. m. ISSN 0021-4949

**Shinrigaku Hyoron Kankokai**
c/o Dept. of Psychology, Faculty of Letters, Kyoto University, Sakyo-ku, Kyoto 606, Japan.
- Shinrigaku Hyoron. s-a.

**Shinseikatsu Undo Kyokai**
1-3 Hibiya Koen, Chiyoda-ku, Tokyo, Japan.
- Jumin Katsudo. q.

**Shinshu Konchu Gakkai**
see **Entomological Society of Shinshu**

**Shinshu University. Faculty of Engineering**
Wakasoto, Nagano 500, Japan.
- Shinshu University. Faculty of Engineerinig. Journal/Shinshu Daigaku Kogakubu Kiyo. s-a. ISSN 0037-3818

**Shinshu University. Faculty of Medicine**
3-1-1 Asahi-machi, Matsumoto, Nagano 390, Japan.
- Shinshu Medical Journal/Shinshu Igaku Zasshi. q. ISSN 0037-3826 (Nagano Medical Society)

**Shinshu University. Faculty of Science**
3-1-1 Asahi, Matsumoto, Nagano 390, Japan.
- Shinshu University. Faculty of Science. Journal/ Shinshu Daigaku Rigakubu Kiyo. s-a.

**Shinshu University. Faculty of Textile Science and Technology**
3-15-1 Tokida, Ueda, Nagano 386, Japan.
- Shinshu University. Faculty of Textile Science and Technology. Journal. Series A: Biology. irreg. ISSN 0583-0648
- Shinshu University. Faculty of Textile Science and Technology. Journal. Series B: Engineering. irreg.
- Shinshu University. Faculty of Textile Science and Technology. Journal. Series C: Chemistry. irreg. ISSN 0559-8621

- Shinshu University. Faculty of Textile Science and Technology. Journal. Series D: Arts. irreg. ISSN 0583-0664
- Shinshu University. Faculty of Textile Science and Technology. Journal. Series E: Agriculture and Sericulture. irreg.
- Shinshu University. Faculty of Textile Science and Technology. Journal. Series F: Physics and Mathematics. irreg.

**Ship Research Institute**
see **Japan. Ship Research Institute**

**Shiryo Yushutsunyu Kyogikai**
see **Japan Feed Trade Association**

**Shizuoka University. Faculty of Science**
836 Oya, Shizuoka-shi 420, Japan.
- Shizuoka University. Faculty of Science. Reports/ Shizuoka Daigaku Rigakubu Kenkyu Hokoku. irreg. ISSN 0583-0923

**Shokokusha Publishing Co., Inc.**
25 Sakamachi, Shinjuku-ku, Tokyo 160, Japan.
- Architecture Culture/Kenchiku Bunka. m. ISSN 0003-8490
- Detail/Diteru; magazine for architects and engineers. q. ISSN 0012-4133

**Shokubai Kenkyusho Kiyo**
see **Hokkaido University. Research Institute for Catalysis**

**Shokubutsu Bunri Chiri Gakkai**
see **Phytogeographical Society**

**Shokuryo Keizai Shimbun Sha**
35-12 Ishigatsujimachi, Tennoji-ku, Osaka 543, Japan.
- Food Economics Yearbook/Shokuryo Keizai Nenkan. a.

**Shokuryo Kogaku Kenkyusho**
see **Kyoto University. Research Institute for Food Science**

**Shomei Gakkai**
see **Illuminating Engineering Institute of Japan**

**Shoni Aiiku Kyokai**
see **Association for the Care of the Child**

**Showa Medical Association**
c/o Showa University, School of Medicine, 1-5-8 Hatanodai, Shinagawa-ku, Tokyo 142, Japan.
- Showa Medical Association. Journal/Showa Igakkai Zasshi. m. ISSN 0037-4342

**Showa University. School of Medicine**
1-5-8 Hatanodai, Shinagawa-ku, Tokyo 142, Japan.
- Electrophysiology/Denki Seirigaku. irreg.

**Shuppan News Co. Ltd.**
3-2-4 Misaki-cho, Chiyoda-ku, Tokyo, Japan.
- Shuppan News; Shuppan news, publications news and reviews. 3 per mo.

**Sinological Society of Hiroshima**
c/o Hiroshima University, Faculty of Literature, 1-1-89 Higashi-Senda-machi, Hiroshima, Japan.
- Journal of Sinological Studies/Shinagaku Kenkyu. s-a.

**Small Business Information Centre**
c/o Small Business Promotion Corporation, Sankaido Bldg., 1-9-13 Akasaka, Minato-ku, Tokyo, Japan.
- Information and Investigation Report/Joho Chosa Report. irreg.
- Management Information Journal/Keiei Joho-shi. 3 per mo.
- Technological Information Journal/Gijutsu Joho-shi. m.

**Snow Brand Milk Products Co. Ltd.**
Research Laboratory, 1-1-2 Minamidai, Kawagoe, Saitama 350, Japan.
- Snow Brand Milk Products Co., Ltd. Research Laboratory. Reports/Yukijirushi Nyugyo Gijutsu Kenkyusho Hokoku. irreg., approx. 1 per year. ISSN 0082-4763

**Social Development Research Institute**
3-3-4 Kasumigaseki, Chiyoda-ku, Tokyo 100, Japan.
- Social Development Research Institute. Organization and Activities. irreg. ISSN 0559-698X

**Socialist Party of Japan**
1-8-1 Nagata-cho, Chiyoda-Ku, Tokyo, Japan.
- Gekkan Shakaito. m. ISSN 0435-1754
- Japan Socialist Review. m. ISSN 0021-4655
- Shakai Shimpo. s-w.

**Societas Anatomica Nipponica**
see **Japanese Anatomical Association**

**Societas Paediatrica Japonica**
see **Japan Pediatric Society**

**Societas Phytogeographica**
see **Phytogeographical Society**

**Societatis Histochemicae Japonicae**
see **Japan Society of Histological Documentation**

**Societe Franco-Japonaise de Medecine**
2-3 Kanda Surugadai, Chiyoda-ku, Tokyo 101, Japan.
- Bulletin Medical Franco-Japonais/Nichifutsu Igaku. q. ISSN 0007-4705

**Societe-Franco-Japonaise des Techniques Industrielles**
2-3 Kanda Surugadai, Chiyoda-ku, Tokyo 101, Japan.
- Techniques Industrielles du Japon. a.

**Societe Japonaise de Psychopathologie de l'Expression**
c/o Neuropsychiatric Research Institute, 91 Bentencho, Shinjuku-ku, Tokyo 162, Japan.
- Japanese Bulletin of Art Therapy. a.

**Society for Asian Folklore**
c/o M. Eder, 1 Nanzan-cho, Showa-ku, Nagoya 466, Japan.
- Asian Folklore Studies. a.

**Society for Near Eastern Studies in Japan**
9th Floor, Tokyo-Tenrikyokan, 9 Kanda Nishiki-cho 1-chome, Chiyoda-ku, Tokyo 101, Japan.
- Orient. q. ISSN 0030-5219

**Society for Rapid Publication of Medical and Biological Papers**
c/o Ogata Institute for Medical and Chemical Research, 2-3-5 Nihonbashi Bakurocho Chuo, Tokyo 103, Japan.
- Medicine and Biology/Igaku to Seibutsugaku. m. ISSN 0019-1604 (Ogata Institute for Medical and Chemical Research)

**Society for Science & Technical Documents Utilization Promotion**
c/o Toyama Prefectural Library, 206-3 Chayamachi, Toyama 930-01, Japan.
- Toyama Science and Technical Documents/ Kagaku Gijutsu Bunken Toyama. bi-m. ISSN 0022-765X

**Society for the Promotion of International Otorhinolaryngology**
Japan Academic Societies Centre, 2-4-16 Yayoi, Bunkyo-ku, Tokyo 113, Japan.
- Auris. Nasus. Larynx. s-a.

**Society of Agricultural Meteorology of Japan**
c/o National Institute of Agricultural Sciences, 2-1 Nishigahara, Kita-ku, Tokyo 114, Japan.
- Journal of Agricultural Meteorology/Nogyo Kisho. q. ISSN 0021-8588

**Society of Applied Medicine**
108 Shimogamo Miyazakai-cho, Sakyo-ku, Kyoto 606, Japan.
- Journal of Applied Medicine/Oyo Igaku. q.

**Society of Automotive Engineers of Japan**
1-16-15 Takawawa, Minato-ku, Tokyo 108, Japan.
- Society of Automotive Engineers of Japan. Bulletin. a.

**Society of Chemical Engineers**
Kyoritsu Bldg., 4-6-19 Kohinata, Bunkyo-ku, Tokyo 112, Japan
(Order from: Maruzen Co., Ltd., 2-3-10 Nihonbashi, Chuo-ku, Tokyo 103, Japan; or Import and Export Department, Box 5050, Tokyo International, Tokyo 100-31, Japan)
- Chemical Engineering/Kagaku Kogaku. m. ISSN 0022-7676
- Journal of Chemical Engineering of Japan/Kagaku Kogaku Zasshi. bi-m. ISSN 0021-9592

**Society of Electrophoresis**
Dept. of General Education, Tokyo Medical and
Dental University, 2-8-30 Kohnodai, Ichikawashi,
Chiba-ken 272, Japan.
- Physico-Chemical Biology/Seibutsu Butsuri
Kagaku. q. ISSN 0031-9082

**Society of Electrophotography of Japan**
c/o Tokyo College of Photography, 2-9-5 Honcho,
Nakano-ku, Tokyo 164, Japan.
- Electrophotography/Denshi Shashin. 3 per yr.
ISSN 0011-8478

**Society of Fiber Science and Technology**
c/o Tokyo Institute of Technology, 2 Oo-Okayama,
Meguro-ku, Tokyo, Japan
(Order from: Japan Publications Trading Co., Ltd.,
Box 5030, Tokyo International, Tokyo 100-31,
Japan; or 1255 Howard St., San Francisco, CA
94103)
- Society of Fiber Science and Technology, Japan.
Journal/Sen'i Gakkaishi. m. ISSN 0037-9875

**Society of Heating, Air Conditioning and Sanitary
Engineers of Japan**
2-9 Kyobashi, Chuo-ku, Tokyo 104, Japan.
- S H A S E. Transactions/Kuki Chowa Eisei
Kogakkai Eibun Ronbunshu. a. ISSN 0081-1610

**Society of Instrument and Control Engineers**
c/o Kotohira Annex, Mori Bldg., 39 Shiba
Kotohira-cho, Minato-ku, Tokyo 105, Japan.
- Society of Instrument and Control Engineers
Journal/Keisoku to Seigyo. m.

**Society of Japanese Virologists**
c/o Institute of Medical Science, University of
Tokyo, Shirokanedai, Minato-ku, Tokyo 108, Japan
(Overseas Distributor: Japan Publications Trading
Co., Ltd., Box 5030, Tokyo International, Tokyo
100-31, Japan; or 1255 Howard St., San Francisco,
CA 94103)
- Virus/Uirusu. q. ISSN 0042-6857

**Society of Mining Geologists of Japan**
Nihon Kogyo Kaikan Bldg., 8-5-4 Ginza, Chuo-ku,
Tokyo 104, Japan.
- Mining Geology/Kozan Chishitsu. bi-m. ISSN
0026-5209

**Society of Nippon Dental College**
1-9-20 Fujimi, Chiyoda-ku, Tokyo 102, Japan.
- Society of Nippon Dental College. Annual
Publications. a.

**Society of Photographic Science and Technology of
Japan**
c/o Tokyo College of Photography, 2-9-5 Honcho,
Nakano-ku, Tokyo 164, Japan.
- Society of Photographic Science and Technology
of Japan. Bulletin/Nihon Shashin Gakkai
Eibungo. q. ISSN 0038-0059

**Society of Plant Protection of North Japan**
c/o Tohoku National Agricultural Experiment
Station, 3 Shimofurumichi, Yotsuya, Omagari 014-
01, Japan.
- Society of Plant Protection of North Japan.
Annual Report/Kitanihon Byogaichu Kenkyukai
Kaiho. a. ISSN 0081-170X

**Society of Political Economy**
c/o Faculty of Economics, Rikkyo University, 3
Ikebukuro, Toshima-ku, Tokyo 171, Japan.
- Journal of Political Economy/Keizaigaku Kenkyu.
bi-m. ISSN 0022-975X

**Society of Polymer Science**
Honshu Bldg., 5-12-8 Ginza, Chuo-ku, Tokyo 104,
Japan.
- Kobunshi Ronbunshu. m.
- Polymer Journal. bi-m. ISSN 0032-3896

**Society of Population Ecology**
c/o Japan Academic Societies Center, 2-4-16 Yayoi,
Bunkyo-ku, Tokyo 113, Japan.
- Researches on Population Ecology/Kotaigun
Seitaigaku no Kenkyu. s-a. ISSN 0034-5466

**Society of Rubber Industry**
1-5-26 Motoakasaka, Minato-ku, Tokyo 107, Japan.
- Society of Rubber Industry. Journal/Nihon Gomu
Kyokaishi. m. ISSN 0029-022X

**Society of Terrestrial Magnetism and Electricity of
Japan**
Geophysical Institute, Faculty of Science, University
of Tokyo, 2-11-16 Yayoi, Bunkyo-ku, Tokyo 113,
Japan.
- Journal of Geomagnetism and Geoelectricity. q.
ISSN 0022-1392

**Society of the Science of Soil & Manure, Japan**
c/o Japan Academic Societies Center, 2-4-16 Yayoi,
Bunkyo-ku, Tokyo 113, Japan.
- Society of the Science of Soil and Manure of
Japan. Journal/Nippon Dojo Hiryogaku Zasshi.
m. ISSN 0029-0610
- Soil Science & Plant Nutrition/Dojo to
Shokubutsu Eiyo. q. ISSN 0038-0768

**Sokka Gakkai**
32 Shinano-machi, Shinjuku-ku, Tokyo 160, Japan.
- Seikyo Times. m. (prep. by its International
Bureau)
- Soka Gakkai News. s-m. (prep. by its
International Bureau)

**Sophia University**
Chiyoda-ku, Kioicho 7, Tokyo 102, Japan.
- Monumenta Nipponica; studies in Japanese
culture. q. ISSN 0027-0741
- Sophia; western civilization and the cultural
interaction of East and West. q.

**Sophia University. Brazilian Center**
Chiyoda-ku, Kioicho 7, Tokyo 102, Japan.
- Anais. a.

**Special Libraries Association, Japan**
c/o National Diet Library, 1-10-1 Nagatacho,
Chiyoda-ku, Tokyo 100, Japan.
- Special Libraries/Semmon Toshokan. q.; 2 per yr.
1969-1970.

**Spectroscopical Society of Japan**
Sanshi-Ken Bldg., 3-25-2 Hyakunin-cho, Shinjuku-
ku, Tokyo 160, Japan.
- Spectroscopical Society of Japan. Journal/Bunko
Kenkyu. bi-m. ISSN 0038-7002

**Sugaku Kyoshitsu**
see Rikkyo University. Institute of Mathematics

**Sugar Beet Institute**
Japan Sugar Beet Improvement Foundation,
Hitsujigaoka 1, Sapporo, Hokkaido 062, Japan.
- Bulletin of Sugar Beet Research. Supplement/
Tensai Kenkyu Hokoku Hokan. a. ISSN 0068-
4090

**Suiken Kagaku Kenkyujo**
see Nagoya University. Water Research Institute

**Suion Chosakan**
3-25-2 Hyakunin-cho, Shinjuku-ku, Tokyo 160,
Japan.
- Water Temperature Research/Suion No Kenkyu.
bi-m. ISSN 0039-484X

**Suiri Kagaku Kenkyusho**
see Water Utilization Research Institute

**Suisan-cho Nihonkai-ku Suisan Kenkyusho**
see Japan. Japan Sea Regional Fisheries Research
Laboratory

**Suisan-cho Tansui-ku Suisan Kenkyusho**
see Japan. Freshwater Fisheries Research
Laboratory

**Suisan-cho Tohoku-ku Suisan Kenkyusho**
see Japan. Tohoku Regional Fisheries Research
Laboratory

**Suisan-cho Tokai-ku Suisan Kenkyusho**
see Japan. Tokai Regional Fisheries Research
Laboratory

**Suisan Kaiyo Kenkyu-Kai**
see Japanese Society of Fisheries and
Oceanography

**Suishitsu Kagaku Kenkyu Shisetsu**
see Nagoya University. Water Research Institute

**Sumitomo Bakelite Co. Ltd.**
Osaka Bldg., 2-2-1 Uchisaiwai-cho, Chiyoda-ku,
Tokyo 100, Japan.
- Beku Nyusu. m. ISSN 0005-8297

**Sumitomo Bank, Ltd.**
Information Department, 1-3-2 Marunouchi,
Chiyoda-ku, Tokyo, Japan.
- Sumitomo Bank Review; economic conditions in
Japan. m. ISSN 0039-4955

**Sumitomo Denki Kogyo**
see Sumitomo Electric Industries Ltd.

**Sumitomo Electric Industries Ltd.**
Shin Sumitomo Bldg., 5-15 Kitahama, Higashi-ku,
Osaka 541, Japan.
- Sumitomo Electric Technical Review. s-a.

**Sumitomo Keikinzoku Kogyo K. K.**
see Sumitomo Light Metal Industries Ltd.

**Sumitomo Light Metal Industries, Ltd.**
3-1-12 Chitose, Minatoku, Nagoya 455, Japan.
- Sumitomo Light Metal Technical Reports/
Sumitomo Keikinzoku Giho. q. ISSN 0039-4963

**Suri Kaiseki Kenkyusho**
see Kyoto University. Research Institute for
Mathematical Sciences

**Swing Journal Co. Ltd.**
9-3 Sakae-cho, Shiba, Minato-ku, Tokyo, Japan.
- Swing Journal. m. ISSN 0039-744X

**Taibundo Publishing Co.**
1-10 Nishiki-cho, Chiyoda-ku, Tokyo, Japan.
- Calamus; Walt Whitman quarterly: international.
s-a. ISSN 0045-382X

**Taikabutsu Gijutsu Kyokai**
see Technical Association of Refractories

**Taiki Osen Kenkyu Zenkoku Kyogikai**
see Japan Society of Air Pollution

**Taiseisha Ltd.**
Publishing Division, 1-5 Kyobashi, Chuo-ku, Tokyo
104, Japan.
- Polymer Friends for Rubber, Plastics and Fiber/
Porima No Tomo. m. ISSN 0032-4779

**Taishitsu Igaku Kenkyusho**
see Kumamoto University. Institute of
Constitutional Medicine

**Taishukan Publishing Co. Ltd.**
3-24 Kanda Nishikicho, Chiyoda-ku, Tokyo 101,
Japan.
- Health and Physical Education/Hoken Taiiku
Kyoshitsu. m. ISSN 0018-3350

**Takenaka Komuten Co., Ltd.**
No. 27, 4-chome, Hommachi, Higashi-ku, Osaka
541, Japan.
- Approach. q. ISSN 0003-7117

**Takii Shubyo Co. Ltd.**
180 Inokuma Higashiiru, Umekoji, Shimogyo-ku,
Kyoto 600, Japan.
- New Flowers/Shin Kaki. q. ISSN 0037-3737
- New Information on Horticulture/Engei Shin
Chishiki. m. ISSN 0013-7634

**Tamagawa University. Faculty of Agriculture**
6-1-1 Tamagawagakuen, Machida, Tokyo 194,
Japan.
- Tamagawa University. Faculty of Agriculture.
Bulletin. a. ISSN 0082-156X

**Tanabe Amino Acid Research Foundation**
3-33 Hirano-machi, Higashi-ku, Osaka, Japan.
- Tanabe Amino Acid Research Foundation. Annual
Report. a. ISSN 0082-1616

**Tanpakushitsu Kenkyusho**
see Osaka University. Institute for Protein
Research

**Tazuke Kofukai Medical Research Institute**
Kitano Hospital, 23 Nishogimachi, Kitaku, Osaka
530, Japan.
- Kitano Hospital Journal of Medicine/Kitano
Byoin Kiyo. q. ISSN 0023-1916

**Technical Association of Graphic Arts of Japan**
5-6-2 Ginza, Chuo-ku, Tokyo 104, Japan.
- Japan Printer/Insatsu Zasshi. m. ISSN 0020-1758
- Technical Association of Graphic Arts of Japan.
Bulletin/Nihon Insatsu Gakkai Robunshu. q.
ISSN 0040-0874
- Technical Association of Graphic Arts of Japan.
Bulletin (Overseas Edition) q.

**Technical Association of Refractories**
c/o New Ginza Bldg., 7-3-13 Ginza, Ginza Chuo-ku, Tokyo 104, Japan.
- Refractories/Taikabutsu. m. ISSN 0039-8993

**Telecommunications Association (Denki Tsushin Kyokai)**
New Yurakucho Bldg., 1-11 Yurakucho, Chiyoda-ku, Tokyo 100, Japan.
- Japan Telecommunications Review. q. ISSN 0021-4744 (Japan Telegraph and Telephone Public Corporation)

**Tenri University**
1050 Somanouchi-cho, Tenri, Nara 632, Japan.
- Untei. a. ISSN 0566-2680

**Tenri University Press**
Tenri Central Library, Tenri City, Nara 632, Japan.
- Biblia. 3 per yr. ISSN 0006-0860

**Tenrikyo Overseas Mission Department**
Tenri, Nara, Japan.
- Tenrikyo. m. ISSN 0040-3482

**Tensor Society**
Kawaguchi Institute of Mathematical Sciences, Matsu-ga-oka 2-7-15, Chigasaki 253, Japan.
- Tensor. 3 per yr. ISSN 0040-3504

**Tetsudo Gijutsu Kenkyusho (Railway Technical Research Institute)**
see under **Japanese National Railways**

**Tetsudo Tosho Kankai**
New Kokusai Bldg., 3-4-1 Marunouchi, Chiyoda-ku, Tokyo 100, Japan.
- Railway Pictorial/Tetsudo Pikutoriaru. m. ISSN 0040-4047

**Textile Journal and Book Pub. Co.**
1-7-9 Ohnodai, Sayamacho, Osaka 589, Japan.
- Textile Review/Sen'i Kogyo Zasshi; Boshokukai. bi-m. ISSN 0037-2064

**Textile Machinery Society of Japan**
1-8-4 Utsubo-honmachi, 1-118 Utsubo, Nishi-ku, Osaka 550, Japan.
- Textile Machinery Society of Japan. Journal. q. ISSN 0040-5043

**Toa Kumo Gakkai**
see **Arachnological Society of East Asia**

**Todai Shuppankai**
see **University of Tokyo Press**

**Toho Daigaku Igakubu Igakkai**
see **Toho University Medical Society**

**Toho Gakkai**
see **Institute of Eastern Culture**

**Toho University Medical Society**
c/o Library, School of Medicine, 5-21-16 Omori Nishi, Ota-ku, Tokyo 143, Japan.
- Toho University Medical Society. Journal/Toho Igakkai Zasshi. bi-m. (2 nos. in English, s-a.; 4 nos. in Japanese, q.) ISSN 0040-8670

**Tohokai, Inc.**
Shinsekai Bldg., 2-2 Kandajinbo-cho, Chiyoda-ku, Tokyo 101, Japan.
- Tohokai. m.
- Young East; a quarterly on Buddhism and Japanese culture. q. ISSN 0513-5974 (Young East Association)

**Tohoku Daigaku**
see **Tohoku University**

**Tohoku Daigaku Hogakkai**
see **Tohoku University. Association of Law and Political Science**

**Tohoku Daigaku Kagaku Keisoku Kenkyusho**
see **Tohoku University. Research Institute for Scientific Measurements**

**Tohoku Daigaku Kenkyusho Rengokai**
see **Tohoku University. Association of the Research Institutes**

**Tohoku Daigaku Kosankinbyo Kenkyusho**
see **Tohoku University. Research Institute for Tuberculosis, Leprosy and Cancer**

**Tohoku Daigaku Nogaku Kenkyusho**
see **Tohoku University. Institute for Agricultural Research**

**Tohoku Medical Society**
2-1 Seiryo-machi, Sendai 980, Japan.
- Tohoku Medical Journal/Tohoku Igaku Zasshi. bi-m. ISSN 0040-8700

**Tohoku Regional Fisheries Research Laboratory**
see **Japan. Tohoku Regional Fisheries Research Laboratory**

**Tohoku Societe de Ortopedia kaj Akcidenti Hirugio**
c/o Dept. of Orthopaedic Surgery, Tohoku University, School of Medicine, 1-1 Seiryo-machi, Sendai 980, Japan.
- Tohoku Archivo Por Orthopedia kej Akcidenta Hirurgio/Tohoku Seikei Saigai Geka Kiyo. s-a. ISSN 0040-8751

**Tohoku University. Association of Law and Political Science**
c/o Institute of Law, Faculty of Law, Tohoku University, 2-1-1 Katahira, Sendai 980, Japan.
- Journal of Law and Political Science/Hogaku. q.

**Tohoku University. Association of the Research Institutes**
2-1-1 Katahira, Sendai 980, Japan.
- Tohoku University. Science Reports of the Research Institutes. Series A: Physics, Chemistry, and Metallurgy/Tohoku Daigaku Kenkyusho Hokoku. A-shu: Butsurigaku, Kagaku, Yakingaku. bi-m. ISSN 0040-8808
- Tohoku University. Science Reports of the Research Institutes. Series C: Medicine/Tohoku Daigaku Kenkyusho Hokoku, C-shu, Igaku. 4 per yr.

**Tohoku University. Department of Psychology**
Faculty of Arts & Letters, 2-1-1 Katahira, Sendai 980, Japan.
- Tohoku Psychologica Folia. s-a. ISSN 0040-8743

**Tohoku University. Faculty of Agriculture**
1-1 Tsutsumi-tori Amamiya-cho, Sendai 980, Japan.
- Tohoku Journal of Agricultural Research. q. ISSN 0040-8719

**Tohoku University. Faculty of Engineering**
Aoba, Aramaki, Sendai 980, Japan.
- Tohoku University. Faculty of Engineering. Technology Reports/Tohoku Daigaku Kogaku Hokoku. s-a. ISSN 0040-8816

**Tohoku University. Faculty of Science**
2-1-1 Katahira, Sendai 980, Japan.
- Tohoku University. Science Reports. Series 1: Physics, Chemistry, Astronomy/Tohoku Daigaku Rika Hokoku, Dai-1-shu, Butsurigaku, Kagaku, Tenmongaku. q. ISSN 0040-8778
- Tohoku University. Science Reports. Series 4: Biology/Tohoku Daigaku Rika Hokoku Dai-4-shu, Seibutsugaku. q. ISSN 0040-8786 (prep. by its Biological Institute)
- Tohoku University. Science Reports. Series 5: Geophysics/Tohoku Daigaku Rika Hokoku, Dai-5-shu, Chikyu Butsurigaku. 3-4 per yr. ISSN 0040-8794 (prep. by its Geophysical Institute)
- Tohoku University. Science Reports. Series 7: Geography/Tohoku Daigaku Rika Hokoku, Dai-7-shu, Chirigaku. s-a. ISSN 0563-6523

**Tohoku University. Institute for Agricultural Research**
2-1-1 Katahira, Sendai 980, Japan.
- Tohoku University. Institute for Agricultural Research. Bulletin/Tohoku Daigaku Nogaku Kenkyusho Hokoku. s-a. ISSN 0040-8697
- Tohoku University. Institute for Agricultural Research. Reports/Tohoku Daigaku Nogaku Kenkyusho Hokoku. a.

**Tohoku University. Institute of Geology and Paleontology**
Aobayama, Sendai 980, Japan.
- Tohoku University. Institute of Geology and Paleontology. Contributions/Tohoku Daigaku Rigakubu Chishitsugaku Koseibutsugaku Kyoshitsu Kenkyu Hobun Hokoku. irreg., no. 75, 1975. ISSN 0082-4658
- Tohoku University. Institute of Geology and Paleontology. Science Reports. Second Series. irreg., vol. 45, no. 2, 1975. ISSN 0082-464X

**Tohoku University Mathematical Institute**
2-1-1 Katahira, Sendai 980, Japan.
- Tohoku Mathematical Journal/Tohoku Sugaku Zasshi. q. ISSN 0040-8735

**Tohoku University. Research Institute for Scientific Measurements**
19-1 Sanjo-machi, Sendai 980, Japan.
- Tohoku University. Research Institute for Scientific Measurements. Bulletin/Tohoku Daigaku Kagaku Keisoku Kenkyusho Hokoku. 3 per yr. ISSN 0040-8689

**Tohoku University. Research Institute for Strength and Fracture of Materials**
Aoba, Aramaki, Sendai 980, Japan.
- Tohoku University. Research Institute for Strength and Fracture of Materials. Reports/Tohoku Daigaku Kogakubu Zairyo Kyodo Kenkyu Shisetsu Hokoku. s-a. ISSN 0563-6590

**Tohoku University. Research Institute for Tuberculosis, Leprosy and Cancer**
4-12 Hirose-machi, Sendai 980, Japan.
- Tuberculosis, Leprosy and Cancer. q.

**Tohoku University. Research Institute of Electrical Communication**
2-1-1 Katahira, Sendai 980, Japan.
- Tohoku University. Research Institute of Electrical Communication. Technical Report. irreg.

**Tohoku University. Research Institute of Mineral Dressing and Metallurgy**
2-1-1 Katahira, Sendai 980, Japan.
- Tohoku University. Research Institute of Mineral Dressing and Metallurgy. Bulletin/Tohoku Daigaku Senko Seiren Kenkyusho Iho. s-a. ISSN 0040-876X

**Tohoku University. School of Medicine**
2-1 Seiryomachi, Sendai 980, Japan.
- Tohoku Journal of Experimental Medicine/Tohoku Jikken Igaku. m. ISSN 0040-8727

**Tokai Bank Ltd.**
3-21-24 Nishiki, Naka-ku, Nagoya, Japan.
- Tokai Monthly Economic Letter. m.

**Tokai Daigaku**
see **Tokai University**

**Tokai Daigaku Shuppankai**
see **Tokai University Press**

**Tokai Regional Fisheries Research Laboratory**
see **Japan. Tokai Regional Fisheries Research Laboratory**

**Tokai Research Establishment**
see under **Japan Atomic Energy Research Institute**

**Tokai University. Faculty of Literature**
1117 Kitakaname, Hiratsuka, Kanagawa 259-12, Japan.
- Tokai University. Faculty of Literature. Bulletin. s-a.

**Tokai University Press**
3-27-4 Shinjuku, Shinjuku-ku, Tokyo 160, Japan (Distributed by: Orion Books, Export Dept., 1-58 Kanda Jimbocho, Chiyoda-ku, Tokyo, Japan)
- Pacific Geology. s-a. ISSN 0552-7333

**Tokei Kagaku Kenkyukai**
see **Kyushu University. Research Association of Statistical Sciences**

**Tokei Suri Kenkyusho**
see **Japan. Institute of Statistical Mathematics**

**Tokita Seed Co. Ltd.**
1069 Nakagawa, Omiya, Saitama, Japan.
- Shubyo to Engei. m. ISSN 0037-4407

**Tokushima Daigaku**
see **Tokushima University**

**Tokushima Medical Association**
School of Medicine, Tokushima University, 3 Kurate-machi, Tokushima 770, Japan.
- Shikoku Acta Medica/Shikoku Igaku Zasshi. bi-m. ISSN 0037-3699

**Tokushima University. Faculty of Education**
1-4 Minamijosanjimi-cho, Tokushima 770, Japan.
- Journal of Mathematics. a. ISSN 0075-4293

● Journal of Natural Science. a. ISSN 0075-4307

**Tokushima University. Faculty of Engineering**
2-1 Nanjo Mishima-machi, Tokushima 770, Japan.
● Tokushima University. Faculty of Engineering.
Bulletin. a. ISSN 0040-8883

**Tokushima University. School of Medicine**
3-18-15 Kuramoto-cho, Tokushima 770, Japan.
● Tokushima Journal of Experimental Medicine. s-a.
ISSN 0040-8875

**Tokyo. Bureau of Public Cleansing**
3-8-1 Marunouchi, Chiyoda-ku, Tokyo 100, Japan.
● Public Cleansing Service in Tokyo/Seiso Jigyo
Gaiyo. a.

**Tokyo. Council on Liaison with Foreign Cities**
Bureau of General Affairs, External Affairs and
Tourist Division, 3-5-1 Marunouchi, Tokyo, Japan.
● Tokyo Municipal News. m. ISSN 0040-893X
(prep. by its Liaison and Protocol Section)

**Tokyo. Port and Harbor Bureau**
3-8 Marunouchi, Chiyoda-ku, Tokyo, Japan.
● Port of Tokyo. a.

**Tokyo Astronomical Observatory**
University of Tokyo, 2-21-1 Osawa, Mitaka, Tokyo
181, Japan.
● Tokyo Astronomical Bulletin. Second Series. irreg.
ISSN 0082-4690
● Tokyo Astronomical Observatory. Annals. Second
Series. irreg. ISSN 0082-4704
● Tokyo Astronomical Observatory. Report. irreg.
● Tokyo Astronomical Observatory. Reprints. irreg.
ISSN 0082-4712

**Tokyo Ato Direkutazu Kurabu**
see Art Directors Club of Tokyo

**Tokyo Chigaku Kyokai**
see Tokyo Geographical Society

**Tokyo College of Domestic Science**
1-18-1 Kaga, Itabashi-ku, Tokyo 173, Japan.
● Tokyo College of Domestic Science. Bulletin/
Tokyo Kasei Daigaku Kenkyu Kiyo. a.

**Tokyo College of Economics. Institute of Industrial
and Commercial Research**
1-7 Minami-cho, Kokubunji, Tokyo 185, Japan.
● Industry and Commerce/Sangyo Boeki Kenkyu. q.
ISSN 0558-4779

**Tokyo Consolidated Fire Prevention Association**
c/o Tokyo Shobo-cho, 1-11-39 Nagata-cho,
Chiyoda-ku, Tokyo 100, Japan.
● Disaster Prevention/Bosai. bi-m. ISSN 0006-7873

**Tokyo Daigaku**
see University of Tokyo

**Tokyo Daigaku Bussei Kenkyusho**
see University of Tokyo. Institute for Solid State
Physics

**Tokyo Daigaku Genshikaku Kenkyusho**
see University of Tokyo. Institute for Nuclear
Study

**Tokyo Daigaku Ikagaku Kenkyusho**
see University of Tokyo. Institute of Medical
Science

**Tokyo Daigaku Jishin Kenkyusho**
see University of Tokyo. Earthquake Research
Institute

**Tokyo Daigaku Kaiyo Kenkyusho**
see University of Tokyo. Ocean Research Institute

**Tokyo Daigaku Oyo Biseibutsu Kenkyusho**
see University of Tokyo. Institute of Applied
Microbiology

**Tokyo Daigaku Rigakubu Fuzoku Rinkai Jikkensho**
see University of Tokyo. Misaki Marine Biological
Station

**Tokyo Daigaku Seisan Gijutsu Kenkyusho**
see University of Tokyo. Institute of Industrial
Science

**Tokyo Daigaku Shakai Kagaku Kenkyusho**
see University of Tokyo. Institute of Social Science

**Tokyo Daigaku Uchu Koku Kenkyusho**
see University of Tokyo. Institute of Space and
Aeronautical Science

**Tokyo Dental College**
2-9-18 Misaki-cho, Chiyoda-ku, Tokyo 101, Japan.
● Tokyo Dental College. Bulletin/Tokyo Shika
Daigaku Obun Kiyo. q. ISSN 0040-8891

**Tokyo Dental College Society**
Tokyo Dental College, 2-9-18 Misaki-cho, Chiyoda-
ku, Tokyo 101, Japan
(Order from: Maruzen Co., Ltd., 2-3-10 Nihonbashi,
Chuo-ku, Tokyo 103, Japan; or their Import and
Export Department, Box 5050, Tokyo International,
Tokyo 100-31, Japan)
● Tokyo Dental College Society. Journal/Shika
Gakuho. m. ISSN 0037-3710

**Tokyo Economic Information Service Co.**
Taiso Bldg., 1-9-1 Takaracho, Chuo-ku, Tokyo 104,
Japan.
● Japanese General Trading Companies Yearbook/
Sogo-Shosha. a.

**Tokyo Gaikogu Daigaku**
see Tokyo University of Foreign Studies

**Tokyo Geographical Society**
12-2 Niban-cho, Chiyoda-ku, Tokyo 102, Japan.
● Journal of Geography/Chigaku Zasshi. bi-m. ISSN
0022-135X

**Tokyo Ika Daigaku**
see Tokyo Medical College

**Tokyo Ika Shika Daigaku**
see Tokyo Medical and Dental University

**Tokyo Ika Shika Daigaku Iyo Kizai Kenkyusho**
see Tokyo Medical and Dental University. Institute
for Medical and Dental Engineering

**Tokyo Institute of Technology**
2-12-1 Okayama, Meguro-ku, Tokyo 152, Japan.
● Kodai Mathematical Seminar Reports/Tokyo
Kogyo Daigaku Gakuho. q. ISSN 0023-2599
(prep. by its Department of Mathematics)
● Tokyo Institute of Technology. Bulletin. irreg.
ISSN 0495-8020

**Tokyo Institute of Technology. Research Laboratory
of Resources Utilization**
2-2-1 Okayama, Meguro-ku, Tokyo 145, Japan.
● Tokyo Institute of Technology. Research
Laboratory of Resources Utilization. Report/
Shigen Kagaku Kenkyusho. a. ISSN 0495-8055

**Tokyo Jikekai Ika Daigaku**
see Jikei University School of Medicine

**Tokyo Joshi Ika Daigaku**
see Tokyo Women's Medical College Society

**Tokyo Kasei Daigaku**
see Tokyo College of Domestic Science

**Tokyo Keizai Daigaku Sangyo Boeki Kenkyusho**
see Tokyo College of Economics. Institute of
Industrial and Commercial Research

**Tokyo Kogyo Daigaku**
see Tokyo Institute of Technology

**Tokyo Kokuritsu Hakubutsukan**
see Tokyo National Museum

**Tokyo Kyoiku Daigaku**
see Tokyo University of Education

**Tokyo Kyoiku Daigaku Kikogaku Danwakai**
see Tokyo University of Education. Laboratory of
Climatology

**Tokyo Kyoiku Daigaku Kikogaku Kyoshitsu**
see Tokyo University of Education. Laboratory of
Climatology

**Tokyo Kyoiku Daigaku Kogaku Kenkyusho**
see Tokyo Kyoiku University. Institute for Optical
Research

**Tokyo Kyoiku University. Institute for Optical
Research**
3-22-17 Hyakunin-cho, Shinjuku-ku, Tokyo 160,
Japan.
● Science of Light/Hikari No Kagaku. irreg. (2-3
issues per year); 1970, Mar., vol. 19, no. 1. ISSN
0080-7583

**Tokyo Lincoln Book Center**
Japan Publications Trading Co. Bldg., 1-2-1
Sarugaku-cho, Chiyoda-ku, Tokyo 101, Japan.
● Tokyo Lincoln Book Center. Report. a. ISSN
0495-811X

**Tokyo Medical and Dental University**
1-5-45 Yushima, Bunkyo-ku, Tokyo 113, Japan.
● Tokyo Medical and Dental University. Bulletin/
Tokyo Ika Shika Daigaku Kiyo. q. ISSN 0040-
8921

**Tokyo Medical and Dental University. Department of
Human Genetics**
1-5-45 Yushima, Bunkyo-ku, Tokyo 113, Japan.
● Japanese Journal of Human Genetics/Jinrui
Idengaku. q. ISSN 0021-5074 (Japan Society of
Human Genetics)

**Tokyo Medical and Dental University. Institute for
Medical and Dental Engineering**
1-5-45 Yushima, Bunkyo-ku, Tokyo 113, Japan.
● Tokyo Medical and Dental University. Institute
for Medical and Dental Engineering. Reports/Iyo
Kizai Kenkyusho Hokoku. a. ISSN 0082-4739

**Tokyo Medical and Dental University. School of
Dentistry**
Dept. of Preventive Dentistry, 1-5-45 Yushima,
Bunkyo-ku, Tokyo 113, Japan.
● Journal of Dental Health/Koku Eisei Gakkai
Zasshi. q. ISSN 0023-2831 (Japanese Society for
Dental Health)

**Tokyo Medical Association**
2-5 Kanda Surugadai, Chiyoda-ku, Tokyo 101,
Japan.
● Tokyo Medical Association. Journal/Tokyo-to
Ishikai Zasshi. m. ISSN 0040-8956

**Tokyo Medical College**
1-412 Higashi Okubo, Shinjuku-ku, Tokyo 160,
Japan.
● Tokyo Medical College. Journal/Tokyo Ika
Daigaku Zasshi. bi-m. ISSN 0040-8905

**Tokyo Metropolitan Agricultural Experiment Station,
Itsukaichi Office**
853 Tokura, Itsukaichi-machi, Nishitama-gun,
Tokyo 190-01, Japan.
● Tokyo Metropolitan Agricultural Experiment
Station, Itsukaichi Office. Forestry Experimental
Bulletin/Ringyo Shiken Kenkyu Hokoku. irreg.
(8-10 vols. per year) ISSN 0082-4720

**Tokyo Metropolitan Institute for Neurosciences**
2-6 Musashidai, Fuchu-shi, Tokyo 183, Japan.
● Tokyo Metropolitan Institute of Neurosciences.
Annual Report/Tokyo-to Shinkei Kagaku Sogo
Kenkyujo Nempo. a.

**Tokyo Metropolitan Research Institute for
Environmental Protection**
2-5 Yuraku-cho, Chiyoda-ku, Tokyo 100, Japan.
● Tokyo Metropolitan Research Institute for
Environmental Protection. Annual Report. a.

**Tokyo Metropolitan Research Laboratory of Public
Health**
3-24-1 Hyakunin-cho, Shinjuk-ku, Tokyo 160,
Japan.
● Tokyo Metropolitan Research Laboratory of
Public Health, Annual Report/Tokyo-toritsu Eisei
Kenkyusho Kenkyu Nenpo. a. ISSN 0082-4771

**Tokyo Metropolitan University**
1-1-1 Yakumo, Meguro-ku, Tokyo 152, Japan.
● Report on Urban Research/Toshi Kenkyu
Hokoku. irreg.

**Tokyo Metropolitan University. Department of
Geography**
2-1-1 Fukazawa, Setagaya-ku, Tokyo 158, Japan.
● Tokyo Metropolitan University. Department of
Geography. Geographical Reports/Tokyo-toritsu
Daigaku Chirigaku Hokoku. a.

**Tokyo Metropolitan University. Faculty of Technology**
2-1-1 Fukazawa, Setagaya-ku, Tokyo 158, Japan.
- Tokyo Metropolitan University. Faculty of Technology. Memoirs/Tokyo-toritsu Daigaku Kogakubu Hokoku. a. ISSN 0082-4747

**Tokyo Metropolitan University. Institute for Social Sciences and Humanity**
591 Fusuma-machi, Meguro-ku, Tokyo 158, Japan.
- Social and Human Sciences Journal/Jinbun Gakuho. q.

**Tokyo Metropolitan University. Shakai-jinruigakkai**
- Shakai-jinruigaku Nenpo. (pub. by Kobundo)

**Tokyo National Museum**
13-9 Ueno Park, Daito-ku, Tokyo 110, Japan.
- Museum. (pub. by Bijutsu Shuppan-sha)
- Tokyo National Museum News. m. ISSN 0040-8948

**Tokyo News Service, Ltd.**
Kosoku Doro Bldg., 8-10 Ginza Nishi, Chuo-ku, Tokyo 104, Japan.
- Shipbuilding/Zosen. m. ISSN 0044-5347
- Shipbuilding Yearbook/Zosen Yearbook. a. ISSN 0084-5671
- Tour Companion. w.

**Tokyo Nyusa Tsushinsha**
see Tokyo News Service Ltd.

**Tokyo Rengo Boka Kyokai**
see Tokyo Consolidated Fire Prevention Association

**Tokyo Rinkan Bukka Senta**
see Tokyo Lincoln Book Center

**Tokyo Shibaura Electric Co., Ltd.**
1-1 Uchisaiwaicho, Chiyoda-ku, Tokyo, Japan.
- Toshiba Review. bi-m. ISSN 0040-9642

**Tokyo Shika Daigaku**
see Tokyo Dental College

**Tokyo Shika Daigaku Gakkai**
see Tokyo Dental College Society

**Tokyo Shuppan Hanbai Co., Ltd.**
53 Higashigoken-cho, Shinjuku-ku, Tokyo 162, Japan.
- Shinkan News for Readers/Shinkan Nyusu. s-m. ISSN 0037-3788

**Tokyo Suisan Daigaku**
see Tokyo University of Fisheries

**Tokyo Tanabe Co., Ltd.**
2-7-3 Nihonbashi Hon-cho, Chuo-ku, Tokyo 103, Japan.
- Tokyo Tanabe Quarterly. q.

**Tokyo Tenmondai**
see Tokyo Astronomical Observatory

**Tokyo-to Ishikai**
see Tokyo Medical Association

**Tokyo-to Kogai Kenkyusho**
see Tokyo Metropolitan Research Institute for Environmental Protection

**Tokyo-to Kyoiku Iinkai**
3-8-1 Marunouchi, Chiyoda-ku, Tokyo, Japan.
- Shakai Kyoiku Gyosei Kihon Shiryo Shu.

**Tokyo-to Nogyo Shikenjo Itsukaichi Bunjo**
see Tokyo Metropolitan Agricultural Experiment Station, Itsukaichi Office

**Tokyo-to Sangyo Rodo Kaikan**
1-1-6 Hashiba, Taito-ku, Tokyo, Japan.
- Leather & Footwears/Kawa to Hakimono. irreg.

**Tokyo-to Seihon Kogyo Kumiai**
2-5 Kanda, Nishiki-cho, Chiyoda-ku, Tokyo, Japan.
- Bookbinding Industry/Seihonkai. m. ISSN 0037-1009

**Tokyo-to Seiso-kyoku Kikaku-bu**
see Tokyo. Bureau of Public Cleansing

**Tokyo-to Shinkei Kagaku Sogo Kenkyujo Nempo**
see Tokyo Metropolitan Institute for Neurosciences

**Tokyo-toritsu Daigaku**
see Tokyo Metropolitan University

**Tokyo-toritsu Daigaku Jinbun Gakkai**
see Tokyo Metropolitan University. Institute for Social Sciences and Humanity

**Tokyo-toritsu Eisei Kenkyusho**
see Tokyo Metropolitan Research Laboratory of Public Health

**Tokyo-toritsu Koka Tanki Daigaku Gakujutsu Kenkyu Un'Eikai**
see Metropolitan Technical College

**Tokyo-toritsu Kyoiku Kenkyujo**
1-1-14 Meguro, Meguro-ku, Tokyo 153, Japan.
- Tokyo-toritsu Kyoiku Kenkyujo Nempo.

**Tokyo University**
see University of Tokyo

**Tokyo University of Education. Faculty of Science**
3-29-1 Otsuka, Bunkyo-ku, Tokyo 112, Japan.
- Tokyo University of Education. Faculty of Science. Science Reports. Section A: Mathematics and Physics/Tokyo Kyokai Daigaku Rigakubu Kiyo A. a.
- Tokyo University of Education. Faculty of Science. Science Reports. Section B: Zoology and Botany/Tokyo Kyoiku Daigaku Rika Kiyo B, Dobutsugaku to Shokubutsugu. irreg.
- Tokyo University of Education. Faculty of Science. Science Reports. Section C: Geography, Geology and Mineralogy. irreg.

**Tokyo University of Education. Laboratory of Climatology**
3-29-1 Otsuka, Bunkyo-ku, Tokyo 112, Japan.
- Japanese Progress in Climatology/Nippon no Kikogaku no Shinpo. a. ISSN 0075-3467 (Japanese Climatological Seminar)
- Tokyo Journal of Climatology/Tokyo Kiko Gakkai Zasshi. s-a. ISSN 0040-8913

**Tokyo University of Fisheries**
4-5-7 Konan, Minato-ku, Tokyo 108, Japan.
- Tokyo University of Fisheries. Journal/Tokyo Suisan Daigaku Tokubetsu Kenkyu Hokoku. s-a. ISSN 0040-9014
- Tokyo University of Fisheries. Report/Tokyo Suisan Daigaku Ronshu. a. ISSN 0563-8372
- Tokyo University of Fisheries. Transactions. irreg., 1968, vol. 9, no. 2.

**Tokyo University of Foreign Studies**
4-51 Nishigahara, Kitaku, Tokyo, Japan.
- Tokyo University of Foreign Studies. Summary. a. ISSN 0082-4844

**Tokyo Women's Medical College Society**
c/o the Library, 10 Kawada-cho, Shinjuku-ku, Tokyo 160, Japan.
- Tokyo Women's Medical College. Journal/Tokyo Joshi Ika Daigaku Zasshi. m. ISSN 0040-9022

**Toshi Keikaku Kyokai**
see City Planning Association of Japan

**Tottori University. Faculty of Agriculture**
1-1 Koyama-cho, Tottori 680, Japan.
- Tottori University. Faculty of Agriculture. Journal. a. ISSN 0082-5360

**Tottori University. School of Medicine**
86 Nishi-machi, Yonago 683, Japan.
- Yonago Acta Medica. 3 per yr. ISSN 0513-5710

**Tottori University Forests**
1-1 Koyama-cho, Tottori 680, Japan.
- Tottori University Forests. Bulletin/Tottori Daigaku Nogakubu Fuzoku Enshurin Hokoku. biennial. ISSN 0082-5379

**Toyama Mercantile Marine College**
1-2 Ebie Neriai, Shinminato, Toyama 933-02, Japan.
- Toyama Mercantile Marine College. Journal/ Toyama Shosen Koto Senmon Gakko Kenkyu Shuroku. a.

**Toyama Prefecture. Welfare Department**
1-7 Shinsogawa, Toyama 930, Japan.
- Toyama Prefecture. Annual Report of Public Health/Toyama-ken Eisei Tokei Nenpo. a.

**Toyama Shosen Koto Senmon Gakko**
see Toyama Mercantile Marine College

**Toyo Bunko**
see Oriental Library

**Toyo Communication Equipment Company**
3-484 Tsukagoshi, Saiwai-ku, Kawasaki-shi 210, Japan.
- Toyo's Technical Bulletin/Toyo Tsushinki Giho. a.

**Toyo Keizai Shinposha**
see Oriental Economist

**Toyo Soda Kogyo K. K.**
see Toyo Soda Manufacturing Co., Ltd.

**Toyo Soda Manufacturing Co., Ltd.**
4560 Tonda, Shinnanyo-shi 746, Yamaguchi-ken 746, Japan.
- Toyo Soda Manufacturing Company, Ltd. Scientific Report/Toyo Soda Kenkyu Hokoku. s-a. ISSN 0041-0144 (prep. by its Research and Development Division)

**Toyo Tsushinki K. K.**
see Toyo Communication Equipment Company

**Toyoda Machine Works Ltd.**
1-1 Asahi-cho, Kariya, Aichi 448, Japan.
- Toyoda Technical Review/Toyoda Giho. q. ISSN 0041-0152

**Toyota Motor Sales Co. Ltd.**
Public Relations Department, 2-3-18 Kudan Minami, Chiyoda-ku, Tokyo 102, Japan.
- Toyota in Brief. a.
- Wheel Extended; a Toyota quarterly review. q. ISSN 0049-755X

**Tropical Agriculture Research Association of Japan**
c/o Faculty of Agriculture, Tokyo University of Education, 2-19-1 Komaba, Meguro-ku, Tokyo 153, Japan.
- Japanese Journal of Tropical Agriculture/Nettai Nogyo. q. ISSN 0021-5260

**Tropical Agriculture Research Center**
see Japan. Tropical Agriculture Research Center

**Tsuda-Juku Women's College**
11491 Tsuda-machi, Kodaira City, Tokyo, Japan.
- Tsuda Review. a. ISSN 0496-3547

**Tsumura Junten-do Co. Ltd.**
Tsumura Laboratory, 1421 Izumi, Komae-shi, Tokyo 182, Japan.
- Journal of Japanese Botany/Shokubutsu Kenkyu Zasshi. m. ISSN 0022-2062

**Tsushin Kikai Kogyokai**
see Communication Industries Association of Japan

**Tsusho Sangyo-cho Kogyo Gijutsu-in Hokkaido Kogyo Kaihatsu Shikenjo**
see Japan. Government Industrial Development Laboratory, Hokkaido

**Tsusho Sangyo-cho Kogyo Gijutsu-in Kogai Shigen Kenkyusho**
see Japan. National Research Institute for Pollution and Resources

**Tsusho Sangyo-sho Gijutsu-in Tokyo Kogyo Shikensho**
see Japan. National Chemical Laboratory for Industry

**Tsusho Sangyo-sho Kogyo Gijutsu-in Chishitsu Chosasho**
see Japan. Geological Survey of Japan

**Tsusho Sangyo-sho Kogyo Gijutsu-in Keiryo Kenkyusho**
see Japan. National Research Laboratory of Metrology

**Tsusho Sangyo-sho Kogyo Gijutsu-in Kyushu Kogyo Gijutsu Shikenjo**
see Japan. Government Industrial Research Institute, Kyushu

**Tusho Sangiyo Chosakai**
see Research Institute of International Trade and Industry

**Uchu Koku Kenkyusho**
see University of Tokyo. Institute of Space and Aeronautical Science

**Uchusen Boenkyo**
see Nagoya University. Cosmic-Ray Research
Laboratory

**Uirusu Kenkyusho**
see Kyoto University. Institute for Virus Research

**Un'Yu Chosakyoku**
see Institute of Transportation Economics

**Un'Yu-sho Daijin Kanbo Joho Kanri-bu**
see Japan. Ministry of Transport

**Un'Yu-sho Kowan Gijutsu Kenkyusho**
see Japan. Port and Harbour Technical Research
Institute

**Un'Yu-sho Senpaku Gijutsu Kenkyusho**
see Japan. Ship Research Institute

**Union of Japanese Scientists and Engineers**
5-10-11 Sendagaya, Shibuya-ku, Tokyo 151, Japan.
- Engineers/Enjiniasu. m. ISSN 0013-8444
- Statistical Quality Control/Hinshitsu Kanri. m.
  ISSN 0018-1951
- Union of Japanese Scientists and Engineers.
  Reports of Statistical Application Research. q.
  ISSN 0034-4842

**United Nations Centre for Regional Development**
For publications of this agency see section for
UNITED NATIONS

**U. S. Embassy**
see Embassy of the United States in Japan

**United States Embassy**
see Embassy of the United States in Japan

**University of Chiba**
see Chiba University

**University of Electro-Communications**
1-5-1 Chofugaoka, Chofu-shi, Tokyo 182, Japan.
- University of Electro-Communications. Report/
  Denki Tsushin Daigaku Gakuho. s-a. ISSN 0493-
  4253

**University of Fukui**
see Fukui University

**University of Fukuoka**
see Fukuoka University

**University of Hirosaki**
see Hirosaki University

**University of Hiroshima**
see Hiroshima University

**University of Hokkaido**
see Hokkaido University

**University of Iwate**
see Iwate University

**University of Kagoshima**
see Kagoshima University

**University of Kanazawa**
see Kanazawa University

**University of Kobe**
see Kobe University

**University of Kumamoto**
see Kumamoto University

**University of Kurume**
see Kurume University

**University of Kyoto**
see Kyoto University

**University of Nagasaki**
see Nagasaki University

**University of Okayama**
see Okayama University

**University of Osaka**
see Osaka University

**University of Osaka Prefecture**
4-804 Mozuume-machi, Sakai-shi 591, Osaka, Japan.
- University of Osaka Prefecture. Bulletin. Section
  A: Engineering and Natural Sciences/Osaka-
  furitsu Daigaku. Kiyo, A, Kogaku, Shizenagaku. s-
  a. ISSN 0474-7844
- University of Osaka Prefecture. Bulletin. Section
  B: Agriculture and Biology/Osaka-furitsu Daigaku
  Kiyo, B Nogaku, Seibutsugaku. a. ISSN 0474-
  7852
- University of Osaka Prefecture. Bulletin. Section
  D: Sciences of Economy, Commerce and Law. a.
  ISSN 0473-4637

**University of Osaka Prefecture. Department of
Mathematics**
4-804 Mozuume-Machi, Sakai-shi 591, Osaka,
Japan.
- Mathematica Japonicae. s-a. ISSN 0025-5513 (Co-
  sponsor: Osaka Kyoiku University. Department of
  Mathematics)

**University of the Ryukyus. College of Agriculture**
3-1 Tonokura-cho, Shuri, Naha 903, Okinawa,
Japan.
- University of the Ryukyus. College of Agriculture.
  Science Bulletin/Ryukyu Daigaku Nogakubu
  Gakujutsu Hokoku. a. ISSN 0485-7828

**University of the Sacred Heart**
Hiroo, 4-3-1 Shibuya-ku, Tokyo, Japan.
- Seishin Studies. s-a. ISSN 0037-1084

**University of Tokushima**
see Tokushima University

**University of Tokyo. Center for American Studies**
153 Komaba, Meguro-ku, Tokoyo 153, Japan.
- American Review. irreg; 1973, no. 7. (Japanese
  Association of American Studies)

**University of Tokyo. College of General Education**
865 Komaba-cho, Meguro-ku, Tokyo 153, Japan.
- University of Tokyo. College of General
  Education. Scientific Papers/Tokyo Daigaku
  Kyoyogakubu Shizenkagaku Kiyo. s-a. ISSN
  0040-8964

**University of Tokyo. Computer Center**
2-11-6 Yayoi, Bunkyo-ku, Tokyo 113, Japan.
- University of Tokyo. Computer Center. Report. a.
  ISSN 0564-8742

**University of Tokyo. Department of Geography**
7-3-1 Hongo, Bunkyo-ku, Tokyo 113, Japan.
- University of Tokyo. Department of Geography.
  Bulletin/Tokyo Daigaku Chirigaku Kyoshitsu
  Kaiho. a. ISSN 0082-478X

**University of Tokyo. Earthquake Research Institute**
1-1-1 Yayoi, Bunkyo-ku, Tokyo 113, Japan.
- Seismological Society of Japan. Journal/Zisin. q.
  ISSN 0037-1114
- University of Tokyo. Earthquake Research
  Institute. Bulletin/Tokyo Daigaku Jishin
  Kenkyujo.

**University of Tokyo. Faculty of Engineering**
7-3-1 Hongo, Bunkyo-ku, Tokyo 113, Japan.
- University of Tokyo. Faculty of Engineering.
  Journal: Series B/Tokyo Daigakubu Kogakubu
  Kiyo, B. s-a. ISSN 0563-7937

**University of Tokyo. Faculty of Medicine**
7-3-1 Hongo, Bunkyo-ku, Tokyo 113, Japan.
- Japanese Heart Journal. bi-m. ISSN 0021-4868
  (prep. by its Department of Internal Medicine)

**University of Tokyo. Faculty of Science**
7-3-1 Hongo, Bunkyo-ku, Tokyo 113, Japan
(Order from: Maruzen Co., Ltd., 2-3-10 Nihonbashi,
Chuo-ku, Tokyo 103, Japan; or their Import and
Export Department, Box 5050, Tokyo International,
Tokyo 100-31, Japan)
- University of Tokyo. Faculty of Science. Journal.
  Section 1A: Mathematics/Tokyo Daigaku
  Rigakubu Kiyo, Dai-1-rui A, Sugaku. 3 per yr.
  ISSN 0040-8980
- University of Tokyo. Faculty of Science. Journal.
  Section 2: Geology, Mineralogy, Geography,
  Geophysics/Tokyo Daigaku Rigakubu Kiyo, Dai-
  2-rui, Chishitsugaku, Kobutsugaku, Chirigaku,
  Chiyu Butsurigaku. a. ISSN 0040-8999
- University of Tokyo. Faculty of Science. Journal.
  Section 3: Botany/Tokyo Daigaku Rigakubu Kiyo,
  Dai-3-rui, Shokubutsugaku. a.

- University of Tokyo. Faculty of Science. Journal.
  Section 4: Zoology/Tokyo Daigaku Rigakubu
  Kiyo Dai-4-rui, Dobutsugaku. a.
- University of Tokyo. Faculty of Science. Journal.
  Section 5: Anthropology/Tokyo Daigaku
  Rigakubu Kiyo, Dai-5-rui, Jinruigaku. a.

**University of Tokyo. Institute for Nuclear Study**
3-2-1 Midori-cho, Tanashi-shi, Tokyo 188, Japan.
- International Symposium on High Energy Physics.
  Proceedings. a.
- University of Tokyo. Institute for Nuclear Study.
  Annual Report. a.
- University of Tokyo. Institute for Nuclear Study.
  INS-J. irreg. ISSN 0495-7814
- University of Tokyo. Institute for Nuclear Study.
  INS-PH. irreg.
- University of Tokyo. Institute for Nuclear Study.
  INS-PT. irreg. ISSN 0563-7848
- University of Tokyo. Institute for Nuclear Study.
  INS-TCA. irreg. ISSN 0563-7856
- University of Tokyo. Institute for Nuclear Study.
  INS-TCB. irreg. ISSN 0563-7864
- University of Tokyo. Institute for Nuclear Study.
  INS-TCH. irreg.
- University of Tokyo. Institute for Nuclear Study.
  INS-TEC. irreg.
- University of Tokyo. Institute for Nuclear Study.
  INS-TH. irreg. ISSN 0563-7872
- University of Tokyo. Institute for Nuclear Study.
  INS-TL. irreg. ISSN 0563-7880
- University of Tokyo. Institute for Nuclear Study.
  INS-TS. irreg.
- University of Tokyo. Institute for Nuclear Study.
  Report. irreg. ISSN 0495-7822

**University of Tokyo. Institute for Solid State Physics**
7-22-1 Roppongi, Minato-ku, Tokyo 106, Japan.
- University of Tokyo. Institute for Solid State
  Physics. Technical Report. Series A. irreg.
  (approx. 60 issues per year), 1973, no. 622. ISSN
  0082-4798
- University of Tokyo. Institute for Solid State
  Physics. Technical Report. Series B. irreg.
  (approx. 1 no. per year), 1973, no. 15. ISSN
  0082-4801

**University of Tokyo. Institute of Applied
Microbiology**
1-1-1 Yayoi, Bunkyo-ku, Tokyo 113, Japan.
- University of Tokyo. Institute of Applied
  Microbiology. Reports. a. ISSN 0082-481X

**University of Tokyo. Institute of Industrial Science**
7-22-1 Roppongi, Minato-ku, Tokyo 106, Japan.
- Production Research/Seisan Kenkyu. m. ISSN
  0037-105X
- University of Tokyo. Institute of Industrial
  Science. Report/Tokyo Daigaku Seisan Gijutsu
  Kenkyusho Hokoku. 6-8 nos.per yr. ISSN 0040-
  9006

**University of Tokyo. Institute of Medical Science**
4-6-1 Shirokanedai, Minato-ku, Tokyo 108, Japan
- Japanese Journal of Experimental Medicine/
  Jikken Igaku Zasshi. bi-m. ISSN 0021-5031
  (Distr. by: Kinokuniya Book-Store Co., Ltd., 3-
  17-7 Shinjuku, Shinjuku-ku, Tokyo 160, Japan)
- Japanese Journal of Tuberculosis and Chest
  Diseases/Nippon Kekkaku Kyobushikka Zasshi. s-
  a. ISSN 0021-5279 (Association of the Research
  Institutes for Tuberculosis of National Universities
  in Japan)

**University of Tokyo. Institute of Social Science**
7-3-1 Hongo, Bunkyo-ku, Tokyo 113, Japan.
- Social Sciences Journal/Shakai Kagaku Kenkyu.
  (pub. by Yuhikaku Publishing Co. Ltd.)
- University of Tokyo. Institute of Social Science.
  Annals. a. ISSN 0563-8054

**University of Tokyo. Institute of Space and
Aeronautical Science**
3-7-6 Komaba, Meguro-ku, Tokyo 153, Japan.
- University of Tokyo. Institute of Space and
  Aeronautical Science. Report. irreg., 1970, vol.
  35, no. 15. ISSN 0082-4828

**University of Tokyo. Misaki Marine Biological
Station**
1024 Koajiro Misaki-cho, Miura-shi 238-02, Japan.
- University of Tokyo. Faculty of Science. Misaki
  Marine Biological Station. Contributions. a. ISSN
  0493-4334

**University of Tokyo. Ocean Research Institute**
1-15-1 Minamidai, Nakano-ku, Tokyo 164, Japan.
- University of Tokyo. Ocean Research Institute.
  Bulletin/Tokyo Daigaku Kaiyo Kenkyusho. irreg.
  ISSN 0564-6898

**University of Tokyo Press**
7-3-1 Hongo, Bunkyo-ku, Tokyo 113, Japan
- Advances in Biophysics. a. ISSN 0065-227X
  (Biophysical Society of Japan) (Dist. In. U.S. by
  University Park Press, Chamber of Commerce
  Bldg., Baltimore, MD 21202)
- Current Contents of Academic Journals in Japan.
  a. (Distributed in U.S. & Canada by ISBS, Inc.,
  P.O. Box 4347, Portland, OR 97208)
- Journal of Economics/Keizaigaku Ronshu. q.
  ISSN 0022-9768 (University of Tokyo Society of
  Economics)
- University of Tokyo. Research Institute of
  Logopedics and Phoniatrics. Annual Bulletin. a.
  ISSN 0564-7630

**University of Tokyo. Research Institute of Logopedics
and Phoniatrics**
- University of Tokyo. Research Institute of
  Logopedics and Phoniatrics. Annual Bulletin.
  (pub. by University of Tokyo Press)

**University of Tokyo. School of Medicine**
Dept. of Ophthalmology, 7-3-1- Hongo, Bunkyo-ku,
Tokyo 113, Japan.
- Japanese Journal of Ophthalmology. q. ISSN
  0021-5155

**University of Tokyo Society of Economics**
- Journal of Economics/Keizaigaku Ronshu. (pub.
  by University of Tokyo Press)

**University of Tokyo. Tokyo Astronomical
Observatory**
see Tokyo Astronomical Observatory

**Shigeo Urabe, Ed. & Pub.**
50 Okado-machi, Hachioji-shi, Tokyo, Japan.
- Japan Forum. q. ISSN 0024-127X

**Urasenke Foundation**
Ogawa Teranouchi Agaru, Kamikyo-ku, Kyoto 602,
Japan.
- Chanoyu; tea and the arts of Japan. q. ISSN 0009-
  1537 (Co-sponsor: Urasenke Foundation of
  Hawaii)

**Vitamin Society of Japan**
Japan Academic Societies Centre, 2-4-16 Yayoi,
Bunkyo-ku, Tokyo 113, Japan.
- Journal of Nutritional Science and Vitaminology.
  6 per yr. ISSN 0301-4800 (Co-sponsor: Japanese
  Society of Food and Nutrition)

**Volcanological Society of Japan**
c/o Earthquake Research Institute, University of
Tokyo, 1-1-1 Yayoi, Bunkyo-ku, Tokyo 113, Japan.
- Bulletin of Volcanic Eruptions. irreg.; no. 13,
  1975. ISSN 0525-1524 (Co-sponsor: International
  Association of Volcanology and Chemistry of the
  Earth's Interior)

**Vou**
8 chome, 13-24-406, Akasaka, Minato-ku, Tokyo
107, Japan.
- Vou. bi-m. ISSN 0042-8981

**Wakayama Chiho Kishodai**
see Wakayama Local Meteorological Observatory

**Wakayama Daigaku Keizai Gakkai**
see Wakayama University. Economic Society

**Wakayama Igakkai**
see Wakayama Medical Society

**Wakayama-kenritsu Ika Daigaku**
see Wakayama Medical College

**Wakayama Local Meteorological Observatory**
4 Onoshiba-cho, Wakayama 640, Japan.
- Wakayama Prefecture. Annual Report of
  Meteorology/Wakayama-ken Kisho Nenpo. a.
- Wakayama Prefecture. Monthly Report of
  Meteorology/Wakayama-ken Kisho Geppo. m.
  ISSN 0043-0021

**Wakayama Medical College**
Wakayama Medical College Library, Wakayama
640, Japan.
- Wakayama Medical Reports. q. ISSN 0511-084X

**Wakayama Medical Society**
c/o Wakayama Medical College, 9 Kyuban-cho,
Wakayama 640, Japan.
- Wakayama Medicine/Wakayama Igaku. q. ISSN
  0043-0013

**Wakayama University. Economic Society**
278 Sekido, Wakayama-shi, Japan.
- Economic Theory/Keizai Riron. 7 per yr. ISSN
  0451-6222

**Waksman Foundation of Japan**
c/o Keio Daigaku Igakubu, 30-8 Daikyo-machi,
Shinjuku-ku, Tokyo 106, Japan.
- Waksman Foundation of Japan. Report. a. ISSN
  0509-5832

**Waseda Daigaku**
see Waseda University

**Waseda Daigaku Imono Kenkyushitsu**
see Waseda University. Casting Research
Laboratory

**Waseda Daigaku Rikogaku Kenkyusho**
see Waseda University. Science and Engineering
Research Laboratory

**Waseda Daigaku Shakaigakkai**
c/o Waseda Daigaku Bungakubu, 42 Toyamacho,
Shinjuku-ku, Tokyo, Japan.
- Shakaigaku Nenshi.

**Waseda University. Casting Research Laboratory**
1-500 Totsuka-cho, Shinjuku-ku, Tokyo 160, Japan.
- Waseda University. Casting Research Laboratory.
  Report. a. ISSN 0511-1927

**Waseda University. Commercial Study Society**
Totsuka-machi, Shinjuku-ku, Tokyo 160, Japan.
- Waseda Commercial Review/Waseda Shogaku. 7
  per yr.

**Waseda University. Graduate Division of Commerce**
1-6-1 Nishi-Waseda, Shinjuku-ku, Tokyo 160, Japan.
- Waseda Business and Economic Studies. a.

**Waseda University. Graduate Division of Political
Science**
Totsuka-machi, Shinjuku-ku, Tokyo 160, Japan.
- Waseda Political Studies. irreg. ISSN 0511-196X

**Waseda University. Political and Economic Science
Society**
Totsuka-machi, Shinjuku-ku, Tokyo 160, Japan.
- Waseda Journal of Political Science and
  Economics/Waseda Seiji Keizagaku Zasshi. bi-m.

**Waseda University. School of Science and
Engineering**
4-170 Nishiokubo, Shinjuku-ku, Tokyo 160, Japan.
- Waseda University. School of Science and
  Engineering. Memoirs/Waseda Daigaku
  Rikogakubu Kiyo. a.

**Waseda University. Science and Engineering Research
Laboratory**
17 Kikui-cho, Shinjuku-ku, Tokyo 162, Japan.
- Waseda University. Science and Engineering
  Research Laboratory. Bulletin/Waseda Daigaku
  Rikogaku Kenkyusho Hokoku. m.
- Waseda University. Science and Engineering
  Research Laboratory. Report. irreg.

**Waseda University. Socio-Economic History Society**
- Socio-Economic History/Shakai Keizai Shigaku.
  (pub. by Yuhikaku Publishing Co. Ltd.)

**Water Research Institute**
see under Nagoya University

**Water Utilization Research Institute**
1-7-12 Koraku, Bunkyo-ku, Tokyo 112, Japan.
- Water Science/Suiri Kagaku. bi-m. ISSN 0039-
  4858

**West-Japanese Society of Orthopedics &
Traumatology**
c/o Dept. of Orthopedic Surgery, Kyushu
University, 1276 Katakasu, Fukuoka 812, Japan.
- Orthopedics and Traumatology/Seikei Geka to
  Saigai Geka. s-a. ISSN 0037-1033

**Whales Research Institute**
1-3-1 Etchujima, Kota-ku, Tokyo 135, Japan.
- Whales Research Institute, Tokyo, Japan.
  Scientific Reports/Geirui Kenkyusho Eibun
  Hokoku. a. ISSN 0083-9086

**Women Eros**
6-205 Yagawa-kita, 6665 Yaho, Kunitachi City,
Tokyo, Japan.
- Women Eros/Onna Eros. q.

**Wood Research Institute**
Kyoto University, Gokansho, Uji, Kyoto 611, Japan.
- Wood Research/Mokuzai Kenkyu. s-a. ISSN
  0049-7916

**Wood Technological Association of Japan**
1-1-23 Shiba Daimon, Minato-ku, Tokyo 105,
Japan.
- Wood Industry/Mokuzai Kogyo. m. ISSN 0026-
  8917

**World Economic Information Services**
WTC Bldg., 2-4-1 Hamamatsu-cho, Minato-ku,
Tokyo 105, Japan.
- Economic Information File: Japan. biennial.

**World Petroleum Congress. Japanese National
Committee**
Kasahara Bldg., 1-6-10 Uchi Kanda, Chiyoda-ku,
Tokyo 101, Japan.
- Petroleum Industry in Japan. a.

**World Trade Center of Japan, Inc.**
Box 57, 2-4-1 Hamamatsu-cho, Minato-ku, Tokyo
105, Japan.
- World Traders. q. (World Trade Centers
  Association of Japan)

**World Trade Centers Association of Japan**
- World Traders. (pub. by World Trade Center of
  Japan, Inc.)

**World United Formosans for Independence**
Mannen Bldg. No. 33, Tomihisacho, Shinjukuku,
Tokyo 168, Japan.
- Taiwan Chenglian. m. ISSN 0039-9094

**Yakugaku Kenkyusho**
see Pharmaceutical Research Institute

**Yakugyo Jiho Co. Ltd.**
2-36 Kanda Jinbo-cho, Chiyoda-ku, Tokyo 101,
Japan.
- Pharma; Japan drug industry news. s-w.
- Pharmaceutical Monthly/Gekkan Yakuji. m. ISSN
  0016-5980 (Pharmaceutical Research Association)

**Yakugyo Kenkyukai**
see Pharmaceutical Research Association

**Yakuji Nippo Ltd.**
1 Kanda Izumicho, Chiyoda-ku, Tokyo 101, Japan.
- J A P T A List: Japanese Drug Directory. irreg.
  (Japan Pharmaceutical Traders' Association)
- Japan Medical Gazette. m. ISSN 0021-4507

**Yakuji Nyususha**
c/o Indo Bldg., Dosho-machi, Higashi-ku, Osaka
541, Japan.
- Doctor. w.

**Yama-to-Keikoku Sha Co. Ltd.**
1-1-33 Shiba Daimon, Minato-ku, Tokyo 105,
Japan.
- Sangaku Shashin Nenkan.

**Yamagata University**
Main Library, 1-4-12 Koshirakawa-machi, Yamagata
City, Japan.
- Yamagata University. Bulletin. a. ISSN 0085-
  834X

**Yamaguchi Daigaku**
see Yamaguchi University

**Yamaguchi University. Faculty of Engineering**
Tokiwadai, Ube-shi 755, Japan.
- Yamaguchi University. Faculty of Engineering.
  Technology Reports. a.

**Yamaguchi University. School of Medicine**
Kogushi, Ube-Shi 755, Japan.
- Yamaguchi Medical School. Bulletin/Yamaguchi
  Daigaku Igakubu Kiyo. 4 per yr.

**Yamanouchi Pharmaceutical Co. Ltd.**
2-5 Nihonbashi Hon-cho, Chuo-ku, Tokyo 103,
Japan.
- Pharmacy Companion/Yakkyoku No Tomo. m.
  ISSN 0044-0043

**Yamanouchi Seiyaku K. K., Ltd.**
*see* Yamanouchi Pharmaceutical Co.

**Yamashina Institute for Ornithology**
8-20 Nampeidai-machi, Shibuya-ku, Tokyo 150, Japan.
- Yamashina Institute for Ornithology. Miscellaneous Reports/Yamashina Chorui Kenkyusho Hokoku. s-a. ISSN 0044-0183

**Yogyo Kyokai**
*see* Yamanouchi Pharmaceutical Co., Ltd.

**Yokendo Ltd.**
5-30-15 Hongo, Bunkyo-ku, Tokyo 113, Japan.
- Animal Husbandry/Chikusan No Kenkyu. m. ISSN 0009-3874

**Yokkaichi. Yokkaichi City Library**
1-2-42 Kubota, Yokkaichi, Mie 510, Japan.
- Industrial and Technological Information of Yokkaichi City/Sangyo Gijutsu Joho Yokkaichi. m. ISSN 0036-4371

**Yokkaichi-shiritsu Toshokan**
*see* Yokkaichi. Yokkaichi City Library

**Yokohama. Port and Harbor Bureau**
Industry and Trade Center Bldg., Yamashita-cho, Nakaku, Yokohama, Japan.
- Guide to the Port of Yokohama. irreg.
- Port of Yokohama. Annual Report. a.
- Port of Yokohama. Monthly Statistics. m. ISSN 0032-4876

**Yokohama City University. Department of Mathematics**
4646 Mutsuura-cho, Kanazawa-ku, Yokohama 236, Japan.
- Yokohama Mathematical Journal. s-a. ISSN 0044-0523

**Yokohama City University. School of Medicine**
2-33 Urafune-cho, Minami-ku, Yokohama 232, Japan.
- Yokohama Medical Bulletin. bi-m. ISSN 0044-0531

**Yokohama Kokuritsu Daigaku**
*see* Yokohama National University

**Yokohama National University. Department of Sociology**
41 Shimizugaoka, Minami-ku, Yokohama 232, Japan.
- Yokohama National University. Humanities. Section 1: Philosophy and Social Sciences/ Yokohama Kokuritsu Daigaku Jimbun Kiyo Dai-1-rui, Tetsugaku, Shakai Kagaku. a. ISSN 0513-5621

**Yokohama National University. Faculty of Education**
Library, Tokiwadai 156, Hodogaya-ku, Yokohama 240, Japan.
- Yokohama National University. Science Reports. Section I: Mathematics, Physics, Chemistry/ Yokohama Kokuritsu Daigaku Rika Kiyo, Dai-1-rui, Sugaku, Butsurigaku, Kagaku. a. ISSN 0085-8366
- Yokohama National University. Science Reports. Section II: Biological Sciences/Yokohama Kokuritsu Daigaku Rika Kiyo, Dai-2-rui, Seibutsugaku, Chigaku. a. ISSN 0513-5613

**Yokohama National University. Faculty of Engineering**
2-31-1 Ooka, Minami-ku, Yokohama-shi 233, Japan.
- Yokohama National University. Faculty of Engineering. Bulletin/Yokohama Kokuritsu Daigaku Kogakubu Kiyo. a. ISSN 0513-2592

**Yokohama National University. Society for Economics and Business Administration**
156 Tokiwadai, Hodogayaku, Yokohama, Japan.
- Economia. q. ISSN 0012-9712

**Yokohama Plant Protection Station**
*see* Japan. Yokohama Plant Protection Station

**Yokohama-shiritsu Daigaku**
*see* Yokohama City University

**Yokufukai Geriatric Hospital**
1-12-1 Nishi Takaido, Suginami-ku, Tokyo 168, Japan.
- Acta Gerontologica Japonica/Yokufukai Chosa Kenkyu Kiyo. a. ISSN 0001-5768

**Yonago Igakkai**
*see* Yonago Medical Association

**Yonago Medical Association**
Tottori University School of Medicine, 86 Nishi-machi, Yonago 683, Japan.
- Yonago Medical Association. Journal/Yonago Igaku Zasshi. bi-m. ISSN 0044-0558

**Yosetsu Gakkai**
*see* Japan Welding Society

**Young East Association**
- Young East. (pub. by Tohokai, Inc.)

**Yubin Chokin Shinkokai Shuppanbu**
6-19 Azabudai, Minato-ku, Tokyo 106, Japan.
- Yubin Chokin. m.

**Yugyo Hochi Shinbunsha**
2-15-19 Shinkawa, Chuo-ku, Tokyo 104, Japan.
- Monthly Journal of Gasoline Service Stations/ Gekkan Kyusho Nihon. m. ISSN 0016-5964

**Yuhikaku Publishing Co. Ltd.**
2-17 Kanda Jimbo-cho, Chiyoda-ku, Tokyo 101, Japan.
- Annales Criminologie Japonicae/Hanzai Gaku Nenpo. a. ISSN 0517-8460
- Comparative Law Journal/Hikaku Ho Kenkyo. s-a. ISSN 0439-1365 (Japanese Society of Comparative Law)
- Nihon Kyoikuho Gakkai Nempo. a.
- Public Law Review/Koho Kenkyu. q. (Japan Public Law Association)
- Social Sciences Journal/Shakai Kagaku Kenkyu. bi-m. (University of Tokyo. Institute of Social Science)
- Socio-Economic History/Shakai Keizai Shigaku. bi-m. (Waseda University. Socio-Economic History Society)

**Yuki Gosei Kagaku Kyokai**
*see* Society of Synthetic Organic Chemistry

**Yukijirushi Nyugyo K. K.**
*see* Snow Brand Milk Products Co. Ltd.

**Yuri Shuppan**
26-10 Hongo, Bunkyo-ku, Tokyo 113, Japan.
- Nihon No Minken Kyoiku. q. ISSN 0302-0282 (Nihon Minkan Kyoiku Kenkyu Dantai Renrakukai)

**Yusei-sho Denpa Kenkyusho**
*see* Japan. Ministry of Posts and Telecommunications. Radio Research Laboratories

**Yushodo Booksellers Ltd.**
29 Sanei-cho, Shinjuku-ku, Tokyo 160, Japan.
- Hon: a Book-Bin for Scholars. q. ISSN 0046-7839

**Zaikeo Shoho Sha**
1-2-14 Higashi Shimbashi, Minato-ku, Tokyo, Japan (Dist. in U.S. by Fred B. Rothman & Co., 57 Leuning St., South Hackensack, NJ 07606)
- Guide to Japanese Taxes. a. ISSN 0072-8551

**Zen-chu**
*see* Central Union of Agricultural Co-operatives

**Zen Kokutetsu Shinshosa Kyokai**
*see* Handicapped Persons Association of Japan National Railways

**Zenkoku Kensetsu Gyomukai**
*see* Associated General Contractors of Japan Inc.

**Zenkoku Shakai Fukushi Kyogikai**
*see* National Council of Social Welfare

**Zenkoku Shinrin Byochu Jugai Bojo Kyokai**
c/o Kobu Bldg., 1-1-12 Uchi-Kanda, Chiyoda-ku, Tokyo 100, Japan.
- Forest Protection/Shinrin Boeki. (Japan. Forestry Agency)

**Zinbum Kagata Kenkynsyo**
*see* Kyoto University. Research Institute for Humanistic Studies

**Zisin Gakkai**
*see* Seismological Society of Japan

**Zoological Society of Japan**
c/o Oriental Library, 2-28-21 Honkomagome, Tokyo 113, Japan.
- Annotationes Zoologica Japonenses/Nippon Dobutsugaku Iho. q. ISSN 0003-5092
- Zoological Magazine/Dobutsugaku Zasshi. m. ISSN 0044-5118

# JORDAN

**Amman in the Evening**
Box 522, Amman, Jordan.
- Amman in the Evening/Amman-al Masa'a. w.

**Catholic Bureau of Press and Publication**
Box 1317, Amman, Jordan.
- Voice of the Holy Land/Sawt El-Ard El-Mukaddash. m.

**Central Bank of Jordan**
Box 37, Amman, Jordan.
- Central Bank of Jordan. Annual Report/Bank Al-Markazi Al-Urduni. Annual Report. a. ISSN 0069-1550 (prep. by its Department of Research and Studies)
- Central Bank of Jordan. Monthly Statistical Bulletin. m. (prep. by its Department of Research and Studies)

**Club of Arts Amateurs**
Box 6370, Amman, Jordan.
- Arts Amateurs/Huwat Al-Funoun. m.

**General Federation of the Labourers Union**
Box 1065, Amman, Jordan.
- Voice of Jordanian Labourers/Sawt Ummal Al-Urdon. m.

**Jordan**
Box 6194, Amman, Jordan.
- Jordan/Urdon. w.

**Jordan. Armed Forces**
Army Headquarters, Amman, Jordan.
- Military Journal/Majallah Al-Askariyyah. q.

**Jordan. Department of Agricultural Marketing**
Box 2097, Amman, Jordan.
- Agricultural Marketing/Taswiq Al-Ziraiy. q.

**Jordan. Department of Culture and Arts**
Box 6140, Amman, Jordan.
- Ideas/Afkar. bi-m.

**Jordan. Department of Statistics**
Amman, Jordan.
- Jordan. Department of Statistics. Agricultural Statistical Yearbook and Agricultural Sample Survey. a.
- Jordan. Department of Statistics. Annual Statistical Yearbook. a. ISSN 0075-4013
- Jordan. Department of Statistics. Consumer Price Index. m.
- Jordan. Department of Statistics. Employment Survey for Establishments Engaging Five Persons or More. 3 per yr.
- Jordan. Department of Statistics. External Trade Statistics. a. ISSN 0075-4021
- Jordan. Department of Statistics. External Trade Statistics and Shipping Activities in Aqaba Port. q. ISSN 0449-1483
- Jordan. Department of Statistics. Hotel Statistics. a.
- Jordan. Department of Statistics. Morbidity Statistics. a.
- Jordan. Department of Statistics. Multi-Purpose Household Survey. a.
- Jordan. Department of Statistics. National Accounts. a. ISSN 0449-1513
- Jordan Economy in Figures. m. ISSN 0449-1491

**Jordan. Ministry of Agriculture**
Box 2178, Amman, Jordan.
- Agriculture in Jordan/Zira'at Fi El-Urdon. q.

**Jordan. Ministry of Culture and Information**
Amman, Jordan.
- Development/Tanmiyah. m.

**Jordan. Ministry of Education**
Educational Publications Division, Amman, Jordan.
- Message of the Teacher/Risalat al-Mu'allim. q. ISSN 0040-0505

**Jordan. Ministry of Health**
Amman, Jordan.
- Health/Sihhah. m.

**Jordan. Ministry of National Economy**
Box 2019, Amman, Jordan.
- Jordanian Economy/Iktisad Al-Urdony. m.

**Jordan. Ministry of National Economy. Department of Agricultural Marketing**
*see* Jordan. Department of Agricultural Marketing

**Jordan. Ministry of Tourism & Antiquities**
Box 224, Amman, Jordan.
- Jordan. Ministry of Tourism and Antiquities. Travel Statistics. a.
- Jordan Tourism Bulletin. m.
- Jordan Tourism Magazine/Assiyaha al Urdiniah. s-a.
- Jordan Travel News. m.
- Tourism Research Bulletin/Nashrat el-Abhath el Siahiyah. q.

**Jordan Bar Association**
Box 588, Amman, Jordan.
- Syndicate of Lawyers/Nakabat-Ul-Muhamin. m.

**Jordan Cooperative Organization**
Box 1343, Amman, Jordan.
- Voice of Cooperation/Sawt Ul-Ta'wun. m.

**Jordan Library Association**
Box 6289, Amman, Jordan.
- Message of the Library/Risalat al-Maktaba. q.

**Jordan Medical Association**
Box 915, Amman, Jordan.
- Jordan Medical Journal/Majallat-Al-Tibbiyyal Al-Urdoniyyah. s-a. (Co-sponsor: Royal Jordanian Medical Services)

**Jordan University. Accounting Society**
Amman, Jordan.
- Colours/Alwan. m.

**Jordan University. Department of Information & Public Relations**
Box 1682, Amman, Jordan.
- Jordan University Newsletter/Anba Al-Jamiah. fortn.

**Jordan University. Economic Studies Society**
Amman, Jordan.
- Economic Journal/Majallat El-Iktissadiyyah. m.

**Jordan University. Public Administration and Political Sciences Society**
Amman, Jordan.
- Debate/Hiwar. m.

**Jordanian Youth and Sports Organization**
Box 1794, Amman, Jordan.
- Youth/Shabab. m.

**Labour Culture Institution**
Box 9137, Amman, Jordan.
- Labour Culture/Thakafat Al-Ummaliyyah. m.

**League of Islamic Sciences**
Box 1829, Amman, Jordan.
- Theology/Sharia. m.

**Abdul Hafez Mohammad, Ed. & Pub.**
Box 605, Amman, Jordan.
- News of the Week/Akhbar-Al-Usbou. w.

**Morning**
Box 2396, Amman, Jordan.
- Morning/Sabah. w.

**Psychiatry Association**
Box 1317, Amman, Jordan.
- Psychiatry Journal/Majallat-Al-Sihhah Al-Nafsiyyah. bi-m.

**Student's Message**
Box 2087, Amman, Jordan.
- Student's Message/Risalat al-Talib. m.

# KENYA

**Africa Bibliographic Center**
Box 5089, Nairobi, Kenya.
- A B C Newsletter. irreg., no. 7, 1975.

**Africa Inland Mission**
- Africa Ya Kesho. (pub. by Kesho Publications)
- Kesho. (pub. by Kesho Publications)
- Today. (pub. by Kesho Publications)

**Amecea Pastoral Institute**
- A F E R. (pub. by Gaba Publications)

**Architectural Association of Kenya**
- Build Kenya. (pub. by Peter Moll Africa Ltd.)

**Automobile Association of East Africa**
- Official Touring Guide to East Africa. (pub. by News Publishers Ltd.)

**T.A. Bhatt, Ed. & Pub.**
Box 41237, Nairobi, Kenya.
- Africa Samachar. w. ISSN 0001-9860

**British Institute of History & Archaeology in East Africa**
P.O. Box 30710, Nairobi, Kenya.
- Azania. a. ISSN 0067-270X

**Central Bank of Kenya**
Box 30463, Nairobi, Kenya.
- Central Bank of Kenya. Annual Report. a. ISSN 0069-1569
- Central Bank of Kenya. Economic and Financial Review. q.

**Cibis Publishers**
Box 10028, Nairobi, Kenya.
- Kenya Review. 3 per yr.

**Commercial Syndicate Ltd.**
P.O. Box 48057, Nairobi, Kenya.
- Children's Own. fortn.

**Corcoran & Tyrrell Ltd.**
Box 44365, Nairobi, Kenya.
- Kenya Media Advertising Review. irreg.

**Development Finance Company of Kenya**
P.O. Box 30483, Bima House, Nairobi, Kenya.
- Industry in Kenya. bi-m.

**East Africa Natural History Society**
c/o Library, Box 40656, Nairobi, Kenya.
- E A N H S Bulletin. m.

**East Africa Womens League**
- Women in Kenya. (pub. by English Press)

**East African Academy**
Research Information and Publications Services, Box 47288, Nairobi, Kenya.
- E A R I C Information Circular. irreg. ISSN 0070-8011 (East African Research Information Centre)
- East African Academy. Foundation Lectures. irreg, no. 6, 1974.
- East African Academy. Proceedings. irreg. ISSN 0070-7945

**East African Agricultural and Forestry Research Organization**
Box 30148, Nairobi, Kenya.
- East African Agricultural and Forestry Journal. q. ISSN 0012-8325

**East African Community. Statistical Department**
Box 30462, Nairobi, Kenya.
- East African Community. Economic and Statistical Review. q. ISSN 0012-9992
- Statistical Survey of the East African Community Institutions. a; latest vol. 1974 per 75.

**East African Directory Company**
P.O. Box 41237, Nairobi, Kenya.
- Kenya, Uganda, Tanzania, East African Community Directory; Trade Commerce Index. irreg.

**East African Harbours Corporation**
P.O. Box 95009, Mombasa, Kenya.
- Gateways of Eastern Africa. bi-m.

**East African High Commission. Customs and Excise Department**
Box 90601, Mombasa, Kenya.
- Annual Trade Report of Tanzania, Uganda and Kenya. a.
- Monthly Trade Statistics for Tanzania, Uganda and Kenya. m.

**East African Institute of Social and Cultural Affairs**
Box 30492, Nairobi, Kenya.
- Contemporary African Monographs. irreg. ISSN 0069-9330
- East Africa Journal. m.

**East African Literature Bureau**
P.O. Box 30022, Nairobi, Kenya.
- African Review; a journal of African politics, development and international affairs. q. ISSN 0002-0117 (University of Dar es Salaam. Department of Political Science TZ)
- Dhana. s-a. (Makerere University. Department of Literature UG)
- East African Journal of Medical Research. q. ISSN 0302-4261 (East African Medical Research Council)
- Eastern Africa Economic Review. s-a. ISSN 0012-866X
- Eastern Africa Law Review; a journal of law and development. 3 per yr. ISSN 0012-8678
- Education in Eastern Africa. s-a. ISSN 0046-1423 (Regional Council for Education)
- Johari za Kiswahili. irreg, vol. 13, 1975. ISSN 0449-0738
- Journal of Eastern African Research & Development. s-a.
- Kenya Historical Review. s-a. (Historical Association of Kenya)
- Kenyan Geographer. s-a. (Geographical Society of Kenya)
- Language Association of Eastern Africa. Journal. s-a. ISSN 0023-8325
- Makerere Historical Journal. s-a. (Makerere University. Department of History UG)
- Maktaba. s-a. ISSN 0070-7988 (Kenya Library Association)
- Pan-African Journal. q. ISSN 0031-0565 (Pan-African Institute US)
- Someni. s-a. ISSN 0038-1292 (Tanzania Library Association TZ)
- Thought and Practice. s-a. (Philosophical Association of Kenya)
- Umma; a magazine of original writing. 2 per yr. ISSN 0011-6696 (University of Dar es Salaam. Department of Literature TZ)
- Utafiti. (University of Dar es Salaam. Faculty of Arts and Social Science TZ)

**East African Medical Research Council**
- East African Journal of Medical Research. (pub. by East African Literature Bureau)

**East African Publishing House**
Box 30571, Lusaka Close, off Lusaka Rd., Nairobi, Kenya.
- East African Studies. irreg. ISSN 0424-0928 (Makerere University. East African Institute of Social Research UG)
- Historical Association of Tanzania. Papers. irreg. ISSN 0440-9264
- Peoples of East Africa.
- Transafrican Journal of History. 2 per yr. ISSN 0041-106X

**East African Research Information Centre**
- E A R I C Information Circular. (pub. by East African Academy)

**East African Staff College**
Box 30005, Nairobi, Kenya.
- Some Current Research in East Africa. irreg.

**East African Standard (Newspapers) Ltd.**
Box 30080, Nairobi, Kenya.
- Baraza. w. ISSN 0005-5875

**East African Venture Co.**
Box 72839, Tom Mboya St., Nairobi, Kenya.
- Target. w. ISSN 0039-9655

**Embassy of the Arab Republic of Egypt**
Press Office, Box 30285, Nairobi, Kenya.
- Voice of Egypt. irreg.

**English Press**
Box 30127, Nairobi, Kenya.
- Nairobi Handbook. m. ISSN 0047-8636
- Women in Kenya. q. ISSN 0049-7800 (East Africa Womens League)

**Equatorial Publishers Ltd.**
Mercury House, Rm. No. 11 & 12, 2nd Fl., Victoria St., Nairobi, Kenya.
- Kenya Teacher Journal. q. ISSN 0023-0464 (Kenya National Union of Teachers)

**Family Planning Association of Kenya**
Phoenix House, Kenyatta Ave., Box 30581, Nairobi, Kenya.
- Family Planning Association of Kenya. Annual Report. a.

**Gaba Publications**
Box 908, Eldoret, Kenya.
- A F E R. (African Ecclesiastical Review) bi-m. ISSN 0001-1134 (Amecea Pastoral Institute)

**Geographical Society of Kenya**
- Kenyan Geographer. (pub. by East African Literature Bureau)

**D. A. Hawkins Ltd.**
Box 2768, Nairobi, Kenya.
- Kenya Weekly News. w. ISSN 0023-0472

**Historical Association of Kenya**
- Kenya Historical Review. (pub. by East African Literature Bureau)

**Industrial Development Bank Limited**
Bima House, P.O. Box 44036, Nairobi, Kenya.
- Industrial Development Bank Limited. Annual Report and Accounts. a; latest 1975.

**International Centre of Insect Physiology and Ecology**
Box 30772, Nairobi, Kenya.
- African Scientist and Technology.
- International Centre of Insect Physiology and Ecology. Annual Report. a.

**International Council on Archives. East and Central African Regional Branch**
c/o Kenya National Archives, Jogoo House "A", P.O. Box 30520, Nairobi, Kenya.
- E C A R B I C A Journal. s-a.
- International Council on Archives. East and Central Africa Regional Branch. General Conference Proceedings. irreg.

**International Planned Parenthood Federation. Africa Regional Office**
Box 30234, Nairobi, Kenya.
- Africa-Link. q.

**Kenya. Board of Adult Education**
Box 30117, Nairobi, Kenya.
- Kenya Journal of Adult Education. 4 per yr. ISSN 0047-3340

**Kenya. Central Bureau of Statistics**
Ministry of Finance and Planning, Box 30266, Nairobi, Kenya
(Orders to: Government Printing and Stationery Office, Box 30128, Nairobi, Kenya)
- Kenya. Central Bureau of Statistics. Agricultural Census (Large Farm Areas)
- Kenya. Central Bureau of Statistics. Development Estimates. a.
- Kenya. Central Bureau of Statistics. Directory of Industries. irreg., latest 1974.
- Kenya. Central Bureau of Statistics. Economic Survey. a.
- Kenya. Central Bureau of Statistics. Employment and Earnings in the Modern Sector. a, latest 1972 per 73.
- Kenya. Central Bureau of Statistics. Estimates of Recurrent Expenditures. a.
- Kenya. Central Bureau of Statistics. Estimates of Revenue Expenditures. a.
- Kenya. Central Bureau of Statistics. Migration and Tourism Statistics. irreg., latest 1973 (covers 1968-71)
- Kenya. Central Bureau of Statistics. Register of Manufacturing Firms. irreg.
- Kenya. Central Bureau of Statistics. Statistical Abstract. a.
- Kenya Statistical Digest. q. ISSN 0453-6002
- Social Perspectives. irreg. (prep. by its Social Statistics Section)

**Kenya. Coffee Board**
Plantation House, Haile Selassie Ave., Box 30566, Nairobi, Kenya.
- Kenya Coffee. m.

**Kenya. Dairy Board**
Nairobi, Kenya.
- Kenya. Dairy Board. Annual Report. a. ISSN 0453-5944

**Kenya. Director of Aerodromes**
P.O. Box 19001, Nairobi, Kenya.
- Nairobi Airport. Annual Report. a. ISSN 0077-2666

**Kenya. Government Printing and Stationery Department**
P.O. Box 30128, Nairobi, Kenya.
- Kenya. Government Printing and Stationery Department. Catalogue of Government Publications. a. or biennial.
- Kenya. Ministry of Education. Annual Report. a, latest 1974. ISSN 0075-5869
- Kenya. Ministry of Housing. Annual Report. a.
- Kenya. Public Accounts Committee. Annual Report. a; latest 1974 per 75. ISSN 0075-5931
- Kenya. Public Service Commission. Annual Report. a. ISSN 0075-594X

**Kenya. Mines and Geological Department**
Box 30009, Nairobi, Kenya
(Orders to: Government Printing and Stationery Department, Box 30128, Nairobi, Kenya)
- Kenya. Mines and Geological Department. Annual Report. a. ISSN 0075-580X

**Kenya. Ministry of Commerce and Industry**
Nairobi, Kenya.
- Guide to Industrial Investment. irreg.

**Kenya. Ministry of Finance and Planning**
Box 30007, Nairobi, Kenya
(Orders to: Government Printing and Stationery Department, Box 30128, Nairobi, Kenya)
- Kenya. Ministry of Finance and Planning. Budget Speech by Minister for Finance and Planning. a.

**Kenya. Ministry of Finance and Planning. Central Bureau of Statistics**
*see* **Kenya. Central Bureau of Statistics**

**Kenya. Ministry of Information and Broadcasting**
Box 30025, Nairobi, Kenya.
- Inside Kenya Today. q. ISSN 0020-1863
- Kenya. Ministry of Information and Broadcasting. Annual Report. a. (Orders to: Government Printing and Stationery Department, Box 30128, Nairobi, Kenya)

**Kenya. Ministry of Tourism and Wildlife**
Box 30027, Nairobi, Kenya.
- Kenya Fisheries Reports. irreg.

**Kenya. National Housing Corporation**
Box 30257, Nairobi, Kenya.
- Kenya. National Housing Corporation. Annual Report. a.

**Kenya. National Irrigation Board**
Lenana Rd., P.O. Box 30372, Nairobi, Kenya.
- Kenya. National Irrigation Board. Reports and Accounts. irreg; latest issue, 1973-74. ISSN 0075-5915

**Kenya. National Library Service Board**
P.O. Box 30573, Nairobi, Kenya.
- Kenya. National Library Service Board. Annual and Audit Report. a. ISSN 0075-5923

**Kenya. National Museum**
Box 40658, Nairobi, Kenya.
- Journal of the East Africa Natural History Society and National Museum. s-a. ISSN 0012-8317 (Co-sponsor: East Africa Natural History Society)

**Kenya Education Journal**
Box 2768, Nairobi, Kenya.
- Kenya Education Journal. q. ISSN 0023-0413

**Kenya Institute of Administration**
P.O. Lower Kabete, Nairobi, Kenya.
- K I A Occasional Papers. irreg., 1970, no. 3. ISSN 0075-5761
- Kenya Institute of Administration. Journal. a. ISSN 0065-1966

**Kenya Library Association**
- Maktaba. (pub. by East African Literature Bureau)

**Kenya Medical Association**
Box 41632, Nairobi, Kenya.
- East African Medical Journal. m. ISSN 0012-835X

**Kenya Museum Society**
c/o National Museum, P.O. Box 40658, Nairobi, Kenya.
- Kenya Past and Present. irreg.

**Kenya National Chamber of Commerce and Industry**
Nairobi, Kenya.
- Kenya National Chamber of Commerce and Industry. Annual Report. a.

**Kenya National Union of Teachers**
- Kenya Teacher Journal. (pub. by Equatorial Publishers Ltd.)

**Kenya Press Centre**
Box 44464, Nairobi, Kenya.
- Mambo. fortn.

**Kenya Railways**
Box 30121, Nairobi, Kenya.
- Kenrail. m.

**Kesho Publications**
Box 60, Kijabe, Kenya.
- Africa Ya Kesho. m. (Africa Inland Mission)
- Kesho. m. ISSN 0023-0723 (Africa Inland Mission)
- Today. m. ISSN 0040-8387 (Africa Inland Mission)

**Language Association of Eastern Africa**
- Language Association of Eastern Africa. Journal. (pub. by East African Literature Bureau)

**Marketing & Publishing Ltd.**
Tom Mboya St., Box 49010, Nairobi, Kenya.
- Africana. q. ISSN 0002-0281

**Medical Research Centre**
Box 20752, Nairobi, Kenya.
- Medical Research Centre, Nairobi. Annual Report. a. ISSN 0076-5988

**Peter Moll Africa Ltd.**
Box 40106, Nairobi, Kenya.
- Build Kenya. m. (Architectural Association of Kenya)

**Nation Newspapers Ltd.**
Nation House, Tom Mboya St., Box 49010, Nairobi, Kenya.
- Daily Nation. d.
- Sunday Nation. w.
- Taifa Leo. d.
- Taifa Weekly. w.

**National Housing Corporation**
*see* **Kenya. National Housing Corporation**

**National Nurses Association of Kenya**
P.O. Box 49422, Nairobi, Kenya.
- Kenya Nursing Journal. s-a. ISSN 0301-0333

**Nelson Africa Ltd.**
Box 73146, Nairobi, Kenya.
- Musical Instruments of East Africa. irreg.

**News Publishers Ltd.**
P.O. Box 30339, Nairobi, Kenya.
- Official Touring Guide to East Africa. a. ISSN 0078-3897 (Automobile Association of East Africa)
- Safari; tourist magazine for East Africa. bi-m. ISSN 0036-2352

**Newspread International**
Box 46854, Nairobi, Kenya.
- New Era; the magazine for young Kenyans. 9 per yr. ISSN 0028-5013
- Uhuru Kenya Yearbook. a.

**Oxford University Press (East African Branch)**
Box 72532, Nairobi, Kenya.
- Gandhi Memorial Lectures. irreg., 1969, series 1. ISSN 0072-0143
- Studies in the Development of African Resources. irreg.

**Philosophical Association of Kenya**
- Thought and Practice. (pub. by East African Literature Bureau)

**Police Training College**
P.O. Kiganjo, Kenya.
- Kenya Police Review. q. ISSN 0023-0448

**Pyrethrum Bureau**
Pyrethrum Board of Kenya, Box 420, Nakuru, Kenya.
- Pyrethrum Post. s-a. ISSN 0048-6043

**Regional Council for Education**
- Education in Eastern Africa. (pub. by East African Literature Bureau)

**Salvation Army**
Box 40575, Nairobi, Kenya.
- Sauti Ya Vita. m.

**Shia Imami Ismailia Association for Kenya**
Box 30606, Nairobi, Kenya.
- Africa Ismaili. w.

**Tea Research Institute of East Africa**
Box 91, Kericho, Kenya.
- Tea in East Africa. s-a.

**Transafrica Publishers Ltd.**
Box 42990, Nairobi, Kenya.
- Transafrica Historical Papers. irreg.

**Unesco. Regional Office of Science and Technology for Africa**
For publications of this agency see section for UNITED NATIONS

**United Africa Press Ltd.**
Box 1237, Nairobi, Kenya.
- Industry in East Africa. a. ISSN 0073-781X

**United Nations Environment Programme**
For publications of this agency see section for UNITED NATIONS

**University of Nairobi. Institute for Development Studies**
Box 30197, Nairobi, Kenya.
- University of Nairobi. Institute for Development Studies. Occasional Paper. irreg.; latest issue, 1974.
- University of Nairobi. Institute for Development Studies. Research and Publications. a.

**University of Nairobi. Library**
Box 30197, Nairobi, Kenya.
- Periodicals in Eastern African Libraries: a Union List. biennial.

# KOREA, NORTH

**Central Committee of the Union of Agricultural Working People of Korea**
Pyonggang, N. Korea.
- Agricultural Working People of Korea. m.

**Foreign Trade Publishing House**
Oesong District, Pyonggang, N. Korea.
- Foreign Trade of the Democratic People's Republic of Korea. m.

**General Federation of Trade Unions of Korea. Central Committee**
Pyongyang, N. Korea.
- Korean Trade Unions. m. ISSN 0454-4196

**Jeon la Bug-do Gyo Yug Yeon Gu Won**
(Jeon la Bug-do Education Research Institute), Jeon Ju, N. Korea.
- Yeon-Gu Weolbo. m. ISSN 0044-0345

**Korean Association for Conservation of Nature**
Pyongyang, N. Korea.
- Korean Nature. q. ISSN 0023-4036

**Korean Democratic Women's Union. Central Committee**
Pyongyang, N. Korea.
- Women of Korea. bi-m. ISSN 0512-1817

**Philatelists Union of the Democratic People's Republic of Korea**
Pyongyang, N. Korea.
- Korean Stamps. m. ISSN 0452-5914

# KOREA, SOUTH

**Academy of Korean Studies**
Yonsei University, Box 3410, Seoul, S. Korea.
- Korea Observer. q. ISSN 0023-3919

**American Studies Association of Korea**
c/o Hankuk University of Foreign Studies, Seoul, S. Korea.
- Papers of American Studies. s-a.

**American Women's Club of Korea**
Mrs. Ross D. James, I.P.O. Box 1825, Seoul, S. Korea.
- A W C Journal.

**Asian and Pacific Council. Cultural and Social Centre**
I.P.O. Box 3129, Seoul, S. Korea.
- A S P A C Newsletter of Cultural and Social Affairs. m. ISSN 0001-2580
- A S P A C Seminar on Audio-Visual Education. Proceedings. irreg., 1970, 3rd. ISSN 0066-8311
- Asian and Pacific Council. Cultural and Social Centre. Annual Report. irreg.; latest issue, 1973. ISSN 0066-8303
- Asian and Pacific Council. Museum Conference. Proceedings. irreg.
- Asian Pacific Quarterly of Cultural and Social Affairs. q.

**Asiatic Research Center**
Korea University, Seoul, S. Korea.
- Journal of Asiatic Studies. q. ISSN 0021-9126

**Bank of Korea**
Library, Research Dept., Seoul, S. Korea.
- Bank of Korea. Annual Report. a. ISSN 0067-3706
- Bank of Korea. Monthly Economic Statistics. m.
- Economic Progress in Korea. a. ISSN 0070-8607

**Catholic Medical College. Graduate School**
Kyongwoon-Dong, Chongno-Koo, Seoul 110, S. Korea.
- Catholic Medical College Journal. q.

**Chin-Tan Society**
c/o National Museum of Korea, Seoul, S. Korea.
- Chin-Tan Society. Chin-Tan Hak-po. a.

**Chung-Ang Herald**
Chung-Ang Univ., Seoul, S. Korea.
- Chung-Ang Herald. m. ISSN 0009-6253

**Council on Korean Affairs**
P.O. Box Central 717, Seoul, S. Korea.
- Korean Affairs. bi-m.

**Cultural and Social Centre for the Asian and Pacific Region**
Public Relations and Information Office, I.P.O. 3129, Seoul, S. Korea.
- Newsletter of Cultural and Social Affairs. bi-m.

**Democratic Republican Party (S. Korea)**
Publicity Dept., Central Office, Central P.O. Box 196, Seoul, S. Korea.
- D R P Bulletin. m. ISSN 0011-5134

**Ewha Women's University. College of Law and Politcal Science**
11-1 Dai-Hyun Dong, Seodaimoon Ku, Seoul, S. Korea.
- Law and Political Review. a.

**Fine Instruments Center**
222-13 Kuro-Dong, Youngdeunapo-Ku, Seoul, S. Korea.
- Korea Electronics Manufacturers Directory. irreg.

**Han'guk Chungdung Kyoyukhoe**
25 L-Ka Sinmullo, Chongno-Ku, Seoul, S. Korea.
- Chungdung Kyoyukui Kisu. irreg.

**Hapdong News Agency**
108-4, Soosong-Dong, Chongro-Ku, Box Kwangwhamoon 145, Seoul, S. Korea.
- Hapdong Yongam. a. ISSN 0073-0335

**Institute for Communication Research**
Readership Research Center, Seoul National University, Dong Song-Dong, Seoul, S. Korea.
- Asian Press. a.

**Institute of East Asian Studies**
130-3-Ga Chong-Ro, Chongru-Ku, Seoul, S. Korea.
- East Asian Review. q.

**Institute of Forest Genetics**
Director, Suwon, S. Korea.
- Institute of Forest Genetics, Suwon, Korea. Research Report. a. ISSN 0073-9294

**International Advertising Association**
Korea Chapter, I.P.O. Box 3562, Seoul, S. Korea.
- Comprehensive Media Guide: Korea. a. ISSN 0069-8067

**International Friendship Society**
P.O. Box 100, Seoul, S. Korea.
- Friendship. q.

**International Research Centre**
Central P. O. Box 891, Seoul, S. Korea.
- Koreana Quarterly. q. ISSN 0023-4060

**Kang-Jae Chang**
14 Chunghak-Dong, Chongno-Gu, Seoul, S. Korea.
- Korea Times. d. ISSN 0023-3935

**Korea Amateur Sports Association**
19 Mugyodong, Seoul, S. Korea.
- Taehan Cheykhoe. Cheyuk Chongso. irreg.

**Korea Development Bank**
Research Dept., Box 28, Seoul, S. Korea.
- Korea Development Bank. Monthly Economic Review. m. ISSN 0017-744X
- Korea Development Bank; Its Functions and Activities. a. ISSN 0075-6806

**Korea Directory Co.**
P.O. Box 242 Kwanghwamoon, Seoul, S. Korea.
- Korea Directory. a. ISSN 0075-6814

**Korea Exchange Bank**
Seoul, S. Korea.
- Korea Exchange Bank. Monthly Review. m. ISSN 0023-3889

**Korea Information Service Inc.**
31 I-Ga, Taepyong-No Chung-Gu, Seoul, S. Korea.
- Korea Herald. d. ISSN 0023-3897

**Korea Institute of Science and Technology**
Box 131, Dongdaemun, Seoul, S. Korea.
- Korea Institute of Science and Technology. Newsletter. q.

**Korea Photo News, Inc.**
C.P.O. Box 2147, Seoul, S. Korea.
- Korea Photo News. q.

**Korea, Republic. Bureau of Planning**
Ministry of Construction, Seoul, S.Korea.
- Quarterly Construction Statistics. q. ISSN 0033-5452

**Korea, Republic. Bureau of Statistics**
Economic Planning Board, Seoul, S. Korea.
- Korea (Republic) Bureau of Statistics. Annual Report of the Price Survey/Mulga Yonbo. a. ISSN 0075-6830
- Korea (Republic) Bureau of Statistics. Annual Report on the Family Income and Expenditure Survey/Tosi Gagye Yonbo. a. ISSN 0075-6822
- Korea (Republic) Bureau of Statistics. Report on Mining and Manufacturing Survey/Kwanggongup Tonggye Zo Sa Bogo Seo. a. ISSN 0075-6849
- Korea (Republic) Bureau of Statistics. Wholesale and Retail Trade Census Report/Tosomaeup Census Bogo Seo. triennial. ISSN 0075-6857
- Korea Statistical Yearbook/Hanguk Tonggye Yongam. a. ISSN 0075-6873
- Monthly Statistics of Korea. m. ISSN 0027-0563
- Statistical Handbook of Korea/Tonggye Suchup. a. ISSN 0081-4806

**Korea, Republic. Central Meteorological Office**
Seoul, S. Korea.
- Korea. Central Meteorological Office. Monthly Weather Report. m.

**Korea, Republic. Economic Planning Board**
Bureau of Statistics, Seoul, S. Korea.
- Korea (Republic) Economic Planning Board. Annual Report on Current Industrial Production Survey. a.
- Korea (Republic) Economic Planning Board. Annual Report on the Economically Active Population. a. ISSN 0454-7543
- Korea (Republic) Economic Planning Board. Monthly Statistics. m.
- Korea (Republic) Economic Planning Board. Yearbook of Migration Statistics. a.

**Korea, Republic. Ministry of Agriculture & Fishery. Office of Rural Development**
Seodun-Dong, Suweon, S. Korea.
- Korea (Republic) Office of Rural Development. Agricultural Research Report/Korea (Republic) Nongch'on Chinhungch'ong. Nongsa Sihom Yon'gu Pogo. a. ISSN 0075-6865

**Korea, Republic. Ministry of Education**
Seoul, S. Korea.
- Korea (Republic). Ministry of Education. Basic
  Statistics of Eduction. a.
- Korea (Republic). Ministry of Education.
  Educational Development in Korea; a graphic
  presentation. irreg.

**Korea, Republic. Ministry of Science and Technology**
Seoul, S. Korea.
- Kwahak Kisul Yoram/Handbook of Science and
  Technology. a.

**Korea Scientific and Technological Information Center**
I.P.O. Box 1229, Seoul, S. Korea.
- Current Contents of Foreign Journals:
  Management & Economics. m.
- Current Contents of Foreign Journals: Medical
  Sciences. m.
- Current Index to Journals in Science &
  Technology: Biology, Agriculture, Pharmacy. m.
- Current Index to Journals in Science &
  Technology: Chemistry & Chemical Engineering.
  m.
- Current Index to Journals in Science &
  Technology: Electrical Engineering & Electronics.
  m.
- Current Index to Journals in Science &
  Technology: Mathematics & Physics. m.
- Current Index to Journals in Science &
  Technology: Mechanical Engineering &
  Metallurgy. m.
- Current List of Foreign Patents. bi-m.
- Documentation & Information Services. bi-m.
- Korean Medical Abstracts. q. ISSN 0047-360X
- Korean Scientific Abstracts. bi-m. ISSN 0023-
  4052
- Technical Information. m.

**Korea Trade Promotion Corp.**
I.P.O. Box 1621, Seoul, S. Korea.
- Korea Trade. 10-12 per yr. ISSN 0023-3943

**Korea University. College of Science and Engineering**
1 Anam-Dong, Seoul 132, S. Korea.
- Science and Technology. irreg.

**Korean Association of International Law**
37 Suhsomoon-Dong, Suhdaimoon-Ky, Seoul, S.
Korea.
- Korean Journal of International Law. 2 per yr.
  ISSN 0023-3994

**Korean Association of International Relations**
c/oGraduate School of Public Administration, Seoul
National University, 119 Tongsung-Dong, Chongno-
Ku, Seoul, S. Korea.
- Korean Journal of International Relations. irreg.

**Korean Institute for Family Planning**
115, Nokbun-dong, Sudaemun-ku, Seoul 120, S.
Korea.
- Journal of Family Planning Studies. a.
- K. I. F. P. Bulletin. bi-m.
- Korean Institute for Family Planning. Annual
  Report. a.
- Korean Population and Family Planning.
  Bibliography Series. a.

**Korean Institute of International Studies**
K.P.O. 426, Seoul, S. Korea.
- Korean Journal of International Studies. q.

**Korean Library Association**
6, Sokong-Dong, Chung-Ku, Seoul, S. Korea.
- K L A Bulletin. m. ISSN 0022-7358

**Korean Library Science Society**
c/o Ewha Women University Library, Seoul 120, S.
Korea.
- Tosoguian Hak. a.

**Korean Medical Association**
Box 2062, Seoul, S. Korea.
- Korean Medical Association. Journal. m. ISSN
  0023-4028

**Korean Micro-Library Association**
Central National Library Bldg, 6 Sogong-Dong,
Jung-Gu, Seoul, S. Korea.
- Micro-Library Bulletin. m. ISSN 0026-2536

**Korean National Commission for UNESCO**
Box Central 64, Seoul, S. Korea.
- Korea Journal. m. ISSN 0023-3900
- Korean National Commission for UNESCO.
  Social Science Journal. a.

- Review of Educational Studies in Korea. irreg.
- Revue de Coree. q.

**Korean Nurses' Association**
88-7 Sanglim-Dong, Choong Ku, Seoul, S. Korea.
- Korean Nurse/Taehan Kanho. bi-m. ISSN 0047-
  3618

**Korean Otolaryngological Society**
c/o Catholic Medical College & Centre, No. 1, 2 ka
Myung Dong, Choong-Ku, Seoul, S. Korea.
- Korean Otolaryngological Society. Journal. q.

**Korean Overseas Information Service**
Seoul, S. Korea.
- Korea Policy Series. irreg?

**Korean Physiological Society**
Department of Physiology, College of Medicine,
Seoul National University, 28 Yebnkun-Dong,
Chongno-Ku, Seoul 110, S. Korea.
- Korean Journal of Physiology. s-a. ISSN 0300-
  4015

**Korean Publishers Association**
105-2 Sagan-Dong, Chongno-Ku, Seoul, S. Korea.
- Ch'ulp'an Munhwa/Korean Book Journal. m.
  ISSN 0009-6245
- Korean Publications Yearbook/Han'quk Ch'ulp;
  an Yon'gam. a. ISSN 0075-6881

**Korean Reconstruction Bank**
Hanguk Saneub Enhang, Seoul, S. Korea.
- Korean Reconstruction Bank. Monthly Review. m.

**Korean Research Center**
90-1, 1-Ga, Chungjong-Ro, Sudaemun-Gu, Seoul, S.
Korea.
- Journal of Social Sciences and Humanities. s-a.
  ISSN 0023-4044
- Korean Research Center. Bulletin. s-a.

**Korean Social Science Research Institute**
18 d'Ang-Su-Dong, Tjong-Lo-Ku, Seoul, S. Korea.
- Korean Social Science Review. irreg.

**Korean Society for Future Studies**
Graduate School of Environmental Studies, Rm. 13-
212, Seoul National University, Seoul 151, S. Korea.
- Inquiry into the Future. a.

**Korean Standards Association**
41-1 Chodong Chung-Ku, Seoul, S. Korea.
- Annual List of Korean Industrial Standards. a.
- Quality Control. bi-m. ISSN 0033-5193

**Korean Studies Institute**
- International Journal of Korean Studies. (pub. by
  Yonsei University Press)

**Medium Industry Bank**
Seoul, S. Korea.
- Medium Industry Bank, Seoul. Report. a. ISSN
  0076-6143

**National Assembly Library**
Processing & Reference Bureau, Yoido-Dong 1,
Yeongdeungpo-Gu, Seoul, S. Korea.
- Korean Periodicals Index/Jeong-Gi Kanhaengmul
  Kisa Saegin. q.
- National Assembly Library Review. m. ISSN
  0027-8572

**Public Relations Association of Korea**
P.O. Box 2147, Seoul, S. Korea.
- Korea Film Catalog. a.
- Korea Newsreview. w.
- South-North Dialogue in Korea. irreg.

**Pulgyo Munhwa**
382 Sonhwa-dong, Taejon, S. Korea.
- Pulgyo Munhwa/Buddhist Civilization. m.

**Research Institute of Asian Economies**
147-21, Kye-Dong, Chongro-Ku, Seoul, S. Korea.
- Asian Economies. q.

**Save the Nation**
National Council, I.P.O. 3385, Seoul, S. Korea.
- Korean Signal. q.

**Secretariat of the National Assembly**
Compiling Section, 61 1-Ka, Tae Pyong-Ro, Chung-
Ku, Seoul, S. Korea.
- National Assembly Review. m. ISSN 0027-8580

**Seoul Journal of Medicine**
c/o E. Huock Kwan, College of Medicine, Seoul
National Univ., Seoul, S. Korea.
- Seoul Journal of Medicine/Soul Uidae Chapchi. q.

**Seoul National University**
College of Dentistry, 28-1, Yenkum-Dong,
Chongro-Ku, Seoul, S. Korea.
- Korea Research Society for Dental Materials.
  Journal. q. ISSN 0023-3927
- Seoul National University. Faculty Papers. a.
- Seoul National University. Faculty Papers. Biology
  and Agriculture Series. a.

**Seoul National University. College of Commerce**
Institute of Economic Research, 19 Jongam-Dong
Sungbuk-Gu, Seoul, S. Korea
(Subscr. to: Publishing Center of Seoul National
University, 199 Dongsung-Dong Jongro-Gu, Seoul,
S. Korea)
- Seoul National University. Economic Review. a.

**Seoul National University. Institute of Economic Research**
Seoul, S. Korea.
- Korean Economic Journal. q. ISSN 0023-3978

**Seoul National University. Institute of Management Research**
56 Shinrim-Dong, Kwanak-Ku, Sungbook-Ku, Seoul,
S. Korea.
- Korean Business Journal. q. ISSN 0023-396X

**Seoul National University. Population and Development Studies Center**
Seoul, S. Korea.
- Seoul National University. Population and
  Development Studies Center. Bulletin. a.

**Seoul National University. School of Public Health**
28 Yun Kun-Dong, Chongro-Ku, Seoul, S. Korea.
- Korean Journal of Public Health/Kong Jung po
  Gon Zap Zi. s-a. ISSN 0023-401X

**Society of Pharmacology**
28 Yeon-Kun Dong, Chong-Ro Ku, Seoul 110, S.
Korea.
- Korean Journal of Pharmacology. irreg.

**Taehan Sanggong Hoeuiso**
Korea Chamber of Commerce & Industry, Seoul, S.
Korea.
- Chonguk Kiopche Chongnam/Directory of
  Korean Business. irreg.

**Tongil Chuche Kungmin Hoeui Samucho**
88 Kyongun-Dong, Chongno-Gu, Seoul, S. Korea.
- Korea (Republic). Tongil Chuche Kungmin Hoeui.
  Kungmin Hoeui Bo/National Conference Review.
  irreg.

**World Anti-Communist League**
San 5-1 Chang Chung-Dong, Chung-Ku, Seoul, S.
Korea.
- Asian Peoples' Anti-Communist League. Charts
  About Chinese Communists on the Mainland.
  irreg. ISSN 0571-2939
- W A C L Bulletin. q. ISSN 0042-9449

**Yonsei University College of Medicine**
Box 71, Seoul, S. Korea.
- Yonsei Journal of Medical Science. s-a.
- Yonsei Medical Journal. s-a.
- Yonsei Reports on Tropical Medicine. a.

**Yonsei University. Graduate School**
Seoul, S. Korea.
- Yonsei University. Graduate School. Abstracts of
  Faculty Research Reports. a.

**Yonsei University. Industrial Management Research Centre**
College of Business and Economics, 134 Sinchon-
Dong, Sudaemoon-ku, Seoul, S. Korea.
- Sanop Kwa Kyongyong/Yonsei Business Review.
  s-a. ISSN 0036-4487

**Yonsei University. Institute of East and West Studies**
134 Shinchon-Dong, Seodaemoon-gu, Seoul, S.
Korea.
- Journal of East and West Studies/Tongso Yongu.
  s-a.

**Yonsei University. Institute of Humanistic Studies**
- Journal of Humanistic Studies/Inmun Kwahak.
  (pub. by Yonsei University Press)

**Yonsei University Press**
Yonsei University, Seoul 120, S. Korea.
- International Journal of Korean Studies. s-a. ISSN 0303-3007
- Journal of Humanistic Studies/Inmun Kwahak. s-a. ISSN 0537-7137 (Yonsei University. Institute of Humanistic Studies)

# KUWAIT

**Arab Fund for Economic and Social Development**
P.O. Box 21923, Kuwait.
- Arab Fund for Economic and Social Development. Annual Report. a. ISSN 0304-6729

**Central Bank of Kuwait**
Box 526, Kuwait.
- Central Bank of Kuwait. Quarterly Statistical Bulletin. q. (prep. by its Research Department)

**Kuwait. Central Statistical Office**
P. O. Box 15, Kuwait.
- Kuwait. Central Statistical Office. Annual Statistical Abstract. m.

**Kuwait. Ministry of Guidance & Information**
Box 193, Kuwait.
- Kuwait Al-Yawm. w. ISSN 0023-575X

**Kuwait Medical Association**
c/o Secretary General, Solaibikhat, Box 1202, Kuwait.
- Kuwait Medical Association Journal. q. ISSN 0023-5776

**Kuwait Oil Co. Ltd.**
Ahmadi, Kuwait.
- Kuwaiti. fortn. (Arabic edt.); q. (English edt.) ISSN 0023-5792

**Organization of Arab Petroleum Exporting Countries**
Box 20501, Kuwait.
- O A P E C News Bulletin. m. (prep. by its Information and Public Relations Department)
- Oil and Arab Cooperation. q. (prep. by its Informaton and Public Relations Department)

**University of Kuwait. Faculty of Science**
P.O. Box 5969, Kuwait.
- University of Kuwait. Journal (Science) a.

# LEBANON

**Albert Adib, Ed. & Pub.**
Box 878, Beirut, Lebanon.
- Adib. m. ISSN 0001-091X

**Advertising Research & Marketing Services Ltd.**
P.O. Box 6615, Beirut, Lebanon.
- Middle East and North Africa Markets Review. a.

**American University of Beirut**
Box 1786, Beirut, Lebanon.
- Al-Abhath. q. ISSN 0002-3973
- Berytus: Archeological Studies. a. ISSN 0067-6195

**American University of Beirut. Economic Research Institute**
Beirut, Lebanon.
- Middle East Economic Papers. a. ISSN 0076-8510

**Arab Film & Television Centre**
see under Lebanon. Ministry of Information

**Arab Petroleum Research Center**
Box 7167, Beirut, Lebanon.
- Arab Oil & Gas Directory. a.
- Petrole et le Gaz Arabes/Arab Oil & Gas. fortn. ISSN 0031-6369

**Armenian Catholic Patriarchate**
Place Debbas, Beirut, Lebanon.
- Avedik. m. ISSN 0005-1950
- Massis. w. ISSN 0025-4975

**Armenian Evangelical Brotherhood Church**
Box 4944, Beirut, Lebanon.
- Tchahert. 5 per yr. ISSN 0040-0297

**Association of Banks in Lebanon**
Rue de l'Armee, Box 967, Beirut, Lebanon.
- Association des Banques du Liban. Bilans des Banques. irreg.

- Association des Banques du Liban. Rapport du Conseil. irreg.

**Atlas Publishing Co.**
Spears St., Beirut, Lebanon.
- Pjichk. m. ISSN 0032-0404

**Aztag Shapatoriag-Troshag**
Salim Bustany St., Beirut, Lebanon
- Aztag Shapatoriag-Troshag. w. (U.S. dist. to: Haig Gakavian, 9417 Curren Rd., Silver Spring, MD 20901)

**B. A. K. Publications**
Hashem A 1 Babon Bldg., Mneime St., P.O. Box 7367, Beirut, Lebanon.
- Middle East Sketch. w.

**Bagin**
Rue Selim Boustany, Beirut, Lebanon.
- Bagin. m. ISSN 0005-3910

**Simon Bakht, Ed. & Pub.**
Tabbara Bldg., Manara, 466 Eliss St., Beirut, Lebanon.
- Africa Middle East Business Digest. m.

**Bible Land Mission**
Box 4115, Beirut, Lebanon.
- Evangelist. q. ISSN 0014-3626

**Bureau of Lebanese and Arab Documentation**
176 rue Monot, B. P. 3000, Beirut, Lebanon.
- Argus de la Legislation Libanaise. q. ISSN 0570-8915

**Center for Economic, Financial and Social Research and Documentation**
Box 11-6068, Clemenceau Str., Gefinor Tower, Bloc B-5th Floor, Beirut, Lebanon.
- Center for Economic, Financial and Social Research and Documentation; monthly survey of Arab economies. m. ISSN 0013-0664
- Economie des Pays Arabes. m.

**Centre Culturel Universitaire, Beirut**
- Travaux et Jours. (pub. by Imprimerie Catholique)

**Chambre de Commerce et d'Industrie de Beyrouth**
Rue Allenby, Immeuble Ayass, Beirut, Lebanon.
- Economie Libanaise et Arabe. bi-m. ISSN 0013-0540

**Conferences du Cenacle**
Box 1145, Beirut, Lebanon.
- Conferences du Cenacle. m. ISSN 0010-5589

**Joseph F. Dahdah, Ed. & Pub.**
Box 4689, Beirut, Lebanon.
- Assurances Banques Transports; revue mensuelle de doctrine, de jurisprudence et d'information. m. ISSN 0004-6035

**Dar-al Kifah**
Box 1462, Beirut, Lebanon.
- Al-Ahad. w. ISSN 0002-3981

**Dar Assayad S.A.L.**
Box 1038, Beirut, Lebanon.
- Assayad. w. ISSN 0004-5012

**Deutsche Morgenlaendische Gesellschaft Beirut. Orient-Institut**
- Beiruter Texte und Studien. (pub. by Franz Steiner Verlag GmbH GW)

**Economic Commission for Western Asia**
For publications of this agency see section for UNITED NATIONS

**Editions Orientales S.A.L.**
Box 1404, Beirut, Lebanon.
- Al-Usbua al-Arabi. w. ISSN 0002-3965

**Gallery One Publishing Company**
Box 1760-11, Beirut, Lebanon.
- Majallat Shi'r; magazine for modern arabic poetry. q. ISSN 0025-1046

**Al-Hawadess Press & Publishing Co. S.A.L.**
Shiyah, Box 1281, Beirut, Lebanon.
- Hawadess. w. ISSN 0017-8527

**Immeuble Azarie**
Rue de Syrie, Beirut, Lebanon.
- Edjer Grakanutian Yev Arvesdi. s-a. ISSN 0013-0990

**Immeuble Chidiac**
Rue Said Akl, Beirut, Lebanon.
- Cahiers de l'Oronte. q. ISSN 0007-991X

**Imprimerie Catholique**
B.P. 946, Beirut, Lebanon.
- Travaux et Jours. q. ISSN 0041-1930 (Centre Culturel Universitaire, Beirut)

**Institut de Recherches Agronomiques. Laboratoire Regional Veterinaire**
Fanar, Lebanon.
- Magon. Serie Scientifique. irreg., 1970, no. 33. ISSN 0076-2369
- Magon. Serie Technique. irreg., 1970, no. 11. ISSN 0076-2377

**Institute for Palestine Studies**
Box 11-7164, Beirut, Lebanon
(Dist. in U. S. by: Institute for Palestine Studies, Box 329A, R. D. 1, Oxford, PA 19363)
- Institute for Palestine Studies. Anthology Series. irreg., 1970, no. 5. ISSN 0073-8786
- Institute for Palestine Studies. Arabic Annual Documentary Series. a.
- Institute for Palestine Studies. Basic Documents Series. irreg., 1970, no. 8. ISSN 0073-8794
- Institute for Palestine Studies. International Annual Documentary Series. a. ISSN 0073-8808
- Institute for Palestine Studies. Monograph Series. irreg., 1970, no. 26. ISSN 0073-8816
- Institute for Palestine Studies. Yearbook Series. a.
- Journal of Palestine Studies; a quarterly on Palestinian affairs and the Arab-Israeli conflict. ISSN 0047-2654 (Co-sponsor: Kuwait University)

**Al-Jamhour - al-Jadid**
c/o Farid Abu Shahla, Box 1834, Beirut, Lebanon.
- Al-Jamhour - al-Jadid. w.

**Johnston International Publishing Corporation**
Strand Bldg, Hamra St, Beirut, Lebanon.
- Alam Attijarat; the business magazine of the Arab world. 10 per yr. ISSN 0002-4392

**Dr. Artin Kazandjian, Pub.**
Spears St., Box 4176, Beirut, Lebanon.
- Pakin. m. ISSN 0030-9613

**Lebanese Association of Armenian University Graduates**
11, rue Negib Haddad, Beirut, Lebanon.
- Armenian Studies/Etudes Armeniennes. irreg.

**Lebanese Dental Council**
Sodeco Bldg., Nasra Sta., Box 2266, Beirut, Lebanon.
- Revue Dentaire Libanaise/Lebanese Dental Journal. q. ISSN 0035-1873

**Lebanese Journal of Political Science**
Box 3865, Beirut, Lebanon.
- Lebanese Journal of Political Science. s-a.

**Lebanon. Direction Centrale de la Statistique**
Ministere du Plan, Beirut, Lebanon.
- Lebanon. Direction Centrale de la Statistique. Bulletin Statistique Mensuel. m. ISSN 0023-9860
- Lebanon. Direction Centrale de la Statistique. Comptes Economiques. a. ISSN 0075-837X
- Lebanon. Direction Centrale de la Statistique. Recueil de Statistiques Libanaises. a. ISSN 0075-8388

**Lebanon. Direction General des Transports**
Beirut, Lebanon.
- Bulletin des Transports Maritimes et Terrestres. s-a.

**Lebanon. Ministry of Information. Arab Film & Television Centre**
Box 3434, Beirut, Lebanon.
- Arab Film and Television Center News. s-m. ISSN 0003-7397

**Imprimerie Leteyf**
Rue Bechara el Khoury, Box 4206, Beirut, Lebanon.
- Cines d'Orient. w. ISSN 0009-7195

**Librairie Orientale**
Place de l'Etoile, P.O.B. 1986, Beirut, Lebanon.
- Universite Saint-Joseph. Institut de Lettres Orientales. Recherches. irreg. ISSN 0067-4923

**Mid-East Commerce**
Fouad Chehab Str., Kubi Bldg., Box 3868, Beirut, Lebanon.
- Mid-East Commerce. m. ISSN 0026-301X

**Middle East Commercial Information Center**
P.O. Box 6466, Beirut, Lebanon
(Dist. by International Publications Service, 114 E. 32 St., New York, NY 10016)
- Lebanese Industrial and Commercial Directory. biennial. ISSN 0075-8353
- Lebanese Joint Stock Companies. Year Book. a. ISSN 0075-8361
- Lebanese Limited Liability Companies. Year Book. a.

**Middle East Petroleum and Economic Publications**
P.O. Box 1224, Beirut, Lebanon.
- International Crude Oil and Product Prices. s-a.

**Middle East Research and Publishing Center**
Box 1224, Beirut, Lebanon.
- Middle East Economic Survey. w.

**National Council for Scientific Research**
Beirut, Lebanon.
- National Council for Scientific Research. Annual Report. a.

**Near East Council of Churches**
Box 5376, Beirut, Lebanon.
- Near East Council of Churches. News Bulletin. 3 per yr. ISSN 0028-1743

**Order of Physicians in Lebanon**
Bechara el-Khoury, Box 640, Beirut, Lebanon.
- Lebanese Medical Journal/Journal Medical Libanais. bi-m. ISSN 0023-9852

**Painter AVO**
c/o A. Toumayan, Box 80179, Beirut, Lebanon.
- Heghapoghagan Albom. every 2-3 per m. ISSN 0017-9566

**Publitec Publications**
Gedeon House. 21-23 Syria St., P.O. Box 5936, Beirut, Lebanon
(Dist. in U.S. by International Publications Service, 214 E. 32 St., New York, N.Y. 10016)
- Who's Who in Lebanon. biennial. ISSN 0083-9612
- Who's Who in the Arab World. biennial. ISSN 0083-9752

**Societe de la Presse Economique (S. A. L.)**
Rue Kantari, Box 687, Beirut, Lebanon.
- Commerce du Levant. m. ISSN 0010-2814
- Middle East Express. m. ISSN 0026-3117

**Spurk**
Box 2669, Beirut, Lebanon.
- Spurk. w. ISSN 0038-8696

**Syrian Documentation Papers**
P.O. Box 50320, Beirut, Lebanon.
- Damascus Economic Letter. q.
- Syrian Documentation Papers. irreg.

**United Nations Economic Commission for Western Asia**
For publications of this agency see section for UNITED NATIONS

**Universite Saint Esprit Kaslik**
Journieh, Lebanon.
- Parole de l'Orient. s-a.

**Universite Saint Joseph**
B.P. 293, Beirut, Lebanon.
- Universite Saint-Joseph. Melanges. irreg., vol. 47, 1972.

**Universite St. Joseph. Faculte de Droit et des Sciences Economiques**
Rue Huvelin, Box 293, Beirut, Lebanon
(Foreign Subscription Address: Editions Sirey, 22 rue Soufflot, 75 Paris (5e), France)
- Proche-Orient Etudes Economiques. s-a. ISSN 0032-9630
- Proche Orient Etudes Juridiques. 3 per yr. ISSN 0032-9649

**Universite Saint Joseph. Institut de Lettres Orientales**
- Universite Saint-Joseph. Institut de Lettres Orientales. Recherches. (pub. by Librairie Orientale)

## LESOTHO

**English Society**
National University of Lesotho, P. O. Roma, Lesotho.
- Expression. s-a. ISSN 0014-5343

**Lesotho. Auditor General**
Box 502, Maseru, Lesotho.
- Report by the Auditor General on the Accounts of Lesotho. a; latest issue, 1972-73. ISSN 0085-2740

**Lesotho. Ministry of Education and Culture**
Maseru, Lesotho.
- Lesotho. Ministry of Education and Culture. Annual Report of the Permanent Secretary. a.

**Lesotho. Treasury**
P.O. Box 401, Maseru, Lesotho.
- Lesotho. Treasury. Report on the Finances and Accounts. a. ISSN 0075-8817

**Mazenod Institute**
Mazenod, Lesotho.
- Moeletsi Oa Basotho/Counsellor of Basotho. w. (Missionary Oblates of Mary Immaculate)

**Missionary Oblates of Mary Immaculate**
- Moeletsi Oa Basotho/Counsellor of Basotho. (pub. by Mazenod Institute)

**National University of Lesotho. School of Education**
Roma, Lesotho.
- Education in Botswana, Lesotho, and Swaziland. irreg (2-4 per yr.); no. 7, 1974.

## LIBERIA

**A & A Enterprises Inc.**
Box 103, Monrovia, Liberia.
- Directory and Who's Who in Liberia. irreg.

**A.M. Dogliotti College of Medicine**
see under **University of Liberia**

**African Publishing House, Ltd.**
Monrovia, Liberia
- Africa International Perspective; African review of international affairs. m. (Subscr. to: Ave. Marc Monnieri, Box 244, 1211 Geneva 12, Switzerland)

**Dogliotti College of Medicine**
see under **University of Liberia**

**First National City Bank**
P.O. Box 280, Monrovia, Liberia.
- First National City Bank, Liberia. Annual Report. a.

**Grimes School of Law**
see under **University of Liberia**

**Lamco J.V. Operating Company**
Box 69, Monrovia, Liberia.
- Lamco News. bi-m.

**Liberia. Bureau of the Budget**
Monrovia, Liberia.
- Budget of the Government of Liberia. a.

**Liberia. Department of State**
Monrovia, Liberia.
- Liberia. Department of State. Newsletter. m. ISSN 0300-2241

**Liberia. General Services Agency**
Box 9027, Monrovia, Liberia.
- Liberia. General Services Agency. Annual Report. a.

**Liberia. Ministry of Agriculture**
Monrovia, Liberia.
- Liberia. Ministry of Agriculture. National Rice Production Estimates. irreg. (Co-sponsor: Ministry of Planning and Economic Affairs)

**Liberia. Ministry of Commerce, Industry and Transportation**
Box 9041, Monrovia, Liberia.
- Journal of Commerce, Industry & Transportation. (pub. by Palm Publications Co.)
- Liberia. Ministry of Commerce, Industry and Transportation. Annual Report. a.
- Liberian Trade Directory; basic trade information, exporters & importers. irreg. (prep. by its Director of Foreign Trade)

**Liberia. Ministry of Finance**
Monrovia, Liberia.
- Liberia. Ministry of Finance. Annual Report. a. ISSN 0304-727X

**Liberia. Ministry of Foreign Affairs**
Monrovia, Liberia.
- Liberia. Ministry of Foreign Affairs. Annual Report. a.

**Liberia. Ministry of Information, Cultural Affairs and Tourism**
Monrovia, Liberia.
- Liberia. Ministry of Information, Cultural Affairs & Tourism. Annual Report to the Session of the Legislature. a.
- Liberia: Political, Economics and Social Monthly. m.

**Liberia. Ministry of Justice**
Monrovia, Liberia.
- Liberia. Ministry of Justice. Annual Report to the Legislature. a.

**Liberia. Ministry of Labour, Youth & Sports**
Monrovia, Liberia.
- Liberia. Ministry of Labour, Youth & Sports. Annual Report. a.

**Liberia. Ministry of Local Government, Rural Development & Urban Reconstruction**
Monrovia, Liberia.
- Liberia. Ministry of Local Government, Rural Development & Urban Reconstruction. Annual Report. a. ISSN 0304-730X

**Liberia. Ministry of National Defense**
Monrovia, Liberia.
- Liberia. Ministry of National Defense. Annual Report. a.

**Liberia. Ministry of Planning and Economic Affairs**
Box 9016, Monrovia, Liberia.
- Economic Survey of Liberia. irreg.
- External Trade of Liberia: Imports. irreg.
- Liberia. Ministry of Planning and Economic Affairs. Activity Report. irreg.
- Liberia. Ministry of Planning and Economic Affairs. Annual Report to the Session of the Legislature of the Republic of Liberia. a. ISSN 0459-2182
- Public Sector Accounts of Liberia.
- Quarterly Statistical Bulletin of Liberia. q.

**Liberia. Ministry of Public Works**
Monrovia, Liberia.
- Liberia. Ministry of Public Works. Annual Report. a. ISSN 0304-7326

**Liberia Baptist Missionary and Educational Convention**
Bentol City, Liberia.
- Liberia Baptist Missionary and Educational Convention. Yearbook. a.

**Louis Arthur Grimes School of Law**
see under **University of Liberia**

**Lutheran Church in Liberia**
Loma LLL Center, Wozi, Box 1046, Monrovia, Liberia.
- Loma Weekly Paper. w.

**National Bank of Liberia**
Box 2048, E. G. King Plaza, Broad St., Monrovia, Liberia.
- National Bank of Liberia. Annual Report. a.
- National Bank of Liberia. Research Department. Statistical Bulletin. m.

**Palm Publications Co.**
Suite 219-321, Bank of Liberia Bldg., Monrovia 1, Liberia
- Journal of Commerce, Industry & Transportation. q. (Liberia. Ministry of Commerce, Industry and Transportation) (Also avail. from: African Development, Wheatsheaf House, Carmelite St., London EC4Y 0AX, England)

**Revelation**
c/o Ed. Vittorio A. Jesus Weeks, University of
Liberia, Monrovia, Liberia.
- Revelation; social, political, economic and cultural
monthly. m.

**Torch Services**
Box 1394, Monrovia, Liberia.
- Torch. irreg.

**True Whig Party**
Box 286, Monrovia, Liberia.
- Liberian Age. s-w. ISSN 0024-1962

**Tubman Teachers College**
*see under* University of Liberia

**University of Liberia**
Research Institute, Monrovia, Liberia.
- University of Liberia Journal. s-a. ISSN 0041-9745

**University of Liberia. A. .M. Dogliotti College of
Medicine**
Monrovia, Liberia.
- University of Liberia. A. M. Dogliotti College of
Medicine. Annual Report of the Dean. a.

**University of Liberia. College of Business and Public
Administration**
Monrovia, Liberia.
- Liberian Economic and Management Review. s-a.
(prep. by its Economic and Management
Research Institute)

**University of Liberia. Division of Science**
Monrovia, Liberia.
- U. L. Science Magazine. s-a.

**University of Liberia. Louis Arthur Grimes School of
Law**
Monrovia, Liberia.
- Liberian Law Journal. s-a. ISSN 0024-1970

**University of Liberia. William V. S. Tubman Teachers
College**
Monrovia, Liberia.
- Julius C. Stevens Annual Lectures in Education.
irreg.

**West Africa Rice Development Association**
Box 1019, Monrovia, Liberia.
- World Rice References for West Africa. s-a.

**William V. S. Tubman Teachers College**
*see under* University of Liberia

# LIBYA

**Alfateh University. Faculty of Science**
Box 656, Tripoli, Libya.
- Libyan Journal of Sciences; an international
journal. a.

**Arab Oil Review**
4 Sharia Omar Ibn Abdulaziz, Tripoli, Libya.
- Arab Oil Review. bi-m. ISSN 0003-7435

**Bank of Libya**
Box 1103, Tripoli, Libya.
- Bank of Libya. Annual Report of the Board of
Directors. a. ISSN 0067-3714 (prep. by its
Economic Research Division)
- Bank of Libya. Balance of Payments. a. ISSN
0075-921X
- Bank of Libya. Economic Research Division.
Economic Bulletin. bi-m. ISSN 0005-5271 (prep.
by its Economic Research Division)

**Libya. Census and Statistical Department**
Tripoli, Libya.
- Libya. Census and Statistical Department.
Monthly Cost of Living Index for Tripoli Town.
m. ISSN 0023-1630
- Libya. Census and Statistical Office. External
Trade Statistics. q & a. ISSN 0075-9228
- Libya. Census and Statistical Office. General
Population Census. decennial. ISSN 0075-9236
- Libya. Census and Statistical Office. Industrial
Census. decennial. ISSN 0075-9244
- Libya. Census and Statistical Office. Report of the
Annual Survey of Large Manufacturing
Establishments. a. ISSN 0075-9252
- Libya. Census and Statistical Office. Report of the
Annual Survey of Petroleum Mining Industry. a.
ISSN 0075-9260

- Libya. Census and Statistical Office. Report of the
Survey of Licensed Construction Units. a. ISSN
0075-9279
- Libya. Census and Statistical Office. Statistical
Abstract. a. ISSN 0075-9287
- Libya. Census and Statistical Office. Wholesale
Prices in Tripoli Town. q. ISSN 0075-9295

**Libya. Ministere de l'Information et de la Culture**
Tripoli, Libya.
- Realites Libyennes. bi-m. ISSN 0034-0936

**University of Garyounis. Faculty of Economics and
Commerce**
Benghazi, Libya.
- Dirassat; Libyan economic and business review. s-
a. (prep. by its Center of Economic and Business
Research)

# LIECHTENSTEIN

**Botanisch-Zoologische Gesellschaft Liechtenstein-
Sargans-Werdenberg**
Vaduz, Liechtenstein.
- Liechtenstein. Botanisch-Zoologische Gesellschaft
Sargans-Werdenberg. Bericht. irreg.

**Comite International des Sciences Historiques**
9491 Nendeln, Liechtenstein.
- Bibliographie Internationale des Travaux
Historiques Publies dans les Volumes de
"Melanges.". irreg. ISSN 0067-7019

**Editions du Marche Commun**
P.O. Box 43202, FL-9490 Vaduz, Liechtenstein.
- Banker's World Directory. a.

**International Society for Prospektive Medicine**
- Datenjournal. (pub. by Mecudo)

**Leben Verlag AG**
9490 Vaduz FL, Liechtenstein.
- Bewusstes Leben; Zeitschrift fuer positive Lebens-
und Arbeitsgestaltung, gesunde Ernaehrung und
natuerliche Lebensweise. m. ISSN 0006-0429

**Liechsteinsteinische Akademische Gesellschaft**
Vaduz, Liechtenstein.
- Liechtenstein. Politische Schriften. irreg.

**Liechtenstein. Press and Information Office**
Government Palace, FL-9490 Vaduz, Liechtenstein.
- Liechtenstein. Press and Information Office. Press
Folder. triennial.
- Liechtenstein Economy. triennial.
- Principality of Liechtenstein: a Documentary
Handbook. triennial. ISSN 0048-5306

**Mecudo**
Vaduz, Liechtenstein.
- Datenjournal. q. ISSN 0011-7005 (International
Society for Prospektive Medicine)

**NIFRA Publishers**
FL 9497 Triesenberg, Liechtenstein.
- International Background. m (except Jul. & Aug.)

# LUXEMBOURG

**Association des Instituteurs Reunis du Grand-Duche
de Luxembourg**
5 rue des Ardennes, Boite Postale 2437,
Luxembourg, Luxembourg.
- Ecole et Vie. q.

**Association Luxembourgeoise des Ingenieurs et
Industriels**
4 Bd. Grande-Duchesse Charlotte, Luxembourg,
Luxembourg.
- Revue Technique Luxembourgeoise. q. ISSN
0035-4260

**Banque Internationale a Luxembourg**
2 Boulevard Royal, Luxembourg, Luxembourg.
- Banque Internationale a Luxembourg. Cahiers
Economiques. irreg.

**Imprimerie J. Beffort**
18 rue de la Post, Luxembourg, Luxembourg.
- Societe des Sciences Medicales du Grand-Duche
de Luxembourg. Bulletin. 2-3 per yr. ISSN 0037-
9247

**Bourg-Bourger**
Bertrange, Case Postale 2002, Luxembourg-Gare,
Luxembourg.
- Revue; Letzeburger illustreirt (Luxembourg's
weekly magazine) w. ISSN 0035-0729

**Conseil Luxembourgeois du Mouvement Europeen**
20 B, rue Louvigny, B. P. 105, Luxembourg,
Luxembourg.
- Federaliste Europeen. s-a. ISSN 0014-9268

**Consociato Internationalis Musicae Sacrae**
18 Ave. Guillaume, Luxembourg, Luxembourg.
- Musicae Sacrae Ministerium. q. ISSN 0027-4569

**Europaeisches Bau-Forum**
19 Ave. Monterey, Luxembourg, Luxembourg.
- Europaeisches Bau-Forum; forum Europeen
d'architecture. m. ISSN 0046-2683

**Federation des Artisans**
41, rue Glesener, Luxembourg, Luxembourg.
- Handwierk. m.

**Federation Internationale de Philatelie**
*see* International Philatelic Federation

**Institut Grand-Ducal de Luxembourg. Section de
Linguistique, de Folklore et de Toponymie**
5 rue Large, Luxembourg, Luxembourg.
- Beitraege zur Luxemburgischen Sprach- und
Volkskunde. irreg., no. 10, 1974.
- Bulletin Linguistique et Ethnologique. irreg. ISSN
0068-4066

**International Philatelic Federation**
38 rue du Cure, Luxembourg, Luxembourg.
- International Philatelic Federation. General
Assembly. Proces-Verbal. 5-6 per year. ISSN
0074-7343

**Luxembourg. Administration de l'Emploi**
32, Ave. de la Porte-Neuve, B. P. 23, Luxembourg,
Luxembourg.
- Luxembourg. Administration de l'Emploi. Rapport
Annuel. a.

**Luxembourg. Bibliotheque Nationale**
37, Boulevard F.-D. Roosevelt, Luxembourg,
Luxembourg.
- Bibliographie zur Geschichte Luxemburgs/
Bibliographie d'Histoire Luxemourgeoise. a. ISSN
0067-7043

**Luxembourg. Caisse d'Epargne de l'Etat**
1, Place de Metz, Luxembourg, Luxembourg.
- Luxembourg. Caisee d'Epargne de l'Etat. Rapports
et Bilans. a.

**Luxembourg. Inspection Generale de la Securite
Sociale**
Ministere du Travail et de la Securite Sociale,
Luxembourg, Luxembourg.
- Luxembourg. Inspection Generale de la Securite
Sociale. Rapport General sur la Securite Sociale
au Grand-Duche de Luxembourg. irreg.

**Luxembourg. Ministere des Finances**
Luxembourg, Luxembourg.
- Luxembourg. Ministere des Finances. Budget de
l'Etat. a. ISSN 0076-1559

**Luxembourg. Ministere du Travail et da la Securite
Sociale. Inspection Generale de la Securite Sociale**
*see* Luxembourg. Inspection Generale de la Securite
Sociale

**Luxembourg. Service Central de la Statistique et des
Etudes Economiques**
B.P. 304, Luxembourg, Luxembourg.
- Luxembourg. Service Central de la Statistique et
des Etudes Economiques. Annuaire Statistique. a.
ISSN 0076-1575
- Luxembourg. Service Central de la Statistique et
des Etudes Economiques. Annuaire Statistique
Retrospectif. irreg.
- Luxembourg. Service Central de la Statistique et
des Etudes Economiques. Bulletin du Statec. 8-10
per year. ISSN 0076-1583
- Luxembourg. Service Central de la Statistique et
des Etudes Economiques. Cahiers Economiques.
Serie A: Economic Luxembourgeoise. a. ISSN
0070-881X
- Luxembourg. Service Central de la Statistique et
des Etudes Economiques. Cahiers Economiques.
Serie B: Comptes Nationaux. a.

- Luxembourg. Service Central de la Statistique et des Etudes Economiques. Cahiers Economiques. Serie C: Apercus sur l'Industrie. irreg.
- Luxembourg. Service Central de la Statistique et des Etudes Economiques. Cahiers Economiques. Serie D: Etudes Diverses. irreg.
- Luxembourg. Service Central de la Statistique et des Etudes Economiques. Collection D et M: Definitions et Methodes. irreg. ISSN 0076-1591
- Luxembourg. Service Central de la Statistique et des Etudes Economiques. Collection RP: Recensements de la Population. irreg. ISSN 0076-1613
- Luxembourg. Service Central de la Statistique et des Etudes Economiques. Indicateurs Rapides. m. ISSN 0019-6916
- Luxembourg. Service Central de la Statistique et des Etudes Economiques. La Situation Economique au Grand-Duche. q.

**Publi-Lux**
8, rue de la Greve, Luxembourg, Luxembourg.
- Annuaire Luxembourgeois; Annuaire LUX pour l'Industrie, le Commerce et l'Artisant. biennial. ISSN 0066-328X

**Imprimerie Saint Paulus, S. A.**
Case Postale 1908, 6-8, rue Jean Origer, Luxembourg, Luxembourg.
- Hemecht; Zeitschrift fuer Luxemburger Geschichte. q. ISSN 0018-0270

**Societe des Sciences Medicales du Grand-Duche de Luxembourg**
- Societe des Sciences Medicales du Grand-Duche de Luxembourg. Bulletin. (pub. by Imprimerie J. Beffort)

**STATEC**
see **Luxembourg. Service Central de la Statistique et des Etudes Economiques**

# MACAO

**Imprensa Nacional**
Macau, Macao.
- Macao. Servico Meterologico. Resultados das Observacoes Meterologicas de Macau. b-m. ISSN 0460-3060

# MALAGASY REPUBLIC

**Automobile Club de Madagascar**
Service du Guide Routier, B.P. 571, Tananarive, Malagasy Republic.
- Guide Routier et Touristique: Madagascar, Reunion, Maurice, Comores et Seychelles. a.

**Banque Centrale de la Republique Malgache**
B.P. 550, Tananarive, Malagasy Republic.
- Banque Centrale de la Republique Malgache . Bulletin Mensuel de Statistiques. m.
- Banque Centrale de la Republique Malgache. Rapport d'Activite. a.

**Banque Nationale Malagasy de Developpement**
B.P. 365, Tananarive, Malagasy Republic.
- Banque Nationale Malagasy de Developpement. Rapport d'Activite. ISSN 0067-401X

**Centre National de la Recherche Appliquee au Developpement Rural. Departement de Recherches Agronomiques**
B. P. 1690, Tananarive, Malagasy Republic.
- Centre National de Recherches Appliques au Developpement Rural. Departement de Recherches Agronomiques. Rapport Annuel. a.
- Centre National de Recherches Appliques au Developpement Rural. Departement de Recherches Agronomiques. Rapport d'Activite. irreg.

**Institut Pasteur de Madagascar**
B.P. 1274, Tananarive, Malagasy Republic.
- Institut Pasteur de Madagascar. Archives. s-a. ISSN 0020-2495

**Kianja**
B.P. 3153, Tananarive, Malagasy Republic.
- Kianja. irreg.

**Malagasy Republic. Bibliotheque Nationale**
B.P. 257, Tananarive, Malagasy Republic.
- Ny Boky No Loharanom-Pandrosoana. q. ISSN 0029-6724

**Malagasy Republic. Direction de la Recherche Scientifique et Technique. Section de Demographie**
B.P. 4096, Tananarive, Malagasy Republic.
- Ny Mponin'i Madagasikara. irreg.

**Malagasy Republic. Institut National de la Statistique et de la Recherche Economique**
Ministere des Finances et du Plan, B.P. 485, Tananarive, Malagasy Republic.
- Malagasy Republic. Institut National de la Statistique et de la Recherche Economique. Recensement Industriel. a.
- Statistiques du Commerce Exterieur de Madagascar. a. ISSN 0081-5306

**Malagasy Republic. Ministere des Finances et du Plan. Institut National de la Statistique et de la Recherche Economique**
see **Malagasy Republic. Institut National de la Statistique et de la Recherche Economique**

**Musee d'Art et Archeologie de l'Universite de Madagascar**
B.P. 564, Tananarive, Malagasy Republic.
- Taloma. irreg.

**Publi-Service Fandrosoana**
23, rue Bereni, Tananarive, Malagasy Republic.
- Taridalana. m.

**Societe Malgache d'Edition**
B.P. 659, Tananarive, Malagasy Republic.
- L'Economie. a.

**Union des Syndicats d'Interet Economique de Madagascar**
Place Roland Garros, Tananarive, Malagasy Republic.
- Union Economique.

**Universite de Madagascar. Bibliotheque Universitaire**
B.P. 908, Tananarive, Malagasy Republic.
- Bibliographie Annuelle de Madagascar. a. ISSN 0067-6926

**Universite de Madagascar. Faculte des Lettres et Sciences Humaines**
- Civilisation Malgache. (pub. by Editions Cujas FR)

**Universite de Madagascar. Laboratoire de Geographie**
B.P. 907, Tananarive, Malagasy Republic.
- Madagascar; Revue de Geographie. s-a. ISSN 0047-5416 (Co-sponsor: Centre National de la Recherche Scientifique; Association de Geographes de Madagascar)

**Zava Misy**
Ed. Richard Claude Ratovonarivo, Rue No 13, Ankadifotsy, Tananarive, Malagasy Republic.
- Zava Misy. m.

# MALAWI

**Agricultural Development and Marketing Corporation**
Box 5052, Limbe, Malawi.
- Agricultural Development and Marketing Corporation. Annual Report and Statement of Accounts. a.

**Agricultural Research Council of Malawi**
Makoka Research Sta., Private Bag 3, Thondwe, Malawi.
- Agricultural Research Council of Malawi. Annual Report. a. ISSN 0065-4515

**Association for the Advancement of Science of Malawi**
Box 280, Zomba, Malawi.
- Malawi Journal of Science. a.

**Blantyre Printing & Publishing Co. Ltd.**
Private Bag 39, Blantyre, Malawi.
- Malawi News. w. ISSN 0047-5580

**Blantyre Water Board**
Box 30369, Chichiri, Blantyre 3, Malawi.
- Blantyre Water Board. Annual Report and Statement of Accounts. a. ISSN 0084-7925

**Bunda College of Agriculture**
Research and Publications Committee, Box 219, Lilongwe, Malawi.
- Bunda College of Agriculture. Research Bulletin. a.

**Chancellor College**
Box 280, Zomba, Malawi.
- Journal of Social Science. a. ISSN 0302-3060

**Chancellor College. Geographical Society**
Box 280, Zomba, Malawi.
- Dziko; the geographical magazine. s-a. ISSN 0420-2392

**Chancellor College. Writers' Group**
Box 280, Limbe, Malawi.
- Odi. q.

**Diocese of Lilongwe**
- African. (pub. by Likuni Press and Publishing House)

**G.P.A.**
Ginnery Corner, P. O. Box 30125, Chichiri, Blantyre 3, Malawi.
- OK Magazine. m.

**General Publications**
Development House, Victoria Ave., Box 829, Blantyre 33328, Malawi.
- Business and Development News. m.

**Likuni Press and Publishing House**
Box 133, Lilongwe, Malawi.
- African. fortn. ISSN 0300-4651 (Diocese of Lilongwe)

**Malawi. Department of Agricultural Research**
Extensions Aids Branch, Box 30134, Lilongwe 3, Malawi.
- Malawi. Department of Agricultural Research. Research Bulletin. irreg.

**Malawi. Department of Information**
Box 494, Blantyre, Malawi.
- Boma Lathu. m.
- Malawi. Department of Information. Year in Review. a.
- This Is Malawi. m. ISSN 0563-4784

**Malawi. Fisheries Department**
Ministry of Agriculture and Natural Resources, Capital City, Box 30134, Lilongwe 3, Malawi.
- Malawi. Fisheries Department. Fisheries Bulletin. irreg.

**Malawi. Geological Survey**
Box 27, Zomba, Malawi
(Orders to: Government Printer, Box 37, Zomba, Malawi)
- Malawi. Geological Survey. Annual Report. a. ISSN 0076-311X
- Malawi. Geological Survey. Bulletin. irreg. ISSN 0076-3128
- Malawi. Geological Survey. Memoir. irreg. ISSN 0076-3136
- Malawi. Geological Survey. Records. irreg., no. 8, 1975. ISSN 0076-3144

**Malawi. Government Printer**
P.O. Box 37, Zomba, Malawi.
- Malawi. Accountant General. Report. a. ISSN 0076-3020
- Malawi. Department of Agriculture. Annual Report. a, latest 1972-73. ISSN 0076-3047
- Malawi. Department of Civil Aviation. Annual Report. a, latest 1968. ISSN 0076-3055
- Malawi. Department of Customs and Excise. Annual Report. a. ISSN 0076-3063
- Malawi. Department of Forestry and Game. Report. irreg.(approx. a) ISSN 0076-3071
- Malawi. Department of Police. Annual Report. a, latest 1971-72. ISSN 0076-308X
- Malawi. Judicial Department. Annual Report. a. ISSN 0076-3152
- Malawi. Lands Department. Annual Report. a. ISSN 0076-3179
- Malawi. Ministry of Finance. Budget Statement. a. ISSN 0076-3195
- Malawi. Ministry of Finance. Financial Statement. a.
- Malawi. Ministry of Justice. Annual Report. a. ISSN 0076-3160
- Malawi. Ministry of Local Government. Annual Report. a. ISSN 0076-3225
- Malawi. Ministry of Works. Annual Report. a. ISSN 0076-3233

- Malawi. Office of the Auditor General. Report. a. ISSN 0076-3314
- Malawi. Registrar of Insurance. Report. a. ISSN 0076-3349
- Malawi. Veterinary Department. Annual Report. a. ISSN 0076-3365
- Malawi Economic Report. a. ISSN 0076-3101
- Malawi Patent Journal and Trade Marks Journal. m. ISSN 0025-1267
- Malawi Treaty Series. a, latest ed. 1969. ISSN 0076-3357

**Malawi. Meteorological Services**
Box 587, Blantyre, Malawi
(Avail. from: Government Printer, Box 37, Zomba, Malawi)
- Malawi. Meteorological Services. Monthly Summaries. m.
- Malawi. Meteorological Services. Totals of Monthly and Annual Rainfall. a; latest issue 1974 per 1975.

**Malawi. National Library**
Box 30074, Chichiri, Blantyre 3, Malawi.
- Malawi. National Library. Annual Report. a. ISSN 0581-0906

**Malawi. National Statistical Office**
P.O. Box 333, Zomba, Malawi.
- Malawi. National Statistical Office. Annual Statement of External Trade. a. ISSN 0076-325X
- Malawi. National Statistical Office. Annual Survey of Economic Activities. a. ISSN 0076-3241
- Malawi. National Statistical Office. Balance of Payments. a. ISSN 0085-3003
- Malawi. National Statistical Office. Census Report. a. ISSN 0076-3039
- Malawi. National Statistical Office. Compendium of Agricultural Statistics. irreg. ISSN 0085-3011
- Malawi. National Statistical Office. Household Income and Expenditure Survey. irreg. ISSN 0076-3276
- Malawi. National Statistical Office. National Accounts Report. a. ISSN 0076-3284
- Malawi. National Statistical Office. National Sample Survey of Agriculture. irreg. ISSN 0076-3292
- Malawi. National Statistical Office. Population Census Final Report. irreg. (probably every 10 yrs) ISSN 0076-3306
- Malawi. National Statistical Office. Reported Employment and Earnings: Annual Report. a.
- Malawi. National Statistical Office. Sample Survey of Agricultural Small Holdings. irreg. ISSN 0085-2996
- Malawi Statistical Yearbook. a. (after 1972)
- Malawi Tourism Report. a.

**Malawi. Post Office Savings Bank**
Box 521, Blantyre, Malawi
(Orders to: Government Printer, Box 37, Blantyre, Malawi)
- Malawi. Post Office Savings Bank. Annual Report. a. ISSN 0076-3322

**Malawi Railways, Ltd.**
P.O. Box 5144, Limbe, Malawi.
- Malawi Railways. Annual Reports and Accounts. a. ISSN 0076-3330

**Malawi Young Pioneers**
Youth News Magazine, P.O. Box 5694, Limbe, Malawi.
- Malawi Youth News. q.

**Popular Publications**
P.O. Box 5592, Limbe, Malawi.
- Moni. m.

**Reserve Bank of Malawi**
Box 565, Blantyre, Malawi.
- Reserve Bank of Malawi. Economic and Financial Review. q. ISSN 0034-5520 (prep. by its Research Department)

**Society of Malawi**
Box 125, Blantyre, Malawi.
- Society of Malawi Journal. s-a. ISSN 0037-993X

**Tea Research Foundation of Central Africa**
Box 51, Mulanje, Malawi.
- Tea Research Foundation of Central Africa. Quarterly Newsletter. q. ISSN 0040-0378

**University of Malawi. Bunda College of Agriculture**
see Bunda College of Agriculture

**University of Malawi. Centre for Extension Studies**
Box 86, Zomba, Malawi.
- University of Malawi. Centre for Extension Studies. Annual Report. a.

**University of Malawi. Chancellor College**
see Chancellor College

**University of Malawi. Library Committee**
Box 280, Zomba, Malawi.
- University of Malawi. Library Committee. Report to the Senate on the University Libraries. a. ISSN 0085-3038

# MALAYSIA

**Academic Publishers**
Kuala Lumpur, Malaysia.
- Economic Bulletin. m.

**Asian Beacon Fellowship**
Box 105, Melaka, Malaysia.
- Asian Beacon. m. ISSN 0044-9180

**Association of Veterinary Surgeons Malaysia**
c/o Dr. Ahmad Mustaffa B. Hj. Babjee, Faculty of Veterinary Medicine & Animal Science, University of Agriculture Malaysia, Serdang, Selangor, Malaysia.
- Kajian Veterinar. s-a. ISSN 0047-309X

**Automobile Association of Malaya**
- A A M News. (pub. by Technical Publications Malaya)
- Motoring in Malaya. (pub. by Technical Publications Malaya)

**Bank Negara Malaysia**
Box 922, Jalan Kuching, Kuala Lumpur, Malaysia.
- Bank Negara Malaysia. Quarterly Economic Bulletin. q. ISSN 0005-5115

**Berita Publishing Sdn. Bhd.**
31 Jalan Riong, Kuala Lumpur, Malaysia.
- Malayan Business. m.
- Malaysian Business. m.
- Puspaniaga. m.
- Straits Times Directory of Malaysia. a.

**Buddhist Missionary Society**
Jalan Berhala, Kuala Lumpur, Malaysia.
- Voice of Buddhism. s-a. ISSN 0042-8094

**Democratic Action Party of Malaysia**
77 Jalan, 20-9 Paramount Garden, Petaling Jaya, Selangor, Malaysia.
- Rocket. bi-m. ISSN 0048-8461

**Dewan Bahasa dan Pustaka Malaysia. Cawangan Sarawak**
Box 1390, Kuching, Sarawak, Malaysia.
- Dewan Pemadah. m.

**Dunlop Estates Berhad**
Box 55, Bastion House, Jalan Kota, Malacca, Malaysia.
- Dunlop Estates News. q.

**Economic Association of Malaysia**
Faculty of Economics and Administration, University of Malaya, Kuala Lumpur, Malaysia.
- Malaysian Economic Studies/Malaysian Economic Studies. s-a. ISSN 0022-782X

**Educational Journal Press**
Box 53, Petaling Jaya, Selangor, Kuala Lumpur, Malaysia.
- Malaysian Journal of Education. s-a. ISSN 0025-133X

**Esso Malaysia Berhad**
Box 601, Kuala Lumpur, Malaysia.
- Esso Dealer. bi-m. ISSN 0014-1003
- Esso News. m. ISSN 0014-102X
- Pelita. q. ISSN 0031-417X

**Geological Society of Malaysia**
c/o Department of Geology, University of Malaya, Kuala Lumpur, Malaysia.
- Geological Society of Malaysia. Bulletin. irreg., no. 7, 1974, in prep. no. 8 and 9. ISSN 0072-1093
- Geological Society of Malaysia. Newsletter. bi-m.

**Gereja Methodist Malaysia**
Tingkat 8, Wisma Methodist, Lorong Davidson, Kuala Kumpur 05-05, Malaysia.
- Pelita Methodist. m.

**Syed Hussain Publications (Sdn) Bhd.**
Penthouse, 6th Fl., Bangunan Bakti, Box 838, 91, Jln. Campbell, Kuala Lumpur, Malaysia.
- Asian Defence Journal. bi-m.
- Asian Trade and Industry. m.
- Malaysian Building & Construction. bi-m.

**Incorporated Society of Planters**
No. 29, 31 & 33, Jalan Taman u Thant, Box 262, Kuala Lumpur, Malaysia.
- Planter. m. ISSN 0032-0951

**Institiut Teknoloji Mara**
see Mara Institute of Technology

**Institution of Engineers, Malaysia**
P.O. Box 223, Petaling Jaya, Selangor, Malaysia.
- Institution of Engineers, Malaysia. Bulletin. m.
- Institution of Engineers, Malaysia. Journal. s-a. ISSN 0538-0057

**Institution of Surveyors (Malaysia)**
P.O. 2524, Kuala Lumpur, Malaysia.
- Surveyor. q.

**Inter-Grafik**
68, Jalam Ampang, Kuala Lumpur, Malaysia.
- Malaysian Finance & Development. irreg.

**International Council on Archives. Southeast Asian Regional Branch**
c/o National Archives of Malaysia, Federal Government Building, Jalan Sultan, Petaling Jaya, Malaysia.
- Southeast Asian Archives. a. ISSN 0085-6509

**International Planned Parenthood Federation. East & South East Asia and Oceania Region**
246 Jalan Ampang, Kuala Lumpur 16-03, Malaysia.
- Concern. q.

**Islamic Political Party of Malaysia**
214-1A Jalan Pahang, Kuala Lumpur, Malaysia.
- Berita Pas; parti Islam se-Malaysia. m.

**Islamic Students' Union of the University of Malaya**
Kuala Lumpur, Malaysia.
- Sejahtera. a.

**Melville Jayathissa, Ed. & Pub.**
No. 19, Road SS 1/7, Sungei Way - Subang, Selangor, Malaysia.
- Library Industry. irreg.; latest issue, no. 4.

**Karate Association of Malaysia**
- Karate International Annual. (pub. by Karate Budokan International Inc.)

**Karate Budokan International Inc.**
44 Pudu Road, Kuala Lumpur, Malaysia.
- Karate International Annual. a. ISSN 0085-2481 (Karate Association of Malaysia)

**Kerala Sree**
Ed. R. S. Mony, Mullakkal, Alleppey 1, Kerala, Malaysia.
- Kerala Sree. m. ISSN 0023-0537

**Kuala Lumpur Stock Exchange**
Damansara Centre, 4th Fl., Block C, Damansara Heights, Kuala Lumpur 23-04, Malaysia.
- Kuala Lumpur Stock Exchange. Companies Handbook. a.

**M P R C (Asia) Sdn. Berhad**
7 Jalan Baiduri, Box 706, Kuala Lumpur 01-02, Malaysia.
- M P R C Report on Finance, Commerce, Industry - Indonesia. irreg.
- M P R C Report on Finance, Commerce, Industry - Singapore. irreg.
- M P R C Report on Finance, Commerce, Industry - Thailand. irreg.

**Majlis Pengeluar-Pengeluar Getah Tanah Melayu**
see Rubber Producers Council of Malaysia

**Majlis Pengeluar-Pengeluar Getah Tanah Melayu**
Box 272, Bangunan Getah Asli, Jalan Ampang, Kuala Lumpur, Malaysia.
- Rubber Producers' Council of Malaysia. Annual Report/Majlis Pengeluar-Pengeluar Getah Tanah Melayu. Lapuran Tahunan. a.

**Malaya Railway Administration**
Box 1, Kuala Lumpur, Malaysia.
- Keretapi. q. ISSN 0047-3375

**Malayan Nature Society**
Box 750, Kuala Lumpur, Malaysia.
- Malayan Nature Journal. q. ISSN 0025-1291

**Malayan Pineapple Industry Board**
Pineapple Research Station, Box 101, Pekan Nenas,
Johor, Malaysia.
- Malaysian Pineapple. irreg, latest vol. 2, 1972.

**Malaysia. Bahagian Perikanan**
*see* **Malaysia. Fisheries Division**

**Malaysia. Department of Statistics**
Jalan Young, Kuala Lumpur, Malaysia.
- Malaysia. Department of Statistics. Annual
Bulletin of Statistics. a. ISSN 0542-3570
- Malaysia. Department of Statistics. Survey of
Construction Industries. a. ISSN 0085-3046
- Malaysia. Department of Statistics. Vital Statistics.
a.
- Monthly Statistical Bulletin of West Malaysia/
Siaran Perangkaan Bulanan Bagi Malaysia Barat.
m. ISSN 0542-3686
- West Malaysia Annual Statistics of External
Trade. a. ISSN 0085-8080

**Malaysia. Department of Tourism**
P.O. Box 328, Kuala Lumpur, Malaysia.
- Around Malaysia. bi-m.

**Malaysia. Federal Agricultural Marketing Authority**
17 & 19 Jalan Selangor, Petaling Jaya, Selangor,
Malaysia.
- Review of Agricultural Economics Malaysia. irreg.
ISSN 0034-6403

**Malaysia. Fisheries Division**
Kuala Lumpur, Malaysia.
- Malaysia. Bahagian Perikanan. Perangkaan
Tahunan Perikanan. Annual Fisheries Statistics. a.

**Malaysia. Geological Survey**
Kuching, Sarawak, Malaysia.
- Malaysia. Geological Survey. Annual Report. a.
ISSN 0542-3767

**Malaysia. Government Printer**
Jalan Chan Sow Ling, Kuala Lumpur, Malaysia.
- Malaysia Official Year Book. a. ISSN 0076-3373
(Prepared by: Federal Department of Information)

**Malaysia. Jabatan Galian**
*see* **Malaysia. Mines Department**

**Malaysia. Kementerian Buroh dan Tenaga Raayat**
*see* **Malaysia. Ministry of Labour and Manpower**

**Malaysia. Kementerian Luar Negeri**
*see* **Malaysia. Ministry of Foreign Affairs**

**Malaysia. Kementerian Pertanian dan Tanah**
*see* **Malaysia. Ministry of Agriculture and Lands**

**Malaysia. Kementerian Pertanian dan Tanah.
Bahagian Perikanan**
*see* **Malaysia. Fisheries Division**

**Malaysia. Lembaga Pemasara Pertanian Persekutuan**
*see* **Malaysia. Federal Agricultural Marketing
Authority**

**Malaysia. Meteorological Service**
Jalan Sultan, Petaling Jaya, Selangor, Malaysia.
- Malaysia. Meteorological Service. Summary of
Observations for Malaysia. a.
- Monthly Abstract of Meteorological Observations
of Malaysia. m.

**Malaysia. Mines Department**
Jalan Gurney, Kuala Lumput, Malaysia.
- Quarterly Bulletin of Statistics Relating to the
Mining Industry of Malaysia. q. ISSN 0025-1313

**Malaysia. Ministry of Agriculture and Lands**
Publications Officer, Swettenham Rd., Kuala
Lumpur, Malaysia.
- Malaysia. Ministry of Agriculture and Lands.
Technical Bulletins. irreg.
- Malaysian Agricultural Journal. s-a. ISSN 0025-
1321

**Malaysia. Ministry of Agricultural and Lands.
Fisheries Division**
*see* **Malaysia. Fisheries Division**

**Malaysia. Ministry of Foreign Affairs**
Jalan Wisma Putra, Kuala Lumpur, Malaysia.
- Foreign Affairs Malaysia. q. ISSN 0015-7147
- Malaysia in Brief. irreg.
- Malaysian Digest. fortn. ISSN 0047-5629

**Malaysia. Ministry of Labour and Manpower**
Jalan Raja, Kuala Lumpur, Malaysia.
- Malaysia. Kementerian Buroh Dan Tenaga
Raayat. Monthly Report. m.

**Malaysia. National Archives**
Federal Government Building, Jalan Sultan, Petaling
Jaya, Malaysia.
- National Archives of Malaysia. Annual Report/
Arkib Negara Malaysia. Penyata Tahunan. a.
ISSN 0076-3381

**Malaysia. National Family Planning Board**
Box 416, Ipoh Road, Kuala Lampur, Malaysia.
- Malaysia. National Family Planning Board.
Bulletin Kejuarga. m.

**Malaysia. National Library**
U.M.B.C. Building, 7th Fl., Jalan Sultan Sulaiman,
Kuala Lampur 01-33, Malaysia.
- Current Malaysian Serials: Government/Majalah
Kini Malaysia: Kerajaan. irreg.
- Malaysian National Bibliography/Bibliografi
Negara Malaysia. q (with annual cumulative issue)
ISSN 0076-3403
- Malaysian Periodicals Index/Indeks Majalah
Malaysia. a.

**Malaysia. Perbendaharaan**
*see* **Malaysia. Treasury**

**Malaysia. Perkhidmatan Kajicuaca Malaysia**
*see* **Malaysia. Meteorological Service**

**Malaysia. Survey Department**
Kuala Lumpur, Malaysia.
- Malaysian Surveyor. irreg.

**Malaysia. Treasury**
Jalan Chan Sow Lin, Kuala Lumpur, Malaysia.
- Malaysia. Perbendaharaan. Anggaran Belanjawan.
irreg.
- Malaysia. Treasury. Economic Report. a.

**Malaysia Inter-Religious Organisation**
16 Road 49E, Petaling Jaya, Selangor, Malaysia.
- Malaysia Inter-Religious Organisation. Suara. q.

**Malaysia. Jabatan Perangkaan**
*see* **Malaysia. Department of Statistics**

**Malaysian Agricultural Research and Development
Institute**
Box 208, Sungei Besi, Serdang, Selangor, Malaysia.
- M A R D I Research Bulletin. s-a.

**Malaysian Branch of the Royal Asiatic Society**
c/o the National Archives, Petaling Jaya, Malaysia.
- Royal Asiatic Society. Malaysian Branch. Journal.
s-a. ISSN 0304-2251

**Malaysian Centre for Development Studies**
Prime Minister's Department, Banganun Komplek
Kerajaan, Blok K 11 8 12, Jalan Duta, Kuala
Lumpur, Malaysia.
- Development Forum. s-a. ISSN 0012-1584
- Foram Pembangunan. s-a.

**Malaysian Chinese Association**
67, Jln. Ampang, 5th Fl., Kuala Lumpur, Malaysia.
- Guardian. m.
- Malaysian Chinese Association. Annual Report. a.
ISSN 0542-397X

**Malaysian Forester**
c/o Forest Research Institute, Kepong, Selangor,
Malaysia.
- Malaysian Forester. q. ISSN 0302-2935

**Malaysian Historical Society**
c/o Muzium Negara, Jalan Petalawati, Kuala
Lumpur, Malaysia.
- Malaysia in History. q. ISSN 0047-5610

**Malaysian Industrial Development Finance Berhad**
Bangunan MIDF, Jalan Ampang, Kuala Lumpur,
Malaysia.
- M I D F Melaporkan/M I D F Reports. 3 per yr.

**Malaysian Institute of Chemistry**
c/o Chemistry Department, Jalan Sultan, Petaling
Jaya, Selangor, Malaysia.
- Kimia. a.

**Malaysian Institute of Management**
Fitzpatrick's Building, 15th Fl., 86, Jalan Raja
Chulan, Kuala Lumpur 05-10, Malaysia.
- Malaysian Management Review. 3 per yr. ISSN
0025-1348

**Malaysian Mathematical Society**
c/o Department of Mathematics, University of
Malaya, Kuala Lumpur, Malaysia.
- Malaysian Mathematical Society. Bulletin. 3 per
yr.

**Malaysian Medical Association**
MMA House, (4th Floor), 124 Jalan Pahang, Kuala
Lumpur, Malaya.
- Malaysian Medical Association. Medical
Directory. triennial.

**Malaysian Multi-Purpose Cooperative Society**
67 Jalan Ampang, Kuala Lumpur, Malaysia.
- Malaysian Multi-Purpose Cooperative Society.
Review. irreg.

**Malaysian Press Institute**
Kuala Lumpur, Malaysia.
- Leader. irreg.

**Malaysian Rubber Research and Development Board**
- Natural Rubber News. (pub. by Malaysian Rubber
Bureau US)

**Malaysian Society of Applied Biology**
c/o Faculty of Agriculture, University of Malaya,
Kuala Lumpur, Malaysia.
- Malaysian Applied Biology Journal. s-a.

**Malaysian Sociological Research Institute**
Box 2112, Kuala Lumpur, Malaysia.
- Intisari; research journal of wider Malaysia. irreg.

**Malaysian Timber Industry Board**
150 Jalan Ampang, Box 887, Kuala Lumpur,
Malaysia.
- Maskayu; a news bulletin on the timber industry
in west malaysia and singapore. m.
- Timber Trade Review/Warta Perdaganan Kayu. q.
ISSN 0302-5802

**Malaysian Trades Union Congress**
120 Jalan Semangat, Petaling Jaya, Malaysia.
- Suara Buroh. m.

**Malaysian Veterinary Association**
c/o Central Animal Facility, Faculty of Medicine,
University of Malaya, Kuala Lumpur, Malaysia.
- Malaysian Veterinary Journal. a. ISSN 0460-8518

**Mara Institute of Technology**
Shah Alam, Selangor, Malaysia.
- Institut Teknoloji Mara. Quarterly Journal. q.

**Medical Practitioners Laboratory and Stores
Cooperative Society**
643-1 Jalan Ipoh, Kuala Lumpur, Malaysia.
- Doctor's Coop Newsletter. irreg.

**J. Victor Morais, Ed. & Pub.**
Box 266, B.P. House, Jalan Davidson, Kuala
Lumpur 0505, Malaysia
(Dist. by International Publications Service, 114 E.
32nd St., New York, N.Y. 10016)
- Who's Who in Malaysia and Singapore. biennial.
ISSN 0083-9620

**National Press Ltd.**
Box 260, Penang, Malaysia.
- Tic-Tac's Malayan Raceguide. m. ISSN 0040-6724

**National Union of Bank Employees**
61 Jalan Ampang, Kuala Lumpur, Malaysia.
- Suara N U B E. m.

**National Union of Plantation Workers**
Plantation House, Box 73, Petaling Jaya, Selangor,
Malaysia.
- Union Herald. m. ISSN 0049-528X

**National Union of Teachers of Malaysia**
Box 169, Taiping, Perak, Malaysia.
- Educator. m. ISSN 0013-2012

**National University of Malaysia**
Jalan Pantai Baru, Kuala Lumpur, Malaysia.
- Humanisma. a.
- Sains Malaysiana: Jernal Sains Alam Semula. s-a.
- Universiti Kebangsaan Malaysia. Lapurau Tahunan/Annual Report. a.

**National University of Malaysia, Department of Geography**
P.O. Box 1124, Jalan Pantai Baru, Kuala Lumpur 22-12, Malaysia.
- Ilmu Alam. a. (Co-sponsor: Geographical Society of the National University of Malaysia)

**National University of Malaysia. Historical Society**
c/o Jabatan Sejarah, Jalan Pantai Baru, Kuala Lumpur, Malaysia.
- Jebat. a.

**National University of Malaysia. Persatuan Kajimanusia Dan Kajimasharakat**
Jalan Pantai Baru, Kuala Lumpur, Malaysia.
- Jernal Antropolojj Dan Sosioloji. a.

**New Straits Times Press (Malaysia) Berhad**
No. 31, Jalan Riong, Kuala Lumpur, Malaysia (Dist. in U.S. by International Publications Service, 303 Park Ave. South, New York, N.Y. 10010)
- Information Malaysia. a.

**Perkhidmatan Kajicuaca Malaysia**
*see* Malaysia. Meteorological Service

**Persatuan Economi Malaysia**
*see* Economic Association of Malaysia

**Persatuan Mahasiswa Islam Universiti Malaya**
*see* Islamic Students' Union of the University of Malaya

**Persatuan Perpustakaan Malaysia**
Box 2072, Kuala Lumpur, Malaysia.
- Majallah Perpustakaan Malaysia. a.

**Pertadbiran Keretapi Tanah Malaya**
*see* Malaya Railway Administration

**Pure Life Society**
Batu 6, Jalan Puchong, Petaling P.O., Kuala Lumpur, Malaysia.
- Dharma; a quarterly devoted to universal religion, righteousness & culture. q. ISSN 0012-1746

**Pusat Pengajian Pembangunan Malaysia**
*see* Malaysian Centre for Development Studies

**A. Ragunathan**
5-15e Jalan Chantek, Petaling Java, Kuala Lumpur, Malaysia.
- Who's Who in the Labour Movement. irreg.

**Regional Centre for Education in Science and Mathematics**
Glugor, Penang, Malaysia.
- R E C S A M Annual Report. a.
- R E C S A M Newsletter. q.

**Rubber Producers' Council of Malaysia**
Peti Surat 272, Bangunan Getah Asli, Jalan Ampang, Kuala Lumpur, Malaysia.
- Rubber Producers' Council of Malaysia. Monthly Statistical Bulletin. m.

**Rubber Research Institute of Malaysia**
Box 150, Kuala Lumpur, Malaysia.
- Planters Bulletin. bi-m. ISSN 0032-096X
- Rubber Research Institute of Malaysia. Journal. 5 nos. per vol.(1 vol. every 2 yrs.) ISSN 0035-953X
- Rubber Research Institute of Malaysia. Planters Conference Proceedings. a.

**Sabah. Department of Agriculture. Agricultural Economics Division**
Kota Kinabalu, Sabah, Malaysia.
- Agricultural Statistics of Sabah. a.

**Sabah. Department of Statistics**
P.O. Box 500, Kota Kinabalu, Sabah, Malaysia.
- Sabah. Department of Statistics. Annual Bulletin of Statistics. a. ISSN 0080-5203

**Sabah. Forest Department**
Sandakan, Sabah, Malaysia.
- Sabah. Forest Department. Annual Report. a. ISSN 0080-5211

**Sabah. Marine Department**
Kota Kinabalu, Sabah, Malaysia.
- Sabah. Marine Department. Annual Report. a. ISSN 0080-522X

**Sabah Society**
Box 547, Kota Kinabalu, Sabah, Malaysia.
- Sabah Society. Journal. irreg. ISSN 0036-2131

**Sambandan International Press**
Post Box 172, Johore Bahru, Malaysia.
- Asian Almanac; weekly abstracts of Asian affairs. w. ISSN 0004-4520

**Sarawak. Department of Agriculture. Research Branch**
P.O. Box 977, Kuching, Sarawak, Malaysia.
- Sarawak. Department of Agriculture. Research Branch. Annual Report. a. ISSN 0080-6420

**Sarawak. Department of Statistics**
Jalan Badrudin, Kuching, Sarawak, Malaysia.
- Annual Statistical Bulletin Sarawak. a. ISSN 0080-6439
- Sarawak External Trade Statistics. a. ISSN 0080-6455
- Sarawak Vital Statistics. a. ISSN 0080-6447
- Statistical Handbook of Sarawak. a. ISSN 0081-4814

**Sarawak. Government Printing Office**
Kuching, Sarawak, Malaysia.
- Sarawak Gazette. m. ISSN 0036-4762

**Sarawak Economic Development Corporation**
Electra House, 2nd Fl., Box 400, Kuching, Sarawak, Malaysia.
- Sarawak Economic Development Corporation. Annual Report and Statement of Account. a.

**Sarawak Electricity Supply Corporation**
Kuching, Sarawak, Malaysia.
- Sarawak Electricity Supply Corporation. Report. a.

**Sound of Malaysian's Musician**
18 Dato Koyah Rd., Penang, Malaysia.
- Sound of Malaysian's Musician/Ta Ma Ko Yu Chih Sheng. s-a.

**Southeast Asia Development Corporation Berhad**
G.P.O. Box 2171, Kuala Lumpur 01-20, Malaysia.
- Southeast Asia Development Corporation Berhad. Reports and Accounts. a.

**States of Malaya Chamber of Mines**
Wisma Doshi, 1st Fl., 12, Jalan Tuanku Abdul Rahman, Box 2560, Kuala Lumpur, Malaysia.
- States of Malaya Chamber of Mines. Council Report. a.
- States of Malaya Chamber of Mines. Yearbook. a.

**Technical Association of Malaysia**
46 Jalan 52/4, New Town Centre, Petaling Jaya, Malaysia.
- Technical Association of Malaysia. Journal. q. ISSN 0040-0882

**Technical Publications Malaya**
10 Clove Hall Rd., Penang, Malaysia.
- A A M News. m. ISSN 0001-0146 (Automobile Association of Malaya)
- Motoring in Malaya. every 18 mos. ISSN 0077-1694 (Automobile Association of Malaya)

**Tin Industry (Research and Development) Board**
Wisma Doshi, 1st Fl., 12, Jalan Tuanku Abdul Rahman, Box 2560, Kuala Lumpur, Malaysia.
- Timah. q.

**United Malayan Banking Corp. Berhad**
42 Jalan Mountbatten, Kuala Lumpur, Malaysia.
- U M B C Economic Review. q. ISSN 0041-5197

**United Malays National Organisation**
Jl. T. Ab. Rahman, Bangunan UMNO, Kuala Lumpur, Malaysia.
- United Malays National Organisation. Penvata. irreg.

**United Planting Association of Malaysia**
Box 272, Kuala Lumpur, Malaysia.
- United Planting Association of Malaysia. Annual Report. a.

**Universiti Kebangsaan Malaysia**
*see* National University of Malaysia

**Universiti Kebangsaan Malaysia. Persatuan Sejarah**
*see* National University of Malaysia. Historical Society

**Universiti Malaya**
*see* University of Malaya

**Universiti Malaya. Persatuan Antropologi dan Sosiologi**
*see* University of Malaya. Anthropology and Sociology Society

**Universiti Malaya. Persatuan Sejarah**
*see* University of Malaya. Historical Society

**Universiti Sains Malaysia. Pusat Pengajian Ilmu Kemanusiaan**
*see* University of Science of Malaya. School of Humanities

**University of Malaya Accounting Club**
Faculty of Economics and Administration, University of Malaya, Lembah Pantai, Kuala Lumpur 22-11, Malaysia.
- Accounting Journal. a.

**University of Malaya. Agricultural Graduates Alumni**
c/o Faculty of Agriculture, Lembah Pantai, Kuala Lumpur 22-11, Malaysia.
- Agricultural Directory of Malaysia. a.
- Tumbuh. s-a. (Subscr. to: Jalan 11/6, No. 21, Petaling Jaya, Selangor, Malaysia)

**University of Malaya. Anthropology and Sociology Society**
Lembah Pantai, Kuala Lumpur 22-11, Malaysia.
- Man and Society/Manusia dan Masyarakat. irreg.

**University of Malaya Business Club**
Kuala Lumpur, Malaysia.
- Businesscope. irreg.

**University of Malaya. Chinese Language Society**
Kuala Lumpur, Malaysia.
- University of Malaya. Chinese Language Society. Journal/Majallah Pantai/Pan T'ai Hsueh Pao. irreg. ISSN 0553-0644

**University of Malaya. Department of Engineering**
Lembah Pantai, Kuala Lumpur 22-11, Malaysia.
- University of Malaya. Department of Engineering. Journal. a.

**University of Malaya. English Department**
Kuala Lumpur, Malaysia.
- Tenggara. s-a.

**University of Malaya. Faculty of Economics & Administration**
Lembah Pantai, Kuala Lumpur, Malaysia.
- Monograph Series on Malaysian Economic Affairs. a.

**University of Malaya. Faculty of Education**
Kuala Lumpur 22-11, Malaysia.
- Journal of Educational Research/Jurnal Pendidekan. a.

**University of Malaya. Faculty of Law**
Lembah Pantai, Kuala Lumpur 22-11, Malaysia.
- Journal of Malaysian and Comparative Law/Jernal Undang-Undang. s-a.

**University of Malaya. Faculty of Science**
Lembah Pantai, Kuala Lumpur 22-11, Malaysia.
- Malaysian Journal of Science/Jernal Sains Malaysia. a.

**University of Malaya. Geographical Society**
Kuala Lumpur, Malaya.
- Geographica. a.

**University of Malaya. Historical Society**
Lembah Pantai, Kuala Lumpur 22-11, Malaysia.
- Jernal Sejarah. a.

**University of Malaya. Law Society**
Lembah Pantai, Kuala Lumpur 22-11, Malaysia.
- Neraca. a.

**University of Science of Malaya. School of Humanities**
Minden, Malaysia.
- University of Science of Malaysia History Forum/Universiti Sains Malaysia Foram Sejarah. irreg.

**Utusan Melayu (Malaysia) Berhad**
46 M Jalan Chan Sow Lin, Kuala Lumpur,
Malaysia.
- U F F. (Utusan Filem dan Feshen) m.
- Wanita. m.

# MALI

**Chambre de Commerce et d'Industrie du Mali**
B.P. 46, Bamako, Mali.
- Annuaire Administratif de la Republique du Mali.
  a. ISSN 0066-2453
- Annuaire des Entreprises du Mali. irreg. ISSN
  0080-0988
- Chambre de Commerce et d'Industrie du Mali.
  Bulletin Trimestriel. m.
- Chambre de Commerce et d'Industrie du Mali.
  Precis Fiscal, Commercial, des Changes et des
  Echanges. a. ISSN 0067-3110
- Elements du Bilan Economique. irreg., latest issue,
  1965. ISSN 0071-0008
- Repertoire des Principaux Textes Legislatifs et
  Reglementaires Promulgues en Republique du
  Mali. a. ISSN 0080-1011

**Institut des Sciences Humaines**
- Etudes Maliennes. (pub. by Impremerie M.E.N.)

**Impremerie M.E.N.**
B.P. 1596, Bamako, Mali.
- Etudes Maliennes. q. (Institut des Sciences
  Humaines)

**Mali. Ministere de l'Enseignement Superieur
Secondaire et de la Recherche Scientifique. Institut
Pedagogique National**
B.P. 1583, Bamako, Mali.
- Contact: Bulletin Pedagogique. q.

**Mali. Service de la Statistique Generale, de la
Comptabilite Nationale et de la Mecanographie**
Bamako, Mali.
- Mali. Service de la Statistique Generale, de la
  Comptabilite Nationale et de la Mecanographie.
  Annuaire Statistique. a. ISSN 0076-3411
- Mali. Service de la Statistique Generale, de la
  Comptabilite Nationale et de la Mecanographie.
  Bulletin Mensuel de Statistique. m.
- Mali. Service de la Statistique Generale, de la
  Comptabilite Nationale et de la Mecanographie.
  Statistiques Douanieres du Commerce Exterieur.

**Sankore**
B.P. 1596, Bamako, Mali.
- Sankore; revue de vulgarisation scientifique. s-a.

# MALTA

**Central Bank of Malta**
Castille Square, Valletta, Malta.
- Central Bank of Malta. Annual Report. ISSN
  0577-0653
- Central Bank of Malta. Quarterly Review. q. ISSN
  0008-9273

**General Workers Union**
- It-Torca. (pub. by Union Press)

**Malta. Central Office of Statistics**
Auberge de Castille, Valletta, Malta
(Subscr. to: Department of Information, Auberge de
Castille, Valletta, Malta)
- Malta. Central Office of Statistics. Annual
  Abstract of Statistics. a. ISSN 0081-4733
- Malta. Central Office of Statistics. Census of
  Agriculture and Fisheries. a.
- Malta. Central Office of Statistics. Census of
  Production Report. a. ISSN 0076-3462
- Malta. Central Office of Statistics. Demographic
  Review. a. ISSN 0076-3470
- Malta. Central Office of Statistics. Education
  Statistics. a. ISSN 0076-3489
- Malta. Central Office of Statistics. Quarterly
  Digest of Statistics. q. ISSN 0025-1437
- Malta Trade Statistics. q.
- National Accounts of the Maltese Islands. a. ISSN
  0077-295X
- Shipping and Aviation Statistics of the Maltese
  Islands. a. ISSN 0080-9268

**Malta. Department of Health**
Auberge de Castille, Valletta, Malta.
- Report on the Health Conditions of the Maltese
  Islands and on the Work of the Department of
  Health. a.

**Malta Chamber of Commerce**
The Exchange, Republic St., Valletta, Malta.
- Commercial Courier. every 3 weeks. ISSN 0010-
  2938
- Malta Trade Directory. a, latest issue 1976 per 77.
  ISSN 0076-3446

**Malta Library Association**
Students' Union, 220 St. Paul St., Valletta, Malta.
- Malta Library Association. Yearbook. biennial.

**Malta Union of Teachers**
Teachers' Institute, Merchants St., Valletta, Malta.
- Teacher. q. ISSN 0040-0416

**Royal University Students' Theological Association**
Tal-Qroqq, Msida, Malta.
- Melita Theologica. a.

**St. Luke's Hospital**
Bacteriology Department, Malta.
- St. Luke's Hospital Gazette. s-a. ISSN 0036-3081

**Sovereign Order of Saint John of Jerusalem**
Russian Grand Priory of Malta, Officier
d'Academie, 5-3 Scerberras Sq., Floriana, Malta.
- O. S. J. Bulletin. q.

**Union Press**
South St., Valletta, Malta.
- It-Torca. w. ISSN 0021-2725 (General Workers
  Union)

**University of Malta. Department of Maltese and
Oriental Languages**
Msida, Malta.
- Journal of Maltese Studies. irreg. ISSN 0075-4285

**Welcome to Malta League**
20312 Old Bakery St., Valletta, Malta.
- This Malta. m. ISSN 0040-6236

# MARTINIQUE

**Chambre de Commerce et d'Industrie de la
Martinique**
Rue Victor Hugo, Fort de France, Martinique.
- Promotion. bi-m.

**Societe Medicale des Antilles et Guyane Francaise**
Section Martiniquaise, 35 rue Victor Severe, Fort de
France, Martinique.
- Caraibe Medical. q.
- Congress International Medical de Pays de
  Langue Francaise de l'Hemisphere American
  Rapports et Communications. biennial. ISSN
  0414-4406

# MAURITANIA

**Mariemou**
B.P. 47, Nouakchott, Mauritania.
- Mariemou; revue de la jeune fille et de la femme
  Mauritaniennes. q. ISSN 0047-5920

**Mauritania. Direction de la Statistique et des Etudes
Economiques**
B.P. 240, Nouakchott, Mauritania.
- Mauritania. Direction de la Statistique et des
  Etudes Economiques. Bulletin Mensuel
  Statistique. m. ISSN 0543-1433

# MAURITIUS

**Association of Urban Authorities**
Port Louis, Mauritius.
- Association of Urban Authorities. Annual Bulletin.
  a. ISSN 0304-6451

**Bank of Mauritius**
P.O. Box 29, Port Louis, Mauritius.
- Bank of Mauritius. Annual Report. a. ISSN 0067-
  3722
- Bank of Mauritius. Quarterly Review. q. ISSN
  0005-5301

**Bureau des Relations Publiques de l'Industrie
Sucriere**
*see* **Public Relations Office of the Sugar Industry**

**J. Clency Dinan, Ed. & Pub.**
113 Boundary Rd., Rosehill, Mauritius.
- I O A Friendship Directory. s-a.

**Mauritius. Archives**
Sauray Hotel, Coromandel, Beau-Bassin, Mauritius.
- Mauritius. Archives. Annual Report. a. ISSN
  0076-5481
- Memorandum of Books Printed in Mauritius. q.

**Mauritius. Central Electricity Board**
Curepipe, Mauritius.
- Mauritius. Central Electricity Board. Annual
  Report. a.

**Mauritius. Central Statistical Office**
Rose Hill, Mauritius.
- Mauritius. Central Statistical Office. International
  Travel and Tourism. irreg.
- Mauritius. Central Statistical Office. Semi-Annual
  Digest of Statistics. s-a. ISSN 0025-6056

**Mauritius. Customs and Excise Department**
Port Louis, Mauritius.
- Mauritius. Customs and Excise Department.
  Annual Report. a, latest 1975. ISSN 0076-549X
- Mauritius. Customs and Excise Department.
  Quarterly Statistical Report. q.

**Mauritius. Government Printing Office**
Elizabeth II Ave., Port Louis, Mauritius.
- Mauritius. Legislative Assembly. Sessional Paper.
  irreg. ISSN 0076-5503
- Mauritius. Meteorological Services. Report. a;
  latest issue 1973 per 74. ISSN 0076-5511
- Mauritius. Ministry of Housing, Lands and Town
  and Country Planning. Annual Reports. a. ISSN
  0076-552X
- Mauritius. Ministry of Works and Internal
  Communications. Report. a. ISSN 0076-5554
- Mauritius. Public Accounts Committee. Report. a.
  ISSN 0076-5562

**Mauritius. Ministry of External Affairs, Tourism and
Immigration**
Port Louis, Mauritius
(Subscr. to: Government Printing Office, Elizabeth
II Ave., Port Louis, Mauritius)
- Mauritius Directory of the Diplomatic Corps. a.
  ISSN 0085-3194

**Mauritius. Ministry of Social Security**
Port Louis, Mauritius.
- Mauritius. Ministry of Social Security. Annual
  Report. a, latest 1973-74. ISSN 0076-5538

**Mauritius. Registrar of Insurance**
Treasury Building, Port Louis, Mauritius.
- Mauritius. Registrar of Insurance. Annual Report.
  a.

**Mauritius People's Progressive Party**
Box 545, Port Louis, Mauritius.
- Travailleur. bi-w.

**Mauritius Times Publication**
23 Bourbon St., Port-Louis, Mauritius.
- Mauritius Times. w. ISSN 0025-6064

**Public Relations Office of the Sugar Industry**
Plantation House, Port Louis, Mauritius.
- Bureau des Relations Publiques de l'Industrie
  Sucriere. Bulletin Mensuel. m.
- P R O S I. m.

**Young Mens Muslim Association**
53 Magon St., P.O. Box 292, Port Louis, Mauritius.
- Youth Mirror. m. ISSN 0049-8459

**Zamana**
c/o B. Bucktowarsingh, Ed., 14 Vallonville St., Port
Louis, Mauritius.
- Zamana. s-m.

# MEXICO

**A I M**
Apdo. Postal 31-70, Guadalajara, Mexico.
● A I M. (Adventures in Mexico Newsletter); a
newsletter on retirement and living in mexico. bi-
m.

**Ediciones A. L. P. E.**
Av. Morelos No. 58-702, Mexico D.F., Mexico.
● Boletin Radiofonico T. V. w (with special editions
monthly) ISSN 0006-6494

**Abside**
c/o Sergio Delmar Junco, Damas 73, Mexico 19, D.
F., Mexico.
● Abside; revista de cultura mejicana. q. ISSN 0001-
3382

**Academia de Historia Potosina**
● Archivos de Historia Potosina. (pub. by
Universidad Autonoma de San Luis Potosi)

**Academia Mexicana de Cirugia**
Apdo. Postal 7994, Mexico 1, D. F., Mexico.
● Cirugia y Cirujanos. bi-m. ISSN 0009-7411
● Surgery Yearbook. a.

**Academia Nacional de Estomatologia**
● Estomatologia. (pub. by Editorial Meteci, S.A.)

**Academia Nacional de Medicina**
Unidad de Congresos del Centro Medico Nacional,
Bloque B, Av. Cuauhtemoc 330, Mexico 7, D.F.,
Mexico.
● Gaceta Medica de Mexico. m. ISSN 0016-3813

**Acero**
Emparan 35, Mexico 1, D.F., Mexico.
● Acero. bi-m.

**Aeromexico**
Blvd. A. Caliente 705, Tijuana, Mexico.
● Aeromexico. m.

**Aeropuertos y Servicios Auxiliares**
Insurgentes sur, 1216, Mexico 12, D.F., Mexico.
● Aeropuertos. m.

**Agro-Sintesis**
Correos 19, Mexico, D.F., Mexico.
● Agro-Sintesis. m.

**Francisco Aguera Cenarro, Ed. & Pub.**
Independencia 72, Mexico 1, D.F., Mexico.
● Revista Internacional y Diplomatica; documentos
y temas de politica internacional. m. ISSN 0034-
9720

**American Chamber of Commerce of Mexico**
Lucerna 78, Mexico 6, D.F., Mexico.
● Mexican-American Review. m. ISSN 0026-1696

**American-Mexican Medical Association**
Calle Pte.73-No.4, Col.16 de Septiembre, Mexico
City 18, D.F., Mexico.
● American-Mexican Medical Association. Journal.
q. ISSN 0003-0015
● Compendio Medico/Medical Compendium. q.
ISSN 0010-4221
● Compendio Pediatrico/Pediatric Compendium. q.
ISSN 0010-423X
● Thoracic Medicine and Surgery. q. ISSN 0040-
6368

**American Society for Horticultural Science**
Londres 40, Mexico 6, D.F., Mexico.
● American Society for Horticultural Science.
Tropical Region. Proceedings of the Annual
Meeting. a. ISSN 0066-0116

**American Society of Mexico, A.C.**
Apartado 555, Mexico 1, D.F., Mexico.
● Amistad. m.

**Amoxtli**
c/o Yolanda Mercader Martinez, Tintoreto 115-401,
Mexico 19, D. F., Mexico.
● Amoxtli; revista de informacion bibliotecologica.
q.

**Anglo American Directory of Mexico**
Apartado (P.O. Box) 27-210, Mexico 7, D. F.,
Mexico.
● Anglo American Directory of Mexico. a.

**Editorial Ano dos Mil, S. A.**
Indianapolis 4-501, Mexico 18 D.F., Mexico.
● Agro-Sintesis; agricultura-ganaderia-avicultura. bi-
m.

**Antigua Libreria Robredo**
Guatemala y Argentina, Mexico 1 D. F., Mexico.
● Sesenta. q. ISSN 0037-2811

**Arquitectura Mexico**
Reforma, 369, Mexico 5, D.F., Mexico.
● Arquitectura Mexico. bi-m.

**Artes de Mexico y del Mundo S.A.**
Amores 262, Mexico 12 D.F., Mexico.
● Artes de Mexico. m. ISSN 0300-4953

**Asociacion de Guias de Mexico**
Praga 60, 3er. Piso, Mexico 6, D.F., Mexico.
● Muchachas. m. ISSN 0300-3779

**Asociacion de Ingenieros de Minas, Metalurgistas y
Geologos de Mexico**
Ap. Postal 22-087, Mexico 22, D.F., Mexico.
● Geomimet. bi-m.

**Asociacion de Ingenieros Petroleros de Mexico, A.D.**
Apartado Postal 53-199, Mexico 17, D.F., Mexico.
● Ingenieria Petrolera. m.

**Asociacion de Ingenieros y Arquitectos de Mexico**
3A Calle del Puente de Alvarado 58, Mexico D.F.,
Mexico.
● Revista Mexicana de Ingenieria y Arquitectura. q.
ISSN 0035-0028

**Asociacion de Medicina Interna de Mexico**
Paseo de las Facultades 26, Frac Copilco-
Universidad, Mexico 20, D.F., Mexico.
● Prensa Medica Mexicana. bi-m. ISSN 0032-7468

**Asociacion de Tecnicos en Alimentos de Mexico, A.C.**
● Tecnologia de Alimentos. (pub. by Editorial
Ciencias y Tecnologia, S.A.)

**Asociacion Dental Mexicana**
Apdo. Postal 7-961, Mexico 7, D.F., Mexico.
● A D M. bi-m. ISSN 0001-0944

**Asociacion Franco-Mexicana de Ingenieros y Tecnicos**
Liverpool 67, Mexico 6, D.F., Mexico.
● Asociacion Franco-Mexicana de Ingenieros y
Tecnicos. Boletin. 4 per yr. ISSN 0004-4814

**Asociacion Latinoamericana de Escuelas de
Bibliotecologia y Ciencias de la Informacion**
Colegio de Bibliotecologia, Universidad Nacional
Autonoma de Mexico, Mexico 20, D.F., Mexico.
● A L E B C I; Boletin Informativo. q.

**Asociacion Latinoamericano de Patologos**
● Patologia. (pub. by Libreria Internacional)

**Asociacion Medica de los Ferrocarriles Nacionales de
Mexico**
Hospital Colonia, Villalongin 117, Mexico 5, D.F.,
Mexico.
● Hospital Colonia. Revista Medica. bi-m. ISSN
0018-5604

**Asociacion Mexicana de Bibliotecarios, A.C.**
Apartado Postal 127-132, Mexico 7 D.F., Mexico.
● A M B A C. Noticiero. q. ISSN 0001-186X

**Asociacion Mexicana de Caminos**
Tiber 103, Mexico 5 D.F., Mexico.
● Caminos; por un sistema integral de transportes.
m. ISSN 0008-2236

**Asociacion Mexicana de Facultades y Escuelas de
Medicina**
Av. V. Carranza 870 Despacho 15, Apdo. Postal
836, San Luis Potosi, Mexico.
● Asociacion Mexicana de Facultades y Escuelas de
Medicina. Boletin. irreg. ISSN 0004-4857

**Asociacion Mexicana de Hoteles y Moteles**
Av. Juarez No. 97-102, Mexico City 1, Mexico.
● Hoteles Mexicanos. m.

**Asociacion Mexicana de Orquideologia AC**
Apdo. Postal 53-123, Mexico 7, D.F., Mexico.
● Orquidea (Mexico) m. ISSN 0300-3701

**Asociacion Mexicana de Restaurantes**
Paseo Reforma 12-404, Mexico 1, D.F., Mexico.
● Restaurante. m. ISSN 0034-5792

**Asociacion Mexicana de Sociologia**
Providencia 330, Col. del Valle, Mexico 12, D. F.,
Mexico.
● Revista Interamericana de Sociologia. 3 per yr.
ISSN 0557-8558

**Asociacion Nacional Automovilistica, A.C.**
Miguel E. Schultz 140, Apdo. Postal 1720, Mexico
4, D.F., Mexico.
● Panorama. m.

**Asociacion Nacional de Contratistas de Instalaciones
Sanitarias e Hidraulicas**
Pilares 758-101, Mexico D.F., Mexico.
● Hidro Mecanica en la Construccion Mexicana. bi-
m. ISSN 0018-1315

**Asociacion Nacional de la Industria Quimica**
Vicente Suarez No.13, Mexico City 11, Mexico.
● Quimiconoticias. w.

**Asociacion Nacional de Universidades e Institutos de
Ensenanza Superior**
Apartado Postal 70-230, Mexico 20 D.F., Mexico.
● Revista de la Educacion Superior. q.

**Asociacion para Evitar la Gequera en Mexico**
Dr. Luis Marque, Queretaro No. 128, Mexico D.F,
Mexico.
● Asociacion para Evitar la Geguera en Mexico.
Archivos. q. ISSN 0004-489X

**Asociacion Periodistica Uruapense**
Av. Cupatitzio 175, Uruapan, Michoacan, Mexico.
● Sol de Uruapan. w. ISSN 0038-0857

**Asociacion Turistica y Deportiva Nacional**
Insurgentes sur 724, Mexico 12, D.F., Mexico.
● Diners; revista de distincion. bi-m. ISSN 0034-
9186

**Editores Asociados**
Angel Urraza 1322, Col. del Valle, Mexico 12, D.F.,
Mexico.
● Boletin S A C M. ISSN 0049-0989 (Sociedad de
Autores y Compositores de Musica)

**Automatic Car Wash Association-International**
Violeta 43, Coyocan, Mexico 21, D. F., Mexico.
● Carwash Journal. m. ISSN 0008-7092

**Autotransportes "Tres Estrellas de Oro"**
Baute 21, 102 Piso, Mexico 1 D.F., Mexico.
● Autotransportes "Tres Estrellas de Oro". ISSN
0005-1780

**Avicultura Tecnica**
Gabriel Mancera 1121, Mexico 12, D.F., Mexico.
● Avicultura Tecnica; la revista que pone ... ideas.
m. ISSN 0567-2848

**Balnearios**
Agustin Melgar, 44-5, Mexico 11, D.F., Mexico.
● Balnearios; donde ir a nadar. q.

**Banca y Comercio**
Reforma 202, Mexico 6, D.F., Mexico.
● Banca y Comercio. q.

**Banco de Mexico**
Subdireccion de Investigacion Economica y
Bancaria, Apartado 98 Bis, Mexico 1, D.F., Mexico.
● Banco de Mexico. Indicadores Economicos. m.
● Banco de Mexico. Informe Anual. a. ISSN 0067-
3374
● Bibliografia Economica de Mexico. q. ISSN 0006-
100X

**Banco de Mexico. Departamento de Investigaciones
Industriales**
Bolivar 15, Mexico 1, D.F., Mexico.
● Banco de Mexico. Servicio Bibliografico y Archivo
Tecnico. Boletin Bibliografico Mensual. m. (prep.
by its Servicio Bibliografico y Archivo Tecnico)

**Banco Nacional de Comercio Exterior, S.A.
Departamento de Publicaciones**
Av. Chapultepec 230, Mexico 7, D.F., Mexico.
● Anuario de Comercio Exterior de Mexico. m.
● Banco Nacional de Comercio Exterior, S.A.,
Mexico. Annual Report. a; latest edt. 1975.
● Mexico; facts, figures, trends. irreg; latest issue
1976. ISSN 0543-7741

**Banco Nacional de Mexico, S.A.**
Departamento de Apoyos Promocionales, Av.
Juarez 42, Apdo Postal 95, Mexico 1, D.F., Mexico.
- Examen de la Situacion Economica de Mexico. m.
ISSN 0014-3960

**Banco Nacional Hipotecaria Urbano y de Obras Publicas**
Avenida Madero 32, Mexico, D.F., Mexico.
- Estudios. bi-m. ISSN 0421-5338

**Bienvenidos - Welcome**
Av. la Paz 1095, Guadalajara, Mexico.
- Bienvenidos - Welcome; turismo internacional. m.

**Boletia Diplomatico**
Morelos 58, Mexico 1, D.F., Mexico.
- Boletin Diplomatico. m.

**Bolsa de Valores de Mexico**
Uruguay 68, Mexico 1, D.F., Mexico.
- Bolsa de Valores de Mexico. Daily Bulletin. d.
- Bolsa de Valores de Mexico. Monthly Newspaper. m.
- Bolsa de Valores de Mexico. Weekly Bulletin. w. ISSN 0006-6915

**Libreria y Ediciones Botas S. A.**
Just Sierra No. 52, Apartado No. 941, Mexico D.F., Mexico.
- Letras; publicacion literaria y bibliografica. bi-m. ISSN 0024-1210

**British Chamber of Commerce in Mexico**
Tiber 103, Mexico 5, D.F, Mexico.
- Intercambio. m. ISSN 0020-5192

**Calli Internacional**
Colima 319, Mexico 7, D.F., Mexico.
- Calli Internacional; revista analytica de arquitectura contemporanea. bi-m.

**Ed. & Pub. Heladio G. Camacho**
Gutenberg 303 O, Apdo Postal 334, Cuernavaca, Mor., Mexico.
- Correo del Sur; semanario regional. w. ISSN 0010-910X

**Camara Belga de Comercio y de Industria en Mexico, A.C.**
Florencia No. 37 - 104. Col. Juarez, Mexico 6. D.F., Mexico.
- Revista Belga. q.

**Camara Nacional de la Industria de Transformacion**
Apdo Postal 60-468, Av. San Antonio 256, Mexico 19, D.F., Mexico.
- Camara Nacional de la Industria de Transformacion. Boletin Informativo. m.
- Transformacion. m. ISSN 0041-1124

**Camara Nacional de la Industria del Hierro y del Acero**
Amores 338, Mexico 12. D.F., Mexico.
- Hierro y Acero. m. ISSN 0018-1374

**Campo**
Mar Negro No. 147, Apdo. Postal 17-506, Mexico 17 D.F., Mexico.
- Campo; revista mensual agricola y ganadera. m. ISSN 0008-2473

**Capilla Alfonsina. Boletin**
Avenida Benjamin Hill, 122, Mexico 11, D.F., Mexico.
- Capilla Alfonsina. Boletin. s-a. ISSN 0576-6931

**Editora Cautitlan S.A.**
Louisiana No. 50, Mexico 18, D.F., Mexico.
- Actualidades Medicas. m.

**Central de Numismatica y Medallistica**
Carranza No. 50, Venustiano, Mexico.
- Monedas. q. ISSN 0026-9603

**Centro de Estudios Educativos**
Revolucion 1291, Mexico 20, D.F., Mexico.
- Centro de Estudios Educativos. Revista. q. ISSN 0045-6128

**Centro de Estudios Historicos del Movimiento Obrero Mexicano**
Av. Dr. Jose Maria Vertiz 96, Mexico City, Mexico.
- Historia Obrera. q.

**Centro de Estudios Monetarios Latinoamericanos**
Durango No. 54, Mexico 7, D. F., Mexico.
- Centro de Estudios Monetarios Latinoamericanos. Boletin Bimensual. bi-m.
- Centro de Estudios Monetarios Latinoamericanos. Ensayos. irreg. ISSN 0577-2451

**Centro de Investigaciones Agrarias**
Aquiles Serdan 28, Mexico, D. F., Mexico.
- Estudios Agrarios. irreg (1-2 per yr) ISSN 0425-3442

**Centro de Investigaciones Agricolas de el Bajio**
Apdo. 112, Celaya Gto, Mexico.
- C I A B.Circular. 4 per yr. ISSN 0047-701X

**Centro de Investigaciones Agricolas de Tamaulipas**
Apartado Postal 172, Rio Bravo, Tamaulipas, Mexico.
- Centro de Investigaciones Agricolas de Tamaulipas. Circular CIAT. a. ISSN 0084-8689
- Centro de Investigaciones Agricolas de Tamaulipas. Informe Anual de Labores. a. ISSN 0084-8697

**Centro Internacional de Mejoramiento de Maiz y Trigo**
Londres 40, Apdo. Postal 6-641, Mexico 6, D.F., Mexico.
- C I M M Y T Information Bulletin. irreg. ISSN 0304-551X
- C I M M Y T Report on Maize Improvement. a. ISSN 0304-548X
- C I M M Y T Report on Wheat Improvement. a. ISSN 0304-5439
- C I M M Y T Review. a. ISSN 0304-5463
- C I M M Y T Today. irreg. ISSN 0304-5447
- International Maize and Wheat Improvement Center. Research Bulletin. irreg. ISSN 0074-6878

**Centro Mexicano de Escritores**
San Francisco No. 12, Mexico, Mexico.
- Recent Books in Mexico. bi-m.

**Centro Nacional de Productividad de Mexico A.C.**
Anillo Periferico sur, 2143, Nazas 23-901, Mexico.
- Productividad y Desarrollo. q.

**Centro Regional de Construcciones Escolares para America Latina**
Apartado Postal 41-518, Mexico 10, D.F., Mexico.
- C O N E S C A L. q. ISSN 0007-8794
- Centro Regional de Construcciones Escolares para America Latina. Documentos Asesoria. irreg.
- Centro Regional de Construcciones Escolares para America Latina. Documentos Tecnicos. irreg.

**Centro Regional Latinoamericano de Estudios para la Conservacion y Restauracion de Bienes Culturales**
Antiguo Convento de Churubusco, Mexico, D.F., Mexico.
- Boletin Informativo - CEdOclA. irreg.

**Editorial Ciencias y Tecnologia, S.A.**
Indianapolis No. 63-2, Mexico 18, D.F., Mexico.
- Tecnologia de Alimentos. bi-m. ISSN 0564-6758 (Asociacion de Tecnicos en Alimentos de Mexico, A.C.)

**Clinica Mexicana de Cirugia y Radioterapie**
Marsella 11, Mexico 6, D.F., Mexico.
- Revista Mexicana de Cirugia, Ginecologia y Cancer. m. ISSN 0034-9984

**Colegio de Ingenieros Agronomos de Mexico, A.C.**
Sindicalismo 92, Mexico 18, D.F., Mexico.
- Ingenieria Agronomica. q.

**Colegio de Mexico**
Dpto. de Publicaciones, Camino al Ajusco 20, Mexico 20, D.F., Mexico.
- Demografia y Economia. 3 per yr. ISSN 0011-8257
- Dialogos; artes, letras, ciencias humanas. bi-m. ISSN 0012-2114
- Estudios de Asia y Africa. 3 per yr. ISSN 0014-1534
- Foro Internacional. q. ISSN 0015-7821
- Historia Mexicana. q. ISSN 0018-2338
- Nueva Revista de Filologia Hispanica. s-a. ISSN 0029-5868

**Colegio de Mexico. Biblioteca**
Apartado Post No. 7-977, Mexico 7, D. F., Mexico.
- Colegio de Mexico. Biblioteca Lista de Obras en Canje Publicaciones Periodicas. q.

**Colegio de Postgraduados**
Chapingo, Estado de Mexico, Mexico.
- Agrociencia. q. ISSN 0568-3025

**Colegio Nacional de Economistas**
Maestro Antonio Caso 86, Apdo. Postal 30-525, Mexico 4, D.F., Mexico.
- Economista Mexicano. m. ISSN 0424-3374

**Colegio Nacional de Enfermeras**
Av. Guauhtemac 300, Mexico, D.F., Mexico.
- Colegio Nacional de Enfermeras. Revista. bi-m. ISSN 0045-7329
- Enfermeras. (pub. by Texto e Imagen S.A.)

**Comerciante Moderno**
Homero 136, Mexico 5,D.F., Mexico.
- Comerciante Moderno. bi-m.

**Comision Nacional Mexicana de la Asociacion del Congreso Panamericano de Ferrocarriles**
Navarra 210, Mexico, D.F., Mexico.
- Ferrocarriles; revista tecnica. q. ISSN 0015-0177

**Compania Mexicana de Aviacion**
Balderas 36-1208, Mexico D.F., Mexico.
- Caminos del Aire; revista inter-americana de turismo y aviacion. m. ISSN 0008-2244

**Comunidad Latinoamericana de Escritores**
Calle Comunal 17 (San Angel), Mexico 20, D.F., Mexico.
- Comunidad Latinoamericana de Escritores. Revista. irreg; continues numbering under new title, with no. 15.

**Confederacion de Asociaciones Agricolas del Estado de Sinaloa**
Zaragoza y Juan Carrasco, Culiacan, Mexico.
- Analisis de la Situacion Agricola de Sinaloa. bi-m. ISSN 0517-6956

**Confederacion de Camaras Nacionales de Comercio**
Balderas No. 144, Mexico 1 D.F., Mexico.
- Confederacion de Camaras Nacionales de Comercio. Carta Semanal. w. ISSN 0010-549X

**Confederacion Internacional de Organizaciones Sindicales Libres**
Plaza de la Republica 30, Apdo. Postal 7039, Mexico, D.F., Mexico.
- Mundo del Trabajo Libre. m. ISSN 0027-3260

**Confederacion Nacional Campesina**
Mariano Azuela 121, Mexico 13 D.F, Mexico (Orders from: Libreria Mexico Agraria, Apdo. Postal 59-007, Mexico 1, D.F., Mexico)
- Revista del Mexico Agrario. 6 per yr. ISSN 0034-9097

**Confederacion Nacional Ganadera**
Mariano Escobedo 714, Mexico 5, D.F., Mexico.
- Mexico Ganadero. m. ISSN 0047-7036

**Editorial Confidencias, S. A.**
Av. Juarez 64-511, Mexico 1, D. F., Mexico.
- Confidencias; la revista que le comunica con el amor. w. ISSN 0010-5635

**Consejo Nacional de Ciencia y Tecnologia**
Insurgentes sur 1677, Mexico 20, D.F., Mexico.
- Ciencia y Desarrollo. bi-m.

**Consejo Nacional para la Ensenanza de la Biologia**
Apdo. Postal 70-268, Mexico 20, D.F., Mexico.
- Biologia. q.

**Consejo Nacional para la Ensenanza e Investigacion en Psicologia**
c/o Sra. Josefina Torres, Cerro de las Torres 395, Mexico 21, D.F., Mexico.
- Ensenanza e Investigacion en Psicologia. s-a.

**Consejo Nacional Tecnico de la Educacion**
Calle Luis Gonzalez Obregon No. 21, Mexico 1, D.F., Mexico.
- Educacion. bi-m.

**Conservatorio Nacional de Musica**
Av. Presidente Masaryk 582, Mexico 5, D.F., Mexico.
- Revista de Conservatorio. 3 per yr. ISSN 0034-7833

**Consorcio Mexicano de Informacioni S.A. Comisa**
Av. Juarez 64-708, Mexico 1, D.F., Mexico.
- Comisa y Comisa Lania. w.

**Editorial Contenido, S. A.**
Morelos 16, Mexico 1, D.F., Mexico.
- Contenido. m. ISSN 0010-7581

**Publicaciones Continentales de Mexico, S. A.**
Av. Insurgentes sur No. 421, Edificio B, Mexico 11,
D.F., Mexico.
- Buenhogar. bi-w.
- Cosmopolitan. m.

**Control Economico de Obras, S.A.**
Av. Chapultepec No. 350-4 piso, Mexico City 6,
Mexico.
- Manual S-Inco. m.

**Editorial Cormor S.A.**
Insurgentes sur 686, Mexico 12, D.F., Mexico.
- Horizontes Financieros. m.

**Corporacion Editorial, S.A.**
Rubens No. 33, Apdo. Postal 19-365, Mexico 19,
D.F., Mexico.
- El. m.
- Genesis; revista universal. m.
- Jet Set; revista del gran mundo. m.
- Sonido; revista musical. m.

**Editorial Cosmos**
Espana 396, Col. Granjas Estrella, Mexico 13, D.F.,
Mexico.
- Alimentaria. a.
- Automotriz. a.
- Envase y Embalaje. a.
- Equipo; materiales y servicio. a.
- Laboratorios de Especialidades y Control. a.
- Metalmecanica; metalurgia, electricidad y
electronica. a.
- Petro Quimica; petroleo y mineria. a.
- Plasticos y Resinas (Annual) a.
- Produccion Quimica Mexicana. irreg.
- Productos Quimicos. a.

**Creatividad**
Monte Palatino 103, Monterrey, Mexico.
- Creatividad. bi-m.

**Cuadernos Americanos**
Avenida Coyoacan, No. 1035, Apdo. Postal 965,
Mexico, D.F., Mexico.
- Cuadernos Americanos; revista del nuevo mundo.
bi-m. ISSN 0011-2356

**Cuento**
Division del Norte No. 521-101, Mexico 12, D. F.,
Mexico.
- Cuento; revista de imaginacion. bi-m. ISSN 0011-
2674

**Cultura y Ciencia Politica**
Patricio Sanz 751, Mexico 12 D.F., Mexico
(Subscr. to: Mexican Academic Clearing House,
Apdo. 7-854, Mexico 7, D.F., Mexico)
- Pensamiento Politico; revista de Afirmacion
Mexicana. m. ISSN 0031-4757

**Ediciones Culturales Mexicanas, S.A.**
Aptdo. Postal 73-032, Mexico 12, D.F., Mexico.
- Archivos de Investigacion Medica. 3 per yr. ISSN
0066-6769 (Instituto Mexicano del Seguro Social.
Departamento de Investigacion Científica)

**Editorial Cumbre, S. A.**
Depto. de Publicidad, Insurgentes sur 933, Mexico
City, Mexico.
- Vendedor Profesional. m.

**D'Pastrana Editores, S.A.**
Kepler 147, Mexico 5, D.F., Mexico.
- En Concreto. q. (Instituto Nacional de
Planificacion)
- Ingenieria de Costos. 4 per yr. (Sociedad
Mexicana de Ingenieria de Costos, A.C.)

**Desarrollo Economico**
Departamento de Circulacion, Hamburgo 20,
Mexico 6, D.F., Mexico.
- Desarrollo Economico; revista para el profesional
del desarrollo. q.

**Diccionario de Especialidades Farmaceuticas**
Medellin 184, Mexico 7 D.F., Mexico.
- Diccionario de Especialidades Farmaceuticas. a.

**Diseno**
Saturno 44, Mexico 14, D.F., Mexico.
- Diseno. m.

**Distrito de Riego No. 38, Rio Mayo**
Pesqueira y Jimenez, Navojoa, Sonora, Mexico.
- Mayo Agricola. q.

**Eco de Nayarit**
Calle Allende Num. 12 Pte., Acaponeta, Nayarit,
Mexico.
- Eco de Nayarit; bisemanario popular portavoz de
la region. s-w. ISSN 0012-9445

**Editorial Elizondo, S. A.**
Granada 126, Col. Morelos, Mexico 2,D. F.,
Mexico.
- Calzado y Teneria. fortn. ISSN 0008-1817

**Embajada de U R S S**
Calzada de Tacubaya 204, Zona 11, Apdo. 11-379,
Admon de Correos No. 11, Mexico D.F., Mexico.
- U R S S Embajada. Bolletin de Informacion. m.

**Ediciones Era**
Avena 102, Apdo. Postal 74-092, Mexico 13, D.F.,
Mexico.
- Cuadernos Politicos. q.

**Escuela Bancaria y Comercial**
Paseo de la Reforma 202, Mexico 6, D. F., Mexico.
- Banca y Comercio. q. ISSN 0005-4615

**Escuela Magnetico Espiritual de la Comuna Universal**
Avenida Morelos No. 37, Despacho No. 210,
Mexico 1, D. F., Mexico.
- Renovacion. bi-m. ISSN 0034-4478

**Escuela Nacional de Antropologia e Historia**
Apdo. Postal 11-425, Mexico 11, D.F., Mexico.
- Nueva Antropologia. q.

**Escuela Nacional de Biblioteconomia y Archivonomia**
Viaducto M. Aleman 155, Col. Alamos, Mexico 13,
D.F., Mexico.
- Bibliotecas y Archivos. a.

**Escuela Normal Superior de Nuevo Leon**
Seccion Editorial, Apdo. Postal 2035, Monterrey,
N.L., Mexico.
- Dialogo. bi-m' ISSN 0012-2092
- Ensayo. q. ISSN 0013-855X

**Fidel Estrada Navarro, Ed. & Pub.**
Balderas 44- 201 - 202, Mexico 1, D.F., Mexico.
- Telegrama Politico. m. ISSN 0040-2567

**Compania Editorial Excelsior S. C. L.**
Paseo de la Reforma 18, Mexico D.F., Mexico.
- Excelsior. d.
- Plural; critica-arte-literatura. m.

**Expansion**
Homero 136, Mexico 5, D.F., Mexico.
- Expansion; revista de negocios de mexico y
centroamerica. fortn.

**Editorial Extemporaneos**
Apdo. Postal 78-048, Mexico 14, D.F., Mexico.
- Cambio. q (with annual cumulation)

**Editorial Fama**
Calle Rio Balsas 107-201, Col. Cuahute Moc,
Mexico 5, D.F., Mexico.
- Alto Peinado; peinados, modas y belleza. m.

**Federacion Latinamericana de Quimica**
Apartado Postal 4644, Sucursal de Correos "J",
Monterrey, Mexico.
- Revista Latinoamericana de Quimica. q. (Co-
Sponsor: Sociedad Fitoquimica de Mexico)

**Ferrocarriles Nacionales de Mexico**
Depto.de Relaciones Publicas, Estacion C. de
Pasajeros, Ala Oriente 20 Piso, Buenavista, Mexico.
- Ferronales. m. ISSN 0015-0207

**Figaro**
Ave. Morelos 45, Mexico City, Mexico.
- Figaro; semanario popular. w. ISSN 0015-0835

**Editorial Finanzas**
Av. Hidalgo No. 5, Mexico 1. D.F., Mexico.
- Finanzas y Contabilidad; revista de divulgacion
financiera y contable. m. ISSN 0015-2234

**Fondo de Cultura Economica**
Av. Universidad 975, Mexico 12, D.F., Mexico.
- Fondo de Cultura. Serie de Lecturas. q.
- Gaceta; fondo de cultura economica. m. ISSN
0016-3716
- Trimestre Economico. q. ISSN 0041-3011

**Frente de Afirmacion Hispanista A.C.**
Lago Ginebra No. 47 C, Mexico 17 D.F., Mexico.
- Norte; revista Hispano Americano. bi-m.

**Gaceta Agricola**
Apdo. Postal 5-225, Guadalajara, Mexico.
- Gaceta Agricola. irreg.

**Geografia Universal**
Kepler 82, Mexico 5, D.F., Mexico.
- Geografia Universal. m.

**Grupo Juventud S.A.**
Saturno 44, Nueva Industria Vallejo, Mexico 14,
Df., Mexico.
- Kena. w.

**Publicaciones Herrerias, S.A.**
Morelos 16, Mexico 1, D. F., Mexico.
- Capricho. w.
- Ciencia para Todos. m.
- Novela Musical. w.
- Novelas de Amor. w.
- Ultima Moda. s-m. ISSN 0041-6223

**Heterofonia**
Heriberto Frias 514, Apdo. 12-808, Mexico 12,
D.F., Mexico.
- Heterofonia; revista musical bimestral. bi-m. ISSN
0018-1137

**Hospital Infantil de Mexico**
- Hospital Infantil de Mexico. Boletin Medico. (pub.
by Ediciones Medicas)

**Hospital Oftalmologico de Nuestra Senora de la Luz**
Ezequiel Montes 135, Mexico 4, D.F., Mexico.
- Hospital Oftalmologico de Nuestra Senora de la
Luz. Boletin. q. ISSN 0018-5760

**Ediciones I N A P**
Av. Country Club 208, Mexico 21, D.F., Mexico.
- Revista de Administracion Publica. 4 per yr. ISSN
0482-5209 (Instituto Nacional de Administracion
Publica)

**Iglesia Metodista de Mexico. Secretaria de Educacion
Cristiana**
Balderas 47, Mexico City, Mexico.
- Comino. bi-m. ISSN 0010-2385

**Iglesia Metodista el Mesias**
Balderas 47, Mexico D. F., Mexico.
- Mesias; boletin semanal de la iglesia Metodista. w.
ISSN 0026-0185

**Publicaciones Importantes S.A.**
Bolivar 8-601, Mexico 1, D.F., Mexico.
- Sus Hijos; la revista papa los padres de familia. m.
ISSN 0039-6362

**Impresiones, S.A.**
Matamoros 813 Ote, Apdo No. 44, Monterrey N.L.,
Mexico.
- Provincia Social. m. ISSN 0033-1929

**Editorial Industria, S. de R. C.**
Filomeno Nata 13-11, Mexico, D.F, Mexico.
- Industria; al servicio del Mexico Industrial. m.
ISSN 0019-7394

**Industria y Laboratorios Farmaceutico**
Uruguay 35-306, Mexico 1, D.F., Mexico.
- Mexico Farmaceutico. m. ISSN 0026-1785

**Informacion Farmaceutica**
Dinamarca 51-102, Mexico 6, D.F., Mexico.
- Informacion Farmaceutica. m. ISSN 0019-9796

**Informacion Nacional y Publicidad**
Mirto No. 25, Mexico 4, D.F., Mexico.
- Correo Economico. w. ISSN 0010-9118

**Informaciones Tecnicas, S.A.**
San Francisco No. 356, Mexico 12, D.F., Mexico.
- Catalogo Informaciones Tecnicas para le
Construccion. a.

**Informador del Hogar S.A.**
Insurgentes sur 300, Mexico 7, D.F., Mexico.
- Casa. m.

**Institute of Electrical and Electronics Engineers.
Seccion Mexico**
- Revista Mexicana de Electricidad. (pub. by
Mexico. Comision Federal de Electricidad)

**Instituto de Ciencias y Artes de Chiapas**
2A Av. sur y 5a, Tuxtla, Gutierrez, Chiapas,
Mexico.
- I C A C H; organo de divulgacion cultural. s-a.
  ISSN 0536-2571

**Instituto de Estudios Oaxaquenos**
Aptdo. 464, Oaxaca, Oax., Mexico.
- Boletin de Estudios Oaxaquenos/Bulletin of
  Oaxaca Studies. irreg. ISSN 0006-6257

**Instituto de Estudios Politicos Economicos y Sociales**
Insurgentes Norte, 59, Mexico, D.F., Mexico.
- Temas Nacionales. irreg.

**Instituto de Investigaciones Sociales y Economicas A.C.**
Plaza 20 de Noviembre, 27, Mexico 1, D.F.,
Mexico.
- Espejo. bi-m. ISSN 0014-0597
- Hoja de Informacion Economica. fortn. ISSN
  0018-3288
- Temas Contemporaneos. m. ISSN 0040-2885

**Instituto de Tonantzintla**
Apartados Postales Nos. 216 y 51, Puebla, Mexico,
Mexico.
- Instituto de Tonantzintla. Boletin. irreg. ISSN
  0303-7584

**Instituto Indigenista Interamericano**
Calle de Ninos Heroes 139, Mexico 7, D.F.,
Mexico.
- America Indigena. q. ISSN 0002-7081
- Antropologia Social. irreg. ISSN 0570-3697
- Anuario Indigenista/Indianist Yearbook. a.
- Instituto Indigenista Interamericano Serie de
  Ediciones Especiales. irreg. (3-4 per yr)
- Inter-American Conference on Indian Life. Acta/
  Congresos Indigenistas Interamericanos. Acta.
  every 4 yrs., 7th, 1972, Brasilia, brazil. ISSN
  0074-0810

**Instituto Internacional de Filosofia, A.C.**
Cordoba 17, Apdo. 24-550, Mexico 7, D. F.,
Mexico.
- Almas. m. ISSN 0002-628X

**Instituto Jalisciense de Antropologia e Historia**
Biblioteca "Lic. Jose Parres Arias", Calle de Escorza
No. 130, Guadalajara, Mexico.
- Eco. 3 per yr. ISSN 0422-2555

**Instituto Mexicano de Contadores Publicos**
Rio Danubio 80, Mexico 5, D.F., Mexico.
- Contaduria Publica. m.

**Instituto Mexicano de Control de Calidad. Division de Divalgacion**
Thiers No. 251-Penthouse, Mexico 5, D.F., Mexico.
- Sistemas de Calidad. bi-m.

**Instituto Mexicano de Estudios Sociales**
A. C. Londres 40, Mexico 6, D. F., Mexico.
- Desarrollo; estudios sobre estructuracion social.
  irreg. ISSN 0011-9199

**Instituto Mexicano de Ingenieros Quimicos**
Londres No. 188-302, Mexico City 6, Mexico.
- Instituto Mexicano de Ingenieros Quimicos.
  Revista. m.

**Instituto Mexicano del Cafe**
Paseo de la Reforma No. 300, Mexico D.F.,
Mexico.
- Boletin Tecnico Cafetalero. bi-m.

**Instituto Mexicano del Cemento y del Concreto, A. C.**
Insurgentes sur No. 1846, Mexico 20, D.F., Mexico.
- I M C Y C. Revista. bi-m. ISSN 0034-9607

**Instituto Mexicano del Petroleo**
Av. Cien Metros No. 152, Mexico 14, D.F.,
Mexico.
- Instituto Mexicano del Petroleo. Revista. q. ISSN
  0538-1428

**Instituto Mexicano del Seguro Social**
San Jeronimo Lidice, Mexico 20, D.F., Mexico.
- Revista Mexicana de Seguridad Social. irreg. ISSN
  0482-6876

**Instituto Mexicano del Seguro Social. Departamento de Investigacion Cientifica**
- Archivos de Investigacion Medica. (pub. by
  Ediciones Culturales Mexicanas, S.A.)

**Instituto Mexicano del Seguro Social. Subdireccion General Medica**
Jefatura de Servicios de Medicina Preventiva, San
Jeronimo Lidice, Mexico 20, D.F., Mexico.
- Boletin Epidemiologico Anual. a.

**Instituto Nacional de Administracion Publica**
- Revista de Administracion Publica. (pub. by
  Ediciones I N A P)

**Instituto Nacional de Antropologia e Historia**
Cordoba 45, Mexico 7, D.F.
- Atlas Arqueologico de la Republica Mexicana.
  irreg. ISSN 0067-0243
- Corpus Antiquitatum Americanensium. irreg.
  ISSN 0070-0312
- Cuadernos del Mexico Prehispanico. irreg. ISSN
  0070-1750
- Historia. irreg. ISSN 0073-2443
- Instituto Nacional de Antropologia e Historia.
  Anales. irreg. ISSN 0076-7557
- Instituto Nacional de Antropologia e Historia.
  Boletin. q. ISSN 0020-4102
- Instituto Nacional de Antropologia e Historia.
  Coleccion Breve. irreg. ISSN 0076-7565
- Instituto Nacional de Antropologia e Historia.
  Investigaciones. irreg., 1970, no. 24. ISSN 0076-7573
- Instituto Nacional de Antropologia e Historia.
  Libros de Homenaie. irreg. ISSN 0076-7581
- Instituto Nacional de Antropologia e Historia.
  Memorias. irreg., 1968, no. 14. ISSN 0076-759X
- Instituto Nacional de Antropologia e Historia.
  Obras Varias. irreg. ISSN 0076-7603
- Instituto Nacional de Antropologia e Historia.
  Serie Cientifica. irreg., 1968, no. 10. ISSN 0076-7611
- Instituto Nacional de Antropologia e Historia.
  Serie Culturas del Mundo. irreg. ISSN 0076-762X
- Instituto Nacional de Antropologia e Historia.
  Sociedad de Alumnos. (Publicaciones) irreg. ISSN
  0076-7549
- Investigaciones Antropologicas. irreg. ISSN 0075-0204

**Instituto Nacional de Antropologia e Historia. Departamento de Monumentos Coloniales**
Consejo de Publicaciones, Administracion de
Correos No. 55, Apdo. Postal 55483 y 55495,
Mexico.
- Instituto Nacional de Antropologia e Historia.
  Departamento de Monumentos Coloniales.
  (Publicaciones) irreg. ISSN 0076-7506

**Instituto Nacional de Antropologia e Historia. Departamento de Monumentos Prehispanicos**
Consejo de Publicaciones, Administracion de
Correos No. 55, Apdo. Postal 55483 y 55495,
Mexico 13, D.F, Mexico.
- Instituto Nacional de Antropologia e Historia.
  Departamento de Monumentos Prehispanicos.
  (Publicaciones) irreg. ISSN 0076-7514

**Instituto Nacional de Bellas Artes. Museo de Arte Moderno**
Paseo de la Reforma y Gandhi, Chalpultepec,
Mexico 5, D.F., Mexico.
- Artes Visuales. q.

**Instituto Nacional de Cancerologia**
Ninos Heroes 151, Mexico 7, D.F., Mexico.
- Instituto Nacional de Cancerologia, Mexico.
  Revista. irreg. ISSN 0076-7131 (Co-Sponsor:
  Sociedad Mexicana de Estudios Oncologicos)

**Instituto Nacional de Cardiologia**
- Instituto de Cardiologia de Mexico. Archivos.
  (pub. by Nueva Editorial Interamericana, S. A. de
  C. V.)

**Instituto Nacional de Energia Nuclear. Department of Libraries and Documentation Services**
Insurgentes sur 1079, Mexico, D.F., Mexico.
- Instituto Nacional de Energia Nuclear.
  Publication. irreg. ISSN 0076-7476

**Instituto Nacional de Investigaciones Agricolas. Departamento de Divulgacion Tecnica**
Apdo. Postal 6-882, Mexico 6, D.F., Mexico.
- Agricultura Tecnica en Mexico. s-a. ISSN 0568-2517

**Instituto Nacional de Investigaciones Pecuarias. Rancho Experimental la Campana**
Apdo. 682, Chihuahua, Mexico.
- Pastizales. bi-m.

**Instituto Nacional de Planificacion**
- En Concreto. (pub. by D'Pastrana Editores, S.A.)

**Instituto Nacional Indigenista**
Av Revolucion 1279, Mexico 20, D.F., Mexico.
- Accion Indigenista. m. ISSN 0044-5908
- Mexico Indigena. m.

**Instituto Panamericano de Geografia e Historia**
see also **Listings in Bolivia, Ecuador and Peru**

**Instituto Panamericano de Geografia e Historia**
Ex-Arzobispado 29, Mexico 18, D.F., Mexico.
- Boletin Bibliografico de Antropologia Americana.
  a. (prep. by its Servicios Bibliograficos)
- Geofisica. s-a. (prep. by its Commission on
  Geophysics)
- Instituto Panamericano de Geografia e Historia
  Boletin Aereo. bi-m. ISSN 0020-4188
- Pan American Institute of Geography and
  History. Commission on History. Bibliografias.
  irreg., 1970, vol. 4. ISSN 0078-8813
- Pan American Institute of Geography and
  History. Commission on History. Guias. irreg.,
  1967, vol. 4. ISSN 0078-8821 (prep. by its
  Commission on History)
- Pan American Institute of Geography and
  History. Commission on History. Historiografias
  Americanas. irreg.; 1977, vol. 9. ISSN 0078-883X
- Pan American Institute of Geography and
  History. Commission on History. Historiadores de
  America. irreg., 1967, vol. 12. ISSN 0078-8848
  (prep. by its Commission on History)
- Pan American Institute of Geography and
  History. Commission on History. Monumentos
  Historicos y Arqueologicos. irreg.; 1974 vol. 17.
  ISSN 0078-8856 (prep. by its Commission on
  History)
- Revista Cartografica. s-a. ISSN 0080-2085 (prep.
  by its Servicios Bibliograficos)
- Revista de Historia de America. s-a. ISSN 0034-8325 (prep. by its Servicios Bibliograficos)
- Revista Geofisica. irreg.
- Revista Geografica. s-a. ISSN 0031-0581 (prep. by
  its Servicios Bibliograficos)

**Instituto Panamericano de Geografia e Historia. Comite del Folklore**
Servicios Bibliograficos, Ex-Arzobispado 29, Mexico
18, D.F., Mexico.
- Folklore Americano. s-a. ISSN 0071-6774

**Instituto Politecnico Nacional. Comision de Operacion y Fomento de Actividades Academicas**
Prolongacion de Diaz Miron y Plan de San Luis,
Mexico 17, D.F., Mexico.
- Acta Mexicana de Ciencia y Tecnologia. 3 per yr.
  ISSN 0567-7785
- Acta Politecnica Mexicana. q. ISSN 0515-3085

**Instituto Politecnico Nacional. Escuela National de Ciencias Biologicas**
Departamento de Publicaciones, Carpio y Plan de
Ayaya, Box 42-186, Mexico 17, D.F., Mexico.
- Instituto Politecnico Nacional. Escuela National
  de Ciencias Biologicas. Revista Anales. a. ISSN
  0026-1777

**Instituto Politecnico Nacional. Escuela Superior de Economia**
Plan de Agua Prieta 66, 17, Mexico City, Mexico.
- Economia Politica. q. ISSN 0531-8203

**Instituto Politecnico Nacional. Escuela Superior de Medicina**
Prolongacion de Diaz Miron y Plan de San Luis,
Mexico 17, D. F., Mexico.
- Acta Medica. q. ISSN 0001-5997

**Instituto Politecnico Nacional. Unidad Professional de Zacatenco**
Depto. de Divulgacion y Publicaciones, Mexico 14,
D.F., Mexico.
- Gaceta Politecnica. s-m. ISSN 0016-3848

**Instituto Tecnologico y de Estudios Superiores de Monterrey**
Sucursal de Correos "J", Monterrey, N.L., Mexico.
- Instituto Tecnologico y de Estudios Superiores.
  Publicaciones. Serie: Catalogos de Biblioteca.
  irreg., 1969, no. 3. ISSN 0074-0306
- Instituto Tecnologico y de Estudios Superiores.
  Publicaciones. Serie Historia. 1970, no. 12. ISSN
  0077-1228
- Instituto Tecnologico y de Estudios Superiores.
  Publicaciones. Serie Letras. irreg., 1970, no. 4.
  ISSN 0077-1236
- Temos de Negocios. q.

**Instituto Tecnologico y de Estudios Superiores de Monterrey. Departamento de Seguridad Industrial**
Sucursal de Correos "J", Monterrey N.L., Mexico.
- Seguinotas. m.

**Instituto Tecnologico y de Estudios Superiores de Monterrey. Division de Ciencias Agropecuarias y Maritimas**
Sucursal de Correos J, Monterrey N.L., Mexico.
- Agronomia. bi-m. ISSN 0002-1903

**Inter American Regional Organisation of Workers**
*see* **Organizacion Regional Interamericana de Trabajadores**

**Interamerican Association of Sanitary Engineers**
- Ingenieria Sanitaria. (pub. by Ramon Sanchez Contreras, Ed.)

**International Conference on Soil Mechanics and Foundation Engineering. Proceedings**
Sociedad Mexicana de Mecanica de Suelos, Londres 44, Coyoacan, Mexico 21, D. F., Mexico.
- International Conference on Soil Mechanics and Foundation Engineering. Proceedings. biennial; 7th, 1974. ISSN 0074-3313

**International Maize and Wheat Improvement Center**
*see* **Centro Internacional de Mejoramiento de Maiz y Trigo**

**Intersistemas, S.A. de C.V.**
Fernando Alencastre No. 110-Lomas Virreyes, Mexico City 10, Mexico.
- Atencion Medica. m.
- Universidad Nacional Autonoma de Mexico. Facultad de Medicina. Nueva Revista. m.

**Istmo**
Goya 73-102, Mexico City 16, Mexico.
- Istmo. bi-m. ISSN 0021-261X

**Jalisco. Comision Forestal del Estado de Jalisco**
Lopez Cotilla 285-2, Guadalajara, Jalisco, Mexico.
- Revista Forestal del Estado de Jalisco. m.

**Jus**
Mejia 19, Mexico, D.F, Mexico.
- Jus; revista de derecho y ciencias sociales. q.

**Editorial Jus, S. A.**
Plaza de Abasolo 14, Colonia Guerrero, Mexico 3, D.F., Mexico.
- Mexico Heroico. m. ISSN 0026-1793

**Letras Potosinas**
Apdo 273, San Luis Potosi, S.L.P., Mexico.
- Letras Potosinas; vocero de cultura. q. ISSN 0024-1245

**Libreria de Porrua Hermanos y Cia S.A.**
Argentina y Justo Sierra, Mexico 1. D.F., Mexico.
- Boletin Bibliografico Mexicano. bi-m. ISSN 0006-6168

**Libreria Internacional**
Av. Sonora 206, Mexico 11, D.F., Mexico.
- Patologia. q. (Asociacion Latinoamericano de Patologos) (Co-sponsor: Asociacion Mexicano de Patalogos)

**Publicaciones Llergo**
Manuel Ma. Contreras 30, Mexico 4, D.F., Mexico.
- Impacto. w. ISSN 0019-2880

**Manana**
Amberes 38, Mexico 6, D.F., Mexico.
- Manana. w. ISSN 0034-9844

**Editorial Manila**
Independencia 72-306, Mexico 1, D.F., Mexico.
- Dulcelandia-Industrias Alimenticias. m.

**Dr. Alfredo Marquez Campos, Ed. & Pub.**
Queretaro 183, Mexico 7 D.F., Mexico.
- Semana Medica de Centroamerica y Panama. fortn. ISSN 0037-1815
- Semana Medica de Mexico. w. ISSN 0037-1823

**Publicaciones Marynka, S. A.**
Sinaloa-9-501, Mexico 7, D.F., Mexico.
- Mexican Financial Report. m.

**Ediciones Medicas**
Calle Dr. Marquez 162, Mexico 7 D.F., Mexico.
- Hospital Infantil de Mexico. Boletin Medico. bi-m. (Hospital Infantil de Mexico)

**Medicina**
Avda. Yucatan 29, Mexico 7, D.F., Mexico.
- Medicina; revista mexicana. m. ISSN 0025-7702

**Medios Publicitarios Mexicanos, S.A.**
Av. Mexico No. 99-303, Mexico 11, D.F., Mexico.
- Directorio M P M-Agencias y Anunciantes; personal y cuentas. s-a.
- Directorio M P M - Medios Audiovisuales; tarifas y Datos - Cine, Radio y Television. q.
- Directorio M P M-Medios Impresos; tarifas y datos-anuncio exterior, periodicos y revistas. q.

**Mensajero Forestal**
Apdo Postal 113, Durango, DGO, Mexico.
- Mensajero Forestal. m. ISSN 0025-9586

**Mercado Comun Latino-Americano**
Apartado Postal 170, Admon 1, Mexico 1, D.F., Mexico.
- Mercado Comun Latino-Americano. m.

**Editorial Meridiano, S. A.**
Angel Urraza St. 1324, Mexico D.F., Mexico.
- Supermachos. w. ISSN 0039-5773

**Editorial Meteci, S.A.**
Ezequiel Montes, No. 92, Mexico 4, D.F., Mexico.
- Estomatologia. s-a. ISSN 0014-1356 (Academia Nacional de Estomatologia)

**Editorial Mex-Ameris, S.A.**
Av. Morelos 16, Mexico 1, D.F., Mexico.
- Automundo. m.
- Bienestar. m.
- Claudia. m. ISSN 0009-8515
- Rutas de Pasion; photo novels. fortn. ISSN 0036-0430

**Mexican Academic Clearing House**
P.O. Box 7-854, Mexico 7, D.F., Mexico.
- Tematica-Economica Politica y Social. bi-m.

**Mexican Air Line Pilots Association**
c/o V.M.O. Camposeco, Av. Palomas 110, Lomas de Sotelo, Mexico 10, D.F., Mexico.
- Helice. m.

**Mexican Investor**
Reforma 398-203, Mexico 6, D. F., Mexico.
- Mexican Investor. s-m.

**Mexican Society for Soil Mechanics**
Londres 44, Coyoacan, Mexico 21, D.F., Mexico.
- Mexican Society for Soil Mechanics Meeting. Proceedings. biennial.

**Mexican Society of Behavior Analysis**
- Revista Mexicana de Analisis de la Conducta/ Mexican Journal of Behavior Analysis. (pub. by Editorial Trillas, S. A.)

**Editora Mexico**
Arteaga 33, Apdo. Postal 3-628, Mexico 3, D.F, Mexico.
- Alerta. w.

**Mexico. Archivo General de la Nacion**
Mexico, D.F., Mexico.
- Mexico. Archivo General de la Nacion. Archivo Historico de Hacienda. Coleccion Documental. irreg.
- Mexico. Archivo General de la Nacion. Boletin. q. ISSN 0026-1734

**Mexico. Comision Federal de Electricidad**
Av. Sonora No. 206, Despacho 403, Mexico 11, D.F., Mexico.
- Revista Mexicana de Electricidad; organo de difusion de: la electricidad, la electronica y la industria en general. m. ISSN 0035-0001 (Institute of Electrical and Electronics Engineers. Seccion Mexico)

**Mexico. Comision Nacional Bancaria y de Seguros**
Republica de el Salvador No. 47, Mexico 1 D.F., Mexico.
- Mexico. Comision Nacional Bancaria y de Seguros. Anuario Estadistico de Seguros. a.
- Mexico. Comision Nacional Bancaria y de Seguros. Boletin Estadistico. m.

**Mexico. Comision Nacional de Valores**
Paseo de la Reforma 77, Piso 12, Mexico 4 D.F, Mexico.
- Comision Nacional de Valores. Boletin Bimestral. bi-m. ISSN 0010-2393

- Mexico. Comision Nacional de Valores. Informe de Actividades. a.

**Mexico. Comison Nacional de los Salarios Minimos**
Mexico, Mexico.
- Mexico. Comison Nacional de los Salarios Minimos. Informe de Labores. a.

**Mexico. Consejo Nacional de Ciencia y Tecnologia**
Insurgentes sur 1814, Mexico 20, D.F., Mexico.
- Folleto de Difusion. irreg.
- Mexico. Consejo Nacional de Ciencia y Tecnologia. Serie Documentos. irreg.

**Mexico. Direccion de Estadistica y Estudios Economicos**
Antonio Caso 19, 20. Piso, Mexico 4, D.F., Mexico.
- Mexico. Direccion de Estadistica y Estudios Economicos. Memorandum Tecnico. m. ISSN 0025-9152

**Mexico. Direccion General de Estadistica**
Secretaria de Programacion y Presupuesto, Balderas 71, Agencia de Correos 245, Mexico 1, D. F., Mexico.
- Mexico. Direccion de Estadistica. Estadistica Industrial Mensual. a.
- Mexico. Direccion General de Estadistica. Estadistica Industrial Anual. irreg.; latest 1974. ISSN 0071-1543
- Mexico. Direccion General de Estadistica. Estadistica Minerometalurgica: Produccion y Exportacion. irreg.; latest 1972.
- Mexico. Direccion General de Estadistica. Revista de Estadistica. m. ISSN 0026-1769
- Principales Indicadores Economicos de Mexico. m. ISSN 0543-6915

**Mexico. Direccion General de Estadistica. Departamento de Estadisticas Economicas Basicas**
Balderas 71, Mexico 1, D.F., Mexico.
- Mexico. Departamento de Estadisticas Economicas Basicas. Estadistica de Trabajo y Salarios Industriales. ISSN 0076-7492

**Mexico. Direccion General de Investigacion en Salud Publica**
Amores 1240, Mexico 12, D.F., Mexico.
- Revista de Investigacion en Salud Publica. q. ISSN 0034-8384

**Mexico. Direccion General de la Prensa, Memorias, Bibliotecas y Publicaciones. Departmento de Asuntos Internacionales**
Mexico, D.F., Mexico.
- Mexico. Direccion General de Prensa, Memorias, Bibliotecas y Publicaciones. Coleccion: Documentos Economicos de la Administracion Publica. irreg.; 1971, no. 7. ISSN 0076-7530

**Mexico. Direction General de Estatistica**
Av. Balderas 71, Mexico 1, D.F., Mexico.
- Agenda Estadistica.

**Mexico. Ministerio de Hacienda y Credito Publico**
Ignacio Ramirez No. 20, 1 piso, Mexico, Mexico.
- Mexico. Ministerio de Hacienda y Credito Publico. Difusion Fiscal. m.

**Mexico. Secretaria de Agricultura y Ganaderia. Departamento de Divulgacion Forestal y de la Fauna**
Secretaria de Agricultura y Ganaderia, Av. Mexico 190, Coyoacan, Mexico 21, D.F., Mexico.
- Bosques y Fauna. bi-m.

**Mexico. Secretaria de Agricultura y Ganaderia. Direccion General de Sanidad Vegetal**
Secretaria de Agricultura y Ganaderia, Calle Guillermo Perez Valenzuela, 127, Mexico 21, D. F., Mexico.
- Fitofilo. w. ISSN 0046-399X

**Mexico. Secretaria de Educacion Publica**
Mexico, D. F., Mexico.
- Estadistica Basica del Sistema Educativo Nacional. irreg.
- Mexico. Secretaria de Educacion Publica. Informe de Labores. irreg.

**Mexico. Secretaria de Industria y Comercio**
Mexico City, Mexico.
- Ingresos y Egresos de las Familias en la Republica Mexicana. irreg.

**Mexico. Secretaria de Industria y Comercio. Direccion General de Estadistica**
Ave Cuauhtemoc 80, Mexico D.F., Mexico.
- Anuario Estadistico de Comercio Exterior de los Estados Unidos Mexicanos. a.

**Mexico. Secretaria de la Defensa Nacional**
Mexico City, Mexico.
- Boletin Juridico Militar. bi-m. ISSN 0006-6419
- Revista del Ejercito. m. ISSN 0034-9046

**Mexico. Secretaria de la Defensa Nacional. Departamento de la Industria Militar**
Mexico City, Mexico.
- Industria Militar. m. ISSN 0019-7688

**Mexico. Secretaria de la Presidencia**
Palma No. 40-5 Piso, Mexico 1 D.F., Mexico.
- Mexican Newsletter. m. ISSN 0047-6994

**Mexico. Secretaria de Obras Publicas**
Avenidas Universidad y Xola, Mexico, D.F., Mexico.
- Mexico. Secretaria de Obras Publicas. m.

**Mexico. Secretaria de Recursos Hidraulicos**
Apartado 783, Mexico 1, D.F., Mexico.
- Recursos Hidraulicos. q.

**Mexico. Secretaria de Recursos Hidraulicos. Instituto Nacional de Investigaciones Pecuarias**
K&M 15, (Carr. Mexico-Toluca), Palo Alto, Mexico D.F., Mexico.
- Tecnica Pecuaria en Mexico. s-a. ISSN 0040-1889 (Co-sponsor: Mexico. Secretaria de Agricultura y Ganaderia)

**Mexico. Secretaria de Salubridad y Asistencia**
Mexico City, Mexico.
- Reunion Nacional Sobre Problemas de Contaminacion Ambiental. Memoria. irreg. (prep. by its Direccion General de Planeacion)
- Salud Publica de Mexico/Public Health of Mexico. bi-m. ISSN 0036-3634

**Mexico. Secretaria del Trabajo y Prevision Social**
Colima 367, Mexico 7, D.F., Mexico.
- Mexico. Secretaria del Trabajo y Prevision Social. Subdireccion de Documentacion. Resena Laboral. m. ISSN 0302-5004
- Panorama; asuntos laborales internacaionales. m.
- Revista Mexicana del Trabajo. q. ISSN 0035-0095

**Mexico. Servicio Nacional A R M O**
*see* Mexico. Servicio Nacional de Adiestramiento Rapido de la Mano de Obra en la Industria

**Mexico. Servicio Nacional de Adiestramiento Rapido de la Mano de Obra en la Industria. Centro de Informacion Tecnica y Documentacion**
Calzada Atzcapotzalco-la Villa 209, Mexico 16, D.F., Mexico.
- Adiestramiento. w.
- Centro de Informacion Tecnica y Documentacion. Indice Bibliografico. q.
- Centro de Informacion Tecnica y Documentacion. Indice de Articulos Sobre Educacion y Adiestramiento. q.
- Centro de Informacion Tecnica y Documentacion. Indice de Revistas. Seccion de Ciencia y Tecnologia. w.
- Centro de Informacion Tecnica y Documentacion. Indice de Revistas. Seccion de Educacion y Communicacion. w.
- Centro de Informacion Tecnica y Documentacion. Indice de Revistas. Seccion de Humanidades y Ciencias Sociales. w.
- Pedagogia para el Adiestramiento. q.

**Mexico Agricola**
Ave. Juarez 30-318, Mexico 1, D.F., Mexico.
- Mexico Agricola; revista mensual de divulgacion agricola, ganadera e industrias derivadas. m. ISSN 0026-1726

**Mexico Industrial**
Rio Danubio 68, Mexico 5, D. F., Mexico.
- Mexico Industrial. w. ISSN 0026-1807

**Mexletter Investment Counsel**
Hamburgo 159, Mexico 6, D.F., Mexico.
- Mexletter; a Mexican investment advisory service. m. ISSN 0026-1858

**Mignon**
6 Norte No. 3, Puebla, Pue., Mexico.
- Mignon. m.

**Militancia: Temas del Socialismo**
Milan 28-104, Mexico 6, D.F.
- Militancia: Temas del Socialismo. b-m.

**Mission Archeologique et Ethnologique Francaise au Mexique**
Virreyes No. 135, Mexico 10, D.F., Mexico.
- Etudes Mesoamericaines. s-a.

**Editorial Monex S. de R.L. y C.V.**
Ave. Insurgentes Centro 132-204, Mexico 4, D.F., Mexico.
- Gazer/Miron. w. ISSN 0016-5379

**Mundo Gastronomico**
Donceles 28, Mexico 1, D.F., Mexico.
- Mundo Gastronomico. m.

**Ediciones Mundo Marina S.A.**
Illinois 57, Mexico 18, D.F., Mexico.
- Tecnica Pesquera. m.

**Mundo Medico**
San Lorenzo 153, Mexico 12, D.F., Mexico.
- Mundo Medico. m.

**Roberto Murillo Rocha, Ed. & Pub.**
Manuel Ocaranza 13 B., Uruapan, Michoacan, Mexico.
- Cruzado; si lo leyo en el cruzado es veridico. d. ISSN 0011-2208

**Museo de Historia Natural de la Ciudad de Mexico**
Apartado Postal 18-845, Mexico 18, D.F., Mexico.
- Acta Zoologica Mexicana. irreg.(6 issues per year) ISSN 0065-1737

**Museu Nacional de Antropologia**
Calz. de la Milla y Reforma, Mexico 7, D. F., Mexico.
- Museu Nacional de Antropologia. Cuadernos. irreg., 1967, no. 4. ISSN 0076-7158

**Nacion**
Serapio Rendou 8, 2 Piso, Mexico 4 D.F., Mexico.
- Nacion; organo de accion nacional. w. ISSN 0027-7509

**Nacional Financiera, S.A.**
Gerencia de Informacion Tecnica, I. la Catolica 51, Mexico 1 D. F., Mexico.
- Mercado de Valores. w. ISSN 0025-9756

**Negocios**
Indiana, 25, Mexico 18, D.F., Mexico.
- Negocios. m. ISSN 0548-1422

**Negocios y Bancos**
Bolivar 8-601, Apdo. Postal 1907, Mexico 1, D.F., Mexico.
- Negocios y Bancos. fortn. ISSN 0028-2456

**Arcadio Noguera, Ed. & Pub.**
Tepeyac No. 292, Mexico 14 D.F., Mexico.
- Letras de Ayer y de Hoy. m. ISSN 0024-1229

**Nosotros**
Morelos 37, Apdo. Postal 9343, Mexico, D.F., Mexico.
- Nosotros; el magazine de mexico para latinoamerica. w. ISSN 0029-375X

**Notitas Musicales**
Alfonso Esparza Oteo 32, Mexico 20, D.F., Mexico.
- Notitas Musicales. fortn.

**Novaro Internacional, S.A.**
Calle 4, No. 27, Naucalpan, Mexico.
- Construccion Mexicana. m.

- Industria Mexicana. m.

**Nueva Editorial Interamericana, S. A. de C. V.**
Av. Puente de Alvarado 42-Apartado M-2977, Mexico 1, D.F., Mexico.
- Clinicas Obstetricas y Ginecologicas. 4 per yr. ISSN 0009-9333
- Instituto de Cardiologia de Mexico. Archivos. bi-m. ISSN 0020-3785 (Co-sponsor: Sociedad Mexican de Cardiologia)

**P y S**
Carpartado 484, Monterrey, Mexico.
- P y S; Prevision y Seguridad. a.

**Pan**
Bolivar 567, Mexico 13, D.F., Mexico.
- Pan. m. ISSN 0479-3013

**Partido Revolucionario Institucional**
Insurgentes sur 11, 3 piso, Colonia Juarez, Mexico 6, D.F., Mexico.
- Linea; organo teorico del P. R. I. bi-m.

**Perfumeria Moderna**
Bolivar 567, Mexico 13, D.F., Mexico.
- Perfumeria Moderna. m.

**Periodismo Especializado, S.A.**
Presidentes 187, Col. Portales, Mexico, 13, D.F., Mexico.
- Balon; futbol mundial. w. ISSN 0005-4410
- Box y Lucha; el mundo del ring. w. ISSN 0006-8470
- Feminidades; para la mujer moderna. m. ISSN 0014-9888
- Hit; lo mejor en beisbol. w. ISSN 0018-2761

**Periodistas y Publicistas Asociados de Mexico, S.A.**
Rio Danubio 68 Col. Cuautemoc, Mexico 5, D. F., Mexico.
- Mexico Mercantil. w. ISSN 0026-1815

**Editorial Posada**
Jose M. Rico, 204, Mexico 12, D.F., Mexico.
- Coleccion Ideas Politicas. irreg.

**Prensa Mexicana, S.A.**
Cipres 295, Mexico 4, D.F., Mexico.
- Gente. fortn. ISSN 0016-6952

**Publi - Representaciones S.A.**
Tlacotalpan 109, Mexico 7, D.F., Mexico.
- Reportero Industrial. m.

**Publicaciones Importantes, S. A.**
Bolivar 8, 601, Apdo. Postal 1907, Mexico 1, D.F., Mexico.
- Reporte Financiero. 12 per yr.

**Publicaciones y Promociones Impresas**
Melchor Ocampo 156, 1er Piso, Box 30-526, Mexico 4 D.F., Mexico.
- Revista Tecnica Textil-Vestido. m.
- Tecnica en Agricultura y Ganaderia. bi-m.

**Publicidad Profesional y Revistas S.A.**
Dinamarca 51-102, Mexico 6, D.F., Mexico.
- Hospitales y Clinicas. m. ISSN 0018-5906

**David Rangel Medina, Ed. & Pub.**
Cerrada de Xitle No. 19, Pedregal San Angel, Mexico 20, D.F., Mexico.
- Revista Mexicana de la Propiedad Industrial y Artistica. s-a. ISSN 0035-0044

**Resumen**
Apartado Postal 53-946, Mexico D.F., Mexico.
- Resumen; ideas, sucesos y opiniones del pensamiento libre de Mexico. m.

**Revista Latinoamericana de Microbiologia**
Apartado Postal 4-862, Mexico 4, D.F., Mexico.
- Revista Latinoamericana de Microbiologia. q. ISSN 0034-9771

**Revista Mexicana de Fianzas**
Calle de Puebla 383, Col. Roma, Mexico 7, D.F., Mexico.
- Revista Mexicana de Fianzas. s-a.

**Revista Mexicana del Petroleo**
Morelos 31, Mexico 1, D.F., Mexico.
- Revista Mexicana del Petroleo. bi-m.

**Editora Revista Tamaulipas**
Juarez y F. I. Madero, Apdo Postal 460, Tampico, Tam., Mexico.
- Revista Tamaulipas. m. ISSN 0035-0486

**Revista Tecnica Iem**
Octavio R. Pacheco, Constitucion 13a, Tacubaya 18, Mexico, D.F., Mexico.
- Revista Tecnica Iem. q. ISSN 0035-0494

**Editorial "Alfonso Reyes"**
Adolfo Prieto 2407 Oriente, Monterrey, N.L., Mexico.
- Salamandra; revista de cultura. 3 per yr. ISSN 0300-3388

**Editorial Salcedo, S. A.**
Calle de Hamburgo 36, Colonia Juarez, Mexico 6, D.F., Mexico.
- Todo. fortn. ISSN 0040-8603

**Ramon Sanchez Contreras, Ed.**
Alfonso Herrera St. 11-103, Mexico 4,D.F, Mexico.
- Ingenieria Sanitaria. q. ISSN 0446-2424
  (Interamerican Association of Sanitary Engineers)

**Luis C. Sanchez Fogarty, Ed. & Pub.**
Av. Cuauhtemoc 1338, Mexico 13, D.F., Mexico.
- Autoindustria. fortn.

**Servicio de Transmisiones del Ejercito**
Mexico City, Mexico.
- Transmisiones; una revista de radio, television, electronica. m. ISSN 0041-1272

**Sindicato de Trabajadores Ferrocarrileros de la Republica Mexicana**
Calzada de Nonolco No. 206, Mexico D.F., Mexico.
- Unificacion. m.

**Sistema Bancos de Comercio**
Venustiano Carranza 44, Mexico 1, D.F., Mexico.
- Panorama Economico. m. ISSN 0479-4346

**Publicaciones Sociales Mexicanas**
Doctor Vertiz No. 1295-202, Mexico 13, D.F., Aptdo Postal 73-206, Mexico.
- Estrategia; revista de analisis politico. b-m.

**Sociedad Astronomica de Mexico**
Jardin Felipe Xicotencatl, Mexico 13, D.F., Mexico 1, D. F., Mexico.
- Universo. q.

**Sociedad Chihuahuense de Estudios Historicos**
Calle 2A, Num. 600, Despachos 103 Y 109, Chihuahua, Chih, Mexico.
- Sociedad Chihuahuense de Estudios Historicos. Boletin. q.

**Sociedad de Autores y Compositores de Musica**
- Boletin S A C M. (pub. by Editores Asociades)

**Sociedad de Industriales de las Artes Graficas**
Calle de Londres No. 190, Mexico 6 D.F., Mexico.
- Artes Graficas en Mexico. bi-m. ISSN 0004-3508

**Sociedad Folklorica de Mexico**
Avenida Amsterdam 130, Mexico 11, D. F., Mexico.
- Sociedad Folklorica de Mexico. Anuario. a.

**Sociedad Forestal Mexicana A.C.**
Jesus Teran N. 11, Mexico 1, D.F., Mexico.
- Mexico Forestal. bi-m. ISSN 0047-7028

**Sociedad Matematica Mexicana**
Aptdo. 14-70, Mexico 14, D. F., Mexico.
- Matematicas y Ensenanza. q.
- Miscelanea Matematica. m.
- Sociedad Matematica Mexicana. Boletin. s-a. ISSN 0037-8615

**Sociedad Medica del Centro Materno-Infantil Gral. Maximino Avila Camacho**
Av. de los Constituyentes No. 240, Mexico 18 D.F., Mexico.
- Ticitl. q. ISSN 0040-6732

**Sociedad Medica del Hospital de Mexico, S.S.A.**
Dr. Balmis 148, 1. piso, Mexico, D.F., Mexico.
- Revista Medica del Hospital General de Mexico S.S.A. m. ISSN 0034-9925

**Sociedad Mexicana de Alergia e Inmunologia, A.C.**
Fuente Emperador 6, Tecamachalco, Mexico 10, D.F., Mexico.
- Alergia. q. ISSN 0002-5151

**Sociedad Mexicana de Fisica**
Apdo 20364, Mexico 20, D.F., Mexico.
- Revista Mexicana de Fisica. 4 per yr. ISSN 0035-001X

**Sociedad Mexicana de Fotogrametria, Fotointerpretacion y Geodesia**
Tacuba No. 5, Corredores Entrada No. 4, Salon No. 39, Mexico-1, Mexico.
- Fotogrametria, Fotointerpretacion y Geodesia. irreg.

**Sociedad Mexicana de Geografia y Estadistica**
Justo Sierra No. 19, Apdo. 10739, Mexico D.F., Mexico.
- Sociedad Mexicana de Geografia y Estadistica. Boletin. s-a. ISSN 0049-1004

**Sociedad Mexicana de Historia de la Ciencia y de la Tecnologia**
Mexico City, Mexico.
- Sociedad Mexicana de Historia de la Ciencia y de la Tecnologia. Anales. irreg.

**Sociedad Mexicana de Ingenieria de Costos, A.C.**
- Ingenieria de Costos. (pub. by D'Pastrana Editores, S.A.)

**Sociedad Mexicana de Micologia**
Dept. Botanica, Escuela Nacional de Ciencias Biologicas, I.P.N., Apartado Postal 42-186, Mexico 17, D.F., Mexico.
- Sociedad Mexicana de Micologia. Boletin. a. ISSN 0085-6223

**Sociedad Mexicana de Neumologia y Cirugia de Torax**
M. Schulz, Av. Oaxaca 23, Mexico 7, D.F., Mexico.
- Revista de Neumologia y Cirugia de Torax. bi-m. ISSN 0034-8589

**Sociedad Mexicana de Neurologia y Psiquiatria**
Patricio Saenz 37, Mexico 16, D.F., Mexico.
- Neurologia-Neurocirugia-Psiquiatria. q. ISSN 0028-3851 (Co-sponsors: Sociedad Mexicana de Electroencefalografia y Neurofisiologia Clinica, Sociedad Neuropsiquiatrica "Bernardino Alvarez", Sociedad de Medicina Psicosomatica de Monterrey)

**Sociedad Mexicana de Ortopedia**
Ejercito Nacional 475, 1Er Piso, Mexico 17, D.F., Mexico.
- Anales de Ortopedia y Traumatologia. q. ISSN 0044-8184

**Sociedad Mexicana de Pediatria**
Calzada de Maderos 240, Mexico D.F., Mexico.
- Revista Mexicana de Pediatria. m. ISSN 0035-0052

**Sociedad Mexicana de Planificacion**
Insurgentes sur 1991, Desp. 706, 20, Mexico.
- Planificacion. bi-m.

**Sociedad Nuevoleonesa de Historia, Geografia y Estadistica**
Washington y Dr. Coss, Monterrey, Mexico.
- Roel. m.

**Juan Solorzano Gomez, Ed. & Pub.**
Filomeno Mata 13-11, Mexico 1, D.F., Mexico.
- Hule Mexicano y Plasticos; revista technica industrial. m. ISSN 0018-7127

**Suenos**
Puebla, Mexico.
- Suenos/Dreams. s-a. ISSN 0039-4645

**Teatro Clasico de Mexico**
A.C. Apartado 61-077, Mexico, D.F., Mexico.
- Teatro Clasico de Mexico. Boletin. Notas y Comentarios. irreg., 1970, no. 27. ISSN 0082-2256

**Telefonos de Mexico, S.A.**
Via Parque 198, Mexico 5, D.F., Mexico.
- Voces de Telefonos de Mexico. m.

**Editorial Television S.A.**
Velazquez de Leon 104, Mexico 4, D. F., Mexico.
- Tele Guia; primera revista de la television Mexicana. w.

**Textil Vestido**
Melchor Ocampo 156, Mexico 4, D.F., Mexico.
- Textil Vestido. m.

**Texto e Imagen S.A.**
Insurgentes sur 1673, Mexico 20, D.F., Mexico.
- Enfermeras. q. (Colegio Nacional de Enfermeras)

**Editorial This Is Mexico**
Calle Londres 166, Apdo. 6-728, Mexico 6, D.F., Mexico.
- Now in Mexico; travel retailers' news. w.
- This Is Mexico; Mexico's weekly visitor's pocket guide. w.

**Tiempo S.A. de C.V.**
Barcelona 32, Mexico 6 D.F., Mexico.
- Hispano Americano; seminario de la vida y la verdad. w. ISSN 0018-2192
- Tiempo; semanario de la vida y la verdad. w. ISSN 0040-7275

**Tierra**
Calle S. Diaz Miron No. 58, Mexico 4, D. F., Mexico.
- Tierra. m. ISSN 0040-733X

**Tlalocan**
Casa de Tlaloc, Madrid No. 5-301, Mexico 4, D.F., Mexico.
- Tlalocan; revista de fuentes para el conocimiento de las culturas indigenas de mexico. irreg. ISSN 0040-8239

**Editorial Trillas, S. A.**
Apartado Postal 69-716, Mexico 21, D. F., Mexico.
- Revista Mexicana de Analisis de la Conducta/ Mexican Journal of Behavior Analysis. s-a. (Mexican Society of Behavior Analysis)

**Turismo**
Sonora 119, Mexico 7, D.F, Mexico.
- Turismo. m.

**Union de Universidades de America Latina**
Apdo. Postal 70232, Ciudad Universitaria, Mexico 20 D.F., Mexico.
- Universidades. q. ISSN 0041-8935

**Union Geofisica Mexicana. Centro de Ciencias de la Atmosfera**
Circuito Exterior, Ciudad Universitaria, Mexico 20, D.F., Mexico.
- Geofisica Internacional. q. ISSN 0016-7169

**Union Nacional de Comerciantes de Calzado A.C.**
Bolivar No. 15-102, Altos, Mexico 1, D.F., Mexico.
- Zapatos y Zapaterias. m. ISSN 0044-1783

**Universidad Autonoma de Guadalajara**
Paseo de las Aquilas 7000, Lomas del Valle, 3A Seccion, Guadalajara, Mexico.
- Docencia. bi-m.

**Universidad Autonoma de San Luis Potosi**
Biblioteca Publica, Av Damian Carmona 130, San Luis Potosi S.L.P., Mexico.
- Archivos de Historia Potosina. q. ISSN 0004-055X (Academia de Historia Potosina)

**Universidad Autonoma de San Luis Potosi. Instituto de Geologia y Metalurgia**
Avenida de los Poetas 5, San Luis Potosi, Mexico.
- Geologia y Metalurgia. s-a. ISSN 0016-7533

**Universidad Autonoma de Sinaloa. Escuela de Economia**
Culiacan, Mexico.
- Temas Economicos.

**Universidad Autonoma del Estado de Mexico. Instituto de Investigaciones Historicas**
Constituyentes, 100 Oriente, Apartado Postal 65-A, Toluca, Mexico.
- Historica. q.

**Universidad de Guadalajara. Escuela Superior de Agricultura**
Apdo. Postal 129, Zapopan, Jalisco, Mexico.
- Universidad de Guadalajara. Instituto de Botanica. Boletin Informativo. irreg. (prep. by its Instituto de Botanica)

**Universidad de Guadalajara. Instituto de Astronomia y Meteorologia**
Av. Vallarta Num. 2602, Guadalajara, Mexico.
- Universidad de Guadalajara. Instituto de Astronomia y Meteorologi Informacion. m. ISSN 0041-8404

**Universidad de Nuevo Leon. Centro de Investigaciones Economicas**
5 de Mayo 523 Ote. (Altos), Monterrey, N.L., Mexico.
- Universidad Autonoma de Nuevo Leon. Centro de Investigaciones Economicas. Boletin Bimestral. bi-m. ISSN 0041-8498

**Universidad de Yucatan**
Calle 60 Con 57, Apdo. Postal 201, Merida, Yucatan, Mexico.
- Universidad de Yucatan. Revista. bi-m. ISSN 0041-8536

**Universidad Iberoamericana**
Cerro de las Torres 395, Mexico 21 D.F., Mexico.
- Comunidad. q. ISSN 0010-5023
- Comunidad. Suplementos. irreg., 1976, no. 6. ISSN 0069-8210
- Cuadernos de Literatura. irreg. (prep. by its Departamento de Letras)
- Humanidades. a. (prep. by its Instituto de Investigaciones Humanisticas)
- Juridica. a. (prep. by its Departamento de Derecho)

**Universidad Nacional Autonoma de Mexico**
Ciudad Universitaria, Mexico, D.F., Mexico.
- Economia Informa. m.
- Universidad Nacional Autonoma de Mexico. Revista. m. ISSN 0026-1750 (prep. by its Direccion General de Difusion Cultural)

**Universidad Nacional Autonoma de Mexico. Biblioteca Nacional e Instituto de Investigaciones Bibliograficas**
Apdo. Postal 29124, Mexico 1, D.F., Mexico.
- Bibliografia Mexicana. bi-m. ISSN 0006-1069
- Boletin de Estudios Medicos y Biologicos. irreg.; latest issue, 1974. ISSN 0067-9666
- Estudios Medicos y Biologicos. Boletin. q. ISSN 0020-3858
- Universidad Nacional Autonoma de Mexico. Instituto de Investigaciones Bibliografica. Boletin. q. ISSN 0006-1719
- Universidad Nacional Autonoma de Mexico. Instituto de Investigaciones Bibliografica. Instrumenta Bibliographica. irreg.

**Universidad Nacional Autonoma de Mexico. Centro de Estudios Mayas**
Torre de Humanidades, Ciudad Universitaria, Mexico 20, D.F., Mexico.
- Estudios de Cultura Maya. a. ISSN 0071-1667
- Universidad Nacional Autonoma de Mexico. Centro de Estudios Mayas. Cuadernos. irreg. ISSN 0076-7166

**Universidad Nacional Autonoma de Mexico. Direccion General de Difusion Cultural**
Ciudad Universitaria, Villa Obregon, Mexico 20 D.F., Mexico.
- Punto de Partida. bi-m. ISSN 0033-4367

**Universidad Nacional Autonoma de Mexico. Facultad de Ciencias Politicas y Sociales**
Facultad de Ciencias Politicas y Sociales, Universidad Nacional Autonoma de Mexico, Ciudad Universitaria, Mexico 20, D.F., Mexico.
- Acta Sociologica. Serie Promocion Social. a. (prep. by its Centro de Estudios del Desarrollo)
- Anuario Politico de America Latina. a.
- Estudios Politicos.
- Relaciones Internationales. q. (prep. by its Centro de Relaciones Internacionales) (Subscr. to: Servi-Libros, Apdo. Postal 25-328, Mexico 13, D.F., Mexico)
- Revista Mexicana de Ciencias Politicas y Sociales. q.

**Universidad Nacional Autonoma de Mexico. Facultad de Comercio y Adminstracion**
Ciudad Universitaria, Mexico, D.F., Mexico.
- Contabilidad Administracion. bi-m. ISSN 0010-7212

**Universidad Nacional Autonoma de Mexico. Facultad de Contaduria Administracion**
Mexico D.F., Mexico.
- Contaduria Administracion. bi-m.

**Universidad Nacional Autonoma de Mexico. Facultad de Derecho**
Mexico City, Mexico.
- Derecho Penal Contemporaneo. bi-m. ISSN 0045-9992

**Universidad Nacional Autonoma de Mexico. Facultad de Filosofia y Letras**
Insurgentes 299, Mexico 7, D.F., Mexico.
- Anuario de Bibliotecologia, Archivologia e Informatica. a.
- Asia. Anuario del Centro de Estudios Orientales. a. ISSN 0066-8249

**Universidad Nacional Autonoma de Mexico. Facultad de Ingenieria**
Apdo. Postal 70-223, Mexico 20, D.F., Mexico.
- Ingenieria. q. ISSN 0020-0999

**Universidad Nacional Autonoma de Mexico. Facultad de Medicina**
Mexico 20, D.F., Mexico.
- Archivalia Medica. irreg. ISSN 0066-6521
- Universidad Nacional Autonoma de Mexico. Facultad de Medicina. Nueva Revista. (pub. by Intersistemas, S.A. de C.V.)

**Universidad Nacional Autonoma de Mexico. Facultad de Medicina Veterinaria y Zootecnia**
Ciudad Universitaria, Mexico 20, D.F., Mexico.
- Veterinaria Mexico. q.

**Universidad Nacional Autonoma de Mexico. Instituto de Astronomia**
Apdo. Postal 70-264, Mexico 20, D.F., Mexico.
- Revista Mexicana de Astronomia y Astrofisica. s-a.

**Universidad Nacional Autonoma de Mexico. Instituto de Biologia**
Ciudad Universitaria, Villa Obregon, Mexico 20, D.F., Mexico.
- Universidad Nacional Autonoma de Mexico. Instituto de Biologia. Anales. a. ISSN 0076-7174

**Universidad Nacional Autonoma de Mexico. Instituto de Geofisica**
Circuito Exterior, Ciudad Universitaria, Mexico 20, D.F., Mexico.
- Universidad Nacional Autonoma de Mexico. Instituto de Geofisica. Anales. a; vol. 20, 1974. ISSN 0076-7182
- Universidad Nacional Autonoma de Mexico. Instituto de Geofisica. Monografias. irreg. ISSN 0076-7204
- Universidad Nacional Autonoma de Mexico. Instituto de Geofisica. Noticiario. q.

**Universidad Nacional Autonoma de Mexico. Instituto de Geografia**
Ciudad Universitaria, Mexico 20, D.F., Mexico.
- Universidad Nacional Autonoma de Mexico. Instituto de Geografia. Anuario de Geografia.
- Universidad Nacional Autonoma de Mexico. Instituto de Geografia. Boletin. a. ISSN 0076-7190

**Universidad Nacional Autonoma de Mexico. Instituto de Geologia**
Apdo. 70-296, Ciudad Universitaria, Mexico 20, D.F., Mexico.
- Universidad Nacional Autonoma de Mexico. Instituto de Geologia. Revista. a.
- Universidad Nacional Autonoma de Mexico. Instituto de Geologia. Serie: Divulgacion. a.

**Universidad Nacional Autonoma de Mexico. Instituto de Investigaciones Antropologicas**
Ciudad Universitaria, Villa Obregon, Mexico 20 D.F., Mexico.
- Universidad Nacional Autonoma de Mexico. Instituto de Investigaciones Historicas. Anales de Anttropologia. ISSN 0020-3947
- Universidad Nacional Autonoma de Mexico. Instituto de Investigaciones Historicas. Cuadernos Serie Antropologica. irreg. 1969, no. 23. ISSN 0076-7263
- Universidad Nacional Autonoma de Mexico. Instituto de Investigaciones Historicas. Serie Antropologica. irreg., 1969, no. 11. ISSN 0076-7298

**Universidad Nacional Autonoma de Mexico. Instituto de Investigaciones Esteticas**
Torre de Humanidades 6 piso, Ciudad Universitaria, Mexico 20, D.F., Mexico
- Cuadernos de Historia del Arte. irreg. (Subscr. to: Libreria Universitaria, Insurgentes sur 299, Mexico 7, D.F., Mexico)
- Estudios de Arte Moderno. irreg.; latest issue, 1971. ISSN 0071-1640
- Estudios de Arte y Estetica. irreg; latest issue, 1972. ISSN 0071-1659
- Estudios de Folklore. irreg; latest issue, 1971. ISSN 0071-1683
- Estudios de Literatura. irreg; latest issue, 1976. ISSN 0071-1691
- Estudios y Fuentes del Arte en Mexico. irreg; latest issue, 1976. ISSN 0071-1748
- Historia del Arte en Mexico. irreg., latest issue, 1970. ISSN 0073-2451
- Problemas del Desarrollo; revista latinoamericana de economia. q. ISSN 0301-7036
- Universidad Nacional Autonoma de Mexico. Instituto de Investigaciones Esteticas. Anales. a. ISSN 0076-7239
- Universidad Nacional Autonoma de Mexico. Instituto de Investigaciones Esteticas. Anales. Suplemento. irreg; latest issue, 1972. ISSN 0076-7247
- Universidad Nacional Autonoma de Mexico. Instituto de Investigaciones Esteticas. Publicaciones Especiales. irreg; latest issue, 1974. ISSN 0076-7255

**Universidad Nacional Autonoma de Mexico. Instituto de Investigaciones Filosoficas**
Apdo Postal 27-414, Mexico, D.F., Mexico.
- Critica; revista Hispanoamericana de Filosofia. 3 per yr. ISSN 0011-1503

**Universidad Nacional Autonoma de Mexico. Instituto de Investigaciones Historicas**
Departamento de Distribucion de Libros Universitarias, Insurgentes sur, 299, Mexico 11, D.F., Mexico.
- Devenir. Cuadernos del Seminario de Historia. irreg., 1966, no. 14.
- Estudios de Historia Moderna y Contemporanea de Mexico. irreg; vol. 5, 1976. ISSN 0014-147X
- Fuentes Indigenas de la Cultura Nahuatl. irreg; 1969, no. 7. ISSN 0071-9773
- Universidad Nacional Autonoma de Mexico. Instituto de Investigaciones Historicas. Serie Bibliografica. irreg., 1969, no. 5. ISSN 0076-7301
- Universidad Nacional Autonoma de Mexico. Instituto de Investigaciones Historicas. Serie Documental. irreg; no. 11, 1974. ISSN 0076-731X
- Universidad Nacional Autonoma de Mexico. Instituto de Investigaciones Historicas. Serie de Culturas Mesoamericanas. irreg; no. 2, 1968. ISSN 0076-7328
- Universidad Nacional Autonoma de Mexico. Instituto de Investigaciones Historicas. Serie de Cultura Nahuatl. Fuentes. irreg., 1969, no. 7. ISSN 0076-7212
- Universidad Nacional Autonoma de Mexico. Instituto de Investigaciones Historicas. Serie de Cultura Nahuatl. Monografias. irreg; no. 19, 1975. ISSN 0076-7344
- Universidad Nacional Autonoma de Mexico. Instituto de Investigaciones Historicas. Serie de Historia General. irreg; no. 8, 1972. ISSN 0076-7352
- Universidad Nacional Autonoma de Mexico. Instituto de Investigaciones Historicas. Serie de Historia Novohispana. irreg; no. 26, 1976. ISSN 0076-7379
- Universidad Nacional Autonoma de Mexico. Instituto de Investigaciones Historicas. Serie de Historiadores y Cronistas. irreg; no. 6, 1977. ISSN 0076-7387
- Universidad Nacional Autonoma de Mexico. Instituto de Investigueiones Historicas. Cuadernos Serie Documental. irreg., 1968, no. 6. ISSN 0076-7271
- Universidad Nacional Autonoma de Mexico Instituto de Investigaciones Historicas Serie de Cultura Nahuatl. Estudios de Cultura Nahuatl. irreg; 1976, vol. 12. ISSN 0071-1675

**Universidad Nacional Autonoma de Mexico. Instituto de Investigaciones Juridicas**
Torre de Humanidades, 3 Er. Piso, Ciudad Universitaria, Mexico 20, D.F., Mexico.
- Boletin Mexicano de Derecho Comparado. 3 per yr. ISSN 0041-8633
- Gaceta Informativa de Legislacion, Jurisprudencia y Bibliografia. q.

**Universidad Nacional Autonoma de Mexico. Instituto de Investigaciones Sociales**
Ciudad Universitaria, Torre de Humanidades, Coyoacan 20, Mexico, D.F., Mexico.
- Revista Mexicana de Sociologia. q. ISSN 0035-0087

**Universidad Nacional Autonoma de Mexico. Instituto de Matematicas**
Torre de Ciencias 60 piso, Ciudad Universitaria, Mexico 20, D.F., Mexico.
- Universidad Nacional Autonoma de Mexico. Instituto de Matematicas. Anales. a; vol. 13, 1973. ISSN 0076-7441

**Universidad Nacional Autonoma de Mexico. Seminario de Investigaciones Bibliotecologicas**
Torre de Ciencias, Ciudad Universitaria, Mexico 20, D.F., Mexico.
- Universidad Nacional Autonoma de Mexico. Seminario de Investigaciones Bibliotecologica. Publicaciones. Serie B. Bibliografia. irreg., 1967, no. 4. ISSN 0076-7468

**Universidad Veracruzana**
Departamento Editorial, Bravo No. 11, Xalapa, Veracruz, Mexico.
- Palabra y el Hombre. q. ISSN 0031-014X

**Vacaciones**
Av. Juarez 76, Mexico 1, D.F., Mexico.
- Vacaciones; ideas para su viajes de placer. m.

**Vida de la Piedad**
Matamoros No. 100, La Piedad, Michoacan, Mexico.
- Vida de la Piedad. s-w. ISSN 0042-5249

**Vigilancia**
Av. 16 de Septiembre No. 6, Apdo. Postal M-7962, Mexico 1, D.F., Mexico.
- Vigilancia. bi-m. ISSN 0042-5974

**Periodicos Villagran, S. A.**
Av. Chapultepec No. 197, Mexico 6, D. F., Mexico.
- Auto Noticias; informador de la industria y del comercio automovilisticos. w. ISSN 0005-0814

**Editorial Vision, S. A.**
Hamburgo 20, Mexico City, D.F., Mexico (U. S. Distrib: Vision, 641 Lexington Ave., New York, N. Y. 10022)
- Progreso; comercio - industria - finanzas - desarrollo. 9 per yr. ISSN 0555-3768

**Who's Who in Mexico**
Apartado Postal 1311, Mexico 1, D.F., Mexico.
- Who's Notable in Mexico; Who's Who in Mexico. quinquennial. ISSN 0300-208X

**Xaloc**
Ave.Uruguay 40-202, Mexico 1 D.F., Mexico.
- Xaloc. bi-m. ISSN 0043-986X

**3A Editores S.A.**
Kepler 82, Mexico, D.F., Mexico.
- Revista de Geografia Universal. m.

## MONACO

**Academie Internationale du Tourisme**
4, rue des Iris, Monte Carlo, Monaco.
- Academie Internationale du Tourisme. Revue. q. ISSN 0001-4060

**Editions du Cap**
Palais de la Scala, Monte Carlo, Monaco.
- Liens. m. ISSN 0024-2942

**Centre International d'Etude des Problems Humains**
17 rue de Millo, Monte Carlo, Monaco.
- Centre International d'Etude des Problems Humains. Bulletins. irreg. ISSN 0577-1730

**International Hydrographic Organization**
7, Ave. President J. F. Kennedy, Monte Carlo, Monaco.
- International Hydrographic Bulletin. m. ISSN 0020-6938
- International Hydrographie Conference. Reports of Proceedings. quinquennial; latest issue, 1975 (for 1972 meeting) ISSN 0074-6274

- International Hydrographic Organization. Yearbook. a.
- International Hydrographic Review. s-a. ISSN 0020-6946

## MOROCCO

**Achaab Publishing**
12 rue Pormentier, Avenue Temara, Rabat, Morocco.
- Achaab/People; serving the people, the throne, Arabism and Islam. s-w. ISSN 0001-4869

**American Chamber of Commerce in Morocco**
27 Av. de l'Armee Royale, Hotel El Mansour, Casablanca, Morocco.
- A M C H A M Morocco. a. ISSN 0065-7689

**Banque du Maroc**
277 Ave. Mohammed V, Rabat, Morocco.
- Banque du Maroc. Rapport Annuel. a. ISSN 0067-396X

**Banque Marocaine du Commerce Exterieur**
241, Bd. Mohammed V, Casablanca, Morocco.
- Banque Marocaine du Commerce Exterieur. Monthly Information Review. m. (prep. by its Studies and Foreign Relations Department)

**Banque Nationale pour le Developpement Economique**
B.P. 407, Place des Alaouites, Rabat, Morocco.
- Banque Nationale pour le Developpement Economique. Rapport Annuel. a.

**Centre Africain de Formation et de Recherche Administratives pour le Developpement**
Box 310, Tangier, Morocco.
- African Administrative Abstracts. q.
- African Administrative Studies. s-a.

**Centre de Recherches et d'Etudes Demographiques.**
Rabat, Morocco.
- Centre de Recherches et d'Etudes Demographiques. Etudes.

**Centre National de Documentation**
B.P. 826, Rabat, Morocco.
- Index Documentation-Economie-Science-Technique. 2-3 per yr.

**Institut des Peches Maritimes**
Rue de Tiznit, Casablanca, Morocco.
- Institut des Peches Maritimes. Bulletin. irreg., July 1969, no. 17. ISSN 0069-0821

**Journal de Tanger**
43 rue Shakespeare, Tangiers, Morocco.
- Journal de Tanger. w. ISSN 0047-2174

**Kompass Maroc-Veto**
Boite Postale 5117, MA Casablanca, Morocco (Dist. by Iliffe NTP Inc., 300 E. 42 St., New York, N.Y. 10017)
- Kompass Maroc; register of Moroccan industry and commerce. a. ISSN 0075-6695 (Foundation for Promoting International Economic Information SZ)

**Morocco. Direction de la Statistique**
B.P. 178, Rabat, Morocco.
- Annuaire Statistique du Maroc. a. ISSN 0066-3719
- Maroc en Chiffre. a. ISSN 0076-4655
- Morocco. Direction de la Statistique. Bulletin Mensuel des Statistiques. m. ISSN 0545-0489
- Morocco. Direction de la Statistique. Bulletin Methodologique Trimestriel. q.
- Morocco. Direction de la Statistique. Comptes de la Nation. a.
- Morocco. Direction de la Statistique. Etude de Conjoncture. q.
- Morocco. Direction de la Statistique. Indice du Cout de la Vie. m.
- Morocco. Direction de la Statistique. Statistiques Retrospectives. a.
- Parc Automobile du Maroc. a.
- Situation Economique du Maroc. a. ISSN 0080-9845

**Morocco. Direction des Mines et de la Geologie**
Rabat, Morocco.
- Morocco. Direction des Mines et de la Geologie. Activite du Secteur Petrolier. irreg.

**Morocco. Division des Antiquites**
23 rue al Brihi, Rabat, Morocco.
- Bulletin d'Archelolgie Marocaine. a. ISSN 0068-4015
- Etudes et Travaux d'Archeologie Marocaine. irreg. ISSN 0071-2027

**National Moroccan Tourist Office**
22 rue d'Alger, Rabat 10013, Morocco.
- Morocco Tourism. q. ISSN 0027-1160

**Johanny Peillon**
B.P. 5054, Dakar-Fann, Morocco.
- Memento Therapeutique du Maroc. a.
- Memento Therapeutique pour l'Afrique Noire Francophone. a.

**Perspectives Euro Africaines**
36 rue d'Argeles, Casablanca, Morocco.
- Perspectives Euro Africaines. bi-m. ISSN 0048-3516

**Societe d'Etudes Economiques Sociales et Statistiques du Maroc**
B.P. 535, Rabat-Chellah, Morocco.
- Bulletin Economique et Social du Maroc. irreg. (4 nos. per subscr.) ISSN 0007-4586

**Societe de Geographie de Maroc**
Faculte des Lettres, Universite de Rabat, Rabat, Morocco.
- Revue de Geographie du Maroc. s-a. ISSN 0035-1156

**Societe des Sciences Naturelles et Physiques du Maroc**
Institut Scientifique Cherifiens, Ave. Moulay Cherif, Rabat, Morocco.
- Societe des Sciences Naturelles et Physiques du Maroc. Bulletin. s-a. ISSN 0037-9255

**Souffles**
10 rue Jouinet Gambetta, Rabat, Morocco.
- Souffles/Anfas; revue culturelle. m. ISSN 0049-1357

**Union Marocaine du Travail**
222,Ave. des Far, Casablanca, Morocco.
- Avant-Garde; attalia. w. ISSN 0005-190X

**Universite Mohammed V. Faculte des Lettres et des Sciences Humaines**
Avenue Moulay Cherif, B.P. 447, Rabat, Morocco.
- Hesperis - Tamuda. 3 per yr. ISSN 0018-1005 (prep. by its Association des Sciences de l'Homme)

## MOZAMBIQUE

**Associacao Africana de Mocambique**
Avda. 24 du Julho 315, Box 461, Maputo, Mozambique.
- Brado Africano. w.

**Associacao Comercial de Lourenco Marques**
Box 1166, Maputo, Mozambique.
- Associacao Comercial de Lourenco Marques. Boletim. m. ISSN 0004-5209

**Centro Africano de Manica e Sofala**
Rua D. Joao de Mascarenhas, Beira, Mozambique.
- Voz Africana. w.

**Instituto de Investigacao Agronomica de Mocambique. Centro de Documentacao Agraria**
C. P. 3658, Maputo 11, Mozambique.
- Agronomia Mocambicana. irreg. ISSN 0044-6858
- Instituto de Investigacao de Mocambique. Centro de Documentacao Agraria. Memorias. irreg. ISSN 0077-1791

**Instituto de Investigacao Cientifica de Mocambique. Centro de Documentacao Cientifica**
C.P. 1780, Maputo, Mozambique.
- Instituto de Investigacao Cientifica de Mocambique. Centro de Documentacao Cientifica. Boletim. q. ISSN 0008-9915
- Instituto de Investigacao Cientifica de Mocambique. Memorias. Series A (Ciencias Biologicas) irreg.; latest edt., vol. 11, 1971. ISSN 0076-1168
- Instituto de Investigacao Cientifica de Mocambique. Memorias. Serie B (Ciencias Geograficas-Geologicas) a. ISSN 0076-1176

- Instituto de Investigacao Cientifica de
  Mocambique. Memorias. Serie C (Ciencias
  Humanas) irreg.; vol. 10, 1973. ISSN 0076-1184
- Novos Taxa Entomologicos. irreg.; no. 102, 1973.
  ISSN 0078-2564
- Revista de Entomologia de Mocambique. irreg.
  ISSN 0034-8139

**Instituto de Investigacao Veterinaria de Mocambique**
Caixa Postal 1922, Maputo, Mozambique.
- Veterinaria Mocambicana. s-a. ISSN 0042-482X

**Laboratorio de Engenharia de Mocambique**
Box 1918, Maputo, Mozambique.
- Laboratoria de Engenharia de Mocambique.
  Boletin Tecnico. q.
- Laboratorio de Engenharia de Mocambique.
  Boletin Bibliografico. bi-m.

**Mozambique. Direccao dos Services das Alfandegas**
Maputo, Mozambique.
- Mozambique. Direccao dos Servicos das
  Alfandegas. Boletim das Alfandegas. 2-4 per yr.

**Mozambique. Direccao dos Servicos dos Portos,
Caminhos de Ferro e Transportes**
P.O.Box 19, Maputo, Mozambique.
- Portos e Caminhar de Ferro de Mocambique. m.
  ISSN 0006-5978

**Mozambique. Harbours, Railways and Transports
Administration**
*see* Mozambique. Direccao dos Servicos dos
Portos, Caminhos de Ferro e Transportes

**Mozambique. Inspeccao Provincial de Educacao**
Avenida da Republica, 882-7, C. P. 1406, Maputo,
Mozambique.
- Humus; revista pedagogica. irreg.

**Mozambique. Servico Meteorologico**
C. P. 256, Maputo, Mozambique.
- Mozambique. Servico Meteorologico. Boletim
  Geomagnetico Preliminar. m. ISSN 0006-6001
- Mozambique. Servico Meteorologico. Boletim
  Meterologico para a Agricultura. 3 per m. ISSN
  0006-6044
- Mozambique. Servico Meteorologico. Boletim
  Seismique. m. ISSN 0006-6095
- Mozambique. Servico Meteorologico. Resumos.
  Meteorologicas para a Aeronautica. m. ISSN
  0034-5946

**Radio Clube de Mozambique**
Caixa Postal No. 594, Maputo, Mozambique.
- Radio Mozambique. m. ISSN 0033-7943

**Sociedade de Estudos de Mocambique**
C.P. 1138, Maputo, Mozambique.
- Sociedade de Estudos de Mocambique. Boletim. q.

**Tempografica, S. A. R. L.**
Av. Ahmed Sekou Toure 1078, Box 2917, Maputo,
Mozambique.
- Tempo. w.

**Universidade Eduardo Mondlane**
C.P. 257, Maputo, Mozambique.
- Revista de Ciencias Agronomicas. Serie A. a.
  ISSN 0080-2123
- Revista de Ciencias Agronomicas. Serie B. irreg.
  ISSN 0080-2131
- Revista de Ciencias Biologicas. Serie A. a. ISSN
  0080-214X (prep. by its Laboratorio de Zoologia)
- Revista de Ciencias Biologicas. Serie B. irreg.
  ISSN 0080-2158 (prep. by its Laboratorio de
  Zoologia)
- Revista de Ciencias do Homen. Serie A. a. ISSN
  0080-2166 (prep. by its Faculdade de Letras)
- Revista de Ciencias do Homen. Serie B. irreg.
  ISSN 0080-2174 (prep. by its Faculdade de
  Letras)
- Revista de Ciencias Geologicas. Serie A. a. ISSN
  0080-2182 (prep. by its Laboratorio de
  Mineralogia e Geologia)
- Revista de Ciencias Geologicas. Serie B. irreg.
  ISSN 0080-2190 (prep. by its Laboratorio de
  Mineralogia e Geologia)
- Revista de Ciencias Matematicas. Serie A. a.
  ISSN 0080-2204
- Revista de Ciencias Matematicas. Serie B. irreg.
  ISSN 0080-2212
- Revista de Ciencias Medicas. Serie A. a. ISSN
  0080-2220 (prep. by its Faculdade de Medicina)
- Revista de Ciencias Medicas. Serie B. irreg. ISSN
  0080-2239 (prep. by its Faculdade de Medicina)
- Revista de Ciencias Veterinarias. Serie A. a. ISSN
  0080-2247 (prep. by its Faculdade de Veterinaria)

- Revista de Fisica, Quimica e Engenharia. Serie A.
  a. ISSN 0080-2263
- Revista de Fisica, Quimica e Engenharia. Serie B.
  irreg. ISSN 0080-2271

**Universidade Eduardo Mondlane. Faculdade de
Medicine**
Caixa Postal 257, Maputo, Mozambique.
- Congresso Nacional de Anatomia Patologicas.
  Actas. irreg.

# NAMIBIA

**Mrs. M.D. Badenhorst, Ed. & Pub.**
5 Conradie St., Box 706, Windhoek, South West
Africa.
- S.W.A. Boer/S.W.A. Farmer. m. ISSN 0049-1543

**Namib Desert Research Station**
Private Bag 13186, Windhoek 9100, South West
Africa.
- Namib Desert Research Station. Scientific Papers.
  irreg.; (approx. 1-2 per yr.) (Council for Scientific
  and Industrial Research. Department of Nature
  Conservation SA)

**S.W.A. Scientific Society**
Box 67, Windhoek, South West Africa.
- Botanische Mitteilungen. m.
- Dinteria; contributions to the flora and vegetation
  of South West Africa. ISSN 0012-3013
- Ornithologische Arbeitsgruppe Mitteilungen. m.
  ISSN 0030-5731
- S.W.A. Scientific Society. Journal. a.
- South West Africa Scientific Society. Newsletter/
  S. W. A. Wetenskaplike Vereniging. Nuusbrief/S.
  W. A. Wissenschaftliche Gesellschaft.
  Mitteilungen. m. ISSN 0036-2069

**South West Africa. Administration**
Private Bag 13186, Windhoek, South West Africa.
- South West Africa Administration: White Paper
  on the Activities of the Different Branches. irreg.

**South West Africa. Administration on Nature
Conservation & Tourism**
Private Bag 13186, Windhoek, South West Africa.
- Madoqua. irreg.

**Southwest Africa. Department of National Education.
State Museum**
*see* Southwest Africa. State Museum

**South West Africa. State Museum**
Box 1203, Windhoek, South West Africa.
- Cimbebasia. Series A: Natural History. irreg; vol.
  4, no. 4, 1975. ISSN 0590-6342
- Cimbebasia. Series B: Cultural History. irreg.

**South West Africa Scientific Society**
*see* S.W.A. Scientific Society

**State Museum**
*see* Southwest Africa. State Museum

# NEPAL

**Centre for Economic Development and Administration**
Box 797, Kirtipur Campus, Kathmandu, Nepal.
- Nepal Documentation; occasional bibliography.
  irreg.

**Family Planning Association of Nepal**
Box 486, Kathmandu, Nepal.
- Nepal Family Planning and Maternal Child
  Health Board. Annual Report. a.

**Gorkhapatra Corporation**
Kathmandu, Nepal.
- Nepalese Perspective. m. ISSN 0047-9349

**Himalangue**
1/11 Bhotebahal, Kathmandu, Nepal.
- Himalangue; discussions on linguistics. 3 per yr.
  ISSN 0302-1599

**Himalayan Economist**
21-694-1 Dillibazar, Kathmandu, Nepal.
- Himalayan Economist. bi-m.

**Management Consultants**
41 Onhaikantala Tole, Kathmandu 12, Nepal.
- Nepal Journal of Management. q.

**Nepal. Central Bureau of Statistics**
Kathmandu, Nepal.
- Nepal. Central Bureau of Statistics. Statistical
  Pocket Book. irreg.

**Nepal. Department of Agricultural Education and
Research**
Lalitpur, Nepal.
- Nepal. Department of Agricultural Education and
  Research. Annual Report. a.

**Nepal. Department of Archaeology**
Kathmandu, Nepal.
- Ancient Nepal.

**Nepal. Department of Commemoration**
Royal Palace, Kathmandu, Nepal.
- Ramjham. q.

**Nepal. Department of Electricity**
Kathmandu, Nepal.
- Power Statistics Journal of Nepal. irreg.

**Nepal. National Planning Commission**
Secretariat, Kathmandu, Nepal.
- Vikas: Nepal Journal of Development. s-a.

**Nepal Bank Limited**
Dharma Path, Kathmandu, Nepal.
- Nepal Bank Patrika/Nepal Bank Bulletin. bi-m.

**Nepal Digest Publication**
6177 Puranobhansar, Pako, Kathmandu, Nepal.
- Nepal Digest. bi-m. ISSN 0047-9330

**Nepal Economic and Commerce Research Centre**
G.P.O. No. 171, 7-358 Kohity Bahal, Kathmandu,
Nepal.
- Commerce. m.

**Nepal Geographical Society**
Tribhuvan University, Dept. of Geography,
Tripureswar, Kathmandu, Nepal.
- Himalayan Review. a.

**Nepal Industrial Development Corporation**
N.I.D.C. Bldg., Durbar Marg, Box 10, Kathmandu,
Nepal.
- Nepal Industrial Development Corporation.
  Annual Report. a. ISSN 0077-6548
- Nepal Industrial Development Corporation.
  Industrial Digest. a. ISSN 0077-6556
- Nepal Industrial Development Corporation.
  Statistical Abstracts. irreg. ISSN 0077-6564

**Nepal Medical Association**
Siddhi Sadan, Exhibition Road, Kathmandu, Nepal.
- Nepal Medical Association. Journal. bi-m. ISSN
  0028-2715

**Nepal Nature Conservation Society**
Box 229, Kathmandu, Nepal.
- Nepal Nature Conservation Society. Newsletter. s-
  a.

**Nepal Press Digest (Pvt) Ltd.**
Lazimpat, Kathmandu, Nepal.
- Nepal Gazette Translation Service. irreg. (2-3 per
  mo.) ISSN 0028-2707
- Nepal Law Translation Series. irreg. ISSN 0077-
  6572
- Nepal Press Digest. w. ISSN 0028-2723

**Nepal Rastra Bank**
Research Department, Baluwatar, Kathmandu,
Nepal.
- Nepal Rastra Bank. Annual Report. a.
- Nepal Rastra Bank. Quarterly Economic Bulletin.
  q. ISSN 0028-274X

**Nepal Red Cross Society**
P.O. 217, Kathmandu, Nepal.
- Red Cross Quarterly/Reda Krasa Traimasika. q.
  ISSN 0048-7023

**Nepalese Association for World Understanding**
21-485 Dilli Bazar, Kathmandu, Nepal.
- Everest Review. q.

**Nepalese Journal of Science**
S. C. Singh, Samepa, Lalitpur 2, Kathmandu, Nepal.
- Nepalese Journal of Science. irreg.

**Nepali Janavadi Krantikari Samskritika Sangha**
Ghantaghar, Kathmandu, Nepal.
- Mukti-Morca. q.

**Ratna Pustak Bhandar**
Bhotahitit, Kathmandu, Nepal.
• Kailash; journal of Himalayan studies. q.

**Regmi Research (Pvt) Ltd.**
Lazimpat, Kathmandu, Nepal.
• Nepal Press Report. d (M-F) ISSN 0028-2731
• Regmi Research Series. m. ISSN 0034-348X

**Sirjana**
1-202 Dilli Bazar, Kathmandu, Nepal.
• Sirjana; an English journal of Nepal's economic, social and political developments, reviews and excerpts. m. ISSN 0049-0628

**Tribhuvan University**
Kirtipur, Nepal.
• Voice of History. a. (Tribhuvan University History Association)

**Tribhuvan University. Centre for Economic Development and Administration**
*see* Centre for Economic Development and Administration

**Tribhuvan University History Association**
• Voice of History. (pub. by Tribhuvan University)

**Tribhuvan University. Institute of Nepal and Asian Studies**
Kirtipur, Nepal.
• Contributions to Nepalese Studies. s-a.

**Vasudha Publication**
8-535 Makhangalli New Rd., Kathmandu, Nepal.
• Vasudha Monthly. m. ISSN 0042-2878

# NETHERLANDS

**A B C voor Handel en Industrie C. V.**
Koningin Wilhelminalaan 16, P.O. Box 190, Haarlem, Netherlands.
• Holland Exports. a. ISSN 0073-3032

**A D A-Vakpers**
Herengracht 294, Amsterdam, Netherlands.
• Spectrum der Herenmode. q. ISSN 0038-7096

**Uitgeverij Aarde en Kosmos**
P.O. Box 108, Huizen N. H., Netherlands.
• Aarde en Kosmos/Earth and Cosmos. m.

**Abdij van Berne**
Abdijstraat 53, Heeswijk- Dinther, Netherlands.
• Rond de Tafel; liturgisch tijdschrift. bi-m. ISSN 0035-8169
• Zondagsmis. m (14 per yr.) ISSN 0044-5002

**Academie de Droit International de la Haye**
• Academie de Droit International de la Haye. Recueil des Cours. (pub. by A. W. Sijthoff International Publishing Co.)

**Academie de Droit International de la Haye. Groupe Francais des Anciens Auditeurs**
• Annuaire Francais de Droit International. (pub. by Centre National de la Recherche Scientifique FR)

**Academie de Marine**
• Academie de Marine. Mededelingen. Communications. (pub. by Uitgeverij de Sikkel N.V.)

**Academie Internationale d'Histoire de la Pharmacie**
Postbus 2250, Rotterdam 3015, Netherlands.
• Acta Pharmacie Historica. irreg. ISSN 0065-1494

**Actuarieel Genootschap**
Box 202, The Hague, Netherlands.
• Actuarieel Genootschap. Mededelingenblad. 6 per yr.

**Adex, C. V.**
Postbus 187, Baarn, Netherlands.
• Automatie; maandblad voor meet- en regeltechniek, mechanisering en automatisering. m. ISSN 0005-1128

**Aeropress**
Pieter Stockmanslaan 53, Eindhoven 4508, Netherlands.
• Planeur. bi-m. ISSN 0304-0704

**Afrika-Studiecentrum**
Stationsplein 10, Leiden, Netherlands.
• African Perspectives. s-a.

• Afrika-Studiecentrum. Communications. (pub. by Mouton Publishers)
• Afrika Studiecentrum. Documentatieblad. m. ISSN 0002-0419
• Change and Continuity in Africa. (pub. by Mouton Publishers)

**Agence Industrielle et Economique**
Postbus 376, The Hague, Netherlands.
• A G E C O - Documentation Siderurgique. 3 per m. ISSN 0001-1320

**Uitgeverij Agraar**
Postbus 73, Deventer, Netherlands.
• Veevoeding; kritisch voorlichtingsblad voor veehouderij en veredelingslandbouw. 9 per yr. ISSN 0042-3041

**Ahmadiyya Muslim Mission**
De Mobarak-Moskee, Oostduinlaan 79, The Hague, Netherlands.
• Islam. m. ISSN 0021-180X

**Ahold N.V.**
P.O.B. 33, Zaandam, Netherlands.
• Flitsen. 9 per yr. ISSN 0001-141X

**Algemeen Nederlands Verbond**
Surinamestraat 28, The Hague, Netherlands.
• Neerlandia. 6 per yr. ISSN 0028-2383

**Algemeen Publiciteitskantoor B.V.**
Keizersgracht 188, Amsterdam C, Netherlands.
• Consudel. m. ISSN 0010-7042

**Algemeen Verbond Bouw Bedrijf**
• Bouwbelangen. (pub. by Ten Hagen B. V.)

**Algemeen Verbond van Ondernemers in het Schildersbedrijf**
Groot Hertoginnelaan 38, Box 1530, The Hague, Netherlands.
• Intrex; vakblad voor verzorgers van interieur en exterieur. 10 per yr.

**Algemeen Verbond van Volkstuinders Vereenigingen in Nederland**
Centrale Markt, Kamer 85, Amsterdam 1015, Netherlands.
• Amateurtuinder. m (11 per yr.) ISSN 0002-6875 (Co-sponsor: Rijkstuinbouwvoorlichtingsdienst)

**Algemeene Vereeniging "Radio Omroep"**
Keizersgracht 107, Postbus 1290, Amsterdam, Netherlands.
• TeleVizier. w. ISSN 0049-3325

**Algemene Bank Nederland**
Postbus 669, Amsterdam, Netherlands.
• A. B. N. Economic Review. bi-m. ISSN 0044-7269
• Algemene Bank Nederland. Annual Report. a. ISSN 0065-6224
• Ankertros. 11 per yr. ISSN 0003-3693

**Algemene Bond van Onderwijzend Personeel**
Herengracht 56, Amsterdam, Netherlands.
• Schoolblad. w. ISSN 0036-6889

**Algemene Conferentie der Nederlandse Letteren**
Steenvoordelaan 370, Rijswijk (Z.H.), Netherlands.
• Gedeeld Domein. s-a. ISSN 0016-5778

**Algemene Nederlandse Bond van Schoonheidsinstituten**
• Estheticienne. (pub. by B. V. Uitgeversmaatschappij Reflex)

**Algemene Nederlandse Grafische Bond**
Koninginneweg 20, Amsterdam 1007, Netherlands.
• Grafia. fortn. ISSN 0017-2871

**Algemene Nederlandse Unie van Muziekverenigingen**
• Musica. (pub. by Tijdschriftenfonds J.J. Lispet)

**Algemene Nederlandse Vereniging voor Sociale Geneeskunde**
• Tijdschrift voor Sociale Geneeskunde. (pub. by B. V: Uitgeversmaatschappij Reflex)

**Algemene Nederlandse Vredesactie**
Postbus 385, Amsterdam, Netherlands.
• Vredesactie; radicaal-pacifistisch maandblad. bi-m. ISSN 0042-9112

**Algemene Speeltuinvereniging Prinsejagt**
Van Aitzemastraat 31, Eindhoven, Netherlands.
• Prinsejagt. m. ISSN 0032-8499

**Algemene Vereniging van Naaimachinehandelaren**
• Naaimachine-Nieuws. (pub. by Stichting Naaimachine-Nieuws)

**Algemene Vereniging van Ondernemers in het Loodgieters- , Sanitair- en Gasverwarmingsinstallatiebedrijf**
• Installatie. (pub. by Uitgeversmaatschappij de Gelderlander Vakpers BV)

**Algemene Vereniging van Zeevarenden**
• Peiling. (pub. by Federatie van Werknemersorganisaties in de Zeevaart)

**Algemene Vereniging voor de Centrale Verwarmings- en Luchtbehandelingsindustrie**
Surinamestraat 24, The Hague, Netherlands.
• Verwarming en Ventilatie. m. ISSN 0042-451X

**Alliance-Zendings-Centrum Parousia**
Rijksstraatweg 426, Wassenaar, Netherlands.
• Pionier. m. ISSN 0032-0056

**Amaco**
Egelantiersgracht 75-79, Amsterdam, Netherlands.
• In de Waagschaal. fortn. ISSN 0019-316X

**American Chamber of Commerce in the Netherlands**
Carnegieplein 5, The Hague, Netherlands.
• A M C H A M Newsletter. m. ISSN 0001-1878
• Netherlands-American Trade Directory. a.

**Amerika Instituut**
University of Amsterdam, c/o A.N.J. den Hollander, Oudezijds Achterburgwal 185, Amsterdam, Netherlands.
• E A A S Newsletter. biennial. ISSN 0423-6645 (European Association for American Studies)

**Amsterdam. Bureau van Statistiek**
O.Z. Achterburgwal 185, Amsterdam, Netherlands.
• Amsterdam. Bureau van Statistiek. Maandbericht. m. ISSN 0028-2871

**Amsterdam. Gemeentelijke Sociale Dienst**
Vlaardingenlaan 15, Amsterdam (Ov. Veld), Netherlands.
• Socioscoop. m. ISSN 0038-0458

**Amsterdam. Stadsdrukkerij**
Voormalige Stadstimmertuin 4 - 6, Amsterdam, Netherlands.
• Gemeenteblad van Amsterdam. s-w. ISSN 0016-6049

**Amsterdam-Rotterdam Bank N.V.**
Herengracht 595, Amsterdam, Netherlands.
• Amro Beursnieuws/Amro Stock Market News. fortn. ISSN 0003-2050
• Amsterdam-Rotterdam Bank. Economisch Kwartaaloverzicht. q.
• Amsterdam-Rotterdam Bank. Report. a. ISSN 0066-1309
• Industrial Kaleidoscope. 3 per yr.
• Kerngetallen van Europese Effecten. q. ISSN 0023-0650
• Kerngetallen van Nederlandse Effecten. bi-m. ISSN 0023-0669
• Relais. w. ISSN 0034-3773

**Angola Comite**
Da Costrastraat 88, Amsterdam, Netherlands.
• Angola Comite. Facts and Reports; press cuttings on Angola, Mozambique, Guinea-Bissau, Portugal and southern Africa. fortn. ISSN 0046-3116

**Uitgeverij Ankh-Hermes B.V.**
Menstr. 17-21, Deventer, Netherlands.
• Prana; tijdschrift voor geestelijke verruiming en randgebieden der wetenschappen. q.

**Anthropological Publications**
Wagenaarstraat 36, Oosterhout, Netherlands.
• Institut fuer Menschen- und Menschheitskunde, Rengsdorf. Studien und Materialien. irreg.

**Anti-Revolutionaire Partij**
Dr. Kuyperstraat 3, The Hague, Netherlands.
• Nederlandse Gedachten. w. ISSN 0028-2278

**APA-Holland University Press**
Postbus 1850, 1000 BW Amsterdam, Netherlands.
• LIAS; Sources and Documents Relating to the Early Modern History of Ideas. s-a. (Stichting Lias)

**Apostolaat van het Gebed**
Graafseweg 11, Nijmegen, Netherlands.
• Jonge Kerk. m. ISSN 0021-7395

**Aramco**
Laan van Meerdervoort 55, The Hague,
Netherlands.
• Aramco World. bi-m. ISSN 0003-7567

**B. V. de Arbeiderspers**
Singel 252, Amsterdam, Netherlands.
• Maatstaf. 10 per yr.

**Architectuur en Beeldende Kunsten**
Nobelstraat 21, Heerlen, Netherlands.
• Architectuur en Beeldende Kunsten. m. ISSN
0044-8664

**Uitgeverij Ariadne B.V.**
Keizersgracht 54, Postbus 8360, Amsterdam,
Netherlands.
• M M D/Ariadne; management report. w.

**Arnhem. Gemeentearchief**
Koningstraat 32 II, Arnhem, Netherlands.
• Bijdragen tot de Geschiedenis van Arnhem. irreg.,
1972, no. 4. ISSN 0067-8554

**Associatie SMK**
*see* Associatie voor Stenografie, Machineschrijven
en Kantoorpraktijk

**Associatie voor Stenografie, Machineschrijven en
Kantoorpraktijk**
Sophia van Wurtemberglaan 17, Eindhoven,
Netherlands.
• Pen en Toets; algemeen tijdschrift voor
stenografie. machineschrijven en kantoorpraktijk.
bi-m.

**Association for Symbolic Logic**
• Annals of Mathematical Logic. (pub. by North-
Holland Publishing Co.)
• Journal of Philosophical Logic. (pub. by D. Reidel
Publishing Co.)

**Association of Attenders and Alumni of the Hague
Academy of International Law**
Koninginnegracht 43, The Hague, Netherlands.
• Association of Attenders and Alumni of the
Hague Academy of International Law. Yearbook.
a. ISSN 0066-8923

**Association of European Operational Research
Societies**
• European Journal of Operational Research. (pub.
by North-Holland Publishing Co.)

**Association of Exploration Geochemists**
• Journal of Geochemical Exploration. (pub. by
Elsevier Scientific Publishing Co.)

**Atlantische Commissie**
Nassau Zuilensteinstraat 9, The Hague, Netherlands.
• Atlantische Tijdingen. irreg., no. 206, 1975. ISSN
0067-0235

**Automobiel Sport Club "de Kempenrijders"**
Helmerslaan 27, Eindhoven, Netherlands.
• Kemphaan. m. ISSN 0022-9881

**B D U**
Postbus 67, Barneveld, Netherlands.
• Cartonnagebedrijf. m. ISSN 0008-705X
(Vereniging van Kartonnagefabrikanten)

**B E N E L U X Merkenbureau**
Bankastraat 149-151, The Hague, Netherlands.
• Merkenblad B E N E L U X/Marques Benelux
Recueil. m. ISSN 0026-007X

**Baarns Lyceum**
Torenlaan 77, Baarn, Netherlands.
• Animo. bi-m. ISSN 0003-3669

**Joost Baljeu, Ed. & Pub.**
Van Boshuizenstr. 59, Amsterdam, Netherlands
(U.S. Subscriptions To: Wittenborn & Cie, 1018
Madison Ave., New York, N.Y. 10021)
• Structure; magazine on constructive plastic
expression. 2 nos. per series. ISSN 0039-257X

**Drukkerij Banda B.V.**
Voorstraat 32, Kollum (Fr.), Netherlands.
• Landeigenaar; maandblad ter behartiging van de
belangen van de landelijke eigendom. m.
(Nederlandse Vereniging voor de Landelijke
Eigendom)

**Bank Mees en Hope N.V.**
Amsterdam, Netherlands.
• Economic Developments in the Common Market
Countries. q.

**Bank voor Nederlandsche Gemeenten N. V.**
Paleisstraat 5, The Hague, Netherlands.
• B & G. (Bank en Gemeenten) m. (Co-sponsor:
Vereniging van Nederlandse Gemeenten)

**Bayer Nederland B.V.**
Postbus 105, Arnhem, Netherlands
(Main Office: Bayer Pflanzenschutz, Leverkusen, W.
Germany (B.R.D.))
• Agro Chemie-Koerier. irreg.

**Bedrijfschap voor de Lederwarenindustrie**
Reitseplein 1, Tilburg, Netherlands.
• Bedrijfschap voor de Lederwarenindustrie.
Jaarverslag. a. ISSN 0067-4834

**Bedrijfslaboratorium voor Grond- en Gewasonderzoek**
Mariendaal, Oosterbeek, Netherlands.
• Boor. q. ISSN 0006-758X

**Uitgeversmaatschappij L.A. van Beek B.V.**
Postbus 53, Berkel ZH, Netherlands.
• Isolatie; voor handel, bouw, industrie en
scheepvaart. m.
• Uit Europoortkringen; maandblad voor het
bedrijfsleven in Rotterdam/Botlek/Europoort/
Delta. m. ISSN 0041-588X

**John Benjamins B. V.**
Amsteldijk 44, Amsterdam, Netherlands.
• Amsterdam Studies in the Theory and History of
Linguistic Science. Series 1: Amsterdam Classics
in Linguistics, 1800-1925. irreg., vol. 12, 1977.
• Amsterdam Studies in the Theory and History of
Linguistic Science. Series 2: Classics in
Psycholinguistics. irreg.
• Amsterdam Studies in the Theory and History of
Linguistic Science. Series 3: Studies in the History
of Linguistics. irreg. vol. 14, 1977.
• Amsterdam Studies in the Theory and History of
Linguistic Science. Series 4: Current Issues in
Linguistic Theory. irreg.
• Amsterdam Studies in the Theory and History of
Linguistic Science. Series 5: Library and
Information Sources in Linguistics. irreg.
• Analecta Linguistica; informational bulletin of
linguistics. 2 per yr. ISSN 0044-8176 (Magyar
Tudomanyos Akademia HU)
• Historiographia Linguistica; international journal
for the history of linguistics. 3 per yr. ISSN 0302-
5160
• Lingvisticae Investigationes; revue internationale
de linguistique francaise et de linguistique
generale. s-a. (Universite de Paris VIII (Paris-
Vincennes). Departement de Linguistique FR)
(Co-sponsor: Laboratoire d'Automatique
Documentaire et Linguistique (C.N.R.S.))

**Drukkerij Bergmans-MCH**
Box 508, Tilburg, Netherlands.
• Noord-Brabant. bi-m. ISSN 0029-1145
(Economisch Technologisch Instituut voor Noord-
Brabant)

**Berlage Lyceum School Alliance**
Stationslaan 17, Stadskanaal, Netherlands.
• Schakel. m. ISSN 0036-5858

**De Bezige Bij**
Van Miereveldstraat 1, Amsterdam, Netherlands.
• Gedicht. q.

**Bibliotheca Rosenthaliana**
• Studia Rosenthaliana. (pub. by Van Gorcum)

**Bijenhuis-Wageningen**
Grintweg 273, Wageningen, Netherlands.
• Maandschrift voor Bijenteelt. m. ISSN 0024-8681
(Vereniging tot Bevordering der Bijenteelt in
Nederland)

**Biologia Maritima**
Burg. Herckenrathlaan 37, Amerzoden, Netherlands.
• Kor. m.

**Biometeorological Research Centre**
Jan Steenlaan 3, Leyden, Netherlands.
• Biometeorological Research Centre, Leyden.
Monograph Series. irreg. ISSN 0067-8872
• Biometeorological Research Centre, Leyden.
Reports. irreg., no. 14, 1970. ISSN 0000-0299
• Biometeorological Research Centre, Leyden.
Special Monograph Series. irreg. ISSN 0067-8880

**Blindenbibliotheek "Le Sage ten Broek"**
Panovenlaan 1, Nijmegen, Netherlands.
• Rondom het Boek; gesproken periodiek over
boeken en schrijvers. 3 per yr. ISSN 0035-8177

**H. W. Blok Uitgeverij B.V.**
Schiedamsevest 51, Rotterdam, Netherlands.
• Geneeskundig Adresboek Met Rijksdelen Overzee
en Nederlandse Artsen in Het Buitenland. irreg.
• Geneeskundig Jaarboek Medicijnen. irreg.

**Boekencentrum B.V.**
Scheveningseweg 72, Box 5176, The Hague,
Netherlands.
• Herkenning; tijdschrift voor joden en christenen.
bi-m.
• Hervormd Nederland. w. ISSN 0018-0939
• Nederlands Theologisch Tijdschrift. q. ISSN 0028-
212X
• Open Deur. m. ISSN 0030-3402 (Co-Sponsors:
Dutch Reformed Church; Lutheran Church;
Roman Catholic Church; Geref. Foundation)
• Open Venster; maandblad voor ouderen. m. ISSN
0030-3453
• Wending; maandblad voor evangelie en cultuur.
m. ISSN 0043-2695
• Woord en Dienst. fortn.

**Drukkerij G.W. den Boer**
Markt 51, Middelburg, Netherlands.
• Metaalbewerking. fortn. ISSN 0026-0487

**C. de Boer Jr. N. V.**
Box 507, Hilversum, Netherlands.
• Bejaarden. s-m. ISSN 0005-822X
• Blauwe Wimpel; maandblad voor scheepvaart en
scheepsbouw in de lage landen. m. ISSN 0006-
4661
• Chronos. s-m. ISSN 0009-6180
• Hockey Sport. w. 36 per yr. ISSN 0018-3032
(Royal Netherlands Hockey Association)
• Lawn Tennis. m. ISSN 0023-9429 (Royal
Netherlands Lawn Tennis Association)
• Marineblad. 8 per yr. ISSN 0025-3340
(Vereniging van Marine-Officieren)
• Nederlandse Chemische Industrie. 24 per yr.
ISSN 0470-6021 (Vereniging van de Nederlandse
Chemische Industrie)
• Vakblad voor Biologen. s-m. ISSN 0042-2215

**Bohn, Scheltema en Holkema**
Box 10697, Amsterdam, Netherlands.
• Index to Plant Chromosome Numbers. irreg. ISSN
0073-6007 (International Association for Plant
Taxonomy)
• International Union of Crystallography. Structure
Reports. a. ISSN 0074-9397
• Molecular Structures and Dimensions. a.
(International Union of Crystallography) (Co-
Sponsor: Crystallographic Data Center)
• Nederlands Tijdschrift voor Geneeskunde. w.
ISSN 0028-2162
• Netherlands Journal of Medicine. 6 per yr. ISSN
0015-5624 (Nederlandse Internisten Vereniging)
• Organic and Organometallic Crystal Structures;
Bibliography. irreg. (Dist. by Polycrystal Book
Service, Box 11567, Pittsburgh, PA. 15238)
• Regnum Vegetabile; A series of publications for
the use of plant taxonomists and plant
geographers. irreg. ISSN 0080-0694 (International
Association for Plant Taxonomy)
• Tijdschrift voor Kindergeneeskunde. m.
• Tropical and Geographical Medicine. q. ISSN
0041-3232 (Foundation Documenta de Medicina
Geographica et Tropica)

**Drukkerij Bolhuis B.V.**
Postbus 3, Ermelo, Netherlands.
• Veluws Kerkblad. w. ISSN 0042-3262
(Gereformeerde Kerken in Classis Harderwijk en
Nijkerk)

**B.V. Uitgeversmaatschappij Bonaventura**
Postbus 152, Amsterdam, Netherlands.
• Elegance. m.
• Elsevier Select. q. ISSN 0013-6409
• Elseviers Magazine. w. ISSN 0013-6395
• F E M. (Financieel-Economisch Magazine) fortn.
(Orders to: Jan van Galenstraat 335, Amsterdam,
Netherlands)
• Tussen de Rails. m. ISSN 0041-4379

**Bond Heemschut**
• Heemschut. (pub. by Drukkerij t Koggeschip B.V.)

**Bond Nederlands Israel**
Box 45, Mijdrecht, Netherlands.
- Nieuw Geluid. m. ISSN 0028-9833

**Bond van Nederlandse Fotodetailhandelaren**
- Foto-Visie. (pub. by Uitgeversmaatschappij de Gelderlander Vakpers BV)

**Bond van Politieambtenaren in Nederland tot Bescherming van Dieren**
Theresialaan 51, Vught, Netherlands.
- Politie-Dierenbescherming; tijdschrift voor dieren- en natuurbescherming. m. ISSN 0032-3322

**Bond voor Materialenkennis**
- Papierwereld. (pub. by Voorns' Papierwereld)

**Bond voor Staatspensionering**
- Staatspensioenen. (pub. by S. Sytema)

**Boom-Pers**
Postbus 58, Meppel, Netherlands.
- Boom-Pers Combinatie. d. ISSN 0006-7571
- Mens en Onderneming/Man and Industry. bi-m. ISSN 0025-9470
- Nederlands Tijdschrift voor Criminologie. q. ISSN 0028-2154
- Nederlands Tijdschrift voor Psychiatrie. m. ISSN 0028-2197 (Nederlandse Vereniging voor Psychiaters in Dienstverband)
- Sociologische Gids; tijdschrift voor sociologie en sociaal onderzoek. bi.-m. ISSN 0038-0334

**Uitgeversmaatschappij Born B. V.**
Esstraat 10, Box 22, Assen, Netherlands.
- Gezinsblad; de vertrouwde koopgids voor de hele week in Assen en wijde omgeving. w. ISSN 0016-9498

**Bosch en Keuning N. V.**
Box 1, Baarn, Netherlands.
- Onze Vacatures; Christelijk schoolblad. w. ISSN 0009-515X

**J. Bout en Zoon**
Ceintuurbaan 32-34, Huizen, Netherlands.
- Huizer Kerkblad. w. ISSN 0018-7119

**Brandenburgh en Co.**
Ged. Poortezijlen 6, Sneek, Netherlands.
- Pompebledden; tydskrift foar underwiis en Fryske studzje. 10 per yr. ISSN 0032-4205

**Bres'**
Madoerastraat 10, The Hague, Netherlands.
- Bres' bi-m.

**E. J. Brill**
Oude Rijn 33a-35, Leiden, Netherlands.
- Abr-Nahrain. a. ISSN 0065-0382 (University of Melbourne. Department of Middle Eastern Studies AT)
- Abr-Nahrain. Supplements. irreg. ISSN 0065-0390 (University of Melbourne. Department of Middle Eastern Studies AT)
- Acta Theologica Danica. irreg., vol. 11, 1973. ISSN 0065-1672
- Altbabylonische Briefe im Umschrift und Uebersetzung. irreg., no. 6, 1974. ISSN 0065-6593
- American Journal of Arabic Studies.
- Analecta Boerhaaviana. irreg., no. 7, 1973. ISSN 0066-1368
- Arabica; revue d'etudes Arabes. 3 per yr. ISSN 0003-7508
- Arbeiten zur Geschichte des Antiken Judentums und des Urchristentums. irreg., 1972, no. 12. ISSN 0066-5681 (Institutum Iudaicum, Tuebingen GW)
- Archives Bakounine/Bakunin- Archiv. irreg., vol. 5, 1974. ISSN 0066-6548 (International Institute for Social History)
- Arena; Zeitschrift fuer Geschichte des Sports und Korperkultur. s-a.
- Astin Bulletin; international journal for actuarial studies in non-life insurance and risk theory. s-a. ISSN 0515-0361 (International Actuarial Association. Astin Section)
- Behaviour; an international journal of comparative ethology. irreg., no. 55, 1975. ISSN 0005-7959
- Columbia Studies in the Classical Tradition. irreg.
- Contributions to Asian Studies. irreg., vol. 8, 1975. (Canadian Association for South Asian Studies CN)
- Crustaceana; international journal of crustacean research. bi-m. ISSN 0011-216X (Universiteit van Amsterdam. Zoologisch Museum)

- Delta Onderzoek Hydrobiologisch Instituut. Communication. irreg. (Rijksmuseum van Natuurlijke Historie. Delta Onderzoek Hydrobiologisch Institut)
- International Journal of Comparative Sociology. q. ISSN 0020-7152 (York University. Department of Sociology CN)
- International Organization for the Study of the Old Testament. Proceedings of the International Congress. triennial, 8th, 1974, Edinburgh. ISSN 0074-719X
- International Ornithological Congress. Proceedings. quadrennial, 1970, 15th, The Hague. ISSN 0074-7211
- International Studies in Sociology and Social Anthropology. irreg. no. 16, 1975. ISSN 0074-8684
- Iranica Antiqua; dealing with archaeology, history, religion, art and literature of ancient Persia. irreg. ISSN 0021-0870
- Journal for the Study of Judaism. 2 per yr. ISSN 0047-2212
- Journal of Arabic Literature. q. ISSN 0085-2376
- Journal of Asian and African Studies. q. ISSN 0021-9096
- Journal of Northwest Semitic Languages. a. ISSN 0085-2414
- Journal of Religion in Africa/Religion en Afrique. 3 per yr. ISSN 0022-4200
- Journal of the Economic and Social History of the Orient/Journal de l'Histoire Economique et Sociale de l'Orient. 3 per yr. ISSN 0022-4995
- Lutra. irreg., vol. 14, 1972. ISSN 0024-7634 (Vereniging voor Zoogdierkunde)
- Medieval Iberian Penninsula. irreg., 1971, no. 4. ISSN 0076-6100
- Mittellateinische Studien und Texte. irreg., no. 9, 1974. ISSN 0076-9754
- Mnemosyne; bibliotheca classica batava. q. ISSN 0026-7074
- Nederlands Archief voor Kerkgeschiedenis. 2 per yr.; vol. 55, N.S. 1975. ISSN 0028-2030
- Nematologica; international journal of nematological research. 4 per yr. ISSN 0028-2596
- Netherlands Journal of Zoology. q. ISSN 0028-2960
- New Testament Tools and Studies. irreg., 1969, vol. 9. ISSN 0077-8842
- Novum Testamentum. irreg., vol. 39, 1974. ISSN 0048-1009
- Oriens. irreg., vol. 24, 1974. ISSN 0078-6527 (Internationale Gesellschaft fuer Orientforschung)
- Philosophia Antiqua. irreg., no. 26, 1973. ISSN 0079-1687
- Pseudepigrapha Veteris Testamenti Graece. irreg., 1970, no. 3. ISSN 0079-7197 (Rijksuniversiteit te Leiden)
- Semitic Study Series. irreg.
- Social, Economic and Political Studies of the Middle East. irreg., 1972, no. 5. ISSN 0085-6193 (Dist. in U.S. by: Humanities Press, Inc., 171 First Ave., Atlantic Highlands, NJ 07716)
- Studia Ad Corpus Hellenisticum Novi Testamenti. irreg.
- Studia Iranica. bi-m.
- Studien zur Geschichte Osteuropas/Studies in East European History. irreg., 1972, no. 15. ISSN 0081-7317 (Dist. in U.S. by: Humanities Press, Inc., 171 First Ave., Atlantic Highlands, NJ 07716)
- Studies in Semitic Languages and Linguistics. irreg., 1971, no. 4. ISSN 0081-8461
- Studies in the History of Christian Thought. irreg., 1968, vol. 4. ISSN 0081-8607
- Theokratia; Jahrbuch des Institutum Judaicum Delitzschianum. a. ISSN 0082-3899 (Institutum Judaicum Delitzschianum)
- Tijdschrift voor Economische en Sociale Geografie/Netherlands Journal of Economic and Social Geography. bi-m. ISSN 0040-747X (Koninklijk Nederlands Aardrijkskundig Genootschap)
- Tijdschrift voor Nederlandse Taal- en Letterkunde. 4 per yr. ISSN 0040-7550 (Maatschappij der Nederlandse Letterkunde)
- T'oung Pao. irreg., 1973, vol. 59. ISSN 0082-5433
- Verzameling van Middelnederlandse Bijbelteksten, Kleine Reeks. Afdeling V: Psalters. irreg.
- Vetus Testamentum. 23 vols. per yr. (4 nos. per vol.) ISSN 0042-4935 (International Organization of Old Testament Scholars)
- Vetus Testamentum. Supplements. irreg., 1972, no. 23. ISSN 0083-5889 (International Organization of Old Testament Scholars)

- Welt des Islams/World of Islam; international journal for the historical development of contemporary islam. a.

**J. B. van den Brink en Co. B.V.**
Postbus 14, Lochem, Netherlands.
- Interaktie. 11 per yr. (Stichting Begeleiding Edukatieve Voorzieningen)

**J.D. Ter Brugge, Ed. & Pub.**
Wijk aan Zeerweg 48, IJmuiden, Netherlands.
- Akrides. q. ISSN 0002-3698 (Velser Basketball Club)

**Budo Bond Nederland**
Laan van Meerdervoort 239, The Hague, Netherlands.
- Budo Echo. 6 per yr.

**Buijten en Schipperheijn, B. V.**
Valkenburgerstraat 106, Amsterdam C, Netherlands.
- Kerkbode van Gereformeerde Kerken in Noord en Zuid-Holland. fortn. ISSN 0023-0618

**Buitenlandse Boek**
Prinsengracht 1083, Amsterdam, Netherlands.
- Buitenlandse Boek. q. ISSN 0007-3741

**Bureau Dienstverlening Overlegorganen**
Koninginnegracht 100, The Hague, Netherlands.
- Sociaal Den Haag. 4-5 per yr.

**Bureau Dit**
Wilhelminalaan 4, Soestdijk 2650, Netherlands.
- D I T. (Documentatie en Informatie over Toerisme) fortn. ISSN 0012-4109

**Bureau Ellens**
Postbus 5323, The Hague, Netherlands.
- Innovatie; informatiebulletin ter bevordering van de industriele vernieuwing in ons land. q.

**Bureau van Vliet B.V.**
Postbus 20, Zandvoort, Netherlands.
- Patrimonium. m. ISSN 0031-3149 (Landelijk Verbond Patrimonium)

**J. H. de Bussy**
Keizersgracht 810, Amsterdam, Netherlands.
- Gids bij de Prijscourant. a. ISSN 0072-4467
- Van Oss' Effectenboek. a. ISSN 0083-5153

**De Bussy, Eilerman Harms N. V.**
Warmoesstraat 151, Amsterdam-C, Netherlands.
- Duitse Kroniek; orgaan voor culturele betrekkingen met Duitsland. q. ISSN 0012-7051
- Genootschap Amstelodamum. Jaarboek. a.

**Capuchin Fathers of the Pokrof-Monastery**
Oosteinde 100, Voorburg, Netherlands.
- Pokrof; bi-monthly review about Russia and its christianity. bi-m. ISSN 0032-2415

**Catholic Parents Organisation voor het Zorgenkind**
Box 103, Maarssen-2570, Netherlands.
- Raakpunt. 8 per yr.

**Centraal Bureau van de Tuinbouwveilingen in Nederland**
- Groenten en Fruit. (pub. by B. V. Uitgeversbedrijf voor de Tuinbouw)

**Centraal Bureau van Sobrietas**
Mgr. Nolensstraat 7, Venray, Netherlands.
- Verantwoord Levensverkeer. q. ISSN 0028-999X

**Centraal Bureau voor de Schapenfokkerij**
- Schaap. (pub. by Uitgeversmaatschappij C. Misset B.V.)

**Centraal Bureau voor de Varkensfokkerij**
Oranjesingel 74, Postbus 1159, Nijmegen, Netherlands
- Maandblad voor de Varkensfokkerij en -Mesterij. m.

**Centraal Bureau voor het Katholiek Onderwijs**
Bezuidenhoutseweg 275, The Hague, Netherlands.
- School en Godsdienst. (pub. by Hoger Katechetisch Instituut, Nijmegen)
- Schoolbestuur. m. ISSN 0036-6870

**Centraalbureau voor Schimmelcultures**
Box 273, Baarn, Netherlands.
- Centraalbureau voor Schimmelcultures. List of Cultures. irreg., latest suppl. 1975.

- Studies in Mycology. irreg.

**Central National Organization for Applied Scientific Research in the Netherlands**
- Applied Scientific Research. (pub. by Martinus Nijhoff)

**N.V. Centrale Suiker Maatschappij**
Postbus 349, Amsterdam, Netherlands.
- C S M Informatie. 9 per yr.

**Centrale Uitgeverijen Adviesbureau B.V.**
Postbus 415, Maastricht, Netherlands.
- Natuur en Techniek/Nature and Technics; natuurwetenschappelijk en technisch maandblad/ scientific and technical monthly. m. ISSN 0028-1093

**Centre d'Etudes de Presse**
- Centre d'Etudes de Presse. Travaux. (pub. by Mouton Publishers)

**Centre d'Etudes des Espaces Urbains**
- Centre d'Etudes des Espaces Urbains. Travaux. (pub. by Mouton Publishers)

**Centre for Agricultural Publishing and Documentation**
P.O. Box 4, Marijkeweg 17, Wageningen, Netherlands.
- Air Pollution. irreg., 1968, 1st, Wageningen, Netherlands (pub. 1969) ISSN 0065-4833
- Animal Blood Groups and Biochemical Genetics. q. ISSN 0003-3480 (International Society for Animal Blood Group Research)
- Center for Agricultural Publishing and Documentation. Agricultural Research Reports. irreg., approx. 20 per year. ISSN 0069-2212
- Horticultural Research International; directory of horticultural research institutes and their activities in 54 countries. irreg. ISSN 0441-7461
- Landbouwdocumentatie. w. ISSN 0023-7760
- Mushroom Science. triennial, 1968, 2nd Symposium and 7th Congress, Hamburg. ISSN 0077-2364
- Netherlands Milk and Dairy Journal/Nederlands Melk en Zuiveltijdschrift. q. ISSN 0028-209X

**Centrex Publishing Co.**
Box 76, Eindhoven, Netherlands.
- Philips Research Reports; a journal of theoretical and experimental research in physics, chemistry and allied fields. bi-m. ISSN 0031-7918
- Philips Technical Review. m. ISSN 0031-7926

**Centrum voor Astrologische Statistiek**
- Astrologische Gids. (pub. by G. V. W. F. Goelst)

**Centrum voor Staatkundige Vorming**
Mauritskade 25, The Hague, Netherlands.
- Politiek Perspectief. bi-m.

**Uitgeverij "Ceres"**
Eendrachtstraat 2, Meppel, Netherlands.
- Openbaar Vervoer; monthly railways journal. m. ISSN 0030-3461

**Chevron Petroleum Maatschappij (Nederland) N.V**
- Chevron Motor. (pub. by Leo Schepman)

**Christelijk-Historische Jongeren Organisatie**
Algemeen Secretariaat, Postbus 370, Haarlem, Netherlands.
- Stakkato. bi-m. ISSN 0021-7417

**Christelijk Jongeren Verbond**
Postbus 115, Driebergen, Netherlands.
- Inklusief. m (10 per yr.) ISSN 0041-2562

**Christelijk Nationaal Vakverbond in Nederland**
Postbus 2475, Utrecht, Netherlands.
- Evangelie en Maatschappij. bi-m. ISSN 0014-3383

**Christelijk-Sociale Jeugd Organisatie-Werkende Jeugd**
Ravellaan 1, Utrecht, Netherlands.
- Warempel. m(10 per yr.)

**Christelijke Blindenbibliotheek**
Box 31, 3850 AC Ermelo, Netherlands.
- Boekenband. bi-m. ISSN 0006-5560

**Christelijke Bond van Schoenmakers-Patroons in Nederland**
Van der Duynstraat 3, Utrecht, Netherlands.
- Schoenwereld. m. ISSN 0036-6307

**Christelijke Gereformeerde Kerken in Nederland. Zendingsdeputaten**
Zendingshuis, Simon Stevinweg 144, Hilversum, Netherlands.
- Uw Koninkrijk Kome. 8 per yr. ISSN 0042-1650

**Church of Jesus Christ of Latter-Day Saints**
- Ster. (pub. by Nederlandse Zending)

**Churches of Christ**
Meloenstraat 86, The Hague, Netherlands.
- Levende Woord/Living Word; devoted to the restoration of New Testament Christianity. m. ISSN 0024-1547

**Cincinnati Milacron B.V.**
Box 98, Vlaardingen 3170, Netherlands.
- Milacroniek. m.

**Hans Clavin, Ed. & Pub.**
Plein 1945 Nr. 16, IJmuiden, Netherlands.
- Subvers; tijdschrift voor visuele poezie. irreg., approx. 4 per yr.

**Coca-Cola Export Corporation (Holland Branch)**
Prof. J. H. Bavinklaan 5, Amstelveen, Netherlands.
- Pauze. m. ISSN 0031-3270

**Cockpit-Uitgeverij**
Postbus 21, Bennekom, Netherlands.
- Vliegtuigencyclopaedie. 4 per yr.
- Vliegtuigparade. bi-m.

**Comite B E N E L U X**
Nassauplein 38, The Hague, Netherlands.
- Nouvelles B E N E L U X Nieuws. bi-m. ISSN 0029-4861

**Commissie voor de Ontwikkeling van Beleidsanalyse**
Kneuterdijk 22, The Hague, Netherlands.
- Beleidsanalyse. q.

**Confederatio Internationalis Ad Qualitates Plantarum Edulium Perquirendas (CIQ)**
- Qualitas Plantarum/Plant Food for Human Nutrition. (pub. by Dr. W. Junk B.V. Publishers)

**N. V. Consultass**
Bernhardstraat 1, Box 319, Zwolle, Netherlands.
- Pensioen Bulletin. m.(except July-Aug.) ISSN 0031-4854 (Co-Sponsor: Amsterdam-Rotterdam Bank N.V.)

**Consumentenbond**
Leeghwaterplein 26, The Hague, Netherlands.
- Consumenten Reisgids. q.

**Continental Iron and Steel Publishing Co.**
Postbus 168, The Hague, Netherlands.
- Continental Iron and Steel Trade Reports. 3 per mo. ISSN 0010-7719

**Cooperative Centrale Raiffeisen-Boerenleenbank B.A.**
Beneluxlaan 31, Utrecht, Netherlands.
- Rabobank. m.

**Drukkerij-Uitgeverij de Courier**
Box 24, Putten 2950, Netherlands.
- Koerier; t postzegelblad voor de jeugd. m.

**Criminologica Foundation**
- Abstracts on Criminology and Penology. (pub. by Kluwer B.V.)
- Abstracts on Police Science. (pub. by Kluwer B.V.)

**Cultureel Jongeren Paspoort Noord-Holland**
Oranje Nassaulaan 51, Amsterdam, Netherlands.
- Plug; maandelijks informatieblad van het cultureel jongeren paspoort. m. ISSN 0032-1621

**Cultuurtechnische Vereniging**
Griffioenlaan 2, Box 20021, 3202 LA Utrecht, Netherlands.
- Cultuurtechnisch Tijdschrift. bi-m. ISSN 0045-9267

**DAF Nederland Bedrijfswagen B.V.**
*see* Doorne's Bedrijfswagenfabriek DAF B.V.

**Dekker en Van de Vegt**
Fransestraat 30, Nijmegen, Netherlands.
- Graecitas Christianorum Primaeva; studia ad sermonem graecum christianum pertainentia. irreg., 1970, vol. 4. ISSN 0072-5293
- Graecitas et Latinitas Christianorum Primaeva. Supplementa; studia ad sermonem christianum pertinentia. irreg., 1970, vol. 3. ISSN 0072-5307

**Delft University Press**
Mijnbouwplein 11, Delft, Netherlands
(Subscr. address: Academic Book Services Holland, P.O. Box 66, Groningen, Netherlands)
- Delft Progress Report. q.

**Delfts Bouwkundig Studenten Gezelschap Stylos**
Berlageweg 1, Delft, Netherlands.
- Delfts Bouwkundig Studenten Gezelschap Styles. Mededelingen. w.(Sept.-June) ISSN 0011-782X

**G. Delwel, B. V.**
Rijksstraatweg 775-777, Wassenaar, Netherlands.
- Maandblad voor Bedrijfsadministratie en Organisatie. m. ISSN 0005-7622

**Deventer Landbouwers Vereniging Nji Sri**
Postbox 27, Deventer, Netherlands.
- Orang Peladang. bi-m. ISSN 0030-4239

**Dierenpark Wassenaar Zoo**
Rijksstraatweg 667, Wassenaar, Netherlands.
- Dierenpark Wassenaar Zoo. Parknieuws. 6 per yr. ISSN 0031-2207

**Drukkerij Dijkstra Niemeyer B.V.**
Peizerweg 138, Groningen, Netherlands.
- Culturele Maandblad Groningen. 10 per yr. ISSN 0011-2941 (Stichting Groninger Culturele Gemeenschap)

**Uitgeversmaatschappij Diligentia B. V.**
Tesselschadestraat 18-22, Box 6332, Amsterdam, Netherlands.
- Bedrijf en Techniek; vakblad voor de bedrijfsleiding in industriele ondernemingen. fortn. ISSN 0005-7614
- Chempress; economisch en technisch weekblad voor de chemische- en metaalindustrie in de Benelux. w. ISSN 0009-3173
- Computable; electronic and technical monthly on electronic data processing. fortn. ISSN 0010-4450
- Electro Radio Mercuur. fortn. ISSN 0013-4619
- Elektronica en Elektrotechniek. m.
- Foodpress. w. ISSN 0015-6701
- Frigotherma; technisch en economisch vakblad voor Koelen, Verwarmen, Luchtbehandeling, Drogen en Isoleren. m.
- Technische Gids voor Ziekenhuis en Instelling. m. ISSN 0040-1404
- Terra; vakblad voor tuin, perk en park. m.
- Texpress; economisch en technisch blad voor de textiel- en kledingindustrie in de Benelux. w. ISSN 0040-4772
- Textiel Adresboek. triennial. ISSN 0082-3619
- Textilia. w. plus 4 special editions. ISSN 0040-5264

**Documentation Centre for Modern Indonesia**
Koninklijk Instituut voor Taal-, Land- en Volkenkunde, Stationsplein 10, Leiden, Netherlands.
- E I. (Excerpta Indonesica) s-a. ISSN 0046-0885

**Dolfinarium Harderwijk**
Harderwijk, Netherlands.
- Aquatic Mammals. irreg. (3 per yr)

**Donemus Foundation**
Jacob Obrechtstr. 51, Amsterdam, Netherlands.
- Key Notes; musical life in the Netherlands. s-a.

**Van Doorne's Bedrijfswagenfabriek DAF B.V.**
Geldropseweg 303, Eindhoven, Netherlands.
- DAF Trucks Magazine. q. ISSN 0011-5282

**Dr. Abrahram Kuyperstichting ter Bevordering van de Studie der Antirevolutionaire Beginselen**
- Anti-Revolutionaire Staatkunde. (pub. by J. H. Kok B. V.)

**Draka Kabel B.V.**
Hamerstraat 2, Box 1013, Amsterdam, Netherlands.
- Draka Omroep. m.

**Drentse Genootschap**
Postbus 174, Assen, Netherlands.
- Maandblad Drenthe. m (10 per yr.) ISSN 0024-8592

**B. V. Drogistenpers**
Sarphatistraat 77, Amsterdam, Netherlands.
- Drogist. fortn. ISSN 0012-6330

**Duiker Apparatenfabriek N.V.**
De Bruyn Kopsstraat. 2, Rijswijk (Z.H), Netherlands.
- Duiker Krant. m. ISSN 0012-7043

**Dutch College of Surgeons**
- Archivum Chirurgicum Neerlandicum. (pub. by H. Veenman en Zonen)

**Dutch Handball Federation**
- Handbal. (pub. by G.U.Z.)

**Dutch Historical Association**
- Acta Historiae Neerlandicae. (pub. by Martinus Nijhoff)

**Dutch Liberal Reformed Association**
see Vereniging van Vrijzinnig Hervormden in Nederland

**Dutch Volkswagen Organization**
Roemer Visscherstraat 2-4, Amsterdam, Netherlands.
- Auto Toeruit. m.

**E. O. Kroon Levensmiddelenorganisatie N.V.**
- Kroonkroniek. (pub. by Gelderlander Pers)

**East-West Foundation**
- East-West Perspectives. (pub. by A. W. Sijthoff International Publishing Co.)

**Economisch Instituut voor het Midden- en Kleinbedrijf**
Neuhuyskade 94, Postbus 2818, The Hague, Netherlands.
- E. I. M. Mededelingen. 10 per yr. ISSN 0012-768X
- Economisch Instituut voor Het Midden- en Kleinbedrijf. Bedrijfsgegevens over de Detailhandel in Koffers en Lederwaren. irreg.
- Economisch Instituut voor Het Midden- en Kleinbedrijf. Kengetallen Betreffende Arbeids- en Vloerproduktiviteit in Het Midden- en Kleinbedrijf. irreg.
- Economisch Instituut voor Het Midden- en Kleinbedrijf. Verslag. a. ISSN 0070-8836
- Samenvattend Beeld Midden- en Kleinbedrijf. irreg.

**Economisch Technologisch Instituut voor Noord-Brabant**
- Noord-Brabant. (pub. by Drukkerij Bergmans-MCH)

**Economisch Technologisch Instituut voor Zuid-Holland**
Beursgebouw, P.O. 30021, Rotterdam-1, Netherlands.
- Industrie-Adresboek voor Zuid-Holland. biennial. ISSN 0073-7704

**Economisch-Technologische Dienst voor Noord-Holland**
Stolbergstraat 9, Haarlem, Netherlands.
- Industrie Adresboek van Noord-Holland. irreg.

**Eigen Huis en Interieur B.V.**
Watteaustraat 29, Amsterdam-Z, Netherlands.
- Eigen Huis en Interieur. m.

**N. V. Electriciteitsmaatschappij Aeg**
Box 1816, Amsterdam, Netherlands.
- A E G - Schakels. bi-m. ISSN 0001-1053
- Ontladingen. bi-m. ISSN 0030-3135

**Uitgeversmaatschappij Elektuur B.V.**
Postbus 75, 6190 AB Beek LB, Netherlands.
- Elektuur. m. ISSN 0013-5895

**Elsevier Scientific Publishing Co.**
Box 211, Amsterdam, Netherlands
(Dist. in the U.S. and Canada by: Elsevier North-Holland, Inc., New York, 52 Vanderbilt Ave., New York, NY 10017)
- Advances in Colloid and Interface Science; an international journal devoted to experimental and theoretical developments in interfacial and colloidal phenomena and their implications in chemistry, physics, technology and biology. q. ISSN 0001-8686
- Advances in Gas Chromatography. irreg. ISSN 0065-2652
- Advances in Molecular Relaxation and Interaction Processes; an international journal devoted to the study of the phenomena of viscoelasticity and acoustic, dielectric and magnetic relaxation. q.
- Agricultural Meteorology; an international journal. 6 per yr. ISSN 0002-1571
- Agricultural Water Management.

- Agriculture and Environment; an international journal for scientific research into the relationships between agriculture, food production and the management of the biosphere. q.
- Agro-Ecosystems. q. ISSN 0304-3746 (International Association for Ecology)
- Analytica Chimica Acta; international journal devoted to all branches of analytical chemistry. 16 per yr. ISSN 0003-2670
- Animal Feed Science and Technology. q.
- Animal Regulation Studies. q. (World Federation for the Protection of Animals)
- Animal Reproduction Science. q.
- Applied Animal Ethology; an international scientific journal reporting on the application of ethology to animals used by man. q.
- Aquaculture; an international journal devoted to research on the exploration and improvement of all aquatic food resources, both floristic and faunistic, from freshwater, brackish and marine environments, related directly or indirectly to human consumption. 8 per yr (in 2 vols.) ISSN 0044-8486
- Aquatic Botany; an international scientific journal dealing with applied and fundamental research on submerged, floating and emergent plants in marine and fresh water ecosystems. q.
- B B A-Bioenergetics. (Biochemica & Biophysica Acta) 16 per yr. (5 vols. per yr.) ISSN 0005-2728
- B B A-Biomembranes. (Biochemica & Biophysica Acta) 28 per yr. (9 vols. per yr.) ISSN 0005-2736
- B B A-Enzymology. (Biochemica & Biophysica Acta) 12 per yr. ISSN 0005-2744
- B B A-General Subjects. (Biochemica & Biophysica Acta) m.
- B B A Library; Biochemica Biophysica Acta. irreg., vol. 13, 1974. ISSN 0067-2734
- B B A-Lipids & Lipid Metabolism. (Biochemica & Biophysica Acta) 12 per yr. ISSN 0005-2760
- B B A-Nucleic Acids and Protein Synthesis. (Biochemica & Biophysica Acta) 24 per yr. ISSN 0005-2787
- B B A-Protein Structure. (Biochemica & Biophysica Acta) 12 per yr. ISSN 0005-2795
- B B A Reviews on Bioenergetics. (Biochemica & Biophysica Acta) q.
- B B A-Reviews on Biomembranes. (Biochemica & Biophysica Acta) q.
- B B A-Reviews on Cancer. (Biochemica & Biophysica Acta) q.
- Behavioural Processes; an international journal of comparative and physiological ethology. 8 per yr. ISSN 0376-6357
- Biochimica et Biophysica Acta; international journal of biochemistry and biophysics. 120 per yr. ISSN 0006-3002
- Brain Research; international multidisciplinary journal devoted to fundamental research in the brain sciences. 48 per yr. (20 vols. per yr.) ISSN 0006-8993
- Carbohydrate Research; an international journal. m. ISSN 0008-6215
- Chemical Geology; an international journal. 12 per yr (3 vols.) ISSN 0009-2541
- Chromatography of Environmental Hazards. irreg., vol. 3, 1975.
- Clinica Chimica Acta; international journal of clinical chemistry. 24 per yr. (8 vols. per yr.) ISSN 0009-8981
- Coastal Engineering. q.
- Comprehensive Biochemistry. irreg., vol. 31, 1975. ISSN 0069-8032
- Comprehensive Chemical Kinetics. irreg., vol. 18, 1977. ISSN 0069-8040
- Computer Techniques and Optimization. q.
- Contemporary Crises; crime, law, welfare. q.
- Coordination Chemistry Reviews; an international journal. 9 per yr (3 vols. per yr.) ISSN 0010-8545
- Developments in Geomathematics. irreg., vol. 13, 1977.
- Developments in Geotechnical Engineering. irreg., vol. 16, 1977.
- Developments in Geotectonics. irreg., vol. 12, 1977. ISSN 0419-0254
- Developments in Landscape Management and Urban Planning. irreg., vol. 3, 1976.
- Developments in Palaeontology and Stratigraphy. irreg., vol. 6, 1977.
- Developments in Petroleum Science. irreg., vol. 6, 1977.
- Developments in Petrology. irreg., vol. 5, 1977.
- Developments in Sedimentology. irreg., vol. 23, 1977. ISSN 0070-4571
- Developments in Soil Science. irreg., vol. 6, 1977.
- Developments in Solar System and Space Science. irreg., vol. 3, 1976.
- Developments in Solid Earth Geophysics. irreg., vol. 11, 1977. ISSN 0070-458X

- Developments in Water Science. irreg., vol. 6, 1976.
- Dialectical Anthropology. q.
- Dynamics of Atmospheres and Oceans. 10 per yr.
- Early Human Development; an international journal concerned with the continuity of foetal and postnatal life. q. (Co-publisher: North-Holland Publishing Co.)
- Earth and Planetary Science Letters. m. ISSN 0012-821X
- Earth Science Reviews; the international geological journal bridging the gap between research articles and text books. q. ISSN 0012-8252
- Ecological Modelling; international journal on ecological modelling and engineering and systems ecology. q. ISSN 0304-3800
- Elsevier Lexica. irreg., 1966, L. 8. ISSN 0422-9878
- Elsevier Materials Science Series. irreg.
- Elsevier Oceanography Series. irreg., vol. 19, 1977. ISSN 0078-3226
- Elsevier's Dictionary of Television and Video Recording. irreg.
- Engineering and Process Economics. q.
- Engineering Geology; an international journal. q. ISSN 0013-7952
- European Brewery Convention. Proceedings of the International Congress. biennial. ISSN 0071-2531
- European Journal of Engineering Education. q. (European Association for Engineering Education)
- European Journal of Political Research. q. (European Consortium for Political Research)
- F E M S-Microbiology Letters. m. (Federation of European Microbiological Societies) (Co-publisher: North-Holland Publishing Co.)
- Federation of European Biochemical Societies. (Proceedings of Meeting) irreg., 1973, 6th, vol. 24. ISSN 0071-4402
- Field Crops Research. q.
- Fluid Phase Equilibria. q.
- Forest Ecology and Management. q.
- Fuel Processing Technology. q.
- Gene; an international journal devoted to gene cloning and recombinant nucleic acids. bi-m. (Co-publisher: North-Holland Publishing Co.)
- Geoderma; an international journal of soil science. m. ISSN 0016-7061
- Geoexploration; international journal of mining and technical geophysics and related subjects. q. ISSN 0016-7142
- Glossaria Interpretum. irreg., 1971, no. 16. ISSN 0072-4750
- Higher Education; an international journal of higher education and educational planning. q. ISSN 0018-1560
- Hydrometallurgy; international journal devoted to all aspects of the aqueous processing of metals. q.
- Industrial Marketing Management; an international journal of industrial marketing and marketing research. bi-m. ISSN 0019-8501 (European Association for Industrial Marketing Research)
- Inorganic Perspectives in Biology and Medicine. q. (Co-publisher: North-Holland Publishing Co.)
- Instructional Science; an international journal. q. ISSN 0020-4277
- International Journal of Mass Spectrometry and Ion Physics. m. ISSN 0020-7381
- International Journal of Mineral Processing. q.
- Isotopes in Organic Chemistry. irreg.
- Journal of Applied Science and Engineering Section A. Electrical Power and Information Systems. q. (Royal Institution of Engineers in the Netherlands) (Co-Sponsor: Netherlands Electronic and Radio Institution (NERG))
- Journal of Chromatography; international journal on chromatography, electrophoresis and related methods. 38 per yr (15 vols. per yr.) ISSN 0021-9673
- Journal of Chromatography-Biomedical Applications; an international journal devoted to new developments and advances in biomedical applications of chromatography and electrophoresis. bi-m.
- Journal of Electron Spectroscopy. m. (in 2 vols.)
- Journal of Electrostatics. q.
- Journal of Geochemical Exploration. 6 per yr. (Association of Exploration Geochemists)
- Journal of Hazardous Materials. q.
- Journal of Hydrology. 16 per yr. ISSN 0022-1694
- Journal of Industrial Aerodynamics; international journal of engineering related to wind effects. q.
- Journal of Mechanical Working Technology. q.
- Journal of Membrane Science. irreg.
- Journal of Molecular Structure. m. ISSN 0022-2860
- Journal of Non-Newtonian Fluid Mechanics. q.

- Journal of Occupational Accidents. 4 per yr.
- Journal of the Neurological Sciences. m. ISSN 0022-510X (World Federation of Neurology)
- Journal of Volcanology and Geothermal Research; an international journal on the geogphysical, geochemical, petrological and economic aspects of geothermal and volcanological research. q.
- Landscape Planning; an international journal on landscape ecology, reclamation and conservation, outdoor recreation and land-use management. q.
- Livestock Production Science. q. ISSN 0301-6226 (European Association for Animal Production)
- Marine Chemistry; an international journal for studies of all chemical aspects of the marine environment. 8 per yr.
- Marine Geology; international journal of marine geology, geochemistry and geophysics. m. ISSN 0025-3227
- Marine Micropaleontology. q.
- Mass Emergencies; international journal of theory, planning and practice. q.
- Mass Energies. irreg.
- Membrane Science and Desalination; the international journal on the science and technology of desalting and water purification. m.
- Methods in Geochemistry and Geophysics. irreg., vol. 12, 1976. ISSN 0076-6895
- Methods in Geomathematics. irreg.
- Mutation Research; international journal on mutagenesis, chromosome breakage and related subjects (incl. section on environmental mutagenesis and related subjects) 29 per yr. (8 vols. per yr.) ISSN 0027-5107
- Netherlands' Journal of Sociology. s-a. (Netherlands Sociological Society)
- Nobel Prize Lectures - Chemistry. irreg., approx. every 3 yrs.
- Nobel Prize Lectures - Peace. irreg., approx. every 3 yrs.
- Nobel Prize Lectures - Physics. irreg., ca. every 3 yrs.
- Nobel Prize Lectures-Physiology of Medicine. irreg., approx. every 3 yrs.
- Ocean Management. q. ISSN 0302-184X
- Oxidation and Combustion. s-a. ISSN 0030-7696
- Pain; international disciplinary journal devoted to research on pain. q. (International Association for the Study of Pain)
- Palaeogeography, Palaeoclimatology, Palaeoecology; an international journal for the geo-sciences. 12 per yr. ISSN 0031-0182
- Photogrammetria. bi-m. ISSN 0031-8663 (International Society for Photogrammetry)
- Physical Inorganic Chemistry. irreg., 1974, mon.2.
- Physics of the Earth and Planetary Interiors; a journal devoted to observational and experimental studies of the earth and planetary interiors and their theoretical interpretation by the physical sciences. 8 per yr. ISSN 0031-9201
- Policy Sciences; an international journal devoted to the improvement of policy making. q. ISSN 0032-2687
- Precambrian Research. 8 per yr.
- Prix Nobel. Nobel Prizes. a. (Nobel Foundation SW)
- Progress in Brain Research. irreg., 1973, vol. 40. ISSN 0079-6123
- Progress in Mathematical Social Sciences. irreg., vol. 8, 1976.
- Protection Ecology. q.
- Quality and Quantity; European journal of methodology. q. ISSN 0033-5177
- Reaction Kinetics and Catalysis Letters. q.
- Reaction Mechanisms in Organic Chemistry. irreg., vol. 10, 1975. ISSN 0079-9823
- Research Progress in Organic, Biological and Medicinal Chemistry. irreg. ISSN 0486-5111
- Resource Recovery and Conservation. q.
- Review of Palaeobotany and Palynology; an international journal. 10 per yr. ISSN 0034-6667
- Rodd's Chemistry of Carbon Compounds. irreg. ISSN 0080-3758
- Science of the Total Environment; an international journal for scientific research into the environment and its relationship with man. 6 per yr. ISSN 0048-9697
- Scientia Horticulturae. 8 per yr. ISSN 0304-4238 (International Society for Horticultural Science)
- Sedimentary Geology; international journal of pure and applied sedimentology. m. ISSN 0037-0738
- Studies on Education. irreg., vol. 6, 1975.
- Sugar Technology Reviews. irreg. ISSN 0081-9204
- Supplements to Electroencephalography and Clinical Neurophysiology. irreg., no. 33, 1973.
- Tectonophysics; international journal of geotectonics and the geology and physics of the interior of the earth. 28 per yr. ISSN 0040-1951

- Textile Chemistry. irreg.; vol. 3, 1975. ISSN 0082-3635
- Theory and Society. q.
- Thermochimica Acta. m. ISSN 0040-6031
- Topics in Inorganic and General Chemistry. irreg., vol. 15. ISSN 0082-495X
- Toxicology Letters. bi-m. (Co-publisher: North-Holland Publishing Co.)
- Transportation; an international journal devoted to the improvement of transportation planning and practice. q. ISSN 0049-4488
- Trends in Biochemical Sciences. m. (International Union of Biochemistry) (Co-publisher: North-Holland Publishing Co.)
- Urban Ecology. q. (International Association for Ecology)
- Veterinary Microbiology. 8 per yr.
- Veterinary Parasitology. q. ISSN 0304-4017
- Veterinary Science Communications; an international journal publishing topical reviews and research letters on all aspects of the veterinary sciences. q.
- Wave Electronics. q.
- West-European Symposia on Clinical Chemistry. irreg. ISSN 0511-568X
- Wilson & Wilson's Comprehensive Analytical Chemistry. irreg., vol. 8, 1976. ISSN 0069-8024
- World Economy. q.
- World Survey of Climatology. irreg., vol. 7, 1977. ISSN 0084-2265

**Energieonderzoek Centrum Nederland**
- Energie-Spectrum. (pub. by Tijl Media B.V.)

**Eska Tijdschriften B. V.**
Lijnmarkt 41-43, Utrecht, Netherlands.
- Ariadne; maandblad voor handwerken. m.
- Lien Wallon; journal de l'eglise Wallonne d'Utrecht. q. ISSN 0024-2934 (Huguenot Society of Utrecht)
- Marion; fashion and home sewing patterns. m. ISSN 0025-3383
- Na Vijven; hobbies for the whole family. m. ISSN 0027-7320

**Esser Scientific Press**
Beelslaan 20, Haarlem, Netherlands.
- Methodology and Science; interdisciplinary journal for the empirical study of the foundations of science and their methodology. q. ISSN 0543-6095 (International Society for the Study of Significs)

**Esso Nederland B. V.**
Zuid-Hollandlaan 7, Box 110, The Hague, Netherlands.
- Essobron. bi-m. ISSN 0014-1046
- Essofoon. bi-w. ISSN 0014-1054

**Euro Fair B. V.**
Gerrit van der Veenstraat 94, Amsterdam-Z, Netherlands.
- Expovisie; maandblad voor tentoonstellingen, congressen en hotellerie. m. ISSN 0014-5254

**Europa Instituut**
*see under* **Universiteit van Amsterdam**

**European Association for American Studies**
- E A A S Newsletter. (pub. by Amerika Instituut)

**European Association for Animal Production**
- Livestock Production Science. (pub. by Elsevier Scientific Publishing Co.)

**European Association for Engineering Education**
- European Journal of Engineering Education. (pub. by Elsevier Scientific Publishing Co.)

**European Association for Industrial Marketing Research**
- Industrial Marketing Management. (pub. by Elsevier Scientific Publishing Co.)

**European Association for Potato Research**
Box 20, Wageningen, Netherlands.
- European Association for Potato Research. Proceedings of the Triennial Conference. triennial. ISSN 0071-2507
- Potato Research. q. ISSN 0014-3065

**European Association for Research on Plant Breeding.**
Secretariat, P.O. Box 128, NL-6140 Wageningen, Netherlands.
- Eucarpia. triennial, 1974, 7th,Budapest, Hungary. ISSN 0071-2221

**European Association of Exploration Geophysicists**
Carel van Bylandtlaan 30, The Hague, Netherlands.
- European Association of Exploration Geophysicists. Constitution and By-Laws, Membership List. a. ISSN 0531-2728
- Geophysical Prospecting. q. ISSN 0016-8025

**European Brewery Convention**
- European Brewery Convention. Proceedings of the International Congress. (pub. by Elsevier Scientific Publishing Co.)

**European Bureau of Adult Education**
P.O. Box 367, Nieuweweg 4, Amersfoort, Netherlands.
- European Bureau of Adult Education. Notes & Studies. q. ISSN 0423-6777

**European Centre for Population Studies**
Pauwenlaan 17, The Hague, Netherlands.
- European Demographic Information Bulletin. q. ISSN 0046-2756

**European Community Information Service**
Lange Voorhout 29, The Hague, Netherlands.
- Europese Gemeenschap. m. ISSN 0014-3200

**European Consortium for Political Research**
- European Journal of Political Research. (pub. by Elsevier Scientific Publishing Co.)

**European Coordination Centre for Research and Documentation in Social Sciences**
- European Coordination Centre for Research and Documentation in Social Sciences. Publications. (pub. by Mouton Publishers)

**European Peptide Symposium**
- Peptides. (pub. by North-Holland Publishing Co.)

**European Scientific Association of Applied Economics**
- European Economic Review. (pub. by North Holland Publishing Co.)

**European Society for Opinion and Marketing Research**
Raadhuisstraat 15, Amsterdam, Netherlands.
- Annuaire E S O M A R/E S O M A R Yearbook. a. ISSN 0071-3074
- Papers from the E S O M A R Congress. a, 1974, Hamburg. ISSN 0071-3082

**European Society for Rural Sociology**
- Sociologia Ruralis. (pub. by Van Gorcum)

**European Society for the Study of Drug Toxicity**
- European Society for the Study of Drug Toxicity. Proceedings. (pub. by Excerpta Medica)

**Europese Bibliotheek**
Gasthuisstraat 12, Zaltbommel, Netherlands.
- Spiegel der Historie; maandblad voor de geschiedenis der Nederlanden. m. ISSN 0038-7460
- Zwischen Hausmannsturm und Walbecker Warte. irreg.

**Eurosell B. V.**
Van Welderenstraat 97, Nijmegen, Netherlands.
- Brug; weekblad voor Nijmegen en omgeving. w. ISSN 0007-2648

**Evangelisatie-Boekhandel en Uitgeverij Horizont**
Box 77, Hoogeveen (Dr.), Netherlands.
- Uitzicht. m. ISSN 0041-5944 (Reformed Presbyterian Fellowship in the Great Congregation (Ps.40,10))

**Evangelische Maatschappij**
Jodichemdreef 28, Odijk (U.), Netherlands.
- Tenminste. m.

**Excerpta Medica**
Box 211, Amsterdam, Netherlands
(Dist. in the U.S. and Canada by: Elsevier North-Holland, Inc., New York, 52 Vanderbilt Ave., New York, NY 10017)
- Advances in Planned Parenthood. ISSN 0065-3179
- Advances in Tumour Prevention, Detection and Characterization. irreg.
- Drug-Induced Diseases. irreg. ISSN 0586-2779
- European Journal of Applied Physiology and Occupational Physiology. 4 per yr. ISSN 0301-4711
- European Journal of Cardiology. q.
- European Journal of Obstetrics, Gynecology and Reproductive Biology. 6 per yr.

- European Ophthalmological Society. Congress. Abstracts. quadrennial, 1968, 3rd, Amsterdam. ISSN 0071-2965 (Inquire: Jules Francois, De Smet de Naeyerpl. 15, 9000 Ghent, Belgium)
- European Society for the Study of Drug Toxicity. Proceedings. irreg. ISSN 0071-3090 (Inquire: Dr. E. Eichenberger, Wander AG, 3001 Berne, Switzerland)
- Excerpta Medica. Section 1: Anatomy, Anthropology, Embryology & Histology. 10 per yr. ISSN 0014-4053
- Excerpta Medica. Section 2: Physiology. 30 per yr. ISSN 0014-4061
- Excerpta Medica. Section 3: Endocrinology. 20 per yr. ISSN 0014-407X
- Excerpta Medica. Section 3b: Health Economics and Hospital Management. 20 per yr. ISSN 0300-5321
- Excerpta Medica. Section 4: Microbiology, Bacteriology, Mycology and Parasitology. 20 per yr.
- Excerpta Medica. Section 5: General Pathology and Pathological Anatomy. 30 per yr. ISSN 0014-4096
- Excerpta Medica. Section 6: Internal Medicine. 20 per yr. ISSN 0014-410X
- Excerpta Medica. Section 7: Pediatrics and Pediatric Surgery. 20 per yr.
- Excerpta Medica. Section 8: Neurology and Neurosurgery. 30 per yr. ISSN 0014-4126
- Excerpta Medica. Section 9: Surgery. 20 per yr. ISSN 0014-4134
- Excerpta Medica. Section 10: Obstetrics and Gynecology. 20 per yr. ISSN 0014-4142
- Excerpta Medica. Section 11: Otorhinolaryngology. 20 per yr. ISSN 0014-4150
- Excerpta Medica. Section 12: Ophthalmology. 10 per yr. ISSN 0014-4169
- Excerpta Medica. Section 13: Dermatology and Venereology. 10 per yr. ISSN 0014-4177
- Excerpta Medica. Section 14: Radiology. 20 per yr. ISSN 0014-4185
- Excerpta Medica. Section 15: Chest Diseases, Thoracic Surgery and Tuberculosis. 20 per yr. ISSN 0014-4193
- Excerpta Medica. Section 16: Cancer. 30 per yr. ISSN 0014-4207
- Excerpta Medica. Section 17: Public Health, Social Medicine & Hygiene. 20 per yr. ISSN 0014-4215
- Excerpta Medica. Section 18: Cardiovascular Diseases and Cardiovascular Surgery. 20 per yr. ISSN 0014-4223
- Excerpta Medica. Section 19: Rehabilitation and Physical Medicine. 10 per yr. ISSN 0014-4231
- Excerpta Medica. Section 20: Gerontology and Geriatrics. 10 per yr. ISSN 0014-424X
- Excerpta Medica. Section 21: Developmental Biology and Teratology. 10 per yr. ISSN 0014-4258
- Excerpta Medica. Section 22: Human Genetics. 20 per yr. ISSN 0014-4266
- Excerpta Medica. Section 23: Nuclear Medicine. 20 per yr. ISSN 0014-4274
- Excerpta Medica. Section 24: Anesthesiology. 10 per yr. ISSN 0014-4282
- Excerpta Medica. Section 25: Hematology. 20 per yr. ISSN 0014-4290
- Excerpta Medica. Section 26: Immunology, Serology and Transplantation. 20 per yr. ISSN 0014-4304
- Excerpta Medica. Section 27: Biophysics, Bio-Engineering and Medical Instrumentation. 10 per yr. ISSN 0014-4312
- Excerpta Medica. Section 28: Urology and Nephrology. 10 per yr. ISSN 0014-4320
- Excerpta Medica. Section 29: Clinical Biochemistry. 30 per yr. ISSN 0300-5372
- Excerpta Medica. Section 30: Pharmacology and Toxicology. 30 per yr.
- Excerpta Medica. Section 31: Arthritis and Rheumatism. 10 per yr. ISSN 0014-4355
- Excerpta Medica. Section 32: Psychiatry. 20 per yr. ISSN 0014-4363
- Excerpta Medica. Section 33: Orthopedic Surgery. 10 per yr. ISSN 0014-4371
- Excerpta Medica. Section 34: Plastic Surgery. 10 per yr. ISSN 0014-438X
- Excerpta Medica. Section 35: Occupational Health and Industrial Medicine. 10 per yr. ISSN 0014-4398
- Excerpta Medica. Section 37: Drug Literature Index. 24 per yr.
- Excerpta Medica. Section 38: Adverse Reactions Titles; a monthly bibliography of titles from approximately 3500 biomedical journals published throughout the world. 12 per yr. ISSN 0001-8848

- Excerpta Medica. Section 40: Drug Dependence. m. (Netherlands. Ministerie van Volksgezondheid en Milieuhygiene)
- Excerpta Medica. Section 46: Environmental Health and Pollution Control. 20 per yr.
- Excerpta Medica. Section 47: Virology. 10 per yr. ISSN 0031-6520
- Excerpta Medica. Section 48: Gastroenterology. 20 per yr. ISSN 0031-3580
- Excerpta Medica. Section 49: Forensic Science Abstracts. 10 per yr.
- Excerpta Medica. Section 50: Epilepsy Abstracts. 12 per yr. ISSN 0031-0743
- Excerpta Medica. Section 61: Transplantation Immunology Literature Index. m.
- Excerpta Medica. Section 62: Lymphocyte Literature Index. m.
- Excerpta Medica. Section 63: Congenital Defects Literature Index. m.
- Excerpta Medica. Section 64: Diabetes Mellitus Literature Index. m.
- Excerpta Medica. Section 65: Cancer Immunology Literature Index. m.
- Forensic Medicine Abstracts. 10 per yr.
- Forensic Science Abstracts. 10 per yr.
- International Conference on Congenital Malformations. Proceedings. irreg., 1969, 3rd, The Hague. ISSN 0074-3038 (National Foundation-March of Dimes)
- International Conference on Intra-Uterine Contraception. Proceedings. irreg., 1964, 2nd, New York. ISSN 0074-3135 (Population Council US)
- International Congress for Child Psychiatry. Proceedings. quadrennial, 1970, 7th, Jerusalem. ISSN 0074-3372 (Inquire: Prof. D. J. Duche, 54 Blvd. Emile Dugier, 75-Paris, France)
- International Congress of Allergology. Abstracts of Reports of Discussion and of Communications. irreg. ISSN 0443-8604 (International Association of Allergology) (Inquire: Dr. C. E. Arbesman, 50 High St., Buffalo, N.Y.)
- International Congress of Cell Biology. Summaries of Reports and Communications. irreg., 1968, 12th, Brussels. ISSN 0074-3550 (International Federation of Cell Biology) (Inquire: Dr. L. A. Franks, Imperial Cancer Research Fund, Lincoln's Inn Fields, London WC2, England)
- International Congress of Endocrinology. Proceedings. irreg. ISSN 0538-6462 (International Society of Endocrinology) (Inquire: Dr. John C. Beck, McIntyre Medical Sciences Center, Montreal, Canada)
- International Congress of Human Genetics. Abstracts. quinquennial.
- International Congress of Neurological Sciences. Abstracts and Descriptions of Contributions of the Scientific Program. irreg. ISSN 0534-9109
- International Congress of Neurological Surgery. Abstracts of Papers. irreg, 5th, published in 1973. ISSN 0074-3801 (World Federation of Neurological Societies)
- International Congress of Physical Medicine. Abstracts of Papers Presented. quadrennial. ISSN 0074-3887 (International Federation of Physical Medicine and Rehabilitation) (Inquire: the Federation, c/o A.P.M. van Gestel, Rehabilitation Centre, Eindhoven, Kempense Baan 96, Eindhoven, Netherlands)
- International Congress of Plastic and Reconstructive Surgery. Transactions. irreg. ISSN 0579-3785 (Inquire: John Watson, 122 Harley St., London WIN 1AN, England)
- International Congress on Hormonal Steroids. Abstracts of Papers Presented. irreg., 1970, 3rd, Hamburg. ISSN 0074-4107
- International Congress on Medical Librarianship. Proceedings. irreg.
- International Congress on Muscle Diseases. Abstracts. irreg., 1st, Milan, 1969.
- International Congress Series. irreg., no. 360, 1975. ISSN 0531-5131
- International Diabetes Federation. Proceedings of Congress. triennial, 1970, 7th Buenos Aires. ISSN 0074-4522 (Inquire: the Federation, Dinkeziekenhuis, Losser, Netherlands)
- International Symposium on Growth Hormone. Abstracts. irreg., 1967, 1st, Milan.
- International Symposium on Pharmacological Treatment in Burns. Proceedings. irreg., 1st, Milan, 1968. (International Society for Burn Injuries) (Inquire: A. B. Wallace, Royal College of Surgeons, 18 Nicolson St., Edinburgh EH8 9DW, Scotland)

- International Union against Tuberculosis. Conference Proceedings. biennial, 1969, 20th, New York. (Inquire: International Union Against Tuberculosis, 20 rue Greuze, 75-Paris 16e, France)
- Journal of Vertigo. s-a. ISSN 0362-4412
- Monographs in Anaesthesiology. irreg.
- Neuro-Psychopharmacology. biennial.
- Side Effects of Drugs. irreg. ISSN 0583-1881
- Swiss Society of Plastic and Reconstructive Surgeons. Proceedings (Of) Annual Meeting. a. ISSN 0082-0482 (And New York Academy of Medicine, 2 E. 103 St., New York, N.Y. 10029)
- World Congress of Anaesthesiologists. Proceedings. irreg., 1968, 4th, London. ISSN 0084-1595 (World Federation of Societies of Anaesthesiologists)

**Exp-Press**
P.O. Box 14012, Utrecht, Netherlands.
- Specimen. irreg.

**F. van Landschot Bankiers**
Box 1021, S-Hertogenbosch, Netherlands.
- Financiele Flitsen; financial & economic information. s-m. ISSN 0015-2080

**Uitgeverij FED B. V.**
Polstraat 10, Deventer, Netherlands.
- Fed's Fiscale Brochures. irreg., approx. 6 per yr.

**Federacio de Esperanto-Organizoj en Nederlando**
Nieuwe Binnenweg 176, Rotterdam 3002, Netherlands.
- Komuna Esperanto-Gazeto. m. ISSN 0023-317X

**Federatie Goud en Zilver**
Van der Spiegelstraat 3, The Hague, Netherlands.
- Edelmetaal Uurwerken Edelstenen. m.

**Federatie van Bedrijfsverenigingen**
Postbus 8300, Amsterdam, Netherlands.
- Federatie van Bedrijfsverenigingen. Jaarverslag. a. ISSN 0071-4151

**Federatie van Bevoegde Nederlandse Sportleiders**
Carmenstraat 9, Apeldoorn, Netherlands.
- Konkreet. bi-m. ISSN 0023-3501

**Federatie van Nederlandse Organisaties voor het Personenvervoer**
Joh. van Oldenbarneveltlaan 11, The Hague, Netherlands.
- Personenvervoer. m. ISSN 0031-5680

**Federatie van Nederlandse Slagerspatroonsbonden**
- Slager. (pub. by Uitgeversmaatschappij de Gelderlander Vakpers BV)

**Federatie van Nederlandse Verenigingen voor de Kantoorboekhandel**
De Lairessestr. 109, Amsterdam-Z, Netherlands.
- Band; stationers trade journal. fortn. ISSN 0005-4909

**Federatie van Organisaties van Groothandelsbedrijven in Levensmiddelen en Aanverwante Artikelen**
- Groothandel/Weekly. (pub. by Uitgeversmaatschappij de Gelderlander Vakpers BV)

**Federatie van Verenigingen van Handelaren in Oude Materialen en Afvalstoffen**
Bachlaan 6, Voorschoten, Netherlands.
- Recuperatie; vakblad voor de herwinning (recuperatie) van grondstoffen. q. ISSN 0034-1916

**Federatie van Werknemersorganisaties in de Zeevaart**
Heemraadssingel 323, Rotterdam 3006, Netherlands.
- Peiling. m. ISSN 0031-4099 (Algemene Vereniging van Zeevarenden)

**Federation Internationale des Ingenieurs Conseils** see International Federation of Consulting Engineers

**Federation of Dutch Naturist-Organisations**
Box 564, The Hague, Netherlands.
- Naturisme. q. ISSN 0028-0968

**Federation of European Biochemical Societies**
- European Journal of Biochemistry. (pub. by Springer-Verlag US)
- F E B S Letters. (pub. by North-Holland Publishing Co.)

• Index of Biochemical Reviews. (pub. by North Holland Publishing Co.)

**Federation of European Microbiological Societies**
• F E M S-Microbiology Letters. (pub. by Elsevier Scientific Publishing Co.)

**Fibula-Van Dishoeck**
Postbus 17, Bussum, Netherlands
• Spiegel Historiael; maandblad voor geschiedenis en archeologie. m(11 per yr.) ISSN 0038-7487 (Subscr. to C. de Boer Jr. N.V., Box 507, Hilversum, Netherlands)

**Filmcentrum Foundation**
Postbus 515, Hilversum, Netherlands.
• Drie D. Filmkompas. q.

**Financieele Koerier N.V.**
Postbox 3906, Amsterdam, Netherlands.
• Financiele Koerier. w. ISSN 0015-2099

**Fokker-VFW B.V. Bedrijf Drechtsteden**
Postbus 1, Papendrecht, Netherlands.
• Informatiekrant Drechtsteden/I D. 13 per yr. ISSN 0017-6818

**Foton Publishing B.V.**
Lijnmarkt 41-43, Utrecht, Netherlands.
• Fototribune; maandblad voor fotografie, smalfilm en geluid. m. ISSN 0015-8925

**Foundation "de Paladijn"**
Nassau Odijckstraat 4, The Hague, Netherlands.
• Paladijn. m. ISSN 0031-0166

**Foundation Documenta de Medicina Geographica et Tropica**
• Tropical and Geographical Medicine. (pub. by Bohn, Scheltema en Holkema )

**Foundation Euphytica**
Lawickse Allee 166, Wageningen, Netherlands.
• Euphytica; Netherlands journal of plant breeding. 3 per yr. ISSN 0014-2336

**Foundation Flora Malesiana**
• Flora Malesiana. Series 2: Pteridophyta. (pub. by Noordhoff International Publishing)
• Flora Malesiana Bulletin. (pub. by Noordhoff International Publishing)

**Foundation for the Promotion of the Translation of Dutch Literary Works**
Singel 450, Amsterdam-C, Netherlands.
• Writing in Holland and Flanders. q.

**Foundation Janus**
Joh. Verhulststraat 185, Amsterdam, Netherlands.
• Janus; revue internationale de l'histoire des sciences, de la medecine, de la pharmacie et de la technique. 4 per yr. ISSN 0021-4264

**Foundation Prometheus**
Box 784, Amsterdam, Netherlands.
• International Lighting Review. q. ISSN 0020-7853 (N.V. Philips Gloeilampenfabrieken) (Co-sponsor: North American Philips Lighting Corporation)

**Fries Instituut**
see under **Rijksuniversiteit Te Groningen**

**Friesch Rundvee-Stamboek en Bond van K. I.**
Verenigingen in Friesland, Post Box 202, Leeuwarden, Netherlands.
• Friese Veefokkerij. m.

**Friese Maatschappij van Landbouw**
Willemskade 11, Box 613, Leeuwarden, Netherlands.
• Fries Landbouwblad; vakblad voor veehouderij en akkerbouw. w. ISSN 0016-1373

**Frysk Orkest**
J.W. Frisostraat 3, Postbus 666, Leeuwarden, Netherlands.
• Paukenslag. ISSN 0031-3246

**Fryske Akademy**
Doelestrjitte 8, Ljouwert/Leeuwarden, Netherlands.
• Beaken. bi-m. ISSN 0005-738X
• Ut de Smidte fan de Fryske Akademy. q. ISSN 0042-1367

**G.U.Z.**
St. Jansstraat 1 - 3, Groningen, Netherlands.
• Handbal. fortn. ISSN 0017-7180 (Dutch Handball Federation)

**Koninklijke Drukkerij van de Garde N. V.**
Zaltbommel, Netherlands.
• Pyttersen's Nederlandse Almanak; annually published directory of persons and organizations in the Netherlands. a. ISSN 0079-8223

**Gaudeamus Foundation**
Postbus 30, Bilthoven, Netherlands.
• Gaudeamus Information. English Edition. bi-m. ISSN 0533-9235

**Geillustreerde Pers B.V.**
Stadhouderskade 85, Amsterdam, Netherlands.
• Avenue. m. ISSN 0005-1985
• Knip. m. ISSN 0023-2289
• Margriet. w. ISSN 0025-2956

**Uitgeversmaatschappij de Gelderlander Vakpers BV**
Doddendaal 24, Postbus 16, Nijmegen, Netherlands.
• A.G.F. Magazine; vakblad voor de handel in aardappelen, groenten, en fruit. fortn.
• Bakker. w. (Nederlandse Bakkerij)
• Food-Magazine; vakblad voor de detailhandel in levensmiddelen. w. (Vereniging van Levensmiddelenhandelaren ANKB) (Co-sponsor: Nederlandse Katholieke Kruidenierbond; Christelijke Kruideniersbond)
• Foto-Visie. m. (Bond van Nederlandse Fotodetailhandelaren)
• Groothandel/Weekly. w. (Federatie van Organisaties van Groothandelsbedrijven in Levensmiddelen en Aanverwante Artikelen)
• Installatie. fortn. ISSN 0020-2096 (Algemene Vereniging van Ondernemers in het Loodgieters- , Sanitair- en Gasverwarmingsinstallatiebedrijf)
• Kroonkroniek; kontaktorgaan europese organisatie. m. ISSN 0023-4931 (E. O. Kroon Levensmiddelenorganisatie N.V.)
• Melk en Zuivel. fortn. ISSN 0025-8970 (Nederlandse Melkhandelaren Organisatie)
• Metaal en Techniek. m. ISSN 0026-0479 (Metaalunie) (Co-sponsor: Katholieke Bond Metaalbewerkingsbedrijven)
• Schoen - Visie. m. ISSN 0036-6269
• Slager; vakblad voor de vleesspecialist. w. ISSN 0037-6698 (Federatie van Nederlandse Slagerspatroonsbonden)
• Slagersambacht. bi-m. ISSN 0037-671X (Vereniging tot Bevordering van Slagersvakonerwijs S.V.O.)
• Stijl. m. ISSN 0039-1425
• Tweewieler. fortn.
• Vleesdistributie en Vleestechnologie. m. ISSN 0042-7691
• Voet-Visie. bi-m. (Landelijke Organisatie Voetverzorging)
• Zelfstandig Ondernemerschap. m. (Koninklijk Verbond van Ondernemers) (Co-sponsors: Nederlands Katholiek Ondernemers Verbond; Nederlands Christelijk Ondernemers Verbond)

**Uitgeverij van Gennep**
Nes 128, Amsterdam, Netherlands.
• Tijdschrift voor Sociale Geschiedenis. 3 per yr. (Nederlandse Vereniging tot Beoefening van de Sociale Geschiedenis)

**Genootschap Amstelodamum**
• Genootschap Amstelodamum. Jaarboek. (pub. by De Bussy, Eilerman Harms N. V.)

**Gereformeerd Historisch Instituut**
Zestienhovensekade 409, Rotterdam 3008, Netherlands.
• Gereformeerd Kerkhistorisch Tijdschrift. q.

**Gereformeerd Maatschappelijk Verbond**
• Ambt en Plicht. (pub. by Uitgeverij De Vuurbaak)

**Gereformeerd Politiek Verbond**
Box 439, Amersfoort, Netherlands.
• Ons Burgerschap. fortn.

**Gereformeerde Kerken in Classis Harderwijk en Nijkerk**
• Veluws Kerkblad. (pub. by Drukkerij Bolhuis B.V.)

**Gereformeerde Persvereniging, Rotterdam**
Pasteursingel 29-B, Rotterdam 3007, Netherlands.
• Opbouw; weekblad tot opbouw van het gereformeerde leven. w. ISSN 0030-3356

**Gerlach en Co. B. V.**
Art Section, Schiphol-Center, Amsterdam, Netherlands.
• Prent 190; new circle of collectors of modern graphic art. m.(Sept.-June) ISSN 0032-7476

**H. Gianotten B.V.**
Bredaseweg 61, Tilburg, Netherlands.
• Gedrag; Tijdschrift voor psychologie. bi-m.
• Maandschrift Economie; tijdschrift voor algemeen economische bedrijfseconomische en sociale vraagstukken. m. ISSN 0024-8673 (Stichting Maandschrift Economie)
• Speling. q. ISSN 0038-7320

**G. V. W. F. Goelst**
Poortstraat 11, Utrecht, Netherlands.
• Astrologische Gids; tijdschrift ten dienste van studerenden en belangstellenden in de astrologie. q. ISSN 0004-6167 (Centrum voor Astrologische Statistiek)

**Gooi en Sticht B.V.**
Postbox 17, Hilversum, Netherlands.
• Kerugma. bi-m. ISSN 0023-0685
• Trans-Actie. bi-m.
• Tussen Ons in. 4 per yr.

**Van Gorcum**
Box 43, Assen, Netherlands.
• Algemeen Nederlands Tijdschrift voor Wijsbegeerte. 4 per yr. ISSN 0002-5275
• Amersfoortse Stemmen. bi-m. ISSN 0003-1666 (Internationale School voor Wijsbegeerte)
• Apocrypha Novi Testamenti. irreg., latest 1965. ISSN 0066-5320
• Clinical Neurology and Neurosurgery. q.
• Compendia Rerum Iudaicarum Ad Novum Testamentum. irreg.
• International Review of Social History. 3 per yr. ISSN 0020-8590 ( International Institute for Social History )
• Kerk en Wereld/Church & World. every 3 wks. ISSN 0023-0588 (Vereniging van Vrijzinnig Hervormden in Nederland)
• Monographs on Clinical Neurology and Neurosurgery. irreg.
• Neerlandica Extra Muros; halfjaarlijks contact en inlichtingenblad. s-a. ISSN 0047-9276 (Internationale Vereniging voor Nederlandistiek)
• Organisations, People, Society/O P S. irreg.
• Philosophia Spinozae Perennis. irreg.
• Phronesis; a journal for ancient philosophy. s-a. ISSN 0031-8868
• Planning and Development in the Netherlands. s-a. ISSN 0032-0692 (Netherlands Universities Foundation for International Cooperation)
• Polemologische Studien. irreg., vol. 16, 1972. ISSN 0079-2926 (Rijksuniversiteit te Groningen. Polemologisch Instituut)
• Publications on Social History. irreg., no. 8, 1974. ISSN 0079-7804 ( International Institute for Social History ) (Dist. by ISBS, P.O. Box 4347, Portland, OR 97208)
• Rapports Franse Boek. q. (Vereniging tot Bevordering van de Studie van het Frans) (Subscr. to: Oostelijk Halfrond 64, Amstelveen, Netherlands)
• Semitic Texts with Translations. irreg. ISSN 0080-8881
• Sociaal-Geografische Studien. irreg., no. 13, 1974. ISSN 0081-0398
• Sociaal-Historische Studien. irreg., no. 6, 1973. ISSN 0081-0401 (International Institute for Social History)
• Sociologia Ruralis. 4 per yr. ISSN 0038-0199 (European Society for Rural Sociology)
• Studia Rosenthaliana; tijdschrift voor Joodse wetenschap en geschiedenis in Nederland/journal for Jewish literature and history in the Netherlands. s-a. ISSN 0039-3347 (Bibliotheca Rosenthaliana)
• Studia Semitica Neerlandica. irreg., no. 16, 1974. ISSN 0081-6914 (Dist. by ISBS, P.O. Box 4347, Portland, OR 97208)
• Studia Theodisca. irreg., no. 13, 1974. ISSN 0081-6957
• Studies in Neuro-Anatomy. irreg., no. 10, 1971. ISSN 0081-8305 (Dist. by ISBS, P.O. Box 4347, Portland, OR 97208)
• Studies of Developing Countries. irreg., no. 17, 1974. ISSN 0081-8771 (Dist. by: Humanities Press, Inc., 171 First Ave., Atlantic Highlands, NJ 07716)

- Wijsgerige Teksten en Studies/Philosophical Texts and Studies. irreg., no. 23, 1975. ISSN 0084-0106 (Rijksuniversiteit te Utrecht) (Dist. by Humanities Press, Inc., 171 First Ave, Atlantic Highlands, N.J. 07716)

**Gouda Quint B.V.**
Box 1148, Arnhem, Netherlands.
- Delikt en Delinkwent; tijdschrift voor strafrecht. 10 per yr. ISSN 0045-9879
- Tijdschrift voor de Politie. m.

**Van der Graaf en Co's Uitgeversmaatschappij B. V.**
Helmholtzstraat 61, Amsterdam 0, Netherlands.
- Handelsbelangen; wekelijks kommercieel, dokumentair en financieel nieuwsblad. w. ISSN 0017-7288

**N. V. Uitgeversmaatschappij de Graafschap**
Heyenoordseweg 5, Arnhem, Netherlands.
- Vrienden Kring. q. ISSN 0042-9163 (Johanna Stichting Revalidatie Centrum)

**Grafische Industrie van Eerd B.V.**
Postbus 8010, Lange Nieuwstraat 237, Tilburg, Netherlands.
- Franciscaans Leven; tijdschrift tot verdieping en vernieuwing van de Franciscaanse beweging. bi-m. ISSN 0015-9794 (Stichting Franciscaanse Samenwerking te Utrecht)

**Grand East of the Netherlands**
Fluwelenburgwal 22, The Hague, Netherlands.
- Algemeen Maconniek Tijdschrift. m. ISSN 0002-5267

**Graphic Export Centre**
Prinsengracht 668, Amsterdam, Netherlands.
- Bookmill. q.

**Grasso's Koninklijke Machinefabrieken N.V.**
Parallelweg 27, S-Hertogenbosch, Netherlands.
- Grassortiment. bi-m.

**Griekenland Werkgroepen in Nederland en Belgie**
Van't Santstraat 32, Nijmegen, Netherlands.
- Internationale Korrespondentie; samenwerkende bedrijfs- en onderzoeksgroepen in Nederland en Belgie. q.

**B.V. Drukkerij J. J. Groen en Zoon**
Pieterskerk Choorsteeg 18, Postbus 31, Leiden, Netherlands.
- Vriend van Oud en Jong; Christelijk weekblad. w. ISSN 0042-9155

**Groen van Prinsterer Kweekschool**
Julianeplein 2, Doetinchem, Netherlands.
- Meteoor. ISSN 0026-1092

**Groene Amsterdammer N.V.**
Westeinde 16, Box 353, Amsterdam, Netherlands.
- Groene Amsterdammer; onafhankelijk weekblad. w. ISSN 0017-4483

**Groninger Maatschappij van Landbouw**
Martinikerkhof 32, Groningen, Netherlands.
- Groninger Landbouwblad. w. ISSN 0017-4521

**Group for the Study of Atoms and Molecules from Radio-Electric Research**
- Colloque A M P E R E. (pub. by North Holland Publishing Co.)

**B. R. Gruener B.V.**
Box 70020, Amsterdam, Netherlands.
- Dialectics and Revolution. irreg.
- Poetica; Zeitschrift fuer Sprach- und Literaturwissenschaft. q. ISSN 0032-2016 (Deutsche Forschungsgemeinschaft GW)
- Poznan Studies in the Philosophy of the Sciences and the Humanities. 4 per yr. ISSN 0303-8157
- Revolutionary World; an international journal of philosophy. irreg., approx. 5 per yr.
- Studien zur Antiken Philosophie. irreg.

**H.T.S. Corps**
Box 1037, S-Hertogenbosch, Netherlands.
- Korrelatief. 8 per yr. ISSN 0017-6281

**Haagse Jazz Club**
Laan van Heldenburg 7, Voorburg, Netherlands.
- Haagse Jazz Club. m. ISSN 0017-632X

**Haentjens Dekker en Gumbert**
Achter Sint Pieter 14, Utrecht, Netherlands.
- Bibliotheca Emblematica. irreg. ISSN 0067-7930

- Orbis Artium; Utrechtse kunsthistorische studien. irreg., 1970, vol. 12. ISSN 0078-5563 (Rijksuniversiteit te Utrecht. Kunsthistorisch Instituut)

**Hafenkurier**
c/o Nieuwe Rotterdamse Courant N.V., Box 601, Rotterdam, Netherlands.
- Hafenkurier. w. ISSN 0017-6591

**Ten Hagen B. V.**
Box 34, The Hague, Netherlands.
- Architect. m. ISSN 0044-8621
- Bouwbelangen. w. ISSN 0006-8330 (Algemeen Verbond Bouw Bedrijf)
- C M. (Cobouw Magazine) fortn.
- Cobouw; dagblad voor de bouwwereld. d. ISSN 0010-0064
- Land and Water International; a Netherlands review on international hydraulic and agricultural engineering. q.
- Land en Water; maandelijks vakblad voor wegenbouwkunde, waterbouwkunde en cultuurtechniek, overkoepelend orgaan van de waterstaat. m. ISSN 0023-7582
- Machinepark. m.
- Renovatie en Onderhoud; maandblad voor stadsvernieuwing, vernieuwbouw, bedrijfsrenovatie, onderhoud en beheer. m.

**The Hague. Afdeling Voorlichting**
City Hall, Burg. de Monchyplein 12, The Hague, Netherlands.
- Den Haag. m.

**Hague Conference on Private International Law. Permanent Bureau**
Javastraat 2C, The Hague, Netherlands.
- Hague Conference on Private International Law. Actes et Documents. quadrennial since 1951; 1972, 12th. ISSN 0072-9272

**Hand Vol Pluis**
Morsestraat 24, The Hague, Netherlands.
- Hand Vol Pluis. ISSN 0017-7148

**B.V. de Handelsdrukkerij van 1874**
Celsiusweg 37, Box 340, Leeuwarden, Netherlands.
- Eisma's Schildersblad; algemeen vakblad voor het schildersbedrijf. w. ISSN 0013-287X
- Silk Screen; Nederlands vaktijdschrift voor zeefdruk. m. ISSN 0037-5268

**W. P. P. Hartman**
Rembrandtkade 260, Rijswijk (Z. H.), Netherlands.
- Koninklijke Officiers Schermbond. Kos-Gebeuren. ISSN 0047-3561

**Havenloods**
Prins Hendrikkade 14, Rotterdam-3001, Netherlands.
- Havenloods. s-w. ISSN 0017-8519

**G. en W. Heijboer, Ed. & Pub.**
Postbus 5, Sint-Annaland, Netherlands.
- Eendrachtbode. w. ISSN 0013-211X

**Firma J. Heijnis Tsz**
Lagedijk 158, Zaandijk, Netherlands.
- Norte; revista hispanica de Amsterdam. m. ISSN 0029-2354

**Helpt Elkander**
Timmermanslaan 2, P.O.B. 103, Maarssen, Netherlands.
- Onze Taak. bi-m.

**Hemelspleet**
Bilderdijkstraat 45a, Rotterdam, Netherlands.
- Hemelspleet; literair - filosofisch tijdschrift in Nederland. m. ISSN 0046-7227

**Henry Dunant Institute**
- Henry Dunant Institute. Scientific Collection. (pub. by A.W. Sijthoff International Publishing Co.)

**Hervormd Opleidingscentrum**
Hoofdstraat 88, Box 28, Driebergen, Netherlands.
- Nieuw Ruimzicht. m. ISSN 0028-9841

**Hervormde Bond voor Inwendige Zending**
Johan van Oldenbarneveltlaan 10, Amersfoort, Netherlands.
- Echo; Hervormd blad. 16 per yr. ISSN 0012-9119

**Hervormde Gemeente Arnhem**
- Hervormd Arnhem. (pub. by Drukkerij J.C. Willemsen)

**Hervormde Gemeente, Hoenderloo**
Hervormde Pastorie, Heldringseweg 8, Hoenderloo, Netherlands.
- Wegwijzer; maandblad voor Hoenderloo. m. ISSN 0043-2105

**Hervormde Gemeente Kerkelijk Bureau**
Markt 17, Wageningen, Netherlands.
- Hervormd Wageningen. fortn. ISSN 0018-0947

**Hervormde Jeugdraad**
Postbus 114, Driebergen, Netherlands.
- M.3. (Materiaal, Metodiek, Mededelingen) 9 per yr.

**Hervormde Vereniging**
A. Paulownastraat 38, Dordrecht, Netherlands.
- Calvijn. m. ISSN 0008-1787

**Hilversum. Bureau voor Sociaal-Wetenschappelijk Onderzoek**
Oude Enghweg 7, Hilversum, Netherlands.
- Statistisch Kwartaaloverzicht Hilversum. q. ISSN 0028-291X

**G. W. Hissink and Co.**
Postbox 806, Amsterdam 1000, Netherlands.
- Scripta Artis Monographia. irreg. ISSN 0080-8350

**Van der Hoeven Foundation for Theoretical Biology**
*see* **Prof. Dr. Jan van der Hoeven Foundation for Theoretical Biology**

**Hofstad Vakpers B.V.**
Box 5303, The Hague, Netherlands.
- Bouwbestek. m.
- Coiffure. m.
- Constructeur. m. ISSN 0010-6658
- Gieterij. m. ISSN 0016-982X
- Hotelrevue. m. ISSN 0010-6666
- Raadgevend-Ingenieur. m. ISSN 0033-7226

**Hoger Katechetisch Instituut, Nijmegen**
Oranjesingel 2, Nijmegen, Netherlands.
- School en Godsdienst; catechetical periodical for elementary school teachers. m. ISSN 0036-6544 (Centraal Bureau voor het Katholiek Onderwijs)

**Hogeschool te Tilburg. Instituut voor Arbeidsvraagstukken**
Hogeschoollaan 225, Tilburg, Netherlands.
- Sociale Wetenschappen. q. ISSN 0037-8097

**Hogeschool te Tilburg. John F. Kennedy Institute**
- John F. Kennedy Institute Series: a Collection of Studies Relating to International Economics. (pub. by A. W. Sijthoff International Publishing Co.)

**Holec NV**
Box 62, Steenbakkersweg 25, Hengelo (O), Netherlands.
- Holecpost. 6 per yr. ISSN 0037-7295
- Holecpost (English Edition) 2 per yr.

**Holland University Press**
*see* **APA-Holland University Press**

**Hollands Diep**
Van Eeghenstraat 66, Amsterdam, Netherlands.
- Hollands Diep. s-m.

**Hollandsche Molen**
Reguliersgracht 9, Amsterdam, Netherlands.
- Molennieuws/Mill-News. q. ISSN 0026-8992

**Honeywell B.V.**
Rijswijkstraat 175, 1062 EV Amsterdam, Netherlands.
- Honeywell Instrumentatie Nieuws. q. ISSN 0020-4358
- Micro Tips. 6 per yr. ISSN 0026-2560
- Regelrecht. bi-m. ISSN 0034-3218

**Hoofdbedrijfschap Ambachten**
Badhuisweg 108, The Hague, Netherlands.
- Kroniek van het Ambacht/Klein- en Middenbedrijf. bi-m. ISSN 0023-4907

**Hoofdproduktschap voor Akkerbouwprodukten**
Stadhoudersplantsoen 12, The Hague, Netherlands.
- Persoverzicht. fortn. ISSN 0031-5869

**De Horstink**
Box 400, 3800 AK Amersfoort, Netherlands.
- Archief van de Kerken. fortn. ISSN 0022-9342
- Nederlands Bibliotheek en Lektuurcentrum. Index. 6 per yr.

**Huguenot Society of Utrecht**
- Lien Wallon. (pub. by Eska Tijdschriften B.V.)

**N. V. Uitgeverij "Het Huis van Linnaeus"**
Amstel 157, Amsterdam, Netherlands.
- Onze Eigen Tuin. q. ISSN 0030-3194

**Humanistisch Verbond**
Postbus 114, Utrecht, Netherlands.
- Humanist. fortn. ISSN 0025-9489
- Rekenschap; tijdschrift voor wetenschap en cultuur. q. ISSN 0034-3749 (Humanistische Stichting Socrates)

**Humanistische Stichting Socrates**
- Rekenschap. (pub. by Humanistisch Verbond)

**I B M Nederland N.V.**
Johan Huizingalaan 257, P.O. Box 9999, Amsterdam, Netherlands.
- I B M Monitor. q.

**I H C Holland**
Marconistraat 2, Box 6141, Rotterdam, Netherlands.
- Ports and Dredging & Oil Report. q. ISSN 0477-6801

**IG-TNO Research Institute for Environmental Hygiene**
Box 214, Schoemakerstraat 97, Delft, Netherlands.
- IG-TNO Research Institute for Environmental Hygiene. Annual Report. a.

**In Search**
Catsheuvel 6, Suite 101, The Hague, Netherlands.
- In Search; in search of a relevant progressivism. s-m.

**Industriebond NKV**
Postbus 8256, Utrecht, Netherlands.
- Industrie Revu. fortn.

**Industriebond NVV**
Postbus 8107, Amsterdam, Netherlands.
- Actie. w. (Cosponsor: Industriebond NKV)
- W I K. (Wekelijkse Industrie Krant) w.

**Industriele Maatschappij- Genaamd Oranje-Nassau Mijnen B. V.**
Kloosterweg 1, Heerlen, Netherlands.
- Oranje-Nassau Post. m. ISSN 0030-4328

**Institute for Atomic Sciences in Agriculture**
Keyenbergseweg 6, Postbus 48, Wageningen, Netherlands.
- Association Euratom-Ital. Annual Report. a. ISSN 0066-9040

**Institute for Land and Water Management Research**
*see* **Instituut voor Cultuurtechniek en Waterhuishouding**

**Institute for Phytopathological Research**
*see* **Instituut voor Plantenziektenkundig Onderzoek**

**Institute of Social Studies, The Hague**
- Institute of Social Studies, The Hague. Publications. Paperback Series. (pub. by Mouton Publishers)
- Institute of Social Studies, The Hague. Publications. Series Major. (pub. by Mouton Publishers)

**Institute of the Science of the Press**
- Gazette. (pub. by Kluwer B.V.)

**Institutum Judaicum Delitzschianum**
- Theokratia; Jahrbuch des Institutum Judaicum Delitzschianum. (pub. by E. J. Brill)

**Instituut Schoevers B.V.**
Cornelis de Wittlaan 17, The Hague, Netherlands.
- Schoevers Koerier. q. ISSN 0036-6315

**Instituut voor Byzantijnse en Oecumenische Studies te Nijmegen**
Louiseweg 12, Nijmegen, Netherlands.
- Christelijk Oosten. q. ISSN 0009-5141

**Instituut voor Cultuurtechniek en Waterhuishouding**
P.O. Box 35, Wageningen, Netherlands.
- Instituut voor Cultuurtechniek en Waterhuishouding. Mededeling. irreg., no. 153, 1976. ISSN 0074-0411
- Instituut voor Cultuurtechniek en Waterhuishouding. Technical Bulletin/Institute for Land and Water Management Research. Technical Bulletin. irreg., no. 101, 1976. ISSN 0074-042X
- Instituut voor Cultuurtechniek en Waterhuishouding. Verspreide Overdrukken/ Institute for Land and Water Management Research. Miscellaneous Reprints. irreg., no. 192, 1976. ISSN 0074-0438

**Instituut voor de Veredeling van Tuinbouwgewassen**
Box 16, Wageningen, Netherlands.
- Instituut voor de Veredeling van Tuinbouwgewassen. Mededelingen/I. V. T. Mededelingen. irreg. ISSN 0020-4250

**Instituut voor Doven**
St. Michielsgestel, Netherlands.
- Vriend. m. ISSN 0042-9139

**Instituut voor Grafische Techniek TNO**
Box 4150, Amsterdam, Netherlands.
- Grafische Literatuur Centrale. m. ISSN 0017-2952
- I G T - Nieuws. bi-m. ISSN 0018-9790

**Instituut voor Kernphysisch Onderzoek**
Amsterdam, Netherlands.
- Instituut voor Kernphysisch Onderzoek. Progress Report. a.

**Instituut voor Landbouwcooperatie in Friesland**
Langemarktstraat 14, Postbus 710, Leeuwarden, Netherlands.
- Bolwerk; maandblad voor de boer. 9 per yr. ISSN 0006-6958

**Instituut voor Nederlandse Lexicologie**
Afdeling Thesaurus, Plantsoen 41-43-45, Box 132, Leiden, Netherlands.
- Informatie Nederlandse Lexikologie. irreg.

**Instituut voor Plantenziektenkundig Onderzoek**
P.O. Box 42, Wageningen, Netherlands.
- Instituut voor Plantenziektenkundig Onderzoek. Jaarverslag. a. ISSN 0074-0446
- Instituut voor Plantenziektenkundig Onderzoek. Mededeling/Institute of Phytopathological Research. Communications. irreg., no. 670, 1974. ISSN 0019-0349

**Instituut voor Pluimveeonderzoek "Het Spelderholt"**
Spelderholt 9, Beekbergen, Netherlands.
- Uit de Pluimveepers. m. ISSN 0041-5863

**Instituut voor Veevoedingsonderzoek "Hoorn"**
Runderweg 2, Lelystad, Netherlands.
- Instituut voor Veevoedingsonderzoek "Hoorn". Jaarverslag. a. ISSN 0074-0489

**Uitgeverij Intermediair B.V.**
Box 3434, Keizersgracht 391, Amsterdam-C, Netherlands.
- Intermediair. w. ISSN 0020-5605

**International Academy of the History of Medicine**
- Clio Medica. (pub. by N.V. Boekhandel en Antiquariaat B.M. Israel B.V.)

**International Actuarial Association. Astin Section**
- Astin Bulletin. (pub. by E. J. Brill)

**International Agricultural Aviation Congress**
- International Agricultural Aviation Congress. Report. (pub. by P U D O C)

**International Agricultural Centre**
P.O. Box 88, Wageningen 6140, Netherlands.
- Agricultural Science in the Netherlands. triennial.

**International Association for Child Psychiatry and Allied Professions**
- International Congress for Child Psychiatry. Proceedings. (pub. by Excerpta Medica)

**International Association for Dutch Studies**
- Dutch Studies. (pub. by Martinus Nijhoff)

**International Association for Ecology**
- Agro-Ecosystems. (pub. by Elsevier Scientific Publishing Co.)
- Oecologia. (pub. by Springer-Verlag US)
- Urban Ecology. (pub. by Elsevier Scientific Publishing Co.)

**International Association for Hydraulic Research**
Rotterdamseweg 185, P.O. Box 177, Delft, Netherlands.
- International Association for Hydraulic Research. Congress Proceedings. irreg., 16th, 1975, sao paulo. ISSN 0074-1477
- Journal of Hydraulic Research. q. ISSN 0022-1686

**International Association for Life Saving and First Aid to the Injured**
Statenlaan 81, The Hague, Netherlands.
- Interrescue Information. 3-4 per yr.

**International Association for Patristic Studies**
- Association Internationale d'Etudes Patristiques. Bulletin d'Information et de Liaison. (pub. by North Holland Publishing Co.)

**International Association for Plant Taxonomy**
- Index to Plant Chromosome Numbers. (pub. by Bohn, Scheltema en Holkema)
- Regnum Vegetabile. (pub. by Bohn, Scheltema en Holkema)

**International Association for Plant Taxonomy. International Bureau for Plant Taxonomy and Nomenclature**
Tweede Transitorium, Kamer 1902, Uithof, Utrecht, Netherlands.
- Taxon. 6-9 per yr. ISSN 0040-0262

**International Association for Semiotic Studies**
- Semiotica. (pub. by Mouton Publishers)

**International Association for the History of Religions**
Churchill-laan 290 I, Amsterdam-Z, Netherlands.
- Numen; international review for the history of religions. 3 per yr. ISSN 0029-5973

**International Association for the Study of Pain**
- Pain. (pub. by Elsevier Scientific Publishing Co.)

**International Association of Agricultural Librarians and Documentalists**
Hullerpad 14, Lunteren 6160, Netherlands.
- International Association of Agricultural Librarians and Documentalists. Quarterly Bulletin. q. ISSN 0020-5966

**International Association of Allergology**
- International Congress of Allergology. Abstracts of Reports of Discussion and of Communications. (pub. by Excerpta Medica)

**International Association of Dredging Companies**
Duinweg 21, The Hague, Netherlands.
- Terra et Aqua. 2 per yr.

**International Association of Sound Archives**
Secretariat: Documentationcentre S.F.W., Hengeveldstraat 29, Utrecht, Netherlands.
- Phonographic Bulletin. irreg.

**International Astronomical Union**
- International Astronomical Union. Finding List for Observers of Eclipsing Variables. (pub. by University of Pennsylvania. Department of Astronomy US)
- International Astronomical Union. General Assembly. Proceedings. (pub. by D. Reidel Publishing Co.)
- International Astronomical Union. Proceedings of Symposia. (pub. by D. Reidel Publishing Co.)
- International Astronomical Union. Transactions and Highlights. (pub. by D. Reidel Publishing Co.)

**International Broadcasters Society**
Zwaluwlaan 78, Bussum, Netherlands.
- Broadcasters Bulletin. m. ISSN 0007-201X

**International Bureau of Fiscal Documentation**
Muiderpoort, Sarphatistraat 124, Amsterdam-C, Netherlands.
- African Tax Systems. q. updating service. (United Nations Economic Commission for Africa UN)

- Bulletin for International Fiscal Documentation. m. ISSN 0007-4624
- Corporate Taxation in Latin America. q. update service.
- European Taxation. m. ISSN 0014-3138
- Guide to European Taxation. Taxation of Companies in Europe. q updating service.
- Guide to European Taxation. Taxation of Patent Royalties, Dividends, Interest in Europe. s-a. updating service.
- Guide to European Taxation. Taxation of Private Investment in Europe. q. updating service.
- Guide to European Taxation. Value Added Taxation in Europe. q. updating service.
- Handbook on the U.S.-German Tax Convention. irreg.
- International Bureau of Fiscal Documentation. Annual Report. a. ISSN 0074-2104
- International Bureau of Fiscal Documentation. Publication. irreg., 1970, no. 22. ISSN 0074-2112
- International Fiscal Harmonization Series. irreg., no. 3, 1975.
- Selected Monographs on Taxation. irreg. (Co-sponsor: Harvard University Law School, Tax Program)
- Studies on Taxation and Economic Development. irreg., no. 3, 1973. ISSN 0071-2191
- Supplementary Service to European Taxation. m. updating service. ISSN 0039-5927
- Tax News Service. s-m. ISSN 0040-0076

**International Business Contacts**
Kl.Gartmanplantsoen 21, 7Th Floor, Box 5091, Amsterdam, Netherlands.
- International Business Contacts/I B C; international monthly for the promotion of world-wide foreign trade. m. ISSN 0020-627X

**International Centre for Local Credit**
Lange Vijverberg 10, The Hague, Netherlands
- Local Finance; international bimonthly journal. bi-m. ISSN 0020-6296 (U.S. and Canadian Subscr. to: Municipal Finance Officers Association, 1313 E. 60th St., Chicago IL 60637)

**International Cliff Richard Movement**
Box 4164, Amsterdam, Netherlands.
- Dynamite/International. bi-m. ISSN 0012-7418

**International Committee for Social Sciences Documentation**
- Confluence. Etats des Recherches en Sciences Sociales: Surveys of Research in the Social Sciences. (pub. by Mouton Publishers)

**International Conference of Human Genetics**
Herengracht 121, Amsterdam, Netherlands.
- International Conference of Human Genetics. (Rapports et des Communications) irreg; 1951 no. 2. ISSN 0534-8587

**International Council for Building Research, Studies and Documentation**
Weena 704, Box 20704, Rotterdam, Netherlands.
- Batiment International/Building Research and Practice. bi-m.
- C I B Directory of Building Research Information and Development Organizations. irreg., latest issue 1971. ISSN 0419-2281
- International Council for Building Research, Studies and Documentation. Congress Reports. triennial, latest issue 1977. ISSN 0074-428X

**International Council of Home Help Services**
c/o Dr. J. M. B. Scholten, Cornelis Houtmanstr. 21, Utrecht, Netherlands.
- International Council of Homehelp Services. Reports of Congress. every 3-4 yrs., 1975, 6th, Stockholm. ISSN 0074-4360

**International Court of Justice**
For publications of this agency see section for UNITED NATIONS

**International Diabetes Federation**
- International Diabetes Federation. Proceedings of Congress. (pub. by Excerpta Medica)

**International Federation for Documentation**
Hofweg 7, 2511 AA The Hague, Netherlands.
- Extensions and Corrections to the U D C. a. ISSN 0014-5424
- F I D Annual Report. a. ISSN 0074-5820
- F I D News Bulletin. m. ISSN 0014-5874
- F I D Publications Catalogue. a. ISSN 0538-7302
- F I D Yearbook. a. ISSN 0074-5839
- International Federation for Documentation. P-Notes. 30-40 per yr.

- International Federation for Documentation. Proceedings of Congress. irreg.; latest issue 1976. ISSN 0074-5812
- International Forum on Information and Documentation. q. ISSN 0304-9701
- Library, Documentation and Archives Serials. irreg., 4th ed., 1975.
- R & D Projects in Documentation and Librarianship. bi-m. ISSN 0301-4436

**International Federation for Documentation. Committee on Classification Research**
Hofweg 7, 2511 AA The Hague, Netherlands
- F I D/C R Newsletter. q. (Orders to: F I D/C R Secretariat, Indian Statistical Institute, Documentation and Training Centre, 112 Cross Road 11, Bangalore, India)
- F.I.D./C.R. Report Series. irreg; no. 14, 1974. ISSN 0074-5804 (Orders to: FID/CR Secretariat, c/o Indian Statistical Institute, Documentation Research and Training Centre, 112 Cross Rd. 11, Bangalore, India)

**International Federation for Documentation. Committee on Developing Countries**
Hofweg 7, 2511 AA The Hague, Netherlands
- F I D/D C News. 3 per yr. (Orders to: F I D/D C Secretariat, c/o IRANDOC, Box 11-1387, Teheran, Iran)
- F I D/D C Occasional Publications. irreg. (And Orszagos Mezogazdasagi Konyvtar es Dokumentacios Kozpont, Box 12, Budapest, Hungary)

**International Federation for Documentation. Committee on Education and Training**
Hofweg 7, 2511 AA The Hague, Netherlands.
- F I D/E T Occasional Papers. irreg., no. 2, 1975.

**International Federation for Documentation. Committee on Linguistics in Documentation**
Hofweg 7, 2511 AA the Hague, Netherlands
- Linguistics in Documentation; Current Abstracts. 3 per yr. ISSN 0075-9651 (Orders to: FID/LD Secretariat, Center for Applied Linguistics, 1611 N. Kent St., Arlington, VA 22209)

**International Federation for Documentation. Committee on Research on the Theoretical Basis of Information**
Hofweg 7, 2511 AA The Hague, Netherlands
- F I D/R I Series of Collected Articles. irreg., no. 4, 1976. (And Vsesoyuznyi Institut Nauchno-Tekhnicheskoi Informatsii, Ul. Baltiiskaya 14, Moscow, U.S.S.R.)

**International Federation for Housing and Planning**
Wassenaarseweg 43, The Hague, Netherlands.
- International Federation for Housing and Planning. News Sheet. 6 per yr.
- International Federation for Housing and Planning. Yearbook. irreg.
- P A /Planning and Administration. s-a.

**International Federation for Information Processing. Applied Information Processing Group**
Paulus Potterstraat 40, Amsterdam, Netherlands.
- I A G Communications. 6 per yr. ISSN 0538-7353

**International Federation of Automatic Control**
- I F A C Symposium on Multivariable Technical Control Systems. Proceedings. (pub. by North Holland Publishing Co.)

**International Federation of Cell Biology**
- International Congress of Cell Biology. Summaries of Reports and Communications. (pub. by Excerpta Medica)

**International Federation of Consulting Engineers**
Carel v. Bylandtlaan 9, The Hague, Netherlands.
- International Federation of Consulting Engineers. Annual Reports of F I D I C Member Associations. a. ISSN 0538-7396

**International Federation of Library Associations and Institutions**
Box 9128, Hague, Netherlands.
- I F L A Directory. a. ISSN 0074-6002
- International Federation of Library Association and Institutions. Progress Report. irreg.

**International Federation of Operational Research Societies**
- International Abstracts in Operations Research. (pub. by North-Holland Publishing Co.)

**International Federation of Pedestrians**
Passage 61 III, The Hague, Netherlands.
- Voice of the Pedestrian. s-a.

**International Federation of Physical Medicine and Rehabilitation**
- International Congress of Physical Medicine. Abstracts of Papers Presented. (pub. by Excerpta Medica)

**International Fiscal Association**
c/o General Secretariat, P.O. Box 1738, Burg. Oudlaan 50, Rotterdam 3016, Netherlands.
- International Fiscal Association. Yearbook. a.

**International Friendship League**
Nederlandlaan 1, Heerlen, Netherlands.
- I. F. L. Nieuws. 12 per yr. ISSN 0018-9707

**International Humanist and Ethical Union**
Oudegracht 152, Utrecht, Netherlands.
- International Humanism. q. ISSN 0020-692X
- International Humanist and Ethical Union. Proceedings of the Congress. irreg.; 6th Amsterdam, 1974. ISSN 0074-6258

**International Institute for Aerial Survey and Earth Sciences**
Box 6, Enschede, Netherlands.
- I T C Information Booklets. irreg. ISSN 0536-2113
- I T C Journal. q.
- I T C - Publications. Series A (Photogrammetry) (International Training Centre for Aerial Survey) irreg.; latest issue, 1974. ISSN 0074-915X
- Symposium on Integrated Surveys of Environment. Proceedings. a. ISSN 0080-8830

**International Institute for Human Rights**
- Teneat Lex Gladium. (pub. by A. W. Sijthoff International Publishing Co.)

**International Institute for Land Reclamation and Improvement**
P.O. Box 45, Wageningen, Netherlands.
- International Institute for Land Reclamation and Improvement. Annual Report. a. ISSN 0074-6428
- International Institute for Land Reclamation and Improvement. Bibliography. irreg. ISSN 0074-6436
- International Institute for Land Reclamation and Improvement. Bulletin. irreg. ISSN 0074-6444
- International Institute for Land Reclamation and Improvement. Publication. irreg. ISSN 0074-6452

**International Institute for Social History**
Herengracht 262-266, Amsterdam, Netherlands.
- Archives Bakounine/Bakunin- Archiv. (pub. by E. J. Brill)
- International Institute for Social History. Annual Report. a.
- International Review of Social History. (pub. by Van Gorcum)
- Publications on Social History. (pub. by Van Gorcum)
- Quellen und Untersuchungen zur Geschichte der Deutschen und Oesterreichischen Arbeiterbewegung. Neue Folge. (pub. by Mouton Publishers)
- Russian Series on Social History. (pub. by D. Reidel Publishing Co.)
- Sociaal-Historische Studien. (pub. by Van Gorcum)

**International League of Antiquarian Booksellers**
Zuideinde 40, Nieuwkoop 2479, Netherlands.
- International Directory of Antiquarian Booksellers/Repertoire International de la Librairie Ancienne. irreg. ISSN 0538-7159

**International Marketing Federation**
c/o Arnold F. van Goch, Secretary-General, Parkstraat 18, The Hague, Netherlands.
- Asian and Pacific Marketing Conference. Proceedings. irreg. ISSN 0066-8346

**International News, Photo, Correspondence & Hobby Club**
Box 7, Badhoevedorp 1132, Netherlands.
- Newsseeker. a. ISSN 0028-9582 (Tie of Friendship)

**International Organization for the Study of the Old Testament**
- International Organization for the Study of the Old Testament. Proceedings of the International Congress. (pub. by E. J. Brill)

- Vetus Testamentum. (pub. by E. J. Brill)
- Vetus Testamentum. Supplements. (pub. by E. J. Brill)

**International Organization of Consumers Unions**
Emmastraat 9, The Hague, Netherlands.
- Consumer Directory. biennial. ISSN 0069-9284
- Consumer Review. q.
- International Consumer. irreg (approx. a) ISSN 0020-6431
- International Organization of Consumers Unions. Proceedings. irreg., 8th 1975, Sydney. ISSN 0538-8988

**International Ornithological Congress**
- International Ornithological Congress. Proceedings. (pub. by E. J. Brill)

**International Pharmaceutical Federation**
Alexanderstraat 11, The Hague, Netherlands
- International Congress of Pharmaceutical Sciences. Proceedings. s-a, 35th, 1975, Rome. ISSN 0074-3879 (Orders to: Elsevier Scientific Publishing Co., Box 211, Amsterdam, Netherlands)

**International Pharmaceutical Students Federation**
Oudegracht 141 Bis, Utrecht, Netherlands.
- I P S F News Bulletin. q. ISSN 0019-039X

**International Social Science Council**
- International Social Science Council. Publications. (pub. by Mouton Publishers)
- Social Sciences Information/Information sur les Sciences Sociales. (pub. by Mouton Publishers)

**International Society for Animal Blood Group Research**
- Animal Blood Groups and Biochemical Genetics. (pub. by Centre for Agricultural Publishing and Documentation)

**International Society for Burn Injuries**
- International Symposium on Pharmacological Treatment in Burns. Proceedings. (pub. by Excerpta Medica)

**International Society for Horticultural Science**
C/O Dr. G. de Bakker, Bezuidenhoutseweg 73, The Hague, Netherlands.
- International Horticultural Congress. Proceedings. quadrennial; 19th Warsaw, 1974. ISSN 0074-6231
- Scientia Horticulturae. (pub. by Elsevier Scientific Publishing Co.)

**International Society for Photogrammetry**
- Photogrammetria. (pub. by Elsevier Scientific Publishing Co.)

**International Society for the Study of Significs**
- Methodology and Science. (pub. by Esser Scientific Press)

**International Society of Biometeorology**
Inquire: Dr. S. W. Tromp. Sec. Gen., Hofbrouckerlaan 54, Oegstqueest, Leiden, Netherlands.
- Biometeorology; Proceedings. (pub. by Swets en Zeitlinger B. V.)
- International Biometeorological Congress. Summaries and Reports Presented to the Congress. triennial, 1975, 6th, College Park, MD, U.S.A. ISSN 0074-2082
- International Journal of Biometeorology. (pub. by Swets en Zeitlinger B. V.)
- International Journal of Speleology. (pub. by Swets en Zeitlinger B. V.)

**International Society of Endocrinology**
- International Congress of Endocrinology. Proceedings. (pub. by Excerpta Medica)

**International Statistical Institute**
Prinses Beatrixlaan 428, Voorburg, Netherlands.
- International Association for Statistics in Physical Sciences. Proceedings (of Meetings) biennial. ISSN 0074-1507
- International Statistical Institute. Bulletin. Proceedings of the Biennial Sessions. biennial, 40th, 1975, warsaw. ISSN 0074-8609
- International Statistical Yearbook of Large Towns/Annuaire de Statistique Internationale des Grandes Villes. biennial. ISSN 0074-8617
- World Fertility Survey. Basic Documentation. irreg. (6-8 per yr)
- World Fertility Survey. Occasional Papers. irreg.
- World Fertility Survey. Report. irreg.
- World Fertility Survey. Scientific Reports. irreg.

**International Textiles BV**
Overschiestraat 170, Box 9111, Amsterdam 17, Netherlands.
- Fashion Flash. bi-w.
- International Textiles. m. ISSN 0020-8914
- International Textiles Interior. 3 per yr. ISSN 0020-8922
- Sir; men's international fashion and textile trade journal. q. ISSN 0037-5845
- Textiel-Visie: Damesmodevakblad. q. ISSN 0011-5924 (Stichting Mitex)
- Textiel-Visie: Herenmodevakblad. q. (Stichting Mitex)
- Textiel-Visie: Kindermodevakblad. q. ISSN 0023-1525 (Stichting Mitex)
- Textiel-Visie: Lingerie en Foundations. q. (Stichting Mitex)
- Textiel-Visie/Weekly; general textile trade journal. w. ISSN 0040-4810 (Stichting Mitex)

**International Translations Centre**
Doelenstraat 101, Delft, Netherlands.
- Translation News. irreg. ISSN 0046-2837
- World Index of Scientific Translations and List of Translations Notified to the International Translations Centre. m.(8 per yr. plus quarterly and annual cumulations) ISSN 0376-6381

**International Union of Biochemistry**
- Trends in Biochemical Sciences. (pub. by Elsevier Scientific Publishing Co.)

**International Union of Biological Sciences**
Publications Office, Tweede Transitorium, Withof, Utrecht, Netherlands.
- International Union of Biological Sciences. Reports of General Assemblies. irreg., 1970, 17th, Washington, D.C. ISSN 0074-9362

**International Union of Crystallography**
- International Union of Crystallography. Structure Reports. (pub. by Bohn, Scheltema en Holkema)
- Molecular Structures and Dimensions. (pub. by Bohn, Scheltema en Holkema)

**International Union of Geological Sciences**
Secretary General, Box 379, Haarlem, Netherlands.
- International Union of Geological Sciences. Geological Newsletter. q. ISSN 0047-1267

**International Union of Local Authorities**
Wassenaarseweg 45, The Hague-2018, Netherlands.
- Bibliographia I U L A- I F H P; new publications in the library. bi-m. ISSN 0006-1182 (Co-Sponsor: International Federation for Housing and Planning)
- I U L A (Publication) irreg. ISSN 0539-1083
- I U L A Newsletter/I U L A Nouvelles/I U L A Nachrichten. m. ISSN 0019-087X
- International Union of Local Authorities. Reports of Congress. irreg.; 20th, vienna, 1971. ISSN 0074-9443
- Planning & Administration. s-a.
- Renewal of Town and Village. irreg. ISSN 0486-3887

**Internationale Gemeenschap van Christenen**
Drakenstein 39, Amsterdam, Netherlands.
- Oorspronkelijk Christendom. m. ISSN 0030-3267

**Internationale Gesellschaft fuer Orientforschung**
- Oriens. (pub. by E. J. Brill)

**Internationale School voor Wijsbegeerte**
- Amersfoortse Stemmen. (pub. by Van Gorcum)

**Internationale Uitlotingsdienst**
Beursstraat 31, Amsterdam C, Netherlands.
- Uitlotings-Archief. d. ISSN 0041-5936

**Internationale Vereinigung Beratender Ingenieure**
*see* **International Federation of Consulting Engineers**

**Internationale Vereniging Bellamy**
- Bellamy - Nieuws. (pub. by Stichting Centrale Administratie Bellamy)

**Internationale Vereniging voor Nederlandistiek**
- Neerlandica Extra Muros. (pub. by Van Gorcum)

**Interuniversitair Centrum voor Studie en Documentatie van Latijns Amerika**
Nieuwe Doelenstraat 16, Amsterdam (C), Netherlands.
- Boletin de Estudios Latinoamericanos y del Caribe. s-a.

**Intramurale Gezondheidszorg**
Romeostr. 64, Amersfoort, Netherlands.
- Intramurale Gezondheidszorg. m.

**N. Israel**
Keizersgracht 526, Amsterdam C, Netherlands.
- Bibliotheca Australiana. irreg., 1967, no. 11. ISSN 0067-7876
- Terrae Incognitae. a. ISSN 0082-2884 (Society for the History of Discoveries)

**N.V. Boekhandel en Antiquariaat B.M. Israel B.V.**
N.Z. Voorburgwal 264, Amsterdam-C, Netherlands.
- Clio Medica. q. ISSN 0045-7183 (International Academy of the History of Medicine)

**JALA Internationaal B.V.**
H. van Borsselenkade 19, Amstelveen, Netherlands.
- Gereedschap. m. ISSN 0016-8602

**Jhr. Mr. A. F. de Savornin Lohman Stichting**
Wassenaarseweg 7, The Hague, Netherlands.
- Christelijk-Historisch Tijdschrift. 6 per yr. ISSN 0009-5133

**Joachimsthal Publishers**
Box 2238, Utrecht, Netherlands.
- Bibliographia Musicologica; a bibliography of musical literature. a. ISSN 0084-7844

**Johanna Stichting Revalidatie Centrum**
- Vrienden Kring. (pub. by N. V. Uitgeversmaatschappij de Graafschap)

**Dr. W. Junk B. V. Publishers**
Box 3713, The Hague, Netherlands.
- Biogeographica. irreg., vol. 8, 1977.
- Documenta Ophthalmologica; advances in ophthalmology. 3-4 per yr. (2 vols.) ISSN 0012-4486
- Documenta Ophthalmologica Proceedings Series. irreg., vol. 12, 1977.
- Environmental Biology of Fishes. 3 per yr.
- Genetica; Netherlands journal of genetics. 3 per yr. ISSN 0016-6707
- Hydrobiologia. 5 per yr. ISSN 0018-8158
- Iconographia Mycologica. irreg., vols. 40-41, 1977. ISSN 0073-4411
- Molecular and Cellular Biochemistry; acta biocatalytica. 12 per yr. ISSN 0300-8177
- Monographiae Biologicae. irreg., nos. 29-30, 1976. ISSN 0077-0639
- Mycopathologia. 9 per yr. (in 3 vols.)
- Photosynthesis Bibliography. a.
- Qualitas Plantarum/Plant Food for Human Nutrition. 4 per yr. (Confederatio Internationalis Ad Qualitates Plantarum Edulium Perquirendas (CIQ)) (Co-Sponsors: Deutsche Gesellschaft fuer Qualitaetsforschung (DGQ); Vegetary Nutritional Research Center)
- Series Entomologica. irreg., vol. 13, 1977. ISSN 0080-8954
- Vegetatio; international review of plant-sociology, ecology and plant-geography. 6 per yr. (2 vols.) ISSN 0042-3106

**Drukkerij Juten**
Parade 17, S-Hertogenbosch, Netherlands.
- Brabantse Leeuw. bi-m. ISSN 0006-8632 (Provinciaal Genootschap van Kunsten en Wetenschappen in Noord-Brabant)

**K E M A**
- Elektrotechniek. (pub. by N.V. Noord Nederlandse Drukkerij)

**K L M Royal Dutch Airlines**
Box 7700, Schiphol Airport 1148, Netherlands.
- K L M Literatuuroverzicht. m. ISSN 0022-7366 (prep. by its Information and Documentation Department)
- K L M News. 3 per m. ISSN 0022-7374 (prep. by its Public Relations Bureau)
- Literatuurinformatie Personeelsaangelegenheden. fortn.
- Wolkenridder. fortn. ISSN 0043-7212

**Kamer van Koophandel Nederland-Israel**
Spui 3, Box 10, The Hague, Netherlands.
- Nederland-Israel. bi-m. ISSN 0028-2014

**Kamerlingh Onnes Laboratory**
Universiteit van Leiden, Nieuwsteg. 18, Leiden, Netherlands.
- Kamerlingh Onnes Laboratory. Communications. irreg(about 7 nos. each yr.) ISSN 0022-8141

**B. V. Erven B. van der Kamp**
St. Jansstraat 1-3, Groningen, Netherlands.
- Nederlands Archievenblad. 4 per yr. ISSN 0028-2049 (Vereniging van Archivarissen in Netherland)

**Kantoor-School-Huis**
Waldecklaan 41, Hilversum, Netherlands.
- Kantoor-School-Huis; voorlichtingsblad voor gebruikers van kantoorartikelen. bi-m. ISSN 0022-8907

**Karmel**
Bloemgracht 90, Amsterdam C, Netherlands (Subscr. Address: Karmel, Rijksweg N. 35, Geleen, Netherlands)
- Tegenwoordig. bi-m. ISSN 0040-2133

**Katholiek Documentatie Centrum**
Erasmuslaan 36, Nijmengen, Netherlands.
- Katholiek Documentatie Centrum. Jaarboek. a.

**Katholiek Onderwijs Verbond**
- Katholieke Kleuterschool. (pub. by Thom. F. Wolfs)

**Katholieke Artsenvereniging**
- Metamedica. (pub. by Samsom Uitgeverij B.V.)

**Katholieke Nederlandse Boeren- en Tuindersbond**
Scheveningseweg 46, The Hague, Netherlands.
- Boer en Tuinder. w. ISSN 0006-5609

**Katholieke Vereniging van Directies, Docenten en Consulten bij het Beroepsonderwijs en het Leerlingwezen**
Stationsweg 56, The Hague, Netherlands.
- Sint Bernardus; blad voor school en beroep. 3 per mo. ISSN 0005-9390

**Katholieke Vereniging van Leerkrachten in de Lichamelijke Oefening "St. Thomas van Aquino"**
Willem van Oranjelaan 33, S-Hertogenbosch, Netherlands.
- Thomas; maandblad voor lichamelijke opvoeding. m. ISSN 0049-3805

**Kellogg Continental B. V.**
De Boelelaan 589, Amsterdam, Netherlands.
- Doorkijk. fortn. ISSN 0012-5482

**Kerk en Vrede**
Utrechtseweg 159, Amersfoort, Netherlands.
- Militia Christi. m. ISSN 0026-4156

**Kerkeraad Hervormde Gemeente**
Marktstraat 13, Musselkanaal, Netherlands.
- Hervormde Gemeente Musselkanaal. Kerkblad. m. ISSN 0018-0955

**Kern Institute**
Eerste Binnenvestgracht 33, Leiden, Netherlands.
- Annual Bibliography of Indian Archaeology. irreg., 1972, vol. 21. ISSN 0066-3794

**Kijk op het Noorden**
Engelandlaan 160, Haarlem, Netherlands.
- Kijk op het Noorden/Outlook on the North; signalement van de economische ontwikkeling in de provincies Groningen, Friesland en Drente. q. ISSN 0023-1363

**Kluwer B.V.**
Box 23, Deventer, Netherlands.
- Abstracts on Criminology and Penology. bi-m. ISSN 0001-3684 (Criminologica Foundation)
- Abstracts on Police Science. bi-m. ISSN 0301-0112 (Criminologica Foundation)
- Accountant-Adviseur. m except July and August. (Nederlandse Orde van Accountants-Administratieconsulenten)
- Air Law. q.
- Autotechnisch Tijdschrift. m. ISSN 0005-1764 (Olyslager Organisation)
- Bedrijfskunde; tijdschrift voor modern management. q.
- Data Juridica. m.
- Gazette; international journal for mass communication studies. q. ISSN 0016-5492 (Institute of the Science of the Press)
- In- en Uitvoer Nieuws. m. ISSN 0019-3178
- Intertax. 8-10 per yr. (Co-publisher: Wilhelm Stollfuss Verlag (Bonn, W. Germany))
- Intertax (Dutch Edition) q.
- Legal Issues. s-a. (Universiteit van Amsterdam. Europa Instituut)
- Nederlands Tijdschift voor Gerontologie. q.
- Nederlandse Vereniging voor Internationaal Recht. Mededelingen. biennial. ISSN 0077-6440

- Open; vaktijdschrift voor bibliothecarissen, literatuuronderzoekers bedrijfsarchivarissen en documentalisten. m. ISSN 0030-3372
- Openbare Uitgaven; zin en omvang van de overheidsuitgaven. q. ISSN 0030-3488
- Radio Electronica. s-m. ISSN 0033-7854
- Sociaal-en Arbeidsrechtelijke Reeks. irreg.
- T.V.V.S. Maandblad voor Ondernemingsrecht. m.
- Toon en Beeld. m. ISSN 0005-495X
- U. T. C. (Uitspraken van de Tariefcommissie) 5 per yr. ISSN 0041-5588 (Netherlands. Tariefcommissie) (Co-publisher: Samsom Uitgeverij B. V.)
- Vakstudie Nieuws; dokumentatie op het gebied van het fiscaal recht. fortn. ISSN 0042-2258
- Weekblad voor Fiscaal Recht. w. ISSN 0043-1796

**Kluwer Schoolboeken B.V.**
Industrieweg 1, Culemborg, Netherlands.
- Attentie; voor opvallende toestanden en gebeurtenissen in de samenleving. m.

**Uitgeverij Frits Knuf B. V.**
Postbox 20, Buren 2707, Netherlands.
- Organ Yearbook; a journal for the players and historians of keyboard instruments. a. ISSN 0078-6098

**Drukkerij t Koggeschip B.V.**
Postbus 1198, Amsterdam, Netherlands.
- Heemschut. m. ISSN 0017-9515 (Bond Heemschut)

**J. H. Kok B. V.**
Oudestraat 5-11, Kampen, Netherlands.
- Anti-Revolutionaire Staatkunde. m. ISSN 0003-5602 (Dr. Abrahram Kuyperstichting ter Bevordering van de Studie der Antirevolutionaire Beginselen)
- Gereformeerd Theologisch Tijdschrift. q. ISSN 0016-8610 (Subscr. to: Ds. S. van Bekkum, Sportlaan 211, The Hague 7, Netherlands)
- Philosophia Reformata. q. ISSN 0031-8035 (Vereniging voor Calvinistische Wijsbegeerte)

**Kompass Nederland N.V.**
Van Stolkweg 6, The Hague, Netherlands.
- Kompass Holland; informatiewerk over het Nederlandse Bedrijfsleven. a. ISSN 0075-6660 (Foundation for Promoting International Economic Information SZ)

**Koninklijk Genootschap voor Landbouwwetenschap**
Postbus 79, Wageningen, Netherlands.
- Netherlands Journal of Agricultural Science. q. ISSN 0028-2928
- Plant and Soil. (pub. by Martinus Nijhoff)

**Koninklijk Instituut voor de Tropen**
Mauritskade 63, Amsterdam, Netherlands.
- Abstracts on Tropical Agriculture. m. (prep. by its Afdeling Agrarisch Onderzoek)
- Koninklijk Instituut voor de Tropen. Afdeling Agrarisch Onderzoek. Bulletin. irreg.
- Koninklijk Instituut voor de Tropen. Afdeling Agrarisch Onderzoek. Communication. irreg.
- Koninklijk Instituut voor de Tropen. Afdeling Agrarisch Onderzoek. Landendocumentatie. 7 per yr. ISSN 0023-7841 (prep. by its Afdeling Agrarisch Onderzoek)
- Selected Studies on Indonesia. (pub. by Mouton Publishers)

**Koninklijk Instituut voor Taal-, Land- en Volkenkunde**
- Bibliotheca Indonesica. (pub. by Martinus Nijhoff)
- Bijdragen tot de Taal-, Land- en Volkenkunde. (pub. by Martinus Nijhoff)
- Koninklijk Instituut voor Taal-, Land- en Volkenkunde. Bibliographical Series. (pub. by Martinus Nijhoff)
- Koninklijk Instituut voor Taal-, Land- en Volkenkunde. Translation Series. (pub. by Martinus Nijhoff)
- Koninklijk Instituut voor Taal-, Land- en Volkenkunde. Verhandelingen. (pub. by Martinus Nijhoff)

**Koninklijk Nederlands Aardrijkskundig Genootschap**
Mauritskade 63, Amsterdam, Netherlands.
- Geografisch Tijdschrift. 5 per yr. ISSN 0016-7215
- Tijdschrift voor Economische en Sociale Geografie/Netherlands Journal of Economic and Social Geography. (pub. by E. J. Brill)

**Koninklijk Nederlands Geologisch Mijnbouwkundig Genootschap**
Postbus 37, Wageningen, Netherlands.
- Geologie en Mijnbouw/Geology and Mining. (pub. by Princo B.V.)
- K. N. G. M. G. Nieuwsbrief. 8 per yr.
- Koninklijk Nederlands Geologisch Mijnbouwkundig Genootschap. Verhandelingen. irreg., no. 31, 1974. ISSN 0075-6741

**Koninklijk Nederlands Korfbal Verbond**
Postbus 1000, Zeist, Netherlands.
- Nederlands Korfbalblad. fortn. ISSN 0028-2073

**Koninklijk Nederlandsch Genootschap voor Geslacht- en Wapenkunde**
Bleijenburg 5, The Hague, Netherlands.
- Nederlandsche Leeuw. m. ISSN 0028-226X

**Koninklijk Technicum PBNA**
Velperbuitensingel 6, Arnhem, Netherlands.
- Dimensie; populair maandblad gewijd aan techniek en wetenschap. m. ISSN 0018-4691

**Koninklijk Verbond van Ondernemers**
- Zelfstandig Ondernemerschap. (pub. by Uitgeversmaatschappij de Gelderlander Vakpers BV)

**Koninklijke Algemeene Vereeniging voor Bloembollencultuur**
- Bloembollencultuur. (pub. by Spoor en Partners B.V.)

**Koninklijke Marine**
Ministerie van Defensie, Koninginnegracht 60, The Hague, Netherlands.
- Alle Hens. m. ISSN 0002-5674

**Koninklijke Nationale Bond voor Reddingwezen en Eerste Hulp Bij Ongelukken "Het Oranje Kruis"**
Statenlaan 81, The Hague, Netherlands.
- Reddingwezen. bi-m. ISSN 0034-2114

**Koninklijke Nederlandsche Athletiek-Unie**
Nachtegaalstraat 67, P.O.B. 14444, Utrecht, Netherlands.
- Athletiekwereld. fortn. ISSN 0004-668X

**Koninklijke Nederlandsche Cricket Bond**
Willem de Zwijgerlaan 96, The Hague, Netherlands.
- Cricket. w.(during the summer) ISSN 0011-1236

**Koninklijke Nederlandsche Maatschappij Tot Bevordering der Geneeskunst**
- Medisch Contact. (pub. by B. V. Uitgeversmaatschappij Reflex)

**Koninklijke Nederlandsche Roeibond**
Joh. Verhulststr. 192, Amsterdam, Netherlands.
- Roeien. m. ISSN 0048-8518

**Koninklijke Nederlandsche Voetbalbond**
Woudenbergseweg 5b, Zeist, Netherlands (European Subscr. Address: Misset Grafische Bedrijven B. V., Doetinchem, Netherlands; U.S. Subscr. Address: IPC Business Press Inc., 205 E. 42nd St., New York, NY 10017)
- K N V Ber. w.

**Koninklijke Nederlandse Akademie van Wetenschappen**
- Koninklijke Nederlandse Akademie van Wetenschapen. Afdeling Natuurkunde, Verhandelingen. Eerste Reeks. (pub. by North-Holland Publishing Co.)
- Koninklijke Nederlandse Akademie van Wetenschappen. Afdeling Letterkunde. Verhandelingen. Nieuwe Reeks. (pub. by North-Holland Publishing Co.)
- Koninklijke Nederlandse Akademie van Wetenschappen. Afdeling Natuurkunde. Verhandellingen. Tweede Reeks. (pub. by North-Holland Publishing Co.)
- Koninklijke Nederlandse Akademie van Wetenschappen. Afdeling Natuurkunde. Verslag van de Gewone Vergadering. (pub. by North-Holland Publishing Co.)
- Koninklijke Nederlandse Akademie van Wetenschappen. Series A: Mathematical Sciences. Proceedings. (pub. by North-Holland Publishing Co.)
- Koninklijke Nederlandse Akademie van Wetenschappen. Series B. Physical Sciences. Proceedings. (pub. by North-Holland Publishing Co.)

- Koninklijke Nederlandse Akademie van Wetenschappen. Series C: Biological and Medical Sciences. Proceedings. (pub. by North-Holland Publishing Co.)

**Koninklijke Nederlandse Akademie van Wetenschappen. Sociaal-Wetenschappelijk Informatie en Documentatiecentrum**
- Koninklijke Nederlandse Akademie van Wetenschappen. Sociaal-Wetenschappelijk Informatie en Documentatiecentrum. Dissertaties Maatschappijwetenschappen. (pub. by North-Holland Publishing Co.)
- Koninklijke Nederlandse Akademie van Wetenschappen. Sociaal-Wetenschappelijk Informatie- en Documentatiecentrum. Register van Sociaal-Wetenschappelijk Onderzoek. (pub. by North-Holland Publishing Co.)
- Steinmetz Archives. (pub. by North-Holland Publishing Co.)

**Koninklijke Nederlandse Akademie van Wetenschappen. Sociaal-Wetenschappelijke Raad**
- Koninklijke Nederlandse Akademie van Wetenschappen. Sociaal-Wetenschappelijke Raad. Handelingen. (pub. by North-Holland Publishing Co.)
- Koninklijke Nederlandse Akademie van Wetenschappen. Sociaal-Wetenschappelijke Raad. Informatie Omtrent Lopend Onderzoek in de Sociale Wetenschappen. (pub. by North-Holland Publishing Co.)
- Koninklijke Nederlandse Akademie van Wetenschappen. Sociaal-Wetenschappelijke Raad. Register van Lopend Onderzoek in de Sociale Wetenschappen. (pub. by North-Holland Publishing Co.)
- Koninklijke Nederlandse Akademie van Wetenschappen. Sociaalwetenschappelijke Raad. Werkdocumenten. (pub. by North-Holland Publishing Co.)

**Koninklijke Nederlandse Baseball en Softball Bond**
Box 3971, Amsterdam, Netherlands.
- Inside. m. ISSN 0046-9610

**Koninklijke Nederlandse Bosbouw Vereniging**
Lovinklaan 1, Arnhem, Netherlands.
- Nederlands Bosbouw Tijdschrift. m. ISSN 0028-2057

**Koninklijke Nederlandse Botanische Vereniging**
Schelpenkade 6, Leiden, Netherlands.
- Acta Botanica Neerlandica. bi-m. ISSN 0044-5983

**Koninklijke Nederlandse Centrale Vereniging tot Bestrijding der Tuberculose**
Box 146, The Hague, Netherlands
(Subscr. to: Box 146, The Hague, Netherlands)
- Tegen de Tuberculose. bi-m. ISSN 0040-2125

**Koninklijke Nederlandse Chemische Vereniging**
Burnierstraat 1, The Hague, Netherlands.
- Chemisch Weekblad. (pub. by Stichting Uitgeverij Sigma Chemie)
- Koninklijke Nederlandse Chemische Vereniging. Chemisch Jaarboek. a.
- Recueil des Travaux Chimiques des Pays-Bas. m. ISSN 0034-186X

**Koninklijke Nederlandse Dambond**
Frankenslag 69, The Hague, Netherlands.
- Damspel. m. ISSN 0011-5959

**Koninklijke Nederlandse Maatschappij Ter Bevordering der Pharmacie**
Alexanderstraat 11, The Hague, Netherlands.
- Pharmaceutisch Weekblad. w. ISSN 0031-6911

**Koninklijke Nederlandse Maatschappij voor Diergeneeskunde**
Julianalaan 10, Box 14031, Utrecht, Netherlands.
- Tijdschrift voor Diergeneeskunde/Netherlands Journal of Veterinary Science. 24 per yr. (including quarterly issues in English) ISSN 0040-7453

**Koninklijke Nederlandse Maatschappij voor Tuinbouw en Plantkunde**
- Groei en Bloei. (pub. by B.V. Koninklijke Drukkerijen Roelants-Schiedam)

**Koninklijke Nederlandse Militaire Bond pro Rege**
Nieuwe Gracht 90, Utrecht, Netherlands.
- Nederlandse Krijgsman. m. ISSN 0047-9241

**Koninklijke Nederlandse Natuurhistorische Vereniging**
Hoogenboomlaan 24, 1718 BJ Hoogwoud, Netherlands.
- Natura. m. ISSN 0028-0631

**Koninklijke Nederlandse Natuurhistorische Vereniging. Bryology Group**
c/o Rijksherbarium, Schelpenkade 6, Leiden, Netherlands.
- Lindbergia. 1-2 per yr. (Co-Sponsor: Nordic Bryological Society)

**Koninklijke Nederlandse Oudheidkundige Bond**
De Poorterstraat 22, The Hague, Netherlands.
- Koninklijke Nederlandse Oudheidkundige Bond. Bulletin. 5 per yr.

**Koninklijke Nederlandse Redersvereniging**
- Zee. (pub. by Stam Tijdschriften B. V.)

**Koninklijke Nederlandse Schaakbond**
Passerdersgracht 32, Amsterdam, Netherlands.
- Schakend Nederland. m. ISSN 0036-5890

**Koninklijke Nederlandse Schutters Associatie**
Bondsbureau KNSA, Bezuidenhoutseweg 205, The Hague, Netherlands.
- Schietsport. m. ISSN 0048-9344

**Koninklijke Nederlandse Toeristenbond ANWB**
Wassenaarseweg 220, Postbus 2200, The Hague, Netherlands.
- Autokampioen. w. ISSN 0005-0997
- Kampeer en Caravankampioen. m.
- Kampioen. m. ISSN 0022-8265
- Toeristenkampioen. 20 per yr.
- Verkeerskunde. m.
- Verkeersrecht; juridical monthly for the road traffic. m. ISSN 0042-398X
- Waterkampioen. fortn. ISSN 0043-1451

**Koninklijke Nederlandse Vereniging "Ons Leger"**
- Ons Leger. (pub. by Wijt en Zn. B.V.)

**Koninklijke Nederlandse Vereniging Onze Vloot**
Lange Voorhout 13, The Hague 3005, Netherlands
- Zeewezen; opiniblad: marine, koopvaardij, zeetechniek en havens. m. (Subscr. to: Dekker & Nordemann B.V., O.Z. Voorburgwal 239, Amsterdam-1001 Netherlands)

**Koninklijke Nederlandse Vereniging van Leraren en Onderwijzers in de Lichamelijke Opvoeding**
Zinzendorflaan 9, Zeist, Netherlands.
- Lichamelijke Opvoeding/White Sisters. 20 per yr. ISSN 0024-2810

**Koninklijke Nederlandse Vereniging van Transportondernemingen**
- Nederlands Transport. (pub. by Tijl Media B.V.)

**Koninklijke Nederlandse Vereniging voor Luchtvaart**
- Avia. (pub. by Wijt en Zn. B.V.)

**Koninklijke Nederlandse Vereniging voor Luchtvaart. Afdeling Parachutespringen**
Jozef Israelsplein 8, The Hague, Netherlands.
- Sportparachutist. bi-m.

**Koninklijke Nederlandse Vereniging voor Luchtvaart. Afdeling Zweefvliegen**
c/o Nationaal Zweefvliegcentrum Terlet, Apeldoornseweg 203, Arnhem, Netherlands.
- Thermiek. bi-m. ISSN 0040-6023

**Koninklijke Notariele Broederschap**
Postbus 2827, The Hague, Netherlands.
- Weekblad voor Privaatrecht, Notariaat en Registratie.

**Koninklijke Vereniging "Het Nederlandsche Rundvee-Stamboek"**
Stadhouders-Plantsoen 24, The Hague, Netherlands.
- Keurstamboeker. s-m.

**Koninklijke Vereniging "Onze Luchtmacht"**
Zwanenlaan 17, Ter Aar (Z.H.), Netherlands.
- Onze Luchtmacht/Our Airforce. 3 per m. ISSN 0030-3208

**Koninklijke Vereniging ter Beoefening van de Krijgswetenschap**
Nassaulaan 6, Zoetermeer, Netherlands.
- Mars in Cathedra. q. ISSN 0025-4029
- Militaire Spectator. m. ISSN 0026-3869 (Netherlands. Ministerie van Defensie)

**Koninklijke Vereniging van Gasfabrikanten in Nederland**
Postbus 137, Apeldoorn, Netherlands.
- Gas. m. ISSN 0016-4828

**Koninklijke Vereniging voor Facultatieve Crematie**
Surinamestraat 34, The Hague, Netherlands.
- Crematienieuws. s-a. ISSN 0011-1163

**Kooperatieve Utjowery**
Postbus 1069, Leeuwarden, Netherlands.
- Trotwaer; letterkunde in de Friese taal. bi-m. ISSN 0041-3348

**Drukkerij Korthuis**
Marnixstraat 16, The Hague, Netherlands.
- Jaarboek/Vademecum voor het Verzekeringswezen. a.

**Van Kouteren's Publishing Co.**
Box 4115, Rotterdam 16, Netherlands.
- Barid Hollanda. 3 per yr. ISSN 0005-5956 (Netherlands Institute for the Middle East) (Co-sponsor: Africa Institute)
- Holland Shipping and Trading. m. ISSN 0018-358X

**Kracht van Omhoog**
Postbus 84, Gorkum, Netherlands.
- Kracht van Omhoog. every 3 weeks. ISSN 0023-4389

**Kristlik Fryske Folsbibleteek**
Hid Heroplantsoen 1, Bolsward, Netherlands.
- Fleanende Krie. 3 per yr. ISSN 0015-3540

**Kroon Levensmiddelenorganisatie N.V.**
see E. O. Kroon Levensmiddelenorganisatie N.V.

**Krul's Maandblad voor Stoom- en Chemische Wasserijen Ververijen en Wassalons**
Box 1332, Rotterdam, Netherlands.
- Krul's Maandblad voor Stoom- en Chemische Wasserijen Ververijen en Wassalons. m. ISSN 0023-4958

**Uitgeversmaatschappij Kruyt**
Groot Hertoginnelaan 28, Bussum, Netherlands.
- Arts en Sociale Verzekering. q. ISSN 0004-3974
- Huisarts en Wetenschap. m. ISSN 0018-7070

**Kuyperstichting ter Bevordering van de Studie der Antirevolutionaire Beginselen**
see Dr. Abraham Kuyperstichting ter Bevordering van de Studie der Antirevolutionaire Beginselen

**Laboratorium voor Grondmechanica**
Stieltjesweg 2, Box 69, Delft, Netherlands.
- L G M Mededelingen. q. ISSN 0023-6276

**Drukkerij-Uitgeverij Lakerveld B.V.**
Postbus 6023, Newtonstraat 441, The Hague, Netherlands.
- Meubel; vakblad voor meubelindustrie en woninginrichting. w.

**Land van Valkenburg**
De Guascostraat 8-10, Valkenburg (L.), Netherlands.
- Land van Valkenburg. w. ISSN 0023-7698

**Landbouw-Economisch Instituut**
Conradkade 175, The Hague, Netherlands.
- Akkerbouw. irreg. (prep. by its Afdeling Landbouw)
- Landbouw-Economisch Instituut. Afdeling Landbouw. Bedrijfsuitkomsten in de Landbouw. a. (prep. by its Afdeling Landbouw)
- Landbouw-Economisch Instituut. Agrarisch Weekoverzicht. w. ISSN 0002-1075
- Landbouw-Economisch Instituut. Prijsstatistiek. m. ISSN 0032-8219
- Landbouw-Economisch Instituut. Stafafdeling. Landbouw-Economisch Bericht. a.
- Landbouw-Economisch Instituut. Tuinbouwcijfers. a.

**Landbouwhogeschool**
Gen. Foulkesweg 1a, Wageningen, Netherlands.
- Landbouwhogeschool, Wageningen. Miscellaneous Papers. irreg., 1971, no. 10. ISSN 0083-6990

**Landbouwhogeschool. Laboratory of Plant Taxonomy and Geography**
Gen. Foulkesweg 1a, Wageningen, Netherlands.
- Belmontia. irreg.

**Landelijk Centrum voor Gereformeerd Jeugdwerk**
Postbus 99, Driebergen, Netherlands.
• Bijblijven. s-m. ISSN 0006-226X
• Jeugd. 8 per yr. ISSN 0021-6038
• Toesj/Combo. bi-m. ISSN 0010-2156
• Weerwoord. 10 per yr. (Co-sponsor: Christelijk
Jongeren Verbond)
• Wimpel. m. ISSN 0043-5678

**Landelijk Verbond Patrimonium**
• Patrimonium. (pub. by Bureau van Vliet B.V.)

**Landelijke Organisatie DIBEVO**
Oldemarktseweg 180, Steenwijk, Netherlands.
• Dibevo. m (11 per yr) ISSN 0012-2416

**Landelijke Organisatie Voetverzorging**
• Voet-Visie. (pub. by Uitgeversmaatschappij de
Gelderlander Vakpers BV)

**Landschot Bankiers**
*see* F. van Landschot Bankiers

**Lecturis B.V. Eindhoven**
Stadhuisplein 1, Eindhoven, Netherlands.
• Jaarboek Eindhoven. a.

**Leger des Heils**
Damstr. 15, Amsterdam, Netherlands.
• Jonge Kampvechter. m. ISSN 0021-7387

**Leiden University Press**
Box 269, Lange Voorhout 9-11, The Hague,
Netherlands
• Acta Biotheoretica. 4 per yr. ISSN 0001-5342
(Prof. Dr. Jan van der Hoeven Foundation for
Theoretical Biology) (Subscr. to: Dr. W. Junk B.
V. Publishers, Box 3713, The Hague,
Netherlands)
• Analecta Praehistorica Leidensia. irreg. ISSN
0569-9843 (Rijksuniversiteit te Leiden. Institute
for Prehistory)
• Boerhaave Series for Postgraduate Medical
Education. irreg.
• Codices Manuscripti, Bibliotheca Universitatis
Leidensis. irreg.
• Leiden Botanical Series. irreg.
• Leidse Germanistische en Anglistische Reeks.
irreg. ISSN 0458-9971
• Leidse Historische Reeks. irreg. ISSN 0458-998X
• Leidse Juridische Reeks. irreg. ISSN 0458-9998
• Leidse Kunsthistorische Reeks. irreg., vol. 2, 1969.
ISSN 0460-2048
• Leidse Voordrachten. irreg.
• Leidse Wijsgerige Reeks. irreg. ISSN 0459-0007
• Rechtshistorische Studies. irreg.
• Thorbecke-Colleges. irreg.

**Leidsche Drukkerij B.V.**
Box 223, Leiden, NETHERLANDS.
• Chemie & Instrument. m. (Stichting tot
Bevordering van de Belangen van Analisten,
Laboratorium-Assistenten en Hogere Chemici)

**Lennards-Instituut**
Steegstraat 16, Roermond, Netherlands.
• Ex Ore Infantium. q. ISSN 0014-3928

**Lepetit Colloquia on Biology and Medicine**
• Lepetit Colloquia on Biology and Medicine.
Proceedings. (pub. by North-Holland Publishing
Co.)

**Lichthoeve**
Oude Barnevelderweg 7, Garderen, Netherlands.
• Lichthoeve-Kinderwerk; prot. chr. kindertehuis. m.
ISSN 0024-2853

**Limburgs Geschied- en Oudheidkundig Genootschap**
Bogaardenstraat 43, Maastricht, Netherlands.
• Societe Historique et Archeologique dans le
Limbourg. Publications. a. ISSN 0085-6266

**L. A. van der Linden**
Norenburg 33, The Hague 2020, Netherlands.
• Niet Zo Benauwd. a. (Stichting Familieclub
Johannes van der Linden)

**Linders-Adremo B.V.**
Stationsweg 44, Postbus 83, Oosterbeek,
Netherlands.
• Levende Natuur; Nederlands tijdschrift voor
veldbiologie. m. ISSN 0024-1520

**Tijdschriftenfonds J.J. Lispet**
Postbus 338, Bussum, Netherlands.
• Musica. m. ISSN 0027-450X (Algemene
Nederlandse Unie van Muziekverenigingen)

• Muziek Mercuur; radio-TV wereld. m. ISSN 0027-
5298

**Liturgical Ecumenical Center Trust**
P.B. 25088, Rotterdam, Netherlands.
• Studia Liturgica; an international ecumenical
quarterly for liturgical research and renewal. q.
ISSN 0039-3207

**Van Loghum Slaterus**
Polstraat 10, Deventer, Netherlands.
• Opbouwwerk. 10 per yr. (Nederlands Instituut
voor Maatschappelijke Opbouw)

**Drukkerij Joh. Luijk N.V.**
Postbus 548, Eindhoven, Netherlands.
• Gereformeerde Kerken in Noord-Brabant en
Limburg. Kerkblad. w. ISSN 0016-8629

**N. V. Drukkerij-Uitgeverij Lumax**
Ondiep 6, Utrecht, Netherlands.
• Bazuin. w. ISSN 0005-7312

**Maatschappij der Nederlandse Letterkunde**
• Tijdschrift voor Nederlandse Taal- en
Letterkunde. (pub. by E. J. Brill)

**B.V. Maatschappij voor Bedrijfswetenschappelijke
Uitgaven**
Parkstraat 5, Postbus 191, Baarn, Netherlands.
• Kantoor en Efficiency. m. ISSN 0022-8893

**L.C.G. Malmberg B.V.**
Leeghwaterlaan 16, S-Hertogenbosch, Netherlands.
• Jippo. w.
• Okki. w. ISSN 0030-1612
• Pedagogisch Forum. 10 per yr. ISSN 0031-3823
• Primo. fortn.
• Taptoe. w. ISSN 0039-9604

**Markos Publicity N. V.**
Rutger Jan Schimmelpennicklaan 1, The Hague,
Netherlands.
• Report; facts & figures, news & unusual
applications of batteries. q. ISSN 0034-4656

**Mathematical Programming Society**
• Mathematical Programming Study. (pub. by
North-Holland Publishing Co.)

**Uitgeverij H. Medema**
Koninginnelaan 34, Apeldoorn, Netherlands.
• Blijde Boodschap. 2 per m. ISSN 0006-4777
• Bode van het Heil in Christus. m. ISSN 0006-
5439

**Medianet B.V.**
Postbus 118, Haarlem, Netherlands.
• Muziek Expres. m. ISSN 0027-528X

**Memisa Nieuws**
Perziklaan 21, The Hague 2025, Netherlands.
• Memisa Nieuws; medische missie post. bi-m. ISSN
0025-9063

**N V V-Bond Mercurius**
Box 550, Woerden, Netherlands.
• Mercurius. fortn. ISSN 0025-9950

**Metaalcompagnie "Brabant" B.V.**
Aalsterweg 137, Eindhoven, Netherlands.
• Wagenbouwnieuws. 3 per yr. ISSN 0042-9953

**Metaalunie**
• Metaal en Techniek. (pub. by
Uitgeversmaatschappij de Gelderlander Vakpers
BV)

**Meulenhoff-Bruna B.V.**
Box 197, Amsterdam, Netherlands.
• Gids. m(10 per yr.) ISSN 0016-9730 (Stichting de
Gids)
• Wijsgerig Perspectief op Maatschappij en
Wetenschap/Philosophical Perspective on Society
and Science. bi-m. ISSN 0043-5414

**Microfiche Foundation**
Delft Technological University Library, Doelenstraat
101, Delft, Netherlands.
• Microfiche Foundation. Newsletter. irreg., approx.
3-4 per yr. ISSN 0076-8480

**Micrography**
c/o Dick Bakker, Ed, Stevinstraat 14, Alphen aan
den Rijn, Netherlands.
• Micrography; jazz and blues on microgroove. q.

**Midden Noord-Holland Combinatie**
Postbox 7, Leeuwarderweg 78, Amsterdam-Noord,
Netherlands.
• Noord-Amsterdammer; editie nieuwe Noord-
Hollandse courant. 3 per w. ISSN 0029-1137

**Midden Oosten Instituut**
Postbus 10, The Hague 2076, Netherlands.
• Midden Oosten. s-m.

**Misset-Amersfoort**
Koningin Wilhelminalaan 12, Postbus 26,
Amersfoort, Netherlands.
• Autovisie; independent automobile magazine.
fortn. ISSN 0005-0873
• Disk; kritisch maandblad voor discofielen. m.
ISSN 0012-3722
• Focus; tijdschrift voor de gehele fotografie. m.
ISSN 0015-4997
• Foto. m. ISSN 0015-8682
• Fotohandel; vakblad voor de gehele fotohandel. m.
ISSN 0015-8852

**Uitgeversmaatschappij C. Misset B. V.**
Box 4, Doetinchem, Netherlands.
• Akkerbouw. every 3 wks.
• Auto en Motor Techniek. m.
• Avicultura. m. ISSN 0005-223X
• Bakkerswereld. w. ISSN 0026-5934
• Banketbakkerij. w. ISSN 0005-5484
• Boerderij. w. ISSN 0006-5617
• Bouwmachines. m. ISSN 0006-8373
• Bouwwereld. fortn. ISSN 0026-5942
• Camera Palet. bi-m.
• Eigen Vervoer; magazine voor eigen vervoerders
en verladers. m.
• Fonoweek; platen/tapes/apparatuur. w.
• Gastrovin. m.
• H L. (Levensmiddelenbedrijf) w. ISSN 0024-1555
(U.S. Subscr. to: IPC America, Inc., 205 E. 42nd
St., New York, NY 10017)
• Horeca. w. ISSN 0026-5950
• IJzerwaren en Doe het Zelf Mix. m.
• Industrieel Verpakken. m.
• Instellingen. m(10 per yr)
• Metaal & Kunststof. fortn. ISSN 0026-0460
• Pluimveehouderij. w. (Nederlandse Organisatie
van Pluimveehouders)
• Schaap. bi-m. (Centraal Bureau voor de
Schapenfokkerij)
• Supermarkt; independent monthly for the
managers of the foodstuffs retail trade. m.
• Technische Revue. fortn.
• Transport en Opslag. m.
• Tuinderij. s-m. ISSN 0041-3984
• Vakblad voor de Bloemisterij. w. ISSN 0042-2223
• Varkenshouderij. every 3 wks.
• Veehouderij. every 3 wks.
• Vlees en Vleeswaren. w.
• Wegvervoer. fortn. ISSN 0043-2083 (Nederlandse
Bond van Protestants-Christelijke Beroeps-
Goederenvervoerders)

**Missiezusters van Sint Petrus Claver**
Bouillonstraat 4, Maastricht, Netherlands.
• Echo uit Afrika en Andere Werelddelen. bi-m.

**Missionarissen van Scheut**
Sparrendaal, Vught, Netherlands.
• Hier en Elders. q. ISSN 0026-5985

**Mouton Publishers**
P.O. Box 482, The Hague, Netherlands.
• Academia Reprints. irreg.
• Afrika-Studiecentrum, Leiden. Communications;
paperback series, communications. irreg. ISSN
0065-4159
• Anglica Germanica. British Studies in Germanic
Languages and Literatures. irreg. ISSN 0066-1791
• Annales de Demographie Historique. a. ISSN
0066-2062 (Societe de Demographie Historique)
• Annual Review of the Social Sciences of Religion.
a.
• Approaches to Semiotics. irreg. ISSN 0066-5576
• Approaches to Semiotics. Paperback Series. irreg.
• Approaches to Translation Studies. irreg.
• Archivum Ottomanicum. a.
• Archontes. irreg. ISSN 0336-2698
• Art in Its Context: Studies in Ethno-Aesthetics.
Field Reports. irreg. ISSN 0066-7978
• Art in Its Context: Studies in Ethno-Aesthetics.
Museum Series. irreg. ISSN 0066-7986
• Asie du Sud-Est et Monde Insulindien. q. (Centre
de Documentation et de Recherche sur l'Asie du
Sud-Est et le Monde Insulindien FR)
• Atlas des Structures Agraires au Sud du Sahara.
irreg. ISSN 0067-0286 (Maison des Sciences de
l'Homme FR)

- Atlas des Structures Agraires de Madagascar. irreg. (Maison des Sciences de l'Homme FR)
- Bibliographies on the Near East. irreg. ISSN 0067-7116
- Cahiers d'Etudes Africaines. q. ISSN 0008-0055 (Ecole des Hautes Etudes en Sciences Sociales FR)
- Canadiana Avant 1867. irreg. (Maison des Sciences de l'Homme FR) (Dist. by: Johnson Reprint Corporation)
- Central Asiatic Studies; a monograph series devoted to the culture, history, and languages of Central Asia and its peoples. irreg. ISSN 0069-1488
- Centre Culturel International de Cerisy-La-Salle. Decades. Nouvelle Serie. irreg. ISSN 0069-1739
- Centre d'Etudes de Presse. Travaux. irreg. (Co-sponsor: Maison des Sciences de l'Homme, Paris)
- Centre d'Etudes des Espaces Urbains. Travaux. irreg.
- Centre des Sciences Sociales d'Athenes. Publications/Social Sciences Center, Athens. Publications. irreg. ISSN 0067-0103
- Change and Continuity in Africa. irreg. (Afrika-Studiecentrum)
- Classiques de la Renaissance en France. Deuxieme Serie. Les Oeuvres de Jacques Lefevre d' Etaples/ French Renaissance Classics. Second Series. Works of Jacques Lefevre d'Etaples. irreg. (Dist. by: Johnson Reprint Corporation, 111 Fifth Ave., New York, NY 10003)
- Classiques de la Renaissance en France. Premiere Serie/French Renaissance Classics. First Series. irreg. ISSN 0069-4541 (Dist. by: Johnson Reprint Corporation, 111 Fifth Ave., New York, NY 10003)
- Collection Dictionnaires des Idees dans les Litteratures Occidentales. Litterature Francaise. irreg. ISSN 0069-5351 (Dist. by Adler Foreign Books, 162 Fifth Ave., New York, NY 10010)
- Comparative Studies in Society and History. irreg. ISSN 0069-7907
- Confluence. Etats des Recherches en Sciences Sociales: Surveys of Research in the Social Sciences. irreg. ISSN 0069-8814 (International Committee for Social Sciences Documentation)
- Connaissance et Langage. irreg. (Ecole des Hautes Etudes en Sciences Sociales FR)
- Contributions to the Sociology of Language. irreg.
- De Propietattbus Litterarum Series Didactica. irreg.
- De Proprietatibus Litterarum. Series Major. irreg. ISSN 0070-3060
- De Proprietatibus Litterarum. Series Minor. irreg. ISSN 0070-3079
- De Proprietatibus Litterarum. Series Practica. irreg. ISSN 0070-3087
- Description and Analysis of Contemporary Standard Russian. irreg. ISSN 0070-3826
- Disputationes Rheno-Trajectinae. irreg., 1970, no. 11. ISSN 0083-4998 (Rijksuniversiteit te Utrecht. Instituut voor Oosterse Talen)
- Documents pour Servir a l'Histoire de l'Afrique Equatoriale Francaise. Deuxieme Serie. Brazza et la Fondation du Congo Francaise. irreg. ISSN 0419-5736 (Ecole des Hautes Etudes en Sciences Sociales FR)
- Dutch Studies in Russian Literature. irreg. ISSN 0070-7783
- Ecole des Hautes Etudes en Sciences Sociales. Section des Sciences Economiques et Sociales. Memoires et Travaux. irreg.
- Etudes Rurales; revue trimestrielle d'histoire, geographie, sociologie et economie des campagnes. q. ISSN 0014-2182 (Ecole des Hautes Etudes en Sciences Sociales FR)
- European Coordination Centre for Research and Documentation in Social Sciences. Publications. irreg. ISSN 0071-271X
- European Journal of Social Psychology. q. ISSN 0046-2772
- European Review of Agricultural Economics. q.
- Harvard Germanic Studies. irreg. ISSN 0440-3428 (Harvard University. Department of Germanic Languages and Literatures US)
- Histoire des Sciences et des Techniques. irreg. (Ecole des Hautes Etudes en Sciences Sociales FR)
- Homme; revue Francaise d'anthropologie. q. ISSN 0046-7790 (Ecole des Hautes Etudes en Sciences Sociales FR)

- Humaniora Islamica; an annual publication of Islamic studies and the humanities. a.
- Indiana University. Folklore Institute. Monograph Series. irreg., 1970, vol. 23. ISSN 0073-6996 (Dist. by: Humanities Press, 303 Park Ave. S., New York, N.Y. 10010)
- Indiana University. Research Center for the Language Sciences. African Series. irreg. ISSN 0073-7062 (Dist. by: Humanities Press, Inc., 1171 First Ave., Atlantic Highlands, NJ 07716)
- Indiana University. Research Center for the Language Sciences. Uralic and Altaic Series. irreg., 1970, vol. 109. ISSN 0073-7097 (Dist. by: Humanities Press, Inc., 1171 First Ave., Atlantic Highlands, NJ 07716)
- Indiana University. Research Center in Anthropology, Folklore, and Linguistics. Publications. irreg.
- Indo-Iranian Monographs. irreg. ISSN 0073-7224
- Indo-Iranian Reprints. irreg. ISSN 0537-3638
- Institut Africain de Geneve. Etudes et Travaux. irreg.
- Institut de Litterature et de Techniques Artistiques de Masse. Travaux et Recherches. irreg. (Co-sponsor: Maison des Sciences de l'Homme, Paris)
- Institute of Social Studies, The Hague. Publications. Paperback Series. irreg. ISSN 0073-9693
- Institute of Social Studies, The Hague. Publications. Series Major. irreg. ISSN 0073-9707
- Interaction. l'Homme et Son Environnement Social. irreg.
- Inter-American Music Monograph Series. irreg. ISSN 0074-0934 (Indiana University. Research Center for the Language Sciences US)
- International Journal of the Sociology of Language. q.
- International P.E.N. Books. irreg.
- International Social Science Council. Publications. irreg. ISSN 0074-8404
- Issues in Contemporary Politics. irreg.
- Janua Linguarum. Series Anastatica. irreg.
- Janua Linguarum. Series Critica. irreg. ISSN 0075-3092
- Janua Linguarum. Series Didactica. irreg. ISSN 0075-3106
- Janua Linguarum. Series Major. irreg. ISSN 0075-3114
- Janua Linguarum. Series Minor. irreg. ISSN 0075-3122
- Janua Linguarum. Series Practica. irreg. ISSN 0075-3130
- Journal of Folklore Studies. 3 per yr. (Indiana University. Folklore Institute US)
- Language Science Monographs. irreg., 1970, Sep., vol. 6. ISSN 0075-7969 (Indiana University. Research Center for the Language Sciences US) (Dist. by Humanities Press, Inc., 303 Park Ave. South, New York, NY 10010)
- Linguistic Structures. irreg. ISSN 0075-9635
- Linguistics; an international review. 18 per yr. ISSN 0024-3949
- Maison des Sciences de l'Homme. Collection de Reeditions. irreg. ISSN 0076-2806 (Co-sponsor: Ecole des Hautes Etudes en Sciences Sociales, Paris)
- Materiaux pour le Manuel de l'Histoire des Song. irreg. ISSN 0553-2361 (Ecole des Hautes Etudes en Sciences Sociales FR)
- Methods and Models in the Social Sciences. irreg. ISSN 0076-6828
- Monda Lingvo Problemo. 3 per yr. ISSN 0026-9344
- Monographs on Linguistic Analysis. irreg. ISSN 0077-1031 (Ohio State University. Project on Linguistic Analysis US)
- Near and Middle East Monographs. irreg.
- New Babylon: Studies in the Social Sciences. irreg. ISSN 0077-801X
- Nova Americana. irreg. ISSN 0550-1555 (Ecole des Hautes Etudes en Sciences Sociales FR)
- Oeuvre Sociologique. irreg. (Ecole des Hautes Etudes en Sciences Sociales FR)
- Papers on Formal Linguistics. irreg. ISSN 0078-9194 (University of Pennsylvania. Department of Linguistics US)
- Psychological Studies. irreg.
- Publications in Near and Middle East Studies. Series A. irreg. ISSN 0079-7707 (Columbia University. Department of Middle East Languages and Cultures US) (Co-sponsor: Middle East Institute)
- Publications in Near and Middle East Studies. Series B. irreg. ISSN 0079-7715 (Columbia University. Department of Middle East Languages and Cultures US) (Co-sponsor: Middle East Institute)

- Quellen und Untersuchungen zur Geschichte der Deutschen und Oesterreichischen Arbeiterbewegung. Neue Folge. irreg., no. 5, 1974. ISSN 0079-9130 (International Institute for Social History)
- Recherche Urbaine. irreg. (Ecole des Hautes Etudes en Sciences Sociales FR)
- Recherches Mediterraneennes. Bibliographies. irreg. ISSN 0080-0090 (Maison des Sciences de l'Homme FR)
- Religion and Reason; Method and Theory in the Study and Interpretation of Religion. irreg. ISSN 0080-0848
- Religion and Society. irreg.
- Revue Bibliographique de Sinologie. a. ISSN 0080-2484 (Ecole des Hautes Etudes en Sciences Sociales. Centre d'Etudes Chinoise FR)
- Rijksuniversiteit te Utrecht. Geografisch Instituut. Bulletin. Serie 1: Sociale Geografie. irreg. ISSN 0083-498X
- Romance Languages and Their Structures. First Series. F: (French) irreg. ISSN 0080-3820
- Romance Languages and Their Structures. First Series. I: (Italian) irreg.
- Romance Languages and Their Structures. First Series. R: (Rumanian) irreg. ISSN 0080-3839
- Romance Languages and Their Structures. First Series. S: (Spanish) irreg. ISSN 0080-3847
- Russian Reprint Series. irreg.
- Savoir Geographique. irreg. (Ecole des Hautes Etudes en Sciences Sociales FR)
- Savoir Historique. irreg. (Ecole des Hautes Etudes en Sciences Sociales FR)
- Selected Studies on Indonesia. irreg. ISSN 0080-8628 (Koninklijk Instituut voor de Tropen)
- Semiotica. 4 per yr. ISSN 0037-1998 (International Association for Semiotic Studies)
- Service d'Echange d'Informations Scientifiques. Serie A: Bibliographies. irreg. ISSN 0080-9039 (Maison des Sciences de l'Homme FR)
- Service d'Echange d'Informations Scientifiques. Serie B: Guides et Repertoires. irreg. ISSN 0080-9047 (Maison des Sciences de l'Homme FR)
- Service d'Echange d'Informations Scientifiques. Serie C: Catalogues et Inventaires. irreg. ISSN 0080-9055 (Maison des Sciences de l'Homme FR)
- Service d'Echange d'Informations Scientifiques. Serie D: Methodes et Techniques. irreg. ISSN 0080-9063 (Maison des Sciences de l'Homme FR)
- Slavistic Printing and Reprintings. irreg. ISSN 0081-0029
- Social Praxis; international and interdisciplinary quarterly of social science. 4 per yr.
- Social Sciences Information/Information sur les Sciences Sociales. bi-m. ISSN 0037-7864 (International Social Science Council)
- Societe des Etudes Juives. Memoires. irreg. ISSN 0560-5296
- Stanford Studies in Germanics and Slavics. irreg. ISSN 0081-4342
- Studia Judaica. irreg. ISSN 0081-668X
- Studies in African History, Anthropology, and Ethnology. irreg. ISSN 0081-749X
- Studies in American History. irreg. ISSN 0081-7503
- Studies in American Literature. irreg. ISSN 0081-752X
- Studies in Ancient History. irreg. ISSN 0081-7546
- Studies in Anthropology. irreg.
- Studies in Art. irreg. ISSN 0081-7562
- Studies in Classical Literature. irreg. ISSN 0081-7724
- Studies in English Literature. irreg. ISSN 0081-7899
- Studies in European History. irreg. ISSN 0081-7910
- Studies in European Society. irreg.
- Studies in Folklore. irreg.
- Studies in French Literature. irreg. ISSN 0081-7937
- Studies in General and Comparative Literature. irreg. ISSN 0081-7945
- Studies in General Anthropology. irreg. ISSN 0081-7953
- Studies in German Literature. irreg. ISSN 0081-797X
- Studies in Italian Literature. irreg. ISSN 0081-8119
- Studies in Philosophy. irreg. ISSN 0081-8399
- Studies in Social Anthropology. irreg. ISSN 0081-8496
- Studies in Spanish Literature. irreg. ISSN 0081-8534
- Studies in the Social Sciences. irreg. ISSN 0081-8674
- Universite de Liege. Laboratoire d'Analyse Statistique des Langues Anciennes. Travaux Publies. irreg. ISSN 0075-9368

- Universite des Sciences Sociales de Grenoble.
  Centre de Recherche d'Histoire Economique,
  Sociale et Institutionnelle. Collection. Serie
  Histoire Institutionnelle. irreg. ISSN 0072-7539
- Universite des Sciences Sociales de Grenoble.
  Centre de Recherche d'Histoire Economique,
  Sociale et Institutionnelle. Collection. Serie
  Histoire Sociale. irreg. ISSN 0072-7547
- Universite des Sciences Sociales de Grenoble.
  Centre de Recherche Economique et Sociale.
  Collection. Serie Agriculture et Devenir Social.
  irreg. ISSN 0072-7555
- Universite des Sciences Sociales de Grenoble.
  Centre de Recherche Economique et Sociale.
  Collection. Serie Economie du Developpement.
  irreg. ISSN 0072-758X
- Universite des Sciences Sociales de Grenoble.
  Centre de Recherche Economique et Sociale.
  Collection. Serie Etudes d'Economie de l'Energie.
  irreg. ISSN 0072-7571
- Universite des Sciences Sociales de Grenoble.
  Centre de Recherche Economique et Sociale.
  Collection. Serie Economie du Financement.
  irreg. ISSN 0072-7563
- Universite des Sciences Sociales de Grenoble.
  Centre de Recherche Juridique. Collection. Serie
  Droit de la Propriete Industrielle. irreg. ISSN
  0072-7598
- Universite des Sciences Sociales de Grenoble.
  Centre de Recherche Juridique. Collection. Serie
  Droit du Tourisme. irreg. ISSN 0072-7601
- Universite des Sciences Sociales de Grenoble.
  Centre de Recherche Juridique. Collection. Serie
  Droits Etrangers et Droit Compare. irreg. ISSN
  0072-761X
- Universite des Sciences Sociales de Grenoble.
  Collection Generale. irreg. ISSN 0072-7628
- Universite des Sciences Sociales de Grenoble.
  Institut d'Etudes Politiques. Serie Essais et
  Travaux. irreg. ISSN 0072-7636
- Universite des Sciences Sociales de Grenoble.
  Institut d'Etudes Politiques. Serie Textes et
  Documents. irreg. ISSN 0072-7644

**Muiderkring B.V.**
Nijverheidswerf 17-21, Bussum, Netherlands.
- Hobby Bulletin. m. ISSN 0018-2931

**Museum Boymans-van Beuningen**
Mathenesserlaan 18-20, P.O. Box 2277, Rotterdam,
Netherlands.
- Museum Boymans-van Beuningen. Agenda-Diary.
  a. ISSN 0077-2275
- Museum Boymans-van Beuningen. Bulletin. q.
  ISSN 0027-4038

**J. Muusses B.V.**
Postbus 13, Purmerend, Netherlands.
- Maandblad voor Accountancy en
  Bedrijfshuishoudkunde. m(11 per yr.) ISSN 0024-
  8622
- Onderwijs en Media. 6 per yr. ISSN 0030-2473
- Vernieuwing van Opvoeding, Onderwijs en
  Maatschappij. m.(11 per yr) (Werkgemeenschap
  voor Vernieuwing van Opvoeding, Onderwijs en
  Maatschappij)

**Muziek Expres B. V.**
Box 63, Haarlem, Netherlands.
- Popfoto. m.

**N. V. Tot Keuring van Elektrotechnische Materialen**
see K E M A

**Nationaal Centrum voor Geestelijke Volksgezondheid**
Postbus 14084, Utrecht, Netherlands.
- M G V. (Maandblad Geestelijke Volksgezondheid)
  11 per yr.

**Nationaal Rheumafonds**
1E Sweelinckstraat 62, The Hague, Netherlands.
- Reuma Bulletin. q. ISSN 0034-6217

**National Christian Temperance Movement**
Kraaiensteinlaan 10, Arnhem, Netherlands.
- Blauwe Kruis. m. ISSN 0006-4653

**National Foundation-March of Dimes**
- International Conference on Congenital
  Malformations. Proceedings. (pub. by Excerpta
  Medica)

**Nationale Commissie tegen het Alkoholisme**
Willem Barentszstraat 39, Utrecht, Netherlands.
- A en D. (Alcohol en Drugs) q. ISSN 0006-4645

**Nationale Cooperatieve Raad voor Land- en Tuinbouw.**
Groenhovenstraat 3, The Hague, Netherlands.
- Cooperatie. m. ISSN 0009-9783

**Nationale Kruisvereniging**
Box 3200, Utrecht, Netherlands.
- Maatschappelijke Gezondheidszorg. m.

**Nationale Nederlanden Insurance**
Prinses Beatrixlaan 15, The Hague, Netherlands.
- Nationale-Nederlanden. Annual Report. a. ISSN
  0077-5975
- 2 N. m. ISSN 0041-4581

**Nationale Organisatie voor Buurtwerk**
Postbus 14029, Utrecht, Netherlands.
- Attak. 10 per yr. ISSN 0044-9962

**Natuurhistorisch Genootschap in Limburg**
Bosquetplein 7, Maastricht, Netherlands.
- Natuurhistorisch Maandblad. m.

**Natuurhistorisch Museum, van Sambeekstichting**
M. H. Tromplaan 19, Enschede, Netherlands.
- Natuur en Museum. q. ISSN 0028-1085

**Natuurwetenschappelijke Studiekring voor Suriname en de Nederlandse Antillen**
c/o Dr. P. Wagenaar Hummelinck, Sweelinckstraat
84, Bilthoven, Netherlands.
- Studies on the Fauna of Suriname and Other
  Guyanas. irreg.

**Nederland-U S S R Instituut**
Spui 3, Box 10, The Hague, Netherlands.
- Ekonomicheskii Byulleten Niderlandov/
  Exporttijdschrift voor de Sovjetunie. bi-m. ISSN
  0013-3000
- Nederland-U S S R Instituut. Maandberichten. m.
  ISSN 0028-2022

**Nederlands-Belgische Vereniging van Liefhebbers van Cactussen en Andere Vetplanten**
Koningsweg 2, Beekbergen, Netherlands.
- Succulenta. m. ISSN 0039-4467

**Nederlands Bibliotheek en Lektuurcentrum**
Taco Scheltemastraat 5, Postbox 2054, The Hague,
Netherlands.
- Bibliotheek en Samenleving. 11 per yr.
- N B L C Info Bulletin. w.
- Nederlands Bibliotheek en Lektuurcentrum. Index.
  (pub. by De Horstink)

**Nederlands Centrum voor het Amateurtoneel**
Zandpad 28, Maarssen, Netherlands.
- Samenspel. m. ISSN 0036-3766

**Nederlands-Duitse Kamer van Koophandel**
Nassauplein 30, The Hague, Netherlands.
- Profit; Nederlands-Duitse handelscourant. bi-m.
  ISSN 0019-9206

**Nederlands Economisch Instituut**
Burg. Oudlaan 50, Box 4224, Rotterdam 3016,
Netherlands.
- Economisch-Statistische Berichten. w. ISSN 0013-
  0583

**Nederlands Filmmuseum**
Vondelpark 3, Amsterdam, Netherlands.
- Filmmuseum-Cinemateek-Journaal. 5 per yr.

**Nederlands Genootschap voor Document Reproductie**
Ambachtsherenlaan 1096, Zoetermeer, Netherlands.
- Document Reproductie. 4 per yr. ISSN 0012-4478

**Nederlands Genootschap voor Informatica**
c/o Mrs. T. Poortenaar-Sikkema, Overboslaan 49,
3722 BK Bilthoven, Netherlands.
- Informatie. m. ISSN 0019-9907 (Co-sponsor:
  Belgisch Studiecentrum voor Automatische
  Informatieverwerking)

**Nederlands Genootschap voor Internationale Zaken**
Alexanderstraat 2, The Hague, Netherlands.
- Internationale Spectator. m. ISSN 0020-9317
- Wereldwijzer; buitenlandse persstemmen. d. ISSN
  0043-275X

**Nederlands Genootschap voor Landmeetkunde**
Werumeus Buninglaan 9, Waddinxveen,
Netherlands.
- Geodesia. m (except Jul.) ISSN 0016-707X

**Nederlands Historisch Genootschap**
- Bijdragen en Mededelingen Betreffende de
  Geschiedenis der Nederlanden. (pub. by Martinus
  Nijhoff)

**Nederlands Instituut van Psychologen**
Nicolaas Maesstraat 122, Amsterdam, Netherlands.
- Psychologen Adresboek. a. ISSN 0079-7324
- Psycholoog. m. ISSN 0033-3115

**Nederlands Instituut van Registeraccountants**
Mensinge 2, Amsterdam-Buitenveldert, Netherlands.
- Accountant. 11 per yr. ISSN 0001-4729

**Nederlands Instituut voor het Bank- en Effectenbedrijf**
Herengracht 136, Amsterdam 1002, Netherlands.
- Bank- en Effectenbedrijf. m. ISSN 0005-5018

**Nederlands Instituut voor het Nabije Oosten**
Noordeindsplein 4a, Leiden, Netherlands.
- Anatolica. a. ISSN 0066-1554
- Bibliotheca Orientalis; international bibliographical
  and reviewing bi-monthly for Near Eastern and
  Mediterranean Studies. bi-m. ISSN 0006-1913
- Institut Historique et Archeologique Neerlandais
  de Stamboull. Publications. irreg., 1974, vol. 36.
  ISSN 0073-8549
- Jaarbericht "Ex Oriente Lux; annuaire de la
  Societe Orientale Neerlandaise "Ex Oriente Lux".
  a. ISSN 0075-2118 (Vooraziatisch-Egyptisch
  Genootschap "Ex Oriente Lux")
- Scholae Adriani de Buck Memoriae Dicatae.
  irreg., 1970, no. 5 (vol. 6 in prep.) ISSN 0080-
  6854
- Studia Francisci Scholten Memoriae Dicata. irreg.,
  1973, vol. 4. ISSN 0081-6396
- Vooraziatisch-Egyptisch Genootschap "Ex Oriente
  Lux". Mededelingen en Verhandelingen. irreg.,
  1968, no. 17. (Vooraziatisch-Egyptisch
  Genootschap "Ex Oriente Lux")

**Nederlands Instituut voor Lastechniek**
- Lastechniek. (pub. by Wijt en Zn. B.V.)

**Nederlands Instituut voor Maatschappelijke Opbouw**
- Opbouwwerk. (pub. by Van Loghum Slaterus)

**Nederlands Instituut voor Ruimtelijke Ordening en Volkshuisvesting.**
Van Speijkstraat 25, The Hague, Netherlands.
- Stedebouw en Volkshuisvesting. m. ISSN 0039-
  0879

**Nederlands Instituut voor Volksontwikkeling en Natuurvriendenwerk**
P.C. Hooftstraat 163, Amsterdam 1007,
Netherlands.
- Stuwing. 10 per yr. ISSN 0039-4211

**Nederlands Interuniversitair Demografisch Instituut**
Prinses Beatrixlaan 428, Voorburg, Netherlands.
- Bevolking en Gezin. (pub. by Uitgeverij de Sikkel
  N.V. BE)
- Bulletin Demografie. bi-m.
- Nederlands Interuniversitair Demografisch
  Instituut. Working Papers. irreg.
- Nederlands Interuniversitair Demographisch
  Instituut. Publications. (pub. by Martinus Nijhoff)
- Selected Annotated Bibliography of Population
  Studies in the Netherlands. a. (Co-sponsor:
  Netherlands Demographic Society)

**Nederlands Letterkundig Museum en Documentatiecentrum**
Juffrouw Idastraat 11, The Hague, Netherlands.
- Achter het Boek. irreg. (approx. 1-3 nos. per yr.)
  ISSN 0084-5892
- Bibliografie van de Nederlandse Taal- en
  Literatuur Wetenschap. a. ISSN 0045-186X
- Schrijvers Prentenboek. irreg.(approx. 1 issue per
  year) ISSN 0080-7192

**Nederlands Normalisatie-Instituut**
Polakweg 5, Rijswijk (ZH), Netherlands.
- Normalisatie. m.

**Nederlands Tandartsenblad**
Lomanlaan 103, Utrecht, Netherlands.
- Nederlands Tandartsenblad. fortn. ISSN 0028-
  2111

**Nederlands Verbond van Grafische Ondernemingen**
Van Eeghenstraat 70, Amsterdam 2, Netherlands.
- Repro en Druk. w.

**Nederlands Verbond van PTT- ,Sport- ,Ontspannings-**
**en Ontwikkelingsverenigingen**
Nvptt, Riouwstraat 210, The Hague, Netherlands.
● In Vrije Tijd/In Spare Time. m. ISSN 0019-3305

**Nederlands Verpakkingscentrum**
● Verpakking. (pub. by B. V. Uitgeversmaatschappij
Reflex)

**Nederlands Volkskundig Genootschap**
Bankastraat 104, The Hague, Netherlands.
● Neerlands Volksleven. q. ISSN 0028-2405

**Nederlands-Zuidafrikaanse Vereniging**
Keizersgracht 141, Amsterdam C, Netherlands.
● Nederlands-Zuidafrikaanse Vereniging. Verslag. a.
ISSN 0077-6416

**Nederlandsch Maandblad voor Philatelie**
c/o A. van der Flier, Tortellaan 69, The Hague,
Netherlands.
● Nederlandsch Maandblad voor Philatelie. m. ISSN
0028-2081

**Nederlandsch-Turksche Vereeniging**
Postbus 10, Spui No. 3, The Hague, Netherlands.
● Nederlandsch-Turksche Vereeniging. Berichten/
Holanda-Turk Cemiyeti. Haberler. q. ISSN 0028-
2251

**Nederlandsche Bond van Boekbinders-Patroons**
Vondelstraat 172, Amsterdam, Netherlands.
● Magnus. fortn. ISSN 0025-0023

**Nederlandsche Maatschappij voor Nijverheid en**
**Handel**
Florapark 11, Box 205, Haarlem 1501, Netherlands
(Subscr. Address: Uitgevers Wyt & Zonen B.V.,
Pieter de Hoochweg 111, Rotterdam, Netherlands)
● Maatschappijbelangen. m. ISSN 0024-8843

**N. V. Nederlandsche Schoenenunie**
Bloch & Stibbe Hollandia, Nieuwstraat 9, Waalwijk,
Netherlands.
● Hollandia Varia. s-m. ISSN 0018-3598

**Nederlandsche Stichting voor Moreele**
**Herbewapening**
Amaliastraat 10, The Hague, Netherlands.
● Nieuw Wereld Nieuws. fortn. ISSN 0028-9876
(Nieuwsdienst Morele Herbewapening)

**Nederlandsche Vereniging van Technici Op**
**Scheepvaartgebied**
● Schip en Werf. (pub. by Wijt en Zn. B.V.)

**Nederlandsche Zondagsschool Vereeniging**
Bloemgracht 65, Amsterdam, Netherlands.
● Kind en Zondag. m. ISSN 0023-1444

**Nederlandse Aannemersvereniging van Afbouw- en**
**Stukadoorswerken**
Leliegracht 5, Amsterdam, Netherlands.
● N A V A S. m (11 per yr.)

**Nederlandse Algemene Keuringsdienst van Groente-**
**en Bloemzaden**
● Zaadbelangen. (pub. by Stichting Vakblad
Zaadbelangen)

**Nederlandse Bakkerij**
● Bakker. (pub. by Uitgeversmaatschappij de
Gelderlander Vakpers BV)

**Nederlandse Baksteenindustrie**
Sonsbeekweg 12, Postbus 51, Arnhem, Netherlands.
● Baksteen. bi-m. ISSN 0005-4186

**Nederlandse Basketball Bond**
Herengracht 570, Amsterdam, Netherlands.
● Basketbal. m. ISSN 0005-6154

**Nederlandse Beatles Fanclub**
Box 1675, Amsterdam, Netherlands.
● Beatles Playback; tijdschrift rond het Beatle-
gebeuren. m.

**Nederlandse Bergsportvereniging**
Laan van Meerdervoort 503, The Hague,
Netherlands.
● Bergvriend. bi-m. ISSN 0005-898X

**Nederlandse Blindenbond**
Boslaan 13, Schaesberg, Netherlands.
● Blindenbode. q. ISSN 0006-484X

**Nederlandse Boek**
Prinsengracht 1083, Amsterdam, Netherlands.
● Nieuwe Pockets en Paperbacks. bi-m. ISSN 0048-
0355

**Nederlandse Boekenclub**
● Gouden Uren. (pub. by B. V.
Uitgeversmaatschappij Succes)

**Nederlandse Boekverkopersbond**
Waalsdorperweg 119, The Hague, Netherlands.
● Boekverkoper. q. ISSN 0006-5587

**Nederlandse Bond "Aqua-Terra"**
Havenstraat 83, Hilversum, Netherlands.
● Aquarium; maandblad voor aquarium-. terrarium-
en insektariumkunde. m. ISSN 0003-729X

**Nederlandse Bond van Huis- en Grondeigenaren**
● Vrije Bouw en Exploitatie. (pub. by Nieuwe
Rotterdamse Courant N.V.)

**Nederlandse Bond van Makelaars in Onroerende**
**Goederen**
Soestdijkseweg 247, Bilthoven, Netherlands.
● Vastgoed. m.

**Nederlandse Bond van Onbezoldigde**
**Opsporingsambtenaren en Bewakingspersoneel**
Metiuslaan 1, Eindhoven, Netherlands.
● N. B. O. B. Orgaan. m. ISSN 0027-6146

**Nederlandse Bond van Protestants-Christelijke**
**Beroeps-Goederenvervoerders**
● Wegvervoer. (pub. by Uitgeversmaatschappij C.
Misset B.V.)

**Nederlandse Bond van Timmerfabrikanten**
● Timmerfabrikant. (pub. by Uitgeverij Wijlhuizen)

**Nederlandse Bond van Vogelliefhebbers**
Postbox 74, Bergen Op Zoom, Netherlands.
● Onze Vogels. m. ISSN 0030-3224

**Nederlandse Bridge Bond**
c/o A. Boekhorst, Ed., Emmapark 9, The Hague,
Netherlands.
● Bridge. m. ISSN 0006-9825

**Nederlandse Centrale Organisatie voor Toegepast-**
**Natuurwetenschappelijk Onderzoek. Technisch-**
**Physische Dienst**
Stieltjesweg 1, Delft, Netherlands.
● Nederlandse Centrale Organisatie voor Toegepast-
Natuurwetenschappelijk Onderzoek. Technisch-
Physische Dienst. Annual Report. a.

**Nederlandse Christelijke Boeren- en Tuindersbond**
Postbus 1510, Sweelinckstraat 30, The Hague,
Netherlands.
● Ons Platteland. w. ISSN 0030-2732

**Nederlandse Christelijke Bond van**
**Overheidspersoneel**
● Welzijn. (pub. by Vanderveer B. V.)

**Nederlandse Christelijke Plattelands Jongeren Bond**
Stationsweg 65, Ede, Netherlands.
● Ons Jonge Platteland. m. ISSN 0030-2708

**Nederlandse Christen Studenten Vereniging**
Woudschoten, Zeist, Netherlands.
● Beet; magazine for scholars. 9 per yr. ISSN 0005-
7789
● Eltheto. 3 per yr. ISSN 0013-6468

**Nederlandse Club voor Chef-Koks**
Postbus 1198, Amsterdam, Netherlands.
● Keuken. bi-m. ISSN 0023-0731

**Nederlandse Economische Hogeschool**
● Studies in Development and Planning. (pub. by
Rotterdam University Press)

**Nederlandse Entomologische Vereniging**
Plantage Middenlaan 64, Amsterdam 1004,
Netherlands.
● Entomologische Berichten. m. ISSN 0013-8827
● Nederlandsche Entomologische Vereniging.
Monographs. irreg., no. 7, 1973. ISSN 0548-1163
● Tijdschrift voor Entomologie. a. ISSN 0040-7496

**Nederlandse Federatie Jeugd en Jongerenwerk**
Henri Polaklaan 14, Amsterdam 04, Netherlands.
● J N. (Jeugdwerk Nu); nieuwsblad over jeugdwerk
en jongerenactiviteiten. s-m. ISSN 0021-6070

**Nederlandse Federatie van Christelijke**
**Muziekbonden**
c/o H.K.W. Frenkel, Ed., Tjaerdaweg 46,
Rinsumageest, Netherlands.
● Christelijke Muziekbode; maandblad voor
Christelijke harmonie-, fanfare- en
tamboerkorpsen in Nederland. m. ISSN 0009-
5176

**Nederlandse Federatie voor Bejaardenbeleid**
Eisenhowerlean 114, The Hague, Netherlands.
● Leef Tijd. 11 per yr.

**Nederlandse Federatie voor de Handel in**
**Pootaardappelen**
Van Stolkweg 31, The Hague, Netherlands.
● Pootaardappelwereld. m.

**Nederlandse Fruittelers Organisatie**
Schiefbaanstraat 29, The Hague, Netherlands.
● Fruitteelt. w. ISSN 0016-2302

**Nederlandse Genealogische Vereniging**
Postbus 976, Amsterdam C, Netherlands.
● Gens Nostra, "Ons Geslacht". m. ISSN 0016-6936

**Nederlandse Genetische Vereniging**
c/o Department of Animal Cytogenetics,
Rijksuniversiteit te Utrecht, Padualaan 8, Utrecht,
Netherlands.
● Genen en Phaenen. q. ISSN 0016-6472

**Nederlandse Geologische Vereniging**
Hogeweg 35, Losser, Netherlands.
● Grondboor en Hamer. bi-m. ISSN 0017-4505

**Nederlandse Golf Federatie**
● Golf. (pub. by B. V. Uitgeversmaatschappij Reflex)

**Nederlandse Handenarbeid Federatie**
Eikenweg 28, Amsterdam, Netherlands.
● Beeldpraat. m.

**Nederlandse Hervormde Kerk. Gereformeerde**
**Zendingsbond**
Utrechtseweg 117, Zeist, Netherlands.
● Alle den Volcke; maandblad van de gereformeerde
zendingsbond in de N. H. kerk. m. ISSN 0002-
5666

**Nederlandse Hervormde Kerk. Persbureau**
Javastraat 100, Box 85932, 2508 CP The Hague,
Netherlands.
● Nederlandse Hervormde Kerk. Persbureau.
Weekbulletin. w. ISSN 0031-5567

**Nederlandse Hotelportiers Vereniging**
Postbus 10571, Amsterdam, Netherlands.
● Gouden Sleutels. bi-m. ISSN 0017-2529

**Nederlandse Houtbond**
Keizersgracht 298, Amsterdam, Netherlands.
● Nederlandse Houtbond. Jaarverslag.

**Nederlandse Ingenieursvereniging**
● Polytechnisch Tijdschrift: Bouwkunde, Wegen- en
Waterbouw. (pub. by Stam Tijdschriften B.V.)
● Polytechnisch Tijdschrift: Elektrotechniek/
Elektronica. (pub. by Stam Tijdschriften B.V.)
● Polytechnisch Tijdschrift: Procestechniek. (pub. by
Stam Tijdschriften B.V.)
● Polytechnisch Tijdschrift: Werktuigbouw. (pub. by
Stam Tijdschriften B.V.)

**Nederlandse Internisten Vereniging**
● Netherlands Journal of Medicine. (pub. by Bohn,
Scheltema en Holkema)

**Nederlandse Judo Ju-Jutsu Associatie**
Boomstraat 153, Tilburg, Netherlands.
● Budo Koerier. bi-m.

**Nederlandse Kamer van Koophandel voor Amerika**
Postbus 1717, Koninginnegracht 143, The Hague,
Netherlands.
● Nederlandse Kamer van Koophandel voor
Amerika. Jaarverslag. a. ISSN 0077-6424

**Nederlandse Katholieke Sportfederatie**
Vughterweg 1, S-Hertogenbosch, Netherlands.
● Sportparade. m. ISSN 0038-8130

**Nederlandse Kermisbond**
Oudegracht 186, Alkmaar, Netherlands.
● N K B. s-m. ISSN 0027-6766

**Nederlandse Klokkenspel-Vereniging**
Versterplein 8, Vught, Netherlands
(Subscr. address: Tafelbergdreef 120, Utrecht, Netherlands)
- Klok en Klepel. s-a. ISSN 0023-2181

**Nederlandse Kring voor Wetenschap der Politiek**
c/o Dr. J. van Putten, Sociaalwetenschappelijk Instituut, Vrije Universiteit, Koningslaan 13, Amsterdam z, Netherlands
- Acta Politica; tijdschrift voor politicologie. q. ISSN 0001-6810 (Subscr. to: Boom-Meppel, Gasgracht 10, Meppel, Netherlands)

**Nederlandse Malacologische Vereniging**
c/o Dr. H. E. Coomans, Zoologisch Museum, Plantage Middenlaan 53, Amsterdam, Netherlands.
- Basteria. 3 per yr. ISSN 0005-6219
- Nederlandse Malacologische Vereniging. Correspondentieblad. bi-m. ISSN 0077-6432

**Nederlandse Melkhandelaren Organisatie**
- Melk en Zuivel. (pub. by Uitgeversmaatschappij de Gelderlander Vakpers BV)

**Nederlandse Natuurkundige Vereniging. Fysisch Laboratorium**
Princetonplein 5, Utrecht, Netherlands.
- Nederlands Tijdschrift voor Natuurkunde. s-m. ISSN 0028-2189

**Nederlandse Onderwatersport Bond**
Balistraat 96, The Hague, Netherlands.
- Onderwatersport. m. ISSN 0048-1696

**Nederlandse Operastichting**
Stadsschouwburg, Marnixstraat 427, Amsterdam, Netherlands.
- Opera Journaal. m. (Sep.-Apr)

**Nederlandse Orchideeen Vereniging**
- Orchideeen. (pub. by Drukkerij Schmitz B.V.)

**Nederlandse Orde van Accountants-Administratieconsulenten**
- Accountant-Adviseur. (pub. by Kluwer B.V.)

**Nederlandse Organisatie van Pluimveehouders**
- Pluimveehouderij. (pub. by Uitgeversmaatschappij C. Misset B. V.)

**Nederlandse Organisatie van Tijdschriftuitgevers**
Herengracht 257, Amsterdam, Netherlands.
- N O T U-Mededelingen. m.

**Nederlandse Organisatie voor Internationale Ontwikkelingssamenwerking**
Amaliastraat 5-7, The Hague, Netherlands.
- Onze Wereld. fortn. ISSN 0030-3232

**Nederlandse Organisatie voor Zuiver-Wetenschappelijk Onderzoek**
Juliana van Stolberglaan 148, The Hague, Netherlands.
- Current Research in the Netherlands: Humanities. irreg.
- Forum der Letteren. (pub. by Smits-N. V.)

**Nederlandse Ornithologische Unie**
Doeffstraat 148, Arnhem, Netherlands.
- Limosa. s-a. ISSN 0024-3620

**Nederlandse Planteziektenkundige Vereniging**
Postbus 31, Wageningen, Netherlands.
- Netherlands Journal of Plant Pathology. bi-m. ISSN 0028-2944

**Nederlandse Rode Kruis**
Prinsessegracht 27, The Hague, Netherlands.
- Ligament. m(10 per yr.) ISSN 0024-3264

**Nederlandse Spaarbankbond**
Singel 236, Box 3861, Amsterdam 1000, Netherlands.
- Bondsspaarbanken. m. ISSN 0006-7091

**N. V. Nederlandse Spoorwegen**
Moreelsepark 1, Utrecht, Netherlands.
- Koppeling. w. ISSN 0023-3870

**Nederlandse Sport Federatie**
Burg. van Karnebeeklaan 6, The Hague, Netherlands.
- Nederlandse Sport Federatie. Technische Mededelingen.
- Sport in de Pers. w. ISSN 0038-7894
- Wegwijs in de Sportliteratuur. q. ISSN 0043-2091

**Nederlandse Stikstofmestoffen Industrie. Landouwkundig Bureau**
Thorbeckelaan 360, Postbus 6695, The Hague 2025, Netherlands.
- Netherlands Nitrogen Technical Bulletin. irreg. ISSN 0077-7595

**Nederlandse Toeristen Kampeerclub**
c/o W. H. Egge, Ed., Weidebloemstraat 23, Berkenwoude Z.H., Netherlands.
- Buitenspoor. m. ISSN 0007-3768

**Nederlandse Unie van Opticiens**
Honthorststraat 12, Amsterdam-z, Netherlands.
- Oculus; vakblad gewijd aan de belangen der Nederlandse opticiens. m. ISSN 0029-8328

**Nederlandse Vacuumvereiniging**
c/o A. van Silfhout, Applied Physics Department, T. H. Twente, Box 217, Enschede, Netherlands.
- Nederlands Tijdschrift voor Vacuumtechniek/ Dutch Journal of Vacuum Technology. bi-m. ISSN 0047-9233

**Nederlandse Vereniging Bescherming Voetgangers**
Passage 61 III, The Hague, Netherlands.
- Voetganger. 2 per yr.

**Nederlandse Vereniging "de Rijwiel- en Automobiel Industrie"**
Europaplein 2, Amsterdam 1010, Netherlands.
- R. A. I. Actueel. w.

**Nederlandse Vereniging ter Bevordering van het Levensverzekeringwezen**
- Verzekerings-Archief. (pub. by Martinus Nijhoff)

**Nederlandse Vereniging tot Beoefening van de Sociale Geschiedenis**
- Tijdschrift voor Sociale Geschiedenis. (pub. by Uitgeverij van Gennep)

**Nederlandse Vereniging tot Steun aan het Koningin Wilhelmina Fonds voor de Kankerbestrijding**
Koninginneweg 28, Amsterdam, Netherlands.
- K. W. F.-Nieuws. s-a. ISSN 0022-7447

**Nederlandse Vereniging van Assurantieadviseurs**
Postbus 235, Amersfoort, Netherlands.
- Reflector. m. ISSN 0034-2947

**Nederlandse Vereniging van Belangstellenden in het Spoor- en Tramwegwezen**
Meppelweg 299, The Hague 2033, Netherlands.
- Op de Rails. m. ISSN 0030-3321

**Nederlandse Vereniging van Bouwondernemers**
Statenlaan 21, The Hague, Netherlands.
- Bouwondernemer. bi-m. ISSN 0006-8381

**Nederlandse Vereniging van Elektroencefalografie Laboranten**
Donker Curtiusstraat 43, Wassenaar, Netherlands.
- Hoofdlijnen. q. ISSN 0018-4705

**Nederlandse Vereniging van Handelaren in Verwarmings- en Huishoudelijke Artikelen**
- Schouw. (pub. by Vanderveer B. V.)

**Nederlandse Vereniging van Huisvrouwen**
Jan van Nassaustraat 89, The Hague, Netherlands.
- Denken en Doen. m. ISSN 0011-8370

**Nederlandse Vereniging van Journalisten**
Johannes Vermeerstraat 55, Amsterdam, Netherlands.
- Journalist. a. ISSN 0022-555X

**Nederlandse Vereniging van Maatschappelijk Werkers**
Wittevrouwenstraat 34, Utrecht, Netherlands.
- N V M W Nieuws. m.

**Nederlandse Vereniging van Modelbouwers**
Du Perronlaan 28, Uithoorn 1220, Netherlands.
- Modelbouwer; tijdschrift voor modelbouw. m. ISSN 0026-7384

**Nederlandse Vereniging van Ondernemers in het Carosseriebedrijf**
Box 1050, Oestgeest, Netherlands.
- Carrosserie. m. ISSN 0008-6940

**Nederlandse Vereniging van Radiologisch Laboranten**
- Gamma. (pub. by Drukkerij J. Valkenburg N.V.)

**Nederlandse Vereniging van Rubberfabrikanten**
Balistraat 97, Postbox 1806, The Hague, Netherlands.
- Nederlandse Rubberindustrie. m.

**Nederlandse Vereniging van Veiligheidstechnici**
- Veilig Werken/Working Safely. (pub. by Veiligheidsinstituut)

**Nederlandse Vereniging van Vrijzinnige Zondagsscholen en Leidraad voor de Leiding**
Molenstr. 14, Lith (N.Br.), Netherland.
- Kandelaar. m. ISSN 0022-8354

**Nederlandse Vereniging van Vrouwen met Academische Opleiding**
c/o Waldeck Pyrmontlaan 7, Oestgeest, Netherlands.
- Nederlandse Vereniging van Vrouwen met Academische Opleiding. Mededelingen. 5 per yr. ISSN 0028-2332

**Nederlandse Vereniging van Wasserijen**
c/o Administration, Reitseplein 1, Tilburg, Netherlands.
- Vakblad voor Textielreiniging. m. ISSN 0042-224X (Co-sponsor: Vereniging van Werkgevers in de Chemische Wasserijen en Ververijen)

**Nederlandse Vereniging voor de Landelijke Eigendom**
- Landeigenaar. (pub. by Drukkerij Banda B.V.)

**Nederlandse Vereniging voor de Verenigde Naties**
Koninginnegracht 140, The Hague, Netherlands.
- N V Informatie.

**Nederlandse Vereniging voor Geodesie**
Thijsseweg 11, Delft, Netherlands.
- Nederlands Geodetisch Tijdschrift. m. ISSN 0040-7526

**Nederlandse Vereniging voor Herpetologie en Terrariumkunde**
c/o Dr. O. H. Blaauw, Sec., Biltstraat 146, Utrecht, Netherlands.
- Lacerta. m. ISSN 0023-7051

**Nederlandse Vereniging voor Internationaal Recht**
- Nederlandse Vereniging voor Internationaal Recht. Mededelingen. (pub. by Kluwer B.V.)

**Nederlandse Vereniging voor Koeltechniek**
- Koeltechniek. (pub. by Uitgeverij P. C. Noordervliet B. V.)

**Nederlandse Vereniging voor Management (Nive)**
Van Alkemadelaan 700, The Hague, Netherlands.
- Bedrijfsvoering. m.
- Inkoop. m. ISSN 0020-1413
- Management Facetten. m.
- N I V E Nieuws. m (11 per yr.)
- Personeelbeleid. m. ISSN 0031-5656 (Nederlandse Vereniging voor Personeelbeleid)
- Tijdschrift voor Effectief Directiebeleid. m. ISSN 0040-7488
- Tijdschrift voor Marketing. m.

**Nederlandse Vereniging voor Personeelbeleid**
- Personeelbeleid. (pub. by Nederlandse Vereniging voor Management (NIVE))

**Nederlandse Vereniging voor Psychiaters in Dienstverband**
- Nederlands Tijdschrift voor Psychiatrie. (pub. by Boom Pers)

**Nederlandse Vereniging voor Revalidatie**
Eisenhowerlaan 142, The Hague, Netherlands.
- Revalidatie. m.

**Nederlandse Vereniging voor Sexuele Hervorming**
Prinses Beatrixlaan 11, Box 64, The Hague, Netherlands.
- Sekstant. m. ISSN 0037-3087

**Nederlandse Vereniging voor Slechthorenden**
Postbus 166, Zutphen, Netherlands.
- Omega; maandblad voor auditieve communicatie. m.

**Nederlandse Vereniging voor Zeegeschiedenis**
Kruipbrem 27, Rotterdam 23014, Netherlands.
- Nederlandse Vereniging voor Zeegeschiedenis. Mededelingen. s-a. ISSN 0028-2340

**Nederlandse Volksdansvereniging**
Proveniersstraat 9b, Rotterdam, Netherlands.
- Nevo-Nieuws. m.

**Nederlandse Volleybal Bond**
Eemwijkstraat 28, Voorburg, Netherlands.
- Volleybal. m.

**Nederlandse Waterski Bond**
Postbus 821, Haarlem, Netherlands.
- Aqua Vite; kritisch tijdschrift voor moderne watersport en buiten-recreatie. bi-m. ISSN 0003-7222

**Nederlandse Zending**
Waldecklaan 3, Hilversum, Netherlands.
- Ster. m. ISSN 0039-1204 (Church of Jesus Christ of Latter-Day Saints)

**Nederlandse Zendingsraad**
Prins Hendriklaan 37, Amsterdam, Netherlands.
- Wereld en Zending; tijdschrift voor opbouw van de missionaire gemeente. q.

**Neerlands Postduiven Orgaan**
Postbus 256, Nieuwe Fellenoord 12, Eindhoven, Netherlands.
- Neerlands Postduiven Orgaan. w. ISSN 0028-2391

**Netherlands. Bureau voor de Industriele Eigendom. Octrooiraad**
Patentlaan 2, Rijswijk (ZH), Netherlands.
- Industriele Eigendom. 3 per mo. ISSN 0019-9249
- Industriele Eigendom. Bijblad. m. ISSN 0006-2251

**Netherlands. Centraal Bureau voor de Statistiek**
Prinses Beatrixlaan 428, Voorburg, Netherlands (Orders to: Staatsuitgeverij, Christoffel Plantijnstraat, The Hague, Netherlands)
- Belastingdruk in Nederland/Burden of Taxes in the Netherlands. a. ISSN 0077-670X
- Compendium Gezondheidsstatistiek Nederland/Compendium Health Statistics of the Netherlands. a. (Co-sponsor: Ministry of Public Health and Environmental Hygiene)
- Kosten en Financiering van de Gezondheidzorg in Nederland/Cost of Health Care in the Netherlands. irreg. ISSN 0075-6954
- Nederlandse Bosstatistiek. irreg., latest 1971 (covers 1964-68)
- Nederlandse Jeugd en Haar Onderwijs/Netherlands Youth and Its Education. irreg. ISSN 0077-6750
- Nederlandse Schadeverzekeringsmaatschappijen/Netherlands Non-Life Insurance Companies. a. ISSN 0077-6874
- Netherlands. Centraal Bureau voor de Statistiek. Beleggingen van Institutionele Beleggers. Investments of Institutional Investors. a. ISSN 0077-6718
- Netherlands. Centraal Bureau voor de Statistiek. Bezoek aan Vermakelijkheidsinstellingen. Attendance at Public Entertainments. a. ISSN 0077-6688
- Netherlands. Centraal Bureau voor de Statistiek. Bibliografie van Regionale Onderzoekingen Op Sociaalwetenschappelijk Terrein. Bibliography of Regional Studies in the Social Sciences. irreg., 1971 latest supplement. ISSN 0077-6726
- Netherlands. Centraal Bureau voor de Statistiek. Conjunctuurtest. m. ISSN 0470-6641
- Netherlands. Centraal Bureau voor de Statistiek. Criminele Statistiek. Criminal Statistics. a. ISSN 0077-6734
- Netherlands. Centraal Bureau voor de Statistiek. Diagnosestatistiek Bedrijfsverenigingen (Omslagleden). Social Insurance Sickness Statistics. a. ISSN 0077-6742
- Netherlands. Centraal Bureau voor de Statistiek. Faillissementsstatistiek. Bankruptcies. a. ISSN 0077-6793
- Netherlands. Centraal Bureau voor de Statistiek. Gevangenisstatistiek. Statistics of Prisons. a. ISSN 0077-6815
- Netherlands. Centraal Bureau voor de Statistiek. Hypotheken en Hypotheekbanken. Statistics of Mortgages and Mortgage Banks. a. ISSN 0077-6823
- Netherlands. Centraal Bureau voor de Statistiek. Jaaroverzicht Bevolking en Volksgezondheid. Population and Health Statistics. a.
- Netherlands. Centraal Bureau voor de Statistiek. Justitiele Statistiek. Judicial Statistics. a. ISSN 0077-684X
- Netherlands. Centraal Bureau voor de Statistiek. Maandcijfers van de Invoer, Uitvoer en Assemblage van Motorrijtuigen. m. ISSN 0548-1910

- Netherlands. Centraal Bureau voor de Statistiek. Maandcijfers van de Visserij. m.
- Netherlands. Centraal Bureau voor de Statistiek. Maandschrift. m. ISSN 0028-2898
- Netherlands. Centraal Bureau voor de Statistiek. Maandstatistiek Financiewezen. m.
- Netherlands. Centraal Bureau voor de Statistiek. Maandstatistiek Politie en Justitie. ISSN 0548-1937
- Netherlands. Centraal Bureau voor de Statistiek. Maandstatistiek van de Binnenlandse Handel. m. ISSN 0024-872X
- Netherlands. Centraal Bureau voor de Statistiek. Maandstatistiek van de Buitenlandse Handel per Goederensoort. m. ISSN 0024-8738
- Netherlands. Centraal Bureau voor de Statistiek. Maandstatistiek van de Buitenlandse Handel per Land. m. ISSN 0024-8746
- Netherlands. Centraal Bureau voor de Statistiek. Maandstatistiek van de Industrie. m. ISSN 0470-6684
- Netherlands. Centraal Bureau voor de Statistiek. Maandstatistiek van de Landbouw. m. ISSN 0024-8754
- Netherlands. Centraal Bureau voor de Statistiek. Maandstatistiek Verkeer en Vervoer. m. ISSN 0024-8770
- Netherlands. Centraal Bureau voor de Statistiek. Maanstatistiek van Bevolking en Volksgezondheid. m. ISSN 0024-8711
- Netherlands. Centraal Bureau voor de Statistiek. Naamlijsten voor de Statistiek van de Buitenlandse Handel. List of Goods for the Statistics of Foreign Trade. irreg. ISSN 0077-6882
- Netherlands. Centraal Bureau voor de Statistiek. Naamlijsten voor de Statistiek van de Buitenlandse Handel. Supplement. List of Goods for the Statistics of Foreign Trade. Supplement. a. ISSN 0077-6890
- Netherlands. Centraal Bureau voor de Statistiek. Nationale Rekeningen. National Accounts. a. ISSN 0077-6866
- Netherlands. Centraal Bureau voor de Statistiek. Nederlandse Energiehuishouding. q.
- Netherlands. Centraal Bureau voor de Statistiek. Productie Statistiek van de Zuivel Industrie. Production Statistics of the Dairy Industry. irreg.
- Netherlands. Centraal Bureau voor de Statistiek. Produktiestatistieken: Distileerderijen en Likeurstokerijen. irreg.
- Netherlands. Centraal Bureau voor de Statistiek. Produktiestatistieken: Papier- en Kartonindustrie. irreg.
- Netherlands. Centraal Bureau voor de Statistiek. Produktiestatistieken. Production Statistics of Individual Industries. a. ISSN 0077-6912
- Netherlands. Centraal Bureau voor de Statistiek. Produktiestatistieken: Rijwiel-en Motorrijwielindustrie. irreg.
- Netherlands. Centraal Bureau voor de Statistiek. Produktiestatistieken: Suikerfabrieken. irreg.
- Netherlands. Centraal Bureau voor de Statistiek. Produktiestatistieken: Veevoederindustrie. irreg.
- Netherlands. Centraal Bureau voor de Statistiek. Regionaal Statistisch Zakboek. irreg.
- Netherlands. Centraal Bureau voor de Statistiek. Sociale Maandstatistiek. m.
- Netherlands. Centraal Bureau voor de Statistiek. Statistical Studies. irreg. ISSN 0077-7064
- Netherlands. Centraal Bureau voor de Statistiek. Statistiek der Branden. Fire Statistics. irreg. ISSN 0077-6955
- Netherlands. Centraal Bureau voor de Statistiek. Statistiek der Lonen in de Landbouw. Statistics of Wages in Agriculture. a. ISSN 0077-6963
- Netherlands. Centraal Bureau voor de Statistiek. Statistiek der Motorrijtuigen. Statistics of Motor Vehicles. a. ISSN 0077-698X
- Netherlands. Centraal Bureau voor de Statistiek. Statistiek der Spaarbanken. Statistical View of the Savings Bank. a. ISSN 0077-7005
- Netherlands. Centraal Bureau voor de Statistiek. Statistiek der Verkiezingen. Gemeenteraden. Election Statistics. Municipal Councils. irreg. ISSN 0077-7013
- Netherlands. Centraal Bureau voor de Statistiek. Statistiek der Verkiezingen. Provinciale Staten. Election Statistics. Provincial Councils. irreg. ISSN 0077-7021
- Netherlands. Centraal Bureau voor de Statistiek. Statistiek der Verkiezingen. Tweede Kamer der Staten-Generaal. Election Statistics. Second Chamber of the States-General. irreg. ISSN 0077-703X

- Netherlands. Centraal Bureau voor de Statistiek. Statistiek van de Algemene Bijstand. Statistics of Public Assistance. a. ISSN 0077-7072
- Netherlands. Centraal Bureau voor de Statistiek. Statistiek van de Bejaardenoorden. Homes for the Aged. a. ISSN 0077-7099
- Netherlands. Centraal Bureau voor de Statistiek. Statistiek van de Gemeentewege per Leerling Beschikbaar Gestelde Bedragen ter Bestrijding van de Materiele Exploitatiekosten der Lagere Scholen. Statistics of the Amounts per Pupil Provided by the Municipality to Meet the Material Cost of Elementary Education. a. ISSN 0077-7226
- Netherlands. Centraal Bureau voor de Statistiek. Statistiek van de Internationale Binnenvaart. Statistics of the International Inland Shipping. a. ISSN 0077-7102
- Netherlands. Centraal Bureau voor de Statistiek. Statistiek van de Investeringen in Vaste Activa in de Industrie. Statistics on Fixed Capital Formation in Industry. a. ISSN 0077-7110
- Netherlands. Centraal Bureau voor de Statistiek. Statistiek van de Investeringen in Vaste Activa in de Nijverheid. irreg.
- Netherlands. Centraal Bureau voor de Statistiek. Statistiek van de Koopvaardijvloot. Statistics of the Merchant Marine. a. ISSN 0077-7129
- Netherlands. Centraal Bureau voor de Statistiek. Statistiek van de Luchtvaart. Civil Aviation Statistics. a. ISSN 0077-7137
- Netherlands. Centraal Bureau voor de Statistiek. Statistiek van de Land- en Tuinbouw. Statistics of Agriculture. a. ISSN 0077-7145
- Netherlands. Centraal Bureau voor de Statistiek. Statistiek van de Openbare Bibliotheken. irreg.
- Netherlands. Centraal Bureau voor de Statistiek. Statistiek van de Spaargelden. Statistics of Savings. irreg.
- Netherlands. Centraal Bureau voor de Statistiek. Statistiek van de Uitgaven der Overheid voor Cultuur en Recreatie. Statistics of Government Expenditure on Culture and Recreation. a. ISSN 0077-7196
- Netherlands. Centraal Bureau voor de Statistiek. Statistiek van de Uitgaven der Overheid voor Onderwijs. Statistics of the Expenditure of the State, the Provinces and the Municipalities on Education. a. ISSN 0077-7188
- Netherlands. Centraal Bureau voor de Statistiek. Statistiek van de Uitgaven der Overheid voor Onderwijs, Wetenschap en Cultuur. Statistics of the Expenditure of the State, the Provinces and the Municipalities on Education, Science and Culture. a. ISSN 0077-720X
- Netherlands. Centraal Bureau voor de Statistiek. Statistiek van de Voorlichting bij Beroepskeuze en Personeelselectie. Statistics of Vocational Guidance and Selection of Personnel. a. ISSN 0077-7218
- Netherlands. Centraal Bureau voor de Statistiek. Statistiek van de Verkeersongevallen op de Openbare Weg. Statistics of Road-Traffic Accidents. a. ISSN 0077-7234
- Netherlands. Centraal Bureau voor de Statistiek. Statistiek van de Visserij. Statistics of Fisheries. a. ISSN 0077-7242
- Netherlands. Centraal Bureau voor de Statistiek. Statistiek van de Zeevaart. Statistics of Seaborne Shipping. a. ISSN 0077-7250
- Netherlands. Centraal Bureau voor de Statistiek. Statistiek van Het Beroepsonderwijs: Beroepsbegeleidend Onderwijs Leerlingwezen. irreg.
- Netherlands. Centraal Bureau voor de Statistiek. Statistiek van Het Binnenlands Goederenvervoer. Statistics of Internal Goods Transport in the Netherlands. a. ISSN 0077-7269
- Netherlands. Centraal Bureau voor de Statistiek. Statistiek van Het Buitengewoon Onderwijs. Statistic of Special Education. irreg.
- Netherlands. Centraal Bureau voor de Statistiek. Statistiek van Het Beroepsonderwijs. Statistics on Vocational Training. a. ISSN 0077-7285
- Netherlands. Centraal Bureau voor de Statistiek. Statistiek van Het Gesubsidieerde Toneel.
- Netherlands. Centraal Bureau voor de Statistiek. Statistiek van Het Internationaal Goederenvervoer. Statistics of the International Goods Traffic. a. ISSN 0077-7293
- Netherlands. Centraal Bureau voor de Statistiek. Statistiek van het internationaal zeehavenvervoer. q.
- Netherlands. Centraal Bureau voor de Statistiek. Statistiek van Het Kunstonderwijs. Statistics on Art Colleges. a. ISSN 0077-7307

- Netherlands. Centraal Bureau voor de Statistiek. Statistiek van Het Kleuteronderwijs. Statistics of Nursery Schools. irreg. ISSN 0077-7315
- Netherlands. Centraal Bureau voor de Statistiek. Statistiek van Het Kweekschoolonderwijs. Statistics on Teacher Training Colleges. a. ISSN 0077-7323
- Netherlands. Centraal Bureau voor de Statistiek. Statistiek van Het Land- en Tuinbouwonderwijs. Statistics Concerning Agricultural and Horticultural Education. a. ISSN 0077-7331
- Netherlands. Centraal Bureau voor de Statistiek. Statistiek van Het Nijverheidsonderwijs. Statistics of Technical and Home Economics Training. a. ISSN 0077-734X
- Netherlands. Centraal Bureau voor de Statistiek. Statistiek van Het Personenvervoer. Statistics of Passenger Transport. a. ISSN 0077-7358
- Netherlands. Centraal Bureau voor de Statistiek. Statistiek van Het Schriftelijk Onderwijs. Statistics on Correspondence Courses. irreg. ISSN 0077-7366
- Netherlands. Centraal Bureau voor de Statistiek. Statistiek van Het Sociaal-Pedagogisch Onderwijs. Statistics on Socio-Pedagogic Training. a. ISSN 0077-7374
- Netherlands. Centraal Bureau voor de Statistiek. Statistiek van Het Toneel. Statistics on Theatre Performances. a. ISSN 0077-7382
- Netherlands. Centraal Bureau voor de Statistiek. Statistiek van Het Uitgebreid Lager Onderwijs. Statistics of Continued Elementary Education. a. ISSN 0077-7390
- Netherlands. Centraal Bureau voor de Statistiek. Statistiek van het Voorbereidend Hoger en Middelbaar Onderwijs. Leraren. Statistics of Secondary Education. Teachers. a. ISSN 0077-7404
- Netherlands. Centraal Bureau voor de Statistiek. Statistiek van Het Wetenschappelijk Onderwijs. Statistics of University Education. a. ISSN 0077-7439
- Netherlands. Centraal Bureau voor de Statistiek. Statistiek Vreemdelingenverkeer. Tourism Statistics. a. ISSN 0077-7447
- Netherlands. Centraal Bureau voor de Statistiek. Statistiek Werkzame Personen. irreg.
- Netherlands. Centraal Bureau voor de Statistiek. Statistisch Bulletin. irreg. ISSN 0077-6947
- Netherlands. Centraal Bureau voor de Statistiek. Statistisch Zakboek. Pocket Yearbook. a. ISSN 0077-7463
- Netherlands. Centraal Bureau voor de Statistiek. Statistische en Econometrisch Onderzoekingen. Statistical and Econometric Studies. irreg. ISSN 0077-7048
- Netherlands. Centraal Bureau voor de Statistiek. Toepassing der Kinderwetten. Application of Juvenile Law. irreg. ISSN 0077-7471
- Netherlands. Centraal Bureau voor de Statistiek. Toepassing der Wegenverkeerswet. Statistics of the Application of the Road Traffic Act. irreg. ISSN 0077-748X
- Netherlands. Centraal Bureau voor de Statistiek. Vermogensverdeling. Regionale Gegevens. Distribution of Personal Wealth. Regional Data. irreg. ISSN 0077-7498
- Netherlands. Centraal Bureau voor de Statistiek. Voortgezet Onderwijs Regionaal Bezien. a.
- Netherlands. Centraal Bureau voor de Statistiek. Voortgezet Onderwijs Regionaal Bezien. Regional Aspects of Post-Elementary Education. irreg. ISSN 0077-6831
- Netherlands. Centraal Bureau voor de Statistiek. Voorziening in de Behoefte aan Onderwijzers Bij het Lager Onderwijs. Supplying the Need for Teachers in Elementary Education. a. ISSN 0077-6785
- Netherlands. Centraal Bureau voor de Statistiek. Winststatiek der Grotere Naamloze Vennootschappen. Profit-Statistics of the Limited Liability Companies. a. ISSN 0077-751X
- Omvang der Vakbeweging in Nederland/Statistics of the Trade Unions in the Netherlands. a. ISSN 0077-6904
- Ontwikkeling van het Onderwijs in Nederland/ Development of Education in the Netherlands. irreg. ISSN 0077-6769
- Population of the Municipalities of the Netherlands. a. ISSN 0079-3930
- Speur- en Ontwikkelingswerk in Nederland/ Research and Development Activities in the Netherlands. irreg. ISSN 0077-7056
- Sportaccommodatie in Nederland/Sports; Public Accommodation. irreg. ISSN 0077-6777
- Statistical Yearbook of the Netherlands. a. ISSN 0077-6858

- Statistiek der Rijksfinancien/Statistics of the State Finances of the Netherlands. irreg. ISSN 0077-6998
- Statistiek van de Gasvoorziening in Nederland. a. ISSN 0081-5225
- Statistiek van de Scheepvaartbeweging in Nederland/Census of Inland Shipping in the Netherlands at Locks and Bridges. a. ISSN 0077-7161
- Vakantiebesteding van de Nederlandse Bevolking/ Spending of Holidays of the Netherlands' Population. irreg. ISSN 0077-7501

**Netherlands. Commissie Zeehavenoverleg**
Koningskade 4, The Hague, Netherlands.
- Netherlands. Commissie Zeehaven Overleg. Jaarverslag. a. ISSN 0077-7552

**Netherlands. Gevangeniswezen. Centraal Wervings- en Opleidingsinstituut**
Ministerie van Justitie, Pompstationsweg 34, The Hague, Netherlands.
- Balans; maandblad voor gevangeniswezen en t.b.r.-stelling. m. ISSN 0005-4259

**Netherlands. Hydrografisch Bureau**
The Hague, Netherlands.
- Netherlands. Hydrografisch Bureau. Catalogus van Nederlandse Zeekaarten en Andere Hydrografische Publikaties /Catalogue of Charts and Other Hydrographic Publications. irreg.

**Netherlands. Inspectie voor het Brandweerwezen**
Spui 49-49, The Hague, Netherlands.
- Netherlands. Inspectie voor het Brandweerwezen. Maandelijkse Mededelingen. m. ISSN 0020-2045

**Netherlands. Kabinet Nederlandse Antillen**
Afdeling Voorlichting, Badhuisweg 175, The Hague, Netherlands.
- Antilliaanse Nieuwsbrief. bi-w. ISSN 0003-5718

**Netherlands. Koninklijke Landmacht**
Ministerie van Defensie, Spui 32, The Hague, Netherlands.
- Legerkoerier. m. ISSN 0024-0389

**Netherlands. Koninklijke Luchtmacht**
Prins Clauslaan 8, The Hague, Netherlands.
- Herkenning; journal for aircraft-, ship and A.F.V. recognition. bi-m. ISSN 0018-0734
- Vliegende Hollander. m. ISSN 0042-7705

**Netherlands. Koninklijke Luchtmacht. Afdeling Bedrijfsveiligheid Koninklijke Luchtmachtstaf**
Prins Clauslaan 8, The Hague, Netherlands.
- Veilig Vliegen; flight, ground and maintenance safety journal. m. ISSN 0042-3122

**Netherlands. Ministerie van Binnenlandse Zaken**
Binnenhof 19, The Hague, Netherlands.
- R. P. A. Bulletin; mededelingen over rijkspersoneelsaangelegenheden. m. ISSN 0033-7056
- Het Torentje; personeelsblad van het Ministerie van Binnenlandse Zaken. m. ISSN 0018-1129

**Netherlands. Ministerie van Binnenlandse Zaken. Inspectie voor het Brandweerwezen**
*see* Netherlands. Inspectie voor het Brandweerwezen

**Netherlands. Ministerie van Buitenlandse Zaken. Voorlichtingsdienst Ontwikkelingssamenwerking**
Herengracht 3a, The Hague, Netherlands.
- Netherlands. Ministerie van Buitenlandse Zaken. Voorlichtingsdienst Ontwikkelingssamenwerking/ Implementation and Vindication of Policy. 2 per yr

**Netherlands. Ministerie van Cultuur Recreatie en Maatschappelijk Werk**
Steenvoordelaan 370, Rijswijk (Z.H.), Netherlands.
- Berichten van de Afdeling Volkskredietwezen. irreg., no. 26, 1976. ISSN 0005-9110
- Dutch Film. irreg.
- Netherlands. Ministerie van Cultuur, Recreatie en Maatschappelijk Werk. Centrale Afdeling Internationale Betrekkingen. Informatie Bulletin. q. ISSN 0028-2979
- Netherlands. Ministerie van Cultuur, Recreatie en Maatschappelijk Werk. Openluchtrecreatie. irreg.
- Trefpunt; tijdschrift van het Ministerie van Cultuur, Recreatie en Maatschappelijk Werk. 11 per yr.

**Netherlands. Ministerie van Defensie**
- Militaire Spectator. (pub. by Koninklijke Vereniging Ter Beoefening van de Krijgswetenschap)

**Netherlands. Ministerie van Economische Zaken. Economische Voorlichtingsdienst**
Bezuidenhoutseweg 151, The Hague, Netherlands.
- Economic Titles. (pub. by Martinus Nijhoff)
- Exportmarkten. q. ISSN 0014-5211
- Key to Economic Science. (pub. by Martinus Nijhoff)

**Netherlands. Ministerie van Justitie.**
Raamweg 47, The Hague, Netherlands.
- Algemeen Politieblad van het Koninkrijk der Nederlanden. fortn. ISSN 0002-5283
- Directie Kinderbescherming. biennial.

**Netherlands. Ministerie van Justitie. Gevangeniswezen**
*see* Netherlands. Gevangeniswezen

**Netherlands. Ministerie van Justitie. Wetenschappelijk Onderzoek- en Documentatiecentrum**
Plein 2b, The Hague, Netherlands.
- Netherlands. Ministerie van Justitie. Wetenschappelijk Onderzoek- en Documentatiecentrum. Onderzoekbulletin / Research Bulletin. a.

**Netherlands. Ministerie van Landbouw en Visserij**
Bezuidenhoutseweg 73, The Hague, Netherlands.
- Bedrijfsontwikkeling; maandblad voor agrarische productie, verwerking en afzet. 11 per yr.
- Landbouwwereldnieuws. bi-m. ISSN 0023-7825
- Visserij; voorlichtingsblad voor de Nederlandse visserij. 8-9 per yr. ISSN 0042-7047 (Subscr. to: Staatsuitgeverij, Christoffel Prantijnstraat 1, The Hague, Netherlands)

**Netherlands. Ministerie van Landbouw en Visserij. Statistics and Documentation Section**
Kon. Julianaplein 3, The Hague, Netherlands.
- E E G Vademecum/Selected Agri-Figures of the E.E.C. biennial.

**Netherlands. Ministerie van Sociale Zaken. Library and Documentation Service**
Anna Paulownastraat 38, The Hague, Netherlands.
- Uitgelezen. m. ISSN 0041-591X

**Netherlands. Ministerie van Volksgezondheid en Milieuhygiene**
The Hague, Netherlands.
- Excerpta Medica. Section 40: Drug Dependence. (pub. by Excerpta Medica)
- Netherlands. Ministerie van Volksgezondheid en Milieuhygiene. Verslag Levensmiddelen en Keuring van Waren. irreg.

**Netherlands. Ministerie van Volkshuisvesting en Ruimtelijke Ordening. Afdeling Voorlichting**
The Hague, Netherlands.
- Netherlands. Ministerie van Volkshuisvesting en Ruimtelijke Ordening. Afdeling Voorlichting. Current Trends and Policies in Housing and Building. irreg.

**Netherlands. Persraad**
The Hague, Netherlands.
- Netherlands. Persraad. Jaarverslag. a.

**Netherlands. Raad voor de Beroepskeuzevoorlichting**
Volmerlaan 1, Rijswijk, Netherlands.
- Netherlands. Raad voor de Beroepskeuzevoorlichting. Verslag van de Werkzaamheden. a.

**Netherlands. Rijks Geologische Dienst**
Spaarne 17, P.O. Box 157, Haarlem, Netherlands.
- Netherlands. Rijks Geologische Dienst. Jaarverslag/Netherlands Geological Survey. Annual Report. a. ISSN 0077-7617

**Netherlands. Rijkscommissie voor Geodesie**
Kanaalweg 4, Delft, Netherlands.
- Netherlands. Rijkscommissie voor Geodesie. Publications on Geodesy. New Series. irreg. ISSN 0077-7625

**Netherlands. Rijksmuseum**
Stadhouderskade 42, Amsterdam, Netherlands.
- Netherlands. Rijksmuseum. Bulletin. q. ISSN 0028-3002

**Netherlands. Rijksmuseum voor Volkenkunde**
Steenstraat 1, Postbus 212, Leiden, Netherlands.
- Verre Naasten Naderbij. 3 per yr. ISSN 0042-
4323

**Netherlands. Rijksvoorlichtingsdienst**
The Hague, Netherlands.
- Netherlands. Rijksvoorlichtingsdienst. Hoofpunten
van het Regeringsbeleid. irreg.

**Netherlands. Sociaal en Cultureel Planbureau**
J. C. van Markenlaan 3, Rijswijk, Netherlands.
- Netherlands. Sociaal en Cultureel Planbureau.
Social and Cultural Report. a.

**Netherlands. Sociale Verzekeringsraad**
President Kennedylaan 21, The Hague, Netherlands.
- Netherlands. Sociale Verzekeringsraad.
Jaarverslag. a.
- Netherlands. Sociale Verzekeringsraad. Verslag
van de Stand der Ziekengeldverzekering. irreg.
ISSN 0489-2992

**Netherlands. Staatsbedrijf der Posterijen Telegrafie
en Telefonie**
Kortenaerkade 12, The Hague, Netherlands.
- P T T Bedrijf. (Posterijen Telegrafie en Telefonie);
denkbeelden, methoden, onderzoekingen. 3-4 per
yr. ISSN 0030-8366

**Netherlands. Staatsuitgeverij**
Chr. Plantijnstr., The Hague, Netherlands
- Deltawerken. q. ISSN 0011-8079 (Prepared by:
Deltadienst Rijkswaterstaat)
- Handelingen der Staten-Generaal. w. ISSN 0017-
7253
- Netherlands. Centraal Planbureau. Central
Economic Plan. a. ISSN 0077-7536 (Prepared by:
Centraal Planbureau)
- Netherlands. Ministerie van Onderwijs en
Wetenschappen. Documentatieblad. m. ISSN
0012-4540 (Prepared by: Ministerie van
Onderwijs en Wetenschappen)
- Netherlands. Ministerie van Onderwijs en
Wetenschappen. Onderwijsverslag. a. (Prepared
by: Ministerie van Onderwijs en Wetenschappen)
- Netherlands. Ministerie van Onderwijs en
Wetenschappen. Pedagogische Bibliografie. m.
ISSN 0028-2987 (Prepared by: Ministerie van
Onderwijs en Wetenschappen)
- Oud-Holland; driemaandelijks tijdschrift voor
Nederlandse kunstgeschiedenis. q. ISSN 0030-
672X (Prepared by: Rijksbureau voor
Kunsthistorische Documentatie)
- Tentoonstellingsagenda. fortn. ISSN 0040-3520
(Prepared by: Rijksbureau voor Kunsthistorische
Documentatie)
- Tractatenblad van het Koninkrijk der
Nederlanden. 200 per yr(approx.) ISSN 0023-
3412 (Prepared by: Ministerie van Buitenlandse
Zaken)
- Woningbouwstudies. irreg., 1971, no. 13. ISSN
0084-1072 (Prepared by: Stichting Research
Instituut voor de Woningbouw)

**Netherlands. Tariefcommissie**
- U. T. C. (pub. by Kluwer B. V.)

**Netherlands A D P Research Centre**
Stadhouderskade 6, Amsterdam, Netherlands.
- International Computer Bibliography; a guide to
books on the use, application and effect of
computers in scientific, commercial, industrial and
social environments. irreg. ISSN 0074-283X (Co-
sponsor: National Computing Center, England)

**Netherlands Association of Journalists**
*see* **Nederlandse Vereniging van Journalisten**

**Netherlands Cement Industry B.V.**
Herengracht 507, Postbus 10, Amsterdam-C,
Netherlands.
- Cement; Tijdschrift gewijd aan cement en beton.
m. ISSN 0008-8811

**Netherlands Central Organization for Applied
Scientific Research TNO**
Public Relations Department, P.O. Box 297, The
Hague, Netherlands.
- International T N O Conference. Proceedings. a.
ISSN 0074-8951

**Netherlands Centre of the International Theatre
Institute**
Nieuwe Uitleg 15, The Hague, Netherlands.
- International Congress of Libraries and Museums
of the Performing Arts. Acts. Actes. irreg. ISSN
0538-6527

**Netherlands Council for Trade Promotion. Economic
Information Service**
Westblaak 180, Rotterdam-2, Netherlands.
- Wereldmarkt. w. ISSN 0043-2741

**Netherlands Electronics and Radio Society.**
Box 39, Leidschendam, Netherlands.
- Elektronica en Telecommunicatie; containing the
proceedings of the Nederlands Elektronica en
Radiogenootschap. 12 per yr. ISSN 0013-5623
(Co-Sponsor: Royal Institution of Engineers)

**Netherlands Emigration Service**
Groot Hertoginnelaan 258, The Hague, Netherlands.
- Elders; een kroniek van zaken buiten de grenzen.
m. ISSN 0013-4082

**Netherlands Federation of Trade Unions**
Plein 40-45, Nr. 1, Amsterdam, Slotermeer,
Netherlands.
- Netherlands Federation of Trade Unions.
Information Bulletin. q. ISSN 0466-7530

**Netherlands Grain Centre**
Box 47, Wageningen, Netherlands.
- Literatuur-Mededeling. q. ISSN 0024-4880

**Netherlands Hydrobiological Society**
c/o Ed. Jaap Dorgelo, University of Amsterdam,
Limnological Laboratory, Kruislaan 320,
Amsterdam-0, Netherlands.
- Hydrobiological Bulletin. 3-4 per yr.

**Netherlands Institute for Sea Research**
P.O. Box 59, Texel, Netherlands.
- Netherlands Journal of Sea Research. 4 per yr.
ISSN 0077-7579

**Netherlands Institute for the Middle East**
- Barid Hollanda. (pub. by Van Kouteren's
Publishing Co.)

**Netherlands Institute of Transport**
Treubstraat 35, Rijswijk (Z-H), Netherlands.
- Documentatie Verkeerseconomie en Aanverwante
Onderwerpen. m. ISSN 0012-4524
- Tijdschrift voor Vervoerswetenschap/Magazine for
Transport Science. q. ISSN 0040-7623

**Netherlands Investment Bank for Developing
Countries**
The Hague, Netherlands.
- Netherlands Investment Bank for Developing
Countries. Annual Report. a. ISSN 0077-7560

**Netherlands-Ireland Institute**
Nassau Zuilensteinstraat 9, The Hague, Netherlands.
- Documentatie; sociaal, economisch en fiscaal. w.
ISSN 0012-4516
- Ireland Today. s-m. (Ireland. Department of
External Affairs. Information Section IE)

**Netherlands Maritime Institute. Maritime Economic
Research Centre**
Hofplein 19, Box 1555, Rotterdam-3001,
Netherlands.
- Manual of Maritime Statistics. s-a.

**Netherlands Organisation for Applied Scientific
Research**
- Project. (pub. by B. V. Uitgeversmaatschappij
Reflex)

**Netherlands Royal Army**
*see* **Netherlands. Koninklijke Landmacht**

**Netherlands Society of Royal Navy Officers**
*see* **Vereniging van Marine-Officieren**

**Netherlands Sociological Society**
- Netherlands' Journal of Sociology. (pub. by
Elsevier Scientific Publishing Co.)

**Netherlands Universities Foundation for International
Cooperation**
Box 90734, 2509 LS The Hague, Netherlands.
- Higher Education and Research in the
Netherlands/Ensenanza Superior e Investigacion
Cientifica en Holanda. q. ISSN 0018-1587
- Netherlands Universities Foundation for
International Cooperation. Overzicht. m.
- Planning and Development in the Netherlands.
(pub. by Van Gorcum)

**Netherlands Youth Council**
*see* **Nederlandse Federatie Jeugd en Jongerenwerk**

**N. V. Uitgeversmij. Nieuwe Limburger**
Wolfstraat 17, Maastricht, Netherlands.
- Duivengazet. w. ISSN 0012-706X

**Nieuwe Rotterdamse Courant N.V.**
Westblaak 180, Rotterdam, Netherlands
(Subscr. to: Tournooiveld 3, The Hague,
Netherlands)
- Vrije Bouw en Exploitatie; bezit en beheer. m.
(Nederlandse Bond van Huis- en Grondeigenaren)

**Nieuwe Vereniging van Aannemers Grootbedrijf**
Benoordenhoutseweg 43, The Hague, Netherlands.
- NIVAG Contour. m(11 per yr)

**Nieuwsdienst Morele Herbewapening**
- Nieuw Wereld Nieuws. (pub. by Nederlandsche
Stichting voor Moreele Herbewapening)

**Martinus Nijhoff**
Lange Voorhout 9-11, The Hague, Netherlands.
- Acta Historiae Neerlandicae. a. ISSN 0065-129X
(Dutch Historical Association)
- Annual Bibliography of the History of the Printed
Book and Library. a.
- Applied Scientific Research. bi-m. ISSN 0003-
6994 (Central National Organization for Applied
Scientific Research in the Netherlands)
- Aquila; Chestnut Hill studies in modern languages
and literatures. irreg. ISSN 0587-3428 (Boston
College US)
- Archives Internationales d'Histoire des Idees/
International Archives of the History of Ideas.
irreg. ISSN 0066-6610
- Bibliotheca Indonesica. irreg. ISSN 0067-8023
(Koninklijk Instituut voor Taal-, Land- en
Volkenkunde)
- Bijdragen en Mededelingen Betreffende de
Geschiedenis der Nederlanden. 3 per yr.
(Nederlands Historisch Genootschap)
- Bijdragen tot de Taal-, Land- en Volkenkunde. q.
ISSN 0006-2294 (Koninklijk Instituut voor Taal-,
Land- en Volkenkunde.)
- Boston College Studies in Philosophy. irreg. ISSN
0524-112X (Boston College US)
- Dutch Studies. a. (International Association for
Dutch Studies)
- Economic Titles; semi-monthly providing concise
information of interest to business, trade, industry,
economic libraries and research institutes. s-m.
(Netherlands. Ministerie van Economische Zaken.
Economische Voorlichtingsdienst)
- European Convention on Human Rights.
Yearbook. a., except 1964. ISSN 0071-2701
(Council of Europe FR)
- European Yearbook. a., except 1964. ISSN 0071-
3139 (Council of Europe FR)
- Husserliana. irreg. ISSN 0439-9714 (Centre
d'Archives Husserl BE)
- International Journal for Philosophy of Religion.
q. ISSN 0020-7047
- International Review of Education. q. ISSN 0020-
8566 (Unesco Institute for Education UN)
- Iowa Publications in Philosophy. irreg. ISSN
0075-0395 (University of Iowa US)
- Journal of Value Inquiry. q. ISSN 0022-5363
- Key to Economic Science; semi-monthly review of
abstracts on economics, finance, trade, industry,
foreign aid, management, marketing, labour. s-m.
(Netherlands. Ministerie van Economische Zaken.
Economische Voorlichtingsdienst)
- Koninklijk Instituut voor Taal-, Land- en
Volkenkunde. Bibliographical Series. irreg. ISSN
0074-0462
- Koninklijk Instituut voor Taal-, Land- en
Volkenkunde. Translation Series. irreg. ISSN
0074-0470
- Koninklijk Instituut voor Taal- , Land- en
Volkenkunde. Verhandelingen. irreg.
- Man and World; an international philosophical
review. q. ISSN 0025-1534
- Melbourne International Philosophy Series. irreg.
(University of Melbourne. Philosophy Department
AT)
- Monumenta Lexicographica Neerlandia. Reek 3:
Studies. irreg.
- Nederlands Interuniversitair Demographisch
Instituut. Publications. irreg. (Nederlands
Interuniversitair Demografisch Instituut) (Co-
sponsor: Population and Family Study Centre)
- Nijhoff Information; books and periodicals from
the Netherlands in foreign languages. bi-m. ISSN
0029-0459
- Phaenomenologica. irreg. ISSN 0079-1350 (Centre
d'Archives Husserl BE)

- Plant and Soil; international journal of plant nutrition, plant chemistry, soil microbiology and soil-borne plant diseases. bi-m. ISSN 0032-079X (Koninklijk Genootschap voor Landbouwwetenschap)
- Research Group for European Migration Problems. Publications. irreg. ISSN 0080-1623
- Rijksinstituut voor Oorlogsdocumentatie. Documenten. irreg. ISSN 0066-1287
- Rijksinstituut voor Oorlogsdocumentatie. Monografieen. irreg. ISSN 0066-1295
- Selected Studies in Phenomenology and Existential Philosophy. irreg.
- Series on the Development of Societies. irreg.
- Spiegel der Letteren; tijdschrift voor Nederlandse literatuurgeschiedenis en voor literatuurwetenschap. 4 per yr. ISSN 0038-7479
- Studies in Social Life. irreg. ISSN 0081-8518
- Tulane Studies in Philosophy. irreg. ISSN 0082-6766 (Tulane University. Department of Philosophy US)
- Verzekerings-Archief. q. ISSN 0042-4528 (Nederlandse Vereniging ter Bevordering van het Levensverzekeringwezen)

**N.V. Noord Nederlandse Drukkerij**
Postbus 6, Meppel, Netherlands.
- Elektrotechniek; leading paper on electrical and nuclear engineering. m. ISSN 0013-4627 (K E M A)

**Uitgeverij P.C. Noordervliet B.V.**
Box 268, Zeist, Netherlands.
- Klimaatbeheersing; tijdschrift voor verwarming, luchtbehandeling en milieuverzorging. m.
- Koeltechniek. m. ISSN 0023-2661 (Nederlandse Vereniging voor Koeltechniek)
- Voedingsmiddelentechnologie. w. ISSN 0042-7934

**Noordhoff International Publishing**
Schuttersveld 9, Box 26, Leiden, Netherlands.
- Compositio Mathematica. 2 vols. per yr.(3 nos. per vol.) ISSN 0010-437X
- Flora Malesiana. Series 2: Pteridophyta. irreg., 1969, vol. 1, pt. 2. ISSN 0071-5786 (Foundation Flora Malesiana) (Co-Sponsor: Rijksherbarium) (Avail. from Foundation at: Schelpenkade 6, Leiden, Netherlands)
- Flora Malesiana Bulletin. irreg.(approx. 1 per year) ISSN 0071-5778 (Foundation Flora Malesiana) (Co-sponsor: Rijksherbarium) (Avail. from Foundation at: Schelpenkade 6, Leiden, Netherlands)
- International Journal of Fracture. q.
- Journal of Elasticity. q.
- Journal of Engineering Mathematics. q. ISSN 0022-0833
- Mechanics of Fracture. irreg.
- Solid Mechanics Archives. q.

**North Atlantic Treaty Organization**
- Atlantic Series. (pub. by A. W. Sijthoff International Publishing Co.)

**North Atlantic Treaty Organization. Scientific Affairs Division**
- N A T O Advanced Study Institutes Series D: Behavioural and Social Sciences. (pub. by A. W. Sijthoff International Publishing Co.)

**North-Holland Publishing Co.**
Box 211, Amsterdam, Netherlands
(Dist. in the U.S. and Canada by: Elsevier North-Holland, Inc., New York, 52 Vanderbilt Ave., New York, NY 10017)
- Acta Philosophica Fennica. q.
- Acta Psychologica; international journal of psychonomics. bi-m. ISSN 0001-6918
- Advanced Textbooks in Economics. irreg., vol. 5, 1974.
- Alternatives; journal for world policy. q.
- Annals of Mathematical Logic. 9 per yr. ISSN 0003-4843 (Association for Symbolic Logic)
- Artificial Intelligence. bi-m. ISSN 0004-3702
- Association Internationale d'Etudes Patristiques. Bulletin d'Information et de Liaison. q. (International Association for Patristic Studies)
- Biological Psychology. 4 per yr. ISSN 0301-0511
- Biophysical Chemistry; an international journal devoted to the physical chemistry of biological phenomena. bi-m. ISSN 0301-4622
- Carnegie-Rochester Conference Series on Public Policy. irreg.
- Chemical Physics; a journal devoted to the experimental and theoretical research involving problems of both a chemical and a physical nature. 24 per yr. ISSN 0301-0104

- Chemical Physics Letters. 24 per yr. ISSN 0009-2614
- Clinical Studies. irreg., vol. 5, 1974.
- Colloque A M P E R E. irreg., vol. 18, 1975. ISSN 0533-3180 (Group for the Study of Atoms and Molecules from Radio-Electric Research)
- Computer Methods in Applied Mechanics and Engineering. 9 per yr. ISSN 0045-7825
- Computer Networks; international journal of distribution informatique. bi-m.
- Computer Physics Communications; an international journal devoted to computational physics and computer programs in physics. bi-m. ISSN 0010-4655
- Computer Programs in Biomedicine. q. ISSN 0010-468X
- Contributions to Economic Analysis. irreg., vol. 93, 1975. ISSN 0573-8555
- Data Resources Series. irreg.
- Defects in Crystalline Solids. irreg., 1973, vol. 8. ISSN 0070-3230
- Discrete Mathematics. m. ISSN 0012-365X
- Dynamic Economics Series. irreg.
- Entomologia Experimentalis et Applicata. bi-m. ISSN 0013-8703
- European Economic Review. bi-m. ISSN 0014-2921 (European Scientific Association of Applied Economics)
- European Journal of Operational Research. bi-m. (Association of European Operational Research Societies)
- European Journal of Pharmacology; an international journal. 24 per yr. ISSN 0014-2999
- F E B S Letters; an international journal established for the most rapid publication of essentially final short papers in the fields of biochemistry, biophysics, and molecular biology. 24 per yr. (12 vols. per yr.) ISSN 0014-5793 (Federation of European Biochemical Societies)
- Frontiers of Biology. irreg., vol. 42, 1975. ISSN 0071-965X
- Fundamental Studies in Computer Science. irreg., vol. 3, 1975.
- General Topology and Its Applications; a journal devoted to set theoretic, axiomatic and geometric topology. bi-m. ISSN 0016-660X
- Handbook of Clinical Neurology. irreg., vol. 24, 1975. ISSN 0072-9752
- Hyperfine Interactions. bi-m.
- I F A C Symposium on Multivariable Technical Control Systems. Proceedings. irreg., 2d, Duesseldorf, 1971. (International Federation of Automatic Control) (Inquire: Kenneth Derbyshire, Dunraven St., Park Lane, London W1, England)
- Index of Biochemical Reviews. a. (Federation of European Biochemical Societies)
- Information Processing Letters. bi-m. ISSN 0020-0190
- International Abstracts in Operations Research. q. ISSN 0020-580X (International Federation of Operational Research Societies)
- International Conference on Few Body Problems in Nuclear and Particle Physics. Proceedings. a.
- International Congress for Logic, Methodology and Philosophy of Science. Proceedings. quadrennial, 1973, 4th Amsterdam. ISSN 0074-3402
- Journal of Crystal Growth. 18 per yr. ISSN 0022-0248
- Journal of Development Economics. q.
- Journal of Econometrics. bi-m.
- Journal of Experimental Marine Biology and Ecology. m (4 vols. per yr.) ISSN 0022-0981
- Journal of Financial Economics. q.
- Journal of Immunological Methods. 20 per yr (5 vols. per yr.) ISSN 0022-1759
- Journal of International Economics. q. ISSN 0022-1996
- Journal of Luminescence; a journal devoted to all luminescent phenomena and all luminescent materials. q. ISSN 0022-2313
- Journal of Magnetism and Magnetic Materials. 9 per yr. ISSN 0304-8853
- Journal of Mathematical Economics. 3 per yr.
- Journal of Medieval History. q.
- Journal of Monetary Economics. q.
- Journal of Non-Crystalline Solids; a journal devoted to glasses and amorphous materials. m. ISSN 0022-3093
- Journal of Nuclear Materials; on metallurgy, ceramics and solid state physics in the nuclear energy industry. m. ISSN 0022-3115
- Journal of Pragmatics. q.
- Journal of Public Economics. bi-m. ISSN 0047-2727
- Journal of Pure and Applied Algebra. 6 per yr. (2 nos. per vol) ISSN 0022-4049
- Journal of Statistical Planning and Inference. bi-m.

- Koninklijke Nederlandse Akademie van Wetenschappen. Afdeling Letterkunde. Verhandelingen. Nieuwe Reeks. irreg., vol. 90, 1975. ISSN 0065-5511
- Koninklijke Nederlandse Akademie van Wetenschapen. Afdeling Natuurkunde. Verhandelingen. Eerste Reeks. irreg., vol. 28, 1975. ISSN 0065-5503
- Koninklijke Nederlandse Akademie van Wetenschappen. Afdeling Natuurkunde. Verhandelingen. Tweede Reeks. irreg., vol. 66, 1975. ISSN 0065-552X
- Koninklijke Nederlandse Akademie van Wetenschappen. Afdeling Natuurkunde. Verslag van de Gewone Vergadering. q. ISSN 0023-3382
- Koninklijke Nederlandse Akademie van. Wetenschappen. Series A: Mathematical Sciences. Proceedings. 5 per yr. ISSN 0023-3358
- Koninklijke Nederlandse Akademie van Wetenschappen. Series B. Physical Sciences. Proceedings. bi-m.(except Aug.) ISSN 0023-3366 (Koninklijke Nederlandse Akademie van Wetenschappen)
- Koninklijke Nederlandse Akademie van Wetenschappen. Series C: Biological and Medical Sciences. Proceedings. 5 per yr. ISSN 0023-3374
- Koninklijke Nederlandse Akademie van Wetenschappen. Sociaal-Wetenschappelijk Informatie en Documentatiecentrum. Dissertaties Maatschappijwetenschappen. a. ISSN 0065-549X
- Koninklijke Nederlandse Akademie van Wetenschappen. Sociaal-Wetenschappelijk Informatie- en Documentatiecentrum. Register van Sociaal-Wetenschappelijk Onderzoek. irreg. ISSN 0065-5473
- Koninklijke Nederlandse Akademie van Wetenschappen. Sociaal-Wetenschappelijke Raad. Handelingen. irreg., no. 6, 1975. ISSN 0065-5449
- Koninklijke Nederlandse Akademie van Wetenschappen. Sociaal-Wetenschappelijke Raad. Informatie Omtrent Lopend Onderzoek in de Sociale Wetenschappen. irreg. ISSN 0065-5465
- Koninklijke Nederlandse Akademie van Wetenschappen. Sociaal-Wetenschappelijke Raad. Register van Lopend Onderzoek in de Sociale Wetenschappen. irreg. (1-2 per yr.) ISSN 0065-5481
- Koninklijke Nederlandse Akademie van Wetenschappen. Sociaalwetenschappelijke Raad. Werkdocumenten. irreg., no. 4, 1974.
- Laboratory Techniques in Biochemistry and Moïecular Biology. irreg., vol. 4, 1975. ISSN 0075-7535
- Lepetit Colloquia on Biology and Medicine. Proceedings. irreg., 5th, 1975, Madrid. ISSN 0075-8779
- Life Sciences and Space Research. a. ISSN 0075-9422 (Committee on Space Research FR)
- Lingua; international review of general linguistics. 9 per yr (3 vol) ISSN 0024-3841
- Mathematical Programming Study. bi-m. (Mathematical Programming Society)
- Mathematics and Computers in Simulation. q. (International Association for Mathematics and Computers in Simulation US)
- Nederlands Tijdschrift voor de Psychologie en Haar Grensgebieden. 9 per yr. ISSN 0028-2235
- North-Holland Linguistic Series. irreg., vol. 18, 1975. ISSN 0078-1592
- North-Holland Mathematical Library. irreg., vol. 13, 1974.
- North-Holland Mathematics Studies. irreg., vol. 17, 1975.
- North-Holland Series in Applied Mathematics and Mechanics. irreg., vol. 21, 1975. ISSN 0066-5460
- North-Holland Series in Crystal Growth. irreg., 1973, vol. 1.
- North-Holland Series in Low Temperature Physics. irreg., vol. 3, 1974.
- North-Holland Studies in Theoretical Poetics. irreg.
- North-Holland/T I M S Studies in the Management Sciences. 3 per yr.
- North-Holland Texts in Advanced Mathematics. irreg.
- Nuclear Engineering and Design; an international journal devoted to the thermal, mechanical and structural problems of nuclear energy. m. ISSN 0029-5493
- Nuclear Instruments and Methods; a journal on accelerators, instrumentation and techniques in nuclear physics. 24 per yr. ISSN 0029-554X
- Nuclear Physics, Section A; devoted to the experimental and theoretical study of the fundamental constituents of matter and their interactions. w.

- Nuclear Physics, Section B; a journal devoted to the experimental and theoretical study of the fundamental constituents of matter and their interactions. w. ISSN 0550-3213
- Optics Communications; a journal devoted to the rapid publication of short contributions in the field of optics and interaction of light with matter. m. ISSN 0030-4018
- P T L; journal for descriptive poetics and theory of literature. 3 per yr.
- Peptides. irreg., 12th, 1973, west germany. ISSN 0079-0753
- Physica; europhysics journal. m. ISSN 0031-8914
- Physics Letters. Section A: General, Atomic and Solid State Physics. 26 per yr.
- Physics Letters. Section B: Nuclear, Elementary Particle and High-Energy Physics. 26 per yr.
- Physics Letters. Section C: Physics Reports. 24 per yr.
- Poetics; international review for the theory of literature. q. ISSN 0048-4571
- Practical Methods in Electron Microscopy. irreg., vol. 4, 1975.
- Progress in Elementary Particle and Cosmic Ray Physics. irreg., 1971, vol. 10. ISSN 0079-6247
- Progress in Low Temperature Physics. irreg., 1970, vol. 6. ISSN 0079-6417
- Progress in Optics. irreg., vol. 12, 1974. ISSN 0079-6638
- Progress in Solid Mechanics. irreg., 1963, vol. 4. ISSN 0555-4276
- Regional Science & Urban Economics. q.
- Research Policy; a journal devoted to research policy, research management and planning. q. ISSN 0048-7333
- Respiration Physiology. 9 per yr. (3 nos. per vol.) ISSN 0034-5687
- Review of Economics and Statistics. q. ISSN 0034-6535 (Harvard University US)
- Selected Topics in Solid State Physics. irreg., vol. 14, 1975. ISSN 0080-8636
- Space Research. a. ISSN 0081-3273 (Committee on Space Research FR)
- Steinmetz Archives; catalog and guide. a. (Koninklijke Nederlandse Akademie van Wetenschappen. Sociaal-Wetenschappelijk Informatie- en Documentatiecentrum)
- Stochastic Processes and Their Applications. bi-m.
- Studies in Financial Economics. irreg.
- Studies in Logic and the Foundations of Mathematics. irreg., vol. 82, 1975. ISSN 0049-237X
- Studies in Mathematical and Managerial Economics. irreg., vol. 21, 1975. ISSN 0081-8194
- Surface Science; devoted to the physics and chemistry of interfaces. 18 per yr. ISSN 0039-6028
- Theoretical Computer Science. bi-m.
- Theory of Molecular Spectroscopy. irreg.
- Ultramicroscopy; journal devoted to the technical and theoretical advancement of structural research. q.
- Vigiliae Christianae; a review of early Christian life and language. q. ISSN 0042-6032

**Nortier en Harmsze B.V.**
Pomstationsweg 7, The Hague, Netherlands.
- Autorevue. fortn. ISSN 0005-1713
- Motor. w. ISSN 0027-1721 (Royal Dutch Motorcycle Union (KNMV))

**Uitgeverij Numismatica Nederland N. V.**
Darwinplantsoen 26, Amsterdam 6, Netherlands.
- European Numismatics. bi-m. ISSN 0014-3030

**Olyslager Organisation**
- Autotechnisch Tijdschrift. (pub. by Kluwer B. V.)

**Drukkerij Onnes B.V.**
Postbus 43, Amersfoort, Netherlands.
- Luister. m. ISSN 0024-7286

**Uitgeverij "Ons Huis"**
Biltstraat 443, Postbus 13060, Utrecht, Netherlands.
- Ons Huis. m. ISSN 0030-2686

**Ons Vee**
Past. van Akenstraat 8, Roosendaal, Netherlands.
- Ons Vee; maandblad voor de veehouderij. m. ISSN 0030-2775

**Oost en West**
Dr. Kuyperstraat 5, The Hague, Netherlands.
- Oost en West; het tijdschrift over tropische en subtropische gebieden. m. ISSN 0030-3275

**Oostenrijkse Handelsdelegatie in Nederland**
Lange Voorhout 58a, The Hague, Netherlands.
- Oostenrijkse Handelsdelegatie in Nederland. m. ISSN 0030-3291

**Uitgeverij A. J. Oranje**
Smitstraat 92-94, The Hague, Netherlands.
- Soteria. m. ISSN 0038-1667 (Protestants-Christelijke Artsen-Organisatie in Nederland)

**Organon Nederland B.V.**
Nieuwe Hescheweg 9, Oss, Netherlands.
- Organorama. bi-m. ISSN 0030-5162

**Ornitologia Rondo Esperantlingva**
Floraplein 23, Eindhoven, Netherlands
(Subscr. To: Roger A. Budnick, 9722 Robinson Ave., Cleveland, Ohio 44125)
- Mevo; internacia revuo ornitologia. 4 per yr. ISSN 0026-1688

**Oude Paden**
Dorpsstraat 19, Oegstgeest, Netherlands.
- Oude Paden. s-m. ISSN 0030-6746

**P U D O C**
Box 4, Wageningen, Netherlands.
- International Agricultural Aviation Congress. Report. irreg., 1969, 4th, Kingston, Canada. ISSN 0074-1280
- P U D O C Bulletin. q. ISSN 0030-8404

**Paper Publications Society**
Nieuwe Prinsengracht 57, Amsterdam, Netherlands.
- Monumenta Chartae Papyraceae Historiam Illustrantia/Collection of Works and Documents Illustrating the History of Paper. irreg., vol. 13, 1973. ISSN 0077-1414

**Partij van de Arbeid. Federatie van Jongerengroepen**
Tesselschadestraat 31, Amsterdam, Netherlands.
- Linksaf. 12 per yr.

**Paters Camillianen Sint Camillushuis**
Heinsbergerweg 176, Roermond, Netherlands.
- Camillusbode. q. ISSN 0008-221X

**Paters Montfortanen**
Heilige Land Stichting 14, Nijmegen, Netherlands.
- Schrift; populaire bijbeltijdschrift. m.

**Uitgeverij Pegasus**
Leidsestraat 25, Amsterdam, Netherlands.
- Politiek en Cultuur. fortn. ISSN 0032-3349

**Permanent International Committee of Linguists**
c/o Prof. Chr. Mohrmann, Sint-Annastraat 40, Nijmegen, Netherlands.
- International Congress of Linguistics. Proceedings. quinquennial since 1962, 1967, 10th, Bucharest. ISSN 0074-3755

**N.V. Philips Gloeilampenfabrieken**
Eindhoven, Netherlands
(U.S. Address: Philips Electronic Equipment, 750 South Fulton Ave., Mount Vernon, N.Y. 10550)
- Electronic Applications Bulletin. q. ISSN 0013-4821 (prep. by its Electronic Components and Materials Division)
- International Lighting Review. (pub. by Foundation Prometheus)
- Medicamundi. q. ISSN 0025-7664 (prep. by its Medical Systems Division)
- Philips Professional Profile. q.
- Science and Industry. bi-m. ISSN 0036-8180 (prep. by its Scientific and Industrial Equipment Division)
- Sound & Image. 4 per yr. ISSN 0038-1802

**Philips' Telecommunicatie Industrie B.V.**
Box 32, Hilversum 1301, Netherlands.
- P T R. (Philips' Telecommunication Review); dedicated to the art of telecommunication. ISSN 0031-7934
- Range; a publication for all those whose interests lie in the field of telecommunications. s-a. ISSN 0033-9199

**Phonogram International B.V.**
Postbus 23, Baarn, Netherlands.
- World Pop News. bi-m.

**Uitgeverij Pi B.V.**
Box 1693, The Hague, Netherlands.
- HTS'er. m. ISSN 0017-629X (Stichting het Landelijk H.T.S.-Orgaan)

**Polak en Van Gennep Uitgeversmaatschappij B.V.**
Keizersgracht 608, Amsterdam, Netherlands.
- Revisor. bi-m. ISSN 0302-8852

**Poland Music Association**
Mauritsweg 34, Dordrecht 3405, Netherlands
(Polish Subscr. Address: Muzilo, Zabrze/SK. Pt. 68, Poland)
- Muzilo; simplified music-notes system. 2-4 per yr. ISSN 0027-5328

**Polytechnic**
Singel 112, Amsterdam, Netherlands.
- Polytechnic-Window of the Netherlands; review of industrial Holland. m. ISSN 0032-6119

**Portugees-Israelietische Gemeente**
Gerrit van der Veenstr. 141, Amsterdam (Nieuw-Zuid), Netherlands.
- Habinjan; de opbouw. q. ISSN 0017-6346
- Reconstruction. m. ISSN 0034-1487

**B. V. Uitgeverij "de Postiljon"**
Adenauerlaan 268, Utrecht, Netherlands.
- Mijn Stokpaardje; maandblad voor filatelisten. m. ISSN 0026-3605

**Prenatal Moeder en Kind N.V.**
Zoutkeetsgracht 10, Amsterdam, Netherlands.
- Prenatal; prenatal gids. s-a. ISSN 0032-7425

**Princo B.V.**
Postbus 9, Culemborg, Netherlands.
- Geologie en Mijnbouw/Geology and Mining. q. ISSN 0016-7746 (Koninklijk Nederlands Geologisch Mijnbouwkundig Genootschap)

**Produktschap voor Siergewassen**
Stadhoudersplantsoen 12-18, Postbus 361, The Hague, Netherlands.
- Produktschap voor Siergewassen. Jaarverslag. a. ISSN 0077-7609
- Produktschap voor Siergewassen. Statistiek. a. ISSN 0556-543X

**Proefstation de voor Groenten- en Fruitteelt onder Glas**
Postbox 8, Naaldwijk, Netherlands.
- Proefstation voor de Groenten- en Fruitteelt onder Glas. Mededelingen. m. ISSN 0033-0019

**Prof. Dr. Jan van der Hoeven Foundation for Theoretical Biology**
- Acta Biotheoretica. (pub. by Leiden University Press)

**Professional Players Union of Holland**
Laan van Meerdervoort 565, The Hague, Netherlands.
- Contractspeler. bi-m. ISSN 0045-8406 (Co-sponsors: Professional Trotter and Jockey Union of Holland; Professional Cyclists Union of Holland)

**Protestants-Christelijke Artsen-Organisatie in Nederland**
- Soteria. (pub. by Uitgeverij A. J. Oranje)

**Protestants Christelijke Onderwijsvakorganisatie**
Postbus 5868, The Hague, Netherlands.
- Beroepsonderwijs. fortn. (22 per yr)

**Protestantse Stichting tot Bevordering van het Bibliotheekwezen en de Lektuurvoorlichting in Nederland**
Parkweg 20a, Voorburg, Netherlands.
- Media-Informatiedienst. bi-m. ISSN 0025-6919
- Prisma Lectuurvoorlichting /Book Reviews for Public Libraries. w. ISSN 0032-8804

**Provinciaal Genootschap van Kunsten en Wetenschappen in Noord-Brabant.**
Box 1104, S-Hertogenbosch, Netherlands.
- Brabantia. bi-m. ISSN 0006-8624
- Brabantse Leeuw. (pub. by Drukkerij Juten)

**Provinciale Vereniging Het Limburgse Groene Kruis**
Kleine Steeg 7, Postbus 12, Sittard, Netherlands.
- Gezond Limburg. m (10 per yr) ISSN 0016-9501

**Uitgeversbedrijf "Publiciteit" Schiedam**
Postbus 42, Schiedam, Netherlands.
- Handboek van de Nederlandse Pers en Publiciteit. s-a. ISSN 0440-1875

**N. V. Publico**
Spaarnestraat 4-8, The Hague, Netherlands.
- Paardesport in Ren en Draf. s-w. ISSN 0039-1387

**Quadriga-Drukwerken**
Amstel 21, Amsterdam C, Netherlands.
- Museologia. s-a.

**Radio-Holland B. V.**
Postbus 9094, Jan Rebelstraat 20, Amsterdam, Netherlands.
- Elektronaut. 3 per yr. ISSN 0013-5615

**Radio Nederland Wereldomroep**
P.O. Box 222, Hilversum, Netherlands.
- Radio Nederland. s-a. ISSN 0033-7951

**Uitgeverij C. E. Radius en P. Gruppelaar**
Box 277, Dordrecht 3400, Netherlands.
- Holland Shipbuilding. m.

**Railway Research Index Division**
Burg. Eijssenstr. 1, Wijnandsrade (Limburg) 5236, Netherlands.
- Railway Research & Engineering News. Section A. 3 per yr. ISSN 0033-894X
- Railway Research & Engineering News. Section B. m. ISSN 0033-8958
- Railway Research & Engineering News. Sections D,E,F and G. ISSN 0033-8966

**Rath en Doodeheefver N. V.**
Prinsengracht 730-736, Amsterdam, Netherlands.
- Variator. m. ISSN 0042-272X

**Uitgeversmaatschappij The Reader's Digest N.V.**
Assumburg 73-75, Amsterdam-Buitenveldert, Netherlands.
- Het Beste uit Reader's Digest (Dutch Edition) m. ISSN 0005-9692

**Reclame Technische Uitgevers Maatschappij NZ**
Voorburgwal 288, Amsterdam, Netherlands.
- Kontekst. s-m.

**Redemptorist Fathers**
Parklaan 3, Roermond, Netherlands.
- Biddend Nazareth. m. ISSN 0006-2081
- Frontlijn; voor katholieken in en buiten de kerk. m. ISSN 0016-2175

**B. V. Uitgeversmaatschappij Reflex**
Mathenesserlaan 310, Rotterdam, Netherlands.
- Estheticienne. bi-m. ISSN 0014-1321 (Algemene Nederlandse Bond van Schoonheidsinstituten)
- Golf. m. ISSN 0017-1727 (Nederlandse Golf Federatie)
- Medisch Contact. w. ISSN 0025-8245 (Koninklijke Nederlandsche Maatschappij Tot Bevordering der Geneeskunst)
- Nederlands Tijdschrift voor Tandheelkunde. 11 per yr. ISSN 0028-2200
- Oppervlaktetechnieken van Metalen. m. ISSN 0030-3844 (Vereniging voor Oppervlaktetechnieken van Metalen)
- Plastica; monthly review on plastics. m. ISSN 0032-1095
- Project; orgaan voor toegepaste wetenschappen. m. (Netherlands Organisation for Applied Scientific Research)
- Tijdschrift voor Oppervlaktetechnieken van Metalen. m. ISSN 0040-7569
- Tijdschrift voor Sociale Geneeskunde. fortn. ISSN 0040-7607 (Algemene Nederlandse Vereniging voor Sociale Geneeskunde)
- Verpakking. m. ISSN 0042-4315 (Nederlands Verpakkingscentrum)
- Weg en Waterbouw. m. ISSN 0043-2016

**Reformed Presbyterian Fellowship in the Great Congregation (Ps.40,10)**
- Uitzicht. (pub. by Evangelisatie-Boekhandel en Uitgeverij Horizont)

**D. Reidel Publishing Co.**
Box 17, 3300 AA Dordrecht, Netherlands
(and Lincoln Building, 160 Old Derby St., Hingham, MA 02043)
- Analecta Husserliana; yearbook of phenomenological research. irreg.
- Aspects of Homogeneous Catalysis: a Series of Advances. biennial.
- Astrophysics and Space Science; an international journal of cosmic physics. m. ISSN 0004-640X
- Astrophysics and Space Science Library. irreg. ISSN 0067-0057
- Boston Studies in the Philosophy of Science; Boston colloquium for the philosophy of science. irreg. ISSN 0068-0346

- Boundary-Layer Meteorology; an international journal of physical and biological processes in the atmospheric boundary layer. 8 per yr. ISSN 0006-8314
- Celestial Mechanics; an international journal of space dynamics. 8 per yr. ISSN 0008-8714
- Climatic Change; an interdisciplinary, international journal devoted to the description, causes and implications of climatic change. q.
- Cultural Hermeneutics. 4 per yr. ISSN 0011-2860
- Culture, Medicine and Psychiatry; an international journal of comparative cross-cultural research. q.
- Educational Studies in Mathematics. 4 per yr. ISSN 0013-1954
- Episteme; a series in the foundational, methodological, philosophical, psychological, sociological and historical aspects of the sciences, pure and applied. irreg.
- Erkenntnis; an international journal of analytical philosophy. 3 per yr.
- Formal Linguistics Series. irreg. ISSN 0071-7592
- Geometriae Dedicata. q. ISSN 0046-5755
- Geophysical Surveys; an international journal of geophysics. q. ISSN 0046-5763
- Geophysics and Astrophysics Monographs; an international series of fundamental textbooks. irreg.
- Homogeneous Catalysis in Organic and Inorganic Chemistry. irreg.
- Indo-Iranian Journal. 4 per yr. ISSN 0019-7246
- International Astronomical Union. General Assembly. Proceedings. irreg., 15th, 1974.
- International Astronomical Union. Proceedings of Symposia. irreg., 66th, 1974. ISSN 0074-1809
- International Astronomical Union. Transactions and Highlights. triennial, 1973, 15th, Sydney, Australia. ISSN 0080-1372
- International Congress of Quantum Chemistry. Proceedings. irreg.
- International Studies in Economics and Econometrics. irreg.
- Jerusalem Symposia on Quantum Chemistry and Biochemistry. irreg. ISSN 0075-3696 (Israel Academy of Sciences and Humanities IS. Section on Sciences)
- Journal of Chinese Philosophy. q. ISSN 0301-8121
- Journal of Indian Philosophy. q. ISSN 0022-1791
- Journal of Philosophical Logic. q. ISSN 0022-3611 (Association for Symbolic Logic)
- Journal of Texture Studies; an international journal of rheology psychorheology, physical and sensory testing of foods and pharmaceuticals. q. ISSN 0022-4901
- Journal of the History of Biology. s-a. ISSN 0022-5010
- L M P. (Letters in Mathematical Physics); a journal for the rapid dissemination of short contributions in the field of mathematical physics. 6 per yr.
- Linguistics and Philosophy. bi-m.
- Marine Geophysical Researches; an international journal for the study of the earth beneath the sea. q. ISSN 0025-3235
- Mathematical Physics and Applied Mathematics. irreg.
- Molecular Biology Reports; an international journal for rapid communications in molecular biology. 6 per yr. ISSN 0301-4851
- Moon; an international journal of lunar studies. 8 per yr. ISSN 0027-0903
- N A T O Advanced Study Institute Series. C: Mathematical and Physical Sciences. irreg. (North Atlantic Treaty Organization. Scientific Affairs Division BE)
- Natural Resources Forum. q. (United Nations. Centre for Natural Resources, Energy and Transport UN) (Or United Nations, Sales Section, NY 10017)
- Origins of Life. q.
- Philosophical Studies; an international journal for philosophpy in the analytic tradition. m. ISSN 0031-8116
- Philosophical Studies Series in Philosophy. irreg.
- Philosophy and Medicine. irreg.
- Physics and Chemistry of Materials with Layered Structures. irreg.
- Problems of the Science of Science. a. (Polska Akademia Nauk. Committee on the Science of Science PL)
- Russian Linguistics; international journal for the study of the Russian language. q.
- Russian Series on Social History. irreg. ISSN 0080-4916 ( International Institute for Social History )
- Series on Food Material Science. irreg.

- Social Indicators Research; an international and interdisciplinary journal for quality-of-life measurement. q.
- Sociology of the Sciences. a.
- Solar Physics; a journal for solar research and the study of solar terrestrial physics. m. ISSN 0038-0938
- Sovietica. Publications and Monographs. irreg. (Universite de Fribourg. Institute of East-European Studies SZ)
- Space Science Instrumentation; an international journal of scientific instruments for aircraft, balloons, sounding rockets, and spacecraft. q.
- Space Science Reviews. 9 per yr.(approx.) ISSN 0038-6308
- Studies in Soviet Thought. q. ISSN 0039-3797
- Studies in the History of Modern Science. irreg.
- Synthese; an international journal for epistemology, methodology and philosophy of science. 2 vols. per year (4 nos. per vol.) ISSN 0039-7857
- Synthese Historical Library; texts and studies in the history of logic and philosophy. irreg., no. 15, 1975. ISSN 0082-111X
- Synthese Library; monographs on epistemology, logic. methodology, philosophy of science and of knowledge, and the mathematical methods of social and behavioral sciences. irreg. ISSN 0082-1128
- Theory and Decision; an international journal for philosophy and methodology of the social sciences. q. ISSN 0040-5833
- Theory and Decision Library; an international series in the philosophy and methodology of the social and behavioral sciences. irreg.
- University of Western Ontario Series in Philosophy of Science. irreg. (University of Western Ontario CN)
- Vienna Circle Collection. irreg.
- Water, Air, and Soil Pollution; an international journal of environmental pollution. q. ISSN 0049-6979

**A. Reiman**
Elandsgracht 33, Amsterdam, Netherlands.
- Camping & Caravaning; revue for camping, caravaning and tourism. m. ISSN 0008-2384

**Reisbureau de Magneet N.V.**
Handelsgebouw, Alkmaar, Netherlands.
- Magneet-Revue. 3 per yr(approx.) ISSN 0024-9963

**Remonstrantse Gemeente Groningen**
Burchtdam 3, Haren, Netherlands.
- Gemeenteleven. m. ISSN 0016-6065

**N.V. Res**
Prinsengracht 463, Amsterdam, Netherlands.
- Nieuwe Linie. w. ISSN 0028-9892

**Research Group for European Migration Problems**
- Research Group for European Migration Problems. Publications. (pub. by Martinus Nijhoff)

**Peter de Ridder Press**
Box 168, 2160 AD Lisse, Netherlands.
- Archivum Eurasiae Medii Aevi. irreg.
- Harvard Ukrainian Studies. irreg. (Harvard Ukrainian Research Institute US)
- International Journal of Romanian Studies. irreg.
- International Journal of Slavic Linguistics and Poetics. irreg. ISSN 0020-7632 (University of California, Los Angeles. Department of Slavic Languages US)
- Italian Linguistics. s-a.
- PdR Press Publications in Literary Systems. irreg, no. 2, 1976.
- Recherches sur le Surrealisme. irreg.
- Studia Caucasica. irreg. ISSN 0081-6345

**Rijksherbarium**
Schelpenkade 6, Leiden, Netherlands.
- Blumea; a journal of plant-taxonomy and plant-geography. 2 per yr. ISSN 0006-5196
- Gorteria; tijdschrift ten dienste van de floristiek, de plantenoecologie en het vegetatie-onderzoek van Nederland. bi-m. ISSN 0017-2294
- Persoonia; a mycological journal. s-a. ISSN 0031-5850

**Rijksinstituut voor het Rassenonderzoek van Cultuurgewassen**
Postbus 32, Wageningen, Netherlands.
- Rassenbericht. 12 per yr.
- Rijksinstituut voor het Rassenonderzoek van Cultuurgewassen. Jaarverslag. a.

● Rijksinstituut voor het Rassenonderzoek van
Cultuurgewassen. Mededelingen. irreg., 1969, no.
57.

**Rijksinstituut voor Oorlogsdocumentatie**
● Rijksinstituut voor Oorlogsdocumentatie.
Documenten. (pub. by Martinus Nijhoff)
● Rijksinstituut voor Oorlogsdocumentatie.
Monografieen. (pub. by Martinus Nijhoff)

**Rijkslandbouwconsulentschap voor Plantenziekten**
Geertjesweg 15, Wageningen, Netherlands.
● Landbouw en Plantenziekten. s-a. ISSN 0023-
7752

**Rijksmuseum Kroeller-Mueller**
Stichting Kunstpublicaties, Otterlo, Netherlands.
● Museumjournaal. bi-m. ISSN 0027-4143

**Rijksmuseum van Geologie en Mineralogie**
Hooglandse Kerkgracht 17, Leiden, Netherlands.
● Scripta Geologica. irreg.

**Rijksmuseum van Natuurlijke Historie**
Postbus 9517, 2300 RA Leiden, Netherlands.
● Rijksmuseum van Natuurlijke Historie.
Zoologische Mededelingen. irreg. ISSN 0024-0672
● Rijksmuseum van Natuurlijke Historie.
Zoologische Verhandelingen. 10 per yr. ISSN
0024-1652

**Rijksmuseum van Natuurlijke Historie. Delta
Onderzoek Hydrobiologisch Institut**
● Delta Onderzoek Hydrobiologisch Instituut.
Communication. (pub. by E. J. Brill)

**Rijkstuinbouwconsulentschap**
● Rijkstuinbouwconsulentschap. Mededelingen. (pub.
by N. V. Drukkerij West-Friesland)

**Rijksuniversiteit te Groningen. Fries Instituut**
Westersingel 28-30, Groningen, Netherlands.
● Us Wurk. 4 per yr. ISSN 0042-1235

**Rijksuniversiteit te Groningen. Polemologisch
Instituut**
● Polemologische Studien. (pub. by Van Gorcum)

**Rijksuniversiteit te Groningen. Stichting Gronings
Universiteitsblad**
Oude Boteringestraat 42, Groningen, Netherlands.
● Rijksuniversiteit te Groningen. Universiteitskrant.
w.

**Rijksuniversiteit te Leiden**
● Pseudepigrapha Veteris Testamenti Graece. (pub.
by E. J. Brill)

**Rijksuniversiteit te Leiden. Documentation Office for
East European Law**
● Law in Eastern Europe. (pub. by A. W. Sijthoff
International Publishing Co.)
● Review of Socialist Law. (pub. by A.W. Sijthoff
International Publishing Co.)

**Rijksuniversiteit te Leiden. Geologisch en
Mineralogisch Instituut**
Garenmarkt 1b, Leiden, Netherlands.
● Leidse Geologische Mededelingen. irreg. ISSN
0075-8639

**Rijksuniversiteit te Leiden. Institute for Prehistory**
● Analecta Praehistorica Leidensia. (pub. by Leiden
University Press)

**Rijksuniversiteit te Utrecht**
● Wijsgerige Teksten en Studies/Philosophical Texts
and Studies. (pub. by Van Gorcum)

**Rijksuniversiteit te Utrecht. Archaeological Institute**
● Archaeologica Traiectina. (pub. by Wolters-
Noordhoff B.V.)

**Rijksuniversiteit te Utrecht. Bibliotheek**
● Catalogus van Academische Geschriften in
Nederland Verschenen. (pub. by Swets en
Zeitlinger B. V.)

**Rijksuniversiteit te Utrecht. Department of
Stratigraphy and Paleontology**
c/o T. van Schaik, Odijk, Netherlands.
● Utrecht Micropaleontological Bulletins. irreg., no.
12, 1975. ISSN 0083-4963

**Rijksuniversiteit te Utrecht. Geografisch Instituut**
Heidelberglaan 2, Utrecht, Netherlands.
● Rijksuniversiteit te Utrecht. Geografisch Instituut.
Bulletin. Serie 1: Sociale Geografie. (pub. by
Mouton Publishers)
● Utrechtse Geografische Studies. irreg. ISSN 0376-
4001

**Rijksuniversiteit te Utrecht. Geologisch Instituut**
Oude Gracht 320, Utrecht, Netherlands.
● Geologica Ultraiectina. irreg., 1973, no. 16. ISSN
0072-1026

**Rijksuniversiteit te Utrecht. Instituut de Vooys voor
Nederlandse Taal- en Letterkunde**
Emmalaan 29, Utrecht, Netherlands.
● Ruygh-Bewerp. irreg. (every 2-3 yrs.)

**Rijksuniversiteit te Utrecht. Instituut voor Oosterse
Talen**
● Disputationes Rheno-Trajectinae. (pub. by Mouton
Publishers)

**Rijksuniversiteit te Utrecht. Kunsthistorisch Instituut**
● Orbis Artium. (pub. by Haentjens Dekker en
Gumbert)

**Rijnlands Lyceum**
Backershagenlaan 5, Wassenaar, Netherlands.
● Krant. 8 per yr.

**Editions Rodopi N.V.**
Keizersgracht 302-304, Amsterdam, Netherlands.
● Amsterdamer Beitraege zur Neueren Germanistik.
irreg.
● Amsterdamer Publikationen zur Sprache und
Literatur. irreg., approx. 20 per yr.
● Beschreibende Bibliographien. irreg.
● Chemie en Techniek; tijdschrift voor laboratorium
en industrie. m. ISSN 0009-2827
● Costerus; essays in English and American
language and literature. 3 per yr.
● Deutsche Buecher. q.
● Dutch Quarterly Review of Anglo American
Letters. q. ISSN 0046-0842
● Grazer Beitraege; Zeitschrift fuer klassische
Altertumswissenschaft. s-a.
● Perspektiven der Philosophie. a.

**B. V. Koninklijke Drukkerijen Roelants-Schiedam**
Postbox 42, Schiedam, Netherlands.
● Beleggers-Belangen; financieel economisch
weekblad. w. ISSN 0005-8343
● Beroepsvervoer. w. ISSN 0005-9447
● Groei en Bloei. m. ISSN 0017-4475 (Koninklijke
Nederlandse Maatschappij voor Tuinbouw en
Plantkunde)
● Houtwereld. fortn. ISSN 0018-6732
● Kosmetiek; vakblad voor de parfumerie,
kosmetische, bijouterie en toiletartikelenbranche.
m.

**B. V. Rotadruk**
Postbus 16, Axel, Netherlands.
● Advertentieblad. w. ISSN 0001-8856

**Rotterdam. Havenbedrijf**
Europoort III, Marconistraat 12, Rotterdam - 3007,
Netherlands.
● Rotterdam - Europoort - Delta. q. ISSN 0035-
8487

**Rotterdam Cotton Association**
*see* **Vereeniging voor den Katoenhandel, Rotterdam**

**Rotterdam University Press**
Box 1474, Rotterdam, Netherlands.
● Mens en Maatschappij; Driemaandelijks tijdschrift
voor sociale wetenschappen. 4 per yr (plus special
issue) ISSN 0025-9454
● Modern Approaches to the Diagnosis and
Instruction of Multi-Handicapped Children. irreg.,
vol. 14, 1975. ISSN 0076-9916
● Studies in Development and Planning. irreg., vol.
5, 1974. (Nederlandse Economische Hogeschool)
(Dist. in U.S. by International Scholarly Book
Services, Inc., P.O. Box 4347, Portland, OR
97208)

**Royal Dutch Geographical Society**
*see* **Koninklijk Nederlands Aardrijkskundig
Genootschap**

**Royal Dutch Motorcycle Union (KNMV)**
● Motor. (pub. by Nortier en Harmsze B.V.)

**Royal Geological and Mining Society of the
Netherlands**
*see* **Koninklijk Nederlands Geologisch
Mijnbouwkundig Genootschap**

**Royal Institute for Linguistics and Anthropology**
*see* **Koninklijk Instituut voor Taal- , Land- en
Volkenkunde**

**Royal Institution of Engineers in the Netherlands**
● Journal of Applied Science and Engineering
Section A. Electrical Power and Information
Systems. (pub. by Elsevier Scientific Publishing
Co.)

**Royal Netherlands Association of Architects**
● Plan/Architectural Review. (pub. by Stam
Tijdschriften B.V.)

**Royal Netherlands Hockey Association**
● Hockey Sport. (pub. by C. de Boer Jr. N.V.)

**Royal Netherlands Lawn Tennis Association**
● Lawn Tennis. (pub. by C. de Boer Jr. N.V.)

**Royal Netherlands Meterological Institute**
De Bilt, Netherlands.
● Yearbook Geomagnetism: Paramaribo, Surinam. a.
ISSN 0077-7587 (Co-sponsors: Surinam
Department of Public Works and Traffic; Surinam
Department of Development)

**Royal Netherlands Shipowners Association**
*see* **Koninklijke Nederlandse Redersvereniging**

**Royal Netherlands Society for Agricultural Science**
*see* **Koninklijk Genootschap voor
Landbouwwetenschap**

**Royal Tropical Institute**
*see* **Koninklijk Instituut voor de Tropen**

**SALCO**
Maliebaan 20, Utrecht, Netherlands.
● Salcofoon. bi-m. ISSN 0009-9678

**Samsom Uitgeverij B. V.**
Box 4, Alphen aan den Rijn, Netherlands.
● D B-Tijdschrift voor Doelmatig Bedrijfsbeheer. m.
● Gemeentewerken. m. ISSN 0046-5577 (Vereniging
van Directeuren van Gemeentewerken, Openbare
Werken, Bouw- en Woningtoezicht en
Woningdienst)
● Maandblad Belasting Beschouwingen;
onafhankelijk maandblad voor belastingrecht en
belastingpraktijk. m. ISSN 0005-8335
● Metamedica; blad voor metamedische
vraagstukken. m. ISSN 0022-9350 (Katholieke
Artsenvereniging)
● Noodzaak. 8 per yr.
● Sociaal Maandblad Arbeid; tijdschrift voor sociaal
recht en sociaal beleid. m. ISSN 0037-7600
● T M W. (Tijdschrift voor
Maatschappijvraagstukken en Welzijnswerk) m.

**De Savornin Lohman Stichting**
*see* **Jhr. Mr. A. F. de Savornin Lohman Stichting**

**Schaafsma en Brouwer**
Box 10, Dokkum, Netherlands.
● Rijkspolitie. m (11 per yr.)

**Leo Schepman**
Box 1808, The Hague, Netherlands.
● Chevron Motor. bi-m. (Chevron Petroleum
Maatschappij (Nederland) N.V)

**Drukkerij Schmitz B.V.**
Wijkerstraatweg 160, Velsen Noord, Netherlands.
● Orchidee. bi-m. ISSN 0030-4484 (Nederlandse
Orchideeen Vereniging)

**Uitgeverij L.C.E. Schnitger-Noyon**
Venloonstraat 31, Box 31, 5175 ZG Loon Op Zand,
Netherlands.
● Sport en Spel. m. ISSN 0038-7851

**Schriks' Drukkerij B. V.**
Burg. Wijnenstraat 44, Postbus 8, Asten (NB),
Netherlands.
● Hondenwereld. s-m. ISSN 0018-4527

**Uitgeverij Semper Agendo**
Hoofdstraat 46, Postbox 327, Apeldoorn,
Netherlands.
● Ministerium; periodical on practical theology and
pastoral practice. m. ISSN 0026-5306

**Shell Nederland B.V.**
Raamweg 34, The Hague, Netherlands.
- Shell Post. fortn.
- Shell Venster. m.

**Shell Nederland Raffinaderij B.V.**
Postbus 7000, Rotterdam, Netherlands.
- Onder de Vlam. w. ISSN 0030-2457 (Co-sponsor: Shell Nederland Chemie B.V.)

**Showunie**
Box 2100, Amsterdam, Netherlands.
- Pop-Telescoop. w.

**A. W. Sijthoff International Publishing Co.**
Schuttersveld 9, Box 26, Leiden, Netherlands.
- Academie de Droit International de la Haye. Recueil des Cours. 3 per yr. ISSN 0001-401X
- Atlantic Series. a. ISSN 0571-7868 (North Atlantic Treaty Organization)
- Collection de Droit International. s-a. (Universite de Geneve. Institut Universitaire de Hautes Etudes Internationales SZ) (Subscriptions to: A.B.S.H., P.O.B. 66, Groningen)
- Collection de Relations Internationales. s-a. (Universite de Geneve. Institut Universitaire de Hautes Internationales SZ) (Subscriptions to: A.B.S.H., P.O.B. 66, Groningen)
- Common Market Law Review. q. ISSN 0010-3292 (British Institute of International and Comparative Law UK) (Co-Sponsor: Europa Institute, University of Leyden)
- Earth Law Journal. q.
- East-West Perspectives. irreg. (East-West Foundation)
- Henry Dunant Institute. Scientific Collection. irreg. (one vol. per yr.)
- John F. Kennedy Institute Series: a Collection of Studies Relating to International Economics. s-a. (Hogeschool te Tilburg. John F. Kennedy Institute) (Subscriptions to: A.B.S.H., P.O.B. 66, Groningen)
- Law in Eastern Europe. irreg., no. 19, 1975. ISSN 0075-823X (Rijksuniversiteit te Leiden. Documentation Office for East European Law)
- Monographs on Industrial Property and Copyright Law. irreg.
- N A T O Advanced Study Institutes Series D: Behavioural and Social Sciences. s-a. (North Atlantic Treaty Organization. Scientific Affairs Division) (Subscr. to: A.B.S.H., P.O. Box 66, Groningen, Netherlands)
- Netherlands International Law Review/ Nederlands Tijdschrift voor International Recht. q. ISSN 0028-2138 (T. M. C. Asser Institute)
- Netherlands Yearbook of International Law. a. (T.M.C. Asser Institute)
- Review of Socialist Law. q. (Rijksuniversiteit te Leiden. Documentation Office for East European Law)
- Teneat Lex Gladium. s-a. (International Institute for Human Rights) (Co-Sponsor: Henry Dunant Institute) (Subscr. to: A.B.S.H., Box 66, Groningen, Netherlands)
- Universite de Geneve. Institut Universitaire de Hautes Etudes Internationales. Economics Series. s-a. (Subscriptions to: A.B.S.H., P.O.B. 66, Groningen)

**Uitgeverij de Sikkel N.V.**
Kapelsestraat 222, 2080 Kapellen, Netherlands.
- Academie de Marine. Mededelingen. Communications. a.

**Sint-Adelbertabdij**
Egmond-Binnen, Netherlands.
- Benediktijns Tijdschrift; voor Evangelische bezinning. q. ISSN 0005-8734

**Sint-Bernardinuscollege**
Akerstraat 95, Heerlen, Netherlands.
- Binden en Bouwen. bi-m. ISSN 0006-2812

**Sint Ignatiuscollege**
Govert Flinckstraat 294a, Amsterdam, Netherlands.
- Harpoen. 9 per yr. ISSN 0017-7911

**Sint Janscollege**
Colijnplein 9, The Hague, Netherlands.
- Adelaar. bi-m. ISSN 0001-8139

**Sjaloom**
De Vork 2, Odijk, Netherlands.
- Achtergrond. w.

**Skolta Esperanto Ligo**
Box 433, Zaandam, Netherlands
(Subscr. to: D.H. Withey, 21 Brookfield Ave., Waterloo, Liverpool L22 3YE, Eng.)
- Skolta Mondo. q. ISSN 0037-6558

**Smeets International Publications**
Transformatorweg 37, Amsterdam, Netherlands.
- Holland Herald; magazine of the Netherlands. m. ISSN 0018-3563

**Smits-N. V.**
Westeinde 135, The Hague, Netherlands.
- Forum der Letteren. q. ISSN 0015-8496 (Nederlandse Organisatie voor Zuiver-Wetenschappelijk Onderzoek)

**Smitweld N.V.**
Box 253, Groenestraat 310, Nijmegen, Netherlands.
- Smitweld Reportage. bi-m (Dutch edition); 3 per yr. (French and German edition)

**P. Snelders-Beckmann**
Roggestr. 42, 3081 XD Rotterdam, Netherlands.
- Tarwewijk. bi-m. ISSN 0039-9736 (Speeltuinvereniging)

**Sociaal Economische Raad**
Bezuidenhoutseweg 60, The Hague, Netherlands.
- Mededelingenblad Bedrijfsorganisatie. w. ISSN 0025-6862
- Sociaal-Economische Raad. Informatie- en Documentatie Bulletin. w. ISSN 0037-7589
- Sociaal-Economische Raad. Verslag. a. ISSN 0560-3641

**Socialistische Uitgeverij Nijmegen**
Bijleveldsingel 9, Nijmegen, Netherlands.
- Recht en Kritiek. q.

**Societe de Demographie Historique**
- Annales de Demographie Historique. (pub. by Mouton Publishers)

**Societe Internationale des Maitres d'Hotel**
Bernhardlaan 20, Sittard, Netherlands.
- Journal d'Hotel. m. ISSN 0021-8138

**Societe Neerlando-Iranienne**
c/o A. A. Kampman, Ed., St. Antoniusbank 26, 5040 Bemelen(L), Netherlands.
- Persica. a. ISSN 0079-0893

**Society for the History of Discoveries**
- Terrae Incognitae. (pub. by N. Israel)

**Society Oud Utrecht**
Alex. Numankade 199, Utrecht, Netherlands.
- Oud Utrecht. m. ISSN 0030-6738

**Uitgeverij Spaarnestad N.V.**
P.B. 1, Haarlem, Netherlands.
- Panorama. w. ISSN 0031-0867

**Uitgeverij Het Spectrum B. V.**
Post Box 2073, Utrecht, Netherlands.
- Mens en Melodie. m. ISSN 0025-9462

**Speeltuinvereniging**
- Tarwewijk. (pub. by P. Snelders-Beckmann)

**Spoor en Partners B.V.**
Postbus 143, Caspar Fagellaan 10, Heemstede, Netherlands.
- Bloembollencultuur. w. (Koninklijke Algemeene Vereeniging voor Bloembollencultuur)

**Sprenger Institute**
Haagsteeg 6, Wageningen, Netherlands.
- Sprenger Instituut. Jaarverslag Annual Report. a. ISSN 0081-3850

**Stam-Robijns**
Industrieweg 1, Culemborg, Netherlands.
- Maandblad voor het Land- en Tuinbouwonderwijs. m. ISSN 0024-8657

**Stam Tijdschriften B.V.**
Postbox 375, The Hague, Netherlands.
- Landbouwkundig Tijdschrift. m. ISSN 0023-7787

**Plan/Architectural Review; monthly for design and environment. m. ISSN 0006-8357 (Royal Netherlands Association of Architects)
- Polytechnisch Tijdschrift: Bouwkunde, Wegen- en Waterbouw. m. ISSN 0032-4078 (Nederlandse Ingenieursvereniging)
- Polytechnisch Tijdschrift: Elektrotechniek/ Elektronica. m. ISSN 0032-4086 (Nederlandse Ingenieursvereniging)
- Polytechnisch Tijdschrift: Procestechniek. m. ISSN 0032-4094 (Nederlandse Ingenieursvereniging)
- Polytechnisch Tijdschrift: Werktuigbouw. m. ISSN 0032-4108 (Nederlandse Ingenieursvereniging)
- Zee. m. (Koninklijke Nederlandse Redersvereniging) (Co-sponsor: Vereniging van Kapiteins en Officieren Ter Koopvaardij; Nederlandse Vereniging van Kapiteins Grote Vaart; Koninklijk Nederlands Meteorologisch Instituut)

**Stamex B.V.**
Box 505, Hilversum, Netherlands.
- Documentation - Europe Post. 12 per yr. ISSN 0012-4575
- International Chemical Register; a monthly buyers' guide. m. ISSN 0020-6326
- International Food Register; a monthly buyers' guide. m. ISSN 0020-6776

**H. E. Stenfert Kroese**
Pieterskerkhof 38, Leiden, Netherlands.
- Economist. q. ISSN 0013-063X

**Stichting Amandla**
Da Costastraat 88, Amsterdam, Netherlands.
- Amandla; maandblad over zuidelijk Afrika. m.

**Stichting Amsterdam Aktief**
Kon. Wilhelminaplein 13, 1017 Amsterdam, Netherlands.
- Amsterdam Aktief. m.

**Stichting Antonie van Leeuwenhoek**
Julianalaan 67A, Delft, Netherlands.
- Antonie van Leeuwenhoek Journal of Microbiology and Serology. q. ISSN 0003-6072

**Stichting Ars Aequi**
Box 1043, Nijmegen, Netherlands.
- Ars Aequi; juridisch studentenblad. m. ISSN 0004-2870

**Stichting Begeleiding Edukatieve Voorzieningen**
- Interaktie. (pub. by J. B. van den Brink en Co. B.V.)

**Stichting Bijdragen**
Keizersgracht 105, Amsterdam-1002, Netherlands.
- Bijdragen; tijdschrift voor filosofie en theologie. 4 per yr. ISSN 0006-2278

**Stichting Bisdomblad Roermond**
Mariastraat 4, Postbus 357, Maastricht (L.), Netherlands.
- Bisdomblad. w. ISSN 0006-3819

**Stichting Bouwcentrum**
Weena 700, Box 299, Rotterdam, Netherlands.
- Bouwliteratuur Documentatie. fortn. ISSN 0006-8365

**Stichting Bouwen aan de Nieuwe Aarde**
Box 7639, Eindhoven, Netherlands.
- Bouwen aan de Nieuwe Aarde. m. ISSN 0006-8349

**Stichting Bovag Orgaan**
Eisenhowerlaan 126, Postbus 5043, The Hague, Netherlands.
- Bovagblad. fortn. ISSN 0006-839X

**Stichting Burgerschapskunde**
Box 349, Leiden, Netherlands.
- Politiek Overzicht. m.

**Stichting Castrum Peregrini**
P.O. Box 645, Amsterdam, Netherlands.
- Castrum Peregrini; deutschsprachige Zeitschrift fuer Literatur- und Kunst- und Geistesgeschichte. 5 per yr. ISSN 0008-7556

**Stichting Centraal Orgaan voor het Scheppend Ambacht**
Oude Delft 145, Delft, Netherlands.
- Scheppend Ambacht. bi-m. ISSN 0036-5998

**Stichting Centrale Administratie Bellamy**
Kromhoutstraat 196 IV, Rotterdam, Netherlands.
- Bellamy - Nieuws. m. ISSN 0005-8610
(Internationale Vereniging Bellamy)

**Stichting China Studie Comite**
Bibliotheek TH, Doelenstraat 101, Delft,
Netherlands.
- China Informatie. q. ISSN 0577-8832 (Co-
sponsor: Stichting voor Moeilijk Toegankelijke
Wetenschappeijke Literatuur)

**Stichting Civis Mundi**
Van Stolkweg 10, The Hague, Netherlands.
- Civis Mundi. m. ISSN 0030-3283

**Stichting Contact van Gelderse Oudheidkundige
Verenigingen en Musea**
Hogestraat 7, Dieren, Netherlands.
- Gelders Oudheidkundig Contactbericht. q. ISSN
0016-6014

**Stichting de Gids**
- Gids. (pub. by Meulenhoff-Bruna B.V.)

**Stichting "De Koepel"**
Nieuwe Gracht 15, Utrecht, Netherlands.
- Zenit. m.

**Stichting Doneto**
Vandelstraat 90, Amsterdam, Netherlands.
- Nederlands Theater- en Televisie Jaarboek. a.

**Stichting Elisabethbode**
Tuinstraat 1, Lochem, Netherlands.
- Elisabethbode. w. ISSN 0013-6212

**Stichting Evangelische Omroep**
- Visie. (pub. by Vanderveer B. V.)

**Stichting Familieclub Johannes van der Linden**
- Niet Zo Benauwd. (pub. by L. A. van der Linden)

**Stichting Film en Wetenschap**
Hengeveldstraat 29, Utrecht, Netherlands.
- S F W Scientific Films-Holland. irreg.

**Stichting Franciscaanse Samenwerking te Utrecht**
- Franciscaans Leven. (pub. by Grafische Industrie
van Eerd B.V.)

**Stichting Geestelijke Weerbaarheid**
Zomerstraat 1, Heerlen, Netherlands.
- Basis. s-m. ISSN 0005-6146

**Stichting Gelders Tijdschrift**
Markt 11, Arnhem 6001, Netherlands.
- Gelderland Nu. m.

**Stichting Gemeenschappelijk Zuivelsekretariaat**
Laan van Meerdervoort 18, Box 1810, The Hague,
Netherlands.
- Zuivelnieuws. w. ISSN 0044-5436

**Stichting Gemengde Branche**
Toussaintkade 70, Box 90, The Hague, Netherlands.
- Vakblad Gemengde Branche; vakblad voor de
huishoudelijke, luxe en speelgoedbranche. m.

**Stichting Gezamenlijke Missiepubliciteit**
Postbox 33, Deurne, Netherlands.
- Bijeen. m (11 per yr.) ISSN 0006-2308

**Stichting Groninger Culturele Gemeenschap**
Martinikerkhof 27, Groningen, Netherlands.
- Culturele Maandblad Groningen. (pub. by
Drukkerij Dijkstra Niemeyer B.V.)

**Stichting het Landelijk H.T.S.-Orgaan**
- HTS'er. (pub. by Uitgeverij Pi B.V.)

**Stichting Het Vogeljaar**
c/o J. Mulder, Laan van Altena 30, Delft,
Netherlands.
- Vogeljaar. bi-m. ISSN 0042-7985

**Stichting In de Rechte Straat**
Boulevard 11, Velp, Netherlands.
- In de Rechte Straat/On the Road to Damascus/
En la Calle Recta. m.(Dutch & Eng. edts.);
q.(Spanish edt.) ISSN 0019-3151

**Stichting Industriele Vormgeving**
Beurs, Damrak 622, Amsterdam, Netherlands.
- Vorm. 10 per yr.

**Stichting IVIO-AO-Reeks**
Postbus 37, Lelystad, Netherlands.
- Actuele Onderwerpen-Reeks. w. ISSN 0001-7841

**Stichting Jeugd en Samenleving**
Maliesingel 27, Utrecht, Netherlands.
- Jeugd en Samenleving. m. ISSN 0047-1976

**Stichting Koninklijke Rotterdamse Diergaarde**
Van Aerssenlaan 49, Rotterdam, Netherlands.
- Blijdorp Geluiden. m. ISSN 0006-4785

**Stichting Landbouwmechanisatie Pers**
Dr. S.L. Mansholtlaan 12, Wageningen,
Netherlands.
- Landbouwmechanisatie. m. ISSN 0023-7795

**Stichting Lias**
- LIAS; Sources and Documents Relating to the
Early Modern History of Ideas. (pub. by APA-
Holland University Press)

**Stichting Liberaal Reveil**
Prins Hendrikplein 4a, The Hague, Netherlands.
- Liberaal Reveil. q.

**Stichting Maandschrift Economie**
- Maandschrift Economie. (pub. by H. Gianotten
B.V.)

**Stichting Macro**
Postbus 281, Haarlem, Netherlands.
- Macro. m.

**Stichting Mathematisch Centrum**
c/o Dhr. F. Barning, Tweede Boerhavestraat 49,
Amsterdam-1005, Netherlands.
- Nieuw Archief voor Wiskunde. 3 per yr. ISSN
0028-9825 (Wiskundig Genootschap)

**Stichting Mitex**
- Textiel-Visie: Damesmodevakblad. (pub. by
International Textiles BV)
- Textiel-Visie: Herenmodevakblad. (pub. by
International Textiles BV)
- Textiel-Visie: Kindermodevakblad. (pub. by
International Textiles BV)
- Textiel-Visie: Lingerie en Foundations. (pub. by
International Textiles BV)
- Textiel-Visie/Weekly. (pub. by International
Textiles BV)

**Stichting Naaimachine-Nieuws**
Postbus 224, Leiden, Netherlands.
- Naaimachine-Nieuws. m. ISSN 0027-7339
(Algemene Vereniging van
Naaimachinehandelaren)

**Stichting "Natuur en Jeugd"**
Parkweg 95, Voorburg, Netherlands.
- Jeugdnatuurwachter. m. ISSN 0021-6062

**Stichting Natuur en Milieu**
Noordereinde 60, S-Graveland, Netherlands.
- Natuur en Milieu. m.

**Stichting Nederlands Studiecentrum voor
Zeevarenden**
Veerkade 8, Rotterdam, Netherlands.
- Wacht te Kooi; seaman's digest. w. ISSN 0042-
9902

**Stichting Nederlandse Landbouwers**
Prins Mauritsplein 23, The Hague, Netherlands.
- Landbode; Nederlands landbouwweekblad. w.
ISSN 0023-7736

**Stichting Nieuwe West-Indische Gids**
Zoologisch Laboratorium, Plompetorengracht 9-11,
Utrecht, Netherlands.
- Nieuwe West Indische Gids. 3 per yr. ISSN 0028-
9930

**Stichting "Ons Leekenspel"**
Gudelalaan 2, Bussum, Netherlands.
- D O E. bi-m. ISSN 0038-7258

**Stichting Opvoeding en Lichamelijke Oefening**
Helmerslaan 13, Hilversum, Netherlands.
- Richting; maandblad voor lichamelijke opvoeding,
sport en gezondheidszorg. m. ISSN 0035-5135

**Stichting Opwenteling**
St. Lambertusstraat 10, Eindhoven, Netherlands.
- Naar Morgen. q. ISSN 0027-7355

**Stichting Plurale Samenlevingen**
Box 3566, The Hague, Netherlands.
- Plural Societies. q. ISSN 0048-4482

**Stichting Proefstation voor de Champignoncultuur**
Peelheideweg 1, Horst (L), Netherlands.
- Champignoncultuur. 10 per yr. ISSN 0009-1316

**Stichting Propria Cures**
O. Z. Voorburgwal 87-89, Amsterdam, Netherlands.
- Propria Cures (PC) w. ISSN 0033-1414

**Stichting Redactie Tijdschriften voor
Verpleegkundigen en Verzorgenden**
- Tijdschrift voor Ziekenverpleging. (pub. by
Uitgeversmaatschappij de Tijdstroom)

**Stichting Skoop**
Box 11377, Amsterdam, Netherlands.
- Skoop; krities filmblad. 10 per yr.

**Stichting Skrien Filmschrift**
Postbus 318, Amsterdam 1000, Netherlands.
- Skrien. 8 per yr.

**Stichting Stedelijke Raad voor Maatschappelijk
Welzijn**
Oude Boteringestraat 65, Groningen, Netherlands.
- Stichting Stedelijke Raad voor Maatschappelijk
Welzijn. Informatie-Bulletin. q. ISSN 0039-1395

**Stichting Tijdschriften voor Jeugdbescherming en
Jeugdwelzijn**
W. Barentszstraat 33, Utrecht, Netherlands.
- Sjow. s-m(except Jun. Jul. Aug. when m)

**Stichting tot Bevordering van de Belangen van
Analisten, Laboratorium-Assistenten en Hogere
Chemici**
- Chemie & Instrument. (pub. by Leidsche
Drukkerij B.V.)

**Stichting tot Instandhouding van de Diergaarde van
het Koninklijk Zoologisch Genootschap Natura
Artis Magistra**
Plantage Kerklaan 40, Amsterdam, Netherlands.
- Artis. bi-m. ISSN 0004-3834 (Zoological Society
Amsterdam)

**Stichting tot Wetenschappelijke Voorlichting op
Voedingsgebied**
Laan Copes van Cattenburch 44, The Hague,
Netherlands.
- Voeding; Netherlands journal of nutrition. m.
ISSN 0042-7926

**Stichting Uitgeverij Sigma Chemie**
Riouwstraat 153, The Hague, Netherlands.
- Chemisch Weekblad. w. ISSN 0009-2932
(Koninklijke Nederlandse Chemische Vereniging)

**Stichting Vakblad voor de Groothandel in
Aardappelen, Groenten en Fruit**
Bezuidenhoutseweg 82, The Hague, Netherlands.
- Vakblad voor de Groothandel in Aardappelen,
Groenten en Fruit. w.

**Stichting Vakblad Zaadbelangen**
Jan van Nassaustraat 109, The Hague, Netherlands.
- Zaadbelangen. m. (Nederlandse Algemene
Keuringsdienst van Groente- en Bloemzaden)

**Stichting Vakontwikkeling Verzekeringsbedrijf**
Witte Vrouwensingel 1, 3581-GA-Utrecht,
Netherlands.
- Beursbengel. m.(bi-m. July & Aug.) ISSN 0006-
0313 (Co-sponsor: Federatie van Verenigingen tot
Bevordering van de Assurantie-Wetenschap)

**Uitgeverij Stichting Vam**
Papelaan 85, Voorschoten, Netherlands.
- Auto Service; maandblad voor
motorvoertuigtechniek. m. ISSN 0005-0849

**Stichting voor Het Bevolkingsonderzoek in de
Drooggelegde Zuiderzee Polders**
- Stichting voor het Bevolkingsonderzoek in de
Drooggelegde Zuiderzee Polders. Publikaties.
(pub. by Swets en Zeitlinger B. V.)

**Stichting Vrienden van het Brabants Orkest**
Postbox 442, S-Hertogenbosch, Netherlands.
- Klank en Weerklank. 3-4 per yr. ISSN 0030-3836

**Stokvis Lindeteves B.V.**
Press Office, Box 426, Rotterdam, Netherlands.
- Inzicht. bi-m.

**Studiecentrum Informatica**
Stadhouderskade 6, Amsterdam, Netherlands.
- New Literature on Automation. m. ISSN 0028-6095

**B. V. Uitgeversmaatschappij Succes**
Prinsevinkenpark 2, The Hague, Netherlands.
- Gouden Uren. q. ISSN 0017-2537 (Nederlandse Boekenclub)
- Succes. m.

**Suiker Unie**
Secretariaat, Postbus 3411, Breda, Netherlands.
- Maandblad Suiker Unie. m. ISSN 0024-8606

**Suikerstichting Nederland**
Box 7498, Amsterdam, Netherlands.
- Kwartaalblad Suiker. q.

**Swets en Zeitlinger B. V.**
Heereweg 347B, Lisse, Netherlands.
- Acta Morphologica Neerlando-Scandinavica. 4 per yr. ISSN 0001-6225
- Biometeorology; Proceedings. triennial, 7th, 1975, College Park, Maryland. ISSN 0067-8902 (International Society of Biometeorology)
- Catalogus van Academische Geschriften in Nederland Verschenen. irreg. (Rijksuniversiteit te Utrecht. Bibliotheek)
- English Studies; a journal of English language and literature. bi-m. ISSN 0013-838X
- Interface; journal of new music research. s-a.
- International Journal of Biometeorology. 4 per yr. ISSN 0020-7128 (International Society of Biometeorology)
- International Journal of Speleology. q. ISSN 0020-7691 (International Society of Biometeorology)
- Journal of Interdisciplinary Cycle Research. q. ISSN 0022-1945
- Neurolinguistics; international series devoted to speech physiology and speech pathology. irreg. ISSN 0301-6412
- Progress in Biometeorology. irreg.
- Quarterly Journal of Crude Drug Research.
- R E A P. (Research Exchange and Practice in Mental Retardation) 4 per yr.
- Stichting voor het Bevolkingsonderzoek in de Drooggelegde Zuiderzee Polders. Publikaties. irreg., no. 37, 1973. ISSN 0081-5527
- Studies on the Neotropical Fauna and Environment. q.
- Vehicle System Dynamics; international journal of vehicle mechanics and mobility. q. ISSN 0042-3114

**S. Sytema**
Narcisstr. 3, Assen, Netherlands.
- Staatspensioenen. m. ISSN 0038-8882 (Bond voor Staatspensionering)

**T. M. C. Asser Institute**
- Netherlands International Law Review/ Nederlands Tijdschrift voor International Recht. (pub. by A. W. Sijthoff International Publishing Co.)
- Netherlands Yearbook of International Law. (pub. by A. W. Sijthoff International Publishing Co.)

**T V Z**
Prinsengracht 474, Amsterdam C, Netherlands.
- T V Z. (Tijdschrift voor Ziekenverpleging) s-m. ISSN 0049-2809

**N. V. Drukkerij V. H. G. Taconis**
Hoofdstraat W. 10-14, Wolvega, Netherlands.
- Stellingwerf. w. ISSN 0039-1123

**Technisch Film Centrum**
Arnhemsestraatweg 17, Velp, Netherlands.
- T F C Nieuws. 4 per yr. ISSN 0039-8330

**Technische Hogeschool te Delft. Bibliotheek**
Box 98, Delft, Netherlands.
- Technische Hogeschool te Delft. Bibliotheek. Aanwinsten. m. ISSN 0006-1948
- Technische Hogeschool, Delft. Bibliotheek. Lijst van Lopende Tijdschriftabonnementen. a.

**Technische Hogeschool Te Delft. Department of Civil Engineering**
c/o L. van Zetten, Box 49, Delft, Netherlands.
- Heron. q. ISSN 0046-7316 (prep. by its Stevin-Laboratory) (Co-Sponsor: I.B.B.C. Institute TNO for Building Materials and Building Structures)

**Technische Hogeschool Twente. Department of Physics**
P.O. 217, Enschede, Netherlands.
- Physical Communications. irreg.

**Christa van Tellingen, Ed. & Pub.**
Schoolstraat 36, Utrecht, Netherlands.
- Kelderblom. m. ISSN 0022-9784

**Tendens**
Herengracht 247, Amsterdam, Netherlands.
- Tendens. bi-m.

**J. Terpstra.**
Sarphatipark 7 III, Amsterdam, Netherlands.
- Ad Fontes. 10 per yr. ISSN 0001-7930

**Theatrum Orbis Terrarum**
Keizersgracht 526, Amsterdam, Netherlands.
- Quaerendo; a quarterly journal from the low countries devoted to manuscripts and printed books. q. ISSN 0014-9527

**Theosofische Stichting H. P. Blavatsky**
- Levende Gedachten. (pub. by E. Tillema Jr. Ed. and Pub.)

**Theosofische Vereniging. Nederlandse Afdeling**
Kruisstraat 7, Utrecht, Netherlands.
- Theosofia. bi-m. ISSN 0040-5868

**Thespa Uitgeverij**
Koninginneweg 164, Amsterdam, Netherlands.
- Vestdijk Kroniek. q. (Vestdijkkring)

**W.J. Thieme en Cie B.V.**
Postbus 7, Zutphen, Netherlands.
- Vacature; nieuws- en advertentieblad voor het onderwijs. 3 per m. ISSN 0042-2053

**Tie of Friendship**
- Newsseeker. (pub. by International News, Photo, Correspondence & Hobby Club)

**Uitgeversmaatschappij de Tijdstroom**
Box 14, Lochem, Netherlands.
- Antiek; tijdschrift voor liefhebbers en kenners van oude kunst en kunstnijverheid. 10 per yr. ISSN 0003-5653
- Antiekwereld; maandelijks informatiemagazine voor de antiek- en kunstliefhebber. m.
- Geneeskunde en Sport. bi-m. ISSN 0016-6448 (Vereniging voor Sportgeneeskunde) (Co-Sponsor: Federatie van Bureaus voor Medische Sportkeuring)
- Tijdschrift voor Bejaarden- ,Kraam- en Ziekenverzorging. m. ISSN 0049-3880
- Tijdschrift voor Ziekenverpleging. fortn. (Stichting Redactie Tijdschriften voor Verpleegkundigen en Verzorgenden)
- Ziekenhuis. fortn. ISSN 0044-4715

**Tijl Media B. V.**
Texelstraat 76-80, Amstelveen, Netherlands.
- Arts en Auto. fortn. ISSN 0004-3966 (Vereniging van Artsen-Automobilisten)
- Energie-Spectrum. m. (Energieonderzoek Centrum Nederland)
- Gastvrij. s-m.
- Nederlands Militair Geneeskundig Tijdschrift. bi-m. ISSN 0028-2103
- Nederlands Transport. fortn. ISSN 0028-2219 (Koninklijke Nederlandse Vereniging van Transportondernemingen)

**E. Tillema Jr. Ed. and Pub.**
Hortensiastr. 20, Capelle a/d IJssel, Netherlands.
- Levende Gedachten. m (11 per yr.) ISSN 0047-4444 (Theosofische Stichting H. P. Blavatsky)

**Tjeenk Willink-Noorduijn B. V.**
Industrieweg 1, Box 48, Culemborg, Netherlands.
- Knippenberg's Histokrant; de geschiedenis als aktualiteit. m.

**Tong-Tong B.V.**
Pr. Mauritslaan 36, The Hague, Netherlands.
- Tong-Tong. s-m. ISSN 0040-9189

**Uitgeverij De Toorts**
Nijverheidsweg 1, Haarlem, Netherlands.
- Repertorium Verpakte Geneesmiddelen Periodiek Overzicht voor Artsen. s-a. ISSN 0034-463X

**Totalcreative Intercontinental Service Ltd**
Postbox 876, The Hague 2076, Netherlands.
- Iets. m. ISSN 0019-1531

**Trade Channel Organisation**
Helmholtzstraat 61, Amsterdam-1006, Netherlands.
- Trade Channel Journal; monthly review of original offers & demands covering the leading centers of import & export in more than 170 countries. m. ISSN 0041-0403

**Drukkerij Trio**
Nobelstraat 27, The Hague, Netherlands.
- Hollands Maandblad. m. ISSN 0018-3601

**Tros**
Box 450, Hilversum, Netherlands.
- Tros-Kompas; weekly TV-guide. w. ISSN 0041-3321

**Tutmonda Esperantista Junulara Organizo**
Nieuwe Binnenweg 176, NL-3015 BJ Rotterdam, Netherlands.
- Kontakto. q. ISSN 0023-3692

**Uitgave M.S.C**
Bredaseweg 204, Tilburg, Netherlands.
- Ons Geestelijk Leven; tijdschrift voor informatie, bezinning en gesprek. bi-m. ISSN 0030-2678

**B. V. Uitgeversbedrijf voor de Tuinbouw**
Javastraat 82, The Hague, Netherlands.
- Groenten en Fruit. w. ISSN 0017-4491 (Centraal Bureau van de Tuinbouwveilingen in Nederland)

**Unie van Baptisten Gemeenten**
c/o "de Vinkenhof", Biltseweg 10, Bilthoven, Netherlands.
- Zaaier. m. ISSN 0044-1562

**Unie van Waterschappen**
Statenplein 1, The Hague, Netherlands.
- Waterschapsbelangen. s-m. ISSN 0043-1486

**Unieboek B.V.**
Box 17, Bussum, Netherlands.
- Simiolus; kunsthistorisch tijdschrift. q. ISSN 0037-5411

**Union International de Interlinguistik Servicie**
Amstel 113, Amsterdam, Netherlands.
- Union; inter lingual review. q.

**Union Mundial pro Interlingua**
Beeckzanglaan 84, Beverwijk, Netherlands
- Currero International de Interlingua. q. (Inquiries to: H. P. Frodelund, Ed., Eckersbergsvej 46, DK-5000 Odense, Denmark)

**Universala Esperanto-Asocio**
Nieuwe Binnenweg 176, NL-3015-BJ-Rotterdam, Netherlands.
- Esperanto. m. ISSN 0014-0635
- Esperanto Documents. New Series. irreg.
- Jarlibro. a. ISSN 0075-3491
- Kongresa Libro. a. ISSN 0083-3851

**Universiteit van Amsterdam. Commissie voor de Artis Bibliotheek**
Plantage Middenlaan 45A, Amsterdam C, Netherlands.
- Bijdragen tot de Dierkunde. s-a. ISSN 0067-8546 (Co-sponsor: Koninklijk Zoologisch Genootschap Natura Artis Magistra)

**Universiteit van Amsterdam. Europa Instituut**
- Legal Issues. (pub. by Kluwer B.V.)

**Universiteit van Amsterdam. Fysisch Geografish en Bodemkundig Laboratorium**
Dapperstraat 115, Amsterdam, Netherlands.
- Universiteit van Amsterdam. Fysisch Geografisch en Bodemkundig Laboratorium. Publikaties. irreg. ISSN 0066-1317

**Universiteit van Amsterdam. Mathematisch Instituut**
Roetersstraat 15, 1004 Amsterdam, Netherlands.
- Universiteit van Amsterdam. Mathematisch Instituut. Report. irreg. (approx. 6 per yr.)

**Universiteit van Amsterdam. Zoologisch Museum**
Plantage Middenlaan 53, Amsterdam-C,
Netherlands.
• Beaufortia; series of miscellaneous publications.
  irreg., vol. 25, 1977. ISSN 0067-4745 (prep. by its
  Instituut voor Taxonomische Zoologie)
• Crustaceana. (pub. by E. J. Brill)
• Universiteit van Amsterdam. Zoologisch Museum.
  Bulletin. irreg., vol. 6, 1977. ISSN 0066-1325

**Utrechts Mechanisch Technologisch Corps**
Oudenoord 70, Utrecht, Netherlands.
• Sigma-T. 7 per yr. ISSN 0037-4865

**Mellie Uyldert, Ed. & Pub.**
Lomanlaan 7, Bussum, Netherlands.
• Kaarsvlam. m. ISSN 0022-7463

**V. E. G. Gasinstituut**
P.O. Box 164, Rijswijk, Netherlands.
• Gids van de Nederlandse Gasindustrie. a. ISSN
  0072-4475

**V. V. V.**
• Uit in West-Brabant. (pub. by Wegwijs
  Tijdschriften Exploitatie)

**Drukkerij Vada B.V., Gebr. Zomer en Keuning**
Wageningen, Netherlands.
• Vandaar. 10 per yr. (Zendingscentrum van de
  Gereformeerde Kerken in Nederland) (Co-
  sponsor: Raad voor de Zending van de
  Nederlandse Hervormde Kerk)

**Vaktechnische Uitgeverij Sri**
Hemonystraat 11, Amsterdam Z, Netherlands.
• Slijtersvakblad; trades magazine for wines, spirits,
  beer and other beverages. m. ISSN 0037-6841

**Drukkerij J. Valkenburg N.V.**
Bovenstestraat 6, Echt, Netherlands.
• Gamma. m. ISSN 0016-4380 (Nederlandse
  Vereniging van Radiologisch Laboranten)

**Vanderveer B. V.**
Postbus 62, Leiderdorp, Netherlands.
• Schouw; trade magazin for heating, domestic
  appliances, household articles, sanitary a.s.o. m.
  ISSN 0036-6927 (Nederlandse Vereniging van
  Handelaren in Verwarmings- en Huishoudelijke
  Artikelen)
• Visie. w. (Stichting Evangelische Omroep)
• Welzijn; league issue for nurses and other people
  working the health field. fortn. (Nederlandse
  Christelijke Bond van Overheidspersoneel)

**H. Veenman en Zonen**
Box 7, Wageningen, Netherlands.
• Archivum Chirurgicum Neerlandicum. q. ISSN
  0004-0657 (Dutch College of Surgeons)

**Veiligheidsinstituut**
Hobbemastraat 22, Amsterdam, Netherlands.
• Operatie Veiligheid. m (11 per yr.)
• Veilig Werken/Working Safely. bi-m. ISSN 0042-
  3130 (Nederlandse Vereniging van
  Veiligheidstechnici)
• Veiligheid/Safety. m. ISSN 0042-3149
• Veiligheidsjaarboek. a. ISSN 0083-534X

**Velser Basketball Club**
• Akrides. (pub. by J.D. Ter Brugge, Ed. & Pub.)

**Verbond van Nederlandse Ondernemingen**
Prinses Beatrixlaan 5, Postbox 2110, The Hague,
Netherlands.
• Onderneming. w.

**Verbond van Wetenschappelijke Onderzoekers**
Box 165, Maarssen, Netherlands.
• Wetenschap en Samenleving. m (10 per yr.) ISSN
  0043-4442 (Co-sponsor: Bond voor
  Wetenschappelijke Arbeiders)

**Vereeniging ter Bevordering van de Belangen des
Boekhandels**
Lassusstraat 9, Box 5475, Amsterdam Z,
Netherlands.
• Nieuwsblad voor de Boekhandel. w. ISSN 0028-
  9965

**Vereeniging voor den Katoenhandel, Rotterdam**
Kipstraat 3-5, Rotterdam, Netherlands.
• Monthly Cotton Report. m. ISSN 0027-0326

**Vereeniging Zuid-Afrikaansche Stichting Moederland**
Keizersgracht 141, Amsterdam-C, Netherlands.
• Zuid-Afrika; maandblad voor de culturele en
  economische betrekkingen tussen Nederland en
  Zuid-Afrika. m. ISSN 0044-5428

**Verenigde Grafische Industrie B.V.**
De Bruyn Kopsstraat 10, Rijswijk ZH, Netherlands.
• Electra; onafhankelijk tijdschrift voor toegepaste
  elektrotechnick. fortn. ISSN 0013-4104
• Graficus; onafhankelijk weekblad voor de grafische
  industrie. w. ISSN 0017-2936
• Stationer's/Kantoorboekhandel. m. ISSN 0039-
  0364

**Vereniging Het Maastrichts Mannenkoor**
Karbindersdreef 27, Maastricht, Netherlands.
• Gaudeamus. m. ISSN 0016-5239

**Vereniging Het Nederlandsche Wegencongres**
Postbus 2200, The Hague, Netherlands.
• Wegen; maandblad gewijd aan de weg, het
  luchtvaartterrein en het verkeer. m. ISSN 0043-
  2067

**Vereniging Kinderverzorging en Opvoeding**
Burg. Patijnlaan 65, The Hague, Netherlands.
• K en O. q. ISSN 0022-9970
• Kinderverzorging/Jeugdverzorging. bi-m.

**Vereniging Klei Industrie**
Box 1057, Rijswijk Z. H., Netherlands.
• Klei en Keramiek. m. ISSN 0023-2041 (Co-
  Sponsor: Nederlandse Keramische Vereniging)

**Vereniging Koninklijke Nederlandsche
Heidemaatschappij**
Lovinklaan 1, Arnhem, Netherlands.
• Vereniging Koninklijke Nederlandsche
  Heidemaatschappij. Tijdschrift. 11 per yr. ISSN
  0040-7410

**Vereniging Leraren Schoolmuziek**
Box 158, Roermond, Netherlands.
• Muziek en Onderwijs. q. ISSN 0378-0651

**Vereniging Milieudefensie**
Herengracht 109, Amsterdam, Netherlands.
• Zondertag Krant. m.

**Vereniging Numaga**
Van Berchenstraat 31, Nijmegen, Netherlands.
• Numaga; tijdschrift gewijd aan heden en verleden
  van Nijmegen en omgeving. q. ISSN 0029-5949

**Vereniging ter Bestrijding van de Kwakzalverij**
Oranjelaan 6, Hilversum, Netherlands.
• Maanblad tegen de Kwakzalverij. m. ISSN 0024-
  8614

**Vereninging tot Bevordering der Bijenteelt in
Nederland**
• Maandschrift voor Bijenteelt. (pub. by Bijenhuis-
  Wageningen)

**Vereniging tot Bevordering der Homeopathie in
Nederland**
Dompvloedslaan 50, Overveen, Netherlands.
• Homeopathisch Tijdschrift. bi-m.

**Vereniging tot Bevordering van de Studie van het
Frans**
• Rapports Franse Boek. (pub. by Van Gorcum)

**Vereniging tot Bevordering van Slagersvakonerwijs
S.V.O.**
• Slagersambacht. (pub. by Uitgeversmaatschappij de
  Gelderlander Vakpers BV)

**Vereniging van Archivarissen in Nederland**
• Nederlands Archievenblad. (pub. by B. V. Erven
  B. van der Kamp)

**Vereniging van Artsen-Automobilisten**
• Arts en Auto. (pub. by Tijl Media B. V.)

**Vereniging van Comptabele Ambtenaren**
• Financieel Overheidsbeheer. (pub. by Vuga B.V.)

**Vereniging van de Nederlandse Chemische Industrie**
• Nederlandse Chemische Industrie. (pub. by C. de
  Boer Jr. N.V.)

**Vereniging van Directeuren van Gemeentewerken,
Openbare Werken, Bouw- en Woningtoezicht en
Woningdienst**
• Gemeentewerken. (pub. by Samsom Uitgeverij
  B.V.)

**Vereniging van Exploitanten van Gasbedrijven in
Nederland**
Postbus 137, Apeldoorn - 6704, Netherlands.
• Jaarboek van de Openbare Gasvoorziening. (Co-
  sponsor: VEG-Gasinstituut N.V.)

**Vereniging van Franciscaanse Tertiarissen**
Malakkastraat 55, The Hague, Netherlands.
• Doortocht; Franciscaans Evangelisch opinieblad. 8
  per yr. ISSN 0012-5504

**Vereniging van Kartonnagefabrikanten**
• Cartonnagebedrijf. (pub. by B D U)

**Vereniging van Leraren in Levende Talen**
• Levende Talen. (pub. by Wolters-Noordhoff B.V.)

**Vereniging van Levensmiddelenhandelaren ANKB**
• Food-Magazine. (pub. by Uitgeversmaatschappij
  de Gelderlander Vakpers BV)

**Vereniging van Marine-Officieren**
• Marineblad. (pub. by C. de Boer Jr. N.V.)

**Vereniging van Medische Analisten**
Nieuwe Achtergracht 73, Amsterdam, Netherlands.
• Tijdschrift voor Medische Analisten. m.

**Vereniging van Muziekhandelaren en -Uitgevers in
Nederland**
Amstel 52, Amsterdam, Netherlands.
• Muziekhandel. m. ISSN 0027-5301

**Vereniging van Uitgevers Vertegenwoordigers.**
Westerstraat 62, Wormerveer, Netherlands.
• Vertegenwoordiger. 3 per yr. ISSN 0042-4412

**Vereniging van Verf- en Drukinktfabrikanten**
Groot Haesebroekseweg 1, Postbus 71, Wassenaar,
Netherlands.
• Verfkroniek. m. ISSN 0042-3904

**Vereniging van Vrienden van de Nederlandse
Ceramiek**
Prinsengracht 586, Amsterdam, Netherlands.
• Vereniging van Vrienden van de Nederlandse
  Ceramiek. Mededelingenblad. q. ISSN 0042-3858

**Vereniging van Vrijzinnig Hervormden in Nederland**
• Kerk en Wereld/Church & World. (pub. by Van
  Gorcum)

**Vereniging voor Calvinistische Wijsbegeerte**
• Philosophia Reformata. (pub. by J. H. Kok B. V.)

**Vereniging voor de Effectenhandel**
Beursplein 5, Amsterdam 1001, Netherlands.
• Amsterdam Stock Exchange. a.

**Vereniging voor de Metaal- en de Elektrotechnische
Industrie (FME).**
Nassaulaan 25, The Hague, Netherlands.
• Metalektro Visie. m. ISSN 0026-0738

**Vereniging voor Experimenteel Radio Onderzoek in
Nederland**
Postbox 1166, Arnhem, Netherlands.
• Electron; maandblad voor de Nederlandse radio-
  amateur. m. ISSN 0013-4767

**Vereniging voor Huismuziek**
Catharynesingel 85, Utrecht, Netherlands.
• Huismuziek. bi-m. ISSN 0018-7097

**Vereniging voor Mulo**
Herengracht 56, Amsterdam, Netherlands.
• Nieuw Zicht. s-m.

**Vereniging voor Nederlandse Muziekgeschiedenis**
Steenvoordelaan 94, Rijswijk Z. H., Netherlands.
• Vereniging voor Nederlandse Muziekgeschiedenis.
  Tijdschrift. s-a. ISSN 0042-3874

**Vereniging voor Onderwijsadviezen**
Van Neckstraat 7, The Hague, Netherlands.
• Informa. m. ISSN 0019-9710

**Vereniging voor Openbaar Onderwijs**
Jan Luykenstraat 29, Amsterdam, Netherlands.
• Inzicht. 8 per yr. ISSN 0021-0307

**Vereniging voor Oppervlaktetechnieken van Metalen**
Soestdijkseweg 246a, P.B. 120, Bilthoven,
Netherlands.
- Oppervlaktetechnieken van Metalen. (pub. by B.
  V. Uitgeversmaatschappij Reflex)
- Vereniging voor Oppervlaktetechnieken van
  Metalen. Documentatieservice. m. ISSN 0042-
  3882

**Vereniging voor Sportgeneeskunde**
- Geneeskunde en Sport. (pub. by
  Uitgeversmaatschappij de Tijdstroom)

**Vereniging voor Statistiek**
Weena 700, Rotterdam, Netherlands.
- Statistica Neerlandica. q.(first no. entirely in
  English) ISSN 0039-0402

**Vereniging voor Zoogdierkunde**
- Lutra. (pub. by E. J. Brill)

**Stichting Uitgeverij "Veritas"**
Postbus 630, The Hague, Netherlands.
- Advent. m. (Zevende-Dags Adventisten)
- Bijbellessen voor de Kinderen. q. ISSN 0006-2235
  (Zevende-Dags Adventisten)
- Bijbellessen voor de Sabbatschool. q. ISSN 0006-
  2243 (Zevende-Dags Adventisten)
- Houvast. m (10 per yr.) (Zevende-Dags
  Adventisten)
- Leven en Gezondheid. m (11 per yr.)

**Vermande Zonen B.V.**
Ir. Justus Dirksstr. 12, Postbus 548, IJmuiden,
Netherlands.
- Bijvoorbeeld. q.
- Brand en Brandweer. m.
- Wereld van het Jonge Kind. m.

**Vestdijkkring**
- Vestdijk Kroniek. (pub. by Thespa Uitgeverij)

**Vooraziatisch-Egyptisch Genootschap "Ex Oriente
Lux"**
Noordeindsplein 4a, Leiden, Netherlands.
- Jaarbericht "Ex Oriente Lux". (pub. by Nederlands
  Instituut voor Het Nabije Oosten)
- Phoenix. s-a. ISSN 0031-8329
- Vooraziatisch-Egyptisch Genootschap "Ex Oriente
  Lux". Mededelingen en Verhandelingen. (pub. by
  Nederlands Instituut voor Het Nabije Oosten)

**Voorns' Papierwereld**
Spreeuwenplaats 18, Leiden, Netherlands.
- Papierwereld; maanblad voor de papier- en
  papierverwerkende industrie. m. ISSN 0031-1413
  (Bond voor Materialenkennis)

**Vrije Pers Nederland N.V.**
Darwinplantsoen 9, Amsterdam, Netherlands.
- Vrije Pers; weekblad voor de zwijgende
  meerderheid. fortn. ISSN 0049-6812

**Vrije Universiteit, Amsterdam**
De Boelelaan 1115, Amsterdam, Netherlands.
- Pharetra. m. ISSN 0031-6822

**Vuga B.V.**
Box 81, Arnhem, Netherlands.
- Financieel Overheidsbeheer; tijdschrift gewijd aan
  de financien van de overheid, haar bedrijven en
  diensten. m. ISSN 0015-2072 (Vereniging van
  Comptabele Ambtenaren) (Co-Sponsor:
  Vereniging van Gemeente-Accountants)

**N. V. Vuil Afvoer Maatschappij**
Stadhouderskade 40, Postbus 5380, 1007
Amsterdam, Netherlands.
- V A M Mededelingen. 4 per yr. ISSN 0042-1715

**Uitgeverij De Vuurbaak**
Box 189, Groningen, Netherlands.
- Ambt en Plicht. m. ISSN 0002-6999
  (Gereformeerd Maatschappelijk Verbond)

**Waalse Gemeente Nederland**
Rooseveltlaan 191, Amsterdam, Netherlands.
- Echo des Eglises Wallonnes. m. ISSN 0012-9275

**Richard Wagner, Ed. & Pub.**
Box 8077, The Hague, Netherlands.
- Antiekrevue. m.
- Sales Results Holland. irreg.
- Veilingberichten. w. ISSN 0042-3157

**Wapen der Koninklijke Marechaussee**
Raamweg 4, The Hague, Netherlands.
- Ons Wapen. bi-m. ISSN 0030-2783

**Weekbladpers**
Raamgracht 4, Amsterdam, Netherlands.
- Voetbal International. w. ISSN 0042-7977

**Wegwijs Tijdschriften Exploitatie**
Box 157, IJmuiden, Netherlands.
- Uit in West-Brabant. m. ISSN 0006-9558 (V. V.
  V.)

**Van der Weij Periodieken B.V.**
Post Box 285, Hilversum, Netherlands.
- D W; drogisten weekblad. w.

**Wereldverbond van Bouwvakarbeiders- en
Houtbewerkersorganisaties**
Postbus 414, Kromme Nieuwe Gracht 22, Utrecht,
Netherlands.
- Wereldverbond van Bouwvakarbeiders- en
  Houtbewerkersorganisaties. Bulletin. 3 per yr.

**Van der Werff en Hubrecht N. V.**
Rokin 75, Box 3446, Amsterdam, Netherlands.
- Van der Werff & Hubrecht N.V. Beursoverzicht. s-
  m. ISSN 0042-2452

**Werkgemeenschap voor Vernieuwing van Opvoeding,
Onderwijs en Maatschappij**
- Vernieuwing van Opvoeding, Onderwijs en
  Maatschappij. (pub. by J. Muusses B. V.)

**N. V. Drukkerij West-Friesland**
Kleine Noord 7-9, Hoorn, Netherlands.
- Rijkstuinbouwconsulentschap. Mededelingen. m.
  ISSN 0035-5321

**Uitgeverij Wijlhuizen**
Elzenkamp 13, Beek(by Nijmegen), Netherlands.
- Timmerfabrikant. m. ISSN 0040-7933
  (Nederlandse Bond van Timmerfabrikanten)

**Wijt en Zn. B.V.**
Postbus 268, Rotterdam, Netherlands.
- Avia; maandblad voor lucht- en ruimtevaart. m.
  ISSN 0005-2035 (Koninklijke Nederlandse
  Vereniging voor Luchtvaart)
- Lastechniek. m. ISSN 0023-8694 (Nederlands
  Instituut voor Lastechniek)
- Ons Leger. m. ISSN 0030-2724 (Koninklijke
  Nederlandse Vereniging "Ons Leger")
- Schip en Werf. fortn. ISSN 0036-6099
  (Nederlandsche Vereniging van Technici Op
  Scheepvaartgebied) (Co-sponsor: Centrale Bond
  van Scheepsbouwmeesters in Nederland;
  Nationaal Instituut voor Scheepvaart en
  Scheepsbouw. Nederlandsch Scheepsbouw-Kundig
  Proefstation)
- Telecommunicatie; informatieblad voor handel en
  industrie. m. ISSN 0030-8382

**Drukkerij J.C. Willemsen**
Postbus 79, Amersfoort, Netherlands
(Subscr. Address: Breyers Boekhandel, Looierstraat
1, Arnhem, Netherlands)
- Hervormd Arnhem. w. ISSN 0018-0920
  (Hervormde Gemeente Arnhem)

**Uitgeversmaatschappij Williams Nederland B. V.**
Energiestraat 29, Postbus 5028, Naarden,
Netherlands.
- Mad. bi-m. ISSN 0024-9300

**H. Wilts, Ed. & Pub.**
Stationsplein 90, Velp (G), Netherlands.
- Genadeklanken. s-m. ISSN 0016-6324

**Wiskundig Genootschap**
- Nieuw Archief voor Wiskunde. (pub. by Stichting
  Mathematisch Centrum)

**Thom. F. Wolfs**
Velseroordstraat 3, Velsen, Netherlands.
- Katholieke Kleuterschool. m. ISSN 0022-9334
  (Katholiek Onderwijs Verbond)
- Uit in Utrecht. w. ISSN 0041-5898

**Wolters-Noordhoff B.V.**
Box 58, Groningen, Netherlands.
- Archaeologica Traiectina. biennial. ISSN 0066-
  5959 (Rijksuniversiteit te Utrecht. Archaeological
  Institute)
- Archimedes. 5 per yr. ISSN 0003-8377

- Drie Talen; maandblad voor de studie van Frans,
  Duits en Engels. 10 per yr. ISSN 0012-6187
- Euclides; maandblad voor de didactiek van de
  wiskunde. 10 per yr.
- Infolt; berichten en mededelingen van de
  Verenging van Leraren in Levende Talen. bi-m.
- Levende Talen. 6 per yr. ISSN 0024-1539
  (Vereniging van Leraren in Levende Talen)
- Neophilologus. q. ISSN 0028-2677
- Nieuw Tijdschrift voor Wiskunde. bi-m. ISSN
  0028-985X
- Nieuwe Taalgids; tijdschrift voor neerlandici. 6 per
  yr. ISSN 0028-9922
- Pythagoras; wiskundig tijdschrift voor jongeren. 5
  per yr. ISSN 0033-4766
- Toneel Teatraal. 10 per yr. ISSN 0040-9170
- Voordrachten Gehouden voor de Gelderse
  Leergangen te Arnhem. irreg, vol. 10, 1965. ISSN
  0504-7250

**World Association of World Federalists**
Leliegracht 21, Amsterdam-C, Netherlands.
- Transnational Perspectives. 4 per yr. (Co-sponsor:
  World Ferderalist Youth)

**World Collectors Publishers**
P.O. Box 263, Voorburg 2111, Netherlands.
- World Collectors Annuary. a. ISSN 0084-1498

**World Esperantist Youth Organization**
*see* Tutmonda Esperantista Junulara Organizo

**World Federation for the Protection of Animals**
- Animal Regulation Studies. (pub. by Elsevier
  Scientific Publishing Co.)

**World Federation of Neurological Societies**
- International Congress of Neurological Surgery.
  Abstracts of Papers. (pub. by Excerpta Medica)

**World Federation of Neurology**
- Journal of the Neurological Sciences. (pub. by
  Elsevier Scientific Publishing Co.)

**World Federation of Societies of Anaesthesiologists**
- World Congress of Anaesthesiologists.
  Proceedings. (pub. by Excerpta Medica)

**World Fertility Survey**
- World Fertility Survey. Basic Documentation.
  (pub. by International Statistical Institute)
- World Fertility Survey. Report. (pub. by
  International Statistical Institute)

**Y W C A Nederland**
F.C. Donderstraat 23, Utrecht, Netherlands.
- Contour. m.

**Youth for Christ**
Hoofdstraat 260, Driebergen, Netherlands.
- Aktie. 11 per yr. ISSN 0002-3744

**Zeeland. Provinciale Waterstaatsdienst**
Rouaansekaai 43, Middelburg, Netherlands.
- Verslag Onderzoek Kwaliteit Oppervlaktewater in
  Zeeland. a.

**Zendingscentrum van de Gereformeerde Kerken in
Nederland**
- Vandaar. (pub. by Drukkerij Vada B.V., Gebr.
  Zomer en Keuning)

**Zendingsgenootschap der Evangelische
Broedergemeente**
Box 19, 3700 AA Zeist, Netherlands.
- Suriname Zending. q. ISSN 0039-6141

**Zevende Dags Adventisten**
Pr. Alexanderweg 1, Huis Ter Heide, Netherlands.
- Advent. (pub. by Stichting Uitgeverij "Veritas")
- Bijbellessen voor de Kinderen. (pub. by Stichting
  Uitgeverij "Veritas")
- Bijbellessen voor de Sabbatschool. (pub. by
  Stichting Uitgeverij "Veritas")
- Contactblad; voor cursisten en oud-cursisten van
  de stem der profetie. q. ISSN 0010-731X
- Houvast. (pub. by Stichting Uitgeverij "Veritas")

**Zomer en Keuning Tijdschriften**
Costerweg 5, Wageningen, Netherlands.
- School. m.

**Zoological Society Amsterdam**
- Artis. (pub. by Stichting tot Instandhouding van
  de Diergaarde van het Koninklijk Zoologisch
  Genootschap Natura Artis Magistra)

**Zoologisch Museum**
*see under* Universiteit van Amsterdam

**Zuidafrikaanse Ambassade**
Wassenaarseweg 40, The Hague, Netherlands.
• Zuidafrikaanse Koerier. m. ISSN 0049-8785

**Drukkerij Uitgeverij Zuijderduijn**
Kerkplein 1, Woerden, Netherlands.
• Theologia Reformata. q. ISSN 0040-5612

**Zusters Augustinessen van Sint Monica**
Soestdijkerstraatweg 151, Hilversum, Netherlands.
• Stad Gods. m. ISSN 0038-8904

# NETHERLANDS ANTILLES

**Citroen-Daal**
Malmokweg 2, Curacao, Netherlands
Antilles.
• Curacao Trade and Industry Directory. a.

**Netherlands Antilles. Bureau voor de Statistiek**
Departement Sociale and Economische Zaken,
Willemstad, Cuaraco.
• Jaarstatistiek van de in-en Uitvoer per
Goederensoort van de Nederlandse Antillen. a.
ISSN 0077-6653
• Jaarstatistiek van de in-en Uitvoer per Land van
de Nederlandse Antillen. a. ISSN 0077-6645
• Netherlands Antilles. Bureau voor de Statistiek.
Statistiek van de Meteorologische Waarnemingen
in de Nederlandse Antillen. irreg. ISSN 0077-
667X
• Netherlands Antilles. Bureau voor de Statistiek.
Statistisch Jaarboek. a. ISSN 0077-6661

**Netherlands Antilles. Departement Sociale and
Economische Zaken**
Fort Amsterdam, Netherlands Antilles.
• Netherlands Antilles. Departement Sociale and
Economische Zaken. Economische Notities. q.

**Stichting Tot Bevordering van de
Rechtswetenschappen in Nederlandse Antillen**
Emanstraat 68, Oranjestad, Aruba.
• Justicia; Rechtsgeleerd Periodiek voor de
Nederlandse Antillen. q. ISSN 0022-7056

**Trade and Industry of Curacao. Monthly Publication**
19f Columbusstraat, Willemstad, Curacao,
Netherlands Antilles.
• Trade and Industry of Curacao. Monthly
Publication. m.

# NEW CALEDONIA

**Chambre de Commerce et d'Industrie de Nouvelle
Caledonie**
B.P. 13, Noumea, New Caledonia.
• Chambre de Commerce et d'Industrie de Nouvelle
Caledonie. Bulletin. q.

**New Caledonia. Service de la Statistique**
B.P. No 6, Noumea, New Caledonia.
• New Caledonia. Service de la Statistique.
Informations Statistiques Rapides.

**New Caledonia. Service des Mines**
Noumea, New Caledonia.
• New Caledonia. Service des Mines et de la
Geologia. Rapport Annuel. a.

**O.R.S.T.O.M.**
Oceanographie, B.P. a5, Noumea, New Caledonia.
• Recueil de Travaux. ORSTOM. Section
Oceanographie. a. ISSN 0078-2130

**Societe d'Etudes Historiques de la Nouvelle-Caledonie**
BP G1 Cedex, Noumea, New Caledonia.
• Societe d'Etudes Historiques de la Nouvelle-
Caledonie. Bulletin. q.

**South Pacific Commission**
Anse Vata, B. P. D5, Noumea, New Caledonia.
• Regional Conference of Directors of Agriculture
and Livestock Production. Report. a.
• South Pacific Commission. Annual Report. a.
• South Pacific Commission. Handbook. irreg.,
1973, no. 8. ISSN 0081-2811
• South Pacific Commission. Information Circular.
irreg.; no. 52, 1973. ISSN 0081-282X
• South Pacific Commission. Information
Document. irreg.; no. 29, 1972. ISSN 0081-2838

• South Pacific Commission. Report of S P C
Technical Meetings. irreg. ISSN 0081-2846
• South Pacific Commission. Statistical Bulletin.
irreg.
• South Pacific Commission. Technical Paper. irreg.,
1972, no. 165. ISSN 0081-2862
• South Pacific Conference. Report of the
Conference and Proceedings of the Session. a.
ISSN 0081-2870

# NEW HEBRIDES

**New Hebrides. Condominium Bureau of Statistics**
Port Vila, New Hebrides.
• New Hebrides. Condominium Bureau of Statistics.
Business Licences. Patents Delivrees. a.
• New Hebrides. Condominium Bureau of Statistics.
Overseas Migration/Echanges Migratoire Avec
l'Exterieur. q.
• New Hebrides. Condominium Bureau of Statistics.
Overseas Shipping and Aircraft Statistics.
Statistiques de Navigation Maritime et Aerienne
Internationales. a.

**New Hebrides. Condominium Geological Survey**
British Residency, Port Vila, New Hebrides.
• New Hebrides. Condominium Geological Survey.
Reports. irreg., ISSN 0077-8443
• New Herbides. Condominium Geological Survey.
Annual Reports. a.

# NEW ZEALAND

**Adis Press (Australasia) Pty. Ltd.**
P.O. Box 34-030, Birkenhead, Auckland 10, New
Zealand.
• Patient Management; a journal of patient
management and therapy. m.

**Aeronautical Press Ltd.**
Box 173, Wellington, New Zealand.
• Wings. m. ISSN 0043-5899

**Agricultural and Industrial Surveys Ltd.**
P.O. 3511 Wellington, New Zealand.
• Te Awatea. bi-m. (New Zealand Theatre Trust)

**Agricultural Promotion Associates**
Box 11-137, Wellington, New Zealand.
• Young Country. m?

**Air New Zealand Ltd**
Private Bag, Auckland, New Zealand
(U. S. Address: Suite 1000, 510 W. 6th St., Los
Angeles, CA 90014)
• Air New Zealand. Annual Report. a. ISSN 0065-
4817

**Akaroa Mail Co. Ltd.**
Box 9, Rue Balguerie, Akaroa, Canterbury, New
Zealand.
• Akaroa Mail. 2 per w. ISSN 0002-3612

**Akron Consolidated Ltd.**
Box 51-182, Auckland 6, New Zealand.
• New Zealand Hardware Journal. m. ISSN 0028-
8160 (New Zealand Wholesale Hardware Guilds'
Federation) (Co-Sponsor: N. Z. Retail Hardware
Federation)
• New Zealand Plumbing Review; heating and
ventilation. m. ISSN 0028-8594 (Modern
Productions Ltd.)

**Rex W. Alding, Ed. & Pub.**
Box 941, Rotorua, New Zealand.
• Spotlight; on the book, stationery, magazine,
greeting cards, & toys trades in N.Z. m. ISSN
0038-8386

**G. R. Allen, Ed. & Pub.**
P.O. Box 1367, Wellington, New Zealand.
• New Zealand Financial Times; New Zealand's
foremost investment and business journal. m.
ISSN 0028-8101

**Apparel Publishing Ltd.**
Box 39-014, Auckland, New Zealand.
• Apparel; to all clothing, textile and footwear
manufacturers and retail clothing outlets. m.

**Archives and Records Association**
Private Bag, Wellington, New Zealand.
• Archifacts. q. (New Zealand Library Association.
Archives Committee.)

**Auckland. City Council**
Auckland, New Zealand.
• Auckland City Council. Directory of Social
Services. irreg.

**Auckland City Art Gallery**
Kitchener St., Auckland 1, New Zealand.
• Auckland City Art Gallery Quarterly. 4 per yr.
ISSN 0004-7422

**Auckland Institute and Museum**
Private Bag, Auckland 1, New Zealand.
• Auckland Institute and Museum. Bulletin. irreg.;
no. 10, 1975. ISSN 0067-0456
• Auckland Institute and Museum. Records. a. since
1970 (vol. 7) ISSN 0067-0464

**Auckland Institute and Museum. Conchology Section**
c/o N. & N. Gardner, Ed. & Pub., 6 Tui Glen Rd.,
Birkenhead, Auckland, New Zealand.
• Poirieria. q. ISSN 0032-2377

**Auckland Rugby League**
Box 1287, Auckland, New Zealand.
• Auckland Rugby League. League News. 30 per
yr.(Apr.-Oct.) ISSN 0004-7430

**Auckland University Field Club**
c/o Botany Department, University of Auckland,
Private Bag, Auckland, New Zealand.
• Tane. a. ISSN 0496-8026

**Auckland University Law Students Society, Inc.**
Private Bag, Auckland, New Zealand.
• Auckland University Law Review. a. ISSN 0067-
0510

**Australia & New Zealand Teachers of the Visually
Handicapped**
Homai College, Box 67, Manurewa, New Zealand.
• A. N. Z. A. T. V. H. Newsletter. q.

**Automatic Control and Instrumentation Society
(N.Z.)**
• Automations and Control. (pub. by Magazine
Press Ltd.)

**Aviation Historical Society of New Zealand**
Box 2694, Christchurch, New Zealand.
• Aviation Historical Society of New Zealand.
Journal. q. ISSN 0005-2124

**Bank of New Zealand**
P. O. Box 2392, Wellington, New Zealand.
• New Zealand Economic Statistics. irreg.

**Baptist Union of New Zealand**
Box 6212, Wellington, New Zealand.
• N. Z. Baptist. m. ISSN 0027-7177

**Berl Publications Ltd.**
Box 10010, Wellington, New Zealand.
• Equity Investment. a.
• New Zealand Economist. m (except Jan.) ISSN
0028-8055

**Bible College of New Zealand, Inc.**
221 Lincoln Rd., Henderson, Auckland 8, New
Zealand.
• Reaper; New Zealand's Evangelical monthly. m.
ISSN 0034-107X

**Biological Society**
Victoria University, Private Bag, Wellington, New
Zealand.
• Tuatara. 3 per yr. ISSN 0041-3860

**Blundell Bros. Ltd.**
Willis St., Wellington 1, New Zealand.
• War Cry. w. ISSN 0043-0242 (Salvation Army)

**Broadcasting Council of New Zealand**
Box 3140, Wellington, New Zealand.
• New Zealand Listener. w. ISSN 0028-839X

**Broadsheet Collective**
Box 47261, Auckland, New Zealand.
• Broadsheet; New Zealand feminist magazine. 10
per yr.

**Butterworths of New Zealand Ltd.**
26-28 Waring Taylor St., Wellington, New Zealand.
• Butterworths Current Law. irreg. ISSN 0110-070X
• New Zealand Law Journal. s-m. ISSN 0028-8373

**Canterbury Botanical Society**
P.O.B. 2443, Christchurch, New Zealand.
• Canterbury Botanical Society. Journal. a.

**Canterbury Chamber of Commerce**
Box 187, Christchurch, New Zealand.
- Canterbury Chamber of Commerce. Economic Bulletin. m. ISSN 0008-5685

**Canterbury Horticultural Society, Inc.**
Box 369, Christchurch, New Zealand.
- City Beautiful. bi-m. ISSN 0009-7705

**Care**
Box 2794, Auckland, New Zealand.
- Care. 5 per yr.

**Carlton Printing Co. Ltd.**
139 Madras St., Box 1023, Christchurch, New Zealand.
- New Zealand Trotting Calendar; Official calendar of New Zealand Trotting Conference. w. ISSN 0028-8799

**Caxton Press**
119 Victoria St., Christchurch, New Zealand.
- Landfall; a New Zealand literary magazine. q. ISSN 0023-7930

**Cockerel Print**
Box 2538, Wellington, New Zealand.
- Cock. 5-8 per yr. ISSN 0010-0080

**Comment Publishing Co.**
Box 1746, Wellington, New Zealand.
- Comment. q. ISSN 0010-2555

**Concrete Publications**
Securities House, 126 the Terrace, P. O. 3644, Wellington, New Zealand.
- New Zealand Concrete Construction. m. (except Jan.) (New Zealand Portland Cement Association)

**Corriedale Sheep Society (Inc.)**
Box 13250, Christchurch, New Zealand.
- Corriedale. biennial.

**Cranwell Publishing Co. Ltd.**
419 Queen St., Auckland, New Zealand.
- Australasian Environment. bi-m.

**J. B. Cronin, Ed. & Pub.**
Box 1198, Wellington, New Zealand.
- Junior Student. 10 per yr. ISSN 0022-670X
- Students' Digest. 10 per yr. ISSN 0039-2863

**Daily Telegraph Ltd.**
Napier, New Zealand.
(Subscr. Address: Box 10322, Wellington, New Zealand)
- N. Z. Valuer. q. ISSN 0027-7282 (New Zealand Institute of Valuers)

**V. V. Donald**
Box 236, Masterdon, New Zealand.
- New Zealand Outdoor. m. ISSN 0028-8543

**Robin Dudding, Ed. & Pub.**
4 Sealy Rd., Torbay, Auckland 10, New Zealand.
- Islands; a New Zealand quarterly of arts and letters. q. ISSN 0110-0858

**Earwig Graphics**
10 Norfolk St., Auckland 2, New Zealand.
- Earwig. s-a.

**Editorial Services Ltd.**
Box 6443, Wellington, New Zealand.
- New Zealand Journal of Physiotherapy. s-a. (New Zealand Society of Physiotherapists)
- New Zealand Veterinary Journal. m. ISSN 0048-0169 (New Zealand Veterinary Association)
- Social Behavior and Personality; an international journal. s-a. ISSN 0301-2212 (Society for Personality Research Inc.)

**Electric Supply Authority Engineers' Institute**
- New Zealand Energy Journal. (pub. by Technical Publications Ltd.)

**Electrical Supply Authorities Association of New Zealand**
Box 1017, Wellington, New Zealand.
- Live Lines. m. ISSN 0024-5143

**Entomological Society of New Zealand**
P.O. Box 77004, Mt. Albert, Auckland, New Zealand.
- Entomological Society of New Zealand. Bulletin. irreg.
- New Zealand Entomologist. a. ISSN 0077-9962

**F E P Productions Ltd.**
P.O. Box 2798, Wellington, New Zealand.
- New Zealand Business Who's Who. a. ISSN 0077-9571

**Far East Oceania Information Services, Ltd.**
P.O. 3981, Auckland, New Zealand.
- Sun. m. ISSN 0039-5102

**Federated Farmers of New Zealand. Women's Division**
- New Zealand Countrywoman. (pub. by Kerslake, Billens & Humphrey, Ltd.)

**Forest Research Institute**
Private Bag, Rotorua, New Zealand.
- What's New in Forest Research. m. ISSN 0110-1048

**Fourman Holdings Ltd.**
Box 883, Wellington, New Zealand.
- Motorman. m. ISSN 0027-2345
- New Zealand Hospital. q. ISSN 0028-8217 (Hospital Boards' Association of New Zealand, Inc.)

**Fourth Estate Publishing Co.**
Box 1449, Wellington, New Zealand.
- National Business Review. w.

**Fragments**
Ed. David Young, 18 Maxell St., Christchurch, New Zealand.
- Fragments. bi-m.

**Friends of the Turnbull Library**
Alexander Turnbull Library, Box 12-349, Wellington, New Zealand.
- Turnbull Library Record. s-a.

**Garratt Printing Co. Ltd.**
Box 6402, Wellington, New Zealand.
- New Zealand Electrician. m. ISSN 0028-8071 (New Zealand Institute of Electricians Inc)

**Gay Publishing Collective**
Box 835, Auckland 1, New Zealand.
- New Zealand Gay News. bi-m.

**Health of the People**
Box 5896, Auckland, New Zealand.
- Health of the People. q. ISSN 0301-0384

**Noel Farr Hoggard, Ed. & Pub.**
Box 6188, Te Aro, Wellington, New Zealand.
- Arena; a literary magazine. ISSN 0004-0959

**Hospital Boards' Association of New Zealand, Inc.**
- New Zealand Hospital. (pub. by Fourman Holdings Ltd.)

**Hotel Association of New Zealand**
- N. Z. Licensee. (pub. by New Zealand Licensee Co. Ltd.)

**I. N. L. Print Ltd.**
Box 1034, Wellington, New Zealand.
- N. Z. Sports Digest. m. ISSN 0027-7258
- New Zealand Horse & Pony. m. ISSN 0028-8209 (New Zealand Pony Clubs Association)
- New Zealand Yachting & Rower Boating. m.

**Institute of New Zealand Health Inspectors Inc.**
Box 510, Taupo, New Zealand.
- New Zealand Sanitarian. q. ISSN 0048-0142

**Institute of the New Zealand Motor Industry Inc.**
Box 9244, Courtenay Place, Wellington, New Zealand.
- Service Side. m.

**David F. Jones Ltd.**
P.O. Box 6117, Wellington, New Zealand.
- New Zealand Gardener. m. ISSN 0028-8136

**Kerslake, Billens & Humphrey, Ltd.**
Box 352, Levin, New Zealand.
- New Zealand Countrywoman. bi-m. ISSN 0028-8039 (Federated Farmers of New Zealand. Women's Division)
- New Zealand Nursing Journal; Kai Tiaki. m. ISSN 0028-8535 (New Zealand Nurses Association)

**Legion of the Frontiersmen of the Commonwealth. New Zealand Division**
Box 459, Wanganui, New Zealand.
- Frontiersman. q. ISSN 0046-5216

**Len Jury Ltd.**
Box 174, New Plymouth, New Zealand.
- New Zealand Stamp Monthly. m. ISSN 0028-8721

**Lincoln College**
Canterbury, New Zealand.
- Lincoln College. Agricultural Economics Research Unit. Discussion Paper. irreg., no. 37, 1976. ISSN 0069-3782
- Lincoln College. Agricultural Economics Research Unit. Research Report. irreg., no. 76, 1976. ISSN 0069-3790
- Lincoln College. Agricultural Economics Research Unit. Technical Paper. irreg., 1972, no. 17. ISSN 0069-3804
- Lincoln College. Farmers' Conference. Proceedings. a. ISSN 0069-3839

**Lincoln College. Department of Farm Management and Rural Valuation**
Canterbury, New Zealand.
- Lincoln College. Department of Farm Management and Rural Valuation. Farm Management Papers. irreg., no. 4, 1971. ISSN 0071-397X
- Lincoln College. Department of Farm Management and Rural Valuation. Farm Management Studies. irreg., no. 4, 1973. ISSN 0071-3988

**Lincoln College. Department of Horticulture**
Canterbury, New Zealand.
- Lincoln College. Department of Horticulture. Bulletin. irreg., 1969, no. 10. ISSN 0069-3820

**Lincoln College. New Zealand Agricultural Engineering Institute**
Canterbury, New Zealand.
- Lincoln College. Lincoln Papers in Water Resources. irreg., no. 12, 1974. ISSN 0075-952X
- Lincoln College. New Zealand Agricultural Engineering Institute. Annual Report. a. ISSN 0077-9520
- Lincoln College. New Zealand Agricultural Engineering Institute. Extension Bulletin. irreg., no. 9, 1971. ISSN 0077-9539
- Lincoln College. New Zealand Agricultural Engineering Institute. Project Report. irreg., no. 15, 1977. ISSN 0077-9547
- Lincoln College. New Zealand Agricultural Engineering Institute. Public Test Report. irreg., no. 61, 1977. ISSN 0077-9555

**Magazine Press Ltd.**
157-161 Khyber Pass, Box 1365, Auckland, New Zealand.
- Automations and Control. bi-m. (Automatic Control and Instrumentation Society (N.Z.))
- Home and Building. m. ISSN 0018-392X

**Maori Education Foundation**
P.O. Box 8006, Wellington, New Zealand.
- Maori Education Foundation. Annual Report. a. ISSN 0076-4280

**Massey University. Geography Department**
Palmerston North, New Zealand.
- Geography of New Zealand. irreg. ISSN 0072-0984

**Massey University. School of Business**
Palmerston North, New Zealand.
- Massey University. School of Business. Occasional Papers. bi-m (approx.) (prep. by its Department of Business Studies)

**Mate**
Box 10153, The Terrace, Wellington, New Zealand.
- Mate; a magazine of New Zealand writing. 2 per yr. ISSN 0025-5130

**Medical Association of New Zealand**
26 The Terrace, Wellington, New Zealand.
- Medical Association of New Zealand. Annual Handbook. a. ISSN 0076-5910
- New Zealand Medical Journal. (pub. by Otago Daily Times, Ltd.)

**Medical Council of New Zealand**
P.O. Box 5135, Wellington, New Zealand.
- Medical Council of New Zealand. Publication. irreg.(every 3-5 yrs.) ISSN 0076-5937
- New Zealand Register of Specialists. a.

**Mercantile Gazette of New Zealand Ltd.**
Box 20-034, Christchurch 5, New Zealand.
- Insurance Directory of New Zealand. a.

- Mercantile Gazette of New Zealand. fortn. ISSN 0025-9799
- New Zealand Company Director & Executive; with sharemarket survey. m.
- New Zealand Shipping Directory. a. ISSN 0545-7866
- New Zealand Shipping Gazette. w. ISSN 0027-724X
- New Zealand Tenders Gazette. w. ISSN 0028-8756
- Travel Executives of New Zealand. a.

**Modern Medicine of New Zealand Ltd.**
20 Fort St., Aukland 1, New Zealand.
- Modern Medicine of New Zealand; the journal of diagnosis and treatment. m. ISSN 0026-8119

**Modern Productions Ltd**
Box 3159, Auckland 1, New Zealand.
- Forest Industries Review. m.
- Management; for business and industrial executives. m. ISSN 0025-1658 (New Zealand Institute of Management)
- New Zealand Plumbing Review. (pub. by Akron Consolidated Ltd.)

**Modern Publications Ltd.**
P.O. Box 3159, Auckland 1, New Zealand.
- Whites Air Directory & Who's Who in New Zealand Aviation. a.

**N.Z. Forest Products Ltd.**
Private Bag, Auckland, New Zealand.
- Forest Products News. q. ISSN 0429-0917

**National Library of New Zealand**
Private Bag, Wellington, New Zealand.
- Index to New Zealand Periodicals. a. ISSN 0073-5957
- New Zealand Library School, Wellington. Bibliographical Series. irreg., no. 12, 1975. ISSN 0078-009X
- New Zealand National Bibliography. m(annual cumulations) ISSN 0028-8497

**National Library of New Zealand. General Services Division**
Private Bag, Wellington, New Zealand.
- Interface N.Z. irreg., no. 1, 1975.

**National Museum. Trustees Board**
Wellington, New Zealand.
- Dominion Museum Records. q.

**New Zealand. Broadcasting Council**
Wellington, New Zealand.
- New Zealand. Broadcasting Council. Report. a.

**New Zealand. Central Advisory Committee**
c/o Department of Education, Private Bag, Government Buildings, Wellington, New Zealand.
- New Zealand. Central Advisory Committee on the Appointments and Promotion of Primary Teachers. Report to the Minister of Education. quinquennial. ISSN 0077-958X

**New Zealand. Council for Recreation and Sport**
Wellington, New Zealand.
- New Zealand. Council for Recreation and Sport. Report. a.

**New Zealand. Customs Department**
Wellington, New Zealand.
- New Zealand. Customs Department. Customs Bulletin. m. ISSN 0548-9962

**New Zealand. Dairy Board**
P.O. Box 417, Wellington, New Zealand.
- New Zealand. Dairy Board. Annual Report and Statement of Accounts. a.
- New Zealand Dairy Exporter. (pub. by New Zealand Dairy Produce Exporter Newspaper Co. Ltd.)

**New Zealand. Department of Education. Public Relations Section**
Wellington, New Zealand.
- Directory of Special Education and Guidance Services in New Zealand. irreg.

**New Zealand. Department of Education. School Publications Branch**
Box 4146, Government Bldgs., Wellington, New Zealand
- Education. 10 per yr. ISSN 0013-1199 (Subscr to: Government Printer, Private Bag, Wellington, N.Z.)

**New Zealand. Department of Health**
Box 5013, Wellington, New Zealand.
- Health. q. ISSN 0017-887X

**New Zealand. Department of Health. National Health Statistics Centre**
Box 6314, Le Aro, Wellington 1, New Zealand.
- Cancer Data: Deaths and Cases Reported a.
- New Zealand. Department of Health. Hospital Management Data. a.

**New Zealand. Department of Internal Affairs. Wildlife Service**
Wellington, New Zealand.
- Wildlife - a Review. a.

**New Zealand. Department of Labour**
Private Bag, Wellington, New Zealand.
- Labour and Employment Gazette. q. ISSN 0023-6896

**New Zealand. Department of Lands and Survey**
Wellington, New Zealand.
- Farming Statistics. a.

**New Zealand. Department of Maori Affairs**
Box 2390, Wellington, New Zealand.
- Te Ao Hou; the Maori Magazine. q. ISSN 0040-0300

**New Zealand. Department of Scientific and Industrial Research**
Box 9741, Wellington, New Zealand.
- New Zealand. Department of Scientific and Industrial Research. Annual Report. a. ISSN 0077-9601
- New Zealand. Department of Scientific and Industrial Research. Bulletin. irreg. ISSN 0077-961X
- New Zealand. Department of Scientific and Industrial Research. Information Series. irreg. ISSN 0077-9636
- New Zealand. Soil Bureau. Bulletin. irreg. ISSN 0077-9644
- New Zealand Journal of Agricultural Research. q. ISSN 0028-8233
- New Zealand Journal of Botany. q. ISSN 0028-825X
- New Zealand Journal of Experimental Agriculture. q.
- New Zealand Journal of Geology and Geophysics. 6 per yr. ISSN 0028-8306
- New Zealand Journal of Marine and Freshwater Research. q. ISSN 0028-8330
- New Zealand Journal of Science. q. ISSN 0028-8365
- New Zealand Journal of Zoology. q.
- New Zealand Wheat Review. a, 1965-67, no. 10. ISSN 0078-0219
- Studies of Cultivated Plants in New Zealand. irreg. ISSN 0081-8763
- Wellington, New Zealand. Oceanographic Institute. Memoir. ISSN 0083-7903

**New Zealand. Department of Scientific and Industrial Research. Geophysics Division**
Wellington, New Zealand.
- New Zealand. Department of Scientific and Industrial Research. Geophysics Division. Report. irreg.

**New Zealand. Department of Statistics**
Private Bag, Wellington, New Zealand
(Subscr. to: Government Printing Office, Publications, Private Bag, Wellington, New Zealand)
- New Zealand. Department of Statistics. Agricultural Statistics. a.
- New Zealand. Department of Statistics. Annual Report of the Government Statistician. a. ISSN 0077-9652
- New Zealand. Department of Statistics. Building Statistics. quinquennial.
- New Zealand. Department of Statistics. Exports. a. ISSN 0077-9660
- New Zealand. Department of Statistics. External Trade. Country Analyses. q. ISSN 0545-7157
- New Zealand. Department of Statistics. Household Sample Survey. a.
- New Zealand. Department of Statistics. Imports. a. ISSN 0077-9679
- New Zealand. Department of Statistics. Incomes and Income Tax Statistics. a. ISSN 0077-9849
- New Zealand. Department of Statistics. Industrial Injuries. a. ISSN 0077-9857
- New Zealand. Department of Statistics. Industrial Production. a. ISSN 0077-9865
- New Zealand. Department of Statistics. Justice Statistics. a. ISSN 0077-9873

- New Zealand. Department of Statistics. Local Authority Statistics. a. ISSN 0077-9881
- New Zealand. Department of Statistics. Monthly Abstract of Statistics. m (except Jan.) ISSN 0027-0180
- New Zealand. Department of Statistics. National Income and Expenditure. a. ISSN 0077-989X
- New Zealand. Department of Statistics. Population and Migration. a.
- New Zealand. Department of Statistics. Population Census: Ages and Marital Status. quinquennial, vol. 2, 1974. ISSN 0077-9687
- New Zealand. Department of Statistics. Population Census: Birthplaces and Ethnic Origin. quinquennial, 1971, issued 1975.
- New Zealand. Department of Statistics. Population Census: Dwellings. quinquennial, 1971 issued 1976. ISSN 0077-9695
- New Zealand. Department of Statistics. Population Census: Education and Birthplaces. quinquennial, 1971 issued 1976. ISSN 0077-9709
- New Zealand. Department of Statistics. Population Census: General Report. quinquennial, 1971 issued 1977. ISSN 0077-9717
- New Zealand. Department of Statistics. Population Census: Households, Families & Fertility. quinquennial, 1971, issued 1976.
- New Zealand. Department of Statistics. Population Census: Incomes. quinquennial, 1971, issued 1975. ISSN 0077-9733
- New Zealand. Department of Statistics. Population Census: Increase and Location of Population. quinquennial, 1971 issued 1972. ISSN 0077-9792
- New Zealand. Department of Statistics. Population Census: Industries and Occupations. quinquennial, 1971 issued 1975. ISSN 0077-9741
- New Zealand. Department of Statistics. Population Census: Maori Population and Dwellings. quinquennial, vol. 8, 1975. ISSN 0077-975X
- New Zealand. Department of Statistics. Population Census: Provisional Population and Dwelling Statistics. quinquennial.
- New Zealand. Department of Statistics. Population Census: Religious Professions. quinquennial, 1971 issued 1974. ISSN 0077-9784
- New Zealand. Department of Statistics. Prices, Wages and Labour. a. ISSN 0077-9911
- New Zealand. Department of Statistics. Report and Analysis of External Trade. a. ISSN 0077-9806
- New Zealand. Department of Statistics. Report on the Survey of Household Electricity Consumption. irreg. (Dist. by: N. Z. Electricity Department, Private Bag, Wellington, New Zealand)
- New Zealand. Department of Statistics. Sheep Returns. a. (Dist. by: Ministry of Agriculture & Fisheries, Private Bag, Wellington, New Zealand)
- New Zealand. Department of Statistics. Transport Statistics. a. ISSN 0077-992X
- New Zealand. Department of Statistics. Vital Statistics. a. ISSN 0077-9938
- New Zealand, Department of Statistics. Balance of Payments. a. ISSN 0077-9814
- New Zealand, Department of Statistics. Insurance Statistics. a. ISSN 0077-9830
- New Zealand Official Year-Book. a. ISSN 0078-0170
- Pocket Digest of New Zealand Statistics. a. ISSN 0079-2411

**New Zealand. Department of Tourist and Publicity**
Box 95, Wellington, New Zealand.
- New Zealand Visitor Statistics. a.

**New Zealand. Department of Trade and Industry**
Wellington, New Zealand.
- New Zealand. Department of Trade and Industry. Import Licensing Schedule. irreg.

**New Zealand. Department of Trade and Industry. Productivity Centre**
Wellington, New Zealand.
- Productivity & Technology. q.

**New Zealand. Forest Service**
Forest Research Institute, Private Bag, Rotorua, New Zealand.
- New Zealand. Forest Service. Forest Research Institute. Report. a. ISSN 0080-4096
- New Zealand. Forest Service. Forest Research Institute. Technical Paper. irreg., no. 64, 1977. ISSN 0080-4118
- New Zealand Journal of Forestry Science. 3 per yr. ISSN 0048-0134

- What's New in Forest Research; semi-technical newsletter. m. ISSN 0110-1048

**New Zealand . Geological Survey**
P.O. Box 30368, Lower Hutt, New Zealand.
- New Zealand. Department of Scientific and Industrial Research. Geological Survey. Bulletin. irreg., no. 91, 1975. ISSN 0077-9628
- Paleontological Bulletins. irreg., no. 46, 1975. ISSN 0078-8589

**New Zealand. Geophysical Observatory**
Box 2111, Christchurch, New Zealand.
- Ionospheric Data. m. ISSN 0021-0374

**New Zealand. Government Printing Office**
Publications Branch, Private Bag, Wellington, New Zealand.
- Education Gazette. s-m.
- New Zealand. Department of Social Welfare. Report. a.
- New Zealand. Department of Trade & Industry. Report. a.
- New Zealand. Forest Service. Report of the Director General of Forests. a. ISSN 0078-0014
- New Zealand. Government Printing Office. Government Publications. 6 per yr. ISSN 0545-7289
- New Zealand. Industrial Research and Development Grants Advisory Committee. Report. a.
- New Zealand. Law Revision Commission. Report. a.
- New Zealand. Maori Affairs Department. Report of the Maori Affairs Department and the Maori Trust Office and the Board of Maori Affairs. irreg.
- New Zealand. Ministry of Transport. Annual Report. a. ISSN 0085-4123
- New Zealand. National Research Advisory Council. Report. a. ISSN 0078-0162
- New Zealand Gazette. w.
- New Zealand Patent Office Journal. m. ISSN 0028-856X

**New Zealand. Lottery Board of Control**
Wellington, New Zealand.
- New Zealand. Lottery Board of Control. Report. a. ISSN 0545-7297

**New Zealand. Marine Department**
P.O. Box 10142, Wellington, New Zealand.
- New Zealand. Marine Department. Annual Report on Fisheries. a. ISSN 0078-0111

**New Zealand. Meat and Wool Boards' Economic Service**
P.O. Box 5179, Wellington, New Zealand.
- New Zealand. Meat and Wool Boards' Economic Service. Annual Review of the Sheep Industry; review of physical and economic conditions in sheepfarming in New Zealand. a. ISSN 0078-0138

**New Zealand. Mines Department**
P.O. Box 6342, Te Aro, Wellington, New Zealand.
- New Zealand. Mines Department. Mines Statement. a.
- New Zealand Mines Department. Annual Returns of Production from Quarries and Mineral Production Statistics. a.

**New Zealand. Ministry of Agriculture and Fisheries**
P.O. Box 19062, Wellington, New Zealand.
- New Zealand. Ministry of Agriculture and Fisheries. Fisheries Research Division. Bulletin. irreg.
- New Zealand. Ministry of Agriculture and Fisheries. Fisheries Research Division: Information Leaflet. irreg.
- New Zealand. Ministry of Agriculture and Fisheries. Fisheries Technical Report. irreg.
- New Zealand Journal of Agriculture. (pub. by Wilson and Horton Ltd.)

**New Zealand. Ministry of Defence**
Wellington, New Zealand.
- New Zealand. Ministry of Defence. Review of Defence Policy. irreg.

**New Zealand. Ministry of Energy Resources**
Wellington, New Zealand.
- New Zealand. Ministry of Energy Resources. Report. irreg.

**New Zealand. Ministry of Foreign Affairs**
Wellington, New Zealand.
- Annual Aid Review, Memorandum of New Zealand. a.

- New Zealand. Ministry of Foreign Affairs. Publication. irreg.
- New Zealand. Ministry of Foreign Affairs. Report. a.
- New Zealand. Ministry of Foreign Affairs. United Nations Handbook. irreg.
- New Zealand Diplomatic Corps and Consular and Other Representatives. s-a.
- New Zealand Foreign Affairs Review. q. ISSN 0014-5440
- New Zealand Representatives Overseas. s-a.

**New Zealand. Ministry of Transport. Civil Aviation Division**
Private Bag, Wellington 1, New Zealand.
- Flight Safety. irreg. (prep. by its Flight Operations Branch)
- New Zealand Aircraft Operators. a.
- New Zealand Civil Aviation Statistics. a.

**New Zealand. Ministry of Works and Development**
Box 12-041, Wellington North, New Zealand.
- People & Planning. q.
- Work News. (pub. by Percival Publishing Co.)

**New Zealand. Ministry of Works and Development. Town & Country Planning Division**
P.O. Box 12041, Wellington North, New Zealand.
- Planning Research Index. a.

**New Zealand. Ministry of Works. Water and Soil Division**
Box 12041, Wellington, New Zealand.
- New Zealand. Water and Soil Division. Hydrological Research Annual Report & Series. ISSN 0085-414X
- Soil & Water. bi-m. ISSN 0038-0695

**New Zealand. National Development Council**
Wellington, New Zealand.
- New Zealand. National Development Council. Progress Report of the Targets Advisory Group. irreg.

**New Zealand. National Research Advisory Council**
P.O. Box 8004, Wellington, New Zealand.
- New Zealand. National Research Advisory Council. Senior and Post Doctoral Research Fellowship Awards for Research in New Zealand Government Departments. a. ISSN 0078-0154

**New Zealand. Nature Conservation Council**
Box 12-200, Wellington, New Zealand.
- New Zealand. Nature Conservation Council. Newsletter. 5 per yr.

**New Zealand. Railways Department**
Wellington, New Zealand.
- New Zealand. Railways Department. Annual Report. a.

**New Zealand. Soil Bureau**
Private Bag, Lower Hutt, New Zealand.
- New Zealand. Soil Bureau. Bibliographic Report. irreg.
- New Zealand. Soil Bureau Scientific Report. irreg.

**New Zealand Agricultural Engineering Institute**
Lincoln College, Canterbury, New Zealand.
- N Z A E I Newletter. 3 per yr.

**New Zealand Antarctic Society**
Box 1223, Christchurch, New Zealand.
- Antarctic; a news bulletin. q. ISSN 0003-5327

**New Zealand Archaeological Association**
Box 447, Hawera, New Zealand.
- New Zealand Archaeological Association. Newsletter. q. ISSN 0028-7962

**New Zealand Association of Economists**
P.O. Box 568, Wellington, New Zealand.
- New Zealand Economic Papers. a; biennial until 1971 (1970, vol. 4, no. 1) ISSN 0077-9954

**New Zealand Association of Health, Physical Education and Recreation**
University of Otago, Dunedin, New Zealand.
- New Zealand Journal of Health, Physical Education and Recreation. 3 per yr. ISSN 0028-8314

**New Zealand Association of Radio Transmitters, Inc.**
Box 1733, Christchurch, New Zealand.
- Break-In; for the radio amateur. m. ISSN 0006-9523

- N. Z. A. R. T. Amateur Radio Callbook. a.

**New Zealand Association of Scientists**
Box 1874, Wellington, New Zealand.
- New Zealand Science Review. bi-m. ISSN 0028-8667

**New Zealand Camellia Society, Inc.**
Box 313, Putaruru, New Zealand.
- New Zealand Camellia Bulletin. 3 per yr. ISSN 0028-7989

**New Zealand Cartographic Society Inc.**
P.O. 9331 Courtenay Place, Wellington, New Zealand.
- New Zealand Cartographic Journal. 2 per yr.

**New Zealand Chambers of Commerce**
Box 1071, Wellington, New Zealand.
- New Zealand Commerce. m. ISSN 0028-8012

**New Zealand Christian Pacifist Society**
Box 2400, Wellington C.1, New Zealand.
- Peace Bulletin. q.

**New Zealand Coal Mining Districts Welfare & Research Council**
Box 2990, Wellington, New Zealand.
- New Zealand Coal. q. ISSN 0028-8004

**New Zealand Council for Educational Research**
Box 3237, Wellington, New Zealand.
- N Z C E R Newsletter. 3 per yr.
- New Zealand Council for Educational Research. Research Information.
- New Zealand Journal of Educational Studies. s-a. ISSN 0028-8276

**New Zealand Country Women's Institutes**
1 Collina Terrace, Box 12007, Wellington, New Zealand.
- Home & Country. bi-m. ISSN 0018-3938

**New Zealand Dairy Produce Exporter Newspaper Co. Ltd.**
Box 1001, Wellington, New Zealand.
- New Zealand Dairy Exporter. m. (New Zealand. Dairy Board)

**New Zealand Dairy Research Institute**
Private Bag, Palmerston North, New Zealand.
- New Zealand Journal of Dairy Science and Technology. q. ISSN 0300-1342

**New Zealand Deerstalkers' Association Inc.**
Box 6514, Wellington, New Zealand.
- New Zealand Wildlife. q. ISSN 0028-8802

**New Zealand Dental Association**
- New Zealand Dental Journal. (pub. by Otago Daily Times Ltd.)

**New Zealand Ecological Society, Inc.**
P.O. Box 1887, Willington, New Zealand.
- New Zealand Ecological Society. Proceedings. a. ISSN 0077-9946

**New Zealand Economic News Service**
- Economic News Bulletin. (pub. by Universe Press Agency Ltd.)

**New Zealand Educational Institute**
Box 466, Wellington 1, New Zealand.
- Nat Ed Newsletter. fortn. (feb. through Nov.)
- National Education. 6 per yr. ISSN 0027-9188

**New Zealand Electrical Contractors Federation Inc.**
- N. Z. Electrical Industry. (pub. by Ward Publishing Co.)

**New Zealand Employers Federation**
Research & Information Services Division, Federation House, 95-99 Molesworth St., Wellington, New Zealand.
- Employer. 10 per yr. ISSN 0046-1903

**New Zealand Export-Import Corporation**
Wellington, New Zealand.
- New Zealand Export-Import Corporation. Report. a.

**New Zealand Federation of Labour**
Box 6161, Lukes Lane, Wellington, New Zealand.
- New Zealand Federation of Labour. Bulletin. m. ISSN 0549-0294
- New Zealand Federation of Labour. Official Trade Union Directory. a.

**New Zealand Federation of Parachute Clubs, Inc.**
P.O. Box 56, 009 Dominion Rd., Auckland, New Zealand.
- Free Fall Kiwi. bi-m.

**New Zealand Ferro Cement Marine Association**
c/o Secretary, P.O. Box 26-073, Auckland 3, New Zealand.
- Journal of Ferrocement. q.

**New Zealand Folklore Society**
26 Buckingham St., Lyall Bay, Wellington, New Zealand.
- Maoriland. ISSN 0047-5831
- Penny Post. q.

**New Zealand Geographical Society (Inc.) Manawatu Branch**
c/o Dept. of Geography, Massey University, Palmerston North, New Zealand.
- J. T. Stewart Lecture in Planning. a. ISSN 0075-210X
- Perspective. irreg. ISSN 0553-738X

**New Zealand Geographical Society Inc.**
Dept. of Geography, Univ. of Canterbury, Christchurch, New Zealand.
- New Zealand Geographer. s-a. ISSN 0028-8144
- New Zealand Geographical Society. Miscellaneous Series. irreg., 1970, no. 11. ISSN 0078-0022
- New Zealand Geography Conference Proceedings Series. biennial; up to 1971 triennial; 1971, no. 6. ISSN 0078-0030
- New Zealand Journal of Geography. s-a. ISSN 0028-8292

**New Zealand Horological Institute**
- New Zealand Horological Journal. (pub. by Otago Daily Times Ltd.)

**New Zealand Hydrological Society**
c/o David L. Murray, Ed., Univ. of Otago, Dept. of Geography, Dunedin, New Zealand
(Subscr. to: P.O. Box 12-300, Wellington North, New Zealand)
- Journal of Hydrology (N.Z.). s-a. ISSN 0022-1708

**New Zealand Industrial Design Council**
Private Bag, Te Aro, Wellington, New Zealand.
- Designscape. m(except Jan.) ISSN 0011-944X

**New Zealand Institue of Foresters Inc.**
Box 468, Tokoroa, New Zealand.
- New Zealand Journal of Forestry. s-a. ISSN 0028-8284

**New Zealand Institute of Architects**
P.O. 438, Wellington S.W., New Zealand.
- New Zealand Institute of Architects Journal. 6 per yr. ISSN 0027-7207

**New Zealand Institute of Chemistry**
Box 250, Wellington, New Zealand.
- Chemistry in New Zealand. bi-m.

**New Zealand Institute of Economic Research**
P.O. Box 3479, Wellington 1, New Zealand.
- New Zealand Institute of Economic Research. Discussion Paper. irreg. ISSN 0078-0049
- New Zealand Institute of Economic Research. Report. a. ISSN 0078-0057
- New Zealand Institute of Economic Research. Research Paper. irreg., 1973, no. 19. ISSN 0078-0065
- New Zealand Institute of Economic Research. Technical Memorandum. irreg., 1969, no. 14. ISSN 0078-0073
- Quarterly Predictions of National Income and Expenditure. q. ISSN 0033-5711

**New Zealand Institute of Electricians Inc**
- New Zealand Electrician. (pub. by Garratt Printing Co. Ltd.)

**New Zealand Institute of Food Science & Technology**
- Food Technology in New Zealand. (pub. by Trade Publications Ltd.)

**New Zealand Institute of Local Authority Administration**
P.O.B. 278, Wellington, New Zealand.
- Local Authority Administration. s-a.

**New Zealand Institute of Management**
- Management. (pub. by Modern Productions Ltd.)

**New Zealand Institute of Medical Laboratory Technology**
c/o Diagnostic Laboratories, Dunedin Hospital, Dunedin, New Zealand.
- New Zealand Journal of Medical Laboratory Technology. 3 per yr. ISSN 0028-8349

**New Zealand Institute of Public Administration**
Box 5032, Wellington, Lambton Quay, New Zealand.
- New Zealand Journal of Public Administration. s-a. ISSN 0028-8357

**New Zealand Institute of Surveyors**
Box 831, Wellington, New Zealand.
- New Zealand Surveyor. s-a. ISSN 0048-0150

**New Zealand Institute of Valuers**
- N. Z. Valuer. (pub. by Daily Telegraph Ltd.)

**New Zealand Institution of Engineers**
- New Zealand Engineering. (pub. by Technical Publications Ltd.)

**New Zealand Library Association**
P.O. Box 12-212, Wellington 1, New Zealand.
- N Z L A Newsletter. 10 per yr. ISSN 0027-7215
- New Zealand Libraries. bi-m. ISSN 0028-8381

**New Zealand Library Association. Archives Committee.**
- Archifacts. (pub. by Archives and Records Association)

**New Zealand Licensee Co. Ltd.**
Box 1198, Wellington, New Zealand.
- N. Z. Licensee. m. ISSN 0027-7223 (Hotel Association of New Zealand)

**New Zealand Marine Sciences Society. Fisheries Research Division**
P.O. Box 19062, Wellington, New Zealand.
- New Zealand Marine Sciences Newsletter. a. ISSN 0028-842X

**New Zealand Medical Records Officers' Association**
Box 2656, Auckland, New Zealand.
- New Zealand Medical Records Officers' Association. Conference Proceedings. biennial. ISSN 0078-0146

**New Zealand Merchant Engineers**
- Engineering Management. (pub. by Stone Publications (NZ) Ltd.)

**New Zealand Military Historical Society**
c/o B. Delahunt, Ed., 44 Wynyard Road, Mt. Eden, Auckland, New Zealand.
- Volunteers. q.

**New Zealand Model Railway Guild Inc.**
Box 108, Wellington, New Zealand.
- New Zealand Model Railway Journal. bi-m. ISSN 0028-8470

**New Zealand Monthly Review Society Inc.**
Box 345, Christchurch, New Zealand.
- New Zealand Monthly Review. m. ISSN 0028-8489

**New Zealand National Society for Earthquake Engineering**
P.O. Box 1818, Wellington, New Zealand.
- New Zealand National Society for Earthquake Engineering. Bulletin. q. ISSN 0550-6743

**New Zealand National Travel Association**
- New Zealand Holiday. (pub. by Shortland Publications)

**New Zealand Newspapers Ltd.**
Box 3697, 20 Shortland St., Auckland 1, New Zealand.
- Auckland Star. d. ISSN 0004-7449
- Eight O'Clock; weekend edition of The Auckland Star. w. ISSN 0013-2551
- New Zealand Farmer. fortn. ISSN 0028-8098
- New Zealand Woman's Weekly. w. ISSN 0028-8829

**New Zealand Nurses Association**
- New Zealand Nursing Journal. (pub. by Kerslake, Billens & Humphrey, Ltd.)

**New Zealand Oceanographic Institute**
P.O. Box 12-346, 177 Thorndon Quay, Wellington North, New Zealand.
- N Z O I Records. 8 per yr.
- N Z O I Records. irreg.
- New Zealand Oceanographic Institute. Collected Reprints. a. ISSN 0083-789X

**New Zealand Operational Research Society**
Box 904, Wellington, New Zealand.
- New Zealand Operational Research. s-a.

**New Zealand Planning Institute**
Box 8789, Auckland, New Zealand.
- Town Planning Quarterly. q. ISSN 0041-0012

**New Zealand Pony Clubs Association**
- New Zealand Horse & Pony. (pub. by I. N. L. Print Ltd.)

**New Zealand Portland Cement Association**
- New Zealand Concrete Construction. (pub. by Concrete Publications)

**New Zealand Potter**
Box 12-162, Wellington North, New Zealand.
- New Zealand Potter. s-a. ISSN 0028-8608

**New Zealand Pottery and Ceramics Research Association**
Private Bag, Lower Hutt, New Zealand.
- New Zealand Pottery and Ceramics Research Association. Technical Report. irreg., no. 25, 1974. ISSN 0078-0189

**New Zealand Poultry Board**
Express Company Buildings, 56 Victoria St., P.O. Box 379, Wellington, New Zealand.
- New Zealand Poultry Board. Report and New Zealand Marketing Authority Report and Statement of Accounts. a. ISSN 0078-0197
- New Zealand Poultry World. (pub. by John Paul Productions, Ltd.)

**New Zealand Printing & Related Trades Industrial Union of Workers**
Labour Party Building, 101 Vivian St., Box 6413, Wellington, New Zealand.
- Imprint. m. ISSN 0019-3054

**New Zealand Pschological Society**
Victoria University of Wellington, Dept. of Psychology, Private Bag, Wellington, New Zealand.
- New Zealand Psychologist. s-a.

**New Zealand Railway and Locomotive Society, Inc**
P.O. Box 5134, Wellington, New Zealand.
- New Zealand Railway and Locomotive Society. N Z R Locomotives and Railcars. irreg., no. 3, 1977.
- New Zealand Railway Observer. q. ISSN 0028-8624
- Pantograph. m. ISSN 0031-1014

**New Zealand Rationalist Association Inc.**
64 Symonds St., Auckland 1, New Zealand.
- New Zealand Rationalist and Humanist; a journal on philosophy, science, religion, literature & society. q. ISSN 0028-8632

**New Zealand Red Cross Society Inc.**
P.O. Box 12-140, Wellington North, New Zealand.
- Red Cross. New Zealand. New Zealand Red Cross Society. Report. a. ISSN 0080-0392

**New Zealand Socialist Unity Party**
Box 1987, Auckland, New Zealand.
- Socialist Politics. m.

**New Zealand Society of Accountants**
Box 10046, Wellington, New Zealand.
- Accountants' Journal. m. ISSN 0001-4745
- New Zealand Society of Accountants. Cost and Management Accounting Division. C M A Bulletin. irreg., no. 11, 1974.

**New Zealand Society of Periodontology**
1A Wootton Rd., Remuera, Auckland 5, New Zealand.
- New Zealand Society of Periodontology. Bulletin. s-a. ISSN 0028-8705

**New Zealand Society of Physiotherapists**
- New Zealand Journal of Physiotherapy. (pub. by Editorial Services Ltd.)

**New Zealand Speech Therapists Association**
- New Zealand Speech Therapists Journal. (pub. by Speech Therapy Clinic)

**New Zealand Student Christian Movement**
Box 9792, Wellington, New Zealand.
- Charisma. 5 per yr. ISSN 0009-1715

**New Zealand Tablet Co. Ltd.**
24 Filleni St., Dunedin, New Zealand.
- New Zealand Tablet; New Zealand's national Catholic weekly. w. ISSN 0028-8748 (Roman Catholic Church)

**New Zealand Teachers' Colleges' Association**
Christchurch Teachers' College, Dovedale Avenue, Christchurch 4, New Zealand.
- N Z T C A Journal. 3 per yr. ISSN 0027-7266

**New Zealand Theater Federation**
Box 9441, Wellington, New Zealand.
- Act. q.

**New Zealand Theatre Trust**
- Te Awatea. (pub. by Agricultural and Industrial Surveys Ltd.)

**New Zealand Urban Public Passenger Transport Council**
Wellington, New Zealand.
- New Zealand. Urban Public Passenger Transport Council. Report. a.

**New Zealand Veterinary Association**
- New Zealand Veterinary Journal. (pub. by Editorial Services Ltd.)

**New Zealand Wholesale Hardware Guilds' Federation**
- New Zealand Hardware Journal. (pub. by Akron Consolidated Ltd.)

**New Zealand Wool Marketing Corporation**
18 Brandon St., Wellington, New Zealand.
- Statistical Analysis of New Zealand Wool Production and Disposal. a.

**News Media Ownership Ltd.**
23-27 Garrett St., Wellington, New Zealand.
- N. Z. Truth. w. ISSN 0027-7274

**Northland Magazine Inc.**
Box 694, Whangarei, New Zealand.
- Northland; a regional magazine. q. ISSN 0029-3261

**Nurses Reform Association of New Zealand**
Box 24-118, Auckland 3, New Zealand.
- Nursing Forum. q.

**Onslow Historical Society**
Box 2456, Wellington, New Zealand.
- Onslow Historian. q.

**Ornithological Society of New Zealand Inc.**
Box 3011, Dunedin, New Zealand.
- Checklist of New Zealand Birds. (pub. by A.H. & A.W. Reed)
- Notornis. q. ISSN 0029-4470

**Otago Daily Times Ltd.**
Box 181, Dunedin, New Zealand.
- New Zealand Camera. bi-m. ISSN 0048-0118 (Photographic Society of New Zealand)
- New Zealand Dental Journal. q. ISSN 0028-8047 (New Zealand Dental Association)
- New Zealand Horological Journal. m.(11 nos.) ISSN 0028-8195 (New Zealand Horological Institute)
- New Zealand Medical Journal. m. ISSN 0028-8446 (Medical Association of New Zealand)
- Pharmaceutical Journal of New Zealand. m. ISSN 0031-6881 (Pharmacy Board of New Zealand)
- R. A. C. S. Newsletter. q. ISSN 0033-6696 (Royal Australasian College of Surgeons)

**Otago Law Review Trust Board**
c/o Faculty of Law, University of Otago, Dunedin, New Zealand
- Otago Law Review. a. ISSN 0078-6918 (Dist. in U.S. by: Wm. M. Gaunt & Sons, Inc., Gaunt Bldg., 3011 Gulf Drive, Holmes Beach, FL 33510)

**Otago Museum Trust Board**
Great King St., Dunedin, New Zealand.
- Otago Museum. Records. Anthropology. irreg., no. 6, 1972. ISSN 0474-8603

- Otago Museum. Records. Zoology. irreg., no. 2, 1965. ISSN 0474-8611

**Otago University. Science Students' Association**
P.O. Box 56, Dunedin, New Zealand.
- Science Record. a. ISSN 0080-7605

**Outrigger Publications Ltd.**
1 von Tempsky St., Hamilton, New Zealand.
- Miorita. ISSN 0110-0068 (University of Rochester. New Zealand Romanian Cultural Association)
- New Quarterly Cave; an international review of arts and ideas. q. ISSN 0110-0076
- Outrigger. 6 per yr.

**Pacific Stamp Journal**
c/o John J. Bishop Ltd., Box 2782, Auckland 1, New Zealand.
- Pacific Stamp Journal. m.

**Paeroa and District Historical Society**
c/o Mrs M. Townsend, 16 Taylor's Ave., Paeroa, New Zealand.
- Ohinemuri; regional history journal. s-a.

**John Paul Productions Ltd.**
P.O. Box 9405, Wellington, New Zealand.
- New Zealand Bookworld; journal of the New Zealand book trade. m.
- New Zealand Poultry World. m. ISSN 0028-8616 (New Zealand Poultry Board)
- Soccer News; magazine of New Zealand Association football. m (except Jan.) ISSN 0110-0394

**Pegasus Press**
c/o Dept. of English, Victoria University of Wellington, Wellington, New Zealand.
- Poetry New Zealand. biennial.

**People's Voice**
Box 2197, Auckland, New Zealand.
- People's Voice. w. ISSN 0048-3354

**Percival Publishing Co.**
P.O. 6004, Auckland, New Zealand.
- Work News. q. (New Zealand. Ministry of Works and Development)

**Pharmacy Board of New Zealand**
- Pharmaceutical Journal of New Zealand. (pub. by Otago Daily Times Ltd.)

**Photographic Society of New Zealand**
- New Zealand Camera. (pub. by Otago Daily Times Ltd.)

**Polynesian Society, Inc.**
Box 10323 the Terrace, Wellington 1, New Zealand.
- Polynesian Society. Journal; a study of the native peoples of the Pacific area. q. ISSN 0032-4000

**Post Office Association**
- Katipo. (pub. by Standard Press Ltd.)

**Presbyterian Church of New Zealand**
c/o Ed. Rev. C. L. Gosling, 236 Hereford St., Box 320, Christchurch, New Zealand.
- Outlook. m. ISSN 0048-2463

**Printing Industries Federation of New Zealand (Inc.)**
Box 1422, Wellington, New Zealand.
- Printers News. m. ISSN 0048-5330

**Railway Enthusiasts Society, Inc.**
Box 2429, Auckland, New Zealand.
- Yarn (Your Auckland Railway News) 11 per yr. ISSN 0044-023X

**A.H. & A.W. Reed**
182 Wakefield St., Wellington, New Zealand (and Box 3511, Hollywood, Calif. 90028)
- Checklist of New Zealand Birds. irreg. ISSN 0069-2816 (Ornithological Society of New Zealand Inc.)
- Mobil New Zealand Travel Guide: North Island. irreg.
- Mobil New Zealand Travel Guide: South Island. irreg.
- New Zealand Shipwrecks. irreg.
- Story of New Zealand. irreg., 8 edt. 1975.
- Who's Who in New Zealand. triennial. ISSN 0083-9655
- Youth Writes.

**Reserve Bank of New Zealand**
Wellington, New Zealand.
- New Zealand News Review. s-m. ISSN 0545-7785
- Reserve Bank of New Zealand. Bulletin. m(Mar.-Dec.); bi-m(Jan.-Feb.) ISSN 0034-5539
- Reserve Bank of New Zealand. Research Papers. irreg.

**Roman Catholic Bishop of Auckland**
2 St. Patricks Square, Auckland, New Zealand.
- Zealandia; the Catholic newspaper. w. ISSN 0044-202X

**Roman Catholic Church**
- New Zealand Tablet. (pub. by New Zealand Tablet Co. Ltd.)

**Royal Astronomical Society of New Zealand (Inc.)**
P.O. Box 3181, Wellington, New Zealand.
- Southern Stars. q. ISSN 0049-1640

**Royal Australasian College of Surgeons**
- R. A. C. S. Newsletter. (pub. by Otago Daily Times Ltd.)

**Royal Forest and Bird Protection Society of New Zealand Inc.**
Box 631, Wellington, New Zealand.
- Forest and Bird. q. ISSN 0015-7384

**Royal New Zealand Institute of Horticulture**
c/o M. B. Thomas, Horticulture Dept., Lincoln College, Canterbury, New Zealand
- Royal New Zealand Institute of Horticulture. Annual Journal. a. (Subscr. Address: P.O. Box 450, Wellington, New Zealand)

**Royal Numismatic Society of New Zealand, Inc.**
G.P.O. Box 23, Wellington, New Zealand.
- New Zealand Numismatic Journal. irreg. ISSN 0028-8527

**Royal Philatelic Society of New Zealand**
Box 1269, Wellington, New Zealand.
- New Zealand Stamp Collector. q.

**Royal Society of New Zealand**
Box 12249, Wellington, New Zealand.
- International Union for Quaternary Research. Congress Proceedings. quadrennial, 1973, 9th, Christchurch, New Zealand. ISSN 0074-932X
- Royal Society of New Zealand. Journal. q. ISSN 0303-6758

**Salvation Army**
- War Cry. (pub. by Blundell Bros. Ltd.)

**Shortland Publications**
Box 1209, Auckland, New Zealand.
- New Zealand Holiday. q. ISSN 0028-8179 (New Zealand National Travel Association)

**Sisters of Homophile Equality**
Box 427, Wellington, New Zealand.
- Circle. m.

**Socialist Action Publishing Association**
Box 1663, Wellington, New Zealand.
- Socialist Action. fortn. ISSN 0037-816X

**Society for Personality Research Inc.**
- Social Behavior and Personality. (pub. by Editorial Services Ltd.)

**Sociological Association of Australia and New Zealand**
Department of Sociology, University of Canterbury, Christchurch, New Zealand.
- Australian & New Zealand Journal of Sociology. 3 per yr. ISSN 0004-8690

**Soil Association of New Zealand**
38 Arran Crescent, Linwood, Christchurch 6, New Zealand.
- Soil & Health Journal. a. ISSN 0038-0687

**South Asian Association of Australia and New Zealand**
c/o Dept. of History, Univ. of Canterbury, Christchurch, New Zealand.
- South Asian Studies Association of Australia and New Zealand. Newsletter. s-a.

**Southern Cross Books**
5 Pencarrow Ave., Auckland 3, New Zealand.
- Wine Review. q. ISSN 0043-5805

**Southern Press Ltd**
Box 11-272, Wellington, New Zealand.
• Rails. m.

**Speech Therapy Clinic**
Saunders House, 44 Peterborough St., Christchurch
1, New Zealand.
• New Zealand Speech Therapists Journal. s-a.
ISSN 0028-8713 (New Zealand Speech Therapists
Association)

**Standard Press Ltd.**
Marion St., Wellington, New Zealand.
• Katipo. m. (combined issues: Nov.-Dec. & Jan.-
Feb.) ISSN 0022-9423 (Post Office Association)

**Stock Exchange Association of New Zealand**
Box 639, Christchurch, New Zealand.
• Stock Exchanges of New Zealand. Official
Record. m. ISSN 0039-1611

**Stockton House Publishers**
Box 46, Albany, New Zealand.
• English in New Zealand. q.
• Multi-Cultural School. q.

**Stone Publications (NZ) Ltd.**
Box 18-218, Glen Innes, Auckland, New Zealand.
• Building Materials News. m. ISSN 0007-3539
• Engineering Management. 6 per yr. ISSN 0019-
8226 (New Zealand Merchant Engineers)
• N. Z. Meat Trades Journal. bi-m. ISSN 0027-7231
• Plastics & Packaging. bi-m.
• Road Transport and Contracting. m. ISSN 0035-
7294

**Sweet & Maxwell (N.Z.) Ltd.**
Box 5043, Wellington, New Zealand
(Dist. by Carswell Co. Ltd., 2330 Midland Avenue,
Agincourt 742, Ont., Canada)
• Guide to New Zealand Income Tax Practice. a.
ISSN 0072-8616
• New Zealand Law Register. a. ISSN 0078-0081
• New Zealand Universities Law Review. q. ISSN
0549-0618
• Taxation Tables. a. ISSN 0082-2175

**Alister Taylor, Ed. & Pub.**
Whole Earth Mail Order Dept., Box 87,
Martinborough, New Zealand.
• New Zealand Whole Earth Catalogue. a.

**Technical Publications Ltd.**
127 Molesworth St., C.P.O. Box 3047, Wellington,
New Zealand.
• New Zealand Energy Journal. m. (Electric Supply
Authority Engineers' Institute)
• New Zealand Engineering. m. ISSN 0028-808X
(New Zealand Institution of Engineers)

**Theosophical Society, New Zealand Section**
10 Belvedere St., Epsom, Auckland 3, New Zealand.
• Theosophy in New Zealand. q. ISSN 0049-3708

**Totalisator Agency Board**
304 Lambton Quay, Wellington, New Zealand.
• Totalisator Agency Board. Annual Report. a.

**Trade Publications Ltd.**
1 Emily Place, Auckland, New Zealand.
• Chemistry and Industry in New Zealand. q. ISSN
0009-3076
• Food Technology in New Zealand; production-
processing-packaging-storage-distribution-
marketing. m. ISSN 0015-6655 (New Zealand
Institute of Food Science & Technology)
• New Zealand Local Government. m. ISSN 0028-
8403

**Trans-Tasman News Service Ltd.**
Box 377, Wellington, New Zealand.
• Trans Tasman. w. ISSN 0049-4380

**United Nations Association of New Zealand**
Box 1011, Wellington, New Zealand.
• World Affairs. q. ISSN 0043-8189

**Universal Business Directories Ltd.**
U B D Center, 360 Dominion Rd., Auckland, New
Zealand.
• Sea Spray. m. ISSN 0037-0037

**Universe Press Agency Ltd.**
Box 1026, Wellington, New Zealand.
• Economic News Bulletin. w. ISSN 0013-0168
(New Zealand Economic News Service)

**University of Auckland**
Private Bag, Auckland, New Zealand.
• Prudentia. s-a.
• University of Auckland News. 9 per yr.

**University of Auckland. Department of Art History**
Private Bag C. 1, Auckland, New Zealand.
• Bulletin of New Zealand Art History. a.

**University of Auckland. Department of Geography**
Private Bag, Auckland, New Zealand.
• University of Auckland. Department of
Geography. Occasional Papers. irreg., no. 9, 1973.

**University of Auckland. Department of History**
Private Bag, Auckland, New Zealand.
• New Zealand Journal of History. 2 per yr. ISSN
0028-8322
• University of Auckland Historical Society.
Annual. a. ISSN 0067-0480

**University of Auckland. Department of Mathematics**
Private Bag, Auckland, New Zealand.
• Mathematical Chronicle. irreg. ISSN 0581-1155
• University of Auckland. Department of
Mathematics. Report Series. irreg., no. 104, 1976.

**University of Auckland. Department of Sociology**
Private Bag, Auckland, New Zealand.
• University of Auckland. Department of Sociology.
Papers in Comparative Sociology. irreg., no. 3,
1975.

**University of Auckland. Fine Arts Library**
Private Bag, Auckland, New Zealand.
• University of Auckland. Fine Arts Library.
Bulletin. q. ISSN 0041-9400

**University of Auckland. Law Students Association**
see Auckland University Law Students Society,
Inc.

**University of Auckland. Library**
Auckland, New Zealand.
• University of Auckland. Library. Bibliographical
Bulletin. irreg., no. 9, 1973. ISSN 0067-0499

**University of Canterbury**
Christchurch, New Zealand
(Proceedings published by host)
• Australasian Conference on Hydraulics and Fluid
Mechanics. Proceedings. triennial; 5th
Christchurch, N.Z., 1974. ISSN 0571-9291

**University of Canterbury. Biological Society**
Private Bag, Christchurch, New Zealand.
• Mauri Ora. a. ISSN 0302-086X

**University of Canterbury. Department of History**
Private Bag, Christchurch, New Zealand.
• Commonwealth and Colonial History Newsletter.
s-a. ISSN 0045-7620

**University of Canterbury. Department of Psychology**
Christchurch, New Zealand.
• University of Canterbury. Department of
Psychology and Sociology. Research Projects.
irreg. (2-3 per yr); no, 24, 1975. ISSN 0069-3774

**University of Canterbury. School of Engineering**
Private Bag, Christchurch, New Zealand.
• Canterbury Engineering Journal. irreg., 1972, no.
3. ISSN 0069-0201

**University of Otago**
Geography Students Assn., c/o Geography Dept.,
Box 56, Dunedin, New Zealand.
• Otago Geographer. a. ISSN 0078-690X

**University of Otago. Hocken Library**
P.O. Box 56, Dunedin, New Zealand.
• Hocken Lecture. irreg.

**University of Rochester. New Zealand Romanian
Cultural Association**
• Miorita. (pub. by Outrigger Publications Ltd.)

**University of Waikato. Antarctic Research Unit**
Hamilton, New Zealand.
• University of Waikato. Antarctic Research Unit.
Report. irreg.

**Urban Development Association (Inc.)**
Box 5175, Wellington, New Zealand.
• Town and Countryside. q. ISSN 0049-4291

**Veterinary Surgeons Board of New Zealand**
Government Printing Office, Mulgrave St,
Thorndon, Wellington, New Zealand.
• Veterinary Surgeons in New Zealand; registered
under the Veterinary Surgeons Act 1956 &
persons entitled to use the title or description of
veterinary practitioner. a.

**Victoria University of Wellington**
Dept. of Accountancy, P.O. Box 196, Wellington,
New Zealand.
• Advanced Accountancy Seminar. Proceedings. a.
ISSN 0065-2075
• New Zealand Slavonic Journal. s-a. ISSN 0028-
8683
• Occasional Papers in Industrial Relations. irreg.
ISSN 0078-3064
• Pacific Viewpoint; specialises in the study of
development, change and underdevelopment. s-a.
ISSN 0030-8978
• Victoria University of Wellington. Awards
Handbook. a. ISSN 0083-6036
• Victoria University of Wellington. Vice-
Chancellor's Report. a.
• Victoria University of Wellington Law Review. s-
a. ISSN 0042-5117
• Words: Wai-Te-Ata Studies in Literature. irreg.
ISSN 0084-1250

**Victoria University of Wellington. Department of
Psychology**
Private Bag, P.O. Box 196, Wellington, New
Zealand.
• Publications in Psychology. irreg., 1972, no. 26.
ISSN 0079-7731

**Victoria University of Wellington. Faculty of
Commerce & Administration**
Private Bag, Wellington, New Zealand.
• Occasional Papers in Accountancy. irreg.

**Victoria University of Wellington. School of Political
Science**
Box 196, Wellington, New Zealand
• Political Science. s-a. ISSN 0032-3187

**Victoria University of Wellington. Zoology
Department**
Private Bag, Wellington, New Zealand.
• Victoria University of Wellington Zoology
Publications. irreg., no, 65, 1974. ISSN 0083-6060

**Ward Publishing Co.**
156 Ward St., Box 1136, Hamilton, New Zealand.
• N. Z. Electrical Industry. m. ISSN 0027-7185
(New Zealand Electrical Contractors Federation
Inc.)

**Wellington. Department of Education**
School Publications Branch, Wellington, New
Zealand.
• New Zealand School Journal. q. ISSN 0028-8659

**Wellington Publishing Co. Ltd.**
Box 1297, Wellington, New Zealand.
• Sunday Times. w. ISSN 0039-5323

**Wellington Regional Employers Association (Inc.)**
Federation House, 6th Floor, 95-99 Molesworthy
St., Box 1087, Wellington, New Zealand.
• Wellington Regional Employers Association
Newsletter. m.

**Whakatane & District Historical Society**
Box 203, Whakatane, New Zealand.
• Historical Review. s-a. ISSN 0018-2516

**Wilson and Horton Ltd.**
149 Queen St., Auckland, New Zealand.
• New Zealand Annual. a.
• New Zealand Journal of Agriculture. m. ISSN
0028-8241 (New Zealand. Ministry of Agriculture
and Fisheries)

# NICARAGUA

**Asociacion de Bibliotecas Universitarias y
Especializadas de Nicaragua**
Apartado 68, Leon, Nicaragua.
• Asociacion de Bibliotecas Univesitarias y
Especializadas de Nicaragua. Boletin. a.
• Boletin de la a B U E N. a.

**Banco Central de Nicaragua**
Apartados 2252-2253, Managua, Nicaragua.
- Banco Central de Nicaragua. Carta Quincenal. fortn.
- Banco Central de Nicaragua. Informe Anual. a; latest issue, 1971. ISSN 0067-3226

**Banco Central de Nicaragua. Biblioteca y Servicios de Informacion**
Managua, Nicaragua.
- Banco Central de Nicaragua. Boletin Semestral. s-a.
- Boletin Nicaraguense de Bibliografia y Documentacion.

**Banco Central de Nicaragua. Departamento de Estudios Economicos**
Managua, Nicaragua.
- Banco Central de Nicaragua. Departmento de Estudios Economicos. Indicadores Economicos. irreg.

**Banco de la Vivienda de Nicaragua. Caja Central de Ahorro y Prestamo**
Managua, Nicaragua.
- B V N. Boletin Informativo. m. ISSN 0005-3457

**Camara Nacional de Comercio de Managua**
Managua, Nicaragua.
- Camara Nacional de Comercio de Managua Boletin. m. ISSN 0008-1922

**Centro de Investigaciones y Actividades Culturales**
Apto. 2108, Managua, Nicaragua.
- Revista del Pensamiento Centroamericano. q.

**Colegio de Medicos y Cirujanos de Nicaragua**
Ed. Dr. Gerardo Peralta, Apdo. 942, Primera Calle S.O. 413, Managua, Nicaragua.
- Nicaragua Medica. q. ISSN 0028-968X

**Consejo Superior Universitario Centroamericano**
- Consejo Superior Universitario Centroamericano. Publicaciones. (pub. by Editorial Universitaria de la U N A N)

**Instituto Indigenista Nacional**
3 Calle N.O. 505, Managua, Nicaragua.
- Nicaragua Indigena. s-a.

**Nicaragua. Direccion General de Aduanas**
Managua, Nicaragua.
- Nicaragua. Direccion General de Aduanas. Memoria. a. ISSN 0078-0510

**Nicaragua. Guardia Nacional de Nicaragua. Oficina del Encargado General de Abastos**
Loma de Tiscapa, Managua, Nicaragua.
- Guardia Nacional. irreg. ISSN 0017-5005

**Nicaragua. Oficina Ejecutiva de Encuestos y Censos**
Aptado 4031, Managua, Nicaragua.
- Nicaragua. Oficina Ejecutiva de Encuestos y Censos. Compendio Estadistico. a.

**Nicaragua. Secretaria de Informacion y Prensa**
Managua, Nicaragua.
- Nicaragua. Secretaria de Informacion y Prensa. Carta Informativo. m.

**Pez y la Serpiente**
Apdo Postal 192, Managua, Nicaragua.
- Pez y la Serpiente; revista de cultura. s-a. ISSN 0031-6652

**Prensa Literaria Centroamericana**
Apartado 192, Managua, Nicaragua.
- Prensa Literaria Centroamericana; una universidad de bolsillo. m.

**Revista Comercial de Nicaragua**
Box 136, Managua, Nicaragua.
- Revista Comercial de Nicaragua. m. ISSN 0034-7469

**Universidad Centroamericana**
Aptdo 69, Managua, Nicaragua.
- Universidad Centroamericana. Revista Encuentro. irreg., 1971, vol. 4.

**Universidad Nacional Autonoma de Nicaragua**
- Cuadernos Universitarios. (pub. by Editorial Universitaria de la u N A N)
- Taller. (pub. by Editorial Universitaria de la u N A N)

**Universidad Nacional Autonoma de Nicaragua. Biblioteca Central**
Apartado 68, Leon, Nicaragua.
- Universidad Nacional de Nicaragua. Biblioteca Central. Boletin. bi-m. ISSN 0545-9249

**Editorial Universitaria de la U N A N**
Leon, Nicaragua.
- Consejo Superior Universitario Centroamericano. Publicaciones. irreg. ISSN 0589-4360
- Cuadernos Universitarios. 4 per yr. ISSN 0011-2569 (Universidad Nacional Autonoma de Nicaragua)
- Taller. 3 per yr. ISSN 0039-9221 (Universidad Nacional Autonoma de Nicaragua)

# NIGER

**Institut Fondamental d'Afrique Noire. Centre du Niger**
B.P. 48, Niamey, Niger.
- Etudes Nigeriennes. irreg.

**Niger. Direction de la Statistique et des Comptes Nationaux**
Ministere du Plan, Niamey, Niger.
- Niger. Direction de la Statistique et des Comptes Nationaux. Bulletin de Statistique. q.

**Niger. Ministere de l'Information**
B.P. 368, Niamey, Niger.
- Niger. q. ISSN 0550-6891
- Niger; Fraternite-Travail-Progres. w. ISSN 0545-9532

**Niger. Office des Postes et Telecommunications**
Niamey, Niger.
- Niger. Office des Postes et Telecommunications. Annuaire Officiel des Telephones. a.

**Organization of African Unity. Scientific Technical and Research Commission**
Publications Bureau, Maison de l'Afrique, B.P. 878, Niamey, Niger.
- Organization of African Unity. Scientific Technical and Research Commission. Publication. irreg. ISSN 0474-6171

# NIGERIA

**Abdullahi Bayero College**
- Kano Studies. (pub. by Oxford University Press (Nigerian Branch))

**African Cultures Publications Ltd.**
Mile 2 Ubulunor Rd., Box 20, Ogwashi Uku, Nigeria.
- Afro Image. m.

**African Education Press**
Box 4061, Ibadan, Nigeria.
- African Historian. a. ISSN 0568-1332 (University of Ife. Historical Society)

**African Literary and Scientific Publications Ltd.**
9 Kodesho St., Ikeja, Lagos, Nigeria.
- Nigerian Medical Directory. a. ISSN 0078-0782

**African Newspapers of Nigeria Ltd.**
212 Broad St., Box 2416, Ibadan, Nigeria.
- Irohin Yoruba. w. ISSN 0021-1494

**Africanus Publishers & Co.**
Rational Building, 6 Ijebu Bye Pass, Oke-Bola, Ibadan, Nigeria.
- Social Reformer. ISSN 0049-0881

**Agricultural Society of Nigeria**
c/o Dr. T. I. Ashaye, P. M. B. 5029, Ibadan, Nigeria.
- Agricultural Society of Nigeria. Proceedings. a. ISSN 0065-454X
- Nigerian Agricultural Journal. s-a. ISSN 0300-368X

**Ahmadiyya Muslim Mission**
45, Idumagbo Ave., Box 418, Lagos, Nigeria.
- Truth; the first muslim weekly newspaper in Nigeria. w.

**Ahmadu Bello University**
P.M. Box 5, Samaru, Zaria, Nigeria.
- Savanna; a journal of the environmental & social sciences. s-a.

**Ahmadu Bello University. Abdullahi Bayero College**
*see* Abdullahi Bayero College

**Ahmadu Bello University. Centre for the Study of Nigerian Languages**
Private Bag 3011, Zaria, Nigeria.
- Harsunan Nijeriya. a.

**Ahmadu Bello University. Centre of Islamic Legal Studies**
P.M.B. 1013, Zaria, Nigeria
- Ahmadu Bello University. Centre of Islamic Legal Studies. Journal. irreg., vol. 5, 1974. ISSN 0065-468X (Overseas orders to: Wildy & Sons Ltd., Lincoln's Inn Archway, Carey St., London W.C. 2, England)

**Ahmadu Bello University. Department of Geography**
Zaria, Nigeria.
- Ahmadu Bello University. Department of Geography. Occasional Paper. irreg. ISSN 0065-4698

**Ahmadu Bello University. Institute for Agricultural Research**
P.M.B. 1044, Zaria, Nigeria.
- Ahmadu Bello University. Institute for Agricultural Research. Annual Report. a. ISSN 0065-471X
- Ahmadu Bello University. Institute for Agricultural Research. Soil Survey Bulletin. irreg. 1969, no. 39. ISSN 0065-4728
- Samaru Agricultural Newsletter. bi-m. ISSN 0036-3731
- Samaru Miscellaneous Paper. irreg., 1968, no. 28. ISSN 0080-5769
- Samaru Research Bulletin. ISSN 0080-5777

**Ahmadu Bello University. Institute of Administration**
Zaria, Nigeria.
- Ahmadu Bello University. Institute of Administration. Traditional Land Tenure Surveys. irreg. ISSN 0065-4744

**Ahmadu Bello University. Institute of Education**
Zaria, Nigeria.
- Ahmadu Bello University. Institute of Education. Paper. irreg. ISSN 0065-4752

**Ahmadu Bello University. Law Society**
Zaria, Nigeria.
- Law in Society. irreg (1-2 per yr.) ISSN 0458-8592

**Ahmadu Bello University. Northern History Research Scheme**
Zaria, Nigeria.
- Ahmadu Bello University. Northern History Research Scheme. Papers. irreg.; 3rd forthcoming, 1975. ISSN 0065-4760 (Co-sponsor: University of Ibadan)

**Alpha Publications**
46, Raufu Williams Crescent, P.M.B. 3122, Surulere, Lagos, Nigeria.
- Message; quarterly for marketing and mass communications. q.

**Ambasciata d'Italia**
Commercial Office, Box 2161, Lagos, Nigeria.
- Italy and Nigeria. q. ISSN 0021-308X

**Association for Teacher Education in Africa. Western Council**
Lagos, Nigeria.
- Association for Teacher Education in Africa. Western Council. Report of the Annual Conference. a.

**Association of History Teachers**
- Association of History Teachers in Nigeria. (pub. by Educational Research Institute)

**Fred Atoki Publishing Co. Ltd.**
50 Olatunde Labinjo Ave., Ikorodu Rd., Box 7313, Lagos, Nigeria.
- Journal of Medical and Pharmaceutical Marketing. bi-m.

**Bendel State. Ministry of Home Affairs and Information**
Printing and Stationery Division, P.M.B. 1099, Benin City, Nigeria.
- Bendel State. Ministry of Home Affairs and Information. Mid-Western State Estimates. irreg.
- Bendel State Gazette. w.

**Biafra Time Ltd.**
Ogbo-Hill, Box 218, Aba, Nigeria.
- Biafra Time. m. ISSN 0006-0569

**Carmen & Co. Ltd.**
17, Ikosi Road, Oregun Industrial Estate, P.M.B.
1292, Ikeja, Nigeria.
- African Spark. m.

**Caxton Press**
Eleiyele Rd., Box 5009, Ibadan, Nigeria.
- Journal of Rural Economics & Development. s-a.
(University of Ibadan. Department of Agricultural
Economics) (Co-sponsor: Department of
Agricultural Extension Services)

**Central Bank of Nigeria**
P.M.B. 12194, Tinubu Square, Lagos, Nigeria.
- Central Bank of Nigeria. Annual Report and
Statement of Accounts. a. ISSN 0069-1577
- Central Bank of Nigeria. Economic and Financial
Review. irreg., vol. 12, 1974. ISSN 0008-9281
- Central Bank of Nigeria. Monthly Report. m.
ISSN 0008-929X

**Christian Council of Nigeria**
- Nigerian Christian. (pub. by Daystar Press)

**Conference of Muslim Lecturers and Senior Staff of
All Nigerian Universities**
- Nigerian Journal of Islam. (pub. by University of
Ife Bookshop Ltd.)

**Daily Times of Nigeria Ltd.**
Box 139, Lagos, Nigeria.
- Lagos Weekend. w. ISSN 0023-7272
- Nigeria Year Book. a. ISSN 0078-0685
- Spear. m. ISSN 0038-6634
- Times Trade and Industrial Directory. irreg.

**Daystar Press**
Box 1261, Ibadan, Nigeria.
- Nigerian Christian. m. ISSN 0029-005X
(Christian Council of Nigeria)
- Nigerian Names. irreg.

**Drum Publications (Nigeria) Ltd.**
37, Ibadah St. West, Ebute Metta, P.M.B. 2128,
Lagos, Nigeria.
- Drum (Nigerian Edition) m. ISSN 0419-7682
- Truck and Car (West African Edition) q.
- Trust. m.

**E C W A Productions Ltd.**
P.M. Bag 2010, Jos, Nigeria.
- Today's Challenge. m. (Evangelical Churches of
West Africa)

**Eagle**
c/o E.A. Etudo, Ed., 89 New Market Rd., Onitsha,
Nigeria.
- Eagle. ISSN 0012-8112

**Educational Research Institute**
Box 277, Ibadan, Nigeria.
- Association of History Teachers in Nigeria. a.

**Entomological Society of Nigeria**
Ibadan, Nigeria.
- Nigerian Journal of Entomology. s-a.

**Ethiope Publishing Corporation**
34 Murtala Mohammed Street, PMB 1192, Benin
City, Nigeria.
- Benin Review. s-a.
- Ethiope Law Series. irreg.

**Evangelical Churches of West Africa**
- Today's Challenge. (pub. by E C W A
Productions Ltd.)

**Federal Institute of Industrial Research, Oshodi**
see **Nigeria. Federal Institute of Industrial
Research, Oshodi**

**Forestry Association of Nigeria**
Box 4185, Ibadan, Nigeria.
- Nigerian Journal of Forestry. s-a.

**Historical Society of Nigeria**
c/o Department of History, University of Ibadan,
Ibadan, Nigeria.
- Historical Society of Nigeria. Journal. s-a. ISSN
0018-2540
- Tarikh. (pub. by Humanities Press, Inc. US)

**I C I C (Directory Publishers) Ltd.**
P.M.B. 3204, Surulere, Lagos, Nigeria.
- Directory of Incorporated (Registered) Companies
in Nigeria. a. ISSN 0084-9952
- Nigerian Office and Quarters Directory. a. ISSN
0085-4190

**Ibadan Renaissance Society**
University College, Ibadan, Nigeria.
- Horizon. a. ISSN 0073-3385

**Ibadan University Geographical Society**
Ibadan, Nigeria.
- University Geographer. a. ISSN 0083-3975

**Ibadan University Library**
see **University of Ibadan. Library**

**Ibadan University Press**
University of Ibadan, Ibadan, Nigeria.
- Abacus. s-a. ISSN 0001-3099 (Mathematical
Association of Nigeria)

**Ideal Companion**
SW 8-980 Adeniji St., Oke-Ado, Ibadan, Nigeria.
- Ideal Companion. m. ISSN 0019-1345

**Igbo Philosophical Association**
Bigard Memorial Seminary, P.M.B. 921, Enugu,
East Central State, Nigeria.
- Igbo Philosophy. a.

**Insight**
Box 139, 3 Kakawa St., Lagos, Nigeria.
- Insight. q. ISSN 0020-1936

**Institute of Chartered Accountants of Nigeria**
60 Marina, Box 1580, Lagos, Nigeria.
- Nigerian Accountant. q. ISSN 0048-0371

**Institute of Medical Laboratory Technology of
Nigeria**
Lagos University Teaching Hospital, Department of
Microbiology, P.M.B. 12003, Lagos, Nigeria.
- Nigerian Journal of Medical Laboratory
Technology. q.

**International Association for Cultural Freedom**
- Ch'indaba. (pub. by University of Ife Press)

**International Confederation of Free Trade Unions.
African Regional Organisation**
85 Simpson St., Ebute Metta, Lagos, Nigeria.
- African Labour News. w. ISSN 0002-0044

**International Grain Legume Information Centre**
- Tropical Grain Legume Bulletin. (pub. by
International Institute of Tropical Agriculture)

**International Institute of Tropical Agriculture**
Oyo Rd., P.M.B. 5320, Ibadan, Nigeria.
- Tropical Grain Legume Bulletin. q. (International
Grain Legume Information Centre) (Co-sponsor:
International Development Research Centre of
Canada)

**International Society of United Modern Enterprise**
60 A Campbell St., P.O. Box 1944, Lagos, Nigeria.
- World Peace. q. ISSN 0300-225X

**J. M. P. Services (West Africa) Ltd.**
Private Mail Bag 12002, Lagos, Nigeria.
- West African Builder and Architect. 6 per yr.
ISSN 0043-2970
- West African Medical Journal. 6 per yr. ISSN
0043-3004

**Kano State. Ministry of Home Affairs and
Information. Information Division**
Kano, Nigeria.
- Kano State of Nigeria Today. m.

**Kwara State. Ministry of Home Affairs and
Information**
Ilorin, Nigeria.
- Kwara News. q.

**Lagos Chamber of Commerce and Industry**
Lagos, Nigeria.
- Commerce in Nigeria. a. ISSN 0069-6633

**Lagos State. Department of Petroleum Resources**
Ministry of Mines and Power, P.M.B. 12574, Lagos,
Nigeria.
- Lagos State. Department of Petroleum Resources.
Monthly Petroleum Information. m. ISSN 0549-
2513

**Lagos State Today**
24A Oil Mill St., P.O. 3738, Lagos, Nigeria.
- Lagos State Today. m.

**Literamed Publications Nigeria, Ltd.**
Oregun Village, P.M.B. 1068, Ikeja, Nigeria.
- West African Journal of Pharmacology and Drug
Research. biennial. (West African Society for
Pharmacology)

**Manufacturers Association of Nigeria**
37, Marina, Box 3835, Lagos, Nigeria.
- Nigeria Industrial Directory. irreg.

**Mathematical Association of Nigeria**
- Abacus. (pub. by Ibadan University Press)

**Modern Publications Co. Ltd.**
Box 2583, Marina, Lagos, Nigeria.
- Apollo; magazine for young Nigerians. m.
- Modern Woman. m. ISSN 0047-7761

**Nara Advertising Ltd.**
30 Idoluwo St., Box 4236, Lagos, Nigeria.
- Nigerian Insurance Monitor. m. ISSN 0048-0398

**New Breed Organization Ltd.**
35 Ogunlana Drive, P.O. 5414, Lagos, Nigeria.
- Newbreed. fortn.
- President. m.

**New Nigeria Development Company Ltd.**
P.M.B. 2120, Kaduna, Nigeria.
- New Nigeria Development Company Limited.
Annual Report and Accounts. a.

**Nigeria**
P.O.B. 2099, Lagos, Nigeria.
- Nigeria. q. ISSN 0029-0033

**Nigeria. Anti-Inflation Task Force**
Lagos, Nigeria.
- Nigeria. Anti-Inflation Task Force. Report. a.

**Nigeria. Federal Department of Fisheries**
P.M.B. 12529, Lagos, Nigeria.
- Nigeria. Federal Department of Fisheries. Federal
Fisheries Occasional Paper. irreg.; latest issue,
1974.

**Nigeria. Federal Department of Forest Research**
Private Mail Bag No. 5054, Ibadan, Nigeria.
- Nigeria. Federal Department of Forest Research.
Research Paper. irreg., 1969, no. 14.

**Nigeria. Federal Institute of Industrial Research,
Oshodi**
Private Mail Bag 1023, Murtala Mohammed
Airport, Ikeja, Lagos State, Nigeria.
- F I I R O Technical Information Bulletin for
Industry. q.

**Nigeria. Federal Ministry of Industries. Federal
Institute of Industrial Research, Oshodi**
see **Nigeria. Federal Institute of Industrial
Research, Oshodi**

**Nigeria. Federal Ministry of Labour**
Independence Bldg., P.M. Box 12576, Ikoyi, Lagos,
Nigeria.
- Nigeria. Federal Ministry of Labour. Quarterly
Review. q. ISSN 0549-2351 (prep. by its
Inspectorate, Research & Training Division)

**Nigeria. Federal Office of Statistics**
Lagos, Nigeria.
- Nigeria. Federal Office of Statistics. Annual
Abstract of Statistics. a. ISSN 0078-0626
- Nigeria. Federal Office of Statistics. Digest of
Statistics. q. ISSN 0029-0017
- Nigeria. Federal Office of Statistics. Review of
External Trade. a. ISSN 0078-0634
- Nigeria. Federal Office of Statistics. Trade Report.
a. ISSN 0078-0642

**Nigeria. Meteorological Service**
Headquarters, Lagos, Nigeria.
- Agro-Meteorological Bulletin for Nigeria. m. ISSN
0545-9923

**Nigeria. National Electric Power Authority**
Electricity Headquarters, 24/25 Marina, Lagos,
Nigeria.
- Nigeria. National Electric Power Authority.
Annual Report and Accounts. a.

**Nigeria. National Library**
4 Wesley St., P.M.B. 12626, Ibadan, Nigeria.
- Index to Nigeriana in Selected Periodicals. a. ISSN 0073-5965
- Libraries in Nigeria: A Directory. a. ISSN 0075-8981
- National Bibliography of Nigeria. m (s-a and a. cumulations)
- National Library of Nigeria. Annual Report. a. ISSN 0075-7624
- National Library of Nigeria. National Library Occasional Publication. irreg. ISSN 0075-7632
- Nigerbiblios. q.
- Nigerian Books in Print. a. ISSN 0078-0693
- Theses and Dissertations Accepted for Higher Degrees in Nigerian Universities. a. ISSN 0082-4100

**Nigeria. National Manpower Board**
5 Oil Mills St., Lagos, Nigeria.
- Nigeria. National Manpower Board. Manpower Studies. irreg (1-2 per yr)

**Nigeria. Nigerian National Advisory Council for the Blind**
Federal Ministry of Labour, P.O. Box 2145, Lagos, Nigeria.
- Nigerian National Advisory Council for the Blind. Annual Report. a. ISSN 0078-0804

**Nigeria. Nigerian Ports Authority**
Headquarters, Marina, Lagos, Nigeria.
- N P A News. s-a. ISSN 0547-0730

**Nigeria Business Directory**
7 Coates Street, Ebute-Metta, Lagos, Nigeria.
- Nigeria Business Directory. a. ISSN 0078-0596

**Nigeria Civil Service Union. Western State Branch**
Box 1640, Ibadan, Nigeria.
- Civil Servant. m.

**Nigeria Confidential Co.**
83 Palm Ave., Mushin, Lagos, Nigeria.
- Nigeria Confidential; so that the people may know. w. ISSN 0048-0363

**Nigeria English Studies Association**
c/o Ibadan, Ibadan, Nigeria.
- Nigeria English Studies Association Journal. s-a. ISSN 0029-0009

**Nigeria Lawyers' Quarterly**
11 Williams St., Lagos, Nigeria.
- Nigeria Lawyers' Quarterly. q. ISSN 0029-0025

**Nigeria Union of Teachers**
Box 1044, 29 Commercial Ave., Yaba, Nigeria.
- Nigerian Schoolmaster. 3 per yr. ISSN 0029-0157

**Nigerian Association of French Teachers**
c/o A. Iwara, Ed., Department of Modern Languages, University of Ibadan, Ibadan, Nigeria.
- Francais au Nigeria. q. ISSN 0015-9387

**Nigerian Broadcasting Corporation**
Box 12504, Lagos, Nigeria.
- Nigerian Radio - Television Times. m.

**Nigerian Chamber of Mines**
P.O. Box 454, Jos, Benue-Plateau State, Nigeria.
- Nigerian Chamber of Mines. Annual Review. a. ISSN 0078-0707

**Nigerian Current Affairs Society**
Faculty of the Social Sciences, University of Ibadan, Ibadan, Nigeria.
- Nigerian Opinion. q. ISSN 0029-0130

**Nigerian Economic Society**
c/o Dept. of Economics, University of Ibadan, Ibadan, Nigeria.
- Nigerian Economic Society. Proceedings of the Annual Conference. a.
- Nigerian Journal of Economics & Social Studies. 3 per yr. ISSN 0029-0092

**Nigerian Geographical Association**
c/o Department of Geography, University of Ibadan, Ibadan, Nigeria.
- Nigerian Geographical Journal. s-a. ISSN 0029-0084

**Nigerian Industrial Development Bank**
Mandilar House, Yakubu Gowen St., Box 2357, Lagos, Nigeria.
- Nigerian Industrial Development Bank. Annual Report and Accounts. a. ISSN 0549-2734

**Nigerian Institute for Oil Palm Research**
P.M.B. 1030, Benin City, Nigeria.
- Nigerian Institute for Oil Palm Research. Journal. irreg. ISSN 0078-0715

**Nigerian Institute of International Affairs**
Kofo Abayomi Rd., G.P.O. Box 1727, Lagos, Nigeria.
- Nigeria Bulletin on Foreign Affairs. m.
- Nigerian Institute of International Affairs. Lecture Series. m. ISSN 0078-0731
- Nigerian Journal of International Affairs. s-a.

**Nigerian Institute of Management**
145 Yakubu Gowon St., Box 2557, Lagos, Nigeria.
- Management in Nigeria. m. ISSN 0025-178X

**Nigerian Institute of Social and Economic Research**
Private Mail Bag 5, University of Ibadan, Ibadan, Nigeria.
- Nigerian Institute of Social and Economic Research. Annual Report. a. ISSN 0078-074X
- Nigerian Institute of Social and Economic Research. Bulletin. s-a.
- Nigerian Institute of Social and Economic Research. Library. List of Accessions. q. ISSN 0078-0766

**Nigerian Library Association**
P.M.B. 12655, Lagos, Nigeria.
- Nigerian Libraries. 3 per yr. ISSN 0029-0122

**Nigerian Library Association. Lagos Division**
c/o University of Lagos, Akaka, Yaba, Lagos, Nigeria.
- Lagos Librarian. q. ISSN 0047-3901

**Nigerian Medical Association**
Box 1108, Lagos, Nigeria.
- Nigerian Medical Journal. q.

**Nigerian Mining, Geological and Metallurgical Society**
c/o Geology Dept., University of Ife, Ile-Ife, Nigeria.
- Journal of Mining and Geology. s-a. ISSN 0022-2763

**Nigerian National Advisory Council for the Blind**
see Nigeria. Nigerian National Advisory Council for the Blind

**Nigerian Pharmaceutical & Medical Company**
21 Wharf Rd., Box 399, Apapa, Nigeria.
- African Journal of Pharmacy and Pharmaceutical Sciences. m. ISSN 0044-6564

**Nigerian Ports Authority**
see Nigeria. Nigerian Ports Authority

**Nigerian Society of International Affairs**
c/o Department of Political Science, University of Ibadan, Ibadan, Nigeria.
- Nigerian Journal of International Studies. s-a.

**Nigerian Tobacco Company**
Lagos, Nigeria.
- Nigerian Tobacco Company. Report. a. ISSN 0078-0820

**Nigerian Tourist Association**
47, Marina, P.O. Box 2944, Lagos, Nigeria.
- Nigeria Tourist Guide/Guide du Tourisme Nigerien. irreg.

**North-Central State. Ministry of Works**
Kaduna, Nigeria.
- North-Central State. Ministry of Works. Report. a. ISSN 0078-1762

**O A B Press Service Ltd.**
P.O. Box 802, Lagos, Nigeria.
- Nigeria Annual and Trading Directory. a. ISSN 0078-057X

**Okike**
Box 53, Nsukka, Nigeria.
- Okike; an African journal of new writing. 3 per yr.

**Old Calabar and Ogoja Youth Organization**
Box 3564, Lagos, Nigeria.
- Brush. 2-3 per yr. ISSN 0045-3269

**Oma Press**
Orlu Division, Awo-Omamma, Nigeria.
- Oma. q. ISSN 0030-218X

**Onibonoje Press**
Box 3109, Ibadan, Nigeria.
- Yoruba. s-a. (Yoruba Studies Association of Nigeria)

**Oxford University Press (Nigerian Branch)**
P.M.B. 5095, Oxford House, Iddo Gate, Ibadan, Nigeria.
- Kano Studies; journal of Saharan and Sudanic research. a. (Abdullahi Bayero College)
- West African Journal of Archaeology. a. ISSN 0083-8160

**Pan-Afriscope (Nigeria) Ltd.**
45 Salami Saibu St., P.M.B. 1119, Lagos, Nigeria.
- Afriscope; Africa's social economic development. m. ISSN 0044-667X

**People's Publishing Co. Ltd.**
Box 3121, Lagos, Nigeria.
- People. m. ISSN 0048-329X
- Prosperity; Nigeria's business quarterly. q. ISSN 0048-5608

**Political Student's Association**
University of Ibadan, Ibadan, Nigeria.
- Statesman. bi-m.

**Prestige Publication Co.**
P.O. Box 416, Lagos State, Nigeria.
- Nigeria Tourist and Motorist. q.

**Professional Association of Trained Nurses of Nigeria**
Speedwell House, Private Mail Bag 12016, Lagos, Nigeria.
- Nigerian Nurse. q.

**Punch (Nigeria) Ltd.**
Kudeti Street, P. M. B. 1204, Ikeja, Lagos, Nigeria.
- Happy Home & Family Health. m.

**Rivers State. Ministry of Agriculture and Natural Resources**
Port Harcourt, Rivers State, Nigeria.
- Rivers State. Ministry of Agriculture and Natural Resources. Agricultural Newsletter. q. (prep. by its Publicity, Information and Library Service Section)

**Rivers State. Ministry of Information**
Port Harcourt, Rivers State, Nigeria.
- Rivers State. Ministry of Information. Quarterly Journal. q.

**Rivers State Council for Arts & Culture**
74/76 Bonny St., P.M.B. 5156, Port Harcourt, Nigeria.
- Oduma. s-a.

**Rota Publishing Co. Ltd.**
A.C. 5 Lagos St. (2nd Floor), P.O. Box 497, Kaduna, Nigeria.
- Northern States Review; review of life in the North. q.
- Rota Trade and Industrial Directory. North Central State. s-a.

**Salvation Army**
Box 125, Lagos, Nigeria.
- War Cry. m. ISSN 0049-688X

**Savanna Forestry Research Station**
Department of Forest Research, Samaru, Nigeria.
- Savanna Forestry Research Station, Nigeria. Annual Report. a. (Co-sponsors: Food and Agriculture Organization of the United Nations; United Nations Development Programme)

**Science Association of Nigeria**
Box 4039, Ibadan, Nigeria.
- Directory of Scientific Research in Nigeria. a. ISSN 0070-6280
- Nigerian Journal of Science. s-a. ISSN 0029-0114

**Society of Health of Nigeria**
227 Herbert Maculay St., Box 1061, Lagos, Nigeria.
- Society of Health of Nigeria. Journal. q. ISSN 0037-9905

**South-Eastern State. Ministry of Economic Development and Reconstruction**
Calabar, Nigeria
(Dist. by South-Eastern State Government Printer, Calabar, Nigeria)
- South-Eastern State. Ministry of Economic Development and Reconstruction. State Development Plan. irreg.

**Standing Conference of African University Libraries**
Box 46, University of Lagos Post Office, Akoka,
Yaba, Lagos, Nigeria.
- S C A U L Newsletter. s-a. ISSN 0563-0924

**Teen Topics Publications**
Box 14, Ikeja, Lagos State, Nigeria.
- Teen and Twenty; Africa's youth magazine. m.

**Tree Club**
University of Ibadan, Department of Forest
Resources Management, Ibadan, Nigeria.
- Obeche. a. ISSN 0078-2912

**U.S. Information Service**
Box 554, Lagos, Nigeria.
- Interlink; Nigerian-American magazine. 5 per yr.
ISSN 0020-5559

**Universal Publications Ltd.**
115 Griffith St., Ebute-Metta, Box 1959, Lagos,
Nigeria.
- Nigerian Business Digest. m. ISSN 0048-038X

**University of Benin. Library**
P.M.B. 1154, Eken Wan Rd., Benin City, Nigeria.
- University of Benin. Library. Annual Report. a.

**University of Ibadan**
Ibadan, Nigeria.
- Anvil. s-m. ISSN 0003-6226
- Ibadan. q. ISSN 0019-0969
- Nigerian X-Ray. q.

**University of Ibadan. Department of Agricultural
Economics**
- Journal of Rural Economics & Development. (pub.
by Caxton Press)

**University of Ibadan. Department of Education**
Ibadan, Nigeria.
- African Journal of Educational Research. s-a.

**University of Ibadan. Department of Linguistics and
Nigerian Languages**
Ibadan, Nigeria
- Journal of West African Languages. s-a. ISSN
0022-5401 (Outside Africa, orders to: Bentley
House, 200 Euston Rd., London N.W. 1,
England)
- University of Ibadan. Department of Linguistics
and Nigerian Languages. Research Notes. irreg.
ISSN 0041-9613

**University of Ibadan. Department of Religious
Studies**
Ibadan, Nigeria.
- Orita; Ibadan journal of religious studies. s-a.
ISSN 0030-5596

**University of Ibadan. Institute of African Studies**
Ibadan, Nigeria.
- African Notes. s-a. ISSN 0002-0087

**University of Ibadan. Institute of Education**
Ibadan, Nigeria.
- University of Ibadan. Institute of Education.
Occasional Publications. irreg. ISSN 0073-4314
- West African Journal of Education. 3 per yr.
ISSN 0043-2997

**University of Ibadan. Library**
Ibadan, Nigeria.
- University of Ibadan. Library. Annual Report. a.
ISSN 0073-4322
- University of Ibadan. Library. Bibliographical
Series. irreg., no. 2, 1970. ISSN 0073-4330
- University of Ibadan. Library. Library Record. m.
ISSN 0046-8436

**University of Ibadan Medical Students' Association**
Alexander Brown Hall, University College Hospital,
Ibadan, Nigeria.
- Dokita. s-a. ISSN 0046-0508

**University of Ibadan. Nigerian Institute of Social and
Economic Research**
*see* **Nigerian Institute of Social and Economic
Research**

**University of Ibadan. Sociological Society**
Ibadan, Nigeria.
- Sociologist. a. ISSN 0081-1807

**University of Ibadan. Student Affairs Office**
Ibadan, Nigeria.
- University of Ibadan. Student Affairs Office.
Student Handbook of Information on University
Policies and Practices. irreg.

**University of Ife**
Ile-Ife, Nigeria.
- Bronze. m. ISSN 0007-2281
- Odu; a journal of West African studies. s-a. ISSN
0029-8522
- Second Order. (pub. by University of Ife Press)

**University of Ife. Department of Education**
Ile-Ife, Nigeria.
- Abstracts of Educational Studies and Research. w.

**University of Ife. Economics Society**
Ile-Ife, Nigeria.
- Social Scientist. a. ISSN 0081-0487

**University of Ife. Faculty of Agriculture**
- University of Ife. Faculty of Agriculture. Annual
Research Report. (pub. by University of Ife Press)

**University of Ife. Faculty of Arts**
Ile-Ife, Nigeria.
- University of Ife. Faculty of Arts. Lecture Series.
irreg.

**University of Ife. Faculty of Law**
- University of Ife. Faculty of Law. Law Report.
(pub. by University of Ife Press)

**University of Ife. Geographical Society**
Ile-Ife, Nigeria.
- Geographica. q. ISSN 0016-7290

**University of Ife. Historical Society**
- African Historian. (pub. by African Education
Press)

**University of Ife. Institute of Administration**
P.M.B. 5246, Ibadan, Nigeria.
- Quarterly Journal of Administration. q. ISSN
0001-8333
- University of Ife. Institute of Administration.
Annual Report. a. ISSN 0536-3454

**University of Ife. Institute of African Studies**
Ile-Ife, Nigeria.
- Ife African Studies. s-a.

**University of Ife Bookshop Ltd.**
Ibadan Branch, Ibadan, Nigeria.
- Nigerian Journal of Islam. s-a. ISSN 0029-0106
(Conference of Muslim Lecturers and Senior Staff
of All Nigerian Universities)

**University of Ife Press**
Ile-Ife, Nigeria.
- Ch'indaba. q. (International Association for
Cultural Freedom)
- Second Order; an African journal of philosophy. s-
a. ISSN 0048-9964 (University of Ife)
- University of Ife. Faculty of Agriculture. Annual
Research Report. a. ISSN 0579-7195
- University of Ife. Faculty of Law. Law Report. q.

**University of Lagos**
Yaba, Lagos, Nigeria.
- Black Orpheus; journal of African and Afro-
American literature. s-a. ISSN 0067-9100
- University of Lagos. Humanities Series. irreg.
ISSN 0075-7675
- University of Lagos. Inaugural Lecture Series. a.
ISSN 0075-7659
- University of Lagos. Scientific Monograph Series.
irreg. ISSN 0075-7713

**University of Lagos. Continuing Education Centre**
Yaba, Lagos, Nigeria.
- University of Lagos. Continuing Education
Centre. Occasional Papers. irreg., no. 2, 1971.
ISSN 0075-7667

**University of Lagos. Faculty of Law**
Lagos, Nigeria.
- Nigerian Journal of Contemporary Law. 3 per yr.
ISSN 0048-0401

**University of Lagos. Human Resources Research Unit**
Yabu, Lagos, Nigeria.
- University of Lagos. Human Resources Research
Unit. Monograph. irreg.

**University of Lagos. Law Society**
Yaba, Lagos, Nigeria.
- Lawyer. 2-3 per yr. ISSN 0023-9437

**University of Lagos. Library**
Yaba, Lagos, Nigeria.
- University of Lagos. Library. Annual Report. a.
ISSN 0075-7705

**University of Lagos. School of Administration and
Social Sciences**
Yaba, Lagos, Nigeria.
- Journal of Business & Social Studies. s-a. ISSN
0021-9428

**University of Lagos. School of African Studies**
Faculty of Arts, Lagos, Nigeria.
- Lagos Notes and Records; a journal of African
studies. irreg., vol. 5, 1974. ISSN 0075-7640

**University of Nigeria. Department of Economics**
Nsukka, Nigeria.
- Small-Scale Industries: South Eastern and Benue
Plateau States of Nigeria. a.

**University of Nigeria. Department of English**
Nsukka, East Central State, Nigeria.
- Nsukka Studies in African Literature. s-a.
- Omabe; poetry from Nsukka. bi-m.

**University of Nigeria. Department of Religion**
Nsukka, East Central State, Nigeria.
- West African Religion. s-a. ISSN 0083-8187

**University of Nigeria. English Association**
Nsukka, Nigeria.
- Muse. irreg.

**University of Nigeria. Institute of African Studies**
Nsukka, East Central State, Nigeria.
- Ikenga. s-a.
- Ikorok. s-a. ISSN 0046-8592

**University of Nigeria. Law Student's Association**
Nsukka, East Central State, Nigeria.
- Barrister. irreg.

**University of Nigeria. Library**
Nsukka, Nigeria.
- Nsukka Library Notes. irreg.

**University of Nigeria. University Research Committee**
Nsukka, Nigeria.
- University of Nigeria. Report on Research. irreg.
ISSN 0078-0677

**West African Book Publishers Ltd.**
Box 3445, Lagos, Nigeria.
- Atoka; Yoruba photoplay series. s-m. ISSN 0004-
7007

**West African Classical Association**
Department of Classics, University of Ibadan,
Ibadan, Nigeria
- Museum Africum; West African journal of
classical and related studies. a.; vol. 3, 1974.
(Dist. by: Rudolf Habelt Verlag GmbH, Am
Buchenhang 1, 53 Bonn 5, West Germany
(B.R.D.))

**West African Examinations Council. Test
Development and Research Division**
P.M.B. 1076, Yaba, Lagos, Nigeria.
- West African Journal of Educational and
Vocational Measurement. s-a. ISSN 0331-0515

**West African Journal of Biological and Applied
Chemistry**
c/o Biochemistry Department, University of Ibadan,
Ibadan, Nigeria.
- West African Journal of Biological and Applied
Chemistry. q. ISSN 0043-2989

**West African Modern Languages Association**
c/o University of Ibadan, Ibadan, Nigeria.
- West African Journal of Modern Languages/
Revue Ouest Africaine des Langues Vivantes. s-a.

**West African Science Association**
c/o Department of Zoology, University of Ibadan,
Ibadan, Nigeria.
- Nigerian Journal of Science. s-a.

**West African Society for Pharmacology**
- West African Journal of Pharmacology and Drug
Research. (pub. by Literamed Publications
Nigeria, Ltd.)

**John West Publications Ltd.**
212 Yakutsu Gowen Street, Lagos, Nigeria
- West Africa Annual. a. ISSN 0083-8144 (Dist. in U.S. by: International Publications Service, 114 E. 32nd St., New York, NY 10016)

**Western Nigeria Development Corporation**
P.M.B. 5085, Cocoa House, Ibadan, Nigeria.
- Western Nigeria Development Corporation. Industrial Directory. irreg.

**Western State. Government Printer**
Ibadan, Nigeria.
- Western State. Estimates Including Budget Speech and Memorandum. irreg.
- Western State. Gazette. irreg.

**Western State. Ministry of Economic Planning and Community Development**
Ibadan, Nigeria
(Orders to: Western State Government Printer, Ibadan, Nigeria)
- Western State. Ministry of Economic Planning and Community Development. Annual Report. a.

**Western State. Ministry of Education**
General Publications Section, P.M.B. 5052, Ibadan, Nigeria.
- Teachers' Forum. bi-m.

**Western State. Ministry of Home Affairs and Information**
Ibadan, Nigeria
- Gangan; a Western Nigerian magazine. q. ISSN 0016-4453

**Western State. Ministry of Local Government and Chieftancy Affairs**
Ibadan, Nigeria
(Orders to: Western State Government Printer, Ibadan, Nigeria)
- Western State. Ministry of Local Government and Chieftancy Affairs. Local Government Circulars. irreg.

**Yoruba Studies Association of Nigeria**
- Yoruba. (pub. by Onibonoje Press)

# NORWAY

**A-S Allers Familie-Journal**
Persveien 20, Postboks 250, Oslo 5, Norway.
- Allers. w. ISSN 0002-5771
- Kvinner og Klaer/Women & Clothes. w. ISSN 0023-5857

**Amagasinet**
c/o Sigurd B. Hennum, Ed., Postboks 415 Sentrum, Oslo, Norway.
- Amagasinet. w.

**Andaktsbokselskapet**
Munchs Gate 2, Oslo 1, Norway.
- Aarbok for den Norske Kirke. a. ISSN 0400-227X (Bispedoemmeraadenes Fellesraad--Kirkeraadet)

**Andelsselskap av Lastbileiere**
Storgt. 39 III, Oslo 1, Norway.
- Lastebileieren; organ for lastebileiere i norge. m. ISSN 0047-4126

**John A. Antonsen A-S**
Postboks 78, Sentrum, Oslo 1, Norway.
- Tre og Moebler. m (10 per yr) (Norske Trevarefabrikkers Landsforbund) (Co-sponsor: Moebelprodusentenes Landsforbund)

**Arkeologisk Museum i Stavanger**
Storgatan 27, 4000 Stavanger, Norway.
- Arkeologisk Museum i Stavanger. Skrifter. irreg.
- Fra Haug og Heidni. q. ISSN 0015-9255 (Rogalands Arkeologiske Forening)

**H. Aschehoug & Co. (W. Nygaard) A-S**
Sehestedsgt. 3, Oslo 1, Norway
(Subscr. to: Box 6005, Etterstad, Oslo 6, Norway)
- Aschehougs Leksikonservice. q. ISSN 0004-4288
- Samtiden; tidsskrift for politikk, litteratur og samfunnsspoersmaal. m.(Sept-June) ISSN 0036-3928
- Statsoekonomisk Tidsskrift. s-a. ISSN 0039-0720 (Statsoekonomisk Forening)

**Association of Norwegian Road Engineers**
- Vaare Veger/Road Engineering. (pub. by Ingenioerforlaget A-S)

**Avholdsfolkets Opplysningsraad**
Moellergt. 38, Oslo 1, Norway.
- Norsk Tidsskrift Om Alkoholspoersmaalet. 4 per yr. ISSN 0029-2249 (Co-sponsor: Statens Edruskapsdirektorat)

**Baatliv**
Drammensveien 230, Oslo 2, Norway.
- Baatliv. m (10 per year)

**Baker-og Konditormestrenes Landsforening**
Akersgt. 16, Oslo 1, Norway.
- Baker-Konditor. m. ISSN 0005-4062

**Bedriftsoekonomens Forlag**
Kaj Munksvei 41B, Oslo 8, Norway.
- Bedriftsoekonomen. 10 per yr. ISSN 0005-7606 (Norwegian Federation of Business Economists)

**Bergen Bank**
P.O. Box 826, 5001 Bergen, Norway.
- Bergen Banks Kvartalsskrift. q.

**Bergen Turlag**
C. Sundtsgt. 3, 5000 Bergen, Norway.
- Sti og Varde. q. ISSN 0049-2248

**Bergens Kjoepmannsforening**
Taarnplass 3, 5000 Bergen, Norway.
- Kjoepmannen. m (11 per yr)

**Bergens Sjoefart Museum**
Box 2636, 5010 Bergen, Norway.
- Sjoefartshistorisk Aarbok/Norwegian Yearbook of Maritime History. a. ISSN 0080-9888

**Bergverks-Nytt**
Box 1438, 7001 Trondheim, Norway.
- Bergverks-Nytt; the Scandinavian journal of mining and quarrying. m.(except July) ISSN 0005-8971

**Det Beste A-S**
Lilleakerveien 31, Oslo 2, Norway.
- Det Beste fra Reader's Digest (Norwegian Edition) m. ISSN 0005-9684

**Bilgummiverkstedenes Landsforbund**
Waldemar Thranes Gate 1A, Oslo 1, Norway.
- Gummi for All Transport. bi-m.

**Kaare Messel Birkelund, Ed. & Pub.**
Parkveien 5, Oslo 3, Norway.
- Filmjournalen. m. ISSN 0015-1556

**Bispedoemmeraadenes Fellesraad--Kirkeraadet**
- Aarbok for den Norske Kirke. (pub. by Andaktsbokselskapet)

**Bladkompaniet A-S**
Postbox 148, Kaldbakken, Oslo 9, Norway.
- Romantikk. w. ISSN 0035-8142
- Western. fortn. ISSN 0043-3454

**Forlaget Bonytt AS**
Bygdoey Alle 9, Oslo 2, Norway.
- Nye Bonytt/Design for Living; Norsk spesialblad for hus, hjemog boliginnredning. 10 per yr. ISSN 0029-6783

**S.M. Bryde Forlag**
Tordenskjoldsgate 4, Oslo 1, Norway
(Dist. in U.S. by International Publications Service, 114 E. 32nd St., New York, N.Y. 10016)
- Norges Handels-Kalender; Adressbok for Handel, Handverk og Industri. a. ISSN 0078-1215

**Buhre's Forlag**
Drammensvn. 140 L, Oslo, Norway.
- Norsk Motorblad. m. ISSN 0029-2036

**Byggenytt**
Hausmannsgate 21,4, Oslo 1, Norway.
- Byggenytt. s-m (20 per yr)

**J. W. Cappelens Forlag**
Postboks 6005, Etterstad, Oslo, Norway.
- Basar. q.

**Creditreformforeningen for Norge**
Postboks 5387, Oslo 3, Norway.
- Creditreform. s-m. ISSN 0011-1104

**E.K.B. Boktrykkeri**
Platousgate 9, Oslo 1, Norway.
- Revmatikeren. q. (Norsk Revmatike Forbund)

**Egede Institute**
- Norsk Tidsskrift for Misjon. (pub. by Universitetsforlaget)

**Elektroinstallatoerernes Landsforbund**
St. Olavs Gatan 28 , 4, Oslo 1, Norway.
- El-Installasjon og Handel. m (10 per yr)

**A-S Emballering**
Postboks 1754, Vika, Oslo 1, Norway.
- Emballering. m. ISSN 0013-6581

**Entreprenoerernes Landssammenslutning**
Holtegate 26, Oslo 3, Norway.
- Byggeindustrien. m.

**European Consortium for Political Research. Data Information Service**
Gamle Kalvedalsveirn 12, N-5000 Bergen, Norway.
- European Political Data Newsletter. q.

**Export Council of Norway**
Drammensveien 40, Oslo 2, Norway.
- Norway Exports. s-a. ISSN 0029-3628

**Fabritius og Soenner Forlag**
Box 352, Oslo 1, Norway.
- Husmorbladet. m. ISSN 0018-8034 (Norges Husmorforbund)
- Over Alle Grenser. m. ISSN 0030-7335 (Norges Roede Kors)

**A-S Fagpresseforlaget**
P.O. Box 175, 1321 Stabekk, Norway.
- Campingboken. a.

**Fakultetsforeningen Veneficus**
Universitetets Farmasoeytiske Institutt, Oslo 3, Norway.
- Veneficus; tidsskrift for farmasistudenter. m.(Sept-June) ISSN 0042-3351

**Forlaget Familien A-S**
Lille Grensen 3, Oslo 1, Norway.
- Familien. 3 per yr. ISSN 0014-7141

**Farmand**
Roald Amundsensgt. 1, Oslo 1, Norway.
- Farmand; norsk forretningsblad. w. ISSN 0014-8334

**Fearnly & Egers Chartering Co. Ltd.**
Oslo, Norway.
- World Bulk Fleet. irreg.(1-2 per yr)

**Federation of Engineering Industries**
- Maskin. (pub. by Ingenioerforlaget A-S)

**Fellesorganisasjonen Norsk Politiforbund**
Arbeidersamfunnets Pl. 1, Oslo 1, Norway.
- Politibladet. m. (Co-sponsor: Politiets Sentralorganisasjon)

**Feltartillerioffiserenes Forening**
FO/HST/ARTINSP, Oslo-Mil/Huseby, Norway.
- Norsk Artilleri-Tidsskrift. 3 per yr. ISSN 0029-1854 (Co-sponsors: Kystartillinets Offisers Forening; Luftvernartillinets Befalsforbund)

**A-S Fiskaren**
Slottsgt. 3, Box 4053, N-5015 Bergen-Dreggen, Norway.
- Fiskaren. s-w. ISSN 0015-3095

**Fiskeribladet**
Boks 562, 9401 Harstad, Norway.
- Fiskeribladet. d.

**Fiskerinytt A-S**
Veiten 2, 5000 Bergen, Norway.
- Fiskerinytt. m (10 per yr)

**Folkeuniversitetet**
Oevre Slottsgate 6, Oslo 1, Norway.
- Tidsskrift for Voksenopplaering. 6 per yr. ISSN 0040-7216

**Forbrukerraadet**
Boks 8104, Oslo 1, Norway.
- Forbruker-Rapporten. 10 per yr. ISSN 0046-449X

**Foreningen Nordens Forbund**
Arbiensgt. 7, Oslo 2, Norway.
- Vi i Norden. q. ISSN 0506-8339

**Foreningen til Norske Fortidsminnesmerkers Bevaring**
Dronningensgt. 11, Oslo, Norway.
- Foreningen til Norske Fortidsminnesmerkers
  Bevaring. Annual. a. ISSN 0071-7436

**Foreningen til Ski-Idrettens Fremme**
Storgt. 2, Oslo 1, Norway.
- Snoe og Ski. q.

**Forretningsbankenes Konjunkturinstitutt**
Oslo, Norway.
- Norwegian Commercial Banks Financial Review.
  q. ISSN 0029-3660

**A-S Forsikringsletteratur**
Box 2473, Solli, Oslo 2, Norway.
- Forsikringstidende. 10 per yr. ISSN 0015-7929

**Fotografisk Forlag**
2070 Raaholt, Norway.
- Fotografi. m. ISSN 0046-4805

**Fraktefartoyenes Rederiforening**
Boks 198, Bergen, Norway.
- Fraktemann. 6 per yr. ISSN 0015-9352

**Frisporg**
Universitetsgt 14, Oslo 1, Norway.
- Frisporg; radio, literatur, kunst. 20 per yr.

**Frukt og Tobakkhandlernes Landsforbund**
Torvgt. 30, Oslo 1, Norway.
- Tobakk-Frukt-Sjokolade. 8 per yr. ISSN 0049-
  3961

**Futurum Forlag A-S**
Hjelmsgate 3, Oslo 3, Norway.
- Gateavisa. m.

**Gauldal Historielag**
Melhus, Norway.
- Gauldalsminne; arbok for bygdehistorie og
  folkeminne. irreg.

**Grafiske Bedrifters Landsforening**
Akersgt. 16, Oslo 1, Norway.
- Norsk Grafisk Tidsskrift. m. ISSN 0029-1978

**Groendahl og Soens Boktrykkeri**
Munkedamsveien 35, Oslo 2, Norway.
- Veterinaerer. a. (Norway. Veterinaerdirektoratet)

**Gyldendal Norsk Forlag**
Universitetsgt. 16, Oslo 1, Norway.
- Kirke og Kultur. m (10 per yr.) ISSN 0023-186X
- Kunst og Kultur. q. ISSN 0023-5415
- Vinduet; Gyldendals tidsskrift for litteratur. q.
  ISSN 0042-6288

**Handelens Samarbeidsorgan for Jordbruksvarer**
Karl Johansgate 1, Oslo 1, Norway.
- Tun og Torg. q.

**Handelsbestyrer Forbundet**
Arbeidersamfundets Plass 1, Oslo 1, Norway.
- Handelsbestyreren. m (11 per yr)

**Hedmark Slektshistorielag**
Box 2, 2314 Espa, Norway.
- Hedmark Slektshistorielags Tidsskrift. s-a. ISSN
  0046-7170

**Heimevernsbladet**
Oslo Mil/Huseby, Oslo 1, Norway.
- Heimevernsbladet. 11 per yr. ISSN 0017-985X

**A-S Hjemmet**
Kristian IV. Gt. 13, Oslo 1, Norway.
- Donald Duck & Co. w.
- Hjemmet. w. ISSN 0018-2842
- Oekonomisk Rapport. 22 per yr.

**Holmes Forlag**
Sandbrugate 3, 5015 Bergen-Dreggen, Norway.
- Maritime News. q.

**I K O'S Laeremidler A-S**
Munchsgate 2, Oslo 1, Norway.
- Prismet; pedagogisk tidsskrift. 10 per yr. ISSN
  0032-8847 (Institutt for Kristen Oppeding)

**A-S Informativ Reklame**
Akersgaten 64, Oslo 1, Norway.
- Hjem og Fritid. s-a.
- Huset Vaart. 3 per yr. ISSN 0018-7976

**Ingenioerforlaget A-S**
Ingenioerenes Hus, P.O. Box 2476, Solli, Oslo 2,
Norway.
- Elektro; elektroteknisk tidsskrift. 22 per yr. ISSN
  0013-550X (Norwegian Electro-technical Society)
  (Co-sponsor: Association of Norwegian Electricity
  Supply Undertakers)
- Kjemi; tidsskrift for kjemi, bergvesen og
  metallurgi. m. ISSN 0023-1983 (Norsk Kjemisk
  Selskap) (Co-sponsors: Norwegian Metallurgical
  Society; Norwegian Society of Professional
  Engineers; Polytechnic Society)
- Maskin; mechanical, production and marine
  engineering. m. ISSN 0025-4614 (Federation of
  Engineering Industries) (Co-sponsor: Norwegian
  Association of Industrial Engineering)
- Norsk Oljerevy/Norwegian Oil Review. 10 per yr.
  (Norwegian Society of Professional Engineers)
  (Co-sponsors: Association of Norwegian
  Engineers; Polytechnic Society)
- Plan/Bygg; Tidsskrift for bygg og anlegg. 10 per
  yr. (Norwegian Society of Professional Engineers)
  (Co-sponsor: Polytechnic Society)
- Stud-Teknikk/Students-Technology. 6 per yr.
  (Norwegian Association for Students of
  Technology)
- Teknisk Ukeblad-TU; the engineer's weekly. 75
  per yr. ISSN 0040-2354 (Norske Sivilingenioerers
  Forening) (Co-Sponsors: Polytekniske Forening;
  Norges Ingenioerorganisasjon NITO)
- Vaare Veger/Road Engineering. 10 per yr.
  (Association of Norwegian Road Engineers) (Co-
  sponsor: Norwegian Society of Professional
  Engineers)

**Institutt for Kristen Oppeding**
- Prismet. (pub. by I K O'S Laeremidler A-S)

**Instituttet for Markedsfoering**
Kronprinsensgt. 9, Oslo, Norway.
- Markedskommunikasjon; periodical for marketing.
  3 per yr. ISSN 0025-3510

**Instituttet for Merkantil Informasjon A-S**
N. Kirkebyvei 11, 1350 Lommedalen, Norway.
- Skipsfartens Innkjoepsbok. a.

**Interflora Norge AS**
Motzfeldtsgate 1, Oslo 1, Norway.
- Blomsterbinderen. m (11 per yr.) (Co-sponsor:
  Norsk Blomsterhandlerforbund)

**International Committee on Laboratory Animals**
National Institute of Public Health, Postuttak, Oslo
1, Norway.
- I C L A Bulletin. s-a. ISSN 0018-8956
- International Committee on Laboratory Animals.
  Proceedings of Symposium. quadrennial, 1969,
  4th, Washington, D.C. ISSN 0074-2805

**International Palaeontological Association**
- Lethaia. (pub. by Universitetsforlaget)

**International Seaweed Symposium**
c/o Dr. A. Jensen, Norwegian Institute of Seaweed
Research, 7034 Trondheim NTH, Norway.
- International Seaweed Symposium. Proceedings.
  irreg., 1974, 8th, Bangor, UK. ISSN 0074-7874

**International Seed Testing Association**
Box 68, N-1432 Aas-NLH, Norway.
- I S T A News Bulletin. q. ISSN 0019-0713
- Seed Science and Technology. q.

**International Union of Forest Research Organizations**
c/o Ivar Samset, Pres., Norwegian Forest Research
Institute, N-1432 Aas-NLH, Norway.
- International Union of Forest Research
  Organizations. Congress Proceedings. Rapports du
  Congres. Kongressberichte. irreg., 16th, 1973,
  Oslo. ISSN 0074-9400

**K N A Forlaget A-S**
Hansteensgt. 9, Oslo 2, Norway.
- Motorliv; Norsk bilmagasin. 10 per yr. ISSN
  0027-2337 (Kongelig Norsk Automobilklub)

**Kjoettbransjens Landsforbund**
St. Olavsgate 28, Oslo, Norway.
- Kjoettbransjen. m.

**Knudsens Reklamebyraa**
Oevre Slottsgate 5, Oslo 1, Norway.
- Pulsen. q. ISSN 0552-5934 (Rikshospitalet)

**Kommunale Kinematografers Landsforbund**
Nedre Vollgate 9, Oslo 1, Norway.
- Film og Kino; Norsk filmblad. 8-10 per yr. ISSN
  0015-1351

**Kompass Norge A-S**
Steinkargt. 10, N-4000 Stavanger, Norway
(Dist. by Iliffe NTP Inc., 300 E. 42 St., New York,
N.Y. 10017)
- Kompass Norge; indeks over Norges industri og
  Naeringsliv. a. ISSN 0075-6709 (Foundation for
  Promoting International Economic Information
  SZ)

**Kongelig Norsk Automobilklub**
- Motorliv. (pub. by K N A Forlaget A-S)

**Kongelig Norsk Motorbaat Forbund**
Box 576, 5001 Bergen, Norway.
- Sjoesport. 8 per yr. ISSN 0037-6000

**Kongelige Norske Videnskabers Selskab**
Erling Skakkes Gt. 47, 7000 Trondheim, Norway.
- Kongelige Norske Videnskabers Selskab.
  Forhandlinger. (pub. by Universitetsforlaget)
- Kongelige Norske Videnskabers Selskab. Museet.
  Miscellanea. irreg. (approx. 5 per yr.)
- Kongelige Norske Videnskabers Selskab. Skrifter.
  (pub. by Universitetsforlaget)

**Kontorteknisk Landsforening**
Tidemandsgt. 43a, Oslo 2, Norway.
- Kontorteknikk. bi-m. ISSN 0023-3730

**Kraftfornytt**
Postboks 326, 5001 Bergen, Norway.
- Kraftfornytt. q.

**Krigsskoleutdannede Offiserers Landsforening**
Postboks 5338, Majorstuen, Oslo 3, Norway.
- Vaart Vern. bi-m. ISSN 0042-2037

**Kristelig Folkeparti**
Skedsmogate 25, Oslo 6, Norway.
- Folkets Framtid. s-w.

**Kristelig Legeforening i Norge**
Rikshospitalet, Oslo 1, Norway.
- Inter Medicos. q. (Co-sponsor: Kristelig
  Medisinerkrets i Oslo)

**Kunstindustrimuseet i Oslo**
St. Olavs Gate, Oslo 1, Norway.
- Kunstindustrimuseet i Oslo. Aarbok. irreg.

**A-S Landbruksforlaget**
Boks 3647, Gamlebyen, Oslo 1, Norway.
- Norsk Landbruk. s-m.

**A-S Landbrukstidende**
Boendernes Hus, 7000 Trondheim, Norway.
- Landbrukstidende; tidsskrift for landbruket i
  Troendelag. w. ISSN 0023-7833

**A-L Landbrukstidsskriftet Norden**
Boks 355, 8001 Bodoe, Norway.
- Norden; nord-norges landbrukstidsskrift. fortn.
  ISSN 0029-1226

**Landslaget for Bygde- og Byhistorie**
- Heimen. (pub. by Universitetsforlaget)
- Landslaget for Bygde- og Byhistorie. Skrifter.
  (pub. by Universitetsforlaget)

**Landslaget for Reiselivet i Norge**
H. Heyerdahlsgt 1, Oslo 1, Norway.
- Reiseliv. m. (Co-sponsor: Norske
  Reisebyraaforening)

**Landslaget Forming i Skolen**
Eventyrvejen 4, 2800 Gjoevik, Norway.
- Ide og Form. q. ISSN 0046-8525

**Landslaget Musikk i Skolen**
Eckersbergsgate 57a, Oslo 3, Norway.
- Musikk i Skolen. 5 per yr.

**Landsorganisasjonen i Norge**
Youngsgt. 11, Oslo 1, Norway.
- Fri Fagbevegelse. s-m. ISSN 0046-5089
- Trade Union News Bulletin from Norway. m.
  ISSN 0041-0519

**Lunde Forlag og Bokhandel A-S**
Boks 540, C. Sundtsgt. 2, Bergen, Norway.
- Fast Grunn. bi-m. ISSN 0014-8733

**Harald Lyche og Co. A-S**
N. Strandgate 7, 3000 Drammen, Norway.
- Sykehuset. 8 per yr. (Norske Sykehusforening)

**Malermestrenes Landsforbund**
St. Olavsgate 28, Oslo, Norway.
- Maleren. m (11 per yr)

**Maskinentreprenoerenes Forbund**
Postboks 1570, Vika, Oslo, Norway.
- Anleggsmaskinen. m. ISSN 0003-3715

**Matematisk Institutt**
Blindern, Oslo 3, Norway.
- Nordisk Mathematisk Tidskrift. q. ISSN 0029-1412

**Mekaniske Verksteders Landsforening**
Oscars Gate 20, Box 7072-H, Oslo 3, Norway.
- Jernindustri; bransjetidsskrift for Norsk verkstedsindustri. m. ISSN 0021-5899

**Mental Barnehjelp**
Arbiens Gt. 1, Oslo 2, Norway.
- Sinnets Helse. 8 per yr. ISSN 0049-0563

**Moderne Databehandling**
Box 107, N-1701 Sarpsborg, Norway.
- Moderne Databehandling. q.

**Moebelhandlernes Landsforbund**
Postboks 3, 1343 Elksmarka, Norway.
- Moebelhandleren. m (10 per yr)

**Ernst G. Mortensens Forlag**
Soerkedalsveien 10 A, Oslo 3, Norway.
- Norsk Ukeblad. w. ISSN 0029-2257
- Det Nye. w. ISSN 0048-122X
- Vi Menn. w. ISSN 0042-4951

**Motorfoerernes Avholdsforbund**
Storgt. 38, Oslo 1, Norway.
- Motorfoereren. m. ISSN 0027-2213

**Naa**
Oscarsgate 53, Oslo 2, Norway.
- Naa. w.

**Nasjonalforeningen for Folkehelsen**
Postboks 7139, Homansbyen, Oslo 3, Norway.
- Helsenytt. bi-m. ISSN 0018-0157

**A-S Nordanger-Bergen og Park Forlag**
Postboks 731, 5001 Bergen, Norway.
- Norsk Fiskaralmanakk. a. (Selskabet for de Norske Fiskeriers Fremme)

**Nordic Association for American Studies**
- American Studies in Scandinavia. (pub. by Universitetsforlaget)
- Nordiske Sallskapet foer Amerikstudier. Publications/Nordic Association for American Studies. Publications. (pub. by Universitetsforlaget)

**Nordic Committee for the Study of International Politics**
- Cooperation and Conflict. (pub. by Universitetsforlaget)

**Nordisk Forlag A-S**
Thv. Meyersgate 72, Oslo 5, Norway.
- Alle Kvinner; magazine for women. w. ISSN 0002-5682
- Alle Menn. w.
- Alt Om Mat. m (13 per yr.)
- Novelle Journalen. fortn.

**Nordisk Kriminalteknisk Tidsskrift**
c/o Lars l'Abee-Lund, Box 8017, Oslo, Norway.
- Nordisk Kriminalteknisk Tidsskrift. q. ISSN 0029-1390

**Nordisk Skibsrederforening**
Kristinelundvei 22, Oslo 2, Norway.
- Nordiske Domme i Sjofartsanliggender. irreg. ISSN 0085-4220

**Nordiske Jordbrugsforskeres Forening**
Wergelandsvein 15, Oslo 1, Norway.
- Nordisk Jordbrugsforskning. q. ISSN 0048-0495

**Nordiske Sallskapet Foer Amerikstudier**
*see* **Nordic Association for American Studies**

**Nordmanns-Forbundet**
Raadhusgt. 23 B, Oslo, Norway.
- Norseman; a review of current events. bi-m. ISSN 0029-1846

**Norges Almenvitenskapelige Forskningsraad**
Munthesgate 29, Oslo 2, Norway.
- Maal og Minne. (pub. by Norske Samlaget)
- Norges Almenvitenskapelige Forskiningsraad. Forskningsnytt/Norwegian Research Council for Science and the Humanities. Research News. (pub. by Universitetsforlaget)
- Research in Norway. a.

**Norges Apotekerforening**
Box 2566, Solli, Oslo 2, Norway.
- Norges Apotekerforenings Tidsskrift. s-m. ISSN 0029-1668

**Norges Astma- og Allergiforbund**
Prinsensgate 22, Oslo 1, Norway.
- Astma-og Allergi-Nytt. 5 per yr. ISSN 0004-6086

**Norges Automobil-Forbund**
Storgaten 2, Postboks 494, Oslo 1, Norway.
- Med Bil i Europa; samt Algerie, Marokko og Tunisia. a.
- Motor. m. ISSN 0027-173X

**Norges Bank**
Box 336, Oslo 1, Norway.
- Norges Bank. Economic Bulletin. q. ISSN 0029-1676 (prep. by its Pengepolitisk Avdeling)
- Norges Bank. Report and Accounts. a. ISSN 0078-1185
- Penger og Kreditt. q. (prep. by its Pengepolitisk Avdeling)

**Norges Bilbransjeforbund**
Drammensv. 97, Oslo 2, Norway.
- Bilbransjen/Bilteknisk Fagblad. m. ISSN 0006-2367
- Oljebladet. m. ISSN 0030-2120

**Norges Bondelag**
Postboks 3747, Gamlebyen, Oslo 1, Norway.
- Bondebladet. w. (fortn. in summer) (Co-sponsor: Landbrukets Sentralforbund)

**Norges Colonialgrossisters Forbund**
Karl Johansgt. 1, Postboks 639, Oslo 1, Norway.
- Fritt Kjoepmannskap. fortn. ISSN 0016-1519

**Norges Dame og Herrefrisoermestres Forbund**
Rosenkrantzgate 7, Oslo 1, Norway.
- Norske Dame- og Herrefrisoer. (8 per year)

**Norges Drosjeeier Forbund**
Trondhjemsveien 100, Postboks 6538, Oslo 5, Norway.
- Norsk Drosjeeierblad. m. ISSN 0048-0584

**Norges Eksportraad**
Drammensvn. 40, Oslo 2, Norway.
- Norges Utenrikshandel. m. ISSN 0029-1722

**Norges Elektrohandlerforbund**
Fagertunveien 23, 1340 Bekkestua, Norway.
- Elektro-Handel; merkantilt og teknisk tidsskrift for elektrobransjen. m. ISSN 0046-1776

**Norges Farmaceutiske Forening**
Lille Grensen 5, Oslo 1, Norway.
- Norsk Farmaceutisk Tidsskrift. bi-m. ISSN 0029-1935

**Norges Fiskarlag**
Postboks 519, 7001 Trondheim, Norway.
- Me'a. m.

**Norges Forsvarsforening**
Sporveisgaten 29, Oslo 3, Norway.
- Norges Forsvar. m. ISSN 0029-1692

**Norges Fotohandlerforbund**
Revesporet 4 B, 1347 Hosle, Norway.
- Norsk Fag Foto. m.(except Jan. & Aug) ISSN 0029-1900 (Co-sponsor: Norges Fotografforbund)

**Norges Geotekniske Institutt**
P.O. Box 40 Taasen, Oslo-8, Norway.
- Norges Geotekniske Institutt. Publikasjon. irreg., no. 115, 1977. ISSN 0078-1193
- Norges Geotekniske Institutt. Technical Report. irreg., no. 14, 1976. ISSN 0078-1207

**Norges Glass- og Stentoeihandleres Forbund**
Dronningensgt. 13, Oslo 1, Norway.
- Glassposten; fagblad for glass- , porselen og stentoeybransjen. m. 10 per yr. ISSN 0046-6018

**Norges Grossistforbund**
Annonseavdeling, Rosenborggt. 26, Oslo 3, Norway.
- Norge Grossisttidende. m (10 per yr)

**Norges Gullsmedforbund**
Storgaten 14., Oslo 1, Norway.
- Gullsmedkunst. m (11 per yr.) ISSN 0046-6603

**Norges Gymnastikk- og Turnforbund**
Hauger Skolevei 1, 1346 Gjettum, Norway.
- Gymnastikk og Turn. 10 per yr. ISSN 0017-596X

**Norges Handelsstands Forbund**
- Naeringsrevyen. (pub. by Bjarne H. Reenskaug A-S)

**Norges Husflidslag**
Oevre Slottsgt.8, Oslo 1, Norway.
- Norsk Husflid. bi-m. ISSN 0048-0592

**Norges Husmorforbund**
- Husmorbladet. (pub. by Fabritius og Soenner Forlag)

**Norges Idrettsforbund**
Hauger Skolevei 1, 1351 Rud, Norway.
- Norsk Idrett. m. ISSN 0029-1994

**Norges Industriforbund**
Drammensveien 40, Oslo 2, Norway.
- Norges Industri. fortn. ISSN 0029-1706

**Norges Jeger- og Fiskerforbund**
Hvalstadaasen 7, Box 98, 1364 Hvalstaad, Norway.
- Jakt-Fiske-Friluftsliv. m. ISSN 0021-4051

**Norges Jernvarehandlerforbund**
Drammensveien 30, Oslo 2, Norway.
- Jernvare Bygg Hobby. m.

**Norges Jordskiftedommer- og Landmaalersamband**
Postboks 29, 1432 Aas-NLH, Norway.
- Kart og Plan. q. ISSN 0047-3278

**Norges Juristforbund**
Grev Wedelsplass 5, Oslo 1, Norway.
- Jurist-Kontakt. m (10 per yr)

**Norges Kjoebannsblad A-S**
Postboks 2518, Solli, Oslo 2, Norway.
- Norges Kjoebmannsblad. w (45 per yr)

**Norges Kobber-og Blikkenslagermesteres Landsforbund**
Rosenkrantzgt. 7, Oslo 1, Norway.
- Kobber- og Blikkenslagermesteren. m. ISSN 0023-2505

**Norges Kooperative Fellesforbund**
Revierstredet 2, Oslo 1, Norway.
- Forbrukeren; periodical for the consumer cooperation in Norway. 10 per yr. ISSN 0015-6930

**Norges Kooperative Landsforening**
Revierstredet 2, Oslo 2, Norway.
- Vaart Blad. bi-w (25 per yr)

**Norges Laererhoegskole**
*see under* **Universitetet i Trondheim**

**Norges Landbrukshoegskole. Institutt for Bygningsteknikk**
Box 15, N-1432 Aas-NLH, Norway.
- Norges Landbrukshoegskole. Institutt for Bygningsteknikk. Aarsmelding. Annual Report. a. ISSN 0065-0226
- Norges Landbrukshoegskole. Institutt for Bygningsteknikk. Hyggekostanadsindeks for Driftsbygninger i Jordbruket. Prisutviklingen. a. ISSN 0065-0218
- Norges Landbrukshoegskole. Institutt for Bygningsteknikk. Melding. irreg., no. 89, 1977. ISSN 0065-0234

**Norges Landbrukshoegskole. Institutt for Jordskifte og Eizndomsutforming**
Box 15, N-1432 Aas-NLH, Norway.
- Norges Landbrukshoegskole. Institutt for Jordskifte og Eizndomsutforming. Melding. irreg., no. 17, 1974. ISSN 0065-0242

**Norges Landbruksoekonomiske Institutt**
Postboks 8024 Oslo-Dep, Oslo 1, Norway.
- Norges Landbruksoekonomiske Institutt.
Driftsgranskinger i Jordbruker. a. ISSN 0078-1223

**Norges Lastebileier-Forbund**
Chr. Krohgsgt. 32A, Oslo 1, Norway.
- Lastebilen. m. ISSN 0023-8686

**Norges Lotteforbund**
Oslo Mil/Akershus, Oslo 1, Norway.
- Lottebladet. m (10 per yr.)

**Norges Markedsforbund**
Sandakerveien 56 A, Oslo 4, Norway.
- Markedsfoering. m(11 per yr.) ISSN 0025-3502

**Norges Pedagogiske Landslag**
Pedagogisk Institutt, Norges Laererhoegskole, 7000
Trondheim, Norway.
- Norsk Pedagogisk Tidskrift. 10 per yr. ISSN
0029-2052

**Norges Pelsdyravlsag**
Oekerntorgvei 13, Oslo 5, Norway.
- Norsk Pelsdyrblad. m.

**Norges Rederforbund**
Raadhusgaten 25, Oslo 1, Norway.
- Sjoemann. bi-m. (Co-sponsor: Skibsfartens
Arbeidsgiverforening)

**Norges Roede Kors**
- Over Alle Grenser. (pub. by Fabritius og Soenner
Forlag)

**Norges Rutebileierforbund**
Postboks 6708, St. Olavs Plass, Oslo 1, Norway.
- Rutebiltidende. m. ISSN 0048-8836

**Norges Seilforbund**
- Sejlsport. (pub. by Seilsport Maritimt Forlag)

**Norges Skibsfoererforbund**
Hafrsfjordgate 11, Oslo 2, Norway.
- Norsk Skibsfoerertidende. m. ISSN 0048-0606

**Norges Skipsforskningsinstitutt**
7034 Trondheim-NTH, Norway.
- Norges Skipsforskningsinstitutt. Aarsberetning. a.
- Ship Abstracts; information service on ship
technology, ship operation and ocean engineering.
10 per yr. ISSN 0346-1025 (Co-sponsors:
Netherland Maritime Institute; Swedish Ship
Research Foundations; Association of Finnish
Shipbuilders)

**Norges Skogeierforbund**
Stortingsgaten 30, Oslo 1, Norway.
- Skogeieren. m. ISSN 0037-6396

**Norges Skogtekniskforbund**
Bogstadvejen 8, Oslo 3, Norway.
- Skogteknikeren. 5 per yr.

**Norges Skokjoepmenns Forbund**
Haakon 7 Gt. 2, Oslo 1, Norway.
- Skotoey. 14 per yr. ISSN 0049-0679 (Co-sponsor:
Norske Skofabrikkers Landssammenslutning)

**Norges Skomakermesterforbund**
Grensen 3, Oslo, Norway.
- Norsk Skomakertidende. 10 per yr. ISSN 0029-
2125

**Norges Sportshandleres Forbund**
Drammensvn. 30, Oslo 2, Norway.
- Sport. m.

**Norges Standardiseringsforbund**
Haakon VII'sGate 2, Oslo 1, Norway.
- Standardisering. bi-m. ISSN 0038-9625

**Norges Statsautoriserte Revisorers Forening**
Uranienborg Terrasse 9, Oslo 3, Norway.
- Revisjon og Regnskap. 8 per yr.

**Norges Stoperitekniske Forening**
Box 1717 H, Oslo 2, Norway.
- Stoperitidende. 6 per yr. ISSN 0039-1824

**Norges Tapetser- og Salmakermestres Landsforening**
Rosenkrantzgt. 7, Oslo 1, Norway.
- Tapetsereren. q. ISSN 0039-9574

**Norges Teknisk-Naturvitenskapelige Forskningsraad**
Gaustadalleen 30, Oslo 3, Norway.
- Norges Teknisk-Naturvitenskapelige
Forskningsraad. Aarsberetning. a. ISSN 0078-
1231
- Norwegian Maritime Research. (pub. by Selvigs
Forlag A-S)

**Norges Teknisk-Naturvitenskapelige Forskningsraad.
Transportoekonomisk Institutt**
Stasjonsveien 4, Slemdal/Oslo 3, Norway.
- Norges Teknisk-Naturvitenskapelige
Forskningsraad. Transportoekonomisk Institutt.
Aarsberetning. a. ISSN 0078-124X

**Norges Tekniske Hoegskole**
see under **Universitetet i Trondheim**

**Norges Unge Venstre**
Mollergt. 16, Oslo 1, Norway.
- Populist. q.

**Norges Urmakerforbund**
Drammensveien 49, Oslo 2, Norway.
- Ur. m.

**Norges Veterinarhoegskole**
Postboks 8146, Oslo-Dep, Oslo 1, Norway.
- Norges Veterinarhoegskole. Aarsberetning/
Veterinary College of Norway. Annual Report. a.
ISSN 0078-6713
- Norges Veterinarhoegskole. Publikasjoner/
Veterinary College of Norway. Publications. a.
ISSN 0078-6721

**Norigon A-S**
Postboks 693, 5001 Bergen, Norway.
- Skips Revyen. 8 per yr.

**Noroil Publishing House Ltd.**
P.O. Box 480, 4001 Stavanger, Norway.
- Noroil; Norwegian oil and gas journal. m.

**Norsk Aero Klubb**
Nedre Slottsgate 17, Oslo 1, Norway.
- Fly-Nytt. m (10 per yr)

**Norsk Apoteknikerforbund**
Snorresgate 10, Oslo 1, Norway.
- Apotek - Teknikeren. m (11 per yr)

**Norsk Arbeidsgiverforening**
Kr. Augustsgate 23, Oslo 1, Norway.
- Arbeidsgiveren. s-m.

**Norsk Arkeologisk Selskap**
Frederiksgt. 2-3, Oslo 1, Norway.
- Viking; tidsskrift for Norron arkeologi/journal of
Norse archaeology. a.

**Norsk Baatinformasjon**
Postboks 317, 1601 Fredrikstad, Norway.
- Norsk Baatindustri. bi-m.

**Norsk Botanisk Forening**
- Blyttia. (pub. by Universitetsforlaget)

**Norsk Brannvern Forening**
Postboks 7132, Homansbyen, Oslo 3, Norway.
- Mot Brann. 8 per yr.

**Norsk Bygningsindustriarbeiderforbund**
Henrik Ibsens Gate 7, Oslo 1, Norway.
- Bygningsarbeideren. m (9 per yr)

**Norsk Dampkjelforening**
Hoffsveien 13, Oslo 2, Norway.
- Norsk Dampkjelforening. Meddelelser. q. ISSN
0048-0576

**Norsk Elektriker- og Kraftstasjonforbund**
Youngsgate 11, Oslo, Norway.
- Elektrikeren. 10 per yr. ISSN 0013-5410

**Norsk Entomologisk Forening**
- Norwegian Journal of Entomology/Norsk
Entomologisk Tidsskrift. (pub. by
Universitetsforlaget)

**Norsk Esperanto- Forbund**
see **Norvega Esperantista Ligo**

**Norsk Faktorforbund**
- Norsk Faktortidende. (pub. by Oslo
Faktorforening)

**Norsk Farmaceutisk Selskap**
Soerli Gt. 8, Oslo 5, Norway.
- Norsk Farmaceutisk Selskap. Meddelelser. q.
ISSN 0029-1927

**Norsk Filatelistforbund**
P.O. Box 875, Sentrum, Oslo 1, Norway.
- Norsk Filatelistisk Tidsskrift. 10 per yr.

**Norsk Fjoerfeavlslag**
Sandakerveien 104 B, Oslo 4, Norway.
- Fjoerfe. m. ISSN 0015-3354

**Norsk Folkemuseum**
Bygdoey, Oslo 2, Norway.
- By og Bygd; Norsk Folkemuseums aarbok. a.
ISSN 0084-8212

**Norsk Forening for Luftrett**
- Arkiv for Luftrett/Scandinavian Journal of Air
Law. (pub. by Universitetsforlaget)

**Norsk Forening for Sosialt Arbeide**
Boks 225, Oekern, Oslo 5, Norway.
- Sosialt Forum/Sosialt Arbeid. 10 per yr.

**Norsk Forening for Varme- , Ventilasjon- og
Sanitaerteknikk**
- Norsk V V S. (pub. by Skarland Press A-S)

**Norsk Forstmannsforening**
- Norsk Skogbruk. (pub. by Norske Skogselskap)

**Norsk Galvano Teknisk Landsforening**
Rosenkrantzgt. 7, Oslo 1, Norway.
- Galvano Teknisk Tidsskrift. q. ISSN 0046-5372

**Norsk Gartnerforbund**
Motzfeldtsgt. 1, Oslo 1, Norway.
- Gartneryrket. w. ISSN 0046-5437

**Norsk Geologisk Forening**
- Norsk Geologisk Tidsskrift/Norwegian Journal of
Geology. (pub. by Universitetsforlaget)

**Norsk Hotell og Restaurantforbund**
Karl Johansgate 21, Oslo 1, Norway.
- Norsk Hotell og Restaurantblad. bi-w.

**Norsk Innkjoepslederforbund**
Trondheimsvn. 80, Oslo 5, Norway.
- Innkjoep. m.(except July) ISSN 0020-160X

**Norsk Institutt for By- og Regionforskning**
Brekkev. 22-24, Oslo 8, Norway.
- N I B R Rapport. irreg. ISSN 0085-4263

**Norsk Institutt for Vannforskning**
Postboks 333, Blindern, Oslo 3, Norway.
- Norsk Institutt for Vannforskning. Aarsbok. a.

**Norsk Instituut for Kosmisk Fysikk**
Nordlysobservatoriet, N-9000 Tromsoe, Norway.
- Norske Instituut for Kosmisk Fysikk. Publications.
irreg.

**Norsk Journalistag**
Rosenkrantzgate 3, Oslo 1, Norway.
- Journalisten. m (11 per yr) (Co-sponsor: Norsk
Redaktoer Forening)

**Norsk Kafeforbund**
Kongensgate 31, Oslo 1, Norway.
- Kafebladet. m.

**Norsk Kennel Klub**
Teglverksgate 8, Oslo 5, Norway.
- Hundesport. m (10 per yr)

**Norsk Kjemisk Selskap**
- Kjemi. (pub. by Ingenioerforlaget A-S)

**Norsk Laererlag**
Rosenkrantzgt. 15, Oslo 1, Norway.
- Norsk Skoleblad. w. ISSN 0029-2117
- Vaar Skole/Our School. 4 per yr. ISSN 0042-2029

**Norsk Landbruksakademikerforbund**
Postbok 7051, Homansbyen, Oslo 3, Norway.
- N L F-Nytt. m (10 per yr)

**Norsk Lektorlag**
Wergelandsveren 15, Oslo 1, Norway.
- Skoleforum. fortn.

**Norsk Musikerforbund**
- Norsk Musikerblad. (pub. by A-S Penn-Inform)

**Norsk Musikksamling**
Observatoriegt. 1, Oslo 2, Norway.
- Norsk Musikkgranskning. Aarbok. irreg.

**Norsk Ornitologisk Forening**
- Sterna. (pub. by Stavanger Museum)

**Norsk Pedagogikklag**
- Pedagogisk Forskning. (pub. by Universitetsforlaget)

**Norsk Plastforening**
- Plastnytt. (pub. by Skarland Press A-S)

**Norsk Polarinstitutt**
Postboks 158, 1330 Oslo Lufthavn, Norway
- Norsk Polarinstitutt. Aarbok. a. ISSN 0085-4271 (Dist. in the U.S. by: Universitetsforlaget, Box 142, Boston, MA 02113)

**Norsk Psykologforening**
Bjorn Farmannsgate 16, Oslo 2, Norway.
- Norsk Psykologforening. Tidsskrift. m.

**Norsk Revmatike Forbund**
- Revmatikeren. (pub. by E.K.B. Boktrykkeri)

**Norsk Rikskringkasting**
Bjoernstjerne Bjoernsons Plass 1, Oslo 3, Norway.
- Norsk Rikskringkasting. Programbladet. w. ISSN 0033-0353

**Norsk Sau- og Geitalslag**
Parkveien 71, Oslo 2, Norway.
- Sau og Geit. bi-m. ISSN 0036-5009

**Norsk Senter for Informatikk**
Forskningsveien 1, Oslo 3, Norway.
- Ajour-Industri-Teknikk. m.
- Norsk Senter for Informatikk. Artikkel Indeks. m (10 per yr)

**Norsk Sjoefartsmuseum**
Bygdoeynesveien 37, Oslo 2, Norway.
- Norsk Sjoefartsmuseum. Aarsberetning. a.

**Norsk Sjoemannsforbund**
Grev Wedels Plass 7, Oslo 1, Norway.
- Norsk Sjoemannsforbund. Medlemsblad. m.(11 per yr.) ISSN 0029-2079

**Norsk Skattebetaleforening**
Kongensgate 6, Oslo 1, Norway.
- Skatt og Budsjett. 8 per yr.

**Norsk Skog- og Landarbeiderforbund**
Arbeidersambunnets Plass 1, Oslo 1, Norway.
- Skog- og Landarbeideren. bi-m.

**Norsk Skogindustri**
Drammensveien 30, Oslo 2, Norway.
- Norsk Skogindustri; journal for the Norwegian paper, pulp, timber and wallboard industries. m. ISSN 0029-2095

**Norsk Slektshistorisk Forening**
Oevre Slottsgate 17, Oslo, Norway.
- Norsk Slektshistorisk Tidsskrift. s-a. ISSN 0029-2141

**Norsk Speidergutforbund**
Moellergate 43, Oslo 1, Norway.
- Speideren. bi-m.

**Norsk Spraakraad**
Postboks 8107 Dep, Oslo 1, Norway.
- Spraaknytt. q.

**Norsk Styrmandsforening**
Arbiensgt. 11, Oslo 2, Norway.
- Norsk Styrmandsblad. m (11 per yr.) ISSN 0029-215X

**Norsk Sveiseteknisk Forening**
Kr. Augustsgt. 5, Oslo 1, Norway.
- Sveiseteknikk. bi-m. ISSN 0039-6427

**Norsk Sykepleierforbund**
Postboks 3649, Gamlebyen, Oslo 1, Norway.
- Sykepleien. s-m. ISSN 0039-7628

**Norsk Tannvern**
Brockmannsgt. 9, Oslo 4, Norway.
- Munnpleien. 4 per yr. ISSN 0047-8377

**Norsk Teknisk Museum.**
Fyrstikkalleen 1, Oslo 6, Norway.
- Norsk Teknisk Museum. Yearbook. a. ISSN 0048-2277

**Norsk Tekstil Teknisk Forbund**
Lars Hillesgt. 34, 5000 Bergen, Norway.
- Norsk Tekstiltidende. m. ISSN 0029-2168

**Norsk Tidsskrift for Sjakk**
Box 121, N-1346 Gjettum, Norway.
- Norsk Tidsskrift for Sjakk. 9 per yr. ISSN 0048-0614

**Norsk Utenrikspolitisk Institutt**
Bygdoey Alle 3, Postboks 8159, Oslo Dep., Oslo 1, Norway.
- Internasjonal Politikk. q. ISSN 0020-577X
- Norsk Utenrikspolitisk Arbok. irreg.

**Norsk Yrkes- og Husstellaererlag**
Fridtjof Nansenspl. 8, Oslo 1, Norway.
- Yrke. m. ISSN 0049-8475

**Norsk Zoologisk Forening**
Universitetet i Oslo, Zoologisk Museum, Sarsgt. 1, Oslo 5, Norway.
- Fauna. q. ISSN 0014-8881

**Norske Advokatforening**
Kongensgt. 6, Oslo 1, Norway.
- Norsk Advokatblad. m (10 per yr)
- Norsk Retstidende. 22-24 per yr. ISSN 0029-2060
- Rettens Gang. m (12-13 per yr.) ISSN 0034-6187

**Norske Arbeiderparti**
Youngstorget 2, Oslo, Norway.
- Sosialistisk Perspektiv. bi-m. ISSN 0049-1330

**Norske Arkitekters Landsforbund**
Josefinesgt. 34, Oslo 3, Norway.
- Arkitektnytt. fortn.(20 per yr) ISSN 0004-1998 (Co-sponsor: Norske Landskapsarkitekters Landsforbund)
- Byggekunst; arkitektur, form og miljoe. bi-m. ISSN 0007-7518 (Co-sponsors: Norske Landskapsarkitekters Forening; Norske Interioerarkitekters Landsforening)

**Norske Avisers Landsforbund**
Rosenkrantzgate 3, Oslo 1, Norway.
- Dagspressen. m. ISSN 0011-5304

**Norske Baatbyggeriers Landsforening**
Boks 137, 1601 Fredrikstad, Norway.
- Baatbyggeren. bi-m.
- Norske Baatbyggeriers Landsforening. Maanesskrift. m.

**Norske Bankforening**
Oslo, Norway.
- Okonomisk Revy. m. ISSN 0030-1914

**Norske Baptistsamfunn**
Hausmannsgt. 22, Oslo 1, Norway.
- Banneret. w. ISSN 0005-5565

**Norske Bokhandlerforening**
Oevre Vollgt. 15, Oslo 1, Norway.
- Bok og Samfunn. m (11 per yr.)-Edition A; 36 per yr.-Edition B (published on weeks when Edition A not published)
- Norsk Bokfortegnelse Aarskatalog. a. ISSN 0029-1870 (Universitetet i Oslo. Biblioteket. Norske Avdeling)

**Norske Boligbyggelags Landsforbund**
- Bo. (pub. by Scandinavian Media Service)

**Norske Doeves Landsforbund**
Postboks 97, 5000 Bergen, Norway.
- Doeves Tidsskrift. s-m.

**Norske Elverksjefers Forening**
Torshovgate 15 E, Oslo 4, Norway.
- Elverksjefen. m (10 per yr)

**Norske Flyktningeraad**
Professor Dahls Gate 1, Oslo 3, Norway.
- NY Fremtid/New Future. q. ISSN 0029-6732

**Norske Fysioterapeuters Forbund**
Motzfeldtgate 3, Oslo 1, Norway.
- Fysioterapeuten; tidsskrift for Norske fysioterapeuter. 11 per yr. ISSN 0016-3384

**Norske Geografiske Selskab**
- Norsk Geografisk Tidsskrift/Norwegian Journal of Geography. (pub. by Universitetsforlaget)

**Norske Gutters Forlag**
Postboks 557, Sentrum, Oslo 1, Norway.
- Norske Gutter. m.

**Norske Hageselskap**
Motzfeldtsgt. 1, Oslo 1, Norway.
- Norsk Hagetidend. m. ISSN 0029-1986

**Norske Handelsreisende**
Pilestredet 17, Oslo 1, Norway.
- Norske Handelsreisende. m (10 per year)

**Norske Handverks og Industribedrifters Forbund**
Rosenkrantzgaten 7, Oslo 1, Norway.
- Handverk Industri. bi-m. ISSN 0046-6816

**Norske Historiske Forening**
- Historisk Tidsskrift. (pub. by Universitetsforlaget)

**A-S Norske Husdyrtidsskrifter**
Storgaten 1, 2800 Gjoevik, Norway.
- Buskap og Avdraatt. bi-m. ISSN 0007-7194

**Norske Jord- og Myrselskap**
Rosenkrantzgt. 8, Oslo 1, Norway.
- Jord og Myr. bi-m.

**Norske Jordmorforening**
Dovregt.4, Oslo 1, Norway.
- Tidsskrift for Jordmoedre; hvori er opptatt jordmorbladet. m. ISSN 0040-7089

**Norske Kokkemesteres Landsforening**
Hr. Tage Clausen Hansen, Oddfellow Engene 6, 3000 Drammen, Norway.
- Mat. bi-m.

**Norske Kommuners Sentralforbund**
UNIREC, Bernhard Getzgate 3B, Oslo 1, Norway.
- Kommunalt Tidsskrift. m. ISSN 0047-3537

**Norske Kunst- og Kulturhistoriske Museer**
Pilestredet 15, Oslo 1, Norway.
- Museumsnytt. s-a. ISSN 0027-4186

**Norske Laegeforening**
Inkognitogt. 26, Oslo 2, Norway.
- Norske Lageforening. Tidsskrift/Norwegian Medical Association. Journal; tidsskrift for praktisk medisin. 3 per m. ISSN 0029-2001

**Norske Maskinistforbund**
Arbiensgate 1, 3, Oslo 2, Norway.
- Norsk Maskin-Tidende/Norwegian Marine Engineers' Magazine. m.

**Norske Mejerifolks Landsforening**
Boks 398, Oslo 1, Norway.
- Meieriposten. fortn. ISSN 0025-8776

**Norske Meteorologiske Institutt**
see Norway. Norske Meteorologiske Institutt

**Norske Murmesteres Landsforening**
Nedre Vollgate 1, Oslo 1, Norway.
- Murmesteren. m. ISSN 0027-3678 (Co-sponsor: Norske Murmesteres Landsforening)

**Norske Musikklaereres Landsforbund**
Schoeningsgt. 42, Oslo 3, Norway.
- Norsk Musikktidsskrift. q.

**Norske Papirhandleres Landsforbund**
Tollbugt. 4, Oslo 1, Norway.
- Papirhandleren. m.

**Norske Radio - TV Handlereslandsforbund**
Postboks 5657, Briskeby, Oslo 2, Norway.
- Radiobransjen. m (11 per yr)

**Norske Roerleggerbedrifters Landsforening**
- Roerfag. (pub. by Skarland Press A-S)

**Norske Samlaget**
Trondheimsvn. 15, Oslo 5, Norway.
- Maal og Minne. s-a. ISSN 0024-855X (Norges Almenvitenskapelige Forskningsraad)
- Norsk Litteraer Aarbok. a. ISSN 0078-1266
- Syn og Segn. 10 per yr. ISSN 0039-7717

**Norske Sivilingenioerers Forening**
- Teknisk Ukeblad-TU. (pub. by Ingenioerforlaget A-S)

**Norske Sjoeretts-Forening**
Arkiv for Sjoerett/Scandinavian Journal of
Maritime Law. (pub. by Universitetsforlaget)

**Norske Skogselskap**
Wergelandsvn. 23 B, Oslo 1, Norway.
- Norsk Skogbruk. m. ISSN 0029-2087 (Norsk
  Forstmannsforening) (Co-sponsor: Norges
  Skogteknikerforbund)
- Skogen. q.
- Tidsskrift for Skogbruk. q. ISSN 0040-7178

**Norske Socialoekonomers Forening**
Storgt. 26, Oslo 1, Norway.
- Socialoekonomen. 10 per yr. ISSN 0038-1624

**Norske Sykehusadministrasjons Landsforbund**
Pilestredet 1, Oslo 1, Norway.
- Norsk Sykehustidende. m (11 per yr)

**Norske Sykehusforening**
- Sykehuset. (pub. by Harald Lyche og Co. A-S)

**Norske Tannlaegeforening**
Kronprinsens Gate 9, Oslo 2, Norway.
- Acta Adontologica Scandinavica. bi-m. ISSN
  0001-6357
- Norske Tannlaegeforenings Tidende. m. ISSN
  0029-2303

**Norske Trevarefabrikkers Landsforbund**
- Tre og Moebler. (pub. by John A. Antonsen A-S)

**Norske Veritas**
Box 300, 1322 Hoevik, Norway.
- Norske Veritas Classification and Registry of
  Shipping. Publication. irreg., no. 85, 1974.
- Veritas. s-a. (Norwegian edt.); q.(English edt.)
  ISSN 0042-3963

**Norske Veterinaerforening**
Sognsveien 4, Oslo 4, Norway.
- Norsk Veterinaertidsskrift. m. ISSN 0029-2273

**Norske Videnskaps-Akademi**
Drammensveien 70, Oslo 2, Norway.
- Hvalraadets Skrifter/Scientific Results of Marine
  Biological Research. (pub. by Universitetsforlaget)
- Norske Videnskaps-Akademi. Historisk-Filosofisk
  Klasse. Avhandlinger Two. (pub. by
  Universitetsforlaget)
- Norske Videnskaps-Akademi. Matematisk-
  Naturvidenkapelig Klasse. Skrifter. (pub. by
  Universitetsforlaget)
- Physica Norvegica. 4 per yr. ISSN 0031-8930

**Norvega Esperantista Ligo**
Box 942, Oslo 1, Norway.
- Norvega Esperantisto; Esperantobladet. bi-m.
  ISSN 0029-361X

**Norway. Arbeidsdirektoratet**
Postboks 8127, Oslo 1, Norway.
- Norway. Arbeidsdirektoratet. Aarsmelding. a.
  ISSN 0078-1835
- Norway. Arbeidsdirektoratet. Nasjonalbudsjettet:
  Arbeidsmarkedet. a. (prep. by its Kontoret for
  Statistikk og Utredninger)
- Plan og Arbeid; labour market policy and regional
  planning. 6 per yr. ISSN 0032-0609

**Norway. Bureau of International Whaling Statistics**
3201 Sandefjord, Norway.
- International Whaling Statistics. 2 per yr. ISSN
  0020-9090

**Norway. Direktoratet for Sivilt Beredskap**
Postboks 8136, Oslo Dep., Oslo - 1, Norway.
- Sivilforsvarsbladet. m. (Co-sponsor: Norges
  Sivilforsvarsforbund)

**Norway. Direktoratet for Utviklingshjelp**
Box 8142, Oslo 1, Norway.
- Norges Samarbeid Med Utviklingslandene. a.
- Norkontakt. 6-8 per yr. ISSN 0048-0541

**Norway. Fiskeridirektoratet**
Postboks 185/186, N-5001 Bergen, Norway.
- Aarsberetning Vedkommende Norges Fiskerier. a.
- Fisken og Havet. irreg. ISSN 0071-5638
- Fiskets Gang. fortn. ISSN 0015-3133
- Norway. Fiskeridirektoratet. Fiskeflaaten. a.
- Norway. Fiskeridirektoratet. Skrifter. Serie
  Ernaering. irreg.
- Norway. Fiskeridirektoratet. Skrifter. Serie Fiskeri.
  irreg., 1971, vol. 5, no. 3. ISSN 0078-1843

**Norway. Fiskeridirektoratet. Skrifter. Serie**
Havundersoekelser. irreg., vol. 16, no. 5, 1974.
ISSN 0015-3117

**Norway. Forsvarets Bygningstekniske Korps**
Oslo, Norway.
- M T T. bi-m. ISSN 0024-8517 (Co-sponsors:
  Ingenioervaapenet; Haerens Samband)

**Norway. Forsvarets Forskningsinstitutt**
Box 25, N-2007 Kjeller, Norway.
- Fallout in Norway. irreg. ISSN 0071-3724 (prep.
  by its Avdeling for Fysikk)
- Norway. Forsvarets Forskningsinstitutt. N D R E
  Report. irreg., no. 68, 1976. ISSN 0085-4301

**Norway. Forsvarets Psykologitjeneste**
Oslo Mil, Oslo 1, Norway.
- Militaerpsykologiske Meddelelser. irreg. ISSN
  0026-3842

**Norway. Forsvarets Rekrutterings- og**
**Opplysningstjeneste**
Biskop Gunnerusgate 2, Oslo 1, Norway.
- Mannskabs Avisa. fortn. ISSN 0025-2352

**Norway. Institutt for Atomenergi**
P.O. Box 40, N-2007 Kjeller, Norway.
- Kjeller Report. irreg. ISSN 0534-4050

**Norway. Komite for Romforskning**
Blindern, Oslo, Norway.
- Norway. Komite for Romforskning. N.S.R.C.
  Report. irreg. ISSN 0452-3687

**Norway. Landbruksdepartementet**
Akersgt. 42, Oslo 1, Norway.
- Norway. Landbruksdepartementet.
  Landbruksdirektoerens Aarsmelding. irreg.

**Norway. Ministry of Church and Education**
Akersgt. 42, Box 8119, Dep., Oslo 1, Norway.
- Norsk Skole; Opplysnings-og Kunngjoringsblad for
  Skoleverket. 20 per yr. ISSN 0029-2109

**Norway. Ministry of Finance**
Oslo - Dep., Oslo 11, Norway.
- National Budget of Norway. a. ISSN 0077-3573

**Norway. Norges Almenvitenskapelige Forskningsraad**
*see* Norges Almenvitenskapelige Forskningsraad

**Norway. Norges Geologiske Undersokelse**
Leiv Erikssons vei 39, Trondheim 7000, Norway.
- N G U Bulletin/Geological Survey of Norway.
  (pub. by Universitetsforlaget)
- N G U Skrifter. (pub. by Universitetsforlaget)
- Norges Geologiske Underskelse. Arsmelding. a.

**Norway. Norges Teknisk-Naturvitenskapelige**
**Forskningsraad**
*see* Norges Teknisk-Naturvitenskapelige
Forskningsraad

**Norway. Norske Meteorologiske Institutt**
Blindern, Oslo 3, Norway.
- Meteorologiske Annaler. m.

**Norway. Postdirektoratet**
Box 1051 Sentrum, Oslo 1, Norway.
- Bladlista. q.

**Norway. Riksbibliotektjenesten**
P.O. Box 2439, Solli, Oslo 2, Norway.
- Synopsis; informasjon om informasjon. bi-m.

**Norway. Sjoekartverket**
Box 60, Stavanger, Norway.
- Norway. Sjoekartverket. Katalog over Norske
  Sjoekart og Nautiske Publicasjoner/Catalogue of
  Norwegian Charts and Nautical Publications.
  ISSN 0546-6482

**Norway. Sprengstoffinspeksjonen**
Postboks 355, Tonsberg 3101, Norway.
- Norway. Sprengstoffinspeksjonen.
  Sprengstoffinspeksjonen om Verksomheten. a.

**Norway. Statens Arbeidstilsyn Direktoratet**
Fr. Nansens vei 14, Box 8103, Oslo, Norway.
- Arbeidervern. q.
- Norway. Statens Arbeidstilsyn Direktoratet.
  Verneregler. irreg., no. 36, 1976.

**Norway. Statens Bibliotektilsyn**
Munkedamsvn. 62, Oslo-Dep, Norway.
- Bok og Bibliotek; tidsskrift for biblioteker og
  bokvenner. 8 per yr. ISSN 0006-5811

- Bokbladet; tidsskrift for skole- og barnebiblioteker.
  q. ISSN 0006-582X

**Norway. Statens Institutt for Alkoholforskning**
- Norway. Statens Institutt for Alkoholforskning.
  Skrifter. (pub. by Universitetsforlaget)

**Norway. Statistisk Sentralbyraa**
Dronningensgt. 16, Oslo-Dep., Oslo 1, Norway.
- Norway. Statistisk Sentralbyraa. Alkohol og
  Andre Rusmidler/Alcohol and Drugs. a.
- Norway. Statistisk Sentralbyraa.
  Arbeidsmarkedstatistikk/Labour Market Statistics.
  a. ISSN 0078-1878
- Norway. Statistisk Sentralbyraa. Artikler/Articles.
  irreg. ISSN 0085-431X
- Norway. Statistisk Sentralbyraa. Familie
  Statistikk/Family Statistics. irreg.
- Norway. Statistisk Sentralbyraa.
  Finansinstitusjoner/Financial Institutions. a. ISSN
  0085-4328
- Norway. Statistisk Sentralbyraa. Folkemengden
  Etter Ålder og Ekteskapelig Status/Population by
  Age and Marital Status. a. ISSN 0550-7170
- Norway. Statistisk Sentralbyraa. Framskriving Av
  Folkemengden: Regionale Tall/Population
  Projections: Regional Figures. irreg.
- Norway. Statistisk Sentralbyraa. Handboeker/
  Manuals. irreg. ISSN 0085-4336
- Norway. Statistisk Sentralbyraa. Industristatistikk/
  Industrial Statistics. a. ISSN 0078-1886
- Norway. Statistisk Sentralbyraa.
  Jordbruksstatistikk/Agricultural Statistics. a. ISSN
  0078-1894
- Norway. Statistisk Sentralbyraa. Kommunevalget/
  Municipal Elections. quadrennial.
- Norway. Statistisk Sentralbyraa. Kredittmarked
  Statistikk/Credit Market Statistics. a. ISSN 0078-
  1908
- Norway. Statistisk Sentralbyraa. Kriminalstatistikk:
  Fanger/Criminal Statistics: Prisoners. a.
- Norway. Statistisk Sentralbyraa. Kriminalstatistikk:
  Reeksjoner/Criminal Statistics: Sanctions. a.
- Norway. Statistisk Sentralbyraa. Levekaar/Level
  of Living. irreg.
- Norway. Statistisk Sentralbyraa. Loennsstatistikk/
  Wage Statistics. a. ISSN 0078-1916
- Norway. Statistisk Sentralbyraa. Oekonomisk
  Utsyn/Economic Survey. a. ISSN 0078-1924
- Norway. Statistisk Sentralbyraa.
  Samfunnsoekonomiske Studier/Social Economic
  Studies. irreg. ISSN 0085-4344
- Norway. Statistisk Sentralbyraa.
  Sjoeulykkesstatistikk/Marine Casualties. irreg.
- Norway. Statistisk Sentralbyraa. Statistisk
  Aarbok/Statistical Yearbook. a. ISSN 0078-1932
- Norway. Statistisk Sentralbyraa. Statistisk
  Fylkeshefte. irreg.
- Norway. Statistisk Sentralbyraa. Statistisk
  Maanedshefte /Monthly Bulletin of Statistics. m.
  ISSN 0029-3636
- Norway. Statistisk Sentralbyraa. Statistisk
  Ukehefte/Weekly Bulletin of Statistics. w. ISSN
  0550-0567
- Norway. Statistisk Sentralbyraa.
  Utdanningsstatistikk: Grunnskolar/Educational
  Statistics: Primary Schools/Educational Statistics:
  Primary Schools. a.
- Norway. Statistisk Sentralbyraa.
  Utdanningsstatistikk: Universiteter og Hoegskoler/
  Educational Statistics: Universities and Other
  Institutions of Higher Education. a.
- Norway. Statistisk Sentralbyraa.
  Utdanningsstatistikk: Vaksenopplaering og
  Folkeopplysning/Educational Statistics: Adult
  Education and Popular Education. a.
- Norway. Statistisk Sentralbyraa.
  Utdanningsstatistikki Videregaende Skoler/
  Educational Statistics: Upper Secondary Schools.
  a.
- Norway. Statistisk Sentralbyraa. Utenrikshandel/
  External Trade. a. ISSN 0078-1940
- Norway. Statistisk Sentralbyraa.
  Varehandelsstatistikk/Wholesale and Retail Trade
  Statistics. irreg. ISSN 0078-1959

**Norway. Teledirektoratet**
Box 6701, Oslo 1, Norway.
- Norway. Televerket. Statistikk. a.
- Telektronikk; televerkets tekniske tidsskrift. q.
  ISSN 0085-7130

**Norway. Velferdstjenesten for Handelsflaaten**
- Frivakt. (pub. by Soelberg Trykk A-S)

**Norway. Veterinaerdirektoratet**
- Veterinaerer. (pub. by Groendahl og Soens Boktrykkeri)

**Norway-America Association**
Drammensvn. 20C, Oslo 2, Norway.
- Norge-Amerika Foreningen. Yearbook. a.

**Norwegian Agency for International Development**
see Norway. Direktoratet for Utviklingshjelp

**Norwegian Association for Students of Technology**
- Stud-Teknikk/Students-Technology. (pub. by Ingenioerforlaget A-S)

**Norwegian Electro-technical Society**
- Elektro. (pub. by Ingenioerforlaget A-S)

**Norwegian Federation of Business Economists**
- Bedriftsoekonomen. (pub. by Bedriftsoekonomens Forlag)

**Norwegian Geotechnical Institute**
see Norges Geotekniske Institutt

**Norwegian Institute of Technology**
see Universitetet i Trondheim. Norges Tekniske Hoegskole

**Norwegian Police Athletic and Sports Association**
Postboks 7177, Homansbyen, Oslo 3, Norway.
- Politiidrett. bi-m. ISSN 0032-3357

**Norwegian Research Council for Science and the Humanities**
see Norges Almenvitenskapelige Forskningsraad

**Norwegian Society of Professional Engineers**
- Norsk Oljerevy/Norwegian Oil Review. (pub. by Ingenioerforlaget A-S)
- Plan/Bygg. (pub. by Ingenioerforlaget A-S)

**Norwegian Technical Press**
see Teknisk Presse A-S

**Norwegian Textile Retailers Association**
Box 1333, Oslo 1, Norway.
- Norges Tekstilkjoepmenns Forbund. fortn.

**Nyegaard & Co. A-S**
Nycoveien 2, Oslo 4, Norway.
- Farmakoterapi. 4 per yr. ISSN 0014-8326

**Officers Association of the Royal Norwegian Air Forces**
FO/LST, Oslo Mil/Huseby, Oslo 1, Norway.
- Norsk Luftmilitaert Tidsskrift. 8 per yr. ISSN 0029-201X

**Organisasjonen Vern og Velferd**
Munchsgate 4, Oslo 1, Norway.
- Vern og Velferd; tidsskriftet for vernearbeid og arbeidsmiljoe. bi-m. ISSN 0049-5964

**Oslo Boers**
Tollbugt. 2, Oslo 1, Norway.
- Oslo Boers. Beretning. a. ISSN 0085-4565

**Oslo Brannkorpsforening**
Arne Garborgs Plass 1, Oslo 1, Norway.
- Brannmannen. m. ISSN 0045-2696

**Oslo Bymuseum**
Frognervn. 67, Oslo 2, Norway.
- Byminner. q. ISSN 0007-7631

**Oslo City Hospital Ward**
c/o Ullevall Hospital, Oslo, Norway.
- Journal of the Oslo City Hospitals. m. ISSN 0030-6207

**Oslo Faktorforening**
Oslo, Norway
(Subscr. to: Finn Halvorsen, Boelersvingen 14, Bryn, Norway)
- Norsk Faktortidende. m. ISSN 0029-1919 (Norsk Faktorforbund)

**Oslo Import- og Export- Agenter Forening**
Drammensveien 30, Oslo 2, Norway.
- Agentur. 6 per yr. ISSN 0017-7261

**Oslo Kamera Klubb**
Postboks 5231, Majorstua, Oslo 3, Norway.
- Objektivet. q.

**Oslo Kjoepmannsforening**
Karl Johansgate 37, Oslo 1, Norway.
- Kjoepmannsnytt. 7 per yr.

**Oslo Militaere Samfund**
Oevre Slottsgate 5, Oslo 1, Norway.
- Norsk Militaert Tidsskrift. m. ISSN 0029-2028

**Oslo og Omegns Vaktmesterforening**
Postboks 692, Sentrum, Oslo 1, Norway.
- Vaktmesteren. m (11 per yr)

**Parfymehandlernes Landsforbund**
- Parfyme og Portefoelje. (pub. by Soelberg Trykk A-S)

**Pax Forlag**
Boks 100, Skoeyen, Oslo 2, Norway.
- Kontrast; tidsskrift for politikk, kultur, kritikk. irreg. ISSN 0085-2597

**A-S Penn-Inform**
Bygdoey Alle 37, Oslo 2, Norway.
- Norsk Musikerblad. 10 per yr. ISSN 0029-2044 (Norsk Musikerforbund)

**R. S. Platou A-S**
Box 1357, Vika, Oslo 1, Norway.
- Platou Report. irreg.

**Politiembetsmennenes Landsforening**
Trondheim, Norway.
- Politiembetsmennenes Blad. m.

**PR-Teknisk A-S**
Postboks 5049, Majorstua, Oslo 3, Norway.
- Seilas. m.
- Trivsel. bi-m. ISSN 0041-3143

**Bjarne H. Reenskaug A-S**
Karl Johans Gate 8, Oslo 1, Norway.
- Naeringsreyen. w. ISSN 0027-7533 (Norges Handelsstands Forbund)
- Skip; maritimt/teknisk tidsskrift. m (10 per yr.) ISSN 0300-3310
- Storkjoekken; tidsskrift for storhusholdning og reiseliv. 10 per yr. ISSN 0039-1956

**Rikshospitalet**
- Pulsen. (pub. by Knudsens Reklamebyraa)

**Rock 'n' Roll Society of Scandinavia**
Asv. 8, N- 1400 Ski, Norway.
- Whole Lotta Rockin. 4 per yr.

**Rogalands Arkeologiske Forening**
- Fra Haug og Heidni. (pub. by Arkeologisk Museum i Stavanger)

**Royal Norwegian Council for Scientific and Industrial Research**
see Norges Teknisk-Naturvitenskapelige Forskningsraad

**Royal Norwegian Society of Science**
see Kongelige Norske Videnskabers Selskab

**Scandinavian Media Service**
Sognsvejen 70, Oslo 8, Norway.
- Bo. q. (Norske Boligbyggelags Landsforbund)

**Scandinavian Oil Gas Magazine**
Box 6855, St. Olavs Plass, Oslo 1, Norway.
- Scandinavian Oil Gas Magazine. 9 per yr.

**Scandinavian Society for Clinical Chemistry and Clinical Physiology**
- Scandinavian Journal of Clinical & Laboratory Investigation. (pub. by Universitetsforlaget)
- Scandinavian Journal of Clinical and Laboratory Investigation. Supplement. (pub. by Universitetsforlaget)

**Scandinavian Sociological Association**
- Acta Sociologica. (pub. by Universitetsforlaget)

**Scanpet (Scandinavian Petroleum) A-S**
Box 1779, Oslo 1, Norway.
- Norwegian Offshore Index. irreg. (Co-sponsors: Federation of Norwegian Industries; Export Council of Norway)

**Seilsport Maritimt Forlag**
Eiksveien 63, 1345 Oesteraas, Norway.
- Sejlsport. 5 per yr. (Norges Seilforbund)

**Selskabet for de Norske Fiskeriers Fremme**
- Norsk Fiskaralmanakk. (pub. by A-S Nordanger-Bergen og Park Forlag)

**Selskabet for Oslo Byes Vel**
Stortingsgaten 16, Oslo, Norway.
- St. Hallvard. 4 per yr. ISSN 0036-2859

**Selvigs Forlag A-S**
Raadhusgaten 4, Box 162-Sentrum, Oslo 1, Norway.
- Northern Offshore; journal of oil and gas. m.
- Norwegian Maritime Research. q. (Norges Teknisk-Naturvitenskapelige Forskningsraad)
- Norwegian Shipping News. 30 per yr. ISSN 0029-3709
- Skandinavisk Smaaskipsfart/Scandinavian Indigenous Shipping. m.
- Skipsteknikk. m.(except July & Dec) ISSN 0037-6361

**Senterpartiets Hovedorganisasjon**
Boks 524, 5001 Bergen, Norway.
- Senterpartiets Hovedorganisasjon Informasjon. 5 per yr.

**Ship Research Institute of Norway**
see Norges Skipsforskningsinstitutt

**Sirene**
Postboks 6893, St. Olavsplass, Oslo 1, Norway.
- Sirene. 8 per yr.

**Sjakkstikka**
Box 88, 1346 Gjettum, Norway.
- Sjakkstikka; blad for skole og ungdomssjakk. m.

**Sjoemannsforeningen**
Joergen Loevlandsgate 25, Oslo 5, Norway.
- Sjoemannsforeningens Medlemsblad. m (10 per yr)

**Sjomilitaere Samfund**
Haakonsvern, Bergen, Norway.
- Norsk Tidsskrift for Sjovesen. 10 per yr. ISSN 0029-2222

**A-S Skagerak**
Postboks 338, Arendal, Norway.
- Skagerak. fortn. ISSN 0037-6035

**Skarland Press A-S**
Hansteensgt. 5, Postboks 1602, Vika-Oslo 1, Norway.
- Naeringsmiddelindustrien. m (10 per yr) ISSN 0040-7127
- Norsk V V S. m. ISSN 0029-2265 (Norsk Forening for Varme- , Ventilasjon- og Sanitaerteknikk)
- Plastnytt. m.(except July) ISSN 0032-1311 (Norsk Plastforening)
- Roerfag. m. ISSN 0048-8526 (Norske Roerleggerbedrifters Landsforening)

**T. Skjel Annonsebyraa**
Odvar Solbergsv 104, Oslo 9, Norway.
- USBL Nytt. q. (Ungdomen Selvbyggerlag)

**Skogbrukets og Skogindustrienes Forskningsraad**
Box 250, Vinderen, Oslo 3, Norway.
- Skogbrukets og Skogindustrienes Forskningsraad. Aarbok. a.

**Socialist Left Party**
Rosenkrantzgt. 18, Oslo 1, Norway.
- Ny Tid; sosialistisk ukeavis. w.

**Societatis Graeco-Latinae**
- Symbolae Osloenses. (pub. by Universitetsforlaget)

**Soelberg Trykk A-S**
Oevre Slottsgt. 12, Oslo 1, Norway.
- Frivakt. m. (except Aug.) ISSN 0046-5143 (Norway. Velferdstjenesten for Handelsflaaten)
- Parfyme og Portefoelje. bi-m. (Parfymehandlernes Landsforbund) (Co-sponsor: Laedervarehandlernes Landsforening)

**Sosialoekonomisk Samfunn**
Frederiksgate 3, Oslo, Norway.
- Stimulator et Fagblad for Socialoekonomer. m.

**Sparebankforeningen i Norge**
Kirkegt 14-18, Oslo, Norway.
- Sparebankbladet. m. ISSN 0038-6502

**Statsoekonomisk Forening**
- Statsoekonomisk Tidsskrift. (pub. by H. Aschehoug & Co. (W. Nygaard) A-S)

**Stavanger Museum**
4000 Stavanger, Norway.
- Stavanger Museum. Aarbok. a.
- Stavanger Museum. Skrifter. irreg., vol. 9, 1975.
- Sterna. q. ISSN 0039-1247 (Norsk Ornitologisk Forening)

**Studieselskapet for Nord-Norsk Naeringsliv**
Sjoegaten 15, 8001 Bodoe, Norway.
- Naering i Nord. bi-m. ISSN 0047-8601
- Nord-Norge Naeringsliv og Oekonomi. irreg., 1973, no. 41. ISSN 0078-1029

**Styret for det Industrielle Rettsvern**
Middelthunsgt. 15 B, Box 8160, Oslo-Dep., Oslo 1, Norway.
- Norsk Tidende for det Industrielle Rettsvern. Del I: Patenter. w. ISSN 0029-2206
- Norsk Tidende for det Industrielle Rettsvern. Del II: Varemerker. 40 per yr. ISSN 0029-2192
- Norsk Tidende for det Industrielle Rettsvern. Del III: Moenstre. 25 per yr. ISSN 0029-2184

**Sunnhetsbladet Trykkeri**
Akersgate 74, Oslo 1, Norway.
- Sunnhetsbladet. m (11 per yr)

**Johan Grundt Tanum Forlag**
Kr. Augustsgt. 7A, Oslo 1, Norway.
- Forretnings- og Bedriftslederen. a. ISSN 0071-7630
- Landbrukets Aarbok. Jordbruk, Hagebruk, Skogbruk. a. ISSN 0075-7853
- Skolens Aarbok. a. ISSN 0080-9950

**Teknisk Presse A-S**
Hovfaret 17, Skoeyen, Oslo 2, Norway.
- Elektronikk. m. ISSN 0013-5690
- Ingenioer - Nytt. s-w (92 per yr)
- Kampanje; bedriftsledelse, markedsforing, public relations. 10 per yr. ISSN 0022-8214
- Korrosjons-Nytt. bi-m. ISSN 0047-3634
- Moderne Transport. s-m (20 per yr)
- Norsk Plast. m (11 per yr)
- Samferdsel/Transport. 10 per yr. ISSN 0036-3774 (Transportoekonomisk Institutt)

**Transportoekonomisk Institutt**
- Samferdsel/Transport. (pub. by Teknisk Presse A-S)

**Tromsoe Museum**
9000 Tromsoe, Norway.
- Acta Borealia A. Scientia. (pub. by Universitetsforlaget)
- Ottar. 6 per yr. ISSN 0030-6703
- Tromsoe Museum. Skrifter. (pub. by Universitetsforlaget)

**Trygdekontorenes Landsforening**
Stortingsgt. 6, Oslo 1, Norway.
- Sosial Trygd. m (11 per yr.) ISSN 0038-1608

**Undervisnings- og Velferdsoffiserenes Forening**
Bergen, Norway.
- Undervisning og Velferd/Education and Welfare. 10 per yr. ISSN 0041-6584

**Ungdomen Selvbyggerlag**
- USBL Nytt. (pub. by T. Skjel Annonsebyraa)

**Universitetet i Bergen**
- Sarsia. (pub. by Universitetsforlaget)

**Universitetet i Bergen. Department of Applied Mathematics**
Avd. B Allegt. 53-55, 5014 Bergen-U, Norway.
- University of Bergen. Department of Applied Mathematics. Report. irreg. ISSN 0084-778X

**Universitetet i Bergen. Institute of Psychology**
Box 25, 5014 Bergen-U, Norway.
- University of Bergen. Institute of Psychology. Report. irreg.(6-8 per yr)

**Universitetet i Bergen. Radiation Observatory**
Geophysical Institute, Bergen, Norway.
- Monthly Radiation Values for Bergen, Norway. m. ISSN 0027-0490
- Radiation Observations in Bergen; radiation yearbook. a.

**Universitetet i Oslo. Biblioteket**
- Norsk Bokfortegnelse Aarskatalog. (pub. by Norske Bokhandlerforening)

**Universitetet i Oslo. Britisk Institutt**
- Norwegian Studies in English. (pub. by Universitetsforlaget)

**Universitetet i Oslo. Etnografiske Museum**
Frederiksgate 2, Oslo, Norway.
- Universitetet i Oslo. Etnografiske Museum. Aarbok/University of Oslo. Ethnological Museum. Yearbook. a. ISSN 0078-6748
- Universitetet i Oslo. Etnografiske Museum. Bulletin/University of Oslo. Ethnological Museum. Bulletin. irreg., 1971, no. 14. ISSN 0078-6756

**Universitetet i Oslo. Institutett for Statsvitenskap**
Box 1071, Blindern, Oslo 3, Norway
(U.S. address: Box 142, Boston, MA 02113)
- Universitetet i Oslo. Institutett for Statsvitenskap. Skrifter/University of Oslo. Institute of Political Science. Papers. irreg., 1966, no. 6. ISSN 0078-6772

**Universitetet i Oslo. Institutt for Bibelvitenskap**
Blindern, Oslo 3, Norway.
- Universitetet i Oslo. Institutt for Bibelvitenskap. Smaarskrifter. irreg. ISSN 0078-6764

**Universitetet i Oslo. Institutt for Teoretisk Astrofysikk**
- Astrophysica Norvegica/Norwegian Journal of Theoretical Astrophysics. (pub. by Universitetsforlaget)

**Universitetet i Oslo. Institutt for Teoretisk Fysikk**
Blindern, Oslo 3, Norway.
- Physica Mathematica Universitatis Osloensis. irreg. ISSN 0078-6780

**Universitetet i Oslo. Slavisk-Baltisk Institutt**
Postboks 1028, Blindern, Oslo 3, Norway.
- Universitetet i Oslo. Slavisk-Baltisk Institutt. Meddelelser. s-a.

**Universitetet i Oslo. Sosialoekonomissie**
- Universitetet i Oslo. Sosialoekonomissie Institutt. Memoranda. (pub. by Universitetsforlaget)

**Universitetet i Tromsoe**
- Astarte. (pub. by Universitetsforlaget)

**Universitetet i Trondheim. Norges Laererhoegskole**
Trondheim, Norway.
- Fra Fysikkens Verden. q. ISSN 0015-9247

**Universitetet i Trondheim. Norges Tekniske Hoegskole. Biblioteket**
7034 Trondheim-NTH, Norway.
- Universitetet i Trondheim. Norges Tekniske Hoegskole. Biblioteket. Litteraturliste. irreg; 1973, no. 46. ISSN 0085-4247
- Universitetet i Trondheim. Norges Tekniske Hoegskole. Biblioteket. Meldinger og Boklister. 5-6 per yr. ISSN 0029-1714

**Universitetet i Trondheim. Norges Tekniske Hoegskole. Vassdrags- og Havnelaboratoriet**
Klaebuveien 153, 7034 Trondheim, Norway.
- Universitetet i Trondheim. Norges Tekniske Hoegskole. Vassdrags- og Havnelaboratoriet. Meddelelse. a. ISSN 0082-6618

**Universitetets Botaniske Museum**
- Naturen. (pub. by Universitetsforlaget)

**Universitetets Paleontologiske Museum**
Sarsgate 1, Oslo 5, Norway.
- Trilobite News. a. ISSN 0085-7386

**Universitetsforlaget**
Box 7508, Skillebekk, Oslo 2, Norway
(U.S. address: Box 142, Boston, MA 02113)
- Acta Borealia A. Scientia. irreg. ISSN 0065-1109 (Tromsoe Museum)
- Acta Sociologica. q. ISSN 0001-6993 (Scandinavian Sociological Association)
- Ambio; a journal of the human environment research and management. bi-m. ISSN 0044-7447 (Kungliga Svenska Vetenskapsakademien SW)
- Ambio. Special Reports. irreg. (Kungliga Svenska Vetenskapsakademien SW)
- American Studies in Scandinavia. s-a. ISSN 0044-8060 (Nordic Association for American Studies)
- Arkiv for Luftrett/Scandinavian Journal of Air Law. irreg. ISSN 0004-2072 (Norsk Forening for Luftrett)
- Arkiv for Sjoerett/Scandinavian Journal of Maritime Law. irreg. ISSN 0004-2102 (Norske Sjoeretts-Forening)

- Astarte; journal of arctic biology. s-a. ISSN 0044-9768 (Universitetet i Tromsoe)
- Astrophysica Norvegica/Norwegian Journal of Theoretical Astrophysics. irreg., 1968, no. 28. ISSN 0067-0030 (Universitetet i Oslo. Institutt for Teoretisk Astrofysikk)
- Blyttia. q. ISSN 0006-5269 (Norsk Botanisk Forening)
- Boreas; an international journal of quaternary geology. q. ISSN 0300-9483
- Bulletin of Peace Proposals. q. ISSN 0007-5035 (International Peace Research Association FI)
- Cooperation and Conflict; Nordic journal of international politics. q. ISSN 0010-8367 (Nordic Committee for the Study of International Politics)
- Edda; Nordisk tidsskrift for litteraturforskning. 6 per yr. ISSN 0013-0818
- Geophysica Norvegica - Geofysiske Publikasjoner/Norwegian Journal of Geophysics. irreg. ISSN 0072-1174
- Heimen. q. ISSN 0017-9841 (Landslaget for Bygde- og Byhistorie)
- Historisk Tidsskrift. q. ISSN 0018-263X (Norske Historiske Forening)
- Hvalraadets Skrifter/Scientific Results of Marine Biological Research. irreg. ISSN 0073-4128 (Norske Videnskaps-Akademi)
- Ibsen Aarboken/Ibsen Yearbook. a. ISSN 0073-4365 (Dist. by: Humanities Press, Inc., 171 First Ave., Atlantic Highlands, NJ 07716)
- Inquiry; an interdisciplinary journal of philosophy and the social sciences. 4 per yr. ISSN 0020-174X
- Journal of Peace Research. 4 per yr. ISSN 0022-3433 (International Peace Research Institute FI)
- Jussens Venner. 10 per yr. ISSN 0022-6971
- Kongelige Norske Videnskabers Selskab. Forhandlinger. a.
- Kongelige Norske Videnskabers Selskab. Skrifter. irreg.
- Landslaget for Bygde- og Byhistorie. Skrifter. irreg. ISSN 0458-7073
- Lethaia; an international journal of palaeontology & stratigraphy. q. ISSN 0024-1164 (International Palaeontological Association)
- Lithos; an international journal of mineralogy, petrology, and geochemistry. q. ISSN 0024-4937
- Lov og Rett; Norsk juridisk tidsskrift. 10 per yr. ISSN 0024-6980
- N G U Bulletin/Geological Survey of Norway. irreg., no. 322, 1977. (Norway. Norges Geologiske Undersokelse)
- N G U Skrifter. irreg., no. 331, 1977. (Norway. Norges Geologiske Undersokelse)
- Naturen. 6 per yr. ISSN 0028-0887 (Universitetets Botaniske Museum)
- Nordisk Domssamling; a collection of cases from the Supreme Courts of the Scandinavian countries. 4 per yr. ISSN 0029-1315
- Nordiske Sallskapet foer Amerikstudier. Publications/Nordic Association for American Studies. Publications. irreg. ISSN 0078-1118
- Norges Almenvitenskapelige Forskiningsraad. Forskningsnytt/Norwegian Research Council for Science and the Humanities. Research News. 8 per yr. ISSN 0015-7945
- Norsk Bibliografisk Bibliotek. ISSN 0029-1862
- Norsk Filosofisk Tidsskrift. q. ISSN 0029-1943
- Norsk Geografisk Tidsskrift/Norwegian Journal of Geography. q. ISSN 0029-1951 (Norske Geografiske Selskab)
- Norsk Geologisk Tidsskrift/Norwegian Journal of Geology. q. ISSN 0029-196X (Norsk Geologisk Forening)
- Norsk Teologisk Tidsskrift. 4 per yr. ISSN 0029-2176
- Norsk Tidsskrift for Misjon. 4 per yr. ISSN 0029-2214 (Egede Institute)
- Norske Videnskaps-Akademi. Historisk-Filosofisk Klasse. Avhandlinger Two. irreg. ISSN 0029-2311
- Norske Videnskaps-Akademi. Matematisk-Naturvidenkapelig Klasse. Skrifter. irreg. ISSN 0029-2338
- Norveg; journal of Nordic ethnology. a. ISSN 0029-3601
- Norway. Statens Institutt for Alkoholforskning. Skrifter. irreg., 1971, no. 10. ISSN 0078-673X (Norway. Statens Institutt for Alkoholforskning) (Dist. by: Rutgers University Center of Alcohol Studies, New Brunswick, NJ 08903)
- Norwegian Archaeological Review. s-a. ISSN 0029-3652
- Norwegian Journal of Botany. q. ISSN 0300-1156
- Norwegian Journal of Entomology/Norsk Entomologisk Tidsskrift. s-a. ISSN 0029-1897 (Norsk Entomologisk Forening)
- Norwegian Journal of Linguistics/Norsk Tidsskrift for Sprogvidenskap. s-a. ISSN 0029-2230

- Norwegian Studies in English. irreg. no. 19, 1974.
  ISSN 0078-1991 (Universitetet i Oslo. Britisk
  Institutt) (Co-sponsor: Universitetet i Bergen;
  Universitet i Trondheim)
- Ornis Scandinavica/Scandinavian Journal of
  Ornithology. s-a. ISSN 0030-5693
- Pedagogisk Forskning; Nordisk tidsskrift for
  pedagogikk. q. (Norsk Pedagogikklag)
- Sarsia. irreg. ISSN 0036-4827 (Universitetet i
  Bergen)
- Scandinavian Journal of Clinical & Laboratory
  Investigation. 8 per yr. ISSN 0036-5513
  (Scandinavian Society for Clinical Chemistry and
  Clinical Physiology)
- Scandinavian Journal of Clinical and Laboratory
  Investigation. Supplement. irreg. ISSN 0085-591X
  (Scandinavian Society for Clinical Chemistry and
  Clinical Physiology)
- Scandinavian Journal of Educational Research. 4
  per yr. ISSN 0031-3831
- Scandinavian Journal of Gastroenterology. 8 per
  yr. ISSN 0036-5521
- Scandinavian Journal of Gastroenterology.
  Supplement. irreg. ISSN 0085-5928
- Scandinavian Journal of Immunology. 12 per yr.
  ISSN 0300-9475
- Scandinavian Political Studies. 4 per yr. ISSN
  0080-6757
- Scandinavian Studies in Criminology. irreg. ISSN
  0085-5936
- Studia Norvegica Ethnologica et Folkloristica.
  irreg.
- Studia Theologica; Scandinavian Journal of
  Theology. s-a. ISSN 0039-338X
- Symbolae Osloenses. a. ISSN 0039-7679
  (Societatis Graeco-Latinae)
- Tidsskrift for Rettsvitenskap. 5 per yr. ISSN 0040-
  7143
- Tidsskrift for Samfunnsforskning/Norwegian
  Journal of Social Research. 6 per yr. ISSN 0040-
  716X
- Tidsskrift for Teologi og Kirke. 4 per yr. ISSN
  0040-7194
- Tradisjon; tidsskrift for folkeminnevitenskap. s-a.
- Tromsoe Museum. Skrifter. irreg., 1968, vol. 13.
  ISSN 0085-7394
- Universitas. fortn.
- Universitetet i Oslo. Sosialoekonomissie Institutt.
  Memoranda. irreg.
- Yrkesopplaering; tidsskrift for praktisk og teoretisk
  opplaering i handverk og industri. 10 per yr. ISSN
  0044-1317

**Valdres Historielag**
2967 Lomen, Norway.
- Valdres Historielag. Aarbok. a.

**Valo Forlag A-S**
Postboks 1777, Vika, Oslo 1, Norway.
- Ide. q. ISSN 0046-8517

**Verden og Vi**
Boks 3715, Oslo 1, Norway.
- Verden og Vi. 10 per yr.

**Vernepligtige Officerers Forening**
Postboks 7525, Skillebekk, Oslo 2, Norway.
- Pro Patria. 6 per yr. ISSN 0032-910X

**Vestlandske Felleskjoep**
C. Sundsgate 9, Bergen, Norway.
- Vestlandsk Landbruk. bi-w.

# PAKISTAN

**Agricultural Development Bank of Pakistan**
Shafi Court, Merewether Rd., Karachi, Pakistan.
- Agricultural Development Bank of Pakistan.
  Annual Report and Statement of Accounts. a.
  ISSN 0065-4426

**Agricultural Economics Society of Pakistan**
154 Government Quarters, Lawrence Rd., Karachi,
Pakistan.
- Agricultural Economist. irreg. ISSN 0065-4469

**Albert Press**
Jinnah Rd., Quetta, Baluchistan, Pakistan.
- Quetta Times. w. ISSN 0033-6386

**All-Pakistan Islamic Education Conference**
7 Friends Colony, Multan Road, Lahore, Pakistan.
- Islamic Education. bi-m. ISSN 0578-8056

**All Pakistan Women's Association**
Information and Research Bureau, 67-B Garden
Rd., Karachi 3, Pakistan.
- A P W A Newsletter. 3 per yr. ISSN 0001-2262

**Archbishop of Karachi**
St. Patrick's Cathedral, Karachi 3, Pakistan.
- Christian Voice; a weekly newspaper and review.
  w. ISSN 0009-5699

**Armed Forces Medical College**
Rawalpindi, Pakistan.
- Pakistan Armed Forces Medical Journal. q. ISSN
  0030-9648

**Association of Pediatricians of Pakistan**
111-D 27-7 Nazimabad, Karachi 18, Pakistan.
- Pakistan Pediatric Journal. q. ISSN 0048-2722

**Bankinsurance News**
4 Amil St. off Robson Rd., Karachi 1, Pakistan.
- Bankinsurance News. w. ISSN 0005-5522

**Barque & Company**
Barque Chambers, Barque Square, 87 Shahrah e-
Liaquat Ali, Box 201, Lahore, Pakistan.
- Barque's Pakistan Trade Directory and Who's
  Who. a. ISSN 0067-4230
- Who's Who in Pakistan. a. ISSN 0083-9671

**Biographical Research Institute**
Lahore, Pakistan.
- Biographical Encyclopedia of Pakistan. irreg. ISSN
  0067-8732

**Biological Society of Pakistan**
Biological Laboratories, Government College,
Lahore, Pakistan.
- Biologia. s-a. ISSN 0006-3096

**Central Cotton Committee**
*see* Pakistan. Pakistan Central Cotton Committee

**Chamber of Commerce and Industry**
Aiwan-e-Tijarat, Box 4158, Nicol Rd., Karachi 2,
Pakistan.
- Karachi. Chamber of Commerce and Industry.
  Report. a. ISSN 0075-5079
- Karachi. Chamber of Commerce and Industry.
  Trade Journal. s-m. ISSN 0047-3197

**Chronicle Publications**
Box 5257, Iftikhar Chambers, Altaf Hussain Rd.,
Karachi 0203, Pakistan.
- Trade Chronicle; Pakistan's leading magazine of
  commerce, industry and public affairs. m. ISSN
  0041-0411

**Combat**
81-82 Farid Chambers, Abdullah Haroon Rd.,
Karachi 3, Pakistan.
- Combat; an independent news weekly. w. ISSN
  0010-2121

**Cricketer**
Box 7698, 19 Rehamam Court, Grieg St., Karachi,
Pakistan.
- Cricketer.

**Current**
Sheika Building, Faiz Mohd Fatehali Road, Box
789, Karachi, Pakistan.
- Current. w.

**Darut-Tasnif Ltd.**
Iqbal Mansion, Shahrah-e-Liaquat, Saddar, Karachi
3, Pakistan.
- Yaqeen International. s-m. ISSN 0044-0213

**Defence Journal**
16-B 7th Central St., Defence Housing Society,
Karachi 4, Pakistan.
- Defence Journal. m.

**Diplomat**
442/2 Jauharabad, Karachi 38, Pakistan.
- Diplomat. m.

**Dogar Bros.**
Santnagar, Lahore, Pakistan.
- Dogar's General Knowledge Digest. m. ISSN
  0012-4907

**Economic and Industrial Publications**
Al-Masiha, 47 Abdullah Haroon Rd., Box 7843,
Karachi 0303, Pakistan.
- E. I. P. Industrial Research Service. w.
- E. I. P. Investors Service. w.

- Economic Review. m. ISSN 0531-8955

**Enterprise**
South Napier Rd., Karachi, Pakistan.
- Enterprise. m. ISSN 0013-8681

**Environmental Research Association**
Bait-ul-Fazal, Darul Rehmat Sharki, Rabwah,
District Jhang, Pakistan.
- Environment Information Bulletin. m.

**Family Planning Association of Pakistan**
3-A Temple Rd., Lahore, Pakistan.
- Family Planning Association of Pakistan. Annual
  Report. a. ISSN 0071-3759

**Federation of Pakistan Chambers of Commerce and
Industry**
Lalji Lakhmidas Bldg., Bellasis St., Karachi,
Pakistan.
- Federation of Pakistan Chambers of Commerce
  Industry. Brief Report of Activities. a. ISSN
  0071-4429

**Ferozsons Ltd.**
60-Shara-e-Quaid-e-Azam, Lahore, Pakistan.
- Talim-O-Tarbiat. m. ISSN 0039-9175

**Finance and Industry Ltd.**
Cotton Exchange Bldg., 3rd Floor, I. I. Chundrigar
Rd., P.O. Box 4447, Karachi 2, Pakistan.
- Pakistan Economist. w. ISSN 0030-9745

**Finance Taxation & Company Law**
11 Dilkusha Chambers, Marston Rd., Karachi 3,
Pakistan.
- Finance Taxation & Company Law; Pakistan's
  pioneer monthly business law reporter. m. ISSN
  0015-1971

**Freedom**
c/o Mohammed Arif, Tabbani Market, Nazimabad
No. 3, Karachi 18, Pakistan
- Freedom. m. (Subscr. to: al Qamar, V-B
  Nazimabad, Karachi 18, Pakistan)

**Government College. Department of Economics**
Lahore, Pakistan.
- Government College. Economic Journal. s-a.

**Government College. Department of English Language
and Literature**
Lahore, Pakistan
(Dist. by: Co-Opera Book Shop & Art Gallery, 70
Shahrah-e-Quaid-e-Azam, Lahore, Pakistan)
- Explorations. s-a. ISSN 0014-4975

**Government College. Department of History and
Political Science**
Lahore, Pakistan.
- Journal of History and Political Science. a.

**Government College. Department of Psychology**
Lahore, Pakistan.
- Psychology Quarterly. q. ISSN 0033-3093

**Government College. Research Council**
Lahore, Pakistan.
- Journal of Natural Sciences and Mathematics. s-a.
  ISSN 0022-2941

**Hamdard Foundation**
*see under* Institute of Health and Tibbi Research

**Hamid & Co.**
21 Inder St., Multan Rd., Lahore 4, Pakistan.
- Industry & Trade Review. m. ISSN 0019-9451

**Henna**
108 Depot Lines, M. A. Jinnah Rd., Karachi 1,
Pakistan.
- Henna; woman and home journal. m. ISSN 0046-
  726X

**Homeo Doctor**
Saddar Bazar, Hyderabad, Pakistan.
- Homeo Doctor. m. ISSN 0046-7782

**Industrial Development Bank of Pakistan**
State Life Bldg., Wallace Rd., Karachi, Pakistan.
- Industrial Development Bank of Pakistan. Report.
  a. ISSN 0073-7399

**Institute of Bankers**
Karachi, Pakistan.
- Institute of Bankers in Pakistan. Council. Report
  and Accounts. s-a. ISSN 0073-8999

**Institute of Chartered Accountants of Pakistan**
5 Mall Mansion, 30 Shahrah-e-Quaid-e-Azam,
Lahore, Pakistan.
- Pakistan Accountant. q. ISSN 0030-9621

**Institute of Cost and Management Accountants of Pakistan**
Box 7284, Soldier Bazar, Karachi 3, Pakistan.
- Industrial Accountant. q. ISSN 0019-7793

**Institute of Health and Tibbi Research. Hamdard National Foundation**
Hamdard, Nazimabad, Karachi 18, Pakistan.
- Hamdard; voice of Eastern medicine. q.
- Medical Times. m.

**Institute of Hygiene and Preventive Medicine**
6 Birdwood Rd., Lahore, Pakistan.
- Pakistan Journal of Health. q. ISSN 0030-9834

**Institute of Islamic Culture**
Club Rd., Lahore 3, Pakistan.
- Al-Ma'arif. m. ISSN 0002-4015

**Interwing Group Ltd.**
125 Reza Shah Pehlavi Rd., Rawalpindi, Pakistan.
- Interwing Weekly Review. w. ISSN 0020-9783

**Investment & Marketing**
10-B Pak Chambers, West Wharf Rd., Box 7578,
Karachi, Pakistan.
- Investment & Marketing. m. ISSN 0021-0064

**Iqbal Academy Pakistan**
90-B-2 Gulberg III, Lahore, Pakistan.
- Iqbal Review. q. ISSN 0021-0773

**Islamic Research Academy**
No. 10-C-163 Mansura, Karachi 3805, Pakistan.
- Criterion. m. ISSN 0011-1481

**Islamic Research Institute**
see Pakistan. Ministry of Religious Affairs. Islamic Research Institute

**Jamiyat-ul-Falah Karachi**
Box 7141, Karachi 3, Pakistan.
- Voice of Islam. m. ISSN 0042-8132

**Karachi Cotton Association**
Cotton Exchange, I.I. Chundrigar Rd., Karachi,
Pakistan.
- Karachi Cotton Annual. a. ISSN 0075-5087

**Karachi Geographers Association**
328/9 Federal B Area, Karachi 38, Pakistan.
- Third World Review. 3 per yr.

**Karachi Port Trust**
Karachi, Pakistan.
- K. P. T. News Bulletin. s-m.
- Karachi Port Trust. Year Book of Information,
Port of Karachi, Pakistan. a. ISSN 0075-5109

**Karachi Poultry Producers Trade Group**
3/A Mohammad Ali Society, Main Drigh Rd.,
Karachi, Pakistan.
- Poultry News. m.

**Karachi University**
see University of Karachi

**Karachi University Library Science Alumni Association**
Karachi 32, Pakistan.
- K U L S A A Newsletter. q. ISSN 0022-7412

**Mohammad Yusef Kureshy, Ed. & Pub.**
14 Japan Mansion, Preedy St., Saddar, Karachi 3,
Pakistan.
- Engineering Forum. m. ISSN 0013-7936
- Engineering News. w. ISSN 0013-8061

**Lahore Chamber of Commerce & Industry. Research and Statistical Department**
Box 597, 11 Race Course Rd., Lahore, Pakistan.
- Lahore Chamber of Commerce and Industry.
Research and Statistical Department. Statistical Report. m.

**M.M. Publications Ltd.**
P.I.I.A. Bldg., Third Floor, Havelock Rd., Sadar,
Karachi, Pakistan.
- Pakistan Medical Review. m. ISSN 0031-0018

**M O T A M A R**
see World Muslim Congress

**Market Bulletin**
Box 4553, Karachi 2, Pakistan.
- Market Bulletin. s-w. ISSN 0464-9974

**Mashoor Press**
Karachi, Pakistan.
- Nairang Da'ijist/Nairang Digest. m. ISSN 0047-8628

**Maulai Enterprise**
118/1 Sharifabad, Karachi 19, Pakistan.
- Pakistan Business and Shopping Guide. a.

**Medical News Ltd.**
Aiwan-e-Saddar Rd., Havelock Rd., Karachi,
Pakistan.
- Medical News Fortnightly; Pakistan's first medical
newspaper. fortn. ISSN 0047-6528

**Memon Youths Organisation**
O.T. 9/145,Kagazi Bazar, Box 5097, Karachi 2,
Pakistan.
- Memon Alam. m. ISSN 0025-9144

**G. Rabbani Mirza, Ed. & Pub.**
2 McLeod Rd., Lahore, Pakistan.
- Educator. m. ISSN 0013-2020

**Modern Book Depot**
Sialkot Cantt, Pakistan.
- Digest of World Events. a. ISSN 0070-4873

**Monthly Guardian**
c/o Rana N. Parveze, 4 Shara-I-Fatima, Jinnah,
Lahore, Pakistan.
- Monthly Guardian. m. ISSN 0027-0423

**Motamar**
see World Muslim Congress

**Motamar al-Alam al-Islam**
see World Muslim Congress

**Museums Association of Pakistan**
Victoria Memorial Hall, Peshawar, Pakistan.
- Museums Journal of Pakistan. a. ISSN 0077-2348

**Muslim Intellectuals' International**
Box 5294, Karachi, Pakistan.
- Muslim Intelectuals' International. M.I.I. Series.
irreg. ISSN 0541-5462

**Muslim News International**
Box 7659, G.E.M. Chambers, Zaibunnisa St.,
Karachi 3, Pakistan.
- Muslim News International. m.

**National Bank of Pakistan**
I. I. Chundrigar Rd., Karachi 2, Pakistan.
- National Bank of Pakistan. Report and Statement
of Accounts. a. ISSN 0077-3522

**National Book Council of Pakistan**
Theosophical Hall, M. A. Jinnah Rd., Karachi,
Pakistan.
- Books from Pakistan. a. ISSN 0068-0206
- Literary Prizes in Pakistan. a. ISSN 0075-9929

**National Institute of Public Administration**
University Rd., Karachi 32, Pakistan.
- Pakistan Journal of Public Administration. s-a.

**National Institute of Public Administration. Regional Office**
78 Upper Mall, Lahore, Pakistan.
- Public Administration Review. q. ISSN 0033-3344

**National Institute of Social and Economic Research**
Box 5659, Karachi 2, Pakistan.
- N I S E R Newsletter. m.

**National Publications Service**
Box 3431, Karachi, Pakistan.
- Banker and Businessman. m.

**Orient**
13/C-C, P.E.C.H.S., Block 2, Karachi, Pakistan.
- Orient; a socio, economic, cum literary journal. m.
ISSN 0048-220X

**Mohammad Owais, Ed. & Pub.**
1260-C Commercial Area, P.E.C.H.S., Karachi 29,
Pakistan.
- Statesman; week-end review. w. ISSN 0039-0313

**P A S T I C**
see Pakistan Scientific and Technological
Information Centre

**P C S I R**
see Pakistan Council of Scientific and Industrial
Research

**P.E.C.H. Society**
187-3b-2 P.E.C.H. Society, Karachi 29, Pakistan.
- Flyer International; aviation and tourism. m. ISSN
0046-4236

**P. L. D. Publishers**
Church Rd., Lahore 1, Pakistan.
- All Pakistan Legal Decisions. m. ISSN 0030-9958
- Pakistan Annual Law Digest. a. ISSN 0078-785X
- Pakistan Criminal Law Journal; monthly reporter
of criminal laws. m.
- Pakistan Labour Cases. m. ISSN 0030-994X
- Pakistan Tax Decisions. m. ISSN 0031-0115
- Supreme Court Monthly Review. m. ISSN 0585-9794

**Pak Publishers**
Urdu Bazar, Lahore, Pakistan.
- Pak Jamhuriat. w. ISSN 0030-9591

**Pakistan. Agricultural Research Council**
Block No. 79, Pakistan Secretariat, Karachi,
Pakistan
- Agriculture Pakistan. q. ISSN 0002-1776 (Order
from: Manager of Publications, Government of
Pakistan, 2nd Floor, Ahmad Chamber, Tariq Rd.,
P.E.C.H.S., Karachi 29, Pakistan)

**Pakistan. Air Force**
Air Headquarters, Karachi 13, Pakistan.
- Shaheen. q. ISSN 0037-3176

**Pakistan. Bureau of Labour Publications**
Zam Zam Chambers, Dunolly Rd., Box 5833,
Karachi 2, Pakistan.
- Eastern Worker. bi-m. ISSN 0012-8953
- Labour Law Cases. m. ISSN 0458-6026

**Pakistan. Central Bureau of Education**
Sector H-9, Cultural Area, Islamabad, Pakistan.
- Pakistan. Central Bureau of Education.
Educational Statistics Bulletin Series. irreg. ISSN
0078-7914

**Pakistan. Central Statistical Office**
see Pakistan. Statistical Division

**Pakistan. Department of Archaeology and Museums**
5-B Pakistan Secretariat, Karachi 1, Pakistan.
- Pakistan Archaeology. a. ISSN 0078-7868

**Pakistan. Department of Civil Aviation**
Karachi 4, Pakistan.
- Civil Aviation in Pakistan: Half-Yearly
Newsletter. s-a.

**Pakistan. Department of Insurance**
Karachi, Pakistan
- Pakistan Insurance Year Book. a. ISSN 0078-8236
(Order from: Manager of Publications,
Government of Pakistan, 2nd Floor, Ahmad
Chamber, Tariq Rd., P.E.C.H.S., Karachi 29,
Pakistan)

**Pakistan. Directorate of Livestock Farms**
Lahore, Pakistan.
- Pakistan. Directorate of Livestock Farms. Report.
a. ISSN 0083-8292

**Pakistan. Directorate of Rural Works Programme**
Lahore, Pakistan.
- Pakistan. Directorate of Rural Works Programme.
Evaluation Report. a. ISSN 0083-8306

**Pakistan. Export Promotion Bureau**
National Assembly Bldg., Court Rd., Karachi,
Pakistan.
- Pakistan. Export Promotion Bureau. Export Guide
Series. irreg. ISSN 0078-8104
- Pakistan. Export Promotion Bureau. Fresh Fruits.
a. ISSN 0078-8112
- Pakistan Export Directory. (pub. by Trade and
Industry Publications Limited)
- Pakistan Exports. m. ISSN 0030-977X

**Pakistan. Finance Division**
Islamabad, Pakistan.
- Budget of the Government of Pakistan. Demands
for Grants and Appropriations. a.
- Pakistan. Finance Division. Budget in Brief. a.

- Pakistan. Finance Division. Economic Analysis of the Budget. a.
- Pakistan Economic Survey. a. ISSN 0078-8082 (Order from: Manager of Publications, Government of Pakistan, 2nd Floor, Ahmad Chamber, Tariq Rd., P.E.C.H.S., Karachi 29, Pakistan)

**Pakistan. Geological Survey of Pakistan**
c/o Chief Librarian, Box 15, Quetta, Pakistan.
- Pakistan. Geological Survey. Memoirs; Paleontologia Pakistanica. irreg. ISSN 0078-8155
- Pakistan. Geological Survey. Records. irreg. ISSN 0078-8163

**Pakistan. Krishi Gabe Shona Parishad**
*see* **Pakistan. Agricultural Research Council**

**Pakistan. Meteorological Department**
Headquarters Office, 34-J Block No. 6, P.E.C.H.S., Karachi 29, Pakistan.
- Monthly Frequency Tables of Visibility, Cloud & Wind. m. ISSN 0027-0415
- Pakistan Weather Review-Monthly Weather Report. m. ISSN 0031-0123
- Weekly Weather Report of Pakistan & Kashmir. w. ISSN 0043-1982

**Pakistan. Military Training Directorate**
General Staff Branch, General Headquarters, Rawalpindi, Pakistan.
- Military Digest. q. ISSN 0026-3974
- Pakistan Army Journal. s-a. ISSN 0030-9656

**Pakistan. Ministry of Commerce**
Karachi, Pakistan
- Pakistan Customs Tariff. irreg. ISSN 0078-8058 (Order from: Manager of Publications, Government of Pakistan, 2nd Floor, Ahmad Chamber, Tariq Rd., P.E.C.H.S., Karachi 29, Pakistan)

**Pakistan. Ministry of Commerce. Trade Marks Registry**
*see* **Pakistan. Trade Marks Registry**

**Pakistan. Ministry of Education. Central Bureau of Education**
*see* **Pakistan. Central Bureau of Education**

**Pakistan. Ministry of Education. Directorate of Archives and Libraries**
Karachi, Pakistan.
- Pakistan. Ministry of Education. Directorate of Archives and Libraries. Accessions List. s-a.

**Pakistan. Ministry of Education. Documentation Section**
Curriculum Wing, Sector H-9, P.O. Shaigan, Industrial Area, Islamabad, Pakistan.
- Development of Education in Pakistan. a. ISSN 0080-1321
- Directory of Pakistani Scholars Abroad. a. ISSN 0070-606X
- Pakistan. Ministry of Education. Yearbook. a. ISSN 0078-8287

**Pakistan. Ministry of Finance**
*see also* **Pakistan. Finance Division**

**Pakistan. Ministry of Finance**
*see also* **Pakistan. Office of the Economic Adviser**

**Pakistan. Ministry of Finance**
*see also* **Pakistan. Statistical Division**

**Pakistan. Ministry of Finance**
Islamabad, Pakistan.
- Pakistan. Ministry of Finance. Estimates of Foreign Assistance. irreg. ISSN 0555-8786
- Taxation Structure of Pakistan. a.

**Pakistan. Ministry of Finance, Planning and Economic Affairs. Statistical Division**
*see* **Pakistan. Statistical Division**

**Pakistan. Ministry of Food, Agriculture and Rural Development. Food and Agriculture Division**
Agriculture Wing, Planning Unit, 139-H, G 6-3, Islamabad, Pakistan.
- Pakistan. Food and Agriculture Division. Yearbook of Agricultural Statistics. a. ISSN 0078-8139

**Pakistan. Ministry of Food, Agriculture and Rural Development. Rural Development Division**
Rural Development Wing, 316, F-6-3 Islamabad, Pakistan.
- Integrated Rural Development Review. q.

**Pakistan. Ministry of Food and Agriculture. Pakistan Central Cotton Committee**
*see* **Pakistan. Pakistan Central Cotton Committee**

**Pakistan. Ministry of Foreign Affairs**
Islamabad, Pakistan.
- Foreign Affairs Pakistan. bi-m.

**Pakistan. Ministry of Religious Affairs. Islamic Research Institute**
Box 1035, Islamabad, Pakistan.
- Al-Dirasat al-Islamiyah. a. ISSN 0002-399X
- Fikr-o-Nazar. m. ISSN 0430-4055

**Pakistan. National Assembly**
Islamabad, Pakistan
- Pakistan. National Assembly. Debates. Official Report. irreg. ISSN 0078-8333 (Order from: Manager of Publications, Government of Pakistan, 2nd Floor, Ahmad Chamber, Tariq Rd., P.E.C.H.S., Karachi 29, Pakistan)

**Pakistan. Office of the Economic Adviser**
Islamabad, Pakistan.
- Pakistan. Office of the Economic Adviser. Government Sponsored Corporations and Other Institutions. a. ISSN 0078-8392
- Pakistan Basic Facts. a. ISSN 0078-7892

**Pakistan. Official Language Committee**
Lahore, Pakistan.
- Pakistan. Official Language Committee. Urdu Translation of Official Terms and Phraseology. a. ISSN 0083-8322

**Pakistan. Pakistan Central Cotton Committee**
Secretary, Moulvi Tamizuddin Khan Rd., Karachi 1, Pakistan.
- Cotistics Quarterly Cotton Statistical Bulletin. q. (prep. by its Marketing and Economic Research Section)
- Pakistan Central Cotton Committee. Agricultural Survey Report. irreg. ISSN 0078-7930
- Pakistan Central Cotton Committee. Monthly Cotton Review. m. ISSN 0027-0334
- Pakistan Central Cotton Committee. Technological Bulletin. Series A. irreg. ISSN 0078-7949
- Pakistan Central Cotton Committee. Technological Bulletin. Series B. irreg. ISSN 0078-7957
- Pakistan Cottons. q. ISSN 0030-9699
- World Cotton Markets Review. m. (prep. by its Marketing and Economic Research Section)

**Pakistan. Planning Commission**
Islamabad, Pakistan.
- Pakistan. Planning Commission. Development Programme. a. ISSN 0078-8414

**Pakistan. Post Office Department**
Karachi, Pakistan.
- Pakistan Postage Stamps. irreg., latest issue, 1966. ISSN 0078-8422

**Pakistan. State Bank of Pakistan**
Central Directorate, Public Relations Department, I.I. Chundrigar Rd., Box 4456, Karachi, Pakistan.
- Banking Statistics of Pakistan. a. ISSN 0067-3811
- Pakistan's Balance of Payments. a. ISSN 0078-852X (prep. by its Department of Statistics)
- State Bank of Pakistan. Bulletin. m. ISSN 0039-0011
- State Bank of Pakistan. Department of Statistics. Index Numbers of Stock Exchange Securities. s-a. ISSN 0081-4466 (prep. by its Department of Statistics)
- State Bank of Pakistan. Department of Statistics. Statistics on Co-operative Banks. q. ISSN 0039-0569 (prep. by its Department of Statistics)
- State Bank of Pakistan. Department of Statistics. Statistics on Scheduled Banks. q. ISSN 0039-0577 (prep. by its Department of Statistics)

**Pakistan. Statistical Division**
63 Muslim Abab, Karachi 5, Pakistan
(Order from: Manager of Publications, Government of Pakistan, 2nd Flo, Ahamd Chamber, Tariq Rd., P.E.C.H.S., Karachi 29, Pakistan)
- Foreign Trade Statistics of Pakistan. s-a. ISSN 0071-7428

- Pakistan. Statistical Division. Consumer Price Index: Scope and Limitations. a. ISSN 0078-7981
- Pakistan. Statistical Division. Foreign Trade. m.
- Pakistan. Statistical Division. Household Income & Expenditure Survey. a.
- Pakistan. Statistical Division. Key to Official Statistics. irreg. ISSN 0078-799X
- Pakistan. Statistical Division. Monthly Statistical Bulletin. m.
- Pakistan. Statistical Division. N S S Series. irreg. ISSN 0078-8007
- Pakistan. Statistical Division. Statistical Yearbook. a.
- Statistical Pocket-Book of Pakistan. a. ISSN 0081-5004

**Pakistan. Supreme Court**
Lahore, Pakistan.
- Law Quarterly. q.

**Pakistan. Survey of Pakistan**
Rawalpindi, Pakistan.
- Pakistan. Survey of Pakistan. General Report. a. ISSN 0078-8481

**Pakistan. Trade Marks Registry**
Ministry of Commerce, Karachi, Pakistan
- Trade Marks Journal. m. ISSN 0041-0454 (Order from: Manager of Publications, Government of Pakistan, 2nd Floor, Ahmad Chamber, Tariq Rd., P.E.C.H.S., Karachi 29, Pakistan)

**Pakistan Academy of Sciences**
c/o Pakistan Council of Scientific and Industrial Research, 39 Garden Rd., Karachi 0310, Pakistan.
- Pakistan Academy of Sciences. Proceedings. s-a.

**Pakistan Administrative Staff College**
Shahrah-e-Quaid-e-Azam, Lahore, Pakistan.
- Pakistan Administrative Staff College Journal. s-a.

**Pakistan Association for the Advancement of Science**
14 Shah Jamal Scheme, Lahore 12, Pakistan.
- Pakistan Journal of Science. bi-m. ISSN 0030-9877
- Pakistan Journal of Scientific Research. q. ISSN 0552-9050
- Pakistan Science Conference. Proceedings. a. ISSN 0078-8430

**Pakistan Atomic Energy Commission**
Box 1114, Islamabad, Pakistan.
- Nucleus. q. ISSN 0029-5698

**Pakistan Botanical Society**
Dept. of Botany, University of Karachi, Karachi 32, Pakistan.
- Pakistan Journal of Botany. s-a.

**Pakistan Boy Scouts Association**
Amin House, Off Moulvi Tamizuddin Khan Road, Karachi 1, Pakistan.
- Pak-Scout. m. ISSN 0030-9605

**Pakistan Cardiac Society**
c/o Dept. of Cardiology, Jinnah Post Graduate Medical Centre, Karachi, Pakistan.
- Pakistan Heart Journal. q. ISSN 0048-2706

**Pakistan Central Cotton Committee**
*see* **Pakistan. Pakistan Central Cotton Committee**

**Pakistan Co-operative Fruit Development Board**
Lyallpur, Pakistan.
- Punjab Fruit Journal. q. ISSN 0033-4316

**Pakistan Council of Scientific and Industrial Research**
39 Garden Rd., Karachi 0310, Pakistan.
- Pakistan Council of Scientific and Industrial Research. Report. a. ISSN 0078-804X
- Pakistan Journal of Scientific and Industrial Research. bi-m. ISSN 0030-9885
- Science Chronicle. q.

**Pakistan Dental Review**
26 Shahrah-e-Quaid-e-Azam, Lahore, Pakistan.
- Pakistan Dental Review. q. ISSN 0030-9710

**Pakistan Economic Association**
University of the Punjab, Department of Economics, New Campus, Lahore, Pakistan.
- Pakistan Economic Journal. s-a.

**Pakistan Forest Institute**
Peshawar, Pakistan.
- Pakistan Forest Institute, Peshawar. Annual Progress Report. a. ISSN 0078-8147
- Pakistan Journal of Forestry. q. ISSN 0030-9818

**Pakistan Group for the Study of Local Government**
14 Japan Mansion, Preedy St., Karachi, Pakistan.
● Local Government. m.

**Pakistan Herald Publications**
Haroon House, Kutchery Rd., Karachi 4, Pakistan.
● Dawn; overseas weekly issue. w.
● Herald. m. ISSN 0018-0467
● Illustrated Weekly of Pakistan. w. ISSN 0019-2449

**Pakistan Historical Society**
30 New Karachi Co-operative Housing Society, Karachi 5, Pakistan.
● Pakistan Historical Society. Journal. q. ISSN 0030-9796
● Pakistan Historical Society. Memoir. a. ISSN 0078-8171
● Pakistan Historical Society. Proceedings of the Pakistan History Conference. a. ISSN 0078-818X

**Pakistan Industrial Credit and Investment Corporation**
Jubilee Insurance House, McLeod Rd., Karachi 2, Pakistan.
● P I C I C News. q. ISSN 0030-8005
● Pakistan Industrial Credit and Investment Corporation. Report. a. ISSN 0078-8198

**Pakistan Industrial Development Corporation**
PIDC House, Dr. Ziauddin Ahmad Rd., Karachi 4, Pakistan.
● Industrial Development. bi-m.
● Pakistan Industrial Development Corporation. Report. a. ISSN 0078-8201

**Pakistan Institute of Development Economics**
Box 1091, Islamabad, Pakistan.
● Monographs in the Economics of Development. irreg. ISSN 0544-8433
● Pakistan Institute of Development Economics. Report. irreg., latest issue, 1969. ISSN 0078-821X
● Pakistan Institute of Development Economics. Research Report. irreg. ISSN 0078-8228
● Pakistan Institute of Development Economics. Statistical Papers. irreg.
● Readings in Development Economics. irreg. ISSN 0557-8280

**Pakistan Institute of Management**
P.I.D.C., Shahrah-Iran, Clifton, Karachi 6, Pakistan.
● Pakistan Management Review. q. ISSN 0030-9974

**Pakistan Insurance Corporation**
Pakistan Insurance Bldg., Bunder Rd., Karachi 2, Pakistan.
● Insurance Review. q. ISSN 0020-4811

**Pakistan Journal of Surgery, Gynaecology, and Obstetrics**
9 Braganza House, Mir Karamali Talpur Rd., Saddar, Karachi, Pakistan.
● Pakistan Journal of Surgery, Gynaecology, and Obstetrics. m. ISSN 0030-9907

**Pakistan Law House**
Pakistan Chowk, Box 90, Karachi 1, Pakistan.
● Karachi Law Journal. a. ISSN 0075-5095

**Pakistan Library Association**
Box 3412, Karachi, Pakistan.
● P L A Newsletter. m. ISSN 0048-2714

**Pakistan Medical Association**
P. M. A. House, Garden Rd., Karachi 3, Pakistan.
● Pakistan Medical Association. Journal. m. ISSN 0030-9982

**Pakistan Medical Research Council**
12-A Mohd. Ali Housing Society, Karachi, Pakistan.
● Pakistan Journal of Medical Research. q. ISSN 0030-9842

**Pakistan National Tuberculosis Association**
Block No. 55, Pakistan Secretariat, Karachi, Pakistan.
● Challenge. q.

**Pakistan Nurses Federation**
c/o College of Nursing, Jinnah Postgraduate Medical Centre, Karachi 35, Pakistan.
● Pakistan Nursing and Health Review. q. ISSN 0078-8376

**Pakistan Paint Manufacturers' Association**
Box 3602, Block 14, Federal B Area, Karachi 16, Pakistan.
● Paints in Pakistan. q.

**Pakistan Petroleum Ltd.**
PIDC House, Dr. Ziauddin Ahmad Rd., Karachi 4, Pakistan.
● Progress. m. ISSN 0033-0574

**Pakistan Philatelic Association**
● Pakistan Stamps. (pub. by M. Sharif Qurshi, Ed. & Pub.)

**Pakistan Philosophical Congress**
Narsingdas Garden, Club Rd., Lahore 3, Pakistan.
● Pakistan Philosophical Congress. Proceedings. a. ISSN 0078-8406
● Pakistan Philosophical Journal. s-a.

**Pakistan Press International**
Saifee House, Dr. Ziauddin Ahmed Rd., Karachi 2, Pakistan.
● Economic Outlook. m.
● Pakistan Courier. m.

**Pakistan Publications**
Box 183, Shahrah Iraq, Karachi 1, Pakistan.
● Pakistan Pictorial. bi-m.
● Perspective. m.

**Pakistan Publishers & Booksellers Association**
Y.M.C.A. Bldg., Shara-e-Quaid-e-Azam, Lahore, Pakistan.
● Bookseller. m. ISSN 0006-7547

**Pakistan Railways**
Moghalpura, Pakistan.
● Pakistan Railways. Yearbook of Information. a.

**Pakistan Scientific and Technological Information Centre**
House No. 6, Street No. 22, Sector F-7/2, Box 1217, Islamabad, Pakistan.
● Directory of Scientific Periodicals of Pakistan. irreg.
● Lists of P A S T I C Bibliographies. a.
● P A S T I C Translations. irreg.
● Pakistan Science Abstracts. q. ISSN 0031-0085
● Union Catalog of Scientific and Technical Periodicals in the Libraries of Pakistan. irreg., latest issue, 1975.

**Pakistan Society of Biochemists**
University of Punjab, Lahore, Pakistan.
● Pakistan Journal of Biochemistry. s-a. ISSN 0300-8185

**Pakistan Society of Leather Technologists**
16 Bambino Chambers, Box 7821, Saddar, Karachi 3, Pakistan.
● Pakistan Leather Trade Journal. q.
● Pakistan Leather Year Book. a. ISSN 0078-8252

**Pakistan Standards Institution**
39 Garden Road, Karachi 3, Pakistan.
● Pakistan Standards Institution. Report. a. ISSN 0078-8457

**Pakistan Statistical Association**
Institute of Statistics, University of the Punjab, Lahore, Pakistan.
● Pakistan Statistical Association. Proceedings. a. ISSN 0078-8473

**Pakistan University of Engineering and Technology**
Grand Trunk Rd., Lahore 31, Pakistan.
● Pakistan University of Engineering and Technology. Research Bulletin. q.

**Pakistan Water and Power Development Authority**
WAPDA House, Shara-e-Quaid-e-Azam, Lahore, Pakistan.
● Barqab. m. ISSN 0522-4314
● Indus. m. ISSN 0537-4715
● Pakistan. Water and Power Development Authority. Report. a. ISSN 0083-8349

**Panjab University**
*see* **University of the Punjab**

**Pashto Academy**
Peshawar, Pakistan.
● Pushto. m. ISSN 0555-8158

**Peshawar (City) Pakistan Academy for Rural Development**
Peshawar, Pakistan.
● Journal of Rural Development and Administration. q. ISSN 0047-2751

**Peshawar University**
*see* **University of Peshawar**

**Pictorial News Review Publications**
1 Victoria Chambers, Abdullah Haroon Rd., Karachi 3, Pakistan.
● Pictorial News Review. m. ISSN 0031-9651

**Printoff Printers & Publishers**
94-96 Central Commercial Area, P.E.C.H.S., Karachi 29, Pakistan.
● Independent Weekly. w. ISSN 0046-8851

**Progressive Papers Limited**
Progressive Papers Bldg., Rattan Chand Rd., Lahore 7, Pakistan.
● Sportimes; the magazine for sportsmen. m. ISSN 0038-7991

**Punjab. Bureau of Education**
Lahore, Punjab, Pakistan.
● Educational Statistics of Punjab. a.

**Punjab. Department of Agriculture**
50 Aryanagar, Samnabad, Lahore, Pakistan.
● Journal of Agricultural Research. q.

**Punjab Punch**
1 McLeod Rd., Lahore, Pakistan.
● Punjab Punch; a views weekly. w. ISSN 0048-6027

**Punjab University**
*see* **University of the Punjab**

**Q I M P Quarterly**
Salma Mansion, Napier St., Saddar, Karachi, Pakistan.
● Q I M P Quarterly. (Quick Index of Medical Preparations) q. ISSN 0033-4790

**Quaid-i-Azam University**
● Quaid-i-Azam University. Journal of Mathematics and Sciences. (pub. by Quaid-i-Azam University Press)

**Quaid-i-Azam University. Department of Pakistan Studies**
● Sirius. (pub. by Quaid-i-Azam University Press)

**Quaid-i-Azam University. International Forum**
● Scrutiny. (pub. by Quaid-i-Azam University Press)

**Quaid-i-Azam University Press**
Bookshop, Bookbank and Publication Cell, Islamabad, Pakistan.
● Quaid-i-Azam University. Journal of Mathematics and Sciences. s-a.
● Scrutiny. s-a. (Quaid-i-Azam University. International Forum)
● Sirius. s-a. (Quaid-i-Azam University. Department of Pakistan Studies)

**M. Sharif Qurshi, Ed. & Pub.**
42 the Mall, Lahore, Pakistan.
● Pakistan Stamps. m. ISSN 0031-0093 (Pakistan Philatelic Association)

**Research Society of Pakistan**
University of the Punjab, 2 Narsingdas Garden, Club Rd., Lahore, Pakistan.
● Research Society of Pakistan. Journal. q. ISSN 0034-5431

**Review of Religions**
c/o M. G. Ahmad, Rabwah, Pakistan.
● Review of Religions. m. ISSN 0034-6721

**Sanaullah Publications**
Box 4186, Karachi, Pakistan.
● Pakistan Banking Directory. a. ISSN 0078-7884

**Scientific Society of Pakistan**
University of Karachi, Dept. of Zoology, Karachi 32, Pakistan.
● Jadeed Science. bi-m. ISSN 0021-3888

**Shivaji University**
Registrar, Kolhapur 4, Pakistan.
● Shivaji University, Kolhapur, India. Journal. Humanities and Sciences. a.(in 2 parts) ISSN 0080-9314

**Sind University**
*see* **University of Sind**

**Sind University Press**
Jamshoro, Hyderabad 6, Pakistan.
- Sind University Journal of Education. a. ISSN 0560-0871 (University of Sind. Institute of Education & Research)

**Smar International**
6 Afshan Chambers, Tariq Rd., P.E.C.H.S., Karachi 29, Pakistan.
- Smar's Industrial Directory of Pakistan. a.

**Society and Screen**
45-E Block 6, P.E.C.H.S., Karachi 29, Pakistan.
- Society and Screen. m.

**Society for the Advancement of Agricultural Sciences**
Lyallpur, Pakistan.
- Pakistan Journal of Agricultural Sciences. q. ISSN 0552-9034

**State Bank of Pakistan**
see Pakistan. State Bank of Pakistan

**Student Times Publications**
185 H-Z, P.E.C.H.S., Karachi, Pakistan.
- Student Times International. ISSN 0039-2790

**Sunday Post**
4-5 Amil St., Off Robson Rd., Karachi 1, Pakistan.
- Sunday Post. w. ISSN 0039-5277

**Sunrise Publications**
Victoria Hotel Bldg., Nicol Rd., Karachi, Pakistan.
- Aviation, Shipping and Tourism Fortnightly. fortn.
- Banking and Insurance. m.

**T V and Advertising**
No. 2 Commercial Area, Block A, Sindhi Muslim Housing Society, Karachi, Pakistan.
- T V and Advertising. m.

**Taxation Publishers**
6 Liaqat Rd., Lahore 6, Pakistan.
- Customs Imports and Exports Journal. m. ISSN 0011-4154
- Taxation. m. ISSN 0040-0157

**Teenager Monthly**
145-C-2 Hali Rd., P.E.C.H.S., Karachi 29, Pakistan.
- Teenager Monthly. m. ISSN 0049-321X

**Textile Industry Publications**
V.E. 15/16 Nazimabad, Karachi, Pakistan.
- Journal of Textile Industry. m.

**Trade and Industry Publications Limited**
Trade and Industry House, 14 West Wharf Road, Box 4611, Karachi 2, Pakistan.
- Pakistan Export Directory. a. ISSN 0078-8090 (Pakistan. Export Promotion Bureau)
- Pakistan Journal of Pharmacy. m. ISSN 0030-9850
- Trade and Industry; the pioneer monthly economic journal of Pakistan. m. ISSN 0041-0373

**Umma Publishing House**
Bahadurabad Commercial Area, Karachi 0511, Pakistan.
- World Muslim Gazetteer. biennial. ISSN 0084-2060 (World Muslim Congress)

**Unesco. Regional Office for Culture and Book Development in Asia**
For publications of this agency see section for UNITED NATIONS

**United Bank Limited**
State Life Bldg., I.I. Chundrigar Rd., Karachi, Pakistan.
- United Bank Limited. Monthly Economic Newsletter. m. (prep. by its Research Department)

**University of Karachi. Department of English**
University Rd., Karachi 32, Pakistan.
- Venture; bi-annual review of English language and literature. s-a. ISSN 0042-3483

**University of Karachi. Department of Journalism**
University Rd., Karachi 32, Pakistan.
- Karachi University Gazette. m. ISSN 0022-8974

**University of Karachi. Department of Library Science**
University Rd., Karachi 32, Pakistan.
- Pakistan Library Bulletin. q. ISSN 0030-9966 (prep. by its Library Promotion Bureau)

**University of Karachi. Department of Psychology**
University Rd., Karachi 32, Pakistan.
- Pakistan Journal of Psychology. a. ISSN 0030-9869

**University of Peshawar. College of Education**
Peshawar, Pakistan.
- New Teacher. a. ISSN 0077-8826

**University of Peshawar. Department of Archaeology**
Peshawar, Pakistan.
- Ancient Pakistan. irreg. ISSN 0066-1600

**University of Sind. Faculty of Arts**
Jamshoro, Hyderabad 6, Pakistan.
- University of Sind. Research Journal. Arts Series: Humanities and Social Sciences. a. ISSN 0080-9616

**University of Sind. Institute of Education & Research**
- Sind University Journal of Education. (pub. by Sind University Press)

**University of the Punjab. Arabic and Persian Society**
Lahore, Pakistan.
- University of the Punjab. Arabic and Persian Society. Journal. a. ISSN 0079-8029

**University of the Punjab. Department of Economics**
New Campus, Lahore, Pakistan.
- Pakistan Economic and Social Review. q.

**University of the Punjab. Department of Geography**
New Campus, Lahore, Pakistan.
- Pakistan Geographical Review. s-a. ISSN 0030-9788

**University of the Punjab. Department of Geology**
New Campus, Lahore, Pakistan.
- University of the Punjab. Department of Geology. Geological Bulletin. irreg., no. 11, 1974. ISSN 0079-8037

**University of the Punjab. Department of Zoology**
New Campus, Lahore, Pakistan.
- University of the Punjab. Department of Zoology. Bulletin. New Series. irreg., 1972, no. 6. ISSN 0079-8045

**Urdu Development Board**
D-41 Block B, Teymuriya, Karachi 33, Pakistan.
- Urdu Namah. q. ISSN 0042-1065

**Weekly al-Fatah**
87-D, Nursery Commercial Area, P.E.C.H.S., Karachi 29, Pakistan.
- Weekly al-Fatah. w.

**West Pakistan Bar Council**
Lahore, Pakistan.
- Pakistan Law Journal. m.

**Wildfields**
15 Dayaram Gidumac Road, Karachi 3, Pakistan.
- Wildfields. m.

**World Federation of Islamic Missions**
B-Block, North Nazimabad, Karachi 33, Pakistan.
- Minaret Monthly International. m.

**World Muslim Congress**
Box 5030, Karachi 2, Pakistan.
- Muslim World; weekly review of the Motamar. w.
- World Muslim Conference. Proceedings. biennial. ISSN 0084-2052
- World Muslim Gazetteer. (pub. by Umma Publishing House)

**Mazhar Yusuf, Ed. & Pub.**
505 Qamar House, Bunder Rd., Karachi, Pakistan.
- Pakistan Textile Journal. m. ISSN 0048-2757
- This Fortnight in Pakistan. ISSN 0049-3759

**Zartaj Publications**
59 Farid Chambers, Abdullah Haroon Rd., Saddar, Karachi, Pakistan.
- Travelogue International. q.

**Z. I. Zobairy, Ed. & Pub.**
Box 7442, Karachi 3, Pakistan.
- Karachi Commerce Weekly. w. ISSN 0022-8966

**Zoological Society of Pakistan**
c/o Department of Zoology, University of the Punjab, New Campus, Lahore, Pakistan.
- Pakistan Journal of Zoology. s-a. ISSN 0030-9923

# PANAMA

**Asociacion Panamena para el Planeamiento de la Familia. Departamento de Informacion y Educacion**
Apartado Postal 4637, Panama 5, Panama.
- Conciencia. m.

**Banco Nacional de Panama**
Plaza Belisario Porras, Apartado Postal 5220, Panama, Panama.
- Banco Nacional de Panama. Cuadernos. a. ISSN 0522-1986

**Banco Nacional de Panama. Asesoria Economica y Planificacion**
Casa Matriz, Apdo. 5520, Panama 5, Panama.
- Banco Nacional de Panama. Asesoria Economica y Planificacion. Carta Economica. q (approx.)

**Casa del Periodista**
John K. Sloan, Apdo. 2096, Panama City, Panama.
- Trabajador del Periodismo/Newspaper Worker. bi-m. ISSN 0028-9566

**Centro de Capacitacion Social**
Apdo 9a-192, Panama, Panama.
- Dialogo Social; la revista de inquietud social. m. (except Jan.) ISSN 0046-0206

**Focus Guide Magazine Group**
Apartado 7656, Panama 5, Panama.
- Focus on Central America. s-a. (Promociones Turisticas de Panama y el Caribe, S.A.)
- Focus on Panama. s-a. (Promociones Turisticas de Panama y el Caribe, S.A.)
- Focus on the Dominican Republic. s-a.

**Instituto de Vivienda y Urbanismo**
Panama City, Panama.
- Instituto de Vivienda y Urbanismo. Memoria Presentada Por el Director General. a.

**Inter-American Center of Tax Administrators**
Apartado Postal 215, Zona 1, Panama, Panama.
- Inter-American Center of Tax Administrators. Informativo/Newsletter. m.
- Studies on Tax Administration Series. irreg.

**Panama. Contraloria General. Direccion de Contabilidad**
Panama City, Panama.
- Panama. Contraloria General. Informe Trimestral de Rentas y Gastos. q.

**Panama. Departamento de Beneficencia Cultural. Loteria Nacional de Beneficencia**
Via Espana No. 13, Panama 1, Panama.
- Loteria. m. ISSN 0024-662X

**Panama. Direccion de Estadistica y Censos**
Contraloria General, Apartado 5213, Panama 5, Panama.
- Estadistica Panamena. Estadistica Electoral. quadriennial. ISSN 0078-897X
- Estadistica Panamena. Indicadores Economicos y Sociales. Seccion 011. Indicadores Economicos y Sociales. a (with quarterly supplements)
- Estadistica Panamena. Inversiones Directas Extranjeras en Panama. irreg.
- Estadistica Panamena. Seccion 221. Movimiento de Poblacion. a (Estadistica Vitales); s-a (Cifras preliminares) ISSN 0078-8902
- Estadistica Panamena. Situacion Cultural. Seccion 511. Educacion. a.
- Estadistica Panamena. Situacion Demografica. Seccion 231. Migracion Internacional. a.
- Estadistica Panamena. Situacion Economica, Industria. a.
- Estadistica Panamena. Situacion Economica. Seccion 331-Comercio. Comercio Exterior. a. ISSN 0553-0660
- Estadistica Panamena. Situacion Economica. Secciones 333 y 334. Transportes y Comunicaciones. a. ISSN 0078-8945
- Estadistica Panamena. Situacion Economica. Seccion 341. Balanza de Pagos. a. ISSN 0078-8929
- Estadistica Panamena. Situacion Economica. Seccion 342. Cuentas Nacionales. a. ISSN 0078-8910
- Estadistica Panamena. Situacion Economica: Seccion 351-Precios, Agropecuario. irreg.
- Estadistica Panamena. Situacion Fisica. Seccion 121-Clima. Meteorologia. a. ISSN 0078-8953

- Estadistica Panamena. Situacion Social. Seccion 441-Trabajo y Salarios. Estadisticas del Trabajo. a.
- Panama. Direccion de Estadistica y Censo. Estadistica Panamena. Serie F. Industrias-Encuestas. a. ISSN 0078-8937
- Panama en Cifras. a. ISSN 0078-8996

**Panama. Direccion General de Recursos Naturales Renovables**
Ministerio de Desarrollo Agropecuario, Panama, Panama.
- Panama. Direccion General de Recursos Naturales Renovables. Memoria. irreg.

**Panama. Ministerio de Agricultura y Ganaderia**
Apartado 5390, Panama 5, Panama.
- Panama. Ministerio de Agricultura y Ganaderia. Boletin Tecnico. irreg. ISSN 0085-4654

**Panama Canal Co.**
U.S. Government, Balboa Heights, Canal Zone, Panama.
- Panama Canal Review. s-a. ISSN 0031-0646

**Panama Canal Co. Engineering Division**
Box M, Balboa Heights, Panama.
- Panama Canal Company. Meteorological and Hydrographic Branch. Climatological Data: Canal Zone and Panama. a. ISSN 0078-8899

**Panama Tribune**
Apartado 3407, Panama 4, Panama.
- Panama Tribune. w. ISSN 0031-0654

**Promociones Turisticas de Panama y el Caribe, S.A.**
- Focus on Central America. (pub. by Focus Guide Magazine Group)
- Focus on Panama. (pub. by Focus Guide Magazine Group)

**Tierra y dos Mares**
c/o Ana Coltilde Barraza, Ed., Apdo. Postal 4927, Panama 5, Panama.
- Tierra y dos Mares. bi-m. ISSN 0040-7348

**Universidad de Panama**
Biblioteca, Estafeta Universitaria, Panama, Panama.
- Voz de la Biblioteca Universitaria. q. ISSN 0042-9082

**Universidad de Panama. Centro de Investigacion Juridica**
Estafeta Universitaria, Panama, Panama.
- Revista Juridica Panamena. 1-2 per yr. ISSN 0302-6655

**Universidad de Panama. Centro de Investigaciones Sociales y Economicas**
- Anales de Ciencias Humanas. (pub. by Editorial Universitaria)

**Universidad de Panama. Escuela de Bibliotecologia**
Apdo 3277, Panama 3, Panama.
- Universidad de Panama. Escuela de Bibliotecologia. Boletin. q. ISSN 0014-0422

**Universidad de Panama. Facultad de Administracion Publica y Comercio**
Panama City, Panama.
- Universidad de Panama. Facultad de Administracion Publica y Comercio. Revista. q.

**Universidad de Panama. Facultad de Derecho y Ciencias Politicas**
Oficina de Informacion y Publicaciones, Panama City, Panama.
- Universidad de Panama. Facultad de Derecho y Ciencias Politicas. Cuadernos. irreg.

**Editorial Universitaria**
Apartado 3368, Panama City 4, Panama.
- Anales de Ciencias Humanas. s-a. ISSN 0302-6957 (Universidad de Panama. Centro de Investigaciones Sociales y Economicas)

# PAPUA NEW GUINEA

**Australian National University**
New Guinea Research Unit, Box 1238, Boroko, Port Moresby, Papua New Guinea.
- Luksave. irreg., latest issue, 1974. ISSN 0085-2902

**Bank of Papua New Guinea**
Port Moresby, Papua New Guinea.
- Bank of Papua New Guinea. Report and Financial Statements. a.

**Girl Guides Association of Papua New Guinea**
Box 2079, Konedobu, Papua New Guinea.
- Drum. 3 per yr.

**Highland Farmers & Settlers Association**
- New Guinea Bulletin. (pub. by Producers Publications (Pty) Ltd.)

**Institute of Papua and New Guinea Studies**
Box 1432, Boroko, Papua New Guinea.
- Gigibori: Magazine of New Guinea Cultures. q.

**Medical Society of Papua New Guinea**
Box 1174, Boroko, Port Moresby, Papua New Guinea.
- Papua New Guinea Medical Journal. q. ISSN 0031-1480

**New Guinea News Service (Pty.) Ltd.**
Box 5050-Boroko, Papua New Guinea.
- Focus-New Guinea. m.

**Papua & New Guinea Scientific Society**
C/O Dept. of Agriculture, Stock & Fisheries, Konedobu, Papua New Guinea.
- Papua and New Guinea Scientific Society. Annual Report and Proceedings. a. ISSN 0085-4697
- Papua and New Guinea Scientific Society. Transactions. a. ISSN 0085-4700

**Papua New Guinea. Bureau of Statistics**
P.O. Wards Strip, Papua New Guinea.
- Building Statistics. q.
- Consumer Price Index. q. ISSN 0094-8616
- Papua New Guinea. Abstract of Statistics. q.
- Papua New Guinea. Bureau of Statistics. Capital Expenditure by Private Businesses. a. ISSN 0078-9259
- Papua New Guinea. Bureau of Statistics. Industrial Accidents. a. ISSN 0078-9267
- Papua New Guinea. Bureau of Statistics. International Trade Statistics. a.
- Papua New Guinea. Bureau of Statistics. Private Overseas Investment. a. ISSN 0078-9283
- Papua New Guinea. Bureau of Statistics. Rural Industries. a. ISSN 0078-7701
- Papua New Guinea. Bureau of Statistics. Rural Industries. Preliminary Statement. a. ISSN 0078-9321
- Papua New Guinea. Bureau of Statistics. Secondary Industries. a. ISSN 0078-933X
- Papua New Guinea. Bureau of Statistics. Secondary Industries (Factories and Works). Preliminary Statement. a. ISSN 0078-9313
- Papua New Guinea. Bureau of Statistics. Statistical Bulletin: Building Statistics. q.
- Papua New Guinea. Bureau of Statistics. Statistical Bulletin: Registered Motor Vehicles. irreg.
- Papua New Guinea. Bureau of Statistics. Statistical Bulletin: Survey of Retail Sales and Selected Services. irreg.
- Papua New Guinea. Bureau of Statistics. Statistics of Religious Organisations. a. ISSN 0078-9356
- Papua New Guinea. Bureau of Statistics. Summary of Statistics. irreg.
- Papua New Guinea. Bureau of Statistics. Taxation Statistics. Preliminary Bulletin. a. ISSN 0078-9372
- Papua New Guinea. Bureau of Statistics. Workers' Compensation Statistics. irreg.
- Papua New Guinea Overseas Migration. q. ISSN 0031-1510
- Population Census of Papua New Guinea. Population Characteristics Bulletin Series. irreg., latest issue, 1971. ISSN 0079-3868

**Papua New Guinea. Department of Agriculture, Stock and Fisheries**
Konedobu, Papua New Guinea.
- Papua and New Guinea Agricultural Journal. irreg. ISSN 0031-1464

**Papua New Guinea. Department of Business Development**
P.O. Box 3383, Port Moresby, Papua New Guinea.
- Bisnis Newsletter. q.

**Papua New Guinea. Department of Education**
Konedobu, Papua New Guinea.
- Papua and New Guinea Education Gazette. m(exc. Jan.) ISSN 0048-2919

- Papua New Guinea. Department of Education. Recent Developments in Education. a.

**Papua New Guinea. Department of Education. Curriculum Branch**
Box 793, Lae, Papua New Guinea.
- Mathsnews. 3 per yr. ISSN 0310-6357

**Papua New Guinea. Department of Information and Extension Services**
Port Moresby, Papua New Guinea.
- Progress and Growth of Papua New Guinea. a. ISSN 0085-5170

**Papua New Guinea. Department of Labour**
Konedobu, Papua New Guinea.
- Papua New Guinea. Department of Labour. Industrial Review. irreg. ISSN 0085-4719

**Papua New Guinea. Department of Social Development and Home Affairs**
Port Moresby, Papua New Guinea.
- Papua New Guinea. Department of Social Development and Home Affairs. Social Science Research. a. ISSN 0310-8147

**Papua New Guinea. Government Printer**
Box 2150, Konedobu, Papua New Guinea.
- Papua and New Guinea Journal of Education. 3 per yr. ISSN 0031-1472
- Papua New Guinea. Public Service Board. Report. a. ISSN 0078-9399

**Papua-New Guinea. Literature Bureau**
Office of Informatin, Box 2312, Konedobu, Papua New Guinea.
- Papua New Guinea Writing. q.

**Papua, New Guinea. Manpower Planning Unit. Manpower Studies**
P. O. 3618, Port Moresby, Papua New Guinea.
- Papua, New Guinea. Manpower Planning Unit. Manpower Studies. 2-3 per yr.

**Papua New Guinea. Office of Local Government**
Box 1179, Boroko, Papua New Guinea.
- Papua New Guinea Office of Local Government. Local Government Bulletin. irreg. ISSN 0085-4727

**Papua-New Guinea Cave Exploration Group**
c/o Michael Bourke, Ed., D.A.S.F., Keravat, E.N.B., Papua New Guinea.
- Niugini Caver. q. ISSN 0310-3773

**Papua New Guinea Institute of Medical Research**
P.O. Box 60, Goroka, Papua New Guinea.
- Papua New Guinea Institute of Medical Research. Monograph Series. irreg.

**Papua New Guinea University of Technology**
Box 793, Lae, Papua New Guinea.
- Spectrum. 3 per yr. ISSN 0310-7442

**Producers Publications (Pty) Ltd.**
Box 75, Goroka, Papua New Guinea.
- New Guinea Bulletin. q. ISSN 0028-5153 (Highland Farmers & Settlers Association)

**University of Papau New Guinea. Biology Department**
P.O. Box 4820, Boroko, Papua New Guinea.
- Science in New Guinea. irreg. ISSN 0310-4303

**University of Papua & New Guinea. Department of Anthropology & Sociology**
Box 4820 University, Papua New Guinea.
- Research in Melanesia; a newsletter of anthropological and sociological research in Papua & New Guinea. q.

**University of Papua and New Guinea. The Library**
Box 4819, University Post Office, Papua New Guinea.
- New Guinea Bibliography. a.
- New Guinea Periodical Index; guide to current periodical literature about New Guinea. q.(with annual cumulation) ISSN 0028-5161

**University of Papua New Guinea. Department of Geography**
Box 4820, University P.O., Papua New Guinea.
- University of Papua New Guinea. Department of Geography. Occasional Papers in Geography. irreg. (2-3 per yr)

**Univ. of Papua New Guinea. Department of History**
P.O. 4820, Papua New Guinea.
- Oral History. m.

**University of Papua New Guinea. Department of Physics**
Box 4820, Univeristy P.O, Papua New Guinea.
- University of Papua New Guinea. Department of Physics. Technical Paper. irreg. ISSN 0085-4735

**University of Papua New Guinea. Teaching Methods and Materials Centre**
Box 4820, University, Papua New Guinea.
- Teaching Methods and Materials Bulletin. irreg.

**Wantok Publications**
Box 386, Wewak, Papua New Guinea.
- Wantok. s-m.

# PARAGUAY

**Accion**
Calle Colon 1236, Casilla 1072, Asuncion, Paraguay.
- Accion; revista paraguaya de reflexion y dialogo. 4 per yr. ISSN 0001-4605

**Arte-Literatura**
Iturbe 870, Asuncion, Paraguay.
- Alcor. q. ISSN 0002-5062

**Asociacion de Agencias de Viajes y Turismo**
Apdo 959, Asuncion, Paraguay.
- Guia Guarani. m. ISSN 0017-5153

**Asociacion de Bibliotecarios del Paraguay**
Casilla de Correo 1505, Asuncion, Paraguay.
- Bibliotecologia y Documentacion Paraguaya. irreg.

**Banco Central del Paraguay**
Independencia Nacional y 25 de Mayo, Paraguay.
- Banco Central del Paraguay. Memoria. a. ISSN 0067-3285

**Centro Paraguayo de Estudios de Poblacion**
Coronel Bogado 1053 Esq. Juan de Mena, Asuncion, Paraguay.
- Temas de Poblacion. bi-m.

**Centro Paraguayo de Estudios Sociologicos**
Eligio Ayala 973, Asuncion, Paraguay.
- Revista Paraguaya de Sociologia. 3 per yr. ISSN 0035-0354

**Jose Venancio Duarte Sosa, Ed. & Pub.**
Casilla de Correos 900, Asuncion, Paraguay.
- Paraguay Industrial y Comercial. m. ISSN 0031-1685 (Paraguay. Ministerio de Industria y Comercio)

**Epoca**
Natalicio Talavera No. 336, Asuncion, Paraguay.
- Epoca; revista de cultura. bi-m. ISSN 0013-9726

**Eladio Gonzalez Nunez, Ed. & Pub.**
Anotado Punto 4, Casilla de Correo 1056, Asuncion, Paraguay.
- Sintesis; revista paraguaya. m. ISSN 0049-0598

**Instituto de Prevision Social**
Asuncion, Paraguay.
- Instituto de Prevision Social. Boletin. bi-m. ISSN 0020-4005

**Instituto Femenino de Investigaciones Historicas**
Asuncion, Paraguay.
- Instituto Femenino de Investigaciones Historicas. Anuario. irreg.

**Museo Etnografico**
Edificio Museum Andres Barbero, Espana y Mompox, Asuncion, Paraguay.
- Boletin de la Sociedad Cientifica del Paraguay y del Museo Etnografico. irreg. ISSN 0560-4168 (Co-sponsor: Sociedad Cientifica del Paraguay)

**Editorial Nande**
Alberdi 1393, Asuncion, Paraguay.
- Aqui. w. ISSN 0044-8524

- Nande. fortn. ISSN 0047-8644

**Paraguay. Armada Nacional**
Asuncion, Paraguay.
- Boletin Naval. bi-m. ISSN 0006-646X

**Paraguay. Centro Militar y Naval**
Asuncion, Paraguay.
- Revista del Ejercito y Armada. m. ISSN 0034-9054

**Paraguay. Direccion General de Estadistica y Censos**
Humaita 463, Casilla de Correo 1118, Asuncion, Paraguay.
- Paraguay. Direccion General de Estadistica y Censos. Boletin Estadistico. s-a. ISSN 0031-1677

**Paraguay. Ministerio de Industria y Comercio**
- Paraguay Industrial y Comercial. (pub. by Jose Venancio Duarte Sosa, Ed. & Pub.)

**Paraguay. Ministerio de Industria y Comercio. Division de Registro y Estadistica Industrial**
Av. Espana 475, Asuncion, Paraguay.
- Paraguay. Ministerio de Industria y Comercio. Division de Registro y Estadistica Industrial. Encuesta Industrial. irreg. ISSN 0085-4743

**Sociedad de Pediatria y Puericultura del Paraguay**
25 de Mayo y Tacuai, Asuncion, Paraguay.
- Revista Medica del Paraguay. q. ISSN 0034-9933

**Universidad Catolica Nuestra Senora de la Asuncion**
Casilla de Correo 1718, Asuncion, Paraguay.
- Estudios Paraguayos. s-a.

**Universidad Catolica Nuestra Senora de la Asuncion. Centro de Estudios Antropologicos**
Independencia Nacional y Comuneros, Asuncion, Paraguay.
- Revista del Ateneo Paraguayo. irreg. ISSN 0084-6929

**Universidad Nacional de Asuncion. Facultad de Ciencias Medicas**
Casilla de Correo 1102, Asuncion, Paraguay.
- Revista Paraguaya de Microbiologia. a. ISSN 0556-6908 (prep. by its Catedra de Bacteriologia y Parasitologia)

# PERU

**A-F Producciones Ltda**
Jr. Soledad, 247, Of. 103, Lima 14, Peru.
- Imera.

**Academia Militar de Chorrillos**
Chorrillos, Peru.
- Academia Militar de Chorrillos. Revista. q. ISSN 0001-3811

**Academia Peruana de Cirugia**
Camana 773, Lima, Peru.
- Academia Peruana de Cirugia Revista. q. ISSN 0001-3854

**Adela Investment Company S.A.**
Paseo de la Republica 3101, P.O. Box 207, Lima, Peru.
- Adela Monthly Bulletin. m.

**Andean Report**
Apartado 2484, Lima, Peru.
- Andean Report. m.

**Asociacion de Exportadores**
Casilla Postal 1806, Las Flores 346 - San Isidro, Lima, Peru.
- Peru Exporta. m.

**Asociacion Peruana de Derechos Sociales**
Jiron de la Union No. 1011, Of. 3, 3er. Piso, Lima, Peru.
- Derechos Sociales. irreg.

**Banco Central de Reserva del Peru. Seccion Publicaciones**
Apdo. 1958, Lima, Peru.
- Banco Central de Reserva del Peru. Boletin. m. ISSN 0005-4712

**Banco de Credito de Peru**
Economic Research Dept., Lima, Peru.
- Peruvian Foreign Trade News. irreg.; (1-2 per yr), latest issue, no. 1, 1974. ISSN 0556-3747

**Banco Minero del Peru. Division de Planeamiento**
Lima, Peru.
- Exportaciones Mineras del Peru. irreg.

**Camara Algodonera del Peru**
Apdo. 1605, Lima, Peru.
- Algodon. m. ISSN 0002-5356

**Camara de Comercio de Lima**
Av. Abancay 291, 2O. Piso, Lima 1, Peru.
- Camara de Comercio de Lima. Boletin Semanal. w. ISSN 0008-1884
- Camara de Comercio de Lima. Informativo Legal. fortn.
- Comercio y Produccion. bi-m. ISSN 0008-1892

**Colegio Medico del Peru**
Avenida Santa Cruz 315, Miraflores, Lima, Peru.
- Acta Medica Peruana. q.

**Colegio Salesiano**
Box 999, Lima, Peru.
- Biota. 4 per yr. ISSN 0006-3584

**Confederacion Nacional de Comerciantes**
- Directorio Industrial Comercial del Peru. (pub. by Estudios Comerciales s.r.l.)

**Creacion y Critica**
Alfonso Vagarte No. 284, Lima 32, Peru.
- Creacion y Critica. q.

**Empresa Editorial Cusco S.A.**
San Andres 240, Cusco, Peru.
- Comercio. d. ISSN 0010-2253

**Dispensario Antituberculoso "Max Arias Schreiber"**
Raymondi 2da Cuadra (La Victoria), Lima, Peru.
- Centro de Salud "Max Arias Schreiber", Lima. Congreso Nacional de Tuberculosis y Enfermedades Respiratorias. irreg., 1970, 9th. ISSN 0069-2166

**Escuela de Peritos Agricolas de Tacna. Grupo Cultural "Mario Vargas Llosa"**
8 via Calientes, Apdo 545, Tacna, Peru.
- Cauce. irreg.

**Estudios Comerciales s.r.l.**
Lima, Peru.
- Directorio Industrial Comercial del Peru. (Confederacion Nacional de Comerciantes)

**Juan Fanning, Ed. & Pub.**
354 Miraflores, Lima 18, Peru.
- Asociacion Peruana de Astronomia. Boletin. q. ISSN 0044-9318

**Federacion Nacional de Camaras de Comercio de Peru**
Avenida Abancay 291, 2 Piso, Lima, Peru.
- Integracion. fortn.

**Livio Gomez, Ed. & Pub.**
Francisco Cornejo 847, Tacna, Peru.
- In Terris; revista de poesia. s-a. ISSN 0300-4031

**Grupo Poesia**
Casilla 151, Trujillo, Peru.
- Cuadernos Trimestrales de Poesia. q. ISSN 0011-2550

**Hablemos de Cine**
Libertadores 199, San Isidro, Lima 97, Peru.
- Hablemos de Cine. 3 per yr. ISSN 0046-6697

**Mario Herrera Gray, Ed. & Pub.**
Calle Mariano Carranza 306, Lima, Peru.
- Conferencias; conferencias, discursos, reportajes, articulos, tesis, notas culturales. m. ISSN 0010-5600

**Editorial Horizonte**
Camana 878, Lima, Peru.
- Realidad Peruana. irreg.

**Empresa Editora Huaral Magazine S.A.**
Av. Solar 217, Jr. Camana 984, Lima, Peru.
- Huaral; el periodico del pueblo. 3 per yr. ISSN 0018-6953

**I E P Ediciones**
Horacio Urteaga 694, Lima 11, Peru.
- America - Problema. irreg.; no. 8, 1973. ISSN 0065-6763 (Instituto de Estudios Peruanos)
- Instituto de Estudios Peruanos. Analisis Economico. irreg.
- Instituto de Estudios Peruanos. Coleccion Minima. irreg.

- Instituto de Estudios Peruanos. Estudios de la
  Sociedad Rural. irreg.
- Instituto de Estudios Peruanos. Historia Andina.
  irreg.
- Instituto de Estudios Peruanos. Proyecto de
  Estudios Etnologicos del Valle de Chancay.
  Monografia. irreg.
- Peru - Problema. irreg.; no. 15,1976. ISSN 0079-
  1075 (Instituto de Estudios Peruanos)

**I. T. F. Regional Office**
Av. Tacna 359, Of. 111, Lima, Peru.
- Transporte. bi-m. ISSN 0041-168X

**Independent Peruvian Association**
Aptdo. 5594, Lima, Peru.
- Latinamerica Press; English language news from
  Noticias Aliadas. w.

**Ingeniero Andino**
Jiron Carabaya 928, Casilla Postal 2484, Lima,
Peru.
- Ingeniero Andino. m. ISSN 0020-1111

**Inspeccion General de Instruccion Pre Militar**
Lima, Peru.
- Gaceta Pre Militar. irreg. ISSN 0016-3856

**Institut Francais d'Etudes Andines**
153 Franklin Roosevelt, Lima, Peru.
- Institut Francais d'Etudes Andines. Bulletin/
  Instituto Frances de Estudios Andinos. Boletin. s-
  a.

**Instituto Cultural Peruano Norteamericano**
Jiron Cuzco 446, Box 304, Lima, Peru.
- Instituto Cultural Peruano Norteamericano.
  Boletin. m. ISSN 0020-3718

**Instituto de Estudios Peruanos**
- America - Problema. (pub. by I E P Ediciones)
- Instituto de Estudios Peruanos. Analisis
  Economico. (pub. by I E P Ediciones)
- Instituto de Estudios Peruanos. Coleccion
  Minima. (pub. by I E P Ediciones)
- Instituto de Estudios Peruanos. Estudios de la
  Sociedad Rural. (pub. by I E P Ediciones)
- Instituto de Estudios Peruanos. Historia Andina.
  (pub. by I E P Ediciones)
- Instituto de Estudios Peruanos. Proyecto de
  Estudios Etnologicos del Valle de Chancay.
  Monografia. (pub. by I E P Ediciones)
- Peru - Problema. (pub. by I E P Ediciones)

**Instituto de Ingenieros de Minas del Peru**
Box 1302, Lima, Peru.
- Mineria. bi-m. ISSN 0026-4679

**Instituto de Pastoral Andina**
Apartado 11, Cusco, Peru.
- Allpanchis. s-a.

**Instituto del Mar del Peru**
Biblioetca, Apartado 3734, Lima, Peru.
- Instituto del Mar del Peru. Boletin. irreg (4-5 per
  year) ISSN 0458-7766
- Instituto del Mar del Peru. Informe. irreg (4-5 per
  year) ISSN 0458-7774

**Instituto Linguistico de Verano**
see also under **United States Summer Institute of
Linguistics**

**Instituto Linguistico de Verano**
see also under **Colombia. Ministerio de Gobierno.
Instituto Linguistico de Verano**

**Instituto Linguistico de Verano**
Casilla 2492, Lima 100, Peru.
- Comunidades y Culturas Peruanas. irreg. no. 10,
  1976. (prep. by its Departamento de Estudios
  Linguisticos)
- Datos Etno-Linguisticos. irreg. no. 60, 1977.
- Instituto Linguistico de Verano. Documentos de
  Trabajo. irreg. no. 13, 1976. (prep. by its
  Departamento de Estudios Linguisticos)
- Serie Linguistica Peruana. irreg. no. 15, 1976.

**Instituto Nacional de Cultura. Museo Nacional de
Historia**
Apartado 1992, Lima, Peru.
- Historia y Cultura. a. ISSN 0073-2486

**Instituto Nacional de Enfermedades Neoplasicas**
Av. Alfonso Ugarte 825, Lima, Peru.
- Instituto Nacional de Enfermedades Neoplasicas.
  Trabajos de Investigacion Clinica y Experimental.
  a. ISSN 0079-1083

**Instituto Panamericano de Geografia e Historia**
see also **Listings in Bolivia, Ecuador and Mexico**

**Instituto Panamericano de Geografia e Historia**
Comision de Historia, Lima, Peru.
- Boletin Bibliografico de Antropologia Americana.
  a. ISSN 0067-9658

**Instituto Peruano de Administracion de Empresas**
Camino Real No. 111 Of. 205, Apartado 4075,
Lima, Peru.
- Gerencia. bi-m. ISSN 0016-8637

**Jovenes Educadores del Peru**
Casilla N. 2213, Lima, Peru.
- Nueva Educacion. m.(Sept-June) ISSN 0029-5817

**Junta del Acuerdo de Cartagena**
Centro de Documentacion, Casilla 3237, Correo
Central, Lima, Peru.
- Leyes Economicas de los Paises Miembros. q.

**Junta del Acuerdo de Cartagena. Unidad
Administrativa**
Casilla 3237, Lima, Peru.
- Junta del Acuerdo de Cartagena. Grupo Andino.
  Carta Informativa. m.

**Ediciones Juridicas**
Monzon 234, Lima, Peru.
- Revista Juridica del Peru. q. (Sociedad de
  Legislacion Comparada. Comite Peruano)

**Editorial Jus**
Paseo Colon 270, Of. 202, Lima, Peru.
- Jus; revista peruana de derecho. m.

**Latinoamericana Editores**
Avenida Benavides 3074, Urbanizacion la
Castellana, Lima, Peru.
- Revista de Critica Literaria Latinoamericana. s-a.

**Imprenta Editorial Lumen S.A.**
Casilla 1589, Lima, Peru.
- Revista de Neuro-Psiquiatria. q. ISSN 0034-8597

**Melibea**
Casimiro Ulloa, 125, Lima, Peru.
- Melibea. irreg.

**Movimiento Internacional de Estudiantes Catolicos**
Aptdo 3564, Lima 1, Peru.
- M I E C Servico de Documentacion. bi-m.

**Museo Nacional de Antropologia y Arqueologia**
Casilla 3640, Lima, Peru.
- Arqueologicas. irreg. latest, no. 15, 1974. ISSN
  0066-7803

**Oiga**
Av. Salaverry 674, Lima, Peru.
- Oiga; semanario de actualidades. castellano. w.
  ISSN 0030-1280

**Organization of the Cooperatives of America**
Baltazar la Torre 10, Apartado 4657, San Isidro,
Lima, Peru.
- Cooperative America. m. ISSN 0002-7057

**Peru. Archivo General de la Nacion**
- Archivo General de la Nacion. Revista. (pub. by
  Peru. Instituto Nacional de Cultura)

**Peru. Biblioteca Nacional**
Apartado 2335, Lima, Peru.
- Fenix; revista. a; no. 23, 1973. ISSN 0015-0002
- Gaceta Bibliotecaria del Peru. a.; latest issue, no.
  21, 1973. ISSN 0433-0730
- Peru. Biblioteca Nacional. Boletin. q. ISSN 0031-
  6067

**Peru. Caja Nacional de Seguro Social**
Hospital Obrero, Lima, Peru.
- Anales del Servicio de Psiquiatria. bi-m. ISSN
  0003-2549
- Informaciones Sociales. q. (prep. by its
  Departamento de Estudios Sociales y
  Economicos)

**Peru. Centro Nacional de Productividad**
Jiron Zepita 423, P. O. Box 5442, Edificio Ferrand,
5 Piso, Lima, Peru.
- Productividad. a. ISSN 0032-9908

**Peru. Consejo Nacional de Justicia**
Lima, Peru.
- Peru. Consejo Nacional de Justicia. Memoria.
  irreg.

**Peru. Empresa Nacional de Telecomunicaciones**
Las Begonias 375, San Isidro, Lima, Peru.
- Empresa Nacional de Telecommunicaciones del
  Peru. Memoria Anual. a.

**Peru. Escuela Naval del Peru**
Callao, Peru.
- Revista de Marina del Peru. m. ISSN 0034-8538

**Peru. Fuerza Aerea**
Edificio Ministerio de Aeronautica, 28 de Julio,
Campo de Marte, Lima, Peru.
- Aviacion. m. ISSN 0005-2078

**Peru. Instituto Nacional de Cultura**
Casilla No 3124, Lima, Peru.
- Archivo General de la Nacion. Revista. a.

**Peru. Ministerio de Educacion Publica. Oficina
Sectorial de Planificacion**
Lima, Peru.
- Peru. Ministerio de Educacion Publica. Oficina
  Sectorial de Planificacion.Plan Bienal. irreg.

**Peru. Ministerio de Guerra y Marina**
Apartado Postal 2483, Lima, Peru.
- Infanteria. q. ISSN 0019-9524
- Revista Militar del Peru. m. ISSN 0035-0141

**Peru. Ministerio de Relaciones Exteriores**
Lima, Peru.
- Peru. Ministerio de Relaciones Exteriores. Boletin
  Trimestral. q.

**Peru. Ministerio de Salud**
Instituto de Zoonosis e Investigacion Pecuaria,
Bibliotecaria, Apartado 1128, Lima, Peru.
- Instituto de Zoonosis e Investigacion Pecuaria
  Revista. s-a. ISSN 0020-3963

**Peru. Ministerio del Interior. Direccion de Sanidad**
Casilla 1683, Lima, Peru.
- Ministerio del Interior. Revista de la Sanidad. bi-
  m.

**Peru. Oficina Regional de Desarrollo del Norte**
Av. Luis Gonzalez No 1915, Chiclayo, Peru.
- Peru. Oficina Regional de Desarrollo del Norte.
  Analisis General de Situacion de la Region Norte.
  irreg. ISSN 0085-4840

**Peru Indigena**
Avda. Salaverry, Lima, Peru.
- Peru Indigena. irreg (aprox. 2 per yr)

**Ediciones Peruanas**
Apdo. 2142, Lima, Peru.
- Arquitecto Peruano. bi-m. ISSN 0004-2676

**Peruvian Society of Cancerology**
Alfonso Ugarte 825, Lima, Peru.
- Acta Cancerologica. 3 per yr. ISSN 0001-5377

**Revista Peruana de Ciencias Juridicas y Sociales**
Carabaya 1126, Lima, Peru.
- Revista Peruana de Ciencias Juridicas y Sociales.
  q.

**H.G. Rozas, S.A.**
Cuzco, Peru.
- Archivos Peruanos de Folklore. s-a. (Universidad
  Nacional del Cuzco. Sociedad Peruana de
  Folklore)

**Selecciones Tauro S.A.**
Jr. Huancavelica 421, Of. 402, Lima, Peru.
- Almanaque del Peru. a.

**Sociedad de Legislacion Comparada. Comite Peruano**
- Revista Juridica del Peru. (pub. by Ediciones
  Juridicas)

**Sociedad Entomologica del Peru**
Apartado 4796, Lima, Peru.
- Revista Peruana de Entomologia. a. ISSN 0080-
  2425

**Sociedad Geografica de Lima**
Jiron Puno 456, Apartado 1176, Lima, Peru.
- Anuario Geografico del Peru. a. ISSN 0066-5223
- Sociedad Geografica de Lima, Peru. Boletin. q.
  ISSN 0037-8585

**Sociedad Geologica del Peru**
Apartado 2559, Lima, Peru.
- Sociedad Geologica del Peru. Boletin. irreg. ISSN
  0079-1091

**Sociedad Peruana de Derecho Internacional**
Box 686, Lima, Peru.
- Revista Peruana de Derecho Internacional. s-a.
  ISSN 0035-0370

**Sociedad Quimica del Peru**
Presidente de la Comision de Publicaciones, Apdo
891, Lima, Peru.
- Sociedad Quimica del Peru. Boletin. q. ISSN
  0037-8623

**Sociedad y Derecho**
Jiron Huancavelica No. 470-Of. 308, Lima, Peru.
- Sociedad y Derecho. q.

**Universidad de San Marcos**
Av. Javier Prado s/n., Monterico, Lima, Peru.
- Scientia et Praxis. ISSN 0559-1414

**Universidad Nacional Agraria**
Apdo. 456, Lima, Peru.
- Anales Cientificos. q. ISSN 0003-2484
- Informativo del Maiz. bi-m. (prep. by its Programa
  Cooperativo de Investigaciones en Maiz)
- Universidad Agraria. Programa Cooperativo de
  Investigaciones en Maiz. Boletin. irreg. ISSN
  0075-7403

**Universidad Nacional de San Agustin**
Siglo XX 227, Apdo. 23, Arequipa, Peru.
- Inedita. irreg.
- Universidad Nacional de San Agustin. Revista de
  Investigacion. irreg. (prep. by its Direccion
  Universitaria de Investigacion)

**Universidad Nacional de San Marcos**
Ave. Republica de Chile, 295, Of. 504, Lima, Peru.
- San Marcos. q.

**Universidad Nacional de Trujillo**
Departamento de Idiomas y Linguistica, Trujillo,
Peru.
- Lenguaje y Ciencias. q. ISSN 0024-0796
- Revista de Pedagogia Cibernetica e Instruccion
  Programada. s-a. ISSN 0034-866X (prep. by its
  Seccion de Pedagogia Cibernetica y Tecnologia
  Educacional)

**Universidad Nacional del Centro del Peru.
Departamento de Publicaciones e Impresiones**
c/o Secretaria de Publicaciones, Calle Real 160,
Huancayo, Peru.
- Universidad Nacional del Centro del Peru. Anales
  Cientificos. a.

**Universidad Nacional del Cuzco. Sociedad Peruana de
Folklore**
- Archivos Peruanos de Folklore. (pub. by H.G.
  Rozas, S.A.)

**Universidad Nacional Federico Villareal.
Departamento de Ciencias Historico Sociales**
Lima, Peru.
- Universidad Nacional Federico Villareal.
  Departamento de Ciencias Historico Sociales.
  Publicaciones. irreg.

**Universidad Nacional Federico Villareal. Facultad de
Derecho**
Av. Nicolas de Pierota 1128, Lima, Peru.
- Universidad Nacional Federico Villareal. Facultad
  de Derecho. Revista. s-a.

**Universidad Nacional Mayor de San Marcos.
Departamento de Sociologia**
Casilla 1985, Lima, Peru.
- Universidad Nacional Mayor de San Marcos.
  Departamento de Sociologia. Revista. s-a.

**Universidad Nacional Mayor de San Marcos.
Facultad de Ciencias Economicas y Comerciales**
Casilla 2631, Lima, Peru.
- Universidad Nacional Mayor de San Marcos.
  Facultad de Ciencias Economicas y Comerciales.
  Revista. irreg.

**Universidad Nacional Mayor de San Marcos.
Facultad de Derecho**
Apdo. 524, Lima, Peru.
- Revista de Derecho Y Ciencias Politicas. 3 per yr.
  ISSN 0034-7949

**Universidad Nacional Mayor de San Marcos.
Instituto de Biologia Andina**
Direccion Universitaria de Biblioteca y
Publicaciones, Box 454, Lima, Peru.
- Instituto de Biologia Andina. Archivos. s-a. ISSN
  0020-3750

**Universidad Nacional Mayor de San Marcos.
Instituto Veterinario de Investigaciones Tropicales
y de Altura**
Aptdo. 4270, Lima, Peru.
- Revista de Investigaciones Pecuarias. s-a.

**Universidad Nacional San Luis Gonzaga. Facultad de
Odontologia**
Bolivar 232, Lima, Peru.
- Educacion Dental. s-a. ISSN 0013-1083

**Angel Eduardo Valdivia Rodriguez, Ed. & Pub.**
Miro Quesada No. 309 Of. 302, Lima, Peru.
- Guia Judicial de Lima. a. ISSN 0072-7911

# PHILIPPINES

**Emilio L. Abarico, Ed. & Pub.**
Lozano Building, 2nd Fl., Rm. 203, C. M. Recto
Ave, Davao City 1901, Philippines.
- Mindanao Mail. s-w. ISSN 0300-3906

**Academy of Nursing of the Philippines**
College of Nursing, University of the Philippines,
Diliman, Quezon City, Philippines.
- A N P H I Papers. irreg. ISSN 0065-0676

**Acquarius Publications**
Segundina Building, 5th Fl., 464 United Nations
Ave., Ermita, Manila, Philippines.
- Agriculture Time. w.
- Infrastructure Time. s-m.

**Constantino F. Agbayani, Ed. & Pub.**
404 Garcia Bldg., Rizal Ave., Manila, Philippines.
- Philippine Architecture & Building Journal. q.
  ISSN 0031-7462

**American Association of the Philippines. American
Historical Committee**
422 Arquiza St., Manila, Philippines.
- American Historical Collection. Bulletin. q.

**American Chamber of Commerce of the Philippines**
Security Bank Building, 6th Fl., 6778 Ayala Ave.,
Makati, Rizal, Manila 2801, Philippines.
- American Chamber of Commerce of the
  Philippines. Journal. m. ISSN 0044-7579

**Ang Bayani**
Box 1253, Makati Commercial Center, Makati,
Rizal, Philippines.
- Ang Bayani. w.

**Archdiocesan Major Seminary**
Vigan, Ilocos sur B-435, Philippines, Philippines.
- Ilocos Review. a. ISSN 0019-2538

**Arellano University**
2600 Legarde St., Manila 2806, Philippines.
- Philippine Education Quarterly; journal of fact
  and opinion. q.

**Asian Development Bank**
P.O. Box 789, Manila 2800, Philippines.
- A D B Quarterly Newsletter. q. (prep. by its
  Information Office)
- Asian Development Bank. Annual Report. a.
  ISSN 0066-8370
- Asian Development Bank. Board of Governors.
  Summary of Proceedings (of the) Annual
  Meeting. a. ISSN 0066-8389
- Asian Development Bank. Key Indicators of
  Developing Member Countries of ADB. s-a.
  (prep. by its Economic Office)
- Asian Development Bank. Occasional Papers.
  irreg., 1972, no. 6. ISSN 0066-8397
- Trends in Developing Asia. a. (prep. by its
  Economic Office)

**Asian Labor Education Center**
University of the Philippines, Diliman, Rizal,
Philippines.
- A L E C Report. q. ISSN 0001-1762

**Asian-Pacific Dental Federation**
Manila Doctors Hospital, United Nations Ave., Box
373, Manila, Philippines.
- A P D F Newsletter. 4 per yr. ISSN 0001-2173

**Association of Special Libraries of the Philippines**
San Beda College Library, Mendiola St., Manila
2806, Philippines.
- A S L P Bulletin. q. ISSN 0001-2548

**Association of Theological Schools in South East Asia**
Box 841, Manila, Philippines.
- South East Asia Journal of Theology. s-a. ISSN
  0038-3406

**Ateneo de Manila University**
- Philippine Studies. (pub. by Ateneo de Manila
  University Press)

**Ateneo de Manila University. Institute of Philippine
Culture**
Box 154, Manila, Philippines.
- I P C Monographs. irreg. ISSN 0073-9537
- I P C Papers. irreg. ISSN 0073-9545

**Ateneo de Manila University. Loyola School of
Theology**
Box 4082, Manila, Philippines
- Logos; a series of monographs in scripture,
  theology, philosophy. irreg., no. 10, 1974. ISSN
  0076-0471 (Dist. by: Cellar Book Shop, 18090
  Wyoming, Detroit, MI 48221)

**Ateneo de Manila University Press**
Box 154, Manila, Philippines.
- Philippine Studies. q. ISSN 0031-7837 (Ateneo de
  Manila University)

**Balthazar Publishing House**
1782 M. Adriatico, Malate, Manila, Philippines.
- Balthazar. m. ISSN 0005-4429

**Biology Teachers Association of the Philippines**
De la Salle College, 2401 Taft Ave., Manila,
Philippines.
- Philippine Biota. q.

**Bernadita Bringcula**
P.O. Box 308, Cebu, Philippines.
- Cebu Commercial Guide.

**Business Masters International**
55 U.E. Tech. Avenue, University Hills, Subdivision
Malabon, Rizal, Philippines.
- Philippine Fishing Journal. m. ISSN 0031-7543
- Philippine Mining & Engineering Journal. m. ISSN
  0048-3842
- Philippine Mining and Engineering Journal.
  Mining Annual and Directory. a. ISSN 0085-4875

**Business Trends**
Baello Building, 2nd Fl., 434 A. Mabini St.,
Caloocan, Philippines.
- Business Trends. bi-m.

**Bustamante Press, Inc.**
Espana Quezon City, Philippines.
- P Ch C Journal of Educational Research. q. ISSN
  0030-7858 (Philippine Christian College)

**Central Bank of the Philippines**
A. Mabini corner Vito Cruz Streets, Manila,
Philippines.
- Bond Line. q. ISSN 0006-7059
- C. B. Review. w. (prep. by its Department of
  Economic Research)
- Central Bank of the Philippines. Annual Report. a.
  ISSN 0069-1585 (prep. by its Department of
  Economic Research)
- Countryside Banking. m.
- Philippine Financial Statistics. q. ISSN 0008-9303
  (prep. by its Department of Economic Research)

**Central Philippine University**
Box 231, Iloilo City, Philippines.
- Centralite. irreg.

**Chamber of Commerce of the Philippines**
Magallanes Dr., Manila, Philippines.
- Commerce; voice of Philippine business. m. ISSN
  0010-2776

**Chemical Society of the Philippines**
Bureau of Plant Industry, Malate, Manila,
Philippines.
- Chemists' Quarterly. q. ISSN 0045-6527 (prep. by
  its Laboratory Services Division)

**Child and Youth Research Center**
940 Quezon Blvd. Extension, Quezon City,
Philippines.
- Philippine Journal of Child-Youth Development.
  s-a. ISSN 0031-7616

**Christian Institute for Ethnic Studies in Asia**
Box 3167, Manila, Philippines.
- Christian Institute for Ethnic Studies in Asia.
  Bulletin. 2-3 per yr. ISSN 0045-6810

**De la Salle University**
P.O. Box 3819, Manila D-406, Philippines.
• Dialogue. s-a.

**Development Academy of the Philippines**
Taqaytay, Philippines.
• Development Academy of the Philippines. Annual Report. a. (prep. by its Office of Special Services)

**Divine Word University**
Tacloban City, Philippines.
• Leyte - Samar Studies. s-a. ISSN 0024-1679

**East Asian Pastoral Institute**
Box 1815, Manila, Philippines.
• Teaching All Nations; a quarterly on mission catechetics and liturgy. q. ISSN 0040-0564

**Economic Development Foundation**
J.M.T. Building, 6764 Ayala Avenue, Box 1896, Makati, Rizal, Philippines.
• Trends in Technology. q.

**Enterprise Publications Inc.**
113 W. Ave., Quezon City, Philippines.
• Business Day. w. ISSN 0007-6635

**Far Eastern University**
Box 609, Manila 2806, Philippines.
• Far Eastern University Journal; a quarterly of cultural perspectives. q. ISSN 0014-7605

**Far Eastern University. Institute of Law**
N. Reyes, Sr. St., Manila, Philippines.
• Far Eastern Law Review. 2 per yr. ISSN 0046-3272

**Federation of Asian Pharmaceutical Associations**
29 Hizon Bldg., Quezon Blvd., Quezon City, Philippines.
• Asian Journal of Pharmacy. a. ISSN 0066-8419

**Filipino Teacher**
49 Quezon Blvd. Ext., Quezon City, Philippines.
• Filipino Teacher. m. (except Apr.-May) ISSN 0015-1009

**Focolare Movement for Men**
Box 332, Manila, Philippines.
• New City. bi-m.

**Focus Philippines**
Med-D I's Bldg., 3rd Fl., Real and Solana Streets Intramuros, Manila, Philippines.
• Focus Philippines. w.

**Food and Nutrition Research Institute**
see Philippines. Food and Nutrition Research Institute

**Forest Products Research and Industries Development Commission**
see Philippines. Forest Products Research and Industries Development Commission

**FORPRIDECOM**
see Philippines. Forest Products Research and Industries Development Commission

**Foundation University**
Dumaguete City 6501, Philippines.
• Foundation Time. m. ISSN 0015-8984
• Horizons Unlimited. q. ISSN 0018-5019

**Foundation University. School of Law**
Dumaguete City 6501, Philippines.
• Foundation Law Review. q. ISSN 0015-8968

**Fund for Assistance to Private Education**
Box 947 M. C. C., Makati, Rizal, Philippines.
• F A P E Review. q.

**General Motors, Philippines**
PPL Building, United Nations Ave., Manila, Philippines.
• Goodman. bi-m.

**Geological Society of the Philippines**
Bureau of Mines Building, Pedro Gil St., Manila, Philippines.
• Geological Society of the Philippines. Journal. q.

**Historical Conservation Society**
Manila, Philippines
• Historical Conservation Society. Publications. irreg., latest issue, 1975. ISSN 0073-2613 (Dist. by: Cellar Book Shop, 18090 Wyoming, Detroit, MI 48221)

**Institute for the Study of Human Reproduction**
see under University of Santo Tomas

**Institute of Export Development**
P.O. Box 181 Greenhills, San Juan, Rizal, Philippines.
• Philippine Export Directory. a.

**Institute of Maternal and Child Health**
National Training Center for Maternal Health Services, 11 Banawe, Quezon City, Philippines.
• I M C H Newsletter. m.

**Institute of Philippine Culture**
see under Ateneo de Manila University

**Integrated Bar of the Philippines**
955 Quezon Boulevard Extension, Quezon City, Philippines.
• Integrated Bar of the Philippines. Journal. q.

**International Federation of Asian and Western Pacific Contractors Associations**
Padilla Building, 3rd Fl., Ortigas Community Center, Emerald Ave., Pasig, Rizal, Philippines.
• International Federation of Asian and Western Pacific Contractors' Associations. Proceedings of the Annual Convention. biennial; 1975, 14th, Seoul. ISSN 0074-588X

**International Rice Research Institute**
Box 933, Manila, Philippines.
• I R R I Annual Report. a. ISSN 0074-7793
• International Bibliography of Rice Research. Supplement. a. ISSN 0074-2031 (prep. by its Library and Documentation Center)

**Jesuit East Asian Assistancy**
Box 4132, Manila, Philippines.
• Asian Report. m.

**Kalikasan Press**
P.O. Box 29, University of the Philippines Post Office, Diliman, Quezon City 3004, Philippines.
• Kalikasan; Philippine Journal of Biology. 3 per yr. (Synergistic Consultants, Inc.)

**Knights of Columbus in the Philippines**
P.O. Box 510, Manila, Philippines.
• Cross; national Catholic magazine. bi-m.

**Land Bank of the Philippines**
B.F. Condominium, 6th Fl., Aduana St., Manila, Philippines.
• Land Bank of the Philippines. Annual Report. a.

**Leprosy Research Laboratory and Training Center**
see Philippines. Leprosy Research Laboratory and Training Center

**Linguistic Society of the Philippines**
Box 154, Manila, Philippines.
• Philippine Journal of Linguistics. s-a. ISSN 0048-3796

**Loyola School of Theology**
see under Ateneo de Manila University

**Makabayan Publishing Corp.**
Box 60, Quezon City, Philippines.
• Weekly Nation. w. ISSN 0049-7061

**Manila. Department of Public Works & Communications**
Manila, Philippines.
• D P W & C Bulletin. q.

**Manila Central University**
Caloocan Campus, Caloocan City, Philippines.
• Philippine Scientific Journal. q. ISSN 0031-7799

**Manila Secondary Teachers**
Division of City Schools, Manila, Philippines.
• M S T English Quarterly. q. ISSN 0047-5289

**Markaz al-Istilamat al-Islami al- Filibbini**
L and S Building, 1414 Roxas Blvd., Manila, Philippines.
• Majallat Salam. irreg.

**Mindanao State University. Research Center**
Marawi City M-206, Philippines.
• Mindanao Journal. q.

**Mushroom Media Inc.**
Marietta Apartments, Jorge Bocobo Street, Ermita, Manila, Philippines.
• Ermita. bi-m.

**National Commission for Unesco**
1580 Taft Ave., Manila, Philippines.
• U N E S C O Philippines. m. ISSN 0041-5294

**National Defense College of the Philippines**
Fort Bonifacio, Rizal, Philippines.
• National Security Review. q.

**National Institute of Science and Technology**
see Philippines. National Institute of Science and Technology

**National Museum of the Philippines**
Rizal Park, Manila, Philippines.
• National Museum of the Philippines. Monograph Series. irreg., no. 4, 1971. ISSN 0076-3772
• National Museum of the Philippines. Museum Publications (Pamphlet Series) irreg., no. 8, 1975. ISSN 0076-3764
• Philippines. National Library. T N L Research Guide Series. a. ISSN 0076-3756

**National Research Council of the Philippines**
Quezon City, Philippines.
• N R C P Research Bulletin. irreg.

**National Science Development Board**
see Philippines. National Science Development Board

**Notre Dame of Jolo College**
Jolo, Sulu 7601, Philippines
(Orders to: Philippine Social Science Council, Box 655, Greenhills, Rizal 3113, Philippines)
• Sulu Studies. a.

**Notre Dame University. Graduate School**
Cotabato City, Philippines.
• Notre Dame Journal; articles, critiques, reports, abstracts. s-a. ISSN 0048-0932

**P. N. C.**
Taft Ave., Manila, Philippines.
• Philippine Health Journal. m. ISSN 0031-7578

**Paencor, Inc.**
Scout Reyes St., Corner Ceba Ave., Roxas District, Quezon City, Philippines.
• Philippine Architecture, Engineering & Construction Record. m. ISSN 0031-7470

**Panamin Foundation**
Makati, Rizal, Philippines.
• Panamin Foundation Research Series. irreg.

**Philippine Airlines, Inc.**
Box 954, Manila, Philippines.
• PALiner. m.

**Philippine Association, Inc.**
702 JMT Bldg., Ayala Ave., Makati, Rizal, Philippines.
• Perspective; a magazine dedicated to enlightening the Filipino on the issues that affect his country. m. ISSN 0031-5915

**Philippine Association of Entomologists**
Department of Entomology, University of the Philippines College, Laguna, Philippines.
• Philippine Entomologist. s-a. ISSN 0048-3753

**Philippine Association of Social Workers**
Department of Social Welfare Building, San Rafael, Manila, Philippines.
• Social Work. q.

**Philippine Atmospheric, Geophysical and Astronomical Services Administration**
see Philippines. Philippine Atmospheric, Geophysical and Astronomical Services Administration

**Philippine Atomic Energy Commission**
see Philippines. Philippine Atomic Energy Commission

**Philippine Cancer Society**
310 San Rafael, Manila, Philippines.
• Philippine Journal of Cancer. q. ISSN 0031-7608

**Philippine Center for Advanced Studies**
see under University of the Philippines

**Philippine Chamber of Industries**
Box 3873, Manila, Philippines.
• Industrial Philippines. m. ISSN 0019-8587

**Philippine Chinese Historical Association**
Box 3131, Manila, Philippines.
• Philippines Chinese Historical Association. Annals. a.

**Philippine Christian College**
• P Ch C Journal of Educational Research. (pub. by Bustamante Press, Inc.)

**Philippine Coconut Authority. Agricultural Research Department**
see Philippines. Philippine Coconut Authority. Agricultural Research Department

**Philippine Commercial and Industrial Bank.**
Antonio Building, T. M. Kalaw St., Manila, Philippines.
• Philippine Commercial and Industrial Bank. Investment Information Folio. m.

**Philippine Council of Management**
Rm. 310, Filoil Bldg., Taft Ave. & T. M. Kalaw St., Manila, Philippines.
• Philippine Manager. q. ISSN 0031-773X

**Philippine Dental Association**
Box 1142, Manila, Philippines.
• Philippine Dental Association. Journal. q. ISSN 0031-7497

**Philippine Economic Society**
Box 1764, Manila, Philippines.
• Philippine Economic Journal. q. ISSN 0031-7500

**Philippine Federation of Private Medical Practitioners**
Geriatrics Center Bldg., Arroceros St., Manila, Philippines.
• Philippine Federation of Private Medical Practitioners. Journal. q. ISSN 0031-7535

**Philippine Geographical Society**
P.O. Box 2116, Manila, Philippines.
• Philippine Geographical Journal. q. ISSN 0031-7551

**Philippine Index Service, Inc.**
Box 4156, Manila, Philippines.
• Philippine Business Index. q. ISSN 0031-7489

**Philippine Institute of Certified Public Accountants**
PICPA House, 7000 Shaw Blvd., Mandaluyong, Rizal, Philippines.
• Accountants' Journal. q. ISSN 0001-4753
• Newsette. m. ISSN 0028-9418

**Philippine Inventors Commission**
see Philippines. Philippine Inventors Commission

**Philippine Journal of Education Co., Inc.**
161 15th Ave., Cubao, Quezon City, Philippines.
• Philippine Journal of Education. m. ISSN 0031-7624

**Philippine Journalists Inc.**
P.O. 557, Greenhills Post Office, Mandaluyong, Rizal D-738, Philippines.
• Manila Journal. w.

**Philippine Library Association**
c/o the National Library, T.M. Kalaw St., Manila, Philippines.
• Philippine Library Association. Bulletin. a.

**Philippine Lumberman, Inc.**
Scout Reyes St., Corner Cebu Ave., Roxas District, Quezon City, Philippines.
• Philippine Lumberman. bi-m.

**Philippine Marketing Association**
• Marketing Horizons. (pub. by Vision Publishing Corporation)

**Philippine Medical Association**
P M A House, North Avenue, Diliman, Quezon City, Philippines.
• Philippine Medical Association. Journal. bi-m. ISSN 0031-7748

**Philippine Medical-Dental Publications**
124 15th Ave., Cubao, Quezon City, Philippines.
• Dental Mirror; journal of Philippine dentistry. s-a. ISSN 0011-8699

**Philippine Mental Health Association**
Box 40, 18 East Ave., Quezon City, Philippines.
• Focus on Mental Health. bi-m. ISSN 0046-4317

• Philippine Journal of Mental Health. s-a. ISSN 0048-380X

**Philippine National Red Cross**
860 United Nations Ave., Manila, Philippines.
• Philippine Junior Red Cross Magazine; ages 10-16. 6 nos. during school year. ISSN 0031-7713

**Philippine Normal College. Community-School Health Education Center**
Taft Ave., Manila, Philippines.
• School Health Bulletin. q. ISSN 0048-9417

**Philippine Normal College. Language Study Center**
Manila D-406, Philippines.
• Philippine Education Abstracts. irreg. ISSN 0079-1423
• Philippine Normal College. Language Study Center. Occasional Paper. irreg., 1971, no. 10. ISSN 0076-3780

**Philippine Nurses Association**
1663 Kansas Ave., Manila, Philippines.
• Philippine Journal of Nursing. q. ISSN 0048-3818

**Philippine Pediatric Society**
Box 3527, Manila, Philippines.
• Philippine Journal of Pediatrics. bi-m. ISSN 0031-7667

**Philippine Public School Teachers Association**
Teachers Bldg., 27 Banawe St., Quezon City, Philippines.
• P P S T A Herald. m. ISSN 0030-8218

**Philippine Society of International Law**
University of the Phillipines, College of Law, Diliman, Quezon City, Philippines.
• Philippine Yearbook of International Law. a.

**Philippine Society of Ophthalmology**
Philippine General Hospital, Taft Ave., Manila D-406, Philippines.
• Philippine Journal of Ophthalmology. q. ISSN 0031-7659

**Philippine Sociological Society**
Box 154, Manila 2801, Philippines.
• Philippine Sociological Review. q. ISSN 0031-7810

**Philippine Statistical Association**
Box 3223, Manila, Philippines.
• Philippine Statistician. q. ISSN 0031-7829

**Philippine Sugar Association**
• Sugar News. (pub. by Sugar News Press, Inc.)

**Philippine Sugar Institute**
North Avenue, Diliman, Quezon City, Philippines.
• Philippine Sugar Institute Quarterly. q. ISSN 0048-3869
• Sugarcane Farmers' Bulletin. bi-m.

**Philippine Tax Journal**
R-203 University Center Bldg., 1985 Recto Ave., Manila, Philippines.
• Philippine Tax Journal; the magazine for lawyers, accountants and businessman. m. ISSN 0031-7845

**Philippine Women's University**
Taft Ave., Manila 2801, Philippines.
• Philippine Educational Forum. s-a. ISSN 0031-7527
• Philippine Women's University Administrative News. q. ISSN 0031-7853
• Philwomenian. m. ISSN 0031-8272
• University (Philippines) q. ISSN 0042-0360

**Philippines. Agricultural Meteorology Division**
Pagasa (Weather Bureau), Quezon City, Philippines.
• Philippine Agricultural Meteorology Bulletin. m.

**Philippines. Board of Investments**
Ortigas Building, Ortigas Avenue, Box 676, Rizal, Philippines.
• Foreign Investment Opportunities in the Philippines. a. ISSN 0085-0802
• Philippine Progress. q. ISSN 0031-7764 (prep. by its Business Information Section)
• Philippines (Republic). Board of Investments. Annual Report. a. ISSN 0079-1504

**Philippines. Bureau of Agricultural Economics**
Casman Bldg., Quezon Blvd. Ext., Quezon City, Philippines.
• Bureau of Agricultural Economics Reporter. q. ISSN 0007-6155

• Philippine Agricultural Situation. q. ISSN 0031-7446
• Philippines (Republic). Bureau of Agricultural Economics. Crop, Livestock and Natural Resources Statistics. a. ISSN 0079-1512
• Philippines (Republic). Bureau of Agricultural Economics. Report. a. ISSN 0079-1520

**Philippines. Bureau of Animal Industry**
Diliman, Quezon City, Philippines.
• Philippine Journal of Animal Industry. s-a. ISSN 0048-3761

**Philippines. Bureau of Disease Control. Leprosy Research Laboratory and Training Center**
see Philippines. Leprosy Research Laboratory and Training Center

**Philippines. Bureau of Mines**
Manila, Philippines.
• Philippines (Republic). Bureau of Mines. Annual Report. a.

**Philippines. Bureau of National and Foreign Information**
Tuazon Bldg., Solana St., Intramuros, Manila, Philippines.
• Archipelago. m.
• Manila Review; Philippines journal of literature and the arts. q.
• Philippine Prospect. m.

**Philippines. Bureau of Plant Industry**
San Andres St., Manila, Philippines.
• Philippine Journal of Plant Industry. q. ISSN 0048-3826

**Philippines. Bureau of Vocational Education**
Manila, Philippines.
• Philippines (Republic) Bureau of Vocational Education. Agricultural Education Program: Information and Statistical Guide. irreg.

**Philippines. Civil Service Commission**
Quezon City D-502, Philippines.
• Philippines. Civil Service Commission. Civil Service Reporter. m. ISSN 0300-3620

**Philippines. Department of Agrarian Reform. Planning Service**
Manila, Philippines.
• Philippines (Republic). Department of Agrarian Reform. Planning Service. Annual Report. a.

**Philippines. Department of Agriculture and Natural Resources. Agricultural Information Division**
Diliman, Quezon City, Philippines.
• Philippine Journal of Soils. q. ISSN 0048-3834

**Philippines. Department of Agriculture and Natural Resources. Bureau of Animal Industry**
see Philippines. Bureau of Animal Industry

**Philippines. Department of Agriculture and Natural Resources. Fisheries Commission**
see Philippines. Fisheries Commission

**Philippines. Department of Commerce and Industry**
Ermita Center Bldg., Roxas Blvd., P.O. Box 3164, Manila D-404, Philippines.
• Philippines (Republic). Department of Commerce and Industry Annual Report. a. ISSN 0079-1539

**Philippines. Department of Foreign Affairs. Office of Press and Public Affairs**
Manila, Philippines.
• Foreign Affairs Review. m.

**Philippines. Department of Natural Resources**
Diliman, Quezon City, Philippines.
• Philippines (Republic). Department of Natural Resources. Annual Report. a.
• Philippines (Republic). Department of Natural Resources. Plans and Programs. a.

**Philippines. Department of Trade. Research and Information Division**
Arcadia Building, 860 Quezon Blvd. Ext., Quezon City, Philippines.
• Philippines (Republic). Department of Trade. Annual Report. a.
• Philippines (Republic). Department of Trade. Dimension of Philippine Exports. a.
• Philippines (Republic). Department of Trade. Trend Analysis of the Twenty Leading Exports and Prospects in the Year Ahead. irreg.
• Philippines (Republic). Department of Trade. Twenty Leading Imports. irreg.

**Philippines. Fisheries Commission**
Diliman, Quezon City, Philippines.
- Philippine Journal of Fisheries. s-a? ISSN 0048-377X

**Philippines. Food and Nutrition Research Institute**
727 Pedro Gil St., Box 774, Ermita, Manila, Philippines.
- Food and Nutrition Research Institute. Annual Report. a.
- Philippine Journal of Nutrition. q. ISSN 0031-7640 (Co-sponsor: Philippine Association of Nutrition)

**Philippines. Forest Products Research and Industries Development Commission**
College, Laguna E-109, Philippines.
- FORPRIDECOM Technical Notes. (Forest Products Research & Industries Development Commission) m.

**Philippines. Forest Research Institute**
College, Laguna 3720, Philippines.
- Canopy. m.

**Philippines. Government Printing Office**
Boston St., Port Area, Manila, Philippines.
- Philippines (Republic). Government Printing Office. Itemization of Personal Services and Organizational Charts. a.
- Philippines (Republic). Public Information Office. Official Gazette. w.

**Philippines. Labor Statistics Service**
Manila, Philippines.
- Philippines (Republic). Labor Statistics Service. Year Book of Labor Statisitcs. irreg.

**Philippines. Leprosy Research Laboratory and Training Center**
Bureau of Disease Control, Department of Health, Manila, Philippines.
- Philippine Journal of Leprosy. s-a. ISSN 0031-7632

**Philippines. National Archives. Bureau of Records Management**
c/o National Library Building, T.M. Kalaw St., Ermita, Manila, Philippines.
- Philippines (Republic). National Archives. Bureau of Records Management. Archiviniana. a.

**Philippines. National Census and Statistics Office**
Ramon Magsaysay Blvd., Manila, Philippines.
- Journal of Philippine Statistics. q. ISSN 0022-3603
- Philippines (Republic). National Census and Statistics Office. Yearbook. biennial.
- Social Indicators of the Philippines. a.

**Philippines. National Economic and Development Authority**
Box 1116, Manila, Philippines.
- N E D A Journal of Development. irreg.
- N E D A Statistical Yearbook. a.
- Philippines (Republic). National Economic and Development Authority. National Income Accounts. irreg.
- Philippines (Republic). National Economic and Development Authority. Report on the Economy. a.

**Philippines. National Grains Authority**
Quezon City, Philippines.
- Philippines (Republic). National Grains Authority. Grains Journal. bi-m.

**Philippines. National Institute of Science and Technology**
Box 774, Manila, Philippines.
- Philippine Journal of Science. q. ISSN 0031-7683

**Philippines. National Library**
T. M. Kalaw St., Manila, Philippines.
- Philippines. National Library. T N L Research Guide Series. irreg., approx. 2 per yr. (prep. by its Bibliography Division)

**Philippines. National Media Production Center**
2255 Pasong Tamo, Makati, Rizal, Philippines.
- New Philippines. bi-m.
- Philippines Quarterly. q. ISSN 0048-3877
- Philippines Today. 4 per yr. ISSN 0085-4883

**Philippines. National Science Development Board**
Box 3596, Manila, Philippines.
- Science Review. m. ISSN 0036-8520

**Philippines. National Science Development Board. Food and Nutrition Research Institute**
*see* Philippines. Food and Nutrition Research Institute

**Philippines. National Science Development Board. Forest Products Research and Industries Development Commission**
*see* Philippines. Forest Products Research and Industries Development Commission

**Philippines. National Science Development Board. National Institute of Science and Technology**
*see* Philippines. National Institute of Science and Technology

**Philippines. National Science Development Board. Philippine Inventors Commission**
*see* Philippines. Philippine Inventors Commission

**Philippines. National Science Development Board. Scientific Library and Documentation Division**
Box 3596, Bicutan, Tagig, Manila, Philippines.
- Philippine Abstracts; a quarterly classified summary of the latest Philippine publications in the field of science and its application. q. ISSN 0031-7438

**Philippines. National Tax Research Center**
First BF Condominium, Aduana St., Intramuros, Manila, Philippines.
- Philippines (Republic). National Tax Research Center. Report. a. ISSN 0079-1547
- Philippines (Republic). National Tax Research Center. Tax Monthly. m. ISSN 0040-0068

**Philippines. Office of Press and Public Affairs**
*see under* Philippines. Department of Foreign Affairs

**Philippines. Philippine Atmospheric, Geophysical and Astronomical Services Administration**
Box 2277, Manila, Philippines.
- Almanac for Geodetic Engineers. a. ISSN 0569-0838
- Philippine Astronomical Handbook. a.

**Philippines. Philippine Atomic Energy Commission**
Commonwealth Ave., Diliman, Quezon City, Phillipines.
- Philippine Atomic Energy Commission. Semi-Annual Report. s-a.
- Philippines Nuclear Journal. irreg. ISSN 0079-1490

**Philippines. Philippine Coconut Authority. Agricultural Research Department**
Box 295, Davao, Philippines.
- Philippine Coconut Authority. Agricultural Research Department. Annual Report. a.

**Philippines. Philippine Inventors Commission**
Publications Staff, 1424 Quezon Blvd., QCDB Bldg. Annex., Quezon City, Philippines.
- Philippine Inventors Bulletin. m.

**Philippines. Population Commission**
Quezon City, Philippines.
- Philippines (Republic). Population Commission. Annual Report. a.

**Philippines Daily Express Publishing Corp.**
371 Bonifacio Drive, Port Area, Manila, Philippines.
- Expressweek. w.

**Philippines Labor Relations Journal**
40 Gasan St., Quezon City D-502, Philippines.
- Philippines Labor Relations Journal. m. ISSN 0031-787X

**Press Foundation of Asia**
Box 1843, Manila, Philippines.
- Asian Press and Media Directory. a.
- Data Asia. w.
- Data Fil. fortn.
- Depthnews. m.

**Private Development Corporation of the Philippines**
P.O. Box 757, Rizal 3117, Philippines.
- Private Development Corporation of the Philippines. Monthly Economic Letter. m.

**Professional Training & Review Academy**
Suite 201, Manufacturers Bank Bldg., Plaza Sta. Cruz, Manila, Philippines.
- Philippine Journal of Business and Finance. m. ISSN 0031-7594

**Psychological Association of the Philippines**
c/o Department of Psychology, University of the Philippines, Diliman, Quezon City, Philippines.
- Philippine Journal of Psychology. s-a.

**Responsible Parenthood Council**
1000 United Nations Ave., Manila, Philippines.
- R P C Monthly. m.

**Saint Louis University**
Box 71, Baguio City 0216, Philippines.
- Builder of Progress. a.
- Saint Louis Chronicle. m. ISSN 0048-8992

**Saint Louis University. Graduate School of Arts and Sciences**
Box 71, Baguio City, Philippines.
- Saint Louis University Research Journal; an interdisciplinary journal in the sciences and the humanities. q. ISSN 0036-3014

**Saint Mary's College**
Bayombong, Nueva Vizcaya, Philippines.
- Journal of Northern Luzon; a semi-annual research forum. s-a.

**San Beda College**
Mendiola St., Manila, Philippines.
- San Beda Review. q. ISSN 0036-3987

**Sanve Publishing, Inc.**
May Building, Suite 316-317, 834 Rizal Ave., Manila, Philippines.
- Philippine Economy and Industrial Journal. bi-m. ISSN 0048-3745

**Science Foundation of the Philippines**
1913 Taft Ave., Manila, Philippines.
- Out of School Science Magazine. q.
- Science Bulletin. q. ISSN 0036-8261
- Science for Schools. m. ISSN 0036-8385

**Select**
c/o Rizal Library, Box 154, Manila, Philippines.
- Select; Philippine publications for college use. q. ISSN 0049-0083

**Silliman University**
Dumaguete City, Philippines.
- Selected Philippine Periodical Index. s-a. ISSN 0037-1335
- Silliman Journal; a quarterly of investigation and discussion in the humanities and in the sciences. q. ISSN 0037-5284

**Social Impact Foundation**
Box 2950, Manila, Philippines.
- Impact; a monthly Asian magazine for human development. m. ISSN 0300-4155

**Sociedad de Escritores Hispano-Filipinos**
Herald Building, 61 Muralla, Intramuros, Manila, Philippines.
- Nueva Horizonte. w.

**Society of St. Paul**
7708 St. Paul Rd., Makati, Rizal, Philippines.
- Home Life; the Philippines' family magazine. m.

**Solidaridad Publishing House**
531 Padre Faura, Ermita, Manila, Philippines.
- Solidarity; current affairs, ideas and the arts. m. ISSN 0038-1160

**Soller Press & Publishing House, Inc.**
45 E. Jacinto St., E. Rodriguez, Sr. Blvd., Box 121, Quezon City, Philippines.
- Fina. m.

**Southeast Asian Fisheries Development Center**
Manila, Philippines.
- Southeast Asian Fisheries Development Center. Report of the Meeting. a.

**Sugar News Press, Inc.**
316 Dona Salud Building, Box 514, Manila, Philippines.
- Sugar News; voice of the Philippine sugar industry. m. ISSN 0049-2477 (Philippine Sugar Association)

**Sugarland Publications**
Box 13, Bacolod City, Philippines.
- Sugarland; a magazine for the sugar industry of the Philippines. m. ISSN 0039-4777

**Sylip, Gorres, Velayo & Co.**
6760 Ayala Ave., Makati, Metro Manila,
Philippines.
- S G V Group Journal. q.

**Synergistic Consultants, Inc.**
- Kalikasan; Philippine Journal of Biology. (pub. by
  Kalikasan Press)

**Tala Publishing Corporation**
P.O. Box 95, University of the Philippines, Quezon
City, Philippines.
- Tala Industrial Relations Bulletin. m.

**Times Journal of Manila (International Edition)**
Chronicle Bldg., Meralco Ave., Pasig, Rizal,
Philippines.
- Times Journal of Manila (International Edition). w.

**Trinity College of Quezon City**
E. Rodriguez Sr. Blvd., Quezon City, Philippines.
- Trinity College Journal. s-a.

**U.S. Information Agency**
c/o American Embassy, Box 15, Manila,
Philippines.
- Free World Horizons. m. ISSN 0016-0482

**University of Eastern Philippines**
Research Center, University Town, Northern Samar,
Philippines.
- Researcher. s-a. ISSN 0048-7341
- University of Eastern Philippines. Research
  Center. Report. irreg., latest issue, 1970. ISSN
  0070-8259

**University of Manila**
546 Dr. M. V. de los Santos St., Manila D-403,
Philippines.
- Campus Leader. m. ISSN 0008-252X
- Journal of East Asiatic Studies. s-a. ISSN 0022-
  0450
- University of Manila Law Gazette. s-a. ISSN
  0041-9796

**University of San Carlos**
Cebu City 6401, Philippines
- Philippine Quarterly of Culture and Society. q.
  (Dist. by: Cellar Book Shop, 18090 Wyoming,
  Detroit, MI 48221)
- Philippine Scientist. a. ISSN 0079-1466 (Dist. by:
  Cellar Book Shop, 18090 Wyoming, Detroit, MI
  48221)
- University of San Carlos. San Carlos Publications.
  Series A: Humanities. irreg., no. 10, 1975. ISSN
  0069-1321 (Dist. by: Cellar Book Shop, 18090
  Wyoming, Detroit, MI 48221)
- University of San Carlos. San Carlos Publications.
  Series D: Occasional Monographs. irreg., no. 3,
  1976. ISSN 0069-1356 (Dist. by: Cellar Book
  Shop, 18090 Wyoming, Detroit, MI 48221)
- University of San Carlos. University Bulletin. bi-
  m. ISSN 0041-9990

**University of Santo Tomas**
Espana St., Manila, Philippines.
- Boletin Eclesiastico de Fillipinas; official organ of
  the Catholic hierarchy of the Philippines. m.
- Unitas; a quarterly review for the arts and
  sciences. q. ISSN 0041-7149

**University of Santo Tomas. College of Architecture
and Fine Arts**
Espana St., Manila, Philippines.
- Vision. s-a. ISSN 0042-692X

**University of Santo Tomas. College of Nursing**
Espana St., Manila, Philippines.
- Santo Tomas Nursing Journal. q. ISSN 0048-9123

**University of Santo Tomas. Ecclesiastical Faculties**
Central Seminary, Espana St., Manila, Philippines.
- Benavides. s-a. ISSN 0005-8696

**University of Santo Tomas. Faculty of Civil Law**
Espana St., Manila, Philippines.
- University of Santo Tomas. Faculty of Civil Law.
  Law Review. ISSN 0047-5734

**University of Santo Tomas. Faculty of Medicine**
Espana St., Manila, Philippines.
- Santo Tomas Journal of Medicine. bi-m.

**University of Santo Tomas. Graduate School**
Espana St., Manila, Philippines.
- University of Santo Tomas. Graduate School.
  Journal of Graduate Research. 1 or 2 nos. per
  semester. ISSN 0047-5742

**University of Santo Tomas. Institute for the Study of
Human Reproduction**
Faculty of Medicine, Espana St., Manila,
Philippines.
- Reproductions. irreg. (15-20 per yr.)

**University of the East. College of Business
Administration**
Sampaloc, Manila, Philippines.
- U E Business Review; a magazine for business
  leaders. 3 per yr. ISSN 0042-0158

**University of the East. Faculty of the Graduate
School**
Sampaloc, Manila, Philippines.
- Economic Research Journal. q.

**University of the Philippines**
Diliman, Quezon City, Philippines.
- Conference on Population, Quezon. Proceedings.
  (pub. by University of the Philippines Press)
- Philippine Law Journal. 5 per yr. ISSN 0031-7721
- University of the Philippines Gazette. m.

**University of the Philippines. Asian Centre**
Diliman, Quezon City, Philippines.
- Lipunan Journal. irreg. ISSN 0459-4835
- University of the Philippines. Asian Centre.
  Monograph Series. irreg., 1969, no. 4. ISSN 0079-
  9238

**University of the Philippines. College of Arts and
Sciences**
Diliman, Quezon City D-505, Philippines.
- Diliman Review. q. ISSN 0012-2858
- General Education Journal. s-a.
- Natural and Applied Science Bulletin. q. ISSN
  0028-0682
- Philippine Social Sciences and Humanities
  Review. q. ISSN 0031-7802

**University of the Philippines. College of Dentistry**
Diliman, Quezon City, Philippines.
- U P College of Dentistry Journal. s-a. ISSN 0041-
  5391

**University of the Philippines. College of Education**
Diliman, Quezon City, Philippines.
- Education Quarterly. q.

**University of the Philippines. College of Medicine**
Pedro Gil St., Manila, Philippines.
- Acta Medica Philippina. q. ISSN 0001-6071 (Co-
  sponsor: Institute of Public Health)

**University of the Philippines. College of Public
Administration**
Box 474, Manila, Philippines.
- Local Government Bulletin. q. ISSN 0024-5526
  (prep. by its Local Government Center)
- Philippine Journal of Public Administration. q.
  ISSN 0031-7675
- University of the Philippines. College of Public
  Administration. Local Government Studies. irreg.
  (prep. by its Local Government Center)
- University of the Philippines. College of Public
  Administration. Public Administration and Special
  Studies Series. a.

**University of the Philippines. College of Veterinary
Medicine**
Diliman, Quezon City, Philippines.
- Philippine Journal of Veterinary Medicine. s-a.
  ISSN 0031-7705

**University of the Philippines. Community
Development Research Council**
Rm. 207, Education Bldg., Diliman, Quezon City,
Philippines.
- University of the Philippines. Community
  Development Research Council. Study Series.
  irreg., 1969, no. 27. ISSN 0079-9246

**University of the Philippines. Institute of
Environmental Planning**
Diliman, Quezon City 3004, Philippines.
- Philippine Planning Journal. s-a. ISSN 0048-3850

**University of the Philippines. Institute of Library
Science**
Diliman, Quezon City 3004, Philippines.
- Journal of Philippine Librarianship. s-a. ISSN
  0022-359X
- University of the Philippines. Institute of Library
  Science. Newsletter. q. ISSN 0300-3612

**University of the Philippines. Institute of Mass
Communications**
Diliman, Quezon City, Philippines.
- Philippine Journal of Communications Studies. s-a.

**University of the Philippines. Institute of Public
Administration**
Rizal Hall, P. Faura, Manila, Philippines.
- University of the Philippines. Institute of Public
  Administration. (Publication) irreg. ISSN 0079-
  9254

**University of the Philippines. Interdepartmental
Reference Service**
Box 474, Manila, Philippines.
- Index to Philippine Periodicals. a. ISSN 0073-
  599X

**University of the Philippines. Law Center**
Diliman, Quezon City, Philippines.
- Law Practice for the Senior Lawyer. irreg.

**University of the Philippines. Library**
Gonzalez Hall, Diliman, Quezon City, Philippines.
- Philippine Union Catalog. q.

**University of the Philippines. Office of Alumni
Relations**
Diliman, Quezon City, Philippines.
- U.P. Alumni Newsletter. s-a.
- University of the Philippines. Office of Alumni
  Relations. Alumni Directory. a.

**University of the Philippines. Philippine Center for
Advanced Studies**
Diliman, Quezon City 3004, Philippines.
- Asian Studies. 3 per yr. ISSN 0004-4679
- University of the Philippines. Philippine Center
  for Advanced Studies. Bibliography. irreg.

**University of the Philippines Press**
Quezon City, Philippines.
- Conference on Population, Quezon. Proceedings.
  irreg. ISSN 0069-861X (University of the
  Philippines) (Co-sponsor: Population Institute and
  Population Council, New York)

**University of the Philippines. School of Economics**
Diliman, Quezon City, Philippines.
- Philippine Review of Business and Economics. s-a.
  ISSN 0031-7780 (Co-sponsor: University of the
  Philippines Business Research Foundation, Inc.)

**University of the Philippines at Los Banos. Agrarian
Reform Institute**
Laguna 3720, Philippines.
- University of the Philippines at Los Banos.
  Agrarian Reform Institute. Occasional Papers.
  irreg.

**University of the Philippines at Los Banos. College of
Agriculture**
College, Laguna 3720, Philippines.
- Agriculture at Los Banos. q.
- Philippine Agriculturist. m.(except Apr-May)
  ISSN 0031-7454 (Co-sponsor: Central Experiment
  Station)

**University of the Philippines at Los Banos. College of
Forestry**
College, Laguna 3720, Philippines.
- Forestry Digest; a magazine about public
  appreciation for forests. q. (prep. by its
  Department of Forestry Extension)
- University of the Philippines at Los Banos.
  College of Forestry. Conservation Circular. m.
  (prep. by its Department of Forestry Extension)

**University of the Philippines at Los Banos. Rodent
Research Center**
Laguna E-109, Philippines.
- University of the Philippines at Los Banos.
  Rodent Research Center. Annual Report. a.

**Manuel Vijungco, Ed. & Pub.**
Box 998, Manila, Philippines.
- Philippines Transportation. m. ISSN 0031-7888

**Vision Publishing Corporation**
Box 4314, Manila, Philippines.
- Business Prospects; proceedings of the annual
  Business Prospects Conference. a.
- Marketing Horizons; the marketing magazine for
  marketing men by marketing men. m. ISSN 0025-
  3715 (Philippine Marketing Association)

**World Health Organization. Regional Office for the Western Pacific**
For publications of this agency see section for
UNITED NATIONS

**World Scout Bureau. Asia-Pacific Region**
Box 4480, Manila, Philippines.
● Asia-Pacific Scouting. bi-m.

**Xavier University**
Cagayan de Oro City, Philippines.
● Xavier University. Museum and Archives
Publications. irreg., no. 18, latest issue. ISSN
0084-3229

# POLAND

**Agencja Autorska**
Hipoteczna 2, 00-068 Warsaw, Poland
(Dist. by: Ars Polona-Ruch, Krakowskie
Przedmiescie 7, Warsaw, Poland)
● Polish Art Review. q.
● Polish Literature/Litterature Polonaise. q. ISSN
0032-289X
● Polish Music/Polnische Musik. q. ISSN 0032-
2946

**Akademia Ekonomiczna, Krakow**
Ul. Rakowicka 27, 35-510 Krakow, Poland.
● Akademia Ekonomiczna, Krakow. Zeszyty
Naukowe. irreg., no. 65, 1975.

**Akademia Ekonomiczna, Poznan**
Marchlewskiego 146, 60-967 Poznan, Poland.
● Akademia Ekonomiczna, Poznan. Zeszyty
Naukowe .Seria 1. irreg. ISSN 0079-4546
● Akademia Ekonomiczna, Poznan. Zeszyty
Naukowe. Seria 2. Prace Habilitacyjne i
Doktorskie. irreg. ISSN 0079-4554

**Akademia Ekonomiczna, Wroclaw**
Komandorska 118-120, 50-950 Wroclaw, Poland.
● Akademia Ekonomiczna we Wroclawiu. Prace
Naukowe. irreg.

**Akademia Gorniczo-Hutnicza im. Stanislawa Staszica**
● Akademia Gorniczo-Hutnicza im. Stanislawa
Staszica. Instytut Ceramiki Specjalnej i
Ogniotrwalej. Prace Naukowe. (pub. by
Panstwowe Wydawnictwo Naukowe)
● Akademia Gorniczo-Hutnicza im. Stanislawa
Staszica. Instytut Gornictwa Podziemnego. Prace.
(pub. by Panstwowe Wydawnictwo Naukowe)
● Akademia Gorniczo-Hutnicza im. Stanislawa
Staszica. Instytut Maszyn Hutniczych i
Automatyki. Prace. (pub. by Panstwowe
Wydawnictwo Naukowe)
● Akademia Gorniczo-Hutnicza im. Stanislawa
Staszica. Zeszyty Naukowe. Gornictwo. (pub. by
Panstwowe Wydawnictwo Naukowe)
● Akademia Gorniczo-Hutnicza Im. Stanislawa
Staszica. Zeszyty Naukowe. Hutnictwo. (pub. by
Panstwowe Wydawnictwo Naukowe)
● Elektryfikacja i Mechanizacja Gornictwa i
Hutnictwa/Electrification and Mechanization in
Mining and Metallurgy. (pub. by Panstwowe
Wydawnictwo Naukowe)
● Metalurgia i Odlewnictwo. (pub. by Panstwowe
Wydawnictwo Naukowe)

**Akademia Medyczna, Bialystok**
Ul. Kilinskiego 1, 15-089 Bialystok, Poland.
● Akademia Medyczna, Bialystok. Rocznik. (pub. by
Panstwowy Zaklad Wydawnictw Lekarskich)
● Annales Academiae Medicae Bialostocensis. irreg.
ISSN 0066-1929

**Akademia Medyczna, Krakow**
Ul. Sw. Anny 12, 31-008 Krakow, Poland
(Dist. by Ars Polona-Ruch, Krakowskie
Przedmiescie 7, Warsaw, Poland)
● Annales Academiae Medicae Cracoviensis. Index
Dissertationum Editarum. a. ISSN 0066-1937

**Akademia Medyczna, Warsaw**
Filtrowa 30, 02-032 Warsaw, Poland
(Dist. by: Ars Polona-Ruch, Krakowskie
Przedmiescie 7, Warsaw, Poland)
● Kardiologia Polska. bi-m. ISSN 0022-9032

**Akademia Medyczna, Wroclaw**
● Akademia Medyczna, Wroclaw. Prace Naukowe.
(pub. by Panstwowe Wydawnictwo Naukowe)

**Akademia Rolnicza, Krakow**
Al. Mickiewicza 21, 30-120 Krakow, Poland.
● Akademia Rolnicza, Krakow. Rolnictwo. irreg.,
1975, no. 15.

**Akademia Rolnicza, Poznan**
Ul. Wojska Polskiego 28, 60-637 Poznan, Poland.
● Akademia Rolnicza, Poznan. Rocznik. Algorytmy
Biometryczne i Statistyczne. irreg.
● Akademia Rolnicza, Poznan. Rocznik. Lesnictwo.
irreg.
● Akademia Rolnicza, Poznan. Rocznik. Melioracje
Wodne. irreg.
● Akademia Rolnicza, Poznan. Rocznik.
Ogrodnictwo. irreg.
● Akademia Rolnicza, Poznan. Rocznik. Ornitologia
Stosowana. irreg.
● Akademia Rolnicza, Poznan. Rocznik. Prace
Habilitacyjne. irreg.
● Akademia Rolnicza, Poznan. Rocznik. Rolnictwo.
irreg.
● Akademia Rolnicza, Poznan. Rocznik.
Technologia Drewna. irreg.
● Akademia Rolnicza, Poznan. Rocznik.
Technologia Rolno-Spozywcza. irreg.
● Akademia Rolnicza, Poznan. Rocznik.
Zootechnika. irreg.

**Akademia Rolnicza, Szczecin**
Janosika 8, 71-424 Szczecin, Poland
(Dist. by: Ars Polona-Ruch, Krakowskie
Przedmiescie 7, Warsaw, Poland)
● Akademia Rolnicza, Szczecin. Zeszyty Naukowe.
irreg., vol. 4, 1975. ISSN 0082-1233

**Akademia Rolnicza, Warsaw**
Ul. Rakoviecka 41, Warsaw, Poland
(Dist. by Ars Polona-Ruch, Krakowskie
Przedmiescie 7, Warsaw, Poland)
● Akademia Rolnicza, Warsaw. Zeszyty Naukowe.
Ogrodnictwo. irreg. ISSN 0083-7288
● Akademia Rolnicza, Warsaw. Zeszyty Naukowe.
Seria Historyczna. irreg. ISSN 0083-7296
● Akademia Rolnicza, Warsaw. Zeszyty Naukowe.
Technologia Drewna. irreg., no. 6, 1975.
● Akademia Rolnicza, Warsaw. Zeszyty Naukowe.
Zootechnika. irreg., 1973, vol. 9.

**Akademia Rolnicza, Wroclaw**
Norwida 25, 50-375 Wroclaw, Poland.
● Akademia Rolnicza, Wroclaw. Rolnictwo. a.

**Akademia Rolniczo-Techniczna**
Blok 21, 10-957 Olsztyn-Kortowo, Poland
(Dist. by Ars Polona-Ruch, Krakowskie
Przedmiescie 7, Warsaw, Poland)
● Akademia Rolniczo-Techniczna. Zeszyty
Naukowe. a.
● Mechanika i Budownictwo/Mechanics and
Building Engineering. irreg.

**Wydawnictwo Arkady**
Ul. Sienkiewicza 14, 00-950 Warsaw, Poland
(Dist. by: Ars Polona-Ruch,Krakowskie
Przedmiescie 7, Warsaw, Poland)
● Architektura. m. ISSN 0003-8814 (Stowarzyszenie
Architektow Polskich-SARP)
● Cement, Wapno, Gips. m. ISSN 0008-8897
(Zjednoczenie Przemyslu Cementowego,
Wapienniczego i Gipsowego, Sosnowiec)
● Magazyn Fotograficzny FOTO. q.

**Wydawnictwa Artystyczne i Filmowe**
Ul. Pulawska 61, Warsaw, Poland
(Dist. by Ars Polona-Ruch, Krakowskie
Przedmiescie 7, Warsaw, Poland)
● Almanach Sceny Polskiej. a. ISSN 0065-6526
(Polska Akademia Nauk. Instytut Sztuki)
● Katalog Zabytkow Sztuki w Polsce. pub'd. by
regions; 1976, vol. 8, pt. 2 and vol. 11, pt. 4.
ISSN 0075-5257 (Polska Akademia Nauk.
Instytut Sztuki)

**Wydawnictwa Artystyczno-Graficzne RSW "Prasa-Ksiazka-Ruch"**
Ul. Smolna 10, Warsaw, Poland
(Dist. by: Ars Polona-Ruch, Krakowskie
Przedmiescie 7, Warsaw, Poland)
● Dialog; miesiecznik poswiecony dramaturgii
wspolczesnej teatralnej, filmowej, radiowej i
telewizyjnej. m. ISSN 0012-2041
● Dookola Swiata; illustrated weekly of the socialist
youth union. w. ISSN 0012-5458
● Ekran. w. ISSN 0013-3299
● Fakty 77; tygodniowy magazyn kulturalny. w.
● Forum. w. ISSN 0015-8402
● Fundamenty. w. ISSN 0429-8918

● Glos Nauczycielski. w. ISSN 0017-1263 (Zwiazek
Nauczycielstwa Polskiego)
● Kino. m. ISSN 0023-1673
● Kobieta i Zycie. w. ISSN 0023-2548
● Literatura na Swiecie. m.
● Magazyn Polski. m. ISSN 0024-9866
● Miesiecznik Literacki. m. ISSN 0026-3567
● Nasze Problemy. m.
● Panorama Polnocy. w. ISSN 0031-0964
(Stowarzyszenie Spoleczno-Kulturalne
"Pojezierze")
● Perspektywy. w. ISSN 0031-6059
● Pielegniarka i Polozna. m. ISSN 0048-4148
(Zwiazek Zawodowy Pracownikow Sluzby
Zdrowia)
● Poezja. m. ISSN 0032-2237
● Polityka. w. ISSN 0032-3500
● Problemy; miesiecznik popularno-naukowy. m.
ISSN 0032-9487 (Towarzystwo Wiedzy
Powszechnej)
● Projekt; sztuka wizualna i projektowanie. bi-m.
ISSN 0033-0957 (Krajowa Agencja Wydawnicza)
● Przekroj. w. ISSN 0033-2488
● Przyjaciolka; popular women's journal. w. ISSN
0033-2534
● Rada Narodowa, Gospodarka, Administracja.
fortn.
● Radar; international magazine for creativity. m.
ISSN 0033-7501
● Ruch Muzyczny; a musical review. fortn. ISSN
0035-9610
● Sportowiec. w. ISSN 0038-8122
● Stolica. w. ISSN 0039-1689
● Szachy. m.
● Szpilki; illustrated satirical weekly. w. ISSN 0039-
8152
● Sztuka. bi-m.
● Teatr. fortn. ISSN 0040-0769
● Tworczosc. m. ISSN 0041-4727
● Widnokregi. m. ISSN 0043-5244
● Zeszyty "Argumentow". bi-m. ISSN 0514-342X
● Zeszyty Prasoznawcze. q. ISSN 0555-0025
(Osrodek Badan Prasoznawczych)
● Zycie i Zdrowie. fortn.

**Bialostockie Towarzystwo Naukowe**
Dom Technika, Sklodowskiej - Curie 2, 15-097
Bialystok, Poland
(Dist by Ars Polona-Ruch, Krakowskie Przedmiescie
7, Warsaw, Poland)
● Bialostockie Towarzystwo Naukowe. Prace. irreg.
ISSN 0067-6470

**Biblioteka Kornicka**
● Biblioteka Kornicka. Pamietnik. (pub. by
Ossolineum, Publishing House of the Polish
Academy of Sciences)

**Biblioteka Narodowa**
Ul. Hankiewicza 1, 00-973 Warsaw, Poland.
● Bibliografia Analityczna Bibliotekoznawstwa i
Informacji Naukowej. q. ISSN 0033-233X
● Biblioteka Narodowa. Biuletyn Informacyjny. q.
ISSN 0006-3983
● Biblioteka Narodowa. Rocznik. a. ISSN 0083-
7261

**Biblioteka Narodowa. Instytut Bibliograficzny**
Ul. Hankiewicza 1, 00-973 Warsaw, Poland
(Dist. by Ars Polona - Ruch, Krakowskie
Przedmiescie 7, Warsaw, Poland)
● Bibliografia Zawartosci Czasopism. m. ISSN 0006-
1093
● Literatura Piekna. Adnotowany Rocznik
Bibliograficzny. (pub. by Stowarzyszenie
Bibliotekarzy Polskich)
● Przewodnik Bibliograficzny; urzedowy wykaz
drukow wydanych w Polskiej Rzeczypospolitej
Ludowej. w. ISSN 0033-2518

**Biblioteka Slaska**
Ul. Francuska 12, 40-015 Katowice, Poland.
● Biblioteka Slaska. Biuletyn Informacyjny. a.

**Bydgoskie Towarzystwo Naukowe**
Jezuicka 4, Bydgoszcz, Poland
(Dist. by Ars Polona-Ruch, Krakowskie
Przedmiescie 7, Warsaw, Poland)
● Bydgoskie Towarzystwo Naukowe. Wydzial Nauk
Humanistycznych. Prace. Seria B (Jezyk i
Literatura) irreg. ISSN 0068-4570
● Bydgoskie Towarzystwo Naukowe. Wydzial Nauk
Humanistycznych. Prace. Seria C (Historia i
Archeologia) irreg. ISSN 0068-4589
● Bydgoskie Towarzystwo Naukowe. Wydzial Nauk
Humanistycznych. Prace. Seria D: (Sztuka) irreg.,
1965, no. 3. ISSN 0067-947X

- Bydgoskie Towarzystwo Naukowe. Wydzial Nauk
Technicznych. Prace. Seria Z: (Prace Zbiorowe)
irreg. ISSN 0068-4597
- Z Dziejow Muzyki Polskiej. irreg. ISSN 0084-
442X
- Zrodla do Dziejow Bydgoszczy. irreg. ISSN 0084-
568X

**Centrala Rolnicza Spoldzielni "Samopomoc Chlopska"
Zaklad Wydawnictw**
Ul. Czackiego 21/23, Pok. 7, Warsaw, Poland
(Dist. by: Ars Polona - Ruch, Krakowskie
Przedmiescie 7, Warsaw, Poland)
- Polish Co-Operative Review. q. ISSN 0032-2822
(Naczelna Rada Spoldzielcza)
- Trybuna Spoldzielcza; miestecznik problemowy
naczelnej rady spoldzielczej. m. ISSN 0041-3720
(Naczelna Rada Spoldzielcza)

**Centralne Muzeum Morskie, Gdansk**
- Transport Museums. (pub. by Ossolineum,
Publishing House of the Polish Academy of
Sciences)

**Centralny Instytut Ochrony Pracy**
- Ochrona Pracy. (pub. by Wydawnictwa Czasopism
Technicznych, N.O.T.)

**Centralny Osrodek Badan i Rozwoju Techniki
Kolejnictwa**
Chlopickiego 50, 04-275 Warsaw, Poland.
- Centralny Osrodek Badan i Rozwoju Techniki
Kolejnictwa. Prace COBiRTK. (pub. by
Wydawnictwa Komunikacji i Lacznosci)
- Przeglad Dokumentacyjny Polskiego i
Zagranicznego Pismiennictwa Kolejowego. m.
ISSN 0033-2070

**Centralny Osrodek Badawczo-Projektowy Gornictwa
Odkrywkowego "Poltegor"**
- Gornictwo Odkrywkowe. (pub. by Panstwowe
Wydawnictwo Naukowe)

**Centralny Osrodek Informacji Budownictwa**
Ul. Senatorska 27, 00-099 Warsaw, Poland.
- Centralny Osrodek Informacji Budownictwa.
Biuletyn-Informacja. m. ISSN 0008-9591
- Polish Building Abstracts/Documentation
Polonaise de la Construction/Polnische
Dokumentation fuer Bauwesen. m. ISSN 0032-
2814

**Centralny Osrodek Metodyczny Studiow Nauk
Politycznych**
- Studia Nauk Politycznych. (pub. by Panstwowe
Wydawnictwo Naukowe)

**Centralny Urzad Geologii**
- Przeglad Geologiczny/Geological Review. (pub.
by Wydawnictwa Geologiczne)
- Technika Poszukiwan Geologicznych/Technique
of Geological Prospecting. (pub. by Wydawnictwa
Geologiczne)

**Centralny Zarzad Przemyslu Skorzanego**
- Przeglad Skorzany. (pub. by Wydawnictwa
Czasopism Technicznych, N.O.T.)

**Centralny Zwiazek Spoldzielni Spozywcow**
Grazyny 13, Warsaw, Poland.
- Spolem. s-m. ISSN 0038-7746

**Centrum Medyczne Ksztalcenia Podyplomowego**
- Materia Medica Polona. (pub. by Wydawnictwa
Handlu Zagranicznego Polexportpress)

**Chrzescijanskie Stowarzyszenie Spoleczne**
Marszalkowska 4, 00-590 Warsaw, Poland
(Dist. by: Ars Polona - Ruch, Krakowskie
Przedmiescie 7, Warsaw, Poland)
- Hejnal Mariacki; miesiecznik o tematyce religijno-
kulturalno-spoleczna. m. ISSN 0017-9914
- Za i Przeciw; tygodnik ilustrowany. w. ISSN
0044-1538

**Wydawnictwa Czasopism Technicznych, N.O.T.**
Czackiego 3-5, Warsaw, Poland
(Dist. by: Ars Polona-Ruch, Krakowskie
Przedmiescie 7, Warsaw, Poland)
- ABC Techniki; magazine for children. 3 per yr.
- Aura. m.

- Budownictwo Okretowe. m. ISSN 0007-2990
(Stowarzyszenie Inzynierow i Technikow
Mechanikow Polskich)
- Chemik. m. ISSN 0009-2886 (Stowarzyszenie
Inzynierow i Technikow Przemyslu Chemicznego)
(Co-sponsor: Ministerstwo Przemyslu
Chemicznego)
- Chlodnictwo. m. ISSN 0009-4919
- Cieplownictwo, Ogrzewnictwo, Wentylacja. m.
(Polskie Zrzeszenie Inzynierow i Technikow
Sanitarnych)
- Cuprum. bi-m. (Zaklad Projektowych Miedzi
"Cuprum")
- Elektronika. m. ISSN 0033-2089 (Polska
Akademia Nauk. Komitet Elektroniki i
Telekomunikacji) (Co-sponsor: Stowarzyszenia
Elektrykow Polskich)
- Energetyka. m. ISSN 0013-7294 (Stowarzyszenie
Elektrykow Polskich)
- Gaz, Woda i Technika Sanitarna. m. ISSN 0016-
5352 (Polskie Zrzeszenie Inzynierow i Technikow
Sanitarnych)
- Gazeta Cukrownicza. m. ISSN 0016-5395
(Stowarzyszenie Technikow Cukrownikow) (Co-
sponsor: Zjednoczenie Przemyslu Cukrowniczego)
- Gospodarka Miesna. m.
- Gospodarka Paliwami i Energia/Fuel and Energy
Management. m. ISSN 0017-2413 (Poland.
Ministerstwo Gornictwa i Energetyki) (Co-
sponsor: Stowarzyszenie Elektrykow Polskich)
- Gospodarka Wodna. m. ISSN 0017-2448
- Horyzonty Techniki. m. (Naczelna Organizacja
Techniczna) (Co-sponsor: Towarzystwo Wiedzy
Powszechnej)
- Informatyka. m. ISSN 0542-9951 (Polski Komitet
Automatycznego Przetwarzania Informacji NOT)
(Co-sponsor: Krajowy Biuro Informatyki)
- Innowacje; przeglad techniczny. w. (Naczelna
Organizacja Techniczna) (Co-sponsor: Polskie
Towarzystwo Ekonomiczne)
- Inzynieria i Aparatura Chemiczna. bi-m.
(Stowarzyszenie Inzynierow i Technikow
Przemyslu Chemicznego) (Co-sponsors:
Stowarzyszenie Inzynierow i Technikow
Mechanikow Polskich, Zjednoczenie Budowy i
Remontow Urzadzen Chemicznych)
- Kalejdoskop Techniki. m.
- Konfrontacje. m. (Naczelna Organizacja
Techniczna. Oddzial w Rzeszowie) (Co-sponsor:
Polskie Towarzystwo Ekonomiczne)
- Maszyny i Ciagniki Rolnicze. m. ISSN 0465-2592
(Stowarzyszenie Inzynierow i Technikow
Mechanikow Polskich. Sekcja Maszyn i
Ciagnikow Rolniczych)
- Materialy Budowlane. m.
- Mechanik; miesiecznik naukowo- techniczny. m.
ISSN 0025-6552
- Ochrona Powietrza. bi-m. (Stowarzyszenie
Inzynierow i Technikow Przemyslu Hutniczego)
- Ochrona Pracy. m. ISSN 0029-8220 (Centralny
Instytut Ochrony Pracy) (Co-sponsor: Naczelna
Organizacja Techniczna)
- Ochrona przed Korozja. m. ISSN 0473-7733
(Stowarzyszenie Inzynierow i Technikow
Przemyslu Chemicznego) (Co-sponsor: Polski
Komitet Ochrony przed Korozja NOT)
- Odziez. m. ISSN 0471-0320 (Stowarzyszenie
Wlokiennikow Polskich)
- Ogrodnictwo. m. ISSN 0030-0756
- Opakowanie. m. ISSN 0030-3348
- Poligrafika. m. (Stowarzyszenie Inzynierow i
Technikow Mechanikow Polskich. Sekcja
Poligrafow)
- Polish Technical Review. m. ISSN 0032-3012
- Pomiary-Automatyka-Kontrola. m. ISSN 0032-
4140 (Polski Komitet Pomiarow i Automatyki)
(Co-sponsor: Sekcja Metrologii Automatyki i
Mechaniki Precyzyjnej SIMP)
- Prasa Techniczna. bi-m. (Rada Prasy Technicznej)
- Przeglad Budowlany/Building Review. m. ISSN
0033-2038 (Polski Zwiazek Inzynierow i
Technikow Budownictwa)
- Przeglad Elektrotechniczny. m. ISSN 0033-2097
(Stowarzyszenie Elektrykow Polskich)
- Przeglad Gastronomiczny. m. ISSN 0033-2119
- Przeglad Geodezyjny. m. ISSN 0033-2127
(Stowarzyszenie Geodetow Polskich)
- Przeglad Gospodarczy. m. (Polskie Towarzystwo
Ekonomiczne. Oddzial we Wroclawiu) (Co-
sponsor: Naczelna Organizacja Techniczna)
- Przeglad Mechaniczny. s-m. ISSN 0033-2259
(Stowarzyszenie Inzynierow i Technikow
Mechanikow Polskich)
- Przeglad Odlewnictwa. m. ISSN 0033-2275
- Przeglad Papierniczy/Polish Paper Review. m.
ISSN 0033-2291
- Przeglad Piekarski i Cukierniczy. m. ISSN 0033-
2313

- Przeglad Skorzany. m. (Centralny Zarzad
Przemyslu Skorzanego)
- Przeglad Spawalnictwa. m. ISSN 0033-2364
(Stowarzyszenie Inzynierow i Technikow
Mechanikow Polskich)
- Przeglad Techniczny Tygodnik. w. ISSN 0033-
2380 (Naczelna Organizacja Techniczna)
- Przeglad Telekomunikacyjny. m. ISSN 0033-2399
(Stowarzyszenie Elektrykow Polskich)
- Przeglad Wlokienniczy. m. ISSN 0033-2410
(Stowarzyszenie Wlokiennikow Polskich)
- Przeglad Zbozowo-Mlynarski. m. ISSN 0033-2461
- Przemysl Chemiczny. m. ISSN 0033-2496
(Poland. Ministerstwo Przemyslu Chemicznego)
(Co-sponsor: Stowarzyszenie Inzynierow i
Technikow Przemyslu Chemicznego)
- Przemysl Drzewny. m. ISSN 0478-6726
(Stowarzyszenie Inzynierow i Technikow
Lesnictwa i Drzewnictwa)
- Przemysl Fermentacyjny i Rolny. m. ISSN 0555-
5264 (Stowarzyszenie Naukowotechniczne
Inzynierow i Technikow Przemyslu Spozywczego)
- Przemysl Spozywczy. m. ISSN 0033-250X
(Stowarzyszenie Naukowo-Techniczne Inzynierow
i Technikow Przemyslu Spozywczego)
- Rynek i Uslugi. s-m. (Stowarzyszenie Inzynierow i
Technikow Mechanikow Polskich. Sekcja
Przemyslu Drobnego) (Co-Sponsor: Ministerstwo
Handlu Wewnetrznego i Uslug)
- Szklo i Ceramika. m. ISSN 0039-8144
- Technik Wlokienniczy. m. ISSN 0492-4851
(Stowarzyszenie Wlokiennikow Polskich)
- Technika Lotnicza i Astronautyczna. m. ISSN
0040-1145
- Technika Motoryzacyjna. m. ISSN 0040-1153
- TEMAT - Wynalazczosc i Racjonalizacja; pismo
poswiecone tworczosci technicznej. s-m.
- Wiadomosci Elektrotechniczne. s-m. ISSN 0043-
5112 (Stowarzyszenie Elektrykow Polskich)
- Wiadomosci Melioracyjne i Lekarskie. m. ISSN
0510-4262 (Stowarzyszenie Inzynierow i
Technikow Wodnych i Melioracyjnych)
- Wiadomosci Produkcyjne-Wlokno, Odziez, Skora.
s-m. (Stowarzyszenie Wlokiennikow Polskich)
- Wiadomosci Tytoniowe. m. ISSN 0508-7104
(Stowarzyszenie Naukowo-Techniczne Inzynierow
i Technikow Przemyslu Spozywczego)
- Wiadomosci Warsztatowe. fortn. ISSN 0043-521X
(Stowarzyszenie Inzynierow i Technikow
Mechanikow Polskich)
- Wiadomosci Zielarskie. m. (Stowarzyszenie
Naukowotechniczne Inzynierow i Technikow
Przemyslu Spozywczego) (Co-sponsors:
Zrzeszenie Producentow Roslin Zielarskich,
Zjednoczenie Przemyslu Zielarskiego "Herbapol")

**Dolnoslaskie Towarzystwo Oswiatowe**
- Rocznik Dolnoslaski. (pub. by Ossolineum,
Publishing House of the Polish Academy of
Sciences)

**Express Wieczorny**
Al. Jerozolimskie 125, Warsaw, Poland.
- Kulisy. w. ISSN 0023-5083

**Film Polski**
Ul. Mazowiecka 6-8, 00-048 Warsaw, Poland
(Dist. by: Ars Polona - Ruch, Krakowskie
Przedmiescie 7, Warsaw, Poland)
- Polish Film/Film Polonais. bi-m. ISSN 0015-136X

**Filmowy Osrodek Badawczo-Rozwojowy "Techfilm".
Branzowy Osrodek Informacji Technicznej i
Ekonomicznej**
Ul Dominikanska 9, 02-738 Warsaw, Poland.
- Filmowy Osrodek Badawczo - Rozwojowy
"Techfilm". Przeglad Dokumentacyjny. m. ISSN
0015-1653

**Gdanskie Towarzystwo Naukowe**
- Acta Biologica Societatis Scientiarum Gedanensis.
(pub. by Ossolineum, Publishing House of the
Polish Academy of Sciences)
- Acta Technica Gedanensia. (pub. by Ossolineum,
Publishing House of the Polish Academy of
Sciences)
- Gdanskie Towarzystwo Naukowe. Wydzial I.
Nauk Spolecznych i Humanistycznych. Komisja
Archeologiczna. Prace. (pub. by Ossolineum,
Publishing House of the Polish Academy of
Sciences)
- Gdanskie Towarzystwo Naukowe. Wydzial I.
Nauk Spolecznych i Humanistycznych. Seria
Monografii. (pub. by Ossolineum, Publishing
House of the Polish Academy of Sciences)

- Gdanskie Towarzystwo Naukowe. Wydzial I.
  Nauk Spolecznych i Humanistycznych. Seria
  Popularnonaukowa "Pomorze Gdanskie". (pub. by
  Ossolineum, Publishing House of the Polish
  Academy of Sciences)
- Gdanskie Towarzystwo Naukowe. Wydzial I.
  Nauk Spolecznych i Humanistycznych. Seria
  Zrodel. (pub. by Ossolineum, Publishing House of
  the Polish Academy of Sciences)
- Pomorskie Monografie Toponomastyczne. (pub.
  by Ossolineum, Publishing House of the Polish
  Academy of Sciences)
- Rocznik Gdanski. (pub. by Ossolineum, Publishing
  House of the Polish Academy of Sciences)

**Gdanskie Towarzystwo Przyjaciol Sztuki**
- Rocznik Kulturalny Ziemi Gdanskiej. (pub. by
  Wydawnictwo Morskie)

**Wydawnictwa Geologiczne**
Ul. Rakowiecka 4, Warsaw, Poland
(Dist. by Ars Polona-Ruch, Krakowskie
Przedmiescie 7, Warsaw, Poland)
- Archiwum Mineralogiczne. irreg., 1971, vol. 29,
  no. 1-2. ISSN 0066-6912 (Polska Akademia
  Nauk. Komitet Nauk Geologicznych)
- Przeglad Geologiczny/Geological Review. m.
  ISSN 0033-2151 (Centralny Urzad Geologii)
- Studia Geologica Polonica. irreg. ISSN 0081-6426
  (Polska Akademia Nauk. Oddzial w Krakowie.
  Komisja Nauk Geologicznych)
- Technika Poszukiwan Geologicznych/Technique
  of Geological Prospecting. bi-m. (Centralny Urzad
  Geologii)

**Glowna Biblioteka Lekarska**
Ul. Chocimska 22, Warsaw, Poland
(Dist. by: Ars Polona - Ruch, Krakowskie
Przedmiescie 7, Warsaw, Poland)
- Glowna Biblioteka Lekarska. Biuletyn. m. ISSN
  0017-1344
- IB-1. Informacja Biezaca; przeglad zawartosci
  obcojezycznych czasopism medycznych. s-m.
- IB-2. Informacja Biezaca; przeglad zawartosci
  czasopism polskich i obcojezycznych z zakresu
  medycyny spolecznej i organizacji ochrony
  zdrowia. q.
- IB-3. Informacja Biezaca; przeglad pismiennictwa
  lekarskiego polskiego. m. ISSN 0033-2321

**Glowny Instytut Gornictwa**
- Przeglad Gorniczy. (pub. by Wydawnictwo
  "Slask")

**Wydawnictwo Idisz Buch**
Nowogrodzka 5, Warsaw, Poland.
- Idisze Szriftn/Jewish Cultural Affairs. m. ISSN
  0019-1507

**Instytut Automatyki Systemow Energetycznych**
Wystawowa 1, 51-618 Wroclaw, Poland.
- Instytut Automatyki Systemow Energetycznych.
  Prace. irreg., 1972, no. 24. ISSN 0084-2788

**Instytut Badan Jadrowych. Zaklad Radiobiologii i
Ochrony Zdrowia**
- Instytut Badan Jadrowych. Zaklad Radiobiologii i
  Ochrony Zdrowia. Prace Doswiadczaine. (pub. by
  Osrodek Informacji o Energii Jadrowej)

**Instytut Badania Prawa Sadowego**
- Instytut Badania Prawa Sadowego. Zeszyty
  Naukowe. (pub. by Wydawnictwo Prawnicze)

**Instytut Badawczy Drog i Mostow**
- Instytut Badawczy Drog i Mostow. Prace. (pub.
  by Wydawnictwa Komunikacji i Lacznosci)

**Instytut Balneoklimatyczny**
Slowackiego 8/10, Poznan, Poland.
- Balneologia Polska. q. ISSN 0005-4402

**Instytut Ciezkiej Syntezy Organicznej**
47-232 Kedzierzyn, Poland.
- Instytut Ciezkiej Syntezy Organicznej. Zeszyty
  Naukowe. 4-6 per yr. ISSN 0020-4447

**Instytut Doskonalenia Kadr Kierowniczych
Administracji Panstwowej**
Ul. Wawelska 56, 02-067 Warsaw, Poland.
- Organizacja - Metody - Technika. m. ISSN 0030-
  5057

**Instytut Ekonomiki Uslug i Drobnej Wytworczosci**
Al Jerozolimskie 87, Warsaw, Poland.
- Instytut Ekonomiki Uslug i Drobnej
  Wytworczosci. Studia i Informacje. irreg.

**Instytut Elektrotechniki**
Ul. Pozaryskiego 28, 04-703 Warsaw, Poland
(Dist. by: Ars Polona-Ruch, Krakowskie
Przedmiescie 7, Warsaw, Poland)
- Instytut Elektrotechniki. Prace. ISSN 0032-6216
- Przeglad Dokumentacyjny Elektrotechniki. m.
  ISSN 0033-2062

**Instytut Geologiczny**
Rakowiecka 4, Warsaw, Poland
(Dist by: Ars Polona - Ruch, Krakowskie
Przedmiescie 7, Warsaw, Poland)
- Kwartalnik Geologiczny/Geological Quarterly. q.
  ISSN 0023-5873

**Instytut Informacji Naukowej, Technicznej i
Ekonomicznej**
Al. Niepodleglosci 188, 00-931 Warsaw, Poland
(Dist. by: Ars Polona - Ruch, Krakowskie
Przedmiescie 7, Warsaw, Poland)
- Aktualne Problemy Informacji i Dokumentacji. bi-
  m. ISSN 0002-3787
- Karty Dokumentacyjne/Documentation Cards. s-
  m. ISSN 0022-9172
- Polish Technical and Economic Abstracts. q.
  ISSN 0032-3004
- Przeglad Pismiennictwa Zagadnien Informacji. m.
  ISSN 0033-2348

**Instytut Koniunktur i Cen Handlu Zagranicznego**
- Problemy Handlu Zagranicznego. (pub. by
  Panstwowe Wydawnictwo Ekonomiczne)

**Instytut Lacznosci**
- Instytut Lacznosci. Prace. (pub. by Wydawnictwa
  Komunikacji i Lacznosci)

**Instytut Lotnictwa**
Al. Krakowska 110-114, Warsaw, Poland
(Dist. by Ars Polona - Ruch, Krakowskie
Przedmiescie 7, Warsaw, Poland)
- B I I L/Biuletyn Informacyjny Instytutu
  Lotnictwa. bi-m. ISSN 0005-3112

**Instytut Maszyn Matematycznych**
Krzywickiego 34, 02-078 Warsaw, Poland.
- Instytut Maszyn Matematycznych. Prace. 3 per
  yr.

**Instytut Materialow Ogniotrwalych**
Ul. Toszecka 99, 44-101 Gliwice, Poland
(Dist. by: Ars Polona - Ruch, Krakowskie
Przedmiescie 7, Warsaw, Poland)
- Przeglad Dokumentacyjny Materialow
  Ogniotrwalych. m. ISSN 0033-2046

**Instytut Mechaniki Precyzyjnej**
Duchnicka 3, 00-967 Warsaw, Poland
(Dist. by: Ars Polona- Ruch, Krakowskie
Przedmiescie 7, Warsaw, Poland)
- Powloki Ochronne. bi-m.

**Instytut Medycyny Morskiej i Tropikalnej w Gdyni**
Ul. Starowiejska 50, 81-356 Gdynia, Poland.
- Instytut Medycyny Morskiej i Tropikalnej w
  Gdyni. Bulletin/Institute of Maritime and
  Tropical Medicine in Gdynia. Bulletin. q.

**Instytut Medycyny Pracy i Higieny Wsi**
Szkolna 16, 20-950 Lublin, Poland
(Dist. by: Ars Polona - Ruch, Krakowskie
Przedmiescie 7, Warsaw, Poland)
- Medycyna Wiejska/Rural Medicine. q. ISSN
  0025-8636

**Instytut Metali Niezelaznych**
Ul. Sowinskiego 5, 44-101 Gliwice, Poland
(Dist. by: Ars Polona-Ruch, Krakowskie
Przedmiescie 7, Warsaw, Poland)
- Instytut Metali Niezelaznych. Biuletyn. q. ISSN
  0030-2317
- Instytut Metali Niezelaznych. Prace. q.
- Instytut Metali Niezelaznych. Przeglad
  Dokumentacyjny. m. ISSN 0020-4471

**Instytut Meteorologii i Gospodarki Wodnej**
Ul. Podlesna 61, 01-673 Warsaw, Poland
(Dist. by: Ars Polona - Ruch, Krakowskie
Przedmiescie 7, Warsaw, Poland)
- Instytut Meteorologii i Gospodarki Wodnej.
  Gazeta Obserwatora IMGW. m.
- Instytut Meteorologii i Gospodarki Wodnej. Prace.
  irreg., 1976, no. 4.
- Wiadomosci Meteorologii i Gospodarki Wodnej.
  q.

**Instytut Naftowy**
- Instytut Naftowy. Prace. (pub. by Wydawnictwo
  "Slask")
- Nafta. (pub. by Wydawnictwo "Slask")

**Instytut Naukowy Kultury Fizycznej**
- Wychowanie Fizyczne i Sport. Studia i Materialy.
  (pub. by Panstwowe Wydawnictwo Naukowe)

**Instytut Obrobki Plastycznej**
Zamenhofa 2/4, 61-120 Poznan, Poland
(Dist. by: Ars Polona - Ruch, Krakowskie
Przedmiescie 7, Warsaw, Poland)
- Polimery; macromolecular materials, chemistry
  and technology of polymers. m. ISSN 0032-2725

**Instytut Obrobki Skrawaniem**
Ul Wroclawska 37A, 30-011 Krakow, Poland.
- Informacja Ekspresowa. s-m. ISSN 0019-9834
- Instytut Obrobki Skrawaniem. Zeszyty Naukowe.
  q. ISSN 0020-4528

**Instytut Ochrony Roslin**
Miczurina 20, 60-318 Poznan, Poland.
- Instytut Ochrony Roslin. Biuletyn. irreg. ISSN
  0020-448X

**Instytut Onkologii**
Wawelska 15, 00-973 Warsaw, Poland.
- Nowotwory. (pub. by Panstwowy Zaklad
  Wydawnictw Lekarskich)
- Polish Oncological Abstracts. q.

**Instytut Organizacji, Zarzadzania i Ekonomiki
Przemyslu Budowlanego**
Ul. Filtrowa 1, 00-611 Warsaw, Poland.
- Problemy Inwestowania i Rozwoju/Building
  Problems. bi-m. ISSN 0032-9517

**Instytut Przemyslu Zielarskiego**
Libelta 27, 61-707 Poznan, Poland
(Dist. by: Ars Polona Ruch, Krakowskie
Przedmiescie 7, Warsaw, Poland)
- Herba Polonica. q. ISSN 0018-0599

**Instytut Slaski.**
Ul. Luboszycka 3, 45-036 Opole, Poland
(Dist. by Ars Polona, Krakowskie Przedmiescie 7,
Warsaw, Poland)
- Instytut Slaski. Komunikaty. Seria
  Niemcoznawcza. irreg. ISSN 0074-0616
- Instytut Slaski. Wydawnictwa. irreg. ISSN 0074-
  0632 (Distributed by: Ars Polona-Ruch,
  Krakowskie Przedmiescie 7, Warsaw, Poland)
- Studia Geograficzno-Fizyczne z Obszaru
  Opolszczyzny. irreg. ISSN 0081-6418
- Studia Spoleczno-Ekonomiczne. irreg. ISSN 0081-
  6930
- Ziema Kozielska. Studia i Materialy. irreg. ISSN
  0084-5493

**Instytut Technologii Drewna**
- Instytut Technologii Drewna. Prace. (pub. by
  Panstwowe Wydawnictwo Naukowe)

**Instytut Technologii Elektronowej**
- Electron Technology. (pub. by Panstwowe
  Wydawnictwo Naukowe)

**Instytut Tele-i Radiotechniczny**
Ratuszowa 11, 03-450 Warsaw, Poland.
- Instytut Tele- i Radiotechniczny. Prace. q. ISSN
  0032-6259

**Instytut Transportu Samochodowego**
Stalingradzka 40, Warsaw, Poland.
- Instytut Transportu Samochodowego. Zeszyty
  Naukowe. irreg., (approx 4-6 per year)

**Instytut Warzywnictwa**
Ul. 22 Lipca 1/3, 96-100 Skierniewice, Poland.
- Biuletyn Warzywniczy. irreg.

**Instytut Weterynarii**
Al. Partyzantow 55, Pulawy, Poland.
- Veterinary Institute, Pulawy. Bulletin. q. ISSN
  0042-4870

**Instytut Wydawniczy "Nasza Ksiegarnia"**
Ul. Spasowskiego 4, 00-389 Warsaw, Poland
(Dist. by: Ars Polona-Ruch, Krakowskie
Przedmiescie 7, Warsaw, Poland)
- Poznaj Swoj Kraj; miesiecznik krajoznawczo-
  turystyczny. m. ISSN 0032-6151
- Psychologia Wychowawcza/Educational
  Psychology. 5 per yr. ISSN 0033-2860

**Instytut Wydawniczy Znak**
Wislna 12, Krakow, Poland.
- Znak. m. ISSN 0044-488X

**Instytut Zachodni**
Stary Rynek 78/79, 61-772 Poznan, Poland
(Dist. by Ars Polona-Ruch, Krakowskie
Przedmiescie 7, Warsaw, Poland)
- Dzieje Polskiej Granicy Zachodniej. irreg. ISSN 0070-7791
- Polish Western Affairs; to scholars interested in present-day economic, social and political problems of Germany and Central Europe. s-a. ISSN 0032-3039
- Pologne et les Affaires Occidentales; to scholars interested in present-day economic, social and political problems of Germany and Central Europe. s-a. ISSN 0032-3675
- Przeglad Zachodni. bi-m. ISSN 0033-2437
- Studia nad Zagadnieniami Gospodarczymi i Spolecznymi Ziem Zachodnich. irreg. ISSN 0081-6752
- Studium Niemcoznawcze. irreg., vol. 26, 1975. ISSN 0081-8941
- Ziemie Zachodnie. Studia i Materialy. irreg. ISSN 0084-5507

**Instytut Zachodnio - Pomorski**
Rycerska 3, 70-537 Szczecin, Poland
(Dist. by: Ars Polona - Ruch, Krakowskie
Przedmiescie 7, Warsaw, Poland)
- Przeglad Zachodnio - Pomorski. q. ISSN 0552-4245

**Instytut Ziemniaka, Bonin**
- Ziemniak/Kartofel/Potato. (pub. by Panstwowe Wydawnictwo Rolnicze i Lesne)

**Instytut Zywnosci i Zywienia**
- Zywienie Czlowieka. (pub. by Panstwowy Zaklad Wydawnictw Lekarskich)

**International Organizing Committee of World Mining Congresses**
c/o Ing. M. Najberg, Secretary-General, Al.
Ujazdowskie 1-3, Warsaw, Poland
(Order 8th Report from: World Mining Congress, Camino Real 159, Ysidro, Lima, Peru)
- International Organizing Committee of World Mining Congresses. Report. biennial since 1963; 8th, Lima, Peru, 1974. ISSN 0074-2775

**International Theatre Institute. Polish Center**
Ul. Moliera 1, 00-072 Warsaw, Poland.
- Theatre en Pologne/Theatre in Poland. m. ISSN 0040-5493

**Polska Agencja Interpress**
Ul. Bagatela 12, Warsaw, Poland
(Dist. by: Ars Polona-Ruch, Krakowskie
Przedmiescie 7, Warsaw, Poland)
- Contemporary Poland. s-m. ISSN 0010-7522
- Panorama Polska. m. ISSN 0027-8327
- Poland/American edition. m. ISSN 0032-244X
- Poland-Tourism. m.

**Panstwowe Przedsiebiorstwo Wydawnictw Kartograficznych**
Ul. Solec 18-20, 00-410 Warsaw, Poland
(Dist. by: Ars Polona-Ruch, Krakowskie
Przedmiescie 7, Warsaw, Poland)
- Polski Przeglad Kartograficzny/Polish Cartographical Review. q. (Polskie Towarzystwo Geograficzne)

**Katolicki Uniwersytet Lubelski**
Al. Raclawickie 14, Lublin, Poland.
- Acta Mediaevalia. irreg.
- Katolicki Uniwersytet Lubelski. Zeszyty Naukowe. q. ISSN 0044-4405
- Roczniki Filozoficzne. ISSN 0035-7685
- Roczniki Nauk Spolecznych. irreg. (prep. by its Towarzystwo Naukowe)
- Roczniki Teologiczno-Kanoniczne. 6 per yr. ISSN 0035-7723

**Wydawnictwa Komunikacji i Lacznosci**
Ul. Kazimierzowska 52, Warsaw, Poland
(Dist. by: Ars Polona- Ruch, Krakowskie
Przedmiescie 7, Warsaw, Poland)
- Centralny Osrodek Badan i Rozwoju Techniki Kolejnictwa. Prace COBiRTK. irreg (approx 4-5 per yr)
- Drogownictwo. m. ISSN 0012-6357
- Instytut Badawczy Drog i Mostow. Prace. q.
- Instytut Gospodarki Wodnej. Prace. irreg., 1971, no. 4, vol. 6. ISSN 0074-0586
- Instytut Lacznosci. Prace. irreg. ISSN 0020-451X

- Medycyna Komunikacyjna. bi-m. ISSN 0025-861X (Zwiazek Zawodowy Pracownikow Sluzby Zdrowia)
- Przeglad Kolejowy Drogowy. m. ISSN 0033-2208
- Przeglad Kolejowy Elektrotechniczny. m. ISSN 0033-2216
- Przeglad Kolejowy Mechaniczny. m. ISSN 0033-2224 (Stowarzyszenie Inzynierow i Technikow Komunikacji)
- Przeglad Kolejowy Przewozowy. m. ISSN 0552-4199
- Przeglad Komunikacyjny; miesiecznik ekonomiczno-techniczny. m. ISSN 0033-2232
- Wiadomosci Telekomunikacyjne. m. ISSN 0043-5198 (Poland. Ministerstwo Komunikacji) (Cosponsor: Stowarzyszenie Elektrykow Polskich)

**Krajowa Agencja Wydawnicza**
- Projekt. (pub. by Wydawnictwa Artystyczno-Graficzne RSW "Prasa-Ksiazka-Ruch")

**Krajowe Wydawnictwo Czasopism**
Noakowskiego 14, Warsaw, Poland
(Dist. by: Ars Polona - Ruch, Krakowskie
Przedmiescie 7, Warsaw, Poland)
- Film. w. ISSN 0015-1033
- Jazz. m. ISSN 0021-5600
- Kinotechnik. bi-m. ISSN 0023-169X

**Krakowskie Wydawnictwo Prasowe RSW "Prasa - Ksiazka - Ruch"**
Ul. Wislna 2, 31-007 Krakow, Poland
(Dist. by: Ars Polona - Ruch, Krakowskie
Przedmiescie 7, Warsaw, Poland)
- Zycie Literackie. w. ISSN 0591-2369

**Wydawnictwo Ksiazka i Wiedza**
Ul. Smolna 13, Warsaw, Poland
(Dist. by: Ars Polona-Ruch, Krakowskie
Przedmiescie 7, War Saw, Poland)
- Archiwum Ruchu Robotniczego. irreg., 1975, vol. 2. (Polska Zjednoczona Partia Robotnicza. Komitet Centralny. Centralne Archiwum) (Subcr. to: Ars Polona-Ruch, Krakowskie Przedmiescie 7, Warsaw, Poland)
- Dokumenty i Materialy do Historii Stosunkow Polsko-Radzieckich. several times a year. ISSN 0012-5199 (Polska Akademia Nauk. Zaklad Historii Stosunkow Polsko - Radzieckich) (Cosponsor: Akademiya Nauk, Ssr. Institut Slowianowiedenija)
- Historia Powszechna. irreg., 1975, vol. 10.
- Informator Robotniczy. a.
- Proza. Poezja. irreg. ISSN 0079-7103
- Studia Religioznawcze. irreg., 1971, vol. 3, no. 4. ISSN 0081-6868 (Polska Akademia Nauk. Instytut Filozofii i Socjologii)
- Z Dziejow Stosunkow Polskoradziekich. Studia i Materialy. irreg., 1975, vol. 11-12. ISSN 0084-4438 (Polska Akademia Nauk. Instytut Krajow Socjalistycznych)
- Z Pola Walki. q. ISSN 0044-149X
- Zeszyty Teoretyczno-Polityczne; wybor artykolow z prasy zagranicznej. m. ISSN 0044-443X

**Legnickie Towarzystwo Przyjaciol Nauk**
- Szkice Legnickie. (pub. by Ossolineum, Publishing House of the Polish Academy of Sciences)

**Lodzkie Towarzystwo Naukowe**
Sienkiewicza 29, Lodz, Poland
(Dist. by: Ars Polona-Ruch, Krakowskie
Przedmiescie 7, Warsaw, Poland)
- Acta Archaeologica Lodziensia. (pub. by Ossolineum,Publishing House of the Polish Academy of Sciences)
- Acta Geographica Lodziensia. (pub. by Ossolineum, Publishing House of the Polish Academy of Sciences)
- Biuletyn Peryglacjalny. (pub. by Ossolineum, Publishing House of the Polish Academy of Sciences)
- Lodzkie Towarzystwo Naukowe. Komisji Jezykowej. Rozprawy. (pub. by Ossolineum, Publishing House of the Polish Academy of Sciences)
- Lodzkie Towarzystwo Naukowe. Wydzial I. Prace. (pub. by Ossolineum, Publishing House of the Polish Academy of Sciences)
- Lodzkie Towarzystwo Naukowe. Wydzial III. Nauk Matematyczno-Przyrodniczych. Prace. (pub. by Panstwowe Wydawnictwo Naukowe)
- Lodzkie Towarzystwo Naukowe. Wydzial IV. Nauk Lekarskich. Prace. (pub. by Panstwowe Wydawnictwo Naukowe)
- Lodzkie Towarzystwo Naukowe. Wydzial V. Nauk Technicznych. Prace. (pub. by Panstwowe Wydawnictwo Naukowe)

- Prace Polonistyczne. (pub. by Ossolineum, Publishing House of the Polish Academy of Sciences)
- Societatis Scientiarum Lodziensis. Acta Chimica. (pub. by Panstwowe Wydawnictwo Naukowe)
- Societe des Sciences et des Lettres de Lodz. Bulletin. s-a. ISSN 0459-6854
- Studia Prawno - Ekonomiczne. (pub. by Ossolineum, Publishing House of the Polish Academy of Sciences)
- Zagadnienia Rodzajow Literakich/Les Problems des Genres Litteraires. (pub. by Ossolineum, Publishing House of the Polish Academy of Sciences)

**Wydawnictwo Lubelskie**
Okopowa 7, Lublin, Poland
(Dist. by Ars Polona-Ruch, Krakowskie
Przedmiescie 7, Warsaw, Poland)
- Dzieje Lublina. irreg. ISSN 0419-8816
- Rocznik Lubelski. a. ISSN 0080-3510 (Polskie Towarzystwo Historyczne. Oddzial w Lublinie)

**Materialy Zrodlowe do Dziejow Kosciola w Polsce**
Al. Raclawickie 14, Lublin, Poland
(Dist. by Ars Polona-Ruch, Krakowskie Przedmiecie 7, Warsaw, Poland)
- Materialy Zrodlowe do Dziejow Kosciola W Polsce. irreg. ISSN 0076-5244

**Wydawnictwo Ministerstwa Obrony Narodowej**
Ul. Grzybowska 77, 00-950 Warsaw, Poland.
- Wojskowy Przeglad Historyczny. q. ISSN 0043-7182 (Wojskowy Instytut Historyczny)

**Morski Instytut Rybacki**
Al. Zjednoczenia 1, Gdynia, Poland
(Dist. by Ars Polona-Ruch, Krakowskie
Przedmiescie 7, Warsaw, Poland)
- Morski Instytut Rybacki, Gdynia. Prace. Seria A: Oceanograficzno - Ichtiologiczna. a. ISSN 0072-0496
- Morski Instytut Rybacki, Gdynia. Prace. Seria B: Technika Rybacka i Technologia Ryb. a. ISSN 0072-050X
- Morski Instytut Rybacki, Gdynia. Prace. Seria C: Ekonomika Rybacka. a. ISSN 0072-0518

**Wydawnictwo Morskie**
Szeroka 38/40, 80-835 Gdansk, Poland
(Dist. by: Ars Polona - Ruch, Krakowskie
Przedmiescie 7, Warsaw, Poland)
- Rocznik Kulturalny Ziemi Gdanskiej. irreg., 1973, vol. 6. (Gdanskie Towarzystwo Przyjaciol Sztuki)
- Technika i Gospodarka Morska. m. ISSN 0040-1137 (Poland. Ministerstwo Handlu Zagranicznego i Gospodarki Morskiej)

**Muzeum Archeologiczne, Gdansk**
- Pomarania Antiqua. (pub. by Ossolineum, Publishing House of the Polish Academy of Sciences)

**Muzeum Archeologiczne i Etnograficzne, Lodz**
- Muzeum Archeologiczne i Etnograficzne, Lodz. Prace i Materialy. Seria Archeologiczna. (pub. by Panstwowe Wydawnictwo Naukowe)
- Muzeum Archeologiczne i Etnograficzne, Lodz. Prace i Materialy. Seria Etnograficzna. (pub. by Panstwowe Wydawnictwo Naukowe)

**Muzeum Archeologiczne, Krakow**
Poselska 3, 31-002 Krakow, Poland.
- Muzeum Archeologiczne, Krakow. Materialy Archeologiczne. irreg., 1972, no. 13. ISSN 0075-7039

**Muzeum Archeologiczne, Poznan**
Ul. Wodna 27, Palac Gorkow, 61-781 Poznan, Poland
(Dist. by Ars Polona-Ruch, Krakowskie
Przedmiescie 7, Warsaw, Poland)
- Fontes Archaeologici Posnanienses/Annales Musei Archaeologici Posnaniensis. a. ISSN 0071-6863
- Wiadomosci Archeologiczne. (pub. by Ossolineum, Publishing House of the Polish Academy of Sciences)

**Muzeum Archeologiczne, Wroclaw**
- Silesia Antiqua. (pub. by Ossolineum, Publishing House of the Polish Academy of Sciences)

**Muzeum Etnograficzne, Wroclaw**
Kazimierza Wielkiego 33, 50-077 Wroclaw, Poland.
- Muzeum Etnograficzne, Wroclaw. Zeszyty Etnograficzne. a. ISSN 0084-2796

**Muzeum Gornoslaskie**
Pl. Thaelmanna 2, 41-902 Bytom, Poland
(Dist. by Ars Polona-Ruch, Krakowskie
Przedmiescie 7, Warsaw, Poland)
- Muzeum Gornoslaskie w Bytomiu. Rocznik. Seria
Archeologia. irreg. ISSN 0068-4635
- Muzeum Gornoslaskie w Bytomiu. Rocznik. Seria
Etnografia. irreg. ISSN 0068-4643
- Muzeum Gornoslaskie w Bytomiu. Rocznik. Seria
Historia. irreg. ISSN 0068-4651
- Muzeum Gornoslaskie w Bytomiu. Rocznik. Seria
Przyroda. irreg. ISSN 0068-466X
- Muzeum Gornoslaskie w Bytomiu. Rocznik. Seria
Sztuka. irreg. ISSN 0068-4678

**Muzeum Historii Polskiego Ruchu Rewolucyjnego**
Plac Dzierzynskiego 1, 00-139 Warsaw, Poland
(Dist. by: Ars Polona-Ruch, Krakowskie
Przedmiescie 7, Warsaw, Poland)
- Muzea Walki. a. ISSN 0077-2577

**Muzeum Mazurskie**
Ul. Zamkowa 2, 10-074 Olsztyn, Poland
(Dist. by Ars Polona-Ruch, Krakowskie
Przedmiescie 7, Warsaw, Poland)
- Rocznik Olsztynski. a. ISSN 0080-3537

**Muzeum Narodowe, Szczecin**
Staromlynska 27, 70-561 Szczecin, Poland
(Dist. by: Ars Polona- Ruch, Krakowskie
Przedmiescie 7, Warsaw, Poland)
- Materialy Zachodnio-Pomorskie. a. ISSN 0076-
5236

**Muzeum Narodowe, Warsaw**
Al. Jerozolimskie 3, 00-495 Warsaw, Poland
(Dist. by: Ars Polona-Ruch, Krakowskie
Przedmiescie 7, Warsaw Poland)
- Musee National de Varsovie. Bulletin. q. ISSN
0027-3791

**Muzeum Narodowe, Wroclaw**
Pl Powstancow Warszawy 5, 50-153 Wroclaw,
Poland.
- Wspolczesne Malarstwo Wroclawskie. irreg. ISSN
0084-3032

**Muzeum w Bialymstoku**
- Rocznik Bialostocki. (pub. by Panstwowe
Wydawnictwo Naukowe)

**Polskie Wydawnictwo Muzyczne**
Al. Krasinskiego 11, Krakow, Poland
(Dist. by Ars Polona-Ruch, Krakowskie
Przedmiescie 7, Warsaw, Poland)
- Biblioteka Sluchacza Koncertowego. Seria
Wprowadzajaca. irreg. ISSN 0067-7779
- Mala Biblioteka Baletowa. irreg. ISSN 0076-2989
- Musica Medii Aevi. irreg. ISSN 0077-247X
(Polska Akademia Nauk. Instytut Sztuki)
- Polska Piesn i Muzyka Ludowa. Zrodla i
Materialy. irreg. ISSN 0079-3612 (Polska
Akademia Nauk. Instytut Sztuki)
- Zrodla do Historii Muzyki Polskiej. irreg. ISSN
0084-571X

**Naczelna Dyrekcja Archiwow Panstwowych**
- Archeion. (pub. by Panstwowe Wydawnictwo
Naukowe)

**Naczelna Organizacja Techniczna**
- Horyzonty Techniki. (pub. by Wydawnictwa
Czasopism Technicznych, N.O.T.)
- Innowacje. (pub. by Wydawnictwa Czasopism
Technicznych, N.O.T.)
- Przeglad Techniczny Tygodnik. (pub. by
Wydawnictwa Czasopism Technicznych, N.O.T.)

**Naczelna Organizacja Techniczna. Oddzial w
Rzeszowie**
- Konfrontacje. (pub. by Wydawnictwa Czasopism
Technicznych, N.O.T)

**Naczelna Rada Spoldzielcza**
- Polish Co-Operative Review. (pub. by Centrala
Rolnicza Spoldzielni "Samopomoc Chlopska"
Zaklad Wydawnictw)
- Trybuna Spoldzielcza. (pub. by Centrala Rolnicza
Spoldzielni "Samopomoc Chlopska" Zaklad
Wydawnictw)

**Wydawnictwa Normalizacyjne**
Nowogrodzka 22, Warsaw, Poland
(Dist. by: Ars Polona-Ruch, Krakowskie
Przedmiescie 7, Warsaw, Poland)
- Normalizacja. m. ISSN 0029-179X (Polski
Komitet Normalizacji i Miar)

- Problemy Jakosci; dwumiesiecznik naukowo-
techniczny. bi-m. (Polski Komitet Normalizacji i
Miar)

**Opolskie Towarzystwo Przyjaciol Nauk**
Ul. Zamkowa 2, 45-016 Opole, Poland
(Dist. by: Ars Polona-Ruch, Krakowskie
Przedmiescie 7, Warsaw, Poland)
- Kwartalnik Opolski. q. ISSN 0023-592X

**Osrodek Badan Prasoznawczych**
- Zeszyty Prasoznawcze. (pub. by Wydawnictwa
Artystyczno-Graficzne RSW "Prasa-Ksiazka-
Ruch")

**Osrodek Informacji o Energii Jadrowej**
Palac Kultury i Nauki, Warsaw, Poland
- Instytut Badan Jadrowych. Zaklad Radiobiologii i
Ochrony Zdrowia. Prace Doswiadczaine. irreg.,
vol. 4, 1973. ISSN 0074-0640

**Ossolineum, Publishing House of the Polish Academy
of Sciences**
Rynek 9, Wroclaw, Poland
(Dist. by: Ars Polona-Ruch, Krakowskie
Przedmiescie 7, Warsaw, Poland)
- Acta Archaeologica Carpathica. a. ISSN 0001-
5229 (Polska Akademia Nauk. Oddzial w
Krakowie. Komisja Archeologiczna)
- Acta Archaeologica Lodziensia. irreg., 1976, no.
25. ISSN 0065-0986 (Lodzkie Towarzystwo
Naukowe)
- Acta Baltico-Slavica. irreg., 1976, vol. 10. (Polska
Akademia Nauk. Zaklad Slowianoznawstwa)
- Acta Biologica Cracoviensia. Botanica. s-a. ISSN
0001-5296 (Polska Akademia Nauk. Oddzial w
Krakowie. Komisja Biologiczna)
- Acta Biologica Cracoviensia. Zoologia. s-a. ISSN
0001-530X (Polska Akademia Nauk. Oddzial w
Krakowie. Komisja Biologiczna)
- Acta Biologica Societatis Scientiarum Gedanensis.
irreg., no. 3, 1977. (Gdanskie Towarzystwo
Naukowe)
- Acta Geographica Lodziensia. irreg., 1976, no. 38.
ISSN 0065-1249
- Acta Poloniae Historica. s-a. ISSN 0001-6829
(Polska Akademia Nauk. Instytut Historii)
- Acta Technica Gedanensia. irreg., 1976, no. 11.
ISSN 0065-1664 (Gdanskie Towarzystwo
Naukowe)
- Analizy i Proby Technik Badawczych w
Socjologii. irreg., 1975, vol.5. (Polska Akademia
Nauk. Instytut Filozofii i Socjologii)
- Annales Silesiae. irreg, 1976, vol. 6. ISSN 0066-
2224 (Wroclawskie Towarzystwo Naukowe)
- Archaeologia Polona. a. ISSN 0066-5924 (Polska
Akademia Nauk. Instytut Historii Kultury
Materialnej)
- Archeologia. a. ISSN 0066-605X (Polska
Akademia Nauk. Instytut Historii Kultury
Materialnej)
- Archeologia Polski. s-a. ISSN 0003-8180 (Polska
Akademia Nauk. Instytut Historii Kultury
Materialnej)
- Archivum Iuridicum Cracoviense. irreg., 1976,
vol. 9. ISSN 0066-6882 (Polska Akademia Nauk.
Oddzial w Krakowie. Komisja Nauk Prawnych)
- Archiwum Dziejow Oswiaty. irreg., vol. 6, 1974.
ISSN 0066-6831 (Polska Akademia Nauk.
Pracownia Dziejow Oswiaty)
- Archiwum Elektrotechniki. q. ISSN 0004-0746
- Archiwum Filologiczne. irreg., vol. 30, 1974. ISSN
0066-6866 (Polska Akademia Nauk. Komitet
Nauk o Kulturze Antycznej)
- Archiwum Historii Filozofii i Mysli Spolecznej.
irreg., 1976, vol. 22. ISSN 0066-6874 (Polska
Akademia Nauk. Instytut Filozofii i Socjologii)
- Archiwum Kryminologii. irreg., 1976, vol. 7. ISSN
0066-6890 (Polska Akademia Nauk. Instytut
Nauk Prawnych)
- Archiwum Literackie. irreg. ISSN 0066-6904
(Polska Akademia Nauk. Instytut Badan
Literackich)
- Archiwum Ochrony Srodowiska. irreg., 1976, no.
2. (Polska Akademia Nauk. Instytut Podstaw
Inzynierii Srodowiska)
- Astronautyka. bi-m. ISSN 0004-623X (Polskie
Towarzystwo Astronautyczne) (Co-sponsor:
Polska Akademia Nauk)
- Bibliografia Historii Polskiej. irreg., bibliography
for 1974 published in 1976. ISSN 0067-6721
(Polska Akademia Nauk. Instytut Historii)
- Biblioteka Archeologiczna. irreg., vol. 23, 1974.
ISSN 0067-7639 (Polskie Towarzystwo
Archeologiczne)
- Biblioteka Etnografii Polskiej. irreg., 1971, no. 23.
ISSN 0067-7655 (Polska Akademia Nauk.
Instytut Historii Kultury Materialnej)

- Biblioteka Klasykow Pedagogiki. irreg. ISSN
0067-7671 (Polska Akademia Nauk. Komitet
Nauk Pedagogicznych i Psychologicznych)
- Biblioteka Kornicka. Pamietnik. irreg., 1976, vol.
12. ISSN 0067-768X
- Biblioteka Pisarzow Polskich. irreg. ISSN 0067-
7736 (Polska Akademia Nauk. Instytut Badan
Literackich)
- Bibliotheca Latina Medii et Recentiori Aevi. irreg.
ISSN 0067-8031 (Polska Akademia Nauk.
Komitet Nauk o Kulturze Antycznej)
- Biuletyn Historii Sztuki. q. ISSN 0006-3967
(Polska Akademia Nauk. Instytut Sztuki)
- Biuletyn Peryglacjalny. irreg., 1976, no. 26. ISSN
0067-9038 (Lodzkie Towarzystwo Naukowe) (Co-
sponsor: Polska Akademia Nauk)
- Biuletyn Polonistyczny. q. ISSN 0067-902X
(Polska Akademia Nauk. Instytut Badan
Literackich)
- Dokumentacja Geograficzna. bi-m. ISSN 0012-
5032 (Polska Akademia Nauk. Instytut Geografii i
Przestrzennego Zagospodarowania)
- Droit Polonais Contemporain. q. ISSN 0070-7325
(Polska Akademia Nauk. Instytut Panstwa i
Prawa)
- Dzieje Najnowsze; kwartalnik poswiecony historii
XX wieku. q. ISSN 0419-8824 (Polska Akademia
Nauk. Instytut Historii)
- Eos; commentarii societatis philologae polonorum.
s-a. ISSN 0012-7825 (Polskie Towarzystwo
Filologiczne)
- Estudios Latinoamericanos. irreg., 1976, vol. 3.
(Polska Akademia Nauk. Instytut Historii)
- Etnografia Polska. s-a. ISSN 0071-1861 (Polska
Akademia Nauk. Instytut Historii Kultury
Materialnej)
- Folia Geographica. Geographica-Oeconomica. a.
ISSN 0071-6707 (Polska Akademia Nauk.
Oddzial w Krakowie. Komisja Nauk
Geograficznych)
- Folia Geographica. Geographica-Physica. a. ISSN
0071-6715 (Polska Akademia Nauk. Oddzial w
Krakowie. Komisja Nauk Geograficznych)
- Folia Medica Cracoviensia. q. ISSN 0015-5616
(Polska Akademia Nauk. Oddzial w Krakowie)
- Folia Oeconomica Cracoviensia. irreg., 1976, vol.
20. ISSN 0071-674X (Polska Akademia Nauk.
Oddzial w Krakowie. Komisja Nauk
Ekonomicznych)
- Folia Orientalia. a. ISSN 0015-5675 (Polska
Akademia Nauk. Oddzial w Krakowie. Komisja
Orientalistyczna)
- Folia Quaternaria. irreg., 1976, no. 48. ISSN
0015-573X (Polska Akademia Nauk. Oddzial w
Krakowie)
- Gdanskie Towarzystwo Naukowe. Wydzial I.
Nauk Spolecznych i Humanistycznych. Komisja
Archeologiczna. Prace. irreg., 1974, no. 8. ISSN
0072-0410 (Gdanskie Towarzystwo Naukowe)
- Gdanskie Towarzystwo Naukowe. Wydzial I.
Nauk Spolecznych i Humanistycznych. Seria
Monografii. irreg., 1976, no. 57. ISSN 0433-230X
(Gdanskie Towarzystwo Naukowe)
- Gdanskie Towarzystwo Naukowe. Wydzial I.
Nauk Spolecznych i Humanistycznych. Seria
Popularnonaukowa "Pomorze Gdanskie". irreg.,
1974, nr. 9. ISSN 0072-0429 (Gdanskie
Towarzystwo Naukowe)
- Gdanskie Towarzystwo Naukowe. Wydzial I.
Nauk Spolecznych i Humanistycznych. Seria
Zrodel. irreg., 1976, no. 10. ISSN 0072-0437
(Gdanskie Towarzystwo Naukowe)
- Gdanskie Towarzystwo Naukowe. Wydzial III.
Nauk Matematyczno-Przyrodnichych. Rozprawy.
irreg. ISSN 0072-0445
- Geologia Sudetica. a. ISSN 0072-100X (Polska
Akademia Nauk. Zaklad Nauk Geologicznych)
- Historyka; Studia Metodologiczne. irreg., 1976,
vol. 6. ISSN 0073-277X (Polska Akademia Nauk.
Oddzial w Krakowie. Komisja Nauk
Historycznych)
- Humanizacja Pracy/Humanization of Work. bi-m.
(Polska Akademia Nauk) (Co-sponsors:
Ministerstwo Nauki, Szkolnictwa Wyzszego i
Techniki; Instytut Organizacji i Kierowania)
- Krakowskie Studia Prawnicze. a. ISSN 0023-4478
(Polska Akademia Nauk. Oddzial w Krakowie.
Komisja Nauk Prawnych)
- Ksiazka w Dawnej Kulturze Polskiej. irreg. ISSN
0075-7179 (Polska Akademia Nauk. Instytut
Badan Literackich)
- Kwartalnik Historii Prasy Polskiej. q. (Polska
Akademia Nauk. Instytut Badan Literackich)
- Litteraria; teoria literatury-metodologia-kultura-
humanistyka. irreg., 1976, vol. 8. ISSN 0084-3008
(Wroclawskie Towarzystwo Naukowe)

- Lodzkie Towarzystwo Naukowe. Komisji Jezykowej. Rozprawy. irreg., 1976, vol. 22. ISSN 0076-0390 (Co-sponsor: Polska Akademia Nauk)
- Lodzkie Towarzystwo Naukowe. Wydzial I. Prace. irreg. ISSN 0076-0404 (Co-sponsor: Polska Akademia Nauk)
- Mediaevalia Philosophica Polonorum. irreg., 1976, vol. 22. ISSN 0076-5880 (Polska Akademia Nauk. Instytut Filozofii i Socjologii)
- Memorabilia Zoologica. irreg.(1-2 per yr.) ISSN 0076-6372 (Polska Akademia Nauk. Instytut Zoologii)
- Monografie Psychologiczne. irreg. ISSN 0077-0515 (Polska Akademia Nauk. Komitet Nauk Psychologicznych)
- Monografie Slaskie Ossolineum. irreg. ISSN 0077-0523
- Monografie Slawistyczne. irreg. ISSN 0077-0531 (Polska Akademia Nauk. Komitet Slowianoznawstwa)
- Monografie z Dziejow Nauki i Techniki. irreg. ISSN 0077-054X (Polska Akademia Nauk. Zaklad Historii Nauki i Techniki)
- Monografie z Dziejow Oswiaty. irreg. ISSN 0077-0558 (Polska Akademia Nauk. Zaklad Historii Nauki, Oswiaty i Techniki. Pracownia Dziejow Oswiaty)
- Muzyka; kwartalnik poswiecony historii i teorii muzyki. q. ISSN 0027-5344 (Polska Akademia Nauk. Instytut Sztuki)
- Nauka Polska. m. ISSN 0028-1271 (Polska Akademia Nauk)
- Nautologia. q. ISSN 0548-0523 (Polskie Towarzystwo Nautologiczne)
- New Books. q. ISSN 0028-4300
- Oceanologia. irreg., 1976, no. 6. ISSN 0078-3234 (Polska Akademia Nauk. Komitet Badan Morza)
- Odrodzenie i Reformacja w Polsce. irreg., 1976, vol. 21. ISSN 0029-8514 (Polska Akademia Nauk. Instytut Historii)
- Onomastica; pismo poswiecone nazewnictwu geograficznemu i osobowemu. a. ISSN 0078-4648 (Polska Akademia Nauk. Komitet Jezykoznawstwa)
- Paideia; miedzynarodowy rocznik pedagogiczny. irreg., 1976, vol. 5. (Polska Akademia Nauk. Komitet Nauk Pedagogicznych)
- Pamietnik Literacki. q. ISSN 0031-0514 (Polska Akademia Nauk. Instytut Badan Literackich)
- Pamietnik Slowianski. a. ISSN 0078-866X (Polska Akademia Nauk. Komitet Slowianoznawstwa)
- Pamietnik Teatralny; poswiecony historii i krytyce teatru. q. ISSN 0031-0522 (Polska Akademia Nauk. Instytut Sztuki)
- Poetyka. Zarys Encyklopedyczny. irreg. ISSN 0079-2527 (Polska Akademia Nauk. Instytut Badan Literackich)
- Polish Academy of Sciences. Review. q. ISSN 0032-2776 (Polska Akademia Nauk)
- Polish Archaeological Abstracts. a. (Polska Akademia Nauk. Instytut Historii Kultury Materialnej. Zaklad Archeologii Wielkopolski)
- Polish Round Table. a. ISSN 0079-3000 (Polskie Towarzystwo Nauk Politycznych)
- Polish Sociological Bulletin. s-a. ISSN 0032-2997 (Polskie Towarzystwo Socjologiczne)
- Polish Sociology. a. (Polskie Towarzystwo Socjologiczne)
- Polish Yearbook of International Law. a. ISSN 0554-498X (Polska Akademia Nauk. Instytut Nauk Prawnych)
- Polonia Typographica Saeculi Sedecimi. irreg. ISSN 0079-3132 (Polska Akademia Nauk. Instytut Badan Literackich)
- Polonica. irreg., 1976, vol. 2. (Polska Akademia Nauk. Instytut Jezyka Polskiego)
- Polska Adakemia Nauk. Centrum Badan Naukowych w Wojewodztwie Katowickim. Prace i Studia. irreg., 1971, vol. 10. ISSN 0079-3582
- Polska Akademia Nauk. Biblioteka, Krakow. Rocznik. a. ISSN 0079-3140
- Polska Akademia Nauk. Instytut Geografii. Prace Geograficzne. irreg. ISSN 0554-5749
- Polska Akademia Nauk. Instytut Podstaw Inzynierii Srodowiska. Prace i Studia. irreg., 1976, no. 17.
- Polska Akademia Nauk. Oddzial w Krakowie. Komisja Archeologiczna. Prace. irreg. ISSN 0079-3256
- Polska Akademia Nauk. Oddzial w Krakowie. Komisja Ceramiczna. Prace: Ceramika. irreg., 1976, no. 25. ISSN 0079-3264
- Polska Akademia Nauk. Oddzial w Krakowie. Komisja Filologii Klasycznej. Prace. irreg., 1976, no. 15. ISSN 0079-3272
- Polska Akademia Nauk. Oddzial w Krakowie. Komisja Gorniczo-Geodezyjna. Prace: Gornictwo. irreg., 1976, no. 22. ISSN 0079-3280

- Polska Akademia Nauk. Oddzial w Krakowie. Komisja Gorniczo-Geodezyjna. Prace: Geodezja. irreg., 1976, no. 23. ISSN 0079-3299
- Polska Akademia Nauk. Oddzial w Krakowie. Komisja Historycznoliteracka. Prace. irreg., 1976, no. 35. ISSN 0554-579X
- Polska Akademia Nauk. Oddzial w Krakowie. Komisja Historycznoliteracka. Rocznik. a. ISSN 0079-3302
- Polska Akademia Nauk. Oddzial w Krakowie. Komisja Jezykoznawstwa. Prace. irreg., 1976, no. 44. ISSN 0079-3310
- Polska Akademia Nauk. Oddzial w Krakowie. Komisja Jezykoznawstwa. Wydawnictwazrodlowe. irreg. ISSN 0079-3329
- Polska Akademia Nauk. Oddzial w Krakowie. Komisja Mechaniki Stosowanej. Prace: Mechanika. irreg., 1976, no. 9. ISSN 0079-3337
- Polska Akademia Nauk. Oddzial w Krakowie. Komisja Metalurgiczno-Odlewnicza. Prace: Metalurgia. irreg., 1976, no. 24. ISSN 0079-3345
- Polska Akademia Nauk. Oddzial w Krakowie. Komisja Nauk Ekonomicznych. Prace. irreg. ISSN 0079-3353
- Polska Akademia Nauk. Oddzial w Krakowie. Komisja Nauk Historycznych. Prace. irreg., 1976, no. 41. ISSN 0079-3388
- Polska Akademia Nauk. Oddzial w Krakowie. Komisja Nauk Historycznych. Materialy. irreg. ISSN 0079-337X
- Polska Akademia Nauk. Oddzial w Krakowie. Komisja Nauk Mineralogicznych. Prace Mineralogiczne. irreg., 1976, no. 50. ISSN 0079-3396
- Polska Akademia Nauk. Oddzial w Krakowie. Komisja Nauk Pedagogicznych. Rocznik. a. ISSN 0079-3418
- Polska Akademia Nauk. Oddzial w Krakowie. Komisja Nauk Pedagogicznych. Prace. irreg. ISSN 0079-340X
- Polska Akademia Nauk. Oddzial w Krakowie. Komisja Naukowych. Sprawozdania z Posiedzen. irreg. ISSN 0079-354X
- Polska Akademia Nauk. Oddzial w Krakowie. Komisja Orientalistyczna. Prace. irreg., 1976, no. 14. ISSN 0079-3426
- Polska Akademia Nauk. Oddzial w Krakowie. Komisja Slowianoznawstwa. Prace. irreg., 1976, no. 36. ISSN 0079-3434
- Polska Akademia Nauk. Oddzial w Krakowie. Komisja Socjologiczna. Prace. irreg., 1976, no. 40. ISSN 0079-3442
- Polska Akademia Nauk. Oddzial w Krakowie. Komisja Urbanistyki i Architektury. Teka. irreg., vol. 9, 1975. ISSN 0079-3450
- Polska Akademia Nauk. Oddzial w Krakowie. Osrodek Dokumentacji Fizjograficznej. Studia. irreg., 1976, vol. 5.
- Polska Akademia Nauk. Oddzial w Krakowie. Rocznik. a. ISSN 0079-3531
- Polska Akademia Nauk. Zaklad Narodowy im. Ossolinskich. Rocznik. a.
- Polska Sztuka Ludowa. q. ISSN 0032-3721 (Polska Akademia Nauk. Instytut Sztuki)
- Polska 2000. irreg., 3-4 per year. ISSN 0079-3620 (Polska Akademia Nauk. Komitet Badan i Prognoz "Polska 2000")
- Polskie Towarzystwo Cybernetyczne. Biuletyn. irreg. ISSN 0079-3655
- Polskie Towarzystwo Jezykoznawcze. Biuletyn. irreg., 1976, vol. 34.
- Pomarania Antiqua. irreg., 1976, vol. 7. (Muzeum Archeologiczne, Gdansk)
- Pomorskie Monografie Toponomastyczne. irreg., 1976, vol. 2. (Gdanskie Towarzystwo Naukowe)
- Postepy Astronautyki. q. ISSN 0554-839X (Polskie Towarzystwo Astronautyczne)
- Powstanie Styczniowe. Materialy i Dokumenty. irreg. ISSN 0079-4465 (Polska Akademia Nauk. Instytut Historii)
- Prace Geologiczne. irreg., 1976, no. 102. ISSN 0079-3361 (Polska Akademia Nauk. Oddzial w Krakowie. Komista Nauk Geologicznych)
- Prace Jezykoznawcze. irreg. ISSN 0079-3485 (Polska Akademia Nauk. Komitet Jezykoznawstwa)
- Prace Literackie. irreg. ISSN 0079-4767 (Uniwersytet Wroclawski)
- Prace Onomastyczne. irreg., 1971, vol. 18. ISSN 0079-4775 (Polska Akademia Nauk. Komitet Jezykoznawstwa)
- Prace Polonistyczne. a. ISSN 0079-4791 (Lodzkie Towarzystwo Naukowe) (Co-sponsor: Polska Akademia Nauk)
- Problemy Polonii Zagranicznej. irreg., vol. 9, 1975. ISSN 0079-5798 (Polska Akademia Nauk. Komitet Badania Polonii Zagranicznej)

- Problemy Rad Narodowych. Studia i Materialy. irreg., 1976, vol. 35. ISSN 0079-5801 (Polska Akademia Nauk. Instytut Panstwa i Prawa)
- Przeglad Archeologiczny. irreg., 1976, vol. 24. ISSN 0079-7138 (Polska Akademia Nauk. Instytut Historii Kultury Materialnej)
- Przeglad Polonijny. s-a. (Polska Akademia Nauk. Komitet Badania Problemow Polonii)
- Przeglad Psychologiczny/Psychological Review. q. ISSN 0048-5675 (Polskie Towarzystwo Psychologiczne)
- Przeglad Zagranicznej Literatury Geograficznej. q. ISSN 0079-7170 (Polska Akademia Nauk. Instytut Geografii i Przestrzennego Zagospodarowania)
- Rocznik Dolnoslaski. irreg. (Dolnoslaskie Towarzystwo Oswiatowe)
- Rocznik Gdanski. irreg., 1976, vol. 34-35. ISSN 0080-3456 (Gdanskie Towarzystwo Naukowe)
- Rocznik Historii Sztuki. a. ISSN 0080-3472 (Polska Akademia Nauk. Instytut Sztuki)
- Rocznik Jeleniogorski. a. ISSN 0080-3480 (Towarzystwo Przyjaciol Ziemi Jeleniogorskiej)
- Rocznik Krakowski. irreg., vol. 45, 1974. ISSN 0080-3499 (Towarzystwo Milosnikow Historii i Zabytkow Krakowa)
- Rocznik Pedagogiczny. irreg., 1976, vol. 3. (Polska Akademia Nauk. Komitet Nauk Pedagogicznych)
- Rocznik Slawistyczny. a. ISSN 0080-3588 (Polska Akademia Nauk. Komitet Slowianoznawstwa)
- Rocznik Wroclawski. a. ISSN 0080-3618 (Towarzystwo Milosnikow Wroclawia)
- Rocznik Ziemi Klodzkiej. a. (Towarzystwo Milosnikow Ziemi Klodzkiej)
- Roczniki Socjologii Wsi. Studia i Materialy. irreg., 1976, vol. 13. ISSN 0080-3731 (Polska Akademia Nauk. Instytut Filozofii i Socjologii)
- Rozprawy z Dziejow Oswiaty. a. ISSN 0080-4754 (Polska Akademia Nauk. Zaklad Historii Nauki, Oswiaty i Techniki. Pracownia Dziejow Oswiaty)
- Ruch Literacki. bi-m. ISSN 0035-9602 (Polska Akademia Nauk. Oddzial w Krakowie) (Co-sponsor: Towarzystwo Literackie Im. A. Mickiewicza)
- Semiotic-Historical Studies. irreg., 1976, vol. 3. (Polska Akademia Nauk. Zaklad Historii Nauki, Oswiaty i Techniki)
- Silesia Antiqua. irreg., 1976, vol. 18. ISSN 0080-9594 (Muzeum Archeologiczne, Wroclaw)
- Slaski Kwartalnik Historyczny "Sobotka". q. ISSN 0037-7511 (Wroclawskie Towarzystwo Milosnikow Historii)
- Sovremennoe Polskoe Pravo. q. ISSN 0081-3214 (Polska Akademia Nauk. Instytut Panstwa i Prawa)
- Sprawozdania Archeologiczne. irreg., 1976, vol. 28. ISSN 0081-3834 (Polska Akademia Nauk. Instytut Historii Kultury Materialnej)
- Studia Copernicana. irreg., 1976, vol. 14. (Polska Akademia Nauk. Zaklad Historii Nauki, Oswiaty i Techniki)
- Studia Geomorphologica Carpatho-Balcanica. irreg., 1976, vol. 10. ISSN 0081-6434 (Polska Akademia Nauk. Oddzial w Krakowie. Komisja Nauk Geograficznych)
- Studia Historyczne. q. ISSN 0025-1429 (Polska Akademia Nauk. Oddzial w Krakowie)
- Studia i Materialy z Dziejow Slaska. irreg. ISSN 0081-6639 (Slaski Instytut Naukowy)
- Studia i Materialy z Dziejow Teatru Polskiego. irreg. ISSN 0081-6647 (Polska Akademia Nauk. Instytut Teatru)
- Studia Logica. q. ISSN 0039-3215 (Polska Akademia Nauk. Instytut Filozofii i Socjologii)
- Studia o Ksiazce. s-a. (Uniwersytet Wroclawski)
- Studia Pedagogiczne. irreg., 1976, vol. 38. ISSN 0081-6795 (Polska Akademia Nauk. Komitet Nauk Pedagogicznych)
- Studia Polono-Slavica Orientalia. Acta Litteraria. irreg., 1976, vol. 3. (Polska Akademia Nauk. Komitet Slowianoznawstwa)
- Studia Prawnicze. q. ISSN 0039-3312 (Polska Akademia Nauk. Instytut Nauk Prawnych)
- Studia Prawno - Ekonomiczne. irreg., 1976, vol. 17. ISSN 0081-6841 (Lodzkie Towarzystwo Naukowe) (Co-sponsor: Polska Akademia Nauk)
- Studia Psychologiczne. s-a. ISSN 0081-685X (Polska Akademia Nauk. Komitet Nauk Psychologicznych)
- Studia Semiotyczne. irreg., 1976, vol. 7. (Polskie Towarzystwo Semiotyczne)
- Studia Socjologiczne. q. ISSN 0039-3371 (Polska Akademia Nauk. Instytut Filozofii i Socjologii) (Co-sponsor: Komitet Nauk Socjologicznych)
- Studia Staropolskie. irreg. ISSN 0081-6949 (Polska Akademia Nauk. Instytut Badan Literackich)

- Studia z Dziejow Gornictwa i Hutnictwa. irreg. ISSN 0081-704X (Polska Akademia Nauk. Instytut Historii Kultury Materialnej)
- Studia z Dziejow Osadnictwa. irreg. ISSN 0081-7058 (Polska Akademia Nauk. Instytut Historii Kultury Materialnej)
- Studia z Dziejow ZSRR i Europy Srodkowej. irreg., 1976, vol. 12. ISSN 0081-7082 (Polska Akademia Nauk. Instytut Historii)
- Studia z Historii Sztuki. irreg. ISSN 0081-7104 (Polska Akademia Nauk. Instytut Sztuki)
- Studia z Okresu Oswiecenia. irreg., 1976, vol. 14. ISSN 0081-7112 (Polska Akademia Nauk. Instytut Badan Literackich)
- Szkice Legnickie. irreg., 1976, vol. 9. (Legnickie Towarzystwo Przyjaciol Nauki)
- Teksty. bi-m. (Polska Akademia Nauk. Instytut Badan Literackich) (Co-sponsor: Komitet Nauk O Literaturze Polskiej)
- Towarzystwo Literackie im. A. Mickiewicza. Biblioteka. irreg. ISSN 0067-7787
- Transport Museums. irreg., 1976, vol. 2. (Centralne Muzeum Morskie, Gdansk) (Co-sponsor: International Association of Transport Museums)
- Wiadomosci Archeologiczne. q. ISSN 0043-5082 (Muzeum Archeologiczne, Poznan)
- Wroclawskie Towarzystwo Naukowe. Komisja Historii Sztuki. Rozprawy. irreg. ISSN 0084-2982
- Wroclawskie Towarzystwo Naukowe. Komisja Jezykowa. Rozprawy. irreg. ISSN 0084-2990
- Wroclawskie Towarzystwo Naukowe. Prace. Seria A. Humanistyka. irreg. ISSN 0084-3016
- Wroclawskie Towarzystwo Naukowe. Prace. Seria B. Nauki Scisle. irreg. ISSN 0084-3024
- Wroclawskie Towarzystwo Naukowe. Sprawozdania. Seria A. irreg.
- Z Dziejow Form Artystycznych w Literaturze Polskiej. irreg. ISSN 0084-4411 (Polska Akademia Nauk. Instytut Badan Literackich)
- Z Naszej Oficyny. bi-m. ISSN 0044-1473
- Z Otchlani Wiekow. q. ISSN 0044-1481 (Polskie Towarzystwo Archeologiczne i Numizmatyczne)
- Zagadnienia Naukoznawstwa; studia i materialy. q. ISSN 0044-1619 (Polska Akademia Nauk. Komitet Naukoznawstwa)
- Zagadnienia Rodzajow Literackich/Les Problems des Genres Litteraires. s-a. ISSN 0084-4446 (Lodzkie Towarzystwo Naukowe) (Co-sponsor: Polska Akademia Nauk)
- Ze Skarbca Kultury. irreg., 1976, vol. 27. ISSN 0084-5221 (Polska Akademia Nauk. Biblioteka. Zaklad Narodowy Im. Ossolinskich)
- Zeszyty Problemowe Nauki Polskiej. irreg. ISSN 0084-5469
- Zrodla do Dziejow Mysli Pedagogicznej. irreg. ISSN 0084-5698 (Polska Akademia Nauk. Komitet Nauk Pedagogicznych)
- Zrodla do Dziejow Nauki i Techniki. irreg. ISSN 0084-5701 (Polska Akademia Nauk. Zaklad Historii Nauki i Techniki)

**Panstwowa Wyzsza Szkola Muzyczna**
Ul. 27 Stycznia 33, 40-025 Katowice, Poland.
- Archiwum Slaskie Kultury Muzycznej. irreg.

**Panstwowe Przedsiebiorstwo "Skladnica Ksiegarska"**
Ul. Mazowiecka 9, Warsaw, Poland
(Dist. by: Ars Polona-Ruch, Krakowskie Przedmiescie 7, Warsaw, Poland)
- Kartkowy Katalog Nowosci. w. ISSN 0324-8003

**Panstwowe Wydawnictwo Ekonomiczne**
Niecala 4a, 00-098 Warsaw, Poland
(Dist. by: Ars Polona-Ruch, Krakowskie Przedmiescie 7, Warsaw, Poland)
- Ekonomista. bi-m. ISSN 0013-3205 (Polska Akademia Nauk. Komitet Nauk Ekonomicznych) (Co-sponsor: Polskie Towarzystwo Ekonomiczne)
- Finanse. m.
- Gospodarka Materialowa. s-m. ISSN 0017-2405
- Gospodarka Planowa; miesiecznik poswiecony problemom planowania i rozwoju gospodarki narodowej. m. ISSN 0017-2421
- Handel Wewnetrzny. bi-m. ISSN 0438-5403
- Praca i Zabezpieczenia Spoleczne. m. ISSN 0032-6186
- Problemy Handlu Zagranicznego. irreg. (Instytut Koniunktur i Cen Handlu Zagranicznego)
- Przeglad Bibliograficzny Pismiennictwa Ekonomicznego. bi-m. ISSN 0032-8138
- Przeglad Ustawodawstwa Gospodarczego/ Economic Legislation Review. m.

- Rachunkowosc. m. ISSN 0481-5475 (Stowarzyszenie Ksiegowych w Polsce)

**Panstwowe Wydawnictwo Naukowe**
Miodowa 10, Warsaw, Poland
(Dist. by: Ars Polona-Ruch, Krakowskie Przedmiescie 7, Warsaw, Poland)
- Academie Polonaise des Sciences. Bulletin. Serie des Sciences Biologiques. m. ISSN 0001-4087 (Polska Akademia Nauk. Prezydium)
- Academie Polonaise des Sciences. Bulletin. Serie des Sciences Chimiques. m. ISSN 0001-4095 (Polska Akademia Nauk. Prezydium)
- Academie Polonaise des Sciences. Bulletin. Serie des Sciences de la Terre. q. ISSN 0001-4109 (Polska Akademia Nauk. Prezydium)
- Academie Polonaise des Sciences. Bulletin. Serie des Sciences Mathematiques, Astronomiques et Physiques. m. ISSN 0001-4117 (Polska Akademia Nauk. Prezydium)
- Academie Polonaise des Sciences. Bulletin. Serie des Sciences Techniques. m. ISSN 0001-4125 (Polska Akademia Nauk. Prezydium)
- Acta Agraria et Silvestria. Series Agraria. irreg., 1972, vol. 12. ISSN 0065-0919 (Polska Akademia Nauk. Oddzial w Krakowie. Komisja Nauk Rolniczych i Lesnych)
- Acta Agraria et Silvestria. Series Silvestris. irreg., 1975, vol. 15. ISSN 0065-0927 (Polska Akademia Nauk. Oddzial w Krakowie. Komisja Nauk Rolniczych i Lesnych)
- Acta Agraria et Silvestria. Series Zootechnica. s-a. ISSN 0065-0935 (Polska Akademia Nauk. Oddzial w Krakowie. Komisja Nauk Rolniczych i Lesnych)
- Acta Agrobotanica. irreg., 1972, vol. 25. ISSN 0065-0951 (Polskie Towarzystwo Botaniczne)
- Acta Alimentaria Polonica. q. (Polska Akademia Nauk. Komitet Technologii i Chemii Zywnosci)
- Acta Arithmetica. irreg., 1976, vol. 29. ISSN 0065-1036 (Polska Akademia Nauk. Instytut Matematyczny)
- Acta Astronomica. q. ISSN 0001-5237 (Polska Akademia Nauk. Komitet Astronomii)
- Acta Geologica Polonica. q. ISSN 0001-5709 (Polska Akademia Nauk. Komitet Nauk Geologicznych)
- Acta Geophysica Polonica. q. ISSN 0001-5725 (Polska Akademia Nauk. Komitet Geofizyki)
- Acta Hydrobiologica. irreg., 1975, vol. 17, no. 3. ISSN 0065-132X (Polska Akademia Nauk. Zaklad Biologii Wod)
- Acta Microbiologica Polonica. q. ISSN 0001-6195 (Polskie Towarzystwo Mikrobiologow)
- Acta Mycologica. 1-2 vols. per yr., 1972, vol. 8, fasc. 2. ISSN 0001-625X (Polskie Towarzystwo Botaniczne)
- Acta Neurobiologiae Experimentalis. bi-m. ISSN 0065-1400 (Polska Akademia Nauk. Instytut Biologii Doswiadczalnej im. M. Nenckiego)
- Acta Ornithologica. irreg., 1975, vol. 14, fasc. 6. ISSN 0001-6454 (Polska Akademia Nauk. Instytut Zoologii)
- Acta Palaeobotanica. 2-3 yr. ISSN 0001-6594 (Polska Akademia Nauk. Instytut Botaniki)
- Acta Palaeontologica Polonica. q. ISSN 0567-7920 (Polska Akademia Nauk. Zaklad Paleozoologii)
- Acta Parasitologica Polonica. irreg., 1975, vol. 22, fasc. 22-23. ISSN 0065-1478 (Polska Akademia Nauk. Zaklad Parazytologii)
- Acta Physica Polonica. m. ISSN 0001-673X (Polska Akademia Nauk. Instytut Fizyki) (Co-sponsor: Polskie Towarzystwo Fizyczne)
- Acta Protozoologica. q. ISSN 0065-1583 (Polska Akademia Nauk. Instytut Biologii Doswiadczalnej im. M. Nenckiego)
- Acta Societatis Botanicorum Poloniae. q. ISSN 0001-6977 (Polskie Towarzystwo Botaniczne)
- Acta Theriologica. 3-5 per yr.; 1975, vol. 20, no. 32-34. ISSN 0001-7051 (Polska Akademia Nauk. Zaklad Badania Ssakow)
- Acta Zoologica Cracoviensia. irreg., 1972, vol. 17. ISSN 0065-1710 (Polska Akademia Nauk. Zaklad Zoologii Systematycznej i Doswiadczalnej)
- Akademia Gorniczo-Hutnicza im. Stanislawa Staszica. Instytut Ceramiki Specjalnej i Ogniotrwalej. Prace Naukowe. irreg.
- Akademia Gorniczo-Hutnicza im. Stanislawa Staszica. Instytut Gornictwa Podziemnego. Prace. irreg.
- Akademia Gorniczo-Hutnicza im. Stanislawa Staszica. Instytut Maszyn Hutniczych i Automatyki. Prace. 2 per yr.
- Akademia Gorniczo-Hutnicza im. Stanislawa Staszica. Zeszyty Naukowe. Gornictwo. irreg., no. 44, 1972. ISSN 0075-6997

- Akademia Gorniczo-Hutnicza Im. Stanislawa Staszica. Zeszyty Naukowe. Hutnictwo. irreg. ISSN 0075-7004
- Akademia Medyczna, Wroclaw. Prace Naukowe. q. ISSN 0084-277X
- Annales Polonici Mathematici. irreg., 1976, vol. 31, no. 3. ISSN 0066-2216 (Polska Akademia Nauk. Instytut Matematyczny)
- Annales Zoologici. 20-26 per yr; 1972, vol. 29. ISSN 0003-4541 (Polska Akademia Nauk. Instytut Zoologii)
- Arboretum Kornickie. a. ISSN 0066-5878 (Polska Akademia Nauk. Zaklad Dendrologii) (Co-sponsor: Arboretum Kornickie)
- Archeion; czasopismo naukowe poswiecone sprawom archiwalnym. irreg., vol. 62, 1975. ISSN 0066-6041 (Naczelna Dyrekcja Archiwow Panstwowych)
- Archives of Mechanics. bi-m. (Polska Akademia Nauk. Instytut Podstawowych Problemow Techniki)
- Archiwum Akustyki. q. ISSN 0066-6823 (Polska Akademia Nauk. Komitet Akustyki) (Co-sponsor: Polskie Towarzystwo Akustyczne)
- Archiwum Automatyki i Telemechaniki. q. ISSN 0004-072X (Polska Akademia Nauk. Komitet Automatyki i Cybernetyki Technicznej)
- Archiwum Energetyki. q. ISSN 0066-684X (Polska Akademia Nauk. Komitet Energetyki)
- Archiwum Gornictwa. q. ISSN 0004-0754 (Polska Akademia Nauk. Komitet Gornictwa)
- Archiwum Hutnictwa. q. ISSN 0004-0770 (Polska Akademia Nauk. Komitet Hutnictwa)
- Archiwum Hydrotechniki. q. ISSN 0004-0789 (Polska Akademia Nauk. Instytut Budownictwa Wodnego)
- Archiwum Inzynierii Ladowej. q. ISSN 0004-0797 (Polska Akademia Nauk. Komitet Inzynierii Ladowej i Wodnej)
- Archiwum Procesow Spalania/Archives of Combustion Processes. q. ISSN 0044-8761 (Polska Akademia Nauk. Komitet Termodynamiki i Spalania)
- Artificial Satellites. s-a. ISSN 0571-205X (Polska Akademia Nauk. Committee on Research and Peaceful Uses of Outer Space)
- Atlas Flory Polskiej i Ziem Osciennych. irreg., 1975, vol. 2, no. 4. ISSN 0067-0294 (Polska Akademia Nauk. Instytut Botaniki)
- Atlas Rozmieszczenia Drzew i Krzewow w Polsce. irreg., 1976, no. 18. ISSN 0067-0324 (Polska Akademia Nauk. Zaklad Dendrologii)
- Badania Fizjograficzne nad Polska Zachodnia. Seria A. Geografia Fizyczna. irreg., vol. 26, 1973. ISSN 0067-2807 (Poznanskie Towarzystwo Przyjaciol Nauk)
- Badania Fizjograficzne nad Polska Zachodnia. Seria B. Biologia. irreg., vol. 27, 1974. ISSN 0067-2815 (Poznanskie Towarzystwo Przyjaciol Nauk)
- Badania Fizjograficzne nad Polska Zachodnia. Seria C. Zoologia. irreg. (Poznanskie Towarzystwo Przyjaciol Nauk)
- Badania z Dziejow Spolecznych i Gospodarczych. irreg. ISSN 0067-2793 (Poznanskie Towarzystwo Przyjaciol Nauk)
- Biblioteka Kopernikanska. irreg. ISSN 0067-7558 (Towarzystwo Naukowe w Toruniu)
- Biblioteka Mechaniki Stosowanej. irreg. ISSN 0067-7701 (Polska Akademia Nauk. Instytut Podstawowych Problemow Techniki)
- Biblioteka Pisarzy Reformacyjnych. irreg. ISSN 0519-8658 (Polska Akademia Nauk. Instytut Filozofii i Socjologii)
- Biuletyn Biblioteki Jagiellonskiej. s-a. ISSN 0006-3940 (Uniwersytet Jagiellonski)
- Biuletyn Fonograficzny/Bulletin Phonographique. irreg; 1972, no. 13. ISSN 0067-8996 (Poznanskie Towarzystwo Przyjaciol Nauk)
- Chemia Analityczna. bi-m. ISSN 0009-2223 (Polska Akademia Nauk. Oddzial w Krakowie. Komisja Chemii Analitycznej)
- Chemia Stosowana. q. (Polska Akademia Nauk. Komitet Nauk Chemicznych)
- Chronmy Przyrode Ojczysta. bi-m. ISSN 0009-6172 (Polska Akademia Nauk. Zaklad Ochrony Przyrody) (Co-sponsor: Panstwowa Rada Ochrony Przyrody)
- Colloquium Mathematicum. irreg., 1975, vol. 34, no. 1. ISSN 0010-1354 (Polska Akademia Nauk. Instytut Matematyczny)
- Control and Cybernetics. q. (Polska Akademia Nauk. Instytut Organizacji i Kierowania)
- Czasopismo Geograficzne/Geographical Journal. q. ISSN 0045-9453 (Polskie Towarzystwo Geograficzne)

- Czasopismo Prawno-Historyczne. irreg., 1972, vol. 24. ISSN 0070-2471 (Polska Akademia Nauk. Instytut Historii. Komisja Historii Panstwa i Prawa)
- Dissertationes Mathematicae/Rozprawy Matematyczne. irreg., 1976, vol. 130. ISSN 0012-3862 (Polska Akademia Nauk. Instytut Matematyczny)
- Dydaktyka Szkoly Wyzszej. q. ISSN 0420-2384 (Poland. Ministerstwo Nauki, Szkolnictwa Wyzszego i Techniki. Instytut Polityki Naukowej i Szkolnictwa Wyzszego)
- Ekologia Polska/Polish Ecology. q. ISSN 0070-9557 (Polska Akademia Nauk. Instytut Ekologii)
- Electron Technology. q. ISSN 0070-9816 (Instytut Technologii Elektronowej)
- Elektryfikacja i Mechanizacja Gornictwa i Hutnictwa/Electrification and Mechanization in Mining and Metallurgy. irreg. ISSN 0070-9964 (Akademia Gorniczo-Hutnicza im. Stanislawa Staszica)
- Etyka. a. ISSN 0014-2263 (Polska Akademia Nauk. Instytut Filozofii i Socjologii)
- Euhemer; przeglad religioznawczy. q. ISSN 0014-2298 (Polskie Towarzystwo Religioznawcze)
- Fauna Slodkowodna Polski. irreg. ISSN 0071-4089 (Polska Akademia Nauk. Instytut Zoologii. Oddzial w Poznaniu)
- Filomata. m. ISSN 0015-1815
- Flora Polska; Rosliny Naczyniowe Polski i Ziem Osciennych. irreg., 1971, vol. 13. ISSN 0071-5816 (Polska Akademia Nauk. Instytut Botaniki)
- Fluid Dynamics Transactions. irreg., 1976, vol. 8, pt. 2. (Polska Akademia Nauk. Instytut Podstawowych Problemow Techniki)
- Folia Biologica; quarterly journal of biological research. q. ISSN 0015-5497 (Polska Akademia Nauk. Instytut Zoologii)
- Folia Forestalia Polonica. Series A. Lesnictwo. a. ISSN 0071-6677 (Polska Akademia Nauk)
- Folia Forestalia Polonica. Series B. Drzewnictwo. irreg.; 1975, no. 12. ISSN 0071-6685 (Polska Akademia Nauk. Oddzial w Krakowie. Komisja Drzewnictwa)
- Folia Histochemica et Cytochemica. q. ISSN 0015-5586 (Polskie Towarzystwo Histochemikow i Cytochemikow)
- Folia Historiae Artium. irreg., 1974, vol. 10. ISSN 0071-6723 (Polska Akademia Nauk. Oddzial w Krakowie. Komisja Teorii i Historii Sztuki)
- Fragmenta Faunistica. 20-26 nos. per yr., 1972, vol. 18. ISSN 0015-9301 (Polska Akademia Nauk. Instytut Zoologii)
- Fragmenta Floristica et Geobotanica. q. ISSN 0015-931X (Polska Akademia Nauk. Instytut Botaniki)
- Fundamenta Mathematicae. 11-12 per yr., 1976, vol. 90, no. 2. ISSN 0016-2736 (Polska Akademia Nauk. Instytut Matematyczny)
- Genetica Polonica; Polish journal of theoretical and applied genetics. q. ISSN 0016-6715 (Polska Akademia Nauk. Instytut Genetyki Roslin)
- Geodezja i Kartografia. q. ISSN 0016-7134 (Polska Akademia Nauk. Komitet Geodezji)
- Geographia Polonica. 2-4 per yr; 1975, no. 31. ISSN 0016-7282 (Polska Akademia Nauk. Instytut Geografii)
- Gornictwo Odkrywkowe. q. ISSN 0043-2075 (Centralny Osrodek Badawczo-Projektowy Gornictwa Odkrywkowego "Poltegor")
- Immunologia Polska. q. (Poznanskie Towarzystwo Przyjaciol Nauk)
- Informator dla Kandydaton na Studia Podyplomowe i Doktoranckie. a. (Poland. Ministerstwo Nauki. Szkolnictwa Wyzszego i Techniki)
- Informator Nauki Polskiej. a. ISSN 0537-667X
- Instytut Technologii Drewna. Prace. q. ISSN 0032-6240
- Inzynieria Chemiczna. q. (Polska Akademia Nauk. Komitet Inzynierii Chemicznej)
- Journal of Juristic Papyrology. irreg., vol. 18, 1974. ISSN 0075-4277 (Uniwersytet Warszawski. Instytut Papirologii i Prawa Antycznego)
- Journal of Technical Physics. q. ISSN 0032-9576 (Polska Akademia Nauk. Instytut Podstawowych Problemow Techniki)
- Katalog Fauny Pasozytniczej Polski. irreg. ISSN 0075-5230 (Polskie Towarzystwo Parazytologiczne)
- Katalog Fauny Polski. irreg. ISSN 0075-5249 (Polska Akademia Nauk. Instytut Zoologii)
- Klucze do Oznaczania Owadow Polski. irreg., nos. 69-72, 1974. ISSN 0075-6350 (Polskie Towarzystwo Entomologiczne)
- Kosmos. Series A. Biologia. bi-m. ISSN 0023-4249 (Polskie Towarzystwo Przyrodnikow im. Kopernika)

- Kultura i Spoleczenstwo. q. ISSN 0023-5172 (Polska Akademia Nauk. Komitet Nauk Socjologicznych)
- Kwartalnik Architektury i Urbanistyki. q. ISSN 0023-5865 (Polska Akademia Nauk. Komitet Architektury i Urbanistyki)
- Kwartalnik Historii Kultury Materialnej. q. ISSN 0023-5881 (Polska Akademia Nauk. Instytut Historii Kultury Materialnej)
- Kwartalnik Nauki i Techniki/Quarterly Journal of the History of Science and Technology. q. ISSN 0023-589X (Polska Akademia Nauk. Zaklad Historii Nauki i Techniki)
- Kwartalnik Historyczny. q. ISSN 0023-5903 (Polska Akademia Nauk. Instytut Historii)
- Kwartalnik Neofilologiczny. q. ISSN 0023-5911 (Polska Akademia Nauk. Komitet Neofilologiczny)
- Kwartalnik Pedagogiczny. q. ISSN 0023-5938 (Uniwersytet Warszawski. Instytut Pedagogiki)
- Lodzkie Studia Etnograficzne. irreg.; 1972, vol. 14. ISSN 0076-0382 (Polskie Towarzystwo Ludoznawcze. Oddzial w Lodzki)
- Lodzkie Towarzystwo Naukowe. Wydzial III. Nauk Matematyczno-Przyrodniczych. Prace. irreg. ISSN 0076-0412
- Lodzkie Towarzystwo Naukowe. Wydzial IV. Nauk Lekarskich. Prace. irreg. ISSN 0076-0420
- Lodzkie Towarzystwo Naukowe. Wydzial V. Nauk Technicznych. Prace. irreg. ISSN 0076-0439
- Lustracje Dobr Krolewskich XVI-XVIII Wieku. irreg. ISSN 0076-1516 (Polska Akademia Nauk. Instytut Historii)
- Materialy i Prace Antropologiczne. irreg., 1972, no. 84. ISSN 0076-521X (Polska Akademia Nauk. Zaklad Antropologii)
- Meander; miesiecznik poswiecony kulturze swiata starozytnego. m. ISSN 0025-6285 (Polska Akademia Nauk. Komitet Nauk o Kulturze Antycznej)
- Mechanika Teoretyczna i Stosowana. q. ISSN 0079-3701 (Polskie Towarzystwo Mechaniki Teoretycznej i Stosowanej)
- Metalurgia i Odlewnictwo. q. (Akademia Gorniczo-Hutnicza im. Stanislawa Staszica)
- Monografie Biochemiczne. irreg. ISSN 0077-0485 (Polskie Towarzystwo Biochemiczne)
- Monografie Fauny Polski. irreg., 1-3 per yr. (Polska Akademia Nauk. Zaklad Zoologii Systematycznej)
- Monografie Matematyczne. irreg., 1976, vol. 57. ISSN 0077-0507 (Polska Akademia Nauk. Instytut Matematyczny)
- Monographiae Botanicae. irreg., 1972, vol. 37. ISSN 0077-0655 (Polskie Towarzystwo Botaniczne)
- Monumenta Musicae in Polonia. irreg. ISSN 0077-1465 (Polska Akademia Nauk. Instytut Sztuki)
- Muzeum Archeologiczne i Etnograficzne, Lodz. Prace i Materialy. Seria Archeologiczna. irreg., 1975, no. 21. ISSN 0458-1520
- Muzeum Archeologiczne i Etnograficzne, Lodz. Prace i Materialy. Seria Etnograficzna. irreg., no. 18, 1975. ISSN 0076-0315
- Nauka dla Wszystkich. irreg. ISSN 0077-6181 (Polska Akademia Nauk. Oddzial w Krakowie)
- Nukleonika. m. ISSN 0029-5922 (Polska Akademia Nauk. Komitet Fizyki) (Co-sponsor: Urzad Energii Atomowej)
- Obraz Literatury Polskiej. irreg. ISSN 0078-2963 (Polska Akademia Nauk. Instytut Badan Literackich)
- Obserwatorium Krakowski. Rocznik Astronomiczny. Dodatek Miedzynarodowy. irreg., 1973, no. 44. ISSN 0075-7047 (Polska Akademia Nauk. Komitet Astronomii)
- Ochrona Przyrody. a, ISSN 0078-3250 (Polska Akademia Nauk. Zaklad Ochrony Przyrody)
- Opolskie Roczniki Ekonomiczne. a. ISSN 0474-2893 (Polskie Towarzystwo Ekonomiczne. Oddzial w Opolu)
- Organon. a. ISSN 0078-6500 (Polska Akademia Nauk. Zaklad Historii Nauki i Techniki) (Dist. by Ars Polona-Ruch, Krakowskie Przedmiescie 7, Warsaw, Poland)
- Orzecznictwo Sadow Polskich i Komisji Arbitrazowych. m. ISSN 0030-6061 (Polska Akademia Nauk. Instytut Nauk Prawnych)
- Palaeontologia Polonica. irreg., 1973, no. 29. ISSN 0078-8562 (Polska Akademia Nauk. Zaklad Paleozoologii)
- Polish Academy of Sciences. Institute of Fundamental Technological Research. Scientific Activities. a. ISSN 0079-323X (Polska Akademia Nauk. Instytut Podstawowych Problemow Techniki)

- Polish Academy of Sciences. Mathematical Institute. Banach Center Publications. irreg.
- Polish Ecological Studies. bi-m. (Polska Akademia Nauk. Instytut Ekologii)
- Polish Journal of Soil Science. irreg., 1971, vol. 4, no. 2. ISSN 0079-2985 (Polska Akademia Nauk. Komitet Gleboznawstwa i Chemii Rolnej)
- Polish Psychological Bulletin. q. ISSN 0079-2993 (Polska Akademia Nauk. Komitet Nauk Psychologicznych)
- Polska Akademia Nauk. Instytut Geofizyki. Materialy i Prace. irreg., 1973, no. 71. ISSN 0079-3574
- Polska Akademia Nauk. Instytut Maszyn Przeplywowych. Prace. irreg. ISSN 0079-3205
- Polska Akademia Nauk. Komitet Gospodarki Wodnej. Prace i Studia. irreg., vol. 11, 1972. ISSN 0079-3477
- Polska Akademia Nauk. Komitet Przestrzennego Zagospodarowania Kraju. Biuletyn. irreg., 1971, no. 65. ISSN 0079-3493
- Polska Akademia Nauk. Komitet Przestrzennego Zagospodarowania Kraju. Studia. irreg., 1973, vol. 43. ISSN 0079-3507
- Polska Akademia Nauk. Zaklad Archeologii Srodziemnomorskiej. Etudes et Travaux. irreg., 1975, vol. 16. ISSN 0079-3566
- Polska Bibliografia Analityczna Mechaniki/Polish Scientific Abstracts on Mechanics. q. ISSN 0032-3713 (Polska Akademia Nauk. Instytut Podstawowych Problemow Techniki)
- Polska Bibliografia Literacka. irreg., 1976 (for the year 1973) ISSN 0079-3590 (Polska Akademia Nauk. Instytut Badan Literackich)
- Polska Klasa Robotnicza. Studia Historyczna. irreg., 1976, vol. 7. (Polska Akademia Nauk. Instytut Historii)
- Polskie Archiwum Hydrobiologii/Polish Archives of Hydrobiology. q. ISSN 0032-3764 (Polska Akademia Nauk. Instytut Biologii Doswiadczalnej im. M. Nenckiego)
- Polskie Archiwum Weterynaryjne. irreg., 1972, vol. 15, fasc. 4. ISSN 0079-3647 (Polska Akademia Nauk. Komitet Nauk Weterynaryjnych)
- Polskie Pismo Entomologiczne/Bulletin Entomologique de Pologne. q. ISSN 0032-3780 (Polskie Towarzystwo Entomologiczne)
- Polskie Towarzystwo Botaniczne. Sekcja Dendrologiczna. Rocznik. irreg. ISSN 0080-357X
- Polskie Towarzystwo Geologiczne. Rocznik/ Societe Geologique de Pologne. Annales. q. ISSN 0079-3663
- Polskie Towarzystwo Matematyczne. Roczniki. Seria I: Commentationes Mathematicae. Prace Matematyczne. irreg., 1975, vol. 18, no. 2. ISSN 0079-368X
- Postepy Astronomii. q. ISSN 0032-5414 (Polskie Towarzystwo Astronomiczne)
- Postepy Biochemii. q. ISSN 0032-5422 (Polskie Towarzystwo Biochemiczne)
- Postepy Biologii Komorki. q. (Polskie Towarzystwo Anatomiczne)
- Postepy Fizyki. bi-m. ISSN 0032-5430 (Polskie Towarzystwo Fizyczne)
- Postepy Mikrobiologii. q. ISSN 0079-4252 (Polska Akademia Nauk. Komitet Mikrobiologii)
- Postepy Napedu Elektrycznego. irreg. ISSN 0079-4260 (Polska Akademia Nauk)
- Poznaj Swiat; magazyn geograficzny. m. ISSN 0032-6143 (Polskie Towarzystwo Geograficzne)
- Poznanskie Towarzystwo Przyjaciol Nauk. Komisja Budownictwa i Architektury. Prace. irreg., 1972, vol. 2, no. 1. ISSN 0079-4597
- Poznanskie Towarzystwo Przyjaciol Nauk. Komisja Elektrotechniki. Prace. irreg., 1972, vol. 1, no. 2. ISSN 0079-4627
- Poznanskie Towarzystwo Przyjaciol Nauk. Komisja Filozoficzna. Prace. irreg., 1970, vol. 12, no.2. ISSN 0079-4635
- Poznanskie Towarzystwo Przyjaciol Nauk. Komisja Geograficzno-Geologiczna. Prace. irreg., 1976, vol. 16. ISSN 0079-4643
- Poznanskie Towarzystwo Przyjaciol Nauk. Komisja Historyczna. Prace. irreg., 1976, vol. 29. ISSN 0079-4651
- Prace Orientalistyczne. irreg. ISSN 0079-4783 (Polska Akademia Nauk. Zaklad Orientalistyki)
- Prace Popularnonaukowe. irreg. ISSN 0079-4805 (Towarzystwo Naukowe w Toruniu)
- Prakseologia. q. ISSN 0079-4872 (Polska Akademia Nauk. Zaklad Prakseologii)
- Problemy Rejonow Uprzemyslawianych. irreg. ISSN 0079-581X (Polska Akademia Nauk)
- Przeglad Antropologiczny. s-a. ISSN 0033-2003 (Polskie Towarzystwo Antropologiczne) (Co-sponsor: Polskie Zaklady Antropologii)

- Przeglad Geofizyczny; review of geophysics. q. ISSN 0033-2135 (Polskie Towarzystwo Geofizyczne)
- Przeglad Geograficzny/Polish Geographical Review. q. ISSN 0033-2143 (Polska Akademia Nauk. Instytut Geografii)
- Przeglad Humanistyczny. m. ISSN 0033-2194 (Poland. Ministerstwo Nauki, Szkolnictwa Wyzszego i Techniki)
- Przeglad Naukowej Literatury Rolniczej i Lesnej. Gleboznawstwo. Chemia Rolna. Ogolna Uprawa Roli i Roslin i Siedliska Lesne. a. ISSN 0079-7154
- Przeglad Orientalistyczny. q. ISSN 0033-2283 (Polskie Towarzystwo Orientalistyczne)
- Przeglad Statystyczny/Statistical Review. q. ISSN 0033-2372 (Polskie Towarzystwo Ekonomiczne. Sekcja Statystyki)
- Przeglad Zoologiczny. q. ISSN 0033-247X (Polskie Towarzystwo Zoologiczne)
- Przeszlosc Demograficzna Polski. Materialy i Studia. irreg., 1974, no. 6. ISSN 0079-7189 (Polska Akademia Nauk. Komitet Nauk Demograficznych)
- Reports on Mathematical Logic. s-a. (Uniwersytet Jagiellonski) (Co-sponsor: Uniwersytet Slaski w Katowicach)
- Reports on Mathematical Physics. q. (Uniwersytet Mikolaja Kopernika. Zaklad Fizyki) (Co-sponsor: Polskie Towarzystwo Fizyczne)
- Rocznik Bialostocki. a. ISSN 0080-3421 (Muzeum w Bialymstoku)
- Rocznik Ekonomiczny. a. ISSN 0080-343X
- Rocznik Elektrycznosci Atmosferycznej i Meteorologii. irreg. ISSN 0080-3448 (Polska Akademia Nauk. Instytut Geofizyki)
- Rocznik Lodzki. a. ISSN 0080-3502 (Polskie Towarzystwo Historyczne. Oddzial w Lodzki)
- Rocznik Magnetyczny/Annuaire Magnetique. irreg. ISSN 0082-0458 (Polska Akademia Nauk. Instytut Geofizyki)
- Rocznik Orientalistyczny. irreg., 1976, vol. 38. ISSN 0080-3545 (Polska Akademia Nauk. Komitet Nauk Orientalistycznych)
- Roczniki Biblioteczne; organ naukowy bibliotek szkol wyzszych. s-a. ISSN 0080-3626 (Poland. Ministerstwo Nauki, Szkolnictwa Wyzszego i Techniki. Komisja do Spraw Bibliotek i Informacji Naukowej)
- Roczniki Chemii. m. ISSN 0035-7677 (Polska Akademia Nauk. Komitet Nauk Chemicznych)
- Roczniki Dziejow Spolecznych i Gospodarczych. irreg, 1972, vol. 33. ISSN 0080-3634 (Poznanskie Towarzystwo Przyjaciol Nauk)
- Roczniki Gleboznawcze. q. ISSN 0080-3642 (Polskie Towarzystwo Gleboznawcze)
- Roczniki Nauk Rolniczych. Seria A. Produkcja Roslinna. irreg., 1975, vol. 101, no. 2. ISSN 0080-3650 (Polska Akademia Nauk. Komitet Uprawy i Hodowli Roslin)
- Roczniki Nauk Rolniczych. Seria B. Zootechniczna. irreg., 1976, vol. 97, no. 3. ISSN 0080-3669 (Polska Akademia Nauk. Komitet Nauk Zootechnicznych)
- Roczniki Nauk Rolniczych. Seria C.Technika Rolnicza. irreg., 1975, vol. 72, no. 1. ISSN 0080-3677 (Polska Akademia Nauk. Komitet Techniki Rolniczej)
- Roczniki Nauk Rolniczych. Seria D. Monografie. irreg., 1976, vol. 158. ISSN 0080-3685 (Polska Akademia Nauk. Wydzial Nauk Rolniczych i Lesnych)
- Roczniki Nauk Rolniczych. Seria E. Ochrona Roslin. irreg., 1976, vol. 5, no. 2. ISSN 0080-3693 (Polska Akademia Nauk. Komitet Ochrony Roslin)
- Roczniki Nauk Rolniczych. Seria F. Melioracji i Vzytkow Zielonych. irreg., 1970, vol. 77. ISSN 0080-3707 (Polska Akademia Nauk. Komitet Melioracji, Lakarstwa i Torfoznawstwa)
- Roczniki Nauk Rolniczych. Seria G. Ekonomika Rolnictwa. irreg., 1975, vol. 80, no.4. ISSN 0080-3715 (Polska Akademia Nauk. Komitet Ekonomiki Rolnictwa)
- Roczniki Nauk Rolniczych. Seria H. Rybactwo. irreg., 1975, vol. 97, no. 1. ISSN 0080-3723 (Polska Akademia Nauk. Komitet Nauk Zootechnicznych)
- Rozprawy Elektrotechniczne. q. ISSN 0035-9386 (Polska Akademia Nauk. Komitet Elektrotechniki) (Co-sponsor: Komitet Elektroniki i Telekomunikacji)
- Rozprawy Hydrotechniczne. irreg., 1976, no. 36. ISSN 0035-9394 (Polska Akademia Nauk. Instytut Budownictwa Wodnego)
- Rozprawy Inzynierskie/Engineering Transactions. q. ISSN 0035-9408 (Polska Akademia Nauk. Instytut Podstawowych Problemow Techniki)

- Ruch Prawniczy, Ekonomiczny i Socjologiczny. q. ISSN 0035-9629 (Uniwersytet im. Adama Mickiewicza)
- Slavia Antiqua; rocznik poswiecony starozytnosciom slowianskim. a. ISSN 0080-9993 (Uniwersytet im. Adama Mickiewicza. Katedra Archeologii) (Co-sponsor: Uniwersytet Warszawski. Zaklad Archeologii Slowianskiej. Katedra Archeologii Pradziejowej i Wczesnosredniowiecznej)
- Slavia Orientalis. q. ISSN 0037-6744 (Polska Akademia Nauk. Komitet Slowianoznawstwa)
- Societatis Scientiarum Lodziensis. Acta Chimica. irreg., 1972, vol. 17. ISSN 0081-0711 (Lodzkie Towarzystwo Naukowe)
- Studia Archeologiczne. irreg., 1976, vol. 9. ISSN 0081-6302 (Uniwersytet Wroclawski)
- Studia Cywilistyczne/Studies in Civil Law. s-a. ISSN 0039-3126 (Uniwersytet Jagiellonski)
- Studia Demograficzne. q. ISSN 0039-3134 (Polska Akademia Nauk. Komitet Nauk Demograficznych)
- Studia Estetyczne. irreg., 1975, vol. 12. ISSN 0081-637X (Polska Akademia Nauk. Instytut Filozofii i Socjologii)
- Studia Filozoficzne. m. ISSN 0039-3142 (Polska Akademia Nauk. Instytut Filozofii i Socjologii)
- Studia Geograficzne. irreg., 1976, vol. 22. ISSN 0081-640X (Uniwersytet Wroclawski)
- Studia i Materialy do Dziejow Wielkopolski i Pomorza. irreg. ISSN 0081-654X (Polskie Towarzystwo Historyczne. Oddzial w Poznaniu)
- Studia i Materialy do Teorii i Historii Architektury i Urbanistyki. irreg. ISSN 0081-6566 (Polska Akademia Nauk)
- Studia i Materialy z Dziejow Nauki Polskiej. Seria A. Historia Nauk Spolecznych. irreg. ISSN 0081-6574 (Polska Akademia Nauk. Zaklad Historii Nauki i Techniki)
- Studia i Materialy z Dziejow Nauki Polskiej. Seria B. Historia Nauk Biologicznych i Medycznych. irreg., 1972, vol. 23. ISSN 0081-6582 (Polska Akademia Nauk. Zaklad Historii Nauki i Techniki)
- Studia i Materialy z Dziejow Nauki Polskiej. Seria C. Historia Nauk Matematycznych, Fizyko-Chemicznych i Geologiczno-Geograficznych. irreg., 1972, vol. 16. ISSN 0081-6590 (Polska Akademia Nauk. Zaklad Historii Nauki i Techniki)
- Studia i Materialy z Dziejow Nauki Polskiej. Seria D. Historia Techniki i Nauk Technicznych. irreg. ISSN 0081-6604 (Polska Akademia Nauk. Zaklad Historii Nauki i Techniki)
- Studia i Materialy z Dziejow Nauki Polskiej. Seria E. Zagadnienia Ogolne. irreg., 1970, no. 4. ISSN 0081-6612 (Polska Akademia Nauk. Zaklad Historii Nauki i Techniki)
- Studia i Materialy z Dziejow Polski w Okresie Oswiecenia. irreg. ISSN 0081-6620 (Polska Akademia Nauk. Instytut Historii)
- Studia Mathematica. irreg., 1975, vol. 54, no. 2. ISSN 0039-3223 (Polska Akademia Nauk. Instytut Matematyczny)
- Studia Naturae. Seria A. Wydawnictwa Naukowe. irreg. (Polska Akademia Nauk)
- Studia Naturae. Seria B. Wydawnictwa Popularno-Naukowe. irreg. (Polska Akademia Nauk)
- Studia Nauk Politycznych. q. (Centralny Osrodek Metodyczny Studiow Nauk Politycznych)
- Studia Societatis Scientiarum Torunensis. Sectio B (Chemia) irreg. ISSN 0082-5530 (Towarzystwo Naukowe w Toruniu)
- Studia Societatis Scientiarum Torunensis. Sectio C (Geografia et Geologia) irreg., 1976, vol. 8, no. 4-6. ISSN 0082-5549 (Towarzystwo Naukowe w Toruniu)
- Studia Societatis Scientiarum Torunensis. Sectio D (Botanika) irreg. ISSN 0082-5557 (Towarzystwo Naukowe w Toruniu)
- Studia Societatis Scientiarum Torunensis. Sectio E (Zoologia) irreg. ISSN 0082-5565 (Towarzystwo Naukowe w Toruniu)
- Studia Societatis Scientiarum Torunensis. Sectio F. (Astronomia) irreg., 1976, vol. 5, no. 6. ISSN 0082-5573 (Towarzystwo Naukowe w Toruniu)
- Studia Societatis Scientiarum Torunensis. Sectio G (Physiologia) irreg. ISSN 0082-5581 (Towarzystwo Naukowe w Toruniu)
- Studia Ubezpieczeniowe. irreg., 1976, vol./3.
- Studia Warszawskie. irreg., 1971, vol. 9, no. 2. ISSN 0081-7023 (Polska Akademia Nauk. Instytut Historii)
- Studia z Automatyki. irreg., 1970, vol. 1, no. 2. (Poznanskie Towarzystwo Przyjaciol Nauk. Komisja Automatyki)

- Studia z Filologii Polskiej i Slowianskiej. irreg., 1976, vo!. 15. ISSN 0081-7090 (Polska Akademia Nauk. Komitet Slawistyczny)
- Studia z Zakresu Inzynierii. irreg. (Polska Akademia Nauk. Komitet Inzynierii Ladowej i Wodnej)
- Studia Zrodloznawcze. irreg. ISSN 0081-7147 (Polska Akademia Nauk. Instytut Historii)
- Studies in Physical Anthropology. s-a. (Polska Akademia Nauk. Zaklad Antropologii)
- Szczecinskie Towarzystwo Naukowe. Wydzial Nauk Matematyczno Technicznych. Prace. irreg. ISSN 0082-1268
- Szczecinskie Towarzystwo Naukowe. Wydzial Nauk Spolecznych. Prace. irreg. ISSN 0082-1284
- Szczecinskie Towarzystwo Naukowe. Wydzial Nauk Spolecznych. Wydawnictwa. irreg. ISSN 0082-1292
- Szkice o Kulturze Muzycznej XIX Wieku. Studia i Materialy. irreg., 1976, vol. 3. (Polska Akademia Nauk. Instytut Sztuki)
- Towarzystwo Naukowe w Toruniu. Fontes. irreg., 1968, vol. 60. ISSN 0082-5506
- Towarzystwo Naukowe w Toruniu. Komisja Historii Sztuki. Teka. irreg. ISSN 0082-5514
- Towarzystwo Naukowe w Toruniu. Roczniki. a. ISSN 0082-5522
- Uniwersytet Jagiellonski. Zeszyty Naukowe. Prace Archeologiczne. irreg., 1972, vol. 14. ISSN 0083-4300
- Uniwersytet Jagiellonski. Zeszyty Naukowe. Prace Botaniczne. irreg.
- Uniwersytet Jagiellonski. Zeszyty Naukowe. Prace Chemiczne. irreg., 1972, vol. 17. ISSN 0083-4319
- Uniwersytet Jagiellonski. Zeszyty Naukowe. Prace Etnograficzne. irreg. ISSN 0083-4327
- Uniwersytet Jagiellonski. Zeszyty Naukowe. Prace Fizyczne. irreg., 1972, vol. 10. ISSN 0083-4335
- Uniwersytet Jagiellonski. Zeszyty Naukowe. Prace Geograficzne. irreg., 1972, vol. 28. ISSN 0083-4343
- Uniwersytet Jagiellonski. Zeszyty Naukowe. Prace Geograficzne. Prace z Geografii Ekonomicznej. irreg. ISSN 0083-4289
- Uniwersytet Jagiellonski. Zeszyty Naukowe. Prace Historyczne. irreg., 1972, vol. 39. ISSN 0083-4351
- Uniwersytet Jagiellonski. Zeszyty Naukowe. Prace Historycznoliterackie. a. ISSN 0083-436X
- Uniwersytet Jagiellonski. Zeszyty Naukowe. Prace Jezykoznawcze. a. ISSN 0083-4378
- Uniwersytet Jagiellonski. Zeszyty Naukowe. Prace Matematyczne. irreg. ISSN 0083-4386
- Uniwersytet Jagiellonski. Zeszyty Naukowe. Prace Prawnicze. irreg., no. 65, 1975. ISSN 0083-4394
- Uniwersytet Jagiellonski. Zeszyty Naukowe. Prace Psychologiczno-Pedagogiczne. irreg., 1972, vol. 18. ISSN 0083-4408
- Uniwersytet Jagiellonski. Zeszyty Naukowe. Prace z Biologii Molekularnej. irreg.
- Uniwersytet Jagiellonski. Zeszyty Naukowe. Prace z Historii Sztuki. irreg., 1972, vol. 10. ISSN 0083-4424
- Uniwersytet Jagiellonski. Zeszyty Naukowe. Prace z Nauk Politycznych. irreg., 1972, vol. 3.
- Wiadomosci Botaniczne. q. ISSN 0043-5090 (Polskie Towarzystwo Botaniczne)
- Wiadomosci Chemiczne. m. ISSN 0043-5104 (Polskie Towarzystwo Chemiczne)
- Wiadomosci Ekologiczne. q. ISSN 0013-2969 (Polska Akademia Nauk. Instytut Ekologii)
- Wiadomosci Parazytologiczne. bi-m. ISSN 0043-5163 (Polskie Towarzystwo Parazytologiczne)
- Wszechswiat/Universe. m. ISSN 0043-9592 (Polskie Towarzystwo Przyrodnikow im. Kopernika)
- Wychowanie Fizyczne i Sport. Studia i Materialy. q. ISSN 0043-9630 (Instytut Naukowy Kultury Fizycznej)
- Zagadnienia Drgan Nieliniowych. irreg. ISSN 0044-1597 (Polska Akademia Nauk. Instytut Podstawowych Problemow Techniki)
- Zagadnienia Eksploatacji Maszyn/Exploitation Problems of Machines. q. ISSN 0084-4454 (Polska Akademia Nauk. Komitet Budowy Maszyn)
- Zapiski Historyczne; poswiecone historii pomorza i krajow baltyckich. q. ISSN 0044-1791 (Towarzystwo Naukowe w Toruniu)
- Zastosowania Matematyki/Applications Mathematicae. 3 per year. ISSN 0044-1899 (Polska Akademia Nauk. Instytut Matematyczny)
- Zeszyty Problemowe Gornictwa. s-a. ISSN 0044-4383 (Polska Akademia Nauk. Komitet Gornictwa)

- Zeszyty Problemowe Postepow Nauk Rolniczych. irreg., 1970, vol. 110. ISSN 0084-5477 (Polska Akademia Nauk. Wydzial Nauk Rolniczych i Lesnych)
- Zoologica Poloniae; archivum Societatis Zoologorum Poloniae. q. ISSN 0044-510X (Polskie Towarzystwo Zoologiczne)
- Zycie Szkoly Wyzszej. m. ISSN 0591-2377 (Poland. Ministerstwo Nauki, Szkolnictwa Wyzszego i Techniki)
- Zydowski Instytut Historyczny w Polsce. Biuletyn. q. ISSN 0006-4033

**Panstwowe Wydawnictwo Naukowe. Oddzial we Wroclawiu**
Ul. Wierzbowa 15, Wroclaw, Poland
(Dist by Ars Polona-Ruch, Krakowskie Przedmiescie 7, Warsaw, Poland)
- Acta Universitatis Wratislaviensis. Prace Pedagogiczne. irreg. (Uniwersytet Wroclawski)
- Wroclawski Rocznik Ekonomiczny. a. ISSN 0084-2974 (Polskie Towarzystwo Ekonomiczne)

**Panstwowy Zaklad Higieny**
- Medycyna Doswiadczalna i Mikrobiologia. (pub. by Panstwowy Zaklad Wydawnictw Lekarskich)
- Panstwowy Zaklad Higieny. Roczniki. (pub. by Panstwowy Zaklad Wydawnictw Lekarskich)

**Panstwowy Zaklad Wydawnictw Lekarskich**
Ul. Dluga 38/40, Warsaw, Poland
(Dist. by: Ars Polona- Ruch, Krakowskie Przedmiescie 7, Warsaw, Poland)
- Acta Haematologica Polonica. q. ISSN 0001-5814 (Polskie Towarzystwo Hematologiczne) (Co-sponsor: Instytut Hematologii)
- Acta Medica Polona. q. ISSN 0001-608X (Polska Akademia Nauk. Wydzial Nauk Medycznych)
- Akademia Medyczna, Bialystok. Rocznik. a. ISSN 0067-6489
- Annales Academiae Medicae Stetinensis. a. ISSN 0066-1945
- Archiwum Historii Medycyny. q. ISSN 0004-0762 (Polskie Towarzystwo Historii Medycyny)
- Biblioteka Pediatry. irreg.
- Bromatologia i Chemia Toksykologiczna. q. (Polskie Towarzystwo Farmaceutyczne)
- Chirurgia Narzadow Ruchu i Ortopedia Polska. bi-m. ISSN 0009-479X (Polskie Towarzystwo Ortopedyczne i Traumatologiczne)
- Czasopismo Stomatologiczne. m. ISSN 0011-4553
- Diagnostyka Laboratoryjna. bi-m. ISSN 0012-1932 (Polskie Towarzystwo Diagnostyki Laboratoryjnej)
- Farmacja Polska. m. ISSN 0014-8261 (Polskie Towarzystwo Farmaceutyczne)
- Ginekologia Polska. m. ISSN 0017-0011 (Polskie Towarzystwo Ginekologiczne)
- Inzynieria i Budownictwo. m. ISSN 0021-0315 (Polski Zwiazek Inzynierow i Technikow Budownictwa)
- Klinika Oczna. m. ISSN 0023-2157
- Medycyna Doswiadczalna i Mikrobiologia. q. ISSN 0025-8601 (Panstwowy Zaklad Higieny) (Co-sponsor: Polskie Towarzystwo Mikrobiologow)
- Medycyna Pracy. bi-m.
- Neurologia i Neurochirurgia Polska. bi-m. ISSN 0028-3843
- Neuropatologia Polska. q. ISSN 0028-3894
- Nowotwory. q. ISSN 0029-540X (Instytut Onkologii) (Co-sponsor: Polskie Towarzystwo Onkologiczne)
- Panstwowy Zaklad Higieny. Roczniki. bi-m. ISSN 0035-7715
- Patologia Polska. q. ISSN 0031-3114 (Polskie Towarzystwo Anatomopatologow)
- Pediatria Polska. m. ISSN 0031-3939 (Polskie Towarzystwo Pediatryczne) (Co-sponsor: Instytut Matki i Dziecka)
- Pneumonologia Polska. m.
- Polish Journal of Pharmacology and Pharmacy. bi-m. ISSN 0301-0244 (Polska Akademia Nauk. Instytut Farmakologii)
- Polska Akademia Nauk. Wydzial Nauk Medycznych. Annals/Polish Academy of Sciences. Medical Section. Annals. q. ISSN 0048-4733
- Polska Akademia Nauk. Wydzial Nauk Medycznych. Rozprawy. irreg. ISSN 0079-3558
- Polski Przeglad Chirurgiczny. m. ISSN 0032-373X (Towarzystwo Chirurgow Polskich)
- Polski Tygodnik Lekarski; Polish medical weekly. w. ISSN 0032-3756
- Polskie Archiwum Medycyny Wewnetrznej/Polish Archives of Internal Medicine. m. ISSN 0032-3772 (Towarzystwo Internistow Polskich)
- Postepy Pediatrii. a. ISSN 0079-4279
- Problemy Rodziny. bi-m.

- Problemy Uczelni i Instytutow Medycznych. q. ISSN 0032-9541 (Poland. Ministerstwo Zdrowia i Opieki Spolecznej)
- Protetyka Stomatologiczna. bi-m. ISSN 0033-1783
- Przeglad Dermatologiczny. bi-m. ISSN 0033-2526 (Polskie Towarzystwo Dermatologiczne)
- Przeglad Epidemiologiczny. q. ISSN 0033-2100
- Przeglad Lekarski. m. ISSN 0033-2240
- Psychiatria Polska. bi-m. ISSN 0033-2674 (Polskie Towarzystwo Psychologiczne)
- Reumatologia. q. ISSN 0034-6233 (Polska Akademia Nauk. Instytut Reumatologiczny) (Co-sponsor: Polskie Towarzystwo Reumatologiczne)
- Szczecinskie Towarzystwo Naukowe. Wydzial Nauk Lekarskich. Prace. irreg. ISSN 0082-125X
- Wiadomosci Lekarskie. bi-w. ISSN 0043-5147
- Zdrowie Publiczne. m. ISSN 0044-2011
- Zywienie Czlowieka. q. (Instytut Zywnosci i Zywienia)

**Instytut Wydawniczy "Pax"**
Mokotowska 43, Warsaw, Poland
(Dist. by: Ars Polona-Ruch, Krakowskie Przedmiescie 7, Warsaw, Poland)
- Zycie i Mysl/Life and Thought. m. ISSN 0044-5584

**Poland. Glowne Biuro Studiow i Projektow Gorniczych**
Plac Grunwaldzki 8-10, 40-950 Katowice, Poland.
- Projekty-Problemy. Budownictwo Weglowe. irreg., 1976, vol. 21, no. 5.

**Poland. Glowny Urzad Statystyczny**
Al. Niepodleglosci 208, Warsaw, Poland
(Dist. by: Ars Polona Ruch, Krakowskie Przedmiescie 7, Warsaw, Poland)
- Biblioteka Wiadomosci Statystycznych. irreg. ISSN 0067-7795
- Poland. Glowny Urzad Statystyczny. Atlas Statystyczny. Statistical Atlas. irreg. ISSN 0079-2586
- Poland. Glowny Urzad Statystyczny. Biuletyn Statystyczny. m. ISSN 0006-4025
- Poland. Glowny Urzad Statystyczny. Budzet Panstwa. State Budget. a. ISSN 0079-2594
- Poland. Glowny Urzad Statystyczny. Kultura. irreg. ISSN 0079-2713
- Poland. Glowny Urzad Statystyczny. Maly Rocznik Statystyczny. Concise Statistical Yearbook. a. ISSN 0079-2608
- Poland. Glowny Urzad Statystyczny. Maly Rocznik Statystyki Miedzynarodowej. irreg.
- Poland. Glowny Urzad Statystyczny. Rocznik Demograficzny. a. ISSN 0079-2616
- Poland. Glowny Urzad Statystyczny. Rocznik Statystyczny Budownictwa. Yearbook of Construction Statistics. irreg. ISSN 0079-2632
- Poland. Glowny Urzad Statystyczny. Rocznik Statystyczny Finansow. Yearbook of Finance Statistics. irreg. ISSN 0079-2640
- Poland. Glowny Urzad Statystyczny. Rocznik Statystyczny Gornictwa. Yearbook of Mining Statistics. irreg. ISSN 0079-2675
- Poland. Glowny Urzad Statystyczny. Rocznik Statystyczny Gospodarki Morskiej. Yearbook of Sea Economy Statistics. irreg. ISSN 0079-2667
- Poland. Glowny Urzad Statystyczny. Rocznik Statystyczny Gospodarski Mieszkaniowej i Komunalnej. irreg. ISSN 0079-2659
- Poland. Glowny Urzad Statystyczny. Rocznik Statystyczny Handlu Wewnetrznego/Yearbook of International Trade Statistics. irreg. ISSN 0079-2683
- Poland. Glowny Urzad Statystyczny. Rocznik Statystyczny Handlu Zagranicznego. Yearbook of Foreign Trade Statistics. ISSN 0079-2691
- Poland. Glowny Urzad Statystyczny. Rocznik Statystyczny Inwestycji i Srodkow Trwalych. Yearbook of Investment and Fixed Assets Statistics. a. ISSN 0079-2705
- Poland. Glowny Urzad Statystyczny. Rocznik Statystyczny Lesnictwa. Yearbook of Forestry Statistics. irreg. ISSN 0079-2721
- Poland. Glowny Urzad Statystyczny. Rocznik Statystyczny Ochrony Zdrowia. Yearbook of Public Health Statistics. irreg. ISSN 0079-2748
- Poland. Glowny Urzad Statystyczny. Rocznik Statystyczny Powiatow. Statistical Yearbook of Counties. a. ISSN 0079-2756
- Poland. Glowny Urzad Statystyczny. Rocznik Statystyczny Pracy. Yearbook of Labour Statistics. irreg. ISSN 0079-2772
- Poland. Glowny Urzad Statystyczny. Rocznik Statystyczny Przemyslu. Yearbook of Industry Statistics. a. ISSN 0079-2764

- Poland. Glowny Urzad Statystyczny. Rocznik Statystyczny. Statistical Yearbook. a. ISSN 0079-2780
- Poland. Glowny Urzad Statystyczny. Rocznik Statystyczny Szkolnictwa. Yearbook of Education Statistics. a. ISSN 0079-2799
- Poland. Glowny Urzad Statystyczny. Rocznik Statystyczny Transportu. Yearbook of Transport Statistics. irreg. ISSN 0079-2802
- Poland. Glowny Urzad Statystyczny. Rocznik Statystyki Miedzynarodowej. Yearbook of International Statistics. irreg. ISSN 0079-273X
- Poland. Glowny Urzad Statystyczny. Rolniczy Rocznik Statystyczny. Yearbook of Agricultural Statistics. irreg. ISSN 0079-2810
- Poland. Glowny Urzad Statystyczny. Statystyka Zegluci Srodladowej i Drog Wodnych Srodladowych. a. ISSN 0079-2837
- Poland. Glowny Urzad Statystyczny. Studia i Prace Statystyczne. q. ISSN 0079-2845
- Poland. Glowny Urzad Statystyczny. Turystyka. a.
- Poland. Glowny Urzad Statystyczny. Ubezpieczenia Majatkowe i Osobowe. Property and Personal Insurance. a. ISSN 0079-2853
- Poland. Glowny Urzad Statystyczny. Uzytkowanie Gruntow i Powierzchnia Zasiewow Oraz Zwierzeta Gospodarskie. a. ISSN 0079-2861
- Poland. Glowny Urzad Statystyczny. Wiadomosci Statystyczne. m. ISSN 0043-518X
- Poland. Glowny Urzad Statystyczny. Wypadki Drogowe. a. ISSN 0079-287X
- Poland. Glowny Urzad Statystyczny. Wypadki Przy Pracy. Accidents at Work. a. ISSN 0079-2888
- Poland. Glowny Urzad Statystyczny. Zatrudnienie w Gospodarce Narodowej. a. ISSN 0079-2896
- Poland. Glowny Urzad Statystyczny. Zeszyty Metodologiczne. irreg., no. 7, 1974. ISSN 0079-2829
- Poland. Glowny Urzad Statystyczny. Zwierzeta Gospodarskie. Livestock. s-a. ISSN 0079-290X

**Poland. Ministerstwo Gornictwa i Energetyki**
- Gospodarka Paliwami i Energia/Fuel and Energy Management. (pub. by Wydawnictwa Czasopism Technicznych N.O.T.)

**Poland. Ministerstwo Handlu Zagranicznego i Gospodarki Morskiej**
- Technika i Gospodarka Morska. (pub. by Wydawnictwo Morskie)

**Poland. Ministerstwo Komunikacji**
- Wiadomosci Telekomunikacyjne. (pub. by Wydawnictwa Komunikacji i Lacznosci)

**Poland. Ministerstwo Kultury i Sztuki. Generalny Konserwator Zabytkow**
Ul. Brzozowa 35, 00-258 Warsaw, Poland
(Dist. by: Ars Polona-Ruch, Krakowskie Przedmiescie 7, Warsaw, Poland)
- Ochrona Zabytkow. q. ISSN 0029-8247 (prep. by its Osrodek Dokumentacji Zabytkow)

**Poland. Ministerstwo Nauki, Szkolnictwa Wyzszego i Techniki**
- Dydaktyka Szkoly Wyzszej. (pub. by Panstwowe Wydawnictwo Naukowe)
- Informator dla Kandydaton na Studia Podyplomowe i Doktoranckie. (pub. by Panstwowe Wydawnictwo Naukowe)
- Przeglad Humanistyczny. (pub. by Panstwowe Wydawnictwo Naukowe)
- Roczniki Biblioteczne. (pub. by Panstwowe Wydawnictwo Naukowe)
- Zycie Szkoly Wyzszej. (pub. by Panstwowe Wydawnictwo Naukowe)

**Poland. Ministerstwo Oswiaty i Wychowania**
- Badania Oswiatowe. (pub. by Wydawnictwa Szkolne i Pedagogiczne)
- Biologia w Szkole. (pub. by Wydawnictwa Szkolne i Pedagogiczne)
- Chemia w Szkole. (pub. by Wydawnictwa Szkolne i Pedagogiczne)
- Fizyka w Szkole. (pub. by Wydawnictwa Szkolne i Pedagogiczne)
- Geografia w Szkole. (pub. by Wydawnictwa Szkolne i Pedagogiczne)
- Jezyk Rosyjski. (pub. by Wydawnictwa Szkolne i Pedagogiczne)
- Jezyki Obce w Szkole. (pub. by Wydawnictwa Szkolne i Pedagogiczne)
- Matematyka. (pub. by Wydawnictwa Szkolne i Pedagogiczne)
- Oswiata Doroslych. (pub. by Wydawnictwa Szkolne i Pedagogiczne)

- Polonistyka. (pub. by Wydawnictwa Szkolne i Pedagogiczne)
- Problemy Opiekunczo- Wychowawcze. (pub. by Wydawnictwa Szkolne i Pedagogiczne)
- Przysposobienie Obronne w Szkole. (pub. by Wydawnictwa Szkolne i Pedagogiczne)
- Szkola Specjalna. (pub. by Wydwnictwa Szkolne i Pedagogiczne)
- Wiadomosci Historyczne. (pub. by Wydawnictwa Szkolne i Pedagogiczne)
- Wychowanie Fizyczne i Higiena Szkolna. (pub. by Wydawnictwa Szkolne i Pedagogiczne)
- Wychowanie Myzyczne w Szkole. (pub. by Wydawnictwa Szkolne i Pedagogiczne)
- Wychowanie Obywatelskie. (pub. by Wydawnictwa Szkolne i Pedagogiczne)
- Wychowanie Techniczne w Szkole. (pub. by Wydawnictwa Szkolne i Pedagogiczne)
- Wychowanie w Przedszkolu. (pub. by Wydawnictwa Szkolne i Pedagogiczne)
- Zbiorcza Szkola Gminna. (pub. by Wydawnictwa Szkolne i Pedagogiczne)
- Zycie Szkoly. (pub. by Wydawnictwa Szkolne i Pedagogiczne)

**Poland. Ministerstwo Przemyslu Chemicznego**
- Przemysl Chemiczny. (pub. by Wydawnictwa Czasopism Technicznych N.O.T.)

**Poland. Ministerstwo Zdrowia i Opieki Spolecznej**
- Problemy Uczelni i Instytutow Medycznych. (pub. by Panstwowy Zaklad Wydawnictw Lekarskich)

**Poland. Urzad Patentowy**
Al. Niepodleglosci 188, Warsaw, Poland
(Dist. by: Ars Polona-Ruch, Krakowskie Przedmiescie 7, Warsaw, Poland)
- Poland. Urzad Patentowy. Biuletyn. bi-w.
- Poland. Urzad Patentowy. Wiadomosci/News of the Patent Office. m. ISSN 0043-5201

**Wydawnictwa Handlu Zagranicznego Polexportpress**
Ul. St. Kierbedzia 4, Warsaw, Poland
(Dist. by: Ars Polona- Ruch, Krakowskie Przedmiescie 7, Warsaw, Poland)
- Food from Poland; review of exports of agricultural products and foodstuffs from Poland. q. ISSN 0015-6418
- Holidays in Poland/Vacances en Pologne/Touristisches Magazin. m.
- Kristina. q.
- Materia Medica Polona; the Polish journal of medicine and pharmacy. q. ISSN 0025-5246 (Centrum Medyczne Ksztalcenia Podyplomowego)
- New Polish Publications; a monthly review of Polish books. m. ISSN 0028-6486
- Novelties of Pharmacology and Medicine. bi-m.
- Polish Economic Survey. fortn. ISSN 0032-2849
- Polish Engineering. bi-m.
- Polish Export-Import. m. ISSN 0032-2865
- Polish Fair Magazine. q.
- Polish Foreign Trade. m. ISSN 0032-2881
- Polish Machine Industry Offers. m.
- Soon to Appear. m.

**Polish Society of Anaesthesiologists**
- Anaesthesia, Resuscitation and Intensive Therapy. (pub. by Karger Libri AG SZ)

**Politechnika Czestochowska**
Ul. Deglera 35, 42-200 Czestochowa, Poland
(Dist. by: Ars Polona-Ruch, Krakowskie Przedmiescie 7, Warsaw, Poland)
- Politechnika Czestochowska. Zeszyty Naukowe. Nauki Podstawowe. s-a. ISSN 0574-9069
- Politechnika Czestochowska. Zeszyty Naukowe. Nauki Spoleczno-Ekonomiczne. s-a. ISSN 0574-9077
- Politechnika Czestochowska. Zeszyty Naukowe. Nauki Techniczne. Elektrotechnika. s-a.
- Politechnika Czestochowska. Zeszyty Naukowe. Nauki Techniczne. Hutnictwo. s-a.
- Politechnika Czestochowska. Zeszyty Naukowe. Nauki Techniczne. Mechanika. s-a.

**Politechnika Gdanska**
Majakowskiego 11/12, Gdansk 6, Poland
(Dist. by: Ars Polona-Ruch, Krakowskie Przedmiescie 7, Warsaw, Poland)
- Politechnika Gdanska. Zeszyty Naukowe. Architektura. irreg.
- Politechnika Gdanska. Zeszyty Naukowe. Budownictwo Ladowe. irreg.
- Politechnika Gdanska. Zeszyty Naukowe. Budownictwo Okretowe. irreg. ISSN 0416-7287
- Politechnika Gdanska. Zeszyty Naukowe. Budownictwo Wodne. irreg. ISSN 0416-7295

- Politechnika Gdanska. Zeszyty Naukowe. Chemia. irreg. ISSN 0416-7309
- Politechnika Gdanska. Zeszyty Naukowe. Ekonomia. irreg.
- Politechnika Gdanska. Zeszyty Naukowe. Elektronika. irreg. ISSN 0418-3614
- Politechnika Gdanska. Zeszyty Naukowe. Elektryka. irreg.
- Politechnika Gdanska. Zeszyty Naukowe. Fizyka. irreg. ISSN 0072-0364
- Politechnika Gdanska. Zeszyty Naukowe. Matematyka. irreg. ISSN 0072-0372
- Politechnika Gdanska. Zeszyty Naukowe. Mechanika. irreg. ISSN 0072-0380

**Politechnika Krakowska**
Ul. Warszawska 24, Krakow, Poland
(Dist. by: Ars Polona-Ruch, Krakowskie Przedmiescie 7, Warsaw, Poland)
- Czasopismo Techniczne. m. ISSN 0011-4561
- Politechnika Krakowska. Zeszyty Naukowe. Chemia. irreg. ISSN 0075-7055

**Politechnika Lodzka**
Ul. Zwirki 36, 90-924 Lodz, Poland
(Dist by Ars Polona-Ruch, Krakowskie Przedmiescie 7, Warsaw, Poland)
- International Symposium on Switching Arc Phenomena. Proceedings. irreg., 1973, 2nd. (Cosponsor: Stowarzyszenie Elektrykow Polskich)
- Politechnika Lodzka. Zeszyty Naukowe. Budownictwo. irreg. ISSN 0076-0323
- Politechnika Lodzka. Zeszyty Naukowe. Chemia. irreg. ISSN 0458-1555
- Politechnika Lodzka. Zeszyty Naukowe. Chemia Spozywcza. irreg. ISSN 0528-9254
- Politechnika Lodzka. Zeszyty Naukowe. Cieplne Maszyny Przeplywowe. irreg.
- Politechnika Lodzka. Zeszyty Naukowe. Elektryka. irreg. ISSN 0459-682X
- Politechnika Lodzka. Zeszyty Naukowe. Fizyka. irreg.
- Politechnika Lodzka. Zeszyty Naukowe. Inzynieria Chemiczna. irreg.
- Politechnika Lodzka. Zeszyty Naukowe. Matematyka. irreg.
- Politechnika Lodzka. Zeszyty Naukowe. Mechanika. irreg. ISSN 0458-1563
- Politechnika Lodzka. Zeszyty Naukowe. Nauki Spoleczno-Ekonomiczne. irreg.
- Politechnika Lodzka. Zeszyty Naukowe. Wlokiennictwo. irreg. ISSN 0076-0331
- Politechnika Lodzka. Zeszyty Naukowe. Zeszyty Specjalny. irreg. ISSN 0458-1547

**Politechnika Poznanska**
Pl. Curie Sklodowskiej 5, Poznan, Poland.
- Fasciculi Mathematici. irreg. ISSN 0044-4413
- Politechnika Poznanska. Materialy Historyczno-Metodyczne. Studia Filozoficzne. irreg. ISSN 0079-4481 (Dist. by: Ars Polona-Ruch, Krakowskie Przedmiescie 7, Warsaw, Poland)
- Politechnika Poznanska. Zeszyty Naukowe. Bibliografia. irreg., no. 10, 1972. ISSN 0551-651X
- Politechnika Poznanska. Zeszyty Naukowe. Budownictwo Ladowe. irreg. ISSN 0079-449X
- Politechnika Poznanska.Zeszyty Naukowe. Chemia Techniki Zastosowan. irreg., 1972, no. 11. ISSN 0079-4473
- Politechnika Poznanska. Zeszyty Naukowe. Ekonomika i Organizacja Przemyslu. irreg.
- Politechnika Poznanska. Zeszyty Naukowe. Elektryka. irreg. ISSN 0079-4503
- Politechnika Poznanska. Zeszyty Naukowe. Fizyka. irreg. ISSN 0079-4511
- Politechnika Poznanska. Zeszyty Naukowe. Maszyny Roboczei i Pojazdy. irreg., no. 12, 1972.
- Politechnika Poznanska. Zeszyty Naukowe. Mechanika. irreg. ISSN 0079-4538

**Politechnika Slaska**
Katowicka 7, Gliwice, Poland
(Dist. by Ars Polona-Ruch, Krakowskie Przedmiescie 7, Warsaw, Poland)
- Politechnika Slaska. Zeszyty Naukowe. Elektryka. irreg. ISSN 0072-4688
- Politechnika Slaska. Zeszyty Naukowe. Inzynieria Sanitarna. irreg. ISSN 0072-4696
- Politechnika Slaska. Zeszyty Naukowe. Matematyka-Fizyka. irreg. ISSN 0072-470X
- Politechnika Slaska. Zeszyty Naukowe. Nauki Spoleczne. irreg. ISSN 0072-4718

**Politechnika Warszawska**
Plac Jednosci Robotniczei 1, 00-661 Warsaw, Poland.
- Politechnika Warszawska. Instytut Fizyki. Prace. irreg., 1975, no. 13. (prep. by its Instytut Fizyki)

- Politechnika Warszawska. Instytut Technologii i Organizacji Produkcji Budowlanej. Prace. irreg.

**Politechnika Wroclawska**
Wybrzeze Wyspianskiego 27, 50-370 Wroclaw, Poland
(Dist. by: Ars Polona-Ruch, Krakowskie Przedmiescie 7, Warsaw, Poland)
- Acta Polytechnicae Wratislaviensis. s-a.
- Environment Protection Engineering. s-a.
- Materials Science. s-a.
- Optica Applicata. q. ISSN 0078-5466
- Politechnika Wroclawska. Biblioteka Glowna i Osrodek Informacji Naukowo-Technicznej. Prace Naukowe. Konferencje. irreg.
- Politechnika Wroclawska. Biblioteka Glowna i Osrodek Informacji Naukowo-Technicznej. Prace Naukowe. Prace Bibliograficzne. irreg., no. 2,1976.
- Politechnika Wroclawska. Biblioteka Glowna i Osrodek Informacji Naukowo-Technicznej. Prace Naukowe. Studia i Materialy. irreg., no. 2, 1977.
- Politechnika Wroclawska. Instytut Architektury i Urbanistyki. Prace Naukowe. Studia i Materialy. irreg., no. 4, 1974.
- Politechnika Wroclawska. Instytut Budownictwa. Prace Naukowe. Konferencje. irreg., no. 3, 1976.
- Politechnika Wroclawska. Instytut Budownictwa. Prace Naukowe. Monografie. irreg., 1977, no. 7.
- Politechnika Wroclawska. Instytut Budownictwa. Prace Naukowe. Studia i Materialy. irreg., 1976, no. 12.
- Politechnika Wroclawska. Instytut Chemii i Technologii Nafty i Wegla. Prace Naukowe. Konferencje. irreg., 1975, no. 2.
- Politechnika Wroclawska. Instytut Chemii i Technologii Nafty i Wegla. Prace Naukowe. Monografie. irreg., 1977, no. 9.
- Politechnika Wroclawska. Instytut Chemii i Technologii Nafty i Wegla. Prace Naukowe. Studia i Materialy. irreg., 1976, no. 19. ISSN 0084-2818
- Politechnika Wroclawska. Instytut Chemii Nieorganicznej i Metalurgii Pierwiastkow Rzadkich. Prace Naukowe. Konferencje. irreg., no. 9, 1975.
- Politechnika Wroclawska. Instytut Chemii Nieorganicznej i Metalurgii Pierwiastkow Rzadkich. Prace Naukowe. Monografie. irreg., 1976, no. 11.
- Politechnika Wroclawska. Instytut Chemii Nieorganicznej i Metalurgii Pierwiastkow Rzadkich. Prace Naukowe. Studia i Materialy. irreg., no. 15, 1975.
- Politechnika Wroclawska. Instytut Chemii Organicznej i Fizycznej. Prace Naukowe. Konferencje. irreg., 1975, no. 2.
- Politechnika Wroclawska. Instytut Chemii Organicznej i Fizycznej. Prace Naukowe. Monografie. irreg., no. 2, 1974.
- Politechnika Wroclawska. Instytut Chemii Organicznej i Fizycznej. Prace Naukowe. Studia i Materialy. irreg., no. 7, 1975.
- Politechnika Wroclawska. Instytut Cybernetyki Technicznej. Prace Naukowe. Konferencje. irreg., 1976, no. 13.
- Politechnika Wroclawska. Instytut Cybernetyki Technicznej. Prace Naukowe. Studia i Materialy. irreg., 1977, no. 24.
- Politechnika Wroclawska. Instytut Energoelektryki. Prace Naukowe. Konferencje. irreg., 1974, no. 2.
- Politechnika Wroclawska. Instytut Energoelektryki. Prace Naukowe. Monografie. irreg., 1976, no. 6.
- Politechnika Wroclawska. Instytut Energoelektryki. Prace Naukowe. Studia i Materialy. irreg., 1977, no. 29. ISSN 0084-2826
- Politechnika Wroclawska. Instytut Fizyki. Prace Naukowe. Monografie. irreg., 1977, no. 3.
- Politechnika Wroclawska. Instytut Fizyki. Prace Naukowe. Studia i Materialy. irreg., 1976, no. 7.
- Politechnika Wroclawska. Instytut Geotechniki. Prace Naukowe. Konferencje. irreg., 1976, no. 7.
- Politechnika Wroclawska. Instytut Geotechniki. Prace Naukowe. Monografie. irreg., no. 3, 1974. ISSN 0084-2834
- Politechnika Wroclawska. Instytut Geotechniki. Prace Naukowe. Studia i Materialy. irreg., 1976, no. 9. ISSN 0084-2842
- Politechnika Wroclawska. Instytut Gornictwa. Prace Naukowe. Konferencje. irreg., 1975, no. 2.
- Politechnika Wroclawska. Instytut Gornictwa. Prace Naukowe. Monografie. irreg., no. 7, 1976.
- Politechnika Wroclawska. Instytut Gornictwa. Prace Naukowe. Studia i Materialy. irreg.
- Politechnika Wroclawska. Instytut Historii Architektury, Sztuki i Techniki. Prace Naukowe. Monografie. irreg., 1975, no. 7.

- Politechnika Wroclawska. Instytut Historii Architektury, Sztuki i Techniki. Prace Naukowe. Studia i Materialy. irreg., 1974, no. 3.
- Politechnika Wroclawska. Instytut Inzynieri Ochrony Srodowska. Prace Naukowe. Monografie. irreg., 1976, no. 12. ISSN 0084-2869
- Politechnika Wroclawska. Instytut Inzynierii Chemicznej i Urzadzen Cieplnych. Prace Naukowe. Konferencje. irreg., 1974, no. 3.
- Politechnika Wroclawska. Instytut Inzynierii Chemicznej i Urzadzen Cieplnych. Prace Naukowe. Monografie. irreg., 1977, no. 18. ISSN 0572-6913
- Politechnika Wroclawska. Instytut Inzynierii Chemicznej i Urzadzen Cieplnych. Prace Naukowe. Studia i Materialy. irreg., 1976, no. 13. ISSN 0084-2850
- Politechnika Wroclawska. Instytut Inzynierii Ladowej. Prace Naukowe. Konferencje. irreg., no. 4, 1975.
- Politechnika Wroclawska. Instytut Inzynierii Ladowej. Prace Naukowe. Monografie. irreg., no. 3, 1975.
- Politechnika Wroclawska. Instytut Inzynierii Ladowej. Prace Naukowe. Studia i Materialy. irreg., 1973, no. 10.
- Politechnika Wroclawska. Instytut Inzynierii Ochrony Srodowiska. Prace Naukowe. Konferencje. irreg., no. 4, 1975.
- Politechnika Wroclawska. Instytut Inzynierii Ochrony Srodowiska. Prace Naukowe. Studia i Materialy. irreg., 1976, no. 18. ISSN 0084-2877
- Politechnika Wroclawska. Instytut Konstrukcji i Eksploatacji Maszyn. Prace Naukowe. Konferencje. irreg., no. 4, 1975.
- Politechnika Wroclawska. Instytut Konstrukcji i Eksploatacji Maszyn. Prace Naukowe. Monografie. irreg., 1976, no. 7.
- Politechnika Wroclawska. Instytut Konstrukcji i Eksploatacji Maszyn. Prace Naukowe. Studia i Materialy. irreg., no. 21, 1974.
- Politechnika Wroclawska. Instytut Matematyki. Prace Naukowe. Monografie. irreg., 1975, no. 2.
- Politechnika Wroclawska. Instytut Matematyki. Prace Naukowe. Studia i Materialy. irreg., 1977, no. 13.
- Politechnika Wroclawska. Instytut Materialoznawstwa i Mechaniki Technicznej. Prace Naukowe. Konferencje. irreg., no. 2, 1974.
- Politechnika Wroclawska. Instytut Materialoznawstwa i Mechaniki Technicznej. Prace Naukowe. Monografie. irreg., no. 10, 1977.
- Politechnika Wroclawska. Instytut Materialoznawstwa i Mechaniki Technicznej. Prace Naukowe. Studia i Materialy. irreg., 1977, no. 24.
- Politechnika Wroclawska. Instytut Metrologii Elektrycznej. Prace Naukowe. Konferencje. irreg., no. 3, 1976.
- Politechnika Wroclawska. Instytut Metrologii Elektrycznej. Prace Naukowe. Monografie. irreg., no. 2, 1976.
- Politechnika Wroclawska. Instytut Metrologii Elektrycznej. Prace Naukowe. Przemysl. irreg., 1975, no. 1.
- Politechnika Wroclawska. Instytut Metrologii Elektrycznej. Prace Naukowe. Studia i Materialy. irreg., 1977, no. 5. ISSN 0084-2958
- Politechnika Wroclawska. Instytut Nauk Spolecznych. Prace Naukowe. Monografie. irreg., 1976, no. 8.
- Politechnika Wroclawska. Instytut Nauk Spolecznych. Prace Naukowe. Studia i Materialy. irreg., no. 7, 1975.
- Politechnika Wroclawska. Instytut Organizacji i Zarzadzania. Prace Naukowe. Konferencje. irreg., 1976, no. 3.
- Politechnika Wroclawska. Instytut Organizacji i Zarzadzania. Prace Naukowe. Monografie. irreg., no. 3, 1975.
- Politechnika Wroclawska. Instytut Organizacji i Zarzadzania. Prace Naukowe. Studia i Materialy. irreg., 1977, no. 8.
- Politechnika Wroclawska. Instytut Podstaw Elektrotechniki i Elektrotechnologii. Prace Naukowe. Konferencje. irreg., 1976, no. 3.
- Politechnika Wroclawska. Instytut Podstaw Elektrotechniki i Elektrotechnologii. Prace Naukowe. Monografie. irreg., no. 5, 1975.
- Politechnika Wroclawska. Instytut Podstaw Elektrotechniki i Elektrotechnologii. Prace Naukowe. Studia i Materialy. irreg., no. 7, 1975.
- Politechnika Wroclawska. Instytut Techniki Cieplnej i Mechaniki Plynow. Prace Naukowe. Konferencje. irreg., 1974, no. 1.
- Politechnika Wroclawska. Instytut Techniki Cieplnej i Mechaniki Plynow. Prace Naukowe. Monografie. irreg., no. 3, 1974.

- Politechnika Wroclawska. Instytut Techniki Cieplnej i Mechaniki Plynow. Prace Naukowe. Studia i Materialy. irreg., 1977, no. 10.
- Politechnika Wroclawska. Instytut Technologii Budowy Maszyn. Prace Naukowe. Konferencje. irreg., 1975, no. 1.
- Politechnika Wroclawska. Instytut Technologii Budowy Maszyn. Prace Naukowe. Monografie. irreg.
- Politechnika Wroclawska. Instytut Technologii Budowy Maszyn. Prace Naukowe. Studia i Materialy. irreg., 1976, no. 13.
- Politechnika Wroclawska. Instytut Technologii Elektronowej. Prace Naukowe. Konferencje. irreg., no. 2, 1975.
- Politechnika Wroclawska. Instytut Technologii Elektronowej. Prace Naukowe. Monografie. irreg., no. 4, 1975. ISSN 0084-280X
- Politechnika Wroclawska. Instytut Technologii Elektronowej. Prace Naukowe. Studia i Materialy. irreg., no. 10, 1974. ISSN 0084-2885
- Politechnika Wroclawska. Instytut Technologii Nieorganicznej i Nawozow Mineralnych. Prace Naukowe. Konferencje. irreg.; 1973, no. 3.
- Politechnika Wroclawska. Instytut Technologii Nieorganicznej i Nawozow Mineralnych. Prace Naukowe. Monografie. irreg., no. 3, 1975. ISSN 0084-2907
- Politechnika Wroclawska. Instytut Technologii Nierorganicznej i Nawozow Mineralnych. Prace Naukowe. Studia i Materialy. irreg., 1977, no. 4. ISSN 0084-2915
- Politechnika Wroclawska. Instytut Technologii Organicznej i Tworzyw Sztucznych. Prace Naukowe. Konferencje. irreg., 1976, no. 7.
- Politechnika Wroclawska. Instytut Technologii Organicznej i Tworzyw Sztucznych. Prace Naukowe. Monografie. irreg., 1977, no. 4.
- Politechnika Wroclawska. Instytut Technologiii Organicznej i Tworzyw Sztucznych. Prace Naukowe. Studia i Materialy. irreg., 1977, no. 16.
- Politechnika Wroclawska. Instytut Telekomunikacji i Akustyki. Prace Naukowe. Konferencje. irreg., 1976, no. 7.
- Politechnika Wroclawska. Instytut Telekomunikacji i Akustyki. Prace Naukowe. Monografie. irreg., 1977, no. 10.
- Politechnika Wroclawska. Instytut Telekomunikacji i Akustyki. Prace Naukowe. Studia i Materialy. irreg., no. 10, 1975.
- Politechnika Wroclawska. Instytut Ukladow Elektromaszynowich. Prace Naukowe. Konferencje. irreg., 1976, no. 5. ISSN 0084-2931
- Politechnika Wroclawska. Instytut Ukladow Elektromaszynowych. Prace Naukowe. Monografie. irreg. ISSN 0084-2923
- Politechnika Wroclawska. Instytut Ukladow Elektromaszynowych. Prace Naukowe. Przemysl. irreg., no. 5, 1973.
- Politechnika Wroclawska. Instytut Ukladow Elektromaszynowych. Prace Naukowe. Studia i Materialy. irreg., 1977, no. 12. ISSN 0084-294X
- Politechnika Wroclawska. Osrodek Badan Prognostycznych. Konferencje. irreg., 1977, no. 6.
- Politechnika Wroclawska. Osrodek Badan Prognostycznych. Prace Naukowe. Konferencje. irreg., 1975, no. 3.
- Politechnika Wroclawska. Prace Naukoznawcze i Prognostyczne. s-a.
- Politechnika Wroclawska. Studium Praktycznej Nauki Jezykow Obcych. Prace Naukowe. Studia i Materialy. irreg., no. 6, 1977.
- Politechnika Wroclawska Instytut Architektury i Urbanistyki. Pace Naukowe. Monografie. irreg., 1975, no. 4.
- Studia Geotechnica. s-a.
- Systems Science. q. (Dist. by: Wissenschaftliche Verbandbuchhandlung Harry Munchberg, Postfach, 3394 Langelscheim 2, E. Germany (D.D.R.))

**Wydawnictwo Polonia**
Koszykowa 6a, Warsaw, Poland
(Dist. by: Ars Polona-Ruch, Krakowskie Przedmiescie 7, Warsaw, Poland)
- Kontynenty. m. ISSN 0023-3765
- Literatura. w.

**Polska Agencja Prasowa**
Al. Jerozolimskie 7, 00-950 Warsaw, Poland
- Polish Weekly. w. ISSN 0032-3020 (Subscr. to: Ars Polona-Ruch, Krakowskie Przedmiescie 7, 00-068 Warsaw, Poland)

**Polska Akademia Nauk**
Palac Kultury i Nauki, 00-901 Warsaw, Poland
(Subscr. Address: Ars Polona Ruch, Krakowskie Przedmiescie 7, 00-068 Warsaw, Poland)
- Dialectics and Humanism; the Polish philosophical quarterly. q.
- Folia Forestalia Polonica. Series A. Lesnictwo. (pub. by Panstwowe Wydawnictwo Naukowe)
- Humanizacja Pracy/Humanization of Work. (pub. by Ossolineum, Publishing House of the Polish Academy of Sciences)
- Nauka Polska. (pub. by Ossolineum, Publishing House of the Polish Academy of Sciences)
- Polish Academy of Sciences. Review. (pub. by Ossolineum, Publishing House of the Polish Academy of Sciences)
- Postepy Napedu Elektrycznego. (pub. by Panstwowe Wydawnictwo Naukowe)
- Problemy Rejonow Uprzemyslawianych. (pub. by Panstwowe Wydawnictwo Naukowe)
- Studia i Materialy do Teorii i Historii Architektury i Urbanistyki. (pub. by Panstwowe Wydawnictwo Naukowe)
- Studia Naturae. Seria A. Wydawnictwa Naukowe. (pub. by Panstwowe Wydawnictwo Naukowe)
- Studia Naturae. Seria B. Wydawnictwa Popularno-Naukowe. (pub. by Panstwowe Wydawnictwo Naukowe)

**Polska Akademia Nauk. Biblioteka**
- Ze Skarbca Kultury. (pub. by Ossolineum, Publishing House of the Polish Academy of Sciences)

**Polska Akademia Nauk. Biblioteka Gdanska**
Walowa 15, Gdansk, Poland.
- Libri Gedanenses. a. ISSN 0075-9163

**Polska Akademia Nauk. Biblioteka, Krakow**
- Polska Akademia Nauk. Biblioteka, Krakow. Rocznik. (pub. by Ossolineum, Publishing House of the Polish Academy of Sciences)

**Polska Akademia Nauk. Centrum Obliczeniowe**
Palac Kultury i Nauki, Pok. 1050, 00-901 Warsaw, Poland.
- Polska Akademia Nauk. Centrum Obliczeniowe. Prace. irreg., 1973, no. 100. ISSN 0079-3175

**Polska Akademia Nauk. Committee on Research and Peaceful Uses of Outer Space**
- Artificial Satellites. (pub. by Panstwowe Wydawnictwo Naukowe)

**Polska Akademia Nauk. Committee on the Science of Science**
- Problems of the Science of Science. (pub. by D. Reidel Publishing Co. NE)

**Polska Akademia Nauk. Instytut Badan Literackich**
Nowy Swiat 72, Palac Staszica, 00-330 Warsaw, Poland.
- Archiwum Literackie. (pub. by Ossolineum, Publishing House of the Polish Academy of Sciences)
- Biblioteka Pisarzow Polskich. (pub. by Ossolineum, Publishing House of the Polish Academy of Sciences)
- Biuletyn Polonistyczny. (pub. by Ossolineum, Publishing House of the Polish Academy of Sciences)
- Ksiazka w Dawnej Kulturze Polskiej. (pub. by Ossolineum, Publishing House of the Polish Academy of Sciences)
- Kwartalnik Historii Prasy Polskiej. (pub. by Ossolineum, Publishing House of the Polish Academy of Sciences)
- Obraz Literatury Polskiej. (pub. by Panstwowe Wydawnictwo Naukowe)
- Pamietnik Literacki. (pub. by Ossolineum, Publishing House of the Polish Academy of Sciences)
- Poetyka. Zarys Encyklopedyczny. (pub. by Ossolineum, Publishing House of the Polish Academy of Sciences)

- Polonia Typographica Saeculi Sedecimi. (pub. by Ossolineum, Publishing House of the Polish Academy of Sciences)
- Polska Bibliografia Literacka. (pub. by Panstwowe Wydawnictwo Naukowe)
- Sredniowiecze.Studia o Kulturze/Etudes sur la Culture Medievale/Middle Ages Studies in Culture. a. ISSN 0079-3183
- Studia Staropolskie. (pub. by Ossolineum, Publishing House of the Polish Academy of Sciences)
- Studia z Okresu Oswiecenia. (pub. by Ossolineum, Publishing House of the Polish Academy of Sciences)
- Teksty. (pub. by Ossolineum Publishing House of the Polish Academy of Sciences)
- Z Dziejow Form Artystycznych w Literaturze Polskiej. (pub. by Ossolineum, Publishing House of the Polish Academy of Sciences)

**Polska Akademia Nauk. Instytut Biologii Doswiadczalnej im. M. Nenckiego**
- Acta Neurobiologiae Experimentalis. (pub. by Panstwowe Wydawnictwo Naukowe)
- Acta Protozoologica. (pub. by Panstwowe Wydawnictwo Naukowe)
- Polskie Archiwum Hydrobiologii/Polish Archives of Hydrobiology. (pub. by Panstwowe Wydawnictwo Naukowe)

**Polska Akademia Nauk. Instytut Botaniki**
Lubicz 46, Krakow, Poland.
- Acta Palaeobotanica. (pub. by Panstwowe Wydawnictwo Naukowe)
- Atlas Flory Polskiej i Ziem Osciennych. (pub. by Panstwowe Wydawnictwo Naukowe)
- Flora Polska; Rosliny Naczyniowe Polski i Ziem Osciennych. (pub. by Panstwowe Wydawnictwo Naukowe)
- Flora Polska: Rosliny Zarodnikowe Polski i Ziem Osciennych. irreg., 1970, vol. IV. ISSN 0071-5824
- Flora Slodkowodna Polski. irreg., 1969, vol. 11. ISSN 0071-5840
- Fragmenta Floristica et Geobotanica. (pub. by Panstwowe Wydawnictwo Naukowe)

**Polska Akademia Nauk. Instytut Budownictwa Wodnego**
- Archiwum Hydrotechniki. (pub. by Panstwowe Wydawnictwo Naukowe)
- Rozprawy Hydrotechniczne. (pub. by Panstwowe Wydawnictwo Naukowe)

**Polska Akademia Nauk. Instytut Chemii Fizycznej**
Kasprzaka 44/52, 01-224 Warsaw, Poland.
- International Conference on Calorimetry and Thermodynamics. Proceedings. irreg., 1st, Warsaw, 1969.

**Polska Akademia Nauk. Instytut Ekologii**
- Ekologia Polska/Polish Ecology. (pub. by Panstwowe Wydawnictwo Naukowe)
- Polish Ecological Studies. (pub. by Panstwowe Wydawnictwo Naukowe)
- Wiadomosci Ekologiczne. (pub. by Panstwowe Wydawnictwo Naukowe)

**Polska Akademia Nauk. Instytut Farmakologii**
- Polish Journal of Pharmacology and Pharmacy. (pub. by Panstwowy Zaklad Wydawnictw Lekarskich)

**Polska Akademia Nauk. Instytut Filozofii i Socjologii**
Nowy Swiat 72, Warsaw, Poland.
- Analizy i Proby Technik Badawczych w Socjologii. (pub. by Ossolineum, Publishing House of the Polish Academy of Sciences)
- Archiwum Historii Filozofii i Mysli Spolecznej. (pub. by Ossolineum, Publishing House of the Polish Academy of Sciences)
- Biblioteka Pisarzy Reformacyjnych. (pub. by Panstwowe Wydawnictwo Naukowe)
- Etyka. (pub. by Panstwowe Wydawnictwo Naukowe)
- Mediaevalia Philosophica Polonorum. (pub. by Ossolineum, Publishing House of the Polish Academy of Sciences)
- Roczniki Socjologii Wsi. Studia i Materialy. (pub. by Ossolineum, Publishing House of the Polish Academy of Sciences)
- Studia Estetyczne. (pub. by Panstwowe Wydawnictwo Naukowe)
- Studia Filozoficzne. (pub. by Panstwowe Wydawnictwo Naukowe)
- Studia Logica. (pub. by Ossolineum, Publishing House of the Polish Academy of Sciences)

- Studia Mediewistyczne/Mediaevistic Studies. ISSN 0039-3231
- Studia Religioznawcze. (pub. by Wydawnictwo Ksiazka i Wiedza)
- Studia Socjologiczne. (pub. by Ossolineum, Publishing House of the Polish Academy of Sciences)

**Polska Akademia Nauk. Instytut Fizyki**
- Acta Physica Polonica. (pub. by Panstwowe Wydawnictwo Naukowe)

**Polska Akademia Nauk. Instytut Genetyki Roslin**
- Genetica Polonica. (pub. by Panstwowe Wydawnictwo Naukowe)

**Polska Akademia Nauk. Instytut Geofizyki**
- Polska Akademia Nauk. Instytut Geofizyki. Materialy i Prace. (pub. by Panstwowe Wydawnictwo Naukowe)
- Rocznik Elektrycznosci Atmosferycznej i Meteorologii. (pub. by Panstwowe Wydawnictwo Naukowe)
- Rocznik Magnetyczny/Annuaire Magnetique. (pub. by Panstwowe Wydawnictwo Naukowe)

**Polska Akademia Nauk. Instytut Geografii**
- Dokumentacja Geograficzna. (pub. by Ossolineum, Publishing House of the Polish Academy of Sciences)
- Geographia Polonica. (pub. by Panstwowe Wydawnictwo Naukowe)
- Polska Akademia Nauk. Instytut Geografii. Prace Geograficzne. (pub. by Ossolineum, Publishing House of the Polish Academy of Sciences)
- Przeglad Geograficzny/Polish Geographical Review. (pub. by Panstwowe Wydawnictwo Naukowe)
- Przeglad Zagranicznej Literatury Geograficznej. (pub. by Ossolineum, Publishing House of the Polish Academy of Sciences)

**Polska Akademia Nauk. Instytut Historii**
- Acta Poloniae Historica. (pub. by Ossolineum, Publishing House of the Polish Academy of Sciences)
- Bibliografia Historii Polskiej. (pub. by Ossolineum, Publishing House of the Polish Academy of Sciences)
- Czasopismo Prawno-Historyczne. (pub. by Panstwowe Wydawnictwo Naukowe)
- Dzieje Najnowsze. (pub. by Ossolineum, Publishing House of the Polish Academy of Sciences)
- Estudios Latinoamericanos. (pub. by Ossolineum, Publishing House of the Polish Academy of Sciences)
- Kwartalnik Historyczny. (pub. by Panstwowe Wydawnictwo Naukowe)
- Lustracje Dobr Krolewskich XVI-XVIII Wieku. (pub. by Panstwowe Wydawnictwo Naukowe)
- Odrodzenie i Reformacja w Polsce. (pub. by Ossolineum, Publishing House of the Polish Academy of Sciences)
- Polska Klasa Robotnicza. Studia Historyczna. (pub. by Panstwowe Wydawnictwo Naukowe)
- Powstanie Styczniowe. Materialy i Dokumenty. (pub. by Ossolineum, Publishing House of the Polish Academy of Sciences)
- Studia i Materialy z Dziejow Polski w Okresie Oswiecenia. (pub. by Panstwowe Wydawnictwo Naukowe)
- Studia Warszawskie. (pub. by Panstwowe Wydawnictwo Naukowe)
- Studia z Dziejow ZSRR i Europy Srodkowej. (pub. by Ossolineum, Publishing House of the Polish Academy of Sciences)
- Studia Zrodloznawcze. (pub. by Panstwowe Wydawnictwo Naukowe)

**Polska Akademia Nauk. Instytut Historii Kultury Materialnej**
Ul. Swierczewskiego 105, Warsaw, Poland.
- Archaeologia Polona. (pub. by Ossolineum, Publishing House of the Polish Academy of Sciences)
- Archeologia. (pub. by Ossolineum, Publishing House of the Polish Academy of Sciences)
- Archeologia Polski. (pub. by Ossolineum, Publishing House of the Polish Academy of Sciences)
- Biblioteka Etnografii Polskiej. (pub. by Ossolineum, Publishing House of the Polish Academy of Sciences)

- Etnografia Polska. (pub. by Ossolineum, Publishing House of the Polish Academy of Sciences)
- Informator Archeologiczny. a. ISSN 0085-1876 (Co-sponsor: Ministerstwo Kultury i Sztuki)
- Kwartalnik Historii Kultury Materialnej. (pub. by Panstwowe Wydawnictwo Naukowe)
- Polish Archaeological Abstracts. (pub. by Ossolineum, Publishing House of the Polish Academy of Sciences)
- Przeglad Archeologiczny. (pub. by Ossolineum, Publishing House of the Polish Academy of Sciences)
- Sprawozdania Archeologiczne. (pub. by Ossolineum, Publishing House of the Polish Academy of Sciences)
- Studia z Dziejow Gornictwa i Hutnictwa. (pub. by Ossolineum, Publishing House of the Polish Academy of Sciences)
- Studia z Dziejow Osadnictwa. (pub. by Ossolineum, Publishing House of the Polish Academy of Sciences)

**Polska Akademia Nauk. Instytut Immunologii i Terapii Doswiadczalnej**
Czerska 12, 53-114 Wroclaw, Poland
(Dist. by Ars Polona-Ruch, Krakowskie Przedmiescie 7, Warsaw, Poland)
- Postepy Higieny i Medycyny Doswiadczalnej. bi-m. ISSN 0032-5449

**Polska Akademia Nauk. Instytut Jezyka Polskiego**
- Polonica. (pub. by Ossolineum, Publishing House of the Polish Academy of Sciences)

**Polska Akademia Nauk. Instytut Krajow Socjalistycznych**
Palac Kultury i Nauki, Pok. 1706, 00-901 Warsaw, Poland.
- Polska Akademia Nauk. Instytut Krajow Socjalistycznych. Biuletyn Informacyjny. q. ISSN 0006-3991
- Z Dziejow Stosunkow Polskoradzieckich. Studia i Materialy. (pub. by Wydawnictwo "Ksiazka i Wiedza")

**Polska Akademia Nauk. Instytut Maszyn Przeplywowych**
- Polska Akademia Nauk. Instytut Maszyn Przeplywowych. Prace. (pub. by Panstwowe Wydawnictwo Naukowe)

**Polska Akademia Nauk. Instytut Matematyczny**
- Acta Arithmetica. (pub. by Panstwowe Wydawnictwo Naukowe)
- Annales Polonici Mathematici. (pub. by Panstwowe Wydawnictwo Naukowe)
- Colloquium Mathematicum. (pub. by Panstwowe Wydawnictwo Naukowe)
- Dissertationes Mathematicae/Rozprawy Matematyczne. (pub. by Panstwowe Wydawnictwo Naukowe)
- Fundamenta Mathematicae. (pub. by Panstwowe Wydawnictwo Naukowe)
- Monografie Matematyczne. (pub. by Panstwowe Wydawnictwo Naukowe)
- Polish Academy of Sciences. Mathematical Institute. Banach Center Publications. (pub. by Panstwowe Wydawnictwo Naukowe)
- Studia Mathematica. (pub. by Panstwowe Wydawnictwo Naukowe)
- Zastosowania Matematyki/Applicationes Mathematicae. (pub. by Panstwowe Wydawnictwo Naukowe)

**Polska Akademia Nauk. Instytut Nauk Prawnych**
Nowy Swiat 72, Palac Staszica, Warsaw, Poland
(Dist. by: Ars Polona-Ruch, Krakowskie Przedmiescie 7, Warsaw, Poland)
- Archiwum Kryminologii. (pub. by Ossolineum, Publishing House of the Polish Academy of Sciences)
- Orzecznictwo Sadow Polskich i Komisji Arbitrazowych. (pub. by Panstwowe Wydawnictwo Naukowe)
- Panstwo i Prawo. m. ISSN 0031-0980
- Polish Yearbook of International Law. (pub. by Ossolineum, Publishing House of the Polish Academy of Sciences)
- Przeglad Ustawodawstwa i Czasopism Prawniczych Socjalistycznych Krajow Europy. q. ISSN 0033-2402 (prep. by its Zaklad Dokumentacji i Informacji)
- Przeglad Wybranych Czasopism Prawniczych Krajow Zachodnich. q. ISSN 0033-2429 (prep. by its Zaklad Dokumentacji i Informacji)
- Studia Prawnicze. (pub. by Ossolineum, Publishing House of the Polish Academy of Sciences)

**Polska Akademia Nauk. Instytut Organizacji i Kierowania**
- Control and Cybernetics. (pub. by Panstwowe Wydawnictwo Naukowe)

**Polska Akademia Nauk. Instytut Panstwa i Prawa**
- Droit Polonais Contemporain. (pub. by Ossolineum, Publishing House of the Polish Academy of Sciences)
- Problemy Rad Narodowych. Studia i Materialy. (pub. by Ossolineum, Publishing House of the Polish Academy of Sciences)
- Sovremennoe Polskoe Pravo. (pub. by Ossolineum, Publishing House of the Polish Academy of Sciences)

**Polska Akademia Nauk. Instytut Podstaw Inzynierii Srodowiska**
- Archiwum Ochrony Srodowiska. (pub. by Ossolineum, Publishing House of the Polish Academy of Sciences)
- Polska Akademia Nauk. Instytut Podstaw Inzynierii Srodowiska. Prace i Studia. (pub. by Ossolineum, Publishing House of the Polish Academy of Sciences)

**Polska Akademia Nauk. Instytut Podstawowych Problemow Techniki**
- Archives of Mechanics. (pub. by Panstwowe Wydawnictwo Naukowe)
- Biblioteka Mechaniki Stosowanej. (pub. by Panstwowe Wydawnictwo Naukowe)
- Fluid Dynamics Transactions. (pub. by Panstwowe Wydawnictwo Naukowe)
- Journal of Technical Physics. (pub. by Panstwowe Wydawnictwo Naukowe)
- Polish Academy of Sciences. Institute of Fundamental Technological Research. Scientific Activities. (pub. by Panstwowe Wydawnictwo Naukowe)
- Polska Bibliografia Analityczna Mechaniki/Polish Scientific Abstracts on Mechanics. (pub. by Panstwowe Wydawnictwo Naukowe)
- Rozprawy Inzynierskie/Engineering Transactions. (pub. by Panstwowe Wydawnictwo Naukowe)
- Zagadnienia Drgan Nieliniowych. (pub. by Panstwowe Wydawnictwo Naukowe)

**Polska Akademia Nauk. Instytut Reumatologiczny**
- Reumatologia. (pub. by Panstwowy Zaklad Wydawnictw Lekarskich)

**Polska Akademia Nauk. Instytut Sztuki**
- Almanach Sceny Polskiej. (pub. by Wydawnictwa Artystyczne i Filmowe)
- Biuletyn Historii Sztuki. (pub. by Ossolineum, Publishing House of the Polish Academy of Sciences)
- Katalog Zabytkow Sztuki w Polsce. (pub. by Wydawnictwa Artystyczne i Filmowe)
- Monumenta Musicae in Polonia. (pub. by Panstwowe Wydawnictwo Naukowe)
- Musica Medii Aevi. (pub. by Polskie Wydawnictwo Muzyczne)
- Muzyka. (pub. by Ossolineum, Publishing House of the Polish Academy of Sciences)
- Pamietnik Teatralny. (pub. by Ossolineum, Publishing House of the Polish Academy of Sciences)
- Polska Piesn i Muzyka Ludowa. Zrodla i Materialy. (pub. by Polskie Wydawnictwo Muzyczne)
- Polska Sztuka Ludowa. (pub. by Ossolineum, Publishing House of the Polish Academy of Sciences)
- Rocznik Historii Sztuki. (pub. by Ossolineum, Publishing House of the Polish Academy of Sciences)
- Studia z Historii Sztuki. (pub. by Ossolineum, Publishing House of the Polish Academy of Sciences)
- Szkice o Kulturze Muzycznej XIX Wieku. Studia i Materialy. (pub. by Panstwowe Wydawnictwo Naukowe)

**Polska Akademia Nauk. Instytut Teatru**
- Studia i Materialy z Dziejow Teatru Polskiego. (pub. by Ossolineum, Publishing House of the Polish Academy of Sciences)

**Polska Akademia Nauk. Instytut Zoologii**
- Acta Ornithologica. (pub. by Panstwowe Wydawnictwo Naukowe)
- Annales Zoologici. (pub. by Panstwowe Wydawnictwo Naukowe)
- Fauna Slodkowodna Polski. (pub. by Panstwowe Wydawnictwo Naukowe)

- Folia Biologica. (pub. by Panstwowe Wydawnictwo Naukowe)
- Fragmenta Faunistica. (pub. by Panstwowe Wydawnictwo Naukowe)
- Katalog Fauny Polski. (pub. by Panstwowe Wydawnictwo Naukowe)
- Memorabilia Zoologica. (pub. by Ossolineum, Publishing House of the Polish Academy of Sciences)

**Polska Akademia Nauk. Komitet Akustyki**
- Archiwum Akustyki. (pub. by Panstwowe Wydawnictwo Naukowe)

**Polska Akademia Nauk. Komitet Architektury i Urbanistyki**
- Kwartalnik Architektury i Urbanistyki. (pub. by Panstwowe Wydawnictwo Naukowe)

**Polska Akademia Nauk. Komitet Astronomii**
- Acta Astronomica. (pub. by Panstwowe Wydawnictwo Naukowe)
- Obserwatorium Krakowski. Rocznik Astronomiczny. Dodatek Miedzynarodowy. (pub. by Panstwowe Wydawnictwo Naukowe)

**Polska Akademia Nauk. Komitet Automatyki i Cybernetyki Technicznej**
- Archiwum Automatyki i Telemechaniki. (pub. by Panstwowe Wydawnictwo Naukowe)

**Polska Akademia Nauk. Komitet Badan i Prognoz "Polska 2000"**
- Polska 2000. (pub. by Ossolineum, Publishing House of the Polish Academy of Sciences)

**Polska Akademia Nauk. Komitet Badan Morza**
- Oceanologia. (pub. by Ossolineum, Publishing House of the Polish Academy of Sciences)

**Polska Akademia Nauk. Komitet Badania Polonii Zagranicznej**
- Problemy Polonii Zagranicznej. (pub. by Ossolineum, Publishing House of the Polish Academy of Sciences)

**Polska Akademia Nauk. Komitet Badania Problemow Polonii**
- Przeglad Polonijny. (pub. by Ossolineum, Publishing House of the Polish Academy of Sciences)

**Polska Akademia Nauk. Komitet Budowy Maszyn**
- Zagadnienia Eksploatacji Maszyn/Exploitation Problems of Machines. (pub. by Panstwowe Wydawnictwo Naukowe)

**Polska Akademia Nauk. Komitet Ekonomiki Rolnictwa**
- Roczniki Nauk Rolniczych. Seria G. Ekonomika Rolnictwa. (pub. by Panstwowe Wydawnictwo Naukowe)

**Polska Akademia Nauk. Komitet Elektroniki i Telekomunikacji**
- Elektronika. (pub. by Wydawnictwa Czasopism Technicznych, N.O.T.)

**Polska Akademia Nauk. Komitet Elektrotechniki**
- Rozprawy Elektrotechniczne. (pub. by Panstwowe Wydawnictwo Naukowe)

**Polska Akademia Nauk. Komitet Energetyki**
- Archiwum Energetyki. (pub. by Panstwowe Wydawnictwo Naukowe)

**Polska Akademia Nauk. Komitet Fizyki**
- Nukleonika. (pub. by Panstwowe Wydawnictwo Naukowe)

**Polska Akademia Nauk. Komitet Geodezji**
- Geodezja i Kartografia. (pub. by Panstwowe Wydawnictwo Naukowe)

**Polska Akademia Nauk. Komitet Geofizyki**
- Acta Geophysica Polonica. (pub. by Panstwowe Wydawnictwo Naukowe)

**Polska Akademia Nauk. Komitet Gleboznawstwa i Chemii Rolnej**
- Polish Journal of Soil Science. (pub. by Panstwowe Wydawnictwo Naukowe)

**Polska Akademia Nauk. Komitet Gornictwa**
- Archiwum Gornictwa. (pub. by Panstwowe Wydawnictwo Naukowe)
- Zeszyty Problemowe Gornictwa. (pub. by Panstwowe Wydawnictwo Naukowe)

**Polska Akademia Nauk. Komitet Gospodarki Wodnej**
- Polska Akademia Nauk. Komitet Gospodarki Wodnej. Prace i Studia. (pub. by Panstwowe Wydawnictwo Naukowe)

**Polska Akademia Nauk. Komitet Hutnictwa**
- Archiwum Hutnictwa. (pub. by Panstwowe Wydawnictwo Naukowe)

**Polska Akademia Nauk. Komitet Inzynierii Chemicznej**
- Inzynieria Chemiczna. (pub. by Panstwowe Wydawnictwo Naukowe)

**Polska Akademia Nauk. Komitet Inzynierii Ladowej i Wodnej**
- Archiwum Inzynierii Ladowej. (pub. by Panstwowe Wydawnictwo Naukowe)
- Studia z Zakresu Inzynierii. (pub. by Panstwowe Wydawnictwo Naukowe)

**Polska Akademia Nauk. Komitet Jezykoznawstwa**
- Onomastica. (pub. by Ossolineum, Publishing House of the Polish Academy of Sciences)
- Prace Jezykoznawcze. (pub. by Ossolineum, Publishing House of the Polish Academy of Sciences)
- Prace Onomastyczne. (pub. by Ossolineum, Publishing House of the Polish Academy of Sciences)

**Polska Akademia Nauk. Komitet Melioracji, Lakarstwa i Torfoznawstwa**
- Roczniki Nauk Rolniczych. Seria F. Melioracji i Vzytkow Zielonych. (pub. by Panstwowe Wydawnictwo Naukowe)

**Polska Akademia Nauk. Komitet Mikrobiologii**
- Postepy Mikrobiologii. (pub. by Panstwowe Wydawnictwo Naukowe)

**Polska Akademia Nauk. Komitet Nauk Chemicznych**
- Chemia Stosowana. (pub. by Panstwowe Wydawnictwo Naukowe)
- Roczniki Chemii. (pub. by Panstwowe Wydawnictwo Naukowe)

**Polska Akademia Nauk. Komitet Nauk Demograficznych**
- Przeszlosc Demograficzna Polski. Materialy i Studia. (pub. by Panstwowe Wydawnictwo Naukowe)
- Studia Demograficzne. (pub. by Panstwowe Wydawnictwo Naukowe)

**Polska Akademia Nauk. Komitet Nauk Ekonomicznych**
Pl. Trzech Krzyzy 3/5 (Komisja Planowania), 00-507 Warsaw, Poland
(Dist. by: Ars Polona-Ruch, Krakowskie Przedmiescie 7, Warsaw, Poland)
- Ekonomista. (pub. by Panstwowe Wydawnictwo Ekonomiczne)
- Oeconomica Polona. q. (Co-sponsor: Polskie Towarzystwo Ekonomiczne)

**Polska Akademia Nauk. Komitet Nauk Geologicznych**
- Acta Geologica Polonica. (pub. by Panstwowe Wydawnictwo Naukowe)
- Archiwum Mineralogiczne. (pub. by Wydawnictwa Geologiczne)

**Polska Akademia Nauk. Komitet Nauk o Kulturze Antycznej**
- Archiwum Filologiczne. (pub. by Ossolineum, Publishing House of the Polish Academy of Sciences)
- Bibliotheca Latina Medii et Recentiori Aevi. (pub. by Ossolineum, Publishing House of the Polish Academy of Sciences)
- Meander. (pub. by Panstwowe Wydawnictwo Naukowe)

**Polska Akademia Nauk. Komitet Nauk Orientalistycznych**
- Rocznik Orientalistyczny. (pub. by Panstwowe Wydawnictwo Naukowe)

**Polska Akademia Nauk. Komitet Nauk Pedagogicznych**
- Biblioteka Klasykow Pedagogiki. (pub. by Ossolineum, Publishing House of the Polish Academy of Sciences)
- Paideia. (pub. by Ossolineum, Publishing House of the Polish Academy of Sciences)
- Rocznik Pedagogiczny. (pub. by Ossolineum, Publishing House of the Polish Academy of Sciences)

- Studia Pedagogiczne. (pub. by Ossolineum, Publishing House of the Polish Academy of Sciences)
- Zrodla do Dziejow Mysli Pedagogicznej. (pub. by Ossolineum, Publishing House of the Polish Academy of Sciences)

**Polska Akademia Nauk. Komitet Nauk Psychologicznych**
- Monografie Psychologiczne. (pub. by Ossolineum, Publishing House of the Polish Academy of Sciences)
- Polish Psychological Bulletin. (pub. by Panstwowe Wydawnictwo Naukowe)
- Studia Psychologiczne. (pub. by Ossolineum, Publishing House of the Polish Academy of Sciences)

**Polska Akademia Nauk. Komitet Nauk Socjologicznych**
- Kultura i Spoleczenstwo. (pub. by Panstwowe Wydawnictwo Naukowe)

**Polska Akademia Nauk. Komitet Nauk Weterynaryjnych**
- Polskie Archiwum Weterynaryjne. (pub. by Panstwowe Wydawnictwo Naukowe)

**Polska Akademia Nauk. Komitet Nauk Zootechnicznych**
- Roczniki Nauk Rolniczych. Seria B. Zootechniczna. (pub. by Panstwowe Wydawnictwo Naukowe)
- Roczniki Nauk Rolniczych. Seria H. Rybactwo. (pub. by Panstwowe Wydawnictwo Naukowe)

**Polska Akademia Nauk. Komitet Naukoznawstwa**
- Zagadnienia Naukoznawstwa. (pub. by Ossolineum, Publishing House of the Polish Academy of Sciences)

**Polska Akademia Nauk. Komitet Neofilologiczny**
- Kwartalnik Neofilologiczny. (pub. by Panstwowe Wydawnictwo Naukowe)

**Polska Akademia Nauk. Komitet Ochrony Roslin**
- Roczniki Nauk Rolniczych. Seria E. Ochrona Roslin. (pub. by Panstwowe Wydawnictwo Naukowe)

**Polska Akademia Nauk. Komitet Organizacji Produkcji Rolnej i Wyzwienia Kraju**
- Zagadnienia Ekonomiki Rolnej. (pub. by Panstwowe Wydawnictwo Rolnicze i Lesne)

**Polska Akademia Nauk. Komitet Przestrzennego Zagospodarowania Kraju**
- Polska Akademia Nauk. Komitet Przestrzennego Zagospodarowania Kraju. Biuletyn. (pub. by Panstwowe Wydawnictwo Naukowe)
- Polska Akademia Nauk. Komitet Przestrzennego Zagospodarowania Kraju. Studia. (pub. by Panstwowe Wydawnictwo Naukowe)

**Polska Akademia Nauk. Komitet Slowianoznawstwa**
- Monografie Slawistyczne. (pub. by Ossolineum, Publishing House of the Polish Academy of Sciences)
- Pamietnik Slowianski. (pub. by Ossolineum, Publishing House of the Polish Academy of Sciences)
- Rocznik Slawistyczny. (pub. by Ossolineum, Publishing House of the Polish Academy of Sciences)
- Slavia Orientalis. (pub. by Panstwowe Wydawnictwo Naukowe)
- Studia Polono-Slavica Orientalia. Acta Litteraria. (pub. by Ossolineum, Publishing House of the Polish Academy of Sciences)
- Studia z Filologii Polskiej i Slowianskiej. (pub. by Panstwowe Wydawnictwo Naukowe)

**Polska Akademia Nauk. Komitet Techniki Rolniczej**
- Roczniki Nauk Rolniczych. Seria C.Technika Rolnicza. (pub. by Panstwowe Wydawnictwo Naukowe)

**Polska Akademia Nauk. Komitet Technologii i Chemii Zywnosci**
- Acta Alimentaria Polonica. (pub. by Panstwowe Wydawnictwo Naukowe)

**Polska Akademia Nauk. Komitet Termodynamiki i Spalania**
- Archiwum Procesow Spalania/Archives of Combustion Processes. (pub. by Panstwowe Wydawnictwo Naukowe)

**Polska Akademia Nauk. Komitet Uprawy i Hodowli Roslin**
- Roczniki Nauk Rolniczych. Seria A. Produkcja Roslinna. (pub. by Panstwowe Wydawnictwo Naukowe)

**Polska Akademia Nauk. Muzeum Ziemi**
Al. na Skarpie 20-26, 00-488 Warsaw, Poland.
- Muzeum Ziemi. Prace. irreg. ISSN 0032-6275

**Polska Akademia Nauk. Oddzial w Krakowie**
- Acta Agraria et Silvestria. Series Agraria. (pub. by Panstwowe Wydawnictwo Naukowe)
- Acta Agraria et Silvestria. Series Silvestris. (pub. by Panstwowe Wydawnictwo Naukowe)
- Acta Agraria et Silvestria. Series Zootechnica. (pub. by Panstwowe Wydawnictwo Naukowe)
- Acta Archaeologica Carpathica. (pub. by Ossolineum, Publishing House of the Polish Academy of Sciences)
- Acta Biologica Cracoviensia. Botanica. (pub. by Ossolineum, Publishing House of the Polish Academy of Sciences)
- Acta Biologica Cracoviensia. Zoologia. (pub. by Ossolineum, Publishing House of the Polish Academy of Sciences)
- Archivum Iuridicum Cracoviense. (pub. by Ossolineum, Publishing House of the Polish Academy of Sciences)
- Chemia Analityczna. (pub. by Panstwowe Wydawnictwo Naukowe)
- Folia Forestalia Polonica. Series B. Drzewnictwo. (pub. by Panstwowe Wydawnictwo Naukowe)
- Folia Geographica. Geographica-Oeconomica. (pub. by Ossolineum, Publishing House of the Polish Academy of Sciences)
- Folia Geographica. Geographica-Physica. (pub. by Ossolineum, Publishing House of the Polish Academy of Sciences)
- Folia Historiae Artium. (pub. by Panstwowe Wydawnictwo Naukowe)
- Folia Medica Cracoviensia. (pub. by Ossolineum, Publishing House of the Polish Academy of Sciences)
- Folia Oeconomica Cracoviensia. (pub. by Ossolineum, Publishing House of the Polish Academy of Sciences)
- Folia Orientalia. (pub. by Ossolineum, Publishing House of the Polish Academy of Sciences)
- Folia Quaternaria. (pub. by Ossolineum, Publishing House of the Polish Academy of Sciences)
- Historyka; Studia Metodologiczne. (pub. by Ossolineum, Publishing House of the Polish Academy of Sciences)
- Krakowskie Studia Prawnicze. (pub. by Ossolineum, Publishing House of the Polish Academy of Sciences)
- Nauka dla Wszystkich. (pub. by Panstwowe Wydawnictwo Naukowe)
- Polska Akademia Nauk. Oddzial w Krakowie Komisja Archeologiczna. Prace. (pub. by Ossolineum, Publishing House of the Polish Academy of Sciences)
- Polska Akademia Nauk. Oddzial w Krakowie. Komisja Ceramiczna. Prace: Ceramika. (pub. by Ossolineum, Publishing House of the Polish Academy of Sciences)
- Polska Akademia Nauk. Oddzial w Krakowie. Komisja Filologii Klasycznej. Prace. (pub. by Ossolineum, Publishing House of the Polish Academy of Sciences)
- Polska Akademia Nauk. Oddzial w Krakowie. Komisja Gorniczo-Geodezyjna. Prace: Gornictwo. (pub. by Ossolineum, Publishing House of the Polish Academy of Sciences)
- Polska Akademia Nauk. Oddzial w Krakowie. Komisja Gorniczo-Geodezyjna. Prace: Geodezja. (pub. by Ossolineum, Publishing House of the Polish Academy of Sciences)
- Polska Akademia Nauk. Oddzial w Krakowie. Komisja Historycznoliteracka. Prace. (pub. by Ossolineum, Publishing House of the Polish Academy of Sciences)
- Polska Akademia Nauk. Oddzial w Krakowie. Komisja Historycznoliteracka. Rocznik. (pub. by Ossolineum, Publishing House of the Polish Academy of Sciences)
- Polska Akademia Nauk. Oddzial w Krakowie. Komisja Jezykoznawstwa. Prace. (pub. by Ossolineum, Publishing House of the Polish Academy of Sciences)

- Polska Akademia Nauk. Oddzial w Krakowie. Komisja Jezykoznawstwa. Wydawnictwazrodlowe. (pub. by Ossolineum, Publishing House of the Polish Academy of Sciences)
- Polska Akademia Nauk. Oddzial w Krakowie. Komisja Mechaniki Stosowanej. Prace: Mechanika. (pub. by Ossolineum, Publishing House of the Polish Academy of Sciences)
- Polska Akademia Nauk. Oddzial w Krakowie. Komisja Metalurgiczno-Odlewnicza. Prace: Metalurgia. (pub. by Ossolineum, Publishing House of the Polish Academy of Sciences)
- Polska Akademia Nauk. Oddzial w Krakowie. Komisja Nauk Ekonomicznych. Prace. (pub. by Ossolineum, Publishing House of the Polish Academy of Sciences)
- Polska Akademia Nauk. Oddzial w Krakowie. Komisja Nauk Historycznych. Prace. (pub. by Ossolineum, Publishing House of the Polish Academy of Sciences)
- Polska Akademia Nauk. Oddzial w Krakowie. Komisja Nauk Historycznych. Materialy. (pub. by Ossolineum, Publishing House of the Polish Academy of Sciences)
- Polska Akademia Nauk. Oddzial w Krakowie. Komisja Nauk Mineralogicznych. Prace Mineralogiczne. (pub. by Ossolineum, Publishing House of the Polish Academy of Sciences)
- Polska Akademia Nauk. Oddzial w Krakowie. Komisja Nauk Pedagogicznych. Rocznik. (pub. by Ossolineum, Publishing House of the Polish Academy of Sciences)
- Polska Akademia Nauk. Oddzial w Krakowie. Komisja Nauk Pedagogicznych. Prace. (pub. by Ossolineum, Publishing House of the Polish Academy of Sciences)
- Polska Akademia Nauk. Oddzial w Krakowie. Komisja Naukowych. Sprawozdania z Posiedzen. (pub. by Ossolineum, Publishing House of the Polish Academy of Sciences)
- Polska Akademia Nauk. Oddzial w Krakowie. Komisja Orientalistyczna. Prace. (pub. by Ossolineum, Publishing House of the Polish Academy of Sciences)
- Polska Akademia Nauk. Oddzial w Krakowie. Komisja Slowianoznawstwa. Prace. (pub. by Ossolineum, Publishing House of the Polish Academy of Sciences)
- Polska Akademia Nauk. Oddzial w Krakowie. Komisja Socjologiczna. Prace. (pub. by Ossolineum, Publishing House of the Polish Academy of Sciences)
- Polska Akademia Nauk. Oddzial w Krakowie. Komisja Urbanistyki i Architektury. Teka. (pub. by Ossolineum, Publishing House of the Polish Academy of Sciences)
- Polska Akademia Nauk. Oddzial w Krakowie. Osrodek Dokumentacji Fizjograficznej. Studia. (pub. by Ossolineum, Publishing House of the Polish Academy of Sciences)
- Polska Akademia Nauk. Oddzial w Krakowie. Rocznik. (pub. by Ossolineum, Publishing House of the Polish Academy of Sciences)
- Prace Geologiczne. (pub. by Ossolineum, Publishing House of the Polish Academy of Sciences)
- Ruch Literacki. (pub. by Ossolineum, Publishing House of the Polish Academy of Sciences)
- Studia Geologica Polonica. (pub. by Wydawnictwa Geologiczne)
- Studia Geomorphologica Carpatho-Balcanica. (pub. by Ossolineum, Publishing House of the Polish Academy of Sciences)
- Studia Historyczne. (pub. by Ossolineum, Publishing House of the Polish Academy of Sciences)

**Polska Akademia Nauk. Osrodek Informacji Naukowej**
Ul. Nowy Swiat 72, 00-330 Warsaw, Poland.
- Zagadnienia Informacji Naukowej. s-a.

**Polska Akademia Nauk. Pracownia Dziejow Oswiaty**
- Archiwum Dziejow Oswiaty. (pub. by Ossolineum, Publishing House of the Polish Academy of Sciences)

**Polska Akademia Nauk. Prezydium**
- Academie Polonaise des Sciences. Bulletin. Serie des Sciences Biologiques. (pub. by Panstwowe Wydawnictwo Naukowe)
- Academie Polonaise des Sciences. Bulletin. Serie des Sciences Chimiques. (pub. by Panstwowe Wydawnictwo Naukowe)
- Academie Polonaise des Sciences. Bulletin. Serie des Sciences de la Terre. (pub. by Panstwowe Wydawnictwo Naukowe)

- Academie Polonaise des Sciences. Bulletin. Serie des Sciences Mathematiques, Astronomiques et Physiques. (pub. by Panstwowe Wydawnictwo Naukowe)
- Academie Polonaise des Sciences. Bulletin. Serie des Sciences Techniques. (pub. by Panstwowe Wydawnictwo Naukowe)

**Polska Akademia Nauk. Wydzial Nauk Medycznych**
- Acta Medica Polona. (pub. by Panstwowy Zaklad Wydawnictw Lekarskich)
- Polska Akademia Nauk. Wydzial Nauk Medycznych. Annals/Polish Academy of Sciences. Medical Section. Annals. (pub. by Panstwowy Zaklad Wydawnictw Lekarskich)
- Polska Akademia Nauk. Wydzial Nauk Medycznych. Rozprawy. (pub. by Panstwowy Zaklad Wydawnictw Lekarskich)

**Polska Akademia Nauk. Wydzial Nauk Rolniczych i Lesnych**
- Roczniki Nauk Rolniczych. Seria D. Monografie. (pub. by Panstwowe Wydawnictwo Naukowe)
- Zeszyty Problemowe Postepow Nauk Rolniczych. (pub. by Panstwowe Wydawnictwo Naukowe)

**Polska Akademia Nauk. Zaklad Antropologii**
- Materialy i Prace Antropologiczne. (pub. by Panstwowe Wydawnictwo Naukowe)
- Studies in Physical Anthropology. (pub. by Panstwowe Wydawnictwo Naukowe)

**Polska Akademia Nauk. Zaklad Archeologii Srodziemnomorskiej**
- Polska Akademia Nauk. Zaklad Archeologii Srodziemnomorskiej. Etudes et Travaux. (pub. by Panstwowe Wydawnictwo Naukowe)

**Polska Akademia Nauk. Zaklad Badania Ssakow**
- Acta Theriologica. (pub. by Panstwowe Wydawnictwo Naukowe)

**Polska Akademia Nauk. Zaklad Biologii Wod**
- Acta Hydrobiologica. (pub. by Panstwowe Wydawnictwo Naukowe)

**Polska Akademia Nauk. Zaklad Dendrologii**
- Arboretum Kornickie. (pub. by Panstwowe Wydawnictwo Naukowe)
- Atlas Rozmieszczenia Drzew i Krzewow w Polsce. (pub. by Panstwowe Wydawnictwo Naukowe)

**Polska Akademia Nauk. Zaklad Genetyki Roslin**
Palac Kultury i Nauki, Warsaw, Poland.
- Przeglad Zagranicznej Literatury Naukowej z Zakresu Genetyki i Hodowli Roslin. s-a. ISSN 0033-2453

**Polska Akademia Nauk. Zaklad Historii Nauki i Techniki**
- Kwartalnik Historii Nauki i Techniki/Quarterly Journal of the History of Science and Technology. (pub. by Panstwowe Wydawnictwo Naukowe)
- Monografie z Dziejow Nauki i Techniki. (pub. by Ossolineum, Publishing House of the Polish Academy of Sciences)
- Organon. (pub. by Panstwowe Wydawnictwo Naukowe)
- Studia i Materialy z Dziejow Nauki Polskiej. Seria A. Historia Nauk Spolecznych. (pub. by Panstwowe Wydawnictwo Naukowe)
- Studia i Materialy z Dziejow Nauki Polskiej. Seria B. Historia Nauk Biologicznych i Medycznych. (pub. by Panstwowe Wydawnictwo Naukowe)
- Studia i Materialy z Dziejow Nauki Polskiej. Seria C. Historia Nauk Matematycznych, Fizyko-Chemicznych i Geologiczno-Geograficznych. (pub. by Panstwowe Wydawnictwo Naukowe)
- Studia i Materialy z Dziejow Nauki Polskiej. Seria D. Historia Techniki i Nauk Technicznych. (pub. by Panstwowe Wydawnictwo Naukowe)
- Studia i Materialy z Dziejow Nauki Polskiej. Seria E. Zagadnienia Ogolne. (pub. by Panstwowe Wydawnictwo Naukowe)
- Zrodla do Dziejow Nauki i Techniki. (pub. by Ossolineum, Publishing House of the Polish Academy of Sciences)

**Polska Akademia Nauk. Zaklad Historii Nauki, Oswiaty i Techniki**
- Monografie z Dziejow Oswiaty. (pub. by Ossolineum, Publishing House of the Polish Academy of Sciences)

- Rozprawy z Dziejow Oswiaty. (pub. by Ossolineum, Publishing House of the Polish Academy of Sciences)
- Semiotic-Historical Studies. (pub. by Ossolineum, Publishing House of the Polish Academy of Sciences)
- Studia Copernicana. (pub. by Ossolineum, Publishing House of the Polish Academy of Sciences)

**Polska Akademia Nauk. Zaklad Historii Stosunkow Polsko - Radzieckich**
- Dokumenty i Materialy do Historii Stosunkow Polsko-Radzieckich. (pub. by Wydawnictwo Ksiazka i Wiedza)

**Polska Akademia Nauk. Zaklad Narodowy im. Ossolinskich**
- Polska Akademia Nauk. Zaklad Narodowy im. Ossolinskich. Rocznik. (pub. by Ossolineum, Publishing House of the Polish Academy of Sciences)

**Polska Akademia Nauk. Zaklad Nauk Ekonomicznych**
Palac Kultury i Nauki, Warsaw, Poland.
- Biblioteki Z. N. E. P.A.N. Biuletyn Informacyjny. s-a. ISSN 0006-1859
- Przeglad Zachodnich Czasopism Ekonomicznych. 2-3 per yr. ISSN 0033-2445
- Z Prac Zakladu Nauk Ekonomicznych PAN. 1-2 per yr. ISSN 0044-1503

**Polska Akademia Nauk. Zaklad Nauk Geologicznych**
- Geologia Sudetica. (pub. by Ossolineum, Publishing House of the Polish Academy of Sciences)

**Polska Akademia Nauk. Zaklad Ochrony Przyrody**
- Chronmy Przyrode Ojczysta. (pub. by Panstwowe Wydawnictwo Naukowe)
- Ochrona Przyrody. (pub. by Panstwowe Wydawnictwo Naukowe)

**Polska Akademia Nauk. Zaklad Orientalistyki**
- Prace Orientalistyczne. (pub. by Panstwowe Wydawnictwo Naukowe)

**Polska Akademia Nauk. Zaklad Paleozoologii**
- Acta Palaeontologica Polonica. (pub. by Panstwowe Wydawnictwo Naukowe)
- Palaeontologia Polonica. (pub. by Panstwowe Wydawnictwo Naukowe)

**Polska Akademia Nauk. Zaklad Parazytologii**
- Acta Parasitologica Polonica. (pub. by Panstwowe Wydawnictwo Naukowe)

**Polska Akademia Nauk. Zaklad Prakseologii**
- Prakseologia. (pub. by Panstwowe Wydawnictwo Naukowe)

**Polska Akademia Nauk. Zaklad Slowianoznawstwa**
- Acta Baltico-Slavica. (pub. by Ossolineum, Publishing House of the Polish Academy of Sciences)

**Polska Akademia Nauk. Zaklad Zoologii Systematycznej**
- Acta Zoologica Cracoviensia. (pub. by Panstwowe Wydawnictwo Naukowe)
- Monografie Fauny Polski. (pub. by Panstwowe Wydawnictwo Naukowe)

**Polska Izba Handlu Zagranicznego**
Ul. Trebacka 4, 00-074 Warsaw, Poland
(Dist. by: Ars Polona-Ruch, Krakowskie Przedmiescie 7, Warsaw, Poland)
- Handel Zagraniczny/Foreign Trade. m.(plus special numbers) ISSN 0017-7245
- Rynki Zagraniczne/Foreign Markets. 156 per yr. ISSN 0036-052X

**Polska Izba Handlu Zagranicznego. Maritime Branch**
Pulaskiego 6, 81-368 Gdynia, Poland
(Dist. by: Ars Polona-Ruch, Krakowskie Przedmiescie 7, Warsaw, Poland)
- Polish Maritime News. m. ISSN 0032-2911

**Polska Zjednoczona Partia Robotnicza. Komitet Centralny**
Nowy Swiat 6, 00-920 Warsaw, Poland.
- Archiwum Ruchu Robotniczego. (pub. by Wydawnictwo Ksiazka i Wiedza)
- Ideologia i Polityka. m.

- Nowe Drogi. m. ISSN 0029-5388 (Dist. by: Ars Polona-Ruch, Krakowskie Przedmiescie 7, Warsaw, Poland)

**Polski Instytut Spraw Miedzynarodowych**
Warecka 1a, 00-950 Warsaw, Poland
(Dist. by: Ars Polona-Ruch, Krakowskie Przedmiescie 7, Warsaw, Poland)
- Polish Perspectives. m: ISSN 0032-2962
- Sprawy Miedzynarodowe. m. ISSN 0038-853X
- Studies on International Relations. s-a.
- Studies on the Developing Countries. s-a.
- Zbior Dokumentow/Recueil de Documents. m. ISSN 0044-1929

**Polski Komitet Automatycznego Przetwarzania Informacji NOT**
- Informatyka. (pub. by Wydawnictwa Czasopism Technicznych, N. O. T.)

**Polski Komitet Normalizacji i Miar**
- Normalizacja. (pub. by Wydawnictwa Normalizacyjne)
- Problemy Jakosci. (pub. by Wydawnictwa Normalizacyjne)

**Polski Komitet Pomiarow i Automatyki**
- Pomiary-Automatyka-Kontrola. (pub. by Wydawnictwa Czasopism Technicznych, N.O.T.)

**Polski Zwiazek Esperantystow**
Jasna 6, Warsaw, Poland
(Dist. by: Ars Polona-Ruch, Krakowskie Przedmiescie 7, Warsaw, Poland)
- Pola Esperantisto/Esperantist's Magazine. bi-m. ISSN 0032-2431

**Polski Zwiazek Filatelistow**
Ul. Mokotowska 4/6, Od. Nr. 18, Warsaw, Poland
(Dist. by: Ars Polona-Ruch, Krakowskie Przedmiescie 7, Warsaw, Poland)
- Filatelista. fortn. ISSN 0015-0975

**Polski Zwiazek Inzynierow i Technikow Budownictwa**
- Inzynieria i Budownictwo. (pub. by Panstwowy Zaklad Wydawnictw Lekarskich)
- Przeglad Budowlany/Building Review. (pub. by Wydawnictwa Czasopism Technicznych, N.O.T.)

**Polski Zwiazek Krotkofalowcow**
Ul. Nowy Zjazd 1, Warsaw, Poland.
- Polski Zwiazek Krotkofalowcow. Biuletyn. irreg.

**Polskie Towarzystwo Anatomiczne**
- Postepy Biologii Komorki. (pub. by Panstwowe Wydawnictwo Naukowe)

**Polskie Towarzystwo Anatomopatologow**
- Patologia Polska. (pub. by Panstwowy Zaklad Wydawnictw Lekarskich)

**Polskie Towarzystwo Antropologiczne**
- Przeglad Antropologiczny. (pub. by Panstwowe Wydawnictwo Naukowe)

**Polskie Towarzystwo Archeologiczne**
- Biblioteka Archeologiczna. (pub. by Ossolineum, Publishing House of the Polish Academy of Sciences)

**Polskie Towarzystwo Archeologiczne i Numizmatyczne**
Jezuicka 6, 00-281 Warsaw, Poland
(Dist. by: Ars Polona-Ruch, Krakowskie Przedmiescie 7, Warsaw, Poland)
- Biuletyn Numizmatyczny/Numismatic Bulletin. m (except July and August) ISSN 0006-4017
- Wiadomosci Numizmatyczne. q. ISSN 0043-5155
- Z Otchlani Wiekow. (pub. by Ossolineum, Publishing House of the Polish Academy of Sciences)

**Polskie Towarzystwo Archeologiczne i Numizmatyczne. Oddzial w Lodzki**
Plac Wolnosci 14, Lodz, Poland.
- Lodzki Numizmatyk. q. ISSN 0024-5771 (prep. by its Gabinet Numizmatyczny MAIE)

**Polskie Towarzystwo Astronautyczne**
- Astronautyka. (pub. by Ossolineum, Publishing House of the Polish Academy of Sciences)
- Postepy Astronautyki. (pub. by Ossolineum, Publishing House of the Polish Academy of Sciences)

**Polskie Towarzystwo Astronomiczne**
- Postepy Astronomii. (pub. by Panstwowe Wydawnictwo Naukowe)

**Polskie Towarzystwo Biochemiczne**
- Monografie Biochemiczne. (pub. by Panstwowe Wydawnictwo Naukowe)
- Postepy Biochemii. (pub. by Panstwowe Wydawnictwo Naukowe)

**Polskie Towarzystwo Botaniczne**
- Acta Agrobotanica. (pub. by Panstwowe Wydawnictwo Naukowe)
- Acta Mycologica. (pub. by Panstwowe Wydawnictwo Naukowe)
- Acta Societatis Botanicorum Poloniae. (pub. by Panstwowe Wydawnictwo Naukowe)
- Monographiae Botanicae. (pub. by Panstwowe Wydawnictwo Naukowe)
- Polskie Towarzystwo Botaniczne. Sekcja Dendrologiczna. Rocznik. (pub. by Panstwowe Wydawnictwo Naukowe)
- Wiadomosci Botaniczne. (pub. by Panstwowe Wydawnictwo Naukowe)

**Polskie Towarzystwo Chemiczne**
- Wiadomosci Chemiczne. (pub. by Panstwowe Wydawnictwo Naukowe)

**Polskie Towarzystwo Cybernetyczne**
- Polskie Towarzystwo Cybernetyczne. Biuletyn. (pub. by Ossolineum, Publishing House of the Polish Academy of Sciences)

**Polskie Towarzystwo Dermatoiogiczne**
- Przeglad Dermatologiczny. (pub. by Panstwowy Zaklad Wydawnictw Lekarskich)

**Polskie Towarzystwo Diagnostyki Laboratoryjnej**
- Diagnostyka Laboratoryjna. (pub. by Panstwowy Zaklad Wydawnictw Lekarskich)

**Polskie Towarzystwo Ekonomiczne**
Nowy Swiat 49, 00-042 Warsaw, Poland
(Dist. by: Ars Polona-Ruch, Krakowskie Przedmiescie 7, Warsaw, Poland)
- Problemy Ekonomiczne. q. ISSN 0079-578X
- Wroclawski Rocznik Ekonomiczny. (pub. by Panstwowe Wydawnictwo Naukowe. Oddzial we Wroclawiu)

**Polskie Towarzystwo Ekonomiczne. Oddzial w Opolu**
- Opolskie Roczniki Ekonomiczne. (pub. by Panstwowe Wydawnictwo Naukowe)

**Polskie Towarzystwo Ekonomiczne. Oddzial we Wroclawiu**
- Przeglad Gospodarczy. (pub. by Wydawnictwa Czasopism Technicznych, N.O.T)

**Polskie Towarzystwo Ekonomiczne. Sekcja Statystyki**
- Przeglad Statystyczny/Statistical Review. (pub. by Panstwowe Wydawnictwo Naukowe)

**Polskie Towarzystwo Entomologiczne**
- Klucze do Oznaczania Owadow Polski. (pub. by Panstwowe Wydawnictwo Naukowe)
- Polskie Pismo Eutomologiczne/Bulletin Entomologique de Pologne. (pub. by Panstwowe Wydawnictwo Naukowe)

**Polskie Towarzystwo Farmaceutyczne**
- Bromatologia i Chemia Toksykologiczna. (pub. by Panstwowy Zaklad Wydawnictw Lekarskich)
- Farmacja Polska. (pub. by Panstwowy Zaklad Wydawnictw Lekarskich)

**Polskie Towarzystwo Filologiczne**
- Eos. (pub. by Ossolineum, Publishing House of the Polish Academy of Sciences)

**Polskie Towarzystwo Filozoficzne**
Palac Kultury i Nauki, Pok. 22-21, 00-901 Warsaw, Poland
(Dist. by: Ars Polona-Ruch, Krakowskie Przedmiescie 7, Warsaw, Poland)
- Ruch Filozoficzny. q. ISSN 0035-9599

**Polskie Towarzystwo Fizyczne**
- Postepy Fizyki. (pub. by Panstwowe Wydawnictwo Naukowe)

**Polskie Towarzystwo Geofizyczne**
- Przeglad Geofizyczny. (pub. by Panstwowe Wydawnictwo Naukowe)

**Polskie Towarzystwo Geograficzne**
- Czasopismo Geograficzne/Geographical Journal. (pub. by Panstwowe Wydawnictwo Naukowe)
- Polski Przeglad Kartograficzny/Polish Cartographical Review. (pub. by Panstwowe Przedsiebiorstwo Wydawnictw Kartograficznych)

- Poznaj Swiat. (pub. by Panstwowe Wydawnictwo Naukowe)

**Polskie Towarzystwo Geologiczne**
- Polskie Towarzystwo Geologiczne. Rocznik/ Societe Geologique de Pologne. Annales. (pub. by Panstwowe Wydawnictwo Naukowe)

**Polskie Towarzystwo Ginekologiczne**
- Ginekologia Polska. (pub. by Panstwowy Zaklad Wydawnictw Lekarskich)

**Polskie Towarzystwo Gleboznawcze**
- Roczniki Gleboznawcze. (pub. by Panstwowe Wydawnictwo Naukowe)

**Polskie Towarzystwo Hematologiczne**
- Acta Haematologica Polonica. (pub. by Panstwowy Zaklad Wydawnictw Lekarskich)

**Polskie Towarzystwo Histochemikow i Cytochemikow**
- Folia Histochemica et Cytochemica. (pub. by Panstwowe Wydawnictwo Naukowe)

**Polskie Towarzystwo Historii Medycyny**
- Archiwum Historii Medycyny. (pub. by Panstwowy Zaklad Wydawnictw Lekarskich)

**Polskie Towarzystwo Historyczne. Instytut Mazurski**
Al. Zwyciestwa 32, 10-578 Olsztyn, Poland
(Dist. by: Ars Polona-Ruch, Krakowskie Przedmiescie 7, Warsaw, Poland)
- Komunikaty Mazursko-Warminskie; czasopismo poswiecone przeszlosci ziem Polski polnocne- wschodniej. q. ISSN 0023-3196

**Polskie Towarzystwo Historyczne. Oddzial w Grudziadzu**
Murowa 29, Grudziadz, Poland
(Dist. by Ars Polona-Ruch, Krakowskie Przedmiescie 7, Warsaw, Poland)
- Rocznik Grudziadzki. a. ISSN 0080-3464

**Polskie Towarzystwo Historyczne. Oddzial w Lodzki**
- Rocznik Lodzki. (pub. by Panstwowe Wydawnictwo Naukowe)

**Polskie Towarzystwo Historyczne. Oddzial w Lublinie**
- Rocznik Lubelski. (pub. by Wydawnictwo Lubelskie)

**Polskie Towarzystwo Historyczne. Oddzial w Nowy Sacz**
Rynek Ratusz, Nowy Sacz, Poland.
- Rocznik Sadecki. a. ISSN 0080-3561

**Polskie Towarzystwo Historyczne. Oddzial w Pila**
- Rocznik Nadnotecki. (pub. by Wydawnictwo Poznanskie)

**Polskie Towarzystwo Historyczne. Oddzial w Poznaniu**
- Studia i Materialy do Dziejow Wielkopolski i Pomorza. (pub. by Panstwowe Wydawnictwo Naukowe)

**Polskie Towarzystwo Jezykoznawcze**
- Polskie Towarzystwo Jezykoznawcze. Biuletyn. (pub. by Ossolineum, Publishing House of the Polish Academy of Sciences)

**Polskie Towarzystwo Lesne**
- Sylwan. (pub. by Panstwowe Wydawnictwo Rolnicze i Lesne)

**Polskie Towarzystwo Ludoznawcze**
Ul. Szewska 36, 50-139 Wroclaw, Poland
(Dist. by Ars Polona-Ruch, Krakowskie Przedmiescie 7, Warsaw, Poland)
- Archiwum Etnograficzne. irreg. ISSN 0066-6858
- Atlas Polskich Strojow Ludowych. irreg. ISSN 0067-0316
- Biblioteka Popularnonaukowa. irreg. ISSN 0067-7760
- Literatura Ludowa. bi-m. ISSN 0024-4708
- Lud. a. ISSN 0076-1435
- Prace Etnologiczne. irreg.
- Prace i Materialy Etnograficzne. irreg. ISSN 0079-4759

**Polskie Towarzystwo Ludoznawcze. Oddzial w Lodzki**
- Lodzkie Studia Etnograficzne. (pub. by Panstwowe Wydawnictwo Naukowe)

**Polskie Towarzystwo Matematyczne**
Ul. Sniadeckich 8, 00-950 Warsaw, Poland.
- Annales Societatis Mathematicae Polonae. Series 1: Commentationes Mathematicae. s-a. ISSN 0032-3799
- Annales Societatis Mathematicae Polonae. Series 3: Matematyka Stosowana. 3-4 per yr.
- Delta; matematyczno-fizyczny miesiecznik popularny. m. (Co-Sponsor: Polskie Towarzystwo Fizyczne) (Dist. by: Ars Polona-Ruch, Krakowskie Przedmiescie 7, Warsaw, Poland)
- Polskie Towarzystwo Matematyczne. Roczniki. Seria I: Commentationes Mathematicae. Prace Matematyczne. (pub. by Panstwowe Wydawnictwo Naukowe)
- Polskie Towarzystwo Matematyczne. Roczniki. Seria II. Wiadomosci Matematyczne. 3-4 per yr. ISSN 0079-3698 (Dist. by: Ars Polona-Ruch, Krakowskie Przedmiescie 7, Warsaw, Poland)

**Polskie Towarzystwo Mechaniki Teoretycznej i Stosowanej**
- Mechanika Teoretyczna i Stosowana. (pub. by Panstwowe Wydawnictwo Naukowe)

**Polskie Towarzystwo Mikrobiologow**
- Acta Microbiologica Polonica. (pub. by Panstwowe Wydawnictwo Naukowe)

**Polskie Towarzystwo Milosnikow Astronomii**
Ul. Solskiego 30, Krakow, Poland
(Dist. by: Ars Polona - Ruch, Krakowskie Przedmiescie 7, Warsaw, Poland)
- Urania. m. ISSN 0042-0794

**Polskie Towarzystwo Mineralogiczne**
Al. Mickiewicza 30, Krakow, Poland.
- Mineralogia Polonica. q. ISSN 0032-6267

**Polskie Towarzystwo Nauk Politycznych**
- Polish Round Table. (pub. by Ossolineum, Publishing House of the Polish Academy of Sciences)

**Polskie Towarzystwo Nauk Weterynaryjnych**
- Medycyna Weterynaryjna. (pub. by Panstwowe Wydawnictwo Rolnicze i Lesne)

**Polskie Towarzystwo Nautologiczne**
- Nautologia. (pub. by Ossolineum, Publishing House of the Polish Academy of Sciences)

**Polskie Towarzystwo Orientalistyczne**
- Przeglad Orientalistyczny. (pub. by Panstwowe Wydawnictwo Naukowe)

**Polskie Towarzystwo Ortopedyczne i Traumatologiczne**
- Chirurgia Narzadow Ruchu i Ortopedia Polska. (pub. by Panstwowy Zaklad Wydawnictw Lekarskich)

**Polskie Towarzystwo Otolaryngologiczne**
Nowogrodzka 59, 02-006 Warsaw, Poland
(Dist. by: Ars Polona-Ruch, Krakowskie Przedmiescie 7, Warsaw, Poland)
- Otolaryngologia Polska. s-m. ISSN 0030-6657

**Polskie Towarzystwo Parazytologiczne**
Norwida 29, 50-375 Wroclaw, Poland.
- International Commission on Trichinellosis. Proceedings. irreg. ISSN 0074-3356
- Katalog Fauny Pasozytniczej Polski. (pub. by Panstwowe Wydawnictwo Naukowe)
- Wiadomosci Parazytologiczne. (pub. by Panstwowe Wydawnictwo Naukowe)

**Polskie Towarzystwo Pediatryczne**
- Pediatria Polska. (pub. by Panstwowy Zaklad Wydawnictw Lekarskich)

**Polskie Towarzystwo Przyrodnikow im. Kopernika**
- Kosmos. Series A. Biologia. (pub. by Panstwowe Wydawnictwo Naukowe)
- Wszechswiat/Universe. (pub. by Panstwowe Wydawnictwo Naukowe)

**Polskie Towarzystwo Psychologiczne**
- Przeglad Psychologiczny/Psychological Review. (pub. by Ossolineum, Publishing House of the Polish Academy of Sciences)
- Psychiatria Polska. (pub. by Panstwowy Zaklad Wydawnictw Lekarskich)

**Polskie Towarzystwo Religioznawcze**
- Euhemer. (pub. by Panstwowe Wydawnictwo Naukowe)

**Polskie Towarzystwo Semiotyczne**
- Studia Semiotyczne. (pub. by Ossolineum, Publishing House of the Polish Academy of Sciences)

**Polskie Towarzystwo Socjologiczne**
- Polish Sociological Bulletin. (pub. by Ossolineum, Publishing House of the Polish Academy of Sciences)
- Polish Sociology. (pub. by Ossolineum, Publishing House of the Polish Academy of Sciences)

**Polskie Towarzystwo Szpitalnictwa**
Mokotowska 14, 00-561 Warsaw, Poland
(Dist. by: Ars Polona-Ruch, Krakowskie Przedmiescie 7, Warsaw, Poland)
- Szpitalnictwo Polskie. bi-m.

**Polskie Towarzystwo Zoologiczne**
Sienkiewicza 21, 50-335 Wroclaw, Poland
(Dist. by: Ars Polona-Ruch, Krakowskie Przedmiescie 7, Warsaw, Poland)
- Przeglad Zoologiczny. (pub. by Panstwowe Wydawnictwo Naukowe)
- Ring; international ornithological bulletin. q. ISSN 0035-5429
- Zoologica Poloniae. (pub. by Panstwowe Wydawnictwo Naukowe)

**Polskie Zrzeszenie Inzynierow i Technikow Sanitarnych**
- Cieplownictwo, Ogrzewnictwo, Wentylacja. (pub. by Wydawnictwa Czasopism Technicznych, N.O.T)
- Gaz, Woda i Technika Sanitarna. (pub. by Wydawnictwa Czasopism Technicznych, N.O.T)

**Wydawnictwo Poznanskie**
Ul. Fredry 8, Poznan, Poland.
- Rocznik Kaliski. irreg.
- Rocznik Nadnotecki. irreg. ISSN 0557-2088 (Polskie Towarzystwo Historyczne. Oddzial w Pila)

**Poznanskie Towarzystwo Przyjaciol Nauk**
Mielzynskiego 27/29, 61-725 Poznan, Poland
(Dist. by Ars Polona-Ruch, Krakowskie Przedmiescie 7, Warsaw, Poland)
- Badania Fizjograficzne nad Polska Zachodnia. Seria A. Geografia Fizyczna. (pub. by Panstwowe Wydawnictwo Naukowe)
- Badania Fizjograficzne nad Polska Zachodnia. Seria B. Biologia. (pub. by Panstwowe Wydawnictwo Naukowe)
- Badania Fizjograficzne nad Polska Zachodnia. Seria C. Zoologia. (pub. by Panstwowe Wydawnictwo Naukowe)
- Badania z Dziejow Spolecznych i Gospodarczych. (pub. by Panstwowe Wydawnictwo Naukowe)
- Biuletyn Fonograficzny/Bulletin Phonographique. (pub. by Panstwowe Wydawnictwo Naukowe)
- Immunologia Polska. (pub. by Panstwowe Wydawnictwo Naukowe)
- Lingua Posnaniensis. a. ISSN 0079-4740
- Poznanskie Towarzystwo Przyjaciol Nauk. Komisja Biologiczny. Prace. irreg., 1972, vol. 35, no. 5. ISSN 0079-4619
- Poznanskie Towarzystwo Przyjaciol Nauk. Komisja Budownictwa i Architektury. Prace. (pub. by Panstwowe Wydawnictwo Naukowe)
- Poznanskie Towarzystwo Przyjaciol Nauk. Komisja Elektrotechniki. Prace. (pub. by Panstwowe Wydawnictwo Naukowe)
- Poznanskie Towarzystwo Przyjaciol Nauk. Komisja Filozoficzna. Prace. (pub. by Panstwowe Wydawnictwo Naukowe)
- Poznanskie Towarzystwo Przyjaciol Nauk. Komisja Geograficzno-Geologiczna. Prace. (pub. by Panstwowe Wydawnictwo Naukowe)
- Poznanskie Towarzystwo Przyjaciol Nauk. Komisja Historii Sztuki. Prace. irreg. ISSN 0079-466X (prep. by its Komisja Historii Sztuki)
- Poznanskie Towarzystwo Przyjaciol Nauk. Komisja Historyczna. Prace. (pub. by Panstwowe Wydawnictwo Naukowe)
- Poznanskie Towarzystwo Przyjaciol Nauk. Komisja Jezykoznawcza. Prace. irreg. ISSN 0079-4678
- Poznanskie Towarzystwo Przyjaciol Nauk. Komisja Matematyczno-Przyrodnicza. Prace. irreg. ISSN 0079-4686
- Poznanskie Towarzystwo Przyjaciol Nauk. Komisja Nauk Rolniczych i Komisja Nauk Lesnych. Prace. irreg., 1972, vol. 34. ISSN 0079-4708 (Co-sponsor: Komisja Nauk Lesnych)
- Poznanskie Towarzystwo Przyjaciol Nauk. Komisja Nauk Spolecznych. Prace. irreg. ISSN 0079-4716

- Poznanskie Towarzystwo Przyjaciol Nauk. Komisja Technologii Drewna. Prace. a. ISSN 0079-4724
- Roczniki Dziejow Spolecznych i Gospodarczych. (pub. by Panstwowe Wydawnictwo Naukowe)
- Slavia Occidentalis. irreg. ISSN 0081-0002
- Societe des Amis des Sciences et des Lettres de Poznan. Bulletin. Serie D: Sciences Biologiques. irreg., 1972, vol. 12-13. ISSN 0079-4570
- Studia z Automatyki. (pub. by Panstwowe Wydawnictwo Naukowe)

**Wydawnictwo Prawnicze**
Ul. Wisniowa 50, 02-520 Warsaw, Poland
(Dist. by: Ars Polona-Ruch, Krakowskie Przedmiescie 7, Warsaw, Poland)
- Instytut Badania Prawa Sadowego. Zeszyty Naukowe. s-a.
- Nowe Prawo. m.
- Palestra/Bar. m. ISSN 0031-0344

**Przemyslowy Instytut Elektroniki**
Ul. Dluga 44/50, 00-241 Warsaw, Poland.
- Przemyslowy Instytut Elektroniki. Prace. q. ISSN 0509-7053

**Przemyslowy Instytut Maszyn Rolniczych. Branzowy Osrodek Informacji Naukowej, Technicznej i Ekonomicznej**
Starolecka 31, 61-361 Poznan, Poland.
- Przeglad Dokumentacyjny Ciagnikow i Maszyn Rolniczych. m. ISSN 0033-2054
- Przemyslowy Instytut Maszyn Rolniczych. Prace. q. ISSN 0030-8021

**Przemyslowy Instytut Telekomunikacji**
Poligonowa 30, 00-991 Warsaw, Poland
(Dist. by: Ars Polona-Ruch, Krakowskie Przedmiescie 7, Warsaw, Poland)
- Przemyslowy Instytut Telekomunikacji. Prace. q. ISSN 0032-6283

**Rada Prasy Technicznej**
- Prasa Techniczna. (pub. by Wydawnictwa Czasopism Technicznych, N.O.T)

**Panstwowe Wydawnictwo Rolnicze i Lesne**
Al. Jerozolimskie 28, Warsaw, Poland
(Dist. by: Ars Polona-Ruch, Krakowskie Przedmiescie 7, Warsaw, Poland)
- Agrochemia; poradnik nawozenia i ochrony roslin. m. ISSN 0002-1849
- Budownictwo Rolnicze. m.
- Gospodarka Rybna. m. ISSN 0017-243X
- Hodowla Roslin, Aklimatyzacja i Nasiennictwo. bi-m. ISSN 0018-3040
- Las Polski. s-m. ISSN 0023-8538 (Stowarzyszenie Inzynierow i Technikow Lesnictwa i Drzewnictwa)
- Medycyna Weterynaryjna. m. ISSN 0025-8628 (Polskie Towarzystwo Nauk Weterynaryjnych)
- Miedzynarodowe Czasopismo Rolnicze. bi-w. ISSN 0026-3540
- Nowe Rolnictwo. s-m. ISSN 0029-5396
- Ochrona Roslin. m. ISSN 0029-8239
- Postepy Nauk Rolniczych. bi-m. ISSN 0032-5457
- Przeglad Naukowej Literatury Zootechnicznej. a (4 fasc.) ISSN 0079-7162
- Sylwan. m. ISSN 0039-7660 (Polskie Towarzystwo Lesne)
- Zagadnienia Ekonomiki Rolnej. bi-m. ISSN 0044-1600 (Polska Akademia Nauk. Komitet Organizacji Produkcji Rolnej i Wyzwienia Kraju)
- Ziemniak/Kartofel/Potato. irreg. (Instytut Ziemniaka, Bonin)

**Panstwowe Przedsiebiorstwo "Skladnica Ksiegarska"**
Ul. Mazowiecka 9, Warsaw, Poland
(Dist. by: Ars Polona-Ruch, Krakowskie Przedmiescie 7, Warsaw, Poland)
- Zapowiedzi Wydawnicze. w. ISSN 0044-1813

**Wydawnictwo "Slask"**
Ul. Armii Czerwonej 51, 40-014 Katowice, Poland
(Dist. by: Ars Polona - Ruch, Krakowskie Przedmiescie 7, Warsaw, Poland)
- Hutnik. m. ISSN 0018-8077 (Stowarzyszenie Inzynierow i Technikow Przemyslu Hutniczego)
- Instytut Naftowy. Prace. 5-7 per yr. ISSN 0032-6232 (Co-sponsor: Ministerstwo Gornictwa i Energetyki)
- Koks, Smola, Gaz. m. ISSN 0023-2823
- Nafta. m. ISSN 0027-7541 (Instytut Naftowy) (Co-sponsor: Stowarzyszenie Inzynierow i Technikow Przemyslu Naftowego)
- Przeglad Gorniczy. m. ISSN 0033-216X (Glowny Instytut Gornictwa) (Co-Sponsor: Stowarzyszenie Inzynierow i Technikow Gornictwa)

- Rudy i Metale Niezelazne. m. ISSN 0035-9696
- Wiadomosci Gornicze. m. ISSN 0043-5120 (Stowarzyszenie Inzynierow i Technikow Gornictwa)
- Wiadomosci Hutnicze. m. ISSN 0043-5139

**Slaski Instytut Naukowy**
Ul. Francuska 12, Katowice, Poland
(Dist. by Ars Polona-Ruch, Krakowskie Przedmiescie 7, Warsaw, Poland)
- Gornoslaskie Studia Socjologiczne. irreg. ISSN 0072-5013
- Pisarze Slascy XIX i XX Wieku. irreg. ISSN 0079-211X
- Studia i Materialy z Dziejow Slaska. (pub. by Ossolineum, Publishing House of the Polish Academy of Sciences)
- Zaranie Slaskie. q. ISSN 0044-183X

**Spoldzielnia Wydawnicza "Czytelnik"**
Ul. Wiejska 12a, Warsaw, Poland
(Dist. by: Ars Polona- Ruch, Krakowskie Przedmiescie 7, Warsaw, Poland)
- Kultura; tygodnik spoleczno-kulturalny. w. ISSN 0023-5156

**Spoleczny Komitet Przecialkoholonego**
Lwowska 5, 00-660 Warsaw, Poland.
- Problemy Alkoholizmu. m. ISSN 0032-9495
- Zdrowie i Trzezwosc. m.

**Stowarzyszenie Architektow Polskich-SARP**
- Architektura. (pub. by Wydawnictwo Arkady)

**Stowarzyszenie Archiwistow Polskich**
Palac Staszica, Nowy Swiat 72, Warsaw, Poland
(Dist. by: Ars Polona-Ruch, Krakowskie Przedmiescie 7, Warsaw, Poland)
- Archiwista; biuletyn Stowarzyszenia Archiwistow Polskich. q. ISSN 0004-0711 (Co-sponsor: Polska Akademia Nauk. Archiwum)

**Stowarzyszenie Ateistow i Wolnomyslicieli**
Oddzial Wojewod w Krakowie, Krakow, Poland.
- Biblioteczka Ateisty. irreg. ISSN 0067-754X

**Stowarzyszenie Bibliotekarzy Polskich**
Konopczynskiego 5/7, 00-953 Warsaw, Poland
(Dist. by: Ars Polona-Ruch, Krakowskie Przedmiescie 7, Warsaw, Poland)
- Bibliotekarz. m.
- Literatura Piekna. Adnotowany Rocznik Bibliograficzny. a. ISSN 0075-9945 (Biblioteka Narodowa. Instytut Bibliograficzny)
- Poradnik Bibliotekarza. m. ISSN 0032-4752
- Przeglad Biblioteczny. q. ISSN 0033-202X

**Stowarzyszenie Elektrykow Polskich**
- Energetyka. (pub. by Wydawnictwa Czasopism Technicznych N.O.T.)
- Przeglad Elektrotechniczny. (pub. by Wydawnictwa Czasopism Technicznych, N.O.T)
- Przeglad Telekomunikacyjny. (pub. by Wydawnictwa Czasopism Technicznych, N.O.T)
- Wiadomosci Elektrotechniczne. (pub. by Wydawnictwa Czasopism Technicznych, N.O.T)

**Stowarzyszenie Geodetow Polskich**
- Przeglad Geodezyjny. (pub. by Wydawnictwa Czasopism Technicznych, N.O.T.)

**Stowarzyszenie Inzynierow i Technikow Gornictwa**
- Wiadomosci Gornicze. (pub. by Wydawnictwo "Slask")

**Stowarzyszenie Inzynierow i Technikow Komunikacji**
- Przeglad Kolejowy Mechaniczny. (pub. by Wydanictwa Komunikacji i Lacznosci)

**Stowarzyszenie Inzynierow i Technikow Lesnictwa i Drzewnictwa**
- Las Polski. (pub. by Panstwowe Wydawnictwo Rolnicze i Lesne)
- Przemysl Drzewny. (pub. by Wydawnictwa Czasopism Technicznych, N.O.T.)

**Stowarzyszenie Inzynierow i Technikow Mechanikow Polskich**
- Budownictwo Okretowe. (pub. by Wydawnictwa Czasopism Technicznych, N.O.T.)
- Maszyny i Ciagniki Rolnicze. (pub. by Wydawnictwa Czasopism Technicznych, N.O.T)
- Poligrafika. (pub. by Wydawnictwa Czasopism Technicznych, N.O.T.)
- Przeglad Mechaniczny. (pub. by Wydawnictwa Czasopism Technicznych, N.O.T)
- Przeglad Spawalnictwa. (pub. by Wydawnictwa Czasopism Technicznych N.O.T.)

- Rynek i Uslugi. (pub. by Wydawnictwa Czasopism Technicznych, N.O.T.)
- Wiadomosci Warsztatowe. (pub. by Wydawnictwa Czasopism Technicznych, N.O.T)

**Stowarzyszenie Inzynierow i Technikow Przemyslu Chemicznego**
- Chemik. (pub. by Wydawnictwa Czasopism Technicznych, N.O.T)
- Inzynieria i Aparatura Chemiczna. (pub. by Wydawnictwa Czasopism Technicznych, N.O.T)
- Ochrona przed Korozja. (pub. by Wydawnictwa Czasopism Technicznych N. O. T.)

**Stowarzyszenie Inzynierow i Technikow Przemyslu Hutniczego**
- Hutnik. (pub. by Wydawnictwo "Slask")
- Ochrona Powietrza. (pub. by Wydawnictwa Czasopism Technicznych, N.O.T.)

**Stowarzyszenie Inzynierow i Technikow Wodnych i Melioracyjnych**
- Wiadomosci Melioracyjne i Lekarskie. (pub. by Wydawnictwa Czasopism Technicznych, N.O.T)

**Stowarzyszenie Ksiegarzy Polskich**
Ul. Mokotowska 4/6, Warsaw, Poland
(Dist by: Ars Polona-Ruch, Krakowskie Przedmiescie 7, Warsaw, Poland)
- Ksiegarz. q.

**Stowarzyszenie Ksiegowych w Polsce**
- Rachunkowosc. (pub. by Panstwowe Wydawnictwo Ekonomiczne)

**Stowarzyszenie Naukowo-Techniczne Inzynierow i Technikow Przemyslu Spozywczego**
- Przemysl Fermentacyjny i Rolny. (pub. by Wydawnictwa Czasopism Technicznych, N.O.T.)
- Przemysl Spozywczy. (pub. by Wydawnictwa Czasopism Technicznych, N.O.T)
- Wiadomosci Tytoniowe. (pub. by Wydawnictwa Czasopism Technicznych, N.O.T.)
- Wiadomosci Zielarskie. (pub. by Wydawnictwa Czasopism Technicznych, N.O.T.)

**Stowarzyszenie Spoleczno-Kulturalne "Pojezierze"**
- Panorama Polnocy. (pub. by Wydawnictwa Artystyczno-Graficzne RSW "Prasa-Ksiazka-Ruch")

**Stowarzyszenie Technikow Cukrownikow**
- Gazeta Cukrownicza. (pub. by Wydawnictwa Czasopism Technicznych, N.O.T)

**Stowarzyszenie Wlokiennikow Polskich**
- Odziez. (pub. by Wydawnictwa Czasopism Technicznych, N.O.T.)
- Przeglad Wlokienniczy. (pub. by Wydawnictwa Czasopism Technicznych N.O.T.)
- Technik Wlokienniczy. (pub. by Wydawnictwa Czasopism Technicznych, N.O.T.)
- Wiadomosci Produkcyjne-Wlokno, Odziez, Skora. (pub. by Wydawnictwa Czasopism Technicznych, N.O.T.)

**Szczecinskie Towarzystwo Naukowe**
Rycerska 3, 70-537 Szczecin, Poland.
- Szczecinskie Towarzystwo Naukowe. Sprawozdania. irreg. ISSN 0082-1241
- Szczecinskie Towarzystwo Naukowe. Wydzial Nauk Lekarskich. Prace. (pub. by Panstwowy Zaklad Wydawnictw Lekarskich)
- Szczecinskie Towarzystwo Naukowe. Wydzial Nauk Matematyczno Technicznych. Prace. (pub. by Panstwowe Wydawnictwo Naukowe)
- Szczecinskie Towarzystwo Naukowe. Wydzial Nauk Przyrodniczo-Rolniczych. Prace. irreg. ISSN 0082-1276 (prep. by its Wydzial Nauk Przyrodniczo-Rolniczych) (Dist. by: Ars Polona-Ruch, Krakowskie Przedmiescie 7, Warsaw, Poland)
- Szczecinskie Towarzystwo Naukowe. Wydzial Nauk Spolecznych. Prace. (pub. by Panstwowe Wydawnictwo Naukowe)
- Szczecinskie Towarzystwo Naukowe. Wydzial Nauk Spolecznych. Wydawnictwa. (pub. by Panstwowe Wydawnictwo Naukowe)

**Szefostwo Sluzby Zdrowia MON**
Warsaw, Poland.
- Lekarz Wojskowy. m. ISSN 0024-0745

**Szkola Glowna Planowania i Statystyki. Instytut Gospodarstwa Spolecznego**
Al. Niepodleglosci 162, Warsaw, Poland
(Dist. by: Ars Polona-Ruch, Krakowskie Przedmiescie 7, Warsaw, Poland)
- Instytut Gospodarstwa Spolecznego. Biuletyn. q. ISSN 0020-4455

**Wydawnictwa Szkolne i Pedagogiczne**
Ul. Grazyny 15, 02-548 Warsaw, Poland
(Dist. by: Ars Polona-Ruch, Krakowskie Przedmiescie 7, Warsaw, Poland)
- Badania Oswiatowe. q. (Poland. Ministerstwo Oswiaty i Wychowania)
- Biologia w Szkole. 5 per yr. (Poland. Ministerstwo Oswiaty i Wychowania)
- Chemia w Szkole. 5 per yr. ISSN 0411-8634 (Poland. Ministerstwo Oswiaty i Wychowania)
- Fizyka w Szkole. bi-m. ISSN 0426-3383 (Poland. Ministerstwo Oswiaty i Wychowania)
- Geografia w Szkole. 5 per yr. (Poland. Ministerstwo Oswiaty i Wychowania)
- Jezyk Rosyjski; czasopismo dla nauczycieli. 5 per yr. (Poland. Ministerstwo Oswiaty i Wychowania)
- Jezyki Obce w Szkole. 5 per yr. ISSN 0446-7965 (Poland. Ministerstwo Oswiaty i Wychowania)
- Matematyka; czasopismo dla nauczycieli matematyki. bi-m. (Poland. Ministerstwo Oswiaty i Wychowania)
- Oswiata Doroslych. 10 per yr. ISSN 0472-2191 (Poland. Ministerstwo Oswiaty i Wychowania)
- Polonistyka. bi-m. (Poland. Ministerstwo Oswiaty i Wychowania)
- Problemy Opiekunczo- Wychowawcze. 10 per yr. ISSN 0552-2188 (Poland. Ministerstwo Oswiaty i Wychowania)
- Przysposobienie Obronne w Szkole. bi-m. (Poland. Ministerstwo Oswiaty i Wychowania)
- Rodzina i Szkola. m. ISSN 0485-3504
- Szkola Specjalna. q. (Poland. Ministerstwo Oswiaty i Wychowania)
- Wiadomosci Historyczne. bi-m. ISSN 0511-9162 (Poland. Ministerstwo Oswiaty i Wychowania)
- Wychowanie Fizyczne i Higiena Szkolna. 10 per yr. ISSN 0510-9868 (Poland. Ministerstwo Oswiaty i Wychowania)
- Wychowanie Myzyczne w Szkole. 5 per yr. ISSN 0512-4255 (Poland. Ministerstwo Oswiaty i Wychowania)
- Wychowanie Obywatelskie. 10 per yr. ISSN 0512-4263 (Poland. Ministerstwo Oswiaty i Wychowania)
- Wychowanie Techniczne w Szkole. 10 per yr. ISSN 0510-9884 (Poland. Ministerstwo Oswiaty i Wychowania)
- Wychowanie w Przedszkolu. m. (Poland. Ministerstwo Oswiaty i Wychowania)
- Zbiorcza Szkola Gminna. 5 per yr. (Poland. Ministerstwo Oswiaty i Wychowania)
- Zycie Szkoly. m. (Poland. Ministerstwo Oswiaty i Wychowania)

**Towarzystwo Chirurgow Polskich**
- Polski Przeglad Chirurgiczny. (pub. by Panstwowy Zaklad Wydawnictw Lekarskich)

**Towarzystwo Internistow Polskich**
- Polskie Archiwum Medycyny Wewnetrznej/Polish Archives of Internal Medicine. (pub. by Panstwowy Zaklad Wydawnictw Lekarskich)

**Towarzystwo Milosnikow Historii i Zabytkow Krakowa**
Ul. Sw. Jana 12, 31-018 Krakow, Poland
(Dist. by: Ars Polona-Ruch, Krakowskie Przedmiescie 7, Warsaw, Poland)
- Biblioteka Krakowska. irreg., 1976, vol. 116. ISSN 0067-7698
- Krakow Dawniej i Dzis. irreg., 1975, vol. 19. ISSN 0075-7020
- Rocznik Krakowski. (pub. by Ossolineum, Publishing House of the Polish Academy of Sciences)

**Towarzystwo Milosnikow Historii w Warszawie**
Krakowskie Przedmiescie 26/28, Warsaw, Poland
(Dist. by: Ars Polona- Ruch, Krakowskie Przedmiescie 7, Warsaw, Poland)
- Przeglad Historyczny. q. ISSN 0033-2186

**Towarzystwo Milosnikow Jezyka Polskiego**
Straszewskiego 27, 31-113 Krakow, Poland
(Dist. by: Ars Polona- Ruch, Krakowskie Przedmiescie 7, Warsaw, Poland)
- Jezyk Polski. 5 per yr. ISSN 0021-6941

**Towarzystwo Milosnikow Wroclawia**
- Rocznik Wroclawski. (pub. by Ossolineum, Publishing House of the Polish Academy of Sciences)

**Towarzystwo Milosnikow Ziemi Klodzkiej**
- Rocznik Ziemi Klodzkiej. (pub. by Ossolineum, Publishing House of the Polish Academy of Sciences)

**Towarzystwo Naukowe Plockie**
Plac Narutowicza 8, 09-402 Plock, Poland
(Dist. by: Ars Polona-Ruch, Krakowskie Przedmiescie 7, Warsaw, Poland)
- Notatki Plockie; pismo regionalne Mazowsza Plockiego. q. ISSN 0029-389X

**Towarzystwo Naukowe w Toruniu**
Ul. Slowackiego 8, 87-100 Torun, Poland
- Biblioteka Kopernikanska. (pub. by Panstwowe Wydawnictwo Naukowe)
- Prace Popularnonaukowe. (pub. by Panstwowe Wydawnictwo Naukowe)
- Studia Iuridica. irreg. ISSN 0081-6671 (Dist. by: Ars Polona-Ruch, Krakowskie Przedmiescie 7, Warsaw, Poland)
- Studia Societatis Scientiarum Torunensis. Sectio B (Chemia) (pub. by Panstwowe Wydawnictwo Naukowe)
- Studia Societatis Scientiarum Torunensis. Sectio C (Geografia et Geologia) (pub. by Panstwowe Wydawnictwo Naukowe)
- Studia Societatis Scientiarum Torunensis. Sectio D (Botanika) (pub. by Panstwowe Wydawnictwo Naukowe)
- Studia Societatis Scientiarum Torunensis. Sectio E (Zoologia) (pub. by Panstwowe Wydawnictwo Naukowe)
- Studia Societatis Scientiarum Torunensis. Sectio F. (Astronomia) (pub. by Panstwowe Wydawnictwo Naukowe)
- Studia Societatis Scientiarum Torunensis. Sectio G (Physiologia) (pub. by Panstwowe Wydawnictwo Naukowe)
- Towarzystwo Naukowe w Toruniu. Fontes. (pub. by Panstwowe Wydawnictwo Naukowe)
- Towarzystwo Naukowe w Toruniu. Komisja Historii Sztuki. Teka. (pub. by Panstwowe Wydawnictwo Naukowe)
- Towarzystwo Naukowe w Toruniu. Prace Archeologiczne. irreg., 1974, vol. 7.
- Towarzystwo Naukowe w Toruniu. Roczniki. (pub. by Panstwowe Wydawnictwo Naukowe)
- Zapiski Historyczne. (pub. by Panstwowe Wydawnictwo Naukowe)

**Towarzystwo Przyjaciol Ziemi Jeleniogorskiej**
- Rocznik Jeleniogorski. (pub. by Ossolineum, Publishing House of the Polish Academy of Sciences)

**Towarzystwo Wiedzy Powszechnej**
- Problemy. (pub. by Wydawnictwa Artystyczno-Graficzne RSW "Prasa-Ksiazka-Ruch")

**Ukrayins'ke Suspil'no-Kul'turne Tovarystvo**
Ul. Nowogrodzka 15, 00-511 Warsaw, Poland.
- Nashe Slovo. w. ISSN 0027-8254

**Uniwersytet Gdanski**
Ul. Czerwonej Armii 110, 81-824 Sopot, Poland
(Dist. by: Ars Polona-Ruch, Krakowskie Przedmiescie 7, Warsaw, Poland)
- Uniwersytet Gdanski. Wydzial Biologii i Nauk o Ziemi. Zeszyty Naukowe. Geografia. irreg.
- Uniwersytet Gdanski. Wydzial Ekonomiki Produkcji. Zeszyty Naukowe. Zagadnienia Ekonomiki Przemyslu. irreg.
- Uniwersytet Gdanski. Wydzial Ekonomiki Transportu. Zeszyty Naukowe. Ekonomika Transportu Ladowego. irreg.
- Uniwersytet Gdanski. Wydzial Ekonomiki Transportu. Zeszyty Naukowe. Ekonomika Transportu Morskiego. irreg.
- Uniwersytet Gdanski. Wydzial Ekonomiki Transportu. Zeszyty Naukowe. Instytut Ekonomii Politycznej. Prace i Materialy. irreg.
- Uniwersytet Gdanski. Wydzial Ekonomiki Transportu. Zeszyty Naukowe. Instytut Handlu Zagranicznego. Prace i Materialy. irreg.
- Uniwersytet Gdanski. Wydzial Humanistyczny. Zeszyty Naukowe. Filozofia i Socjologia. irreg. ISSN 0072-0453
- Uniwersytet Gdanski. Wydzial Humanistyczny. Zeszyty Naukowe. Historia. irreg. ISSN 0072-0461

- Uniwersytet Gdanski. Wydzial Humanistyczny. Zeszyty Naukowe. Pedagogika, Psychologia, Historia Wychowania. irreg. ISSN 0072-047X
- Uniwersytet Gdanski. Wydzial Humanistyczny. Zeszyty Naukowe. Prace Historyczno-Literackie. irreg. ISSN 0072-0488
- Uniwersytet Gdanski. Wydzial Matematyki, Fizyki, Chemii. Zeszyty Naukowe. Chemia. irreg.
- Uniwersytet Gdanski. Wydzial Matematyki, Fizyki, Chemii. Zeszyty Naukowe. Fizyka. irreg.
- Uniwersytet Gdanski. Wydzial Matematyki, Fizyki, Chemii. Zeszyty Naukowe. Matematyka. irreg.
- Uniwersytet Gdanski. Wydzial Prawa i Administracji. Zeszyty Naukowe. Prawo.

## Uniwersytet im. Adama Mickiewicza
Ul. Stalingradzka 1, Poznan, Poland
- Glottodidactica; an International Journal of Applied Linguistics. irreg., 1975, vol. 8. ISSN 0072-4769 (Dist. by: Ars Polona-Ruch, Krakowskie Przedmiescie 7, Warsaw, Poland)
- Neodidagmata. irreg., vol. 7, 1975. ISSN 0077-653X (prep. by its Miedzywydzialowy Zaklad Nowych Technik Nauczania)
- Quaestiones Geographicae. a.
- Ruch Prawniczy, Ekonomiczny i Socjologiczny. (pub. by Panstwowe Wydawnictwo Naukowe)
- Slavia Antiqua. (pub. by Panstwowe Wydawnictwo Naukowe)
- Studia Anglica Posnaniensia; an International Review of English Studies. irreg., 1976, vol. 8. ISSN 0081-6272 (Dist. by: Ars Polona-Ruch, Krakowskie Przedmiescie 7, Warsaw, Poland)
- Studia Historiae Oeconomica. irreg., 1976, vol. 11. ISSN 0081-6485 (Dist. by: Ars Polona-Ruch, Krakowskie Przedmiescie 7, Warsaw, Poland)
- Studia Metodologiczne. Dissertationes Methodologicae. s-a. ISSN 0039-324X
- Studia Polonistyczne. irreg., 1973. vol. 1.
- Studia Rossica Posnaniensia. irreg., 1976, vol. 7. ISSN 0081-6884 (Dist. by: Ars Polona-Ruch, Krakowskie Przedmiescie 7, Warsaw, Poland)
- Uniwersytet im. Adama Mickiewicza. Wydzial Biologii i Nauk o Ziemi. Prace. Seria Geologia. irreg. ISSN 0083-4238
- Uniwersytet im. Adama Mickiewicza. Wydzial Filologiczny. Seria Filologia Angielska. irreg.
- Uniwersytet im. Adama Mickiewicza. Wydzial Filozoficzno-Historyczny. Prace. Seria Filozofia i Logika. irreg. ISSN 0083-4246
- Uniwersytet im. Adama Mickiewicza. Wydzial Historyczny. Prace. Seria Psychologia, Pedagogika. irreg. ISSN 0083-4254
- Uniwersytet im. Adama Mickiewicza. Wydzial Matematyki, Fizyki i Chemii. Prace. Seria Matematyka. irreg., 1975, vol. 2. ISSN 0551-6625
- Uniwersytet im. Adama Mickiewicza. Wydzial Prawa. Prace. irreg. ISSN 0083-4262
- Uniwersytet im. Adama Mickiewicza. Zeszyty Naukowe. Geografia. biennial. ISSN 0554-8063
- Uniwersytet im. Adama Mickiewicza. Zeszyty Naukowe.Historia z Sztuki. irreg. ISSN 0083-4270 (Dist. by: Ars Polona-Ruch, Krakowskie Przedmiescie 7, Warsaw, Poland)

## Uniwersytet Jagiellonski
Golebia 24, Krakow, Poland
(Dist. by Ars Polona-Ruch, Krakowskie Przedmiescie 7, Warsaw, Poland)
- Biuletyn Biblioteki Jagiellonskiej. (pub. by Panstwowe Wydawnictwo Naukowe)
- Reports on Mathematical Logic. (pub. by Panstwowe Wydawnictwo Naukowe)
- Studia Cywilistyczne/Studies in Civil Law. (pub. by Panstwowe Wydawnictwo Naukowe)
- Uniwersytet Jagiellonski. Zeszyty Naukowe. Prace Archeologiczne. (pub. by Panstwowe Wydawnictwo Naukowe)
- Uniwersytet Jagiellonski. Zeszyty Naukowe. Prace Botaniczne. (pub. by Panstwowe Wydawnictwo Naukowe)
- Uniwersytet Jagiellonski. Zeszyty Naukowe. Prace Chemiczne. (pub. by Panstwowe Wydawnictwo Naukowe)
- Uniwersytet Jagiellonski. Zeszyty Naukowe. Prace Etnograficzne. (pub. by Panstwowe Wydawnictwo Naukowe)
- Uniwersytet Jagiellonski. Zeszyty Naukowe. Prace Fizyczne. (pub. by Panstwowe Wydawnictwo Naukowe)
- Uniwersytet Jagiellonski. Zeszyty Naukowe. Prace Geograficzne. (pub. by Panstwowe Wydawnictwo Naukowe)
- Uniwersytet Jagiellonski. Zeszyty Naukowe. Prace Geograficzne. Prace z Geografii Ekonomicznej. (pub. by Panstwowe Wydawnictwo Naukowe)

- Uniwersytet Jagiellonski. Zeszyty Naukowe. Prace Historyczne. (pub. by Panstwowe Wydawnictwo Naukowe)
- Uniwersytet Jagiellonski. Zeszyty Naukowe. Prace Historycznoliterackie. (pub. by Panstwowe Wydawnictwo Naukowe)
- Uniwersytet Jagiellonski. Zeszyty Naukowe. Prace Jezykoznawcze. (pub. by Panstwowe Wydawnictwo Naukowe)
- Uniwersytet Jagiellonski. Zeszyty Naukowe. Prace Matematyczne. (pub. by Panstwowe Wydawnictwo Naukowe)
- Uniwersytet Jagiellonski. Zeszyty Naukowe. Prace Prawnicze. (pub. by Panstwowe Wydawnictwo Naukowe)
- Uniwersytet Jagiellonski. Zeszyty Naukowe. Prace Psychologiczno-Pedagogiczne. (pub. by Panstwowe Wydawnictwo Naukowe)
- Uniwersytet Jagiellonski. Zeszyty Naukowe. Prace z Biologii Molekularnej. (pub. by Panstwowe Wydawnictwo Naukowe)
- Uniwersytet Jagiellonski. Zeszyty Naukowe. Prace z Historii Sztuki. (pub. by Panstwowe Wydawnictwo Naukowe)
- Uniwersytet Jagiellonski. Zeszyty Naukcwe. Prace z Nauk Politycznych. (pub. by Panstwowe Wydawnictwo Naukowe)
- Uniwersytet Jagiellonski. Zeszyty Naukowe. Prace Zoologiczne. a. ISSN 0083-4416

## Uniwersytet Lodzki
Narutowicza 65, Lodz, Poland
(Dist. by Ars Polona-Ruch, Krakowskie Przedmiescie 7, Warsaw, Poland)
- Acta Universitatis Lodziensis. Zeszyty Naukowe. Seria 3: Nauki Ekonomiczne. irreg.
- Uniwersytet Lodzki. Prace. irreg. ISSN 0076-034X
- Uniwersytet Lodzki. Zeszyty Naukowe. Seria 2: Nauki Matematyczno-Przyrodnicze. irreg. ISSN 0076-0366

## Uniwersytet Marii Curie-Sklodowskiej
Plac Litewski 5, Lublin, Poland.
- Annales Universitatis Mariae Curie-Sklodowska. Sectio A. Mathematica. a.
- Annales Universitatis Mariae Curie-Sklodowska. Sectio B. Geographia, Geologia, Mineralogia et Petrographia. a.
- Annales Universitatis Mariae Curie-Sklodowska. Sectio C. Biologia. a. ISSN 0066-2232
- Annales Universitatis Mariae Curie-Sklodowska. Sectio D. Medicina. a. ISSN 0066-2240
- Annales Universitatis Mariae Curie-Sklodowska. Sectio E. Agricultura. a.
- Annales Universitatis Mariae Curie-Sklodowska. Sectio F. Humaniora. a.
- Annales Universitatis Mariae Curie-Sklodowska. Sectio G. Ius. a.
- Annales Universitatis Mariae Curie-Sklodowska. Sectio I. Philosophia-Sociologia. a.
- Annales Universitatis Mariae Curie-Sklodowska. Sectio M. Oeconomia. a.
- Annales Universitatis Mariae Curie-Sklodowska. Sectio SD. Medicina Veterinaria. a.

## Uniwersytet Mikolaja Kopernika
Fosa Staromiejska 3, Torun, Poland
(Dist. by Ars Polona-Ruch, Krakowskie Przedmiescie 7, Warsaw, Poland)
- Reports on Mathematical Physics. (pub. by Panstwowe Wydawnictwo Naukowe)
- Uniwersytet Mikolaja Kopernika, Torun. Katedra Historii Polski i Powszechnej XIX i XX Wieku. Prace. irreg. ISSN 0083-4459
- Uniwersytet Mikolaja Kopernika, Torun. Nauki Humanistyczno-Spoleczne. Archeologia. irreg. ISSN 0083-4467
- Uniwersytet Mikolaja Kopernika, Torun. Nauki Humanistyczno-Spoleczne. Filozofia. irreg. ISSN 0083-4475
- Uniwersytet Mikolaja Kopernika, Torun. Nauki Humanistyczno-Spoleczne. Filologia Polska. irreg. ISSN 0083-4483
- Uniwersytet Mikolaja Kopernika, Torun. Nauki Humanistyczno-Spoleczne. Historia. irreg. ISSN 0083-4491
- Uniwersytet Mikolaja Kopernika, Torun. Nauki Humanistyczno-Spoleczne. Prawo. irreg. ISSN 0083-4513
- Uniwersytet Mikolaja Kopernika, Torun. Nauki Humanistyczno-Spoleczne. Nauka o Ksiazce. irreg. ISSN 0083-4505
- Uniwersytet Mikolaja Kopernika, Torun. Nauki Humanistyczno-Spoleczne. Socjologia. a.
- Uniwersytet Mikolaja Kopernika, Torun. Nauki Matematyczno-Przyrodnicze. Biologia. irreg. ISSN 0083-4521

## Uniwersytet Slaski w Katowicach
Ul. Bankowa 14, 40-007 Katowice, Poland.
- Acta Biologica. irreg.
- Linguistica Silesiana. irreg., 1975, vol. 1.
- Slaskie Studia Historyczne. irreg., 1975, vol. 1. (prep. by its Slaski Instytut Naukowy)
- Uniwersytet Slaski w Katowicach. Physics Papers. irreg.
- Uniwersytet Slaski w Katowicach. Prace Chemiczne. irreg., 1975, vol. 5.
- Uniwersytet Slaski w Katowicach. Prace Dydaktyczne. irreg.
- Uniwersytet Slaski w Katowicach. Prace Historyczne. irreg., 1975, no. 4.
- Uniwersytet Slaski w Katowicach. Prace Historycznoliterackie. irreg., 1976, vol. 4.
- Uniwersytet Slaski w Katowicach. Prace Jezykoznawcze. irreg.
- Uniwersytet Slaski w Katowicach. Prace Matematyczne. irreg.
- Uniwersytet Slaski w Katowicach. Prace Pedagogiczne. irreg., 1976, vol. 4.
- Uniwersytet Slaski W Katowicach. Prace Prawnicze. irreg., 1975, no. 6.
- Uniwersytet Slaski w Katowicach. Prace Psychologiczne. irreg.
- Uniwersytet Slaski w Katowicach. Prace z Nauk Spolecznych. irreg., 1976, no. 3.
- Uniwersytet Slaski w Katowicach. Wydzial Techniki. Prace. irreg., 1975, vol. 5.

## Uniwersytet Warszawski
Krakowskie Przedmiescie 26/28, Warsaw, Poland
- Acta Philologica. irreg., 1970, vol. 2. ISSN 0065-1524 (prep. by its Wydzial Filologii Obcych) (Dist. by: Ars Polona-Ruch, Krakowskie Przedmiescie 7, Warsaw, Poland)
- Biuletyn Geologiczny. irreg. ISSN 0067-9003 (prep. by its Katedra Geologii)
- Fasciculi Historici. irreg., vol. 7, 1974. ISSN 0071-4038 (prep. by its Instytut Historyczny) (Dist. by: Ars Polona-Ruch, Krakowskie Przedmiescie 7, Warsaw, Poland)
- Fotointerpretacja w Geografii. irreg., 1976, vol. 11. ISSN 0071-8076 (Co-sponsors: Uniwersytet Gdanski, Uniwersytet Slaski)
- Journal of Juristic Papyrology. (pub. by Panstwowe Wydawnictwo Naukowe)
- Kwartalnik Pedagogiczny. (pub. by Panstwowe Wydawnictwo Naukowe)
- Studia Palmyrenskie. irreg., 1970, no. 4. ISSN 0081-6787 (prep. by its Katedra Archeologii Srodziemnomorskiej) (Dist. by: Ars Polona-Ruch, Krakowskie Przedmiescie 7, Warsaw, Poland)
- Swiatowit. irreg., 1971, vol. 32. ISSN 0082-044X (prep. by its Katedra Archeologii Pradziejowaj i Wczesnosredniowiecznej) (Dist. by: Ars Polona-Ruch, Krakowskie Przedmiescie 7, Warsaw, Poland)
- Uniwersytet Warszawski. Instytut Geograficzny. Katedra Klimatologii. Biuletyn/Warsaw University. Geographical Institute. Chair of Climatology. Bulletin. m. ISSN 0042-0433
- Uniwersytet Warszawski. Instytut Geograficzny. Prace i Studia. irreg. ISSN 0083-7326 (Subscription to: Ars Polona-Ruch, Krakowskie Przedmiescie 7, Warsaw, Poland)
- Uniwersytet Warszawski. Katedra Klimatologii. Prace i Studia. a. ISSN 0083-7334
- Uniwersytet Warszawski. Roczniki/Annales Universitatis Varsoviensis. a. ISSN 0083-7342

## Uniwersytet Warszawski. Studium Afrykanistyczne
Al. Zwirki i Wigury 93, 02-089 Warsaw, Poland.
- Africana Bulletin. s-a. ISSN 0002-029X
- Informatory Regionalne. 2-3 per yr.
- Przeglad Informacji o Afryce. q. (Dist. by: Ars Polona-Ruch, Krakowskie Przedmiescie 7, Warsaw, Poland)

## Uniwersytet Wroclawski
Plac Uniwersytecki 1, Wroclaw, Poland.
- Acta Universitatis Wratislaviensis. Prace Pedagogiczne. (pub. by Panstwowe Wydawnictwo Naukowe. Oddzial we Wroclawiu)
- Prace Literackie. (pub. by Ossolineum, Publishing House of the Polish Academy of Sciences)
- Studia Archeologiczne. (pub. by Panstwowe Wydawnictwo Naukowe)
- Studia Geograficzne. (pub. by Panstwowe Wydawnictwo Naukowe)
- Studia o Ksiazce. (pub. by Ossolineum, Publishing House of the Polish Academy of Sciences)

- Uniwersytet Wroclawski. Instytut Geograficzne. Prace. Seria A: Geografia Fizyczna. irreg., 1974, no. 236.
- Uniwersytet Wroclawski. Instytut Geograficzne. Prace. Seria B: Geografia Spoleczna i Ekonomiczna. irreg.

**Wojewodzka i Miejska Biblioteka Publiczna-Biblioteka Glowna im. S. Staszica**
Dworcowa 8, 70-952 Szczecin, Poland.
- Bibliografia Pomorza Zachodniego. irreg, 1975, vol. 8. ISSN 0409-3453
- Bibliotekarz Zachodniopomorski. q.

**Wojsko Polskie. Glowny Zarzad Polityczny**
Grzybouska 77, 00-950 Warsaw, Poland
(Dist. by: Ars Polona- Ruch, Krakowskie Przedmiescie 7, Warsaw, Poland)
- Wojsko Ludowe. m. ISSN 0043-7174
- Zolnierz Polski. w. ISSN 0044-4979

**Wojskowy Instytut Historyczny**
- Wojskowy Przeglad Historyczny. (pub. by Wydawnictwo Ministerstwa Obrony Narodowej)

**Wroclawskie Towarzystwo Milosnikow Historii**
- Slaski Kwartalnik Historyczny "Sobotka". (pub. by Ossolineum, Publishing House of the Polish Academy of Sciences)

**Wroclawskie Towarzystwo Naukowe**
- Annales Silesiae. (pub. by Ossolineum, Publishing House of the Polish Academy of Sciences)
- Litteraria. (pub. by Ossolineum, Publishing House of the Polish Academy of Sciences)
- Wroclawskie Towarzystwo Naukowe. Komisja Historii Sztuki. Rozprawy. (pub. by Ossolineum, Publishing House of the Polish Academy of Sciences)
- Wroclawskie Towarzystwo Naukowe. Komisja Jezykowa. Rozprawy. (pub. by Ossolineum, Publishing House of the Polish Academy of Sciences)
- Wroclawskie Towarzystwo Naukowe. Prace. Seria A. Humanistyka. (pub. by Ossolineum, Publishing House of the Polish Academy of Sciences)
- Wroclawskie Towarzystwo Naukowe. Prace. Seria B. Nauki Scisle. (pub. by Ossolineum, Publishing House of the Polish Academy of Sciences)
- Wroclawskie Towarzystwo Naukowe. Sprawozdania. Seria A. (pub. by Ossolineum, Publishing House of the Polish Academy of Sciences)

**Wyzsza Szkola Morska. Instytut Nawigacji**
Czerwonych Kosynierow 83, 81-225 Gdynia, Poland
(Dist. by Ars Polona-Ruch, Krakowskie Przedmiescie 7, Warsaw, Poland)
- Biblioteka Nawigatora. irreg. ISSN 0067-7728

**Wyzsza Szkola Pedagogiczna, Katowice**
Ul. Szkolna 9, Katowice, Poland.
- Wyzsza Szkola Pedagogiczna, Katowice. Zeszyty Naukowe. Sekcja Jezykoznawstwa. a. ISSN 0075-5281

**Wyzsza Szkola Pedagogiczna, Krakow**
Podchorazych 2, 30-084 Krakow, Poland.
- Wyzsza Szkola Pedagogiczna, Krakow. Prace Jezykoznawcze. irreg.
- Wyzsza Szkola Pedagogiczna, Krakow. Prace Zoologiczne. irreg.

**Wyzsza Szkola Pedagogiczna, Opole**
Oleska 48, Opole, Poland
(Dist. by Ars Polona-Ruch, Krakowskie Przedmiescie 7, Warsaw, Poland)
- Wyzsza Szkola Pedagogiczna, Opole. Zeszyty Naukowe. Serie A. Fizyka. irreg., 1973, vol. 14. ISSN 0078-5385
- Wyzsza Szkola Pedagogiczna, Opole. Zeszyty Naukowe. Serie A. Matematyka. irreg., 1973, vol. 11. ISSN 0078-5431
- Wyzsza Szkola Pedagogiczna, Opole. Zeszyty Naukowe. Filologia Polska. irreg., 1975, no. 13.
- Wyzsza Szkola Pedagogiczna, Opole. Zeszyty Naukowe. Seria A. Historia. irreg., no. 12, 1974. ISSN 0078-5393
- Wyzsza Szkola Pedagogiczna, Opole. Zeszyty Naukowe. Seria A. Historia Slaska. irreg., 1966, vol. 1. ISSN 0078-5415
- Wyzsza Szkola Pedagogiczna, Opole. Zeszyty Naukowe. Seria A. Historia Literatury. irreg., no. 12, 1974. ISSN 0078-5407
- Wyzsza Szkola Pedagogiczna, Opole. Zeszyty Naukowe. Seria A. Jezykoznawstwo. irreg., no. 5, 1974. ISSN 0078-5423

- Wyzsza Szkola Pedagogiczna, Opole. Zeszyty Naukowe. Seria B. Studia i Monografie. irreg., no. 42, 1975. ISSN 0078-544X

**Zaklad Projektowych Miedzi "Cuprum"**
- Cuprum. (pub. by Wydawnictwa Czasopism Technicznych, N. O. T.)

**Zjednoczenie Przemyslu Cementowego, Wapienniczego i Gipsowego, Sosnowiec**
- Cement, Wapno, Gips. (pub. by Wydawnictwo "Arkady")

**Spoleczny Instytut Wydawniczy "Znak"**
Ul. Wislna 12, Cracow, Poland
(Dist. by: Ars Polona-Ruch, Krakowskie Przedmiescie 7, Warsaw, Poland)
- Tygodnik Powszechny; katolickie pismo spolecznokulturalne. w. ISSN 0041-4808

**Zrzeszenie Miedzynarodowych Przewoznikow Drogowych**
Grojecka 17, 02-021 Warsaw, Poland.
- Z M P D. Kwartalny Biuletyn Informacyjny. q. ISSN 0514-809X

**Zrzeszenie Polskich Hoteli Turystycznych**
Karowa 22, 00-324 Warsaw, Poland.
- Hotelarz. m.

**Zwiazek Nauczycielstwa Polskiego**
- Glos Nauczycielski. (pub. by Wydawnictwa Artystyczno-Graficzne RSW "Prasa-Ksiazka-Ruch")

**Zwiazek Zawodowy Gornikow**
Ul. Dabrowskiego 23, Katowice, Poland.
- Gornik. s-m. ISSN 0017-226X

**Zwiazek Zawodowy Pracownikow Sluzby Zdrowia**
- Medycyna Komunikacyjna. (pub. by Wydawnictwa Komunikacji i Lacznosci)
- Pielegniarka i Polozna. (pub. by Wydawnictwa Artystyczno-Graficzne RSW "Prasa-Ksiazka-Ruch")

**Zydowski Instytut Historyczny w Polsce**
- Zydowski Instytut Historyczny w Polsce. Biuletyn. (pub. by Panstwowe Wydawnictwo Naukowe)

# PORTUGAL

**Academia das Ciencias de Lisboa**
Rua da Academia das Ciencias, 19, Lisbon-2, Portugal.
- Academia das Ciencias de Lisboa. Boletim. q. ISSN 0001-3781

**Academia Portuguesa da Historia**
Palacio da Rosa-Largo da Rosa, Lisbon 2, Portugal.
- Academia Portuguesa da Historia. Anais. a; latest issue, 1974.

**Actualidades Economicas**
Av. Aem. Gago Coutimho 33, Lisbon 5, Portugal.
- Actualidades Economicas; revista Portuguesa de informacao e cultura. bi-m. ISSN 0001-7876

**Administracao-Geral do Porto de Lisboa**
Servico de Relacoes Publicas, Cais do Sodre, Lisbon 2, Portugal.
- Boletim do Porto de Lisboa. b-m. ISSN 0006-596X

**Aero Club de Portugal**
Avenida da Liberdade 226, Lisbon, Portugal.
- Revista do Ar. m. ISSN 0034-9208

**Agencia Geral do Ultramar**
Praca do Comercio, Lisbon, Portugal.
- Boletim Geral do Ultramar. m.

**Agencia Internacional de Livraria e Publicacoes Lda.**
R.S. Pedro de Alcantara, 63-1 D. Lisbon, Portugal.
- Peninsula; cadernos culturais. q. ISSN 0031-4285

**R. Aquiles**
Monteverde 32, Lisbon, Portugal.
- Jornal Portugues de Economia e Financas. s-m.

**Arquivo de Bibliografia Portuguesa**
Rua Ferreira Borges 103-111, Coimbra, Portugal.
- Arquivo de Bibliografia Portuguesa. s-a. ISSN 0571-1223

**Arquivos de Tisiologia. Estancia Sanatorial**
Caramulo, Portugal.
- Arquivos de Tisiologia. approx. a. ISSN 0066-7862

**Casa Publicadoradas Assembleias de Deus**
Rua Neves Ferreira 13, Lisbon 1, Portugal.
- Avivamento. q.
- Boa Semente. m.
- Caminho. bi-m.
- Expositor Dominical. q.
- Novas de Alegria. m. ISSN 0029-5116

**Associacao Comercial de Lisboa**
Camara de Comercio, Rua das Portas de Santo Antao 89, Lisbon 2, Portugal.
- Comercio Portugues. q. ISSN 0010-2334

**Associacao dos Estudantes de Agronomia**
Lisbon 3, Portugal.
- Agros. 6 per yr. ISSN 0002-1970

**Associacao Industrial Portuense**
Rua Mousinho da Silveira No 228, Porto, Portugal.
- Associacao Industrial Portuense. Boletim de Documentacao Economica e Tecnologica. q. ISSN 0044-9377
- Industria do Norte. m. ISSN 0019-7572

**Associacao Portuguesa**
Largo de Andaluz 16-1oe, Lisbon, Portugal.
- Livros de Portugal. m. ISSN 0024-5364

**Associacao Portuguesa de Bibliotecarios Arquivistas e Documentalistas**
Edificio da Biblioteca Nacional, Campo Grande 83, Lisbon 1, Portugal.
- Associacao Portuguesa de Bibliotecarios Arquivistas e Documentalistas. Noticia; boletim informativo interno. m.

**Associacao Portuguesa de Empresas Cinematograficas**
Av. Duque de Loule 86, Lisbon 1, Portugal.
- Jornal das Actividades Cinematograficas. q.

**Associacao Portuguesa de Fundicao**
Rua do Campo Alegre 672, Porto, Portugal.
- Fundicao. m.

**Editorial Aster**
Largo D. Estefania 8, Lisbon 1, Portugal.
- Rumo; revista de problemas actuais Portuguese. m. ISSN 0035-984X

**Editorial Avante S A R L**
Central Distribuidora Livreira, Rua Pedro Nunes 9-A, Lisbon, Portugal.
- Economia E. C; questoes economicos e sociais. bi-m.

**Bayer Portugal S A R L**
Apartado 2365, Lisbon, Portugal
(Main Office: Bayer Pflanzenschutz, Leverkusen, W. Germany (B.R.D.))
- Correio Agricola (Portugal) irreg.

**Livraria Bertrand S A R L**
Rua Garrett 75, Lisbon, Portugal.
- Economia e Socialismo; revista mensal de economia politica. m.

**British-Portuguese Chamber of Commerce**
Rua da Estrela 8, Lisbon 2, Portugal.
- British-Portuguese Chamber of Commerce. Monthly Magazine. m (10 per yr)

**Broteria: Ciencias Naturais**
Rua Maestro Antonio Taborda 14, Caixa Postal 2364, Lisbon, Portugal.
- Broteria: Ciencias Naturais. q. ISSN 0007-2427

**Cadernos de Biblioteconomia, Arquivistica e Documentacao**
Apartado 103, Coimbra, Portugal.
- Cadernos de Biblioteconomia, Arquivistica e Documentacao. q. ISSN 0007-9421

**Calouste Gulbenkian Foundation**
- Imago Mvndi. (pub. by Imago Mundi Ltd. UK)

**Camara de Comercio Luso-Americana**
Rua Dona Estefania 155-5 Esq., Lisbon, Portugal.
- Camara de Comercio Luso-Americana. Boletim. 9 per yr. ISSN 0008-1906

**Camara Municipal de Braga**
- Bracara Augusta. (pub. by Livraria Cruz)

**Cartaz**
Avenida de Roma 72, 1 Esq. Frente, Lisbon, Portugal.
- Cartaz; revista mensal de cultura e informacao e turismo. m.

**Joaquim de Carvalho**
Rua S. Francisco Xavier, 49, Lisbon 3, Portugal.
- Fazenda do Ultramar. q.

**Casa do Alentejo**
Rua das Portas de Santo Antao 58, Lisbon 2, Portugal.
- Revista Alentejana. m. ISSN 0034-6977

**Casa do Castelo**
Rua da Sofia 47, Coimbra, Portugal.
- Revista Portuguesa de Filologia. a (2nos. per vol.) ISSN 0080-2433

**Casa do Gaiato**
Paco de Sousa, Portugal.
- Gaiato; obra de rapazes, para rapazes, pelos rapazes. s-m. ISSN 0016-3910

**Celuloide**
Rua David Manuel da Fonseca 88, Rio Maior, Portugal.
- Celuloide; revista Portuguesa de cinema. m. ISSN 0008-8781

**Centro de Caridade Nossa Senhora do Perpetuo Socorro**
Rua D. Joao 4, 390, Porto, Portugal.
- Caridade. m. ISSN 0008-655X

**Centro de Documentacao e Informacao da Maternidade Dr. Alfredo da Costa**
Imprensa Nacional, Rua Viriato, Lisbon, Portugal.
- Maternidade Dr. Alfredo da Costa, Lisbon. Arquivo Clinico. 2 vols. per yr.(4 nos. per vol.) ISSN 0302-4326

**Centro de Estudos Filologicos**
Av. Cinco de Octubro 85, 50 Lisbon 2, Portugal.
- Boletim de Filologia. q.

**Centro de Estudos Geograficos. Faculdade de Letras de Lisboa**
Livraria Portugal, Rua do Carmo 70, Lisbon, Portugal.
- Finisterra; revista Portuguesa de geografia. s-a.

**Cineclube do Porto**
Rua do Rosario, 5-10, Oporto, Portugal.
- Cineclube. 1-2 per yr.

**Circulo Fraternal de Cooperacao Escotista**
T. Vitorino de Freitas 9, Lisbon 3, Portugal.
- Sempre Pronto; mensario escotista. m. ISSN 0037-203X

**Clinica Pediatrica Universitaria de Lisboa**
Hospital de Santa Maria, Lisbon, Portugal.
- Revista Portuguesa de Pediatria e Puericultura. ISSN 0048-7880

**Clube de Campismo de Lisboa**
Rua de Misericordia 137, 2 Andar, Lisbon, Portugal.
- Companheiros. 6 per yr. ISSN 0010-3969

**Clube Filatelico de Portugal**
Apartado 2869, Lisbon, Portugal.
- Clube Filatelico de Portugal. Boletim. m. ISSN 0009-9651

**Clube Militar Naval**
Praca Marques de Pombal 2, Lisbon, Portugal.
- Clube Militar Naval. Anais. q. ISSN 0009-966X

**Coimbra Editora**
Rua Ferrira Borges, Coimbra, Portugal.
- Universidade de Coimbra. Faculdade de Direito. Boletim. a.
- Universidade de Coimbra. Faculdade de Direito. Boletim de Ciencias Economicas. 3 per yr.

**Colegio Ibero-Latino-Americano de Dermatologia**
Avenida da Liberdade, 90, 1, Lisbon 2, Portugal.
- Medicina Cutanea Ibero-Latino-Americana. bi-m.

**Convencao Baptista Portuguesa**
Rua Goncalves Crespo 33, 3 Frente, Lisbon 1, Portugal.
- Semeador Baptista. m. ISSN 0037-1874

**Correios e Telecomunicacoes de Portugal. Servicos Culturais**
Rua Alexandre Herculano 100, Lisbon 2, Portugal.
- Correios e Telecomunicacoes de Portugal. Boletim Oficial. d.

**Livraria Sa da Costa**
Rua Garrett 102, Lisbon, Portugal.
- Hospitais Civis de Lisboa. Boletim Clinico. 4 per yr. ISSN 0046-8037

**Livraria Cruz**
Rua D. Diogo de Sousa, Braga, Portugal.
- Bracara Augusta; revista cultural de Regionalismo e historia. irreg. ISSN 0006-8640 (Camara Municipal de Braga)

**Cruz Vermelha Portuguesa**
Rua das Flores 85-1, Lisbon 2, Portugal.
- Humanidade. q.

**Cruzada Eucaristica**
5 Largo de Sta. Teresa, Braga, Portugal.
- Cruzada Eucaristica. m. ISSN 0011-2194

**Dr. Jose Dias, Ed. & Pub.**
Av. da Republica, 23,R/C, Lisbon 1, Portugal.
- Jornal de Estomatologia. s-a. ISSN 0021-7522

**Divulgotecnica. Agencia Publicitaria de Investimentos e Representacoes**
Av. Almirante Reis, 188- 4, Lisbon, Portugal.
- A Cooperacao. m.

**Dominican Convent Friars-Fatima. Secretariado Nacional do Rosario**
Fatima, Portugal.
- Rosario de Maria; publicacao mensalde espiritualidade rosario mariana. m. ISSN 0035-8274

**Empresa Editorial Electrotecnica, Ltda.**
Rua de Dona Estefania 48, 3 Esq, Lisbon 1, Portugal.
- Electricidade. bi-m. ISSN 0013-4465

**Empresa Editora de Estudos Medicos, Ltda.**
Rua de Sa da Bandeira 245-2, Porto, Portugal.
- Jornal do Medico. w. ISSN 0021-7573

**Faculdade de Ciencias de Lisbon. Laboratorio de Fisica**
Rua da Escola Politecnica, 58, Lisbon - 2, Portugal.
- Portugaliae Physica. s-a. ISSN 0048-4903

**Faculdade de Filosofia, Braga**
Braga, Portugal.
- Revista Portuguesa de Filosofia. q. ISSN 0035-0400

**Federacao Nacional dos Sindicatos dos Tipografos**
Litografos e Oficios Correlativos, Rua da Barroca 107, - 1o, Lisbon, Portugal.
- Grafico. 4 per yr. ISSN 0017-2928

**M. G. Tomaz Ferreira**
Largo da Ajuda, Penafiel, Portugal.
- Tempo. s-m. ISSN 0049-335X

**Livraria Figueirinhas**
Praca da Liberdade 67, Porto, Portugal.
- Livraria Figueirinhas Catalogo. a.

**Edicoes Maria da Fonte**
Rua da Fe, 26,-2, Lisboa 2, Portugal.
- Que Fazer; cadernos marxistas-leninistas. irreg.

**Editorial Franciscana**
Montariol, Braga, Portugal.
- Itinerarium; revista trimestral de cultura. q. ISSN 0021-3209 (Portuguese Franciscans)
- Paz e Alegria. m. (Portuguese Franciscans)

**Fundacao Calouste Gulbenkian**
Avenida de Berna 56, Lisbon 1, Portugal.
- Arquivo do Instituto Gulbenkian de Ciencia; estudos de economia e financas. 2 per yr. (prep. by its Centro de Economia e Financas)
- Coloquio/Artes; revista de artes visuais musica e bailado. 5 per yr. ISSN 0010-1451 (Subscr. to: Editorial Noticias, Rua Rodrigues Faria 103, Lisbon 3, Portugal)

- Fundacao Calouste Gulbenkian Centro de Investigacao Pedagogica. Boletin Bibliografia e Informacao. s-a. (prep. by its Centro de Investigacion Pedagogica)
- Fundacao Calouste Gulbenkian Centro de Investigacao Pedagogica. Estudos. a. (prep. by its Centro de Investigacion Pedagogica)

**Gabinete de Estudos das Pescas**
R. S. Bento 644, Lisbon, Portugal.
- Boletim da Pesca. q. ISSN 0006-5870

**Gracas do Servo de Deus: Padre Cruz**
Apartado 2661, Lisbon 2, Portugal.
- Gracas do Servo de Deus: Padre Cruz. bi-m. ISSN 0017-2758

**Gremio dos Industriais do Transportes Em Automoveis**
Rua Dr. Antonio Candido 8, Lisbon, Portugal.
- G I T A. m. ISSN 0016-3546

**Gremio Nacional dos Bancos e Casas Bancarias**
Av. Liberdade 258-3, Lisbon 2, Portugal.
- Revista Bancaria. q.

**Grupo de Trabalho Permanente para a Documentacao e Informacao Economico Social**
Av. D. Carlos I 126-3, Lisbon 2, Portugal.
- Noticias Sobre I C T (Informacao Cientifica e Tecnica) m.

**Guimaraes, Portugal. Arquivo Municipal "Alfredo Pimenta"**
Largo Conego Jose Maria Gomes, Guimaraes, Portugal.
- Guimaraes. Arquivo Municipal "Alfredo Pimenta." Boletim Detrabalhos Historicos; elementos para a historia Vimaranese. a.

**Livros Horizonte**
Rua das Chagas, 17, Lisbon 2, Portugal.
- Biblioteca do Educador Profissional. irreg. ISSN 0067-7469
- Perspectivas. q. (Unesco UN)

**Iniciativas Editoriais**
Av. Rio de Janeiro 6, Lisbon, Portugal.
- Cadernos Politicos de Educacao Popular. irreg.

**Instituto de Arqueologia. Faculdade de Letras**
Coimbra, Portugal.
- Conimbriga. a. ISSN 0084-9189

**Instituto de Botanica "Dr. Goncalo Sampaio"**
Rua do Camho Alegre, 1191 - Porto, Portugal.
- Instituto de Botanica "Dr. Goncalo Sampaio". Publicacoes. 3 Serie. irreg. (approx. 2 per yr.) ISSN 0473-0658

**Instituto de Higiene e Medicina Tropical**
Rua da Junqueira, 96, Lisbon 3, Portugal.
- Instituto de Higiene e Medicina Tropical, Lisbon. Anais. irreg.; vol. 1, nos. 1-4, 1973. ISSN 0075-9767

**Instituto de Soldadura**
R. Tomas de Figueiredo, 16-A, Lisbon, Portugal.
- Instituto de Soldadura. Boletim. bi-m. ISSN 0046-9955

**Instituto do Azeite e Produtos Oleaginosos**
Av. de Sidonio Pais, 10, 10 Lisbon 1, Portugal.
- Instituto do Azeite e Produtos Oleaginosos. Boletim. irreg.

**Instituto dos Produtos Florestais**
Rua Filipe Folque 10-J, Lisbon, Portugal.
- Instituto dos Produtos Florestai⁺- Cortica. Boletim. m.
- Instituto dos Produtos Florestais-Madeira. Boletim. q.
- Instituto dos Produtos Florestais-Resinosos. Boletim. q.

**Instituto Geofisico do Infante D. Luis**
R. Escola Politecnica, Lisbon 2, Portugal.
- Station Seismographique de Lisboa. Bulletin Seismique. 6 per yr. ISSN 0039-0356

**Instituto Gregoriano de Lisboa**
Campo dos Martires da Patria 96-2, Lisbon, Portugal.
- Canto Gregoriano. q. ISSN 0008-5731

**Instituto Italiano di Cultura in Portogallo**
- Estudos Italianos em Portugal. (pub. by Papelaria Fernandes)

**Instituto Portugues de Heraldica**
c/o Marques de Abrantes, Rua Tenete Ferreira
Durado 2, Lisbon 3, Portugal.
- Armas e Trofeus; revista de historia, heraldica,
  genealogie ede arte. q.

**Instituto Portugues de Oncologia de Francisco Gentil**
Palhava, Lisbon, Portugal.
- Arquivo de Patologia. 3 per yr. ISSN 0004-2714

**Instituto Superior Economico e Social**
Rua Vasco da Gama 15, Evora, Portugal.
- Economica e Sociologia. a.

**Instituto Superior Tecnico**
Associacao dos Estudantes, Avda. Rovisco Pais,
Lisbon 1, Portugal.
- Tecnica; revista de engenharia. m.(Oct-July) ISSN
  0040-1714

**International Society for Rock Mechanics**
Laboratorio Nacional de Engenharia Civil, Avenida
do Brasil, Lisbon 5, Portugal
(Order proceedings of 3rd meeting from National
Academy of Sciences, Washington D.C. 20418)
- International Society for Rock Mechanics.
  Congress. Proceedings. every 4 years since 1966;
  3rd, Washington, D.C., 1974. ISSN 0074-848X

**Jornal de Letras e Artes**
Rua Vitor Bastos 14 A, Lisbon 1, Portugal.
- Jornal de Letras e Artes. w. ISSN 0021-7530

**Empresa do Jornal do Comercio**
Rua Dr. Luis Almeida e Albuquerque 5, Lisbon 1,
Portugal.
- Binario; revista de arquitectura, construcao e
  equipamento. m. ISSN 0006-2804
- Jornal do Comercio. d.
- Revista de Marinha. m. ISSN 0034-8546

**Jornal Portugues de Economic e Financas**
c/o A. Valdez dos Santos, Ed., Rua Aquiles
Monteverde 32, Lisbon-3, Portugal.
- Jornal Portugues de Economic e Financas. s-m.
  ISSN 0449-1750

**Junta da Accao Social. Centro de Estudos Sociais e
Corporativos**
Alameda D. Alfonso Henriques, 82, Lisbon,
Portugal.
- Estudos Sociais e Corporativas. q.

**Junta de Colonizacao Interna**
R. do Salitre 171-1, Lisbon 2, Portugal.
- Temas Economico-Sociais Agrarios. 6-7 per yr.
  ISSN 0040-2893

**Junta de Investigacaoes do Ultramar**
Rua de Jau 54, Lisbon 3, Portugal.
- Garcia de Orta. 4 per yr. ISSN 0016-4569

**Junta de Investigacaoes do Ultramar. Centro de
Estudos Historicos Ultramarinos**
Rua da Jan Queira 86, Lisbon, Portugal.
- Filmoteca Ultramarina Portuguesa. Boletim. irreg.,
  1971, no. 44. ISSN 0430-4497

**Junta de Investigacoes do Ultramar. Centro de
Documentacao Cientifica Ultramarina**
Av. de Ilha da Madeira, Restelo, Lisbon 3, Portugal.
- Bibliografia Cientifica da Junta de Investigacoes
  do Ultramar. irreg.
- Documentacao e Informacao Cientificas. a.

**Laboratorio Nacional de Engenharia Civil**
Avenida do Brasil, Lisbon 5, Portugal.
- Bibliografia Portuguesa de Construcao Civil. a.
  ISSN 0067-6756
- Laboratorio Nacional de Engenharia Civil.
  Boletim Mensal de Informacao. m. ISSN 0032-
  5090

**Missao de Estudos Agronomicos do Ultramar**
Apdo. 3014, Lisbon, Portugal.
- Estudos Agronomicos. q. ISSN 0014-1585

**Mobil Oil Portuguesa**
Edificio Mobil, Rua Castilho, 165, Apartado 1925,
Lisbon 1, Portugal.
- Gazeta Mobil. q. ISSN 0016-5468

**Museu de Etnografia e Historia**
Largo de Sao Joao Novo, Porto, Portugal.
- Revista de Etnografia. 2 per yr.

**Museu e Laboratorio Zoologico e Antropologico,
(Museu Bocage)**
Faculdade de Ciencias de Lisboa, Rua da Escola
Politechnica, Lisbon, Portugal.
- Museu Bocage. Arquivos. 4 per yr. ISSN 0027-
  3988

**Empresa Nacional de Publicidade**
Avenida da Liberdade 266, Lisbon 2, Portugal.
- Coloquio-Letras. bi-m.

**Francisco Ferretra Neves, Ed. & Pub.**
Avda. Dr. Lourenco Peixinho 133-1, Aveiro,
Portugal.
- Arquivo do Distrito de Aveiro. q. ISSN 0004-
  2722

**News**
Rua de S. Pedro, De Alcantara 45, Lisbon, Portugal.
- News. fortn. ISSN 0028-8934

**Jose Soares de Oliveira, Ed. & Pub.**
Rua de S. Jose 34, Lisbon, Portugal.
- Defesa Nacional. 12 yr. ISSN 0011-765X (Jose
  Soares de Oliveira, Ed. & Pub.)

**Oporto, Portugal. Camara Municipal, Oporto**
Gabinete de Historia de Cidade, Casa do Infante,
Oporto, Portugal.
- Camara Municipal, Oporto. Boletin Cultural. irreg.

**Palacio Foz**
Praca dos Restauradores, Lisbon, Portugal.
- Panorama; revista Portuguesa de arte e turismo. q.
  ISSN 0031-0875

**Papelaria Fernandes**
L. do Rato, 13, Lisbon 2, Portugal.
- Estudos Italianos em Portugal. irreg., 1968-69, no.
  31-32. (Instituto Italiano di Cultura in Portogallo)

**Pathe Baby Portugal**
R.S. Nicolau 22, Lisbon 2, Portugal.
- Cinema de Amadores. q. ISSN 0009-708X
  (Portuguese Club of Cine Amateurs)

**Plasticos**
Rua de D. Estefania 32, 2-Esq., Lisbon, Portugal.
- Plasticos; revista da industria de materias plasticas.
  q. ISSN 0554-291X

**Policia Portuguesa**
Rua 1 de Maio, 1-1 Lisbon, Portugal.
- Policia Portuguesa Revista Ilustrada. bi-m. ISSN
  0032-2628

**Portugal. Centro de Estudos de Historia Eclesiastica**
Campo dos Martires da Patria, 45, Lisbon-1,
Portugal.
- Lusitania Sacra. a. ISSN 0076-1508

**Portugal. Comissariado Nacional da Mocidade
Portuguesa Feminina**
Rua Artilharia Um 105, Lisbon, Portugal.
- Menina e Moca. m. ISSN 0025-9276

**Portugal. Departamento Nacional de Obras Contra as
Secas**
Rua Senador Pompeu No 713, Fortaleza-Ceara
60000, Portugal.
- Portugal. Departamento Nacional de Obras
  Contra as Secas. Relatorio Anual. a.

**Portugal. Direccao Geral da Informacao**
Secretaria de Estado da Informacao e Turismo,
Palacio Foz, Lisbon, Portugal.
- Portugal Hoje. m.

**Portugal. Direccao-Geral da Marinha do Comercio**
Junta Nacional da Marinha Mercante, Praca Luis de
Camoes 22-1 Dt., Lisbon 2, Portugal.
- Direccao-Geral de Marinha do Comercio.
  Boletim. 3 per yr.

**Portugal. Direccao-Geral de Minas e Servicos
Geologicos**
Rua Antonio Enes 7, Lisbon 1, Portugal.
- Boletim de Minas. q. ISSN 0006-5935

**Portugal. Direccao Geral de Minas e Servicos
Geologicos. Servicos Geologicos de Portugal**
Rua Academia das Ciencias 19-2, Lisbon 2,
Portugal.
- Servicos Geologicos de Portugal. Comunicacoes.
  1-2 per yr. ISSN 0037-2730

**Portugal. Estacao Agronomica Nacional**
Oeiras, Portugal.
- Agronomia Lusitana. 4 per yr. ISSN 0002-1911

**Portugal. Federacao Nacional das Instituicoes de
Proteccao a Infancia**
Direccao-Geral dos Servicos Tutelares de Menores,
Lisbon, Portugal.
- Infancia e Juventude. q. ISSN 0019-9508

**Portugal. Gabinete de Recursos Humanos e
Prevencao. Instituto Nacional de Seguros**
Rua Almirante Barroso,13-4, Lisbon, Portugal.
- Seguranca. q. ISSN 0049-0059

**Portugal. Imprensa Geral**
Rua das Chagas, 2, Lisbon, Portugal.
- Rua. w.

**Portugal. Imprensa Nacional-Casa da Moeda**
Livraria do Estado, Rua do Marques de Sa da
Bandeira, 16-a, 1, Lisbon, Portugal.
- Portugal. Instituto Nacional de Estatistica.
  Servicos Centrais. Sinopse de Dados Estatisticos:
  Continente e Ilhas Adjacentes. irreg; latest issue,
  1974.

**Portugal. Instituto Nacional de Estatistica**
Av. Antonio Jose de Almeida, Lisbon 1, Portugal.
- Bibliografia Sobre a Economia Portuguesa. irreg.
  ISSN 0067-6764
- Estado das Culturas e Previsao de Colheitas. m.
  ISSN 0014-1178
- Estatisticas da Energia: Continente e Ilhas
  Adjacentes. irreg. (prep. by its Servicos Centrais)
- Portugal. Estatisticas Industriais: Continente e
  Ilhas Adjacentes. a. ISSN 0079-418X
- Portugal. Instituto Nacional de Estatistica.
  Anuario Estatistico. a. ISSN 0079-4112
- Portugal. Instituto Nacional de Estatistica.
  Boletim Mensal. m. ISSN 0032-5082
- Portugal. Instituto Nacional de Estatistica.
  Boletim Mensal das Estatisticas da Agricultura e
  da Pesca. Continente e Ilhas Adjacentes. m.
- Portugal. Instituto Nacional de Estatistica.
  Boletim Mensal das Estatisticas Industrias. m.
- Portugal. Instituto Nacional de Estatistica.
  Boletim Mensal Estatistica. m.
- Portugal. Instituto Nacional de Estatistica.
  Boletim Trimestral das Estatisticas Monetarias e
  Financeiras. q.
- Portugal. Instituto Nacional de Estatistica.
  Estatisticas Agricolas. a. ISSN 0079-4139
- Portugal. Instituto Nacional de Estatistica.
  Estatisticas da Pesca/Statistiques de la Peche;
  continente e ilhas adjacentes. a.
- Portugal. Instituto Nacional de Estatistica.
  Estatisticas das Financas Publicas. a. ISSN 0079-
  4171
- Portugal. Instituto Nacional de Estatistica.
  Estatisticas das Organizacoes Sindicais. a. ISSN
  0079-4163
- Portugal. Instituto Nacional de Estatistica.
  Estatisticas de Educacao. a. ISSN 0079-4155
- Portugal. Instituto Nacional de Estatistica.
  Estatisticas Demograficas. a.
- Portugal. Instituto Nacional de Estatistica.
  Estatisticas do Comercio Externo. a. ISSN 0079-
  4147
- Portugal. Instituto Nacional de Estatistica.
  Estatisticas do Turismo. a.
- Portugal. Instituto Nacional de Estatistica.
  Estatisticas das Contribucoes e Impostos. a.
  ISSN 0079-4120
- Portugal. Instituto Nacional de Estatistica.
  Indicadores Economics-Sociais/Social-Economic
  Indicators.
- Portugal. Instituto Nacional de Estatistica. Seri
  Estatisticas Regionais. irreg.
- Portugal. Instituto Nacional de Estatistica.
  Servicos Centrais. Recenseamento da Habitacao:
  Continente e Ilhas Adjacentes. irreg. (prep. by its
  Servicos Centrais)
- Resumo Meteorologico. irreg. (prep. by its Servios
  Centrais)

**Portugal. Instituto Nacional de Estatistica. Centro de
Estudos Demograficos**
Lisbon, Portugal.
- Portugal. Instituto Nacional de Estatistica. Centro
  de Estudos Demograficos. Caderno. irreg.
- Portugal. Instituto Nacional de Estatisticas.
  Centro de Estudos Demograficos. Revista. irreg.
  ISSN 0079-4082

**Portugal. Instituto Nacional de Estatistica. Delegacao do Funchal**
Edificio de Junta Geral, Avenida Arriaga, Funchal, Madeira, Portugal.
- Portugal. Instituto Nacional de Estatistica. Delegacao do Funchal. Boletim Trimestral de Estatistica - Arquipelago de Madeira. q.

**Portugal. Instituto Nacional de Meteorologia e Geofisica**
Rua Saraiva de Carvalho 2, Lisbon 1, Portugal.
- Resumos Meteorologicos para a Aeronautica. m. ISSN 0034-5954

**Portugal. Medical Association of Portugal**
Ave. de Liberdade 65, Lisbon, Portugal.
- Ordem dos Medicos. Boletim. m. ISSN 0030-4506

**Portugal. Ministerio da Educacao Nacional**
Campo Grande 83, Lisbon 5, Portugal.
- Bibliotecas e Arquivos de Portugal. irreg. (prep. by its Direccao-Geral do Patrimonio Cultural)

**Portugal. Ministerio da Educacao Nacional. Biblioteca Nacional de Lisboa**
Campo Grande-83, Lisbon 5, Portugal.
- Boletim de Bibliografia Portuguesa. m. ISSN 0006-5897

**Portugal. Ministerio da Justica**
c/o Director Se Servicos dos Cofres, Praca do Comercio, Lisbon, Portugal.
- Portugal. Ministerio da Justicia. Boletin. a.

**Portugal. Ministerio da Saude e Assistencia. Direccao Geral da Assistencia**
Largo do Rato, Lisboa 1, Portugal.
- Informacao Social. q.

**Portugal. Ministerio das Corporacoes e Previdencia Social. Gabinete de Planeamento**
Lisbon, Portugal.
- Portugal. Ministerio das Corporacoes e Previdencia Social. Gabinete de Planeamento. Inguerito Emprego. irreg.

**Portugal. Ministerio das Financas**
Lisbon 2, Portugal.
- Ciencia e Tecnica Fiscal. bi-m. (prep. by its Dirrecao Geral de Contribuicoes e Impostos)
- Portugal. Departamento Central de Planeamento. Plano de Desenvolvimento. a. (prep. by its Departamento Central de Planeamento)
- Portugal. Ministerio das Financas. Relatorio do Orcamento Geral do Estado. a. ISSN 0079-4201

**Portugal. Ministerio do Equipamento Social e do Ambiente. Comissao Nacional do Ambiente**
Carlos I No. 126, Lisbon 2, Portugal.
- Portugal. Comissao Nacional do Ambiente. Relatorio de Actividades. a.

**Portugal. Ministerio do Exercito**
Larga da Graca 94, Lisbon, Portugal.
- Jornal do Exercito. m. ISSN 0447-8819

**Portugal. Ministerio do Plano e da Coordenacao Economica. Departamento Central de Planemente**
Lisbon, Portugal.
- Portuguese Economic Situation from an External Relationship Point of View. irreg.

**Portugal. Ministerio do Ultramar**
Lisbon 3, Portugal.
- Portugal. Ministerio do Ultramar. Centro de Documentacao Tecnico-Economica. Boletim Bibliografico. m. ISSN 0008-9931 (prep. by its Centro de Documentacao Tecnico-Economica)
- Portugal. Ministerio do Ultramar. Relatorio das Actividades. a.

**Portugal. Ministry of Mass Communication. Directorate for Publications and Information**
Palacio Foz, Praca dos Restauradores, Lisbon 2, Portugal.
- Portugal Information. m.

**Portugal. Secretaria de Estado da Agricultura**
Direccao-Geral dos Servicos Florestais e Aquicolas, Lisbon, Portugal.
- Portugal. Direccao-Geral dos Servicos Florestais e Aquicolas. Gabinete de Estudos Economicos e Estatisticos. Cadernos. q. ISSN 0032-504X

**Portugal. Secretaria de Estado da Informacao e Turismo**
Direccao Geral da Informacao, Palacio Foz, Lisbon, Portugal.
- N P/Noticias de Portugal. w. ISSN 0047-8563
- Portugal-an Information Review. m. ISSN 0032-5031

**Portugal. Secretaria de Estado das Pescas**
Lisbon-2, Portugal.
- Notas e Estudos. Serie Recursos e Ambiente Aquaticos. s-a.

**Portugal. Servico de Administracao Militar**
Rua Rodrigo da Fonseca, No. 180, Lisbon, Portugal.
- Portugal. Servico de Administracao Militar. Revista Bimestral. bi-m.
- Servico de Administracao Militar. m. ISSN 0037-2714

**Portugal. Servico Meteorologico Nacional**
Rua Saraiva de Carvalho 2, Lisbon 3, Portugal.
- Boletim Geoelectrico. m. ISSN 0006-5994
- Boletim Meteorologico para a Agricultura. m. ISSN 0006-6052

**Portugaliae Mathematica**
Rua do Diario de Noticias, 134-1, S. Lisbon 2, Portugal.
- Portugaliae Mathematica. q. ISSN 0032-5155

**Portuguese Club of Cine Amateurs**
- Cinema de Amadores. (pub. by Pathe Baby Portugal)

**Portuguese Franciscans**
- Itinerarium. (pub. by Editorial Franciscana)
- Paz e Alegria. (pub. by Editorial Franciscana)

**Portuguese Methodist Church**
Igreja do Mirante, Praca Coronel Pacheco, Porto, Portugal.
- Portugal Evangelico. m. ISSN 0032-5066 (Co-Sponsor: Presbyterian Church in Portugal)

**Procuradoria das Estudantes Ultramarinos**
Av. da Republica 8-6, Lisbon 1, Portugal.
- Ultramar; revista da comunidade portuguesa e da actualidade ultramarina internacional. q. ISSN 0041-6231

**Reparticao de Assistencia Tecnica e Vulgarizacao**
Av.Antonio Serpa No 26, Lisbon 1, Portugal.
- Boletim de Vulgarizacao Veterinaria. m. ISSN 0045-2386

**Revista de Economia**
Rua Rodrigo da Fonseca, 76, Lisbon 1, Portugal.
- Revista de Economia. q.

**Empresa de Publicidade Seara Nova, S.A.R.L.**
Rua Bernardo Lima 23, Lisbon 1, Portugal.
- Seara Nova. m. ISSN 0037-0177

**Servico de Publicacoes da M.P.**
Rua Artilharia 1, 101, 7-0, Lisbon, Portugal.
- Camarada. fortn. ISSN 0008-1957

**Sindicato Nacional dos Oficiais Maquinistas da Marinha Mercante**
Av. D. Carlos 1, Lisbon, Portugal.
- Propulsor. bi-m.

**Jose Soares de Oliveira, Ed. & Pub.**
- Defesa Nacional. (pub. by Jose Soares de Oliveira, Ed. & Pub.)

**Sociedade das Ciencias Medicas de Lisboa**
Avenida da Republica, 34, 1 Lisbon, Portugal.
- Sociedade das Ciencias Medicas. Jornal. m.

**Sociedade de Lingua Portuguesa**
Rua de S. Jose 41, 20 Lisbon, Portugal.
- Bem Lingua Portuguesa. bi-m.
- Lingua e Cultura. 3 per yr. ISSN 0047-4703
- Sociedade de Lingua Portuguesa. Boletim. bi-m. ISSN 0049-1039

**Sociedade Farmaceutica Lusitana**
Rua da Sociedade Farmaceutica, No. 18, Lisbon-1, Portugal.
- Revista Portuguesa de Farmacia. q.

**Sociedade Industrial Farmaceutica**
Trav. da Espera 3, Apdo. 2072, Lisbon, Portugal.
- Anais Azevedos. a. ISSN 0003-2425

**Sociedade Martins Sarmento**
Rua de Paio Galvao, Guimaraes, Portugal.
- Revista de Guimaraes. s-a. ISSN 0034-8295

**Sociedade Portuguesa de Antropologia e Etnologia**
Universidade de Oporto, Oporto, Portugal.
- Trabalho de Antropologia e Etnologia. 2 per yr (some double issues) (Co-sponsor: Instituto de Antropologia. Centro de Estudos de Etnologia Peninsular)

**Sociedade Portuguesa de Ciencias Veterinarias**
Rua de D. Dinis 2-A, Lisbon 2, Portugal.
- Revista Portuguesa de Ciencias Veterinarias. q. ISSN 0035-0389

**Sociedade Portuguesa de Estomatologia**
Av. Rainha D. Amelia36-R/C.Dt, Lisbon-5, Portugal.
- Revista Portuguesa de Estomatologia e Cirurgia Maxilo-Facial. ISSN 0035-0397

**Sociedade Portuguesa de Numismatica**
Rua de Costa Cabral, 664, Porto, Portugal.
- N U M U S Numismatica, Medalhistica, Argueologia. a. ISSN 0085-364X

**Sociedade Portuguesa de Quimica**
Instituto Superior Tecnico, Lisbon 1, Portugal.
- Apcadec. Boletim do Comprador. q.
- Revista Portuguesa de Quimica. q. ISSN 0035-0419

**Sociedade Portuguesa de Reumatologia**
Rua de Dona Estefania, 187-189, Lisbon-1, Portugal.
- Acta Reumatologica Portuguesa. q.
- Sociedade Portuguesa de Reumatologia. Boletim Informativo. q.

**South African Embassy, Lisbon**
Av. Antonio Augusto de Aguiar 88-3, Lisbon, Portugal.
- Noticias da Africa do Sul; revista de cultura, turismo e economia. m. ISSN 0048-0886

**Sport Lisboa e Benfica**
Rua Jardim do Regedor, 19-3, Lisbon, Portugal.
- Benfica. w. ISSN 0005-8785

**Tertulia Edipica**
Rua de Arroios, 11-R-C-E, Lisbon 1, Portugal.
- Charadista. q. ISSN 0300-4368

**Uniao das Associacoes de Espectaculos e Diversoes**
Avenida Duque de Loule 86-2dt, Lisbon, Portugal.
- Jornal dos Espectaculos. m.

**Universidade Catolica Portuguesa. Faculdade de Teologia**
Palma de Cima, Lisbon 4, Portugal.
- Didaskalia. s-a.

**Universidade de Coimbra. Arquivo**
Paco das Escolas, Coimbra, Portugal.
- Universidade de Coimbra. Boletim do Arquivo. irreg.

**Universidade de Coimbra. Departamento de Zoologia**
Coimbra, Portugal.
- Ciencia Biologica: Biologia Molecular e Celular. a.

**Universidade de Coimbra. Faculdade de Direito**
- Universidade de Coimbra. Faculdade de Direito. Boletim. (pub. by Coimbra Editora)
- Universidade de Coimbra. Faculdade de Direito. Boletim de Ciencias Economicas. (pub. by Coimbra Editora)

**Universidade de Coimbra. Faculdade de Farmacia**
Rua do Norte and Couraca des Apostolos, 51 - R/C E, Coimbra, Portugal.
- Coimbra. Universidade. Faculdade de Farmacia. Boletin. Edicao Didactica. Noticias Farmaceuticas. a.

**Universidade de Coimbra. Faculdade de Letras**
Coimbra, Portugal.
- Biblos. a.

**Universidade de Coimbra. Faculdade de Medicina**
Coimbra, Portugal.
- Arquivos de Patologia Geral e Anatomia Patologia da Universidade de Coimbra. a. ISSN 0066-7854

**Universidade de Coimbra. Instituto Botanico**
Arcos do Jardim, Coimbra, Portugal.
- Sociedade Broteriana, Coimbra. Anuario. a.
- Sociedade Broteriana, Coimbra. Boletim. a. ISSN 0081-0657
- Sociedade Broteriana, Coimbra. Memorias. irreg., approx. 1 per year. ISSN 0081-0665

**Universidade de Coimbra. Instituto de Antropologia**
Rua da Ilha, Coimbra, Portugal.
- Contribuicoes para o Estudo da Antropologia Portuguesa. irreg.

**Universidade de Lisboa. Faculdade de Ciencias**
Lisbon 2, Portugal.
- Portugaliae Acta Biologica. irreg. ISSN 0032-5147 (prep. by its Instituto Botanico) (Co-sponsor: Laboratorio de Patologia Vegetal Verissimo de Almeida)
- Revista de Biologia. q. ISSN 0034-7736 (prep. by its Museo, Laboratorio e Jardim Botanico)
- Universidade de Lisboa. Faculdade de Ciencias. Instituto Botanico. Artigo de Divulgacao. irreg. ISSN 0066-8079 (prep. by its Instituto Botanico)

**Universidade de Lisboa. Faculdade de Direito**
Lisbon, Portugal.
- Universidade de Lisboa. Faculdade de Direito. Revista. a.

**Universidade de Lisboa. Faculdade de Farmacia**
Avenida 28 de Maie, Lisbon, Portugal.
- Universidade de Lisboa. Faculdade de Farmacio. Boletim. irreg.

**Universidade de Lisboa. Faculdade de Letras**
Lisbon, Portugal.
- Universidade de Lisboa. Faculdade de Lisboa. Revista. irreg.; 1971, 3rd series, no. 13.

**Universidade de Lisboa. Instituto de Anatomia Normal**
Avda. Egas Moniz, Lisbon 4, Portugal.
- Arquivo de Anatomia e Antropologia. a. ISSN 0066-7811

**Universidade do Porto**
Instituto de Zoologia "Dr. Augusto Nobre", Faculdade de Ciencias, Porto, Portugal.
- Instituto de Zoologia "Dr. Augusto Nobre" Publicacoes. 3-5 per yr. ISSN 0020-4021

**Universidade do Porto. Instituto Geofisico**
Sierra do Pilar, Villa Nova de Gaia, Portugal.
- Boletim Microssismico. irreg.
- Boletim Sismico. a. ISSN 0006-6109

**Universidade Tecnica de Lisboa**
Instituto Superior de Ciencias Sociais e Politica Ultramarina, Rua da Junqueira 86, Lisbon, Portugal.
- Estudos Politicos e Sociais. q. ISSN 0014-1623

**Universidade Tecnica de Lisboa. Gabinete de Investigacoes Sociais**
R. do Quelhas 6, Lisbon 2, Portugal.
- Analise Social. q. ISSN 0003-2573

**Universidade Tecnica de Lisboa. Instituto Superior de Ciencias Economicas e Financeiras**
Lisbon, Portugal.
- Economia e Financas. a.

**Vertice**
Rua das Fangas 55-A-2. D.O, Coimbra, Portugal.
- Vertice; revista de cultura e arte. m. ISSN 0042-4447

**Voz do Operario**
R. da Voz do Operaro, 13, Lisbon-2, Portugal.
- Voz do Operario. m.

# PUERTO RICO

**Academia de Artes y Ciencias de Puerto Rico**
Condominio Balmoral Ofic. 1D, Calle Parque 110, Santurce, PR 00911.
- Academia de Artes y Ciencias de Puerto Rico. Boletin. q. ISSN 0001-379X

**Aquarius**
Box 613, Old San Juan, PR 00902.
- Aquarius. q.

**Artes Visuales**
Box 5718, Pta. de Tierra, San Juan, PR 00906.
- Artes Visuales. ISSN 0092-489X

**Asociacion de Maestros de Puerto Rico**
Av. Ponce de Leon 452, Hato Rey, PR 00918.
- Sol. 10 per yr. ISSN 0034-933X

**Asociacion Medica de Puerto Rico**
Avenida Fernandez Juncos, No. 1305, Apdo. de Correo 9387, Santurce, PR 00908.
- Asociacion Medica de Puerto Rico. Boletin. m. ISSN 0004-4849

**Asociacion Puertorriquena de la Unesco**
Box 1361, San Juan, PR 00902.
- Boletin de Arte. q. ISSN 0006-6206

**Association of Caribbean Universities and Research Institutes**
Box 11532, Caparra Heights Station, San Juan, PR 00922.
- Caribbean Educational Bulletin/Boletin Educacional del Caribe. 3 per yr.

**Association of Caribbean University and Research Libraries**
Box S, Estacion de la Universidad, San Juan, PR 00931.
- Association of Caribbean University and Research Libraries. Carta Informativa de ACURIL/A C U R I L Newsletter. q.

**Association of Island Marine Laboratories of the Caribbean**
University of Puerto Rico, Dept. of Marine Sciences, Mayaguez, Puerto Rico.
- Association of Island Marine Laboratories of the Caribbean. Proceedings. irreg., 1973, no. 9. ISSN 0066-9571

**Barba**
Calle Asomante 1736, Summit Hills, Rio Piedras, PR 00920.
- Barba; the rock newspaper of Puerto Rico. m. ISSN 0005-5883

**Chamber of Commerce of Puerto Rico**
Box 3789, San Juan, PR 00904.
- Comercio y Produccion. bi-m. ISSN 0010-2350

**Colegio de Abogados de Puerto Rico**
Box 1900, San Juan, PR 00903.
- Colegio de Abogados de Puerto Rico. Revista. q. ISSN 0010-0579

**Colegio de Cirujanos Dentistas de Puerto Rico**
Box 9023, Santurce, PR 00908.
- Revista Odontologica de Puerto Rico. ISSN 0035-0281

**Colegio de Ingenieros Arquitectos y Agrimensores de Puerto Rico**
- Colegio de Ingenieros Arquitectos y Agrimensores de Puerto Rico. Revista. (pub. by Insular Publishers Corp)

**Commercial Fisheries Laboratory**
Box 3665, Mayaguez, PR 00708.
- Puerto Rico. Department of Agriculture. Agricultural and Fisheries Contributions/Puerto Rico. Departamento de Agricultura. Contribuciones Agropecuarias y Pesqueras. irreg.

**Cooperativa Cafeteros de Puerto Rico**
Ponce, Puerto Rico.
- Revista del Cafe; al servicio de la agricultura en general. m. ISSN 0034-9011

**Editorial Cordillera, Inc.**
Ave. F.D. Roosevelt, 237, Hato Rey, Puerto Rico.
- Almanaque Boricua; libro de informacion general sobre Puerto Rico. a.

**Economic Development Administration**
- Puerto Rico Official Industrial Directory. (pub. by Witcom Group)

**Facultad de la Escuela de Trabajo Social**
Rosa C. Marin, Apdo 6679, Santurce, PR 00907.
- Revista de Servicio Social. irreg. ISSN 0034-8937

**Government Development Bank for Puerto Rico**
see **Puerto Rico. Banco Gubernamenta de Fomento**

**Guajana**
Las Palmas 1059, Santurce, PR 00907.
- Guajana. 3 per yr. ISSN 0017-498X

**Guia Industrial y Comercial de Puerto Rico, Inc.**
Box 8789, Fernandez Juncos Sta., Santurce, PR 00907.
- Guia Industrial y Comercial de Puerto Rico/ Puerto Rico Industrial & Commercial Guide. irreg.

**Instituto de Cultura Puertorriquena**
Apartado 4184, San Juan, PR 00905.
- Instituto de Cultura Puertorriquena. Revista. q. ISSN 0020-3815
- Serie Literatura Hoy. irreg.

**Insular Publishers Corp**
Box GA, Caparra Heights, Puerto Rico, PR 00922.
- Colegio de Ingenieros Arquitectos y Agrimensores de Puerto Rico. Revista. 4 per yr. ISSN 0010-0609

**Inter American University of Puerto Rico**
- Revista/Review Interamericana. (pub. by Inter American University Press)

**Inter American University of Puerto Rico. Alumni Association**
Box 3255, Hato Rey, PR 00936.
- Polygraph-I A U News. q.

**Inter American University Press**
Box 3255, San Juan, PR 00936.
- Readings in Spanish-English Contrastive Linguistics. irreg.
- Revista/Review Interamericana. q. (Inter American University of Puerto Rico)

**Liga Socialista Puertorriquena**
Cerra 628 PDA, 15 Bajos Santurce, Apdo 283, Guaynabo, PR 00657.
- Socialista. m. ISSN 0037-8283

**Municipio de San Juan**
San Juan, Puerto Rico.
- Capital en Accion. m. ISSN 0008-5871

**Partido Socialista Puertorriqueno**
Calle Toscanio 1153 Urb. Villa Capri, Rio Piedras, PR 00632.
- Claridad; el periodico de la independencia. s-w.

**Publishers Group**
406 Ponce de Leon Ave., San Juan, PR 00901.
- Industrial Puerto Rico. bi-m. ISSN 0019-8633
- Te-ve Guia. w. ISSN 0040-0327

**Puerto Rico. Banco Gubernamental de Fomento**
Centro Gubernamental Minillas, G.P.O. 4748, San Juan, PR 00905.
- Banco Gubernamental de Fomento para Puerto Rico. Carta Trimestral. q.
- Government Development Bank for Puerto Rico. Report of Activities. a.
- Quarterly Report to Investors in Puerto Rican Securities. q. ISSN 0033-572X

**Puerto Rico. Bureau of Labor Statistics. Wage Analysis and Occupational Studies Division**
San Juan, Puerto Rico.
- Puerto Rico. Bureau of Labor Statistics. Salarios, Horas Semanales Trabajadas y Otras Condiciones de Trabajo. Earnings, Weekly Hours Worked and Other Working Conditions. irreg.

**Puerto Rico. Bureau of the Budget**
Box 3228, San Juan, PR 00904.
- Puerto Rico. Bureau of the Budget. Boletin de Gerencia Administrativa. irreg. (approx. 4-6 per yr.)
- Puerto Rico. Bureau of the Budget. Resoluciones Conjuntas del Presupuesto General y de Presupuestos Especiales. a. ISSN 0079-7863

**Puerto Rico. Comision de Derechos Civiles**
Aptdo 1016, Estacion de Hato Rey, Hato Rey, San Juan, PR 00919.
- Puerto Rico. Comision de Derechos Civiles. Estudios y Monografias. irreg.
- Puerto Rico. Comision de Derechos Civiles. Informe Anual. a.

**Puerto Rico. Departamento de la Vivienda. Urban Renewal and Housing Corporation**
San Juan, Puerto Rico.
- Puerto Rico. Departamento de la Vivienda. Secretaria Auxiliar de Planificacion y Programacion. Informe Anual. a.

**Puerto Rico. Department of Agriculture**
P.O. Box 10163, Santurce, PR 00908.
- Agricultura al Dia. bi-m. ISSN 0002-1342
- Puerto Rico. Department of Agriculture. Agricultural and Fisheries Contributions/Puerto Rico. Departamento de Agricultura. Contribuciones Agropecuarias y Pesqueras. (pub. by Commercial Fisheries Laboratory)
- Puerto Rico. Oficina de Estadisticas Agricolas. Boletin Mensual de Estadisticas Agricolas. m. (prep. by its Agricultural Statistics Office)
- Revista de Agricultura de Puerto Rico. s-a.

**Puerto Rico. Department of Education**
Ave. Cesar Gonzalez, Hato Rey, PR 00918.
- Educacion. 3 per yr. ISSN 0013-1067

**Puerto Rico. Department of Health. Cancer Control Program**
Central Cancer Registry, Santurce, PR 00908.
- Cancer in Puerto Rico. a.

**Puerto Rico. Department of Health. Division of Health Facilites**
Stop 19, Santurce, PR 00907.
- Puerto Rico. Division of Health Facilities. Plan for Hospital and Medical Facilites. a.

**Puerto Rico. Department of Labor**
Hato Rey, PR 00917.
- Empleo y Desempleo en Puerto Rico/ Employment and Unemployment in Puerto Rico: Calendar Years.

**Puerto Rico. Department of Labor. Bureau of Labor Statistics**
414 Barbosa Ave., Hato Rey, PR 00917.
- Census of Manufacturing Industries of Puerto Rico. a. ISSN 0552-5276
- Establecimientos Manufactureras en Puerto Rico. a.
- Indice de Precios al Consumidor para Familias Obreras en Puerto Rico. m. ISSN 0019-7017
- Noticias del Trabajo. m. ISSN 0029-4195
- Puerto Rico. Department of Labor. Bureau of Labor Statistics. Employment Hours and Earnings in the Manufacturing Establishments Promoted by the Economic Development Administration of the Puerto Rican Industrial Development Company. m.
- Puerto Rico. Department of Labor. Directorio de Organizaciones del Trabajo. a.
- Regularidad de Trabajo en Puerto Rico/Work Experiences in Puerto Rico. irreg; latest issue, 1975.

**Puerto Rico. Department of State**
Fortaleza 54, San Juan, PR 00904.
- Carta de Puerto Rico. s-m.

**Puerto Rico. Department of State. Caribbean Regional Library**
Av. Ponce de Leon 452, Apdo. 1050, Hato Rey, PR 00919.
- Current Caribbean Bibliography/Bibliografia Actual del Caribe/Bibliographie Courante de la Caraibe. a. ISSN 0070-1866

**Puerto Rico. Department of the Treasury**
Box 4515, San Juan, PR 00905.
- Consolidated Report of the Condition of Banks Operating in Puerto Rico. m. ISSN 0045-8163 (prep. by its Bureau of Bank and Financial Institutions)
- Puerto Rico. Department of the Treasury. Economy & Finances. a. ISSN 0079-7871 (prep. by its Economics Division)
- What You Should Know about Taxes in Puerto Rico. a. ISSN 0083-9132 (prep. by its Office of Economic Research)

**Puerto Rico. Division of Demographic Registry and Vital Statistics**
San Juan, PR 00901.
- Puerto Rico. Division of Demographic Registry and Vital Statistics. Annual Vital Statistics Report. a. ISSN 0555-6511
- Puerto Rico. Division of Demographic Registry and Vital Statistics. Quarterly Vital Statistics Report. q.

**Puerto Rico. Planning Board. Economic Indices Section**
Box 41119, Santurce, PR 00940.
- Indicadores Economicos Mensuales de Puerto Rico/Monthly Economic Indicators of Puerto Rico. m.

**Puerto Rico. Planning Board. Statistics Coordination Section**
Box 41119, Santurce, PR 00940.
- Puerto Rico. Planning Board. Statistics Coordination Section. Programas Estadisticos/ Puerto Rico. Junta de Planificacion. Seccion de Coordinacion de Estadisticas. Programas Estadisticos. s-a. ISSN 0555-6562

**Puerto Rico. Ports Authority. Office of Economic Research**
G.P.O. Box 2829, San Juan, PR 00936.
- Puerto Rico. Ports Authority. Office of Economic Research. Statistical Report. m.

**Puerto Rico Living**
Box 6756 , Loiza Sta., Santurce, PR 00914.
- Puerto Rico Living. a. ISSN 0033-4049

**Editorial Ramallo**
Calle Duarte 227, Hato Rey, PR 00917.
- Infantil. m.

**Sala Foundation**
43 Concordia St., Ponce, PR 00731.
- Ciencia/Science; boletin cientifico del sur. q.

**San Juan. Gobierno Municipal**
San Juan, PR 00936.
- Dialogo. m.

**Sin Nombre, Inc.**
55 Cordero St., Santurce, PR 00911.
- Sin Nombre; quarterly literary review. q. ISSN 0037-5527

**Sociedad de Autores Puertorriquenoes**
San Juan, Puerto Rico.
- Sociedad de Autores Puertorriquenoes. Boletin. q.

**Sociedad de Bibliotecarios de Puerto Rico**
Box 22898, University Sta., San Juan, PR 00931.
- Sociedad de Bibliotecarios de Puerto Rico. Boletin. 3 per yr. ISSN 0037-8496

**Publicaciones Torregrosa**
Apartado 1807, Hato Rey, PR 00919.
- Angela Luisa. m.

**Tourism Company of Puerto Rico**
G.P.O. Box BN, San Juan, PR 00936.
- Que Pasa; official visitors guide to Puerto Rico. m.
- Selected Statistics of the Tourism Industry in Puerto Rico. a; latest issue, 1975-76.

**U. S. Geological Survey**
Water Resources Div., District Chief, Box 34168, Fort Buchanan, Puerto Rico 00934.
- Water Resources Data for Puerto Rico. a. (Co-Sponsor: Puerto Rico Aqueduct and Sewer Authority)

**U.S. Institute of Tropical Forestry**
P. P. Box AQ, Rio Piedras, PR 00928.
- U.S. Institute of Tropical Forestry. Annual Letter. a.

**Universidad Catolica de Puerto Rico**
Ponce, PR 00731.
- Horizontes. s-a. ISSN 0018-5027

**Universidad Catolica de Puerto Rico. School of Law**
Ponce, PR 00731.
- Revista de Derecho Puertorriqueno. q. ISSN 0034-7930

**Universidad de Puerto Rico**
- Puerto. (pub. by Editorial Universitaria)
- Torre. (pub. by Editorial Universitaria)

**Universidad de Puerto Rico. Administracion de Colegios Regionales**
Colegio Regional de Ponce, Ponce, PR 00731.
- Ceiba. s-a.

**Universidad de Puerto Rico. Agricultural Experimental Station**
Box H, Rio Piedras, PR 00928.
- University of Puerto Rico. Journal of Agriculture. q. ISSN 0041-994X

**Universidad de Puerto Rico. Animal Husbandry Division**
Box AR, Rio Piedras, PR 00928.
- Universidad de Puerto Rico. Servicio de Extension Agricola. Boletin Ganadero. q. ISSN 0041-8528 (prep. by its Cooperative Extension Service)

**Universidad de Puerto Rico. Center for Educational Research**
Recinto de Rio Piedras, PR 00928.
- Universidad de Puerto Rico. Centro de Investigaciones Pedagogicas. Boletin. q.

**Universidad de Puerto Rico. Centro de Investigaciones Sociales**
Rio Piedras, PR 00931.
- Universidad de Puerto Rico. Centro de Investigaciones Sociales. Informe Anual. a.

**Universidad de Puerto Rico. Escuela de Derecho**
Rio Piedras, PR 00931.
- Universidad de Puerto Rico. Escuela de Derecho. Revista Juridica. q. ISSN 0041-851X

**Universidad de Puerto Rico. Escuela Graduada de Planificacion**
Apartado B. E., Rio Piedras, PR 00931.
- P L E R U S. (Planning-Economic, Regional, Urban, Social) s-a. ISSN 0048-4466

**Universidad de Puerto Rico. Facultad de Humanidad**
P.O. Box 21572, U.P.R. Station, Rio Piedras, PR 00931.
- Dialogos. s-a. ISSN 0012-2122 (prep. by its Department of Philosophy)
- Revista de Estudios Hispanicos. a. (prep. by its Departamento de Estudios Hispanicos)

**Universidad de Puerto Rico. Facultad de Pedagogia**
- Pedagogia. (pub. by Editorial Universitaria)

**Universidad de Puerto Rico. Graduate School of Social Work**
Rio Piedras, PR 00931.
- Humanidad. a. ISSN 0441-4144
- Revista de Ciencias Sociales. q. ISSN 0034-7817

**Universidad de Puerto Rico. Institute of Caribbean Studies**
Rio Piedras, PR 00931.
- Caribbean Bibliography. irreg. ISSN 0069-0465
- Caribbean Documents. irreg. ISSN 0069-0473 (Co-sponsor: Institute of International Relations, University of the West Indies)
- Caribbean Monograph Series. irreg. ISSN 0069-0511
- Caribbean Scholars' Conference. Proceedings. biennial. ISSN 0069-052X
- Caribbean Studies. q. ISSN 0008-6533
- Universidad de Puerto Rico. Institute of Caribbean Studies. Special Studies. irreg. ISSN 0079-788X

**Universidad de Puerto Rico. Mayaguez Campus**
Mayaguez, PR 00708.
- Atenea. q. ISSN 0044-9849 (prep. by its College of Arts and Sciences)

**Universidad de Puerto Rico. Medical Sciences Campus Library**
G.P.O. Box 5067, San Juan, PR 00936.
- List of Current Serial Publications Being Received at the University of Puerto Rico Medical Sciences Campus Library. a; latest issue, 1972.

**Universidad de Puerto Rico. School of Medicine**
Box 5067, San Juan, PR 00936.
- Buhiti. q. ISSN 0045-3374
- Escalpelo. 4 per yr. ISSN 0014-0341

**Universidad de Puerto Rico. School of Public Administration**
Apartado 21839, Estacion U.P.R, Rio Piedras, PR 00931.
- Revista de Administracion Publica. s-a. ISSN 0034-7620

**Editorial Universitaria**
Apartado Postal X, San Juan, PR 00931.
- Pedagogia. 2 per yr. (Universidad de Puerto Rico. Facultad de Pedagogia)
- Puerto. q. ISSN 0033-4022 (Universidad de Puerto Rico)
- Torre; revista general de la Universidad de Puerto Rico. q. ISSN 0040-9588 (Universidad de Puerto Rico)

**University of Puerto Rico**
see **Universidad de Puerto Rico**

**Witcom Group**
210 Ponce de Leon, San Juan, PR 00901
- Commercial Directory of Puerto Rico-Virgin
  Islands. a. ISSN 0092-1297 (U.S. Distrib.: Dun &
  Bradstreet International, Box 3224 Church St.
  Sta., New York, Ny 10008)
- Puerto Rico Official Industrial Directory. a. ISSN
  0090-3612 (Economic Development
  Administration) (U.S. Distrib: Dun & Bradstreet
  International, Box 3224 Church St. Sta., New
  York, Ny 10008)

# REUNION

**Imprimerie Librairie Cazal**
42 rue Alexis-de-Villeneuve, Saint-Denis, Reunion.
- Combat National; bi-mensuel reunionnais. bi-m.
- Journal de l'Ile de la Reunion. d.

**Centre Universitaire de la Reunion**
12 rue de la Victoire, 97489 Saint-Denis, Reunion.
- Centre Universitaire de la Reunion. Cahier. irreg.

**Fondation pour la Recherche et le Developpement
dans l'Ocean Indien**
Bibliotheque Departementale, Rue Roland Garros,
St. Denis, Reunion.
- Fondation pour la Recherche et le Developpement
  dans l'Ocean Indien. Documents et Recherches.
  irreg.

**Museum d'Histoire Naturelle**
B.P. 1012, Saint-Denis, Reunion.
- Info-Nature. irreg. (Societe Reunionnaise pour
  l'Etude et la Protection de la Nature)

**Societe Reunionnaise pour l'Etude et la Protection de
la Nature**
- Info-Nature. (pub. by Museum d'Histoire
  Naturelle)

# RHODESIA

**African National Council**
Machipisa Shopping Center, Salisbury, Zimbabwe,
Rhodesia.
- Zimbabwe Star. w.

**Air Rhodesia Corporation**
P.O. Box AP. 1, Salisbury Airport, Salisbury,
Rhodesia.
- Air Rhodesia Annual Report. a.
- Air Rhodesia Time Table. q.

**Association of Afrikaans Rhodesians**
Box 2783, Salisbury, Rhodesia.
- Rhodesier. m.

**Automobile Association of Rhodesia**
P.O. Box 585, Salisbury, Rhodesia.
- Automobile Association of Rhodesia. Quarterly
  Bulletin. q.

**British South Africa Police**
Box HG 106, Highlands, Salisbury, Rhodesia.
- Outpost. m. ISSN 0030-7289

**Candour League of Rhodesia**
P.O. Box 1871, Salisbury, Rhodesia.
- Rhodesia and World Report. m. ISSN 0035-4694

**Central Africa Historical Association**
University College, Box MP 167, Salisbury,
Rhodesia.
- Central Africa Historical Association. Local Series
  Pamphlets. irreg. ISSN 0577-036X
- Rhodesian History. a.

**Central African Journal of Medicine**
Box 2073, Salisbury, Rhodesia.
- Central African Journal of Medicine. m. ISSN
  0008-9176

**Central African Power Corporation**
P.O. Box 630, Salisbury, Rhodesia.
- Central African Power Corporation. Annual
  Report and Accounts. a. ISSN 0069-147X

**Central African Zionist Organisation**
Box 1162, Bulawayo, Rhodesia.
- Central African Zionist Digest. m. ISSN 0008-
  9184

**Chamber of Mines of Rhodesia**
- Chamber of Mines Journal. (pub. by Thomson
  Newspapers Rhodesia)

**Chirimo**
Box A 294, Avondale, Salisbury, Rhodesia.
- Chirimo; review of Rhodesian and international
  poetry. 3 per yr. ISSN 0009-4684

**City Printers and Stationers (Pty) Ltd.**
Box 1943, Salisbury, Rhodesia.
- Assegai; the magazine of the Rhodesian Army. m.
  ISSN 0004-5020 (Rhodesia. Army)

**Contemporary Publishers (Pvt.) Ltd.**
Box 3793, Salisbury, Rhodesia.
- Hotel Tourama of Rhodesia. m. (Hotel
  Association of Rhodesia) (Co-sponsor:
  Association of Rhodesian Travel Agents)
- You. m. ISSN 0044-0701

**Cotton Research Institute, Gatooma**
Department of Research and Specialist Services,
Box 8108, Causeway, Salisbury, Rhodesia.
- Cotton Research Institute, Gatooma. Annual
  Report. a.

**Federation of African Women's Clubs**
Box UA 339, Salisbury, Rhodesia.
- Federation of African Women's Clubs. Newsletter.
  s-a.

**Fort Victoria-Zimbabwe Publicity Association**
P. O. Box 340, Fort Victoria, Rhodesia.
- Fort Victoria Diary. m.

**Graham Publishing Co. (Pvt.) Ltd.**
Box 2931, Salisbury, Rhodesia.
- Illustrated Life Rhodesia. fortn. ISSN 0019-2414

**Hotel Association of Rhodesia**
- Hotel Tourama of Rhodesia. (pub. by
  Contemporary Publishers (Pvt.) Ltd.)
- Rhodesian Hotel & Catering Gazette. (pub. by
  Roblaw Publishers (Pvt.) Ltd.)

**Independent Newspapers**
Box 1160, Salisbury, Rhodesia.
- National Observer. w.

**Industrial Press (Pvt.) Ltd.**
Manica Rd., Box 638, Salisbury, Rhodesia.
- Rhodesian Industrialist. m. ISSN 0035-4791

**Insurance Institute, Rhodesia**
- Rhodesian Insurance Review. (pub. by Thomson
  Newspapers Rhodesia)

**Litho Services (Pvt.) Ltd.**
Box 3625, Salisbury, Rhodesia.
- Rhodesia Science News. m. ISSN 0035-4732

**Mambo Press**
Box 779, Gwelo, Rhodesia.
- Mambo Occasional Papers. Socio-Economic
  Series. irreg.

**Modern Publications**
P.O. Box 1183, Bulawayo, Rhodesia.
- Bulawayo This Month.

**Modus Publications (Pvt.) Ltd.**
Elgin House, 6th Fl., Union Ave., Box 1819,
Salisbury, Rhodesia.
- Development. m.

**National Free Library of Rhodesia**
P.O. Box 1773, Bulawayo, Rhodesia.
- National Free Library of Rhodesia. Annual
  Report. a. ISSN 0068-3612
- Shelfmark. bi-m. ISSN 0037-3494

**National Gallery of Rhodesia**
Box 8155, Causeway, Salisbury, Rhodesia.
- National Gallery of Rhodesia. Annual Report and
  Balance Sheet and Income and Expenditure
  Account. a.

**National Museums and Monuments of Rhodesia**
P.O. Box 8540, Causeway, Salisbury, Rhodesia.
- Arnoldia Rhodesia. irreg. ISSN 0066-7781
- Kariba Studies. irreg., no. 6, 1976. ISSN 0085-
  249X
- Museum Memoir. irreg; no. 8, 1976. ISSN 0304-
  5323
- National Museums and Monuments of Rhodesia.
  Occasional Papers. Series A: Human Sciences.
  irreg. ISSN 0304-5307

- National Museums and Monuments of Rhodesia.
  Occasional Papers. Series B: Natural Sciences.
  irreg. ISSN 0304-5315

**Parade Publications (Pty) Ltd.**
Travlos House, 3rd. Floor, 34 Stanley Ave., Box
3798, Salisbury, Rhodesia.
- Parade and Foto-Action. m. ISSN 0031-1618

**Radio Society of Rhodesia**
Box 2377, Salisbury, Rhodesia.
- Q U A. m.

**Rhodesia. Army**
- Assegai. (pub. by City Printers and Stationers
  (Pty) Ltd.)

**Rhodesia. Central Statistical Office**
P.O. Box 8063, Causeway, Salisbury, Rhodesia.
- National Accounts and Balance of Payments of
  Rhodesia. a. ISSN 0077-2941
- Rhodesia. Central Statistical Office. Agricultural
  Production in African Purchase Lands. Part 1.
  National and Provincial Totals. a, latest 1975.
- Rhodesia. Central Statistical Office. Agricultural
  Production in European Areas. Part 1. Livestock.
  National and Provincial Totals. a, latest 1976.
- Rhodesia. Central Statistical Office. Population
  Census. irreg; latest issue, 1969. ISSN 0085-5685

**Rhodesia. Department of Meteorological Services**
Box BE 150, Belvedere, Salisbury, Rhodesia.
- Rhodesia. Department of Meteorological Services.
  Rainfall Report. a. ISSN 0085-5693
- Rhodesia. Department of Meteorological Services.
  Report. a. ISSN 0085-5707

**Rhodesia. Government Printer**
Box 8062, Causeway, Salisbury, Rhodesia.
- Economic Survey of Rhodesia. a. ISSN 0070-8739
- Rhodesia. Department of Works. Report of the
  Controller of Works. a; latest issue, 1973.
- Rhodesia. Ministry of Education. African
  Education Report. a. ISSN 0080-2859
- Rhodesia. Ministry of Lands and Natural
  Resources. Report of the Secretary for Lands and
  Natural Resources. a.
- Rhodesia Government Gazette. fortn.
- Rhodesia Research Index; register of current
  research in Rhodesia. a. (Co-sponsors: University
  of Rhodesia; Department of the Prime Minister,
  Scientific Liaison)

**Rhodesia. Ministry of Agriculture**
Box 8108, Causeway, Salisbury, Rhodesia.
- Rhodesia Agricultural Journal. bi-m. ISSN 0035-
  4686
- Rhodesian Journal of Agricultural Research. s-a.
  ISSN 0035-4813 (prep. by its Department of
  Research and Specialist Services)

**Rhodesia. Ministry of Education. Branch of
Community Development Training**
Private Bag 7724, Causeway, Salisbury, Rhodesia.
- People and Projects. irreg., no. 11, 1976.

**Rhodesia. Ministry of Finance**
Box 8062, Causeway, Rhodesia.
- Rhodesia. Ministry of Finance. Budget Statement.
  a.

**Rhodesia. Ministry of Information, Immigration and
Tourism**
Box 8122, Causeway, Rhodesia.
- African Times; the Rhodesian people's paper.
  fortn.
- Focus on Rhodesia. fortn. (English edition); m
  (other editions)

**Rhodesia. Ministry of Internal Affairs**
Private Bag 7702, Causeway, Salisbury, Rhodesia.
- NADA. a. ISSN 0085-3658 (prep. by its
  Management Committee)

**Rhodesia. Ministry of Water Development**
c/o Chief Hydrological Engineer, P.O. Box 8132,
Causeway, Salisbury, Rhodesia.
- Rhodesia. Ministry of Water Development.
  Hydrological Summaries. quinquennial; latest
  1969-70. ISSN 0080-2832
- Rhodesia. Ministry of Water Development.
  Hydrological Year Book. a. ISSN 0080-2840

**Rhodesia. National Archives**
Private Bag 7729, Causeway, Salisbury, Rhodesia.
- National Archives of Rhodesia. Annual Report. a.
- National Archives of Rhodesia. Occasional Papers.
  irreg. ISSN 0035-4716

- Rhodesia National Bibliography. a. ISSN 0085-5677

**Rhodesia. Registrar of Insurance**
Private Bag 7705, Causeway, Salisbury, Rhodesia, Rhodesia.
- Rhodesia. Registrar of Insurance. Report. a. ISSN 0556-8692

**Rhodesia. Tobacco Research Board**
P.O. Box 1909, Salisbury, Rhodesia.
- Rhodesia. Tobacco Research Board. Annual Report and Accounts. a. ISSN 0080-2875

**Rhodesia, a Field for Investment**
c/o H.C.P. Anderson, Box 1566, Salisbury, Rhodesia.
- Rhodesia, a Field for Investment. a; latest issue, 1974.

**Rhodesia Broadcasting Corporation**
Box HG 444, Highlands, Salisbury, Rhodesia.
- Look & Listen. w. ISSN 0024-6352

**Rhodesia Calls (Pvt.) Ltd.**
Box 8045, Causeway, Salisbury, Rhodesia.
- Rhodesia Calls. bi-m. ISSN 0035-4708 (Rhodesia National Tourist Board)

**Rhodesia Library Association**
Box 3133, Salisbury, Rhodesia.
- Rhodesian Librarian. q. ISSN 0035-4848

**Rhodesia National Farmers' Union**
- Rhodesian Farmer. (pub. by Rhodesian Farmer Publications)

**Rhodesia National Tourist Board**
- Rhodesia Calls. (pub. by Rhodesia Calls (Pvt.) Ltd.)

**Rhodesia Nurses Association**
P.O. Box 3502, Salisbury, Rhodesia.
- Rhodesian Nurse. a. ISSN 0080-2883

**Rhodesia Railway Worker's Union**
Box 556, Bulawayo, Rhodesia.
- Rhodesian Railway Review. m. ISSN 0035-4872

**Rhodesia Railways**
Box 596, Bulawayo, Rhodesia.
- Rhodesia Railways Magazine. m. ISSN 0035-4724
- Sitima. m.

**Rhodesia Teachers' Association**
16-18 St. Andrews House, Jameson Ave., Salisbury, Rhodesia
- R T A Journal. 3 per yr. ISSN 0033-7137 (Subscr. to: Box 411, Marandellas, Rhodesia)

**Rhodesian Caravan Association**
- Rhodesian Caravaner. (pub. by Roblaw Publishers (Pvt.) Ltd.)

**Rhodesian Economic Society**
Treasurer, Private Bag 167H, Salisbury, Rhodesia.
- Rhodesian Journal of Economics. q. ISSN 0035-4821

**Rhodesian Farmer Publications**
Farmers Mutual House, Moffat St., Box 1622, Salisbury, Rhodesia.
- Modern Farming. q. ISSN 0026-7716
- Rhodesian Farmer. w. ISSN 0035-4775 (Rhodesia National Farmers' Union) (Co-sponsor: Rhodesia Tobacco Association)

**Rhodesian Financial Gazette**
Kingstons Ltd., Box 2374, Salisbury, Rhodesia.
- Rhodesian Financial Gazette. w.

**Rhodesian Journals Ltd.**
Lister Building, Stanley Ave., Box 2266, Salisbury, Rhodesia.
- Rhodesian Property & Finance. m. ISSN 0035-4864

**Rhodesian Motor Trade Association**
- Motor Trader and Fleet Operator. (pub. by Thomson Newspapers Rhodesia)

**Rhodesian Ornithological Society**
Box 8382, Causeway, Salisbury, Rhodesia.
- Honeyguide. q. ISSN 0018-456X

**Rhodesian Philatelic Agencies (Pvt) Ltd.**
Box 3415, Salisbury, Rhodesia.
- Rhodesian Stamp Catalogue. a.

**Rhodesiana Society**
Box 8268, Causeway, Salisbury, Rhodesia.
- Rhodesiana. s-a. ISSN 0556-9605

**Roblaw Publishers (Pvt.) Ltd.**
P.O. Box 8045, Causeway, Salisbury, Rhodesia.
- Rhodesian Caravaner; and outdoor life. bi-m. ISSN 0048-8232 (Rhodesian Caravan Association)
- Rhodesian Hotel & Catering Gazette. m. (Hotel Association of Rhodesia) (Co-sponsor: Catering Employers Association of Rhodesia; Bottle Liquor Licensees Association of Rhodesia)

**Thomson Newspapers Rhodesia**
Box 1683, Salisbury, Rhodesia.
- Chamber of Mines Journal. m. ISSN 0009-1162 (Chamber of Mines of Rhodesia)
- Mining in Rhodesia. a. ISSN 0076-8987
- Motor Trader and Fleet Operator. m. ISSN 0027-2051 (Rhodesian Motor Trade Association) (Co-sponsor: Rhodesian Motor Industry Employers' Association)
- Rhodesian Insurance Review. m. ISSN 0035-4805 (Insurance Institute, Rhodesia)
- Rhodesian Tobacco Journal. m. ISSN 0035-4880

**Tobacco Research Board of Rhodesia**
*see* **Rhodesia. Tobacco Research Board**

**Two Tone**
Box MP 79, Mt. Pleasant, Salisbury, Rhodesia.
- Two Tone; a quarterly of Rhodesian poetry. q. ISSN 0049-4917

**University of Rhodesia**
Publications Department, Box MP 45, Mt. Pleasant, Salisbury, Rhodesia.
- Zambezia; the Journal of the University of Rhodesia. a.

**University of Rhodesia. Department of Law**
Box MP 167, Mt. Pleasant, Salisbury, Rhodesia.
- Rhodesian Law Journal. s-a. ISSN 0035-483X

**Wildlife Society of Rhodesia**
P.O. Box 3497, Salisbury, Rhodesia.
- Wild Rhodesia. 4 per yr.

**Wilrey Publications**
P.O. Box 3430, Salisbury, Rhodesia.
- Jumbo Guide to Rhodesia.

# RUMANIA

**Academia de Stiinte Agricole si Silvice. Institutul de Cercetari Pentru Imbunatatiri Funciare**
B-dul Marasti Nr. 61, Bucharest, Romania
(Subscr. to: ILEXIM, Calea Grivitei 64-66, P.O. Box 136-137, Bucharest, Romania)
- Studii de Hidraulica. a.
- Studii de Irigatii Si Desecari. a.

**Academia de Stiinte Medicale**
- Revue Roumaine de Medecine. Serie Endocrinologie/Romanian Journal of Medicine. Series Endocrinology. (pub. by Editura Academiei Republicii Socialiste Romania)
- Revue Roumaine de Medecine. Serie Medicine Interne. (pub. by Editura Academiei Republicii Socialiste Romania)
- Revue Roumaine de Medecine. Serie Neurologie et Psychiatrie/Romanian Journal of Medicine. Neurology and Psychiatry. (pub. by Editura Academiei Republicii Socialiste Romania)
- Revue Roumaine de Medecine. Serie Virologie/ Romanian Journal of Medicine. Virology Series. (pub. by Editura Academiei Republicii Socialiste Romania)
- Revue Roumaine de Morphologie, d'Embryologie et Physiologie. Serie Morphologie et Embryologie/Romanian Journal of Morphology, Embriology and Physiology. Morphology and Embriology Series. (pub. by Editura Academiei Republicii Socialiste Romania)
- Revue Roumaine de Morphologie, d'Embryologie et Physiologie. Serie Physiologie/Romanian Journal of Morphology, Embryology and Physiology. Physiology Series. (pub. by Editura Academiei Republicii Socialiste Romania)

**Academia de Stiinte Sociale din Cluj. Centrul de Stiinte Sociale din Cluj**
- Centrul de Stiinte Sociale Din Cluj. Seria Drept. (pub. by Editura Academiei Republicii Socialiste Romania)

**Academia de Stiinte Sociale si Politice**
Str. Gutenberg Nr. 3 bis, Bucharest, Romania
(Subscr. to: ILEXIM, Calea Grivitei 64-66, P.O. Box 136-137, Bucharest, Romania)
- Arheologia Moldovei/Archeologie de la Moldavie. (pub. by Editura Academiei Republicii Socialiste Romania)
- Documente Istorice. (pub. by Editura Academiei Republicii Socialiste Romania)
- Magazin Istoric. m.
- Probleme de Logica. (pub. by Editura Academiei Republicii Socialiste Romania)
- Revista de Filozofie. (pub. by Editura Academiei Republicii Socialiste Romania)
- Revista de Istorie. (pub. by Editura Academiei Republicii Socialiste Romania)
- Revista de Istorie si Teorie Literara. (pub. by Editura Academiei Republicii Socialiste Romania)
- Revista de Psihologie. (pub. by Editura Academiei Republicii Socialiste Romania)
- Revue Roumaine d'Histoire de l'Art. Serie Beaux-Arts. (pub. by Editura Academiei Republicii Socialiste Romania)
- Revue Roumaine d'Histoire de l'Art. Serie Theatre, Musique, Cinematographie. (pub. by Editura Academiei Republicii Socialiste Romania)
- Revue Roumaine des Sciences Sociales. Serie de Philosophie et de Logique. (pub. by Editura Academiei Republicii Socialiste Romania)
- Revue Roumaine des Sciences Sociales. Serie de Psychologie. (pub. by Editura Academiei Republicii Socialiste Romania)
- Revue Roumaine des Sciences Sociales. Serie de Sciences Economiques. (pub. by Editura Academiei Republicii Socialiste Romania)
- Revue Roumaine des Sciences Sociales. Serie de Sciences Juridiques. (pub. by Editura Academiei Republicii Socialiste Romania)
- Revue Roumaine des Sciences Sociales. Serie de Sociologie. (pub. by Editura Academiei Republicii Socialiste Romania)
- Romanian Scientific Abstracts. m. ISSN 0035-8096
- Studii si Cercetari de Documentare; a quarterly journal for scientific documentation. q. ISSN 0039-3916 (Co-sponsor: Ministerul Educatie si Invatamintului)
- Studii si Cercetari de Istoria Artei. Seria Arta Plastica. (pub. by Editura Academiei Republicii Socialiste Romania)
- Studii si Cercetari de Istoria Artei. Seria Teatru-Muzica-Cinematografie. (pub. by Editura Academiei Republicii Socialiste Romania)
- Studii si Cercetari Juridice. (pub. by Editura Academiei Republicii Socialiste Romania)
- Studii si Materiale de Istorie Medie. (pub. by Editura Academiei Republicii Socialiste Romania)
- Viitorul Social. (pub. by Editura Academiei Republicii Socialiste Romania)

**Academia de Stiinte Sociale si Politice. Centrul de Stiinte Sociale Sibiu**
- Forschungen zur Volks- und Landeskunde. (pub. by Editura Academiei Republicii Socialiste Romania)

**Academia de Stiinte Sociale si Politice. Institutul de Istorie "N. Iorga"**
- Biblioteca Istorica. (pub. by Editura Academiei Republicii Socialiste Romania)
- Documenta Romaniae Historica. Serie A: La Moldavie. (pub. by Editura Academiei Republicii Socialiste Romania)
- Documenta Romaniae Historica. Serie B: La Valachie. (pub. by Editura Academiei Republicii Socialiste Romania)
- Studii si Materiale de Istorie Moderna. (pub. by Editura Academiei Republicii Socialiste Romania)

**Academia de Stiinte Sociale si Politice. Institutul de Istorie si Arheologie "A. D. Xenopol"**
- Institutul de Istorie si Arheologie "A. D. Xenopol". Anuarul. (pub. by Editura Academiei Republicii Socialiste Romania)

**Academia de Stiinte Sociale si Politice. Institutul de Istorie si Arheologie Cluj-Napoca**
- Academia de Stiinte Sociale si Politice. Institutul de Istorie si Arheologie Cluj-Napoca. Anuarul. (pub. by Editura Academiei Republicii Socialiste Romania)

**Academia de Stiinte Sociale si Politice. Institutul de Istorie si Teorie Literara "G. Calinescu"**
- Documente si Manuscrise Literare. (pub. by Editura Academiei Republicii Socialiste Romania)

## Academia Republicii Socialiste Romania

- B I: Filosofie-Logica. (pub. by Editura Academiei Republicii Socialiste Romania)
- Bibliografia Analitica a Periodicelor Romanesti. (pub. by Editura Academiei Republicii Socialiste Romania)
- Bibliotheca Historica Romaniae. Monographies. (pub. by Editura Academiei Republicii Socialiste Romania)
- Bibliotheca Historica Romaniae. Studies. (pub. by Editura Academiei Republicii Socialiste Romania)
- Bibliotheca Oeconomica. (pub. by Editura Academiei Republicii Socialiste Romania)
- Cercetari de Lingvistica. (pub. by Editura Academiei Republicii Socialiste Romania)
- Istoria Limbii Romane. (pub. by Editura Academiei Republicii Socialiste Romania)
- Istorie si Civilizatie. (pub. by Editura Academiei Republicii Socialiste Romania)
- Ocrotirea Naturii si a Mediului Inconjurator. (pub. by Editura Academiei Republicii Socialiste Romania)
- Revue Roumaine de Biochimie. (pub. by Editura Academiei Republicii Socialiste Romania)
- Revue Roumaine de Biologie. Serie Biologie Animale. (pub. by Editura Academiei Republicii Socialiste Romania)
- Revue Roumaine de Biologie. Serie Biologie Vegetale. (pub. by Editura Academiei Republicii Socialiste Romania)
- Revue Roumaine de Chimie. (pub. by Editura Academiei Republicii Socialiste Romania)
- Revue Roumaine de Geologie, Geophysique et Geographie. Geographie. (pub. by Editura Academiei Republicii Socialiste Romania)
- Revue Roumaine de Geologie, Geophysique et Geographie. Geologie. (pub. by Editura Academiei Republicii Socialiste Romania)
- Revue Roumaine de Geologie, Geophysique et Geographie. Geophysique. (pub. by Editura Academiei Republicii Socialiste Romania)
- Revue Roumaine de Mathematiques Pures et Appliquees. (pub. by Editura Academiei Republicii Socialiste Romania)
- Revue Roumaine des Sciences Techniques. Serie de Mecanique Appliquee. (pub. by Editura Academiei Republicii Socialiste Romania)
- Revue Roumaine des Sciences Techniques. Serie Electrotechnique et Energetique. (pub. by Editura Academiei Republicii Socialiste Romania)
- Studii si Cercetari de Antropologie. (pub. by Editura Academiei Republicii Socialiste Romania)
- Studii si Cercetari de Bibliologie. Serie Noua. (pub. by Editura Academiei Republicii Socialiste Romania)
- Studii si Cercetari de Biochimie. (pub. by Editura Academiei Republicii Socialiste Romania)
- Studii si Cercetari de Fizica. (pub. by Editura Academiei Republicii Socialiste Romania)
- Studii si Cercetari de Mecanica Aplicata. (pub. by Editura Academiei Republicii Socialiste Romania)
- Studii si Cercetari de Numismatica. (pub. by Editura Academiei Republicii Socialiste Romania)
- Studii si Cercetari Matematice. (pub. by Editura Academiei Republicii Socialiste Romania)

## Academia Republicii Socialiste Romania. Centrul de Cercetari Fonetice si Dialectale

- Fonetica si Dialectologie. (pub. by Editura Academiei Republicii Socialiste Romania)

## Academia Republicii Socialiste Romania. Institutul de Arheologie

- Biblioteca de Arheologie. (pub. by Editura Academiei Republicii Socialiste Romania)
- Materiale si Cercetari Arheologice. (pub. by Editura Academiei Republicii Socialiste Romania)
- Studii si Cercetari de Istorie Veche si Arheologie. (pub. by Editura Academiei Republicii Socialiste Romania)

## Academia Republicii Socialiste Romania. Institutul de Cercetari Etnologice si Dialoctologice

- Revista de Etnografie si Folclor. (pub. by Editura Academiei Republicii Socialiste Romania)

## Academia Republicii Socialiste Romania. Institutul de Lingvistica

- Limba Romana/Romanian Language. (pub. by Editura Academiei Republicii Socialiste Romania)
- Revue Roumaine de Linguistique. (pub. by Editura Academiei Republicii Socialiste Romania)
- Studii de Slavistica. (pub. by Editura Academiei Republicii Socialiste Romania)
- Studii si Cercetari Lingvistice. (pub. by Editura Academiei Republicii Socialiste Romania)

## Academia Republicii Socialiste Romania. Institutul de Speologie "Emil Racovita"

- Institutul de Speologie Emil Racovitza. Travaux. (pub. by Editura Academiei Republicii Socialiste Romania)

## Agerpres the Romanian News Agency

Piata Scinteii Nr. i, Bucharest, Romania
(Subscr. to: ILEXIM, Calea Grivitei 64-66, P.O. Box 136-137, Bucharest, Romania)
- Lumea. w. (Uniunea Ziaristilor din Republica Socialista Romania)
- News from Romania. fortn. ISSN 0028-9116
- Romania: Articles-Features-Information. m.
- Romania; Documents-Events. w. ISSN 0048-8658

## Arhiva Nationala de Filme

Bd. Gh. Gheorgiu Dej, Nr. 65, Bucharest, Romania.
- Anul Cinematografic. a.
- Bibliografia Internationala Cinema/Bibliographie Internationale Cinema. a. ISSN 0084-7828
- Caiet de Documentare Cinematografica. m. ISSN 0008-0519

## Asociatia Crescatorilor de Albine din Republica Socialista Romania

Str. J. Fucik Nr. 17, Bucharest, Romania.
- Meheszet Romaniaban. m.

## Asociatia de Drept International si Relatii Internationale

- Revue Roumaine d'Etudes Internationales. (pub. by Editura Academiei Republicii Socialiste Romania)

## Asociatia Filatelistilor din Republica Socialista Romania

Strada Boteanu Nr.6, Bucharest 1, Romania
(Subscr. to: ILEXIM, Calea Grivitei 64-66, P.O. Box 136-137, Bucharest, Romania)
- Filatelia. m. ISSN 0428-3341

## Asociatia Juristilor din Republica Socialista Romania

- Revista Romana de Drept. (pub. by Editura Academiei Republicii Socialiste Romania)

## Association Internationale d'Etudes du Sud-Est Europeen

Str. I.C. Frimu Nr. 9, Bucharest, Romania
(Subscr. to: ILEXIM, Calea Grivitei 64-66, P.O. Box 136-137, Bucharest, Romania)
- Association Internationale d'Etudes du Sud-Est Europeen. Bulletin. s-a. ISSN 0004-5551
- Bulletin d'Archeologie Sud-Est Europeenne.

## Biblioteca Centrala de Stat a Republicii Socialiste Romania

Str. Ion Ghica 4, Bucharest, Romania.
- Buletin de Informare in Bibliologie. m. ISSN 0007-3784
- Revista de Referate in Bibliologie. q. ISSN 0034-8783

## Biblioteca Centrala Pedagogica

Str. Zalomit Nr. 12, Bucharest, Romania.
- Probleme de Pedagogie Contemporana. 3-4 per yr.

## Biblioteca Judeteana Constanta

B-dul Republicii nr. 7 bis, Constanta, Romania.
- Bibliografia Dobrogei. a.

## Centrala Editoriala

Piata Scinteii Nr. 1, Bucharest, Romania
(Subscr. to: ILEXIM, Calea Grivitei 64-66, P.O. Box 136-137, Bucharest, Romania)
- Romanian Books. q. ISSN 0035-8045

## Centrul de Documentare Tehnica Pentru Economia Forestiera

Soseaua Pipera Nr. 46, Bucharest, Romania.
- Mobila; mobilier, interioare, decor. s-a. ISSN 0026-7104

## Chamber of Commerce and Industry of the Socialist Republic of Romania

Bd. N. Balcescu Nr. 22, Bucharest, Romania
(Subscr. to: ILEXIM, Calea Grivitei 64-66, P.O. Box 136-137, Bucharest, Romania)
- Foresta; Romanian wood and furniture review. q. ISSN 0015-7503
- Romanian Engineering. q. ISSN 0035-8061
- Romanian Foreign Trade. q. ISSN 0035-807X
- Romanian Journal of Chemistry; a quarterly on trade and industry. q. ISSN 0048-8577

## Comitetul Central al Uniunii Tineretului Comunist

- Stiinta si Tehnica. (pub. by Editura Scinteia)

## Comitetul de Cultura si Educatie Socialista al Judetului Brasov

Str. Mihail Sadoveanu Nr. 3, Brasov, Romania
(Subscr. to: ILEXIM, Calea Grivitei 64-66, P.O. Box 136-137, Bucharest, Romania)
- Astra. q. ISSN 0004-6108

## Comitetul de Cultura si Educatie Socialista al Judetului Iasi

Str. V. Alecsandri Nr. 8, Jassy, Romania
(Subscr. to: ILEXIM, Calea Grivitei 64-66, P.O. Box 136-137, Bucharest, Romania)
- Cronica. w.

## Comitetul de Cultura si Educatie Socialista al Judetului Mures

Str. Primariei, Nr. 1, Tirgu-Mures, Romania
(Subscr. to: ILEXIM, Calea Grivitei 64-66, P.O. Box 136-137, Bucharest, Romania)
- Vatra; revista social-culturala. m.

## Comitetul de Cultura si Educatie Socialista al Judetului Sibiu

B-Dul Victoriei Nr. 1-3, Sibiu, Romania
(Subscr. to: ILEXIM, Calea Grivitei 64-66, P.O. Box 136-137, Bucharest, Romania)
- Transilvania. m.

## Comitetul National Pentru Apararea Pacii din Republica Socialista Romania

Str. Stefan Gheorghiu, Bucharest, Romania.
- Comitetul National Pentru Apararea Pacii din Republica Socialista Romania. Information Bulletin. q. ISSN 0547-5090

## Comitetul Pentru Cultura si Educatie Socialista a Municipiului Bucuresti

Bucharest, Romania
(Subscr. to: ILEXIM, Calea Grivitei 64-66, P.O. Box 136-137, Bucharest, Romania)
- Saptamina Culturala a Capitalei. w.

## Conservatorul "George Dima"

Str. 23 August Nr. 25, Cluj-Napoca, Romania.
- Lucrari de Muzicologie. a.

## Consiliul Culturii si Educatiei Socialiste

Bucharest, Romania
(Subscr. to: ILEXIM, Calea Grivitei 64-66, P.O. Box 136-137, Bucharest, Romania)
- Cahiers Roumains d'Etudes Litteraires. (pub. by Editura Univers)
- Indrumatorul Cultural. m.
- Revista Muzeelor si Monumentelor. Monumente. s-a.
- Revista Muzeelor si Monumentelor. Muzee. q.
- Teatrul. m. ISSN 0040-0815
- Urzica. m. ISSN 0042-1200
- Volk und Kultur. m.

## Consiliul General A.R.L.U.S.

Piata Scinteii Nr. 1, Bucharest, Romania
(Subscr. to: ILEXIM, Calea Grivitei 64-66, P.O. Box 136-137, Bucharest, Romania)
- Veac Nou. m.

## Consiliul National al Apelor

Bd. Republicii Nr. 34, Bucharest, Romania
(Subscr. to: ILEXIM, Calea Grivitei 64-66, P.O. Box 136-137, Bucharest, Romania)
- Hidrotehnica. 6 per yr.

## Consiliul National al Femeilor din Republica Socialista Romania

- Femeia. (pub. by Editura Scinteia)

## Consiliul Suprem al Dezvoltarii Economice si Sociale. Institutul Central de Cercetari Economice

Calea Dorobantilor Nr. 11-25, Bucharest, Romania
(Subscr. to: ILEXIM, Calea, Grivitei 64-66, P.O. Box 136-137, Bucharest, Romania)
- Revista Economica. w.

## Editura Academiei Republicii Socialiste Romania

Calea Victoriei 125, Bucharest, Romania
(Subscr. to: ILEXIM, Calea Grivitei 64-66, P.O. Box 136-137, Bucharest, Romania)
- Academia de Stiinte Sociale si Politice. Institutul de Istorie si Arheologie Cluj-Napoca. Anuarul. a. ISSN 0065-048X
- Arheologia Moldovei/Archeologie de la Moldavie. irreg. ISSN 0066-7358 (Academia de Stiinte Sociale si Politice) (Co-Sponsor: Institutul de Istorie si Arheologie A.D. Xenopol)
- B I: Filosofie-Logica; buletin de informare stiinsifica. bi-m. (Academia Republicii Socialiste Romania)

- Bibliografia Analitica a Periodicelor Romanesti. irreg. ISSN 0067-6551 (Academia Republicii Socialiste Romania)
- Biblioteca de Arheologie. irreg. ISSN 0067-7388 (Academia Republicii Socialiste Romania. Institutul de Arheologie)
- Biblioteca Istorica. irreg. ISSN 0067-7493 (Academia de Stiinte Sociale si Politice. Institutul de Istorie "N. Iorga)
- Bibliotheca Historica Romaniae. Monographies. irreg. ISSN 0067-799X (Academia Republicii Socialiste Romania) (Co-sponsor: Academia de Stiinte Sociale si Politice)
- Bibliotheca Historica Romaniae. Studies. irreg. ISSN 0067-7981 (Academia Republicii Socialiste Romania) (Co-sponsor: Academia de Stiinte Sociale si Politice)
- Bibliotheca Oeconomica. irreg. ISSN 0067-8082 (Academia Republicii Socialiste Romania)
- Cellulose Chemistry and Technology; international journal for physics, chemistry and technology of cellulose and lignin. bi-m. ISSN 0576-9787
- Centrul de Stiinte Sociale Din Cluj. Seria Drept. irreg.
- Cercetari de Lingvistica. s-a. (Academia Republicii Socialiste Romania)
- Dacia; Revue d'Archeologie et d'Histoire Ancienne. a. ISSN 0070-251X
- Documenta Romaniae Historica. Serie A: La Moldavie. irreg. ISSN 0070-6825 (Academia de Stiinte Sociale si Politice. Institutul de Istorie "N. Iorga")
- Documenta Romaniae Historica. Serie B: La Valachie. irreg. ISSN 0070-6833 (Academia de Stiinte Sociale si Politice. Institutul de Istorie "N. Iorga")
- Documente Istorice. irreg. ISSN 0070-6884 (Academia de Stiinte Sociale si Politice)
- Documente si Manuscrise Literare. irreg. ISSN 0070-6892 (Academia de Stiinte Sociale si Politice. Institutul de Istorie si Teorie Literara "G. Calinescu")
- Fonetica si Dialectologie. irreg. ISSN 0071-6855 (Academia Republicii Socialiste Romania. Centrul de Cercetari Fonetice si Dialectale)
- Forschungen zur Volks- und Landeskunde. s-a. ISSN 0015-7902 (Academia de Stiinte Sociale si Politice. Centrul de Stiinte Sociale Sibiu)
- Institutul de Istorie si Arheologie "A. D. Xenopol". Anuarul. a. ISSN 0074-039X
- Institutul de Speologie Emil Racovitza. Travaux. a. ISSN 0065-0498
- Istoria Limbii Romane. irreg. ISSN 0075-160X (Academia Republicii Socialiste Romania)
- Istorie si Civilizatie. irreg. ISSN 0075-1626 (Academia Republicii Socialiste Romania)
- Latin Language Mathematicians Group. Actes et Travaux du Congres. irreg. ISSN 0075-8175 (Latin Language Mathematicians' Group)
- Limba Romana/Romanian Language. 6 per yr. ISSN 0024-3523 (Academia Republicii Socialiste Romania. Institutul de Lingvistica)
- Materiale si Cercetari Arheologice. irreg. ISSN 0076-5147 (Academia Republicii Socialiste Romania. Institutul de Arheologie)
- Observatorul Astronomic din Bucuresti. Anuarul. a. ISSN 0068-3086
- Observatorul Astronomic din Bucuresti. Observations Solaires. a. ISSN 0068-3094
- Ocrotirea Naturii si a Mediului Inconjurator. s-a. ISSN 0029-8263 (Academia Republicii Socialiste Romania)
- Probleme de Automatizare. bi-m.
- Probleme de Logica. bi-m. (Academia de Stiinte Sociale si Politice)
- Revista de Etnografie si Folclor. s-a. ISSN 0034-8198 (Academia Republicii Socialiste Romania. Institutul de Cercetari Etnologice si Dialoctologice)
- Revista de Filozofie. 6 per yr. ISSN 0034-8260 (Academia de Stiinte Sociale si Politice)
- Revista de Istorie. m. ISSN 0567-6304 (Academia de Stiinte Sociale si Politice)
- Revista de Istorie si Teorie Literara. q. ISSN 0034-8392 (Academia de Stiinte Sociale si Politice)
- Revista de Psihologie. q. ISSN 0034-8759 (Academia de Stiinte Sociale si Politice)
- Revista Romana de Drept. m. ISSN 0035-0435 (Asociatia Juristilor din Republica Socialista Romania)
- Revue des Etudes Sud-Est Europeennes. q. ISSN 0035-2063 (Institutul de Studii Sud-Est Europene)
- Revue Roumaine d'Etudes Internationales. q. ISSN 0048-8178 (Asociatia de Drept International si Relatii Internationale)

- Revue Roumaine d'Histoire de l'Art. Serie Beaux-Arts. a. ISSN 0080-262X (Academia de Stiinte Sociale si Politice)
- Revue Roumaine d'Histoire de l'Art. Serie Theatre, Musique, Cinematographie. a. ISSN 0080-2638 (Academia de Stiinte Sociale si Politice)
- Revue Roumaine de Biochimie. 4 per yr. ISSN 0001-4214 (Academia Republicii Socialiste Romania)
- Revue Roumaine de Biologie. Serie Biologie Animale. q. (Academia Republicii Socialiste Romania)
- Revue Roumaine de Biologie. Serie Biologie Vegetale. q. (Academia Republicii Socialiste Romania)
- Revue Roumaine de Chimie. 10 per yr. ISSN 0035-3930 (Academia Republicii Socialiste Romania)
- Revue Roumaine de Geologie, Geophysique et Geographie. Geographie. 2 per yr. ISSN 0556-8099 (Academia Republicii Socialiste Romania)
- Revue Roumaine de Geologie, Geophysique et Geographie. Geologie. a. ISSN 0556-8102 (Academia Republicii Socialiste Romania)
- Revue Roumaine de Geologie, Geophysique et Geographie. Geophysique. a. ISSN 0556-8110 (Academia Republicii Socialiste Romania)
- Revue Roumaine de Linguistique. 6 per yr. ISSN 0035-3957 (Academia Republicii Socialiste Romania. Institutul de Lingvistica)
- Revue Roumaine de Mathematiques Pures et Appliquees. 10 per yr. ISSN 0035-3965 (Academia Republicii Socialiste Romania)
- Revue Roumaine de Medecine. Serie Endocrinologie/Romanian Journal of Medicine. Series Endocrinology. q. (Academia de Stiinte Medicale)
- Revue Roumaine de Medecine. Serie Medicine Interne. q. (Academia de Stiinte Medicale)
- Revue Roumaine de Medecine. Serie Neurologie et Psychiatrie/Romanian Journal of Medicine. Neurology and Psychiatry. q. (Academia de Stiinte Medicale)
- Revue Roumaine de Medecine. Serie Virologie/Romanian Journal of Medicine. Virology Series. s-a. (Academia de Stiinte Medicale)
- Revue Roumaine de Morphologie, d'Embryologie et Physiologie. Serie Morphologie et Embryologie/Romanian Journal of Morphology, Embriology and Physiology. Morphology and Embriology Series. q. ISSN 0035-4007 (Academia de Stiinte Medicale)
- Revue Roumaine de Morphologie, d'Embryologie et Physiologie. Serie Physiologie/Romanian Journal of Morphology, Embryology and Physiology. Physiology Series. q. (Academia de Stiinte Medicale)
- Revue Roumaine de Physique. 10 per yr. ISSN 0035-4090 (Institutul de Fizica Atomica)
- Revue Roumaine des Sciences Sociales. Serie de Philosophie et de Logique. 4 per yr. ISSN 0035-4031 (Academia de Stiinte Sociale si Politice)
- Revue Roumaine des Sciences Sociales. Serie de Psychologie. s-a. ISSN 0035-3892 (Academia de Stiinte Sociale si Politice)
- Revue Roumaine des Sciences Sociales. Serie de Sciences Economiques. s-a. ISSN 0035-404X (Academia de Stiinte Sociale si Politice)
- Revue Roumaine des Sciences Sociales. Serie de Sciences Juridiques. s-a. ISSN 0035-4023 (Academia de Stiinte Sociale si Politice)
- Revue Roumaine des Sciences Sociales. Serie de Sociologie. a. ISSN 0080-2646 (Academia de Stiinte Sociale si Politice)
- Revue Roumaine des Sciences Techniques. Serie de Mecanique Appliquee. 4 per yr. ISSN 0035-4074 (Academia Republicii Socialiste Romania)
- Revue Roumaine des Sciences Techniques. Serie Electrotechnique et Energetique. 4 per yr. ISSN 0035-4066 (Academia Republicii Socialiste Romania)
- Scriptores Byzantini. irreg. ISSN 0080-8385
- Seminar de Fizica Teoretica. irreg. ISSN 0080-8806 (Institutul de Fizica, Bucharest)
- Studii Clasice. a. ISSN 0081-8844 (Societatea de Studii Clasice din Republica Socialista Romania)
- Studii de Literatura Universala si Comparata. irreg. ISSN 0081-8852
- Studii de Slavistica. irreg. ISSN 0081-8860 (Academia Republicii Socialiste Romania. Institutul de Lingvistica)
- Studii Istorice Sud-Est Europene. irreg. (Institutul de Studii Sud-Est Europene)
- Studii si Cercetari de Antropologie. s-a. ISSN 0039-3886 (Academia Republicii Socialiste Romania)

- Studii si Cercetari de Bibliologie. Serie Noua. irreg. ISSN 0081-8879 (Academia Republicii Socialiste Romania)
- Studii si Cercetari de Biochimie. 2 per yr. ISSN 0049-2396 (Academia Republicii Socialiste Romania)
- Studii si Cercetari de Fizica. 10 per yr. ISSN 0039-3940 (Academia Republicii Socialiste Romania)
- Studii si Cercetari de Geologie, Geofizica si Geografie. Geografie. s-a. ISSN 0039-3967
- Studii si Cercetari de Istoria Artei. Seria Arta Plastica. s-a. ISSN 0039-3983 (Academia de Stiinte Sociale si Politice)
- Studii si Cercetari de Istoria Artei. Seria Teatru-Muzica-Cinematografie. a. ISSN 0039-3991 (Academia de Stiinte Sociale si Politice)
- Studii si Cercetari de Istorie Veche si Arheologie. 4 per yr. (Academia Republicii Socialiste Romania. Institutul de Arheologie)
- Studii si Cercetari de Mecanica Aplicata. 4 per yr. ISSN 0039-4017 (Academia Republicii Socialiste Romania)
- Studii si Cercetari de Numismatica. irreg., 1971, vol. 5. ISSN 0081-8887 (Academia Republicii Socialiste Romania)
- Studii si Cercetari Juridice. q. ISSN 0039-4041 (Academia de Stiinte Sociale si Politice)
- Studii si Cercetari Lingvistice. 6 per yr. ISSN 0039-405X (Academia Republicii Socialiste Romania. Institutul de Lingvistica)
- Studii si Cercetari Matematice. 6 per yr. ISSN 0039-4068 (Academia Republicii Socialiste Romania)
- Studii si Materiale de Istorie Medie. irreg. (Academia de Stiinte Sociale si Politice)
- Studii si Materiale de Istorie Moderna. irreg. (Academia de Stiinte Sociale si Politice. Institutul de Istorie "N. Iorga")
- Synthesis; Bulletin du Comite National Roumain de Litterature Comparee. a.
- Viitorul Social; revista de sociologie Si stiinte politice. q. (Academia de Stiinte Sociale si Politice)

**Editura Medicala**
Str. 13 Decembrie Nr. 14, Bucharest, Romania (Subscr. to: ILEXIM, Calea Grivitei 64-66, P.O. Box 136-137, Bucharest, Romania)
- Archives Roumaines de Pathologie Experimentale et de Microbiologie. q. ISSN 0004-0037 (Institutul de Microbiologie, Parazitologie si Epidemiologie "Dr. I. Cantacuzino")
- Sante Publique. q. ISSN 0048-9107

**Editura Tehnica**
Str. Stirbei Voda Nr. 37, Bucharest, Romania.
- Lucrari de Cercetare. (Institutul de Cercetari si Proiectari Alimentare)

**Federatia Comunitatilor Evreiesti din Republica Socialista Romania**
Str. Sf. Vineri Nr. 9, Bucharest, Romania.
- Revista Cultului Mozaic. bi-m. ISSN 0034-754X

**Foreign Languages Press**
Piata Scinteii Nr. 1, Bucharest, Romania (Subscr. to: ILEXIM, Calea Grivitei 64-66, P.O. Box 136-137, Bucharest, Romania)
- Romania Today. m. ISSN 0035-9815
- Romanian Review. q. ISSN 0035-8088

**Frontul Unitatii Socialiste**
Piata Scinteii Nr. 1, Bucharest, Romania (Subscr. to: ILEXIM, Calea Grivitei 64-66, P.O. Box 136-137, Bucharest, Romania)
- Flacara. w. ISSN 0015-3362

**Gradina Botanica a Universitatii Bucuresti**
Soseaua Cotroceni Nr. 32, Bucharest, Romania.
- Acta Botanica Horti Bucurestiensis. a. ISSN 0068-3329

**Institutul Agronomic "Dr. Petru Groza"**
Str. Manastur No. 3, Cluj-Napoca, Romania.
- Institutul Agronomic "Dr. Petru Groza". Buletinul. a.

**Institutul Agronomic "Ion Ionescu de la Brad"**
Aleea M. Sadoveanu, Nr. 3, Jassy, Romania.
- Institutul Agronomic "Ion Ionescu de la Brad". Lucrari Stiintifice. I. Agronomie - Horticultura. irreg. ISSN 0075-3505
- Institutul Agronomic "Ion Ionescu de la Brad" Lucrari Stiintifice II Zootehnie - Medicina Veterinara. irreg. ISSN 0075-3513

**Institutul Central de Cercetari Chimice**
Calea Plevnei 139, Bucharest, Romania
(Subscr. to: ILEXIM, Calea Grivitei 64-66, P.O.
Box 136-137, Bucharest, Romania)
- Materiale Plastice. 3 per yr. ISSN 0025-5289
- Revista de Chimie. m. ISSN 0034-7752

**Institutul de Cercetari Pedagogice si Psihologice**
Str. Sfintii Apostoli Nr. 14, Bucharest, Romania
(Subscr. to: ILEXIM, Calea Grivitei 64-66, P.O.
Box 136-134, Bucharest, Romania)
- Revista de Pedagogie. m. ISSN 0034-8678

**Institutul de Cercetari Pentru Cultura Cartofului si Sfeclei de Zahar**
Str. Fundaturii, Nr. 2, Brasov, Romania.
- Institutul de Cercetari Pentru Cultura Cartofului si Sfeclei de Zahar, Brasov. Anale. Cartoful. a. ISSN 0074-0373
- Institutul de Cercetari Pentru Cultura Cartofului si Sfeclei de Zahar, Brasov. Anale. Sfecla de Zahar. a. ISSN 0074-0381

**Institutul de Cercetari si Proiectari Alimentare**
- Lucrari de Cercetare. (pub. by Editura Tehnica)

**Institutul de Fizica Atomica**
Soseaua Magurele, Bucharest, Romania.
- Institutul de Fizica Atomica. Sesiunea Stiintifica Anuala de Comunicari; Program si Rezumate. a.
- Revue Roumaine de Physique. (pub. by Editura Academiei Republicii Socialiste Romania)

**Institutul de Fizica, Bucharest**
- Seminar de Fizica Teoretica. (pub. by Editura Academiei Republicii Socialiste Romania)

**Institutul de Geologie si Geofizica**
Str. Caransebes, Nr. 1, Bucharest, Romania.
- Institutul de Geologie si Geofizica. Anuarul. a.
- Institutul de Geologie si Geofizica. Dari de Seama ale Sedintelor. 5 per yr. ISSN 0068-306X
- Institutul de Geologie si Geofizica. Studii Tehnice si Economice. irreg.
- Institutul Geologie si Geofizica. Memoire. 3 per yr. ISSN 0020-4234

**Institutul de Medicina si Farmacie din Tirgu-Mures**
Str. Gh. Marinescu Nr. 38, Tirgu-Mures, Romania
(Subscr. to: ILEXIM, Calea Grivitei 64-66, P.O.
Box 136-137, Bucharest, Romania)
- Revista Medicala/Medical Review. s-a. ISSN 0034-995X

**Institutul de Meteorologie si Hidrologie**
Soseaua Bucuresti-Ploiesti 97, Bucharest, Romania.
- Institutul de Meteorologie si Hidrologie. Studii de Climatologie. irreg.
- Meteorology and Hydrology. s-a.

**Institutul de Microbiologie, Parazitologie si Epidemiologie "Dr. I. Cantacuzino"**
- Archives Roumaines de Pathologie Experimentale et de Microbiologie. (pub. by Editura Medicala)

**Institutul de Mine Petrosani**
Str. Institutului Nr. 20, Petrosani, Romania.
- Institutul de Mine Petrosani. Lucrari Stiintifice. irreg.

**Institutul de Studii, Cercetari si Proiectari Pentru Gospodarirea Apelor**
Splaiul Indepentei 294, Bucharest, Romania.
- Institutul de Studii, Cercetari si Proiectari Pentru Gospodarirea Apelor. Studii de Economia Apelor. irreg.

**Institutul de Studii Istorice si Social Politice**
Str. Ministerului Nr. 4, Bucharest, Romania.
- Anale de Istorie. bi-m.

**Institutul de Studii si Proiectari Energetice**
Bd. Lacul Tei Nr. 1, Bucharest, Romania.
- Institutul de Studii si Proiectari Energetice. Buletinul. q.

**Institutul de Studii Sud-Est Europene**
- Revue des Etudes Sud-Est Europeennes. (pub. by Editura Academiei Republicii Socialiste Romania)
- Studii Istorice Sud-Est Europene. (pub. by Editura Academiei Republicii Socialiste Romania)

**Institutul National de Informare si Documentare Stiintifica si Tehnica**
Str. Cosmonautilor Nr. 27-29, Bucharest, Romania
(Subscr. to: ILEXIM, Calea Grivitei 64-66, P.O.
Box 136-137, Bucharest, Romania)
- Abstracts of Romanian Scientific and Technical Literature. s-a. ISSN 0001-365X
- Bulletin Analytique de la Litterature Scientifique et Technique Roumaine. q.
- Fotografia. bi-m.
- Institutul Central de Documentare Tehnica. Revista de Titluri: Transport Intern. Ambalare. Depozitare. m. ISSN 0047-0333
- Institutul National de Informare si Documentare Stiintifica si Tehnica. Revista de Titluri: Scientica. Cercetare. Proiectare. Estetica Indusriala. m. ISSN 0047-0368
- Probleme de Documentare si Informare. bi-m. ISSN 0018-9111
- Standardizarea Romana. m.

**Institutul Pedagogic Oradea**
Calea Armatei Rosii Nr. 5, Oradea, Romania.
- Institutul Pedagogic Oradea. Lucrari Stiintifice Seria Biologic. a.
- Institutul Pedagogic Oradea. Lucrari Stiintifice Seria Chimie. a.
- Institutul Pedagogic Oradea. Lucrari Stiintifice Seria Educatie Fizica si Sport. a.
- Institutul Pedagogic Oradea. Lucrari Stiintifice: Seria Fizica. a.
- Institutul Pedagogic Oradea. Lucrari Stiintifice: Seria Geografie. a.
- Institutul Pedagogic Oradea. Lucrari Stiintifice: Seria Istorie. a.
- Institutul Pedagogic Oradea. Lucrari Stiintifice: Seria Lingvistica. a.
- Institutul Pedagogic Oradea. Lucrari Stiintifice: Seria Literatura. irreg.
- Institutul Pedagogic Oradea. Lucrari Stiintifice: Seria Matematica. a.
- Institutul Pedagogic Oradea. Lucrari Stiintifice: Seria Pedagogie, Psihologie, Metodica. irreg.
- Institutul Pedagogic Oradea. Lucrari Stiintifice: Seria Stiinte Sociale. a.

**Institutul Politehnic "Gheorghe Asachi" din Iasi**
Calea 23 August 11, Jassy, Romania.
- Institutul Politehnic Iasi. Buletinul. Sectia I: Matematica, Mecanica Teoretica, Fizica. q.
- Institutul Politehnic Iasi. Buletinul. Sectia II: Chimie. q.
- Institutul Politehnic Iasi. Buletinul. Sectia III: Electrotehnica, Electronica, Automatizari. q.
- Institutul Politehnic Iasi. Buletinul. Sectia IV: Mecanica Tehnica. q.
- Institutul Politehnic Iasi. Buletinul. Sectia V: Constructi. Arhitectura. q.
- Institutul Politehnic Iasi. Buletinul. Sectia VI: Imbunatatiri Funciare. q.
- Institutul Politehnic Iasi. Buletinul. Sectia VII: Textile, Pielarie. s-a.
- Institutul Politehnic Iasi. Buletinul. Sectia VIII. Stiinte Social-Economice. q.

**Institutul Politehnic "Gheorghe Gheorghiu-Dej"**
Calea Grivitei 132, Bucharest, Romania.
- Institutul Politehnic "Gheorghe Gheorghiu-Dej." Buletin. 3 per yr. ISSN 0020-4242

**Institutul Politehnic "Traian Vuia"**
Str. 30 Decembrie Nr. 2, Timisoara, Romania.
- Institutul Politehnic "Traian-Vuia". Buletinul Stiintific si Tehnic. s-a.

**International Federation of Beekeepers' Associations "Apimondia"**
Str. Pitar Mos Nr. 20, Bucharest, Romania.
- Apiacta. q. ISSN 0003-6455
- International Beekeeping Congress. Reports. biennial since 1963; 24th, Buenos Aires, Argentina, 1973. ISSN 0074-2007

**Latin Language Mathematicians' Group**
- Latin Language Mathematicians Group. Actes et Travaux du Congres. (pub. by Editura Academiei Republicii Socialiste Romania)

**Muzeul Banatului**
Piata Huniade Nr. 1, Timisoara, Romania.
- Tibiscus. Seria Arta.
- Tibiscus. Seria Etnografie. a.
- Tibiscus. Seria Istorie. a.
- Tibiscus. Seria Stiintele Naturii. a.

**Muzeul de Istorie Naturala "Gr. Antipa"**
Soseaua Kiseleff Nr. 1, Bucharest, Romania.
- Muzeul de Istorie Naturala "Gr. Antipa." Travaux. irreg. ISSN 0068-3078

**Muzeul de Istorie si Arheologie Alba Julia**
Str. Mihai Vieazul nr. 12-14, Alba Julia, Romania.
- Apulum. a.

**Muzeul Literaturii Romane**
Str. Fundatiei Nr. 4, Bucharest, Romania
(Subscr. to: ILEXIM, Calea Grivitei 64-66, P.O.
Box 136-137, Bucharest, Romania)
- Manuscriptum. q.

**Observatorul Astronomic din Bucuresti**
- Observatorul Astronomic din Bucuresti. Anuarul. (pub. by Editura Academiei Republicii Socialiste Romania)
- Observatorul Astronomic din Bucuresti. Observations Solaires. (pub. by Editura Academiei Republicii Socialiste Romania)

**Partidul Comunist Roman. Comitetul Central**
Piata Scinteii Nr. 1, Bucharest, Romania
(Subscr. to: ILEXIM, Calea Grivitei 64-66, P.O.
Box 136-137, Bucharest, Romania)
- Era Socialista. s-m.
- Munca de Partid. m.
- Probleme ale Pacii si Socialismului. m.

**Romania. Arhivele Statului. Directia Generala**
Bd. Gheorghe Gheorghiu-Bej 29, Bucharest, Romania
(Subscr. to: ILEXIM, Calea Grivitei 64-66, P.O.
Box 136-137, Bucharest, Romania)
- Revista Arhivelor. q. ISSN 0034-7043

**Romania. Directia Centrala de Statistica**
Str. Stavropoleos Nr. 6, Bucharest, Romania
(Subscr. to: ILEXIM, Calea Grivitei 64-66, P.O.
Box 136-137, Bucharest, Romania)
- Revista de Statistica. m. ISSN 0035-8037

**Romania. Ministerul Apararii Nationale**
Str. Cobalcescu Nr. 28, Bucharest, Romania
(Subscr. to: ILEXIM, Calea Grivitei 64-66, P.O.
Box 136-137, Bucharest, Romania)
- Viata Militara/Military Life. m. ISSN 0042-5044

**Romania. Ministerul Comertului Exterior**
B-dul N. Balcescu Nr. 22, Bucharest, Romania
(Subscr. to: ILEXIM, Calea Grivitei 64-66, P. O.
Box 136-137, Bucharest, Romania)
- Informatii de Comert Exterior. w.

**Romania. Ministerul Economiei Forestiere si Materialelor de Constructii**
Soseaua Pipera Nr. 46, Bucharest, Romania
(Subcr to: ILEXIM, Calea Grivitei 64-66,P.O. Box 136-137, Bucharest, Romania)
- Revista Padurilor - Industria Lemnului, Celuloza si Hirtie. Celuloza si Hirtie. q.
- Revista Padurilor-Industria Lemnului, Celuloza si Hirtie. Industria Lemnului. q.
- Revista Padurilor-Industria Lemnului, Celuloza si Hirtie, Silvicultura si Exploatarea Padurilor. q.

**Romania. Ministerul Educatiei si Invatamintului**
Str. Spiru Haret Nr. 12, Bucharest, Romania
(Subscr. to: ILEXIM, Calea Grivitei 64-66, P.O.
Box 136-137, Bucharest, Romania)
- Forum - Revista Invatamintului Superior. m. ISSN 0015-8453
- Invatamintul Liceal si Tehnic Profesional. m (10 per yr.)

**Romania. Ministerul Industriei Constructiilor de Masini**
Str. Ion Ghica Nr. 3, Bucharest, Romania
(Subscr. to: ILEXIM, Calea Grivitei 64-66, P.O.
Box 136-137, Bucharest, Romania)
- Electrotehnica, Electronica si Automatica. Automatica si Electronica. q.
- Electrotehnica, Electronica si Automatica. Electrotehnica. 8 per yr.

**Romania. Ministerul Industriei Constructiilor de Masini Grele**
Calea Victoriei, Bucharest, Romania
(Subscr. to: ILEXIM, Calea Grivitei 64-66, P.O.
Box 136-137, Bucharest, Romania)
- Constructia de Masini. m.

**Romania. Ministerul Industriei Usoare**
Bucharest, Romania
(Subscr. to: ILEXIM, Calea Grivitei 64-66, P.O.
Box 136-137, Bucharest, Romania)
- Industria Usoara-Pielarie, Confectii de Piele,
Prelucrarea Cauciucului si Maselor Plastice,
Sticla, Ceramica Fina, Articole Casnice, Utilaje
Pentru Industria Usoara. m.
- Industria Usoara-Textile, Tricotaje, Confectii
Textile. m.

**Romania. Ministerul Minelor Petrolului si Geologiei.**
**Oficiul de Informare Documentara**
Str. Mendeleev 36-38, Sector 1, Bucharest,
Romania.
- Mine, Petrol si Gaze. m.

**Romania. Ministerul Transporturilor si**
**Telecomunicatiilor**
Calea Grivitei 193b, Bucharest, Romania
(Subscr. to: ILEXIM, Calea Grivitei 64-66, P.O.
Box 136-137, Bucharest, Romania)
- Revista Transporturilor si Telecomunicatiilor. m.

**Romania. Ministerul Turismului**
Bd. Poligrafiei Nr. 3, Bucharest, Romania
(Subscr. to: ILEXIM, Calea Grivitei 64-66, P.O.
Box 136-137, Bucharest, Romania)
- Holidays in Romania. m. ISSN 0018-3555
- Romania Pitoreasca. m.

**Romanian Olympic Committee**
Str. Vasile Conta Nr. 16, Bucharest, Romania
(Subscr. to: ILEXIM, Calea Grivitei 64-66, P.O.
Box 136-137, Bucharest, Romania)
- Sport en Roumanie/Sports in Romania. q. ISSN
0007-5191

**Editura Scinteia**
Piata Scinteii Nr. 1, Bucharest, Romania
(Subscr. to: ILEXIM, Calea Grivitei 64-66, P.O.
Box 136-137, Bucharest, Romania)
- Femeia; revista social politica si culturala. m.
ISSN 0046-3655 (Consiliul National al Femeilor
din Republica Socialista Romania)
- Stiinta si Tehnica. m. ISSN 0039-1417 (Comitetul
Central al Uniunii Tineretului Comunist)

**Societatea de Medici si Naturalisti din Iasi**
Str. Ghiorghi Dimitrov 72, Jassy, Romania
(Subcr. to: ILEXIM, Calea Grivitei 64-66, P.O. Box
136-137, Bucharest, Romania)
- Revista Medico-Chirurgicala. q. ISSN 0048-7848

**Societatea de Stiinte Biologice din Republica**
**Socialista Romania**
Bd. Schitu Magureanu Nr. 9, Bucharest, Romania.
- Natura. bi-m. ISSN 0028-0674

**Societatea de Stiinte Filologice din Republica**
**Socialista Romania**
Bd. Republicii Nr. 55, Bucharest, Romania.
- Limba si Literatura. irreg. ISSN 0583-8045

**Societatea de Stiinte Fizice si Chimice din Republica**
**Socialista Romania**
Str. Spiru Haret Nr. 12, Bucharest, Romania
(Subscr. to: ILEXIM, Calea Grivitei 64-66, P.O.Box
136-137, Bucharest, Romania)
- Revista de Fizica si Chimie. m.

**Societatea de Stiinte Istorice din Republica Socialista**
**Romania**
Bd. Republicii Nr. 55, Bucharest, Romania.
- Studii si Articole de Istorie. irreg.

**Societatea de Stiinte Matematice din Republica**
**Socialista Romania**
Str. Academiei 14, Bucharest, Romania
(Subscription to: ILEXIM, Calea Grivitei 64-66,
P.O. Box 136-137, Bucharest, Romania)
- Bulletin Mathematique. q. ISSN 0007-4691
- Gazeta Matematica; publicatie punara pentru
tineret. m.
- Mathematica; revue d'analyse numerique et de
theorie de l'approximation. s-a. ISSN 0025-5505

**Societatea de Studii Clasice din Republica Socialista**
**Romania**
- Studii Clasice. (pub. by Editura Academiei
Republicii Socialiste Romania)

**Union Medicale Balkanique**
Str. Gabriel Peri Nr. 1, Bucharest, Romania
(Subscr. to: ILEXIM, Calea Grivitei 64-66, P.O.Box
136-137, Bucharest, Romania)
- Union Medicale Balkanique. Archives. bi-m. ISSN
0041-6940

**Uniunea Arhitectilor din Republica Socialista**
**Romania**
Str. Academiei Nr. 18-20, Bucharest, Romania
(Subscr. to: ILEXIM, Calea Grivitei 64-66, P.O.
Box 136-137, Bucharest, Romania)
- Arhitectura. bi-m. ISSN 0300-5356

**Uniunea Artistilor Plastici din Republica Socialista**
**Romania**
Calea Victoriei 155, Bucharest, Romania
(Subscription to: ILEXIM, Calea Grivitei 64-66,
P.O. Box 136-137, Bucharest, Romania)
- Arta. m. ISSN 0004-3354

**Uniunea Compozitorilor din Republica Socialista**
**Romania**
Str. 13 Decembrie Nr. 24, Bucharest, Romania
(Subscr. to: ILEXIM, Calea Grivitei 64-66, P.O.
Box 136-137, Bucharest, Romania)
- Muzica. m. ISSN 0580-3713 (Co-sponsor:
Consiliul Culturii si Educatiei Socialiste)

**Uniunea Generala a Sindicatelor din Romania.**
**Consiliul Central**
St. Stefan Gheorghiu Nr. 14, Bucharest, Romania.
- Syndicats de Roumanie. q. ISSN 0049-2736

**Uniunea Scriitorilor din Republica Socialista**
**Romania**
Calea Victoriei 115, Bucharest, Romania
(Subscr. to: ILEXIM, Calea Grivitei 64-66, P.O.
Box 136-137, Bucharest, Romania)
- Convorbiri Literare. m. ISSN 0010-8243
- Romania Literara. w. ISSN 0048-8550
- Secolul 20; revista de literatura universala. m.
ISSN 0037-0517
- Steaua. m. ISSN 0039-0852
- Viata Romineasca. m. ISSN 0042-5052

**Uniunea Scriitorilor din Republica Socialista**
**Romania (Timisoara)**
Str. Rodnei Nr. 1, Timisoara, Romania.
- Orizont. m. ISSN 0030-560X

**Uniunea Societatilor De Stiinte Medicale Din**
**Republica Socialista Romania**
Str. Progresului No. 8, Bucharest, Romania
(Subscr. to: ILEXIM, Calea Grivitei 64-66, P.O.
Box 136-137, Bucharest, Romania)
- Farmacia/Pharmacy. 4 per yr. ISSN 0014-8237
- Oto-Rino Laringologie. 4 per yr. ISSN 0030-6649
- Revista de Chirurgie, Oncologie, O.R.L.,
Radiologie, Oftalmolgie, Stomatologie. Oncologie.
4 per yr.
- Revista de Chirurgie, Oncologie, O.R.L.,
Radiologie, Oftalmologie, Stomatologie.
Radiologie. 4 per yr. ISSN 0481-6684
- Revista de Chirurgie, Oncologie, O.R.L.,
Radiologie, Oftalmologie, Stomatologie.
Stomatologie. 4 per yr. ISSN 0039-1719
- Revista de Chirurgie, Oncologie, O.R.L.,
Radiologie, Stomatologie. Oftalmologie. 4 per yr.
ISSN 0030-0667
- Revista de Chirurgie, Oncologie, Radiologie,
O.R.L., Oftalmologie, Stomatologie. Chirurgia/
Surgery. 6 per yr.
- Revista de Igiena, Bacteriologie, Virusologie,
Parazitologie, Pneumoftiziologie. Bacteriologie,
Virusologie, Parazitologie, Epidemiologie. 4 per
yr. ISSN 0301-7338
- Revista de Igiena, Bacteriologie, Virusologie,
Parazitologie, Pneumoftiziologie. Igenia. 4 per yr.
ISSN 0019-1620
- Revista de Igiena, Bacteriologie, Virusologie,
Parazitologie, Pneumoftiziologie.
Pneumoftiziologie. 4 per yr.
- Revista de Medicina Interna, Neurologie,
Psihiatrie, Neuro-Chirurgie, Dermato-Venerologie.
Medicina Interna. 6 per yr. ISSN 0025-7869
- Revista de Medicina Interna, Neurologie,
Psihiatrie, Neuro-Chirurgie, Dermato-Venerologie.
Neurologie, Psihiatrie, Neuro-Chirurgie. 4 per yr.
ISSN 0028-386X
- Revista de Medicina Interna, Neurologie,
Psihiatrie, Neurochirurgie, Dermato-Venerologie.
Dermato-Venerologie. 6 per yr.
- Revista de Pediatrie, Obstetrica, Ginecologie.
Obstetrica si Ginecologie. 4 per yr. ISSN 0029-
781X
- Revista de Pediatrie, Obstetrica, Ginecologie.
Pediatrie. 4 per yr. ISSN 0031-3904
- Viata Medicala-Cadre Medii. 12 per yr.
- Viata Medicala - Cadre Superioare. m. ISSN
0042-5036

**Uniunea Ziaristilor din Republica Socialista Romania**
Calea Victoriei Nr. 163, Bucharest, Romania
(Subscr. to: ILEXIM, Calea Grivitei 64-66, P.O.
Box 136-137, Bucharest, Romania)
- Lumea. (pub. by Agerpres the Romanian News
Agency)
- Presa Noastra. m.

**Editura Univers**
Piata Scinteii 1, Bucharest, Romania
(Subscr. to: ILEXIM, Calea Grivitei 64-66, P.O.
Box 136-137, Bucharest, Romania)
- Cahiers Roumains d'Etudes Litteraires. q.
(Consiliul Culturii si Educatiei Socialiste)

**Universitatea "Al. I. Cuza" din Iasi**
Calea 23 August Nr. 11, Jassy, Romania
(Subscr. to: ILEXIM, Calea Grivitei 64-66, P.O.
Box 136-137, Bucharest, Romania)
- Universitatea "Al. I. Cuza" din Iasi. Analele
Stiintifice. Sectiunea 1A: Matematica. s-a. ISSN
0041-9109
- Universitatea "Al. I. Cuza" din Iasi. Analele
Stiintifice Sectiunea 1b: Fizica. s-a. ISSN 0041-
9141
- Universitatea "Al. I. Cuza" din Iasi. Analele
Stiintifice. Sectiunea 1c: Chimie. s-a. ISSN 0041-
9117
- Universitatea "Al. I. Cuza" din Iasi. Analele
Stiintifice. Sectiunea 2a: Biologie. s-a. ISSN 0041-
9133
- Universitatea "Al. I. Cuza" din Iasi. Analele
Stiintifice. Sectiunea 2B: Geologie. a. ISSN 0075-
3521
- Universitatea "Al. I. Cuza" din Iasi. Analele
Stiintifice. Sectiunea 2c: Geografie. a.
- Universitatea "Al. I. Cuza" din Iasi. Analele
Stiintifice. Sectiunea 3a: Istorie. s-a. ISSN 0041-
9125
- Universitatea "Al. I. Cuza" din Iasi. Analele
Stiintifice. Sectiunea 3b: Stiinte Filozofice. a.
ISSN 0075-353X
- Universitatea "Al. I. Cuza" din Iasi. Analele
Stiintifice. Sectiunea 3c: Stiinte Economice. a.
- Universitatea "Al. I. Cuza" din Iasi. Analele
Stiintifice. Sectiunea 3d: Stiinte Juridice. a.
- Universitatea "Al. I. Cuza" din Iasi. Analele
Stiintifice. Sectiunea 3e: Lingvistica. a.
- Universitatea "Al. I. Cuza" din Iasi. Analele
Stiintifice. Sectiunea 3f. : Literatura. a.

**Universitatea "Babes-Bolyai". Biblioteca Centrala**
**Universitara**
Str. Clinicilor Nr. 2, Cluj-Napoca, Romania.
- Studia Universitatis "Babes-Bolyai". Biologia. s-a.
ISSN 0039-3398
- Studia Universitatis "Babes-Bolyai". Chemia. s-a.
ISSN 0039-3401
- Studia Universitatis "Babes-Bolyai". Geologia.
Geographia. s-a. ISSN 0039-341X
- Studia Universitatis "Babes-Bolyai". Historia. s-a.
ISSN 0039-3428
- Studia Universitatis Babes-Bolyai. Iurisprudentia.
s-a. ISSN 0578-5464
- Studia Universitatis "Babes-Bolyai". Mathematica.
s-a.
- Studia Universitatis Babes-Bolyai. Oeconomica. s-
a. ISSN 0578-5472
- Studia Universitatis "Babes-Bolyai". Philologia. s-a.
ISSN 0039-3444
- Studia Universitatis Babes-Bolyai. Philosophia. s-a.
ISSN 0578-5480
- Studia Universitatis Babes-Bolyai. Physica. s-a.

**Universitatea Babes-Bolyai. Gradina Botanica**
Str. Republicii nr. 42, Cluj-Napoca, Romania.
- Contributii Botanice. a. ISSN 0069-9616

**Universitatea Bucuresti**
Bulevardul Gh. Gheorghiu Dej 64, Bucharest,
Rumania
(Dist. by Cartimex, Str. 13 Decemvrie 3-5, P.O.
Box 134-145, Bucharest, Rumania)
- Analele Universitatii Bucuresti. Acta Logica. a.
ISSN 0068-3116
- Universitatea Bucuresti. Analele. Filologie. a.
- Universitatea Bucuresti. Analele. Filozofie. Istorie.
Drept. a.
- Universitatea Bucuresti. Analele. Stiintele Naturii.
a.

**Universitatea din Brasov**
Bd. Gh. Gheorghiu-Dej, Nr. 29, Brasov, Romania.
- Universitatea din Brasov. Buletinul. Seria A.
Mecanica Aplicata-Constructii de Masini. a.

- Universitatea din Brasov. Buletinul. Seria a/3.
  Mecanica Aplicata - Constructii de Masini.
  Constructia de Masini si Tehnologia Prelucrarii
  Metalelor. a.
- Universitatea din Brasov. Buletinul Seria C. Stiinte
  Ale Naturii si Pedagogie. a.

**Universitatea din Craiova**
Str. Al.I. Cuza Nr. 13, Craiova, Romania
(Subscr. to: ILEXIM, Calea Grivitei 64-66, P.O.
Box 136-137, Bucharest, Romania)
- Universitatea Din Craiova. Analele: Seria Istorie,
  Geografie, Filologie. irreg.

**Universitatea din Timisoara**
Bd. Vasile Pirvan Nr. 4, Timisoara, Romania
(Subscr. to: ILEXIM, Calea Grivitei 64-66, P.O.
Box 136-137, Bucharest, Romania)
- Universitatea din Timisoara. Analele. Stiinte
  Filologice. a. ISSN 0082-4461
- Universitatea din Timisoara. Analele. Stiinte
  Fizico-Chimice. s-a. ISSN 0082-4453

**Universitatea din Timisoara. Facultatea de Stiinte ale
Naturii**
Bd. Vasile Pirvan Nr. 4, Timisoara, Romania.
- Universitatea din Timisoara. Facultatea de Stiinte
  ale Naturii. Analele: Stiinte Matematice. s-a.

# RWANDA

**Banque Nationale de Rwanda**
B.P. 531, Kigali, Rwanda.
- Banque Nationale de Rwanda. Rapport Annuel. a.

**Office Rwandais d'Information**
see Rwanda. Office Rwandais d'Information

**Rwanda. Bureau de l'Enseignement Familial**
Ministere de l'Education Nationale, B.P. 622, Kigali,
Rwanda.
- Vie Familiale. q.

**Rwanda. Direction de la Documentation et des
Statistiques**
B.P. 46, Kigali, Rwanda.
- Rwanda. Direction de la Documentation et des
  Statistiques. Bulletin de Statistique. q.
- Rwanda. Direction de la Documentation et des
  Statistiques. Etat d'Execution du Plan de
  Developpement. a. ISSN 0080-5017
- Rwanda. Direction de la Documentation et des
  Statistiques. Produit Interieur Brut. a. ISSN 0080-
  5025
- Rwanda. Direction de la Documentation et des
  Statistiques. Rapport Annuel de Ministeres. a.
  ISSN 0080-5033

**Rwanda. Office Rwandais d'Information**
B.P. 83, Kigali, Rwanda.
- Releve. w.

**Universite Nationale du Rwanda**
Rectorat, B.P. 117, Butare, Rwanda.
- Etudes Rwandaises. 3 per yr.

# RYUKYU ISLANDS, SOUTHERN

**Bank of the Ryukyus Ltd.**
Research Dept., 1-13-1 Kumoji, Naha, Okinawa,
Ryukyu Islands.
- Kinyu Keizai. q. ISSN 0023-1711

# SAINT LUCIA

**Castries Catholic Chronicle**
Bishop's House, Castries, St. Lucia, W. Indies.
- Castries Catholic Chronicle. s-m.

# SAINT VINCENT

**St. Vincent. Government Information Service**
Kingstown, St. Vincent, West Indies.
- St. Vincent Government Information Service
  News Bulletin. m.

# SAN MARINO

**San Marino. Segreteria di Stato per gli Affari Esteri**
San Marino.
- San Marino (Repubblica) Bollettino Ufficiale. 6
  per yr. ISSN 0036-4223

# SAO TOME E PRINCIPE

**Sao Tome e Principe. Reparticao Provincial dos
Servicos de Estatistica**
Caixa Postal No. 256, Sao Tome, Sao Tome e
Principe.
- Sao Tome e Principe. Reparticao Provincial dos
  Servicos de Estatistica. Boletin Trimestral de
  Estatistica. q.

# SAUDI ARABIA

**Arabian American Oil Co.(ARAMCO)**
Box 1389, Dhahran, Saudi Arabia.
- Oil Caravan Weekly. w. ISSN 0030-1418

**ARAMCO**
see Arabian American Oil Co. (ARAMCO)

**Muslim World League**
Mecca, Saudi Arabia.
- Muslim World League. Journal/Rabetat al-Alam
  al-Islami. Journal. m. (prep. by its Press and
  Publications Department)

**Saudi Arabia. Central Department of Statistics**
P. O. Box 3735, Riyadh, Saudi Arabia.
- Saudi Arabia. Central Department of Statistics.
  Statistical Indicator. irreg.

**Saudi Arabia. Ministry of Finance and National
Economy. Central Department of Statistics**
see Saudi Arabia. Central Department of Statistics

**Saudi Arabia. Ministry of Hajj and Aukaf**
Mecca, Saudi Arabia.
- Majallat Al-Tadamun Al-Islami. m.

**Saudi Arabian Monetary Agency**
Box 394, Jeddah, Saudi Arabia.
- Saudi Arabian Monetary Agency. Statistical
  Summary. a. ISSN 0581-8672 (prep. by its
  Research and Statistics Department)

# SENEGAL

**African Institute for Economic Development and
Planning**
- African Institute for Economic Development and
  Planning. Programme. (pub. by Nouvelles
  Editions Africaines)
- African Institute for Economic Development and
  Planning. Series in Economic and Social
  Development. (pub. by Nouvelles Editions
  Africaines)

**Afrique Mon Pays**
B. P. 2469, Dakar, Senegal.
- Afrique Mon Pays. m. ISSN 0002-0524

**Association des Universites Partiellement Ou
Entierement de Langue Francaise. Bureau Africain**
B.P. 10017, Liberte, Dakar, Senegal.
- A U P E L F Nouvelles Universitaires Africaines.
  4 per yr.

**Association Generale des Psycholoques Francophones
d'Afrique et de Madagascar**
c/o Secretariat Technique Permanent de la
Conference des Ministeres de l'Education, Union
Senegalaise de Banque, Dakar, Senegal.
- Revue Africaine et Malgache de Psychologie. q.

**Association Inter-Africaine d'Editions**
7 rue de Thiong, Dakar, Senegal.
- Revue Senegalaise de Droit. s-a. ISSN 0035-4112
  (Association Senegalaise d'Etudes et de
  Recherches Juridiques)

**Association Senegalaise d'Etudes et de Recherches
Juridiques**
- Revue Senegalaise de Droit. (pub. by Association
  Inter-Africaine d'Editions)

**Association Senegalaise pour l'Etude du Quaternaire
Africain**
Laboratoire de Geologie, Faculte des Sciences,
Dakar-Fann, Senegal.
- Association Senegalaise pour l'Etude du
  Quaternaire Africain. Bulletin de Liaison. q.

**Banque Centrale des Etats de l'Afrique de l'Ouest**
3 Ave. W. Ponty, B.P. 1398, Dakar, Senegal
(Provisional Address: 29 rue de Colisee, Paris (8e),
France)
- Banque Centrale des Etats de l'Afrique de l'Ouest.
  Notes d'Information et Statistiques. m. ISSN
  0005-559X
- Banque Centrale des Etats de l'Afrique de l'Ouest.
  Rapport Annuel. a. ISSN 0067-3889
- Banque Centrale des Etats de l'Afrique de l'Ouest.
  Rapport d'Activite. a. ISSN 0067-3897

**Librairie Clairafrique**
2 rue Sandiniery, B.P. 2005, Dakar, Senegal
(Dist. by: Livre Africain, 113 rue de Sevres, 75
Paris 6, France)
- Icones Plantarum Africanarum. a. ISSN 0073-
  4403
- Institut Fondamental d'Afrique Noire. Catalogues
  et Documents. irreg. ISSN 0070-2617
- Institut Fondamental d'Afrique Noire. Initiations
  et Etudes Africaines. irreg. ISSN 0070-2625
- Institut Fondamental d'Afrique Noire. Memoires.
  irreg. ISSN 0070-2633

**Council for the Development of Economic and Social
Research in Africa**
B. P. 3186, Dakar, Senegal.
- African Development Research Annual. a.

**Joel Decupper, Ed. & Pub.**
30 Blvd. Pinet Lapade, B.P. 1826, Dakar, Senegal.
- Africa. m. ISSN 0001-9755
- Afrique Medicale. bi-m. ISSN 0002-0516

**Environment Training Programme**
Box 3370, Dakar, Senegal.
- African Environment. q. (Co-sponsor:
  International African Institute)

**Institut Fondamental d'Afrique Noire**
Universite de Dakar, B.P. 206, Dakar, Senegal.
- I F A N Bulletin. Serie A: Sciences Naturelles. q.
  ISSN 0018-9634
- I F A N Bulletin. Series B: Sciences Humaines. s-
  a. ISSN 0018-9642
- Institut Fondamental d'Afrique Noire. Catalogues
  et Documents. (pub. by Librairie Clairafrique)
- Institut Fondamental d'Afrique Noire. Initiations
  et Etudes Africaines. (pub. by Librairie
  Clairafrique)
- Institut Fondamental d'Afrique Noire. Memoires.
  (pub. by Librairie Clairafrique)
- Institut Fondamental d'Afrique Noire. Rapport
  Annuel. a.
- Notes Africaines. q. ISSN 0029-3954

**Institut Fondamental d'Afrique Noire. Centre de
Mauritanie**
Universite de Dakar, B.P. 206, Dakar, Senegal.
- Etudes Mauritaniennes. irreg.

**Institut Fondamental d'Afrique Noire. Centre de
Saint-Louis de Senegal**
Universite de Dakar, B.P. 206, Dakar, Senegal.
- Etudes Senegalaises. irreg.

**International Development Research Centre**
CCP No. 518, Dakar, Senegal.
- Famille et Developpement. q.

**Moniteur Africain**
13 Ave. Jean Jaures, B.P. 1877, Dakar, Senegal.
- Moniteur Africain; mensuel economique des
  cadres d'Afrique noire. w. ISSN 0026-9670

**Nouvelles Editions Africaines**
Dakar, Senegal.
- African Institute for Economic Development and
  Planning. Programme. a.
- African Institute for Economic Development and
  Planning. Series in Economic and Social
  Development. irreg.

**Observateur Africain**
29 rue Paul Holle, Dakar, Senegal.
● Observateur Africain. m. ISSN 0048-1319

**Office de la Recherche Scientifique et Technique Outre-Mer de M'Bour. Centre de Geophysique**
B.P. 50, M'Bour, Senegal.
● Office de la Recherche Scientifique et Technique Outre-Mer de M'Bour. Centre de Goephysique. Bulletin Seismique. m.

**Panorama Africain**
B.P. 135, Dakar, Senegal.
● Panorama Africain. bi-m.

**Parti Democratique Senegalais**
7 rue de Thiong, Dakar, Senegal.
● Le Democrate. m.

**S.A.P.E.F.**
B.P. 176, Dakar, Senegal
(Subscr. to: 11 rue de Teheran, 78008 Paris, France)
● Amina. m.
● Bingo; le mensuel du monde noir. m. ISSN 0005-6499

**Senegal. Archives**
Immeuble Administratif, Av. Roume, Dakar, Senegal.
● Bibliographie du Senegal. q.

**Senegal. Centre d'Etude des Civilisations**
Ministry of Culture, Dakar, Senegal.
● Demb Ak Tey/Yesterday and Today; a journal of myths and legends. q.

**Senegal. Direction de l'Exploitation Meteorologique**
B.P. 3144, Dakar, Senegal.
● Senegal. Direction de l'Exploitation Meteorologique. Publications. Serie 1. irreg.; no. 37, 1974. ISSN 0065-4248 (Co-sponsor: Agence pour la Securite de la Navigation Aerienne en Afrique et a Madagascar)
● Senegal. Direction de l'Exploitation Meteorologique. Publications. Serie 2. irreg.; no. 48, 1974. ISSN 0084-6015

**Senegal. Direction de la Statistique**
B.P. 116, Dakar, Senegal.
● Commerce Exterieur du Senegal. a.
● Senegal. Direction de la Statistique. Bulletin Statistique et Economique Mensuel. m. ISSN 0037-2153
● Situation Economique du Senegal. a. ISSN 0080-9853

**Senegal. Imprimerie Nationale**
Rufisque, Senegal.
● Senegal. Liste du Corps Diplomatique. irreg.

**Senegal. Ministere de l'Information et de Telecommunications. Direction de l'Information**
58 Bd. de la Republique, Dakar, Senegal.
● Carte d'Identite du Senegal. a.

**Senegal. Ministere des Finances et des Affaires Economiques. Direction de la Statistique**
see Senegal. Direction de la Statistique

**Senegal. Office de Radiodiffusion-Television**
58 Blvd. de la Republique, Dakar, Senegal.
● Disoo. irreg.

**Societe Africaine d'Edition**
16 bis, rue de Thiong, Dakar, Senegal
(and 32 rue de l'Echiquier, Paris, France)
● Afrique Litteraire et Artistique. q. ISSN 0002-0508
● Annee Politique Africaine. a. ISSN 0066-2364
● Cote d'Ivoire en Chiffres. a.
● Economie Africaine. a.
● Revue Francaise d'Etudes Politiques Africaines/Mois en Afrique. m. ISSN 0035-3027
● Revue Francaise d'Etudes Politiques Mediterraneennes. m (10 per yr)
● Senegal en Chiffres. a.

**Societe de Psychopathologie et d'Hygiene Mentale de Dakar**
B.P. 5097, Dakar-Fann, Senegal.
● Psychopathologie Africaine. 3 per yr. ISSN 0033-314X

**Societe Medicale d'Afrique Noire de Langue Francaise**
B.P. 450, Dakar, Senegal.
● Societe Medicale d'Afrique Noire de Langue Francaise. Bulletin. q. ISSN 0049-1101

**Societe Nationale d'Etude et de Promotion Industrielle**
14, rue Maunoury, B.P. 100, Dakar, Senegal.
● Guide de l'Investisseur Industriel au Senegal. irreg.
● Societe Nationale d'Etude et de Promotion Industrielle. Bulletin d'Information Industrielle. bi-m.

**Societe Nationale de Presse, d'Edition et de Publicite**
B.P. 2047, Rue de Reims, Dakar, Senegal.
● Ouest Africain. w.

**SONAPRESS**
see Societe Nationale de Presse, d'Edition et de Publicite

**Union Nationale des Travailleurs du Senegal**
48 Rue Vincene, Dakar, Senegal.
● Ouvrier Senegalais. m. ISSN 0048-2498

**Unir: Echo de Saint Louis**
1 Rue Neuville, B.P. 160, Saint Louis, Senegal.
● Unir: Echo de Saint Louis. m.

**Universite de Dakar. Ecole des Bibliothecaires, Archivistes et Documentalistes**
B.P. 3252, Dakar, Senegal.
● BLIBAD; bulletin e liaison a l'intention des bibliothecaires, archivistes et documentalistes africans. 3 per yr.

# SEYCHELLES

**Express Transport Company Ltd.**
Box 239, Mahe, Seychelles.
● Trade Directory of Seychelles. a.

**Seychelles. National Archives and Museum**
Victoria, Seychelles.
● Seychelles National Archives and Museum. Biennial Report. biennial.

**Seychelles Farmers Association**
● Seychellois. (pub. by Seychellois Press Ltd.)

**Seychelles People's United Party**
Victoria St., Box 154, Victoria, Mahe, Seychelles.
● People. fortn. ISSN 0031-4994

**Seychellois Press Ltd.**
Box 32, Victoria, Mahe, Seychelles.
● Seychellois. d. (Seychelles Farmers Association) (Co-sponsor: Seychelles Copra Association)

# SIERRA LEONE

**Ahmadiyya Muslim Mission**
P.O. Box 353, Freetown, Sierra Leone.
● African Crescent. m. ISSN 0044-653X

**Bank of Sierra Leone**
P.O. Box 30, Freetown, Sierra Leone.
● Balance of Payments of Sierra Leone. a. ISSN 0067-2998
● Bank of Sierra Leone. Annual Report. a. ISSN 0067-3730
● Bank of Sierra Leone Economic Review. q.
● Sierra Leone in Figures. a. ISSN 0080-9535

**Chamber of Commerce of Sierra Leone**
P.O. Box 502, Freetown, Sierra Leone.
● Chamber of Commerce of Sierra Leone. Journal. a. ISSN 0080-9527

**Fourah Bay College**
see under University of Sierra Leone

**International Agencies**
26, Liverpool St., Box 1365, Freetown, Sierra Leone.
● Sierra Leone Trade Fairs and Exhibitions. 3 per yr.

**Jamawu Publications**
Freetown, Sierra Leone.
● Focus; a Sierra Leonean international socio-economic political quarterly. q.

**National Development Bank**
Leone House, 21/23 Siaka Stevens St., Freetown, Sierra Leone.
● National Development Bank. Annual Report and Accounts. a.

**Njala University College**
see under University of Sierra Leone

**Sierra Commercial Enterprise**
5 Kissy St., Freetown, Sierra Leone.
● Sierra Trade. bi-m.

**Sierra Leone. Central Statistics Office**
Freetown, Sierra Leone.
● Sierra Leone. Central Statistics Office. Quarterly Statistical Bulletin. q. ISSN 0037-4741

**Sierra Leone. Ministry of Education**
c/o Publications Branch, New England, Freetown, Sierra Leone.
● Sierra Leone. Ministry of Education. Monthly Newsletter. m.
● Sierra Leone. Ministry of Education. Report. a. ISSN 0080-9551
● Sierra Leone Journal of Education. s-a. ISSN 0022-0582

**Sierra Leone. Ministry of Finance**
Freetown, Sierra Leone.
● Sierra Leone. Ministry of Finance. Budget Speech. a.

**Sierra Leone. Ministry of Information and Broadcasting**
Lightfoot Boston St., Freetown, Sierra Leone.
● Sierra Leone Trade Journal. q. ISSN 0037-4768 (prep. by its Government Information Services)

**Sierra Leone Geographical Association**
c/o Fourah Bay College Bookshop, Freetown, Sierra Leone.
● Sierra Leone Geographical Journal. a. ISSN 0583-239X

**Sierra Leone Library Association**
c/o Mrs. A. M. Thomas, Ed., Milton Margai Teachers College, Private Mail Bag, Goderich near Freetown, Sierra Leone.
● Sierra Leone Library Journal. s-a.

**Sierra Leone Society**
● Sierra Leone Studies. (pub. by University of Sierra Leone Press)

**University of Sierra Leone. Fourah Bay College**
Freetown, Sierra Leone.
● African Literature Today. (pub. by Africana Publishing Co. US)
● Africana Research Bulletin. s-a. (prep. by its Institute of African Studies)

**University of Sierra Leone. Njala University College**
Private Mail Bag, Freetown, Sierra Leone.
● Sierra Leone Agricultural Journal. s-a. (prep. by its Educational Services Centre)

**University of Sierra Leone Press**
University of Sierra Leone, Freetown, Sierra Leone.
● Sierra Leone Studies. s-a. ISSN 0037-475X (Sierra Leone Society)

# SIKKIM

**Namgyal Institute of Tibetology**
Gangtok, Sikkim.
● Bulletin of Tibetology. 3 per yr. ISSN 0007-5159

**Youth's Library**
Gangtok, Sikkim.
● Nava Jyoti. s-a. ISSN 0028-1387

# SINGAPORE

**Afro-Asian Trade Union Bureau**
● Afro-Asian Labour Bulletin. (pub. by National Trades Union Congress)

**American Association of Singapore**
American Club, Scotts Rd., Singapore 9, Singapore.
● Singapore American. m.

**Asia Research (Private) Ltd**
● Asia Research Bulletin. (pub. by Times Periodicals Private, Ltd.)

**Asian Federation of Obstetrics and Gynaecology**
c/o University Dept of Obstetrics and Gynaecology,
Kandang Kerbau Hospital for Women, Hampshire
Road, Singapore 8, Singapore.
- Asian Federation of Obstetrics and Gynaecology.
Journal. q.

**Asian Mass Communication Research and
Information Centre**
39 Newton Road, Singapore 11, Singapore.
- Asian Mass Communications Bulletin. q.
- Media Asia. q.

**Association of Southeast Asian Librarians**
- Conference of Southeast Asian Librarians.
Proceedings. (pub. by Chopmen Enterprises)

**Automobile Association of Singapore**
336 River Valley Road, Singapore 9, Singapore.
- Highway. q. ISSN 0439-1292

**Barisan Sosialis Malaya**
436-C Victoria St., Singapore 7, Singapore.
- Plebeian. m. ISSN 0048-444X

**Botanic Gardens**
Cluny Rd., Singapore 10, Singapore.
- Gardens' Bulletin, Singapore. irreg: vol 26, pt. 1,
1972; vol 27, pt. 2, 1975. ISSN 0072-0178

**British Association of Singapore**
F9 Maritime Bldg., Collyer Quay, Singapore,
Singapore.
- Beam. m. ISSN 0005-7398

**Building and Estate Management Society**
Ladyhill Campus, 3 Ladyhill Rd., Singapore,
Singapore.
- Building and Estate Management Society.
Proceedings of the Annual Seminar. a.

**Chinese Pictorial Review Ltd.**
112-120 Robinson Road, Singapore, Singapore.
- Indian Movie News. m. ISSN 0019-5979
- Movie News. m. ISSN 0027-2736

**Chopmen Enterprises**
428-429 Katong Shopping Centre (4th Fl.),
Mountbatten Road, Singapore-15, Singapore.
- Conference of Southeast Asian Librarians.
Proceedings. irreg., 1970, 1st, Singapore.

**Cosmic Media**
P.O. Box 3163, Singapore, Singapore.
- Singapore Shipping 'n' Shipbuilder. m.

**Democratic Socialist Club**
Box 28, Newton, Singapore, Singapore.
- People. ISSN 0048-3303

**Diocese of Singapore**
4 Bishopsgate, Singapore 10, Singapore.
- Diocesan Digest. m. ISSN 0012-3021

**Educational Publications Bureau**
177-a, Outram Park, 3, Singapore, Singapore.
- Language. irreg. (Singapore Linguistic Society)
- Prospect. m. ISSN 0048-5594

**Electrical & Electronic Engineering Society**
Ngee Ann Technical College, 535, Clementi Road,
Singapore 21, Singapore.
- Electro. a.

**F E P International Ltd.**
Jalan Boon Lay, Jurong 22, Singapore, Singapore.
- Journal of Southeast Asian Studies. s-a. ISSN
0022-4634 (University of Singapore. History
Department)
- Southeast Asian Affairs. a. (Institute of Southeast
Asian Studies)

**Fraser & Co.(Pte)**
Box 789, Singapore, Singapore.
- Fraser's Circular. m. ISSN 0016-0083

**Margo V. Gill, Ed. & Pub.**
226, Tanglin Shopping Centre, Singapore 10,
Singapore.
- Eastern Trade. fortn.

**Golf Singapore Review**
455-a East Coast Rd., 15 Singapore, Singapore.
- Golf Singapore Review. q. ISSN 0017-1832

**Government and Public Administration Society**
Nanyang University, Singapore, Singapore.
- Government and Public Administration Society.
Journal. a.

**Graphic Publications**
Singapore Professional Centre, Block 23, 2nd Floor,
Outram Park 3, Singapore 3, Singapore.
- Institution of Engineers, Singapore. Journal. irreg.

**Historical Society of Nanyang University**
- Historical Miscellany. (pub. by Nanyang
University)

**Immedia Pte. Ltd.**
2213 International Plaza, 10 Anson Rd., Singapore
2, Singapore.
- Singapore Shipping and Air Gazette. s-m.

**Institute of Southeast Asian Studies**
8 Cluny Road, Singapore 10, Singapore.
- Institute of Southeast Asian Studies. Annual
Report. a.
- Institute of Southeast Asian Studies. Library
Accessions List. m. ISSN 0046-984X
- Institute of Southeast Asian Studies. Library
Bulletin. irreg., 1972, no. 5. ISSN 0073-9723
- Institute of Southeast Asian Studies. Newsletter.
irreg.
- Institute of Southeast Asian Studies. Occasional
Paper. irreg. ISSN 0073-9731
- Southeast Asia Microfilms Newsletter. s-a.
- Southeast Asian Affairs. (pub. by F E P
International Ltd.)
- Trends in Southeast Asia. irreg., 1972, no. 4.
ISSN 0082-6316

**Institution of Engineers, Singapore**
- Institution of Engineers, Singapore. Journal. (pub.
by Graphic Publications)

**International Development Research Centre**
Tanglin P. O. Box 160, Singapore 10, Singapore.
- Technonet Asia Newsletter; Asian network for
industrial technology information and extension.
q.

**James Cowan Associates (S.E. Asia) Pte Ltd.**
9Th Floor, Grand Building, Phillip, Singapore 1,
Singapore.
- J C A Market Digest. w.

**Kandang Kerbau Hospital**
Singapore, Singapore.
- Kandang Kerbau Hospital Bulletin. s-a. ISSN
0022-8346

**Kesatuan Akademis Universiti Singapura**
Singapore, Singapore.
- Kesatuan Bulletin. m. ISSN 0047-3383

**Lee Foundation**
- University of Singapore Science Journal. (pub. by
University of Singapore Science Society)

**Lee Kong Chian Museum of Asian Culture**
Nanyang University, Singapore, Singapore.
- Journal of Asian Art. a.

**Library Association of Singapore**
c/o National Library, Stamford Road, Singapore 6,
Singapore.
- Singapore Libraries. a. ISSN 0085-6118

**Malayan Law Journal (Pte) Ltd.**
1302-1304 (13th Floor) Shenton House, Shenton
Way, Singapore 1, Singapore.
- Malayan Law Journal. m. ISSN 0025-1283

**Malayan Medical Association**
- Medical Journal of Malaya. (pub. by Young
Advertising & Marketing Ltd.)

**Medical Centre**
4A College Rd., Singapore, Singapore.
- Academy of Medicine, Singapore. Annals. q.

**Nanyang Orchid Association**
33 Phillip St., Singapore 1, Singapore.
- Nanyang Orchid. a.

**Nanyang Univ. Nan-Yang ta Hsueh Chung-Kuo Yu
Wen Hsueh Hui**
Jurong Road, 22, Singapore, Singapore.
- Hsin Sheng. q.

**Nanyang University**
Jurong Road, Singapore 22, Singapore.
- Historical Miscellany. a. (Historical Society of
Nanyang University)
- Nanyang University. Bulletin. q. ISSN 0027-7797
- Nanyang University Journal. a. ISSN 0077-2747

**Nanyang University. Biology Society**
Jurong Road, Singapore 22, Singapore.
- Biosphere Bulletin. irreg.

**Nanyang University. Lee Kong Chian Institute of
Mathematics**
22 Singapore, Singapore.
- Nanta Mathematica. irreg., 2-3 per yr. ISSN
0077-2739

**National Book Development Council of Singapore**
c/o National Library, Stamford Road, Singapore 6,
Singapore
(Subscr to: Chopmen Enterprises, 428-429 Katong
Shopping Center, Singapore)
- Singapore Book World. a. ISSN 0080-9659

**National Library**
Stamford Road, Singapore 6, Singapore.
- Books about Singapore. biennial. ISSN 0068-0176
- Singapore. National Library. Annual Report. a.
ISSN 0080-9721
- Singapore. National Library. Board Report. a.
ISSN 0080-973X
- Singapore National Bibliography. a. ISSN 0080-
9713

**National Trades Union Congress**
Trade Union House, Shenton Way, Singapore,
Singapore.
- Afro-Asian Labour Bulletin. m. ISSN 0002-063X
(Afro-Asian Trade Union Bureau)
- N. T. U. C. Perjuangan. m. ISSN 0031-5443

**National Youth Leadership Training Institute**
South Buona Vista, Rd., Singapore 5, Singapore.
- N Y L T I Journal. s-a.

**Orchid Society of South East Asia**
- Malayan Orchid Review. (pub. by Times
Periodicals Private Ltd.)

**Salvation Army in Malaysia and Singapore**
207 Clemenceau Ave., Singapore-9, Singapore.
- War Cry. m. ISSN 0049-6898

**Shell Eastern Petroleum Ltd.**
UOB Building, No. 1 Bonham Street, 1 Singapore,
Singapore.
- Berita Shell. m. ISSN 0005-9153

**Sima Publishers**
76F/78F, Boon Keng Road, Block 4, 12, Singapore,
Singapore.
- International Trade and Singapore. irreg.

**Singapore Armed Forces Education Dept. Personnel
Research & Education Department**
Manpower Division, Ministry of Defense, Tanglin,
Singapore 10, Singapore
(Subscr. to: MPH Book Co., 71-77 Stamford Rd.,
Singapore 6, Singapore)
- Pioneer; Singapore armed forces news. m. ISSN
0048-4199

**Singapore. Department of Statistics**
c/o Government Publications Bureau, Fullerton
Bldg., Singapore, Singapore.
- Singapore. Department of Statistics. Monthly
Digest of Statistics. m. ISSN 0037-5640
- Singapore. Department of Statistics. Report on the
Census of Industrial Production. a. ISSN 0080-
9675
- Singapore. Department of Statistics. Report on the
Household Expenditure Survey. a.
- Singapore. Department of Statistics. Report on the
Labour Force Survey. a.
- Singapore. Department of Statistics. Singapore
Balance of Payments. biennial.

**Singapore. Economic Development Board**
P.O. Box 2692, Singapore, Singapore.
- Singapore. Economic Development Board. Annual
Report. a. ISSN 0080-9683

**Singapore. Family Planning and Population Board**
Singapore, Singapore.
- Report of National Survey on Family Planning in
Singapore. a.

**Singapore. Government Printing Office**
Singapore, Singapore.
- Singapore Trade Classification & Customs Duties. irreg.

**Singapore. Housing and Development Board**
National Development Bldg., Maxwell Road, Singapore 1, Singapore.
- Our Home. bi-m.
- Singapore. Housing and Development Board. Annual Report. a.

**Singapore. Metrication Board**
Ministry of Science and Technology, Anson Road, Singapore 2, Singapore.
- Singapore. Metrication Board. Annual Report. a.

**Singapore. Ministry of Culture**
3Rd Floor, Govt. Offices, St. Andrew's Road, Singapore, 6, Singapore.
- Singapore Bulletin. m.
- Singapore Facts and Pictures. a. ISSN 0080-9691

**Singapore. Ministry of Finance**
Singapore, Singapore.
- Economic Survey of Singapore. a.

**Singapore. Ministry of Health**
Palmer Road, Singapore 2, Singapore.
- Singapore Public Health Bulletin. a. (Co-Sponsor: Singapore Ministry of Environment)

**Singapore. Ministry of Labour**
Havelock Rd., Singapore 1, Singapore.
- Singapore. Ministry of Labour. Annual Report. a.

**Singapore. Ministry of Science and Technology**
Singapore, Singapore.
- Singapore. Ministry of Science and Technology. National Survey of Scientific Manpower. a.

**Singapore. Ministry of the Environment**
Princess House, Alexandra Rd., Singapore 3, Singapore.
- Singapore. Ministry of the Environment. Annual Report. a.

**Singapore. Monetary Authority**
S I A Bldg., 77 Robinson Rd., Singapore 1, Singapore.
- Singapore. Monetary Authority. Quarterly Bulletin. q.

**Singapore. National Maritime Board**
Singapore, Singapore.
- Singapore. National Maritime Board. Report. q.

**Singapore. National Statistical Commission**
P.O. Box 3010, Singapore 1, Singapore.
- Singapore Statistical Bulletin. s-a.

**Singapore. National Statistical Commission. Library-Cum-Archive**
31-B Goldhill Plaza, Off Newton Road, Singapore, Singapore.
- Annotated Bibliography of Statistical Publications. a.

**Singapore. Primary Production Department**
7Th Floor National Development Bldg., Maxwell Road, Singapore 2, Singapore.
- Singapore Journal of Primary Industries. s-a.

**Singapore. Science Council**
Singapore, Singapore.
- Singapore. Science Council. Annual Reports. a.

**Singapore Buddhist Youth Organisations Joint Celebrations Committee**
83 Silat Road, Singapore 3, Singapore.
- Young Buddhist. a.

**Singapore Chinese Chamber of Commerce**
47 Hill Street, Singapore 6, Singapore.
- Singapore Chinese Chamber of Commerce. Economic Monthly. m.

**Singapore Cine Club**
38a Orchard Rd., 9 Singapore, Singapore.
- Cine News. m. ISSN 0009-6954

**Singapore Computer Society**
P.O. Box 2570, Singapore, Singapore.
- Singapore Computer Society. Journal. irreg.

**Singapore Guppy Club**
5 Chancery Lane, Singapore, Singapore.
- Guppy Digest. q. ISSN 0046-6638

**Singapore Indian Chamber of Commerce**
55-a, Robinson Road, Box 1038, Singapore, Singapore.
- Singapore Indian Chamber of Commerce. Directory. irreg.

**Singapore Institute of Architects**
Publications Board, 395A/397A Block 23, Outram Park, Singapore 3, Singapore.
- S I A Journal. bi-m. ISSN 0049-0520

**Singapore Institute of Planners**
Box 3600, Singapore, Singapore.
- Planews. irreg., latest issue, 1975.

**Singapore International Chamber of Commerce**
Denmark House, Singapore 1, Singapore.
- Singapore International Chamber of Commerce. Economic Bulletin. m. ISSN 0037-5659
- Singapore International Chamber of Commerce. Report. a. ISSN 0583-3736

**Singapore Investor**
50-J Armenian St., Singapore 8, Singapore.
- Singapore Investor. w.

**Singapore Linguistic Society**
- Language. (pub. by Educational Publications Bureau)

**Singapore Manufacturers' Association**
P.O. Box No. 213, Colombo Court Post Office, North Bridge Road, Singapore, 6, Singapore.
- Directory of Singapore Manufacturers. a. ISSN 0070-6337

**Singapore National Institute of Chemistry**
c/o Singapore Professional Centre, Block 23, 129B, Outram Park, Singapore 3, Singapore.
- Singapore National Institute of Chemistry. Bulletin. a.

**Singapore National Printers Ltd.**
303 Upper Serangoon Road, Box 485, Singapore 13, Singapore.
- Singapore National Printers. Publications Catalogue. irreg.

**Singapore Police Academy**
Thomson Rd., Singapore 11, Singapore.
- Singapore Police Journal. 2 per yr.

**Singapore Polytechnic Building Society**
Prince Edward Rd., Singapore 2, Singapore.
- Quantibuild. a.

**Singapore Polytechnic Draughting Society,**
Singapore Polytechnic, Princess Mary Campus, Dover Rd, Singapore, Singapore.
- Technographics. a.

**Singapore Polytechnic Engineering Society**
c/o Singapore Polytechnic Students Union, 9 Prince Edward Rd., Singapore, Singapore.
- Singapore Polytechnic Engineering Society. Journal. a.

**Singapore Polytechnic Polymer Society**
c/o Singapore Polytechnic Students Union, 9, Prince Edward Rd, Singapore 2, Singapore.
- Polymer Journal. a.

**Singapore Securities Research Institute**
6Th Floor, Clifford Centre, Raffles Place, Singapore 1, Singapore.
- Securities Industry Review. s-a.

**Singapore Society of Accountants**
Rooms 3 & 8, 15-B Amber Mansions, Orchard Rd., Singapore 9, Singapore.
- Singapore Accountant. a. ISSN 0080-9640

**Singapore Sports Council**
National Stadium, Kallang, Singapore 14, Singapore.
- Sports. m.

**Singapore Tourist Promotion Board**
Tudor Court, Tanglin Road, Singapore 10, Singapore.
- Singapore Tourist Promotion Board. Annual Statistical Report on Visitor Arrivals. a.
- Singapore Tourist Promotion Board. Monthly Statistical Report on Visitor Arrivals. m.
- Singapore Travel News. m. ISSN 0037-5713

**Singapore Trained Nurses' Association**
Singapore Professional Centre, Block 23, Outram Park, Singapore 3, Singapore.
- Nursing Journal of Singapore/Berita Jururawat. s-a. ISSN 0067-5814

**South Seas Society**
Box 709, Singapore, Singapore.
- Nanyang Quarterly; review of Southeast Asian studies. q.
- South Seas Society. Journal. s-a. ISSN 0081-2889
- South Seas Society. Monograph. irreg., no. 17, 1976. ISSN 0081-2897

**South East Asia Iron and Steel Institute**
Tower 1003, Dbs Building, 6 Shenton Way, Singapore-1, Singapore.
- S E A I S I Quarterly. q.

**Southeast Asia Union Mission of Seventh-Day Adventists**
251 Upper Serangoon Rd, Singapore, Singapore.
- Messenger. bi-m. ISSN 0026-0371

**Southeast Asian Fisheries Development Center**
Marine Fisheries Research Department, Changi Point, Singapore 17, Singapore.
- Southeast Asian Fisheries Development Center Marine Fisheries Research Department. Annual Report. a.

**Southeast Asian Ministers of Education Organization. Regional Language Centre**
30 Orange Grove Road, Singapore 10, Singapore.
- R L C Annual Report. a.
- R L C Journal; a journal of language teaching and research in Southeast Asia. s-a. ISSN 0033-6882

**Southeast Asian Research Centre**
167-B, MacPherson Rd., Singapore 13, Singapore.
- Journal of Southeast Asian Researches. a. ISSN 0075-4382

**Stamford College**
72 the Arcade, Raffles Place, Singapore, Singapore.
- Stamford Journal. m.

**Stock Exchange of Malaysia & Singapore**
3A/E, Clifford House, Collyer Quay, 1, Singapore, Singapore.
- Stock Exchange of Malaysia & Singapore. Company Reports. irreg. ISSN 0583-3981

**C. K. Tang Ltd.**
310 Orchard Rd., Singapore 9, Singapore.
- House of Tang Family News. m. ISSN 0018-6481

**Telecommunication Authority of Singapore**
15/33, Hill St., Singapore 6, Singapore.
- Telecommunication Authority of Singapore. T A S Annual Report. a.

**Times International**
G.P.O. Box 1857, 1 Singapore, Singapore.
- Construction Review. q.

**Times Periodicals Private, Ltd.**
390 Kim Seng Rd., Singapore 9, Singapore.
- Asia Research Bulletin; monthly economic reports with monthly political supplement. m. ISSN 0044-9172 (Asia Research (Private) Ltd)
- Fanfare. w. ISSN 0046-3248
- Her World. m. ISSN 0046-7278
- Malayan Orchid Review. s-a. ISSN 0047-5602 (Orchid Society of South East Asia)
- Singapore Business. m.
- Singapore Trade & Industry Yearbook. a.
- Strait Times Directory of Singapore. a.

**Times Publishing Sdn Bhd.**
Magazines and Periodicals Division, 442 Thomson Road, Singapore 11, Singapore.
- Straits Times Annual. a. ISSN 0585-3923

**University Education Press**
Newton P.O. Box 96, Singapore 11, Singapore.
- Contemporary Asia Review. s-a.
- Journal of International Education and Development. s-a.

**University of Singapore**
c/o Lewis L. T. Au, Prince Edward Rd., Singapore 2, Singapore.
- Engineering News. q.

**University of Singapore. Chinese Society**
c/o Dept. of Chinese Studies, Cluny Rd.,
Singapore 10, Singapore.
● University of Singapore. Chinese Society. Journal.
a. ISSN 0080-9667

**University of Singapore. Department of English**
Bukit Timah Rd., 10 Singapore, Singapore
(Subscr. Address: P.O. Box 4060, Bukit Timah Post
Office, 21 Singapore)
● Poetry Singapore. 3 per yr. ISSN 0032-2164

**University of Singapore. Department of Geography**
Bukit Timah Rd., 10 Singapore, Singapore.
● Journal of Tropical Geography. s-a. ISSN 0022-
5290 (Co-Sponsor: University of Malaya, Dept. of
Geography)

**Univ. of Singapore. Department of Sociology**
Bukit Timah Road, Singapore, Singapore
(Subscr. to: Chopmen Enterprises, 428 Katong
Shopping Centre, Singapore 15, Singapore)
● Sociology Working Papers. m.

**University of Singapore. Economic Research Centre**
Bt. Timah Rd., Singapore, Singapore.
● Malayan Economic Review. s-a. ISSN 0047-5599

**University of Singapore. Economics Society**
Singapore 10, Singapore.
● University of Singapore. Economics Society.
Journal/Suara Ekonomi. q.

**University of Singapore. Faculty of Engineering**
Prince Edward Rd., Singapore 2, Singapore.
● Engineering Journal of Singapore. a.

**University of Singapore Historical Society**
History Dept., University, Bukit Timah Road,
Singapore, 10, Singapore.
● University of Singapore. Historical Society.
Journal. a. ISSN 0085-610X

**University of Singapore. History Department**
● Journal of Southeast Asian Studies. (pub. by F E
P International Ltd.)

**University of Singapore. Law Society**
c/o Law Faculty, Singapore 10, Singapore.
● Singapore Law Review. a. ISSN 0080-9705

**University of Singapore. Muslim Society**
c/o Union House, Cluny Rd., Singapore 10,
Singapore.
● Sedar; journal of Islamic studies. a. ISSN 0559-
2674

**University of Singapore Political Science Society**
University of Singapore, Singapore, Singapore.
● University of Singapore Political Science Society.
Journal. irreg.

**University of Singapore Science Society**
Union House, Bukit Timah Rd., Singapore 10,
Singapore.
● University of Singapore Science Journal. irreg.
ISSN 0083-405X (Lee Foundation) (Co-sponsor:
Asia Foundation)

**University of Singapore Society**
Guild House, 15 Evans Rd., Singapore 10,
Singapore.
● Commentary. 4 per yr. ISSN 0084-8956

**University of Singapore. Students' Union**
Bukit Timah Rd, Singapore 10, Singapore.
● Singapore Undergrad. m. ISSN 0049-0547

**Wesley Methodist Church**
5 Fort Canning Rd., Singapore 6, Singapore.
● Wesleyan. q. ISSN 0043-2881

**Workers' Party**
92-A Hill St., Singapore 6, Singapore.
● Hammer. m.

**Yamaha Music (Asia) Pte.**
Singapore, Singapore.
● Music Bulletin/Yin Yueh Tsa Chih. bi-m.

**Young Advertising & Marketing Ltd.**
Box 664, Singapore, Singapore.
● Medical Journal of Malaya. q. ISSN 0025-7303
(Malayan Medical Association)

# SOMALIA

**Banca Nazionale Somala**
*see* Somali National Bank

**Dalka**
Box 388, Mogadishu, Somalia.
● Dalka; monthly of current affairs. m. ISSN 0045-
9542

**Somali Institute of Public Administration**
Mogadishu, Somali.
● Somali Institute of Public Administration
Newsletter. q.

**Somalia. Ministry of Education. Department of
Planning**
Mogadishu, Somalia.
● Statistics of Education in Somalia. irreg.

**Somalia National Bank**
Box 11, Mogadishu, Somalia.
● Somali National Bank. Bulletin/Banca Nazionale
Somala. Bollettino. q. ISSN 0038-1268 (prep. by
its Economic Research and Statistics Department)
● Somalia National Bank. Annual Report and
Statement of Accounts. a. (prep. by its Economic
Research and Statistics Department)
● Somalia National Bank. Economic Report. a.
ISSN 0067-317X

# SOUTH AFRICA

**A E C I Ltd.**
Box 1122, Johannesburg 2000, South Africa.
● Prospect. q. ISSN 0033-1481

**Addressograph-Multigraph (Pty.) Ltd.**
Box 282, Johannesburg 2000, South Africa.
● A M News - Southern Africa. q. ISSN 0001-1932

**Adlodorum**
Box 3194, Pretoria, South Africa.
● Hospital R. S. A. bi-m. ISSN 0018-5833 (Hospital
Employees Association)

**Africa Evangelistic Band**
Private Bag, Mowbray, Cape Town, South Africa.
● Pilgrim/Pelgrim. m. ISSN 0031-9805

**Africa Institute of South Africa**
P. O. Box 630, Pretoria, South Africa.
● Africa at a Glance: A Quick Reference of Facts
and Figures on Africa. irreg. ISSN 0065-3829
● Africa Institute. Annual Report. a. ISSN 0065-
3853
● Africa Institute. Communications. irreg. ISSN
0065-3861
● Africa Institute. Special Publications. irreg. ISSN
0065-3888
● Africa Institute of South Africa. Bulletin. 10 per
yr. ISSN 0568-1138
● South African Journal of African Affairs. a. ISSN
0085-638X

**African Insurance Record**
Box 2651, Cape Town, South Africa.
● African Insurance Record. m. ISSN 0002-001X

**African International Publishing Co. (Pty.) Ltd.**
Box 78440, Johannesburg, South Africa
(U.S. dist. to: Harry C. Thompson, 45 Owenoke
Park, Westport, CT 06880)
● To the Point: World News in Depth. w.

**African Library Association of South Africa**
c/o Mamelodi Branch Library, P.O. Mamelodi,
Pretoria, South Africa.
● African Library Association of S.A. Newsletter. q.

**African Music Society**
P.O. Box 138, Roodepoort, Transvaal 1725, South
Africa.
● African Music. a. ISSN 0065-4019 (International
Library of African Music)

**African Oxygen Ltd**
Box 5404, Johannesburg 2000, South Africa.
● Afrox News. q. ISSN 0002-0672

**Africana Museum**
Public Library, Market Square, Johannesburg 2001,
South Africa.
● Africana Notes and News/Africana Aantekeninge
en Nuus. q. ISSN 0002-032X (Africana Society)

**Africana Society**
● Africana Notes and News/Africana Aantekeninge
en Nuus. (pub. by Africana Museum)

**Afrika-Spiegel Verlag**
P.O.Box 3099, Pretoria, South Africa.
● Afrika-Spiegel. bi-m. ISSN 0002-0400

**Afrikaans-Duitse Kultuurunie**
Box 2308, Pretoria 0001, South Africa.
● A D K Nuusbrief/A D K Mitteilungen. q. ISSN
0001-0928

**Afrikaanse Christen-Studentevereniging van Suid-
Afrika**
Box 25, Stellenbosch, South Africa.
● Ons Bou. bi-m. ISSN 0030-2643

**Afrikaanse Leesgenot (Edms.) Bpk**
P.O. Box 4532, Cape Town, South Africa.
● Motor. m. ISSN 0027-1756

**Afrikaanse Taal en Kultuurvereniging**
Box 4585, Johannesburg 2000, South Africa.
● Taalgenoot. m. ISSN 0039-8705

**Alcoholics Anonymous in South Africa & South-West
Africa**
General Service Office of Alcholics Anonymous,
Box 23005, Joubert Park, Johannesburg, South
Africa.
● Regmaker. bi-m. ISSN 0034-3471

**All Saints' Church, Plumstead**
● Parish News. (pub. by Samuel Griffiths and Co.
(Pty) Ltd.)

**Allied Publishing Ltd.**
39 Gale St., Durban, South Africa.
● Ilanga. 2 per wk. ISSN 0019-1779

**Amalgamated Engineering Union**
Box 3387, Johannesburg, South Africa.
● Metal Worker/Metaal Werker. m. ISSN 0026-
072X

**Amalgamated Press (Pty) Ltd.**
Box 494, Benoni, South Africa.
● Benoni City Times en Oosrandse Nuus. w. ISSN
0005-8831

**Amalgamated Society of Woodworkers of South
Africa**
Box 1095, Johannesburg, South Africa.
● Woodworker/Houtwerker. q.

**Amanzimtoti Printing & Publishing Co. (Pty) Ltd.**
202 Lagoon Centre, Bjorseth Crescent,
Amanzimtoti, South Africa.
● South Coast Sun. w. ISSN 0049-1519

**Amanzimtoti Zulu Training School**
P.O. Adams Mission, Durban 4100, Natal, South
Africa.
● Imbongi. s-a. ISSN 0019-2716

**Anglican Diocese of Kimberley and Kuruman**
c/o Rev. G.N. Pressly, Ed, Box 567, Kimberley,
South Africa.
● Highway. m. ISSN 0018-1684

**Anglo American Corporation**
44 Main St., Johannesburg, South Africa.
● Optima. q. ISSN 0030-4050

**Angora Goat Stud Breeders Society**
Box 50, Jansenville, South Africa.
● Angora Goat & Mohair Journal/Angorabok- en
Sybokhaarblad. s-a. ISSN 0003-3464

**Animal Anti-Cruelty League**
P.O. Box 49007, Rosettenville, Transvaal, South
Africa.
● Animal Anti-Cruelty League. Chairman's Report.
a.
● Animal Times. bi-m.

**Apple Publishers, Designers and Photographers (Pty)
Ltd.**
Box 78317, Sandton, Johannesburg, South Africa.
● Artlook. bi-m. ISSN 0004-3915
● Watersport Southern Africa. m.

**Aquarius**
University of Cape Town, Rondebosch, Cape Town,
South Africa.
- Scan. 2 per yr.

**Arcade Stamp Shop**
Investment Bldg., 97 Commissioner St.,
Johannesburg, South Africa.
- R. S. A. Postage Stamp Catalogue. irreg.

**Artisan Staff Association**
- Artisan Staff Association Magazine. (pub. by Leon
Maister (Pty) Ltd.)

**Associated Scientific and Technical Societies of South
Africa**
Box 61019, 2 Hollard St., Marshalltown,
Johannesburg 2107, South Africa.
- Mine Ventilation Society of South Africa. Journal.
m. ISSN 0026-4504
- South African Association of Consulting
Engineers. Directory of Registered Firms/Gids
van Geregistreede Firmas. irreg.

**Association for French Studies in Southern Africa**
University of Cape Town, Department of Romance
Studies, Private Bag, Rondesbosch, Cape Town,
South Africa.
- French Studies in Southern Africa. a.

**Association of Chambers of Commerce of South Africa**
Box 10211, Johannesburg, South Africa.
- Commerce/Handel. m.

**Association of Hebrew Writers of Southern Africa**
55-60 Shakespeare House, 116 Commissioner St.,
Johannesburg, South Africa.
- Barkai. fortn. ISSN 0005-5964

**Association of Law Societies of the Republic of South
Africa**
Box 1428, Pretoria, South Africa.
- De Rebus Procuratoriis. m. ISSN 0045-9755

**Association of Metal Sprayers**
- Metal Industries. (pub. by Thomson Publications
S.A. (Pty) Ltd.)

**Association of Surgeons of South Africa**
- South African Journal of Surgery/Suid-Afrikaanse
Tydskrif vir Chirurgie. (pub. by J. A. Fisch
Associates Pty. Ltd.)

**Astronomical Society of Southern Africa**
University of Cape Town, Department of
Astronomy, Box 594, Rondebosch, Cape Town,
South Africa.
- Astronomical Society of Southern Africa. Monthly
Notes. bi-m. ISSN 0024-8266

**Aviation Centre**
Box 20, Pretoria, South Africa.
- General Aviation. m. ISSN 0016-6502

**Aviation Publications (Pty) Ltd.**
Box 33011, 308 Fox St., Jeppe 2047, South Africa.
- Wings over Africa. m. ISSN 0043-5910

**Avonwold Publishing Co. (Pty.) Ltd.**
24 Baker St., Rosebank, Johannesburg, South Africa.
- Municipal Engineer/Munisipale Ingenieur. bi-m.
ISSN 0047-8369
- Planning & Building Developments. bi-m.

**Sheila Baille & Associates**
75 Howard House, Loveday St., Johannesburg,
South Africa.
- South African Architectural Record. m. ISSN
0038-1977 (Institute of South African Architects)

**A. A. Balkema Ltd.**
P.O. Box 3117, Cape Town 8000, South Africa
(and Box 1675, Rotterdam, Netherlands; dist. in
U.S. and Canada by: ISBS, Box 555, Forest Grove,
OR 97116)
- Acta Classica. a. ISSN 0065-1141 (Classical
Association of South Africa)
- Acta Germanica; jahrbuch des Sudafrikansichen
Germanistenverbandes. a. ISSN 0065-1273 (S.A.
Germanistenverband)
- Albany Series of Plays. irreg., 1972, no. 4.
(Rhodes University. Speech and Drama
Department)
- Contributions to the Development of the Piano
Sonata. irreg, 1970, no. 2.
- Graham's Town Series. irreg.; no. 3, 1974.
(Rhodes University)

- Palaeoecology of Africa and the Surrounding
Islands and Antarctica. a. ISSN 0078-8538
(Council for Scientific and Industrial Research)
(Co-sponsor: University of the Orange Free State)
- South African Biographical and Historical Studies.
irreg., no. 22, 1975. ISSN 0085-6363
- South African Pollen Grains and Spores. irreg.,
1970, no. 4. ISSN 0081-251X (Council for
Scientific and Industrial Research)
- Zoologica Africana. s-a. ISSN 0044-5096
(Zoological Society of Southern Africa)

**Bantu Investment Corporation of South Africa**
179A Skinner St., Karel Schoeman Building,
Pretoria 0002, South Africa.
- Bantu Investment Corporation of South Africa.
Annual Report/Bantoe Beleggingskorporasie van
Suid- Afrika. Jaarverslag. a.

**Barclays National Bank**
Head Office, Box 1153, Johannesburg, South Africa.
- Barclays National Review. q. ISSN 0302-6809

**Bernard Price Institute for Palaeontological Research**
*see under* **University of the Witwatersrand,
Johannesburg**

**Bethal Printing Works**
P.O. Box 99, Bethal, Transvaal, South Africa.
- Echo(Bethal) w. ISSN 0012-9127

**Bethlehem Express Printing & Publishing Co. (Pty)
Ltd.**
Box 555, Bethlehem, South Africa.
- Bethlehem Express. w. ISSN 0005-9838

**Bible Society of South Africa**
Box 6215, Roggebaai, Cape Town 8012, South
Africa.
- Sower/Saaier. q. ISSN 0038-5980

**Black Community Programmes**
86 Beatrice St., Durban, South Africa.
- Black Review. irreg.

**Black Literature and Arts Congress**
1 Long St., Mowbray, South Africa.
- B L A C. irreg.

**Black Sash**
503 Lestar House, 58 Marshall Street, Johannesburg
2001, South Africa.
- Sash. q. ISSN 0036-4843

**Blesston Printers & Publishers**
Box 39387, Bramley, Johannesburg, South Africa.
- South African Rider; a journal for horsemen. m.
ISSN 0038-2655

**Bloemfontein. Development Officer**
Box 288, Bloemfontein, South Africa.
- Bloemfontein Nuusbrief/Bloemfontein. Newsletter.
m. ISSN 0006-4939

**Bolton Publications (Pty) Ltd.**
Box 35281, Northcliff 2115, South Africa.
- Ford Fleetowner. q.
- South African Transport; the independent
transport journal. m. ISSN 0038-2760

**Botanical Research Institute**
Private Bag X101, Pretoria, South Africa.
- Bothalia. a.; vol. 11, nos. 1-2, 1973. ISSN 0006-
8241

**Botanical Society of South Africa**
Kirstenbosch, Claremont, Cape Town 7735, South
Africa.
- Veld & Flora. q.

**Simon Brooke and Associates**
Private Bag 1, Garden View, South Africa.
- Certificated Engineer/Gediplomeerde Ingenieur.
m. ISSN 0009-0409 (Institution of Certificated
Mechanical and Electrical Engineers)

**S.E.D. Brown, Ed. & Pub.**
Box 2401, Pretoria, South Africa.
- South African Observer; a journal for realists. m.
ISSN 0038-2515

**Bruecke**
18 Kelly Rd., Amalinda, East London, South Africa.
- Bruecke; Vierteljahrschrift fuer evangelische
Mission im Suedlichen Afrika. q. ISSN 0007-2583

**Building Industries Federation (South Africa)**
- Building and Allied Industries Official Handbook.
(pub. by South African Builder (Pty) Ltd.)
- South African Builder. (pub. by South African
Builder (Pty) Ltd.)

**T.V. Bulpin**
1004 Cape of Good Hope Savings Bank Building,
St. Georges St., Box 1516, Cape Town, South
Africa.
- Southern Africa; its natural wonders, interesting
people and coming events. irreg.

**Business Week Holdings Ltd**
Sakers Corner, 34 Eloff St., Johannesburg, South
Africa.
- Expansion. m.

**Butterworth & Co. (South Africa) (Pty.) Ltd.**
152-4 Gale St., Durban, Natal, South Africa.
- Butterworths Consolidated Legislation Service of
South Africa. Monthly Bulletin. m. ISSN 0007-
7321
- S.A. Journal for Criminal Law and Criminology/
S.A. Tydskrif vir Strafreg en Kriminologie. 3 per
yr. (National Institute for Crime Prevention and
Rehabilitation of Offenders)

**Caledon Venster Printing Works (Pty.) Ltd.**
Box 40, Caledon 7230, South Africa.
- Caledon Venster. w. ISSN 0008-0713

**Campaign Publications**
(Subsidiary of: Songee (Pty.) Ltd.)
62 Davies St., Doornfontein, Johannesburg 2001,
South Africa.
- Graphix; the monthly journal for the graphic
communications industry. m.

**Cape of Good Hope. Cape School Board**
P.O. Box 1252, Cape Town, South Africa.
- Cape of Good Hope. Cape School Board. Annual
Report. a.

**Cape of Good Hope. Department of Nature
Conservation**
Wale St., Cape Town, South Africa.
- Cape of Good Hope. Department of Nature
Conservation. Annual Report. a.

**Cape Piscatorial Society**
Westminister House, 122 Longmarket St., Cape
Town 8001, South Africa.
- Piscator. 3 per yr. ISSN 0032-0277

**Cape Provincial Library Service**
Box 2108, Cape Town, South Africa.
- Cape Librarian/Kaapse Bibliotekaris. m(except
July & Dec.) ISSN 0008-5790

**Cape Town Photographic Society**
Box 2431, Cape Town, South Africa.
- Cape Town Photographic Society Syllabus. m.
ISSN 0008-5820

**Caravan Publications (Pty) Ltd.**
P.O. Box 751, Cape Town, South Africa.
- Caravan. m.

**Cathcart Chronicle**
Box 29, Cathcart, Cape Province, South Africa.
- Cathcart Chronicle. w. ISSN 0008-7866

**Cathedral Church of St. George**
Wale St., Cape Town, South Africa.
- Gateway. m. ISSN 0016-5204

**Cathedral of St. Mary the Virgin**
Box 2029, Johannesburg, South Africa.
- Parishioner. m. ISSN 0031-2088

**Catholic Newspaper and Publishing Co. Ltd.**
12 Bouquet St., Box 2372, Cape Town, South
Africa.
- Southern Cross. w. ISSN 0038-4011 (Southern
African Catholic Bishops' Conference)

**Central Council of Land Surveyors of South Africa**
Department of Land Surveying, University of Cape
Town, Private Bag, Rondebosch 7700, South Africa.
- South African Survey Journal/Suid-Afrikaanse
Opmetings Tydskrif. 3 per yr. ISSN 0038-2736

**Central News Agency Ltd.**
Cor. Rissik and Commissioner Sts., Johannesburg, South Africa.
- Central News; the trade magazine for retail newsagents, booksellers, stationers and publishers in Southern Africa. m. ISSN 0008-9494

**Tom Chalmers Enterprises (Pty) Ltd.**
Box 35082, Northway, Durban 4065, Natal, South Africa
(and 88-89 High St., Winchester, Hampshire, England)
- World Airnews. w.

**Chamber of Mines of South Africa**
Box 809, Johannesburg, South Africa.
- Chamber of Mines of South Africa. Mining Survey. q. ISSN 0026-5268
- Chamber of Mines of South Africa. Research Review. a. ISSN 0069-245X
- Gold Bulletin; a quarterly review of research on gold and its applications in industry. q. ISSN 0017-1557

**Chartered Institute of Transport. Southern Africa Division**
- Transport & Traffic/Vervoer & Verkeer. (pub. by Moxxom Magazines (Pty) Ltd.)

**Christian Booksellers of Southern Africa**
- Intercom. (pub. by Church of Christ Literature Services)

**Christian Institute of Southern Africa**
- Pro Veritate. (pub. by Pro Veritate (Pty) Ltd.)

**Church of Christ Literature Services**
11 Jasmay Place, Nahoon Valley, East London 5201, South Africa.
- Intercom. q. (Christian Booksellers of Southern Africa)

**Church of Scientology in South Africa (Pty) Ltd.**
9 Lowcliffe House, Main St., Port Elizabeth, South Africa.
- Dynamic. m. ISSN 0012-737X

**Church of the Nazarene**
Box 15, Acornhoek, East Transvaal 1360, South Africa.
- Lebone la Kgalalelo. q.

**Church of the Province of South Africa**
Box 1932, Cape Town 8000, South Africa.
- Seek. m. ISSN 0037-0827

**Citrum**
Box 8774, Johannesburg, South Africa.
- Swaziland Recorder. q. ISSN 0039-7229

**Classic Publishing (Pty.) Ltd.**
16, Birkett Rd., Rondebosch, Cape Town, South Africa.
- South African Racehorse. s-a. ISSN 0038-2590

**Classical Association of South Africa**
- Acta Classica. (pub. by A. A. Balkema Ltd.)

**College of Medicine of South Africa**
17 Milner Rd., Rondebosch, Cape Town 7700, South Africa.
- College of Medicine of South Africa. Transactions. s-a.

**Combined Publishers (Pty.) Ltd.**
5th floor, Star Building, 47 Sauer St., Johannesburg, South Africa
(Dist. by International Publications Service, 114 E. 32nd St., New York NY 10016)
- Who's Who of Rhodesia, Mauritius, Central and East Africa. a. ISSN 0083-9868
- Who's Who of Southern Africa. a. ISSN 0083-9876

**Committee of Civil Rights League**
Box 3807, Cape Town, South Africa.
- Civil Rights News Letter. every 5 weeks. ISSN 0045-706X

**Company Publications (Pty.) Ltd.**
Private Bag 3, Motortown 2111, Transvaal, South Africa.
- Communika. bi-m. ISSN 0045-7698 (Public Relations Institute of South Africa)

**Computer Society of South Africa**
- Systems/Stelsels. (pub. by Systems Publishers (Pty.) Ltd.)

**Constructional Engineering Association**
- Construction in Southern Africa. (pub. by Pithead Press (Pty.) Ltd.)

**Council for Scientific and Industrial Research**
Publishing Division, Box 395, Pretoria 0001, South Africa.
- C S I R Annual Report. a. ISSN 0081-2382
- C S I R Organization and Activities. irreg. ISSN 0081-2390
- C S I R Publications; computer-produced list of publications arising from work undertaken or supported by C S I R, with keyword (KWIC) and author index. q.
- Calendar of Scientific and Technical Meetings in South Africa/Kalender voor Wetenskaplike en Tegniese Byeenkomste in Suid-Afrika. s-a.
- Palaeoecology of Africa and the Surrounding Islands and Antarctica. (pub. by A. A. Balkema Ltd.)
- Scientiae. q. ISSN 0036-8717
- Scientific and Technical Periodicals Published in South Africa/Wetenskaplike en Tegniese Tydskrifte in Suid-Afrika Uitgegee. a. ISSN 0080-7702
- Scientific and Technical Societies in South Africa/Wetenskaplike en Tegniese Verenigings in Suid-Afrika. a. ISSN 0080-7710
- Scientific Progress/Wetenskaplike Vordering; science and technology in South Africa. q. ISSN 0036-8814
- Scientific Research Organizations in South Africa/Wetenskaplike Navorsingsorganisasies in Suid-Afrika. a. ISSN 0080-7761
- South African Pollen Grains and Spores. (pub. by A. A. Balkema Ltd.)
- T. I. (Technical Information for Industry) m. ISSN 0040-0955

**Council for Scientific and Industrial Research. Department of Nature Conservation**
- Namib Desert Research Station. Scientific Papers. (pub. by Namib Desert Research Station SX)

**Council for Scientific and Industrial Research. National Building Research Institute**
*see* **National Building Research Institute**

**Council for Scientific and Industrial Research. National Institute for Personnel Research**
*see* **National Institute for Personnel Research**

**Council for Scientific and Industrial Research. National Institute for Transport and Road Research**
*see* **National Institute for Transport and Road Research**

**Council for Scientific and Industrial Research. National Institute for Telecommunication Research**
*see* **National Institute for Telecommunication Research**

**Council for Scientific and Industrial Research. National Mechanical Engineering Research Institute**
*see* **National Mechanical Engineering Research Institute**

**Council for Scientific and Industrial Research. National Research Institute for Mathematical Sciences**
*see* **National Research Institute for Mathematical Sciences**

**Council for Scientific and Industrial Research. Scientific Committee for Antarctic Research**
National Scientific Programmes Unit, P.O. Box 395, Pretoria 0001, South Africa.
- Report to S C A R on South African Antarctic Research Activities. a. ISSN 0081-2412
- South African Journal of Antarctic Research/Suid-Afrikaanse Tydskrif vir Antarktiese Navorsing. a. ISSN 0081-2455

**Council for Scientific and Industrial Research. South African Wool and Textile Research Institute**
*see* **South African Wool and Textile Research Institute**

**Cycling Publications**
105 Church St., Box 201, Pietermaritzburg 3200, South Africa.
- South African Cyclist. m. (South African Cycling Federation)

**Da Gama Publishers (Pty) Ltd.**
311 Locarno House, 20 Loveday St., Box 61464, Johannesburg, South Africa.
- Southern Africa and the Indian Ocean Islands Travel Trade Directory. a.
- State of South Africa; economic, financial and statistical yearbook for the Republic of South Africa. a. ISSN 0585-1289 (Dist. in U.S. by: W. S. Heinman, Imported Books, 400 E. 72nd St., New York, NY 10021)
- Travel Times. m. ISSN 0041-204X
- Travelgram. fortn. ISSN 0300-3108

**Democratic National Party**
P.O. Box 2931, Pretoria, South Africa.
- Demokraat. m. ISSN 0011-829X

**Dental Association of South Africa**
- Dental Association of South Africa. Journal/Tandheelkundige Vereniging van Suid Afrika. Tydskrif. (pub. by M.I.M.S. (Pty) Ltd)

**Rufus Dercksen, Ed. & Pub.**
Bank St., Box 64, Beaufort West, South Africa.
- Courier. w. ISSN 0011-0426

**Deutscher Lehrerverein Sued- und Suedwestafrikas**
Boerenstr. 87, 3100 Vryheid, South Africa.
- D L V Information. s-a.

**Dialogue**
P.O. Box 102, Wynberg 7824, South Africa.
- Dialogue; a literary annual for young writers. a.

**Diamond News (Pty.) Ltd.**
317/8 Flaxley House, Box 361, Kimberley 8300, South Africa.
- Diamond News and South African Jeweller. m. ISSN 0012-2300 (South African Jewellery Council)

**Dickinson Robinson Group Africa (Pty.) Ltd.**
Box 932, Cape Town, South Africa.
- Impact-Africa; digest of modern packaging. bi-m. ISSN 0019-2864

**Dolphin Press**
Box 3145, Durban, South Africa
(Subscr. Address: American - Southern Africa Council, Suite N-1, 800 4th St., Washington, D.C. 20024)
- Behind the News; A Southern African bulletin. m. ISSN 0002-0109

**Dramatic Artistic & Literary Rights Organisation (Pty) Ltd.**
SAMRO House, Cor. de Beer & Juta Streets, Braamfontein, South Africa.
- Wat Kan Ons Opvoer/What Can We Stage. s-a.(approx.) ISSN 0043-1036

**Duff's Turf Guide (Pty.) Ltd.**
401 Union Club, Boilding Smith St., Durban, South Africa.
- Duff's Turf Guide (Incorporating Computaform) w.

**Duiwebenodigdhede (Edms) Bpk**
Posbus 594, Pietersburg, Transvaal, South Africa.
- Vedvlugduif. m.

**Dunlop Industrial Products (Pty.) Ltd**
Private Bag 1027, Benoni, South Africa.
- Dunlop Industrial Rubber News. 3-4 per yr. ISSN 0012-7159

**Durban High School Old Boys' Club**
20 Gainsborough Dr., Box 6092, Durban North, South Africa.
- Durban High School Old Boys' Club. Bulletin. bi-m. ISSN 0012-7221

**Durban Museum**
City Hall, Smith St., Durban, South Africa.
- Durban Museum Novitates. 6 per yr. ISSN 0012-723X

**Durban Progressive Jewish Congregation**
369 Ridge Rd., Durban, South Africa.
- Temple David Bulletin. s-m. ISSN 0040-2966

**Dutch Reformed Mission Church**
*see* **Nederduitse Gereformeerde Sendingkerk**

**East London Photographic Society**
Box 147, East London 5200, South Africa.
- Perspective. m. ISSN 0012-8473

**Economic Society of South Africa**
Box 31213, Braamfontein, Transvaal, South Africa.
- South African Journal of Economics/Suid-Afrikaanse Tydskrif vir Ekonomie. q. ISSN 0038-2280

**Educum Publishers Ltd.**
Box 9573, Johannesburg, South Africa.
- Bona. m. ISSN 0006-7016

**Eland Press (Pty) Ltd**
Box 202, Aliwal North, South Africa.
- Front. m. ISSN 0016-2019

**Engineers' Association of South Africa**
Box 26189, Arcadia 0007, South Africa.
- Professional Engineer/Professionele Ingenieur. q. (Federation of Societies of Professional Engineers)

**Entomological Society of Southern Africa**
Box 103, Pretoria, South Africa.
- Entomological Society of Southern Africa. Journal. s-a. ISSN 0013-8789
- Entomological Society of Southern Africa. Proceedings of the Congress. irreg.

**Ernest Oppenheimer Institute of Portuguese Studies**
1 Jan Smuts Ave., Johannesburg 2001, South Africa.
- Ernest Oppenheimer Institute of Portuguese Studies. Publications. irreg. ISSN 0071-1209

**Ethical Publishing Co. (Pty.) Ltd.**
Box 10466, Johannesburg, South Africa.
- South African Retail Chemist. m. ISSN 0038-2639

**Evangelical Lutheran Church in South Africa. Western Diocese**
- Mosupa - Tsela. (pub. by Lutheran Book Depot)

**Faith for Daily Living Foundation**
Box 3737, Durban, Natal, South Africa.
- Faith for Daily Living; a guide to confident Christian living. m. ISSN 0014-7044

**Federasie van Afrikaanse Kultuurvereniginge**
Posbus 8711, Johannesburg, South Africa.
- Handhaaf. m.

**Federated Caledonian Society of Southern Africa**
Box 31424, Braamfontein 2017, South Africa.
- Caledonian. m. ISSN 0045-3870

**Federation of Civil Engineering Contractors**
- Civil Engineering Contractor. (pub. by Felstar Publishers (Pty.) Ltd)

**Federation of Societies of Professional Engineers**
- Professional Engineer/Professionele Ingenieur. (pub. by Engineers' Association of South Africa)

**Federation of South African Gem & Mineral Societies**
Box 31701, Braamfontein 2017, Transvaal, South Africa.
- South African Lapidary Magazine/Suid-Afrikaanse Lapidere Tydskrif. 3 per yr. ISSN 0038-237X

**Federation of Synagogues of South Africa**
24 Raleigh St., Yeoville, Johannesburg, South Africa.
- Federation of Synagogues of South Africa. Federation Chronicle. m. ISSN 0014-9314

**Federation of the Covenant People**
Box 3178, Johannesburg, South Africa.
- News of the New World. bi-m. ISSN 0048-0231

**Federation of Women's Institutes**
Fraser Building, 1st Fl., Fraser Lane, Pietermaritzburg 3201, South Africa.
- F. W. I. News. m. ISSN 0014-9489

**Felstar Publishers (Pty.) Ltd**
Box 6977, Johannesburg, South Africa.
- Civil Engineering Contractor. m. ISSN 0009-7888 (Federation of Civil Engineering Contractors)
- Hi-Fidelity & Video Review. m. ISSN 0046-7332
- Radio, Electrical & Furniture Merchandiser. m. ISSN 0033-7846 (Radio, Electricity & Furniture Association)
- Underground Official. m. ISSN 0041-6525 (Underground Officials' Association of South Africa)

**Ficksburg Press (Pty) Ltd.**
Box 380, Ficksburg, Orange Free State, South Africa.
- Free State Educational News/Vrystaatse Onderwysnuus. s-a. ISSN 0042-9228 (Orange Free State. Education Department)

**Financial Gazette Ltd.**
P.O. Box 8161, Johannesburg, South Africa.
- South African Financial Gazette. w. ISSN 0049-1403

**Financial Mail (Pty) Ltd.**
Box 9959, Johannesburg, South Africa.
- Financial Mail. w. ISSN 0015-2013
- Top Companies. irreg. ISSN 0563-8895 (South African Associated Newspapers)

**Findiver Association**
Box 251, New Germany 3620, Durban, Natal, South Africa.
- Findiver. q. ISSN 0015-1904

**J. A. Fisch Associates Pty. Ltd.**
Box 10003, Johannesburg, South Africa.
- South African Journal of Surgery/Suid-Afrikaanse Tydskrif vir Chirurgie. q. ISSN 0038-2361 (Association of Surgeons of South Africa)

**Flesch Financial Publications (Pty) Ltd**
P.O. Box 3473, Cape Town, South Africa.
- Johannesburg Stock Exchange. Handbook. a. ISSN 0075-3793

**Fondation de l'Afrique du Sud**
*see* South Africa Foundation

**Fort Hare University Press**
Private Bag 322, Alice, Cape Province, South Africa.
- Fort Hare Papers. 2-3 per yr. ISSN 0015-8054

**Foundation for Education, Science and Technology**
211 Skinner St., Box 1758, Pretoria, South Africa.
- Archimedes; popular science journal for high school pupils. q. ISSN 0003-8385
- Crux. q.
- Klasgids. q.
- Lantern; journal for knowledge and culture. q. ISSN 0023-8422
- Spectrum; mathematical journal for universities and schools. q.

**Friesland Cattle Breeder's Association of South Africa**
Box 544, Bloemfontein 9300, South Africa.
- South African Friesland Journal/Suid-Afrikaanse Friesland Joernaal. q. ISSN 0036-0724

**Genealogical Society of South Africa**
Box 4839, Cape Town, South Africa.
- Familia. q. ISSN 0014-7117

**General Dealer (Pty) Ltd.**
(Subsidiary of: Langham House Group)
Langham House, 59 Long St., Cape Town, South Africa.
- Supermarket and Retailer. m. ISSN 0049-2590

**General Enterprises**
Box 67, Hibberdene, Natal, South Africa.
- Christian Family. m. ISSN 0009-5346

**Genootskap vir Afrikaanse Volkskunde**
Box 4585, Johannesburg 2000, South Africa.
- Tydskrif vir Volkskunde en Volkstaal. q. ISSN 0049-4933

**Geological Society of South Africa**
P.O. Box 61019, Marshalltown, Transvaal, South Africa.
- Geological Society of South Africa. Quarterly News Bulletin/Geologiese Vereniging van Suid-Afrika. Kwartaallikse Nuusbulletin. q. ISSN 0016-7657
- Geological Society of South Africa. Special Publication. irreg; latest issue, 1976.
- Geological Society of South Africa. Transactions. 3 per yr.

**Gereformeerde Kerk in Suid-Afrika**
*see* Reformed Church in South Africa

**Golden Film Productions (Edms) Bpk**
Dunwell-Gebou 112, Jorrissenstraat, Braamfontein, Johannesburg, South Africa.
- Lara Lamont. m. ISSN 0023-8481

**Good News Missionary Society**
Box 7848, Johannesburg, South Africa.
- Good News/Goeie Nuus; the magazine with a message. bi-m. ISSN 0017-2146
- Zions Freund. bi-m. ISSN 0028-3568

**Grassland Society of Southern Africa**
Private Bag X 179, Pretoria, South Africa.
- Grassland Society of Southern Africa. Proceedings of the Congress. a. ISSN 0072-5560

**Samuel Griffiths and Co. (Pty.) Ltd.**
Fir St., Observatory, Cape Province, South Africa.
- Parish News. m. ISSN 0031-207X (All Saints' Church, Plumstead)

**H.A.U.M.**
Box 460, Pretoria, South Africa.
- Mens en Gemeenskap. q. ISSN 0539-3337 (University of Pretoria)

**Heraldry Society of Southern Africa**
Box 4839, Cape Town, South Africa.
- Arma. q. ISSN 0004-2145

**Heron Publishing Co. (Pty) Ltd.**
Box 9737, Johannesburg, South Africa.
- South African Draughtsman/S. A. Tekenaar. q. ISSN 0036-0643 (South African Institute of Draughtsmen)

**Highway Mail (Pty) Ltd.**
174-176 Old Main St., Box 16, Pinetown, Natal 3600, South Africa.
- Highway Mail. w. ISSN 0018-1722
- Highway Reporter. m.

**Historical Firearms Society of South Africa**
c/o B. M. Berkovitch (Secretary), "Minden", 11 Buchan Rd., Newlands 7700, Cape Province, South Africa.
- Historical Firearms Society of South Africa. Journal/Historiese Vuurwapenvereniging van Suid-Afrika. Tydskrif. s-a. ISSN 0018-2451

**Historical Society of Cape Town**
P.O. Box 2615, Cape Town, South Africa.
- Cabo. a.

**Historical Society of Port Elizabeth**
Box 12070, Port Elizabeth, South Africa.
- Looking Back/Kykies in Die Verlede. q. ISSN 0024-6417

**Historical Society of South Africa**
Box 409, Springs 1560, South Africa.
- Historia. 2 per yr. ISSN 0018-229X
- Historia Junior. q. ISSN 0439-2116 (Subscr. to: Box 3002, Three Rivers, South Africa)

**Holiness Union Mission**
- Ubaqa. (pub. by Mission Press)

**Hospital Employees Association**
- Hospital R. S. A. (pub. by Adlodorum)

**Huisvrou Press (Pty) Ltd.**
Box 662, Cape Town, South Africa.
- Huisvrou. m. ISSN 0018-7100

**Huletts Aluminum Ltd.**
Box 2430, Johannesburg 2000, South Africa.
- Aluminum Review. q.

**Human Sciences Research Council**
Private Bag X41, Pretoria 0001, South Africa.
- Human Sciences Research Council. General Information. irreg.
- Human Sciences Research Council. Newsletter/Raad vir Geesteswetenskaplike Navorsing. Nuusbrief. m.
- Human Sciences Research Council. Research Bulletin/Raad vir Geesteswetenskaplike Navorsing. Navorsingsbulletin. 10 per yr.
- Human Sciences Research Council: Annual Report. a.
- Humanitas. s-a. ISSN 0046-8258

**Human Sciences Research Council. Institute for Historical Research**
Private Bag X41, Pretoria 0001, South Africa.
- Contree; journal for South African urban and regional history/tydskrif vir Suid-Afrikaanse stedelike en streekgeskiedenis. s-a. (prep. by its Section for Regional History)

**Human Sciences Research Council. Institute of Manpower Research**
Private Bag X41, Pretoria, South Africa.
- Human Sciences Research Council. Institute for Manpower Research. Project Talent Survey: Research Findings. a.

**Ichud Habonim S.A.**
Zionist Centre, 84 de Villiers St., Johannesburg, South Africa. .
- Aleh. 4 per yr.(approx.) ISSN 0002-5127
- Habinyan. 4 per yr.(approx.) ISSN 0017-6354

**Ikon Publications**
Box 1343, Pietermaritzburg, South Africa.
- Ikon. 5 per yr. ISSN 0019-1752

**Illovo Sugar Estates Ltd.**
Box 3130, Durban, South Africa.
- Illovo Digest. q. ISSN 0019-2325 (Co-sponsors: Doornkop Sugar Company, Noodsberg Sugar Company)

**Independent Cultural Association**
Box 8380, Johannesburg, South Africa.
- Union Contemporary Cultural Review. q. ISSN 0049-5247

**Inspan Publishers (Pty) Ltd.**
Box 3835, Johannesburg 2000, South Africa.
- Volkstem. m. (United South African National Party)

**Institute for Historical Research**
see under Human Sciences Research Council

**Institute for Industrial Education**
Box 18109, Dalbridge, Durban, South Africa.
- South African Labour Bulletin. irreg (8-10 per yr.)

**Institute for Manpower Research**
see under Human Sciences Research Council

**Institute for the Study of English in Africa**
see under Rhodes University

**Institute for the Study of Man in Africa**
Medical School, Hospital St., Johannesburg 2001, South Africa.
- I S M A Occasional Papers. irreg., no. 6, 1969. ISSN 0073-893X
- I S M A Papers. irreg. ISSN 0073-8921
- Raymond Dart Lecture. (pub. by Witwatersrand University Press)

**Institute of Administration & Commerce of South Africa**
- Business and Administration/Bedryf en Bestuur. (pub. by Johnston & Neville (Pty) Ltd.)

**Institute of Bankers in South Africa**
Box 10335, Johannesburg, South Africa.
- South African Banker/Suid-Afrikaanse Bankier. q. ISSN 0038-2000

**Institute of Mine Surveyors of South Africa**
Box 62339, Marshalltown, Transvaal 2107, South Africa.
- Institute of Mine Surveyors of South Africa. Journal/Instituut van Mynopmeters van Suid-Afrika. Joernaal. q. ISSN 0020-2983

**Institute of Municipal Treasurers and Accountants South Africa**
Box 1450, Johannesburg, South Africa.
- South African Treasurer/Suid-Afrikaanse Tesourier. m. ISSN 0038-2779

**Institute of Park & Recreation Administration (Southern Africa)**
613 Volkskas Building, 76 Market St., Johannesburg, South Africa.
- Park Administration. q. ISSN 0031-2118

**Institute of Public Health**
Box 4623, Johannesburg, South Africa.
- Public Health/Volksgesondheid. m. ISSN 0033-3492

**Institute of Purchasing**
- Purchasing South Africa. (pub. by George Warman Publications (Pty) Ltd.)

**Institute of Shipping and Forwarding Agents of Southern Africa**
Box 767, Port Elizabeth, South Africa.
- Portcullis. q. ISSN 0032-4892

**Institute of South African Architects**
- South African Architectural Record. (pub. by Sheila Baille & Associates)

**Institution of Certificated Mechanical and Electrical Engineers**
- Certificated Engineer/Gediplomeerde Ingenieur. (pub. by Simon Brooke and Associates)

**International Library of African Music**
- African Music. (pub. by African Music Society)

**Islamic Missionary Society**
P. O. 54125, Vrededorp, Transvaal, South Africa.
- Muslim Africa. m. ISSN 0027-4860

**J.L.B. Smith Institute of Ichthyology**
see under Rhodes University

**Jeppe High Schools' Quondam Club**
c/o M. D. Sparke, Box 24, Bedfordview, Transvaal, South Africa.
- Quondam. q. ISSN 0033-6661

**Jersey Cattle Breeders' Society of S.A.**
Box 928, Bloemfontein, South Africa.
- South African Jersey/Suid-Afrikaanse Jersey. q. ISSN 0038-2264

**Jewish Herald (Pty) Ltd.**
Box 4474, Johannesburg, South Africa.
- Jewish Herald; national Jewish weekly. w. ISSN 0021-647X (Zionist Revisionist Organisation of South Africa)

**Johannesburg. Produce Market Department**
Johannesburg, South Africa.
- National Fresh Produce Market, Johannesburg. Annual Report of the Director. a.
- National Fresh Produce Market, Johannesburg. Annual Trading Results/Jaarlikse Handelsyfers. a.

**Johannesburg College of Education**
17 Hoofd St., Braamfontein, Johannesburg, South Africa.
- Symposium; journal of education for southern Africa. a. ISSN 0082-0792

**Johannesburg Drukkery**
25 Davies Str., Doornfontein, Johannesburg, South Africa.
- African Jewish Newspaper; Africa's only Yiddish newspaper. w. ISSN 0044-6556

**Johannesburg Film Society**
Box 10849, Johannesburg, South Africa.
- Johannesburg Film Society. Programme News. m. ISSN 0033-0388

**Johannesburg Jaycees**
Box 11, Johannesburg, South Africa.
- On the Agenda. m.

**Johannesburg Laundry & Dry Cleaners Association**
- South African Laundry and Cleaning Review. (pub. by G. Warman Publications (Pty) Ltd.)

**Johannesburg Stock Exchange**
P.O. Box 1174, Johannesburg, South Africa.
- Johannesburg Stock Exchange. Handbook. (pub. by Flesch Financial Publications (Pty) Ltd)
- Johannesburg Stock Exchange Monthly Bulletin. m. ISSN 0021-7182

**Johnston & Neville (Pty) Ltd.**
3, Dorp Street, Box 2981, Cape Town, South Africa.
- Business and Administration/Bedryf en Bestuur. 4 per yr. ISSN 0007-6449 (Institute of Administration & Commerce of South Africa)

**Juta & Co. Ltd.**
Box 30, Cape Town, South Africa.
- Acta Juridica. irreg., latest issue 1975. ISSN 0065-1346 (University of Cape Town. Faculty of Law)
- Businessman's Law. 8 per yr. ISSN 0045-3668
- Geneeskunde. m. ISSN 0016-643X
- Income Tax Reporter. 8 per yr.
- South African Law Journal. q. ISSN 0038-2388
- South African Law Reports. m. ISSN 0038-2396
- South African Tax Cases. 8 per yr. ISSN 0038-2752

**Kelvin Publications (Pty) Ltd.**
Box 2988, Johannesburg, South Africa.
- South African Institute of Electrical Engineers. Transactions. m. ISSN 0038-2221

- South African Mechanical Engineer. m. ISSN 0038-2442 (South African Institution of Mechanical Engineers)

**Kerkjeugvereniging**
Nederduitse Gereformeerde Kerk, Box 2406, Pretoria, South Africa.
- Ons Jeug. m. ISSN 0030-2694

**Ko-Operatieve Wijnbouwers Vereniging van Z.A.**
Box 528, Suider-Paarl 7624, South Africa.
- Wynboer. m. ISSN 0043-9657

**Konservatorium-Vereniging**
Konservatorium vir Musiek, Private Bag 315, Pretoria, South Africa.
- Konservatorium Nuus. s-a. ISSN 0023-3579

**Langham House (Pty) Ltd.**
P.O. Box 4605, Cape Town, South Africa.
- Bowls. m.

**Leather Industries Research Institute**
see under Rhodes University

**Leo Publications (Pty) Ltd.**
Box 37032, Overport 4067, South Africa.
- Sharp Shoot Soccer. m.

**Liberal Party of South Africa**
268 Longmarket St., Pietermaritzburg, Natal, South Africa.
- Liberal Opinion. q. ISSN 0024-1830

**Life Underwriters Association of South Africa**
- S. A. Insurance. (pub. by Thomson Publications S. A. (Pty) Ltd.)

**Limnological Society of Southern Africa**
Department of Botany, University of the Orange Free State, Bloemfontein, South Africa.
- Limnological Society of Southern Africa. Journal. 2 per yr.

**Lorton Publications**
Box 17805, Hillbrow 2038, Johannesburg, South Africa.
- Photography and Travel. m. ISSN 0031-8817

**Lower Albany Historical Society**
24 Colgate St., Port Alfred, South Africa.
- Toposcope. a.

**Lutheran Book Depot**
Box 76, Rustenburg, Transvaal, South Africa.
- Mosupa - Tsela. m. ISSN 0027-1454 (Evangelical Lutheran Church in South Africa. Western Diocese)

**M.I.M.S. (Pty) Ltd**
Box 2059, Pretoria 0001, South Africa.
- Dental Association of South Africa. Journal/Tandheelkundige Vereniging van Suid Afrika. Tydskrif. m. ISSN 0011-8516
- I V S. (Index of Veterinary Specialists) q. ISSN 0019-0918
- M I M S. (Monthly Index of Medical Specialities) m. ISSN 0027-0431
- M I M S Desk Reference. a. ISSN 0076-8847
- South African Journal of Medical Laboratory Technology/Suid-Afrikaanse Tydskrif vir Mediese Laboratorium Tegnologie. q. ISSN 0038-2302 (Society of Medical Laboratory Technologists of South Africa)
- South African Optometrist/Suid- Afrikaanse Oogkundige. q. (South African Optometric Association)
- South African Pharmaceutical Journal/Suid-Afrikaanse Tydskrif vir Apteekwese. m. ISSN 0038-2558 (Pharmaceutical Society of South Africa)

**Mafeking Mail (Pty) Ltd.**
2 First Ave., Industrial Township, Mafeking, Cape Province, South Africa.
- Mafeking Mail and Botswana Guardian. w. ISSN 0024-9718

**Magistrates' Association of South Africa and South-West Africa**
Private Bag 1, Johannesburg, South Africa.
- Magistrate/Landdros. q. ISSN 0024-9939

**Leon Maister (Pty) Ltd.**
Langham House, 59 Long St, Box 4385, Cape Town, South Africa.
- Artisan Staff Association Magazine. m. ISSN 0004-3869

**Makki Publications**
100 Brickfield Rd., Durban, South Africa.
● Muslim Digest; international monthly of Muslim affairs. m. ISSN 0027-4887

**Mariannhill Mission Society**
The Monastery, P.O.Mariannhill, Natal, South Africa.
● Umafrika. w. ISSN 0041-6274

**Market Indicators Digest**
Box 17389, Johannesburg 2038, South Africa (and Box 576, Florida 1710, South Africa)
● Gold. every 3 wks.
● Macaskill Letter. every 3 wks.

**Market Research Africa (Pty) Ltd.**
P.O. Box 10483, Johannesburg, South Africa.
● Listening Index; a report on radio listening habits in the Republic of South Africa and South West Africa. q. ISSN 0047-4762 (South African Broadcasting Corporation)

**Mead & McGrouther (Pty) Ltd.**
P.O. Box 741, Johannesburg, South Africa.
● Agricultural Machinery Dealers' Digest. s-m.
● Auto Data Digest. a.
● Auto Dealers' Digest. m. ISSN 0005-0733
● Automobil. m. ISSN 0304-8721 (Motor Industries Federation)

**Medical Association of South Africa**
Box 643, Cape Town 8000, South Africa.
● South African Journal of Obstetrics and Gynaecology/Suid-Afrikaanse Tydskrif vir Obstetrie en Ginekologie. 1963. ISSN 0038-2329 (South African Society of Obstetricians and Gynaecologists) (Co-sponsor: Royal College of Obstetricians and Gynaecologists, South African Regional Council)
● South African Medical Journal/Suid-Afrikaanse Mediese Tydskrif. w. ISSN 0038-2469

**Megakor Publishers**
Box 17077, Groenkloof, Pretoria, South Africa.
● Farm Mechanisation/Landboumeganisasie. m. ISSN 0014-8067

**Merck Sharp & Dohme (Pty) Ltd.**
Box 7748, Johannesburg 2000, Transvaal, South Africa.
● Merck Sharp & Dohme Review. 3 per yr. ISSN 0025-9918

**Merino Stud Breeders' Association of South Africa**
Box 109, Graaff-Reinet, South Africa.
● Merino Breeders' Journal/Merinotelers Se Kwartaalblad. q. ISSN 0026-0045

**Methodist Church of South Africa**
Box 10376, Johannesburg, Transvaal, South Africa.
● Dimension. m. ISSN 0046-0265

**Mine Medical Officers' Association of South Africa**
Box 61809, Marshalltown, Transvaal, South Africa (and Chamber of Mines, Hollard St., Johannesburg, South Africa)
● Mine Medical Officers' Association of South Africa. Proceedings. 3 per yr. ISSN 0026-4490

**Mine Surface Officials' Association of South Africa**
41 Biccard St., Braamfontein, Johannesburg, South Africa.
● M S O A Journal. m. ISSN 0024-8428

**Mine Ventilation Society of South Africa**
● Mine Ventilation Society of South Africa. Journal. (pub. by Associated Scientific and Technical Societies of South Africa)

**Mission Press**
Box 37088, Overport, Natal 4067, South Africa.
● Ubaqa. m. ISSN 0041-5626 (Holiness Union Mission)

**Modern Newspapers (Pty) Ltd.**
Box 58, 1B Victoria St., Somerset West, South Africa.
● District Mail/Distrikspos. w. ISSN 0012-4028

**Motor Industries Federation**
● Automobil. (pub. by Mead & McGrouther (Pty) Ltd.)

**Motor Transport Owners' Association in South Africa**
● Commercial Transport and Freight. (pub. by Thomson Publications S.A. (Pty) Ltd.)

**Moxxom Magazines (Pty) Ltd.**
Box 1884, Johannesburg 2000, South Africa.
● Transport & Traffic/Vervoer & Verkeer. s-a. (Chartered Institute of Transport. Southern Africa Division)

**Namib Times**
Box 706, Walvis Bay, South Africa.
● Namib Times. s-w. ISSN 0027-7746

**Nasionale Tydskrifte**
Box 1802, Cape Town 8000, South Africa.
● Huisgenoot. w. ISSN 0018-7089
● Landbouweekblad. w. ISSN 0023-7779

**Natal. Education Department**
Private Bag 9044, Pietermaritzburg, South Africa.
● N.E.O.N. (Natal Education/Onderwys in Natal) 3 per yr.

**Natal. Parks, Game & Fish Preservation Board**
P.O. Box 662, Pietermaritzburg 3200, South Africa.
● Lammergeyer. irreg. (approx. 2 numbers per year) ISSN 0075-7780

**Natal. Provincial Library Services**
Private Bag 9016, Pietermaritzburg 3200, South Africa.
● Libri Natales. m.

**Natal Agricultural Union**
Box 186, Pietermaritzburg, South Africa.
● N A U N L U. m. ISSN 0028-128X

**Natal Hunters & Game Conservation Association**
Box 23, Pietermaritzburg, Natal, South Africa.
● Inyala News. 3 per yr. ISSN 0021-0269

**Natal Society**
Box 415, Pietermaritzburg, Natal, South Africa.
● Natalia. a. ISSN 0085-3674

**Natale Onderwysersunie**
P.O. Box 1122, Pietermaritzburg, Natal, South Africa.
● NOU-Blade; vir christelike en nasionale onderwys en opvoeding. s-a.

**National African Chamber of Commerce**
Box 28, Dube, Johannesburg, South Africa.
● African Trader. q. ISSN 0002-0249

**National Botanic Gardens of South Africa**
Kirstenbosch Botanic Garden, Private Bag X7, Claremont, South Africa.
● Journal of South African Botany. q. ISSN 0022-4618

**National Building Research Institute**
Box 395, Pretoria 0001, South Africa.
● N B R I Information Sheet. bi-m. ISSN 0027-6162
● National Building Research Institute. Complete List of N B R I Publications. a. ISSN 0077-3581

**National Cancer Association of South Africa**
Box 2000, Johannesburg, South Africa.
● South African Cancer Bulletin/Suid-Afrikaanse Kankerbulletin. q. ISSN 0038-2043

**National Conference of South African Surveyors**
Institute of Land Surveyors of the Cape Province, Box 462, Cape Town, South Africa.
● National Conference of South African Surveyors. Proceedings/Nasionale Konferensie van Suid-Afrikaanse Opmeters. Verrigtinge. irreg.

**National Council for Chartered Accountants**
Box 964, Johannesburg, South Africa.
● S A C A. (South African Chartered Accountant)/Suid-Afrikaanse Geoktrooieerde Rekenmeester. m. ISSN 0038-206X

**National Council for Social Research. Department of Education, Arts and Science**
Private Bag 122, Pretoria, South Africa.
● Journal for Social Research/Tydskrif vir Maatskaplike Navorsing. s-a. ISSN 0449-203X
● Research Educational and Social. s-a.

**National Council for the Care of Cripples in South Africa**
Box 10173, Johannesburg 2000, South Africa.
● Cripple Care News/Kreupelsorgnuus. q. ISSN 0011-1392
● South African Cerebral Palsy Journal/S. A. Tydskrif vir Serebraalverlamming. q. ISSN 0036-0600

**National Council of Women of South Africa**
532-3 CTC Bldgs., Plein St., Cape Town, South Africa.
● N. C. W. News. m(except Dec) ISSN 0027-6367

**National Funeral Directors' Association of Southern Africa**
Box 3155, Cape Town, South Africa.
● Funeral Forum. m. ISSN 0016-2787

**National Industrial Council of the Printing and Newspaper Industry of South Africa**
Electrical House, Loop and Waterkant St., Cape Town, South Africa.
● National Industrial Council of the Printing and Newspaper Industry of South Africa. Monthly Record. m.

**National Institute for Crime Prevention and Rehabilitation of Offenders**
● S.A. Journal for Criminal Law and Criminology/S.A. Tydskrif vir Strafreg en Kriminologie. (pub. by Butterworth & Co. (South Africa) (Pty.) Ltd.)

**National Institute for Metallurgy**
Private Bag X 3015, Randburg 2125, South Africa.
● Minerals Science and Engineering. q. ISSN 0026-4660
● N I M Reports. irreg.
● N I M Research Digest. q.

**National Institute for Personnel Research**
P.O. Box 10319, Johannesburg 2000, South Africa.
● National Institute for Personnel Research. Annual Report. a. ISSN 0077-4758
● National Institute for Personnel Research. List of N I P R Publications. a; latest issue 1976. ISSN 0077-4766
● Psychologia Africana. irreg., vol. 17, 1977. ISSN 0079-7332
● Psychologia Africana. Monograph Supplement. irreg., no. 8, 1975. ISSN 0079-7340

**National Institute for Telecommunications Research**
Box 3718, Johannesburg, South Africa.
● Monthly Bulletin of Ionospheric Characteristics Recorded at Johannesburg and Hermanus/Maandelikse Bulletin van Ionosferiese Karakteristieke Soos Waargeneem in Johannesburg en Hermanus. m.
● Radio Propagation Predictions for Southern Africa. m. ISSN 0033-7986

**National Institute for Transport and Road Research**
P.O. Box 395, Pretoria 0001, South Africa.
● National Institute for Transport and Road Research. Annual Report/Nasionale Instituut vir Vervoer- en Padnavorsing. Jaarverslag. a.
● Via. s-a. ISSN 0042-4978

**National Magazines Ltd.**
Box 1802, Cape Town, South Africa.
● Fair Lady. fortn. ISSN 0014-6927

**National Mechanical Engineering Research Institute**
P.O. Box 395, Pretoria, South Africa.
● Index to N M E R I Publications. irreg., 1971 covering 1952-70. ISSN 0077-5207

**National Museum, Bloemfontein**
Box 266, Bloemfontein, South Africa.
● National Museum, Bloemfontein. Memoirs. irreg. ISSN 0067-9194
● National Museum, Bloemfontein. Researches. irreg. ISSN 0067-9208

**National Occupational Safety Association**
Cor.Proes & Beatrix Sts., Box 26434, Arcadia 0007, Pretoria, South Africa.
● Safety Management/Veiligheidsbestuur. m.

**National Publishing Co. (Pty) Ltd.**
P.O. Box 335, Cape Town, South Africa.
● Advertising and Press Annual of Africa. a. ISSN 0065-3594
● Architects, Builders, and Contractors Blue-Book. a. ISSN 0084-6708
● Building Equipment & Materials for South Africa. m. ISSN 0007-344X
● Business Blue-Book of Southern Africa. a. ISSN 0068-4406
● Business Systems & Equipment. m. ISSN 0007-6732
● Factory Equipment & Materials for Southern Africa. m. ISSN 0014-6552
● National Trade-Index of Southern Africa. a. ISSN 0077-5894

**National Research Institute for Mathematical Sciences**
P.O. Box 395, Pretoria 0001, South Africa.
- National Research Institute for Mathematical Sciences. Computing Centre Bulletin. irreg. (approx. 5 per yr.)

**National Road Safety Council**
Private Bag X147, Pretoria, South Africa.
- Robot. bi-m. ISSN 0035-7391

**National Union of Southern African Students**
202 Film Centre, 17 Jamieson St., Cape Town, South Africa.
- Dissent. m.

**National Zoological Gardens of South Africa**
Box 754, Pretoria, South Africa.
- Zoon. irreg. ISSN 0044-5274

**Nederduitse Gereformeerde Kerk, Bloemfontein**
Bloemheuwel, 15 General Hertzog Str., Bloemfontein, South Africa.
- Bloemheuwel-Nuus. q. ISSN 0006-4947

**Nederduitse Gereformeerde Kerk in Afrika**
Posbus 19, Bloemfontein, South Africa.
- Lehlasedi. m. ISSN 0024-0575
- Ligstraad; Lehlasedi: Umsebe: Umtha. m. ISSN 0024-3442
- Sendingnuus. s-a. ISSN 0037-2137

**Nederduitse Gereformeerde Kerk in Suid-Afrika**
Box 433, Pretoria 0001, South Africa.
- D R C Africa News. (Dutch Reformed Church) m. (prep. by its Ecumenical Department)
- Nederduitse Gereformeerde Teologiese Tydskrif. (pub. by Nederduitse Gereformeerde Kerk Uitgewers en -Boekhandel)

**Nederduitse Gereformeerde Kerk, Paarl**
Hoofstraat 144, Paarl, South Africa.
- Strooidak. q.

**Nederduitse Gereformeerde Kerk Uitgewers en - Boekhandel**
Box 4539, Cape Town, South Africa.
- Nederduitse Gereformeerde Teologiese Tydskrif. q. ISSN 0028-2006 (Nederduitse Gereformeerde Kerk in Suid-Afrika. Faculties of Theology)

**Nederduitse Gereformeerde Kerk van Natal Gemeentevryheid**
Smalstraat 82, Vryheid, Natal, South Africa.
- Nederduitse Gereformeerde Kerk van Natal Gemeente Vryheid. Maandbrief. m. ISSN 0024-8665

**Nederduitse Gereformeerde Sendingkerk**
Box 169, Worcester 6850, Cape Province, South Africa.
- Ligdraer. fortn. ISSN 0024-3272

**New Chemical Publications (Pty) Ltd.**
Box 3080, Johannesburg 2000, South Africa.
- Chemsa. m. (South African Institution of Chemical Engineers) (Co-sponsors: South African Chemical Institute; Transvaal Chemical Manufacturers Association)

**New Nation Publications**
Box 3039, Pretoria, South Africa.
- New Nation. m. ISSN 0028-6370

**Newspaper Representations (S.A.) (Pty.)**
Box 549, Johannesburg, South Africa.
- Medical Chronicle. m. ISSN 0025-7117

**Nieuws Uit Zuid-Afrika**
Postbus 1847, Pretoria, South Africa.
- Nieuws Uit Zuid-Afrika. m. ISSN 0028-9949

**C. & J. Mackie Niven**
30 Pallinghurst Rd., Westcliff, Johannesburg, South Africa.
- South African Citrus and Sub-Tropical Fruit Journal; the citrus grower. m.

**Nuwe Protestantse Kerk in Afrika**
Box 18348, Hercules 0030, Pretoria, Transvaal, South Africa.
- Nuwe Protestant. m. ISSN 0029-6708

**Old Rhodian Union**
- Rhodes Review. (pub. by Rhodes University)

**Oostelike Transvaalse Kooperasie Beperk**
Box 100, Bethal 2310, South Africa.
- O. T. Kaner. q. ISSN 0029-7321

**Op Safari (Pty) Ltd.**
80 Bosman St., Pretoria, Transvaal, South Africa.
- Op Safari. m. ISSN 0048-1890

**Orange Free State. Director of Hospital Services**
Box 517, Bloemfontein 9300, South Africa.
- Orange Free State. Director of Hospital Services. Report/Orange Free State, South Africa. Direkteur van Hospitaldienste. Verslag. a. ISSN 0078-5547

**Orange Free State. Education Department**
- Free State Educational News/Vrystaatse Onderwysnuus. (pub. by Ficksburg Press (Pty) Ltd.)

**Orange Free State. Library Service**
Private Bag X20606, Bloemfontein 9300, South Africa.
- Free State Libraries/Vrystaatse Biblioteke. q. ISSN 0016-0458

**Orange Free State. Nature Conservation Division**
P.O. Box 517, Bloemfontein, South Africa.
- Orange Free State. Nature Conservation Division. Annual Report. a.
- Orange Free State. Nature Conservation Division. Miscellaneous Publications Series. irreg.

**Order of St. John. Priory for South Africa**
Box 7137, Johannesburg, South Africa.
- Call of St. John/Stem van St. John. m.

**Oudtshoorn Courant (Pty) Ltd.**
Box 240, Oudtshoorn, Cape Province, South Africa.
- Suidwestern. w. ISSN 0049-2485

**Outlook Publications Pty. Ltd.**
1 Long St., Mowbray 7700, South Africa.
- South African Outlook; a journal dealing with ecumenical and racial affairs. m. ISSN 0038-2523

**P T P Publishing Services (Pty) Ltd**
Box 33011, Jeppestown 2043, Johannesburg, South Africa.
- Management. m. ISSN 0047-5653

**Paarl Printing Co. (Pty.) Ltd**
New Street, Box 248, Paarl, South Africa.
- Paarl Post. s-w. ISSN 0030-8447

**Pan Africanist Congress of Azania (South Africa)**
- Azania Combat. (pub. by Pan Africanist Congress UK)

**S. R. Pather, Ed. & Pub**
Box 1233, Durban, Natal, South Africa.
- 1860 Settler. bi-m. ISSN 0013-2578

**Patrys**
Posbus 8124, Johannesburg, South Africa.
- Patrys; maanblad vir die jeug. m. ISSN 0031-3181

**Pentecostal Protestant Church**
Box 180, Isando, Transvaal, South Africa.
- Pinkster Protestant. 4 per yr. ISSN 0031-9902

**Performing Arts Council, Orange Free State**
P.O. Box 1292, Bloemfontein, South Africa.
- P A C O F S News/S U K O V S Nuus. irreg.

**Performing Arts Council Transvaal**
Box 566, Pretoria 0001, South Africa.
- T R U K-P A C T. (Transvaalse Raad vir die Uitvoerende Kunste-Performing Arts Council Transvaal) irreg. ISSN 0085-7416

**Perskorporasie van S.A. (Edms) Bpk.**
Box 845, Johannesburg, South Africa.
- Rooi Rose. fortn. ISSN 0035-8207

**Pharmaceutical Society of South Africa**
- South African Pharmaceutical Journal/Suid-Afrikaanse Tydskrif vir Apteekwese. (pub. by M.I.M.S. (Pty) Ltd.)

**Philatelic Federation of Southern Africa**
Box 375, Johannesburg, South Africa.
- South African Philatelist. m. ISSN 0038-2566

**Photogrammetric Society of South Africa**
P.O. Box 3954, Johannesburg, South Africa.
- South African Journal of Photogrammetry. a. ISSN 0085-6398

**Pithead Press (Pty) Ltd.**
Box 9002, Johannesburg, South Africa.
- Coal, Gold and Base Minerals of Southern Africa. m.
- Construction in Southern Africa. m. ISSN 0010-6690 (Constructional Engineering Association) (Co-sponsors: South African Reinforced Concrete Engineers Association; Materials Handling and Construction Plant Association of South Africa)
- Heating, Air Conditioning & Refrigeration. bi-m. ISSN 0017-9353 (South African Institute of Refrigeration and Air Conditioning)
- South African Tunnelling. q.

**Plastics Institute of South Africa**
- Plastics Southern Africa. (pub. by G. Warman Publications (Pty) Ltd.)

**Political Science Association of South Africa**
Department of Political Science, University of Pretoria, Pretoria, South Africa.
- Politikon. s-a.

**Postal and Telegraph Association of South Africa**
Box 9186, Johannesburg 2000, South Africa.
- Postal and Telegraph Herald/Pos- en Telegraafherald. m. ISSN 0032-5317

**Potchefstroom University for Christian Higher Education**
Potchefstroom, South Africa.
- Abstracts of Theses and Dissertations Accepted for Higher Degrees in the Potchefstroom University for Christian Higher Education. a. ISSN 0079-4317
- Koers; Maandblad vir Calvinistiese Denke. 6 per yr. ISSN 0023-270X
- Potchefstroom University for Christian Higher Education. Wetenskaplike Bydraes. Reeks A: Geesteswetenskappe. irreg. ISSN 0079-4333
- Potchefstroom University for Christian Higher Education. Wetenskaplike Bydraes. Reeks B: Natuurwetenskappe. Series. irreg. ISSN 0079-4341
- Potchefstroom University for Christian Higher Education. Wetenskaplike Bydraes. Reeks H: Inougurele Redes. irreg.
- Union Catalogue of Theses and Dissertations of the South African Universities. a. ISSN 0079-4325

**Potchefstroom University for Christian Higher Education. Centre for International Politics**
Potchefstroom 2520, South Africa.
- Wereld in Oenskou. m.

**Potchefstroom University for Christian Higher Education. Department Kosteberekening**
Posbus 368, Bedryfsrekeningkunde, Potchetstroom, South Africa.
- Bestuurlike Informasie/Managerial Information. a. ISSN 0067-6349

**Potchefstroom University for Christian Higher Education. Department of Development**
Posbus 156, Potchefstroom, South Africa.
- P. U.-Kaner. m. ISSN 0030-8412

**Presbyterian Church of Southern Africa**
Box 11269, Johannesburg, South Africa.
- Christian Leader. m. ISSN 0010-5848 (Co-sponsor: United Congregational Church of South Africa)

**Pretoria College for Advanced Technical Education**
420 Church St., East, Pretoria, South Africa.
- Pretoria College for Advanced Technical Education. Annual/Jaarblad. a. ISSN 0079-5062
- Trompie; weekikse studente koerant/weekly newspaper. w. ISSN 0041-316X

**Pretoria Horticultural Society**
Box 1186, Pretoria, South Africa.
- Gardener/Tuinier. m.

**Pretoria Photographic Society**
Box 1065, Pretoria, South Africa.
- Flash. m. ISSN 0015-3494

**Price Institute for Palaeontological Research**
see under **University of the Witwatersrand, Johannesburg**

**Pro Rege Pers**
Box 343, Potchefstroom, South Africa.
- Nuus Oor Afrika; nuusopsomming en-kommentaar oor Afrikaaangeleenthede. 10 per yr. ISSN 0029-6694

**Pro Veritate (Pty) Ltd.**
Box 31135, Braamfontein 2017, Transvaal, South Africa.
- Pro Veritate; Christian monthly for Southern Africa. m. ISSN 0032-9142 (Christian Institute of Southern Africa)

**Psychological Institute of the Republic of South Africa**
Box 2729, Pretoria, South Africa.
- Psychological Institute of the Republic of South Africa. Proceedings/Sielkundige Instituut van die Republiek van Suid-Afrika. Verrigtings. a.
- South African Psychologist. s-a.

**Psychology Society**
University of Natal, c/o Department of Psychology, King George V Ave., Durban, South Africa.
- Journal of Behavioural Science. 2 per yr. ISSN 0075-4145

**Public Relations Institute of South Africa**
- Communika. (pub. by Company Publications (Pty) Ltd.)

**Public Servants Association of South Africa**
P.S.A. Bldg., 125 Vermeulen St., Room 706, Pretoria, South Africa.
- Public Servant/Staatsamptenaar. m. ISSN 0033-376X

**Quarry**
c/o A. Donker, Craighall Mews, Jan Smuts Ave., Craighall Park, Johannesburg 2196, South Africa.
- Quarry; new South African writing. a.

**Quill Publications**
Box 41419, Craighill 2024, South Africa.
- Marketing Research and Media. q. (South African Market Research Association) (Co-sponsors: Media Association of South Africa; Bureau of Market Research)

**R S A World**
Box 2660, Pretoria, South Africa.
- R S A World; South African affairs in their world context. 8 per yr. ISSN 0033-7099

**Raad vir Geesteswetenskaplike Navorsing**
*see* **Human Sciences Research Council**

**Radha Soami Satsang Beas**
c/o Sam Busa, Box 9513, Johannesburg, South Africa.
- Science of the Soul. q. ISSN 0036-8466

**Radio, Electricity & Furniture Association**
- Radio, Electrical & Furniture Merchandiser. (pub. by Felstar Publishers (Pty) Ltd.)

**Ramsay, Son & Parker (Pty) Ltd.**
405 Tulbagh Centre, Hans Strijdom Ave., Cape Town, South Africa.
- Buyer. m. ISSN 0007-7372
- Car; the motoring journal of Southern Africa. m. ISSN 0008-5995
- Hotelier & Caterer. m. ISSN 0018-6295
- South African Licensee's Guardian. a. ISSN 0489-8567

**Rand Afrikaans University**
Box 524, Johannesburg 2000, South Africa.
- R A U-Rapport. q. ISSN 0033-6785
- Randse Afrikaanse Universiteit. Jaarboek. a.
- Randse Afrikaanse Universiteit. Op en Om die Kampus. a.
- Randse Afrikaanse Universiteit. Opsommings van Proefskrifte en Verhandelinge/Abstracts of Dissertations and Theses. a.
- Randse Afrikaanse Universiteit. Prospektus. a.

**Randse Afrikaanse Universiteit**
*see* **Rand Afrikaans University**

**Ravan Press (Pty.) Ltd.**
Box 31136, Braamfontein 2017, Transvaal, South Africa.
- Snarl; a critical review of the arts.

**Reader's Digest Association Ltd.**
Box 2677, Cape Town, South Africa.
- Reader's Digest (South African Edition) m. ISSN 0034-0456

**Reality**
Box 1104, Pietermaritzburg 2000, South Africa.
- Reality; a journal of liberal and radical opinion. bi-m. ISSN 0034-0979

**Reformed Church in South Africa**
Box 20008, Noordbrug 2522, Potchefstroom, South Africa.
- Gereformeerde Vroueblad. m.
- Imbongi Yenkosi. m (11 per yr.)
- Kerkblad. w. ISSN 0023-0596
- Molaetsa-Molaetsa. 8 per yr.
- Murhumiwa. bi-m.
- Murumiwa. bi-m.
- My Volk. q. ISSN 0027-5468
- Oes. q. ISSN 0029-8727
- Quo Vadis. 3 per yr. ISSN 0033-6637
- Slingervel; publication for the youth. m. ISSN 0037-685X
- Umthombo Wamandla. bi-m.

**C. V. Rensburg Publications**
P.O. Box 25272, Marshalltown, South Africa.
- Guide to the Hotels in South Africa. irreg. ISSN 0533-5450

**Republican News Agency (Pty) Ltd.**
Box 32083, Mobeni 4060, Natal, South Africa.
- Darling. fortn.
- Family Radio & TV. w.
- Farmers Weekly. w. ISSN 0014-8482
- Scope. w. ISSN 0036-9012
- South African Garden & Home. m. ISSN 0038-2183
- Tempo. w.

**Res Publica (Pty) Ltd.**
Box 2045, Pretoria, South Africa.
- Stuurwiel. m. ISSN 0039-4203

**Reunert & Lenz Ltd.**
Box 92, Johannesburg, South Africa.
- R. & L. News. q. ISSN 0033-6815

**Rhodes University**
Box 94, Grahamstown, South Africa.
- Graham's Town Series. (pub. by A. A. Balkema Ltd.)
- Rhodes Review. s-a. (Old Rhodian Union)

**Rhodes University. Department of Philosophy**
Grahamstown 6140, South Africa.
- Rhodes University. Department of Philosophy. Philosophical Papers. s-a.

**Rhodes University. Institute for the Study of English in Africa**
Box 93, Grahamstown 6140, South Africa.
- English in Africa. s-a. ISSN 0425-0508
- New Coin. s-a. ISSN 0028-4459

**Rhodes University. J. L. B. Smith Institute of Ichthyology**
Grahamstown 6140, South Africa.
- J. L. B.Smith Institute of Ichthyology. Ichthyological Bulletin. irreg. ISSN 0073-4381 (Co-sponsor: South African Council for Scientific and Industrial Research)
- J. L. B. Smith Institute of Ichthyology. Occasional Paper. irreg. ISSN 0075-207X (Co-sponsor: South African Council for Scientific and Industrial Research)
- J. L. B. Smith Institute of Ichthyology. Special Publication. irreg. ISSN 0075-2088 (Co-sponsor: South African Council for Scientific and Industrial Research)

**Rhodes University. Leather Industries Research Institute**
Box 185, Grahamstown 6140, South Africa.
- L I R I Monthly Circular. m. ISSN 0023-9755
- L. I. R. I. Research Bulletin. irreg. ISSN 0085-2724

**Rhodes University. Speech and Drama Department**
- Albany Series of Plays. (pub. by A. A. Balkema Ltd.)

**Rhodes University. Students' Representative Council**
Grahamstown, South Africa.
- Rhodeo. w. ISSN 0035-466X

**Roman Catholic Diocese of Kimberly**
Box 309, Kimberly, South Africa.
- Kehilwenyane; Dikgang tsa badumedi le merafe. m. ISSN 0022-9687

**Rondalia Touring Club**
Box 2290, Pretoria, South Africa.
- Mylpaal/Milepost. bi-m. ISSN 0027-5565

**Rotary in Africa, Ltd.**
Box 3509, Durban, South Africa.
- Rotary in Africa. m.

**Royal Society of South Africa**
University of Cape Town, Rondebosch, South Africa.
- Royal Society of South Africa. Transactions. irreg (1-4 per yr.) ISSN 0035-919X

**S.A. Blind Workers Organisation**
Box 2360, Johannesburg 2000, South Africa.
- Braillorama. m.

**S.A. Engine Driver's, Firemen's and Operators' Association**
Box 8991, Johannesburg 2000, South Africa.
- Indicator. m. ISSN 0019-6932

**S.A. Germanistenverband**
- Acta Germanica. (pub. by A. A. Balkema Ltd.)

**S. A. Scientific Committee for Antarctic Research**
*see* **Council for Scientific and Industrial Research. Scientific Committee for Antarctic Research**

**S.E.G. Public Relations (Pty) Ltd.**
Box 10122, Johannesburg, South Africa.
- Safe and Security News. q. ISSN 0036-2360

**S H A W C O**
*see* **University of Cape Town. Students Health and Welfare Centres Organisation (SHAWCO)**

**S.R.C. Press**
Students Union, Rondebosch, Cape Town, South Africa.
- Varsity. w. ISSN 0042-2797 (University of Cape Town. Students Representative Council)

**Safety First Association**
Box 56400, Johannesburg, South Africa.
- National Safety/Nasionale Veiligheid. m. ISSN 0028-0097

**St. Vincent de Paul Superior Council for Southern Africa**
Box 1027, Cape Town, South Africa.
- Society of St. Vincent de Paul. Bulletin for Southern Africa. q. ISSN 0036-2034

**St. Wilfrid's Church**
96 Duxbury Rd., Pretoria, South Africa.
- St. Wilfrid's Notes and News. m. ISSN 0036-3235

**Saiva Sithantha Sungum of South Africa (Universal Mission)**
37 Derby Street, Box 4677, Durban, Natal, South Africa.
- Gracious Light. q.

**Salvation Army**
Box 707, Cape Town, South Africa.
- War Cry/Strydkreet. w. ISSN 0043-0250

**SARP Uitgewers**
Box 828, Pretoria 0001, South Africa.
- Sarp; tydskrif vir die S.A. polisie/magazine for the S.A. police. m. ISSN 0036-4819 (South African Police Force)

**School of Truth Ltd.**
South African Centre, 5th Fl., 253 Bree St., Johannesburg, South Africa.
- Path of Truth. m. ISSN 0031-2932
- Young Ideas. m. ISSN 0044-0787

**Scientific Committee for Antarctic Research**
*see under* **Council for Scientific and Industrial Research**

**Scott Publications (Pty) Ltd.**
Scott House, 41 Church St., Box 4532, Cape Town, South Africa.
- South Africa Motor. m.
- South African Motor-Cyclist. m. ISSN 0038-2485

**Seal Publishing Co. (Pty) Ltd.**
P.O. Box 4960, Johannesburg, South Africa.
- Industrial South Africa. every 4 yrs. ISSN 0073-7658
- Skyways. s-a. ISSN 0037-6671 (South African Airways)

**Sentinel Publishing Association**
Rosmead Ave., Kenilworth, Cape Town, South Africa.
- Home and Health/Gesin en Gesondheid. bi-m. ISSN 0018-3962 (Seventh-Day Adventist Church) (Co-Sponsor: Better Living League)
- Signs of the Times/Tekens van Die Tye. m. ISSN 0037-5071 (Seventh-Day Adventist Church)
- South African Union Lantern/Suid-Afrikaanse Unie-Lantern. m. ISSN 0038-2795 (South African Union Conference of Seventh-Day Adventists)
- Trans-Africa Division Outlook. m. (Seventh-Day Adventist Church. Trans-Africa Division)

**Seventh-Day Adventist Church**
- Home and Health/Gesin en Gesondheid. (pub. by Sentinel Publishing Association)
- Signs of the Times/Tekens van Die Tye. (pub. by Sentinel Publishing Association)

**Seventh-Day Adventist Church. Trans-Africa Division**
- Trans-Africa Division Outlook. (pub. by Sentinel Publishing Association)

**J. Sharpe Publications (Pty) Ltd.**
Box 61569, Marshalltown, Johannesburg, South Africa.
- Business South Africa. m. ISSN 0007-7070

**SHAWCO**
*see* University of Cape Town. Students Health and Welfare Centres Organisation (SHAWCO)

**Shell Southern Africa (Pty) Ltd.**
Box 2231, Cape Town 8000, South Africa.
- Shell Chronicle. bi-m. ISSN 0037-3524
- Shell Dealer News. bi-m. ISSN 0037-3532

**Sielkundige Instituut van die Republiek van Suid-Afrika**
*see* Psychological Institute of the Republic of South Africa

**Simon van der Stel Foundation**
Box 1743, Pretoria 0001, South Africa.
- Restorica. a.

**Simon's Town Historical Society**
Box 56, Simon's Town 7995, South Africa.
- Simon's Town Historical Society Bulletin. s-a. ISSN 0037-5470

**Sivananda School of Yoga**
Embassy Place, 240 Bree St., 3rd Fl., Johannesburg, Johannesburg.
- Illumination Annual. a. ISSN 0019-235X

**Smith Institute of Ichthyology**
*see under* Rhodes University

**Social Work**
Box 223, Stellenbosch, South Africa.
- Social Work/Maatskaplike Werk; a professional journal for the social worker. q. ISSN 0037-8054

**Society for Geography**
Box 2031, Dennesig 7601, Stellenbosch, Cape Province, South Africa.
- South African Geographer/Suid-Afrikaanse Geograaf. s-a.

**Society for the Protection of the Environment**
Box 370, Stellenbosch, South Africa.
- Society for the Protection of the Environment Newsletter. q.

**Society of Medical Laboratory Technologists of South Africa**
- South African Journal of Medical Laboratory Technology/Suid-Afrikaanse Tydskrif vir Mediese Laboratorium Tegnologie. (pub. by M.I.M.S. (Pty) Ltd.)

**Society of Opticians (S.A.)**
342 Giovanetti St., Pretoria, South Africa.
- South African Refractionist/Suid-Afrikaanse Gesigkundige. q. ISSN 0038-2612

**Society of St. Vincent de Paul**
- Society of St. Vincent de Paul. Bulletin for Southern Africa. (pub. by St. Vincent de Paul Superior Council for Southern Africa)

**South Africa. Atomic Energy Board**
Private Bag X256, Pretoria 0001, South Africa.
- Nuclear Active. s-a. ISSN 0048-1025

**South Africa. Bureau of Standards**
Private Bag X191, Pretoria 0001, South Africa.
- Brief; brief on design. m. (prep. by its Design Institute)
- South Africa. Bureau of Standards. S A B S Bulletin. m. ISSN 0038-2698
- South Africa. Bureau of Standards. S A B S Yearbook. a. ISSN 0081-2137
- South African Metrication News. m. ISSN 0049-1411

**South Africa. Deciduous Fruit Board**
Mobil House, Hans Strijdom Ave., Box 1298, Cape Town 8000, South Africa.
- Deciduous Fruit Grower/Sagtevrugteboer. m. ISSN 0011-7285
- South Africa. Deciduous Fruit Board. Report. a.

**South Africa. Department of Agricultural Economics and Marketing**
Private Bag 250, Pretoria, South Africa.
- Agrekon. q. ISSN 0002-113X

**South Africa. Department of Agricultural Economics and Marketing. Division of Agricultural Marketing Research**
Private Bag 250, Pretoria 0001, South Africa.
- South Africa. Department of Agricultural Economics and Marketing. Division of Agricultural Marketing and Research. Trends in the Agricultural Sector. s-a.
- South Africa. Department of Agricultural Economics and Marketing. Division of Agricultural Marketing Research. Abstract of Agricultural Statistics. a; latest issue 1977.

**South Africa. Department of Agricultural Technical Services**
Private Bag X144, Pretoria, South Africa.
- Agroanimalia; animal sciences. q.
- Agrochemophysica; soil, chemical and physical sciences. q.
- Agroplantae; plant sciences. q.
- Flowering Plants of Africa. 2 per yr. ISSN 0015-4504
- Guide to the Use of Insecticides and Fungicides in South Africa. a.
- Onderstepoort Journal of Veterinary Research. q. ISSN 0030-2465
- Phytophylactica; plant protection sciences and microbiology. q.
- South Africa. Department of Agricultural Technical Services. Agricultural Bulletins. 10-12 per yr. ISSN 0002-1393
- South Africa. Department of Agricultural Technical Services. Agricultural Research. a. ISSN 0081-2145
- South Africa. Department of Agricultural Technical Services. Entomology Memoirs. 4 per yr(approx) ISSN 0013-8940
- South Africa. Department of Agricultural Technical Services. Official List of Professional Research Workers, Lecturing Staff and Extension Workers in the Agricultural Field. a.
- South Africa. Department of Agricultural Technical Services. Report of the Secretary for Agricultural Technical Services. a. ISSN 0081-2153
- South Africa. Department of Agricultural Technical Services. Science Bulletins. irreg. ISSN 0038-1934
- South Africa. Department of Agricultural Technical Services. Special Publication. irreg. ISSN 0081-2161
- South Africa. Department of Agricultural Technical Services. Technical Communication. irreg.; no. 118, 1974. ISSN 0081-217X

**South Africa. Department of Bantu Education**
Private Bag X212, Pretoria 0001, South Africa.
- Bantu Education Journal/Bantoe-Onderwysblad. 10 per yr. ISSN 0005-5662
- South Africa. Department of Bantu Education. Annual Report. irreg. ISSN 0081-2188 (Orders to: Government Printer, Bosman St., Pretoria, South Africa)

**South Africa. Department of Customs and Excise**
Pretoria, South Africa.
- South Africa. Department of Customs and Excise. Foreign Trade Statistics. a. ISSN 0081-2196

**South Africa. Department of Defense**
Cape Town, South Africa.
- South Africa. Department of Defense. White Paper on Defence and Armament Production. irreg.

**South Africa. Department of Indian Affairs**
Private Bag X54332, Durban, South Africa.
- Fiat Lux. m. ISSN 0015-0495

**South Africa. Department of Information**
Private Bag X152, Pretoria, South Africa.
- Alpha. m. ISSN 0002-6379
- Muelaphanda. m. ISSN 0025-6242
- Nhluvuko. m. ISSN 0028-9647
- South African Digest Incorporating Comment and Opinion. w.
- South African Panorama. m (Afrikaans, English); others bi-m. ISSN 0038-254X
- Tswelopele. m. ISSN 0041-3828

**South Africa. Department of Labour**
Private Bag X117, Pretoria 0001, South Africa.
- My Career/My Loopbaan. q. ISSN 0027-5425
- Rehabilitation in South Africa/Rehabilitasie in Suid-Afrika. q. ISSN 0034-3501

**South Africa. Department of Statistics**
Private Bag X44, Pretoria, South Africa
(Subscr. to: Government Printer, Bosman St., Private Bag X85, Pretoria 0001, South Africa)
- South Africa. Department of Statistics. Annual Report of the Statistics Council and of the Secretary of Statistics. a.
- South Africa. Department of Statistics. Bulletin of Statistics. q. ISSN 0038-1926
- South Africa. Department of Statistics. Census of Cinemas, Cafe-Bioscopes and Drive-in Theatres. irreg.
- South Africa. Department of Statistics. Census of Construction. a.
- South Africa. Department of Statistics. Census of Electricity, Gas and Steam. a.
- South Africa. Department of Statistics. Census of Fisheries. a.
- South Africa. Department of Statistics. Census of Transport and Allied Services/Sensus van Vervoer- en Verwante Dienste. a.
- South Africa. Department of Statistics. Manufacturing Statistics, Products Manufactured./Fabriekswesestatistieke, Produkte Vervaardig. m.
- South Africa. Department of Statistics. Road Traffic Accidents/Padverkeerongelukke. irreg, latest 1974. ISSN 0584-195X
- South Africa. Department of Statistics. Short Term Economic Indicators/Korttermyn Ekonomiese Aanwysers. m.
- South Africa. Department of Statistics. Statistics of Flats, Eleven Principal Urban Areas of South Africa. irreg, latest 1975.
- South Africa. Department of Statistics. Statistieke van Motorvoertuie: Nuwe Voertuie Gelisensieer/Motor Vehicle Statistics: New Vehicles Licensed. a, latest covers 1970-1974.
- South Africa. Department of Statistics. Survey of Accounts of Companies in Secondary and Tertiary Industries. irreg, latest 1974 per 75.
- South Africa. Department of Statistics. Verslag Oor Huwelike en Egskeidings: Suid Afrika/Report on Marriages and Divorces: South Africa. irreg.
- South African Statistics. biennial. ISSN 0081-2544

**South Africa. Department of Transport. Weather Bureau**
*see* South Africa. Weather Bureau

**South Africa. Directorate of Hydrography**
Youngsfield, Kenwyn 7790, South Africa.
- South African Tide Tables/Suid--Afrikaanse Getytafels. a.

**South Africa. Geological Survey**
Private Bag 112, Pretoria, South Africa
(Orders to: Government Printer, Bosman St., Private Bag X85, Pretoria 0001, South Africa)
- Catalogue of Earth Tremors in Southern Africa and Surrounding Oceans. a.
- South West Africa Series. irreg.

**South Africa. Government Printer**
Bosman St., Private Bag X85, Pretoria 0001, South Africa.
- Bibliography of South African Government Publications. irreg. ISSN 0067-7256 (Prepared by: Department of National Education, Division of Library Sciences)
- Economic Development Programme for the Republic of South Africa. irreg. ISSN 0070-8518 (Prepared by: Department of Planning)
- Patent Journal Including Trademarks and Models. m. ISSN 0031-286X
- South Africa. Department of Coloured Relations and Rehoboth Affairs. Annual Report. a. ISSN 0584-2166

- South Africa. Department of Higher Education. Annual Report. a. ISSN 0081-220X
- South Africa. Department of National Education. Jaarverslag/Annual Report. a.
- South Africa. Law Commission. Jaarverslag van die Suid-Afrikaanse Regskommissie/Annual Report of the South African Law Commission. a.
- South Africa. Philatelic Services. Philatelic Bulletin/Filateliebulletin. 10 per yr. ISSN 0031-7349
- South Africa. Prisons Department. Annual Statistics by the Commissioner of Prisons/Jaarlikse Statistieke Deur die Kommissaris van Gevangenisse. a.
- South Africa. Prisons Department. Report of the Commissioner of Prisons/Verslag van die Kommissaris van Gevangenisse. a.
- South West Africa Survey. a. (Prepared by: Department of Foreign Affairs)

**South Africa. Livestock and Meat Industries Control Board**
Meat Board Bldg., Hamilton & Vermeulen Sts., Box 1357, Pretoria, South Africa.
- Meat Industry/Vleisnywerheid. q. ISSN 0025-6374

**South Africa. Maize Board**
Box 669, Pretoria 0001, South Africa.
- Maize News/Mielienuus. m. ISSN 0026-3559
- South Africa. Maize Board. Report on Grain Sorghum and Buckwheat for the Financial Year. a.
- South Africa. Maize Board. Report on Maize for the Financial Year. a.
- South African Maize and Grain Sorghum News. irreg.

**South Africa. Milk Board**
Box 2682, Pretoria, South Africa.
- Milk Producer. bi-m. ISSN 0026-4199

**South Africa. National Parks Board of Trustees**
P.O. Box 787, Pretoria 0001, South Africa.
- Custos. m.
- Koedoe; research journal for National Parks in the Republic of South Africa. a; no. 16, 1972. ISSN 0075-6458
- Koedoe. Monographs. irreg. ISSN 0075-6466
- South Africa. National Parks Board of Trustees. Annual Report. a.

**South Africa. Office of the Director of Archives**
Private Bag X236, Union Buildings, Pretoria 0001, South Africa.
- South Africa. Office of the Director of Archives. Jaarverslag van die Direkteur van Argiewe. a.

**South Africa. Office of the Scientific Advisor to the Prime Minister**
P.B. X420, Pretoria 0001, South Africa.
- National Register of Research Projects: Natural and Human Sciences.

**South Africa. State Library**
Box 397, Pretoria, South Africa.
- S A N B. (South African National Bibiography) q (annual cumulation) ISSN 0036-0864
- S. A. Unicat. bi-m.
- South Africa. State Library Council. Report/Verslag. irreg.

**South Africa. Tobacco Board**
P.O. Box 934, Pretoria, South Africa.
- South Africa. Tobacco Board. Annual Report/Jaarverslag. a.

**South Africa. Unemployment Insurance Fund**
Box 1851, Pretoria 0001, South Africa.
- South Africa. Unemployment Insurance Fund. Report. irreg.

**South Africa. Water Research Commission**
Box 824, Van der Stel Building, Pretorius St., Pretoria 0001, South Africa.
- South Africa. Water Research Commission. Annual Report. a.

**South Africa. Weather Bureau**
Department of Transport, Private Bag X193, Pretoria 0001, South Africa.
- South Africa. Weather Bureau. Annual Radiation Bulletin/Jaarlikse Stralingsbulletin. a.
- South Africa. Weather Bureau. Daily Weather Bulletin/Daaglikse Weerbulletin. d. ISSN 0011-5517

- South Africa. Weather Bureau. Monthly Weather Report/Maandelikse Weerverslag. m. ISSN 0038-1942
- South Africa. Weather Bureau. Newsletter/Nuusbrief. m. ISSN 0032-7948
- South Africa. Weather Bureau. Radiosonde Rawin Data. irreg., latest issue 1974. ISSN 0081-2315
- South Africa. Weather Bureau. Report on Meteorological Data of the Year/Verslag Oor Weerkundige Data van die Jaar. irreg., latest issue 1973. ISSN 0081-2323
- South Africa. Weather Bureau. Technical Paper/Tegniese Verhandelinge. irreg., no. 4, 1976.
- South Africa. Weather Bureau. W.B. Series. irreg. no. 38, 1975. ISSN 0081-2331
- South Africa. Weather Bureau. Weekly Rainfall Report. w.

**South Africa. Wheat Board**
P.O. Box 908, Pretoria 0001, South Africa.
- South Africa. Wheat Board. Annual Report. a.

**South Africa. Wool Board**
Pretoria, South Africa.
- South Africa. Wool Board. Review of the Wool Season. irreg.; latest issue, 1974.

**South Africa Foundation**
Box 7006, Johannesburg 2000, South Africa.
- South Africa Foundation News. m.
- South Africa International. q. ISSN 0015-5055

**South Africa National Sunday School Association**
P.O. Box 1547, Cape Town 8000, South Africa.
- Christian Education Advance. q.

**South African Academy of Arts and Sciences**
see **Suid-Afrikaanse Akademie vir Wetenskap en Kuns**

**South African Airways**
- Skyways. (pub. by Seal Publishing Co.(Pty.) Ltd.)

**South African Aloe and Succulent Society**
Box 1193, Pretoria 0001, South Africa.
- Aloe. q. ISSN 0002-6301

**South African Amateur Athletics Union**
Box 1261, Pretoria 0001, South Africa.
- S.A. Athlete/S.A. Atleet; track and field news. m. ISSN 0049-1381

**South African Antarctic Association**
32 Park Ave., Bordeaux, Randburg, South Africa.
- Antarktiese Bulletin/Antarctic Bulletin. q. ISSN 0003-5351

**South African Archaeological Society**
P.O. Box 31, Claremont 7735, Cape Town, South Africa.
- Goodwin Series. biennial.
- South African Archaeological Bulletin/Suid-Afrikaanse Argeologiese Bulletin. s-a. ISSN 0038-1969

**South African Associated Newspapers**
- Top Companies. (pub. by Financial Mail (Pty) Ltd.)

**South African Association for Marine Biological Research**
Centenary Aquarium, 2 West St., Durban, Natal, South Africa.
- South African Association for Marine Biological Research. Bulletin. a; no. 10, 1973. ISSN 0081-234X

**South African Association for Technical and Vocational Education**
Box 945, Middleburg, Transvaal 1050, South Africa.
- Journal for Technical and Vocational Education in South Africa/Tydskrif vir Tegniese en Beroepsonderwys in Suid-Afrika. q. ISSN 0021-8278

**South African Association for the Advancement of Science**
Box 61019, Marshalltown, Transvaal 2107, South Africa.
- South African Association for the Advancement of Science. Newsletter/Suid-Afrikaanse Genootskap vir Die Bevordering van Die Wetenskap. Newsletter. m. ISSN 0038-1985
- South African Journal of Science/Suid-Afrikaanse Tydskrif vir Wetenskap. m. ISSN 0038-2353

**South African Association of Botanists**
Private Bag X101, Pretoria 0001, South Africa.
- Forum Botanicum. m. ISSN 0015-847X

**South African Association of Business Management**
Box 2502, Pretoria, South Africa.
- Bedryfsleiding/Business Management. q. ISSN 0045-1614

**South African Association of Consulting Engineers**
- South African Association of Consulting Engineers. Directory of Registered Firms/Gids van Geregistreede Firmas. (pub. by Associated Scientific and Technical Societies of South Africa)

**South African Association of Municipal Employees. Pretoria Branch**
City Hall, 1st Floor, Pretoria, South Africa.
- Festina Lente. q. ISSN 0015-0347
- Municipal Administration & Engineering/Munisipale Administrasie en Ingenieurwese. m. ISSN 0027-3422

**South African Association of Occupational Therapists**
Box 17289, Hillbrow, Johannesburg 2038, South Africa.
- South African Journal of Occupational Therapy. s-a. ISSN 0038-2337

**South African Bridge Federation**
Box 42038, Fordsburg, Johannesburg 2033, South Africa.
- Bridge Bulletin. m. ISSN 0006-9841

**South African Broadcasting Corporation**
- Listening Index. (pub. by Market Research Africa (Pty) Ltd.)

**South African Builder (Pty) Ltd.**
Federated Insurance House, 1 de Villiers St., Box 11359, Johannesburg 2000, South Africa.
- Building and Allied Industries Official Handbook. a. (Building Industries Federation (South Africa))
- South African Builder. m. ISSN 0038-2027 (Building Industries Federation (South Africa))

**South African Bureau of Racial Affairs**
Box 2768, Pretoria, South Africa.
- Tydskrif vir Rasse-Aangeleenthede/Journal of Racial Affairs. q. ISSN 0041-4794

**South African Chemical Institute**
Box 61019, Marshalltown 2107, Transvaal, South Africa.
- South African Journal of Chemistry/Suidafrikaanse Joernaal van Chemie. q.

**South African Chessplayer**
Box 4513, Cape Town, South Africa.
- South African Chessplayer. m. ISSN 0038-2094

**South African Copper Development Association (Pty.) Ltd.**
Box 3701, Johannesburg, South Africa.
- Copper Information. Architectural Series. 4 per yr.
- Copper Information. Engineering Series. 8 per yr.

**South African Corrosion Institute**
- Corrosion and Coatings. (pub. by George Warman Publications (Pty) Ltd.)

**South African Council of Churches**
P.O. Box 31190, Braamfontein, Transvaal, South Africa.
- Journal of Theology for Southern Africa. q. ISSN 0047-2867
- Kairos. m. ISSN 0022-7765

**South African Cycling Federation**
- South African Cyclist. (pub. by Cycling Publications)

**South African Defence Force**
Private Bag 158, Pretoria, South Africa.
- Paratus. m.

**South African Dog Breeders and Dog Lovers**
Box 462, East London, South Africa.
- Dog Review of Southern Africa. q. ISSN 0012-4877

**South African Esperanto Association**
P.O. Box 1227, Cape Town 8000, South Africa.
- Bona Espero. q. ISSN 0006-7024

**South African Federation of Beekeepers' Associations**
P.O. Box 48, Irene 1675, South Africa.
- South African Bee Journal. bi-m. ISSN 0038-2019

**South African Fire Services Institute**
Fire Department, Nigel, South Africa.
- South African Fire Services Institute. Quarterly/ Suid-Afrikaanse Brandweerinstitut Kwartaalblad. q. ISSN 0038-2159

**South African Footplate Staff Association**
105 Simmonds St., Braamfontein, Johannesburg, South Africa.
- Footplate/Voetplaat. m. ISSN 0015-6809

**South African Foreign Trade Organization**
Box 9039, Johannesburg 2000, South Africa.
- S A F T O Annual Report/Suid-Afrikaanse Buitelandse Handelsorgonisasie Jaarverslag. a. ISSN 0081-2552
- S A F T O Exporter. m. ISSN 0036-0716

**South African Forestry Association**
62 Lurgan Rd., Parkview, Johannesburg, South Africa.
- South African Forestry Journal/Suid-Afrikaanse Bosboutydskrif. q. ISSN 0038-2167

**South African Genetic Society**
c/o Department of Genetics, University of Stellenbosch, Stellenbosch, South Africa.
- Genetics Newsletter/Genetika Nuusbrief. q.

**South African Geographical Society**
Box 31201, Braamfontein 2017, Transvaal, South Africa.
- South African Geographical Journal. s-a.

**South African Guernsey Cattle Breeders Society**
P.O. Box 248, Humansdorp, South Africa.
- Suid-Afrikaanse Guernsey. a. ISSN 0081-9220

**South African Historical Society**
University of the Orange Free State, Department of History, Bloemfontein, South Africa
- South African Historical Journal. a. (Subscr. to: Nasionale Boekwinkels Beperk, Box 1047, Bloemfontein 9300, South Africa)

**South African Institute for Public Administration**
Box 2752, Pretoria 0001, South Africa.
- S A I P A; journal for public administration/ tydskrif vir publieke administrasie. q. ISSN 0036-0767

**South African Institute of Assayers and Analysts**
Box 61019, Marshalltown, Transvaal, South Africa.
- South African Institute of Assayers and Analysts. Journal. q. ISSN 0038-2213

**South African Institute of Draughtsmen**
- South African Draughtsman/S. A. Tekenaar. (pub. by Heron Publishing Co. (Pty) Ltd.)

**South African Institute of Electrical Engineers**
- South African Institute of Electrical Engineers. Transactions. (pub. by Kelvin Publications (Pty) Ltd.)

**South African Institute of Foundrymen**
Box 31548, Braamfontein 2017, South Africa.
- F. W. P. Journal. (Founding, Welding, Production Engineering) m. ISSN 0015-9026 (Co-sponsors: South African Institute of Welding; South African Institute for Production Engineering)

**South African Institute of International Affairs**
Box 31596, Braamfontein, Transvaal 2017, South Africa.
- International Affairs Bulletin. 3 per yr.
- Southern Africa Record. irreg.

**South African Institute of Materials Handling**
- S. A. Materials Handling News. (pub. by Thomson Publications S.A. (Pty) Ltd.)

**South African Institute of Mining and Metallurgy**
Box 61019, Marshalltown, Transvaal, South Africa.
- South African Institute of Mining and Metallurgy. Journal. m. ISSN 0038-223X

**South African Institute of Organization and Methods**
Box 693, Pretoria, South Africa.
- O & M; the magazine for organization and methods. q. ISSN 0029-6937

**South African Institute of Photographers**
Box 8380, Johannesburg, South Africa.
- Profoto. bi-m. ISSN 0033-0329

**South African Institute of Race Relations**
Auden House, 68 de Korte St., Johannesburg, South Africa.
- Race Relations News. m. ISSN 0033-734X
- South African Institute of Race Relations. (Publication) RR. irreg.
- Survey of Race Relations in South Africa. a. ISSN 0081-9778
- Thought; a journal of opinion expressed in the press in South Africa. q. ISSN 0040-6465

**South African Institute of Refrigeration and Air Conditioning**
- Heating, Air Conditioning & Refrigeration. (pub. by Pithead Press (Pty.) Ltd.)

**South African Institution of Chemical Engineers**
- Chemsa. (pub. by New Chemical Publications (Pty) Ltd.)

**South African Institution of Civil Engineers**
Box 61019, Marshalltown 2107, South Africa.
- Civil Engineer in South Africa/Siviele Ingenieur in Suid-Afrika. m. ISSN 0009-7845

**South African Institution of Mechanical Engineers**
- South African Mechanical Engineer. (pub. by Kelvin Publications (Pty) Ltd.)

**South African Iron and Steel Industrial Corp., Ltd.**
H.Q. Bldg., Wagonwheel Circle, Box 450, Pretoria 0001, South Africa.
- Iscor News/Yskornuus. m. ISSN 0019-0594

**South African Iron, Steel and Allied Industries Union**
430 Church St. West, Box 19299, Pretoria, South Africa.
- S. A. Worker/S. A. Werker. m. ISSN 0036-1011

**South African Jewellery Council**
- Diamond News and South African Jeweller. (pub. by Diamond News (Pty) Ltd.)

**South African Jewish Board of Deputies**
Box 1180, Johannesburg, South Africa.
- Jewish Affairs. m. ISSN 0021-6313

**South African Jewish Ex-Service League**
Box 7309, Johannesburg, South Africa.
- Judean. s-a. ISSN 0022-5770

**South African Legion**
306 Duncan House, 11 de Villiers St., Johannesburg, South Africa.
- Springbok. m.

**South African Library**
Queen Victoria St., Cape Town 8001, South Africa.
- South African Library. Quarterly Bulletin/Suid-Afrikaanse Biblioteek. Kwartaalblad. q. ISSN 0038-2418

**South African Library Association**
c/o Ferdinand Postma Library, Potchefstroom University for Christian Higher Education, Potchefstroom, South Africa.
- S A L A Newsletter/S A B V Nuusbrief. m. ISSN 0036-0783
- South African Libraries/Suid-Afrikaanse Biblioteke. q. ISSN 0038-240X
- South African Library Association. Annual Report/Suid-Afrikaanse Biblioteekvereniging. Jaarverslag. a.

**South African Literary Journal Ltd.**
3 Scott Road, Box 3841, Claremont, Cape Town, South Africa.
- Contrast; South African literary journal. 3 per yr.

**South African Maize Producers Institute**
Box 88, Bothaville, South Africa.
- Landman. m. ISSN 0023-7965

**South African Market Research Association**
- Marketing Research and Media. (pub. by Quill Publications)

**South African Medical & Dental Council**
P.O. Box 205, Pretoria 0001, South Africa.
- Register of Medical Practitioners. Interns and Dentists for the Republic of South Africa. a.

**South African Medical Research Council**
P.O. Box 70, Parowvallei 7503, South Africa.
- South African Medical Research Council. Annual Report/Suid-Afrikaanse Mediese Navorsingsraad. Jaarverslag. a.; latest issue, 1973. ISSN 0081-248X

**South African Museums Association**
South African Museum, Box 61, Cape Town 8000, South Africa.
- S A M A B; a journal of museology. q. ISSN 0036-0791

**South African National Council for the Aged**
Box 2335, Cape Town 8000, South Africa.
- Senatus. bi-m.
- Senior News/Senior Nuus. q. ISSN 0037-2234

**South African National Council for the Blind**
Box 26211, Arcadia 0007, South Africa.
- Difofu; a monthly braille magazine in Bantu languages/'n braille maanblad in Bantoetale. m. ISSN 0012-2688
- Imfama (Braille Edition) bi-m.
- Imfama (Inkprint Edition) bi-m. ISSN 0019-2724
- South African National Council of the Blind. Biennial Report. biennial.

**South African National Council for the Deaf**
Box 31663, Braamfontein, Transvaal, South Africa.
- Silent Messenger/Stille Boodskapper. q. ISSN 0037-5195

**South African National Museum of Military History**
Box 52090, Saxonwold, Transvaal, South Africa.
- Military History Journal/Krygshistoriese Tydskrif. s-a. ISSN 0026-4016 (Co-sponsor: South African Military History Society)

**South African National Tuberculosis Association**
621 Leisk House, 195 Bree St., Johannesburg 2001, South Africa.
- S A N T A Annual Report. a, latest issue 1975. ISSN 0081-2501
- S A N T A Health Magazine/S A N T A Gesondheidstydskrif. bi-m.
- S A N T A News. m. ISSN 0036-0872

**South African Nursing Association**
Private Bag X105, Pretoria, South Africa.
- South African Nursing Journal/S. A. Verplegingstydskrif. m. ISSN 0038-2507

**South African Optometric Association**
- South African Optometrist/Suid- Afrikaanse Oogkundige. (pub. by M.I.M.S. (Pty.) Ltd.)

**South African Ornithological Society**
Box 9081, Cape Town, South Africa.
- Bokmakierie; a magazine for birdwatchers. q. ISSN 0006-5838
- Ostrich. 4 per yr. ISSN 0030-6525

**South African Photographic Trade Association Ltd.**
Box 10425, Johannesburg 2000, South Africa.
- Golden Eye. m. ISSN 0017-1581

**South African Police Force**
- Sarp. (pub. by SARP Uitgewers)

**South African Postal Association**
Box 2004, Johannesburg, South Africa.
- Postal Journal/Posjoernaal. q. ISSN 0032-535X

**South African Progressive Reform Party**
601 Garmor House, 121 Plein St., Cape Town 8000, South Africa.
- Progress. bi-m. ISSN 0033-0582

**South African Psychological Association**
P.O. Box 4292, Johannesburg, South Africa.
- South African Journal of Psychology. a. ISSN 0081-2463

**South African Radio League**
Box 3911, Cape Town, South Africa.
- Radio Z S. m. ISSN 0033-815X

**South African Railways and Harbours Employees' Union**
Box 1125, Cape Town, South Africa.
- Emplo Review/Tydskrif. m.

**South African Railways and Harbours Magazine Association**
Box 1111, Johannesburg, South Africa.
- SASSAR; S A R and H Magazine/Tydskrif van die Suid Afrikaanse Spoorwee en Hawens. m. ISSN 0036-0953

**South African Red Cross Society (Cape Region)**
Box 32, Wynberg 7824, Cape Town, South Africa.
- South African Red Cross Society (Cape Region). Newsletter/Suid-Afrikaanse Rooikruisvereniging (Kaapse Streek). Nuusbrief. m.

**South African Reserve Bank**
Box 427, Pretoria 0001, South Africa.
- South African Reserve Bank. Annual Economic Report/Suid-Afrikoanse Reserwebank. Jaarlikse Ekonomiese Verslag. a. ISSN 0081-2528
- South African Reserve Bank. Monthly Release of Money and Banking Statistics/Suid-Afrikaanse Reserwebank. Maandelikse Vrystelling van Geld- en Bankwesestatistiek. m. ISSN 0584-3073
- South African Reserve Bank. Quarterly Bulletin/Suid-Afrikaanse Reserwebank. Kwartaalblad. q. ISSN 0038-2620
- South African Reserve Bank. Report of the Ordinary General Meeting. a.

**South African Society of Animal Production**
Box 4196, Pretoria 0001, South Africa.
- South African Journal of Animal Science. 3 per yr.

**South African Society of Archivists**
c/o Treasurer, Government Archives, Union Buildings, Private Bag X236, Pretoria 0001, South Africa.
- Suid-Afrikaanse Argiefblad/South African Archives Journal. a.

**South African Society of Bank Officials**
Box 31537, Braamfontein, South Africa.
- S A S B O News/S A S B O Nuus. m.
- South African Banking. m. ISSN 0036-0570

**South African Society of Music Teachers**
20 Erica Place, Bergvliet 7800, South Africa.
- South African Music Teacher/Suid-Afrikaanse Musiekonderwyser. s-a. ISSN 0038-2493

**South African Society of Obstetricians and Gynaecologists**
- South African Journal of Obstetrics and Gynaecology/Suid-Afrikaanse Tydskrif vir Obstetrie en Ginekologie. (pub. by Medical Association of South Africa)

**South African Society of Physiotherapy**
Box 11151, Johannesburg 2000, South Africa.
- South African Journal of Physiotherapy. q.

**South African Sociological Association**
University of Pretoria, Department of Sociology, Pretoria, South Africa.
- South African Journal of Sociology. s-a.

**South African Speech & Hearing Association**
Box 31782, Braamfontein 2017, South Africa.
- South African Speech and Hearing Association. Journal. a. ISSN 0081-2471

**South African Statistical Association**
Box 27321, Sunnyside, Pretoria, South Africa.
- South African Statistical Journal/Suid-Afrikaanse Statistiese Tydskrif. s-a. ISSN 0038-271X

**South African Students' Organization**
86 Beatrice St., Box 2346, Durban, South Africa.
- S A S O Newsletter. bi-m.

**South African Sugar Association**
Box 507, Durban, South Africa.
- South African Sugar Journal. m. ISSN 0038-2728

**South African Table Tennis Union**
Box 3194, Cape Town, South Africa.
- South African Table Tennis News. bi-m. ISSN 0038-2744

**South African Teachers' Association**
15 Grove Buildings, Grove Ave., Claremont 7700, Cape Province, South Africa.
- Education. m. ISSN 0013-1202

**South African Typographical Union**
Box 1993, 166 Visagie St., Pretoria, South Africa.
- South African Typographical Journal/Suid-Afrikaanse Tipografiese Joernaal. m. ISSN 0038-2787

**South African Union Conference of Seventh-Day Adventists**
- South African Union Lantern/Suid-Afrikaanse Unie-Lantern. (pub. by Sentinel Publishing Association)

**South African Union of Jewish Students at Wits**
P.O. Box 31542, Braamfontein, Johannesburg 2017, South Africa.
- Genesis 2. q.

**South African Veterinary Association**
Box 2460, Pretoria, South Africa.
- South African Veterinary Association. Journal/Suid-Afrikaanse Veterinere Vereniging. Tydskrif. q. ISSN 0301-0732

**South African Water Information Centre**
Council for Scientific and Industrial Research, Box 395, Pretoria 0001, South Africa.
- Current Literature on Water. m. (Water Research Commission)
- S.A. Waterabstracts. q.
- Selected Journals on Water. bi-w.

**South African Wool and Textile Research Institute**
Box 1124, Port Elizabeth 6000, South Africa.
- S A W T R I Technical Report. irreg. ISSN 0081-2560
- South African Wool and Textile Research Institute. Annual Report. a. ISSN 0560-9941
- South African Wool and Textile Research Institute. Bulletin/Suid-Afrikaanse Woltekstielnavorsingsinstituut. Bulletin. q. ISSN 0036-1003

**South African Zionist Federation**
- Zionist Record and S. A. Jewish Chronicle. (pub. by Zionist Record (Pty) Ltd.)

**South Coast Herald (Pty) Ltd.**
36 Reynolds St, Port Shepstone, Natal, South Africa.
- South Coast Herald. w. ISSN 0038-3228

**Southern Africa Commercial Travellers' Association**
Box 828, Cape Town, South Africa.
- On the Road. m. ISSN 0030-2368

**Southern Africa Stainless Steel Development Association**
Box 8954, Johannesburg, South Africa.
- Stainless Steel. bi-m. ISSN 0038-917X

**Southern African Catholic Bishops' Conference**
- Southern Cross. (pub. by Catholic Newspaper and Publishing Co. Ltd.)

**Southern African Wildlife Management Association**
Box 413, Pretoria, South Africa.
- South African Journal of Wildlife Research. q.

**Southern Universities Nuclear Institute**
P.O. Box 17, Faure 7131, South Africa.
- Southern Universities Nuclear Institute. Annual Research Report. a.

**Souvenir Publishers**
Box 89, Northlands, Transvaal, South Africa.
- Rugby. m. ISSN 0035-9726

**Springs Advertiser (Pty.) Ltd.**
Box 138, Springs, South Africa.
- Springs & Brakpan Advertiser. w. ISSN 0038-8629

**Stage and Cinema Newspapers (Pty) Ltd.**
Box 1556, Johannesburg, South Africa.
- Cinema & T V. fortn.

**Stigting vir Onderwys, Wetenskap en Tegnologie**
see Foundation for Education, Science and Technology

**C. Struik Africana Publishers**
P.O. Box 1144, Cape Town, South Africa.
- Africana Collectanea Series. irreg.(approx. 4 vols. per year) ISSN 0065-4116

**Suedafrikanischer Germanistenverband**
University of Stellenbosch, German Department, Stellenbosch 7600, South Africa
(or University of the Orange Free State, German Department, Box 339, Bloemfontein 9300, South Africa)
- Deutschunterricht in Suedafrika. s-a. ISSN 0012-1487

**Suid-Afrikaanse Aalwyn- en Vetplantvereniging**
see South African Aloe and Succulent Society

**Suid-Afrikaanse Akademie vir Wetenskap en Kuns**
Box 538, Pretoria 0001, South Africa.
- Christiaan de Wet Annale. s-a.
- Suid-Afrikaanse Akademie vir Wetenskap en Kuns. Nuusbrief. 4 per yr. ISSN 0039-4807
- Tegnikon. q. ISSN 0040-215X
- Tydskrif vir Geesteswetenskappe. q. ISSN 0041-4751
- Tydskrif vir Natuurwetenskappe. q. ISSN 0041-4786

**Suid-Afrikaanse Genootskap vir die Bevordering van die Wetenskap**
see South African Association for the Advancement of Science

**Systems Publishers (Pty) Ltd.**
Box 31720, Braamfontein, Transvaal, South Africa.
- Systems/Stelsels. m. ISSN 0049-2795 (Computer Society of South Africa)

**T.C.M. Publishing Co. (Pty) Ltd.**
Estella House, 47A Main Rd., Claremont, Cape Town, South Africa.
- Christian Minister. m. ISSN 0009-5486

**Tafelberg Publishers**
Box 879, Cape Town, South Africa.
- Standpunte. 6 per yr. ISSN 0038-9730

**Taxpayer (Pty.) Ltd.**
Box 3191, 302 French Bank Bldg., 4 Church Square, Cape Town, South Africa.
- Taxpayer; a monthly journal devoted to the law, practice and incidence of income tax and death duties. m. ISSN 0040-0270

**Thomson Publications S.A. (Pty) Ltd.**
Box 8308, Johannesburg 2000, South Africa.
- Chemical Industry Buyers' Guide for S. A. biennial.
- Commercial Transport and Freight. m. (Motor Transport Owners' Association in South Africa)
- Commercial Transport Handbook and Buyers Guide for S. A. a. ISSN 0069-6676
- Electrical Engineer. m.
- Electronics and Instrumentation. m. ISSN 0013-5186
- Food Industries of South Africa; processing, refrigeration, packaging. m. ISSN 0015-6450
- Food Industries Yearbook and Buyers' Directory. a.
- Hospital and Nursing Yearbook of Southern Africa. a. ISSN 0441-2613
- Merkels' Builders' Pricing and Management Manual. a.
- Metal Industries. m. (Association of Metal Sprayers)
- Mildex Motor Book. a. ISSN 0076-8766
- Motor World. m.
- New Equipment News. m. ISSN 0028-498X
- Pakprint. bi-m.
- Plastics and Rubber News. m.
- Plastics, Rubber and Paint Yearbook and Buyers' Guide of S.A. a.
- Power & Plant in Southern Africa; incorporating Chemical Processing. m. ISSN 0032-5937
- Public Works, Construction & Transport. m. ISSN 0030-3496
- Railways Southern Africa. bi-m.
- S. A. Building Products News. m. ISSN 0007-3369
- S. A. Fishing Industry Handbook and Buyers Guide. biennial. ISSN 0080-5076
- S. A. Hardware. m. ISSN 0038-2191
- S. A. Insurance. m. ISSN 0038-2256 (Life Underwriters Association of South Africa) (Co-sponsor: South African Registered Insurance Brokers Association)
- S. A. Journal of Hospital Medicine. m.
- S. A. Materials Handling News; what's new in plant methods and industrial automation. m. ISSN 0025-6579 (South African Institute of Materials Handling) (Co-sponsor: Materials Handling and Construction Plant Association)

- S. A. Medical Equipment News. m. ISSN 0038-2205
- S. A. Mining and Engineering Journal. m. ISSN 0038-2477
- S. A. Mining and Engineering Yearbook. a. ISSN 0081-2498
- S. A. Shipping News and Fishing Industry Review. m. ISSN 0038-2671
- S. A. Textiles. m. ISSN 0038-3791
- Security and Protection of South Africa. bi-m.
- Shoes & Views. m.

**Thrust Publications**
Box 47160, Greyville 4023, South Africa.
- Thrust; for youth by youth. 5 per yr. (Young Christian Workers)

**Times of Gonubie**
c/o S. R. Chapman, Ed., 11 Meierist Gonubie, East London, South Africa.
- Times of Gonubie. m.

**Transkei Teachers Association**
Box 197, Umtata, South Africa.
- T. T. A. s-a. ISSN 0039-8497

**Transvaal. Education Department**
Private Bag X76, Pretoria, South Africa.
- Transvaal. Education Department. Education Bulletin/Transvaalse. Onderwysdepartement. Onderwysbulletin. 3 per yr.
- Transvaal. Education Department. Educational News Flashes/Onderwysnuusflitse. 3 per yr. ISSN 0013-1830

**Transvaal. Education Library Service**
- School Library/Skoolbiblioteek. (pub. by Transvaal School Library Association)

**Transvaal. Nature Conservation Division**
Private Bag X209, Pretoria, South Africa.
- Fauna & Flora. irreg. ISSN 0046-3388

**Transvaal Farmer**
c/o Ponie de Wet, Ed., Box 20, Pretoria, South Africa.
- Transvaal Farmer/Transvaalse Boer. q. ISSN 0041-1736

**Transvaal High School Teachers' Association**
72 Julius Jeppe St., Waterkloof, Pretoria, Transvaal, South Africa.
- Journal for Secondary Education/Tydskrif vir Middelbare Onderwys. q. ISSN 0041-4778

**Transvaal Horticultural Society**
Box 7616, Johannesburg, South Africa.
- Transvaal Gardener. m. ISSN 0041-1744

**Transvaal Museum**
Box 413, Pretoria, Transvaal, South Africa.
- Transvaal Museum. Bulletin. irreg. ISSN 0496-1102
- Transvaal Museum Annals/Transvaal Museum Annale. irreg. ISSN 0041-1752

**Transvaal Provincial Golf Association**
Box 4645, Johannesburg, South Africa.
- Golfer. q. ISSN 0017-1913

**Transvaal School Library Association**
Private Bag X290, Pretoria 0001, South Africa.
- School Library/Skoolbiblioteek. s-a. ISSN 0036-6617 (Transvaal. Education Library Service)

**Transvaal Teachers' Association**
38 Honey St., Berea, Johannesburg 2198, Transvaal, South Africa.
- Transvaal Educational News. m. ISSN 0041-1728

**Transvaal Women's Agricultural Union**
Box 11226, Brooklyn, Pretoria 0011, South Africa.
- T. W. A. U. News/T. V. L. U. Nuus. m. ISSN 0039-8640

**Transvaalse Raad vir die Uitvoerende Kunste**
see Performing Arts Council Transvaal

**Tree Society of Southern Africa**
Box 4116, Johannesburg, South Africa.
- Trees in South Africa/Bome in Suid-Afrika. q. ISSN 0041-2236

**Trio-Rand Publishers**
Pinelands, Cape Province, South Africa.
- Matieland. 3 per yr. ISSN 0025-5947 (University of Stellenbosch)

**Tydskrif vir Letterkunde**
Posbus 1758, Pretoria, South Africa.
- Tydskrif vir Letterkunde. q. ISSN 0041-476X

**Tydskriftemaatskappy van die Nederduitse Gereformeerde Kerk**
Box 2406, Pretoria 0001, Johannesburg, South Africa.
- Voorligter. m. ISSN 0042-8728

**Underground Officials' Association of South Africa**
- Underground Official. (pub. by Felstar Publishers (Pty.) Ltd.)

**Union Acceptances Ltd.**
Box 582, Johannesburg 2000, South Africa.
- U A L Executive Guide to the Economy. m. (prep. by its Nedsual Economic Unit)

**Union Bible Institute**
Box 50, Hilton 3245, South Africa.
- Ubaqa Lwabantwana. s-m. ISSN 0041-5634

**United South African National Party**
- Volkstem. (pub. by Inspan Publishers (Pty) Ltd.)

**University of Cape Town**
Private Bag, Rondebosch 7700, South Africa.
- T. B. Davie Memorial Lecture. a. ISSN 0082-1330
- University of Cape Town. Fact Paper. irreg. (prep. by its News and Infromation Bureau)

**University of Cape Town. Centre for Intergroup Studies**
Rondebosch, South Africa.
- University of Cape Town. Centre for Intergroup Studies. Annual Report. a.

**University of Cape Town. Department of English**
Rondebosch 7700, South Africa.
- U C T Studies in English. irreg.

**University of Cape Town. Department of Geology**
Rondebosch 7700, South Africa.
- University of Cape Town. Department of Geology. Precambrian Research Unit. Bulletin. 2-3 per yr. ISSN 0041-9478

**University of Cape Town. Department of Obstetrics and Gynaecology**
Observatory C.P., Cape Town, South Africa.
- University of Cape Town. Department of Obstetrics and Gynaecology. Annual Report. a.

**University of Cape Town. Department of Sociology**
Rondebosch, Cape Town 7700, South Africa.
- Social Dynamics. irreg.

**University of Cape Town. Faculty of Law**
- Acta Juridica. (pub. by Juta & Co. Ltd.)

**University of Cape Town. Science Students' Council**
Rondebosch, Cape Province, South Africa.
- Impulse. 3 per yr.

**University of Cape Town. Student Law Society**
Cape Town 7700, South Africa.
- Responsa Meridiana; an annual law review. a. ISSN 0486-5588 (Co-sponsor: University of Stellenbosch, Student Law Society)

**University of Cape Town. Students Health and Welfare Centres Organisation (SHAWCO)**
12th Ave., Kensington, Cape Town, South Africa.
- Shawcover. 3 per yr. ISSN 0037-3362

**University of Cape Town. Students Representative Council**
- Varsity. (pub. by S.R.C. Press)

**University of Durban-Westville**
Private Bag X54001, Durban 4000, South Africa.
- University of Durban-Westville. Journal. a. ISSN 0070-7740

**University of Fort Hare. Faculty of Law**
Fort Hare, South Africa.
- Speculum Juris. a. ISSN 0584-8652

**University of Natal**
2 West St., Durban, Natal, South Africa.
- Natal Regional Survey. Additional Report. (pub. by Lawrence Verry, Inc. (U.S. Distrib.) US)

- University of Natal. Oceanographic Research Institute. Investigational Report. irreg, 3-4 per yr. ISSN 0078-320X (University of Natal. Oceanographic Research Institute) (Co-sponsor: South African Association for Marine Biological Research)

**University of Natal. Faculty of Arts**
- Theoria. (pub. by University of Natal Press)

**University of Natal. Faculty of Medicine**
P.O. Box 39, Congella, Durban, Natal, South Africa.
- Amoeba. irreg. ISSN 0066-1279

**University of Natal. Institute for Social Research**
Durban, South Africa.
- University of Natal. Institute for Social Research. Annual Report. a. ISSN 0070-7759

**University of Natal. Oceanographic Research Institute**
- University of Natal. Oceanographic Research Institute. Investigational Report. (pub. by University of Natal)

**University of Natal Press**
Box 375, Pietermaritzburg, South Africa.
- Theoria; a journal of studies in the arts, humanities and social sciences. s-a. ISSN 0040-5817 (University of Natal. Faculty of Arts)

**University of Natal. Students Engineering Society**
King George IV Ave., Durban 4001, South Africa.
- Pulse. a. ISSN 0555-6945
- Throb. 5 per yr. ISSN 0040-6589

**University of Natal. Students Geographical Society**
Durban, South Africa.
- Isizwe. a.

**University of Natal. Students Representative Council**
Box 375, Pietermaritzburg, South Africa.
- Edgar Brookes Academic and Human Freedom Lecture. a. ISSN 0070-8976
- Nux. 12 per yr. ISSN 0029-6716

**University of Port Elizabeth**
Private Bag 6058, Port Elizabeth 6000, South Africa.
- Libra. a. since 1972. ISSN 0024-2101 (prep. by its Library)
- U P E N. (University of Port Elizabeth Newspaper) fortn. ISSN 0041-5405
- University of Port Elizabeth. Publications. General Series. irreg., no. A 13, 1975. ISSN 0079-3957
- University of Port Elizabeth. Publications. Inaugural and Emeritus Addresses. irreg., no. D 12, 1976. ISSN 0085-5022
- University of Port Elizabeth. Publications. Research Papers. irreg., no. C 13, 1977. ISSN 0079-3965
- University of Port Elizabeth. Publications. Symposia, Seminars, and Lectures. irreg., no. B 4, 1977.

**University of Port Elizabeth. Institute for Planning Research**
Box 1600, Port Elizabeth 6000, South Africa.
- University of Port Elizabeth. Institute for Planning Research. Annual Report. a, latest 1972.

**University of Pretoria**
Director of Public Relations, Hillcrest, Pretoria, South Africa.
- Link-Up. 1-3 per yr. ISSN 0024-4015
- Mens en Gemeenskap. (pub. by H.A.U.M.)
- Skakelblad. a. ISSN 0037-6051
- Universiteit van Pretoria. Publikasies. Nuwe Reeks. irreg.

**University of Pretoria. Departement Bantoetale**
Pretoria, South Africa.
- Studies in Bantoetale. a.

**University of Pretoria. Deutsch-Africanischen Studentenbundes**
Pretoria, South Africa.
- D A S U P. (Deutsch-Africanischen Studentenbundes, Universitaet Pretoria) s-a. ISSN 0011-4731

**University of Pretoria. Faculty of Education**
Pretoria, South Africa.
- Suid-Afrikaanse Tydskrif vir Die Pedagogiek/South African Journal of Pedagogy. s-a. ISSN 0039-4815

**University of Pretoria Student Publishers**
Student Council Office, 84 Tindall Rd., Box 3194, Pretoria, South Africa.
- Venturi. 7 per yr. ISSN 0042-3572

**University of South Africa**
Box 392, Pretoria 0001, South Africa.
- Iter. s-a. ISSN 0301-7788
- Semitics. a.

**University of South Africa. Department of Art History and Fine Arts**
Box 392, Pretoria 0001, South Africa.
- De Arte. a. ISSN 0004-3389

**University of South Africa. Department of Bantu Languages**
Box 392, Pretoria 0001, South Africa.
- Limi. a. ISSN 0024-3558

**University of South Africa. Department of Development Administration and Politics**
P.O. Box 392, Pretoria 0001, South Africa.
- Africanus. a. ISSN 0304-615X

**University of South Africa. Department of English**
Box 392, Pretoria 0001, South Africa.
- English Usage in Southern Africa. s-a. ISSN 0046-2098
- U N I S A English Studies. s-a. ISSN 0041-5359

**University of South Africa. Department of History**
Box 392, Pretoria 0001, South Africa.
- Kleio. a. ISSN 0023-2084

**University of South Africa. Department of Library Science**
Box 392, Pretoria 0001, South Africa.
- Mousaion; library science contributions. irreg. ISSN 0027-2639 (Co-sponsor: University Library)

**University of South Africa. Faculty of Education**
P. O. Box 392, Pretoria 0001, South Africa.
- Educare. a.

**University of South Africa. Faculty of Law**
Box 392, Pretoria 0001, South Africa.
- Codicillus. s-a. ISSN 0010-020X

**University of South Africa. Institute of Foreign and Comparative Law**
Box 392, Pretoria 0001, South Africa.
- Comparative and International Law Journal of Southern Africa. 3 per yr. ISSN 0010-4051

**University of Stellenbosch**
- Matieland. (pub. by Trio-Rand Publishers)

**University of Stellenbosch. Bureau for Economic Research**
Stellenbosch, South Africa.
- University of Stellenbosch. Bureau for Economic Research. Building Survey; report on business conditions in the building industry. q. ISSN 0045-3447
- University of Stellenbosch. Bureau for Economic Research. Opinion Survey Report. q.
- University of Stellenbosch. Bureau for Economic Research. Survey of Contemporary Economic Conditions and Prospects. a. ISSN 0081-5454
- University of Stellenbosch. Bureau for Economic Research. Survey of Investment Intentions. irreg.

**University of Stellenbosch. Department of Latin**
Stellenbosch 7600, South Africa.
- Akroterion. q. ISSN 0023-2033 (Co-sponsor: Classical Association of South Africa)

**University of the North. Department of Bantu Languages**
P.O. Sovenga, Pietersburg, South Africa.
- University of the North. Department of Bantu Languages. Communications. a.

**University of the Orange Free State**
P.O. Box 339, Bloemfontein, South Africa.
- University of the Orange Free State. Opsommings van Proefskrifte en Verhandelinge. Abstracts of Dissertations and Theses. a. ISSN 0067-9216

**University of the Orange Free State. Institute for Contemporary History**
P.O. Box 2320, Bloemfontein, South Africa.
- Acta Diurna Historica. s-a. ISSN 0301-6129

**University of the Witwatersrand, Johannesburg**
Jan Smuts Ave., Johannesburg, South Africa.
- University of the Witwatersrand, Johannesburg. University Gazette. s-a. ISSN 0042-0182

**University of the Witwatersrand, Johannesburg. Bernard Price Institute for Palaeontological Research**
Jan Smuts Ave., Johannesburg, South Africa.
- Palaeontologia Africana. irreg.; (approx. a) vol. 16, 1973. ISSN 0078-8554

**University of the Witwatersrand, Johannesburg. Faculty of Medicine**
- Pulse Beat. (pub. by Alex White and Co. (Pty) Ltd.)

**University of the Witwatersrand, Johannesburg. Library**
Jan Smuts Ave., Johannesburg 2001, South Africa.
- University of the Witwatersrand, Johannesburg. Libraries. Annual Report. a. ISSN 0075-3807

**University of the Witwatersrand, Johannesburg. Medical School**
7A Esselen St., Hillbrow, Johannesburg, South Africa.
- Auricle. m. ISSN 0004-8070 (prep. by its Students Medical Council)

**University of the Witwatersrand, Johannesburg. School of Mechanical Engineering**
Jan Smuts Ave., Johannesburg, South Africa.
- University of Witwatersrand, Johannesburg. School of Mechanical Engineering. Reports. irreg.

**University of the Witwatersrand, Johannesburg. Student Engineers Council**
South West Engineering Block, Room B1, 1 Jan Smuts Ave., Johannesburg 2001, South Africa.
- Fulcrum. a. ISSN 0071-979X

**Veer**
Post Box 1600, Port Elizabeth, South Africa.
- Veer.

**Veteran Car Club of South Africa**
Box 1204, Durban, Natal, South Africa.
- Veterantics. q. ISSN 0042-4811

**Volkskas- Amptenarevereniging**
Box 578, Pretoria, Johannesburg, South Africa.
- Opsaal. q. ISSN 0030-3879

**Volkskas Ltd.**
Box 578, Pretoria, South Africa.
- Finance and Trade Review. q. ISSN 0015-1955

**Laurie Wale (Pty) Ltd.**
Box 4591, Cape Town, South Africa.
- Architect & Builder. m. ISSN 0003-8407

**George Warman Publications (Pty) Ltd.**
Box 3847, Cape Town 8000, South Africa.
- Corrosion and Coatings. bi-m. (South African Corrosion Institute)
- Dyers Digest. bi-m.
- Plastics Southern Africa. bi-m. ISSN 0048-4385 (Plastics Institute of South Africa)
- Purchasing South Africa. bi-m. (Institute of Purchasing)
- S. A. Hairdressing and Beauty Culture. m. ISSN 0036-0759
- South African Bakery and Confectionery Review. bi-m.
- South African Laundry and Cleaning Review. bi-m. (Johannesburg Laundry & Dry Cleaners Association)
- South African Machine Tool Review. m. ISSN 0036-0848
- STATS - Statistical Review. m.

**Watch Tower Bible & Tract Society**
Private Bag 2, Elandsfontein 1406, Transvaal, South Africa.
- Galamukani. m. ISSN 0016-3988
- I-Mboniselo. s-m. ISSN 0019-008X
- I Nqabayokulinda. s-m. ISSN 0019-0241
- Molula-Qhooa. s-m. ISSN 0026-9093
- Morokami. m. ISSN 0027-1179
- Nharireyomurindi. s-m. ISSN 0028-9639
- Nsanja Ya Olonda. s-m. ISSN 0029-5442
- Ontwaak. s-m. ISSN 0030-316X
- Phaphama. s-m. ISSN 0031-6806
- Tora Ya Tebelo. m. ISSN 0040-9391

**Water Research Commission**
Van der Stel Building, Box 824, Pretorius Street, Pretoria, South Africa.
- Current Literature on Water. (pub. by South African Water Information Centre)
- Water Research Commission. Report. a.

**White and Boughton (Pty) Ltd.**
Box 90, Cradock, South Africa.
- Nuwe Afrikaner. w. ISSN 0048-119X

**Alex White and Co. (Pty) Ltd.**
Box 4886, Johannesburg, South Africa.
- Dairy Industry Journal of Southern Africa/ Suiwelnywerheidsjoernaal van Suidelike Afrika. q. ISSN 0011-5630
- Pulse Beat. m. ISSN 0033-4200 (University of the Witwatersrand, Johannesburg. Faculty of Medicine)

**Wildlife Society of Southern Africa**
Box 44189, Linden 2104, South Africa.
- African Wildlife. bi-m. ISSN 0002-0273

**Wildlife Society of Southern Africa. E. P. Branch**
2C Lawrence St., Port Elizabeth 6001, South Africa.
- Eastern Cape Naturalist. 3 per yr. ISSN 0012-8724

**Wildlife Society of Southern Africa. Natal Branch**
100 Brand Rd., Durban 4001, South Africa.
- Natal Wildlife. m. ISSN 0027-8343

**Wildlife Society of Southern Africa. Transvaal Branch**
Box 61365, Marshalltown 2107, Transvaal, South Africa.
- Chat. m. ISSN 0045-6365

**Witwatersrand University Press**
Jan Smuts Ave., Johannesburg 2001, South Africa.
- African Studies; a biannual journal devoted to the study of african anthropology, government and languages. s-a. ISSN 0002-0184
- Bantu Treasury. irreg. ISSN 0067-4044
- English Studies in Africa; a journal of the humanities. s-a. ISSN 0013-8398
- Raymond Dart Lecture. a. ISSN 0079-9815 (Institute for the Study of Man in Africa)

**Women's Zionist Council of South Africa**
Zionist Centre, Box 18, Johannesburg 2000, South Africa.
- Women's Zionist Council of South Africa. News and Views. 5 per yr. ISSN 0043-7603

**I.J.A. Wood, Pub.**
Box 44, 12 Miller St., De Aar, South Africa.
- Echo (De Aar). w. ISSN 0011-7161 (Co-publishers: C. Wood, R. E. Wood)

**World Printing and Publishing Co. (Pty) Ltd**
P.O. Box 1491, Durban, South Africa.
- Weekend World. w.
- World. d. ISSN 0043-8162

**Yachting News (Pty) Ltd.**
Van der Stel Bldg., 58 Burg St., Cape Town, South Africa.
- South African Yachting-Power, Waterski & Sail. m.

**Yomtov Bletter**
65 Seventh Ave., Highlands North, Box 7690, Johannesburg 2000, South Africa.
- Yomtov Bletter. q. ISSN 0044-054X

**Young Christian Workers**
- Thrust. (pub. by Thrust Publications)

**Zionist Record (Pty) Ltd.**
84 De Villiers St., Johannesburg, South Africa.
- Zionist Record and S. A. Jewish Chronicle; the organ of South African Jewry. w. ISSN 0044-4782 (South African Zionist Federation)

**Zionist Revisionist Organisation of South Africa**
- Jewish Herald. (pub. by Jewish Herald (Pty) Ltd.)

**Zoological Society of Southern Africa**
c/o South African Museum, Box 61, Cape Town, South Africa.
- Zoologica Africana. (pub. by A. A. Balkema Ltd.)
- Zoological Society of Southern Africa. Occasional Bulletin. irreg.

**1820 Settler's Association of South Africa**
415 Union Centre, 55 Harrison St., Johannesburg, South Africa.
- 1820; the settlers' magazine on South Africa. m. ISSN 0013-256X

# SPAIN

**Publicaciones de l' Abadia de Montserrat**
Ausias March 92-98, Ap. 244, Barcelona 13, Spain.
- Documents d'Esglesia. fortn.
- Questions de Vida Cristiana. 5 per yr.
- Serra d'Or. m. ISSN 0037-2501
- Studia Monastica; commentarium ad rem monasticam historice investigandam. s-a. ISSN 0039-3258

**Abadia de Santo Domingo de Silos**
Burgos, Spain.
- Studia Silensia. a.

**Antonio Abarca Benito, Ed. & Pub.**
Ave Jose Antonio, 410, Barcelona 15, Spain.
- Revitec; revista tecnica tintoreria y lavanderia. m.
- Revitec 2; revista tecnica lavanderia clinicas, hospitales, colegios, conunidades y hoteles. m.

**Academia de Ciencias Exactes, Fisico-Quimicas y Naturales. Facultad de Ciencias**
Zaragoza, Spain.
- Academia de Ciencias Exactas, Fisico-Quimicas y Naturales, Zaragoza. Revista. q.

**Academia de Ciencias Medicas de Bilbao**
Lersundi 11, Bilbao 9, Spain.
- Gaceta Medica de Bilbao. m.

**Academia de Ciencias Medicas de Cataluna y Baleares**
551 Paseo de la Bonanova 47, Barcelona 6, Spain.
- Anales de Medicina. Especialidades. ISSN 0517-6832
- Anales de Medicina. Medicina. ISSN 0517-6824

**Academia de Jurisprudencia y Legislacion. Colegio de Abogados de Barcelona**
Mallorca 283, Barcelona, Spain.
- Revista Juridica de Cataluna. q.

**Academia Espanola de Dermatologia y Sifiliografia**
- Actas Dermo-Sifiliograficas. (pub. by Editorial Garsi)

**Academia ROCOSA**
- Boletin Tecnico Sartorial. (pub. by D. Emilio Oromi, Ed. & Pub.)

**Accion Catolica Olot**
Paseo Blay 13, Girona, Spain.
- Olot - Mision. w.

**Accion Social Empresarial Comision Nacional**
Alfonso XI 4, Madrid 14, Spain.
- Accion Empresarial; la revista del directivo. m. ISSN 0044-5894

**Acta Iberica Radiologica-Cancerologica**
Vitrubio 11, Madrid 6, Spain.
- Acta Iberica Radiologica-Cancerologica. q. ISSN 0001-589X

**Acta Obstetrica y Ginecologica Hispano-Lusitania**
c/o Manuel Usandizaga, Santalo 11, Barcelona, Spain.
- Acta Obstetrica y Ginecologica Hispano-Lusitania. 9 per yr. ISSN 0001-5784

**Acta Pediatrica Espanola**
Ayala 45, Madrid 1, Spain.
- Acta Pediatrica Espanola. 10 per yr. ISSN 0001-6640

**Actualidad Filatelica**
Plaza Mayor, 29, Madrid-12, Spain.
- Actualidad Filatelica. m.

**Aeroguia S.A.**
Concha Espina 8, Madrid-16, Spain.
- Guia Espanola del Transporte. q.

**Agencia Espanola I S B N**
Santiago Rusinol 10, Madrid 3, Spain.
- Libros Espanoles I S B N. (Instituto Nacional del Libro Espanol)

**Editorial Agricola Espanola, S.A.**
Cabellero de Gracia 24, Madrid 14, Spain.
- Agricultura; revista agropecuaria. m. ISSN 0002-1334

**Agrupacion Astronomica de Sabadell**
Cardenal Goma 1, Sabadell (Barcelona), Spain.
- Astrum. irreg.; approx. q.

**Agrupacion de Periodistas de Informacion Economica**
Plaza del Callao 4, Madrid 13, Spain.
- Agrupacion de Periodistas de Informacion Economica. Informe. a.

**Agrupacion Nacional Autonoma de Industriales de Plasticos**
Sindicato Nacional de Industrias Quimicas, San Bernardo, 62, Madrid, Spain.
- Guia Catalogo Plasticos Espanoles. irreg.

**Agrupacion National de Tecnicos de Turismo**
Lopez de Hayos 78, Madrid 2, Spain.
- Posada y Camino. bi-m. ISSN 0032-518X

**Agrupacion Sindical de Productores**
see **Uniespana**

**Antonio Agudo Izquierdo, Ed. & Pub.**
Cana 59, Madrid 24, Spain
(Subscrip. Address: Sagasta, 19, Madrid -4- Spain)
- Petrogas. m.

**Editorial Alas**
Valencia 234, Barcelona 7, Spain.
- Revista de las Artes Marciales. m.

**P. Francisco Albarracin Pascual, S.J.**
Claudio Coello 129, Madrid 6, Spain.
- Unidad Cristiana-Oriente Cristiano. q. ISSN 0041-6711

**Ediciones Alcala S.A.**
Colombia 18, Madrid 16, Spain.
- Iberoromania; Zeitschrift fuer die Sprachen und Literaturen von Spanien, Portugal und Iber-Amerika. 3 per yr.

**Editorial Alcion**
Pedro de Valdivia 29, Madrid 6, Spain.
- M I. (Montajes e Instalaciones); revista mensual sobre ingenieria de instalaciones. m.

**Alemas**
Seccion Publicidad, Quinones 15-1, Madrid 8, Spain.
- Alemas; revista espanola de alquitranes, emulsiones, asfaltos e impermeabilizantes. m. ISSN 0002-5143

**Ediciones Alfaguara S.A.**
Avenida de America, 37, Madrid 2, Spain.
- Estudios de Literatura Contemporanea. irreg. ISSN 0071-1705

**Alter S.A.**
Mateo Inrria 3, Madrid 16, Spain.
- Publicaciones Cientificas Alter. bi-m. ISSN 0033-3867

**Ediciones Jose Luis Alvarez**
Nueva Zelanda 50. Torre Montserrat, Madrid 35, Spain.
- A L S A R. (Al Servicio de Una Agricultura Rentable) m.
- Canciones Cifradas-J L A. m.
- Fono 2; la revista de los jovenes y de la musica. m.

**Ama**
Calle las Fuentes 13, Madrid 13, Spain.
- Ama. s-m.

**Andalan**
Aznar Molina 15-17, Zaragoza, Spain.
- Andalan; periodico quincenal aragones. s-m.

**Antena de Telecommunicacion**
c/o Jamie Ruiz de Infante, Ed., Hermanos Miralles, No. 14, Madrid-1, Spain.
- Antena de Telecommunicacion. q.

**Antibioticos, S.A.**
Bravo Murillo, 38, Madrid, Spain.
- Tribuna Medica. w.

**Editorial Aranzadi**
Pamplona, Spain.
- Spain. Tribunal Central de Trabajo. Repertorio de Sentencias. s-a.

**Ediciones Ariel, S.A.**
134-138 Esplugas de Llobregat, Barcelona, Spain.
- Acero y Energia; revista tecnica de ingenieria industrial. bi-m. ISSN 0001-4850
- Crol. m. ISSN 0011-1694 (Federacion Espanola de Natacion)
- Revista Iberica de Endocrinologia. bi-m. ISSN 0034-9615

**Arte Fotografico S.L.**
Calle D. Ramon de la Cruz 53, Madrid-1, Spain.
- Arte Fotografico. bi-m. ISSN 0514-9193

**Arteguia**
Paseo de la Castellana 53, Madrid 1, Spain.
- Arteguia. m., Oct.-may.

**Arzobispado de Madrid-Alcala**
c/o Bailen 8, Madrid-13, Spain.
- Archidiocesis de Madrid-Alcala. Boletin Oficial. s-m.

**Arzobispado de Sevilla. Oficina Diocesana de Informacion**
Apartado Postal 6, Sevilla, Spain.
- Arzobispado de Sevilla. Boletin Oficial Eclesiastico. m.

**Asociacion Asturiana de Amigos de la Naturaleza**
Santa Susana, 35, Oviedo, Spain.
- Asturnatura. irreg.

**Asociacion Comercial Hispano-Sueca**
Marques de Casa Riera, 4, Madrid-14, Spain.
- Asociacion Comercial Hispano-Sueca. Circular Informativa. s-m.

**Asociacion de Academias de la Lengua Espanola Comision Permanente. Boletn**
Calle de Felipe IV 4, Madrid 14, Spain.
- Asociacion de Academias de la Lengua Espanola Comision Permanente. Boletn. s-a.

**Asociacion de Centros Farmaceuticos de Espana S.A.**
General Oraa 70, Madrid 6, Spain.
- Monitor de la Farmacia y de la Terapeutica. m.

**Asociacion de Estudios Cooperativos**
Heroes del 10 de Agosto 5, 4 Andar, Madrid-1, Spain.
- Boletin de Formacion Cooperativa. bi-m. ISSN 0006-6273
- Estudios Cooperativos. 3 per yr. (Co-sponsor: Universidad de Madrid. Catedra Libre de Cooperacion)

**Asociacion de Hidalgos a Fuero de Espana**
Atocha, 91 Madrid 12, Spain.
- Gacetilia del Estado de Hidalgos. m.

**Asociacion de Ingenieros Aeronauticos**
Departamento de Publiciadad, Juan Bta. de Toledo 30, Madrid-2, Spain.
- Ingenieria Aeronautica y Astronautica. bi-m. ISSN 0020-1006

**Asociacion de Ingenieros de Montes**
Jorge Juan 39- 2, Madrid-1, Spain.
- Montes. bi-m. ISSN 0027-0105

**Asociacion de Ingenieros del I. C. A. I.**
Reina 31, Madrid, Spain.
- Anales de Mecanica y Electricidad. bi-m. ISSN 0003-2506

**Asociacion de Ingenieros Navales**
Apdo. Correos 457, Madrid, Spain.
- Ingenieria Naval. m. ISSN 0020-1073

**Asociacion de Investigacion Industrial Electrica**
Francisco Gervas 3, Madrid, Spain.
- Boletin ASINEL. 3 per yr.

**Asociacion de Investigacion Tecnica de la Industria Papelera Espanola**
Avda. Padre Huidobro, s/n, Carr. de la Coruna, Km. 7, Madrid 35, Spain.
- Investigacion y Tecnica del Papel. q.

**Asociacion de Investigacion Tecnica de las Industrias de la Madera**
Flora 1, Madrid 13, Spain.
- A I T I M Boletin de Informacion Tecnica. s-m. ISSN 0044-9261

**Asociacion de Investigacion Textil Algodonera**
Avda. Jose Antonio, 670, Barcelona, Spain.
- Asociacion de Investigacion Textil Algodonera. Coleccion de Manuales Tecnicos. irreg. ISSN 0571-3609
- Asociacion de Investigacion Textil Algodonera. Estudios y Documentos. irreg.
- Serie de Ingenieria de la Calidad.

**Asociacion de la Prensa de Lugo**
Jose A. Primo de Rivera, 12, Lugo, Spain.
- Hoja del Lunes de Lugo. w. ISSN 0018-3296

**Asociacion de la Prensa Medica Espanola**
Carlos Caamano 5, Madrid 16, Spain.
- Gaceta Medica Espanola. m. ISSN 0016-3821
- Odontoiatria; revista Ibero-Americana de medicina de la boca. m. ISSN 0029-8395

**Asociacion de Maestros Pintores de Barcelona**
Diputacion 297, Pral., Barcelona, Spain.
- Pintores. m. ISSN 0031-9945

**Asociacion de Obstetricia y Ginecologia**
- Revista Espanola de Obstetricia y Ginecologia. (pub. by Editorial Facta)

**Asociacion de Quimicos y Coloristas Textiles**
- Revista de Quimica Textil. (pub. by Editecnia, S.A.)

**Asociacion de San Jorge de Alcoy**
- Alcoy; Fiesta de Moros y Cristianos. (pub. by Casa de Escritores)

**Asociacion Espanola Contra el Cancer**
Calle Amador de los Rios 5, Madrid 4, Spain.
- Asociacion Espanola Contra el Cancer. Memoria de la Asamblea General. a. ISSN 0066-8540

**Asociacion Espanola de Amigos de los Castillos**
Genova 23, 30 D CHA, Madrid 4, Spain.
- Castillos de Espana. q. ISSN 0008-7505

**Asociacion Espanola de Cirujanos**
- Cirugia Espanola. (pub. by Editorial Garsi)

**Asociacion Espanola de la Carretera**
Serrano 57, Madrid 6, Spain.
- C A. bi-m.
- Carreteras. m. ISSN 0008-6908

**Asociacion Espanola de la Prensa Tecnica**
Paseo de Gracia, 50, Barcelona, Spain.
- Asociacion Espanola de la Prensa Tecnica. Catalogo de Publicaciones Asociadas. irreg.

**Asociacion Espanola de Lucha Contra el Fuego**
Sepulveda, 162, Barcelona 9, Spain.
- A S E L F. bi-m. ISSN 0571-3684

**Asociacion Espanola de Lucha Contra la Contaminacion Ambiental**
c/o Raimundo Fernandez Villaverde, 19 Madrid-3, Spain.
- Medio Ambiente. q.

**Asociacion Espanola de Orientalistas**
- Asociacion Espanola de Orientalistas. Boletin. (pub. by F. M. Pareja, Ed. & Pub.)

**Asociacion Espanola de Technicos de Cerveza y Malta**
Juan de la Cierva, 3, Madrid 6, Spain.
- Cerveza y Malta. q. ISSN 0300-4481

**Asociacion Espanola de Tecnicos de Maquinaria para la Construccion y Obras Publicas**
Cruz del sur 3, Madrid 30, Spain.
- Revista A T E M C O P. m (10 per yr)

**Asociacion Espanola de Urologia**
- Archivos Espanoles de Urologia. (pub. by Editorial Garsi)

**Asociacion Espanola Hematologia y Hemoterapia**
Av. Marina Moreno 10, Zaragoza, Spain.
- Sangre; revista de biologia y patologia sanguineas y hemoterapia. bi-m. ISSN 0036-4355

**Asociacion Espanola para el Control de la Calidad**
- Cero Defectos. (pub. by Julian Yebenes Guerrero)

**Asociacion Espanola para el Progreso de las Ciencias**
Valverde 22, Madrid (13), Spain.
- Ciencias. q. ISSN 0009-6776

**Asociacion Nacional de Bibliotecarios, Archiveros y Arqueologos**
Avda. de Calvo Sotelo 22, Apart. 14.281, Madrid 1, Spain.
- A. N. A. B. A. Boletin. q. ISSN 0044-9288
- Congreso Nacional de Bibliotecas. Ponencias, Comunicaciones y Cronica. irreg.

**Asociacion Nacional de Ingenieros Industriales. Agrupacion de Tataluna**
Via Layetana 39, Barcelona 3, Spain.
- Novatecnia. bi-m.

**Asociacion Nacional de Ingenieros Industriales de Espana**
Alda. Mazarredo, 69, 5D, Apdo. 646, Bilbao, Spain.
- Dyna. m. ISSN 0012-7361

**Asociacion Nacional de Medicos Forenses**
Goya 99, Madrid 9, Spain.
- Revista Espanola de Medicina Legal. bi-m.

**Asociacion Nacional de Peritos e Ingenieros Tecnico Industriales**
Av. Dr. Federico Rubio y Gali, 2, Madrid-3, Spain.
- Tecnica Industrial. bi-m. ISSN 0040-1838

**Asociacion Nacional de Quimicos de Espana**
Lagasca 83, Madrid 6, Spain.
- Quimica e Industria. m. ISSN 0033-6521

**Asociacion Numismatica Espanola**
Avda. Jose Antonio 627, Barcelona 10, Spain.
- Gaceta Numismatica. q.

**Asociacion "Omnium Cultural"**
Montcada 20 Pral (Palau Dalmases), Barcelona 3, Spain.
- Asociacion "Omnium Cultural." Bullet: Interior Informatiu. q.

**Asociacion para el Desarrollo Hospitalario**
Apdo. 14041, Barcelona, Spain.
- Estudios Sobre Hospitales. 8 per yr. ISSN 0014-1569

**Asociacion para el Fomento de Estudios Sobre la Patata**
Avenida Jose Antonio, 70, Madrid-13, Spain.
- Aspas de la Patata. q. ISSN 0403-5542

**Asociacion para la Prevencion de Accidentes**
Camino 1, San Sebastian, Spain.
- Revista de Prevencion. q. ISSN 0034-8732

**Asociacion Tecnica y de Investigacion de Fundicion**
Avda. de la Moncloa s/n, Madrid-3, Spain.
- Colada. m. ISSN 0010-0544

**Augustinian Fathers Recollets**
Gral. Davila, 5, Madrid 3, Spain.
- Augustinus; quarterly review of The Father Recollets. q. ISSN 0004-802X

**Auto Mecanica**
c/o Enrique Hernandez Munoz, Isaac Peral, 42, Madrid 15, Spain.
- Auto Mecanica. m.

**Avila. Camara Oficial de la Propiedad Provincia**
Martin Carramolino 10, Spain.
- Camara Oficial de la Propiedad Urbana de la Provincia de Avila. Boletin Informativo. q.

**Antonio Aysa Rodriguez, Ed. & Pub.**
Ercilla 24-4, Bilbao 11, Spain.
- Bilbao Maritimo. w.

**Ayuntamiento de Barcelona. Instituto Municipal de Ciencias Naturales**
- Museo de Zoologia. Barcelona. Miscelanea Zoologica. (pub. by Museo de Zoologia)

**Ayuntamiento de Madrid**
Plaza la Villa, Madrid, Spain.
- Villa de Madrid; revista del Excmo. Ayuntamiento. q. ISSN 0042-6164

**Ayuntamiento de Vitoria**
Vitoria (Alava), Spain.
- Boletin Municipal de Vitoria. s-a.

**Azucarera Cooperativa "Onesimo Redondo"**
Paseo Isabel la Catolica, 1, Valladolid, Spain.
- Revista A C O R. q.

**Ediciones Bahia**
Fray Bartolome Bloque 1, 6a, Algeciras, Spain.
- Bahia; pliegos poeticos del campo de Gibraltar. 8 per yr.
- Coleccion "Bahia". irreg.

**Banco Central**
Alcala, 49, Madrid, Spain.
- Banco Central. Boletin Informativo. m.

**Banco de Alicante**
Alfonso el Sabio 11, Alicante, Spain.
- Banco de Alicante. Noticias. m.

**Banco de Bilbao**
Bilbao, Spain.
- Banco de Bilbao. Informacion Semanal de Valores. w.
- Banco de Bilbao. Memoria. a.
- Campo; boletin de informacion agraria del Banco de Bilbao. bi-m.
- Servex; el seminario del comercio exterieur. w. ISSN 0488-3721

**Banco de Espana. Servicio de Estudios**
Seccion de Publicaciones, Alcala 50, Madrid 14, Spain.
- Banco de Espana. Boletin Estadistico. m. ISSN 0005-4798
- Banco de Espana, Madrid. Informe Anual. a. ISSN 0067-3315
- Estudios Economicos. irreg.

**Banco de Financiacion Industrial**
Servicio de Estudios, Plomo 19, Madrid, Spain.
- Banco de Financiacion Industrial. la Banca Privada. irreg.

**Banco de Santander. Publicidad y Estudios**
Paseo de Pereda, 9/12, Santander 2, Spain.
- Business Opportunities in Spain. a.
- Informe Economico.

**Banco de Vizcaya**
Gran Via 1, Bilbao, Spain.
- Banco de Vizcaya. Noticiario Economico. m. ISSN 0005-4852

**Banco Exterior de Espana**
36 Carrera de San Jeronimo, Madrid 14, Spain.
- Extebank Monthly Economic Report. m. ISSN 0014-5378
- Last Week in Spain. w.

**Banco Guipuzcoano**
Departamento Internacional, Servicios Centrales, Ave. de Espana 21, San Sebastian, Spain.
- Intercoqui; boletin internacional. w.

**Banco Hispano Americano**
Canalejas 1, Madrid 7, Spain.
- Guia Bursatil. m

**Feliciano Baratech Alfaro, Pub.**
Casanova 57, Barcelona, Spain.
- Fomento de la Produccion; revista de la industria, el comercio y las finanzas. s-m. ISSN 0015-6035

**Jose Luis Barbero, Ed. & Pub.**
Antonio Acuna, 13, Madrid 9, Spain.
- Cineguia; directorio Espanol de cine, teatro y television. a. ISSN 0069-4134

**Barcelona. Delegacion de Servicios de Cultura del Ayuntamiento de Barcelona. Museo de Historia de la Ciudad**
Plaza del Rey, Barcelona 2, Spain.
- Miscellanea Barcinonensia. 3 per yr. ISSN 0026-5861
- Museo de Historia, Barcelona. Cuadernos de Arqueologia e Historia de la Cuidad; "seminario de investigacion". irreg. ISSN 0067-415X

**Barcelona. Patronato Municipal de la Vivienda**
Plaza F. de Lesseps, 12, Barcelona 6, Spain.
- Patronato Municipal de la Vivienda de Barcelona. Memoria. a. ISSN 0067-4168
- Vivienda. q. ISSN 0042-756X

**Carlos Barros, Ed. & Pub.**
Hilarion Eslava 29, Madrid 15, Spain.
- Alimentaria; revista de tecnologia e higiene de los alimentos. m. ISSN 0300-5755

**Publicaciones Bayarri**
Angel Guimeja 8, Valencias 8, Spain.
- Bayarri Internacional; guia nacional de la exportacion and importacion. s-a.

**Bibliografia Medica Internacional**
Calle Claudio Coello 76, Madrid 1, Spain.
- Bibliografia Medica Internacional. m. ISSN 0006-1050

**Biblioteca de Menendez Pelayo**
Santander, Spain.
- Biblioteca de Menendez Pelayo. Boletin. q. ISSN 0006-1646

**Biblioteca Universitaria y Provincial de Barcelona**
Avda. Jose Antonio, 585, Barcelona-7, Spain.
- Biblioteca Universitaria y Provincial, Barcelona. Boletin de Noticias. m.
- Universidad de Barcelona. Biblioteca. Memoria Annual. a.

**Editorial Blume**
Tuset 17, Barcelona 6, Spain.
- Nuevo Ambiente/Habitat/New Interiors. q.

**Boixareu Editores, S.A.**
Avda. Jose Antonio, 594, Barcelona 7, Spain.
- Mundo Electronico. m. (except Aug.) ISSN 0300-3787

**Botanical Institute of Barcelona**
Av. Muntanyans - Montjuic, Barcelona 4, Spain.
- Collectanea Botanica. irreg. (1-2 per yr) ISSN 0010-0730

**British Chamber of Commerce in Spain**
Paseo de Gracia 11, Barcelona - 7, Spain.
- Trade Review. q.

**Ediciones C E A C**
Via Layetanam 17, Barcelona 3, Spain.
- Cupula; revista de construccion y arquitectura. m. ISSN 0011-3050
- Ohmio; revista de electricidad y electronica. m. ISSN 0030-1264
- Tecnica Mecanica; revista de mecanica, motor y automovil. m. ISSN 0040-1854

**C E T I S A**
*see* **Compania Espanola de Editoriales Technologicas Internacionales, S.A.**

**Cabildo Insular de Gran Canaria, las Palmas**
- Cuadernos de Botanica Canaria. (pub. by Finca Llano de la Piedra)
- Monographiae Biologicae Canarienses/Biological Monographs of the Canary Islands. (pub. by Finca Llano de la Piedra)

**Caja de Ahorros de Ronda**
Virgen de la Paz, 18, Ronda (Malaga), Spain.
- Estudia y Ahorra. q.

**Caja de Ahorros y Monte de Piedad de las Baleares**
Palma de Mallorca, Spain.
- Caja de Ahorros y Monte de Piedad de las Baleares. Memoria. irreg. ISSN 0409-9192

**Caja de Ahorros y Monte de Piedad de Zaragoza**
Aragon y Rioja, Calle San Jorge No. 8, Zaragoza, Spain.
- Remanso. bi-m. ISSN 0034-4184

**Camara de Directores y Mayordomos del Arte Textil**
- Revista de la Industria Textil. (pub. by Editecnia S. A.)

**Camara Oficial de Comercio e Industria de Alava**
General Alavazz, Vitoria, Spain.
- Camaras Oficiales de Comercio, Industria y Navegacion de la Region Vasconavarra. Coyuntura Industrial Regional. q.

**Camara Oficial de Comercio e Industria de Madrid**
Huertas 13, Madrid 12, Spain.
- Comercio e Industria. m. ISSN 0019-7432
- Comercio e Industria. Suplemento Quincenal. fortn.
- Guia del Comercio y de la Industria de Madrid. biennial.

**Camara Oficial de Comercio e Industria de Zaragoza**
D. Jaime I. No. 18., Zaragoza-1, Spain.
- Camara Oficial de Comercio e Industria de Zaragoza. Boletin Informativo de Legislacion. s-m.

**Camara Oficial de Comercio, Industria y Navegacion de Aviles**
Pz. Camposagrado, 1, Aviles (Oviedo), Spain.
- Camara de Comercio, Industria y Navegacion de Aviles. Boletin Informativo. bi-m.

**Camara Oficial de Comercio, Industria y Navegacion de Barcelona**
General Primo de Rivera, 11-13, Barcelona, Spain.
- Boletin de Estadistica y Coyuntura. m.
- Camara Oficial de Comercio, Industria y Navegacion de Barcelona. Boletin. m. ISSN 0008-1930
- Cataluna Exporta. a. ISSN 0069-1178
- Informacion Economica Mundial. m.
- Noticiario de Comercio Exterior. 3 per m.

**Camara Oficial de Comercio, Industria y Navegacion de Bilbao**
Rodriguez Arias, 6, Bilbao (Vizcaya), Spain.
- Camara Oficial de Commercio Informacion. m (with supplements)
- Informe Sobre la Coyuntura Industrial Vizcaina. m.
- Informe Sobre Utilizacion de la Capacidad Productiva de Vizcaya. q.

**Camara Oficial de Comercio, Industria y Navegacion de Guipuzcoa**
Calle Camino, 1, San Sebastian, Spain.
- Economia Guipuzconan. bi-m.

**Camara Oficial de Comercio Industria y Navegacion de Valencia**
Poeta Querol 15, Valencia, Spain.
- Comercio Industria y Navegacion. m.

**Camara Oficial Sindical Agraria**
Avenida Manuel Agustin Heredia No 26, Malaga, Spain.
- Campo Malagueno. fortn.

**Camaras Oficiales de Comercio, Industria y Navegacion de la Region Vasconavarra**
- Camaras Oficiales de Comercio, Industria y Navegacion de la Region Vasconavarra. Coyuntura Industrial Regional. (pub. by Camara Oficial de Comercio e Industria de Alava)

**Camp de l'Arpa**
Valencia 72, Entlo. 4a, Barcelona 15, Spain.
- Camp de l'Arpa; revista de literatura. m.

**Campana Contra el Hambre en el Mundo**
Alfonso XI, 4, Madrid 14, Spain.
- Campana Contra el Hambre en el Mundo. Boletin. q.

**Dr. J.A. Canut, Ed. & Pub.**
Grabador Esteve. 10, Valencia 4, Spain.
- Revista Espanola de Ortodoncia. q.

**Carabela**
General Sanjuro 53, Dpto 50, Barcelona 12, Spain.
- Verde Yerba; antologia Hispanoamericana de poesia. irreg.

**Caracola**
Larios 5, Malaga, Spain.
- Caracola; revista Malaguena de poesia. m. ISSN 0008-6118

**Carga Util**
Edificio Pegaso, General Sanjuro 2, Madrid 25, Spain.
- Carga Util. bi-m.

**Pere Cartanya Aleu, Ed. & Pub**
Apartado 168, Roig 8. Reus, Spain.
- B. N. A. Informes Tecnicos; informes tecnicos sobre ganaderia. m.
- Reus Avicola y Agricola. m. ISSN 0034-6241

**Casa de Escritores**
Calle San Miguel, 60, Alcoy (Alicante), Spain.
- Alcoy; Fiesta de Moros y Cristianos. a. ISSN 0065-6127 (Asociacion de San Jorge de Alcoy)
- Estudios Eclesiasticos. q.
- Manresa; revista de investigacion e informacion ascetica y mistica. q.
- Resena de Literatura, Arte, y Espectaculos. m. ISSN 0080-1763
- Revista de Fomento Social; ciencias sociales. q. ISSN 0015-6043

**Casa de Escritores SJ**
Avenida de las Universidades 13, Apartado 73, Bilbao, Spain.
- Mensajero; del corazon de Jesus. m.

**Casa de Velaquez**
- Casa de Velaquez, Madrid. Melanges/Casa de Velasquez, Madrid. Miscellanies. (pub. by Diffusion de Boccard FR)

**Editorial Catolica Espanola**
Gravina 29, Seville, Spain.
- Hispalis Medica; revista Sevillana de medicina y cirugia. m. ISSN 0018-2125

**Caza y Pesca**
General Sanjurjo, 24, 1 Izqda., Madrid-3, Spain.
- Caza y Pesca; revista mensual de caza, pesca, tiro, armas y guaderia. m.

**Ediciones CEDEL**
Calle Mallorca 257, Barcelona, Spain.
- Anuario de Relojeria y Arte en Metal para Espana e Hispanoamerica. a. ISSN 0066-510X
- Pinturas y Acabados Industriales. q. ISSN 0031-9953
- Vivir; consejos para vivir con salud. bi-m. ISSN 0042-7578

**Camilo Jose Cela Trulock**
La Bonanova, Palma de Mallorca, Spain.
- Papeles de Son Armadans. m. ISSN 0031-1065

**Cemento-Hormigon**
Calle Maignon 26, Barcelona 12, Spain.
- Cemento-Hormigon; revista technica. m. ISSN 0008-8919

**Centro de Documentacion**
Glorieta de Quevedo 8, Madrid 10, Spain.
- Centro de Documentacion. Boletin. q. ISSN 0008-994X (Patronato de Obras Docentes del Movimiento)

**Centro de Documentacion de Historia de la Medicina**
Decano BAHI 59-67, Barcelona, Spain.
- Medicina e Historia. m. ISSN 0300-8169

**Centro de Estudios e Investigacion San Isidoro**
Leon, Plaza de Regla, 6, Leon, Spain.
- Archivos Leoneses; Estudios y documentacion de los Reinos Hispanos Occidentales. s-a. ISSN 0004-0630
- Colligite; sintesis de pensamiento y vida de la Iglesia. q. ISSN 0531-0008

**Centro de Estudios Interplanetarios de Barcelona**
Apto. 282, Barcelona, Spain.
- Stendek. 4 per yr.

**Centro de Estudios Judeo-Cristianos**
- Coleccion Senda Abierta. Serie II (Azul): Judaismo. (pub. by Studium Ediciones)

**Centro de Estudios Sociales**
Calle Baileu s/n, Palacio de Oriente, Madrid 13, Spain.
- Revista de Estudios Sociales. 3 per yr.

**Centro de Estudios Sociales de la Santa Cruz del Valle de los Caidos**
Madrid, Spain.
- Anales de Moral Social y Economica. irreg. ISSN 0066-1473
- Centro de Estudios Sociales de la Santa Cruz del Valle de los Caidos. Revista de Estudios Sociales. (pub. by Fragua)

**Centro de Estudios y Asesoramiento Metalurgico**
Jose Anselmo Clave 4, Barcelona 2, Spain.
- C E A M; revista de economia industrial. bi-m.

**Centro de Etnologia Peninsular**
Egipciacas 9, Barcelona 1, Spain.
- Ethnica. s-a.

**Centro de Informacion y Documentacion Economica**
Evaristo San Miguel, 20, Madrid-8, Spain.
- I N - C I D E. s-m.

**Centro de Iniciativa y Turismo**
Plaza Calvo Sotelo, Jaca, Spain.
- Jacetania. bi-m. ISSN 0021-3810

**Centro de Investigacion y Promocion de Exportaciones**
Via Augusta 143, Barcelona 6, Spain
(Subscr. to Ediciones la Poligrafa, Balmes 54, Barcelona, 7, Spain)
- Mercado Comun Internacional; servicio de documentacion, informacion y asesoramiento sobre comercio internacional. s-m.

**Centro de Investigaciones Fisica "L. Torres Quevedo"**
Serrano 144, Madrid 6, Spain.
- Electronica y Fisica Aplicada/Electronics and Applied Physics. q. ISSN 0013-5054

**Centro de la Informatica, Tecnica y Material Administrativos**
Plaza Conde del Valle de Suchil, 8, Madrid 15, Spain.
- Congreso Hispano-Luso de Informatica. Actas. irreg.

**Centro de Lectura**
Major, 15, Reus, Spain.
- Centro de Lectura, Reus. Revista. m.

**Centro Informativo de la Construccion**
Lauria, 117, Barcelona-9, Spain.
- C I C Informacion. bi-m.

**Centro Josefino Espanol**
c/o Fray Jose Antonio Carrasco, Pp. Carmelitas Descalzos, Valladolid, Spain.
- Estudios Josefinos. s-a.

**Centro Nacional de Educacion Cooperativa**
Palacio de la Cooperacion, Apdo. de Correos 15, San Felix 9, Zaragoza, Spain.
- Documentos de Education Cooperativa. 3 per yr. ISSN 0046-0486 (Escuela de Gerentes de Cooperativas)
- Educacion Cooperativa. q.
- Escuela de Gerentes de Cooperativas. Cartillas de Cooperacion. irreg.; latest issue, 1974. ISSN 0084-5132 (Escuela de Gerentes de Cooperativas)

**Centro Nacional de Investigaciones Metalurgicas**
Ciudad Universitaria, Madrid 3, Spain.
- Resumenes de Articulos de Metalurgia. Serie C. m. ISSN 0034-5938
- Revista de Metalurgia. bi-m. ISSN 0034-8570
- Revista de Soldadura. q. ISSN 0048-7759

**Libreria Cientifica Medinaceli**
Duque de Medinaceli 4, Madrid 14, Spain.
- Cuadernos Informativos de Desarrollo Economico-Social. bi-m. ISSN 0011-2518
- Hispania Sacra; revista de historia eclesiastica. s-a. ISSN 0018-215X
- Instituto Cajal de Investigaciones Biologicas. Trabajos. q' ISSN 0020-3696
- Revista Internacional de Sociologia. (pub. by Libreria Cientifica Medinaceli)

**Publicaciones de el Ciervo, S.A.**
Calvet 56, Apdo. 12121, Barcelona 6, Spain.
- Ciervo. bi-m. ISSN 0045-6896

**Editorial Ciguena**
Paseo General Martinez Campos 19, Madrid, Spain.
- Arte y Hogar. m.

**Cimas**
Santa Teresa, 10, Madrid, 4, Spain.
- Cimas. 11 per yr.

**CIMBRA**
Miguel Angel 16, Madrid 10, Spain.
- CIMBRA; revista de la ingeniera technica de obras publicas. m.

**Cine-Asesor**
Plaza Marina Espanola, 6, Madrid, Spain.
- Resumen Cinematografico. a.

**Cinestudio**
Hermosilla 20, Madrid 1, Spain.
- Cinestudio. m. ISSN 0009-7217

**Circulo de Bellas Artes**
La Chesta, Santa Cruz de Tenerife, Canary Islands.
- Ganigo. q. ISSN 0016-447X

**Ciudadano**
Villanueva 8, Madrid 1, Spain.
- Ciudadano; revista de informacion al consumidor. m.

**Claretian Fathers**
C. Buen Suceso N. 22, Madrid 8, Spain.
- Ephemerides Mariologicae; international revue of mariology. q. ISSN 0425-1466

**Clima y Ambiente**
Santisima Trinidad, 30-1 No. 7, Madrid 3, Spain.
- Clima y Ambiente. m.

**Club Atletico de Madrid**
Barquillo, 22, Madrid 4, Spain.
- Revista Atletico de Madrid. m.

**Club de Radiorama**
- Radiorama. (pub. by Ediciones Tecnicas R.E.D.E.)

**Club del Ejecutivo de Seguros**
Magallanes 5, Madrid, Spain.
- Actualidad Aseguradora; el eco del seguro. m.
- Anuario Espanol de Seguros. a.

**Club International Alhambra**
P.O. Box 109, Granada, Spain.
- Alhambra; revista filatelica internacional. m. ISSN 0401-3689

**Club Juventud Panadera**
Gobernador Viejo 9, Valencia-3, Spain.
- Juventud Panadera. m. ISSN 0022-7218

**Cointra, S.A.**
Alcala de Henares (Madrid), Spain.
- Cointra Press. q.

**Colegio de Abogados de Zaragoza.**
Zaragoza, Spain.
- Jurisprudencia Aragonesa. a.

**Colegio de Agentes de Cambio y Bolsa de Barcelona. Servicio de Estudios e Informacion**
Paseo Isabel II, s/n, Barcelona-3, Spain.
- Colegio de Agentes de Cambio y Bolsa de Barcelona. Servicio de Estudios e Informacion. Boletin Financiero. q. ISSN 0522-3822
- Estadisticas de la Bolsa de Barcelona. q.

**Colegio de Ingenieros de Caminos, Canales y Puertos**
C /Montalban, 3-4 Izquieroa, Madrid, Spain.
- Colegio de Ingenieros de Caminos, Canales y Puertos. Boletin de Informacion. m. ISSN 0010-0617
- Relacion de Ingenieros de Caminos, Canales y Puertos.

**Colegio de San Ignacio. Asociacion Antiguos Alumnos**
c/o Dr. Amigant, 32 Barcelona 17, Spain.
- Estol; circular de los antiguos alumnos del colegio de san ignacio. bi-m.

**Colegio Nacional General Primo de Rivera**
Calle Leon 7, Albacete, Spain.
- Forja. q.

**Colegio Oficial de Arquitectos de Cataluna y Baleares**
Plaza Nueva Num.5, Barcelona 2, Spain
(Dist. by: Libreria Internacional, Corcega 428, Barcelona 9, Spain)
- Cuadernos de Arquitectura. q. ISSN 0011-2364

**Colegio Oficial de Arquitectos de Madrid**
Barquillo 12, Madrid, Spain.
- Arquitectura. m. ISSN 0004-2706

**Colegio Oficial de Farmaceuticos de la Provincia de Barcelona**
Via Layetana 94, Barcelona 10, Spain.
- Butlleti Informatiu de Circular Farmaceutica. m.
- Colegio Oficial de Farmaceutico. Circular Farmaceutica. q. ISSN 0009-7314

**Colegio Oficial de Ingenieros Tecnicos en Topografia**
Avda. del Generalisimo, 96-11, Madrid 16, Spain.
- Tecnica Topografica. bi-m.

**Colegio Sindical Nacional de Agentes de Seguros**
- Aseguradores. (pub. by Ediciones y Publicaciones Populares)

**Colegio Teologado "Felipe Scio"**
- Analecta Calasanctiana. (pub. by Orden de las Escuelas Pias)

**Colores y Pinturas**
65 Av. Jose Antonio, Madrid 13, Spain.
- Colores y Pinturas; revista tecnica de pinturas y afines. m. ISSN 0010-1788

**Comercial Madera Pla S. A.**
Espronceda, Barcelona, Spain.
- Mercado de la Madera. m.

**Comisaria General de Excavaciones Arqueologicas**
Serrano 13, Madrid, Spain.
- Excavaciones Arqueologicas en Espana. irreg. ISSN 0071-3279

**Comision Asesora de Editores de Libros de Ensenanza**
Santiago Rusinol, 8, Madrid-3, Spain.
- Libros y Material de Ensenanza. a. ISSN 0075-9201

**Comision Episcopal de Misiones y Cooperacion Entre las Iglesias**
Jose Maranon 3, Madrid 10, Spain.
- Comision Episcopal de Misiones y Cooperacion Entre las Iglesias. Mensaje Iberoamericano. m.

**Comision Espanola de Cooperacion Con la UNESCO**
Secretaria General, Escuela de Diplomatica, Ciudad Universitaria, Madrid, Spain.
- Comision Espanola de Cooperacion Con la UNESCO. Revista de Informacion. q.

**Comision Mixta de Coordinacion Estadistica de Barcelona**
Urgel, 187, 11, Barcelona, Spain.
- Comision Mixta de Coordinacion Estadistica de Barcelona. Estadisticas de Ensenanza de la Provincia de Barcelona.

**Comite Nacional Lechero**
Alberto Alcocer 46, Madrid 16, Spain.
- Revista Espanola de Lecheria. q. ISSN 0300-5550

**Compania de Jesus**
Plaza de San Marcos, 1,1, Leon, Spain.
- Boletin Intimo de Compania; evangelio y mision. m.

**Compania de Santa Teresa de Jesus**
Ganduxer, 85, Barcelona-6, Spain.
- Jesus Maestro. m.

**Compania Espanola de Editoriales Technologicas Internacionales, S.A.**
Concepcion Arenal 5 y 7, Barcelona 16, Spain
(U.S. Distributor: Illife N.T.P. Ltd., 205 E. 42 St., New York, N.Y. 10017)
- Manutencion y Almacenaje; logistica de la distribucion. 10 per yr. ISSN 0025-2646 (Federation Europeenne de la Manutention. Comite Nacional Espanol)
- Oficinas; instalacion, equipos y organizacion. 8 per yr.
- Tecnica de la Regulacion y Mando Automatico; automacion, instrumentacion, sistemas, tratamiento de la informacion. 10 per yr (with supplement) ISSN 0040-1722 (International Federation of Automatic Control. Comite Espanol)

**Comunidad Parroquial de Duenas**
Duenas (Palencia), Spain.
- Luz de Antorcha; boletin de la comunidad parroquial de duenas. m.

**Confederacion Espanola de Cajas de Ahorros**
Distribuidora 6000, Juan Hurtado de Mendoza 14, Madrid 16, Spain.
- Ahorro. q. ISSN 0002-2055
- Coyuntura Economica. m.
- Fondo para la Investigacion Economica y Social. Boletin de Documentacion. q. ISSN 0015-6132 (prep. by its Fonda para la Investigacion Economica y Social)
- Indicadores Socio-Economicos del Campo Espanol. irreg. (prep. by its Fonda para la Investigacion Economica y Social)

**Consejo Economico Sindical Nacional**
Paseo del Prado, 18, Madrid, Spain.
- De Economia; revista de temas economicos. q.

**Consejo General de Colegios de Odontologos y Estomatologos**
Villanueva 11, Madrid 1, Spain.
- Boletin de Informacion Dental. m. ISSN 0006-6311

**Consejo Nacional de Ayudantes Tecnicos Sanitarios**
Cuesta de Santo Domingo, 6, Madrid, Spain.
- Medicina y Cirugia Auxiliar. m.

**Consejo Nacional de Enfermeras**
Buen Suceso 6, Madrid, Spain.
- Caridad, Ciencia y Arte. m. ISSN 0069-0546

**Consejo Superior de Colegios de Ingenieros de Minas**
Almagro, 11, Madrid-4, Spain.
- Industria Minera. m.

**Consejo Superior de Colegios Oficiales de Aparejadores y Arquitectos Tecnicos**
Avda. Generalisimo, 73, Madrid 16, Spain.
- Cercha. q.

**Consejo Tecnico de Telecomunicacion**
Apdo. de Correos No. 936, Madrid, Spain.
- Revista de Telecomunicacion. q. ISSN 0034-8961

**Control de Publicidad y Ventas**
Calle Fetraz 11, Madrid 8, Spain.
- Control de Publicidad y Ventas. m. ISSN 0573-8636

**Cooperativa de Ensenanza Antonio Machado**
Apdo. 309, Salamanca, Spain.
- Aldaba. s-a.
- Ciencia y Naturaleza. s-a.

**Cruz Roja Espanola**
- Revista de Reumatologia. (pub. by Julio Garcia Peri Editor)

**Cruzada Espanol**
c/o Jose Oriol Cuffi Canadell, Ed., Via Layetana 103, 3, 1, Barcelona 9, Spain.
- Cruzada Espanol. s-m. ISSN 0574-5101

**Editorial Cuadernos para el Dialogo, S.A.**
Jarama 19, Madrid 2, Spain.
- Cuadernos para el Dialogo. w. ISSN 0011-2534

**Cuerpo Medico Beneficencia Provincia de Madrid**
- Hospital General. (pub. by Editorial Garsi)

**Ediciones Cutor S. A.**
Plaza Nunez de Arce, 1, Barcelona 6, Spain.
- Athena; cuadernos de medicina, arte y coleccionismo. s-m.
- Oncologia /80. bi-m. (Sociedad Espanola de Oncologia)
- Practica Diaria; educacion medica continuada. bi-m.

**John Deere S.A.**
Apartado 10, Getafe (Madrid), Spain.
- Campo y Mecanica. bi-m.

**Delegacion Vallvidrera del C. E. A.**
Mont d'Orsa 17, Barcelona 17, Spain.
- Brots de Collcerola.

**Editoriales de Derecho Reunidas, S.A.**
Caracas 21, Apdo. 4032, Madrid 4, Spain.
- Revista de Derecho Privado. 11 per yr. ISSN 0034-7922
- Revista de Economia y Hacienda Local. 3 per yr.

**Diaz de Santos**
Lagasca 95, Madrid, 6, Spain.
- Ciencia y Tecnia; boletin bibliografico nacional y extranjero. m.

**Ediciones Didascalia**
Madreselva 64 D, Madrid, Spain.
- Didascalia; revista de orietacion didactica e investigacion pedagogica. m.

**Diputacion Foral de Navarra. Institucion Principe de Viana**
Av. Carlos III, No. 2, Pamplona, Spain.
- Cuadernos de Etnologia y Etnografia de Navarra. 3 per yr. ISSN 0590-1871
- Estudios Americanos; revista de sintesis e interpretacion. m. ISSN 0014-1410
- Fontes Linguae Vasconum. 3 per yr. ISSN 0046-435X
- Institucion Principe de Viana. Coleccion Historia. irreg.
- Principe de Viana. s-a. ISSN 0032-8472

**Diputacion Provincial de Barcelona. Instituto de Ciencias Sociales**
Calle Urgel 187, Barcelona 11, Spain.
- Instituto de Ciencias Sociales. Revista. s-a. ISSN 0020-3807

**Diputacion Provincial de Barcelona. Servicios de Bibliotecas**
Biblioteca de Catalunya, Carmen, No. 47, Barcelona 1, Spain.
- Anuario de la Biblioteca de la Cataluna y de las Populares y Especiales de Barcelona. a.

**Diputacion Provincial de Caceres**
Plaza Santa Maria, Caceres, Spain.
- Alcantara; revista de cultura extremena. q.

**Direccion Central de la Accion Catolica Espanola**
4 Alfonso 11, Madrid, Spain.
- Ecclesia. s-a. ISSN 0012-9038

**Direccion General de Archivos y Bibliotecas**
Av. Calvo Sotelo, 22, Madrid, Spain.
- Revistas Espanolas en Curso de Publicacion. a. (Instituto Bibliografico Hispanico. Departamento de Informacion Cientifica y Tecnica)

**Direccion General de Seguridad**
Miguel Angel, Num. 5, Madrid-10, Spain.
- Policia Espanola. m. ISSN 0048-4709

**Discobolo**
Sagasta 23, Madrid 4, Spain.
- Discobolo; revista de musica y discos. w. ISSN 0012-3528

**Discos Colombia. Promotion Department**
Plaza Vazquez de Mella 5, Madrid, Spain.
- Flash Musical. bi-w.

**Divultec S. A.**
Breton de los Herreros, 57, Madrid 3, Spain.
- Catalogo Nacional del Envase, Embalaje y Artes Graficas Aplicadas. s-a. ISSN 0008-7610 (Instituto Espanol del Envase y Embalaje)

**Documentacion Espanola Contemporanea, S.L.**
Castello 36, Madrid, Spain.
- Documentacion Espanola. m.

**Dominicos de Andalucia. Studium Generale**
Apartado 820, Seville, Spain.
- Communio; commentarii Internationales de Ecclesia et Theologia. 3 per yr. ISSN 0010-3705

**Ediciones Don Bosco**
Paseo San Juan Bosco 62, Barcelona-17, Spain.
- J-20. (Juventud Siglo XX) m.

**Dopress**
Jose Ortego y Gasset, 29, Madrid 6, Spain.
- Revista de Revistas. w. ISSN 0034-8880

**Ediciones Doyma, S.A.**
Aribau 282-284,3,4, Barcelona-6, Spain.
- Archivos de Bronoconeumologia. bi-m. (Sociedad de Patologia Respiratoria)
- Clinica e Investigacion en Ginecologia y Obstetricia. q.
- Diario de Congresos Medicos. irreg.
- Jano Arquitectura; revista de arquitectura, interiorismo y diseno. m.
- Jano "Medicina y Humanidades". w.
- Medicina Clinica. s-m. ISSN 0025-7753 (Universidad de Barcelona. Facultad de Medicina) (Co-sponsors: Hospitales y Sociedades Medicas de Barcelona)
- Pediatrics. m.
- Revista Quirurgica Espanola. bi-m.

**Miguel Duran-Loriga, Ed. & Pub.**
Francisco Suarez 16, Madrid 16, Spain.
- T. A. (Temas de Arquitectura y Urbanismo) m.

**E S - Espana Cultural**
Avda. del Generalisimo, 39, Madrid, Spain.
- E S - Espana Cultural. m.

**E U N S A**
*see* **Ediciones Universidad de Navarra S.A.**

**Eco del Seguro**
Muntaner 318, Barcelona, Spain.
- Eco del Seguro. m. ISSN 0012-947X

**Editorial ECO, S.A.**
Calle de la Cruz 44, Barcelona 17, Spain.
- Eikonos; revista de la imagen y el sonido. m.
- Fundacion Puigvert. Anales. q.

**Economia Internacional**
Balmes, 213, Barcelona 6, Spain.
- Economia Internacional. m. ISSN 0012-9801

**Economia Mundial**
Quintana 15, Apdo. de Correos 757, Madrid 8, Spain.
- Economia Mundial. w. ISSN 0012-9844

**Economia Nacional Internacional de la Empresa**
Via Layetana 32-34, Barcelona, Spain.
- Economia Nacional Internacional de la Empresa. m.

**Economista**
Calle del Conde de Aranda 8, Apdo. 1024, Madrid 1, Spain.
- Economista; revista financiera. w. ISSN 0013-0656

**Edilerner**
P. de la Castellana, 63-2 Izquierda, Madrid-3, Spain.
- Consulta. m.
- Tiempos Medicos. s-m.

**Edimedica S.A.**
Comadante Zorita 13-5, Madrid 20, Spain.
- Cuestiones de Internado.
- Vie Medicale. m.

**Edipress**
Tallers 62, Barcelona 1, Spain.
- Garbo. w.

**Edisport, S.I.**
Isaac Peral 12, Madrid, Spain.
- Ano del Transporte. a.
- Autopista. w. ISSN 0567-2392

**Editecnia, S.A.**
Provenza, 260, 4, Barcelona-8, Spain.
- Revista de la Industria Electrica. bi-m. (Gremio Sindical de la Electricidad)
- Revista de la Industria Textil. m(except July-Aug.) (Camara de Directores y Mayordomos del Arte Textil)
- Revista de Quimica Textil. q. ISSN 0300-9718 (Asociacion de Quimicos y Coloristas Textiles)

**Editepsa**
Avda. Jose Antonio, 38, 9, Madrid-13, Spain.
- Profesiones y Empresas; revista de orientacion e investigacion profesional. bi-m.

**Embajada Argentina**
Departamento Cultural, Castellana, 63, Madrid 6.
- Cuaderno Cultural. 3 per yr. ISSN 0011-2348

**Embalajes**
San Romualdo, s/n (Edificio Astygi,Planta 7), Madrid-17, Spain.
- Embalajes; revista envase, embalaje, manutencion y transporte. m.

**En Punta**
Jardin de San Federico, No. 5, Bajo, Madrid 9, Spain.
- En Punta. m.

**Publicaciones Ensenanza, S.A.**
Corcega 272, Barcelona-8, Spain.
- Promoventas; revista de marketing y administracion de empresas. m. (Escuela Superior de Marketing y Administracion)

**Escelicer S.A.**
Comandante Azcarraga s/n, Madrid 16, Spain.
- Biblioteca Estudios Escelicer. irreg.

**Escuela de Bibliotecarias**
Diputacion Provincial de Barcelona, Calle Hospital, 56 Barcelona 1, Spain.
- Biblioteconomia. s-a. ISSN 0006-1778

**Escuela de Gerentes de Cooperativas**
Palacio de la Cooperacion, Apdo. de Correos 15, San Felix 9, Zaragoza, Spain.
- Documentos de Education Cooperativa. (pub. by Centro Nacional de Educacion Cooperativa)
- Escuela de Gerentes de Cooperativas. Cartillas de Cooperacion. (pub. by Centro Nacional de Educacion Cooperativa)
- Escuela de Gerentes de Cooperativas. Coleccion Textos. irreg. ISSN 0084-5159 (Co-sponsor: Centro Nacional de Educacion)
- Escuela de Gerentes de Cooperativas. Cuadernos de Practicas. irreg. ISSN 0084-5167 (Co-sponsor: Centro Nacional de Educacion)
- Escuela de Gerentes de Cooperativas. Serie Especial. irreg. ISSN 0084-5175 (Co-sponsor: Centro Nacional de Educacion Cooperativa)

**Escuela de Ingenieros de Caminos, Canales y Puertos**
Ciudad Universitaria, Madrid-3, Spain.
- Revista de Obras Publicas. m. ISSN 0034-8619 (Ingenieros de Caminos, Canales y Puertos)

**Escuela Diplomatica**
Paseo de Juan 23, No. 5, Madrid 3, Spain.
- Madrid. Escuela Diplomatica. Cuadernos. irreg. ISSN 0464-3755

**Escuela Nacional de Administracion. Biblioteca**
Antigua Universidad de Cisneros, Alcala Henares, Madrid, Spain.
- Antigua Universidad de Cisneros. Escuela Nacional de Administration. Biblioteca. Boletin Informativo. q.

**Escuela Nacional de Administracion Publica. Instituto de Desarrollo Economico**
Madrid, Spain.
- Revista Espanola de Economia. 3 per yr.

**Escuela Radio Maymo**
Pelayo 1⁹, Barcelona-1, Spain.
- Electrotecnia Popular. m. ISSN 0013-5313

**Escuela Superior de Marketing y Administracion**
- Promoventas. (pub. by Publicaciones Ensenanza, S.A.)

**Escuela Superior de Musica Sagrada**
Victor Pradera 65, Madrid 8, Spain.
- Melodias; revista de musica liturgica. bi-m.
- Tesoro Sacra Musical. q.

**Escuela Superior de Tecnica Empresarial**
Paseo del Urumea - Mundiaz, San Sebastian, Spain.
- Estudios Empresariales. 3 per yr.

**Prensa Espanola**
Serrano 61, Madrid 6, Spain.
- Blanco y Negro. w. ISSN 0006-4572

**Espasa-Calpe, S.A.**
Carretera de Irun, Num. 12200, Apartado 547, Madrid 34, Spain.
- Coleccion Austral. irreg. ISSN 0069-5041
- Coleccion Boreal. irreg.
- Grandes Biografias. irreg. ISSN 0072-5390
- Historia y Filosofia de la Ciencia. Serie Mayor. Encuadernada. irreg. ISSN 0073-2494
- Historia y Filosofia de la Ciencia. Serie Menor. Rustica. irreg. ISSN 0073-2508
- Monografias de Psicologia, Normal y Patologica. irreg. ISSN 0077-0469
- Nueva Ciencia. Nueva Tecnica. irreg. ISSN 0078-2661
- Summa Artis; historia general del artes. irreg. ISSN 0081-9298

**Estudio Teologico Agustiniano**
Paseo de Filipinos, 7, Valladolid, Spain.
- Estudio Agustiniano. 3 per yr.

**Estudio Teologico de San Esteban**
Convento de San Estaban., Apartado 17, Salamanca, Spain.
- Ciencia Tomista. q.

**Euramerica, S.A.**
Mateo Inurria, 15, Madrid-16, Spain.
- Coleccion Fundacion Foessa. Serie Estudios. irreg.

**Libreria Europa**
Calle de Arriaza 16, Madrid 8, Spain.
- Instituto de Estudios Politicos. Boletin. bi-m. ISSN 0020-3866 (Instituto de Estudios Politicos)
- Revista de Economia Politica. 3 per yr. ISSN 0034-8058 (Instituto de Estudios Politicos)

**European Congress of Anaesthesiology**
Inquire: Professor Arias, Arapiles 16, Madrid, Spain.
- European Congress of Anaesthesiology. Proceedings. quadrennial, 4th, Madrid, 1974. ISSN 0071-2671 (World Federation of Societies of Anaesthesiologists)

**Editorial Everest**
Carretera Leon-Astorga Km. 4, Leon 500, Spain.
- Everfoto. a.

**Editorial Facta**
Avellanas, No 4, Valencia- 3, Spain.
- Medicina Espanola; revista nacional de medicina, cirugia y especialidades. m. ISSN 0025-7842
- Revista Espanola de Cirugia Osteoarticular. bi-m.
- Revista Espanola de Obstetricia y Ginecologia. 10 per yr. ISSN 0034-9445 (Asociacion de Obstetricia y Ginecologia)
- Revista Espanola de Oto-Neuro-Oftalmologia y Neurocirugia. bi-m. ISSN 0034-9453 (Sociedad Luso-Espanola de Neurocirugia)

**Facultad de Teologia, Granada**
Apartado 2002, Granada, Spain.
- Proyeccion; teologia y mundo actual. q. ISSN 0478-6378

**Facultad de Teologia San Federico de Borja**
- Actualidad Bibliografica de Filosofia y Teologia. (pub. by Ediciones Mensajero)

**Facultad Teologica del Norte de Espana. Facultad de Teologia**
Martinez del Compo 7, Burgos, Spain.
- Burgense; collectanea scientifica. s-a. ISSN 0521-8195

**Facultades de Filosofia de la Compania de Jesus en Espana**
Pablo Aranda 3, Madrid, 6, Spain.
- Pensamiento; revista de investigacion e informacion filosofica. q. ISSN 0031-4749

**J. Faura - Soler, Ed. & Pub.**
Rocafort 123, Barcelona-15, Spain.
- Oro y Hora. m. ISSN 0030-5758

**Federacion Catalana de Montanismo**
Ramblas 61, 1-2, Barcelona 12, Spain.
- Vertex. bi-m. ISSN 0042-4420

**Federacion de Asociaciones de Maestros Industriales de Espana**
Ronda de Valencia 3, Madrid 5, Spain.
- Maestria Industrial. bi-m.

**Federacion Espanola Boxeo**
Ferraz 16, Madrid-8, Spain.
- Febox-Boxeo. m.

**Federacion Espanola de Actividades Subacuaticas. Departamento de Actividades Cientificas**
Santalo 15, Barcelona 16, Spain.
- Inmersion y Ciencia. irreg.

**Federacion Espanola de Halterofilia**
Alberto Aguilera, 3-7 Izda., Madrid, Spain.
- Boletin Informativo de Halterofilia. q.

**Federacion Espanola de Natacion**
Conde Penalver 61, Madrid-6, Spain.
- Crol. (pub. by Ediciones Ariel, S.A.)
- Federacion Espanola de Natacion. Anuario. a.

**Federacion Espanola de Religiosos de la Ensenanza**
Conde de Penalver, 45-4, Madrid-6, Spain.
- Educadores. bi-m. ISSN 0013-1113
- Guia de Centros Docentes de la Iglesia. a. (prep. by its Servicio Estadistico de Centros Docentes de la Iglesia)

**Federacion Espanola Galguera**
Barquillo 19, Madrid, Spain.
- Federacion Espanola Galguera. Anuario y Memoria Deportiva. a. ISSN 0071-4119

**Federacion Nacional del Tiro Olimpico Espanol**
Barquillo 21, Madrid 4, Spain.
- Federacion Nacional del Tiro Olimpico Espanol. Revista Informativa. m. ISSN 0040-8093

**Federacion Taquigrafica Espanola**
Cruz Num.5, Madrid, Spain.
- Mundo Taquigrafico. q. ISSN 0047-8342

**Federation Europeenne de la Manutention. Comite Nacional Espanol**
- Manutencion y Almacenaje. (pub. by Compania Espanola de Editoriales Technologicas Internacionales, S.A.)

**Feju**
Marva 32, 30 Valencia 7, Spain.
- Feju. m. ISSN 0014-973X

**Miguel Ferrer Sureda**
Troncoso, 9, Palma de Mallorca, Spain.
- Cort; revista Mallorquina. s-m.

**Ferrocarriles y Tranvias**
Paseo del Prado 12, Madrid, Spain.
- Ferrocarriles y Tranvias. m. ISSN 0015-0185

**Editorial Financiera Alfa Omega**
Castello, 45, Madrid, 1, Spain.
- Anuario Espanol de Empresas. a.

**Financiero**
Conde de Penalver 94, Madrid, Spain.
- Financiero; revista internacional de economia, comercio e industria. m. ISSN 0015-2102

**Finca Llano de la Piedra**
Santa Lucia de Tirajana, Gran Canaria, Spain.
- Cuadernos de Botanica Canaria; comunicaciones sobre flora y vegetacion del Archipielago Canario. 3 per yr. ISSN 0011-2372 (Cabildo Insular de Gran Canaria, las Palmas)
- Monographiae Biologicae Canarienses/Biological Monographs of the Canary Islands. a. ISSN 0077-0647 (Cabildo Insular de Gran Canaria, las Palmas)

**Jorge Foix, Ed. & Pub.**
Londres 93, Barcelona-11, Spain.
- Oficina Moderna; revista de papeleria, material, maquinas y mobiliario de oficinas. s-a. ISSN 0030-0624
- Revista de Ferreteria. 7 per yr. (Gremio de Ferreteria de Barcelona)

**Fomento de las Artes Decorativas. Agrupacion de Diseno Industrial**
Barcelona, Spain.
- Fomento de las Artes Decorativas, Barcelona. Agrupacion de Diseno Industrial. Guia de Asociados. irreg.

**Fomento del Trabajo Nacional**
Via Layetana, 32-34 Pral., Barcelona-3, Spain.
- Fomento del Trabajo Nacional; economia nacional, internacional y de la empresa -servicio sindical de alta cultura, economica. m. ISSN 0041-0233

**Fomento Martinense. Grupo Espeleologico**
Calle Provenza, 595, Barcelona - 13, Spain.
- GOURS. irreg.

**Fragua**
Andres Mellado, 64 y Gaztambide, 77, Madrid 15, Spain.
- Centro de Estudios Sociales de la Santa Cruz del Valle de los Caidos. Revista de Estudios Sociales. 3 per yr. ISSN 0008-9966 (Centro de Estudios Sociales de la Santa Cruz del Valle de los Caidos)

**Franciscanos Espanoles**
Joaquin Costa 38, Madrid 6, Spain.
- Archivo Ibero-Americano; revista de estudios historicos. q. ISSN 0004-0452
- Verdad y Vida; revista de las ciencias del espiritu. q. ISSN 0042-3718

**Fuerza Nueva**
Nunez de Balboa, 31, Madrid 1, Spain.
- Fuerza Nueva. w. ISSN 0016-2477

**Laureano Fueyo**
Arturo Soria, 151 (Chalet), Madrid-33, Spain.
- Mecametal. m.

**Fundacion Foessa**
- Coleccion Fundacion Foessa. Serie Estudios. (pub. by Euramerica, S.A.)

**Fundacion Jimenez Diaz**
- Fundacion Jimenez Diaz. Boletin. (pub. by Publicaciones Controladas, S.A.)

**Fundacion Juan March**
Castello, 77, Madrid-6, Spain.
- Fundacion Juan March. Boletin Informativo. m.
- Hoja Informativa de Literatura y Filologia. m.

**Fundacion Lazaro Galdiano**
Serrano 122, Madrid, Spain.
- Goya; revista de arte. bi-m. ISSN 0017-2715

**Fundacion Puigvert**
- Fundacion Puigvert. Anales. (pub. by Editorial Eco, S.A.)

**Gaceta Ilustrada, S.A.**
Juan Bravo 49 Dpcho. 7, Madrid 6, Spain.
- Gaceta Ilustrada. w. ISSN 0016-3783
- Historia y Vida. m. ISSN 0018-2354

**Ediciones Gaisa**
Gran via Marques del Turia, 64, Valencia.
- Guia de Valencia: Turistica, Urbana, Comercial. irreg., 1974, latest issue.

**Editorial Galaxia**
Reconquista 1, Vigo, Spain.
- Grial; revista galega de cultura. q. ISSN 0017-4181

**Luis Gallego, Ed. & Pub.**
Orense 26, Madrid 20, Spain.
- Cimas-Ski; sports de ski y montana. m.

**Editorial Gama Moda**
Caspe 118-120,5p., Barcelona-13, Spain.
- C Y L Corseteria y Lenceria. q.

**Ganado**
Apartado 188, Saragossa, Spain.
- Ganado. m.

**Joaquin Garcia Morato**
39 Apdo. 756, Madrid 10, Spain.
- Metalurgia y Electricidad. m. ISSN 0026-0991

**Julio Garcia Peri Editor**
Sanchez Pacheco 83, Madrid 2, Spain.
- Acta Ginecologica. m. ISSN 0001-5776
- Boletin de Ginecologia. m. (Sociedad Ginecologica Espanola)
- Indice de Actualidad Farmacologica. a.
- Mundo Pediatrico. w.
- Noticias Medicas; el periodico de la medicina espanola. d. ISSN 0029-4225
- Revista de Reumatologia. q. (Cruz Roja Espanola)
- Sociedad Espanola de Oftalmologia. Archivos. m.

**Editorial Garsi**
Londres 17, Madrid 2, Spain.
- Acta Medica de Tenerife. bi-m. ISSN 0001-6020
- Acta Otorrinolaringologica Espanola. bi-m. ISSN 0001-6519 (Sociedad Espanola de Otorrinolaringologia)
- Actas Dermo-Sifiliograficas. bi-m. ISSN 0001-7310 (Academia Espanola de Dermatologia y Sifiliografia)
- Actas Luso Espanolas de Neurologia Psiquiatria y Ciencias Afines. bi-m. ISSN 0300-5062
- Allergologia et Immunopathologia. bi-m. ISSN 0301-0546 (Sociedad Espanola de Alergia) (Co-Sponsors: Sociedad Latinoamericana de Alergia Einmunologia; Association of Asthnology (Interasthna))
- Anales Espanoles de Pediatrica. bi-m.
- Anestesiologia Pediatrica. q.
- Archivos de Neurobiologia. bi-m. ISSN 0004-0576
- Archivos Espanoles de Urologia. bi-m. ISSN 0004-0614 (Asociacion Espanola de Urologia)
- Avances en Alimentacion y Mejora Animal. m. ISSN 0005-1896
- Ciencias Neurologicas. q. ISSN 0009-6792 (Instituto de Ciencias Neurologicas)
- Cirugia Espanola. bi-m. ISSN 0009-739X (Asociacion Espanola de Cirujanos)
- Contaminacion y Prevencion. bi-m.
- Corrosion Y Proteccion. m. ISSN 0045-8678
- Explotacion Agraria; revista agricola, ganadera y forestal. m. ISSN 0531-755X
- Explotacion Agraria. bi-m.
- Hospital General; revista de medicina y cirugia, beneficencia provincial de Madrid. bi-m. ISSN 0018-568X (Cuerpo Medico Beneficencia Provincia de Madrid)
- Radiologia. bi-m. ISSN 0033-8338 (Sociedad Espanola de Radiologia y Electrologia Medicas y de Medicina Nuclear)
- Revista Espanola de Gerontologia. q. ISSN 0034-9410 (Sociedad Espanola de Gerontologia)
- Revista Espanola de las Enfermedades del Aparato Digestivo. fortn. ISSN 0034-9437 (Sociedad Espanola de Patologia Digestiva)
- Revista Espanola de Pediatria. bi-m. ISSN 0034-947X (Universidad de Sevilla. Catedra de Pediatria y Puericultura)
- Sociedad Canaria de Pediatria. Boletin. q. ISSN 0037-8410
- Sociedad Vasco-Navarra de Pediatria. Boletin. q. ISSN 0037-8658
- Toko-Ginecologia Practica. fortn. ISSN 0040-8867 (Universidad de Sevilla. Catedra de Obstetrica y Ginecologia)
- Veterinaria Espanola. q.
- Zootechnia; acta societatis internationalis veterinariorum zootechnicorum. q. ISSN 0044-5312 (International Veterinary Association for Animal Production) (Co-Sponsor: Spanish Veterinary Assn. for Zootechnics)

**Gaya Ciencia**
Barcelona, Spain.
- Cuadernos de la Gaya Ciencia. irreg.

**General Espanola de Seguros, S.A.**
Plaza de las Cortes, 2, Madrid-14, Spain.
- General Espanola de Seguros, S.A. Boletin de Informacion. q.

**Editorial Gustavo Gili, S.A.**
Rosellon 87-89, Barcelona 15, Spain.
- Coleccion Arquitectura/Perspectivas. irreg.
- Coleccion Arquitectura y Critica. irreg.
- Coleccion Ciencia Urbanistica. irreg. ISSN 0069-5068 (Laboratorio de Urbanismo de la Escuela Tecnica Superior de Arquitectura de Barcelona)
- Coleccion Comunicacion Visual. irreg.
- Coleccion Estructuras y Formas. irreg. ISSN 0071-1632
- Coleccion Proyecto y Planificacion. irreg.
- Coleccion Punto y Linea. m.
- Coleccion Temas Basicos de Ingenieria. irreg.
- Coleccion Temas de Arquitectura Actual. irreg. ISSN 0082-2701
- Color y Decoracion en el Hogar. irreg.
- Materiales de la Ciudad. irreg.

**Editorial Glarma, S.A.**
Muntaner, 33, Barcelona 6, Spain.
- Folia Humanistica; ciencias, artes, letras. 11 per yr. ISSN 0015-5594

**Diego Gomez Florez, Ed. & Pub.**
Travesera de las Cortes, 305, Barcelona, 14, Spain.
- Catalogo de Libros Antiguos y Modernos. s-a.

**Miguel J. Goni Fernandez, Ed. & Pub.**
Ardemans 64, Madrid, Spain.
- Nueva Lente; publicacion mensual de fotografia y cine. m.

**Fernando Gordillo Escudero, Ed. & Pub.**
San Bernabe, 18, Madrid 5, Spain.
- Cuadernos de Fotografia. q.

**Editorial Gredos**
Sanchez Pacheco 81, Madrid, Spain.
- Revista Espanola de Linguistica. s-a. (Sociedad Espanola de Linguistica)

**Gremio de Ferreteria de Barcelona**
- Revista de Ferreteria. (pub. by Jorge Foix, Ed. & Pub.)

**Gremio Sindical de la Electricidad**
- Revista de la Industria Electrica. (pub. by Editecnia, S.A.)

**Gremio Sindical de Libreros de Barcelona**
Mallorca 274, Barcelona-9, Spain.
- Libreria. m (with supplements) ISSN 0024-2659

**Gremio Sindical Nacional de Detallistas de Alimentacion**
Paseo del Prado 18-20, Madrid 14, Spain.
- Detalle. m. ISSN 0418-7830

**Grupo Espeleologico Vizcaino**
P.O. Box 53, Bilbao, Spain.
- KOBIE. a.

**Grupo Local de Panaderia de Barcelona**
Via Layetana, 134, Barcelona-9, Spain.
- Actualidad Panadera de Cataluna; G P B-organo oficial panaderia de Barcelona, Tarragona, Lerida y Gerona. 14 per yr.

**Demetrio Guitierrez Alarcon**
Teodoro Camino 2, Albacete, Spain.
- Cronica de Albacete; periodico de informacion general. 15 per yr.

**Ediciones H Y M S A**
see Hogar y la Moda, S.A.

**Miguel de Haro Serrano, Ed. & Pub**
Fernando el Catolico 15, Madrid 15, Spain.
- Distribucion Actualidad. m.
- I.P./Mark. (Informacion de Publicidad y Marketing) m.
- Marketing Actualidad. m.

**Hechos y Dichos**
Pablo Aranda 3, Madrid 6, Spain.
- Hechos y Dichos; revista de pensamiento y actualidad Cristiana. m. ISSN 0017-9485

**Lorenzo Herranz, Ed. & Pub**
Sanchez Barcaiztegui, 38, Madrid-7, Spain.
- S P I C; revista de aviacion comercial y turismo. m. ISSN 0036-1852 (S P I C)

**Hogar del Libro, S. A.**
Pelayo, 11, 4, Barcelona, Spain.
- Informacion Librera. m.

**Hogar y Arquitectura**
Francisco de Rojas 9, Madrid 10, Spain.
- Hogar y Arquitectura. bi-m. ISSN 0018-3237

**Hogar y la Moda, S.A.**
Diputacion 211, Barcelona 11, Spain.
- Algo; revista de divulgacion cientifica, tecnica y cultural. s-m. ISSN 0002-5348
- Cocina y Hogar. m. ISSN 0045-7248
- Hogar y la Moda. s-m. ISSN 0046-7723
- Labores del Hogar. m. ISSN 0047-3863
- Lecturas. w. ISSN 0047-4304

**Ediciones I N A P P**
Habana 66, Madrid 16, Spain.
- Parapsicologia; divulgacion cientifica - el misterio al luz de la ciencia. m.
- Psicodeia; revista de psicologia. m.

**Iberflora**
Apartado 13, Valencia, Spain.
- Iberflora. m.

**Iberico Europea de Ediciones, S.A.**
Serrano, 44, Madrid, 1, Spain.
- Anuario del Arte Espanol. a.

**Ibero-American Bureau of Education**
Avenida de los Reyes Catolicos, Ciudad Universitaria, Madrid 3, Spain.
- Ibero-American Bureau of Education. Information and Publications Department Series V: Technical Seminars and Meetings. ISSN 0536-2512

**IGA Iberica**
Coslada 15, 1-a, Madrid-28, Spain.
- Hablemos....de IGA. bi-m.

**Ilustre Colegio Provincial de Abogados de San Sebastian**
San Martin, 41 (Palacio de Justicia), Guipuzcoa, Spain.
- Boletin de Pequena Jurisprudencia. bi-m.

**Impresa Mossen Alcover**
Palma de Mallorca, Spain.
- Coleccion Siurell. Serie de Cocina. irreg.

**Impresos y Ediciones, S.A.**
Caspe, No 6, Barcelona (10), Spain.
- Ondas; revista de Radio, TV y actualidad. s-m. ISSN 0030-2422

**Indice, S.A.**
Magallanes 3, Madrid 15, Spain.
- Indice. s-m. ISSN 0019-6975

**Industria de la Carne**
Archa 2, Malaga, Spain.
- Industria de la Carne. m.

**Industria Juegetera Espana**
San German, 5, Barcelona 4, Spain.
- Juguetes y Juegos de Espana. q. ISSN 0022-6157

**Ediciones Informativas y Deportivas**
Avda. del Generalisimo, 60, Madrid, Spain.
- Golfinformacion. irreg.

**Informes Union S.A.**
Sevilla, Spain.
- Ideas Tecnicas. m.

**Ingenieria**
General Martinez Campos 3, Madrid 10, Spain.
- Ingenieria; revista de informacion tecnica. q. ISSN 0446-2378

**Ingenieria Quimica S.A.**
Pedro de Valdivia 29, Madrid 6, Spain.
- Ingenieria Quimica. m.

**Ingenieros de Caminos, Canales y Puertos**
- Revista de Obras Publicas. (pub. by Escuela de Ingenieros de Caminos, Canales y Puertos)

**Institucion Fernan Gonzalez**
Palacio de la Diputacion Provincial, Burgos, Spain.
- Institucion Fernan-Gonzalez. Boletin. s-a.

**Institucion Fernando el Catolico**
Pl. de Espana 2, Zaragoza, Spain.
- Caesaraugusta. a. ISSN 0007-9502 (Seminario de Argueologia y Numismatica Aragonesas)
- Zaragoza. s-a. ISSN 0044-1821
- Zurita; cuadernos de historia. q. ISSN 0044-5517

**Institucion "Fray Bernardino de Sahagun"**
Edificio Fierro, Puerta de la Reina, 1, Leon, Spain.
- Provincia; coleccion de poesia. irreg.
- Tierras de Leon. q. ISSN 0495-5773

**Institucion "Mila y Fontanals". Departamento de Sociologia**
Egipciacas 15, Barcelona, Spain.
- Anales de Sociologia. s-a. ISSN 0003-2522

**Institution Jakin**
Cuartel, 2, Tolosa, Guipuzcoa, Spain
(Subscr. to: Pelota 4-1, Bilbao-5, Spain)
- Anaitasuna. s-m. (National Council of the Third Order of Saint Francis)

**Instituto Agricola Catalan de San Isidro**
Plaza de San Jose Oriol,4, Barcelona, Spain.
- Instituto Agricola Catalan de San Isidro. Revista. m. ISSN 0046-9890

**Instituto Antituberculoso Francisco Moragas**
Paseo de San Juan 20, Barcelona, Spain.
- Instituto Antituberculoso Francisco Moragas. Publicaciones. biennial.

**Instituto "Antonio de Nebrija"**
Consejo Superior de Investigaciones Cientificas, Francisco Rodriguez Adrados, Duque de Medinaceli 4, Madrid, Spain.
- Emerita; Revista de Linguistica y Filologia Classica. s-a. ISSN 0013-6662

**Instituto Arnaldo de Vilanova**
Duque de Medinaccli, Madrid-14, Spain.
- Asclepiu; archivo iberoamericana de historia de la medicina y antropologia medica. a.

**Instituto Barraquer**
Laforja 88, Barcelona, Spain.
- Instituto Barraquer. Anales. q. ISSN 0020-3645

**Instituto Bibliografico Hispanico**
Calle de Atocha 106, Apartado 12311, Madrid 12, Spain.
- Bibliografia Espanola. m.
- Revistas Espanolas en Curso de Publicacion. (pub. by Direccion General de Archivos y Bibliotecas)

**Instituto Catolico de Estudios Sociales de Barcelona**
Enrique Granados, 2, Barcelona 7, Spain.
- Cuadernos de Orientacion Familiar. q. ISSN 0011-2453
- Perspectiva Social. s-a.

**Instituto Corachan**
Buigas 19, Barcelona, Spain.
- Anales del Instituto Corachan. q. ISSN 0003-2530

**Instituto de Aclimatacion**
General Segura-1, Almeira, Spain.
- Instituto de Aclimatacion. Archives. s-a.

**Instituto de Administracion Local. Centro de Estudios Urbanos**
- Secretariado Iberoamericano de Municipios. Boletin de Informacion. (pub. by Instituto de Estudios de Administracion Local)

**Instituto de Agroquimica y Tecnologia de Alimentos**
Jaime Roig 11, Valencia 10, Spain.
- Revista de Agroquimica y Tecnologia de Alimentos. q. ISSN 0034-7698

**Instituto de Antropologia de Barcelona**
Espana 15, Hospitalet L1, Barcelona, Spain.
- Anthropoligica. s-a. ISSN 0301-6587

**Instituto de Biologia Sueroterapia, S.A.**
Bravo Murillo, 53, Madrid, Spain.
- Instituto de Biologia y Sueroterapia. Oficina de Informacion Sanitaria. Boletin; suplemento de la revista IBYS. m.

**Instituto de Ciencias Neurologicas**
- Ciencias Neurologicas. (pub. by Editorial Garsi)

**Instituto de Cultura Hispanica**
Avda. de los Reyes Catolicos s/n, (Ciudad Universitaria), Madrid-3, Spain.
- Cuadernos Hispanoamericanos; revista mensual de cultura Hispanica. m. ISSN 0011-250X
- Sintesis Informativa Iberoamericana. a. (prep. by its Centro de Documentacion Iberoamericana)
- Sumario Actual de Revistas. bi-m. (prep. by its Biblioteca) (Co-sponsor: Instituto Bibliografico Hispanico)

**Instituto de Derecho Canonico "San Raimundo de Penafort"**
Compania 1, Salamanca, Spain.
- Revista Espanola de Derecho Canonico. 3 per yr. ISSN 0034-9372

**Instituto de Derecho Internacional "Francisco de Vitoria"**
Duque de Medinaceli 4, Madrid 14, Spain.
- Revista Espanola de Derecho Internacional. q. ISSN 0034-9380

**Instituto de Estructura de la Materia. Laboratorio de Quimica Cuantica**
Serrano, 119, Madrid, Spain.
- F C T L. (Folia Chimica Theoretica Latina); boletin informativo de los quimicos cuanticos de expresion latina. q.

**Instituto de Estudios Africanos**
Paseo de la Castellana 5, Madrid, Spain.
- Africa. m. ISSN 0001-9763
- Archivo del Instituto de Estudios Africanos. q.
- Coleccion Monografica Africana. irreg. ISSN 0069-5130
- Revista Africa. bi-m.

**Instituto de Estudios Agro-Sociales**
Calle de Los Madrazo 11, Madrid 14, Spain.
- Revista de Estudios Agro-Sociales. q. ISSN 0034-8155

**Instituto de Estudios Alicantinos**
Diputacion Provincial, Alicante, Spain.
- Instituto de Estudios Alicantinos. Revista. 3 per yr.

**Instituto de Estudios Asturianos**
Plaza Porlier 5, Oviedo, Spain.
- Instituto de Estudios Asturianos. Boletin. q. ISSN 0020-384X

**Instituto de Estudios de Administracion Local**
Joaquin Garcia Morato, 7, Madrid 10, Spain.
- Secretariado Iberoamericano de Municipios. Boletin de Informacion. bi-m. (Instituto de Administracion Local. Centro de Estudios Urbanos. Secretariado Iberoamericano de Municipios)

**Instituto de Estudios de Administracion Local. Centro de Estudios Urbanos**
Garcia Morata 7, Madrid, Spain.
- Ciudad y Territorio. q.
- Revista de Ciencia Urbana. 4 per yr.
- Revista de Estudios de la Vida Local. q. ISSN 0034-8163
- Vida Local. Boletin de Informacion. bi-m.

**Instituto de Estudios de Jardineria y Arte Paisajista**
Alfonso XII, 48, Madrid, 14, Spain.
- Jardin y Paisaje; revista de jardineria y animales. bi-m.

**Instituto de Estudios Electronicos**
- Transistor. (pub. by Vasan, S.L. Ediciones Tecnica)

**Instituto de Estudios Gerundenses**
Plaza Aceite 7, Gerona, Spain.
- Instituto de Estudios Gerundenses. Anales. a.

**Instituto de Estudios Giennenses**
c/o Palacio Provincial, Jaen, Spain.
- Instituto de Estudios Giennenses Boletin. q.

**Instituto de Estudios Hebraicos Sefardies y de Oriente Proximo "Arias Montano"**
Duque de Medicaneli 4, Madrid, Spain.
- Sefarad. s-a. ISSN 0037-0894

**Instituto de Estudios Politicos**
Plaza de la Marina Espanola, 8, Madrid 13, Spain.
- Instituto de Estudios Politicos. Boletin. (pub. by Libreria Europa)
- Revista de Administracion Publica. 3 per yr. ISSN 0034-7639
- Revista de Economia Politica. (pub. by Libreria Europa)
- Revista de Estudios Politicos. bi-m. ISSN 0048-7694
- Revista de Politica Internacional. bi-m. ISSN 0034-8716
- Revista de Politica Social. q. ISSN 0034-8724

**Instituto de Estudios Sindicales de Madrid**
Lope de Vega 38, 8A Planta, Madrid-14, Spain.
- Revista de Estudios Sindicales. q.

**Instituto de Estudios Sindicales, Sociales y Cooperativos**
Lope de Vega 38, Madrid 3, Spain.
- Anuario de Sociologia de los Pueblos Ibericos. a.
- Communidades. 3 per yr. ISSN 0010-3691
- Estudios Sindicales y Cooperativos. q. ISSN 0014-1542

**Instituto de Estudios Sobre Armas Antiguas**
P.O. Box 4, Jarandilla (Caceres), Spain.
- Gladius; etudes sur les armes anciennes, l'armement, l'art militaire et la vie culturelle en Orient et Occident. a. ISSN 0436-029X

**Instituto de Estudios Tarraconenses Ramon Berenguer IV**
Tarragona, Spain.
- Instituto de Estudios Tarraconenses Ramon Berenguer IV. Publicacion. irreg. ISSN 0534-3364
- Instituto de Estudios Tarraconenses Ramon Berenguer IV. Seccion de Estudios Juridicos. Publicacion. irreg.

**Instituto de Farmacologia Espanola**
Fundacion Marques de Urquijo, Ciudad Universitaria, Madrid, Spain.
- Instituto de Farmacologia Espanola. Anales. a. ISSN 0074-0071

**Instituto de Filologia Hispanica "Miguel de Cervantes". Departamento de Dialectologia y Tradiciones Populares**
Duque de Medinaceli 4, Madrid 14, Spain.
- Revista de Dialectologia y Tradiciones Populares. q. ISSN 0034-7981 (Consejo Superior de Investigaciones Cientificas)

**Instituto de Filosofia "Luis Vives"**
Serrano 127, Madrid 6, Spain.
- Revista de Filosofia. q. ISSN 0034-8244

**Instituto de Genetica y Antropologia**
Velazquez 144, Madrid 6, Spain.
- Genetica Iberica. q. ISSN 0016-6693 (Consejo Superior de Investigaciones Cientificas)

**Instituto de Geografia Aplicada**
Serrano 115, Madrid-6, Spain.
- Fuentes Cartograficas Espanolas. irreg.

**Instituto de Historia "Jeronimo Zurita"**
Duque de Medinaceli 4, Madrid 14, Spain.
- Hispania; revista espanola de historia. q. ISSN 0018-2141

**Instituto de Informacion y Documentacion en Biomedicina**
Paseo al Mar 17, Valencia 10, Spain.
- Indice Medico Espanol. q. ISSN 0019-7068 (Universidad de Valencia. Facultad de Medicina)

**Instituto de Informacion y Documentacion en Ciencia y Tecnologia**
Joaquin Costa 22, Madrid - 6, Spain.
- Resumenes de Articulos Cientificos y Tecnicos. Serie A: Quimica Industrial. m. ISSN 0034-5881 (Spain. Consejo Superior de Investigaciones Cientificas. Patronato Juan de la Cierva)
- Resumenes de Articulos Cientificos y Tecnicos. Serie B: Fisica Aplicada. m. ISSN 0034-589X (Spain. Consejo Superior de Investigaciones Cientificas. Patronato Juan de la Cierva)
- Resumenes de Articulos Cientificos y Tecnicos. Serie C: Ciencia y Tecnica de los Metales. m. ISSN 0034-5903 (Spain. Consejo Superior de Investigaciones Cientificas. Patronato Juan de la Cierva)
- Resumenes de Articulos Cientificos y Tecnicos. Serie D: Ingenieria y Tecnologias Varias. m. ISSN 0034-5911 (Spain. Consejo Superior de Investigaciones Cientificas. Patronato Juan de la Cierva)
- Resumenes de Articulos Cientificos y Tecnicos. Serie E: Economia de la Empresa. m. ISSN 0034-592X (Spain. Consejo Superior de Investigaciones Cientificas. Patronato Juan de la Cierva)
- Revista Espanola de Documentacion Cientifica. q.

**Instituto de Investigacion Operativa y Estadistica**
Serrano 123, Madrid 6, Spain.
- Trabajos de Estadistica e Investigacion Operativa. q. ISSN 0041-0241

**Instituto de Investigacion Textil y de Cooperacion Industrial**
Escuela Tecnica Superior de Ingenieros Industriales, Colon 11, Tarrasa, Spain.
- Instituto de Investigacion Textil y de Cooperacion Industrial. Boletin. q.

**Instituto de la Caza Fotografica y Ciencias de la Naturaleza.**
Castello, 59, Madrid, Spain.
- Caza Fotografica. bi-m.

**Instituto de la Grasa y sus Derivados**
Avda. Padre Garcia Tejero 4, Seville 12, Spain.
- Grasas y Aceites. bi-m. ISSN 0017-3495

**Instituto de la Opinion Publica**
Calle Pedro Teixeira 8, Madrid 20, Spain.
- Revista Espanola de la Opinion Publica. (pub. by Editora Nacional)
- Revista Espanola de la Opinion Publica. q. ISSN 0034-9429 (Spain. Presidencia del Gobierno)

**Instituto de Optica "Daza de Valdes"**
- Optica Pura y Aplicada. (pub. by Sociedad Espanola de Optica)

**Instituto de Parasitologia, "Lopez-Neyra"**
Ventanilla 11, Granada, Spain.
- Revista Iberica de Parasitologia. 4 per yr. ISSN 0034-9623 (Co-sponsor: Asociacion de Parasitologos Espanoles)

**Instituto de Pedagogia**
Duque de Medinaceli 4, Madrid, Spain.
- Revista Espanola de Pedagogia. q. ISSN 0034-9461

**Instituto de Plastico y Caucho**
Juan de la Cierva 3, Madrid 6, Spain.
- Revista de Plasticos Modernos. m. ISSN 0034-8708

**Instituto de Prehistoria y Arqueologia de la Diputacion Provincial de Barcelona**
Palacio del Museo Arqueologico, Parque de Montjuich, Barcelona 4, Spain.
- Ampurias; revista de prehistoria, arqueologia y etnologia. a.
- Informacion Arqueologica. 3 per yr.

**Instituto de Sociologia Aplicada**
Claudio Coello 141, Madrid, Spain.
- Cuadernos de Realidades Sociales. 3 per yr.

**Instituto de Sociologia y Desarrollo del Area Iberica**
Fernandez de la Hoz, 7-20 Madrid,4, Spain.
- Instituto de Sociologia y Desarrollo del Area Iberica.Boletin Informativo. bi-m.

**Instituto de Tecnicas Sociales de la Fundacion Fondo Social Universitario**
Apartado Num. 502 F.D., Madrid, Spain.
- Sistema. q.

**Instituto de Teologia "Francisco Suarez"**
Duque de Medinaceli 4, Madrid 14, Spain.
- Estudios Biblicos. q. ISSN 0014-1437 (Spain. Consejo Superior de Investigaciones Cientificas)

**Instituto de Zootecnica. Facultad de Veterinaria**
Avda. de Medina Azahara, 9, Cordoba, Spain.
- Archivos de Zootecnia. q. ISSN 0004-0592
- Instituto de Zootecnica. Facultad de Veterinaria. Catalogo de Publicaciones. irreg.

**Instituto Dexeus**
- Clinica Ginecologica. (pub. by Salvat Editores, S.A.)

**Instituto Diego Velazquez**
Duque de Medinaceli 4, Madrid 14, Spain.
- Archivo Espanol de Arte. q. ISSN 0004-0428
- Revista de Ideas Esteticas. q. ISSN 0034-8333

**Instituto Eduardo Torroja de la Construccion y del Cemento**
Costillares (Chamartin) Apdo. 19002, Madrid 33, Spain.
- Informes de la Construccion; revista de informacion tecnica. m. ISSN 0020-0883
- Materiales de Construccion. q.

**Instituto Espanol de Arqueologia**
Medinaceli 4, Madrid 14, Spain.
- Archivo Espanol de Arqueologia. a. ISSN 0066-6742

**Instituto Espanol de Emigracion**
Paseo del Pintor Rosales 44-46, Madrid 8, Spain.
- Carta de Espana; la revista para los espanoles en el extranjero. m.

**Instituto Espanol de Entomologia**
J. Gutierrez Avascal 2, Madrid 6, Spain.
- EOS; revista espanola de entomologia. a. ISSN 0013-9440

**Instituto Espanol de Estudios Mediterraneos**
Pomaret 21, Torre, Barcelona 8, Spain.
- Instituto Espanol de Estudios Mediterraneos. Cuadernos. q.

**Instituto Espanol de Medicina Tropical**
Pabellon 2, Facultad de Medicina (Ciudad Universitaria), Madrid 3, Spain.
- Medicina Tropical. bi-m. ISSN 0025-7958

**Instituto Espanol de Oceanografia**
Alcala 27, Madrid 14, Spain.
- Instituto Espanol de Oceanografia. Boletin. irreg., 1969, no. 171. ISSN 0074-0195
- Instituto Espanol de Oceanografia. Trabajos. irreg. ISSN 0074-0209

**Instituto Espanol del Envase y Embalaje**
Breton de los Herreros, 57, Madrid 3, Spain.
- Catalogo Nacional del Envase, Embalaje y Artes Graficas Aplicadas. (pub. by Divultec S. A.)
- I D E. (Informacion de Embalaje) m. ISSN 0300-4171
- Instituto Espanol del Envase y Embalaje. BIU. Boletin Informativo de Urgencia. m.
- Instituto Espanol del Envase y Embalaje. RBM. Resumen Bibliografico Mundial. m.

**Instituto Filologia Hispanica "Miguel de Cervantes"**
Duque de Medinaceli 4, Madrid 14, Spain.
- Boletin de Filologia Espanola. q. ISSN 0006-6265 (Consejo Superior de Investigaciones Cientificas)

**Instituto Filosofico de Balmesiana**
Apdo 1382, Duran y Bas 9, Barcelona 2, Spain.
- Espiritu. s-a. ISSN 0014-0716

**Instituto Francisco de Vitoria. Escuela de Estudios Juridicos del Ejercito**
Calle Tambre No. 35, Madrid-2, Spain.
- Revista Espanola de Derecho Militar. s-a. ISSN 0034-9399

**Instituto Gemologico Espanol**
Victor Hugo 1, Madrid 4, Spain.
- Instituto Gemologico Espanol. Boletin. 3 per yr.

**Instituto Geografico y Catastral. Seccion de Geomagnetismo y Aeronomia**
Apdo. 3007, Madrid 3, Spain.
- Anuarios del Servicio de Geomagnetismo y Aeronomia.

**Instituto IBYS**
Bravo Murillo 53, Madrid 3, Spain.
- Revista Ibys. 4 per yr. ISSN 0034-9658

**Instituto Ingenieros Civiles de Espana**
General Goded 38, Madrid 4, Spain.
- Instituto Ingenieros Civiles de Espana. Boletim Informativo. ISSN 0020-4048

**Instituto Internacional de Genealogia y Heraldica y Federacion de Corporacion es Afines**
Apdo de Correos 12079, Madrid, Spain.
- Hoja Informativa. m. ISSN 0018-3318

**Instituto Jaime Ferran de Microbiologia**
Joaquin Costa 32, Madrid 6, Spain.
- Microbiologia Espanola. q. ISSN 0026-2595 (Co-sponsor: Sociedad Espanola de Microbiologia)

**Instituto Jorge Juan de Matematicas**
Serrano 123, Madrid 6, Spain.
- Estructuras. 10 per yr.
- Gaceta Matematica. q. ISSN 0016-3805 (Co-sponsor: Real Sociedad Matematica Espanola)

**Instituto Jose Celestino Mutis**
Serrano 113, Madrid 6, Spain.
- Farmacognosia. q. ISSN 0014-8288

**Instituto Juan Sebastian Elcano**
Vitrubio 8, Madrid 6, Spain.
- Estudios Geograficos. q. ISSN 0014-1496 (Consejo Superior de Investigaciones Cientificas)

**Instituto Nacional de Edafologia y Agrobiologia**
Serrano 115, Madrid 6, Spain.
- Anales de Edafologia y Agrobiologia. m. ISSN 0003-3987

**Instituto Nacional de Educacion Fisica**
Av. Martin Fierro s/n, Madrid-3, Spain.
- Citius Altius Fortius; revista de estudios deportivos. q.

**Instituto Nacional de Ensenanza Media "Alfonso X el Sabio"**
Vista Alegre, Murcia, Spain.
- Brisas Alfonsinas; revista literaria escolar del instituto.

**Instituto Nacional de Estudios Juridicos**
Seccion de Publicaciones, Duque de Medinaceli, 6, Madrid 14, Spain.
- Anuario de Filosofia del Derecho. a.
- Anuario de Historia del Derecho Espanol. a.
- Instituto Internacional de Historia del Derecho Indiano. Actas y Estudios. triennial.

**Instituto Nacional de Geofisica**
Serrano 123, Madrid 6, Spain.
- Revista de Geofisica. q. ISSN 0034-8279

**Instituto Nacional de Geologia**
Avenida Jose Antonio 585, Facultad de Ciencias, Universidad Barcelona, Spain.
- Acta Geologica Hispanica. bi-m. ISSN 0567-7505

**Instituto Nacional de Industria**
Plaza de Salamanca, 8, Madrid, Spain.
- Instituto Nacional de Industria. Resumen de Actividades. irreg.

**Instituto Nacional de Investigaciones Agrarias**
General Sanjurjo 56, Madrid 3, Spain.
- Instituto Nacional de Investigaciones Agrarias. Anales. Serie: Economia Sociologia Agrarias. irreg (approx 1 per yr)
- Instituto Nacional de Investigaciones Agrarias. Anales. Serie: General. irreg (approx 1-2 per yr)
- Instituto Nacional de Investigaciones Agrarias. Anales Serie: Higiene y Sanidad Animal. irreg.
- Instituto Nacional de Investigaciones Agrarias. Anales. Serie: Produccion Animal. irreg (approx 1-2 per yr)
- Instituto Nacional de Investigaciones Agrarias. Anales. Serie: Produccion Vegetal. irreg.
- Instituto Nacional de Investigaciones Agrarias. Anales. Serie: Proteccion Vegetal. irreg (approx 1-2 per yr)
- Instituto Nacional de Investigaciones Agrarias. Anales. Serie: Recursos Naturales. irreg.
- Instituto Nacional de Investigaciones Agrarias. Anales. Serie: Technologia Agraria. irreg.

**Instituto Nacional de la Vivienda**
Documentacion, Plaza de San Juan de la Cruz No. 3, Madrid, Spain.
- Instituto Nacional de la Vivienda. Boletin Interior de Informacion. q. ISSN 0020-4145

**Instituto Nacional del Libro Espanol**
Santiago Rusinol 8, Madrid 3, Spain.
- Guia de Editores y de Libreros de Espana. irreg. ISSN 0072-7903
- Libro Espanol. m. ISSN 0024-273X
- Libros Espanoles I S B N. (pub. by Agencia Espanola I S B N)

**Instituto Quimico de Sarria**
Barcelona 17, Spain.
- I.Q.S; trabajos de fin de carrera. a.

**Instituto Quimico de Sarria. Asociacion de Quimicos**
Barcelona 17, Spain.
- Afinidad; revista de quimica teorica y aplicada. 10 per yr. ISSN 0001-9704

**Instituto Salazar y Castro**
Calle de Atocha 91, Madrid 12, Spain.
- Hidalguia; revista de genealogia, nobleza y armas. bi-m. ISSN 0018-1285

**Instituto Sancho de Moncado**
Duque de Medinaceli 4, Madrid, Spain.
- Anales de Economia. q.

**Instituto Sindical de Formacion Cooperativa**
Paseo del Prado, 18, Madrid, Spain.
- Cuadernos de Estudios Cooperativos. 4 per yr.

**Instituto Superior de Ciencias Morales**
Felix Boix, 13, Madrid, Spain.
- Penetecostes. q.

**Instituto Superior de Filosofia**
Apartado 100, Guadalajara, Spain.
- Estudios Filosoficos. 3 per yr.

**Ediciones y Publicaciones de Insula**
Benito Gutierrez 26, Madrid 8, Spain.
- Insula; revista bibliografica de ciencias y letras. m.
ISSN 0020-4536

**International Association for Shell and Spatial Structures.**
Alfonson XII 3, Madrid 7, Spain.
- International Association for Shell and Spatial Structures. Bulletin. irreg. ISSN 0538-4400

**International Commission for the Conservation of Atlantic Tunas.**
Calle General Molla 17, Madrid 1, Spain.
- International Commission for the Conservation of Atlantic Tunas. Report. biennial.

**International Federation of Automatic Control. Comite Espanol**
- Tecnica de la Regulacion y Mando Automatico. (pub. by Compania Espanola de Editoriales Technologicas Internacionales S.A.)

**International Olive Growers Federation**
c/o Alfredo Jiminez-Millas, Agustina de Aragan 11, 2e, Madrid 6, Spain.
- International Olive Growers Federation. Congress Reports. irreg., 1969, 21st, Madrid. ISSN 0074-7173

**International Olive Oil Council**
C/Juan Bravo, 10, Madrid, 6, Spain.
- Feuille d'Information du C O I/Hoja de Informacion del C O I. s-m.

**International Veterinary Association for Animal Production**
- Zootechnia. (pub. by Editorial Garsi)

**Itinerario-Guia del Viajero**
Principe 9, Madrid-12, Spain.
- Itinerario-Guia del Viajero; mercancias y transportes en general. 7 per yr. ISSN 0021-3195

**Ediciones Joker**
San Leonardo 12, Madrid 8, Spain.
- Meridiano; sintesis de la prensa mundial al gusto Espanol. m. ISSN 0026-0037

**Junta Central de Fiestas**
Palacio Municipal, Villena, Alicante, Spain.
- Dia Cuatro Que Fuera. . . m.

**Junta de Energia Nuclear**
Ciudad Universitaria, Madrid 3, Spain.
- Energia Nuclear. bi-m. ISSN 0013-7324
- Junta de Energia Nuclear, Spain. Informes J.E.N. irreg., 40-50 per yr. ISSN 0081-3397

**Kirolak**
c/o Jose Acosta Montoro, Ed., Villa Cord, Miraconcha, San Sebastian, Spain.
- Kirolak; revista deportiva del pais Vasco. m.

**Kompass Espana SA**
Av. del General Peron 26, Madrid, 20, Spain (Dist. by Iliffe NTP Inc., 300 E. 42 St., New York, N.Y. 10017)
- Kompass Espana; repertorio general de la economie espanola. a. ISSN 0075-6644 (Foundation for Promoting International Economic Information SZ)

**Kurpil**
Apartado 570 Marina, 4, San Sebastian, Spain.
- Kurpil; revista mensual de literatura. m.

**Ignacio H. de La Mota, Ed. & Pub.**
Recoletos, 1, Madrid-1, Spain.
- Guia de los Medios. m.

**Laboratorio**
c/o Eduardo Suarez Peregrin, Hoteles de Beln, Calle B, Granada, Spain.
- Laboratorio. m. ISSN 0023-6691

**Laboratorio Aldo-Union**
Angel Guimera, 123-125, Esplugas (Barcelona), Spain.
- Leguas. bi-m.

**Laboratorio de Urbanismo de la Escuela Tecnica Superior de Arquitectura de Barcelona**
- Coleccion Ciencia Urbanistica. (pub. by Editorial Gustavo Gili, S.A.)

**Laboratorio Lafarquim S. A.**
Rufino Gonzalez 4, Madrid-17, Spain.
- F A C: Revista Practica del Estudiante de Medicina. 9 per yr.

**Laboratorios y Talleres**
c/o Rafael Fuentes Guerra, Ed., Alcala 31-7, Madrid-14, Spain.
- Laboratorios y Talleres. s-a.

**LECTO Libreria**
General Rodrigo, 5, Madrid, Spain.
- Anuario de Ciencia Economica. a.

**Editorial Lectura y Estudio S.A.**
Barcelona-6, Spain.
- Anuario Medico Farmaceutico Nacional. a. ISSN 0304-8500

**Leon. Ayuntamiento de Leon**
c/o Juan Pastrana Garcia, Director, Legio Vii, 1, Leon, Spain.
- Leon. Boletin de Informacion Municipal. q.

**Libreria Cientifica Medinaceli**
Duque de Medinaceli, 4 Madrid 14, Spain.
- Revista Internacional de Sociologia. q. ISSN 0034-9712

**Magda Llohis Serra, Ed. & Pub.**
Tuset, 21, Barcelona 6, Spain.
- Revista Recepcion. bi-m.

**Luis Llongueras Batlle, Ed. & Pub.**
Alcolea, 43, Barcelona 14, Spain.
- Peluquerias de Gran Seleccion; revista tecnica del peinado. m.

**Lluvia de Rosas**
c/o Fray Carmelo Corbella de la Inmaculada O.C.D., Apartado 112, Lerida, Spain.
- Lluvia de Rosas. bi-m.

**Lookout Publications**
Loma de los Riscos 1, Torremolinos (Malaga), Spain.
- Lookout; the magazine about living in Spain. m. ISSN 0024-6433

**Francisco Lopez Canis**
Puerto Rico, 5, Madrid, 33, Spain.
- A N E S M O. (Anuario Espanol del Motor) a.

**Jose Lopez del Arco y Soler, Ed. & Pub.**
Av. Generalisimo 88-5, Madrid 16, Spain.
- Economia. fortn. ISSN 0012-9720

**Los Yebenes, Spain. Ayuntamiento**
Toledo, Spain.
- Heraldo de los Yebenes. m.

**Editorial Macrometrica**
Paseo Calvo Sotelo 29, Madrid 4, Spain.
- Cuadernos Universitarios de Planificacion Empresarial y Marketing. q. (Universidad Autonoma de Madrid. Fundacion Universidad Empresa)

**Magisterio Espanol, S.A.**
c/o Jose Luis Sastre Fernandez-Rey, Quevedo, 1-3 y 5, Madrid, Spain.
- Escuela en Accion. m.
- Magisterio Espanol. w.
- Pinon. m.

**Maioricensis Schola Lullistica**
c/o Garcias Palou, Apartado 17, Palma de Mallorca, Spain.
- Estudios Lulianos. 3 per yr. ISSN 0425-3752

**Malaga. Camara Oficial de la Propiedad Urbana de la Provincia**
Carreteria, 7, Malaga, Spain.
- Camara Oficial de la Propiedad Urbana de la Provincia de Malaga. Hoja Informativa. m.

**Malaga. Diputacion Provincial**
Palacio Provincial, Plaza Queipo de Llano, Malaga, Spain.
- Jabega. q.

**Publicaciones Men-Car**
Paseo de Colon, 24, Barcelona, Spain.
- Men-Car, Guia de Medios de Transporte Internacional. w.
- Men-Car, Informaciones Maritimas de Importacion y Exportacion. w.

**Ediciones Mensajero**
S. Cugat del Valles, Barcelona, Spain.
- Actualidad Bibliografica de Filosofia y Teologia; selecciones del libros. s-a. (Facultad de Teologia San Federico de Borja)
- Selecciones de Teologia. q. ISSN 0037-119X (Universidad de Deusto. Facultad de Teologia)

**Ediciones Mercantiles Especializadas, S.A.**
Via Layetana, 30, Barcelona 3, Spain.
- Anuario General de Ingenieria Sanitaria y Ambiental de Espana. a.

**Merksa-Servicio de Estudios de Mercado, S.A.**
Escorial 118-122, Barcelona 12, Spain.
- Boletin Merksa de Estudios de Mercado. q.

**Raul M. Mir Rague, Ed. & Pub.**
Via Augusta 158-6, 4, Barcelona 6, Spain.
- Cultivador Moderno; revista mensual teorica-practica de agricultura y ganaderia. m. ISSN 0011-2747

**Misioneros Combonianos. Congregacion Misionera**
Arturo Soria, 101, Madrid-33, Spain.
- Mundo Negro; revista misional africana. m.

**Misioneros del Sagrado Corazon**
Avenida Pio XII, 31, Madrid, 16, Spain.
- Madre y Maestra. m.

**Misioneros Hijos del Corazon de Maria (Claretianos)**
Buen Suceso, 22, Madrid, 8, Spain.
- Vida Religiosa. s-m.

**Misioneros Javerianos**
San Mateo 12-1, Madrid-4, Spain.
- Misioneros Javerianos. m.

**Editorial Moneda y Credito**
Modesto la Fuente 68, Madrid, Spain.
- Moneda y Credito; revista de economia. q. ISSN 0026-959X
- Seminario Xavier Zubiri. Trabajos. irreg. (Seminario Xavier Zubiri)

**Juan A. Monroy**
Apartado 2 029, Madrid 2, Spain.
- Primera Luz. m.
- Restauracion. m.

**Monsalvat**
Edificio Autopistas, Plaza Gala Placidia 1, Barcelona, Spain.
- Monsalvat; revista wagneriana y de informacion musical. irreg.

**Empresa Editorial Federico Montagud de Miguel**
Avd. Generalisimo Franco 321, 1 Piso, Barcelona 9, Spain.
- Confiteria Espanola. m.
- Molineria y Panaderia. m. ISSN 0026-900X

**Montaneros de Aragon**
Calvo Sotelo 11, Zaragoza, Spain.
- Montaneros de Aragon. q. ISSN 0027-0032

**Montepio de Perfumistas y Drogueros**
Av. Jose Antonio 34, No. 12, Madrid 13, Spain.
- Realidad. m.

**D. Antonio Morales Rodriguez, Ed. & Pub.**
Desengano, 12, Madrid, 13, Spain.
- Medios Audiovisuales. m.

**Ignacio H. de la Mota, Ed. & Pub.**
Recoletos, 1, Madrid, Spain.
- Banca Espanola. m.

**Motor Mundial, S.A.**
c/o Ardemans, 63.-Madrid-28, Spain.
- Motor Mundial. m.

**Ediciones del Movimiento**
Gaztambide, 61, Madrid, Spain.
- Panorama de la Economia Espanola. irreg.

**Prensa del Movimiento**
Ave. Generalisimo 142, Madrid 16, Spain.
- Ruedo; semanario grafico de los toros. w. ISSN 0035-9661

**Publicaciones Mundial**
Consejo de Ciento 201, Barcelona 11, Spain.
- Cuadernos de Pedagogia; revista mensual de educacion. m.
- Femme Elegante. bi-m.

**Mundo Financiero**
Box N. 6-119, Madrid, Spain.
- Mundo Financiero; gran revista grafica de economia y finanzas. m. ISSN 0300-3884

**Ediciones Mundo Hispanico**
Av. Reyes Catolicos, Ciudad Universitaria, Apdo. de Correos 245, Madrid 3, Spain.
- Mundo Hispanico. m. ISSN 0027-3309

**Ediciones Mundo, S. A.**
Infanta Carlota, 123-5, Barcelona-15, Spain.
- Dossier. m.

**Municipalia**
Calle Serrano No. 7, Madrid 1, Spain.
- Municipalia; revista de administracion local. m.

**Museo Arqueologico Nacional**
Serrano, 13, Madrid 1, Spain.
- Biblioteca Praehistorica Hispana. irreg. ISSN 0067-7507
- Mision Arqueologica Espanola en Nubia. Memorias. irreg. ISSN 0076-9371
- Noticiario Arqueologico Hispanico. s-a. ISSN 0078-205X
- Trabajos de Prehistoria. Nueva Serie. a. ISSN 0082-5638 (Universidad Complutense de Madrid. Departamento de Prehistoria) (Co-sponsor: Instituto Espanol de Prehistoria)

**Museo de Zoologia**
Apartado 593 (3), Barcelona, Spain.
- Museo de Zoologia. Barcelona. Miscelanea Zoologica. a, vol. 3, 1974. (Ayuntamiento de Barcelona. Instituto Municipal de Ciencias Naturales)

**Mutua Sabadellense de Seguros**
Cruz, 92, Sabadell (Barcelona), Spain
- Centro de Cirugia Experimental de la Mutua Sabadellense. Anales. a. (Subscr to: Centro Cirugia Exp., Clinica Santa Fe, Sabadell, Barcelona)

**Editora Nacional**
Torregalindo, 10, Madrid 16, Spain.
- Estafeta Literaria. s-m. ISSN 0014-1186
- Estudios de Informacion. q. (Spain. Ministerio de Informacion y Turismo)
- Estudios Turisticos. q. ISSN 0423-5037
- Poesia Hispanica. m. ISSN 0048-4547
- Revista Espanola de la Opinion Publica. q. (Instituto de la Opinion Publica)

**National Council of the Third Order of Saint Francis**
- Anaitasuna. (pub. by Institution Jakin)

**Ediciones Nauta S.A.**
Loreto 16, Barcelona 15, Spain.
- Alta Direccion; revista a nivel de los problemas de gestion. bi-m. ISSN 0002-6549

**Nautilus**
Principe 9, Apdo. de Correos 658, Madrid 12, Spain.
- Nautilus; revista general del mar. bi-m. ISSN 0028-1352

**Vinko Nikolic**
Apdo. Correos 14030, Barcelona 17, Spain.
- Hrvatska Revija/Kroatische Rundschau. q. ISSN 0018-6902

**Novographos, S.A.**
Enamorados 138, Barcelona 13, Spain.
- Novographos; industria grafica, envase, embalaje. m. (except Aug. & Jan.)
- 2C: Construccion de la Ciudad. irreg.

**Nueva Forma**
Avda. de America 37, Edificio Torres Blancas, Apdo. 50-935, Madrid 2, Spain.
- Nueva Forma. m. ISSN 0029-5825

**Nuevas Ediciones, S.A.**
Avda. Jose Antonio, 32-2, Madrid-13, Spain.
- Gran Musical. m. (Sociedad Espanola de Radiodifusion)

**Obispado de la Diocesis de Salamanca**
Prior, 2, Salamanca, Spain.
- Comunidad; semanario de la Iglesia Diocesana, Salamanca. w.

**Obispado de Tortosa**
Cruera, 9, Tortosa, Spain.
- Obispado de Tortosa. Boletin Oficial. m.

**Editorial Ofice**
German Perez Carrasco 63, Madrid 27, Spain.
- A. F. R E; African trade review. m. ISSN 0001-1207
- Bar. fortn.
- Comestible. fortn.
- E U R O - U S A. m.
- East Trade Directory. irreg. ISSN 0531-8912
- Euromueble. m.
- Fundicion. m.
- IBAR - Iberoamerican Trade Directory. biennial.
- Industria Siderometalurgica. m.
- Mercado Mundial/World Market. m. ISSN 0539-3728
- SLAM: Trade Year Book of Africa. irreg.; no, 7, 1975. ISSN 0080-9985
- T E T (The East Trade) m.

**Oficina de Educacion Iberoamericana**
Avenida Reyes Catolicas, Ciudad Universitaria, Madrid, Spain.
- I R E B I. (Indices de Revistas de Bibliotecologia) q. (Co-Sponsors: Instituto Bibligrafico Hispanico (IBH)-Spain; Centro de Documentacion Bibliotecologica (CDB)-Argentina)
- Impacto. (pub. by Ediciones de Promocion Cultural, S.A.)
- Plana. m. ISSN 0476-9465

**Oficina Informativa de Comercio Exterior**
Madrid, Spain.
- Anuario Comercial Iberoamericano. a. ISSN 0570-3980

**Oficina Internacional de Informacion y Observacion del Espanol**
Avda. Reyes Catolicos S/N, Madrid, Spain.
- Espanol Actual. q. ISSN 0425-2772

**Oilgas S.A.**
Paseo de la Habana 48, Madrid 16, Spain.
- C y F. m.
- Enciclopedia Nacional del Petroleo Petrolquimica y Gas. a.
- Frio Calor Aire Acondicionado. m.
- Oilgas. m. (Spanish Petroleum Association)

**Oleo**
Fernando VI, 27, Madrid 4, Spain.
- Oleo; anuario espanol de aceites y grasas e industrias auxiliares. biennial. ISSN 0472-8807
- Oleo - Semanal. w.

**Orden de las Escuelas Pias**
c/o Jesus M. Lecea, Paseo de Canalejas 75, Salamanca, Spain.
- Analecta Calasanctiana. s-a. ISSN 0569-9789 (Colegio Teologado "Felipe Scio")

**Organizacion Sindical Espanola**
Casa Sindical, Paseo del Prado 18, Madrid, Spain.
- Anuario de Empresas Exportadoras. a. (prep. by its Servicio de Accion Exterior Empresarial)
- Evolucion Socioeconomica de Espana. (prep. by its Secretariado Central de Asuntos Economicos)

**Organizacion Sindical Leridana**
Plaza 18 de Julio s/n, Lerida, Spain.
- Tarea. m.

**Oriflama Edicions, S.A.**
Canalejas, 65, Barcelona-14, Spain.
- Oriflama. bi-m.

**D. Emilio Oromi, Ed. & Pub.**
Ronda Universidad 31, Barcelona 10, Spain.
- Boletin Tecnico Sartorial. q. (Academia ROCOSA)
- Dandy; mens fashions. q. ISSN 0011-6068

**Padres Carmelitas Descalzas**
Rioja 23, Apdo. 72, Seville, Spain.
- Revista de Espiritualidad. q. ISSN 0034-8147

**F. M. Pareja, Ed. & Pub.**
Juan 23, 5, Madrid 3, Spain
(Subscr. to: Limite 5, Madrid 3, Spain)
- Asociacion Espanola de Orientalistas. Boletin. a. ISSN 0571-3692 (Asociacion Espanola de Orientalistas)

**Parroquia Immaculada Concepcion**
c/o Sebastian Oliver Balaguer, Espartero, 9, Palma de Mallorca, Baleares, Spain.
- Hoja Parroquial. s-m.

**Pastoral Misionera**
Bola 3, Bajo Derecha, Madrid 13, Spain.
- Pastoral Misionera. 8 per yr.

**Patronato de Obras Docentes del Movimiento**
- Centro de Documentacion. Boletin. (pub. by Centro de Documentacion)

**Editorial Pedeca**
Maria Auxiliadora 5, Madrid 20, Spain.
- Cambus; actualidad tecnica del vehiculo industrial. m.
- Canteras y Explotaciones; revista tecnica de maquinaria para canteras, minas, cementos y obras hidraulicas. m. ISSN 0008-5677
- Clave; informatica y mecanizacion. m. ISSN 0045-7116
- Potencia; revista mensual para tecnicos y usuarios de Maguinara de Construccion y Obras Publicas. m. ISSN 0032-5600
- Rotacion; actualidad tecnica de maquinaria y equipos para buques. m.

**Prensa Periodica, S.A.**
Plaza Conde Valle Suchil 20, Madrid 15, Spain.
- Triunfo. w.

**Editorial Perpetuo Socorro**
Covarrubias, 19, Madrid-10, Spain.
- P. S. m.

**Editorial Planeta S. A.**
Calvet 51-53, Barcelona 6, Spain.
- Novedades; servicio de informacion bibliografica. irreg.

**Plaza y Janes S.A.**
21-33 Virgen de Guadeloupe, Esplugas de Llobregat, Barcelona, Spain.
- Testigos de Espana. irreg.

**Pontificial University of Salamanca**
- Imagenes de la Fe. (pub. by Promocion Popular Cristiana)

**Ediciones y Publicaciones Populares**
Nunez de Balboa, 101, Madrid-6, Spain.
- Aseguradores. m. ISSN 0004-430X (Colegio Sindical Nacional de Agentes de Seguros)
- Asi; la revista de Alicante. m. ISSN 0004-4385
- Revista Sindical de Estadistica. q. ISSN 0035-046X (Spain. Servicio Sindical de Estadisticas)

**Pregon**
Conde Oliveto, 5, Pamplona, Spain.
- Pregon; revista grafica Navarra. q.

**Presencia, S.A.**
Forga-4-2-2, Girona, Spain.
- Presencia. w. ISSN 0032-7689

**Press Export, S.A.**
1371 Avenida Generalismo, Madrid 16, Spain.
- From Spain. bi-m.

**Primer Acto, S.A.**
Virgen del Lluc, 42, Port. H, 1 B, Madrid, Spain.
- Primer Acto. m. ISSN 0032-8367

**Prodace, S. A.**
Ferraz 11, Madrid 8, Spain.
- Proceso de Datos; revista tecnica de mecanizacion. m.

**Prodei**
Goya 73, Madrid, Spain.
- Prodei; catalogue of Spanish Manufacturers, Exporters and Importers. biennial. ISSN 0079-5836

**Progresos de Obstetricia y Ginecologia**
Avda. Jose Antonio 300, Barcelona 4, Spain.
- Progresos de Obstetricia y Ginecologia. bi-m.

**Prointer-Ediciones**
Peurta del Sol 11, Madrid, Spain.
- Quien Vende en Espana los Productos Extranjeros/Who Sells Foreign Products in Spain. biennial.

**Ediciones de Promocion Cultural, S.A.**
Ciudad Universitaria, Madrid, Spain.
- Impacto; ciencia y sociedad. q. (Oficina de Educacion Iberoamericana)

**Promocion Popular Cristiana**
Apartado 19049, Madrid 16, Spain.
- Imagenes de la Fe. m. (Pontificial University of Salamanca)

**Promotora de Publicaciones, S.A.**
Velazquez 92, Madrid 6, Spain.
- Aduanas; revista de tecnicas aduaneras, comercio exterior y transportes. bi-m.

**Dr. J. R. Prous, Ed. & Pub**
Apdo. de Correos 540, Barcelona, Spain.
- Drugs of the Future. m.
- Drugs of Today. m. ISSN 0012-6691
- Medicamentos de Actualidad. m. ISSN 0025-7656

**Publiart S.A.**
Avenida Principe de Asturias, No. 16, Pral. 1, Barcelona 12, Spain.
- Batik; panorama general de las artes - arte, diseno, arquitectura. m.

**Publibanif S.A.**
Juan Bravo 2, Madrid 6, Spain.
- Banif's Investment Bulletin. m. ISSN 0005-4992

**Publica S.A.**
Travesera de las Corts 354, Barcelona 15, Spain.
- Arte Regalo. 5 per yr.
- Fluidos; hidraulica, neumatica, lubricacion. bi-m.
- Tecnica Ceramica. bi-m.
- Tecnicas de Laboratorio. bi-m.
- Tecnicas de los Prefabricados de Hormigon. q.
- Textiles para el Hogar. bi-m.

**Publicaciones Controladas, S.A.**
Sanchez Pacheco 83, Madrid 2, Spain.
- Fundacion Jimenez Diaz. Boletin. m. ISSN 0016-2698
- Historia Internacional. m.

**Publicaciones Espanolas**
Planta 8, Avenida de Generalisimo 39, Madrid 16, Spain.
- Boletin de Orientacion Bibliografica. m.

**Publicaciones Especializadas Internacionales, S.A.**
Corcega, 89, Barcelona-15, 88 Barcelona, Spain.
- Mundo Industrial. m.

**Publicaciones Internacionales S.A.**
Generalisimo 96, Madrid 16, Spain.
- Industria Internacional. m.
- Manipulacion de Materiales en la Industria. m.

**Publicaciones y Revistas, S.A.**
Consejo de Ciento 425-5a, Barcelona 9, Spain.
- Destino. w. ISSN 0011-9563

**Publicidad Delta**
Avda Generalisimo 108, Amposta, Spain.
- Amposta; boletin de informacion local. m. ISSN 0003-2034

**Publicisa**
Calvet 56, Apdo 12121, Barcelona 6, Spain.
- Foc Nou; Revista de serveis cristians. bi-m.

**Pulsar, S.A.**
Felipe de Paz 4, Barcelona 14, Spain.
- Novamaquina 2000. m.

**Editorial Quiris S.A.**
Avda. Jose Antonio 140, Esplugues de Llobregat (Barcelona), Spain.
- Belleza y Moda; la gran revista femenina. m. ISSN 0005-8629
- Mueble; la gran revista del hogar. m. ISSN 0027-2930

**RECOEX**
Avda. Jose Antonio 57, Madrid, Spain.
- R E C O E X. (Recopilacion Tecnica de Comercio Exterior) m.

**Editorial Razon y Fe S.A.**
Pablo Aranda, 3, Madrid 6, Spain.
- Razon y Fe; revista mensual hispano-americana. m. ISSN 0034-0235

**Real Academia de Ciencias Exactas, Fisicas y Naturales**
Valverde 22, Madrid 13, Spain.
- Real Academia de Ciencias Exactas, Fisicas y Naturales. Revista. q. ISSN 0034-0596

**Real Academia de Cordoba de Ciencias, Bellas Letras y Nobles Artes**
Pedro Lopez 7, Cordoba, Spain.
- Real Academia de Cordoba de Ciencias, Bellas Letras y Nobles Artes. Boletin. q. ISSN 0034-060X

**Real Academia de Farmacia**
Calle de Farmacia 11, Madrid 4, Spain.
- Real Academia de Farmacia. Anales. q. ISSN 0034-0618

**Real Academia de la Historia**
Calle de Leon 21, Madrid 14, Spain.
- Real Academia de la Historia. Boletin. q. ISSN 0034-0626

**Real Academia Espanola**
Calla de Felipe IV, Num. 4, Madrid 14, Spain.
- Academia Espanola, Madrid. Anejos del Boletin. irreg; latest issue, no. 35. ISSN 0065-0455
- Real Academia Espanola. Boletin. 3 per yr.

**Real Academia Nacional de Medicina**
Prof. Dr. D. Valentin Matilla y Gomez, Arrieta 12, Madrid, Spain.
- Real Academia Nacional de Medicina. Anales. q. ISSN 0034-0634

**Real Aero Club de Espana**
Arlaban 10, Madrid, Spain.
- Avion. m (with supplements) ISSN 0005-2272

**Real Conservatorio Superior de Musica**
Plaza de Isabel II, Madrid 13, Spain.
- Madrid. Conservatorio de Musica. Anuario. a. ISSN 0076-2318

**Real Escuela Oficial y Superior de Avicultura**
Arenys de Mar, Barcelona, Spain.
- Selecciones Avicolas. m. ISSN 0582-4818
- Selecciones Ganaderas. bi-m.

**Real Monasterio del Escorial**
Madrid, Spain.
- Ciudad de Dios; revista Agustiniana. 3 per yr. ISSN 0009-7756

**Real Sociedad Arquelogica Tarraconense**
Museo Arqueologico, Tarragona, Spain.
- Real Sociedad Arqueologica. Boletin Arqueologico. q. ISSN 0034-0863

**Real Sociedad Espanola de Fisica y Quimica**
Facultad de Ciencias, Ciudad Universitaria, Madrid 3, Spain.
- Real Sociedad Espanola de Fisica y Quimica. Anales de Fisica. q.
- Real Sociedad Espanola de Fisica y Quimica. Anales. Serie B: Quimica. m.

**Real Sociedad Espanola de Historia Natural**
Facultad de Ciencias. Pabellon IIIi, Ciudad Universitaria, Madrid 3, Spain.
- Real Sociedad Espanola de Historia Natural. Boletin de Geologia y Biologia. a.

**Real Sociedad Vascongada de los Amigos del Pais**
Museo de San Telmo, San Sebastian, Spain.
- EGAN; suplemento de literatura, del boletin de la real sociedad vascongada de los amigo del pais. s-a.
- Estudios Historicos Sobre San Sebastian. Boletin. ISSN 0014-150X

**Recien Nacido**
Av. del Jordan s/n, Edificio B-2, Barcelona 16, Spain.
- Recien Nacido; guta de los papas. s-m.

**Editorial Reddis S.A.**
Baja del Carmen, 23, Reus (Tarragona), Spain.
- Reus; semanario de la ciudad. w.

**Region**
Cardenal Quiroga 11 y 15, Orense, Spain.
- Hoja del Lunes de Orense. w. ISSN 0018-330X

**Relaciones Publicas**
Ed. Fernando Lozano Domiguez, Jose Ortega y Gasset, 50-Madrid-6, Spain.
- Relaciones Publicas. bi-m.

**Repress, S.A.**
27, O'Donnell, Madrid-9, Spain.
- Communicacion XXI. m.

**Revista Clinica Espanola**
Jorge Juan 127, Madrid, Spain.
- Revista Clinica Espanola. fortn. ISSN 0014-2565

**Revista de Cultura Brasilena**
c/o Angel Crespo, Ponzano 26, Madrid 3, Spain.
- Revista de Cultura Brasilena. q. ISSN 0034-785X

**Revista de Menorca**
c/o Conde de Cifuentes, 25-Mahon, Minorca, Spain.
- Revista de Menorca. s-a.

**Revista de Occidente, S.A.**
General Mola, 11, Madrid 1, Spain.
- Revista de Occidente. m. ISSN 0034-8635

**Revista Espanola de Seguros**
D. Ramon de la Cruz, 1, Apartado 9063, Madrid 9, Spain.
- Revista Espanola de Seguros. q. ISSN 0034-9488

**Revista Financiera**
Puerta del Sol 6, Madrid, Spain.
- Revista Financiera. 3 per mo. ISSN 0034-9518

**Revista Literaria Azor**
C. Borell, 128, 1.2A, Barcelona-15, Spain.
- Revista Literaria Azor. q. ISSN 0034-981X

**Raimundo de los Reyes, Ed. & Pub.**
Almirante 9, Madrid 4, Spain.
- Panorama Harinero; revista del mundo de la harina y sus derivados. m.

**Ritena**
P.O.B. 466, Barcelona, Spain.
- International Meeting of Animal Nutrition Experts. Proceedings. irreg., 1970, Majorca, Spain. ISSN 0074-6959

**Editorial Roca**
Calle Amigo, 47, Barcelona 6, Spain.
- Gine Dips; revista hispano americana de obstetricia y ginecologia. m.

**Editorial Rocas**
Avenida Generalisimo 580, Barcelona, Spain.
- Angiologia; publicacion dedicada al estudio de las enfermedades vasculares. bi-m. ISSN 0003-3170

**Editorial Rocas y Minerales**
Arturo Soria 166, Madrid-33, Spain.
- Rocas y Minerales. m.

**Romargraf S.A.**
Juventud 55, Hospitalet del Llobregat, Barcelona, Spain.
- N C P. (Noticias de Cosmetica y de Perfumeria) m. (Sociedad Espanola de Quimicos Cosmeticos)
- N C P Documenta. (Noticias de Cosmetica y de Perfumeria) 3 per yr. (Sociedad Espanola de Quimicos Cosmeticos)

**Ediciones Rondas**
C. Borrell, 128, Barcelona 15, Spain.
- Cuadernos Literarios Azor. q.

**Juan Ruiz Pena, Ed. & Pub.**
Plaza del Claudillo 1, Salamanca, Spain.
- Alamo; revista de poesia. bi-m. ISSN 0002-4422

**Editora Rural, S.A.**
Paseo de la Castellana 63, Madrid 1, Spain.
- Gaceta Rural; semanario de informacion agropecuaria. w. ISSN 0016-3864

**Rutas de Cataluna**
Calle de Guardia, Barcelona 1, Spain.
- Rutas de Cataluna; boletin catalogo comercial. a.

**S.A.R.P.E**
Lazaro Galdiano, 6, Madrid 16, Spain
(U.S. Distrib.: AHRE, Inc., 505 Fifth Ave., New York, N.Y. 10017)
- Actualidad Economica. w. ISSN 0001-7655
- Mundo Cristiano. m. ISSN 0027-3252
- Telva. bi-w.
- Tria; una revista para el campo. fortn.

**Editorial S O P E C S.A.**
Villanueva, 24, Madrid-1, Spain.
- Anuario Financiero y de Sociedades Anonimas de Espana. a.

**S P I C**
- S P I C. (pub. by Lorenzo Herranz, Ed. & Pub)

**Editorial Sal Terrae**
Guevara 20, Santander, Spain.
- Almanaque Misal. a.
- Homiletica. 3 per yr. ISSN 0439-4208
- Sal Terrae. m.

**Salvat Editores, S.A.**
Mallorca 41-49, Barcelona, Spain.
- Avances en Obstetricia y Ginecologia. a.
- Avances en Terapeutica. a. (Universidad Autonoma de Barcelona)
- Clinica Anestesiologica. 4 per yr.
- Clinica Endocrinologica. 3 per yr.
- Clinica Gastroenterologica. 3 per yr.
- Clinica Ginecologica. 3 per yr. (Instituto Dexeus)
- Clinica Hematologica. 3 per yr.
- Clinica Radiologica. 3 per yr.

**Javier San Roman, Ed. & Pub.**
Arga, 4 (el Viso), Madrid 2, Spain.
- Control; de publicidad y ventas. m.

**Ediciones Secretariado Trinitario**
Heroes de Brunete, 34, Salamanca, Spain.
- Estudios Trinitarios. 3 per yr.

**Sedmay Ediciones**
Fleming 51, Madrid 16, Spain.
- Forges. irreg.

**Selecciones del Reader's Digest (Iberia) S.A.**
Edificio de Selecciones, Avenida de America, Madrid 27, Spain.
- Selecciones del Reader's Digest(Iberian Edition) m. ISSN 0037-1246

**Semana, S.A.**
Paseo de Onesimo Redondo, 26, Apdo. 383, Madrid 8, Spain.
- A S; diario grafico deportivo. d.
- Semana. w. ISSN 0037-1793

**Semana Vitivinicola**
Maestre Racional 8, P.O.B. 642, Valencia 5, Spain.
- Semana Vitivinicola. w. ISSN 0037-184X

**Ediciones Semanales Gallegas, S.A.**
Ave. Camelias, 28-10, Vigo, Spain.
- Galicia Deportiva; semanario de deportes y espectaculos. w.

**Seminario de Argueologia y Numismatica Aragonesas**
- Caesaraugusta. (pub. by Institucion Fernando el Catolico)

**Seminario de Filologia Vasca Julio de Urquijo**
Palacio de la Diputacion de Guipuzcoa, San Sebastian (Guipuzcoa), Spain.
- Seminario de Filologia Vasca Julio de Urquijo. Anuario. a.

**Seminario de Historia Social y Economica**
Facultad de Filosofia y Letras, Ciudad Universitaria, Madrid 3, Spain.
- Anuario de Historia Economica y Social. a. ISSN 0066-5088

**Seminario Matematico Garcia de Galdeano. Facultad de Ciencias**
Zaragoza, Spain.
- Seminario Matematico Garcia de Galdeano. Publicaciones. irreg. ISSN 0085-6029

**Seminario Xavier Zubiri**
- Seminario Xavier Zubiri. Trabajos. (pub. by Editorial Moneda y Credito)

**Servicio Comercial de la Industria Textil Algodonera**
Ave. Jose Antonio, 670, Barcelona-10, Spain.
- Algodon Hace Sus Cuentas. biennial.

**Servicio de Extension Agraria**
Ministerio de Aricultura, Bravo Murillo 101, Madrid 20, Spain.
- Spain. Servicio de Extension Agraria. Serie Tecnica. irreg; latest issue, no. 52, 1974. ISSN 0081-3478

**Servicio de Publicaciones Agrarias**
Paseo Infanta Isabel, 1, Madrid, Spain.
- Spain. Ministerio de Agricultura. Boletin Informativo de la Bibloteca Central. s-a. (Spain. Ministerio de Agricultura. Secretario General Tecnica)

**Servicio Informativo Espanol**
Apdo. de Correos 19101, Madrid, Spain.
- Espana Hoy/Espana Semanal. w.

**Servicio Municipal de Parques y Jardines de Barcelona**
Parque Zoologico, Barcelona-5, Spain.
- Zoo; revista del Parque Zoologico de Barcelona. q. ISSN 0044-5037

**Servicios Industriales Pesqueros S.A.**
Policarpo Sanz 21-2, Vigo (Pontevedra), Spain.
- Industrias Pesqueras; revista maritima quincenal. s-m.

**Siemens, S.A.**
Calle Orense No. 2, Madrid 20, Spain.
- Mini Data Report; boletin informativo de proceso de datos. q.

**Sindicato Nacional de Industria Quimicas**
San Bernardo 62, Madrid, Spain.
- Anuario de la Industria Quimica Espanola. biennial.
- I Q. (Industria Quimica en Desarrollo) m.
- Ion; revista espanola de quimica aplicada. m. ISSN 0021-034X
- Quimica Analitica; pura y aplicada. bi-m.

**Sindicato Nacional de la Pesca**
Paseo del Prado 18-20, Madrid, Spain.
- Sindicato Nacional de la Pesca Boletin de Informacion. m. ISSN 0037-556X

**Sindicato Nacional de la Piel**
Avenida de Jose Antonio 32-5, Madrid 13, Spain.
- Revista de la Piel. m.

**Sindicato Nacional del Metal**
C. Diego de Leon 50, Madrid 6, Spain.
- Metal; revista espanola de mineria metalica y siderometalurgia. m. ISSN 0047-682X
- Sindicato Nacional del Metal, Madrid. Informe-Economico y Social. a; latest issue, 1975. ISSN 0085-6096

**Sindicato Nacional Textil**
Avda. Jose Antonio 32, Madrid, Spain.
- Sindicato Nacional Textil. Boletin de Informacion. 9 per yr. ISSN 0037-5578
- Textil; boletin de informacion. 9 per yr. ISSN 0049-3546

**Sociedad Canaria de Pediatria**
- Sociedad Canaria de Pediatria. Boletin. (pub. by Editorial Garsi)

**Sociedad Castellano-Astur-Leonosa de Pediatria**
c/o Prof. Dr. E. Sanchez Villares, Miguel Iscar 13, 3 Valladolid, Spain.
- Sociedad Castellano-Astur-Leonosa de Pediatria. Boletin. bi-m. ISSN 0037-8429

**Sociedad Castellonense de Cultura**
Calle Mayor 103, Aptdo de Correos 16, Castellon de la Plana, Spain.
- Sociedad Castellonense de Cultura. Boletin. q.

**Sociedad Catalana de Seguridad y Medicina del Trabajo**
Tapineria, 10, 2, Barcelona 2, Spain.
- Medicina de Empresa; publicacion dedicada a la seguridad y medicina del trabajo. q.

**Sociedad Cultural Amigos del Arte de Baena**
Plaza G. Cascajo 5, Baena, Spain.
- Tambor. m. ISSN 0049-2922

**Sociedad de Ciencias Naturales Aranzadi**
Museo San Telmo, Plaza de I. Zuloago, San Sebastian, Spain.
- Anuario de Eusko-Folklore; etnografia y paletnografia. a; latest issue, 1971-72.
- Munibe. q. ISSN 0027-3414

**Sociedad de Fomento de la Cria Caballar de Espana**
6, Fernanflor, Madrid, Spain.
- Guia de los Caballos Verificadas en Espana. a. ISSN 0085-1337

**Sociedad de Historia Natural de Baleares**
San Roque, 8, Estudio General Luliano, Palma de Mallorca, Spain.
- Sociedad de Historia Natural de Baleares. Boletin. a; no. 19, 1974. ISSN 0583-7405

**Sociedad de Patologia Respiratoria**
- Archivos de Bronconeumologia. (pub. by Ediciones Doyma, S.A.)

**Sociedad Espanola de Acustica**
Serrano 144, Madrid 6, Spain.
- Revista de Acustica. q.

**Sociedad Espanola de Alergia**
- Allergologia et Immunopathologia. (pub. by Editorial Garsi)

**Sociedad Espanola de Anatomia Patologica**
Velazquez 144, Madrid-6, Spain.
- Patologia. q. ISSN 0031-3106

**Sociedad Espanola de Anestesiologia y Reanimacion**
Mallorca 189, Barcelona 11, Spain.
- Revista Espanola de Anestesiologia y Reanimacion. bi-m. ISSN 0034-9356

**Sociedad Espanola de Bromatologia**
Edificio Facultad de Farmacia, Ciudad Universitaria, Madrid 3, Spain.
- Anales de Bromatologia. q. ISSN 0003-2492

**Sociedad Espanola de Ceramica y Vidrio**
Carretera de Valencia, Km. 24, 3 Arganda del Rey, Madrid, Spain.
- Sociedad Espanola de Ceramica y Vidrio. Boletin. bi-m.

**Sociedad Espanola de Gerontologia**
- Revista Espanola de Gerontologia. (pub. by Editorial Garsi)

**Sociedad Espanola de Historia de la Medicina**
Duque de Medinaceli 4, Madrid-14, Spain.
- Sociedad Espanola de Historia de la Medicina. Boletin. a. ISSN 0583-7480

**Sociedad Espanola de Linguistica**
- Revista Espanola de Linguistica. (pub. by Editorial Gredos)

**Sociedad Espanola de Oftalmologia**
- Sociedad Espanola de Oftalmologia. Archivos. (pub. by Julio Garcia Peri Editor)

**Sociedad Espanola de Oncologia**
- Oncologia /80. (pub. by Ediciones Cutor S. A.)

**Sociedad Espanola de Optica**
Serrano 121, Madrid -6, Spain.
- Optica Pura y Aplicada. 3 per yr. ISSN 0030-3917 (Instituto de Optica "Daza de Valdes")

**Sociedad Espanola de Otorrinolaringologia**
- Acta Otorrinolaringologica Espanola. (pub. by Editorial Garsi)

**Sociedad Espanola de Patologia Digestiva**
- Revista Espanola de las Enfermedades del Aparato Digestivo. (pub. by Editorial Garsi)

**Sociedad Espanola de Problemistas de Ajedrez**
Av. Principe Asturias 35, Barcelona (12), Spain.
- Problemas. q. ISSN 0032-9223

**Sociedad Espanola de Quimicos Cosmeticos**
- N C P. (pub. by Romargraf S.A.)
- N C P Documenta. (pub. by Romargraf S.A.)

**Sociedad Espanola de Radiodifusion**
- Gran Musical. (pub. by Nuevas Ediciones, S.A.)

**Sociedad Espanola de Radiologia y Electrologia Medicas y de Medicina Nuclear**
- Radiologia. (pub. by Editorial Garsi)

**Sociedad Espanola de Rehabilitacion**
Villanueva 11, Madrid-1, Spain.
- Rehabilitacion. q. ISSN 0048-7120

**Sociedad Ginecologica Espanola**
- Boletin de Ginecologia. (pub. by Julio Garcia Peri Editor)

**Sociedad Ibero-American de Estudios Numismaticos**
Jorge Juan 106, Madrid 9, Spain.
- Numisma. bi-m. ISSN 0029-6015

**Sociedad Luso-Espanola de Neurocirugia**
- Revista Espanola de Oto-Neuro-Oftalmologia y
Neurocirugia. (pub. by Editorial Facta)

**Sociedad Petrolifera Espanola, Shell, S.A.**
Alcala 45, Madrid 14, Spain
(Subscription Address: Barquillo, 17, Madrid 4,
Spain)
- Agrishell; revista de fitopatalogia. q.

**Sociedad Vasco Navarra de Pediatria**
- Sociedad Vasco-Navarra de Pediatria. Boletin.
(pub. by Editorial Garsi)

**Sonda, Juventudes Musicales**
San Bernardo 44, Madrid 8, Spain.
- Sonda; problema y panorama de la musica
contemporania. q.

**Spain. Boletin Oficial del Estado**
Eloy Gonzalo, 19, Madrid 10, Spain.
- Boletin Oficial del Estado; gaceta de madrid. d
(except sun)
- Disposiciones Generales. s-a.
- Documentacion Administrativa. m. ISSN 0012-
4494 (Spain. Gabinete Tecnico)
- O y M. irreg. (Spain. Servicio Central de
Organizacion y Metodos)
- Recopilacion de Doctrina Legal. a. (Spain.
Consejo de Estado)
- Revista Internacional de Ciencias Administrativas.
q. (International Institute of Administrative
Sciences BE)
- Spain. Servicio Central de Publicaciones de la
Presidencia del Gobierno. Coleccion Informe.
irreg. (Spain. Presidencia del Gobierno. Servicio
Central de Publicaciones)

**Spain. Comisaria General de Excavaciones
Arqueologicas**
Palacio del Museo Arqueologico National, Serrano,
13 (1), Madrid, Spain.
- Noticiario Arqueologico Hispanico: Arqueologia.
a.

**Spain. Consejo de Estado**
- Recopilacion de Doctrina Legal. (pub. by Spain.
Boletin Oficial del Estado)

**Spain. Consejo Superior de Investigaciones Cientificas**
Serrano 117, Madrid, Spain.
- Anuario de Estudios Americanos. a; no. 31
forthcoming.
- Arbor; revista general de investigacion y cultura.
m.
- Consejo Superior de Investigaciones Cientificas.
Grupo de Montana de Accion Cultural. Boletin
Informativo. s-a. (prep. by its Grupo de Montana
de Accion Cultura)
- Cuadernos Bibliograficos. irreg.
- Estudios Biblicos. (pub. by Instituto de Teologia
"Francisco Suarez")
- Investigacion e Informacion Textil y des
Tensioactivos. q. ISSN 0302-5268
- Kemixon Reporter; noticiario tecnico-quimico. m.
ISSN 0022-9873
- Spain. Consejo Superior de Investigaciones
Cientificas. Cuadernos de Economia. 3 per yr.

**Spain. Consejo Superior de Investigaciones
Cientificas. Departamento de Investigaciones
Fisiologicas**
Apdo. 273, Pamplona, Spain.
- Revista Espanola de Fisiologia. q. ISSN 0034-
9402

**Spain. Consejo Superior de Investigaciones
Cientificas. Instituto de Investigaciones Pesqueras**
Paseo Nacional, Barcelona 3, Spain.
- Instituto de Investigaciones Pesqueras. Datos
Informativos. 7-8 per yr.
- Instituto de Investigaciones Pesqueras. Informes
Tecnicos. 10-12 per yr.
- Investigacion Pesquera. 2-3 per yr. ISSN 0020-
9953

**Spain. Consejo Superior de Investigaciones
Cientificas. Instituto de Medicine Experimental**
Apdo. 8248, Ciudad Universitaria, Madrid, Spain.
- Archivos de Medicina Experimental. q. ISSN
0004-0568

**Spain. Consejo Superior de Investigaciones
Cientificas. Instituto G. Fernandez de Oviedo**
Duque de Medinaceli, 4, Madrid 14, Spain.
- Revista de Indias. s-a. ISSN 0034-8341

**Spain. Consejo Superior de Investigaciones
Cientificas. Patronato Juan de la Cierva**
- Resumenes de Articulos Cientificos y Tecnicos.
Serie A: Quimica Industrial. (pub. by Instituto de
Informacion y Documentacion en Ciencia y
Tecnologia)
- Resumenes de Articulos Cientificos y Tecnicos.
Serie B: Fisica Aplicada. (pub. by Instituto de
Informacion y Documentacion en Ciencia y
Tecnologia)
- Resumenes de Articulos Cientificos y Tecnicos.
Serie C: Ciencia y Tecnica de los Metales. (pub.
by Instituto de Informacion y Documentacion en
Ciencia y Tecnologia)
- Resumenes de Articulos Cientificos y Tecnicos.
Serie D: Ingenieria y Tecnologias Varias. (pub. by
Instituto de Informacion y Documentacion en
Ciencia y Tecnologia)
- Resumenes de Articulos Cientificos y Tecnicos.
Serie E: Economia de la Empresa. (pub. by
Instituto de Informacion y Documentacion en
Ciencia y Tecnologia)

**Spain. Consejo Superior de Investigaciones
Cientificas. Patronato Menedez Pelayo**
Duque de Medinaceli 4, Madrid 14, Spain.
- Estudios Clasicos. 3 per yr. ISSN 0014-1453

**Spain. Cortes Espanolas. Grupo Espanol de la Union
Interparlimentaria**
- Grupo Espanol de la Union Interparlamentaria.
Boletin de Informacion.

**Spain. Departamento de Fomento y Difusion
Internacional**
Arenal 22, Madrid 13, Spain.
- Spain. Departamento de Fomento y Difusion
Internacional. Documentacion; revista de
informacion general y tecnica para la industria
turistica y hotelera. m. ISSN 0038-6375

**Spain. Direccion de Pesca Maritima**
Madrid, Spain.
- Spain. Direccion General de Pesca Maritima.
Anuario de Pesca Maritima. a.

**Spain. Direccion General de Banca, Bolsa e
Inversiones**
Serrano 69, Madrid, Spain.
- Banca y Seguros. 3 per yr.

**Spain. Direccion General de Bellas Artes**
Murcia, Spain.
- Spain. Direccion General de Bellas Artes. Semana
de Musica en la Navidad. irreg.

**Spain. Direccion General de Cooperacion Tecnica
Internacional**
Madrid, Spain.
- Spain. Direccion General de Cooperacion Tecnica
Internacional. Sintesis de Informacion Sobre
Organismos Internacionales. m.

**Spain. Direccion General de Correos y
Telecomunicacion**
Madrid, Spain.
- Spain. Direccion General de Correos y
Telecomunicacion. Boletin Oficial de Correos y
Telecomunicacion. s-w.

**Spain. Direccion General de Empresas y Actividades
Turisticas**
Madrid-16, Spain.
- Guia de Hoteles: Espana. a.

**Spain. Direccion General de Ensenanza Primaria.
Campana Nacional de Promocion Cultural de
Adultos**
Alcala 104, Madrid, Spain.
- Alba; hablar y escribir, para saber, para amar, para
vivir. s-m. ISSN 0002-4635

**Spain. Direccion General de Sanidad**
Apdo. 1281, Madrid, Spain.
- Revista de Sanidad e Higiene Publica. m. ISSN
0034-8899
- Spain. Direccion General de Sanidad. Resumen
Cronologico de la Legislacion del Estado Que
Afecta a Servicos de Sanidad. irreg.

**Spain. Direccion General de Trafico. Gabinete de
Estudios**
Amador de los Rios, 7, Madrid 4, Spain.
- Spain. Direccion General de Trafico. Anuario
Estadistico de Accidentes. Boletin Informativo. a.
ISSN 0085-655X
- Spain. Direccion General de Trafico. Anuario
Estadistico General. a. ISSN 0085-6568
- Spain. Direccion General de Trafico. Boletin
Informativo. m.

**Spain. Gabinete Tecnico**
- Documentacion Administrativa. (pub. by Spain.
Boletin Oficial del Estado)

**Spain. Instituto Geografico y Catastral. Observatorio
Astronomico Nacional**
Alfonso XII No. 3, Madrid 7, Spain.
- Observatorio Astronomico de Madrid. Anuario. a.
- Observatorio Astronomico de Madrid. Boletin
Astronomico. s-a.

**Spain. Instituto Geologico y Minero**
Claudio Coello, 44, Madrid, Spain.
- Spain. Instituto Geologico y Minero. Catalogo de
Ediciones. irreg.

**Spain. Instituto Nacional de Educacion Fisica y
Deportes**
Martin Fierro, Madrid-3, Spain.
- Deporte 2000. m.

**Spain. Instituto Nacional de Estadistica**
Avda. Generalisimo 91, Madrid 16, Spain.
- Anuario Estadistico de Espana. a. ISSN 0066-
5177
- Contabilidad Nacional de Espana. a. ISSN 0069-
9292
- Estadistica de la Ensenanza en Espana. a.
- Estadisticas de Turismo; viajeros en hoteles y
acampamentos. a.
- Movimiento Natural de la Poblacion de Espana. a.
ISSN 0077-1767
- Spain. Instituto Nacional de Estadistica. Boletin
Mensual de Estadistica. m. ISSN 0038-6391
- Spain. Instituto Nacional de Estadistica.
Estadistica de Transporte. a. ISSN 0081-3346
- Spain. Instituto Nacional de Estadistica.
Estadistica Espanola. q. ISSN 0014-1151
- Spain. Instituto Nacional de Estadistica.
Estadistica Industrial. a. ISSN 0081-3354
- Spain. Instituto Nacional de Estadistica. Indice del
Coste de la Vida. a.
- Spain. Instituto Nacional de Estadistica. Industrias
Derivadas de la Pesca. a. ISSN 0081-3362
- Spain. Instituto Nacional de Estadistica. Informe
Sobre la Distribucion de las Rentas. a. ISSN
0081-3370
- Spain. Instituto Nacional de Estadistica. Poblacion
Activa. a. ISSN 0081-3389

**Spain. Instituto Nacional de Industria. Direccion
Financiera**
Recursos Financieros, Madrid, Spain.
- Instituto Nacional de Industria. Direccion
Financiera. Boletin de Informacion Financiera. m.
ISSN 0534-3844

**Spain. Instituto Nacional de Prevision**
Alcala 56, Madrid, Spain.
- Revista Iberoamericana de Seguridad Social. bi-m.
ISSN 0034-964X

**Spain. Ministerio de Agricultura. Direccion General
de la Produccion Agraria**
Madrid, Spain.
- Spain. Direccion General de la Produccion
Agraria. Campana Algodonera. irreg.

**Spain. Ministerio de Agricultura. Estacion Central de
Ecologia**
Madrid, Spain.
- Spain. Ministerio de Agricultura Estacion Central
do Ecologia. Boletin. s-a.

**Spain. Ministerio de Agricultura. Secretaria General
Tecnica**
Paseo Infante 1, Madrid 7, Spain.
- Agricultura Espanola. a. ISSN 0065-440X
- Informacion Agraria. s-a.
- Producto Neto de la Agricultura Espanola. a.
ISSN 0079-5895
- Spain. Ministerio de Agricultura. Boletin Mensual
de Estadistica Agraria. m.
- Spain. Ministerio de Agricultura. Boletin Semanal
de Precios Agrarios. w.

- Spain. Ministerio de Agricultura. Secretaria General Tecnica. Anuario de Estadistica Agraria. a.

**Spain. Ministerio de Agricultura. Secretario General Tecnica**
- Spain. Ministerio de Agricultura. Boletin Informativo de la Bibloteca Central. (pub. by Servicio de Publicaciones Agrarias)

**Spain. Ministerio de Agricultura. Servicio de Extension Agraria**
Bravo Murillo, 101, Madrid 20, Spain.
- Hojas Divulgadoras. m.
- Spain. Ministerio de Agricultura. Direccion General de Capacitacion y Extension Agrarias. Resumen de Actividades. irreg. ISSN 0085-6541

**Spain. Ministerio de Comercio**
Goya 73, Madrid, Spain.
- Informacion Comercial Espanola. Boletin Semanal. w. ISSN 0019-9761
- Informacion Comercial Espanola. Revista Mensual. m. ISSN 0019-977X
- Prodei. a.

**Spain. Ministerio de Comercio. Servicio de Estudios**
Madrid, Spain.
- Balanza de Pagos de Espana. a. ISSN 0067-3021

**Spain. Ministerio de Comercio. Subsecretaria de la Marina Mercante**
Madrid, Spain.
- Spain. Direccion General de Pesca Maritima. Publicaciones Tecnicas. irreg. (prep. by its Direccion General de Pesca)

**Spain. Ministerio de Educacion y Ciencia**
Servicio de Publicaciones, Madrid 3, Spain.
- Datos y Cifras de la Ensenanza en Espana. a. ISSN 0070-2897 (prep. by its Secretaria General Tecnica)
- Revista de Archivos, Bibliotecas y Museos. s-a. ISSN 0034-771X
- Revista de Educacion. bi-m. ISSN 0034-8082 (prep. by its Secretaria General Tecnica)
- Spain. Ministerio de Educacion y Ciencia. Guia. irreg.
- Spain. Ministerio de Education y Ciencia. Boletin Official: Colleccion Legislativa. m.
- Universidad Internacional Menendez Pelayo. Publicaciones. (pub. by Universidad Internacional Menendez Pelayo)

**Spain. Ministerio de Educacion y Ciencia. Junta Nacional Contra el Analfabetismo**
Los Madrazo 17, Madrid, Spain.
- Junta Nacional Contra el Analfabetismo. Boletin. a. ISSN 0561-4619

**Spain. Ministerio de Hacienda**
Direccion General de Aduanas, Madrid, Spain.
- Estadistica del Comercio Exterior de Espana. a. ISSN 0071-1527
- Spain. Direccion General de Aduanas. Informe Mensuel Sobre el Comercio Exterior. m. ISSN 0584-6544 (Distrib. by: Promotora de Publicaciones, Velazquez 92, Madrid 6, Spain)
- Spain. Ministerio de Hacienda. Informacion Estadistica. a. ISSN 0081-3435
- Spain. Ministerio de Hacienda. Memoria; estadistica seguros privados. a. ISSN 0081-3443
- Spain. Ministerio de Hacienda. Subdireccion General de Organizacion e Informacion. Estadistica de la Informacion al Publico. irreg.

**Spain. Ministerio de Hacienda. Instituto de Credito Oficial**
Madrid, Spain.
- Instituto de Credito Oficial. Memoria del Credito Oficial. a. ISSN 0081-3451

**Spain. Ministerio de Hacienda. Instituto de Estudios Fiscales**
Casado del Alisal 6, Madrid 14, Spain.
- Cronica Tributaria. q.
- Hacienda Publica Espanola. bi-m.

**Spain. Ministerio de Industria**
Servicio de Publicaciones, Claudio Coello, 44, Madrid 1, Spain.
- Economia Industrial. m.
- Estadisticas Minera y Metalurgica de Espana. a. ISSN 0071-156X
- Spain. Ministerio de Industria. Boletin Estadistico. q.
- Spain. Ministerio de Industria. Boletin Estadistico. m.

- Spain. Ministerio de Industria. Secretaria General Tecnica. Comercio Exterior de Productos Industriales. irreg.
- Spain. Ministerio de Industria. Secretaria General Tecnica. Informe Sobre Infrautilizacion de la Capacidad Productiva. q.
- Spain. Ministerio de Industria. Secretaria General Tecnica. Resultados de la Encuesta de Coyuntura Industrial: Sector Industrial. irreg.

**Spain. Ministerio de Industria. Instituto Geologico y Minero**
Servicio de Publicaciones, Claudio Coello 44, Madrid 1, Spain.
- Spain. Instituto Geologico y Minero. Boletin Geologico y Minero. bi-m.
- Spain. Instituto Geologico y Minero. Colleccion Memorias. irreg.

**Spain. Ministerio de Industria. Registro de la Propriedad Industrial**
Pradilla 66, Madrid, Spain.
- Spain. Ministerio de Industria. Registro de la Propreidad Industrial. Boletin Oficial. fortn. ISSN 0038-6413

**Spain. Ministerio de Informacion y Turismo**
Secretaria General Technica, Seccion de Planification y Documentation, Madrid, Spain.
- Anuario de la Prensa Espanola. a. ISSN 0084-6643
- Estudios de Informacion. (pub. by Editora Nacional)
- Spain. Junta Central de Informacion, Turismo y Educacion Popular. Memoria Annual. a. ISSN 0085-6576
- Spain. Ministerio de Informacion y Turismo. Estadisticas de Turismo. a. ISSN 0081-346X

**Spain. Ministerio de Justicia. Secretaria General Tecnica**
Gabinete de Documentacion y Publicaciones, Calle de San Bernardo, 66-2. B, Madrid, Spain.
- Spain. Ministerio de Justicia. Secretaria General Tecnica. Documentacion Juridica. q.

**Spain. Ministerio de la Vivienda**
Servicio Central de Publicaciones, Plaza de San Juan de la Cruz 1, Madrid, Spain.
- Spain. Ministerio de la Vivienda. Boletin de Jurisprudencia y Resoluciones Administrativas Sobre Urbanismo y Vivienda. q. (prep. by its Secretaria General Tecnica)
- Spain. Ministerio de la Vivienda . Boletin Oficial. m. ISSN 0490-3323
- Spain. Ministerio de la Vivienda. Serie 3: Vivienda. irreg.

**Spain. Ministerio de Marina**
Montalban, 2, Madrid 14, Spain.
- Revista General de Marina. m. ISSN 0034-9569

**Spain. Ministerio de Marina. Instituto y Observatorio de Marina**
San Fernando (Cadiz), Spain.
- Almanaque Nautico. a. ISSN 0080-5963
- Boletin Astronomico.
- Instituto y Observatorio de Marina. Efemerides Astronomicas. a; no. 185, 1975. ISSN 0080-5971
- Instituto y Observatorio de Marina. Observaciones Meteorologicas, Magneticas y Sismicas. Anales. a. ISSN 0080-5955 (prep. by its Seccion de Geofisica)

**Spain. Ministerio de Obras Publicas**
Servicio de Publicaciones, Nuevos Ministerios, Madrid, Spain.
- Spain. Ministerio de Obras Publicas.Boletin de Informacion. m. ISSN 0490-334X

**Spain. Ministerio de Trabajo**
Servicio de Publicaciones, Plaza San Juan de la Cruz, (Nueva Ministerios), Madrid, Spain.
- Revista de Trabajo. q. ISSN 0034-897X

**Spain. Ministerio de Trabajo. Servicio del Mutualismo Laboral**
Calle Padre Damian, 4, Madrid, 16, Spain.
- Boletin del Mutualismo Laboral. m. (prep. by its Seccion de Relaciones Publicas)

**Spain. Ministerio del Aire**
Princesa, 88, Madrid, 8, Spain.
- Revista de Aeronautica y Astronautica. m. ISSN 0034-7647

- Spain. Ministerio del Aire. Boletin Oficial. 3 per yr. ISSN 0038-6405

**Spain. Ministerio del Aire. Subsecretaria de Aviacion Civil**
Madrid, Spain.
- Estadisticas de la Aviacion Civil en Espana. a. ISSN 0421-4986

**Spain. Ministerio del Ejercito**
Alcala 18, Madrid, Spain.
- Ejercito; revista de las armas y servicios. m. ISSN 0013-2918
- Guion; revista ilustrada de los mandos subalternos. m. ISSN 0017-5455

**Spain. Ministerio Espanol de Asuntos Exteriores**
Cultural Relations Dept., Palacio de Santa Cruz, Madrid, Spain.
- Spanish Cultural Index. m. ISSN 0038-6456

**Spain. Presidencia del Gobierno**
- Revista Espanola de la Opinion Publica. (pub. by Instituto de la Opinion Publica)
- Spain. Servicio Central de Publicaciones de la Presidencia del Gobierno. Coleccion Informe. (pub. by Spain. Boletin Oficial del Estado)

**Spain. Servicio Central de Organizacion y Metodos**
- O y M. (pub. by Spain. Boletin Oficial del Estado)

**Spain. Servicio de Relaciones Exteriores Sindicals**
Servicio de Relaciones Exteriores Sindicales, Paseo del Prado, 18-20, Madrid-14, Spain.
- Sindicalismo en Espana/Trade Unionism in Spain. bi-m.

**Spain. Servicio Meteorologico Nacional**
Ciudad Universitaria, Apdo 285, Madrid, Spain.
- Boletin Mensual Climatologico. m. ISSN 0006-6435
- Spain. Ministerio del Aire. Revista de Meteorologia Maritima. q. (prep. by its Seccion Meteorologia Maritima)

**Spain. Servicio Sindical de Estadisticas**
Huertas 73, Madrid, Spain.
- Estadisticas de Produccion Industrial; analisis y resultados. a.
- Revista Sindical de Estadistica. (pub. by Ediciones y Publicaciones Populares)
- Spain. Servicio Sindical de Estadistica. Existencias e Inversiones. irreg.

**Spain. Tribunal Central de Trabajo**
- Spain. Tribunal Central de Trabajo. Repertorio de Sentencias. (pub. by Editorial Aranzadi)

**Spanish Petroleum Association**
- Oilgas. (pub. by Oilgas S.A.)

**SPARCO**
SPAR Espanola, S.A., Carretera de Andalucia, Kilometro 12,700, Madrid, Spain.
- SPARCO; revista tecnica mensual de la distribucion. m.

**Studium Ediciones**
Bailen 19, Madrid 13, Spain.
- Coleccion Senda Abierta. Serie II (Azul): Judaismo. irreg. (Centro de Estudios Judeo-Cristianos)

**Subdireccion de Estudios Economicos y Marketing**
Avda. del Generalisimo, 146 Madrid-16, Spain.
- Informe S E A T; boletin economico financiero destinado a accionistas de la empresa. s-a.
- 132 Expres. a.

**Sucesores de Rivadeneyra, S.A.**
Paseo de Onesimo Redondo, 36, Madrid, Spain.
- Boletin de Legislacion Extranjera. q.
- Boletin Oficial de la Cortes Espanolas. s-w.

**Sucro S.A.**
Hernan Cortes, 5, Valencia 4, Spain.
- Anuario Hortofruticola Espanol. a.

**Tabapress S.A.**
Infantas 27, Madrid 4, Spain.
- Actualidad Tabaquera; revista del tabaco. m.

**Tapicerias Gancedo**
Jose Gancedo Bago, Ed., Velazques 21, Madird 1, Spain.
- T.G; revista de las artes decorativas. bi-m.

**Tecnica e Invencion**
Princesa 14, Madrid-8, Spain.
- Tecnica e Invencion. m. ISSN 0040-179X

**Editorial Tecnica Espanola, S.A.**
Antonio Arias, 11, Madrid 9, Spain.
- Espana Agricola. fortn.
- Espana Ganadera. m.
- Estudios Economicos. q. ISSN 0014-1488
- Nueva Planta. fortn. ISSN 0029-5841

**Prensa Tecnica, S.A.**
Caspe 118-120, Barcelona 13, Spain.
- Confeccion Industrial. m.
- Guia de la Moda del Calzado. s-a.
- Jersey. q.
- Marroquineria Espanola. s-a.
- Modapiel. s-a.
- Revista Tecnica de la Industria de Generos de Punto. m.
- Tecnica del Calzado. bi-m.

**Ediciones Tecnicas Doria**
Ronda S. Pedro, 8, Barcelona-10, Spain.
- Pinker Moda. m (10 per yr)

**Ediciones Tecnicas Especializadas**
Travesera de Gracia 15, 4, Barcelona-6, Spain.
- Nueva Estetica. s-m.
- Tecnica Textil Internacional. bi-m. ISSN 0040-1900

**Publicaciones Tecnicas Periodicas**
Principe 9, Apartado 658, Madrid-12, Spain.
- Mineria y Metalurgia, Plasticos y Electricidad. bi-m. ISSN 0047-7443

**Ediciones Tecnicas R.E.D.E.**
Aptdo 19061, Barcelona, Spain.
- Radiorama; practica electronica/t.v./radio/hi-fi/ciencia. m. (Club de Radiorama)

**Editorial Teide**
Viladomat 291, Barcelona 15, Spain.
- Bibliografia Historica de Espana e Hispanoamerica; Indice Historico Espanol. 3 per yr. ISSN 0006-1026 (Universidad de Barcelona. Facultad de Filosofia y Letras. Centro de Estudios Historicos Internacionales)

**Telepublicaciones**
Luisa Fernanda, 3, 4E. Madrid (8), Spain.
- Teleprograma. w. ISSN 0040-2672

**Telva**
6 (Edificio Azul), Madrid 16, Spain.
- Telva. s-m.

**Terror Fantastic**
Pje. Pla, 11-13, Barcelona, Spain.
- Terror Fantastic. m.

**Tertulia Flamenca de Ceuta**
P.O. Box 344, Ceuta, Spain.
- Flamenco; boletin de informacion. 2-3 per yr.

**Tiradores**
Ardemans, 63, Madrid-28, Spain.
- Tiradores; tiro-caza-pesca. m.

**Tucar Ediciones S.A.**
Almagro 44, Madrid 4, Spain.
- Partido Socialista Popular. Congreso. (Actas) irreg.

**Turisport**
Pasaje Bocabella 13 Pral 29, Apdo 80611, Barcelona-13, Spain.
- Turisport. bi-m.

**Ediciones Turisticas, S. A.**
Gran via Carlos III 86, Barcelona-14, Spain.
- Editur; semanario de informacion y documentacion turisticas. w. ISSN 0422-6186
- Tecno Hotel; vida colectiva. m.

**Uinversidad de Granada. Departamento de Historia Medieval**
Facultad de Filosofia y Letras, Granada, Spain.
- Cuadernos de Estudios Medievales. a.

**Uniespana**
Castello 18, Madrid 1, Spain.
- Uniespana-Cine Espanol. a. ISSN 0082-7576

**Union de Fabricantes de Conservas de Galicia**
Filipe Sanchez, 152, Vigo, Spain.
- Industria Conservera. m.

**Universidad Autonoma de Barcelona**
- Avances en Terapeutica. (pub. by Salvat Editores, S.A.)

**Universidad Autonoma de Madrid. Fundacion Universidad Empresa**
- Cuadernos Universitarios de Planificacion Empresarial y Marketing. (pub. by Editorial Macrometrica)

**Universidad Complutense de Madrid**
Madrid, Spain.
- Universidad de Madrid. Seminario de Metafisica. Anales. irreg. ISSN 0580-8650

**Universidad Complutense de Madrid. Centro de Calculo**
Avda. Complutense, Madrid 3, Spain.
- Madrid. Universidad Centro de Calculo. Boletin. q.

**Universidad Complutense de Madrid. Consejo Superior de Investigaciones Cientificas**
Ciudad Universitaria, Madrid 3, Spain
- Anales de Literatura Hispanoamericana. a; nos. 2-3. 1973-74. (Subscrip. to: Catedra de Literatura Hispanoamericana, Same Address as Above)

**Universidad Complutense de Madrid. Departamento de Prehistoria**
- Trabajos de Prehistoria. Nueva Serie. (pub. by Museo Arqueologico Nacional)

**Universidad Complutense de Madrid. Departmento de Botanica y Fisiologia Vegetal.**
Madrid, Spain.
- Universidad de Madrid. Departamento de Botanica y Fisiologia Vegetal. Trabajos. irreg. ISSN 0580-468X

**Universidad Complutense de Madrid. Facultad de Ciencias**
111 Pabellon, Madrid-3, Spain.
- Cuadernos de Geologia Iberica. a; latest issue, 1974. (prep. by its Departamento de Economicas Geologicas)
- Seminarios de Estratigrafia. 2 per yr. (prep. by its Departamento de Estratigrafia)

**Universidad Complutense de Madrid. Facultad de Ciencias Politicas y Sociologia**
Seminario 18, Madrid, Spain.
- Boletin Informativo de Ciencia Politica; publicacion de la 2a catedra de teoria del estado y derecho constitucional. q.

**Universidad Complutense de Madrid. Facultad de Farmacia**
Madrid 3, Spain.
- Galenica Acta. bi-m. ISSN 0016-4011

**Universidad Complutense de Madrid. Facultad de Filologia**
Ciudad Universitaria, Madrid 3, Spain.
- Cuadernos de Filologia Clasica. s-a.
- Revista Filologia Moderna. ISSN 0046-3841

**Universidad Complutense de Madrid. Facultad de Filosofia y Letras**
Ciudad Universitaria, Madrid 3, Spain.
- Universidad Complutense de Madrid. Revista. bi-m.

**Universidad Complutense de Madrid. Facultad de Medicina**
Pabellon, Madrid 3, Spain.
- Spain. Consejo Superior de Investigaciones Cientificas. Instituto de Farmacologia Experimental. Archivos. irreg. ISSN 0024-9629 (prep. by its Departamento de Farmacologia Experimental)

**Universidad de Barcelona**
Departamento Farmacia Galenica, Nucleo Universitario Pedralbes, Barcelona (14), Spain.
- Ciencia e Industria Farmaceutica. 12 per yr.
- Revista de Geografia. s-a. ISSN 0048-7708
- Universidad de Barcelona. Facultad de Farmacia. Memoria. biennial. ISSN 0067-4176
- Universidad de Barcelona. Instituto de Arqueologia y Prehistoria. Publicaciones Eventuales. irreg., 1970, no. 16. ISSN 0067-4184

**Universidad de Barcelona. Biblioteca Central**
Barcelona, Spain.
- Universidad de Barcelona. Biblioteca Central. Catalogos de la Production Editorial Barcelonesa. a. ISSN 0067-4141

**Universidad de Barcelona. Departamenta de Pediatria**
Casanova 143, Barcelona-11, Spain.
- Archivos de Pediatria. bi-m. ISSN 0402-9054

**Universidad de Barcelona. Departamento de Arte**
Av Jose Antonio 585, Barcelona 11, Spain.
- D'Art. irreg.

**Universidad de Barcelona. Departamento de Historia Economica**
Prof. Dr. Pedro Voltes, Santa Lucia 1., Barcelona, Spain.
- Cuadernos de Historia Economica de Cataluna. s-a. ISSN 0045-9186 (Co-sponsor: Instituto Municipal de Historia)

**Universidad de Barcelona. Departmento de Psicologia**
Nucleo Universitario, Barcelona 14, Barcelona, Spain.
- Anuario de Psicologia. a.(in 2 pts) ISSN 0066-5126

**Universidad de Barcelona. Facultad de Biologia**
Barcelona, Spain.
- Acta Geobotanica Barcinonensia. irreg. ISSN 0065-1222 (prep. by its Departamento de Botanica)
- Acta Phytotaxonomica Barcinonensia. irreg. ISSN 0065-1575 (prep. by its Departamento de Botanica)

**Universidad de Barcelona. Facultad de Ciencias**
Barcelona, Spain.
- Collectanea Mathematica. q. ISSN 0010-0757 (prep. by its Seminario Matematico)

**Universidad de Barcelona. Facultad de Filologia**
Barcelona, Spain.
- Universidad de Barcelona. Facultad de Filologia. Annuario. a.

**Universidad de Barcelona. Facultad de Filosofia y Letras**
Avda. Jose Antonio 585, Barcelona 7, Spain.
- Bibliografia Historica de Espana e Hispanoamerica. (pub. by Editorial Teide)
- Convivium, Filosofia, Psicologia, Humanidades. 3 per yr. ISSN 0010-8235
- Pyrenae: Cronica Arqueologica; annual scientific journal. a. ISSN 0079-8215 (prep. by its Instituto de Arqueologia)

**Universidad de Barcelona. Facultad de Medicina**
- Medicina Clinica. (pub. by Ediciones Doyma, S.A.)

**Universidad de Barcelona. Instituto de Historia Medieval de Espana**
Barcelona, Spain.
- Anuario de Estudios Medievales. a. ISSN 0066-5061

**Universidad de Barcelona. Instituto de Historia Medievales**
Departamento de Estudios Medievales, Egipciacas 15, Barcelona 1, Spain.
- Miscelanea de Textos Medievales. a.

**Universidad de Deusto**
Apdo. 153, Aguirre 2, Bilbao, Spain.
- Boletin de Estudios Economicos. 3 per yr. ISSN 0006-6249 (Co-sponsor: Asociacion Licenciados en Ciencias Economicas)
- Estudios de Deusto. s-a. ISSN 0423-4847

**Universidad de Deusto. Facultad de Filosofia y Letras**
Apartado 1, Bilbao, Spain.
- Letras de Deusto. s-a.

**Universidad de Deusto. Facultad de Teologia**
- Selecciones de Teologia. (pub. by Ediciones Mensajero)

**Universidad de Granada**
Secretariado de Publicaciones, Rectorado, Granada, Spain.
- Archivo de Derecho Publico. a (some double issues)
- Cuadernos Geograficos. a.
- Universidad de Granada. Catedra Francisco Suarez. Anales. a. ISSN 0008-7750
- Universidad de Granada. Coleccion Monografica. irreg; no. 34, 1974. ISSN 0072-5382

**Universidad de Granada. Facultad de Ciencias**
Hospital Real, Granada, Spain
- Universidad de Granada. Facultad de Ciencias. Boletin de Obras Ingresadas. q.

**Universidad de Granada. Facultad de Derecho**
Granada, Spain.
- Monografias de Filosofia Juridica y Social/ Monographs of Social and Legal Philosophy. a. ISSN 0077-0442

**Universidad de Granada. Facultad de Farmacia**
Granada, Spain.
- Ars Pharmaceutica. q. ISSN 0004-2927

**Universidad de Granada. Facultad de Filosofia y Letras**
Avda. Cervantes 12-3A, Granada, Spain.
- Cuadernos de Historia del Islam. Serie Monografica Islamica Occidentalia. a; no. 4, 1972. ISSN 0070-1696 (prep. by its Seminario de Historia del Islam)

**Universidad de Granada. Secretariado de Publicaciones**
Granada, Spain.
- Cuadernos de Ciencias Biologicas. s-a.

**Universidad de la Laguna**
Secretariado de Publicaciones, Laguna, Canary Islands, Spain.
- Universidad de la Laguna. Facultad de Ciencias. Anales. a. ISSN 0075-7721
- Universidad de la Laguna. Facultad de Derecho. Anales. a. ISSN 0075-773X

**Universidad de Navarra**
- Biblioteca de Teologia. (pub. by Ediciones Universidad de Navarra, S.A.)
- Scripta Theologica. (pub. by Ediciones Universidad de Navarra, S.A.)

**Universidad de Navarra. Departamento de Derecho Internacional**
- Anuario de Derecho Internacional. (pub. by Ediciones Universidad de Navarra, S.A.)

**Universidad de Navarra. Departamento de Historia Antigua**
- Mundo Antiguo. (pub. by Ediciones Universidad de Navarra, S.A.)

**Universidad de Navarra. Departamento de Historia Medieval**
- Cuadernos de Trabajo de Historia. (pub. by Ediciones Universidad de Navarra, S.A.)

**Universidad de Navarra. Departamento de Literatura Espanola**
- Universidad de Navarra. Departamento de Literatura Espanola. Publicaciones. (pub. by Ediciones Universidad de Navarra S.A.)

**Universidad de Navarra. Escuela de Arquitectura**
- Universidad de Navarra. Escuela de Arquitectura. Manuales: Arquitectura. (pub. by Ediciones Universidad de Navarra, S.A.)

**Universidad de Navarra. Escuela de Asistentes Sociales**
- Cuadernos de Trabajo Social. (pub. by Ediciones Universidad de Navarra, S.A.)

**Universidad de Navarra. Escuela de Bibliotecarias**
- Universidad de Navarra. Escuela de Bibliotecarias. Manuales: Bibliotecarias. (pub. by Ediciones Universidad de Navarra, S.A.)

**Universidad de Navarra. Facultad de Ciencias de la Educacion**
- Universidad de Navarra. Instituto de Ciencias de la Educacion. Coleccion I C E. (pub. by Ediciones Universidad de Navarra, S.A.)

**Universidad de Navarra. Facultad de Ciencias de la Informacion**
- Universidad de Navarra. Facultad de Ciencias de la Informacion. Cuadernos de Trabajo. (pub. by Ediciones Universidad de Navarra, S.A.)
- Universidad de Navarra. Facultad de Ciencias de la Informacion. Manuales: Periodismo. (pub. by Ediciones Universidad de Navarra, S.A.)

**Universidad de Navarra. Facultad de Derecho.**
- Coleccion Juridica. (pub. by Ediciones Universidad de Navarra, S.A.)

**Universidad de Navarra, Facultad de Derecho Canonico**
- Coleccion Canonica. (pub. by Ediciones Universidad de Navarra, S.A.)
- Universidad de Navarra. Departamento de Derecho Canonico. Manuales: Derecho Canonico. (pub. by Ediciones Universidad de Navarra, S.A.)

**Universidad de Navarra. Facultad de Filosofia y Letras**
- Anuario Filosofico. (pub. by Ediciones Universidad de Navarra, S.A.)
- Coleccion Filosofica. (pub. by Ediciones Universidad de Navarra, S.A.)
- Coleccion Historica. (pub. by Ediciones Universidad de Navarra, S.A.)

**Universidad de Navarra. Facultad de Medicina**
- Coleccion Medicina. (pub. by Ediciones Universidad de Navarra, S.A.)

**Universidad de Navarra. Facultad de Teolgia**
Plaza de los Sauces 1 y 2, Baranain, Pamplona, Spain.
- Coleccion Teologica. irreg; no. 8, 1974.

**Universidad de Navarra. Instituto de Estudios Superiores de la Empresa**
- Empresa y Su Entorno. Serie AC. (pub. by Ediciones Universidad de Navarra, S.A.)
- Empresa y Su Entorno. Serie L. (pub. by Ediciones Universidad de Navarra, S.A.)

**Universidad de Navarra. Instituto Martin de Azpilcueta**
- Ius Canonicum. (pub. by Ediciones Universidad de Navarra, S.A.)

**Ediciones Universidad de Navarra, S.A.**
Plaza de los Sauces, 1 y 2, Baranain, Pamplona, Spain.
- Anuario de Derecho Internacional. a. (Universidad de Navarra. Departamento de Derecho Internacional)
- Anuario Filosofico. s-a. ISSN 0066-5215 (Universidad de Navarra. Facultad de Filosofia y Letras)
- Biblioteca de Teologia. irreg; 1976, no. 13. ISSN 0067-740X (Universidad de Navarra)
- Coleccion Canonica. irreg; 1976, no. 60. ISSN 0069-505X (Universidad de Navarra, Facultad de Derecho Canonico)
- Coleccion Ciencias Biologicas. irreg; 1976, no. 5.
- Coleccion de Economia. irreg; 1976, no. 3.
- Coleccion Filosofica. irreg; 1976, no. 23. ISSN 0069-5076 (Universidad de Navarra. Facultad de Filosofia y Letras)
- Coleccion Historica. irreg; 1976, no. 31. ISSN 0069-5106 (Universidad de Navarra. Facultad de Filosofia y Letras)
- Coleccion Juridica. irreg; 1976, no. 70. ISSN 0069-5122 (Universidad de Navarra. Facultad de Derecho.)
- Coleccion Medicina. irreg; 1976, no. 3. (Universidad de Navarra. Facultad de Medicina)
- Cuadernos de Trabajo de Historia. irreg; 1976, no. 6. (Universidad de Navarra. Departamento de Historia Medieval)
- Cuadernos de Trabajo Social. irreg; 1976, no. 4. (Universidad de Navarra. Escuela de Asistentes Sociales)
- Direccion de Empresas y Organizaciones. irreg; 1976 no. 4.
- Empresa y Su Entorno. Serie AC. irreg; 1976; no. 7.
- Empresa y Su Entorno. Serie L. irreg; 1976, no. 11.
- Historia de la Iglesia. irreg; 1976, no. 8.
- Ius Canonicum. 2 per yr. ISSN 0021-325X (Universidad de Navarra. Instituto Martin de Azpilcueta)
- Jurisprudencia y Textos Legales. irreg; 1976, no. 2.
- Mundo Antiguo. irreg; 1976, no. 4. ISSN 0077-2054 (Universidad de Navarra. Departamento de Historia Antigua)
- Nuestro Tiempo; revista mensual de cuestiones actuales. m. ISSN 0029-5795
- Orientacion Familiar. irreg; 1976, no. 5.
- Persona y Derecho. a.
- Scripta Theologica. s-a. ISSN 0036-9764 (Universidad de Navarra)
- Temas N T; coleccion cultural de bolsillo. irreg; 1976, no. 40.
- Universidad de Navarra. Departamento de Derecho Canonico. Manuales: Derecho Canonico. irreg; 1976, no. 3. ISSN 0078-8759

- Universidad de Navarra. Departamento de Literatura Espanola. Publicaciones. irreg; 1976, no. 4.
- Universidad de Navarra. Escuela de Arquitectura. Manuales: Arquitectura. irreg; 1976, no. 4. ISSN 0078-8732
- Universidad de Navarra. Escuela de Bibliotecarias. Manuales: Bibliotecarias. irreg; 1976, no. 4. ISSN 0078-8740
- Universidad de Navarra. Facultad de Ciencias de la Informacion. Cuadernos de Trabajo. irreg; 1976, no. 23. ISSN 0078-8724
- Universidad de Navarra. Facultad de Ciencias de la Informacion. Manuales: Periodismo. irreg; 1976, no. 4. ISSN 0078-8783
- Universidad de Navarra. Instituto de Ciencias de la Educacion. Coleccion I C E. irreg; 1976; no. 17. ISSN 0078-8686
- Universidad de Navarra. Manuales de Derecho. irreg; 1976, no. 4.
- Universidad de Navarra. Revista de Medicina. q. ISSN 0556-6177

**Universidad de Oviedo**
San Francisco, Oviedo, Spain.
- Asturiensia Medievalia. (prep. by its Departamento de Historia Medieval)
- Breviora Geologica Asturica. q. ISSN 0520-9455 (prep. by its Instituto de Geologia Aplicada)
- Universidad de Oviedo. Centro de Estudios del Siglo XVIII. Boletin. irreg. (prep. by its Centro de Estudios del Siglo XVIII)
- Universidad de Oviedo. Departamento de Prehistoria y Arqueologia. Publicaciones. irreg. (prep. by its Departamento de Prehistoria y Arqueologia)

**Universidad de Salamanca. Seminario de Derecho**
Salamanca, Spain.
- Salamanca. Universidad. Seminario de Derecho Politico. Boletin Informativo. q.

**Universidad de Sevilla**
Secretariado de Publicaciones, Seville, Spain.
- Habis.
- Universidad de Seville. Seminario de Antropologia Americana. Publicaciones. irreg.; vol. 12, 1974. ISSN 0080-9101
- Universidad Hispalense. Anales. Series: Filosofia y Letras, Derecho, Medicina, Ciencias, y Veterinaria. 3-4yr. ISSN 0041-8552

**Universidad de Sevilla. Catedra de Obstetrica y Ginecologia**
- Toko-Ginecologia Practica. (pub. by Editorial Garsi)

**Universidad de Sevilla. Catedra de Pediatria y Puericultura**
- Revista Espanola de Pediatria. (pub. by Editorial Garsi)

**Universidad de Valencia**
Paseo al Mar, Valencia, Spain.
- Cuadernos de Filologia. s-a. (prep. by its Seccion de Filologia Moderna)
- Cuadernos Hispanicos de Historia de la Medicina y de la Ciencia. irreg. (2-3 nos. per yr) (prep. by its Facultad de Medicina) (Co-sponsor: Catedra Historia de la Medicina de Valencia)
- Indice Medico Espanol. (pub. by Instituto de Informacion y Documentacion en Biomedicina)
- Teorema. q. (prep. by its Departamento de Logica y Filosofia de Ciencia)
- Valencia (City). Universidad. Catedra de Derecho del Trabajo. Cuadernos. s-a.

**Universidad de Valencia. Facultad de Filosofia y Letras**
Nave 2, Valencia, Spain.
- Cuadernos de Geografia. s-a. (prep. by its Departamento de Geografia)

**Universidad de Valladolid. Facultad de Medicina**
Plaza de Santa Cruz, No. 9, Valladolid, Spain.
- Universidad de Valladolid. Facultad de Medicina. Biblioteca. Boletin de Obras Ingresadas. a. (prep. by its Biblioteca)

**Universidad de Zaragoza. Facultad de Medicina**
Ciudad Universitaria, Zaragoza, Spain.
- Facultad de Medicina de Zaragoza. Archivos. bi-m. ISSN 0014-6730
- Facultad de Medicina, Zaragoza. Departamento Anatomico. Anales de Anatomia. 3 per yr. (prep. by its Departamento Anatomico)

**Universidad Internacional Menendez Pelayo**
Santander, Spain.
- Universidad Internacional Menendez Pelayo.
  Publicaciones. biennial, no. 43, 1974. ISSN 0080-
  6145 (Spain. Ministerio de Educacion y Ciencia)

**Universidad Politecnica de Barcelona**
Avda. Gregorio Maranon s/n, Barcelona 14, Spain.
- Universidad Politecnica de Barcelona. Publicacion.
  a.

**Universidad Politecnica de Barcelona. Instituto de
Investigacion Textil y de Cooperacion Industrial.**
Avda. Gregorio Maranon s/n, Barcelona 14, Spain.
- Universidad Politecnica de Barcelona. Instituto de
  Investigacion Textil y de Cooperacion Industrial.
  Boletin. q.

**Universidad Politecnica de Madrid. Escuela Tecnica
Superior de Ingenieros de Montes**
Madrid 3, Spain.
- Escuela Tecnica Superior de Ingenieros de
  Montes. Biblioteca. Boletin Bibliografico y
  Documental. (prep. by its Biblioteca)

**Universidad Pontificia de Salamanca**
Compania 1, Salamanca, Spain.
- Colectanea de Jurisprudencia Canonica. a.
- Cuadernos Salmantinos de Filosofia. a.
- Helmantica; revista de filologia clasica y hebrea. 3
  per yr. ISSN 0018-0114
- Salmanticensis. 3 per yr. ISSN 0036-3537

**Universidad Pontificia Salamanca. Centro Estudios
Orientales y Ecumenicos**
Calle Compania 1, Salamanca, Spain.
- Dialogo Ecumenico. 3 per yr.

**Universidad, Santiago de Compostela. Seminario de
Arqueologia**
- Studia Archaeologica. (pub. by Rudolf Habelt
  Verlag GW)

**Valencia Filatelica**
c/o Jose M. Gomis Segui, Ed., Box 912, Valencia 9,
Spain.
- Valencia Filatelica; cuadernos de filatelia. m.

**Vasan, S.L. Ediciones Tecnica**
Marcenado 7, Apto. 2179, Madrid-2, Spain.
- Transistor. m. ISSN 0041-1140 (Instituto de
  Estudios Electronicos)

**Enrique Vicente de Vera, Ed. & Pub.**
Avenida de Espana 7-2, San Sebastian (Guipuzcoa),
Spain.
- Economia Vascongada; revista de la industria, el
  comercio, y la navegacion. m.

**Editorial Veterinaria, S.A.**
Galileo, 288, 1e, Barcelona-14, Spain.
- Veterinaria; revista tecnica. bi-m.

**Vicariato General Castrense**
Nuncio 13, Madrid-5, Spain.
- Boletin Oficial de la Jurisdiccion Eclesiastica
  Castrense. m.

**Angel Villatoro, Ed. & Pub.**
G. V. Marques del Turia 26, Valencia, Spain.
- Aficion Espanola. s-m. ISSN 0001-9690

**World Federation of Societies of Anaesthesiologists**
- European Congress of Anaesthesiology.
  Proceedings. (pub. by European Congress of
  Anaesthesiology)

**World Tourism Organization**
Avenida del Generalisimo, 59, Madrid-16, Spain.
- Economic Review of World Tourism. biennial.
  ISSN 0070-864X
- International Travel Statistics. a. ISSN 0074-9184
- International Union of Official Travel
  Organizations. Minutes of the IUOTO General
  Assemblies. a. ISSN 0074-9451
- Tourist Bibliography. a. ISSN 0082-5468
- Travel Abroad: Frontier Formalities. a. ISSN
  0082-6103
- Travel Research Journal. a. with irreg. suppls.
  ISSN 0082-6197
- World Tourism. biennial. ISSN 0084-2354
- World Tourism Organization. Collection of
  Technical Bulletins. 30 per yr.
- World Travel/Tourisme Mondial. bi-m. ISSN
  0043-9169

**Yate y Motonautica**
Diputacion 304-4, Barcelona-9, Spain.
- Anuario de la Industria Nautica Espanola. a.
- Yate y Motonautica; revista espanola de la mar.
  m.

**Julian Yebenes Guerrero**
Fernando VI, 27, Madrid-4, Spain.
- Agricultor Practico. m.
- Aral; semanario de articulos alimenticios y
  bebidas. w.
- Auto Revista; semanario del motor. w. ISSN
  0005-1691
- Cero Defectos. m. (Asociacion Espanolo para el
  Control de la Calidad)
- Jomar; boletin de informacion de comercio
  exterior. d., 5 per wk.
- Laboreo; revista de la nueva agricultura espanola.
  m.
- Metales y Maquinas. m.
- Nuestra Cabana; revista de la nueva ganaderia
  espanola. m.
- Oleo; revista semanal de aceites y grasas. w. ISSN
  0472-8807
- Proyectos Quimicos. w.
- R.E.S. (Relacion de Empresas Suspensas en Pagos,
  Embargos y Subastas) w.

**Yelmo**
Apdo 877, Madrid, Spain.
- Yelmo; la revista del profesor de espanol. q. ISSN
  0006-6966

**Zona Abierta**
Argueso 8, Madrid, Spain.
- Zona Abierta. q.

**1 del Metal de Valencia**
Ave. Baron de Carcer, 36, Valencia 1, Spain.
- Val Metal. bi-m.

# SRI LANKA

**Afro Asian Writers Bureau**
73 Castle St., Colombo 8, Sri Lanka.
- Call. q. ISSN 0045-401X

**Aquinas College of Higher Studies**
Colombo 8, Sri Lanka.
- Aquinas Law Journal. irreg.

**Asian Regional Institute for School Building Research**
Box 1368, Colombo 7, Sri Lanka.
- Asian Regional Institute for School Building
  Research. Newsletter. q. ISSN 0007-3733

**Associated Newspapers of Ceylon Ltd.**
Box 1195, Lake House, Colombo 10, Sri Lanka.
- Ferguson's Ceylon Directory. a.

**Buddhist Publication Society**
Box 61, Kandy, Sri Lanka.
- Bodhi Leaves. q. ISSN 0520-3325
- Buddhist Publication Society. Report. a. ISSN
  0068-3345
- Wheel; a series of Buddhist publications. q. ISSN
  0049-7541

**Buddhist Publications**
153-3 Dutugemunu St., Nugegoda, Sri Lanka.
- World Buddhism. m. ISSN 0043-8286
- World Buddhism. Vesak Annual. a. ISSN 0084-
  1447

**Central Bank of Ceylon**
Deputy Director of Information, Janadhipathi
Mawatha, Colombo 1, Sri Lanka.
- Central Bank of Ceylon. Annual Report. a. ISSN
  0069-1496
- Central Bank of Ceylon. Bulletin. m. ISSN 0008-
  9222 (prep. by its Department of Economic
  Research)
- Central Bank of Ceylon. Staff Studies. s-a. (prep.
  by its Department of Economic Research)

**Ceylon Chamber of Commerce**
Lower Chatham St., Box 274, Colombo 1, Sri
Lanka.
- Enterprise. bi-m.

**Ceylon Institute of Scientific and Industrial Research**
- Directory of Scientific Research Projects in
  Ceylon. (pub. by National Science Council of Sri
  Lanka)

**Ceylon National Chamber of Industries**
2-1-12A Bristol Bldg., Box 133, Colombo 1, Sri
Lanka.
- Industrial Ceylon. q. ISSN 0019-8064

**Ceylon Rationalist Association**
89 Pamankada Lane, Colombo 6, Sri Lanka.
- Ceylon Rationalist Ambassador. a. ISSN 0577-
  4772

**Ceylon Tourist Board**
25 Galle Face Center Rd., Box 1504, Colombo 3,
Sri Lanka.
- Tourmaline. q.

**Ceylon Veterinary Association**
School of Veterinary Science, University of Sri
Lanka, Peradeniya, Sri Lanka.
- Ceylon Veterinary Journal. q. ISSN 0009-0891

**Ceylon Workers' Congress**
Box 1294, 72 Ananda Coomaraswamy Mawatha,
Colombo 7, Sri Lanka.
- Congress News. s-m. ISSN 0045-6217

**Coconut Research Institute**
Bandirippuwa Estate, Lunuwila, Sri Lanka.
- Ceylon Coconut Planter's Review. irreg. ISSN
  0009-0816
- Ceylon Coconut Quarterly. q. ISSN 0009-0824

**Colombo Plan Bureau**
12 Melbourne Ave., Box 596, Colombo 4, Sri
Lanka.
- Colombo Plan Bureau. Technical Cooperation
  under the Colombo Plan. Report. a. ISSN 0069-
  5947
- Colombo Plan for Co-operative Economic
  Development in South and South-East Asia;
  Report of the Consultative Committee. a. ISSN
  0069-5963
- Colombo Plan Newsletter. m. ISSN 0010-1419

**Colombo Publications**
235-2/2 Olcott Mawatha, Colombo 11, Sri Lanka.
- Tutor. m.

**Dental Students' Association**
University of Sri Lanka, University Park,
Peradeniya, Sri Lanka.
- Mirror and Probe. a.

**Hansa Publishers Ltd.**
Clifford Ave., Colombo 3, Sri Lanka.
- Colombo Law Review. a. ISSN 0069-5939 (Sri
  Lanka University Law Review Association)

**Income Tax Payers' Association of Ceylon**
54 3/2 Australia Bldg., Colombo 1, Sri Lanka.
- Ceylon Tax Payer. q.

**Incorporated Law Society of Sri Lanka**
129/5 Hultsdorf St., Colombo 12, Sri Lanka.
- Incorporated Law Society of Sri Lanka. Annual
  Report. a. ISSN 0073-5728
- Incorporated Law Society of Sri Lanka. Journal.
  irreg. ISSN 0073-5736

**Institute of Chartered Accountants of Sri Lanka**
30A Longden Place, Colombo 7, Sri Lanka.
- Accountant. s-a.

**Institute of Criminology of Sri Lanka**
Buddhist Academy of Ceylon, 109 Rosmead Place,
Colombo, Sri Lanka.
- Criminology Journal of Sri Lanka. s-a.

**Institution of Engineers, Sri Lanka**
Lower Chatham Street, Colombo 1, Sri Lanka.
- Engineer. q.
- Institution of Engineers, Sri Lanka. Year Book. a.

**Leisure**
No. 42 32nd Lane, Colombo 6, Sri Lanka.
- Leisure; Ceylon's own monthly magazine. m.
  ISSN 0047-4363

**Marga Institute (Sri Lanka Centre for Development
Studies)**
Box 601, 61 Issipathana Mawatha, Colombo 5, Sri
Lanka.
- Marga. q. ISSN 0047-5912
- Marga Institute. Progress Report. biennial.

**Metro Printers**
19 Austin Place, Borella, Colombo 8, Sri Lanka.
- National Education Society of Sri Lanka. Journal.
  a. ISSN 0085-3747

**National Agricultural Society of Ceylon**
Faculty of Agriculture, University of Sri Lanka, Peradeniya, Sri Lanka.
- National Agricultural Society of Ceylon. Journal. a. ISSN 0547-3616

**National Education Society of Sri Lanka**
- National Education Society of Sri Lanka. Journal. (pub. by Metro Printers)

**National Science Council of Sri Lanka**
147/5 Maitland Place, Colombo 7, Sri Lanka.
- Directory of Scientific Research Projects in Ceylon. irreg. (Ceylon Institute of Scientific and Industrial Research)

**Outlook**
60-2 Barnes Place, Colombo 7, Sri Lanka.
- Outlook; perspectives for Christian living. bi-m.

**Pix/Film Monthly**
Box 758, Colombo 15, Sri Lanka.
- Pix/Film Monthly. m.

**Rubber Research Institute of Sri Lanka**
Dartonfield, Agalawatta, Sri Lanka.
- Rubber Research Institute of Sri Lanka. Journal. irreg.

**Soil Science Society of Ceylon**
Faculty of Agriculture, University of Sri Lanka, Peradeniya, Sri Lanka.
- Soil Science Society of Ceylon. Journal. a.

**Spicy Isle**
23 Rajamalwatte Rd., Colombo 15, Sri Lanka.
- Spicy Isle. q.

**Sri Aurobindo Centenary Committee**
47 Galle Face Court, Galle Rd., Colombo 3, Sri Lanka.
- Sri Aurobindo Centenary Annual. a.

**Sri Lanka. Department of Agriculture**
102 Union Place, Box 636, Colombo 2, Sri Lanka.
- Tropical Agriculturist; agricultural journal of Ceylon. q. ISSN 0041-3224

**Sri Lanka. Department of Archaeology**
Sir Marcus Fernando Rd., Colombo 7, Sri Lanka.
- Ancient Ceylon. irreg.

**Sri Lanka. Department of Census and Statistics**
Box 563, Colombo 7, Sri Lanka.
(Order from: Superintendent, Government Publications Bureau, Colombo, Sri Lanka)
- Sri Lanka Yearbook. a.
- Statistical Abstract of Sri Lanka. a. ISSN 0081-4636
- Statistical Pocket Book of Sri Lanka. a.

**Sri Lanka. Department of Labour**
Assistant Commissioner of Labour, Labour Secretariat, Colombo 5, Sri Lanka.
- Sri Lanka Labour Gazette. m.

**Sri Lanka. Department of National Archives. National Bibliography Branch**
7 Reid Ave., Colombo 7, Sri Lanka.
- Sri Lanka National Bibliography. m.

**Sri Lanka. Department of National Museums**
Box 854, Sir Marcus Fernando Mawatha, Colombo 7, Sri Lanka.
- Journal of the National Museums of Ceylon. q.
- Spolia Zeylanica/Bulletin of the National Museums of Sri Lanka. a. ISSN 0081-3745
- Sri Lanka. Department of National Museums. Translations Series. irreg. ISSN 0069-2352
- Sri Lanka Periodicals Index. bi-m. (prep. by its National Museum Library)

**Sri Lanka. Forest Department**
Box 509, Colombo 2, Sri Lanka.
- Sri Lanka Forester. s-a.

**Sri Lanka. Government Information Department**
7 Sir Baron Jayatilleke Mawatha, Colombo 1, Sri Lanka.
- Sri Lanka. m. ISSN 0490-6381

**Sri Lanka. Irrigation Department. Hydrology Division**
Bauddhaloka Mawatha, Colombo 7, Sri Lanka.
- Sri Lanka. Irrigation Department. Hydrology Division. Hydrological Annual. a.

**Sri Lanka. Ministry of Commerce and Trade**
Colombo, Sri Lanka.
- Sri Lanka Export Directory. a. ISSN 0069-2360

**Sri Lanka Academy of Administrative Studies**
28-10 Longdon Place, Colombo 7, Sri Lanka.
- Journal of Development Administration. s-a. ISSN 0047-2360

**Sri Lanka Historical and Social Studies Publication Board**
University Park, Peradeniya, Sri Lanka.
- Sri Lanka Journal of Historical and Social Studies. s-a. ISSN 0009-0832

**Sri Lanka Library Association**
University of Sri Lanka, Colombo Campus, Box 1698, Colombo 7, Sri Lanka.
- Sri Lanka Library Review. s-a. ISSN 0009-0867

**Sri Lanka Medical Association**
S. L. M. A. House, 6 Wijerama Mawatha, Colombo 7, Sri Lanka.
- Sri Lanka Medical Journal. q.

**Sri Lanka Meteorological Society**
26 Clifford Place, Colombo 4, Sri Lanka.
- Sri Lanka Meteorological Society. Journal. q.

**Sri Lanka University Law Review Association**
- Colombo Law Review. (pub. by Hansa Publishers Ltd.)

**Study Centre for Religion and Society**
490-5 Havelock Rd., Colombo 6, Sri Lanka.
- Dialogue. 3 per yr. ISSN 0012-2181

**Tea Research Institute of Sri Lanka**
St. Coombs, Talawakele, Sri Lanka.
- Tea Quarterly & Annual Reports. q. ISSN 0040-036X

**Tisara Prakaskayo Ltd**
137 Dutugemunu St., Dehiwala, Sri Lanka.
- Ceylon Historical Journal. irreg. ISSN 0577-4691

**Tribune**
43 Dawson St., Colombo 2, Ceylon.
- Tribune; Ceylon news review. s-m. ISSN 0493-9042

**University of Sri Lanka**
Senate House, Box 1406, Bauddhaloka Mawatha, Colombo 7, Sri Lanka.
- Sigma. a. ISSN 0080-956X

**University of Sri Lanka, Colombo Campus**
Faculty of Medicine, Kynsey Rd., Colombo 8, Sri Lanka.
- Ceylon Journal of Medical Science. 2 per yr. ISSN 0011-2232

**University of Sri Lanka, Peradeniya Campus**
University Park, Peradeniya, Sri Lanka.
- Ceylon Journal of Science. Biological Sciences. irreg. ISSN 0069-2379
- Modern Ceylon Studies. s-a. ISSN 0026-7570
- Sri Lanka Journal of the Humanities. s-a.

**Wildlife & Nature Protection Society of Ceylon**
Chaitiya Rd., Fort, Colombo 1, Sri Lanka.
- Loris; a journal on Ceylon wildlife. s-a. ISSN 0024-6514

# SUDAN

**Bank of Sudan**
Box 313, Khartoum, Sudan.
- Bank of Sudan. Economic and Financial Bulletin. q. ISSN 0005-5336 (prep. by its Economic Research Department)
- Bank of Sudan. Foreign Trade Statistical Digest. a. ISSN 0522-246X (prep. by its Economic Research Department)
- Bank of Sudan. Report. a. ISSN 0067-3749

**Cotton Public Corporation**
Box 1672, Khartoum, Sudan.
- Sudan Cotton Bulletin. m. ISSN 0562-5033 (prep. by its Department of Research and Statistics)

**Industrial Bank of Sudan**
United Nations Sq., P.O. Box 1722, Khartoum, Sudan.
- Industrial Bank of Sudan. Board of Directors. Annual Report. a. ISSN 0073-7356

**Institute of Public Administration**
P.O. Box 1492, Khartoum, Sudan.
- Institute of Public Administration, Khartoum. Occasional Papers. irreg. ISSN 0073-9618
- Institute of Public Administration, Khartoum. Proceedings of the Annual Round Table Conference. irreg. ISSN 0073-9626

**Khartoum University Press**
Box 321, Khartoum, Sudan.
- Adab. a. (University of Khartoum. Faculty of Arts)
- Sudan Medical Journal. q. ISSN 0491-4481 (Sudan Medical Association)

**National Council for Research**
see Sudan. National Council for Research

**Philosophical Society of the Sudan**
P.O. Box 526, Khartoum, Sudan.
- Philosophical Society of the Sudan. Proceedings of the Annual Conference. a. ISSN 0079-1695

**Regional Educational Building Institute of Africa**
B.P. 1720, B.P. 1720, Khartoum, Sudan.
- Regional Educational Building Institute for Africa. Letter/Institut Regional pour les Constructions Scolaires en Afrique. Lettre. q.

**Sudan. Department of Statistics**
Box 700, Khartoum, Sudan.
- Sudan. Department of Statistics. Internal Trade and Other Statistics. a.

**Sudan. Idarat al-Bahuth al-Iqtisadiyah Wa-al-Maliyah**
see Sudan. Ministry of Finance and National Economy. Economic and Financial Research Section

**Sudan. Maslahat al-'ihsa**
see Sudan. Department of Statistics

**Sudan. Ministry of Finance and National Economy. Economic and Financial Research Section**
Box 2092, Khartoum, Sudan.
- Sudan. Ministry of Finance and National Economy. Economic and Financial Research Section. Economic Survey. a. ISSN 0081-9050

**Sudan. Ministry of People's Local Government**
Box 94, Khartoum, Sudan.
- People's Local Government Journal/Al-Hukm al-Shabi al-Mahalli. m.

**Sudan. Mufawadiyat al-Takhtit al-Qawmi. Department of Statistics**
see Sudan. Department of Statistics

**Sudan. Mufawadiyat al-Takhtit al-Qawmi. National Income Division**
see Sudan. National Planning Commission. National Income Division

**Sudan. National Council for Research**
Box 2404, Khartoum, Sudan.
- Sudan. National Council for Research. Science Policy and Annual Report. a.

**Sudan. National Income Division**
see under Sudan. National Planning Commission

**Sudan. National Planning Commission. Department of Statistics**
see Sudan. Department of Statistics

**Sudan. National Planning Commission. National Income Division**
Box 700, Khartoum, Sudan.
- Sudan. National Planning Commission. National Income Division. National Income Accounts and Supporting Tables. a.

**Sudan. Wizarat al-Hukumah al-Mahalliyah**
see Sudan. Ministry of People's Local Government

**Sudan Engineering Society**
Box 759, Khartoum, Sudan.
- Sudan Engineering Society. Journal. s-a. ISSN 0049-2469

**Sudan Food Research Centre**
P.O. Box 213, Khartoum, Sudan.
- Sudan Journal of Food Science and Technology.

**Sudan Medical Association**
- Sudan Medical Journal. (pub. by Khartoum University Press)

**Sudan News Agency**
P.O. Box 1506, Gamaa Avenue, Khartoum, Sudan.
- Wakatlat al-Sudan Lil-Anba. Weekly Review/
Sudan News Agency. Weekly Review. w.

**Sudanese Socialist Union**
Box 1850, Khartoum, Sudan.
- Al-Ishtiraki. m.

**University of Khartoum. Faculty of Arts**
- Adab. (pub. by Khartoum University Press)

**Wakatkat al-Sudan Lil-Anba**
see Sudan News Agency

## SURINAM

**Centre for Agricultural Research in Surinam.**
P.O. Box 1914, Paramaribo, Surinam.
- C E L O S Bulletins. irreg. ISSN 0069-1909

**Surinam. Algemeen Bureau voor de Statistiek**
Paramaribo, Surinam.
- Surinam. Algemeen Bureau voor de Statistiek.
Kwartaal Statistiek van de Industriele Produktie.
irreg.

**Surinam. Centraal Bureau Luchtkartering**
Paramaribo, Surinam.
- Surinam. Centraal Bureau Luchtkartering.
Jaarverslag. irreg.

**Surinam. Department of Agriculture and Fisheries**
Box 160, Paramaribo, Surinam.
- Landbouwproefstation Suriname. Jaarverslag/
Agricultural Experiment Station Surinam. Annual
Report. (prep. by its Landbouwproefstation)
- Surinaamse Landbouw/Surinam Agriculture. 2-3
per yr. ISSN 0039-6133

## SWAZILAND

**Swaziland. Central Statistical Office**
P.O. Box 456, Mbabane, Swaziland.
- Swaziland. Central Statistical Office. Annual
Statistical Bulletin. a. ISSN 0586-1357
- Swaziland. Central Statistical Office. Annual
Survey of Swazi Nation Land. a, latest 1973-74.
- Swaziland. Central Statistical Office. Balance of
Payments. a.
- Swaziland. Central Statistical Office. Census of
Commerical Timber Plantations and Wood and
Wood Products. a.
- Swaziland. Central Statistical Office. Census of
Individual Tenure Farms. a.
- Swaziland. Central Statistical Office. National
Accounts. a.
- Swaziland. Central Statistical Office. Quarterly
Digest of Statistics. q.

**Swaziland. Economic Planning Office**
Mbabane, Swaziland.
- Swaziland. Economic Planning Office. Economic
Review. a.

**Swaziland. Geological Survey and Mines Department**
P.O. Box 9, Mbabane, Swaziland.
- Swaziland. Geological Survey and Mines
Department. Annual Report. a; latest 1960. ISSN
0081-9999
- Swaziland. Geological Survey and Mines
Department. Bulletin. a. ISSN 0082-0008

**Swaziland. Ministry of Agriculture**
Mbabane, Swaziland.
- Swaziland. Ministry of Agriculture. Annual
Report. a.

**Swaziland. Ministry of Education**
P.O. Box 39, Mbabane, Swaziland.
- Swaziland Teachers Journal: Education Today. a.

**Swaziland. Ministry of Finance**
Box 443, Mbabane, Swaziland.
- Swaziland. Ministry of Finance. Capital Fund
Estimates for the Financial Year. a.
- Swaziland. Ministry of Finance. Financial
Statement Supporting the Estimates of Recurrent
and Capital Expenditure. a.

**Swaziland National Centre**
Box 100, Lobamba, Swaziland.
- Swaziland National Centre. Yearbook. a.

**University of Botswana, Lesotho and Swaziland.**
**Faculty of Agriculture**
Swaziland Campus, P.O. Luyengo, Swaziland.
- University of Botswana, Lesotho and Swaziland.
Faculty of Agriculture. Research Division. Annual
Report. a.

## SWEDEN

**Aahlens och Aakerlunds Foerlag AB**
Torsgatan 21, 105 44 Stockholm, Sweden.
- Damernas Vaerld. w. ISSN 0011-5916
- Fib-Aktuellt. w. ISSN 0015-0509
- Husmodern. w. ISSN 0018-8026
- Kamratposten. fortn. ISSN 0022-8273
- Min Vaarld. w.
- Vecko-Journalen. w. ISSN 0042-2940
- Vecko Revyn. m.

**Paul Aastroems Foerlag**
Soedra Vaegen 61, S-412 54 Goeteborg, Sweden.
- Studies in Mediterranean Archaeology.
Monograph Series. irreg., no. 49, 1977. ISSN
0081-8232

**Acta Radiologica**
Vasagatan 12, S-111 20 Stockholm, Sweden.
- Acta Radiologica. Series 1: Diagnosis. bi-m. ISSN
0567-8056
- Acta Radiologica. Series 2: Therapy, Physics,
Biology: bi-m. ISSN 0567-8064

**Acta Universitatis Gothoburgensis**
Box 5096, S-402 22 Goeteborg 5, Sweden
(Dist. in U. S., Canada, and Mexico by: Humanities
Press, Inc., 171 First Ave., Atlantic Highlands, NJ
07716)
- Botanica Gothoburgensia. irreg., 1968, no. 6.
ISSN 0068-0370
- Goeteborger Germanistische Forschungen. irreg.,
no. 15, 1976. ISSN 0072-4793
- Gothenburg Studies in English. irreg., no. 34,
1976. ISSN 0072-503X
- Gothenburg Studies in Philosophy. irreg., 1964,
no. 3. ISSN 0072-5048
- Nordistica Gothoburgensia. irreg., no. 9, 1976.
ISSN 0078-1134
- Romanica Gothoburgensia. irreg., no. 15, 1974.
ISSN 0080-3863
- Slavica Gothoburgensia. irreg., no. 6, 1974. ISSN
0081-0010
- Studia Graeca et Latina Gothoburgensia. irreg.,
no. 34, 1976. ISSN 0081-6450
- Zoologica Gothoburgensia. irreg. ISSN 0084-5590

**Aeronautical Research Institute of Sweden**
see Flygtekniska Foersoeksanstalten

**Foerlags AB Affaersekonomi**
Box 45056, S-104 30 Stockholm, Sweden.
- Affaerekonomi-Management Nu. 8 per yr.
- Transport och Hantering. m.

**African Clarion**
Box 4037, 422 04 Hisings Backa, Sweden.
- African Clarion. 6 per yr.

**Afrikagrupperna i Sverige**
Box 1143, S-221 05 Lund, Sweden.
- Soedra Afrika. Informations Bulletin. 4-6 per yr.
ISSN 0038-0490

**Agrifack**
Kommendoersgatan 35, S-114 58 Stockholm,
Sweden.
- Agrifack. s-m. ISSN 0044-6831

**Agro Tekniska Foerlaget**
Box 3175, S-103 63 Stockholm 3, Sweden.
- Traktor Journalen; maskinteknik i jord och skog.
14 per yr. ISSN 0021-7433
- Transport Teknik; maskiner och hantering. 10 per
yr. ISSN 0041-154X

**Akademifoerlaget**
(Subsidiary of: Esselte Studium AB)
Fack, S-400 10 Goeteborg, Sweden.
- Studies in the Theory of Science. irreg, no. 6,
1977. ISSN 0081-8704 (Goeteborgs Universitet)

**Akvariet Publications**
Box 22020, S-400 72 Goeteborg 22, Sweden.
- Akvariet. 10 per yr. ISSN 0002-3922

**Allers Foerlag AB**
S-251 85 Helsingborg, Sweden.
- Allers. w. ISSN 0002-578X
- Femina. w. ISSN 0014-9861

**Allmaenna Foerlaget**
see Liber Foerlag

**Allmaenna Foersvarsfoereningen**
Karlavaegen 65, 114 49 Stockholm, Sweden.
- Vaart Foersvar. 5 per yr. ISSN 0042-2800

**Kommanditbolaget Allt om Hobby AB och Co.**
Aarsta Skolgraend 8a, Box 9185, S-102 73
Stockholm 9, Sweden.
- Allt om Hobby. 8 per yr. ISSN 0002-6190

**Almqvist and Wiksell International**
26 Gamla Brogatan, S-101 20 Stockholm, Sweden.
- Abstracts of Uppsala Dissertations in Science. 20
per yr. ISSN 0001-3676
- Acta Chirurgica Scandinavica. 8 per yr. ISSN
0001-5482
- Acta Dermato-Venereologica. 6 per yr. ISSN
0001-5555
- Acta Medica Scandinavica. m.(2 vols a yr) ISSN
0001-6101
- Acta Obstetricia et Gynecologica Scandinavica. 5
per yr. ISSN 0001-6349 (Scandinavian
Association of Obstetricians and Gynaecologists)
- Acta Oto-Laryngologica. m.(2 vols. per yr.) ISSN
0001-6489
- Acta Paediatrica Scandinavica. 6 per yr. ISSN
0001-656X
- Ars Suecica. irreg, vol. 3, 1974. ISSN 0066-7919
(Uppsala Universitet. Institute of Art History)
- Arv/Journal of Scandinavian Folklore; journal of
Scandinavian folklore/tidskrift foer nordisk
folkminnesforskning. a. ISSN 0066-8176
(Kungliga Gustav Adolfs Akademien)
- Chemica Scripta; an international journal on
progress in methodology and basic knowledge. 10
per yr. ISSN 0004-2056 (Kungliga Svenska
Vetenskapsakademien)
- Demografiska Forskargruppen, Goeteborg.
Reports. irreg., 1969, no. 5. ISSN 0072-5064
- Figura. Nova Series; Uppsala studies in the history
of art. irreg., no. 17, 1976. ISSN 0071-481X
(Uppsala Universitet. Institute of Art History)
- Fornvaennen; tidskrift foer svensk antikvarisk
forskning/journal of Swedish antiquarian research.
4 per yr. ISSN 0015-7813 (Kungliga Vitterhets-,
Historie- och Antikvitets Akademien)
- Geografiska Annaler. Series A. Physical
Geography. 4 per yr. ISSN 0435-3676 (Svenska
Saellskapet Foer Antropologi och Geografi)
- Geografiska Annaler. Series B. Human
Geography. 4 per yr. ISSN 0435-3684 (Svenska
Saellskapet Foer Antropologi och Geografi)
- Goeteborgs Universitet. Statistiska Institutionen.
Skriftserie. Publications. irreg., no. 16, 1974. ISSN
0072-5110
- Grana; international journal of palynology. 3 per
yr. ISSN 0017-3134
- International Journal of Gynaecology and
Obstetrics. bi-m. ISSN 0020-7292 (International
Federation of Gynaecology and Obstetrics)
- Lychnos-Bibliotek. Studies och Kaellskrifter
Udgivna av Laerdomshistoriska Samfundet.
Studies and Sources Published by the Swedish
History of Science Society. irreg. ISSN 0076-
163X (Laerdomshistoriska Samfundet)
- Lychnos-Laerdomshistoriska Samfundets Aarsbok.
Annual of the Swedish History of Science
Society. a. ISSN 0076-1648 (Laerdomshistoriska
Samfundet)
- Nobel Symposium Series. irreg., vol. 24, no. 22.
ISSN 0078-0901
- Nordisk Tidskrift Foer Bok- och Biblioteksvaesen/
Scandinavian Journal of Libraries. 4 per yr. ISSN
0029-148X
- Nova Acta Regiae Societatis Scientiarum
Upsaliensis. irreg. ISSN 0029-5000 (Kungliga
Vetenskaps-Societeten)
- Orientalia Suecana. a. ISSN 0078-6578 (Uppsala
Universitet)
- Physica Scripta. m. ISSN 0031-8949 (Kungliga
Svenska Vetenskapsakademien)
- Scandinavian Actuarial Journal. q. (Swedish
Society of Actuaries) (Co-sponsors: Danish
Society of Actuaries; Actuarial Society of Finland;
Norwegian Society of Actuaries)
- Scandinavian Audiology. q. ISSN 0048-9271
(Nordisk Audiologisk Selskab)

- Scandinavian Institute of African Studies. Annual Seminar Proceedings. a. ISSN 0080-6706 (Nordiska Afrikainstitutet) (Dist. in U.S. by: Africana Publishing Co., 101 Fifth Ave., New York, NY 10003)
- Scandinavian Journal of Economics. q. (Stockholms Universitet. Institutionen Foer Nationalekonomi)
- Scandinavian Journal of History. 4 per yr. (Historical Association of Sweden) (Co-sponsors: Historical Association of Denmark; Historical Association of Finland; Historical Association of Norway)
- Scandinavian Journal of Infectious Diseases. q. ISSN 0036-5548
- Scandinavian Journal of Metallurgy. bi-m. (Jernkontoret)
- Scandinavian Journal of Plastic and Reconstructive Surgery. 3 per yr. ISSN 0036-5556 (Scandinavian Association of Plastic Surgeons)
- Scandinavian Journal of Psychology. q. ISSN 0036-5564
- Scandinavian Journal of Rehabilitation Medicine. q. ISSN 0036-5505
- Scandinavian Journal of Rheumatology. 4 per yr. ISSN 0300-9742 (Scandinavian Society of Rheumatologists)
- Scandinavian Journal of Social Medicine. 3 per yr. ISSN 0300-8037 (Nordisk Socialmedicinsk Foerening)
- Scandinavian Journal of Statistics; theory and applications. 4 per yr.
- Scandinavian Journal of Thoracic and Cardiovascular Surgery. 3 per yr. ISSN 0036-5580 (Scandinavian Association for Thoracic and Cardiovascular Surgery)
- Scandinavian Journal of Urology and Nephrology. 3 per yr. ISSN 0036-5599 (Scandinavian Association of Urology)
- Scandinavian Studies in Law. a. ISSN 0085-5944 (Stockholms Universitet)
- Stockholm Studies in English. irreg.
- Studia Anlistica Upsalienses. irreg. ISSN 0562-2719
- Studia Ethnographica Upsaliensia. a. ISSN 0491-2705 (Universitet i Uppsala. Institutionen Foer Allmaen och Jaemfoerande Ethnografi)
- Studia Historica Upsaliensia. irreg., vol. 63, 1975. ISSN 0081-6531 (Uppsala Universitet. Historiska Institutionen)
- Studia Musicologica Upsaliensia. Nova Series. irreg., 1973, vol. 5. ISSN 0081-6744 (Uppsala Universitet)
- Studia Neophilologica; a journal of Germanic and Romance philology. s-a. ISSN 0039-3274
- Studia Philologiae Scandinavicae Upsaliensia. irreg., vol. 11, 1977. ISSN 0081-6809 (Uppsala Universitet)
- Studia Uralica et Altaica Upsaliensia. irreg., vol. 11, 1976. ISSN 0081-7015 (Uppsala Universitet)
- Svensk Visarkiv. Handlingar. irreg. ISSN 0081-9824
- Svensk Visarkiv. Meddelanden. irreg. ISSN 0081-9832
- Svensk Visarkiv. Skrifter. irreg., 1967, no. 4. ISSN 0081-9840
- Swedish Journal of Agricultural Research. 4 per yr. ISSN 0049-2701 (Lantbrukshoegskolan)
- Swedish Nutrition Foundation. Symposia. a. ISSN 0082-0415
- Symbolae Botanicae Upsalienses. irreg., vol. 22, 1975. ISSN 0082-0644 (Botaniske Institutionerna, Uppsala)
- Uppsala Universitet. Geological Institution. Bulletin. irreg.
- Upsala Journal of Medical Sciences. 3 per yr. ISSN 0300-9734 (Uppsala Laekarefoerening)
- Zoologica Scripta; an international journal of evolutionary zoology. 4 per yr. ISSN 0300-3256 (Kungliga Svenska Vetenskapsakademien)
- Zoon, a Journal of Zoology. 2 per yr. (Uppsala Universitet. Institute of Zoology)

**Ana-Maskin Aktiebolag**
(Subsidiary of: Saab-Scania)
Box 185, 611 01 Nykoeping 1, Sweden.
- Teg och Teknik; med industri- och entreprenadnytt. s-a. ISSN 0040-2109

**Annonsoerfoereningens Service AB**
Rosenlundsgatan 13, S-116 53 Stockholm, Sweden.
- Info. q ISSN 0019-9656

**Ansgarsfoerbundet Inom Svenska Kyrkan**
Prostvaegen 15, 171 64 Solna, Sweden.
- Ansgarsledaren. bi-m. ISSN 0003-5254
- Ansgarsposten. 4 per yr. ISSN 0003-5262

**Apotekarsocieteten**
Box 1136, Stockholm, Sweden.
- Svensk Farmaceutisk Tidskrift. s-m. ISSN 0039-6524

**Arbetaren**
Sveavaegen 98, 113 50 Stockholm, Sweden.
- Arbetaren; veckotidning for frihetlig politik ekonomi och kultur. w.

**Arbetarnas Bildningsfoerbund**
Box 11044, 100 61 Stockholm 11, Sweden.
- Foenstret. 16 per yr. ISSN 0015-6167

**Aret Runt**
Box 3263, Stockholm 3, Sweden.
- Aret Runt. w.

**Argument for Frihet och Raett**
Box 40001, 103 41 Stockholm 40, Sweden.
- Argument for Frihet och Raett. q. ISSN 0004-1149

**Armestaben**
S-100 45 Stockholm 90, Sweden.
- Armenytt. 6 per yr. ISSN 0004-2404

**Artilleriklubben**
Fack, 103 60 Stockholm, Sweden.
- Artilleri-Tidskrift. 4 per yr. ISSN 0004-3788

**Asea AB**
S-721 83 Vasteras, Sweden.
- A S E A Journal. bi-m. ISSN 0001-2459

**Foerlags AB ASK**
171 78 Solna, Sweden.
- Fri Koepenskap. w. ISSN 0016-1217

**Association of Environmental Hygiene**
c/o Goeteborgs Universitet, Bio-Medicinska Biblioteket, Fack, 400 33 Goeteborg 33, Sweden.
- Scandinavian Journal of Work, Environment & Health. q. ISSN 0355-3140 (Co-sponsors: Swedish National Board of Occupational Safety and Health; Occupational Health Foundation (Finland))

**Association of Swedish Automobile Manufacturers and Wholesalers**
- Motor Traffic in Sweden. (pub. by A B Bilstatistik)

**Association of Var Naring**
Box 559, Stockholm 1, Sweden.
- Var Naring; tidskrift foer upplysning om livsmelden, kosten och haelsan. 4 per yr. ISSN 0042-2681

**Atlas Copco AB**
105 23 Stockholm, Sweden.
- Tryckluft. 3-4 per yr. ISSN 0041-3739

**A B Atomenergi**
Fack, S-611 01 Nykoeping 1, Sweden.
- A E. irreg.
- Reaktorn. q. ISSN 0034-057X
- Studsvik Technical News. q.

**Auktoriserade Fastighetsmaeklares Riksfoerbund**
Box 397, 101 25 Stockholm, Sweden.
- Fastighetsmaeklaren/Real Estate Broker. q. ISSN 0345-3278

**B P A Byggproduction AB**
Tegnergat 23, Box 45126, Stockholm 45, Sweden.
- Svenska Riksbyggen Byggteknisk Information. a. ISSN 0068-0613

**Bayer (Sverige) AB, Agro-Kemi**
Bjuroegatan 42, S-211 24 Malmoe, Sweden.
- Vaextskydds-Kuriren. irreg.

**AB Wilh. Becker**
Fack, 102 70 Stockholm, Sweden.
- Faerg och Fernissa. q. ISSN 0427-9107

**Beklaednadsarbetarnes Foerbund**
Box 1120, 111 81 Stockholm, Sweden.
- Beklaednadsfolket. every 3 wks. ISSN 0005-8262

**Bibliotekstjaenst AB**
Fack, 221 01 Lund 1, Sweden.
- Barn och Kultur/Children and Culture. 6 per yr. ISSN 0037-6477
- Biblioteket Presenterar Nya Boecker. 10 per yr. ISSN 0006-1840
- Bokrevy. q. ISSN 0005-2833

- Kommunal Litteraturtjaenst. bi-m. ISSN 0023-3056
- Skolans Artikelservice. 12 per yr. ISSN 0037-6469
- Studiekamraten. 10 per yr. ISSN 0039-3452
- Svenska Tidningsartiklar. m (cum. yrly.) ISSN 0039-6907
- Svenska Tidskriftsartiklar. m (cum. q. and yrly.) ISSN 0039-6915

**A B Bilstatistik**
Box 5514, S-114 85 Stockholm, Sweden.
- Motor Traffic in Sweden. a. ISSN 0077-1619 (Association of Swedish Automobile Manufacturers and Wholesalers)

**Blabandsrorelsens Barnversamhet**
Kortebovagen 14, 552 58 Jonkoping, Sweden.
- Blaklint. 7-8 per yr. ISSN 0006-4556

**Blue Book of Europe AB**
P.O. Box 3013, Goeteborg, Sweden
(Dist. by: International Publications Service, 114 E. 32nd St., New York, NY 10016)
- Blue Book of Europe; European Export Directory. irreg., 1970, 2nd ed. ISSN 0067-9267

**Bokcafet**
Stt. Petri Kyrkogata 7, 222 21 Lund, Sweden.
- Boc Klubben. m.

**Albert Bonniers Foerlag AB**
Box 3159, 103 63 Stockholm 3, Sweden.
- B L M. (Bonniers Litteraera Magasin) 6 per yr. ISSN 0005-3198

**Botaniske Institutionerna, Uppsala**
- Symbolae Botanicae Upsalienses. (pub. by Almqvist & Wiksell International)

**Branschtidningsfoerlaget**
Nybrokajen 7, 111 48 Stockholm, Sweden.
- Aktuellt Maaleri. m (11 per yr.)
- Gjuteriet. m. ISSN 0017-0682 (Sveriges Gjuteritekniska Foerening)

**British-Swedish Chamber of Commerce in Sweden**
Birger Jarlsgatan 6B, S-114 34 Stockholm, Sweden.
- B S C C Bulletin. m(plus irreg. supplements)

**Budo-Centrum AB**
S. Larmgatan 4, 411 16 Goeteborg, Sweden.
- Budo-Sport. 7 per yr. ISSN 0007-2982

**Foerlaget By och Bygd**
Box 102, 311 01 Falkenberg, Sweden.
- Politisk Tidskrift; centerroerelsens ide- och debatttidskrift. bi-m. ISSN 0032-3489

**Byggfoerlaget**
Maria Skolgatan 81, Box 17087, 104 62 Stockholm, Sweden.
- Byggmaestaren; journal of Swedish building. m (10 per yr) ISSN 0007-7550 (Svenska Arkitektfoereningen)
- Byggnadsindustrin. 40 per yr. ISSN 0007-7577

**AB Byggmaestarens Foerlag**
Box 1742, 111 87 Stockholm, Sweden.
- Swedish Review of Architecture. 10 per yr. ISSN 0004-2021 (Svenska Arkitektfoereningen) (Co-sponsor: Building Association of Stockholm)

**Byggnadsingenjoren- Team**
Observatoriegatan 12, 113 29 Stockholm, Sweden.
- Byggnadsingenjoren- Team; teknik, ekonomi, arkitektur, material. m. ISSN 0007-7585

**Foerlags AB Tidning Foer Byggnadskonst**
Sveavaegen 74, 113 59 Stockholm, Sweden.
- Byggnadskonst; tidskrift foer arkitektur, bostaeder, byggteknik. s-m. ISSN 0007-7593

**Byggnadsvaerlden AB**
Kungsgatan 42, Stockholm C, Sweden.
- Byggnadsvaerlden. w. ISSN 0007-7615

**C B I**
see Cement- och Betonginstitutet

**Caravan Club of Sweden**
Traengkaarsvaegen 39, 703 57 Oerebro, Sweden.
- Caravan Bladet. bi-m. ISSN 0008-6169

**J. E. Carlstedt Foerlag AB**
Maester Samuelsgatan 1, 111 44 Stockholm, Sweden.
- Longitude; a magazine of the Seven Seas. a. ISSN 0024-6328

**Cement- och Betonginstitutet**
Fack, S-100 44 Stockholm 7, Sweden.
- C B I Forskning/Research. irreg (approx. 4 per yr.)
- C B I Rapporter/Reports. m.
- C B I Rekommendationer/Recommendations. irreg (approx. 3 per yr.)

**Center for Bibliographical Studies, Uppsala**
- Text. (pub. by Dahlia Books)

**Centralfoerbundet Foer Alkohol- och Narkotikaupplysning**
Karlavaegen 117, 115 26 Stockholm, Sweden.
- Alkohol och Narkotika/Alcohol and Other Drugs. 9 per yr.

**Centralfoerbundet Folk och Foersvar**
Grev Turegatan 2, S-114 35 Stockholm, Sweden.
- Foersvar i Nutid. bi-m. ISSN 0046-4643

**Centralforbundet for Befaelsutbildning**
Box 5034, 102 41 Stockholm, Sweden.
- F B U-Befael. (Frivilliga Befaelsutbildningsroerelsen) 6 per yr. ISSN 0005-7797

**Centralorganisationen S A C O-S R**
Box 5902, 114 89 Stockholm, Sweden.
- S A C O/S R-Tidningen. 10 per yr.

**Cewe-Foerlaget**
Box 77, 2890 10 Bjaesta, Sweden.
- Friidrott. 10 per yr. ISSN 0046-5135 (Svenska Fri-Idrottsfoerbundet)
- Hockey. 10 per yr. ISSN 0345-4347 (Svenska Ishockeyfoerbundet)
- Nya Cyklisten. 9 per yr. ISSN 0048-1211 (Cykelfoerbundet)
- Svensk Skidsport. 14 per yr. ISSN 0049-2671 (Svenska Skidfoerbundet)

**Chalmers Tekniska Hoegskola**
Fack, S-402-20 Goeteborg 5, Sweden.
- Chalmers Tekniska Hoegskola. Handlingar/ Chalmers University of Technology. Transactions. irreg. ISSN 0069-2417

**Chalmers Tekniska Hoegskola. Division of Ship Hydromechanics**
S-402 20 Goeteborg 5, Sweden.
- Chalmers University of Technology. Division of Ship Hydromechanics. Report. irreg. ISSN 0009-112X

**Chalmers Tekniske Hoegskola. Institutionen Foer Vattenfoersoerjnings och Avloppsteknik**
Fack, S-402 20 Goeteborg 5, Sweden.
- Chalmers Tekniska Hogskola. Institutionen Foer Vattenfoersoerjnings och Avloppsteknik. Publikationsserie B; Current reports on research in water supply and sewage disposal. irreg. ISSN 0009-1111

**Chalmers University of Technology**
*see* Chalmers Tekniske Hoegskola

**Civilfoersvarsfoerbundets Foerlags AB**
Sturegatan 6, S-114 35 Stockholm, Sweden.
- Civilt Foersvar. m. ISSN 0009-8159 (Sveriges Civilfoersvarsfoerbund)

**Civilingenjoersfoerbundets Tidskrift**
Box 40223, Stockholm 40, Sweden.
- Civilingenjoersfoerbundets Tidskrift. 14 per yr. ISSN 0009-8132

**Cobra Foerlags**
Box 66, 162 11 Vaellingby 1, Sweden.
- Vaegnytt; vagar, trafik, maskiner. 9 per yr. ISSN 0042-2185

**Cykel-och Mopedfraemjandet**
Box 2085, 103 12 Stockholm 2, Sweden.
- Cykel-och Mopednytt. 4 per yr. ISSN 0011-4391

**Cykel- och Sporthandlarnes Riksfoerbund Serviceaktiebolag**
Box 2170, 103 14 Stockholm 2, Sweden.
- Cykel- och Sporthandlaren. m (11 per yr.) ISSN 0011-4383

**Cykelfoerbundet**
- Nya Cyklisten. (pub. by Cewe-Foerlaget)

**Dag Hammarskjoeld Foundation**
Oevre Slottsgatan 2, 752 20 Uppsala, Sweden.
- Development Dialogue. irreg., 2 per year.

**Dahlia Books**
P.O. Box 23037, S-750 23 Uppsala 23, Sweden.
- Text; svensk tidskrift foer bibliografi. q. ISSN 0345-0112 (Center for Bibliographical Studies, Uppsala)

**Dance Museum**
Box 27109, Stockholm, Sweden.
- Dans; tidskrift foer dansvetenskap. q.

**Demografiska Forskargruppen**
- Demografiska Forskargruppen, Goeteborg. Reports. (pub. by Almqvist & Wiksell International)

**Development Dialogue**
Dag Hammarskjold Centre, Oevre Slottsgatan 2, 752 20 Uppsala, Sweden.
- Development Dialogue. s-a.

**Dordius AB**
Djurgaardsslaetten 92, S-115 21 Stockholm, Sweden.
- Militaer Teknisk Tidskrift. q. ISSN 0047-7354 (Militaertekniska Foereningen)

**E F S**
Tegnergaton 34, 113 59 Stockholm, Sweden.
- E F S Paa Vaeg; tidskrift foer ungdoms ledare. 5 per yr.
- E F S Start; tidskrift foer barn ledare. 5 per yr.

**M. Edenlund, Ed. & Pub.**
Box 4050, Goeteborg 4, Sweden.
- Dessa Mina Minsta; kamporgan foer etisk kristendom och individens maenniskovaerde. q. ISSN 0011-9490

**Eesti Keele Ja Kirjanduse Instituut**
Stockholm, Sweden.
- Eesti Keele Ja Kirjanduse Instituut. Aastaraamat/ Institute of Estonian Language and Literature. Year Book. a.

**El Branschen**
Kungsbroplan 1, 112 27 Stockholm, Sweden.
- El Branschen. m. ISSN 0013-4007

**Elanders Boktryckeri AB**
Box 238, 434 01 Kungsbacha, Sweden.
- Etnologiska Studier. a. (Goeteborgs Museer. Etnografiska Museet)
- Nordisk Psykiatrisk Tidsskrift. 8 per yr. ISSN 0029-1455 (Nordiske Psykiatriske Foreninger)

**Elektriska Installatoersorganisationen**
Box 1723, S-111 87 Stockholm, Sweden.
- Elinstallatoeren. m. ISSN 0013-6190

**Engstroem och Nilson Maskin AB**
Fack, S-172 20 Sundbyberg, Sweden.
- Schakt-Bladet; tidning om entreprenad-och transportmaskiner. q. ISSN 0036-5904

**Eranos Foerlag**
c/o Universitetsbiblioteket, Box 510, 751 20 Uppsala 1, Sweden
(Dist. by: Almqvist & Wiksell International, 26 Gamla Brogatan, Box 62, S-101 20 Stockholm, Sweden)
- Eranos; Acta philologica suecana. 4 per yr. ISSN 0013-9947

**Ericstambolagen**
Essingeringen 24 B, 112 64 Stockholm, Sweden.
- Aktuellt Foer Kontor. m (10 per yr.)

**ESAB**
Fack, 402 70 Goeteborg, Sweden.
- Svetsaren; a welding review. 3 per yr. ISSN 0039-7083

**Esselte Kartfoerlagen**
Box 22069, S-104 22 Stockholm, Sweden.
- Globen. 4 per yr. ISSN 0017-1220

**Esselte Studium AB**
Scheelegatan 24, S-112 85 Stockholm, Sweden.
- Lund Studies in International History. irreg., vol. 5, 1974. ISSN 0076-1494
- Ordets Makt. q.

- Spraakvaard. q. ISSN 0038-8440 (Svenska Spraaknaemnden)

**Estlandssvenskarna i Sverige**
Eknaesvaegen 2, S-112 64 Stockholm, Sweden.
- Kustbon. q.

**Estonian Information Centre**
Box 450, 104 30 Stockholm, Sweden.
- Newsletter from behind the Iron Curtain. ISSN 0028-9442
- Problems of the Baltic. irreg., 1973, no. 3. ISSN 0552-2005

**Etnografiska Museet**
S-115 27 Stockholm, Sweden.
- Ethnographical Museum of Sweden. Monograph Series. irreg., 1968, no. 14. ISSN 0081-5632
- Ethnos. 4 per yr. ISSN 0014-1844

**Eureka**
c/o Allan Burgis, Ed., Tellusborgsv. 45B, 3TR, 126 33 Hagersten, Sweden.
- Eureka. q.

**European Abstracts Service**
Box 12035, S-402 41 Goeteborg 12, Sweden.
- Laser and Unconventional Optics Journal. bi-m. ISSN 0458-7871

**European Grassland Federation**
c/o E. Aberg, Pres., Institute of Plant Husbandry, Royal Agricultural College, 750 07 Uppsala 7, Sweden.
- European Grassland Federation. Proceedings of the General Meeting. irreg., 5th, Uppsala, 1973. ISSN 0071-2825

**Evangeliipress**
Box 329, 70105 Oerebro, Sweden.
- Hemmets Vaen; kristlig veckotidning. w. ISSN 0018-0335

**F F A**
*see* Flygtekniska Foersoeksanstalten

**Fackliga Vaerldsrorelsen**
Box 9144, S-102 72 Stockholm, Sweden.
- Fackliga Vaerldsrorelsen. m. ISSN 0014-6471

**Fahlbeckska Stiftelsen**
Fack, S-220 05 Lund 5, Sweden.
- Statsvetenskaplig Tidskrift. 4 per yr. ISSN 0039-0747

**Foerlags AB Thorsten Fahlskog**
Box 25, 162 11 Vaellingby 1, Sweden.
- Nord-Emballage. m. ISSN 0039-6494

**Farmaceutiska Fakultetsfoereningen**
Box 8036, S-750 08 Uppsala, Sweden.
- Farmis - Reptilen. 8 per yr. ISSN 0014-8520

**Flygfoerlaget AB**
Fack, S-161 10 Bromma, Sweden.
- Flyghorisont. 9 per yr. ISSN 0015-475X (Svenska Allmaenflygfoereningen)

**Flygtekniska Foersoeksanstalten**
S-161 11 Bromma 11, Sweden
- Flygtekniska Foersoeksanstalten. Meddelande/ Report. irreg. ISSN 0081-5640 (Dist. by Almqvist & Wiksell International, 26 Gamla Brogatan, S-101 20 Stockholm, Sweden)

**Focus Foerlag**
Foerraadsgatan 22, 171 32 Solna, Sweden.
- Aakerifoeretagaren-Transportoeren. m. ISSN 0001-298X

**Foerbundet Svenska Finlandsfrivilliga**
Box 40042, S-103 42 Stockholm, Sweden.
- Foerbundet Svenska Finlandsfrivilliga. Tidning. q. ISSN 0015-5225

**Foereningen Flottans Maen**
Teatergatan 3, 111 48 Stockholm, Sweden.
- Flottans Maen. q. ISSN 0015-4431

**Foereningen Foer Arbetarskydd**
Kungsholms Hamnplan 3, S-112 20 Stockholm, Sweden.
- Arbetsmiljoe. m.(except July & Aug.) ISSN 0003-7834

**Foereningen Foer Inre Vattenvaegar**
c/o Olle Renck, Ed., Pyrolavaegen 38, 181 60
Lidingoe, Sweden.
- F I V Meddalanden. irreg., approx. (2-5 per yr.)
  ISSN 0015-5268

**Foereningen Foer Samhaellsplanering**
Bagaregatan 10, 216 18 Malmoe, Sweden.
- Plan; the Swedish town and country planning
  review. bi-m. ISSN 0032-0560

**Foereningen Foer Svensk Kulturhistoria**
Nordiska Museet, S-115 21 Stockholm, Sweden.
- Rig. q. ISSN 0035-5267 (Co-sponsor: Nordiska
  Museet och Folkslivarkivet i Lund)

**Foereningen Foer Vaestgoetalitteratur**
Malma, 460 40 Nossebro, Sweden.
- Vaestgoetalitteratur. s-a. ISSN 0042-2150

**Foereningen Foer Vattenhygien**
Nyckelkroken 22, S-222 47 Lund, Sweden.
- Vatten/Water; tidskrift foer vattenvaard/periodical
  on water conservation. q. ISSN 0042-2886

**Foereningen Heimdal**
Box 2043, S-750 02 Uppsala, Sweden.
- Tidskriften Heimdal. 8 per yr. ISSN 0040-6988

**Foereningen Kurskamraterna**
Box 696, S-101 29 Stockholm 1, Sweden.
- Postmaennens Tidning. 7 per yr. ISSN 0032-5503

**Foereningen NEFA-Norden**
Box 10 106, S-100 55 Stockholm, Sweden.
- Nord Nytt. m. ISSN 0008-1345

**Foereningen Norden**
Box 1130, 111 81 Stockholm, Sweden.
- Nordisk Tidskrift for Vetenskap, Konst och
  Industri. q. ISSN 0029-1501 (Letterstedtska
  Foereningen)

**Foereningen Opuscula Medica**
Soedersjukhuset, 100 64 Stockholm 38, Sweden.
- Opuscula Medica. 6 per yr. ISSN 0030-414X

**Foereningen Svensk Fjaederfaeskoetsel**
Gamla Brogatan 29, 111 20 Stockholm, Sweden.
- Fjaederfae. m. ISSN 0015-3338

**Foereningen Svensk Form**
Box 7047, S-103 82 Stockholm 7, Sweden.
- Form. 8 per yr. ISSN 0015-766X

**Foereningen Svenska Tonsattares Internationella
Musikbyra**
Tegnerlunden 3, Box 1539, 111 85 Stockholm,
Sweden.
- Ord och Ton. s-a.

**Foereningen Svenska Verktygsmaskintillverkare**
Box 5506, S-114 85 Stockholm, Sweden.
- Swedish Machine Tools/Machines Outils
  Suedoises/Machines Utiles Suedoises. irreg., vol.
  6, 1973.

**Foereningen Sveriges Flotta**
Birger Jarlsgatan 18, 114 34 Stockholm, Sweden.
- Sveriges Flotta. m. ISSN 0039-6966

**Foereningen Sveriges Saendareamafoerer**
Oestmarksgatan 43, S-123 42 Farsta, Sweden.
- Q T C. 11 per yr. ISSN 0033-4820

**Foereningen Unga Filosoter**
Box 5220, S-102 45 Stockholm, Sweden.
- Kommentar. m. ISSN 0023-3013

**Tidskriftaktiebolaget Foeretagsekonomi**
Linnegatan 36A, 413 04 Goeteborg, Sweden.
- Foeretagsekonomi Bok Foeraren-Revisorn. m.
  ISSN 0015-7619

**Foersikringsbranschens Serviceaktiebolag**
Strandvaegen 5 B, 111 51 Stockholm, Sweden.
- Foersikringstidningen. 10 per yr. ISSN 0015-7880

**Foersvarets Civila Tjaenstemannafoerbund**
Box 5328, 102 46 Stockholm, Sweden.
- Foersvarstjaenstemannen. 10 per yr. ISSN 0015-
  5306

**Foersvarets Forskningsanstalt**
S-104 50 Stockholm 80, Sweden.
- Froe Foersvarsforskningsreferat; oeppen del. q.
  ISSN 0016-1543

**Folkbildningsfoerbundet**
Drottninggatan 77, 111 60 Stockholm, Sweden.
- Folkbildningsarbetet. 10 per yr. ISSN 0046-4341

**Folkparkernas Centralorganisation**
Svedenborgsgatan 1, S-116 48 Stockholm, Sweden.
- Scen och Salong. m. ISSN 0036-5718

**Folkpartiet Riksorganisation**
Box 6508, 113 83 Stockholm, Sweden.
- Utsikt. m. ISSN 0346-3788

**Folkpartiets Ungdomsfoerbund**
Box 6508, 113 83 Stockholm, Sweden.
- Liberal Ungdom. bi-m. ISSN 0024-1857

**Fornminnesfoereningen i Goeteborg**
- Studier i Nordisk Arkeologi/Studies in North
  European Archaeology. (pub. by Wettergren)

**Forskningsbiblioteksraadet**
Odengatan 59, Box 6404, S-113 82 Stockholm,
Sweden.
- F B R Aktuellt. 2 per yr. ISSN 0345-3286

**Forskningsraadens Naemnd Foer
Forskningsinformation**
Box 45 143, Drottninggatan 102/IV, S-104 30
Stockholm, Sweden.
- Forskning och Framsteg. 8 per yr. ISSN 0015-
  7937

**Fredrika-Bremer Foerbundet**
Biblioteksgatan 12, S-111 46 Stockholm, Sweden.
- Hertha. bi-m. ISSN 0018-0912

**Frihetlig Socialistisk Tidskrift**
Kammakargatan 35, 111 60 Stockholm, Sweden.
- Frihetlig Socialistisk Tidskrift. bi-m. ISSN 0345-
  3685

**Fritidsfiskarna**
Fack, 104 40 Stockholm 14, Sweden.
- Fiske. a.
- Svenskt Fiske. m. ISSN 0039-694X (Sveriges
  Fritidsfiskares Riksfoerbund)

**General Church of the New Jerusalem**
- Nova Ecclesia. (pub. by Bokfoerlaget Nova
  Ecclesia)

**Generalstabens Lithografiske Anstalt**
Box 22069, S-104 22 Stockholm, Sweden.
- Folkl-Liv; Acta Ethnologica et Folkloristica
  Europea. a. (Kungliga Gustav Adolfs Akademien)
- Ymer. a. ISSN 0044-0477 (Svenska Saellskapet
  Foer Antropologi och Geografi)

**Geografilararnas Riksfoerening**
c/o Knut Norborg, Ed., Department of Geography,
223 62 Lund, Sweden.
- Geografiska Notiser. 4 per yr. ISSN 0016-724X

**Geological Survey of Sweden**
see Sweden. Sveriges Geologiska Undersoekning

**Geologiska Foereningen i Stockholm**
104 05 Stockholm, Sweden.
- Geologiska Foereningens i Stockholm
  Foerhandlingar (G F F) q. ISSN 0016-786X

**Gillelije Sten och Grus**
Havnen, 3250, Gilleleje, Sweden.
- Moving; kundtidning med aktuelle information. q.

**Glasforskningsinstitutet**
Box 3093, S-350 03 Vaxjo 3, Sweden.
- Glassteknisk Tidskrift. q. ISSN 0017-1093

**Goetabanken**
Ostra Hamngatan 16, S-405 09 Goeteborg, Sweden.
- Geotabanken. Economic Survey. 10 per yr. ISSN
  0013-0370 (prep. by its Economic Intelligence
  Department)

**Goeteborg. Stadskontor**
Utredningsavdelningen, Fack 1510, 401 10
Goeteborg 1, Sweden.
- Geoteborg. Stadskontor. Statistiska Meddelanden.
  q. ISSN 0039-7237

**Goeteborgs Kungliga Segelsaellskap**
Box 7115, S-402 32 Goeteborg 7, Sweden.
- Seglarbladet. r1. ISSN 0037-0916

**Goeteborgs Kungliga Vetenskaps- och Vitterhets-
Samhaelle**
Goeteborgs Universitetsbibliotek, P.O. Box 5096, S-
402 22 Goeteborg 5, Sweden
(Dist. in U.S., Canada and Mexico by: Humanities
Press, Inc., 171 First Ave., Atlantic Highlands, NJ
07716)
- Acta Regiae Societatis Scientiarum et Litterarum
  Gothoburgensis. Geophysica. irreg., 1969, no. 2.
  ISSN 0072-4815
- Acta Regiae Societatis Scientiarum et Litterarum
  Gothoburgensis. Humaniora. irreg., no. 11, 1976.
  ISSN 0072-4823
- Acta Regiae Societatis Scientiarum et Litterarum
  Gothoburgensis. Zoologica. irreg., no. 11, 1977.
  ISSN 0072-4807

**Goeteborgs Museer. Etnografiska Museet**
- Etnologiska Studier. (pub. by Elanders Boktryckeri
  AB)

**Goeteborgs Tandlaekare Saellskap**
Erik Dahlbergsgatan 9, 411 26 Goeteborg, Sweden.
- Goeteborgs Tandlaekare-Saellskap. Aarsbok. a.
  ISSN 0072-4831

**Goeteborgs Universitet**
Box 5096, S-402 22 Goeteborg 5, Sweden.
- Goeteborg Studies in Politics. irreg.
- Studia Historica Gothoburgensia. irreg., 1971, no.
  13. ISSN 0081-6515
- Studies in the Theory of Science. (pub. by
  Akademifoerlaget)

**Goeteborgs Universitet. Bibliotek**
P.O. Box 5096, S-402 22 Goeteborg 5, Sweden
- Acta Bibliothecae Universitatis Gothoburgensis.
  irreg., no. 18, 1976. ISSN 0065-1079 (Dist. in
  U.S., Canada and Mexico by: Humanities Press,
  Inc., 171 First Ave., Atlantic Highlands, NJ
  07716)
- Goeteborgs Universitets. Bibliotek. Aarsberattelse.
  a.
- Goeteborgs Universitets. Bibliotek.
  Kvinnohistoriskt Arkiv. Foerteckning Oever
  Nyutkommen Litteratur. q.

**Goeteborgs Universitet. Demographic Research
Institute**
Viktoriagatan 13, S-411 25 Goeteborg, Sweden
(Dist. by: Almqvist & Wiksell International, 26
Gamla Brogatan, S-111 20 Stockholm, Sweden)
- Goeteborgs Universitet. Demographic Research
  Institute. Reports. irreg.

**Goeteborgs Universitet. Department of Psychology**
Fack, S-400 20 Goeteborg 14, Sweden.
- Acta Psychologica-Gothoburgensia. irreg. ISSN
  0065-1605
- Goeteborgs Psychological Reports. 20 per yr. ISSN
  0301-0996

**Goeteborgs Universitet. Ekonomisk-Historiska
Institutionen**
Stora Nygatan 23-25, S-411 08 Goeteborg, Sweden.
- Goeteborgs Universitet. Economisk-Historiska
  Institutionen. Meddelanden. irreg., 1973, no. 26.
  ISSN 0072-5080

**Goeteborgs Universitet. Sociologiska Institutionen**
Karl Johansgatan 27, S-414 59 Goeteborg, Sweden.
- Goeteborgs Universitet. Sociologiska Institutionen.
  Forsknings-Rapport. irreg. ISSN 0072-5099
- Goeteborgs Universitet. Sociologiska Institutionen.
  Monografier. irreg., 1970, no. 3. ISSN 0072-5102

**Goeteborgs Universitet. Statistiska Institutionen**
- Goeteborgs Universitet. Statistiska Institutionen.
  Skriftserie. Publications. (pub. by Almqvist &
  Wiksell International)

**Gothenburg Chamber of Commerce**
Storgatan 26, S-411 38 Goeteborg, Sweden.
- Trade Directory of Western Sweden. a.

**Gothenburg Retail Association**
P.O. Box 53 200, 400 15 Goeteborg 53, Sweden.
- Goeteborgs-Koepmannen. m. ISSN 0046-6050

**Gotlands Historical Museum**
Box 83, S-62101 Visby, Sweden.
- Acta Visbyensia; Visby-symposiet foer historiska
  vetenskaper. biennial, 1971, no. 4.

**Graenges AB**
P.O. Box, S-103 26 Stockholm 16, Sweden.
- Graengeskontakten. q. (prep. by its Information
  Department)

**Grafiska Arbetsgivare-och Industriorganisationerna**
Blasieholmsgatan 4 A, Box 16383, 103 27
Stockholm, Sweden.
- Grafiskt Forum. m. ISSN 0017-3002

**Grafiska Fackfoerbundet**
Box 1101, S-111 81 Stockholm, Sweden.
- Grafia. s-m.(m.June-Aug) ISSN 0017-288X

**Grafiska Faktors- och Tjaenstemannafoerbundet**
Box 12069, 102 22 Stockholm 12, Sweden.
- Grafisk Faktorstidning. m. ISSN 0017-2979

**Gummessons Bokfoerlag**
Box 6302, 113 81 Stockholm, Sweden.
- Nordisk Ekumenisk Aarsbok. a. ISSN 0085-4212
  (Nordiska Ekumeniska Institutet)

**H S B Riksfoerbund**
- Att Bo. (pub. by Hyresgaesternas Foerlags AB)

**Haaken Ohlssons Foerlag**
S-T Annegatan 4, 221 04 Lund, Sweden.
- Kyrkofoerfattningar. 10 per yr. ISSN 0023-6136
- Socialfoerfattningar. 20 per yr. ISSN 0037-8100

**Foerlags AB Habit**
Humlegaardsgatan 19, 114 46 Stockholm, Sweden.
- Habit; herr- och dammodebranschen. 14 per yr.
  ISSN 0017-6362

**Handelsanstaelldas Foerbund**
Fack, 200 70 Malmoe, Sweden.
- Handelsnytt. m. ISSN 0017-7326

**Handelshoegskolan i Stockholm. Bibliotek**
Dokumentationstjaensten, Box 6501, S-113 83
Stockholm, Sweden.
- Ekonomisk Dokumentation. Ser. A. Ny Litteratur
  i Urval. m.
- Ekonomisk Dokumentation. Ser. FS.
  Foeretagsekonomi-Samhaellskonomi. m.
- Ekonomisk Dokumentation. Ser. T.
  Transportekonomi. m.

**Handelshoegskolan i Stockholm. Ekonomiska
Forskningsinstitutet**
Box 6501, 113 83 Stockholm, Sweden.
- E F I Nytt. irreg.

**Handikappinstitutet**
Fack, S-161 25 Bromma 1, Sweden.
- Information Om Rehabilitering. 8 per yr. ISSN
  0020-0174

**Lennart Hansson**
Munkbron 7, Stockholm, Sweden.
- Svensk Tidskrift for Industriellt Rattsskydd. s-m.
  ISSN 0039-6788

**Helgelsefoerbundet**
Box 67, 692 01 Kumla, Sweden.
- Trons Segrar. w. ISSN 0041-3178

**Hemmets Journal AB**
Fack, S-200 22 Malmoe 3, Sweden.
- Hemmets Journal. w. ISSN 0018-0327

**Hemvaernets Stiftelse**
Box 5345, 102 46 Stockholm, Sweden.
- Hemvaernet. 6 per yr. ISSN 0018-0351

**Hermods Foundation**
Fack, 205 10 Malmoe, Sweden.
- Korrespondens /Utbildningskontakt. irreg (from
  no. 3, 1975) ISSN 0023-4125

**Historical Association of Sweden**
- Scandinavian Journal of History. (pub. by
  Almqvist & Wiksell International)

**Horselframjandets Riksforbund**
Skoeldungagatan 7, Box 5615, 114 86 Stockholm,
Sweden.
- Auris. 8 per yr. ISSN 0045-0030

**Hushaallslaerarnas Riksfoerening**
Stureplan 6, 114 35 Stockholm, Sweden.
- Hushaallslaeraren. m. ISSN 0018-7992

**Husmodersfoerbundet Hem och Samhaelle**
Drottninggatan 77, 111 60 Stockholm, Sweden.
- Hem och Samhaelle; husmodersfoerbundets
  tidskrift. 5 per yr. ISSN 0018-0254

**Hyresgaesternas Foerlags AB**
Fleminggatan 41, S-112 32 Stockholm, Sweden.
- Att Bo; HSB's tidskrift foer bostadspolitik och
  samhaellsdebatt. 6 per yr. ISSN 0004-7244 (H S
  B Riksfoerbund)
- Hyresgaesten. bi-m. ISSN 0018-8360
  (Hyresgaesternas Riksfoerbund)
- Vaar Bostad/Our Dwelling. m. ISSN 0042-2002

**Hyresgaesternas Riksfoerbund**
Norrlandsgatan 7, S-111 43 Stockholm, Sweden.
- Hyresgaesten. (pub. by Hyresgaesternas Foerlags
  AB)
- Miljoespegeln. q. ISSN 0026-4164

**I C A-Foerlaget AB**
Storagatan 41, 721 85 Vaesteraas, Sweden.
- Hem och Fritid. m. ISSN 0018-0246
- Supermarket. m. ISSN 0039-5781

**Industrifackpress AB**
Box 12006, 250 12 Helsingborg, Sweden.
- Plastforum Scandinavia; journal for the Swedish
  plastics and rubber industry. 10 per yr.

**Foerlags AB Information**
Parkgatan 42, S-224 00 Hoerby, Sweden.
- Information-Ekonomi och Miljoe, Vetenskap och
  Humanism. q.
- International Management Information Business
  Digest. q. ISSN 0020-7896

**Ingenioersvetenskapsakademien**
Box 5073, S-102 42 Stockholm 5, Sweden
- Directory of International Congresses and
  Symposia in 1976-1980. 3 per yr. (Dist. by:
  Almqvist & Wiksell International, 26 Gamla
  Brogatan, Box 62, S-101 20 Stockholm, Sweden)
- I V A. 8 per yr. ISSN 0039-8535

**Ingenjoersfoerbundet T L I**
Fack, S-103 10 Stockholm, Sweden.
- T L I-Ingenjoeren. m.

**Ingenjoersfoerlaget AB**
Box 5703, 114 87 Stockholm, Sweden.
- Cellulosa. q.
- Elteknik Med Aktuell Elektronik; Swedish journal
  for electrical power, teletechnics and electronics.
  16 per yr.
- Kemisk Tidskrift. m. ISSN 0039-6605 (Svenska
  Kemistsamfundet) (Co-sponsors: Svenska
  Kemiingenjoerers Riksfoering; Sveriges Kemiska
  Industrikontor)
- Medicinsk Teknik; Scandinavian journal for
  medical technique. 4 per yr.
- Ny Teknik. m. ISSN 0550-8754
- Sweden Now. bi-m. (Svenska
  Arbetsgivarefoereningen) (Co-sponsor: Federation
  of Swedish Industries) (U.S. Subscr. to: Box 2919,
  Grand Central Sta., N.Y. 10017)
- Teknisk Tidskrift. 20 per yr. ISSN 0040-2346
  (Sveriges Civilingenjoersfoerbund) (Co-Sponsor:
  Swedish Association of Engineers & Architects)

**Institute for Water and Air Pollution Research**
*see* **Sweden. Institutet Foer Vatten- och
Luftvaardsforskning**

**Institute of Estonian Language and Literature**
*see* **Eesti Keele ja Kirjanduse Instituut**

**Institute of Freshwater Research**
S-170 11 Drottningholm, Sweden.
- Institute of Freshwater Research, Drottningholm.
  Report. irreg., no. 54, 1975. ISSN 0082-0032

**Institutet Foer Byggdokumentation**
Haelsingegatan 49, S-113 31 Stockholm, Sweden.
- Byggreferat. 10 per yr. ISSN 0345-1941

**Institutet Foer Lederskap och Loensamhet**
Box 1151, 111 81 Stockholm, Sweden.
- Ledarskap och Loensamhet/Management for
  Profitability; ideskrift om ekonomisk
  foeretagsstyrning. 8 per yr. ISSN 0024-0168

**Institutet Foer Vatten- och Luftvaardsfoskning**
*see* **Sweden. Institutet Foer Vatten- och
Luftvaardsforskning**

**Institututet Foer Metallforskning**
Drottning Kristinas Vag 48, S-114 28 Stockholm,
Sweden.
- Institutet Foer Metallforskning.
  Forskningsverksamheten. a. ISSN 0015-7953

**Interflora Sweden**
Per Ekstroems Vaeg 1, 161 55 Bromma, Sweden.
- Blomster-Branschen. m. ISSN 0006-4963

**International Association for Accident and Traffic
Medicine**
Box 10043, S-100 55 Stockholm 10, Sweden.
- Journal of Traffic Medicine; I A A T M
  newsletter. q. ISSN 0345-5564

**International Association of Art Critics**
c/o Sven Sandstroem, Ed., Institute of the History
of Art, P.B. 1135, S-221 04 Lund, Sweden.
- A I C A R C Bulletin. s-a.

**International Association of Logopedics and
Phoniatrics**
c/o Dr. B. Fritzell, S-146 00 Tullinge, 416 78
Gothenberg, Sweden.
- Folia Phoniatrica. (pub. by S. Karger AG SZ)
- International Association of Logopedics and
  Phoniatrics. Reports of Congress. triennial; 1974,
  16th, Interlaken. ISSN 0074-1655

**International Federation of Gynaecology and
Obstetrics**
- International Journal of Gynaecology and
  Obstetrics. (pub. by Almqvist & Wiksell
  International)

**International Mathematical Union**
c/o Otto Frostman, Baltzar von Platens Gatan 1,
112 42 Stockholm, Sweden.
- World Directory of Mathematicians. irreg., 5th
  ed., 1974. ISSN 0512-2740 (Co-sponsor: National
  Committees of Mathematics)

**International Meteorological Institute in Stockholm**
S-104 05 Stockholm, Sweden.
- International Meteorological Institute in
  Stockholm. Annual Report. a.

**Internationella Kvinnofoerbundet foer Fred och
Frihet. Svenska Sektionen**
*see* **Women's International League for Peace and
Freedom. Swedish Section**

**IOGT-NTO**
Bolidenvaegen 14, 121 63 Johanneshov, Sweden.
- Accent. fortn.

**B. O. Jahnsson, Ed. & Pub.**
Jakobsbergsplatsen 1, 724 61 Vaesteraas, Sweden.
- Jaktmaker och Fiskevatten. m. ISSN 0021-406X

**Jannersten Foerlag AB**
Box 66, S-122 21 Enskede, Sweden.
- Bridge Tidningen. 10 per yr. ISSN 0006-9906

**Acke Janson, Ed. & Pub.**
Postgatan 5-7, S-411 13 Goeteborg, Sweden.
- Paletten. q. ISSN 0031-0352
- Reflexer. q.

**Jernkontoret**
Box 1721, S-111 87 Stockholm, Sweden.
- Jernkontorets Annaler; tidskrift for nordisk
  bergshantering. q. ISSN 0021-5902
- Scandinavian Journal of Metallurgy. (pub. by
  Almqvist & Wiksell International)
- Swedish Steel Manual. irreg.

**Jiells Bokfoerlag**
Box 137, 701 03 Oerebro, Sweden.
- Lediga Platser. w. ISSN 0024-0230

**Journal of Contemporary Asia**
Box 49010, Stockholm 49, Sweden.
- Journal of Contemporary Asia. q. ISSN 0047-
  2336

**Jurist- och Samhaellsvetare Foerbundet**
Box 5167, S-102 44 Stockholm, Sweden.
- J U S. (Juristnytt-Samhaellsvetaren) m. ISSN
  0022-6947

**K-Konsult**
117 80 Stockholm, Sweden.
- K-Kontur. s-a. ISSN 0022-7331 (prep. by its
  Information Department)
- Va-Nytt; literaturoeversikt om miljoevaard. 10 per
  yr. ISSN 0042-1995

**Bernard Kangro, Ed. & Pub.**
Skoerdevaegen 1, 222 38 Lund, Sweden.
- Tulimuld; eesti kirjanduse ja kultuuri ajakiri. q.
  ISSN 0041-4034

**Karolinska Institutet**
104 01 Stockholm, Sweden.
- Acta Physiologica Scandinavica. m. ISSN 0001-6772 (Scandinavian Physiological Society)
- List Bio-Med; Biomedical Serials in Scandinavian Libraries. irreg., 4th edt. in prep. ISSN 0075-9813 (prep. by its Bibliotek)

**KFUK-KFUM's Riksfoerbund**
Box 1722, 111 87 Stockholm, Sweden.
- Ung Vaerld. 9 per yr. ISSN 0346-363X

**Kiruna Geophysical Institute**
981 01 Kiruna 1, Sweden.
- Kiruna Geophysical Data. q.
- Kiruna Geophysical Institute. Report. irreg.

**Kockums AB**
201 10 Malmoe, Sweden.
- Kockums Info. 6-8 per yr.

**Koepmannens Foerlags AB**
Kungsgatan 19, 105 61 Stockholm, Sweden.
- Koepmannen. w. ISSN 0023-2688 (Sveriges Koepmannafoerbund)

**Koettbranschens Riksfoerbund**
Slakthusplan 5, 121 62 Johanneshov, Sweden.
- Koettbranschen. m. ISSN 0047-3510

**Kommunalarbetarefoerbundet**
Postbox 19039, 104 32 Stockholm, Sweden.
- Kommunalarbetaren. fortn.

**Kommunistiska Foerbundet**
Kvrkkullen Vaksala, c/o Frycklund, 755 90 Uppsala, Sweden.
- Marxistiskt Forum. bi-m. ISSN 0047-6072

**Kompass Sweden**
Malmvaegen 80, S-191 04 Sollentuna, Sweden
- Kompass Sverige; handbok oever Sveriges industri og Naeringsliv. a. ISSN 0075-6725 (Foundation for Promoting International Economic Information SZ) (Dist. by: Iliffe NTP Inc., 300 E. 42 St., New York, NY 10017)

**Konsthistoriska Saellskapet**
Institutionen Foer Konstvetenskap, Department of the History of Art, University of Stockholm, Fack, 104 05 Stockholm 5, Sweden.
- Konsthistorisk Tidskrift; revy for konst och konstforskning. q. ISSN 0023-3609

**Kontrollraadet foer Betongvaror**
S: T Eriksgatan 58, 112 34 Stockholm, Sweden.
- Kontrollraadet foer Betongvaror, Stockholm. Meddelande. a. ISSN 0075-6776

**Kooperativa Foerbundet**
Fack, S-104 65 Stockholm, Sweden.
- Kooperativa Foerbundet. International Department. Newsletter. q.
- Kooperatoeren. m. ISSN 0023-3846

**Kooperativa Ledares Foerbund**
Fack, 104 65 Stockholm 15, Sweden.
- Ledarforum. 8 per yr. ISSN 0024-015X

**Kristen Demokratisk Samling**
Box 451, S-101 26 Stockholm, Sweden.
- Samhaellsgemenskap. 15 per yr. ISSN 0036-3782

**Kristliga Esperantofoerbund**
Eyragatan 16, S-702 27 Oerebro, Sweden.
- Kristliga Esperantofoerbundets Medlemsblad. q. ISSN 0023-4796

**Kristna Samfundens Nykterhetsroerelse**
Vaestmannagatan 15, 111 24 Stockholm, Sweden.
- Folkets-Vael/DKSN-RIA Informerar. q.

**Kulturhistoriska Foereningen Foer Soedra Sverige**
Lund, Sweden.
- Kulturen. a.

**Kungliga Armemuseum**
Riddargatan 13, Stockholm 7, Sweden.
- Kungliga Armemuseum. Meddelande. a.

**Kungliga Automobil Klubben**
Wahrendorfsgatan 1, Fack, S-103 20 Stockholm 16, Sweden.
- S M T. (Svensk Motor Tidning) 9 per yr. ISSN 0039-6664

**Kungliga Gustav Adolfs Akademien**
Klostergatan 2, Uppsala, Sweden.
- Acta Academiae Regiae Gustavi Adolphi. irreg., no. 55, 1977. ISSN 0065-0897
- Arv/Journal of Scandinavian Folklore. (pub. by Almqvist & Wiksell International)
- Folkl-Liv. (pub. by Generalstabens Lithografiske Anstalt)
- Folklivsskildringar och Bygdesstudier. irreg., no. 9, 1973. ISSN 0071-6766
- Namn och Bygd. (pub. by Lundequistka Bokhandeln)

**Kungliga Krigsvetenskapsakademien**
100 45 Stockholm, Sweden.
- Kungliga Krigsvetenskapsakademien. Handlingar och Tidskrift. bi-m. ISSN 0023-5369

**Kungliga Oerlogsmannasaellskapet**
Karlskrona, Sweden.
- Tidskrift i Sjovasendet. 6 per yr. ISSN 0040-6945

**Kungliga Skogs- och Lantbruksakademien**
Box 6806, S-113 86 Stockholm, Sweden.
- Acta Agriculturae Scandinavica. 4 per yr. ISSN 0001-5121
- Kungliga Skogs- och Lantbruksakademien. Tidskrift. 6 per yr. ISSN 0023-5350

**Kungliga Skogshoegskolan. Institutionen Foer Virkeslaera**
Fack, S-104 05 Stockholm, Sweden.
- Kungliga Skogshoegskolan. Institutionen Foer Virkeslaera. Rapporter. irreg., no. 97, 1976. ISSN 0082-0040
- Kungliga Skogshoegskolan. Institutionen Foer Virkeslaera. Uppsatser. irreg., no. 42, 1973. ISSN 0082-0059
- Studia Forestalia Suecica. (pub. by Liber Foerlag)

**Kungliga Svenska Aeroklubben**
Box 1212, Skeppsbron 40, S-111 82 Stockholm, Sweden.
- Flygrevyn. 9 per yr. ISSN 0015-4784

**Kungliga Svenska Vetenskapsakademien**
- Ambio. (pub. by Universitetsforlaget NO)
- Ambio. Special Reports. (pub. by Universitetsforlaget NO)
- Chemica Scripta. (pub. by Almqvist & Wiksell International)
- Physica Scripta. (pub. by Almqvist & Wiksell International)
- Zoologica Scripta. (pub. by Almqvist & Wiksell International)

**Kungliga Tekniska Hoegskolan**
100 44 Stockholm 70, Sweden.
- Power Systems Computation Conference. P S C C Proceedings. irreg.; latest issue, 1975.

**Kungliga Tekniska Hoegskolan. Division of Photogrammetry**
S-100 44 Stockholm, Sweden.
- Fotogrammetriska Meddelanden/Photogrammetric Information. irreg., vol. 6, no. 6, 1974. ISSN 0071-8068

**Kungliga Tekniska Hoegskolan. Flygtekniska Institutionen**
S-100 44 Stockholm 70, Sweden.
- Kungliga Tekniska Hoegskolan. Flygtekniska Institutionen. K T H Aero Memo F I. irreg.

**Kungliga Vetenskaps-Societeten**
- Nova Acta Regiae Societatis Scientiarum Upsaliensis. (pub. by Almqvist & Wiksell International)

**Kungliga Vetenskapsakademien**
S-104 05 Stockholm, Sweden.
- Documenta. 3-5 per yr. ISSN 0347-5719
- Kungliga Svenska Vetenskapsakademiens Bidrag till Kungliga Vetenskapsakademiens Historia. irreg., vol.17, 1976. ISSN 0081-9956

**Kungliga Vitterhets-, Historie- och Antikvitets Akademien**
Villagatan 3, 114 32 Stockholm, Sweden.
- Fornvaennen. (pub. by Almqvist & Wiksell International)
- Kungliga Vitterhets- , Historie- och Antikvitets Akademien. Aarsbok. a. ISSN 0083-6796
- Kungliga Vitterhets- , Historie- och Antikvitets Akademien. Antikvariskt Arkiv. irreg., no. 64, 1977. ISSN 0083-6737

- Kungliga Vitterhets- , Historie- och Antikvitets Akademien. Filologiskt Arkiv. irreg., no. 19, 1974. ISSN 0083-6745
- Kungliga Vitterhets- , Historie- och Antikvitets Akademien. Handlingar. Antikvariska Serien/Royal Academy of Letters, History and Antiquities. Proceedings. Antiquarian Series. irreg., no. 28, 1974. ISSN 0083-6761
- Kungliga Vitterhets- ,Historie- och Antikvitets Akademien. Handlingar. Filologisk-Filosofiska Serien/Royal Academy of Letters, History and Antiquities. Proceedings. Philological-Philosophical Series. irreg., no. 15, 1975. ISSN 0083-677X
- Kungliga Vitterhets- , Historie- och Antikvitets Akademien. Handlingar. Historiska Serien/Royal Academy of Letters, History and Antiquities. Proceedings. Historical Series. irreg., no. 18, 1972. ISSN 0083-6788
- Kungliga Vitterhets- , Historie- och Antikvitets Akademien. Historiskt Arkiv. irreg., no. 16, 1975. ISSN 0083-6753
- Nordisk Numismatisk Aarsskrift/Scandinavian Numismatic Journal. a. ISSN 0078-107X (Co-sponsor: Nordisk Numismatisk Union)

**Kustartilleriklubben**
Fack, 104 50 Stockholm 80, Sweden.
- Tidskrift Foer Kustartilleriet. q. ISSN 0040-683X

**Kvaekarna**
*see* Vaenner Samfund i Sverige

**Kvidinge Sockens Hembygdsfoerening**
Kvidinge, Sweden.
- Kvidinge Sockens Hembygdsfoerening Skriftserie. a.

**Kyrkomusikernas Riksfoerbund**
c/o Jan Rostroem, Turingevaegen 77, S-125 41 Aelvsjoe, Sweden.
- Svensk Kyrkomusik. (Edition AB for Church Musicians) m(Jan.-June; Sept.-Dec.) (Co-Sponsor: Sveriges Kyrkosaangs Foerbund)
- Svensk Kyrkomusik (Edition B for Choir Members) m (Jan.-June; Sept.-Dec.) (Co-Sponsor: Sveriges Kyrkosaangs Foerbund)

**L K B-Produkter AB**
Box 76, Bromma 1, Sweden.
- Science Tools; the L K B instrument journal. 3 per yr. ISSN 0036-8598

**Ladugaardsfoermannens Riksfoerfund**
Leif Lindwalk Pl 2409, 311 00 Falkenberg, Sweden.
- Ladugaardsfoermannen. m. ISSN 0023-7159

**Laerarhoegskolan i Malmoe. Pedagogisk-Psykologiska Institutionen**
Fack, S-200 45 Malmoe, Sweden.
- Didakometry and Sociometry. s-a. ISSN 0346-5020
- Educational and Psychological Interactions. irreg. ISSN 0070-9263

**Laerarhoegskolan i Moelndal. Pedagogiska Institutionen**
431 20 Moelndal, Sweden.
- Laerarhoegskolan i Moelndal. Pedagogiska Institutionen. Rapport. irreg.

**Laerarinnornas Missionsfoerening**
Vasaplatsen 4, 411 34 Goeteborg, Sweden.
- Laerarinnornas Missionsfoerening. Meddelande till L M F. 9 per yr. ISSN 0023-6322

**Laerarnas Riksfoerbund**
Fack, 103 60 Stockholm, Sweden.
- Skolvaerlden. w. ISSN 0037-6566

**Laerdomshistoriska Samfundet**
- Lychnos-Bibliotek. Studies och Kaellskrifter Udgivna av Laerdomshistoriska Samfundet. Studies and Sources Published by the Swedish History of Science Society. (pub. by Almqvist & Wiksell International)
- Lychnos-Laerdomshistoriska Samfundets Aarsbok. Annual of the Swedish History of Science Society. (pub. by Almqvist & Wiksell International)

**Landsorganisationen i Sverige**
Barnhusgatan 18, 105 53 Stockholm, Sweden.
- L O-Tidningen Fackfoereningsroerelsen. 36 per yr.
- Landsorganisationen i Sverige. Yttranden till Offentlig Myndighet. irreg.

**Landstingsfoerbundet**
Box 6606, S-113 84 Stockholm, Sweden.
- Landstingens Tidskrift. 14 per yr. ISSN 0023-8074

**Lantbrukarnas Ekonomi AB**
Fack, S-105 33 Stockholm, Sweden.
- Lantmannen; tidskrift foer lantmaen. fortn.

**Lantbrukarnas Riksfoerbund**
Klara Oestra Kyrkogate 12, S-105 33 Stockholm, Sweden.
- Land. w. ISSN 0023-7531
- Nya Perspektiv; journal of agricultural co-operatives. q. ISSN 0550-4112

**Lantbrukshoegskolan**
S-750 07 Uppsala 7, Sweden.
- Lantbrukshoegskolan. Meddelanden. Serie A. irreg., (20 per 30 per yr), no. 221, 1974. ISSN 0083-4653
- Swedish Journal of Agricultural Research. (pub. by Almqvist & Wiksell International)

**Lantbrukshoegskolan. Institutionen Foer Markvetenskap**
S-750 07 Uppsala, Sweden.
- Grundfoerbaettring; journal of agricultural land improvement. 4 per yr. ISSN 0017-4904 (prep. by its Avdelning Foer Lantbrukets Hydroteknik)

**Lantbruksnytt**
Box 165, 20121 Malmoe 1, Sweden.
- Lantbruksnytt. 16 per yr. ISSN 0345-7001

**Lantmannens Tryckeri-Forening**
Box 22, 721 03 Vaesteraas 1, Sweden.
- Kvallsstunden. w. ISSN 0023-5822

**Latinamerika-Institutet**
Odengatan 61, S-102 30 Stockholm, Sweden.
- Ibero-Americana. s-a. ISSN 0046-8444 (Scandinavian Association for Research on Latin America)
- Instituto de Estudios Iberoamericanos. Publicaciones. Serie C: Informes. a.
- Instituto de Estudios Iberoamericanos. Publicaciones. Serie B: Informes. irreg.

**Lattbetong AB**
Skeppargaton 8, 114 52 Stockholm, Sweden.
- Lattbetong; publication for information and debate in building questions. 4 per yr. ISSN 0023-8872

**Legitimerade Sjukgymnasters Riksfoerbund**
Birger Jarlsgatan 13, 111 45 Stockholm, Sweden.
- Sjukgymnasten. m. ISSN 0037-6019

**Lerums Boktryckeri AB**
LBA Publications, Fack, 443 01 Lerum 1, Sweden.
- Illustrerad Motor Sport. m. ISSN 0019-249X
- M C-Nytt. m. ISSN 0024-7995
- Soldat & Teknik. m.
- Start & Speed. 10 per yr. ISSN 0038-9943

**Letterstedtska Foereningen**
- Nordisk Tidskrift for Vetenskap, Konst och Industri. (pub. by Foereningen Norden)

**Liber Foerlag**
Fack, S-162 89 Vaellingby, Sweden.
- Aarsbok Foer Sveriges Kommuner. a. ISSN 0065-020X (Sweden. Statistiska Centralbyraan)
- Cancer Incidence in Sweden. a. ISSN 0069-0155 (Sweden. Swedish Cancer Registry)
- Humanistisk Forskning. s-a. (Statens Humanistiska Forskningsraad)
- Konjunkturlaget. q. ISSN 0023-3463 (Sweden. Konjunkturinstitutet)
- R A K-Information. 2 per yr. ISSN 0033-6726 (Sweden. Lantmaeteriverket)
- Register over Gaellande SFS-Foerfattningar. irreg.
- Statistisk Aarsbok Foer Sverige. a. ISSN 0081-5381 (Sweden. Statistiska Centralbyraan)
- Studia Forestalia Suecica. irreg., no. 117, 1974. ISSN 0039-3150 (Kungliga Skogshoegskolan. Institutionen Foer Virkeslaera)
- Sverige-EG. a. (Sweden. Utrikesdepartementet) (Co-sponsor: Handelsdepartementet)
- Sweden. Finansdepartementet. Regeringens Budgetfoerslag. a.
- Sweden. Riksrevisionsverket. Statens Finanser; Riksrevisionsverkets aarsbok. a. ISSN 0079-7561
- Sweden. Socialstyrelsen. Redoviser. irreg. (5-8 per yr)
- Sweden. Socialstyrelsen. Legitimerade Laekare. Authorized Physicians. a.
- Sweden. Statens Naturvaardsverk. Publikationer. 12 per yr. ISSN 0039-0259

- Sweden. Statistiska Centralbyraan. Allmaan Fastighetstaxering. a.
- Sweden. Statistiska Centralbyraan. Allmaan Maanadsstitistik/Monthly Digest of Swedish Statistics. m. ISSN 0039-7253
- Sweden. Statistiska Centralbyraan.Arbetskraftsundersoekningen. Arsmedeltal. irreg.
- Sweden. Statistiska Centralbyraan. Befolkningsfoeraendringar. a. ISSN 0082-0156
- Sweden. Statistiska Centralbyraan. Folkmaengd. a. ISSN 0082-0164
- Sweden. Statistiska Centralbyraan. Industri. a. ISSN 0082-0172
- Sweden. Statistiska Centralbyraan. Information i Prognosfragor/Forecasting Information. irreg. ISSN 0082-0180
- Sweden. Statistiska Centralbyraan. Jordbruksstatistik Aarsbok. a. ISSN 0082-0199
- Sweden. Statistiska Centralbyraan. Kommunal Personal. a. ISSN 0082-0202
- Sweden. Statistiska Centralbyraan. Levnadsfoerhaallanden Aarsbok/Living Conditions Yearbook. a.
- Sweden. Statistiska Centralbyraan. Loener. a. ISSN 0082-0210
- Sweden. Statistiska Centralbyraan. Meddelanden i Samordningsfraagor. irreg. ISSN 0082-0229 (Sweden. Statistiska Centralbyraan)
- Sweden. Statistiska Centralbyraan. S C B Manadens Tryck. m. (Subscr. to: Box 902, S-701 22 Oerebro, Sweden)
- Sweden. Statistiska Centralbyraan. Statistisk Tidskrift. 6 per yr. ISSN 0039-7261
- Sweden. Statistiska Centralbyraan. Statistiska Meddelanden. Subgroup Am (Labor Market) irreg. ISSN 0082-0237
- Sweden. Statistiska Centralbyraan. Statistiska Meddelanden. Subgroup Be (Population) irreg. ISSN 0082-0245
- Sweden. Statistiska Centralbyraan. Statistiska Meddelanden. Subgroup Bo (Housing and Construction) irreg. ISSN 0085-6991
- Sweden. Statistiska Centralbyraan. Statistiska Meddelanden. Subgroup H (Trade) irreg. ISSN 0082-0261
- Sweden. Statistiska Centralbyraan. Statistiska Meddelanden. Subgroup I (Manufacturing) irreg. ISSN 0082-027X
- Sweden. Statistiska Centralbyraan. Statistiska Meddelanden. Subgroup J (Agriculture) irreg. ISSN 0082-0288
- Sweden. Statistiska Centralbyraan. Statistiska Meddelanden. Subgroup N (National Accounts and Finance) irreg. ISSN 0082-0296
- Sweden. Statistiska Centralbyraan. Statistiska Meddelanden. Subgroup P (Prices and Price Indices) irreg. ISSN 0082-030X
- Sweden. Statistiska Centralbyraan. Statistiska Meddelanden. Subgroup R (Judicial Statistics. Law and Social Welfare) irreg. ISSN 0082-0318
- Sweden. Statistiska Centralbyraan. Statistiska Meddelanden. Subgroup S (Social Welfare Statistics) irreg. ISSN 0082-0326
- Sweden. Statistiska Centralbyraan. Statistiska Meddelanden. Subgroup T (Transport and Other Forms of Communication) irreg. ISSN 0082-0334
- Sweden. Statistiska Centralbyraan. Statistiska Meddelanden. Subgroup U (Education and Culture) irreg. ISSN 0082-0342
- Sweden. Statistiska Centralbyraan. Urval Skriftseries/Selection Series. irreg., 1970, no. 3. ISSN 0082-0350
- Sweden. Statistiska Centralbyraan. Utbildningsstatistik/Swedish Educational Statistics. irreg.
- Sweden. Statistiska Centralbyraan. Utrikeshandel/Foreign Trade. m. ISSN 0082-0369
- Sweden. Statistiska Centralbyraan. Utrikeshandel. Kvartalsstatistik. q. ISSN 0039-727X
- Sweden. Statistiska Centralbyraan. Utrikeshandel. Maanadsstatistik. m. ISSN 0039-7288
- Swedish Economy. q. ISSN 0039-7296 (Sweden. Konjunkturinstitutet)
- Yrke och Framtid. a. (Sweden. Yrksev Agledningsenheten)

**LiberLaeromedel**
Box 1205, S-221 05 Lund, Sweden.
- Acta Archaelogica Lundensia: Monographs of Lunds Universitets Historiska Museum. Series in 4. irreg., no. 11, 1977. ISSN 0065-1001
- Acta Archaelogica Lundensia: Monographs of Lunds Universitets Historiska Museum. Series in 8. irreg., no. 11, 1977. ISSN 0065-0994
- Arkiv for Nordisk Filologi/Archives for Scandinavian Philology. a. ISSN 0066-7668

- Coniectanea Biblica. New Testament Series. irreg., no. 9, 1977. ISSN 0069-8946
- Coniectanea Biblica. Old Testament Series. irreg., no. 10, 1977. ISSN 0069-8954
- Lund Studie in English. irreg., no. 51, 1977. ISSN 0069-.451
- Lund Studies in Geography. Series A. Physical Geography. irreg., no. 56, 1977. ISSN 0076-146X (Lunds Universitet. Department of Geography)
- Lund Studies in Geography. Series B. Human Geography. irreg., no. 44, 1977. ISSN 0076-1478 (Lunds Universitet. Department of Geography)
- Lund Studies in Geography. Series C. General and Mathematical Geography. irreg; 1971, no. 12. ISSN 0076-1486 (Lunds Universitet. Department of Geography)
- Studia Linguistica; revue de linguistique generale et comparee. s-a. ISSN 0039-3193
- Svensk Exegetisk Aarsbok. a. (Uppsala Exegetiska Saellskap)
- Svensk Geografisk Aarsbok. a. ISSN 0081-9808 (South-Swedish Geographical Society)
- Svensk Teologisk Kvartalskrift. q. ISSN 0039-6761
- Theoria; a Swedish journal of philosophy. irreg (1-3 per yr.) ISSN 0040-5825

**LiberLaeromedel, Malmoe**
205 10 Malmoe, Sweden.
- Skolvaerldens Aarsbok. a.

**Lions International**
Nybrokajen 7, 111 48 Stockholm, Sweden.
- Lion; Nordisk upplaga. bi-m. ISSN 0024-4198

**Ljudtekniska Saellskapet**
Fack, S-100 71 Stockholm 36, Sweden.
- Musik och Ljudteknik. q. ISSN 0027-4720

**Ljuskultur**
Skepparg 27, Box 5512, 114 85 Stockholm, Sweden.
- Ljuskultur. q.

**Lundequistka Bokhandeln**
Tiundagatan 39, 752 30 Uppsala, Sweden.
- Namn och Bygd; journal for Nordic place-name research. a. ISSN 0077-2704 (Kungliga Gustav Adolfs Akademien)

**Lunds Universitet. Department of Geography**
- Lund Studies in Geography. Series A. Physical Geography. (pub. by LiberLaeromedel)
- Lund Studies in Geography. Series B. Human Geography. (pub. by LiberLaeromedel)
- Lund Studies in Geography. Series C. General and Mathematical Geography. (pub. by LiberLaeromedel)

**Lunds Universitet. Faculty of Odontology**
214 21 Malmoe, Sweden.
- University of Lund. School of Dentistry. Faculty of Odontology. Annual Publications. a. ISSN 0076-3438

**Lunds Universitet. Historiska Museum**
- Acta Archaelogica Lundensia: Monographs of Lunds Universitets Historiska Museum. Series in 4. (pub. by LiberLaeromedel)
- Acta Archaelogica Lundensia: Monographs of Lunds Universitets Historiska Museum. Series in 8. (pub. by LiberLaeromedel)

**Lunds Universitet. Institute of Art History**
Box 1135, S-221 04 Lund, Sweden.
- A R I S. (Art Research in Scandinavia) a. ISSN 0044-5711

**Lunds Universitet. Institute of Economic History**
Finngatan 16, S-223 62 Lund, Sweden.
- Economy and History. biennial. ISSN 0070-8852

**Lunds Universitet. Institutionen Foer Nordiska Spraak**
Helgonabacken 14, S-223 62 Lund, Sweden.
- Lundastudier i Nordisk Spraakvetenskap. Serie D: Meddelanden. irreg.

**Lunds Universitet. Psychological Laboratory**
Paradisgatan 223, Lund, Sweden.
- Psychological Research Bulletin. Monograph Series. irreg.

**Lunds Universitet. Slaviska Institutionen**
Finngatan 12, S-223 62 Lund, Sweden.
- Lunds Universitet. Slaviska Institutionen. Aarsbok. irreg.
- Slavica Lundensia. a.

- Spraakliga Bidrag; meddelanden fraan seminariera slaviska spraak, jaemfoerande spraakforskning, finskae-ugriska spraak och oestasiatiska spraak. s-a.

**Lunds Universitet. Tandlaekarhoegskolan. Odontologiska Fakulteten**
see **Lunds Universitet. Faculty of Odontology**

**M S Foerbundet**
David Bagares Gatan 3, 111 38 Stockholm, Sweden.
- M S-Brevet. (Multiple Sclerosis) bi-m. ISSN 0024-8371

**Sven Magnusson, Ed. and Pub.**
Box 3063, S-103 61 Stockholm 3, Sweden.
- Soekaren. 10 per yr. ISSN 0038-0504

**Malmborg och Hedstrom Foerlags AB**
Karlsbodavaegen 14, S-161 70 Bromma, Sweden.
- Baat Foer Alla. 14 per yr.

**Marinnytt**
S-104 50 Stockholm, Sweden.
- Marinnytt. bi-m. ISSN 0025-3375

**Marxist-Leninistiska Kampforbundet**
Box 450 40, S-104 30 Stockholm, Sweden.
- Stormklockan. w. ISSN 0039-1980

**Maskinkontakt AB**
Box 419, 531 01 Lidkoeping, Sweden.
- Maskin Kontakt. m (10 per yr.) ISSN 0345-7788

**A B Mecman**
Box 32 035, S-126 11 Stockholm 32, Sweden.
- Mecman-Technique. irreg. ISSN 0025-6609

**Medicinhistoriska Museet**
Aasoegatan 146, 116 32 Stockholm, Sweden.
- Nordisk Medicinhistorisk Aarsbok. a. ISSN 0078-1061

**Medicinska Foereningarna i Sverige**
c/o Goeran Petersson, Winstrupsgatan 14, 222 22 Lund, Sweden.
- Motpol; tidskrift foer haelsa och politik. 8 per yr.

**Meie Post**
Box 6057, 102 31 Stockholm 6, Sweden.
- Meie Post. m. ISSN 0025-875X

**Mendelian Society**
Institute of Genetics, Lund, Sweden
- Hereditas; a periodical devoted to the publication of original research in genetics and cytology. q. ISSN 0018-0661 (Scandinavian Association of Geneticists) (Subscr. to: J.L. Toernquists Bokhandel, 261 31 Landskrons, Sweden)

**Metodistkyrkans i Sverige**
- Metodistkyrkans i Sverige. Aarsbok. (pub. by Nya Bokfoerlags AB)

**Militaertekniska Foereningen**
- Militaer Teknisk Tidskrift. (pub. by Dordius AB)

**Missionssaellskapet Bibeltrogna Vaenner**
Upplandsgatan 43, S-113 28 Stockholm, Sweden.
- Bibeltrogna Vaenner Missionstidning. m. ISSN 0006-0658

**Mittag- Lefflers Matematiska Stiftelse**
Auravaegen 17, S-182 62 Djursholm, Sweden.
- Acta Mathematica. 2 vols.per yr. ISSN 0001-5962
- Arkiv Foer Matematik. s-a. ISSN 0004-2080

**Moderata Samlingspartiets Riksorganisation**
Box 1246, 111 82 Stockholm, Sweden.
- Medborgaren. 12 per yr. ISSN 0025-665X

**Moderata Ungdomsfoerbundet**
Box 1243, 111 82 Stockholm, Sweden.
- Moderat Debatt. m. ISSN 0026-7449

**Modern Byggteknik Team**
Observatoriegatan 12, 113 29 Stockholm, Sweden.
- Modern Byggteknik Team; teknik-ekonomi-arkitektur-material. m.

**Modern Language Teachers Association of Sweden**
see **Riksfoereningen Foer Laerarna i Moderna Sprak**

**Moebelindustrins Service AB**
Box 140 12, S-104 40 Stockholm 14, Sweden.
- Interior. s-a. ISSN 0047-049X (Swedish Furniture Manufacturers Association)

**R. Moellerfors, Ed. & Pub.**
Saangarvaegen 4, S-183 40 Taeby, Sweden.
- Storkoek/Catering. m. ISSN 0039-1964

**Mosaiska Forsamlingens Committee for Judar i Sovjet**
Box 7057, S-103 82 Stockholm, Sweden.
- Judar i Sovjet. m.

**Motorbranschens Foerlag**
Karlavaegen 14 A, Box 5611, S-114 86 Stockholm, Sweden.
- Motorbranschen; official journal of the motor trade and repair organization in Sweden. 15 per yr. ISSN 0027-2140 (Motorbranschens Riksfoerbund) (Co-sponsor: Daeckspecialisternas Riksfoerbund)

**Motorbranschens Riksfoerbund**
- Motorbranschen. (pub. by Motorbranschens Foerlag)

**Motortidningen Kart**
Skiljemyntsgatan 18 F, 414 80 Goeteborg, Sweden.
- Motortidningen Kart. 5 per yr. ISSN 0027-2388

**Museum of Varberg**
Varberg, Sweden.
- Musuem of Varberg. Aarsbok. a. ISSN 0083-5536

**Musikhistoriska Museet**
Slottsbacken 6, S-111 30 Stockholm, Sweden.
- Musikhistoriska Museet, Stockholm. Skrifter. irreg. ISSN 0081-5675

**N R F**
see **Sweden. Statens Naturvetenskapliga Forskningsraad**

**Naeringslivets Arkivraad**
Klubbacken 16, 126 56 Haegersten, Sweden.
- Arkivinformation. irreg. (3 per yr.) ISSN 0571-0731

**Naeringslivets Tidningsstiftelse**
Box 1760, 111 87 Stockholm, Sweden.
- Affaersvaerlden. w.

**National Council for Consumer Goods and Consumer Information**
see **Sweden. Statens Konsumentraad**

**National Defense Research Institute**
see **Sweden. Foersvarets Forskningsanstalt**

**Nationalekonomiska Foereningen**
- Ekonomisk Debatt/Economic Debate. (pub. by Sparfraemjandet)

**Naturhistoriska Riksmuseet**
104 05 Stockholm 50, Sweden.
- Fauna och Flora; populaer tidskrift foer biologi. bi-m. ISSN 0014-8903

**Navigationssaellskapet**
Soedra Hamnvaegen Vaegen 42, 115 41 Stockholm, Sweden.
- Navis. m. ISSN 0028-1603

**Aktiebolaget NIBO**
Drottninggatan 65, 111 36 Stockholm, Sweden.
- Tidskriften Bostadsnaemnden. m. ISSN 0040-6961
- Tidskriften Landsstaten. m. ISSN 0040-7003
- Tidskriften Taxeringsnaemden. m. ISSN 0040-7011

**Nobel Foundation**
- Prix Nobel. Nobel Prizes. (pub. by Elsevier Scientific Publishing Co. NE)

**Nordisk Audiologisk Selskab**
- Scandinavian Audiology. (pub. by Almqvist & Wiksell International)

**Nordisk Avis-Teknisk Samarbetsnaemnd**
- Tidningsteknik. (pub. by TU: S Foerlags AB)

**Nordisk Filateli AB**
Box 40200, 103 44 Stockholm 40, Sweden.
- Nordisk Filateli. m. ISSN 0029-134X

**Nordisk Mejeriindustri AB**
Muskoetgatan 23, Box 12037, S-250 12 Helsingborg, Sweden.
- Nordisk Mejeriindustri/Scandinavian Journal of Dairy Technology. m. (Svenska Mejeriernas Riksfoerening) (Co-sponsors: Norske Melkeprodusenters Landsfoerbund, Mejeriernas Centrallag Valio, Centrallaget Enigheten)

**Nordisk Skrottidning**
Jaerntorget 83, 119 29 Stockholm, Sweden.
- Nordisk Skrottidning/Scandinavian Reclamation Industries Review. m.

**Nordisk Socialmedicinsk Foerening**
- Scandinavian Journal of Social Medicine. (pub. by Almqvist & Wiksell International)

**Nordisk Tidskrift for Fotografi**
c/o John-Ake Anderzon, Ed., Skogsvaegen 14, Enebyberg, Sweden.
- Nordisk Tidskrift for Fotografi. 10 per yr. ISSN 0029-1498

**Nordisk Violinbyggarefoerening**
Box 131, Stockholm 1, Sweden.
- Sloejd och Ton. bi-m. ISSN 0037-6892

**Nordiska Afrikainstitutet**
Box 2126, S-750 02 Uppsala, Sweden.
- Africana i Nordiska Vetenskapliga Bibliotek/ Africana in Scandinavian Research Libraries/ Africana dans les Bibliotheques de Recherche Scandinaves. s-a. ISSN 0044-6645
- Scandinavian Institute of African Studies. Annual Seminar Proceedings. (pub. by Almqvist & Wiksell International)
- Scandinavian Institute of African Studies. Newsletter. m. ISSN 0549-6330
- Scandinavian Institute of African Studies. Research Report. irreg., no. 38, 1977. ISSN 0080-6714

**Nordiska Betongfoerbundet**
Fack, 100 44 Stockholm 70, Sweden.
- Nordisk Betong. 6 per yr. ISSN 0029-1307

**Nordiska Branschtidskrifter AB**
Box 34, 191 21 Sollentuna 1, Sweden.
- Tvaettnytt; Scandinavian laundry and dry cleaning journal. m (10 per yr.) ISSN 0049-4887 (Sveriges Tvaetterifoerbund) (Co-sponsor: Tvaettbranschens Riksfoerbund)

**Nordiska Ekumeniska Institutet**
- Nordisk Ekumenisk Aarsbok. (pub. by Gummessons Bokfoerlag)

**Nordiska Jaernvaegsmannasaellskapet**
SJ Centralfoervaltning, S-105 50 Stockholm C, Sweden.
- Nordisk Jaernbane Tidskrift. bi-m. ISSN 0029-1382

**Nordiska Raadet**
Fack, S-103 10 Stockholm 2, Sweden.
- Nordisk Statistisk Aarsbok/Yearbook of Nordic Statistics. a. ISSN 0078-1088
- Nordisk Statutsamling. a. ISSN 0300-3094

**Nordiska Samarbetskommitten foer Namnfforskning**
S: T Johannesgatan 11, S-752 21 Uppsala, Sweden.
- NORNA - Rapporter. irreg.

**Nordiska Samfundet mot Plaagsamma Djurfoersoek**
Drottninggatan 102, 111 60 Stockholm, Sweden.
- Djurens Raett/Right of the Animals. q.

**Nordiske Psykiatriske Foreninger**
- Nordisk Psykiatrisk Tidsskrift. (pub. by Elanders Boktryckeri AB)

**Norrlandsfoerbundet**
Box 294, 851 05 Sundsvall, Sweden.
- Norrlaendsk Tidskrift. 8 per yr. ISSN 0029-1838

**Norstedts Tryckeri AB**
Box 2080, S-103 12 Stockholm, Sweden.
- Foervaltningsraettslig Tidskrift. 6 per yr. ISSN 0015-8585
- Gronkopings Veckoblad. m.(10 per yr) ISSN 0017-4548
- Svensk Juristtidning. 10 per yr. ISSN 0039-6591

**Bokfoerlaget Nova Ecclesia**
Aladdinsvaegen 27, 161 38 Bromma, Sweden.
- Nova Ecclesia. bi-m. ISSN 0029-5019 (General Church of the New Jerusalem)

**Nya Bokfoerlags AB**
Sibyllegatan 18 III, 114 42 Stockholm, Sweden.
● Metodistkyrkans i Sverige. Aarsbok. a. ISSN
0543-6206

**Nykterhetsroerelsens Scoutfoerbund**
Bolidenvaegen 14, S-121 63 Johanneshov, Sweden.
● Scoutledaren. 6 per yr. ISSN 0036-9519

**Oceanografiska Institutet**
Goeteborg, Sweden.
● Oceanografiska Institutet, Goeteborg.
Meddelanden. irreg. ISSN 0072-5072

**Odontologiska Foreningen**
Hollandargatan 17, 111 60 Stockholm, Sweden.
● Odontologiska Foreningens Tidskrift. q. ISSN
0029-8468

**Oerebromissionens Foerlag**
Box 330, S-701 05 Oerebro 1, Sweden.
● Missionsbaneret. w. ISSN 0026-6132

**Oestasiatiska Museet**
Skeppsholmen, Stockholm 100, Sweden
● Oestasiaska Museet. Bulletin. a. ISSN 0081-5691
(Dist. by: George Wittenborn, Inc., 1018 Madison
Ave., New York, NY 10021)

**Office of the Chancellor of the Swedish Universities**
*see* Sweden. Universitetskanslersaembetet

**Lillies Ohlsson, Ed. & Pub.**
Box 8014, S-720 08 Vaesteraas, Sweden.
● Kountry Korral; Scandinavia's country music
magazine. bi-m. ISSN 0023-429X

**Orkester Journalen AB**
Drottninggatan 14, 111 51 Stockholm, Sweden.
● Orkester Journalen. m. ISSN 0030-5642

**Ortodox Kyrkotidnings Foerlag**
Box 3154, S-103 63 Stockholm, Sweden.
● Ortodox Kyrkotidning. m. ISSN 0030-5952
(Stockholms Ortodoxa Institut)

**Pax**
Jungfrugatan 30, 3tr., 114 44 Stockholm, Sweden.
● Pax; tidskrift for fredsdebatt. q. ISSN 0048-3087

**Personhistoriska Samfundet**
Kungliga Biblioteket, S-102 41 Stockholm 5,
Sweden.
● Personhistorisk Tidskrift. q. ISSN 0031-5699

**Bengt Pleijel, Ed. & Pub.**
Jaerntorgsgatan 4, 111 29 Stockholm, Sweden.
● Jorden Runt; lander, folk, resor. m. ISSN 0021-
7476
● Musikrevy; nordisk tidskrift for musik och
grammofoh. 6 per yr. ISSN 0027-4844

**Polisidrott**
Ostermalmsgatan 66, 114 50 Stockholm 5, Sweden.
● Polisidrott. m.

**Reader's Digest AB**
Box 6064, 102 31 Stockholm 6, Sweden.
● Det Baesta ur Reader's Digest (Swedish Edition)
m. ISSN 0005-3864

**Riksfoerbundet DX-Alliansen**
Box 3108, S-103 62 Stockholm 3, Sweden.
● Eter-Aktuellt. 10 per yr. ISSN 0014-1658

**Riksfoerbundet Foer Hembygdsvaard**
Rutger Fuchsgatan 4, Box 20031, S-104 60
Stockholm, Sweden.
● Bygd och Natur. 6 per yr.

**Riksfoerbundet foer Hjaert- och Lungsjuka**
Box 3196, 103 63 Stockholm, Sweden.
● Status. 10 per yr. ISSN 0085-6738

**Riksfoerbundet Hem och Skola**
Rosenlundsgatan 54, 116 53 Stockholm, Sweden.
● Barn i Hem-Skola-Samhaelle. m. ISSN 0005-6006

**Riksfoerbundet Mot Alkoholmissbruk**
Box 17136, S-104 62 Stockholm 17, Sweden.
● Alkoholdebatt. q. ISSN 0002-550X

**Riksfoerbundet mot Allergi**
Box 45153, S-104 30 Stockholm, Sweden.
● Allergia. bi-m. ISSN 0002-5747

**Riksfoerbundet Mot Reumatism**
Vanadisvaegen 4, 113 85 Stockholm, Sweden.
● Reuma. q. ISSN 0034-6209

**Riksfoerbundet Svensk Traedgaard**
Sibyllegatan 69, 114 43 Stockholm, Sweden.
● Hemtraedgaarden. 4 per yr. ISSN 0018-0343

**Riksfoereningen Foer Laerarna i Moderna Spraak**
c/o B. Henningsson, Treasurer, Saegengatan 7, S-
422 46 Hisings Backa, Sweden
● L M S-Lingua. q. ISSN 0023-6330 (Editorial
information to: Martin Oeman, Kolfatsvaegen 10,
S-752 47 Uppsala, Sweden)
● Moderna Spraak. 4 per yr. ISSN 0026-8577
(Editorial information to: Majken Korten, Box 41,
S-130 11 Saltsjoe-Duvnaes, Sweden)

**Riksfoereningen Foer Svenskhetens Bevarande i
Utlandet**
Teaterg. 4, S-411 35 Goeteborg, Sweden.
● Sverigekontakt. m.

**Riksidrottsfoerbundets Foerlags AB**
Box 34, 123 21 Farsta, Sweden.
● Svensk Idrott. s-m. ISSN 0049-2663 (Sveriges
Riksidrottsfoerbund)

**Roerfirmornas Riksfoerbund**
Storgatan 36, 114 55 Stockholm, Sweden.
● V V S-Forum. m.

**Torgil Rosenberg AB**
Box 4016, 183 04 Taby, Sweden.
● Musiktidningen. bi-m. ISSN 0345-7699

**Royal Academy of Letters, History and Antiquities**
*see* Kungliga Vitterhets-, Historie-, och Antikvitets
Akademien

**Royal Armed Forces Staff College**
*see* Sweden. Kungliga Militaerhoegskolan

**Royal Swedish Academy of Agriculture and Forestry**
*see* Kungliga Skogs- och Lantbruksakademien

**Royal Swedish Academy of Engineering Sciences**
*see* Ingenioersvetenskapsakademien

**Royal Swedish Academy of Sciences**
*see* Kungliga Vetenskapsakademien

**Ryska Bibelsaellskapet**
Box 412, Oerebro, Sweden.
● Bibel-Journalen. bi-m. ISSN 0006-0607

**S A F O**
*see* Swedish Atomic Forum

**S E R-Schaktkonsult AB**
Kungsgatan 70, S-111 22 Stockholm, Sweden.
● S E R Tidningen. m.(Sept.-June); bi-m.(July-Aug.)
ISSN 0037-2080 (Sveriges Schaktentreprenoerers
Riksfoerbund)

**SAAB-SCANIA**
S-581 88 Linkoeping, Sweden.
● SAAB Technical Notes. irreg., 1972, no. 68. ISSN
0080-5149

**SAAB-SCANIA. SCANIA Division**
Information Department, 151 87 Soedertaelje,
Sweden.
● Mil. q. ISSN 0026-3710

**Saellskapet Bokvaennera**
Ulvsatervaegen 18, S-181 62 Lidingoe, Sweden.
● Bokvaennen. 9 per yr. ISSN 0006-5846

**Saellskapet Foer Studier i Arbetarroerelsens Historia**
Box 16 393, Stockholm, Sweden.
● Studier i Arbetarroerelsens Historia. irreg.

**Samfundet de Nio**
c/o Anders Oehman, Smaalandsgatan 14, 111 46
Stockholm, Sweden.
● Svensk Litteraturtidskrift. q. ISSN 0039-663X

**Karl Sandels, Ed. & Pub.**
Kungstensgatan 20, S-113 57 Stockholm, Sweden.
● Fotonyheterna. 10 per yr. ISSN 0015-8909

**Saxon och Lindstroems Foerlags AB**
Sveavaegen 145, 106 53 Stockholm, Sweden.
● Saxons Veckotidning. w. ISSN 0036-5211
● Svensk Dam Tidning. w. ISSN 0039-6486
● Viola-Traedgaardsvaerlden. s-w. ISSN 0042-6407

**Scandia**
c/o Rosen, O. Vallgatan 41, 223 61 Lund, Sweden.
● Scandia; tidskrift foer historisk forskning. s-a.
ISSN 0036-5483

**Scandinavian Airlines**
S-161 87 Bromma, Sweden.
● Scanorama. bi-m.

**Scandinavian Association for Research on Latin
America**
● Ibero-Americana. (pub. by Latinamerika-Institutet)

**Scandinavian Association for Thoracic and
Cardiovascular Surgery**
● Scandinavian Journal of Thoracic and
Cardiovascular Surgery. (pub. by Almqvist &
Wiksell International)

**Scandinavian Association of Geneticists**
● Hereditas. (pub. by Mendelian Society)

**Scandinavian Association of Obstetricians and
Gynaecologists**
● Acta Obstetricia et Gynecologica Scandinavica.
(pub. by Almqvist & Wiksell International)

**Scandinavian Association of Plastic Surgeons**
● Scandinavian Journal of Plastic and
Reconstructive Surgery. (pub. by Almqvist &
Wiksell International)

**Scandinavian Association of Urology**
● Scandinavian Journal of Urology and Nephrology.
(pub. by Almqvist & Wiksell International)

**Scandinavian Blues Association**
c/o Tommy Loefgren, Skoerdevaegen 5, 186 00
Vallentuna, Sweden.
● Jefferson; Nordisk tidskrift foer blues och
folkmusik. 5 per yr.

**Scandinavian Institute of African Studies**
*see* Nordiska Afrikainstitutet

**Scandinavian Physiological Society**
● Acta Physiologica Scandinavica. (pub. by
Karolinska Institutet)

**Scandinavian Society of Rheumatologists**
● Scandinavian Journal of Rheumatology. (pub. by
Almqvist & Wiksell International)

**Selektiv Reklam AB**
Box 68, 183 21 Taby 1, Sweden.
● Hon & Han. s-a. ISSN 0018-4500

**SIDA**
*see* Sweden. Styrelsen Foer Internationell
Utveckling

**Skandinavisk Byggfackpress AB**
Observatoriegatan 12, Box 6114, S-102 32
Stockholm 6, Sweden.
● Byggnadstidningen/Building News. w. ISSN 0007-
7607

**Skandinavisk Emballage- och Transport- Tidskrift**
Box 15023, 161 15 Bromma, Sweden.
● Skandinavisk Emballage- och Transport- Tidskrift.
m. ISSN 0037-6078

**Skandinaviska Enskilda Banken**
Kungstraedgaardsgatan 8, S-106 40 Stockholm,
Sweden.
● Skandinaviska Enskilda Banken Quarterly Review.
q. ISSN 0347-3120

**Skattebetalarnas Foerening**
Box 7087, S-103 82 Stockholm, Sweden.
● Sunt Foernuft. 10 per yr. ISSN 0039-5455

**Aktiebolaget SKF**
S-415 50 Goeteborg, Sweden.
● Kullagertidningen. q. ISSN 0347-1748

**Georg P. Skogberg**
Sveavaegen 74, 113 59 Stockholm, Sweden.
● Mat Foer Millioner; organ foer storhushaall. bi-m.
● Traktoeren; tidning foer hotell, restaurang- och
noejesliv. m (10 per yr.) ISSN 0041-0969

**Skolledarfoerbundet**
Sveavaegen 98, 113 50 Stockholm, Sweden.
● Skolledaren. m. ISSN 0037-6515

**Spraakfoerlaget Skriptor**
Fack, 104 65 Stockholm, Sweden.
- SMIL (Journal of Linguistic Calculus) q.

**Socialmedicinsk Tidskrift**
Fack, 104 01 Stockholm 60, Sweden.
- Socialmedicinsk Tidskrift. m.(10 per yr.) ISSN 0037-833X

**Society for the Promoting of Emigration Research**
Box 331, S-651 05 Karlstad, Sweden.
- Bridge/Bryggan. q.

**Soedra Skogsaegarna**
S-351 89, Vaxjo 1, Sweden.
- Soedra-Kontakt. m.

**South-Swedish Geographical Society**
- Svensk Geografisk Aarsbok. (pub. by LiberLaeromedel)

**Sparfraemjandet**
Fack, S-103 20 Stockholm 16, Sweden.
- Ekonomisk Debatt/Economic Debate. 8 per yr. (Nationalekonomiska Foereningen)
- Sparbankerna. 15 per yr. ISSN 0346-1602 (Svenska Sparbanksfoereningen)

**Specialtidningsfoerlaget AB**
Sveavaegen 53, S-105 44 Stockholm, Sweden.
- Allt i Hemmet. m. ISSN 0002-6182
- Allt Om Mat/All About Food and Cooking. 16 per yr. ISSN 0002-6204
- Baatnytt/Boating News. 15 per yr. ISSN 0005-6308
- Dagens Industri. s-w (86 per yr) ISSN 0346-640X
- Radio & Television. 11 per yr. ISSN 0033-7749
- Sveriges 1000 Stoersta Foeretag/1000 Largest Companies in Sweden. a.
- Teknikens Vaerld; allt om bilen. fortn.
- Veckans Affaerer; den aktuella affarstidningen. w. ISSN 0506-4406

**Statens Geotekniska Institut**
Fack, 581 01 Linkoeping, Sweden.
- Statens Geotekniska Institut. Rapports/Swedish Geotechnical Institute. Reports. irreg.

**Statens Humanistiska Forskningsraad**
- Humanistisk Forskning. (pub. by Liber Foerlag)

**Statens Naturvetenskapliga Forskningsraad**
*see* Sweden. Statens Naturvetenskapliga Forskningsraad

**Statsanstaelldas Foerbund**
Barnhusgatan 8, Stockholm, Sweden.
- Statsanstaelld. w (40 per yr.) ISSN 0039-0712

**Statsfoeretag AB**
Fack, S-103 40 Stockholm, Sweden.
- Statsfoeretag. Aarsredovisning. a.

**Frank Stenvalls Foerlag**
Malmgatan 3, S-211 32 Malmoe, Sweden.
- Nordens Jaernvaegar. a.
- Railway Scene. bi-m. ISSN 0347-030X

**Stiftelsen Biblicum**
S. Rudbecksgatan 6, 752 36 Uppsala, Sweden.
- Biblicum; tidskrift foer biblisk tro och forskning. q (plus 3 supplements) ISSN 0345-1453

**Stiftelsen Elementa**
Stabby Alle 13, S-752 29 Uppsala, Sweden.
- Elementa; tidskrift for matematik, fysik och kemi. q. ISSN 0013-5933

**Stiftelsen Kyrkligt Forum**
Box 12041, S-750 12 Uppsala 12, Sweden.
- Svensk Pastoral Tidskrift. s-w. ISSN 0039-6699

**Stiftelsen Ord och Bild**
Box 15116, 104 65 Stockholm, Sweden.
- Ord och Bild/Words and Pictures. 8 per yr. ISSN 0030-4492

**Stiftelsen Svensk Livsmedelsteknik**
Katarinavaegen 20, 116 48 Stockholm, Sweden.
- Livsmedelsteknik; tidskrift foer livsmedelsfoeraedling och naeringsfraagor. 9 per yr. ISSN 0024-5399

**Stockholm Concert Hall Foundation**
Box 40083, S-103 42 Stockholm, Sweden.
- Konsertnytt. fortn. ISSN 0023-3560

**Stockholm International Peace Research Institute**
Sveavaegen 166, S-113 46 Stockholm, Sweden.
- Stockholm International Peace Research Institute. Report of Activities. irreg.

**Stockholms Handelskammare**
Vaestra Traedgaardsgatan 9, Box 16050, S-103 22 Stockholm, Sweden.
- Handelskammartidningen. fortn. ISSN 0345-4495

**Stockholms Ortodoxa Institut**
- Ortodox Kyrkotidning. (pub. by Ortodox Kyrkotidnings Foerlag)

**Stockholms Universitet**
Fack, 104 05 Stockholm, Sweden
- Gaudeamus. fortn.(Sept.-June) ISSN 0016-5247 (Orders to: Box 6801, 113 86 Stockholm, Sweden)
- Scandinavian Studies in Law. (pub. by Almqvist & Wiksell International)
- Stockholm Studies in Russian Literature. irreg. (Orders to: Bibliotek, Odengatan 59, Box 6404, Stockholm, Sweden)

**Stockholms Universitet. Department of Political Science**
Fack, S-104 05 Stockholm 5, Sweden.
- Stockholm Studies in Politics. irreg., no. 7, 1975. ISSN 0085-6762

**Stockholms Universitet. Institute of Linguistics**
Drottninggatan 116, Box 6801, S-113 86 Stockholm, Sweden.
- Stockholms Universitet. Institute of Linguistics. Monographs. irreg, vol. 2, 1975.

**Stockholms Universitet. Institutionen Foer Nationalekonomi**
- Scandinavian Journal of Economics. (pub. by Almqvist & Wiksell International)

**Stockholms Universitet. Psykologiska Institutionen**
Box 6706, S-113 85 Stockholm, Sweden.
- Stockholms Universitet. Psykologiska Institutionen. Report Series. irreg. (approx. 30 per yr.) ISSN 0081-5756
- Stockholms Universitet. Psykologiska Institutionen. Reports. Supplement Series. irreg. (approx. 5 per yr.) ISSN 0345-021X

**Stockholms Universitet. Socialantropologiska Institutionen**
Fack, S-104 05 Stockholm 50, Sweden.
- Antropologiska Studier. q. (Co-sponsor: Antropologfoereningen)

**Stroembergs Idrottsboecker**
Vittangigatan 27, Vaellingby, Stockholm, Sweden.
- Aarets Ishockey. irreg. (Svenska Ishockeyfoerbundet)

**Styrelsen Foer Svenska Kyrkan i Utlandet**
Box 22047, 104 22 Stockholm 22, Sweden.
- Ute och Hemma; tidning for Svenskt sjoefolk. m. ISSN 0042-1553

**Svensk Bergs- och Brukstidning**
Kungsbroplan 1, 112 27 Stockholm, Sweden.
- Svensk Bergs- och Brukstidning. irreg. (10-12 per yr.) ISSN 0039-6435

**Tidnings AB Svensk Bokhandel**
Klara Norra Kyrkogatan 34, S-111 22 Stockholm, Sweden.
- Svensk Bokforteckning/Swedish National Bibliography. m. ISSN 0039-6443 (Sweden. Kungliga Biblioteket. Bibliografiska Institutet)
- Svensk Bokhandel. w. ISSN 0039-6451 (Svenska Bokfoerlaeggarefoereningen) (Co-sponsor: Svenska Bokhandlarefoereningens)

**Svensk Bridge**
Box 106, 733 00 Sala, Sweden.
- Svensk Bridge. m. ISSN 0039-6478

**Svensk Handelstidning Justita**
Box 16141, 103 23 Stockholm 16, Sweden.
- Svensk Handelstidning Justita. w. ISSN 0039-6575

**Svensk Husdjursskoetsel**
633 84 Eskilstuna, Sweden.
- Husdjur. 11 per yr. ISSN 0046-8339

**Svensk Leveranstidning AB**
Sorterargatan 9-11, Box 144, 162 12 Vaellingby, Sweden.
- Leveranstidningen Entreprenad. w. ISSN 0345-7133

**AB Svensk Papperstidning**
Villagatan 1, S-114 32 Stockholm, Sweden.
- Svensk Papperstidning; Swedish paper journal. 18 per yr. ISSN 0039-6680 (Svenska Cellulosa- och Papperbruksfoereningen) (Co-sponsor: Svenska Papers- och Cellulosaingenioersfoereningen)

**Foerlags AB Svensk Tidskrift**
Linnegatan 28-30, IV, 114 47 Stockholm, Sweden.
- Svensk Tidskrift. 10 per yr. ISSN 0039-677X

**AB Svensk Traevarutidning**
Box 1724, 111 87 Stockholm, Sweden.
- Handbook of the Northern Wood Industries. biennial. ISSN 0072-9922
- Saagverken/Sawmills. m. ISSN 0036-259X
- Svensk Traevaru- och Papersmassetidning/Swedish Timber and Wood Pulp Journal. m. ISSN 0039-6796
- Traeindustrin/Woodworking Industry. m.

**Svensk Visarkiv**
- Svensk Visarkiv. Handlingar. (pub. by Almqvist & Wiksell International)
- Svensk Visarkiv. Meddelanden. (pub. by Almqvist & Wiksell International)
- Svensk Visarkiv. Skrifter. (pub. by Almqvist & Wiksell International)

**Svenska Aakerifoerbundet**
Fack, 100 41 Stockholm 26, Sweden.
- Lastbilen. m. ISSN 0023-8678

**Svenska Allmaenflygfoereningen**
- Flyghorisont. (pub. by Flygfoerlaget AB)

**Svenska Arbetsgivarefoereningen**
Box 16 120, 103 23 Stockholm 16, Sweden.
- Arbetsgivaren. w. ISSN 0044-8567
- Ekonomiska Laeget. s-a. ISSN 0013-3175
- Sweden Now. (pub. by Ingenjoersfoerlaget AB)

**Svenska Arkitekters Riksfoerbund**
Odengatan 3, 114 24 Stockholm, Sweden.
- A T. (Arkitekttidningen) 20 per yr. ISSN 0004-2005

**Svenska Arkitektfoereningen**
- Byggmaestaren. (pub. by Byggfoerlaget)
- Swedish Review of Architecture. (pub. by AB Byggmaestarens Foerlag)

**Svenska Arkivsamfundet**
Riksarkivet, Fack, 100 26 Stockholm 34, Sweden.
- Svenska Arkivsamfundet. Skriftserie. a., no. 17, 1975. ISSN 0562-7451

**Svenska Armens och Flygvapnets Reserfofficersfoerbund**
Karlavaegen 65, 114 49 Stockholm, Sweden.
- Reservbefal; tidskrift for reservofficerare. bi-m. ISSN 0034-5490

**Svenska Bankfoereningen**
Box 16143, S-103 23 Stockholm, Sweden.
- Svensk Obligationsbok. a.
- Svenska Bank Foereningen. Ekonomisk Revy. 10 per yr. ISSN 0013-3167
- Svenska Bankfoereningen. Ekonomiska Meddelanden. w.

**Svenska Bankmannafoerbundet**
Box 7009, 103 81 Stockholm 7, Sweden.
- Bankvaerlden. m. ISSN 0005-5549

**Svenska Barnmorskefoerbundet**
Flintbacken 30, 117 42 Stockholm, Sweden.
- Jordemodern. m. ISSN 0021-7468

**Svenska Bibliotekariesamfundet**
c/o Hallberg, Linkoping University Library, Fack, S-581 83 Linkoeping, Sweden.
- Bibliotekariesamfundet Meddelar. 4 per yr.

**Svenska Blaa Stjaernan**
Torstenssonsgatan 12, 114 56 Stockholm, Sweden.
- Blaa Stjaernan. q. ISSN 0006-4076

**Svenska Bokfoerlaeggarefoereningen**
Klara Norra Kyrkogatan 34, S-111 22 Stockholm,
Sweden.
- Svensk Bokhandel. (pub. by Tidnings AB Svensk
Bokhandel)
- Svenska Bokfoerlaeggarefoereningen. Matrikel. a.
ISSN 0081-9859

**AB Svenska Bostaeder**
Box 95, 162 12 Vaellingby 1, Sweden.
- Fasaden. q.

**Svenska Botaniska Foereningen**
Universitetets Botaniska Institution, Lilla Frescati,
S-104 05 Stockholm 50, Sweden.
- Svensk Botanisk Tidskrift. q. ISSN 0039-646X

**Svenska Brandfoersvarsfoereningen**
Kungsholms Hamnplan 3, S-112 20 Stockholm,
Sweden.
- Brandfoersvar. m. ISSN 0006-9051

**Svenska Bustrafikfoerbundet**
Nybrogatan 7, S-114 34 Stockholm, Sweden.
- Svensk Omnibustidning. 10 per yr. ISSN 0039-
6672

**Svenska Byggnadsarbetarefoerbundet**
Box 19013, 104 32 Stockholm 19, Sweden.
- Byggnadsarbetaren. 35 per yr. ISSN 0007-7569

**Svenska Byggnadsingenjoerers Riksfoerbund**
Box 1717, 111 87 Stockholm, Sweden.
- Husbyggaren. m. ISSN 0018-7968

**Svenska Cellulosa Aktiebolaget**
Skepparplatsen 1, 851 88 Sundsvall, Sweden.
- S C A-Tidningen. m. ISSN 0036-1119

**Svenska Cellulosa- och Papperbruksfoereningen**
- Svensk Papperstidning. (pub. by AB Svensk
Papperstidning)

**Svenska Civilekonomfoereningen**
Arsenalsgatan 4, 111 47 Stockholm, Sweden.
- Ekonomen. m. ISSN 0013-2977

**Svenska Curlingfoerbundet**
Grevturegatan 18, S-114 46 Stockholm, Sweden.
- Curling. 4 per yr. ISSN 0011-3107

**Svenska Djurskddsfoereningen**
Birger Jarlsgatan 36, 114 29 Stockholm, Sweden.
- Djur-Expressen. 4 per yr. ISSN 0012-432X

**Svenska Doevlaerarsaellskapet**
Svampvaegen 167, 122 33 Enskede, Sweden.
- Nordisk Tidskrift Foer Doevundervisningen. q.
ISSN 0029-1471

**Svenska Ekumeniska Naemnden**
190 30 Sigtuna, Sweden.
- Social Debatt i Tidningar och Tidskrifter. 5 per yr.
ISSN 0037-7708

**Svenska Eldbegaengelsefoereningen**
Box 19071, 104 32 Stockholm 19, Sweden.
- Ignis. m. ISSN 0019-1698

**Svenska Elverksfoereningen**
Box 6405, 113 82 Stockholm, Sweden.
- E R A. m. ISSN 0013-9939
- El. 3 per yr. ISSN 0013-399X

**Svenska Esperanto-Foerbundet**
Fack, S-122 04 Stockholm-Enskede, Sweden.
- Espero; Svenska Esperanto-tidningen. 8 per yr.
ISSN 0014-0694

**Svenska Faangvaardssaellskapet**
Box 418, 801 05 Gavle, Sweden.
- Tidskrift Foer Kriminalvaard. q. ISSN 0040-6821

**Svenska Faaravelsfoerbundet**
Parkgatan 14, S-112 30 Stockholm, Sweden.
- Faarskoetsel. 10 per yr. ISSN 0014-8598

**Svenska Fabriksarbetarefoerbundet**
Box 1114, 111 81 Stockholm, Sweden.
- Fabriksarbetaren. 19 per yr. ISSN 0014-6234

**Svenska Facklaerarfoerbundet**
Box 15023, 161 15 Bromma, Sweden.
- Facklaeraren. s-m. ISSN 0014-6463

**Svenska Faunistiska Saellskapet**
Box 6038, 113 86 Stockholm 6, Sweden.
- Zoologisk Revy. q. ISSN 0044-5258

**Svenska Filminstitutet**
P.O. Box 27126, S-102 52 Stockholm, Sweden.
- Chaplin. bi-m. ISSN 0045-6349
- Filmaarsboken/Swedish Film Annual. a. ISSN
0071-4925
- Svenska Filminstitutet.
Dokumentationsavdelningen. Skrifter. irreg., no.
20, 1976. ISSN 0081-9867

**A B Svenska Flaktfabriken**
Box 20-040, S-104 60 Stockholm 20, Sweden.
- Flakten. a. ISSN 0015-3400

**Svenska Flottledsfoerbundet**
Aaraasvaegen 7, 680 30 Raada, Sweden.
- Svenska Flottledsfoerbundet. Aarsbok. a. ISSN
0081-9875

**Svenska Foeretagares Riksfoerbund**
Odengatan 87, S-113 22 Stockholm, Sweden.
- Foeretagaren/Enterpriser. 15 per yr. ISSN 0015-
5276

**Svenska Foersaekringsfoereningen**
Birger Jarlsgatan 5, S-111 45 Stockholm, Sweden.
- Nordisk Foersaekringstidskrift/Scandinavian
Insurance Journal. q. ISSN 0029-1358
- Svensk Foersaekrings-Aarsbok. a. ISSN 0081-9794

**Svenska Folkhoegskolans Laerarfoerbund**
821 00 Bollanes, Sweden.
- Tidskrift Foer Svenska Folkhoegskolan. q. ISSN
0040-6899

**Svenska Forskningsinstitutet Foer Cement och Betong**
see Cement- och Betonginstitutet

**Svenska Fotografernas Foerbund**
Nytorgsgatan 17, S-116 22 Stockholm, Sweden.
- Svensk Fotografisk Tidskrift. 8 per yr. ISSN 0039-
6540

**Svenska Fraelsningsarmen**
Sibyllegatan 18, S-114 42 Stockholm, Sweden.
- Vaar Fana. s-m. ISSN 0042-2010

**Svenska Fri-Idrottsfoerbundet**
- Friidrott. (pub. by Cewe-Foerlaget)

**Svenska Gaangfoerbundet**
Fack, 104 40 Stockholm, Sweden.
- Gaangsport. m. ISSN 0016-3678

**Svenska Gasfoereningen**
Norrtullsgatan 6, Box 6405, S-113 82 Stockholm 6,
Sweden.
- Gasnytt. q. ISSN 0039-6834

**Svenska Geofysiska Foerening**
- Tellus. (pub. by Munksgaard DK)

**Svenska Gymnastikfoerbundet**
Box 22076, 104 22 Stockholm, Sweden.
- Gymnastikledaren. 10 per yr. ISSN 0017-5978

**Svenska Handelsbanken**
Arsenalsgatan 11, Box 12128, S-102 24 Stockholm,
Sweden.
- Svenska Handelsbanken. Annual Report. a. ISSN
0081-9913

**Svenska Industritjaenstemanna Foerbundet**
Box 5104, 102 43 Stockholm 5, Sweden.
- Industritjaenstemannen. m. ISSN 0019-9427

**Svenska Institutet**
Hamngatan 27, Box 7072, S-103 82 Stockholm,
Sweden
- Current Sweden; environment planning and
conservation. 8 per yr. (U.S. Distributor: Swedish
Information Service, 825 Third Ave., New York,
NY 10022)
- New Swedish Books. irreg.

**Svenska Ishockeyfoerbundet**
- Aarets Ishockey. (pub. by Stroembergs
Idrottsboecker)
- Hockey. (pub. by Cewe-Foerlaget)

**Svenska Jaegarefoerbundet**
Box 39049, S-100 54 Stockholm 39, Sweden.
- Svensk Jakt. m. ISSN 0039-6583

**Svenska Jaernvaegsklubben**
Klackvaegen 43, S-126 39 Haegersten, Sweden.
- Taag/Trains. m.(10 per yr) ISSN 0039-8683

**Svenska Journalistforbundet**
Vegagatan 4, 113 29 Stockholm, Sweden.
- Journalisten. m. ISSN 0022-5592

**Svenska Kanotfoerbundet**
Sveavaegen 25-27, 111 34 Stockholm, Sweden.
- Kanot-Nytt. m. ISSN 0022-8397

**Svenska Kemistsamfundet**
- Kemisk Tidskrift. (pub. by Ingenjoersfoerlaget AB)

**Svenska Kennel Klubben**
Box 1308, 111 83 Stockholm, Sweden.
- Hundsport. m. ISSN 0018-7690

**Svenska Kommunaltekniska Foreningen**
Kungsgatan 65, III, S-111 22 Stockholm C, Sweden.
- Stadsbyggnad. 12 per yr. ISSN 0038-8963

**Svenska Kommunfoerbundet**
Hornsgatan 15, 116 47 Stockholm, Sweden.
- Hygien och Miljoe; tidskrift foer
haelsovaardsnaemnder. m.(except July & Aug.)
- Kommunal Skoltidning/Municipal Educational
Review; tidskrift foer skolstyrelser och skolledare.
m.(except Jan., July & Aug.) ISSN 0023-3064
- Kommunal Tidskrift/Municipal Review. 20 per yr.
ISSN 0023-3072
- Paa Fritid/In Leisure Time. m(9 per yr)
- Socialt Forum. 10 per yr. ISSN 0049-0970

**Svenska Kraftverksfoereningen**
Box 1704, 111 87 Stockholm, Sweden.
- Svenska Kraftverksfoereningens Publikationer. 12
per yr. ISSN 0039-6931

**Svenska Kryssarklubben**
Lillaengsvaegan 10A, 114 49 Stockholm, Sweden.
- Paa Kryss och till Rors. 11 per yr. (Co-sponsors:
Royal Swedish Yachting Association; Swedish
Boat Union)

**Svenska Kyrkans Centralraad**
Fack, 104 32 Stockholm 19, Sweden.
- Vaar Kyrka. w. ISSN 0042-2673

**Svenska Kyrkans Foersamlings- och
Pastoratsfoerbund**
Box 1737, S-111 87 Stockholm, Sweden.
- Foersamlings- och Pastoratsfoervaltning. 10 per yr.
ISSN 0015-5284

**Svenska Kyrkohistoriska Foereningen**
Box 511, 751 20 Uppsala, Sweden.
- Kyrkohistorisk Aarsskrift. a. ISSN 0085-2619

**Svenska Laboratorieassistentfoereningen**
Fack, S-100 41 Stockholm, Sweden.
- Laboratoriet. m. except Jul-Aug.
- Tidskriften Laboratoriet. m.(except July & Aug.)
ISSN 0040-6996

**Svenska Livsmedelsinstitutet**
Fack, S-400 21 Goeteborg 16, Sweden.
- S I K Information. irreg.

**Svenska Lokaltrafikfoereningen**
Box 6301, S-113 81 Stockholm, Sweden.
- Svensk Lokaltrafik. 8 per yr. ISSN 0039-6648

**Svenska Maskinbefaelsfoerbundet**
Barnhusgatan 3, Box 3157, 103 63 Stockholm,
Sweden.
- Maskinbefaelet. 9 per yr. ISSN 0025-4622

**Svenska Mejeriernas Riksfoerening**
Postfack, S-101 10 Stockholm 1, Sweden.
- Nordisk Mejeriindustri/Scandinavian Journal of
Dairy Technology. (pub. by Nordisk
Mejeriindustri AB)
- Svenska Mejeriernas Riksfoerening. Meddelande.
irreg., no. 94, 1973. ISSN 0039-6869

**Svenska Metallindustriarbetarefoerbundet**
Vasagatan 11, Box 1144, 111 81 Stockholm,
Sweden.
- Metallarbetaren. w. ISSN 0026-0754

**Svenska Missionsfoerbundet**
Box 6302, 113 81 Stockholm, Sweden.
- Svensk Veckotidning. w. ISSN 0039-6826

**Svenska Mongol- och Japanmissionen**
Brunnsgatan 4, 111 38 Stockholm, Sweden.
- Ljusglimtar. m (10 per yr.) ISSN 0024-5410

**Svenska Museifoereningen**
c/o Stockholms Stadsmuseum, Peter Myndes Backe
6, S-116 46 Stockholm, Sweden.
- Svenska Museer. 4 per yr. ISSN 0039-6885

**Svenska Musikerfoerbundet**
Box 102, S-126 22 Haegersten 1, Sweden.
- Musikern. 11 per yr. ISSN 0027-478X

**Svenska Naturskyddsfoereningen**
Kungsholms Strand 125, S-112 34 Stockholm,
Sweden.
- Sveriges Natur. bi-m (plus yearbook) ISSN 0039-6974

**Svenska Numismatiska Foereningen**
Oestermalmsgatan 81, 114 50 Stockholm, Sweden.
- Numismatiska Meddelanden/Numismatic
Communications. irreg. ISSN 0078-2734

**Svenska Oesterbottens Litteraturfoerening**
c/o Harry Jaerv, Fyrverkarbacken 32, S-112 60
Stockholm, Sweden.
- Horisont. 6 per yr. ISSN 0018-4950

**Svenska Pappershandlarefoereningen**
Skeppargatan 27, S-114 52 Stockholm, Sweden.
- Pappershandlaren. fortn. ISSN 0031-1456

**Svenska Ponnyavelsforbundet**
Tjaerbyhus, S-312 00 Laholm, Sweden.
- Vaar Ponny. q. ISSN 0346-4687

**AB Svenska Pressbyraan**
Fack, 104 25 Stockholm 30, Sweden.
- Tidnings Nytt. m. ISSN 0040-6805

**Svenska Reklambyraa Foerbundet**
Box 3160, Luntmakargatan 66, 103 63 Stockholm 3,
Sweden.
- S R F Resume. m. ISSN 0036-1887

**Svenska Restauratoerfoerbundet**
Rehnsgatan 21 NB, 113 57 Stockholm, Sweden.
- Comple. bi-m. ISSN 0010-4299

**Svenska Riksteatern**
Raasundav 150, S-171 30 Solna, Sweden.
- Entre; teatertidskrift. 6 per yr.
- Teatern. 4 per yr. ISSN 0040-0750

**Svenska Roeda Korset**
Box 143, 162 12 Vaellingby 1, Sweden.
- Vaart Roeda Kors. q. ISSN 0042-2819

**Svenska Saellskapet Foer Antropologi och Geografi**
- Geografiska Annaler. Series A. Physical
Geography. (pub. by Almqvist & Wiksell
International)
- Geografiska Annaler. Series B. Human
Geography. (pub. by Almqvist & Wiksell
International)
- Ymer. (pub. by Generalstabens Lithografiske
Anstalt)

**Svenska Saellskapshundklubben**
Bergtallsvaegen 1, S-752 56 Uppsala, Sweden.
- Vaara Hundar. m. ISSN 0042-269X

**Svenska Samfundet foer Musikforskning**
Strandvaegen 82, 115 27 Stockholm, Sweden.
- Monumenta Musicae Suecicae. irreg., vol. 8, 1977.
ISSN 0077-1473
- Svensk Tidskrift foer Musikforskning/Swedish
Journal of Musicology. s-a. ISSN 0081-9816

**Svenska Skidfoerbundet**
- Svensk Skidsport. (pub. by Cewe Foerlaget)

**Svenska Socialvaardsfoerbundet**
Hornsgatan 15, Stockholm, Sweden.
- Svenska Socialvaardsfoerbundets Tidskrift. bi-m.

**Svenska Sockerfabriks AB**
Box 17050, S-200 10 Malmoe 17, Sweden.
- Socker Handlingar/Sugar; communications from
the Swedish Sugar Corporation. irreg. ISSN 0038-0466

**Svenska Sparbanksfoereningen**
- Sparbankerna. (pub. by Sparfraemjandet)

**Svenska Spraaknaemnden**
- Spraakvaard. (pub. by Esselte Studium AB)

**Svenska Svinavelsfoereningen**
Bondgaardsgatan 3 C, S-692 00 Kumla, Sweden.
- Svinskoetsel. m (10 per yr.) ISSN 0346-2471

**Svenska Taxifoerbundet**
Raadmannsgatan 48, 113 57 Stockholm, Sweden.
- Taxitrafiken. m. ISSN 0040-022X

**Svenska Tennisfoerbundets**
Box 19022, 104 32 Stockholm, Sweden.
- Tennis Tidningen. 10 per yr. ISSN 0040-3431

**Svenska Tidningsutgivarefoereningen**
- Pressens Tidning. (pub. by TU: S Foerlags AB)

**Svenska Traeforskningsinstitutet**
Box 5604, S-114 86 Stockholm, Sweden.
- Svenska Traeforskningsinstitutet. Meddelande.
Series A. irreg. ISSN 0085-6983

**Svenska Traeskyddsinstitutet**
Drottning Kristinas Vaegen 47 C, S-114 280
Stockholm, Sweden.
- Svenska Traeskyddinstitutet. Meddelanden.
Reports. irreg., no. 111, 1974. ISSN 0081-5748

**Svenska Transportarbetarefoerbundet**
Vasagatan 11, Box 158, 101 22 Stockholm, Sweden.
- Transportarbetaren. m (11 per yr.) ISSN 0492-004X

**Svenska Turistfoereningen**
Stureplan 2, 103 80 Stockholm, Sweden.
- Turist. 6 per yr. ISSN 0041-4190

**Svenska U N Foerbundet**
Box 15050, S-104 65 Stockholm 15, Sweden.
- Vaerldshorisont. bi-m. ISSN 0042-2134

**Svenska Ungdomsringen Foer Bygdekultur**
Box 4030, S-102 61 Stockholm, Sweden.
- Hembygden; tidning foer folkdans och folkmusik.
6 per yr. ISSN 0018-0262

**Svenska Utbildningsfoerlaget Liber**
Norr Maalarstrand 24, Fack, 104 22 Stockholm,
Sweden.
- Sweden. Universitetskanslersaembetet. Hoegre
Utbildning och Forskning. a.

**Svenska Vaeg- och Vattenbyggares Riksfoerbund**
Box 1334, S-111 83 Stockholm, Sweden.
- Vaeg- och Vattenbyggaren. 9 per yr. ISSN 0042-2177

**Svenska Vaegfoereningens Foerlags AB**
Fridhemsgatan 15, 112 40 Stockholm K, Sweden.
- Svenska Vaegfoereningens Tidskrift. bi-m. ISSN
0039-6923

**Svenska Vaextgeografiska Saellskapet**
c/o Vaextbiologiska Institutionen, Box 559, 751 22
Uppsala, Sweden.
- Acta Phytogeographica Suecica. irreg., vol. 62,
1975. ISSN 0084-5914
- Vaextekologiska Studier. irreg., no. 10, 1977.

**Svenska Yrkesutbildningsfoereningen**
Box 172, 771 01 Ludvika 1, Sweden.
- Tidskrift Foer Yrkesutbildning. 9 per yr. ISSN
0040-6856

**Svenskt Musikhistoriskt Arkiv**
Strandvaegen 82, S-115 27 Stockholm, Sweden.
- Musik i Sverige/Music in Sweden. irreg. ISSN
0077-2518 (Co-sponsor: Svenska Samfundet Foer
Musikforskning)
- Svensk Musikhistorisk Arkiv. Bulletin. irreg
(approx. 1 per yr.) ISSN 0586-0709

**Aktiebolaget Sverige-Nytt**
Skeppargatan 37, S-114 52 Stockholm, Sweden.
- Sverige-Nytt/Swedish Digest. w. ISSN 0039-6958

**Sveriges Advokatsamfund**
Box 1339, 111 83 Stockholm, Sweden.
- Foerteckning Oever Advokater och
Advokatbyraer. a.
- Sveriges Advokatsamfund. Tidskrift. 10 per yr.
ISSN 0040-6902

**Sveriges Allmaenna Biblioteksfoerening**
Fack, 221 01 Lund 1, Sweden.
- Biblioteksbladet/Library Journal. 18 per yr. ISSN
0006-1867

**Sveriges Arbetsledarefoerbund**
Box 12069, 102 22 Stockholm 12, Sweden.
- Arbetsledaren. m. ISSN 0003-7842

**Sveriges Bagerifoerbund**
Hovslagargatan 5, 111 48 Stockholm, Sweden.
- Broed-Konditorn; facktidskrift foer bagare och
konditorer. m (11 per yr.) ISSN 0345-181X

**Sveriges Biodlares Riksforbund**
Box 91, 590 20 Mantorp, Sweden.
- Bitidningen. m. ISSN 0006-3886

**Sveriges Civilfoersvarsfoerbund**
- Civilt Foersvar. (pub. by Civilfoersvarsfoerbundets
Foerlags AB)

**Sveriges Civilingenjoersfoerbund**
- Teknisk Tidskrift. (pub. by Ingenjoersfoerlaget
AB)

**Sveriges Djurskyddsfoereningars Riksfoerbund**
Markvardsgatan 10, S-113 53 Stockholm, Sweden.
- Djurskyddet. bi-m. ISSN 0012-4346

**Sveriges Doevas Riksfoerbund**
Fack, 793 01 Leksand, Sweden.
- S D R-Kontakt. bi-m. ISSN 0036-1194

**Sveriges Exportraad**
Box 5513, S-114 85 Stockholm, Sweden.
- Svensk Export. 6 per yr. ISSN 0039-6508

**Sveriges Faerghandlares Riksfoerbund**
105 61 Stockholm, Sweden.
- Svensk Faerghandel. 9 per yr. ISSN 0039-6516

**Sveriges Farmacevtfoerbund**
Nybrogatan 30, Box 5182, S-102 44 Stockholm,
Sweden.
- Farmacevtisk Revy. 24 per yr. ISSN 0014-8210

**Sveriges Fartygsbefaelsfoerening**
Skeppsbron 32, S-111 30 Stockholm, Sweden.
- Nautisk Tidskrift. m.(except July & Aug.) ISSN
0028-1379

**Sveriges Fastighetsaagarefoerbund**
Sveavaegen 24, 5 Tr., 111 57 Stockholm, Sweden.
- Svensk Fastighetstidning. m (11 per yr.) ISSN
0346-2064

**Sveriges Filatelist-Foerbund**
Birger Jarlsgatan 18 B, 114 34 Stockholm, Sweden.
- Svensk Filatelistisk Tidskrift. m. ISSN 0039-6532

**Sveriges Fiskares Riksfoerbund**
Box 4036, S-400 40 Goeteborg 4, Sweden.
- Yrkesfiskaren. s-m. ISSN 0347-4275

**Sveriges Foerenade Filmstudios**
Ringvaegen 54, S-181 34 Lidingoe, Sweden.
- Filmrutan. q. ISSN 0015-1661

**Sveriges Foereningsbankers Foerbund**
Fack, S-102 40 Stockholm, Sweden.
- Foereningsbankerna. bi-m. ISSN 0346-9670

**Sveriges Foerfattarfoerbund**
Box 5252, 102 45 Stockholm 5, Sweden.
- Foerfattaren. ISSN 0025-8547
- Sveriges Foerfattarfoerbund. Medlemsfoerteckning.

**Sveriges Foerskollaerares Riksfoerbund**
Box 5522, 114 85 Stockholm, Sweden.
- Foerskolan. 10 per yr. ISSN 0015-5292

**Sveriges Fritidsfiskares Riksfoerbund**
- Svenskt Fiske. (pub. by Fritidsfiskarna)

**Sveriges Froeodlarefoerbund**
Box 161, 201 21 Malmoe, Sweden
(Subscr. to: Grubbensgatan 2, S-702 25 Oerebro,
Sweden)
- Svensk Froetidning. m (11 per yr.) ISSN 0346-2099 (Co-sponsor: Sveriges Oljevaextodlares
Central Foerening)

**Sveriges Gjuteritekniska Foerening**
- Gjuteriet. (pub. by Branschtidningsfoerlaget)

**Sveriges Glas- och Porslinshandlarefoerbund**
Jakobsbergsgatan 23, S-111 44 Stockholm, Sweden.
- Glas och Porslin. m. ISSN 0017-078X

**Sveriges Grossistfoerbund**
Box 5512, 114 85 Stockholm, Sweden.
- Svensk Handel. q. ISSN 0039-6567

**Sveriges Handelsagenters Foerbund**
Hantverkargatan 46, S-112 21 Stockholm, Sweden.
- Vaerldsmarknad. q. ISSN 0042-2142

**Sveriges Hotell- och Restaurangfoerbund**
Kungsgatan 62, 2 tr., 111 22 Stockholm, Sweden.
- Restauratoeren. m. ISSN 0034-5814 (Co-sponsor:
  Sveriges Arbetsgivarefoerening Foer Hotell och
  Restauranger)

**Sveriges Jaernhandlarefoerbund**
Tortenssonsgatan 12, 114 56 Stockholm, Sweden.
- Jaernhandlaren. s-m. ISSN 0021-552X

**Sveriges Juvelerare- och Guldsmedsfoerbund**
Nytorgsgatan 170, S-116 22 Stockholm, Sweden.
- Svensk Guldsmeds-Tidning. m. ISSN 0039-6559

**Sveriges Koepmannafoerbund**
- Koepmannen. (pub. by Koepmannens Foerlags
  AB)

**Sveriges Kontoristfoerening**
Box 1341, S-111 83 Stockholm, Sweden.
- Kontorsvaerlden. q. ISSN 0023-3722

**Sveriges Korfoerbund**
Grev Magnigatan 9, 114 55 Stockholm, Sweden.
- Musiklivet-Vaar Sang. q. ISSN 0027-4836

**Sveriges Laekarfoerbund**
Box 5610, S-114 86 Stockholm, Sweden.
- Laekartidningen. w. ISSN 0023-7205

**Sveriges Laerarfoerbund**
Box 12239, S-102 26 Stockholm 12, Sweden.
- Aarsbok foer Skolan. a. ISSN 0065-0196
- Laerartidningen; Svensk skoltidning. w. ISSN
  0023-849X

**Sveriges Lantbruksuniversitet. Institutionen Foer
Vaextskydd**
Konsulentavdelningen/Vaextskydd, S-171 07 Solna,
Sweden.
- Vaextskyddsnotiser. 6 per yr. ISSN 0042-2169

**Sveriges Lantmaestarfoerbund**
Vaangavaegen 30, S-260 40 Viken, Sweden.
- Lantmaestaren. q. ISSN 0023-8430

**Sveriges Lantmaetarefoerening**
Box 40037, 103 41 Stockholm, Sweden.
- Svensk Lantmaeteritidskrift/Swedish
  Landsurveying Journal. bi-m. ISSN 0039-6613

**Sveriges Leksakshandlares Riksfoerbund**
Box 3103, 103 62 Stockholm 3, Sweden.
- Svensk Leksaksrevy. 10 per yr. ISSN 0039-6621

**Sveriges Livsmedelshandlarefoerbund**
Box 1311, S-111 83 Stockholm, Sweden.
- Livs. m. ISSN 0024-5380

**Sveriges Maestarefoerening**
Saelgstigen 18, 125 31 Aalvsjae, Sweden.
- Maaleri. 5 per yr. ISSN 0025-1232

**Sveriges Marknadsfoerbund**
Ludvigsbergsgatan 20, 117 26 Stockholm, Sweden.
- Marknaden. 10 per yr. ISSN 0025-3855

**Sveriges Moebelhandlares Centralfoerbund**
Kungsgatan 19, S-105 61 Stockholm, Sweden.
- Moebler och Miljoe. 10 per yr. ISSN 0345-7737

**Sveriges Ornitologiska Foerening**
Runebergsgat. 8, 114 29 Stockholm, Sweden.
- Vaar Faagelvaerld. 4 per yr. ISSN 0042-2649

**Sveriges Paelsdjursuppfoedares Riksfoerbund**
Fack, S-100 31 Stockholm, Sweden.
- Vaara Paelsdjur/Our Furred Animals. 10 per yr.
  ISSN 0042-2703

**Sveriges Radio**
S-105 10 Stockholm, Sweden.
- Audience and Programme Research. 5 per yr.
  ISSN 0044-9989 (prep. by its Audience and
  Program Research Department)
- Nutida Musik/Contemporary Music. q. ISSN
  0029-6597 (Co-sponsor: Institutet foer
  Rikskonserter)
- Roester i Radio-TV. w. ISSN 0035-7839

**Sveriges Radiohandlares Riksfoerbund**
Kloerup, S-231 00 Trelleborg, Sweden.
- Rateko. m. ISSN 0033-9962

**Sveriges Redarefoerening**
Box 53090, S-400 14 Goeteborg 53, Sweden.
- Svensk Sjoefarts Tidning/Swedish Shipping
  Gazette. w. ISSN 0039-6702

**Sveriges Riksbank**
Box 2119, S-103 13 Stockholm 2, Sweden.
- Sveriges Riksbank. Aarsbok. a. ISSN 0081-9972

**Sveriges Riksidrottsfoerbund**
- Svensk Idrott. (pub. by Riksidrottsfoerbundets
  Foerlags AB)

**Sveriges Schackfoerbund**
Box 7123, S-402 32 Goeteborg 7, Sweden.
- Tidskrift Foer Schack. 10 per yr. ISSN 0040-6848

**Sveriges Schaktentreprenoerers Riksfoerbund**
- S E R Tidningen. (pub. by S E R-Schaktkonsult
  AB)

**Sveriges Skogsaegarefoereningars Riksfoerbund**
S-T Eriksgatan 20, Box 12 199, 102 25 Stockholm
12, Sweden.
- Skogsaegaren. m. ISSN 0037-6426

**Sveriges Skogsvaardsfoerbund**
Wallingatan 5, Box 45 166, 104 30 Stockholm,
Sweden.
- Skogen. 15 per yr. ISSN 0037-640X
- Swedish Forestry Association. Magazine. 6 per yr.
  ISSN 0039-730X

**Sveriges Skohandlarfoerbund**
Kungsgatan 19, 111 43 Stockholm, Sweden.
- Skohandlaren. 20 per yr. ISSN 0346-1300

**Sveriges Skorstensfejaremaestares Riksfoerbund**
Styrmansgatan 19, 114 54 Stockholm, Sweden.
- Skorstensfejarmaestaren; tidning for
  sotningsvaesendet. bi-m. ISSN 0346-1351

**Sveriges Skraedderiidkarefoerbund**
Box 16116, 103 23 Stockholm, Sweden.
- Skraedderi. bi-m.

**Sveriges Socialdemokratiska Arbetareparti**
Sveavaegen 68, 105 60 Stockholm, Sweden.
- Aktuellt i Politiken. 20 per yr. ISSN 0345-0635
- Tiden. 10 per yr. ISSN 0040-6759

**Sveriges Socialdemokratiska Kvinnofoerbund**
Box 1317, 111 83 Stockholm, Sweden.
- Morgonbris. 8 per yr. ISSN 0027-1101

**Sveriges Socialdemokratiska Ungdomsfoerbund**
Fack, 121 20 Johanneshov, Sweden.
- Frihet. m. ISSN 0016-142X

**Sveriges Socionomeres Riksfoerbund**
Fack, S-104 32 Stockholm 5, Sweden.
- Socionomen. w. ISSN 0038-044X

**Sveriges Socionomfoerbund**
Box 16195, S-103 24 Stockholm, Sweden.
- Socionomfoerbundets Tidskrift. 20 per yr.

**Sveriges Standardiseringskommission**
Box 3295, S-103 66 Stockholm 3, Sweden.
- Standard. 10 per yr. ISSN 0037-5861

**Sveriges Tandlaekarfoerbund**
Nybrogatan 53, S-114 40 Stockholm, Sweden.
- Swedish Dental Journal. bi-m.
- Tandlaekartidningen. s-m. ISSN 0039-6982

**Sveriges Tapetseraremaestare Centralfoerening**
Box 22064, 104 22 Stockholm, Sweden.
- Svensk Tapetserartidning. m. ISSN 0039-6753

**Sveriges Tegelindustrifoerening**
Birger Jarlsgatan 58, S-111 29 Stockholm, Sweden.
- Tegel. q. ISSN 0040-2117

**Sveriges Textilhandlarefoerbund**
Kungsgatan 19, 105 61 Stockholm, Sweden.
- Textilbranschen. m. ISSN 0040-4888

**Sveriges Trae- och Byggvaruhandlares
Centralfoerbund**
Box 14019, 104 40 Stockholm 14, Sweden.
- S T C Matrikel. a.
- Trae och Byggvaruhandlaren. m. (11 per yr.)

**Sveriges Tvaetterifoerbund**
- Tvaettnytt. (pub. by Nordiska Branschtidskrifter
  AB)

**Sveriges Universitets och Hoegskoleamanuensers
Foerbund**
Nyaengsvaegen 21-23, 161 37 Bromma, Sweden.
- S U H A F Tidningen. 4 per yr. ISSN 0036-2018

**Sveriges Urmakare- och Optikerfoerbund**
Box 16104, S-103 23 Stockholm, Sweden.
- Svensk Ur- Optik Tidning. m. ISSN 0039-680X

**Sveriges Utsaedesfoerening**
S-260 00 Svaloev, Sweden.
- Sveriges Utsadesfoerenings Tidskrift. 4 per yr.
  ISSN 0039-6990

**Sveriges Verkstadsfoerening**
Box 5510, S-114 85 Stockholm, Sweden.
- Verkstaederna. 16 per yr. ISSN 0042-4056

**Sveriges Veterinaerfoerbund**
Kungsholms Hamnplan 7, S-112 20 Stockholm,
Sweden.
- Svensk Veterinaertidning. fortn.

**Sveriges Yngre Lakares Foerening**
Box 5610, S-114 86 Stockholm, Sweden.
- Sylf Nytt. 7 per yr. ISSN 0039-7636

**Sveriges Yrkesfruktodlares Riksfoerbund**
Box 35, S-162 11 Vaellingby 1, Sweden.
- S Y R-Information Med Fruktodlaren. 8 per yr.
  ISSN 0036-2093

**Sveriges 4H**
Box 19072, S-104 32 Stockholm 19, Sweden.
- 4H-Journalen. bi-m. ISSN 0016-335X

**Svetstekniska Foereningen**
Box 5073, S-102 42 Stockholm 5, Sweden.
- Svetsen. bi-m. ISSN 0039-7091

**Sweden. Arbetsmarknadsstyrelsen**
Box 1235, S-171 24 Solna, Sweden.
- Arbetsmarknaden. w. ISSN 0003-7850

**Sweden. Byggnadsstyrelsen**
Development Division, S-106 43 Stockholm 27,
Sweden.
- K B S Anvisning/K B S Directions. irreg. (5-10
  per yr.) ISSN 0022-7285
- K B S-Rapporter. irreg. (5-15 per yr.) ISSN 0022-
  7293

**Sweden. Central Bureau of Statistics**
*see* Sweden. Statistiska Centralbyraan

**Sweden. Finansdepartementet**
- Sweden. Finansdepartmentet. Regeringens
  Budgetfoerslag. (pub. by Liber Foerlag)

**Sweden. Finansdepartementet. Budget Department**
S-103 10 Stockholm 2, Sweden.
- Swedish Budget; a summary. a. ISSN 0082-0393

**Sweden. Fiskeristyrelsen. Institute of Marine
Research**
S-45300 Lysekil, Sweden.
- Sweden. Institute of Marine Research. Series:
  Biology. Reports. irreg., 1972, no. 20. ISSN 0346-
  8666

**Sweden. Foersvarets Forskningsanstalt**
S-104 50 Stockholm 80, Sweden.
- F O A Orienterar Om. ISSN 0014-6013

**Sweden. Folksams Sociala Raad**
Folksam Fack, 104 60 Stockholm, Sweden.
- Sweden. Folksams Sociala Raad. Var Trygghet. a.

**Sweden. Geological Survey of Sweden**
*see* Sweden. Sveriges Geologiska Undersoekning

**Sweden. Inrikesdepartement**
Postbox 1406, S-111 84 Stockholm, Sweden.
- Invandrartidningen Information. 45 per yr. ISSN
  0345-4983

**Sweden. Institute for Water and Air Pollution
Research**
*see* Sweden. Institutet Foer Vatten- och
Luftvaardsforskning

**Sweden. Institute of Marine Research**
*see* Sweden. Fiskeristyrelsen. Institute of Marine
Research

**Sweden. Institutet Foer Vatten- och
Luftvaardsforskning**
Box 21060, S-100 31 Stockholm, Sweden.
- I V L Bulletin. 2 per yr.
- I V L Nytt. q. ISSN 0019-0896

**Sweden. Konjunkturinstitutet**
Box 1756, 111 87 Stockholm, Sweden.
- Konjunkturlaget. (pub. by Liber Foerlag)
- Sweden. Konjunkturinstitutet. Occasional Paper.
  irreg., no. 7, 1973. ISSN 0082-0067
- Swedish Economy. (pub. by Liber Foerlag)

**Sweden. Konsumentverket**
Fack, 162 10 Vaellingby, Sweden.
- Konsument- Raett och Ekonomi. bi-m.
- Raad och Roen/Advice and Discovery. 10 per yr.
  ISSN 0035-7235

**Sweden. Kungliga Biblioteket**
Box 5039, 102 41 Stockholm, Sweden.
- Accessionskatalog over Utlandsk Litteratur i
  Svenska Forskningsbibliotek/Union Catalogue of
  Foreign Literature in Swedish Research Libraries.
  a. with cumulations every 5 years. ISSN 0065-
  0811
- Acta Bibliothecae Regiae Stockholmiensis. irreg.
  ISSN 0065-1060
- Suecana Extranea; books on Sweden and Swedish
  literature in foreign languages. s-a. ISSN 0039-
  4599 (prep. by its Bibliografiska Institutet)
- Svensk Bokforteckning/Swedish National
  Bibliography. (pub. by Tidnings AB Svensk
  Bokhandel)
- Sweden. Riksbibliotekarien. Notiser. 2 per yr.
  ISSN 0035-5364

**Sweden. Kungliga Livrustkammaren**
Kungliga Slottet, Slottsbacken, 111 30 Stockholm,
Sweden.
- Livrustkammaren. q. ISSN 0024-5372

**Sweden. Kungliga Militaerhoegskolan.
Militaerhistoriska Avdelningen**
100 45 Stockholm 90, Sweden.
- Aktuellt och Historiskt. a. ISSN 0065-5619
- Carl X Gustaf-Studier. irreg., no. 6, 1974. ISSN
  0069-0597

**Sweden. Lantmaeteriverket**
- R A K-Information. (pub. by Liber Foerlag)

**Sweden. Luftfartsverket**
Fack, S-601 01 Norrkoeping, Sweden.
- Sweden. Luftfartsverket. Aarsbok. a. ISSN 0586-
  1632
- Sweden. Luftfartsverket. Charterstatistik. s-a.
- Sweden. Luftfartsverket. Flygplatsstatistik. m.

**Sweden. Ministry of Finance**
see Sweden. Finansdepartementet

**Sweden. Ministry of Foreign Affairs**
see Sweden. Utrikesdepartementet

**Sweden. Ministry of Labour and Housing**
see Sweden. Inrikesdepartementet

**Sweden. National Agricultural Marketing Board**
see Sweden. Statens Jordbruksnaemd

**Sweden. National Audit Bureau**
see Sweden. Riksrevisionsverket

**Sweden. National Board of Health and Welfare**
see Sweden. Socialstyrelsen

**Sweden. National Board of Public Building**
see Sweden. Byggnadsstyrelsen

**Sweden. National Civil Aviation Administration**
see Sweden. Luftfartsverket

**Sweden. National Collective Bargaining Office**
see Sweden. Statens Avtalsverk

**Sweden. National Consumer Institute**
see Sweden. Statens Institut Foer
Konsumentfraagor

**Sweden. National Council for Consumer Goods and
Consumer Information**
see Sweden. Statens Konsumentraad

**Sweden. National Debt Office**
see Sweden. Riksgaeldskontoret

**Sweden. National Defense Research Institute**
see Sweden. Foersvarets Forskningsanstalt

**Sweden. National Environment Protection Board**
see Sweden. Statens Naturvaardsverk

**Sweden. National Labour Market Board**
see Sweden. Arbetsmarknadsstyrelsen

**Sweden. National Record Office**
see Sweden. Riksarkivet

**Sweden. National Social Insurance Board**
see Sweden. Riksfoersaekringsverket

**Sweden. Nationalmuseum**
Biblioteket, 103 24 Stockholm, Sweden.
- Sweden. Nationalmuseum. Skriftserie. irreg., no.
  17, 1973. ISSN 0081-5683

**Sweden. Office of the Chancellor of the Swedish
Universities**
see Sweden. Universitetskanslersaembetet

**Sweden. Patent- och Registreringsverket**
Box 5055, S-102 42 Stockholm 5, Sweden.
- Registreringstidning Foer Varumaerken. Part A
  (Publications for Opposition) w. ISSN 0347-3449
- Registreringstidning Foer Varumaerken. Part B
  (Publications of Registrations) w. ISSN 0347-3465
- Registreringstidning Foer Varumaerken. Part C
  (Renewals, Changes of Ownership) w. ISSN
  0347-3457
- Svenskt Varumaerkeslexikon/Swedish Trade Mark
  Dictionary. q. updates to base vol.
- Sweden. Patent- och Registreringsverket.
  Aarsberaettelse/Annual Report. a.

**Sweden. Postverket**
Marknadsavdelningen, MPT, 105 00 Stockholm,
Sweden.
- Inlaendsk Tidningstaxa; list of Swedish
  newspapers and reviews. a. ISSN 0020-1448

**Sweden. Riksarkivet**
Fack, 100 26 Stockholm, Sweden.
- R A-Nytt. 3-4 per yr. ISSN 0347-4585
- Sweden. Riksarkivet. Meddelanden. irreg. ISSN
  0039-6893

**Sweden. Riksdagen**
Riksdagens Tryckeriexpedition, S-100 12 Stockholm,
Sweden.
- Sweden. Riksdagen. Foerteckning Oever
  Riksdagens Ledamoeter. a.
- Sweden. Riksdagen. Riksdagen Aarsbok. a.

**Sweden. Riksfoersaekringsverket**
Fack, S-103 60 Stockholm 3, Sweden.
- Sweden. Riksfoersaekringsverket. Allmaen
  Foersaekring. a. ISSN 0082-0075
- Swedish Social Security Scheme. a. ISSN 0082-
  0083 (Orders to: Liber Foerlag, Fack, S-162 89
  Vaellingby, Sweden)

**Sweden. Riksgaeldskontoret**
Box 16306, 103 26 Stockholm, Sweden.
- Sweden. Riksgaeldskontoret. Budgataaret.
  Aarsbok. a. ISSN 0082-0091

**Sweden. Riksrevisionsverket**
- Sweden. Riksrevisionsverket. Statens Finanser.
  (pub. by Liber Foerlag)

**Sweden. Royal Armoury**
see Sweden. Kungliga Livrustkammaren

**Sweden. Royal Library**
see Sweden. Kungliga Biblioteket

**Sweden. Royal Patent and Registration Office**
see Sweden. Patent- och Registreringsverket

**Sweden. Sjukvaardens och Socialvaardens Planerings-
och Rationaliseringsinstitut**
Fack, S-102 50 Stockholm, Sweden.
- Sweden. Sjukvaardens och Socialvaardens
  Planerings- och Rationaliseringsinstitut. S P R I
  Raad. irreg. ISSN 0082-0113
- Sweden. Sjukvaardens och Socialvaardens
  Planerings- och Rationaliseringsinstitut. S P R I
  Specifikationer. irreg. ISSN 0082-0105

**Sweden. Socialstyrelsen**
106 30 Stockholm, Sweden.
- Social-Nytt. m (11 per yr.) ISSN 0037-7619
- Sweden. Socialistyrelsen. Redoviser. (pub. by
  Liber Foerlag)
- Sweden. Socialstyrelsen. Legitimerade Laekare.
  Authorized Physicians. (pub. by Liber Foerlag)

**Sweden. State Railways Central Administration**
see Sweden. Statens Jaernvaegars
Centralfoervaltning

**Sweden. Statens Avtalsverk**
Fack, 103 10 Stockholm, Sweden.
- Sweden. Statens Avtalsverk. Information Fraan S
  A V. 4-6 per yr. ISSN 0036-0996
- Sweden Statens Avtalsverk. Foereskrifter Om
  Statlig Tjaenstepensionering; F S P. a.

**Sweden. Statens Humanistiska Forskningsraad**
see Statens Humanistiska Forskningsraad

**Sweden. Statens Institut Foer Konsumentfraagor**
Raalambsvaegen 8, 112 59 Stockholm, Sweden.
- Sweden. Statens Institut Foer Konsumentfraagor.
  Meddelar. irreg. ISSN 0082-0121

**Sweden. Statens Jaernvaegars Centralfoervaltning**
S-105 50 Stockholm, Sweden.
- S J Nytt. fortn. ISSN 0037-5985
- Sveriges Jaernvaegar/Railways of Sweden. a. ISSN
  0081-9964
- Sweden. Statens Jaernvaegars Centralfoervaltning.
  Geotekniska Kontoret. Meddelanden.
- Transport-Journalen. 4 per yr. ISSN 0041-1507
  (prep. by its Commercial Department)

**Sweden. Statens Jordbruksnaemd**
Box 16384, S-103 27 Stockholm 16, Sweden.
- Jordbruksekonomiska Meddelanden/Journal of
  Agricultural Economics. m. ISSN 0021-7441

**Sweden. Statens Konsumentraad**
Lund, Sweden.
- Sweden. Statens Konsumentraad.
  Verksamhetsberaettelse. irreg.

**Sweden. Statens Lantmaeteriverk**
801 12 Gavle, Sweden.
- Sweden. Statens Lantmaeteriverk. L M V
  Information. bi-m.

**Sweden. Statens Livsmedelsverk**
Box 622, S-751 26 Uppsala, Sweden.
- Vaar Foeda. 10 per yr. ISSN 0042-2657

**Sweden. Statens Naturvaardsverk**
Fack, S-171 20 Solna 1, Sweden.
- Environmental Research. a (Swedish edition);
  biennial (English edition)
- Sweden. Statens Naturvaardsverk. Publikationer.
  (pub. by Liber Foerlag)

**Sweden. Statens Naturvetenskapliga Forskningsraad**
Box 23136, S-104 35 Stockholm, Sweden.
- Acta Zoologica; international journal for zoology.
  4 per yr. ISSN 0001-7272
- Botaniska Notiser. 4 per yr. ISSN 0006-8195 (Co-
  sponsor: Lund Botanical Society)
- Entomologisk Tidskrift. q. ISSN 0013-886X (Co-
  sponsor: Entomologiska Foereningen)
- Opera Botanica. irreg., no. 38, 1975. ISSN 0078-
  5237 (Co-sponsor: Lund Botanical Society)
- Opera Botanica. Series B. Flora of Ecuador. irreg.
  (Co-sponsor: Lund Botanical Society)
- Swedish Natural Science Research Council.
  Ecological Bulletins. irreg. (2-3 per yr.) ISSN
  0587-1433 (prep. by its Ecological Research
  Committee)
- Swedish Natural Science Research Council.
  Swedish Committee on Research Economics.
  FEK Reports. irreg. (2-3 per yr.)

**Sweden. Statens Offentliga Utredningar**
Stockholm, Sweden.
- Svensk Industri Delrapport. irreg.

**Sweden. Statens Planverk**
Box 22027, 104 22 Stockholm, Sweden.
- Plan- och Byggklipp. fortn.
- Sweden. Statens Planverk. Statens Planverk
  Aktuellt. bi-m. ISSN 0039-0267

**Sweden. Statens Raad Foer Byggnadsforskning**
Sankt Goeransgatan 66, S-112 30 Stockholm,
Sweden
(Orders to: Svensk Byggjaenst, Box 1403, 111 84
Stockholm, Sweden)
- Sweden. Statens Raad foer Byggnadsforskning.
  Document. irreg., no. 4, 1975. ISSN 0586-6766
- Sweden. Statens Raad Foer Byggnadsforskning.
  Fraan Byggnadsforskningen. 9 per yr.
- Sweden. Statens Raad foer Byggnadsforskning.
  Informationsblad. irreg. ISSN 0585-3400
- Sweden. Statens Raad foer Byggnadsforskning.
  Rapport. irreg., no. 60, 1975.

- Sweden. Statens Raad Foer Byggnadsforskning. Verksamhetsplan. a.

**Sweden. Statens Vaeg- och Trafikinstitut**
Documentation and Information Department, Fack, S-581 01 Linkoeping, Sweden.
- Sweden. Statens Vaeg- och Trafikinstitut. Rapport. irreg. (10-15 per yr.) ISSN 0373-4706

**Sweden. Statistiska Centralbyraan**
- Aarsbok Foer Sveriges Kommuner. (pub. by Liber Foerlag)
- Statistisk Aarsbok Foer Sverige. (pub. by Liber Foerlag)
- Sweden. Statistiska Centralbyraan. Allmaan Fastighetstaxering. (pub. by Liber Foerlag)
- Sweden. Statistiska Centralbyraan. Allmaan Maanadsstitistik/Monthly Digest of Swedish Statistics. (pub. by Liber Foerlag)
- Sweden. Statistiska Centralbyraan.Arbetskraftsundersoekningen. Arsmedeltal. (pub. by Liber Foerlag)
- Sweden. Statistiska Centralbyraan. Befolkningsfoeraendringar. (pub. by Liber Foerlag)
- Sweden. Statistiska Centralbyraan. Folkmaengd. (pub. by Liber Foerlag)
- Sweden. Statistiska Centralbyraan. Industri. (pub. by Liber Foerlag)
- Sweden. Statistiska Centralbyraan. Information i Prognosfragor/Forecasting Information. (pub. by Liber Foerlag)
- Sweden. Statistiska Centralbyraan. Jordbruksstatistisk Aarsbok. (pub. by Liber Foerlag)
- Sweden. Statistiska Centralbyraan. Kommunal Personal. (pub. by Liber Foerlag)
- Sweden. Statistiska Centralbyraan. Levnadsfoerhaallanden Aarsbok/Living Conditions Yearbook. (pub. by Liber Foerlag)
- Sweden. Statistiska Centralbyraan. Loener. (pub. by Liber Foerlag)
- Sweden. Statistiska Centralbyraan. Meddelanden i Samordningsfraagor. (pub. by Liber Foerlag)
- Sweden. Statistiska Centralbyraan. S C B Manadens Tryck. (pub. by Liber Foerlag)
- Sweden. Statistiska Centralbyraan. Statistisk Tidskrift. (pub. by Liber Foerlag)
- Sweden. Statistiska Centralbyraan. Statistiska Meddelanden. Subgroup Am (Labor Market) (pub. by Liber Foerlag)
- Sweden. Statistiska Centralbyraan. Statistiska Meddelanden. Subgroup Be (Population) (pub. by Liber Foerlag)
- Sweden. Statistiska Centralbyraan. Statistiska Meddelanden. Subgroup Bo (Housing and Construction) (pub. by Liber Foerlag)
- Sweden. Statistiska Centralbyraan. Statistiska Meddelanden. Subgroup H (Trade) (pub. by Liber Foerlag)
- Sweden. Statistiska Centralbyraan. Statistiska Meddelanden. Subgroup I (Manufacturing) (pub. by Liber Foerlag)
- Sweden. Statistiska Centralbyraan. Statistiska Meddelanden. Subgroup J (Agriculture) (pub. by Liber Foerlag)
- Sweden. Statistiska Centralbyraan. Statistiska Meddelanden. Subgroup N (National Accounts and Finance) (pub. by Liber Foerlag)
- Sweden. Statistiska Centralbyraan. Statistiska Meddelanden. Subgroup P (Prices and Price Indices) (pub. by Liber Foerlag)
- Sweden. Statistiska Centralbyraan. Statistiska Meddelanden. Subgroup R (Judicial Statistics. Law and Social Welfare) (pub. by Liber Foerlag)
- Sweden. Statistiska Centralbyraan. Statistiska Meddelanden. Subgroup S (Social Welfare Statistics) (pub. by Liber Foerlag)
- Sweden. Statistiska Centralbyraan. Statistiska Meddelanden. Subgroup T (Transport and Other Forms of Communication) (pub. by Liber Foerlag)
- Sweden. Statistiska Centralbyraan. Statistiska Meddelanden. Subgroup U (Education and Culture) (pub. by Liber Foerlag)
- Sweden. Statistiska Centralbyraan. Urval Skriftseries/Selection Series. (pub. by Liber Foerlag)
- Sweden. Statistiska Centralbyraan. Utbildningsstatistisk/Swedish Educational Statistics. (pub. by Liber Foerlag)
- Sweden. Statistiska Centralbyraan. Utrikeshandel/Foreign Trade. (pub. by Liber Foerlag)
- Sweden. Statistiska Centralbyraan. Utrikeshandel. Kvartalsstatistik. (pub. by Liber Foerlag)
- Sweden. Statistiska Centralbyraan. Utrikeshandel. Maanadsstatistik. (pub. by Liber Foerlag)

**Sweden. Statistiska Centralbyraan. Biblioteket**
Fack, S-102 50 Stockholm, Sweden.
- Sweden. Statistiska Centralbyraan. Biblioteket. Ny Foervaer/List of New Acquisitions. q.

**Sweden. Styrelsen Foer Internationell Utveckling**
S-105 25 Stockholm, Sweden.
- S I D A Development Studies. 2-3 per yr.

**Sweden. Sveriges Geologiska Undersoekning**
Fack, 104 05 Stockholm, Sweden.
- Sweden. Sveriges Geologiska Undersoekning. Serie C. Avhandlingar och Uppsatser/Memoirs and Notices. irreg., no. 713, 1975. ISSN 0082-0024
- Sweden. Sveriges Geologiska Undersoekning.Serie Ca. Avhandlingar och Uppsatser i Kvarto/Notices in Quarto and Folio. irreg., no. 48, 1974. ISSN 0082-0016

**Sweden. Sveriges Geologiska Undersoekning. Section of Regional Geophysics**
Fack, S-102 50 Stockholm 27, Sweden.
- Geomagnetic Observatory, Lovoe. Year Book. a. ISSN 0076-1354
- Sweden. Sveriges Geologiska Undersoekning Jordmagnetiska Publikationer /Geomagnetic Publications. irreg., 1967 no. 20. ISSN 0075-403X

**Sweden. Swedish Air Staff**
Fack, S-104 50 Stockholm, Sweden.
- FlygvapenNytt. 4 per yr. ISSN 0015-4792 (Co-sponsor: Foersvaret)

**Sweden. Swedish Cancer Registry**
- Cancer Incidence in Sweden. (pub. by Liber Foerlag)

**Sweden. Swedish Planning and Rationalization Institute of the Health and Social Services**
Fack, S-102 50 Stockholm, Sweden.
- Sweden. Sjukvaardens och Socialvaardens Planerings- och Rationaliseringsinstitut. S P R I Litteraturtjaenst. 10 per yr. ISSN 0036-1879

**Sweden. Telecommunications Administration**
see Sweden. Televerket

**Sweden. Televerket**
Central Archives, Marbackagatan 11, S-123 86 Farsta, Sweden.
- TELE (English Edition) 2 per yr. ISSN 0495-0127
- TELE (Swedish Edition) 4 per yr. ISSN 0040-2427

**Sweden. Universitetskanslersaembetet**
Box 16334, S-103 26 Stockholm, Sweden.
- Sweden. Universitetskanslersaembetet. Hoegre Utbildning och Forskning. (pub. by Svenska Utbildningsfoerlaget Liber)
- Sweden. Universitetskanslersaembetet. R & D in Higher Education. bi-m.

**Sweden. Utrikesdepartementet**
- Sverige-EG. (pub. by Liber Foerlag)

**Sweden. Yrksev Agledningsenheten**
- Yrke och Framtid. (pub. by Liber Foerlag)

**Swedish Academy of Pharmaceutical Sciences**
Box 1136, S-111 81 Stockholm, Sweden.
- Acta Pharmaceutica Suecica; Svensk farmaceutisk tidskrift. 6 per yr. ISSN 0001-6675

**Swedish Air Line Pilots Association**
Olofsgatan 10, 111 36 Stockholm, Sweden.
- Flygposten. m. ISSN 0015-4776

**Swedish Association for Mental Health**
St. Goransgatan 114, S-112 45 Stockholm, Sweden.
- Psykisk Haelsa/Mental Health. q. ISSN 0033-3212

**Swedish Atomic Forum**
Box 5506, S-114 85 Stockholm, Sweden.
- Swedish Nuclear News. m.

**Swedish Cancer Registry**
see Sweden. Swedish Cancer Registry

**Swedish Cement and Concrete Research Institute**
see Cement- och Betonginstitutet

**Swedish Collector's Society Northern Star**
Jungfrugatan 13, S-575 00 Eksjoe, Sweden.
- Samlarnytt. 10 per yr. ISSN 0036-3790

**Swedish Cooperative Centre**
Fack, S-104 65 Stockholm, Sweden.
- S C C News. q. ISSN 0346-0762

**Swedish Council for Building Research**
see Sweden. Statens Raad Foer Byggnadsforskning

**Swedish Engineers' Press Ltd.**
see Ingenjoersfoerlaget AB

**Swedish Furniture Manufacturers Association**
- Interior. (pub. by Moebelindustrins Service AB)

**Swedish Humanistic Research Council**
see Statens Humanistiska Forskningsraad

**Swedish Industrial Publications**
Box 5501, Stockholm, Sweden.
- Economic Research Reports. Series A. irreg.

**Swedish Institute for Nationwide Concerts**
Box 1225, 111 82 Stockholm, Sweden.
- Tonfallet. 22 per yr. ISSN 0346-329X

**Swedish Institute of International Affairs**
see Utrikespolitiska Institutet

**Swedish International Development Authority**
see Sweden. Styrelsen Foer Internationell Utveckling

**Swedish Jazz Federation**
Box 73, 570 40 Aneby, Sweden.
- Jazznytt. 5 per yr. ISSN 0092-0525

**Swedish-Korean Society**
Box 32 59, S-103 65 Stockholm 3, Sweden.
- Koreansk Journal. 4-6 per yr. ISSN 0023-4079

**Swedish Natural Science Research Council**
see Sweden. Statens Naturvetenskapliga Forskningsraad

**Swedish Nutrition Foundation**
- Swedish Nutrition Foundation. Symposia. (pub. by Almqvist & Wiksell International)

**Swedish Plastics and Chemicals Suppliers Association**
Box 5512, S-114 85 Stockholm, Sweden.
- P K L Plaster. triennial.

**Swedish Society of Actuaries**
- Scandinavian Actuarial Journal. (pub. by Almqvist & Wiksell International)

**Swedish Sociological Association**
S-752 20 Uppsala, Sweden
- Sociologisk Forskning. q. ISSN 0038-0342 (Inquiries to: c/o Crona, Sandelsgatan 23 Aiv, S-115 33 Stockholm, Sweden)

**Swedish Spiritualistic Federation**
Krutkallervaegen 1, 722 20 Vasteraas, Sweden.
- Utan Grans. bi-m. ISSN 0042-1537

**Swedish Sportdivers Federation**
Box 925, 101 33 Stockholm 1, Sweden.
- Sportdykaren. bi-m. ISSN 0038-7967

**Swedish Textile Employers' Association**
Box 7007, S-103 81 Stockholm 7, Sweden.
- Textil och Konfektion; organ for den svenska textil och konfektionsindustrin samt laeder- och skoindustrin. 9 per yr. ISSN 0040-4845

**Swedish Veteran Car Club**
Box 485, 651 08 Karlstad, Sweden.
- Autoveteranen. 10 per yr. ISSN 0005-1799

**Synpunkt**
Arstaskolgrand 18, Box 43011, 100 72 Stockholm 43, Sweden.
- Synpunkt; popular tidskrift for konst. 7 per yr. ISSN 0039-7849

**Tekniska Litteratursaellskapet**
c/o Ingenjoersvetenskapsakademien, Box 5073, S-102 42 Stockholm 5, Sweden.
- Tidskrift foer Dokumentation/Scandinavian Documentation Journal. bi-m. ISSN 0040-6872

**Tekniska Museet**
S-115 27 Stockholm, Sweden.
- Daedalus. a. ISSN 0070-2528

**Tekniska Nomenklaturcentralen**
Box 43041, S-100 72 Stockholm, Sweden.
- T N C - Aktuellt. 6 per yr. ISSN 0039-8438

- Tekniska Nomenklaturcentralen Publikationer.
  irreg., no. 64, 1977. ISSN 0081-573X

**Telefornaktiebolaget L.M. Ericsson**
Fack, S-126 25 Stockholm, Sweden.
- Ericsson Review. 4 per yr. ISSN 0014-0171
- Ericsson Technics. q. ISSN 0014-018X

**Theosophical Society in Sweden**
Nybrogatan 24, S-114 39 Stockholm, Sweden.
- Teosofi i Norden. bi-m. ISSN 0040-3628 (Co-
  sponsors: Theosophical Society of Denmark;
  Theosophical Society of Norway)

**Tibnur AB**
Box 9100, 102 72 Stockholm, Sweden.
- Trenden. q. ISSN 0041-2325

**Tidskrift i Fortifikation**
Box 16371, Stockholm 16, Sweden.
- Tidskrift i Fortifikation; foer fortifikationskaaren,
  Ingenjoertrupperna, samt Vaeg- och
  vattenbyggradskaaren. 4 per yr. ISSN 0040-6937

**Foerlags AB Tifa**
N. Bulltoftavaegen 65, 212 20 Malmoe, Sweden.
- Allas Veckotidning. w.
- Hemmets Veckotidning. w.

**Tjaenstemaennens Centralorganisation**
Linnegatan 14, Box 5252, 104 45 Stockholm,
Sweden.
- Tjaenstemaennens Centralorganisation.
  Verksamhetsaret. a. ISSN 0082-4542

**Transport-Nytt Foerlags AB**
Box 11021, S-100 61 Stockholm 11, Sweden.
- Transport-Nytt. m. ISSN 0041-1523

**Trelleborgs Gummifabriks AB**
231 01 Trelleborg, Sweden.
- Trelleborgs Nyheter. q (Swedish edt.); 3 per yr.
  (english edt.) ISSN 0493-8348

**TU: S Foerlags AB**
Box 45136, 104 30 Stockholm 45, Sweden.
- Pressens Tidning. m (10 per yr.) ISSN 0032-7883
  (Svenska Tidningsutgivarefoereningen\
- Tidningsteknik. q. (Nordisk Avis-Teknisk
  Samarbetsnaemnd)

**Umeaa Universitet**
Bibliotek, Box 718, S-901 10 Umeaa, Sweden.
- Umeaa Studies in the Humanities. irreg no. 8,
  1975.

**Umeaa Universitet. Department of Education**
S-901 87 Umeaa, Sweden.
- Educational Reports Umeaa. irreg., no. 13, 1977.
- Pedagogisk Debatt Umeaa. irreg., no. 17, 1977.
- Pedagogiska Monografier. irreg., no. 18, 1976.
- Pedagogiska Rapporter Umeaa. irreg., no. 60,
  1977.

**Unga Filosofers Foerlag**
Brunnsgatan 28, 111 38 Stockholm, Sweden.
- Haften for Kritiska Studier. 8 per yr.

**Unga Oernars Riksfoerbund**
Box 1149, S-111 81 Stockholm, Sweden.
- Unga Oernar. 8 per yr. ISSN 0041-6657

**United NFL Groups of Sweden**
Fack, 104 32 Stockholm 19, Sweden.
- Vietnambulletinen. bi-m. ISSN 0042-5788

**Universitet i Uppsala. Institutionen Foer Allmaen och
Jaemfoerande Ethnografi**
- Studia Ethnographica Upsaliensia. (pub. by
  Almqvist & Wiksell International)

**University of Lund. School of Dentistry. Faculty of
Odontology**
*see* **Lunds Universitet. Faculty of Odontology**

**Uppsala Exegetiska Saellskap**
- Svensk Exegetisk Aarsbok. (pub. by
  LiberLaeromedel)

**Uppsala Laekarefoerening**
- Upsala Journal of Medical Sciences. (pub. by
  Almqvist & Wiksell International)

**Uppsala Universitet**
- Orientalia Suecana. (pub. by Almqvist & Wiksell
  International)
- Studia Musicologica Upsaliensia. Nova Series.
  (pub. by Almqvist and Wiksell International)

- Studia Philologiae Scandinavicae Upsaliensia.
  (pub. by Almqvist & Wiksell International)
- Studia Uralica et Altaica Upsaliensia. (pub. by
  Almqvist & Wiksell International)

**Uppsala Universitet. Geological Institution**
- Uppsala Universitet. Geological Institution.
  Bulletin. (pub. by Almqvist & Wiksell
  International)

**Uppsala Universitet. Historiska Institutionen**
- Studia Historica Upsaliensia. (pub. by Almqvist &
  Wiksell International)

**Uppsala Universitet. Institute of Art History**
- Ars Suecica. (pub. by Almqvist & Wiksell
  International)
- Figura. Nova Series. (pub. by Almqvist & Wiksell
  International)

**Uppsala Universitet. Institute of Education**
Box 256, S-751 05 Uppsala, Sweden.
- Studia Scientiae Paedagogicae Upsaliensia. irreg.,
  no. 12, 1973. ISSN 0081-6892

**Uppsala Universitet. Institute of Zoology**
- Zoon, a Journal of Zoology. (pub. by Almqvist &
  Wiksell International)

**Uppsala Universitet. Institutionen Foer Nordiska
Spraak**
Box 256, S-751 05 Uppsala, Sweden.
- Uppsala Universitet. Institutionen Foer Nordiska
  Spraak. Skrifter. irreg., 1967, no. 15. ISSN 0083-
  4661

**Utbildningstidningen AB**
Ringvaegen 23, 116 52 Stockholm, Sweden.
- Undervisningsteknologi. 4 per yr.
- Utbildningstidningen. 8 per yr. ISSN 0049-5735

**Utrikespolitiska Institutet**
Lilla Nygatan 23, 111 28 Stockholm, Sweden.
- Archives 69; a selection of articles from the world
  press since 1969. d.
- Internationella Studier. bi-m. ISSN 0020-952X
- Vaerldspolitikens Dagsfragor. 12 per yr. ISSN
  0042-2754

**Vaenner Samfund i Sverige**
Varvsgatan 15, 117 29 Stockholm, Sweden.
- Kvaekartidskrift. q. ISSN 0345-6005

**Vaesterbottens Norra Fornminnesfoerening. Skelleftea
Museum**
Skelleftea, Sweden.
- Vaesterbottens Norra Fornminnesfoerening.
  Skelleftea Museum. Meddelande. irreg.

**Valiseesti**
Box 2171, 103 14 Stockholm, Sweden.
- Valiseesti. s-m. ISSN 0049-5808

**Var Konst**
Box 43011, 100 72 Stockholm 43, Sweden.
- Var Konst; medlemsblad for Konstframjandet. q.
  ISSN 0042-2665

**Vi Bilaegare Med Hem och Hobby**
S-113 87 Stockholm, Sweden.
- Vi Bilaegare Med Hem och Hobby. 22 per yr.
  ISSN 0042-4943

**Foerlags AB Villa och Hem**
Kungsgatan 6, Box 1739, 111 87 Stockholm,
Sweden.
- Villa & Hem i Sverige. 10 per yr. ISSN 0042-6156

**Volvo Flygmotor AB**
Trollhaettan, Sweden.
- Flygmotor. 6 per yr. ISSN 0015-4768

**Weibullsholm Plant Breeding Institute**
S-261 20 Landskrona, Sweden.
- Agri Hortique Genetica. 1-2 per yr. ISSN 0002-
  1172

**Wettergren**
Skaargaardsgatan 4, S-414 58 Goeteborg, Sweden.
- Studier i Nordisk Arkeologi/Studies in North
  European Archaeology. irreg., no. 13, 1975. ISSN
  0081-7414 (Fornminnesfoereningen i Goeteborg)
  (Co-sponsor: Goeteborgs Arkeologiska Museum)

**Women's International League for Peace and
Freedom. Swedish Section**
Hovslagargatan 2, 111 48 Stockholm, Sweden.
- Fred och Frihet/Pax et Libertas. 4-5 per yr. ISSN
  0016-0288

**World Health Organization. Research and Training
Centre on Human Reproduction**
For publications of this agency see section for
UNITED NATIONS

**Tidskriftsfoereningen Zenit**
Box 1156, S-221 05 Lund, Sweden.
- Zenit; nordisk socialistisk tidskrift. bi-m. ISSN
  0044-3980

**Zoologisk Institut**
c/o Lennart Cederholm, Service Center for
Taxonomic Zoology, S-223 62 Lund, Sweden.
- Entomologica Scandinavica. 4 per yr. ISSN 0013-
  8711

## SWITZERLAND

**Aargauer Tagblatt AG**
Bahnhofstr. 39-43, 5001 Aarau, Switzerland.
- Auto-Technik; der Automobil-Mechaniker. m.
  ISSN 0005-0857

**Absintenten-Verkehrsverband**
Zentralsekretariat, Haldenstr. 55, Biel-Bienne,
Switzerland.
- 0/00 Freie Fahrt/Route et Sobriete. m.

**Editions Adversaires**
27 Ch. de la Vendee, 1213 Petit-Lancy, Geneva,
Switzerland.
- Editions Adversaires. Cahiers. bi-m.

**Aero-Club der Schweiz**
Postfach, CH-4002 Basel, Switzerland.
- Aero-Revue. m. ISSN 0001-9186

**Afrique Economique**
Ave. du Lignon, B.P. 313, 1219 Lignon,
Switzerland.
- Afrique Economique; magazine Africain de
  l'economie et des finances. bi-m.

**Editions l' Age d'Homme-la Cite**
10, Metropole, 1003 Lausanne, Switzerland.
- Travail Theatral. q. ISSN 0049-4534

**Agifa Verlag**
Universitaetstrasse 120, Postfach 257, 8033 Zurich,
Switzerland.
- European Organization for Quality Control.
  Proceedings of Conference. a 1970, 14th,
  Lausanne. ISSN 0071-2981
- Microtecnic. q. ISSN 0026-2854

**H. Akerets Erben AG**
Postfach, 8600 Duebendorf, Switzerland.
- Amtlicher Anzeiger. w. ISSN 0003-2115

**ALA Schweizerische Gesellschaft fuer Vogelkunde und
Vogelschutz**
*see* **Schweizerische Gesellschaft fuer Vogelkunde
und Vogelschutz**

**Albert Steffen Stiftung**
- Therapeutische Dichtung. (pub. by Verlag fuer
  Schoene Wissenschaften)

**Allgemeine Anthroposophische Gesellschaft**
CH-4143 Dornach, Switzerland.
- Goetheanum. w.

**Allgemeine Geschichtsforschende Gesellschaft der
Schweiz**
- Schweizerische Zeitschrift fuer Geschichte/Revue
  Suisse d'Histoire/Rivista Storica Svizzera. (pub.
  by Buchdruckerei und Verlag Leemann AG)

**Alliance Internationale de Tourisme**
*see* **International Touring Alliance**

**Alma Verlag**
Postfach 6766, 8953 Dietikon, Zurich, Switzerland.
- Foto - Film - Ton; Magazin fuer Foto, Film und
  Tonaufzeichnung. 10 per yr. ISSN 0015-8690

**Anthropos Institut**
- Anthropos. (pub. by Editions Saint-Paul)

**Arbeitsgemeinschaft Cinema**
Postfach 1049, CH-8022 Zurich, Switzerland.
• Cinema; unabhaengig schweizerische
Filmzeitschrift /revue cinematographique
independent suisse. q.

**Arbeitsgemeinschaft fuer Elektrische
Nachrichtentechnik**
Postfach, Zurich, Switzerland.
• Arbeitsgemeinschaft fuer Elektrische
Nachrichtentechnik. Mitteilungen. irreg., no. 19,
1975.

**Arbeitsstelle Jugend- und Bildungsdienst**
Auf der Mauer 13, 8001 Zurich, Switzerland.
• Ancilla; Monatszeitschrift der weltoffenen Frau.
m. ISSN 0003-2867

**Archives Suisses d'Anthropologie Genérale**
12, rue Gustave-Revilliod, CH-1227 Acacias,
Geneva, Switzerland.
• Archives Suisses d'Anthropologie Generale;
anthropologie, archeologie, ethnographie. a. ISSN
0066-6653

**Artibus Asiae Publishers**
CH-6612 Ascona, Switzerland
(U.S. address: Institute of Fine Arts, New York
University, 1 E. 78th St., NY 10021)
• Artibus Asiae; quarterly of Asian art and
archaeology for scholars and connoisseurs. q.
ISSN 0004-3648 (New York University. Institute
of Fine Arts US)
• Artibus Asiae Supplementa. a.

**Asia Documentation and Research Center**
*see under* Universite de Geneve

**Association d'Humanisme et Renaissance**
• Bibliotheque d'Humanisme et Renaissance. (pub.
by Librarie Droz)

**Association d'Interpretes et de Traducteurs**
Case Strand 388, Geneva, Switzerland.
• Interprete. q. ISSN 0047-1291

**Association d'Organisation Scientifique du Travail**
14 rue de l'Ancien-Port, 1201 Geneva, Switzerland.
• Chefs; revue suisse du management. m. ISSN
0009-2177

**Association de Etablissements Canton aux
d'Assurances Contre l'Incendie**
*see* Vereinigung Kantonaler
Feuerversicherungsanstalten

**Association de la Revue Militaire Suisse**
c/o Col. Montort, 39 Av. de la Gare, CH-1000
Lausanne, Switzerland.
• Revue Militaire Suisse. m. ISSN 0035-368X

**Association des Anciens Eleves des Ecoles Techniques
Superieures de Geneve**
Case Postale 9, 1211 Geneva 1, Switzerland.
• Association des Anciens Eleves des Ecoles
Techniques Superieures de Geneve. Bulletin
Technique. 10 per yr. ISSN 0004-5349

**Association des Horticulteurs de la Suisse Romande**
2 Avenue Agassiz, 1001 Lausanne, Switzerland.
• Horticulteurs et Maraichers Romands. m. (Co-
sponsors: Association Romande des Fleuristes;
Union Maraichere Romande; Groupement des
Paysagistes Romands)

**Association des Universitaires de Geneve**
4 rue de Candolle, 1211 Geneva 4, Switzerland.
• Bastions de Geneve. s-a. ISSN 0408-6392

**Association Internationale d'Experts Scientifiques du
Tourisme**
*see* International Association of Scientific Experts
in Tourism

**Association Internationale de la Securite Sociale**
*see* International Social Security Association

**Association Internationale des Ponts et Charpentes**
*see* International Association for Bridge and
Structural Engineering

**Association Internationale pour la Defence de la
Liberte Religieuse**
*see* International Association for the Defence of
Religious Liberties

**Association of Institutes for European Studies**
European Cultural Centre, 122 rue de Lausanne,
Geneva, Switzerland.
• Association of Institutes for European Studies.
Annuaire. a. ISSN 0571-6322
• Association of Institutes for European Studies.
Year-Book. a. ISSN 0571-6330

**Association of Swiss Ironmongers**
Talstrasse 70, CH-8001 Zurich, Switzerland.
• Perspective. s-m. ISSN 0031-5923

**Association of Swiss Macaroni Manufacturers**
Aegertenstrasse 6, Postfach 18, 3000 Berne 6,
Switzerland.
• Hornli Post.

**Association Suisse Chateaux et Ruines**
Laubisserstr. 74, 8105 Watt/Regensdorf ZH,
Switzerland.
• Schweizerischen Burgenvereins. bi-m.

**Association Suisse de Science Politique**
c/o Centre de Recherche de Politique Suisse,
Universitaet Bern, Neubrueckstr. 10, 3012 Berne,
Switzerland.
• Annee Politique Suisse/Schweizerische Politik/
Swiss Politics. a. ISSN 0066-2372

**Association Suisse des Electriciens**
• Association Suisse des Electriciens. Bulletin. (pub.
by FABAG und Druckerei Winterthur AG)

**Association Suisse des Geologues et Ingenieurs**
*see* Vereinigung Schweizerischer Petroleum-
Geologen und -Ingenieure

**Association Suisse des Magasins d'Horlogerie
Specialises**
*see* Verband Schweizerischer Uhrenfachgeschaefte

**Associazione dei Librai della Svizzera Italiana**
*see* Schweizerischer Buchhaendler- und Verleger-
Verband

**Atar SA**
Case Postale, 1211 Geneva 17, Switzerland.
• Maky/Rataplan. m.

**Automobil-Clubs der Schweiz**
Falkenplatz 14, 3000 Berne, Switzerland.
• Automobil-Clubs der Schweiz. Juristiche
Publikationen. a. ISSN 0084-7666

**Automotosport**
Case Postale 199, 2002 Neuchatel, Switzerland.
• Automotosport; revue mensuelle des sports
motorises. m.

**B.A.K. Publications**
Ramistr. 7, 8001 Zurich, Switzerland.
• Sketch; the Middle East news magazine. w.

**B B C Brown, Boveri & Co., Ltd.**
Baden, Switzerland
• Brown Boveri Review. m. ISSN 0007-2486 (U.S.
subscr. addr: Brown Boveri Corp. 1460
Livingstone Ave., North Brunswick, NJ 08902)

**Editions de la Baconniere S. A.**
2017 Boudry, Switzerland.
• Journal of World History. 4 per yr. ISSN 0022-
5436
• Mandragore Qui Chante. irreg., latest vol. 29.
ISSN 0076-3748

**O. Baldinger, Ed. & Pub.**
Aarestr. 83, 5222 Umiken, Switzerland.
• Betriebstechnik. m. (Swiss Federation of Plant
Engineers)
• Industriearchaeologie; zeitschrift fuer
technikgeschichte. q. (Schweizerische Gesellschaft
pro Technorama)

**Ballistocardiography Research Society**
• Ballistocardiography Research Society.
Proceedings of the Annual Meeting of the U.S.
(pub. by S. Karger AG)

**Bank for International Settlements**
7 Centralbahnstrasse, Case Postale 262, CH-4002
Basel, Switzerland.
• Bank for International Settlements. Annual
Report. a. ISSN 0067-3560
• Bank for International Settlements. Monetary and
Economic Department. International Commodity
Position. General Survey. irreg. ISSN 0408-4284

**Bank Julius Baer and Company**
Postfach, 8022 Zurich, Switzerland.
• Bank Julius Baer and Company. Bulletin. w.

**Banque Populaire Suisse**
Bundesgasse 26, 3001 Berne, Switzerland.
• Balance Sheet Prospectus. s-a. ISSN 0005-4240
• Banque Populaire Suisse. Informations. irreg.,
latest 1974. ISSN 0067-4028
• Fragments. q(English edt.); m(French, German
and Italian edts) ISSN 0015-9336

**Bargezzi AG**
Wasserwerkgasse 19, 3011 Berne, Switzerland.
• Maria; marianischer digest. 6 per yr. ISSN 0025-
2972

**Basel (Canton) Staatsarchiv**
• Quellen und Forschungen zur Basler Geschichte.
(pub. by Friedrich Reinhardt Verlag)

**Basel Institute for Immunology**
Postfach, CH-4005 Basel, Switzerland.
• Basel Institute for Immunology. Annual Report. a.

**Basler Afrika Bibliographien**
Postfach 235, CH-4001 Basel, Switzerland.
• Basler Afrika Bibliographien. Mitteilungen/Basel
Africa Bibliography. Communications. irreg., no.
12, 1975.

**Basler Botanische Gesellschaft**
Postfach, Basel 20, Switzerland.
• Bauhinia. irreg., 1969, vol. 4. ISSN 0067-4605

**Basler Effektenboerse**
Freie Str. 3, Postfach 940, 4001 Basel, Switzerland.
• Basler Effektenboerse. Jahresbericht/Rapport
Annuel/Annual Report. a.

**Oscar Bauer Verlag**
Aeschengraben 16, CH-4051 Basel, Switzerland.
• International Fruit World; review of the
international fruit and vegetable wholesale trade.
3 per yr.

**Bayer (Schweiz) AG**
Postfach 189, 3052 Zollikofen, Switzerland
(Main Office: Bayer Pflanzenschutz, Leverkusen, W.
Germany (B.R.D.))
• Courrier Phytosanitaire. irreg.
• Pflanzenschutz-Kurier (Swiss/German edition)
irreg.

**Beaux-Arts et Culture**
Hotel Municipal, Geneva, Switzerland.
• Musees de Geneve; revue des musees et
collections de la ville de geneve. m. ISSN 0027-
3821

**Verlag Beltz Basel**
Postfach 494, CH-4002 Basel, Switzerland.
• Universite de Fribourg. Paedagogisches Institut.
Arbeitspapiere und Kurzberichte. irreg. (Co-
sponsor: Freiburger Arbeitsgruppe fuer
Lehrplanforschung)
• Universite de Fribourg. Paedagogisches Institut.
Studien und Forschungsberichte. irreg. ISSN
0071-9552 (Co-sponsor: Freiburger Arbeitsgruppe
fuer Lehrplanforschung)

**Benteli-Verlag**
3018 Berne, Switzerland.
• Reformatio; Evangelische Zeitschrift fuer Kultur
und Politik. m. ISSN 0034-3021 (Evangelisch-
Kirchliche Vereinigung in der Schweiz)
• Schweizer Buch. s-m. ISSN 0036-732X
(Schweizerischer Buchhaendler- und Verleger-
Verband) (Co-Sponsor: Schweizerische
Landesbibliothek)
• Schweizerische Landwirtschaftliche Forschung/
Recherche Agronomique in Suisse. q. ISSN 0036-
763X (Switzerland. Eidgenoessisches
Volkswirtschaftsdepartement. Abteilung fuer
Landwirtschaft)
• Schweizerische Landwirtschaftliche Monatshefte.
m. ISSN 0036-7648 (Gesellschaft Schweizerischer
Landwirte)

**Verlagsgenossenschaft Beobachter AG**
CH-8152 Glattbrugg, Switzerland.
• Schweizerische Beobachter. s-m. ISSN 0036-7532

**Verlag Berichthaus**
Postfach, Zwingliplatz 3, 8022 Zurich, Switzerland.
• Schweisstechnik/Soudure. m. ISSN 0036-7206
(Schweizerischer Verein fuer Schweisstechnik)

- Schweizerische Monatsschrift fuer Zahnheilkunde. m. ISSN 0036-7702
- Zeitschrift fuer Schweizerische Archaeologie und Kunstgeschichte/Revue Suisse d'Art et d'Archeologie. q. ISSN 0044-3476 (Schweizerisches Landesmuseum)
- Zeitschrift fuer Unfallmedizin und Berufskrankheiten/Revue de Medecine des Accidents et des Maladies Professionelles. 4 per yr. ISSN 0044-3603

**Berne (Canton) Kantonale Steuerverwaltung**
- Neue Steuerpraxis. (pub. by Paul Haupt AG)

**Berner Boersenverein**
Aarbergergasse 30, 3000 Berne, Switzerland.
- Berner Boersenverein. Jahresbericht. a.

**Beste aus Reader's Digest AG**
Raeffelstr. 11, Gallushof, 8021 Zurich, Switzerland.
- Beste aus Reader's Digest (Swiss-German Edition) m. ISSN 0005-9676
- Selection du Reader's Digest (Swiss-French Edition) m. ISSN 0037-1394

**Biblioteca Cantonale Lugano**
Viale Carlo Cattaneo, CH-6900 Lugano, Switzerland.
- Bibliografia Ticinese. a. ISSN 0067-6772

**Bibliotheque Nationale Suisse**
see Switzerland. Bibliotheque Nationale Suisse

**Verlag Max Binkert AG**
CH-4335 Laufenburg, Switzerland.
- Foerdermittelkatalog; Foerdern-Lagern-Verteilen. a.
- Grafiscope. 6 per yr. ISSN 0017-2960
- Laborscope; laboratoriumstechnik-verfahrenstechnik. bi-m.
- Polyscope Automatik und Elektronik. 16 per yr. ISSN 0032-4035
- Schweizer Verpackungskatalog. a.
- Sysdata und Buerotechnik. m.

**Bircher-Benner Verlag Dr. Ralph Bircher und Co.**
CH-8703 Erlenbach-Zurich, Switzerland.
- Wendepunkt. m. ISSN 0043-2687

**Birkhaeuser Verlag**
Elisabethenstr. 19, CH-4010 Basel, Switzerland.
- Aequationes Mathematicae. 3 per yr. ISSN 0001-9054 (University of Waterloo. Faculty of Mathematics CN)
- Agents and Actions. 6 per yr. ISSN 0065-4299 (European Biological Research Association)
- Algebra Universalis. 3 per yr. ISSN 0002-5240 (University of Manitoba CN)
- Archiv der Mathematik/Archives of Mathematics/Archives Mathematiques. bi-m. ISSN 0003-889X
- Basler Drucke. irreg. ISSN 0067-4494
- Bioelectrochemistry and Bio-Energetics. q. ISSN 0302-4598 (Istituto Superiore de Sanita IT)
- Commentarii Mathematici Helvetici. 4 per yr. ISSN 0010-2571 (Schweizerischen Mathematischen Gesellschaft)
- Contributions to Current Research in Geophysics. irreg.
- Eclogae Geologicae Helvetiae. 3 per yr. ISSN 0012-9402 (Schweizerische Geologische Gesellschaft)
- Electroanalytical Abstracts; international journal dealing with the documentation of all aspects of electroanalytical chemistry including fundamental electrochemistry. bi-m. ISSN 0013-4775
- Elemente der Mathematik/Revue de Mathematiques Elementaires/Rivista di Matematica Elementare. s-m. ISSN 0013-6018
- Experientia; monthly journal of pure and applied science. m. ISSN 0014-4754
- Experientia. Supplementum. irreg. ISSN 0071-335X
- Forschungsinstitut der Eidgenoessischen Turn- und Sportschule Magglingen. Wissenschaftliche Schriftenreihe. irreg.
- Fortschritte der Arzneimittelforschung/Progress in Drug Research/Progres des Recherches Pharmaceutiques. irreg., (1-2 per yr.), vol. 18, 1974. ISSN 0071-786X
- Helvetica Physica Acta. 6 per yr. ISSN 0018-0238 (Schweizerischen Physikalischen Gesellschaft)
- Journal of Geometry. 4 per yr. ISSN 0047-2468
- Naturforschende Gesellschaft, Basel. Verhandlungen/Society for Natural Sciences, Basel. Proceedings. irreg. (approx. 2 per yr.) ISSN 0077-6122

- Pure and Applied Geophysics. 6 per yr. ISSN 0033-4553
- Schweizerische Naturforschende Gesellschaft. Verhandlungen/Societe Helvetique des Sciences Naturelles. Actes/Societa Elvetica dei Scienze Naturali. Atti. a. ISSN 0080-7362
- Schweizerische Palaeontologische Abhandlungen/Memoires Suisse de Paleontologie. irreg. ISSN 0080-7389 (Schweizerische Naturforschende Gesellschaft)
- Schweizerische Zeitschrift fuer Hydrologie/Revue Suisse d'Hydrologie/Swiss Journal of Hydrology. s-a. ISSN 0036-7842
- Scientia Electrica. 4 per yr. ISSN 0036-8695 (Eidgenoessische Technische Hochschule Zuerich. Abteilung fuer Elektrotechnik)
- Statistisches Jahrbuch der Schweiz/Annuaire Statistique de la Suisse. a. ISSN 0081-5330 (Switzerland. Statistisches Amt.)
- Technica; international technical review. s-m. ISSN 0040-0866
- Zeitschrift fuer Angewandte Mathematik und Physik/Journal of Applied Mathematics and Physics/Journal de Mathematiques Ed de Physique Appliquees. bi-m. ISSN 0044-2275

**Blaukreuz-Verlag**
Lindenrain 5A, 3001 Berne, Switzerland.
- Blaue Kreuz. fortn. ISSN 0006-4629 (Blue Cross of Switzerland)
- Familienblatt; Monatszeitschrift des Blauen Kreuzes. m. ISSN 0014-715X

**Blue Cross of Switzerland**
- Blaue Kreuz. (pub. by Blaukreuz-Verlag)

**Verlag Jacques Bollmann AG**
Heinrichstrasse 177, CH-8031 Zurich, Switzerland.
- Bau; Fachzeitschrift fuer Bautechnik, Baupraxis, und Baumaschinen. s-m. ISSN 0005-6391 (Schweizerischer Baukaderverband)
- Bau; Fachzeitschrift fuer Betriebsfuehrung und Kalkulation. m.

**Verlag Bouer und Wohner**
Postfach, 8033 Zurich, Switzerland.
- Bauen und Wohnen. m. ISSN 0005-6529

**Brass Bulletin**
Box 12, CH-1510 Moudon, Switzerland.
- Brass Bulletin; international brass chronicle. q. ISSN 0303-3848

**British-Swiss Chamber of Commerce in Switzerland**
Dufourstr. 51, CH-8008 Zurich, Switzerland.
- British-Swiss Bulletin. 10 per yr.

**Brown, Boveri & Co., Ltd.**
see B B C Brown, Boveri & Co., Ltd.

**Brunner Verlag AG**
Stauffacherstr. 5, CH-8036 Zurich, Switzerland.
- Alimenta. bi-m. ISSN 0002-5402
- Chimia. m. ISSN 0009-4293 (Schweizerischer Chemiker-Verband)
- Kosmetika; internationales Fachorgan fuer Kosmetik industrie. bi-m.

**Verlag C.J. Bucher AG**
Zurichstrasse 3, CH-6002 Lucerne, Switzerland.
- Camera; international magazine for photography. m. ISSN 0008-2074
- Schweizerisches Ortslexikon. every 4-5 yrs.

**Hugo Buchser S.A.**
4 Tour de l'Ile, CH-1211 Geneva 11, Switzerland
- Belora; revista Portuguesa de relojoaria, optica, modas e perfumaria. 6 per yr. ISSN 0005-867X (Also avail. from: Americo Marinho, Apdo. 793, Lisbon 2, Portugal)
- Europa Star. bi-m. ISSN 0014-2603
- Eurotec; European technical news. bi-m. ISSN 0014-3243
- Guide des Acheteurs: Horlogerie, Bijouterie et Branches Annexes/Buyers' Guide: Watch Industry, Jewellery and Allied Trades. a.
- Guide International des Machines, Appareils, Outils. a. ISSN 0072-8136

**Buechler und Co. AG**
Seftigenstr. 310, CH-3084 Wabern, Switzerland.
- Schweizerische Technische Zeitschrift; revue technique suisse. w. ISSN 0040-151X (Schweizerischer Technischer Verband)
- Yachting/Yachting Suisse. m. ISSN 0043-9959 (Unione Suisse de Yachting)

**Buri Druck und Verlag**
Eigerstr. 71, 3001 Berne, Switzerland.
- Berner Wochen Bulletin/This Week in Berne/Semaine a Berne. w. ISSN 0005-9412 (Verkehrsverein der Stadt Bern)
- Papeterist/Papetier/Cartolaio. m. ISSN 0031-1316 (Verband Schweizerischer Papeteristen)

**Business International S.A.**
7 rue Versonnex, Geneva, Switzerland.
- Survey of Living Costs in Major Cities Worldwide. irreg.

**C E D I P S**
Case Postale, 1000 Lausanne 17, Switzerland.
- Breche. bi-m. (Ligue Marxiste Revolutionaire)

**C E R N**
see European Organization for Nuclear Research

**C I R P**
see International Institution for Production Engineering Research

**C R E**
see Standing Conference of Rectors and Vice-Chancellors of the European Universities

**Cahiers de la Renaissance Vaudoise**
18 Petit-Chene, 1003 Lausanne, Switzerland.
- Cahiers de la Renaissance Vaudoise. 3-6 per yr. ISSN 0007-9847

**Edizioni Casagrande SA**
Casella Postale 489, CH-6501 Bellinzona, Switzerland.
- Archivio Storico Ticinese. q. ISSN 0004-0371
- Materiali e Documenti Ticinesi. q.
- Rivista di Bellinzona. m.

**Caux Verlag**
Postfach 218, CH-6002 Lucerne, Switzerland.
- Caux Information; moralische aufrustung informationdienst. m.

**Cenobio**
Casella Postale 6655, 6901 Lugano, Switzerland.
- Cenobio; rivista bimestrale di cultura. bi-m. ISSN 0008-896X

**Center for Immunology**
- International Convocation in Immunology. Papers. (pub. by S. Karger AG)

**Centralverband Schweizerischen Schneidermeister**
- Intermode. (pub. by Intermode Verlag)

**Centre Europeen d'Etudes Burgondo-Medianes**
Birfeldstr. 4, CH 4132 Muttenz, Switzerland.
- Centre Europeen d'Etudes Burgondo-Medianes. Publication. a. ISSN 0069-1895

**Centre Europeen de la Culture**
Villa Moynier, 122, rue de Lausanne, Geneva, Switzerland.
- Centre Europeen de la Culture. Bulletin. q.

**Centre International de la Tapisserie Ancienne et Moderne**
4 Av. Villamont, 1005 Lausanne, Switzerland.
- Biennale Internationale de la Tapisserie. biennial. ISSN 0067-849X

**Centre International de Recherches sur l'Anarchisme**
C.P. 51, CH-1211 Geneva 13, Switzerland.
- C I R A Bulletin. s-a.

**Centre Medico-Social de pro Familia**
Av. Georgette 1, 1003 Lausanne, Switzerland.
- Bulletin d'Information des Animateurs de Cours; educations sexuelle de la jeunesse. irreg. (approx. 3 per yr.)

**Centre Suisse de Documentation en Matiere d'Enseignement et d'Education**
Palais Wilson, CH-1211 Geneva 14, Switzerland.
- Centre Suisse de Documentation en Matiere d'Enseignement et d'Education. Bulletin. q.

**Cerberus Ltd.**
CH-8708 Maennedorf, Switzerland.
- Cerberus Alarm. q. ISSN 0528-5984
- Cerberus Electronic. q.
- Cerberus Sercurity. q.

**Cercle Ferdinand de Saussure**
- Cahiers Ferdinand de Saussure. (pub. by Librarie Droz)

**Chambre Francaise de Commerce et d'Industrie en Suisse**
32 Av. de Frontenex, 1211 Geneva 6, Switzerland.
- Commerce Franco-Suisse. m. ISSN 0010-2830

**Chambre Suisse de l'Horlogerie**
Leopold-Robert 65, 2801 la Chaux-de-Fonds, Switzerland.
- Suisse Horlogere et Revue Europeenne de l'Horlogerie-Bijouterie. q.

**Choisir**
14 bis Avenue du Mail, 1205 Geneva, Switzerland.
- Choisir; revue de reflexion chretienne. m. ISSN 0009-4994

**CIBA-Geigy Ltd.**
4002 Basel, Switzerland.
- CIBA-Geigy Journal. q.

**Editions Claspy Zurich**
Jacob-Burckhardt-Str. 32, CH-8049 Zurich, Switzerland.
- Rendez-Vous de la Mode; vedettes du pret-a-porter Europeen. 3 per yr. ISSN 0034-4397
- Tout pour Vous. s-a. ISSN 0040-9820

**Club Alpin Suisse**
- Alpen/Alpes. (pub. by Staempfli und Cie AG)

**Club de la Grammaire**
c/o M.J. Degiorgis, 6 Ch. Betems, Geneva, Switzerland.
- Club de la Grammaire. Cahiers. q. ISSN 0008-0128

**Verlag B. Cohn**
Rebbergstr. 45, 8049 Zurich, Switzerland.
- Flughafen - Revue; Kloten, Tor zur Schweiz Tor zur Welt. s-a. ISSN 0015-4555

**Collections Baur**
8 Rue Munier-Romilly, Geneva, Switzerland.
- Collections Baur. Bulletin. s-a. ISSN 0010-0781

**College International pour l'Etude Scientifique des Techniques de Production Mecanique**
see **International Institution for Production Engineering Research**

**Collegium Internationale Allergologicum**
- Allergologicum; Transactions of the Collegium Internationale. (pub. by S. Karger AG)

**Collegium Romanicium Helvetiorum a Curatoribus Vocis Romanicae**
- Romanica Helvetica. (pub. by Francke Verlag)

**Comite Intergouvernemental pour les Migrations Europeenes**
see **Intergovernmental Committee for European Migration**

**Comite International de la Croix Rouge**
see **International Committee of the Red Cross**

**Comite International Olympique**
see **International Olympic Committee**

**Commission Interuniversitaire Suisse de Linguistique Appliquee**
Universite de Neuchatel, Institut de Linguistique, CH-2000 Neuchatel, Switzerland.
- Bulletin C I L A. s-a.

**Committee for International Cooperation in Information Retrieval Among Examining Patent Offices**
32 Chemin des Colombettes, 1211 Geneva 20, Switzerland.
- Committee for International Cooperation in Information Retrieval Among Patent Offices. Bulletin. irreg. ISSN 0069-6838
- Committee for International Cooperation in Information Retrieval Among Patent Offices. Proceedings of Annual Meetings. a. ISSN 0069-6846

**Imprimerie la Concorde**
Case Postale 330, CH-1010 Lausanne, Switzerland.
- Bulletin Technique de la Suisse Romande. fortn.(bulletin); m.(supplement) ISSN 0007-5744 (Societe Suisse des Ingenieurs et des Architectes)
- Documentation du Batiment. a. ISSN 0070-6868 (Societe Suisse des Ingenieurs et des Architectes)

**Conference Permanente des Recteurs et Vice Chanceliers des Universites Europeennes**
see **Standing Conference of Rectors and Vice-Chancellors of the European Universities**

**Conference Universitaire Suisse**
Waaghaus-Passage 8, 3011 Berne, Switzerland.
- Conference Universitaire Suisse. Rapport Annuel. a.

**Conseil Europeen pour la Recherche Nucleaire**
see **European Organization for Nuclear Research**

**Conseil International des Agences Benevoles**
see **International Council of Voluntary Agencies**

**Conseil International sur les Problemes de l'Alcoolisme et des Toxicomanies**
see **International Council on Alcohol and Addictions**

**Conseil Oecumenique des Eglises**
see **World Council of Churches**

**Conservatoire Botanique de la Ville de Geneve**
Case Postale 21, CH-1211 Geneva 21, Switzerland.
- Exsiccatorum Genavensium; a conservatorio botanico distributorum fasciculus. a.

**Conservatoire de Musique de Geneve**
Place Neuve, 1204 Geneva, Switzerland.
- Conservatoire de Musique de Geneve. Bulletin. m (10 per yr.) ISSN 0010-6550

**Conzett und Huber AG**
Baslerstr. 30, Postfach, 8048 Zurich, Switzerland.
- Bulletin Technique; photogravure, lithographie, heliogravure. 5 per yr. ISSN 0007-5736 (Schweizerische Lithographenbund) (Co-sponsor: Verein Schweizerischer Lithographiebesitzer)
- Du; Europaeische Kunstzeitschrift. m. ISSN 0012-6837
- Fachhefte fuer Chemigraphie, Lithographie und Tiefdruck. 5 per yr. ISSN 0014-6374 (Schweizerischer Lithographenbund) (Co-sponsor: Verein Schweizerischer Lithographiebesitzer)

**Coop Schweiz**
Postfach 1285, CH-4002 Basel, Switzerland.
- Coop Fachblatt fuer Unternehmungsfuehrung/ Revue d'Economie d'Enterprise. m.

**Imprimerie Corbaz S. A.**
Av. des Planches 22, 1820 Montreux, Switzerland.
- Educateur et Bulletin Corporatif. w. ISSN 0013-1148 (Societe Pedagogique de la Suisse Romande)

**Council for International Organizations of Medical Sciences**
c/o World Health Organization, 20 Ave. Appia, CH-1211 Geneva 27, Switzerland.
- Calendar of International and Regional Congresses of Medical Sciences. a.

**Credit Suisse**
Paradeplatz 8, 8021 Zurich, Switzerland.
- Credit Suisse. Bulletin. 9 per yr (French & German edts.); 4 per yr. (English & Italian edts.); s-a (Spanish edt.) ISSN 0011-1023 (prep. by its Economic Research Department)
- Dollar-Bonds & Euro-Bonds. m. ISSN 0012-5237

**Credito Svizzero**
see **Credit Suisse**

**Cryophysics S.A.**
39 rue Rothschild, 1202 Geneva, Switzerland.
- Cryophysics Newsletter. q.

**Data Information Services S. A.**
81, Route de l'Aire, CH-1211 Geneva 26, Switzerland.
- Repertoire de la Presse Suisse/Leitfaden der Schweizer Presse. a.

**Destin**
13B Golette, Meyrin-Geneva, Switzerland.
- Destin. m. ISSN 0011-9555

**Deutschschweizerischer Sprachverein**
Alpenstr. 7, CH-6004 Lucerne, Switzerland.
- Sprachspiegel; Schweizerische Zeitschrift fuer die deutsche Muttersprache. bi-m. ISSN 0038-8513

**Dialectica**
c/o Association F. Gonseth, Case Postale 1081, 2501 Bienne, Switzerland.
- Dialectica; international review of philosophy of knowledge. q. ISSN 0012-2017

**Editions Diplomatiques Africaines**
Ave. du Lignon, Box 313, 1219 le Lignon/Geneva, Switzerland.
- Africa Diplomatica. m.

**Dokumentationsstelle fuer Schul- und Bildungsfragen**
see **Centre Suisse de Documentation en Matiere d'Enseignement et d'Education**

**Dorec Verlags AG**
Voltastr. 50a, CH-6005 Lucerne, Switzerland.
- Kunststoff Dokumentum. m. ISSN 0023-5539

**Drapalik Verlag**
Eichstrasse 24, CH-8045 Zurich, Switzerland.
- Radio-T V-Electronic Service. 12 per yr.

**Drehpunkt**
Postfach 794, CH-4002 Basel, Switzerland.
- Drehpunkt. 4 per yr. ISSN 0012-6055

**Librarie Droz**
11, rue Massot, 1211 Geneva 12, Switzerland.
- Bibliographie Internationale de l'Humanisme et de la Renaissance. a. ISSN 0067-7000 (International Federation of Societies and Institutes for the Study of the Renaissance)
- Bibliotheca Africana Droz. irreg. ISSN 0067-7825
- Bibliotheca Helvetica Romana. irreg., 1973, no. 12. ISSN 0067-7965 (Institut Suisse de Rome IT)
- Bibliotheque d'Humanisme et Renaissance; travaux et documents. 3 per yr. ISSN 0006-1999 (Association d'Humanisme et Renaissance)
- Bibliotheque de l'Ecole des Chartes; revue d'erudition. 2 per yr. ISSN 0006-1980 (Societe de l'Ecole des Chartes)
- Cahiers Ferdinand de Saussure; review de linguistique general. irreg., no. 30, 1976. ISSN 0068-516X (Cercle Ferdinand de Saussure)
- Cahiers Vilfredo Pareto; revue europeenne d'histoire des sciences sociales. 5 per yr. ISSN 0008-0497
- Classiques de la Pensee Politique. irreg., 1968, no. 5. ISSN 0069-4533
- Diderot Studies. a. ISSN 0070-4806
- Ecole Pratique des Hautes Etudes. Quatrieme Section. Historiques et Philologiques. Annuaire. a. ISSN 0078-964X
- Entretiens sur l'Antiquite Classique. irreg., vol. 22, 1976. ISSN 0071-0822 (Fondation Hardt pour l'Etude de l'Antiquite Classique)
- Etudes de Philologie et d'Histoire. irreg., no. 30, 1976. ISSN 0071-1934
- Hautes Etudes du Monde Greco-Romain. irreg., 1966, no. 2. ISSN 0073-0939 (Ecole Pratique des Hautes Etudes. Centre de Recherches d'Histoire et de Philologie FR)
- Hautes Etudes Islamiques et Orientales d'Histoire Comparee. irreg. ISSN 0073-0947 (Ecole Pratique des Hautes Etudes. Centre de Recherches d'Histoire et de Philologie FR)
- Hautes Etudes Medievales et Modernes. irreg. ISSN 0073-0955 (Ecole Pratique des Hautes Etudes. Centre de Recherches d'Histoire et de Philologie FR)
- Hautes Etudes Numismatiques. irreg., 1967, no. 2. ISSN 0073-0963 (Ecole Pratique des Hautes Etudes. Centre de Recherches d'Histoire et de Philologie FR)
- Hautes Etudes Orientales. irreg. ISSN 0073-0971 (Ecole Pratique des Hautes Etudes. Centre de Recherches d'Histoire et de Philologie FR)
- Histoire des Idees et Critique Litteraire. irreg., no. 161, 1977. ISSN 0073-2397
- Histoire et Civilisation du Livre. irreg., no. 9, 1976. ISSN 0073-2419 (Ecole Pratique des Hautes Etudes. Centre de Recherches d'Histoire et de Philologie FR)
- Koelner Romanistische Arbeiten. irreg., no. 49, 1976. ISSN 0075-6520 (Universitaet zu Koeln. Romanisches Seminar GW)
- Langue et Cultures; etudes et documents. irreg., no. 8, 1977. ISSN 0085-2678
- Publications Romanes et Francaises. irreg., no. 143, 1977. ISSN 0079-7812
- Revue Internationale d'Histoire de la Banque. a. ISSN 0080-2611 (Banco di Napoli IT)
- Societe de l'Ecole des Chartes. Memoires et Documents. irreg. ISSN 0078-9518
- Textes Litteraires Francais. irreg, no. 236, 1977.
- Travaux d'Histoire Ethico-Politique. irreg., no. 30, 1976. ISSN 0082-6073

- Travaux d'Humanisme et Renaissance. irreg., no. 154, 1977. ISSN 0082-6081
- Travaux de Droit, d'Economique de Sociologie et de Sciences Politiques. irreg. ISSN 0082-6022
- Universite de Geneve. Institut Universitaire de Hautes Etudes Internationales. Etudes et Travaux. irreg., no. 14, 1973. ISSN 0073-859X
- Universite de Geneve. Institut Universitaire de Hautes Etudes Internationales. Publication. irreg., no. 51, 1973. ISSN 0073-8603
- Universite de Geneve. Section d'Histoire. Documents. irreg., no. 10, 1976. ISSN 0072-0836
- Universite de Lausanne. Ecole des Sciences Sociales et Politiques. Publications. irreg., no. 9, 1972. ISSN 0075-8191
- Universite de Lausanne. Faculte des Lettres. Publications. irreg. ISSN 0041-915X
- Universite de Neuchatel. Faculte des Lettres. Recueil de Travaux. irreg., no. 81, 1975. ISSN 0077-7633

**Drusberg Verlag**
8053 Zurich, Switzerland.
- Holzbau. m. ISSN 0018-3814

**Ecole de Danse Simone Suter**
Caroline 7, CH-1003 Lausanne, Switzerland.
- Cahiers de la Danse. q.

**Ecole Polytechnique Federale de Lausanne**
33 Ave. de Cour, 1007 Lausanne, Switzerland.
- Ecole Polytechnique Federale de Lausanne. Publication. irreg.

**Ecole Polytechnique Federale de Lausanne. Chaire de Systemes Logiques**
16, chemin de Bellrive, 1007 Lausanne, Switzerland.
- Systemes Logiques; cahiers de la C S L. irreg., no. 6, 1975.

**Ecole Polytechnique Federale de Lausanne. Institut d'Entomologie**
2 rue de l'Universite, 8006 Zurich, Switzerland.
- Liste d'Identification des Entomophages. irreg. (International Organization of Biological Control)

**Economic Commission for Europe**
For publications of this agency see section for United Nations

**EDISAFRIC**
see Editions Diplomatiques Africaines

**Edita S.A.**
7 rue de Geneve, Lausanne, Switzerland.
- Automobile Year/Annee Automobile/Auto-Jahr. a. ISSN 0084-7674

**Editions Fempol**
Socinstrasse 2, CH-4051 Basel, Switzerland.
- Editions Fempol; blaetter fuer feministisches Bewusstsein und politische Aktion. q.

**Editions Imprimerie Federative SA**
see Buchverlag Verbandsdruckerei AG

**Editions Universitaires de Fribourg**
36 Bd. de Perolles, CH-1700 Fribourg, Switzerland.
- Colloques Economiques. irreg.
- Freiburger Zeitschrift fuer Philosophie und Theologie. 2 per yr. ISSN 0016-0725 (Universite de Fribourg. Dominikaner-Professoren der Theologischen Fakultaet)
- Methodes de la Cartographie Thematique. irreg.
- Nova et Vetera. q. ISSN 0029-5027
- Universite de Fribourg. Historische Schriften. irreg.

**Effektenboersenverein Zuerich**
Bleicherweg 5, 8001 Zurich, Switzerland.
- Zuercher Boerse: Jahresbericht. a. (Zuercher Boerse)

**Eglises Protestantes de la Suisse Romande. Department Missionaire**
Ch. des Cedres 5, 1000 Lausanne 9, Switzerland.
- Actualite Missionnaire. 5 per yr. ISSN 0001-7744

**Eidgenoessische Sternwarte**
Schmelzbergstr. 25, 8006 Zuerich, Switzerland.
- Eidgenoessische Sternwarte, Zurich. Astronomische Mitteilungen. irreg., no. 353, 1977. ISSN 0085-8420
- Eidgenoessische Sternwarte, Zurich. Taetigkeitsbericht. a.
- Quarterly Bulletin on Solar Activity. q. ISSN 0048-6167 (International Astronomical Union)

**Eidgenoessische Technische Hochschule Zuerich**
- Eidgenoessische Technische Hochschule Zuerich. Mitteilungen. Aerodynamik. (pub. by Buchdruckerei und Verlag Leemann AG)
- Eidgenoessische Technische Hochschule Zuerich. Mitteilungen. Photoelastizitaet. (pub. by Buchdruckerei und Verlag Leemann AG)
- Eidgenoessische Technische Hochschule Zuerich. Mitteilungen. Textilmaschinenbau und Textilindustrie. (pub. by Buchdruckerei und Verlag Leemann AG)

**Eidgenoessische Technische Hochschule Zuerich. Abteilung fuer Elektrotechnik**
- Scientia Electrica. (pub. by Birkhaeuser Verlag)

**Eidgenoessische Technische Hochschule Zuerich. Bibliothek**
Raemistr. 101, 8006 Zurich, Switzerland.
- Eidgenoessische Technische Hochschule Zuerich. Bibliothek. Schriftenreihe. irreg. ISSN 0514-0668

**Eidgenoessische Technische Hochschule Zuerich. Gesellschaft zur Foerderung des Betriebswissenschaftlichen Institutes**
- I O. (pub. by Verlag Industrielle Organisation)

**Eidgenoessische Technische Hochschule Zuerich. Institut fuer Baustatik**
Raemistrasse 101, 8006 Zurich, Switzerland.
- Eidgenoessische Technische Hochschule Zuerich. Institut fuer Baustatik. Bericht. irreg.

**Eidgenoessische Technische Hochschule Zuerich. Institut fuer Geophysik**
Postfach 266, CH-8049 Zurich, Switzerland.
- Eidgenoessische Technische Hochschule Zuerich. Institut fuer Geophysik.Schweizerische Erdbebendienst. Jahresbericht. irreg. ISSN 0084-5779

**Eidgenoessische Technische Hochschule Zuerich. Institut fuer Orts- , Regional- und Landesplanung**
Hoenggerberg, CH-8093 Zurich, Switzerland.
- Bibliographie der Orts-, Regional- und Landesplanung. a.
- Dokumente und Informationen zur Schweizerischen Orts- ,Regional- und Landesplanung. q.
- Vademecum. biennial.

**Eidgenoessische Technische Hochschule Zuerich. Versuchsanstalt fuer Wasserbau, Hydrologie und Glaziologie**
Gloriastrasse 37-39, CH-8006 Zurich, Switzerland.
- Eidgenoessische Technische Hochschule Zuerich: Versuchsanstalt fuer Wasserbau, Hydrologie und Glaziologie. Jahresbericht. a.

**Electrowatt Engineering Services Ltd.**
Postfach, 8022 Zurich, Switzerland.
- Literaturrundschau. m. ISSN 0024-4872

**Verlag der Elektromonteur AG**
Postfach 68, CH-5000 Aarau, Switzerland.
- Elektromonteur. 9 per yr. ISSN 0046-1784

**Elektrowirtschaft**
Bahnhofplatz 9, 8028 Zurich, Switzerland.
- Elektrizitaet. q. ISSN 0013-5461
- Elektrizitaetsverwertung/Electrique/Electrical Service; internationale zeitschrift fuer elektrizitaetsverwertung. m. ISSN 0013-5488 (International Union of Producers and Distributors of Electrical Energy FR)

**Elsevier Sequoia S.A.**
Box 851, 1001 Lausanne 1, Switzerland.
- Chemical Engineering Journal; an international journal of research and development. bi-m. ISSN 0009-2487
- Cognition; an International journal of Cognitive Psychology. 4 per yr. ISSN 0010-0277
- Current Awareness in Particle Technology. m. (Particle Science and Technology Information Service UK)
- Current Titles in Electrochemistry. m.
- Drug and Alcohol Dependence; an international journal on biomedical and psychosocial approaches. bi-m. (International Council on Alcohol and Addictions)
- Electric Power Systems Research; an international journal devoted to research and new applications in generation, transmission, distribution and utilization of electric power. q.
- Elsevier Sequoia Patent Reports. irreg.
- Energy and Building; an international journal on energy efficiency in the building environment. q.

- Environmental Conservation. q. (Foundation for Environmental Conservation)
- Environmental Policy and Law. 4 per yr. (International Council for Environmental Law)
- Fire Research. bi-m.
- Forensic Science. bi-m. ISSN 0300-9432
- Inorganica Chimica Acta. m. ISSN 0020-1693
- Journal of Electroanalytical Chemistry and Interfacial Electrochemistry; international journal dealing with all aspects of electroanalytical chemistry, including fundamental electrochemistry. 24 per yr. ISSN 0022-0728
- Journal of Fluorine Chemistry. m. ISSN 0022-1139
- Journal of Molecular Catalysis. bi-m.
- Journal of Organometallic Chemistry. w. ISSN 0022-328X
- Journal of Photochemistry; an international journal devoted to the study of the quantitative aspects of photochemistry and energy transfer. m. ISSN 0047-2670
- Journal of Power Sources; an international journal on the science, technology and application of non-mechanical, electrical power storage, generation and conversion. q.
- Journal of Radioanalytical Chemistry; an international journal dealing with all aspects of nuclear analytical methods. m. ISSN 0022-4081 (Co-publisher: Akademiai Kiado, Publisher of the Hungarian Academy of Sciences)
- Journal of the Less-Common Metals; an international journal of their science and application. m (6 vols. per yr.) ISSN 0022-5088
- Marxist Anthropology. irreg.
- Materials Science and Engineering; an international journal. m. (5 vols. per yr.) ISSN 0025-5416
- Mechanisms of Ageing and Development. bi-m. ISSN 0047-6374
- Powder Technology; an international journal on the science and technology of wet and dry particulate systems. bi-m. ISSN 0032-5910
- Progress in Organic Coatings; an international review journal. 3 per yr. ISSN 0033-0655
- Psychological Reader's Guide. m. ISSN 0300-0443 (Institut de Documentation Scientifique)
- Radiochemical and Radioanalytical Letters. 24 per yr. ISSN 0079-9483 (Co-publisher: Akademiai Kiado, Publisher of the Hungarian Academy of Sciences)
- Surface Technology. bi-m.
- Thin Solid Films; an international journal on the science and technology of thin and thick films. s-m. ISSN 0040-6090
- Wear; international journal on the science and technology of friction, lubrication and wear. m. ISSN 0043-1648

**Emmentaler Druck**
Alleestrasse 11, CH-3550 Langnau, Switzerland.
- Blaue, Alpwirtschaftliche Monatsblaetter. m. ISSN 0006-4610 (Schweizerischer Alpwirtschaftlicher Verein)
- Conversation et Traduction; franzoesisch-deutsche Sprach- und Unterhaltungszeitschrift. m. ISSN 0010-8170
- Nadel Faden Fingerhut. m. ISSN 0027-7525

**Ensemble - l'Information d'Action Sociale**
Case Postale 121, CH-1000 Lausanne, Switzerland.
- Ensemble - l'Information d'Action Sociale. 6 per yr. ISSN 0046-2128

**Escherbund**
47A Ottenbergstr., 8049 Zurich, Switzerland.
- Neue Bund. q. ISSN 0028-3134

**EUROFIMA**
see European Company for the Financing of Railway Rolling Stock

**Europa Verlag AG**
Raemistrasse 5, 8001 Zurich, Switzerland.
- Thomas Mann Gesellschaft. Blaetter. a. ISSN 0082-4186

**European Association of Endocrinology**
- Hormone Research. (pub. by S. Karger AG)

**European Association of Perinatal Medicine**
- European Congress of Perinatal Medicine. Proceedings. (pub. by S. Karger AG)

**European Association of Urology**
- European Urology. (pub. by S. Karger AG)

**European Biological Research Association**
- Agents and Actions. (pub. by Birkhaeuser Verlag)

**European Broadcasting Union**
Case Postale 193, CH-1211 Geneva 20, Switzerland.
- E B U Monographs, Legal and Administrative Series. irreg.
- E B U Review. Geneva Edition (Programmes, Adminstration, Law) bi-m.
- E B U Seminars for Producers and Directors of Educational Television for Schools and Adults. a.
- E B U Workshops for Producers and Directors of Television Programmes for Children and Young People. biennial.
- International Forum of Light Music in Radio. biennial.

**European Company for the Financing of Railway Rolling Stock**
Rittergasse 20, Basel, Switzerland.
- EUROFIMA. Rapport Annuel. a. ISSN 0071-2264

**European Federation for the Protection of Waters**
Kuerbergstr. 19, 8049 Zurich, Switzerland.
- European Federation for the Protection of Waters. Information Bulletin. 1-2 per yr. ISSN 0014-293X

**European Free Trade Association**
9-11 rue de Varembe, 1211 Geneva 20, Switzerland.
- E F T A Bulletin. m. ISSN 0012-7655
- E F T A Trade. a. ISSN 0531-4119
- European Free Trade Association. Annual Report. a. ISSN 0531-4127

**European Organization for Caries Research**
- Caries Research. (pub. by S. Karger AG)

**European Organization for Nuclear Research**
CH-1211 Geneva 23, Switzerland.
- C E R N Annual Report. a. ISSN 0304-2901
- C E R N Courier. m. ISSN 0304-288X
- C E R N-H E R A Reports. irreg. ISSN 0366-5690
- C E R N Reports. irreg. ISSN 0007-8328
- C E R N School of Computing. Proceedings. biennial. ISSN 0304-2898
- C E R N School of Physics. Proceedings. irreg. ISSN 0531-4283
- European Organization for Nuclear Research. List des Publications Scientifiques/List of Scientific Publications. a. ISSN 0304-2871

**European Organization for Quality Control**
Box 2613, CH-3001 Berne, Switzerland.
- European Organization for Quality Control. Proceedings of Conference. (pub. by Agifa Verlag)
- Quality. 5 per yr. ISSN 0033-5169

**European Physical Society**
Box 39, CH-1213 Petit-Lancy 2, Switzerland.
- Europhysics Conference Abstracts. a.
- Europhysics News. m. ISSN 0531-7479

**European Society for Experimental Surgery**
- European Surgical Research. (pub. by S. Karger AG)

**European Society of Ophthalmology**
- European Society of Ophthalmology. Proceedings of the Congress. (pub. by S. Karger AG)

**European Society on Microcirculation**
- European Conference on Microcirculation. Proceedings. (pub. by S. Karger AG)

**Evangelisch-Kirchliche Vereinigung in der Schweiz**
- Reformatio. (pub. by Benteli-Verlag)

**Ex Libris et Guilde du Disque**
Place de la Palud 22, C.P. 605, Lausanne 17, Switzerland.
- Ex Libris. m.

**Exakt-Verlag**
8280 Kreuzlingen TG, Switzerland.
- S K M. (Schweizer Kontakt) bi-m.

**EXIM-INDEX Dr. E. Goldberger**
Box 525, Grellingerstrusse 53, CH-4002 Basel, Switzerland.
- Swisstrade; current business opportunities with Switzerland. m(10 per yr) (Swissexport Cooperation Alliance)

**Fachgruppe Ladenbau**
- Ladenbau. (pub. by Forster-Verlag AG)

**Federation des Societes d'Agriculture de la Suisse Romande**
- Revue Suisse d'Agriculture. (pub. by Presses Centrales Lausanne S.A.)
- Revue Suisse de Viticulture, Arboriculture et Horticulture. (pub. by Presses Centrales Lausanne S.A.)

**Federation Horlogere Suisse**
*see* **Federation of Swiss Watch Manufacturers**

**Federation Internationale de Football Association**
*see* **International Federation of Association Football**

**Federation Internationale de Gymnastique**
*see* **International Gymnastic Federation**

**Federation Internationale des Societes et Instituts pour l'Etude de la Renaissance**
*see* **International Federation of Societies and Institutes for the Study of the Renaissance**

**Federation Internationale Motocycliste**
19 Chemin William-Barbey, 1292 Chamesy-Geneva, Switzerland.
- Federation Internationale Motocycliste. Annuaire. a. ISSN 0071-4283

**Federation Mondiale pour la Protection des Animaux**
*see* **World Federation for the Protection of Animals**

**Federation of Migros Cooperatives**
Limmastr. 152, 8031 Zurich, Switzerland.
- Federation of Migros Cooperatives. Abridged Annual Report; summary of the report of the Board of Directors to the Assembly of Delegates. a. ISSN 0071-4410

**Federation of Swiss Physicians**
*see* **Schweizerische Aerzteorganisation**

**Federation of Swiss Watch Manufacturers**
6 Silbergasse, 2501 Bienne, Switzerland
- Federation Horlogere Suisse. Annual Report. a. ISSN 0071-4259 (Dist. by Watchmakers of Switzerland Information Center, Inc., 608 Fifth Ave., New York, NY 10020)

**Federation Romande de Metiers du Batiment**
10 rue de Beaumont, Case 339, 1211 Geneva 25, Switzerland.
- Construire. m. ISSN 0010-7034

**Federation Romande Immobiliere**
- Bulletin Immobilier. (pub. by Presses Centrales Lausanne S.A.)

**Federation Romandes des Maitres Menuisiers, Ebenistes, Charpentiers, Fabricants de Meubles et Parqueteurs**
Ave. Jomini 8, C. P. 66, CH-1000 Lausanne 9, Switzerland.
- Industriel sur Bois. m.

**Federation Suisse des Avocats**
*see* **Schweizerischer Anwaltsverband**

**Federation Suisse des Cheminots**
*see* **Schweizerischer Eisenbahnerverband**

**Federation Suisse des Marchands de Tabacs**
*see* **Verband Schweizerischer Tabakhaendler**

**Federation Suisse des Typographes**
Case 577, 2301 la Chaux-de-Fonds, Switzerland.
- Gutenberg. w. ISSN 0017-5811

**Federation Suisse-Liechtentein des Sports Populaires**
2400 le Locle, Switzerland.
- Schweizer Volksport/Sport Populaire Suisse. 5 per yr.

**Federazione Svizzera dei Ferrovieri**
*see* **Schweizerischer Eisenbahnerverband**

**Federazione Svizzera dei Negozianti in Tabacchi**
*see* **Verband Schweizerischer Tabakhaendler**

**Fehr'sche Buchhandlung AG**
Schmiedgasse 16, 9001 St. Gallen, Switzerland.
- Historischer Verein des Kantons St. Gallen. Neujahrsblatt. a.

**Finanz-Revue A.G.**
Loewenstr. 11, 8021 Zurich, Switzerland.
- Finanz-Revue; Schweizerisches Wirtschaftsblatt. w. ISSN 0015-2188

**Verlag Finanz und Wirtschaft AG**
Baeckerstrasse 7, Postfach, CH-8021 Zurich, Switzerland.
- Finanz und Wirtschaft. 2 per wk. ISSN 0015-220X

**AG Buchdruckerei B. Fischer**
3110 Munsingen, Switzerland.
- Schwyzerluet; schriftenreihe fuer veses schwyzerduetsch. q.

**James Fitzsimmons, Ed. & Pub.**
Via Maraini 17-A, Lugano, Switzerland.
- Art International: the Art Spectrum. bi-m. ISSN 0004-3230
- New Lugano Review; devoted to exhibition reviews, monographs on contemporary artists and articles on current and perennial problems in arts: also short stories, poems and articles on modern European and American literature. q. ISSN 0024-7278

**Focus-Verlag**
Postfach 161, 8033 Zurich, Switzerland.
- Focus; das politische magazin. m. ISSN 0046-4287

**Fondation Hardt pour l'Etude de l'Antiquite Classique**
- Entretiens sur l'Antiquite Classique. (pub. by Librarie Droz)

**Forschungsinstitut der Eidgenoessischen Turn- und Sportschule Magglingen**
- Forschungsinstitut der Eidgenoessischen Turn- und Sportschule Magglingen. Wissenschaftliche Schriftenreihe. (pub. by Birkhaeuser Verlag)

**Forschungsstelle fuer Politische Wissenschaft**
- Annuaire Suisse de Science Politique/ Schweizerisches Jahrbuch fuer Politische Wissenschaft/Swiss Political Science Yearbook. (pub. by Paul Haupt AG)

**Forster-Verlag AG**
Ottikerstr. 59, Postfach 295, CH-8033 Zurich, Switzerland.
- Hotel- und Gastgewerbe-Rundschau; unabhaengiges fachorgan fuer gastronomie, betriebs- und kuechentechnische praxis. m. ISSN 0035-9920
- Ladenbau; schweizerische fachzeitschrift fuer modernen ladenbau schaufenster und display. bi-m. ISSN 0458-6123 (Fachgruppe Ladenbau)
- Lebensmittel Technologie; fachzeitschrift fuer lebensmittel- und genussmittel-industrie maschinen-apparate-geraete-verfahren. 4 per yr.
- Lebensmittel-Wissenschaft und Technologie/Food Science and Technology/Science et Technologie Alimentaire; international journal for chemistry, biochemistry, microbiology, and technology of food processing. bi-m. ISSN 0023-6438 (Schweizerische Gesellschaft fuer Lebensmittelwissenschaft und- Technologie)
- Oberflaeche/Surface; internationale fachzeitschrift fuer das gesamte gebiet der oberflaechentechnik und des korrosionsschutzes von metallen und anderen werkstoffen. m. ISSN 0048-1270 (Schweizerische Galvanotechnische Gesellschaft) (Co-sponsor: Verband Galvanischer Anstalten des Schweiz)
- Temperatur Technik; fachzeitschrift fuer das gesamte Gebiet Kaelteerzeugung und Kaelteanwendung, Kuehl und tiefkuehltransport, klimatechnik, lueftung, isolierung und Heizung. bi-m. (Schweizerischer Verein fuer Kaeltetechnik)
- Transport und Lagertechnik; Schweizerische Fachzeitschrift fuer rationellen Gueterumschlag, Transport, Lagerhaltung und Foerdertechnik. m. ISSN 0041-1574
- Verpackung; schweizerische Fachzeitschrift fuer Verpackung, Technologie, Verpackungspsycholigie, Package Design, Marketing. m. ISSN 0042-4277

**Fotorotar AG**
Gewerbestr. 18, 8132 Egg, Switzerland.
- Schweizerische Entomologische Gesellschaft. Mitteilungen/Societe Entomologique Suisse. Bulletin. q. ISSN 0036-7575

**Foundation for Environmental Conservation**
- Environmental Conservation. (pub. by Elsevier Sequoia S.A.)

**Foundation for Promoting International Economic Information**
- Kompas Danmark. (pub. by Forlaget Kompas-Denmark DK)

- Kompass Belgium/Luxembourg. (pub. by Kompass Belgium S.A. BE)
- Kompass Espana. (pub. by Kompass Espana SA SP)
- Kompass Holland. (pub. by Kompass Nederland N.V. NE)
- Kompass Maroc. (pub. by Kompass Maroc-Veto MR)
- Kompass Norge. (pub. by Kompass Norge A-S NO)
- Kompass Schweiz/Liechtenstein. (pub. by Kompass International AG)
- Kompass Sverige. (pub. by Kompass Sweden SW)

**Francke Verlag**
Postfach, CH-3000 Berne 26, Switzerland.
- Antike Kunst. s-a. ISSN 0003-5688 (Vereinigung der Freunde Antiker Kunst)
- Antike Kunst. Beihefte. irreg., vol. 10, 1976. ISSN 0066-4782 (Vereinigung der Freunde Antiker Kunst)
- Asiatische Studien/Etudes Asiatiques. 1-2 per yr. ISSN 0004-4717 (Schweizerische Gesellschaft fuer Asienkunde)
- Basler Studien zur Deutschen Sprache und Literatur. irreg., vol. 52, 1976. ISSN 0067-4508
- Bibliotheca Germanica. Handbuecher, Texte und Monographien aus dem Gebiete der Germanischen Philologie. irreg., vol. 18, 1975. ISSN 0067-7477
- Bibliotheca Romanica. irreg., vol. 5, 1975. ISSN 0067-7515
- Colloquia Germanica; an international journal for Germanic philology and literary criticism. 4 per yr. ISSN 0010-1338 (University of Kentucky. Department of Germanic and Classical Languages US)
- Cooper Monographs on English and American Language and Literature. irreg., vol. 25, 1976. ISSN 0069-9780
- Helvetia Politica; Schriften des Forschungszentrums fuer Geschichte und Soziologie der schweizerischen Politik. irreg. ISSN 0073-182X
- Romanica Helvetica. irreg., vol. 86, 1976. ISSN 0080-3871 (Collegium Romanicium Helvetiorum a Curatoribus Vocis Romanicae)
- Sammlung Dalp. irreg., vol. 105, 1976. ISSN 0080-5807
- Schweizer Anglistische Arbeiten/Swiss Studies in English. irreg., vol. 91, 1976. ISSN 0080-7214
- Schweizerische Geisteswissenschaftliche Gesellschaft. Schriften. irreg., 1971, vol. 13. ISSN 0080-729X
- Vox Romanica; annales helvetici explorandis linguis romanicis destinati. s-a. ISSN 0042-899X

**Verlag H. G. Franke**
8126 Zumikon, Switzerland.
- Modernes Wohnen/Habitation Moderne. q. ISSN 0026-8712

**Freidenker-Vereinigung der Schweiz**
c/o E. C. Geissmann, Buch Otz, Aarauerstr 3, 5600 Lenzberg, Switzerland.
- Freidenken. q.

**Freisinnig-Demokratische Partei der Schweiz**
Postfach 2642, Bahnhofplatz 10, 3001 Berne, Switzerland.
- Politische Rundschau/Revue Politique; Zeitschrift fuer Kultur, Politik und Wirtschaft. q.

**Verlag Gebrueder Fretz**
Postfach, 8032 Zurich, Switzerland.
- Graphia. m. ISSN 0017-3266

**Verlag Jean Frey AG**
Staffelstr. 12, 8021 Zurich, Switzerland.
- Annabelle. fortn. ISSN 0003-3774
- Weltwoche. w. ISSN 0043-2660

**Hans Frey, Ed. & Pub.**
Kreuzstr. 11, 8712 Staefa, Switzerland.
- Schweizer Hotel Journal. s-a. ISSN 0048-9514
- Schweizer Journal. m. ISSN 0036-7370

**Buchdruckerei K. Furter**
Scheidgasse 48, 3800 Unterseen-Interlaken, Switzerland.
- Uhrenfachgeschaeft/Magasin d'Horlogerie Specialise. bi-m. ISSN 0049-5042 (Verband Schweizerischer Uhrenfachgeschaefte)

**Editions Bertil Galland**
29 rue du Lac, CH-1800 Vevey, Switzerland.
- Ecriture; l'annnee litteraire en suisse romande. a. ISSN 0070-8879

**Gartenbau-Verlag**
Gaertnerstrasse, Gaertnerhof Nord, Postfach, 4500 Solothurn 1, Switzerland.
- Gartenbau/Horticulture Suisse. w. ISSN 0016-4747

**E.F. Gasser**
Fach 26, CH-3017 Berne, Switzerland.
- Rampenlicht; Artisten Zeitschrift. irreg. ISSN 0079-9599

**Buchdruckerei Gassmann AG**
Werkhofstr. 17, 4500 Solothurn, Switzerland.
- Wirtschaft und Technik im Transport/Economie et Technique des Transports. bi-m. ISSN 0049-6820

**General Agreement on Tariffs and Trade**
For publications of this agency see section for
UNITED NATIONS

**Genossenschaftliche Zentralbank AG**
- Kyklos. (pub. by Kyklos-Verlag)

**Geographisch-Ethnographische Gesellschaft Zurich**
- Geographica Helvetica. (pub. by Kuemmerly und Frey AG)

**Georgi Publishing Co.**
CH-1813 St.-Saphorin, Switzerland.
- Colloquium Internationale. bi-m. ISSN 0304-2863 (Society for Human Ecology)
- Digital Processes; an international journal on the theory and design of digital systems. q.

**Gesellschaft der Freunde Alter Musikinstrumente**
Walleraustr. 44, CH-8807 Freienbach, Switzerland.
- Glareana. q.

**Gesellschaft des Schweizerische Hals- Nasen- und Ohrenaerzte**
- O R L. (pub. by S. Karger AG)

**Gesellschaft fuer das Schweizerischen Volkstheater**
Berne 30, Switzerland.
- Laientheater. m.

**Gesellschaft fuer Militaerische Bautechnik**
Auf der Mauer 2, CH-8001 Zurich, Switzerland.
- Technische Mitteilungen fuer Sappeure, Pontoniere und Mineure. q.

**Gesellschaft fuer Volkskunde, Basel. Abteilung Film**
- Altes Handwerk. (pub. by Rudolf Habelt Verlag GW)

**Gesellschaft pro Vindonissa**
Vindonissa Museum, 5200 Brugg, Switzerland.
- Gesellschaft pro Vindonissa. Jahresbericht. a. ISSN 0072-4270
- Gesellschaft pro Vindonissa. Veroeffentlichungen. irreg. ISSN 0072-4289

**Gesellschaft Schweizer Monatshefte**
Stockerstr. 14, 8002 Zurich, Switzerland.
- Schweizer Monatshefte; Zeitschrift fuer Politik, Wirtschaft, Kultur. m. ISSN 0036-7400

**Gesellschaft Schweizerische Musikzeitung**
- Schweizerische Musikzeitung/Revue Musicale Suisse. (pub. by Musikverlag Hug und Co.)

**Gesellschaft Schweizerischer Landwirte**
- Schweizerische Landwirtschaftliche Monatshefte. (pub. by Benteli-Verlag)

**Gesellschaft Schweizerischer Maler, Bildhauer und Architekten**
Rigistrasse 28, 8006 Zurich, Switzerland.
- Schweizer Kunst/Art Suisse/Arte Suizzera. m.

**Gesellschaft Schweizerischer Tieraerzte**
- G S T Bulletin/Bulletin S V S. (pub. by Orell Fuessli Graphische Betriebe AG)
- Schweizer Archiv fuer Tierheilkunde. (pub. by Orell Fuessli Graphische Betriebe AG)

**Gesellschaft Schweizerischer Zeichenlehrer**
c/o Bernhard Wyss, Ed., Bodenacker, CH-3033 Wohlen, Switzerland.
- Zeichnen und Gestalten. q.

**Gesellschaft zur Domprobstei**
Lange Gasse 20, 4052 Basel, Switzerland.
- Tip; Sportmagazin. w. ISSN 0040-8018 (Sport-Toto- Gesellschaft) (Co-sponsor: Gesellschaft Schweizer Zahlenlotto)

**Glasblaeser-Vereinigung**
Probusweg 10, Zurich 11/57, Switzerland.
- Glasblaeser. bi-m. ISSN 0017-0836

**Gotthelf Verlag**
Postfach, CH-8026 Zurich, Switzerland.
- Musik und Gottesdienst. bi-m. ISSN 0027-4763

**Gottlieb Duttweiler Institute for Economic & Social Studies**
CH-8803 Ruschlikon Zurich, Switzerland.
- G D I Information. fortn. ISSN 0016-3457

**Graduate Institute of International Studies**
*see* Universite de Geneve. Institut Universitaire de Hautes Etudes Internationales

**Graf und Neuhaus**
Bachtoldstr. 4, 8044 Zurich, Switzerland.
- Anthos; vierteljahres-Zeitschrift fuer Garten- und Landschaftsgestaltung. q. ISSN 0003-5424 (International Federation of Landscape Architects)
- Armee-Motor. m. ISSN 0004-2269
- Petri-Heil; unabhaengige sportfischerzeitung. m. ISSN 0031-6318
- Protector. q.

**Groupe d'Etude du Film**
C.P. 2876, CH-1002 Lausanne, Switzerland.
- Travelling; revue de cinema. 3 per yr. ISSN 0041-2120 (Co-sponsor: Cinematheque Suisse)

**Groupe Voie Lactee**
Case Postale 209, 1000 Lausanne 9, Switzerland.
- Ergot. 8 per yr. ISSN 0046-2454

**Groupes Bibliques Universitaires de Suisse Romande**
31 Rue de l'Ale, 1003 Lausanne, Switzerland.
- Chantiers. q. ISSN 0009-1588

**Guilde du Livre**
5, rue de l'Ecole Superieure, 1005 Lausanne, Switzerland.
- Guilde du Livre. m. ISSN 0017-5412

**Habegger Verlag**
CH-4552 Derendingen-Solothurn, Switzerland.
- Film & Foto; Ihr Bild- und Ton-hobby. m(10 per yr.) ISSN 0015-1076
- Ski-Schweizer Skisport/Sci Suisse. 10 per yr. ISSN 0037-623X

**Hallwag AG**
Nordring 4, CH-3001 Berne, Switzerland.
- C. I. R. P. Annals. q. ISSN 0007-8506 (International Institution for Production Engineering Research)
- Neue Columbus; das grosse Jahrbuch von Spiel und Sport von Erfindungen, Entdeckungen und Abenteuern aus aller Welt. a.
- Orbis Pictus. irreg. ISSN 0078-5571 (Dist. by: Hippocrene Books, 171 Madison Ave., New York, NY 10016)
- Revue Automobile; journal suisse de l'automobile. w. ISSN 0005-1314
- Schweizerische Rundschau fuer Medizin Praxis/ Revue Suisse de Medecine. w.
- Technische Rundschau; Europaeische Industrie- und Handelszeitung. w. ISSN 0040-148X
- Tier; internationale Tierillustrierte. m. ISSN 0040-7291

**Hasler Ltd.**
Belpstr. 23, CH-3000 Berne 14, Switzerland.
- Hasler-Mitteilungen. q. ISSN 0017-8306

**Hauenstein-Verlag**
Dornacherstr. 10, CH-4600 Olten, Switzerland.
- Ring-Post; Ausblick vom hauenstein. m.

**Paul Haupt AG**
Falkenplatz 14, CH-3001 Berne, Switzerland.
- Annuaire Suisse de Science Politique/ Schweizerisches Jahrbuch fuer Politische Wissenschaft/Swiss Political Science Yearbook. a. ISSN 0066-3727 (Forschungsstelle fuer Politische Wissenschaft)
- Aus dem Schweizerischen Landesmuseum. irreg., no. 40, 1976. ISSN 0067-0618 (Schweizerisches Landesmuseum)

- Bankwirtschaftliche Forschungen. irreg., vol. 41, 1977. ISSN 0067-382X (Universitaet Zuerich. Institut fuer Schweizerisches Bankwesen) (Cosponsor: Hochschule St. Gallen fuer Wirtschafts- und Sozialwissenschaften, Institut fuer Bankwirtschaft)
- Berner Beitraege zur Nationaloekonomie. irreg., vol. 30, 1976. ISSN 0067-6128
- Berner Beitraege zur Soziologie. irreg., vol. 17, 1976. ISSN 0067-6136 (Universitaet Bern. Institut fuer Soziologie und Sozio-Oekonomische Entwicklungsfragen)
- Berner Kriminologische Untersuchungen. irreg., 1973, vol. 8. ISSN 0067-6144
- Betriebswirtschaftliche Mitteilungen. irreg. ISSN 0067-639X (Hochschule St. Gallen fuer Wirtschafts- und Sozialwissenschaften. Institut fuer Betriebswirtschaft)
- Eidgenoessische Zukunft: Bausteine fuer Die Kommende Schweiz. irreg., no. 14, 1976. ISSN 0070-9514
- Erziehung und Unterricht. irreg., no. 21, 1976. ISSN 0071-125X
- Fuehrung und Organisation der Unternehmung. irreg. ISSN 0071-9765 (Hochschule St. Gallen fuer Wirtschafts- und Sozialwissenschaften. Institut fuer Betriebswirtschaft)
- Grosse Heimatbuecher. irreg. ISSN 0072-7725
- Hochschule St. Gallen fuer Wirtschafts- und Sozialwissenschaften. Forschungsinstitut fuer Absatz und Handel. Schriftenreihe. irreg., vol. 16, 1976. ISSN 0080-603X
- Koerpererziehung/Education Physique. m. ISSN 0023-2696 (Schweizerischer Turnverein)
- Neue Steuerpraxis. m. ISSN 0028-338X (Berne (Canton) Kantonale Steuerverwaltung)
- Noctes Romanae; Forschungen ueber die Kultur der Antike. irreg., vol. 15, 1977. ISSN 0078-0936
- Partnerberatung; Zentralblatt fuer Ehe- und Familienkunde. q. (Institut fuer Ehe- und Familienwissenschaft)
- Planung und Kontrolle in der Unternehmung. irreg., vol. 6, 1976. ISSN 0079-2276 (Hochschule St. Gallen fuer Wirtschafts- und Sozialwissenschaften. Institut fuer Betriebswirtschaft)
- Praktische Betriebswirtschaft. irreg., 1973, vol. 7. ISSN 0079-4880 (Hochschule St. Gallen fuer Wirtschafts- und Sozialwissenschaften. Institut fuer Betriebswirschaft)
- Pruefen und Entscheiden. irreg., no. 7, 1977. ISSN 0079-7111 (Universitaet Bern. Institut fuer Betriebswirtschaft)
- Sankt Galler Beitraege Zum Fremdenverkehr und zur Verkehrswirtschaft: Reihe Verkehrswirtschaft. irreg. ISSN 0080-6048 (Hochschule St. Gallen fuer Wirtschafts- und Sozialwissenschaften. Institut fuer Fremdenverkehr und Verkehrswirtschaft)
- Schweizer Hundesport. fortn. ISSN 0036-7354 (Schweizerischen Kynologischen Gesellschaft)
- Schweizerische Musikforschende Gesellschaft. Publikationen. Serie II. irreg., no. 30, 1977. ISSN 0080-7354
- Schweizerische Zeitschrift fuer Sportmedizin/Revue Suisse de Medecine des Sports/Revista Svizzera di Medicina Dello Sport. 4 per yr. ISSN 0036-7885 (Schweizerische Gesellschaft fuer Sportmedizin)
- Soziale Sicherheit; Beitraege zu ihrer Erforschung in Vergangenheit, Gegenwart und Zukunft. irreg., 1969, no. 2. ISSN 0081-3249
- Sprache und Dichtung. Neue Folge. irreg., vol. 26, 1977. ISSN 0081-3826
- Staat und Politik. irreg., vol. 16, 1976. ISSN 0081-4105
- Studientage fuer Die Pfarrer; eine Sammlung von Vortraegen. irreg., 1968, no. 6. ISSN 0081-7406 (Synodalrat der Evangelisch-Reformierten Landeskirche des Kantons Bern)
- Unternehmung; Schweizerische Zeitschrift fuer Betriebswirtschaft Organisation und modernes Foerderwesen. q. ISSN 0042-059X (Vereinigung Schweizerischer Betriebswirtschafter)
- Unternehmung und Unternehmungsfuehrung. irreg. ISSN 0083-4548 (Hochschule St. Gallen fuer Wirtschafts- und Sozialwissenschaften. Institut fuer Betriebswirtschaft)

**Helbing und Lichtenhahn Verlag AG**
Steinentorstr. 13, CH-4010 Basel, Switzerland.
- Basler Beitraege zur Geographie. irreg. ISSN 0067-4486
- Basler Beitraege zur Geschichtswissenschaft. irreg.
- Basler Studien zur Rechtswissenschaft. irreg.
- Bibliographie des Schweizerischen Recht. a.
- Institut fuer Internationales Recht und Internationale Beziehungen. Schriftenreihe. irreg.

- Praxis des Bundesgerichts. m.
- Regio Basiliensis; Basler Zeitschrift fuer Geographie/Revue de Geographie de Bale. s-a. ISSN 0034-3293
- Zeitschrift fuer Schweizerisches Recht/Revue de Droit Suisse. irreg; 8-10 per yr. ISSN 0084-540X

**Helioda-Verlag**
CH-5014 Gretzenbach, Switzerland.
- Form und Geist; illustrierte blaetter fuer angewandte Menschenkenntnis und Sozialreform. m. ISSN 0015-7694

**Verlag Helvetica Chimica Acta**
P.O. Box 273, 4002 Basel, Switzerland.
- Helvetica Chimica Acta. 9 per yr. ISSN 0018-019X (Schweizerische Chemische Gesellschaft)

**Herausgeberkommission und Historischer Verein des Kantons Bern**
Stadt- und Universitaetsbibliothek Bern, Muenstergasse 61, CH-3000 Berne 11, Switzerland.
- Berner Zeitschrift fuer Geschichte und Heimatkunde. q. ISSN 0005-9420

**Walter Herdeg Graphis Press**
Dufourstrasse 107, CH-8008 Zurich, Switzerland.
- Graphis; international journal for graphic and applied art. bi-m. ISSN 0017-3452
- Graphis Annual; international annual of advertising and editorial graphics. a. ISSN 0072-5528 (Dist. by Hastings House Publishers, Inc., 10 East 40 St., New York, NY 10016)
- Graphis Packaging; an international survey of package design. irreg., 3rd. edt. 1977. ISSN 0072-5536 (Dist. by Hastings House Publishers, Inc., 10 East 40 St., New York, NY 10016)
- Graphis Posters; international annual of poster art. a. (Dist. by Hastings House Publishers, Inc., 10 East 40th St., New York, NY 10016)
- Photographis; international annual of advertising and editorial photography. a. ISSN 0079-1830 (Dist. by Hastings House Publishers, Inc., 10 E. 40 St., New York NY 10016)

**Historisch-Antiquarischer Verein Obwalden**
Sarnen, Switzerland.
- Obwaldner Geschichtsblaetter. irreg., no. 12, 1974.

**Historische und Antiquarische Gesellschaft zu Basel**
Universitaetsbibliothek, Schoenbeinstr. 18-20, CH-4056 Basel, Switzerland.
- Basler Zeitschrift fuer Geschichte und Altertumskunde. irreg. (1-2 nos per year) ISSN 0067-4540

**Historischer Verein des Kantons St. Gallen**
- Historischer Verein des Kantons St. Gallen. Neujahrsblatt. (pub. by Fehr'sche Buchhandlung AG)

**Verlag Hoch und Tiefbau**
Weinbergstr. 49, Zurich 6, Switzerland.
- Hoch und Tiefbau. s-m. ISSN 0046-7677 (Schweizerischen Baumeisterverbandes)
- Schweizer Bauwirtschaft/Journal Suisse des Entrepreneurs/Giornale Suizzero degli Impresari Costrutori. bi-w.

**Hochschule St. Gallen fuer Wirtschafts- und Sozialwissenschaften. Forschungsinstitut fuer Absatz und Handel**
- Hochschule St. Gallen fuer Wirtschafts- und Sozialwissenschaften. Forschungsinstitut fuer Absatz und Handel. Schriftenreihe. (pub. by Paul Haupt AG)

**Hochschule St. Gallen fuer Wirtschafts- und Sozialwissenschaften. Institut fuer Betriebswirtschaft**
- Betriebswirtschaftliche Mitteilungen. (pub. by Paul Haupt AG)
- Fuehrung und Organisation der Unternehmung. (pub. by Paul Haupt AG)
- Planung und Kontrolle in der Unternehmung. (pub. by Paul Haupt AG)
- Praktische Betriebswirtschaft. (pub. by Paul Haupt AG)
- Unternehmung und Unternehmungsfuehrung. (pub. by Paul Haupt AG)

**Hochschule St. Gallen fuer Wirtschafts- und Sozialwissenschaften. Institut fuer Fremdenverkehr und Verkehrswirtschaft**
- Sankt Galler Beitraege Zum Fremdenverkehr und zur Verkehrswirtschaft: Reihe Verkehrswirtschaft. (pub. by Paul Haupt AG)

**Hochschule St. Gallen fuer Wirtschafts- und Sozialwissenschaften. Schweizerisches Institut fuer Aussenwirtschafts-, Struktur- und Marktforschung**
Dufourstrasse 48, 9000 St. Gallen, Switzerland. (Subscr. to: Schulthess Polygraphischer Verlag AG, Zwingliplatz 2, 8001 Zurich, Switzerland)
- Aussenwirtschaft; Zeitschrift fuer internationale Wirtschaftsbeziehungen. q. ISSN 0004-8216

**Hochuli AG**
Box 4132, Mutteuz, Switzerland.
- Jazz. m.

**F. Hoffmann-La Roche & Co., Ltd.**
Basel, Switzerland.
- Hexagon Roche. 8 per yr.

**Hospitalis Verlag AG**
Kreuzstr.72, 8032 Zurich 8, Switzerland.
- Hospitalis. m. ISSN 0018-5930

**Verlag Hans Huber**
Laenggassstr. 76 und Marktgasse 9, CH-3000 Berne 9, Switzerland
- Aktuelle Probleme in der Chirugie. irreg. ISSN 0065-5589 (Dist. by Williams & Wilkins Company, 428 E. Preston St., Baltimore, MD 21202)
- Aktuelle Probleme in der Klinischen Biochemie/Current Problems in Clinical Biochemistry. irreg. ISSN 0065-5597 (Dist. by Williams & Wilkins Company, 428 E. Preston St., Baltimore, MD 21202)
- Aktuelle Probleme in der Psychiatrie, Neurologie, Neurochirurgie. irreg. ISSN 0065-5600 (Dist. by Williams & Wilkins Company, 428 E. Preston St., Baltimore, MD 21202)
- Beitraege zur Heilpaedagogik und Heilpaedagogischen Psychologie. irreg. ISSN 0067-5075 (Dist. by Williams & Wilkins Company, 428 E. Preston St., Baltimore, MD 21202)
- Internationale Zeitschrift fuer Vitamin- und Ernaehrungsforschung/International Review of Vitamin and Nutrition Research. q. ISSN 0300-9831
- Jahrbuch der Psychoanalyse. irreg., latest 1974. ISSN 0075-2363 (Dist. by Williams & Wilkins Company, 328 E. Preston St., Baltimore, MD 21202)
- Krankenhaus-Probleme der Gegenwart. irreg. ISSN 0075-708X (Dist. by Williams & Wilkins Company, 328 E. Preston St., Baltimore, MD 21202)
- Monographs on Standardization of Cardioangiological Methods. irreg. (International Committee for the Standardization of Angiological Methods) (Co-sponsor: Council on Clinical Science of the International Society of Cardiology)
- Schriften zur Sozialpsychologie. irreg. ISSN 0080-7079 (Dist. by Williams & Wilkins Company, 328 Preston St., Baltimore, MD 21202)
- Schweizerische Aerztezeitung/Bulletin des Medecins Suisses/Bollettino dei Medici Svizzeri. w. ISSN 0036-7486 (Schweizerische Aerzteorganisation)
- Schweizerische Zeitschrift fuer Psychologie und ihre Anwendungen/Revue Suisse de Psychologie Pure et Appliquee. 4 per yr. ISSN 0036-7869 (Societe Suisse de Psychologie et de Psychologie Appliquee)
- Schweizerischer Ernaehrungsbericht. irreg.
- Therapeutische Umschau/Revue Therapeutique; Monatsschrift fuer praktische Medizin/revue mensuelle de medecine pratique. m. ISSN 0040-5930
- Vasa; Zeitschrift fuer Gefaesskrankheiten/Journal for vascular disease. q. ISSN 0301-1526
- Zeitschrift fuer Kinder-und Jugendpsychiatrie. q. ISSN 0301-6811
- Zeitschrift fuer Sozialpsychologie. q. ISSN 0049-867X

**Huber und Co. AG**
Promenadenstr. 16, 8500 Frauenfeld, Switzerland.
- Allgemeine Schweizerische Militaerzeitschrift. m. ISSN 0002-5925 (Schweizerische Offiziersgesellschaft)

- Feldweibel/Sergent-Major/Sergente Maggiore. m.
  ISSN 0014-9780 (Schweizerischer
  Feldweibelverband)
- Schweizerische Gesellschaft fuer Ur- und
  Fruehgeschichte. Institut fuer Ur- und
  Fruehgeschichte der Schweiz. Jahrbuch. a. ISSN
  0080-7311

**Hudson-Fachpresse**
CH-9403 Goldach, Switzerland.
- Marche Suisse des Machines. fortn. ISSN 0025-
  2840
- Motor Service; Fachzeitschrift fuer das Automobil
  und den Transport. s-m. ISSN 0027-1985
- Output; die schweizerische EDV-zeitschrift fuer
  den Manager und den Fachmann/la revue suisse
  d'information pour le manager et l'information. w.
- Schweizer Maschinenmarkt; die praxisnahe
  technische Fachzeitschrift. w. ISSN 0036-7397

**Huethig und Wepf Verlag**
Eisengasse 5, CH-4001 Basel, Switzerland.
- Angewandte Makromolekulare Chemie. 9 per yr.
  ISSN 0003-3146
- Makromolekulare Chemie. m. ISSN 0025-116X

**Musikverlag Hug und Co.**
Limmatquai 28, 8022 Zurich, Switzerland.
- Schweizerische Musikzeitung/Revue Musicale
  Suisse; Schweizer musikpaedagogische blaetter/
  feuillets suisses de pedagogie musicale. bi-m. ISSN
  0036-7710 (Gesellschaft Schweizerische
  Musikzeitung) (Co-Sponsors: Schweizerischer
  Tonkuenstlerverein; Schweizerischer
  Musikpaedagogischer Verband; Schweizerische
  Gesellschaften der Urheber und Verleger)

**Hug-Verlag AG**
Hohenrainweg 1, CH-8802 Kilchberg/Zurich,
Switzerland.
- Junior. m. ISSN 0022-6475

**I C E M**
*see* **Intergovernmental Committee for European
Migration**

**Verlag Industrielle Organisation**
Zurichbergstr. 18, 8028 Zurich, Switzerland.
- I O. (Industrielle Organisation); Management-
  Zeitschrift. m. ISSN 0019-9281 (Eidgenoessische
  Technische Hochschule Zuerich. Gesellschaft zur
  Foerderung des Betriebswissenschaftlichen
  Institutes)

**Information Research and Data Selection Ltd.**
Box 497, CH-6830 Chiasso, Switzerland.
- I.R.D.S. (International Register of Department
  Stores) a.

**Inspiration Verlag AG**
CH-8903 Birmensdorf, Switzerland.
- Inspiration; internationale publikation fuer visuelle
  faszination im display/international publication for
  visual fascination display/publication
  internationale pour la fascination visuelle dans le
  display. bi-m. ISSN 0020-2061

**Institut Africain de Geneve**
- Institut Africain de Geneve. Etudes et Travaux.
  (pub. by Mouton Publishers NE)

**Institut d'Etudes du Developpement**
24, rue Rothschild, CH-1202 Geneva, Switzerland.
- Geneve-Afrique/Acta Africana. s-a. ISSN 0016-
  6774
- Institut d'Etudes du Developpement. Cahiers. a.

**Institut de Documentation Scientifique**
- Psychological Reader's Guide. (pub. by Elsevier
  Sequoia S.A.)

**Institut de Mathematiques**
2-4, rue du Lievre, Case Postale 124, 1211 Geneva
24, Switzerland.
- Enseignement Mathematique. q. ISSN 0013-8584

**Institut fuer Bueroorganisation**
- Moderne Sekretarin. (pub. by Union Druck und
  Verlag)

**Institut fuer Ehe- und Familienwissenschaft**
- Partnerberatung. (pub. by Paul Haupt AG)

**Institut fuer Heilpaedagogik**
Loewenstr. 5, 6000 Lucerne, Switzerland.
- Vierteljahresschrift fuer Heilpaedagogik und ihre
  Nachbargebiete. q. ISSN 0017-9655

**Institut fuer Internationales Recht und Internationale
Beziehungen**
- Institut fuer Internationales Recht und
  Internationale Beziehungen. Schriftenreihe. (pub.
  by Helbing und Lichtenhahn Verlag AG)

**Institut fuer Politologische Zeitfragen**
Postfach 2720, 8023 Zurich, Switzerland.
- I P Z Information. Reihe S: Subversion. q.

**Institut fuer Weltanschauliche Fragen**
Scheideggstr. 45, CH-8002 Zurich, Switzerland.
- Orientierung; katholische Blaetter fuer
  weltanschauliche Information. s-m. ISSN 0030-
  5502

**Institut International de Psychagogie et de
Psychotherapie**
5 Rue Maupertuis, 1260 Nyon, Switzerland.
- Action et Pensee; revue de psychanalyse. q. ISSN
  0001-7426

**Institut Konsumenten- und Sozialanalysen**
Steinernng 49, 4002 Basel, Switzerland.
- Konsonanz; Quartalshefte zur Markt- und
  Sozialanalyse. q. ISSN 0023-3595

**Institut National Genevois**
1, Promenade du Pin, Geneva, Switzerland.
- Institut National Genevois. Rapport Administratif.
  irreg.

**Institut Suisse de Recherche sur les Pays de l'Est**
*see* **Schweizerisches Ost-Institut**

**Institut Universitaire de Hautes Etudes
Internationales**
*see under* **Universite de Geneve**

**Institut Universitaire de Hautes Etudes
Internationales. Asia Documentation and Research
Center**
*see* **Universite de Geneve. Asia Documentation and
Research Center**

**Institute for Consumer and Social Research**
*see* **Institut Konsumenten- und Sozialanalysen**

**Interavia S.A.**
86, Avenue Louis Casai, Case Postale 162, 1216
Cointrin-Geneva, Switzerland.
- Interavia A B C; world directory of aviation and
  astronautics. a. ISSN 0074-1116
- Interavia Air Letter; world aviation, space and
  electronics day by day. d. ISSN 0020-5176
- Interavia Data; military avionic equipment. irreg.
- Interavia: World Review of Aviation-Astronautics-
  Avionics. m. ISSN 0020-5168
- International Defense Review. bi-m. ISSN 0020-
  6512

**Interconair**
Via Brentani 7, 6900 Lugano, Switzerland.
- Defense. m (11 per yr)
- Interconair "Addifa Wal-Amn Fil-Aalam". 11 per
  yr.
- Interconair "Armies & Weapons". bi-m.
- Interconair "Aviation & Marine International"
  (Atlantic Edition) 11 per yr.
- Interconair "Aviation & Marine International"
  (Middle East Edition) 11 per yr.
- Interconair Aviazione e Marina Internazionale. m.
  ISSN 0020-529X
- Interconair "Eserciti e Armi". bi-m.

**Inter-Documentation Company**
Poststrasse 14, Zug, Switzerland.
- English Legal Manuscripts. irreg.
- Guide to the Sources of the History of the
  Nations. B: Africa. irreg.
- Inter-Documentation Company. Newsletter. irreg.
  ISSN 0074-1019

**Interessengemeinschaft der Schweizerischen
Aluminium,-Huetten, -Walz- und -Presswerke**
Dufourstrasse 31, CH-8008 Zurich, Switzerland.
- Schweizer Aluminium Rundschau/Revue Suisse
  de l'Aluminum. bi-m. ISSN 0036-7257

**Intergovernmental Committee for European Migration**
16 Ave. Jean Trembley, Case Postale 100, CH-1211
Geneva 19, Switzerland.
- Intergovernmental Committee for European
  Migration. Review of Achievements. a.
- International Migration. q. ISSN 0020-7985
- Migration Bulletin. 4 per yr. (U.S. addr: Mrs.
  Ruth Tropin, I CE M, Lincoln Building, Suite
  2127, 60 East 42 St., New York, NY 10017)

**Interkantonale Kontrollstelle fuer Heilmittel**
Erlachstr. 8, CH-3000 Berne 9, Switzerland.
- Interkantonale Kontrollstelle fuer Heilmittel.
  Monatsbericht/Office Intercantonal de Controle
  de Medicaments. Bulletin Mensuel/Ufficio
  Intercantonale di Controllo dei Medicamenti.
  Bolletin Mensile. m. ISSN 0026-9212

**Editiones Interlingua**
CH-1110 Morges, Switzerland.
- Revista de Interlingua. m.

**Interlingue Institute**
CH-1033 Cheseaux, Switzerland.
- Cosmoglotta. q. ISSN 0010-9533

**Intermode Verlag**
Zurich, Switzerland.
- Intermode. m. (Centralverband Schweizerischen
  Schneidermeister) (Co-sponsors: Schweizerischer
  Frauengewerbeverband; Schweizerische
  Bekleidungsfachschule)

**International Air Transport Association**
P.O. Box 315, 1215 Geneva 15 Airport,
Switzerland.
- World Air Transport Statistics. a. ISSN 0084-1366

**International Association for Analytical Psychology**
c/o Alice Maurer, Adm. Sec., Sihlberg 32, 8002
Zurich, Switzerland.
- International Congress for Analytical Psychology.
  Proceedings. irreg., 1974, 6th, London. ISSN
  0074-3364

**International Association for Bridge and Structural
Engineering**
ETH-Hoenggerberg, CH-8093 Zurich, Switzerland.
- International Association for Bridge and Structural
  Engineering. Final Report (of Congress)
  quadrennial, 11th, 1980, Vienna. ISSN 0074-1418
- International Association for Bridge and Structural
  Engineering. Preliminary Report (of Congress)
  quadrennial. ISSN 0074-1434
- International Association for Bridge and Structural
  Engineering. Reports of the Working
  Commissions. irreg., no. 25, 1977. ISSN 0074-
  1442

**International Association for the Defence of Religious
Liberties**
Schosshaldenstr., CH-3006 Berne, Switzerland.
- Conscience et Liberte. 2 per yr.

**International Association of Hail Insurers**
61 Seilergraben, 8001 Zurich, Switzerland.
- International Association of Hail Insurers.
  Congress Report. biennial, 13th Copenhagen,
  1975. ISSN 0074-1647

**International Association of Labor History
Institutions**
- International Association of Labour History
  Institutions. Bibliographische Information. (pub.
  by Pinkus-Genossenschaft)

**International Association of Microbiological Societies.
Virology Section**
- Intervirology. (pub. by S. Karger AG)

**International Association of Scientific Experts in
Tourism**
- Zeitschrift fuer Fremdenverkehr/Revue de
  Tourisme/Tourist Review. (pub. by Staempfli und
  Cie AG)

**International Association of State Lotteries**
c/o Loterie Intercantonale, Nueschelerstr. 45, Case
644, 8021 Zurich, Switzerland.
- International Association of State Lotteries.
  (Reports of Congress) biennial, 8th, 1970, Athens.
  ISSN 0074-1744

**International Astronomical Union**
- Quarterly Bulletin on Solar Activity. (pub. by
  Eidgenoessische Sternwarte)

**International Automobile Parade**
10 Pfadackerstr., CH-8957 Spreitenbach,
Switzerland
(Dist. by International Publications Service, 114 E.
32nd St., New York, N.Y. 10016)
- Auto-Universum. a. ISSN 0067-2416

**International Baccalaureate Office**
Palais Wilson, 1211 Geneva 14, Switzerland.
- International Baccalaureate Office. Annual
  Bulletin. a. ISSN 0074-1973

**International Bureau of Education**
For publications of this agency see section for
UNITED NATIONS

**International Catholic Migration Commission**
65 rue de Lausanne, Geneva, Switzerland.
• Migration News; an international bi-monthly on
migration, population, land settlement, refugees.
bi-m. ISSN 0026-3583

**International Catholic Movement for Intellectual and
Cultural Affairs**
General Secretariat, B.P. 1062, 1 Rte. de Jura, 1701
Fribourg, Switzerland.
• Convergence. q. ISSN 0010-8154
• Pax Romana. irreg., 22nd, 1975. ISSN 0079-0281

**International Centre of Fertilizers**
Beethovenstr. 24, 8002 Zurich, Switzerland.
• International Centre of Fertilizers. World
Congress. Acts. irreg., 1972, 7th, Vienna and
Baden. ISSN 0074-2171

**International Civil Defence Organization**
Information Service, 10-12 Chemin de Surville,
1213 Petit-Lancy/Geneva, Switzerland.
• International Civil Defence. m. ISSN 0020-6369

**International College of Pediatrics**
• Paediatrician. (pub. by S. Karger AG)

**International College of Psychosomatic Medicine**
• International College of Psychosomatic Medicine.
Proceedings of the Congress. (pub. by S. Karger
AG)

**International Commission of Jurists**
109 Route de Chene, 1224 Chene-Bougeries,
Geneva, Switzerland.
• International Commission of Jurists. Review. s-a.
ISSN 0020-6393

**International Committee for the Standardization of
Angiological Methods**
• Monographs on Standardization of
Cardioangiological Methods. (pub. by Verlag
Hans Huber)

**International Committee of the Red Cross**
17 Avenue de la Paix, 1211 Geneva 1, Switzerland.
• International Committee of the Red Cross.
Annual Report/Rapport d'Activite/Informe de
Actividad/Taetigkeitsbericht. a.
• International Review of the Red Cross. m. ISSN
0020-8604

**International Confederation for Agricultural Credit**
24 Beethovenstr., 8002 Zurich, Switzerland.
• International Confederation for Agricultural
Credit. Assembly and Congress Reports. irreg.,
1973, 5th Congress, Milan. ISSN 0074-2856

**International Congress of Psychopathology of
Expression**
• Psychiatry and Art. (pub. by S. Karger AG)

**International Council for Environmental Law**
• Environmental Policy and Law. (pub. by Elsevier
Sequoia S.A.)

**International Council of Nurses**
Box 42, 1211 Geneva 20, Switzerland.
• International Nursing Review. 6 per yr. ISSN
0020-8132

**International Council of Voluntary Agencies**
17 Av. de la Paix, 1202 Geneva, Switzerland.
• I C V A News. q. ISSN 0018-9065
• International Council of Voluntary Agencies.
Documents Series. irreg. ISSN 0074-4395
• International Council of Voluntary Agencies.
General Conference. Record of Proceedings. irreg.
ISSN 0074-4409

**International Council on Alcohol and Addictions**
C.P. 140, 1001 Lausanne, Switzerland.
• Drug and Alcohol Dependence. (pub. by Elsevier
Sequoia S.A.)
• I.C.A.A. News. (pub. by V L E Verlag GmbH)
• International Congress on Alcoholism and Drug
Dependence. Proceedings. triennial, 31st, 1975,
Bangkok, Thailand.
• International Institute on the Prevention and
Treatment of Alcoholism. Selected Papers. a; 21st,
1975, Helsinki, Finland. ISSN 0074-6622
• International Institute on the Prevention and
Treatment of Drug Dependence. Selected Papers.
a; 6th, 1976, Hamburg, W. Germany.

**International Creative Center**
20, Ch. Coladon, CH-1211 Geneva, Switzerland.
• Futurology. q.

**International Electrotechnical Commission**
1 rue Varembe, 1211 Geneva 20, Switzerland
(Dist. in the U.S. by: American National Standards
Institute, 1430 Broadway, New York, NY 10018)
• I E C Bulletin. bi-m. ISSN 0018-9138
• I E C Catalogue of Publications. a. with
supplements twice per year.
• International Electrotechnical Commission.
Annuaire/International Electrotechnical
Commission. Handbook. a.
• International Electrotechnical Commission. Report
on Activities. a. ISSN 0074-4697

**International Federation for Information Processing**
Secretariat, 3 rue du Marche, CH-1204 Geneva,
Switzerland.
• I F I P Information Bulletin. irreg (approx. 2 per
yr.)

**International Federation for Medical Psychotherapy**
11-bis rue Caroline, CH-1000 Lausanne, Switzerland
• International Congress of Psychotherapy.
Proceedings/Verhandlungen/Comptes Rendus.
(pub. by S. Karger AG)
• International Federation for Medical
Psychotherapy. Congress Reports. triennial, 8th,
1970, Milan: 10th, 1976, Paris. ISSN 0074-5847
(Order 8th report from: S. Karger AG, Arnold-
Boecklin-Str. 25, CH-4011 Basel, Switzerland)
• Psychotherapy and Psychosomatics. (pub. by S.
Karger AG)

**International Federation of Air Traffic Controllers
Associations**
P.O.B. 196, 1215 Geneva 15, Switzerland.
• International Federation of Air Traffic Controllers
Associations. Annual Conference Proceedings. a.
ISSN 0074-5871

**International Federation of Association Football**
P.B. 136, CH-8030 Zurich, Switzerland.
• F I F A News. m.

**International Federation of Associations of Textile
Chemists and Colorists**
c/o Max Peter, Sec., Handrenterweg 18, CH-4125
Biehen, Switzerland.
• International Federation of Associations of Textile
Chemists and Colorists. Reports of Congress.
irreg., 1972, 14th, Munich. ISSN 0074-5898

**International Federation of Building and
Woodworkers**
27-29, rue de la Coulouvreniere, CH-1204 Geneva,
Switzerland.
• Building and Wood. q.

**International Federation of Clinical Chemistry**
• International Congress on Clinical Chemistry.
Abstracts. (pub. by S. Karger AG)
• International Congress on Clinical Chemistry.
Proceedings. (pub. by S. Karger AG)

**International Federation of Commercial Clerical and
Technical Employees**
15, Avenue de Balexert, 1270 Chatelaine-Geneva,
Switzerland.
• International Federation of Commerical Clerical
and Technical Employees. Newsletter. 10 per yr.

**International Federation of Cotton and Allied Textile
Industries**
Am Schanzengraben 29, Postfach 289, 8039 Zurich,
Switzerland.
• Cotton and Allied Textile Industries. a. ISSN
0574-2315
• I F C A T I Directory. irreg. ISSN 0445-0698
• I F C A T I Newsletter. bi-m.
• International Cotton Industry Statistics. a. ISSN
0538-6829
• International Cotton Industry Statistics.
Supplement. a.
• International Cotton-System Fibre Consumption
Statistics. q.
• International Man-Made Fibre Production
Statistics. q.
• Structure of the Cotton and Allied Textile
Industries. every 4 yrs.

**International Federation of Gynaecology and
Obstetrics**
c/o H. de Watteville, Sec'y. Gen., Maternite, Rue
Alcide Jentzer 1211, Geneva 4, Switzerland.
• International Federation of Gynaecology and
Obstetrics. Journal. q. ISSN 0020-6695

**International Federation of Landscape Architects**
• Anthos. (pub. by Graf und Neuhaus)

**International Federation of Plantation, Agricultural
and Allied Workers**
17 rue Necker, Geneva, Switzerland.
• International Federation of Plantation,
Agricultural and Allied Workers. Report of the
Secretariat to the I F P A A W World Congress.
irreg. ISSN 0538-7477

**International Federation of Societies and Institutes
for the Study of the Renaissance**
• Bibliographie Internationale de l'Humanisme et de
la Renaissance. (pub. by Librarie Droz)

**International Graphical Federation**
Monbijoustr. 73, CH-3007 Berne, Switzerland.
• I G F-Journal; journal of the printing, bookbinding
and paper workers in all countries. s-a. ISSN
0018-9782
• International Graphical Federation. Report of
Activities. triennial. ISSN 0074-6177

**International Gymnastic Federation**
c/o Max Bangerter, Secretary, Juraweq 12, 3250
Lyss, Switzerland.
• Federation Internationale de Gymnastique.
Bulletin. q. ISSN 0428-1659

**International Institute for Labour Studies**
For publications of this agency see section for
UNITED NATIONS

**International Institution for Production Engineering
Research**
• C. I. R. P. Annals. (pub. by Hallwag AG)

**International Labour Organization**
For publications of this agency see section for
UNITED NATIONS

**International Metalworkers Federation**
54 bis, Rte. des Acacias, CH-1227 Geneva,
Switzerland.
• I M F News. fortn.
• I M F Studies. irreg.
• International Metalworkers' Congress. Reports.
triennial, 23rd, 1974, Stockholm. ISSN 0074-6983

**International Musicological Society**
Box 1561, CH-4001 Basel, Switzerland.
• Acta Musicologica. 2 per yr. ISSN 0001-6241

**International Narcotics Control Board**
For publications of this agency see section for
UNITED NATIONS

**International Olympic Committee**
Chateau De Vidy, Lausanne 1007, Switzerland.
• Olympic Review. m. ISSN 0010-2431

**International Organization for Standardization**
1 rue de Varembe, 1211 Geneva 20, Switzerland
(Dist. in U.S. by: American National Standards
Institute, 1430 Broadway, New York, NY 10018)
• I S O Annual Review. a. ISSN 0303-3317
• I S O Bulletin. m. ISSN 0303-805X
• I S O Catalogue. a. ISSN 0303-3309
• I S O International Standards. irreg.
• I S O Memento. a. ISSN 0536-2067
• I S O Participation. 3 per yr.

**International Organization of Biological Control**
• Liste d'Identification des Entomophages. (pub. by
Ecole Polytechnique Federale de Lausanne.
Institut d'Entomologie)

**International Potash Institute**
Postfach, CH-3048 Worblaufen-Berne, Switzerland.
• International Potash Institute. Colloquim. Compte
Rendu. irreg., 13th, 1977. ISSN 0074-7491
• International Potash Institute. Congress Report.
irreg., 10th, 1974, Brussels. ISSN 0074-7505
• Potash Review. m. ISSN 0032-5546

**International Publishers Association**
Ave. Miremont 3, 1206 Geneva, Switzerland.
• International Publishers Association. Proceedings
of Congress. irreg., 1976, 20th. ISSN 0074-7556

**Editions International Registry of Who's Who S.A. (Geneva)**
23, Ch. du Levant, CH-1005 Lausanne, Switzerland.
- Annuaire Suisse du Monde et des Affaires/Wer Ist Wer in der Schweiz/Swiss Biographical Index of Prominent Persons/Chi e Svizzeria e nel Liechtenstein? biennial.

**International Road Transport Union**
1 rue de Varembe, 1211 Geneva 20, Switzerland.
- World Transport Data/Statistiques Mondiales de Transport. biennial.

**International Savings Banks Institute**
1-3 rue Albert-Gos, 1206 Geneva, Switzerland.
- International Savings Banks Institute. Report. biennial.

**International Secretariat for Volunteer Service**
10 Chemin de Surville, 1213 Petit-Lancy, Geneva, Switzerland.
- I S V S Flash. s-a.

**International Skating Union**
Postfach, 7270 Davos-Platz, Switzerland.
- I S U Constitution. biennial.
- I S U Regulations. biennial; latest issue 1977.
- International Skating Union. Bestimmungen ueber das Eistanzen. biennial. ISSN 0539-0168
- International Skating Union. Minutes of Congress. biennial, latest 1977, Paris. ISSN 0535-2479

**International Social Security Association**
Box 1, 1211 Geneva 22, Switzerland.
- African Social Security Series. irreg. ISSN 0065-4043
- Automatic Data Processing Information Bulletin. 3 per yr. ISSN 0074-8412
- International Social Security Association. Etudes et Recherches/Studies and Research. irreg. (1-2 per yr.)
- International Social Security Association. Technical Reports of Assemblies. triennial since 1964, 18th, 1973, Abidjan. ISSN 0074-8439
- International Social Security Review. q. ISSN 0020-871X
- World Bibliography of Social Security/ Bibliographie Universelle de Securite Sociale. q. ISSN 0006-1476 (prep. by its Documentation Service)
- World Congress on the Prevention of Occupational Accidents and Diseases. Proceedings. triennial, 1971, 6th, Vienna. ISSN 0084-165X

**International Society for Business Education**
Chemin de la Croix, 1052 le Mont-Sur-Lausanne, Switzerland.
- International Review for Business Education/ Revue Internationale pour l'Enseignement Commercial/Internationale Zeitschrift fuer Kaufmaennisches Bildungswesen/Rivista Internazionale per la Cultura Commerciale/ Revista Internacional la Ensenanza Comercial. s-a. ISSN 0035-354X

**International Society for Labour Law and Social Legislation**
4, Place du Molard, CH-1204 Geneva, Switzerland.
- International Society for Labour Law and Social Legislation. Proceedings of Congress. triennial; 8th, 1974, Selva di Fasano, Italy. ISSN 0074-8455

**International Society for Paediatric Neurosurgery**
- Child's Brain. (pub. by S. Karger AG)

**International Society of Art and Psychopathology**
- Confinia Psychiatrica/Borderlands of Psychiatry/ Grenzgebiete der Psychiatrie/Confins de la Psychiatrie. (pub. by S. Karger AG)

**International Society of Audiology**
- Audiology. (pub. by S. Karger AG)

**International Society of Blood Transfusion**
- Vox Sanguinis. (pub. by S. Karger AG)

**International Society of Cardiology**
c/o Pierre Moret, Sec.-Gen., Box 127, CH-1211 Geneva 12, Switzerland.
- International Symposium on Atherosclerosis. Proceedings. irreg., 1962, 2nd, Chicago. ISSN 0074-8765

**International Society of Digestive Endoscopy**
- European Congess of Digestive Endoscopy. Proceedings. (pub. by S. Karger AG)

**International Society of Geographical Pathology**
- International Society of Geographical Pathology. Proceedings of the Conference. (pub. by S. Karger AG)

**International Society of Hematology**
- Bibliotheca Haematologica. (pub. by S. Karger AG)

**International Society of Hematology. European Division**
- Acta Haematologica. (pub. by S. Karger AG)

**International Society of Internal Medicine**
c/o Dr. Philippe C. Frei, Hospital Nestle, Lausanne, Switzerland.
- International Society of Internal Medicine. Congress Proceedings. biennial, 1974, 12th, Tel Aviv. ISSN 0074-8544

**International Society of Nephrology**
- International Congress of Nephrology. Proceedings. (pub. by S. Karger AG)

**International Society of Neuroendocrinology**
- Neuroendocrinology. (pub. by S. Karger AG)

**International Society of Phonetic Sciences**
- Phonetica. (pub. by S. Karger AG)

**International Society of Radiology**
c/o Prof. Dr. W. A. Fuchs, University Hospital, Department of Diagnostic Radiology, Inselspital, CH-3010 Berne, Switzerland.
- International Congress of Radiology. (Reports) irreg., 1973, 13th, Madrid; 1977, 14th, Rio de Janeiro. ISSN 0074-3933

**International Society on Biotelemetry**
- Biotelemetry and Patient Monitoring. (pub. by S. Karger AG)

**International Solid Waste and Public Cleansing Association**
Veberlandstr. 133, CH-8600 Duebendorff, Switzerland.
- International Solid Waste and Public Cleansing Association. Information Bulletin. 3 per yr.

**International Telecommunication Union**
For publications of thiis agency see section for
UNITED NATIONS

**International Touring Alliance**
2 Quai Gustave Ador, Geneva, Switzerland.
- International Touring Alliance. Minutes of the General Assembly. a. ISSN 0074-9133

**International Union Against Cancer**
3 rue de Conseil-General, 1205 Geneva, Switzerland.
- International Journal of Cancer. m. ISSN 0020-7136
- International Union against Cancer. Manual/ Union Internationale Contre le Cancer. Manuele. irreg; latest 1975. ISSN 0074-9192
- International Union against Cancer. Proceedings of Congress. quadrennial since 1958, 11th, 1974, Florence. ISSN 0074-9206
- U I C C Bulletin. q. ISSN 0041-5111
- U I C C Technical Report Series. irreg, latest vol. 25. ISSN 0074-9222

**International Union for Child Welfare**
1 rue Varembe, 1211 Geneva 20, Switzerland.
- International Child Welfare Review. q. ISSN 0020-6342
- Union Internationale de Protection de l'Enfance. Bibliotheque. Liste. q.

**International Union for Conservation of Nature and Natural Resources**
1110 Morges, Switzerland.
- Environmental Policy and Law Papers. approx. 3 per yr.
- I U C N Bulletin. m. ISSN 0020-9058
- I U C N Publications. New Series. irreg., 1970, no. 16. ISSN 0074-9273
- I U C N Yearbook. a. ISSN 0074-9265
- International Union for Conservation of Nature and Natural Resources. Proceedings and Reports of the Technical Meeting. triennial; 12th meeting with 11th general assembly, 1972, Banff, Canada. ISSN 0074-9281
- International Union for Conservation of Nature and Natural Resources. Proceedings of the General Assembly. triennial; 11th, Banff, Canada, 1972. ISSN 0074-929X

- Taraxacum. 3 per yr. ISSN 0496-8859

**International Union for Health Education**
3 Rue Viollier, 1207 Geneva, Switzerland.
- International Conference on Health and Health Education. Proceedings. triennial. ISSN 0074-3100
- International Journal of Health Education. q. ISSN 0020-7306

**International Union of Alpine Associations**
29, rue des Delices, 1211 Geneva, Switzerland.
- International Union of Alpine Associations. Bulletin/Union Internationale des Associations d'Alpinisme. Bulletin. 5 per yr.

**International Union of Food and Allied Workers' Associations**
Secretariat, Rampe du Pont-Rouge 8, CH-1213 Petit-Lancy/Geneva, Switzerland.
- International Union of Food and Allied Workers' Associations. Meeting of the Executive Committee. I. Documents of the Secretariat. II. Summary Report. a. ISSN 0579-8299
- International Union of Food and Allied Workers' Associations. News Bulletin. m. ISSN 0020-9074
- International Union of Food and Allied Workers' Associations. Tobacco Workers' Trade Group Board. Meeting. irreg. ISSN 0579-8302

**International Union of Speleology**
c/o Institut de Geologie, Universite de Neuchatel, 11 rue Emile-Argand, CH-2000 Neuchatel, Switzerland.
- Speleological Abstracts/Bulletin Bibliographique Speleologique. 2 per yr. (prep. by its Bibliographical Commission)

**Internationale Vereinigung Christlicher Geschaeftsleute. Gruppe Zurich**
Box 29, 8034 Zurich, Switzerland.
- Geschaeftsmann und Christ. m. ISSN 0016-9021

**Internationale Vereinigung fuer Brueckenbau und Hochbau**
see **International Association for Bridge and Structural Engineering**

**Internationale Vereinigung fuer Soziale Sicherheit**
see **International Social Security Association**

**Internationaler Rat zur Bekaempfung des Alkoholismus und der Suchtgefahren**
see **International Council on Alcohol and Addictions**

**Inter-Parliamentary Union**
Place du Petit-Saconnex, 1209 Geneva, Switzerland.
- Constitutional and Parliamentary Information. (pub. by Association of Secretaries General of Parliaments FR)
- Inter-Parliamentary Bulletin. q. ISSN 0020-5079
- Inter-Parliamentary Union. Chronicle of Parliamentary Elections. a. ISSN 0074-1043 (prep. by its International Center for Parliamentary Documentation)
- Inter-Parliamentary Union. Conference Proceedings. Comptes Rendus des Conferences. a. ISSN 0074-1051

**W. Jaeggi AG**
Freie Str. 40, CH-4001 Basel, Switzerland.
- Art/Kunst. a.

**Jeunnesses Musicales de Suisse Romande et Italienne**
Case 157, 1401 Yverdon, Switzerland.
- Revue Musicale de Suisse Romande; courrier suisse du disque. q. ISSN 0035-3744

**Journal de la Construction de la Suisse Romande**
Av. Jomini 8, Lausanne, Switzerland.
- Journal de la Construction de la Suisse Romande. s-m. ISSN 0021-776X

**Journal Europeen du Collectionneur d'Ordres et Decorations**
CH-1141 Yens, Switzerland.
- Journal Europeen du Collectionneur d'Ordres et Decorations. q.

**Judaica Verlag**
Rotelstrasse 96, CH-8057 Zurich, Switzerland.
- Judaica; beitraege zum Verstaendnis des juedischen Schicksals in Vergangenheit und Gegenwart. ISSN 0022-572X

**Kalt-Zehnder Editions**
Postfach 250, CH-6301 Zug, Switzerland.
- Schweizer Schule. s-m. ISSN 0036-7443

**Kantonal Zuercher Vereinigung fuer Sozialberatung**
Postfach 231, 8034 Zurich, Switzerland.
- Zeitschrift fuer Sozialberatung. bi-m. ISSN 0044-3522

**S. Karger AG**
Arnold-Boecklin-Str. 25, CH-4011 Basel,
Switzerland.
- Acta Anatomica; international archives of anatomy, histology, embryology and cytology. m.(3 vols. per year) ISSN 0001-5180
- Acta Haematologica. m.(2 vols.per yr) ISSN 0001-5792 (International Society of Hematology. European Division)
- Advances in Cardiology. irreg (approx. 2 per yr.) ISSN 0065-2326
- Advances in Microcirculation. irreg (approx. 1 per yr.) ISSN 0065-2938
- Advances in Ophthalmology/Fortschritte der Augenheilkunde/Progres en Ophtalmologie. irreg (approx. 2 per yr.) ISSN 0065-3004
- Advances in Oto-Rhino-Laryngology. irreg. (approx 1 per yr.) ISSN 0065-3071
- Advances in Psychosomatic Medicine. irreg (approx. 1 per yr.) ISSN 0065-3268
- Advances in Stereoencephalotomy. irreg (approx. 1 per yr.) ISSN 0065-3381
- Advances in Tuberculosis Research. irreg (approx. 1 per yr.) ISSN 0065-3500
- Allergologicum; Transactions of the Collegium Internationale. irreg., 10th, 1975, Copenhagen. ISSN 0065-6372 (Collegium Internationale Allergologicum)
- Analytische Psychologie; Zeitschrift fuer Analytische Psychologie und ihre Grenzgebiete. q. ISSN 0302-8925
- Antibiotics and Chemotherapy. irreg (approx. 1 per yr.) ISSN 0066-4758
- Applied Neurophysiology. q. ISSN 0302-2773 (World Society for Stereotactic and Functional Neurosurgery)
- Arbeitsmedizinische Fragen in der Ophthalmologie/Problems of Industrial Medicine in Ophthalmology. irreg (approx. 1 per yr.) ISSN 0066-5851
- Audiology; journal of auditory communication. bi-m. ISSN 0020-6091 (International Society of Audiology)
- Ballistocardiography Research Society. Proceedings of the Annual Meeting of the U.S. a, 17th, 1973, Atlantic City. ISSN 0067-3056
- Bibliotheca Anatomica. irreg (approx. 1 per yr.) ISSN 0067-7833
- Bibliotheca Cardiologica. irreg (approx. 2 per yr.) ISSN 0067-7906
- Bibliotheca Haematologica. irreg. (approx. 1 per yr.) ISSN 0067-7957 (International Society of Hematology)
- Bibliotheca Nutritio et Dieta. irreg (approx. 1 per yr.) ISSN 0067-8198
- Bibliotheca Ophthalmologica. irreg. (approx. 1 per yr.) ISSN 0067-8090
- Bibliotheca Phonetica. irreg (approx. 1 per yr.) ISSN 0067-8120
- Bibliotheca Psychiatrica. irreg. (approx. 1 per yr.) ISSN 0067-8147
- Bibliotheca Radiologica. irreg (approx. 1 per yr.) ISSN 0067-8155
- Biology of the Neonate; fetal and neonatal research. m.(2 vols. per year) ISSN 0006-3126
- Biosciences Communications; an international interdisciplinary journal of communications research and theory in the biosciences and fields of health care delivery. bi-m. ISSN 0302-2781
- Biotelemetry and Patient Monitoring. q. ISSN 0378-309X (International Society on Biotelemetry)
- Blood Vessels; international journal of blood and lymphatic vessels. bi-m. ISSN 0302-2765
- Brain, Behavior and Evolution. bi-m. ISSN 0006-8977
- Canadian Society for Immunology. International Symposium. Proceedings. irreg., 5th, 1970, Univ. of guelph. ISSN 0301-3146
- Cardiology. bi-m. ISSN 0008-6312
- Caries Research. bi-m. ISSN 0008-6568 (European Organization for Caries Research)
- Chemotherapy; international journal of experimental and clinical chemotherapy. bi-m. ISSN 0009-3157
- Child's Brain. bi-m. ISSN 0302-2803 (International Society for Paediatric Neurosurgery)

- Comparative Animal Nutrition. irreg (approx. 1 per yr.) ISSN 0304-5374
- Confinia Psychiatrica/Borderlands of Psychiatry/Grenzgebiete der Psychiatrie/Confins de la Psychiatrie. q. ISSN 0010-5686 (International Society of Art and Psychopathology)
- Contributions to Epidemiology and Biostatistics. irreg (approx. 1 per yr.) ISSN 0377-3574
- Contributions to Gynecology and Obstetrics. irreg (approx. 1 per yr.) ISSN 0304-4246
- Contributions to Human Development. irreg (approx. (1 per yr.) ISSN 0073-3849
- Contributions to Microbiology and Immunology. irreg (approx. 1 per yr.) ISSN 0301-3081
- Contributions to Nephrology. irreg (approx. 2 per yr.) ISSN 0302-5144
- Contributions to Primatology. irreg (approx. 1 per yr.) ISSN 0301-4231
- Contributions to Vertebrate Evolution. a.
- Current Problems in Dermatology. irreg (approx. 1 per yr.) ISSN 0070-2064
- Current Topics in Critical Care Medicine. irreg (approx. 1 per yr.) ISSN 0376-4249
- Cytogenetics and Cell Genetics. m (2 vol. per year) ISSN 0301-0171
- Data Processing in Medicine/Datenverarbeitung in der Medizin. irreg (approx. 1 per yr.) ISSN 0070-2889
- Dermatologica. m (2 vol. per yr) ISSN 0011-9075 (Swiss Society of Dermatology and Venerology) (Co-sponsor: Nederlandse Vereniging van Dermatologen; Belgian Society for Dermatology and Syphiligraphy)
- Developments in Biological Standardization. irreg (approx. 2 per yr.)
- Digestion; international journal of gastroenterology. bi-m. ISSN 0012-2823
- Enzyme; metabolism, experimental and clinical enzymology. bi-m. ISSN 0013-9432
- European Conference on Microcirculation. Proceedings. irreg., 8th, 1974, Le toquet. ISSN 0071-2655 (European Society on Microcirculation)
- European Congess of Digestive Endoscopy. Proceedings. irreg., 1st, Prague. ISSN 0071-2663 (International Society of Digestive Endoscopy)
- European Congress of Perinatal Medicine. Proceedings. irreg., 1971, 3rd, Lausanne. ISSN 0071-2698 (European Association of Perinatal Medicine) (Inquire: Dr. K. Polacek, Institute for the Care of the Mother and Child, Prague, CSSR)
- European Congress on Ballistocardiography and Cardiovascular Dynamics. Proceedings. irreg. ISSN 0302-511X
- European Congress on Sleep Research. Proceedings. irreg. ISSN 0302-5128
- European Neurology. bi-m. ISSN 0014-3022
- European Society of Ophthalmology. Proceedings of the Congress. irreg. ISSN 0301-326X
- European Surgical Research; clinical and experimental surgery. bi-m. ISSN 0014-312X (European Society for Experimental Surgery)
- European Urology. bi-m. ISSN 0302-2838 (European Association of Urology)
- Experimental Biology and Medicine. irreg (approx. 1 per yr.) ISSN 0071-3384
- Experimental Cell Biology; international journal of basic pathology, microbiology and immunology. q. ISSN 0304-3568
- Folia Phoniatrica; international journal of phoniatrics, speech therapy and communication pathology. q. ISSN 0015-5705 (International Association of Logopedics and Phoniatrics SW)
- Folia Primatologica; international journal of primatology. 8 per yr. ISSN 0015-5713
- Fortbildungskurse fuer Rheumatologie. irreg (approx. 1 per yr.) ISSN 0071-7851
- Frontiers of Gastrointestinal Research. irreg (approx. 1 per yr.) ISSN 0067-7949
- Frontiers of Hormone Research. irreg (approx. 1 per yr.) ISSN 0077-0868
- Frontiers of Matrix Biology. irreg (approx. 1 per yr.) ISSN 0301-0155
- Frontiers of Oral Physiology. irreg (approx. 1 per yr.) ISSN 0301-536X
- Frontiers of Radiation Therapy and Oncology. irreg (approx. 1 per yr.) ISSN 0071-9676
- Gastroenterologische Fortbildungskurse fuer die Praxis. irreg.(approx 1 issue per year) ISSN 0071-7843
- Gerontology; international journal of experimental and clinical gerontology. bi-m. ISSN 0304-324X
- Gynaekologische Rundschau. q. ISSN 0017-6001 (Schweizerische Gesellschaft fuer Gynaekologie) (Co-sponsor: Oesterreichische Gesellschaft fuer Gynaekologie und Geburtshilfe)

- Gynecologic Investigation; international journal of the science of reproduction. bi-m. ISSN 0017-5986
- Haemostasis; international journal on haemostasis and thrombosis research. bi-m. ISSN 0301-0147
- Hormone Research; international journal of experimental and clinical endocrinology. q. ISSN 0301-0163 (European Association of Endocrinology)
- Human Development. bi-m. ISSN 0018-716X
- Human Heredity. bi-m. ISSN 0001-5652
- Infusionstherapie und Klinische Ernaehrung; forschung und praxis. bi-m. ISSN 0301-3243
- Institut de Droit International. Annuaire. biennial. ISSN 0073-8182
- Interdisciplinary Topics in Gerontology. irreg (approx. 1 per yr.) ISSN 0074-1132
- International Archives of Allergy and Applied Immunology. m.(2 vols.per year) ISSN 0020-5915
- International College of Psychosomatic Medicine. Proceedings of the Congress. irreg. ISSN 0302-5136
- International Congress for Virology. Proceedings. irreg., 3rd, 1975, Madrid. ISSN 0074-9567
- International Congress of Life Assurance Medicine. Proceedings. irreg, 9th, 1967, Tel Aviv. ISSN 0074-3747 (Permanent International Committee for the Study of Life Assurance Medicine)
- International Congress of Nephrology. Proceedings. irreg., 1975, 6th, Florence. ISSN 0074-378X (International Society of Nephrology)
- International Congress of Physchosomatic Medicine in Obstetrics and Gynaecology. Proceedings. irreg., 1974, 4th, Tel Aviv. ISSN 0302-5152
- International Congress of Psychotherapy. Proceedings/Verhandlungen/Comptes Rendus. triennial since 1964; 1976, 10th, Paris. ISSN 0074-3917 (International Federation for Medical Psychotherapy)
- International Congress on Clinical Chemistry. Abstracts. triennial since 1963; 1975, 9th, Toronto. ISSN 0074-4042 (International Federation of Clinical Chemistry) (Inquire: P.M.G. Broughton, Sec., University Department of Chemical Pathology, General Infirmary, Leeds LS1 3EX, England)
- International Congress on Clinical Chemistry. Proceedings. triennial since 1963; 1975, 9th, Toronto. ISSN 0074-4050 (International Federation of Clinical Chemistry) (Inquire: P.M.G. Broughton, Sec., University Department of Chemical Pathology, General Infirmary, Leeds LS1 3EX, England)
- International Convocation in Immunology. Papers. biennial, 4th, Buffalo, June 1974. ISSN 0074-4220 (Center for Immunology)
- International Pharmacopsychiatry. q. ISSN 0020-8272
- International Seminar on Reproductive Physiology and Sexual Endocrinology. Proceedings. irreg., 1975, 5th, Brussels. ISSN 0074-7920
- International Society of Geographical Pathology. Proceedings of the Conference. irreg., 1975, 12th, Zurich. ISSN 0074-8536 (International Society of Geographical Pathology) (Inquire: Prof. J.R. Ruettner, Kantonsspital, Schmelzbergstr. 10, CH-8006 Zurich, Switzerland)
- International Symposium on Brain-Endocrine Interaction. Proceedings. irreg. ISSN 0301-309X
- International Symposium on Comparative Leukemia Research. Proceedings. irreg., 7th, 1975, Copenhagen. ISSN 0074-879X
- Intervirology. bi-m. ISSN 0300-5526 (International Association of Microbiological Societies. Virology Section)
- Journal of Medical Primatology. bi-m. ISSN 0047-2565
- Journal of Submicroscopic Cytology. q. ISSN 0022-4782 (Istituto di Microscopia Elettronica Clinica Policlinico S. Orsola IT)
- Medicine and Sport. irreg (approx. 1 per yr.) ISSN 0076-6070
- Mental Health and Society; an international journal of community mental health. bi-m. ISSN 0302-2811
- Methods and Achievements in Experimental Pathology. irreg (approx. 1 per yr.) ISSN 0076-681X
- Mineral and Electrolyte Metabolism. bi-m. ISSN 0378-0392
- Modern Problems in Ophthalmology/Moderne Probleme der Ophthalmologie/Problemes Actuels en Ophthalmologie. irreg. (approx. 2 per yr.) ISSN 0077-0078
- Modern Problems in Paediatrics. irreg (approx. 2 per yr.) ISSN 0077-0086

- Modern Problems of Pharmacopsychiatry. irreg (approx. 1 per yr.) ISSN 0077-0094
- Monographs in Allergy. irreg. (approx. 1 per yr.) ISSN 0077-0760
- Monographs in Clinical Cytology. irreg (approx. 1 per yr.) ISSN 0077-0809
- Monographs in Developmental Biology. irreg (appox. 1 per yr.) ISSN 0077-0825
- Monographs in Human Genetics. irreg (approx. 1 per yr.) ISSN 0077-0876
- Monographs in Neural Sciences. irreg (approx. 1 per yr.) ISSN 0077-0779
- Monographs in Oral Science. irreg. (approx. 1 per yr.) ISSN 0077-0892
- Monographs in Paediatrics. irreg (approx. 1 per yr.) ISSN 0077-0914
- Monographs in Virology. irreg (approx. 1 per yr.) ISSN 0077-0965
- Monographs on Atherosclerosis. irreg. (approx. 1 per yr.) ISSN 0077-099X
- Monographs on Drugs. irreg. ISSN 0301-3057
- Nephron. m (2 vol. per year) ISSN 0028-2766
- Neuroendocrinology; international journal for basic and clinical studies on neuroendocrine relationships. m.(2 vols. per yr) ISSN 0028-3835 (International Society of Neuroendocrinology)
- Neuropsychobiology; international journal for basic and clinical studies in psychiatric research. q. ISSN 0302-282X
- Nutrition and Metabolism; journal of nutrition, metabolic diseases and dietetics. bi-m. ISSN 0029-6678
- O R L; journal for oto-rhino-laryngology and its borderlands. bi-m. ISSN 0301-1569 (Gesellschaft des Schweizerische Hals- Nasen- und Ohrenaerzte) (Co-sponsor: Nederlandse Keel-Neus-Oorheelkundige Vereniging)
- Oncology; international journal of cancer research and treatment. bi-m. ISSN 0030-2414
- Ophthalmic Microsurgery Study Group. Proceedings of the Symposium. irreg. ISSN 0302-5101
- Ophthalmic Research; journal for research in experimental and clinical ophthalmology. bi-m. ISSN 0030-3747
- Ophthalmologica; international journal of ophthalmology. m.(2 vols. per yr.) ISSN 0030-3755
- Paediatrician; international journal for the paediatrician in practice. bi-m. ISSN 0300-1245 (International College of Pediatrics)
- Paediatrische Fortbildungskurse fuer die Praxis/ Cours de Perfectionnement en Pediatric pour le Praticien. irreg (approx. 2 per yr.) ISSN 0078-7795
- Pediatric and Adolescent Endocrinology. irreg (approx. 2 per yr.) ISSN 0304-4254
- Perspectives in Medicine. irreg (approx 1 per yr.) ISSN 0301-3014
- Pharmacology; international journal of experimental and clinical pharmacology. bi-m. ISSN 0031-7012
- Phonetica; international journal of phonetics. bi-m. ISSN 0031-8388 (International Society of Phonetic Sciences)
- Pigment Cell. irreg (approx. 1 per yr.) ISSN 0301-0139
- Primates in Medicine. irreg. (approx. 1 per yr.) ISSN 0079-5119
- Primatologia. irreg (approx 1 per yr.) ISSN 0079-5127
- Progress in Allergy. irreg (approx. 1 per yr.) ISSN 0079-6034
- Progress in Biochemical Pharmacology. irreg (approx. 1 per yr.) ISSN 0079-6085
- Progress in Experimental Tumor Research. irreg. (approx. 1 per yr.) ISSN 0079-6263
- Progress in Medical Virology. irreg (approx. 1 per yr.) ISSN 0079-645X
- Progress in Neurological Surgery. irreg (approx. 1 per yr.) ISSN 0079-6492
- Progress in Nuclear Medicine. irreg (approx. 1 per yr.) ISSN 0079-6573
- Progress in Pediatric Radiology. irreg (approx. 1 per yr.) ISSN 0079-6646
- Progress in Reproductive Biology. irreg (approx. 1 per yr.) ISSN 0304-4262
- Progress in Respiration Research. irreg (approx. 1 per yr.) ISSN 0079-6751
- Progress in Surgery. irreg (approx. 1 per yr.) ISSN 0079-6824
- Psychiatria Clinica. q. ISSN 0033-264X
- Psychiatry and Art. irreg (aprox. 1 per yr.) ISSN 0079-7286 (International Congress of Psychopathology of Expression)
- Psychologische Praxis. irreg (approx. 2 per yr.) ISSN 0079-7413

- Psychopathology and Pictorial Expression. irreg. ISSN 0555-5795
- Psychotherapy and Psychosomatics; international journal of psychotherapy and psychosomatics. q. ISSN 0033-3190 (International Federation for Medical Psychotherapy)
- Radiologia Clinica. bi-m.
- Reconstruction Surgery and Traumatology. irreg (approx. 1 per yr.) ISSN 0080-0260
- Research and Clinical Studies in Headache. irreg (approx. 1 per yr.) ISSN 0080-1453
- Respiration; international review of thoracic diseases. bi-m. ISSN 0025-7931
- Rheumatology. irreg (approx. 1 per yr.) ISSN 0080-2727
- Schweizerische Gesellschaft fuer Psychiatrie. Fortbildungskurse/Societe Suisse de Psychiatrie. Cours de Perfectionnement. irreg (approx. 1 per yr.) ISSN 0080-7303
- Sozialmedizinische und Paedagogische Jugendkunde. irreg (approx. 1 per yr.) ISSN 0076-6186
- Symposia Angiologica Santoriana. irreg., 4th, 1972, Fribourg. ISSN 0082-0687
- Synthetic Methods of Organic Chemistry. irreg (approx. 1 per yr.) ISSN 0082-1136
- Urologia Internationalis. bi-m. ISSN 0042-1138
- Vox Sanguinis; journal of blood transfusion, immunohaematology and immunopathology. m (2 vols. per yr.) ISSN 0042-9007 (International Society of Blood Transfusion) (Dist. in U. S. by: J. B. Lippincott Co., East Washington Sq., Philadelphia, PA 19105)
- World Congress on Ballistocardiography and Cardiovascular Dynamics. Proceedings. irreg., 4th, 1975, Amsterdam. ISSN 0084-1633
- World Review of Nutrition and Dietetics. irreg (approx. 2 per yr.) ISSN 0084-2230

**Karger Libri AG**
Petersgraben 15, CH-4000 Basel 11, Switzerland
- Anaesthesia, Resuscitation and Intensive Therapy. q. ISSN 0301-0864 (Polish Society of Anaesthesiologists PL) (Eastern European subscr. to: Panstwowy Zoklad Wydawnictw Lekarskich (Polish Medical Publishers), Ul. Dluga 38/40, Warsaw, Poland)
- ChemBooks; a bibliography of new and forthcoming books in chemistry. a. ISSN 0069-2875
- MedBooks; a bibliography of new and forthcoming books in human and dental medicine. s-a. ISSN 0025-6641
- ZooBooks; a bibliography of new and forthcoming books in veterinary medicine and zoology. a. ISSN 0084-5574

**Keller und Co., Druckerei und Verlag**
Baselstr. 11-13, 6002 Lucerne, Switzerland.
- Jahrbuch fuer Umweltschutz. a.

**Keramik-Freunde der Schweiz**
- Keramik-Freunde der Schweiz. Mitteilungsblatt. (pub. by Schweizerisches Landesmuseum)

**Kompass International AG**
Neuhausstrasse 4, CH-8044 Zurich, Switzerland
- Kompass Schweiz/Liechtenstein; informationswerk der Schweizerischen. Wirtschaft. a. ISSN 0075-6717 (Foundation for Promoting International Economic Information) (Dist. by: Iliffe NTP Inc., 300 E. 42 St., New York, NY 10017)

**Lisbet Konfeld**
Munstergasse 41, CH-3011 Berne, Switzerland.
- Loewe. 3 per yr.

**Kooperation Evangelischer Kirchen und Missionen**
Missionstr. 21, 4003 Basel, Switzerland.
- Auftrag. 6 per yr. ISSN 0004-7880

**Verlag Karl Kraemer und Co.**
CH-8867 Niederurnen, Switzerland.
- A C; international asbestos-cement review/revue internationale d'amiente-ciment/internationale asbestcement-revue. q. ISSN 0001-0731

**G. Krebs Verlagsbuchhandlung AG**
St. Alban-Vorstadt 56, CH-4006 Basel, Switzerland.
- Folklore Suisse/Folclore Svizzero. bi-m. ISSN 0015-5969 (Schweizerische Gesellschaft fuer Volkskunde.)
- Schweizer Volkskunde. bi-m. ISSN 0048-9522 (Schweizerische Gesellschaft fuer Volkskunde)
- Schweizerisches Archiv fuer Volkskunde. q. ISSN 0036-794X (Schweizerische Gesellschaft fuer Volkskunde)

**Michael Kuehnle, Ed. & Pub.**
Honggerstr. 80, CH-8037 Zurich, Switzerland.
- Chess Express/Schach Express; international chess magazine. irreg (2 per yr.)

**Kuemmerly und Frey AG**
Hallestr. 6-10, CH-3001 Berne, Switzerland.
- Geographica Helvetica; Schweizerische Zeitschrift fuer Laender- und Voelkerkunde. q. ISSN 0016-7312 (Geographisch-Ethnographische Gesellschaft Zurich)
- Itinera Romana; Beitraege zur Strassengeschichte des roemischen Reiches. irreg. ISSN 0075-2002

**Verlag Kunst und Stein**
Gmeimeriweg 1, 8047 Zurich, Switzerland.
- Kunst und Stein. bi-m. ISSN 0023-5458 (Verband Schweizerischer Bildhauer- und Steinmetzmeister)

**Verlag Kunstkreis AG**
Alpenstr. 5, Lucerne, Switzerland.
- Kunstnachrichten. bi-m. ISSN 0023-5512

**Kunstmuseum Bern**
Hodlerstrasse 12, CH-3011 Berne, Switzerland.
- Berner Kunstmitteilungen. 8 per yr. (Co-sponsors: Bernische Kunstgesellschaft; Verein der Freunde des Berner Kunstmuseums; Verein Kunsthalle Bern)

**Kyklos-Verlag**
Petersgraben 29, CH-4000 Basel 2, Switzerland.
- Kyklos; internationale Zeitschrift fuer Sozialwissenschaften. q. ISSN 0023-5962 (Genossenschaftliche Zentralbank AG) (Co-Sponsor: List Society)

**L G Z Landis und Gyr Zug AG**
CH-6301 Zug, Switzerland.
- Landis und Gyr Mitteilungen/Revue Landis et Gyr/Landis & Gyr Review. irreg. ISSN 0023-7949

**Labor et Fides S.A.**
1 Rue Beauregard, 1204 Geneva, Switzerland.
- Cahiers du Renouveau. 2 per yr. ISSN 0008-0187

**Editions Emile-M. et Rene Lambelet**
1, rue du Vieux-Billard, 1205 Geneva, Switzerland.
- Indicateur Industriel; revue de la technique Europeenne. m.

**Landis und Gyr Zug AG**
see L G Z Landis und Gyr Zug AG

**Peter Lang Publishers**
Muengraben 2, CH-3011 Berne, Switzerland.
- Anglo-American Forum. irreg.
- Augsburger Schriften zum Staats- und Voelkerrecht. irreg.
- Beitraege zur Kommunikationswissenschaft und Medienforschung. irreg.
- Berner Studien zum Fremdenverkehr. irreg., 17th, 1974, Lausanne. ISSN 0067-6152 (Universitaet Bern. Forschungsinstitut fuer Fremdenverkehr)
- Ethnologische Zeitschrift. s-a. ISSN 0014-181X (Universitaet Zuerich)
- Forum Linguisticum. irreg.
- Jahrbuch fuer International Germanistik. s-a.
- Schriftenriehe Risikopolitik. irreg.
- Schweizerische Versicherungszeitschrift/Revue Suisse d'Assurances. m.
- Verfassungsgeschichte. irreg.

**League of Red Cross Societies**
17 Chemin des Crets, Petit-Saconnex, C.P. 2099, 1211 Geneva 19, Switzerland.
- League of Red Cross Societies. Rapport Annuel. a. ISSN 0458-9033
- League of Red Cross Societies Report. irreg. ISSN 0458-9041
- Panorama. 8 per yr. ISSN 0034-1991

**Buchdruckerei und Verlag Leemann AG**
Arbenzstr. 20, 8034 Zurich, Switzerland.
- Eidgenoessische Technische Hochschule Zuerich. Mitteilungen. Aerodynamik. irreg., 1963, no. 32. ISSN 0084-5744
- Eidgenoessische Technische Hochschule Zuerich. Mitteilungen. Photoelastizitaet. irreg., 1965, no. 10. ISSN 0084-5752
- Eidgenoessische Technische Hochschule Zuerich. Mitteilungen. Textilmaschinenbau und Textilindustrie. irreg., 1967, no. 9. ISSN 0084-5760

- Forschung und Konstruktion im Stahlbau/
  Research and Construction on Steel-Engineering/
  Etude des Ouvrages en Acier et Construction
  Metallique. irreg. ISSN 0071-7649
- Naturforschende Gesellschaft in Zuerich.
  Vierteljahresschrift. q. ISSN 0042-5672
- Schweizerische Mineralogische und
  Petrographische Mitteilungen. s-a. ISSN 0036-
  7699
- Schweizerische Zeitschrift fuer Gemeinnuetzigkeit.
  bi-m. ISSN 0036-7826 (Schweizerische
  Gemeinnuetzige Gesellschaft)
- Schweizerische Zeitschrift fuer Geschichte/Revue
  Suisse d'Histoire/Rivista Storica Svizzera. q. ISSN
  0036-7834 (Allgemeine Geschichtsforschende
  Gesellschaft der Schweiz)
- Schweizerische Zeitschrift fuer Geschichte.
  Beihefte/Revue Suisse d'Histoire. Supplement.
  irreg., no. 16, 1976. ISSN 0080-7397

**Armando Libotte, Ed. & Pub.**
Casella Postale, 6904 Lugano, Switzerland.
- Almanacco Calcistico Svizzero. a.
- Rivista di Lugano; rassegna settimanale illustrata
  per le famiglie. w. ISSN 0035-628X

**Ligue Marxiste Revolutionaire**
- Breche. (pub. by C E D I P S)

**Ligue Suisse pour la Litterature de la Jeunesse**
*see* **Schweizerischer Bund fuer Jugendliteratur**

**E. Loepfe-Benz AG Graphische Anstalt**
9400 Rorschach, Switzerland.
- Nebelspalter; schweizerische humoristisch-
  satirische Wochenschrift. w. ISSN 0028-1786

**Luedin AG**
4410 Leistal, Switzerland.
- Ars Medici; das Organ des praktischen Arztes. m.
  ISSN 0004-2897

**Lutheran World Federation**
150 Route de Ferney, 1211 Geneva 20, Switzerland.
- Lutheran World/Lutherische Rundschau. q. ISSN
  0024-760X

**Luzern (Canton) Staatskanzlei**
- Luzerner Kantonsblatt. (pub. by Raeber AG)

**M L F**
Case Postale 3268, CH-1000 Lausanne, Switzerland.
- La Fronde. irreg.

**Maltzeff**
5 Avenue Bertrand, 1205 Geneva, Switzerland.
- Exil. q.

**Colin Martin, Ed. & Pub.**
1 rue Pepinet, Lausanne, Switzerland.
- Bibliotheque Historique Vaudoise. irreg., 1969,
  vol. 47. ISSN 0067-8406

**Verlag Manfred Marx und Co.**
Florastr. 14, 8034 Zurich, Switzerland.
- Israelitisches Wochenblatt fuer die Schweiz/Revue
  Juive. w. ISSN 0021-2342

**Editions Medecine et Hygiene**
78 Av. de la Roseraie, Case Postale 229, CH-1211
Geneva 4, Switzerland.
- Archives de Psychologie. q. ISSN 0003-9640
  (Universite de Geneve. Faculte de Psychologie et
  des Sciences de l'Education. Section de
  Psychologie)
- Journal de Genetique Humaine. 4 per yr. ISSN
  0021-7743 (World Federation of Neurology.
  Groupe de Travail de Neurogenetique)
- Medecine et Hygiene. w. ISSN 0025-6749
- Revue de Belles-Lettres. q. ISSN 0035-1016
  (Societe de Belles Lettres de Lausanne et Geneve)
- Schweizerische Zeitschrift fuer Militaer- und
  Katastrophenmedizin. q. (Schweizerische
  Gesellschaft der Offiziere der Sanitatstruppen)

**Marcel Meichtry Editions**
Chemin de la Caroline 22, 1213 Petit-Lancy/
Geneva, Switzerland.
- Revue Polytechnique. m.

**Meier und Cie**
Vordergasse 58, 8200 Schaffhausen, Switzerland.
- Feld Wald Wasser; schweizerische Jagdzeitung. m.
  ISSN 0014-9756

**Editions K. Meister**
Case Postale, 1211 Geneva 9, Switzerland.
- Neue Photo-Kino-Berater; Fachzeitschrift fuer
  Foto-und Filmamateure. 9 per yr.
- Nouveau Photo-Cine-Expert; revue de
  photographe et du cine-amateur. 9 per yr.

**Metzgereipersonal-Verband der Schweiz**
Berninastr. 25, CH-8057 Zurich, Switzerland.
- Metzger und Wurster/Boucher-Charcutier/
  Macellaio-Salumiere. fortn. ISSN 0026-1645

**Editions Meyer et Cie**
5 rue Bovy-Lysberg, 1211 Geneva 11, Switzerland.
- Femme d'Aujourd'hui. w.

**Verlag G. Meyers Erben**
Klausstr. 33, CH-8008 Zurich, Switzerland.
- Meyers Modeblatt. w. ISSN 0026-1866

**Montreaux TV Symposium**
Box 97, 1820 Montreaux, Switzerland.
- Symposium International et Exposition Technique
  de Television, Montreux. biennial. ISSN 0082-
  0776

**Buchdruckerei Robert Mueller AG**
6442 Gersau, Switzerland.
- Fourier. m. ISSN 0015-914X (Schweizerischer
  Fourierverband) (Co-sponsor: Verband
  Schweizerischer Fouviergehilfen)

**Muenzen und Medaillen AG**
Malzgasse 25, CH-4000 Basel, Switzerland.
- Muenzen und Medaillen/Monnaies et Medailles.
  m. ISSN 0027-3007

**Musee d'Art et d'Histoire, Geneva**
Rue Charles Galland, 1211 Geneva 3, Switzerland.
- Genava; revue d'archeologie et d'histoire de l'art.
  a. ISSN 0072-0585

**Musee d'Ethnographie de la Ville de Geneve**
65-67 Bd. Carl-Vogt, 1205 Geneva, Switzerland.
- Musee d'Ethnographie de la Ville de Geneve.
  Bulletin Annuel. a. ISSN 0072-0828

**Musee National Suisse**
*see* **Schweizerisches Landesmuseum**

**Musee Neuchatelois**
c/o Jean-Pierre Michaud, 4 rue de la Poste, 2013
Colombier, Switzerland.
- Musee Neuchatelois; revue d'histoire regionale. q.
  ISSN 0027-3805 (Societe d'Histoire et
  d'Archeologie du Canton de Neuchatel)

**Museum d'Histoire Naturelle**
Malagnou, 1211 Geneva 6, Switzerland.
- Revue Suisse de Zoologie. q. ISSN 0035-418X

**Nachrichten fuer Unzufrieden**
Gundeldingerstr. 462, Basel, Switzerland.
- Nachrichten fuer Unzufrieden. 10 per yr.

**Editions Nagel S.A.**
5-7, rue de l'Orangerie, 1211 Geneva 7,
Switzerland.
- Who's Who in Switzerland. biennial. ISSN 0083-
  9736

**Nature Information**
14 Pl. du Tunnel, 1000 Lausanne 17, Switzerland.
- Nature Information. m.

**Naturforschende Gesellschaft, Basel**
- Naturforschende Gesellschaft, Basel.
  Verhandlungen/Society for Natural Sciences,
  Basel. Proceedings. (pub. by Birkhaeuser Verlag)

**Naturforschende Gesellschaft in Bern**
Stadt-und Universitaetsbibliothek, Muenstergasse 61,
CH-3000 Berne 7, Switzerland.
- Naturforschende Gesellschaft in Bern.
  Mitteilungen. a. ISSN 0077-6130

**Naturforschende Gesellschaft in Zuerich**
- Naturforschende Gesellschaft in Zuerich.
  Vierteljahresschrift. (pub. by Buchdruckerei und
  Verlag Leemann AG)

**Naturhistorisches Museum**
Brunnadernstr. 65, CH-3006 Berne, Switzerland.
- Naturhistorisches Museum, Bern. Jahrbuch. a.

**Hans Nesser**
Stockerstr. 43, 8002 Zurich, Switzerland.
- Ariaqua; fachschrift fuer luft und wasser,
  umwelttechnik und umweltschutz. q.

**Neue Religioes-Soziale Vereinigung**
Postfach 1008, 8036 Zurich, Switzerland.
- Aufbau; schweizerische Wochenzeitung fuer
  Recht, Freiheit und Frieden. w. ISSN 0004-7821

**Verlag Neue Technik AG**
Tiefenhoefe 11, CH-8001 Zurich, Switzerland.
- Neue Technik/Nouvelles Techniques/New
  Techniques. m. ISSN 0028-3398

**Neue Zuercher Zeitung**
Box 660, 8021 Zurich, Switzerland.
- Swiss Review of World Affairs. m. ISSN 0039-
  7490

**Nordfinanz-Bank Zuerich**
Bahnhofstr. 1, Postfach 750, CH-8022 Zurich,
Switzerland.
- Scandinavian Market; a business survey of the
  four Scandinavian countries. biennial. ISSN 0080-
  6749 (Co-sponsor: Manufacturers Hanover
  Banque Nordique)

**Observatoire de Geneve**
CH-1290 Sauverny, Switzerland.
- Observatoire de Geneve. Publications. Serie A.
  irreg. ISSN 0085-0942

**Oeffentliche Kunstammlung**
Kunstmuseum Basel, St. Albangraben 16, CH-4010
Basel, Switzerland.
- Oeffentliche Kunstsammlung. Jahresbericht. irreg.
  ISSN 0067-4311

**Emil F. Oesch Verlag AG**
Seestr. 3, CH-8800 Thalwil-Zurich, Switzerland.
- Briefe an den Chef; ein zeitsparender
  Informationsdienst. w. ISSN 0006-9973
- Briefe an den Mitarbeiter. fortn. ISSN 0006-9981
- Briefe an den Mitmenschen. m. ISSN 0006-999X

**Offensiv**
Postfach, 8042 Zurich, Switzerland.
- Offensiv/Offensif; eine Zeitung von Soldaten Fuer
  soldaten gemacht/journal de soldats pour les
  soldats. q.

**Office du Baccalaureat International**
*see* **International Baccalaureate Office**

**Office Forestier Central Suisse**
14 Rosenweg, 4500 Solothurn, Switzerland.
- Foret; revue de sylviculture et d'economie
  forestiere. m. ISSN 0015-7597 (Co-sponsors:
  Societe Forestiere Suisse; Association Suisse
  d'Economie Forestiere)

**Office Intercantonal de Controle de Medicaments**
*see* **Interkantonale Kontrollstelle fuer Heilmittel**

**Office Suisse d'Expansion Commerciale**
*see* **Schweizerische Zentrale fuer
Handelsfoerderung**

**Offset-Haus AG**
Postfach, CH-8021 Zurich, Switzerland.
- Mensuration, Photogrammetrie, Genie Rural/
  Vermessung, Photogrammetrie, Kulturtechnik. m.

**Ordre Souverain de Malte**
3 Place Claparede, Geneva, Switzerland.
- Acta Leprologica. 3 per yr. ISSN 0001-5938

**Orell Fuessli Graphische Betriebe AG**
Dietzingerstr. 3, CH-8036 Zurich, Switzerland.
- Archiv fuer Genetik. 3 per yr. ISSN 0300-984X
- Blaetter fuer Zuercherische Rechtsprechung. 10
  per yr. ISSN 0006-4491
- G S T Bulletin/Bulletin S V S. m. (Gesellschaft
  Schweizerischer Tieraerzte)
- Orella; Monatszeitschrift fuer Mode, Strickmode
  und Handarbeiten. m. ISSN 0030-4867
- Schweizer Archiv fuer Neurologie, Neurochirurgie
  und Psychiatrie. 4 per yr. ISSN 0036-7273
  (Schweizerische Neurologische Gesellschaft) (Co-
  Sponsor: Schweizerische Gesellschaft fuer
  Psychiatrie)
- Schweizer Archiv fuer Tierheilkunde. 12 per yr.
  ISSN 0036-7281 (Gesellschaft Schweizerischer
  Tieraerzte)
- Schweizerische Kartellkommission.
  Veroeffentlichungen/Commission Suisse des
  Cartels. Publications. q. ISSN 0036-7621

- Schweizerische Nationalbank. Monatsbericht. m. ISSN 0036-7729
- Schweizerische Zeitschrift fuer Verkehrswirtschaft. 4 per yr.
- Schweizerisches Zentralblatt fuer Staats-und Gemeindeverwaltung. m. ISSN 0036-7990
- Turicum; kultur, wissenschaft und wirtschaft. q.
- Wir Eltern; fuer Kinderpflege und Erziehung. m.
- Wirtschaft und Recht; Zeitschrift fuer Wirtschaftspolitik und Wirtschaftsrecht mit Einschluss des Sozial- und Arbeitsrechtes. 4 per yr. ISSN 0043-6135
- Zeitschrift fuer Oeffentliche Fuersorge; Monatsschrift fuer oeffentliche Fuersorge und Jugendhilfe. bi-m. ISSN 0044-3204 (Schweizerische Konferenz fuer Oeffentliche Fuersorge)

**Organisation des Communistes de Suisse (M.L.)**
Case Postale 278, 1000 Lausanne 9, Switzerland.
- Octobre. m. ISSN 0029-828X

**Organisations Chretiennes-Sociales**
Rue de l'Abbe Bovet 6, 1700 Fribourg, Switzerland.
- Action Sociale. s-m. ISSN 0001-7507

**Ostkirchenwerk Catholica Unio**
6006 Lucerne, Switzerland.
- Catholica Unio; ostkirchliche Zeitschrift. q. ISSN 0008-851X

**Verlag Ostschweiz**
Oberer Graben 8, Postfach 716, CH-9001 St. Gallen, Switzerland.
- St. Galler Studien Zum Wettbewerbs und Immaterialgueterrecht. irreg.

**Ostschweizerische Gesellschaft fuer Hoehlenforschung**
c/o Rene Scherrer, Bruggwiesenstr. 6, CH-8442 Hettlingen, Switzerland.
- Hoehlenpost. 3 per yr. ISSN 0018-3105

**Parti Radical-Democratique Suisse**
see Freisinnig-Demokratische Partei der Schweiz

**Paulus-Verlag GmbH**
Pilatusstr. 41, 6000 Lucerne, Switzerland.
- Kleine Chorzeitung; Mitteilungsblatt fuer die katholischen Kirchenchoere. 2-3 per yr. ISSN 0023-2068

**Permanent International Committee for the Study of Life Assurance Medicine**
- International Congress of Life Assurance Medicine. Proceedings. (pub. by S. Karger AG)

**Pinkus-Genossenschaft**
Froschaugasse 71, 8001 Zurich, Switzerland.
- International Association of Labour History Institutions. Bibliographische Information. q.

**Verlag Plaedoyer**
Postfach, 8022 Zurich, Switzerland.
- Hey. m. (Schweizerische Organisation der Homophilen)

**Poesie**
Postfach, CH-4001 Basel, Switzerland.
- Poesie; Zeitschrift fuer Literatur. q. ISSN 0378-0643

**Polana AG**
Postfach 1173, 8036 Zurich, Switzerland.
- Horizont; slovensky nezavisly mesacnik. m.

**Postal Telegraph and Telephone International**
36 Avenue du Lignon, Geneva, Switzerland.
- P. T. T. I. Studies. q.

**Postes, Telephones et Telegraphes Suisses**
Viktoriastr. 2, CH-3000 Berne 33, Switzerland.
- Communications Postales Avec l'Etranger Par Voies de Terres de Mer et de l'Air. m.
- P T T Technische Mitteilungen. m. ISSN 0040-1471

**Powerslide AG**
Florastr. 14, CH-8008 Zurich, Switzerland.
- Motorsport Aktuell; Internationaler Motorsport. w.

**Preisberichtstelle des Schweizerisches Bauernverband**
see Union Suisse des Paysans

**Presses Centrales Lausanne S.A.**
17 rue de Geneve, 1003 Lausanne, Switzerland.
- Bulletin Immobilier. s-m. ISSN 0007-4675 (Federation Romande Immobiliere)

- Revue Suisse d'Agriculture. bi-m. (Federation des Societes d'Agriculture de la Suisse Romande) (Co-sponsors: Station Federale de Recherches Agronomiques de Changins; Service Romand de Vulgarisation Agricole)
- Revue Suisse de Viticulture, Arboriculture et Horticulture. bi-m. (Federation des Societes d'Agriculture de la Suisse Romande) (Co-sponsors: Station Federale de Recherches Agronomiques de Changins; Service Romand de Vulgarisation Agricole)

**Progressiven Organisationen**
Postfach 338, 4001 Basel, Switzerland.
- Poch. s-m.

**Psychologische Lehr- und Beratungsstelle**
Susenbergstr. 53, 8044 Zurich, Switzerland.
- Psychologische Menschenkenntnis; Beratung in Ehe-, Erziehungs-, Berufs-, und Lebensfrage. q. ISSN 0033-3034

**Publipress S.A.**
Rue des Armes 20, 2500 Bienne, Switzerland.
- Flair; revue de Madame. s-m. ISSN 0035-1490

**Radical-Democratic Party**
see Freisinning-Demokratische Partei der Schweiz

**Raeber AG**
Frankenstr. 7-9, Lucerne, Switzerland.
- Luzerner Kantonsblatt. w. (Luzern (Canton) Staatskanzlei)

**Raggi Verlag**
Postfach 113, CH-8706 Feldmeilen, Switzerland.
- Antike Welt; zeitschrift fuer Archaeologie und Kulturgeschichte. q.

**Emil Rahm, Ed. & Pub.**
AZ 8215 Hallau, Switzerland.
- Memo Press; aktuelle press- und literatur hinweise mit kommentar. q.

**Editions de la Rampe**
Neuchatel, Switzerland.
- Rampe (Neuchatel) m.

**Reich Verlag AG**
Zinggentorstr. 4, CH-6000 Lucerne 6, Switzerland.
- Internationales Jahrbuch der Fotografie. a. ISSN 0074-9826

**Friedrich Reinhardt Verlag**
Missionsstr. 36, CH-4012 Basel, Switzerland.
- Basler Predigten; eine monatliche Predigtfolge. m. ISSN 0005-6189
- Kirchenblatt fuer die Reformierte Schweiz; fuer die reformierte Schweiz. fortn. ISSN 0023-1797
- Quellen und Forschungen zur Basler Geschichte. irreg., no. 8, 1976. ISSN 0079-9076 (Basel (Canton) Staatsarchiv)
- Schweizerische Beitraege zur Altertumswissenschaft. irreg., no. 14, 1976. ISSN 0080-7273 (Dist. by: Albert J. Phiebig Books, Box 352, White Plains, NY 10602)
- Sonderbaende zur Theologischen Zeitschrift. irreg., no. 8, 1977. ISSN 0067-4907 (Dist. by: Albert J. Phiebig Books, Box 352, White Plains, NY 10602)
- Theologische Dissertationen. irreg., no. 13, 1976. ISSN 0082-3902 (Universitaet Basel. Theologische Fakultaet) (Dist. by Albert J. Phiebig Books, Box 352, White Plains, NY 10602)
- Theologische Zeitschrift. bi-m. ISSN 0040-5701 (Universitaet Basel. Theologische Fakultaet)

**Editions Rencontre Orient Occident**
12 rue Francois-Grast, Geneva, Switzerland.
- Rencontre Orient Occident. bi-m. ISSN 0034-1509

**Editions Rencontre S.A.**
29 Chemin d'Entre-Bois, 1018 Lausanne, Switzerland.
- Bestsellers du Monde Entier. irreg. ISSN 0067-6330
- Bibliotheque Rencontre des Lettres Anciennes et Modernes. irreg. ISSN 0067-8457
- Chefs-d'Oeuvre de la Science-Fiction. irreg. ISSN 0069-2840

**Imprimeries Reunies**
33, Avenue de la Gare, CH-1001 Lausanne, Switzerland.
- Gazette des Beaux-Arts. 10 per yr. ISSN 0016-5530

**Revue de Droit International de Sciences Diplomatiques et Politiques**
Case Postale 138, 1211 Geneva 12, Switzerland.
- Revue de Droit International de Sciences Diplomatiques et Politiques. q. ISSN 0035-1091

**Revue de Theologie et de Philosophie**
7 Chemin des Cedres, Lausanne, Switzerland.
- Revue de Theologie et de Philosophie. q. ISSN 0035-1784

**Revue du Vieux Geneve**
c/o Paul Loosli, Rue Philippe - Plantamour, 1-3, Geneva, Switzerland.
- Revue du Vieux Geneve. a.

**Revue Neuchateloise**
Case Postale 906, 2001 Neuchatel, Switzerland.
- Revue Neuchateloise. q. ISSN 0035-3779

**Paul Richenbacher Verlag**
Kornhausstr. 22, 8840 Einsiedele, Switzerland.
- Zahntechnik. 6 per yr. ISSN 0044-1686 (Schweizerische Zahntechniker-Vereinigung)

**Ringier und Co.**
CH-4800 Zofingen, Switzerland.
- Schweizer Illustrierte. w. ISSN 0036-7362

**Rittmann Ltd.**
Spalentorweg 9, Postfach, 4000 Basel 3, Switzerland.
- Internationale Transport-Zeitschrift/Journal pour le Transport International/International Transport Journal-Overseas Digest. w. ISSN 0020-9341

**Rivista Militare della Svizzera Italiana**
Via Cattedrale 4, 6900 Lugano, Switzerland.
- Rivista Militare della Svizzera Italiana. bi-m. ISSN 0035-6999

**Verlag Dr. Roth AG**
Postfach 34, Seenerstr. 157, CH-8405 Winterthur, Switzerland.
- Neue Produkte; Weltmarkt-Umschau fuer Industrie und Handel. fortn. ISSN 0028-3339

**Russian Petroleum Press Review**
P.O. Box 670, CH-1211 Geneva 1, Switzerland.
- Russian Petroleum Press Review.

**S E V**
see Schweizerischer Eisenbahnerverband

**Sadesi**
39 rue Peillonnex, 1225 Chene-Bourg, Geneva, Switzerland.
- Sciences et Industries Spatiales/Space Research and Engineering/Weltraumforschung Und-Industrie. bi-m. ISSN 0036-8644

**St. Gallen Graduate School of Economics, Business and Public Administration**
see Hochschule St. Gallen fuer Wirtschafts- und Sozialwissenschaften

**Editions Saint-Paul**
36 Perolles, CH-1700 Fribourg, Switzerland.
- Anthropos; revue internationale d'ethnologie et de linguistique. 3 per yr. ISSN 0003-5572 (Anthropos Institut)
- Zeitschrift fuer Schweizerische Kirchengeschichte/ Revue d'Histoire Ecclesiastique Suisse. 2 per yr. ISSN 0044-3484 (Vereinigung fuer Schweizerische Kirchengeschichte)

**Arti Grafiche A. Salvoni e Co., S.A.**
Conto Postale 65-79, Bellinzona, Switzerland.
- Bollettino Storico della Svizzera Italiana. 4 per yr. ISSN 0006-6869

**Sandoz AG**
CH-4002 Basel, Switzerland.
- Triangle; the Sandoz journal of medical science. q. ISSN 0041-2597

**Sankt Gallische Naturwissenschaftliche Gesellschaft**
St. Gallen, Switzerland.
- Sankt Gallische Naturwissenschaftliche Gesellschaft. Bericht ueber Die Taetigkeit. irreg., 1969, vol. 79. ISSN 0080-6056

**Sarganserlaendische Buchdruckerei AG**
8887 Mels, Switzerland.
- Terra Plana. s-a.

**Verlag Sauerlaender**
Laurenzenvorstadt 89, CH-5001 Aarau, Switzerland.
- Berufsschueler. q. (Schweizerischer Verband fuer Beruflichen Unterricht)
- Cockpit; die Luftfahrtzeitschrift fuer die Jugend. m. ISSN 0010-0110 (Schweizerischer Aero-Club)
- Dialog; Monatszeitschrift fuer das Amateurtheater. m. (Zentralverband Schweizer Volksbuehnen) (Co-sponsor: Gesellschaft fuer das Schweizerische Volkstheater)
- Gesnerus; Vierteljahrschrift fuer Geschichte der Medizin und der Naturwissenschaften. 2 per yr. ISSN 0016-9161 (Schweizerische Gesellschaft fuer Geschichte der Medizin und der Naturwissenschaften)
- Gymnasium Helveticum. 6 per yr. ISSN 0017-5951 (Verein Schweizerischer Gymnasiallehrer)
- Schweizer Foerster. m. (Verband Schweizerischer Foerster)
- Schweizerische Bienen-Zeitung. m. ISSN 0036-7540 (Verein Deutschschweizerischer Bienenfreunde)
- Strafvollzug in der Schweiz. q. (Schweizerische Verein fuer Straf- Gefaengniswesen und Schutzaufsicht) (Subscriptions to: Schutzaufsichtsamt Bern, Kramgasse 20, 3011 Berne, Switzerland)

**Verlag Schiffahrt und Weltverkehr AG**
Blumenrain 12, 4001 Basel, Switzerland.
- Strom und See; Zeitschrift fuer Schiffahrt und Weltverkehr. 7 per yr. ISSN 0039-2510 (Schweizerische Schiffahrtsvereinigung)

**Buchdruckerei Schippert und Co.**
Zuerichbergstrasse 22, 8028 Zurich, Switzerland.
- Schweizer Musikerblatt/Bulletin Musical Suisse. m (11 per yr.) (Schweizerischer Musikverband)

**Schoch und Co.**
Schermenweg 190, 3072 Ostermundigen BE, Switzerland.
- Militaer-Kuechenchef. bi-m. ISSN 0026-3907 (Verband Schweizerischer Militaerkuechenchefs)

**Schueck Soehne AG**
Bahnhofstr. 24, CH-8803 Rueschlikon, Switzerland.
- Schweizer Baublatt. s-w. ISSN 0036-7303

**Schulthess Polygraphischer Verlag AG**
Zwingliplatz 2, 8001 Zurich, Switzerland.
- Arbeitsrecht und Arbeitslosenversicherung. 3-4 per yr. ISSN 0003-777X (Switzerland. Bundesamt fuer Industrie, Gewerbe und Arbeit)
- Basler Wirtschaftswissenschaftliche Vortraege. irreg. ISSN 0067-4532 (Universitaet Basel. Wirtschaftswissenschaftliche Institut)
- Schweizerische Juristen-Zeitung/Revue Suisse de Jurisprudence. s-m. ISSN 0036-7613 (Schweizerischer Anwaltsverband)

**Schwabe und Co.**
Steinenforstr. 13, 4010 Basel, Switzerland.
- Acta Paedopsychiatrica; international journal of child psychology. 6 per yr. ISSN 0001-6586
- Acta Tropica; journal of biomedical sciences. 4 per yr. ISSN 0001-706X (Schweizerisches Tropeninstitut)
- Basler Veroeffentlichungen zur Geschichte der Medizin und der Biologie. irreg., 1971, fasc. 29. ISSN 0067-4524
- Helvetica Chirurgica Acta. bi-m. ISSN 0018-0181 (Schweizerische Gesellschaft fuer Chirurgie)
- Helvetica Paediatrica Acta. 6 per yr. ISSN 0018-022X (Swiss Society of Paediatrics)
- Helvetica Paediatrica Acta. Supplementum. irreg. ISSN 0073-1811 (Swiss Society of Paediatrics)
- Museum Helveticum; schweizerische Zeitschrift fuer klassische Altertumswissenschaft. 4 per yr. ISSN 0027-4054
- Publicus; Schweizer Jahrbuch des Oeffentlichen Lebens. a. ISSN 0080-7249
- Schweizerische Akademie der Medizinischen Wissenschaften. Bulletin. 6 per yr. ISSN 0036-7494
- Schweizerische Medizinische Wochenschrift. w. ISSN 0036-7672
- Schweizerisches Medizinisches Jahrbuch. a. ISSN 0080-7400 (Schweizerische Aerzteorganisation)
- Series Paedopsychiatrica. irreg., vol. 4, 1975. ISSN 0080-9012

**Schweizer Brauerei-Rundschau**
Postfach 190, CH-8047 Zurich, Switzerland.
- Schweizer Brauerei-Rundschau. m. ISSN 0036-7311

**Schweizer Heimatschutz**
Postfach 8042, Zurich, Switzerland.
- Heimatschutz. q. ISSN 0017-9817

**Schweizer Heimatwerk**
"Heimethuus", Rudolf Brun-Bruecke, CH-8023 Zurich, Switzerland.
- Heimatwerk; Blaetter fuer Volkskunst und Handwerk. q. ISSN 0017-9833

**Verlag Schweizer Kavallerist**
CH-8330 Pfaeffikon, Switzerland.
- Schweizer Kavallerist. 18 per yr. ISSN 0036-7389

**Schweizer Kneippverband**
Riehenstrasse 88, 4058 Basel, Switzerland
- Kneipp; schweizerische monatsschrift fuer die knieppsche naturgemaesse lebens- und heilweise. m. ISSN 0023-2246 (Subscr. to: Kunzler-Bachmann AG, Postfach 926, 9001 St. Gallen, Switzerland)

**Verlagsgenossenschaft Schweizer Soldat**
Inselstr. 76, 4057 Basel, Switzerland.
- Schweizer Soldat; Die Monatszeitschrift fuer Armee und Kader mit FHD-Zeitung. m.

**Schweizer Spiegel Verlag AG**
Hirschengraben 20, 8001 Zurich, Switzerland.
- Grammatiken und Woerterbuecher des Schweizerdeutschen. irreg., 1969, vol. 3. ISSN 0072-5366

**Schweizer Wirteverband**
Gotthard Str. 61, CH-8027 Zurich, Switzerland.
- Schweizerische Wirte-Zeitung. w. ISSN 0036-780X

**Schweizerische Aerzteorganisation**
- Schweizerische Aerztezeitung/Bulletin des Medecins Suisses/Bollettino dei Medici Svizzeri. (pub. by Verlag Hans Huber)
- Schweizerisches Medizinisches Jahrbuch. (pub. by Schwabe und Co.)

**Schweizerische Akademie der Medizinischen Wissenschaften**
- Schweizerische Akademie der Medizinischen Wissenschaften. Bulletin. (pub. by Schwabe und Co.)

**Schweizerische Aktion fuer Menschenrechte**
Postfach 482, 8021 Zurich, Switzerland.
- Menschenrecht; Ueberkonfessionelles Organ fuer politische und religioese Information. m.

**Schweizerische Amerikanisten-Gesellschaft**
*see* Societe Suisse des Americanistes

**Schweizerische Apotheker-Verein**
*see* Societe Suisse de Pharmacie

**Schweizerische Bibliophilen-Gesellschaft**
Zwingliplatz 3, CH-8001 Zurich, Switzerland.
- Librarium. 3 per yr. ISSN 0024-2152

**Schweizerische Botanische Gesellschaft**
Eidgenoessische Technische Hochschule Zuerich, Institut fuer Spezielle Botanik, 8006 Zurich, Switzerland.
- Schweizerische Botanische Gesellschaft. Berichte. 4 per yr. ISSN 0080-7281

**Schweizerische Chemische Gesellschaft**
- Helvetica Chimica Acta. (pub. by Verlag Helvetica Chimica Acta)

**Schweizerische Entomologische Gesellschaft**
- Schweizerische Entomologische Gesellschaft. Mitteilungen/Societe Entomologique Suisse. Bulletin. (pub. by Fotorotar AG)

**Schweizerische Fahrrad und Motorrad Gewerbe Verband**
Werkstr. 1, 8910 Affoltern A-A, Switzerland.
- F M G-Fachblatt; offizielles Organ der Fahrrad- und Motorrad Branche. fortn. ISSN 0014-5955

**Schweizerische Galvanotechnische Gesellschaft**
- Oberflaeche/Surface. (pub. by Forster-Verlag AG)

**Schweizerische Gefluegelzeitung**
Burgerweg 24, 3052 Zollikofen, Switzerland.
- Schweizerische Gefluegelzeitung. bi-w.

**Schweizerische Geisteswissenschaftliche Gesellschaft**
- Schweizerische Geisteswissenschaftliche Gesellschaft. Schriften. (pub. by Francke Verlag)

**Schweizerische Gemeinnuetzige Gesellschaft**
- Schweizerische Zeitschrift fuer Gemeinnuetzigkeit. (pub. by Buchdruckerei und Verlag Leemann AG)

**Schweizerische Geologische Gesellschaft**
- Eclogae Geologicae Helvetiae. (pub. by Birkhaeuser Verlag)

**Schweizerische Gesellschaft der Offiziere der Sanitatstruppen**
- Schweizerische Zeitschrift fuer Militaer- und Katastrophenmedizin. (pub. by Editions Medecine et Hygiene)

**Schweizerische Gesellschaft der Offiziere des Munitionsdienstes**
Poolstr. 2, CH 4414 Fuellinsdorf, Switzerland.
- Schweizerische Gesellschaft der Offiziere des Munitionsdienstes. Bulletin. m. ISSN 0036-7591

**Schweizerische Gesellschaft fuer Asienkunde**
- Asiatische Studien/Etudes Asiatiques. (pub. by Francke Verlag)

**Schweizerische Gesellschaft fuer Chirurgie**
- Helvetica Chirurgica Acta. (pub. by Schwabe und Co.)

**Schweizerische Gesellschaft fuer Geschichte der Medizin und der Naturwissenschaften**
- Gesnerus. (pub. by Verlag Sauerlaender)

**Schweizerische Gesellschaft fuer Gynaekologie**
- Gynaekologische Rundschau. (pub. by S. Karger AG)

**Schweizerische Gesellschaft fuer Klinische Chemie**
Spalenring 147, CH-4002 Basel, Switzerland.
- Schweizerische Gesellschaft fuer Klinische Chemie. Bulletin. 1-2 per yr.

**Schweizerische Gesellschaft fuer Lebensmittelwissenschaft und- Technologie**
- Lebensmittel-Wissenschaft und Technologie/Food Science and Technology/Science et Technologie Alimentaire. (pub. by Forster-Verlag AG)

**Schweizerische Gesellschaft fuer Marktforschung**
Bleicherweg 21, 8022 Zurich, Switzerland.
- Schweizerische Gesellschaft fuer Marktforschung. Geschaeftsbericht. irreg.

**Schweizerische Gesellschaft fuer Psychiatrie**
- Schweizerische Gesellschaft fuer Psychiatrie. Fortbildungskurse/Societe Suisse de Psychiatrie. Cours de Perfectionnement. (pub. by S. Karger AG)

**Schweizerische Gesellschaft fuer Sportmedizin**
- Schweizerische Zeitschrift fuer Sportmedizin/ Revue Suisse de Medecine des Sports/Revista Svizzera di Medicina Dello Sport. (pub. by Paul Haupt AG)

**Schweizerische Gesellschaft fuer Statistik und Volkswirtschaft**
Hallwylstr. 15, CH-3003 Berne, Switzerland.
- Schweizerische Zeitschrift fuer Volkswirtschaft und Statistik/Revue Suisse d'Economie Politique et de Statistique. q.

**Schweizerische Gesellschaft fuer Theaterkultur**
c/o Edmund Stadler, Ed., Schweizerische Theatersammlung, Hallwylstr. 15, CH-3003 Berne, Switzerland.
- Mimos. q. ISSN 0026-4385
- Schweizerische Gesellschaft fuer Theaterkultur. Jahrbuecher. a.
- Schweizerische Gesellschaft fuer Theaterkultur. Schriften. irreg, no. 31 per 32, 1965 per 66.

**Schweizerische Gesellschaft fuer Ur- und Fruehgeschichte**
Rheinsprung 20, CH-4051 Basel, Switzerland.
- Schweizerische Gesellschaft fuer Ur- und Fruehgeschichte. Mitteilungsblatt. q.

**Schweizerische Gesellschaft fuer Ur- und Fruehgeschichte. Institut fuer Ur- und Fruehgeschichte der Schweiz**
- Schweizerische Gesellschaft fuer Ur- und Fruehgeschichte. Institut fuer Ur- und Fruehgeschichte der Schweiz. Jahrbuch. (pub. by Huber und Co. AG)

**Schweizerische Gesellschaft fuer Vogelkunde und Vogelschutz**
27 Kernstr., 8406 Winterthur, Switzerland.
- Ornithologische Beobachter. 6 per yr. ISSN 0030-5707

**Schweizerische Gesellschaft fuer Volkskunde.**
- Folklore Suisse/Folclore Svizzero. (pub. by G. Krebs Verlagsbuchhandlung AG)
- Schweizer Volkskunde. (pub. by G. Krebs Verlagsbuchhandlung AG)
- Schweizerische Gesellschaft fuer Volkskunde. Schriften. (pub. by Rudolf Habelt Verlag GW)
- Schweizerisches Archiv fuer Volkskunde. (pub. by G. Krebs Verlagsbuchhandlung AG)

**Schweizerische Gesellschaft pro Technorama**
- Industriearchaeologie. (pub. by O. Baldinger, Ed. & Pub.)

**Schweizerische Kartellkommission**
- Schweizerische Kartellkommission. Veroeffentlichungen/Commission Suisse des Cartels. Publications. (pub. by Orell Fuessli Graphische Betriebe AG)

**Schweizerische Katholische Bibelbewegung**
- Biblische Beitraege. (pub. by Verlag Schweizerisches Katholisches Bibelwerk)

**Schweizerische Konferenz fuer Oeffentliche Fuersorge**
- Zeitschrift fuer Oeffentliche Fuersorge. (pub. by Orell Fuessli Graphische Betriebe AG)

**Schweizerische Kreditanstalt**
see Credit Suisse

**Schweizerische Kriminalistische Gesellschaft**
- Rechtsprechung in Strafsachen. (pub. by Staempfli und Cie AG)

**Schweizerische Landesbibliothek**
see Switzerland. Bibliotheque Nationale Suisse

**Schweizerische Lithographenbund**
- Bulletin Technique. (pub. by Conzett und Huber AG)

**Schweizerische Meteorologische Zentralanstalt**
see Switzerland. Schweizerische Meteorologische Zentralanstalt

**Schweizerische Musikforschende Gesellschaft**
- Schweizerische Musikforschende Gesellschaft. Publikationen. Serie II. (pub. by Paul Haupt AG)

**Schweizerische Nationalbank**
- Schweizerische Nationalbank. Monatsbericht. (pub. by Orell Fuessli Graphische Betriebe AG)

**Schweizerische Naturforschende Gesellschaft**
- Schweizerische Naturforschende Gesellschaft. Verhandlungen/Societe Helvetique des Sciences Naturelles. Actes/Societa Elvetica dei Scienze Naturali. Atti. (pub. by Birkhaeuser Verlag)
- Schweizerische Palaeontologische Abhandlungen/Memoires Suisse de Paleontologie. (pub. by Birkhaeuser Verlag)

**Schweizerische Neurologische Gesellschaft**
- Schweizer Archiv fuer Neurologie, Neurochirurgie und Psychiatrie. (pub. by Orell Fuessli Graphische Betriebe AG)

**Schweizerische Offiziersgesellschaft**
- Allgemeine Schweizerische Militaerzeitschrift. (pub. by Huber und Co. AG)

**Schweizerische Organisation der Homophilen**
- Hey. (pub. by Verlag Plaedoyer)

**Schweizerische Public Relations Gesellschaft**
Sekretariat, Kasinoplatz 8, CH-3011 Berne, Switzerland.
- P R Revue. (Public Relations); schweizevische zeitschrift fuer Public Relations/ journal suisse de public relations. q. ISSN 0033-3727

**Schweizerische Rueckversicherungs-Gesellschaft**
Economic Department, Mythenquai 60, Zurich, Switzerland.
- Experiodica. m. ISSN 0014-4932
- Sigma. m. ISSN 0037-4857

**Schweizerische Schiffahrtsvereinigung**
- Strom und See. (pub. by Verlag Schiffahrt und Weltverkehr AG)

**Schweizerische Spenglermeister- und Installateur-Verband**
Auf der Mauer 11, 8001 Zurich, Switzerland.
- Installation. 6 per yr.
- Schweizerische Spenglermeister- und Installateur-Zeitung. 24 per yr.

**Schweizerische Staatsbuergerliche Gesellschaft**
c/o E. F. Bienz, Ed., Hermikonstr. 54, 8600 Duebendorf, Switzerland.
- Staatsbuerger; Zeitschrift fuer politische Bildung und Aufklaerung. bi-m. ISSN 0038-8874

**Schweizerische Stiftung fuer das Alter**
Witikonerstr. 56, CH-8032 Zurich, Switzerland.
- Zeitlupe; das Senioreu-Magazin. q.

**Schweizerische Treuhand- und Revisionskammer**
Limmatquai 120, CH-8001 Zurich, Switzerland.
- Schweizer Treuhander/Expert-Comptable Suisse; zeitschrift fuer revision, betriebswirtschaft und steuer/revue pour la branche fiduciare, l'economie d'entreprise et les imports. m. ISSN 0036-746X

**Schweizerische Verein fuer Straf- Gefaengniswesen und Schutzaufsicht**
- Strafvollzug in der Schweiz. (pub. by Verlag Sauerlaender)

**Schweizerische Vereinigung der Versicherungsmathematiker**
- Schweizerische Vereinigung der Versicherungsmathematiker. Mitteilungen. (pub. by Staempfli und Cie AG)

**Schweizerische Vereinigung fuer Atomenergie**
Box 2613, CH-3001 Berne, Switzerland.
- Nuclear Newsletter from Switzerland. q.
- Schweizerische Vereinigung fuer Atomenergie. Bulletin. s-m. ISSN 0036-777X

**Schweizerische Vereinigung von Textilfachleuten**
Lindenweg 7, 8122 Pfaffhausen-Zurich, Switzerland.
- Mittex: Mitteilungen ueber Textilindustrie; Schweizerische Fachschrift fuer die gesamte Textilindustrie. m.

**Schweizerische Verkehrszentrale**
Talacker 42, 8023 Zurich, Switzerland
- Schweiz, Suisse, Svizzera, Switzerland. m.(Swiss edt.); 2 per yr.(Foreign edt.) ISSN 0036-7230 (U.S. subscr. addr.: Swiss National Tourist Office, 608 Fifth Ave., New York NY 10020 or 661 Market St., San Francisco, CA 94105)

**Schweizerische Volksbank**
see Banque Populaire Suisse

**Schweizerische Zahntechniker-Vereinigung**
- Zahntechnik. (pub. by Paul Richenbacher Verlag)

**Schweizerische Zentrale fuer Handelsfoerderung**
18, rue de Bellefontaine, 1001 Lausanne, Switzerland.
- Nouvelles Economiques de Suisse/Wirtschaftsnachrichten aus der Schweiz/Swiss Economic News/Noticias Economicas de Suiza. m. ISSN 0562-9020
- Textiles Suisses. 4 per yr. ISSN 0040-5248
- Textiles Suisses/Interieur. 2 per yr. ISSN 0082-3708
- Wirtschaftliche Mitteilungen/Informations Economiques. fortn. ISSN 0043-6186

**Schweizerischen Baumeisterverbandes**
- Hoch und Tiefbau. (pub. by Verlag Hoch und Tiefbau)

**Schweizerischen Corrosserie Industrie**
- Carrossier. (pub. by Vogt-Schild AG)

**Schweizerischen Kynologischen Gesellschaft**
- Schweizer Hundesport. (pub. by Paul Haupt AG)

**Schweizerischen Mathematischen Gesellschaft**
- Commentarii Mathematici Helvetici. (pub. by Birkhaeuser Verlag)

**Schweizerischen Physikalischen Gesellschaft**
- Helvetica Physica Acta. (pub. by Birkhaeuser Verlag)

**Schweizerischer Aero-Club**
- Cockpit. (pub. by Verlag Sauerlaender)

**Schweizerischer Alpwirtschaftlicher Verein**
- Blaue, Alpwirtschaftliche Monatsblaetter. (pub. by Emmentaler Druck)

**Schweizerischer Anwaltsverband**
- Schweizerische Juristen-Zeitung/Revue Suisse de Jurisprudence. (pub. by Schulthess Polygraphischer Verlag AG)

**Schweizerischer Arbeitslehrerinnen-Verein**
c/o Margit Goetz-Schlatter, Hohe Winde-Str. 35, CH-4059 Basel, Switzerland.
- Schweizerische Arbeitslehrerinnen-Zeitung. m. ISSN 0036-7214

**Schweizerischer Aufklaerungsdienst**
Bellerivestrasse 209, 8034 Zurich, Switzerland.
- Zur Lage der Schweiz; beitrage zueinem Rueckblick. a. ISSN 0084-5809

**Schweizerischer Bankverein**
1 Aeschenvorstadt, CH-4002 Basel, Switzerland.
- Mois Economique et Financier. m. ISSN 0304-2162
- Prospects; business news survey. 4 per yr.
- S B C Booklet. irreg.

**Schweizerischer Baukaderverband**
- Bau; Fachzeitschrift fuer Bautechnik, Baupraxis, und Baumaschinen. (pub. by Verlag Jacques Bollmann AG)

**Schweizerischer Berufsverband fuer Tanz und Gymnastik**
Zurich, Switzerland.
- Tanz und Gymnastik.

**Schweizerischer Buchdruckerverein**
Carmenstr. 6, Zurich 7, Switzerland.
- Schweizerische Buchdrucker-Zeitung/Journal des Imprimeurs Suisses/Giornale dei Padroni Tipographi Svizzeri. w.

**Schweizerischer Buchhaendler- und Verleger-Verband**
P.O.B. 408, 8034 Zurich, Switzerland.
- Schweizer Buch. (pub. by Benteli Verlag)
- Schweizer Buchhandel/Librairie Suisse/Libreria Svizzera. s-m. ISSN 0036-7338
- Schweizer Buchhandels-Adressbuch. biennial. ISSN 0080-7230

**Schweizerischer Bund fuer Jugendherbergen**
Hochhaus 9, Shopping Center, 8958 Spreitenbach, Switzerland.
- Jugi/Ajiste. bi-m. ISSN 0022-6009

**Schweizerischer Bund fuer Jugendliteratur**
Zentralsekretariat, Herzogstr. 5, 3014 Berne, Switzerland.
- Jugendliteratur/Litterature de la Jeunesse/Litteratura della Gioventu/Litteratura de la Giuventuna. q.
- Schweizerischer Bund fuer Jugendliteratur. Jahresbericht/Rapport Annuel. a.

**Schweizerischer Bund fuer Naturschutz**
CH-4020 Basel, Switzerland.
- Schweizer Naturschutz; protection de la Nature. 8 per yr. ISSN 0036-7427

**Schweizerischer Chemiker-Verband**
- Chimia. (pub. by Brunner Verlag AG)

**Schweizerischer Drogistenverband**
- Schweizerische Drogistenzeitung. (pub. by Zollikofer und Co. AG)

**Schweizerischer Eisenbahnamateur- und Modellbauclubs**
c/o Otto Gerber, Trottenstr. 84, CH-8037 Zurich, Switzerland.
- Eisenbahn-Amateur; Schweizerische Zeitschrift fuer Eisenbahn- und Modellbaufreunde. m. ISSN 0013-2764

**Schweizerischer Eisenbahnerverband**
Steinerstr. 35, Case Postale 36, 3000 Berne, Switzerland.
- Cheminot. w. ISSN 0009-2916
- Ferroviere. w. ISSN 0015-0215

**Schweizerischer Elektrotechnischer Verein**
Seefeldstrasse 301, Postfach, 8034 Zurich, Switzerland.
- Bulletin S E V/V S E. s-m. (Co-sponsor: Verband Schweizerischer Elektrizitaetswerke)

**Schweizerischer Feldpostverein**
Kasparstr.`17-156, CH-3027 Berne, Switzerland.
- Feldpost/Poste de Campagne/Posta de Campo. q. ISSN 0046-3620

**Schweizerischer Feldweibelverband**
- Feldweibel/Sergent-Major/Sergente Maggiore. (pub. by Huber und Co. AG)

**Schweizerischer Feuerwehrverband**
Ensingerstrasse 37, CH-3000 Berne, Switzerland
- Schweizerische Feuerwehr-Zeitung. m. (Subscr. to: Staempfli und Cie AG, Hallerstr. 7-9, 3012 Berne, Switzerland)

**Schweizerischer Floristenverband**
Postfach 302, 8042 Zurich, Switzerland.
- Florist/Fleurist. s-m.

**Schweizerischer Forstverein**
Universitaetstr. 2, 8006 Zurich, Switzerland.
- Schweizerische Zeitschrift fuer Forstwesen/Journal Forestier Suisse. m. ISSN 0036-7818

**Schweizerischer Fourierverband**
- Fourier. (pub. by Buchdruckerei Robert Mueller AG)

**Schweizerischer Gewerbeverband**
Schwarztorstr. 26, 3000 Berne, Switzerland.
- Gewerbliche Rundschau; Zeitschrift fuer Gewerbepolitik, Gewerbefoerderung und gewerbliche Kultur. q. ISSN 0016-9412

**Schweizerischer Gewerkschaftsbund**
Monbijoustr. 61, CH-3000 Berne 23, Switzerland.
- Gewerkschaftliche Rundschau. m. ISSN 0016-9455
- Revue Syndicale Suisse. m. ISSN 0035-421X

**Schweizerischer Jaegerverband zur Hebung der Patentjagd und des Wildschutzes**
Mythenstr. 28, Einsiedeln, Switzerland.
- Schweizerjaeger/Chasseur Suisse/Cacciattore Svizzero. 18 per yr. ISSN 0036-8016

**Schweizerischer Katholischer Anstalter-Verband**
Zaehringerstr. 19, 6003 Lucerne, Switzerland.
- Heim und Anstalt/Homes et Instituts; Zeitschrift fuer schul-Internate, Haeuser religioeser Gemeinschaften und Fuersorgeheime jeder Art. bi-m. ISSN 0017-9671

**Schweizerischer Kaufmaennischer Verein**
Talacker 34, 8001 Zurich, Switzerland.
- Schweizerisches Kaufmaennisches Zentralblatt. w. ISSN 0036-7966

**Schweizerischer Kunstverein**
Baselstr. 11, CH-6002 Lucerne, Switzerland.
- Schweizerischer Kunstverein. Kunst-Bulletin. m.

**Schweizerischer Lehrerverein**
- Schweizerische Lehrerzeitung. (pub. by Buchdruckerei Staefa AG)

**Schweizerischer Lichtspieltheater-Verband**
Postfach 2674, 3001 Berne, Switzerland.
- Film. m.

**Schweizerischer Lithographenbund**
- Fachhefte fuer Chemigraphie, Lithographie und Tiefdruck. (pub. by Conzett und Huber AG)

**Schweizerischer Maler und Gipsermeister Verband**
c/o E. Eckert, Raemistr. 6, 8001 Zurich, Switzerland.
- Applica; zeitschrift fuer das maler und gipsergewerbe. bi-m.

**Schweizerischer Mechanikermeister-Verband**
Langmauerstr. 103, CH-8006 Zurich, Switzerland.
- Schweizerische Mechaniker-Zeitschrift/Revue Suisse des Mecaniciens. s-m. ISSN 0036-7664

**Schweizerischer Metall- und Uhrenarbeitnehmer-Verband**
Monbijoustr. 61, CH-8007 Berne, Switzerland.
- S M U V Zeitung. w.

**Schweizerischer Musikerverband**
- Schweizer Musikerblatt/Bulletin Musical Suisse. (pub. by Buchdruckerei Schippert und Co.)

**Schweizerischer Obstverband Zug**
c/o Rudolf Schumacher, 6300 Zug, Switzerland.
- Fruechte und Gemuese/Fruits et Legumes. w. ISSN 0016-2221 (Co-sponsor: Schweizerischer Gemuese-Union Zuerich)

**Schweizerischer Pfadfinderbund**
Muenstergasse 42, 3011 Berne, Switzerland.
- Trefle /Kim. 9 per yr. (Co-sponsor: Bund Schweizerischer Pfadfinderinnen)

**Schweizerischer Photographenverband**
Postfach 17, 3930 Visp, Switzerland.
- Schweizerische Photorundschau. s-m. ISSN 0036-7737 (Co-sponsor: Schweizerischer Photohandlerverband)

**Schweizerischer Reklameverband**
Kappelergasse 14, CH-8022 Zurich, Switzerland.
- Werbung/Publicite; Schweizerische Zeitschrift fuer Marketing und Kommunikation. 11 per yr.

**Schweizerischer Schachverband**
Zurich, Switzerland.
- Schweizerische Schachzeitung. m. ISSN 0036-7745

**Schweizerischer Studentenverein**
Mythenquai 26, CH-8027 Zurich, Switzerland.
- Civitas; Monatsschrift fuer Politik und Kultur/ revue mensuelle politique et culturelle / mensile di politica e cultura. m.

**Schweizerischer Technischer Verband**
- Schweizerische Technische Zeitschrift. (pub. by Buechler und Co. AG)

**Schweizerischer Tierschutzverband**
Birsfelderstr. 45, CH-4052 Basel, Switzerland.
- Schweizer Tierschutz. bi-m.

**Schweizerischer Turnverein**
- Koerpererziehung/Education Physique. (pub. by Paul Haupt AG)

**Schweizerischer Typographenbund**
- Typographische Monatsblaetter. (pub. by Zollikofer und Co. AG)

**Schweizerischer Verband Angestellter Drogisten**
Thiersteinerstrasse 24/2, CH-4153 Reinach, Switzerland.
- Droga Helvetica. m.

**Schweizerischer Verband des Schmiede, Landmaschinen, Metall und Holzgewerbe**
- S L M H/F B M A. Bulletin. (pub. by FABAG und Druckerei Winterthur AG)

**Schweizerischer Verband Evangelischer Arbeitnehmer**
Hoehenring 29, 8052 Zurich, Switzerland.
- Evangelisch-Soziale Warte. w. ISSN 0014-3405

**Schweizerischer Verband fuer Behindertensport**
Brunaustr. 6, 8002 Zurich, Switzerland.
- Invalidensport; sport-handicap. bi-m. ISSN 0020-9880

**Schweizerischer Verband fuer Beruflichen Unterricht**
- Berufsschueler. (pub. by Verlag Sauerlaender)

**Schweizerischer Verband fuer Berufsberatung**
Eidmattstr. 51, 8032 Zurich, Switzerland.
- Berufsberatung und Berufsbildung/Orientation et Formation Professionnelles. bi-m. ISSN 0005-9501

**Schweizerischer Verband Staatlich Anerkannter Physiotherapeuten**
Steinmuhlegasse 3, CH-8800 Thalwil, Switzerland.
- Physiotherapeut/Physiotherapeute. bi-m.

**Schweizerischer Verband Technischer Betriebskader**
Schaffhauserstr. 2/4, 8006 Zurich, Switzerland.
- Werkmeister und Techniche Arbeitsleiter/ Contremaitre et Agent de Maitrise. fortn. ISSN 0043-2776

**Schweizerischer Verband von Fachleuten fuer Alkoholgefaehrdeten- und Suchtkrankenhilfe**
Lauenenweg 69, 3600 Thun, Switzerland.
- Fuersorger. bi-m. ISSN 0016-3139

**Schweizerischer Verein fuer Kaeltetechnik**
- Temperatur Technik. (pub. by Forster Verlag AG)

**Schweizerischer Verein fuer Schweisstechnik**
- Schweisstechnik/Soudure. (pub. by Verlag Berichthaus)

**Schweizerischer Verein von Gas- und Wasserfachmaennern**
Gruetlistr. 44, CH-8027 Zurich, Switzerland.
- G W A - Gas Wasser Abwasser/G E E U - Gaz Eaux Eaux Usees. m. ISSN 0036-8008

**Schweizerischer Wasserwirtschaftsverband**
Ruetistrasse 3A, CH-5401 Baden, Switzerland.
- Wasser, Energie, Luft/Eau, Energie, Air. m. (Co-sponsor: Schweizerische Vereinigung fuer Gewaesserschutz und Lufthygiene)

**Schweizerischer Wissenschaftsrat**
Wildhainweg 9, Postfach 2732, 3001 Berne, Switzerland.
- Schweizerischer Wissenschaftsrat. Jahresbericht. a.

**Schweizerischer Zeitungsverleger-Verband**
Morgartenstrasse 29, Postfach 1465, 8036 Zurich, Switzerland.
- S Z V Aktualitaten. bi-m.
- Schweizerischer Zeitungsverleger-Verband. Bulletin. m. ISSN 0036-7923

**Schweizerischer Zentralverband des Musikhandels und der Angeschlossen Verbaende**
- Schweizerische Zeitschrift fuer Musik-Handel und Industrie/Journal Suisse du Commerce et de l'Industrie de la Musique. (pub. by K.J. Wyss Erben AG)

**Schweizerisches Bundesarchiv**
see Switzerland. Schweizerisches Bundesarchiv

**Schweizerisches Gutenbergmuseum**
Zeughausgasse 2, 3011 Berne, Switzerland.
- Schweizerisches Gutenbergmuseum/Musee Gutenberg Suisse. q. ISSN 0036-7958

**Schweizerisches Institut fuer Gewerbliche Wirtschaft**
- Internationales Gewerbearchiv. (pub. by Duncker und Humblot GW)

**Schweizerisches Institut fuer Hauswirtschaft**
Nordstr. 31, 8035 Zurich, Switzerland.
- S I H Bulletin. q.

**Verlag Schweizerisches Katholisches Bibelwerk**
Rue de l'Hopital 1, CH-1700 Fribourg, Switzerland.
- Biblische Beitraege. irreg. ISSN 0582-1673 (Schweizerische Katholische Bibelbewegung)

**Schweizerisches Landesmuseum**
Zurich, Switzerland.
- Aus dem Schweizerischen Landesmuseum. (pub. by Paul Haupt AG)
- Keramik-Freunde der Schweiz. Mitteilungsblatt. q. ISSN 0023-0553
- Zeitschrift fuer Schweizerische Archaeologie und Kunstgeschichte/Revue Suisse d'Art et d'Archeologie. (pub. by Verlag Berichthaus)

**Schweizerisches Ost-Institut**
Jubilaeumsstr. 41, CH-3000 Berne 6, Switzerland.
- Etudes Politiques. 10 per yr.
- S O I Bilanz. m.
- T.M. (Tatsachen und Meinungen) irreg., no. 35, 1976. ISSN 0080-7427
- ZeitBild. fortn. ISSN 0044-2100

**Schweizerisches Sozialarchiv**
Neumarkt 28, 8001 Zurich, Switzerland.
- Schweizerisches Sozialarchiv. a. ISSN 0080-7419

**Schweizerisches Tropeninstitut**
- Acta Tropica. (pub. by Schwabe und Co.)

**Sciweizerischer Buchhaendler- und Verleger-Verband**
P.O.B. 408, 8034 Zurich, Switzerland.
- Domino. bi-m. ISSN 0046-0583

**Editions Scriptar S.A.**
23 Ave. de la Gare, 1001 Lausanne, Switzerland.
- Swiss Watch and Jewelry Journal. bi-m. ISSN 0039-7520 (Swiss Watch Fair)

**Sedo S.A**
33 Av.de la Gare, Lausanne, Switzerland.
- Oeil; revue d'art. m.(double no. in summer ) ISSN 0029-862X

**Selection du Reader's Digest S.A.**
see Beste aus Reader's Digest AG

**Senger Annoncen**
Alfred Escher-Str. 82, 8027 Zurich, Switzerland.
- Wirtschaftsrevue. m. ISSN 0510-5528

**SEPEG**
Grand-Saconnex, Switzerland
- Vision; the European business magazine. m (11 per yr.) (Subscr. to: Vision, Inc., 641 Lexington Ave., New York, NY 10022)

**Siemens-Albis**
Albisriederstr. 245, 8047 Zurich, Switzerland.
- Siemens-Albis. Berichte. q.

**Sinter Press**
c/o Ed. D. E. Steward, Spalentorweg 41, 4051 Basel, Switzerland.
- Sinter. irreg (approx. 3 per yr.) no. 9, 1976.

**Socialistes Chretiens de Langue Francaise**
c/o Arthur Maret, 15 Avenue Druey, 1004 Lausanne, Switzerland.
- Espoir du Monde; unite-liberte-oecumenisme. q. ISSN 0014-0732

**Societa di Banca Svizzera**
*see* Schweizerischer Bankverein

**Societe Botanique de Geneve**
Case Postale 21, CH-1211 Geneva 21, Switzerland.
- Saussurea. a.

**Societe d'Etudes Economiques et Sociales**
5 Place de la Cathedrale, 1005 Lausanne, Switzerland.
- Revue Economique et Sociale. q. ISSN 0035-2772

**Societe d'Histoire et d'Archaeologie de Geneve**
c/o Bibliotheque Publique et Universitaire de Geneve, Promenade des Bastions, Geneva, Switzerland.
- Societe d'Histoire et d'Archaeologie de Geneve. Bulletin. a. ISSN 0081-0959

**Societe d'Histoire et d'Archeologie du Canton de Neuchatel**
- Musee Neuchatelois. (pub. by Musee Neuchatelois)

**Societe de Banque Suisse**
*see* Schweizerischer Bankverein

**Societe de Belles Lettres de Lausanne et Geneve**
- Revue de Belles-Lettres. (pub. by Editions Medecine et Hygiene)

**Societe de l'Ecole des Chartes**
- Bibliotheque de l'Ecole des Chartes. (pub. by Librarie Droz)
- Societe de l'Ecole des Chartes. Memoires et Documents. (pub. by Librarie Droz)

**Societe de Physique et d'Histoire Naturelle de Geneve**
Museum d'Histoire Naturelle de Geneve, Geneva, Switzerland.
- Archives des Sciences. 3 per yr. ISSN 0003-9705

**Societe des Carabiniers de Lausanne**
Case Gare, 1001 Lausanne, Switzerland.
- Carabinier de Lausanne. 3 per yr. ISSN 0008-6096

**Societe des Etudes de Lettres**
Rue Cite-Devant 1-3, CH-1005 Lausanne, Switzerland.
- Etudes de Lettres. 4 per yr. ISSN 0014-2026

**Societe des Exportateurs de Vins Suisses**
Avenue Ruchonnet 11, CH-1001 Lausanne, Switzerland.
- Liste des Prix des Vins et Spiritueux Suisses. a.

**Societe des Libraires et Editeurs de la Suisse Romande**
*see* Schweizerischer Buchhaendler- und Verleger-Verband

**Societe Elvetica dei Scienze Naturali**
*see* Schweizerische Naturforschende Gesellschaft

**Societe Helvetique des Sciences Naturelles**
*see* Schweizerische Naturforschende Gesellschaft

**Societe Internationale de Musicologie**
*see* International Musicological Society

**Societe Internationale pour l'Enseignement Commercial**
*see* International Society for Business Education

**Societe Medicale de la Suisse Romande**
2 Bellefontaine, 1000 Lausanne, Switzerland.
- Revue Medicale de la Suisse Romande. m. ISSN 0035-3655

**Societe Pedagogique de la Suisse Romande**
- Educateur et Bulletin Corporatif. (pub. by Imprimerie Corbaz S. A.)

**Societe Romande d'Apiculture**
Aug. Merminod, Sansui 14, 1530 Payerne, Switzerland.
- Journal Suisse d'Apiculture. m. (11 per yr)

**Societe Romande pour l'Etude et la Protection des Oiseaux**
Case Postale 548, CH-1401 Yverdon, Switzerland.
- Nos Oiseaux. q. ISSN 0029-3725

**Societe Suisse d'Astronomie**
c/o W. Luethi, Lorraine 12D/16, CH-3400 Burgdorf, Switzerland.
- Orion. 6 per yr. ISSN 0030-557X

**Societe Suisse d'Heraldique**
c/o Georges-Claude Passavant, 6 Laubeggstr., CH-3013 Berne, Switzerland.
- Archivum Heraldicum. 3-4 per yr. ISSN 0004-0673

**Societe Suisse de Chimie**
*see* Schweizerische Chemische Gesellschaft

**Societe Suisse de l'Industrie du Gaz et des Eaux**
*see* Schweizerischer Verein von Gas und Wasserfachmaennern

**Societe Suisse de Numismatique**
c/o Colin Martin, 1 rue Pepinet, Lausanne, Switzerland.
- Gazette Numismatique Suisse/Schweizer Muenzblaetter. q. ISSN 0016-5565
- Revue Suisse de Numismatique/Schweizerische Numismatische Rundschau. ISSN 0035-4163

**Societe Suisse de Pharmacie**
Marktgasse 52, 3011 Berne, Switzerland.
- Index Nominum. irreg., 8th edt., 1975.
- Pharmaceutica Acta Helvetiae. (pub. by Vogt-Schild AG)
- Schweizerische Apotheker-Zeitung. s-m. ISSN 0036-7508

**Societe Suisse de Philosophie**
- Studia Philosophica. (pub. by Verlag fuer Recht und Gesellschaft AG)

**Societe Suisse de Psychologie et de Psychologie Appliquee**
- Schweizerische Zeitschrift fuer Psychologie und ihre Anwendungen/Revue Suisse de Psychologie Pure et Appliquee. (pub. by Verlag Hans Huber)

**Societe Suisse de Speleologie**
c/o Institut de Geologie, Universite de Neuchatel, 11 rue Emile-Argand, CH-2000 Neuchatel, Switzerland.
- Congres National de Speleologie. Actes. irreg. ISSN 0069-8911
- Stalactite. 2 per yr. ISSN 0038-9226

**Societe Suisse de Statistique et d'Economie Politique**
*see* Schweizerische Gesellschaft fuer Statistik und Volkswirtschaft

**Societe Suisse des Americanistes**
65-67, Boulevard Carl-Vogt, 1205 Geneva, Switzerland.
- Societe Suisse des Americanistes.Bulletin. a. ISSN 0582-1592

**Societe Suisse des Ingenieurs et des Architectes**
- Bulletin Technique de la Suisse Romande. (pub. by Imprimerie la Concorde)
- Documentation du Batiment. (pub. by Imprimerie la Concorde)
- Schweizerische Bauzeitung. (pub. by Verlag der Akademischen Technischen Vereine)

**Societe Suisse des Maitres-Imprimeurs**
*see* Schweizerischer Buchdruckverein

**Societe Vaudoise d'Histoire et d'Archeologie**
4287 Lausanne 10, Switzerland.
- Revue Historique Vaudoise. a.

**Societe Vaudoise des Sciences Naturelles**
Palais de Rumine, 1005 Lausanne, Switzerland.
- Societe Vaudoise des Sciences Naturelles. Bulletin. ISSN 0037-9603
- Societe Vaudoise des Sciences Naturelles. Memoires. irreg. ISSN 0037-9611

**Society for Human Ecology**
- Collioquium Internationale. (pub. by Georgi Publishing Co.)

**Sozialdemokratische Partei der Schweiz**
Pavillonweg 3, 3012 Berne, Switzerland.
- Profil; sozialistische Monatsschrift. m.

**Spektrum-Verlag**
Napfgasse 4, 8001 Zurich, Switzerland.
- Spektrum; vierteljahresschrift fuer dichtung und orginalgrafik. q. ISSN 0038-7274

**Sport- Toto- Gesellschaft**
- Tip. (pub. by Gesellschaft zur Domprobstei)

**Staedtische Sukkulentensammlung**
Mythenquai 88, 8002 Zurich, Switzerland.
- Staedtische Sukkulentensammlung, Zurich. Katalog der in Kultur Stehenden Arten. irreg., 2nd edt. 1967. ISSN 0081-4156

**Buchdruckerei Staefa AG**
8712 Staefa, Switzerland.
- Schweizer Frauenblatt; unabhaengiges Informationsorgan fuer Fraueninteressen u. Konsumentenfragen. s-m. ISSN 0036-7346
- Schweizerische Lehrerzeitung. w. ISSN 0036-7656 (Schweizerischer Lehrerverein)

**Staempfli und Cie AG**
Hallerstr. 7-9, 3012 Berne, Switzerland.
- Acta Bernensia: Beitraege zur Praehistorischen, Klassischen und Juengeren Archaeologie. irreg. ISSN 0065-1052
- Alpen/Alpes. m. ISSN 0002-6336 (Club Alpin Suisse)
- Internationale Kirchliche Zeitschrift. q. ISSN 0020-9252
- Rechtsprechung in Strafsachen. q. ISSN 0034-138X (Schweizerische Kriminalistische Gesellschaft)
- Schweizerische Vereinigung der Versicherungsmathematiker. Mitteilungen. s-a. ISSN 0042-3815
- Schweizerische Zeitschrift fuer Sozialversicherung. 4 per yr. ISSN 0036-7877
- Schweizerische Zeitschrift fuer Strafrecht/Revue Penale Suisse. q. ISSN 0036-7893
- Zeitschrift des Bernischen Juristenvereins. m. ISSN 0044-2127
- Zeitschrift fuer Fremdenverkehr/Revue de Tourisme/Tourist Review. q. ISSN 0044-2755 (International Association of Scientific Experts in Tourism) (Co-sponsors: University of Berne, Tourist Research Institute; University of St. Gallen, Institute for Tourism and Transport Economy)

**Standing Conference of Rectors and Vice-Chancellors of the European Universities**
10 rue de Conseil General, CH-1211 Geneva 4, Switzerland.
- C R E Information. q. ISSN 0007-9049

**Stiftung fuer Kirche und Judentum**
Roetelstrasse 96, 8057 Zurich, Switzerland.
- Judaica; Beitraege zum Verstaendnis des juedischen Schicksals in Vergangenheit und Gegenwart. q. ISSN 0022-572X

**R. Stocker, Ed. & Pub.**
Bahnpostfach 3142, Zurich, Switzerland.
- Schweizer Musiker-Revue. m. ISSN 0036-7419

**Editions Stuessi Ltd.**
Postfach, CH-8121 Benglen, Switzerland.
- Pot-Au-Feu. m. ISSN 0032-5538

**Sulzer Brothers Ltd.**
Winterthur, Switzerland.
- Sulzer Technical Review. 2-4 per yr (depending on language edition) ISSN 0039-4912

**Svisa Esperanto Societo**
Schorenstr 32, CH-4900 Langenthal, Switzerland.
- Svisa Esperanto Revuo. m.

**Swedenborg Verlag**
Postfach 247, CH-8032 Zurich, Switzerland.
- Offene Tore; Beitraege zum neuen christlichen Zeitalter. q. ISSN 0030-0101

**Swiss Alpine Club**
*see* Club Alpin Suisse

**Swiss Association for Atomic Energy**
*see* Schweizerische Vereinigung fuer Atomenergie

**Swiss Association of Graduate Nurses**
- Zeitschrift fuer Krankenpflege/Revue Suisse des Infirmieres. (pub. by Vogt-Schild AG)

**Swiss Bank Corporation**
*see* Schweizerischer Bankverein

**Swiss Eastern Institute**
*see* Schweizerisches Ost- Institut

**Swiss Entomological Society**
*see* Schweizerische Entomologische Gesellschaft

**Swiss Federal Institute of Technology**
*see* Eidgenoessische Technische Hochschule Zuerich

**Swiss Federal Railways**
*see* Switzerland. Chemins de Fer Federaux Suisses

**Swiss Federation of Camping and Caravanning**
Case Postale 24, CH-6000 Lucerne 4, Switzerland.
- Camping-Caravanning-Revue. 10 per yr. ISSN 0008-2414

**Swiss Federation of Plant Engineers**
- Betriebstechnik. (pub. by O. Baldinger, Ed. & Pub.)

**Swiss Federation of Trade Unions**
*see* Schweizerischer Gewerkschaftsbund

**Swiss Meteorological Institute**
*see* Switzerland. Schweizerische Meteorologische Zentralanstalt

**Swiss National Museum**
*see* Schweizerisches Landesmuseum

**Swiss Natural History Society**
*see* Schweizerische Naturforschende Gesellschaft

**Swiss Newspaper Publishers Association**
*see* Schweizerischer Zeitungsverleger-Verband

**Swiss Pharmaceutical Society**
*see* Societe Suisse de Pharmacie

**Swiss Shipping Association**
*see* Schweizerische Schiffahrtvereinigung

**Swiss Society of Dermatology and Venerology**
- Dermatologica. (pub. by S. Karger AG)

**Swiss Society of Engineers and Architects**
*see* Societe Suisse des Ingenieurs et des Architectes

**Swiss Society of Food Science and Technology**
*see* Schweizerische Gesellschaft fuer Lebensmittelwissenschaft und- Technologie

**Swiss Society of Paediatrics**
- Helvetica Paediatrica Acta. (pub. by Schwabe und Co.)
- Helvetica Paediatrica Acta. Supplementum. (pub. by Schwabe und Co.)

**Swiss Society of Plastic and Reconstructive Surgeons**
- Swiss Society of Plastic and Reconstructive Surgeons. Proceedings (Of) Annual Meeting. (pub. by Excerpta Medica NE)

**Swiss Union of Arts and Crafts**
*see* Schweizerischer Gewerbeverband

**Swiss Watch Fair**
- Swiss Watch and Jewelry Journal. (pub. by Editions Scriptar S.A.)

**Swiss Watch Shops Association**
*see* Verband Schweizerischer Uhrenfachgeschaefte

**Swissexport Cooperation Alliance**
- Swisstrade. (pub. by EXIM-INDEX Dr. E. Goldberger)

**Switzerland. Bibliotheque Nationale Suisse**
Hallwylstrasse 15, Berne, Switzerland.
- Bibliographia Scientiae Naturalis Helvetica. a. ISSN 0067-6829

**Switzerland. Bundesamt fuer Industrie, Gewerbe und Arbeit**
- Arbeitsrecht und Arbeitslosenversicherung. (pub. by Schulthess Polygraphischer Verlag AG)

**Switzerland. Bundesamt fuer Sozialversicherung**
Berne, Switzerland.
- Switzerland. Bundesamt fuer Sozialversicherung. Spezialitaeten-Liste/Liste des Specialites/Elenco delle Specialita. s-a. ISSN 0082-0504

**Switzerland. Bundesamt fuer Zivilschutz**
Case Postale 3003, Berne, Switzerland.
- Feuille Officielle de la Protection Civile/Mitteilungsblatt des Zivilschutzes/Foglio d'Informazione della Protezione Civile. s-a. ISSN 0015-0428

**Switzerland. Bureau Federal de Statistique**
*see* Switzerland. Statistisches Amt.

**Switzerland. Chemins de Fer Federaux Suisses**
Hochschulstr. 6, CH-3000 Berne, Switzerland.
- European Passenger Timetable Conference Minutes. a. ISSN 0071-3120

**Switzerland. Commission de Recherches Economiques**
*see* Switzerland. Eidgenoessisches Volkswirtschaftsdepartement. Kommission fuer Konjunkturfragen

**Switzerland. Departement Federal de l'Economie Publique. Commission de Recherches Economiques**
*see* Switzerland. Eidgenoessisches Volkswirtschaftsdepartement. Kommission fuer Konjunkturfragen

**Switzerland. Department Federal de l'Economie Publique**
*see* Switzerland. Eidgenoessisches Volkswirtschaftsdepartement

**Switzerland. Direction Generale des Douanes**
*see* Switzerland. Eidgenoessische Oberzolldirektion

**Switzerland. Directorate General of Customs**
*see* Switzerland. Eidgenoessische Oberzolldirektion

**Switzerland. Eidgenoessische Anstalt fuer das Forstliche Versuchswesen**
CH-8903 Birmensdorf, Switzerland.
- Switzerland. Eidgenoessische Anstalt fuer das Forstliche Versuchswesen. Mitteilungen. irreg., band 50, 1974.

**Switzerland. Eidgenoessische Gesundheitsamt**
3000 Berne, Switzerland.
- Mitteilungen aus dem Gebiete der Lebensmitteluntersuchung und Hygiene/Travaux de Chimie Alimentaire et d'Hygiene. 6 per yr. ISSN 0026-6841 (Co-sponsor: Schweizerische Gesellschaft fuer Analytische und Angewandte Chemie)

**Switzerland. Eidgenoessische Oberzolldirektion**
Monbijoustr. 40, 3003 Berne, Switzerland.
- Statistique Annuelle du Commerce Exterieur de la Suisse. a. ISSN 0081-525X (prep. by its Abteilung Handelsstatistik)
- Swiss Foreign Trade Statistics. m. (plus annual no.) ISSN 0049-2183 (prep. by its Abteilung Handelsstatistik)
- Zoll Rundschau/Rivista della Dogane/Revista della Dogane; Fachzeitschrift des Schweizerischen Zollpersonals. bi-m.

**Switzerland. Eidgenoessisches Amt fuer Geistiges Eigentum**
3003 Berne, Switzerland.
- Schweizerisches Patent-, Muster- und Marken-Blatt/Feuille Suisse des Brevets, Dessins et Marques/Foglio Svizzero dei Brevetti, Disegni e Marchi. s-m. ISSN 0036-7974

**Switzerland. Eidgenoessisches Departement des Innern**
Berne, Switzerland.
- Schoenste Schweizer Buecher. a. ISSN 0080-6838

**Switzerland. Eidgenoessisches Volkswirtschaftsdepartement**
Effingerstr. 3, 3011 Berne, Switzerland.
- Landwirtschaftliches Jahrbuch der Schweiz/Annuaire Agricole de la Suisse. (pub. by Buchverlag Verbandsdruckerei AG)
- Switzerland. Eidgenoessisches Volkswirtschaftsdepartement. Volkswirtschaft. m. ISSN 0042-8590

**Switzerland. Eidgenoessisches Volkswirtschaftsdepartement. Abteilung fuer Landwirtschaft**
- Schweizerische Landwirtschaftliche Forschung/Recherche Agronomique in Suisse. (pub. by Benteli-Verlag)

**Switzerland. Eidgenoessisches Volkswirtschaftsdepartement. Kommission fuer Konjunkturfragen**
Belpstr. 53, 3003 Berne, Switzerland.
- Ertragsbilanz der Schweiz. a.
- Schweizerische Konjunktur und ihre Aussichten. a.
- Switzerland. Kommission fuer Konjunkturfragen. Allfaellige Studien. irreg.
- Switzerland. Kommission fuer Konjunkturfragen. Wirtschaftslage. q.

**Switzerland. Kommission fuer Konjunkturfragen**
*see under* Switzerland. Eidgenoessisches Volkswirtschaftsdepartement

**Switzerland. Office d'Orientation et de Formation Professionelle**
Rue Prevost-Martin 6, Case Postale 226, 1211 Geneva 4, Switzerland.
- Etudes et Carrieres. q.

**Switzerland. Office de la Science et de la Recherche**
P.O. Box 2732, Wildhainweg 9, 3001 Berne, Switzerland.
- Politique de la Science. irreg (5 per yr) ISSN 0085-4980

**Switzerland. Office Federal de la Protection Civile**
*see* Switzerland. Bundesamt fuer Zivilschutz

**Switzerland. Office Federal du Personnel. Service de Placement**
3003 Berne, Switzerland.
- Emploi. w.

**Switzerland. Schweizerische Landesbibliotek**
*see* Switzerland. Bibliotheque Nationale Suisse

**Switzerland. Schweizerische Meteorologische Zentralanstalt**
Kraehbuehlstrasse 58, CH-8044 Zurich, Switzerland.
- Schweizerische Meteorologische Zentralanstalt. Annalen. a. ISSN 0080-7338
- Schweizerische Meteorologische Zentralanstalt. Veroeffentlichungen. irreg., no. 37, 1976. ISSN 0080-7346

**Switzerland. Schweizerisches Bundesarchiv**
Archivstrasse 24, CH-3003 Berne, Switzerland.
- Schweizerisches Bundesarchiv. Studien und Quellen/Etudes et Sources/Studi e Fonti. irreg.

**Switzerland. Statistisches Amt.**
Publikationsdienst, Hallwylstr. 15, CH-3003 Berne, Switzerland.
- Offentliche Finanzen der Schweiz/Finances Publiques en Suisse. a.
- Schweizerische Bibliographie fuer Statistik und Volkswirtschaft. a.
- Statistisches Jahrbuch der Schweiz/Annuaire Statistique de la Suisse. (pub. by Birkhaeuser Verlag)
- Steuerbelastung in der Schweiz/Charge Fiscale en Suisse. irreg.
- Studierenden an den Schweizerischen Hochschulen/Les Etudiants dans les Hautes Ecoles Suisses. a.
- Switzerland. Statistisches Amt. Eingefuehrte Motorfahrzeuge/Vehicules a Moteur Importes. irreg.
- Switzerland. Statistisches Amt. Heiraten, Lebendgeborene und Gestorbene in den Gemeinden/Mariages, Naissances et Deces dans les Communes. irreg.
- Switzerland. Statistisches Amt. In Verkehr Gesetzte Neue Motorfahrzeuge/Vehicules a Moteur Neufs Mis en Circulation. irreg.
- Switzerland. Statistisches Amt. Strassenverkehrsunfaelle/Accidents de la Circulation Routiere en Suisse. a.

**Switzerland. Wildlife Information Service**
Birchstr. 95, CH-8050 Zurich, Switzerland.
- Key Word Index of Wildlife Research. a.

**Synodalrat der Evangelisch-Reformierten
Landeskirche des Kantons Bern**
- Studientage fuer Die Pfarrer. (pub. by Paul Haupt AG)

**Noel Tamini, Ed. & Pub.**
Chalet du Midi, 1922 Salvan, Switzerland.
- Spiridon; revue internationale de course a pied. bi-m.

**Textolux AG**
Fuerstenlandstr. 122, CH-9001 St. Gallen, Switzerland.
- Textil-Revue. w. ISSN 0040-4861

**Editions Theatre et Films de Caux S.A.**
Case Postale 3, CH-1211 Geneva 20, Switzerland.
- Tribune de Caux. m.

**Thomas Mann Gesellschaft**
- Thomas Mann Gesellschaft. Blaetter. (pub. by Europa Verlag AG)

**Thurgauische Museumsgesellschaft**
c/o Thurgauische Museum, CH-8500 Frauenfeld, Switzerland.
- Thurgauische Museum. Mitteilungen. irreg.

**Ticino. Cancelleria Dello Stato**
6500 Bellinzona, Switzerland.
- Rivista Tributaria Ticinese. q. ISSN 0048-8429

**Touring-Club of Switzerland**
- Touring. (pub. by Buchverlag Verbandsdruckerei AG)

**Touristenverein Naturfreunde Schweiz**
Postfach 1277, 8036 Zurich, Switzerland.
- Naturfreund/Ami de la Nature. m (10 per yr.) ISSN 0028-0925

**Editions Trente Jours S.A.**
c/o M. Alfred Loertscher, Ed., 19 Av. de Beaulieu, 1004 Lausanne, Switzerland.
- Trente Jours. m.

**Troxler-Verlag**
Wabernstrasse 64, CH-3007 Berne, Switzerland.
- Gegenwart; Zweimonatsschrift fuer freies Geistesleben und soziale Dreigliederung. bi-m. ISSN 0016-5867

**Ufficio Intercantonale di Controllo dei Medicamenti**
see Interkantonale Kontrollstelle fuer Heilmittel

**Unesco. International Bureau of Education**
For publications of this agency see section for UNITED NATIONS

**Union Bank of Switzerland**
see Union de Banques Suisses

**Union de Banques Suisses**
Bahnhofstr. 45, 8000 Zurich, Switzerland.
- Business Facts and Figures. m. ISSN 0007-6740
- Country Studies; Union Bank of Switzerland reports. irreg.
- Economic Panorama. q.
- Prices and Earnings Around the Globe. irreg, 3rd edt., 1976.

**Union Druck und Verlag**
Werkhofstr. 5, CH-4500 Solothurn, Switzerland.
- Moderne Sekretarin. m. (Institut fuer Bueroorganisation)

**Union Internationale Contre le Cancer**
see International Union Against Cancer

**Union Internationale de Protection de l'Enfance**
see International Union for Child Welfare

**Union Internationale des Associations d'Alpinisme**
see International Union of Alpine Associations

**Union Internationale des Travailleurs de l'Alimentation et des Branches Connexes**
see International Union of Food and Allied Workers' Associations

**Union Interparlementaire**
see Interparliamentary Union

**Union Mondiale des Organisations Syndicales sur Bases Economique et Sociale Liberales**
see World Union of Liberal Trade Union Organizations

**Union of European Football Associations**
33 Jupiter Strasse, Case Postale 16, 3000 Berne 15, Switzerland.
- Union of European Football Associations. Manuel/Handbook/Handbuch of U E F A. irreg. ISSN 0570-2070

**Union of Swiss Short Wave Amateurs**
Postfach, 8607 Seegraeben, Switzerland.
- Old Man. m. ISSN 0030-2007

**Union Suisse des Fabricants de Boites de Montres**
Case Postale 75, 2500 Bienne 4, Switzerland.
- U S F B Informations. m (10 per yr.)

**Union Suisse des Lithographes**
see Schweizerischer Lithographenbund

**Union Suisse des Papetiers**
see Verband Schweizerischer Papeteristen

**Union Suisse des Paysans**
Laurstrasse 10, 5200 Brugg, Switzerland.
- Revue Suisse des Marches Agricoles. w. ISSN 0035-4198

**Union Suisse pour l'Amelioration du Logement**
Avenue de Tivoli 2, Lausanne, Switzerland.
- Habitation. m. ISSN 0017-6419 (Co-sponsors: Association Suisse pour le Plan d'Amenagement; Federation des Architectes Suisses)

**Union Syndicale Suisse**
see Schweizerischer Gewerkschaftsbund

**Unione Suisse de Yachting**
- Yachting/Yachting Suisse. (pub. by Buechler und Co. AG)

**United Nations Economic Commission for Europe**
For publications of this agency see section for UNITED NATIONS

**United Nations High Commissioner for Refugees**
For publications of this agency see section for UNITED NATIONS

**United Nations Research Institute for Social Development**
For publications of this agency see section for UNITED NATIONS

**Universal Postal Union**
For publications of this agency see section for UNITED NATIONS

**Universitaet Basel. Theologische Fakultaet**
- Theologische Dissertationen. (pub. by Friedrich Reinhardt Verlag)
- Theologische Zeitschrift. (pub. by Friedrich Reinhardt Verlag)

**Universitaet Basel. Wirtschaftswissenschaftliche Institut**
- Basler Wirtschaftswissenschaftliche Vortraege. (pub. by Schulthess Polygraphischer Verlag AG)

**Universitaet Bern. Forschungsinstitut fuer Fremdenverkehr**
- Berner Studien zum Fremdenverkehr. (pub. by Peter Lang Publishers)

**Universitaet Bern. Institut fuer Betriebswirtschaft**
- Pruefen und Entscheiden. (pub. by Paul Haupt AG)

**Universitaet Bern. Institut fuer Soziologie und Sozio-Oekonomische Entwicklungsfragen**
- Berner Beitraege zur Soziologie. (pub. by Paul Haupt AG)

**Universitaet Zuerich**
- Ethnologische Zeitschrift. (pub. by Peter Lang Publishers)

**Universitaet Zuerich. Institut fuer Schweizerisches Bankwesen**
- Bankwirtschaftliche Forschungen. (pub. by Paul Haupt AG)

**Universitaet Zuerich. Soziologisches Institut**
Zeltweg 63, 8032 Zurich, Switzerland.
- Bulletin. irreg., latest 1974. (Co-sponsor: Fundacion Bariloche, Departamento de Sociologia)

**Universite de Fribourg**
- Universite de Fribourg. Historische Schriften. (pub. by Editions Universitaires de Fribourg)

**Universite de Fribourg. Dominikaner-Professoren der Theologischen Fakultaet**
- Freiburger Zeitschrift fuer Philosophie und Theologie. (pub. by Editions Universitaires de Fribourg)

**Universite de Fribourg. Institut International des Sciences Sociales et Politiques**
Case Postale 437, CH-1701 Fribourg, Switzerland.
- Bibliographie der Sozialethik; grundsatzfragen des oeffentlichen Lebens. biennial. ISSN 0067-6977

**Universite de Fribourg. Institute of East-European Studies**
- Sovietica. Publications and Monographs. (pub. by D. Reidel Publishing Co. NE)

**Universite de Fribourg. Paedagogisches Institut**
- Universite de Fribourg. Paedagogisches Institut. Arbeitspapiere und Kurzberichte. (pub. by Verlag Beltz Basel)
- Universite de Fribourg. Paedagogisches Institut. Studien und Forschungsberichte. (pub. by Verlag Beltz Basel)

**Universite de Geneve. Asian Documentation and Research Centre**
Institut Universitaire de Hautes Etudes Internationales, 132, rue de Lausanne, 1211 Geneva 21, Switzerland.
- Asian Documentation and Research Center. Studies and Documents. irreg 4-6 per yr)

**Universite de Geneve. Faculte de Psychologie et des Sciences de l'Education**
- Archives de Psychologie. (pub. by Editions Medecine et Hygiene)

**Universite de Geneve. Institut Universitaire de Hautes Etudes Internationales**
- Collection de Droit International. (pub. by A. W. Sijthoff International Publishing Co. NE)
- Collection de Relations Internationales. (pub. by A. W. Sijthoff International Publishing Co. NE)
- Universite de Geneve. Institut Universitaire de Hautes Etudes Internationales. Economics Series. (pub. by A. W. Sijthoff International Publishing Co. NE)
- Universite de Geneve. Institut Universitaire de Hautes Etudes Internationales. Etudes et Travaux. (pub. by Librarie Droz)
- Universite de Geneve. Institut Universitaire de Hautes Etudes Internationales. Publication. (pub. by Librarie Droz)

**Universite de Geneve. Institut Universitaire de Hautes Etudes Internationales Alumni Association**
- Annales d'Etudes Internationales/Annals of International Studies. (pub. by Etablissements Emile Bruylant BE)

**Universite de Geneve. Section d'Histoire**
- Universite de Geneve. Section d'Histoire. Documents. (pub. by Librarie Droz)

**Universite de Lausanne. Ecole des Sciences Sociales et Politiques**
- Universite de Lausanne. Ecole des Sciences Sociales et Politiques. Publications. (pub. by Librarie Droz)

**Universite de Lausanne. Faculte des Lettres**
- Universite de Lausanne. Faculte des Lettres. Publications. (pub. by Librarie Droz)

**Universite de Neuchatel**
Neuchatel, Switzerland.
- Universite de Neuchatel. Annales. a.

**Universite de Neuchatel. Centre de Recherches en Mathematiques Pures**
Ave. du Premier Mars 24, 2002 Neuchatel, Switzerland.
- Universite de Neuchatel. Centre de Recherches en Mathematiques Pures. Publications. Serie 1. Courtes Publications. irreg.
- Universite de Neuchatel. Centre de Recherches en Mathematiques Pures. Publications. Serie 2. Monographies. irreg.

**Universite de Neuchatel. Faculte des Lettres**
- Universite de Neuchatel. Faculte des Lettres. Recueil de Travaux. (pub. by Librarie Droz)

**V L E Verlag GmbH**
C.P. 140, 1001 Lausanne, Switzerland.
- I.C.A.A. News. q. (International Council on Alcohol and Addictions)

**Verband Schweizer Metzgermeister**
Secretariat, CH-8028 Zurich, Switzerland.
- Schweizerische Metzger-Zeitung. w. ISSN 0036-7680

**Verband Schweizerischer Artillerie-Vereine**
Berne, Switzerland.
- Artillerie, Armee & Technik. m. ISSN 0004-3796

**Verband Schweizerischer Bildhauer- und Steinmetzmeister**
- Kunst und Stein. (pub. by Verlag Kunst und Stein)

**Verband Schweizerischer Foerster**
- Schweizer Foerster. (pub. by Verlag Sauerlaender)

**Verband Schweizerischer Gaertnermeister**
Forchstr. 287, CH-8029 Zurich, Switzerland.
- Schweizerische Gaertnerzeitung. w.

**Verband Schweizerischer Heizungs- und Leuftungsfirmen**
- Schweizerische Blatter fuer Heizung und Luftung/ Revue Suisse du Chauffage et de la Ventilation. (pub. by J. H. Waser AG)

**Verband Schweizerischer Lebensmittel-Detaillisten**
Falkenplatz 1, 3001 Berne, Switzerland.
- Lebensmittelhandel. fortn. ISSN 0023-9984

**Verband Schweizerischer Militaerkuechenchefs**
- Militaer-Kuechenchef. (pub. by Schoch und Co.)

**Verband Schweizerischer Papeteristen**
- Papeterist/Papetier/Cartolaio. (pub. by Buri Druck und Verlag)

**Verband Schweizerischer Schreinermeister und Moebelfabrikanten**
Schmelzbergstr. 56, 8044 Zurich, Switzerland.
- Schweizerische Schreiner Zeitung. w. ISSN 0036-7753

**Verband Schweizerischer Tabakhaendler**
Jurastr. 21, 4657 Dulliken, Switzerland.
- Tabak/Tabac/Tabacco. fortn. ISSN 0039-8721

**Verband Schweizerischer Transportunternehmungen des Oeffentlichen Verkehrs**
Daehlhoelzliweg 12, 3000 Berne 6, Switzerland.
- V S T Revue. m. ISSN 0042-1928

**Verband Schweizerischer Uhrenfachgeschaefte**
- Uhrenfachgeschaeft/Magasin d'Horlogerie Specialise. (pub. by Buchdruckerei K. Furter)

**Verband Schweizerischer Vogelschutzvereine**
CH-8840 Einsiedeln, Switzerland.
- Voegel der Heimat; monatsschrift fuer vogelkunde, vogelschutz, natur- und heimatschutz. m. ISSN 0042-7950

**Buchverlag Verbandsdruckerei AG**
Maulbeerstr. 10, CH-3001 Berne, Switzerland.
- Landwirtschaftliches Jahrbuch der Schweiz/ Annuaire Agricole de la Suisse. 4 per yr. ISSN 0023-8171 (Switzerland. Eidgenoessisches Volkswirtschaftsdepartement)
- Touring. w.(French and German edition); fortn. (Italian edition) ISSN 0040-9758 (Touring-Club of Switzerland)

**Verein der Buchbindereibesitzer der Schweiz**
Postfach, 8023 Zurich, Switzerland.
- Schweizerische Fachschrift fuer Buchbindereien/ Relier Suisse. m. ISSN 0036-7583

**Verein Deutschschweizerischer Bienenfreunde**
- Schweizerische Bienen-Zeitung. (pub. by Verlag Sauerlaender)

**Verein Freunde der Milchsuppe**
Flughafenstr. 235, 4000 Basel, Switzerland.
- Milchsuppe. m. ISSN 0026-377X

**Verein fuer Foerderung Wissenschaftlicher Untersuchungen im Graphischen Gewerbe**
c/o EMPA, Postfach 977, 9001 St. Gallen, Switzerland.
- U G R A Mitteilungen. q.

**Verein fuer Krebsforschung**
CH-4144 Arlesheim, Switzerland
(German address: Postfach, D-7000 Stuttgart-Stillenbuch, W. Germany)
- Verein fuer Krebsforschung. Mitteilungen; aus der Behandlung maligner Tumoren mit Viscum Album. 3 per yr. ISSN 0042-3777

**Verein fuer Radiaesthesie St. Gallen**
Postfach, CH-9004 St. Gallen, Switzerland.
- Radiaesthesie - Geopathie - Strahlenbiologie. bi-m. ISSN 0033-7552

**Verein Schweizerischer Gymnasiallehrer**
- Gymnasium Helveticum. (pub. by Verlag Sauerlaender)

**Verein Schweizerischer Lithographiebesitzer**
Postfach 32, Schosshaldenstr. 20, 3000 Berne 32, Switzerland.
- Verein Schweizerischer Lithographiebesitzer. Mitteilungen/Societe Suisse des Patrons Lithographes. Communications. m. ISSN 0042-3831

**Verein zur Foerderung der Missionswissenschaft**
CH-6405 Immensee, Switzerland.
- Neue Zeitschrift fuer Missionswissenschaft/ Nouvelle Revue de Science Missionaire. q. ISSN 0028-3495

**Vereingung Schweizerischer Strassenfachmaenner**
Seefeldstr 9, 8008 Zurich, Switzerland.
- Vereinigung Schweizerischer Strassenfachmaenner. Versuchsbericht. irreg.

**Vereinigung der Freunde Antiker Kunst**
- Antike Kunst. (pub. by Francke Verlag)
- Antike Kunst. Beihefte. (pub. by Francke Verlag)

**Vereinigung fuer Schweizerische Kirchengeschichte**
- Zeitschrift fuer Schweizerische Kirchengeschichte/ Revue d'Histoire Ecclesiastique Suisse. (pub. by Editions Saint-Paul)

**Vereinigung fuer Walsertum**
- Wir Walser. (pub. by Neue Buchdruckerei Visp AG)

**Vereinigung Kantonaler Feuerversicherungen**
Bundesgasse 20, 3011 Berne, Switzerland.
- Vereinigung Kantonaler Feuerversicherungen. Mitteilungen/Association des Establissements Cantonaux d'Assurance Contre l'Incendie. Bulletin.

**Vereinigung pro Sihltal**
Postfach, 8039 Zurich Selnau, Switzerland.
- Vereinigung pro Sihltal. Blaetter. a. ISSN 0083-5641

**Vereinigung Schweizerischer Betriebswirtschafter**
- Unternehmung. (pub. by Paul Haupt AG)

**Vereinigung Schweizerischer Bibliothekare**
Hallwylstrasse 15, Berne, Switzerland.
- Vereinigung Schweizerischer Bibliothekare. Nachrichten/Nouvelles/Notizie. 6 per yr. ISSN 0042-3807 (Co-sponsor: Schweizerischer Vereinigung fuer Dokumentation)

**Vereinigung Schweizerischer Petroleum-Geologen und -Ingenieure**
c/o W. Ruggli, Dir., Shell Switzerland, Bederstr. 66, 8002 Zurich, Switzerland.
- Vereinigung Schweizerischer Petroleum-Geologen und -Ingenieure. Bulletin/Association Suisse des Geologues et Ingenieurs du Petrole. Bulletin. s-a. ISSN 0042-1901

**Vereinigung Schweizerischer Puppenspieler**
c/o Gustav Gysin, Ed., Roggenstr. 1, CH-4125 Riehen, Switzerland.
- Puppenspiel und Puppenspieler; zeitschrift fuer das theater mit Figuren. s-a. ISSN 0033-4405

**Vereinigung Schweizerischer Strassenfachleute**
Seefeldstr. 9, CH-8008 Zurich, Switzerland.
- Strasse und Verkehr. m. ISSN 0039-2189

**Verkauf und Marketing**
Postfach 710, Waisenhausstr. 15, 9001 St. Gallen, Switzerland.
- Verkauf und Marketing. m.

**Verkehrsverein der Stadt Bern**
- Berner Wochen Bulletin/This Week in Berne/ Semaine a Berne. (pub. by Buri Druck und Verlag)

**Verkehrsverein der Stadt St. Gallen**
Bahnhofplatz 1A, CH-9001 St. Gallen, Switzerland.
- St. Gallen; offizielles St. Galler Wochenprogramm. w. ISSN 0036-2832

**Verlag der Akademischen Technischen Vereine**
Postfach 630, 8021 Zurich, Switzerland.
- Schweizerische Bauzeitung; Wochenschrift fuer Architektur, Ingenieurwesen, Maschinentechnik. w. ISSN 0036-7524 (Societe Suisse des Ingenieurs et des Architectes)

**Verlag fuer Internationale Wirtschaftsliteratur GmbH**
P.O.Box 108, CH-8047 Zurich, Switzerland.
- Handbuch der Internationalen Kautschukindustrie/International Rubber Directory/Manuel International de Caoutchouc. irreg. ISSN 0073-0076
- Handbuch der Internationalen Kunstoffindustrie/ International Plastics Directory/Manuel International des Plastiques. irreg. ISSN 0073-0084
- Internationales Firmenregister der Brauindustrie, Malzerien, Mineralwasser und Erfrischungsgetranke/International Brewers' Directory/Registre International des Brasseurs, Malteries, Eaux et Limonades. irreg. ISSN 0074-9796

**Verlag fuer Recht und Gesellschaft AG**
Bundesstr. 15, CH-4054 Basel, Switzerland.
- Studia Philosophica. a. ISSN 0081-6825 (Societe Suisse de Philosophie)

**Verlag fuer Schoene Wissenschaften**
Unterer Zielweg 36, CH-4143 Dornach, Switzerland.
- Therapeutische Dichtung. 2-3 per yr. (Albert Steffen Stiftung)

**Verlag der "Veska"**
Postfach 149, 5001 Aarau, Switzerland.
- Schweizer Spital-Veska; schweizerische spitalzeitschrift/revue hospitaliere suisse. m.

**Neue Buchdruckerei Visp AG**
Kantonsstr. 55, 3930 Visp, Switzerland.
- Wir Walser. s-a. (Vereinigung fuer Walsertum)

**Viva-Kollektiv**
Postfach 66, 7002 Chur, Switzerland.
- Viva. bi-m.

**Verlag A. Vogel**
9053 Teufen AR, Switzerland.
- Gesundheitsnachrichten; vogelin utiset. m. ISSN 0016-9285

**Vogt-Schild AG**
Dornacherstr. 35-39, CH-4500 Solothurn 2, Switzerland.
- Anzeiger Solothurn-Lebern. w. ISSN 0003-6315
- Carrossier. bi-m. (Schweizerischen Corrosserie Industrie)
- Chemische Rundschau; Europaeische Wochenzeitung fuer Chemie, Pharmazeutik, und die Lebensmittelindustrie. w. ISSN 0009-2983
- Dein Kind; elternwegweiser und ratgeber fuer junge muetter. biennial. ISSN 0070-3257
- I N U FA: Internationaler Nutzfahrzeug-Katalog/ International Catalogue for Commercial Vehicles. a. ISSN 0073-4292
- Internationaler Spitalbedarf. a. ISSN 0074-977X
- Kunststoffe-Plastics. m. ISSN 0023-5598
- Montre Suisse. Annuaire. a. ISSN 0077-1309
- Pharmaceutica Acta Helvetiae. m (10 per yr.) ISSN 0031-6865 (Societe Suisse de Pharmacie)

- Plan; Zeitschrift fur Planen, Bauen und Umwelt. m. ISSN 0032-0579
- Schweizerisches Rotes Kreuz/Croix-Rouge Suisse. 8 per yr. ISSN 0036-7982
- Solothurner-Zeitung; Tageszeitung. d. ISSN 0038-1195
- Uhren Rundschau/Watch News/Revue de la Montre/Revista del Reloj. m.(Editions Technique & Europe) bi-m.(Edition Mondiale)
- Zeitschrift fuer Krankenpflege/Revue Suisse des Infirmieres. m. (11 per yr.) ISSN 0044-2941 (Swiss Association of Graduate Nurses)

**J. Vontobel & Co., Bankers**
Bahnhofstrasse 3, CH-8022 Zurich, Switzerland.
- Zurich Stock Exchange. Handbook. a. (Zuercher Boerse)

**Walter Verlag AG**
Amthausquai 21, CH-4600 Olten, Switzerland.
- Schweizer Beitraege zur Kulturgeschichte und Archaeologie des Mittelalters. irreg.

**J. H. Waser AG**
Konradstr. 61, 8005 Zurich, Switzerland.
- Schweizerische Blatter fuer Heizung und Luftung/ Revue Suisse du Chauffage et de la Ventilation; Zeitschrift fuer Heizung Lueftung Klima- und Gesundheitstechnik. q. ISSN 0036-7559 (Verband Schweizerischer Heizungs- und Leuftungsfirmen)

**Welttierschutzbund**
see World Federation for the Protection of Animals

**Werkzeitung der Schweizerischen Industrie**
Kirchenweg 4, 8032 Zurich, Switzerland.
- Werkzeitung der Schweizerischen Industrie. m. ISSN 0043-2830

**Wild-Service**
Neugasse 55, CH-9000 St. Gallen, Switzerland.
- Gute Reise; Kurzinformationen fuer Tourismus und Verkehr. s-m. ISSN 0017-579X

**FABAG und Druckerei Winterthur AG**
Ruedigerstr. 12, Postfach 229, 8021 Zurich, Switzerland.
- Association Suisse des Electriciens. Bulletin. s-m. ISSN 0004-587X (Co-sponsor: Union des Centrales Suisses d'Electricite)
- Pionier; Zeitschrift fuer Verbindung und Uebermittlung. m. ISSN 0032-0064
- S L M H/F B M A. Bulletin. fortn. ISSN 0036-1623 (Schweizerischer Verband des Schmiede, Landmaschinen, Metall und Holzgewerbe)
- Schweizerische Weinzeitung/Journal Vinicole Suisse. w. ISSN 0036-7796

**Women's International League for Peace and Freedom**
1 rue Varembe, 1211 Geneva 20, Switzerland.
- Pax et Libertas. q. ISSN 0031-3327

**World Alliance of Reformed Churches**
150 Route de Ferney, 1211 Geneva 20, Switzerland.
- Reformed World. q. ISSN 0034-3056

**World Alliance of Young Men's Christian Associations**
37 Quai Wilson, 1201 Geneva, Switzerland.
- World Alliance of Y M C A's Directory. biennial. ISSN 0513-6032
- World Alliance of Young Men's Christian Associations. World Communique. bi-m.
- Y M C As of the World. irreg., latest issue 1977.

**World Confederation of Organizations of the Teaching Profession**
5 Chemin du Moulin, 1110 Morges, Switzerland.
- Echo. 4 per yr. ISSN 0012-9143
- W C O I P Theme Study. a. ISSN 0512-252X
- W C O T P Annual Report. a. ISSN 0084-1528

**World Council of Churches**
150 Route de Ferney, 1211 Geneva 20, Switzerland.
- Anticipation; Christian social thought in a future perspective. irreg (2-3 per yr) (prep. by its Department on Church and Society)
- Conseil Oecumenique des Eglises. Etudes. irreg; latest issue, 1970. ISSN 0425-497X (Dist. in U.S.: 475 Riverside Dr., Rm. 439, New York, NY 10027)
- Ecumenical Review. q. ISSN 0013-0796
- Faith and Order Papers. irreg.; no. 71, 1975. ISSN 0512-2589 (Dist. in U.S.: 475 Riverside Dr., Rm. 439, New York, NY 10027)
- International Review of Mission. q. ISSN 0020-8582 (prep. by its Commission on World Mission and Evangelism)

- Migration Today. s-a. ISSN 0544-1188 (prep. by its Refugee and World Service, Division of Inter-Church Aid)
- One World. 10 per yr.
- Risk. q. ISSN 0035-5585
- World Council of Churches. Commission on World Mission and Evangelism. Research Pamphlets. irreg., 1970, no. 18. ISSN 0084-1668 (Dist. in U.S.: 475 Riverside Dr., Rm. 439, New York, NY 10027)
- World Council of Churches. General Assembly. Assembly-Reports. irreg., 1968, 4th. ISSN 0084-1676 (Dist. in U.S.: 475 Riverside Dr., Rm. 439, New York, NY 10027)
- World Council of Churches. Minutes and Reports of the Central Committee Meetings. approx. a; latest issue, 1974. ISSN 0084-1684 (Dist. in U.S.: 475 Riverside Dr., Rm. 439, New York, NY 10027)
- World Council of Churches. Office of Education. Education Newsletter. q.
- World Council of Churches. World Council Studies. irreg., 1970, no. 8. ISSN 0084-1692 (Dist. in U.S.: 475 Riverside Dr., Rm. 439, New York, NY 10027)

**World Federation for the Protection of Animals**
37 Dreikoenigstr., CH-8002 Zurich, Switzerland.
- Animalia. q.

**World Federation of Neurology. Groupe de Travail de Neurogenetique**
- Journal de Genetique Humaine. (pub. by Editions Medecine et Hygiene)

**World Federation of United Nations Associates**
c/o L. H. Horace Perera, Box 54, 1211 Geneva 20, Switzerland.
- W F U N A Newsletter. a. ISSN 0084-1773

**World Health Organization**
For publications of this agency see section for UNITED NATIONS

**World Intellectual Property Organization**
For publications of this agency see section for UNITED NATIONS

**World Meteorological Organization**
For publications of this agency see section for UNITED NATIONS

**World O R T Union**
1, rue de Varembe, 1211 Geneva 20, Switzerland.
- O R T Yearbook. (Organization for Rehabilitation Through Training) a.
- World O R T Union. Congress Report. (Organization for Rehabilitation Through Training) a. ISSN 0510-9175 (Dist. by: American O R T Federation, 817 Broadway, New York, NY 10003)

**World Organization of the Scout Movement**
- World Scout Bureau. Biennial Report. (pub. by World Scout Bureau)
- World Scouting/Scoutisme Mondial. (pub. by World Scout Bureau)
- World Scouting Newsletter/Bulletin du Scoutisme Mondial. (pub. by World Scout Bureau)

**World Scout Bureau**
Case Postale 78, 1211 Geneva 4, Switzerland.
- World Scout Bureau. Biennial Report. biennial. (World Organization of the Scout Movement)
- World Scouting/Scoutisme Mondial. q. ISSN 0043-8995 (World Organization of the Scout Movement)
- World Scouting Newsletter/Bulletin du Scoutisme Mondial. m. ISSN 0043-9002 (World Organization of the Scout Movement)

**World Society for Stereotactic and Functional Neurosurgery**
- Applied Neurophysiology. (pub. by S. Karger AG)

**World Student Christian Federation**
37, Quai Wilson, 1201 Geneva, Switzerland.
- World Student Christian Federation. Dossier. irreg. no. 10, 1975.

**World Union of Liberal Trade Union Organizations**
41 Badenerstrasse, 8004 Zurich, Switzerland.
- Union Mondiale des Organisations Syndicales sur Bases Economique et Sociale Liberales. Conferences: Rapport. a. ISSN 0503-2334

**World Veterinary Association**
70, Rte. du Pont Butin, 1213 Petit-Lancy/GE, Switzerland.
- World Veterinary Association. Catalogue of Veterinary Films and Films of Veterinary Interest. irreg., latest edition 1975. ISSN 0084-2435
- World Veterinary Association. News Items. s-a. ISSN 0510-9477
- World Veterinary Association. News Letter. bi-m.

**World Veterinary Congress**
c/o World Veterinary Association, 70 Route du Pont Butin, 1213 Petit-Lancy/GE, Switzerland
- World Veterinary Congress. Proceedings. quadrennial, 21st, 1979, Moscow, U.S.S.R. ISSN 0084-2443 (Published by the organizing committee of each congress; for 21st Congress, inquire: USSR National Organizing Committee, Bld. B1, Room 404, Orlikov Per. 1/11, Moscow, USSR)

**K.J. Wyss Erben AG**
Effingerstr. 17, 3001 Berne, Switzerland.
- Schweizerische Zeitschrift fuer Musik-Handel und Industrie/Journal Suisse du Commerce et de l'Industrie de la Musique. 8 per yr. ISSN 0036-7850 (Schweizerischer Zentralverband des Musikhandels und der Angeschlossen Verbaende)

**Zentralverband der Schweizerischen Milchproduzenten**
Weststr. 10, 3000 Berne 6, Switzerland.
- Producteur de Lait. w. ISSN 0019-9125

**Zentralverband Schweizer Volksbuehnen**
- Dialog. (pub. by Verlag Sauerlaender)

**Zentralverband Schweizerischer Arbeitgeber-Organisationen**
Florastr. 44, 8034 Zurich, Switzerland.
- Schweizerische Arbeitgeber-Zeitung/Journal des Associations Patronales. w. ISSN 0036-7516

**Zentralverband Schweizerischer Uhrmacher**
Postfach Gare 870, CH-1001 Lausanne, Switzerland.
- Schweizerische Uhrmacher- und Goldschmiede-Zeitung/Journal Suisse des Horlogers et des Bijoutiers-Orfevres. m. (Co-sponsor;: Vereinigung Schweizerischer Juwelen- und Edelmetallbranchen)

**Zollikofer und Co. AG**
Fuerstenlandstr. 122, CH-9001 St. Gallen, Switzerland.
- Druckindustrie. s-m. ISSN 0046-0737
- Schweizerische Drogistenzeitung. w. ISSN 0036-7567 (Schweizerischer Drogistenverband)
- Touring Freizeit/Touring Loisirs. m. ISSN 0040-9766
- Typographische Monatsblaetter; Schweizer Graphische Mitteilungen/Revue suisse de l'imprimerie. m. ISSN 0041-4840 (Schweizerischer Typographenbund)

**Zuercher Boerse**
- Zuercher Boerse: Jahresbericht. (pub. by Effektenboersenverein Zuerich)
- Zurich Stock Exchange. Handbook. (pub. by J. Vontobel & Co., Bankers)

**Zumstein und Cie**
Zeughausgasse 24, CH-3011 Berne, Switzerland.
- Berner Briefmarken-Zeitung/Journal Philatelique de Berne. 10 per yr.(including two double nos.) ISSN 0005-9404

**Zurich (Canton). Amt fuer Raumplanung**
Stampfenbach Str. 14, 8090 Zurich, Switzerland.
- Raumplanung und Umweltschutz im Kanton Zurich. m.

# SYRIA

**Arab Academy of Damascus**
P.O. Box 327, Damascus, Syria.
- Majma al-Lugha la-Arabiyya Bi Dimashg. Majallat. q. ISSN 0002-4031

**Arab Palestinian Resistance**
P.O.B. 3577, Damascus, Syria.
- Arab Palestinian Resistance. m.

**Banque Centrale de Syrie**
see Central Bank of Syria

**Central Bank of Syria**
29 Ayar Square, Damascus, Syria.
- Central Bank of Syria. Quarterly Bulletin. q.
  (prep. by its Research Department)

**Compendium of Laws of the Federation of Arab Republics**
Box 539, Damascus, Syria.
- Compendium of Laws of the Federation of Arab
  Republics. irreg.

**Ittihad al-Kuttab al-Arab**
Shari Murshid Khatir, Damascus, Syria.
- Al-Mawqif al-Adabi. m.

**Office Arabe de Presse et de Documentation**
67 Place Chahbandar, Box 3550, Damascus, Syria.
- Bulletin des Affaires Internationales; traitees par la
  presse arabe. w.
- Numero Economique du Vendredi. w. ISSN 0029-
  6007
- Rapport Annuel sur l'Economie Arabe. a. ISSN
  0079-9688
- Rapport Annuel sur l'Economie Syrienne. a. ISSN
  0079-9696
- Recueil Complet des Budgets de la Syrie. a. ISSN
  0080-0309
- Revue de la Presse Arabe. s-w. ISSN 0035-1245
- Syrie et Monde Arabe; etude mensuelle
  economique, politique et statistique. m. ISSN
  0039-7962

**Syria. Central Bureau of Statistics**
Damascus, Syria.
- Statistics of Foreign Trade of Syria; classified
  according to United Nations standard
  international trade classification. a; latest issue
  1975. ISSN 0081-5136
- Syria. Central Bureau of Statistics. Monthly
  Summary of Foreign Trade. q.
- Syria. Central Bureau of Statistics. Statistical
  Abstract. a; latest edt., 1976. ISSN 0081-4725

**Syrian Documentation Papers**
P.O. Box 2712, Damascus, Syria.
- Bibliography of the Middle East. a. ISSN 0067-
  7302
- General Directory of the Press and Periodicals in
  Jordan and Kuwait. a. ISSN 0072-0690
- General Directory of the Press and Periodicals in
  Syria. a. ISSN 0072-0704

# TANZANIA

**Bank of Tanzania**
Box 2939, Dar es Salaam, Tanzania.
- Bank of Tanzania. Economic and Operations
  Report. a. ISSN 0067-3757 (prep. by its Research
  and Statistics Department)
- Bank of Tanzania. Economic Bulletin. q. ISSN
  0045-1479

**Catholic Publishers Ltd.**
Box 9400, Dar es Salaam, Tanzania.
- Kiongozi/Leader; gazeti la wananchi. fortn.

**Council for the Social Sciences in East Africa. Social Science Conference**
University of Dar-es-Salaam, Faculty of Arts and
Social Science, Box 35091, Dar-es-Salaam,
Tanzania.
- Council for the Social Sciences in East Africa.
  Social Science Conference. Proceedings. a.

**Dar es Salaam University Students' Organisation**
Box 35080, Dar es Salaam, Tanzania.
- University Echo. q.

**Diocese of Songea**
- Mlezi. (pub. by Peramiho Publications)

**Evangelical Lutheran Church of Tanzania. North Western Diocese**
Box 98, Bukoba, Tanzania.
- Ija Webonere. m. ISSN 0019-171X

**Geographical Association of Tanzania**
University of Dar es Salaam, Box 35049, Dar es
Salaam, Tanzania.
- Geographical Association of Tanzania Journal. s-a.
  ISSN 0016-738X

**Historical Association of Tanzania**
Box 35032, Department of History, University of
Dar es Salaam, Dar es Salaam, Tanzania.
- Historical Association of Tanzania. Papers. (pub.
  by East African Publishing House KE)
- Kale. s-a.
- Tanzania Zamani; bulletin of research of general
  history. 2 per yr. ISSN 0039-9507

**Institute of Adult Education**
Box 20679, Dar es Salaam, Tanzania.
- Studies in Adult Education. irreg.

**Institute of Development Management**
Box 604, Morogoro, Mzumbe, Tanzania.
- Institute of Development Management. Report of
  the Activities of the Institute. a.

**Kivukoni College**
Box 9193, Dar es Salaam, Tanzania.
- Mbioni. m. ISSN 0025-6234

**Mathematical Association of Tanzania**
Box 35062, Dar es Salaam, Tanzania.
- Mathematical Association of Tanzania. Bulletin. 2
  per yr. ISSN 0047-6250

**National Bank of Commerce. International Banking Department**
Box 1255, Dar es Salaam, Tanzania.
- Tanzania Import and Export Directory. irreg.

**National Development Corporation**
Box 2669, Dar es Salaam, Tanzania.
- Jenga. 4-5 per yr. ISSN 0021-5872

**National Insurance Corporation of Tanzania**
Insurance House, Box 9264, Dar es Salaam,
Tanzania.
- Ngao. q.

**National Museum of Tanzania**
P.O. Box 511, Dar es Salaam, Tanzania.
- National Museum of Tanzania. Annual Report. a.
  ISSN 0082-1675

**National Swahili Council**
P.O. Box 4766, Dar es Salaam, Tanzania.
- Lugha Yetu. 6 per yr. ISSN 0047-5165

**Organisation of Angolan Women**
Box 20604, Dar es Salaam, Tanzania.
- O. M. A. Quarterly. q.

**People's Movement for the Liberation of Angola**
DIP Delegation, P. O. 20793, Dar es Salaam,
Tanzania.
- Angola in Arms. m.
- War Communiques. ISSN 0043-020X

**Peramiho Publications**
Box 41, Peramiho, Tanzania.
- Mlezi; a journal for teaching religion. bi-m. ISSN
  0047-7583 (Diocese of Songea)

**Serengeti Research Institute**
P.O. Seronera, via Arusha, Arusha, Tanzania.
- Serengeti Research Institute. Annual Report. a,
  latest 1974-75.

**Shamrock Agencies**
Box 977, Moshi, Tanzania.
- Tanzania Directory of Trades. irreg. ISSN 0564-
  724X

**South West Africa People's Organization**
Box 2604, Dar es Salaam, Tanzania.
- Current Events in Namibia. q.
- Namibia. ISSN 0027-7754

**T.M.P. Book Department**
P.O. Box 399, Tabora, Tanzania
- Catholic Directory of Eastern Africa. biennial.
  ISSN 0069-1240 (Dist. by: White Fathers, 777
  Belvidere Ave., Plainfield, NJ 07062)

**Tanzania. Bureau of Statistics**
Box 796, Dar es Salaam, Tanzania
(Orders to: Government Publications Agency, Box
1801, Dar es Salaam, Tanzania)
- Report on Tourism Statistics in Tanzania. irreg.
  ISSN 0564-836X
- Tanzania. Bureau of Statistics. Directory of
  Industries. a (approx.), latest 1975.
- Tanzania. Bureau of Statistics. Employment and
  Earnings. approx. a. ISSN 0049-2973
- Tanzania. Bureau of Statistics. Migration
  Statistics. irreg.

- Tanzania. Bureau of Statistics. Quarterly Statistical
  Bulletin. q. ISSN 0039-9469
- Tanzania. Bureau of Statistics. Survey of Industrial
  Production. a.

**Tanzania. Capital Development Authority**
Box 913, Dodoma, Tanzania.
- Tanzania. Capital Development Authority. Report
  and Accounts. a.

**Tanzania. Geology and Mines Division**
Box 903, Dodoma, Tanzania.
- Review of the Mineral Industry in Tanzania. a.
  ISSN 0082-1659

**Tanzania. Government Publications Agency**
Box 1801, Dar es Salaam, Tanzania.
- Appropriation Accounts, Revenue Statements,
  Accounts of the Funds and Other Public
  Accounts of Tanzania. irreg., latest 1972-73. ISSN
  0496-8492
- Gazette of the United Republic of Tanzania. w.
- Tanzania. Government Publications Agency.
  Catalogue of Government and T A N U
  Publications. Orodha Ya Vitabu Vya T A N U na
  Serikali. irreg.

**Tanzania. Ministry of Agriculture**
Publicity Section, Box 2308, Dar es Salaam,
Tanzania.
- Ukulima Wa Kisasa. m. ISSN 0041-6150

**Tanzania. Ministry of Economic Affairs and Development Planning**
P.O. Box 9242, Dar es Salaam, Tanzania
(Subscr. to: Government Publications Agency, P.O.
Box 1801, Dar es Salaam, Tanzania)
- Tanzania. Ministry of Economic Affairs and
  Development Planning. Hali Ya Uchumi Wa
  Taifa. a.

**Tanzania. Ministry of National Education**
Box 9121, Dar es Salaam, Tanzania.
- Tanzania Education Journal. 3 per yr. ISSN 0039-
  9477

**Tanzania. Ministry of Water, Energy and Minerals**
Box 35066, Dar es Salaam, Tanzania.
- Maji Review. irreg (approx. a) (prep. by its
  Research and Training Division)

**Tanzania. Police Force**
Box 9141, Dar es Salaam, Tanzania.
- Tanzania Police Journal. q. ISSN 0049-2981

**Tanzania. Urban Planning Division**
Box 20671, Dar es Salaam, Tanzania.
- Tanzania. Urban Planning Division. Annual
  Report. a.

**Tanzania Library Association**
- Someni. (pub. by East African Literature Bureau
  KE)

**Tanzania Library Service**
P.O. Box 9283, Dar es Salaam, Tanzania.
- Mapinduzi Katika Uandishi. 3 per yr.

**Tanzania Publishing House**
Box 2138, Dar es Salaam, Tanzania.
- Tanzanian Studies. irreg.

**Tanzania Society**
Box 511, Dar es Salaam, Tanzania.
- Tanzania Notes & Records. s-a. ISSN 0039-9485

**Tanzania Trade and Industry**
Box 234, Dar es Salaam, Tanzania.
- Tanzania Trade and Industry. q. ISSN 0039-9493

**Tropical Pesticides Research Institute**
P.O. Box 3024, Arusha, Tanzania.
- Tropical Pesticides Research Institute. Annual
  Report. a. ISSN 0082-6642

**University of Dar es Salaam**
Box 35094, Dar-es-Salaam, Tanzania.
- Studies in Curriculum Development. irreg.

**University of Dar es Salaam. Botany Department**
P.O. Box 35060, Dar es Salaam, Tanzania.
- University of Dar es Salaam. Botany Department.
  Departmental Herbarium Publications. irreg.

**University of Dar es Salaam. Bureau of Resource Assessment and Land Use Planning**
Box 35097, Dar es Salaam, Tanzania.
- University of Dar es Salaam. Bureau of Resource Assessment and Land Use Planning. Annual Report. a. ISSN 0084-960X
- University of Dar es Salaam. Bureau of Resource Assessment and Land Use Planning. Research Paper. irreg., no. 45, 1976. ISSN 0084-9626
- University of Dar es Salaam. Bureau of Resource Assessment and Land Use Planning. Research Report. irreg., no. 19, 1976. ISSN 0084-9634

**University of Dar es Salaam. Department of Literature**
- Umma. (pub. by East African Literature Bureau KE)

**University of Dar es Salaam. Department of Political Science**
P.O. Box 35042, Dar es Salaam, Tanzania.
- African Review. (pub. by East African Literature Bureau KE)
- Taamuli; a political science forum. s-a. ISSN 0049-2817

**University of Dar es Salaam. Economics Association**
Box 35184, Dar es Salaam, Tanzania.
- Economic Reflections. irreg.

**University of Dar es Salaam. Faculty of Arts and Social Science**
- Utafiti. (pub. by East African Literature Bureau KE)

**University of Dar es Salaam. Faculty of Law**
Box 35034, Dar es Salaam, Tanzania.
- Dar es Salaam University Law Journal. a. ISSN 0418-3770
- Law Reports of Tanzania. q.

**University of Dar es Salaam. Faculty of Medicine**
Box 20693, Dar es Salaam, Tanzania.
- Dar es Salaam Medical Journal. q.

**University of Dar es Salaam. Institute of Swahili Research**
Box 35110, Dar es Salaam, Tanzania.
- Kiswahili. s-a. ISSN 0023-1886
- Mulika. m.

**University of Dar es Salaam. Student's Organization**
see Dar es Salaam University Student's Organization

# THAILAND

**Advertising and Media Consultants Ltd.**
6Th Floor, Thaniya Building, 62 Silom Road, Bangkok, Thailand.
- LookEast. m.

**Agricultural Science Society of Thailand**
Dept. of Agriculture Bldg., Bang Khen, Bangkok 9, Thailand.
- Thai Journal of Agricultural Science. q. ISSN 0049-3589

**Allied Newspapers**
3Rd Floor, U-Chulaing Bldg., 968 Rama IV Rd., Bangkok 5, Thailand.
- Living in Thailand. bi-m.

**American Chamber of Commerce in Thailand**
140 Wireless Rd., Bangkok, Thailand.
- Thai-American Business. bi-m. ISSN 0002-7855

**Applied Scientific Research Corporation of Thailand**
196 Phahonyothin Road, Bangkhen, Bangkok 9, Thailand.
- Scientific and Technical Literature Relating to Thailand. irreg. (Thai National Documentation Centre)
- Thai Abstracts, Series A. Science and Technology. s-a.
- Thai National Documentation Center. List. irreg.

**Asian Development Institute**
For publications of this agency see section for UNITED NATIONS

**Asian Information Center for Geotechnical Engineering**
c/o Asian Institute of Technology, Box 2754, Bangkok, Thailand.
- A G E Current Awareness Series. q. ISSN 0301-4150 (Co-sponsor: International Development Research Centre of Canada)
- A G E Current Awareness Service. q.
- Asian Geotechnical Engineering Abstracts. q.
- Asian Geotechnical Engineering Directory. biennial. (Co-Sponsor: International Development Research Centre of Canada)
- Asian Geotechnical Engineering in Progress. s-a.

**Asian Institute of Technology**
Box 2754, Bangkok, Thailand.
- Asian Institute of Technology. Newsletter. bi-m. ISSN 0004-4598
- Asian Institute of Technology. Research Report. irreg; latest issue, 1973. ISSN 0572-418X
- Asian Institute of Technology. Research Summary. a; latest issue, 1973. ISSN 0572-4198

**Association of Southeast Asian Institutions of Higher Learning**
Ratasastra Building, Chulalongkorn University, Henri Dunant Road, Bangkok, Thailand.
- A S A I H L. Seminar Reports. irreg., latest issue, 1975. ISSN 0587-5587
- Association of Southeast Asian Institutions of Higher Learning. Handbook: Southeast Asian Institutions of Higher Learning. biennial. ISSN 0066-9687
- Association of Southeast Asian Institutions of Higher Learning. Newsletter. irreg. ISSN 0572-4325
- Association of Southeast Asian Institutions of Higher Learning. Seminar Report. irreg., latest issue, 1974. ISSN 0066-9695

**Bamrung Nukoulkit Press**
83 Bamrung Muang Road, Bangkok, Thailand.
- Thai Chamber of Commerce. Journal. m.

**Bangkok Bank Ltd. Economic Research Division**
9 Suapa Rd., Bangkok, Thailand.
- Statistical Data on Commercial Banks in Thailand. a.

**Bangkok Bank Ltd. Planning & Analysis Department**
3-9 Suapa Rd., Box 95, Bangkok, Thailand.
- Bangkok Bank. Monthly Review. m. ISSN 0005-4984

**Bangkok English Language Center**
Rama Vi Road, Bangkok, Thailand.
- Bangkok English Language Center. Bulletin. s-a.

**Bank of Thailand**
Bang Khunprom, Bangkok, Thailand.
- Bank of Thailand. Annual Economic Report. a. ISSN 0067-3773

**Bank of Thailand. Department of Economic Research**
Bangkok, Thailand.
- Bank of Thailand. Monthly Bulletin. m. ISSN 0005-5352

**Business Publicity Ltd.**
P.O. Box 1217, Bangkok, Thailand.
- Business in Thailand. m.
- Siam Scene. bi-m.

**Business Review**
c/o The Nation, 5/5-6 Decho Road, Bangkok, Thailand.
- Business Review. m.

**Chatra Press**
77 Rama V, Bangkok, Thailand.
- Thai Junior Red Cross Magazine. bi-m. ISSN 0040-5361

**Chiang Mai University. Faculty of Medicine**
Nakorn Chiang Mai Hospital, Chiang Mai, Thailand.
- Chiang Mai Medical Bulletin. q. ISSN 0009-3440

**Chulalongkorn University. Institute of Population Studies**
Bangkok 5, Thailand.
- Population Newsletter. irreg. (3-4 per yr.)

**Chulalongkorn University. School of Dentistry**
Henri Dunant Rd., Bangkok, Thailand.
- Dental Association of Thailand. Journal. bi-m. ISSN 0045-9917

**Economic and Social Commission for Asia and the Pacific**
For publications of this agency see section for UNITED NATIONS

**Food and Agriculture Organization of the United Nations. Regional Office for Asia and the Far East**
For publications of this agency see section for UNITED NATIONS

**Houseman & Co.**
Suite 602, Silom Bldg., Silom Rd., Bangkok, Thailand.
- Thai Investment Review. a. ISSN 0082-3783

**International Publishing and Marketing Co.**
B.O.A.C. Building, 5th Floor, Rajaprasong Corner, Bangkok, Thailand.
- Who's Who in Thailand. m.

**Kasetsart University**
Bangkok 9, Thailand.
- Kasetsart Journal. s-a. ISSN 0075-5192

**Kasetsart University. Museum of Fisheries**
Faculty of Fisheries, Bangkok 9, Thailand.
- Kasetsart University, Bangkok, Thailand. Faculty of Fisheries. Notes. irreg., 1969, no. 5. ISSN 0075-5206

**Medical Association of Thailand**
67/9 Soi Soonvichai, New Pechburi Rd., Bangkok 10, Thailand.
- Medical Association of Thailand. Journal. m. ISSN 0025-7036

**Metropolitan Electricity Authority**
121 Chakphet Rd., Bangkok-2, Thailand.
- Khao Kan-Faifa/Electrical News. m. ISSN 0023-1045

**National Institute of Development Administration. Development Document Center**
Klongjan, Bangkapi, Bangkok 24, Thailand.
- Index to Thai Newspapers. irreg.
- Index to Thai Periodical Literature. irreg.

**National Institute of Development Administration. Research Center**
Klongchan, Bangkok 24, Thailand.
- Thai Journal of Development Administration. q. ISSN 0040-5353

**Pracandra Printing Press**
Maharaja Road, Bangkok, Thailand.
- Foreign Affairs Bulletin. bi-m. (Thailand. Ministry of Foreign Affairs. Department of Information)

**Regional Clearinghouse Service for Population Education**
Box 1425, Bangkok 11, Thailand.
- Population Education in Asia Newsletter. 3 per yr.

**SEAMEO Central Coordinating Board for Tropical Medicine & Public Health**
420 6 Rajvithi Rd., Bangkok 4, Thailand.
- Southeast Asian Journal of Tropical Medicine and Public Health. q. ISSN 0038-3619

**Siam Publications Ltd.**
68-3 Pan St, Silom Rd., Bangkok, Thailand.
- Investor. m. ISSN 0021-0153

**Siam Society**
131 Soi Asoke, Sukhumvit 21, Bangkok, Thailand.
- Siam Society. Journal. s-a.

**South East Asia Treaty Organization**
Sri Ayudhaya Road, P.O. Box 517, Bangkok, Thailand.
- Research into Disease. irreg. ISSN 0557-7330
- South-East Asian Spectrum. q.

**Southeast Asian Society of Soil Engineering**
Box 2754, Bangkok, Thailand.
- Geotechnical Engineering. s-a. ISSN 0046-5828

**Suan Sunautha Teacher College**
Samsen, Bangkok 4, Thailand.
- Bangkok, Thailand. College of Education. Thesis Abstract Series. a. ISSN 0067-3498

**Temple Publicity Services**
4Th Floor, British Airways Building, 133/19 Gaysorn Road, P.O. Box 316, Bangkok, Thailand.
- Guide to Thailand. a.
- Thailand Year Book. a. ISSN 0563-3737

**Thai Chamber of Commerce.**
150 Rajbopitre Road, Bangkok, Thailand.
- Thai Chamber of Commerce. Business Directory. irreg. ISSN 0563-3400
- Thai Chamber of Commerce. Journal. (pub. by Bamrung Nukoulkit Press)

**Thai National Documentation Centre**
- Scientific and Technical Literature Relating to Thailand. (pub. by Applied Scientific Research Corporation of Thailand)

**Thailand. Bureau of the Budget**
Bangkok, Thailand.
- Thailand's Budget in Brief. irreg.

**Thailand. Government House Press**
Samsen Rd., Bangkok 3, Thailand.
- Silpakon. bi-m. ISSN 0037-5314

**Thailand. Government Public Relations Department**
Rajdamnern Ave., Bangkok, Thailand.
- Thailand Illustrated. m. ISSN 0040-537X

**Thailand. Ministry of Agriculture. Department of Fisheries**
Rajadamnern Ave., Bangkok, Thailand.
- Thai Fisheries Gazette. q. ISSN 0040-5345

**Thailand. Ministry of Agriculture. Division of Agricultural Chemistry**
Bangkok 9, Thailand.
- Thailand. Division of Agricultural Chemistry. Report on Fertilizer Experiments and Soil Fertility Research. irreg. ISSN 0085-7246

**Thailand. Ministry of Agriculture. Division of Agriculture Economics**
Office of Under-Secretary of State, Bangkok, Thailand.
- Khao Setthakit Kan-Kaset/Agricultural Economic News. m. ISSN 0023-1053

**Thailand. Ministry of Foreign Affairs. Department of Information**
- Foreign Affairs Bulletin. (pub. by Pracandra Printing Press)

**Thailand. National Economic Development Board**
Secretary-General, Krung Kasem Rd., Bangkok, Thailand.
- National Income Statistics of Thailand. a. ISSN 0077-4723

**Thailand. National Research Council of Thailand**
196 Phahonyothin Rd., Bangkhen, Bangkok 9, Thailand.
- National Research Council of Thailand. Journal. s-a. ISSN 0028-0011

**Thailand. National Research Council. Social Science Research Division**
Bangkok, Thailand.
- Directory of Research Institutions in Thailand. irreg.

**Thailand. National Statistical Office**
Lan Luang Rd., Bangkok, Thailand.
- Statistical Handbook of Thailand. irreg. ISSN 0081-4822
- Thailand. National Statistical Office. Quarterly Bulletin of Statistics. q. ISSN 0040-5388
- Thailand. National Statistical Office, Report of Industrial Survey in Northeast Region/Thailand. Samnakngan Sathiti Haeng Chat. irreg.
- Thailand. National Statistical Office. Research Paper. irreg.
- Thailand. National Statistical Office. Statistical Bibliography. irreg. ISSN 0082-3791

**Thailand. Translation & Secretarial Office**
56 Suan Luang I Street, Pathum Wan, Bangkok, Thailand.
- Organizational Directory of the Government of Thailand. irreg. ISSN 0475-2015

**Tourist Organization of Thailand**
Ratchadanoen Ave., Bangkok 2, Thailand.
- Holiday Time in Thailand. q. ISSN 0439-3678

**Unesco. Regional Office for Education in Asia**
For publications of this agency see section for UNITED NATIONS

**United Nations Economic and Social Commission for Asia and the Pacific. Asian Development Institute**
For publications of this agency see section for UNITED NATIONS

**United Nations Economic and Social Commission for Asia and the Pacific**
For publications of this agency see section for UNITED NATIONS

**Vanasarn Forest Journal Office**
Royal Forest Dept., Bangkok, Thailand.
- Wanasan. q. ISSN 0043-0196

**World Fellowship of Buddhists**
41, Phra Athit St., Bangkok-2, Thailand.
- World Fellowship of Buddhists. Book Series. irreg., latest issue, 1975. ISSN 0084-1781
- World Fellowship of Buddhists Review. bi-m. ISSN 0043-8464

# TOGO

**Banque Togolaise de Developpement**
B.P. 65, Lome, Togo.
- Banque Togolaise de Developpement. Rapport Annuel. a; latest issue, 1974. ISSN 0067-4036

**Chambre de Commerce, d'Agriculture et d'Industrie du Togo**
Ave Albert Sarraut, Boite Postale No. 360, Lome, Togo.
- Chambre de Commerce, d'Agriculture et d'Industrie du Togo. Bulletin Mensuel. m.

**Compagnie Africaine d'Editions Techniques**
Boite Postale 1960, Lome, Togo.
- Revue Generale Africaine des Travaux Publics, de l'Industrie et des Mines. bi-m.

**EDITOGO**
*see* Etablissements des Editions du Togo

**Etablissements des Editions du Togo**
B.P. 891, Lome, Togo.
- Espoir de la Nation Togolaise. m. ISSN 0046-2535 (Togo. Ministry of Information)
- Togo Dialogue. m. (Togo. Ministry of Information)

**Institut Togolais des Sciences Humaines**
B.P. 1002, Lome, Togo.
- Etudes Togolaises. irreg. ISSN 0531-2051

**Togo. Conseil Economique et Social**
Lome, Togo.
- Togo. Conseil Economique et Social. Session Annuelle. (Compte Rendu) irreg.

**Togo. Direction de la Meteorologie Nationale**
B.P. 1505, Lome, Togo.
- Togo. Direction de la Meteorologie Nationale. Resume Annuel du Temps. a.
- Togo. Direction de la Meteorologie Nationale. Resume Mensuel du Temps. m.

**Togo. Direction de la Statistique**
Boite Postale 118, Lome, Togo.
- Annuaire des Statistiques du Commerce Exterieur du Togo. a.
- Annuaire Statistique du Togo. a.
- Enquete sur les Enterprises Industrielles et Commerciales du Togo. a.
- Indices des Prix et Cout de la Vie a Lome. irreg.
- Inventaire Economique du Togo. a. ISSN 0075-000X
- Togo. Direction de la Statistique. Bulletin Mensuel de Statistique. m.

**Togo. Ministry of Information**
- Espoir de la Nation Togolaise. (pub. by Etablissements des Editions du Togo)
- Togo Dialogue. (pub. by Etablissements des Editions du Togo)

**Universite du Benin**
B.P. 1515, Lome, Togo.
- Cine Qua Non.

# TONGA

**Dept. of Customs**
Nuku'alofa, Tongatapu, Tonga Islands.
- Tonga. Department of Customs. Statement of Trade and Navigation. a. ISSN 0082-4887

**Tonga Islands. Government Printer**
Nuku-Alofa, Tongatapu, Tonga Islands.
- Tonga. Minister of Health. Report. a. ISSN 0082-4895

# TRINIDAD & TOBAGO

**Agricultural Society of Trinidad & Tobago**
P. O. Box 256, Port-of-Spain, Trinidad, West Indies.
- Agricultural Society of Trinidad & Tobago. Journal. q. ISSN 0368-1327

**Camalas Business Services**
86 Abercromby St., Port of Spain, Trinidad, West Indies.
- Caribbean Medical Journal. bi-m.
- Educator. m.

**Caribbean Congress of Labour**
53-55 Frederick St., Port-of-Spain, Trinidad.
- Caribbean Labour. q. ISSN 0008-6479

**Caribbean Contact**
Box 876, Port-of-Spain, Trinidad, W.I.
- Caribbean Contact. m.

**Caribbean Free Trade Association**
- Caribbean Free Trade Association. Directory. (pub. by International Publications Ltd.)

**Central Bank of Trinidad and Tobago**
Independence Square, Port of Spain, Trinidad.
- Central Bank of Trinidad and Tobago. Quarterly Economic Bulletin. q.
- Central Bank of Trinidad and Tobago. Report. a. ISSN 0069-1593
- Central Bank of Trinidad and Tobago. Statistical Digest. m.

**Central Library of Trinidad and Tobago**
West Indian Reference Section, 20 Queens Park East, Port of Spain, Trinidad.
- Trinidad and Tobago and West Indian Bibliography. Bi-Monthly Accessions. bi-m.

**Commonwealth Institute of Biological Control**
Commonwealth Agricultural Bureaux, Gordon St., Curepe, Trinidad, West Indies.
- Commonwealth Institute of Biological Control. Technical Bulletin. irreg., 1973, no. 16. ISSN 0069-7117

**Commonwealth Institute of Helminthology**
Commonwealth Agricultural Bureaux, Gordon St., Curepe, Trinidad, West Indies.
- Commonwealth Institute of Helminthology. Technical Communications. irreg.; no. 46, 1975. ISSN 0069-696X

**Economic and Business Research Information and Advisory Service**
P.O. Box 780, Port of Spain, Trinidad.
- Caribbean Economic Almanac; a collection of economic and statistical data covering the Caribbean area. irreg. ISSN 0069-0481

**Government Printer**
Tragarete Rd., Port-of-Spain, Trinidad.
- Report of the Auditor General on the Accounts of Trinidad and Tobago. a; latest issue, 1973. (Trinidad and Tobago. Auditor General of Trinidad and Tobago)
- Trinidad and Tobago Gazette. w.

**International Publications Ltd.**
Fernandes Industrial Centre, Eastern Main Rd., Laventville, Trinidad.
- Caribbean Free Trade Association. Directory. a.
- Trinidad and Tobago Directory of Commerce, Industry & Tourism. irreg.

**Library Association of Trinidad and Tobago**
Box 547, Port of Spain, Trinidad.
- Library Association of Trinidad and Tobago. Bulletin. a. ISSN 0521-9590

**New Vision**
5 Bhagoutee Lane, Don Miguel Road, San Juan, Trinidad.
● New Vision. q.

**New Voices**
c/o Ed. Anson Gonzalez, 1 Sapphire Drive, Diego Martin, Trinidad and Tobago.
● New Voices. s-a.

**P. N. M. Publishing Co. Ltd.**
90 Frederick St., Port-Of-Spain, Trinidad.
● Psychological Association of Trinidad and Tobago. Journal. s-a. ISSN 0033-2895

**People's National Movement Publishing Co.**
27 Pembroke St., Port of Spain, Trinidad, W. Indies.
● Nation. w. ISSN 0027-8394

**Psychological Association of Trinidad and Tobago**
● Psychological Association of Trinidad and Tobago. Journal. (pub. by P. N. M. Publishing Co. Ltd.)

**Scope Publishing Co**
1 St. Ann's Ave., St. Ann's, Trinidad & Tobago.
● Scope (St. Ann's) q.

**Sugar Technologists' Association of Trinidad & Tobago**
P.O. Box 230, Port of Spain, Trinidad 62-36106, West Indies.
● Sugar Technologists' Association of Trinidad and Tobago. Proceedings. a.

**Tapia House Publishing Co. Ltd.**
91 Tunapuna Road, Tunapuna, Trinidad & Tobago.
● Tapia. w.

**Trinidad and Tobago. Auditor General of Trinidad and Tobago**
● Report of the Auditor General on the Accounts of Trinidad and Tobago. (pub. by Government Printer)

**Trinidad and Tobago. Central Statistical Office**
Textel Building, 1, Edward Street, Port of Spain, Trinidad
(or Govt. Printery, 2 Victoria Ave., Port of Spain, Trinidad)
● Balance of Payments of Trinidad and Tobago. a; latest issue, 1973. ISSN 0067-3005
● C.S.O. Statistical Bulletins. irreg.
● Trinidad and Tobago. Central Statistical Office. Annual Statistical Digest. a; latest issue, 1971-72. ISSN 0082-6502
● Trinidad and Tobago. Central Statistical Office. Continuous Sample Survey of Population. irreg. ISSN 0564-2612
● Trinidad and Tobago. Central Statistical Office. Digest of Statistics on Education. a. ISSN 0082-6510
● Trinidad and Tobago. Central Statistical Office. Economic Indicators. q.
● Trinidad and Tobago. Central Statistical Office. Estimated Internal Migration. Bulletin.
● Trinidad and Tobago. Central Statistical Office. Financial Statistics. a; latest issue, 1972. ISSN 0082-6529
● Trinidad and Tobago. Central Statistical Office. International Travel Report. a. ISSN 0082-6537
● Trinidad and Tobago. Central Statistical Office. Labour Force by Sex. irreg.; latest issue, 1973.
● Trinidad and Tobago. Central Statistical Office. Monthly Travel. m.
● Trinidad and Tobago. Central Statistical Office. Overseas Trade. Annual Report. a. ISSN 0082-6545
● Trinidad and Tobago. Central Statistical Office. Overseas Trade. Monthly Report. bi-m (covers monthly data) ISSN 0030-7505
● Trinidad and Tobago. Central Statistical Office. Pocket Digest. a.
● Trinidad and Tobago. Central Statistical Office. Population and Vital Statistics; Report. a. ISSN 0082-6553
● Trinidad and Tobago. Central Statistical Office. Quarterly Agricultural Report. q.
● Trinidad and Tobago. Central Statistical Office. Quarterly Economic Report. q. ISSN 0041-3046
● Trinidad and Tobago. Central Statistical Office. Staff Papers. irreg.
● Trinidad and Tobago Today. irreg. ISSN 0082-6561

**Trinidad and Tobago. Department of Petroleum and Mines**
Port of Spain, Trinidad, W.I.
● Caribbean Geological Conference. Proceedings. irreg., 1964, 4th, Port of Spain; 1965, 5th, St. Thomas. ISSN 0069-049X

**Trinidad & Tobago. Management Development Centre. Library**
Salvatori Building, Box 1301, Port-of-Spain, Trinidad.
● M D C Business Journal. s-a.
● M D C News. q.
● Management Abstracts. bi-m.

**Trinidad and Tobago. Ministry of Petroleum and Mines**
Box 96, Port-of-Spain, Trinidad.
● Trinidad and Tobago. Ministry of Petroleum and Mines. Annual Report. a.
● Trinidad and Tobago. Ministry of Petroleum and Mines. Monthly Bulletin. m. ISSN 0026-5322

**Trinidad Naturalist**
Box 309, Port of Spain, Trinidad and Tobago.
● Trinidad Naturalist. bi-m.

**Trinidad Philatelic Society**
78 London Street, San Fernando, Trinidad.
● Trinidad Philatelic Society Bulletin. bi-m.

**Trinidad Publishing Company Ltd.**
Box 122, Port of Spain, Trinidad, West Indies.
● Sunday Guardian. w.
● Trinidad Guardian.

**Unique Services**
17 Cassia Avenue, Pleasantville, San Fernando, Trinidad.
● Calypso.

**University of the West Indies**
St. Augustine, Trinidad.
● University of the West Indies. Annual Report on Cocao Research. a.

**University of the West Indies. Department of Soil Science**
St. Augustine, Trinidad.
● University of the West Indies. Department of Soil Science. Soil and Land Use Surveys. irreg.

**University of the West Indies. Imperial College of Tropical Agriculture**
● Tropical Agriculture. (pub. by I P C Science and Technology Press Ltd. UK)

**University of the West Indies. Institute of International Relations**
St. Augustine, Trinidad and Tobago.
● University of the West Indies. Institute of International Relations. Special Lecture Series. irreg.

**University of the West Indies. Library**
Acquisitions Department, St. Augustine, Trinidad
(Orders to: Central Library of Trinadad and Tobago, P. O. B. 547, Port of Spain, Trinidad)
● Trinidad and Tobago National Bibliography. q.

**West Indies Sugar Association**
Sugar Manufactures' Association Ltd., 80 Abercromby St., Port of Spain, Trinidad.
● Sugar in the West Indies and British Guiana. irreg. ISSN 0081-9182

# TRUST TERRITORY, PACIFIC ISLDS

**Micronitor News and Printing Co.**
Majuro, Marshall Islands.
● Micronesian Independent. w.

**Trust Territory Government Printing Office**
Saipan, Mariana Islands.
● Congress of Micronesia. Senate. Journal. irreg.

**Trust Territory of the Pacific Islands**
Public Information Office, Saipan 96950, Mariana Islands.
● Micronesian Reporter. q. ISSN 0026-2781

**Trust Territory of the Pacific Islands. Congress of Micronesia. House of Representatives**
Capitol Hill, Saipan 96950, Mariana Islands.
● Congress of Micronesia. House of Representatives. Journal. q.

**Trust Territory of the Pacific Islands. Congress of Micronesia. Joint Committee on Program and Budget Planning**
Capitol Hill, Saipan 96950, Mariana Islands.
● Congress of Micronesia. Joint Committee on Program and Budget Planning. Public Hearings on High Commissioner's Preliminary Budget. a.

**Trust Territory of the Pacific Islands. Congress of Micronesia Library**
Capitol Hill, Saipan 96950, Mariana Islands.
● Congress of Micronesia Library. Bibliography. s-a.

**Trust Territory of the Pacific Islands. Congress of Micronesia. Senate**
● Congress of Micronesia. Senate. Journal. (pub. by Trust Territory Government Printing Office)

**Trust Territory of the Pacific Islands. Territorial Housing Commission**
Capitol Hill, Saipan 96950, Mariana Islands.
● Trust Territory of the Pacific Islands. Territorial Housing Commission. Annual Report. a.

# TUNISIA

**Banque Centrale de Tunisie**
7 Place de la Monnaie, Tunis, Tunisia.
● Banque Centrale de Tunisie. Bulletin. irreg. ISSN 0067-3854
● Banque Centrale de Tunisie. Rapport d'Activite. a. ISSN 0067-3862
● Banque Centrale de Tunisie. Statistiques Financieres. m.

**C.E.R.E.S.**
see Universite de Tunis. Centre d'Etudes et de Recherches Economiques et Sociales

**Centre d'Etudes et de Recherches Economiques et Sociales**
see under Universite de Tunis

**Chambre de Commerce de Tunis**
1, rue des Entrepreneurs, Tunis, Tunisia.
● Chambre de Commerce de Tunis. Bulletin. m.

**Chambre de Commerce du Sud de la Tunisie**
21-23 rue Habib Thameur, Sfax, Tunisia.
● Chambre de Commerce du Sud de la Tunisie. Bulletin Economique. m. ISSN 0045-6292

**Ecole Nationale d'Administration. Centre de Recherches et d'Etudes Administratives**
24 Ave. du Dr. Calmette, Mutuelleville, Tunis, Tunisia.
● Servir; revue Tunisienne du service public. s-a. ISSN 0035-4120

**Faculte des Lettres et Sciences Humaines de Tunis**
B.P. 1128, 94 Bd. du 9 Avril, Tunis, Tunisia.
● Cahiers de Tunisie; revue de sciences humaines. q. ISSN 0008-0012

**Information Economique Africaine**
16 rue de Rome, Tunis, Tunisia.
● Information Economique Africaine. m. ISSN 0020-0050

**Institut des Belles Lettres Arabes**
12, rue Jamaa el Haoua, Tunis, Tunisia.
● I B L A. s-a. ISSN 0018-862X

**Institut National de la Recherche Agronomique de Tunisie**
Ariana, Tunisia.
● Institut National de la Recherche Agronomique de Tunisie. Documents Techniques. irreg., no.69, May 1975. ISSN 0020-238X

**Institut Pasteur de Tunis**
13 Place Pasteur, Tunis, Tunisia.
● Institut Pasteur de Tunis. Archives. q. ISSN 0020-2509

**Societe Tunisienne des Sciences Medicales**
18 rue de Russie, Tunis, Tunisia.
● Tunisie Medicale. s-m. ISSN 0041-4131

**Abdeljelil Temimi, Ed. & Pub.**
Rue Habib Thameur-Kheireddine/La Goulette, Tunis, Tunisia.
● Revue d' Histoire Maghrebine/North African Historical Review. 3 per yr.

**Tunisia. Division des Resources en Eau**
Tunis, Tunisia.
- Resources en Eau de Tunisie. irreg.

**Tunisia. Institut National de la Statistique**
Tunis, Tunisia
(Avail. from: Imprimerie Officielle de la Republique
Tunisienne, 42 rue de 18 Janvier 1952, Tunis,
Tunisia)
- Annuaire Statistique de la Tunisie. a. ISSN 0066-
3689
- Economie de la Tunisie en Chiffres. a. ISSN
0070-878X
- Statistiques du Commerce Exterieur de la Tunisie.
a. ISSN 0081-5292
- Tunisia. Institut National de la Statistique.
Bulletin Mensuel de Statistique. m. ISSN 0041-
4115
- Tunisia. Institut National de la Statistique.
Statistiques Industrielles. a. ISSN 0082-6839

**Tunisia. Ministere de l'Equipement**
Cite Jardins, Tunis, Tunisia.
- Revue Tunisienne de l'Equipement. q. (prep. by
its Centre de Documentation)

**Tunisia. Ministere du Plan**
Tunis, Tunisia.
- Tunisia. Ministere du Plan. Rapport sur le Budget
Economique. a. ISSN 0082-6820

**Tunisia. Ministere du Plan. Institut National de la
Statistique**
see Tunisia. Institut National de la Statistique

**Tunisia. Office des Ports Nationaux**
Tunis, Tunisia.
- Tunisia. Office des Ports Nationaux. Bulletin
Annuel des Statistiques. a.

**Union Tunisienne de l'Industrie, du Commerce et de
l'Artisanat**
32 rue Charles de Gaulle, Tunis, Tunisia.
- Annuaire Economique de la Tunisie. a. ISSN
0066-3042
- Economic Yearbook of Tunisia. biennial. ISSN
0070-8747
- Tunisie Economique. q. ISSN 0041-4123

**Universite de Tunis. Centre d'Etudes et de
Recherches Economiques et Sociales**
23 rue d'Espagne, Tunis, Tunisia.
- C. E. R. E. S. Cahiers. Serie Linguistique. q. ISSN
0564-7975
- Carthage; Tunisian quarterly review. q.
- Revue Tunisienne de Sciences Sociales. q. ISSN
0035-4333

# TURKEY

**Ankara Universitesi. Tip Fakultesi**
see University of Ankara. Medical Faculty

**Arkitekt**
Anadolu Han No. 33, Eminonu, Istanbul, Turkey.
- Arkitekt. q. ISSN 0004-1971

**Association of the University Library School
Graduates**
P.K. 440 Kizilay, Ankara, Turkey.
- Yeni Yayinlar; monthly bibliographic journal. m.
ISSN 0513-5303

**Baha Matbaas**
Cagaloglu, Istanbul, Turkey.
- Turkish Medical Association.Journal. bi-m. ISSN
0041-431X

**Bogazici Universitesi**
Box 2, Istanbul, Turkey.
- Bogazici University Journal: Engineering. a.
- Bogazici University Journal: Sciences. a.
- Bogazici University Journal: Social Sciences. a.

**Bogazici University**
see Bogazici Universitesi

**Bosporus University**
see Bogazici Universitesi

**British Chamber of Commerce of Turkey**
P.K. 190, Kara Koy, Istanbul, Turkey.
- British Chamber of Commerce of Turkey. Trade
Journal. m. ISSN 0007-0416

**Celal Tevfik Karasapan**
Tunali Hilmi Cad. 121-5, Kavaklidere, Ankara,
Turkey.
- Orta Dogu. m. ISSN 0030-5812

**Celtut Matbaasi**
Cagaloglu, Istanbul, Turkey.
- Orkestra. m. ISSN 0030-5650 (Istanbul State
Symphony Orchestra)

**Central Bank of the Republic of Turkey**
Bankalar Caddesi: 48, Ankara, Turkey.
- Turikye Cumhuriyet Merkez Bankasi. Aylik
Bulten. m. ISSN 0041-4336

**Central Treaty Organization**
Eski Buyuk Millet, Meclisi Binasi, Ankara, Turkey.
- C E N T O Newsletter. irreg. ISSN 0577-0335

**Chamber of Civil Engineers**
Selanik Caddesi 19-1, 1 Yenisehir-Ankara, Turkey.
- Insaat Muhendisleri Odasi. Teknik Bulten. q.
ISSN 0300-2721
- Turkiye Muhendislik Haberleri. m. ISSN 0049-
4852

**Chamber of Commerce, Izmir**
Izmir, Turkey.
- Chamber of Commerce, Izmir. Review. bi-m.
ISSN 0021-3357

**Chemical Society of Turkey**
Halaskargazi Caddesi No. 53, Uzay Apt. D.8, Box
829, Istanbul, Turkey.
- Kimya ve Sanayi. q.

**Constante Basin Ajansi**
Peykhane Caddesi No. 14, Cemberlitas, Istanbul,
Turkey.
- Turkish Trade Directory & Telex Index/Turk
Ticaret Rehberi. irreg., 1970, 4th ed. ISSN 0082-
6952

**Deprem Arastirma Enstitusu**
see Earthquake Research Institute

**Earthquake Research Institute**
Konur Sokak No. 4-2, Yenisehir/Ankara, Turkey.
- Deprem Arastirma Enstitusu Bulteni. q.

**Ekonomik Basin Ajansi**
Olgunlar Sokak 2-1, Bakanlikar, Ankara, Turkey.
- Briefing: Weekly Inside Perspective on Turkish
Political, Economic and Business Affairs. w.

**Elektrik Muhendisleri Odasi**
see Institute of Electrical Engineers

**Et ve Balik Kurumu**
Balikcilik Muessesesi, Besiktas, Istanbul, Turkey.
- Balik ve Balikcilik. bi-m. ISSN 0404-6811

**Hacettepe Universitesi. Cucak Sagligi Enstitusu**
see University of Hacettepe. Institute of Child
Health

**Hacettepe Universitesi. Nufus Etutleri Enstitusu**
see University of Hacettepe. Institute of
Population Studies

**Hacettepe University Press**
Ankara, Turkey.
- Hacettepe Bulletin of Medicine-Surgery/Hacettepe
Tip-Cerrahi Bulteni. q. ISSN 0017-6451
(University of Hacettepe)
- Hacettepe Fen ve Muhendislik Bilimleri Dergisi.
a. ISSN 0072-9221 (University of Hacettepe)
- Turkish Journal of Pediatrics. q. ISSN 0041-4301
(University of Hacettepe. Institute of Child
Health)

**Industrial Development Bank of Turkey**
Meclisi Mebusan Cad. 137, Box 59, Findikli,
Istanbul, Turkey.
- Industrial Development Bank of Turkey. Annual
Statement. a. ISSN 0073-7402

**Insaat Muhendisleri Odasi**
see Chamber of Civil Engineers

**Institut Historique et Archeologique Neerlandais de
Stamboull**
- Institut Historique et Archeologique Neerlandais
de Stamboull. Publications. (pub. by Nederlands
Instituut voor Het Nabije Oosten NE)

**Institute of Electrical Engineers**
Ihlamur Sokak 10-1 Yenisehir, Ankara, Turkey.
- Elektrik Muhendisligi. m. ISSN 0013-5402

**Istanbul Chamber of Commerce**
c/o Y. Kilkis, P.O. Box 377, Istanbul, Turkey.
- Istanbul Ticaret Odasi Mecmuasi/Istanbul
Chamber of Commerce. Journal. q.

**Istanbul Medical Faculty**
see under Istanbul University

**Istanbul State Symphony Orchestra**
- Orkestra. (pub. by Celtut Matbaasi)

**Istanbul Teknik Universitesi**
see Technical University of Istanbul

**Istanbul Tip Fakultesi**
see Istanbul University. Istanbul Medical Faculty

**Istanbul Universitesi. Islam Tetkikleri Enstitusu**
see Istanbul University. Institute of Islamic
Studies

**Istanbul Universitesi. Istanbul Tip Fakultesi**
see Istanbul University. Istanbul Medical Faculty

**Istanbul Universitesi. Turkiyat Enstitusu**
see Istanbul University. Institute of Turcology

**Istanbul University. Institute of Islamic Studies**
Istanbul, Turkey.
- Islam Tetkikleri Enstitusu Dergist. q.

**Istanbul University. Institute of Turcology**
Ayniyat, Istanbul, Turkey.
- Turkiyat Mecmuasi. irreg. ISSN 0085-7432

**Istanbul University. Istanbul Medical Faculty**
Istanbul, Turkey.
- Istanbul Medical Faculty. Medical Bulletin/
Istanbul Tip Fakultesi. Tip Mecmuasi. q. ISSN
0301-7362

**Istanbul University. Sarkiyat Enstitusu**
Istanbul, Turkey.
- Sarkiyat Mecmuasi. irreg. ISSN 0578-9761

**K. K. K. Istanbul Askeri Basimevi**
Istanbul, Turkey.
- Ordu Dergisi. m. ISSN 0030-4581

**Maden Tetkik ve Arama Enstitusu**
see Mineral Research and Exploration Institute

**Makina Muhendisleri Odasi**
Sumer Sokak 36-1, Demirtepe-Ankara, Turkey.
- Makina Muehendisleri Odasi Haftalik Haberler
Gazetesi. w. ISSN 0025-1135
- Muhendis ve Makina. m. ISSN 0027-304X

**Mensucat Meslek Dergisi**
Eskisehir Rd., Istanbul, Turkey.
- Mensucat Meslek Dergisi. m. ISSN 0025-9624

**Middle East Technical University**
Public Relations and Publications Office, Ismet
Inonu Bulvari, Ankara, Turkey.
- Journal of Pure and Applied Sciences/Temel ve
Uygulamali Bilmler Dergisi. 3 per yr. (approx.)
ISSN 0022-4057 (Co-sponsor: Turk Tarih
Kurumu Basimevi)

**Milli Kutuphane**
see Turkey. National Library

**Mineral Research and Exploration Institute of
Turkey**
Genel Direktorlugu, Ankara, Turkey.
- Mineral Research and Exploration Institute of
Turkey. Bulletin. s-a. ISSN 0026-4563

**Mining Engineering Society of Turkey**
Yeni Oesen Mathuasi, Ibrahim Muteferrika Sok.,
Ankara, Turkey.
- Madencilik; maden muhendisleri odasi dergisi. q.
ISSN 0024-9416

**Ormanci Gazetesi**
Setbasi Hocalizade Caddesi No. 22 A, Bursa,
Turkey.
- Ormanci Gazetesi. m. ISSN 0030-5677

**Orta Dogu Teknik Universitesi**
see Middle East Technical University

**Outlook**
P.K. 210 Kizilay, Ankara, Turkey.
- Outlook; weekly newsmagazine. w. ISSN 0030-7254

**Refik Saydam Merkez Hifzissihha Enstitusuo**
Ankara, Turkey.
- Turkish Bulletin of Hygiene and Experimental Biology/Turk Hijiyen ve Tecrubi Biyoloji Dergisi/Revue Turque d'Hygiene et de Biologie Experimentale. 3 per yr. ISSN 0049-4844

**Selcuklu Tarih ve Medeniyeti Enstitusu**
Posta Kutusu 244, Yenisehir-Ankara, Turkey.
- Journal of Seljuk Studies/Selcuklu Arastirmalari Dergisi. a.

**Technical University of Istanbul. Department of the History of Architecture and Preservation**
Gumussuyu Caddesi 87, Beyoglu, Istanbul, Turkey.
- Anadolu Sanati Arastirmalari/Researches on Anatolian Art. irreg., 1970, vol. 2. ISSN 0066-1333

**TURDOK**
see Turkish Scientific and Technical Documentation Centre

**Turk Belediyecilik Dernegi**
Mithat Pasa Caddesi 45/2, Ankara, Turkey.
- Iller ve Belediyeler; aylik ilim ve meslek dergisi. m.

**Turk Dil Kurumu**
see Turkish Linguistic Society

**Turk Folklor Arastirmalari**
Posta Kutusu 46, Akrasay, Istanbul, Turkey.
- Turk Folklor Arastirmalari; istanbulida ayda bir defa cikar halk kulturu dergisi. q.

**Turk Kulturunu Arastirma Enstitusu**
see Turkish Cultural Research Institute

**Turk Sinematek Dernegi**
Siraselviler Cad. 65, Taksim, Istanbul, Turkey.
- Yeni Sinema; sinema dergisi. 3 per yr. ISSN 0044-0337

**Turk Tarih Kurumu**
see Turkish Historical Society

**Turkey. Devlet Istatistik Enstitusu**
see Turkey. State Institute of Statistics

**Turkey. Devlet Planlama Teskilati**
see Turkey. State Planning Organization

**Turkey. Electricity Authority**
Necatibey Caddesi No. 36, Ankara, Turkey.
- Turkish Electricity Authority. Annual Report. a.

**Turkey. General Directorate of Antiquities and Museums**
Ankara, Turkey.
- Turkish Review of Ethnography/Turk Etnografya Dergisi. a. ISSN 0082-6898

**Turkey. General Directorate of Highways**
Ankara, Turkey.
- Karayollari Teknik Bulteni. q. ISSN 0022-9024

**Turkey. Icisleri Bakanligi**
see Turkey. Ministry of Interior

**Turkey. Mili Kutuphane**
see Turkey. National Library

**Turkey. Ministry of Interior**
Tetkik Kurulu Yayin Mudurlugu, Ankara, Turkey.
- Turk Idare Dergisi. bi-m. ISSN 0041-3925

**Turkey. Ministry of Tourism and Information**
Gazi Mustafa Kemal Bulvari 33, Ankara, Turkey.
- Hotel Guide to Turkey. irreg., latest issue, 1974.

**Turkey. National Library**
Ankara, Turkey.
- Turkish National Bibliography/Turkiye Bibliyografyasi. 4 per yr. ISSN 0041-4328

**Turkey. National Library. Bibliographical Institute**
Ankara, Turkey.
- Bibliography of Articles in Turkish Periodicals/Turkiye Makaleler Bibliyografyasi. 4 per yr. ISSN 0041-4344

**Turkey. State Institute of Statistics**
Ankara, Turkey.
- Turkey. Devlet Istatistik Enstitusu. Aylik Istatistik Bulteni/Monthly Bulletin of Statistics. m. ISSN 0041-4263
- Turkey. Devlet Istatistik Enstitusu. Dis Ticaret Yillik Istatistik/Statistique Annuelle du Commerce Exterieur/Annual Foreign Trade Statistics. a. ISSN 0082-6901
- Turkey. Devlet Istatistik Enstitusu. Istatistik Yillik/Annuaire Statistique. a. ISSN 0082-691X
- Turkey. Devlet Istatistik Enstitusu. Milli Egitim Istatistikleri: Ogretim Yili Basi. a.
- Turkey. Devlet Istatistik Enstitusu. Tarim Istatistikleri Ozeti/Summary of Agricultural Statistics. a. ISSN 0082-6928
- Turkey. Devlet Istatistik Enstitusu. Tarimsal Yapi ve Uretim/Agricultural Structure and Production. a. ISSN 0082-6936

**Turkey. State Planning Organization**
Ankara, Turkey.
- Turkey. Devlet Planlama Teskilati. Annual Program of the Five Year Development Plan. a. ISSN 0082-6944

**Turkey. Turizm ve Tanitma Bakanligi**
see Turkey. Ministry of Tourism and Information

**Turkine Bilimsel ve Teknik Dokumentasyon Merkezi**
see Turkish Scientific and Technical Documentation Centre

**Turkish Chamber of Chemical Engineers**
Konur Sokak 4/2, Yenisehir, Ankara, Turkey.
- Kamya Muhendisligi. bi-m. ISSN 0023-1428

**Turkish Cultural Research Institute**
Box 14, Tunus Caddesi 16, Cankaya, Ankara, Turkey.
- Cultura Turcica. s-a. ISSN 0011-281X
- Turk Kulturu. m. ISSN 0041-4239

**Turkish Historical Society**
Ankara, Turkey.
- Turk Tarih Kurumu. Belgeler. 2 per yr. ISSN 0041-4247
- Turk Tarih Kurumu. Belleten. q. ISSN 0041-4255

**Turkish Librarians' Association**
Box 175, Yenisehir, Ankara, Turkey.
- Turkish Librarians' Association. Bulletin/Turk Kutuphaneciler Bulteni. q.

**Turkish Linguistic Society**
Ankara, Turkey.
- Turk Dili. m. ISSN 0041-4220

**Turkish Medical Association**
- Turkish Medical Association.Journal. (pub. by Baha Matbaas)

**Turkish Phytopathological Society**
Ege Universitesi, Ziraat Fakultesi Fitopatoloji ve Zirai Botanik Kursusu, Bornova-Izmir, Turkey.
- Journal of Turkish Phytopathology. q.

**Turkish Scientific and Technical Documentation Centre**
Ataturk Bulvari 221, Kavaklidere, Ankara, Turkey.
- Current Titles in Turkish Science. m.
- National and International Meetings on Science and Technology. q.

**Turkiye Elekrik Kurumu**
see Turkey. Electricity Authority

**Turkiye Fitopatoloji Dernegi**
see Turkish Phytopathological Society

**Turkiye Is Bankasi**
Ulus Meydani, Ankara, Turkey.
- General Economic Conditions in Turkey. a. (prep. by its Economic Research Department)
- Turkiye Is Bankasi. Review of Economic Conditions. bi-m. ISSN 0034-6500 (prep. by its Economic Research Department)

**Turkiye Kimya Cemiyeti**
see Chemical Society of Turkey

**Turkiye Sinai Kalkinma Bankasi**
see Industrial Development Bank of Turkey

**University of Ankara. Faculty of Veterinary Medicine**
Ankara, Turkey.
- Ankara Universitesi. Veteriner Fakultesi. Dergisi. q. ISSN 0003-3685

**University of Ankara. Medical Faculty**
Yayin Komisyonu, Baskanligi, Sihhiye, Ankara, Turkey.
- Ankara Universitesi. Tip Fakultesi. Mecmuasi. 6 per yr.

**University of Hacettepe**
- Hacettepe Bulletin of Medicine-Surgery/Hacettepe Tip-Cerrahi Bulteni. (pub. by Hacettepe University Press)
- Hacettepe Fen ve Muhendislik Bilimleri Dergisi. (pub. by Hacettepe University Press)

**University of Hacettepe. Institute of Child Health**
Ankara, Turkey.
- Cocuk Sagligi ve Hastaliklari Dergisi. q. ISSN 0010-0161
- Turkish Journal of Pediatrics. (pub. by Hacettepe University Press)

**University of Hacettepe. Institute of Population Studies**
Ankara, Turkey.
- Haceteppe Universitesi. Nufus Etutleri Enstitusu. Bulteni. q.
- Nufus Yayinlari Bulteni. q.
- Turkiye Ozetli Nufus Bibliyografyasi. a.

**Varlik Yayinevi**
Cagaloglu Yokusu 40, Istanbul, Turkey.
- Varlik. m. ISSN 0042-2762

# UGANDA

**Diocese of Arua**
Box 3230, Kampala, Uganda.
- Nile Gazette. m. ISSN 0048-041X

**East African Freshwater Fisheries Research Organization**
Box 343, Jinja, Uganda.
- African Journal of Tropical Hydrobiology and Fisheries. s-a. ISSN 0002-0036
- East African Freshwater Fisheries Research Organization. Annual Report. a. ISSN 0070-7953

**L.D.C. Publications**
Box 7117, Kampala, Uganda.
- Uganda Law Focus. s-a. (Law Development Centre)

**Law Development Centre**
- Uganda Law Focus. (pub. by L.D.C. Publications)

**Leadership Publications**
Box 2522, Kampala, Uganda.
- Leadership; a magazine for Christian leaders in Africa. m. ISSN 0047-424X

**Makerere Institute of Social Research**
P.O. Box 16022, Kampala, Uganda.
- Makerere Institute of Social Research. Research Abstracts and Newsletter; a journal of policy communication. a. ISSN 0302-6736

**Makerere Law Society**
Faculty of Law, Makerere University, Box 7062, Kampala, Uganda.
- Makerere Law Journal. s-a.

**Makerere Political Society**
Political Science Department, Makerere University, Kampala, Uganda.
- Makerere Political Review. irreg.

**Makerere University. Department of Geography**
P.O. Box 7062, Kampala, Uganda.
- Makerere University. Department of Geography. Occasional Paper. irreg. ISSN 0075-4722

**Makerere University. Department of History**
- Makerere Historical Journal. (pub. by East African Literature Bureau KE)

**Makerere University. Department of Literature**
- Dhana. (pub. by East African Literature Bureau KE)

**Makerere University. Department of Religious Studies and Philosophy**
Box 7062, Kampala, Uganda.
- Dini na Mila; revealed religion and traditional custom. 3 per yr.

- Makerere University. Department of Religious Studies and Philosophy. Occasional Research Papers in African Religions and Philosophies. irreg.

**Makerere University. Department of Rural Economy and Extension**
Box 7062, Kampala, Uganda.
- Eastern Africa Journal of Rural Development. s-a. (Co-sponsor: Eastern Africa Agricultural Economics Society)
- Rural Development Research Paper. irreg. ISSN 0080-4851 (Co-sponsor: Makerere Institute of Social Research)

**Makerere University. East African Institute of Social Research**
- East African Studies. (pub. by East African Publishing House KE)

**Makerere University. Faculty of Agriculture**
Box 7062, Kampala, Uganda.
- Makerere University. Faculty of Agriculture. Handbook. irreg. ISSN 0075-4730
- Makerere University. Faculty of Agriculture. Technical Bulletin. irreg. ISSN 0075-4773

**Makerere University. Faculty of Arts & Social Sciences**
Box 7062, Kampala, Uganda.
- Mawazo; the Makerere journal of the arts and social sciences. s-a. ISSN 0047-6293

**Makerere University. Faculty of Education**
Box 7062, Kampala, Uganda.
- Makerere University. Faculty of Education. Handbook. a.

**Makerere University. Faculty of Law**
Box 17062, Kampala, Uganda.
- Makerere University. Faculty of Law. Handbook. a. ISSN 0075-4781

**Makerere University. Library**
Box 16002, Kampala, Uganda.
- Makerere University. Library. Library Bulletin and Accessions List. q. ISSN 0047-3138
- Makerere University. Library. Makerere Library Publications. irreg. ISSN 0075-4854

**Makerere University Medical Students Association**
Box 7072, Kampala, Uganda.
- Makerere Medical Journal. s-a. ISSN 0025-1119

**Makerere University. Science Faculty**
Box 7062, Kampala, Uganda.
- Makerere University. Science Faculty. Handbook. irreg.

**Makerere University. Sociological Society**
Box 7062, Kampala, Uganda.
- Sociological Journal. a.

**Management Training and Advisory Center**
P.O. Box 4655, Kampala, Uganda.
- Management. a. ISSN 0300-2144

**Munno Publications**
Box 1014, Kisubi, Uganda.
- Kizito; children's own magazine. 9 per yr. ISSN 0023-1975

**National Teachers College, Kyambago**
Box 20012, Kampala, Uganda.
- Nanga. s-a.

**P P D Publications**
Kampala, Uganda.
- Uganda Journal of Political Economy. s-a. (Uganda Economic Association)

**Public Health Inspectors' Association**
Box 46, Kampala, Uganda.
- Public Health and Hygiene. a.

**Public Libraries Board**
P.O. 4262, Kampala, Uganda.
- Public Libraries Board, Kampala. Accession List. bi-m.

**Uganda. Forest Department**
P.O. Box 31, Entebbe, Uganda.
- Uganda. Forest Department. Annual Report. a. ISSN 0082-7177
- Uganda. Forest Department. Bulletins. a. ISSN 0082-7185

- Uganda. Forest Department. Technical Note. irreg. ISSN 0082-7193
- Uganda. Forest Department. Timber Leaflets. irreg. ISSN 0082-7207
- Uganda. Forest Department. Working Plans. irreg.

**Uganda. Geological Survey and Mines Department**
P.O. Box 9, Entebbe, Uganda.
- Uganda. Geological Survey and Mines Department. Annual Report. a, latest 1971. ISSN 0082-7215

**Uganda. Government Printer**
Box 33, Entebbe, Uganda.
- Uganda Estimates of Development Expenditures. irreg., latest 1975-76.

**Uganda. Ministry of Information, Broadcasting and Tourism**
Box 7142, Kampala, Uganda.
- Dwon Lwak/People's Voice. w. ISSN 0419-8735
- Uganda Schools Newsletter. m. ISSN 0049-5026

**Uganda. Ministry of Planning and Economic Development. Statistics Division**
P.O. Box 13, Entebbe, Uganda
(Subscr. to: Government Printer, Box 33, Entebbe, Uganda)
- Uganda. Ministry of Planning and Economic Development. Statistics Division. Background to the Budget. a; latest issue, 1970. ISSN 0082-7231
- Uganda. Ministry of Planning and Economic Development. Statistics Division. Enumeration of Employees. a. ISSN 0082-724X
- Uganda. Ministry of Planning and Economic Development. Statistics Division. Monthly Trade Bulletin. m.
- Uganda. Ministry of Planning and Economic Development. Statistics Division. Quarterly Economic and Statistical Bulletin. q. ISSN 0041-5758

**Uganda Church Publications**
Box 14123, Kampala, Uganda.
- New Day. s-m. ISSN 0028-4556

**Uganda Economic Association**
- Uganda Journal of Political Economy. (pub. by P P D Publications)

**Uganda Geographical Association**
P.O. Box 7062, Kampala, Uganda.
- East African Geographical Review. a. ISSN 0070-7961

**Uganda School Leavers Association**
Box 5145, Kampala, Uganda.
- School Leaver. q.

**Uganda Society**
Box 4980, Kampala, Uganda.
- Uganda Journal. s-a. ISSN 0041-574X

# UNITED ARAB EMIRATES

**Abu Dhabi. Council of Ministers Secretariat**
Box 516, Abu Dhabi, United Arab Emirates.
- Abu Dhabi Offical Gazette. irreg.

**Abu Dhabi. Department of Information and Tourism**
Abu Dhabi, United Arab Emirates.
- Abu Dhabi News. w.

**Abu Dhabi Chamber of Commerce and Industry**
Box 662, Abu Dhabi, United Arab Emirates.
- Abu Dhabi Chamber of Commerce and Industry. Review. m.

**United Arab Emirates. Ministry of Education**
Box 80, Doha, United Arab Emirates.
- United Arab Emirates. Ministry of Education. al-Tarbiya. bi-m.

**United Arab Emirates. Ministry of Petroleum and Industry**
Abu Dhabi, United Arab Emirates.
- United Arab Emirates. Ministry of Petroleum and Industry. Akhbar al-Petrol Wall Sinaa. irreg.

# UNITED KINGDOM

**A A R P**
c/o Dalu Jones & George Mitchell, 102 St. Pauls Rd., London N1 2LR, England.
- A A R P. (Art and Archaeology Research Papers) s-a. ISSN 0308-5597
- A A R P Monographs. (Art and Archaeology Research Papers) irreg.

**A B C Historic Publications**
Oldhill, London Rd., Dunstable, Bedfordshire LU6 3EB, England.
- Historic Houses, Castles and Gardens. a. ISSN 0073-2567
- Museum and Galleries. a. ISSN 0077-2267

**A B C Travel Guides Ltd.**
Oldhill, London Rd., Dunstable, Beds. LU6 3EB, Eng.
- A B C Air Cargo Guide. m.
- A B C Air/Rail Europe. m.
- A B C Freight Guide. 2 per yr.
- A B C Guide to Cruises. m.
- A B C Guide to International Travel. q.
- A B C Rail Guide. m. ISSN 0001-0472
- A B C Shipping Guide. m. ISSN 0001-0480
- A B C World Airways Guide. m.

**A. B. E. Publications**
10 Dryden Chambers, 119 Oxford St., London W1R 1PA, England.
- Education and Training. m. ISSN 0040-0912

**A B M R Publications Ltd.**
30 Cornmarket St., Oxford, England.
- Antiquarian Book Monthly Review. m. ISSN 0306-7475

**A C P Publishers Ltd.**
Ayres House, Station Road, Wallingford-on-Thames, Oxon OX10 0LA, England.
- Europe. a.
- Farm Contractor. bi-m.

**A.M.O.**
73 Newman St., London W.1, England.
- Personnel Service News. irreg. (approx. 5 per yr.) (Federation of Personnel Services)

**A.P. Publications Ltd.**
322 St. John St., London EC1V 4QH, England.
- Database Journal. q.
- Small Systems Software. 4 per yr.
- Software World; an international journal of computer programs and packages. 4 per yr. ISSN 0038-0652

**A S I Publications Ltd.**
56/60 Wigmore Street, London W1H 9DG, England.
- All Sports International. bi-m. ISSN 0084-6201

**A S T M S**
15 Half Moon St., London W.1, Eng.
- Medical World. m. ISSN 0025-7621

**A S T M S. Pearl Section Gazette Committee**
Sutton House, 2-4 Homerton High St., London E9 6JT, England.
- Pearl Gazette. bi-m. ISSN 0048-3109

**A V A Magazine**
c/o Mrs. E. Jones, 17 Nether St., North Finchley, London N.12, England.
- A V A Magazine. (Audio-Visual-Aids Magazine) 3 per yr. ISSN 0001-2858

**A Wake Newslitter Press**
c/o University of Essex, Wivenhoe Park, Colchester, Essex CO4 3SQ, Eng.
- A Wake Newslitter; studies of James Joyce's Finnegans Wake. bi-m. ISSN 0049-6847

**A-4 Publications Ltd.**
Press House, 25 High St., Edenbridge, Kent, Eng.
- Architect's & Specifiers Guide Series. a.
- Bathrooms and Kitchens. a.
- Ceilings & Partitions. a.
- Contract Carpeting. a. ISSN 0069-9578
- Doors & Windows. a.

- External Walls. a.
- Fabrics, Wallcoverings & Furniture. a.
- Flooring. a.
- Roofing. a. ISSN 0080-4037

**AAFAQ Monthly**
c/o M.B. Khan, 217 Sussex Way, London N. 19, England.
- AAFAQ Monthly. m. ISSN 0001-2963

**Aarox Publishing Ltd.**
Fielden Square, Todmorden 0L14 7LA, England
(U.S. Address: Box 252, Winchester, MA 01890)
- New Earth Times Quarterly & Catalogue. q.

**Abbey National Building Society**
Abbey House, Baker St., London N.W.1, England.
- Bellman Lecture. biennial.

**Abbey Press**
Stent St., Abingdon, Oxon OX14 3JW, England
- Institute of Animal Technicians. Journal. s-a. ISSN 0020-2711 (Subscr. to: Mrs. J. Beattie, Animal Unit, Western General Hospital, Crewe Rd., Edinburgh EH4 2XU, Scotland)

**Abbotsbury Publications**
Abbotsbury, Weymouth, Dorset, Eng.
- Energy and Character; journal of bio-energetic research. 3 per yr. ISSN 0013-7472

**Aberdeen and District Milk Marketing Board**
Twin Spires Creamery, Bucksburn, Aberdeen, Scotland.
- Milk News. m. ISSN 0047-7400

**Aberdeen-Angus Cattle Society**
Pedigree House, 6 King's Place, Perth, Scotland.
- Aberdeen-Angus Herd Book. a.
- Aberdeen-Angus Review. a. ISSN 0001-317X

**Aberdeen Chamber of Commerce**
15 Union Terrace, Aberdeen AB9 1HF, Scotland.
- Aberdeen Chamber of Commerce Journal. q. ISSN 0001-3188

**Aberdeen College of Education**
Hilton Place, Aberdeen AB9 1FA, Scotland.
- Education in the North. a. ISSN 0424-5512

**Aberdeen University Press**
Farmers Hall, Aberdeen AB9 2XT, Scotland.
- British Journal for the Philosophy of Science. q. ISSN 0007-0882 (British Society for the Philosophy of Science)
- Oceanography and Marine Biology: an Annual Review. a.

**Abertay Historical Society**
c/o Dept. of History, The University, Dundee DD1 4HN, Scotland.
- Abertay Historical Society. Series of Monographs. a.

**Abor Publishing Co. Ltd.**
Samuel House, Taylor Street, Liverpool L5 5AD, England.
- Liverpool Jewish Gazette. m.

**Academic Press Inc. (London) Ltd.**
24 Oval Rd., London N.W.1., England
(Dist. in U.S. by: Academic Press Inc., 111 Fifth Ave., New York, NY 10003)
- A S A Monographs. irreg., 1974, no. 12. ISSN 0066-9679 (Association of Social Anthropologists of the Commonwealth)
- Advances in Botanical Research. irreg. ISSN 0065-2296
- Advances in Drug Research. irreg; 1973, vol. 7. ISSN 0065-2490
- Advances in Ecological Research. irreg. ISSN 0065-2504
- Advances in High Pressure Research. irreg. ISSN 0065-2733
- Advances in Insect Physiology. irreg., 1972, vol. 9. ISSN 0065-2806
- Advances in Marine Biology. irreg., 1973, vol. 11. ISSN 0065-2881
- Advances in Optical and Electron Microscopy. irreg; 1973, vol. 5. ISSN 0065-3012
- Advances in Parasitology. irreg; 1973, vol. 11. ISSN 0065-308X
- Advances in Physical Organic Chemistry. irreg; 1973, vol. 8. ISSN 0065-3160
- Advances in Radio Research. irreg. ISSN 0065-3314
- Annals of Botany. 5 per yr. ISSN 0003-4754
- Annual Review of N M R Spectroscopy. a. ISSN 0066-4235
- Association of Public Analysts. Journal. q. ISSN 0004-5780
- Biochemical Society Symposia. a. ISSN 0067-8694
- British Phycological Journal. q. ISSN 0007-1617
- Cancer Treatment Reviews. q.
- Cancer Treatment Reviews. q.
- Clinical Oncology. q. ISSN 0305-7399 (Society for Clinical Oncology)
- Curtis's Botanical Magazine. 2 per yr. ISSN 0011-4073
- Essays in Biochemistry. a. ISSN 0071-1365 (Biochemical Society (Book Depot))
- Eugenics Society Symposia. irreg. ISSN 0071-223X
- Experimental Eye Research; an international journal devoted to scientific research on the eye. m. (2 vols. per yr.) ISSN 0014-4835
- Ibis. q. ISSN 0019-1019 (British Ornithologists' Union)
- Institute of Mathematics and Its Application. Journal. bi-m(2 vols. per yr.) ISSN 0020-2932
- International Journal of Nautical Archaeology and Underwater Exploration. q. ISSN 0305-7445 (Council for Nautical Archaology)
- International Symposium on Aerobiology. Proceedings. irreg. ISSN 0074-8757
- Journal of Agricultural Engineering Research. q. ISSN 0021-8634 (British Society for Research in Agricultural Engineering)
- Journal of Antimicrobial Chemotherapy. q.
- Journal of Applied Bacteriology. q. ISSN 0021-8847 (Society for Applied Bacteriology)
- Journal of Archaeological Science. q.
- Journal of Archaeological Science. q.
- Journal of Comparative Pathology. q. ISSN 0021-9975
- Journal of Historical Geography. q.
- Journal of Human Evolution. bi-m. ISSN 0047-2484
- Journal of Molecular Biology. every 10 days (9 vols. per yr.) ISSN 0022-2836
- Journal of Sound and Vibration. fortn. ISSN 0022-460X (Institute of Acoustics)
- Journal of Theoretical Biology. m. (6 vols. per yr.) ISSN 0022-5193
- Journal of Zoology. 3 vols.per yr. ISSN 0022-5460 (Zoological Society of London)
- Leprosy Review. q. ISSN 0024-1032 (British Leprosy Relief Association)
- Lichenologist. s-a. ISSN 0024-2829 (British Lichen Society)
- Medical Laboratory Sciences. q. (Institute of Medical Laboratory Technology)
- Physiological Plant Pathology. q. ISSN 0048-4059
- Phytochemical Society Symposia Series. Proceedings. irreg.
- Public Health. bi-m. ISSN 0033-3506 (Society of Community Medicine)
- Quarterly Journal of Experimental Psychology. q. ISSN 0033-555X (Experimental Psychology Society)
- Scandinavica. s-a. ISSN 0036-5653
- Science of Ceramics. irreg. ISSN 0080-7575
- Scottish Universities' Summer School in Physics. Proceedings. a. ISSN 0080-8253
- Spore Research. irreg.
- Zoological Society of London. Symposia. irreg. ISSN 0084-5612

**Academy for Arts**
Ashurstwood Abbey, East Grinstead, Sussex RH19 3SD, England.
- Gold Circle Numismatics. irreg.

**Accolade Publications Ltd.**
99 Dean St., London W1V 5RA, England.
- Style International; fashion and merchandising in menswear. m.

**Accountants' Publishing Co. Ltd.**
27 Queen St., Edinburgh EH2 1LA, Scotland.
- Accountant's Magazine. m. ISSN 0001-4761 (Institute of Chartered Accountants of Scotland)

**Acorn Sporting Publications**
634 River Gardens, Feltham, Middlesex, England.
- Par Golf. m.

**Adam International Review**
28 Emperors Gate, London SW7, England.
- Adam International Review; arts, drama, architecture, music. q. ISSN 0001-8015

**Adam Publishing Ltd.**
The Adelphi, John Adam St., London W.C.2, Eng.
- Groundsman. m. ISSN 0017-4696 (Institute of Groundsmanship)

**Admap Publications Ltd.**
28 Great Queen St., London WC2B 5BB, Eng.
- Admap. m. ISSN 0001-8295

**Advanced Mile-Posts Publications Ltd.**
Empire House, Chiswick, London W4 5TJ, Eng.
- Milestones. q. ISSN 0026-380X (Institute of Advanced Motorists)

**Adverse Drug Reaction Research Unit**
Shotley Bridge General Hosptial, Consett, Co. Durham DH8 0NB, England.
- Adverse Drug Reaction Bulletin. bi-m. ISSN 0044-6394 (Regional Postgraduate Institute for Medicine and Dentistry, Newcastle-Upon-Tyne)

**Advertising Association**
Abford House, 15 Wilton Rd., London SW1V 1NJ, Eng.
- Advertising Quarterly. q. ISSN 0001-8961

**Advertising Data Ltd.**
5 Scrutton St., London EC2A 4SJ, Eng.
- T V Advertising Statistical Review. m.

**Advertising Standards Authority Ltd.**
15-17 Ridgemount St., London WC1E 7AW, England.
- Advertising Standards Authority, London. Annual Report. a. ISSN 0065-3659

**Advisory Centre for Education**
32 Trumpington St., Cambridge CB2 1QY, Eng.
- Where; the education magazine for parents. m. ISSN 0043-4809

**Advisory Information Services Ltd.**
150 Regent St., London W.1, England
(U.S. Subscr. to: 30 E. 42nd St., New York, NY 10017)
- London Gold and Commodity Report. m. (Institute for International Research)

**Africa Bureau**
48 Grafton Way, London W.1., Eng.
- X-Ray on Current Affairs in Southern Africa. bi-m. ISSN 0049-8238

**Africa Contemporary Record Ltd.**
- Africa Contemporary Record, Annual Survey and Documents. (pub. by Rex Collings Ltd.)

**Africa Evangelical Fellowship**
30 Lingfield Rd., London SW19 4PU, Eng.
- Pioneer. q. ISSN 0048-4202

**Africa Journal Ltd.**
Kirkman House, 54a Tottenham Court Rd., London W1P 0BT, England.
- Africa; an international business, economic and political monthly. m. ISSN 0044-6475

**Africa Publications Trust**
48 Grafton Way, London W1P 5LB, Eng.
- Africa Currents. q.

**Africa Research Ltd.**
18 Lower North St., Exeter, Devon, EX4 3EN, Eng.
- Africa Research Bulletin. Series A: Political, Social and Cultural. m. ISSN 0001-9844
- Africa Research Bulletin. Series B: Economic, Financial and Technical. m. ISSN 0001-9852

**African Development Magazine Ltd.**
63 Long Acre, London WC2Y 4JM, England.
- New African Development. m.

**African National Congress of South Africa**
49 Rathbone St., London W1A 4NL, Eng.
- Sechaba. q. ISSN 0037-0509
- South African Studies. irreg. ISSN 0049-142X

**African Studies Association of the United Kingdom**
c/o Centre of West African Studies, P.O. Box 363,
Birmingham B13 2SD, England.
- African Research and Documentation. 3 per yr.
  ISSN 0305-862X (Co-Sponsor: Standing
  Committee on Library Materials on Africa)

**African Succulent Plant Society**
54 Fishponds Rd., Hitchin, Hertfordshire SG5 1NS,
Eng.
- African Succulent Plant Society. Bulletin. q. ISSN
  0002-0222

**Afro-Asian Publications, Ltd.**
1B, Parkfield St., London N1 0PR, England.
- Afro-Asian Affairs. bi-w. (Central Asian Research
  Centre)

**Age Concern England. National Old People's Welfare
Council**
Bernard Sunley House, 60, Pitcairn Road, Mitcham
CR4 3LL, England.
- Age Concern Today. q. ISSN 0308-2792

**Agenda Editions**
5 Cranbourne Court, Albert Bridge Rd., London
SW11 4PE, Eng.
- Agenda. q. ISSN 0002-0796

**Aggie Weston's**
c/o Stuart Mills, Editor, 37 Laund Close, Belper,
Derbyshire, England.
- Aggie Weston's. q.

**Agitprop**
160 N. Gower St., London N.10, Eng.
- Red Notes. m. ISSN 0034-2025

**Agra Europe (London) Ltd.**
Agroup House, 16 Lonsdale Gardens, Tunbridge
Wells, Kent, Eng.
- Agra Europe. w. ISSN 0002-1024

**Agricultural Education Association**
c/o Ed. & Pub. A. R. Staniforth, 5 Capel Close,
Oxford OX2 7LA, England, England.
- Agricultural Progress. a. ISSN 0065-4493

**Agricultural Press Ltd.**
Surrey House, 1 Throwley Way, Sutton, Surrey
SM1 4QQ, England
(Dist. in the U.S. by Iliffe- N.T.P. Inc., Sales
Division, 205 E. 42 St., New York, N.Y. 10017)
- Agricultural Machinery Journal. m. ISSN 0002-
  1539
- Farm and Garden Equipment Guide. a. ISSN
  0071-3880
- Poultry World. w. ISSN 0032-5813

**Agricultural Research Council**
- Grassland Research Institute, Hurley, England
  (Berkshire) Technical Reports. (pub. by Grassland
  Research Institute)
- National Institute for Research in Dairying.
  Biennial Report. (pub. by National Institute for
  Research in Dairying)
- National Institute for Research in Dairying.
  Biennial Reviews. (pub. by National Institute for
  Research in Dairying)
- Plant Breeding Institute, Cambridge. Annual
  Report. (pub. by Plant Breeding Institute)

**Agricultural Research Council. Weed Research
Organization**
- Weed Abstracts. (pub. by Commonwealth
  Agricultural Bureaux)

**Agudas Israel of Great Britain**
97 Stamford Hill, London N16X 5TR, England.
- Jewish Tribune. w.

**Aims for Freedom and Enterprise**
5 Plough Place, Fetter Lane, London EC4A 1AN,
England.
- Stay Free. q.

**Air Age Publications Ltd.**
Temple Chambers, Temple Ave., London E.C.4,
Eng.
- Hovercraft World. 8 per yr. ISSN 0018-6759

**Air Europa Timetable Ltd.**
49 Trinity Rd., London S.W. 17, Eng.
- Air Europa. m. ISSN 0002-2314

**Air Transport and Travel Industry Training Board**
Staines House, 158-162 High Street, Staines,
Middlesex TW18 4AS, England.
- Air Transport and Travel Industry Training Board.
  Report and Statement of Accounts. a.

**Airfix Products Ltd.**
- Airfix. (pub. by P S L Publications Ltd.)

**Airtimetable Publications Ltd.**
49 Trinity Rd., London S.W.17, Eng.
- Airport Times. m. ISSN 0002-2837

**Akros Publications**
14 Parklands Ave., Penwortham, Preston,
Lancashire, Eng.
- Akros; poetry magazine. 3 per yr. ISSN 0002-
  3728
- Parklands Poets Series. irreg; no. 15, 1975. ISSN
  0079-0087

**Alabaster Passamore, Ltd.**
32 Chancery Lane, London W.C.2, England.
- Acrow Review. q. ISSN 0001-5067

**Alba Stamp Group**
34, Gray Street, Glasgow G3 7TY, Scotland.
- Scottish Stamp News. m.

**Albion Village Press**
28 Albion Drive, London E. 8. 4ET, England.
- Albion Village Press Books. q.

**Album**
70 Princedale Rd., London W.11, Eng.
- Album. m. ISSN 0002-4937

**Alden Press (Oxford) Ltd.**
Osney Mead, Oxford, Eng.
- Institute of Actuaries. Journal. 3 per yr. ISSN
  0020-2681
- Institute of Actuaries Students' Society. Journal. 3
  per yr. ISSN 0020-269X

**Aldria Securities Ltd.**
Alert Bldg., 189 de la Warr Rd., Bexhill-on-Sea,
Sussex TN40 2JY, England.
- Stock Market Alert. w.

**All-British Pigeon Racing Publishing Co. Ltd.**
St. Georges Hall, 198 Brooklands Rd., Weybridge,
Surrey KT13 0RJ, Eng.
- Pigeon Racing News & Gazette. m. ISSN 0048-
  4164

**All England Netball Association**
70 Brompton Rd., London SW3 1HD, Eng.
- Netball. q.

**All England Women's Lacrosse Association**
70 Brompton Rd., London SW3 1EQ, Eng.
- Lacrosse. 3 per yr. ISSN 0023-7086

**All in**
c/o Nina Steane, Ed., 31 Headlands, Kettering,
Northants, England.
- All in; wallstickers. s-a.

**Ian Allan Ltd.**
Terminal House, Shepperton, Middlesex TW17 8AJ,
England.
- Air Extra. q.
- Aircraft Illustrated. m. ISSN 0002-2675
- Buses. m. ISSN 0007-6392
- Buses Annual. a. ISSN 0068-4376
- Little Red Book, Classified to All Public
  Transport Fleet Owners and Operators and
  Vehicle Manufacturers. a. ISSN 0076-0013
- Model Railway Constructor. m. ISSN 0026-735X
- Modern Railways. m. ISSN 0026-8356
- Railway World. m. ISSN 0033-9032
- Railway World Annual. a. ISSN 0082-5891

**W. H. Allen & Co. Ltd.**
44 Hill St., London W1X 8LB, England.
- Film Review. a. ISSN 0071-4917

**George Allen & Unwin (Publishers) Ltd.**
40 Museum St., London W. C. 1, England
(U.S. Address: Allen & Unwin Inc., 198 Ash St.,
Reading, MA 01867)
- Historical Problems: Studies and Documents.
  irreg. ISSN 0073-2621
- National Institute Social Services Library. irreg.,
  no. 30, 1976. ISSN 0077-4774 (National Institute
  for Social Work)
- Studies in Economics. irreg., no. 11, 1976. ISSN
  0081-7856

- University of Birmingham. Centre for Urban and
  Regional Studies. Urban and Regional Studies.
  irreg., no. 7, 1976. ISSN 0067-8961

**J. A. Allen Ltd.**
1 Lower Grosvenor Place, Buckingham Palace
Road, London, SW1W OEL, England.
- Baily's Hunting Directory. a. ISSN 0067-2947

**Allens (Clerkenwell) Ltd.**
39 High St., Wheathampstead, Herts AL4 8DG,
England.
- Double Glazing - Domestic, Industrial &
  Commercial. q.
- Electric Vehicles for Industry. q. ISSN 0013-4171
- Energy Digest. bi-m.
- Jeweller. s-m. (British Watch and Clock Makers
  Guild)

**Alliance Party of Northern Ireland**
88 University St., Belfast BT7 1HE, N. Ireland.
- Alliance. m. ISSN 0044-734X

**Allotrope**
Ed. Humphrey Evans, 73 Woodcock Hill, Kenton,
Harrow, Middlesex, Eng.
- Allotrope. q. ISSN 0044-7366

**Alpine Club**
74 S. Audley St., London W1Y 5FF, England.
- Alpine Journal. a. ISSN 0065-6569

**Alpine Garden Society**
c/o D. K. Haselgrove, 278-280 Hoe St.,
Walthamstow, London E17 9PL, England.
- A. G. S. Guides. irreg.
- Alpine Garden Society. Quarterly Bulletin. q.
  ISSN 0002-6476

**Alternative England and Wales**
65 Edith Grove, London SW10, England.
- Alternative England and Wales. biennial (with
  quarterly supplements)

**Amalgamated Union of Engineering Workers.
Engineering Section**
110 Peckham Rd., London S.E. 15, England.
- A U E W E S Journal. m. ISSN 0001-110X

**Amalgamated Union of Engineering Workers. Foundry
Section**
164 Chorlton Rd., Brook's Bar, Manchester 16,
Eng.
- Foundry Worker. m. ISSN 0015-9050

**Amalgamated Union of Engineering Workers.
Technical, Administrative & Supervisory Section**
Onslow Hall, Little Green, Richmond, Surrey, Eng.
- Tass News and Journal. m.

**Amateur Athletic Association**
70 Brompton Rd., London SW3 1EE, England.
- Amateur Athletic Association. Handbook. a. ISSN
  0065-6690

**Amateur Basketball Association of Scotland**
8 Frederick St., Edinburgh EH2 2HB, Scotland.
- Amateur Basketball Association of Scotland.
  Officiating Bulletin. q.
- Coaching Bulletin. q.

**Amateur Entomologists Society**
355 Hounslow Rd., Hanworth, Feltham, Middlesex
TW13 5JH, England.
- Amateur Entomologists Society. Bulletin. q.

**Amateur Fencing Association**
83 Perham Rd., West Kensington, London W14,
England.
- Sword. 3 per yr.

**Amateur Rowing Association**
5 Lower Mall, London W6 9DJ, England.
- British Rowing Almanack. a. ISSN 0068-2446

**Amateur Swimming Association**
- Swimming Times. (pub. by Swimming Times Ltd.)

**Amateur Winemaker Publications Ltd.**
South St., Andover, Hants, England.
- Amateur Winemaker. m. ISSN 0002-6883

**Amateur Yacht Research Society**
Hermitage, Newbury, Berkshire, England.
- A Y R S Airs. 4 per yr.

**Ambassador College Press**
Box 111, Radlett Rd., Colney St. Village, St.
Albans, Herts, Eng.
- Plain Truth. m.

**Ambit**
17 Priory Gardens, London N.6, Eng.
- Ambit; a quarterly of poems, short stories,
drawings and criticism. q. ISSN 0002-6972

**Ambulance Service Institute**
79 Dudsbury Ave., Ferndown, Wimborne, Dorset
BH22 8DY, England.
- Ambulance Journal. bi-m.

**American Chamber of Commerce (United Kingdom)**
75 Brook St., London W1Y 2EB, England.
- Anglo American Trade Directory. 2 per yr. ISSN
0066-1813
- Anglo American Trade News. m. ISSN 0003-3316

**Amnesty International**
53 Theobold's Rd., London WC2X 8SP, England.
- Amnesty International Annual Report. a. ISSN
0569-9495
- Amnesty International Newsletter. m.
- Chronicle of Current Events; a journal of the
soviet human rights movement. bi-m.

**Amon-Ra Fine Art Ltd.**
Meeting House, Frenchay, Bristol BS16 1NT, Eng.
- Blues World. m. ISSN 0006-5161

**Ampleforth Abbey**
York YO6 4EN, Eng.
- Ampleforth Journal. 3 per yr. ISSN 0003-2018

**An Lef Kernewek**
c/o E. G. Hooper, Ed., 93 Mount Pleasant Rd.,
Camborne, Cornwall, England.
- An Lef Kernewek/Cornish Voice. s-a. ISSN 0003-
2360

**Anatomical Society of Great Britain and Ireland**
- Journal of Anatomy. (pub. by Cambridge
University Press)

**Anbar Publications Ltd.**
Box 23, Wembley HA9 8DJ, Eng.
- Accounting & Data Processing Abstracts. 8 per yr
(plus index) ISSN 0001-4796 (Institute of
Chartered Accountants in England & Wales)
- Anbar Management Services Bibliography. a.
ISSN 0003-2808
- Anbar Management Services Joint Index. a. ISSN
0003-2816
- Anbar Yearbook; the compleat Anbar. a.
- Marketing & Distribution Abstracts. 8 per yr (plus
index) ISSN 0305-0661 (Institute of Marketing)
- Personnel & Training Abstracts. 8 per yr (plus
index) ISSN 0305-067X (Institute of Personnel
Management)
- Top Management Abstracts. 8 per yr (plus index)
ISSN 0049-4100 (British Institute of
Management)
- Work Study & O and M Abstracts. 8 per yr (plus
index) ISSN 0305-0653 (Institute of Practitioners
in Work Study, Organization and Methods)

**Ancient Monuments Society**
c/o Jennifer Jenkins, 33 Ladbroke Square, London
W. 1., England.
- Ancient Monuments Society Newsletter. s-a.

**Ancient Order of Foresters Friendly Society**
136 High St., Southampton SO9 1FP, Eng.
- Foresters Miscellany. m. ISSN 0015-7511

**Aneks Press**
61 Dorset Rd., London W5 4HX, England.
- Aneks; kwartalnik polityczny/political quarterly.
q.

**Anglers Cooperative Association**
Midland Bank Chambers, Westgate, Grantham,
Lincs NG31 6LE, England.
- A.C.A. Review. a. ISSN 0044-8257

**Anglesey Antiquarian Society and Field Club**
c/o Hon. Secretary, 22 Lon Ganol, Menai Bridge,
Anglesey, Wales.
- Anglesey Antiquarian Society Transactions. a.
- Studies in Anglesey History. irreg. (approx.
biennial) ISSN 0585-6515

**Anglican & Eastern Churches Association**
137 Liverpool Rd., London N. 1, England.
- Eastern Churches News Letter. s-a. ISSN 0012-
8732

**Anglican Pacifist Fellowship**
St. Mary's Church House, Bayswater Rd.,
Headington, Oxford OX3 9EY, England.
- Challenge (London, 1961) bi-m. ISSN 0009-0999

**Angling Times Ltd.**
Park House, Park Road, Peterborough PE1 2TS,
Eng.
- Tackle & Guns. m. ISSN 0015-3052
- Trout and Salmon; a journal for game fishermen.
m. ISSN 0041-3372

**Anglo Arab Association**
21 Collingham Rd., London SW5 0NU, England.
- Arab World. s-a. ISSN 0518-1852

**Anglo-Byelorussian Society**
230 Strand, London W.C.2, England.
- Journal of Byelorussian Studies. a. ISSN 0075-
4161

**Anglo Chilean Society**
12 Devonshire St., London W1N 2DS, Eng.
- Chilean News. 2 per yr.

**Anglo-Continental Dental Society**
22 Devonshire Place, London W1N 1PD, England.
- Anglo-Continental Dental Society. Journal. s-a.
ISSN 0003-3324

**Anglo-German Association**
2 Henrietta St., London W.C.2, Eng.
- Anglo-German Review. q. ISSN 0003-3340

**Anglo-Israel Chamber of Commerce**
8-12 Brook St., London W1Y 1AB, England.
- Anglo-Israel Trade Journal. m. ISSN 0003-3359

**Anglo-Japanese Economic Institute**
342 Grand Bldgs., Trafalgar Square, London W.C.2,
England.
- Anglo-Japanese Economic Institute Bulletin. m.

**Anglo-Spanish Society**
5 Cavendish Square, London W.1, England.
- Anglo-Spanish Quarterly Review. q. ISSN 0003-
3383

**Animal Health Trust**
24 Portland Pl, London W1N 4HN, Eng
(and 122 E. 55th St., New York, N.Y. 10022)
- Animal Health. a. ISSN 0003-3502

**Anthroposophical Society in Great Britain**
- Golden Blade. (pub. by Rudolf Steiner Press)

**Anti-Apartheid Movement**
89 Charlotte St., London W.1, Eng.
- Anti-Apartheid News. 10 per yr. ISSN 0003-5580

**Antiquarian Horological Society**
New House, High St., Ticehurst, Wadhurst, Sussex
TN5 7AL, England.
- Antiquarian Horology and the Proceedings of the
Antiquarian Horological Society. q. ISSN 0003-
5785

**Antique & General Advertising Ltd.**
Amadines, Coln St. Dennis, Cheltenham, Glos.
GL54 3JY, England.
- Antiques. q.
- Antiques in Britain. a. ISSN 0003-5955

**Antique Collector**
16 Strutton Ground, London SW1P 2HP, Eng.
- Antique Collector; an authoritative in the field of
fine and applied art and antiques. bi-m. ISSN
0003-5858

**Antique Collectors Club**
Clopton, Woodbridge, Suffolk, Eng.
- Antique Collecting. m. ISSN 0003-584X
- Guide to the Antique Shops of Britain. irreg.

**Antique Finder Ltd.**
5 Church St., Woodbridge, Suffolk, England.
- Antique Finder. m. ISSN 0003-5874

**Antiquities Service of the Sudan**
- Kush. (pub. by Daniel Greenaway & Sons Ltd.)

**Antiquity Publications Ltd.**
King's Hedges Rd., Cambridge CB4 2PQ, England.
- Antiquity; a quarterly review of archaeology. 3 per
yr. ISSN 0003-598X

**Anvil Press (Liverpool)**
5 Cases St., 1st Floor, Liverpool L1 1HW, England.
- Profile: an Introduction to Liverpool. a.
- Profile: an Introduction to Manchester. a.

**Apollo Magazine**
22 Davies St., London W.1, Eng.
- Apollo; the international magazine of art and
antiques. m. ISSN 0003-6536

**Apostleship of the Sea**
National Board for England and Wales, Anchor
House, Anlaby Rd., Hull, Yorks, England.
- Anchor. q. ISSN 0003-2840

**Applied Probability Trust**
Department of Probability and Statistics, The
University, Sheffield S3 7RH, England.
- Advances in Applied Probability. q. ISSN 0001-
8678
- Journal of Applied Probability. q. ISSN 0021-9002
- Mathematical Spectrum. 3 per yr. ISSN 0025-
5653

**Applied Science Publishers Ltd.**
Ripple Rd., Barking, Essex, England.
- Agricultural Administration. q.
- Applied Acoustics; an international journal. q.
ISSN 0003-682X
- Applied Energy. q.
- Biological Conservation. 8 per yr. ISSN 0006-
3207
- Environmental Pollution; an international journal.
m. ISSN 0013-9327
- Fibre Science and Technology. q. ISSN 0015-0568
- Food Chemistry; an international journal. 2 per
yr.
- Gas and Liquid Chromatography Abstracts. q.
ISSN 0301-388X (Gas Chromatography
Discussion Group)
- Institute of Petroleum Standards for Petroleum
and Its Products. Part 1: Methods for Analysis
and Testing. a.
- International Journal of Bio-Medical Computing.
q. ISSN 0020-7101
- Meat Science. q.
- Pressure Vessels and Piping. q.
- Royal Institution of Great Britain. Proceedings. a.
ISSN 0035-8959
- World Petroleum Congresses. Proceedings.
quadrennial since 1963; 1967, 7th, Mexico; 1971,
8th, Moscow; 1975, 9th Tokyo. ISSN 0084-2176

**Applied Technology Publications Ltd.**
15 Coombe Rd., New Malden, Surrey KT 3 4PX,
England.
- Hydraulic & Air Engineering. bi-m.

**Aquarius**
c/o Eddie S. Linden, Ed., 116 Sutherland Ave.,
London W.9., England.
- Aquarius; poetry magazine. q. ISSN 0003-7303

**Aquila Publishing Co. Ltd.**
9 Scullamus Breakish, Isle of Skye, IV42 8QB,
Scotland.
- New Poetry News. bi-m.

**Arab Horse Society**
Sackville, Lodge, Lye Green, Crowborough Sussex
TN6 IUU, England.
- Arab Horse Society News. s-a. ISSN 0402-7493
- Arab Horse Stud Book. a.

**Arab Report and Record**
84 Chancery Lane, London WC2A 1DL, Eng.
- A R R. s-m. ISSN 0003-7451

**Arabic Literature Mission**
22 Culverden Park Rd., Tunbridge Wells, Kent TN4
9RA, Eng.
- Crossroads. bi-m. ISSN 0045-9119 (Co-sponsor:
Lebanon Evangelical Mission)

**Arboricultural Association**
c/o Merrist Wood College of Agriculture,
Worplesdon, Guildford, Surrey GU3 3PE, England.
- Arboricultural Journal. s-a. ISSN 0307-1375

**Archaeological Centre**
50 Braidley Rd., Bournemouth, Eng.
- Ago. m.

**Archaeological News Letter**
60 Frederick St., Gray's Inn Rd., London W.C.1, Eng.
- Archaeological News Letter. m. ISSN 0003-8040

**Archaeology Abroad Service**
31-34 Garden Square, London W.C.1., England.
- Archaeology Abroad Service. Newsheet. a.

**Archigram Group**
59, Aberdare Gardens, London N.W.6, England.
- Archigram. irreg., 1970, no. 9. ISSN 0066-6092

**Architectural and Archaeological Society of Durham and Northumberland**
c/o University Library, Durham, England.
- Architectural and Archaeological Society of Durham and Northumberland. Transactions. New Series. a. ISSN 0066-6203

**Architectural Association**
36 Bedford Square, London WC1, England.
- Architectural Association Quarterly. q. ISSN 0001-0189

**Architectural Metalwork Association**
18, Croydon Rd., Caterham, Surrey CR3 6YR, England.
- Architectural Metalwork Association. Members Specialised Products. a.

**Architectural Press Ltd.**
9 Queen Anne's Gate, London SW1H 9BY, Eng.
- Architects' Journal. w. ISSN 0003-8466
- Architectural Review. m. ISSN 0003-861X
- Specification; building methods and products. a. ISSN 0081-3567

**Arena Publications Ltd.**
325 Streatham High Rd., London SW16 3NS, Eng.
- Athletics Arena International; the international track & field athletics magazine. m.

**Argus Books Ltd.**
(Subsidiary of: Fountain Press)
Station Road, Kings Langley, Hertfordshire, England.
- Photography Year Book. a. ISSN 0079-1865

**Argus Press Ltd.**
The Illustrated Publications Co., 12-18 Paul St., London EC2A 4JS, Eng.
- Mother & Baby; the quality magazine for parents. m. ISSN 0047-8172

**Aristotelian Society**
- Aristotelian Society. Proceedings. (pub. by Methuen and Co. Ltd.)

**Arlington Books (Publishers) Ltd.**
38 Bury St., St. James's, London S.W.1, England.
- Careers and Vocational Training. biennial.

**Arlis (Art Libraries Society)**
c/o Ed. Philip Pacey, Preston Polytechnic, Corporation St., Preston, Lancashire, England.
- Art Libraries Journal. q. ISSN 0307-4722

**Arms and Armour Society**
90 Links Rd., Ashtead, Surrey KT21 2HW, Eng.
- Arms and Armour Society. Journal. s-a. ISSN 0004-2439

**Army Cadet Force Association**
58 Buckingham Gate, London S.W.1, Eng.
- Cadet Journal and Gazette. bi-m. ISSN 0007-9456

**Army Quarterly and Defence Journal**
1 West St., Tavistock, Devon, Eng.
- Army Quarterly and Defence Journal. q. ISSN 0004-2552

**Art & Language Press**
13 Milverton Crescent, Leamington Spa, Warwickshire, England.
- Art-Language. irreg. ISSN 0587-3584

**Art Net Ltd.**
14 W. Central St., London WC1A 1JH, England.
- Net. 3 per yr.

**Art Sales Index Ltd.**
Pond House, Weybridge, Surrey, KT13, England.
- Annual Arts Sales Index: Oil Paintings. a. ISSN 0308-5910
- Annual Arts Sales Index: Watercolours and Drawings. a. ISSN 0308-5902
- Monthly Art Sales Index. m.

**Art Workers Guild**
6 Queen Square, London WC1N 3AR, England.
- Art Workers Guild. Annual Report. a.

**Arthritis and Rheumatism Council**
8-10 Charing Cross Rd., London WC2H 0HN, England.
- Arthritis and Rheumatism Council. Magazine. q.
- Reports on Rheumatic Diseases. 3 per yr. ISSN 0048-7279

**Artist Publishing Co. Ltd.**
33 Warwick Square, London SW1, England.
- Artists' Guide. a. ISSN 0066-8087

**Arts Council of Great Britain**
105 Piccadilly, London W1V 0AU, England
(Dist. by H.M.S.O., P.O.B. 569, London S.E.1, England)
- Arts Council of Great Britain. Annual Report and Accounts. a. ISSN 0066-8133
- New Review. (pub. by New Review Ltd.)

**Arts Council of Great Britain. Eastern Arts Association**
c/o Nicholas Zurbrugg, Church Steps, Kersey, Near Ipswich, Suffolk, England.
- Stereo Headphones; an occasional magazine of the new experimental poetries. 2-3 per yr. ISSN 0039-1212

**Asgard Publishing Ltd.**
5A Warwick St., London W1R 5RA, Eng.
- On Call; the newspaper for hospital doctors. fortn. (Junior Hospital Doctors'' Association)

**Ashire Publishing Ltd.**
42 Grays Inn Rd., London WC1X 8LR, Eng.
- Mine and Quarry. m. ISSN 0369-1632

**Ashoka Publications Ltd.**
Wheatsheaf House, 4 Carmelite St., London EC4Y 0BN, Eng.
- India Weekly. w. ISSN 0046-8959

**Asia Christian Colleges Association**
2 Eaton Gate, London SW1W 9BL, England.
- Asia Christian Colleges Association. Bulletin. a. ISSN 0004-444X

**ASLIB**
3 Belgrave Sq., London S.W.1, Eng.
- Aslib Book List; a monthly list of recommended scientific and technical books. m. ISSN 0001-2521
- Aslib Information. m. ISSN 0305-0033
- Aslib Membership List. a. ISSN 0066-8524
- Aslib Occasional Publications. irreg., no. 18, 1976. ISSN 0066-8532
- Aslib Proceedings. m. ISSN 0001-253X
- Forthcoming International Scientific and Technical Conferences. q. ISSN 0046-4686
- Index to Theses Accepted for Higher Degrees in the Universities of Great Britain and Ireland. a. ISSN 0073-6066
- Journal of Documentation; devoted to the recording, organization and dissemination of specialized knowledge. q. ISSN 0022-0418
- Program; news of computers in libraries. q. ISSN 0033-0337
- Technical Translation Bulletin. 3 per yr. ISSN 0497-0489
- Work of Aslib: Annual Report. a. ISSN 0084-1285

**ASLIB. Library Association, Audiovisual Groups**
c/o Miss Frances Thorpe, 35 Primrose Gardens, London NW3 4UL, England.
- Audiovisual Librarian. q.

**ASLIB. Transport and Planning Group**
c/o Kay Henderson, 3 Templar St., London SE5, England.
- Aslib Transport and Planning Group Newsletter. q.

**ASLIB. Youth Libraries Group**
c/o Mrs. C. A. Kloct, Hattersley Comprehensive School, Fields Farm Rd., Hattersley, Hyde, Cheshire, England.
- Y L G News. 3 per yr. ISSN 0459-2476

**Asphalt & Coated Macadam Association**
25 Lower Belgrave St., London SW1W OLS, Eng.
- Queen's Highway. s-a. ISSN 0033-6025

**Assistant Masters' Association**
29 Gordon Square, London WC1H OPT, Eng.
- A. M. A. 8 per yr. ISSN 0001-1819

**Associated British Machine Tool Makers Ltd.**
20 Park St., London W1Y 4NA, Eng.
- Machine Tool Engineering; a journal written for machine tool users by machine tool makers. 3 per yr. ISSN 0024-9165

**Associated Catholic Newspapers Ltd.**
The Universe, Universe House, 21 Fleet St., London EC4Y 1AP, England.
- Catholic Directory. a. ISSN 0069-1224
- Universe. w. ISSN 0041-8226

**Associated Country Women of the World**
50 Warwick Square, Victoria, London SW1V 2AJ, Eng.
- Countrywoman. bi-m. ISSN 0011-0302

**Associated Newspapers Group Ltd.**
Carmelite House, Carmelite St., London EC4Y 0JA, England.
- Daily Mail Motor Show Review. a.
- Daily Mail Year Book. a.
- Weekend. w. ISSN 0043-1818

**Associated Octel Company Ltd.**
20 Berkeley Square, London W.1, Eng.
- Information about the Oil Industry/For the Oil Industry. m. ISSN 0019-9931

**Associated Society of Locomotive Engineers and Firemen**
9 Arkwright Rd., Hampstead, London NW3 6AB, Eng.
- Locomotive Journal. m.

**Association for Group Psychoanalysis and Process**
- Group Process. (pub. by Gordon and Breach Science Publishers Ltd.)

**Association for Literary and Linguistic Computing**
c/o Joan M. Smith, 6 Sevenoaks Ave., Heaton Moor, Stockport, Cheshire SK4 4AW, England.
- Association for Literary and Linguistic Computing Bulletin. 3 per yr. ISSN 0305-9855

**Association for Programmed Learning and Educational Technology**
33 Queen Anne St., London W1M 0AL, England.
- A P L E T Journal. q.
- Ed. Tech. News. q.
- Programmed Learning & Educational Technology. (pub. by Kogan Page Ltd.)

**Association for Psychiatric Treatment of Offenders**
199 Gloucester Place, London NW1 6BU, Eng.
- International Journal of Offender Therapy and Comparative Criminology. 3 per yr. ISSN 0306-624X

**Association for Radical East Asian Studies**
6 Endsleigh St., London W.C.1., Eng.
- A R E A S Bulletin. 3 per yr.

**Association for Research in Vision and Ophthalmology**
- Vision Research. (pub. by Pergamon Press Ltd.)

**Association for Science Education**
College Lane, Hatfield, Herts AL10 9AA, Eng.
- Education in Science. 5 per yr. ISSN 0013-1377
- School Science Review. (pub. by John Murray (Publishers) Ltd.)

**Association for Scottish Literary Studies**
Dept. of English, University of Aberdeen, Old Aberdeen, Scotland.
- Scottish Literary Journal. s-a. ISSN 0305-0785

**Association for the Education of Pupils from Overseas**
- Multiracial School. (pub. by Oxford University Press)

**Association for the Reform of Latin Teaching**
c/o Kenneth F. Cox, King Charles I School, Kidderminster, Worcestershire, England.
- Latin Teaching. s-a. ISSN 0023-8821

**Association for the Study of Animal Behaviour**
- Animal Behaviour. (pub. by Bailliere Tindall)
- Animal Behaviour Abstracts. (pub. by Information Retrieval Ltd.)

**Association for the Study of Medical Education**
- Medical Education. (pub. by Blackwell Scientific Publications Ltd.)

**Association for Therapeutic Education**
c/o Heathlands, 56 Parkside, Wimbledon, London
SW19 5NJ, England.
- Therapeutic Education. 2 per yr. ISSN 0305-7860

**Association of Applied Biologists**
National Vegetable Research Station, Wellesbourne,
Warwick CV35 9EF, England
- Annals of Applied Biology. 9 per yr. ISSN 0003-
4746 (Subscr. to: Biochemical Society Book
Depot, Box 32, Commerce Way, Whitehall
Industrial Estate, Colchester, Essex CO2 8HP,
England)

**Association of Art Historians. Department of Art
History**
University of Manchester, Manchester, England.
- Association of Art Historians. Bulletin. s-a.

**Association of Assistant Librarians**
West Norwood Library, 1 Norwood High St.,
London Borough of Lambeth, London SE 27,
England.
- Assistant Librarian. 11 per yr. ISSN 0004-5152

**Association of British Adoption and Fostering
Agencies**
4 Southampton Row, London WC1B 4AA, England.
- Adoption and Fostering. q.

**Association of British Dental Surgery Assistants**
3 Market Place, Poulton, Blackpool, Lancs, Eng.
- British Dental Surgery Assistant. m. ISSN 0007-
0629

**Association of British Launderers & Cleaners**
Lancaster Gate House, 319 Pinner Rd., Harrow,
Middlesex HA1 4HX, England.
- A B L C News. m. ISSN 0306-1264

**Association of British Riding Schools**
- Horse World: Pony Express. (pub. by Independent
Magazines Ltd.)

**Association of British Spectroscopists**
- European Spectroscopy News. (pub. by Heyden &
Son Ltd.)

**Association of British Travel Agents**
- Cruises, Sea Voyages & Car Ferries. (pub. by
Maclean-Hunter Ltd.)

**Association of British Tree Surgeons & Arborists**
Pembroke Cottage, 11 Wings Rd., Upper Hale,
Farnham, Surrey, England.
- Association of British Tree Surgeons & Arborists.
Newsletter. 3 per yr.

**Association of Broadcasting & Allied Staffs**
King's Court, 2 Goodge St., London WIP 2AE,
Eng.
- Broadcast. m. ISSN 0306-7602

**Association of Burglary Insurance Surveyors**
- Security Surveyor. (pub. by Victor Green
Publications Ltd.)

**Association of Cashiers Ltd.**
1 Ironmonger St., Stamford, Lincs., Eng.
- Cashier. q. ISSN 0008-7319

**Association of Child Psychotherapists**
Burgh House, New End Sq, London N.W.3,
England.
- Journal of Child Psychotherapy. a. ISSN 0075-
417X

**Association of Christian Teachers**
47 Marylebone Lane, London, W1M 6AX, Eng.
- Spectrum; a magazine for Christians in education.
3 per yr. ISSN 0305-7917

**Association of Cinematograph, Television and Allied
Technicians**
2 Soho Sq., London W1V 6DD, Eng.
- Film and Television Technician. m. ISSN 0015-
1106

**Association of Clinical Biochemists**
Administrative Office, 30 Russell Square, London
W.C.1., England.
- Annals of Clinical Biochemistry. (pub. by
Professional & Scientific Publications)
- Association of Clinical Biochemists. News Sheet.
m.

**Association of Clinical Pathologists**
- Journal of Clinical Pathology. (pub. by British
Medical Association)

**Association of Colleges for Further and Higher
Education**
16 Balderton St., London W1Y 1TF, England.
- Association of Colleges for Further and Higher
Education. Year Book. a. ISSN 0066-9539

**Association of Commonwealth Universities**
36 Gordon Square, London WC1H 0PF, Eng.
- A. C. U. Bulletin of Current Documentation
(ABCD) 5 per yr. ISSN 0044-9563
- Association of Commonwealth Universities.
Report of the Council Together with the
Accounts of the Association. a. ISSN 0571-6241
- Commonwealth Universities Yearbook. a. ISSN
0069-7745 (Dist. by International Publications
Service, 114 East 32nd St. New York, N.Y.
10016)
- Compendium of University Entrance
Requirements for First Degree Courses in the
United Kingdom. a. ISSN 0571-625X
- Scholarships Guide for Commonwealth
Postgraduate Students. biennial. ISSN 0306-1736

**Association of Community Schools**
c/o H. D. G. Evans, Mobberley Boys' School,
Knolls Green, Knutsford, Cheshire WA16 7AR,
England.
- Community Schools Gazette. m. ISSN 0010-3896

**Association of Conference Executives**
8 St. John's St., Huntingdon, Cambs. PE18 6DD,
England.
- A C E News. bi-m.

**Association of Contemporary Historians**
c/o Secretary, Prof. D.C. Watt, London School of
Economics, Aldwych, London WC2A 2AE,
England.
- Association of Contemporary Historians. Bulletin.
a.

**Association of Cost Engineers**
33 Ovington Sq., Kensington, London, SW3 1LJ,
Eng.
- Cost Engineer. bi-m. ISSN 0010-9606

**Association of County Councils**
66A Eaton Square, Westminster, London SW1 9BH,
Eng.
- County Councils Gazette. m. ISSN 0011-0310
- Social Services Yearbook. (pub. by Councils &
Education Press Ltd.)

**Association of Dispensing Opticians**
- Dispensing Optician. (pub. by Weald of Kent
Publications (Tonbridge), Ltd.)

**Association of District Councils**
25 Buckingham Gate, London SW1E 6LE, Eng.
- District Councils Review. 11 per yr. ISSN 0306-
3240

**Association of Education Committees**
- Education. (pub. by Councils and Education Press
Ltd.)
- Education Committees Year Book. (pub. by
Councils and Education Press Ltd.)

**Association of Estonians in Great Britain**
11 Campden Hill Mansion, Edge St., London W. 8.
7PL, England.
- Eesti Haal/Estonian Weekly News. w.

**Association of Government Supervisors and Radio
Officers**
90 Borough High Street, London Bridge, London
SE1, England.
- Monitor. m.

**Association of Insurance Brokers**
Lonsdale Chambers, 27 Chancery Lane, London
WC2A 1NF, England.
- Brokers' Chronicle. m.

**Association of International Accountants**
Box 38, Billerican, Essex, Eng.
- International Accountant. 4-6 per yr. ISSN 0020-
5826

**Association of Jewish Ex-Servicemen and Women,
(Cardiff)**
c/o D. Jacobs, Cemmaes Lodge, Ty-Gwyn Road,
Penylan, Cardiff, Wales.
- C A J E X. q.

**Association of Jewish Refugees in Great Britain**
8 Fairfax Mansions, London NW3 6JY, Eng.
- A J R Information. m. ISSN 0001-1681

**Association of Law Teachers**
- Law Teacher. (pub. by Sweet & Maxwell Stevens
Journals)

**Association of Little Presses of Great Britain**
18 Clairview Rd., London S. W. 16, England
(Subscr. National Book League Ltd., 7 Albemarle
St. London W1, England)
- Catalogue of Little Press Books in Print Published
in the UK. a. ISSN 0591-0986
- Getting Your Poetry Published. biennial.

**Association of London Clearing Banks**
- Bank Sorting Code Numbers. (pub. by Thomas
Skinner Directories)

**Association of Metropolitan Authorities**
36 Old Queen St., Westminster, London SW1
H9JE, Eng.
- Municipal Review. m. ISSN 0027-3562

**Association of Mining, Electrical & Mechanical
Engineers**
276-282 The Corn Exchange, Fennel St.,
Manchester M4 3HF, Eng.
- Mining Technology. m. ISSN 0026-5276

**Association of Musical Instrument Industries, London**
- Living Music. (pub. by Music Industry
Publications)

**Association of Occupational Therapists**
20 Rede Place, Bayswater, London W2 4TU,
England.
- British Journal of Occupational Therapy. m. ISSN
0029-800X

**Association of Photographic Laboratories**
- Photographic Processor. (pub. by Henry
Greenwood & Co. Ltd.)

**Association of Physicians of Great Britain and
Ireland**
- Quarterly Journal of Medicine. (pub. by Oxford
University Press)

**Association of Polish Students and Graduates in Exile**
42 Emperor's Gate, London SW7, Eng.
- Merkuriusz Polski-Zycie Akademickie. q. ISSN
0026-0118

**Association of Professional, Executive, Clerical and
Computer Staff**
22 Worple Rd., Wimbledon, London SW19 4DF,
Eng.
- A P E X. 8 per yr.

**Association of Professional Foresters**
Brokerswood House, Brokerswood, Nr. Westbury,
Wiltshire BA13 4EH, England.
- A P F Newsletter. q.

**Association of Public Address Engineers**
47 Windsor Rd., Slough, Berks, England.
- Public Address. m.

**Association of Public Lighting Engineers**
78 Buckingham Gate, Westminster, London SW1E
6PF, Eng.
- Public Lighting. q. ISSN 0033-3603

**Association of Railway Preservation Societies**
Back Clarendon Rd., Blackpool, Lancashire FY1
6EG, England.
- Association of Railway Preservation Societies. A.
R. P. S. Year Book & Steam Preservation Guide.
(pub. by Haraton Ltd.)
- Railway Forum. (pub. by Haraton Ltd.)
- Railway Forum Steam. s-a.

**Association of Recognised English Language Schools**
43 Russell Square, London WC1B 5DH, England.
- A R E L S Journal. 3 per yr.

**Association of Scientific Workers**
10/26 Jamestown Rd., London, N.1, Eng.
- A S T M S Journal. (Association of Scientific, Technical and Managerial Staff) bi-m. ISSN 0001-2653

**Association of Social Anthropologists of the Commonwealth**
- A S A Monographs. (pub. by Academic Press Inc. (London) Ltd.)

**Association of Supervisory and Executive Engineers**
- Executive Engineer. (pub. by Wheatland Journals Ltd.)

**Association of Surgeons of Gt. Britain and Ireland**
- British Journal of Surgery. (pub. by John Wright & Sons Ltd.)

**Association of Teachers in Colleges and Departments of Education**
3 Crawford Place, London W1H 2BN, Eng.
- Education for Teaching. 3 per yr. ISSN 0013-1326
- Handbook of Colleges and Departments of Education. (pub. by Lund Humphries)

**Association of Teachers of Domestic Science**
Hamilton House, Mabledon Place, London WC1H 9BB, England.
- Housecraft. m. ISSN 0018-6503

**Association of Teachers of Management**
c/o M. Greatorex, Polytechnic of Central London, 35 Marylebone Road, London NW1 5LS, England.
- A T M Occasional Papers. irreg. ISSN 0066-9709
- Management Education & Development. 3 per yr. ISSN 0047-5688

**Association of Teachers of Mathematics**
Market St. Chambers, Nelson, Lancs. BB9 7LN, Eng.
- Mathematics Teaching. q. ISSN 0025-5785

**Association of Teachers of Printing and Allied Subjects**
Technical Publications Committee, Bowland, Wood Bank, Lincoln LN6 OUD, Eng.
- A T P A S Printing Education & Training Journal. 3 per yr.

**Association of Teachers of Russian**
c/o Ed. J. Y. Muckle, School of Education, Univ. of Nottingham, University Park, Nottingham NG7 2RO, England.
- Association of Teachers of Russian.Newsletter. s-a. ISSN 0306-7432
- Journal of Russian Studies. s-a. ISSN 0047-276X

**Association of the British Pharmaceutical Industry**
162 Regent St., London W1R 6DD, Eng.
- A B P I News. 6 per yr. ISSN 0001-0561
- Studies on Current Health Problems. (pub. by Office of Health Economics)

**Association of the Guilds of Weavers, Spinners and Dyers**
6 Queen Square, London WC1N 3AR, England.
- Weavers Journal. q.

**Association of Ukranian Former Combatants in Great Britain**
49 Linden Gardens, London W2 4HG, England.
- Surmach. a. ISSN 0491-6204

**Association of Unit Trust Managers**
- Unit Trust Yearbook. (pub. by Fundex Ltd.)

**Association of University Teachers**
United House, Pembridge Rd., London W11 3HJ, Eng.
- A. U. T. Bulletin. bi-m. ISSN 0001-2823

**Atcost Ltd.**
The Pantiles, Turnbridge Wells, Kent, Eng.
- Farm Building Express. q. ISSN 0014-7850

**Athlone Press**
4 Gower St., London WC1E 6DR, England
(Dist. in U.S. by: Humanities Press Inc., 171 First Ave., Atlantic Highlands, NJ 07716)
- Cassal Bequest Lectures. irreg., 1971, 1976 Lectures. ISSN 0069-0961
- London School of Economics Monographs on Social Anthropology. irreg., no. 52, 1975. ISSN 0077-1074

- London School of Economics Papers on Soviet and East European Law, Economics and Politics. irreg., 1967, no. 2. ISSN 0078-9224 (London School of Economics and Political Science)
- Survey of London. irreg., vol. 38, 1975. ISSN 0081-9751
- University of London. Institute of Latin American Studies. Monographs. irreg., no. 7, 1976. ISSN 0076-0846
- University of London Historical Studies. irreg., no. 38, 1975. ISSN 0076-0692
- University of London Legal Series. irreg., no. 11, 1977. ISSN 0076-0714

**Atlanteans Association Ltd.**
42 St. George's St., Cheltenham, GL50 4AF, Eng.
- Atlantean. q.

**Atlantic Education Trust**
37a High St., Wimbledon, London SW19 5BY, Eng.
- World Survey. m. ISSN 0043-9096

**Atlantic Information Centre for Teachers (A I C T)**
37a, High St., Wimbledon, London SW19, Eng
(U.S. Subscr. to: U.S. Office, 1616 H St. N.W., Washington, DC 20006)
- World and the School. 3 per yr. ISSN 0043-8235

**Atlantic Press**
9 Duke St. Mansions, Duke St., London W1M 6JQ, England
(Represented by Atlantic Press International, 520 Fifth Ave., New York, NY 10036)
- New Poetry. irreg., 1971, no. 4. ISSN 0077-8621

**Audenshaw Foundation**
Muker, Richmond, Yorkshire DL11 6QQ, Eng.
- Audenshaw Papers. 6 per yr. ISSN 0004-7481

**Audio Arts**
c/o William J. Furlong, Ed., 92-104 Carnwath Rd., London SW6 3HW, England.
- Audio Arts. q.

**Audio - Visual Language Association**
Dept. of Modern Languages, University of Aston in Birmingham, Gosta Green, Birmingham B4 7ET, Eng.
- Audio-Visual Language Journal; the journal of applied linguistics and language teaching technology. 3-4 per yr. ISSN 0004-7589

**Austin Catelinet Ltd.**
London End, Beaconsfield, Bucks, Eng.
- British Bandsman. w. ISSN 0007-0319

**Auto Camping Club Publications Ltd.**
5 Dunsfold Rise, Coulsdon, Surrey CR3 2ED, Eng.
- Motor Caravan & Camping. m. ISSN 0027-1829

**AutoMetrix Publications**
1A, Manor Rd., Toddington, Dunstable, Beds., England.
- Beetling. m.

**Automobile Association**
Fanum House, Basingstoke, Hants RG21 2EA, England.
- A A/G B Road Atlas. (pub. by Geographia Ltd.)
- Camping and Caravanning U.K. a.
- Drive. (pub. by Drive Publications Ltd.)
- Guide to Guesthouses, Farmhouses and Inns. a.
- Guide to Stately Homes, Museums, Castles, and Gardens. a.
- Hotel and Restaurant Guide. a.
- Touring Guide to England. a.

**Avenue Publishing Co.**
18 Park Ave., London NW11 7SJ, Eng.
- International Journal of Social Psychiatry. q. ISSN 0020-7640

**Aviation Marketing Services**
69 Fleet St., London EC4, England.
- Executive. bi-1m.

**Aviation Studies International**
Sussex House, Parkside, Wimbledon, London S.W. 19, Eng.
- Aircraft Industry Record. several updatings per year. ISSN 0002-2683
- Airline Fleet Record. q. ISSN 0002-2721
- Armament Data Sheets. q. ISSN 0004-2153
- Army, Air Force & Naval Air Statistical Record. 10 per yr. ISSN 0004-2463
- Army Vehicle and Military Aircraft Data Sheets. q. ISSN 0004-2609
- Aviation Reports. s-w. ISSN 0005-2159

- Aviation Studies International. Official Price List. q. ISSN 0005-2167
- Avionics Data Sheets. irreg.
- Civil Transport Data Sheets. q. ISSN 0009-806X
- Engine Data Sheets. q. ISSN 0013-774X
- Forecast Data Bank Cumulative Sheets. ISSN 0015-7082
- Military Aircraft & Missile Data Sheets. q. ISSN 0026-394X
- Military Record of Atomic C B R Happenings. q. ISSN 0026-4121

**Avicultural Society**
20 Bourdon St., London W.1., Eng.
- Avicultural Magazine. q. ISSN 0005-2256

**Axminster Light Centre**
Clinton House, Castle Hill, Axminster, Devonshire, England.
- Logos Focus. q.

**Ayrshire Archaeological & Natural History Society**
Carnegie Library, 12 Main St., Ayr, KA8 8ED, Scotland.
- Ayrshire Collections. s-a.

**Ayrshire Cattle Society**
1 Racecourse Rd., Ayr, Scotland.
- Ayrshire Cattle Society's Journal. q. ISSN 0005-2442

**B.B. Bks**
1 Spring Bank, Salesbury, Blackburn, Lancs BB1 9EU, Eng.
- Global Tapestry Journal; mind-opening & post-underground creativity. 3 per yr.

**B.E.D. Business Journals Ltd.**
Bridge House, Restmoor Way, Wallington, Surrey SM6 7BZ, England.
- Business Equipment Digest. m. ISSN 0007-6708
- Business Equipment Guide. s-a. ISSN 0007-6716
- Instant Information. q.
- Reproduction; for the printing department and drawing office. m. ISSN 0034-4958

**B. K. T. Publishing Co.**
4 Whalley Rd., Accrington, Lancs, Eng.
- Poultry Fancier. m. ISSN 0048-4962

**B. M. G. Publications Ltd.**
20 Earlham St., London W.C.2, Eng.
- B M G. m. ISSN 0005-321X

**B P S Exhibitions**
4 Seaford Court, 220 Great Portland St., London W1, Eng.
- Foodpack; foodpack news and digest and produce packaging. q. ISSN 0015-6698 (International Exhibition for the Food and Allied Industries)

**B W S Publishing Ltd.**
4 Addison Bridge Place, Kensington, London W. 14, England.
- Architect. m. ISSN 0003-8415

**B. Y. B. Ltd.**
c/o Jack Adley, 7 Higher Drive, Purley, Surrey CR2 2HP, England.
- Bottlers Year Book. a. ISSN 0068-0508

**Babani Press**
Shepherds Bush Rd., London W6 7NF, England.
- Bernards and Babani Press Radio & Electronics Books. irreg; no. 5, 1972.

**Badminton Association of England**
44/45 Palace Road, Bromley, Kent BR1 3JU, England.
- Badminton Association of England. Official Handbook. a. ISSN 0067-2882
- Badminton Gazette. 6 per yr. ISSN 0005-3805

**F. Bailey & Son Ltd.**
Long Street, Dursley, Gloucestershire, England
(Subscr. to: I.A.D.C., Eastman Dental Hospital, Gray's Inn Rd., London WC1X 8LD, England)
- Bristol Medico-Chirurgical Journal. q. ISSN 0007-019X (Bristol Medico Chirurgical Society)
- International Association of Dentistry for Children. Journal. s-a.

**Bailliere Tindall**
38 Red Lion Square, London WC1R 4SG, England, Eng.
- Age and Ageing. q. ISSN 0002-0729 (British Geriatric Society) (Co-sponsor: British Society for Research in Ageing)

- Animal Behaviour. 4 per yr. ISSN 0003-3472 (Association for the Study of Animal Behaviour)
- British Journal of Diseases of the Chest. q. ISSN 0007-0971
- British Veterinary Journal. bi-m. ISSN 0007-1935
- International Review of Psycho-Analysis. q. (Institute of Psycho-Analysis)
- Rheumatology and Rehabilitation. q. ISSN 0300-3396 (British Association of Rheumatology and Rehabilitation)

**Bakers Union**
3Rd Floor, Station House, Darkes Lane, Potters Bar, Herts, Eng.
- Bakery Worker. m. ISSN 0045-1339

**Bale Catalogue of Palestine and Israel Postage Stamps**
c/o Michael H. Bale, Ed., 41 High St., Ilfracombe, England
- Bale Catalogue of Palestine and Israel Postage Stamps. a. ISSN 0305-4039

**John Ball Publications Ltd.**
389 Alfred St. N., Nottingham NG 3 1AA, Eng.
- Leeds & Yorkshire Topic. m.
- Nottingham Topic. m. ISSN 0048-0940

**Bananas Publishing**
2 Blenheim Crescent, London W.11, England.
- Bananas. q.

**Banbury Historical Society**
Banbury Museum, Banbury Oxfordshire, Eng.
- Cake and Cockhorse. 3 per yr. ISSN 0008-0535

**Bangor Students' Union**
- Forecast. (pub. by Forecast Publications)

**Bank of England**
London E.C.2, England.
- Bank of England. Report. a. ISSN 0067-3625
- Bank of England Quarterly Bulletin. q. ISSN 0005-5166

**Bank of England. Library and Literary Association**
London E. C. 2, Eng.
- Old Lady of Threadneedle Street. q. ISSN 0030-199X

**Bankers' Magazine**
Holywell House, Worship St., London E.C.2, England.
- Bankers' Magazine. m. ISSN 0005-5441

**Baptist Historical Society**
4 Southampton Row, London W.C.1, Eng.
- Baptist Quarterly. q. ISSN 0005-576X

**Baptist Missionary Society**
93 Gloucester Place, London, W1H 4AA, England.
- Baptist Missionary Society, London. Annual Report. a. ISSN 0067-4060
- Baptist Missionary Society, London. Official Report and Directory of Missionaries. a. ISSN 0067-4079

**Baptist Times Ltd.**
4 Southampton Row, London WC1B 4AB, Eng.
- Baptist Times. w. ISSN 0005-5786

**Baptist Union of Great Britain and Ireland**
4, Southampton Row, London WC1B 4AB, England.
- Baptist Union Directory. a.

**Baptist Union of Ireland**
3 Fitzwilliam St., Belfast BT9 6AW, Northern Ireland.
- Irish Baptist Historical Society. Journal. a. ISSN 0075-0727

**Baptist Union of Scotland**
14 Aytoun Rd., Glasgow GH1 5RT, Scotland.
- Scottish Baptist Magazine. m. ISSN 0036-9136

**Barclays Bank Group. Economic Intelligence Unit**
54 Lombard St., London EC3P 3AA, Eng.
- Barclays Country Reports. irreg.

**Peter H. Barker**
Empire House, 414 High Rd., Chiswick, London W.4, Eng.
- Modern Medicine of Great Britain. m. ISSN 0026-8100

**Barler Publications Ltd.**
2 Basil St., London, S.W.3, Eng.
- Hairdressers' Guide. fortn. ISSN 0017-6753

**Barnes, Newberry & Co.**
Hertford, England.
- Who's Who in Football. irreg

**Barracuda Books Ltd.**
Chesham, Bucks, England.
- Barracuda Guide to County History Series. irreg.

**Barrie and Jenkins Ltd.**
c/o 8 Pembroke St., Cambridge, Eng.
- Cambridge Review; a journal of university life and thought. 6 per yr. ISSN 0008-2007

**Bath & West Southern Counties Society**
The Showground, Shepton Mallet, Somerset BA4 6QN, England.
- Bath & West Show Catalogue. a.

**Batiste Publications Ltd**
Pembroke House, Campsbourne Rd., London N8, Eng.
- Plant Engineers. m. ISSN 0032-0838 (Institution of Plant Engineers)
- Point of Sale News. m. ISSN 0036-9586
- Toys International. m. ISSN 0041-0195

**Battle of Britain Prints International Ltd.**
3 New Plaistow Road, Stratford, London E. 15, Eng (Dist. in U.S. by: Sky Books International, 48 E. 50th St., New York, NY 10022)
- After the Battle. q. ISSN 0306-154X

**Bax Society**
Ed. Paul Podro, 103 Cheyneys Ave., Canons Park, Edgware, Middlesex, Eng.
- Bax Society Bulletin. q.

**Bayer UK Ltd. Agrochem Division**
Eastern Way, Bury St. Edmunds, Suffolk IP32 7AH, England
(Main Office: Bayer AG, Bayer Pflanzenschutz, Leverkusen, W. Germany (B.R.D.))
- Bayer Agrochem Courier. irreg.

**Ernest Bayly, Ed. & Pub**
19 Glendale Rd., Bournemouth BH6 4JA, England.
- Talking Machine Review International. bi-m.

**Beau Geste Press**
Barhatch Farm, Cranleigh, Surrey GU6 7NG, England.
- Schmuck. 3 per yr.
- Spanner. bi-m.

**Beaverbrook Newspapers Ltd.**
Fleet St., London E.C.4, Eng.
- Giles Cartoon Annual. (pub. by Daily Express Books Department)
- Rupert Annual. (pub. by Daily Express Books Department)
- Sunday Express. w. ISSN 0039-5196

**Bedfordshire Area Health Authority**
- Medical Centre Journal. (pub. by Luton & Dunstable Hospital)

**Bedfordshire Historical Record Society**
White Crescent Press, Luton, Beds., England.
- Bedfordshire Historical Record Society. Publications. a. ISSN 0067-4826

**Beecham Foods**
Beecham House, Great West Rd., Brentford, Middlesex, Eng.
- Nutrition Information Bulletin. 6 per yr. ISSN 0029-6627

**De Beers Industrial Diamond Division Pty. Ltd.**
Charters, Sunninghill, Ascot, Berks SL5 9PX, England
- Industrial Diamond Review. m. ISSN 0019-8145 (Subscr. to: Will Kitchen Jr. Ltd., 131 Fleet Street, London EC4A 2BH, England)

**Belfast Natural History and Philosophical Society**
7 College Square North, Belfast, Northern Ireland.
- Belfast History and Philosophical Society. Proceedings and Reports. irreg. ISSN 0067-5350

**Belgian Chamber of Commerce in Great Britain**
6 Belgrave Square, London S.W.1., Eng.
- Belgian Chamber of Commerce in Great Britain. Journal. q. ISSN 0005-8378

**G. Bell & Sons Ltd.**
York House, Portugal St., London WC2A 2NL, Eng.
- Mathematical Gazette. 4 per yr. ISSN 0025-5572 (Mathematical Association)
- Writers and Their Background. irreg.

**Bell Publishing Ltd.**
Hollygate, Chestergate, Stockport SK3 0BD, England.
- Industry Northwest. bi-m.

**Bell's Fashion Bureau (1940) Ltd.**
Kent House, Market Place, London, W1N 8EJ, England.
- Grafton Fashions for Men. a. ISSN 0072-5315

**Belmont-Maitland Ltd.**
188 Piccadilly, London W.1, Eng.
- Tradition. m. ISSN 0041-0594 (International Society of Military Collectors)

**Benn Brothers Ltd.**
25 New Street Square, London EC4A 3JA, England.
- Benn's Hardware Directory; the year book of the Hardware Trade Journal. a. ISSN 0067-5725
- Benn's Hardware Price List. 6 per yr. ISSN 0005-8823
- Benn's International Hardware Exporter. a.
- Bindery Data Index. a.
- Builders' Merchants' Journal. m. ISSN 0007-3288
- Building Board Directory. biennial. ISSN 0068-3523
- Cabinet Maker and Retail Furnisher. w. ISSN 0007-9278
- Carpet and Floor Covering World. m (10 per yr.)
- Chemical Industry Directory. a. ISSN 0069-2980
- Chemist and Druggist; for retailer, wholesaler, manfuacturer. w. ISSN 0009-3033 (Pharmaceutical Society of Ireland IE) (Co-sponsor: Pharmaceutical Society of Northern Ireland)
- Chemist and Druggist Directory. a.
- Directory to the Furnishing Trade; cabinet maker directory. a. ISSN 0070-6604
- Education Equipment. m. ISSN 0013-1296
- Education Equipment, Primary & Middle Schools Edition. 3 per yr.
- European Leather Guide. a. ISSN 0071-2906
- European Woodworking Machinery Directory. a.
- Export Data; export document requirements of all countries. a.
- Fire Protection Directory. a. ISSN 0071-5409
- Fire Protection Review. m. ISSN 0015-2641
- Forestry and Home Grown Timber. bi-m.
- Gas Directory and Who's Who. a. ISSN 0307-3084
- Gas Marketing. m.
- Gas Marketing Pocket Book and Diary. a. ISSN 0072-0259
- Gas World. m. ISSN 0016-5026
- Gifts. m.
- Gifts Annual Buyers' Guide. a.
- Hardware Trade Journal. w. ISSN 0017-7741
- Horticulture Industry. m.
- International Shipping and Shipbuilding Directory. a. ISSN 0074-8358
- Leather. m. ISSN 0023-9739
- Leathergoods; the journal of the British leather goods and allied trades. m. ISSN 0023-9798
- Marine and Air Catering. m. ISSN 0025-3138
- Natural Gas. m.
- Natural Gas for Commerce. q. ISSN 0306-2414
- Newspaper Press Directory. a.
- Nurseryman and Garden Centre. w. ISSN 0029-6430
- Offset Data Index. a.
- Paper. s-m (plus two additional numbers)
- Paper. World Research and Development. a.
- Paper Review of the Year. a.
- Phillips' Paper Trade Directory- Europe-Mills of the World. a. ISSN 0079-158X
- Ports of the World. a. ISSN 0079-4066
- Printing Trades Directory. a. ISSN 0079-5372
- Printing Trades Journal. m. ISSN 0032-8707
- Printing World. w. ISSN 0032-8715
- Shipping Marks on Timber. triennial (approx.) ISSN 0080-9284
- Shipping World & Shipbuilder. m. ISSN 0037-3931
- Sports and Recreation Equipment. 3 per yr. ISSN 0038-8181
- Sports Trader; the British journal of sports goods and equipment. m. ISSN 0038-8254
- Timber Trade Journal. Annual Special Issue. a. ISSN 0082-4364
- Timber Trades Directory. irreg. ISSN 0082-4372

- Timber Trades Journal and Woodworking Machinery. w. ISSN 0040-7798
- University Equipment. bi-m. ISSN 0041-9303
- Woodworking Industry. m. ISSN 0043-7786
- Woodworking Industry /Buyers' Guide. a.

**Bentham-Moxon Trust**
Royal Botanic Gardens, Kew, Richmond, Surrey TW9 3AB, England.
- Hooker's Icones Planetarium. irreg.

**Berkshire Archaeological Society**
"Turstins", High St., Upton, Didcot, Berks OX11 9JE, England.
- Berkshire Archaeological Journal. a.

**Bexley Christadelphians Ecclesia**
- Light. (pub. by Dawn Book Supply)

**Bharat Sevashram Sangha**
17 Stanlake Villas, London, W.12, Eng.
- Hinduism. q. ISSN 0018-1927

**Bibliographic Press Ltd.**
160 North Gower St., London NW1 2ND, Eng.
- British Geological Literature. q.

**Bibliographical Society**
- Library. (pub. by Oxford University Press)

**Billboard Ltd.**
7 Carnaby St., London W1Y 1PG, England.
- Jazz Journal. m. ISSN 0021-5651

**Clive Bingley (Journals) Ltd.**
16 Pembridge Rd., London W.11, Eng.
- New Library World. m.

**Binsted Publications**
Binsted House, 42a Devonshire Close, Devonshire St., London WIN 2DL, Eng.
- International Beverage News. m. ISSN 0020-6148
- International Bottler and Packer. m. ISSN 0020-6199

**Biochemical Society (Book Depot)**
Box 32, Commerce Way, Colchester, Essex C02 8HP, England.
- Biochemical Journal. Cellular Aspects. s-m (8 vols. per year) ISSN 0306-3283
- Biochemical Journal. Molecular Aspects. s-m (8 vols. per year) ISSN 0306-3275
- Biochemical Society, London. Transactions. 6 per yr.
- Essays in Biochemistry. (pub. by Academic Press Inc. (London) Ltd.)
- Essays in Medical Biochemistry. a.
- Journal of Endocrinology. m.(4 vols. per year) ISSN 0022-0795 (Society for Endocrinology)
- Journal of Reproduction and Fertility. m. ISSN 0022-4251

**Biodeterioration Information Centre**
Univ. of Aston in Birmingham, 80 Coleshill St, Birmingham B47 PF, Eng.
- Biodeterioration Research Titles. q. ISSN 0300-5801
- International Biodeterioration Bulletin. q. ISSN 0020-6164

**Biological Engineering Society**
- Journal of Medical Engineering & Technology. (pub. by United Trade Press Ltd.)

**Biomedical Information Service**
The University, Sheffield S10 2TN, Eng.
- Biological Rhythms. m.
- Cell Membranes. m.
- Cyclic Amp. m.
- Enzyme Regulation. m.
- Immunohistochemistry. m.
- Intestinal Absorption. m.
- Nerve Cell Biology. m.
- Neurophysiology. m.
- Radioimmunoassay. m.
- Renal Physiology. m. ISSN 0300-3434
- Renal Transplantation and Dialysis. m.
- Ribosomes. m.

**Biometrika Trust**
Univ. College, Gower St., London WC1E 6BT, Eng.
- Biometrika. 3 per yr. ISSN 0006-3444

**Birds and Country**
79 Surbiton Hill Park, Surbiton, Surrey, Eng.
- Birds and Country. q. ISSN 0006-3673

**Birmingham and Midland Society for Genealogy and Heraldry**
48, Howard Road, Kings Heath, Birmingham B14 7PQ, England.
- Midland Ancestor. q. ISSN 0307-2851

**Birmingham & Warwickshire Archaeological Society**
Birmingham & Midland Institute, Margaret Street, Birmingham, England.
- Birmingham & Warwickshire Archaeological Society. Transactions. a.

**Birmingham Chamber of Industry and Commerce**
75 Harborne Rd., Edgbaston, Birmingham B15 3DH, Eng.
- Midlands Industry and Commerce. m. ISSN 0026-3311

**Birmingham Medical and Dental Schools**
Birmingham 15, Eng.
- Queens Medical Magazine. 3 per yr. ISSN 0033-6033 (Birmingham Medical Society)

**Birmingham Medical Society**
- Queens Medical Magazine. (pub. by Birmingham Medical and Dental Schools)

**Birmingham Post & Mail Ltd.**
Colmore Circus, Birmingham B4 6AZ, Eng.
- Sunday Mercury; and Weekly Post. w. ISSN 0039-5242

**Bit Information Service**
146 Great Western Rd., London W.11, Eng.
- Bitman. q.

**Bizarre Acres Publications**
19 Danesmoor, Ruscote, Banbury, Oxon, England.
- Country Bizarre. q. ISSN 0045-8848

**J. J. Black**
Somerset House, Cranleigh, Surrey, Eng.
- Accordion Times. m. ISSN 0001-4656
- Southern Farmer. m. ISSN 0038-4100

**Black Country Society**
49 Victoria Rd., Tipton, West Midlands, Eng.
- Blackcountryman. q. ISSN 0006-4335

**Black Dwarf**
7 Carlisle St., London W1A 4PZ, Eng.
- Black Dwarf. fortn.

**A. & C. Black Ltd.**
35 Bedford Row, London WC1R 4Jh, England.
- Girls School Year Book. a. ISSN 0072-4564
- Public and Preparatory Schools, London. Year Book; official book of reference of the Headmasters Conference and of the Incorporated Association of Preparatory Schools. a. ISSN 0079-7537
- Who's Who; an Annual Biographical Dictionary. a. ISSN 0083-937X
- Writers' and Artists' Year Book; a directory for writers, artists, playwrights, writers for film, radio and television, photographers and composers. a. ISSN 0084-2664

**Black Watch**
- Red Hackle. (pub. by Holmes McDougall Ltd.)

**Black Wax Magazine**
Flat 3, 108 Greyhound Lane, London SW 16, England.
- Black Wax Magazine. m.

**Blackface Sheep Breeders' Association**
c/o Ed. & Pub. A. W. Bryson, 24 Beresford Terrace, Ayr KA7 2EL, Scotland.
- Blackface Sheep Breeders' Association Journal. a.

**Blackfriars**
Oxford, Eng.
- New Blackfriars. m. ISSN 0028-4289 (English Dominicans)

**Blackfriars Press Periodicals Ltd.**
Box 80, Leicester, Eng.
- Motorists Guide to New & Used Car Prices. m. ISSN 0027-2302

**Blackpool Gazette & Herald Ltd.**
Box 20, Victoria St., Blackpool, Eng.
- West Lancashire Evening Gazette. d. ISSN 0043-3160

**Blackpool Hotel and Guest House Association Ltd.**
87a Coronation St., Blackpool F Y1 4 PD, Lancs., Eng.
- Blackpool Hotel & Guest House Association Ltd. Journal. w. ISSN 0006-4351

**Blackstaff Press Ltd.**
16 Donegall Square South, Belfast BT1 5JF, N. Ireland.
- Irish Booklore. a. ISSN 0044-8346
- Soundings. a.

**Basil Blackwell & Mott Ltd.**
108 Cowley Rd., Oxford OX4 1JF, Eng.
- American Philosophical Quarterly. q. ISSN 0003-0481
- American Philosophical Quarterly. Monograph Series. a. ISSN 0084-6422 (University of Pittsburgh. Department of Philosophy US)
- Analysis. 6 per yr. ISSN 0003-2638
- British Journal of Educational Studies. 3 per yr. ISSN 0007-1005
- Byzantine and Modern Greek Studies. a.
- Didaskalos. a. ISSN 0419-1188 (Joint Association of Classical Teachers)
- German Life and Letters. q. ISSN 0016-8777
- Journal for the Theory of Social Behaviour. s-a. ISSN 0021-8308
- Journal of Common Market Studies. q. ISSN 0021-9886
- Journal of Industrial Economics. q. ISSN 0022-1821
- Journal of Management Studies. 3 per yr. ISSN 0022-2380
- Metaphilosophy. q. ISSN 0026-1068 (State University of New York at Albany. Department of Philosophy US)
- Mind; a quarterly review of philosphy. q. ISSN 0026-4423 (Mind Association)
- New Universities Quarterly. q.
- Oxford Bulletin of Economics and Statistics. q. ISSN 0305-9049
- Philological Society Transactions. a. ISSN 0079-1636
- Philosophy of Education Society of Great Britain Proceedings. a. ISSN 0048-3923
- R & D Management. 3 per yr. ISSN 0033-6807
- Ratio. s-a. ISSN 0034-0006
- Social and Economic Administration. 3 per yr. ISSN 0037-7643 (University of Exeter. Faculty of Social Studies)

**Blackwell Scientific Publications Ltd.**
Osney Mead, Oxford OX2 OEL, Eng.
- African Journal of Medicine & Medical Sciences. q. ISSN 0309-3913
- Anaesthesia. 10 per yr. ISSN 0003-2409
- Australian Journal of Ecology. q. ISSN 0307-692X (Ecological Society of America US)
- Australian Society for Medical Research. Proceedings. a. ISSN 0067-2130
- British Journal of Dermatology. m. ISSN 0007-0963
- British Journal of Haematology. m. ISSN 0007-1048
- Cell & Tissue Kinetics. bi-m. ISSN 0008-8730
- Child: Care, Health and Development. bi-m. ISSN 0305-1862
- Clay Minerals. q. ISSN 0009-8558
- Clinical Allergy. bi-m. ISSN 0009-9090
- Clinical & Experimental Dermatology. q.
- Clinical and Experimental Immunology. m. ISSN 0009-9104 (British Society for Immunology)
- Clinical and Experimental Pharmacy and Physiology. bi-m.
- Clinical Endocrinology. m. ISSN 0300-0664
- Clinical Otolaryngology and Allied Sciences. q. ISSN 0307-7772
- Clinical Science and Molecular Medicine. m. ISSN 0301-0538 (Medical Research Society) (Co-Sponsor: Biochemical Society)
- East African Wildlife Journal. q. ISSN 0070-8038 (East African Wildlife Society)
- Ecological Entomology. q.
- Freshwater Biology. bi-m. ISSN 0046-5070
- Geophysical Journal of the Royal Astronomical Society. m. ISSN 0016-8009
- Histopathology. bi-m. (International Academy of Pathology)
- Immunology. m. ISSN 0019-2805 (British Society for Immunology)
- Journal of Advanced Nursing. bi-m. ISSN 0309-2402
- Journal of Animal Ecology. 3 per yr. ISSN 0021-8790 (British Ecological Society)
- Journal of Applied Chemistry and Biotechnology. m. (Society of Chemical Industry)

- Journal of Applied Ecology. 3 per yr. ISSN 0021-8901 (British Ecological Society)
- Journal of Biogeography. 4 per yr. ISSN 0305-0270
- Journal of Biosocial Science. q. ISSN 0021-9320 (Galton Foundation)
- Journal of Bryology. s-a. ISSN 0373-6687
- Journal of Clinical Pharmacy. q. ISSN 0308-6593
- Journal of Consumer Studies & Home Economics. q.
- Journal of Ecology. 3 per yr. ISSN 0022-0477 (British Ecological Society)
- Journal of Food Technology. bi-m. ISSN 0022-1163 (Institute of Food Science and Technology of the United Kingdom)
- Journal of Immunogenetics. bi-m.
- Journal of Microscopy. 9 per yr. ISSN 0022-2720 (Royal Microscopical Society)
- Journal of Molluscan Studies. 3 per yr.
- Journal of Oral Rehabilitation; clinical dental science and materials. q. ISSN 0305-182X
- Journal of Small Animal Practice. m. ISSN 0022-4510 (British Small Animal Veterinary Association)
- Journal of the Science of Food and Agriculture. m. ISSN 0022-5142 (Society of Chemical Industry)
- Journal of the Society of Cosmetic Chemists. m.
- Mammal Review. q. ISSN 0305-1838 (Mammal Society)
- Medical Education. bi-m. (Association for the Study of Medical Education)
- Neuropathology and Applied Neurobiology. bi-m. ISSN 0305-1846
- New Phytologist. bi-m. ISSN 0028-646X
- Pesticide Science; a journal of international research and technology on crop protection & pest control. bi-m. ISSN 0031-613X (Society of Chemical Industry)
- Phycologia; dedicated to the promotion of phycology. q. ISSN 0031-8884 (International Phycological Society)
- Physiological Entomology. q. ISSN 0307-6962
- Postgraduate Medical Journal. m. ISSN 0032-5473 (Fellowship of Postgraduate Medicine) (Dist. in U.S. by: Williams & Wilkins Co., 428 E. Preston St., Baltimore, MD 21202)
- Royal Astronomical Society. Monthly Notices. m. ISSN 0035-8711
- Royal Astronomical Society. Quarterly Journal. q. ISSN 0035-8738
- Royal Astronomical Society, England. Memoirs. irreg.
- Royal Microscopical Society. Proceedings. bi-m. ISSN 0035-9017
- Science Progress; a quarterly review of current developments in science. q. ISSN 0036-8504 (Dist. in U.S. by: J. B. Lippincott Company, E. Washington Square, Philadelphia, PA 19105)
- Sedimentology. 4 per yr. ISSN 0037-0746 (International Association of Sedimentologists)
- Systematic Entomology. q. ISSN 0307-6970
- Weed Research. q. ISSN 0043-1737 (European Weed Research Council)

**William Blackwood & Sons Ltd.**
32 Thistle St., Edinburgh EH2 1HA, Scotland.
- Blackwood's. m. ISSN 0006-436X
- Scottish Bankers Magazine. q. ISSN 0036-9128 (Institute of Bankers in Scotland)

**Blakeham Publications Ltd.**
Spotlight House, One Benwell Rd., Holloway, London N7 7AX, England.
- Hi-Fi for Pleasure. m.

**Blakes (Norfolk Broads Holidays) Ltd.**
Wroxham, Norwich NR12 8DH, England.
- Blakes Holidays Afloat. a.

**Blandford Business Press**
Pembroke House, Wellesley Rd., Croydon CR9 2BX, England.
- Business Travel World; the commercial house travel journal. m.
- Catering and Hotel Management. m. ISSN 0018-6104
- Catering & Hotel Management Year Book & Diary. a. ISSN 0069-1194
- Freight News Weekly. w.
- Glass Age. m. ISSN 0017-0992
- Industrial Catering. a. ISSN 0073-7364
- Junior Age. m. ISSN 0022-6483 (National Children's Wear Association)
- Junior Age Year Book and Diary. a.
- Shopfitting International; design, construction, equipment, fitting. m. ISSN 0037-4202

- Travel World Year Book and Diary. a. ISSN 0082-6219

**Blandford Press Ltd.**
167 High Holborn, London WC1V 6PH, England.
- Archaeologists' Year Book. a.

**Blink Publications Ltd.**
52 Walsworth Rd., Hitchin, Herts SG4 9SX, England.
- Blues-Link. irreg.

**Bliss Classification Association**
c/o Library, Commonwealth Institute, Kensington High St., London W86NQ, England.
- Bliss Classification Bulletin. a. ISSN 0520-2795

**Bluebell Railway Ltd.**
Sheffield Park Station, Sussex, England.
- Bluebell News. q. ISSN 0520-3015 (Bluebell Railway Preservation Society)

**Bluebell Railway Preservation Society**
- Bluebell News. (pub. by Bluebell Railway Ltd.)

**Blues Unlimited**
38a Sackville Rd., Bexhill-On-Sea, Sussex, Eng.
- Blues Unlimited. m. ISSN 0006-5153

**Board for Social Responsibility of the General Synod**
- Crucible. (pub. by Church of England)

**Board of Celtic Studies**
- Geiriadur Prifysgol Cymru. (pub. by University of Wales Press)
- Llen Cymru. (pub. by University of Wales Press)

**Board of Education of the General Synod**
- Together. (pub. by Church of England)

**Boat Enquiries Ltd.**
7 Walton Well Rd., Oxford, England.
- Lazy Man's Guide to Holidays Afloat. a. ISSN 0075-8272

**Boat World Publications**
39 East St., Epsom, Surrey, England.
- Boat World Guide to Motor Cruisers Under 4500 (Pounds Sterling) a.

**Boc-Murex**
Hertford Rd., Waltham Cross, Herts, Eng.
- Welder. q. ISSN 0043-2237

**Bodleian Library**
Oxford OX1 3BG, England.
- Bodleian Library Record. irreg. ISSN 0067-9488

**Bolton College of Education**
Chadwick St., Bolton, BL2 1JW, England.
- Vocational Aspect of Education. 3 per yr.

**Bond Street Publishers Ltd.**
Ashton Court, 1 Oxford Rd., Aylesbury, Bucks, Eng.
- Writer; the magazine for the freelance writer. m.

**Bondholder's Register (Publishers) Ltd.**
5 the White House, Beacon Rd., Crowborough, Sussex, Eng.
- Bondholder's Register. s-m (plus Interim Rights Supplement in alternate weeks) ISSN 0006-7075

**Books for Your Children**
c/o Anne Wood, Ed., 90 Gillhurst Rd., Harborne, Birmingham 17, England.
- Books for Your Children. q. ISSN 0006-7482

**Booksellers Association of Great Britain & Ireland**
154 Buckingham Palace Rd., London SW1W 9TZ, England.
- Booksellers Association of Great Britain and Ireland. List of Members. a. ISSN 0068-0249
- Booksellers Association of Great Britain and Ireland. Trade Reference Book. irreg. ISSN 0068-0257

**Boosey & Hawkes Music Publishers Ltd.**
295 Regent St., London W1A 1BR, Eng
(U.S. Address: Boosey & Hawkes, Inc., Oceanside, N.Y.)
- Tempo; a quarterly review of modern music. q. ISSN 0040-2982

**Boost**
5 Wharf Lane, Solihull, Warwickshire, Eng.
- Boost. m. ISSN 0006-7601

**Borax Consolidated Ltd**
Borax House, Carlisle Place, London S.W. 1, Eng.
- Boron in Agriculture. q. ISSN 0006-7814
- Boron in Glass. q. ISSN 0006-7822

**Border Press Agency Ltd.**
12 Lonsdale St., Carlisle, Eng.
- Cumbria Business Digest. w.
- Lakescene-What's on in Lakeland. m.

**Borodin Communications Ltd.**
49 Stonegate, York YO1 2AW, Eng.
- York-What's on. w. (Co-Sponsor: York Department of Tourism)

**Botanical Society of Edinburgh**
Royal Botanic Garden, Inverleith Row, Edinburgh EH3 5LR, Scotland.
- Botanical Society of Edinburgh Transactions. a.

**Botanical Society of the British Isles**
c/o Dept. of Botany, British Museum (Natural History), London SW7 5BD, England.
- B S B I Abstracts; abstracts from literature relating to the Vascular plants of the British Isles. a.
- Watsonia. s-a. ISSN 0043-1532

**Bottler & Packer Ltd.**
Binsted House, Devonshire Close, Devonshire St., London, Eng.
- International Paper Board Industry. m. ISSN 0020-8191

**Bourne Society**
c/o 17 Manor Ave., Caterham, Surrey CR3 6AP, England.
- Bourne Society Local History Records. a. ISSN 0520-6790

**Bouverie Publishing Co. Ltd.**
Cliffords Inn, Fetter Lane, London EC4 1PJ, Eng.
- U. K. Press Gazette. w. ISSN 0041-5170

**Bow Publications Ltd.**
240 High Holborn, London W.C.1, Eng.
- Crossbow; a journal of politics. 3 per yr. ISSN 0011-1988

**Bowker Publishing Co. Ltd.**
Erasmus House, Epping, Essex CM16 4BU, England.
- British Music Yearbook. a.

**Bowley Publications**
Box 1, St. Mary's, Isles of Scilly, England.
- Standard Guidebook to the Isles of Scilly. irreg.

**Boys' Brigade, Inc.**
Brigade House, Parsons Green, London SW6 4TH, Eng.
- Boys Brigade Gazette. bi-m. ISSN 0006-8578
- Boys' Brigade, London. Annual Report. a. ISSN 0068-0605
- Junior Stedfast Magazine. (pub. by Stedfast Publishers)
- Stedfast Magazine. (pub. by Stedfast Publishers)

**Bradfield College**
Berkshire RG7 6AY, England, Wilts, Eng.
- Bradfield College Chronicle. 2 per yr. ISSN 0006-8675

**Bradford & Halifax Chambers of Commerce**
- Bradford & Halifax Chambers of Commerce. Chamber of Commerce Journal. (pub. by G. W. Foster Associates Ltd.)
- Bradford and Halifax Chambers of Commerce Members Directory. (pub. by G.W. Foster Associates Ltd.)

**Herbert W. Bradnick**
22 Cross St., Islington, London N.1, Eng.
- Buttons; the journal of the British button industry. m. ISSN 0007-733X

**Bradwell Abbey Field Centre**
Abbey Rd., Bradwell, Milton Keynes MK13 9AP, England.
- Bradwell Abbey Field Centre for the Study of Archaeology, Natural History & Environmental Studies. Occasional Papers. irreg. ISSN 0306-8838

**Branch Line Society**
Hon. General Secretary N. J. Hill, 15 Springwood Hall Gardens, Gledholt, Huddersfield, HD1 4HA, Eng.
- Branch Line News. s-m.

**Brandshare Ltd.**
10 Northburgh St, London EC1V 0AD, England.
- New Psychiatry. fortn.

**Brant Wright Associates Ltd.**
Box No 22, Ashford, Kent, Eng.
- Horological Journal. m. ISSN 0018-5108 (British Horological Institute)

**Breakthru Publications**
38 Penn Crescent, Haywards Heath, Sussex, Eng.
- Breakthru; international poetry magazine. 3 per yr. ISSN 0006-9531

**Brewers Guild Publications Ltd.**
8 Ely Place, Holborn, London EC1N 6SD, Eng.
- Brewer. m. ISSN 0006-9736

**Brewing Research Foundation**
Lyttel Hall, Nutfield, Redhill, Surrey RH1 4RY, Eng.
- Brewing Research Foundation. Bulletin of Current Literature. m.

**Brewster Printing Co.**
Rochester, Kent, Eng.
- Left. m. ISSN 0024-0303

**Bridge West Publications**
56 Harrow Rd., Bristol BS4 3NB, Eng.
- Imprint. s-a. ISSN 0019-3038

**Brighton College**
Brighton BN2 2AL, Sussex, Eng.
- Brightonian. 2 per yr. ISSN 0007-0157

**Brighton Head and Freak Magazine**
c/o John Upton, Ed., 46 Hallett Rd., Brighton, Sussex, Eng.
- Brighton Head and Freak Magazine. irreg. ISSN 0007-0122

**Brimicombe Magazines**
8 St. John's Park, Blackheath, London SE3 7TQ, Eng.
- Paris. 6 per yr. ISSN 0031-1987

**Bristol and Gloucestershire Archaeological Society**
9A Pembroke Rd., Bristol BS8 3AU, England.
- Bristol and Gloucestershire Archaeological Society, Bristol, England. Transactions. a. ISSN 0068-1032

**Bristol & West of England Engineering Manufacturers Association Ltd.**
Royal London House, Queen Charlotte St., Bristol BS1 4EZ, Eng.
- B E M A Bulletin. m. ISSN 0005-304X
- B E M A Engineering Directory. a. ISSN 0067-5709

**Bristol Arts Centre**
415 King Square, Bristol 2, Eng.
- Circle in the Square Broadsheet. 2 per yr.

**Bristol City Museum. Bristol Archaeological Research Group**
Queen Rd., Bristol 8, Eng.
- B A R G Bulletin. 3 per yr.

**Bristol Evening Post**
Temple Way, Bristol BS99 7HD, Eng.
- Green 'un. w. ISSN 0046-6417

**Bristol Industrial Archaeological Society**
c/o Mrs J. Day, Hunters Hill, Oakfield Rd., Keysham, Bristol BS18 1JQ, England.
- B I A S Journal. a.

**Bristol Medico Chirurgical Society**
- Bristol Medico-Chirurgical Journal. (pub. by F. Bailey & Son Ltd.)

**Bristol Naturalists' Society**
City Museum, Bristol 8, England.
- Bristol Naturalists' Society. Proceedings. a. ISSN 0068-1040

**Bristol University Medical Students Club**
Bristol Royal Infirmary, Bristol 2, Eng.
- Black Bag. m. ISSN 0045-2084

**Britain First Press**
50 Pawsons Rd., Croydon, Surrey, England.
- Britain First. m.
- Britain First. m.

**Britain's Sun Club**
- Health and Efficiency. (pub. by Plant News Ltd.)

**British Academy**
- Auctores Britannici Medii Aevi. (pub. by Oxford University Press)
- British Academy, London. Proceedings. (pub. by Oxford University Press)
- Henriette Hertz Trust: Annual Lectures on the Aspects of Art of the British Academy. (pub. by Oxford University Press)
- Henriette Hertz Trust: Annual Master-Mind Lectures of the British Academy. (pub. by Oxford University Press)
- Henriette Hertz Trust: Annual Philosophical Lectures of the British Academy. (pub. by Oxford University Press)
- Schweich Lectures. (pub. by Oxford University Press)

**British Academy of Forensic Sciences**
- Medicine, Science and the Law. (pub. by John Wright & Sons Ltd.)

**British Agents Register**
- British Commercial Agents Review. (pub. by International Commercial Network Ltd.)

**British Agricultural and Garden Machinery Association Ltd.**
Church St., Rickmansworth, Herts WD3 1RQ, Eng.
- A G M Service. (Agricutural and Garden Machinery) m.

**British Agricultural History Society**
Museum of English Rural Life, The University, Whiteknights, Reading, Berks RG6 2AG, Eng.
- Agricultural History Review. s-a. ISSN 0002-1490

**British Air Line Pilots Association**
81 New Rd., Harlington, Hayes, Middlesex, Eng., U.K.
- Log. bi-m. ISSN 0024-5798

**British Aircraft Corp.**
100 Pall Mall, London, Eng.
- Airframe. m. ISSN 0002-2713

**British Airways**
Air Terminal, Victoria, London S.W.1, Eng.
- British Airways News. w.
- High Life. (pub. by Punch Publications Ltd.)

**British Airways. Travel Div.**
Box 115, London SW7 4ED, England.
- British Airways Executive. bi-m.

**British Amateur Athletic Board**
70 Brompton Rd., London SW3 1PE, England.
- British Athletics. a. ISSN 0068-1326

**British Amateur Press Association**
B M- Mono, London W. C. I, Eng.
- British Amateur Journalist. q. ISSN 0007-0238

**British Amateur Scientific Research Association**
Ed.& Pub J. England, Ounsdale Rd., Wombourn, Wolverhampton, Staffs WV5 8BT, Eng.
- B A S R A Journal. q. ISSN 0005-2671

**British & Commonwealth Shipping Co., Ltd.**
Cayzer House, 2 & 4 St. Mary Axe, London EC3A 8BP, Eng.
- Clansman. bi-m. ISSN 0007-0254

**British and Foreign Bible Society**
146 Queen Victoria St., London EC4V 4BX, Eng.
- Word in Action: the Bible in the World. q.

**British and Irish Communist Organisation**
10 Athol St., Belfast BT 12 4GX, Northern Ireland.
- Comment (Belfast) fortn.
- Communist. m.
- Irish Communist. m.
- Problems of Communism. q.

**British Antarctic Survey**
Madingley Rd., Cambridge CB3 0ET, Eng
(Subscr. to: Heffers Printers Ltd., Kings Hedges Rd., Cambridge, Eng.)
- British Antarctic Survey. Bulletin. s-a. ISSN 0007-0262 (Co-sponsor: Natural Environment Research Council)

**British Antique Dealers Association**
20 Rutland Gate, London SW7 1BD, England.
- B A D A Journal. q.

**British Arachnological Society**
c/o Dr. P. Merrett, Ed., Furzebrook Research Station, Wareham, Dorset BH20 5AS, England.
- British Arachnological Society. Bulletin. 3 per yr.

**British Archaeological Association**
61 Old Park Ridings, Winchmore Hill, London, N21 2ET, England.
- British Archaeological Association. Journal. a. ISSN 0068-1288

**British Association for American Studies**
- Journal of American Studies. (pub. by Cambridge University Press)

**British Association for Commercial and Industrial Education**
16 Park Crescent, Regent's Park, London W1N 4AP, Eng.
- B A C I E Journal. m (except Aug.) ISSN 0005-2612

**British Association of Accountants and Auditors, Ltd.**
Stamford House, 2-4 Chiswick High Rd., London W4 1TP, England.
- Registered Accountant. 4 per yr.

**British Association of Americn Square Dance Clubs**
2, Tolmers Gardens, Cuffley, Potters Bar, Herts EN6 4JE, England
- Let's Square Dance. m. ISSN 0301-8881 (Subscr. to:, Mr. S. Nye, 4 Devonshire Gardens, Winchmore Hill, London, N21 2al, England)

**British Association of Chemists**
Hinchley House, 14 Harley St., London W.1, England.
- British Chemist. bi-m. ISSN 0007-0432

**British Association of Colliery Management**
317 Nottingham Rd., Old Basford, Nottingham, Eng.
- National News Letter. q. ISSN 0027-9773

**British Association of Green Crop Driers Ltd.**
Agroup House, 16 Lonsdale Gardens, Tunbridge Wells TN1 1PD, Kent, England.
- Grass. 3 per yr. ISSN 0072-5544

**British Association of Industrial Editors**
2A Elm Bank Gardens, London SW13 0NT, England.
- B. A. I. E. Membership Directory. a.
- B A I E News. m.
- British House Journals; survey. irreg. ISSN 0073-3598

**British Association of Organisers and Lecturers in Physical Education**
c/o Ed. David L. Willey, Polytechnic of North London, Prince of Wales Rd., London N.W.5, England.
- Bulletin of Physical Education. q. ISSN 0007-5043

**British Association of Orientalists**
c/o Dept. of Oriental Manuscripts, British Library, Great Russell St., London WC1, England.
- British Association of Orientalists. Bulletin. biennial.

**British Association of Plastic Surgeons**
- British Journal of Plastic Surgery. (pub. by Longman Group Ltd.)

**British Association of Removers**
279 Grays Inn Rd., London WC1X 8SY, Eng.
- Removals and Storage. m. ISSN 0034-4265

**British Association of Rheumatology and Rehabilitation**
- Rheumatology and Rehabilitation. (pub. by Bailliere Tindall)

**British Association of Social Workers**
16 Kent St., Birmingham B5 6RD, England.
- British Association of Social Workers. Annual Report. a, no. 6, 1976.
- British Journal of Social Work. q. ISSN 0045-3102
- Parliament and Social Work. w. during Parliament session.
- Social Work Today. w. ISSN 0037-8070

**British Association of Teachers of the Deaf**
20 Devonshire Rd., Bolton, Lancashire, Eng.
- Teacher of the Deaf. bi-m. ISSN 0040-0459

**British Association of Urological Surgeons**
● British Journal of Urology. (pub. by Longman Group Ltd.)

**British Astronomical Association**
Burlington House, Piccadilly, London W1V 0NL, England.
● British Astronomical Association. Handbook. a. ISSN 0068-130X
● British Astronomical Association. Journal. 6 per yr. ISSN 0007-0297
● British Astronomical Association. Memoirs. irreg. ISSN 0068-1318

**British Automobile Racing Club**
Thruxton Circuit, Nr. Andover, Hampshire, Eng.
● B A R C News. m. ISSN 0005-2647

**British Bee-Keepers' Association**
13 Orchard Close, Littlebourne, Cantebury, Kent, Eng.
● Bee Craft. m. ISSN 0005-7703

**British Bee Publications Ltd.**
46 Queen St., Geddington, Nr. Kettering, Northants. NN14 1AZ, Eng.
● British Bee Journal. m. ISSN 0007-0327

**British Beer-mat Collectors Society**
142 Leicester St., Wolverhampton WV6 OPS, Staffs., Eng.
● Coasters. m.

**British Blind & Shutter Association**
● Blinds and Shutters. (pub. by Wheatland Journals Ltd.)

**British Boot and Shoe Institution**
The Old School, Station Rd., Cogenhoe, Northampton NN7 1LT, England.
● British Boot and Shoe Institution. Journal. bi-m. ISSN 0007-0351

**British Broadcasting Corp.**
35 Marylebone High St., London W1M 4AA, Eng.
● Ariel. m. ISSN 0004-1335
● British Broadcasting Corporation. B B C Engineering. irreg.(approx. 4 per year) ISSN 0005-2817
● British Broadcasting Corporation. B B C Handbook. a. ISSN 0068-1377
● British Broadcasting Corporation. B B C Lunchtime Lectures. irreg. ISSN 0521-9477
● Listener. w. ISSN 0024-4392
● London Calling. m. ISSN 0024-600X
● Radio Times. w. ISSN 0033-8060

**British Broadcasting Corp. Arabic Service**
Bush House, P.O. Box 76, Strand, London WC2B 4PH, England.
● Huna London; Arabic radio times. m.

**British Bromeliad Society**
c/o R. J. Lucibell, Ed., Queen Mary College, London E1 4NS, England.
● Bromeliads. irreg. (approx. q) ISSN 0084-8107

**British Bureau of Television Advertising**
Knighton House, 52/66 Mortimer St., London W1N 7DG, England.
● British Bureau of Television Advertising. B B T A Bulltein. irreg. (approx. 5-6 per yr.)

**British Caledonian Airways Ltd**
Gatwick Airport-London, Horley, Surrey, Eng.
● British Caledonium International. m.

**British Campaign for the Release of Indonesian Political Prisoners**
103 Tilehurst Rd., Wandsworth Common, London S.W. 18, England.
● Tapol. bi-m.

**British Canoe Union**
● Canoeing. (pub. by Ocean Publications Ltd.)

**British Carbonization Research Association**
Chesterfield, Derbyshire, Eng.
● B C R A Review; a quarterly guide to published literature dealing with coke and coal tar. q. ISSN 0305-8131

**British Cardiac Society**
● British Heart Journal. (pub. by British Medical Association)

**British Carpet Manufacturers Association**
Aykroyd House, Hoo Road, Kidderminster, Worcs. DY10 1NB, England.
● British Carpet Manufacturers' Association. Index of Quality Names. 3 per yr.

**British Cartographic Society**
Dept. of Land Surveying, North East London Polytechnic, Forest Rd., London E17 4JB, Eng.
● Cartographic Journal. s-a. ISSN 0008-7041

**British Cast Iron Research Association (BCIRA)**
Alvechurch, Birmingham, Eng.
● B C I R A Abstracts of Foundry Literature. bi-m. ISSN 0005-2868
● Russian Castings Production. m. ISSN 0036-0201

**British Cave Research Association**
c/o Bryan Ellis, 30 Main Rd., Westonzoyland, Bridgewater, Somerset TA7 0EB, England.
● British Cave Research Association. Bulletin. q.
● British Cave Research Association. Transactions. irreg. (approx 4 per yr) ISSN 0305-859X

**British Ceramic Plant & Machinery Manufacturers' Association**
P.O. Box 9, Sunbury, Middlesex TW16 6BX, England.
● British Ceramic Review. q.

**British Ceramic Research Association**
Queens Rd., Penkhull, Stoke-on-Trent ST4 7LQ, Eng.
● British Ceramic Abstracts. m. ISSN 0300-4570
● British Ceramic Research Association. Special Publications. irreg. (2-3 per yr.) no. 90, 1977.
● In Fact. q.
● Symposium on Special Ceramics, Stoke-On-Trent, England. Special Ceramics, Proceedings. (pub. by Academic Press, Inc US)

**British Ceramic Society**
Shelton House, Stoke Rd., Shelton, Stoke- on- Trent ST4 2DR, England.
● British Ceramic Society. Proceedings. irreg. ISSN 0524-5141
● British Ceramic Society. Publications. 8 per yr. ISSN 0007-0394

**British Chess Federation**
c/o A.R. Gooderson, 43 Roman Road, Steyning, Sussex BN4 3FN, England.
● British Chess Federation. Awards in Problem Tourneys. a.

**British Chess Magazine Ltd.**
9 Market St., St. Leonards on Sea, Sussex TN38 0DQ, Eng.
● British Chess Magazine. m. ISSN 0007-0440

**British Chess Problem Society**
c/o G. W. Chandler, 46 Worcester Rd., Sutton, Surrey, Eng.
● Problemist. bi-m. ISSN 0032-9398

**British Club Year Book & Directory Ltd.**
8 Cavendish Place, London W.1., England.
● British Club Year Book. biennial. ISSN 0524-5168

**British Coke Research Association**
Chesterfield, Derbyshire, England.
● Carbonization Research Report. irreg.

**British Combustion Equipment Manufacturers Association**
● British Combustion. (pub. by Prestige Publications, Ltd.)

**British Computer Society**
29 Portland Place, London W.1, Eng.
● Computer Journal. q. ISSN 0010-4620
● Computing Europe. (pub. by Haymarket Publishing Ltd.)
● Educational Yearbook. a.

**British Correspondence Chess Association**
c/o J. Skipworth, Ed., 3 Pingot Rd., New Mills via Stockport SK12 4JH, England
(Subscr. to: T. Paterson, Whitestones, Maddox Lane, Little Bookham, Leatherhead, Surrey KT23 3BS, Eng.)
● Correspondence Chess. q.

**British Council**
65 Davies St., London W1Y 2AA, Eng.
● British Book News. m. ISSN 0007-0343
● Educational Broadcasting International. (pub. by Peter Peregrinus Ltd.)

● English Language Teaching Journal. (pub. by Oxford University Press)

**British Council. English-Teaching Information Centre**
10 Spring Gardens, London SW1A 2BN, England.
● Academic Courses in Great Britain Relevant to the Teaching of English to Speakers of Other Languages. a.
● English-Teaching Information Centre, London. Information Guides. irreg.

**British Council. Medical Department**
65 Davies St., London W1Y 2AA, England.
● British Medical Bulletin. 3 per yr. ISSN 0007-1420
● British Medicine. m.

**British Council for Rehabilitation of the Disabled**
Tavistock Sq., London W.C.1, Eng.
● Rehabilitation. q. ISSN 0034-3528

**British Council of Churches**
10 Eaton Gate, London SW1W 9BT, England.
● One World/Vision One. 6 per yr. ISSN 0303-125X

**British Country Music Association**
P.O. Box 2, Newton Abbot TQ12 4HT, England.
● British Country Music Association. Yearbook. a. ISSN 0308-4698

**British Cycling Federation**
70 Brompton Rd, London SW3 1EN, England.
● British Cycling Federation. Handbook. a. ISSN 0068-1938

**British Deaf Association**
38 Victoria Place, Carlisle, England.
● British Deaf News. bi-m. ISSN 0007-0602

**British Decorators Association**
6 Haywra St., Harrogate, Yorkshire HG1 5BL, Eng.
● British Decorator. m.
● British Decorators Association. Members Reference Handbook. a.

**British Dental Association**
64 Wimpole St., London W1M 8AL, Eng.
● British Dental Journal. s-m. ISSN 0007-0610

**British Diabetic Association**
3-6 Alfred Place, London WCIE 7EE, Eng.
● Balance. s-a. ISSN 0005-4216

**British Direct Mail Marketing Association**
1 New Burlington St., London W1X 1FD, England.
● B. D. M. M. A. News. 5 per yr.

**British Ecological Society**
● Journal of Animal Ecology. (pub. by Blackwell Scientific Publications Ltd.)
● Journal of Applied Ecology. (pub. by Blackwell Scientific Publications Ltd.)
● Journal of Ecology. (pub. by Blackwell Scientific Publications Ltd.)

**British Educational Administration Society**
Further Education Staff College, Blagdon, Bristol BS18 6RG, England.
● Educational Administration. 3 per yr. ISSN 0305-7496

**British Educational Research Association**
● Research Intelligence. (pub. by Studies in Education Ltd.)

**British Epilepsy Association**
3-6 Alfred Place, London WC1E 7ED, England.
● Epilepsy News. q.

**British Equine Veterinary Association**
93 Mill Lane, Fordham, Ely, Cambridgeshire CB7 SNH, England.
● Equine Veterinary Journal. q. ISSN 0425-1644

**British Esperanto Association**
140 Holland Park Ave., London, Eng.
● Brita Esperantisto. bi-m.
● British Esperantist. m. ISSN 0007-067X
● Esperanto News. bi-m.

**British European Associated Publishers Ltd.**
7 Abingdon Rd., London W8 6AH, England.
● Home and Freezer Digest. m. ISSN 0305-8751

**British Farmer and Stockbreeder Ltd.**
● British Farmer and Stockbreeder. (pub. by I.P.C. Business Press Ltd.)

**British Federation of Film Societies**
81 Dean St., London W.1, Eng.
● Film. m. ISSN 0015-1025

**British Federation of Folk Clubs**
Cecil Sharp House, 2 Regents Park Road, London
NW1 7AY, Eng.
● Folk News. bi-m.

**British Federation of Master Printers**
11 Bedford Row, London, WC1R 4DX, England.
● British Printing Industries Federation. Printing
Industries Annual. a.

**British Federation of Music Festivals**
106 Gloucester Place, London W1H 3DB, England.
● British Federation of Music Festivals. Yearbook.
a.

**British Film Fund Agency**
P.O.B. 569, London S.E.1, England
● British Film Fund Agency. Annual Report. a.
ISSN 0068-2004 (Avail. from: H.M.S.O., c/o
Liaison Officer, Atlantic House, London EC1P
1BW, England)

**British Film Institute**
81 Dean St., London W1V AA, Eng
(U.S. Address: 111 Eighth Ave., New York, NY
10011)
● British National Film Catalogue. q. ISSN 0007-
1552
● Monthly Film Bulletin. m. ISSN 0027-0407
● Sight and Sound; the international film quarterly.
q. ISSN 0037-4806

**British Fire Services Association**
86 London Rd., Leicester LE2 0QR, Eng.
● British Fire Services Association. Journal. q.

**British Flower Industry Association**
281 Flower Market, New Covent Garden Market,
London SW8 5NB, England.
● British Flower. m.

**British Food Manufacturing Industries Research
Association**
Randalls Road, Leatherhead, Surrey, Eng.
● Abstracts from Current Scientific and Technical
Literature. m. ISSN 0001-3439
● Overseas Food Legislation Manual. s-a (updates of
base vol.)

**British Footwear Manufacturers Federation**
72 Dean St., London W1V 5HB, England.
● Footwear Industry Statistical Review. a.

**British Friesian Cattle Society of Great-Britain &
Ireland**
Scotsbridge House, Rickmansworth, Herts, WD3
3BB, England.
● British Friesian Herd Book. a. ISSN 0068-2012
● British Friesian Journal. bi-m. ISSN 0007-0726

**British Frozen Food Federation**
Honeypot Lane, Colsterworth, Grantham,
Lincolnshire NG33 5LY, England.
● British Frozen Food Federation. Year Book. a.

**British Fuchsia Society**
72 Ash Lane, Hale Altrincham, Ches., England.
● Fuchsia Annual. a. ISSN 0071-9730

**British Gas Corporation**
59 Bryanston Street, London, W1A 2AZ, England.
● British Gas Corporation. Report and Accounts. a.
ISSN 0072-0216

**British Geriatric Society**
● Age and Ageing. (pub. by Bailliere Tindall)

**British Glass Industry Research Association**
Northumberland Rd., Sheffield S10 2UA, England.
● British Glass Industry Research Association.
Annual Report. a. ISSN 0068-2020

**British Gliding Association**
Kimberley House, Vaughan Way, Leicester,
England.
● Sailplane and Gliding. bi-m. ISSN 0036-2735

**British Goat Society**
Rougham, Bury St. Edmunds, Suffolk, England.
● British Goat Society. Herd Book. a. ISSN 0068-
2039
● British Goat Society. Monthly Journal. m.(11 per
yr) ISSN 0007-0734

● British Goat Society. Year Book. a. ISSN 0068-
2047

**British Golf Greenkeepers Association**
Chilberton House, Doods Rd., Reigate, Surrey,
England.
● British Golf Greenkeeper. m. ISSN 0007-0742

**British Grassland Society**
c/o Grassland Research Institute, Hurley Nr.
Maidenhead, Berks, Eng.
● British Grassland Society. Journal. q. ISSN 0007-
0750

**British Hardware Federation**
20 Harborne Rd., Edgbaston, Birmingham B15 3AB,
Eng.
● Hardware Today. m.

**British Herpetological Society**
c/o Zoological Society of London, Regents Park,
London N.W.1, Eng.
● British Journal of Herpetology. s-a. ISSN 0007-
1056

**British Homoeopathic Association**
27a Devonshire St, London W1N 1RJ, England.
● Homoeopathy. bi-m.

**British Horological Institute**
● Horological Journal. (pub. by Brant Wright
Associates Ltd.)

**British Hospitals Contributory Schemes Association**
30 Lancaster Gate, London W2 4LT, England.
● British Hospitals Contributory Schemes
Association. Directory of Convalescent Homes
Serving the Provinces. biennial. ISSN 0068-208X
● British Hospitals Contributory Schemes
Association. Directory of Hospitals Contributory
Scheme Benefits. biennial  ISSN 0068-2098
● British Hospitals Contributory Schemes
Association. Report. a. ISSN 0068-2101

**British Hotels, Restaurants and Caterers Association**
13 Cork St., London W1X 2BH, Eng.
● British Hotelier and Restaurateur. m. ISSN 0007-
0807
● Official Guide to Hotels & Restaurants in Great
Britain, Ireland and Overseas. a. ISSN 0307-062X

**British Humanist Association**
13 Prince of Wales Terrace, London W8 5PG, Eng.
● Humanist Newsletter. 12 per yr.

**British Hydromechanics Research Association**
Cranfield, Bedford MK43 0AJ, Eng
(Dist. in U.S. by: Air Science Co., Box 143,
Corning, NY 14830)
● Civil Engineering Hydraulics Abstracts. m. ISSN
0305-9456
● Cranfield Fluidics Conference. Proceedings. irreg.,
7th, 1977. ISSN 0070-1424
● Fluid Flow Measurement Abstracts. bi-m. ISSN
0305-9235
● Fluid Power Abstracts. m. ISSN 0015-4644
● Fluid Power Symposium. Proceedings. irreg., 4th,
1975. ISSN 0071-6278
● Fluid Sealing Abstracts. bi-m. ISSN 0015-4660
● Fluidics Feedback. bi-m. ISSN 0015-4679
● Industrial Aerodynamics Abstracts. bi-m. ISSN
0019-7823
● International Conference on Fluid Sealing.
Proceedings. irreg. (approx. biennial) 7th, 1976.
ISSN 0074-3089
● International Dredging Abstracts. q. (U.S. Orders
to: Air Science Co., P.O. Box 143, Corning, NY
14830)
● Pumps and Other Fluids Machinery Abstracts. bi-
m. ISSN 0302-2870
● Solid-Liquid Flow Abstracts. q. ISSN 0038-1063
● Tribos-Tribology Abstracts. m. ISSN 0041-2694

**British Ichthyological Society**
60, Newfields, Welwyn, Garden City, Herts AL8
6YT, England.
● British Ichthyological Society. Newsletter. bi-m.

**British Independent Steel Producers Association**
5 Cromwell Rd, London S.W. 7 2HX, England.
● British Independent Steel Companies and Their
Products. irreg.

**British Industrial and Scientific International
Translation Service**
● Ferrous and Non-Ferrous Science and Technology
Lists-British Industrial and Scientific International
Translations. (pub. by Metals Society)

**British Industrial Biological Research Association**
● Food and Cosmetics Toxicology. (pub. by
Pergamon Press, Inc. US)

**British Industrial Publicity Overseas Ltd.**
Walter House, Bedford St., London W.C.2, Eng.,
U.K.
● British Industry and Engineering. q. ISSN 0007-
0823

**British Institute in Eastern Africa**
c/o British Academy, Burlington House, Picadilly,
London W1V 0NS, England.
● British Institute in Eastern Africa. Report. a. ISSN
0068-2152

**British Institute of Archaeology at Ankara**
c/o British Academy, Burlington House, Piccadilly,
London W1V 0NS, England.
● Anatolian Studies. a. ISSN 0066-1546

**British Institute of Cleaning Science**
87/89 Central Buildings, London SE1 17Y, London
SE1 17Y, England.
● C I N. (Cleaning Industry News) q.

**British Institute of International and Comparative
Law**
32 Furnival St., London EC4A 1JN, England.
● British Institute of International and Comparative
Law. Comparative Law Series. irreg. ISSN 0068-
2160
● British Institute of International and Comparative
Law. International Law Series. irreg. ISSN 0068-
2179
● British Institute of International and Comparative
Law. Quarterly Newsletter. q.
● British Practice in International Law. irreg. ISSN
0007-1676
● Bulletin of Legal Developments; a fortnightly
survey of U. K., European, foreign,
commonwealth and international legal events.
fortn. ISSN 0007-4969
● Common Market Law Review. (pub. by A. W.
Sijthoff International Publishing Co. NE)
● International and Comparative Law Quarterly. q.
ISSN 0020-5893
● International Commercial Arbitration. (pub. by
Oceana Publications, Inc. US)

**British Institute of Management**
● Top Management Abstracts. (pub. by Anbar
Publications Ltd.)

**British Institute of Management Foundation**
Management House, Parker St., London WC2B
5PT, Eng.
● Management Review & Digest. q.

**British Institute of Non-Destructive Testing**
53-55 London Rd., Southend-on-Sea, England, Eng.
● British Journal of Non-Destructive Testing. bi-m.
ISSN 0007-1137

**British Institute of Radiology**
32 Welbeck St., London W1M 7PG, Eng.
● British Journal of Radiology. m. ISSN 0007-1285

**British Institute of Recorded Sound**
29 Exhibition Rd., London S.W.7, Eng.
● Recorded Sound. q. ISSN 0034-1630

**British Interlingua Society**
14 Ventnor Court, Wostenholm Rd., Sheffield S7
1LB, England
(Subscription Address: c/o P. Berwick, 15 Barnton
Park Gardens, Edinburgh, Scotland)
● Lingua e Vita. q.

**British Internal Combustion Engine Research
Institute**
111/112 Buckingham Ave., Slough, Bucks, Eng.
● Abstracts from Technical and Patent Publications.
w. ISSN 0001-3447

**British Interplanetary Society**
12 Bessborough Gardens, S.W.N. 2JJ, Eng.
● British Interplanetary Society Journal. m. ISSN
0007-084X
● Spaceflight. m. ISSN 0038-6340

**British Iris Society**
72 South Hill Park, London, NW3 2SN, England.
● Iris Year Book. a. ISSN 0075-0700

**British Israel World Federation**
6 Buckingham Gate, London SW1E 6JP, Eng.
- British Israel World Federation. National Message. m. ISSN 0047-8962

**British-Italian Society**
1 Beauchamp Place, London S.W.3, England.
- Rivista; the Journal of the British Italian Society. bi-m.

**British Jazz Society**
10 Southfield Gardens, Twickenham, Middlesex, Eng.
- Jazz Times. m. ISSN 0021-5716

**British Jewellery & Giftware Federation Ltd.**
27 Frederick St., Birmingham B1 3HJ, Eng.
- Britannia. q. ISSN 0007-0203
- British Jeweller & Watch Buyer. m. ISSN 0007-0866

**British Kinematograph Sound and Television Society**
110-112 Victoria House, Vernon Place, London WC1B 4DJ, Eng.
- B K S T S Journal; film, sound, television, audio, visual. m.

**British Leprosy Relief Association**
50 Fitzroy St., London W1P 6AL, England.
- L E P R A News. q.
- Lepra News. 4 per yr.
- Leprosy Review. (pub. by Academic Press Inc. (London) Ltd.)

**British Liberals**
- New Outlook. (pub. by Prism Publications Ltd.)

**British Library**
Store St., London WC1E 7DG, England.
- British Library News. m. ISSN 0307-9481

**British Library. Bibliographic Services Division**
Store St., London WC1E 7DG, Eng.
- Books in English; a bibliography compiled from UK and US MARC sources. bi-m. (plus annual cumulations) ISSN 0045-2572
- British Catalogue of Music. a, with 2 interim issues. ISSN 0068-1407
- British Education Index. a (plus 3 quarterly issues) ISSN 0007-0637
- British Library. Bibliographic Services Division. Newsletter. irreg. ISSN 0308-230X
- British National Bibliography. w. plus 2 interim cumulations and annual vol. ISSN 0007-1544

**British Library. Board**
Store St., London WC1E 7DG, England.
- British Library. Board. Annual Report. a.
- British Library Journal. (pub. by Oxford University Press)

**British Library. Lending Division**
Publications Section, Boston Spa, Wetherby LS23 7BQ, Eng.
- B L L D Announcement Bulletin. m. ISSN 0301-2085
- B L L Review. q. ISSN 0305-6503
- British Library. Lending Division. Index of Conference Proceedings. m (annual cumulations)
- Machines and Tooling. (pub. by Production Engineering Research Association)
- Russian Engineering Journal. (pub. by Production Engineering Research Association)

**British Library. Reference Division**
Great Russell St., London WC1B 3DG, England.
- Checklist of British Official Serial Publications. irreg (approx. annual) ISSN 0084-8085

**British Library. Research and Development Department**
Sheraton House, Great Chapel St., London W1V 4BH, England.
- British Library Research and Development Newsletter. 3 per yr. ISSN 0305-9271
- National Reprographic Centre for Documentation, Hatfield, England. Technical Evaluation Report. irreg. ISSN 0077-541X

**British Library of Political and Economic Science**
Houghton St., London WC2A 2AE, England.
- British Library of Political and Economic Science. Quarterly List of Additions in Russian and East European Languages. q.
- London Bibliography of the Social Sciences. (pub. by Mansell Information - Publishing Ltd.)

**British Lichen Society**
c/o Department of Botany, British Museum (Natural History), Cromwell Road, London SW7 5BD, Eng.
- British Lichen Society Bulletin. s-a. ISSN 0300-4562
- Lichenologist. (pub. by Academic Press Inc. (London) Ltd.)

**British Mahabodhi Society**
(London Buddhist Vihara), 5 Heathfield Gardens, London W4 4JU, Eng.
- Buddhist Quarterly. q. ISSN 0045-3315

**British Medical Association**
B.M.A. House, Tavistock Sq., London WC1H 9JR, Eng.
- Annals of the Rheumatic Diseases. bi-m. ISSN 0003-4967
- Archives of Diseases in Childhood. m. ISSN 0003-9888
- British Heart Journal. m. ISSN 0007-0769 (British Cardiac Society)
- British Journal of Industrial Medicine. q. ISSN 0007-1072
- British Journal of Ophthalmology. m. ISSN 0007-1161
- British Journal of Preventive and Social Medicine. q. ISSN 0007-1242
- British Journal of Venereal Diseases. bi-m. ISSN 0007-134X (Medical Society for the Study of Venereal Diseases)
- British Medical Journal. w. ISSN 0007-1447
- Cardiovascular Research. bi-m. ISSN 0008-6363 (Co-Sponsor: British Cardiac Society)
- Gut. m. ISSN 0017-5749 (British Society of Gastroenterology)
- Journal of Clinical Pathology. m. ISSN 0021-9746 (Association of Clinical Pathologists)
- Journal of Medical Genetics. bi-m. ISSN 0022-2593
- Journal of Neurology, Neurosurgery and Psychiatry. m. ISSN 0022-3050
- Thorax. bi-m. ISSN 0040-6376

**British Midland Airways Limited**
- Voyager. (pub. by Trent Press (Nottingham) Ltd.)

**British Model Soldier Society**
16 Charlton Rd., Kenton, Harrow, Middlesex, Eng.
- British Model Soldier Society. Bulletin. q.

**British Monomarks Ltd.**
Napier House, 24 High Holborn, London WC1, Eng.
- Zero One; magazine of politics and the arts. q. ISSN 0044-4340

**British Mountaineering Council**
- Climber and Rambler. (pub. by Mountain Life Ltd.)

**British Museum (Natural History)**
Cromwell Rd., London SW7 5BD, England.
- British Museum (Natural History) Bulletin. Botany. irreg. ISSN 0068-2292
- British Museum (Natural History) Bulletin. Entomology. irreg. ISSN 0007-1501
- British Museum (Natural History) Bulletin. Geology. irreg. ISSN 0007-1471
- British Museum (Natural History) Bulletin. Historical. irreg. ISSN 0068-2306
- British Museum (Natural History) Bulletin. Mineralogy. irreg. ISSN 0007-148X
- British Museum (Natural History) Bulletin. Zoology. irreg. ISSN 0007-1498

**British Music Information Centre**
10 Stratford Place, London W1N 9AE, Eng.
- Composer. 3 per yr. ISSN 0010-4337 (Composers' Guild of Great Britain)

**British Mycological Society**
Broom's Barn Experimental Sta., Higham, Bury St. Edmunds, Suffolk, Eng.
- British Mycological Society. Bulletin. s-a. ISSN 0007-1528
- British Mycological Society. Transactions. (pub. by Cambridge University Press)

**British National Association for Soviet and East European Studies**
University of Glasgow, 10 South Park Terrace, Glasgow GL2 8LQ, Scotland.
- British National Association for Soviet and East European Studies. Information Bulletin. q.

**British-National Association of Toy Retailers**
- Toy Trader. (pub. by Wheatland Journals Ltd.)

**British National Committee for Geodesy and Geophysics. Geodesy Subcommittee.**
- United Kingdom Geodesy Report. (pub. by Royal Society)

**British National Export Council**
- British Exports. Export Services/Exportations Britanniques/Britischer Export/Exportaciones Britanicas. (pub. by Kompass Publishers Ltd.)

**British Natural Hygiene Society**
c/o Shalimar, First Ave., Frinton-On-Sea, Essex, Eng.
- Hygienist. q. ISSN 0018-8263

**British Naturalists Association**
40 Roundhill, Stone Nr. Aylesbury, Bucks HP 178RD, Eng
(Subscr. to: Mrs. Y. Griffiths, 23 Oak Hill Close, Woodford Green, Essex, Eng.)
- Country-Side; a magazine devoted to nature. 3 per yr. ISSN 0011-023X

**British Naturopathic and Osteopathic Association**
6 Netherhall Gardens, London, NW3, Eng.
- British Naturopathic Journal and Osteopathic Review. q. ISSN 0045-3110

**British-North American Research Association**
6-14 Dean Farrar St., London SW1H 0DZ, England.
- British-North American Research Association. Committee Publications. irreg.
- British-North American Research Association. Occasional Papers. irreg.

**British Nuclear Energy Society**
- British Nuclear Energy Society. Journal. (pub. by Thomas Telford Ltd.)

**British Nuclear Forum**
1 St. Alban's St., London SW1Y 4SL, Eng.
- British Nuclear Forum. Bulletin. m.

**British Numismatic Society**
Warburg Institute, Woburn Square, London WC1H 0AB, England.
- British Numismatic Journal. a.

**British Occupational Hygiene Society**
- Annals of Occupational Hygiene. (pub. by Pergamon Press, Inc. US)

**British Optical Association**
65 Brook St., London W.1, Eng.
- British Journal of Physiological Optics. q. ISSN 0007-1218
- Ophthalmic Optician. fortn. ISSN 0030-3739 (Co-Sponsor: Association of Optical Practitioners)

**British Ornithologists' Club**
c/o Zoological Society, Regent's Park, London NW1 4RY, Eng.
- British Ornithologists' Club. Bulletin. 4 per yr. ISSN 0007-1595

**British Ornithologists' Union**
- Ibis. (pub. by Academic Press Inc. (London) Ltd.)

**British Orthoptic Society**
Tavistock House North, Tavistock Sq., London W.C.1, England.
- British Orthoptic Journal. a. ISSN 0068-2314

**British Paedodontic Society**
33, Weymouth Street, London W1N 3FL, Eng.
- British Paedodontic Society. Proceedings. a.

**British Paper and Board Industry Federation**
Plough Place, Fetter Lane, London EC4A 1AL, England.
- British Paper and Board Industry Federation. Technical Division. Fundamental Research International Symposia. quadrennial. ISSN 0068-2322
- British Paper and Board Industry Federation. Technical Section. Technical Papers. a. ISSN 0068-2330
- British Paper and Board Industry Federation. Technical Section. Yearbook. a. ISSN 0068-2349
- Paper Technology and Industry. bi-m. ISSN 0031-1189

**British Parachute Association**
Kimberley House, 47 Vaughan Way, Leicester LE1 4SG, England.
- Sport Parachutist. bi-m. ISSN 0584-9217

**British Peace Committee**
84 Claverton St., London S.W.1, Eng.
- Peace Monitor. ISSN 0031-353X

**British Pelagorium and Germanium Society**
129 Aylesford Ave, Beckenham, Kent, Eng.
- Pelargonium News. q and annual year-book.

**British Petroleum Co. Ltd.**
Britannic House, Moor Lane, London E.C.2, Eng (U.S. Dist. BP North America Inc., 620 Fifth Ave., New York, NY 10020)
- B P Shield International. (British Petroleum) m. ISSN 0045-1274
- Statistical Review of the World Oil Industry. a. ISSN 0081-5039

**British Pharmacological Society**
- British Journal of Clinical Pharmacology. (pub. by Macmillan Journals Ltd.)
- British Journal of Pharmacology. (pub. by Macmillan Journals Ltd.)

**British Philatelic Federation Ltd.**
1 Whitehall Place, London SW1A 2HE, Eng.
- Philately. q. ISSN 0031-739X

**British Photobiology Society**
Department of Applied Optics, Imperial College, London SW7 2BZ, England.
- British Photobiology Society. Bulletin. a.

**British Phycological Journal**
- British Phycological Journal. (pub. by Academic Press Inc. (London) Ltd.)

**British Plastics Federation**
47 Piccadilly, London W1V 0DN, England.
- Reinforced Plastics Congress. biennial. ISSN 0306-3607

**British Polio Fellowship**
Bell Close, West End Rd., Ruislip, Middlesex HA4 6LP, Eng.
- British Polio Fellowship. Bulletin. q. ISSN 0007-1633

**British Post Office**
Central Headquarters, 23 Howland St., London W1P 6HQ, Eng.
- Courier. m. ISSN 0011-0396

**British Printing Industries Federation**
11 Bedford Row, London WC1R 4DX, Eng.
- Printing Industries. m.
- Printing Industries Annual. a.

**British Property Federation**
35 Catherine Place, London S.W.1, Eng.
- Property Journal. q. ISSN 0033-1309

**British Psychological Society**
St. Andrews House, 48 Princess Rd. East, Leicester LE1 7DR, England.
- British Journal of Mathematical and Statistical Psychology. (pub. by John Wright & Sons Ltd.)
- British Journal of Medical Psychology. (pub. by Cambridge University Press)
- British Journal of Psychology. (pub. by Cambridge University Press)
- British Journal of Social and Clinical Psychology. (pub. by Cambridge University Press)
- British Psychological Society. Bulletin. m. ISSN 0007-1692
- Journal of Occupational Psychology. q. ISSN 0305-8107

**British Pteridological Society**
46 Sedley Rise, Loughton, Essex 1G10 1LT, England.
- British Pteridological Society. Bulletin. a. ISSN 0301-9195
- Fern Gazette. a. ISSN 0308-0838

**British Puppet and Model Theatre Guild**
c/o Gordon Shapley, Hon. Sec., 18 Maple Rd., Yeading, Hayes, Middlesex, England.
- British Puppet and Model Theatre Guild. (Newsletter) m.

**British Quarrying & Slag Federation**
14 Waterloo Place, London SW1Y 4AR, England.
- British Quarrying & Slag Federation. Technical Review. q. ISSN 0309-1449

**British Rabbit Council**
- Fur and Feather, Rabbits and Rabbit Keeping. (pub. by Watmoughs Ltd.)

**British Racing & Sports Car Club**
Empire House, Chiswick High Rd., London W4 5TW, Eng.
- British Racing News. bi-m. ISSN 0045-3137

**British Railways Board**
222 Marylebone Rd., London NW1 6JJ, England.
- British Railways Board. Monthly Review of Technical Literature. m. ISSN 0007-1714
- British Railways Board. Report and Statement of Accounts. a. ISSN 0068-242X (Avail. from: H.M.S.O., c/o Liaison Officer, Atlantic House, London EC1P 1BW, England)
- Rail News. m. ISSN 0033-8745

**British Records Association**
The Charterhouse, Charterhouse Sq., London EC1M 6AU, England.
- Archives and the User. irreg. ISSN 0066-653X
- British Records Association. Archives. s-a. ISSN 0003-9535

**British Rheumatism and Arthritis Association**
6 Grosvenor Crescent, London SW1X 7ER, Eng.
- B R A Review. q. ISSN 0005-3279

**British Rubber Manufacturers' Association Ltd.**
90-91 Tottenham Court Rd., London W1P 0BR, England.
- British Rubber Industry Directory. triennial.

**British Safety Council**
Chancellors Rd., Hammersmith, London W.4, Eng.
- Safety and Rescue. m.

**British Sailors' Society**
680, Commercial Road, London e14 17HF, England.
- Chart and Compass. s-a.

**British School at Athens**
31-34 Gordon Sq., London W.C.1, England.
- British School at Athens. Annual. a. ISSN 0068-2454

**British School at Rome**
1 Lowther Gardens, Exhibition Rd., London SW7 2AA, England.
- British School at Rome. Papers. Archaeology. a. ISSN 0068-2462

**British School of Archaeology in Iraq**
(Gertrude Bell Memorial), 31-34 Gordon Square, London WC1H 0PY, Eng.
- Iraq. s-a. ISSN 0021-0889

**British School of Archaeology in Jerusalem**
2 Hinde Mews, Marylebone Lane, London W1M 5RH, England.
- Levant; Journal of the British School of Archaeology in Jerusalem. a. ISSN 0075-8914

**British Schools Exploring Society**
175 Temple Chamber, Temple Ave., London E.C. 44, England.
- British Schools Exploring Society. Report. a. ISSN 0521-1573

**British Science Fiction Association Ltd.**
72 Kenilworth Ave., Southcote, Reading RG3 3DN, England.
- Vector. bi-m. ISSN 0505-0448

**British Ship Research Association**
Wallsend Research Station, Wallsend, Tyne and Wear NE28 6UY, England.
- British Ship Research Association. B. S. R. A. Bibliographies. irreg.
- British Ship Research Association. Journal. m. ISSN 0007-1765

**British Sign Association**
- Sign World. (pub. by A. E. Morgan Publications Ltd.)

**British Small Animal Veterinary Association**
- Journal of Small Animal Practice. (pub. by Blackwell Scientific Publications Ltd.)

**British Social Biology Council**
69 Eccleston Sq., London S.W.1, Eng.
- Biology and Human Affairs. 3 per yr. ISSN 0006-3355

**British Society for Immunology**
- Clinical and Experimental Immunology. (pub. by Blackwell Scientific Publications Ltd.)
- Immunology. (pub. by Blackwell Scientific Publications Ltd.)

**British Society for Middle East Studies**
- International Journal of Middle East Studies. (pub. by Cambridge University Press)

**British Society for Middle Eastern Studies**
- British Society for Middle Eastern Studies. Bulletin. (pub. by Mansell Information-Publishing Ltd.)

**British Society for Music Therapy**
48 Lanchester Rd., London N6 4TA, Eng.
- British Journal of Music Therapy. 3 per yr. ISSN 0308-244X

**British Society for Phenomenology**
- British Society for Phenomenology. Journal. (pub. by Haigh and Hochland Ltd.)

**British Society for Research in Agricultural Engineering**
- Journal of Agricultural Engineering Research. (pub. by Academic Press Inc. (London) Ltd.)

**British Society for Social Responsibility in Science**
9 Poland St., London W1V 3DG, England.
- Science for People. q.

**British Society for Strain Measurement**
281 Heaton Rd., Newcastle-Upon-Tyne,NE6 5QB, Eng.
- Strain. q. ISSN 0039-2103

**British Society for Surgery of the Hand**
- Hand. (pub. by E. & S. Livingstone)

**British Society for the History of Pharmacy**
36 York Place, Edinburgh EH1 3HU, Scotland.
- British Society for the History of Pharmacy. Transactions. irreg. ISSN 0068-2519
- Pharmaceutical Historian. irreg. (approx. 3 per yr.) ISSN 0079-1393

**British Society for the History of Science**
Halfpenny Furze, Mill Lane, Chalfont St. Giles, Buckinghamshire HP8 4NR, England.
- British Journal for the History of Science. 3 per yr. ISSN 0007-0874

**British Society for the Philosophy of Science**
- British Journal for the Philosophy of Science. (pub. by Aberdeen University Press)

**British Society for the Study of Mental Subnormality**
Monyhull Hospital, Birmingham, Eng.
- British Journal of Mental Subnormality. s-a.

**British Society of Aesthetics**
- British Journal of Aesthetics. (pub. by Oxford University Press)

**British Society of Animal Production**
- Animal Production. (pub. by Longman Group Ltd.)

**British Society of Commerce**
25 Bridgeman Terrace, Wigan, Eng.
- British Society of Commerce. Review. q. ISSN 0007-1781

**British Society of Dowsers**
19 High St., Eydon, Daventry, Northamptonshire, Eng.
- British Society of Dowsers. Journal. q. ISSN 0007-179X

**British Society of Gastroenterology**
- Gut. (pub. by British Medical Association)

**British Society of Rheology**
67 Daniells, Welwyn Garden City, Hertfordshire
AL7 1QT, England.
- British Society of Rheology. Bulletin. q. ISSN
  0045-3145
- Rheology Abstracts. (pub. by Pergamon Press, Inc.
  US)

**British Society of Russian Philately**
c/o John Lloyd, The Retreat, West Bergholt,
Colchester, Essex CO6 3HE, Eng.
- British Journal of Russian Philately. s-a.

**British Society of Soil Science**
- Journal of Soil Science. (pub. by Oxford
  University Press)

**British Society of the Study of Orthodontics**
- British Journal of Orthodontics. (pub. by Longman
  Group Ltd.)

**British Sociological Association**
- Sociology. (pub. by Oxford University Press)

**British Soviet Friendship Society**
36 St. Johns Square, London E.C.1, Eng.
- British-Soviet Friendship. bi-m. ISSN 0007-1803

**British Standards Institution**
2 Park St., London W1A 2BS, Eng.
- B. S. I. News. m. ISSN 0005-3309
- British Standards Year Book. a. ISSN 0068-2578

**British Stationery & Office Products Federation**
6 Wimpole St., London W1M 8AS, Eng.
- New Stationer. m. ISSN 0009-1065

**British Steel Corp.**
151 Gower St, London WC1, Eng.
- British Steel. q. ISSN 0007-182X
- British Steel Corporation. Annual Report and
  Accounts. a. ISSN 0068-2586 (Avail. from:
  H.M.S.O., c/o Liaison Officer, Atlantic House,
  London EC1P 1BW, England)
- Building with Steel. q. ISSN 0045-3455
- International Steel Statistics - World Tables. a.
- Tubular Structures. irreg. (2-3 per yr.) ISSN 0041-
  3909

**British Steel Corp. Corporate Development
Laboratory**
Hoyle St., Sheffield 53 7EY, Eng.
- British Steel Corporation. Corporate Development
  Laboratory. Open Report List. bi-m.

**British Steel Corp. Market Promotion Dept.**
Po Box 35, Bridge Street, Sheffield S3 8az, England.
- Stainless. q. ISSN 0306-8943

**British Steelmaker Ltd.**
5 Pond St., Hampstead, London NW3 2PN, Eng.
- British Steelmaker; a monthly review of the steel
  industry. 6 per yr. ISSN 0007-1838

**British Stock Car Association**
17 Arnesby Rd., Nottingham NG7 2EA, Eng.
- Stock Car. m. ISSN 0049-2272

**British Sugar Corp., Ltd.**
Box 26, Oundle Rd., Peterborough PE2 9QU,
England.
- British Sugar Beet Review. q. ISSN 0007-1854

**British Sulphur Corp. Ltd.**
Parnell House, 25 Wilton Rd., London SW1V 1NH,
Eng.
- Fertilizer International. m. ISSN 0015-0304
- Nitrogen; covers all aspects of world ammonia
  and nitrogen fertilizer industry. bi-m. ISSN 0029-
  0777
- Phosphorus and Potassium; covers all aspects of
  world phosphate and potash fertilizer industry. bi-
  m. ISSN 0031-8426
- Sulphur; covers all aspects of world sulphur and
  sulphuric acid industry. bi-m. ISSN 0039-4890
- World Directory of Fertilizer Manufacturers. irreg.
- World Directory of Fertilizer Products. irreg.
- World Fertilizer Atlas. irreg., 5th edt. 1976. ISSN
  0512-2953
- World Guide to Fertilizer Plant and Equipment.
  irreg.
- World Guide to Fertilizer Processes and
  Constructors. irreg.
- World Guide to Pollution Control in the Fertilizer
  Industry. irreg.
- World Survey of Phosphate Deposits. irreg.
- World Survey of Sulphur Resources. irreg.

**British Surrealist Group**
Transformation, Peeks, Harpford, Sidmouth, Devon
EX10 ONH, Eng.
- Surrealist Transformaction. 3 per yr. ISSN 0039-
  6168

**British Tar Industry Association**
132 Sloane St, London SW1X 9BB, Eng.
- Road Tar. 3 per yr. ISSN 0035-7251

**British Textile Confederation**
- Skinner's British Textile Register. (pub. by
  Thomas Skinner Directories)

**British Theatre Association**
9 Fitzroy Square, London W.1, Eng.
- Drama; the quarterly theatre review. q. ISSN
  0012-5946

**British Theatre Institute**
c/o 125 Markyate Rd., Dagenham, Essex RM8
2LB, England.
- British Theatre Institute. Newsletter & Report. 6
  per yr.

**British Tourist Authority**
64-65 St. James St., London S.W.1, England.
- British Tourist Authority. Annual Report. a. ISSN
  0068-2667
- British Tourist Authority. Digest of Tourist
  Statistics. irreg. ISSN 0068-2616
- British Travel News. q. ISSN 0007-1900
- Hotels and Restaurants in Britain. a. ISSN 0073-
  3512
- In Britain. m. ISSN 0019-3143 (Dist in U.S. by:
  British Tourist Authority, 680 Fifth Ave., New
  York, NY 10019)
- London: Your Sightseeing Guide. a.

**British Toy Manufacturers Association**
80 Camberwell Rd., London SE5 OEG, England.
- B T M A Directory. a. ISSN 0068-2624
- British Toys. m. ISSN 0007-1897

**British Trades Alphabet Ltd.**
Alpha House Main St., East Ardsley, Wakefield,
Yorkshire, England.
- British Trades Alphabet; journal of educational
  projects. a. ISSN 0068-2632

**British Transport Docks Board**
Melbury House, Melbury Terrace, London N.W.1.,
England.
- British Transport Docks Board. Annual Report
  and Accounts. a. ISSN 0068-2659

**British Trust for Ornithology**
Beech Grove, Tring, Herts, Eng.
- B T O News; a bulletin for bird watchers. 7 per
  yr. ISSN 0005-3392
- Bird Study. q. ISSN 0006-3657
- British Trust for Ornithology. Annual Report. a.
  ISSN 0068-2675

**British Unidentified Flying Object Research
Association**
6 Cairn Avenue, London W5, England.
- B U F O R A Journal. bi-m.

**British Union Conference of Seventh-Day Adventists**
- British Advent Messenger. (pub. by Stanborough
  Press Ltd.)

**British Union for the Abolition of Vivisection**
47 Whitehall, London SW1, Eng.
- Animal Welfare. m.

**British Universities Film Council Ltd.**
Royalty House, 72 Dean St., London W1V 5HB,
England.
- B U F C Newsletter; news & comment on audio-
  visual media in higher education. 3 per yr. ISSN
  0308-5376

**British Veterinary Association**
7 Mansfield St, London W1M OAT, Eng.
- Research in Veterinary Science. bi-m. ISSN 0034-
  5288
- Veterinary Record. w. ISSN 0042-4900

**British Watch and Clock Makers Guild**
- Jeweller. (pub. by Allens (Clerkenwell) Ltd.)

**British Water Ski Federation**
- Water Skier. (pub. by Goldhawk Press Ltd.)

**British Waterfowl Association**
111-113 Lambeth Rd., London S.E.1, England.
- Waterfowl. 3 per yr.

**British Waterways Board**
Melbury House, Melbury Terrace, London NW1
6JX, England
- British Waterways Board. Annual Report and
  Accounts. a. ISSN 0068-2683 (Avail. from:
  H.M.S.O., c/o Liaison Officer, Atlantic House,
  London EC1P 1BW, England)

**British Women Pilots Association**
P.O. Box 13, British Airways, Victoria Terminal,
London S.W. 1, Eng.
- B W P A Magazines. q.

**British Women's Temperance Association**
8 North Bank St, Edinburgh EH1 2LP, Scotland.
- Scottish Women's Temperance News. q. ISSN
  0036-9446

**Broadcast Magazine**
111a Wardour St., London W1V 3TD, England.
- Broadcast Yearbook and Diary. a.

**Broadfields (Technical Publishers) Ltd.**
Little Leighs, Chelmsford, Essex CM3 1PF,
England.
- Rail Engineering International. bi-m. ISSN 0048-
  6612

**Broadsheet**
30 Effingham Close, Sutton, Surrey, Eng.
- Broadsheet. 2 per yr. ISSN 0007-2044

**Broadwater Press Ltd.**
Welwyn Garden City, Herts, Eng.
- Economic History Review. q. ISSN 0013-0117
  (Economic History Society)

**Brockhouse Limited**
Victoria Works, Hill Top, West Bromwich B70
OSN, England.
- Forge. q. ISSN 0015-7635

**Bromley Weekly Review Ltd.**
44 East St., Bromley, Kent, Eng.
- Bromley Weekly Review. w. ISSN 0007-2206

**Bronte Parsonage Museum**
Haworth, Keighley, Yorks., Eng.
- Bronte Society Transactions. a.

**Brown, Son and Ferguson Ltd.**
52 Darnley Street, Glasgow G41 2SG, Scotland.
- Brown's Nautical Almanac. a. ISSN 0068-290X
- Nautical Magazine; for those interested in ships
  and the sea. m. ISSN 0028-1336

**Browning Society of London**
29 Southmoor Rd., Oxford OX26RF, Eng.
- Browning Society Notes. 3 per yr. (Subscr. to: R.
  E. Bolton, 9 Lakenheath, Southgate, London NI4
  4RJ, England)

**Brunel University Students Union**
Kingston Lane, Uxbridge, Middlesex UB8 3PH,
England.
- Needle. w.

**Buckley Press Ltd.**
The Butts, Half Acre, Brentford, Middlesex TW8
8BN, Eng.
- Aquarist and Pondkeeper. m. ISSN 0003-7273
- Insurance Directory and Year Book. a. ISSN
  0074-0691
- Post Magazine and Insurance Monitor. w. ISSN
  0032-5252
- Reinsurance; the monthly international
  reinsurance magazine. m. ISSN 0048-7171

**Buddhist Society**
58 Eccleston Square, London S.W.1, Eng.
- Middle Way. q. ISSN 0026-3214

**Budgerigar Society**
12 Abel Close, Hemel Hempstead, Herts, Eng.
- Budgerigar Bulletin. q. ISSN 0045-3323

**Budtail Publishing**
100 Fleet St., London EC4V 1DE, Eng.
- Investors Review and Financial World. fortn.

**Building & Contract Journals Ltd.**
Surrey House, 1 Throwley Way, Sutton, Surrey,
England.
- B and C J Directory. a. ISSN 0068-3507

**Building and Engineering Review**
c/o J. Woods, 10 Kingsberry Park, Rosetta, Belfast BT6 OHT, Northern Ireland.
• Building and Engineering Review. a. ISSN 0084-814X

**Building Centre, Bristol**
26 Store Street, London WC1, Eng.
• Bristol Newsletter. q.

**Building Publishers Ltd.**
Box 135, 4 Catherine St, London WC2B 5JN, Eng.
• Building; for the design and construction team. w. ISSN 0007-3318

**Building Services Research and Information Association**
Old Bracknell Lane, Bracknell, Berks RG12 4AH, England.
• B S R I A Application Guides. Technical Notes. irreg., 1974, no. 83.
• B S R I A Technical Notes. irreg., 1973, no. 38.
• Omnibus; operation manufacture, design and installation or building services. bi-m.
• Thermal Abstracts. bi-m. ISSN 0040-599X

**Building Societies Institute**
Fanhams Hall, Ware, Herts, Eng.
• B. S. I. Quarterly. q. ISSN 0005-3317

**Bulwer Lytton Circle**
High Orchard, 125 Markyate Rd., Dagenham, Essex RM8 2LB, England.
• Bulwer Lytton Circle Chronicle. a.

**Bunhill Publications Ltd.**
127 Standstead Rd., Forest Hill, London S.E. 23, England.
• Aircraft Engineering. m. ISSN 0002-2667

**Bureau for International Language Coordination**
• B I L C Bulletin. (pub. by Institute of Army Education. Foreign Language Section)

**Bureau of Hygiene and Tropical Diseases**
Keppel St., London WC1E 7HT, Eng.
• Abstracts on Hygiene. m. ISSN 0001-3692
• Tropical Diseases Bulletin. m. ISSN 0041-3240

**Bureau of Medical Practitioner Affairs Ltd.**
Francis House, King's Head Yard, Borough High St., London SE1 1NA, England.
• General Practice Team. m.

**Burke House Periodicals Ltd.**
Box 4, 22A London End, Beaconsfield, Bucks., England.
• Auto Accessory Retailer. m. ISSN 0306-2899

**Burke's Peerage Ltd.**
56 Walton St., London SW3 1RB, England (Dist. in U.S. by: Arco Publishing Co. Inc., 219 Park Ave. S., New York, NY 10003)
• Burke's Guide to the Royal Family. irreg.
• Burke's Irish Family Records. irreg.
• Burke's Landed Gentry. irreg., 18th ed, (3 vols.)
• Burke's Peerage and Baronetage.
• Burke's Presidential Families of the USA. every 8 years.
• International Businessmen's Who's Who. triennial. ISSN 0074-2139

**Burleigh Press Ltd.**
Channons Hill, Fishponds, Bristol BS16 2DP, England.
• Catena. m. ISSN 0008-7769 (Catenian Association)

**Burlington Magazine Publications Ltd.**
Elm House, Elm St., London W.C. 1., England.
• Burlington Magazine. m. ISSN 0007-6287

**Burlington Publishing Company(1942) Ltd.**
Cordwallis Estate, Clivemont Rd., Maidenhead, Berkshire, Eng.
• Shooting Times and Country Magazine. w. ISSN 0037-4164

**Burmah Oil Trading Ltd**
Burmah House, Pipers Way, Swindon, Wiltshire, England.
• Burmah International. q. ISSN 0008-7548

**John S. Burns and Sons**
25 Finlas Street, Possilpark, Glasgow, G22 5DS, Scotland.
• Catholic Directory for Scotland. a. ISSN 0306-5677

• Directory of Religious Orders, Congregations & Societies of Great Britain & Ireland. biennial, latest 1972-1974. ISSN 0419-3407
• Innes Review. s-a. ISSN 0020-157X (Scottish Catholic Historical Association)

**Burns Federation**
Dick Institute, Elmbank Avenue, Kilmarnock KAI 3BU, Scotland.
• Robert Burns Chronicle. a.

**J. Burrow & Co. Ltd.**
Publicity House, Streatham Hill, London SW2 4TR, England.
• Schools of England, Wales, Scotland and Ireland. a. ISSN 0080-6919

**Aubrey Bush Publications**
17 Balmoral Rd., Forest Rd., Nottingham NG1 4HX, Eng.
• Poetry Market. irreg. ISSN 0032-2083
• Publicity Review. irreg. ISSN 0033-3921

**Business Books Ltd.**
Mercury House, Waterloo Rd., London SE1 8UL, England
• Applied Chemistry Series. irreg. ISSN 0066-541X (Dist. by: Cahners Books, 89 Franklin St., Boston, MA 02110)

**Business Graduates Association**
Rutland House, Rutland Gardens, London SW7 1BY, England.
• Business Graduate. q.

**Business Surveys Ltd.**
P.O. Box 21, Dorking, RH5 4EE, Surrey, Eng.
• Research Index. fortn. (semi-annual cumulative no.) ISSN 0034-5296

**Business Systems & Equipment**
76 Oxford St., London W.1, Eng.
• Business Systems & Equipment. m. ISSN 0007-7097

**Michael Butler & Kemble Williams, Eds. & Pubs.**
45 Westfields, Catshill, Bromsgrove, Worcs., Eng.
• Samphire; new poetry. q. ISSN 0036-388X

**Butterworth & Co. (Publishers) Ltd.**
88 Kingsway, London WC2B 6AB, England.
• Absorption Spectra in the Infrared Region. s-a.
• All England Law Reports. w. ISSN 0002-5569
• Annual Charities Digest. a. ISSN 0066-3867 (Family Welfare Association)
• Annual Survey of Commonwealth Law. a. ISSN 0570-2658
• British Union Catalogue of Periodicals. q (annual and 5 year cumulations. ISSN 0007-1919
• Butterworths Budget Tax Tables. a. ISSN 0525-3063
• Butterworths Tax Handbook. a. ISSN 0068-452X
• Colston Research Society, Bristol, England. Proceedings of the Symposium. Colston Research Papers. irreg., no. 25, 1974. ISSN 0069-6277 (U.S. Dist. Shoe String Press, 995 Sherman Ave., Hamden, CT 06514)
• Dibden's Index to Double Taxation Agreements. irreg.
• Halsbury's Laws of England Annual Abridgment. a.
• Institute for Research into Mental and Multiple Handicap. Symposium. irreg.
• Journal of African Law. 3 per yr. ISSN 0021-8553 (International African Law Association)
• Modern Trends in Orthopaedics. irreg. ISSN 0077-0159
• Organic Chemistry. Series Two. irreg.
• Paterson's Licensing Acts. a.
• Physical Chemistry. Series Two. irreg.
• Physiology, Series One. irreg.
• Simon's Tax Cases. w.
• Society of Public Teachers of Law. Journal. s-a. ISSN 0038-0016
• Whillan's Tax Tables and Tax Reckoner. a.

**Buzz Christian Ministries**
99a Burlington Rd., New Malden, Surrey KT3 4LR, Eng.
• Buzz. m. ISSN 0045-3692

**Byblos Productions Ltd.**
30-34 Langham St., London W1N 5LB, Eng.
• Angling. m. ISSN 0003-3294
• Boxing News. w. ISSN 0006-8519
• Motor Cyclist Illustrated. m. ISSN 0027-187X
• My Story. m. ISSN 0027-545X

**Byron Society Journal Ltd.**
6 Gertrude St., London SW10 0JN, England.
• Byron Journal. a.

**Byways**
14 Frognal, London N.W.3., Eng.
• Byways. q.

**C.B.D. Research Ltd.**
154 High St., Beckenham, Kent BR3 1EA, England.
• Councils, Committees and Boards; a handbook of advisory, consultative, executive and similar bodies in British public life. biennial. ISSN 0070-1211
• Current African Directories. irreg.
• Current British Directories. irreg., 8th edt. 1977. ISSN 0070-1858
• Current European Directories. irreg. ISSN 0070-1955
• Directory of British Associations. irreg., 5th edt. 1977-1978. ISSN 0070-5152
• Directory of European Associations. Part 1: National Industrial Trade & Professional Associations. irreg. ISSN 0070-5500
• Directory of European Associations. Part 2: National Learned, Scientific & Technical Societies. irreg.
• European Companies; a guide to sources of information. irreg., 1971, 3rd edition. ISSN 0071-2582
• Statistics - Africa; sources for market research. irreg. ISSN 0081-5098
• Statistics - America; sources for market research (North, Central & South America) irreg.
• Statistics - Asia & Australasia: Sources for Market Research. irreg.
• Statistics - Europe; sources for market research. irreg., 3rd edt. 1976. ISSN 0081-5101

**C D P Information and Intelligence Unit**
5 Tavistock Place, London WC1H 9SS, England.
• National Community Development Project Forward Plan. a.

**C.N.A. Publications**
15 Katharine Street, Croydon, Surrey, England.
• Darts World. m.

**C O M A (Year Book) Ltd.**
Waveney House, Adwick Road, Mexborough, Yorks S64 0BS, England.
• Coke Oven Managers' Association. Year Book. a. ISSN 0069-4991

**C. S. Publications Ltd.**
115 Bedford Road, London SW4 7RA, England.
• Cargo Systems. m.

**Cable Television Association of Great Britain**
295 Regent St., London W1R 7YA, Eng.
• Cablevision News. 3 per yr.

**Cactus and Succulent Society of Great Britain**
1A Hardwicke Rd., Richmond, Surrey, England.
• Cactus and Succulent Journal of Great Britain. q. ISSN 0007-9375

**Cactus Place**
C/O David Hooker, Ed., 33 Bridge Ave., Upminster, Essex RM14 2LX, Eng.
• Essex Succulent Review; the magazine for "Essex Cactophiles". q.

**Cadbury Ltd.**
Bournville, Birmingham B30 2LU, Eng.
• Cocoa Growers Bulletin. s-a. ISSN 0045-7256

**Cairngorm Club**
c/o Secretary R. C. Shirreffs, 18 Bon-Accord Square, Aberdeen AB9 1YE, Scotland.
• Cairngorm Club Journal. biennial, no. 95, 1973. ISSN 0068-5267

**John Calder (Publishers) Ltd.**
18 Brewer St., London W1E 4AS, Eng.
• Gambit; an international drama quarterly. q. ISSN 0016-4283

**Calvinistic Methodist Book Agency**
The Bookroom, St. David's Rd., Caernarvon, Gwynedd LL55 1ER, Wales.
• Goleuad/Light. w. ISSN 0017-1700 (Presbyterian Church of Wales)

**Camberwell Council on Alcoholism**
25 Camberwell Grove, London SE 5, Eng.
• C C A Journal on Alcoholism. 4 per yr.

**Cambridge Group for History of Population and Social Structure**
- Cambridge Group for History of Population and Social Structure. Publications. (pub. by Cambridge University Press)

**Cambridge Historical Society**
- Historical Journal. (pub. by Cambridge University Press)

**Cambridge Institute of Education**
Shaftesbury Rd., Cambridge CB2 2BX, Eng.
- Cambridge Journal of Education. 3 per yr. ISSN 0305-764X

**Cambridge Medical Publication Ltd.**
435-437 Wellingborough Rd., Northampton NN1 4EZ, Eng.
- Journal of International Medical Research. bi-m. ISSN 0300-0605

**Cambridge Philological Society**
Museum of Classical Archaeology, Little St. Mary's Lane, Cambridge CB2 1RR, England.
- Cambridge Philological Society. Proceedings. a. ISSN 0068-6735
- Cambridge Philological Society. Proceedings. Supplement. irreg., vol. 4, 1977. ISSN 0068-6743

**Cambridge Philosophical Society**
- Cambridge Philosophical Society. Biological Reviews. (pub. by Cambridge University Press)
- Cambridge Philosophical Society. Mathematical Proceedings. (pub. by Cambridge University Press)

**Cambridge Quarterly**
2 Summerfield, Cambridge CB3 9HE, Eng.
- Cambridge Quarterly. irreg. ISSN 0008-199X

**Cambridge University**
- Cambridge Studies in Applied Econometrics. (pub. by Chapman and Hall Ltd.)

**Cambridge University. Cambridge School of Architecture**
- Cambridge Urban and Architectural Studies. (pub. by Cambridge University Press)

**Cambridge University. Department of Architecture**
Cambridge CB3 9DT, England.
- Cambridge University. Department of Architecture. Autonomous Housing Study Working Papers. irreg.

**Cambridge University Engineering Society**
Dept. of Engineering, Trumpington Street, Cambridge, England.
- Cambridge University Engineering Society. Journal. a. ISSN 0068-6867

**Cambridge University. Institute of Criminology**
Cambridge CB3 9DT, England.
- Cambridge University. Institute of Criminology. Bibliographical Series. irreg., no. 7, 1977. ISSN 0068-6883
- Cropwood Round-Table Conference Papers. irreg., no. 9, 1977.

**Cambridge University. Law Faculty**
- Cambridge Law Journal. (pub. by Cambridge University Press)

**Cambridge University Library**
West Road, Cambridge CB3 9DT, England (and 32 E. 57 St., New York, N.Y. 10022)
- Cambridge Bibliographical Society. Transactions. a. ISSN 0068-6611
- Cambridge Bibliographical Society. Transactions. Monograph Supplements. irreg. ISSN 0068-662X
- Cambridge University Library Librarianship Series. irreg.

**Cambridge University. Library Management Research Unit**
West Rd., Cambridge, England.
- Cambridge University. Library Management Research Unit. Report to the Office for Scientific and Technical Information. irreg.

**Cambridge University Mathematical Society**
Junior Branch of the Mathematical Association, Cambridge, England.
- Eureka; the Archimedean's Journal. a. ISSN 0071-2248

**Cambridge University Medical Society**
Department of Anatomy, Cambridge University, Cambridge, England.
- Murmur. 3 per yr. ISSN 0047-8385

**Cambridge University. Middle East Centre**
- Arabian Studies. (pub. by C. Hurst and Co.)

**Cambridge University Press**
Bentley House, P.O. Box 92, 200 Euston Rd., London NW1 2DB, England
(U.S. Address: 32 E. 57th St., New York, NY 10022)
- African Studies Series. irreg. ISSN 0065-406X
- Anglica Germanica: Series 2. irreg.
- Anglo-Saxon England. a.
- Annals of Human Genetics. q. ISSN 0003-4800 (University College, London)
- Association of University Teachers of Economics. Proceedings of the Annual Conference. a.
- Biological Structure and Function. irreg., no. 5, 1975. ISSN 0520-1853
- British Authors Series. irreg. ISSN 0068-1334
- British Commonwealth Series. irreg. ISSN 0068-189X
- British Journal of Medical Psychology. q. ISSN 0007-1129 (British Psychological Society)
- British Journal of Nutrition. bi-m. ISSN 0007-1145 (Nutrition Society)
- British Journal of Political Science. q. ISSN 0007-1234
- British Journal of Psychology. 4 per yr. ISSN 0007-1269 (British Psychological Society)
- British Journal of Social and Clinical Psychology. q. ISSN 0007-1293 (British Psychological Society)
- British Mycological Society. Transactions. 2 vols. per yr.(3 parts per vol) ISSN 0007-1536
- Cambridge Aeronautical Series. irreg. ISSN 0068-6573
- Cambridge African Studies Series. irreg. ISSN 0068-6581 (Centre for African Studies)
- Cambridge Air Surveys. irreg. ISSN 0068-659X
- Cambridge Authors' and Printers' Guides. irreg. ISSN 0068-6603
- Cambridge Chemistry Texts. irreg.
- Cambridge Classical Studies. irreg.
- Cambridge Classical Texts and Commentaries. irreg. ISSN 0068-6638
- Cambridge Commonwealth Series. irreg.
- Cambridge Computer Science Texts. irreg.
- Cambridge Earth Science Series. irreg.
- Cambridge Economic Handbooks. irreg.
- Cambridge Economic History of Europe. irreg. ISSN 0068-6646
- Cambridge Geographical Studies. irreg. ISSN 0068-6654
- Cambridge Greek and Latin Classics. irreg.
- Cambridge Group for History of Population and Social Structure. Publications. irreg.,, vol. 41, 1970. ISSN 0575-6804
- Cambridge History of Iran. irreg. ISSN 0068-6662
- Cambridge History of the British Empire. irreg. ISSN 0068-6670
- Cambridge Introduction to the History of Mankind. Topic Books. irreg.
- Cambridge Latin American Studies. irreg., no. 17, 1974. ISSN 0068-6689
- Cambridge Latin Texts. irreg.
- Cambridge Law Journal. s-a. ISSN 0008-1973 (Cambridge University. Law Faculty)
- Cambridge Legal Case Book Series. irreg.
- Cambridge Monographs in Experimental Biology. irreg., no. 18, 1971. ISSN 0068-6697
- Cambridge Monographs in Physical Chemistry. irreg.
- Cambridge Monographs on Mathematical Physics. irreg.
- Cambridge Monographs on Mechanics and Applied Mathematics. irreg.
- Cambridge Monographs on Physics. irreg.
- Cambridge Oriental Series. irreg. ISSN 0068-6700
- Cambridge Papers in Social Anthropology. irreg. ISSN 0068-6719
- Cambridge Papers in Sociology. irreg. ISSN 0068-6727
- Cambridge Philosophical Society. Biological Reviews. q. ISSN 0006-3231
- Cambridge Philosophical Society. Mathematical Proceedings. 2 vols per yr., 3 parts per vol.
- Cambridge Readers in Modern Chinese. irreg.
- Cambridge Solid State Science Series. irreg0.
- Cambridge South Asian Studies. irreg., no. 15, 1975. ISSN 0575-6863
- Cambridge Studies in Chinese History, Literature and Institutions. irreg.
- Cambridge Studies in Early Modern History. irreg. ISSN 0084-8336
- Cambridge Studies in Economic History. irreg.

- Cambridge Studies in English Legal History. irreg.
- Cambridge Studies in International and Comparative Law. irreg. ISSN 0068-6751
- Cambridge Studies in Linguistics. irreg. ISSN 0068-676X
- Cambridge Studies in Medieval Life and Thought. New Series. irreg. ISSN 0068-6778
- Cambridge Studies in Medieval Life and Thought. Third Series. irreg. ISSN 0068-6786
- Cambridge Studies in Social Anthropology. irreg. ISSN 0068-6794
- Cambridge Studies in Sociology. irreg. ISSN 0068-6808
- Cambridge Studies in the History and Theory of Politics. irreg. ISSN 0575-6871
- Cambridge Texts and Studies in the History of Education. irreg. ISSN 0068-6816
- Cambridge Tracts in Mathematics. irreg.
- Cambridge University. Department of Applied Economics. Monographs. irreg., no. 24, 1973. ISSN 0068-6832
- Cambridge University. Department of Applied Economics. Occasional Papers. irreg. ISSN 0068-6840
- Cambridge University. Oriental Publications. irreg. ISSN 0068-6891
- Cambridge University Reporter. w.(Sept.-June) ISSN 0008-2015
- Cambridge Urban and Architectural Studies. (Cambridge University. Cambridge School of Architecture)
- Comparative Studies in Society and History; an international quarterly. 4 per yr. ISSN 0010-4175
- Economic and Social Studies. irreg. ISSN 0070-8453 (National Institute of Economic and Social Research)
- Economic History Review. Supplements. irreg. ISSN 0070-8569 (Economic History Society)
- Economic Journal. q. ISSN 0013-0133 (Royal Economic Society)
- European Journal of Sociology/Archives Europeennes de Sociologie. s-a. ISSN 0003-9756
- Experimental Agriculture. q. ISSN 0014-4797
- Genetical Research. 2 vols. per yr.(3 parts each vol.) ISSN 0016-6723
- Geography of the British Isles Series. irreg.
- Geological Magazine. bi-m. ISSN 0016-7568
- Historical Journal. q. ISSN 0018-246X (Cambridge Historical Society)
- International Conference of Applied Linguistics. (Proceedings) irreg., 1969, 2nd, Cambridge, England. ISSN 0074-2910 (International Association of Applied Linguistics)
- International Congress on Mathematical Education. Proceedings. irreg, 2nd, 1973.
- International Journal of Middle East Studies. q. ISSN 0020-7438 (British Society for Middle East Studies)
- Journal of African History. q. ISSN 0021-8537
- Journal of Agricultural Science. bi-m. ISSN 0021-8596
- Journal of American Studies. 3 per yr. (British Association for American Studies)
- Journal of Anatomy. 2 vols. per yr.(3 parts per vol.) ISSN 0021-8782 (Anatomical Society of Great Britain and Ireland)
- Journal of Cell Science. 6 per yr. ISSN 0021-9533 (Company of Biologists, Ltd)
- Journal of Child Language. 3 per yr. ISSN 0305-0009
- Journal of Dairy Research. 3 per yr. ISSN 0022-0299 (National Institute for Research in Dairying) (Cosponsor: Hannah Dairy Research Institute)
- Journal of Ecclesiastical History. q. ISSN 0022-0469
- Journal of Embryology and Experimental Morphology. 6 per yr. ISSN 0022-0752 (Company of Biologists Ltd)
- Journal of Experimental Biology. 6 per yr. ISSN 0022-0949 (Company of Biologists, Ltd)
- Journal of Fluid Mechanics. 6 vols. per yr. (4 parts per vol.) ISSN 0022-1120
- Journal of General Microbiology. bi-m. ISSN 0022-1287 (Society for General Microbiology)
- Journal of General Virology. 4 vol. per yr. (3 parts per vol.) ISSN 0022-1317 (Society for General Microbiology)
- Journal of Hygiene. 2 vols. per yr. (3 parts per vol.) ISSN 0022-1724
- Journal of Latin American Studies. s-a. ISSN 0022-216X (Centres of Latin American Studies at the Universities of Cambridge, Glasgow, Liverpool, London and Oxford)
- Journal of Linguistics. s-a. ISSN 0022-2267 (Linguistics Association of Great Britain)
- Journal of Modern African Studies; a quarterly survey of politics, economics and related topics in contemporary Africa. q. ISSN 0022-278X

- Journal of Physiology. 10 vols. per yr. (3 parts per vol.) ISSN 0022-3751 (Physiological Society, London)
- Journal of Plasma Physics. 2 vols per yr(3 parts per vol.) ISSN 0022-3778
- Journal of Social Policy. q. ISSN 0047-2794 (Social Administration Association)
- Language in Society. 3 per yr. ISSN 0047-4045
- Language Teaching and Linguistics Abstracts. q. ISSN 0306-6304
- London Mathematical Society. Lecture Note Series. irreg. ISSN 0076-0552
- Major European Author Series. irreg.
- Medievalia et Humanistica: Studies in Medieval and Renaissance Culture. a. ISSN 0076-6127
- Microbios Letters. 3 per yr.
- Modern Asian Studies. q. ISSN 0026-749X
- National Institute of Economic and Social Research, London. Occasional Papers. irreg. ISSN 0077-4928
- National Institute of Economic and Social Research, London. Regional Studies. irreg. ISSN 0077-4936
- New Studies in Archaeology. irreg.
- New Testament Studies. q. ISSN 0028-6885 (Studiorum Novi Testamenti Societas)
- Nutrition Society, Proceedings. 3 per yr. ISSN 0029-6651
- Parasitology. 3 per yr. ISSN 0031-1820
- Philosophy. q. ISSN 0031-8191 (Royal Institute of Philosophy)
- Physiological Society. Monographs. irreg., 1967, no. 71. ISSN 0079-2020 (Dist. in U.S. by Williams & Wilkins Co., 428 E. Preston St., Baltimore, MD 21202)
- Princeton-Cambridge Studies in Chinese Linguistics. irreg. ISSN 0079-5178
- Psychological Medicine; a journal for research in psychiatry & the allied sciences. q. ISSN 0033-2917
- Quarterly Reviews of Biophysics. q. ISSN 0033-5835 (International Union for Pure & Applied Biophysics)
- Religious Studies. q. ISSN 0034-4125
- Resources of Music. irreg. ISSN 0080-1828
- Royal Society of London. Royal Society Mathematical Tables. irreg. ISSN 0080-4657
- School Mathematics Project. Computing in Mathematics. irreg.
- School Mathematics Project. Handbooks. irreg.
- Shakespeare Survey. a. ISSN 0080-9152
- Slavonic and East European Review. q. ISSN 0037-6795
- Smuts Memorial Lecture. irreg. ISSN 0085-6150
- Society for Endocrinology (Great Britain) Memoirs. irreg., no. 20, 1973. ISSN 0081-136X
- Society for General Micriobiology. Symposia. irreg., no. 24, 1974. ISSN 0081-1394
- Society for New Testament Studies. Monograph Series. irreg. ISSN 0081-1432
- Studies in the Modern Russian Language. irreg. ISSN 0081-8631
- Studies in the National Income and Expenditure of the United Kingdom. irreg. ISSN 0081-864X (National Institute of Economic and Social Research) (Co-sponsor: Cambridge University, Department of Applied Economics)
- University of London. Contemporary China Institute. Publications. irreg. ISSN 0085-2856
- West African Language Monograph Series. irreg. ISSN 0083-8179
- Wiles Lectures. a. ISSN 0511-9561
- Yale Classical Studies. irreg, vol. 24, 1975. ISSN 0084-330X

**Cambridgeshire & Isle of Ely Naturalists Trust**
1 Brookside, Cambridge CB2 1JF, England.
- Nature in Cambridgeshire. a. ISSN 0466-6046

**Cambridgeshire Life Ltd.**
4&5 Free Church Passage, St. Ives, Huntingdon PE17 4AY, Eng.
- Cambridgeshire, Huntingdon & Peterborough Life. m. ISSN 0008-2023
- Northamptonshire & Bedfordshire Life. m.

**Camden History Society**
St. Pancras Library, London NW1 2AJ, England.
- Camden History Review. a. ISSN 0305-4756

**Camera Club**
8 Great Newport St., London WC2H 7JA, Eng.
- Camera Club Journal. m. ISSN 0008-2104

**Campaign for Comprehensive Education**
17 Granard Ave., London SW15 6HH, England.
- Comprehensive Education. 3 per yr. ISSN 0588-9278

**Campaign for Nuclear Disarmament**
Eastbourne House, Bullards Place, London E2 OPJ, England.
- Sanity. 6 per yr. ISSN 0036-4444

**Campillos Ltd.**
23 Ridgmount St., London W.C.1., Eng.
- Beat Instrumental Songwriting & Recording Magazine. m.

**Camping & Sports Equipment Ltd.**
4 Spring St., London W.2, Eng.
- C S E News. m. ISSN 0008-2406
- Camping Caravanning and Sports Equipment Trades Directory. a. ISSN 0068-6948

**Camping Club of Great Britain and Ireland Ltd.**
11 Lower Grosvenor Place, London SW1W 0EY, Eng.
- Camping & Caravanning. m.
- Camping Club Handbook and Sites List. biennial.

**Canada-United Kingdom Chamber of Commerce**
British Columbia House, 1-3 Lower Regent St., London SW1Y 4NZ, England.
- Canada-U.K. Trade News. m. ISSN 0045-4281

**Canadian High Commission. Counsellor (Public Affairs)**
Canada House, Trafalgar Square, London SA1Y 5BJ, England.
- Canada Today. bi-m.

**Canadian Philatelic Society of Great Britain**
17 Mellish Rd., Walsall, Staffs, Eng.
- Maple Leaves. 5 per yr.

**Cancer Research Campaign**
2 Carlton House Terrace, London SW1Y 5AR, England.
- British Journal of Cancer. (pub. by H. K. Lewis & Co. Ltd.)
- Cancer Research Campaign. Annual Report. a.

**Canoe Camping Club**
11 Lower Grosvenor Place, London S.W.I., England, Eng.
- Canoe-Camper. 4 per yr. ISSN 0008-5626

**Canon Law Society of Great Britain**
St. Andrew's College, Drygrange Melrose TD6 9DH, Scotland
(Subscr. To. Rev. E. Walker, St. Hugh's College, Tellerton Hall, Nottingham NG12 4FZ, England)
- Canon Law Abstracts; half-yearly review of periodical literature in Canon Law. s-a. ISSN 0008-5650

**Canterbury Archaeological Scoiety**
c/o L. D. Lyle, 3 Queen's Ave., Canterbury, Kent CT2 8AY, England.
- Canterbury Archaeological Society. Occasional Papers. irreg., no. 7, 1974. ISSN 0069-0198

**Canterbury Diocesan House**
Canterbury, Kent, Eng.
- Canterbury Diocesan Notes. m. ISSN 0008-5693

**Car Ferry Enquiries Ltd.**
9A Spur Rd., Isleworth, Middlesex, England.
- Lazy Way to Book Your Car Ferries. a.

**Caravan Club**
55 St. James's St., London S.W.1., England.
- En Route. bi-m.

**Carcanet Press Ltd.**
Pin Farm, South Hinksey, Oxford, England.
- Oxford Theatre Texts. irreg.

**Cardiff Area Students Association**
Joint Students Union, Park Place, Cardiff, Wales.
- C A S A. m.

**Cardiff Medical Society**
University Hospital of Wales, Cardiff, Wales.
- Cardiff Medical Society. Scientific Proceedings. m (Oct.-May) ISSN 0069-035X

**Cardinallar Ltd**
11 B Wardour Mews, London W.1, Eng.
- I T. fortn. ISSN 0019-073X

**Career Consultants Ltd.**
20 Fouberts Place, London W1V 1HH, England.
- Degree Course Offers. irreg.

**Careers Research and Advisory Centre**
- British Journal of Guidance and Counselling. (pub. by Hobsons Press)

**Caret**
2 Bakers Mead, Tilbrook, Huntingdon, Cambridge Shire, England.
- Caret; a poetry magazine. 3 per yr.

**Carfax Publishing Co.**
Haddon House, Dorchester-on-Thames, Oxford OX9 8JZ, England.
- C O R E. (Collected Original Resources in Education); an international journal of educational research published in microform. 3 per yr. ISSN 0308-6909
- Comparative Education; an international journal of comparative studies. 3 per yr. ISSN 0305-0068
- Compare; a journal of comparitive education. 2 per yr. ISSN 0305-7925
- Educational Studies. 3 per yr. ISSN 0305-5698
- International Background; international journal of current political, social and economic affairs. 10 per yr.
- Oxford Review of Education. 3 per yr. ISSN 0305-4985
- Studies in Higher Education. s-a. ISSN 0307-5079

**Caribbean Tourism Association**
- Tourism International Research/Caribbean. (pub. by Tourism International Press Ltd.)

**CARL Communications Ltd.**
2 College Hill Terrace, Haslemere, Surrey, England.
- Pensions World. m. ISSN 0307-191X (National Association of Pension Funds)

**William Carling & Co.**
Market Place, Hitchin, Herts SG5 1EA, England.
- Berkshire and Buckinghamshire Countryside. m. ISSN 0306-6614
- Essex Countryside. m. ISSN 0014-0910
- Hertfordshire Countryside. m. ISSN 0306-672X

**Carmarthen County Museum**
County Hall, Carmarthen, England.
- Carmarthen County Museum. Publication. irreg.

**Carnegie School of Physical Education**
Leeds Polytechnic, Beckett Park, Leeds 6, Eng.
- Research Papers in Physical Education. s-a. ISSN 0034-5350

**Carnegie United Kingdom Trust**
Comely Park House, Dunfermline, Fife KY12 7EJ, Scotland.
- Carnegie United Kingdom Trust. Annual Report. a. ISSN 0069-0686

**Carregraff**
Graig Las, Talybont, Brecon, Wales.
- Mainly. 2-4 per yr. ISSN 0025-0848

**Carriers Publishing Co. Ltd.**
Blenheim House, London S.W.11, Eng.
- Roads and Road Construction. m. ISSN 0035-7332

**Carruthers & Sons**
Box 13, 9-11 Bank Lane, Inverness, Scotland.
- Inverness Courier. s-w. ISSN 0020-9929

**Carson and Comerford Ltd.**
19-21 Tavistock St., London WC2E 7PA, England.
- Showcall. a.
- Stage and Television Today. w. ISSN 0038-9099

**Cartophilic Society of Great Britain Ltd.**
c/o R. C. Bongart, Secy, 267 Roding Lane North, Woodford Green, Essex, Eng.
- Cartophilic Notes & News. bi-m. ISSN 0008-7076

**Frank Cass & Co. Ltd.**
Gainsborough House, 11 Gainsborough Rd., London E11 1RS, England
(Dist. in U.S. by: Biblio Distribution Center, 81 Adams Drive, Totowa, N.J. 07512)
- African Language Review. a. ISSN 0065-3977
- Annual Survey of African Law. a. ISSN 0066-4405
- Business History. s-a. ISSN 0007-6791
- Cass Library of African Studies. Africana Modern Library. irreg., no. 18, 1972. ISSN 0069-0880
- Cass Library of African Studies. General Studies. irreg, no. 137, 1973. ISSN 0069-0899
- Cass Library of African Studies. Researches and Travels. irreg., no. 25, 1973. ISSN 0069-0902

- Cass Library of African Studies. South African Studies. irreg., no. 6, 1970. ISSN 0069-0910
- Cass Library of African Studies. Travels and Narratives. irreg., no. 73, 1968. ISSN 0069-0929
- Cass Library of Industrial Classics. irreg., no. 28, 1969. ISSN 0069-0937
- Cass Library of Science Classics. irreg., no. 23, 1971. ISSN 0069-0945
- English Little Magazines. irreg., no. 16, 1971. ISSN 0071-061X
- Journal of Commonwealth & Comparative Politics. 3 per yr. (Institute of Commonwealth Studies)
- Journal of Development Studies; devoted to economic, political and social development. q. ISSN 0022-0388
- Journal of Imperial and Commonwealth History. 3 per yr.
- Journal of Peasant Studies. q.
- Middle Eastern Studies. 3 per yr. ISSN 0026-3206

**Cassell and Co., Ltd.**
35 Red Lion Sq., London WC1R 4SG, England.
- Cassell's Directory of Publishing in Great Britain, the Commonwealth, Ireland, South Africa and Pakistan. biennial. ISSN 0069-097X

**Castle Books**
47 High St., Tonbridge, Kent, England.
- Boatbuilders' & Chandlers' Directory of Suppliers. a. ISSN 0306-3593

**Castle Publishing Co.**
314 Gray's Inn Rd., London W.C. 1, England.
- Castle's Guide to the Fruit, Flower, Vegetable and Allied Trades. biennial. ISSN 0069-0988

**Casualties Union**
1 Grosvenor Crescent, London SW1X 7EE, Eng.
- Casualty Simulation; to stimulate realism in first aid, nursing and rescue training. q. ISSN 0008-7580

**Catenian Association**
- Catena. (pub. by Burleigh Press Ltd.)

**Catholic Biblical Association of Great Britain**
8 Holly Hill Close, Southampton SO1 7EU, Eng.
- Scripture Bulletin. q. ISSN 0036-9780 (Co-Sponsor: Bible Reading Fellowship)

**Catholic Church**
- Clergy Review. (pub. by Tablet Publishing Co.)

**Catholic Fireside Ltd.**
110 Coombe Lane, London SW2O 0AY, Eng.
- Catholic Fireside; the weekly magazine for all the family. w. ISSN 0008-803X

**Catholic Herald Ltd.**
63 Charterhouse St., London EC1M 6LA, Eng.
- Catholic Herald. w. ISSN 0008-8072

**Catholic Missionary Society**
114 W. Heath Rd., London NW3 7TX, Eng.
- Catholic Gazette. m. ISSN 0008-8064

**Catholic Nurses Guild of England and Wales**
St. Winifred's Hospital, Canton, Cardiff, S. Glamorgan, Wales.
- Catholic Nurse. q. ISSN 0008-8269

**Catholic Pictorial Ltd.**
12 Prescot Rd., Liverpool L7 0LQ, Eng.
- Catholic Pictorial. w. ISSN 0008-8293

**Catholic Record Society**
Secretary, c/o 114 Mount St., London W1, Eng.
- Recusant History. 2 per yr. ISSN 0034-1932

**Catholic Study Circle for Animal Welfare**
Ealing Abbey, London W5 2DY, Eng.
- Ark. 3 per yr. ISSN 0004-167X

**Catholic Teachers' Federation**
St. Mary's College, Strawberry Hill, Twickenham TW1 4SX, Middlesex, England.
- Catholic Education Today. q. ISSN 0008-8013 (Co-Sponsor: Catholic Colleges of Education)

**Catholic Truth Society**
38/40 Eccleston Square, London SW1V 1PD, England.
- Catholic Truth. s-a. ISSN 0411-275X

**Catonsville Roadrunner**
c/o Martin Jelfs, Ed., 128 Bethnal Green Rd., London E2 6DG, England.
- Catonsville Roadrunner. 10 per yr. ISSN 0008-8536

**Cats Protection League**
29 Church St., Slough, Bucks, Eng.
- Cat. bi-m. ISSN 0008-7599

**Caution Magazine Ltd.**
18 Imperial Square, Cheltenham, Glos. GL50 1QZ, England.
- Caution Magazine; industrial fire, safety and security. bi-m.

**Paul Cave Publications Ltd.**
13 Portland St., Southampton, Eng.
- Hampshire; the county magazine. m. ISSN 0017-7113

**Caxton Press**
Oswestry, Shropshire, England.
- Country Quest; the magazine for Wales and the border. m. ISSN 0011-0213

**Celebrity Service Ltd.**
10 Dover St., London, W1X 3PH, Eng.
- Celebrity Bulletin. s-w. ISSN 0045-6020

**Cement and Concrete Association**
Wexham Springs, Slough, Bucks SL3 6PL, Eng.
- Concrete. m. ISSN 0010-5317 (Concrete Society)
- Concrete Quarterly. q. ISSN 0010-5376
- Concrete Year Book. a. ISSN 0069-8288
- Magazine of Concrete Research. q. ISSN 0024-9831
- Precast Concrete. m. ISSN 0010-5325
- World Cement Technology. bi-m.

**Central Asian Mission**
Emmaus, Talbot Rd., Maidstone, Kent ME16 OJD, England.
- Dawn in Central Asia. irreg. ISSN 0070-2994

**Central Asian Research Centre**
18 Parkfield St., London N1 OPR, England
(Dist. in U. S. by: Columbia University Press, 136 S. Broadway, Irvington- on- Hudson, NY 10533)
- Afro-Asian Affairs. (pub. by Afro-Asian Publications, Ltd.)
- Soviet - Third World Relations. irreg.
- U S S R and Third World; a survey of Soviet and Chinese relations with Africa, Asia and Latin America. 8 per yr. ISSN 0041-5545

**Central Bureau for Educational Visits and Exchanges**
43 Dorset St., London W1H 3FN, Eng.
- Educational Exchange. 3 per yr. ISSN 0046-1490
- Higher Education Exchange. 3 per yr. ISSN 0305-3253
- Intercommunity - International Community Education. q. ISSN 0308-9231

**Central Council for Agricultural and Horticultural Co-Operation**
Hancock House, Vincent Sq., London SW1P 2PQ, England.
- Farming Business. q.

**Central Council for British Naturism**
Box 35, Enfield, Middlesex, England.
- British Naturism. q. ISSN 0007-1560

**Central Council of Church Bell Ringers**
Penmark House, Woodbridge Meadows, Guildford GU1 1BL, Surrey, Eng.
- Ringing World. w. ISSN 0035-5453

**Central European Federalists**
39 Stanwick Mansions, Stanwick Rd., London W.14, Eng.
- European Bulletin and Press. s-a. ISSN 0046-2713

**Central Literary Magazine**
45 Sandhills Lane, Barnt Green, Nr. Birmingham, England.
- Central Literary Magazine. a. ISSN 0069-164X

**Central London Adult Education Institute**
6 Bolt Court, Fleet St., London E.C.4, England.
- People like That. irreg.

**Central Scotland Chamber of Commerce**
11 Orchard St., Falkirk, Stirlingshire, Scotland.
- Central Scotland Chamber of Commerce Quarterly Bulletin. q.

**Centre for Advanced Land Use Studies**
College of Estate Management, White Knights, Reading RG6 2AW, England.
- Occasional Papers in Estate Management. irreg., no. 9, 1977. ISSN 0078-3048
- Property Studies in the U.K. and Overseas. irreg., no. 8, 1976.

**Centre for African Studies**
- Cambridge African Studies Series. (pub. by Cambridge University Press)

**Centre for English Cultural Tradition and Language**
c/o Dept. of English Language, Sheffield University, Sheffield S10 2TN, England.
- Lore and Language. s-a. ISSN 0307-7144

**Centre for Environmental Studies**
62 Chandos Place, London WC2N 4HH, England.
- Centre for Environmental Studies, London. Conference Paper. irreg. ISSN 0069-1917
- Centre for Environmental Studies, London. Information Paper. irreg. ISSN 0069-1925

**Centre for Information on the Teaching of English**
Moray House College of Education, Holyrood Road, Edinburgh EH8 8AQ, Scotland.
- Teaching English. 3 per yr. ISSN 0305-7755

**Centre for Research and Documentation**
c/o the Director, 77 Grassmere Ave., Wembley, Middlesex HA9 8TF, England.
- Centre for Research and Documentation on the Language Problem. irreg.

**Centre for Scottish Studies**
Director, Taylor Bldg., King's College, Old Aberdeeen AB9 2UB, Scotland.
- Northern Scotland. a.

**Centre for the Study of Religion & Communism**
Keston College, Heathfield Rd., Keston, Kent BR2 6BA, England.
- Religion in Communist Lands. q.

**Centre of Adhyatma Yoga in the West**
29 Chepstow Villas, London W.11, England.
- Self-Knowledge; a quarterly journal devoted to spiritual thought and practice. q. ISSN 0037-1556 (Shanti Sadan)

**Centre Seventeen**
57, Newbiggen St., Thaxted, Essex, Eng.
- Centre Seventeen. q.

**Centres of Latin American Studies at the Universities of Cambridge, Glasgow, Liverpool, London and Oxford**
- Journal of Latin American Studies. (pub. by Cambridge University Press)

**Century Services, Ltd.**
51-59 Donegall St., Belfast BT1 2GB, N. Ireland.
- Belfast and Northern Ireland Directory. a. ISSN 0067-5342

**Ceredigion Antiquarian Society**
26 Alban Square, Aberaeron, Cards., Wales.
- Ceredigion. a. ISSN 0069-2263

**Certified Accountants Educational Trust**
22 Bedford Sq., London WC1B 3HS, Eng.
- Certified Accountant. bi-m.

**Challenger Society**
c/o Institute of Oceanographic Sciences, Wormley, Godalming, Surrey, England.
- Challenger Society. Newsletter. 3 per yr.

**Chalton Publishing Co., Ltd.**
Watermans Oast, Headcorn Nr. Ashford, Kent, England.
- Nigerian Commercial Vehicle User. q. ISSN 0029-0068

**Harry Chambers, Ed. & Pub.**
8 Cavendish Rd., Heaton Mersey, Stockpot, Cheshire SK4 3DN, Eng.
- Phoenix; a poetry magazine. irreg. ISSN 0031-8337 (North West Arts Association)

**Chameleon Press Ltd.**
98 Thornbury Rd., Osterley, Isleworth, Middx., Eng.
- Medical Missionary. q. ISSN 0025-7370

**R. H. Chandler Ltd.**
Box 55, Braintree, Essex, England.
- Automotive Emission Control. q.

- Bibliographies in Paint Technology. irreg. ISSN 0067-7094
- Catalysts in Chemistry. m.
- Continental Paint and Resin News; a digest of company news, articles and patents from the countries of Europe. m. ISSN 0010-7735
- Organometallic Compounds. fortn. ISSN 0030-5138
- Paint and Resin Patents. m. ISSN 0030-946X

**Chandler Publications Ltd.**
Owermoigne, Dorchester, Dorset, Eng.
- Agricultural & Veterinary Chemicals and Agricultural Engineering. m. ISSN 0002-1377
- Disposables and Nonwovens. m. ISSN 0012-3811
- Multihull International. m. ISSN 0027-3155

**Chansitor Publications**
46 Bedford Row, London WC1R 4LR, England.
- Church Pulpit Year Book; sermon outlines. a. ISSN 0069-4002

**John Chapman**
36 Broad St. Haverhill, Suffolk CB9 9HD, Eng.
- Zion's Witness. m. ISSN 0049-8742

**Chapman & Hall Ltd.**
11 New Fetter Lane, London EC4P 4EE, Eng.
- Applied Economics. q. ISSN 0003-6846
- Cambridge Studies in Applied Econometrics. irreg. (Cambridge University)
- Histochemical Journal. bi-m. ISSN 0018-2214
- I M S Monitor; quarterly review of the labour market. q. (Institute of Manpower Studies)
- International Astrophysics. irreg. ISSN 0074-1817 (Dist. in U.S. by Halstead Press, 605 Third Ave., New York, NY 10016)
- Journal of Applied Electrochemistry. q. ISSN 0021-891X
- Journal of Materials Science. m. ISSN 0022-2461
- Journal of Neurocytology. q. ISSN 0300-4864
- Monographs on Applied Probability and Statistics. irreg. ISSN 0076-6976 (Dist. in U.S. by Halstead Press, 605 Third Ave., New York, NY 10016)
- Optical and Quantum Electronics. bi-m. ISSN 0306-8919

**Charities Aid Foundation**
48 Pembury Rd., Tonbridge TN9 2JD, Kent, England.
- Directory of Grant-Making Trusts. irreg. ISSN 0070-5624

**Charles Darwin Foundation for the Galapagos Isles**
c/o G. T. Corley Smith, Greensted Hall, Ongar, Essex, England.
- Noticias de Galapagos. s-a. ISSN 0550-1067

**Alain Charles Publishing Ltd.**
70 Lexham Gardens, London W8, England.
- Media International. 10 per yr.

**Chartered Institute of Patent Agents**
Staple Inn Bldgs., High Holborn, London WC1V 7PZ, England.
- Register of Patent Agents. a.

**Chartered Institute of Public Finance and Accountancy**
1 Buckingham Place, London SW1E 6HS, England.
- Chartered Institute of Public Finance and Accountancy. Education Statistics. a.
- Chartered Institute of Public Finance and Accountancy. Fire Services Statistics. irreg.
- Chartered Institute of Public Finance and Accountancy. Local Health & Social Services Statistics. a.
- Chartered Institute of Public Finance and Accountancy. Public Libraries Statistics. a.
- Public Finance and Accountancy. m.
- Return of Outstanding Debt. a.

**Chartered Institute of Transport**
80 Portland Place, London W1N 4DP, England.
- Chartered Institute of Transport. Handbook. a.
- Chartered Institute of Transport. Journal. bi-m. ISSN 0020-3181

**Chartered Institution of Building Services**
49 Cadogan Sq., London SW1X 0JB, Eng.
- Building Services Engineer. m. ISSN 0301-6536

**Chartered Insurance Institute**
20 Aldermanbury, London EC2V 7HY, England.
- C I I Journal. 3 per yr.

**Chartered Society of Physiotherapy**
14 Bedford Row, London WC1R 4ED, Eng.
- Physiotherapy. m. ISSN 0031-9406

**Charterhouse School**
Godalming, Surrey, Eng.
- Carthusian. 3 per yr. ISSN 0008-7033

**Chatfield Applied Research Laboratories Ltd.**
Croydon, England.
- Chatfield's European Directory of Paints and Allied Products/Annuaire Chatfield European de Peintures et Produits Assimiles/Chatfields Europaeisches Adressbuch fuer Anstrichmittel-und Verwandte Produkte. irreg.

**Cheering Words**
c/o D. Oldham, 22 Victoria Rd., Stamford, Lincs. PE9 1HB, Eng.
- Cheering Words. m. ISSN 0009-2126

**Chelsea College. Students Union**
Manresa Rd., London. SW3 6LX, England.
- Concetto; newspaper of Chelsea College students. fortn.
- Science Chelsea. 2 per yr. ISSN 0300-3361

**Chelsea Speleological Society**
Chelsea Community Centre, 385 Kings Rd., London SW10 0LR, England.
- Chelsea Speleological Society. Records. irreg.
- Chelsea Speleological Society Newsletter. m. ISSN 0045-6381

**Chemical Industries Association Ltd.**
Alembic House, 93 Albert Embankment, London SE1 7TU, England.
- British Chemicals & Their Manufacturers. biennial.
- U K Chemical Industry Statistics Handbook. a.

**Chemical Society**
Burlington House, London W1V 0BN, England (Subscr. to: Blackhorse Road, Letchworth, Herts SG6 1HN, England)
- Alkaloids. a.
- Amino-Acids, Peptides and Proteins. a.
- Analyst. m. ISSN 0003-2654
- Analytical Abstracts. m. ISSN 0003-2689
- Analytical Sciences Monographs. irreg., no. 3, 1975.
- Annual Reports on Analytical Atomic Spectroscopy. a.
- Aromatic and Heteroaromatic Chemistry. a.
- Biosynthesis. a.
- Carbohydrate Chemistry. a. ISSN 0576-7172
- Chemical Society. Analytical Division. Proceedings. m. ISSN 0306-1396
- Chemical Society, London. Annual Reports on the Progress of Chemistry. Section A: Physical and Inorganic Chemistry. a.
- Chemical Society, London. Annual Reports on the Progress of Chemistry. Section B: Organic Chemistry. a. ISSN 0069-3030
- Chemical Society, London. Journal: Dalton Transactions; a journal for inorganic chemists. 24 per yr. ISSN 0300-9246
- Chemical Society, London. Journal: Faraday Transactions 1; a journal of physical chemistry. m. ISSN 0300-9599
- Chemical Society, London. Journal: Faraday Transactions 2; a journal of chemical physics. m. ISSN 0300-9238
- Chemical Society, London. Journal: Perkin Transactions 1; a journal of organic and bio-organic chemistry. fortn. ISSN 0300-922X
- Chemical Society, London. Perkin Transactions 2; a journal of physical organic chemistry. 15 per yr. ISSN 0300-9580
- Chemical Society, London. Reviews. q.
- Chemical Society, London, Annual Report of Council and Accounts. a.
- Chemical Society, London, Monographs for Teachers. irreg.(approx. 3 nos. per year) ISSN 0080-4428
- Chemical Thermodynamics. a.
- Colloid Science. a.
- Dielectric and Related Molecular Processes. biennial.
- Education in Chemistry. bi-m. ISSN 0013-1350
- Electrochemistry. a.
- Electron Spin Resonance; sepcialist periodical reports. a.
- Electronic Structure & Magnetism of Inorganic Compounds. a.
- Environmental Chemistry; specialist periodical reports. biennial.
- Faraday Discussions. s-a. ISSN 0301-7249
- Faraday Symposia. a. ISSN 0301-5696

- Fluorocarbon and Related Chemistry. biennial.
- Foreign Compound Metabolism in Mammals. biennial. ISSN 0300-3493
- Gas Kinetics and Energy Transfer; specialist periodical reports. biennial.
- Index of Reviews in Organic Chemistry. a., with triennial cumulations.
- Inorganic Chemistry of the Main Group Elements. a.
- Inorganic Chemistry of the Transition Elements. a.
- Inorganic Reaction Mechanisms. irreg. (every 18 mos)
- Journal of the Chemical Society. Chemical Communications; a journal for urgent preliminary accounts of important chemical research. s-m. ISSN 0022-4936
- Mass Spectrometry. biennial.
- Molecular Spectroscopy. a.
- Molecular Structure by Diffraction Methods. a.
- Nuclear Magnetic Resonance. a.
- Organic Compounds of Sulphur, Selenium and Tellurium. biennial.
- Organometallic Chemistry. a. ISSN 0301-0074
- Organophosphorus Chemistry. a. ISSN 0475-1582
- Radio Chemistry. biennial.
- Russian Chemical Reviews. m. ISSN 0036-021X
- Russian Journal of Inorganic Chemistry. m. ISSN 0036-0236
- Russian Journal of Physical Chemistry. m. ISSN 0036-0244
- Selected Annual Reviews of the Analytical Sciences. a. ISSN 0300-9963
- Specialist Periodical Reports. 30 vols. per yr.
- Spectroscopic Properties of Inorganic & Organometallic Compounds; specialist periodical reports. a. ISSN 0584-8555
- Statistical Mechanics. biennial.
- Surface and Defect Properties of Solids. a.
- Terpenoids and Steroids. a. ISSN 0300-5992
- Theoretical Chemistry. biennial.

**Cheshire Foundation Homes**
19 Bolton St., London W1Y 8HD, England.
- Cheshire Smile. q. ISSN 0009-3297

**Chess (Sutton Coldfield) Ltd**
Sutton Coldfield B73 6AZ, England.
- Chess. fortn.(double issues monthly) ISSN 0009-3319
- Chess Book List. q. ISSN 0069-3197

**Chess Endgame Study Circle**
c/o A. J. Roycroft, Ed., 17 New Way Rd., London NW9 6PC, England.
- E G. q. ISSN 0012-7671

**Chest and Heart Association. Scottish Branch**
65 North Castle St., Edinburgh EH2 3LT, Scotland.
- Chest and Heart Association. Scottish Branch. Bulletin. s-a.

**Chest Heart and Stroke Association**
Tavistock House, Tavistock Sq., London WC1H 9JE, Eng.
- Chest, Heart and Stroke Journal. q.

**Chetham Society**
- Remains, Historical and Literary, Connected with the Palatine Counties of Lancaster and Chester. (pub. by Manchester University Press)

**Chichester Diocese**
- Chichester News. (pub. by Southern Publishing Co.)

**Chigwell Local History Society**
c/o C. A. Osborne, 3 Parndon House, Valley Hill, Loughton, Essex, Eng.
- Chigwell Local History Society. Transactions. s-a.

**Child Poverty Action Group**
1 Macklin St., London W.C.2, Eng.
- Poverty. q. ISSN 0032-5856

**Children and Youth Aliyah Committee for Great Britain**
- Youth Aliyah Review. (pub. by Youth Aliyah)

**Childrens Book Centre Ltd.**
229 Kensington High St., London W8 6SA, England.
- Children's Book Newsletter. q.

**China Policy Study Group**
62 Parliament Hill, London NW3 2TJ, Eng.
- China Policy Study Group. Broadsheet. m. ISSN 0007-2052

**Christadelphian Magazine and Publishing Association Ltd.**
404 Shaftmoor Lane, Hall Green, Birmingham B28 8SZ, Eng.
- Christadelphian; dedicated wholly to the hope of Israel. m. ISSN 0009-5117

**Christian Education Movement**
2 Chester House, Pages Lane, London N10 1PR, England.
- Learning for Living. q. ISSN 0023-9704

**Christian Endeavour Union of Great Britain and Ireland**
18 Leam Terrace, Royal Leamington Spa, Warwickshire CV31 1BB, England.
- Christian Endeavour Topic Book. a.

**Christian Herald Co. Ltd.**
4 Western Esplanade, Portslade, Brighton, BN4 1WP, Eng.
- Prophetic News and Israel's Watchman. m. ISSN 0033-1333

**Christian News Ltd.**
Centre One, Devonshire House, High St., Birmingham, B12 0LP, Eng.
- Compass. m. ISSN 0045-7809

**Christian Order**
65 Belgrave Rd., London S.W. 1, Eng.
- Christian Order. m. ISSN 0009-5559

**Christian Socialist Movement**
Kingsway Hall, London W.C.2, Eng.
- Christian Socialist. q. ISSN 0009-5648

**Christian Weekly Newspapers Ltd.**
146 Queen Victoria St., London EC4V 4EH, Eng.
- British Weekly. w.
- C E N; Church of England newspaper. w. ISSN 0007-8255
- Christian Record. w.

**Christian Witness to Israel**
44 Lubbock Rd., Chislehurst, Kent BR7 5JX, England.
- C W I Herald.

**Chronicle House**
72-78 Fleet Street, London, England.
- Hospital Life. m.

**Church Army**
C.S.C House, North Circular Rd., London NW10 7UG, England.
- Church Army Review. bi-m. ISSN 0009-6350
- Spearhead. q. ISSN 0038-6650

**Church in Wales Publications**
Woodland Place, Penarth; Glam CF6 2EX, Wales.
- Llan. w. ISSN 0024-5445
- Welsh Churchman. m.

**Church Information Office**
Church House, Westminster, London S.W.1, England.
- York Journal of Convocation. irreg. ISSN 0085-8374 (Convocation of York)

**Church Lads Brigade**
Claude Hardy House, 15 Etchingham Park Rd., Finchley, London N3 2DU, England.
- Brigade. s-a. ISSN 0045-2831

**Church of England**
Church House, Deans Yard, London SW1P 3NZ, England.
- Church of England. General Synod. Report of Proceedings. 3 per yr. ISSN 0307-7225
- Church of England Yearbook. a. ISSN 0069-3987
- Crucible. q. ISSN 0011-2100 (Board for Social Responsibility of the General Synod)
- Together. 9 per yr. ISSN 0307-5982 (Board of Education of the General Synod)

**Church of England. Board for Social Responsibility**
Church House, Deans Yard, London, SW1P 3NZ, England.
- Directory of Church of England Social Services. a. ISSN 0070-5268

**Church of England. Central Readers' Conference**
Church House, Dean's Yard, London SW1P 3NZ, Eng.
- Reader. q. ISSN 0300-3469

**Church of England Children's Society**
Old Town Hall, Kennington, London SE11 4QD, Eng.
- Gateway. q.

**Church of Scientology**
Saint Hill Manor, East Grinstead, Sussex, Eng.
- Auditor; the monthly journal of Scientology. m. ISSN 0004-7651

**Church of Scotland**
Dept. of Publicity and Publication, 121 George St., Edinburgh EH2 4YN, Scotland.
- Church of Scotland. Yearbook. a. ISSN 0069-3995
- Life and Work; the record of the Church of Scotland. m. ISSN 0024-306X

**Church Pastoral Aid Society**
Falcon Court, 32 Fleet St., London EC4Y 1DB, Eng.
- Together. bi-m.

**Church Service Society**
- Liturgical Review. (pub. by Scottish Academic Press Ltd.)

**Church Society**
7 Wine Office Court, Fleet St., London EC4 3DA, England.
- Churchman; a journal of Anglican theology. q. ISSN 0009-661X

**Church Union**
Faith House, 7 Tufton St., London SW1, Eng.
- Church Observer. q. ISSN 0009-6482
- Faith and Unity. q. ISSN 0014-7036

**J. & A. Churchill**
104 Gloucester Place, London, W1, England.
- Ophthalmological Societies of the United Kingdom. Transactions. a. ISSN 0078-5334

**Church's Ministry Among the Jews**
Vincent House, Vincent Square, London SW1P 2PX, England.
- Shalom. q.

**Ciba-Geigy Plastics and Additives Co.**
Plastics Division, Duxford, Cambridge CB2 4QA, Eng.
- Ciba-Geigy Technical Notes. bi-m.

**Cinderella Stamp Club**
c/oL. N. Williams, 30 Dunstan Rd, London NW11 8AB, Eng.
- Cinderella Philatelist. q. ISSN 0009-6911

**Cinema Magazine**
1213 Little Newport St., London WC2, England.
- Cinema. 4 per yr.

**Cinema Organ Society**
45 Turnpike Link, Park Hill, Croydon CR0 5NT, England.
- Cinema Organ. q.

**Circle Books**
16 Davenant Rd., Oxford OX2 8BX, Eng.
- Informer; international poetry magazine. q. ISSN 0020-0840

**Circle of State Librarians**
c/o Civil Service Dept., Whitehall, London SW1A 2A2, England.
- State Librarian. 3 per yr. ISSN 0305-9189

**Circle Publications, Ltd.**
882-4 Eastern Ave., Ilford, Essex, Eng.
- Corsetry and Underwear. bi-m. ISSN 0010-9444

**City and Guilds College Union**
- Spanner. (pub. by Dominion Press Ltd.)

**City Business Library**
Gillet House, 55 Basinghall St., London EC2V 5BX, Eng.
- City Business Courier; news-letter of the City Business Library. s-a. ISSN 0009-7713 (Corporation of London)

**City Magazines Ltd.**
1-3 Wine Office Court, Fleet St., London EC4 3AL, England.
- Antique Dealer and Collectors' Guide. m. ISSN 0003-5866
- Licensed Bookmaker & Betting Office Proprietor. m. ISSN 0024-2772
- Trader. m.

**City of Aberdeen. Public Relations Department**
St. Nicholas House, Broad St., Aberdeen AB9 1DE, Scotland.
- What's on and Where to Shop in Aberdeen. m.

**City of Birmingham Symphony Orchestra**
60 Newhall Street, Birmingham B3 3RP, England.
- City of Birmingham Symphony Orchestra. Annual Prospectus. a.
- City of Birmingham Symphony Orchestra. Prom Prospectus. a.

**City of London Phonograph & Gramophone Society**
148 Nether St., West Finchley, London N3 1PG, England
(Subscr. to: B. A. Williamson, 157 Childwall Valley Rd., Liverpool L16 1LA, England)
- Hill and Dale News. bi-m. ISSN 0018-1846

**City of London Polytechnic. Mansfield Law Club**
London EC2M 6SQ, England.
- City of London Law Review. s-a. ISSN 0306-9788

**City of London Weekly Ltd.**
4 Moorfields, London EC2Y 9AB, England.
- City of London Directory & Livery Companies Guide. a.
- City Press Investment Bulletin. m. ISSN 0308-8316

**City of Westminster Chamber of Commerce**
Mitre House, 177 Regent St., London W1R 8DJ, Eng.
- Westminster Review. m. ISSN 0043-437X

**City of York Art Gallery**
Exhibition Sq., York, Eng.
- Preview. q. ISSN 0032-8103

**City University Union Society**
St. John St., London E.C. 1V 4PB, Eng.
- Beacon. every 3 wks. ISSN 0005-7320

**Civic Trust**
17 Carlton House Terrace, London SW1 5AW, England.
- Civic Trust News. bi-m. ISSN 0306-090X

**Civil and Public Services Association**
215 Balham High Rd., London S.W.17, Eng.
- Red Tape. m. ISSN 0034-2076

**Civil Service National Whitley Council**
19 Rochester Row, London SW1P 1LB, Eng.
- Whitley Bulletin. m. ISSN 0043-5023

**Civil Service Sports Council**
272-274 Vauxhall Bridge Rd., London S.W. 1, Eng.
- Civil Service Sports Quarterly. q. ISSN 0009-8051

**Civil Service Union**
17-21 Hatton Hall, London E.C. 1, Eng.
- Whip. m. ISSN 0043-485X

**Clarendon Press**
Press Rd., Neasden, London NW10 0DD, England.
- Oxford Studies in Social Mobility. irreg.

**James Clarke & Co. Ltd.**
7 All Saints Passage, Cambridge CB2 3LS, England.
- Clegg's International Directory of the World'S Book Trade. irreg. ISSN 0069-4614
- Libraries, Museums and Art Galleries Year Book. irreg. ISSN 0075-899X (Dist. in U.S. and Canada by R. R. Bowker Co., Box 1807, Ann Arbor, MI 48106)
- London Divinity Series. New Testament. irreg. ISSN 0076-0536

**Clarke & Hunter (London) Ltd.**
Armour House, Bridge St., Guildford, Surrey, Eng.
- Parks and Sports Grounds. m. ISSN 0031-224X
- Swimming Pool Review. q. ISSN 0039-7385

**E. W. Classey Ltd.**
Park Rd., Faringdon, Oxon. SN7 7DR, England.
- Entomologist's Gazette. q. ISSN 0013-8894

**Classic Publications Ltd.**
Recorder House, Church St., London, N16, England.
- Careers in Banking, Insurance, Finance. a. ISSN 0069-0430
- Employment Opportunities for Advanced Post-Graduate Scientists and Engineers. a. ISSN 0071-0148

**Classical Association**
c/o Dept. of Classics, University College, Singleton Park, Swansea, Wales.
- Classical Association. Proceedings. a. ISSN 0069-4460
- Greece and Rome. (pub. by Oxford University Press)
- New Surveys in the Classics. (pub. by Oxford University Press)

**Classified Media Ltd.**
Box 356, Addlestone, Weybridge, Surrey, Eng.
- Management by Objectives. q. ISSN 0047-5661

**Clio Press Ltd.**
Woodside House, Hinksey Hill, Oxford OX1 5BE, England
(U.S. Subscr. to: ABC-CLIO, Riviera Campus, 2040 Alameda Padre Serra, Santa Barbara, CA 93103)
- Artbibliographies Current Titles. bi-m. ISSN 0095-1420
- Artbibliographies Modern. s-a. ISSN 0300-466X

**Clique Ltd.**
75 World's End Rd., Handsworth Wood, Birmingham B20 2NS, England.
- Annual Directory of Booksellers in the British Isles Specialising in Antiquarian and Out-Of-Print Books. a. ISSN 0066-3913
- Clique; the antiquarian booksellers' medium. w. ISSN 0009-9422

**Clothing Institute**
Albert Road, Hendon, London NW4 2JS, England.
- Clothing Institute Journal. bi-m. ISSN 0578-5294
- Clothing Institute Year Book. a.
- Clothing Research Journal. 3 per yr.

**CNK International**
37 the Close, Dunmow, Essex, England.
- Cosmology Newslink. q.

**Co-Existence**
9-11 Southpark Terrace, Glasgow G12, Scotland.
- Co-Existence; an international journal. s-a.

**Coaching News**
5 Bentinck St., London W1M 5RN, England.
- Coaching News. q.

**Coastal Anti-Pollution League**
Alverstoke, Greenway Lane, Bath, Somerset, England.
- Golden List of Beaches; believed to be free from sewage pollution. every 10 yrs.

**Cockatrice Press Ltd.**
99 Mortimer St., London W.1, Eng.
- Space. m. ISSN 0038-6219

**Collector Ltd.**
3 Bloomsbury Place, London WC1A 2QA, Eng.
- Book Collector. q. ISSN 0006-7237

**College of Librarianship Wales**
Llanbadarn Fawr, Aberystwyth SY23 3AS, Wales.
- S P E L. (Selected Publications in European Languages); a pointer to selected articles and books in European languages. 5 per yr. ISSN 0307-5354

**College of Preceptors**
Bloomsbury House, 130 High Holborn, London WC1V 6PS, England.
- Education Today. bi-m.

**College of Psychic Studies**
16 Queensberry Pl., London SW7, England.
- C P S Papers. irreg.
- Light; a journal of psychic studies. q. ISSN 0047-4649

**College of Radiographers**
14 Upper Wimpole St., London W1M 8BN, Eng.
- Radiography. m. ISSN 0033-8281 (Society of Radiographers)

**College of Speech Therapists**
47 St. John's Wood High St., London NW8 7NJ, England.
- British Journal of Disorders of Communication. s-a. ISSN 0007-098X
- College of Speech Therapists. Bulletin. m.

**College of Teachers of the Blind**
Royal School for the Blind, Church Rd., Liverpool L15 6TQ, England.
- Teacher of the Blind. q. ISSN 0040-0440

**Rex Collings Ltd.**
6 Paddington St., London, W1, England
(American edition available from: Africana Publishing Corporation, 101 Fifth Ave., New York, NY 10003)
- Africa Contemporary Record, Annual Survey and Documents. a. ISSN 0065-3845

**Colston's School**
Stapleton, Bristol, Eng.
- Colstonian. a. ISSN 0010-1842

**Combined Service Publications Ltd.**
67-68 Jermyn St., London SW1Y 6N2, England.
- Fusilier. s-a. ISSN 0016-3147 (Royal Regiment of Fusiliers)

**Commercial Fishing Enterprises Ltd.**
Fish Trades Bldg., Fish Dock, Fleetwood FY7 6HS, England.
- Commercial Fishing. m.
- Interfish. 4 per yr.

**Commercial Transport Magazine Ltd.**
34 Station Rd., 26 Station Rd. Cambridge, Eng.
- Transport Journal. m. ISSN 0041-1485

**Committee for Babylonian Jewry**
19e Avenmore Rd., London W.14, Eng.
- Scribe; journal of Babylonian Jewry. bi-m.

**Committee for Freedom in Mozambique, Angola and Guinea**
12 Little Newport St., London N.7., England.
- Committee for Freedom in Mozambique, Angola and Guinea. Topics. irreg.
- Guerrilheiros. bi-m.

**Committee of Directors of Polytechnics**
- Handbook of Polytechnic Courses. (pub. by Manningham Press)

**Committee of London Clearing Bankers**
Statistical Unit, London EC3V 9AP, Eng.
- Balances of London Clearing Banks' Groups. m.

**Committee on Invisible Exports**
23 Fenchurch St., London EC3M 3DD, England.
- Committee on Invisible Exports. Annual Report. a.

**Common Law Reports Ltd.**
49 Park Lane, London W1Y 3LB, Eng.
- Eurolaw Commercial Intelligence. s-m.
- European Law Digest. m.

**Common Market Law Reports**
49 Park Lane, London W.1, Eng.
- Common Market Law Reports. m. ISSN 0010-3284

**Common Wealth**
c/o W. J. Taylor, 107 Pilton St., Pilton, Barnstaple, Devon, Eng.
- Libertarian. 4 per yr. ISSN 0024-2004

**Commons, Open Spaces and Foot Paths Preservation Society**
Suite 4, 166 Shaftesbury Ave., London WC2H 8JH, Eng.
- Commons, Open Spaces and Footpaths Preservation Society, Journal. q. ISSN 0010-3322

**Commonwealth Agricultural Bureaux**
Farnham House, Farnham Royal, Slough SL2 3BN, England.
- Agricultural Engineering Abstracts. m.
- Animal Breeding Abstracts; a monthly abstract of world literature. m. ISSN 0003-3499
- Commonwealth Agricultural Bureaux. Executive Council. Annual Report. a. ISSN 0069-6889
- Commonwealth Agricultural Bureaux. List of Research Workers; in the agricultural sciences in the Commonwealth and the Republic of Ireland. a; latest issue 1975. ISSN 0069-6897
- Commonwealth Bureau of Agricultural Economics. Annotated Bibliographies Series A. irreg. ISSN 0305-1552
- Commonwealth Bureau of Agricultural Economics. Annotated Bibliographies. Series B: Agricultural Policy and Rural Development in Africa. irreg. ISSN 0305-1552
- Commonwealth Bureau of Animal Breeding and Genetics. Technical Communications. irreg; no. 10 (revised), 1972. ISSN 0069-6919
- Commonwealth Bureau of Nutrition. Technical Communications. irreg., 1969, no. 25. ISSN 0069-6943

- Commonwealth Institute of Biological Control. Technical Communications. irreg., no. 7, 1976. ISSN 0069-7125
- Cotton and Tropical Fibres Abstracts. m.
- Crop Physiology Abstracts. m.
- Field Crop Abstracts; monthly abstract journal on world annual cereal, legume, root, oilseed and fibre crops. m. ISSN 0015-069X
- Food Science and Technology Abstracts. m. ISSN 0015-6574 (International Food Information Service)
- Herbage Abstracts; monthly abstract journal on grassland husbandry and fodder crop production. m. ISSN 0018-0602
- Irrigation and Drainage Abstracts. q.
- Maize Quality Protein Abstracts. q.
- Nutrition Abstracts and Reviews. m. ISSN 0029-6619
- Ornamental Horticulture. m.
- Plant Growth Regulator Abstracts. m.
- Potato Abstracts. m.
- Poultry Abstracts. m.
- Rural Recreation and Tourism Abstracts. q.
- Small-Animal Abstracts. q.
- Sorghum and Millets Abstracts. m.
- Triticale Abstracts. q.
- Tropical Oil Seeds Abstracts. m.
- Weed Abstracts; compiled from world literature. m. ISSN 0043-1729 (Agricultural Research Council. Weed Research Organization)
- World Agricultural Economics and Rural Sociology Abstracts; abstracts of world literature. m. ISSN 0043-8219

**Commonwealth Air Transport Council**
Shell-Mex House Strand, London W.C.2, England.
- C A T C Electronic News. irreg. ISSN 0526-6122

**Commonwealth & Continental Church Society**
175 Tower Bridge Rd., London SE1 2AQ, Eng.
- Intercom; a magazine for English-speaking expatriates of the world throughout the world. 3 per yr. ISSN 0020-5265

**Commonwealth Broadcasting Association**
Broadcasting House, London W1A 1AA, England.
- Combroad. q.

**Commonwealth Bureau of Animal Health**
Commonwealth Agricultural Bureaux, Central Veterinary Laboratory, New Haw, Weybridge, Surrey, England.
- Commonwealth Bureau of Animal Health. Review Series. irreg. ISSN 0069-6927
- Index Veterinarius; a classified subject and author index produced by computer processes of current literature on veterinary science with approximately 16,000 titles. m (with annual cumulation) ISSN 0019-4123
- Veterinary Bulletin; a monthly abstract journal on veterinary science. m. ISSN 0042-4854

**Commonwealth Bureau of Dairy Science and Technology**
Commonwealth Agricultural Bureaux, Shinfield, Reading, Berks RG2 9AT, Eng.
- Dairy Science Abstracts. m. ISSN 0011-5681

**Commonwealth Bureau of Horticulture and Plantation Crops**
Commonwealth Agricultural Bureaux, East Malling Research Station, Nr. Maidstone, Kent ME19 6BJ, England.
- Commonwealth Bureau of Horticulture and Plantation Crops. Crop Progress Review. m. ISSN 0069-6978
- Commonwealth Bureau of Horticulture and Plantation Crops. Horticultural Review. irreg.; no. 2, 1972. ISSN 0069-6986
- Commonwealth Bureau of Horticulture and Plantation Crops. Research Review. irreg.; no. 4, 1973. ISSN 0069-6994
- Commonwealth Bureau of Horticulture and Plantation Crops. Technical Communications. irreg.; no. 35, 1975. ISSN 0069-7001
- Horticultural Abstracts; compiled from world literature on temperate and tropical fruits, vegetables, ornamentals, plantation crops. m. ISSN 0018-5280

**Commonwealth Bureau of Nutrition**
Aberdeen, AB2 9SB, Scotland.
- Commonwealth Bureau of Nutrition. Annotated Bibliographies. irreg. ISSN 0069-6935

**Commonwealth Bureau of Pastures and Yield Crops**
Commonwealth Agricultural Bureaux, Hurley, Nr.
Maidenhead, Berks. SL6 5LR, England.
- Commonwealth Bureau of Pastures and Field
Crops. Bulletin. irreg. ISSN 0069-701X

**Commonwealth Bureau of Plant Breeding and Genetics**
Commonwealth Agricultural Bureaux, Department
of Applied Biology, Pembroke St., Cambridge CB2
3DX, England.
- Plant Breeding Abstracts. m. ISSN 0032-0803

**Commonwealth Bureau of Soils**
Rothampstead Experimental Station, Harpenden,
Herts AL5 2JQ, England.
- Commonwealth Bureau of Soils. Annotated
Bibliographies. irreg. ISSN 0305-2524
- Commonwealth Bureau of Soils. Technical
Communications. irreg., no. 55, 1975. ISSN 0069-
7036
- Irrigation and Drainage Abstracts. q. ISSN 0306-
7327
- Soils and Fertilizers; abstracts of world literature.
m. ISSN 0038-0792

**Commonwealth Committee on Mineral Resources and Geology. Geological Liaison Office**
38 Parliament St., London S.W.1, England.
- Commonwealth Geological Liaison Office. Liaison
Report. irreg. ISSN 0588-7720
- Commonwealth Geological Liaison Office.
Newsletter. m. ISSN 0588-7739
- Commonwealth Geological Liaison Office. Special
Publication. irreg. ISSN 0588-7763

**Commonwealth Forestry Bureau**
Commonwealth Agricultural Bureaux,
Commonwealth Forestry Institute, South Parks Rd.,
Oxford OX1 3RD, England.
- Commonwealth Forestry Bureau. Card Title
Service. w. ISSN 0008-6266
- Commonwealth Forestry Bureau. Technical
Communication. irreg., 1970, no. 8. ISSN 0069-
7060
- Commonwealth Forestry Bureau Annotated
Bibliographies. irreg., no. 13, 1975. ISSN 0069-
7052
- Forestry Abstracts; compiled from world
literature. m. ISSN 0015-7538
- Forestry Abstracts. Leading Article Series. irreg.,
1970, no. 44. ISSN 0071-7584

**Commonwealth Forestry Institute. Forest Economics Section**
University of Oxford, Oxford, England.
- Commonwealth Forestry Institute. Economic
Survey of Private Forestry, Income and
Expenditure. England and Wales. a.
- Commonwealth Forestry Institute. Survey of
Private Forestry Costs, England and Wales.
Annual Report. a. ISSN 0078-7302
- Economic Survey of Private Forestry in England
& Wales. Establishment Costs. a.
- Economic Survey of Private Forestry in England
& Wales. Income and Expenditure. a.

**Commonwealth Foundation**
Marlborough House, Pall Mall, London, S.W.1,
England.
- Commonwealth Foundation. Occasional Paper.
irreg, no. 39, 1976. ISSN 0069-7087
- Commonwealth Foundation Progress Report.
irreg. ISSN 0069-7095
- Commonwealth Foundation Report. biennial.

**Commonwealth Human Ecology Council**
63 Cromwell Road, London SW7 5BL, Eng.
- C H E C Newsletter. s-a.

**Commonwealth Institute**
Kensington High St., London W.8, England.
- Commonwealth Bibliographies. irreg., no. 1, 1974.
- Commonwealth Institute, London. Annual Report.
a. ISSN 0069-7109

**Commonwealth Institute of Entomology**
Commonwealth Agricultural Bureaux, 56 Queen's
Gate, London SW7 5JR, England.
- Bulletin of Entomological Research; containing
original and review articles on economic
entomology. q. ISSN 0007-4853

- Commonwealth Entomological Conference.
Report. irreg., 10th Conference 1975. ISSN 0069-
7044
- Review of Applied Entomology. Series A:
Agricultural; consisting of abstracts of reviews of
current literature on applied entomology
throughout the world. m.
- Review of Applied Entomology. Series B: Medical
and Veterinary. m.

**Commonwealth Institute of Helminthology**
Commonwealth Agricultural Bureaux, White House,
103 St. Peter's St., St. Albans, Herts AL1 3EW,
England.
- C.I.H. Descriptions of Plant-Parasitic Nematodes.
ISSN 0305-0351
- C I H Keys to the Nematode Parasites of
Vertebrates. s-a. ISSN 0305-2729
- Helminthological Abstracts. Series A: Animal and
Human Helminthology. m. ISSN 0300-8339
- Helminthological Abstracts. Series B: Plant
Nematology. q. ISSN 0300-8320
- Protozoological Abstracts. m.

**Commonwealth Magistrates' Association**
28 Fitzroy Square, London W1P 6DD, England.
- Commonwealth Magistrates' Conference. Report.
irreg.

**Commonwealth Mycological Institute**
Ferry Lane, Kew, Richmond, Surrey TW9 3AF,
Eng.
- Bibliography of Systematic Mycology. s-a. ISSN
0006-1573
- CMI Descriptions of Pathogenic Fungi and
Bacteria. q. ISSN 0009-9716
- CMI Distribution Maps of Plant Diseases. s-a.
ISSN 0012-396X
- Commonwealth Mycological Institute.
Phytopathological Papers. irreg. ISSN 0069-7141
- Index of Fungi. s-a. ISSN 0019-3895
- Mycological Papers. 2-4 per yr. ISSN 0027-5522
- Review of Medical and Veterinary Mycology. q.
ISSN 0034-6624
- Review of Plant Pathology; consisting of abstracts
and reviews of current literature on plant
pathology. m. ISSN 0034-6438

**Commonwealth Parliamentary Association**
General Council, Houses of Parliament, London
SW1P 3JY, Eng.
- Parliamentarian. q. ISSN 0031-2282

**Commonwealth Press Union**
Studio House, 184 Fleet St., London EC4A 2DU,
England.
- C P U Quarterly. q.
- Commonwealth Press Union. Book of
Quinquennial Conference. quinquennial. ISSN
0069-7168
- Commonwealth Press Union. Record of
Quadrennial Conference. quadrennial; 1974, Hong
Kong.

**Commonwealth Producers' Organization**
25 Victoria St., Westminster, London S.W.1, Eng.
- Commonwealth Producer. bi-m. ISSN 0010-342X

**Commonwealth Secretariat. Commonwealth Youth Programme**
Marlborough House, Pall Mall, London, England.
- Youth News Service. q.

**Commonwealth Secretariat. Education Division**
Marlborough House, Pall Mall, London SW1Y
5HX, Eng.
- Commonwealth Education Liaison Committee
Newsletter. q. ISSN 0010-3373
- Education in the Developing Countries of the
Commonwealth: Research Register. biennial.

**Commonwealth Secretariat. General Trade and Commodities Division**
Marlborough House, Pall Mall, London SW1Y
5HX, England.
- Commonwealth Trade. irreg; latest issue, 1972.
ISSN 0588-7933

**Commonwealth Secretariat. Information Division**
Marlborough House, Pall Mall, London SW1Y
5HX, England.
- Commonwealth Diary of Coming Events. q.
- Commonwealth Record of Recent Events. q.

**Communications Board**
- United Free Church of Scotland. Handbook. (pub.
by United Free Church of Scotland)

**Communications Software, Ltd.**
111A Wardour St., London W.1, Eng.
- Broadcast. w. ISSN 0040-2788

**Communist Federation of Britain(M-L)**
- Revolution. (pub. by New Era Books)

**Communist Party of Great Britain**
16 King St., Covent Garden, London WC2 8HY,
Eng.
- Comment (London) (pub. by S.C. Easton)
- Marxism Today; theoretical and discussion journal
of the Communist Party of Great Britain. m.
ISSN 0025-4118
- Our History. q.

**Community Levy for Alternative Projects**
c/o Bit Information Service, 146 Great Western
Rd., London W. 11, England.
- C L A P Handbook. bi-m.

**Community of the Sisters of the Church**
St. Michael's Convent, Ham Common, Richmond,
Surrey TW10 7JH, Eng.
- C S C. Newsletter. s-a. ISSN 0007-9073

**Company of Biologists, Ltd**
- Journal of Cell Science. (pub. by Cambridge
University Press)
- Journal of Embryology and Experimental
Morphology. (pub. by Cambridge University
Press)
- Journal of Experimental Biology. (pub. by
Cambridge University Press)

**Company of Scottish History Ltd.**
c/o Aberdeen University Press, Farmers Hall,
Aberdeen AB9 2T, Scotland.
- Scottish Historical Review. s-a. ISSN 0036-9241

**Company of Veteran Motorists**
- Good Motoring. (pub. by H. I. Thompson Press
Ltd.)

**Comparative Education Society in Europe**
University of London Institute of Education, c/o
Dr. Brian Holmes, Malet St., London WC1E 7HS,
England
(Subscr. to: Prof. Denis Kallen, University of
Amsterdam, Prinsengracht 225, Amsterdam)
- Comparative Education Society in Europe.
Proceedings of the General Meeting. biennial.
ISSN 0588-9049

**Composers' Guild of Great Britain**
- Composer. (pub. by British Music Information
Centre)

**Comprint Ltd.**
157 Hagden Lane, Watford, Herts, England.
- Insulation-Thermal, Acoustic, Vibration. bi-m.
ISSN 0020-4552
- National Federation of Plastering Contractors.
Year Book. a. ISSN 0077-4480

**Computer Arts Society**
4 Binfield Rd., Wokingham, Berkshire, Eng.
- Page. 8 per yr. ISSN 0030-9362

**Computer Education Group**
- Computer Education. (pub. by North Staffordshire
Polytechnic)

**Computer Information Service**
P.O. Box 4, Totnes, Devon TQ4 5HD, Eng.
- Programming Index. bi-m. ISSN 0305-5426

**Computer Publications**
P.O. Box 29, Stevenage SG1 3QD, England.
- Computerware. 9 per yr.

**Computer Users' Year Book**
18 Queens Road, Brighton, Sussex, England.
- Computer Users' Year Book. a.

**Comunn Gaidhealach**
Abertarff House, Inverness IV1 1EU, Scotland.
- Sruth. m. ISSN 0038-8807

**Conchological Society of Great Britain and Ireland**
c/o Ed. Dr. C. R. C. Paul, Dept. of Geology,
Liverpool University L69 3Bx, England.
- Journal of Conchology. s-a. ISSN 0022-0019

**Concilium**
2-10 Jerdan Place, London SW6 5PT, Eng
- Concilium; an international review of theology. 10
per yr. ISSN 0010-5236

**Concrete Society**
- Concrete. (pub. by Cement and Concrete
Association)

**Conde Nast Publications Ltd.**
Vogue House, Hanover Square, London W1R 0AD,
Eng.
- Brides; & setting up home. bi-m.
- House & Garden (London) 10 per yr. ISSN 0043-
5759
- Stitchcraft. m. ISSN 0039-1530

**Cone Publications**
Crondall Cottage, Highclere, Newbury, Berks,
England.
- Commercial Rabbit. q.
- Turkeys. bi-m.

**Confederation Internationale des Accordeonistes**
c/o J. J. Black, Secretary, Somerset House,
Cranleigh, Surrey, England.
- C.I.A. Revue. irreg. ISSN 0574-9468

**Confederation of British Industry**
21, Tothill St., London SW1H 9LP, England.
- Taxation in Western Europe; a guide for
industrialists. irreg. ISSN 0082-2167

**Confederation of Health Service Employees**
Glen House, High St., Banstead, Surrey, England.
- Health Services Journal. m. ISSN 0017-9116

**Conference of Socialist Economists**
Birkbeck College, Department of Economics, 7-15
Gresse St., London W1P 1PA, England.
- Capital and Class. s-a.

**Conferences & Exhibitions Publications Ltd.**
Wardrobe Chambers, 146a Queen Victoria St.,
London EC4V 5DQ, Eng.
- Conferences and Exhibitions. m.

**Confrontation Press**
63-A Brick Lane, London E1, Eng.
- Confrontation.

**Congregational Memorial Hall Trust Ltd.**
22 Fleet Lane, London E.C.4, England.
- Congregational Lectures. irreg. ISSN 0069-8865

**Connolly Books Ltd.**
28 Mercer Rd., London N.19, England.
- Connolly's Suppressed Writings. irreg. ISSN 0069-
908X (Irish Communist Organization)

**Conservative & Unionist Central Office**
32 Smith Square, Westminster SW1P 3HH, London,
England.
- Conservative and Unionist Central Office.
Monthly News. m. ISSN 0010-6518
- Politics Today. fortn.

**Consolidated Publications Co. Ltd.**
11-13 Baker St., Portman Square, London W.1, Eng.
- Liberia; trade, industry and travel. q. ISSN 0024-
1954
- Sierra Leone; trade, industry and travel. bi-m.
ISSN 0037-4733

**Construction Industry Research and Information
Association**
Old Queen St. House, 6 Storey's Gate, London
SW1P 3AU, England.
- C I R I A Annual Report. a. ISSN 0069-9209
- C I R I A Report. irreg., approx 6 per yr. ISSN
0305-408X

**Construction Publications Ltd.**
Elm House, 10-16 Elm Street, London, WC1,
England.
- Consulting Engineer Who's Who and Year Book.
a. ISSN 0069-9225

**Construction Surveyors' Institute**
203 Lordship Lane, East Dulwich, London SE22
8HA, Eng.
- Construction Surveyor. q.

**Consumer Industries Press Ltd.**
40 Bowling Green Lane, London E.C. 1, England.
- Food Processing and Packaging Directory. a.
ISSN 0071-7207

**Consumers Association**
14 Buckingham St., London WC2N 6DS, Eng.
- Drug and Therapeutics Bulletin. fortn. ISSN 0012-
6543
- Good Food Guide. a. ISSN 0072-5005
- Which? m. ISSN 0043-4841

**Consyl Publishing & Publicity Ltd.**
9-10 Little Britain, London EC1A 7LE, England.
- Australian Outlook. m. ISSN 0301-5785

**Contac Arts Magazine**
c/o John Freeman, Ed., 6 Main View, Thorne Rd.,
Stainforth, Nr. Doncaster, Yorks DN7 5BU,
England.
- Contac Arts Magazine. q.

**Contempo International Ltd.**
42 Hanway St., London W.I., Eng.
- Blues & Soul Music Review. fortn. ISSN 0045-
2297

**Contemporary China Institute**
School of Oriental and African Studies, Malet St.,
London W.C.1, England.
- China Quarterly. q. ISSN 0009-4439

**Contemporary Jewish Library Ltd.**
31 Percy St., London W.1, Eng.
- Jews & the Jewish People; collected materials
from the Soviet daily and periodical press. ISSN
0021-6895

**Contemporary Press Ltd.**
21A Alma Square, London NW8 9QA, England.
- Continental Motoring Holidays. a.

**Contemporary Review Co. Ltd.**
61 Carey St., London WC2 2JG, Eng.
- Contemporary Review. m. ISSN 0010-7565

**Continental Hotel Gazetteers**
P.O. Box 24, Beaconsfield, England.
- Agent's Hotel Gazetteer: Tourist Cities of Europe.
irreg.

**Control Magazine**
5 London Mews, London W.2, England.
- Control Magazine. a. ISSN 0069-973X

**Convocation of York**
- York Journal of Convocation. (pub. by Church
Information Office)

**Conway Maritime Press Ltd.**
2-7 Nelson Rd, Greenwich, London SE10, England.
- Model Shipwright; a quarterly journal of ships and
ship models. q.
- Warship. q.

**Coo Press Ltd.**
19 Doughty St., London WC1N 2PT, Eng.
- Creative Camera. m. ISSN 0011-0876
- Creative Camera International Year Book. a.

**J. & J. Cook**
Gazette Office, 18-20 Gordon St., Paisley,
Renfrewshire, Scotland.
- Rod & Line. m. ISSN 0048-8496

**Thomas Cook Group Ltd.**
Berkeley St., Piccadilly, London W.1., England.
- Thomas Cook International Timetable. m.
- Thomas Cook News. bi-m.

**Cookery and Food Association**
Rosaletta House, Charlwood Drive, Oxshott, Surrey
KT22 0HB, England.
- Food and Cookery Review. m. ISSN 0015-6256
- International Food and Cookery Review. m. ISSN
0047-0708

**Cooperative Industrial and Commercial Reference and
Information Service. Acton District Library**
High St., London W3 6NA, England.
- C I C R I S Directory and Guide to Resources.
biennial  ISSN 0069-9829

**Co-Operative Press Ltd.**
Progress House, Chester Rd., Manchester 16, Eng.
- Coop Marketing & Management. m. ISSN 0307-
8604 (National Association of Cooperative
Officials)
- Co-Operative News; official organ of the Co-
operative Movement. w. ISSN 0009-9821
- Co-Operative News (Scottish Edition) w.
- G M W Herald. q. (General and Municipal
Workers' Union)
- G M W Journal. m. (General and Municipal
Workers' Union)

**Co-Operative Union Ltd.**
Holyoake House, Hanover St., Manchester M60
OAS, Eng.
- Co-Operative Review. m. ISSN 0009-9848
- Co-Operative Statistics. a.
- Platform. 9 per yr. ISSN 0032-1370

**Coopercrest Ltd.**
Fleet House, Admirals Walk, Hampstead, London
N.W., England.
- World Food. m.

**Copper Development Association**
Orchard House, Mutton Lane, Potters Bar, Herts.
EN6 3AP, England.
- International Copper Information Bulletin; recent
reports, publications and abstracts on copper, its
alloys and compounds. q. ISSN 0309-2216

**Cornmarket Press Ltd.**
42 Conduit St., London W1R 0NL, Eng.
- After School. q. ISSN 0044-6696

**Cornwall Archaeological Society**
c/o Mrs. V. Harris, Forest House, St. Erme, Truro,
Cornwall, England.
- Cornish Archaeology. a. ISSN 0070-024X
- Cornwall Archaeological Society. Field Guide.
irreg. ISSN 0070-0258

**Corporation of Lloyds**
Lloyd's Bldg., Lime St., London E.C.3, Eng.
- Lloyd's Log. m. ISSN 0024-550X

**Corporation of London**
- City Business Courier. (pub. by City Business
Library)

**Corrosion Prevention and Control**
11a Gloucester Rd., London S.W.7, Eng.
- Corrosion Prevention and Control. bi-m. ISSN
0010-9371

**Cosmatom**
P.O. Box 12, Worthing, Sussex BN14 8BS, BN14
8Bs, England.
- Cosmatom. s-a.

**Cosmetic World News**
7 Bell Yard, Fleet St., London WC2A 2JR,
England.
- Cosmetic World News; the international news
magazine of the perfumery, cosmetics and
toiletries industry. m. ISSN 0305-0319

**Cosmos**
c/o Walter Gillings, Ed., 115 Wanstead Park Rd.,
Ilford, Essex, Eng.
- Cosmos. m. ISSN 0010-9576

**Costume Society**
c/o Mrs. H. Wood, Birtle Edge House, Bury, Lancs,
England.
- Costume. a. ISSN 0590-887⁴

**Cotton Research Corp**
14 Grosvenor Place, London SW1X 7 JL, Eng.
- Cotton Growing Review. q. ISSN 0010-9819

**Council for British Archaeology**
7 Marylebone Rd., London NW1 5HA, England.
- Archaeological Bibliography for Great Britain and
Ireland. a. ISSN 0066-5967
- British Archaeological Abstracts. s-a. ISSN 0007-
0270
- Council for British Archaeology. Current Offprints
and Reports. a. ISSN 0305-5280
- Council for British Archaeology. Newsletter and
Calendar of Excavations. m (Mar.-Sep., Nov.-
Jan.) ISSN 0309-3204

**Council for Educational Technology for the United
Kingdom**
- British Journal of Educational Technology. (pub.
by Councils and Education Press Ltd.)

**Council for Kentish Archaeology**
143 Sturry Rd., Canterbury, Kent, England.
- Kent Archaeological Review. q. ISSN 0023-0014

**Council for Nature**
Zoological Gardens, Regent's Park, London NW1 4RY, Eng.
• Habitat. 10 per yr. ISSN 0028-9043

**Council for Nautical Archaeology**
• International Journal of Nautical Archaeology and Underwater Exploration. (pub. by Academic Press Inc. (London) Ltd.)

**Council for the Protection of Rural England**
4 Hobart Place, London SW1W 0HY, Eng.
• Council for the Protection of Rural England. Quarterly Bulletin. q. ISSN 0010-9916

**Council for the Protection of Rural Wales**
14 Broad St., Welshpool, Powys, Wales.
• Council for the Protection of Rural Wales. Newsletter. 3 per yr.

**Council for World Mission (Congregational and Reformed)**
11 Carteret St., London SW1H 9DL, England.
• C W M Report. a.

**Council of British Manufacturers of Petroleum Equipment**
118 Southwark St., London SE1 0SU, England.
• British Petroleum Equipment and Services. biennial. ISSN 0068-2365

**Council of Christians and Jews**
41 Cadogan Gardens, London SW3 2TD, Eng.
• Common Ground; to combat all forms of religious and racial intolerance. q. ISSN 0010-325X

**Council of Legal Education**
4, Gray's Inn Place, London W.C.1R 5DX, England.
• Council of Legal Education. Calendar. a.

**Council of T A V R Associations**
Duke of York's Headquarters, Chelsea, London S.W.3, Eng.
• T A V R. m. ISSN 0039-8268

**Council of the Scottish Law Agents Society**
61 High St., Dunblane, Scotland.
• Scottish Law Gazette. q. ISSN 0036-9314

**Council of the Stock Exchange**
London EC2N 1HP, England.
• London. Stock Exchange. Stock Exchange Fact Book. q.
• Stock Exchange, London. Members and Firms of the Stock Exchange. a.

**Councils and Education Press Ltd.**
10 Queen Anne St., London W1M 9LD, Eng.
• British Journal of Educational Technology. 3 per yr. ISSN 0007-1013 (Council for Educational Technology for the United Kingdom)
• Education. w. ISSN 0013-1164 (Association of Education Committees)
• Education Committees Year Book. a. ISSN 0070-9158 (Association of Education Committees)
• Social Services Yearbook. a. (Association of County Councils) (Co-sponsor: Association of Metropolitan Authorities)

**Countdown Ltd**
49 Rathbone St., London W1P 1AN, England.
• Countdown Today. q.

**Country and Western Roundabout**
c/o R. F. Benson, Ed., 21 Roseacres, Takeley, Dunmow, Essex, Eng.
• Country and Western Roundabout. q. ISSN 0011-0094

**Country Churchman Ltd.**
Abbey Press, Abingdon, Berkshire, Eng.
• Country Churchman. m. ISSN 0011-0124

**Country Gentlemen's Association Ltd.**
Icknield Way West, Letchworth, Herts SG6 4AP, Eng.
• Country Gentlemen's Magazine. m. ISSN 0011-0132

**Country Landowners Association**
16 Belgrave Square, London SW1X 8PQ, Eng.
• Country Landowner. bi-m. ISSN 0011-0159

**Country Music Enterprises**
68 Golden House, Great Pulteney St., London W.1, Eng.
• Country & Western Express. q. ISSN 0011-0086

• Folk Style. irreg. ISSN 0015-5829

**Country Music People Ltd.**
Powerscroft Road, Footscray, Sidcup, Kent, England.
• Country Music People. m. ISSN 0591-2237

**Country Standard**
c/o J. Dunman, Ed., 27 Bedford St., London W. C. 2., England.
• Country Standard. q. ISSN 0011-0256

**Countryman Ltd.**
Sheep St., Burford, Oxford OX8 4LH, England.
• Countryman; a quarterly illustrated magazine of the British countryside and its people, past & present. q. ISSN 0011-0272

**Courage House**
6 Langley Ave., Surbiton, Surrey KT6 6QL, England.
• Scottishe. s-a.

**Coutts and Company**
440 Strand, London W.C.2, Eng.
• Three Crowns. 3 per yr. ISSN 0040-652X

**Covenant Peoples Fellowship**
Brith Lodge, 87 St. Barnabas Rd., Woodford Green, Essex, Eng.
• Brith. m. ISSN 0007-0211

**Coventry Chamber of Commerce Inc.**
123 St. Nicholas St., Coventry CV1 4FD, England.
• Directory of Engineering Capacity. a.

**Coventry Newspapers Ltd.**
Corporation Street, Coventry CV1 1FP, Warwickshire, England.
• Coventry Evening Telegraph Year Book Who's Who. a.

**Cox-Webster Ltd.**
74 the Street, Ashtead, Surrey, Eng.
• British Medical Register of Holiday Accommodation. s-a. ISSN 0007-1455

**Crafts Advisory Committee**
28 Haymarket, London SW1Y 4SU, Eng.
• Crafts. bi-m.

**Craftsmen Potters Association**
17a Newburgh St., London W.1, England.
• Ceramic Review. bi-m.

**Creative Leisure Ltd.**
249 Lincoln Rd., Enfield, Middlesex, Eng.
• Leisure Painter & Craftsman. m.

**Credit Retailer (Publishers) Ltd.**
1 Kenilworth House, Grosvenor Rd., London W4 4EJ, Eng.
• Credit Retailer; monthly newspaper of retail credit. m. ISSN 0011-1031

**Cremation Society of Great Britain**
Woodcut House, Ashford Rd., Hollingbourne, Maidstone, Kent ME17 IXH, England.
• Cremation Society Handbook and Directory of Crematoria. a. ISSN 0305-9537
• Cremation Society of Great Britain. Conference Report. a. ISSN 0070-1475
• Pharos. (pub. by Pharos Press)

**Crescendo Publications Ltd.**
122 Wardour St., London W.1, Eng
(and Box 187, Williston Park, N.Y. 11596)
• Crescendo International. m. ISSN 0011-118X

**Cricket Quarterly**
c/o Rowland Bower, Ed., The Lantern, Mullion, Nr. Helston, Cornwall, England.
• Cricket Quarterly. q. ISSN 0011-1252

**Cricketer**
Beech Hanger, Ashurst, Nr. Tunbridge Wells, Kent, England.
• Cricketer. m. ISSN 0011-1260

**Crisis & Change**
607A Grand Bldg., Trafalgar Sq., London W.C.2, Eng.
• Crisis & Change. m. ISSN 0011-1430

**Critics' Guild**
9 Compayne Gardens, London N.W. 6, Eng.
• Critic. w. ISSN 0015-1203

**Critique**
31 Cleveden Rd., Glasgow G12 0PH, Scotland.
• Critique; a journal of soviet studies & socialist theory. s-a.

**Paul H. Crompton Ltd.**
638 Fulham Rd., London S.W.6, Eng.
• Karate and Oriental Arts. bi-m. ISSN 0022-9008
• Way of Life. q.

**Cromwell Association**
Combe Lodge, Ringley Park Ave., Reigate, Surrey, England.
• Cromwelliana. a.

**Croner Publications Ltd.**
46-50 Coombe Road, New Malden, Surrey, England.
• Croner's Export Digest. m.
• Croner's Reference Book for Employers. m. ISSN 0070-1580
• Croner's Reference Book for Exporters. m. ISSN 0070-1599
• Croner's Reference Book for Importers. m. ISSN 0070-1602
• Croner's Reference Book for the Self-Employed. m.
• Croner's Reference Book for Value Added Tax. m.
• Croner's Road Transport Operation. m. ISSN 0070-1610
• Croner's World Directory of Freight Conferences. m. ISSN 0070-1629

**Croquet Association**
Hurlingham Club, London SW6 3PR, Eng.
• Croquet Gazette. 4 per yr. ISSN 0011-1880

**Crown Agents for Overseas Governments and Administration**
4 Milbank, London S.W.1, England.
• Crown Agents. Quarterly Review. q.

**Croydon Advertiser Group of Newspapers**
Advertiser House, Brighton Rd., South Croydon CR2 6UB, Eng.
• Croydon Advertiser. w. ISSN 0011-2089

**Croydon Natural History & Scientific Society Ltd.**
96a Brighton Rd., South Croydon, Surrey CR2 6AD, Eng.
• Croydon Bibliographies for Regional Survey. 2 per yr.
• Croydon Natural History & Scientific Society. Bulletin. 3 per yr.
• Croydon Natural History & Scientific Society. Proceedings and Transactions. irreg. (approx. 3-4 per yr.)

**Croydon Weekly Review Ltd.**
44 East St., Bromley, Kent, Eng.
• Croydon Weekly Review. w. ISSN 0011-2097

**Crusade of the Blessed Sacrament**
1 Lambton Road, London SW20 0LN, Eng.
• Crusader. m.(Oct-July)

**Cuckfield Baptist Church**
3 Quarry Hill, Haywards Heath, Sussex, Eng.
• Reformation Today. q. ISSN 0034-3048 (Reformed Baptist Movement)

**William Culross & Son Ltd.**
Queen Street, Coupar Angus, Perthshire, Scotland.
• Scotlands Regions. a. ISSN 0305-6562

**Cumberland Industrial Association**
• Summit. (pub. by G.W. Foster Associates Ltd.)

**Cutlands Press Ltd.**
62 Victoria St., Etchingham, Albans AL1 3XT, England.
• Diecasting & Metal Moulding. bi-m. ISSN 0012-2548

**Cwmni Urdd Gobaith Cymru**
Swyddfa'r Urdd, Aberystwyth, Cardiganshire, Wales.
• Blodau'r Ffair. s-a. ISSN 0006-4912

**Cyclists' Touring Club**
69 Meadrow, Godalming, Surrey, England.
• Cycletouring. bi-m.

**Cygnet Enterprises**
c/o Students Union, Keele Univ., Keele, Staffs ST5
5BJ, Eng.
- Cygnet; the independent student newspaper. 6 per
yr. ISSN 0011-4375

**Cyngor Llyfrau Cymraeg**
Queen's Square, Aberystwyth, Wales.
- Llais Llyfrau /Book News from Wales. q.

**Cyngor Ysgolion Ac Addysg Grefyddol Cymru**
- Antur. (pub. by Welsh Calvinistic Methodist Book
Agency)

**Cypher**
Plovers Barrow, School Road Nomansland,
Salisbury, Wilts, England
- Cypher. irreg., approx. s-a.

**D R Publications Ltd.**
111 St. James's Rd., Croydon, Surrey CR9 2TH,
Eng.
- Water and Waste Treatment. m. ISSN 0043-1133

**Daffodil Society**
c/o D. J. Pearce, 1, Noak's Cross, Cottages, Great
Braxted, Witham, Essex, Eng.
- Daffodil Society. Journal. a.

**Daily Express Books Department**
Standard House, 56 Farringdon Street, London
EC4A 4DY, England.
- Giles Cartoon Annual. a. (Beaverbrook
Newspapers Ltd.)
- Rupert Annual. a. (Beaverbrook Newspapers Ltd.)

**Daily Telegraph Ltd.**
135 Fleet St., London E.C.4, Eng.
- Daily Telegraph Magazine. w. ISSN 0011-5495
- Scientific Exploration Society. Newsletter. irreg.
(approx. 10 per yr.)

**Dalesman Publishing Co. Ltd.**
Clapham, Lancaster, Eng.
- Cumbria; a magazine of Lakeland and Border life.
m. ISSN 0011-2984
- Dalesman; a monthly magazine of Yorkshire and
its people. m. ISSN 0011-5800

**Dallruth Ltd.**
344 S. Lambeth Rd., London SW8, Eng.
- New Witchcraft. m.

**Dance News Ltd.**
22 Shaftesbury Ave., London W1V 8AP, Eng.
- Dance News and Recall. ISSN 0011-6025

**Dancing Times Ltd.**
18 Hand Court, High Holborn, London WC1V 6JF,
Eng.
- Ballroom Dancing Times. m. ISSN 0005-4380
- Dancing Times. m. ISSN 0011-605X
- Lyttons Theatre and Concert Halls Seating Plans.
(pub. by H. Wise & Co. Ltd.)

**Daniel Greenaway & Sons Ltd.**
Runnings Rd., Cheltenham GL5 9NT, England.
- Kush. a. ISSN 0075-7349 (Antiquities Service of
the Sudan)

**Darpon Publications**
1 Adelaide Villas, Copse Rd., St. Johns, Woking,
Surrey, Eng.
- Darpon; the independent and impartial Bengali
quarterly. q. ISSN 0011-6718

**Dartmoor Preservation Association**
c/o Dr. W. F. Beech, 4 Oxford Gardens,
Mannamead, Plymouth PL3 4SF, England.
- Dartmoor Preservation Association Newsletter. q.

**Data Publications Ltd.**
57 Maida Vale, London W9ISN, Eng.
- Radio & Electronics Constructor. m.

**Datr**
c/o John Noyce, Flat 2, 83 Montpelier Rd.,
Brighton, Sussex BN1 3BN, England.
- Datr. irreg.

**David Davies Memorial Institute of International
Studies**
Thorney House, 34 Smith Square, London SW1,
England.
- David Davies Memorial Institute of International
Studies, London. Annual Memorial Lecture. a.
ISSN 0070-2900
- International Relations. s-a. ISSN 0047-1178

**Christopher Davies Publishers Ltd.**
4/5 Thomas Row, Swansea SA1 1NJ, Wales, U.K.
- Poetry Wales; Cylchgrawn Cenedlaethol o
Farddoniaeth Newydd. 4 per yr. ISSN 0032-2202
(Welsh Arts Council)

**Alexander Davis Publications Ltd.**
43 South Hill Rd., Hemel Hempstead, Herts HP1
1JB, England
- Art Design Photo; annual bibliography on modern
art, graphic design & photography. a. ISSN 0306-
817X (Dist. by: Art Book Co., 18 Endell St.,
Covent Garden, London W.C. 2, England)

**Dawn Book Supply**
17 Leegate, London SE12 8SS, Eng.
- Light; on a new world. bi-m. ISSN 0047-4657
(Bexley Christadelphians Ecclesia)

**Wm. Dawson & Sons Ltd.**
Cannon House, Folkestone, Kent CT19 5EE,
England.
- Art Prices Current. a.
- Bar Quarterly. q. ISSN 0307-8647
- Guide to the Press of the World. a. ISSN 0072-
8748

**Dawsons of Pall Mall**
Cannon House, Folkestone, Kent, England.
- Book Auction Records. a. ISSN 0068-0095

**Days Publications and Services Ltd.**
37-45 Paul St., London EC2A 4PB, England.
- Register of Registrars. a., plus periodic updates.
ISSN 0482-1319

**Ddraig Goch**
8 Heol y Dwr, Caerfyrodin, Sir Gaerfyrodin, Wales.
- Ddraig Goch. m. (Plaid Cymru (Welsh Nationalist
Party))

**Decal Press**
52 Dan-y-Coed Rd., Cyncoed, Cardiff, Wales.
- Decal Poetry Review. s-a.

**Decanter Magazine Ltd.**
18 Black Friars Lane, London E.C.4, England.
- Decanter. bi-m.

**Delane Press**
4 Boscombe Ave., London E1O 6HY, Eng.
- Viewpoint. q. ISSN 0042-5834
- Warfare. s-a.

**Delawarr Laboratories Ltd.**
Raleigh Park Road, Oxford, England.
- Delawarr Laboratories Newsletter. q.

**Delphinium Society**
25 Sladbury's Lane, Holland-on-Sea, Essex,
England.
- Delphinium Society Yearbook. a.

**Delta**
c/o Michael Launchbury, Ed., 8 St. Johns Rd.,
Turnchapel, Plymouth, England.
- Delta; a literary review. 3 per yr. ISSN 0011-7986

**Deneway Guides and Travel Ltd.**
P.O. Box 286, Rottingdean, Brighton, BN2 8AY,
England.
- Alan Rogers' Selected Sites for Caravanning and
Camping in Europe. a. ISSN 0065-5686

**J. M. Dent & Sons Ltd.**
26 Albemarle St., London W1X 4OY, England.
- Readings in Economic History and Theory. irreg.

**Benjamin Dent Publications Ltd.**
33 Bedford Place, London WC1B 5JX, Eng.
- Fabric Forecast. 2 per yr. ISSN 0014-620X
- Fashion Forecast. 2 per yr. ISSN 0014-8679
- Textile Forecast; British cloth for international
menswear. 3 per yr.

**Dental Publications Ltd**
172 Kingston Rd., Ewell, Epsom, Surrey, Emgland.
- Year Book and Directory for the Dental
Technician. a.

**Dental Technician Ltd.**
203 Kings Cross Road, London W.C.1, Eng.
- Dental Technician. m. ISSN 0011-8796

**Department for National Savings**
Blythe Road, London W44 1SB, England.
- D N S News. m.

**Derby and Derbyshire Chamber of Commerce**
5-7 St. Mary's Gate, Derby, DE1 3JH, Eng.
- Derby Enterprise. m. ISSN 0011-8982

**Derbyshire Archaeological Society**
35, St. Mary's Gate, Derby DE1 3JU, England.
- Derbyshire Archaeological Journal. a. ISSN 0070-
3788

**Derbyshire Countryside Ltd.**
Lodge Lane, Derby, Eng.
- Derbyshire Life and Countryside. m. ISSN 0011-
8990

**Derwent Publications Ltd.**
Rochdale House, 128 Theobalds Rd., London
WC1X 8RP, Eng.
- Belgian Patents Report. w. ISSN 0011-9121
- British Patents Abstracts. w. ISSN 0007-1609
- British Patents Report. w.
- French Patents Abstracts. w. ISSN 0016-1098
- German Patents Abstracts. w. ISSN 0016-8807
- German Patents Gazette. Section 1: Chemical. w.
- German Patents Gazette. Section 2: Electrical. w.
- German Patents Gazette. Section 3: Mechanical
and General. w.
- German Patents Report: Auslegeschriften. w.
- Japanese Patents Gazette. w.
- Japanese Patents Report. w. ISSN 0011-913X
- Netherlands Patents Report. w. ISSN 0028-2995
- Ringdoc Profile Booklets. 45 per yr. ISSN 0035-
5445
- Soviet Inventions Illustrated. w. ISSN 0038-5441
- United States Patents Report. w.
- World Patents Index Abstracts Journal. w.
- World Patents Index Gazette. Section Ch:
Chemical. w.
- World Patents Index Gazette Section P: General.
w.
- World Patents Index Gazette Section Q:
Mechanical. w.
- World Patents Index Gazette Section R:
Electrical. w.

**Design and Industries Association**
Nash House, 12 Carlton House Terrace, London,
SW1, England.
- D I A Yearbook - Design Action. a. ISSN 0306-
6185

**Design Council**
28 Haymarket, London SW1Y 4SU, Eng.
- Design. m. ISSN 0011-9245
- Engineering. m. ISSN 0013-7782

**Designer Bookbinders Review**
6 Queen Square, London WC1N 3AR, England.
- Designer Bookbinders Review. s-a.

**Development Corp. for Wales**
15 Park Place, Cardiff CF1 3DQ, Wales.
- Industrial Directory of Wales. irreg.
- Progress Wales. q. ISSN 0019-8854

**Devon and Cornwall Notes and Queries Publishing
Co.**
Ed. Mrs. M. Rowe, 4 Aldrin Rd., Exeter, Devon,
Eng.
- Devon and Cornwall Notes and Queries; a journal
devoted to the local history, archaeology,
biography and antiquities of the Counties of
Devon and Cornwall. 2 per yr. ISSN 0012-1681

**Devon Archaeological Society**
c/o the Editor, City Museum, Queen St., Exeter,
England.
- Devon Archaeological Society. Proceedings. a.

**Devon Beekeepers Association**
20 Parkhurst Rd., Torquay, Devon, Eng.
- Beekeeping. 8 per yr. ISSN 0005-7754

**Devon Cattle Breeders' Society**
Court House, the Square, Wiveliscombe, Somerset,
England.
- Davy's Devon Herd Book. a. ISSN 0070-2986

**Dickens Fellowship**
The Dickens House, 48 Doughty St., London
WC1N 2LF, Eng.
- Dickensian. 3 per yr. ISSN 0012-2440

**Dickens Press Ltd.**
121 King St., London W6 9JG, England.
- Holiday Haunts. a. ISSN 0073-3016

**Diocese of Bristol**
23 Great George St., Bristol BS1 5QZ, Eng.
- Bristol Diocesan News. m.

**Diplomatic Press and Publishing Co.**
29 Marsh Lane, London N.W.7, England
(Dist. by: Arthur H. Thrower Ltd., 44-46 South
Ealing Rd., London W. 5, England)
- Directory of Jamaica Including Trade Index and
Biographical Section. a. ISSN 0070-5713
- Directory of the Republic of Cyprus; including
trade index and biographical section. a. ISSN
0070-6493
- Directory of the State of Singapore. a. ISSN 0070-
6507
- Guyana Trade Directory. a.
- Hong Kong Trade Directory. a. ISSN 0073-3261
- Trade Directory of Malta. a. ISSN 0082-5697
- Trade Directory of the Empire of Ethiopia. a.
ISSN 0082-5700
- Trade Directory of the Federal Republic of
Nigeria. a. ISSN 0082-5719
- Trade Directory of the Republic of Ghana. a.
ISSN 0082-5727
- Trade Directory of the Republic of the Sudan. a.
ISSN 0082-5735
- Trinidad and Tobago Trade Directory. a. ISSN
0082-657X
- Uganda Trade Directory. a. ISSN 0082-7274

**Diplomatist Associates Ltd.**
Shooter's Lodge, Windsor Forest, Berks, England.
- At the Court of St. James's. a. ISSN 0067-0065
- Bolivia Information Handbook. a. ISSN 0067-
981X (Embassy of Bolivia, London)
- Defence Attache. q.
- Diplomatist; the review of the diplomatic and
consular world. m. ISSN 0012-3110
- Mexico Today. q. ISSN 0026-184X (Embassy of
Mexico, London)
- Paraguay Today. q. ISSN 0031-1693 (Embassy of
Paraguay, London)

**Diprepu Co. Ltd.**
29 Marsh Lane, London N.W. 7, Eng.
- Diplomatic List of Arrivals & Departures. m.
ISSN 0012-3102

**Director General of the Ordnance Survey**
Romsey Rd., Maybush, Southampton SO9 4DH,
England.
- Ordnance Survey Publication Report. m.

**Directory of Alternative Periodicals**
Flat 2, 83 Montpelier Rd., Brighton BN1 3BD,
England.
- Directory of Alternative Periodicals. a.

**Directory of Somalia**
c/o Arthur H. Thrower, Ed., 44-46 S. Ealing Rd.,
Ealing, London W.5, England.
- Directory of Somalia. irreg. ISSN 0070-6353

**Disabled Driver's Association**
Registered Office, The Hall, Ashwellthorpe, Nr.
Norwich, NR16 1EX, Eng.
- Magic Carpet. q. ISSN 0047-5475

**Disabled Drivers' Motor Club**
- Disabled Driver. (pub. by T. G. Scott and Son
Ltd.)

**Discographical Forum**
c/o Malcolm Walker, Ed., 44 Belleville Rd., London
SW11 6QT, England.
- Discographical Forum. q. ISSN 0012-3544

**Distinctive Publications Ltd.**
Davis House, 69/77 High St., Box 109, Croydon
CR9 1QH, Eng.
- Incentive Marketing & Sales Promotion. 10 per yr.
ISSN 0305-2230

**Ditchley Foundation**
Enstone, Oxon OX7 4ER, England
(U.S. & Canadian subscr. to: American Ditchley
Foundation, 39 E. 51st St., New York, NY 10022)
- Ditchley Journal. s-a. ISSN 0305-4322

**Dobson Books Ltd.**
80 Kensington Church St., London W8 4BZ,
England.
- People from the Past Series. irreg., no. 14, 1973.
ISSN 0079-0729

**Dolmetsch Foundation**
14 Chestnut Way, Godalming, Surrey GU7 1TS,
England.
- Consort; journal of the Dolmetsch foundation. a.

**Domestic Equipment Publications Ltd**
Abbey Walk, Cambridge, Eng., U.K.
- Domestic Equipment Trader. m. ISSN 0012-530X

**Domestic Heating Society**
23 Northaw Rd., Cuffley, Herts, Eng.
- Domestic Heating. q. ISSN 0012-5318

**Dominion Press Ltd.**
Grand Buildings, Trafalgar Sq., London WC2N
5H5, Eng.
- Career; other pursuits for students qualifying in
higher education. 6 per yr.
- Career Advisor. 9 per yr.
- Spanner. a. ISSN 0584-8067 (City and Guilds
College Union)
- Which Course? m.

**Donizetti Society**
56 Harbut Rd., London SW11 2RB, England.
- Donizetti Society. Journal. a.
- Donizetti Society Newsletter. 4-5 per yr.

**Doris Publications**
19 Doris Rd., Norwich, Norfolk NOR 0211,
Norwich NR2 3EJ, Norfolk, England.
- Doris. 6 per yr.

**Dorset County Museum**
Dorchester, Dorset, England.
- Dorset Natural History and Archaeological
Society. Proceedings. a. ISSN 0070-7112
- Dorset Worthies. irreg., no. 13, 1969. ISSN 0070-
7120

**Dorset Down Sheep Breeders' Association**
c/o The Secretary, Brierley House, Summer Lane,
Combe Down, Bath, England.
- Dorset Down Flock Book. a.

**Dorset Natural History and Archaeological Society**
- Dorset Natural History and Archaeological
Society. Proceedings. (pub. by Dorset County
Museum)

**Dorset Publishing Co.**
Knock-na-cre, Milborne Port, Sherborne, Dorset
DT9 5HJ, Eng.
- Dorset; the county magazine. m. ISSN 0046-0621

**Dositey Obradovich Circle**
7 Bonchurch Rd., London W10 5SD, England.
- Guslar.

**Douai Abbey**
Woolhampton, Near Reading, Berkshire, Eng.
- Douai Magazine. s-a. ISSN 0012-5695

**Downhill Only Club**
c/o Ed. & Pub. D.N. Freund, Bannwald, Ballinger,
Great Missenden, Bucks, Eng.
- Downhill Only Journal. a. ISSN 0070-718X

**Dramrite Printers Ltd.**
Kings Hedges Rd., Cambridge CB4 2PQ, England.
- Medico-Legal Journal. q. ISSN 0025-8172
(Medico-Legal Society)

**Drive Publications Ltd.**
Fanum House, Basingstoke, Hampshire RG21 2EA,
Eng.
- Drive; AA motorist's magazine. 6 per yr. ISSN
0046-0710 (Automobile Association)

**Drum Publications (UK) Ltd.**
40-43 Fleet St., London E. C. 4, Eng.
- Drum. m. ISSN 0012-673X
- Trust. m.

**Dudley Public Libraries**
Central Library, St. James's Rd., Dudley, West
Midlands DY1 1HR, England.
- Dudley, England (Worcestershire) Public
Libraries. Archives Department. Transcripts.
irreg., 1973, no. 17. ISSN 0070-7430

**Dumfriesshire and Galloway Natural History and
Antiquarian Society**
c/o James Williams, Hillis Tower, Lochfoot,
Dumfries, Scotland.
- Dumfriesshire and Galloway Natural History and
Antiquarian Society. Transactions. a.

**Dun and Bradstreet Ltd.**
26/32 Clifton Street, London EC2P 2LY, England
(and 99 Church St., New York, N.Y. 10007)
- Guide to Key British Enterprises. a. ISSN 0072-
856X

**Dundee and Tayside Chamber of Commerce and
Industry**
Panmure St., Dundee DD1 1ED, Scotland.
- Dundee and Tayside Chamber of Commerce and
Industry. Buyer's Guide & Trade Directory. a.
- Dundee Tayside; industry in the Tayside region.
q.

**Duodecimal Society of Great Britain**
69 Scotby Road, Carlisle, Cumbria CA4 8BG,
England.
- Duodecimal Review. irreg. (11-2 per yr)

**Durham County Local History Society**
Middleton St. George College of Education, Near
Darlington, County Durham, England.
- Durham County Local History Society. Bulletin.
s-a. ISSN 0012-7272

**Durlacher Press**
Newland, Silecroft, Millom, Cumbria LA18 4NX,
England.
- British Journal of Chiropody. m. ISSN 0007-0939

**Dustbooks**
56 Blakes Lane, New Malden KT3 6NX, England.
- British Directory of Little Magazines and Small
Presses. irreg.

**E. D. Publications Ltd.**
120 Wigmore St., London W1H 0AS, Eng.
- Automation. m. ISSN 0005-1152

**E. M. A. P National Publications Ltd.**
Park House, 117 Park Rd., Peterborough, Eng.
- Garden News. w. ISSN 0016-4593
- Practical Gardening. m. ISSN 0032-6399

**E. M. G. Handmade Gramophones Ltd.**
26 Soho Square, London, W.1, Eng.
- E.M.G. Handmade Gramophones. Monthly
Letter. m. ISSN 0012-7744

**Ealing Publications Ltd.**
70 Chiswick High Rd., London W.4., Eng.
- Stone Industries. bi-m. ISSN 0039-1778

**Ealing Technical College. School of Librarianship**
Woodlands Ave., London W.5, Eng.
- Ealing Occasional Papers in the History of
Libraries. irreg.

**Earby Mine Research Group**
c/o Uplands, Skipton, N. Yorkshire, England.
- Industrial Past; an industrial & transport
archaeology review. q. ISSN 0307-1677

**Earlsport Ltd.**
33 Ludgate Hill, London EC4, England.
- Hospital Engineering. 10 per yr. ISSN 0046-7960
(Institute of Hospital Engineering)

**East African Wildlife Society**
- East African Wildlife Journal. (pub. by Blackwell
Scientific Publications, Ltd.)

**East Anglian Magazine Ltd.**
6 Great Colman St., Ipswich, Eng.
- East Anglian Magazine. m. ISSN 0012-8392

**East London Arts Magazine Society**
28 Commercial St., London E.1, Eng.
- Elam; a magazine for the arts in East London.
ISSN 0013-4058

**East London History Society**
c/o Ed. A. H. French, 36 Parkland Rd., Woodford
Green, Essex, England.
- East London History Society Bulletin. q.

**East Midland Allied Press Ltd.**
Northfield Ave., Kettering, Northamptonshire, Eng.
- Angling Times. w. ISSN 0003-3308
- Bike. m.
- Motor Cycle Mechanics. m.
- Motor Cycle News. w. ISSN 0027-1853
- Motorcycle Mechanics. m. (Mercury House
Publications Ltd.)
- Popular Motoring; and practical car maintenance.
m. ISSN 0032-4574
- Practical Photography. m. ISSN 0032-6445
- Sea Angler. m.

• Two Wheeler Dealer. m. ISSN 0027-5891
(National Association of Cycle Traders)

**East Midlands Arts**
1 Frederick St, Loughborough, Leics. LE11 3BH,
England.
• Artefact; arts tabloid. m.

**East Midlands Geological Society**
Dept. of Geology, The University, Nottingham
NG7 2RD, Eng.
• Mercian Geologist. s-a. ISSN 0025-990X

**East of England Agricultural Society**
East of England Showground, Peterborough PE2
OXE, England.
• East of England Show Catalogue. a.

**East Riding Archaeological Society**
187 Boothferry Rd., Hull HU4 6EY, England.
• East Riding Archaeologist. irreg. ISSN 0012-852X

**East Yorkshire Local History Society**
Purey Cust Chambers, York YO1 2EJ, England.
• East Yorkshire Local History Series. irreg. ISSN
0070-8208

**Eastbourne College**
Eastbourne, Sussex, Eng.
• Eastbournian. 2 per yr. ISSN 0012-8643

**Eastern Counties Newspapers Ltd.**
Prospect House, Rouen Rd., Norwich, Norfolk, Eng.
• Eastern Evening News. d. ISSN 0012-8791

**Eastern Electricity Board**
Box 40, Wherstead, Ipswich, Suffolk, Eng.
• Cable. m. ISSN 0045-3714

**Eastern Esplanade**
Southend- On- Sea, Essex SS1 3AB, Eng.
• Yachts and Yachting. fortn. ISSN 0044-0000

**R. F. Eastern Ltd.**
Cucumber Lane, Brundall, Norwich NR13 5RB,
Norfolk, Eng.
• Norfolk Fair. m. ISSN 0029-165X

**S.C. Easton**
16 King St., Covent Garden, London W.C. 2, Eng
(Subscr. Address: Central Books Ltd., 37 Grays Inn
Rd., London W.C.1 Eng)
• Comment (London); a Communist review. fortn.
ISSN 0010-2547 (Communist Party of Great
Britain)

**Eaton House Publishers Ltd.**
8 Wyndham Place, London W1H 2AY, Eng.
• Arts Review. fortn. ISSN 0004-4091

**Eaton-Williams Publications**
40 Gray's Inn Road, London, W.C.1, Eng.
• Triton; dealing with undersea exploration, diving,
marine research. bi-m. ISSN 0041-3119

**Echidna Epics Co. Ltd.**
301 Portobello Rd., London W1O 5TR, Eng.
• Frendz. bi-w. ISSN 0046-5062

**Eclipse Publications Ltd.**
286 Kilburn High Rd., London NW6, Eng.
• Industrial Relations Law Reports. m.
• Industrial Relations Review and Report. s-m.
ISSN 0046-9246

**Ecologist**
c/o Edward Goldsmith, Ed., 73 Molesworth St.,
Wadebridge, Cornwall PL27 7DS, England.
• Ecologist. m (10 per yr.) ISSN 0012-9631

**Economic and Social History Society of Ireland**
c/o Hon. Treasurer, 66 Balmoral Ave., Belfast BT9
6NY, N. Ireland.
• Irish Economic and Social History. a.

**Economic and Social Science Research Association**
177 Vauxhall Bridge Road, London S.W.1, Eng.
• E S S R A Magazine. 3 per yr. ISSN 0307-1901

**Economic History Society**
• Economic History Review. (pub. by Broadwater
Press Ltd.)
• Economic History Review. Supplements. (pub. by
Cambridge University Press)

**Economic League Ltd.**
Asphalte House, Palace St., London SW1E 5HO,
England.
• Economic League. Notes and Comments. m.
• News and Views: for Young Workers. q.

**Economics Association**
Room 340, Hamilton House, Mabledon Place,
London WC1H 9BH, Eng.
• Economics. 4 per yr. ISSN 0300-4287

**Economist Intelligence Unit, Ltd**
Spencer House, St. James's Place, London SW1A
1NI, England.
• Economist Intelligence Unit. E I U World
Outlook. a. ISSN 0424-3331
• European Trends. q. ISSN 0014-3162
• International Tourism Quarterly. q.
• Marketing in Europe; a monthly bulletin providing
detailed analysis of the European market for
consumer goods. m. ISSN 0025-3723
• Motor Business; a quarterly research bulletin for
the automotive and allied industries. q. ISSN
0027-1802
• Multinational Business. q. ISSN 0300-3922
• Paper and Packaging Bulletin; a quarterly review
of production, markets, etc. q. (U.S. Address:
Lincoln House, 60 E. 42nd St., New York, NY
10017)
• Quarterly Economic Review. q. ISSN 0033-5495
• Retail Business; a monthly bulletin on the British
market for consumer goods. m. ISSN 0034-6012
• Rubber Trends; a quarterly review of production,
markets, prices, etc. q. ISSN 0035-9564 (U.S.
Address: 633 Third Ave., New York, NY 10017)

**Economist Newspaper Ltd.**
25 St. James's St., London SW1A 1HG, Eng.
• Economist. w. ISSN 0013-0613

**Eden Press**
Lunesdale House, Hornby, Lancaster LA2 8NB,
Eng.
• Medical Hypotheses. q. ISSN 0306-9877
(Newcastle University. Department of Physiology)

**Edgar Wallace Society**
4 Bradmore, Oxford, England.
• Edgar Wallace Society Newsletter. q.

**Edinburgh Academy**
Henderson Row, Edinburgh EH3 5BL, Scotland.
• Edinburgh Academy Chronicle. 3 per yr. ISSN
0013-0893

**Edinburgh Architectural Association**
• E A A Review. (pub. by Edinburgh Pictorial Ltd.)

**Edinburgh College of Commerce**
Edinburgh, England.
• North Sea Oil: Select List: Periodical and
Newspaper Articles. a.

**Edinburgh Mathematical Society**
• Edinburgh Mathematical Society. Proceedings.
(pub. by Scottish Academic Press Ltd.)

**Edinburgh Medical Missionary Soceity**
12 Mayfield Terrace, Edinburgh EH9 1SA,
Scotland.
• Healing Hand. 3 per yr. ISSN 0017-8829

**Edinburgh Pictorial Ltd.**
Smith's Place House, Edinburgh 6, Scotland.
• E A A Review. a. ISSN 0307-1634 (Edinburgh
Architectural Association)
• Scottish Building & Civil Engineering Year Book.
a. ISSN 0085-6002

**Edinburgh University Press**
22 George Square, Edinburgh EH8 9LF, Scotland.
• Islamic Surveys. irreg., no. 1976. ISSN 0075-093X
• Regesta Regum Scottorum. irreg. ISSN 0080-0554

**Edinburgh University Student Publications Board**
1 Buccleuch St., Edinburgh EH8 9LW, Scotland.
• Edinburgh Dental Hospital Gazette. 2 per yr.
ISSN 0013-0907

**Editorial Associates**
The Crown, Crown Rd., Wheatley, Oxford, Eng.
• Idler; an entertainment. q.

**Edmund Plowden Trust**
51 High St., Hampton, Middlesex TW12 5SX, Eng.
• Law & Justice. q.

**B. Edsall & Co. Ltd.**
36 Eccleston Square, London S.W.1, Eng.
• British Journal of Alcohol & Alcoholism. q. ISSN
0309-1635 (Medical Council on Alcoholism)
• Health Education Index; and Guide to Voluntary
Social Welfare Organisations. 2 per yr.
• Health Visitor. m. ISSN 0017-9140 (Health
Visitors Association)
• New Baby. a. (Health Visitors Association)

**Edu-Games (U.K.) Ltd.**
11 Tottenham Court Rd., London W1A 4XF,
England.
• Games & Puzzles. m.

**Education Welfare Officers' National Association**
37 Papworth Gardens, London N7 8QP, England,
England.
• Education Welfare Officer. bi-m. ISSN 0013-1598

**Educational Drama Association**
• Creative Drama. (pub. by Stacey Publications)

**Educational Puppetry Association**
The Puppet Centre, Battersea Town Hall, Lavender
Hill, London SW11 5TJ, England.
• Puppet Post. s-a. ISSN 0033-4421
• Spotlight (London, 1943) 8 per yr. ISSN 0038-
8378

**Educational Review**
c/o School of Education, University of Birmingham,
Birmingham B15 3XA, England.
• Educational Review. 3 per yr. ISSN 0013-1911

**Edwardian Studies**
125 Markyate Rd., Dagenham, Essex RM8 2LB,
England.
• Edwardian Studies. a.

**Egon Ronay Organization Ltd.**
Leicester Sq., London W.C.2, England.
• Egon Ronay's Dunlop Guide to Hotels and
Restaurants in the British Isles. a. ISSN 0070-
9468

**Egypt Exploration Society**
2-3 Doughty Mews, London WC1N 2PG, England.
• Journal of Egyptian Archaeology. a. ISSN 0075-
4234

**Electoral Reform Society**
6 Chancel St., London SE1 0UX, Eng.
• Representation. q. ISSN 0034-4893

**Electric Railway Society**
14 Askerfield Ave., Allestree, Derby DE3 2ST,
England.
• Electric Railway Society. Journal. bi-m. ISSN
0013-4147

**Electrical Contractors' Association**
34 Palace Court, London W2 4HY, England.
• E C A Year Book Desk Diary. a.
• Electrical Contractor. m. ISSN 0308-7174

**Electrical Electronic and Telecommunication-
Plumbing Union**
W. Common Rd., Hayes, Bromley, Kent, Eng.
• Contact (Bromley) q. ISSN 0010-7255

**Electrical-Electronic Press Ltd.**
Dorset House, Stamford St., London, SE1 9LU,
England
(Dist. by W. F. Strube, IPC Business Press Inc., 300
E. 42 St., New York, N.Y. 10017)
• Electrical Who's Who. biennial. ISSN 0070-9727

**Electrical Power Engineers' Association**
Fox Lane North, Chertsey, KT16 9HW, Surrey,
Eng.
• Electrical Power Engineer. m. ISSN 0013-4376

**Electricity Council**
30 Millbank, London SW1P 4RD, England.
• Circuit News. m. ISSN 0009-7292

**Electro Medical Trade Association Ltd.**
276 High St., Guildford, Surrey GU1 3JU, Engalnd.
• Electro Medical Trade Association. Products
Directory. irreg.

**Electronic Engineering Association**
Berkeley Square House, Berkeley Sq, London W.1,
England.
• Electronic Engineering Association, London.
Annual Report. a. ISSN 0070-9859

**Electrophysiological Technologists' Association**
c/o Ed. J. W. Osselton, Fleming Memorial Hospital, Newcastle Upon Tyne, NE2 3AX, Eng.
● Journal of Electrophysiological Technology. q. ISSN 0307-5095

**Elek Books Ltd.**
54-58 Caledonian Rd., London N1 9RN, England.
● Architects' Year Book. irreg. ISSN 0066-619X
● Plays of the Year. irreg. no. 45 1975.

**Elektor Publishers Ltd.**
6 Stour Street, Canterbury CT1 2XZ, England.
● Elektor. m.

**Elim Pentecostal Church**
Elim Publications Board, Box 38, Cheltenham, Gloucestershire, England.
● Elim Evangel. w. ISSN 0013-6182
● Young Folk. m. ISSN 0044-0760

**Elliot Brothers (London) Ltd.**
Marconi House, Chelmsford, Essex, Eng.
● Airadio News. q. ISSN 0002-2624

**Elliott Publications Ltd.**
9 Queen Victoria St., Reading RG1 1SY, England.
● Craft & Hobby Dealer. bi-m.
● Craft Teacher News; equipment, materials and resources for all practical subjects in schools. q. ISSN 0306-0462

**Elmfield Press**
Elmfield Rd., Morley, Yorks. LS27 0NN, England.
● World Best SF Short Stories. a.

**Elvy & Gibbs**
11 Best Lane, Canterbury, Kent, England.
● Scientific Horticulture. approx. a. ISSN 0080-7737 (Horticultural Education Association)

**Embankment Press Ltd.**
Bldg. G59, G.E.C. Estate, East Lane, Wembley, Middlesex, England.
● Converter. m. ISSN 0010-8189
● Converter Directory; suppliers and services to the U.K. converting industry. a.
● Data Systems; for management decisions. m. ISSN 0011-6912
● Highways & Road Construction International. m. ISSN 0308-9533
● Industrial Management. m. ISSN 0007-6929 (Institute of Factory Management)
● Transport Engineer. bi-m. ISSN 0020-3122 (Institute of Road Transport Engineers)

**Embassy**
132 Wardour St., London W.I., Eng.
● Embassy. m. ISSN 0046-1857

**Embassy of Bolivia, London**
● Bolivia Information Handbook. (pub. by Diplomatist Associates Ltd.)

**Embassy of Mexico, London**
● Mexico Today. (pub. by Diplomatist Associates, Ltd.)

**Embassy of Paraguay, London**
● Paraguay Today. (pub. by Diplomatist Associates, Ltd.)

**Embassy of the Republic of Vietnam**
12 Victoria Rd., London W.8., Eng.
● Vietnam: Yesterday and Today. m. ISSN 0049-6367

**Ember Press**
6 the Mount, Furzeham, Brixham, Devon, England.
● Littack Supplement; a literary periodical. s-a.

**Embroiderers' Guild**
73 Wimpole St., London W1M 8AX, Eng.
● Embroidery. q. ISSN 0013-6611

**EMI Cinemas Ltd.**
30-31 Golden Sq., London W.1, Eng.
● Film Review. m.

**Emigrante**
47 Palace Court, London W.2., England.
● Emigrante; boletin del trabajador espanol en inglaterra. m.

**Emma (Printers & Publishers)**
South Corner, Burses Way, Brentwood, Essex CM13 2PY, England.
● Civil Service Poetry. a.

**Employment Conditions Abroad Ltd.**
13 Devonshire St., London W1N 1FS, England
(U.S. address: UNIPUB, c/o Wayne Kerwood, Box 433, Murray Hill Station, New York, NY 10016)
● World Employment Report in U.S.A. & Canada. m.

**Encounter Ltd.**
59 St. Martins Lane, London WC2 N 4JS, Eng.
● Encounter. m. ISSN 0013-7073

**Energy Economics Research Ltd.**
Guildgate House Terrace, Wokingham, Berks RG11 1BP, England.
● Oil and Energy Trends. m.

**Andi Engel, Ed. & Pub.**
3 Tottenham St., London W1P 9PB, England.
● Enthusiasm. irreg (1-2 per yr)

**Engineering Industries Association**
3-7 Portman Square, London W.1, Eng.
● Engineering Capacity and Export Review. m. ISSN 0013-7847
● Engineering Industries Journal. m. ISSN 0013-7995

**Engineering Industries Association. Northern Region**
● Northern Executive. (pub. by Pandon Publications, Ltd.)

**Engineering Materials and Design**
33-40 Bowling Green Lane, London EC1R 0NE, England.
● European Design Directory. a.

**Engineering Sciences Data Unit Ltd.**
251-259 Regent St., London W1R 7AD, England.
● Engineering Sciences Data Unit Index. irreg. with supplements. (Co-sponsors: Royal Aeronautical Society; Institutions of Chemical, Mechanical and Structural Engineers)

**Engineers' Digest Ltd.**
120 Wigmore St., London W1H 0AS, England.
● Engineers' Digest/Ingenieur Digest. m. ISSN 0013-8169

**Engineers' Guild Ltd.**
69-70 Evelyn House, 62 Oxford St., London W1N 0BD, Eng.
● Professional Engineer. q. ISSN 0033-006X

**English Association**
● English. (pub. by Oxford University Press)
● Essays and Studies. (pub. by John Murray (Publishers) Ltd.)
● Year's Work in English Studies. (pub. by John Murray (Publishers) Ltd.)

**English Basketball Association**
Calomax House, Lupton Ave., Leeds 9, England.
● Basketball. bi-m. ISSN 0005-6162

**English Ceramic Circle**
● English Ceramic Circle. Transactions. (pub. by W. & J. Mackey Ltd.)

**English Churchman Trust Ltd.**
P.O. Box 217, London SE5 8NP, England.
● English Churchman. fortn. ISSN 0013-8223

**English Congregation of the Order of Saint Benedict**
St. Alban's Priory, Bewsey St, Warrington WA2 7JQ, England.
● Benedictine Yearbook. a. ISSN 0522-8883

**English Dominicans**
● New Blackfriars. (pub. by Blackfriars)

**English Folk Dance and Song Society**
Cecil Sharp House, 2 Regents Park Rd., London NW1 7AY, Eng.
● English Dance and Song. q. ISSN 0013-8231
● Folk Music Journal. a. ISSN 0531-9684

**English Folk Dance and Song Society. Bristol District**
c/o John Maher, Shanboe, Claremont Ave., Bishopston, 7, Bristol, England.
● Bristol Folk News. irreg.

**English Golf Union**
c/o the Secretary, 12a Denmark St., Wokingham, Berkshire RG11 2BE, England.
● Golf News & Fixtures. m.
● Golfing Year. a.

**English Guernsey Cattle Society**
Giggs Hill Green, Thames Ditton, Surrey, England.
● English Guernsey Herd Book. a. ISSN 0071-0571
● Guernsey Breeders' Journal. s-a.

**English Harpsichord Magazine**
c/o Edgar Hunt, Ed., Rose Cottage, 8 Bois Lane, Chesham Bois, Bucks HP6 6BP, England.
● English Harpsichord Magazine; and early keyboard instrument review. s-a. ISSN 0306-4395

**English Jesuits**
● Way. (pub. by Way Publications)

**English National Opera**
London Coliseum, St. Martin's Lane, London WC2, England.
● English National Opera Programme. m.

**English Place-Name Society**
c/o Mrs. G. B. Lucas, 104a Barton Road, Cambridge, England
(and 32 E. 57 St., New York, N.Y. 10022)
● English Place-Name Society. irreg. ISSN 0071-0636

**English Speaking Board (International Ltd.)**
32 Roe Lane, Southport, Lancashire, Eng.
● Spoken English; ideas and developments in oral education. 3 per yr. ISSN 0038-772X

**English-Speaking Union**
Dartmouth House, 37 Charles Street, London, W1X 8AB, Eng.
● Concord. q. ISSN 0300-4384

**English Table Tennis Association**
21 Claremont, Hastings, Sussex, Eng.
● Table Tennis News. 8 per yr. ISSN 0039-8799

**English Westerners' Society**
Clive House, 4 Mays Hill Rd., Bromley, Kent, England.
● English Westerners' Brand Book. q. ISSN 0013-8401
● English Westerners' Tally Sheet. q. ISSN 0013-841X

**Entomologist's Monthly Magazine Ltd.**
7 Thorncliffe Rd., Oxford OX2 7BA, England.
● Entomologist's Monthly Magazine. q. ISSN 0013-8908

**Entomologist's Record**
c/o J. M. Chalmers - Hunt, Ed., 1 Hardcourts Close, West Wickham, Kent, Eng.
● Entomologist's Record. 11 per yr. ISSN 0013-8916

**Environmental Health Officers Association**
19 Grosvenor Place, London S.W.1, Eng.
● Environmental Health. m. ISSN 0013-9270

**Envoi**
c/o J. C. Meredith Scott, Ed., Lagan Nam Bann, Ballachulish, Argyll, Scotland.
● Envoi; a poetry magazine. 3 per yr. ISSN 0013-9394

**Epiphany Philosophy**
● Theoria to Theory. (pub. by Gordon and Breach Science Publishers Ltd.)

**Equipment News Ltd.**
30 Old Burlington St., London W1X 2AE, Eng.
● Domestic Heating & Plumbing: Bathrooms-Kitchens. m.
● Lighting Equipment News. m. ISSN 0024-3418

**Erdesdun Pomes**
10 Greenhaugh Rd., South Wellfield, Whitley Bay, Tyne and Wear NE25 9HF, Eng.
● Ostrich. q.

**Ergonomics Information Analysis Centre**
● Ergonomics Abstracts. (pub. by Taylor & Francis Ltd.)

**Esperanto Teachers Association**
7 Fairacre Rd., Barwell, Leicester LE9 8HH, England.
● Esperanto Teacher. 3 per yr. ISSN 0046-2527

**Essex County Council**
Essex Record Office, County Hall, Essex, Chelmsford CM1 1LX, England.
● Essex Education. (pub. by Essex Education Committee)

● SEAX Series of Teaching Portfolios. a.

**Essex County Library**
Goldlay Gardens, Chelmsford, Essex, England.
● Essex County Library. Union List of Serials.

**Essex Education Committee**
County Hall, Chelmsford Essex, Eng.
● Essex Education. 3 per yr. (Essex County Council)

**Essex Field Club**
Passmore Edwards Museum, Romford Road, Stratford, London, E15, England.
● Essex Naturalist. a. ISSN 0071-1489

**Essex Hall Bookshop**
1 Essex St., Strand, London, WC2R 3HY, England.
● Unitarian and Free Christian Churches. Handbook and Directory of the General Assembly. a. (directory); triennial (handbook) (General Assembly of Unitarian Free Christian Churches)

**Essex Naturalists' Trust Ltd.**
Fingringhoe Wick Nature Reserve, South Green Rd., Fingringhoe, Colchester, Essex CO5 7DN, England.
● Essex Naturalists' Trust Bulletin. s-a.

**Essex Society for Family History**
6 Windsor Way, Rayleigh, Essex, England.
● Essex Family Historian. irreg.

**Esso Petroleum Co., Ltd.**
Victoria St., London S.W.1, Eng.
● Esso Magazine. q. ISSN 0014-1011

**Estates Gazette Ltd.**
151 Wardour St., London W1V 4BN, Eng.
● Estates Gazette; devoted to land, commercial, industrial and residential properties and agriculture. w. ISSN 0014-1240
● Estates Gazette Digest of Land and Property Cases. a. ISSN 0071-1586

**Eugenics Society**
69 Eccleston Square, London SW1V 1PJ, England.
● Eugenics Society Bulletin. q.

**Eurap Publishing Co. Ltd.**
71 Stoke Newington Rd., London N16, England.
● Continental Film Review. m. ISSN 0010-7700

**Euro Publications Ltd.**
31 Churchill Way, Cardiff, Glamorgan CF1 4HE, Wales.
● Business News. South Wales Edition. m.
● Business News. West of England Edition. m.

**Euromed Publications**
97 Moore Park Rd., London SW6 2DA, Eng.
● Russian Pharmacology and Toxicology. bi-m. ISSN 0036-0325

**Euromoney Publications Ltd.**
Tallis House, Tallis St, London EC4Y 0JA, England.
● Euromoney; the monthly journal of international money and capital markets. m. ISSN 0014-2433
● Hambro Euromoney Directory. irreg.

**Euromonitor Publications Ltd.**
Box 115, 41 Russell Square, London WC1B 5DL, England.
● Euromonitor Review: Market Research Europe. bi-m.
● European Marketing Data and Statistics. a. ISSN 0071-2930
● Market Research Great Britain. m.

**Europa Publications Ltd.**
18 Bedford Sq., London WC1B 3JN, England.
● Africa South of the Sahara. a. ISSN 0065-3896
● Europa Year Book; a world survey. a. ISSN 0071-2302
● Far East and Australasia. a. ISSN 0071-3791
● International Who's Who. a. ISSN 0074-9613
● Middle East and North Africa; survey and Directory of Lands of Middle East and North Africa. a. ISSN 0076-8502
● National Trust for Places of Historic Interest or Natural Beauty. Yearbook. a.
● World of Learning. a. ISSN 0084-2117

**Europe House Publishing Ltd.**
1A Whitehall Place, London SW1A 2HA, England.
● Facts. m. (European Movement)
● New Europe. q. (European Movement)

**European Chemoreception Organization**
● Chemoreception Abstracts. (pub. by Information Retrieval Ltd.)

**European Coil Coating Association**
● European Coil Coating Association. Directory. (pub. by Sheet Metal Industries)

**European Data Publishing Co.**
32 St. James's Street, London SW1A 1HR, England.
● Background Data on the Common Market. irreg. ISSN 0305-8689

**European Economic Data Publishing Co., Ltd.**
4 Cleveland Square, London W2 6DH, Eng.
● Common Market News. m. ISSN 0300-4406

**European Federation of Corrosion.**
c/o Society of Chemical Industry, 14 Belgrave Sq., London, SW1X 8PS, England.
● European Federation of Corrosion. Report (of Meeting) irreg. ISSN 0071-2779
● International Congress on Metallic Corrosion. (Proceedings) irreg; 6th, Sydney, Aust., 1975. ISSN 0074-4123

**European Home Study Council**
c/o Keith Rawson-Jones, 44 Hendham Rd., Wandsworth, London S.W. 17, England.
● Epistolodidaktika; a home study periodical. 2 per yr. ISSN 0013-9653

**European Jewish Publications, Ltd.**
31 Perry St., London W. 1, England.
● Insight: Soviet Jews. bi-m.

**European Lead Development Committee**
c/o Lead Development Association, 34 Berkeley Sq., London W1X 6AJ, England.
● International Conference on Lead. Proceedings. irreg., 1968, 3rd, Vienna. ISSN 0074-316X

**European Movement**
● Facts. (pub. by Europe House Publishing Ltd.)
● New Europe. (pub. by Europe House Publishing Ltd.)

**European Orthodontic Society**
64 Wimpole St., London W1M 8AL, England.
● European Orthodontic Society. Transactions. a. ISSN 0071-299X

**European Pressure Die Casting Committee**
● International Pressure Die Casting Conference. Report. (pub. by Zinc Development Association)

**European Society for Opinion Surveys and Market Research**
56 Grosvenor St., London W1X 9DA, Eng.
● European Research. bi-m.

**European Studies Committee**
20 Kensington Palace Gardens, London W8 4QQ, Eng.
● European Studies. q. ISSN 0014-3103

**European Travel Commission**
● Tourism International Research/Europe. (pub. by Tourism International Press Ltd.)

**European Weed Research Council**
● Weed Research. (pub. by Blackwell Scientific Publications Ltd.)

**Evangelical Magazine**
Providence House, 118 Falcon Rd., London S.W.11., Eng.
● Evangelical Magazine. bi-m. ISSN 0046-2853

**Hugh Evans & Sons Ltd.**
350-360 Stanley Rd., Liverpool L20 2AH, Eng.
● Royal Army Medical Corps. Journal. q. ISSN 0035-8665

**Evans Brothers Ltd.**
Montague House, Russell Square, London WC1B 5BX, Eng.
● Art & Craft in Education; a magazine for all teachers of art and craft. m. ISSN 0004-3028
● Child Education; for teachers of young children to 9 years of age. m. ISSN 0009-3947
● Child Education Quarterly. q. ISSN 0045-6640
● Junior Education. m.
● Music Teacher. m. ISSN 0027-4461
● Pictorial Education. m. ISSN 0048-4121
● Pictorial Education Quarterly. q. ISSN 0048-413X
● University of Lagos. Law Series. irreg. ISSN 0075-7691

**Evans-Methuen Educational**
11 New Fetter Lane, London EC4P 4EE, England.
● Great Britain. Schools Council Publications. Curriculum Bulletins. irreg. ISSN 0072-7113
● Great Britain. Schools Council Publications. Examinations Bulletins. irreg. ISSN 0072-7121
● Great Britain. Schools Council Publications. Working Papers. irreg. ISSN 0072-713X

**Everyweek Educational Press Ltd.**
High St., Rickmansworth, Herts. WD3 1EU, Eng.
● Our World. 30 per yr (during school term) ISSN 0030-6975

**Ex-Service (1943) Association**
3 Circus Rd., London N.W.8, Eng.
● Ex-Serviceman. bi-m. ISSN 0014-3936

**Experimental Psychology Society**
● Quarterly Journal of Experimental Psychology. (pub. by Academic Press Inc. (London) Ltd.)

**Export Times Publishing Ltd.**
60 Fleet St., London Ec4, Eng.
● Export Times; the independent journal of international marketing. m. ISSN 0046-2950

**Expression One**
c/o Leslie Surridge, Ed., 5 Avon Rd., Waltham Forest, London E17 3RB, England.
● Expression One. q. ISSN 0014-536X

**F C I News Agency**
4 Holland Rd., London W14 8AZ, Eng.
● Features and News from behind the Iron Curtain. w. ISSN 0046-3396

**Fabian Society**
11 Dartmouth St., London SW1H 9BN, Eng.
● Fabian News. m. ISSN 0014-6196
● Fabian Reserarch Series. m. ISSN 0305-3555
● Fabian Society. Annual Report. a. ISSN 0071-3570
● Fabian Tract. m. ISSN 0307-7535
● Young Fabian Pamphlet. irreg., no. 45, 1976. ISSN 0513-5982

**Faculty of Actuaries in Scotland**
23 St. Andrew Sq., Edinburgh E H2 1 AQ, Scotland.
● Faculty of Actuaries in Scotland. Transactions. irreg. ISSN 0071-3686

**Faculty of Building**
The Secretariat, 10 Manor Way, Boreham Wood WD6 1QQ, Herts., England.
● Faculty of Building. Register of Members. irreg.

**Faculty of Homoeopathy**
Royal London Homoeopathic Hospital, Gt. Ormond St., London WC1N 3HR, England.
● British Homoeopathic Journal. q. ISSN 0007-0785

**Faculty of Radiologists**
● Clinical Radiology. (pub. by Longman Group Ltd.)

**Faculty of Teachers in Commerce Limited**
141 Bedford Rd., Sutton Coldfield, West Midlands B75 6DB, England.
● Teacher in Commerce; national journal of the commerical teaching profession. q.

**Faculty Press**
88 Regent St., Cambridge, Eng.
● Cytobios; a prestige international journal of cell biology. 3 vols. per year. ISSN 0011-4529
● Microbios; a prestige international journal of chemical and general microbiology. 3 vols per year. ISSN 0026-2633
● Microbios Letters; a prestige international journal for the rapid publication of biomedical communications. 3 vols per year. ISSN 0307-5494

**Roy Faiers Ltd.**
8A St. Davids Hill, Exeter, Devon, Eng.
● Chiltern Life. m. ISSN 0009-4277
● Cotswold Life. m. ISSN 0010-9746
● Devon Life. m. ISSN 0012-1703

**Fairplay Publications, Ltd.**
1 Pudding Lane, London EC3R 8AA, Eng.
● Fairplay International Shipping Weekly. w. ISSN 0307-0220
● World Ships on Order. q. ISSN 0043-9010

**Falling Wall Press Ltd.**
79, Richmond Road, Montpelier, Bristol BS6 5EP, England.
- Falling Wall Book Review. 5 per yr.

**Family Planning Association**
27 Mortimer St., London W1A 4QW, Eng.
- Current Literature in Family Planning. bi-m.
- Family Planning Today. bi-m.
- Fertility and Contraception. q.

**Family Welfare Association**
501 Kingsland Rd., London E8, England.
- Annual Charities Digest. (pub. by Butterworth & Co. (Publishers) Ltd.)
- Charities Digest. a.
- Guide to the Social Services. (pub. by Macdonald and Evans Ltd.)

**Farleys (Fareham) Ltd**
West St., Fareham, Hants. PO16 0EF, England.
- Hampshire Poets. 2 per yr. (Southern Arts Association)

**Farm Buildings Information Centre**
National Agricultural Centre, Kenilworth, Warwickshire CV8 2LG, Eng.
- Farm Buildings Digest; a cumulative information service. q. ISSN 0014-7877

**Farm Business Ltd.**
2 Church St., Warwick, Eng.
- Euro-Farm Business. m.

**Farm Holiday Guides Ltd.**
18 High Street, 2Paisley PA1 2BX, Scotland.
- Farm Holiday Guide and Country Guest House. a. ISSN 0071-3902
- Guide to Britain. a. ISSN 0072-825X

**Farm Management Association**
National Agriculture Centre, Kenilworth, Warwickshire CV8 2LG, England.
- Farm Management. 3 per yr. ISSN 0014-8059

**Farmers Club**
3 Whitehall Court, London S.W.1, Eng.
- Farmers Club. Journal. bi-m. ISSN 0014-8393

**Farmers' Union of Wales**
Llys Amaeth, Queens Square, Aberystwyth, Cardiganshire, Wales.
- Tir/Land. bi-m. ISSN 0040-8050
- Y Tir and Welsh Farmer. bi-m.

**Farming Press Ltd.**
Fenton House, Wharfedale Rd., Ipswich, Suffolk, England.
- Arable Farming. m.
- Dairy Farmer. m. ISSN 0011-5576
- Pig Farming. m. ISSN 0031-9759

**Farriers Journal Publishing Co. Ltd.**
674 Leeds Road, Lofthouse Gate, Wakefield WF3 3HJ, England.
- Farriers Journal. m. (National Master Farriers Blacksmiths) (Co-sponsor: Agricultural Engineers Association)

**Fashion Buyer Ltd.**
15 Adamson Rd., London, N.W.3, Eng.
- Speleologist. q. ISSN 0038-7304

**Fauna Preservation Society**
c/o Zoological Society of London, Regent's Park, London NW1 4RY, England.
- Oryx. 3 per yr. ISSN 0030-6053

**Faversham House**
103 Brigstock Rd., Thornton Heath, Surrey, England.
- Air Conditioning, Ventilating and Heating Equipment. a. ISSN 0065-4809

**Faversham Society**
Fleur-De-Lis, Preston St., Faversham, Kent ME13 8NS, Eng.
- Faversham Papers. 2 per yr. ISSN 0014-892X

**Federated Employers Press Ltd.**
82 New Cavendish St., London W1M 8AD, England.
- House Builder & Estate Developer; management journal of a 1500 million pound industry. m;1974, vol 34. (House-Builders' Federation)
- Modern Plastering. q. ISSN 0026-8267 (National Federation of Plastering Contractors)
- National Builder. m. ISSN 0027-8807 (National Federation of Building Trades Employers)

**Federation of British Artists**
17 Carlton House Terrace, London SW1Y 5BD, England.
- F. B. A. Quarterly. q.

**Federation of Children's Book Groups**
Owston Ferry 220, Doncaster, Yorks, England.
- Federation of Children's Book Groups. Yearbook. a.

**Federation of Commonwealth and British Chambers of Commerce**
69 Cannon St., London E.C.4, England.
- Federation of Commonwealth and British Chambers of Commerce. Annual Report. a.

**Federation of Family History Societies**
Peapkin's End, 2 Stella Grove, Tollerton, Notts NG12 4EY, England.
- Family History News and Digest. 4 per yr. ISSN 0309-8559

**Federation of Junior Chambers of Commerce in Scotland**
25 Charlotte Sq., Edinburgh 2, Scotland.
- Scotland Tomorrow; journal of the Federation of Junior Chambers of Commerce in Scotland. a. ISSN 0080-7923

**Federation of Master Builders**
- Master Builders' Journal. (pub. by Trade Press (FMB) Ltd.)

**Federation of Old Cornwall Societies**
Pengarth, Count House Lane, Carbis Bay, St. Ives, Cornwall, England.
- Old Cornwall. s-a.

**Federation of Personnel Services**
- Personnel Service News. (pub. by A.M.O.)

**Federation of Playgoers Society**
27 The Commons, Shrub End, Colchester, Essex, England.
- Federation of Playgoers Societies. Newsletter. q.

**Federation of Women Zionists of Great Britain and Ireland**
107 Gloucester Place, London W1H 4BX, England.
- F.W.Z. Review. q.

**Fellowship for Freedom in Medicine**
86 Harley St., London W. 1, Eng.
- Fellowship for Freedom in Medicine Newletter. 2 per yr.

**Fellowship of Postgraduate Medicine**
- Postgraduate Medical Journal. (pub. by Blackwell Scientific Publications Ltd.)

**Fellowship of Reconciliation**
9 Coombe Rd., New Malden, Surrey KT3 4QA, Eng.
- Newspeace. m (11 per yr) ISSN 0048-0304
- Reconciliation Quarterly. q. ISSN 0034-1479

**Fellowship Party**
- Day by Day. (pub. by Loverseed Press)
- Un-Common Sense. (pub. by Loverseed Press)

**Ferrari Owners' Club**
40 Bartholomew St., Newburg, Berkshire, Eng.
- Ferrari. q. ISSN 0015-0169

**Ferry Pickering Publishers Ltd.**
Eastern Boulevard, Leicester LE2 7BN, England.
- Knitting International. m.

**Ferry Press**
177 Green Lane, London S.E.9, Eng.
- Park. q. ISSN 0031-210X
- Wivenhoe Park Review. 4 per yr. ISSN 0043-7107

**Festiniog Railway Society Ltd.**
Harbour Sta., Porthmadog, Gwynedd, LL49 9NF, Wales.
- Festiniog Railway Magazine. q. ISSN 0015-0355

**Fettes College**
Edinburgh, Scotland.
- Fettesian. a. ISSN 0046-3701

**Fiasco Publications**
31, Bellevue St., Filey, North Yorkshire YO14 9HU, Eng.
- Bogg. q.

**David Field Holdings Ltd.**
42 Berkeley St., London W1X 5FP, England.
- David Field All-World Miniature Sheet Catalogue. a.

**Francis J. Field Ltd.**
Sutton Coldfield, West Midlands B73 6BJ, Eng.
- Aero Field. q. ISSN 0001-9135

**Field Studies Council**
9 Devereux Court, Strand, London WC2R 3JR, England.
- Field Studies. a. ISSN 0428-304X

**Murray Fieldhouse**
Northfields Studio, Northfields, Tring, Herts, England.
- Pottery Quarterly; a review of craft pottery. irreg. ISSN 0032-5678

**Film Dope**
5 Norman Court, Little Heath, Potters Bar, Hertfordshire, EN6 1HY, Eng.
- Film Dope. irreg. (approx. 3 per yr)

**Film Production Association of Great Britain**
25 Green Street, London W1Y 3FD, England.
- Film Product Association of Great Britain. Annual Report. a. ISSN 0071-4895

**Financial Times**
Bracken House, 10 Cannon St., London EC4P 4BY, Eng.
- Banker. m. ISSN 0005-5395
- European Law Newsletter. m. ISSN 0300-2233
- Financial Times International Business Yearbook. a.
- Financial Times Tax Newsletter. m.
- Financial Times World Shipping Yearbook. a.
- History Today. m. ISSN 0018-2753
- Mining International Year Book. a. ISSN 0076-9002
- North Sea and Europe Offshore Year Book and Buyers Guide. a.
- Oil and Gas International Year Book. a. ISSN 0078-4273
- Who's Who in World Oil and Gas. a.

**Financial Times. Business Enterprises Division**
10 Bolt Court, London EC4A 7HL, England.
- British Antiques Year Book. a.
- Business Letter from Europe. w.
- European Community Information. m. ISSN 0046-2748
- Financial Times Who's Who in World Banking. a.
- Financial Times World Hotel Directory. a.
- Insurance. m.
- International Antiques Year Book. a. ISSN 0538-4311

**Findlay Publications Ltd.**
10 Letchworth Drive, Bromley, Kent BR2 9BE, England.
- British Plastics and Rubber. m.
- Works Management. m. (Institution of Works Managers)

**Finescroll Ltd.**
De Worde House, 283 Lonsdale Rd., Barnes, London S.W.13., Eng.
- Air International. m. ISSN 0306-5634

**Finishing Publications Ltd.**
179b High St., Hampton Hill, Middlesex, Eng.
- Metal Finishing Abstracts. bi-m. ISSN 0026-0584
- Metal Finishing Plants and Processes; bi-monthly international market service and product guide. bi-m. ISSN 0026-0606

**Fire Protection Association**
Aldermary House, Queen St., London EC4N 1TJ, Eng.
- Fire Prevention. q.

- Fire Prevention Science and Technology. 2-3 per yr.

**Fiscal Press Ltd.**
Fiscal House, 36 Lattimore Rd., St. Albans, Herts. AL1 3XW, Eng.
- Income Tax Digest and Accountants' Review. m.

**Fish Friers Review Ltd.**
Federation House, 289 Dewsbury Rd., Leeds 11, Eng.
- Fish Friers Review. m. ISSN 0015-2927 (National Federation of Fish Friers)

**Fisheries Laboratory**
Lowestoft, England.
- Fishing Prospects. a.

**Fisheries Organization Society Ltd.**
558 London Rd., North Cheam, Sutton, Surrey SM3 9AA, England.
- F. O. S. Year Book & Annual Report. a.

**Fishpaste**
97 Holywell St., Oxford, Eng.
- Fishpaste; postcard review of art and letters. m. ISSN 0015-3087

**Fitzken Publishers**
45 Rodney Rd., Cheltenham, Eng.
- Report on World Affairs. q. ISSN 0034-4737

**Five Arches Press**
c/o Gillian Clarke, Ed., Knowling Mead, Tenby, Dyfed SA70 8EE, Wales.
- Anglo-Welsh Review. 3 per yr. ISSN 0003-3405 (Welsh Arts Council)

**Fleet Street Letter Ltd.**
72 Fleet St., London EC4Y 1JH, Eng.
- Fleet Street Letter. w. ISSN 0300-4228

**Fleet Street Patent Law Reports Ltd**
Elm House, 10-16 Elm St., London W.C. 1, England.
- Fleet Street Patent Law Reports. m. ISSN 0430-6457

**Flintshire Historical Society**
50, Hafod Park, Mold, Clwyd CH7 1QW, Wales.
- Flintshire Historical Society. Publications, Journal and Record Series. a. ISSN 0071-5727

**Florists Telegraph Delivery Association**
- Mercury. (pub. by Interflora British Unit Ltd.)

**Flour Milling and Baking Research Association**
Chorleywood, Herts WD3 5SH, England.
- Flour Milling and Baking Research Association. Annual Report and Accounts. a. ISSN 0071-6243
- Flour Milling and Baking Research Association Abstracts. bi-m. ISSN 0300-421X

**Flyfishers Club**
86 St. James St., London SW1A 1EG, Eng.
- Fly-Fishers Journal. q. ISSN 0046-4228

**Focus Publications**
13 New Quebec St., London W1, England.
- Church School University Equipment. bi-m.

**Focus Publications Council**
19 Claremont Crescent, Edinburgh EH7 4QD, Scotland.
- Focus on Social Work and Service in Scotland. m.

**Fodens Ltd.**
Elworth Works, Sandbach, Cheshire, Eng.
- Foden News. q. ISSN 0015-5209

**Folio Society Ltd.**
202 Great Suffolk St., London SE1 1PR, Eng.
- Folio. q. ISSN 0015-5772

**Folk Review Ltd.**
c/o Fred Woods, Ed., Austin House, Hospital St., Nantwich, Cheshire, England.
- Folk Review. m.

**Folklore Society**
c/o University College London, Gower St., London WC1E 6BT, Eng.
- Folklore. s-a. ISSN 0015-587X

**Follow up**
200d Railton Road, London SE 24, England.
- Follow up. q.

**Fontessa Publications Ltd.**
Hermit Place, 252 Belsize Road, Kilburn, London, England.
- Knave. m.

**Food Education Society**
c/o Dr. A.N. Howard, 160 Piccadilly, London W1V ONQ, Eng.
- Food Education Society. News Bulletin. q.

**Food Trade Press Ltd.**
29 High St., Green Street Green, Orpington, Kent BR6 6LS, England.
- Binsted'S Directory of Food Trade Marks and Brand Names. biennial. ISSN 0067-8651
- Food Machinery and Ingredients Export News. q. ISSN 0307-1596
- Food Trade Review. m. ISSN 0015-6671

**Football Association**
- Football Association. Official F. A. Year Book. (pub. by Heinmann Pan Books)

**G. W. Foote & Co.**
702 Holloway Rd., London N19 3NL, Eng.
- Freethinker. m. ISSN 0016-0687

**Footnote**
44 High St., Meldreth, Royston, Herts SG8 6JU, England.
- Footnote; the magazine for New Orleans jazz. bi-m.

**Forbes Publications Ltd.**
Hartree House, Queensway, London W2 4SH, England.
- Consumer Education. q.
- Creative Needlecraft. 5 per yr.
- Home Economics. m. ISSN 0307-2053
- Nutrition and Food Science. q. ISSN 0034-6659

**Force Four Motoring Publications Ltd.**
1314 Little Britain, London EC1A 7LP, England.
- Car. m. ISSN 0008-5987

**Ford Motor Co., Ltd. Tractor Operations**
Basildon, Essex, Eng.
- Farm; progress in mechanisation. bi-m. ISSN 0014-7796

**Forecast Publications**
Students' Union, University College of North Wales, Bangor, Caerns, Waies.
- Forecast. 10 per yr. ISSN 0015-7074 (Bangor Students' Union)

**Foreign Affairs Publishing Co.**
139 Petersham, Nr. Richmond, Surrey, Eng.
- East-West Digest. every 2 wks. ISSN 0012-8627

**Foreign Correspondents Ltd.**
58 Paddington St., London W.1, England.
- Africa Annual; the "New Africa" reference book. a. (no edition in 1969) ISSN 0065-3810
- Asian Annual. a.(no edition in 1969) ISSN 0066-8354
- East-West Commerce; dealing with the trade between the Soviet bloc and China and the rest of the world. m. ISSN 0012-8600
- Eastern World; the Asia monthly. m. ISSN 0012-8961
- New Africa. m. ISSN 0028-4157

**Foremost Press Ltd.**
Box 1, Wirral, Merseyside L46 0TS, Eng.
- Home Beer and Winemaking. m. ISSN 0046-7758
- Home Brew Trader. m.

**Forensic Publishing Co.**
Box 18, Bognor Regis PO22 7AA, England.
- Criminologist. q. ISSN 0011-1376

**Forensic Science Society**
Box 41, Harrogate, Yorkshire HG1 2LF, England.
- Forensic Science Society. Journal. q. ISSN 0015-7368

**Foresight Publishing Co.**
29 Beaufort Ave, Birmingham B34 6AD; Birmingham B34 6AD, Eng.
- Foresight. bi-m.

**Fortean Times**
Box 152, London N10 1EP, England.
- Fortean Times; a contemporary record of strange phenomena. bi-m. ISSN 0308-5899

**Forum International**
- Forum. (pub. by Forum Press Ltd.)

**Forum Press Ltd.**
2 Bramber Road, London W14 9PB, Eng. (U.S. Address: Penthouse-Forum, 21st Floor, 909 Third Ave., New York, NY 10022)
- Forum; the journal of human relations. and psycho-sexual studies. m. ISSN 0015-833X (Forum International)

**G. W. Foster Associates Ltd.**
Greek House, 17 Greek St., Stockport SK3 8AB, Eng.
- Bradford & Halifax Chambers of Commerce. Chamber of Commerce Journal. q. ISSN 0006-8683
- Bradford and Halifax Chambers of Commerce Members Directory. a.
- Cumbria Guide Industry and Commerce. a.
- Journal of Industry & Commerce. q. (Co-sponsors: Kirklees, Huddersfield & Spen Valley, Batley & Birstall, Dewsbury Chambers of Commerce)
- Kirklees Chamber of Commerce. Member's Directory. a.
- Manchester Developer. bi-m.
- Staffordshire Guide Industry and Commerce. a. (Staffordshire Development Association)
- Summit. q. (Cumberland Industrial Association)

**W. Foulsham & Co. Ltd.**
Yeovil Road, Slough, Bucks., England.
- Foulsham's Original Old Moore's Almanack. a. ISSN 0071-8084

**Foundation for Business Responsibilities**
5 Plough Place, Fetter Lane, London EC4P 4LT, England.
- Foundation for Business Responsibilities. Dialogues. irreg; 1972, no. 2.
- Foundation for Business Responsibilities. Discussion Paper. irreg. ISSN 0073-7410
- Foundation for Business Responsibilities. Occasional Papers. irreg. ISSN 0073-7429
- Foundation for Business Responsibilities. Research Paper. irreg. ISSN 0073-7437
- Foundation for Business Responsibilities. Seminar Papers. 3 per yr.
- Sir Frederic Hooper Award Essay. a.
- Sir George Earle Memorial Lecture on Industry and Government. a. ISSN 0080-9780

**Foundation for European Judaism**
Kent House, Rutland Gardens, London S.W.7, Eng. (U.S. address: UAHC-European Judaism, 838 Fifth Ave., New York, NY 10021)
- European Judaism. s-a. ISSN 0014-3006

**Foundation Publications Ltd.**
7 Ongar Rd., Brentwood, Essex, Eng.
- Ground Engineering. 8 per yr. ISSN 0017-4653

**Foxlow Publications Ltd.**
19 Harcourt St., London W.1, Eng., U.K.
- Dock and Harbor Authority. m. ISSN 0012-4419

**Fragment**
c/o F. G. Bissenden, Ed., 41 Fabian Rd., Fulham, London SW6 7TY, England.
- Fragment. irreg., (approx. 2-3 per yrs.); no. 24, 1974.

**Frameworks Press**
50 Princes Gate, Exhibition Road, London S.W.7, Eng.
- Frameworks Journal. 3 per yr.

**Francis Bacon Society Inc.**
Canonbury Tower, Islington, London N.1, England.
- Baconiana. a.

**Francis Thompson Society**
3 Kemplay Road, London, NW3, England.
- Francis Thompson Society. Journal. irreg. ISSN 0532-5781

**Franey and Co. Ltd.**
Burgon Street, London, EC4, England.
- Building Societies. Year Book. a. ISSN 0068-3566
- Building Societies' Gazette. m. ISSN 0007-3652

**Fraser Pearce Ltd.**
26, Station Rd., Cambridge CB1 2LB, Eng.
- Film Making. m. ISSN 0013-2543

**Free Church Federal Council**
27 Tavistock Square, London WC1H 9HH, Eng.
- Free Church Chronicle. q. ISSN 0016-0326

**Free Church of Scotland Publications Committee**
15 N. Bank St., Edinburgh EH1 2LS, Scotland.
- Free Church of Scotland. Monthly Record. m. ISSN 0016-0334

**Free Commonwealth Group, Ltd.**
30 Craven St., London W.C.2., Eng.
- Open Secret. q.

**Free Press**
25 Alderney St., London S.W. 1., Eng.
- Free Press. m. ISSN 0046-5011

**Freedom of Vision**
Ashurstwood Abbey, Sussex RH19 35D, England.
- Freedom of Vision. irreg. ISSN 0016-0571

**Freedom Press**
84B White Chapel High St., London E.1, Eng.
- Freedom. w. ISSN 0016-0504

**Freeland Press Ltd.**
112 Westbourne Grove, Oxford OX7 2AP, England.
- Every Man's Own Lawyer. every 4-5 yrs., 70th edt. 1971. ISSN 0071-3228

**Miller Freeman Publications Ltd.**
Circle House North, 69-71 Wembley Hill Rd., Wembley, Middlesex HA9 8BL, England.
- International Hospital Equipment. 7 per yr. ISSN 0301-5580

**Freezer Family Ltd.**
26 Bloomsbury Way, London WC1A 2SP, England.
- Freezer Family.

**Freight Transport Association**
Hermes House, St. John's Rd., Tunbridge Wells TN4 9UZ, Eng.
- Freight. m. ISSN 0016-0849

**French Chamber of Commerce in Great Britain**
96 Sloane St., London S.W.1., England.
- Franco British Trade Directory. a. ISSN 0071-917X
- Franco-British Trade Journal. m.

**French Notes & Queries**
97 Holywell St., Oxford, Eng.
- French Notes & Queries. q. ISSN 0016-108X

**Laurence French Publications Ltd.**
9 Princess Mews, London NW3 5AP, Eng.
- Far East Week by Week. w. ISSN 0046-3264

**Friend Publications Ltd.**
Drayton House, Gordon St., London W.C.1, Eng.
- Friend; a Quaker weekly journal. w. ISSN 0016-1268

**Friends Historical Society**
Friends House, Euston Rd., London NW1 2BJ, England.
- Friends Historical Society. Journal. a. ISSN 0071-9587

**Friends of Covent Garden Ltd.**
Royal Opera House, Covent Garden, London W. C. 2, Eng.
- About the House; the magazine of the Friends of Covent Garden. 3 per yr. ISSN 0001-3242

**Friends of the Western Buddhist Order**
1A Balmore St., London N.19, Eng.
- Freinds of the Western Buddhist Order Newsletter. q.

**Friends Service Council**
Friends House, Euston Road, London NW1 2BJ, England.
- Friends Service Council. Annual Report. a. ISSN 0071-9609
- Quaker Monthly. m. ISSN 0033-507X
- Quaker Service. q.

**Friends World Committee**
Drayton House, 30 Gordon St., London WC1H 0AX, Eng.
- Friends World News. 2 per yr. ISSN 0016-1365

**Fudge & Co. Ltd.**
Sardinia Hse, Sardinia St., London WC2A 3NW, England.
- Bookdealer; the trade weekly for books wanted and for sale. w.

**Fuel and Metallurgical Journals Ltd.**
Queensway House, 2 Queensway, Redhill, Surrey RH1 1QS, England.
- Colliery Guardian. m. ISSN 0010-1281
- European Glass Directory and Buyer's Guide. a. ISSN 0306-204X (Glass Manufacturers Federation)
- Foundry Trade Journal. w. ISSN 0015-9042 (Co-Sponsor: National Society of Master Patternmakers)
- Foundry Yearbook. a.
- Glass; the monthly journal. m. ISSN 0017-0984
- Guide to the Coalfields. a. ISSN 0072-8713
- Industrial Pollution Control Yearbook. a.
- Metal Finishing Journal. m.
- Metallurgia and Metal Forming; the International journal of metals. m.
- Polymers Paint and Colour Journal. fortn.
- Polymers Paint and Colour Year Book. a. ISSN 0078-7817
- Power and Works Engineering. fortn.
- Ryland's Directory. a. ISSN 0080-505X
- Safety at Sea International. m. ISSN 0036-2441
- Sheet Metal Industries. m. ISSN 0037-3435
- Sheet Metal Industries Year Book. a.
- Steel Times. m. ISSN 0039-095X
- Steel Times Annual Review of the Steel Industry. a.
- Water Services. m. ISSN 0301-7028
- Water Services Handbook. a. ISSN 0307-1782

**Fullerton & Lloyd (Publishers) Ltd.**
263a Sydenham Rd., Croydon, Surrey, Eng.
- Span. m. ISSN 0049-1799

**Fund for the Replacement of Animals in Medical Experiments**
312a Worple Rd., London SW20 8QU, England.
- A T L A Abstracts. (Alternatives to Laboratory Animals) s-a. ISSN 0306-2465

**Fundex Ltd.**
30 Finsbury Square, London EC2A 1PJ, England.
- Managed and Property Bonds. a.
- Money Management and Unitholder; the journal of money management. m. ISSN 0028-6052
- Regular Savings Plans. a.
- Unit Trust Yearbook. a. ISSN 0503-2628 (Association of Unit Trust Managers)

**Fur Review Publishing Co.**
27 Garlick Hill, London EC4V 2BA, Eng.
- Fur Review. m.

**Fur Weekly News Ltd.**
87-93 Lambs Conduit St., London WC1N 3NA, Eng.
- Fur Weekly News. w. ISSN 0016-2981

**Furniture History Society**
Victoria and Albert Museum, Dept. of Furniture & Woodworking, London S.W.7, England.
- Furniture History. s-a. ISSN 0016-3058

**Furniture Industry Research Association**
Maxwell Rd., Stevenage, Herts SG1 2EW, England.
- F I R A Bulletin. q. ISSN 0014-5904

**G. E. C.-Marconi Electronics Ltd.**
Baddow Research Laboratories, W. Hanningfield Rd., Great Baddow, Essex, Eng.
- Marconi Review. q. ISSN 0025-2883

**G. K. W. Publications Ltd.**
Staple Inn Bldgs. (South), 335 High Holborn, London WC1V 7QG, Eng.
- Job; newspaper for the men & women of the Metropolitan Police. fortn. ISSN 0021-7026

**Gairm Publications**
29 Waterloo St., Glasgow C.2, Scotland.
- Gairm. q. ISSN 0016-3929

**Galaxy Publication Ltd.**
Hermit Place, 252 Belsize Road, Kilburn, London NW6 4BT, England.
- Fiesta. m.

**Gale & Polden Ltd.**
Wellington Press, Aldershot, Hants, Eng
(Subscr. to: Treasurer, Guards Magazine, Horse Guards, Whitehall, London SW1A 2AX, England)
- Guards Magazine. q. ISSN 0017-503X

**A. R. Gallant**
32, New St., Ashford, Kent TN24 8UX, Eng.
- Dog World. w. ISSN 0012-4885
- Dog World Annual. a. ISSN 0070-7015

**Galleon World Travel Association Ltd.**
Galleon House, King St., Maidstone, Kent ME14 1EG, England, England
(Dist. in U.S. by: Fourways Travel Ltd., 27th Floor, 245 Park Ave., New York, NY 10017)
- Coach Tours in Britain. a. ISSN 0069-4886
- Holidays in Britain. a. ISSN 0073-3024
- Painting Holidays. a. ISSN 0078-7833

**Gallery**
c/o Valerie Sinason, Editor, 15a Alexandra Mansions, West End Lane, London N.W.6, England.
- Gallery. s-a.

**Galloway Cattle Society**
131 King St., Castle Douglas, Kirkcudbrightshire, Scotland.
- Galloway Herd Book. a.
- Galloway Journal. a. ISSN 0430-9928

**Galpin Society**
Rose Cottage, Boislane, Chesham Bois, Bucks HP6 6BP, England.
- Galpin Society Journal; for the Study of Musical Instruments. a. ISSN 0072-0127

**Galton Foundation**
- Journal of Biosocial Science. (pub. by Blackwell Scientific Publications Ltd.)

**Garavi Gujarat Publications**
22 Rosoman St., London EC1R 0NA, England.
- Garavi Gujarat. w.

**Garden History Society**
24 Woodlands North Side, London SW4 0RJ, England.
- Garden History. irreg.

**Gardeners' Sunday Organisation**
White Witches, Claygate Road, Dorking, Surrey, England.
- Gardens to Visit. a. (Co-sponsors: Gardeners' Royal Benevolent Society; Gardeners' Orphan Fund)

**Gas Chromatography Discussion Group**
- Gas and Liquid Chromatography Abstracts. (pub. by Applied Science Publishers Ltd.)

**Gateway Publications**
Foley Trading Estate, Foley St., Hereford HR1 2SN, England.
- Export. 10 per yr. ISSN 0014-5084 (Institute of Export)

**Gauge "O" Guild Gazette**
Mr. E. C. Taylor, Secretary, 37 The Drove, Andover, Hants., Eng.
- Gauge "O" Guild Gazette. q. ISSN 0016-5255

**Gay News Ltd.**
c/o Peter Burton, 1A Normand Gardens, Greyhound Rd., London W14 9SB, England.
- Gay News. s-m.
- Gay News Gay Guide. m.

**Gayre & Nigg**
1 Darnaway St., Edinburgh EH3 6DW, Scotland.
- Armorial; an international annual journal of heraldry, genealogy, names and related names. a. ISSN 0066-7749

**Gee & Co. (Publishers) Ltd.**
151 Strand, London WC1R 1JJ, Eng.
- Accountant; the recognized weekly journal for the accountancy profession throughout the world. w. ISSN 0001-4710

**Gemmological Association of Great Britain**
Saint Dunstan's House, Carey Lane, London EC2V 8AB, Eng.
- Journal of Gemmology and Proceedings of the Gemmological Association of Great Britain. q. ISSN 0022-1252

**Genera**
c/o Colin Simms, Ed., Bessie Surtees' House, Sandhill, Newcastle-on-Tyne 1, England.
- Genera. s-a.

**General and Municipal Workers' Union**
Ruxley Towers, Claygate, Esher, Surrey, Eng.
- G M W Herald. (pub. by Co-Operative Press Ltd.)
- G M W Journal. (pub. by Co-Operative Press Ltd.)
- General and Municipal Workers' Union. m. ISSN 0016-6499

**General Assembly of Unitarian Free Christian Churches**
- Unitarian and Free Christian Churches. Handbook and Directory of the General Assembly. (pub. by Essex Hall Bookshop)

**General Aviation Safety Committee**
Church House, 33 Church St., Henley-on-Thames, Oxfordshire RG9 1SE, Eng.
- Flight Safety Bulletin. q. ISSN 0015-3737

**General Conference of the New Church**
- General Conference of the New Church. Yearbook. (pub. by New Church Press)

**General Council of British Shipping**
30-32 St. Mary Axe, London EC3A 8ET, England.
- British Shipping Statistics. a. ISSN 0590-9775
- General Council of British Shipping. Annual Report. a.

**General Dental Council**
37 Wimpole St., London W1M 8DQ, England.
- General Dental Council. Dentists Register. a. ISSN 0072-0674
- General Dental Council. Minutes of the Proceedings. a. ISSN 0072-0682

**General Electric Co. Ltd. Hirst Research Centre**
Wembley, Middlesex HA9 7PP, Eng.
- G E C Journal of Science & Technology. 3 per yr.

**General Electric Co. Ltd. of England**
Box 53, Coventry CV3 1HJ, Eng.
- G E C Telecommunications. s-a. ISSN 0046-5593

**General Federation of Trade Unions**
Central House, Upper Woburn Place, London W.C.1, Eng.
- Federation News. q. ISSN 0014-9411

**General Gramophone Publications Ltd.**
177-179 Kenton Road, Harrow, Middlesex HA3 0HA, England.
- Cassettes & Cartridges. m.
- Gramophone. m. ISSN 0017-310X
- Gramophone Classical Catalogue. q. ISSN 0309-4367
- Gramophone Popular Catalogue. q. ISSN 0309-4359
- Recommended Recordings. s-a. ISSN 0309-0574

**General Medical Council**
44 Hallam Street, London, W1N 6AE, England.
- General Medical Council, London. Medical Register. a. ISSN 0072-0763

**Genetical Society of Great Britain**
- Heredity. (pub. by Longman Group Ltd.)

**Geo Abstracts Ltd**
University of East Anglia, Norwich NR4 7TJ, England.
- British Geomorphological Research Group. Technical Bulletin. irreg; (2-3 per yr) ISSN 0306-3380
- C A T M O G. (Concepts and Techniques in Modern Geography) irreg. (5 per yr approx.) ISSN 0306-6142
- Ecological Abstracts. bi-m. ISSN 0305-196X
- Geo Abstracts. Annual Index. a.
- Geo Abstracts A (Landforms & the Quaternary) 6 per yr. ISSN 0305-1897
- Geo Abstracts B (Climatology and Hydrology) 6 per yr. ISSN 0305-1900
- Geo Abstracts C (Economic Geography) 6 per yr. ISSN 0305-1919
- Geo Abstracts D (Social & Historical Geography) 6 per yr. ISSN 0305-1927
- Geo Abstracts E (Sedimentology) 6 per yr. ISSN 0305-1935
- Geo Abstracts F (Regional and Community Planning) 6 per yr. ISSN 0305-1943

- Geo Abstracts G (Remote Sensing and Cartography) 6 per yr. ISSN 0305-1951
- Geophysical Abstracts. 6 per yr. ISSN 0309-4332

**Geographia Ltd.**
63 Fleet St., London E.C.4, England.
- A A/G B Road Atlas. (Automobile Association - Great Britain) a. (Automobile Association)

**Geographical Association**
- Geography. (pub. by George Philip & Son Ltd.)
- Teaching Geography. (pub. by Longman Ltd.)

**Geographical Field Group**
University of Nottingham, Dept. of Geography, Nottingham NG7 2RD, Eng.
- Geographical Field Group (Nottingham). Regional Studies. irreg. no. 16, 1973. ISSN 0078-2084

**Geographical Publications Ltd.**
The Keep, Berkhamsted, Herts., HP4 1HQ, England.
- World Land Use Survey. Occasional Papers. irreg. ISSN 0512-3186 (International Geographical Union. World Land Use Survey Commission)
- World Land Use Survey. Regional Monograph. irreg. ISSN 0512-3194 (International Geographical Union. World Land Use Survey Commission)

**Geological Society of London**
- Geological Society. Journal. (pub. by Scottish Academic Press Ltd.)
- Geological Society of London. Special Publications. (pub. by Scottish Academic Press Ltd.)
- Quarterly Journal of Engineering Geology. (pub. by Scottish Academic Press Ltd.)

**Geologists' Association**
c/o Chelsea College, 171-3 King St., London W6 9LZ, England.
- Geologists' Association. Proceedings. q. ISSN 0016-7878

**George Street Press**
Fancy Walk, Stafford, Eng.
- Science and Archaeology. q. ISSN 0586-9668

**Geosystems**
Box 1024, Westminster, London S.W.1, England.
- Bibliography of Vertebrate Paleontology. q. (Society of Vertebrate Paleontology)
- Geocom Bulletin; bibliography of economic geology. bi-m. ISSN 0016-7053
- Geoscience Documentation; a bi-monthly journal for the study of geoscience literature. bi-m. ISSN 0016-8483
- Geoserials. irreg. ISSN 0072-1417
- Geotitles Weekly; geoscience bibliography. w. ISSN 0016-8564

**Gershire Ltd.**
106 Church Rd., London SE19 2UB, England.
- Systems International. m. ISSN 0305-1668

**Gilbert and Sullivan Journal**
c/o Miss N. M. Clark, 37 Frankland Close, Croxley Green, Herts WD3 3AR, England.
- Gilbert and Sullivan Journal. ISSN 0016-9951

**Gilbertson & Page Ltd.**
Corry's, Roestock Lane, Colney Heath, Herts AL4 0QW, England.
- Gamekeeper and Countryside; for people interested in field sports and natural history. m. ISSN 0016-4321

**Gingerbread, Association for One Parent Families**
9 Poland St., London W1V 3DG, England.
- Ginger. bi-m.

**Girl Crusaders' Union**
31 Catherine Place, London S.W.1, Eng.
- Girl Crusader. bi-m. ISSN 0017-0569

**Girl Guides Association**
17-19 Buckingham Palace Rd., London S.W. 1, Eng.
- Brownie. w. ISSN 0007-2524
- Guider. m. ISSN 0017-534X
- Today's Guide. m. ISSN 0017-5234

**Girls' Brigade**
Brigade House, 8 Parsons Green, London S.W. 6, Eng.
- Girls' Brigade Gazette. 10 per yr. ISSN 0017-0593

**Girls Brigade International**
Brigade House, 8 Parsons Green, London SW6 4TH, England.
- Girls Brigade International News. q.

**Glamorgan History Society**
Dept. of History, University College, Cardiff, Glam., Wales.
- Morgannwg. a. ISSN 0545-0373

**Glasgow Archaeological Society**
c/o Dept. of Archaeology, University of Glasgow, Glasgow, Scotland.
- Glasgow Archaeological Journal. biennial. ISSN 0305-8980

**Glasgow Art Gallery**
Kelvingrove, Glasgow, Scotland.
- Scottish Art Review. s-a. ISSN 0036-911X (Glasgow Art Gallery and Museums Association)

**Glasgow Art Gallery and Museums Association**
- Scottish Art Review. (pub. by Glasgow Art Gallery)

**Glasgow Chamber of Commerce**
30 George Square, Glasgow G2 1EQ, Scotland.
- Glasgow Chamber of Commerce. Industrial Index to Glasgow & West of Scotland. a.
- Glasgow Chamber of Commerce. Journal. m. ISSN 0017-0860

**Glasgow Mathematical Society**
- Glasgow Mathematical Journal. (pub. by Scottish Academic Press Ltd.)

**Mary Glasgow Publications Ltd.**
140 Kensington Church St., London W.8, Eng (U.S. Address: Scholastic Magazines, Inc., 50 W. 44th St., New York, N.Y.)
- Boum. m.(during school term) ISSN 0032-0471
- Catch. m.(Oct-June) ISSN 0008-7696
- Club. m. ISSN 0009-9503
- Crown. 9 per yr (Oct.-June) ISSN 0045-9127

**Glass Manufacturers Federation**
- European Glass Directory and Buyer's Guide. (pub. by Fuel & Metallurgical Journals Ltd.)

**Glass's Guide Service Ltd.**
Elgin House, St. George's Avenue, Weybridge, Surrey KT13 0BX, England.
- Glass's Guide to Caravan Values. q.
- Glass's Guide to Used Car Values. m.
- Glass's Guide to Used Commercial Vehicle Values. m.
- Glass's Guide to Used Motor Cycle Values. m.

**Glyndebourne Festival Opera**
- Glyndebourne Festival Programme Book. (pub. by Glyndebourne Productions Ltd.)

**Glyndebourne Productions Ltd.**
Glyndebourne, Lewes, Sussex BN8 5UU, England.
- Glyndebourne Festival Programme Book. a. ISSN 0434-1066 (Glyndebourne Festival Opera)

**George Godwin Ltd.**
Builder House, Catherine St., London WC2B 5JN, Eng.
- Built Environment. q. ISSN 0045-3463
- Directory of Official Architecture and Planning. a.
- Directory of Technical and Further Education. a.

**Golden Years**
Ed. F.R. Bristo, 7 Greenmeadow Close, Cumbran, Monmouthshire NP4 3NR, Wales, UK.
- Golden Years. q.

**Goldhawk Press Ltd.**
3 Heathcock Court, Strand, London WC2, England.
- Dinghy Sailing. m.
- Sub-Aqua. m. ISSN 0039-4327
- Water Skier. m. ISSN 0043-1427 (British Water Ski Federation)

**Golf World Associates Ltd.**
Suite 2, Millstream House, 41 Maltby St., London SE1 3PQ, England.
- Golf Trade Journal; the official magazine of the P.G.A. 10 per yr. ISSN 0017-1859

**Gomer Press**
Llandysul, Dyfed SA44 4BQ, Wales.
- Genhinen. q. ISSN 0046-5623 (Welsh Arts Council)

**Good Road Ltd.**
12, Palace St., London SW1E 5JF, Eng.
• New World News; for moral re-armament. w.

**C. Goodliffe Neale Ltd.**
c/o Goodliffe the Magician, Ed., Arden Forest
Industrial Estate, Alcester, Warwickshire, Eng.
• Abracadabra. w. ISSN 0001-3269

**Gordon and Breach Science Publishers Ltd.**
42 William IV St., London WC2N 4DF, England
(U.S. Address: One Park Ave., New York, NY
10016)
• Applicable Analysis; an international journal. 4
per yr. ISSN 0003-6811
• Astrophysical Letters. m.(2 vols. per year) ISSN
0004-6388
• Automedica. 4 per yr. ISSN 0045-1045
• Cancer Biochemistry - Biophysics. 6 per yr.
• Chemical Engineering Communications. 6 per yr.
• Collective Phenomena. 4 per yr. ISSN 0095-7003
• Combustion Science & Technology. 6 per yr.
ISSN 0010-2202 (Guggenheim Laboratories)
• Comments on Astrophysics. bi-m.
• Comments on Atomic and Molecular Physics. bi-
m. ISSN 0010-2687
• Comments on Earth Sciences: Geophysics. bi-m.
ISSN 0010-2695
• Comments on Nuclear & Particle Physics. 6 per
yr. ISSN 0010-2709
• Comments on Plasma Physics and Controlled
Fusion. 6 per yr.
• Comments on Solid State Physics. 6 per yr. ISSN
0010-2717
• Communication. s-a. ISSN 0305-4233
• Computer Applications Newsletter. bi-m. (System
Consulting Enterpreneurs)
• Connective Tissue Research; an international
journal. 8 per yr. ISSN 0300-8207
• Coordination Chemistry. 4 per yr.
• Crystal Lattice Defects. 4 per yr. ISSN 0011-2305
• Early Child Development and Care. 4 per yr.
ISSN 0300-4430
• Earth and Extraterrestrial Sciences. 8 per yr.
ISSN 0070-7902
• Ecology of Food and Nutrition; an international
journal. 4 per yr.
• Economics Selections; an international
bibliography. 4 per yr. ISSN 0013-046X
• Electrocomponent Science & Technology. 4 per
yr.
• Engineering Optimization. 4 per yr.
• Environmental Biology and Medicine. 4 per yr.
ISSN 0046-2233
• Environmental Times. bi-m.
• Ethnic Groups.
• Ferroelectrics. 6 per yr. ISSN 0015-0193
• Fields and Quanta; a review journal of
contemporary physics. 4 per yr. ISSN 0046-3744
• Fundamentals of Cosmic Physics. 4 per yr. ISSN
0094-5846
• Geophysical Fluid Dynamics; a journal of
atmospheric oceanographic interaction. 4 per yr.
ISSN 0016-7991
• Group Process. 2 per yr. ISSN 0046-6468
(Association for Group Psychoanalysis and
Process)
• International Interactions. m.(Oct-May); bi-
m.(June-Sept)
• International Journal of Chronobiology. 4 per yr.
ISSN 0300-9998
• International Journal of Computer Mathematics. 4
per yr. ISSN 0020-7160
• International Journal of Environmental Analytical
Chemistry. 4 per yr. ISSN 0092-9085
• International Journal of Environmental Studies. bi-
m. ISSN 0020-7233
• International Journal of Ethnic Studies. q.
• International Journal of General Systems; a
comprehensive periodical devoted to general
systems methodology, applications and education.
4 per yr. ISSN 0308-1079
• International Journal of Neuroscience. q. ISSN
0020-7454
• International Journal of Nondestructive Testing. 4
per yr. ISSN 0020-7470
• International Journal of Polymeric Materials. 4
per yr. ISSN 0091-4037
• Intra-Science Chemistry Reports. 4 per yr. ISSN
0020-9848
• Ion Exchange and Membranes. 4 per yr. ISSN
0091-0619
• Journal of Adhesion. 4 per yr. ISSN 0021-8464
• Journal of Color and Appearance. bi-m. ISSN
0091-4452
• Journal of Coordination Chemistry. 4 nos. per vol.
(2 vols. per year)

• Journal of Mathematical Sociology. 2 per yr. ISSN
0022-250X
• Journal of Mechanochemistry and Cell Motility. 4
per yr. ISSN 0091-6552
• Journal of Structural Learning. 4 per yr. ISSN
0022-4774 (International Study Group for
Mathematics Learning)
• Journal of Urban Analysis. 2 per yr. ISSN 0091-
1909
• Kybernetes; international journal of cybernetics
and general systems. 4 per yr.
• Linear and Multilinear Algebra. 4 per yr.
• Magnetic Resonance Reviews. 4 per yr. ISSN
0097-7330
• Magnetism Letters. irreg.
• Marine Behavior and Physiology. 4 per yr.
• Modern Geology. 4 per yr. ISSN 0026-7775
• Molecular Crystals and Liquid Crystals. 4 per yr.
ISSN 0026-8941
• Music and Man. 4 per yr.
• Natural Life Styles; an organic guide to living. q.
ISSN 0047-9160
• New Priorities; a journal devoted to the re-
examination and reordering of national goals. 4
per yr. ISSN 0047-9837
• Particle Accelerators. 4 per yr. ISSN 0031-2460
• Philosophy Forum. q. ISSN 0031-823X
• Phosphorus and Sulfur and Related Elements. q.
(Intra-Science Research Foundation)
• Physics and Chemistry of Liquids. 4 per yr. ISSN
0031-9104
• Polymer News. 6 per yr. ISSN 0032-3918
• Progress of Physics/Forschritte der Physik. m.
ISSN 0033-0671
• Psychoenergetic Systems. 4 per yr. ISSN 0305-
7224
• Radiation Effects; an international journal. 4 per
yr. ISSN 0033-7579
• Semiconductors and Insulators. 4 per yr.
• Statistical Computation and Simulation. 4 per yr.
• Stochastics. 4 per yr. ISSN 0090-9491
• Technology Assessment. 4 per yr. ISSN 0092-
2234
• Texture. 4 per yr.
• Theoria to Theory. q. ISSN 0049-3686 (Epiphany
Philosophy)
• Toxicological and Environmental Chemistry
Review. 4 per yr. ISSN 0092-9867
• Transportation Planning and Technology; reviews
and communications. 4 per yr.
• Videoscope; the magazine of videotape source
information. 4 per yr.
• Women's Studies. 3 per yr. ISSN 0049-7878

**Gospel Standard Publications**
69, Langham Gardens, Grange Park, London 1DL,
Eng.
• Friendly Companion. m. ISSN 0016-1292
• Gospel Standard. m. ISSN 0017-2367

**Gothique Publications**
c/o Stan Nicholls, 5 St. John's Wood Terrace, St.
John's Wood, London N.W.8, Eng.
• Gothique. q. ISSN 0017-2472

**Government and Opposition Ltd.**
London School of Economics and Political Science,
Houghton St., London W.C.2, Eng.
• Government and Opposition. q. ISSN 0017-257X

**Gown Trust. Students' Union**
University Rd., Belfast 7, N. Ireland.
• Gown. bi-w.(during school yr.) ISSN 0017-2693

**Grace Magazine Trust**
Foxtons Farm, Ugley Green, Bishop's Stortford,
Herts CM22 6HH, England.
• Grace. m. ISSN 0046-6239

**Grail**
125 Waxwell Lane, Pinner, Middlesex, Eng.
• In Touch. q. ISSN 0019-3283

**Granite Publications**
9 Wellington Place, Belfast BT1 6GA, N. Ireland.
• Textile Times International. m. (Irish Linen Guild)

**Granta**
21a Silver St., Cambridge CB3 9ER, Eng.
• Granta; the Cambridge University magazine. m.
ISSN 0017-3231

**Graphmitre Ltd.**
1 West St., Tavistock, Devon, England.
• Industrial Archaeology; the journal of the history
of industry and technology. q. ISSN 0019-7971
• Maritime History. s-a.
• Transport History. 3 per yr. ISSN 0041-1469

**Grassland Research Institute**
Hurley, Maidenhead, Berks SL6 5RL, England.
• Grassland Research Institute, Hurley, England
(Berkshire) Technical Reports. irreg. ISSN 0072-
5552 (Agricultural Research Council)

**Gray's Inn Press Ltd.**
Walkden House, 10 Melton St., Euston, London
NW1 2EJ, Eng.
• Transport Salaried Staff Journal. m. ISSN 0041-
1531

**Gt. Brit. Agricultural Development and Advisory
Service**
Whitehall Place, London S.W.1, Eng
(Avail. from H.M.S.O., c/o Liaison Officer, Atlantic
House, Holborn Viaduct, London EC1P 1BW,
England)
• A. D. A. S. Quarterly Review. q. ISSN 0027-5670

**Gt. Brit. Agricultural Research Council. Institute of
Animal Physiology**
160 Great Portland St., London W1N 6DT,
England
(Avail. from H.M.S.O., c/o Liaison Officer, Atlantic
House, Holborn Viaduct, London EC1P 1BN,
England)
• Agricultural Research Council. Institute of Animal
Physiology, Babraham, Cambridge. Report.
biennial. ISSN 0065-4507

**Gt. Brit. Atomic Energy Research Establishment**
Harwell, Oxfordshire OX11 ORA, Eng
(Avail. from H.M.S.O., c/o Liaison Officer, Atlantic
House, Holborn Viaduct, London EC1P 1BN,
England)
• Great Britain. Atomic Energy Research
Establishment. Nondestructive Testing Centre.
Quality Technology. a.
• United Kingdom Atomic Energy Authority. List
of Publications Available to the Public. m. ISSN
0041-7289

**Gt. Brit. Board of Inland Revenue**
Somerset House, London W.C.2., England
(Avail. from H.M.S.O., c/o Liaison Officer, Atlantic
House, Holborn Viaduct, London EC1P 1BN,
England)
• Great Britain. Board of Inland Revenue. the
Survey of Personal Incomes. irreg.

**Gt. Brit. British Airports Authority**
2 Buckingham Gate, London S.W.1, England
(Avail. from H.M.S.O., c/o Liaison Officer, Atlantic
House, Holborn Viaduct, London EC1P 1BN,
England)
• British Airports Authority. Annual Report and
Accounts. a. ISSN 0068-1229

**Gt. Brit. British Antarctic Survey**
30 Gillingham St., London S.W. 1, England
(Avail. from H.M.S.O., c/o Liaison Officer, Atlantic
House, Holborn Viaduct, London EC1P 1BN,
England)
• British Antarctic Survey. Scientific Reports. irreg.,
1970, no. 64. ISSN 0068-1261

**Gt.Brit. Cabinet Office**
10 John Adam St., London WC2N 6HD, England
(Avail. from H.M.S.O., c/o Liaison Officer, Atlantic
House, Holborn Viaduct, London EC1P 1BW,
England)
• Great Britain. Department of Health and Social
Security. Review Body on Doctor's and Dentists'
Remuneration. Report. a. ISSN 0072-6095

**Gt. Brit. Central Health Services Council**
Alexander Fleming House, Elephant and Castle,
London SE1 6BY, England
(Avail. from H.M.S.O., c/o Liaison Officer, Atlantic
House, Holborn Viaduct, London EC1P 1BN,
England)
• Great Britain. Central Health Services Council.
Report. a. ISSN 0072-5714

**Gt. Brit. Central Office of Information**
Hercules Rd., London SE1 7DU, England
(Avail. from H.M.S.O., c/o Liaison Officer, Atlantic
House, Holborn Viaduct, London EC1P 1BN,
England)
- Britain: An Official Handbook. a. ISSN 0068-1075
- Great Britain. Central Office of Information.
  Reference Division. Reference Pamphlets. irreg.
  ISSN 0072-5722 (prep. by its Reference Division)
- Technical and Specialised Periodicals Published in
  Britain. irreg. (Dist. in U.S. by: British
  Publications, Inc., 11-03 46th Ave., Long Island
  City, New York, NY 11101)

**Gt. Brit. Central Statistical Office**
Great George St., London SW1P 3AQ, England
(Avail. from H.M.S.O., c/o Liaison Officer, Atlantic
House, Holborn Viaduct, London EC1P 1BN
England)
- Economic Trends. m. ISSN 0013-0400
- Great Britain. Central Statistical Office. Annual
  Abstract of Statistics. a. ISSN 0072-5730
- Great Britain. Central Statistical Office. Financial
  Statistics. m. ISSN 0015-203X
- Great Britain. Central Statistical Office. Monthly
  Digest of Statistics. m. ISSN 0017-3622
- Great Britain. Central Statistical Office. Regional
  Statistics. a.
- Great Britain. Central Statistical Office. Research
  Series. irreg. ISSN 0072-5757
- Great Britain. Central Statistical Office. Social
  Trends. a. ISSN 0072-5765
- Great Britain. Central Statistical Office. Statistical
  News; developments in British official statistics. q.
  ISSN 0017-3630
- Studies in Official Statistics. irreg. ISSN 0081-
  8313

**Gt. Brit. Civil Aviation Authority**
43-59 Kingsway, London WC2B 6NN, England.
- Accidents to Aircraft on the British Register.
  ISSN 0065-0838
- Great Britain. Board of Trade. Civil Aviation
  Publications. irreg. ISSN 0072-5641
- Great Britain. Civil Aviation Authority. Annual
  Report and Accounts. a.
- Great Britain. Civil Aviation Authority. C A A
  Statistics. m.

**Gr.Brit. Civil Service Department**
Whitehall, London S.W.1, England
(Avail. from H.M.S.O., c/o Liaison Officer, Atlantic
House, Holborn Viaduct, London EC1P 1BN,
England)
- Civil Service Year Book. a.
- Great Britain. Civil Service Department. Report.
  irreg., 3rd report, 1973.
- Management Services in Government. q.

**Gt. Brit. Civil Service Department. Central Computer
Agency**
Whitehall, London SW1A 2AZ, England
(Avail. from H.M.S.O., c/o Liaison Officer, Atlantic
House, London EC1P 1BW, England)
- Great Britain. Civil Service Department. Central
  Computer Agency. Guide. irreg.

**Gt. Brit. Commission on Industrial Relations**
GKN House, 22 Kingsway, London W.C.2, England
(Avail. from H.M.S.O., c/o Liaison Officer, Atlantic
House, Holborn Viaduct, London EC1P 1BN,
England)
- Great Britain. Commission on Industrial
  Relations. Annual Report. a.

**Gt. Brit. Customs and Excise Department**
King's Beam House, 39-41 Mark Lane, London
EC1R 7HE, England
(Avail. from H.M.S.O., c/o Liaison Officer, Atlantic
House, Holborn Viaduct, London EC1P 1BN,
England)
- Annual Statement of the Overseas Trade of the
  United Kingdom. a. ISSN 0072-5846

**Gt. Brit. Department of Agriculture and Fisheries for
Scotland**
Chesser House, 500 Gorgie Rd., Edinburgh,
Scotland
(Avail. from H.M.S.O., 13a Castle St., Edinburgh
EH2 3AR, Scotland)
- Agricultural Statistics, Scotland. a. ISSN 0065-
  4582

- Fisheries of Scotland. a. ISSN 0071-5565
- Fisheries of Scotland Report. a. ISSN 0080-1283
- Fresh Water and Salmon Fisheries Research
  (Scotland) irreg. ISSN 0071-9536
- Great Britain. Director of Fishery Research.
  Annual Report. a. ISSN 0072-6141
- Scotland. Red Deer Commission. Annual Report.
  a. ISSN 0080-7850
- Scottish Agricultural Economics; Some Studies of
  Current Economic Conditions in Scottish
  Farming. a. ISSN 0080-7966
- Scottish Sea Fisheries Statistical Tables. a. ISSN
  0080-8202

**Gt. Brit. Department of Education and Science**
Elizabeth House, York Rd., London SE1 7PH,
England
(Avail. from H.M.S.O., c/o Liaison Officer, Atlantic
House, Holborn Viaduct, London EC1P 1BN,
England)
- Education and Science. a. ISSN 0070-9115
- Education Statistics for the United Kingdom. a.
- Great Britain. Computer Board for Universities
  and Research Councils. Report. irreg. ISSN 0072-
  582X
- Great Britain. Department of Education and
  Science. Building Bulletins. irreg. ISSN 0072-5870
- Great Britain. Department of Education and
  Science. Education Pamphlet. irreg., 1971, no. 58.
  ISSN 0085-1175
- Great Britain. Department of Education and
  Science. Education Surveys. irreg. ISSN 0072-
  5897
- Great Britain. Department of Education and
  Science. Science Policy Studies. irreg. ISSN 0072-
  5919
- Great Britain. Department of Education and
  Science. Statistics of Education. a. in 6 pts. ISSN
  0072-5900
- Project. 3 per yr. ISSN 0033-0914
- Reports on Education. irreg (4-6 per yr.
- Trends in Education. q. ISSN 0041-2392

**Gt. Brit. Department of Employment**
12 St. James's Square, London SW1Y 4LL, England
(Avail. from H.M.S.O., c/o Liaison Officer, Atlantic
House, Holborn Viaduct, London EC1P 1BN,
England)
- British Labour Statistics. Year Book.
- Changes in Rates of Wages and Hours of Work.
  m. ISSN 0009-1405
- Great Britain. Department of Employment.
  Changes in Rates of Wages and Hours of Work.
  m.
- Great Britain. Department of Employment.
  Family Expenditure Survey. a. ISSN 0072-5927
- Great Britain. Department of Employment.
  Gazette. m. ISSN 0013-6859
- Great Britain. Department of Employment. New
  Earnings Survey. a.
- Great Britain. Department of Employment.
  Research. a.
- Industrial Tribunal Reports; reports of decisions of
  the Industrial Tribunals, including reports of
  decisions on appeal. 12 per yr.(approx.) ISSN
  0019-8838

**Gt. Brit. Department of Energy**
Thames House, South Millbank, London SW1P
4QJ, England
(Avail. from H.M.S.O., c/o Liaison Officer, Atlantic
House, London EC1P 1BW, England)
- Digest of United Kingdom Energy Statistics. a.
  ISSN 0307-0603
- Energy Trends. m. ISSN 0308-1222
- Great Britain. Department of Energy. Electricity:
  Report of the Secretary of State for Energy. a.
- Great Britain. Department of Energy. Report on
  Research and Development. a.
- Safety in Mines Research Establishment, Sheffield,
  England. Annual Reports. a. ISSN 0080-5327

**Gt. Brit. Department of Health and Social Security**
10 John Adam St., London WC2N 6HD, England
(Avail. from H. M. S. O., c/o Liaison Officer,
Atlantic House, Holborn Viaduct, London EC1P
1BN, England)
- Abstracts of Efficiency Studies in the National
  Health Service. irreg.
- Digest of Health Statistics for England and Wales.
  irreg. ISSN 0070-4849
- Great Britain. Department of Health and Social
  Security. Annual Report. a. ISSN 0072-596X
- Great Britain. Department of Health and Social
  Security. Capricode Capital Projects Code.
  Hospital Building Procedure Notes. irreg. ISSN
  0072-5978

- Great Britain. Department of Health and Social
  Security. Food Hygiene Codes of Practice. irreg.
  ISSN 0072-5986
- Great Britain. Department of Health and Social
  Security. Health Building Notes. irreg.
- Great Britain. Department of Health and Social
  Security. Hospital In-Patient Inquiry. irreg. ISSN
  0072-6036
- Great Britain. Department of Health and Social
  Security. ON the State of the Public Health. a.
  ISSN 0072-6087
- Great Britain. Department of Health and Social
  Security. Report on Confidential Inquiries into
  Maternal Deaths in England and Wales. triennial.
  ISSN 0072-6109
- Great Britain. Department of Health and Social
  Security. Reports on Public Health and Medical
  Subjects. irreg. ISSN 0072-6117
- Great Britain. Department of Health and Social
  Security. Social Science Research Unit Studies.
  irreg. ISSN 0072-6133
- Great Britain. Department of Health and Social
  Security. Social Security Statistics. a.
- Great Britain. Department of Health and Social
  Security. Statistical Report Series. irreg. ISSN
  0072-6125
- Health Trends. q. ISSN 0017-9132
- Hospital Abstracts; a monthly survey of world
  literature. m. ISSN 0018-5507
- Prescribers' Journal. bi-m. ISSN 0032-7611

**Gt. Brit. Department of Health and Social Security.
Committee on Safety of Medicines**
Alexander Fleming House, Elephant and Castle,
London SE1 6BY, England
(Avail. from H.M.S.O., c/o Liaison Officer, Atlantic
House, Holborn Viaduct, London EC1P 1BN,
England)
- Great Britain. Committee on Safety of Medicines.
  Report. a.

**Gt. Brit. Department of Health and Social Security.
National Health Service**
Alexander Fleming House, Elephant and Castle,
London SE1 6BY, England
(Avail. from H.M.S.O., c/o Liaison Officer, Atlantic
House, Holborn Viaduct, London EC1P 1BN,
England)
- Great Britain. National Health Service. Hospital
  Costing Returns. a. ISSN 0072-6966

**Gt. Brit. Department of Industry**
1 Victoria St., London S.W.1., England
(Avail. from H.M.S.O., c/o Liaison Officer, Atlantic
House, Holborn Viaduct, London EC1P 1BN,
England)
- Business Monitor: Miscellaneous Series. M2
  Cinemas. a. ISSN 0068-4449
- Business Monitor: Miscellaneous Series. M3
  Company Finance. a. ISSN 0068-4457
- Business Monitor: Miscellaneous Series. M4
  Overseas Transactions. a. ISSN 0068-4465

**Gt. Brit. Department of Industry. Business Statistics
Office**
Cardiff Road, Newport, Gwent NPT 1XG, England
(Avail. from H.M.S.O., c/o Liaison Officer, Atlantic
House, Holborn Viaduct, London EC1P 1BN,
England)
- Great Britain. Department of Industry. Business
  Statistics Office Report on the Census of
  Production. a.

**Gt. Brit. Department of the Environment**
2 Marsham St., London SW1P 3EB, England
(Avail. from H.M.S.O., c/o Liaison Officer, Atlantic
House, London EC1P 1BW, England)
- Archaeological Excavations. irreg.
- Great Britain. Department of the Environment.
  Archaeological Reports. irreg. ISSN 0072-6842
- Great Britain. Department of the Environment.
  Engineering Specifications. irreg. ISSN 0072-6850
- Great Britain. Department of the Environment.
  Housing and Construction Statistics. q (with
  annual notes and definitions supplement)
- Great Britain. Department of the Environment.
  Local Government Financial Statistics: England
  and Wales. a.
- Great Britain. Department of the Environment.
  Local Housing Statistics: England and Wales. q.
- Great Britain. Department of the Environment.
  Metrication in the Construction Industry. irreg.,
  1971, no. 3. ISSN 0072-6869
- Great Britain. Department of the Environment.
  Rate Rebates in England and Wales. a.
- Great Britain. Department of the Environment.
  Rates and Rateable Values in England and Wales.
  irreg.

- Great Britain. Department of the Environment. Report on Research and Development. a.
- Great Britain. Department of the Environment. Statistics for Town and Country Planning. Series 1. irreg. ISSN 0072-6818
- Great Britain. Department of the Environment. Statistics for Town and Country Planning. Series 2. irreg. ISSN 0072-6826
- Production of Aggregates in Great Britain. a.
- Road Accidents in Great Britain. a.

**Gt. Brit. Department of the Environment. Ancient Monuments Board**
Fortress House, 23 Savile Row, London W1X 2AA, England
(Avail. from H.M.S.O., c/o Liaison Officer, Atlantic House, Holborn Viaduct, London EC1P 1BN, England)
- Ancient Monuments Board for England. Annual Report. a. ISSN 0072-5625

**Gt.Brit. Department of the Environment. Building Research Establishment**
Garston, Watford WD2 7JR, Hertfordshire, England
(Avail. from H.M.S.O., c/o Liaison Officer, Atlantic House, Holborn Viaduct, London EC1P 1BN, England)
- Building Research Establishment. B R E News. q.
- Building Research Station, Garston, England. Annual Report. a. ISSN 0068-354X
- Great Britain. Department of the Environment. Building Research Establishment. Bulletins. irreg.
- Overseas Building Notes. 8 per yr.(approx.) ISSN 0030-7432
- Tropical Building Studies. irreg. ISSN 0082-6634

**Gt. Brit. Department of the Environment. Committee on Synthetic Detergents**
2 Marsham St., London SW1P 3EB, England
(Avail. from H.M.S.O., c/o Liaison Officer, Atlantic House, Holborn Viaduct, London EC1P 1BN, England)
- Great Britain. Committee on Synthetic Detergents. Progress Report. approx. a. ISSN 0072-5803

**Gt. Brit. Department of the Environment. Fire Research Station**
Boreham Wood, Herts. WD6 2BL, England
(Avail. Fom H. M. S. O., c/o Liaison Officer, Atlantic House, Holborn Viaduct, London EC1P 1BW, England)
- Great Britain. Department of the Environment. Building Research Establishment. Reports. irreg.
- Great Britain. Department of the Environment. Fire Research Station. Proceedings of Symposia. irreg. ISSN 0071-5441
- References to Scientific Literature on Fire. s-a. ISSN 0306-5766
- United Kingdom Fire and Loss Statistics. a. ISSN 0082-7959

**Gt.Brit. Department of the Environment. Headquarters Library, Research Section**
2 Marsham St., London SW1P 3EB, England
(Avail. from H.M.S.O., c/o Liaison Officer, Atlantic House, Holborn Viaduct, London EC1P 1BN, England)
- Index of Current Government and Governmental-Supported Research in Environmental Pollution in Great-Britain. irreg.

**Gt. Brit. Department of the Environment. Housing and Construction**
2 Marsham St., London SW1P 3EB, England
(Avail. from H.M.S.O., c/o Liaison Officer, Atlantic House, Holborn Viaduct, London EC1P 1BN, England)
- Great Britain. Department of the Environment. Housing and Construction. Design Bulletin. irreg.
- Great Britain. Department of the Environment. Housing and Construction. Planning Bulletin. irreg.

**Gt. Brit. Department of the Environment. Property Services Agency**
Whitgift Centre, Wellesley Rd., Croydon CR9 3LY, England
(Avail. from H.M.S.O., c/o Liaison Officer, Atlantic House, Holborn Viaduct, London EC1P 1BN, England)
- Construction References. s-a.
- Current Information in the Construction Industry. fortn. ISSN 0306-1914
- D O E Construction. q.
- Great Britain. Department of the Environment. Property Services Agency. Advisory Leaflets. irreg. ISSN 0072-5951

**Gt. Brit. Department of the Environment. Transport and Road Research Laboratory**
2 Marsham St., London SW1P 3EB, England
(Avail. from H.M.S.O., c/o Liaison Officer, Atlantic House, Holborn Viaduct, London EC1P 1BN, England)
- Transport and Road Research. a.

**Gt. Brit. Department of Trade**
Victoria St., London SW1H OET, Eng
(Avail. from H.M.S.O., c/o Liaison Officer, Atlantic House, Holborn Viaduct, London EC1P 1BN, England)
- Contents of Recent Economics Journals. w. ISSN 0045-8368
- Great Britain. Board of Trade. Bankruptcy: General Annual Report. a. ISSN 0072-5633
- Great Britain. Board of Trade. Companies: General Annual Report. a. ISSN 0072-565X
- Great Britain. Board of Trade. Export of Works of Art. a. ISSN 0072-5668
- Great Britain. Board of Trade. Import Duties Act 1958. Annual Report. a. ISSN 0072-5676
- Great Britain. Board of Trade. Particulars of Dealers in Securities and of Trust Units. a. ISSN 0072-5692
- Great Britain. Department of Trade and Industry. Insurance Business: Annual Report. a.
- Great Britain. Department of Trade and Industry. Patents, Design and Trade Marks (Annual Report) a. ISSN 0072-5706
- Trade and Industry. w. ISSN 0006-5323

**Gt.Brit. Department of Trade. H. M. Coastguard**
Rm. 439 1 Victoria St., London Sw1 OET, England
(Avail. from H.M.S.O., c/o Liaison Officer, Atlantic House, Holborn Viaduct, London EC1P 1BN, England)
- Coastguard. q.

**Gt. Brit. Department of Transport**
2 Marsham St., London SW1P 3EB, England
(Avail. from H.M.S.O., c/o Liaison Officer, Atlantic House, Holborn Viaduct, London EC1P 1BN, England)
- Great Britain. Department of Transport. Highway Statistics. a. ISSN 0072-6893
- Great Britain. Department of Transport. Roads in England. a.
- Transport Statistics Great Britain. a.

**Gt. Brit. Departments of the Environment and Transport**
2 Marsham Street, Room P3/178, London SW1P 3EB, England
(Avail. from H.M.S.O., c/o Liaison Officer, Atlantic House, Holborn Viaduct, London EC1P 1BN, England)
- Great Britain. Departments of the Environment and Transport. Library Services. Annual List of Publications. a. ISSN 0305-3474

**Gt.Brit. Departments of the Environment & Transport. Library**
Room P3/178, 2 Marsham St., London SW1P 3EB, England
(Avail. from H.M.S.O., c/o Liaison Officer, Atlantic House, Holborn Viaduct, London EC1P 1BN, England)
- Great Britain. Departments of the Environment and Transport. Library. Library Bulletin. s-m. ISSN 0306-1043

**Gt. Brit. Electricity Council**
30 Millbank St., London S.W.1., England
(Avail. from H.M.S.O., c/o Liaison Officer, Atlantic House, Holborn Viaduct, London EC1P 1BN, England)
- Great Britain. Electricity Council. Report and Accounts. a. ISSN 0072-615X

**Gt. Brit. Foreign and Commonwealth Office**
Downing St., London SW1A 2AL, England
(Avail. from H.M.S.O., c/o Liaison Officer, Atlantic House, Holborn Viaduct, London EC1P 1BN, England)
- Great Britain. Foreign and Commonwealth Office. Bermuda. Report. a. ISSN 0072-6192
- Great Britain. Foreign and Commonwealth Office. Falkland Islands. Report. a. ISSN 0072-6257
- Great Britain. Foreign and Commonwealth Office. Montserrat. Report. a. ISSN 0072-6303
- Great Britain. Foreign and Commonwealth Office. Overseas Research Publications. irreg. ISSN 0072-632X
- Great Britain. Foreign and Commonwealth Office. Treaty Series. irreg. ISSN 0072-6397
- Yearbook of the Commonwealth. a. ISSN 0084-4047

**Gt. Brit. Foreign and Commonwealth Office. Overseas Development Administration**
Downing St., London SW1A 2AL, England
(Avail. from H. M. S. O., c/o Liaison Officer, Atlantic House, Holborn Viaduct, London EC1P 1BN, England)
- Journal of Administration Overseas. q. ISSN 0021-8472

**Gt. Brit. Forestry Commission**
Alice Holt Lodge, Wrecclesham, Nr. Farnham, Surrey, Eng
(Avail. from H.M.S.O., c/o Liaison Officer, Atlantic House, Holborn Viaduct, London EC1P 1BN, England)
- Forestry Commission Library Review. 3 per yr. ISSN 0015-7554
- Great Britain. Forestry Commission. Leaflets. irreg., no. 68,1976. ISSN 0085-1183

**Gt. Brit. General Register Office, Scotland**
New Register House, Edinburgh 1, Scotland.
- Annual Estimates of the Population of Scotland. a. ISSN 0066-3964

**Gt. Brit. H.M. Nautical Almanac Office**
Royal Greenwich Observatory, Herstmonceux, Sussex, England
(Avail. from H.M.S.O., c/o Liaison Officer, Atlantic House, Holborn Viaduct, London EC1P 1BN, England)
- Air Almanac. 2 per yr.(part 1: Jan.-Jun.; part 2: Jul.-Dec.) ISSN 0002-2160
- Astronomical Ephemeris. a. ISSN 0066-9962 (Co-sponsor: U.S. Naval Observatory, Washington)

**Gt. Brit. H.M.S.O.**
P.O. Box 569, London SE1 9NH, England.
- Great Britain. Aeronautical Research Council. Current Paper Series. irreg. ISSN 0072-5595
- Great Britain. Aeronautical Research Council. Reports and Memoranda Series. irreg. ISSN 0072-5609
- Great Britain. Cinematograph Films Council. Annual Report. a. ISSN 0072-5773
- Great Britain. Department of Employment and Productivity. Safety, Health and Welfare. New Series Booklets. irreg. ISSN 0072-5935
- Great Britain. Department of Employment and Productivity. Statistics Division. Time Rates of Wages and Hours of Work. a.
- Great Britain. Department of Employment and Productivity. Training Information Papers. irreg. ISSN 0072-5943
- Great Britain. Domestic Coal Consumers' Council. Report. a.
- Great Britain. General Register Office. Studies on Medical and Population Subjects. irreg. ISSN 0072-6400
- Great Britain. Government Actuary. Occupational Pension Board. Annual Report. irreg.
- Great Britain. Keeper of Public Records. Annual Report of the Keeper of Public Records on the Work of the Public Record Office and the Report of the Advisory Council on Public Records. a. ISSN 0072-6516
- Great Britain. Laboratory of the Government Chemist. Annual Report of the Government Chemist. a. ISSN 0072-6524
- Great Britain. Manpower Research Unit. Manpower Studies. irreg. ISSN 0072-6532
- Great Britain. Mercantile Navy List. a, with monthly supplements. ISSN 0072-6591
- Great Britain. Ministry of Energy on Electricity. Report. a.
- Great Britain. Ministry of Energy on Gas. Report. a.
- Great Britain. National Board for Prices and Incomes. Report. irreg. ISSN 0072-6931

• Great Britain. National Film Finance Corporation. Annual Report. a. ISSN 0072-6958
• Great Britain. Public Record Office. Handbooks. irreg. ISSN 0072-7016
• Great Britain. Road Research Laboratory. Technical Papers. irreg. ISSN 0072-7059
• Great Britain. Royal Commission on Enviromental Pollution. Report. a.
• Great Britain. Select Committee on Education and Science. Special Report. irreg. ISSN 0072-7156
• Local Housing Statistics: England and Wales. q. ISSN 0076-0250
• London Gazette. 4 per wk.
• Marine Observer; a quarterly journal of maritime meteorology. q. ISSN 0025-3251
• National Coal Board. Report and Accounts. a. ISSN 0077-3786
• Road Notes. irreg. ISSN 0080-3294
• Scotland. Department of Agriculture and Fisheries. Advisory Bulletins. irreg. ISSN 0080-7796
• Scotland. Registrar General. Annual Report. a. ISSN 0080-7869
• Scotland. Scottish Home and Health Department. Hospital Design in Use. irreg. ISSN 0080-7885
• Scottish Social Work Statistics. a.
• Soldier; the British Army magazine. m. ISSN 0038-1004
• Survey of Current Affairs. m. ISSN 0039-6214
• United Kingdom Atomic Energy Authority. Annual Report. a. ISSN 0082-7940

**Gt. Brit. H.M.S.O. (N. Ireland)**
80 Chichester St., Belfast BT1 4JY, N. Ireland.
• Northern Ireland. Ministry of Education. Education Statistics. s-a. ISSN 0048-0770
• Reform in Northern Ireland. irreg. (approx. 1 per yr.)
• Ulster Year Book. a. ISSN 0082-7371

**Gt. Brit. H.M. Treasury**
Parliament St., London SW1P 3AG, England
(Avail. from H.M.S.O., c/o Liaison Officer, Atlantic House, Holborn Viaduct, London EC1P 1BN, England)
• Great Britain. Treasury. Supply Estimates. a.

**Gt. Brit. Herring Industry Board**
Glenfinlas St., Edinburgh 3, Scotland
(Avail. from H.M.S.O., c/o Liaison Officer, Atlantic House, Holborn Viaduct, London EC1P 1BN, England)
• Great Britain. Herring Industry Board. Annual Report. a. ISSN 0072-6419

**Gt. Brit. Home Office**
Whitehall, London S.W.1, England
(Avail. from H.M.S.O., Atlantic House, Holborn Viaduct, London EC1P 1BN, England)
• Great Britain. Home Office. Research Studies. irreg. ISSN 0072-6435
• Great Britain. Home Office. Studies in the Causes of Delinquency and the Treatment of Offenders. irreg. ISSN 0072-6443

**Gt. Brit. Home Office. Police Research Services Unit**
Horseferry House, Dean Ryle St., London, SW1P 2AW, England
(Avail. from H.M.S.O., c/o Liaison Officer, Atlantic House, London EC1P 1BW, England)
• Police Research Bulletin. s-a. ISSN 0556-056X

**Gt. Brit. Home Office. Prison Department**
89 Eccleston Square, London S.W.1., Eng
(Avail. from H.M.S.O., c/o Liaison Officer, Atlantic House, London EC1P 1BW, England)
• Prison Service Journal. q. ISSN 0300-3558

**Gt. Brit. Hydraulics Research Station**
Wallingford, Berkshire, England
(Avail. from H.M.S.O., Atlantic House, Holborn Viaduct, London EC1P 1BN, England)
• Hydraulics Research Station, Wallingford, England. Reports. a. ISSN 0073-4187
• Hydraulics Research Station, Wallingford, England. Research Papers. irreg. ISSN 0073-4195

**Gt. Brit. Institute of Geological Sciences**
Exhibition Rd., London SW7 2DE, England
(Avail. from H.M.S.O., c/o Liaison Officer, Atlantic House, Holborn Viaduct, London EC1P 1BN, England)
• British Regional Geology. irreg.
• Institute of Geological Sciences, London. Annual Report. approx a. ISSN 0073-9308
• Institute of Geological Sciences, London. Bulletin of the Geological Survey of Great Britain. irreg. (approx. 4 issues per yr.) ISSN 0366-4198

• Institute of Geological Sciences, London. Geomagnetic Bulletins. irreg. ISSN 0073-9316
• Institute of Geological Sciences, London. Geophysical Papers. irreg. ISSN 0073-9324
• Institute of Geological Sciences, London. Memoirs of the Geological Survey of Great Britain. irreg. ISSN 0072-6494
• Institute of Geological Sciences, London. Mineral Assessment Report. irreg.
• Institute of Geological Sciences, London. Mineral Monographs. irreg.
• Institute of Geological Sciences, London. Overseas Geology and Mineral Resources. irreg. ISSN 0073-9332
• Institute of Geological Sciences, London. Overseas Memoirs. irreg.
• Institute of Geological Sciences, London. Report. irreg. ISSN 0073-9359
• Institute of Geological Sciences, London. Seismological Bulletins. irreg. ISSN 0308-5082
• Institute of Geological Sciences, London. Water Supply Papers. Hydrogeological Reports. irreg. ISSN 0073-9375
• Institute of Geological Sciences, London. Water Supply Papers. Research Reports. irreg. ISSN 0073-9383
• Institute of Geological Sciences, London. Water Supply Papers. Technical Communications. irreg. ISSN 0073-9391
• United Kingdom Mineral Statistics. a. ISSN 0308-5090
• World Mineral Statistics; world production, exports and imports. a.

**Gt. Brit. Institute of Terrestrial Ecology**
Merlewood Research Station, Grange-over-Sands, Cumbria LA11 6JU, England
(Avail. from H.M.S.O., c/o Liaison Officer, Atlantic House, Holborn Viaduct, London EC1P 1BN, England)
• Institute of Terrestrial Ecology. Report. a.

**Gt. Brit. Medical Research Council**
20 Park Crescent, London W1N 4AL, England
(Avail. from H.M.S.O. c/o Liaison Officer, Atlantic House, Holborn Viaduct, London EC1P 1BN)
• Great Britain. Medical Research Council. Memoranda. irreg., no. 45, 1976. ISSN 0072-6583
• Great Britain. Medical Research Council. Report. a. ISSN 0072-6567
• Great Britain. Medical Research Council. Special Report Series. irreg., no. 310, 1971.
• Medical Research Council. Annual Report. a. (Dist. in U.S. by: Pendragon House Inc., 220 University Ave., Palo Alto, CA 94301)
• Medical Research Council. Handbook. a.

**Gt. Brit. Medical Research Council. Laboratory Animals Centre**
Woodmansterne Rd., Carshalton, Surrey, SM5 4EF, England.
• Guinea-Pig News Letter. s-a. ISSN 0309-1821
• L A C News. (Laboratory Animals Centre) s-a. ISSN 0308-9568
• Rat News Letter. s-a. ISSN 0309-1848

**Gt. Brit. Meteorological Office**
London Rd., Bracknell, Berks., England
(Avail. from H.M.S.O., c/o Liaison Officer, Atlantic House, Holborn Viaduct, London EC1P 1BN, England)
• Great Britain. Meteorological Office. Annual Report. a. ISSN 0072-6605
• Great Britain. Meteorological Office. Geophysical Memoirs. irreg. ISSN 0072-6613
• Great Britain. Meteorological Office. Monthly Weather Report. m. ISSN 0027-0636
• Great Britain. Meteorological Office. Scientific Paper. irreg. ISSN 0072-6621
• Meteorological Magazine. m. ISSN 0026-1149

**Gt. Brit. Ministry of Agriculture, Fisheries and Food**
Whitehall Place, London SW1A 2HH, England
(Avail. from H.M.S.O., c/o Liaison Officer, Atlantic House, Holborn Viaduct, London Ec1p 1bn, England)
• Agricultural Statistics, England and Wales. a. ISSN 0065-4558 (Co-sponsors: Department of Agriculture and Fisheries for Scotland; Ministry of Agriculture, N. Ireland)
• Agricultural Statistics, United Kingdom. a. ISSN 0065-4590
• Experimental Horticulture. irreg. ISSN 0071-3406
• Experimental Husbandry. irreg. ISSN 0071-3414
• Farm Classification in England and Wales. a. ISSN 0071-3848
• Farm Incomes in England and Wales. a. ISSN 0071-3910

• Great Britain. Ministry of Agriculture. Fisheries and Food. Fatstock Guarantee Scheme. a. ISSN 0072-6672
• Great Britain. Ministry of Agriculture. Fisheries and Food. Fishery Investigations. Series II: Sea Fisheries. irreg. ISSN 0072-6680
• Great Britain. Ministry of Agriculture, Fisheries and Food. Research and Development Report. a.
• Great Britain. Ministry of Agriculture, Fisheries and Food. Return of Proceedings under the Diseases of Animals Act, 1950. irreg. ISSN 0072-6745
• Great Britain. Ministry of Agriculture, Fisheries and Food. Safety, Health, Welfare and Wages in Agriculture. Reports. a. ISSN 0072-6710
• Great Britain. Ministry of Agriculture, Fisheries and Food. Sea Fisheries Statistical Tables. a. ISSN 0072-6702
• Great Britain. Ministry of Agriculture, Fisheries and Food. Technical Bulletin. irreg. ISSN 0072-6729
• Great Britain. Ministry of Agriculture, Fisheries and Food. Technical Report FRL. irreg. ISSN 0072-6737
• Plant Pathology; a record of current work on plant diseases and pests. q. ISSN 0032-0862
• Plant Varieties and Seeds Gazette. m. ISSN 0048-4342

**Gt. Brit. Ministry of Agriculture, Fisheries and Food. Pest Infestation Control Laboratory**
Whitehall Place, London SW1A 2HH, England
(Avail. from H.M.S.O., c/o Liaison Officer, Atlantic House, Holborn Viaduct, London EC1P 1BN, England)
• Great Britain. Pest Infestation Control Laboratory. Report. irreg. ISSN 0072-6486

**Gt. Brit. Ministry of Agriculture, Fisheries and Food. White Fish Authority**
Whitehall Place, London SW1A 2HH, England
(Avail. from H.M.S.O., c/o Liaison Officer, Atlantic House, Holborn Viaduct, London EC1P 1BN, England)
• Great Britain. White Fish Authority. Annual Report and Accounts. a. ISSN 0072-7261

**Gt. Brit. Ministry of Defence**
c/o H. M. Naval Base, COB 3, Devonport, England.
• Devonport News; H. M. Naval Base newspaper. m. ISSN 0046-0184

**Gt. Brit. Ministry of Defense (Army) Royal Army Chaplains' Department Centre**
Bagshot Park, Bagshot, Surrey, Eng.
• Royal Army Chaplains' Department. Journal. s-a.

**Gt.Brit. Ministry of Defense. Royal Air Force**
Turnstile House, 97-99 High Holborn, London WC1V 6LL, Eng.
• Royal Air Force News. fortn. ISSN 0035-8614

**Gt.Brit. Ministry of Defense. Royal Navy**
Whitehall, London S.W.1., England.
• Navy News. m. ISSN 0028-1670
• Periscope; Chatham Naval Base newspaper. m. ISSN 0048-3400
• Spotlight (Bath) m. ISSN 0049-2000
• Trident; Portsmouth Naval Base newspaper. m. ISSN 0049-4690

**Gt. Brit. Ministry of Overseas Development**
Stag Place, London SW1E 5DH, England
(Avail. from H.M.S.O., c/o Liaison Officer, Atlantic House, Holborn Viaduct, London EC1P 1BN, England)
• Bibliography of Insecticide Materials of Vegetable Origin. (pub. by Tropical Products Institute)
• British Aid Statistics; Statistics of Economic Aid to Developing Countries. a. ISSN 0068-1210
• Oil Palm News. (pub. by Tropical Products Institute)
• Overseas Development. bi-m. ISSN 0030-7440
• Technical Co-Operation; a monthly bibliography. m.(with quarterly supplements) ISSN 0040-0904
• Tropical Storage Abstracts. (pub. by Tropical Products Institute)
• Tropical Stored Products Information. (pub. by Tropical Products Institute)

**Gt. Brit. Ministry of Overseas Development. Centre for Overseas Pest Research**
PANS Office, College House, Wrights Lane, London W8 5SJ, Eng
(Avail. from H.M.S.O., c/o Liaison Officer, Atlantic House, Holborn Viaduct, London EC1P 1BN, England)
- Centre for Overseas Pest Research. Report. a (approx.)
- P A N S. q. ISSN 0030-7793

**Gt. Brit. Ministry of Overseas Development. Directorate of Overseas Surveys**
Kingston Rd., Tolworth, Surbiton, Surrey KTs 9NS, England
(Subscr. to: Messrs C.F. Hodgson & Son Ltd., 50 Holloway Rd., London N7 8JL, England)
- Survey Review. q. ISSN 0039-6265

**Gt.Brit. National Coal Board**
Hobart House, Grosvenor Place, London SW1X 7AE, Eng., U.K.
- Coal News. m. ISSN 0009-997X
- National Coal Board Statistical Tables. a. ISSN 0307-7691

**Gt. Brit. National Economic Development Office**
Millbank Tower, Millbank St., London S.W.1, England
(Avail. from H.M.S.O., c/o Liaison Officer, Atlantic House, Holborn Viaduct, London EC1P 1BN, England)
- Annual Statistical Survey of the Electronics Industry. a.
- Great Britain. National Economic Development Office. Monographs. irreg. ISSN 0072-694X

**Gt. Brit. National Savings Committee for England and Wales**
Alexandra House, Kingsway, London WC2B 6TS, England
(Avail. from H.M.S.O., c/o Liaison Officer, Atlantic House, Holborn Viaduct, London EC1P 1BN, England)
- Great Britain. National Savings Committee. Report. a. ISSN 0072-6990

**Gt. Brit. Natural Environment Research Council**
Alhambra House, 27-33 Charing Cross Rd., London WC2H 0AX, England
(Avail. from H.M.S.O., c/o Liaison Officer, Atlantic House, Holborn Viaduct, London EC1P 1BN, England)
- Great Britain. Natural Environment Research Council. Report. a. ISSN 0072-7008
- Monks Wood Experimental Station, Huntingdon, England. Symposia. (pub. by Monks Wood Experimental Station)

**Gt. Brit. Office of Fair Trading**
1 Victoria St., London S.W.1, England
(Avail. from H.M.S.O., c/o Liaison Officer, Atlantic House, Holborn Viaduct, London EC1P 1BN, England)
- Great Britain. Office of Fair Trading. Report. a.

**Gt.Brit. Office of Population Censuses and Surveys**
London, England
(Avail. from H.M.S.O., c/o Liaison Officer, Atlantic House, Holborn Viaduct, London EC1P 1BN, England)
- Population Trends. q.

**Gt. Brit. Ministry of Public Building and Works**
London, England.
- National Building Maintenance Conference. Papers. irreg. (Property Services Agency)

**Gt. Brit. Public Works Loan Board**
Royex House, Aldermanbury Square, London EC2V 7LT, England
(Avail. from H.M.S.O., c/o Liaison Officer, Atlantic House, Holborn Viaduct, London EC1P 1BN, England)
- Great Britain. Public Works Loan Board. Report. a. ISSN 0072-7032

**Gt. Brit. Royal Botanic Gardens**
Kew, London, England
(Avail. from H.M.S.O., c/o Liaison Officer, Atlantic House, Holborn Viaduct, London EC1P 1BN, England)
- Kew Bulletin. irreg. ISSN 0075-5974

**Gt. Brit. Royal Botanic Gardens (Edinburgh)**
Edinburgh, Scotland
(Avail. from H.M.S.O., c/o Liaison Officer, Atlantic House, Holborn Viaduct, London EC1P 1BN, England)
- Notes from the Royal Botanic Garden, Edinburgh. irreg., vol. 35, 1976. ISSN 0080-4274

**Gt. Brit. Royal Commission on Historical Manuscripts**
Quality House, Chancery Lane, London WC2A 1HP, England
(Avail. from: H. M. S. O., c/o Liaison Officer, Atlantic House, London EC1P 1BN, England)
- Great Britain. Historical Manuscripts Commission. Secretary's Report to the Commissioners. a. ISSN 0533-9685
- Great Britain. Royal Commission on Historical Manuscripts. Joint Publication. irreg. ISSN 0072-7091
- Great Britain. Royal Historical Manuscripts Commission. Commissioners' Reports to the Crown. irreg. ISSN 0072-7083

**Gt. Brit. Royal Commission on Historical Monuments**
Quality House, Quality Court, Chancery Lane, London WC2A 1HP, England
(Avail. from H.M.S.O., c/o Liaison Officer, Atlantic House, Holborn Viaduct, London EC1P 1BN, England)
- Great Britain. Royal Commission on the Ancient and Historical Monuments and Constructions of England. Interim Report. irreg., 34th, 1977. ISSN 0072-7067
- Great Britain. Royal Commission on the Ancient and Historical Monuments and Constructions of Wales and Monmouthshire. Interim Report. irreg. ISSN 0072-7075

**Gt. Brit. Royal Electrical & Mechanical Engineers**
Moat House, Arborfield, Reading, Berks RG2 9LN, England.
- R E M E Journal. a. ISSN 0432-2924

**Gt. Brit. Royal Greenwich Observatory**
Herstmonceux, Sussex, England
(Avail. from H.M.S.O., c/o Liaison Officer, Atlantic House, Holborn Viaduct, London EC1P 1BN, England)
- Nautical Almanac. a. ISSN 0077-619X (Co-sponsors: H.M. Nautical Almanac Office; National Almanac Office, U.S. Naval Observatory, Washington, D.C.)
- Star Almanac for Land Surveyors. a. ISSN 0081-4377 (Avail. from: H.M.S.O., c/o Liaison Officer, Atlantic House, London EC1P 1BW, England)

**Gt. Brit. Royal Mint**
Tower Hill, London EC3N 4DR, England
(Avail. from H.M.S.O., c/o Liaison Officer, Atlantic House, Holborn Viaduct, London EC1P 1BN, England)
- Great Britain. Royal Mint. Annual Report. a. ISSN 0072-7105

**Gt.Brit. Royal Navy Communications Branch**
- Communicator. (pub. by H.M.S. Mercury)

**Gt. Brit. Science Research Council**
State House, High Holborn, London WC1R 4TA, England
(Avail. from H.M.S.O., c/o Liaison Officer, Atlantic House, Holborn Viaduct, London EC1P 1BN, England)
- Great Britain. Science Research Council. Report. a. ISSN 0072-7148

**Gt. Brit. Scottish Health Service Planning Council**
45-47 Melville St., Edinburgh EH3 7HL, Scotland
(Avail. from H.M.S.O., c/o Liaison Officer, Atlantic House, Holborn Viaduct, London EC1P 1BN, England)
- Scottish Health Services Council. Annual Report. a. ISSN 0080-7877

**Gt. Brit. Scottish Law Commission**
Old College, South Bridge, Edinburgh EH8 9BD, Scotland
(Avail. from H.M.S.O., c/o Liaison Officer, Atlantic House, Holborn Viaduct, London EC1P 1BN, England)
- Scotland. Scottish Law Commission. Annual Report. a. ISSN 0080-7915

**Gt. Brit. Scottish Office**
Dover House, Whitehall, London SW1A 2AU, England
(Avail. from H.M.S.O., c/o Liaison Officer, Atlantic House, Holborn Viaduct, London EC1P 1BN, England)
- Scottish Abstract of Statistics. a.

**Gt. Brit. Social Science Research Council**
State House, High Holborn, London WC1R 4TH, England
(Avail. from H.M.S.O., c/o Liaison Officer, Atlantic House, Holborn Viaduct, London EC1P 1BN, England)
- Social Science Research Council (Great Britain) Report. a. ISSN 0081-0444

**Gt.Brit. Soil Survey**
Rothamsted Experimental Station, Harpenden, Herts AL5 2JQ, England
(Avail. from H.M.S.O., c/o Liaison Officer, Atlantic House, Holborn Viaduct, London EC1P 1BN, England)
- Great Britain. Soil Survey of England and Wales. Records. irreg., no. 43, 1977. ISSN 0072-7180
- Great Britain. Soil Survey of England and Wales. Report. a. ISSN 0072-7199
- Great Britain. Soil Survey of England and Wales. Special Surveys. irreg., no. 10, 1976. ISSN 0072-7202
- Great Britain. Soil Survey of England and Wales. Technical Monographs. irreg., no. 10, 1977. ISSN 0072-7210

**Gt. Brit. University Grants Committee**
14 Park Crescent, London W1N 4DH, England
(Avail. from H.M.S.O., c/o Liaison Officer, Atlantic House, Holborn Viaduct, London EC1P 1BN, England)
- Great Britain. University Grants Committee. Annual Survey. a. ISSN 0072-7237

**Gt. Brit. Victoria and Albert Museum**
South Kensington, London S.W.7, England
(Avail. from H.M.S.O., c/o Liaison Officer, Atlantic House, Holborn Viaduct, London EC1P 1BN, England)
- Victoria and Albert Museum, South Kensington. Illustrated Booklets. irreg. ISSN 0083-5900
- Victoria and Albert Museum, South Kensington. Monographs. irreg. ISSN 0083-5919

**Gt. Brit. Water Pollution Research Laboratory**
Stevenage, Hertfordshire, England
(Avail. from H.M.S.O., c/o Liaison Officer, Atlantic House, Holborn Viaduct, London EC1P 1BN, England)
- Water Pollution Research. a. ISSN 0083-7660
- Water Pollution Research Laboratory, Stevenage, England. Technical Papers. irreg. ISSN 0083-7679

**Gt. Brit. Water Resources Board**
Reading Bridge House, Reading, Berks, England
(Avail. from H.M.S.O., Atlantic House, Holborn Viaduct, London EC1P 1BN, England)
- Great Britain. Water Resources Board. Publication. irreg. ISSN 0072-7245
- Great Britain. Water Resources Board. Report. a. ISSN 0072-7253
- Surface Water Year Book of Great Britain. a. ISSN 0081-959X

**Great Britain Philatelic Society**
c/o R. C. A. Payne, The Shieling, Sibley's Green, Thaxted, Dunmow, Essex CM6 2NU, Eng.
- Great Britain Journal. 6 per yr. ISSN 0017-3657

**Great North of Scotland Railway Association**
c/o N. Forrest, 14 Gordon Rd., Bridge of Don, Aberdeen AB2 8PT, Scotland.
- Great North Review. q. ISSN 0307-3319

**Great Western Society Ltd.**
Didcot, Oxfordshire, Eng.
- Great Western Echo. q.

**Great Works**
c/o Bill Symondson, 47 Windsor St., Hanley, Stoke-on-Trent, Staffs., England.
- Great Works. 3 per yr.

**Greater London Arts Association**
25/31 Tavistock Place, London WC1H 9SG,
England.
- Greater London Arts Association. Annual Report
and Year Book. a.

**Greater London Council**
GLC Bookshop, County Hall, London SE1 7PB,
England.
- Greater London Council. Greater London
Services. irreg.
- Greater London Intelligence Quarterly. q. ISSN
0305-7747
- London Facts and Figures. irreg.
- Looking for Leisure. a. ISSN 0076-0862

**Greater London Council. Department of Public
Health Engineering**
10 Great George St., London SW1P 3AB, England.
- Greater London Council. Department of Public
Health Engineering. Annual Report. a.

**Greater London Council. Intelligence Unit**
County Hall, London SE1 7PB, England.
- Greater London Council. Housing Facts and
Figures. irreg.

**Greater World Association**
3 Lansdowne Rd., Holland Park, London, W.11
3AL, Eng.
- Greater World. w. ISSN 0046-6352

**Greek Institute**
34 Bush Hill Rd., London N21 2DS, England.
- Greek Review. q. ISSN 0307-4536

**Greek Observer**
328 Gray's Inn Rd., London W.C.1, Eng
- Greek Observer; a monthly magazine on Greek
affairs. m. ISSN 0017-3886

**Greek Report**
20 Eccleston, London S.W.I., Eng.
- Greek Report. m. ISSN 0017-3908

**Green & Co.**
Caxton Press, Lowestoft, Suffolk, Eng.
- Immanuel's Witness; a bi-monthly record of the
Barbican Mission to the Jews. bi-m. ISSN 0019-
2759

**W. Green & Son Ltd.**
2 St. Giles St., Edinburgh EH1 6PU, Scotland.
- Juridical Review; Law Journal of Scottish
Universities. 3 per yr. ISSN 0022-6785
- Parliament House Book. a. ISSN 0079-0095
- Scots Law Times. w. ISSN 0036-908X

**Green Island**
c/o David A. Kilburn, Ed., Flat 2, 126 Long Acre,
London WC2E 9PE, England.
- Green Island. s-a. ISSN 0017-3967

**Victor Green Publications Ltd.**
106 Hampstead Rd., London NW1 2LS, England.
- Fire Surveyor. bi-m. (Incorporated Association of
Architects and Surveyors. Fire Surveyors Section)
- Safety Surveyor. bi-m.
- Security Surveyor. bi-m. (Association of Burglary
Insurance Surveyors)

**Henry Greenwood & Co. Ltd.**
24 Wellington St., London WC2E 7DH, Eng.
- British Journal of Photography; technical,
professional, scientific. w. ISSN 0007-1196
- British Journal of Photography Annual. a. ISSN
0068-2217 (Dist. in U.S. by A.M.P.H.O.T.O.,
East Gate & Zeckendorf Blvds., Garden City, NY
11530)
- Photo Trader. fortn.
- Photographic Processor. m. ISSN 0031-8515
(Association of Photographic Laboratories)

**Greyhound Magazine Co. Ltd.**
1-2 Dorset Bldgs., Dorset Rise, London, EC4Y 8ES,
Eng.
- Greyhound. m. ISSN 0017-4157

**Greyhound Owner Ltd.**
8 Greenford Ave., London W7 3QP, Eng.
- Greyhound Owner & Breeder. w. ISSN 0017-4165

**Grocer's Gazette Ltd.**
24 Bruton Lane, London W1X 7LA, Eng.
- Cash & Carry News. m. ISSN 0008-7270
- Grocers Gazette. w. ISSN 0017-4386

**Grosseteste Review Books**
10 Consort Crescent, Commonside, Pensnett,
Staffordshire, Eng.
- Grosseteste Review. 4 per yr. ISSN 0017-4637

**Grower Publications Ltd.**
49 Doughty St., London WC1N 2LP, Eng.
- Grower. w. ISSN 0017-4785

**Growing Point**
c/o Margery Fisher, Ed., Ashton Manor,
Northampton NN7 2JL, England.
- Growing Point. 9 per yr. ISSN 0046-6506

**Gryphon Press**
38 Prince Edward's Rd., Lewes, Sussex, England.
- Tract. q.

**Guardian and Manchester Evening News Ltd.**
164 Deansgate, Manchester M6O 2RR, Eng.
- Manchester Guardian Weekly. w. ISSN 0025-
200X

**Guggenheim Laboratories**
- Combustion Science & Technology. (pub. by
Gordon and Breach Science Publishers Ltd.)

**Guild for the Promotion of Welsh Music**
94 Walter Rd., Swansea SA1 5QA, Wales.
- Welsh Music/Cerddoriaeth Cymru. 3 per yr.
ISSN 0043-244X

**Guild of British Newspaper Editors**
White Friars House, 6 Carmelite St., London EC4Y
0BL, England.
- Guild of British Newspaper Editors Guild Journal.
4 per yr.

**Guild of Catholic Doctors**
Ed. Dr. W.H. Reynolds, Broad Towers, Caerleon,
Newport, Mon., Wales.
- Catholic Medical Quarterly. q. ISSN 0008-8226

**Guild of Freemen of the City of London**
4 Dowgate Hill, London EC4, England.
- Freemen. a.

**Guild of Health**
26 Queen Anne St., London W1M 9LB, Eng.
- Way of Life. q. ISSN 0043-1605

**Guild of Our Lady of Ransom**
31 Southdown Rd., London SW20 8QJ, Eng.
- Ransomer. 3 per yr. ISSN 0033-9245

**Guild of Undergraduates**
Student Union 2 Bedfort St. N., Liverpool 7, Eng.
- Sphinx; the student magazine for Liverpool. /yr.
ISSN 0038-7428

**Guildford Poets Press**
10, Ashcroft, Shalford, Guildford, Surrey, England.
- Weyfarers. 3 per yr.

**Guildhall Library**
Aldermanbury, London E.C.2., England.
- Guildhall Studies in London History. s-a. ISSN
0306-3194

**Guildhall Poets**
19 Rugwood Rd., Flackwell Heath, High Wycombe
HP10 9HA, England.
- Guildhall Poets. a.

**Guilds of Weavers, Spinners and Dyers**
6 Queen's Square, London WC1N 3AR, England.
- Guilds of Weavers,Spinners and Dyers. Quarterly
Journal. q. ISSN 0017-5439

**Guinness Superlatives Ltd.**
2 Cecil Court, London Road, Enfield, England.
- Guinness Book of Records. a. ISSN 0300-1679

**Guitar**
8 Horse and Dolphin Yard, Macclesfield St.,
London W.1, England.
- Guitar; magazine for all guitarists. m. ISSN 0301-
7214

**Guy's Hospital**
Gazette Committee, 16 St. Thomas St., London
S.E.1, Eng.
- Guy's Hospital Gazette. m. ISSN 0017-5870

**Gwasg Y Sir**
Bala, Gwynedd, Wales.
- Y Faner. w.

**H. G. Wells Society**
24 Wellin Lane, Edwalton, England.
- H. G. Wells Society Newsletter. q. ISSN 0306-
5480
- Wellsian. s-a. ISSN 0308-1397

**H.M.S. Mercury**
East Meon, Petersfield, Hampshire, England.
- Communicator. 3 per yr. ISSN 0010-3683
(Gt.Brit. Royal Navy Communications Branch)

**H P A**
47 Belgrave Square, London SW1X 8QX, England.
- H P A Bulletin. q.

**H. Q. Royal Artillery**
Government House, New Road, Woolwich, London
SE18, England.
- Gunner. m.

**Hackney Horse Society**
35 Belgrave Square, London SW1X 8QB, Sussex,
England.
- Hackney Stud Book. triennial.

**Hackney Junior Libraries**
- Preface. (pub. by Hackney Library Services)

**Hackney Library Services**
Mare St., Hackney, London E. 8, Eng.
- Preface; an introduction to books. bi-m. ISSN
0032-7263 (Hackney Junior Libraries)

**Hackney People's Press**
136 Kingsland High St., London, E.8, England.
- Hackney People's Press. m.

**Haigh and Hochland Ltd.**
Precinct Centre, Oxford Rd., Manchester 13, Eng.
- British Society for Phenomenology. Journal. 3 per
yr. ISSN 0007-1773

**Hair and Beauty Publications Ltd.**
Evelyn House, 62 Oxford St., London W.1,
England.
- Hair & Beauty. m. ISSN 0017-6702

**Hakluyt Society**
c/o British Library, Great Russell St., London
WC1B 3DG, England.
- Hakluyt Society. Works in the Ordinary Series.
Second Series. biennial. ISSN 0072-9396

**Alan W. Hall (Publications) Ltd.**
2 Sheepfold Lane, Amersham, Buckinghamshire
HP7 9EL, England.
- Aviation News. fortn.

**Sir John Hall, Ed. & Pub.**
Carradde, 29 Embercourt Rd., Thames Ditton,
Surrey KT7 0LH, England.
- Antique Records. irreg?

**Halle Concerts Society**
30 Cross St., Manchester M2 7BA, England.
- Halle Magazine. q.
- Halle Prospectus. s-a.

**Hambro Life Assurance**
- Hambro Tax Guide. (pub. by Robert Yeatman
Ltd.)

**Hamibantu Publications**
c/o 107 Pevensey Rd., London, E7 0AH, England.
- African Red Family; journal of All-African
Revolutionary Marxist-Leninist Movement. 2-3
per yr.

**Hamish Hamilton Ltd.**
90 Great Russell St, London W.C.1, England.
- Institute of Psychophysical Research. Proceedings.
irreg. ISSN 0073-9561

**Hamlyn Group**
42 The Centre, Feltham, Middlesex, England.
- Motor Manual. irreg. ISSN 0077-1600

**Hampshire Field Club**
c/o Dept. of Adult Education, University of
Southampton, Southampton SO9 5NH, England
(Subscr. to: D.J. Gaukroger, 40 Eastgate St.,
Winchester, England)
- Hampshire Field Club. Proceedings. a.

**Hampshire Genealogical Society**
c/o Mr. R. Asher, 14 Wadham Rd., North End, Portsmouth, England.
- Hampshire Family Historian Quarterly. q. ISSN 0306-6843

**Albert Hand Publications Ltd.**
41-43 Derby Rd., Heanor, Derbyshire, Eng.
- Elvis Monthly. m. ISSN 0013-6484

**Hanover Books Ltd.**
4 Mill St., London, W.1, England.
- British Aviation Year Book. a. ISSN 0068-1342
- Let It Rock. m.

**Hansom Books**
Artillery Mansions, 75 Victoria St., London SW1H 0HZ, Eng.
- Art and Artists. m. ISSN 0004-3001
- Books and Bookmen. m. ISSN 0006-744X
- Dance and Dancers. m. ISSN 0011-5983
- Films and Filming. m. ISSN 0015-167X
- Look and Listen. m.
- Music and Musicians. m. ISSN 0027-4232
- Plays and Players. m. ISSN 0032-1559
- Records and Recording. m. ISSN 0034-169X

**Haraton Ltd.**
Back Clarendon Rd., Blackpool FY1 6EG, England.
- Association of Railway Preservation Societies. A. R. P. S. Year Book & Steam Preservation Guide. a.
- Railway Forum. q. ISSN 0033-8893 (Association of Railway Preservation Societies)

**Hard Cheese**
c/o Ted Bowden, Ed., 95a Shooters Hill Rd., Blackheath, London SE3 8RL, England.
- Hard Cheese; a journal of education. irreg.

**Harmsworth Press Ltd.**
8 Stratton St., London W1X 6AT, Eng.
- Field; the country newspaper. w. ISSN 0015-0649
- Golf Illustrated. w.

**Harper Trade Journals Ltd.**
Southbank House, Black Prince Road, London, SE1, England.
- Harpers Directory and Manual of the Wine and Spirit Trade. a. ISSN 0073-0408
- Harpers Export Wine and Spirit Gazette. 3 per yr. ISSN 0017-7881
- Harpers Guide to Sports Trade. a. ISSN 0073-0416
- Harpers Sports and Camping. fortn.
- Harpers Wine and Spirit Gazette. w. ISSN 0017-7903
- Solid Fuel. fortn. ISSN 0038-1055
- Solid Fuel and Coal Merchant and Shipper. fortn.

**George G. Harrap & Co. Ltd.**
182-184 High Holborn, London WC4 7AX, England.
- American Historical Documents. irreg.

**G. W. Harris**
43 Leopold Road, Willesden, London, NW10, England.
- Institute of Clerk of Works' of Great Britain Incorporated. Year Book. a. ISSN 0073-9073

**Harris Publications Ltd.**
42 Maiden Lane, London WC2E 7LW, Eng.
- Philatelic Magazine. m. ISSN 0031-7357
- Philatelic Trader. fortn.

**Harrison Mayer Ltd.**
Stoke-on-Trent ST3 7PX, England.
- H M Monthly Bulletin for the Ceramic Industry. m.

**Hart-Davis Educational**
Park St., St. Albans, Herts, Eng.
- Use of English. 3 per yr. ISSN 0042-1243

**Harvester Press Ltd.**
2 Stamford Terrace, Hassocks, Brighton, Sussex, England.
- Language and Thought Series. a.
- Royal Historical Society. Annual Bibliography of British and Irish History. a.

**Harvey & Blythe Ltd.**
Lloyds Bank Chambers, 216 Church Rd., Hove, Sussex, Eng.
- British Journal of Clinical Practice. m. ISSN 0007-0947

**Hatra Research Centre for Knitting, Dyeing and Making-up**
7 Gregory Blvd., Nottingham NG7 6LD, Eng.
- Hosiery Abstracts. m. ISSN 0018-537X

**Havering Central Library. London Borough**
St. Edwards Way, Romford, Essex RM1 3AR, Eng.
- L O G A/Local Government Annotations. m. ISSN 0023-6349 (London Boroughs Association)

**Haymarket Publishing Ltd.**
Regent House, 54-62 Regent St., London W1A 4YJ, Eng.
- Accountancy Age. w. ISSN 0001-4672
- Autosport. w.
- Boat World. a. ISSN 0067-933X
- Boat World Guide to Dinghies. a. ISSN 0067-9348
- Boat World Guide to Sailing Cruisers over 4500 (Pounds Sterling) a.
- Campaign; the national weekly of the communications business, embracing advertising, marketing, newspapers and magazines, films and television. w. ISSN 0008-2309
- Caravan & Chalet Sites Guide. a. ISSN 0069-0317
- Careers for School Leavers. a. ISSN 0069-0422
- Carpet Annual. a. ISSN 0069-0767
- Carpet Review Weekly. w.
- Computing Europe. w. ISSN 0307-8965 (British Computer Society)
- Directory of Opportunities for Graduates. a. ISSN 0070-6019
- Fishing Industry Index International. a. ISSN 0071-5557
- Fruit Trades World Directory. a. ISSN 0071-9722
- Gardeners Chronicle/Horticultural Trade Journal. w. ISSN 0016-4682
- General Practitioner. w. ISSN 0046-5607
- Hi-Fi Answers. m.
- Hi-Fi Sound. m. ISSN 0018-1234
- Hi-Fi Sound Annual. a. ISSN 0073-2044
- House Buyer. m. ISSN 0018-6473
- Lithoprinter. m. ISSN 0024-4929
- London Weekly Advertiser. w. ISSN 0024-6182
- Marketing. m. ISSN 0025-3650 (Institute of Marketing)
- Powerboating Yearbook. a.
- Practical Camper. m. ISSN 0032-6356
- Practical Camper's Sites Guide. a.
- Practical Caravan. m.
- S L R Camera. m. ISSN 0036-1631
- Sell's Guide to Touring Caravans & Caravanning. a.
- What Car? m.
- What Hi-Fi? m.
- Which University. a. ISSN 0083-923X (Dist. in U.S. by Barnes & Noble, Inc., 105 Fifth Ave., New York, NY 10003)
- Wine & Spirit. m.

**Headland Publications**
56 Blakes Lane, New Malden, Surrey, KT3 6NX, England.
- Hallamshire & Osgoldcross Poetry Express. 3 per yr.
- Promontory; a magazine of progressive poetry. 3 per yr.

**Headley Bros. Ltd.**
Ashford, Kent TN24 8HH, England.
- British Journal of Psychiatry. 12 per yr. ISSN 0007-1250 (Royal College of Psychiatrists)
- British Journal of Psychiatry. Special Publications. irreg., no. 11, 1975. ISSN 0068-2225 (Royal College of Psychiatrists)
- Friends' Quarterly. q. ISSN 0016-1357
- Journal of Horticultural Science. q. ISSN 0022-1589 (Horticultural and Agricultural Research Station)
- Journal of Laryngology and Otology. m. ISSN 0022-2151
- Register of Early Music. irreg.

**Headmasters Association**
29 Gordon Sq., London, WC1, Eng.
- Headmasters Association Review. 3 per yr. ISSN 0046-6980

**Headmasters' Conference**
c/o the Master, Wellington College, Crowthorne, Berks, England.
- Conference. 3 per yr.

**Headquarters Air Cadets R.A.F.**
Brampton, Huntingdon, England.
- Air Cadet News. m. ISSN 0002-2209

**Healer Publishing Co. Ltd.**
Burrows Lea, Shere, Guildford, Surrey, Eng.
- Spiritual Healer; journal of spiritual healing and philosophy. m. ISSN 0038-7622

**Health and Strength Publishing Co.**
Halton House, 20-23 Holborn, London E.C.4, Eng.
- Health and Strength. m. ISSN 0017-890X

**Health Education Council**
78 New Oxford St., London WC1A 1AH, England.
- Health Education Journal. q. ISSN 0017-8969

**Health Services Manpower Review**
c/o Department of Adult Education, University of Keele, Keele, Staffordshire ST5 5BG, England.
- Health Services Manpower Review. q.

**Health Visitors Association**
- Health Visitor. (pub. by B. Edsall & Co. Ltd.)
- New Baby. (pub. by B. Edsall & Co. Ltd.)

**Heanor Record Centre**
41 Derby Rd., Heanor, Derbyshire, Eng.
- Record Collector. m. ISSN 0034-155X

**Hearts of Oak Benefit Society**
Euston Rd., London NW1 2DL, Eng.
- Hearts of Oak Benefit Society. Journal. q. ISSN 0017-9302

**Heather Society**
c/o Mrs. C. I. Macleod, Yew Trees, Horley, Surrey, England.
- Heather Society. Yearbook. a. ISSN 0440-5757

**Heating and Ventilating Contractors' Association**
Coastal Chambers, 172 Buckingham Palace Road, London SW1W 9TD, England.
- Heating, Ventilating and Air Conditioning Year Book. a. ISSN 0306-3585 (Co-sponsors: H E V A C Association; Institution of Heating and Ventilating Engineers; Heating and Ventilating Research Association)

**Heating and Ventilating Publications Ltd.**
111 St James Rd., Croydon, Surrey CR9 2TH, England.
- Heating and Ventilating Review. m. ISSN 0017-9396

**W. Heffer & Sons Ltd.**
20 Trinity St., Cambridge, England.
- English Philological Studies. a. (University of Birmingham)
- Society of Analytical Chemistry. Chemical Society Division. Proceedings. m.

**Heffers Printers Ltd.**
Kings Hedges Rd., Cambridge CB4 2PQ, Eng.
- Ambix. 3 parts to vol.(1 vol. per year) ISSN 0002-6980 (Society for the Study of Alchemy and Early Chemistry)
- Music Review. q. ISSN 0027-4445
- Preparatory Schools Review. 3 per yr. ISSN 0032-7492 (Incorporated Association of Preparatory Schools)

**Arthur J. Heighway Publications, Ltd.**
Ludgate House, 110 Fleet Streeet, London EC4A 2JL, England.
- Fish Farming International. q.
- Fishing News. w. ISSN 0015-3036
- Fishing News International. m. ISSN 0015-3044

**Heim Gallery (London) Ltd.**
59 Jermyn St., London SW1Y 6LX, Eng.
- Heim Gallery Catalogues. 2 per yr.

**Heinemann Educational Books Ltd.**
48 Charles St., Mayfair, London W 1, England.
- African Writers Series. irreg. ISSN 0065-4108

**Heinemann Medical Books Ltd.**
23 Bedford Square, London WC1B 3H, England (Dist.in U.S. by: Yearbook Medical Publishers Inc., 35 E.Wacker Drive, Chicago, IL 60601)
- New Aspects of Breast Cancer. irreg. ISSN 0307-6695

**Heinmann Pan Books**
33, Tothill St., London SW1, England.
- Football Association. Official F. A. Year Book. a. ISSN 0071-724X

**Hellenic Review**
41 Duke St., London W.1, Eng.
- Hellenic Review. m. ISSN 0018-0041

**Hellenic Shipping International**
26-27 Conduit St., London W.I., Eng.
- Hellenic Shipping International. bi-m. ISSN 0018-005X

**Herald Advisory Services**
23A Brighton Rd, South Croydon Surrey CR2 6UE, England.
- Away from It All in Britain. a. ISSN 0067-2688
- Bed and Breakfast in South and South-West England. a. ISSN 0067-4761
- Bed and Breakfast in Wales, Northern England and Scotland. a.
- Children Welcome; happy Family Holiday Guide. a. ISSN 0069-3456
- Furnished Holiday Homes & Caravans. a. ISSN 0071-996X
- Pets Welcome. a. ISSN 0079-130X
- Recommended Country Hotels of Britain. a.
- Recommended Wayside Inns of Britain. a. ISSN 0080-0252

**Heraldry Society**
28 Museum St., London WC1 1LH, Eng.
- Coat of Arms; a heraldic quarterly magazine. q. ISSN 0010-003X

**Herbarium of the Royal Botanic Gardens, Kew**
- Index Kewensis. Supplement. (pub. by Oxford University Press)

**Alfred Herbert Ltd.**
Box 30, Coventry, Eng.
- Machine-Tool Review. bi-m. ISSN 0024-9173

**Here Now**
22 Torquay Parade, Hebburn Co., Durham NE 31 2AD, Eng.
- Here Now; South Tyneside arts quarterly. q. ISSN 0046-7294

**Hereford Herd Book Society**
Hereford House, 3 Offa Street, Hereford, England.
- Herd Book of Hereford Cattle. a. ISSN 0073-1943
- Hereford Breed Journal. a. ISSN 0073-1951

**Hereford Press**
111 Cheyne Walk, London S. W. 10, England.
- Hereford's Air Cargo. s-a.

**Heriot-Watt University**
Publications Office, Edinburgh EH1 1HX, Scotland.
- Heriot-Watt University Lectures. a.

**E. T. Heron & Co. Ltd.**
9-11, Tottenham St., London, W.1. Eng.
- London College of Music Magazine. 3 per yr.

**Hertfordshire Chamber of Commerce**
Andre House, Salisbury Square, Old Hatfield AL9 5BH, England.
- Law and Parliamentary Digest. m.

**Hertfordshire Local History Council**
- Hertfordshire Local History Council. Occasional Papers. (pub. by Phillimore and Co. Ltd.)

**Peter Hewitt Publications Ltd.**
94 Gray's Inn Rd., London WC1X 8AA, Eng.
- London Hilton Magazine. m. ISSN 0024-6042

**Heyden & Son Ltd.**
Spectrum House, Alderton Crescent, London NW4 3XX, England
(U.S. address: Heyden & Son Inc., Kor. Center East, Bellmawr, NJ 08030)
- Advances in Infrared and Raman Spectroscopy. a.
- Advances in Nuclear Quadropole Resonance. s-a.
- Advances in Raman Spectroscopy. quinquennial.
- B M S -Biomedical Mass Spectrometry; an international journal of mass spectrometry in the biological, environmental and medical sciences. bi-m.
- European Spectroscopy News. q. ISSN 0307-0026 (Association of British Spectroscopists)
- Fire and Materials. q.
- Interdisciplinary Science Reviews. q. ISSN 0308-0188
- Journal of Raman Spectroscopy; the international journal for original work in all aspects of Raman spectroscopy, including higher order processes, and also Brillouin and Rayleigh scattering. bi-m.
- Journal of Thermal Analysis; an international forum for communications on thermal investigations. bi-m. ISSN 0022-5215 (Co-Sponsor: Akademiai Kiado, Budapest)

- Liquid Scintillation Counting; Proceedings of the Symposia on Liquid Scintillation Counting. s-a. ISSN 0302-3354 (Society for Analytical Chemistry)
- Organic Magnetic Resonance; an international journal. m. ISSN 0030-4921
- Organic Mass Spectrometry; an international journal. m. ISSN 0030-493X
- Thermal Analysis Abstracts; a survey of current literature on thermogravimetric analysis and differential thermal analysis. bi-m. (International Confederation of Thermal Analysis)
- X-Ray Spectrometry; an international journal. q. ISSN 0049-8246

**Heythrop College (University of London)**
11 Cavendish Square, London W1M 0AN, Eng.
- Heythrop Journal; a review of philosophy and theology. q. ISSN 0018-1196

**Hi-Fi Trade Journal Limited**
6 Disraeli Gardens, Fawe Park Rd., Putney, London SW15 2QB, Eng.
- Hi-Fi Trade Journal; the retailers' guide to audio. q.

**T. & C. Hicks**
12 Winster Ave., Stretford M32 95E, England.
- Manchester Folk Directory. a.

**High Commissioner for New Zealand in Britain**
Public Relations Officer, New Zealand House, Haymarket, London, SW1, England.
- Forefront: News from New Zealand. m. ISSN 0429-0550

**High Orchard Press**
High Orchard 125 Markyate Rd., Dagenham, Essex RM8 2LB, England.
- Shavian. 3 per yr. ISSN 0037-3346

**Highland Herald Ltd.**
1 Friars St., Inverness, Scotland.
- Highland Hotelkeeper & Touristmaker. m. ISSN 0018-1617

**Highlands and Islands Development Board**
Bridge House, 27 Bank St., Inverness 1V1 1QR, Scotland.
- North 7. 4 per yr.

**Adam Hilger Ltd.**
29 King St., London WC2, England.
- International Spectroscopy Colloquium. Proceedings/Colloquium Spectroscopicum Internationale. Proceedings. biennial; 17th, Florence, 1973. ISSN 0074-8595

**Leonard Hill Books**
Kingswood House, Heath & Reach, Nr. Leighton Buzzard, Beds., Eng
(Dist. in U.S. by: Barnes & Noble Books, 10 E. 53rd St., New York, NY 10022)
- British Initials and Abbreviations. irreg., 3rd ed. 1971. ISSN 0068-2144
- Dictionary of Dairying. Supplement. irreg. ISSN 0070-4725
- Food Industries Manual. irreg., 20th ed., 1969. ISSN 0071-7177

**Hire Purchase Trade Association**
3 Berners St., London W1E 4JZ, England.
- Hire Trading. q.

**Hispanic and Luso-Brazilian Council**
2 Belgrave Square, London SW1X 8PJ, England
(Subscr. to: Bailey Subscription Agents Ltd., Warner House, Folkstone, Kent CT19 6PH, England)
- British Bulletin of Publications on Latin America, the West Indies, Portugal and Spain. s-a. ISSN 0007-036X

**Historic Commercial Vehicle Club**
Iden Grange Farm, Cranbrook Rd., Staplehurst, Kent, England.
- H.C.V.C. Newsletter. m.

**Historic Society of Lancashire and Cheshire**
School of History, University of Liverpool, P.O. Box 147, Liverpool L69 3BX, England
(Subscr. to: Hon. Sec. P. Andrews, 15 Woodley Fold, Penketh, Warrington WA5 2JB, England)
- Historic Society of Lancashire and Cheshire. Transactions. a.

**Historical Association**
59a Kennington Park Rd., London SE11 4JH, England.
- Annual Bulletin of Historical Literature. a. ISSN 0066-3832
- Helps for Students of History. irreg. ISSN 0073-1714
- Historical Association, London. Aids for Teachers. irreg. ISSN 0073-2591
- Historical Association, London. General Series. 3 per yr.
- History. 3 per yr. ISSN 0018-2648
- Teaching History. 3 per yr. ISSN 0040-0610
- Teaching of History. irreg. ISSN 0073-2605

**Historical Breechloading Smallarms Association**
c/o Imperial War Museum, Lambeth Road, London SE1 6HZ, Eng.
- Historical Breechloading Smallarms Association. Journal. a. ISSN 0305-0440

**Historical Metallurgy Society**
147 Whirlowdale Road, Sheffield S7 2NG, Eng.
- Historical Metallurgy Society. Journal. 2 per yr.

**Historical Society of the Church in Wales**
c/o Owen W. Jones, The Vicarage, Builth Wells, Brec, Wales.
- Historical Society of the Church in Wales. Journal. a.

**Historical Society of the Presbyterian Church of Wales**
The Manse, Caradog Rd., Aberystwyth, Dyfed, Wales.
- Historical Society of the Presbyterian Church of Wales. Journal. 3 per yr.

**Historical Times Ltd.**
34 S. Molton St., London, England.
- British History Illustrated. bi-m.

**History of Education Society**
c/o Mrs. B. Starkey, 4 Marydene Dr., Leicester. LE5 6HD, England.
- History of Education Society Bulletin. s-a. ISSN 0018-2699
- Research in the History of Education: A List of Theses for Higher Degrees in the Universities of England and Wales. a. ISSN 0080-1674

**History Workshop Journal**
Box 69, Oxford 0X2 7XA, England.
- History Workshop; a journal of socialist historians. s-a. ISSN 0309-2984

**Hobsons Press**
Bateman Street, Cambridge CB2 1BR, England
- British Journal of Guidance and Counselling. s-a. (Careers Research and Advisory Centre) (U.S. Subscr. to: International Educational Consultants Ltd., 5042 E. Calle Guebabi, Tucson, AR 85718)

**Hockey Association**
70 Brompton Rd., London SW3 1HB, England.
- Hockey Association. Official Handbook. a. ISSN 0085-1566

**William Hodge & Co. Ltd.**
34/6 No. Frederick St., Glasgow G1 2BT, Scotland.
- Scottish Law Directory. a. ISSN 0080-8083

**C. E. Hodge, Ed. & Pub.**
70 Westmount Rd., London SE9 1JE, England.
- Women Speaking. q. ISSN 0049-7827

**Peter Hodgkiss, Ed. & Pub.**
National Poetry Centre, 21 Earls Court Square, London S.W. 5, England.
- Poetry Information. 2 per yr. ISSN 0048-4598

**C. F. Hodgson & Son Ltd.**
150 Holloway Road, London N7, England
(Subscriptions to: 321 Chase Rd., London N14, England)
- N P A Supplement. m. (National Pharmaceutical Association)

**Hogarth Press Ltd.**
40-42 William IV St., London W. C.2, England.
- International Psycho-Analytical Library. irreg. ISSN 0074-7548 (Institute of Psycho-Analysis)

**Holiday Fellowship Ltd**
142 Great North Way, London NW4 1EG, Eng.
- Over the Hills. a. ISSN 0030-7378

**Hollis Directories**
Contact House, Lower Hampton Rd., Sunbury-On-Thames, Middlesex TW16 5HG, England.
- Hollis Press and Public Relations Annual. a. (with quarterly supplements) ISSN 0073-3059

**W. & R. Holmes (Books)**
30 Clydeholm Rd., Glasgow G14 0BJ, Scotland.
- Library Review; a quarterly magazine on libraries and literature. q. ISSN 0024-2535

**Holmes McDougall Ltd.**
36 Tay St., Perth PH1 STT, Scotland.
- Business Scotland; a monthly review of national and international business. m.
- Climber and Rambler. m. ISSN 0009-8973
- Macdonald Countries. irreg.
- Red Hackle. 3 per yr. ISSN 0048-704X (Black Watch)
- Scottish Field. m. ISSN 0036-9209

**Arthur Holmes Society**
University of Durham, Department of Geological Sciences, South Road, Durham DH1 3LE, England.
- Arthur Holmes Society. Journal. a. ISSN 0066-8044

**Holy Childhood Society**
16 Raymond Rd., London S.W.19, Eng.
- Missionland. 3 per yr. ISSN 0021-4167

**Home Words Printing & Publishing Co. Ltd.**
Box 44, Guildford, Surrey GU1 1XL, Eng.
- Church News. m. ISSN 0009-6474

**Homefinders (1915) Ltd.**
10 East Rd., London N.1., Eng.
- Homefinder. m. ISSN 0018-4160
- Homes Overseas. bi-m. ISSN 0018-4241

**Honourable Artillery Company**
Armoury House, London, EC1Y 2BQ, London, EC1Y 2BO, Eng.
- Honourable Artillery Company Journal. q. ISSN 0046-7863

**Honourable Company of Master Mariners**
c/o H. Q. S. Wellington, Temple Stairs, Victoria Embankment, London W.C.2, Eng.
- Honourable Company of Master Mariners. Journal. q. ISSN 0018-4675

**Horizon Publications Ltd.**
Shoemaker's House, Montacute, Somerset TA15 6XQ, England.
- Hovercraft Contact Book and International ACV Directory. a.
- Hoverfoil News. fortn. ISSN 0018-6767
- Hoversport. a.
- New Transport Technology. fortn.

**Horticultural and Agricultural Research Station**
- Journal of Horticultural Science. (pub. by Headley Bros. Ltd)

**Horticultural Education Association**
- Scientific Horticulture. (pub. by Elvy & Gibbs)

**Hoseasons**
Sunway House, Oulton Broad, Lowestoft, England.
- Hoseasons Holidays Boats and Bungalows Hire. a. ISSN 0073-3431
- Norfolk Holiday Handbook. a. ISSN 0078-1150

**Hospital for Sick Children**
Great Ormond St., London W.C.1, England.
- Great Ormond Street Gazette. a. ISSN 0072-7334

**Hospital Medicine Publications Ltd.**
Northwood House, Goswell Rd., London EC1V 7QA, England.
- British Journal of Clinical Equipment. bi-m. ISSN 0307-4730
- British Journal of Hospital Medicine. m. ISSN 0007-1064

**Hotel Catering & Institutional Management Association**
191 Trinity Road, London, SW17 7HN, Eng.
- H C I M A Journal. m.

**House-Builders' Federation**
- House Builder & Estate Developer. (pub. by Federated Employers Press Ltd.)

**House Information Services Ltd.**
1 Cresswell Park, London SE3 9RG, England.
- Construction Industry Europe. biennial.

- Construction Industry U.K. a.

**Housewife's Trust**
c/o Mrs. P. McLaughlin, 92 Iverna Court, London W8 6TU, England.
- Insight. bi-m. ISSN 0020-188X

**Housing Centre Trust**
62 Chandos Place, London WC2N 4HG, Eng.
- Housing Review. bi-m. ISSN 0018-6651

**Housman Society**
- Housman Society Journal. (pub. by Turner and Devereux)

**Hover Club of Great Britain Ltd.**
128 Queens Rd., Portsmouth, Hants. PO2 7NE, England.
- Light Hovercraft. m.

**Howard League for Penal Reform**
125 Kennington Park Rd., London SE11, England.
- Howard Journal of Penology and Crime Prevention. 3 per yr. ISSN 0073-3741
- Howard League for Penal Reform Newsletter. 3 per yr.

**Howard Publications**
112 Lisburn Rd., Belfast BT9 6AA, Northern Ireland.
- Constabulary Gazette; Ulster police magazine. m. ISSN 0010-6607
- Soccer Year Book for Northern Ireland. a. ISSN 0081-038X

**George L. Howe Press Service Ltd.**
85 Elmhurst Dr., Hornchurch, Essex RM11 1PB, Eng.
- Printing and Bookbinding Trade Review; equipment-materials-production. m.

**Howey Foundation**
2A Lebanon Rd., Croydon, Surrey CR0 6UR, England.
- Epoch. q. ISSN 0301-0643

**Hub Publications Ltd.**
Youlgrave, Bakewell, Derbyshire, England.
- Ipse. q. (International Poetry Society)
- Orbis. q. ISSN 0030-4425 (International Poetry Society)

**Hudson Publications Ltd.**
300 Ashley Road, Parkstone, Poole, Dorset BH14 9EF, England.
- British Marine Products. q.
- Chandler & Boatbuilder. m. ISSN 0009-1340

**Hughes, Sanders & Howard Ltd.**
21 Devonshire St., London W.1, Eng.
- Jute Markets and Prices. w. ISSN 0022-7129
- World Fibre News. m. ISSN 0040-5159
- World Jute Directory. irreg. ISSN 0084-1862

**Huguenot Society of London**
c/o Barclay's Bank Ltd., 1 Pall Mall East, London SW1Y 5AX, England
(Subscriptions to: I. Scouloudi, 67 Victoria Road, London W8 5RH, England)
- Huguenot Society of London. Proceedings. a.
- Huguenot Society of London, Quarto Series. every 2-4 per yrs.

**Hulton House**
28-32 Hulton St., London EC4, England.
- Buying Antiques. m.

**Hulton Technical Press Ltd.**
Warwick House, Swanley, Kent, Eng.
- Garage and Transport. m. ISSN 0307-1154
- P E D. (Production & Industrial Equipment Digest) m. ISSN 0030-7904

**Humane Education Society**
Animals' Convalescent Home, Newgate, Wilmslow, Cheshire, Eng.
- Friend of Animals. q. ISSN 0016-1276

**Humberside**
c/o Hull Literary Club, 5 Ferensway House, Prospect St., Hull, Eng.
- Humberside. q. ISSN 0018-7585

**John Humphries**
48 Shacklewell Lane, London E8 2EY, England.
- Music Master. a (with monthly supplements)
- Record Prices; prefixes, labels, companies. m.
- Singles Master. w (monthly supplements)

**Hunter & Barney Ltd.**
20-22 Wellington St., Strand, London W.C.2, Eng.
- Number Three St. Jame's Street. s-a. ISSN 0029-5965

**Hunting Group**
Norwich House, 4 Dunraven St., Park Lane, London W.1, Eng.
- Hunting Group Review; shipping, oil, aviation, survey, engineering. q. ISSN 0018-7887

**Huntingdonshire Local History Society**
7 Post St., Godmanchester, Huntington, Cambs, Eng.
- Records of Huntingdonshire. s-a. ISSN 0034-1738

**Hurad Ltd.**
Christchurch, England.
- Wessex Geographical Year. a. ISSN 0083-8136

**C. Hurst and Co.**
Seager Bldg. Brookmill Rd., London SE8, England.
- Arabian Studies. a. (Cambridge University. Middle East Centre)

**Hutchinson Educational Ltd.**
3 Fitzroy Square, London W1P 6JD, England (Dist in U.S. by Humanities Press Inc., 303 Park Ave. S., New York, N.Y. 10010)
- Psychological Monographs on Cognitive Processes. irreg., 1970, vol. 2. ISSN 0079-7367

**Hyde Chemical Publishing Co. Ltd.**
44 the Keep, London SE3 OAF, England.
- Chemical Insight; Mike Hydes perspective on the international chemical industry. s-m. ISSN 0045-6403

**I B F Publications**
Alton House, Market Street, Clay Cross, Chesterfield, Derbyshire, Eng.
- British Foundryman. m. ISSN 0007-0718 (Institute of British Foundrymen)

**I P C Building and Contract Journals Ltd.**
Surrey House, 1 Throwley Way, Sutton, Surrey SM1 4QQ, England.
- Building Equipment and Materials. m.
- Community Care. (pub. by International Publishing Corp.)
- International Construction. m. ISSN 0020-6415
- Surveyor-Public Authority Technology. w.
- U K Plant Hire Guide. w. ISSN 0307-2630

**I P C Business Press Information Services Ltd.**
Neville House, Eden Street, Kingston Upon Thames KT1 1BY, Surrey, England.
- Laxton's Building Price Book. a., 147th ed. 1975.
- Official Garage Guide. irreg.

**I P C Business Press Ltd.**
33-40 Bowling Green Lane, London EC1R 0NE, England.
- Amateur Photographer. w. ISSN 0002-6840
- British Farmer and Stockbreeder. fortn. ISSN 0007-0688
- Drinks International. 6 per yr. ISSN 0012-625X
- European Chemical Buyer's Guide. a.
- European Chemical News. w. ISSN 0014-2875
- European Plastics Buyers Guide. a.
- Food Policy - Economics, Planning and Politics of Food and Agriculture. q.
- Guide to British Offshore Suppliers. a. ISSN 0306-9192
- International Optical Year Book. a.
- Local Government Chronicle. w. ISSN 0024-5534
- Manufacturing Optics International. m. ISSN 0025-2581
- Motor Cycle. w. ISSN 0027-1837
- Motor Cycle Diary. a. ISSN 0077-1589
- Nursing Mirror. w. ISSN 0029-6511
- Railway Gazette International; a journal of management, engineering and operation. m.
- Railway Magazine. m. ISSN 0033-8923
- Watchmaker, Jeweller & Silversmith. m. ISSN 0043-1079 (National Association of Goldsmiths)
- Wireless World Diary. a. ISSN 0084-0459

**I P C Consumer Industries Press Ltd.**
40 Bowling Green Lane, London E.C.1, Eng.
- C T N. (Confectioner, Tobacconist, Newsagent) w.
- Caterer & Hotelkeeper. w. ISSN 0008-7777
- Fashion Weekly. w. ISSN 0012-6039
- Food Processing Industry. m. ISSN 0015-6531
- Footwear World. m.
- Hairdressers' Journal. w. ISSN 0017-6761
- Laundry and Cleaning. fortn. ISSN 0023-8961

- Laundry & Cleaning International; the European bulletin of the fabric care industry. 6 per yr. ISSN 0023-897X
- Power Laundry & Cleaning News. fortn. ISSN 0032-6038
- Retail Chemist. w. ISSN 0034-6020
- Scottish Licensed Trade News. w. ISSN 0036-9322
- Super Marketing. w.
- Watchmaker, Jeweller and Silversmith Directory of Trade Names and Punch Marks. a. ISSN 0083-7628

**I P C Electrical-Electronic Press Ltd.**
Dorset House, Stamford St., London S.E.1, Eng.
- Computer Weekly. w. ISSN 0010-4787
- Data Processing. bi-m. ISSN 0011-684X
- E R T Price List. (Electrical and Radio Trading) 4 per yr.
- Electrical & Electronic Trader. w. ISSN 0013-418X
- Electrical and Electronic Trader Year Book. a. ISSN 0070-9638
- Electrical and Radio Trading. w. ISSN 0013-4228
- Electrical Export Review. q. ISSN 0013-4341
- Electrical Review. w. ISSN 0013-4384
- Electrical Times. w. ISSN 0013-4414
- Electricity Supply Handbook. a. ISSN 0070-976X
- Electronics Weekly. w. ISSN 0013-5224
- Hi-Fi Year Book. a. ISSN 0073-2060
- International Water Power and Dam Construction. m. ISSN 0306-400X
- Nuclear Engineering International. m. ISSN 0029-5507
- Water Power and Dam Construction. m.
- Wireless World; electronics, radio television. m. ISSN 0043-6062

**I P C Industrial Press Ltd.**
33-39 Bowling Green Lane, London EC1R ONE, England.
- Directory of Shipowners, Shipbuilders and Marine Engineers. a. ISSN 0070-6310
- Engineering Materials and Design; the magazine for engineering designers. m. ISSN 0013-8045
- European Plastics News. m.
- Industrial Equipment News. s-m. ISSN 0019-8277
- Marine Week; news journal of shipbuilding, shipping and marine equipment industries. w.
- Materials Handling News. m. ISSN 0025-5351
- Metrology and Inspection. bi-m. ISSN 0026-1408
- Motor Ship. m. ISSN 0027-2000
- Ocean Energy; industrial offshore journal. q.
- Packaging Review. m. ISSN 0048-2684
- Petroleum Times. fortn. ISSN 0031-6547
- Processing. m. ISSN 0305-439X
- World Fishing. m. ISSN 0043-8480

**I P C Magazines Ltd.**
Tower House, Southampton St., London WC2E 9QX, Eng.
- Amateur Gardening. w. ISSN 0002-6832
- Amateur Gardening Guide; an amateur gardening publication. a.
- Angler's Mail. w. ISSN 0003-3243
- Argosy. m. ISSN 0004-1114
- Country Life. w. ISSN 0045-8856
- Everyday Electronics. m.
- Flair. m. ISSN 0015-3389
- Geographical Magazine. m. ISSN 0016-741X (Royal Geographical Society)
- Hers. m. ISSN 0018-0890
- Homemaker. m. ISSN 0018-4187
- Homes and Gardens. m. ISSN 0018-4233
- Honey. m. ISSN 0018-4551
- Horse and Hound. w. ISSN 0018-5140
- Ideal Home. m. ISSN 0019-1361
- Jinty. w.
- June and Pixie. w.
- Loving. w.
- Mirabelle. w.
- Miracle Library. w. ISSN 0026-5799
- Mother. m. ISSN 0027-1500
- My Home and Family. m. ISSN 0027-5409
- New Musical Express. w. ISSN 0028-6362
- New Society. w. ISSN 0028-6729
- Once upon a Time. w. ISSN 0048-1688
- Petticoat. w. ISSN 0031-6601
- Playhour. w. ISSN 0032-1508
- Power & Sail. m.
- Practical Boat Owner. m. ISSN 0032-6348
- Practical Electronics. m. ISSN 0032-6372
- Practical Hi-Fi & Audio. m. ISSN 0306-6495
- Practical Householder. m.
- Practical Motorist. ISSN 0032-6437
- Practical Woodworking. m. ISSN 0032-6488
- Riding. m. ISSN 0035-516X
- Sewing & Knitting. m.

- Television. m. ISSN 0032-647X
- Tina. w.
- Treasure. w. ISSN 0041-2139
- Woman. w. ISSN 0043-7220
- Woman's Journal. m. ISSN 0043-7344
- Woman's Own. w. ISSN 0043-7360
- Woman's Realm. w. ISSN 0043-7387
- Woman's Weekly. w. ISSN 0043-7417
- Yachting Monthly. m. ISSN 0043-9983

**I P C Newspapers Ltd.**
Sporting Life, 9 New Fetter Lane, London EC4A 1AR, England.
- Ruff's Guide to the Turf and The Sporting Life Annual. a. ISSN 0080-4819

**I P C Science and Technology Press Ltd.**
IPC House, 32 High St., Guildford, Surrey, Eng (U.S. Address: I P C Business Press Ltd., 205 E. 42nd St., New York, NY 10017)
- Applied Ergonomics; man-machine-environment-systems technology. q. ISSN 0003-6870
- Applied Mathematical Modelling. q.
- Composites; the technology of composite materials. q. ISSN 0010-4361
- Computer Aided Design. q. ISSN 0010-4485
- Cryogenics. m. ISSN 0011-2275
- Energy Policy; the economics and planning of energy. q. ISSN 0301-4215
- Fuel; science of fuel and energy. q. ISSN 0016-2361
- Fuel Abstracts and Current Titles; a summary of world literature on all technical and scientific aspects of fuel and power. m. ISSN 0016-2388 (Institute of Fuel)
- Futures; the journal of forecasting and planning. bi-m. ISSN 0016-3287
- Iron and Steel International. 6 per yr. ISSN 0308-9142
- Microprocessors; hardware, software, applications. q.
- N D T International. bi-m. ISSN 0308-9126
- Optics and Laser Technology. q. ISSN 0030-3992
- Policy Publications Review. bi-m. ISSN 0307-4757
- Polymer; the science and technology of polymers and biopolymers. m. ISSN 0032-3861
- Resources Policy. q. ISSN 0301-4207
- Tribology International; lubrication, friction and wear. bi-m. ISSN 0301-679X
- Tropical Agriculture. q. ISSN 0041-3216 (University of the West Indies. Imperial College of Tropical Agriculture TR)
- Ultrasonics; principles and practice of ultrasonics and allied technology. bi-m. ISSN 0041-624X
- Underwater Information Bulletin. bi-m. ISSN 0302-3478
- Welding and Metal Fabrication. 10 per yr. ISSN 0043-2245

**I P C Specialist & Professional Press Ltd.**
Surrey House, 1 Throwley Way, Sutton, Surrey, England.
- Black Music. m.
- Cage & Aviary Birds. w. ISSN 0007-9561
- Cycling. w. ISSN 0011-4316
- Melody Maker. w. ISSN 0025-9012
- Rugby World. m. ISSN 0035-9777

**I P C Transport Press Ltd.**
Dorset House, Stamford St., London SE1 9LU, England.
- Aeroplane Monthly. m.
- Airports International. bi-m. ISSN 0002-2853 (International Civil Airport Association)
- Autocar. w. ISSN 0005-092X
- Commercial Motor. w. ISSN 0010-3063
- Developing Railways. a.
- Flight International. w. ISSN 0015-3710
- Freight Management. m. ISSN 0016-0873
- Historical Transport. irreg.
- International Boat Industry. bi-m. ISSN 0020-6172
- Motor Boat and Yachting. m. ISSN 0027-1780
- Motor Trader. w. ISSN 0027-2043
- Motor Trader Directory. biennial.
- Motor Transport. w. ISSN 0027-206X
- Railway Directory and Yearbook. a. ISSN 0079-9513
- Thoroughbred and Classic Cars. m.
- Travelnews. w. ISSN 0049-4577
- Yachting World. m. ISSN 0043-9991

**I. S. E. Publications Ltd.**
Concorde House, 24, Warwick New Road, Leamington Spa, Warwickshire CV32 5JH, England.
- Buyers and Buying. m. (Institution of Buyers)
- Sales Management. m. (Institute of Sales Management)

**Ice Cream Alliance**
90-94 Gray's Inn Rd, London WC1X 8AH, Eng.
- Ice Cream & Frozen Confectionery. m. ISSN 0019-106X

**Iconolatre Publications**
71 Ryehill Gardens, West Hartlepool, Durham, Eng.
- Iconolatre. q. ISSN 0019-1140

**Ileostomy Association of Great Britain & Ireland**
c/o B. Storey, Ed., 9 South Hanningfield Way, Wickford, Essex, Eng.
- I. A. Quarterly Journal. q.

**Ilford Ltd.**
Christopher Martin Rd., Basildon, Essex, England.
- X-Ray Focus. 3 per yr. ISSN 0374-4809

**Illuminating Engineering Society**
York House, Westminster Bridge Rd., London SE1 7UN, Eng.
- Light and Lighting; and environmental design. bi-m. ISSN 0024-3302
- Lighting Research and Technology. q. ISSN 0024-3426

**Illustrated County Magazine Group Ltd.**
Hogg Lane, Radcliffe-on-Trent, Nottingham, England.
- Bradford Bystander. m.
- East Anglia Life. m. ISSN 0422-0943
- Edinburgh Tatler. m. ISSN 0422-5740
- Glasgow Illustrated. m. ISSN 0017-0887
- Illustrated Bristol News. m. ISSN 0019-2392
- Leeds Graphic. m.
- Tatler & Bystander. m. ISSN 0039-9906

**Illustrated Liverpool News**
Rigby's Building, Liverpool 2, Liverpool 2, England.
- Illustrated Liverpool News. m.

**Imago Mundi Ltd.**
c/o Hary Margary, Lympne Castle, Kent, England.
- Imago Mvndi; a review of early cartography. irreg. (approx. 2 per yr) (Calouste Gulbenkian Foundation PO)

**Immedia Ltd.**
2 Salisbury Court, Fleet St., London EC4Y 8AB, Eng.
- Your Home & Freezer. q.

**Impact**
33 Stroud Green Rd., London N4 3EF, Eng.
- Impact; international fortnightly. s-m. ISSN 0046-8703

**Imperial Cancer Research Fund**
Lincoln's Inn Fields, London, WC2A 3PX, England.
- Imperial Cancer Research Fund. Scientific Report. a.
- Research Using Transplanted Tumours of Laboratory Animals: A Cross Referenced Bibliography. a. ISSN 0080-1747

**Imperial Chemical Industries Ltd. Plant Protection Division**
Jealott's Hill Research Station, Bracknell, Berks RG12 6EY, Eng.
- Outlook on Agriculture. 3 per yr. ISSN 0030-7270

**Imperial Society of Teachers of Dancing**
70 Gloucester Place, London W1H 4AJ, England.
- Dance. bi-m.

**Imperial Tobacco Ltd.**
Research Dept. Library, Raleigh Rd., Bristol BS3 1QX, England.
- Tobacco Bibliography. s-m. ISSN 0563-6140

**Imperial War Museum**
Department of Printed Books, Lambeth Rd., London S.E.1, England.
- Imperial War Museum, London. Department of Printed Books. Accessions List. m.

**IMSWORLD Publications Ltd.**
York House, 37 Queen Square, London WC1N 3BN, England.
- IMS Monitor Report. q.

- IMS Pharmaceutical Marketletter. w. (I M S International Inc. (New York) US)
- New Product Card Index. s-m.
- World Directory of Pharmaceutical Manufacturers. irreg.
- World Pharmaceutical Introductions. q.

**In Particular**
97 Holywell St., Oxford, Eng.
- In Particular. 2-3 per yr. ISSN 0019-3216

**Incept**
c/o Eric Harrison, Ed., 3 Grantley Close, Shalford, Surrey, England.
- Incept. s-a.

**Incomes Data Services Ltd.**
140 Great Portland St., London W.1, Eng.
- Incomes Data Report. s-m. ISSN 0019-3461

**Incorporated Association of Architects & Surveyors**
24 Half Moon St., London W1Y 8BT, Eng.
- Architect & Surveyor. q. ISSN 0003-8431

**Incorporated Association of Architects and Surveyors. Fire Surveyors Section**
- Fire Surveyor. (pub. by Victor Green Publications Ltd.)

**Incorporated Association of Organists**
Kennedy Tower, St. Chad's Queensway, Birmingham B4 6JG, Eng.
- Organists Review. q. ISSN 0048-2161

**Incorporated Association of Preparatory Schools**
- Preparatory Schools Review. (pub. by Heffers Printers Ltd.)

**Incorporated British Institute of Certified Carpenters**
118 Elm Rd., Earley, Nr. Reading, Berks, Eng.
- Incorporated British Institute of Certified Carpenters. Journal. q. ISSN 0019-350X

**Incorporated Council of Law Reporting for England and Wales**
3 Stone Bldgs., Lincoln's Inn, London WC2A 3XN, England.
- Industrial Cases Reports. m.
- Law Reports. m. ISSN 0023-9348
- Weekly Law Reports. w. ISSN 0019-3518

**Incorporated Law Society**
- Incorporated Law Society of Northern Ireland. Gazette. (pub. by Royal Courts of Justice (Ulster))

**Incorporated Practitioners in Radio & Electronics**
32 Kidmore Rd., Caversham, Reading RG4 7LU, Eng.
- I. P. R. E. Review. 3 per yr.

**Incorporated Society of Musicians**
48 Gloucester Place, London W1H 3HJ, England.
- Incorporated Society of Musicians Handbook & Register of Members. biennial.

**Incorporated Society of Organ Builders**
P.O. Box 1, Ruislip, Middlesex HA4 0XS, England.
- Incorporated Society of Organ Builders. Journal. irreg. ISSN 0073-5744

**Incorporated Society of Valuers & Auctioneers**
3 Cadogan Gate, London S.W. 1X 0AS, Eng.
- Valuer. 10 per yr. ISSN 0042-2428

**Ind Coope Hotels (Allied Breweries Ltd.)**
The Brewery, Station St., Burton-on-Trent, Staffs. DE14 1BZ, Eng.
- Guest and Host. q. ISSN 0046-6565

**Indcom Publications Ltd.**
Faversham House, 111 St. James's Rd., Croydon, Surrey CR2 7TH, Eng.
- Hardware Review. m. ISSN 0017-7733

**Independent Broadcasting Authority**
70 Brompton Rd., London SW3 1EY, England
- Guide to Independent Television and Independent Local Radio. a. (Dist. by: Independent Television Publications, 247 Tottenham Court Rd., London W1P 0AU, England)
- I B A Technical Review. irreg., no. 9, 1977. ISSN 0308-423X
- Independent Broadcasting. q. ISSN 0305-6104
- Independent Broadcasting Authority. Annual Report and Accounts. a.

**Independent Magazines Ltd.**
181 Queen Victoria St., London, EC4V 4DD, Eng.
- Art & Antiques Weekly. w. ISSN 0004-2978
- Films Illustrated. m.
- Horse World: Pony Express. m. ISSN 0018-5183 (Association of British Riding Schools)

**Independent Order of Odd Fellows**
Manchester Unity Friendly Society, 40 Fountain St, Manchester M2 2AB, Eng.
- Odd Fellow. m. ISSN 0048-1408

**Independent Order of Rechabites**
Rechabite Bldgs., 1 North Parade, Deansgate, Manchester 3, England.
- Rechabite. q. ISSN 0034-1215

**Independent Schools Association Inc**
Max Gate, BurghHill, Etchingham, Sussex TN19 7PF, Eng.
- Independent School. every 4 mos. ISSN 0019-3747

**Independent Schools Careers Organization**
12a-18a Princess Way, Camberely, Surrey GU15 3SP, England.
- Temporary Occupations and Employment. biennial, 3rd ed. 1974.

**Independent Television Publications Ltd.**
247 Tottenham Court Road, London W1P 0AU, England.
- Look-in. w.
- T V Times. w. ISSN 0039-8624

**India Office Library and Records**
197 Blackfriars Rd., London SE1 8NG, England.
- India Office Library and Records Newsletter. irreg.

**Indochina Solidarity Conference**
101 Gower St., London W.C.1, Eng.
- Indochina. 4-5 per yr.

**Industrial and Professional Careers Research Association Ltd.**
Gillow House, 5 Winsley Street, London, W1N 8AP, England.
- Directory of British Recruitment Services. biennial. ISSN 0070-5160

**Industrial Christian Fellowship**
St. Katherine Cree Church, Leadenhall St., London E.C.3, Eng.
- I. C. F. Quarterly. q. ISSN 0018-8913

**Industrial Diamond Information Bureau**
Charters, Sunninghill, Ascot, Berks. SL5 9PX, England.
- Diamond Research. irreg.(usually annual) ISSN 0070-4679
- Industrial Diamond Buyers Guide. irreg. ISSN 0446-0448

**Industrial Locomotive Society**
Channings Kettlewell Hill, Woking, Surrey, Eng.
- Industrial Locomotive. q.

**Industrial Marketing Research Association**
Room 11-18, Portland House, Stage Place, London S.W. 1, Eng
(Subscr. to: 198 Ashenhurst Rd., Dudley, Worcestershire, Eng.)
- Industrial Marketing Research Association.I M R A Journal. q. ISSN 0019-0039

**Industrial Newspapers Ltd.**
2 Queensway, Redhill, Surrey RH1 1QS, England.
- International Conference on Hot Dip Galvanizing. Proceedings. triennial; 9th, Duesseldorf, 1970. ISSN 0074-3119 (Zinc Development Association)
- Merseyside Chamber of Commerce and Industry. Directory. irreg.
- Where to Buy. a. ISSN 0083-9175

**Industrial Opportunities Ltd.**
13-14 Homewell, Havant, Hants, England.
- Research Disclosure. m.

**Industrial Participation Association**
25/28 Buckingham Gate, London SW1E 6LP, Eng.
- Industrial Participation. 3 per yr.

**Industrial Policy Group**
21 Tothill St., London SW01, England.
- Industrial Policy Group. Papers. irreg.

**Industrial Review of Great Britain**
c/o W. Parr, Rex Bldgs., Alderly Rd., Wilmslow, Cheshire SK9 1H2, England.
- Industrial Review of Great Britain. bi-m.

**Industrial Reviews**
109A High St., Winchester, Hampshire, Eng.
- Cutting Tools. bi-m. ISSN 0011-4197

**Industrial Society**
Box 1BQ, 48 Bryanston Sq., London W1H 1BQ, Eng.
- Industrial Society. bi-m. ISSN 0019-8781
- Industrial Society. Handbook and Diary. a.

**Information Centre on High Temperature Processes**
Department of Fuel Science, Leeds University, Leeds LS2 9T, Eng.
- High Temperature Bulletin. bi-m.

**Information for Education Ltd.**
19 Abercromby Square, Liverpool L69 3BX, Eng.
- Sociology of Education Abstracts. q. ISSN 0038-0415

**Information Retrieval Ltd.**
1 Falconberg Court, London W1V 5FG, Eng
(U.S. Address: Information Retrieval Inc., Suite 907, 1911 Jefferson Davis Highway, Arlington, VA 22202)
- Amino Acids, Peptide & Protein Abstracts. m. ISSN 0044-8125
- Animal Behaviour Abstracts. q. (Association for the Study of Animal Behaviour)
- Applied Ecology Abstracts; studies in renewable natural resources. m.
- Aquatic Sciences & Fisheries Abstracts. m. ISSN 0044-8516
- Biological Membrane Abstracts. m. ISSN 0300-5763
- Calcified Tissue Abstracts. m. ISSN 0008-0586
- Chemical Senses and Flavor; a journal devoted to the chemical senses and to sensory evaluation of the gustatory, olfactory, factile and visual properties of materials. q.
- Chemoreception Abstracts; chemical senses & applied techniques. q. ISSN 0300-1261 (European Chemoreception Organization)
- Entomology Abstracts. m. ISSN 0013-8924
- Feeding-Weight and Obesity Abstracts. m. ISSN 0308-2997
- Footwear and Leather Abstracts. m. ISSN 0532-1042
- Genetics Abstracts. m. ISSN 0016-674X
- Immunology Abstracts. m. ISSN 0307-112X
- Microbiology Abstracts. Section A. Industrial & Applied Microbiology. m. ISSN 0300-838X
- Microbiology Abstracts. Section B. Bacteriology. ISSN 0300-8398
- Microbiology Abstracts. Section C. Algology, Mycology & Protozoology. m. ISSN 0301-2328
- Nucleic Acids Abstracts. m. ISSN 0048-1041
- Nucleic Acids Research. m. ISSN 0301-5610
- Oncology Abstracts; experimental and clinical studies. m. ISSN 0308-7980
- Virology Abstracts. m. ISSN 0042-6830

**Inherited**
Ed. Peter Hoida, 88 Ladbroke Grove, London, W11, Eng.
- Inherited. q. ISSN 0020-1332

**Inkululeko Publications**
39 Goodge St., London W1P 1FD, Eng
(U.S. address: Imported Publications Inc., 320 West Ohio St., Chicago, IL 60610)
- African Communist. q. ISSN 0001-9976 (South African Communist Party)

**Inner London Education Authority**
1-4 King St., London WC2E 8HN, England.
- Floodlight; I L E A guide to evening classes. a.
- I L E A Contact. w. ISSN 0306-1981

**Inner London Teachers' Association (N.U.T.)**
Hamilton House, Mabledon Place, London WC1H 9BD, England.
- Centre Point; the London Teacher (1883) 3 per yr. ISSN 0577-1935

**Inquirer Publishing Co. Ltd.**
1-6 Essex St., London W.C.2, Eng.
- Inquirer. fortn. ISSN 0020-1723

**Insight Magazine Club**
c/o Deric Robert James, Ed., 118 Windham Rd., Bournemouth, Dorset, Eng.
- Insight; journal of the occult. q. ISSN 0020-1987

**INSPEC Institution of Electrical Engineers**
Savoy Place, London WC2R 0BL, England.
- Key Abstracts - Communications Technology. m. ISSN 0306-5588
- Key Abstracts - Electrical Measurements and Instrumentation. m.
- Key Abstracts - Electronic Circuits. m. ISSN 0306-557X
- Key Abstracts - Industrial Power & Control Systems. m. ISSN 0306-5596
- Key Abstracts - Physical Measurements and Instrumentation. m.
- Key Abstracts - Power Transmission & Distribution. m. ISSN 0306-5561
- Key Abstracts - Solid State Devices. m. ISSN 0306-5537
- Key Abstracts - Systems Theory. m. ISSN 0306-5553

**Institute for African Studies**
- Zambian Papers. (pub. by Manchester University Press)

**Institute for Clay Technology**
- EuroClay. (pub. by London and Sheffield Publishing Co. Ltd.)

**Institute for Fiscal Studies**
62 Chandos Place, London WC2N 4HG, England.
- Impact of Tax Changes on Income Distribution. a.

**Institute for International Research**
150 Regent St., London W.1, England
(U.S. Address: 30 E. 42nd St., New York, NY 10017)
- European and Middle East Tax Report; the executive's report on new tax opportunities. fortn.
- International Accounting and Financial Report. fortn.
- London Gold and Commodity Report. (pub. by Advisory Information Services Ltd.)

**Institute for Marine Environmental Research**
Oceanographic Laboratory, 78 Craighall Road, Edinburgh EH6 4RQ, Scotland.
- Bulletins of Marine Ecology. irreg., vol. 8, pt. 3, 1975. ISSN 0068-4198 (Natural Environmental Research Council)

**Institute for the Study and Treatment of Delinquency**
- British Journal of Criminology. (pub. by Sweet & Maxwell Stevens Journals)

**Institute for the Study of Conflict**
17 Northumberland Ave., London WC2N 5BJ, England.
- Annual Power and Conflict. a. (Co-sponsor: National Strategy Information Center, New York)
- Conflict Studies. m. ISSN 0069-8792

**Institute for the Study of Drug Dependence**
Kingsbury House, 3 Blackburn Rd, London NW6 1XA, England.
- Druglink. q. ISSN 0305-4349

**Institute for Workers Control**
Bertrand Russell House, 45 Gamble St., West Nottingham NG7 4ET, England.
- Archives in Trade Union History and Theory Series. irreg. ISSN 0066-6599
- Workers' Control Bulletin. m.

**Institute of Accident Surgery**
- Injury. (pub. by John Wright & Sons Ltd.)

**Institute of Acoustics**
- Journal of Sound and Vibration. (pub. by Academic Press Inc. (London) Ltd.)

**Institute of Actuaries**
Staple Inn Hall, High Holborn, London, WC1V 7QJ, England.
- Institute of Actuaries. Year Book. a. ISSN 0073-8980

**Institute of Administrative Accounting**
418-422 Strand, London W.C.2, Eng.
- Administrative Accounting. q.

**Institute of Advanced Legal Studies**
17 Russell Square, London WC1B 5DR, Eng
(U.S. subscr. to: American Association of Law Libraries, 53 West Jackson Blvd., Suite 1201, Chicago, IL 60604)
- Index to Foreign Legal Periodicals. q(annual and three-year cumulations) ISSN 0019-400X (American Association of Law Libraries US)

**Institute of Advanced Motorists**
- Milestones. (pub. by Advanced Mile-Posts Publications Ltd.)

**Institute of Agricultural Economics**
Dartington House, Little Clarendon Street, Oxford, 0X1 2HP, England.
- International Conference of Agricultural Economists. Proceedings. triennial; 16th 1976, nairobi. ISSN 0074-2902 (International Association of Agricultural Economists)

**Institute of Animal Technicians**
- Institute of Animal Technicians. Journal. (pub. by Abbey Press)

**Institute of Arbitrators**
75 Cannon St., London EC4N 5BH, Eng.
- Arbitration. q. ISSN 0003-7877

**Institute of Army Education. Foreign Language Section**
Eltham, London SE9 5NR, England
(or Defense Language Institute, Presidio of Monterey, CA)
- B I L C Bulletin. irreg.; latest issue, 1974. ISSN 0525-2083 (Bureau for International Language Coordination) (Co-Sponsors: UK Ministry of Defence; Germany (Federal) Republic. Bundessprachenamt)

**Institute of Bankers**
10 Lombard St., London EC3V 9AS, Eng.
- Institute of Bankers. Journal. bi-m. ISSN 0020-2738

**Institute of Bankers in Scotland**
- Scottish Bankers Magazine. (pub. by William Blackwood & Sons Ltd.)

**Institute of Baths Management**
256A Green Lanes, Palmers Green, London N.13, Eng.
- Baths Service. m. ISSN 0005-626X

**Institute of Biology**
41 Queen's Gate, London SW7 5HU, Eng.
- Biologist. q. ISSN 0006-3347
- Journal of Biological Education. bi-m. ISSN 0021-9266

**Institute of Biology. Committee on Biological Information**
41 Queen's Gate, London S.W. 7, England.
- C O B I Newsletter. irreg., no. 3, 1977. ISSN 0307-6407

**Institute of Brewing**
33 Clarges St, London W1Y 8EE, Eng.
- Institute of Brewing, London. Journal. bi-m. ISSN 0046-9750

**Institute of British Carriage and Automobile Manufacturers**
Thames Meadow, 59 Henley Rd., Shillingford 0X9 8EZ, England.
- I B C A M Journal. m.

**Institute of British Foundrymen**
- British Foundryman. (pub. by I B F Publications)

**Institute of British Geographers**
1 Kensington Gore, London SW7 2AR, Eng.
- Area. q. ISSN 0004-0894
- Institute of British Geographers. Special Publication. a. ISSN 0073-9006
- Institute of British Geographers. Transactions. 4 per yr. ISSN 0020-2754

**Institute of Building**
Englemere, Kings Ride, Ascot, Berkshire SL5 8BJ, England.
- Building Management Abstracts. 6 per yr. ISSN 0308-9665
- Building Technology and Management. m. ISSN 0007-3709
- Institute of Building. Estimating Information Service. q. ISSN 0308-8073
- Institute of Building. Site Management Information Service. q. ISSN 0308-8081
- Institute of Building. Year Book and Directory of Members. a. ISSN 0073-9014

**Institute of Burial & Cremation Administration Inc**
Chesterfield & District Crematorium, Brimington, Chesterfield, Derbyshire, Eng.
- Institute of Burial and Cremation Administration. Journal. q. ISSN 0020-2762

**Institute of Certified Ambulance Personnel**
c/o F. Thornley, 64 Pen-y-fro, Dunvant, Wales.
- Ambulance Service Journal; a professional journal for ambulance and first aid personnel. q.

**Institute of Chartered Accountants in England and Wales**
Moorgate Place, London EC2R 6EQ, Eng.
- Accountancy. m. ISSN 0001-4664
- Accounting and Business Research. q. ISSN 0001-4788
- Accounting & Data Processing Abstracts. (pub. by Anbar Publications Ltd.)
- Institute of Chartered Accountants in England and Wales. Management Information Series. irreg. ISSN 0073-9030
- Institute of Chartered Accountants in England and Wales. Practice Administration Series, Exposure Drafts and Statements of Standard Accounting Practice. irreg. ISSN 0073-9049

**Institute of Chartered Accountants of Scotland**
27 Queen Street, Edinburgh, EH2 1LA, Scotland.
- Accountant's Magazine. (pub. by Accountants' Publishing Co. Ltd.)
- Institute of Chartered Accountants of Scotland. Official Directory. a. ISSN 0073-9057

**Institute of Chiropodists**
59 Gloucester Place, London W1H 3PE, Eng.
- Chiropody Review. m. ISSN 0009-4714

**Institute of Civil Defence**
Box No. 229, 3 Little Montague Court, London EC1P 1HN, Eng.
- Institute of Civil Defence. Journal. q. ISSN 0020-2770

**Institute of Commerce**
1, Lincoln's Inn Fields, London, W.C.2, Eng.
- Institute of Commerce, London. Magazine. q. ISSN 0046-9793

**Institute of Commonwealth Studies**
- Journal of Commonwealth & Comparative Politics. (pub. by Frank Cass & Co. Ltd.)

**Institute of Contemporary Arts**
12 Carlton House Terrace, London S.W.1, Eng.
- I C A S M. m.

**Institute of Cost and Management Accountants**
63 Portland Place, London W1N 4AB, Eng.
- Management Accounting. m. ISSN 0025-1682

**Institute of Craft Education**
23 Brinkburn Drive, Darlington, Co. Durham, England.
- Practical Education and School Crafts. m. ISSN 0048-5071

**Institute of Credit Management**
12 Queen Square, Brighton BN1 3FD, Eng.
- Credit Management. q.

**Institute of Data Processing**
418-422 Strand, London W.C.2, Eng.
- Data Processing Practitioner. q. ISSN 0011-6882

**Institute of Directors**
10 Belgrave Square, London S.W.1, Eng.
- Director. m. ISSN 0012-3242

**Institute of Directors. Manchester Branch**
276-282 the Corn Exchange, Fennel Street, Manchester M4 3HF, England.
- Manchester Director. q.

**Institute of Domestic Heating Engineers**
29 Old Bond St., London W1X 4LJ, Eng.
- Domestic Heating Engineer. bi-m. ISSN 0046-0540

**Institute of Economic Affairs**
2 Lord North St., London SW1P 3LB, England
(Dist. in North America by: Transatlantic Arts, Inc., N. Village Green, Levittown, NY 11756)
- Hobart Paperbacks; studies in the translation of economic ideas into practical policy and the economics of government. irreg. ISSN 0309-1783
- Hobart Papers. irreg. ISSN 0073-2818
- Institute of Economic Affairs. Occasional Papers. irreg. ISSN 0073-909X
- Institute of Economic Affairs. Research Monographs. irreg. ISSN 0073-9103
- Reading in Political Economy. irreg., no. 16, 1977. ISSN 0305-814X

**Institute of Electrolysis**
251 Seymour Grove, Manchester M16 ODS, Lancs, England.
- Institute of Electrolysis. List of Qualified Operators. a.

**Institute of Engineers and Technicians**
11-12 Barry Parade, London, Se22 0JA, Eng.
- Institute of Engineers & Technicians Journal. q.

**Institute of Export**
- Export. (pub. by Gateway Publications)

**Institute of Factory Management**
- Industrial Management. (pub. by Embankment Press Ltd.)

**Institute of Fisheries Management**
Dorset Press, 23 High East Street, Dorcheser DT1 1HD, England.
- Fisheries Management. q.

**Institute of Food Science and Technology of the United Kingdom**
- Journal of Food Technology. (pub. by Blackwell Scientific Publications Ltd.)

**Institute of Foresters of Great Britain**
- Forestry. (pub. by Oxford University Press)

**Institute of Freight Forwarders Ltd.**
Suffield House, 9 Paradise Rd., Richmond, Surrey, TW9 1SA, Eng.
- Freight Forwarder. bi-m. ISSN 0046-5046

**Institute of Fuel**
18 Devonshire Street, London W1N 2AU, England.
- Energy World. m.
- Fuel Abstracts and Current Titles. (pub. by I P C Science and Technology Press Ltd.)
- Institute of Fuel. Journal. q. ISSN 0020-2886
- Institute of Fuel. Papers of the National Convention. a.
- Institute of Fuel. Symposium Series. irreg.

**Institute of Fuel. British Flame Research Committee**
18 Devonshire St., London W1N 2AU, England.
- Symposium on Flames and Industry. Proceedings. irreg.

**Institute of Fuel. Northern Ireland Section**
3 Clarence St. W., Belfast, N. Ireland.
- Institute of Fuel. Northern Ireland Section. Year Book. a.

**Institute of Groundsmanship**
- Groundsman. (pub. by Adam Publishing Ltd.)

**Institute of Group Analysis**
1 Bickenhall Mansions, Bickenhall St., London W1H 3LF, England.
- Group Analysis: International Panel and Correspondence. 3 per yr. ISSN 0533-3164

**Institute of Health Education**
35 Victoria Road, Sheffield, South Yorkshire S10 2DJ, England.
- Institute of Health Education. Journal. q.

**Institute of Health Service Administrators**
75 Portland Place, London WIN 4AN, Eng.
- Hospital and Health Service Purchasing; guide to equipment and supplies. m. ISSN 0300-5461
- Hospital and Health Services Review. m.
- Hospitals & Health Services Year Book and Directory of Hospital Suppliers. a. ISSN 0073-3474

**Institute of Heraldic and Genealogical Studies**
Northgate, Canterbury, Kent, Eng.
- Family History. 6 per yr. ISSN 0014-7265

**Institute of Historical Research**
University of London, London WC1E 7HU, England
(Dist. in U.S. by: Humanities Press Inc., 171 First Ave., Atlantic Highlands, NJ 07716)
- Guides to Materials for West African History in European Archives. irreg., 1973, no. 5. ISSN 0072-8942

**Institute of Hospital Engineering**
- Hospital Engineering. (pub. by Earlsport Ltd.)

**Institute of Housing**
c/o Henry Key, Victoria House, Southampton Row, London WLIB 4EB, England.
- Housing Monthly. m.

**Institute of Incorporated Photographers**
87 High Holborn, London WC1, Eng.
- Photographer. m. ISSN 0031-8698

**Institute of Information Scientists**
Top Flat, 19 Anson Rd., Kentish Town, London N.7, England.
- Information Scientist. q. ISSN 0020-0263

**Institute of Jewish Affairs**
13-16 Jacob's Well Mews, George St., London W1H 5PD, Eng.
- Christian Attitudes on Jews and Judaism. 6 per yr. ISSN 0009-5249
- Patterns of Prejudice. 6 per yr. ISSN 0031-322X
- Soviet Jewish Affairs, a Journal on Jewish Problems in the USSR and Eastern Europe. s-a. ISSN 0038-545X (Co-Sponsor: World Jewish Congress)

**Institute of Jewish Studies**
University College, Gower St, London WC1E 6BT, Eng.
- Institute of Jewish Studies. Bulletin.

**Institute of Legal Executives**
Ilex House, Barrhill Rd., London SW2 4RW, Eng.
- Legal Executive. bi-m. ISSN 0024-0362

**Institute of Linguists**
24a Highbury Grove, London N5, England.
- Incorporated Linguist. q. ISSN 0019-3534

**Institute of Local Government Administrators**
127 Lexden Rd., Colchester, Essex CO3 3RJ, England.
- L G A; the journal of the Institute of Local Government Administrators. 6 per yr.

**Institute of Local Government Studies**
Box 363, University of Birmingham, Birmingham B15 2TT, England.
- Corporate Planning; a review of corporate planning and management in local government. 3 per yr. ISSN 0305-3695
- Local Government Studies. 4 per yr. ISSN 0300-3930

**Institute of Manpower Studies**
- I M S Monitor. (pub. by Chapman and Hall Ltd.)

**Institute of Marine Engineers**
- Institute of Marine Engineers Technical Reports. (pub. by Marine Media Management Ltd.)
- Marine Engineers Review. (pub. by Marine Media Management Ltd.)

**Institute of Market Officers**
Markets Dept., The Abattoir, Cricket Inn Road, Sheffield S2 5BD, England.
- Institute of Market Officers. List of Members and Proceedings of the Annual General Meetings. a.

**Institute of Marketing**
- Marketing. (pub. by Haymarket Publishing Ltd.)
- Marketing & Distribution Abstracts. (pub. by Anbar Publications Ltd)
- Quarterly Review of Marketing. (pub. by Marketing House Publishers Ltd)

**Institute of Materials Handling**
- Materials Handling and Management. (pub. by Temprint Press Ltd.)

**Institute of Mathematics and its Applications**
Maitland House, Warrior Sq., Southend-on-Sea, Essex SS1 2JY, England.
- Institute of Mathematics and Its Application. Journal. (pub. by Academic Press Inc. (London) Ltd.)
- Institute of Mathematics and its Applications. Bulletin. m.

**Institute of Measurement and Control**
20 Peel St., London W8 7PD, Eng.
- Measurement and Control. m. ISSN 0020-2940

**Institute of Mechanical Engineers**
1 Birdcage Walk, London SW1H 9JJ, England.
- Automotive Engineer. (pub. by Mechanical Engineering Publications, Ltd.)
- Railway Engineer. bi-m.

**Institute of Medical & Biological Illustration**
- Medical and Biological Illustration. (pub. by Longman Group Ltd.)

**Institute of Medical Laboratory Sciences**
12 Queen Anne St., London W1M 0AU, Eng.
- Institute of Medical Laboratory Sciences. Gazette. m. ISSN 0307-5656
- Institute of Medical Laboratory Sciences. London, Annual Report. a.

**Institute of Medical Laboratory Technology**
- Medical Laboratory Sciences. (pub. by Academic Press Inc. (London) Ltd.)

**Institute of Metal Finishing**
178 Goswell Rd., London EC1V 7DU, Eng.
- Institute of Metal Finishing. Transactions. q. ISSN 0020-2967

**Institute of Naval Medicine**
Alverstoke PO12 2DL, Eng.
- Royal Naval Medical Service. Journal. 3 per yr. ISSN 0035-9033

**Institute of Oceanographic Sciences**
Wormley, Godalming, Surrey GU8 5UB, England.
- Discovery Reports. irreg. ISSN 0070-6698
- Institute of Oceanographic Sciences. Collected Reprints. a.

**Institute of Operation Theatre Technicians**
- Technic. (pub. by Newton Mann Ltd.)

**Institute of Ophthalmology**
Judd St., London WC1H 9QS, Eng.
- Ophthalmic Literature. 6 per yr. ISSN 0030-3720

**Institute of Park and Recreation Administration**
- Parks and Recreation. (pub. by Journal of Park Administration Ltd.)

**Institute of Patentees and Inventors**
Whiteley Building, 165 Queensway, London W2 4SB, England.
- Inventor. q. ISSN 0579-8388

**Institute of Personnel Management**
Central House, Upper Woburn Place, London WC1H 0 HX, Eng.
- I P M Digest. m. ISSN 0019-0330
- Personnel & Training Abstracts. (pub. by Anbar Publications Ltd.)
- Personnel Review. (pub. by Teakfield Ltd.)

**Institute of Petroleum**
61 New Cavendish St., London W1M 8AR, England.
- Institute of Petroleum Standards for Petroleum and Its Products. Part 1: Methods for Analysis and Testing. (pub. by Applied Science Publishers Ltd.)
- Oil World Statistics.
- Petroleum Review. m. ISSN 0020-3076

**Institute of Pharmacy Management International**
- Pharmacy Management. (pub. by Pharmaceutical Business Analysis Service)

**Institute of Physics.**
47 Belgrave Square, London SW1X 8QX, Bristol BS1 6NX, England
(U.S.Address: American Institute of Physics, Dept. N/M, 335 E. 45th St., New York, NY 10017)
- Institute of Physics, London. Conference Booklet. irreg (1-2 per year) ISSN 0085-1906
- Institute of Physics, London. Conference Series. Proceedings. irreg., no. 34, 1977.
- Journal of Physics A: Mathematical and General. m. ISSN 0305-4470
- Journal of Physics B: Atomic and Molecular Physics. 24 per yr. ISSN 0022-3700
- Journal of Physics C: Solid State Physics. 24 per yr. ISSN 0022-3719
- Journal of Physics D: Applied Physics. 18 per yr. ISSN 0022-3727
- Journal of Physics E: Scientific Instruments. m. ISSN 0022-3735
- Journal of Physics F: Metal Physics. m. ISSN 0305-4608 (Co-sponsors: Metals Society; Institution of Metallurgists; American Institute of Physics)
- Journal of Physics G: Nuclear Physics. 12 per yr. ISSN 0305-4616
- Physics Bulletin. m. ISSN 0031-9112
- Physics Education. 7 per yr. ISSN 0031-9120
- Physics in Medicine and Biology. bi-m. ISSN 0031-9155 (American Association of Physicists in Medicine US) (Co-sponsors: Canadian Assn. of Physicists; Hospital Physicists' Assn.)
- Physics in Technology. 6 per yr. ISSN 0305-4624

- Reports on Progress in Physics. m. ISSN 0034-4885
- Research Fields in Physics at United Kingdom Universities and Polytechnics. (pub. by Physics Trust Publications)

**Institute of Plumbing**
Scottish Mutual House, North St., Hornchurch, Essex RM11 1RU, Eng.
- Plumbing. q. ISSN 0032-1656

**Institute of Practitioners in Work Study, Organization and Methods**
9-10 River Front, Enfield, Middlesex, England.
- Management Services. m.
- Work Study & O and M Abstracts. (pub. by Anbar Publications Ltd.)

**Institute of Printing**
10/11 Bedford Row, London WC1R 4DZ, Eng.
- Professional Printer. bi-m. ISSN 0032-8685

**Institute of Psycho-Analysis**
- International Psycho-Analytical Library. (pub. by Hogarth Press Ltd.)
- International Review of Psycho-Analysis. (pub. by Bailliere Tindall)

**Institute of Psychophysical Research**
- Institute of Psychophysical Research. Proceedings. (pub. by Hamish Hamilton Ltd.)

**Institute of Public Relations**
1 Great James St., London W.C.1, Eng.
- Communicator. m. ISSN 0307-9252

**Institute of Purchasing and Supply**
Westminster Bridge Road, London SE1 7UT, England.
- Institute of Purchasing and Supply. Yearbook. a. ISSN 0073-9650
- Procurement Weekly. w.
- Purchasing and Supply. m.

**Institute of Quality Assurance**
146 Cromwell Rd., Kensington, London SW7 4EF, Eng.
- Quality Assurance. q. ISSN 0306-2856

**Institute of Quantity Surveyors**
98 Gloucester Place, London W.1, England.
- Institute of Quantity Surveyors. Year Book. biennial. ISSN 0073-9669

**Institute of Quarrying**
- Quarry Management and Products. (pub. by Quarry Managers' Journal Ltd.)

**Institute of Race Relations**
247 Pentonville Rd., London N. 1, England.
- Race and Class. q.

**Institute of Refrigeration**
272 London Road, Wallington, Surrey, England.
- Institute of Refrigeration, London. Proceedings. a. ISSN 0073-9677

**Institute of Registered Architects**
Faculty of Architects and Surveyors, 68 Gloucester Place, London W1H 3HL, Eng.
- Portico. q. ISSN 0032-4914

**Institute of Road Transport Engineers**
- Transport Engineer. (pub. by Embankment Press Ltd.)

**Institute of Rural Life at Home and Overseas**
27 Northumberland Rd., New Barnet, Herts, Eng.
- Rural Life. q. ISSN 0036-0074

**Institute of Sales Management**
- Sales Management. (pub. by I. S. E. Publications Ltd.)

**Institute of Science Technology**
66 Leggart Terrace, Aberdeen, Scotland.
- Institute of Science Technology. Bulletin. m. ISSN 0020-3130

**Institute of Scientific and Technical Communicators Ltd.**
17 Bluebridge Ave., Brookmans Pk., Hatfield AL9 7RY, England.
- Communication News. 8 per yr.
- Communicator of Scientific and Technical Information. q. ISSN 0308-6925

**Institute of Small Business**
- Business Ideas Letter. (pub. by Lorne, Caldough Ltd.)

**Institute of Social Anthropology**
51 Banbury Rd., Oxford, Eng.
- Anthropological Society of Oxford. Journal. 3 per yr. ISSN 0044-8370

**Institute of Solid Wastes Management**
28 Portland Place, London W.1, Eng.
- Solid Wastes. m. ISSN 0306-6509

**Institute of Statisticians**
- Statistician. (pub. by Longman Group Ltd.)

**Institute of Supervisory Management**
22 Bore St., Lichfield, Staffs WS13 6LP, Eng.
- Supervisory Management. 4 per yr.

**Institute of the Motor Industry, Inc.**
Fanshaws, Brickendon, Hertford, Eng.
- Motor Management. bi-m. ISSN 0020-2746

**Institute of Trading Standards Administration**
Estate House, 319d London Rd., Hadleigh, Benfleet, Essex SS7 2bn, Eng.
- Institute of Trading Standards Administration Monthly Review. m. ISSN 0302-3249

**Institute of Vitreous Enamellers**
Ripley, Nr. Derby DE 5 3EB, Eng.
- Vitreous Enameller. q. ISSN 0042-7519

**Institute of Water Pollution Control**
53 London Rd., Maidstone ME16 8JH, Kent, England.
- I W P C Newsletter. irreg. ISSN 0308-9444
- Water Pollution Control. q. ISSN 0043-129X

**Institute of Welfare Officers**
- Welfare Officer. (pub. by Marylebone Press Ltd.)

**Institute of Wood Science**
62 Oxford St., London, W.1, Eng.
- Institute of Wood Science. Journal. 2 per yr. ISSN 0020-3203

**Institution of Agricultural Engineers**
West End Rd., Silsoe, Bedford MK45 4DU, England.
- Agricultural Engineer. q. ISSN 0308-5732

**Institution of Buyers**
- Buyers and Buying. (pub. by I. S. E. Publications Ltd.)

**Institution of Chemical Engineers**
165-171 Railway Terrace, Rugby CV21 3HQ, England.
- Chemical Engineer and Transactions of the Institution of Chemical Engineers. m. ISSN 0009-2452
- European Federation of Chemical Engineering. Proceedings of Congress. irreg.; latest edt., 1974. ISSN 0071-2760 (Avail. from: European Federation of Chemical Engineering, Theodor Heuss-Allee 25, 6 Frankfurt/Main, W. Germany (B.R.D.))
- Institution of Chemical Engineers. Diary. m. ISSN 0020-3246
- Institution of Chemical Engineers. Transactions. q. ISSN 0046-9858

**Institution of Civil Engineers**
Publications Division, 26-34 Old St., London EC1V 9AD, England.
- British National Committee on Large Dams. New and Views. (pub. by Thomas Telford Ltd.)
- British Nuclear Energy Society. Journal. (pub. by Thomas Telford Ltd.)
- Civil Engineering Technician. (pub. by Thomas Telford Ltd.)
- Geotechnique. (pub. by Thomas Telford Ltd.)
- I.C.E. Abstracts. (pub. by Thomas Telford Ltd.)
- Institution of Civil Engineers. Proceedings. Part 1: Design and Construction. (pub. by Thomas Telford Ltd.)
- Institution of Civil Engineers. Proceedings. Part 2: Research and Theory. (pub. by Thomas Telford Ltd.)
- International Safety Conference. Proceedings. irreg.
- New Civil Engineer. (pub. by Thomas Telford Ltd.)
- Offshore Engineer. (pub. by Thomas Telford, Ltd.)

**Institution of Electrical & Electronics Technician Engineers**
2 Savoy Hill, London WC2R 0BS, Eng.
- Electrotechnology. q. ISSN 0306-8552
- I E E T E Bulletin. m. ISSN 0018-9561

**Institution of Electrical Engineers**
Savoy Place, London WC2R 0BL, Eng
- Computer & Control Abstracts. m. ISSN 0036-8113 (Dist. in U.S. by Institute of Electrical & Electronics Engineers, Inc., 345 E. 45th St., New York, NY 10017)
- Control and Science Record. q. ISSN 0010-8030
- Current Papers in Physics; containing about 65000 titles of research articles from more than 900 of the world's physics journals. fortn. ISSN 0011-3786
- Electrical & Electronic Abstracts. m. ISSN 0036-8105 (Dist. in U.S. by Institute of Electrical & Electronics Engineers Inc., 345 E. 45th St., New York, NY 10017)
- Electronics and Power. 22 per yr. ISSN 0013-5127
- Electronics Letters; an international journal offering speedy dissemination of research and development results in electronics, control and allied subjects. fortn. ISSN 0013-5194
- Electronics Record. q. ISSN 0013-5208
- I E E Medical Electronics Monographs. (pub. by Peter Peregrinus Ltd.)
- I E E Monograph Series. (pub. by Peter Peregrinus Ltd.)
- I. E. E. Reprint Series. (pub. by Peter Peregrinus Ltd.)
- I E E Reviews. (pub. by Peter Peregrinus Ltd.)
- I E E Telecommunications Series. (pub. by Peter Peregrinus Ltd.)
- Inspec Matters. m.
- INSPEC Reports. irreg.
- Institution of Electrical Engineers. Proceedings. m. ISSN 0020-3270
- Physics Abstracts. (Science Abstracts. Section A) bi-w. ISSN 0036-8091 (Dist. in U.S. by American Institute of Physics, 345 E. 45th St., New York, NY 10017)
- Power Record. q. ISSN 0032-6062
- Regulations for the Electrical Equipment of Buildings. irreg; 1966, 14th ed.

**Institution of Electronic & Radio Engineers**
8-9 Bedford Square, London WC1B 3RG, England.
- National Electronics Review; a survey of progress in electronics. bi-m. ISSN 0305-2257
- Radio and Electronic Engineer. m. ISSN 0033-7722

**Institution of Engineers and Shipbuilders in Scotland**
183 Bath St., Glasgow G2 4HT, Scotland.
- Institution of Engineers and Shipbuilders in Scotland. Transactions. 7 per yr. ISSN 0020-3289

**Institution of Engineers-in-Charge**
117 Shooters Hill, London S.E.18, Eng.
- Institution of Engineers-In-Charge. Transactions. bi-m. ISSN 0020-3335

**Institution of Fire Engineers**
148 New Walk, Leicester LE1 7QB, England.
- Fire Engineers Journal. (pub. by Technical Journals Ltd.)
- Institution of Fire Engineers Journal. q.

**Institution of Gas Engineers**
17 Grosvenor Crescent, London SW1X 7ES, Eng.
- Gas Engineering & Management. m.
- Institution of Gas Engineers. Proceedings. s-a.

**Institution of Highway Engineers**
- Highway Engineer. (pub. by Whitehall Press Ltd.)

**Institution of Industrial Safety Officers**
- Protection. (pub. by Alan Osborne & Associates)

**Institution of Mechanical and General Technician Engineers**
33 Ovington Sq., Kensington, London S.W.3, Eng.
- General Engineer. m.

**Institution of Mechanical Engineers**
1 Birdcage Walk, London SW1H 9JJ, England.
- Chartered Mechanical Engineer. (pub. by Mechanical Engineering Publications Ltd.)
- Heat and Fluid Flow. (pub. by Mechanical Engineering Publications Ltd.)
- Institution of Mechanical Engineers. Conference Publication. (pub. by Mechanical Engineering Publications Ltd.)

- Institution of Mechanical Engineers. Post Conference Books. irreg.
- Institution of Mechanical Engineers. Proceedings. (pub. by Mechanical Engineering Publications Ltd.)
- International Journal of Mechanical Engineering Education. (pub. by Mechanical Engineering Publications Ltd.)
- Journal of Mechanical Engineering Science. (pub. by Mechanical Engineering Publications Ltd.)

**Institution of Mechanical Engineers. Tribology Group**
1 Birdcage Walk, London SW1H 9JJ, England.
- Tribology Convention. Proceedings. a. ISSN 0082-6405

**Institution of Metallurgists**
Aero Mill, Church, Accrington, Lancashire, England.
- Metallurgist & Materials Technologist. m.

**Institution of Mining and Metallurgy**
44 Portland Place, London W1N 4BR, Eng.
- I M M Abstracts; a survey of world literature on the economic geology and mining of all minerals (except coal), mineral dressing and non-ferrous extraction metallurgy. bi-m. ISSN 0019-0020
- Institution of Mining and Metallurgy. Bulletin and Transactions. Section A: Mining Industry. q.
- Institution of Mining and Metallurgy. Bulletin and Transactions. Section B: Applied Earth Science. q.
- Institution of Mining and Metallurgy. Bulletin and Transactions. Section C: Mineral Processing & Extractive Metallurgy. q.

**Institution of Mining Engineers**
Hobart House, Grosvenor Place, London SW1X 7AE, England.
- Mining Engineer. m. ISSN 0026-5179

**Institution of Municipal Engineers**
25 Eccleston Square, London SW1 V1NX, Eng.
- Chartered Municipal Engineer. m.

**Institution of Nuclear Engineers**
1 Penerley Rd., London SE6 2LQ, England.
- Institution of Nuclear Engineers. Journal. bi-m. ISSN 0368-2595
- Institution of Nuclear Engineers. Year Book. irreg. ISSN 0073-9812

**Institution of Plant Engineers**
- Plant Engineers. (pub. by Batiste Publications Ltd)

**Institution of Post Office Electrical Engineers**
2-12 Gresham St., London EC2V 7AG, Eng.
- Post Office Electrical Engineers' Journal. q. ISSN 0032-5287

**Institution of Post Office Electrical Engineers. National Committee, Associate Section**
P.O. RETC Kineholm, West Busk Lane, Otley, Yorkshire, England.
- I P O E E National Committee. Associate Section. National News. q.

**Institution of Production Engineers**
146 Cromwell Road, Kensington, London SW7 4EF, Eng.
- Production Engineer. m. ISSN 0032-9851

**Institution of Professional Civil Servants**
3-7 Northumberland St., London WC2N 5BS, Eng.
- State Service. m. ISSN 0039-0151

**Institution of Public Health Engineers**
- Public Health Engineer. (pub. by Municipal Publications)

**Institution of Railway Signal Engineers**
21 Avalon Rd, Earley Reading Berks, England.
- Institution of Railway Signal Engineers. Proceedings. a. ISSN 0073-9839

**Institution of Royal Engineers**
Chatham, Kent ME4 4UG, Eng.
- Royal Engineers Journal. q. ISSN 0035-8878

**Institution of Sales Engineers**
24 Warwick New Rd., Royal Leamington Spa, Warwickshire CV32 5JH, England.
- Sales Engineering (1976) m. ISSN 0306-5618

**Institution of Structural Engineers**
11 Upper Belgrave St., London SW1X 8BH, England.
- Institution of Structural Engineers. Yearbook. a. ISSN 0073-9847

- Structural Engineer. m. ISSN 0039-2553

**Institution of Water Engineers and Scientists**
6-8 Sackville St., Piccadilly, London, W1X 1DD, Eng
(Subscr. to: Lavenham Press Ltd., Water St., Lavenham, Sudbury, Suffolk CO10 9RN, England)
- Institution of Water Engineers and Scientists. Journal. 6 per yr.

**Institution of Works Managers**
- Works Management. (pub. by Findlay Publications

**Insurance and Actuarial Society of Glasgow**
106 Buchanan St., Glasgow G1 2JL, Scotland.
- Insurance and Actuarial Society of Glasgow. Newsletter. 3 per yr. ISSN 0020-4609

**Insurance Publishing & Printing Co.**
Stambermill Industrial Estate, Stourbridge, West Midlands DY9 7BQ, Eng.
- Insurance Brokers' Monthly. m. ISSN 0020-4633

**Intec Press Ltd.**
3 Station Parade, Whyteleafe, Surrey, England.
- Shipcare International. m.
- Tanker & Bulker International. m. ISSN 0306-946X

**Intelligence International Ltd.**
17 Rodney Rd., Cheltenham, Glos. GL5O 1JQ, Eng.
- Intelligence Digest; a review of world affairs. m. ISSN 0020-4900
- Intelligence Digest-Weekly Review; a summary of political and economic intelligence for businessmen and students of world affairs. w.

**Inter Counties Publications Ltd.**
Thames Industrial Estate, Marlow, Bucks., Eng.
- Home Services. fortn.

**Intercity Publications (N. W.) Ltd.**
2A Lloyd St., Altrincham, Cheshire WA14 2DE, England.
- What's on in and around Manchester. m.

**Interface Periodicals Ltd.**
405 Strand, London W.C.2., England.
- Medical Interface. m.

**Interflora British Unit Ltd.**
Interflora House, Sleaford, Lincolnshire, England.
- Mercury. m. (Florists Telegraph Delivery Association)

**Intergovernmental Maritime Consultative Organization**
For publications of this agency see section for UNITED NATIONS

**Interline and Air Travel News**
23-25 Piazza Chambers, Covent Garden, London WC2E 8EL, England.
- Interline and Air Travel News. s-m.

**Intermediate Technology Publications Ltd.**
9 King St., Covent Garden, London WC2E 8HN, England
(Dist. in U. S. by: International Scholarly Book Services, Box 555, Forest Grove, OR 97116)
- Appropriate Technology. q. ISSN 0305-0920

**International Academy of Pathology**
c/o Ed. Dr. Geoffrey Farrer Brown, Bland Sutton Institute of Pathology, Middlesex Hospital, London, England.
- Histopathology. (pub. by Blackwell Scientific Publications Ltd.)
- Monographs in Pathology. q. ISSN 0538-4109

**International Advertising Association. United Kingdom Chapter**
- International Advertising Association. United Kingdom Chapter. Concise Guide to International Markets. (pub. by Leslie Stinton & Partners)

**International African Institute**
210 High Holborn, London WC1V 7BW, Eng.
- Africa. q. ISSN 0001-9720
- African Environment Special Reports. irreg.
- African Languages/Langues Africaines. a.
- Current Africanist Research; an international information bulletin. a.
- Ethnographic Survey of Africa. Central Africa, Belgian Congo. irreg.; latest issue, no. 5, 1960. ISSN 0425-4538

- Ethnographic Survey of Africa. East Central Africa. irreg., 1967, no. 17. ISSN 0071-1802
- Ethnographic Survey of Africa. French Series/ Monographies Ethnologiques Africaines. irreg., 1963, no. 10. ISSN 0071-1810
- Ethnographic Survey of Africa. North Eastern Africa. irreg.; no. 4, 1973. ISSN 0425-4546
- Ethnographic Survey of Africa. Western Africa. irreg., no. 15, 1960. ISSN 0071-1829
- I A I Bulletin; African studies notes and news. q. ISSN 0308-2717
- International African Institute. Africa Bibliography Series B: Special Subjects. irreg.; latest edt., 1972. ISSN 0538-4192

**International African Law Association**
- Journal of African Law. (pub. by Butterworth & Co. (Publishers) Ltd.)

**International Alliance of Women**
47 Victoria St., 3Rd Floor, London SW1H 0EQ, England.
- International Women's News. 5 per yr. ISSN 0020-9120

**International Archery Federation**
46 The Balk, Walton, Wakefield, England.
- International Archery Federation. Bulletin Officiel. biennial; no. 26, 1974. ISSN 0074-137X

**International Arthurian Society**
c/o Prof. Cedric Pickford, The University, French Dept., Hull HU6 7RX, Yorkshire, England.
- International Arthurian Society. Report of Congress/Societe Internationale Arthurienne. Rapports du Congres. a; latest issue, 1974. ISSN 0074-1396

**International Association for Cultural Freedom**
59 St. Martin's Lane, London WC2N 4JS, Eng.
- Minerva; a review of science, policy and learning. q. ISSN 0026-4695
- Survey. (pub. by Oxford University Press)

**International Association for Earthquake Engineering**
- Earthquake Engineering and Structural Dynamics. (pub. by John Wiley & Sons Ltd.)

**International Association for Mass Communication Research**
c/o James D. Halloran, Centre for Mass Communications Research, University of Leicester, 104 Regent Rd., Leicester, England.
- International Association for Mass Communication Research. Letter from the President. irreg. ISSN 0579-3742

**International Association for Plant Tissue Culture**
Botanical Laboratories, University of Leicester, Leicester LE1 TR4, Eng.
- International Association for Plant Tissue Culture. Newsletter. 3 per yr.

**International Association for Reformed Faith and Action**
Milverton Lodge, 3 Ottawa Place, Chapel Allerton, Leeds LS7 4L6, England.
- International Reformed Bulletin. q.

**International Association of Agricultural Economists**
- International Conference of Agricultural Economists. Proceedings. (pub. by Institute of Agricultural Economics)

**International Association of Applied Linguistics**
- International Conference of Applied Linguistics. (Proceedings) (pub. by Cambridge University Press)

**International Association of Applied Psychology**
- Revue Internationale de Psychologie Appliquee/ International Review of Applied Psychology. (pub. by Liverpool University Press)

**International Association of Hydrological Sciences**
Institute of Hydrology, Wallingford, Oxon., Eng
(Subscr. Address 1909 K St., N. W., Washington, D. C. 20006)
- Hydrological Sciences Bulletin/Bulletin des Sciences Hydrologiques. q.

**International Association of Individual Psychology**
6 Vale Rise, London NW 11 8SD, England.
- Individual Psychology News Letter. bi-m. ISSN 0019-7157

**International Association of Museums of Arms and Military History**
c/o William Reid, National Army Museum, London S.W.3, England.
- International Association of Museums of Arms and Military History. Congress Reports. triennial., 1969, 5th, Rome, Naples, Brescia. ISSN 0074-168X

**International Association of Music Libraries (U. K. Branch)**
Central Music Library, Buckingham Palace Rd., London SW1 9UD, England.
- Brio. s-a. ISSN 0007-0173

**International Association of Orientalist Librarians**
c/o the British Library, Great Russell St., London WC1B 3DG, England.
- International Association of Orientalist Librarians. Newsletter. s-a.

**International Association of Papyrologists**
c/o Dr. R. A. Coles, Papyrology Rooms, Ashmolean Museum, Oxford, England.
- International Congress for Papyrology. Proceedings. triennial, 14th Congress 1974, Oxford. ISSN 0074-3429

**International Association of Sedimentologists**
- Sedimentology. (pub. by Blackwell Scientific Publications, Ltd.)

**International Association of Seed Crushers**
8 Salisbury Square, London EC4P 4AN, England.
- International Association of Seed Crushers. Proceedings of the Annual Congress. a. ISSN 0074-1736

**International Association of Technological Universities Libraries**
Univ. of Technology Library, Loughborough, Leicestershire LE11 3TU, England.
- I A T U L Proceedings. irreg. ISSN 0018-8476

**International Association of University Professors & Lecturers**
Ed. Mrs. Jane P. Russell-Gebett, Florence Boot Hall, University Park, Nottingham NG7 2QY, Eng.
- International Association of University Professors & Lecturers. Communication. s-a. ISSN 0018-8492

**International Badminton Federation**
4 Madeira Ave, Bromley, Kent, England.
- International Badminton Federation. Annual Handbook. a. ISSN 0074-1981
- World Badminton. 6 per yr.

**International Bank Note Society**
Ed. Y. L. Beresiner, Liverpool House, 15-17 Eldon St., London E.C.2., Eng.
- International Bank Note Society Magazine. q. ISSN 0020-6121

**International Bar Association**
14 Waterloo Place, London SW1Y 4AR, England.
- International Bar Journal. s-a. ISSN 0047-0589
- International Business Lawyer. q.

**International Bee Research Association**
Hill House, Gerrards Cross, Bucks SL9 ONR, Eng.
- Apicultural Abstracts. q. ISSN 0003-648X
- Bee World. q. ISSN 0005-772X
- Journal of Apicultural Research. q. ISSN 0021-8839

**International Cargo Handling Coordination Association**
Abford House, 15 Wilton Road, London SW1V ILX, England.
- International Cargo Handling Coordination Association. Rapports des Comites Nationaux. a. ISSN 0534-7793
- Progress in Cargo Handling; Proceedings. biennial. ISSN 0079-6131

**International Centre for Training and Research in Development Studies. Institute of Social Studies**
- Development and Change. (pub. by Sage Publications Ltd.)

**International Centre of Free Trade Unionists in Exile**
24 B Clifton Gardens, London W.9, Eng.
- Labour in Exile. bi-m. ISSN 0023-6950

**International Civil Airport Association**
- Airports International. (pub. by I P C Transport Press Ltd.)

**International Co-Operative Alliance**
11 Upper Grosvenor St., London W1X 9PA, Eng.
- Agricultural Co-Operative Bulletin. m. ISSN 0002-1415
- Consumer Affairs Bulletin. m. ISSN 0010-7115
- Co-Operative News Service. m. ISSN 0009-983X
- International Cooperative Alliance. Congress Report. quadrennial; 26th, 1976, paris. ISSN 0074-4247
- Review of International Cooperation/Revue de la Cooperation Internationale/Revista de la Cooperacion Internacional. q. ISSN 0034-6608 (Spanish Edition Available Only from Intercoop, Alberti 191, Buenos Aires, Argentina)

**International Commercial Network Ltd.**
17 Victoria Ave., Harrogate, Yorkshire, Eng.
- British Commercial Agents Review. m. (British Agents Register)
- Worldwide Marketing Opportunities Digest. bi-m.

**International Commission for Uniform Methods of Sugar Analysis**
Box 35, Wharf Rd., Peterborough PE2 9PU, England.
- International Commission for Uniform Methods of Sugar Analysis. Report of the Proceedings of the Session. irreg.

**International Commission on Radiological Protection**
- I C R P Annals. (pub. by Pergamon Press Ltd.)
- I C R P Publications. (pub. by Pergamon Press Ltd.)

**International Committee of Photobiology. King's College**
68 Half Moon Lane, London, SE24 9JE, England.
- International Photobiological Congress. Proceedings. irreg. 1972, 6th Bochum, Germany. ISSN 0074-7351

**International Confederation for Disarmament & Peace**
6 Endsleigh St., London W.C.1, Eng.
- Peace Press; an international information service. m. ISSN 0031-3572
- Vietnam/South East Asia International. a.

**International Confederation of Midwives**
47 Victoria St., London SW1H OEQ, England.
- International Confederation of Midwives. Congress Reports. triennial, 1972, 16th, Washington, D.C. ISSN 0074-2880

**International Confederation of Thermal Analysis**
- Thermal Analysis Abstracts. (pub. by Heyden & Son Ltd.)

**International Congresses of Entomology**
Permanent Committee, c/o British Museum (Natural History), Cromwell Rd., London, S.W. 7, England.
- International Congress of Entomology. quadrennial, 1968, 13th, Moscow. ISSN 0074-364X

**International Council for Bird Preservation**
c/o British Museum (Natural History), Cromwell Rd., London SW7, England.
- International Council for Bird Preservation. Proceedings of Conferences. irreg., 16th. 1974, Canberra, Australia. ISSN 0074-4271

**International Council for Bird Preservation. British Section**
c/o Natural History Museum, Cromwell Rd., London S.W.7, England.
- International Council for Bird Preservation. British Section. Report. a. ISSN 0074-4263

**International Council for Educational Media**
- Educational Media International. (pub. by Modino Press Ltd.)

**International Council of Graphic Design Associations**
7 Templeton Court, Radnor Walk, Croydon CRO 7NZ, Great Britain.
- Icographic. irreg. ISSN 0085-1698

**International Council of Jews from Czechoslovakia**
30 Craven St., Strand, London WC2N 5NT, Eng.
- I C J C Newsletter. bi-m.
- Report on Czechoslovak Jewry. irreg.

**International Council of Societies of Industrial Design**
- Design Abstracts International. (pub. by Pergamon Press Ltd.)

**International Crosby Circle**
c/o Reg Bristo, 7 Greenmeadow Close, Cwmbran, Gwent NP4 3NR, England.
- Bing. q.

**International Currency Review Ltd.**
11 Regency Place, London SW1P 2EA, Eng.
- International Currency Review. bi-m. ISSN 0020-6490
- London Currency Report. 20 per yr. ISSN 0307-0360
- Middle East Currency Reports. 9 per yr. ISSN 0307-0387

**International Dance Teachers Association Ltd**
76 Bennett Road, Brighton BN2 5JL, England.
- Ballroom Dancing Year Book. a. ISSN 0404-6919
- Dance Teacher. m.

**International Dental Federation**
64 Wimpole St., London W1M 8AL, Eng
(U.S. Subscr. to: c/o Miss E. Uttech, 6 Main St., Watertown, WI 53094)
- F. D. I. Newsletter. q. ISSN 0014-5777
- International Dental Journal. (pub. by John Wright & Sons, Ltd.)

**International Diabetes Federation**
3-6 Alfred Place, London WC1E 7EE, England.
- I D F Bulletin. triennial.

**International Epidemiological Association**
- International Journal of Epidemiology. (pub. by Oxford University Press)

**International Exhibition for the Food and Allied Industries**
- Foodpack. (pub. by B P S Exhibitions)

**International Export Association**
North St., Bourne, Lincolnshire, Eng.
- International Export Association. Export News. bi-m. ISSN 0047-0694

**International Federation for Information Processing**
c/o Dr. C. H. Lindsey, Dept. of Computer Science, University of Manchester, Manchester, England.
- ALGOL Bulletin. irreg. (approx. 3 per yr.) ISSN 0084-6198

**International Federation for Medical Electronics and Biological Engineering**
- Medical & Biological Engineering & Computing. (pub. by Peter Peregrinus Ltd.)

**International Federation for Theatre Research**
- Theatre Research International. (pub. by Oxford University Press)

**International Federation of Audit Bureaus of Circulations**
19 Dunraven Street, Park Lane, London W1Y 3FE, England.
- Circulation Auditing Around the World; memorandum report by the secretary-general. a.

**International Federation of Business and Professional Women**
54 Bloomsbury St., London WC1B 3QU, Eng.
- Widening Horizons. q. ISSN 0049-7614

**International Federation of Clinical Chemistry**
c/o P.M.G. Broughton, Sec., University Department of Chemical Pathology, General Infirmary, Leeds LS1 3EX, England.
- International Congress on Clinical Chemistry. Papers. 9th, 1975, Toronto. ISSN 0074-4069

**International Federation of Library Associations. Children's Section**
45 Stephenson Tower, Station St., Birmingham B5 4DR, England.
- Children's Literature Abstracts. q. ISSN 0306-2015

**International Federation of Library Associations. Office for UBC**
c/o Reference Division, British Library, London, WC1B 3DG, Eng.
- International Cataloguing. q. ISSN 0047-0635

**International Federation of Park and Recreation Administration**
c/o Kenneth L. Morgan, The Grotto, Lower Basildon, Reading RG8 9NE, Berkshire, England
- World Congress in Public Park Administration. Programme. irreg., 1977, durban. ISSN 0510-8233

- World Congress in Public Park Administration. Reports. irreg. ISSN 0510-8225

**International Federation of Prestressing**
Wexham Springs, Slough SL3 6PL, England.
- International Federation of Prestressing. Congress Proceedings. quadrennial; 7th. 1974, New York. ISSN 0074-6045

**International Film Collector**
c/o John Walter Skinner, Ed., 15 Wallace Ave., West Worthing, West Sussex BN11 5RA, England
- International Film Collector. q. (Dist. in U. S. by Frank Jones, 34 Walnut St., Lawrence, MA 01841)

**International Fluidics Services Ltd.**
39 High St., Kempston, Bedford MK42 7BT, England.
- Industrial Robot; an international quarterly journal on industrial robot technology. q.

**International Food Information Service**
- Food Science and Technology Abstracts. (pub. by Commonwealth Agricultural Bureaux)

**International Friendship League**
3 Creswick Rd., Acton, London W3 9HE, Eng.
- International Friendship League. Newsletter. 4 per yr. ISSN 0020-6806

**International Gas Union**
Inquire: A. G. Higgins, Gen. Sec., 17 Grosvenor Crescent, London SW1, England
- International Gas Union. Proceedings of Conferences. triennial, 1973, 12th Nice. ISSN 0074-6126 (For Abstracts of Proceedings: Institute of Gas Technology, 3424 South State St., Chicago, IL 60616)

**International Geographical Union. World Land Use Survey Commission**
- World Land Use Survey. Occasional Papers. (pub. by Geographical Publications Ltd.)
- World Land Use Survey. Regional Monograph. (pub. by Geographical Publications Ltd.)

**International Glaciological Society**
Cambridge CB2 1BR, Eng.
- ICE; news bulletin of the International Glaciological Society. 3 per yr. ISSN 0019-1043
- Journal of Glaciology. s-a. ISSN 0022-1430

**International Hebrew Christian Alliance**
Shalom, Brockenhurst Rd., Ramsdate, Eng.
- Hebrew Christian. q. ISSN 0017-9477

**International Hospital Federation**
126 Albert St., London NW1 7NF, England.
- World Hospitals. q. ISSN 0512-3135

**International Hotel Association**
- International Hotel Review/Revue de l'Hotellerie Internationale. (pub. by International Trade Publications Ltd.)

**International Institute for Conservation of Historic and Artistic Works**
6 Buckingham St., London WC2N 6BA, England.
- Studies in Conservation. q. ISSN 0039-3630

**International Institute for Strategic Studies**
18 Adam St., London WC2N 6AL, England
(Subscr. to: Research Publications Services Ltd., Victoria Hall, East Greenwich, London SE 10 ORF, England)
- Adelphi Papers. irreg., no. 131, 1977. ISSN 0567-932X
- International Institute for Strategic Studies. Military Balance. a. ISSN 0459-7222
- International Institute for Strategic Studies. Strategic Survey. a. ISSN 0459-7230
- Survival. bi-m. ISSN 0039-6338

**International Institute of Communications**
Tavistock Hse. East, Tavistock Square, London W.C.1H 9LG, Eng.
- InterMedia. bi-m. ISSN 0309-118X

**International Institute of Social Economics**
- International Journal of Social Economics. (pub. by M C B (Social Economics) Ltd.)

**International Institute of Welding**
54 Princes Gate, Exhibition Rd., London SW7 2PG, Eng.
- Welding in the World/Soudage dans le Monde. bi-m. ISSN 0043-2288 (Co-Sponsor; Institut de Soudure Autogene(Paris))

**International Journal of Forensic Dentistry**
P.O. Box 18, Bognor Regis PO22 7AA, Eng.
- International Journal of Forensic Dentistry. q. ISSN 0306-9419

**International Language Centre**
International House, 40 Shaftesbury Ave., London W1V8HJ, Eng.
- BBC Modern English; a magazine for students of English as a foreign language. 10 per yr. ISSN 0306-9346
- Modern English Teacher; a magazine of practical suggestions for improving the teaching of English as a foreign language. q.

**International Law Association**
3 Paper Bldgs., Temple, London EC4, England.
- International Law Association. Reports of Conferences. biennial 1972, 55th, New York. ISSN 0074-6738

**International Licensing Ltd.**
92 Cannon Lane, Pinner, Middlesex HA5 1HT, Eng.
- International Licensing; a monthly bulletin providing an international forum for the negotiation of manufacturing licenses and joint ventures. m. ISSN 0020-7845

**International Machine Tool Design and Research Conference**
Dept. of Mechanical Engineering, University of Birmingham, P.O. Box 363, Birmingham B15 2TT, England
(Subscr. to: Little Essex St., London W.C.2., England)
- International Machine Tool Design and Research Conference. Proceedings. a., 1974, 15th, Birmingham, England. ISSN 0074-6835

**International Markets Advertising Agency**
Old Court House, Old Court Place, London W 8 4 PD, England
(U.S. Subscr. Address: 711 Third Ave. New York, NY 10017)
- Image. 2 per yr. ISSN 0046-8649

**International Marxist Group(British Section, 4th International)**
- Red Weekly. (pub. by Relgocrest Ltd.)

**International Medical Society of Paraplegia**
- Paraplegia. (pub. by Longman Group Ltd.)

**International Medieval Bibliography**
School of History, University of Leeds, Leeds LS2 9JT, England.
- International Medieval Bibliography. Annual Subject Guide. s-a. ISSN 0074-6940

**International Numismatic Directory**
c/o J. J. Krasnodebski, 9 St. Lawrence Rd., London SW9 GPW, England.
- International Numismatic Directory. irreg.

**International P. E. N.**
62 Glebe Place, London S.W.3, England
(U.S. Address: Stechert-Hafner Inc., 31 E. 10th St., New York, NY 10003)
- International P. E. N. Bulletin of Selected Books. q. ISSN 0020-823X
- International P. E. N. Congress. Report. irreg., 1970, 38th, Dublin. ISSN 0074-722X

**International Phonetic Association**
University College London, Gower St., London WC1E 6BT, England.
- International Phonetic Association. Journal. s-a. ISSN 0025-1003

**International Phycological Society**
- Phycologia. (pub. by Blackwell Scientific Publications Ltd.)

**International Planned Parenthood Federation**
18-20 Lower Regent St., London SW1Y 4PW, England.
- Family Planning in Five Continents. a. ISSN 0538-9089
- I P P F Medical Bulletin. 6 per yr. ISSN 0019-0357

- I P P F News. m. ISSN 0306-4018
- International Conference on Planned Parenthood. Proceedings. irreg., 1967, 8th, Santiago. ISSN 0074-3259
- International Planned Parenthood Federation. Annual Report. a.
- International Planned Parenthood Federation. Library Bulletin. q. ISSN 0047-0880
- International Planned Parenthood Federation. Proceedings of the Conference of the Europe and near East Region. irreg., 1969, 6th, Budapest. ISSN 0074-7386
- International Planned Parenthood Federation. Working Papers. irreg; latest issue, no. 5. ISSN 0074-7394
- People. q. ISSN 0301-5645
- Research in Reproduction. bi-m. ISSN 0034-5253
- Victor-Bostrom Fund. Report. irreg. ISSN 0538-9127
- World List of Family Planning Agencies. irreg. ISSN 0535-1774

**International Planned Parenthood Federation. Europe Region**
64 Sloane St., London SW1X 9SJ, England.
- I P P F Europe. q.

**International Plastic Modellers Society**
17 Hardwick Close, Shefford, Bedfordshire SG17 5DY, Eng.
- I.P.M.S. Magazine. bi-m.

**International Playground Association**
12 Cherry Tree Dr., Sheffield S11 9AE, England.
- International Playground Association. Conference Report. approx. triennial; 6th, Milan, 1976. ISSN 0074-7416

**International Poetry Society**
- Ipse. (pub. by Hub Publications Ltd.)
- Orbis. (pub. by Hub Publications Ltd.)

**International Police Association**
County Police Hqtrs., Sutton Rd., Maidstone, Kent, England.
- International Police Association. Meeting of the International Executive Council. a; latest edition, 1976. ISSN 0579-5567
- International Police Association. Travel Scholarships. a; latest edition, 1976. ISSN 0579-6881

**International Police Association. British Section**
- Police World. (pub. by M and W Publications)

**International Press Institute**
City University, 280 St. John St., London EC1V 4PB, England.
- I P I Report. m. ISSN 0019-0314
- International Press Institute. Survey. irreg., no. 8, 1976. ISSN 0085-2198

**International Press Telecommunications Council**
Studio House, Hen and Chickens Ct., 184 Fleet St., London EC4A 2dU, England.
- I. P. T. C. Newsletter. 3 per yr. ISSN 0579-6903

**International Prospect**
17 Summer Hill, Harbledown, Canterbury, Kent, Eng.
- International Prospect. bi-m. ISSN 0020-8418

**International Psycho-Analytical Association**
49 Croftdown Road, London NW5 1EL, England.
- International Psycho-Analytical Association. Bulletin. a.; latest issue, 1975. ISSN 0074-753X

**International Publishing Corp.**
Surrey House, 1 Throwley Way, Sutton, Surrey, England.
- Community Care. w. (I P C Building and Contract Journals Ltd.)
- Woman and Home. m. ISSN 0043-7247

**International Research Communications System (IRCS)**
St. Leonard's House, St. Leonard's Gate, Lancaster, Eng.
- I R C S Journal of Medical Science. m. ISSN 0305-6481
- I R C S Medical Science: Alimentary System. bi-m. ISSN 0305-6678
- I R C S Medical Science: Anatomy and Human Biology. bi-m. ISSN 0305-6686
- I R C S Medical Science: Biochemistry. m. ISSN 0305-6708
- I R C S Medical Science: Biomedical Technology. bi-m. ISSN 0305-6716

- I R C S Medical Science: Cancer. m. ISSN 0305-6724
- I R C S Medical Science: Cardiovascular System. m. ISSN 0305-6732
- I R C S Medical Science: Cell and Membrane Biology. m. ISSN 0305-6740
- I R C S Medical Science: Classified List. m. ISSN 0305-649X
- I R C S Medical Science: Clinical Biochemistry. q. ISSN 0309-1481
- I R C S Medical Science: Clinical Medicine. m. ISSN 0309-1546
- I R C S Medical Science: Clinical Pharmacology and Therapeutics. m. ISSN 0305-6759
- I R C S Medical Science: Connective Tissue, Skin and Bone. bi-m. ISSN 0305-6767
- I R C S Medical Science: Dentistry and Oral Biology. q. ISSN 0305-6775
- I R C S Medical Science: Developmental Biology and Medicine. q. ISSN 0309-149X
- I R C S Medical Science: Drug Metabolism and Toxicology. q. ISSN 0309-1503
- I R C S Medical Science: Endocrine System. m. ISSN 0305-6783
- I R C S Medical Science: Environmental Biology and Medicine. q. ISSN 0309-1473
- I R C S Medical Science: Experimental Animals. q. ISSN 0309-1562
- I R C S Medical Science: Hematology. m. ISSN 0305-6805
- I R C S Medical Science: Immunology and Allergy. m. ISSN 0305-666X
- I R C S Medical Science: Kidneys and Urinary System. bi-m. ISSN 0305-6813
- I R C S Medical Science: Library Compendium. m. ISSN 0305-6651
- I R C S Medical Science: Metabolism and Nutrition. m. ISSN 0305-6821
- I R C S Medical Science: Microbiology, Parasitology and Infectious Diseases. m. ISSN 0305-683X
- I R C S Medical Science: Nervous System. m. ISSN 0309-1554
- I R C S Medical Science: Pathology. q. ISSN 0309-1511
- I R C S Medical Science: Pharmacology. m. ISSN 0305-6872
- I R C S Medical Science: Physiology. m. ISSN 0305-6880
- I R C S Medical Science: Psychology and Psychiatry. m. ISSN 0309-152X
- I R C S Medical Science: Reproduction, Obstetrics and Gynecology. m. ISSN 0305-6929
- I R C S Medical Science: Respiratory System. bi-m. ISSN 0305-6937
- I R C S Medical Science: Social and Occupational Medicine. bi-m. ISSN 0305-6945
- I R C S Medical Science: Surgery and Transplantation. bi-m. ISSN 0305-6953
- I R C S Medical Science: The Eye. q. ISSN 0305-6791

**International Rubber Study Group**
Brettenham House, 5-6 Lancaster Place, London WC2E 7ET, Eng.
- International Rubber Digest. m. ISSN 0020-8655
- International Rubber Study Group. Summary of Proceedings of the Group Meetings and Assemblies. irreg., 24th, 1974. ISSN 0074-7823
- Rubber Statistical Bulletin. m. ISSN 0035-9548

**International Seismological Centre**
6 South Oswald Rd., Edinburgh EH9 2HX, Scotland.
- International Seismological Centre. Bulletin. m. ISSN 0020-8671
- International Seismological Centre. P-Nodal Solutions for Earthquakes. irreg. ISSN 0538-978X
- International Seismological Centre. Regional Catalogue of Earthquakes. s-a. ISSN 0034-334X

**International Society for Burn Injuries**
- Burns. (pub. by John Wright and Sons Ltd.)

**International Society for Human and Animal Mycology**
- Sabouraudia. (pub. by Longman Group Ltd.)

**International Society for Hybrid Microelectronics**
c/o David Boswell, 20 Hale Lane, London NW 7, England.
- Hybrid Microelectronics Symposium. (Papers) irreg., 1968, 3rd. ISSN 0073-4136

**International Society of Military Collectors**
- Tradition. (pub. by Belmont-Maitland Ltd.)

**International Sociological Association**
- Current Sociology/Sociologie Contemporaine. (pub. by Sage Publications Ltd.)

**International Standing Committee on Physiology and Pathology of Animal Reproduction**
c/o Prof. J. A. Laing, Royal Veterinary College, Hawkshead House, Hawkshead Lane, N. Mymms, Hatfield, Herts., England.
- International Congress on Animal Reproduction and Artificial Insemination. Proceedings. quadrennial; 1972, 7th, Munich; 1976, 8th, Krakow. ISSN 0074-4026

**International Statistical Institute**
- International Statistical Review/Revue Internationale de Statistique. (pub. by Longman Group Ltd.)
- Statistical Theory and Method Abstracts. (pub. by Longman Group Ltd.)

**International Study Group for Mathematics Learning**
- Journal of Structural Learning. (pub. by Gordon & Breach Science Publishers, Ltd.)

**International Sugar Journal Ltd.**
23a Easton St., High Wycombe, Bucks, Eng.
- International Sugar Journal; a technical and commercial periodical devoted entirely to the sugar industry. m. ISSN 0020-8841

**International Sugar Organization**
28 Haymarket, London S.W. 1, England.
- International Sugar Organization. Annual Report. a. ISSN 0074-8706
- International Sugar Organization Statistical Bulletin. m. ISSN 0020-885X

**International Superphosphate and Compound Manufacturers Association Ltd.**
121 Gloucester Pl, London W1, England.
- International Superphosphate and Compound Manufacturers Association Limited. Technical Meeting. Proceedings. biennial. ISSN 0074-8714

**International Telephone and Telegraph Corp.**
190 Strand, London WCR1 RDU, England.
- Electrical Communication. q. ISSN 0013-4252

**International Tin Council**
Haymarket House, 1 Oxendon St., London SW1Y 4EQ, Eng.
- Notes on Tin. m. ISSN 0029-4098
- Tin Statistics. a.

**International Tin Research Council**
- Tin and Its Uses. (pub. by International Tin Research Institute)

**International Tin Research Institute**
Fraser Rd., Perivale, Greenford, Middlesex, UB6 7AQ, England
(and Tin Research Institute, Inc., 483 W. Sixth Ave., Columbus, Ohio 43201)
- International Tin Research Council. Annual Report. a. ISSN 0074-9125
- Tin and Its Uses. q. ISSN 0040-7941 (International Tin Research Council)

**International Trade Publications Ltd.**
Queensway House, Redhill, Surrey RH1 1QS, England.
- Coffee International. q.
- Decorating Contractor Annual Directory. a. ISSN 0070-3192
- International Hotel Review/Revue de l'Hotellerie Internationale. q. ISSN 0020-6911 (International Hotel Association)
- Smoker's Handbook; of recommended retail prices. a. ISSN 0081-0355
- Tableware International. m.
- Tableware Reference Book. a.
- Tobacco; the journal of the tobacco and allied trades. m. ISSN 0040-8271
- Tobacco Trade Year Book and Diary. a. ISSN 0082-4631
- World Tobacco. q. ISSN 0043-9126
- World Tobacco Directory. a. ISSN 0084-2273

**International Transport Workers' Federation**
Maritime House, Old Town, Clapham, London S.W.4, Eng.
- I T F Newsletter. m. ISSN 0019-0799
- International Transport Workers' Federation Report on Activities. irreg. ISSN 0539-0915

**International Trust for Zoological Nomenclature**
c/o British Museum (Natural History), Cromwell Rd., London SW7 5BD, England.
- Bulletin of Zoological Nomenclature. 4 per yr. ISSN 0007-5167

**International Union Against the Venereal Diseases**
Dr. F. J. G. Jefferies, The Pread Street Clinic, St. Mary's Hospital, London WC 2, Eng.
- International Union against the Venereal Diseases and the Treponematoses. Proceedings of Assemblies. irreg., 1975, 28th General Assembly, Malta. ISSN 0074-9230

**International Union Against Tuberculosis**
- Tubercle. (pub. by Longman Group Ltd.)

**International Union for Pure & Applied Biophysics**
- Quarterly Reviews of Biophysics. (pub. by Cambridge University Press)

**International Union for Vacuum Science Technique and Applications**
47 Belgrave Square, London SW1X 8QX, Eng.
- International Union for Vacuum Science, Technique and Applications. News Bulletin. bi-m. ISSN 0020-9066

**International Union of Biochemistry**
9 Hyde Terrace, Leeds LS2 9LS, England.
- Biochemical Education. q.

**International Union of Building Societies and Savings Associations**
14 Park St., Mayfair, London W1Y 4AL, England.
- International Union of Building Societies and Savings Associations. Congress Proceedings. triennial, 1977, 14th, San Francisco. ISSN 0074-9370

**International Union of Pure and Applied Chemistry**
- Carotenoids Other Than Vitamin A. (pub. by Pergamon Press Ltd.)
- Chemistry of Natural Products. (pub. by Pergamon Press Ltd.)
- Coordination Chemistry. (pub. by Pergamon Press Ltd.)
- International Congress of Pure and Applied Chemistry. (Lectures) (pub. by Pergamon Press Ltd.)
- International Newsletter on Chemical Education. (pub. by Pergamon Press Ltd.)
- International Union of Pure and Applied Chemistry. Comptes Rendus of IUPAC Conference. (pub. by Pergamon Press Ltd.)
- International Union of Pure and Applied Chemistry. Information Bulletin. (pub. by Pergamon Press Ltd.)
- Macromolecular Chemistry. (pub. by Pergamon Press Ltd.)
- Pharmaceutical Chemistry. (pub. by Pergamon Press Ltd.)
- Photochemistry. (pub. by Pergamon Press Ltd.)

**International Union of Pure and Applied Physics**
- International Conference on Phenomena in Ionized Gases. Proceedings. (pub. by Donald Parsons & Co. Ltd.)

**International Wages for Housework. London Wages for Housework Committee**
138 Drummond St., London N.W.1, England.
- Power of Women. q.

**International Water Supply Association**
1 Queen Anne's Gate, London SW1H 9BT, Eng.
- Aqua. q. ISSN 0003-7214
- International Water Supply Congress. Proceedings. every 2-3 yrs., 10th, amsterdam, 1976. ISSN 0074-9583

**International Waterfowl Research Bureau**
Slimbridge, Gloucester,GL2 7BX, Eng.
- International Waterfowl Research Bureau Bulletin. s-a.

**International Weightlifting Federation**
4 Godfrey Ave., Twickenham TW2 7PF, Eng.
- International Weightlifting. m.

**International Whaling Commission**
Great Westminster House, Horseferry Rd., London SW1, England.
- International Whaling Commission. Report. a.; latest issue, 1973. ISSN 0074-9591

**International Wheat Council**
Haymarket House, 28 Haymarket, London SW1Y
4SS, England.
- International Wheat Council. Annual Report. a.
- International Wheat Council. Market Report. m.
- International Wheat Council. Record of
  Operations of Member Countries. a. ISSN 0539-
  130X
- International Wheat Council. Review of the World
  Wheat Situation. a.
- International Wheat Council. Secretariat Papers.
  irreg. ISSN 0539-1326
- World Wheat Statistics. a. ISSN 0512-3844

**International Year Book and Statesmen's Who's Who**
Neville House, Eden St., Kingston-upon-Thames,
Surrey KT1 1BY, England.
- International Year Book and Statesmen's Who's
  Who. a. ISSN 0074-9621

**Interplanetary Space Travel Research Association
(United Kingdom)**
15 Nealden St., Stockwell, London SW9 9QX,
England.
- Interplanetary News; Britains space monthly. m.
  ISSN 0020-9597

**Inter-Varsity Press**
39 Bedford Square, London WC1B 3EY, England.
- Tyndale Bulletin. a. ISSN 0082-7118 (Tyndale
  Fellowship for Biblical and Theological Research)

**Intra-Science Research Foundation**
- Phosphorus and Sulfur and Related Elements.
  (pub. by Gordon and Breach Science Publishers
  Ltd.)

**Investors Chronicle Publication**
30 Finsbury Square, London EC2A 1PJ, England.
- World Banking. a.

**Iran Philatelic Study Circle**
99 Moseley Wood Dr, Leeds LS16 7HD, England.
- Iran Philatelic Study Circle Bulletin. 3 per yr.

**Irish Association of Master Bakers**
114 Somerton Rd, Belfast, N. Ireland.
- Master Baker, Confectioner & Caterer. m. ISSN
  0025-4983

**Irish Astronomical Journal**
Armagh Observatory, N. Ireland.
- Irish Astronomical Journal. 4 per yr. ISSN 0021-
  1052

**Irish Communist Organization**
- Connolly's Suppressed Writings. (pub. by
  Connolly Books Ltd.)

**Irish Linen Guild**
- Textile Times International. (pub. by Granite
  Publications)

**Irish National Teachers Organization**
23 College Gardens, Belfast 9, Northern Ireland.
- Northern Teacher. s-a. ISSN 0048-0797 (Co-
  Sponsor: Ulster Teachers Union)

**Irish Naturalists' Journal Committee**
Science Library, Queen's Univ., Belfast BT9 5EQ,
N. Ireland.
- Irish Naturalists' Journal. q. ISSN 0021-1311

**Iron and Steel Statistics Bureau**
P.O. Box No. 230, 12, Addiscombe Rd., Croydon
CR9 6BS, England.
- Iron and Steel. Annual Statistics for the United
  Kingdom. a. ISSN 0075-0867
- Iron and Steel Industry: Monthly Statistics. m.
- U. K. Exports of Iron and Steel (Monthly) m.
- U. K. Imports of Iron and Steel (Quarterly) q.
- World Trade-Steel. q (quantities); a. (values)

**Iron and Steel Trades Confederation**
Swinton House, 324 Gray's Inn Rd., London WC1X
8DD, Eng.
- Man and Metal. m. ISSN 0025-1518

**Iron Press**
5 Marden Terrace, Cullercoats, Northumberland,
England.
- Iron. q.

**Islamic Cultural Centre**
146 Park Rd., London N.W.8, Eng.
- Islamic Quarterly; a review of Islamic Culture. q.
  ISSN 0021-1842

**Isle of Man Examiner Ltd.**
Hill St., Douglas, Isle of Man, U.K.
- Manx Star. w. ISSN 0047-5823

**Isle of Wight County Press Ltd.**
29 High Street, Newport, Isle of Wight PO30 1ST,
England.
- Solent Yearbook; solent cruising & racing
  association year book. a. (Solent Cruising &
  Racing Association)

**Italiano Ltd.**
48 Catherine Place, London SW1E 6HL, England.
- Italiano. m.

**J.E.P. and Associates**
Suite 23, 107-111 Fleet Street, London, EC4,
England.
- Scottish Graduate. a. ISSN 0080-8032 (Scottish
  Union of Students)

**John I. Jacobs & Co. Ltd.**
19 Great Winchester St., London EC2N 2DB, Eng.
- World Tanker Fleet Review. s-a. ISSN 0049-8157

**Jaguar Books**
3 Carlisle Place, London SW1, England.
- Filmlog; index of feature film production and
  casting in Britian. m.
- P C R. (Professional Casting Report) w.

**Derek James, Ed. & Pub.**
118 Wyndham Rd., Bournemouth, Hants., England.
- Gay World. q.

**Japan Society of London**
630 Grand Buildings, Trafalgar Square, London
WC2N 5HN, England.
- Japan Society of London. Bulletin. 3 per yr. ISSN
  0021-4701

**Jazz Journal**
27 Willow Vale, London W12 0PA, England.
- Jazz Catalogue. a. ISSN 0075-3556

**Jehovah's Witnesses**
- Yearbook of Jehovah's Witnesses. (pub. by
  Watchtower Bible and Tract Society)

**Jersey Cattle Society of the U.K.**
Jersey House, 154 Castle Hill Reading RG1 7RP,
Berkshire, England.
- Combined Jersey Herd Book, Directory, & Elite
  Register of the U.K. a.
- Jersey. s-a. ISSN 0021-5929

**Jerusalem and the Middle East Church Association**
24 the Borough, Farnham, Surrey GU9 7NJ, Eng.
- Bible Lands. q. ISSN 0006-0763

**Jetline Schedules Ltd.**
89 Stroud Green Rd., London N4 3EP, England.
- Jetline Schedules. m. ISSN 0021-602X

**Jewish Chronicle Publications**
25 Furnival St., London E.C.4, Eng.
- Jewish Chronicle; the organ of British Jewry. w.
  ISSN 0021-633X
- Jewish Travel Guide. a. ISSN 0075-3750
- Jewish Year Book. a. ISSN 0075-3769

**Jewish Echo Ltd.**
463 Eglinton Street, Glasgow G5 9RT, Scotland.
- Jewish Echo. w.

**Jewish Gazette Ltd.**
18 Cheetham Parade, Manchester M8 6DJ, Eng.
- Jewish Gazette. w. ISSN 0021-6461

**Jewish Historical Society of England**
33 Seymour Pl., London W.1, Eng.
- Anglo-Jewish Art and History. irreg. ISSN 0003-
  3367 (Jewish Museum)
- Jewish Historical Society of England. Annual
  Report and Accounts for the Session. a.

**Jewish Literary Trust Ltd.**
68 Worcester Crescent, London NW7 4NA, Eng.
- Jewish Quarterly. q.

**Jewish Museum**
- Anglo-Jewish Art and History. (pub. by Jewish
  Historical Society of England)

**Jewish Telegraph Ltd.**
Levi House, Bury Old Rd., Manchester M8 6HB,
Eng.
- Jewish Telegraph. w. ISSN 0021-6755

**Jewish Vegetarian & Natural Health Society**
855, Finchley Rd., London N.W.11, Eng.
- Jewish Vegetarian. q. ISSN 0021-681X

**Jim Clarke Foundation**
20 Tudor St., London Ec4, England, Eng.
- New Driver. q. ISSN 0028-4637

**John Player & Sons Ltd.**
- John Player Cricket Yearbook. (pub. by Queen
  Anne Press Ltd.)
- John Player Golf Yearbook. (pub. by Queen Anne
  Press Ltd.)
- John Player Motorsport Yearbook. (pub. by
  Queen Anne Press Ltd.)
- Motor Cycling. (pub. by Queen Anne Press Ltd.)

**John Rylands University Library**
Deansgate, Manchester M3 3EH, Eng.
- John Rylands University Library of Manchester.
  Bulletin. s-a.

**Johnson, Matthey & Co. Ltd.**
78 Hatton Garden, London EC1P 1AE, Eng.
- Platinum Metals Review. q. ISSN 0032-1400

**Johnson Society of London**
Broadmead, Eynsford Rd., Farningham, Kent, Eng.
- New Rambler. a. ISSN 0028-6540

**Johnson's of Hendon Ltd.**
335 Hendon Way, Dendon, London, NW4,
England.
- Johnson Photographic Year Book. a. ISSN 0075-
  3912

**Joint Association of Classical Teachers**
31-34 Gordon Sq., London WC1H 0PY, England.
- Didaskalos. (pub. by Basil Blackwell & Mott Ltd.)
- Joint Association of Classical Teachers. Bulletin. 3
  per yr.

**Joint British Committee for Stress Analysis**
- Journal of Strain Analysis for Engineering Design.
  (pub. by Mechanical Engineering Publications
  Ltd.)

**Jordan Dataquest Ltd.**
Jordan House, 47 Brunswick Place, London N1
6EE, England.
- Britain's Top 1000 Private Companies. a.

**Michael Joseph**
52 Bedford Sq., London W.C. 1, England.
- Let's Halt Awhile in Great Britain. a. ISSN 0075-
  8876

**Journal of Collective Chemistry and Physics**
Drs. L. Zakarias & J. Zakarias, 7 Downside Rd.,
Clifton, Bristol BS8 2XE, Eng.
- Journal of Collective Chemistry and Physics. s-a
  (in double nos.)

**Journal of Commerce and Shipping Telegraph Ltd.**
213 Tower Bldg, Water St., Liverpool L3 1LN, Eng.
- Journal of Commerce. d. ISSN 0021-9851
- New Construction; shipbuilding in British and
  overseas yards. q. ISSN 0028-4491
- Sea Breezes; the magazine of ships and the sea. m.
  ISSN 0036-9977

**Journal of Park Administration Ltd.**
The Adelphi, John Adam St., London W.C.2, Eng.
- Parks and Recreation. m. ISSN 0031-2223
  (Institute of Park and Recreation Administration)

**Journal of Refrigeration Ltd.**
19 Harcourt St., London W.1, Eng., U.K.
- Journal of Refrigeration. m. ISSN 0022-4138

**Joynson-Bruwers Ltd.**
Box 67, Oxford OX1 5JZ, Oxford, Eng.
- Forma; the true informer for planners. q.

**Judo, Ltd.**
28 High St., Tooting, London S.W. 17, Eng.
- Judo. m. ISSN 0022-5819

**Junior Astronomical Society**
58 Vaughan Gardens, Ilford, Essex IG1 3PD, Eng.
- Hermes. q.

**Junior Bookshelf**
Marsh Hall, Thurstonland, Huddersfield HD4 6XB,
Yorkshire, England.
- Junior Bookshelf. 6 per yr. ISSN 0022-6505

**Junior Club Publications Ltd.**
36 Craven St., London WC2N 5NG, Eng.
- Science Teacher. 6 per yr. ISSN 0036-8547

**Junior Hospital Doctors" Association**
- On Call. (pub. by Asgard Publishing Ltd.)

**Juniper Journals Ltd.**
49-50 Hatton Garden, London EC1N 8XS, England.
- Communications International. m.
- New Electronics. fortn. ISSN 0047-9624

**Justice of the Peace (Holdings) Ltd.**
Little London, Chichester, Sussex, Eng
(and Butterworth & Co. Ltd., 14 Curity Ave., Toronto 16, Canada)
- Anglo-American Law Review. q.
- Family Law. 8 per yr. ISSN 0014-7281
- Justice of the Peace. w.
- Local Government Review. w.
- Police Journal; a quarterly review for the police forces of the commonwealth and english-speaking world. q. ISSN 0032-258X

**Justices' Clerks' Society**
c/o Magistrates' Court, Hobson Street, Cambridge CB1 1NS, England
(Subscriptions to: M. Hargreaves, Court House, Dunstable, Beds., England)
- Justices' Clerk. q.

**K. Publications (London) Ltd.**
8 Bloomsbury Way, London W.C. 1, Eng.
- Headlight; the lorry drivers trade paper. m. ISSN 0017-8764

**Kalerghi Publications**
51 Welbeck St., London W1M 7HE, Eng.
- Hovering Craft and Hydrofoil. m. ISSN 0018-6775

**Norman Kark Publications Ltd.**
268-270 Vauxhall Bridge Rd., London S.W.1, Eng.
- London Mystery Selection; a quarterly anthology of the best crime, mystery and detective fact and fiction. q. ISSN 0307-9112

**Karting Magazine Ltd.**
Bank House, Summerhill, Chislehurst, Kent, Eng.
- Karting. m. ISSN 0022-913X

**Keats-Shelley Memorial Association**
Longfield Cottage, Longfield Drive, London S.W.14, England
- Keats-Shelley Memorial Bulletin. a. ISSN 0453-4395 (Avail. from Wm. Dawson & Sons Ltd., Cannon House, Folkestone, Kent, England)

**Keepsake Press**
26 Sydney Rd., Richmond, Surrey TW9 1VB, England.
- Keepsake Poems. irreg.

**Kelly's Directories Ltd.**
Neville House, Eden St., Kingston-upon-Thames, Surrey, England.
- Advertiser's Annual. a. ISSN 0065-3578 (Co-publisher: Media Expenditure Analysis Ltd.)
- British Industry and Services in the Common Market. a.
- Debrett's Peerage and Baronetage. a.
- Flight Directory of British Aviation. a. ISSN 0071-5700
- Kelly's Handbook. a. ISSN 0075-5362
- Kelly's Manufacturers and Merchants Directory; list of manufacturers and merchants (alphabetical and classified) a. ISSN 0075-5370
- Kelly's Post Office London Directory; comprehensive list of trades in London (classified and alphabetical) a. ISSN 0075-5389

**Kemp's Group (Printers & Publishers) Ltd.**
1-5 Bath St., London EC1V 9QA, England.
- Chambers Trades Register. South Wales and South West England. a. ISSN 0069-2506
- Chambers Trades Register of Scotland and North East England. a.
- Chambers Trades Register of the Wirral to the Wash. a.
- Kemps Directory. a. ISSN 0075-5419
- Kemps Film and Television Year Book (International) a. ISSN 0075-5427
- Kemps Harrow and District Local Directory. a. ISSN 0450-0261
- Kemps Music and Record Industry Year Book International. a.
- Kemps Ruislip and Northwood Directory. a.

- Kemps Uxbridge and District Local Directory. a.
- London Directory. a.

**Kendervic Ltd.**
3 Erpingham Rd., London SW15 1BE, England.
- Non-Ionizing Radiation; r.f., microwaves, infra-red, lasers. irreg. ISSN 0550-8398

**Kennedy and Co. Ltd.**
22 Methuen Park, London N1O 2JS, Eng.
- C M M. (Confectionery Manufacture & Marketing) 12 per yr. ISSN 0007-8654
- I C M. (Ice Cream Manufacture) bi-m.

**Kennedy Brothers (Publishing) Ltd.**
Howden Rd., Silsden, Keighley, Yorkshire, Eng
(U.S. Address: 3570 Warrensville Center Rd. Shaker Heights, Ohio 44122)
- International Cycle Sport. m. ISSN 0020-6504

**Kennel Club**
1 Clarges St., London W1Y 8AB, Eng.
- Kennel Gazette. m. ISSN 0022-9962

**Kent Archaeological Society**
The Museum, Saint Faith's St., Maidstone, Kent, England.
- Archaeologia Cantiana. a. ISSN 0066-5894

**Kent County Council**
County Hall, Maidstone, Kent, England.
- Kentish Sources. irreg., 1969, no. 6. ISSN 0075-5486

**Kent Family History Society**
c/o Colin J. Perry, 53 St. Lawrence Forstal, Canterbury, Kent, England.
- Kent Family History Society. Record Publication. irreg. ISSN 0308-9037

**George Kent Ltd.**
Biscot Rd., Luton, Bedfordshire LU3 1AL, England.
- Kent Technical Review. 3 per yr. ISSN 0374-3659

**Kent Messenger**
Head Office, New Hythe Lane, Larkfield, Kent, Eng.
- Incant; independent newspaper for the University of Kent at Canterbury and surrounding colleges. fortn.
- Kent Messenger; county paper of Kent. w. ISSN 0023-0049

**A. S. Kerswill Ltd.**
15 Cochrane Mews, London NW8, Eng.
- Vacher's European Companion. q.
- Vachers Parliamentary Companion. q.

**Kime's International Law Directory, Ltd**
170 Sloane St., London SW1X 9QG, England.
- Kime's International Law Directory. a. ISSN 0075-6040

**Henry Kimpton Ltd.**
205 Great Portland St., London W1N 6LR, England
(Dist. in U.S. by C. V. Mosby Co., 3207 Washington Blvd., St. Louis, Mo. 63103)
- System of Ophthalmology. irreg. ISSN 0082-1195

**King & Hutchings**
Cricketfield Rd., Uxbridge, Middlesex, Eng.
- Funeral Service Journal. m. ISSN 0016-2809

**King Publications Ltd.**
Film House, 142 Wardour Street, London W1V 4BR, England.
- International Film and T. V. Yearbook. a.
- Screen International. w.

**Kings College Hospital Medical School**
Denmark Hill, London SE5 8RX, Eng.
- King's Gazette; the journal of King's College Hospital. irreg. ISSN 0085-2546

**Kings Cross Publishing Co.**
205 Euston Rd., London N.W.1, Eng.
- Transport Review. w.

**Kings Regiment**
T and AVR Center, Townsend Ave., Liverpool L11 5AF, Eng.
- Kingsman. s-a.

**Kingsclere Publications**
40 George Street, Kingclere, Newbury, Berkshire RG15 8NQ, England.
- Out and About Thames & Kennet Valleys. bi-m.

**Kingston Press Services Ltd.**
179b High St., Hampton Hill, Middlesex, Eng.
- Language and Speech. q. ISSN 0023-8309

**Kipling Society**
18 Northumberland Ave., London WC2N 5BJ, Eng.
- Kipling Journal. q. ISSN 0023-1738

**Kirklees Chamber of Commerce Inc. (West Yorkshire)**
- Kirklees Chamber of Commerce. Member's Directory. (pub. by G. W. Foster Associates Ltd.)

**Kiver-Patterson Publishing**
322 St. John St., London E.C.1, England.
- Electronic Production; methods and equipment. m. 10 per yr. ISSN 0306-333X

**Knighton Publications**
151 Pampisford Rd, South Croydon, Surrey, CR2 6DE, Eng.
- Pet Product Marketing and Garden Supplies - the Pet Trade Journal. m. ISSN 0031-6202

**Kogan Page Ltd.**
116a Pentonville Rd., London N1 9JN, England.
- British Qualifications. a.
- European Offshore Oil and Gas Yearbook. a.
- European Offshore Oil & Gas Yearbook. a.
- Programmed Learning & Educational Technology. q. ISSN 0033-0396 (Association for Programmed Learning and Educational Technology)
- Transport Manager's Handbook. a.

**C. C. Kohler**
12 Horsham Rd., Dorking, Surrey RH4 2JL, England.
- Gissing Newsletter. q. ISSN 0017-0615

**Kompass Publishers Ltd.**
Stuart House, 41-43 Perrymount Rd., Haywards Heath, West Sussex, RH16 3DA, Eng.
(Dist. in U.S. by: I.P.C. (America) Inc., 205 E. 42nd St., New York, NY 10017)
- British Exports. Export Services/Exportations Britanniques/Britischer Export/Exportaciones Britanicas. a. ISSN 0305-7682 (British National Export Council)
- Dial Industry. a.
- Kompass United Kingdom; register of British industry and commerce. a.
- U K Trade Names. biennial. ISSN 0082-7142

**Kontexts Publications**
31 Pinhoe Road, Exeter, Devon, England.
- Kontexts. irreg.

**Kosmon Church**
- Kosmon Unity. (pub. by Kosmon Press)

**Kosmon Press**
BM-KCKP, London WC1V 6XX, England
(Dist. in U.S. by: Kosmon Service Center, Box 664, Salt Lake City, UT 84110)
- Kosmon Unity. s-a. (Kosmon Church)

**Kraushar Andrews and Eassie Ltd**
32 Fitzroy Square, London W i, Eng.
- MINTEL. m. ISSN 0305-3504 (Objective Marketing and Intelligence Services Ltd.) (U.S. Subscr. to: International Scholarly Book Services Inc., 10300 S.W. Allen Blvd., Beaverton, OR 97116)

**Krax**
63 Dixon Lane, Leeds LS12 4RR, Yorkshire, England.
- Krax. m.

**Krikos Ltd.**
33 Mapesbury Rd., London NW2 4Ht, Eng.
- Krikos; a bi-monthly international Greek review. bi-m. ISSN 0023-4656

**Kvakera Esperantista Societo**
c/o G. B. Tordoff, 82 Pendennis Park, Bristol BS4 4JN, England.
- Kvakera Esperantisto. q. ISSN 0023-5814

**Kwame Nkrumah Institute of Writers and Journalists**
P.O. Box 23, 101-103 Gower St., London WC1E 6AW, England.
- Liberation Struggle. s-a.
- Zambezi Press International. bi-m.

**Laban Art of Movement Guild**
Raymont Hall, 57/63, Wickham Road, London SE4 1LX, England.
- Laban Art of Movement Guild Magazine. s-a.

**Laboratory Animal Science Association**
- Laboratory Animal Handbooks. (pub. by Laboratory Animals Ltd.)
- Laboratory Animals. (pub. by Laboratory Animals Ltd.)

**Laboratory Animals Ltd.**
7 Warwick Court, London WC1R 5DP, England.
- Laboratory Animal Handbooks. irreg. ISSN 0458-5933 (Laboratory Animal Science Association)
- Laboratory Animals. q. ISSN 0023-6772 (Laboratory Animal Science Association)

**Labour Committee for Europe**
Europe House, 1A Whitehall Place, London SW1A 2HA, Eng.
- Europe Left. m. ISSN 0046-2705

**Labour Party**
Transport House, Smith Square, London SW1P 3JA, Eng.
- Labour Organiser. bi-m. ISSN 0023-6993
- Labour Weekly. w.

**Labour Research Department**
78 Blackfriars Rd., London S.E. 1, Eng.
- Labour Research. m. ISSN 0023-7000
- Labour Research Department Fact Service. fortn. ISSN 0047-388X

**Lady**
39-40 Bedford St., Strand, London WC2E 9ER, Eng.
- Lady. w. ISSN 0023-7167

**Lafarge Aluminous Cement Co.**
Box 13, Fondu Works, 730 London Rd., Grays, Essex RM16 1NJ, Eng.
- Cement Special. q. ISSN 0008-8889

**Lakeland Dialect Society**
c/o Miss N. Dawson, 8 Barras Close, Morton Park, Carlisle CA2 6PR, England.
- Lakeland Dialect Society. Bulletin. a.

**Lakescene Publications**
12 Lonsdale St., Carlisle, Cumbria, England.
- Lakeland Rambler. a.

**Charles Lamb Society**
46 Brookfield, Highgate West Hill, London N6 6AT, Eng.
- Charles Lamb Bulletin. q. ISSN 0308-0951

**Lancashire Authors' Association**
55 Rutland Ave., Poulton-le-Fylde, Blackpool, Lancs. FY6 7RX, Eng.
- Lancashire Authors' Association. Record. q. ISSN 0034-1525

**Lancashire Dialect Society**
c/o G. L. Brook, English Dept., The University, Manchester 13, England.
- Lancashire Dialect Society. Journal. a. ISSN 0075-7799

**Lancaster Archaeological Society**
Lonsdale College, Department of Classics and Archeology, The University, Lancaster, England.
- Contrebis. a. ISSN 0307-5087

**Lancet Ltd.**
7 Adam St., Adelphi, London W.C.2, Eng
- Lancet. a. ISSN 0023-7507 (North American edition published by: Little, Brown and Co., 34 Beacon St., Boston, MA 02106)

**Land & Liberty Press Ltd.**
177 Vauxhall Bridge Rd., London SW1V 1EU, Eng.
- Land & Liberty; bi-monthly journal for land value taxation and free trade. bi-m. ISSN 0023-7574 (United Committee for the Taxation of Land Values)

**Land of Cokaygne**
1 Jesus Terrace, New Square, Cambridge, England.
- Arcana; the magazine of cosmology, eschatology, hermetic science and the occult. 4 per yr.

**Land Worker Publishing Co. (1919) Ltd.**
308 Gray's Inn Rd., London W.C.1, Eng.
- Land Worker. m. ISSN 0023-7701 (National Union of Agricultural Workers)

**Landscape Institute**
12 Carlton House Terrace, London, S.W.1, Eng.
- Landscape Design. q. ISSN 0020-2908

**Landscape Research Group**
Longmoor, 8 Cunningham Rd., Banstead, Surrey SM7 3HG, England.
- Landscape Research News. irreg. (approx. 3 per yr.) ISSN 0458-7014

**Lapidary Publications**
84 High St., Broadstairs, Kent, Eng.
- Gems; the British Lapidary Magazine. bi-m. ISSN 0016-6251 (Rank Xerox-U.K.)

**Laser**
26 Selwood Rd., Addiscombe, Croydon CR0 7JR, Surrey, Eng.
- Laser. irreg.

**Latin America Review of Books, Ltd.**
6-7 New Bridge St., London EC4V 6HR, England.
- Latin America Review. irreg.

**Latin American Newsletters Ltd.**
90-93 Cowcross Rd., London EC1M 6BL, England (U.S. Address: 432 Park Ave. S., New York, N.Y. 10016)
- Latin America Economic Report. fortn. ISSN 0309-443X
- Latin America Political Report. w. ISSN 0309-2992

**Latin American Notaphilic Society**
238-245 Grand Bldgs., Trafalgar Square, London WC2N 5EZ, Eng.
- L A N S A. q.

**Laurence, Scott & Electromotors Ltd.**
Norwich NR1 1JD, Eng.
- L S E Engineering Bulletin. 2-3 per yr. ISSN 0023-6381

**Law and Local Government Publications Ltd.**
27-29 Furnival St., London EC4A 1PS, Eng.
- Health & Social Service Journal. w. ISSN 0300-8347
- Hospital International. bi-m. ISSN 0018-571X
- Residential Social Work. m. (Residential Care Association)

**Law Guardian Publishing Co. Ltd.**
69 Theobald's Rd., London W.C.1, Eng.
- Guardian Gazette. m. ISSN 0306-3348

**Law Notes Lending Library Ltd.**
25-26 Chancery Lane, London WC2A 1NB, England.
- Law Notes. m.

**Law Society**
Chancery Lane, London W.C.2, Eng.
- Law Society's Gazette. w. ISSN 0023-9380

**Law Society of Scotland**
26-27 Drumsheugh Gardens, Edinburgh EH3 7YR, Scotland.
- Law Society of Scotland. Journal. m.

**Lead Development Association (London)**
- Lead Abstracts. (pub. by Zinc-Lead Library and Abstracts Service)

**League of Arab States**
1-11 Hay Hill, London W.1, Eng.
- Arab. m. ISSN 0003-7389

**League of Welldoers**
119/133 Limekiln Lane, Liverpool 5, Eng.
- Welldoer. q. ISSN 0043-2407

**R. D. Leakey, Ed. & Pub.**
Sutcliffe House, Settle, Yorkshire, England.
- Modern Inshore Fishing. irreg.

**Leather Wear**
154 Fleet St., London, E.C.4, Eng.
- Leather Wear. s-m.

**Leeds Arts Collections Fund**
Temple Newsam House, Leeds 15, Yorkshire, England.
- Leeds Arts Calendar. s-a. ISSN 0024-0257

**Leeds Chamber of Commerce and Industry**
9 Quebec St., Leeds LS1 2HD, Eng.
- Leeds Journal. m. ISSN 0024-0273

**Leeds Grammar School**
Moorland Rd., Leeds LS6 1AN, Eng.
- Leodiensian. 3 per yr. ISSN 0024-0923

**Leeds Labour Publishing Society Ltd.**
9 Queen Square, Leeds LS2 8AJ, Yorkshire, Eng.
- Leeds Weekly Citizen. w. ISSN 0047-4339

**Leeds Philosophical and Literary Society**
Central Museum, Calverley St., Leeds 2, England.
- Leeds Philosophical and Literary Society. Proceedings. Literary and Historical Section. 3-4 per yr. ISSN 0024-0281

**Leeds University Union**
Leeds 2, Leeds 2, Yorks, Eng.
- Leeds Student. w. ISSN 0041-6975 (Co-Sponsor: Leeds Polytechnic Union)

**Legal Action Group**
28a Highgate Road, London Nw5 1NS, England.
- L A G Bulletin. m.

**Leicester & County Chamber of Commerce**
4 Horsefair St., Leicester LE1 6EA, Eng.
- Leicester & County Chamber of Commerce Journal. m. ISSN 0024-0648

**Leicester University Press**
2 Univ. Rd., Leicester LEI 7RB, Eng.
- Journal of Transport History. s-a. ISSN 0022-5266
- Occasional Papers in English Local History. irreg., 3rd series, no. 2, 1976. ISSN 0078-303X
- Philosophical Books. 3 per yr. ISSN 0031-8051
- Studies in Early English History. irreg., no. 6, 1975. ISSN 0081-7821 (Dist. by Humanities Press, 171 First Ave., Atlantic Highlands, NJ 07716)
- Urban History Yearbook. a. ISSN 0306-0845

**Leicestershire Local History Council**
White House, Ashby Parva, Lutterworth, Leicestershire, England.
- Leicestershire Historian. a. ISSN 0024-0664

**Leo Baeck Institute**
- Leo Baeck Institute. Year Book. (pub. by Secker & Warburg)

**Leprosy Mission**
50 Portland Place, London W1N 3DG, England.
- Leprosy Mission, London. Annual Report. a. ISSN 0075-8809
- New Day. 3 per yr.
- Partners. s-a. ISSN 0308-745X

**Lepus Books**
7 Leighton Place, Leighton Road, London NW5 2QL, England.
- Journal of Human Movement Studies. q. ISSN 0306-7297

**Lernhurst Publications Ltd.**
Blakeden Drive, Claygate, Surrey, England.
- Pilot. m. ISSN 0300-1695

**Lesterstar Ltd.**
375 Upper Richmond Rd. W., London SW14 7RX, England.
- E C Electronics Components Europe. 3 per yr.
- Electronics Industry. fortn. ISSN 0307-2401

**Leviathan House**
80 East St., Epsom KT17 1HF, Surrey, England.
- Who's Who in Computing. irreg.

**H. K. Lewis & Co. Ltd.**
136 Gower St., London WC1E 6BS, England.
- British Journal of Cancer. m. (2 vols. per yr.) ISSN 0007-0920 (Cancer Research Campaign)
- British Journal of Experimental Pathology. bi-m. ISSN 0007-1021

**Lewis Carroll Society**
69 Ashby Rd., Woodville, Burton-on-Trent, Staffs., England.
- Jabberwocky. q. ISSN 0305-8182

**Lewis Publications Ltd.**
83 Maybury Rd., Woking, Surrey GU21 5JH, England.
- Family Holiday Guide. a. ISSN 0071-3740

**Ley Hunter**
P.O. Box 152, London N1O 1EP, England.
- Ley Hunter; magazine of earth mysteries. bi-m. ISSN 0308-812X

**Liberal Catholic Church**
30 Gordon St., London W.C.1, Eng.
- Liberal Catholic. q. ISSN 0024-1792

**Liberal News**
1 Whitehall Place, London SW1A 2ME, England.
- Liberal News. w.

**Liberal Party Organisation**
Liberal Party Publications Dept., 9 Poland St.,
London WiV 3DG, England.
- Liberal Focus. irreg.
- Liberal Party Organisation. Liberal News. w.
  ISSN 0024-1849
- Liberal Party Organisation. Study Paper. irreg.

**Liberation**
313-5 Caledonian Rd., London N.1, Eng.
- Liberation. bi-m. ISSN 0024-1873

**Liberation News Services**
30 Holland Park Gardens, London W.14, Eng.
- Liberation News Service. w. ISSN 0024-1903

**Library Action Group**
1-Station Terrace, Leeds LS B 3 QR, Eng.
- Library Action. q. ISSN 0047-4525

**Library Association**
7 Ridgmount St., Store St., London, W.C.1, England
- British Humanities Index. 4 quarterly parts and
  annual cumulation. ISSN 0007-0815
- British Librarianship & Information Science.
  quinquennial. ISSN 0071-5662
- British Technology Index; a current subject-guide
  to articles in British technical journals. m.(annual
  cumulation) ISSN 0007-1889
- Guide to Current British Journals. a. ISSN 0017-
  5277 (Dist. in U.S. by: R. R. Bowker Co., 1180
  Ave. of the Americas, New York, NY 10036)
- Guide to Reference Material. irreg., 3rd ed. 1977.
  ISSN 0072-8640
- Journal of Librarianship. q. ISSN 0022-2232
- Library & Information Science Abstracts. bi-m.
  ISSN 0024-2179
- Library Association. Proceedings, Papers and
  Summaries of Discussions at the ... Conference. a.
- Library Association. Year Book. a. ISSN 0075-
  9066
- Library Association Record. m. ISSN 0024-2195
- New Library Buildings. irreg.
- R A D I A L S Bulletin. (Research and
  Development-Information and Library Science) s-
  a. ISSN 0302-2706

**Library Association. Branch and Mobile Libraries
Group**
c/o Ulverston Library, King's Road, Ulverston,
Cumbria LA12 0BT, England.
- Service Point. s-a.

**Library Association. Cataloguing and Indexing Group**
c/o C. J. Koster, 18 Apple Grove, Enfield, Middx.
EN1 3DD, England.
- Catalogue & Index. q. ISSN 0008-7629

**Library Association. Colleges, Institutes and Schools
of Education Group**
West Midlands College, Gorway, Walsall, Staffs.,
England
(Subscr. to: Ms. D. E. Jones, Ed., West London
Institute of Higher Education, Maria Grey College,
300 St. Margaret's Rd., Twickenham, Middlesex
TW1 1PT England)
- C.I.S.E. Newsletter. 3 per yr.

**Library Association. East Midlands Branch**
c/o the Library, Derby Lonsdale College, Kedleston
Rd., Derby DE3 1GB, Eng.
- East Midlands Bibliography. q. ISSN 0029-2885
- NEMCON. s-a.

**Library Association. Eastern Branch**
County Library, March, Cambridgeshire, England.
- Easterner. 3 per yr.

**Library Association. Hospital Libraries and
Handicapped Readers Group**
50 Canadian Ave., Catford, London S.E.6, Eng.
- Health and Welfare Libraries Quarterly. q. ISSN
  0305-9340

**Library Association. Industrial Group**
c/o Mrs. D. Palmer, Technical Librarian, Smith
Kline & French Laboratories Ltd., Welwyn Garden
City, Herts., England.
- Industrial Group Newsletter. q.

**Library Association. International and Comparative
Librarianship Group**
7 Ridgmount St., London WC1, England.
- Focus on International and Comparative
  Librarianship. 3 per yr. ISSN 0305-8468

**Library Association. Library Education Group**
P.N.L., 132 Haverstock Hill, London NW3 ZA4,
Eng.
- L E G News. (Library Education Group) 2 per yr.

**Library Association. Library History Group**
7, Ridgmount St., Store St., London WC1E 7AE,
England
(Orders to: Miss V. A. A. Fletcsher, Law Library,
Kings College, Strand, London WC2R 2LS,
England)
- Library Association. Library History Group.
  Occasional Publication. irreg. ISSN 0075-9031
- Library History. s-a. ISSN 0024-2306

**Library Association. North Western Group**
London, Ridgmount Street, London, W.C.1,
England.
- Library Association. Reference, Special and
  Information Section. North Western Group.
  Occasional Papers. irreg. ISSN 0075-9058

**Library Association of Ireland**
Belfast, Northern Ireland.
- Leabharlann/Irish Library. q. ISSN 0023-9542

**Library Association. Scottish Group**
College & Research Section, University Library,
Stirling FK9 4LA, Scotland.
- Bibliotheck; a Scottish journal of bibliography and
  allied topics. 3 per yr (plus annual supplement)
  ISSN 0006-193X

**Library Association. West Midland Branch**
Central Libraries, Birmingham B3 3HQ, Eng.
- Open Access; a news-sheet for West Midland
  librarians. q. ISSN 0048-1904

**John Liggins Ltd.**
Fleckney, Leicester, Eng.
- Free-Lance Report. fortn. ISSN 0016-0377

**Light Railway Transport League**
49 Acfold Rd., Handsworth Wood, Birmingham
B2O 1HG, Eng.
- Modern Tramway and Rapid Transit Review. m.
- Tramway Review. q. ISSN 0041-1019

**Light Steam Power**
c/o J. N. Walton, Ed., Kirk Michael, Isle of Man,
U. K.
- Light Steam Power. q. ISSN 0024-3388

**Ligue des Bibliotheques Europeennes de Recherche**
c/o Main Library, University of Birmingham, P.O.
Box 363, England.
- L I B E R Bulletin. 2 per yr.

**Limestone Publications**
c/o the City Lt., Stukeley St., Drury Lane, London
WC2B 5LJ, England.
- Limestone Literary Magazine. 3 per yr. ISSN
  0308-4787

**Lincolnshire and South Humberside Arts**
Beaumont Lodge, Beaumont Fee, Lincoln, England.
- Proof. 3 per yr.

**Lincolnshire Life Ltd**
10 Dudley St, Grimsby, Eng.
- Lincolnshire Life. m. ISSN 0024-371X

**Lindsey Press**
1-6 Essex St., Strand, London W.C.2, England
- Unitarian Historical Society, London.
  Transactions. a. ISSN 0082-7800 (Subscr. to: 4
  Allerton Drive, Liverpool 8, England)

**Linguistics Association of Great Britain**
- Journal of Linguistics. (pub. by Cambridge
  University Press)

**Link House Publications Ltd**
Link House, Dingwall Ave, Croydon, CR9 2TA,
England.
- Broads Book. a. ISSN 0068-273X

- Camping. m. ISSN 0032-4469
- Canals Book. a. ISSN 0069-0066
- Caravan. m. ISSN 0008-6142
- Caravan Factfinder. a.
- Caravan Sites. a.
- Coins and Medals. m.
- Coins Market Values. a. ISSN 0069-4983
- Continental Camping & Caravan Sites. a. ISSN
  0069-9527
- Custom Car. m. ISSN 0591-2334
- Do It Yourself; for the practical man about the
  house. m. ISSN 0012-4370
- Do-It-Yourself. Annual; do-it-yourself and home
  improvement. a. ISSN 0070-6779
- Do-It-Yourself Gardening Annual. a. ISSN 0070-
  6787
- Do It Yourself Retailing; the do it yourself trade
  review. m. ISSN 0012-4397
- Exchange and Mart. w. ISSN 0014-4460
- Fishing Waters; where to fish in England,
  Scotland and Wales. a.
- Hi-Fi News & Record Review. m. ISSN 0018-
  1226
- Hi Fi News & Record Review Annual. a.
- Mobile Home & Holiday Caravan. bi-m.
- Modern Caravanning. m.
- Prediction. m. ISSN 0032-7182
- Prediction Annual. a. ISSN 0079-4953
- Small Boat. m. ISSN 0037-718X
- Stamp Magazine. m.
- Studio Sound & Broadcast Engineering. m.
- Thames Book. a. ISSN 0082-3805

**Linnean Society of London**
- Linnean Society. Biological Journal. (pub. by
  Academic Press, Inc. US)
- Linnean Society. Botanical Journal. (pub. by
  Academic Press, Inc. US)
- Linnean Society. Zoological Journal. (pub. by
  Academic Press, Inc. US)
- Synopses of the British Fauna. (pub. by Academic
  Press Inc. US)

**List and Index Society. Public Record Office**
Chancery Lane, London WC2A 1LR, England.
- List and Index Society. Copies Unpublished Lists
  Etc in Public Record Office, London. (pub. by
  Swift Ltd)
- List and Index Society. Special Series.
  Unpublished Lists, Etc. of Archives Other Than
  Public Record Office. a. ISSN 0075-9805

**John Lister Ltd.**
37 Bury Street, St. James's, London S.W.1.,
England.
- John Lister Catalogue of Queen Elizabeth IInd
  Postage Stamps. a.

**Liszt Society Ltd.**
32 Chivelston, 78 Wimbledon Park Side,
Wimbledon, London SW19 5LH, England.
- Liszt Society, London. Journal. irreg.

**Literature & History**
c/o Dr. P. J. Widdowson, Dept. of Humanities,
Thomas Polytechnic, Wellington St, London SE18
3PF, England.
- Literature & History. s-a. ISSN 0306-1973

**Lithuanian House Ltd.**
Nida Press, 1-2, Ladbroke Gardens, London W11,
England
(Dist. in U.S. by Draugas, 4545 W. 63 St., Chicago,
Ill. 60629)
- S W A T H; yearly book of literature. a. ISSN
  0080-5122

**Lithuanian Social Democratic Party in Exile**
1 Ladbroke Gardens, London W11 2PT, England.
- Mintis/Thought; politikos ir kulturos zurnalas. a.

**Little Ship Club**
Bell Wharf Lane, London E.C.4, Eng.
- Little Ship. q. ISSN 0024-5062

**Little Word Machine Publications**
39 Queenswood Rd., Mosley, Birmingham B13
9AX, England.
- Little Word Machine. q.

**Liverpool Corp.**
Liverpool, Eng.
- Liverpool Bulletin. ISSN 0024-5151

**Liverpool Cotton Services Ltd.**
G.01-G.02 Cotton Exchange Buildings, Liverpool
L3 9JR, Eng.
- Cotton Outlook. w.

**Liverpool Council for Voluntary Service**
14 Castle St., Liverpool L2 0NJ, Eng.
- Castle Street Circular. m. ISSN 0045-592X
(Liverpool Council of Social Service)

**Liverpool Council of Social Service**
- Castle Street Circular. (pub. by Liverpool Council
for Voluntary Service)

**Liverpool School of Tropical Medicine**
- Annals of Tropical Medicine and Parasitology.
(pub. by Liverpool University Press)

**Liverpool University Press**
123 Grove St., Liverpool L7 7AF, Eng.
- Annals of Tropical Medicine and Parasitology. q.
ISSN 0003-4983 (Liverpool School of Tropical
Medicine)
- Bulletin of Hispanic Studies. q. ISSN 0007-490X
- Revue Internationale de Psychologie Appliquee/
International Review of Applied Psychology. s-a.
ISSN 0035-340X (International Association of
Applied Psychology)
- Town Planning Review. q. ISSN 0041-0020
(University of Liverpool. Department of Civic
Design, Town and Regional Planning and
Transport Studies)

**E. & S. Livingstone**
43/45 Annandale St., Edinburgh EH 7 4AT,
Scotland.
- Hand. irreg. ISSN 0072-968X (British Society for
Surgery of the Hand)

**Lloyds Bank International Ltd.**
40-66 Queen Victoria St., London EC4P 4EL,
England.
- Bank of London and South America Review. m.
ISSN 0005-5298

**Lloyds Bank Ltd.**
71 Lombard St., London EC3P 3BS, Eng.
- Dark Horse. m. ISSN 0011-667X
- Lloyds Bank Review. q. ISSN 0024-547X

**Lloyd's of London Press Ltd.**
Sheepen Place, Colchester, Essex CO3 3LP,
England
- Lloyd'S Calendar. a. ISSN 0076-0196 (U.S.
Subscr. to: International Scholarly Book Services,
Inc., Box 555, Forest Grove, OR 97116)
- Lloyd's Law Reports. m. ISSN 0024-5488
- Lloyd's Loading List. w. ISSN 0024-5496
- Lloyd'S Maritime Atlas, Including a
Comprehensive List of Ports and Shipping Places
of the World. biennial. ISSN 0076-020X
- Lloyd's Shipbuilding Review.
- Lloyd's Weekly Casualty Reports. w. (4 vols. per
yr.) ISSN 0047-4908

**Lloyd's Register of Shipping**
71 Fenchurch St., London EC3M 4BS, England.
- Annual Summary of Merchant Ships Launched/
Completed in the World. a (plus quarterly
reports)
- Casualty Return Statistical Summary. a (plus
quarterly reports) ISSN 0008-7572
- Lloyd'S Register of Shipping. Statistical Tables. a.
ISSN 0076-0234
- Lloyd's Register of Yachts. a. (plus 2
supplements)
- 100A1. q.

**Llyfrfa's Methodistiaid Calfinaid**
Caernarfon, North Wales.
- Traethodydd; cylchgrawn chwarterol at wasanaeth
Crefydd, Diwinyddiaeth, Athroniaeth a
llenyddiaeth. q.

**Local Government Operational Research Unit**
King's Road, Reading RG1 4LH, England.
- L G O R U Transportation News. s-a.

**Local Population Studies**
Tawney House, Matlock, Derbyshire DE4 3BT,
England
- Local Population Studies. s-a. (Subscr. to: Mrs. M.
H. Charlton, 9 Lisburne Sq., Torquay, Devon,
England)

**Locke Newsletter**
c/o Roland Hall, Editor, Dept. of Philosophy,
University of York, Heslington, York y0L 5DD,
England.
- Locke Newsletter. a.

**Lockwood Press Ltd.**
6-7 Gough Square, Fleet St, London E.C.4, Eng.
- Fruit Trades Journal. w. ISSN 0016-2256

**Locus Science Publishers**
P.O. Box 26, East Grinstead, West Sussex RH19
4NW, Eng.
- Liquid Crystal Abstracts. m. ISSN 0306-2597

**Lolfa**
Talybont, Ceredigion, Cards., Wales.
- Lol. s-a.

**London and Continental Publishing Ltd.**
117-123 King St., Hammersmith, London W6 9JG,
England.
- Goff's Guide to Motels in Great Britain and
Europe. a. ISSN 0072-4890

**London and Home Counties Regional Advisory
Council for Technological Education**
Tavistock House South, Tavistock Square, London
WC1H 9LR, England.
- Science Education in the Region. irreg.

**London and Middlesex Archaeological Society**
c/o Bishopsgate Institute, 230 Bishopsgate, London
EC2M 4QH, England
(and Phillimore & Co. Ltd., Shopwyke Hall,
Chichester, Sussex, England)
- London and Middlesex Archaeological Society.
Transactions. a. ISSN 0076-0501

**London and Sheffield Publishing Co. Ltd.**
5 Pond Street, Hampstead, London NW3 2PN, Eng.
- EuroClay. bi-m. ISSN 0306-1841 (Institute for
Clay Technology)
- International Refractories Handbook & Directory.
a.
- Refractories Journal. bi-m. ISSN 0034-3110
(Refractories Association of Great Britain)

**London Archaeologist Association**
7 Coalecroft Rd., London S.W. 15, Eng.
- London Archaeologist. q. ISSN 0024-5984

**London Borough of Barking**
Central Library, Axe St., Barking, Essex IG11 7NB,
England.
- Barking Record; London borough of Barking. q.

**London Boroughs Association**
Westminster City Hall, Victoria St., London SW1E
6QW, England.
- L B A Handbook. biennial.
- L O G A/Local Government Annotations. (pub.
by Havering Central Library. London Borough)

**London Bureau**
266-272 Kirkdale, London SE26 4RZ, Eng.
- Exhibition Bulletin. m. ISSN 0014-4649

**London Chamber of Commerce & Industry**
69 Cannon St., London E.C.4, Eng.
- Commerce International. m. ISSN 0010-2733
- Eastern Europe. s-m.
- London Chamber of Commerce & Industry.
Directory. a.

**London Cigarette Card Co. Ltd.**
34 Wellesley Rd., Chiswick, London W.4, Eng.
- Cigarette Card News and Trade Card Chronicle.
m. ISSN 0009-6822

**London City Mission**
175 Tower Bridge Rd., London SE1 2AH, Eng.
- Span. bi-m.

**London Corn Circular Ltd.**
52-57 Mark Lane, London EC3R 7NE, Eng.
- London Corn Circular. w. ISSN 0024-6026

**London Diary Publications Ltd.**
26 d'Arblay, London W1V 3FH, Eng.
- London Weekly Diary of Social Events. w. ISSN
0024-6190

**London Hospital League of Nurses**
London Hospital, Whitechapel, London E1,
England.
- London Hospital League of Nurses Review. a.

**London Information (Rowse Muir) Ltd.**
77-79 Charlotte St., London W1P 2AB, Eng.
- London Information. w. ISSN 0024-6069
- London Information, Galleries, Exhibitions,
Museums. m.

**London Institute of World Affairs**
- Yearbook of World Affairs. (pub. by Sweet &
Maxwell Stevens Journals)

**London Letter**
25 Melville Rd., London S.W. 13, Eng.
- London Letter. bi-m. ISSN 0024-6077

**London Magazine**
30 Thurloe Place, London S.W.7, Eng.
- London Magazine. bi-m. ISSN 0024-6085

**London Mathematical Society**
Burlington House, London W. 1, Eng.
- London Mathematical Society. Bulletin. 3 per yr.
ISSN 0024-6093
- London Mathematical Society. Journal. q. ISSN
0024-6107
- London Mathematical Society. Proceedings. (pub.
by Oxford University Press)
- Russian Mathematical Surveys. (pub. by
Macmillan Journals Ltd.)

**London Medieval Society**
c/o Dept. of German, University of London King's
College, Strand, London WC2R 2LS, England.
- Medieval Research Students in London. a.

**London Natural History Society**
110 Meadvale Rd., London W51LR, England.
- London Bird Report. a.
- London Naturalist. a. ISSN 0076-0579

**London Record Society**
Leicester University Library, University Road,
Leicester. LE17RH, England.
- London Record Society. Occasional Publications.
irreg. ISSN 0085-283X
- London Record Society. Publications. a. ISSN
0085-2848

**London Review**
45 Manor Rd., Ashford, Middx., Eng.
- London Review. s-a. ISSN 0024-614X

**London School of Economics**
- British Journal of Sociology. (pub. by Routledge &
Kegan Paul Ltd.)

**London School of Economics and Political Science**
Houghton St., Aldwych, London WC2A 2AE, Eng.
- British Journal of Industrial Relations. 3 per yr.
ISSN 0007-1080
- Clare Market Review. s-a. ISSN 0009-8221
- Economica. q. ISSN 0013-0427
- Greater London Papers; problems of government
of greater London. irreg; 1971, no. 14. ISSN
0072-7350
- Journal of Transport Economics and Policy. 3 per
yr. ISSN 0022-5258
- L S E Magazine. s-a. ISSN 0023-639X
- L S E Research Monographs. (pub. by Weidenfeld
and Nicolson Ltd.)
- London School of Economics and Political
Science. Department of Geography. Geographical
Papers. irreg. no. 6, 1974. ISSN 0076-0641
- London School of Economics Papers on Soviet
and East European Law, Economics and Politics.
(pub. by Athlone Press)

**London School of Economics and Political Science.
Students' Union**
Houghton St., Aldwych, London WC2 2AE, Eng.
- Beaver. bi-w. ISSN 0005-7525

**London School of Hygiene & Tropical Medicine**
Keppel St., London WC1 E7HT, Eng.
- Journal of Helminthology. q. ISSN 0022-149X

**London Society**
4 Carmelite St., London EC4Y 0BN, England.
- London Society. Journal. m. ISSN 0024-6158

**London Welsh Association**
157-163 Gray's Inn Rd., London W.C.1, Eng.
- London Welshman. m. ISSN 0024-6204

**London Writer Circle**
c/o Mrs. Arda Lacey, 48 Lower Camden,
Chislehurst, Kent BR7 51A, England.
- Within the Circle; London writers' circle review. 3
per yr.

**Longmac Ltd.**
Research Publications Services, Victoria Hall, Fingal St., London SE10 ORF, England.
- Recall; review of educational cybernetics and applied linguistics. 3 per yr. ISSN 0034-1150

**Longman Group Ltd.**
Journals Div., 43/45 Annandale St., Edinburgh EH7 4AT, Scotland.
- Animal Production. bi-m. ISSN 0003-3561 (British Society of Animal Production)
- Annual Register World Events. a. ISSN 0066-4057
- British Journal of Addiction. s-a. ISSN 0007-0890 (Society for the Study of Addiction to Alcohol and other Drugs)
- British Journal of International Studies. 3 per yr. ISSN 0305-8026
- British Journal of Oral Surgery. 3 per yr. ISSN 0007-117X
- British Journal of Orthodontics. q. (British Society of the Study of Orthodontics) (Co-Sponsor: British Association of Orthodontists)
- British Journal of Plastic Surgery. q. ISSN 0007-1226 (British Association of Plastic Surgeons) (Dist. in U.S. by: Williams & Wilkins, Inc., 428 E. Preston St., Baltimore, MD 21202)
- British Journal of Urology. 7 per yr. ISSN 0007-1331 (British Association of Urological Surgeons) (Dist. in U.S. by: Williams & Wilkins Co., 428 E. Preston St., Baltimore, MD 21202)
- British Poultry Science. bi-m. ISSN 0007-1668
- Chromosomes Today. irreg., 1973?vol. 3. ISSN 0069-3944
- Clinical Radiology. bi-m. ISSN 0009-9260 (Faculty of Radiologists) (Dist. in U.S. by: Williams & Wilkins, 428 E. Preston St., Baltimore, MD 21202)
- Heredity; an international journal of genetics. bi-m. ISSN 0018-067X (Genetical Society of Great Britain)
- International Statistical Review/Revue International de Statistique. 3 per yr. ISSN 0306-7734 (International Statistical Institute)
- Journal of Medical Microbiology. q. ISSN 0022-2615 (Pathological Society of Great Britain and Ireland)
- Journal of Pathology. m. ISSN 0022-3417 (Pathological Society of Great Britain and Ireland)
- London Journal; review of metropolitan society past and present. s-a.
- Mathematics in School. 5 per yr. (Mathematical Association)
- Medical and Biological Illustration. q. ISSN 0025-6978 (Institute of Medical & Biological Illustration)
- Paraplegia. q. ISSN 0031-1758 (International Medical Society of Paraplegia)
- Practitioner. m. ISSN 0032-6518
- Quarterly Journal of Experimental Physiology and Cognate Medical Sciences. q. ISSN 0033-5541
- Remedial Education. q. ISSN 0034-4214
- Review of Economic Studies. 3 per yr. ISSN 0034-6527
- Sabouraudia. (International Society for Human and Animal Mycology)
- Scottish Journal of Political Economy. 3 per yr. ISSN 0036-9292 (Scottish Economic Society)
- Statistical Theory and Method Abstracts. q. ISSN 0039-0518 (International Statistical Institute)
- Statistician. q. ISSN 0039-0526 (Institute of Statisticians)
- Tissue & Cell. q. ISSN 0040-8166
- Tropical Animal Health and Production. q. ISSN 0049-4747
- Tubercle. q. ISSN 0041-3879 (International Union Against Tuberculosis) (Dist. in U.S. by: Williams & Wilkins, 428 E. Preston St., Baltimore, MD 21202)
- Urban Studies. 3 per yr. ISSN 0042-0980

**Longman Group Ltd. Keesing's Publications**
5 Miles's Bldgs., Bath BA1 2QS, Eng.
- Keesing's Contemporary Archives; weekly record of world events indexed. w. ISSN 0022-9679

**Longman Ltd.**
Longman House, Burnt Mill, Harlow, Essex, England.
- Teaching Geography. q. ISSN 0305-8018 (Geographical Association)

**Lonsdale Publications Ltd.**
120 Lower Ham Rd., Kingston-On-Thames, Surrey, Eng.
- Florist. m. ISSN 0015-4377
- Florist Trade Magazine. m. ISSN 0015-4415

**Lord's Day Observance Society**
47 Parish Lane, London SE2O 7LU, England.
- Happy Day Diary. a.
- Joy & Light; the Lord's Day magazine. s-a. ISSN 0022-5703

**Lorne, Caldough Ltd.**
Tower Suite, 1 White Hall Place, London SW1, England.
- Business Ideas Letter. m. (Institute of Small Business)

**Loughborough University of Technology**
Loughborough, Leics, England.
- Loughborough University of Technology Gazette. 5 per yr. ISSN 0024-6719

**Loughborough University of Technology. Department of Economics**
Loughborough, Leics. LE11 3TU, England.
- Loughborough Occasional Papers in Economics. irreg.

**Loughborough University of Technology. Students Union**
Venture Newspapers, Edward Herbert Bldg., Loughborough, Leics, Eng. U.K.
- Venture. 8 per yr. ISSN 0042-3548

**Loverseed Press**
Woolacombe House, 141 Woolacombe Rd., Blackheath, London S.E.3, Eng.
- Day by Day; news commentary and digest of national and international affairs and review of the arts. m. ISSN 0011-7080 (Fellowship Party)
- Un-Common Sense; the international illustrated review. m. ISSN 0041-6363 (Fellowship Party)

**Robson Lowe Ltd.**
50 Pall Mall, London SW1Y 5JZ, Eng.
- P J G B/Philatelic Journal of Great Britain. q. ISSN 0030-8048
- Philatelist. m. ISSN 0031-7373

**Loxton Publishers Ltd**
82 Caledonian Rd., London N.1, Eng.
- Mashriq; Urdu newsweekly. w. ISSN 0025-4584

**Loyal Order of Ancient Shepherds (Ashton Unity) Friendly Society**
Shepherds' House, 316A Buxton Rd., Great Moor, Stockport, Eng.
- Shepherd's Magazine. m. ISSN 0037-3613

**Lucas Industries Ltd.**
Great King St., Birmingham B19 2XF, Eng., U.K.
- Lucas Engineering Review. s-a. ISSN 0024-7170

**Ludd's Mill Poetry Publishing Co-Operative**
4 Nowell Place, Almondbury, Huddersfield, Yorks HD5 8PB, Eng.
- Ludd's Mill. q. ISSN 0047-5157

**Lund Humphries**
12 Bedford Square, London Wci, England (and George Wittenborn, Inc., 1018 Madison Ave., New York, N.Y. 10021)
- Architectural Association, London. Papers. irreg. ISSN 0066-6211
- Handbook of Colleges and Departments of Education; and other institutions for the training of teachers in England and Wales. a. ISSN 0072-9760 (Association of Teachers in Colleges and Departments of Education)

**Lute Society**
71 Priory Rd., Kew Gardens, Richmond, Surrey TW9 3DH, England.
- Lute Society Journal. a. ISSN 0460-007X

**Luton & Dunstable Hospital**
Medical Centre, Luton, Bedfordshire, Eng.
- Medical Centre Journal. 3 per yr. ISSN 0025-7095 (Bedfordshire Area Health Authority)

**Luton, Dunstable & District Chamber of Commerce**
Luton, Bedfordshire, England.
- C & T. m. ISSN 0007-7909
- Luton Commerce and Trade Journal. bi-m. ISSN 0047-522X

**Luzac & Co., Ltd.**
46 Great Russell St., London, WC1, England.
- African Language Studies. a. ISSN 0065-3985 (University of London. School of Oriental and African Studies)

- Royal Asiatic Society of Great Britain and Ireland. Oriental Translation Fund Series. irreg.; 1972, no. 42.
- University of London. School of Oriental and African Studies. Bulletin. 3 per yr.

**Lyle Publishing**
Glenmayne, Galashiels, Selkirkshire, Scotland.
- Lyle Official Antiques Review. a.

**Lyric Theatre**
55 Ridgeway St., Belfast 9, N. Ireland.
- Threshold. irreg. ISSN 0040-6562

**M and W Publications**
42 Stanley St., Liverpool L1 6AW, England.
- Police College Magazine. s-a.
- Police World. q. ISSN 0032-261X (International Police Association. British Section)
- Warren; magazine of No. 4 Area metropolitan police. 3 per yr.

**M C B (European Marketing & Customer Studies)**
200 Keighley Road, Bradford BD9 4JQ, West Yorkshire, England.
- European Journal of Marketing. 8 per yr. ISSN 0309-0566

**M C B (Management Decision) Ltd.**
200 Keighley Rd., Bradford BD9 4JQ, Yorkshire, England.
- Management Bibliographies and Reviews. a. ISSN 0309-0582
- Management Decision. 8 per yr. ISSN 0025-1747

**M C B (Managerial Finance) Ltd.**
200 Keighley Rd., Bradford BD9 4JQ, Yorkshire, England.
- Managerial Finance. 3 per yr. ISSN 0307-4358

**M C B (Managerial Law) Ltd.**
200 Keighly Road, Bradford, Yorkshire BD9 4JQ, England.
- Managerial Law. m. ISSN 0309-0558

**M C B (Physical Distribution Management) Ltd.**
200 Keighley Rd., Bradford BD9 4JQ, Yorkshire, Eng.
- International Journal of Physical Distribution. 6 per yr. ISSN 0020-7527

**M C B (Social Economics) Ltd.**
200 Keighly Rd., Bradford, Yorkshire, England.
- International Journal of Social Economics. 3 per yr. ISSN 0306-8293 (International Institute of Social Economics)

**M.C.B. (European Training) Ltd.**
200 Keighley Rd., Bradford BD9 4JQ, Yorks., Eng.
- Journal of European Industrial Training; a professional review of theory and practice. 6 per yr. ISSN 0309-0590

**M P R Publishing Services Ltd.**
Box 40, 15 Greenhill Ave., Shrewsbury SY3 8NR, Eng.
- Metal Powder Report. m. ISSN 0026-0657

**M. S. Publishing**
The Adelphi, John Adam St., London WC2N GAP, England.
- Over Twentyone. m.

**M W Publishers**
290A Hale Lane, Edgware, Middlesex HA8 8NP, England.
- Cranes Today. m. ISSN 0307-0018

**M. MacDonald**
Edgefield Rd., Loanhead, Midlothian, Scotland.
- Lines Review. q. ISSN 0459-4541

**Macdonald and Co.**
Paulton House, 8 Shepherdess Walk, London N1 7LW, England (and Purnell Library Service, 850 7th Ave., New York, NY 10019)
- International Conference on Product Development and Manufacturing Techology. Proceedings. irreg., 1st, London, 1969.

**Macdonald and Evans Ltd.**
8 John St., London WC1N 2HY, England.
- Guide to the Social Services. a. ISSN 0072-8756 (Family Welfare Association)

**Macdonald & Jane's Publishers Ltd.**
Paulton House, 8 Shepherdess Walk, London N.1., England.
- Computer Monographs. a.
- Jane's All the World Aircraft. a. ISSN 0075-3017
- Jane's Fighting Ships. a. ISSN 0075-3025
- Jane's Freight Containers. a. ISSN 0075-3033
- Jane's Infantry Weapons. a.
- Jane's Major Companies of Europe. a. ISSN 0075-3041
- Jane's Ocean Technology. a.
- Jane's Surface Skimmers. a. ISSN 0075-305X
- Jane's Weapon Systems. a. ISSN 0075-3068
- Jane's World Railways. a. ISSN 0075-3084
- Radio and Television Servicing. a.

**McDonald Publications of London Ltd.**
268 High St., Uxbridge, Middlesex UB8 1UA, England.
- Environmental Pollution Management. bi-m.
- International Pest Control; crop protection, public health, wood preservation. bi-m. ISSN 0020-8256
- Reinforced Plastics. m. ISSN 0034-3617

**McGraw Hill Book Co. (U.K.) Ltd.**
McGraw Hill House, Shoppenhangers Rd., Maidenhead, Berks SL6 2QL, England.
- Executive Employment Bulletin. w.

**Machinery Market Ltd.**
146a Queen Victoria St., London EC4 V5AR, Eng.
- Machinery Market and the Machinery and Engineering Materials Gazette. w. ISSN 0024-9211

**Machinery Publishing Co. Ltd.**
New England House, New England St., Brighton BN1 4HN, Eng.
- Machinery and Production Engineering; a journal of production engineering and machine tools. w. ISSN 0024-919X
- Machinery's Buyers' Guide. a. ISSN 0305-3121

**George McIntosh**
120 Woodhill Rd., Glasgow G64 1AX, Scotland.
- Scottish Ironmongery and Hardware Review. m.
- Scottish Jeweller and Watchmaker. bi-m.
- Scottish Plumbers' Journal. bi-m.

**Mack Brooks Exhibitions, Ltd.**
62-64 Victoria St., St. Albans, Herts. AL1 3XT, England.
- European Electro-Optics Markets and Technology Conference. Proceedings. a, 2nd. 1974, Montreux, Switzerland.

**Mackenzie & Arthur Ltd.**
53 George St., Edinburgh, Scotland.
- Landowning in Scotland. q. ISSN 0023-799X (Scottish Landowners' Federation)

**W. & J. Mackey Ltd.**
Lordswood, Chatham, Kent, England.
- English Ceramic Circle. Transactions. a. ISSN 0071-0547

**Mackintosh Publications**
Flemington Rd., Glenrothes KYE, Scotland.
- Mackintosh Yearbook of West European Electronics Data. irreg.

**Maclaren Publishers Ltd.**
Box 109, Croydon, Surrey, CR9 1QH, Eng.
- Audio Visual; use of all forms of audio-visual media in industry, commerce, higher education and the public sector; deals with equipment, materials and practical applications. m. ISSN 0305-2249
- Baking Industries Journal; bread, biscuits, cake. m. ISSN 0005-4151
- British Baker. w. ISSN 0007-0300
- European Rubber Directory. biennial.
- European Rubber Journal. m. ISSN 0305-2222
- H & V News. m. ISSN 0017-9396
- Industrial and Commercial Photographer. m. ISSN 0019-784X
- Materials Reclamation Weekly. w. ISSN 0025-5386
- Office Equipment Index. m. ISSN 0305-635X
- Plastics and Rubber Weekly. w. ISSN 0032-1168
- Refrigeration and Air Conditioning. m. ISSN 0026-8364

**Maclean-Hunter Ltd.**
30 Old Burlington St., London W1X 2AE, England.
- Airtrade. m.
- Brad Advertiser & Agency List. 3 per yr.
- Brad Digest. s-a.

- British Printer; leading technical journal of the printing industry. m. ISSN 0007-1684
- British Printer Specification Manual. a. ISSN 0068-239X
- British Rate & Data Directories and Annuals. a.
- Cruises, Sea Voyages & Car Ferries. s-a. (Association of British Travel Agents)
- Domestic Heating and Engineering Product Information Cards. s-a.
- Freight Transport & Handling Enquiry Service. s-a.
- Heating and Air Conditioning Enquiry Card Service. s-a.
- Heating and Air Conditioning Journal. m. ISSN 0307-7950
- Holiday Scanner; an at a glance guide to one centre inclusive holidays. s-a.
- Industrial Equipment & Materials Product Information Cards. 3 per yr.
- International Freighting Weekly; sea, air, rail, road. w. ISSN 0032-5007
- Modern Purchasing. m.
- Offset Printing. m.
- Oilman. w.
- Packaging News. m. ISSN 0030-9133
- Packaging News Product Information Cards. 3 per yr.
- Printing Product Information Cards. 3 per yr. ISSN 0032-8642
- Routes; directory of International Freighting Services. a.
- Travel Agency; Britain's leading business, marketing and sales publication for the travel trade. m. ISSN 0041-1981

**Macmillan Journals Ltd.**
(Subsidiary of: Macmillan Publishers Ltd.)
4 Little Essex St., London WC2R 3LF, Eng.
- British Birds. m. ISSN 0007-0335
- British Journal of Anaesthesia. m. ISSN 0007-0912
- British Journal of Clinical Pharmacology. bi-m. ISSN 0306-5251 (British Pharmacological Society)
- British Journal of Pharmacology. 12 per yr. ISSN 0007-1188 (British Pharmacological Society)
- Music in Education. bi-m. ISSN 0027-433X
- Nature. w. ISSN 0028-0836
- Nursing Times. w. ISSN 0029-6589
- Occupational Health; a journal for the occupational health team. 12 per yr. ISSN 0029-7917
- Russian Mathematical Surveys. 6 per yr. ISSN 0036-0279 (London Mathematical Society)

**Macmillan London Ltd.**
(Subsidiary of: Macmillan Publishers Ltd.)
4 Little Essex St., London W.C.2, England.
- Winter's Tales; an anthology of long short stories. a. ISSN 0084-0394

**Macmillan Press Ltd.**
(Subsidiary of: Macmillan Publishers Ltd.)
4 Little Essex St., London WC2R 3LF, England.
- International Economic Association. Proceedings of the Conferences and Congresses. irreg. ISSN 0074-4646
- International Institute for Labour Studies. Publications. irreg. ISSN 0074-6509
- Statesman's Year Book; statistical and historical annual of the states of the world. a. ISSN 0081-4601

**Macmillan Publishers Ltd.**
4 Little Essex St., London WC2R 3LF, England.
- Differentiation: Research in Biological Diversity. bi-m. ISSN 0301-4681
- Marine Pollution Bulletin. m. ISSN 0025-326X
- Royal Institute of Philosophy. Lectures. a; latest vol. 8, 1973-1973. ISSN 0080-4436

**Macnaughtan and Sinclair Ltd.**
Rosyth Rd., Polmadie Industrial Estate, Glasgow G5 0XX, Scotland.
- Scottish Electrical Engineer. m. ISSN 0036-9187
- Scottish Radio Trade Digest. m. ISSN 0036-9381
- Scottish Radio Trade Directory Yearbook. a. ISSN 0080-8172
- Scottish Stock Exchange Official List. d. ISSN 0036-9403 (Scottish Stock Exchange Association)

**Macniven and Wallace**
Edinburgh, Scotland.
- Scottish Church and University Almanac. irreg.

**Magistrates' Association**
28 Fitzroy Square, London W.1P 6DD, Eng.
- Magistrate. m. ISSN 0024-9920

**Magnum Publications Ltd.**
110-112 Station Rd. E., Oxted, Surrey RH8 0QA, England.
- Furniture Manufacturer; the international journal for the manufacturer. m. ISSN 0306-0519
- Wire Industry; international monthly journal. m. ISSN 0043-6011
- Wire Industry Yearbook. a. ISSN 0084-0424
- Wire Review; international wire machinery review. a. ISSN 0084-0432

**Malago Archives Committee**
c/o Sixth Form Block, Bedminster Down School, Donald Rd., Uplands, Bristol, England.
- Malago. q.

**Malaysian Rubber Producers' Research Association. Malaysian Rubber Research & Development Board**
Brickendonbury, Hertford, England.
- Rubber Developments. q. ISSN 0035-9483

**Mallett & Co.**
26 Chapel St., Bradford 1, Yorks, Eng.
- Weekly Wool Chart. w. ISSN 0043-2008

**Mammal Society**
- Mammal Review. (pub. by Blackwell Scientific Publications Ltd.)

**Man-to-Man**
57 Pembridge Rd., London W.11, England.
- Man-to-Man Quorum. m.

**Management Consultants Ltd.**
200 Keighly Rd., Bradford, Yorks BD9 4J2, England.
- Library Research Occasional Paper. irreg.

**Management Decision Monographs**
200 Keighley Rd., Bradford, Yorkshire BD9 4JZ, England.
- Management Decision Monographs. irreg.

**Management Publications Ltd.**
Regent House, 54-62 Regent St., London W1A 4YJ, Eng.
- Management Today. m. ISSN 0025-1925

**Manchester Association of Engineers**
M.T.A. Office, U.M.I.S.T., Manchester M6O 1QD, England.
- Manchester Association of Engineers. Transactions. a. ISSN 0076-3705

**Manchester Business School**
Booth St. West, Manchester M15 6PB, England.
- Contents Pages in Management. w. ISSN 0306-3224

**Manchester Chamber of Commerce and Industry**
Ship Canal House, King St., Manchester M6O 2HB, England.
- Manchester Chamber of Commerce and Industry. Yearbook. a.
- Manchester Chamber of Commerce Record. bi-m. ISSN 0025-1992

**Manchester College. Old Students' Association**
Oxford, Eng.
(U.S. Address: Meadville College, 5701 Woodlawn Ave, Chicago, IL 60637)
- Faith and Freedom; a journal of progressive religion. 3 per yr. ISSN 0014-701X

**Manchester District Association of Unitarian and Free Christian Churches**
c/o Keith M. Noble, Elbon House, 27 Gladstone Rd., Altrincham, Cheshire, Eng.
- Unitarian. m. ISSN 0049-531X

**Manchester Guardian Society for the Protection of Trade**
47 Mosley St., Manchester, M6O 8AA, England.
- Manchester Guardian Society for the Protection of Trade. Annual Report. a. ISSN 0076-3713

**Manchester Literary and Philosophical Society**
36 George St., Manchester, England.
- Manchester Literary and Philosophical Society. Memoirs and Proceedings. a. ISSN 0076-3721

**Manchester Mensa.**
c/o Andrew White, 212 Buxton Rd., Davenport, Stockport, Ches, Eng.
- Sear. m. ISSN 0048-9905

**Manchester University Folk Song Society**
University Union, Oxford Road, Manchester M13
9PR, England.
- University Folk. 1-2 per yr.

**Manchester University Press**
Oxford Rd., Manchester M13 9PL, Eng.
- African Social Research. s-a. ISSN 0002-0168
(University of Zambia. Institute for African
Studies ZA)
- Critical Quarterly. q. ISSN 0011-1562
- International Journal of Electrical Engineering
Education. q. ISSN 0020-7209
- Journal of Semitic Studies. s-a. ISSN 0022-4480
- Melland Schill Lectures on International Law.
irreg. ISSN 0076-6313
- Remains, Historical and Literary, Connected with
the Palatine Counties of Lancaster and Chester.
irreg. ISSN 0080-0880 (Chetham Society)
- Research in Education. s-a. ISSN 0034-5237
- Statistical Guides in Educational Research. irreg.
ISSN 0081-4784
- Victoria University of Manchester. Faculty of
Arts. Publications. irreg. ISSN 0083-6028
- Zambian Papers. irreg. ISSN 0084-5124 (Institute
for African Studies)

**W.S. Maney & Sons Ltd.**
Hudson Road, Leeds LS9 7DL, England
(Subscr. to: Treasurer, Sunnyside Cottage, Halton
East, Skipton, Yorkshire, Eng)
- Folk Life; a journal of ethnological studies. a.
ISSN 0430-8778 (Society for Folk Life Studies)

**Manifold**
99 Vera Ave., London N.21, Eng.
- Manifold; review of poetry and the arts. q. ISSN
0025-2166

**Mankind Quarterly**
1 Darnaway St., Edinburgh EH3 6DW, Scotland.
- Mankind Monographs. irreg. ISSN 0076-4116
- Mankind Quarterly; an international quarterly
journal dealing with race and inheritance in the
fields of ethnology, ethno- and human genetics,
ethno-psychology, racial history, demography and
anthro-geography. q. ISSN 0025-2344

**Manning Rapley Publishing Ltd.**
42 High St., Croydon, Surrey CRO 1YB, Eng.
- Building Specification. m. ISSN 0045-3439

**Manningham Press**
Drummond Road, Bradford 8, Yorks, England.
- Handbook of Polytechnic Courses. a. (Committee
of Directors of Polytechnics)

**Mansell Information-Publishing Ltd.**
3 Bloomsbury Place, London WC1A 2QA, England
(Dist. in U.S. by: International Scholarly Book
Services, Box 4347, Portland, OR 97208)
- African Books in Print. biennial.
- Archivum Linguisticum; a review of comparative
philology and general linguistics. s-a. ISSN 0004-
0703
- British Society for Middle Eastern Studies.
Bulletin. s-a. ISSN 0305-6139 (British Society for
Middle Eastern Studies)
- Dumbarton Oaks Bibliographies; based on
"Byzantinische Zeitschrift". irreg. (Dumbarton
Oaks Center for Byzantine Studies, Washington,
D.C. US)
- History of Technology. a. ISSN 0307-5451
- International African Bibliography; current books,
articles and papers in African studies. q. ISSN
0020-5877 (School of Oriental and African
Studies, University of London)
- ISIS Cumulative Bibliography. (Smithsonian
Institution. History of Science Society US)
- London Bibliography of the Social Sciences. irreg.
ISSN 0076-051X (British Library of Political and
Economic Science)
- Persian Studies Series. irreg.
- Quarterly Index Islamicus; current books, articles,
and papers on Islamic Studies. q. ISSN 0308-7395
(University of London. School of Oriental and
African Studies)

**Mantatoforos**
c/o School of Hellenic and Roman Studies, Box
363, Birmingham B15 2FT, England.
- Mantatoforos; bulletin on Modern Greek studies.
q.

**Manufacturers Agents Association**
Box 8, Majestic House, Staines, Middlesex TW18
4DF, Eng.
- Manufacturers Agent. m. ISSN 0025-2522

**Manx Museum and National Trust**
Douglas, Isle of Man, England.
- Manx Museum, Douglas, Isle of Man. Journal. a.
ISSN 0076-4264

**Map Collectors Circle**
30 Baker St., London W1M 2DS, England.
- Map Collectors Circle. 10 per yr. ISSN 0542-6243

**Marcham Manor Press**
Appleford, Abingdon, Oxford OX14 4PB, England.
- Latimer House Papers. irreg., 1968, no. 1. ISSN
0075-8043
- Latimer Monographs. irreg., 1972, no. 3. ISSN
0075-8051
- News Extra. m. ISSN 0028-9027

**Marconi Co. Ltd.**
Chelmsford, Essex, Eng.
- Aerial. 3 per yr. ISSN 0001-9062
- Communication & Broadcasting; information,
practice, technique. q. ISSN 0305-3601

**Marconi Instruments Ltd.**
Longacres, St. Albans, Herts AL4 OJN, Eng
(U.S. Subscr. Address: 100 Stonehurst Court,
Northvale, NJ 07647)
- M I Contact; international news bulletin. bi-m.
ISSN 0024-8207
- Marconi Instrumentation. 3 per yr. ISSN 0025-
2875

**Marine Biological Association of the United Kingdom**
- Marine Biological Association of the United
Kingdom. Journal. (pub. by Oxford University
Press)

**Marine Laboratory, Aberdeen. Scotland**
13A Castle St., Edinburgh EH2 3AR, Scotland.
- Marine Research. irreg. ISSN 0076-4493

**Marine Media Management Ltd.**
Memorial Bldg., 276 Park Lane, London EC3R
7JN, England.
- Institute of Marine Engineers Technical Reports.
irreg. ISSN 0309-3948
- Marine Engineers Review. m. ISSN 0047-5955
(Institute of Marine Engineers)

**Marine Pollution Information Centre. Marine
Biological Association of the United Kingdom**
Citadel Hill, Plymouth, Devon PL1 2PB, England.
- Marine Pollution Research Titles. m.

**Maritime World Ltd.**
24 Petworth Rd., Haslemere, Surrey GU27 2HT,
Eng.
- Navy International. m.

**Marjorie Pollard Publications Ltd.**
Whitemilnes, Kencot, Lechlade, Glos.GL7 3QT,
Eng.
- Hockey Field. 14 per yr. (Sept.-April) ISSN 0018-
3008

**Market Intelligence Ltd.**
439 Market Towers, New Convent Garden Market,
London SW8 5NQ, England.
- Eurofruit. m.

**Market Research Society**
15 Belgrave Sq., London SW1X 8PF, England.
- M. R. S. Newsletter. m.
- Market Research Abstracts. s-a. ISSN 0025-3596
- Market Research Society. Journal. q. ISSN 0025-
3618
- Market Research Society. Yearbook. a. ISSN
0076-4523

**Marketing House Publishers Ltd**
Moor Hall, Cookham, Maidenhead, Berks. SL6
9QH, England.
- Quarterly Review of Marketing. q. ISSN 0307-
7667 (Institute of Marketing)

**Markham House Press Ltd.**
58 West St., Brighton, Eng.
- New World Antiquity-Atlantis; for the use of all
interested in the Archaeology and Ethnology of
the new world. m.

**Marquetry Society**
c/o Ed. & Pub. E. Schulkins, St. Annes Park, Bristol
4, Eng.
- Marquetarian. q. ISSN 0025-3944

**Marshall, Morgan & Scott Ltd.**
1Bath St., London EC1V 9LB, Eng.
- Life of Faith. w. ISSN 0024-3175

**Martec Publishing Group Ltd.**
Martec House, 61 Berners St., London W.1., Eng.
- Space-Wise. m. ISSN 0038-6324

**Martonair Ltd.**
Twickenham, Middlesex TW1 1RJ, Eng.
- Applied Pneumatics. q. ISSN 0003-6978

**Marx Memorial Library**
37a Clerkenwell Green, London EC1R 0DY, Eng.
- Marx Memorial Library. Quarterly Bulletin. q.
ISSN 0025-410X

**Marylebone Press Ltd.**
276-282 the Corn Exchange, Fennell St.,
Manchester M4 3HF, Eng.
- Recycling and Waste Disposal. m.
- Training Officer. m. ISSN 0041-090X
- Welfare Officer. m. ISSN 0043-2350 (Institute of
Welfare Officers)

**Kenneth Mason Publications Ltd.**
Homewell, Havant, Hants, England.
- Road Traffic Reports. 9-10 per yr.
- What's Where in London with B.P. irreg. ISSN
0083-9159

**Masonic Record Ltd.**
38 Great Queen St., London, W.C.2, Eng.
- Masonic Record. m. (10 per yr) ISSN 0025-4665

**Librairie Francois Maspero**
1, Place Paul- Painleve, 75005 Paris, France.
- Khamsin. q.

**Masque Enterprises**
Edward Herbert Bldg., Loughborough University,
Leicestershire, Eng.
- Masque. 3 per yr. ISSN 0025-4703

**Mass Spectrometry Data Centre**
AWRE Aldermaston, Reading RG7 4PR, Eng
(Subscr. to: Pendragon House, Inc., 899 Broadway
Ave., Redwood City, CA 94063)
- Mass Spectrometry Bulletin. m. ISSN 0025-4738

**Massenet Society**
c/o Stella J. Wright, Flat 2, 79 Linden Gardens,
London W2 4EU, England.
- Massenet Society. Newsletter. q.

**Massey-Ferguson (United Kingdom) Ltd.**
Banner Lane, Coventry, Eng.
- Modern Farmer. m. ISSN 0047-7699

**Master Photographers Association**
1-2 Lincoln's Inn Fields, London WC2, Eng.
- Master Photographer. q. ISSN 0047-6196

**Mathematical Association**
- Mathematical Gazette. (pub. by G. Bell & Sons
Ltd.)
- Mathematics in School. (pub. by Longman Group
Ltd.)

**Mathematical Pie**
West View, Five Ways, Wroxall, Nr. Warwick, Eng.
- Mathematical Pie. 3 per yr. ISSN 0025-5602

**Mather and Platt Ltd.**
Park Works, Manchester M10 6BA, Eng.
- Sprinkler Bulletin. every 6-9 mos. ISSN 0038-
8637

**Mathilda and Terence Kennedy Institute of
Rheumatology**
Bute Gardens, Hammersmith, London W6 7DW,
England.
- Mathilda and Terence Kennedy Institute of
Rheumatology. Annual Report. a., 8th 1974.

**May & Baker Ltd.**
Dagenham, Essex RM10 7XS, England.
- M & B Pharmaceutical Bulletin; for pharmacists in
hospital practice throughout the world. 4 per yr.
ISSN 0460-2390
- Veterinary Review. 3 per yr.

**May & Brett Ltd.**
23 High St., Dunmow, Essex, England.
- Dunmow Broadcast & District Advertiser. m.

**Mayhew-McCrimmon Ltd.**
10-12 High St., Gt. Wakering, Essex, Eng.
- New Sower. q.

**MD Promotions Ltd.**
27 Sloane Square, London SW1W 8AB, England.
- Current Medical Research and Opinion. a.

**Meal Expenditure Analysis Ltd.**
9 Paddington St., London W.1., Eng.
- New Promotions and Competitions. m. ISSN 0047-9853

**Meat and Livestock Commission**
Queensway House, Bletchley, Milton Keynes MK2 2EF, England.
- Meat and Livestock Commission, Bucks, England. Index of Research. a. ISSN 0076-5716
- Meat and Livestock Commission, Bucks, England. International Market Survey. q. ISSN 0047-634X

**Meat Magazine Ltd.**
2 Woburn St., Ampthill, Beds. MK45 2HP, Eng.
- Meat. 10 per yr.

**Mebyon Kernow Publications**
Trewirgie Hill, Redruth, Cornwall, England.
- An Forth. 1-2 per yr.
- Cornish Nation. q. ISSN 0045-8570

**Mechanical Engineering Publications, Ltd.**
1 Birdcage Walk, London SW1H 9JJ, Eng.
- Automotive Engineer; for designers of cars, vans, trucks, etc. m. (Institute of Mechanical Engineers)
- Chartered Mechanical Engineer. m.(except Aug) ISSN 0009-191X (Institution of Mechanical Engineers)
- Engineering in Medicine. q. ISSN 0046-2039
- Heat and Fluid Flow. s-a. ISSN 0046-7138 (Institution of Mechanical Engineers)
- Institution of Mechanical Engineers. Conference Publication. irreg; no. 14, 1974.
- Institution of Mechanical Engineers. Mechanisms. a.
- Institution of Mechanical Engineers. Proceedings. a. ISSN 0020-3483
- International Journal of Mechanical Engineering Education. q. ISSN 0306-4190 (Institution of Mechanical Engineers)
- Journal of Mechanical Engineering Science. bi-m. ISSN 0022-2542 (Institution of Mechanical Engineers)
- Journal of Strain Analysis for Engineering Design. q. ISSN 0309-3247 (Joint British Committee for Stress Analysis)
- M E N. (Mechanical Engineering News) m. ISSN 0306-9540
- Railway Engineer. bi-m. ISSN 0308-3209
- Thermodynamics and Fluid Mechanics Convention. Proceedings. biennial. ISSN 0085-7254

**Mechanics Institute**
Spring St., Shuttleworth, Nr. Ramsbottom, Lancashire, Eng.
- British Mouthpiece; brass & military band journal. w. ISSN 0007-1463

**Media Expenditure Analysis Ltd.**
2 Cheapside, Reading RG1 7AA, England.
- M E A L Digest. q.

**Media Information Ltd.**
Hale House, 290-296 Green Lanes, London N13 5TP, England.
- P R Planner - Europe. bi-m.
- P R Planner - U.K. m.

**Medical and Scientific Services Ltd.**
226, the Strand, London W.C.2, England.
- Medical Gynaecology, Andrology and Sociology. 4 per yr. ISSN 0300-5828

**Medical Association for Prevention of War**
1 Rodborough Rd., London NW11 8SA, Eng.
- Medical Association for Prevention of War. Proceedings. s-a. ISSN 0025-701X

**Medical Council on Alcoholism**
- British Journal of Alcohol & Alcoholism. (pub. by B. Edsall & Co. Ltd.)

**Medical Education (International)**
Box 271, S. Lindsay House, 7 Gloucester Rd., London 5WF, Eng.
- Medicine (London) m.

**Medical Missionary Association**
6 Canonbury Place, London N1 2NJ, Eng.
- Saving Health. q. ISSN 0036-5106

**Medical News-Tribune Ltd.**
359 Strand, London, WC2R 0HP, England.
- British Journal of Sexual Medicine. bi-m. ISSN 0301-5572
- Medical News. w.

**Medical Protection Society Ltd.**
50 Hallam Street, London W1N 6DE, England.
- Medical Protection Society. Annual Report. a. ISSN 0076-5961

**Medical Records Officers**
c/o N. A. Campion, Scilly Area Hospital Authority, Cornwall and Isles, St. Clement Vean, Truro, England.
- Medical Record. q. ISSN 0025-7478

**Medical Research Society**
- Clinical Science and Molecular Medicine. (pub. by Blackwell Scientific Publications Ltd.)

**Medical Society for the Study of Venereal Diseases**
- British Journal of Venereal Diseases. (pub. by British Medical Association)

**Medical Society of London**
11 Chandos Street, Cavendish Square, London, W1N OEB, England.
- Medical Society of London. Transactions. a. ISSN 0076-6011

**Medicine Digest Ltd.**
17/18 Henrietta Street, London WC2 9JH, England.
- Medicine Digest. m.

**Medico-Legal Society**
- Medico-Legal Journal. (pub. by Dramrite Printers Ltd.)

**Melrose Press Ltd.**
Market Hill, Cambridge CB2 3QP, England.
- Dictionary of African Biography. triennial. ISSN 0070-4709
- Dictionary of International Biography. a. ISSN 0419-1137
- Dictionary of Latin American and Caribbean Biography. triennial. ISSN 0070-4733
- Dictionary of Scandinavaian Biography. triennial.
- International Author's and Writer's Who's Who. biennial.
- International Who's Who in Art and Antiques. triennial.
- International Who's Who in Music and Musicians' Directory. biennial.
- International Who's Who in Poetry. biennial. ISSN 0539-1342
- Men of Achievement. a.
- World Who's Who of Women. a.

**Memory Lane**
40 Merryfield Approach, Leigh-on-Sea, Essex SS9 4HJ, England.
- Memory Lane. q.

**Men of the Trees**
Crawley Down, Crawley, Sussex, Eng.
- Trees; the magazine for tree-lovers. q. ISSN 0041-221X

**Mendip Publishing**
30 Drake Road, Wells, Somerset, Eng.
- Descent; the magazine for cavers. every 8 weeks. ISSN 0046-0036

**Men's Wear Publishing Co. Ltd.**
Knightway House, 20 Soho Square, London, W1V 6DT, England.
- Men's Wear Year Book and Diary. a. ISSN 0076-6437

**John Menzies (Holdings) Ltd.**
Hanover Bldgs., Rose St., Edinburgh 2, Scotland.
- News Trade Weekly. w. ISSN 0028-9353

**Merchant Navy and Airline Officers Association**
Oceanair House, 750-760 High Rd., Leytonstone, London E11 3BB, Eng.
- Telegraph. m. ISSN 0040-2575

**Mercia Publicity**
91 Stourbridge Road, Halesowen, West Midlands B63 3UA, England.
- Black Country Bugle. m.

**Mercury House Publications Ltd.**
Waterloo Rd., London SE1 8UL, Eng.
- Advertising & Marketing. q.
- Car Mechanics. m. ISSN 0008-6037
- Commercial Television and Radio Year Book. a. ISSN 0306-7718
- Council. m.
- Education Equipment Selector. s-a. ISSN 0046-1415
- Electrical Equipment. m. ISSN 0013-4317
- Electrical Equipment Selector. q. ISSN 0046-1679
- Electronic Equipment Monitor. 8 per yr. ISSN 0046-1717
- Electronic Equipment News; monthly journal of electronic and associated equipment for industry. m. ISSN 0013-4910
- Engineering Design Service. 6 per yr.
- Factory & Industrial Equipment. 6 per yr.
- Hot Car. 12 per yr ISSN 0018-6007
- Industrial Relations Journal. q. ISSN 0019-8692
- Journal of General Management. q. ISSN 0306-3070
- Maintenance Engineering. m. ISSN 0025-0902
- Motorcycle Mechanics. (pub. by East Midland Allied Press Ltd.)
- O E M Design. m.
- Office Equipment News. m. ISSN 0030-0187
- Personnel Management. m. ISSN 0031-5761

**Merlin Press**
Suffrance Wharf, 2-4 West Ferry Rd., London E. 14, England.
- Review of African Political Economy. 3 per yr.
- Socialist Register; a survey of movements and ideas. a. ISSN 0081-0606

**Merseyside Arts Association**
c/o J. B. Dearing, 1a Winston Parade, New Milton, Hamps, Eng.
- Contrasts; a magazine of new poetry. s-a. ISSN 0045-8414

**Merseyside Social Credit Association**
Rose Cottage, 17 Hadassah Grove, Lark Lane, Liverpool L17 4XH, England.
- Liverpool Newsletter. m. ISSN 0047-4827

**Metal Bulletin Ltd.**
Park House, 3 Park Terr., Worcester Park, Surrey, Eng.
- European Metals Directory. irreg. ISSN 0071-2949
- Industrial Minerals. m. ISSN 0019-8544
- Iron and Steel Works of the World. irreg. ISSN 0075-0875
- Metal Bulletin. s-w. ISSN 0026-0533
- Metal Bulletin Handbook. a. ISSN 0076-664X
- Metallurgical Plantmakers of the World. irreg.
- Non-Ferrous Metal Works of the World. irreg. ISSN 0078-0987
- Service Center International. fortn.

**Metals Society**
1 Carlton House Terrace, London SW1Y 5DB, Eng (and American Society for Metals, Metals Park, OH 44073)
- Abstracts and Book Title Index Card Service (ABTICS); an iron and steel abstracting service on card format. w. ISSN 0001-3404
- British Corrosion Journal. q. ISSN 0007-0599
- Ferrous and Non-Ferrous Science and Technology Lists-British Industrial and Scientific International Translations. w. (British Industrial and Scientific International Translation Service)
- International Metals Reviews. q. ISSN 0308-4590
- Iron & Steel Industry Profiles. w.
- Ironmaking and Steelmaking. bi-m. ISSN 0301-9233
- Metal Science. m.
- Metals and Materials. m. ISSN 0026-0940
- Metals Technology. m. ISSN 0307-1693
- Powder Metallurgy. q. ISSN 0032-5899
- Steel in the U S S R. m. ISSN 0038-9218
- World Calendar of Forthcoming Meeting: Metallurgical and Related Fields. q.

**Kyriakos H. Metaxas, Ed. & Pub.**
55 Westbourne Grove, London W2 4AA, Eng.
- Greek Gazette. m. ISSN 0017-386X

**Methodist Church. Division of Education and Youth**
2 Chester House, Pages Lane, London N10 1PR, England
(and National Christian Education Council, Robert Denholm House, Nutfield, Redhill RH1 4HW Surrey, England)
- Partners in Learning. a. ISSN 0079-0117

**Methodist Church Music Society**
c/o Ed. Rev. Bryan F. Spinney, 84 Peabody Rd., Farnborough, Hants, Eng.
- Methodist Church Music Society Bulletin. 2 per yr. ISSN 0047-6919

**Methodist Church Overseas Division**
25 Marylebone Rd., London NW1 5JR, England.
- Now. m.
- Window. q.

**Methodist Local Preachers Aid Association**
The Grange, Chorleywood Close, Rickmansworth, Herts WD3 4EG, Eng.
- Local Preachers. q. ISSN 0024-5607

**Methodist Newspaper Co., Ltd.**
176 Fleet St., London E.C.4, Eng.
- Methodist Recorder. w. ISSN 0026-1262

**Methodist Publishing House**
Wellington Rd., Wimbledon, London SW19 8EU, England.
- Worship and Preaching. bi-m. ISSN 0032-7107

**Methuen and Co. Ltd.**
11 New Fetter Lane, London, EC4, England.
- Aristotelian Society. Proceedings. a. ISSN 0066-7374
- British Journal of Teacher Education. 3 per yr. ISSN 0305-8913
- Social History. 3 per yr. ISSN 0307-1022
- Studies in African History. irreg., no. 14, 1976. ISSN 0081-7481

**Metraton Publications**
25 Circle Gardens, Merton Park, London SW19 3JX, England.
- Kabbalist. q.

**Metric Information Service Bulletin**
61 Lee High Road, London SE13 5NS, England.
- Metric Information Service Bulletin. bi-w.

**Metropolitan Police. Traffic Division**
Rm. 1011, New Scotland Yard, London SW1H 0BG, England.
- Clearway; traffic magazine of the metropolitan police. s-a. ISSN 0009-8698

**Michelin Tyre Co.Ltd.**
Tourist Service, 81 Fulham Rd., London SW3 6RD, England.
- Michelin Spain. irreg.

**Microfilm Association of Great Britain**
8 High St., High St., Guildford, Surrey GU2 5N, England.
- Microdoc. q. ISSN 0026-2684

**Microinfo Ltd.**
Hamlet House, High Street, Alton, Hampshire GU34 1EF, England.
- Energy Report; energy policy and technology news bulletin. m.
- Microinfo; micrographics news bulletin. m. ISSN 0047-7192
- Pollution; environmental news bulletin. m. ISSN 0048-4784

**Microscope Publications Ltd.**
2 McCrone Mews, Belsize Lane, London NW3 5BG, Eng.
- Microscope. q. ISSN 0026-282X

**Middle East Economic Consultants**
14 Finsbury Circus, London EC2M 7AB, England.
- An-Nahar Arab Report and Memo. w. ISSN 0003-2379

**Middle East Economic Digest Ltd.**
84-86 Chancery Lane, London WC2A 1DL, Eng.
- Middle East Economic Digest. w. ISSN 0047-7230

**Middle East International Publishers**
21 Collingham Rd., London SW5 0NU, England.
- Middle East International. m. ISSN 0047-7249

**Middle East Magazine Ltd.**
63 Long Acre, London WC2 9JH, England.
- Middle East. m.

**Middle East Research and Action Group**
5 Caledonian Rd., London N.1., England.
- On Target. 4 per yr.

**Middle East Review**
Saffron Walden, England.
- Middle East Annual Review. a.

**Middle East Trade Publications Ltd.**
34 Percy St., London W.1, Eng.
- Middle East Trade. bi-m. ISSN 0026-3192

**Middlesex & Surrey League for the Hard of Hearing**
54 Hemingford Rd., London N1 1DB, Eng.
- Aural News. q. ISSN 0004-8054

**Middlesex Hospital Medical School**
Cleveland St., London W.1, Eng.
- Middlesex Hospital Journal. 3 per yr. ISSN 0026-3222

**Middlesex Publishing Co., Ltd.**
21 New St., London EC2M 4NT, Eng.
- Timber and Plywood. w. ISSN 0040-7739
- Timber and Plywood. Board News Annual. a. ISSN 0082-433X

**Midland Bank Ltd.**
Griffin House, P.O. Box 2, Sheffield S1 3GG, England.
- Midland Bank Review. q. ISSN 0026-3257

**Midland Medical Institute**
36 Harborne Rd., Edgbaston, Birmingham B15 3AF, England.
- Midland Medical Review. s-a. ISSN 0026-3281

**Midland News Association Ltd.**
Queen St., Wolverhampton, WV1 3BU, Staffs., Eng.
- Sporting Star. w. ISSN 0049-1950

**Midlands Club Cricket Conference**
- Midlands Club Cricket Conference Yearbook. (pub. by Read Hudson Organization Ltd.)

**Midlands New Towns Society**
1064 Evesham Rd., Astwood Bank, Redditch, Worcs. B96 6ED, England.
- Midlands New Towns Society Quarterly News Letter. q.

**Migraine Trust**
45 Great Ormond St., London WC1N 3HD, England.
- Migraine News. s-a. ISSN 0544-1153

**Milapweekly**
307a Northend Rd., London W14 9NS, Eng.
- Milap Weekly. w. ISSN 0026-3737

**Militant**
1 Mentmore Terrace, London E8 3PN, England.
- Militant; the Marxist paper for labour and youth. w.
- Militant International Review. q.

**Military Historical Society**
Centre Block, Duke of York's Hq., London S.W. 3, Eng.
- Military Historical Society. Bulletin. q. ISSN 0026-4008

**Milk Marketing Board**
Thames Ditton, Surrey, Eng.
- Better Breeding. q. ISSN 0006-0046
- Better Management. q. ISSN 0006-0186
- Milk Producer. m. ISSN 0026-4180

**Milk Marketing Board for Northern Ireland**
456, Antrin Road, Belfast, N. Ireland.
- Topics. m.

**Millennium Publishing Group**
Houghton St., London WC2A 2AE, England.
- Millennium; journal of international studies. 3 per yr. ISSN 0305-8298

**Millinery and Boutique**
22 Cross St., Islington, London, N.1, Eng.
- Millinery and Boutique. m. ISSN 0026-427X

**Mills and Boon Ltd.**
50 Grafton Way, Fitzroy Sq., London W.1, England.
- Home Made Series. irreg. ISSN 0073-313X

**Milton Publishing Co. Ltd.**
28 Craven St., London WC2N 5PD, England.
- Diagnostics Index. 2 per yr. ISSN 0306-2864
- Electro Optics. q. ISSN 0013-4589
- Laboratory Weekly. w.
- Medical Equipment. q. ISSN 0025-7249

- Science Teaching Equipment. 4 per yr. ISSN 0036-8571

**Mimram Books**
Stephen Austin & Sons Ltd., Caxton Hill, Hertford, Eng.
- Journal of African Languages. 3 per yr. ISSN 0021-8545

**Mind Association**
- Mind. (pub. by Basil Blackwell & Mott Ltd.)

**Mineralogical Society**
41 Queen's Gate, London S.W.7 5HR, Eng.
- Mineralogical Abstracts; a quarterly journal of abstracts in English, covering the world literature of mineralogy and related subjects. 4 parts a year. ISSN 0026-4601 (Mineralogical Society of America US)
- Mineralogical Magazine. q. ISSN 0026-461X
- Mineralogy and Materials News Bulletin for Microscopic Methods. q.

**Miners' International Federation**
75-76 Blackfriars Rd., London S.E.1, England.
- Miners' International Federation. International Information. irreg. ISSN 0544-2621

**Miniature Armoured Fighting Vehicle Association**
15 Berwick Ave., Heaton Mersey, Stockport, Cheshire SK4 3AA, England.
- Tankette. bi-m.

**Mining Journal Ltd.**
15 Wilson St., London EC2M 2TR, Eng.
- Mining. m. ISSN 0026-5233
- Mining Annual Review. a. ISSN 0076-8995
- Mining Journal. w. ISSN 0026-5225

**Minority Rights Group**
36 Craven St., London WC2N 5NG, England.
- Minority Rights Group. Reports. irreg. (5 per yr.) ISSN 0305-6252

**Miramoor Publications Ltd.**
Flat 5, 33 Rutland Gate, London SW7, Eng.
- Africa Confidential. fortn. ISSN 0044-6483

**Missions to Seamen**
St. Michael Paternoster Royal, College Hill, London EC4R 2RL, Eng.
- Flying Angel. q. ISSN 0015-4822
- Missions to Seamen Annual Report. a.

**Mizrachi Federation**
2B Golders Green Rd., London NW11 8LH, Eng.
- Jewish Review. 10 per yr. ISSN 0021-6690

**Model Aeroplane Gazette**
c/o Ronald Firth, Ed., 22 Slayleigh Ave., Sheffield, South Yorkshire S10 3RB, England.
- Model Aeroplane Gazette. bi-m.

**Model & Allied Publications Ltd.**
Box 35, Hemel Hempstead, Herts HP1 1EE, England
- Aero Modeller. m. ISSN 0001-9232 (U.S. Subscr. to: Eastern News Distributors, Inc., 155 W. 15th St., New York, NY 10011)
- Aeromodeller Annual. a. ISSN 0065-3691
- Battle. m.
- Gem Craft. m.
- Military Modelling. m. ISSN 0026-4083
- Model Boats. m.
- Model Engineer. fortn. ISSN 0026-7325
- Model Railways. m. ISSN 0026-7368
- Movie Maker. m. ISSN 0027-2701
- Photography. m. ISSN 0031-8809
- Radio Control Models & Electronics. m. ISSN 0033-7838
- Scale Models. m. ISSN 0036-5432
- Woodworker. m. ISSN 0043-776X
- Woodworker Annual. a. ISSN 0084-1196

**Modern Churchmen's Union**
Marbrae, Balmaha, Stirlingshire, Scotland.
- Modern Churchman. q. ISSN 0026-7597

**Modern Humanities Research Association**
Kings College, London WC2R 2LS, England
- Annual Bibliography of English Language and Literature. a. ISSN 0066-3786 (Vols. 1-39 avail. from: Wm. Dawson & Sons Ltd., Cannon House, Folkstone, Kent, England)
- Modern Humanities Research Association. Monograph. a. ISSN 0076-9983
- Modern Language Review. q. ISSN 0026-7937 (Vols. 1-69 avail. from Wm. Dawson & Sons Ltd., Cannon House, Folkstone, Kent, England)
- Yearbook of English Studies. a.
- Year's Work in Modern Language Studies. a. ISSN 0084-4152 (Vols. 1-29 Avail. from: Wm. Dawson & Sons Ltd., Cannon House, Folkstone, Kent, England)

**Modern Language Association**
35 Lewisham Way, London SE14 6PP, Eng.
- Modern Languages. q. ISSN 0026-7945

**Modern Metals Publications Ltd.**
39 Hillside Gardens, Brockham Betchworth, Surrey, England.
- Stainless Steel Industry. bi-m.

**Modern Poetry in Translation Ltd.**
10 Compayne Gdns., London NW6 3DH, Eng.
- Modern Poetry in Translation. 4 per yr. ISSN 0026-8291

**Modino Press Ltd.**
50 Pine Grove, London N20 8LA, Eng.
- Educational Media International. q. ISSN 0004-7597 (International Council for Educational Media)

**Moffat Publishing Co. Ltd.**
Unit 4 Sewell St., Industrial Estate, Plaistow, London e13 8AT, Eng.
- Resale Weekly. w. ISSN 0034-5105

**Mofussil**
20 Hall Close, Kettering, Northants, Eng.
- Mofussil; a quarterly of poetry. q. ISSN 0026-8860

**Monarchist League**
International Headquarters, 60 Paddington St., London W1M 3NG, Eng.
- Monarchist. q. ISSN 0047-7834

**Monarchist Press Association**
7 Sutherland Rd, West Ealing, London W13 0DX, England.
- Kings of Tomorrow Series. irreg. ISSN 0075-6083
- Monarchist Book Review; an annotated list of new and reprinted books dealing with various aspects of monarchy. a. ISSN 0077-0280
- Monarchist Press Association. Historical Series. irreg. ISSN 0077-0299

**Monitor Consultants**
25 Bedford Row, London WC1R 4HD, Eng.
- China Trade and Economic Newsletter. m.

**Monks Wood Experimental Station**
Abbots Ripton, Huntingdon PE17 2LS, England.
- Monks Wood Experimental Station, Huntingdon, England. Symposia. irreg., 1972, no. 6. ISSN 0077-0426 (Gt. Brit. Natural Environment Research Council)

**Monogram Publications**
63 Old Compton St., London W1V 5PN, England.
- Monogram. s-a.

**Monotype Corp. Ltd.**
Salfords, Redhill RH1 5BR, Eng.
- Monotype Pictorial. s-a. ISSN 0306-7068

**Montagu Ventures Ltd.**
Beaulieu, Hampshire, England.
- National Motor Museum Pictorial Guide. a. (National Motor Museum Trust)

**Monthly Film Making**
Wessex House, 26 Station.Rd., Cambridge, Eng.
- Monthly Film Making. m.

**Moodies Services, Ltd.**
6, 7 & 8 Bonhill St., London EC2A 4BU, England.
- Moodies Australian Review. irreg.
- Moodies Investment Handbook. q. ISSN 0027-0784
- Moodies Review of Investment. w. ISSN 0027-0792

**Moonraker Press**
26 St. Margarets St., Bradford-on-Avon, Wiltshire, England.
- Whitlock's Wessex. a.

**Moonshine**
c/o Tina Fulker, Ed., 6 Oxford Close, Edmonton, London N. 9., England.
- Moonshine. q.

**Moot: Thirkill - Threlkeld Family Newsletter**
c/o Eunice Wilson, Ed., 143 Harbord St., London SW6 6PN, England.
- Moot: Thirkill - Threlkeld Family Newsletter. 3 per yr.

**Moravian Church in Great Britain**
Moravian Book Room, 5 Muswell Hill, London N.10 3TJ, England.
- Daily Watchwords; the Moravian textbook with almanack. a.

**Moray Publications**
28 Clarence Gate Gardens, London N.W. 1, Eng.
- Spica; a review of siderea astrology. q. ISSN 0038-7444

**Morgan-Grampian (Construction Press) Ltd.**
30 Calderwood St., London, SW18 6QH, Eng.
- Building Design. w. ISSN 0007-3423
- Civil Engineering (London) m. ISSN 0305-6473
- Construction Plant and Equipment. m.
- Tunnels & Tunnelling. bi-m. ISSN 0041-414X

**Morgan-Grampian (Professional Press) Ltd.**
Morgan-Grampian House, 30 Calderwood St., London SE18 6QH, Eng.
- Pulse. w. ISSN 0048-6000

**Morgan-Grampian (Publishers) Ltd.**
Morgan-Grampian House, Calderwood St., London SE18 6QH, England.
- Accountants Weekly. w. ISSN 0307-7861
- Business Administration; journal for the chief executive. m. ISSN 0007-6414
- Chemical Age. w. ISSN 0009-2312
- Construction Machines. irreg.
- Control and Instrumentation. m. ISSN 0010-8022
- Daltons Weekly; house, hotel, boarding house & apartment advertiser. w. ISSN 0011-5894
- Design Engineering. m. ISSN 0011-9350
- Electronic Engineering. m. ISSN 0013-4902
- Engineer. w. ISSN 0013-7758
- Engineer Buyers Guide. a. ISSN 0071-0288
- Estates Times. w. ISSN 0014-1259
- Food Manufacture. m. ISSN 0015-6477
- Freight Transport Services. m.
- Industrial Purchasing News. m. ISSN 0019-865X
- Instruments, Electronics and Automation Purchasing Directory. a. ISSN 0074-0578
- Kempe's Engineers Year Book. a. ISSN 0075-5400
- Laboratory Equipment Digest. m. ISSN 0023-6829
- Laboratory Equipment Directory & Buyers Guide. a.
- Manufacturing Chemist and Aerosol News. m. ISSN 0025-2557
- Metalworking Production. m. ISSN 0026-1033
- Music Week. w.
- Process Engineering. m.
- Record Mirror. w. ISSN 0034-1576
- Travel Trade Gazette. w. ISSN 0041-2074

**A. E. Morgan Publications Ltd.**
172 Kingston Rd., Ewell, Epsom, Surrey, Eng.
- Caravan Industry & Park Operator. m. ISSN 0045-5725
- Dental Practice; the journal of modern techniques, equipment and materials. m. ISSN 0011-8710
- Index of Veterinary Specialities. bi-m. ISSN 0019-3941
- M I M S Africa. bi-m.
- Machinery Lloyd; international review of mechanical, electrical and constructional engineering products. m. ISSN 0024-9203
- Medical Technologist and Scientist. m.
- Mims Caribbean. bi-m.
- Mims Middle East. bi-m.
- Sign Makers and Suppliers Year Book and Directory. a.
- Sign World. m. ISSN 0049-0466 (British Sign Association)
- Veterinary Practice. fortn. ISSN 0042-4897

**Nigel Morland, Ed. & Pub.**
Box 18, Bognor Regis, Sussex P022 7AA, England.
- Current Crime. q.

- Forensic Photography. q.

**Morpeth-Northumbrian Gathering Committee**
Westgate House, Dogger Bank, Morpeth, Northumberland Ne61 1RF, England.
- Northumbriana. q.

**William Morris Society**
Kelmscott House, 26 Upper Mall, London W.6, England.
- William Morris Society. Journal. irreg. ISSN 0084-0254
- William Morris Society. Report. a. ISSN 0084-0270
- William Morris Society. Transactions. irreg. ISSN 0084-0289

**Morton Associates Ltd.**
12 Union Row, Aberdeen, Scotland.
- Offshore Oil. w.
- Project Scotland. w.

**Morton Newspapers Ltd.**
Lurgan, N. Ireland.
- Church of Ireland Gazette. w. ISSN 0009-6512

**Morton Publications Ltd.**
Windsor Ave., Lurgan Co., Armagh, N. Ireland.
- Farmweek. w. ISSN 0014-8547

**Moscow Narodny Bank Quarterly Review**
P.O. Box 26, 24/32 King William St., London EC4P 4JS, England.
- Moscow Narodny Bank Quarterly Review. q.

**Moss Side Press**
136 Withington Rd., Manchester 16, England.
- Manchester Free Press. m.

**Mothers' Union**
125 Herne Hill, London SE24 9LY, Eng.
- Home and Family. q. ISSN 0018-3946

**Motor Agents Association Ltd.**
201 Great Portland St., London, W1N 6AB, Eng.
- Motor Trade Executive; with Motor Industry. m. ISSN 0027-2027

**Motor Industry Research Association**
Watling St., Nr. Nuneaton, Warwickshire, Eng.
- M I R A Automobile Abstracts. m. ISSN 0309-0817

**Motor News Market Place**
Arbroath, Angus, Scotland.
- Motor News & Advertiser. w.

**Motor Sport Magazine Ltd.**
Standard House, Bonhill St., London EC2A 4DA, Eng.
- Motor Sport. m. ISSN 0027-2019

**Mountain Life Ltd.**
The Navigators House, River Lane, Richmond, Surrey TW10 7AG, England.
- Climber and Rambler. bi-m. (British Mountaineering Council)

**Mountain Magazine Ltd.**
c/o Sylvester Rd., London N2, England.
- Mountain Magazine. bi-m.

**Mouthpiece Publications**
35 Battledean Rd., London N.5, Eng.
- Mouthpiece. s-a. ISSN 0027-2655

**Movement**
14 Hanley Rd., London N.4, England.
- Movement. m.

**Movie Magazine Ltd.**
3 Cork St., London W.1, Eng.
- Movie. q. ISSN 0027-268X

**Mullard Ltd.**
London Rd., Mitcham, Surrey, Eng.
- Mullard Technical Communications. q. ISSN 0027-3139

**Multi-Science Publishing Co. Ltd.**
The Old Mill, Dorset Place, London, E.15, Eng.
- Acoustics Abstracts. bi-m. ISSN 0001-4974
- Electronics and Communications Abstracts. m. ISSN 0013-5119
- Medical Electronics & Communications Abstracts. q. ISSN 0025-7222
- Noise & Vibration Bulletin. m. ISSN 0029-0947
- Optics Abstracts. bi-m.

- Rare Earth Bulletin. bi-m.
- Renewable Energy Bulletin. q.
- Russian Ultrasonics. q. ISSN 0048-8828
- Surface Wave Abstracts. q. ISSN 0049-2639

**Multiple Sclerosis Society**
4 Tachbrook St., London SW1 1SJ, Eng.
- M. S. News/Multiple Sclerosis News. q. ISSN 0047-5270

**Municipal Engineering Publications Ltd.**
178-202 Great Portland St., London W1N 6NH, Eng.
- Municipal Engineering; and environmental technology. w. ISSN 0027-3457

**Municipal Journal Ltd.**
178-202 Great Portland St., London W1N 6NH, Eng.
- Municipal and Public Services Journal; British public services, local government administrator, contractors' guide, public works engineer, local government journal and baths weekly. w. ISSN 0027-3430

**Municipal Publications**
32 Eccleston Sq., London SWiV 1PB, England.
- Public Health Engineer. bi-m. ISSN 0300-5925 (Institution of Public Health Engineers)

**Munro Barr Publications Ltd.**
113 St. Vincent St., Glasgow G2 5HU, Scotland.
- Golf Monthly. m. ISSN 0017-1816
- Golf Rules Illustrated. quadrennial. ISSN 0072-4963
- Golfer's Handbook. a. ISSN 0072-498X
- Scottish Licensed Trade Guardian. w.

**D. J. Murphy (Publishers) Ltd.**
19 Charing Cross Rd., London WC2H 0EY, Eng.
- Light Horse. m. ISSN 0024-3329
- Pony; horses and horsemastership for children. m. ISSN 0032-4256

**John Murray (Publishers) Ltd.**
50 Albemarle St., London W1X 4BD, England.
- Essays and Studies. a. ISSN 0071-1357 (English Association)
- School Science Review. 4 per yr. ISSN 0036-6811 (Association for Science Education)
- Year's Work in English Studies. a. ISSN 0084-4144 (English Association)

**Muscular Dystrophy Group of Great Britain**
35 Macaulay Rd., London SW4 0QP, Eng.
- Muscular Dystrophy Journal. q. ISSN 0027-3740

**Museums Association**
87 Charlotte St., London W1P 2BX, England.
- Museums Association Information Sheets. irreg.
- Museums Bulletin. m.
- Museums Journal. q. ISSN 0027-416X
- Museums Yearbook. a.

**Mushroom Growers' Association**
Agriculture House, Knightsbridge, London SW1X 7NJ, Eng.
- Mushroom Journal. m.

**Music and Letters Ltd.**
44 Conduit St., London W1R ODE, Eng.
- Music and Letters. q. ISSN 0027-4224

**Music Group of the Communist Party**
C/O Frank Stokes, 11 Fairacres Close, Potters Bar, Hertfordshire, England.
- Music and Life. irreg. ISSN 0085-3607

**Music Industry Publications**
44 Berners St., London W.1, Eng.
- Living Music. q. ISSN 0047-4878 (Association of Musical Instrument Industries, London)
- Music Industry. m. ISSN 0027-4356

**Musical Box Society of Great Britain**
40 Station Approach, Hayes, Bromley, Kent, England.
- Music Box. q. ISSN 0027-4275

**Musical Opinion Ltd.**
3-11 Spring Rd., Bournemouth, Dorset BH1 4QA, Eng.
- Musical Opinion; educational journal. m. ISSN 0027-4623
- Organ; review for its makers, its players and its lovers. q. ISSN 0030-4883

**Muzzle Loaders Association of Great Britain**
73 Broad Lane, Coventry CV5 7AH, England.
- Black Powder. 10 per yr.

**Mysl Polska**
8 Alma Terrace, Allen St., London W8 6QY, England.
- Mysl Polska/Polish Thought; dwutygodnik poswiecony zyciu i kulturze narodu. fortn. ISSN 0027-5581

**Mystery Trader**
c/o Ethel Lindsay, Ed., 6 Langley Ave., Surbiton, Surrey KT6 6QL, England.
- Mystery Trader. irreg.

**N.A.G. Press Ltd.**
Northwood House, 93-99 Goswell Rd., London EC1V 7QA, Eng.
- Retail Jeweller; for retailers, wholesalers and manufacturers of jewelry, clocks, watches, silverware, etc., dealers and designers. fortn. ISSN 0034-6063

**N F E R Publishing Co., Ltd.**
2 Jennings Bldg., Thames Ave., Windsor, Berkshire SL4 1QS, England.
- Journal of Moral Education. 3 per yr.

**N P M**
5 Stone Bldgs., Lincoln's Inn, London WC2A 3XT, England.
- P L I Know How. m.

**Names Society**
Seven Aragon Ave., Surrey KT7 OPY, England.
- Viz. irreg.

**Napoleonic Society**
4 Boscombe Ave., London E10 6HY, Eng.
- Napoleon. s-a. ISSN 0027-7827

**Narod Press**
129-131 Carell St., London E.1, Eng.
- Loshen und Leben. m. ISSN 0024-6611

**Narrow Gauge Railway Society**
c/o M. Swift, 47 Birchington Ave., Birchington, Huddersfield, Yorks HD3 3RD, England.
- Narrow Gauge. q.
- Narrow Gauge News. bi-m.

**National Advanced Drivers' Association**
2 Queensway, Sawston, Cambridge CB2 4DJ, England.
- N.A.D.A. Digest. q.

**National & Commercial Banking Group Ltd.**
3 Bishopsgate, London EC2N 3AA, Eng.
- Three Banks Review. q. ISSN 0040-649X

**National and Local Government Officers Association**
Nalgo House, 1 Mabledon Place, London WC1H 9AJ, England.
- National Executive Council of the National and Local Government Officers Association. Nalgo Annual Report. a. ISSN 0077-4456
- National Executive Council of the National and Local Governments Officers Association. NALGO Annual Report. Statement of Accounts. a. ISSN 0077-4464

**National Anti-Vivisection Society Ltd.**
51 Harley St., London W. 1, Eng.
- Animals: Defender & Anti-Vivisection News. bi-m. ISSN 0003-3634

**National Association for Deaf-Blind and Rubella Children**
c/o Mrs. Jessica Hills, 61 Senneleys Park Road, Northfield, Birmingham B31 1AE, England.
- National Association for Deaf/Blind and Rubella Children. Newsletter. irreg. (approx. 3 per yr.)

**National Association for Environmental Education**
48 Charles St., London W1X 8AH, England.
- Environmental Education. irreg.

**National Association for the Care and Resettlement of Offenders.**
125 Kennington Park Rd., London S.E.11, England
- National Association for the Care and Resettlement of Offenders. Papers and Reprints. irreg., no. 11, 1975. ISSN 0077-3220 (Subscr. to: Barry Rose, Little London, Chichester, Sussex PO19 1PG, England)

**National Association for the Teaching of English**
Fernleigh 10B, Thornhill Rd., Edgerton, Huddersfield HD3 3AU, Eng.
- English in Education. 3 per yr.

**National Association of Almshouses**
Billingbear Lodge, Wokingham, Berkshire RG11 5RU, Eng.
- Almshouses Gazette. q.
- National Association of Almshouses. Yearbook and Statement of Accounts. a.

**National Association of Boys' Clubs**
17 Bedford Square, London WC1B 3JJ, Eng.
- Challenge (London) q. ISSN 0009-1006

**National Association of Cooperative Officials**
- Coop Marketing & Management. (pub. by Co-Operative Press Ltd.)

**National Association of Cycle Traders**
- Two Wheeler Dealer. (pub. by East Midland Allied Press Ltd.)

**National Association of Flower Arrangement Societies**
21A Denbigh St., London SW1, England
(Subscr. to: Mrs. J. Wiggins, Cowpasture Farm, Felixstowe, Suffolk 1P11 9RD, England)
- Flower Arranger. q. ISSN 0046-421X

**National Association of Goldsmiths**
- Watchmaker, Jeweller & Silversmith. (pub. by I P C Business Press Ltd.)

**National Association of Local Councils**
100 Great Russell St., London W.C.1, Eng.
- Local Council Review; a countryside magazine. q.

**National Association of Master Bakers, Confectioners & Caterers**
- Bakers Review. (pub. by Turret Press Ltd.)

**National Association of Pension Funds**
- Pensions World. (pub. by CARL Communications Ltd.)

**National Association of Prison Visitors**
47 Hartington St., Bedford, England.
- N. A. P. V. Newsletter. s-a.

**National Association of Probation Officers**
Ambassador House, Brigstock Rd., Thornton Heath, Surrey CR4 7JG, England.
- Probation Journal. q.

**National Association of Soft Drinks Manufacturers Ltd.**
The Gatehouse, 2 Holly Rd., Twickenham, Middlesex, Eng.
- Soft Drinks Trade Journal. m. ISSN 0038-058X

**National Association of Teachers in Colleges and Departments of Education**
Hamilton House, Mabledon Place, London WC1H 9BH, England.
- Summary of Teacher Training Courses at Colleges and Departments of Education. a. ISSN 0081-9328

**National Association of Teachers in Further and Higher Education**
Hamilton House, Mabledon Place, London WC1H 9BH, Eng.
- British Journal of in-Service Education. (pub. by Studies in Education Ltd.)
- N A T F H E Journal. 9 per yr. ISSN 0308-1907

**National Association of Teachers of the Mentally Handicapped .**
1 Beechfield Ave., Urmston, Manchester 313 RT, Eng.
- Teaching & Training. q. ISSN 0040-0572

**National Association of Theatre Nurses**
- N A T News. (pub. by Newton Mann Ltd.)

**National Auricula & Primula Society**
c/o D. G. Hadfield, 146 Queens Rd., England.
- National Auricula & Primula Society (Northern) Year Book. a. ISSN 0027-8726

**National Awami Party of Bangla Desh**
86 Oakleigh Road, London N.11, England.
- National Awami Party of Bangla Desh (in Great Britian). Bulletin. irreg., 1973, no. 5.

**National Begonia Society**
c/o E. Catterall, Ed., 165 Sunnymead Rd., Yardley, Birmingham B26 1LS, England.
- National Begonia Society Bulletin. 3 per yr.

**National Bible Society of Scotland**
7-8 Hampton Terrace, Edinburgh EH12 5JD, Scotland.
- National Bible Society of Scotland. Annual Report. a. ISSN 0077-3557

**National Book League**
7 Albemarle St., London W IX 4BB, Eng.
- Book News. q.
- British Book Design & Production. a.

**National Book League. Scottish Office**
112k Paisley Road, Glasgow G52 1EQ, Scotland.
- Scottish Small Presses. irreg.

**National British Women's Total Abstinence Union**
Rosalind Carlisle House, 23 Dawson Place, London W.2, Eng.
- White Ribbon Magazine. q. ISSN 0043-4973

**National Children's Bureau**
8 Wakly St., Islington, London EC1V 7QE, England.
- National Children's Bureau. Annual Review. a.

**National Children's Wear Association**
- Junior Age. (pub. by Blandford Business Press)

**National Chrysanthemum Society**
65 St. Margaret's Avenue, Whetstone, London N2O 9HT, England.
- N. C. S. Bulletin. q.

**National Committee for Audio-Visual Aids in Education**
254 Belsize Rd., London NW6 4BY, Eng.
- Visual Education. m. ISSN 0042-7152
- Visual Education Yearbook. a. ISSN 0083-6680

**National Computing Centre Ltd.**
Oxford Rd., Manchester M1 7ED, England, Eng.
- Computing Journal Abstracts. w.
- N C C-Interface. bi-m. ISSN 0027-6243

**National Confederation of Parent Teacher Associations**
1 White Avenue, Northfleet, Gravesend, Kent, England.
- Home and School. 3 per yr. ISSN 0305-1536

**National Council for Civil Liberties**
186 Kings Cross Rd., London WC1X 9DE, England.
- Rights! 6 per yr. ISSN 0308-8227

**National Council for Special Education**
1 Wood St., Stratford-Upon-Avon, Warwickshire CV37 6JE, England.
- Guidelines for Teachers. irreg. ISSN 0072-8918
- Special Education: Forward Trends. q.

**National Council of Building Material Producers**
26 Shore St., London WC1E 7B5, Eng.
- B M P Monthly Statistical Bulletin. (Building Material Producers) m.

**National Council of Social Service Inc.**
26 Bedford Square, London WC1B 3HU, England.
- Dictionary of Social Services. irreg.
- Local Historian. q. ISSN 0024-5585 (Standing Conference for Local History)
- National Council of Social Service. Annual Report. a. ISSN 0077-409X
- Newsletter of Women's Forum and the Standing Conferences of Women's Organisations. q.
- Public Social Service. irreg.
- Social Service Quarterly. q. ISSN 0037-7953
- Village. q. ISSN 0042-6172
- Voluntary Social Services. irreg. ISSN 0083-6907
- Women's Organizations in Great Britain. irreg (every 2 or 3 years)

**National Dahlia Society (Great Britain)**
26 Burns Rd., Lillington, Leamington Spa, Warks, England.
- January Bulletin. a.
- National Dahlia Society Annual. a. ISSN 0077-4189

**National Dairymen's Association, Inc.**
20 Eastbourne Terrace, Paddington, London W2 6LE, England.
- Milk Industry; the journal of diary management. m. ISSN 0026-4172

**National Deaf Childrens Society**
31 Gloucester Place, London W.1, Eng.
- Talk. q. ISSN 0049-2906

**National Defence College**
Latimer, Chesham, Bucks County, England.
- National Defence College Gazette. a. ISSN 0021-7336

**National Documentation Centre for Sport, Physical Education and Recreation**
Box 363, University of Birmingham, Birmingham B15 2TT, England.
- National Documentation Centre for Sport, Physical Education and Recreation. Abstract Journal Holdings. irreg.
- National Documentation Centre for Sport, Physical Education and Recreation. List of Periodical Holdings. irreg.
- National Documentation Centre for Sport, Physical Education and Recreation. Monthly Selection of Recent Publications. m.
- Sports Documentation Monthly Bulletin. m.

**National Dog Owners' Association**
92 High St., Lee-on-Solent, Hants, Eng.
- Dog News and Family Pets. bi-m. ISSN 0309-1031

**National Economic Development Office**
Millbank Tower, Millbank, London SW1P 4QX, England.
- N.E.D.O. in Print. q.

**National Electronics Council**
8-9 Bedford Square, London WC1B 3RG, England.
- National Electronics Review. bi-m.

**National Environmental Research Council**
Alhambra House, 27-33 Charing Cross Rd., London WC2H 0AX, Eng.
- N E R C News Journal. irreg.

**National Equine Defence League**
138 Blackwell Rd., Carlisle CA2 4DL, England.
- National Equine (and Smaller Animals) Defence League. Annual Report. a. ISSN 0077-4448

**National Extension College**
131 Hills Rd., Cambridge, England.
- Home Study; a quarterly magazine from the National Extension College, Cambridge. q. ISSN 0441-7445

**National Farmers' Union**
- Cheshire Farmer. (pub. by Plough Publicity (Hull) Ltd.)
- Cumbria Farmer. (pub. by Plough Publicity (Hull) Ltd.)
- East Riding Farmer. (pub. by Plough Publicity (Hull) Ltd.)
- Lancashire Farmer. (pub. by Plough Publicity (Hull) Ltd.)
- North Riding (No.2) Farmer. (pub. by Plough Publicity (Hull) Ltd.)
- North Riding and Durham Farmer. Durham Edition. (pub. by Plough Publicity (Hull) Ltd.)
- North Riding and Durham Farmer. North Riding Edition. (pub. by Plough Publicity (Hull) Ltd.)
- Northumberland Farmer. (pub. by Plough Publicity (Hull) Ltd.)
- Nottinghamshire Farmers' Journal. (pub. by Plough Publicity (Hull) Ltd.)
- Shropshire N F U Journal. (pub. by Plough Publicity (Hull) Ltd.)
- West Riding Farmer. (pub. by Plough Publicity (Hull) Ltd.)
- Worcestershire Record. (pub. by Plough Publicity (Hull) Ltd.)

**National Farmers' Union County Publications Ltd.**
64A High East St., Dorchester, Dorset, Eng.
- Brecon and Radnor Farmer. m. ISSN 0006-954X
- Carmarthenshire Farmer. m.
- Central Southern Farmer. m.
- Cornish Farmer & Grower. m.
- Derbyshire farmer. m.
- Dorset Farmer. m. ISSN 0012-5598
- East Sussex Farmer. m. ISSN 0012-8546
- Essex Farmers Journal. m. ISSN 0014-0945
- Glamorgan Farmers' Review. m.
- Gloucestershire Farmer. m. ISSN 0017-131X

- Hampshire Farmer. m. ISSN 0017-7121
- Herefordshire Farmer. m. ISSN 0018-0688
- Kent Farmer. m. ISSN 0023-0022
- Leicestershire, Northamptonshire & Rutland Farmer. m.
- Monmouthshire Farmer. m. ISSN 0026-9816
- Norfolk Farmers' Union Gazette. m.
- Oxford & Berkshire Farmer. m.
- Pembrokeshire Farmer. m. ISSN 0031-4226
- Somerset Farmer. m. ISSN 0038-1314
- South Lincolnshire Farmer. m.
- Staffordshire Farmer. m.
- Suffolk Farmer. m.
- Warwickshire Farmer. m.
- Wiltshire Farmer. m. ISSN 0043-566X

**National Federation of Bakery Students Societies**
c/o R. E. Cope, Ed., 2A Collier Lane, Baildon, Shipley, Yorks. BD17 5LN, Eng.
- Student Baker. 5 per yr.

**National Federation of Building Trades Employers**
- National Builder. (pub. by Federated Employers' Press Ltd.)

**National Federation of Fish Friers**
- Fish Friers Review. (pub. by Fish Friers Review Ltd.)

**National Federation of Housing Associations**
86 Strand, London WC2R 0EG, Eng.
- Voluntary Housing. q.

**National Federation of Master Window Cleaners**
Summerfield House, Harrogate Rd., Reddish, Stockport, Cheshire SK5 6HH, Eng.
- Window Talk. q.

**National Federation of Meat Traders**
- Meat Trade Yearbook. (pub. by Wheatland Journals Ltd.)
- Meat Trader. (pub. by Wheatland Journals Ltd.)

**National Federation of Old Age Pensions Associations**
Melling House, 91 Preston New Rd., Blackburn, Lancashire, Eng.
- Pensioners Voice. m. ISSN 0048-3281

**National Federation of Plastering Contractors**
- Modern Plastering. (pub. by Federated Employers Press Ltd)
- National Federation of Plastering Contractors. Year Book. (pub. by Comprint Ltd.)

**National Federation of Retail Newsagents**
2 Bridewell Place, London, EC4, England.
- National Federation of Retail Newsagents. National Federation Yearbook. a. ISSN 0077-4499

**National Federation of Roofing Contractors**
15 Soho Square, London W1V 5FB, England.
- N F R C Yearbook. a.
- Roofing Contractor. bi-m. ISSN 0035-8193

**National Federation of Sub-Postmasters**
Evelyn House, 22 Windlesham Gardens, Shoreham-By-Sea, Sussex, Eng.
- Sub-Postmaster. m. ISSN 0039-4335

**National Federation of Taxicab Associations**
- Steering Wheel & Taxi Trader. (pub. by Steering Wheel Publications Ltd.)

**National Foundation for Educational Research Publishing Co., Ltd.**
Journals Dept, 2 Jennings Bldgs., Thames Ave., Windsor, Berks SL4 1QS, Eng.
- Educational Research. 3 per yr. ISSN 0013-1881

**National Froebel Foundation**
Froebel Institute, Grove House, Roehampton Lane, London SW15 5PJ, England
- Co-Operative Study Scheme on ' Finding Out' Activities. irreg. ISSN 0069-486X (Dist. by C. F. Hodgson & Son Ltd., 50 Holloway Rd., London N7 8JL, England)

**National Gardens Scheme**
57 Lower Belgrave St., London SW1W 0LR, England.
- Gardens of England and Wales Open to the Public. a. ISSN 0072-0186 (Queen's Nursing Institute)

**National Graphical Association**
Graphic House, 63-67 Bromham Rd., Bedford, Eng.
- Print. m. ISSN 0032-8529

**National Hairdressers Federation**
11, Goldington Rd., Bedford, England.
- National Hairdresser. q.

**National Housing and Town Planning Council**
34 Junction Rd., London N19, Eng.
- Housing and Planning Review; the journal of the national housing and town planning council. q. ISSN 0018-6589
- Housing and Planning Year Book. a. ISSN 0073-3644
- National Housing and Town Planning Council. Handbook and Year Book. a. ISSN 0077-4707

**National Industrial Fuel Efficiency Service**
Abford House, 15 Wilton Rd., S.W.1., London, England.
- National Industrial Fuel Efficiency Service, London Progress Survey with Report and Accounts. a. ISSN 0077-4731

**National Industrial Materials Recovery Association**
York House, Westminster Bridge Rd., London SE1 7UT, Eng.
- Industrial Recovery. m. ISSN 0019-8668

**National Institute for Medical Research**
Mill Hill, London N.W.7, England.
- National Institute for Medical Research. Report. a. ISSN 0072-6567

**National Institute for Research in Dairying**
Church Lane, Shinfield, Reading RG2 9AT, England.
- Journal of Dairy Research. (pub. by Cambridge University Press)
- National Institute for Research in Dairying. Biennial Report. biennial. ISSN 0085-3798 (Agricultural Research Council)
- National Institute for Research in Dairying. Biennial Reviews. biennial. ISSN 0085-3801 (Agricultural Research Council)

**National Institute for Social Work**
- National Institute Social Services Library. (pub. by George Allen & Unwin (Publishers) Ltd.)

**National Institute of Adult Education**
De Montfort House, 19B de Montfort St., Leicester LE1 7GH, England.
- Adult Education. bi-m. ISSN 0001-849X
- Calendar of Residential Short Courses. s-a.
- Teaching Adults. s-a. ISSN 0040-0548
- Yearbook of Adult Education. a. ISSN 0084-3601

**National Institute of Adult Education (England and Wales)**
Dept. of Adult Education, Univ. of Leicester, Leicester LE1 7RH, England
(Distr.: Research Publications Services, Victoria Hall, E. Greenwich, London SE 10, Eng.)
- Studies in Adult Education. s-a. ISSN 0039-3525

**National Institute of Agricultural Botany**
Commonwealth Agricultural Bureaux, Huntingdon Rd., Cambridge, England.
- National Institute of Agricultural Botany, Cambridge, England. Annual Report of the Council and Accounts. a. ISSN 0077-4782
- National Institute of Agricultural Botany, Cambridge, England. Journal. a. ISSN 0077-4790

**National Institute of Agricultural Engineering**
Wrest Park, Silsoe, Bedford MK45 4HS, England.
- National Institute of Agricultural Engineering, Silsoe, England. Translations. irreg., no. 372, 1975. ISSN 0077-4812

**National Institute of Economic and Social Research**
2 Dean Trench St., Smith Sq., London SW1P 3HE, Eng.
- Economic and Social Studies. (pub. by Cambridge University Press)
- National Institute Economic Review. q. ISSN 0027-9501
- National Institute of Economic and Social Research. Annual Report. a. ISSN 0077-491X
- Studies in the National Income and Expenditure of the United Kingdom. (pub. by Cambridge University Press)

**National Institute of Industrial Psychology**
14 Welbeck Street, London, W1M 8DR, England.
- N I I P Bulletin. irreg. ISSN 0077-5010

**National League of the Blind and Disabled**
262 Langham Rd., London N15 3NS, Eng.
- Blind Advocate. q. ISSN 0006-4807

**National Library of Wales**
Aberystwyth, Dyfed SY23 3BU, Wales.
- Bibliotheca Celtica; A register of publications relating to Wales and the Celtic peoples. a.(approx.) ISSN 0067-7914
- Cylchgrawn Llyfrgell Genedlaethol Cymru/ National Library of Wales Journal. s-a. ISSN 0011-4421
- Wales. National Library. Handlist on Manuscripts in the National Library of Wales. a. (occasionally irreg.) ISSN 0065-0293

**National Magazine Co., Ltd.**
Chestergate House, Vauxhall Bridge Rd., London SW1V 1HF, Eng
(Subscr. address: Armoury Way, London SW18 1HA, England)
- Connoisseur. 12 per yr. ISSN 0010-6275
- Containerisation International. m. ISSN 0010-7379
- Cosmopolitan: English Edition. m.
- Good Housekeeping. m. ISSN 0017-2081
- Harpers & Queen. m.
- She. m. ISSN 0037-3370
- Womancraft. m.

**National Maritime Board**
Rooms 177-179, 110 Cannon Street, London, EC4N 6BP, England.
- National Maritime Board. (Great Britain) Year Book. a. ISSN 0077-5185

**National Maritime Museum**
Romney Rd., Greenwich S. E. 10 9NF, England.
- Maritime Monographs and Reports. irreg.
- N M M News. 3 per yr.

**National Marriage Guidance Council**
7 Cedar Row, Shirehampton, Bristol BS11 0UH, Eng.
- Marriage Guidance. 6 per yr.

**National Master Farriers Blacksmiths**
- Farriers Journal. (pub. by Farriers Journal Publishing Co. Ltd.)

**National Motor Museum Trust**
- National Motor Museum Pictorial Guide. (pub. by Montagu Ventures Ltd.)

**National Museum of Wales**
Cathays Park, Cardiff CF1 3NP, Wales.
- National Museum of Wales. Annual Report. a.

**National Mutual House**
South Park, Sevenoaks, Kent, England.
- Her Majesty's Consuls List. bi-m.

**National Operatic and Dramatic Association**
1 Crestfield St., London WC1 8AU, Eng.
- N O D A Bulletin. 3 per yr. ISSN 0027-6863

**National Pawnbrokers Association (Inc.)**
Box 15, Southend-on-Sea, Essex SS2 4TU, Eng.
- N. P. A. Journal. bi-m. ISSN 0047-9020

**National Pharmaceutical Association**
- N P A Supplement. (pub. by C. F. Hodgson & Son Ltd.)

**National Philatelic Society**
Room 4, 1 Whitehall Place, London SW1A 2HE, Eng.
- Stamp Lover. q. ISSN 0038-9277

**National Pig Breeders' Association**
49 Clarendon Rd., Watford, Herts, WD1 1HT, England.
- National Pig Breeders' Association Herd Book. a. ISSN 0077-5312
- Pig Breeders Gazette. q. ISSN 0031-9732

**National Radiological Protection Board**
Harwell, Didcot, Oxon, England.
- Radiological Protection Bulletin. q. ISSN 0308-4272

**National Reprographic Centre for documentation**
Hatfield Polytechnic, Hatfield, Hertfordshire, Eng.
- Reprographics Quarterly. q. ISSN 0306-2880

**National Savings Committee for England and Wales**
Alexandra House, Kingsway, London, WC2B 6TS, Eng.
- National Savings Newsletter. 8 per yr. ISSN 0047-9071

**National Small-Bore Rifle Association**
Codrington House, 113 Southwark St, London SE1 0JW, Eng.
- Rifleman. q. ISSN 0035-5224

**National Society for Autistic Children**
1A Golders Green Rd., London N.W.11 8EA, Eng.
- Communication. q. ISSN 0045-7663

**National Society for Clean Air**
136 North St., Brighton BN1 1RG, Eng.
- Clean Air. q. ISSN 0300-5143
- Clean Air Conference (Gt. Brit.) a.
- N. S. C. A. Reference Book; comprehensive guide to all aspects of air pollution control. biennial.
- National Society for Clean Air. Proceedings of the Annual Conference. a. ISSN 0077-5746

**National Society for Mentally Handicapped Children**
Pembridge Hall, 17 Pembridge Square, London W2 4EP, England.
- Journal of Mental Deficiency Research. q. ISSN 0022-264X
- Parents Voice. q. ISSN 0031-1936
- Subnormality in the Seventies. irreg., 2-3 per yr.

**National Society for the Prevention of Cruelty to Children**
1 Riding House St., London W1P 8AA, Eng.
- Child's Guardian. s-a. ISSN 0009-4218
- League of Pity Paper. s-a. ISSN 0047-4258
- National Society for Prevention of Cruelty to Children. Annual Report. a. ISSN 0077-5754

**National Society of Master Patternmakers**
139/143 Deykin Ave., Witton, Birmingham B6 YBG, Eng.
- British Pattern & Mould Maker. q.

**National Traction Engine Club**
19 Bridle Path, Woodcote, Reading R98 OSE, England.
- Steaming. q.

**National Trust for Scotland**
5 Charlotte Sq., Edinburgh EH2 4DU, Scotland.
- National Trust for Scotland Yearbook. a. ISSN 0077-5916

**National Tyre Distributors Association**
- T. A. B/Tyres, Accessories, Batteries. (pub. by Northwood Publications Ltd.)

**National Union of Agricultural Workers**
- Land Worker. (pub. by Land Worker Publishing Co. (1919) Ltd.)

**National Union of Bank Employees**
Sheffield House, Portsmouth Rd., Esher, Surrey, Eng.
- N U B E News; the bank officer. m. ISSN 0027-7088

**National Union of Insurance Workers. Prudential Section**
91-93 Gray's Inn Rd., London WC1X 8TX, England.
- National Union of Insurance Workers. Prudential Section. Gazette. irreg.

**National Union of Journalists**
314-320 Grays Inn Rd., London WC1X 8DP, Eng.
- Journalist. m. ISSN 0022-5541

**National Union of Licensed Victuallers**
Boardman House, 2 Downing St., Farnham, Surrey GU9 7NX, England.
- Licensee. m. ISSN 0024-2802

**National Union of Seamen**
Maritime House, Old Town, Clapham, London S.W.4, Eng.
- Seaman. m. ISSN 0037-0142

**National Union of Sheet Metal Workers, Coppersmiths, Heating and Domestic Engineers**
75-77, West Heath Rd., Hampstead, London NW3 7tL, Eng.
- National Union of Sheet Metal Workers, Coppersmiths, Heating & Domestic Engineers Journal. q.

**National Union of Students**
Press & Publicity Dept., 3 Endsleigh St., London WC1H 0DU, England.
- N U S Grants Handbook and Survey of LEA Awards. triennial.
- N U S Yearbook. a. ISSN 0077-5932

• National Student. m.

**National Union of Students United Kingdom. Health Student Section**
3 Endsleigh St., London WC1H 0DU, England.
• Health Team. 6 per yr.

**National Union of Teachers**
Hamilton House, Mabledon Place, London, WC1H 9BD, England.
• N U T Guide to Careers Work. (pub. by Schoolmaster Publishing Co. Ltd.)
• National Union of Teachers. Annual Report. a. ISSN 0077-5940
• Secondary Education. 2 per yr. ISSN 0018-1595
• Teacher. (pub. by Schoolmaster Publishing Co. Ltd.)

**National Union of the Footwear Leather and Allied Trades**
The Grange, Earls Barton, Northampton NN6 0JH, Eng.
• National Union of the Footwear, Leather and Allied Trades Monthly Journal and Report. m. ISSN 0028-0356

**National Union of Townswomen's Guilds**
2 Cromwell Place, London SW7 2JG, England.
• Townswoman. m.

**National University**
• Monographs in Ethiopia Land Tenure. (pub. by Oxford University Press)

**National Vegetable Society**
288 Northumberland Ave., Welling, Kent, England.
• National Vegetable Society. Newsletter. q.

**National Vulcan Engineering Insurance Group Ltd.**
St. Mary's Parsonage, Manchester M60 9AP, Eng.
• Vigilance. s-a. ISSN 0042-5958

**National Water Council**
1 Queen Anne's Gate, London SW1H 9BT, England.
• Water. q.
• Who's Who in the Water Industry. (pub. by Wheatland Journals Ltd.)

**National Westminster Bank Ltd**
41 Lothbury, London, E.C.2, Eng.
• National Westminster Bank Review. q. ISSN 0028-0399

**National Youth Bureau**
17-23 Albion St., Leicester LE1 6GD, England.
• Youth in Society. bi-m. ISSN 0307-1790
• Youth Social Work Bulletin. bi-m.

**Nationwide Building Society**
Planning Dept., New Oxford House, High Holborn, London WC1V 6PW, England.
• Nationwide Building Society. Occasional Bulletin. irreg. (4-8 per yr.)

**Natural Environmental Research Council**
• Bulletins of Marine Ecology. (pub. by Institute for Marine Environmental Research)

**Natural Food Publications Ltd.**
Box 1, Wirral, Merseyside L46 0TS, Eng.
• Healthy Living. m. ISSN 0017-9167
• Natural Food Retailer. m.

**Natural History Society of Northumbria**
Hancock Museum, Newcastle Upon Tyne NE2 4PT, England.
• Natural History Society of Northumbria. Transactions. 2 parts per yr.

**Naturalists' Trusts of West Wales, North Wales and Radnor**
4 Victoria Place, Haverfordwest, Wales.
• Nature in Wales. s-a.

**Naturist Foundation**
Sheepcote Lane, Orpington, Kent BR5 4ET, England.
• Grove. 3 per yr.

**Navin Weekly**
307A North End Rd., London WI4 9NS, England.
• Navin Weekly. w.

**Navy, Army & Air Force Institutes**
Kennington, London S.E.11, Eng.
• N A A F I News. m. ISSN 0027-5662
• N A A F I Reports. a.

**Navy League**
Broadway House, Broadway, Wimbledon, London, SW19, England.
• Maritime Survey. a. ISSN 0077-6289
• Sea Cadet. m. ISSN 0036-9985 (Sea Cadet Corps of the United Kingdom)

**Nether Press**
25 Whitehall Park, London, N.19, England.
• Nether Press Miscellaneous Series. irreg. (2-3 issues per year) ISSN 0077-6637

**Netherlands-British Chamber of Commerce**
The Dutch House, 307/308 High Holborn, London WC1V 7LS, England.
• Netherlands-British Trade Directory. a.

**Network**
84, High Street, Newport Pagnell, Bucks MK16 8EG, England.
• Journal of A T E. (Automatic Test Equipment); state of the art review. q.

**New Century Publishing Co.Ltd.**
84-88 Great Eastern St., London EC2A 3ED, Eng.
• Shoe and Leather News. w. ISSN 0037-4040
• Shoe Trades Directory. every 2 years. ISSN 0080-9349

**New Christian**
67a Camden, High St., London, N.W. 1, Eng.
• New Christian. fortn. ISSN 0028-4416

**New Church Press**
20 Bloomsbury Way, London WC1A 2TH, England.
• General Conference of the New Church. Yearbook. a. ISSN 0072-0666

**New City Songster**
35 Stanley Ave., Beckenham, Kent BR3 2PU, England.
• New City Songster. irreg. (approx. 2 per yr.)

**New Community Press Ltd.**
Oldbourne Hall, 43 Shoe Lane, London EC4 3BH, England.
• Social Worker. w.

**New Departures**
c/o Michael Horovitz, Ed., Mullions, Piedmont, Bisley, Strond, Glos. GL6 7BU, England.
• New Departures. biennial.

**New Diffusionist Press**
19 Crabtree Rd., Botley, Oxford, Eng.
• National Cactus & Succulent Journal. q. ISSN 0027-8858

**New Directions**
St. Stephen's Lodge, Hankey Place, London S.E.1, Eng.
• New Directions. q. ISSN 0028-4610

**New Era Books**
203 Seven Sisters Rd., London N4, England.
• Revolution. q. (Communist Federation of Britain(M-L))

**New Farm Press (Grimsby) Ltd.**
384-6 Cleethorpe Rd., Grimsby, Lincolnshire, Eng.
• Lincolnshire Agricultural and Industrial Sales and Wants. bi-w. ISSN 0047-4681

**New Fiction Society**
55 High Street, Frimley, Surrey GU16 5JE, England.
• New Fiction. q.

**New Internationalist Publications Ltd.**
62a High St., Wallingford, Oxford, England.
• New Internationalist. m.

**New Journal of Statistics and Operational Research**
c/o Cornelius Mack, Ed., University of Bradford, Bradford 7, Yorkshire, Eng.
• New Journal of Statistics and Operational Research. 3 per yr. ISSN 0028-601X

**New Left Review Ltd.**
7 Carlisle St., London W.1, Eng.
• New Left Review. 6 per yr. ISSN 0028-6060

**New Life Publications**
106 Clapham Rd., London SW9 0JX, Eng.
• New Life. bi-m. ISSN 0028-6079

**New Medical Journals Ltd.**
Clareville House, 26-27 Oxendon St., London SW1Y 4EL, England.
• World Medicine; the medical newsmagazine. fortn. ISSN 0043-8669

**New Property Press**
5 St. Peters St., London N.1, Eng.
• Building & Heating Product Guide; product promotion mailings. s-a. ISSN 0007-3377
• New Building Projects. m.

**New Review Ltd.**
11 Greek Street, London W1V 5LE, England.
• New Review. m. ISSN 0305-8344 (Arts Council of Great Britain)

**New Scientist**
King's Reach Tower, Stamford St., London SE1 9LS, Eng.
• New Scientist. w. ISSN 0028-6664

**New Towns Association**
Glen House, Stag Place, London SW1E 5AJ, England.
• New Towns Bulletin. m. ISSN 0306-1884

**New World Publishers Ltd.**
Surrey House, Throwley Way, Sutton, Surrey, England
(U. S. Address: Cahners Publishing Co. Inc., 5 S. Wabash, Chicago, IL 60603)
• Middle East Construction. 10 per yr.

**New Worlds Publishing**
271 Portobello Road, London, W.11, Eng.
• New Worlds; modern fiction. m. ISSN 0028-7075

**Donald Newby Publications, Ltd.**
Hooker House, Quay St., Halesworth, Suffolk IP19 8AP, Eng.
• World Bowls. m. ISSN 0043-8278

**Newcastle Chronicle and Journal**
Thomson House, Groat Market, Newcastle Upon Tyne, Eng.
• Sunday Sun. w. ISSN 0039-5315

**Newcastle University. Department of Physiology**
• Medical Hypotheses. (pub. by Eden Press)

**Newcastle University Students" Representative Council**
Union Society King's Walk, Newcastle Upon Tyne NE1 8QB, Eng.
• Package. 3 per yr. ISSN 0048-2668

**Newcastle Upon Tyne Polytechnic**
Ed. A. Potts., Dept. of Management, 1 Ellison Place, Newcastle Upon Tyne NE1 8ST, England.
• North East Group for the Study of Labour History Bulletin. a. ISSN 0029-2818

**Newcomen Society for the Study of the History of Engineering and Technology**
Science Museum, London SW7 2DD, England.
• Newcomen Bulletin. 3 per yr.
• Newcomen Society for the Study of the History of Engineering and Technology. Transactions. a.

**Newman Association**
Newman House, 15 Carlisle St., London WV5RE, Eng.
• Newman. s-a. ISSN 0048-0207

**Newman Bookshop**
87 St. Aldates, Oxford OX1 1RB, Eng.
• Downside Review; a quarterly of Catholic thought. q. ISSN 0012-5806

**Newman Publishing Ltd.**
48 Poland St., London W1V 4PP, Eng.
• Factory and Office Selector. m. ISSN 0046-3086
• Food Trades Directory, Food Buyer's Yearbook. biennial. ISSN 0071-7231
• Journal of Human Nutrition. q.
• Plant Foods for Man. q.
• Retail and Distribution Management. bi-m. ISSN 0307-2363
• Shop Property. m. ISSN 0037-4199
• Stores and Shops Retail Directory. a. ISSN 0081-5810
• Stores of the World Directory. biennial. ISSN 0081-5829

**Newnes-Butterworths**
Borough Green, Sevenoaks, Kent, England.
• Wireless World. Guide to Broadcasting Stations.
ISSN 0508-850X

**News & Book Trade Review & Stationers Gazette Ltd.**
21-25 Earl St., London EC2A 2HY, Eng.
• Retail Newsagent; Official journal of National
Federation of Retail Newsagents. w.

**News from Neasden**
Box 30, 197 Kings Cross Rd., London W.C.1,
England.
• News from Neasden. 3 per yr.

**News Group Newspapers Ltd.**
30 Bouverie St., London EC4Y 8EX, Eng.
• News of the World. w. ISSN 0028-9280

**News Publications Ltd.**
Standard House, Bonhill St., London EC2A 4DA,
Eng.
• Motoring News. w. ISSN 0027-2264

**Newspaper Archive Developments Ltd.**
16 Westcote Rd, Reading RG3 2DF, England
(Dist. in U.S. by: Research Publications Inc., 12
Lunar Drive, New Haven, CT 06525)
• Times Index. m.

**Newspaper Society**
Whitefriars House, 6 Carmelite St., London EC4Y
0BL, Eng.
• Production Journal. q. ISSN 0032-9878

**Newton Mann Ltd.**
Sherwood House, Matlock, Derbyshire, Eng.
• N A T News. 9 per yr. ISSN 0027-6049 (National
Association of Theatre Nurses)
• Technic. bi-m. (Institute of Operation Theatre
Technicians)

**Noise Abatement Society**
6 Old Bond St., London W.1, Eng.
• Noise News Digest. m.

**NOP Market Research Ltd.**
76-86 Strand, London WC2R 0DZ, England.
• Political Social Economic Review. bi-m. ISSN
0306-6061

**Norfolk Record Society**
425 Unthank Rd., Norwich NR4 7QB, England.
• Norfolk Record Society. Publications. a. ISSN
0078-1169

**North Cheshire Family History Society**
c/o Mrs P. M. Litton, 34 Bramley Rd., Bramhall,
Stockport, Cheshire SK7 2DP, England.
• North Cheshire Family Historian. q. ISSN 0306-
9206

**North of England Zoological Society**
Zoological Gardens, Upton by Chester, Cheshire,
Eng.
• Chester Zoo News. m. ISSN 0300-4988

**North of Scotland College of Agriculture**
581 King St., Aberdeen AB9 1UD, Scotland.
• North of Scotland College of Agriculture,
Aberdeen. Annual Report. a. ISSN 0550-8525
• North of Scotland College of Agriculture,
Aberdeen. Bulletin. irreg.
• North of Scotland College of Agriculture,
Aberdeen. Guide to Grassland Experiments. a.
ISSN 0078-1614

**North of Scotland Milk Marketing Board**
Ardconell Terrace, Inverness, Scotland.
• Milk Topics. m. ISSN 0047-7419

**North Staffordshire Chamber of Commerce and Industry**
Winton House, Stoke Rd., Shelton, Stoke-On-Trent,
Staffs, Eng.
• Focus on Industry and Commerce. m. ISSN 0015-
5098

**North Staffordshire Polytechnic**
c/o Dr. H. L. W. Jackson, Black Heath Lane,
Stafford, Eng.
• Computer Education; a journal for teachers
(especially of 11-18 age range) interested in
computers & computing. 3 per yr. ISSN 0010-
4590 (Computer Education Group)

**North Thames Gas**
North Thames House, London Rd., Staines,
Middlesex, TW18 4AE, England.
• Modern Living. 3 per yr. ISSN 0026-7988

**Northampton Independent Ltd.**
12 the Parade, Northampton, Eng.
• Northampton and County Independent. m. ISSN
0048-0711

**Northamptonshire and Bedfordshire Life**
4 & 5 Free Church Passage, St. Ives, England.
• Northamptonshire and Bedfordshire Life. m.

**Northamptonshire Natural History Society and Field Club**
c/o S.V.F. Leleux, Treas., 7 Langham Pl.,
Northampton, England.
• Northamptonshire Natural History Society and
Field Club Journal. a.

**Northamptonshire Record Society**
Delapre Abbey, Northampton, Eng.
• Northamptonshire Past and Present. a.

**North-East Atlantic Fisheries Commission**
Room 224, Great Westminster House, Horseferry
Rd., London, S.W.1, England.
• North-East Atlantic Fisheries Commission.
Reports of Meetings. a. ISSN 0078-1584

**North East Coast Institution of Engineers and Shipbuilders**
Bolbec Hall, Westgate Road, Newcastle Upon Tyne,
NE1 1TB, Eng.
• North East Coast Institution of Engineers and
Shipbuilders. Transactions. 6 yr. ISSN 0029-280X

**North East London Polytechnic. Department of Applied Economic Studies**
Longbridge Rd., Dagenham, Essex RM8 2AS,
England.
• Applecon. q. ISSN 0305-9499

**Northern Advertising Agency (Bradford) Ltd.**
7 Tong Lane, Bradford, BD4 0RR, England.
• Engineering Industries Association. Classified
Directory and Buyers Guide. bienniel. ISSN
0071-0342

**Northern House**
58 Queens Road, Newcastle-Upon-Tyne, NE2 2PR,
England.
• Northern House Pamphlet Poets. irreg. ISSN
0078-1738

**Northern Ireland. Department of Agriculture**
Dundonald House, Belfast BT4 3SB, N. Ireland.
• Agriculture in Northern Ireland. m. ISSN 0002-
175X
• Northern Ireland. Department of Agriculture.
Annual Report on Research and Technical Work.
a. ISSN 0078-1746
• Northern Ireland. Department of Agriculture.
Record of Agricultural Research. irreg., vol. 22,
1974. ISSN 0078-1754

**Northern Ireland. Department of Commerce**
21 Linenhall St., Belfast BT2 8BZ, Northern
Ireland.
• Review of the Linen Industry. a.

**Northern Ireland. Office of the Northern Ireland Commissioner for Complaints**
River House, 48 High St., Belfast BT1 2JT,
Northern Ireland
(Orders to H.M. Stationery Office, Chichester
House, Chichester St., Belfast, Northern Ireland)
• Northern Ireland. Commissioner for Complaints.
Annual Report. a.

**Northern Ireland Association for Mental Health**
Beacon House 84, University St., Belfast BT7 1HE,
Northern Ireland.
• Northern Ireland Association for Mental Health.
Newsletter. s-a.

**Northern Ireland Civil Rights Association**
• Civil Rights. (pub. by Printworkshop)

**Northern Ireland Community Relations Commission.**
Bedford House, Bedford St., Belfast 2, Northern
Ireland.
• Northern Ireland Community Relations
Commission. Annual Report. a. ISSN 0085-4298

**Northern Ireland Council of Social Service**
2 Annadale Avenue, Belfast BT7 3JR, N. Ireland.
• Scope: a Review of Voluntary and Community
Work in Northern Ireland. bi-m.

**Northern Ireland Information Service**
Stormont Castle, Belfast, N. Ireland.
• Ulster Commentary. m. ISSN 0041-6185

**Northern Mine Research Society**
41 Windsor Walk, South Anston, Sheffield S31
7EL, England
(Subscr. to: R. G. Guthrie, 186 Station Rd.,
Billingham, Cleveland TS23 2RT, England)
• British Mining; memoirs & monographs. s-a. ISSN
0308-2199

**Northern Naturalists Union**
The Poplars, Chester-le-Street, County Durham
DH3 3LY, England.
• Vasculum. q. ISSN 0049-5891

**Northgate Publications**
1 Wardour Mews, London W17, England.
• Tape and Hi-Fi Test. m.

**North West Arts Association**
• Phoenix. (pub. by Harry Chambers, Ed. & Pub.)

**North West Industrial Development Association**
Brazennose House (West Door), Brazennose St.,
Manchester M2 5A2, England.
• North West Industrial Development Association.
Annual Report. a.
• North West Industrial Development Association.
Newsletter. q.

**North Western Electricity Board**
Cheetwood Rd., Manchester M8 8BA, Eng.
• Norweb News. m.

**Northwood Publications Ltd**
Elm House, 10-16 Elm St., London WC1X 0BP,
England
(Dist. by Hastings House Publishers, Inc., 10 E.
40th St., New York, N.Y. 10016)
• Big Farm Management. m. ISSN 0014-7818
• Brewers' Guardian. m. ISSN 0006-9728
• Brewery Manual and Who's Who in British
Brewing. a. ISSN 0305-8123
• Building Trades Journal. w. ISSN 0306-3194
• Catering Times. w. ISSN 0008-7831
• Consulting Engineer; journal of the professional
engineer. m. ISSN 0010-7093
• Engineering Capacity. m.
• Factory Equipment News. m. ISSN 0014-6579
• Hospital Development. bi-m. ISSN 0300-5720
• Hospital Equipment & Supplies. m. ISSN 0018-
5620
• Meat Trades Journal. w. ISSN 0025-6412
• Paper Facts and Figures. bi-m. ISSN 0031-112X
• Penrose Annual; international review of the
graphic arts. a. ISSN 0079-0710
• Print Buyer. m.
• Printing Equipment & Materials. m. ISSN 0032-
8596
• T. A. B/Tyres, Accessories, Batteries. bi-m. ISSN
0039-8187 (National Tyre Distributors
Association)

**Norwegian Chamber of Commerce (London) Inc.**
Norway House, 21/24 Cockspur St., London S.W.1,
Eng.
• Anglo-Norwegian Trade Journal. bi-m. ISSN
0003-3375
• Norwegian Chamber of Commerce. Year Book
and Directory of Members. a. ISSN 0085-4360

**Notes and Queries for Somerset and Dorset**
c/o L. C. Hayward, 226 Goldcroft, Yeovil,
Somerset, Eng.
• Notes and Queries for Somerset and Dorset. s-a.
ISSN 0029-3989

**Nothing Doing (Formally of London)**
25 Woodhall Drive, London SE21 7HJ, England.
• Literary Supplement. irreg., no. 21, 1975.

**Nottingham & Nottinghamshire Field Club**
50 Selby Rd., West Bridgford, Nottingham,
England.
• Field Fare; quarterly bulletin of the Nottingham &
Nottinghamshire Field Club. q.

**Nottingham and Nottinghamshire Technical Information Service**
Central Library, South Sherwood St., Nottingham NG1 4DA, England.
- N A N T I S Handbook and Directory of Resources. irreg.
- N A N T I S News. m. ISSN 0027-593X

**Nottingham UFO Investigation Society**
443 Meadow Lane, Nottingham NG2 3GB, England.
- U F O Research Review. q.

**Nottingham Union Students Union**
Portland Bldg., University Park, Nottingham, England.
- Gong. 3 per yr. ISSN 0017-1972

**Nottinghamshire Chamber of Commerce and Industry**
395 Mansfield Rd, Nottingham, Eng.
- Industrial Nottingham. m. ISSN 0019-8579

**Nova Hrvatska Ltd.**
30 Fleet St., London EC4Y 1AJ, England.
- Nova Hrvatska. s-m.

**Novello and Co. Ltd.**
1-3 Upper James St., London W1R 4BP, Eng.
- Musical Times. m. ISSN 0027-4666
- Strad; a monthly journal for professionals and amateurs of all stringed instruments played with the bow. m. ISSN 0039-2049

**John L. Noyce, Ed. & Pub.**
Box 450, Brighton, Sussex BN1 8GR, Eng.
- Librarians for Social Change. 3 per yr.
- Studies in Labour History. a.

**Numismatic Directories**
2 The Square, Richmond, Surrey, England.
- Dealers in Coins; directory of dealers in coins and medals in the British Isles. irreg. ISSN 0070-3109

**Numismatic Publishing Co.**
Sovereign House, High St., Brentwood, Essex CM14 4SE, Eng.
- Coin Monthly. m. ISSN 0010-0390
- Coin Yearbook. a.

**Nursery World**
Cliffords Inn, Fetter Lane, London EC4A 1 PJ, Eng.
- Nursery World; devoted to mothercraft, child care, hygiene and pre-school education. w. ISSN 0029-6422

**Nursing Notes Ltd.**
98 Belsize Lane, London NW3 5BB, Eng.
- Midwives Chronicle. m. ISSN 0026-3524 (Royal College of Midwives)

**Nutrition Society**
- British Journal of Nutrition. (pub. by Cambridge University Press)
- Nutrition Society, Proceedings. (pub. by Cambridge University Press)

**O.S. & S. Ltd.**
14 Peterborough Rd., Harrow, Middlesex, Eng.
- Contact Lens Journal. bi-m. ISSN 0306-9575

**Oakham School**
Oakham School, Oakham, Rutland, Eng.
- Oakhamian. s-a. ISSN 0029-7380

**Oakwood Press**
50 York Rd., Leeds, 9, Eng.
- Scooter World. m. ISSN 0036-8954

**Oasis Books**
12 Stevenage Rd., London SW6 6ES, Eng.
- Oasis. 3 per yr.

**Objective Marketing and Intelligence Services Ltd.**
- MINTEL. (pub. by Kraushar Andrews and Eassie Ltd)

**Observer Ltd.**
8 St. Andrew's Hill, London EC4V 5JA, Eng.
- Observer. w. ISSN 0029-7712

**Ocean Publications Ltd.**
34 Buckingham Palace Rd., London SW1W 0RE, England.
- British Ski Magazine. 6 per yr.
- Canoeing. m. ISSN 0008-5634
- Canoeing. bi-m. (British Canoe Union)

**A. S. O'Connor & Co. Ltd.**
26 Sheen Park, Richmond, Surrey TW9 1UW, England.
- Adhesives Directory. a.
- Medical Digest. m. ISSN 0025-7168
- Resin News. m. ISSN 0034-5563

**Odhams Press Ltd.**
Long Acre, London W.C.2, Eng.
- Eagle and Boys' World. w. ISSN 0012-8104

**Off-Licence Journal**
c/o E. A. Brandon, Ed., 66 Queens Rd., Watford, WD1 2LA, England.
- Off-Licence Journal. ISSN 0030-0063

**Office of Health Economics**
162 Regent St., London W1R 6DD, England.
- Early Diagnosis Papers. irreg.
- Studies on Current Health Problems. irreg. (Association of the British Pharmaceutical Industry)

**Officers' Christian Union**
77 High St., Aldershot GU11 1BY, Eng.
- Practical Christianity. q. ISSN 0032-6364

**Officers' Pensions Society Ltd.**
15, Buckingham Gate, London, SW1E 6NS, Eng.
- Pennant. s-a. ISSN 0048-3192

**John Offord (Publications) Ltd.**
Box 64, Eastbourne, East Sussex BN21 3LE, England.
- British Theatre Directory. a.
- Municipal Entertainment. m.

**Offshore Information Literature**
30 Baker St., London W1M 2DS, England.
- Offshore Abstracts. bi-m. ISSN 0305-0513

**Oil & Colour Chemists Association**
Priory House, 967 Harrow Rd., Wembley, Middlesex HA0 2SF, Eng.
- Oil and Colour Chemists' Association. Journal. m. ISSN 0030-1337

**Old Colfeians Association**
Horn Park, Eltham Rd., London S.E. 12, Eng.
- Colfeian. a. ISSN 0010-0676

**Old Contemptible**
c/o Major Darroch, Darmar, Ingham, Lincoln, England.
- Old Contemptible. m. ISSN 0048-1645

**Old Motor Magazine Ltd.**
17 Air St., London W.1, Eng., U.K.
- Old Motor; a North London artists presentation. ISSN 0030-2023 (U. S. Subscr. to: Sky Books International Inc., 520 Fifth Ave., New York, NY 10036)

**Old Time Music**
c/o Tony Russell, Ed., 33 Brunswick Gardens, London W8 4AW, England.
- Old Time Music. q. ISSN 0048-1653

**Oleander Press**
17 Stansgate Ave., Cambridge CB2 2QZ, England (U.S. Address: 210 Fifth Ave., New York, NY 10010)
- Arabia Past & Present Series. irreg. (approx. 2 per yr)
- Arrangement of Documents Series. irreg. ISSN 0066-7889
- Cambridge Town, Gown & County Series. irreg.
- Dramascripts Series. irreg., 1970, no. 4. ISSN 0070-7198
- Herbert Read Series. irreg. ISSN 0073-1927
- Libyan Past and Present Series. irreg., (approx. 2 per year) 1970, vol. 3.

**Oliver & Boyd**
Croythorn House, 23 Ravelston Terrace, Edinburgh EH 4 3TJ, Scotland.
- University of Glasgow. Social and Economic Studies. Occasional Papers. irreg. ISSN 0072-4610

**Oliver's Guides**
37 Amwell St., London EC1, England.
- Oliver's Guide to the City of London. a.

**Omens**
9 Roundhay Rd., Leicester LE3 2BY, England.
- Omens; poetry magazine. q.

**Omnibus Society**
103a Streatham Hill, London S.W.2, England.
- Omnibus Magazine. bi-m. ISSN 0305-9243

**Open-Air Mission**
19 John St., London WC1N 2DL, England.
- Master and the Multitude. q.

**Open University**
Walton Hall, Milton Keynes MK7 6AA, England.
- Sesame; the newspaper of the Open University. m.
- Technical Education Abstracts from British Sources. q. ISSN 0040-0920

**Open University Press**
Walton Hall, Milton Keynes, Bucks, England.
- Systems Behaviour. irreg.

**Opera North**
41 Sandhill, Newcastle- upon- Tyne NE1 3JF, England.
- Opera North. 5 per yr.

**Operational Research Society**
6Th Floor, Neville House, Waterloo Street, Birmingham B2 5TX, England.
- Operational Research Quarterly. (pub. by Pergamon Press Inc. US)
- Operational Research Society. Education and Research Year Book. a.

**Optical World Ltd.**
379 Woodgrange Drive, Southend on Sea, Essex SS1 3DY, Eng.
- Optical World/Optische Welt/Optique dans le Monde. bi-m.

**Orbis Publishing Ltd.**
49 Russell Sq., London WC1, England (U.S. Subscr. to: 6 Commercial St., Hicksville, NY 11801)
- World of Wildlife. w.

**Orbit Books**
72 Beeches Drive, Erdington, Birmingham B24 0DT, England.
- Andromeda. s-a.

**Orcadian**
c/o W. R. Mackintosh, Orcadian Office, Kirkwall, Orkney KW15 1DW.
- Orcadian. w.

**Orchid Review Ltd.**
62 Chaldon Common Rd., Caterham, Surrey CR3 5DD, Eng.
- Orchid Review. m. ISSN 0030-4476

**Order of St. John**
1 Grosvenor Crescent, London S.W.1, England.
- St. John Review. m. ISSN 0036-2883

**Order of the Road**
47 Curzon St., London W.1, Eng.
- Safe Driver. q. ISSN 0036-2387

**Ore**
c/o Ed. Eric Ratcliffe, 7 the Towers, Stevenage, Herts., SG1 1HE, England.
- Ore. irreg. (1-2 per yr.) ISSN 0030-459X

**Organ Club**
c/o Graham R. Bamber, Ed., 93 Lynton Rd., Acton, London W3 9HL, England (Subscr. to: F. C. Symonds, 44a Gayton Rd., Hampstead, London NW3 1TU, England)
- Organ Club Journal. bi-m.

**Oriental Art Magazine Ltd.**
12 Ennerdale Rd., Richmond, Surrey, Eng.
- Oriental Art; devoted to the study of all forms of Oriental art. q. ISSN 0030-5278

**Alan Osborne & Associates**
113 Blackheath Park, London S.E.3, Eng.
- Protection. m. ISSN 0033-1716 (Institution of Industrial Safety Officers)

**Osbornes Advertising Service**
79 St. Lawrence Ave., Worthing, Sussex, Eng.
- Overseas Visitor to United Kingdom. s-a. ISSN 0030-7521

**Other Scenes Inc.**
Bcm-Oscenes, London WC1V, Eng.
- Other Scenes; the international newspaper. irreg. ISSN 0030-6568

**Our Dogs Publishing Co. Ltd.**
5 James Leigh St., Manchester, Eng.
- Our Dogs. w. ISSN 0030-6827

**Outposts Publications**
72 Burwood Road, Walton on Thames, Surrey KT12 4AL, Eng.
- Outposts. q. ISSN 0030-7297

**George Outram & Co. Ltd.**
70 Mitchell Street, Glasgow G13LZ, Scotland.
- Evening Times Wee Red Book; the football annual. a.

**The Overseas American, Inc.**
500 Chesham House, 150 Regent St., London, W1, England.
- Overseas American. fortn.

**Overseas Development Institute**
10-11 Percy St., London W1P 0JB, England.
- O D I Review. s-a. ISSN 0078-7116

**Overseas Newspapers (Agencies) Ltd.**
Bath House, 53 Holborn Viaduct, London EC1A 2FD, Eng.
- West Africa. w. ISSN 0043-2962

**Overseas Press and Media Association**
122 Shaftesbury Ave., London, W1V 8HA, England.
- Overseas Media Guide. a. ISSN 0078-7132

**Overseas Trade Research Fund**
55 Park Lane, London W1Y 3DH, England.
- Britain and Overseas. q. ISSN 0045-2866

**Overspill**
c/o Eric Harrison, Ed., Grantley Close, Shalford, Nr. Guildford, Surrey, England.
- Overspill; for the longer poem. 5 per yr.

**Peter Owen Ltd.**
20, Holland Park Ave, London W.11 3Q V, England
(Dist in U. S. by: Humanities Press Inc., 450 Park Ave. So., New York, NY 10010)
- Contemporary Issues Series. a. ISSN 0069-942X

**Owen's Commerce and Travel Ltd.**
886 High Road, Finchley, London N12 9SB, England.
- Owen's Commerce and Travel and International Register. a. ISSN 0078-7167

**Owner Drivers Society**
1 Buckingham Gate, London S.W.1, Eng.
- Taxinews. m. ISSN 0040-0254

**Owner Publication**
6 The Lawn, St. Leonards on Sea, Sussex, England.
- Rolls Royce Owner. m. ISSN 0035-7952

**Oxfam**
274 Banbury Road, Oxford OX2 7DZ, England.
- Oxfam News. bi-m.

**Oxford and Cambridge Philological Societies**
- Classical Quarterly. (pub. by Oxford University Press)
- Classical Review. (pub. by Oxford University Press)

**Oxford Bibliographical Society**
c/o Bodleian Library, Oxford OX1 3BG, England.
- Oxford Bibliographical Society. Occasional Publications. irreg. ISSN 0078-7175
- Oxford Bibliographical Society. Publications. New Series. irreg. ISSN 0078-7183

**Oxford Centre for Postgraduate Hebrew Studies**
45 St. Giles, Oxford OX1 3LP, Eng.
- Journal of Jewish Studies. s-a. ISSN 0022-2097

**Oxford Consumers Group**
86 Gidley Way, Horspath, Oxford, Eng.
- Oxford Consumer. q. ISSN 0048-2560

**Oxford Mission**
35 Great Peter St., London SW1P 3LR, Eng.
- Oxford Mission. q. ISSN 0048-2579

**Oxford Society**
8 Wellington Square, Oxford OX1 2HY, Eng.
- Oxford. s-a. ISSN 0030-7645

**Oxford Student Publications Ltd.**
St. Michael's St., Oxford OX1 3JB, England.
- Cherwell; the Oxford University newspaper. 24 per yr. ISSN 0308-731X

**Oxford University Press**
Press Rd., Neasden, London N.W. 10, England
(U.S. address: 200 Madison Ave., New York, NY 10016)
- African Affairs. q. ISSN 0001-9909 (Royal African Society)
- Antiquaries Journal. s-a. ISSN 0003-5815 (Society of Antiquaries of London)
- Auctores Britannici Medii Aevi. irreg. ISSN 0067-0529 (British Academy)
- Brain; journal of neurology. q. ISSN 0006-8950
- British Academy, London. Proceedings. a. ISSN 0068-1202
- British Journal of Aesthetics. q. ISSN 0007-0904 (British Society of Aesthetics)
- British Library Journal. s-a. (British Library Board) (Co-publisher: British Museum Publications Ltd.)
- Classical Quarterly. s-a. ISSN 0009-8388 (Oxford and Cambridge Philological Societies)
- Classical Review. 2 per yr. ISSN 0009-840X (Oxford and Cambridge Philological Societies)
- Community Development Journal. 3 per yr. ISSN 0010-3802
- Early Music. q.
- Eastern Churches Review. s-a. ISSN 0012-8740
- English. 3 per yr. ISSN 0013-8215 (English Association)
- English Language Teaching Journal. q. ISSN 0307-8337 (British Council)
- Forestry. s-a (plus supplement on special topic) ISSN 0015-752X (Institute of Foresters of Great Britain)
- Greece and Rome. s-a. ISSN 0017-3835 (Classical Association)
- Henriette Hertz Trust: Annual Lectures on the Aspects of Art of the British Academy. a. ISSN 0073-1854 (British Academy)
- Henriette Hertz Trust: Annual Master-Mind Lectures of the British Academy. a. ISSN 0073-1862 (British Academy)
- Henriette Hertz Trust: Annual Philosophical Lectures of the British Academy. a. ISSN 0073-1870 (British Academy)
- Human Rights Review. s-a.
- Index Kewensis. Supplement. quinquennial. ISSN 0073-5809 (Herbarium of the Royal Botanic Gardens, Kew)
- Index on Censorship. q. ISSN 0306-4220
- International Affairs. q. ISSN 0020-5850 (Royal Institute of International Affairs)
- International Journal of Agrarian Affairs. irreg. ISSN 0074-6649 (University of Oxford. Institute of Agrarian Affairs) (Co-sponsor: International Association of Agricultural Economists)
- International Journal of Epidemiology. q. ISSN 0300-5771 (International Epidemiological Association)
- Journal of Commonwealth Literature. 3 per yr. ISSN 0021-9894 (University of Leeds)
- Journal of Experimental Botany. bi-m. ISSN 0022-0957 (Society for Experimental Biology)
- Journal of Petrology. 3 per yr. ISSN 0022-3530
- Journal of Soil Science. 4 per yr. ISSN 0022-4588 (British Society of Soil Science)
- Journal of Southern African Studies. s-a.
- Journal of Theological Studies. s-a. ISSN 0022-5185
- Library. q. ISSN 0024-2160 (Bibliographical Society)
- London Mathematical Society. Proceedings. 8 per yr. ISSN 0024-6115 (London Mathematical Society)
- London Oriental Series. irreg., no. 29, 1974. ISSN 0076-0625 (University of London. School of Oriental and African Studies)
- Marine Biological Association of the United Kingdom. Journal. q. ISSN 0025-3154
- Maudsley Monographs. irreg., 1972, no. 21. ISSN 0076-5465 (University of London. Institute of Psychiatry)
- Monographs in Ethiopia Land Tenure. irreg. ISSN 0077-0841 (National University)
- Multiracial School. 3 per yr. (Association for the Education of Pupils from Overseas)
- New Surveys in the Classics. a. (Classical Association)
- Notes and Queries; for readers and writers, collectors and librarians. m. ISSN 0029-3970
- Oxford Economic Papers. 3 per yr. ISSN 0030-7653
- Oxford Slavonic Papers. New Series. a. ISSN 0078-7256

- Parliamentary Affairs; devoted to all aspects of parliamentary democracy. q. ISSN 0031-2290
- Political Studies. 4 per yr. ISSN 0032-3217 (Political Studies Association of the United Kingdom)
- Quarterly Journal of Mathematics. q. ISSN 0033-5606
- Quarterly Journal of Mechanics and Applied Mathematics. q. ISSN 0033-5614
- Quarterly Journal of Medicine. q. ISSN 0033-5622 (Association of Physicians of Great Britain and Ireland)
- Review of English Studies; a quarterly journal of English literature and the English language. q. ISSN 0034-6551
- Round Table; the commonwealth journal of international affairs. q. ISSN 0035-8533
- Royal Society of Literature of the United Kingdom. Essays by Divers Hands: Being the Transactions of the Society. irreg., 1972, vol. 37. ISSN 0080-4584 (Royal Society of Literature of the United Kingdom)
- Schweich Lectures. irreg. ISSN 0080-7206 (British Academy)
- Sociology. 3 per yr. ISSN 0038-0385 (British Sociological Association)
- Survey; a journal of East & West studies. q. ISSN 0039-6192 (International Association for Cultural Freedom) (Co-sponsor: Stanford University)
- Theatre Research International. 3 per yr. ISSN 0307-8833 (International Federation for Theatre Research)
- West African History Series. irreg. ISSN 0510-0690
- Wilde Lectures in Natural and Comparative Religion in the University of Oxford. irreg.
- World Today. m. ISSN 0043-9134 (Royal Institute of International Affairs)

**Oxford University Scientific Society**
University Museum, Oxford, England.
- Zenith. a. ISSN 0084-5442

**Oxfordshire Architectural and Historical Society**
Ashmolean Museum, Oxford, England.
- Oxoniensia. a.

**P & J Press**
33 Fairlawnes, Maldon Road, Wallington, Surrey, England.
- Federation of British Tape Recordists. News & Views. q.

**P C A Publications Ltd.**
238-246 King St., London W6 0RF, England.
- Na Antenie; mowi rozglosnia polska radia wolna europa. m. ISSN 0027-7290

**P C V A Publications Ltd.**
171 Battersea Church Rd., London S.W.11, Eng.
- Orzel Bialy/White Eagle. m. ISSN 0030-607X

**P.F. Publications**
554 Garratt Lane, London SW17 0NY, England.
- Petfish Practical Fishkeeping Monthly. m.

**P.H. Press Ltd.**
Waterloo Rd., Stockport SK1 3BN, Eng.
- Policy Holder Insurance Journal. w. ISSN 0032-2679

**P N Review**
c/o Department of English, University of Manchester, Manchester M13 9PL, England.
- P N Review. (Poetry Nation) q.

**P. P. Layouts**
Box A, 240 Camden High St., London NW1, England.
- Other Times. q.

**P R M Science & Technology Agency**
3 Harrington Rd., South Kensington, London, England.
- Activation Analysis Abstracts. q.

**P S L Publications Ltd.**
Bar Hill, Cambridge CB3 8EL, Eng.
- Airfix; for plastic modellers. m. ISSN 0002-2705 (Airfix Products Ltd.)
- Autoworld. 5 per yr. ISSN 0005-1829

**P S W (Educational) Publications**
11 Pendene Rd, Leicester LE2 3DQ, Eng.
- Forum for the Discussion of New Trends in Education. 3 per yr. ISSN 0046-4708

**P V Publications**
4 Wealden Close, Crowborough, Sussex TN6 2ST, England.
- Radix. 3 per yr.

**Pacific Area Travel Association**
- Tourism International Research/Pacific. (pub. by Tourism International Press Ltd.)

**Paddle Steamer Preservation Society**
6 Windermere Rd., Gloucester GL2 ONH, Eng.
- Paddle Wheels. q.

**Pagan Movement in Britain and Ireland**
103 Maindy Rd., Caerdydd, Cymru, Wales.
- Waxing Moon. q. ISSN 0049-7029

**Pages**
23 Wellesley Rd., Chiswick, London W4 4BU, Eng.
- Pages; international magazine of the avant-garde arts. q. ISSN 0030-9389

**Paint Research Association**
Waldegrave Rd., Teddington, Middlesex, Eng.
- Paint Titles. w.

**Pakistan Society**
37 Sloan St., London S.W. 1, England.
- Pakistan Society Bulletin. a.

**Palatinate Office**
Dunelm House, Durham City, County Durham, Eng.
- Phalanx. 3 per yr.

**Palestine Exploration Fund**
2 Hinde Mews, London W1M 5RH, Eng.
- Palestine Exploration Quarterly. s-a. ISSN 0031-0328

**Palgrave Publishing Co. Ltd.**
25 Windsor Street, Chertsey, Surrey, England.
- Technical Service Data. a. ISSN 0082-2329

**Pali Buddhist Union**
c/o Russell Webb, Ed., 51 Wellesley Rd., Ilford, Essex IG1 4JZ, England.
- Pali Buddhist Review. 3 per yr.

**G. J. Palmer & Sons Ltd.**
7 Portugal St., London WC2A 2HP, Eng.
- Church Times. w. ISSN 0009-658X

**Pan Africanist Congress**
Mission to Europe & the Americas, 22a Hillview Gardens, London NW4 2JH, Eng.
- Azania Combat. 6 per yr. (Pan Africanist Congress of Azania (South Africa) SA)

**Pandon Publications, Ltd.**
E Floor, Milburn House, Dean St., Newcastle Upon Tyne NE1 1LE, Eng.
- Northern Executive. 4 per yr. (Engineering Industries Association. Northern Region)

**Paper, Printing & Packaging Industries Research Association**
Randalls Rd., Leatherhead, Surrey KT22 7RU, England.
- P I R A Management and Marketing Abstracts. m. ISSN 0308-2172
- P I R A Newsbrief. fortn.
- Packaging Abstracts. m. ISSN 0030-9087
- Paper and Board Abstracts. m.
- Printing Abstracts. m. ISSN 0031-109X

**Parachute Regiment and Airborne Forces**
Browning Barracks, Aldershot, Hampshire GU11 2BS, England.
- Pegasus Journal. q. ISSN 0031-4080

**Parents National Educational Union**
Murray House, Vandon St., London SW1H OAJ, Eng.
- P N E U Journal. q. ISSN 0030-817X

**Park Street Publishing (London) Ltd.**
International House, 183-185 Askew Rd., London W12 9AX, England.
- Golf International. 25 per yr.
- Tennis World. 10 per yr. ISSN 0040-3474

**S. E. Parker, Ed. & Pub.**
186 Gloucester Terrace, London W. 2., England.
- Minus One; an anarchist individualist review. irreg. ISSN 0026-5721

**Parliamentary Digest Ltd.**
Morgan-Grampian House, Calderwood St., London SE18 6QH, England.
- Review of Parliament and Political Chronicle. w. ISSN 0306-0616

**Parliamentary Research Services**
18 Lincoln Green, Chichester, West Sussex PO19 4DN, Eng.
- Political Companion. s-a. ISSN 0032-3152

**Parochial Clergy Association**
Mildenhall, Marlborough, Eng.
- Parson and Parish; National Church News. q. ISSN 0031-2436

**W. Parr & Co.**
Rex Buildings, Alderley Rd., Wilmslow SK9 1HZ, England.
- European Industrial & Commercial Review. bi-m.

**Parrett & Neves Ltd.**
Crown Quay, Sittingbourne, Kent ME10 3JE, England.
- East Coast Digest. bi-m. ISSN 0309-8273

**Donald Parsons & Co. Ltd.**
6 Brewer St., Oxford, England.
- International Conference on Phenomena in Ionized Gases. Proceedings. biennial; 1971, 10th, London. ISSN 0074-3143 (International Union of Pure and Applied Physics)

**Particle Science and Technology Information Service**
- Current Awareness in Particle Technology. (pub. by Elsevier Sequoia S.A. SZ)

**Pasold Research Fund Ltd.**
Ed. K. G. Ponting, Becketts House, Edington, Near Westbury, Wiltshire, Eng.
- Textile History. a. ISSN 0040-4969

**Past and Present Society**
Corpus Christi College, Oxford, England.
- Past and Present: a Journal of Historical Studies. 4 per yr. ISSN 0031-2746

**Patent Office**
St. Mary Cray, Orpington, Kent BR5 3RD, Eng.
- Official Journal (Patents) w. ISSN 0030-0330
- Reports of Patent, Design, Trade Mark and Other Cases. irreg. ISSN 0080-1364
- Trade Marks Journal. w. ISSN 0041-0446

**Paternoster Press Ltd.**
Paternoster House, 3 Mount Radford Crescent, Exeter EX1 4JW, Eng.
- Emergency Post. m. ISSN 0305-005X
- Evangelical Quarterly. q. ISSN 0014-3367
- Harvester. m. ISSN 0017-8217

**Pathological Society of Great Britain and Ireland**
- Journal of Medical Microbiology. (pub. by Longman Group Ltd.)
- Journal of Pathology. (pub. by Longman Group Ltd.)

**Stanley Paul & Co. Ltd.**
3 Fitzroy Square, London W1P 6JD, England.
- Manchester United Football Book. a.

**Kegan Paul, Trench, Trubner Ltd.**
39 Store St., London WC1E 7DD, Eng.
- African Quarterly. q. ISSN 0002-0125

**Paull & Goode Publishing Ltd.**
Ellington House, Ellington Rd., Ashington, Northumberland, Eng.
- Northern Architect. q. ISSN 0029-3040 (Royal Institute of British Architects. Northern Region)
- Northern Industry. m. ISSN 0048-0762
- Yorkshire Architect. bi-m. ISSN 0044-0582 (Royal Institute of British Architects. Yorkshire Region)

**Pax Christi Centre**
Blackfriars Hall, Southampton Rd., London N.W. 5, England.
- Just Peace. 10 per yr. ISSN 0306-7645

**John Paxton & Associates**
Moss Cottage, Hardway, Bruton, Somerset BA10 0LN, England.
- Euromarket Surveys. a.

**Peace News Ltd.**
5 Caledonian Rd., London N19 DX, Eng.
- Peace News; for nonviolent revolution. w. ISSN 0031-3548

**Peace Pledge Union**
6 Endsleigh St., London, W.C.1, Eng.
- Pacifist. m. ISSN 0048-265X

**Peacemaker**
c/o Guy Otten, Ed., 168 Hamilton Rd., Longsight, Manchester M13 OPG, England.
- Peacemaker. bi-m.

**Peak District Mines Historical Society**
c/o Department of Geology, University of Leicester, Leicester LE1 7RH, England.
- Peak District Mines Historical Society. Bulletin. s-a. ISSN 0031-3637
- Peak District Mines Historical Society. Special Publications. irreg; 1973, no. 3. ISSN 0553-4356

**Peco Publications & Publicity Ltd.**
Beer, Seaton, Devon Ex12 3na, Eng.
- Railway Modeller. m. ISSN 0033-8931

**Pedestrians Association for Road Safety**
Suite 4, 166, Shaftesbury Ave., London WC2H 8JH, Eng.
- Arrive. q. ISSN 0031-3874

**Pelham Books Ltd.**
52 Bedford Sq., London W.C.1, England.
- Pears Cyclopaedia. a. ISSN 0079-0362

**Pembrokeshire Local History Society**
4 Victoria Place, Haverfordwest, England.
- Pembrokeshire Historian. irreg. ISSN 0479-8244

**Pennine Platform**
c/o B. M. Hill, Ed., 4 Insmanthorpe Hall Farm, Wetherby, Yorks LS22 5EQ, England.
- Pennine Platform. s-a. ISSN 0306-140X

**Pension Publications**
30 Queen Anne's Gate, London SW1H 9AW, Eng.
- Benefits International. m. ISSN 0045-172X

**Penthouse Publications Ltd.**
R. C. Guccione, Ed. & Pub., 2 Bramber Rd., London W14 9PB, Eng
(U.S. Subscr. Address: 909 Third Ave., New York, NY 10022)
- Penthouse. m. ISSN 0031-4935

**Peoples Democracy**
Avoca Park, Andersonstown Rd., Belfast 11, Northern Ireland.
- Unfree Citizen; newspaper of peoples democracy. 2 per wk.

**Peoples Dispensary for Sick Animals**
P.D.S.A. House, South St., Dorking, Surrey, Eng.
- Animal Forum. irreg.
- Busy Bees' News. m. ISSN 0007-7232
- People's Dispensary for Sick Animals. Guild News. 3 per yr.

**People's News Service**
182 Upper St., Islington, London N.1., England.
- People's News Service Bulletin. fortn.

**Peter Peregrinus Ltd.**
Box 8, Southgate House, Stevenage, Herts SG1 1HQ, Eng
(U.S. address: International Scholarly Book Services Inc., Box 555, Forest Grove, OR 97116)
- Educational Broadcasting International. q. ISSN 0013-1970 (British Council)
- Electrical and Electronics Trades Directory. a. ISSN 0070-9646
- I E E Medical Electronics Monographs. irreg. (Institution of Electrical Engineers)
- I E E Monograph Series. irreg., no. 18, 1976. ISSN 0073-9766 (Institution of Electrical Engineers)
- I. E. E. Reprint Series. irreg. (Institution of Electrical Engineers)
- I E E Reviews. a. (Institution of Electrical Engineers)
- I E E Telecommunications Series. irreg. (Institution of Electrical Engineers)
- Medical & Biological Engineering & Computing. bi-m. (International Federation for Medical Electronics and Biological Engineering)
- Plastics and Rubber: Materials and Applications. q. (Plastics and Rubber Institute)

● Plastics and Rubber: Processing. q. (Plastics and Rubber Institute)

**Perennial Books Ltd.**
Pates Manor, Bedfont, Middlesex, TW14, 8JP, Eng.
● Studies in Comparative Religion. q. ISSN 0039-3622

**Performing Right Society Ltd.**
29-33 Berners St., London, England.
● Performing Right News. irreg.

**Pergamon Press Ltd.**
Headington Hill Hall, Oxford OX3 0BW, England
(U.S. Address: Maxwell House, Fairview Park, Elmsford, NY 10523)
● Advances in Solid State Physics. irreg. ISSN 0065-3357
● Advances in the Biosciences. q. ISSN 0065-3446
● Annales d'Histochimie. q. ISSN 0003-4355
● Annual Review in Automatic Programming. 4 per yr. ISSN 0066-4138
● Biomaterials Research Communications.
● Carotenoids Other Than Vitamin A. irreg., 1972, 3rd. Cluj, Romania; ISSN 0069-0732 (International Union of Pure and Applied Chemistry)
● Ceramurgia International. q.
● Chemistry of Natural Products. irreg., 1972, 8th New Delhi; 1974, 9th Ottawa. ISSN 0069-3162 (International Union of Pure and Applied Chemistry)
● Coordination Chemistry. irreg., 15th 1973, Moscow; 16th 1974, Dublin. ISSN 0069-9845 (International Union of Pure and Applied Chemistry)
● COSPAR Information Bulletin. 3 per yr. ISSN 0045-8732 (Committee on Space Research FR)
● Design Abstracts International. q. (International Council of Societies of Industrial Design)
● Endeavour. q. ISSN 0013-7162
● European Journal of Cancer. m. ISSN 0014-2964
● I C R P Annals. 4 per yr. (International Commission on Radiological Protection)
● I C R P Publications. irreg. ISSN 0074-2740 (International Commission on Radiological Protection)
● Institute for Research into Mental Retardation. Monograph. irreg. ISSN 0073-8883
● International Congress of Pure and Applied Chemistry. (Lectures) biennial, 1973, 24th Hamburg; 1975, 25th, Jerusalem. ISSN 0074-3925 (International Union of Pure and Applied Chemistry)
● International Newsletter on Chemical Education. s-a. (International Union of Pure and Applied Chemistry)
● International Reviews in Aerosol Physics and Chemistry. q. ISSN 0074-7785
● International Series of Monographs in Electrical Engineering. irreg. ISSN 0074-803X
● International Series of Monographs on Experimental Psychology. irreg. ISSN 0074-8137
● International Union of Pure and Applied Chemistry. Comptes Rendus of IUPAC Conference. biennial since 1947; 1975, 25th, Jerusalem. ISSN 0074-9508
● International Union of Pure and Applied Chemistry. Information Bulletin. irreg. ISSN 0539-1148
● Japanese Miniature Electronic Components Data. irreg., approx a. ISSN 0075-3440
● Macromolecular Chemistry. irreg., 1969, 4th, 5th, 6th, Prague. ISSN 0076-2075 (International Union of Pure and Applied Chemistry)
● Marcellia; the international review of phytopathological morphogenesis and cecidology. q. ISSN 0025-2794
● Monographs in Chemistry in Non-Aqueous Ionizing Solvents. irreg. ISSN 0077-0795
● Omega; international journal of management science. bi-m. ISSN 0305-0483
● Pergamon General Psychology Series. irreg. ISSN 0079-0818
● Pergamon Mathematical Tables Series. irreg. ISSN 0079-0826
● Pergamon Unified Engineering Series. irreg. ISSN 0079-0869
● Pharmaceutical Chemistry. irreg., 1968, 2nd, Munster, B.R.D. ISSN 0079-1385 (International Union of Pure and Applied Chemistry)
● Photochemistry. irreg., 1972, 4th, Baden-Baden, W. Germany; 1974, 5th, Enschede, Netherlands. ISSN 0079-1806 (International Union of Pure and Applied Chemistry)
● Progress in Food & Nutrition Science. m.
● Progress in Heat and Mass Transfer. q. ISSN 0079-631X

● Progress in Neurobiology. 8 per yr. ISSN 0301-0082
● Progress in Physical Chemistry and Chemical Physics. q.
● Progress in Planning. bi-m.
● Progress in Quantum Electronics. q. ISSN 0079-6727
● Progress in Surface Science. bi-m. ISSN 0079-6816
● Research in Protozoology. irreg. ISSN 0080-1658
● Vision Research; an international journal. m. ISSN 0042-6989 (Association for Research in Vision and Ophthalmology)

**Permanent Way Institution**
31, Ockley Way, Keymer, Hassocks, Sussex, Eng.
● Permanent Way Institution. Journal and Report of Proceedings. 3 per yr. ISSN 0031-5524

**Personal Rights Association**
31 Parkside Gardens, London, SW19 5ET, Eng.
● Individualist. bi-m. ISSN 0019-7165

**Peter Warlock Society**
c/o 14 Barlby Rd., London W1O 6AR, England.
● Peter Warlock Society Newsletter. 3 per yr.

**Peterson Publishing Co. Ltd.**
Peterson House, Northbank, Berryhill Industrial Estate, Droitwich, Worcs. WR9 9BL, England.
● British Food Journal. m. ISSN 0007-070X
● Industrial Lubrication & Tribology; a technical journal devoted exclusively to the science and practice of lubrication and tribology. m. ISSN 0036-8792
● Midland Industrialist. bi-m. ISSN 0026-3273
● Plumbing and Heating Equipment News. m.

**Petrine Publications**
4 Boscombe Ave., London E1O 6HY, Eng.
● Keys of Peter. bi-m.

**Petroleum Digests**
8 Waterloo Place, 5th Floor, London 5W1Y 4AN, England.
● North Sea Oil and Gas Monthly Activity Report. m.

**Petroleum Press Bureau Ltd.**
5 Pemberton Row, Fleet St., London EC4A 3DP, Eng.
● Petroleum Economist. m. ISSN 0306-395X

**Petulengro Publications**
11 Ship St. Gardens, Brighton BN1 1AJ, Sussex, Eng.
● Your Horoscope Guide. s-a. ISSN 0049-8424

**Phaidon Press Ltd.**
5 Cromwell Place, London S.W.7, England
(Dist. in U.S. by Praeger Publishers Inc., 111 Fourth Ave., New York, N.Y. 10003)
● Kress Foundation Studies in the History of European Art. a. ISSN 0075-7128

**Pharmaceutical Business Analysis Service**
27 Park View, Hatch End, Pinner, Middlesex, Eng.
● Pharmacy Management; a journal for the progressive pharmacist. q. ISSN 0031-7055 (Institute of Pharmacy Management International)

**Pharmaceutical Promotion Ltd.**
41 Parker St., London WC2B 5NX, Eng.
● Folio Pharmaceutica. bi-m. ISSN 0015-5799

**Pharmaceutical Society of Great Britain**
1 Lambeth High St., London SE1 7JN, Eng.
● Index of New Products; an independent information service on new medicinal preparations. m. ISSN 0019-3925
● Journal of Pharmacy and Pharmacology. m. ISSN 0022-3573
● Martindale: the Extra Pharmacopoeia. every five years. (Dist. in U.S. by: Rittenhouse Book Distributors, Philadelphia, PA 19104)
● Pharmaceutical Journal. w. ISSN 0031-6873

**Pharos Press**
Woodcut House, Ashford Rd., Hollingbourne Maidstone, Kent ME17 IXH, Eng.
● Pharos. q. ISSN 0048-3672 (Cremation Society of Great Britain)

**Philatelic Exporter Ltd.**
Box 4, Edgware, Middlesex, Eng.
● Philatelic Exporter; world's greatest stamp trade journal. m. ISSN 0031-7381

**Philatelic Traders Society Ltd.**
27 John Adam St., London, WC2N 6HZ, Eng.
● P. T. S. Journal. bi-m. ISSN 0048-3729

**George Philip & Son Ltd.**
12-14 Long Acre, London WC2E 9LP, Eng.
● Geography. q. ISSN 0016-7487 (Geographical Association)

**Phillimore & Co. Ltd.**
Shopwyke Hall, Chichester, Sussex, Eng.
● Essex Journal. q. ISSN 0014-0961
● Hertfordshire Local History Council. Occasional Papers. a.
● Sussex Industrial History. s-a.

**Philological Soceity**
● Philological Society Transactions. (pub. by Basil Blackwell & Mott Ltd.)

**Photogrammetric Society**
Department of Photogrammetry & Surveying, University College London, Gower St., London WC1E 6BT, England.
● Photogrammetric Record. s-a. ISSN 0031-868X

**Photojournalist Ltd.**
717 New Bond St., London, W1, England.
● Freelance Photo Journalist. Yearbook. a. ISSN 0071-9374

**Physical Education Association**
Ling House, 10 Nottingham Place, London W1M 4AX, England.
● Outdoors. q. ISSN 0306-5723

**Physical Education Association. M. Hankinson Trust**
10 Nottingham Place, London W1M 4AX, England.
● Bibliographical Index on Physical and Health Education, Sport, and Allied Subjects. q.

**Physical Education Association of Great Britain & Northern Ireland**
Ling House, 10 Nottingham Place, London, W1M 4AX, Eng.
● Bibliography of Articles on Physical and Health Education, Sport and Allied Subjects. q. ISSN 0045-1924
● British Journal of Physical Education. bi-m. ISSN 0007-120X
● Physical Education Association of Great Britain and Northern Ireland. Report. a. ISSN 0079-1903

**Physics Trust Publications**
Blackhorse Road, Letchworth, Herts SG6 1HN, England.
● Research Fields in Physics at United Kingdom Universities and Polytechnics. a. (Institute of Physics)

**Physiological Society, London**
● Journal of Physiology. (pub. by Cambridge University Press)
● Physiological Society. Monographs. (pub. by Cambridge University Press)

**Pick Publications**
43 Edgar Rd., South Croydon, Surrey, England.
● Pick. s-a.

**Pickering & Inglis Ltd.**
26 Bothwell St., Glasgow G 2 6PA, Scotland.
● Boys and Girls. m. ISSN 0006-8551
● Witness; a monthly journal of Biblical literature. m.

**Pig Breeders Weekly**
c/o Bob Powers, 73 Hillbrook Rd., London S.W.17, Eng.
● Pig Breeders Weekly. bi-m. ISSN 0048-4156

**Pion Ltd.**
207 Brondesbury Park, London NW2 5JN, Eng (Dist. by Academic Press Inc. (London) Ltd., 24-28 Oval Rd., London NW1 7DX, England)
● Environment and Planning A. m.
● High Temperatures - High Pressures. bi-m. ISSN 0018-1544
● London Papers in Regional Science. irreg. ISSN 0076-0633
● Perception. bi-m.
● Pion Applied Physics Series. irreg. ISSN 0079-208X

**Pioneer Publications Ltd.**
John Montagu Building, Beaulieu, Hants S04 7ZN,
England.
- Veteran and Vintage Magazine. m. ISSN 0042-
4773

**Pipe Club of Great Britain Ltd.**
Kipling House, 43 Villiers St., London WC2N 6NE,
Eng.
- Pipe Line. q. ISSN 0032-0137

**Pitman Medical Publishing Co. Ltd.**
42 Camden Rd., Tunbridge Wells, Kent TN1 2QD,
England.
- European Dialysis and Transplant Association.
Proceedings of Conference. a. ISSN 0071-2736
- Royal College of Physicians of London. Journal.
q. ISSN 0035-8819 (Sir Isaac Pitman & Sons Ltd.)

**Pitman Periodicals Ltd.**
41 Parker St., London WC2B 5PB, Eng
(and 155 W. 15th St., New York, N.Y., 10011)
- Artist. m. ISSN 0004-3877
- Memo. m. ISSN 0025-9071
- Office Skills for the Business Studies Teacher. m.

**Plaid Cymru (Welsh Nationalist Party)**
- Ddraig Goch. (pub. by Ddraig Goch)
- Welsh Nation. (pub. by Welsh Nation Office)

**Plaistow Press**
c/o Alan Osborne, 3 New Plaistow Rd., Stratford,
London E15 3JA, England.
- On View; guide to museum and gallery
acquisitions in the U.S.A. and U.K. a. ISSN 0474-
1382
- Welsh Secondary Schools Review. s-a. ISSN
0043-2474 (Welsh Secondary Schools
Association)

**Plan Magazines Ltd.**
45 Station Rd., Redhill, Surrey, Eng.
- House & Bungalow; quarterly journal of the
Architectural Service Planning Partnership. q.
ISSN 0018-6392

**Planet**
Llangeitho Tregaron, Dyfed SY25 6TX, Wales.
- Planet. bi-m. ISSN 0048-4288

**Planning and Transport Research and Computation
(International) Co.**
167 Oxford St., London, W1, England.
- Planning and Transport Research and
Computation. Summer Annual Meeting.
Proceedings. a (approx. 20 vols. per yr.)

**Plant and Equipment Publications Ltd.**
The Adelphi, John Adam St., London WC2N 6AY,
Eng.
- Plant Hire. m.

**Plant Assessment (London) Ltd.**
16 N. Pallant, Chichester, Sussex PO19 1TQ,
England.
- Plant & Equipment Guide; the standard reference
for new and used construction equipment values.
irreg.

**Plant Breeding Institute**
Trumpington, Cambridge, England.
- Plant Breeding Institute, Cambridge. Annual
Report. a. ISSN 0079-2225 (Agricultural Research
Council)

**Plant News Ltd.**
38 N. Audley St., London W. 1., Eng.
- Health and Efficiency. 20 per yr. ISSN 0017-8888
(Britain's Sun Club)

**Plastic Aircraft Modellers**
22 Slayleigh Ave., Sheffield S1O 3RB, South
Yorkshire, England.
- P A M News; plastic aircraft modeller's magazine.
q.

**Plastics and Rubber Institute**
11 Hobart Place, London SW1W 0HL, England.
- Plastics and Rubber International. bi-m.
- Plastics and Rubber: Materials and Applications.
(pub. by Peter Peregrinus Ltd.)
- Plastics and Rubber: Processing. (pub. by Peter
Peregrinus, Ltd.)

**Plastics Investigations**
31 Canonsfield Rd, Welwyn, Herts., Eng.
- Plastics Abstracts; a comprehensive abstracting
service covering British patent specifications
dealing with the science, technology and
application of plastics. w. ISSN 0032-115X

**Platt Saco Lowell Bulletin**
Box 55, Accrington BB5 0RN, Lancashire, England.
- Platt Saco Lowell Bulletin. 2-3 per yr.

**Plenhurst Ltd.**
79 Baker Street, London W1M 1AJ, England.
- Football. m.

**Plenum Publishing Co. Ltd.**
Davis House, 8 Scrubs Lane, Harlesden NW10 6SE,
Eng
(U.S. Subscr. Address: 227 W. 17th. St., New York,
N.Y. 10011)
- Foundations of Physics; an international journal
devoted to the conceptual bases of modern
natural science. 6 per yr. ISSN 0015-9018
- Journal of Bioenergetics. bi-m. ISSN 0449-5705
- Journal of Crystal and Molecular Structure. bi-m.
- Progress in Electrochemistry of Organic
Compounds. irreg. ISSN 0079-6239
- Scientific Aesthetics/Sciences de l'Art. s-a.

**Plessey Telecommunications Ltd. Electronic Systems
Ltd.**
Liverpool, Eng.
- Systems Technology; technical coverage of various
aspects in telecommunications, radar and allied
fields. 3 per yr. ISSN 0039-8047

**Plough Publicity (Hull) Ltd.**
Barclay House, 401 Anlaby Rd., Hull HU3 6AF,
England.
- Cheshire Farmer. m. (National Farmers' Union)
- Cumbria Farmer. m. (National Farmers' Union)
- East Riding Farmer. m. (National Farmers'
Union)
- Lancashire Farmer. q. (National Farmers' Union)
- North Riding (No.2) Farmer. m. (National
Farmers' Union)
- North Riding and Durham Farmer. Durham
Edition. m. (National Farmers' Union)
- North Riding and Durham Farmer. North Riding
Edition. m. (National Farmers' Union)
- Northumberland Farmer. m. (National Farmers'
Union)
- Nottinghamshire Farmers' Journal. m. (National
Farmers' Union)
- Shropshire N F U Journal. m. (National Farmers'
Union)
- West Riding Farmer. m. (National Farmers'
Union)
- Worcestershire Record. m. (National Farmers'
Union)

**Pluto Press**
Unit 10 Spencer Court, 7 Chalcot Road, London
NW1 8LH, England.
- Big Red Diary. irreg.

**Plymouth College**
Ford Park, Plymouth, Devonshire, Eng.
- Plymothian. 3 per yr. ISSN 0048-4490

**Poale Zion**
62 Charles Lane, London NW8 7SP, Eng.
- Jewish Vanguard. fortn. ISSN 0021-6801

**Poetry Book Society**
105 Piccadilly, London W1V 0AU, England.
- New Poems. a.

**Poetry Society Inc.**
21 Earls Court Sq., London S.W.5, Eng.
- Poetry Review; The Poetry Society's quarterly for
members. q. ISSN 0032-2156
- Verse Speaking Anthology. every 3 or 4 yrs. ISSN
0083-582X

**Poets' and Painters Press**
146 Bridge Arch, Sutton Walk, London S.E.1, Eng.
- Oficyna Poetow. q. ISSN 0030-0659

**Poets Press of Osgoldcross**
50 Chiltern Drive, Ackworth, Pontefract, Yorks.
WF7 7DW, England.
- Osgoldcross Review. s-a.

**Police College, Bramshill**
- Police College Magazine. (pub. by M and W
Publications)

**Police Federation**
15-17 Langley Rd., Surbiton, Surrey KT6 6LP, Eng.
- Police. m. ISSN 0032-2555

**Police Review Publishing Co. Ltd.**
14 St. Cross St., London EC1N 8FE, Eng.
- Police Review. w.

**Polish Cultural Foundation Ltd. Editorial Committee**
43 Eaton Place, London SW1X 8BX, London
S.W.7, Eng.
- Polish Affairs. q. ISSN 0032-2784

**Polish Embassy in London**
Press Office, 47 Portland Place, London W1N 3AC,
Eng.
- Polish Facts and Figures. 3-4 per yr. ISSN 0032-
2873

**Polish Historical Society in Great Britain**
20 Princes Gate, London SW7 1QA, England.
- Teki Historyczne. a. ISSN 0085-4956

**Polish Institute and Sikorski Museum**
20 Princes Gate, London SW7 1WA, Eng.
- Bellona; kwartalnik. a. ISSN 0005-8645

**Polish Library**
238-246 King St., London W6 ORF, Eng.
- Books in Polish or Relating to Poland. q. ISSN
0006-7512

**Polish Populist Party**
2, Vista Way, Harrow, Middlesex, Eng.
- Jutro Polski/Poland of Tomorrow. fortn. ISSN
0022-7137

**Polish Socialist Party in Exile**
84 Fordhook Ave., London W. 5, England.
- Robotnik. q. ISSN 0483-2027

**Polish Society of Arts and Sciences Abroad**
20 Princes Gate, London, S.W.7, England.
- Bibliography of Works by Polish Scholars and
Scientists Published outside Poland in Languages
Other Than Polish. irreg. ISSN 0067-7310
- Polskie Towarzystwo Naukowe na Obczyznie.
Rocznik. a. ISSN 0079-371X

**Political and Economic Planning**
12 Upper Belgrave St., London SW1X 8BB, Eng.
- P E P; broadsheet series and major reports. irreg.
ISSN 0030-7947

**Political Quarterly Publishing Co. Ltd.**
Elm House, 10-16 Elm St., London W.C.1,
England.
- Political Quarterly. o. ISSN 0032-3179

**Political Studies Association of the United Kingdom**
- Political Studies. (pub. by Oxford University
Press)

**Politics and Money Publishing Co.**
14 South Hill Park Gardens, London N.W.3, Eng.
- Politics and Money. (P & M) m. ISSN 0032-3284

**Pollyhaugh Press Ltd.**
Nealhampton House, Speldhurst, Tunbridge Wells,
Kent, Eng.
- Today. q. ISSN 0040-8360

**Polystyle Publications Ltd.**
Polly Perkins House, 382-386 Edgware Rd, London
W.2., Eng.
- Pippin. w. ISSN 0032-0218
- T V Comic. w. ISSN 0039-8527

**Pontifical Missionary Union**
c/o J. L. Coonan, 23 Eccleston Square, London
SW1V 1NU, Eng.
- Outlook. q. ISSN 0030-7211

**Popular Flying Association**
Terminal Building, Shoreham Airport, Shoreham- by
Sea, Sussex, BN4 5FF, Eng.
- Popular Flying. bi-m. ISSN 0032-4493

**Population Investigation Committee**
London School of Economics, Houghton St.,
London WC2A 2AE, Eng.
- Population Studies. 3 per yr.(1 vol.per yr) ISSN
0032-4728

**Port of Bristol Authority**
St. Andrews Rd., Avonmouth, Bristol BS11 9DQ,
England.
- Port of Bristol. Handbook. a.

**Port of London Authority**
PLA World Trade Centre, London E.1, England.
- Polanews. fortn.
- Port of London. q. ISSN 0030-8064

**Port Publishing Co. Ltd.**
Ludgate House, 107 Fleet St., London E.C.4, Eng.
- Port. fortn. ISSN 0032-4809

**Portsmouth City Council**
Guild Hall, Portsmouth, England.
- Portsmouth Papers. irreg., no. 22, 1974. ISSN 0554-7598

**Portsmouth Polytechnic. Department of Geography**
Ravelin House, Museum Rd., Portsmouth, Hants PO1 2QQ, England.
- Society for Latin America Studies. Bulletin. irreg.

**Portuguese and Colonial Bulletin**
c/o K. Shingler, 10 Fentiman Rd., London S.W.8, England.
- Portuguese and Colonial Bulletin. q.

**Portway Press Ltd.**
Timeform House, Northgate, Halifax, Yorkshire, England.
- Racehorses. a. ISSN 0079-9408

**Post Office Central Headquarters**
23 Howland St., London W1P 6Hq, Eng.
- Post Office Telecommunications Journal. q. ISSN 0032-5309

**Post Office Engineering Union**
Greystoke House, 150 Brunswick Rd., London W5 1AW, Eng.
- Post Office Engineering Union Journal. m. ISSN 0032-5295

**Post Office Management Staffs' Association**
52 Broadway, Bracknell, Berkshire, England.
- New Management. m. ISSN 0548-5924

**Postlib Publications**
Swan House, 630 Kingsbury Rd, London NW9 9HN, Eng.
- Sporting Investor Method Magazine. m. ISSN 0049-1934

**Potato Marketing Board**
50 Hans Crescent, Knightsbridge, London SW1X 0NB, England.
- Potato Marketing Board, London. Annual Report and Accounts. a. ISSN 0079-4309

**Poultry Review**
Graphis House, 15 New North Rd., Exeter, England.
- Poultry Review. m.

**Powder Advisory Centre**
10 St. John's Rd., London NW11 OPG, Eng.
- Particulate Matter. q. ISSN 0031-2487

**Pre-Retirement Association**
19 Undine St., Tooting, London SW17 8PP, England.
- Choice. m.

**Prehistoric Society**
Flat 2, 75 Clarendon Rd., London W11 4JF, England.
- Prehistoric Society, London. Proceedings. a. ISSN 0079-497X

**Premier Publicity Service Ltd.**
14 High St., Chislehurst Kent, Eng.
- New Chislehurst Announcer. m. ISSN 0047-956X
- Petts Wood Post. m. ISSN 0048-3605

**Presbyterian Church in Ireland**
Church House, Fisherwick Place, Belfast BT1 6DW, N. Ireland.
- Daybreak. m. ISSN 0011-7102
- Outward Bound. m. ISSN 0030-7327
- Presbyterian Herald. m. ISSN 0032-7530

**Presbyterian Church of Wales**
- Goleuad/Light. (pub. by Calvinistic Methodist Book Agency)

**Pressdram Ltd.**
34-Greek St., London W.1, Eng.
- Private Eye. fortn. ISSN 0032-888X

**Pressed Curtains**
12 Foster Clough, Hebden Bridge, West Yorkshire HX7 5QZ, England.
- Curtains. s-a.

**Presshouse Publications Ltd.**
30 Wellington Crescent, Kingston Rd., New Malden, Surrey, Eng.
- Infant and Nursery School Equipment. m. ISSN 0019-9516

**Pressmedia Ltd.**
Owermoigne, Dorchester, Dorset, Eng.
- Board Manufacture & Processing; the only journal exclusively covering board materials and finishes for architects, builders, importers and distributors of fibreboard, chipboard, plywood and allied products. m.
- Board Purchasing Guide and Directory. a. ISSN 0067-9313
- Directory of Plant and Tools for the Board Industry. a. ISSN 0070-6108

**Prestige Publications, Ltd.**
59-61 Kensington High St., London W8 5ED, England.
- British Combustion. q. ISSN 0307-1219 (British Combustion Equipment Manufacturers Association)

**Preston and District Chamber of Commerce and Industry**
2 Camden Place, Preston, Lancashire PR1 8BE, Eng.
- Forum. 10 per yr.

**Preston Polytechnic**
Robin House, Fylde St., Preston, Lancs., England.
- Palantir. 3 per yr.

**Priapus**
37 Lombardy Dr., Berkhamsted, Hertfordshire, Eng.
- Priapus. 3 per yr. ISSN 0032-8146

**Printerhall Ltd.**
29 Newman St., London WIP 3PE, Eng.
- Traffic Engineering and Control. m. ISSN 0041-0683

**Printing and Publishing Industry Training Board**
Merit House, Edgware Rd, Colindale, London NW9 5AG, England.
- Contact (London, 1973) m.

**Printing Historical Society**
St. Bride Institute, Bride Lane, Fleet St, London E.C.4, England.
- Printing Historical Society. Journal. a. ISSN 0079-5321
- Printing Historical Society Newsletter. q. ISSN 0556-1515

**Printworkshop**
28 Cooke Street, Belfast 7, N. Ireland
(Subscription Address: 2 Marquis Street, Belfast 1, N. Ireland)
- Civil Rights. (Northern Ireland Civil Rights Association)

**Prism Publications Ltd.**
80 St. Thomas St., Wells, Somerset, Eng.
- New Outlook. m. ISSN 0028-6419 (British Liberals)

**Prison Officers Association**
245 Church St., Edmonton N9, Eng.
- Prison Officers Magazine. m. ISSN 0032-8863

**Private Libraries Association**
Ravelston, South View Road, Pinner, Middlesex, Eng.
- Private Library. q. ISSN 0032-8898
- Private Press Books; a checklist of books issued by private presses in the past year. a. ISSN 0079-5402

**Private Printer & Private Press**
97 Holywell St., Oxford, Eng.
- Private Printer & Private Press. 2-3 per yr. ISSN 0032-8936

**PRM Science & Technology Agency Ltd.**
787 High Rd., North Finchley, London N12 8JT, Eng.
- Atomic Absorption & Emission Spectrometry Abstracts. bi-m.
- Electron Microscopy Abstracts. q.

- Electron Spin Resonance Spectroscopy Abstracts. q. ISSN 0301-7575
- Gas Chromatography-Mass Spectrometry Abstracts. bi-m. ISSN 0046-5461
- Laser Raman & Infrared Spectroscopy Abstracts. q.
- Liquid Chromatography Abstracts. q.
- Neutron Activation Analysis Abstracts. q. ISSN 0047-9446
- Nuclear Magnetic Resonance Spectrometry Abstracts. bi-m. ISSN 0048-1033
- Thin-Layer Chromatography Abstracts. q. ISSN 0049-3724
- X-Ray Diffraction Abstracts. q.
- X-Ray Fluorescence Spectrometry Abstracts. q. ISSN 0043-9851

**Probe**
Cliffords Inn, Fetter Lane, London EC4A 1PJ, Eng.
- Probe. m. ISSN 0032-9185

**Production Engineering Research Association**
Melton Mowbray, Leicester, Eng.
- Machines and Tooling. m. ISSN 0024-922X (British Library Lending Division)
- Russian Engineering Journal. m. ISSN 0036-0228 (British Library Lending Division)

**Professional & Scientific Publications**
B.M.A. House, Tavistock Square, London WC1H 9JR, England
(U.S. address: Professional & Scientific Publications, 117 Commonwealth Ave., Boston, MA 02134)
- Annals of Clinical Biochemistry. bi-m. ISSN 0004-5632 (Association of Clinical Biochemists)
- Journal of Medical Ethics. q. ISSN 0306-6800 (Society for the Study of Medical Ethics)

**Professional Books Ltd.**
6 1/2 Suffolk St., London SW1Y 4HG, Eng.
- British Journal of Law and Society.

**Profile Books Ltd.**
Dial House, 6 Park St., Windsor, Berks SL4 1UU, England.
- Air Pictorial. m. ISSN 0002-2462

**Progressive League**
Albion Cottage, Fortis Green, London N.2, Eng.
- Plan. m. ISSN 0032-0552

**Property Services Agency**
- National Building Maintenance Conference. Papers. (pub. by Ministry of Public Building and Works)

**Prophetic Witness Movement International**
Upperton House, The Avenue, Eastbourne, Sussex BN21 3YB, England.
- Prophetic Witness. m. ISSN 0033-135X

**Prospect**
c/o Dept. of English, University College, Swansea SA2 8PP, Wales.
- Prospect. 3 per yr.

**Protestant Truth Society Inc.**
184 Fleet St., London E.C.4, Eng.
- British Citizen. q. ISSN 0007-0459
- Churchman's Magazine. bi-m. ISSN 0009-6636

**Proud-Bailey Co. Ltd.**
25 Meeting House Lane, Brighton, Sussex BN1 1JS, England.
- Postal History International. m. ISSN 0306-8463

**Provincial Insurance Co. Ltd.**
Stramongate, Kendal, Westmorland, England.
- Cover; a magazine for insurance brokers & agents. irreg. (3 per yr) ISSN 0084-9405

**Provincial Trade Press Ltd.**
320 Higher Lane, Lymm, Cheshire, Eng.
- Club Committee & Northern Free Trade News. m. ISSN 0009-9538

**Psionic Medical Society**
Hindhead, Surrey, Eng.
- Psionic Medicine. s-a. ISSN 0033-2585

**Psychic Press Ltd.**
23 Great Queen St., London WC2B 5BB, Eng.
- Psychic News. w. ISSN 0033-2801

**Psychologist Magazine Ltd.**
Denington Estate, Wellingborough, Northants NN8
2RQ, Eng.
- Psychologist Magazine; giving articles on practical
and applied psychology to meet the needs of
everyday living. m. ISSN 0033-3050

**Psywar Society**
c/o P.H. Robbs, 8 Ridgway Rd., Barton Seagrave,
Kettering, Northants, England.
- Falling Leaf. q.

**Publishing & Distributing Co. Ltd.**
Mitre House, 177 Regent St., London W.1, Eng.
- Far East. m. ISSN 0014-7532
- Indian Exporter Quarterly. q. ISSN 0019-4751
- Overseas Advertising. m. ISSN 0048-251X
- Overseas Books. m. ISSN 0048-2528
- Overseas Directories, Who's Who, Press Guides,
Year Books and Overseas Periodical
Subscriptions. biennial. ISSN 0078-7124
- Overseas Newspapers and Periodicals. biennial.
ISSN 0078-7159
- Overseas Trade Directories. approx. biennial or
triennial.
- Pubdisco News. m. ISSN 0033-3263

**Punch Publications Ltd.**
23 Tudor St., London EC4 YoHR, England.
- High Life. m. (British Airways)
- Punch. w. ISSN 0033-4278

**Punjabi Sahitya**
c/o H. S. Kalra, Ed., 254 Rowley Gardens,
Woodberry Grove, London N4 1HW, England.
- Punjabi Sahitya; magazine of Punjabi life and
letters. q.

**Purnell & Sons Ltd.**
Paulton House, Shepherdess Walk, London N.1,
Eng., U.K.
- Creel; a fishing magazine. m. ISSN 0011-1139
- History of the Second World War. w.
- History of the Twentieth Century. w. ISSN 0018-
2737
- Holiday Book. a. ISSN 0073-2958

**Purnell Books**
Berkshire House, Queen St., Maidenhead, Berkshire
SL6 1NF, England.
- Big Enid Blyton Story Annual. a.

**Q. C. Correspondence Circle Ltd.**
27 Great Queen St., London WC2B 5BB, England.
- Ars Quatuor Coronatorum; transaction of the
Quatuor Coronati Lodge of Research. a. ISSN
0066-7900

**Quaintance & Co. (Publishers) Ltd.**
24A Chertsey St., Guildford, Eng.
- Business Credit and Hire Purchase Journal. m.
ISSN 0007-6627

**Quaker Fellowship of the Arts**
c/o Ed. & Pub. Charles Kohler, Overmist, Yew Tree
Rd., Dorking, Surrey, England
(Subscr. to: 41 Ludlow Road, Guildford, Surrey,
England)
- Reynard. irreg. (1-2 per yr.) ISSN 0484-9035

**Quarry Managers' Journal Ltd.**
7 Regent St., Nottingham NG1 5BY, Eng.
- Quarry Management and Products. m. (Institute
of Quarrying)

**Queen Anne Press Ltd.**
12 Vandy St., London EC2A 2EN, England.
- Athletics. a.
- John Player Cricket Yearbook. a. (John Player &
Sons Ltd.)
- John Player Golf Yearbook. a. (John Player &
Sons Ltd.)
- John Player Motorsport Yearbook. a. (John Player
& Sons Ltd.)
- Motor Cycling. a. (John Player & Sons Ltd.)
- Playfair Book of Sporting Records. a.
- Playfair Cricket Annual. a. ISSN 0079-2314
- Playfair Football Annual. a. ISSN 0079-2322
- Rothmans Football Yearbook. a. ISSN 0080-4088
(Rothmans of Pall Mall Ltd.)
- Rothmans Rugby Yearbook. a. ISSN 0306-9605
(Rothmans of Pall Mall Ltd.)
- William Hill Racing Yearbook. a. (William Hill
Organisation)
- Wills Horse & Rider Yearbook. a. (W. D. & H. O.
Wills)
- World of Squash. a.

**Queen's Nursing Institute**
57 Lower Belgrave St., London SW1W 0LR, Eng.
- Gardens of England and Wales Open to the
Public. (pub. by National Gardens Scheme)
- Queen's Nursing Journal. m. ISSN 0301-0821

**Queens Own Highlanders**
Cameron Barracks, Inverness, Scotland.
- Queens Own Highlander. 2 per yr. ISSN 0048-
6329

**Queens University Medical Library**
Institute of Clinical Science, Grosvenor Rd., Belfast
BT 12 6BJ, N. Ireland.
- Ulster Medical Journal. s-a. ISSN 0041-6193
(Ulster Medical Society)

**Queen's University of Belfast**
Faculty of Law, Belfast BT7 1NN, N. Ireland.
- Northern Ireland Legal Quarterly. q. ISSN 0029-
3105

**Quekett Microscopical Club**
c/o British Museum (Natural Hsitory), Cromwell
Rd., London SW7 5BD, England.
- Microscopy. s-a. ISSN 0026-2838

**Quest Research Publications Ltd.**
P.O. Box 168, London SE26 6PR, England.
- Know Your Training Films. a ( 3 up-dating
supplements)

**R.A.F. Provost Branch**
- Provost Parade. (pub. by Royal Air Force Police
Depot)

**R C C Press**
William Blake House, Marshall St., London W 1,
England.
- Roving Commissions; anthology of cruising logs.
a. ISSN 0485-5175

**R C G Publications Ltd.**
49 Railton Rd., London SE24 0LN, England.
- Hands off Ireland. q. ISSN 0309-2526
- Revolutionary Communist. q. ISSN 0306-5626
(Revolutionary Communist Group)

**R. F. W. W. Publications Ltd.**
Lloyds Bank Chambers, Cirencester, Glos, Eng.
- Safer Motoring. m. ISSN 0036-2417

**R I B A Publications Ltd.**
66 Portland Place, London W1N 4AD, Eng.
- Journal of Architectural Research. 3 per yr.
(American Institute of Architects US) (Co-
Sponsor: Royal Institute of British Architects)

**R. S. P. C. A.**
Causeway, Horsham, Sussex RH12 1HG, England.
- Animal Ways. 5 per yr.
- Animal World. 5 per yr.

**R S V P**
5 Tollet St., Stepney Green, London E. 1, England.
- R S V P; magazine for record collectors. m.

**Race Relations Board**
5 Lower Belgrave St., London SW1W 0NR,
England.
- Equals. b-m.

**Raceform Ltd.**
Raceform House, 29-31 York Road, London SW11
3PZ, England.
- Raceform up-to-Date. w. ISSN 0079-9394

**Racehorse Ltd.**
55 Curzon St., London W.1., Eng.
- Racehorse. w. ISSN 0048-6523

**Racing Pigeon Publishing Co. Ltd**
19 Doughty St., London WC1N 2PT, Eng.
- Racing Pigeon; the British pigeon racing weekly.
w. ISSN 0033-7390
- Racing Pigeon Pictorial. m. ISSN 0033-7404

**Radical Education**
86 Eleanor Rd., London E.8., England.
- Radical Education. q. ISSN 0305-6147

**Radical Science Journal**
9 Poland St., London W1V 3DG, England.
- Radical Science Journal. irreg. ISSN 0305-0963

**Radio and Electronic Officers Union**
Ed. K.A. Murphy, 4-6 Branfill Rd., Upminster,
Essex RM14 2XX, Eng.
- Signal. bi-m. ISSN 0037-4946

**Radio Society of Great Britain**
35 Doughty St., London WC1N 2AE, England.
- R S G B Amateur Radio Call Book. a. ISSN
0079-9475
- Radio Communication. m. ISSN 0033-7803

**Radionic Association**
Field House, Peaslake, Nr. Guildford, Surrey GU5
9SS, England.
- Radionic Quarterly; an approach to health and
harmony. q. ISSN 0481-6722

**Radnorshire Society**
c/o Radnor College of Further Education,
Llandrindd Wells, Radnorshire, England.
- Radnorshire Society. Transactions. a.

**Railway and Canal Historical Society**
Tuborg Halt, 34 Manor Ave, Caterham, Eng.
- Railway and Canal Historical Society Journal. 3
per yr. ISSN 0033-8834

**Railway Development Association**
c/o Jack Ellis, Ed., 25 the Embankment,
Twickenham, Middlesex, England.
- R D A Development Report. q.

**Railway Digest International**
Maple Cottage, Ashburnum Ave., Harrow-on-the-
Hill, Middlesex HA1 2JO, Eng.
- Railway Digest International. bi-m. ISSN 0048-
6647

**Railway Industry Association of Great Britain**
9 Catherine Place, London SW1E 6DX, England.
- Railpower. irreg.

**Railway Invigoration Society**
BM-RIS, London WC1V 6XX, England.
- Railway Invigoration Society. Progress Reports. q.

**Railway Preservation Society of Ireland**
Whitehead Excursion Station, Whitehead, Co.
Antrim, Northern Ireland.
- Five Foot Three. s-a.

**Rainer Foundation**
89a Blackheath Hill, London SE10 8TJ, England.
- Rainer Foundation. Annual Report. a.

**Ramblers' Association**
1-4 Crawford Mews, York St., London W1H 1PT,
Eng.
- Rucksack. 3 per yr. ISSN 0006-7334

**Ramsay Society of Chemical Engineers**
Dept. of Chemical Engineering, University College
London, Torrington Place, London WC1E 7JE,
England.
- Ramsay Society of Chemical Engineers. Journal.
a. ISSN 0456-4804

**Rank and File Teachers Group**
5 Rommany Rd., London S. E. 27, Eng.
- Rank and File; journal of socialist teachers. 8 per
yr. ISSN 0300-3507

**Rank Strand Electric**
32 King St., Covent Garden, London WC2E 8JH,
Eng.
- Tabs. q. ISSN 0306-9389

**Rank Xerox-U.K.**
- Gems. (pub. by Lapidary Publications)

**Ratcliffe College**
Leicester, Eng.
- Ratcliffian. a. ISSN 0048-6809

**Rating and Valuation Association**
115, Ebury Street, Belgravia, London SW1W 9QT,
England.
- Rating and Valuation. 10 per yr.

**Rating Publishers Ltd.**
2 Paper Bldgs., Temple, London E.C.4., Eng.
- Rating and Valuation Reporter. w. ISSN 0048-
6817

**Rationalist Press Association**
88 Islington High St., London N.1, Eng.
- New Humanist. m. ISSN 0306-512X

- Question. a. ISSN 0079-919X (Dist. by Prometheus Books, 923 Kensington Ave., Buffalo, NY 14215)

**Ravenhill Publishing Co. Ltd.**
Standard House, Bonhill St., London EC2A 4DA, Eng.
- Guns Review. m. ISSN 0017-5692
- Motorcycle Sport. m.

**Ravenswood Publications. Ltd.**
Box 24, 205 Croydon Rd., Beckenham, Kent, England.
- Health Services Travelogue. International Series. irreg.

**RDP (Data Services) Ltd.**
42-44 Hoe St., Walthamstow, London E.17, England.
- Book Exchange. m. ISSN 0006-7245

**Read Hudson Organization Ltd.**
Norfolk House, Smallbrook, Queensway, Birmingham B5 4LJ, England.
- Midlands Club Cricket Conference Yearbook. a.

**Reader's Digest Association Ltd.**
25 Berkeley Square, London W1X 6AB, Eng.
- Reader's Digest (British Edition) m. ISSN 0034-0405

**Reading University. Graduate School of Contemporary European Studies**
- Reading University Studies on Contemporary Europe. (pub. by Weidenfeld and Nicolson Ltd.)

**Record Collector**
c/o James Dennis, Ed., 17 St. Nicholas St., Ipswich 1P1 1TW, Suffolk, Eng.
- Record Collector; a magazine for collectors of recorded vocal art. bi-m. ISSN 0034-1568

**Record Mart**
16 London Hill, Rayleigh, Essex, Eng.
- Record Mart. m.

**Recorder Press Ltd.**
Recorder House, 91 Church St., London N.16, Eng.
- Midwife, Health Visitor and Community Nurse. m. ISSN 0306-9699

**Red Candle Press**
3 Abbey Hill, Nocton Fen Rd., Lincolnshire, England.
- Candelabrum. 2 per yr.

**Red House**
Staines Green, Hertford, Herts SG14 2LN, England.
- Journal of Criminal Law. q. ISSN 0022-0183

**Redbridge & Waltham Forest Area Health Authority. East Roding Health District**
17-23 Clements Rd., Ilford, Essex, Eng.
- Rodings Medical Journal. q.

**Redemptorist Publications**
Alphonsus House, Chawton, Alton, Hants., Eng.
- Novena. m. ISSN 0029-5140

**William Reed Ltd.**
19 Eastcheap, London EC3M 1DB, Eng.
- Brewing & Distilling International. m. ISSN 0020-6210
- Grocer. w. ISSN 0017-4351
- Grocer Directory. a.
- Off Licence News. w. ISSN 0043-5775
- Wine and Spirit Trade Review Trade Directory. a. ISSN 0084-0343

**Thomas Reed Publications Ltd.**
Saracen's Head Bldgs., 36-27 Cock Lane, London EC1A 9BY, England.
- Cash & Carry Caterer. m.
- Green Book; the authority on tractors and farm equipment. a. ISSN 0017-3932
- Reed's Nautical Almanac. a. ISSN 0080-0422
- Ship & Boat International. m. ISSN 0037-3834
- Special Ships. m.

**Referees' Association**
c/o Ted Ring, Ed., 23 Fifth Park Rd., Sheffield 55 6WL, Eng.
- Football Referee. bi-m (5 per yr.)

**Reform Synagogues of Great Britain**
33 Seymour Place, London W.1, Eng.
- Living Judaism. q. ISSN 0024-5267
- R S G B Inform. bi-m.

**Reformed Baptist Movement**
- Reformation Today. (pub. by Cuckfield Baptist Church)

**Refractories Association of Great Britain**
- Refractories Journal. (pub. by London and Sheffield Publishing Co. Ltd.)

**Refrigeration Press, Ltd.**
Davis House, 69-77 High St., Croydon CR9 1QH, Surrey, England.
- Refrigeration and Air Conditioning Year Book. a.

**Regency International Publications Ltd.**
Newstone House, 127 Sandgate Rd., Folkestone, Kent, England.
- Regency International Directory; of enquiry agents, private detectives & debt collecting agencies. a. ISSN 0080-0538

**Regency Press**
43 New Oxford St., London WC1A 1BH, England.
- New Poets. irreg.
- Where to Eat in London. a. ISSN 0083-9205

**Regional Postgraduate Institute for Medicine and Dentistry, Newcastle-Upon-Tyne**
- Adverse Drug Reaction Bulletin. (pub. by Adverse Drug Reaction Research Unit)

**Release News**
1 Elgin Ave., London W9, England.
- Release News. q.

**Relgocrest Ltd.**
182 Pentonville Rd., London N.1, Eng.
- Red Weekly. w. (International Marxist Group(British Section, 4th International))

**Reproduction Research Information Service Ltd.**
141 Newmarket Rd., Cambridge CB5 8HA, Eng.
- Bibliography of Reproduction; a classified monthly list of references compiled from research literature. m.(2 vols. of 6 nos. per year) ISSN 0006-1565

**Research and Documentation Centre**
Box 734, London SW11 6PF, Eng.
- Scanner; digest of current events in the South Asian continent. s-m.

**Research in Librarianship**
36 Sagars Rd., Handforth, Cheshire SK9 3EE, England.
- Research in Librarianship. 3 per yr. ISSN 0034-5245

**Research Publications Services Ltd.**
Victoria Hall, East Greenwich, London S.E.10, Eng.
- Modern China Studies. International Bulletin.
- Social Audit. q.
- Soviet Analyst; a fortnightly newsletter. s-m. ISSN 0049-1713

**Residential Care Association**
- Residential Social Work. (pub. by Law & Local Government Publications Ltd.)

**Resurgence Trust**
Pentre Ifan, Felindre Farchog, Crymych, Dyfed, Wales.
- Resurgence; journal of the fourth world. bi-m. ISSN 0034-5970

**Resuscitation Press**
554 Garratt Lane, London SW17 0NY, Eng.
- Resuscitation. q. ISSN 0300-9572

**Retail Credit Federation**
192A Nantwich Road, Crewe, Cheshire CW2 6BP, England.
- Retail Credit Federation. Year Book and Directory. a. ISSN 0080-1852

**Retail Fruit Trade Federation Ltd.**
8-15 Russell Chambers, Covent Garden, London W. C. 2., England.
- Retail Fruit Trade Review. m.

**Retail Journals Ltd**
Queensway House, 2 Queensway, Redhill, Surrey RH1 1QS, Eng.
- Fish Trader. w.
- Frozen Foods. m. ISSN 0016-2205
- Frozen Foods Year Book. a. ISSN 0071-9692

**Retirement Choice Magazine Co. Ltd.**
1-2 Dorset Bldgs., Dorset Rise, London EC4Y 9ES, England.
- Pre Retirement Choice; the monthly magazine for those approaching, planning and enjoying retirement. m. (Co-publisher: J-Jay Publications Ltd.)

**Reveille Newspapers Ltd.**
33 Holborn, London, EC1, England.
- Reveille. w.

**Revelation**
1 Heeley Rd., St. Annes, Lancs., England.
- Revelation. q.

**Review**
72 Westbourne Terrace, London W.2, Eng.
- Review; a magazine of poetry and criticism. q. ISSN 0034-6330

**Revolutionary Communist Group**
- Revolutionary Communist. (pub. by R C G Publications Ltd.)

**Richard 3rd Society**
65 Howard Rd., Upminster, Essex RM14 2UE, Eng.
- Ricardian. q. ISSN 0048-8267

**Richmond Publishing Co. Ltd.**
Orchard Road, Richmond, Surrey TW9 4PD, England.
- Natural History Book Reviews. 3 per yr.

**Ridings Publishing Co.**
33 Beverley Rd., Driffield, Yorks, Eng.
- Yorkshire Ridings; County magazine. m. ISSN 0044-0639

**Ringsport Publications**
5 Stockland St., Caerphilly, Glam., Wales.
- Ringsport. m. ISSN 0037-6310

**Road Haulage Association**
22 Upper Woburn Place, London WC1H OES, England.
- Haulage Manual. a.
- Road Way. m. ISSN 0035-7316

**Martin Robertson & Co. Ltd.**
17 Quick Place, London N1 8HL, England.
- University of Glasgow. Social and Economic Research Studies. irreg. ISSN 0072-4629

**Robson Books**
28 Poland St., London W1V 3DB, England.
- Poetry Dimension; a living record of the poetry year. a.

**Rells House Publishing Co., Ltd.**
Breams Bldgs., London E.C. 4, Eng., U.K.
- New Health. q. ISSN 0028-534X

**Romford and District Historical Society**
c/o Central Library, Romford, Essex, England.
- Romford Record. a.

**Rondo Publications Ltd.**
155-157 the Albany, Old Hall St., Liverpool L3 9EG, England.
- Meridian; poetry magazine. 3 per yr.

**Ronin**
24 Rylett Crescent, London W12, Eng.
- Ronin. m.

**Barry Rose Ltd.**
Little London, Chichester, Sussex, England.
- Crown Court; an index of common penalties and formalities. a. since 1974.

**Rossendale Society for Genealogy**
209 Rochdale Rd., Edenfield, Bury BL0 0RG, England.
- Lancashire. q.

**Rotary International in Great Britian and Ireland**
Sheen Lane House, Sheen Lane, London SW14 8AF, Eng.
- Rotary. bi-m. ISSN 0035-8401

**Rothmans of Pall Mall Ltd.**
- Rothmans Football Yearbook. (pub. by Queen Anne Press Ltd.)
- Rothmans Rugby Yearbook. (pub. by Queen Anne Press Ltd.)

**Rothwell Advertiser Press Ltd.**
39 Commercial St., Rothwell Leeds, Yorkshire, Eng.
- Leeds Weekend Advertiser. w.
- Rothwell Advertiser. w. ISSN 0035-8444

**Routledge & Kegan Paul Ltd.**
Broadway House, Newton Rd., Henley on Thames
RG9 1EN, Eng
(U.S. Orders to: Routledge Journals, 9 Park St.,
Boston, MA 02108)
- British Journal of Sociology. q. ISSN 0007-1315
  (London School of Economics)
- Community Work. a.
- Economy and Society. q.
- Ethnic and Racial Studies. q.
- Greek and Latin Studies Series. irreg.
- Journal of Mithraic Studies. s-a.
- Religion; a journal of religion and religions. s-a.
  ISSN 0048-721X
- Ulster-Scot Historical Series. irreg., 1969, no. 2.
  ISSN 0082-7363
- World Archaeology. 3 per yr. ISSN 0043-8243

**Rowing**
Aylings Boathouse, Embankment, Putney, London
SW15 1IB, England.
- Rowing. 9 per yr. ISSN 0035-8584

**Royal Aeronautical Society**
4 Hamilton Place, London W1V OBQ, Eng.
- Aeronautical Journal. m. ISSN 0001-9240
- Aeronautical Quarterly. q. ISSN 0001-9259
- Aerospace. m. ISSN 0001-933X
- Anglo-American Aeronautical Conference.
  Proceedings. irreg., 15th, London 1977.

**Royal African Society**
- African Affairs. (pub. by Oxford University Press)

**Royal Agricultural Society of England**
National Agricultural Centre, Kenilworth,
Warwickshire, Eng.
- N A C News. 6 per yr. ISSN 0027-8491
- Royal Agricultural Society of England. Journal. a.
  ISSN 0080-4134

**Royal Air Force College**
Cranwell, Sleaford, Lincs, Eng.
- Royal Air Force College Journal. a. ISSN 0035-
  8606

**Royal Air Force Ornithological Society**
110 Edinburgh Drive, Ickenham, Uxbridge,
Middlesex, Eng.
- Royal Air Force Ornithological Society. Journal.
  s-a. ISSN 0035-8622

**Royal Air Force Police Depot**
Debden, Saffron Walden, Essex, Eng.
- Provost Parade. q. ISSN 0033-1945 (R.A.F.
  Provost Branch)

**Royal Air Forces Quarterly Association Ltd.**
Portland Rd., Malvern, Worcestershire WR14 2TA,
Eng.
- Royal Air Forces Quarterly. q. ISSN 0035-8630

**Royal Aircraft Establishment**
Building Q1, Farnborough, Hampshire, Eng.
- R. A. E. News. m. ISSN 0033-6718

**Royal Anthropological Institute of Great Britain and
Ireland**
56 Queen Anne St., London W1M 9LA, Eng.
- Man. q. ISSN 0025-1496
- R A I N: Royal Anthropological Institute News.
  bi-m. ISSN 0307-6776
- Royal Anthropological Index to Current
  Periodicals in the Library of the Museum of
  Mankind. q.

**Royal Archaeological Institute**
304, Addison House, Grove End Road, London,
NW8 9EL, England.
- Archaeological Journal. a. ISSN 0066-5983

**Royal Army Educational Corps**
Eltham Palace, Eltham, London S.E.9, Eng.
- Torch. s-a.

**Royal Army Pay Corps**
Corps Headquarters, Worthy Down, Winchester,
Hants, Eng.
- Royal Army Pay Corps Journal. 3 per yr. ISSN
  0035-8673

**Royal Artillery Institution**
Woolwich, London S.E.18, Eng.
- Journal of the Royal Artillery. s-a. ISSN 0022-
  5134

**Royal Asiatic Society of Great Britain and Ireland**
56 Queen Anne St., London W1M 9LA, Eng.
- Royal Asiatic Society of Great Britain and
  Ireland. Journal. s-a. ISSN 0035-869X

**Royal Astronomical Society**
- Geophysical Journal of the Royal Astronomical
  Society. (pub. by Blackwell Scientific Publications
  Ltd.)
- Royal Astronomical Society. Quarterly Journal.
  (pub. by Blackwell Scientific Publications Ltd.)
- Royal Astronomical Society, England. Memoirs.
  (pub. by Blackwell Scientific Publications Ltd.)

**Royal Botanic Gardens**
Kew, London, England
- Kew Bulletin. Additional Series. irreg. ISSN 0075-
  5982 (Avail. from: H.M.S.O., c/o Liaison Officer,
  Atlantic House, London EC1P 1BW, England)

**Royal British Legion**
National Executive Council, Pall Mall, London,
SW1Y 5JY, England.
- Royal British Legion. Journal. m.

**Royal British Legion Scotland**
23 Drumsheugh Gardens, Edinburgh, Scotland.
- Claymore. m. ISSN 0009-8590

**Royal Caledonian Curling Club**
2 Coates Crescent, Edinburgh, 3, Scotland.
- Royal Caledonian Curling Club. Annual. a. ISSN
  0080-4282

**Royal College of Art**
Exhibition Rd., London S.W.7, England.
- Royal College of Art. Journal. 3 per yr.

**Royal College of Midwives**
- Midwives Chronicle. (pub. by Nursing Notes Ltd.)

**Royal College of Music**
Prince Consort Rd., London S.W.7, Eng.
- R C M Magazine. 3 per yr. ISSN 0033-684X

**Royal College of Nursing**
1A Henrietta Place, Cavendish Square, London
W1M 0AB, Eng.
- Nursing Standard. m. ISSN 0029-6570
- Study of Nursing Care: Research Project Series.
  irreg.

**Royal College of Nursing. Library**
Henrietta Place, Cavendish Square, London W1M
0AB, England.
- Nursing Bibliography. m.

**Royal College of Obstetricians and Gynaecologists**
27 Sussex Place, Regents Park, London NW1 4RG,
Eng.
- British Journal of Obstetrics & Gynaecology. m.
  ISSN 0306-5456

**Royal College of Organists**
Kensington Gore, London SW7 2QS, England.
- Royal College of Organists. Year Book. a. ISSN
  0080-4320

**Royal College of Physicians of Edinburgh**
9 Queen Street, Edinburgh EH2 1JQ, Scotland.
- Royal College of Physicians of Edinburgh.
  Yearbook and Calendar. triennial; with annual
  supplements.

**Royal College of Psychiatrists**
- British Journal of Psychiatry. (pub. by Headley
  Bros. Ltd.)
- British Journal of Psychiatry. Special Publications.
  (pub. by Headley Bros. Ltd.)

**Royal College of Surgeons of Edinburgh**
18 Nicolson St., Edinburgh EH8 9DW, Scotland.
- Royal College of Surgeons of Edinburgh. Journal.
  bi-m. ISSN 0035-8835

**Royal College of Surgeons of England**
Lincolns Inn Fields, London WC2A 3PN, Eng.
- Royal College of Surgeons of England. Annals. bi-
  m. ISSN 0035-8843
- Royal College of Surgeons of England. Faculty of
  Anaesthetists. Newsletter. a.
- Royal College of Surgeons of England. Handbook.
  irreg.

**Royal Commonwealth Society**
Northumberland Ave., London WC2N 5BJ, Eng.
- Commonwealth. bi-m. ISSN 0010-3411
- Royal Commonwealth Society Library Notes. q.
  ISSN 0035-8851

**Royal Corps of Transport**
Regimental Headquarters, Buller Barracks,
Aldershot, England.
- Waggoner. q. ISSN 0042-9961

**Royal Courts of Justice (Ulster)**
Belfast 1, Northern Ireland.
- Incorporated Law Society of Northern Ireland.
  Gazette. q. ISSN 0019-3526

**Royal Economic Society**
- Economic Journal. (pub. by Cambridge University
  Press)

**Royal Entomological Society**
41 Queen's Gate, London S.W.7, England.
- Royal Entomological Society of London.
  Proceedings. a. ISSN 0080-4355
- Royal Entomological Society of London.
  Symposia. a. ISSN 0080-4363 (Nos. 5-8 Published
  by: Blackwell Scientific Publications, Ltd., Osney
  Mead, Oxford, England)

**Royal Forestry Society of England, Wales and
Northern Ireland**
102 High St., Tring, Herts. HP23 4AH, England.
- Quarterly Journal of Forestry. q. ISSN 0033-5568

**Royal Geographical Society**
1 Kensington Gore, London SW7 2AR, Eng.
- Geographical Journal. 3 per yr. ISSN 0016-7398
- Geographical Magazine. (pub. by I P C Magazines
  Ltd.)
- New Geographical Literature and Maps. s-a. ISSN
  0028-5110

**Royal Greenwich Observatory**
Herstmonceux Castle, Hailsham, East Sussex BN27
1RP, Eng.
- Observatory. bi-m. ISSN 0029-7704
- Royal Greenwich Observatory, Herstmonceux,
  England. Royal Observatory Annals. irreg. ISSN
  0080-4371 (Science Research Council)

**Royal Highland and Agricultural Society of Scotland**
Ingliston, Newbridge, Midlothian, Scotland.
- Royal Highland and Agricultural Society of
  Scotland. Show Guide and Review. a.

**Royal Historical Society**
University College London, Gower St., London
WC1E GBT, England.
- Camden Fourth Series. a. ISSN 0068-6905
- Royal Historical Society. Guides and Handbooks.
  irreg. ISSN 0080-4398
- Royal Historical Society. Transactions. Fifth
  Series. a. ISSN 0080-4401

**Royal Horticultural Society**
Vincent Sq., London S.W.1, England.
- Daffodils. a. ISSN 0070-2544 (Co-sponsor:
  Daffodil Society)
- Lilies and Other Liliaceae. a. ISSN 0075-949X
- R. H. S. Gardener's Diary. a. ISSN 0080-441X
- Rhododendrons, with Magnolias and Camellias. a.
  ISSN 0080-2891
- Royal Horticultural Society. Garden Journal. m.

**Royal Humane Society**
Watergate House, York Bldgs, Adelphi, London
WC2N 6LE, England.
- Royal Humane Society. Annual Report. a.

**Royal Institute of British Architects**
66 Portland Place, London WIN 4AD, Eng.
- Architectural Periodicals Index. q(last issue of
  year cumulative)
- R I B A Journal. m. ISSN 0035-8932

**Royal Institute of British Architects. East Midlands
Region**
Midland Design and Building Centre, Mansfield
Rd., Nottingham NG1 3FE, Eng.
- Architecture East Midlands. bi-m. ISSN 0003-
  8709

**Royal Institute of British Architects. Northern
Region**
- Northern Architect. (pub. by Paull & Goode
  Publishing Ltd.)

**Royal Institute of British Architects. West Midlands Region**
Birmingham Building Centre, Broad St., Birmingham B1 2DB, England.
- Architecture West Midlands. q.

**Royal Institute of British Architects. Yorkshire Region**
- Yorkshire Architect. (pub. by Paull & Goode Publishing Ltd.)

**Royal Institute of International Affairs**
- British Year Book of International Law. (pub. by Oxford University Press US)
- International Affairs. (pub. by Oxford University Press)
- Middle Eastern Monographs. (pub. by Oxford University Press US)
- World Today. (pub. by Oxford University Press)

**Royal Institute of Navigation**
- Journal of Navigation. (pub. by Scottish Academic Press Ltd.)

**Royal Institute of Philosophy**
- Philosophy. (pub. by Cambridge University Press)

**Royal Institute of Public Administration**
Hamilton House, Mabledon Place, London WC1H 9BD, Eng.
- Public Administration. q. ISSN 0033-3298

**Royal Institute of Public Health and Hygiene**
- Community Health. (pub. by John Wright & Sons Ltd.)

**Royal Institution of Chartered Surveyors**
12 Great George St., London S.W.1, Eng.
- Chartered Surveyor. m. ISSN 0009-1936
- R I C S Abstracts and Reviews. m. ISSN 0033-6939
- R I C S Library Information Service. Weekly Briefing; a digest of news selected from the press. w.
- Royal Institution of Chartered Surveyors Year Book. (pub. by Thomas Skinner Directories)

**Royal Institution of Great Britain**
21 Albemarle St., London W1X 4BS, England.
- Royal Institution of Great Britain. Proceedings. (pub. by Applied Science Publishers Ltd.)
- Royal Institution of Great Britain. Record. a.
- Royal Institution of Great Britain. Royal Institution Lectures. 3 per yr.

**Royal Institution of Naval Architects**
10 Upper Belgrade St., London SW1X 8BQ, Eng.
- Naval Architect. bi-m.
- Royal Institution of Naval Architects. Supplementary Papers. irreg.
- Royal Institution of Naval Architects. Transactions. a. ISSN 0035-8967

**Royal Life Saving Society**
Desborough House, 14, Devonshire St., London, W.1., Eng.
- Royal Life Saving Society. Quarterly Journal. q. ISSN 0048-8704

**Royal Marines**
Eastney, Southsea, Hants PO4 9PX, Eng.
- Globe and Laurel; the journal of the Royal Marines. 6 per yr. ISSN 0017-1204

**Royal Meteorological Society**
James Glaisher House, Grenville Place, Bracknell, Berks. RG12 1BX, England.
- Royal Meteorological Society. Quarterly Journal. q. ISSN 0035-9009
- Weather. m. ISSN 0043-1656

**Royal Microscopical Society**
- Journal of Microscopy. (pub. by Blackwell Scientific Publications Ltd.)

**Royal Military Police**
Ed. Col. A.G. Akerman, Roussillon Barracks, Chichester, Sussex, Eng.
- Royal Military Police Journal. q. ISSN 0035-9025

**Royal Musical Association**
c/o Hugh Cobbe, Department of Manuscripts, British Library, Great Russell St., London WC1B 3DG, England.
- Musica Britannica. (pub. by Stainer and Bell Ltd.)
- Royal Musical Association, London. Proceedings. a. ISSN 0080-4452

- Royal Musical Association, London. R. M. A. Research Chronicle. a. ISSN 0080-4460

**Royal National Institute for the Blind**
224 Great Portland St., London W1N 6AA, Eng.
- Braille Chess Magazine. q. ISSN 0006-8756
- Braille Digest. m. ISSN 0006-8764
- Braille Journal of Physiotherapy. m. ISSN 0006-8780
- Braille Musical Magazine. (400); containing topical information of interest to blind musicians, teachers, students and music lovers, reviews of new music publications in Braille, etc. m. ISSN 0006-8837
- Braille News Summary. w. ISSN 0006-8853
- Braille Radio Times. w. ISSN 0006-887X
- Braille Rainbow. q. ISSN 0006-8888 (Co-sponsor: National Deaf-Blind Helpers' League)
- Channels of Blessing. bi-m. ISSN 0009-1529
- Fleur de Lys. m.(except Aug.) ISSN 0015-3648
- National Braille Mail. s-w. ISSN 0047-8768
- New Beacon (Braille Edition); the journal of blind welfare. m.
- New Beacon (Inkprint Edition); the journal of blind welfare. m. ISSN 0028-4270
- Physiotherapists' Quarterly. q. ISSN 0048-4083
- Piano-Tuners Quarterly. q. ISSN 0048-4105
- Portland. m. ISSN 0048-4881
- Progress. m. ISSN 0033-0566
- Roundabout. q. ISSN 0048-8666
- Royal National Institute for the Blind. Information Leaflets. irreg. ISSN 0080-4479
- Royal National Institute for the Blind. Law Notes. Extracts. m. ISSN 0023-9291
- Royal National Institute for the Blind. School Magazine. m (except Aug.) ISSN 0048-8712
- Tape Record. m. ISSN 0039-9531
- Theological Times. q. ISSN 0049-3651
- Trefoil Trail; a journal for blind guides. m (except Aug.) ISSN 0049-4615

**Royal National Institute for the Blind. Moon Branch**
Holmesdale Rd., Reigate, Surrey RH2 0BA, England.
- Diane. m. ISSN 0012-236X
- Light of the Moon. m. ISSN 0024-3361
- Moon Magazine. m. ISSN 0027-0911
- Moon Rainbow. q. ISSN 0047-8083

**Royal National Institute for the Deaf**
105 Gower St, London WC1E 6AH, Eng.
- British Journal of Audiology; a quarterly journal for the study of audiology. q. ISSN 0300-5364 (Co-Sponsor: British Society of Audiology)
- Hearing. bi-m. ISSN 0017-9183

**Royal National Life-Boat Institution**
West Quay Rd., Poole, Dorset BH15 1HZ, England.
- Life-Boat. q. ISSN 0024-3086

**Royal National Mission to Deep Sea Fishermen**
43 Nottingham Place, London W1M 4BX, Eng.
- Toilers of the Deep. 3 per yr. ISSN 0040-8824

**Royal National Rose Society**
Chiswell Green Lane, St. Albans, Hertfordshire AL2 3NR, England.
- Rose Annual. a. ISSN 0483-3686

**Royal Naval Engineering College**
Manadon, Plymouth, England.
- Thunderer. a.

**Royal Naval Sailing Association**
RN Club, Pembroke Rd., Portsmouth, Hants, Eng.
- Royal Naval Sailing Association Journal. s-a. ISSN 0035-9041

**Royal Numismatic Society**
British Museum, London, WC1B 3DG, England.
- Numismatic Chronicle and Journal. a. ISSN 0078-2696

**Royal Over-Seas League**
Over-Seas House, Park Place St. James's, London S.W.1, Eng.
- Overseas. q. ISSN 0030-7424

**Royal Philatelic Society**
41 Devonshire Place, London W1N 1PE, Eng.
- London Philatelist. bi-m. ISSN 0024-6131

**Royal Philosophical Society of Glasgow**
26 Dryburgh Ave., Rutherglen, Glasgow G73 3EG, Scotland.
- Philosophical Journal. s-a. ISSN 0031-8078

**Royal Photographic Society of Great Britain**
14 South Audley St., London W1Y 5DP, Eng.
- Journal of Photographic Science. bi-m. ISSN 0022-3638
- Photographic Abstracts. 12 per yr. ISSN 0031-8701
- Photographic Journal. bi-m. ISSN 0031-8736

**Royal Pigeon Racing Association**
26 High St., Welshpool, Powys SY21 7JP, Wales, U.K.
- British Homing World. w. ISSN 0007-0777
- Homing World Stud Book. a. ISSN 0073-3164

**Royal Pioneer Corps and Association**
Simpson Barracks, Wootton, Northampton NN4 0HX, Eng.
- Royal Pioneer. q. ISSN 0035-9076

**Royal Regiment of Fusiliers**
- Fusilier. (pub. by Combined Service Publications Ltd.)

**Royal School of Church Music**
Addington Palace, Croydon CR95AD, Eng.
- Church Music Quarterly. q. ISSN 0307-6334
- English Church Music. a. ISSN 0071-0555

**Royal School of Mines Association**
Prince Consort Road, London, SW7, England.
- Royal School of Mines, London. Journal. a. ISSN 0080-4495

**Royal Scottish Forestry Society**
18 Abercromby Place, Edinburgh EH3 6LB, Scotland.
- Scottish Forestry. q. ISSN 0036-9217

**Royal Scottish Geographical Society**
10 Randolph Crescent, Edinburgh EH3 7TU, Scotland.
- Scottish Geographical Magazine. 3 per yr. ISSN 0036-9225

**Royal Society**
6 Carlton House Terrace, London SW1Y 5AG, England.
- United Kingdom Geodesy Report. irreg. (British National Committee for Geodesy and Geophysics. Geodesy Subcommittee.)

**Royal Society for Asian Affairs**
42 Devonshire St., London W.1, Eng.
- Asian Affairs. 3 per yr. ISSN 0306-8374

**Royal Society for the Prevention of Accidents**
6 Buckingham Place, London SW1E 6HR, England.
- Care in the Home. q. ISSN 0300-5909
- Care on the Road. m.
- Occupational Safety and Health. m. ISSN 0007-1153
- Occupational Safety and Health Supplement. m. ISSN 0029-7992

**Royal Society for the Prevention of Cruelty to Animals**
The Causeway, Horsham, Sussex RH12 1HG, Eng.
- R S P C A Today. s-a. ISSN 0048-8720

**Royal Society for the Protection of Birds**
The Lodge, Sandy, Bedfordshire SG19 2DL, Eng.
- Birds. q. ISSN 0006-3665
- R S P B Annual Report and Accounts. a. ISSN 0080-4509

**Royal Society of Arts**
6 John Adam St., Adelphi, London W.C.2, Eng (Subscr. to: George Bell & Sons Ltd., York House, Portugal St., London W.C.2., England)
- Royal Society of Arts. Journal. m. ISSN 0035-9114

**Royal Society of Edinburgh**
22 George St., Edinburgh EH2 2PQ, Scotland.
- Royal Society of Edinburgh. Communications, Physical Sciences. irreg. ISSN 0308-129X
- Royal Society of Edinburgh. Proceedings. (Mathematics) irreg. ISSN 0308-2105
- Royal Society of Edinburgh. Proceedings. (Natural Environment) irreg. ISSN 0308-2113
- Royal Society of Edinburgh. Transactions. irreg. ISSN 0080-4568
- Royal Society of Edinburgh. Year Book. a. ISSN 0080-4576

**Royal Society of Health**
13 Grosvenor Place, London SW1X 7EN, England.
- Royal Society of Health. Papers. irreg.; 1973, no. 8.
- Royal Society of Health Journal. bi-m. ISSN 0035-9130

**Royal Society of Literature of the United Kingdom**
- Royal Society of Literature of the United Kingdom. Essays by Divers Hands: Being the Transactions of the Society. (pub. by Oxford University Press)

**Royal Society of London**
6 Carlton House Terrace, London S.W.1, England.
- Royal Society of London. Author Index to the Proceedings, Philosophical Transactions, Obituary Notices and Bibliographical Memoirs. irreg. ISSN 0080-4592
- Royal Society of London. Biographical Memoirs of Fellows of the Royal Society. a. ISSN 0080-4606
- Royal Society of London. Notes and Records. s-a. ISSN 0035-9149
- Royal Society of London. Philosophical Transactions. Series A. Mathematical and Physical Sciences. irreg. ISSN 0080-4614
- Royal Society of London. Philosophical Transactions. Series B. Biological Sciences. irreg. ISSN 0080-4622
- Royal Society of London. Proceedings. Series A. Mathematical and Physical Sciences. irreg. ISSN 0080-4630
- Royal Society of London. Proceedings. Series B. Biological Sciences. irreg. ISSN 0080-4649
- Royal Society of London. Year Book. a. ISSN 0080-4673

**Royal Society of London. British National Committee for Geodesy and Geophysics**
6 Carlton House Terrace, London SW1, England.
- Geomagnetism and Aeronomy in the United Kingdom. irreg.

**Royal Society of Medicine**
2 Queen Anne St., London W1M 0BR, England.
- Royal Society of Medicine. Annual Report of the Council. a. ISSN 0080-4681
- Royal Society of Medicine. Proceedings. m. ISSN 0035-9157
- Tropical Doctor; a journal of modern medical practice. q. ISSN 0049-4755

**Royal Society of Tropical Medicine and Hygiene**
Mansion House, 26 Portland Place, London, W1N 4EY, England.
- Royal Society of Tropical Medicine and Hygiene, London. Yearbook. a. ISSN 0080-4711
- Royal Society of Tropical Medicine and Hygiene Transactions. bi-m. ISSN 0035-9203

**Royal Statistical Society**
25 Enford St., London W1H 2BH, Eng.
- Royal Statistical Society. Journal. Series A: General. 4 parts a year. ISSN 0035-9238
- Royal Statistical Society. Journal. Series B: Methodological. 3 parts a year. ISSN 0035-9246
- Royal Statistical Society. Journal. Series C: Applied Statistics. 3 parts a year. ISSN 0035-9254

**Royal Tank Regiment Publications Ltd.**
1 Elverton St., London SW1P 2QJ, Eng.
- Tank. q. ISSN 0039-9418

**Royal Television Society**
Tavistock House East, Tavistock Square, London WC1H 9HR.
- Television. bi-m.

**Royal Town Planning Institute**
26 Portland Place, London W1 N 4BE, Eng.
- Planner. 10 per yr.
- Town and Country Planning Summer School; Report of Proceedings. a. ISSN 0078-2114

**Royal United Service Institute for Defence Studies**
Whitehall, London SW1A 2ET, Eng.
- R U S I. q.

**Royal Yachting Association**
196, Eastern Esplanade, Southend-on-Sea, Essex, England.
- R. Y. A. Magazine. s-a. ISSN 0557-661X

**Royal Zoological Society of Scotland**
Scottish National Zoological Park, Murrayfield, Edinburgh EH12 6TS, Scotland.
- Royal Zoological Society of Scotland. Zoo Guide. irreg.

**Rubber and Plastics Research Association of Great Britain**
Shawbury, Shrewsbury SY4 4NR, Eng.
- Bio-Medical Applications of Polymers. m.
- International Polymer Science and Technology. m.
- New Trade Names in the Rubber and Plastics Industries. a. ISSN 0077-8869
- R A P R A Abstracts. bi-w. ISSN 0033-6750

**Rugby Football League**
180 Chapeltown Road, Leeds, 7, England.
- Rugby Football League Official Guide. a. ISSN 0080-4827

**Rumanian Free Democratic Committee**
2 Mulletsfield, Cromer St., London W.C.1, England.
- East-European Spokesman. s-a. ISSN 0422-1001

**Runnymede Trust**
62 Chandos Place, London WC2N 4HG, England.
- Runnymede Trust Bulletin. m.

**Rural Music Schools Association**
Little Benslow Hills, 1 Ibberson Way, Hitchin, Herts SG4 9RB, England.
- Rural Music Schools Association. Bulletin. 3 per yr (plus supplements)

**Bertrand Russell Peace Foundation**
Bertrand Russell House, 45 Gamble St., Forest Rd. W., Nottingham NG7 4ET, Eng.
- Spokesman. s-a. ISSN 0024-5992

**Rutherford Laboratory. Scientific Administration Department**
Chilton, Didcot, Oxon OX11 0OX, England.
- Rutherford Laboratory, Scientific Administration Department. Report. a.

**S. & H. Publications**
57 Pembridge Rd., London W.11, England.
- Boys International. m.

**S C M Press Ltd.**
56 Bloomsbury St., London WC1 3QX, England.
- Sociological Yearbook of Religion in Britain. irreg. ISSN 0081-1777

**S. P. Technical Publications Ltd.**
2 Walker Street, Edinburgh, EH3 7LB, Scotland.
- Scottish and Northern Ireland Plumbing and Heating. m.

**S R M Foundation of Great Britain**
32 Cranbourn St., London WC2H 7EY, Eng.
- Creative Intelligence; an international publication devoted to the science of creative intelligence. 4 per yr.

**Ralph Sadgrove**
M1 Victoria House, Southampton Row, London WC1B 4EW, England.
- Gift Buyer International. m. ISSN 0016-9854

**Safety in Mines Research Establishment**
Red Hill, Off Broad Lane, Sheffield S3 7HQ, Eng.
- Safety in Mines Abstracts. bi-m. ISSN 0036-2492

**Sage Publications Ltd.**
44 Hatton Garden, London E.C.1., England (and Sage Publications, Inc., 275 S. Beverly Drive, Beverly Hills, CA 90212)
- Current Sociology/Sociologie Contemporaine. 3 per yr. ISSN 0011-3921 (International Sociological Association)
- Development and Change. q. ISSN 0012-155X (International Centre for Training and Research in Development Studies. Institute of Social Studies)
- European Studies Review. q. ISSN 0014-3111
- Journal of Contemporary History. q. ISSN 0022-0094
- Policy and Politics. q. ISSN 0305-5736
- Social Studies of Science; an international review of research in the social dimensions of science and technology. q. ISSN 0306-3127
- Teaching Politics. 3 per yr. ISSN 0305-7771

**St. Anthonys' Press**
St. Anthony's Hall, York YO1 2PW, Eng.
- Borthwick Institute of Historical Research. Borthwick Papers. s-a. ISSN 0524-0913 (University of York)

**St. Bartholomew's Hospital. Students Union**
London E.C.1, Eng., U.K.
- St. Bartholomew's Hospital Journal. q. ISSN 0036-2778

**St. David's University College**
- Trivium. (pub. by University of Wales Press)

**St. Dunstan's for Men and Women Blinded on War Service**
Box 58, 191 Old Marylebone Rd., London NW1 5QN, England.
- Nuggets. m. ISSN 0048-1106
- St. Dunstan's Annual Report. a.
- St. Dunstan's Review. m. ISSN 0036-2808

**St. George's Hospital Medical School**
9 Knightsbridge, London S.W.1., England.
- Saint George's Hospital Gazette. 3 per yr. ISSN 0036-2840

**St. James Press**
3 Percy St., London W1, England
(U.S. Address: St. Martin's Press, 175 Fifth Ave., New York, NY 10010)
- Blue Book: Leaders of the English-Speaking World. a. ISSN 0067-9240
- Contemporary Novelists. triennial.
- Contemporary Poets of the English Language. triennial. ISSN 0069-9470
- Writers Directory. biennial. ISSN 0084-2699

**St. James Press Publications Ltd.**
1 St. James's St., London SW1A 1EF, England.
- A B C Flights. 2 per yr.

**St. Luke's College**
English Dept., Exeter, Eng.
- Accent. 2-3 per yr. ISSN 0001-4486

**St. Martin-In-The-Fields Church**
5 St. Martins Place, London W.C.2, Eng.
- St. Martin's Review; the journal with the international outlook. m. ISSN 0036-3111

**St. Martin's Press**
18 Queen's Rd., Brighton BN1 3XA, Eng.
- Club Mirror; the national trade newspaper. m. ISSN 0045-7213

**St. Mary's Hospital Medical School Students' Union**
Paddington, London W.C.2, Eng.
- St. Mary's Hospital Gazette. 8 per yr. ISSN 0036-312X

**St. Thomas's Hospital Medical School**
c/o Dean's Office, London SE1 7EH, England.
- St. Thomas's Gazette. 3 per yr. ISSN 0306-3860

**Salvation Army**
101 Queen Victoria St., London EC4P 4EP, Eng.
- All the World. q. ISSN 0002-5623
- Deliverer. bi-m. ISSN 0011-7897
- Musical Salvationist. q. ISSN 0027-464X
- Salvation Army Year Book. (pub. by Salvationist Publishing and Supplies, Ltd.)
- War Cry. w. ISSN 0043-0226
- Young Soldier. w. ISSN 0044-0906

**Salvationist Publishing and Supplies, Ltd.**
Judd St., Kings Cross, London WC1H 9NN, England.
- Salvation Army Year Book. a. ISSN 0080-567X (Salvation Army)

**Samizdat**
c/o Bernard J. Kelly, Ed., 68 Parkhill Rd., London N. W. 3., England.
- Samizdat. q.

**Samsom Publications Ltd.**
12/14 Hill Rise, Richmond, Surrey TW10 6UA, England.
- Computer Report. w. ISSN 0306-6886
- Industrial Relations Week. w. ISSN 0306-6894
- Middle East Week. w. ISSN 0306-6908
- Motor Report International. fortn. ISSN 0306-6274

**Sanctuary Press Ltd.**
76A Rochester Row, London, S.W. 1, Eng.
- Action. fortn. ISSN 0044-6068

**Sand and Gravel Association Limited**
48park St., London W1Y 4HE, Eng.
- S A G A Bulletin. q.

**Sandbach Parochial Church Council**
Buttersfield, 66 Manor Rd., Sandbach, Cheshire
CW11 0NB, Eng.
- Challenge (Sandbach); the magazine of St. Mary's
Church, Sandbach. m. ISSN 0009-1014

**Sandes Soldiers' & Airmen's Homes**
3D Belmont Rd., Belfast BT4 2AA, N. Ireland.
- Forward. q. ISSN 0015-8607

**Sappho Publications Ltd.**
B C M/Petrel, London WC1V 6XX, England.
- Sappho; lesbian/feminist magazine. m.

**W. B. Saunders Co. Ltd.**
12 Dyott St., London, England.
- Major Problems in Anaesthesia. irreg., approx. 2
per yr.

**Save the Children Fund**
157 Clapham Rd., London S.W.9, Eng.
- World's Children; international journal of child
care and development. q. ISSN 0043-9290

**Savings Banks Insitute**
Knighton House, 52-66 Mortimer St., London W1N
70G, Eng.
- Savings Banks Institute. Journal. bi-m. ISSN 0048-
9247

**Sawell Publications Ltd.**
127 Stanstead Rd., London SE23 1JE, Eng.
- Anti-Corrosion Methods and Materials; the first
British journal of corrosion control, prevention,
engineering and research. m. ISSN 0003-5599
- Finishing Handbook and Directory. a. ISSN 0071-
5182
- Garden Supplies Retailer. m. ISSN 0016-4623
- Pigment and Resin Technology. m.
- Product Finishing. m. ISSN 0032-9762
- Tooling. m. ISSN 0040-9227
- Work Study. m. ISSN 0043-8022

**Scalabrini Fathers**
20 Brixton Rd., London S.W.9, Eng.
- Voce degli Italiani; British-Italian fortnightly.
fortn. ISSN 0042-7810

**Scandinavia Philatelic Society**
c/o P. S. S. F. Marsden, 87 Hunters Field, Stanford-
in-the-Vale, Faringdon, Oxon. SN7 8ND, Eng.
- Scandinavian Contact. q.

**School Government Publishing Co. Ltd.**
Darby House, Bletchingley Rd., Merstham, Redhill
RH1 3DN, England.
- Education Authorities' Directory and Annual. a.
ISSN 0070-9131

**School Library Association**
Victoria House, 29-31 George St., Oxford OX1
2AY, Eng.
- School Librarian. 4 per yr. ISSN 0036-6595

**School Natural Science Society**
5 Upper Park Rd., Kingston, Surrey, England
(Subscr. to: Miss D. Edwards, 8 Sandy Lane,
Sevenoaks, Kent, Eng.)
- Natural Science in Schools. 3 per yr. ISSN 0028-
0763

**School of Oriental and African Studies, University of
London**
- International African Bibliography. (pub. by
Mansell Information - Publishing Ltd.)

**School of Universal Philosophy & Healing**
6 Phillimore Place, Kensington, London W. 8., Eng.
- Royal Universal Philosophy. q.

**School Yarn Publications, Ltd.**
93 Brownspring Drive, New Eltham, London, S.E.9,
Eng.
- School Yarn Magazine. bi-m. ISSN 0036-6862
- Schoolgirl Story Magazine. fortn. ISSN 0036-6897

**Schoolmaster Publishing Co. Ltd.**
Derbyshire House, Lower Street, Kettering,
Northants, NN16 8BB, England.
- N U T Guide to Careers Work. a. ISSN 0066-
3972 (National Union of Teachers)
- Teacher. w. ISSN 0040-0408 (National Union of
Teachers)

**Schools Council**
- Great Britain. Schools Council Publications.
Curriculum Bulletins. (pub. by Evans-Methuen
Educational)
- Great Britain. Schools Council Publications.
Examinations Bulletins. (pub. by Evans-Methuen
Educational)
- Great Britain. Schools Council Publications.
Working Papers. (pub. by Evans-Methuen
Educational)

**Schott & Co. Ltd.**
48 Great Marlborough St., London W.1, Eng.
- Recorder and Music. q. ISSN 0034-1665

**Science and Technology Agency**
787 High Rd., North Finchley, London N12 8JT,
England.
- Mossbauer Spectroscopy Abstracts. q.
- Polarography Abstracts. q.

**Science Fiction Foundation**
North East London Polytechnic, Longbridge Road,
Dagenham, Essex RM8 2AS, England.
- Foundation; the review of science fiction. 3 per yr.

**Science History Publications Ltd.**
Halfpenny Furze, Mill Lane, Chalfont St. Giles,
Bucks HP8 4NR, England
(U.S. address: Science History Publications, 156
Fifth Ave., Rm. 502, New York, NY 10010)
- Anglo - Irish Studies. a. ISSN 0307-3300
- History of Science; review of literature and
research. 4 per yr. ISSN 0073-2753
- Journal for the History of Astronomy. 3 per yr.
ISSN 0021-8286
- Journal of European Studies. q. ISSN 0047-2441

**Science Museum Library**
South Kensington, London SW7 5NH, Eng.
- List of Accessions to the Science Museum
Library. m. ISSN 0024-4317

**Science Policy Foundation**
32 High St, Guildford, Surrey, England.
- Science and Public Policy. bi-m. ISSN 0302-3427

**Science Research Council**
Herstmonceux Castle, Hailsham, Sussex BN27 1RP,
England.
- Royal Greenwich Observatory. Herstmonceux,
England. Royal Observatory Bulletin. irreg., about
12 nos. per yr. ISSN 0080-438X
- Royal Greenwich Observatory, Herstmonceux,
England. Royal Observatory Annals. (pub. by
Royal Greenwich Observatory)

**Scientific Documentation Centre Ltd.**
Halbeath House, Dunfermline, Fife, Scotland.
- S. D. C. Bulletin. q. ISSN 0036-1178

**Scientific Exploration Society**
- Scientific Exploration Society. Newsletter. (pub.
by Daily Telegraph Ltd.)

**Scientific Indexing & Retrieval Service**
Sangria House, Elm Rd., Tokers Green, Reading
RG4 9EG, Berks, England.
- Commercial Food Information. m.

**Scientific Information Consultants Ltd.**
661 Finchley Rd., London NW2 2HN, Eng
(and Plenum Publishing Corp., 227 W. 17th St.,
New York, N.Y. 10011)
- Automatic Monitoring & Measuring. bi-m. ISSN
0005-1292
- Corrosion Control Abstracts. m. ISSN 0010-9347
- Cybernetics Abstracts. m. ISSN 0011-4243
- Czechoslovak Engineering Sciences Abstracts. bi-
m. ISSN 0011-457X
- Czechoslovak Science & Technology Digest. bi-m.
ISSN 0045-947X
- Index to Forthcoming Russian Books. m. ISSN
0019-4018
- Mechanical Sciences Abstracts. ISSN 0025-6536
- Protection of Metals. bi-m. ISSN 0033-1732
- Russian Metallurgy. bi-m. ISSN 0036-0295
- Soviet Journal of Nondestructive Testing. bi-m.
ISSN 0038-5492

**Scientific Press Ltd.**
11a Gloucester Rd., London S.W.7, England.
- Applied Plastics; the practical uses of plastics in
industry and commerce. m. ISSN 0003-696X

**Scientific Surveys Ltd.**
4 Burkes Parade, Beaconsfield, Bucks, England.
- Natural Gas Manual. triennial.

- Offshore Europe. biennial. ISSN 0078-3692
- Pipes and Pipelines International; hoses, tubes,
pumps, valves. bi-m. ISSN 0032-020X

**Scotia**
33a Huddart St., Wick, Caithness, Scotland.
- Scotia Review; for the Scottish muse and nation. 3
per yr.

**Scots Independent (Newspapers) Ltd.**
9 Upper Bridge St., Stirling, Scotland.
- Scots Independent. m. ISSN 0036-9071

**Scots Philosophical Club**
St. Andrews KY16 9AL, Scotland
- Philosophical Quarterly. q. ISSN 0031-8094
(University of St. Andrews) (Subscr. to:, Scottish
Academic Press, 33 Montgomery St., Edinburgh
EH7 5JX, Scotland)

**Scots Secretariat Pamphlets Organisation**
Jess Cottage, Carlops, Penicuik, Midlothian EH26
9NF, Scotland.
- Scottish Journal of Science. irreg. (approx.1 pt.
per year); 1973, vol. 1., pt.3, no. 15. ISSN 0080-
8075

**T. G. Scott and Son Ltd.**
1 Clement's Inn, London WC2A 2ED, England.
- Disabled Driver. bi-m. (Disabled Drivers' Motor
Club)

**Colin Scott, Ed. & Pub.**
1 St. Paul's Close, Clitheroe, Lancashire BB7 2NB,
Eng.
- European Grocery Letter. 3 per yr. ISSN 0014-
2948

**Scott Polar Research Institute**
Cambridge CB2 1ER, Eng.
- Polar Record. 3 per yr. ISSN 0032-2474

**Scottish Academic Press Ltd.**
33 Montgomery St., Edinburgh EH7 5JX, Scotland.
- British Journal of Educational Psychology. 3 per
yr. ISSN 0007-0998
- Edinburgh Mathematical Society. Proceedings. 2
per yr. ISSN 0013-0915
- Forum for Modern Language Studies. q. ISSN
0015-8518 (University of St. Andrews)
- Geological Society. Journal. 6 per yr. ISSN 0016-
7649
- Geological Society of London. Special
Publications. irreg., approx. biennial. (Geological
Society of London)
- Glasgow Mathematical Journal. 2 per yr. ISSN
0017-0895 (Glasgow Mathematical Society)
- Horticultural Research; a journal for the
publication of scientific work on horticulture. 2
per yr. ISSN 0018-5299
- Journal of Navigation. 3 per yr. (Royal Institute of
Navigation)
- Liturgical Review. s-a. (Church Service Society)
- Quarterly Journal of Engineering Geology. q.
ISSN 0481-2085 (Geological Society of London)
- Scottish Journal of Geology. 4 per yr. ISSN 0036-
9276 (Co-Sponsors: Geological Societies of
Edinburgh & Glasgow)
- Scottish Journal of Theology. 6 per yr. ISSN
0036-9306
- Twentieth Century Studies. s-a. ISSN 0041-4638

**Scottish & Universal Newspapers Ltd.**
146 King St., Castle Douglas, Scotland.
- Galloway News. w. ISSN 0016-4178

**Scottish Area National Union of Mineworkers**
5 Hillside Crescent, Edinburgh7, Scotland.
- Scottish Miner. m. ISSN 0036-9349

**Scottish Association of Master Bakers**
19 Atholl Crescent, Edinburgh, EH3 8HJ, Scotland.
- Scottish Bakers' Year Book. a. ISSN 0080-7974

**Scottish Association of Opticians**
179 West George St., Glasgow G2 2LQ, Scotland.
- Scottish Ophthalmic Practitioner. bi-m. ISSN
0308-7670 (Co-sponsor: Scottish National
Committee of Ophthalmic Opticians)

**Scottish Braille Press**
Craigmillar Park, Edinburgh EH16 5NB, Scotland.
- Braille Science Journal; a record of scientific
progress. m. ISSN 0006-8896
- Braille Sporting Record. w. ISSN 0006-890X
- Madam. m. ISSN 0024-9351

**Scottish Catholic Historical Association**
- Innes Review. (pub. by John S. Burns & Sons)

**Scottish Centre for Ornithology & Bird Protection**
21 Regent Terrace, Edinburgh EH7 5BT, Scotland.
- Scottish Birds. q. ISSN 0036-9144 (Scottish
  Ornithologists Club)

**Scottish Children's League of Pity**
16 Melville St., Edinburgh, Scotland.
- City Sparrows. a.

**Scottish Clubman Ltd.**
57 Evan St., Stonehaven, Kincardinshire, Scotland.
- Motorscot. m.

**Scottish Council for Research in Education**
- Scottish Council for Research in Education.
  Publications. (pub. by University of London Press
  Ltd.)

**Scottish Economic Society**
- Scottish Journal of Political Economy. (pub. by
  Longman Group Ltd.)

**Scottish Episcopal Church**
21 Grosvenor Crescent, Edinburgh EH12 5EE,
Scotland.
- Outlook. m. (Co-Sponsor: Congregational Union
  of Scotland)
- Scottish Episcopal Church Yearbook. a. ISSN
  0080-8016

**Scottish Farmer Publications Ltd.**
39 York St., Glasgow G2 8JL, Scotland.
- Gardener. m.
- Horse & Pony. m.
- Scottish Farmer. w. ISSN 0036-9195

**Scottish Folk Directory**
c/o Sheila Douglas, Ed., 12 Mansfield Rd., Perth,
Scotland.
- Scottish Folk Directory. a.

**Scottish Genealogy Society**
20 Ravelston Garden, Edinburgh EH4 3LE,
Scotland.
- Scottish Genealogist. q. ISSN 0300-337X

**Scottish Georgian Society**
39 Castle St., Edinburgh EH2 3BH, Scotland.
- Scottish Georgian Society. Bulletin. biennial.

**Scottish Graphical Association**
136 West Regent St., Glasgow G2 2RL, Scotland.
- Scottish Graphical Association Journal. m.

**Scottish Grocer**
36 N. Frederick St., Glasgow C.1, Scotland.
- Scottish Grocer. w. ISSN 0036-9233

**Scottish Group of the University. College and
Research Section of the Library Association**
University Library, Stirling, FK9 4LA, Scotland.
- Annual Bibliography of Scottish Literature. a.

**Scottish Hardware and Drysalters Association**
16 Royal Terrace, Glasgow, C3, Scotland.
- Scottish Hardware and Drysalters Association.
  Yearbook. a. ISSN 0080-8059

**Scottish Home and Health Department**
H.M. Stationery Office, Edinburgh, Scotland.
- Criminal Statistics, Scotland.
- Scottish Health Services. irreg.
- Scottish Regional Hospital Boards: Scottish
  Hospital Costs. irreg.

**Scottish Institute of Adult Education**
57 Melville St., Edinburgh EH3 7HL, Scotland.
- Scottish Journal of Adult Education. s-a.
- Stay and Study in Scotland This Summer. a.
- Yearbook of Adult Education in Scotland. a.

**Scottish Institute of Missionary Studies**
Department of Religious Studies, University of
Aberdeen, King's College, Aberdeen AB9 2UB,
Scotland.
- Scottish Institute of Missionary Studies Bulletin. s-
  a. ISSN 0048-9778

**Scottish Landowners' Federation**
- Landowning in Scotland. (pub. by Mackenzie &
  Arthur Ltd.)

**Scottish Library Association**
The Mitchell Library, North St., Glasgow G3 7DN,
Scotland.
- Library Resources in Scotland. irreg.
- S L A News. bi-m. ISSN 0048-9786
- Scottish Libraries. triennial. ISSN 0080-8091

**Scottish Local Authorities Special Housing Group**
83 Melville St., Edinburgh EH3 7HL, Scotland.
- S L A S H Newsletter. irreg.

**Scottish Marine Biological Association**
Dunstaffnage Marine Research Laboratory, P.O.B.
3, OBAN, Argyll, Scotland.
- Fauna of the Clyde Sea Area. irreg. ISSN 0071-
  4062
- S. M. B. A. Collected Reprints. a. ISSN 0080-
  8121

**Scottish Milk Marketing Board**
Underwood Rd., Paisley, Renfrewshire, Scotland.
- Milk Bulletin. m.

**Scottish Mountaineering Club**
12 Newington Rd., Edinburgh, 9, Scotland.
- Scottish Mountaineering Club. Journal. a. ISSN
  0080-813X

**Scottish Opera Club**
Elmbank Crescent, Glasgow G2 4 PT, Scotland.
- Scottish Opera News. m.

**Scottish Ornithologists Club**
- Scottish Birds. (pub. by Scottish Centre for
  Ornithology & Bird Protection)

**Scottish Pharmacist**
5 Loudoun St., Mauchline, Ayrshire, Scotland.
- Scottish Pharmacist. m. ISSN 0036-9357

**Scottish Pipe Band Association**
45, Washington Street, Glasgow, G3 8AZ, Scotland.
- Tutor & Textbook - Elementary Piping &
  Drumming.

**Scottish Planning Exchange**
186 Bath St., Glasgow G2 4HG, Scotland.
- Planning Exchange Information Bulletin. w.
- Planning Exchange News-Sheet. irreg.
- Scottish Planning Appeal Decisions. q.

**Scottish Postmark Group**
David C. Jefferies, 11 Craigcrook Ave., Edinburgh
EH4 3QE, Scotland.
- Scottish Postmark Group. Handbook. irreg. ISSN
  0080-8164

**Scottish Reformation Society**
17 George Fourth Bridge, Edinburgh EH1 1EE,
Scotland.
- Bulwark. 6 per yr. ISSN 0045-3536

**Scottish Rock Garden Club**
c/o R. H. D. Orr, Ed., 70, High Street, Haddington,
East Lothian, Scotland.
- Scottish Rock Garden Club Journal. s-a.

**Scottish Society for Industrial Archaeology**
c/o John R. Hume, Department of History,
University of Strathclyde, Glasgow G1 1XQ,
Scotland.
- Scottish Industrial History. 3 per yr. (Co-sponsors:
  Scottish Society for the Preservation of Historical
  Machinery; Business Archives Council of
  Scotland)

**Scottish Society for Prevention of Vivisection**
10 Queensferry St., Edinburgh, EH2 4pG, Scotland.
- Scottish Society for Prevention of Vivisection.
  Annual Pictorial Review. a. ISSN 0080-8210

**Scottish Stock Exchange Association**
- Scottish Stock Exchange Official List. (pub. by
  MacNaughtan & Sinclair Ltd.)

**Scottish Sub Aqua Club**
16 Royal Crescent, Glasgow G3 7SL, Scotland.
- Scottish Diver. bi-m.

**Scottish Tartans Society**
Broughty Castle Museum, Broughty, Ferry, Dundee
DD5 2BE, Scotland.
- Scottish Tartans Society. Proceedings. a.

**Scottish Temperance Alliance**
244 Bath St., Glasgow, Scotland.
- Scotia Quarterly. q. ISSN 0036-9047

**Scottish Tourist Board**
23 Ravelston Terrace, Edinburgh EH4 3EU,
Scotland.
- Angler's Guide to Scottish Waters. a.
- Camping and Caravan Sites in Scotland; camping
  and caravan sites. a.
- Enjoy Scotland: a World of a Difference. a.
- Scotland by Road. a. ISSN 0080-7788
- Scotland for Hillwalking. irreg.
- Scotland-Home of Golf. a. ISSN 0080-7842
- Scotland: Travel Trade Guide. a.
- Scotland 600 Things to See. a.
- Self Catering Accomodation in Scotland. a.
- Taste of Scotland. irreg.
- Where to Stay in Scotland. a. ISSN 0083-9221
- Winter Sports in Scotland. a. ISSN 0084-0386

**Scottish Tramway Museum Society**
46 Wellshot Dr., Cambuslang, Glasgow, Scotland.
- Scottish Transport. 2 per yr. ISSN 0048-9808

**Scottish Typographical Association**
136 West Regent St., Glasgow, Scotland.
- Scottish Typographical Annual Report. a. ISSN
  0080-8245

**Scottish Union of Students**
- Scottish Graduate. (pub. by J.E.P. and Associates)

**Scottish Wildlife Trust**
8 Dublin St., Edinburgh EH1 3PP, Scotland.
- Scottish Wildlife. 3 per yr.

**Scout Association**
25 Buckingham Palace Rd., London SW1W OPY,
England.
- Cub Scout Handbook. irreg.
- Cub Scout Leader's Handbook. irreg.
- Discovery and Adventure. irreg.
- Enjoy Camping. irreg.
- Notes for Venture Scout Leaders. irreg.
- Patrol Leaders Handbook. irreg.
- Programmed Planning in the Scout Troop. irreg.
- Scout Camping. irreg.
- Scouting; the national magazine of the Scout
  Association. m. ISSN 0036-9489

**Scrip Services**
18-20 Hill Rise, Richmond, Surrey TW10 6UA,
England.
- Scrip - World Pharmaceutical News. w.

**Script Publications**
35, Glenmore Road, London NW3 4PA, England.
- Script; magazine on alternative radio. bi-m.

**Scripture Gift Mission**
Radstock House, 3 Eccleston St., London SW1W
9LZ, Eng.
- S G M News Digest. q. ISSN 0048-9859
- Y S L Magazine. m.

**Scripture Union**
47 Marylebone Lane, London W1M 6AX, England.
- Teaching over 13s. q.
- Teaching Under 5s. q.
- Teaching 5-7. q.
- Teaching 7-10. q.
- Teaching 10-13. q.

**Sea Cadet Corps of the United Kingdom**
- Sea Cadet. (pub. by Navy League)

**Seabird Group**
c/o Zoology Department, Tillydrone Ave, Aberdeen
AB9 2TN, Scotland.
- Seabird Report. a. ISSN 0080-8415

**B. A. Seaby Ltd.**
Audley House, 11 Margaret St., London W1N 8AT,
Eng.
- Seaby's Coin and Medal Bulletin. m. ISSN 0037-
  0053 (American Numismatic Society US)

**Seacoast Newspaper Ltd.**
16 Wolseley Rd., Ashford, Kent, Eng.
- Ashford Advertiser. w. ISSN 0004-4334

**Seafarers Education Service**
Mansbridge House, 207 Balham High Rd., London
SW17 7BH, Eng.
- Seafarer. q. ISSN 0037-007X

**Seaforth Advertising**
8 Lennox Gardens, London SW1X 0DG, England.
- Will to Charity: the Charities' Story Book. a.

**Sean Dorman Manuscript Society**
4 Union Place, Fowey, Cornwall PL23 1BY, Eng.
- Writing. q.

**Seatrade Publications Ltd.**
Fairfax House, Colchester, Essex, Eng.
- Seatrade. m. ISSN 0037-0428

**Secker & Warburg**
14 Carlisle Street, Soho Square, London W. 1,
England
(Dist. by Kraus-Thomson, Route 100, Millwood, N
Y 10546 and Kraus-Thomson, Nendeln,
Liechtenstein)
- Leo Baeck Institute. Year Book. a. ISSN 0075-
8744

**Security Gazette Ltd.**
117 Hatfield Rd., St. Albans, Herts AL1 4JS,
England.
- International Security Directory; world police, fire
and security forces, services, products and
supplies. a. ISSN 0074-7890
- Security Gazette. m. ISSN 0049-0024

**Seed Publications Ltd.**
8A All Saint's Rd., London W. 11, England.
- Seed. m.

**Seel House Press Ltd.**
Seel House, Seel St., Liverpool L1 4AY, England.
- Geological Journal. s-a. ISSN 0072-1050
(University of Liverpool. Department of Geology)

**Selden Society**
Queen Mary College, Faculty of Laws, Mile End
Rd., London E1 4NS, England.
- Selden Society, London. Handbook: Publications,
List of Members and Rules. every 4-5 years.
- Selden Society, London. Lectures. every 2-3 years.
- Selden Society, London. Main (Annual) Series. a.
- Selden Society, London. Supplementary Series.
irreg. ISSN 0582-4788

**A. R. L. Selkirk**
9 Nassington Rd., London NW3 2TX, Eng.
- Current Archaeology. bi-m. ISSN 0011-3212

**Sell's Publications Ltd.**
39 East St., Epsom KT17 1BQ, Surrey, England.
- Scottish National Register of Classified Trades. a.
ISSN 0080-8148
- Sell's British Aviation. a. ISSN 0080-8695
- Sell's British Exporters. a. ISSN 0080-8709
- Sell's Building Index. a. ISSN 0080-8717
- Sell's Directory of Products & Services. a. ISSN
0080-8725
- Sell's Government and Municipal Contractors
Register. a. ISSN 0072-5129
- Sell's Health Service Buyers Guide. a.
- Sell's Hotel, Restaurant and Canteen Supplies. a.
ISSN 0073-3504

**Seminar for Arabian Studies**
31-34 Gordon Square, London WC1H 0PY,
England.
- Seminar for Arabian Studies. Proceedings. irreg.

**Service Station Publications Ltd.**
178-202 Great Portland St., London W1N 6NH,
Eng.
- Service Station. m. ISSN 0037-265X

**Servisads Ltd.**
7/9 Stanmore Hill, Stanmore, Middlesex HA7 3EU,
England.
- Automatic Chemistry Equipment International. bi-
m.
- Equipment and Materials for Industry. 4 per yr.
- Hospital Equipment Service. q. ISSN 0026-5853
- Laboratory Enquiry Service. 10 per yr. ISSN
0024-9475

**William Sessions Ltd.**
c/o Ebor Press, York YO3 9HS, England.
- Quaker Encounters. irreg.

**Seventh-Day Adventist Church in Britain**
- Life and Health. (pub. by Stanborough Press Ltd.)

**Sewing Machine Times Ltd.**
64 Whitechapel High St., London E.1.7., Eng.
- Clothing Machinery Times. bi-m. ISSN 0305-7046
- Sewing Machine Times; news & views for
progressive sewing machine dealers. bi-m. ISSN
0049-030X

**Seymour Press Ltd.**
334 Brixton Road, London S.W.9, Eng.
- Opera. m. ISSN 0030-3526

**Shaftesbury Society**
112 Regency St., London SW1P 4AX, Eng.
- Shaftesbury Review. s-a. ISSN 0037-3168

**Shakespearean Authorship Society**
10 Uphill Grove, Mill Hill, London NW7 4NJ,
England.
- Bard. s-a. ISSN 0307-3408

**Shanti Sadan**
- Self-Knowledge. (pub. by Centre of Adhyatma
Yoga in the West)

**Shaw & Sons Ltd.**
Shaway House, Bell Green Lane, London SE26
5AE, England.
- Shaw's Directory of Courts in England and Wales.
a. ISSN 0085-6061

**Sheet Metal Industries**
John Adam House, John Adam St., London WC2N
6JH, England.
- European Coil Coating Association. Directory.
irreg.

**Sheffield Chamber of Commerce**
Commerce House, 33 Earl St., Sheffield S1 3FX,
England.
- Quality of Sheffield and South Yorkshire. bi-m.

**Sheffield University Metallurgical Society**
Dept. of Metallurgy, Portobello St, Sheffield S1
3JD, England.
- University of Sheffield. Metallurgical Society.
Journal. a. ISSN 0080-9209

**Shell International Petroleum Co. Ltd.**
Shell Centre, London SE1 7NA, Eng.
- Shell Aviation News. 6 per yr. ISSN 0037-3508
- Shell Bitumen Review. q. ISSN 0037-3516

**Shell-Mex. and B.P. Ltd**
- Ad. (pub. by Sonostrips Ltd.)

**Sheppard Press, Ltd.**
P.O. Box 42, Russell Chambers, Covent Garden,
London WC2E 8AX, England.
- Book Dealers in North America. biennial. ISSN
0068-0109
- Bookdealers in India, Pakistan and Sri Lanka. a.
- Directory of Dealers in Secondhand and
Antiquarian Books in the British Isles. biennial.
ISSN 0070-5411
- European Bookdealers; a directory of dealers in
secondhand and antiquarian books on the
continent of Europe. triennial. ISSN 0071-2523

**Sherlock Holmes Society of London**
5 Manor Close, Warlingham, Surrey CR3 9SF,
England.
- Sherlock Holmes Journal. s-a. ISSN 0037-3621

**John Sherratt & Son Ltd.**
Park Rd., Altrincham, Cheshire, Eng.
- Salmon and Trout Magazine. 3 per yr. ISSN
0036-3545

**Shin Buddhist Association**
Mulberry House, Epsom Rd., Ewell Surrey KT17
1JL, England.
- Western Buddhist; journal of the full Buddhist
tradition. 2 per yr. ISSN 0043-3527

**Shire Horse Society**
East of England Showground, Peterborough PE2
0XE, England.
- National Shire Horse Show Catalogue. a.

**Shire Publications**
12B Temple Square, Aylesbury, Buckshire, England.
- Lifelines. irreg.

**Shirley Institute**
Manchester M2Q 8RX, England.
- Digest of English-Language Textile Literature. m.
ISSN 0306-1639
- Textiles. 3 per yr. ISSN 0306-0748
- World Textile Abstracts. s-m. ISSN 0043-9118

**Shoe and Allied Trades Research Association
(SATRA)**
SATRA House, Rockingham Road, Kettering,
Northants, England.
- Footwear Digest. bi-m.

**Short Brothers & Harland Ltd.**
Airport Rd., Belfast BT3 9DZ, N. Ireland.
- Short Story. bi-m. ISSN 0037-4245

**Short Wave Magazine Ltd.**
55 Victoria St., London SW1H OHF, Eng.
- Short Wave Magazine. m. ISSN 0037-4261

**Shorthorn Society of the United Kingdom of Great
Britain and Ireland**
Green Lodge, Great Bowden, Market Harborough,
Leicestershire, England.
- Coates's Herd Book (Beef) a. ISSN 0069-4924
- Coates's Herd Book (Dairy) a. ISSN 0069-4932
- Dairy Shorthorn Journal. bi-m. ISSN 0011-569X

**Shout**
c/o Clive Richardson, Ed., 46 Slades Drive,
Chislehurst, Kent BR7 6JX, England.
- Shout. m. ISSN 0583-1296

**Siecle a Mains**
c/o Michel Couturier, 3 Chalcot Rd., London N.
W. 1., England.
- Siecle a Mains. 2-3 per yr. ISSN 0037-4628

**Sikh Cultural Society of Great Britain**
88 Mollison Way, Edgeware, Middlesex HA8 5QW,
Eng.
- Sikh Courier. q. ISSN 0037-511X

**R. Richard Simmons Ltd.**
30 Knightrider St., London EC4Y 5BL, Eng.
- Games and Toys. m. ISSN 0016-4348
- Games and Toys Year Book. a. ISSN 0072-0135

**Sino-British Trade Council**
25 Queen Annes Gate, London SW1H 9BU,
England.
- Sino-British Trade. m. ISSN 0583-4279

**Sir Isaac Pitman & Sons Ltd.**
39 Parker St., Kingsway, London WC2B 5PB,
England
(Dist. by Pitman Publishing Corp., 6 East 43 St.,
New York, N.Y. 10017)
- Royal College of Physicians of London. Journal.
(pub. by Pitman Medical Publishing Co. Ltd.)
- Who's Who in Theatre. irreg., 1972, 15th ed.
ISSN 0083-9833

**Sir Thomas Beecham Society**
46 Wellington Ave., Westcliff-on-Sea, Essex SS0
9XV, England.
- Sir Thomas Beecham Society Newsletter. bi-m.

**Sira Institute Ltd.**
South Hill, Chislehurst, Kent BR7 5EH, Eng.
- Measurement and Automation News. q.
- Sira Institute. Annual Report. a.

**Sisson and Parker Ltd.**
25 Wheeler Gate, Nottingham, Eng.
- Renaissance and Modern Studies. a. ISSN 0486-
3720 (University of Nottingham)

**Skate Magazine**
1 Strathmore Close, Caterham, Surrey CR3 5EQ,
England.
- Ice and Roller Skate Magazine. m.

**Ski Club of Great Britain**
118 Eaton Sq., London SW1, England.
- Ski Survey. 3 per yr. (Sep., Oct., Dec.,)

**Ski Specialists**
4 Douro Place, London W85PH, England.
- Skier's Holiday Guide. irreg.

**Thomas Skinner Directories**
Stuart House, 41-43 Perrymount Rd., Haywards
Heath, West Sussex RH16 3BS, England
(Dist. in U.S. by: I.P.C. (America) Inc., 205 E. 42nd
St., New York, NY 10017)
- Bank Sorting Code Numbers. a. (Association of
London Clearing Banks)
- Bankers Almanac and Year Book. a. ISSN 0067-
379X
- Directory of Directors. a. ISSN 0070-5438
- Royal Institution of Chartered Surveyors Year
Book. a.
- Skinner's British Textile Register. a. (British
Textile Confederation)
- Stock Exchange, London. Stock Exchange Official
Year Book. a. ISSN 0076-0684
- Willing's Press Guide; British European & U.S.
edition. a. ISSN 0000-0213

**Skota Federacio Esperantista**
16 Woodlands Dr., Coatbridge ML5 1LE, Scotland.
- Esperanto en Skotlando. q. ISSN 0014-0643

**Sleep Learning Association**
14 Belsize Crescent, London NW3 5QU, Eng.
- Sleep-Learning Association. Journal. q. ISSN 0037-6817

**Carl Slienger**
Box 4ST, London W1P 1AA, England.
- Bibliotheca Historico Militaris. irreg.

**Slimming Magazine Ltd.**
4 Clareville Grove, Kensington, London SW7 5AL, Eng.
- Slimming & Nutrition. bi-m. ISSN 0049-075X

**R. A. Slinn Ltd.**
52 Kettering Rd., Northampton NN1 4BR, England.
- Remedial Gymnastics and Recreational Therapy. q. (Society of Remedial Gymnasts)

**J. B. Smith**
Elm Cottage, Chilsham Lane, Herstmonceux, East Sussex, England.
- Dod's Parliamentary Companion. a. ISSN 0070-7007

**Albert E. Smith (Printers) Ltd.**
Longsmith St., Gloucester, Eng.
- Gloucester Diocesan Gazette. m. ISSN 0017-1301

**Bruce Main Smith & Co. Ltd.**
16s Holmdale Rd., London N.S.6, Eng.
- Marxist Studies. q. ISSN 0025-4126

**Smiths Industries Ltd. Aviation Division**
Cricklewood, London NW2 6JN, England.
- Aviation Review. q. ISSN 0374-2490

**Snail Enterprises**
The Flat, Corffe, Tawstock, Barnstaple, North Devon, England.
- Snail. m.

**Soccer File Ltd.**
53, Hampstead High St., London, N.W.3. 1QG, Eng.
- Football News. m. ISSN 0306-1132

**Social Administration Association**
- Journal of Social Policy. (pub. by Cambridge University Press)

**Social Credit Co-Ordinating Centre**
10 Midhope Way, Filey, North Yorkshire, Eng.
- Abundance; quarterly journal of the new economics. q. ISSN 0044-5827

**Social Science Research Council**
1 Temple Ave., London EC4Y 0BD, England.
- S S R C Newsletter. 3 per yr. ISSN 0036-1909
- S S R C Studentship Handbook; postgraduate studentships in the social sciences. a.

**Social Science Research Council. Postgraduate Awards Division**
1 Temple Ave., London EC4Y 0BD, England (and Research Publications Services Ltd., Victoria Hall, East Greenwich, London SE1O 0RF, England)
- Social Science Research Council (Gr. Brit.) Bursary Scheme. a.
- Social Science Research Council (Gr. Brit.) Fellowships. a.
- Social Science Research Council (Great Britain) Research Supported by the Social Science Research Council. a. ISSN 0583-6948

**Socialist Commentary Publications Ltd.**
77 New Bond St., London W1Y 9DB, Eng.
- Socialist Commentary. m. ISSN 0037-8178

**Socialist International**
88 A St. John's Wood High St., London N.W.8, Eng.
- Socialist Affairs. bi-m. ISSN 0049-0946

**Socialist Party of Great Britain**
52 Clapham High St., London SW4 7UN, Eng.
- Socialist Standard. m. ISSN 0037-8259

**Society for African Church History**
c/o Dept. of Religious Studies, Kings College, University of Aberdeen, Aberdeen AB9 2UB, Scotland.
- Society for African Church History. Bulletin. a. ISSN 0081-1297

**Society for Analytical Chemistry**
9/10 Savile Row, London W1X 1AF, England.
- Liquid Scintillation Counting. (pub. by Heyden & Son, Ltd.)
- Society for Analytical Chemistry. Annual Reports on Analytical Atomic Spectroscopy. a.

**Society for Analytical Chemistry. Chemical Society Division**
- Society of Analytical Chemistry. Chemical Society Division. Proceedings. (pub. by W. Heffer & Sons Ltd.)

**Society for Anglo-Chinese Understanding**
152 Camden High St., London NW1 0NE, Eng.
- China Now. 10 per yr. ISSN 0045-6764

**Society for Applied Bacteriology**
- Journal of Applied Bacteriology. (pub. by Academic Press Inc. (London) Ltd.)

**Society for Army Historical Research**
National Army Museum, Royal Hospital Rd., London SW3, Eng.
- Society for Army Historical Research. Journal. q. ISSN 0037-9700

**Society for Clinical Oncology**
- Clinical Oncology. (pub. by Academic Press Inc. (London) Ltd.)

**Society for Cultural Relations with the U.S.S.R.**
320 Brixton Rd., London SW9 6AB, Eng.
- Anglo-Soviet Journal. 3 per yr. ISSN 0044-8265

**Society for Education in Film and Television**
29 Old Compton St., London W1V 5PL, England.
- Screen. q. ISSN 0036-9543
- Screen Education. q. ISSN 0306-0691

**Society for Education Through Art**
131 a Bedford Square Mansions, Bedford Square, London WC1B 3AH, Eng.
- Athene. s-a. ISSN 0004-6582 (Co-Sponsor: International Society for Education Through Art)

**Society for Endocrinology**
- Journal of Endocrinology. (pub. by Biochemical Society (Book Depot))

**Society for Environmental Education**
16 Trinity Road, Enderby, Leicester, Eng.
- S. E. E. Journal. s-a.

**Society for Experimental Biology**
- Journal of Experimental Botany. (pub. by Oxford University Press)

**Society for Folk Life Studies**
- Folk Life. (pub. by W.S. Maney & Sons Ltd.)

**Society for General Microbiology**
Harvest House, 62 London Rd., Reading RG1 5AS, Berkshire, England.
- Journal of General Microbiology. (pub. by Cambridge University Press)
- Journal of General Virology. (pub. by Cambridge University Press)
- Society for General Microbiology Proceedings. 4 per yr.

**Society for Italic Handwriting**
c/o Mrs. Fiona Sturdy, 69 Arlington Rd., London NW1 7ES, England.
- Society for Italic Handwriting. Journal. q. ISSN 0037-9743

**Society for Lincolnshire History & Archaeology**
86 Newland, Lincoln, England.
- Lincolnshire History and Archaeology. a. ISSN 0459-4487

**Society for Medieval Archaeology**
c/o University College, Gower St., London, WCIE 6BT, England.
- Medieval Archaeology. a. ISSN 0076-6097

**Society for Nautical Research**
Lions Wood, Dern Lane, Heathfield, Sussex, Eng.
- Mariner's Mirror. q. ISSN 0025-3359

**Society for Old Testament Study**
University of Hull, Dept. of Theology, Cottingham Rd., Hull HU6 7RX, England.
- Society for Old Testament Study. Book List. a. ISSN 0081-1440

**Society for Post-Medieval Archaeology**
c/o J. H. Ashdown, Treas., 53 Bainton Road, Oxford OX2 7AG, England.
- Post-Medieval Archaeology. a. ISSN 0079-4236

**Society for Promoting Christian Knowledge**
Holy Trinity Church, Marylebone Rd., London NW1 4DU, England.
- Churchman's Pocket Book and Diary. a. ISSN 0069-4029
- Theology. bi-m. ISSN 0040-571X

**Society for Psychical Research**
1 Adam and Eve Mews, London W8 6UQ, Eng.
- Society for Psychical Research. Journal. q. ISSN 0037-9751
- Society for Psychical Research. Proceedings. irreg. ISSN 0081-1475

**Society for Renaissance Studies**
Department of Italian, University College, Gower St., London W.C.1., England.
- Society for Renaissance Studies. Occasional Papers. irreg.

**Society for Research in Psychology of Music and Music Education**
Dept. of Education, University of Manchester, Manchester M13 9PL, England.
- Psychology of Music. s-a.

**Society for Spreading the Knowledge of True Prayer**
Box 29, Woking, Surrey GU21 4AR, Eng.
- Active Service; a magazine devoted to the spreading of the knowledge of divinely scientific thinking. bi-m. ISSN 0001-7558

**Society for the Advancement of Anaesthesia in Dentistry**
53 Wimpole St., London, W.1, Eng.
- S A A D Digest. q. ISSN 0049-1160

**Society for the Bibliography of Natural History**
c/o British Museum (Natural History), Cromwell Rd., London SW7 5BD, England.
- Sherborn Fund Facsimiles. irreg., 1973, no. 4. ISSN 0080-9241
- Society for the Bibliography of Natural History. Journal. s-a. ISSN 0037-9778

**Society for the Promotion of Hellenic Studies**
31-34 Gordon Square, London WC1H 0PP, England.
- Journal of Hellenic Studies. a. ISSN 0075-4269

**Society for the Promotion of Nature Reserves**
The Green, Nettleham, Lincoln LN2 2NR, England.
- Society for the Promotion of Nature Reserves. Technical Publications. irreg. ISSN 0081-1513

**Society for the Promotion of Roman Studies**
31-34 Gordon Sq., London WC1H 0PP, England.
- Britannia. a. ISSN 0068-113X
- Journal of Roman Studies. a. ISSN 0075-4358

**Society for the Protection of Unborn Children**
9A Brechin Place, London SW7 4QB, England.
- Society for the Protection of Unborn Children. Bulletin. irreg (2-3 per yr)

**Society for the Study of Addiction to Alcohol and other Drugs**
- British Journal of Addiction. (pub. by Longman Group Ltd.)

**Society for the Study of Alchemy and Early Chemistry**
- Ambix. (pub. by Heffers Printers Ltd.)

**Society for the Study of Human Biology**
c/o Dr. A. J. Boyce, Anthropology Laboratory, Dept. of Human Anatomy, S. Park Rd., Oxford OX1 3QX, England.
- Annals of Human Biology. (pub. by Taylor & Francis Ltd.)
- Society for the Study of Human Biology. Symposia. irreg., 1970, vol. 9. ISSN 0081-153X

**Society for the Study of Labour History**
c/o University of Sheffield, Department of
Extramural Studies, 85 Wilkinson St., Sheffield S10
2GS, Eng.
- Society for the Study of Labour History. Bulletin.
s-a. ISSN 0049-1179

**Society for the Study of Medical Ethics**
- Journal of Medical Ethics. (pub. by Professional
and Scientific Publications)

**Society for the Study of Welsh Labour History**
c/o Deian Hopkin, Editor, Department of History,
University College, Aberystwyth, Wales.
- Llafur. a.

**Society for Theatre Research**
77 Kinnerton St., London SW1X 8ED, Eng.
- Theatre Notebook; quarterly journal of the history
and technique of the British theatre. 3 per yr.
ISSN 0040-5523

**Society for Underwater Technology**
1 Birdcage Walk, London SW1H 9JJ, England.
- Society for Underwater Technology. Journal. q.

**Society of Analytical Psychology**
30 Devonshire Place, London W.1, Eng.
- Journal of Analytical Psychology. 4 per yr. ISSN
0021-8774

**Society of Antiquaries of London**
Burlington House, London W1V OHS, England.
- Antiquaries Journal. (pub. by Oxford University
Press)
- Archaeologia. biennial.

**Society of Antiquaries of Scotland**
National Museum of Antiquities of Scotland, Queen
Street, Edinburgh, Scotland.
- Society of Antiquaries of Scotland. Proceedings. a.
ISSN 0081-1564

**Society of Archer-Antiquaries**
c/o D. Elmy, 61, Lambert Road, Bridlington,
Yorkshire, England.
- Society of Archer-Antiquaries. Journal. a. ISSN
0560-6152
- Society of Archer-Antiquaries. Newsletter. 2-3 per
yr. ISSN 0049-1187

**Society of Architectural Historians of Great Britain**
8 Belmount Avenue, Melton Park, Newcastle upon
Tyne NE3 5QD, England.
- Architectural History; journal of the Society of
Architectural Historians of Great Britain. a. ISSN
0066-622X
- Society of Architectural Historians of Great
Britain Newsletter. s-a.

**Society of Archivists**
County Record Office, County Hall, Cumbran,
Gwent NP4 2XH, U.K.
- Society of Archivists. Journal. s-a. ISSN 0037-
9816

**Society of Assistants Teaching in Preparatory Schools**
Kilvington, Ringley Ave., Horley, Surrey RH6 7EZ,
England.
- S A T I P S News and Views. 3 per yr.

**Society of Authors**
84 Drayton Gardens, London SW10 9SD, Eng.
- Author. q. ISSN 0005-0628

**Society of Border Leicester Sheep Breeders**
24 Beresford Terrace, Ayr KA7 2eL, Scotland.
- Border Leicester Flock Book. a.

**Society of British Aerospace Companies Ltd.**
29 King St. St. James's, London, SW1Y 6RD,
England.
- Farnborough Air Show (Public Programme)
biennial. ISSN 0071-402X

**Society of Cable Television Engineers**
10 Avenue Rd., Dorridge, Solihull, West Midlands
B93 8LD, Eng.
- Cable Television Engineering. 3 per yr. ISSN
0308-4213

**Society of Chemical Industry**
14 Belgrave Sq., London SW1X 8PS, Eng.
- Chemistry and Industry. s-m. ISSN 0009-3068
- Chemistry and Industry Buyers' Guide. a. ISSN
0069-312X
- Journal of Applied Chemistry and Biotechnology.
(pub. by Blackwell Scientific Publications Ltd.)

- Journal of the Science of Food and Agriculture.
(pub. by Blackwell Scientific Publications Ltd.)
- Pesticide Science. (pub. by Blackwell Scientific
Publications Ltd.)
- Society of Chemical Industry. Bulletin.

**Society of Chiropodists**
8 Wimpole St., London W1M 8BX, Eng.
- Chiropodist. m. ISSN 0009-4706

**Society of Civil and Public Servants**
124-126 Southwark St., London SE1 OTU, Eng.
- Opinion. m.

**Society of Commercial Teachers Ltd.**
Falkland Cottage, Mottram St. Andrew, Nr.
Macclesfield, Cheshire, Eng.
- Commercial Teacher. q. ISSN 0010-311X

**Society of Community Medicine**
- Public Health. (pub. by Academic Press Inc.
(London) Ltd.)

**Society of Dairy Technology**
172A Ealing Rd., Wembley, Middlesex HA0 4QD,
England.
- Society of Dairy Technology. Journal. q. ISSN
0037-9840

**Society of Dyers and Colourists**
Box 244, Perkin House, Grattan Rd., Bradford,
Yorkshire BD1 2JB, Eng.
- Society of Dyers and Colourists. Journal. m. ISSN
0037-9859

**Society of Electronic and Radio Technicians**
Faraday House, 8-10 Charing Cross Rd., London
WC2H OHP, Eng.
- S. E. R. T. Journal. m. ISSN 0013-4805

**Society of Engineers**
21-23 Mossop St., London SW3 2LW, England.
- Society of Engineers. Journal and Transactions. q.
ISSN 0037-9867

**Society of Environmental Engineers**
4 Harmsworth Way, London N20 8JU, England.
- Society of Environmental Engineers. Journal. q.

**Society of Film & Television Arts Ltd.**
195 Piccadilly, London W1V 9LG, Eng.
- Society of Film & Television Arts. Journal. q.
ISSN 0037-9883

**Society of Genealogists**
37 Harrington Gardens, London SW7 4JX, Eng.
- Genealogists' Magazine. q. ISSN 0016-6391

**Society of Glass Technology**
Thornton, 20 Hallam Gate Rd., Sheffield S10 5BT,
Eng.
- Glass Technology. bi-m. ISSN 0017-1050
- Physics and Chemistry of Glasses. bi-m. ISSN
0031-9090

**Society of Indexers**
c/o Barclays Bank, 1 Pall Mall E., London SW1Y
5AX, England.
- Indexer. s-a. ISSN 0019-4131 (Co-Sponsor:
American Society of Indexers)

**Society of Industrial Artists & Designers**
12 Carlton House Terrace, London SW1Y 5AH,
England
(Dist. in U.S. by: New York Graphic Society, 140
Greenwich Ave., Greenwich, CT 06830)
- Designer. m. ISSN 0011-9423
- Designers in Britain. irreg., 1972, vol. 7. ISSN
0084-974X

**Society of Investment Analysts**
211-213 High St., Bromley, Kent BR1 1NY, Eng.
- Investment Analyst. 3 per yr. ISSN 0021-0048

**Society of Jesus. English Province**
114 Mount St., London W1Y 6AH, Eng.
- Month. m. ISSN 0027-0172

**Society of Leather Technologists and Chemists**
52 Crouch Hall Lane, Redbourn, Herts AL3 7EU,
Eng.
- Society of Leather Technologists and Chemists.
Journal. bi-m.

**Society of Licensed Aircraft Engineers and
Technologists**
Grey Tiles, Kingston Hill, Kingston Upon Thames,
Eng.
- Tech Air. m. ISSN 0040-0831

**Society of Lithographic Artists, Designers, Engravers
& Process Workers**
SLADE House, 55 Clapham Common South Side,
London, SW4 9DF, Eng.
- S L A D E Journal. q.

**Society of Master Saddlers**
9 St Thomas Street, London S.E.1, England.
- Master Saddlers Yearbook. a.

**Society of Motor Manufacturers and Traders Ltd.**
Forbes House, Halkin St., London, SW1X 7DS,
England.
- Motor Industry of Great Britain. a. ISSN 0077-
1597

**Society of Occupational Medicine**
- Society of Occupational Medicine. Journal. (pub.
by John Wright & Sons Ltd.)

**Society of Painters in Tempera**
28 Eldon Rd, London W.8, England.
- Tempera; year-book of painters in tempera. a.

**Society of Public Teachers of Law**
- Society of Public Teachers of Law. Journal. (pub.
by Butterworth & Co. (Publishers) Ltd.)

**Society of Radiographers**
- Radiography. (pub. by College of Radiographers)

**Society of Registration Officers**
82 West Ham Lane, Strasford E15 4PT, England.
- Unity. q.

**Society of Remedial Gymnasts**
- Remedial Gymnastics and Recreational Therapy.
(pub. by R. A. Slinn Ltd.)

**Society of St. Gregory**
Addington Place, Croydon CR9 5AD, England.
- Music and Liturgy. q.

**Society of St. John Chrysostom**
Marian House, Holden Ave., London N12 8HY,
Eng.
- Chrysostom. 3 per yr.

**Society of Shipping Executives**
Alderman House, 37 Soho Square, London W.1,
Eng.
- Shipping Executive. q. ISSN 0037-3907

**Society of Teachers of Speech and Drama**
211b Old Dover Rd., Canterbury, England.
- Speech and Drama. 3 per yr. ISSN 0038-7142

**Society of University Cartographers**
Dept. of Geography, Portsmouth Polytechnic,
Portsmouth PO1 3HE, Eng.
- S U C Bulletin. s-a. ISSN 0036-1984

**Society of Vertebrate Paleontology**
- Bibliography of Vertebrate Paleontology. (pub. by
Geosystems)

**Society of Women Writers and Journalists**
45, Basildon Court Devonshire St., London W1N
1RH, Eng.
- Woman Journalist. q. ISSN 0043-731X

**Society Publications Ltd.**
7 W. Halkin St., Belgrave Sq., London S.W.1, Eng.
- Photo Typesetting; and computer-aided
typesetting. m. ISSN 0031-8639

**Sociological Analysis & Theory**
c/o Dr. A. Lahey, University of Sheffield, Sheffield
210 2TN, England.
- Sociological Analysis & Theory; a discussion
journal of research & ideas. q. ISSN 0306-2481

**Soil Association**
Walnut Tree Manor, Haughley, Stowmarket,
Suffolk, Eng.
- Soil Association. Quarterly Review. q.

**Sol Quarterly**
25 First Avenue, Westcliff-on-Sea, Essex SS0 8HS,
England.
- Sol Quarterly. q.

**Solent Cruising & Racing Association**
- Solent Yearbook. (pub. by Isle of Wight County Press Ltd.)

**Solicitors' Law Stationery Society Ltd.**
11-13 Norwich St., London EC4B 1AB, England.
- Solicitors' Journal. w. ISSN 0038-1047

**Solon**
c/o Sir Anthony Meyer, Garden House, Sunningdale, Berkshire, Eng.
- Solon; a right wing journal. q. ISSN 0038-1187

**Solstice**
21A Silver St., Cambridge, Eng.
- Solstice. q. ISSN 0038-1225

**Solway Publications**
4 Buccleuch St., Dumfries, Scotland.
- World Stamps. m. ISSN 0043-9061

**Somerset and Dorset Notes and Queries**
L. C. Hayward, Treasurer, 226 Goldcroft, Yeovil, Somerset, Eng.
- Somerset and Dorset Notes and Queries. 2 per yr. ISSN 0049-1306

**Somerset Archaeological & Natural History Society**
Taunton Castle, Taunton, England.
- Somerset Archaeology and Natural History. a. ISSN 0081-2056

**Somerset Ornithological Society**
Barnfield, Tower Hill Rd., Crewkerne, Somerset, England.
- Somerset Birds. a. ISSN 0081-2048

**Sonostrips Ltd.**
498 Station Rd., Edgware, Middlesex MA 7hX, Eng.
- Ad. q. ISSN 0001-7892 (Shell-Mex. and B.P. Ltd)

**Sorby Natural History Society**
17 Winchester Ave., Sheffield S10 4EA, Eng.
- Sorby Natural History Society Newsletter. m. ISSN 0038-1551

**Sounding Brass Ltd.**
The Old House, London End, Beaconsfield, England.
- Sounding Brass; the conductor. q. ISSN 0308-5554

**South African Communist Party**
- African Communist. (pub. by Inkululeko Publications)

**South American Missionary Society**
Allen Gardiner House, Pembury Rd., Tunbridge Wells, Kent TN2 3QU, England.
- Share. 3 per yr.

**South Asia Church Aid Association**
2 Eaton Gate, London SW1W 9BL, England.
- South Asia Church Aid Association. Annual. a.

**South London Field Studies Society**
11 Clive Court, Babington Rd., London S.W.16, England.
- South London Field Studies Society. Journal. a. ISSN 0081-2803

**South Place Ethical Society**
Conway Hall Humanist Centre, Red Lion Sq., London W. C. 1, Eng.
- Ethical Record. m.(except *aug. & Nov.) ISSN 0014-1690

**South Staffordshire Archaeological and Historical Society**
58 Wednesbury Rd., Walsall, Staffs. WS1 3RS, England.
- South Staffordshire Archaeological and Historical Society. Transactions. a. ISSN 0457-7817

**South Street Publications**
3 South St., Sherborne, Dorset, Eng.
- Aplomb Zero. 5 per yr. ISSN 0003-651X

**South Wales and Monmouthshire Master Printers' Alliance**
67 Queen St., Cardiff, Wales, U.K.
- Impressions. 3 per yr. ISSN 0019-3011

**South Wales Institute of Engineers**
Park Place, Cardiff, Wales, U.K.
- South Wales Institute of Engineers. Proceedings. a. ISSN 0038-3570

**South East Asia Library Group**
c/o University of Hull, Brynmor Jones Library, Yorkshire HU6 7RX, England.
- South East Asia Library Group Newsletter. irreg. (approx. 2 per yr.)

**South East Hampshire Genealogical Society**
21 Lodge Ave., East Cosham, Portsmouth PO6 2JR, England.
- Family History Journal. q (approx.)

**South East Peace Newsletter**
21 Princess Margaret Ave., Margate, Kent CT9 3EQ, England.
- South East Peace Newsletter. bi-m.

**South Eastern Magazines Ltd.**
109 Week St., Maidstone, Kent, England.
- Kent Life. m. ISSN 0023-0030
- Sussex Life. m. ISSN 0039-6397

**Southend Chamber of Trade**
845 London Rd., Westcliff-On-Sea, Essex, Eng.
- Southend-on-Sea & District Chamber of Trade, Commerce & Industry. Monthly Journal. m.

**Southern Arts Association**
- Hampshire Poets. (pub. by Farleys (Fareham) Ltd)

**Southern Electric Group**
6A Purley Parade, High St., Purley, Surrey CR2 2AB, Eng.
- Live Rail. bi-m.

**Southern Publishing Co.**
Robert St., Brighton, Sussex, Eng.
- Chichester News. m. ISSN 0009-3785 (Chichester Diocese)

**South West Arts**
23 Southernhay East, Exeter, Devon, England.
- S W; events in the arts in the South West. bi-m.

**South West Scotland Grassland Society**
Auchincruive, Ayr, Scotland.
- Greensward. a. ISSN 0017-4092

**Souvenir Press Ltd.**
95 Mortimer St., London W.1, England.
- International Football Book. a. ISSN 0074-610X

**Soviet Embassy in London**
Press Dept., 3 Rosary Gardens, London SW7 4NW, Eng.
- Soviet News. w. ISSN 0038-5603
- Soviet Weekly. w. ISSN 0038-5905

**Spanish Chamber of Commerce in Great Britain**
5 Cavendish Square, London W.1., Eng.
- Comercio Hispano Britanico. 6 per yr. ISSN 0010-2326

**Spare Ribs Ltd.**
27 Clerkenwell Close, London EC1R 0AT, England (Subscr. Address: Linda Phillips, 114 George St., Berkhamstead, Herts HP4 2EJ, Eng.)
- Spare Rib. m.

**Robert Spark, Ed. & Pub.**
Evelyn Way, Cobham, Surrey KT11 2SJ, Eng.
- European Railways. q. ISSN 0014-3073

**Spastics International Medical Publications**
5A Netherhall Gardens, London NW3 5RN, England
(Dist. in U.S. by: J.B. Lippincott Co., E. Washington Square, Philadelphia, PA 19105)
- Bibliography of Developmental Medicine and Child Neurology. Books and Articles Received. a. ISSN 0067-7183
- Clinics in Developmental Medicine. irreg.(approx. 4 per year) ISSN 0069-4835
- Developmental Medicine and Child Neurology. bi-m. ISSN 0012-1622 (Spastics Society)

**Spastics Society**
12 Park Crescent, London, W1N 4EQ, Eng.
- Developmental Medicine and Child Neurology. (pub. by Spastics International Medical Publications)
- Spastics News. m. ISSN 0049-1810

**Spearhead Publications**
55-59 Fife Rd., Kingston Upon Thames, Surrey KT1 1TA, England.
- Offshore Services. m.

**Specialized Publications Ltd.**
5 Grove Rd., Surbiton, Surrey, Eng.
- Confectionery Production. m. ISSN 0010-5473

**Spectator Ltd.**
99 Gower St., London WC1E GAE, Eng.
- Spectator. w. ISSN 0038-6952

**Speed and Sports Publications Ltd.**
Acorn House, Victoria Rd., Acton, London. W.3, Eng.
- Automobile Connoisseur. q. ISSN 0045-1061

**Spicebox Books, Ltd.**
37 Soho Square, London W.1., England.
- Zigzag. m.

**Spin Publications**
24 Beresford Rd, Wallasey, Cheshire, Eng.
- Spin; the folksong magazine. q. ISSN 0038-7533

**Spink & Son Ltd.**
5 King St., St. James's, London S.W. 1, Eng.
- Numismatic Circular. m. ISSN 0029-6023

**Spirit**
303 Portobello Rd., London W.10, Eng.
- Spirit. bi-m.

**Spokesman Books, Etc.**
Betrand Russell House, Gamble St., Nottingham, England.
- Trade Union Register. irreg.

**E. & F. N. Spon Ltd.**
11 New Fetter Lane, London EC4P 4EE, England.
- Recreation Management Yearbook. biennial. ISSN 0306-3062
- Spon's Architects' & Builders' Price Book. a. ISSN 0306-3046
- Spon's Landscape Handbook. biennial. ISSN 0306-3054
- Spon's Mechanical & Electrical Services Price Book. a. ISSN 0305-4543

**Sporting Chronicle Publications Ltd.**
Thomson House, Withy Grove, Manchester M60 4BJ, England.
- Raceform up-to-Date Form Book Annual. a. ISSN 0081-377X
- Sporting Chronicle "Horses in Training". a. ISSN 0081-3761

**Sports Council**
70 Brompton Rd., London, SW3 1EX, Eng.
- Sport and Recreation. q. ISSN 0038-7819
- Sports Development Bulletin. q.

**Spotlight Publications Ltd.**
Spotlight House, One Benwell Rd., London N7 7AX, England.
- Hi-Fi Weekly; and record review. w.
- Sounds. w.

**Spry Publications, Ltd.**
119 Ewell Rd., Surbiton, Surrey, Eng.
- Mayfair. m. ISSN 0025-6161

**Spurgeon's Homes**
Park Rd., Birchington, Kent, Eng.
- Within Our Gates. 3 per yr. ISSN 0043-6992

**Squash Rackets Association**
70 Brompton Rd., London SW3 1DX, England.
- Squash Rackets Association. Handbook. a. ISSN 0081-3885

**Stacey Publications**
1 Hawthorndene Rd., Hayes, Bromley, Kent, Eng.
- Amateur Stage. m. ISSN 0002-6867
- Creative Drama. s-a. ISSN 0011-0892 (Educational Drama Association)
- London Drama. s-a.
- Plays. A Classified Guide to Play Selection. a. ISSN 0554-3045
- Theatre Directory. biennial.

**Staffordshire Development Association**
- Staffordshire Guide Industry and Commerce. (pub. by G.W. Foster Associates Ltd.)

**Stainer and Bell Ltd.**
82 High Rd., London N2 9PW, England.
- Musica Britannica; a national collection of music. irreg. ISSN 0580-2954 (Royal Musical Association)

**Stamp Collecting Ltd.**
42 Maiden Lane, London WC2E 7LL, Eng.
- Stamp Collecting. w. ISSN 0038-9269

**Stanborough Press Ltd.**
Alma Park, Grantham, Lincs NG31 9SL, Eng.
- British Advent Messenger. fortn. ISSN 0045-2874
  (British Union Conference of Seventh-Day
  Adventists)
- Life and Health; a family magazine promoting a
  lifestyle of total health within the balance of the
  mental, physical and spiritual dimensions. irreg.
  (Seventh-Day Adventist Church in Britain)

**Stand Magazine**
19 Haldane Terr., Newcastle Upon Tyne NE2 3AN,
Eng.
- Stand. q. ISSN 0038-9366

**Standard Catalogue Co. Ltd.**
26 Bloomsbury Way, London, WC1A 2SS, England.
- Architects Standard Catalogues. a. ISSN 0066-
  6181
- Architectural Design. m. ISSN 0003-8504
- British Building Products Catalogue; A catalogue
  of British building products available to architects
  overseas. a. ISSN 0084-8026
- Foundry Directory and Register of Forges.
  biennial. ISSN 0071-8130

**Standard Chartered Bank Ltd.**
10 Clements Lane, London E.C.4, Eng.
- Standard and Chartered Review. m.

**Standbrook Publications Ltd.**
Elm House, 10-16 Elm St., London WC1X 0BP,
England.
- Family Circle. m.
- Living. m. ISSN 0024-5224

**Standing Conference for Local History**
- Local Historian. (pub. by National Council of
  Social Service, Inc.)

**Standing Conference of Co-Operative Library and
Information Services**
c/o Angela Allott, Ed., Sheffield City Libraries,
Surrey SI 1XZ, England.
- S. C. O. C. L. I. S. News. 3 per yr. ISSN 0307-
  6903

**Standing Conference on National and University
Libraries. Subcommittee on Slavonic and East
European Materials**
c/o J. Freeman, School of Slavonic & East
European Studies, University of London, Malet St.,
London WC1E 7HU, England.
- Solanus. a. ISSN 0038-0903

**Stanley Gibbons Publications Ltd.**
391 Strand, London WC2R OLX, England.
- British Commonwealth Stamp Catalogue. a. ISSN
  0068-1903
- Collect British Stamps. s-a. ISSN 0069-5262
- Elizabethan Stamp Catalogue. a. ISSN 0071-0024
- Flora. q.
- Great Britain Specialised Stamp Catalogue. irreg.
  ISSN 0072-7229
- Stamp Monthly. m. ISSN 0016-9676
- Stamps of the World. a. ISSN 0081-4210

**Stanley Tools Ltd.**
Woodside, Sheffield, England.
- Craft Education. 3 per yr.

**Staples & Staples Ltd.**
94 Wigmore St., London W.1, Eng.
- Journal of Tropical Medicine and Hygiene;
  devoted to medical, surgical and sanitary work in
  warm countries. m. ISSN 0022-5304

**Star and Garter Home for Disabled Sailors Soldiers
and Airmen**
Richmond Upon Thames, Surrey, Eng.
- Star and Garter Magazine. q. ISSN 0038-9846

**Star Research (Publications) Society**
34 Oxford Garden, Chiswick, London W.4,
England.
- Opus. irreg.

**Stardance**
c/o Marek Urbanowicz, Ed., 49 Sheen Park,
Richmond, Surrey, England.
- Stardance. a.

**Stardock**
5 St. Johns Wood Terrace, St. Johns Wood, London
N.W.8, Eng.
- Stardock. 4 per yr approx. ISSN 0038-9919

**Starfish Books Ltd.**
Starfish House, Brook Farm Rd., Cobham, Surrey
KT11 3AY, England.
- Bed, Breakfast and Evening Meal. a. ISSN 0084-
  7755
- Farm & Country Holidays. a.
- Holidays in the Sun, Devon, Cornwall, Somerset
  and Dorset. a.
- Self Catering Holidays. a. ISSN 0080-8679
- Starfish Book of Farm and Country Holidays. a.
  ISSN 0081-4385

**Statesman & Nation Publishing Co.**
10 Great Turnstile, London WC1V 7HJ, Eng.
- New Statesman; an independent political and
  literary review. w. ISSN 0028-6842

**Statistical Record**
59 High St., Ascot, Berkshire, England.
- General Stud Book. Supplement. a. ISSN 0072-
  078X

**Stedfast Publishers**
23 Western Rd., Bletchley, Milton Keynes, Bucks
MK2 2PS, England.
- Junior Stedfast Magazine. m. (Boys' Brigade, Inc.)
- Stedfast Magazine. m. ISSN 0039-0887 (Boys'
  Brigade, Inc.)

**Steel Castings Research and Trade Association**
East Bank Rd., Sheffield S2.3PT, Eng.
- Steel Castings Abstracts. bi-m. ISSN 0039-0909

**Steel Industry Management Association**
Rigby House, 34 The Parade, Watford, Herts WD1
7EA, England.
- Challenge. q.

**Steering Wheel Publications Ltd.**
Imperial Buildings, Kingsway, London W.C. 2, Eng.
- Steering Wheel & Taxi Trader. bi-w. (National
  Federation of Taxicab Associations)

**Rudolf Steiner Press**
35 Park Rd., London NW1 6XT, England.
- Golden Blade. a. (Anthroposophical Society in
  Great Britain)

**Steiner Schools Fellowship**
White Heather, Dale Road, Forest Row, Sussex,
England.
- Child and Man; a journal for contemporary
  education. s-a. ISSN 0009-3890

**Stephenson Locomotive Society**
49, Acfold Rd., Handsworth Wood, Birmingham
B20 1HG, Eng.
- Stephenson Locomotive Society Journal. m. ISSN
  0039-1190

**William Stevens Publications Ltd.**
55 Conduit St., London W.1, Eng.
- This Is London; what, where, and when for the
  visitor. w. ISSN 0040-6198

**Stilt Press**
c/o Alan & Joan Tucker, The Bookshop, Stroud,
Gloucestershire, Eng.
- Format. irreg. ISSN 0015-7740

**Leslie Stinton & Partners**
39A London Rd., Kingston-Upon-Thames, Surrey
KT2 6ND, England.
- International Advertising Association. United
  Kingdom Chapter. Concise Guide to International
  Markets. irreg., latest edt. 1976. ISSN 0538-4168

**Stock Exchange Council, London**
- Stock Exchange, London. Stock Exchange Official
  Year Book. (pub. by Thomas Skinner Directories)

**Stock Market Analysts Ltd.**
58 High St., Esher, Surrey KT10 9QY, England.
- Investment Advisory Service. s-m.

**Stokes & Lindley-Jones Ltd**
Alverstoke House, 21 Montpelier Row, Blackheath,
London, S.E.3, Eng.
- Export Courier; product information for
  international buyers. 17 per yr. ISSN 0014-5122

**Stone & Cox (Publications) Ltd.**
44 Fleet St., London EC4Y 1BS, England
(Subscr. to: 73-75 Gammons Lane, Watford, Herts
WD2 5HU, England)
- Holiday Camps and Centres Directory. a.
- Holiday Chalets and Caravans Directory
  Magazine. a. ISSN 0073-2982
- Insurance Mail. m. ISSN 0020-4773
- Policy. m. ISSN 0032-2652
- Stone & Cox Ordinary Branch Life Assurance
  Tables. m.
- Stone & Cox Unit Linked Assurance & Annuity
  Tables. m.

**Stone Industrial Publications Ltd.**
54/55 Wilton Rd., London SW1V 1DE, England.
- Project South East. bi-w.

**Storage Handling Distribution**
886 High Road, Finchley, London N12 95B,
England.
- Storage Handling Distribution. Materials Handling
  Buyers' Guide. a.

**Storyville Publications & Co. Ltd.**
66 Fairview Drive, Chigwell, Essex 1G7 6HS, Eng.
- Storyville. bi-m. ISSN 0039-2030

**Strathkelvin Press Ltd.**
1 North Claremont St., Glasgow G3 7NR, Scotland.
- What's on in Glasgow. m. ISSN 0043-4655
- Yot; Scotland's yachting news. m.

**Street Research**
86 Railton Rd., London S.E. 24, England.
- Street Research Bulletin. m.

**Street Singer**
Ed. C. Wilson, 54 the Mall, Southgate, London
N.14., Eng.
- Street Singer. bi-m.

**Strode Publications (Holdings) Ltd.**
Map House, 243 Caledonian Rd., London N1 1ED,
England.
- Builder and Decorator. m.
- Decorating Contractor. m. ISSN 0011-7374

**Stuart Phillips Publications**
30 Ringstead Rd., Sutton, Surrey, Eng.
- British Journal of Geriatrics & Psychogeriatrics. q.
- Clinical Trials Journal. q. ISSN 0009-9325
- Orthopaedic Medicine Surgery. q. ISSN 0030-
  5855

**Stubbs Ltd.**
Snow House, 103-109 Southwark St., London SE1,
England.
- Stubbs Buyers' National Guide; professional and
  commercial products and services. a. ISSN 0081-
  6043

**Stud & Stable Ltd.**
59 High St., Ascot, Berkshire, England.
- Directory of the Turf. triennial. ISSN 0419-3806
- Stud & Stable. m. ISSN 0039-2626

**Studies Centre on Polish-German Affairs**
20 Princes Gate, London S.W.7, Eng.
- Poland and Germany (East & West) q. ISSN
  0032-2458

**Studies in Education Ltd.**
Nafferton, Driffield, N. Humberside, England
(and APS Publications, Inc., 150 Fifth Ave., New
York, NY 10011)
- British Journal of in-Service Education. 3 per yr.
  ISSN 0305-7631 (National Association of
  Teachers in Further and Higher Education)
- Education Three-Thirteen. s-a. ISSN 0300-4279
- Research Intelligence. 3 per yr. ISSN 0307-9023
  (British Educational Research Association)
- Studies in Design, Education and Craft. s-a. ISSN
  0305-7666

**Studio International Journal Ltd.**
14 W. Central St., London WC1A 1JH, Eng.
- Studio International. 6 per yr. ISSN 0039-4114

**Studio Vista**
(Subsidiary of: Cassell & Collier Macmillan
Publishers Ltd.)
35 Red Lion Square, London WC1, England
(Dist. in U.S. by: van Nostrand Reinhold Co., 450
W. 33rd St., New York, NY 10010)
- Decorative Art and Modern Interiors. a. ISSN
  0070-3206
- Modern Publicity. a. ISSN 0077-0108

**Studiorum Novi Testamenti Societas**
- New Testament Studies. (pub. by Cambridge University Press)

**Study Centre for Yugoslav Affairs**
4 Audley Square, S. Audley St., London N.1., England.
- Study Centre for Yugoslav Affairs. Review. a. ISSN 0585-7694

**Study Group on Eighteenth-Century Russia**
c/o Dr. A. G. Cross, School of European Studies, University of East Anglia, Norwich N0R 88C, England.
- Study Group on Eighteenth-Century Russia. Newsletter. a.

**Success Magazine**
17 Andrews Crescent, Peterborough PE4 6XL, England.
- Success; magazine for creative writers. q. ISSN 0049-2442

**Sudan United Mission**
75 Granville Rd., Sidcup, Kent, Eng.
- Lightbearer. bi-m. ISSN 0024-3396

**Sun Vale**
Burnley Rd., Luddendenfoot, Yorkshire, Eng.
- Platform; poetry magazine. q. ISSN 0032-1389

**Sunderland Polytechnic Students Union**
Wearmouth Hall, Chester Rd., Sunderland SR1 3SD, Eng.
- Dais. 12 per yr. ISSN 0011-5754

**Supreme Publishing Co. Ltd.**
200 Avenue Rd., London W.3, Eng.
- Race News. m. ISSN 0033-7285

**Surrey Archaeological Society**
Castle Arch, Guildford, Surrey GU1 3SX, England.
- Surrey Archaeological Collections. a.
- Surrey Archaeological Society. Bulletin. m.

**Sussex Archaeological Society**
Barbican House, Sussex, Sussex, Eng.
- Sussex Archaeological Society Newsletter. q.

**Sussex Family History Group**
4-33 Sussex Square, Brighton, Sussex BN2 5AB, England.
- Sussex Family Historian. q.

**Sussex Folk Diary**
c/o Vic Smith, 7 Stanmer Villas, Brighton, Sussex BN1 7HO, England.
- Sussex Folk Diary. bi-m.

**Sutton Courtenay Press**
Appleford, Abingdon, Oxford OX14 4PB, England.
- Courtenay Library of Reformation Classics. irreg., no. 5, 1977. ISSN 0070-1394
- Courtenay Reformation Facsimiles. irreg.
- Courtenay Studies in Reformation Theology. irreg., 1969, no. 2. ISSN 0070-1408

**Sutton-Siebert Publications Ltd.**
8 North St., Guildford, Surrey, Eng.
- Doctor. w. ISSN 0046-0451

**Swain & Co. Ltd.**
High St., Stockport, Cheshire, Eng.
- Alderley and Wilmslow and Knutsford Advertiser. w. ISSN 0002-5097

**Sweet & Maxwell Stevens Journals**
11 New Fetter Lane, London EC4 P4EE, Eng. (Dist. in U.S. & Canada by: Caswell Co. Ltd., 233 Midland Ave., Agincourt, Ont., Canada)
- British Journal of Criminology; delinquency and deviant social behaviour. q. ISSN 0007-0955 (Institute for the Study and Treatment of Delinquency)
- British Tax Review. bi-m. ISSN 0007-1870
- Conveyancer and Property Lawyer. bi-m. ISSN 0010-8200
- Criminal Appeal Reports. irreg. ISSN 0070-1521
- Criminal Law Review. m. ISSN 0011-135X
- Current Accounting Law & Practice. a.
- Current Law. m. ISSN 0011-362X
- Current Legal Problems. a. ISSN 0070-1998 (University College, London)
- European Law Review. 6 per yr.
- Industrial Law Journal. q.
- Journal of Business Law. q. ISSN 0021-9460

- Journal of Planning and Environment Law. m. ISSN 0307-4870
- Law Librarian. 3 per yr. ISSN 0023-9275
- Law List. a.
- Law Quarterly Review. q. ISSN 0023-933X
- Law Teacher. 3 per yr. ISSN 0306-9400 (Association of Law Teachers)
- Modern Law Review. 6 per yr. ISSN 0026-7961
- Nigerian Law Journal. a. ISSN 0078-0774
- Property and Compensation Reports. bi-m. ISSN 0033-1295
- Public Law; the Constitutional and Administrative Law of the Commonwealth. q. ISSN 0033-3565
- Supreme Court Practice. triennial. ISSN 0039-5978
- Yearbook of World Affairs. a. ISSN 0084-408X (London Institute of World Affairs) (Dist. in U.S. by: Praeger Publishers, Inc., 111 Fourth Ave., New York, NY 10003)

**Swift Fleet Ltd.**
19 Westbourne Road, London N7 8AN, England.
- Country Music Review. m.

**Swift Ltd**
1-7 Albion Place, St. John's Lane, London E.C.1, England.
- List and Index Society. Copies Unpublished Lists Etc in Public Record Office, London. 12 per yr.

**Swimming Teachers Association**
National Headquarters, No. 1 Birmingham Rd., West Bromwich, West Midlands, Eng.
- Swimming Teacher. m.

**Swimming Times Ltd.**
Haroud Fern House, Derby Square, Loughborough, Leic's LE11 OAL, Eng.
- Swimming Times. m. ISSN 0039-7423 (Amateur Swimming Association)

**Swinton Conservative College**
Masham, Nr. Ripon, Yorkshire, Eng.
- Swinton Journal. q. ISSN 0049-271X

**Swiss Observer Ltd.**
63/67 Tabernacle St., London E.C. 2, Eng.
- Swiss Observer; official organ of Swiss Colony in Great Britain. m. ISSN 0039-7482

**System Consulting Enterpreneurs**
- Computer Applications Newsletter. (pub. by Gordon and Breach Science Publishers Ltd.)

**Systems Publications Ltd.**
Bugle House, Noel St., London W.1, Eng., U.K.
- Systems & Communications. m. ISSN 0039-8020

**T. and T. Clark**
38 George St., Edinburgh EH2 2LQ, Scotland.
- Expository Times. m. ISSN 0014-5246

**Tablet Publishing Co.**
48 Great Peter St., London S.W. 1, Eng.
- Clergy Review. m. ISSN 0009-8736 (Catholic Church)
- Tablet. w. ISSN 0039-8837

**Tagus Poetry**
242 Ittley Rd., Oxford, Eng.
- Tagus. q. ISSN 0039-8950

**Tail-Waggers' Club (Gt. Britain) Ltd.**
Astral House, Wakering Rd., Barking, Essex, Eng.
- Tail-Wagger and Family Magazine. m. ISSN 0039-9027

**Talyllyn Railway Preservation Society**
Flat One, 25 Gwendolen Ave., London SW15 6ET, Eng.
- Talyllyn News. q. ISSN 0300-3272

**Tantivy Press**
136-148 Tooley St., London SE1 2TT, Eng (Dist. in U.S. by: A.S. Barnes & Co., Forsgate Drive, Cranbury, NJ 08512)
- Focus on Film. q. ISSN 0015-5128
- International Film Guide. a. ISSN 0074-6053

**Tavistock Institute of Human Relations**
- Human Relations. (pub. by Plenum Press US)

**Tavistock Publications Ltd.**
11 New Fetter La., London EC4P 4EE, England (Dist. in U.S. by: Adline-Atherton, Inc., 529 S. Wabash Ave., Chicago, IL 60605)
- International Bibliography of the Social Sciences. Economics. irreg., vol. 24, 1975. ISSN 0085-204X (Unesco UN)
- International Bibliography of the Social Sciences. Political Science. irreg., vol. 24, 1975. ISSN 0085-2058
- International Bibliography of the Social Sciences. Social and Cultural Anthropology. irreg., vol. 21, 1975. ISSN 0085-2074
- International Bibliography of the Social Sciences. Sociology. irreg., vol. 25, 1975. ISSN 0085-2066
- Mind and Medicine Monographs. irreg., 1973, no. 23. ISSN 0076-888X (Dist. in U.S. and Canada by: J.B. Lippincott Co., E. Washington Square, Philadelphia, PA 19105)

**Taxation Publishing Co. Ltd.**
98 Park St., London W1Y 4BR, Eng.
- Taxation; leading authority on the law practice and administration of direct taxation in the U. K. w. ISSN 0040-0149

**Taylor & Francis Ltd.**
10-14 Macklin St., London WC2B 5NF, Eng.
- Advances in Physics. bi-m. ISSN 0001-8732
- Annals of Human Biology. bi-m. ISSN 0301-4460 (Society for the Study of Human Biology)
- Annals of Science; a quarterly review of the history of science since the Renaissance. bi-m. ISSN 0003-3790
- Communications on Physics. irreg. ISSN 0306-9486
- Contemporary Physics; a review of Physics and associated techniques. bi-m. ISSN 0010-7514
- Ergonomics; human factors in work, machine control and equipment design. bi-m. ISSN 0014-0139
- Ergonomics Abstracts. q. ISSN 0046-2446 (Ergonomics Information Analysis Centre)
- History of Education. s-a. ISSN 0046-760X
- History of Photography; an international journal. q. ISSN 0308-7298
- International Conference on Production Research. Proceedings. a; 1973 Copenhagen.
- International Journal of Control; the theory of process control & automation. m. ISSN 0020-7179
- International Journal of Electronics; theoretical and experimental. m. ISSN 0020-7217
- International Journal of Mathematical Education in Science and Technology. q. ISSN 0020-739X
- International Journal of Production Research. bi-m. ISSN 0020-7543 (Co-Sponsors: Institution of Production Engineers; American Institute of Industrial Engineers; Society of Manufacturing Engineers)
- International Journal of Radiation Biology and Related Studies in Physics, Chemistry and Medicine. m.(2 vols.per yr.) ISSN 0020-7616
- International Journal of Systems Science. m. ISSN 0020-7721
- Journal of Curriculum Studies. s-a. ISSN 0022-0272
- Journal of Natural History; international journal of taxonomic and general biology. bi-m. ISSN 0022-2933
- Maritime Policy and Management. 6 per yr. ISSN 0308-8839
- Medical Informatics/Medicine et Informatique. q. ISSN 0307-7640
- Molecular Physics. m(2vols. per yr.) ISSN 0026-8976
- Optica Acta; international journal of optics. m. ISSN 0030-3909
- Philosophical Magazine; a journal of theoretical experimental and applied physics. m. ISSN 0031-8086
- Xenobiotica; the fate of foreign compounds in biological systems. m. ISSN 0049-8254

**Teakfield Ltd.**
1 Westmead, Farnborough, Hants GU14 7RU, England.
- European Financial Almanac. irreg. ISSN 0098-1265
- Personnel Review. q. ISSN 0048-3486 (Institute of Personnel Management)
- U K Chemical Industries Review. irreg.

**Technical Indexes Ltd.**
Easthampstead Rd., Bracknell, Berks RG12 1NS, England.
- British Archer; devoted to the fast growing sport of archery. 6 per yr. ISSN 0007-0289
- Chemical Engineering Index. s-a. ISSN 0308-8391

- Electronic Engineering Index. s-a. ISSN 0308-8375
- Engineering Components and Materials Index. s-a. ISSN 0308-8383
- Laboratory Equipment Index. a. ISSN 0308-8367
- Materials Handling Index. s-a. ISSN 0308-8359

**Technical Journals Ltd.**
32-36 Dudley Road, Tunbridge Wells, Kent TN1 1LH, England.
- Fire Engineers Journal. q. (Institution of Fire Engineers)

**Technicopy Ltd.**
66 High Street, Stonehouse, Glos. GL10 2NA, Eng.
- Soviet Non-Ferrous Metals Research. bi-m.

**Technitrade Journals Ltd.**
886 High Rd. Finchley, London N.12, England
- Heating and Ventilating Engineer and Journal of Air Conditioning. m. ISSN 0017-937X (Subscr. to:, Local Board Rd., Watford WD1 2JS, England)

**Teesside & District Chamber of Commerce & Industry**
Middlesbrough, Cleveland TS1 1DW, England.
- Tees-Side Journal of Commerce. m. ISSN 0040-2095

**Teilhard Centre for the Future of Man**
81 Cromwell Rd., London SW7 5BW, England.
- Teilhard Review. 3 per yr. ISSN 0040-2184

**Thomas Telford Ltd.**
Publications Division, 26-34 Old St., London EC1V 9AD, England.
- British National Committee on Large Dams. News and Views. a. ISSN 0525-4205 (Institution of Civil Engineers)
- British Nuclear Energy Society. Journal. q. ISSN 0007-1587 (Institution of Civil Engineers)
- Civil Engineering Technician. q. ISSN 0307-7713 (Institution of Civil Engineers)
- Geotechnique; international journal of soil mechanics. q. ISSN 0016-8505 (Institution of Civil Engineers)
- I.C.E. Abstracts. m (except Aug. & Dec.) ISSN 0305-2176 (Institution of Civil Engineers)
- Institution of Civil Engineers. Proceedings. Part 1: Design and Construction. q. ISSN 0307-8353
- Institution of Civil Engineers. Proceedings. Part 2: Research and Theory. q. ISSN 0307-8361
- New Civil Engineer. w. ISSN 0307-7683 (Institution of Civil Engineers)
- Offshore Engineer. m. ISSN 0305-876X (Institution of Civil Engineers)

**Temperance Council of Christian Churches**
4 Southampton Row, London WC1B 4AA, England.
- Fact Finder. s. ISSN 0425-5860
- Focus on Drink and Gambling. a. ISSN 0071-6308

**Temprint Press Ltd.**
886 High Rd., Finchley, London N12 9SB, Eng.
- Materials Handling and Management. q. ISSN 0025-5335 (Institute of Materials Handling)

**Tennyson Society**
Tennyson Research Centre, Central Library, Free School Lane, Lincoln, England.
- Tennyson Research Bulletin. a. ISSN 0082-2841
- Tennyson Society, Lincoln, England. Monographs. irreg., no. 7, 1975. ISSN 0082-285X
- Tennyson Society, Lincoln, England. Occasional Papers. irreg.
- Tennyson Society, Lincoln, England. Report. a. ISSN 0082-2868

**Tensor Society of Great Britain**
c/o Imperial College of Science & Technology, Lyon Playfair Library, South Kensington, London SW7 2AZ, England.
- Matrix and Tensor Quarterly. q. ISSN 0025-5998

**Terry Art Ltd.**
19a Air St., London W.1, Eng
(and 643 Yonge St., Toronto 5, Ont., Canada)
- Know Britain. q. ISSN 0023-2440

**Olive Rhodes Teugels, Ed. & Pub.**
6 Clapham Mansions, Nightingale Lane, London SW4 9AQ, England.
- Bedsitter. s-a. ISSN 0005-7673

**Textile Business Press Ltd.**
Statham House, Talbot Rd., Stretford, Manchester, M32 OEP, England
(U.S. address: 205 E. 42nd St., New York, NY 10017)
- Index to Textile Auxiliaries. biennial. ISSN 0073-604X
- International Dyer, Textile Printer, Bleacher and Finisher. s-m. ISSN 0020-658X
- International Textile Machinery. a. ISSN 0074-9087
- Textile Month. m. ISSN 0040-5116
- Tufting Year Book. a. ISSN 0082-674X
- Wool Record & Textile World. fortn. ISSN 0043-7832

**Textile Institute**
10 Blackfriars St., Manchester M3 5DR, Eng.
- Textile Institute. Journal. m. ISSN 0040-5000
- Textile Institute and Industry. m. ISSN 0039-8357
- Textile Institute, Manchester Annual Conference. Papers. a.
- Textile Progress; a critical appreciation of recent developments. q. ISSN 0040-5167

**Textile Mercury Ltd.**
1 Ford Lane, Salford 6, Lancs., Eng.
- Knitting World & Textile Manufacturer. m. ISSN 0307-2517

**Textile Trade Publications Ltd.**
Knightway House, 20 Soho Square, London W.I., Eng.
- British Clothing Manufacturer. m. ISSN 0007-0467
- Drapers' Record. w. ISSN 0012-6020
- Men's Wear. w. ISSN 0025-9519

**Theatre Nights**
3 Goodwin's Court, St. Martin's Lane, London WC2N 4LL, Eng.
- Theatre Nights. bi-m.

**Theatre Organ Review**
127 Stratford St., Leeds LS11 6JG, Yorkshire, Eng
(U.S. subscr. address: Bobby Clark, 939 Green St., Orangeburg, SC 29115)
- Theatre Organ Review. q. ISSN 0040-5558

**Theological Abstracting and Bibliographical Services**
33 Mayfield Grove, Harrogate, North Yorkshire HG1 5HD, England.
- Theological and Religious Index. irreg. ISSN 0306-087X

**Theoretical Chemical Engineering Abstracts**
Box 146, Liverpool L69 2BL, Eng.
- Theoretical Chemical Engineering Abstracts. bi-m. ISSN 0040-5787

**Theosophical Publishing House Ltd.**
68 Great Russell St., London WC1B 3BU, England
(and Box 270, Wheaton, IL 60187)
- Blavatsky Lecture. irreg. ISSN 0067-916X

**Theosophical Society in England**
Astrological Lodge, 50 Gloucester Place, London W.1, Eng.
- Astrology; the astrologer's quarterly. q. ISSN 0004-6183
- Theosophical Journal. bi-m. ISSN 0040-5876

**Thimble Press**
Lockwood, Station Rd., South Woodchester, Nr. Stroud, Glos. GL5 5EQ, England.
- Signal; approaches to children's books. 3 per yr. ISSN 0037-4954
- Young Drama. 3 per yr. ISSN 0307-0395

**Third World Reports**
52 Uplands Rd., London N.8, Eng.
- Third World Reports. m. ISSN 0049-3740

**Thirteen Twenty Club**
Tigh an Uillt, Wilton Dean by Hawick, County Roxburgh, Scotland.
- Catalyst for the Scottish Viewpoint. q. ISSN 0045-5962

**Thirty Press Limited**
19 Draycott Place, London SW3 2SJ, Eng.
- Crusade. m. ISSN 0011-2127
- Thirdway. fortn. ISSN 0309-3492

**This England Ltd.**
Box 52, Cheltenham, Gloucestershire, Eng.
- This England. q. ISSN 0040-6171

**Thomas Paine Society**
443 Meadow Lane, Nottingham, Eng.
- T. P. S. Bulletin. s-a. ISSN 0049-3813

**H. I. Thompson Press Ltd.**
2 Ellis St., Sloane St., London SW1X 9AN, Eng., U.K.
- Garage Management. m.
- Good Motoring. m. ISSN 0017-2111 (Company of Veteran Motorists)

**D. C. Thomson & Co. Ltd.**
185 Fleet St., London EC4 2HS, England.
- Annabel; the magazine women really enjoy. m. ISSN 0003-3758
- Bunty. w.
- Commando; war stories in pictures. 84 per yr. ISSN 0010-2490
- Hornet. w.
- Hotspur. w. ISSN 0018-635X
- Judy. w. ISSN 0022-5851
- Judy Book. a.
- Mandy. w.
- Red Star Weekly. w. ISSN 0034-2068
- Scots Magazine. m. ISSN 0048-9751

**Stuart Thomson Ltd.**
1 Tahoma Lodge, Lubbock Rd., Chislehurst, Kent, Eng.
- Selling. m. ISSN 0037-1599

**Thomson Publications Ltd.**
Elm House, 10-16 Elm St., London WC1X 0BP, Eng.
- Construction News. w. ISSN 0010-6860
- Illustrated London News. m. ISSN 0019-2422

**Thoresby Society**
Claremont, Leeds LS2 9NZ, Leeds L52 29NZ, England.
- Thoresby Society, Leeds, England. Publications. a. ISSN 0082-4232

**Thoroton Society of Nottinghamshire**
Whip Ridding, Kirklington, Newark, Notts., England.
- Thoroton Society of Nottinghamshire. Transactions. a.

**Thoroughbred Publishers Ltd.**
26 Charing Cross Road, London WC2, England.
- Bloodstock Breeders' Review. a. ISSN 0067-9224
- Stallion Review. a.

**Throgmorton Publications Ltd.**
30 Finsbury Square, London E.C.2, Eng.
- Investors Chronicle and Stock Exchange Gazette. w. ISSN 0021-0161
- Statistical World Banking Survey. a.

**Arthur H. Thrower Ltd.**
44 S. Ealing Rd., Ealing, London W.5, Eng.
- Diplomatic Bookshelf & Review. m.
- Liberian Shipping Bulletin and Trading Review. m. ISSN 0024-2136

**Thunderbird Enterprises Ltd.**
102 College Rd., Harrow, Middlesex, Eng.
- Effluent and Water Treatment Journal. m. ISSN 0013-2217

**Timber Growers' Organisation Ltd.**
National Agricultural Centre, Kenilworth, Warwickshire, Eng.
- Timber Grower. q. ISSN 0040-7763

**Time & Tide Ltd.**
13 New Bridge Street, London EC4, England.
- Business World. w.
- Time and Tide; independent monthly. w. ISSN 0040-7828

**Time Machine**
82-90 Seymour Place, London W.1, Eng.
- Time Machine; magazine devoted to literature and the arts. q. ISSN 0040-7852

**Time Out Ltd.**
374 Grays Inn Rd., London WC1X 8BB, Eng.
- Time Out; the living guide to all London's events plus news & reviews. w. ISSN 0049-3910

**Times Newspapers Ltd.**
Box No. 7, New Printing House Square, Gray's Inn Rd., London WC1X 8EZ, England.
- Times Educational Supplement. w. ISSN 0040-7887

- Times Guide to the House of Commons; complete survey of Parliament after a General Election. irreg. ISSN 0082-4399
- Times Higher Education Supplement. w. ISSN 0049-3929
- Times Literary Supplement. w. ISSN 0040-7895
- Times 1000; lists leading companies in Britain and Overseas. a. ISSN 0082-4429

**Tin Publications Ltd.**
7 High Rd, London W4 2NE, Eng.
- Tin International. m. ISSN 0040-795X

**Tobacco Research Council**
Glen House, Stag Place, London S.W.1, England.
- Tobacco Research Council. Research Papers. irreg. ISSN 0082-4607
- Tobacco Research Council. Review of Activities. irreg. ISSN 0082-4615

**Toc H,**
1 Forest Close, Wendover, Aylesbury, Bucks HP22 6BT, England.
- Point Three. m. ISSN 0032-2326

**Tofts and Woolf (Publishers) Ltd.**
64a Lansdowne Road, South Woodford, E18 2BD, England.
- Music Trade Directory. biennial. ISSN 0077-2453

**Tolkien Society**
c/o J. Kemball-Cook, 110 Breakspears Rd., London SE4 1UD, England.
- Amon Hen. bi-m. ISSN 0306-8781
- Mallorn. s-a. ISSN 0308-6674

**Tolley Publishing Co.**
(Subsidiary of: Benn Bros. Ltd.)
44a High St., Croydon CR9 1UU, England.
- Tolley's Corporation Tax. a.
- Tolley's Income Tax. a. ISSN 0305-8921
- Tolley's Tax Tables. a.

**Tolpolski's Chronicle**
Bridge Arch, 158 Sutton Walk, London S.E.1, Eng.
- Tolpolski's Chronicle. 24 per yr. ISSN 0040-9103

**Tom Chalmers Enterprises Ltd.**
88/89 High St., Winchester, Hampshire, England.
- Defence Africa. q.

**Top Sellers Ltd.**
283-289 Cricklewood Broadway, London NW2 6NX, England.
- Flirt N Skirt. q.
- Game. m.
- Look "N" Cook. m. ISSN 0024-6395

**Torc**
3 Jacobs Close, Windmill Hill, Glastonbury, Soms. TA7 9PH, Eng.
- Torc. 3 per m.

**Torquay Natural History Society**
The Museum, Babbacombe Road, Torquay, England.
- Torquay Natural History Society. Transactions and Proceedings. a. ISSN 0082-5344

**Torry Research Station**
P.O. Box 31, 135 Abbey Rd., Aberdeen, Scotland.
- Torry Research Station, Aberdeen, Scotland. Annual Report. a. ISSN 0082-5352

**Tourism International Press Ltd.**
154 Cromwell Rd., London SW7 4EF, Eng.
- Tourism International Airletter. s-m. ISSN 0309-8621
- Tourism International History. q. ISSN 0309-8575
- Tourism International Policy. q. ISSN 0309-8567
- Tourism International Research/Caribbean. q. ISSN 0309-8524 (Caribbean Tourism Association) (Co-sponsors: Caribbean Hotel Association; Caribbean Tourism Research Centre)
- Tourism International Research/Europe. q. ISSN 0309-8605 (European Travel Commission)
- Tourism International Research/Pacific. q. ISSN 0309-8613 (Pacific Area Travel Association)

**Town and Country Planning Association**
17 Carlton House Terrace, London SW1, Eng.
- B E E/Bulletin of Environmental Education. m. ISSN 0045-1266
- Town and Country Planning. m. ISSN 0040-9960
- Town and Country Planning Association. Annual Report. a.
- Town and Country Planning Association. Plan News Review. m (11 per yr.) ISSN 0085-7300

**Toys International Trade News Ltd.**
Pembroke House, Campsbourne Road, Hornsey, London, England.
- Toy Retailing News. m.

**Trade & Technical Press Ltd.**
Crown House, Morden, Surrey SM4 5EW, Eng.
- Church and School Equipment News. bi-m. ISSN 0045-687X
- Church and School Handbook. triennial.
- Hydraulic Pneumatic Mechanical Power. m. ISSN 0306-4069
- Noise Control, Vibration and Insulation. 9 per yr.
- Pumps-Pompes-Pumpen. m. ISSN 0033-426X

**Trade Distributors**
Icon Books Ltd., 9 Down St., London W.1, England.
- Writer's Guide. irreg. ISSN 0084-2702

**Trade Magazines Ltd.**
7 Paddington Street, London, W1, England.
- Architect and Contractors Yearbook. a. ISSN 0066-6114

**Trade Papers (London) Ltd.**
563 High Rd., Chiswick, London W4 3AY, Eng.
- Music Trades International. m.
- Music Trades International Directory. irreg; 1973, 3rd ed.
- Radio and Electrical Retailing. 12 per yr. ISSN 0033-7714

**Trade Press (FMB) Ltd.**
33 John St., Holborn, London W.C.1, Eng.
- Master Builders' Journal. m. ISSN 0025-4991 (Federation of Master Builders)

**Tramway Museum Society**
29 Old Hall Ave., Duffield, Derby, Eng.
- Tramway Museum Society. Journal. q. ISSN 0049-4372

**Transcripta Press**
30 Craven St., London W.C.2., England.
- Aspects of Adhesion. irreg. ISSN 0066-8656

**Transcription Feature Service Ltd.**
Cherry Trees Cottage, Crow End, Bourn, Cambridgeshire CB3 7SY, Eng.
- Cultural Events in Africa. m. ISSN 0011-2844

**Transgravity Press**
176 Pekham Rye, London SE22 9QA, England.
- Mindsleight. q.

**Transport and Distribution Press**
47 Surbiton Road, Kingston on Thames, Surrey, England.
- Freight Industry Yearbook; classified reference and guide for transport vehicle manufacturers, operators and users. a. ISSN 0071-9471

**Transport & General Workers Union**
Transport House, Smith Square, London S.W.1., England.
- Highway. bi-m. ISSN 0018-1676
- T G W U Record. m.

**Transport Studies Group**
Polytechnic of Central London, 35 Marylebone Rd., London NW1 5LS, England.
- Transport Studies Group. Annual Seminar on Rural Public Transport. Papers and Proceedings. a.

**Transport Ticket Society**
4 Princess Court, Harrogate Rd., Leeds LS 17 8BY, England.
- Transport Ticket Society. Journal. m.

**Transworld Publishers Ltd.**
Cavendish House, 57-59 Uxbridge Road, Ealing, London W.5, England.
- Corgi Modern Poets in Focus Series. irreg.

**Travel Aid Services Ltd.**
7A Belsize Park, London N.W.3, England.
- Moneywise Guide to North America. s-a.
- Moneywise Guide to the Lands and Islands of the Mediterranean. s-a.

**Travel and Transport Ltd.**
122 Newgate St., London EC1A 7AD, Eng.
- Coaching Journal and Bus Review. m. ISSN 0009-9899

**Travel Trade Gazette Ltd.**
Morgan Grampian House, Calderwood St., Woolwich, London, SE18 6QH, Eng.
- T T G Europa; Europe's leading international travel trade journal. fortn.
- Travel Trade Directory, U K and Ireland. a. ISSN 0082-7932

**Trefoil Guild**
17 Buckingham Palace Rd., London S.W.1, Eng.
- Trefoil. q. ISSN 0041-2244

**Trent Polytechnic. National Centre for School Technology**
Burton St., Nottingham NG1 4BU, England.
- School Technology. 4 per yr.

**Trent Press (Nottingham) Ltd.**
c/o Roger Milward, Leen Gate, Lenton, Nottingham NG7 2LY, Eng.
- Voyager; the BMA in-flight magazine. 4 per yr. (British Midland Airways Limited)

**Trevithick Society**
c/o Holman's Museum, Camborne, Cornwall, England.
- Trevithick Society. Occasional Publication. irreg.

**Tribune Publications Ltd.**
24 St. John St., London E.C.1, Eng.
- Tribune. w. ISSN 0041-2821

**Robert Trillo Ltd.**
Broadlands, Brockenhurst, Hampshire SO4 7SX, England.
- Air-Cushion and Hydrofoil Systems Bibliography Service. bi-m. ISSN 0306-0594
- High-Speed Ground Transportation and Urban Rapid Transit Systems Bibliography Service. bi-m. ISSN 0306-0586

**Trinidad and Tobago Society**
106 Huddleston Rd., Tufnell Park, London N.7, Eng.
- Enquiry. q. ISSN 0013-8509

**Trinitarian Bible Society**
217 Kingston Rd., London SW19 3NN, England.
- Trinitarian Bible Society. Annual Report. a. ISSN 0082-6588
- Trinitarian Bible Society Quarterly Record. q. ISSN 0049-4712

**Tropical Products Institute**
56-62 Gray's Inn Rd., London WC2X 8LU, England.
- Bibliography of Insecticide Materials of Vegetable Origin. s-a. ISSN 0306-0284 (Gt.Brit. Ministry of Overseas Development)
- Oil Palm News. s-a. ISSN 0048-1580 (Gt.Brit. Ministry of Overseas Development)
- Tropical Science. q. ISSN 0041-3291
- Tropical Storage Abstracts. bi-m. (Gt. Brit. Ministry of Overseas Development)
- Tropical Stored Products Information. s-a. ISSN 0564-3325 (Gt. Brit. Ministry of Overseas Development)

**Truman & Knightley Educational Trust Ltd.**
76-78 Notting Hill Gate, London, W11 3LJ, England.
- Directory of Catholic Schools and Colleges. irreg. ISSN 0070-5233
- Scholarships at Independent Schools. irreg.
- Schools. a. ISSN 0080-6897
- Schools of English in Great Britain. a. ISSN 0080-6927

**Trust for British Archaeology**
15a Bull Plain, Hertford, Herts, England.
- Rescue News. q.

**Trustee Savings Bank Association**
Knishton House, Mortimor St., London W1N 7DG, England.
- T S B Gazette. q.

**Tudor Press Ltd.**
9 Chiswick High Rd., London W4 2ND, Eng.
- Insurance Record. m. ISSN 0020-479X
- Packaging. m. ISSN 0030-9060
- Packaging Directory. irreg. ISSN 0078-768X

**Turf Newspapers Ltd.**
55 Curzon St., London W1Y 7PF, Eng.
- British Racehorse. 5 per yr. ISSN 0007-1706
- Register of Thoroughbred Stallions. biennial. ISSN 0305-5892

**Turner and Devereux**
22a, Baker St., London W.1., England.
- Housman Society Journal. a. ISSN 0305-926X

**Turret Press Ltd.**
4 Local Board Rd., Watford, Herts WD1 2J5,
England.
- Bakers Review. m. ISSN 0005-4100 (National
Association of Master Bakers, Confectioners &
Caterers)
- Baltic Exchange. q. ISSN 0005-4437
- Bulk: Storage, Movement, Control. bi-m. ISSN
0305-3709
- Ceramic Industries Journal. bi-m. ISSN 0305-7623
- Journal of Flour & Animal Feed Milling. m. ISSN
0305-716X
- Manual of Building Maintenance. a.
- Materials Handling Buyers Guide. a. ISSN 0076-
4167
- Storage Handling Distribution; monthly journal of
materials management. m. ISSN 0039-1832

**Tweeddale Press Ltd.**
97 Fleet St., London E.C.4, Eng.
- New Zealand News U.K. w. ISSN 0028-8500

**Twickenham Local History Society**
59 Park House Gardens, Twickenham Middlesex,
England.
- Borough of Twickenham Local History Society.
Papers. irreg. ISSN 0084-7984

**Two Rivers**
28 Tottenham St., London W.1, Eng.
- Two Rivers. q. ISSN 0041-4670

**Two Thousand**
c/o Robert Lloyd George, University College,
Oxford, England.
- Two Thousand. m.

**Two Worlds Publishing Co. Ltd.**
23 Great Queen St., London WC2B 5BB, Eng.
- Two Worlds. m. ISSN 0041-4719

**Tyndale Fellowship for Biblical and Theological
Research**
- Tyndale Bulletin. (pub. by Inter-Varsity Press)

**Tyne & Wear Chamber of Commerce**
4 St. Nicholas Bldgs., Newcastle Upon Tyne NE1
1RR, Eng.
- Industrial Tyne & Wear. m.

**Tyre Industry Publications Ltd.**
136 Valley Rd., Clacton-on-Sea, Essex CO15 6LX,
Eng.
- Tyres and Accessories. m. ISSN 0041-4859

**Tyrrell Burgess Associates Ltd.**
34 Sandilands, Croydon, CRO 5DB, Eng.
- Higher Education Review. 3 per yr. ISSN 0018-
1609

**U. K. Chemical Information Service**
University, Nottingham NG7 2RD, Eng.
- Inforcast. irreg, latest 1975.

**U.K. Publications Ltd.**
11 Tokenhouse Yard, London E.C.2, Eng.
- Public Ledger. d. ISSN 0048-5888

**U.V. Spectrometry Group**
c/o C. J. Timmons, Pye Unicam Ltd., York St.,
Cambridge CB1 2PX, England.
- U.V. Spectrometry Group. Bulletin. a.

**Ukrainian Publishers Ltd.**
200 Liverpool Rd., London N.1., Eng.
- Juni Druzi. q.
- Ukrainian Review. q. ISSN 0041-6029
- Ukrainian Thought. w.
- Vyzvol'nyi Shlyakh/Liberation Path; Ukrainian
political, social, scientific & literary magazine. m.
ISSN 0042-9422

**Ulster Archaeological Society**
c/o N. Ireland Archaeological Survey, 66 Balmoral
Ave., Belfast 9, Northern Ireland.
- Ulster Journal of Archaeology. a. ISSN 0082-7355

**Ulster Folk and Transport Museum**
Cultra Manor, Holywood, County Down BT18
0EU, Northern Ireland.
- Ulster Folklife. a. ISSN 0082-7347

**Ulster Journals Ltd.**
112 Lisburn Rd., Belfast BT9 6AH, N. Ireland.
- Ulster Tatler. m. ISSN 0049-5107

**Ulster Medical Society**
- Ulster Medical Journal. (pub. by Queens
University Medical Library)

**Ulster Motorist**
c/o Ulster Bank Ltd., Waring St., Belfast 1, N.
Ireland.
- Ulster Motorist. m. ISSN 0041-6207

**Undercurrents Ltd.**
213 Archway Rd., London N.6, England.
- Undercurrents; the magazine of radical science
and peoples' technology. bi-m. ISSN 0306-2392

**Underground Alternative Press Service - Europe**
22, Dane Road, Margate, Kent, England.
- Magic Ink. q.

**Union of Construction, Allied Trades and Technicians**
UCATT House, 177 Abbeville Rd., Clapham,
London SW4 9RL, England.
- Viewpoint. q. ISSN 0042-5842

**Union of Post Office Workers**
U.P.W. House, Crescent Lane, Clapham, London
SW4 9RN, Eng.
- Post. fortn. ISSN 0032-5236

**Union of Shop Distributive and Allied Workers**
Oakley, 188 Wilmslow Road Fallowfield,
Manchester, Eng.
- Dawn. m.

**Union of Welsh Independents**
11 St Helen's Rd., Swansea, Wales.
- Porfeydd. bi-m. ISSN 0048-4857
- Tyst. w.

**Union of Women for Liberation**
13 Grove Rd., Hemel Hempstead, Herts HP1 1NG,
England.
- Women's Struggle; journal of the Women's
National Coordinating Committee. q.

**Unisaf Publications Ltd.**
32-36 Dudley Rd., Tunbridge Wells, Kent 7N1
1LH, England.
- Fire; journal of the fire protection profession. m.
- Fire International; the journal of the World's Fire
Protection Services. q. ISSN 0015-2609
- Fltech; the international equipment guide for the
emergency services. q.
- National Fire Prevention Gazette. a. ISSN 0077-
4537
- Securitech; the international guide to security
equipment. a. ISSN 0307-7780

**United Commercial Travellers' Association. Section
ASTMS**
Bexton Lane, Knutsford, Cheshire, Eng.
- Selling Today. m. ISSN 0037-1629

**United Committee for the Taxation of Land Values**
- Land & Liberty. (pub. by Land & Liberty Press
Ltd.)

**United Free Church of Scotland**
11 Newton Place, Glasgow G3 7PR, Scotland.
- United Free Church of Scotland. Handbook. a.
ISSN 0082-7908 (Communications Board)

**United Kingdom Agricultural Supply Trade
Association, Ltd.**
3 Whitehall Court, London SW1A 2EQ, Eng.
- Agricultural Merchant. m. ISSN 0002-1563

**United Kingdom Atomic Energy Authority**
Information Services Branch, 11 Charles 2nd St.,
London SW1P 4QP, England.
- Atom. m. ISSN 0004-7015
- Atom News. m. ISSN 0004-7058

**United Kingdom Automation Council**
Institution of Production Engineers, 10 Chesterfield
St., Mayfair, London W.1, Eng.
- Automation Council News. m. ISSN 0005-1187

**United Kingdom Federation of Business &
Professional Women**
54 Bloomsbury St., London WC1, Eng.
- Business and Professional Woman. q. ISSN 0045-
3595

**United Kingdom Reading Association.**
c/o S. V. Heatlie, 63 Laurel Grove, Sunderland,
Tyne and Wear, Eng.
- Reading; a journal for the study and improvement
of reading and related skills. 3 per yr.(March,
June & Dec.) ISSN 0034-0472

**United Kingdom Temperance Alliance Ltd.**
12 Caxton St., London S.W.1., Eng.
- United Kingdom Temperance Alliance. Alliance
News. m. ISSN 0002-6085

**United Nations Association**
93 Albert Embankment, London S.E.1, Eng.
- New World. m. ISSN 0028-6990

**United Newspapers Publications Ltd**
127 Fishergate, Preston, Lancashire PR1 2DN, Eng.
- Farmers Guardian. w. ISSN 0014-8423

**United Publicity Services Ltd.**
Gray's Inn Road, London, WC1, England.
- Castle's Town and County Trades Directory. a.
ISSN 0069-0996

**United Reformed Church in England and Wales**
86 Tavistock Place, London WC1H 9RT, Eng.
- Reform. 11 per yr. ISSN 0306-7262
- United Reformed Church in England and Wales.
United Reformed Church Year Book. a. ISSN
0069-8849

**United Reformed History Society**
Church House, 86 Tavistock Pl., London WC1H
9RT, Eng.
- United Reformed Church History Society.
Journal. s-a. ISSN 0049-5433

**United Society for Christian Literature**
Luke House, Farnham Rd., Guildford, Surrey, GU1
4XD, England.
- United Society for Christian Literature. Annual
Report. a. ISSN 0082-8564

**United Society for the Propagation of the Gospel**
15 Tufton St., London SW1P 3QQ, Eng.
- Adventurer. 5 per yr. ISSN 0001-8821
- Network. q. ISSN 0028-3037
- United Society for the Propagation of the Gospel.
Annual Report/Review. a. ISSN 0082-8572

**United Trade Press Ltd.**
15 Albert Mews, London W8 5RY, Eng.
- Club Secretary. m. ISSN 0009-9635
- Computer Survey; covering the electronic digital
computer industry in Britain. bi-m. ISSN 0010-
4760
- Dairy Industries International. m. ISSN 0308-
8197
- Hard's Year Book for the Clothing Industry. a.
ISSN 0073-0343
- Industrial Safety. m. ISSN 0019-8757
- International Flavours and Food Additives. bi-m.
ISSN 0306-6517
- Journal of Medical Engineering & Technology. m.
ISSN 0309-1902 (Biological Engineering Society)
- Laboratory Practice; research techniques and
equipment. m. ISSN 0023-6853
- Manufacturing Clothier. m. ISSN 0025-2565
- Review. fortn. ISSN 0034-6349
- Soap, Perfumery and Cosmetics. m. ISSN 0037-
749X

**United Writers Publications**
Trevail Mill, Zennor, St. Ives, Cornwall, Eng.
- Writer's Review. q. ISSN 0043-9568

**Unity Publications (Finchley) Ltd**
134 Ballards Lane, London N3 2PD, Eng.
- Labour Monthly. m. ISSN 0023-6985

**Universities and Colleges Christian Fellowship**
39 Bedford Square, London WC1B 3EY, Eng.
- Christian Graduate; quarterly journal of the
graduates' fellowship. q. ISSN 0045-6802

**University College Cardiff. Faculty of Education**
Senghennydd Road, Cardiff CF2 4AG, Wales.
- Education for Development. s-a. ISSN 0305-7291

**University College Hospital Dental School. Dental
Society**
Mortimer Market, London WC1E, 6JD, Eng.
- Apex. 3 per yr. ISSN 0003-6439

**University College Hospital Medical School**
University St., London W.C. 1, Eng.
- University College Hospital Magazine. 10 per yr.
  ISSN 0041-9273

**University College, London**
- Annals of Human Genetics. (pub. by Cambridge
  University Press)
- Current Legal Problems. (pub. by Sweet &
  Maxwell Stevens Journals)

**University College London. Department of Geography**
c/o Gareth M. Hadley, 25 Gordon St., London,
WC1H OAH, England.
- Bloomsbury Geographer. every 18 mos. ISSN
  0067-9232

**University College London. Department of
Mathematics**
Gower St., London WC1B 6BT, Eng.
- Mathematika; a journal of pure and applied
  mathematics. s-a. ISSN 0025-5793

**University College London. Dramatic Society**
Gower St., London W.C.1, Eng.
- Prompt. 3 per yr. ISSN 0033-1147

**University College London. Institute of Jewish
Studies**
Gower St., London WC1E 6BT, England.
- University College London. Institute of Jewish
  Studies. Bulletin. 1-2 per yr.

**University College London Union**
25 Gordon Street, London WC1A 0AH, Eng.
- Pi; University College London students news. w.

**University College of North Wales. Marine Science
Laboratories**
Menai Bridge, Anglesey, Wales.
- Contributions to Marine Science. a. ISSN 0069-
  9691

**University College of Swansea. Department of
Geography**
Singleton Park, Swansea, Glam. SA2 8PP, Wales.
- Swansea Geographer. a. ISSN 0081-9980

**University College of Swansea. Students Union**
Union House, Singleton Park, Swansea SA2 8PP,
Wales.
- Crefft. m.

**University College of Wales, Aberystwyth.
Department of Geography**
c/o J.A. Taylor, Llandinam Bldg., Penglais,
Aberystwyth, Dyfed SY23 3DB, Wales.
- Aberystwyth Memoranda in Agricultural, Applied
  and Biometeorology. a. ISSN 0065-0285

**University College of Wales, Aberystwyth. Faculty of
Education**
- Welsh Studies in Education Series. (pub. by
  University of Wales Press)

**University College of Wales. Department of Law**
Aberystwyth, Wales.
- Cambrian Law Review. a. ISSN 0084-8328

**University College of Wales. Department of Music**
Cardiff, Wales.
- Soundings: A Music Journal. a. ISSN 0081-2080
  (Co-sponsor: Welsh Arts Council)

**University College of Wales. Students' Union**
Aberystwyth, Cardiganshire, Wales.
- Dragon. a. ISSN 0012-589X

**University of Aberdeen. African Studies Group**
Dept. of History, Kings College, Aberdeen AB9
2UB, Scotland.
- University of Aberdeen. African Studies Group.
  Bulletin. 1-2 per yr. ISSN 0001-3196

**University of Aberdeen. Alumnus Association**
18 Bon-Accord Square, Aberdeen, AB9 1YE,
Scotland.
- University of Aberdeen Review. s-a. ISSN 0001-
  320X

**University of Aberdeen. Centre for Scottish Studies**
Taylor Building, Old Aberdeen AB9 2UB, Scotland.
- Northern Scotland. s-a.

**University of Aberdeen. Department of Economics**
Aberdeen, Scotland.
- Economic Studies. s-a.

**University of Aberdeen. Department of Forestry**
St. Machar Dr., Old Aberdeen AB9 2UU, Scotland.
- University of Aberdeen. Department of Forestry.
  Economic Survey of Private Forestry. a. ISSN
  0065-0277

**University of Aberdeen. Medical Faculty**
University Medical Bldg., Foresterhill, Aberdeen,
Scotland.
- Helix. 3 per yr.

**University of Aston in Birmingham. Department of
Biological Sciences**
Gosta Green, Birmingham B4 7ET, England.
- Waste Materials Biodegradation Research Titles.
  q. (prep. by its Biodeterioration Information
  Centre)

**University of Birmingham**
- English Philological Studies. (pub. by W. Heffer &
  Sons Ltd.)

**University of Birmingham. Centre for Contemporary
Cultural Studies**
Box 563, Birmingham BI5 2TT, Eng.
- Working Papers in Cultural Studies. a. ISSN
  0049-7991

**University of Birmingham. Centre for Urban and
Regional Studies**
J. G. Smith Bldg., Ring Rd. North, Box 363,
Birmingham B15 2TT, England.
- University of Birmingham. Centre for Urban and
  Regional Studies. Occasional Papers. irreg., no.
  35, 1976. ISSN 0067-8953
- University of Birmingham. Centre for Urban and
  Regional Studies. Research Memorandum. irreg.,
  no. 52, 1976.
- University of Birmingham. Centre for Urban and
  Regional Studies. Working Paper. irreg., no. 42,
  1976.

**University of Birmingham. Chemical Engineering
Society**
Dept. of Chemical Engineering, Birmingham BI 5
2TT, Eng.
- University of Birmingham Chemical Engineer. 3
  per yr. ISSN 0006-3746

**University of Birmingham. Communist Group (M - L)**
Birmingham University Students Union,
Birmingham 15, England.
- Communist News. 15 per yr. ISSN 0024-029X

**University of Birmingham. Department of English
Language Research**
Birmingham, England.
- Discourse Analysis Monographs. irreg.

**University of Birmingham. Department of Political
Science**
P.O. Box 363, Birmingham B15 2TT, England.
- University of Birmingham. Faculty of Commerce
  and Social Science. Discussion Papers: Series F:
  Birmingham Society and Politics. irreg. ISSN
  0525-3772

**University of Birmingham. Department of
Transportation & Environmental Plannning**
P.O. Box 363, Birmingham B15 2TT, Great Britain.
- University of Birmingham. Department of
  Transportation and Environmental Planning.
  Research Journal. biennial.

**University of Bradford Library**
Bradford BD7 1DP, Eng.
- A C E/Articles in Civil Engineering. m. ISSN
  0001-0650

**University of Bradford Union**
Richard Rd., Bradford BD7 1DP, Yorks, Eng.
- Javelin. s-m during term. ISSN 0047-1941

**University of Bristol. Department of Extra-Mural
Studies**
Bristol, England.
- Archaeological Review. a. ISSN 0066-5991

**University of Durham**
Durham DH1 3EX, Eng.
- Durham University Journal. 2 per yr. ISSN 0012-
  7280

**University of Durham. Anthropological Society**
South End House, South Rd., Durham DH1 3TG,
England.
- Dyn; the journal of the Durham University
  Anthropological Society. a. or biennial.

**University of Durham. Center for Middle Eastern and
Islamic Studies**
Elvet Hill, Durham City DH1 3TR, England.
- University of Durham. Center for Middle Eastern
  and Islamic Studies. Occasional Papers Series. 2-3
  per yr.

**University of Durham. Institute of Education**
48 Old Elvet, Durham, Eng.
- Durham Research Review. s-a. (Co-Sponsor:
  University of Newcastle upon Tyne, Institute of
  Education)

**University of Edinburgh**
c/o Dept. of Educational Studies, 10 Buccleuch
Place, Edinburgh EH8 9JT, Scotland.
- International Congress of University Adult
  Education. Journal. 3 per yr. ISSN 0074-3992
- Sylva. a. ISSN 0082-0636

**University of Edinburgh. Architecture Research Unit**
55 George Square, Edinburgh EH8 9JU, Scotland.
- University of Edinburgh. Architecture Research
  Unit. Report. irreg. ISSN 0070-8992

**University of Edinburgh. Graduates' Association**
5 Buccleuch Place, Edinburgh EH8 9LN, Scotland.
- University of Edinburgh Journal. s-a. ISSN 0041-
  9567

**University of Edinburgh. School of Scottish Studies**
27 George Square, Edinburgh EH8 9LD, Scotland.
- Scottish Studies. a. ISSN 0036-9411
- Tocher. 3 per yr. ISSN 0049-397X

**University of Edinburgh. Student Publications Board**
1 Buccleuch Place, Edinburgh EH8 9LW, Scotland.
- New Edinburgh Review. 4 per yr. ISSN 0028-
  4645

**University of Essex**
Wivenhoe Park, Colchester CO4 3SQ, England.
- Oral History. irreg.

**University of Exeter**
Northcote House, The Queens Drive, Exeter EX4
4QJ, Eng.
- Exeter University Gazette. 3 per yr. ISSN 0014-
  4622

**University of Exeter. Agricultural Economics Unit**
Exeter EX4 4QJ, England.
- Farm Business Review. a.

**University of Exeter. American Arts Documentation
Centre**
Queens Building, Exeter EX 4QH, England.
- American Arts Pamphlet Series. irreg., (1-2 per
  yr.)

**University of Exeter. Department of Politics**
Exeter EX4 4PU, England.
- West African Journal of Sociology and Political
  Science. q. ISSN 0308-4450

**University of Exeter. Faculty of Social Studies**
- Social and Economic Administration. (pub. by
  Basil Blackwell & Mott Ltd.)

**University of Glasgow**
c/o Publications Officer, University Court, Glasgow
G12 8QQ, Scotland.
- Glasgow University Gazette. irreg. ISSN 0017-
  0909
- Soviet Studies; a quarterly review of the social and
  economic institutions of the U.S.S.R. q. ISSN
  0038-5859
- University of Glasgow. Social and Economic
  Research Studies. (pub. by Martin Robertson &
  Co. Ltd.)

**University of Glasgow. Department of Psychology**
Glasgow G12 8RT, Glasgow W.2, Scotland.
- Feedback; the Glasgow journal of psychology. 2-3
  per yr. ISSN 0014-9608

**University of Glasgow. Institute of Latin American
Studies**
Glasgow GL2 8QH, Scotland.
- University of Glasgow. Institute of Latin
  American Studies. Occasional Papers. bi-m.
- University of Glasgow. Institute of Latin
  American Studies. Occasional Papers. irreg.

**University of Glasgow. Medico-Chirurgical Society**
University Union, 32, University Ave., Glasgow,
G12 8LX, Scotland.
- Surgo. 3 per yr. ISSN 0039-6125

**University of Glasgow Press**
Publications Office, Glasgow G12 8QG, Scotland.
- W. A. Cargill Memorial Lectures in Fine Art. irreg. ISSN 0512-4638

**University of Glasgow. Students' Representative Council**
John McIntyre Bldg., Glasgow G12 8QQ, Scotland.
- Glasgow University Guardian. fortn. ISSN 0017-0917

**University of Hull. Department of Geography**
Hull, Yorkshire HU6 7RX, England.
- University of Hull. Department of Geography. Miscellaneous Series in Geography. irreg. (approx. 2 per yr.) ISSN 0441-4004

**University of Hull. Department of German**
Hull HU6 7RX, England.
- New German Studies. 3 per yr. ISSN 0307-2770

**University of Hull. Institute of Education**
173, Cottingham Rd., Hull HU5 2EH, England.
- Aspects of Education. irreg., no. 18, 1975. ISSN 0066-8672
- University of Hull. Institute of Education. Aids to Research. irreg., no. 2, 1975. ISSN 0073-3806
- University of Hull. Institute of Education. Research Monographs. irreg., 1968, no. 2. ISSN 0073-3814

**University of Hull Publications Committee**
Hull HU6 7RX, England.
- Occasional Papers in Economic and Social History. irreg. ISSN 0078-3013
- Occasional Papers in Geography. irreg. ISSN 0078-3056
- Occasional Papers in Modern Languages. irreg. ISSN 0078-3099

**University of Keele**
Keele, Staffs. ST5 5BG, England.
- Iberian Studies; journal of the Iberian Social Studies Association. s-a.
- North Staffordshire Journal of Field Studies. a. ISSN 0078-1649
- Sociological Review. q. ISSN 0038-0261
- Sociological Review. Monograph. irreg., no. 24, 1977. ISSN 0081-1769

**University of Lancaster. Department of Systems**
Bailrigg, Lancaster LA1 4YR, Eng.
- Journal of Applied Systems Analysis. s-a. ISSN 0308-9541

**University of Lancaster. Library**
Bailrigg, Lancaster LA1 4YH, England.
- University of Lancaster. Library. Bibliographic Guide. irreg.
- University of Lancaster. Library. Occasional Papers. irreg. ,no. 9, 1975. ISSN 0075-7810

**University of Leeds**
Leeds LS2 9JT, England.
- Journal of Commonwealth Literature. (pub. by Oxford University Press)
- University of Leeds Review. s-a. ISSN 0041-9737

**University of Leeds. African Studies Unit**
Leeds LS2 9JT, England.
- Leeds African Studies Bulletin. s-a. ISSN 0024-0249

**University of Leeds. Department of Earth Sciences**
Research Institute of African Geology, Leeds, England.
- University of Leeds. Research Institute of African Geology. Annual Report. a. ISSN 0075-8558

**University of Leeds. Institute of Education**
Leeds, LS2 9JT, England.
- University of Leeds. Institute of Education. Papers. irreg. ISSN 0075-854X

**University of Leeds. Leeds University Union**
Leeds 2, Yorks, Eng.
- Poetry & Audience. bi-m (Oct.-Sep.) ISSN 0032-2040

**University of Leeds. Museum of the History of Education**
Leeds 2, Eng.
- Journal of Educational Administration and History. s-a. ISSN 0022-0620

**University of Leeds. School of Economic Studies**
c/o Eds. Prof. A. J. Brown, C. E. V. Leser, Leeds LS2 9JT, England.
- Bulletin of Economic Research. s-a. ISSN 0044-0590 (Co-Sponsors: Universities of Hull, Leeds, Sheffield, York and Bradford)

**University of Leeds. School of English**
Leeds LS2 9JT, England.
- Leeds Studies in English. a. ISSN 0075-8566
- Leeds Texts and Monographs. a. ISSN 0075-8574

**University of Leeds. School of History**
Leeds, England.
- Northern History; a review of the history of the North of England. a. ISSN 0078-172X

**University of Leicester. Department of Adult Education**
University Rd., Leicester LE1 7RH, England.
- Northamptonshire Archaeology. a.

**University of Leicester. Department of English Local History**
Leicester, England.
- University of Leicester. Department of English Local History. Occasional Papers. Third Series. irreg.

**University of Leicester Geography Society**
University Rd., Leicester, England.
- Confluence. irreg.

**University of Leicester. MRC Microbial Research Unit**
University Rd., Leicester LE1 7RH, England.
- Classification Society Bulletin. a. ISSN 0578-4565

**University of Liverpool. Department of Civic Design, Town and Regional Planning and Transport Studies**
- Town Planning Review. (pub. by Liverpool University Press)

**University of Liverpool. Department of Geography**
Roxby Bldg., Liverpool, England.
- University of Liverpool. Department of Geography. Research Paper. irreg., 1972, no. 9. ISSN 0076-0056

**University of Liverpool. Department of Geology**
- Geological Journal. (pub. by Seel House Press Ltd.)

**University of Liverpool. Guild of Undergraduates**
2 Bedford St., N. Liverpool 7L7 7BD, Eng.
- Guild Gazette. fortn. ISSN 0017-5374

**University of Liverpool. Medical School**
Pembroke Place, Liverpool, Eng.
- Sphincter. 3 per yr. ISSN 0038-741X

**University of London**
- University of London. School of Oriental and African Studies. Bulletin. (pub. by Luzac & Co. Ltd.)

**University of London. Contemporary China Institute**
- University of London. Contemporary China Institute. Publications. (pub. by Cambridge University Press)

**University of London. Institute of Advanced Legal Studies**
London WC1B 5DR, England.
- University of London. Institute of Advanced Legal Studies. List of Current Legal Research. a. ISSN 0076-0706

**University of London. Institute of Archaeology**
31 Gordon Sq., London WC1H OPY, England.
- University of London. Institute of Archaeology. Bulletin. irreg. (approx. a.) ISSN 0076-0722

**University of London. Institute of Classical Studies**
31-34 Gordon Sq, London WC1H 0PY, England.
- Studies in Mycenaean Inscriptions and Dialect. a. ISSN 0081-8275
- University of London. Institute of Classical Studies. Bulletin. a. ISSN 0076-0730
- University of London. Institute of Classical Studies. Bulletin Supplement. irreg., no. 37, 1977. ISSN 0076-0749
- University of London. Institute of Classical Studies. Occasional Publications. irreg. ISSN 0076-0757

**University of London. Institute of Commonwealth Studies**
27 Russell Sq., London WC1B 5DS, England.
- University of London. Institute of Commonwealth Studies. Annual Report. a. ISSN 0076-0781
- University of London. Institute of Commonwealth Studies. Collected Seminar Papers. irreg., no. 20, 1976. ISSN 0076-0773
- University of London. Institute of Commonwealth Studies. Commonwealth Papers. irreg. ISSN 0076-0765

**University of London. Institute of Education Library**
11-13 Ridgmount St., London WC1E 7AH, Eng.
- Education Libraries Bulletin. 3 per yr. ISSN 0013-1407
- University of London. Institute of Education. Library. Education Libraries Bulletin Supplements. irreg., no. 20, 1977. ISSN 0076-079X

**University of London. Institute of Germanic Studies**
29 Russell Sq., London W.C. 1B 5D, England.
- Essays in German Literature. irreg., 1973, vol. 3. ISSN 0071-1403
- Theses in Germanic Studies. quinquennial. ISSN 0082-4119
- University of London. Institute of Germanic Studies. Library. Publications. irreg. ISSN 0076-0803
- University of London. Institute of Germanic Studies. Theses in Progress at British Universities. a. ISSN 0082-4127

**University of London. Institute of Historical Research**
Senate House, London W.C.1., England.
- Bibliography of Historical Works Issued in the United Kingdom. quinquennial. ISSN 0067-7191 (Co-sponsor: Anglo-American Conference of Historians)
- Historical Research for University Degrees in the United Kingdom. a. ISSN 0073-263X
- London. University. Institute of Historical Research. Bulletin. s-a. ISSN 0020-2894
- Teachers of History in the Universities of the United Kingdom. a. ISSN 0085-7114
- University of London. Institute of Historical Research. Bulletin. Special Supplement. irreg., no. 11, 1976. ISSN 0076-082X
- Writings on British History. irreg. ISSN 0084-2753

**University of London. Institute of Jewish Studies**
- University of London. Institute of Jewish Studies. Papers. (pub. by Magnes Press IS)

**University of London. Institute of Latin American Studies**
31 Tavistock Sq., London WC1H 9HA, England.
- Latin American Studies in the Universities of the United Kingdom. a. ISSN 0085-2694
- Latin American Studies in the Universities of the United Kingdom. Staff Research in Progress or Recently Completed in the Humanities and the Social Sciences. a. ISSN 0085-2708

**University of London. Institute of Psychiatry**
- Maudsley Monographs. (pub. by Oxford University Press)

**University of London Press Ltd.**
Saint Paul's House, Warwick Lane, London EC4P 4AH, England.
- London History Studies. irreg. ISSN 0076-0544
- Scottish Council for Research in Education. Publications. irreg. ISSN 0080-8008

**University of London. Royal Postgraduate Medical School**
Hammersmith Hospital, Du Cane Rd., London W12 0HS, England.
- University of London. Royal Postgraduate Medical School. Report. a. ISSN 0076-0854

**University of London. School of Environmental Studies**
Gower St., London WC1E 6BT, England.
- Bartlett Society. Transactions. a (approx.) ISSN 0459-7400

**University of London. School of Oriental and African Studies**
Malet St., London WC1E 7HP, Eng.
- African Language Studies. (pub. by Luzac & Co., Ltd.)
- London Oriental Series. (pub. by Oxford University Press)

- Quarterly Index Islamicus. (pub. by Mansell Information - Publishing Ltd.)
- University of London. School of Oriental and African Studies. Bulletin. 3 per yr. ISSN 0041-977X

**University of Loughborough**
Loughborough, Leicestershire, England.
- History of Economic Thought Newsletter. s-a. ISSN 0440-9884

**University of Manchester. Department of Economics**
Dover St., Manchester M13 9Pl, Eng.
- Manchester School of Economic and Social Studies. 4 per yr. ISSN 0025-2034

**University of Manchester. Department of Italian**
Manchester M13 9PL, England.
- Italian Studies. a. ISSN 0075-1634

**University of Manchester. Institute of Science and Technology**
Chemical Engineering Dept., Sackville St., Manchester M6O 1OD, Eng.
- Mutech Chemical Engineering Journal. s-a. ISSN 0027-5115

**University of Manchester. Medical School**
Manchester, 13, Eng.
- Manchester Medical Gazette. 3 per yr. ISSN 0025-2018

**University of Manchester. School of Education**
Manchester MI3 9PL, England.
- University of Manchester. School of Education. Gazette. a.

**University of Newcastle-Upon-Tyne. Computing Laboratory**
Claremont Tower, Newcastle-Upon-Tyne NE1 7RU, England.
- University of Newcastle-Upon-Tyne. Computing Laboratory. Technical Report. irreg.

**University of Newcastle-Upon-Tyne. Department of Geography**
Newcastle-Upon-Tyne NE1 7RU, England.
- University of Newcastle-Upon-Tyne. Department of Geography. Research Series. irreg., no. 10, 1974. ISSN 0078-026X

**University of Newcastle-Upon-Tyne. Department of Town and Country Planning**
Newcastle-Upon-Tyne NE1 7RU, Eng.
- Planning Outlook. s-a. ISSN 0032-0714 (Co-sponsor: Oxford Polytechnic, Department of Town Planning)

**University of Newcastle-Upon-Tyne. Exploration Society**
Daysh Building, Newcastle-Upon-Tyne NE1 7RO, England.
- University of Newcastle-Upon-Tyne. Exploration Society Journal. a.

**University of Newcastle-Upon-Tyne. Philosophical Society**
Armstrong Bldg., Queen Victoria Rd., Newcastle-Upon-Tyne NE1 7RU, England.
- University of Newcastle-Upon-Tyne. Philosophical Society. Proceedings. irreg., 1969, vol. 1, no. 15. ISSN 0078-0251

**University of Nottingham**
Nottingham, England.
- Nottingham Mediaeval Studies. a. ISSN 0078-2122
- Renaissance and Modern Studies. (pub. by Sisson and Parker Ltd.)

**University of Nottingham. Department of Adult Education**
14-22 Shakespeare St., Nottingham NG1 4FJ, England.
- East Midland Archaeological Bulletin. a. ISSN 0424-1088
- University of Nottingham. Department of Adult Education. Bulletin of Local History, East Midlands Region. a. (prep. by its Library and Publications Unit)

**University of Nottingham. Department of French**
Nottingham, Eng.
- Nottingham French Studies. s-a. ISSN 0029-4586

**University of Nottingham. Department of Geography**
Nottingham NG7 2RD, England.
- Computer Applications in the Natural and Social Sciences. s-a. ISSN 0069-8105
- East Midland Geographer. s-a. ISSN 0012-8481

**University of Nottingham. School of Agriculture**
University Park, Nottingham NG7 2RD, England.
- Farming in the East Midlands. a. ISSN 0071-3961
- Farming in the East Midlands. Financial Results. a.

**University of Oxford. Agricultural Economics Institute**
Dartington House, Little Clarendon St., Oxford, Eng.
- Oxford Agrarian Studies. a.

**University of Oxford. Classical Society**
Worcester College, Oxford, Eng.
- Arepo; Oxford classical journal. 2-3 per yr. ISSN 0004-0967

**University of Oxford. Institute of Agrarian Affairs**
- International Journal of Agrarian Affairs. (pub. by Oxford University Press)

**University of Oxford. Medical School**
Osler House, 43 Woodstock Rd., Oxford OX2 6HE, Eng.
- Oxford Medical School Gazette. 3 per yr. ISSN 0030-7661

**University of Oxford. Research Laboratory for Archeology and the History of Art**
6 Keble Road, Oxford OX1 3QJ, England.
- Archaeometry. s-a. ISSN 0003-813X

**University of Oxford. School of Geography**
Mansfield Road, Oxford OX1 3TB, England.
- University of Oxford. School of Geography. Research Papers. irreg.

**University of Reading. Department of Agricultural Economics**
Reading, England.
- University of Reading. Department of Agricultural Economics and Management. Farm Business Data. a. ISSN 0557-6911
- University of Reading. Department of Agricultural Economics. Miscellaneous Studies. irreg. ISSN 0486-0845

**University of Reading. Department of Agricultural Economics & Management**
Reading, England.
- Reading/Legon Joint Research Project in Village Development, South East Ghana. Report. irreg.

**University of Reading. Department of Geography**
White Knights, Reading RG6 2AB, England.
- Geographical Papers. 10-12 per yr. ISSN 0305-5914
- Reading Geographer. s-a.

**University of Reading. Graduate School of Contemporary European Studies**
Faculty of Letters and Social Sciences, White Knights, Reading, Berks RG6 2AB, England.
- University of Reading. Graduate School of Contemporary European Studies. Occasional Publication. irreg. ISSN 0079-9858

**University of St. Andrews**
- Forum for Modern Language Studies. (pub. by Scottish Academic Press Ltd.)
- Philosophical Quarterly. (pub. by Scots Philosophical Club)

**University of Sheffield**
Sheffield S10 2TN, England.
- University of Sheffield. Newsletter Diary. 10 per yr.

**University of Southampton**
Highfield, Southampton SO9 5NH, England.
- Fawley Foundation Lectures. a. ISSN 0071-4097

**University of Southampton. Library**
Highfield, Southampton, Hants SO9 5NH, England.
- Parkes Library Pamphlets. irreg., 1971, no. 20. ISSN 0079-0052
- University of Southampton. Library. Automation Project Report. irreg., 1972, no. 4. ISSN 0081-2935
- Vine; a very informal newsletter on library automation. 3 per yr. ISSN 0305-5728

**University of Strathclyde. Fraser of Allander Institute for Research on the Scottish Economy**
100 Montrose St., Glasgow G4 OLZ, Scotland.
- University of Strathclyde, Fraser of Allander Institute for Research on the Scottish Economy. Research Monograph. irreg. ISSN 0306-7408

**University of Strathclyde. Politics Department**
Richmond St., Glasgow C1, Scotland, England.
- University of Strathclyde. Survey Research Centre. Occasional Paper. irreg., no. 13, 1975. ISSN 0072-4602

**University of Strathclyde. Students' Association**
S. R. C. Publications, 90 John St, Glasgow C. 1, Scotland.
- Masque. a. ISSN 0025-4711
- Strathclyde Telegraph. fortn. ISSN 0039-2243

**University of Surrey**
Bookshop, Guildford, Surrey GU2 5XH, England.
- Surrey Papers in Economics. irreg., no. 10, 1974. ISSN 0081-9670

**University of Sussex. Center for Contemporary European Studies**
20 Kensington Palace Gardens, London W.8. 4QQ, England.
- European Studies- Teachers' Series. q.

**University of Sussex. Institute of Development Studies**
Andrew Cohen Bldg., Falmer, Brighton, Sussex BN1 9RE, England
- Development Studies. Register of Research in the United Kingdom. biennial. (Subscr. to: Research Publications Services Ltd., Victoria Hall, East Greenwich, London SE10 0RF, England)
- Institute of Development Studies. Annual Report. a.
- Institute of Development Studies Bulletin. q. ISSN 0020-2835

**University of Sussex Union. Unionews Management Board**
Falmer, Brighton, Sussex BN1 9QF, England.
- Unionews. w.

**University of Wales. Board of Celtic Studies**
- Board of Celtic Studies. Bulletin. (pub. by University of Wales Press)
- Studia Celtica. (pub. by University of Wales Press)

**University of Wales. Institute of Science and Technology**
King Edward VII Avenue, Cardiff, CF1 3NU, Wales.
- Iron Industry Housing Papers. irreg. ISSN 0305-4276 (prep. by its Welsh School of Architecture)

**University of Wales Press**
6 Gwennyth St., Cathays, Cardiff CF2 4YD, Wales (Dist. in U.S. by: Lawrence Verry, Inc., Mystic, CT 06355)
- Board of Celtic Studies. Bulletin. s-a. (University of Wales. Board of Celtic Studies)
- Efrydiau Athronyddol. a.
- Geiriadur Prifysgol Cymru. a. ISSN 0072-0542 (Board of Celtic Studies)
- Gwyddonydd. q. ISSN 0017-5897
- Llen Cymru. a. ISSN 0076-0188 (Board of Celtic Studies)
- Studia Celtica. a. ISSN 0081-6353 (University of Wales. Board of Celtic Studies)
- Trivium. a. ISSN 0082-660X (St. David's University College)
- University of Wales. Board of Celtic Studies. Social Science Monographs. irreg.
- Welsh History Review. s-a. ISSN 0043-2431
- Welsh Studies in Education Series. irreg. ISSN 0083-7946 (University College of Wales, Aberystwyth. Faculty of Education)

**University of Warwick. Centre for Industrial Economic & Business Research**
Coventry, Warwickshire CV4 7AL, England.
- Warwick Industrial Economic and Business Research Papers. irreg.

**University of Warwick. Department of Economics**
Coventry CV4 7AL, England.
- Warwick Economic Research Papers. irreg., 1971, no. 14. ISSN 0083-7350

**University of Warwick. Department of English**
Coventry CV4 7AL, Eng.
- Tracks. 3 per yr. ISSN 0041-0349

**University of Warwick. Department of German Studies**
Coventry CV4 4AL, England.
- Occasional Papers in German Studies. 3 per yr. (Co-sponsor: Volkswagen Foundation)

**University of Warwick. Graduate School of Literature**
Coventry, Warwick, England.
- Comparison. 3 per yr.

**University of Warwick Library**
Coventry, Warwickshire, CV4 7AL, England.
- University of Warwick Library. Occasional Publications. irreg.

**University of York**
- Borthwick Institute of Historical Research. Borthwick Papers. (pub. by St. Anthonys' Press)

**University of York. Centre for Southern African Studies**
Heslington, York YO1 5DD, England.
- University of York. Centre for Southern African Studies. Collected Papers. irreg.

**Unservile State Group**
c/o Ed. George Watson, St. John's College, England.
- Unservile State Papers. irreg., no. 21, 1975. ISSN 0566-2672

**Up Against the Law Collective**
66 Yorkway, London N.1, England.
- Up Against the Law. bi-m.

**Update Publications Ltd.**
33-34 Alfred Place, London WC1E 7DP, England.
- Dental Update. bi-m.
- Hospital Update. m.
- Update; the journal for education of postgraduate studies. s-m.

**Uplands Press Ltd.**
1 Katharine St., Croydon, Surrey CR9 1LB, Eng.
- Filtration & Separation. 6 per yr. ISSN 0015-1882

**Urch, Harris & Co. Ltd.**
7 Richmond Hill Ave., Clifton, Bristol BS8 1BQ, England.
- Commonwealth Queen Elizabeth Stamp Catalogue. a.
- U. H. Stamp Digest. m.

**Urdd Gobaith Cymru**
Llanbadarn Rd., Aberystwyth, Wales.
- Bore Da. m.(Sept.-June) ISSN 0006-7709
- Cymru'r Plant. m.(Sept-June) ISSN 0011-4448
- Deryn. m.(Sept-June) ISSN 0011-9148
- Mynd. m.(Sept-June) ISSN 0026-4431

**Vacation-Work**
9 Park End St., Oxford, England
(Dist. in U.S. by National Directory Service, 252 Ludlow Ave., Cincinnati, OH 45220)
- Directory of Overseas Summer Jobs. a. ISSN 0070-6051
- Directory of Summer Jobs in Britain. a.

**Vantasy Press**
31, Heath Lodge Site, Welwyn, Herts., Eng.
- Idiocy Couchant. q.

**Vauxhall Motors Ltd.**
Kimpton Rd., Luton, Bedfordshire, England.
- Bedford Transport. bi-m. ISSN 0005-7584
- Vauxhall Motorist. bi-m. ISSN 0042-2908

**Vedanta Movement**
Batheaston Villa, Batheaston, Bath, Eng.
- Common Life; a newsletter on reconciliation, non-violence, peace and spiritual communism. q. ISSN 0010-3276

**Vedic Publications**
Hindi House, 63 Hanbury St., London E.1, England
(Subscr. to: 2 Chepstow Rd., London W7 2BG, England)
- Amar Deep; Hindi weekly London. w.

**Vegetarian Society**
Parkdale, Dunham Road, Altrincham, Cheshire, England.
- International Vegetarian Health Food Handbook. a.
- New Vegetarian. m.

**Vehicle Builders and Repairers Association**
Belmont House, 102 Finkle Lane, Gildersome, Leeds LS27 7TW, Eng.
- Body. m. ISSN 0006-5501
- Vehicle Builders & Repairers Association. Directory of Members & Buyers. a.

**Ver Poets**
63 Chiswell Green Lane, St. Albans, Herts AL2 3AG, England.
- Poetry Post. s-a.
- Ver Poets Broadsheets. irreg.
- Vermouth. irreg.

**Veratbrite Ltd.**
53 Beak St., London W1R 3LF, England.
- Agricultural Supply Industry. w.

**Veritas Foundation**
12 Praed Mews, London W.2, England.
- Biblioteka Polska. Seria Tomistyczna. irreg. ISSN 0067-7752

**Veteran Car Club of Great Britian**
14 Fitzhardinge St., Portman Square, London, W.I., Eng.
- Veteran Car. 2 per yr. ISSN 0042-4781

**Veterinarians Alliance**
8 Hartington Place, Carlisle CA1 1HL, Cumberland, Eng.
- Veterinary Doctor and Veterinary Digest. 3 per yr. ISSN 0049-6065

**Vickers Ltd.**
Millbank Tower, London S.W.I., Eng.
- Vickers News. m. ISSN 0049-609X

**Victoria Institute**
130 Wood St., Cheapside, London EC2V 6DN, Eng.
- Faith and Thought; a journal devoted to the study of the inter-relation of the Christian revelation and modern research. 3 per yr. ISSN 0014-7028 (Co-Sponsor: Philosophical Society of Great Britain)

**Victoria League**
18 Northumberland Ave., London WC2N 5BJ, England.
- Victoria League for Commonwealth Friendship. Annual Report. a. ISSN 0083-601X

**Victorian Society**
1 Priory Gardens, Bedford Park, London W4 1TT, England.
- Victorian Society. Annual. a. ISSN 0083-6079
- Victorian Society. Conference Reports. irreg. ISSN 0083-6087

**Vietnam Solidarity Committee**
182 Pentonville Rd., London N. 1., Eng.
- Indochina. every 6 weeks. ISSN 0300-4023

**Viewpoint Aquarius**
49 Blandford St., London W.1., England.
- Viewpoint Aquarius. m.

**Viking Society for Northern Research**
c/o Dept. of Scandinavian Studies, University College, London WC1E 6BT, England.
- Viking Society for Northern Research. Saga Book. a.
- Viking Society for Northern Research. Text Series. irreg. ISSN 0083-6257

**Villa Guide Ltd.**
51 Brompton Road, London, SW3, England.
- Villa Guide. a. ISSN 0083-6273

**Vincent Press**
60 Cole Park Rd., Twickenham, Middlesex, Eng.
- Journal of World Trade Law. bi-m. ISSN 0022-5444

**Vintage**
54 Ouseley Rd., Wraysbury, Bucks, Eng.
- Vintage. m. ISSN 0042-6342

**Vintage Jazz Mart**
c/o Trevor H. Benwell, Ed., 4 Hillcrest Gardens, Dollis Hill, London N. W. 2., England.
- Vintage Jazz Mart. 4 per yr. ISSN 0042-6369

**Vintage Record Mart**
16 London Hill, Rayleigh, Essex SS6 7HP, Eng.
- Vintage Record Mart. bi-m.

**Vintage Transport Enthusiasts Club**
140 Abbey House, Victoria St., London S.W.1., Eng.
- Penny Wise Motoring; for advertising anything and everything in prewar motoring. fortn. ISSN 0048-3273

**Viola da Gamba Society**
c/o G. D. Davidson, 2 Northfield, Braughing, Ware, Hertfordshire, England.
- Chelys; journal of the Viola da Gamba Society. a.

**Virgil Society**
c/o F. Robertson, Faculty of Letters, Reading University, Reading, England.
- Virgil Society. Proceedings. a. ISSN 0083-629X

**Vision Inc., S.A.**
Times House, Station Approach, Ruislip, Middlesex, England
(Dist. in U.S. by: Vision, 641 Lexington Ave., New York, NY 10022)
- Vision; revista internacional. fortn. ISSN 0042-6911

**Visual Publications Ltd.**
32 Liverpool Rd., Worthing, West Sussex BN11 1SZ, England
- A P/Advertising Parade. m. ISSN 0044-5703
- Actualite Publicitaire; les faits vus a travers la publicite. m.(11 per yr) ISSN 0001-7760
- Advertisement Parade; A P International Research. m. ISSN 0001-8864

**Vita et Pax-Foundation for Unity**
Benedictine Priory "Regina Pacia", Southgate, London N14 4AT, England.
- One in Christ; a Catholic ecumenical review. q. ISSN 0030-252X

**Voice of Methodism Association**
111 Windsor Rd., Southport, Merseyside PR9 9BX, England.
- Voice of Methodism. q (approx.) ISSN 0042-8167

**Voices of North Devon**
107 Pilton St., Pilton, England.
- Voices of North Devon. bi-m.

**Voltaire Foundation**
Thorpe Manderville House, Banbury, Oxfordshire, England.
- Studies on Voltaire and the Eighteenth Century. 12 per yr.

**Voluntary Committee on Overseas Aid and Development**
Parnell House, 25 Wilton Rd., London SW1V 1JSEng.
- World Hunger/Action for Development. bi-m.

**W A G B I for Shooting and Conservation**
Marford Mill, Chester Rd., Rossett, Wrexham, Clwyd LL12 0HL, England.
- W A G B I Magazine. (Wildfowlers Association of Great Britain and Ireland) q.

**W. D. & H. O. Wills**
- Wills Horse & Rider Yearbook. (pub. by Queen Anne Press Ltd.)

**John Waddington Ltd.**
Wakefield Rd., Leeds 10, Eng.
- Bridge Magazine. m. ISSN 0006-9868

**Arthur Waite Productions**
Forestry Chambers, 67 Bridge St., Manchester M3 3B, Eng.
- Free-Lance Writing & Photography. q. ISSN 0016-0385

**Wales International**
Clydfan, Ael-Y-Garth, Caernarfon, Wales.
- Enfys. q. ISSN 0013-7596

**Wales Publications Ltd.**
40 Heath St., London N.W.3, Eng.
- Wales; the national magazine of literature, the arts and Welsh affairs. q. ISSN 0043-0056

**W. Walker & Sons (Otley) Ltd.**
Victoria Works, Otley, England.
- Walker's Old Moore's Almanac. a. ISSN 0083-7067

**Stephen Wall, Christopher Ricks and F. W. Bateson**
Brill, Aylesbury, Bucks, Eng.
- Essays in Criticism; a quarterly journal of literary criticism. q. ISSN 0014-0856

**Wallpaper Paint & Wallcovering Retailers Association**
14 Birmingham Rd., Walsall WS1 2NA, Eng.
- Wallpaper, Paint & Wallcovering. m. ISSN 0043-0153

**Warburg Institute**
University of London, Woburn Square, London, WC1H 0AB, England.
- Journal of the Warburg and Courtauld Institutes. a. ISSN 0075-4390
- Warburg Institute. Studies. irreg. ISSN 0083-7199

**Alan Ward, Ed. & Pub**
90 St. Julian's Farm Rd., London SE27 ORS, England.
- Traditional Music. 3 per yr. ISSN 0306-7440

**Ward Lock, Ltd.**
Warwick House, 116 Baker St., London W.1, England
(Dist. in U.S. by: International Publications Service, 114 E. 32nd St., New York, NY 10016)
- London Red Guide. irreg. ISSN 0076-0498

**Warner Publicity Ltd.**
11 Old Bond St., London W.1, England.
- Glimpse of London with American Express. a. (American Express International US)

**Warren Spring Laboratory**
P.O. Box 20, Gunnels Wood Rd., Stevenage, Herts. SG1 2BX, England.
- Warren Spring Laboratory, Stevenage, England. Investigation of Air Pollution: National Survey, Smoke and Sulphur Dioxide. a.

**Washington Publishing House**
Littlethorpe, Ripon, North Yorkshire, England.
- Human Experimentation Abstracts. s-a. ISSN 0302-3338

**Watan Publications Ltd.**
261 Hoe St., London E 17, England.
- Akhbar-e-Watan Urdu Newsweekly. w.

**Watchtower Bible and Tract Society**
The Ridgeway, London, NW7, England.
- Yearbook of Jehovah's Witnesses. a. ISSN 0084-3849 (Jehovah's Witnesses)

**Water Research Centre**
Stevenage Laboratory, Elder Way, Stevenage Herts SG1 1TH, England.
- Notes on Water Research. bi-m. ISSN 0307-6652
- W R C Information. w. ISSN 0306-6649

**Waterway Productions Ltd.**
Kottingham House, Dale St., Burton-on-Trent, Staffs DE14 3TD, England.
- Ships Monthly. m. ISSN 0037-394X
- Waterways World. m. ISSN 0309-1422

**Watford and District Industrial History Society**
c/o C. A. Jacques, 9 Parsonage Rd., Rickmansworth, Herts, Eng.
- Watford and District Industrial History Society Bulletin. a.

**Watmoughs Ltd.**
Idle, Bradford, Eng.
- Fur and Feather, Rabbits and Rabbit Keeping. fortn. ISSN 0016-2892 (British Rabbit Council)

**Way Publications**
39 Fitzjohn's Ave., London NW3 5JT, Eng.
- Way; a quarterly review of Christian spirituality. q. ISSN 0043-1575 (English Jesuits)

**Weald of Kent Publications (Tonbridge) Ltd.**
47 High St., Tonbridge, Kent, England.
- Bristow's Book of Yachts. a.
- Dispensing Optician. 8 per yr. ISSN 0012-3773 (Association of Dispensing Opticians)
- Vending International; automatic merchandising & food services. m.

**Wealden Press Ltd.**
South Park Ledge, Mayfield Lane, Wadhurst, East Sussex TN5 6JE, England.
- Pollution Monitor; effluent, sewage, atmosphere, garbage, public cleansing, noise, oil, safety and health at work & energy control. bi-m.

**Webb Society**
Broomfield Lane, Palmers Green, London N13 4HB, England.
- Webb Society Quarterly Journal. q. ISSN 0043-1680

**Websters Publications Ltd.**
79 Temple Chambers, London E.C. 4, Eng.
- Racing & Football Outlook. w. ISSN 0033-7366
- Racing and Football Outlook: Racing Annual. a. ISSN 0079-9424
- Racing Specialist. w. ISSN 0033-7420
- Speedway Star. w. ISSN 0038-724X
- What's on in London. w. ISSN 0043-4671
- World Soccer. m. ISSN 0043-9037

**Wedgwood Society**
c/o Mrs. T.B. Jarvis, Roman Villa, Rockbourne, Fordingbridge, Hants, England.
- Wedgwood Society of London. Proceedings. biennial. ISSN 0511-4063

**Weidenfeld and Nicolson Ltd.**
5 Winsley St., Oxford Circus, London W.1, England (Dist. in U.S. by: Humanities Press, Inc., 303 Park Ave. S., New York, NY 10010)
- L S E Research Monographs. irreg., 1969, no. 4. ISSN 0076-0668 (London School of Economics and Political Science)
- Reading University Studies on Contemporary Europe. irreg., 1970, vol. 4. ISSN 0079-9866 (Reading University. Graduate School of Contemporary European Studies)

**Welding Institute**
Abington Hall, Abington, Cambridge CB1 6AL, Eng.
- Automatic Welding. m. ISSN 0005-108X
- Metal Construction. m. ISSN 0307-7896
- Welding Production. m. ISSN 0043-230X
- Welding Research International. q. ISSN 0306-9427

**Welding Institute. Surfacing Division**
54 Princes Gate, Exhibition Road, London S.W.7, Eng.
- Surfacing Journal. 4 per yr. ISSN 0307-7365

**Wellcome Institute for the History of Medicine**
183 Euston Rd., London NW1 2BP, Eng.
- Current Work in the History of Medicine; an international bibliography. q. ISSN 0011-3999
- Medical History; devoted to the history and bibliography of medicine and the related sciences. q. ISSN 0025-7273

**Wellens Publishing**
The Sun, Guilsborough, Northampton NN6 8PY, England.
- Industrial and Commercial Training; management of human resources. m. ISSN 0019-7858

**Wells Gardner, Darton & Co. Ltd.**
Faygate, Horsham, West Sussex RH12 4SU, England.
- Disco 45. m.

**Welsh Amateur Swimming Association**
Honorary General Secretary, 45 Devon Place, Newport Mon., Wales.
- Welsh Amateur Swimming Association. Handbook. irreg.

**Welsh Arts Council**
- Anglo-Welsh Review. (pub. by Five Arches Press)
- Genhinen. (pub. by Gomer Press)
- Poetry Wales. (pub. by Christopher Davies Publishers Ltd.)

**Welsh Association of Youth Clubs**
Andrews Buildings, 67 Queen Street, Cardiff, Wales.
- Welsh Association of Youth Clubs. Yearbook of Activities; leaders handbook. a.

**Welsh Bibliographical Society**
c/o David Jenkins, National Library of Wales, Aberystwyth, Dyfed SY23 3BU, Wales.
- Welsh Bibliographical Society. Journal. a. ISSN 0083-7911

**Welsh Calvinistic Methodist Book Agency**
Caernarfon, N. Wales.
- Antur. m. ISSN 0003-6161 (Cyngor Ysgolion Ac Addysg Grefyddol Cymru)

**Robin Welsh, Ed. & Pub.**
2 Coates Crescent, Edinburgh EH3 7AL, Scotland.
- Scottish Curler. m.(Sept-May) ISSN 0036-9160

**Welsh Medical Press Ltd.**
23 Blenheim Rd., Cardiff, Wales.
- Welsh Medical Gazette. q.

**Welsh Nation Office**
8 Queen St., Cardiff, Wales.
- Welsh Nation. m. ISSN 0043-2458 (Plaid Cymru (Welsh Nationalist Party))

**Welsh Pony and Cob Society**
c/o T. E. Roberts, 6 Chalybeate St., Aberystwyth, Dyfed, Wales.
- Welsh Pony and Cob Society Journal. a.

**Welsh Secondary Schools Association**
- Welsh Secondary Schools Review. (pub. by Plaistow Press)

**Welsh Soils Discussion Group**
c/o Welsh Plant Breeding Station, Plas Gogerddan, Aberystwyth, Wales.
- Welsh Soils Discussion Group. Report. a. ISSN 0083-7938

**Welshpool Webb-Offset Co.**
17A Castle Gates, Shrewsbury, Eng.
- Shropshire Magazine. m. ISSN 0037-4393

**Wembley History Society**
25 Forty Ave., Wembley, Middlesex HA9 8JL, Eng.
- Wembley History Society Journal. s-a.

**Wesley Historical Society**
Ed. Rev. John C. Bowmer, 25-35 City Rd., London EC1Y 1AA, Eng.
- Wesley Historical Society. Proceedings. 3 per yr. ISSN 0043-2873

**Wessex Cave Club**
Priddy, Wells, Somerset BA5 3AX, England.
- Wessex Cave Club Occasional Publication. irreg.(approx. 1 issue per year) ISSN 0083-811X

**West African Technical Review**
70 Lexham Gardens, London W.8, Eng.
- West African Technical Review. 11 per yr. ISSN 0043-3039

**West Highland Publishing Co. Ltd.**
Breakish, Isle of Skye 1V42 8PY, Scotland.
- Calgacus; the Scottish review of politics, current affairs, history and the arts. q. ISSN 0307-2029

**West India Committee**
18 Grosvenor St., London W1X OHP, Eng.
- West Indies Chronicle. bi-m. ISSN 0043-3152

**West Midland Bird Club**
C/O J. N. Sears, 81 Alcester Rd., Hollywood, Worcestershire, England.
- West Midland Bird Report. a. ISSN 0083-8241

**West Midland Institute of Geriatric Medicine and Gerontology**
c/o Moseley Hall Hospital, Alcester Rd., Moseley, Birmingham B13 8JL, England.
- Symposia on Geriatric Medicine. a.

**West Midlands Arts Association**
c/o Nick Toczek, Ed., Flat 3, 39 Queenswood Rd., Moseley, Birmingham B13 9AX, England.
- Little Word Machine. irreg (2-3 per yr.)

**West of England Newspapers**
Burrington Way, Plymouth, Devon, Eng.
- Western Sunday Independent. w.

**Westbourne Journals Ltd.**
Crown House, Morden, Surrey, Eng.
- Decor and Contract Furnishing. m. ISSN 0010-2946
- Interior Design. m. ISSN 0020-5494
- Kitchens & Bathrooms. bi-m.
- Shop Equipment & Materials Guide. a.
- Shop Equipment & Shopfitting News. m. ISSN 0037-4172
- Shop Fitting and Equipment Monitor. q. ISSN 0037-4180
- Wood & Equipment News. m. ISSN 0043-7646

**Western Counties, Association of Chambers of Commerce**
Clifton Park, Bristol 8, Eng
(Subscr. to: St. Stephen's Bristol Press Ltd., Station Rd., Filton, Bristol, Eng)
- Western Commerce. q. ISSN 0043-3586

**Western Orchestral Society Ltd.**
Westover Mansions, Gervis Place, Bournemouth
BH1 2AW, England.
● Western Orchestral Society. s-a.

**Western Sporting Press Ltd.**
Suite 8, 3rd Floor, St. David's House, Wood St.,
Cardiff, Wales.
● Welsh Rugby. m. ISSN 0043-2466

**Western Temperance League**
89 Alma Rd., Bristol BS8 2DU, Eng.
● Western Temperance Herald. 2 per yr. ISSN
0049-7517

**Westminster Medical School. Student's Union**
Horseferry Rd., London S.W. 1, Eng.
● Broadway; Westminster Hospital gazette. q. ISSN
0007-2133

**Westminster Press Ltd.**
116 Deptford High St., London SE8 4NX, Eng.
● South East London & Kentish Mercury. w. ISSN
0038-3422

**Wheatland Journals Ltd.**
157 Hagden Lane, Watford, Herts WD1 8LW, Eng.
● Blinds and Shutters. q. (British Blind & Shutter
Association)
● Brushes International; journal of the world's brush
industry. m.
● Cordage, Canvas and Jute World. m. ISSN 0010-
8693
● Cordage, Canvas and Jute World Directory. a.
● Directory of Brush and Allied Trades. a. ISSN
0070-5179
● Executive Engineer. bi-m. (Association of
Supervisory and Executive Engineers)
● Finishing Industries. m.
● International Finishing Industries Manual. a. ISSN
0073-747X
● Meat Trade Yearbook. a. ISSN 0082-7967
(National Federation of Meat Traders)
● Meat Trader. m. (National Federation of Meat
Traders)
● Motor Cycle and Cycle Trader. fortn. ISSN 0027-
1845
● Motor Cycle and Cycle Trader Year Book. a.
● Paint Manufacture. 10 per yr. ISSN 0030-9508
● Pram & Nursery Trader. m. ISSN 0032-6844
● Pram and Nursery Trader Year Book. a. ISSN
0306-6541
● Process Biochemistry. m. ISSN 0032-9592
● Toy Trader. m. ISSN 0041-0136 (British-National
Association of Toy Retailers)
● Toy Trader Year Book. a. ISSN 0082-5611
● Who's Who in the Water Industry. a. (National
Water Council)

**Wheel of Yoga.**
c/o Jim Pym, Ed., 37B Rydal Rd., London SW16
1QF, England
● Yoga. q. (Subscriptions to: Ted Lovett, 63 Carlisle
Street. Crewe Cheshire England)

**Where to Go Ltd.**
191 Kings Cross Rd., London W.1, Eng.
● Where to Go in London & Around. w. ISSN
0043-4817

**J. Whitaker & Sons Ltd.**
13 Bedford Sq., London WC1B 3JE, Eng
● Bookseller; the organ of the book trade. w. ISSN
0006-7539
● British Books in Print. a. ISSN 0068-1350
(Dist. in U.S. and Mexico by: R.R. Bowker Co.,
Box 1807, Ann Arbor, MI 48106)
● Paperbacks in Print. a. ISSN 0031-1219
● Publishers in the United Kingdom and Their
Addresses. a. ISSN 0079-7839
● Whitaker's Almanack. a. ISSN 0083-9256
● Whitaker's Books of the Month and Books to
Come. m. ISSN 0043-4868
● Whitaker's Five-Year Cumulative Book List.
quinquennial. ISSN 0000-0183

**White Crescent Press Ltd.**
Harold White, Luton, Bedfordshire, Eng.
● Bedfordshire; a miscellany and review of
Bedfordshire life and history. q. ISSN 0005-7592

**S. S. White Dental Manufacturing Co. Ltd.**
126 Great Portland St., London, W.1, England.
● Dental Delineator. irreg. ISSN 0070-3648

**Whitehall Press Ltd.**
Earl House, 27 Earl St., Maidstone, Kent ME14
1PE, England.
● British Hospitals Home and Overseas. s-a. ISSN
0068-211X
● Cash & Carry Wholesaler. m.
● D. I. Y. Trade. (Do It Yourself) m. ISSN 0011-
4979
● Diesel Engineering. q.
● Freezer Foods. m.
● Highway Engineer. m. (Institution of Highway
Engineers)
● Shipbuilding & Marine Engineering International.
m.
● Stationery Trade Reference Book and Buyer
Guide. a. ISSN 0081-461X
● Stationery Trade Review. m. ISSN 0039-0372

**Whitethorn Press Ltd.**
Thomson House, Withy Grove, Manchester M60
4BL, Eng.
● Cheshire Life Magazine. m. ISSN 0009-3289
● Gloucester and Avon Life. m.
● Lancashire Life. m. ISSN 0023-7469
● Warwickshire and Worcestershire Life. m. ISSN
0043-0390
● Yorkshire Life. m. ISSN 0044-0620

**Whitton Press Ltd.**
50 High St., Eton, Berks, England.
● Defence. m.
● International Broadcast Engineer. 6 per yr. ISSN
0020-6229

**Who Owns Whom Ltd.**
24 Tufton St., London SW1P 3RA, England.
● Who Owns Whom. Australasia and Far East. a.
● Who Owns Whom. Continental Edition. a. ISSN
0083-9302
● Who Owns Whom. North America Edition. a.
ISSN 0083-9310
● Who Owns Whom. United Kingdom Edition. a.
ISSN 0083-9329

**Wiadomosci Trust**
67 Great Russell St., London WC1B 3BS, Eng.
● Wiadomosci. w. ISSN 0043-5074

**Wiener Library Ltd.**
4 Devonshire St., London W.1, Eng.
● Wiener Library Bulletin. s-a. ISSN 0043-5333

**Wildfowl Trust**
Slimbridge, Gloucester GL2 7BT, England.
● Wildfowl. a.

**Wildlife Publications Ltd.**
243 King's Rd., London SW3 5EA, Eng.
● Wildlife; the international wildlife magazine. m.

**John Wiley & Sons Ltd.**
Baffins Lane, Chichester, Sussex, England.
● Earthquake Engineering and Structural Dynamics.
q. ISSN 0098-8847 (International Association for
Earthquake Engineering)
● International Journal for Numerical and
Analytical Methods in Geomechanics. q.
● International Journal for Numerical Methods in
Engineering. m. ISSN 0029-5981
● International Journal of Circuit Theory &
Applications. q. ISSN 0098-9886
● International Journal of Energy Research. q. ISSN
0363-907X
● Journal of Labelled Compounds and
Radiopharmaceuticals. q. ISSN 0362-4803
● Software: Practice & Experience. bi-m. ISSN
0038-0644

**Wilkinson Bros. Ltd.**
12-16 Laystall St., London EC1R 4PB, Eng.
● Handy Shipping Guide. w. ISSN 0017-7423

**William Hill Organisation**
● William Hill Racing Yearbook. (pub. by Queen
Anne Press Ltd.)

**William Pengelly Cave Studies Trust Ltd.**
16 New Road, Kingston Upon Thames, Surrey,
England.
● Studies in Speleology. a. ISSN 0585-718X

**Wynn Williams (Publishers) Ltd.**
Centenary Bldgs., King St., Wrexham, Eng.
● Graduate Careers. q. ISSN 0017-2804

**Williams Publishing Co. Ltd.**
2nd Floor, Warner House, 135 Wardour St., London
W.1., England.
● Carnival. m. ISSN 0008-6703
● Parade. w. ISSN 0031-160X

**W. A. Wilson**
9 Hall St., Llangollen, Wales.
● Llangollen Broadsheet. w. ISSN 0024-5453

**Wiltshire Archaeological and Natural History Society**
41 Long St., Devizes, Wiltshire SN10 1NS,
England.
● Wiltshire Archaeological and Natural History
Magazine. a. ISSN 0084-0335

**Winckelmann Publications**
4 Great St. Thomas Apostle, London E.C.4, Eng.
● Fur Bulletin. w. ISSN 0016-2914

**Wincott Foundation**
2 Lord North Street, London S.W.1, England.
● Wincott Memorial Lecture. a.

**Wine and Spirit Publications Ltd.**
Southbank House, Black Prince Rd., London S.E.1,
Eng.
● Wine Magazine. bi-m. ISSN 0043-5791

**Winsor & Newton Ltd.**
Educational Div., Wealdstone, Harrow, Middlesex,
Eng.
● Colour Review; Art Teachers Journal. 3 per yr.
ISSN 0010-1818

**Wira**
Headingley Lane, Leeds LS6 1BW, England.
● Wira News. bi-m.

**H. Wise & Co. Ltd.**
18 Hand Court, High Holborn, London WC1V 6JF,
England
(Dist. by Meyer Schattner-Stubs Publications, 346
West 44 St., New York, N.Y. 10036)
● Lyttons Theatre and Concert Halls Seating Plans.
irreg., 1967. ISSN 0076-0021 (Dancing Times
Ltd.)

**Witan Publications Ltd**
c/o M.F. Costelloe, Rm. 333a, County Hall,
London S.E.1., Eng.
● London Town; Greater London Council staff
gazette. m. ISSN 0024-6174

**Woking Muslim Mission and Literary Trust**
10 Tremadoc Rd., London SW4 7NE, Eng.
● Islamic Review. m. ISSN 0021-1850

**Woking Review Ltd.**
1 Duke St., Woking, Surrey, Eng.
● Basingstoke Review. m. ISSN 0005-612X
● Guildford & District Outlook. fortn. ISSN 0017-
5420
● Woking Review. w. ISSN 0043-7204

**Women's Employment Publishing Co., Ltd.**
185 Vauxhall Bridge Rd., London S.W.1, Eng.
● Women's Employment. m. ISSN 0043-7530

**Women's Engineering Society**
25 Foubert's Place, London W1V 2AL, Eng.
● Woman Engineer. 4 per yr. ISSN 0043-7298

**Women's International League for Peace and Freedom**
c/o Mrs. B.M. Coppock, Bara Cottage, Tai
Cochion, the Waew, St. Asaph Lliyoag, Clwyd
LL17 0AG, N. Wales.
● Peace and Freedom. q. ISSN 0031-3491

**Women's Liberation Movement National Information Service**
24 Mexborough Drive, Leeds 7, England.
● Women's Liberation Movement National
Information Service. Newsletter. bi-m.

**Women's Liberation Workshop**
42 Earlham St., London W. C. 2., Eng.
● Shrew. irreg.

**Women's Report Collective**
14 Aberdeen Rd., Wealdstone, Harrow, Middlesex,
England.
● Women's Report. bi-m. ISSN 0306-1426

**Women's Squash Rackets Association**
345 Upper Richmond Rd. W., London SW14 8QN, Surrey, England.
- Women's Squash Rackets Association. Handbook. a.

**Woolhope Club**
Hereford Library, Hereford, England.
- Woolhope Naturalists' Field Club, Herefordshire. Transactions. a.

**Wootten Publications Ltd.**
150 Caledonian Rd., London N1 9RD, Eng.
- Planned Savings; a review of personal finance & saving. m. ISSN 0032-0668
- Savings Market. q. ISSN 0308-1729

**Worcester City Museum and Art Gallery**
Foregate St., Worcester WR1 1DT, England.
- Worcestershire Archaeology and Local History Newsletter. s-a. (Co-Sponsor: Worcestershire Archaeological Society)

**Worcestershire Catholic History Society**
243 Jockey Rd., Sutton Coldfield, Warwickshire, England.
- Worcestershire Recusant. s-a.

**Workers Association in Belfast**
10 Athol St., Belfast BT12 4GX, Northern Ireland.
- Workers Weekly. w.

**Worker's Northern Publishing Society Ltd.**
52 Palmerston Rd., London SW19, Eng.
- Labour's Voice. m.
- Voice of the Unions. m. ISSN 0042-8248

**Working Men's Club and Institute Union Ltd.**
Club Union House, 251-256 Upper St., London N.1, Eng.
- Club and Institute Journal. m. ISSN 0009-952X

**Workshop Press Ltd.**
2 Culham Court, Granville Rd., London N4 4JB, England.
- New Poetry. q. ISSN 0308-6283

**World Association of Girl Guides and Girl Scouts**
132 Ebury St., London SW1W 9QQ, Eng.
- Council Fire. q. ISSN 0010-9886
- World Association of Girl Guides and Girl Scouts. Report of Conference. triennial; 22nd., 1975. ISSN 0084-1412
- World Bureau Newsletter. q.

**World Athletics & Sporting Publications Ltd.**
344 High St., Rochester, Kent, Eng.
- Athletics Weekly. w. ISSN 0004-6671

**World Bird Research Station**
Glanton, Northumberland NE66 4AH, England.
- Bird Research. irreg.
- Dawn Song and All Day. irreg. ISSN 0070-3001

**World Bureau of Metal Statistics**
Crest House, 7 Highfield Rd., Edgbaston, Birmingham B15 3ED, England.
- World Metal Statistics. m. ISSN 0043-8758

**World Confederation of Physical Therapy**
20-22 Mortimer St., London W1, England.
- World Confederation of Physical Therapy. Proceedings of the Congress. irreg., 1967, 5th, Melbourne. ISSN 0084-151X

**World Council of Young Men's Service Clubs**
44/46 Orsett Rd., Essex RM 17 5ED, England.
- World Council of Young Mens Service Clubs. Minutes of the General Meeting. a. ISSN 0052-2678

**World Crops Publications Ltd.**
40 Wellington St., London WC2E 7BD, England.
- Livestock International. bi-m.
- World Crops; the journal of international agriculture. bi-m. ISSN 0043-8391

**World Education Fellowship**
c/o William Johnson, 53 Grayshott Rd., London SW11 5TS, England.
- New Era. 6 per yr. ISSN 0028-5048

**World Energy Conference**
34 St. James St., London SW1A 1HD, England.
- World Energy Conference. Directory of Energy Information Centres in the World. triennial.

- World Energy Conference. Plenary Conferences. Transactions. triennial, 9th. 1974, Detroit, Mich. ISSN 0084-1722
- World Energy Conference. Survey of Energy Resources. every 6 years. ISSN 0084-1730
- World Energy Conference. Technical Data on Fuel. every 6 yrs.

**World Federation of Occupational Therapists**
c/o Miss Caroline Henderson, 29 Sherbrooke Ave., Glasgow G41 4ER, Scotland
- International Congress of Occupational Therapy. Proceedings. irreg., 1974, Vancouver. ISSN 0074-3828 (Publisher of proceedings varies)

**World Federation of Scientific Workers**
40 Goodge St., London W1P 1FH, Eng.
- Scientific World. q. ISSN 0036-8857

**World Jersey Cattle Bureau**
Agricultural House, Knightsbridge, London SW1 England.
- World Jersey Cattle Bureau. Conference Reports. irreg. ISSN 0084-1854

**World Jewish Congress**
55 New Cavendish St., London W1M 8BT, Eng.
- Jewish Journal of Sociology. s-a. ISSN 0021-6534

**World League Against Vivisection**
3A North View, Wimbledon Common, London S.W. 19, Eng.
- Animals' Champion and the Way to Health. q. ISSN 0003-3626

**World Media Ltd.**
78 Wigmore St., London W1, Eng.
- Career Accountant. m. ISSN 0306-3429

**World Pentecostal Conference**
The City Temple, Cowbridge Road, Cardiff, Wales.
- World Pentecost. q.

**World Petroleum Congresses**
- World Petroleum Congresses. Proceedings. (pub. by Applied Science Publishers Ltd.)

**World Ploughing Federation**
Foulsyke, Loweswatwer, Cockermouth, Cumberland, England.
- World Ploughing Contest. Official Handbook. a. ISSN 0084-2184

**World Prohibition Federation**
64 Dixon Rd., London S.E. 25, England.
- International Record; for editors, writers, speakers and others. q.

**World Psychiatric Association**
c/o Denis Leigh, Secretary, Maudsley Hospital, Denmark Hill, London SE5 8AZ, England
- World Congress of Psychiatry. Proceedings. irreg., 1971, 5th, Mexico. ISSN 0084-1609 (Proceedings of 5th, 1971 Avail. from: Excerpta Medica Foundation, Box 1126, Amsterdam, Netherlands)
- World Psychiatric Association. Bulletin. biennial. ISSN 0084-2206

**World Refrigeration and Air Conditioning**
11a Gloucester Rd., London S.W. 7, Eng.
- World Refrigeration and Air Conditioning; devoted to the refrigeration and allied industries. bi-m. ISSN 0043-8928

**World Ship Society**
28 Natland Rd., Kendal, Eng.
- Marine News. m. ISSN 0025-3243

**World Touring and Automobile Organization**
32 Chesham Pl., London S.W.1, England.
- International Study Week in Traffic Engineering and International Road Safety Congress. biennial; 12th. Belgrade 1974. ISSN 0074-8692
- World Touring and Automobile Organization. Documentation for Traffic Engineering and Safety Study Weeks. biennial. ISSN 0084-2346

**World Trade Magazines Ltd.**
World Trade House, London E.C.4, Riverhead, Sevenoaks, Kent TN13 2DE, England.
- Achievement. m. ISSN 0001-4907
- British Commercial and Industrial Property. q.

**World Union of Jewish Students**
247 Gray's Inn Rd., London WCT, England.
- Elul. bi-m.

**World's Fair Ltd.**
Times Buildings, Union Street, Oldham, Lancs, England.
- Markets Year Book. a. ISSN 0076-4647
- World's Fair. w. ISSN 0043-9304

**World's Poultry Science Association**
12 Ware Lane, Wyton, Huntingdon PE17 2BZ, England.
- World's Poultry Science Journal. q. ISSN 0043-9339

**World's Woman's Christian Temperance Union**
62 Becmead Ave., London SW16 1UQ, Eng.
- White Ribbon Bulletin. q. ISSN 0043-4965
- World's Woman's Christian Temperance Union. Convention Report. triennial. ISSN 0084-2540

**Worldwide Evangelization Crusade**
Bulstrode, Gerrards Cross, Bucks SL9 8SZ, Eng.
- Warrior. m (except Aug.) ISSN 0049-6901

**Worldwide Knitting Publications, Ltd.**
18 Stannary St., London SE11 4AA, England.
- Modern Knitting. m. ISSN 0026-7880

**Wrangler's Roost**
c/o D. Rowlands, Ed., 53 Patrick Coman House, St. John St., London EC1V 4NQ, England.
- Wrangler's Roost; a news-sheet for the B-Western afficionado. m. ISSN 0043-9452

**John Wright & Sons Ltd.**
42-44, Triangle West, Bristol BS8 1EX, England (U.S. Address: Williams & Wilkins Co., 428 E. Preston St., Baltimore, MD 21202)
- British Journal of Mathematical and Statistical Psychology. s-a. ISSN 0007-1102 (British Psychological Society)
- British Journal of Surgery. m. ISSN 0007-1323 (Association of Surgeons of Gt. Britain and Ireland)
- Burns. q. (International Society for Burn Injuries)
- Community Health. bi-m. ISSN 0010-3837 (Royal Institute of Public Health and Hygiene)
- Dental Practitioner Handbook. irreg., 1973, no. 17. ISSN 0070-3699
- Injury; British journal of accident surgery. q. ISSN 0020-1383 (Institute of Accident Surgery)
- International Dental Federation. News Letter/ Federation Dentaire Internationale. News Letter. q. ISSN 0014-9322
- International Dental Journal. q. ISSN 0020-6539 (Federation Dentaire Internationale)
- Journal of Dentistry. q. ISSN 0300-5712
- Medical Annual; A year book of treatment and practitioners' index. a. ISSN 0076-5899 (Dist. in U.S. by Publishing Sciences Group Inc., 411 Massachusetts Ave., Acton, MA 01720)
- Medicine, Science and the Law. q. ISSN 0025-8024 (British Academy of Forensic Sciences)
- Society of Occupational Medicine. Journal. q. ISSN 0301-0023

**Wye College (University of London) School of Rural Economics and Related Studies**
Nr. Ashford, Kent, England.
- Agrarian Development Studies. irreg. ISSN 0065-4337
- British Isles Tomato Survey. Report. irreg. ISSN 0068-2209
- Economics of Fruit Farming. irreg. ISSN 0070-8763
- Farm Business Statistics for South East England. a. (prep. by its Farm Business Unit)
- Journal of Agricultural Economics. 3 per yr. ISSN 0021-857X
- Studies in Rural Land Use. irreg., 1972, no. 11. ISSN 0081-8453 (prep. by its Countryside Planning Unit)

**Wyevern Astronomical Society**
The Lawns, Churcham, Gloucestershire, Eng.
- Astronomy. q. ISSN 0004-6353

**Wykeham Publications, Ltd., London**
10-14 Macklin St., London WC2B 5NF, England.
- Wykeham Science Series. irreg., 1973, no. 25. ISSN 0084-3113
- Wykeham Technological Series. irreg. ISSN 0084-3121

**Wyndham Lewis Society**
Pollokshields, Glasgow, Scotland.
- Lewisletter. irreg.

**Robert Yeatman Ltd.**
401 Grand Buildings, Trafalgar Square, London
WC2N 5HD, England.
- Hambro Tax Guide. irreg. (Hambro Life
Assurance)

**Yoga Research Association**
79 Addison Way, London N.W. 11, Eng.
- Yoga Quarterly Review. q. ISSN 0049-8327

**York Georgian Society**
Kings, Manor, York YO1 2EW, England.
- York Georgian Society. Annual Report. a.

**Yorkshire Archaeological Society**
Claremont, Clarendon Road, Leeds LS2 9NZ,
England.
- Yorkshire Archaeological Journal. a. ISSN 0084-
4276
- Yorkshire Archaeological Society Parish Register
Series. a.
- Yorkshire Archaeological Society Record Series.
a.

**Yorkshire Dialect Society**
c/o S. Ellis, School of English, University of Leeds,
Leeds LS2 9JT, England.
- Yorkshire Dialect Society. Summer Bulletin. a.
ISSN 0513-2762
- Yorkshire Dialect Society Transactions. a.

**Yorkshire Naturalists' Union**
The University, Leeds LS2 9JT, Eng.
- Naturalist. q. ISSN 0028-0771

**Young Farmers Clubs of Ulster**
10 Kinnaird St., Belfast 14, N. Ireland.
- Ulster Young Farmer. m. ISSN 0041-6215

**Young Ornithologist's Club**
Royal Society for the Protection of Birds, The
Lodge, Sandy, Bedfordshire, Eng.
- Bird Life. bi-m. ISSN 0006-3649

**Young Writer Group**
2A Chertsey Rd., Ashford Common, Middlesex,
Eng.
- Young Writer. m. ISSN 0044-0957

**Youth Aliyah**
233 Baker St., London NW1 6XJ, Eng.
- Youth Aliyah Review. q. ISSN 0044-1155
(Children and Youth Aliyah Committee for Great
Britain)

**Youth Hostels Associations (England & Wales)**
Trevelyan House, St. Albans, Herts., Eng.
- Hostelling News. q. ISSN 0306-8927

**Hans Zell Publishers Ltd.**
P.O. Box 56, Oxford OX1 3EL, England.
- African Book Publishing Record. q.

**Zephyr Records & Magazines**
P.O. Box 6, Wallasey, Merseyside L45 4SJ,
England.
- Zephyr. bi-m.

**Zinc Development Association**
34 Berkeley Square, W1X 6AJ, London, Eng.
- F E & Z N. 1-2 nos.per yr. ISSN 0014-5785
- International Conference on Hot Dip Galvanizing.
Proceedings. (pub. by Industrial Newspapers Ltd.)
- International Pressure Die Casting Conference.
Report. irreg.; 8th. Munich, 1975. ISSN 0074-
7521 (European Pressure Die Casting Committee)
- Zinc Abstracts; a review of recent technical
literature on the uses of zinc and its products. bi-
m. ISSN 0044-4731 (Co-Sponsors: Zinc Institute
Inc; Lead Industry Association Inc.)

**Zinc-Lead Library and Abstracts Service**
34 Berkeley Square, London W1X 6AJ, Eng.
- Lead Abstracts; a review of recent technical
literature on the uses of lead and its products. 6
per yr. ISSN 0023-9569 (Lead Development
Association (London)) (Co-Sponsor: Lead
Industries Association (New York))

**Zionist Federation of Great Britain and Northern
Ireland**
Rex House, 4-12 Regent St., London S.W.1,
England.
- Zionist Year Book. a. ISSN 0084-5531

**Zionist Review Ltd.**
36-38 Whitefriars St., London EC4Y 8BL, Eng.
- Jewish Observer and Middle East Review. w.
ISSN 0021-6623

**Zoo-Centrum**
1 Lyall St., London, W1, England.
- International Zoo-News. 8 per yr. ISSN 0020-
9155

**Zoological Society of London**
Regent's Park, London NW1 4RY, England.
- International Zoo Yearbook. a. ISSN 0074-9664
- Journal of Zoology. (pub. by Academic Press Inc.
(London) Ltd.)
- Nomenclator Zoologicus. irreg., vol. 7, 1975.
ISSN 0078-0952
- Zoological Record. a. ISSN 0084-5604
- Zoological Society of London. Symposia. (pub. by
Academic Press Inc. (London) Ltd.)
- Zoological Society of London. Transactions. irreg.
ISSN 0084-5620

**Zululand Swaziland Association**
c/o Phyllis Sargent, organizing secretary, 4 Crown
St., Bury St. Edmunds, Suffolk, Eng.
- Net. 2 per yr. ISSN 0028-2820

**3M United Kingdom Ltd.**
3M House, Wigmore St., London W1A 1ET,
England.
- Tape Teacher; a magazine of audio visual
teaching. a.

**1745 Association and National Military History
Society**
c/o Ed. Barbara Fairweather, Invevloe House,
Glencoe, Argyll, Scotland
(Subscr. to: M.M. Macdonald, 14 Mountblow
House, Clydebank G81 4QE, Dunbarton, Scotland)
- 1745 Association and National Military History
Society. Quarterly Notes.

# UNITED KINGDOM MISC. ISLANDS

**Anson & Co Ltd.**
9 New St., St. Helier, Jersey, Channel Islands.
- What's on in Jersey. 24 per yr(May-Oct.) ISSN
0043-4663

**Channel Islands Communications (Television) Ltd.**
Television Centre, Rouge Bouillon, St. Helier,
Jersey, Channel Islands.
- Channel Television Times. w.

**Francis Hodgson (F.H. Books Ltd.)**
P.O. Box 74, Guernsey, Channel Islands.
- Agricultural Research Index; including forestry,
fisheries and food. irreg., 6th edt., 1977. ISSN
0065-4531
- Directory of Library Directories. irreg.
- Directory of Scientific Directories. irreg., 3rd edt.,
1975. ISSN 0070-6272
- East European Research Index. a.
- European Research Index (Western Europe) irreg.,
4th edt., 1977. ISSN 0071-304X
- Guide to European Sources of Technical
Information. irreg., 4th edt., 1976. ISSN 0072-
8349
- Guide to Science and Technology in the U.S.A.
irreg.
- Guide to Science and Technology in the U K.
irreg., 2nd edt., 1977. ISSN 0072-8675
- Guide to Science and Technology in the U S S R.
irreg., 2nd edt., 1977. ISSN 0072-8683
- Guide to World Science. irreg., 2nd edt., 1974-76.
ISSN 0072-8780
- Industrial Research in Britain. irreg., 8th edt.,
1976. ISSN 0073-7615
- Medical Research Index. irreg., 5th edt., 1977.
ISSN 0076-6003
- Nuclear Research Index. irreg., 5th edt., 1976.
- Ocean Research Index; including Freshwater
Science. irreg., 2nd edt., 1976. ISSN 0078-3145
- Pollution Research Index. irreg.
- Who's Who in Atoms. irreg., 6th., 1977. ISSN
0083-9434
- Who's Who in Ocean and Fresh Water Science.
irreg.
- Who's Who in Science in Europe. irreg., 3rd edt.,
1977 (4 vols.) ISSN 0083-968X

**Isle of Man Natural History and Antiquarian Society**
c/o Manx Museum, Douglas, Isle of Man.
- Isle of Man Natural History and Antiquarian
Society. Proceedings. biennial.

**Royal Jersey Agricultural & Horticultural Society**
Springfield, St. Helier, Jersey, Channel Islands.
- Jersey at Home. s-a. ISSN 0446-7310

**Shetland Council of Social Service**
4B Market St., Lerwick ZE1 0JN, Shetland Islands,
U.K.
- New Shetlander. q. ISSN 0047-987X

**Societe Guernesiaise**
Guille-Alles Library, Guernsey, C. I., Channel
Islands.
- Societe Guernesiaise. Report and Transactions. a.

**Technical Information Co. Ltd.**
Box 59, St. Helier, Jersey, Channel Islands.
- Computer Abstracts. m. ISSN 0010-4469
- Computer News. m. ISSN 0010-4647

**Toucan Press**
Birling, Mount Durand, St. Peter Port, Guernsey,
Channel Islands.
- Channel Islands Anthology. irreg.
- Literary Repository; devoted to the printing of
unpublished manuscripts and original articles. s-a.
ISSN 0047-4797
- Thomas Hardy Year Book. a. ISSN 0082-416X

**Victoria College. School and Old Victorians'
Association**
Jersey, Channel Islands, U.K.
- Victorian. s-a. ISSN 0042-5125

# UNITED NATIONS

**A I E A**
see **International Atomic Energy Agency**

**Asian Development Bank**
For publications of this agency see section for
PHILIPPINES

**Asian Development Institute**
see under **United Nations Economic and Social
Commission for Asia and the Pacific**

**B I T**
see **International Labour Office**

**Bureau International d'Education**
see **Unesco. International Bureau of Education**

**Bureau International du Travail**
see **International Labour Office**

**C E L A D E**
see **United Nations. Centro Latinoamericano de
Demografia**

**C E P A L**
see **United Nations Economic Commission for Latin
America**

**C I S**
see **International Labour Office. International
Occupational Safety and Health Information
Centre**

**Caribbean Food and Nutrition Institute**
see under **World Health Organization. Pan
American Health Organization**

**Centre International d'Informations de Securite et
d'Hygiene du Travail**
see **International Labour Office. International
Occupational Safety and Health Information
Centre**

**Centre International de Recherche sur le Cancer**
see **International Agency for Research on Cancer**

**Centro Latinoamericano de Demografia**
see under **United Nations**

**Comision Economica America Latina (C E P A L)**
see **United Nations Economic Commission for Latin
America**

Comision Economica de las Naciones Unidas para
America Latina
*see* United Nations Economic Commission for Latin
America

Commission Economique pour l'Afrique
*see* United Nations Economic Commission for
Africa

Consejo Economica y Social de las Naciones Unidas
*see* United Nations Economic and Social Council

E C A
*see* United Nations Economic Commission for
Africa

E C E
*see* United Nations Economic Commission for
Europe

E C L A
*see* United Nations Economic Commission for Latin
America

E C O S O C
*see* United Nations Economic and Social Council

E C W A
*see* United Nations Economic Commission for
Western Asia

E S C A F E
*see* United Nations Economic and Social
Commission for Asia and the Pacific

E S C A P
*see* United Nations Economic and Social
Commission for Asia and the Pacific

Economic and Social Commission for Asia and the
Far East
*see* United Nations Economic and Social
Commission for Asia and the Pacific

Economic and Social Commission for Asia and the
Pacific
*see* United Nations Economic and Social
Commission for Asia and the Pacific

Economic and Social Council
*see* United Nations Economic and Social Council

Economic and Social Council. International Narcotics
Control Board
*see* International Narcotics Control Board

Economic Commission for Africa
*see* United Nations Economic Commission for
Africa

Economic Commission for Europe
*see* United Nations Economic Commission for
Europe

Economic Commission for Latin America
*see* United Nations Economic Commission for Latin
America

Economic Commission for Western Asia
*see* United Nations Economic Commission for
Western Asia

F A O
*see* Food and Agriculture Organization of the
United Nations

Fonds des Nations Unies pour l'Enfance
*see* Unicef

Food and Agriculture Organization of the United
Nations
Distribution and Sales Section, Via delle Terme di
Caracalla, 00100 Rome, Italy
- Agrindex; international information system for the
agricultural sciences and technology. m. (Dist. in
U.S. by: Unipub, Box 433, Murray Hill Station,
New York, NY 10016)
- Animal Health Yearbook. a. ISSN 0066-1872
(Dist. in U.S. by: Unipub, Box 433, Murray Hill
Station, New York, NY 10016)
- Annual Fertilizer Review. a. ISSN 0084-6546
(Dist. in U.S. by: Unipub, Box 433, Murray Hill
Station, New York, NY 10016)
- Ceres; the F A O review on development. bi-m.
ISSN 0009-0379 (Dist. in U.S. by: Unipub, Box
433, Murray Hill Station, New York, NY 10016)
- Codex Committee on Pesticide Residues. Report
of the Meeting. ISSN 0587-5943

- Desert Locust Field Research. irreg.; 1973, no. 12.
(Dist. in U.S. by: Unipub, Box 433, Murray Hill
Station, New York, NY 10016)
- Development Education Exchange. 6 per yr.
(prep. by its Action for Development)
- F A O African Regional Meeting on Animal
Production and Health. Report of the Meeting.
ISSN 0532-0623
- F A O Agricultural Development Papers. irreg.,
1969, no. 91. ISSN 0071-6960 (Dist. in U.S. by:
Unipub, Box 433, Murray Hill Station, New York,
NY 10016)
- F A O Agricultural Studies. irreg., 1973, no. 91.
ISSN 0071-6987 (Dist. in U.S. by: Unipub, Box
433, Murray Hill Station, New York, NY 10016)
- F A O Aquaculture Bulletin. q. ISSN 0014-5599
(prep. by its Fisheries Department)
- F A O Atomic Energy Series. irreg., 1966, no. 6.
ISSN 0071-6979 (Dist. in U.S. by: Unipub, Box
433, Murray Hill Station, New York, NY 10016)
- F A O Commodity Bulletin Series. irreg., 1972,
no. 51. ISSN 0071-6995 (Dist. in U.S. by:
Unipub, Box 433, Murray Hill Station, New York,
NY 10016)
- F A O Commodity Review and Outlook. a. ISSN
0071-7002 (Dist. in U.S. by: Unipub, Box 433,
Murray Hill Station, New York, NY 10016)
- F A O Documentation-Current Bibliography. m.
(supplemented by annual volume cumulating the
author and subject indexes)
- F A O Fisheries Circulars. irreg.; 1973, no. 314.
ISSN 0429-9329 (Dist. in U.S. by: Unipub, Box
433, Murray Hill Station, New York, NY 10016)
- F A O Fisheries Reports. irreg.; 1973, no. 132.
ISSN 0429-9337 (Dist. in U.S. by: Unipub, Box
433, Murray Hill Station, New York, NY 10016)
- F A O Fisheries Studies. irreg., 1966, no. 12.
ISSN 0071-7037 (Dist. in U.S. by: Unipub, Box
433, Murray Hill Station, New York, NY 10016)
- F A O Fisheries Technical Paper. ISSN 0429-
9345
- F A O Food Additive Control Series. irreg., 1969,
no. 8. ISSN 0071-7010 (Dist. in U.S. by: Unipub,
Box 433, Murray Hill Station, New York, NY
10016)
- F A O Forestry and Forest Products Studies.
ISSN 0532-0283 (Dist. in U.S. by: Unipub, Box
433, Murray Hill Station, New York, NY 10016)
- F A O Forestry Development Papers. irreg., 1971,
no. 17. ISSN 0071-7029 (Dist. in U.S. by:
Unipub, Box 433, Murray Hill Station, New York,
NY 10016)
- F A O Legislative Series. irreg., 1970, no. 9. ISSN
0071-7045 (Dist. in U.S. by: Unipub, Box 433,
Murray Hill Station, New York, NY 10016)
- F A O Library List of Recent Accessions. ISSN
0532-0291
- F A O Manuals in Fisheries Science. irreg., 1972,
no. 5. ISSN 0071-7061 (Dist. in U.S. by: Unipub,
Box 433, Murray Hill Station, New York, NY
10016)
- F A O Marketing Guide. irreg., 1966, no. 2. ISSN
0071-7053 (Dist. in U.S. by: Unipub, Box 433,
Murray Hill Station, New York, NY 10016)
- F A O Nutrition Meeting for Europe. Report.
ISSN 0425-5089
- F A O Nutrition Meetings Report Series. irreg.,
1970, no. 46. ISSN 0071-707X (Dist. in U.S. by:
Unipub, Box 433, Murray Hill Station, New York,
NY 10016)
- F A O Nutrition Special Reports. ISSN 0532-
0305
- F A O Nutritional Study. irreg., 1970, no. 24.
ISSN 0071-7088 (Dist. in U.S. by: Unipub, Box
433, Murray Hill Station, New York, NY 10016)
- F A O Papers on Demand Analysis. ISSN 0428-
9625
- F A O Plant Protection Bulletin; a publication of
the world reporting service on plant diseases,
pests, and their control. bi-m. ISSN 0014-5637
(prep. by its Plant Production and Protection
Division) (Dist. in U.S. by: Unipub, Box 433,
Murray Hill Station, New York, NY 10016)
- F A O Regional Conference for Africa. biennial,
1972, 7th, Libreville, Gabon. ISSN 0429-9353
- F A O Regional Conference for Asia and the Far
East. Report. irreg.; 1972, 11th, New Delhi. ISSN
0427-8070
- F A O Regional Conference for Europe. Report of
the Conference. irreg.; 1972, 8th, Munich.
- F A O Regional Conference for Latin America.
Report. irreg.; 1972, 12th, Cali.
- F A O Regional Conference for the Near East.
Report. a.; 1972, 11th, Kuwait. ISSN 0427-8089
- F A O Rice Report. a. ISSN 0071-7096 (Dist. in
U.S. by: Unipub, Box 433, Murray Hill Station,
New York, NY 10016)

- F A O Rice Trade Intelligence. 6 per yr. ISSN
0046-4376 (prep. by its Basic Foodstuffs Service)
- F A O Terminology Bulletin. ISSN 0532-0313
- F A O/W H O Expert Panel on Veterinary
Education. Report of the Meeting. ISSN 0429-
9388
- Food Aid Bulletin; a quarterly information service.
4 per yr. ISSN 0046-4368
- Food and Agricultural Legislation. s-a. ISSN
0015-6221 (prep. by its Legislation Branch) (Dist.
in U.S. by: Unipub, Box 433, Murray Hill Station,
New York, NY 10016)
- Food and Agriculture Organization of the United
Nations. Agricultural Planning Studies. ISSN
0532-0194
- Food and Agriculture Organization of the United
Nations. Animal Health Branch. Animal Health
Monograph. ISSN 0428-9552
- Food and Agriculture Organization of the United
Nations. Basic Texts. ISSN 0532-0208 (Dist. in
U.S. by: Unipub, Box 433, Murray Hill Station,
New York, NY 10016)
- Food and Agriculture Organization of the United
Nations. Cereal Improvement and Production:
Near East Project. Information Bulletin.
- Food and Agriculture Organization of the United
Nations. Committee for Inland Fisheries of
Africa. CIFA Reports. irreg.
- Food and Agriculture Organization of the United
Nations. Committee for Inland Fisheries of
Africa. CIFA Technical Papers. irreg.; 1973, no.
2.
- Food and Agriculture Organization of the United
Nations. Commodity Policy Studies. irreg., 1971,
no. 22. ISSN 0071-6928 (Dist. in U.S. by:
Unipub, Box 433, Murray Hill Station, New York,
NY 10016)
- Food and Agriculture Organization of the United
Nations. Commodity Reference Series. irreg.,
1970, vol. 28. ISSN 0071-6952 (Dist. in U.S. by:
Unipub, Box 433, Murray Hill Station, New York,
NY 10016)
- Food and Agriculture Organization of the United
Nations. European Inland and Fisheries Advisory
Commission. E I F A C Newsletter. ISSN 0532-
9396
- Food and Agriculture Organization of the United
Nations. Fishery Committee for the Eastern
Central Atlantic. Report of the Session. irreg.;
1972, 3rd, Santa Cruz de Tenerife.
- Food and Agriculture Organization of the United
Nations. Forest Tree Seed Directory. irreg., latest
1975. ISSN 0532-0666 (Dist. in U.S. by: Unipub,
Box 433, Murray Hill Station, New York, NY
10016)
- Food and Agriculture Organization of the United
Nations. Forestry and Forest Products Division.
World Forest Products Statistics. irreg. ISSN
0532-0690
- Food and Agriculture Organization of the United
Nations. Forestry Occasional Paper. irreg. ISSN
0428-9374
- Food and Agriculture Organization of the United
Nations. Index of Agricultural Institutions in
Europe. ISSN 0428-9390
- Food and Agriculture Organization of the United
Nations. Interamerican Meeting on Animal
Production and Health. Report. ISSN 0532-0348
- Food and Agriculture Organization of the United
Nations. Irrigation and Drainage Papers. irreg.;
1972, no. 12. (Dist. in U.S. by: Unipub, Box 433,
Murray Hill Station, New York, NY 10016)
- Food and Agriculture Organization of the United
Nations. National Grain Policies. a. ISSN 0071-
710X (Dist. in U.S. by: Unipub, Box 433, Murray
Hill Station, New York, NY 10016)
- Food and Agriculture Organization of the United
Nations. Production Yearbook. a. ISSN 0071-
7118 (Dist. in U.S. by: Unipub, Box 433, Murray
Hill Station, New York, NY 10016)
- Food and Agriculture Organization of the United
Nations.Review of FAO Field Programmes. irreg.
- Food and Agriculture Organization of the United
Nations. Soils Bulletins. irreg.; 1972, no. 17. ISSN
0532-0437
- Food and Agriculture Organization of the United
Nations. Trade Yearbook. a. ISSN 0071-7126
(Dist. in U.S. by: Unipub, Box 433, Murray Hill
Station, New York, NY 10016)
- Food and Agriculture Organization of the United
Nations. World Soil Resources Reports. irreg.
ISSN 0532-0488
- Food and Agriculture Organization of the United
Nations Conference. Report. biennial, 1975, 18th
session. ISSN 0071-6944 (Dist. in U.S. by:
Unipub, Box 433, Murray Hill Station, New York,
NY 10016)

- Food and Nutrition. q. (Dist. in U.S. by: Unipub, Box 433, Murray Hill Station, New York, NY 10016)
- Freedom from Hunger Campaign. Basic Studies. irreg., 1970, no. 24. ISSN 0071-934X (Dist. in U.S. by: Unipub, Box 433, Murray Hill Station, New York, NY 10016)
- Freedom from Hunger Campaign. F F H C Report. ISSN 0532-6370
- Freedom from Hunger Campaign/Action for Development. irreg.
- General Fisheries Council for the Mediterranean. Proceedings and Technical Papers. Debats et Documents Techniques. irreg., 1969, no. 10. ISSN 0072-0747 (Dist. in U.S. by: Unipub, Box 433, Murray Hill Station, New York, NY 10016)
- General Fisheries Council for the Mediterranean. Reports of the Sessions. irreg., no. 12, 1974. ISSN 0072-0755 (Dist. in U.S. by: Unipub, Box 433, Murray Hill Station, New York, NY 10016)
- General Fisheries Council for the Mediterranean. Studies and Reviews. irreg.; 1972, no. 52. ISSN 0433-3519 (Dist. in U.S. by: Unipub, Box 433, Murray Hill Station, New York, NY 10016)
- Ideas and Action Bulletin. 8 per yr. incl. 2 double nos. ISSN 0445-2216
- Indian Ocean Fishery Commission. Report of the Session. irreg., 1972, 3rd, Colombo.
- International Poplar Commission. Session Reports. irreg.; 11th, 1976. ISSN 0074-7475
- International Rice Commission. Newsletter. 4 per yr. ISSN 0538-9550 (prep. by its Agriculture Department)
- Joint F A O/W H O Codex Alimentarius Commission. Report of the Session. irreg.; 1972, 9th. ISSN 0449-122X
- Joint F A O/W H O Expert Committee on Food Additives Report. a. ISSN 0075-3963 (Dist. in U.S. by: Unipub, Box 433, Murray Hill Station, New York, NY 10016)
- Joint F A O/W H O Expert Committee on Nutrition. Report. irreg., 1966, 7th Report (pub. 1967) ISSN 0075-3971 (Dist. in U.S. by: Unipub, Box 433, Murray Hill Station, New York, NY 10016)
- Land Reform, Land Settlement and Cooperatives/ Reforme Agraire, Colonisation et Cooperatives Agricoles/Reforma Agraria, Colonizacion y Cooperativas. 2 per yr. ISSN 0047-3952 (prep. by its Rural Institutions Division) (Dist. in U.S. by: Unipub, Box 433, Murray Hill Station, New York, NY 10016)
- Locust Newsletter. s-a. (prep. by its Locust Control and Emergency Operations Group)
- Marine Science Contents Tables. m. ISSN 0025-3308 (prep. by its Fishery Resources and Environment Division) (Co-sponsor: Unesco Division of Marine Sciences)
- Meeting of International Organizations for the Joint Study of Programs and Activities in the Field of Agriculture in Europe. Report. irreg. ISSN 0532-0402
- Meeting on Soil Correlation for North America. (Report) irreg. ISSN 0543-3770
- Meeting on Soil Survey Correlation and Interpretation for Latin America. Report. irreg. ISSN 0543-3789
- Monthly Bulletin of Agricultural Economics and Statistics (FAO) m. ISSN 0027-0229 (Dist. in U.S. by: Unipub, Box 433, Murray Hill Station, New York, NY 10016)
- Plant Genetic Resources Newsletter. irreg.; latest no. 32, 1976. ISSN 0048-4334 (prep. by its Crop Ecology and Genetic Resources Unit)
- State of Food and Agriculture. a. ISSN 0081-4539 (Dist. in U.S. by: Unipub, Box 433, Murray Hill Station, New York, NY 10016)
- Training for Agriculture and Rural Development. a. (prep. by its Agricultural Education and Training Service) (Dist. in U.S. by:, Unipub, Box 433, Murray Hill Station, New York, NY 10016)
- Unasylva; international journal of forestry and forest products. q. ISSN 0041-6436 (prep. by its Forestry Department) (Dist. in U.S. by: Unipub, Box 433, Murray Hill Station, New York, NY 10016)
- World Animal Review. q. ISSN 0049-8025 (Dist. in U.S. by: Unipub, Box 433, Murray Hill Station, New York, NY 10016)
- World Food Problems. irreg., 1971, no. 14. ISSN 0084-179X (Dist. in U.S. by: Unipub, Box 433, Murray Hill Station, New York, NY 10016)
- World Food Programme News. 6 per yr. ISSN 0049-8084

- World Grain Trade Statistics. a. ISSN 0084-182X (Dist. in U.S. by: Unipub, Box 433, Murray Hill Station, New York, NY 10016)
- Yearbook of Fishery Statistics. a. ISSN 0084-375X (Dist. in U.S. by: Unipub, Box 433, Murray Hill Station, New York, NY 10016)
- Yearbook of Forest Products. a. ISSN 0084-3768 (Dist. in U.S. by: Unipub, Box 433, Murray Hill Station, New York, NY 10016)

**Food and Agriculture Organization of the United Nations. Regional Office for Asia and the Far East**
Maliwan Mansion, Phra Atit Rd., Bangkok 2, Thailand.
- Farm Management Notes for Asia and the Far East. ISSN 0430-084X (prep. by its Regional Working Party on Farm Management for Asia and the Far East)
- Food and Agriculture Organization of the United Nations. Asia and the Far East Commission on Agricultural Statistics. Periodic Report. irreg.
- Food and Agriculture Organization of the United Nations. Plant Protection Committee for Southeast Asia and Pacific Region. Information Letter. irreg.
- Food and Agriculture Organization of the United Nations. Plant Protection Committee for Southeast Asia and Pacific Region. Quarterly Newsletter. q. ISSN 0428-9749
- Food and Agriculture Organization of the United Nations. Plant Protection Committee for Southeast Asia and Pacific Region. Technical Document. 6-8 per yr. ISSN 0428-9765
- Forestry Newsletter of the Asia-Pacific Region. ISSN 0532-0747
- Indo-Pacific Fisheries Council. Regional Studies. irreg. ISSN 0537-3654

**Food and Agriculture Organization of the United Nations. Regional Office for Latin America**
Casilla 10095, Avenida Providencia 871, Santiago, Chile.
- Latin American Land Water Development Bulletin. irreg.

**"Fund"**
*see* **International Monetary Fund**

**G A T T**
*see* **General Agreement on Tariffs and Trade**

**General Agreement on Tariffs and Trade**
Villa le Bocage, Palais des Nations, CH-1211 Geneva 10, Switzerland
- G A T T Studies in International Trade. irreg; 1972 no. 3. (Dist. in U.S. by: Unipub, Box 433, Murray Hill Station, New York, NY 10016)
- General Agreement on Tariffs and Trade. Basic Instruments and Selected Documents Series. Supplement. a. ISSN 0072-0623 (Dist. in U.S. by: Unipub, Box 433, Murray Hill Station, New York, NY 10016)
- General Agreement on Tariffs and Trade. G A T T Activities in (Year) a. ISSN 0072-0615 (Dist. in U.S. by: Unipub, Box 433, Murray Hill Station, New York, NY 10016)
- General Agreement on Tariffs and Trade. International Trade. a. ISSN 0072-064X (Dist. in U.S. by: Unipub, Box 433, Murray Hill Station, New York, NY 10016)
- International Trade Forum. q. ISSN 0020-8957 (prep. by its International Trade Center)

**I A E A**
*see* **International Atomic Energy Agency**

**I A R C**
*see* **International Agency for Research on Cancer**

**I B E**
*see* **Unesco. International Bureau of Education**

**I B R D**
*see* **International Bank for Reconstruction and Development**

**I C A O**
*see* **International Civil Aviation Organization**

**I C J**
*see* **International Court of Justice**

**I D A**
*see* **International Development Association**

**I E R S**
*see* **Unesco. International Bureau of Education. International Educational Reporting Service**

**I F C**
*see* **International Finance Corporation**

**I I E P**
*see* **International Institute for Educational Planning**

**I I E S. Latin American Institute for Economic and Social Planning**
*see* **International Institute for Labour Studies**

**I I L S**
*see* **International Institute for Labour Studies**

**I L O**
*see* **International Labour Office**

**I M C O**
*see* **Intergovernmental Maritime Consultative Organization**

**I M F**
*see* **International Monetary Fund**

**I N C B**
*see* **International Narcotics Control Board**

**I N I S**
*see* **International Atomic Energy Agency. International Nuclear Information System**

**I O S H**
*see* **International Labour Office. International Occupational Safety and Health Information Centre**

**I T U**
*see* **International Telecommunication Union**

**Institut fuer Paedogogik**
*see* **Unesco Institute for Education**

**Institut International d'Etudes Sociales.**
*see* **International Institute for Labour Studies**

**Institute for Education**
*see* **Unesco Institute for Education**

**Instituto de Nutricion de Centro America y Panama**
*see* **United Nations. Institute of Nutrition of Central America and Panama**

**Instituto Latinamericano de Planificacion Economica y Social**
Edificio Naciones Unidas, Av. Dag Hammarskjold, Casilla 1567, Santiago, Chile
(Dist. in U.S. by Economic Commission for Latin America, 1801 K St. N.W., Suite 1261, Washington, DC 20006)
- I L P E S Cuadernos. Serie 1: Apuntes de Clase. irreg.

**Inter-Governmental Maritime Consultative Organization**
101-104 Piccadilly, London W1V 0AE, England.
- I M C O News. 2 per yr.
- Inter-Governmental Maritime Consultative Organization. Annual Report to the Economic and Social Council of the United Nations. a. ISSN 0085-1957

**International Agency for Research on Cancer**
150 cours Albert-Thomas, 69372 Lyon Cedex 2, France
(U.S. Subscr. Address: World Health Organization, Box 5284, Church Street Station, New York, NY 10249)
- I A R C Monographs on the Evaluation of Carcinogenic Risk of Chemicals to Man. irreg.
- I A R C Scientific Publications. irreg; latest 1976.

**International Atomic Energy Agency**
Division of Publications, Kaertner Ring 11, Box 590, A-1011 Vienna, Austria
- Atomic Energy Review/Revue d'Energie Atomique. q. ISSN 0004-7112 (Dist. in U.S. by: Unipub, Box 433, Murray Hill Station, New York, NY 10016)

- C I N D A; an index to the literature on microscopic neutron data. a. (prep. by its Nuclear Data Section) (Co-sponsors: U.S.A. National Neutron Cross-Section Center; U.S.S.R. Nuclear Data Centre; N.E.A. Neutron Data Compilation Centre) (Dist. in U.S. by: Unipub, Box 433, Murray Hill Station, New York, NY 10016)
- Health Physics Research Abstracts. irreg; no. 5, 1974. ISSN 0085-1450
- I A E A Library Film Catalog. a. ISSN 0534-7319
- I A E A Science Feature. q. (prep. by its Public Information Section)
- International Atomic Energy Agency. Annual Report. a. ISSN 0085-2023
- International Atomic Energy Agency. Bibliographical Series. irreg. ISSN 0074-1833 (Dist. in U.S. by: Unipub, Box 433, Murray Hill Station, New York, NY 10016)
- International Atomic Energy Agency. Law Library. Books and Articles in the I A E A Law Library. List. irreg. ISSN 0538-4893 (Dist. in U.S. by: Unipub, Box 433, Murray Hill Station, New York, NY 10016)
- International Atomic Energy Agency. Legal Series. irreg. ISSN 0074-1868 (Dist. in U.S. by: Unipub, Box 433, Murray Hill Station, New York, NY 10016)
- International Atomic Energy Agency. Library. New Acquisitions in the IAEA and UNIDO Libraries. m.
- International Atomic Energy Agency. Panel Proceedings Series. irreg. ISSN 0074-1876 (Dist. in U.S. by: Unipub, Box 433, Murray Hill Station, New York, NY 10016)
- International Atomic Energy Agency. Power Reactors in Member States. a. (Dist. in U.S. by: Unipub, Box 433, Murray Hill Station, New York, NY 10016)
- International Atomic Energy Agency. Proceedings Series. irreg. ISSN 0074-1884 (Dist. in U.S. by: Unipub, Box 433, Murray Hill Station, New York, NY 10016)
- International Atomic Energy Agency. Safety Series. irreg. ISSN 0074-1892 (Dist. in U.S. by: Unipub, Box 433, Murray Hill Station, New York, NY 10016)
- International Atomic Energy Agency. Technical Directories. irreg. ISSN 0074-1906 (Dist. in U.S. by: Unipub, Box 433, Murray Hill Station, New York, NY 10016)
- International Atomic Energy Agency. Technical Report Series. irreg. ISSN 0074-1914 (Dist. in U.S. by: Unipub, Box 433, Murray Hill Station, New York, NY 10016)
- International Atomic Energy Agency Bulletin. bi-m. ISSN 0020-6067
- List of Bibliographies on Nuclear Energy. 3 per yr. ISSN 0020-6075
- Meetings on Atomic Energy. q. ISSN 0047-6641 (Dist. in U.S. by: Unipub, Box 433, Murray Hill Station, New York, NY 10016)
- Nuclear Fusion/Fusion Nucleaire; journal of plasma physics and thermonuclear fusion. 6 per yr. ISSN 0029-5515 (prep. by its Akademische Sexton Graz) (Dist. in U.S. by: Unipub, Box 433, Murray Hill Station, New York, NY 10016)
- Radiation Dosimetry Data; Catalogue. irreg.
- Waste Management Research Abstracts. a. ISSN 0083-761X

**International Atomic Energy Agency. International Centre for Theoretical Physics**
Box 586, Miramare, Trieste 34100, Italy.
- Directory of Theoretical Physicists from Developing Countries. quinquennial.
- International Centre for Theoretical Physics. Annual Report. a. ISSN 0304-7091
- International Centre for Theoretical Physics. Monthly Bulletin. m. ISSN 0020-630X

**International Atomic Energy Agency. International Nuclear Information System**
Kaerntner Ring 11, Box 590, A-1011 Vienna, Austria
- I N I S Atomindex. s-m. ISSN 0004-7139 (Dist. in U.S. by: Unipub, Box 433, Murray Hill Station, New York, NY 10016)
- I N I S Newsletter. 4 per yr. ISSN 0047-0856
- I N I S Reference Series. irreg; no. 15, 1975. (Dist. in U.S. by: Unipub, Box 433, Murray Hill Station, New York, NY 10016)

**International Bank for Reconstruction and Development**
1818 H St., N.W., Washington, DC 20433.
- Facts About the World Bank and the International Development Association. m.
- International Bank for Reconstruction and Development. Economic Development Institute. E D I Seminar Papers. irreg.
- International Bank for Reconstruction and Development. Statement of Loans. 4 per yr. ISSN 0047-0570
- International Bank for Reconstruction and Development. Working Paper. irreg.; no. 201, 1975.
- International Bank for Reconstruction and Development. World Bank Staff Occasional Papers. irreg.; no. 19, 1975. ISSN 0074-199X (Dist. by: Johns Hopkins University Press, Baltimore, Md. 21218)
- World Bank Atlas. a. ISSN 0512-2457
- World Bank Catalog of Publications. irreg.

**International Bureau of Education**
see under **Unesco**

**International Centre for Theoretical Physics**
see under **International Atomic Energy Agency**

**International Civil Aviation Organization**
P.O. Box 400, Succursale: Place de l'Aviation Internationale, 1000 Sherbrooke Street West, Montreal, Quebec H3A 2R2, Canada.
- Aircraft Accident Digest. irreg.; latest issue, no. 20, 1974. ISSN 0065-4876
- European Civil Aviation Conference (Report of Session) triennial since 1961 with intermediate sessions; 8th triennial, Strasbourg, 1973; 6th intermediate, Paris, 1974. ISSN 0071-2558
- I C A O Bulletin. m. ISSN 0018-8778
- I C A O Circulars. irreg. ISSN 0074-2481
- International Civil Aviation Association. Aeronautical Agreements and Arrangements. Annual Supplement. a. ISSN 0074-221X
- International Civil Aviation Organization. Air Navigation Plan. Africa-Indian Ocean Region. irreg; 18th, 1974. ISSN 0074-2287
- International Civil Aviation Organization. Air Navigation Plan. Caribbean Region. irreg; 7th, 1974.
- International Civil Aviation Organization. Air Navigation Plan. European Region. irreg; 9th, 1975. ISSN 0074-2309
- International Civil Aviation Organization. Air Navigation Plan. Middle East and South East Asia Regions. irreg; 9th, 1975. ISSN 0074-2317
- International Civil Aviation Organization. Air Navigation Plan. North Atlantic, North American and Pacific Regions. irreg; 8th, 1975. ISSN 0074-2325
- International Civil Aviation Organization. Airworthiness Committee. Report of Meeting. irreg; 10th, Montreal, 1973. ISSN 0074-2244
- International Civil Aviation Organization. All-Weather Operations Panel. Report of Meeting. irreg; 5th, Montreal, 1973. ISSN 0074-2333
- International Civil Aviation Organization. Assembly. Report and Minutes of the Legal Commission. irreg; 21st, Montreal, 1974. ISSN 0074-2368
- International Civil Aviation Organization. Assembly. Report of the Economic Commission. irreg.; 18th, 1971. ISSN 0074-2376
- International Civil Aviation Organization. Assembly. Report of the Technical Commission. irreg.; 18th, 1971. ISSN 0074-2384
- International Civil Aviation Organization. Assembly. Resolutions. irreg; 21st, Montreal, 1974. ISSN 0074-235X
- International Civil Aviation Organization. Automated Data Interchange Systems Panel. Report of Meeting. irreg; 6th, Montreal, 1975. ISSN 0074-2252
- International Civil Aviation Organization. Council. Annual Report. a; latest, 1974.
- International Civil Aviation Organization. Digests of Statistics. Series AT. Airport Traffic. a; no. 14, 1973. ISSN 0074-2422
- International Civil Aviation Organization. Digests of Statistics. Series F. Financial Data. a; latest issue, no. 28, 1974. ISSN 0074-2430
- International Civil Aviation Organization. Digests of Statistics. Series FP. Fleet, Personnel. a; latest issue, no. 27, 1973. ISSN 0074-2449
- International Civil Aviation Organization. Digests of Statistics. Series R. Civil Aircraft on Register. a; no. 13, 1974. ISSN 0074-2457

- International Civil Aviation Organization. Digests of Statistics. Series T. Traffic. a, no. 33, 1974. ISSN 0074-2465
- International Civil Aviation Organization. Digests of Statistics. Series TF. Traffic Flow. q; no. 67, 1974. ISSN 0074-2473
- International Civil Aviation Organization. Indexes to I C A O Publications. Annual Cumulation. a; latest edition 1974. ISSN 0074-249X
- International Civil Aviation Organization. Legal Committee. Minutes and Documents (of Sessions) irreg.; 21st, Montreal, 1974. ISSN 0074-2503
- International Civil Aviation Organization. Library Information: Recent Accessions and Selected Articles. 4 per yr.
- International Civil Aviation Organization. Obstacle Clearance Panel. Report of Meeting. irreg; 3rd, Montreal, 1971. ISSN 0074-252X
- International Civil Aviation Organization. (Panel On) Application of Space Techniques Relating to Aviation. Report of Meeting. irreg; 4th, Montreal, 1971. ISSN 0074-2228
- International Civil Aviation Organization. Report of the Air Navigation Conference. irreg; 8th, Montreal, 1974. ISSN 0074-2546
- International Civil Aviation Organization. Sonic Boom Panel. Report of the Meeting. irreg; 2nd, Montreal, 1970. ISSN 0074-2562
- International Civil Aviation Organization. Technical Panel on Supersonic Transport. Report of Meeting. irreg; 5th, Montreal, 1974. ISSN 0074-2570
- International Civil Aviation Organization. Visual Aids Panel. Report of Meeting. irreg; 6th, Montreal, 1972. ISSN 0074-2589
- Review of Economic Situation of Air Transport. triennial since 1965. ISSN 0085-5596

**International Court of Justice**
Peace Palace, The Hague 2012, Netherlands (or United Nations Publications, Room LX-2300, New York, NY 10017; or Distribution and Sales Section, Palais des Nations, CH-1211 Geneva 10, Switzerland)
- International Court of Justice. Bulletin. a. ISSN 0085-2147
- International Court of Justice. Yearbook. a. ISSN 0074-445X

**International Development Association**
1818 H Street, N.W., Washington, DC 20433.
- International Development Association. Development Credit Agreement. irreg. ISSN 0074-4492
- International Development Association. Statement of Development Credits. q. ISSN 0085-2155

**International Finance Corporation**
1818 H St. N.W., Washington, DC 20433.
- Facts About the International Finance Corporation. q.
- International Finance Corporation. Report. a. ISSN 0074-6061

**International Institute for Educational Planning**
7-9 rue Eugene Delacroix, 75016 Paris, France (Dist. in U.S. by: Unipub, Box 433, Murray Hill Station, New York, NY 10016)
- Financing Education Systems: Case Studies. irreg; no. 5, 1975.
- Financing Education Systems: National Case Studies. irreg.
- Fundamentals of Educational Planning. irreg. 1973, no. 21. ISSN 0071-9862
- Fundamentals of Educational Planning. Lecture-Discussion Series. irreg., 1973, no. 60. ISSN 0071-9870
- International Institute for Educational Planning. African Research Monographs Series. irreg., 1968, no. 16. ISSN 0074-6398
- International Institute for Educational Planning. Occasional Papers. irreg; no. 35, 1975. ISSN 0074-6401
- Planning the Development of Universities. irreg.; 1973, no. 3.
- Planning the Location of Schools: Case Studies. irreg.

**International Institute for Labour Studies**
C.P.6, CH-1211 Geneva 22, Switzerland.
- Institut International d'Etudes Sociales. Cahiers. (pub. by Librairie Sociale et Economique FR)
- International Institute for Labour Studies. International Educational Materials Exchange. List of Available Materials. irreg.,no.9,1976. ISSN 0074-641X
- International Institute for Labour Studies. Public Lecture Series. irreg.

- International Institute for Labour Studies. Publications. (pub. by Macmillan Press Ltd. UK)
- International Institute for Labour Studies. Research Series. irreg.
- Labour and Society. q.

**International Labour Office**
Publications Sales Service, CH-1211 Geneva 22, Switzerland
(U.S. Distributor: I L O Branch Office, 1750 New York Ave. N.W., Washington, DC 20006)
- Bulletin of Labour Statistics; supplementing the annual data presented in the Year Book of Labour Statistics. 4 per yr (plus 8 supplements) ISSN 0007-4950
- Co-operative Information. 3 per yr. ISSN 0047-0783
- I L O Information. 6 per yr. ISSN 0047-0805 (prep. by its Bureau of Public Information)
- I L O Publications. q.
- International Labour Conference. Reports to the Conference and Record of Proceedings. a. ISSN 0074-6673
- International Labour Documentation. m. ISSN 0020-7756 (prep. by its Central Library and Documentation Branch)
- International Labour Office. Legislative Series. bi-m. ISSN 0020-7764
- International Labour Office. Minutes of the Governing Body. 3-4 per yr. ISSN 0047-0791
- International Labour Office. Official Bulletin. issued in 3 series: Series A 3 per yr., Series B 2-3 per yr.,Series C 2 per yr. ISSN 0020-7772
- International Labour Office. Special Report of the Director-General on the Application of the Declaration Concerning the Policy of Apartheid of the Republic of South Africa. a. ISSN 0538-8333
- International Labour Review. bi-m. ISSN 0020-7780
- Labor Education. 3 per yr. ISSN 0043-8081 (prep. by its Workers' Education Branch)
- Social and Labour Bulletin. 4 per yr.
- T & D Abstracts. (Training & Development) 6 per yr.
- Year Book of Labour Statistics. a. ISSN 0084-3857

**International Labour Office. International Institute for Labour Studies**
see International Institute for Labour Studies

**International Labour Office. International Occupational Safety and Health Information Centre**
Publications Sales Service, CH-1211 Geneva 22, Switzerland
(U.S. Distributor: I L O Branch Office, 1750 New York Ave. N.W., Washington DC 20006)
- Bulletin CIS. (Centre International d'Informations de Securite et d'Hygiene du Travail) 8 per yr.
- C I S Abstracts. (Centre International d'Informations de Securite et d'Hygiene du Travail) 8 per yr. ISSN 0302-7651
- International Catalogue of Occupational Safety and Health Films. irreg. ISSN 0074-2147
- International Directory of Occupational Safety and Health Services and Institutions. a. ISSN 0579-8140
- Occupational Safety and Health Series. irreg. ISSN 0078-3129

**International Labour Organisation**
see International Labour Office

**International Monetary Fund**
H and 19th Sts., N.W., Washington, DC 20431.
- Direction of Trade. m (plus annual no.) ISSN 0012-3226 (Co-sponsor: International Bank for Reconstruction and Development (World Bank))
- Finance and Development. q. ISSN 0015-1947 (Co-sponsor: International Bank for Reconstruction and Development (World Bank))
- I M F Survey. s-m (23 per yr.) ISSN 0047-083X
- International Financial Statistics. m. ISSN 0020-6725
- International Financial Statistics. Supplement. a. ISSN 0535-0492
- International Monetary Fund. Annual Report of the Executive Directors. a (September) ISSN 0085-2171
- International Monetary Fund. Annual Report on Exchange Restrictions. a (August) ISSN 0085-2163
- International Monetary Fund. Balance of Payments Yearbook. 10-12 per yr plus annual bound volume.

- International Monetary Fund. Pamphlet Series. irreg. ISSN 0538-8759
- International Monetary Fund. Selected Decisions of the International Monetary Fund and Selected Documents. irreg. ISSN 0094-1735
- International Monetary Fund. Staff Papers. 3 per yr. ISSN 0020-8027
- International Monetary Fund. Summary Proceedings of the Annual Meeting of the Board of Governors. a. ISSN 0074-7025

**International Narcotics Control Board**
Distributions and Sales Section, Palais des Nations, CH-1211 Geneva 10, Switzerland
(or United Nations Publications, Room LX-2300, New York, NY 10017)
- Estimated World Requirements of Narcotic Drugs. a.; latest, 1975. ISSN 0082-8335
- Estimated World Requirements of Narcotic Drugs, Supplement. irreg.; latest, supp. 5, 1975. ISSN 0082-8327
- International Narcotics Control Board. Comparative Statement of Estimates and Statistics on Narcotic Drugs Furnished by Governments in Accordance with the International Treaties. a.
- United Nations. International Narcotics Control Board. Statistics on Narcotic Drugs Furnished by Governments in Accordance with the International Treaties and Maximum Levels of Opium Stocks. a.; latest issue, 1973 (pub. 1975) ISSN 0566-7658
- United Nations. Permanent Central Narcotics (Opium) Board. Report of the International Narcotics Control Board on Its Work. irreg.

**International Occupational Safety and Health Information Centre**
see under International Labour Office

**International Telecommunication Union**
Place des Nations, 1211 Geneva 20, Switzerland.
- International Telecommunication Union. Central Library. List of Recent Acquisitions/Union Internationale des Telecommunications. Bibliotheque Centrale. Liste de Acquisitions Recentes/Union Internacional de Telecommunicaciones. Biblioteca Central. Lista de Adquisiciones Recientes. q. (prep. by its Central Library)
- International Telecommunication Union. Central Library. Liste des Periodiques. List of Periodicals. Lista de Revistas. a.
- International Telecommunication Union. Central Library. Listes des Publications Annuelles. List of Annuals. Lista de Publicaciones Anuales. a.
- International Telecommunication Union. List of Telegraph Offices Open for International Service. every 5 years. ISSN 0074-9044
- International Telecommunication Union. Operational Bulletin. m. ISSN 0047-1224
- International Telecommunication Union. Report on the Activities. a. ISSN 0085-2201
- List of Cables Forming the World Submarine Network. irreg., 1972, 18th ed. ISSN 0074-9001
- List of Destination Indicators and Telex Identification Codes. triennial; 3rd edt., 1973. ISSN 0074-901X
- List of International Telephone Routes. a.; 16th edt., 1976. ISSN 0074-9028
- Table of International Telex Relations and Traffic. a. ISSN 0074-9052
- Telecommunication Journal. m.
- Telecommunication Statistics. a. ISSN 0074-9060
- Yearbook of Common Carrier Telecommunication Statistics/Annuaire Statistique des Telecommunications du Secteur Public. a.

**Latin American Institute for Economic and Social Planning**
see Instituto Latinamericano de Planificacion Economica y Social

**Naciones Unidas**
see United Nations

**Nations Unies**
see United Nations

**O A C I**
see International Civil Aviation Organization

**O I C S**
see International Narcotics Control Board

**O M P I**
see World Intellectual Property Organization

**O M S**
see World Health Organization

**O S P (Oficina Sanitaria Panamericana)**
see World Health Organization. Pan American Health Organization

**Oficina Sanitaria Panamericana**
see World Health Organization. Pan American Health Organization

**Organe Internationale de Controle des Stupefiants**
see International Narcotics Control Board

**Organisation de l'Aviation Civile Internationale**
see International Civil Aviation Organization

**Organisation des Nations pour l'Education, la Science et la Culture**
see Unesco

**Organisation Intergouvernementale Consultative de la Navigation Maritime**
see Intergovernmental Maritime Consultative Organization

**Organisation Mondiale de la Propriete Intellectuelle**
see World Intellectual Property Organization

**Organisation Mondiale de la Sante**
see World Health Organization

**Organizacion Mundial de la Propriedad Intelectual**
see World Intellectual Property Organization

**P A H O**
see World Health Organization. Pan American Health Organization

**Pan American Health Organization**
see under World Health Organization

**Pan American Sanitary Bureau**
see World Health Organization. Pan American Health Organization

**Protein-Calorie Advisory Group of the United Nations System**
Room 555, 866 United Nations Plaza, New York, NY 10017.
- P A G Bulletin. 4 per yr.

**Regional Center for Demographic Training and Research in Latin America**
see United Nations. Centro Latinoamericano de Demografia

**U I E**
see Unesco Institute for Education

**U I T**
see International Telecommunication Union

**U N C H R**
see United Nations High Commissioner for Refugees

**U N C I T R A L**
see United Nations. Commission on International Trade Law

**U N C R D**
see United Nations Centre for Regional Development

**U N C T A D**
see United Nations Conference on Trade and Development

**U N C T A D - G A T T**
see General Agreement on Tariffs and Trades. International Trade Centre

**U N D P**
see United Nations Development Programme

**U N E P**
see United Nations Environment Programme

**U N E S C O**
see Unesco

**U N F P A**
see United Nations Fund for Population Activities

**UNHCR**
*see* United Nations High Commissioner for Refugees

**UNICEF**
*see* Unicef

**UNIDO**
*see* United Nations Industrial Development Organization

**UNITAR**
*see* United Nations Institute for Training and Research

**UNRISD**
*see* United Nations Research Institute for Social Development

**UNRWA**
*see* United Nations Relief and Works Agency for Palestine Refugees in the Near East

**UPU**
*see* Universal Postal Union

**Unesco**
*see also* Unesco Press

**Unesco**
7-9 Place de Fontenoy, 75700 Paris, France.
- Adult Education Information Notes. bi-m. (prep. by its Adult Education Section)
- Annotated Accessions List of Studies and Reports in the Field of Science Statistics. a. (prep. by its Division of Statistics on Science and Technology)
- Annual Summary of Information on Natural Disasters. irreg; no. 7, 1972. ISSN 0066-4383 (Dist. in U.S. by: Unipub, Box 433, Murray Hill Station, New York, NY 10016)
- Arid Zone Research. irreg., 1970, vol. 30. ISSN 0066-7366 (Dist. in U.S. by: Unipub, Box 433, Murray Hill Station, New York, NY 10016)
- Bibliographie, Documentation, Terminologie. bi-m. ISSN 0006-1433 (prep. by its Department de la Documentation des Bibliotheques et des Archives) (Dist. in U.S. by: Unipub, Box 433, Murray Hill Station, New York, NY 10016)
- Bibliography of Interlingual Scientific and Technical Dictionaries. irreg., 1969, 5th ed. ISSN 0067-7205 (Dist. in U.S. by: Unipub, Box 433, Murray Hill Station, New York, NY 10016)
- Book Promotion News. q. (prep. by its Section of Book Promotion and Development)
- Catalogue of Reproductions of Paintings Prior to 1860. irreg., 1972, 9th ed. ISSN 0069-1135 (Dist. in U.S. by: Unipub, Box 433, Murray Hill Station, New York, NY 10016)
- Catalogue of Reproductions of Paintings, 1860-1973. irreg.; no. 9, 1973. ISSN 0069-1143 (Dist. in U.S. by: Unipub, Box 433, Murray Hill Station, New York, NY 10016)
- Connaissance de l'Orient. Collection Unesco d'Oeuvres Representatives. (pub. by Editions Gallimard FR)
- Connect; Unesco-UNEP environmental education newsletter. q.
- Copyright Bulletin; quarterly review. q. ISSN 0010-8634 (Dist. in U.S. by: Unipub, Box 433, Murray Hill Station, New York, NY 10016)
- Copyright Laws and Treaties of the World. Supplements. a. ISSN 0069-9969 (Co sponsor: World Intellectual Property Organization)
- Cultures. q. (Dist. in U.S. by: Unipub, Box 433, Murray Hill Station, New York, NY 10016)
- Earth Sciences Series. irreg; no. 12, 1974. ISSN 0070-7910 (Dist. in U.S. by: Unipub, Box 433, Murray Hill Station, New York, NY 10016)
- Ecology and Conservation Series. irreg; no. 4, 1976. ISSN 0070-8372 (Dist. in U.S. by: Unipub, Box 433, Murray Hill Station, New York, NY 10016)
- Educational Studies and Documents. irreg; no. 15, 1974. ISSN 0070-9344 (Dist. in U.S. by: Unipub, Box 433, Murray Hill Station, New York, NY 10016)
- Engineering Laboratories Series. irreg. ISSN 0071-0350 (Dist. in U.S. by: Unipub, Box 433, Murray Hill Station, New York, NY 10016)
- General Catalogue of Unesco and Unesco-Sponsored Publications. irreg., 1969, 2nd supp. ISSN 0072-0658 (Dist. in U.S. by: Unipub, Box 433, Murray Hill Station, New York, NY 10016)

- Guide to National Bibliographical Information Centres. irreg., 1970, 3rd ed. ISSN 0072-8608 (Dist. in U.S. by: Unipub, Box 433, Murray Hill Station, New York, NY 10016)
- I. M. S. Newsletter. (International Marine Science) 4 per yr. (prep. by its Division of Marine Sciences)
- Impact of Science on Society. q. ISSN 0019-2872 (Dist. in U.S. by: Unipub, Box 433, Murray Hill Station, New York, NY 10016)
- Index Translationum. a.; vol. 26, 1976. ISSN 0073-6074 (Dist. in U.S. by: Unipub, Box 433, Murray Hill Station, New York, NY 10016)
- Intergovernmental Oceanographic Commission. Technical Series. irreg., 1972, no. 10. ISSN 0074-1175 (Dist. in U.S. by: Unipub, Box 433, Murray Hill Station, New York, NY 10016)
- International Association of Art. Information Bulletin/Association Internationale des Arts Plastiques. Bulletin d'Informations; art-the journal of the professional artist/le porte-narole de l'artiste professionnel. a. ISSN 0004-5535 (Co-sponsor: International Association of Art)
- International Bibliography of the Social Sciences. Economics. (pub. by Tavistock Publications Ltd. UK)
- International Book Year Newsletter. m. ISSN 0047-0619 (prep. by its International Book Year Unit)
- International Indian Ocean Expedition. Collected Reprints. irreg.; vol. 8, 1970. ISSN 0074-6320
- International Social Science Journal. q. ISSN 0020-8701 (Dist. in U.S. by: Unipub, Box 433, Murray Hill Station, New York, NY 10016)
- International Understanding at School. 2 per yr. ISSN 0047-1240 (prep. by its Department of Curriculum, Structure and Methods of Education)
- Monographs on Education. irreg.; vol. 8, 1973. ISSN 0077-1007 (Dist. in U.S. by: Unipub, Box 433, Murray Hill Station, New York, NY 10016)
- Monographs on Oceanographic Methodology. irreg., 1973, no. 3. ISSN 0077-104X (Dist. in U.S. by: Unipub, Box 433, Murray Hill Station, New York, NY 10016)
- Museum. q. ISSN 0027-3996 (Dist. in U.S. by: Unipub, Box 433, Murray Hill Station, New York, NY 10016)
- Museums and Monuments Series. irreg.; vol. 15, 1973. ISSN 0077-233X (Dist. in U.S. by: Unipub, Box 433, Murray Hill Station, New York, NY 10016)
- N A T I S-News. irreg.
- Natural Resources Research. irreg; vol. 12, 1974. ISSN 0077-6092 (Dist. in U.S. by: Unipub, Box 433, Murray Hill Station, New York, NY 10016)
- Nature and Resources; international news about research on environment, resources, and conservation of nature. q. (Dist. in U.S. by: Unipub, Box 433, Murray Hill Station, New York, NY 10016)
- New Trends in Biology Teaching. irreg; vol. 3, 1971. ISSN 0077-8877 (Dist. in U.S. by: Unipub, Box 433, Murray Hill Station, New York, NY 10016)
- New Trends in Chemistry Teaching. irreg; vol. 4 forthcoming. ISSN 0077-8885 (Dist. in U.S. by: Unipub, Box 433, Murray Hill Station, New York, NY 10016)
- New Trends in Integrated Science Teaching. biennial. (Dist. in U.S. by: Unipub, Box 433, Murray Hill Station, New York, NY 10016)
- New Trends in Mathematics Teaching. irreg.; latest issue, 1973. ISSN 0077-8893 (Dist. in U.S. by: Unipub, Box 433, Murray Hill Station, New York, NY 10016)
- New Trends in Physics Teaching. irreg. ISSN 0077-8907 (Dist. in U.S. by: Unipub, Box 433, Murray Hill Station, New York, NY 10016)
- Perspectivas. (pub. by Livros Horizonte PO)
- Perspectives; revue trimestrielle de l'education. q. (Dist. in U.S. by: Unipub, Box 433, Murray Hill Station, New York, NY 10016)
- Prospects; quarterly review of education. q. (Dist. in U.S. by: Unipub, Box 433, Murray Hill Station, New York NY 10016)
- Reports and Papers in the Social Sciences. irreg.; no. 30, 1974. ISSN 0080-1348 (Dist. in U.S. by: Unipub, Box 433, Murray Hill Station, New York, NY 10016)
- Reports and Papers on Mass Communications. irreg.; no. 71, 1974. ISSN 0080-1356 (Dist. in U.S. by: Unipub, Box 433, Murray Hill Station, New York, NY 10016)
- Revue Internationale des Sciences Sociales. q. (Dist. in U.S. by: Unipub, Box 433, Murray Hill Station, New York NY 10016)

- Science Policy Studies and Documents. irreg.; no. 35, 1974. ISSN 0080-7591 (Dist. in U.S. by: Unipub, Box 433, Murray Hill Station, New York, NY 10016)
- Studies and Reports in Hydrology Series. irreg.; no. 18, 1974. ISSN 0081-7449 (Dist. in U.S. by: Unipub, Box 433, Murray Hill Station, New York, NY 10016)
- Studies in Compulsory Education. irreg. ISSN 0081-7783 (Dist. in U.S. by: Unipub, Box 433, Murray Hill Station, New York, NY 10016)
- Study Abroad/Etudes a l'Etranger/Estudios en el Extranjero; international scholarships and courses. biennial; vol. 20, 1975. ISSN 0081-895X (Dist. in U.S. by: Unipub, Box 433, Murray Hill Station, New York, NY 10016)
- Teachers' Associations. Associations d'Enseignants. Asociaciones de Personal Docente. irreg., 1971, 2nd ed. ISSN 0082-2213 (Dist. in U.S. by: Unipub, Box 433, Murray Hill Station, New York, NY 10016)
- Technical Papers in Hydrology Series. irreg.; no. 13, 1974. ISSN 0082-2310 (Dist. in U.S. by: Unipub, Box 433, Murray Hill Station, New York, NY 10016)
- U N I S I S T Boletin de Informacion. (Unesco Programme of International Cooperation in Scientific and Technological Information) q. ISSN 0304-0062 (prep. by its Division of Scientific and Technological Documentation and Information)
- U N I S I S T Newsletter. (Unesco Programme of International Cooperation in Scientific and Technological Information) 4-6 per yr. ISSN 0300-2519 (prep. by its Division of Scientific and Technological Information and Documentation)
- U N I S I S T Newsletter. Russian Edition. (Unesco Programme of International Cooperation in Scientific and Technological Information) q. ISSN 0304-0070 (prep. by its Division of Scientific and Technological Documentation and Information)
- Unesco. Records of the General Conference. Proceedings. irreg.; seventeenth session, 1972, pub. 1974. ISSN 0082-7509 (Dist. in U.S. by: Unipub, Box 433, Murray Hill Station, New York, NY 10016)
- Unesco. Records of the General Conference. Resolutions. irreg.; seventeenth session, 1972, pub. 1974. ISSN 0082-7517 (Dist. in U.S. by: Unipub, Box 433, Murray Hill Station, New York, NY 10016)
- Unesco. Report of the Director-General on the Activities of the Organization. a. ISSN 0082-7525 (Dist. in U.S. by: Unipub, Box 433, Murray Hill Station, New York, NY 10016)
- Unesco. Scientific Maps and Atlases and Other Related Publications. irreg.
- Unesco Bulletin for Libraries. bi-m. ISSN 0041-5243 (Dist. in U.S. by: Unipub, Box 433, Murray Hill Station, New York, NY 10016)
- Unesco Chronicle. 11 per yr. ISSN 0041-526X (Dist. in U.S. by: Unipub, Box 433, Murray Hill Station, New York NY 10016)
- Unesco Courier. m.; bi-m., Aug.-Sept. ISSN 0041-5278 (Dist. in U.S. by: Unipub, Box 433, Murray Hill Station, New York, NY 10016)
- Unesco Earthquake Study Missions. irreg. ISSN 0082-7479 (Dist. in U.S. by: Unipub, Box 433, Murray Hill Station, New York, NY 10016)
- Unesco Features; fortnightly bulletin for the news media. fortn. ISSN 0041-5286
- Unesco Handbook of International Exchanges. biennial, 1967, 2nd ed. ISSN 0082-7487 (Dist. in U.S. by: Unipub, Box 433, Murray Hill Station, New York, NY 10016)
- Unesco List of Documents and Publications. 4 per yr. and annual cum. (prep. by its Computerized Documentation Service)
- Unesco Statistical Reports and Studies. irreg. 1972, no. 18. ISSN 0082-7533 (Dist. in U.S. by: Unipub, Box 433, Murray Hill Station, New York, NY 10016)
- Unesco Statistical Yearbook. a. ISSN 0082-7541 (Dist. in U.S. by: Unipub, Box 433, Murray Hill Station, New York, NY 10016)
- Unesco Technical Papers in Marine Science. irreg. ISSN 0503-4299
- World Cultural Heritage. irreg.; latest issue, 1974. (prep. by its Department for Cultural Heritage)
- World List of Social Science Periodicals. irreg. ISSN 0084-1870 (Dist. in U.S. by: Unipub, Box 433, Murray Hill Station, New York, NY 10016)

**Unesco. Coordinating Committee for International Voluntary Service**
1 rue Miollis, 75015 Paris, France.
● Volunteer Service Bulletin; comprehensive newsheet on current initiatives and actions about voluntary service and relevant youth events. 3 per yr. ISSN 0007-4942

**Unesco Institute for Education**
Feldbrunnenstr. 70, 2000 Hamburg 13, W. Germany (B.R.D.)
● Documents on Educational Research. irreg.; 1973, no. 3. (Dist. in U.S. by: Unipub, Box 433, Murray Hill Station, New York, NY 10016)
● Educational Research and Practice. irreg.; 1972, no. 3. (Dist. in U.S. by: Unipub, Box 433, Murray Hill Station, New York, NY 10016)
● International Review of Education. (pub. by Martinus Nijhoff NE)
● International Studies in Education. irreg.; no. 34, 1973. (Dist. in U.S. by: Unipub, Box 433, Murray Hill Station, New York, NY 10016)
● U I E Monographs. irreg. (Dist. in U.S. by: Unipub, Box 433, Murray Hill Station, New York, NY 10016)

**Unesco. International Bureau of Education**
Palais Wilson, CH-1211 Geneva 14, Switzerland.
● Awareness List/Bulletin Signaletique (U N) bi-m. (prep. by its International Educational Reporting Service)
● Cooperative Educational Abstracting Service. 4 per yr. ISSN 0045-8473
● Educational Documentation and Information/Documentation et Information Pedagogiques. q. ISSN 0303-3899 (Dist. in U.S. by Unipub, Box 433, Murray Hill Station, New York, NY 10016)
● Experiments and Innovations in Education; an Internatinoal Bureau of Education series. 5-6 per yr. (prep. by its International Educational Reporting Service) (Dist. in U.S. by: Unipub, Box 433, Murray Hill Station, New York, NY 10016)
● Innovation; newsletter of the International Educational Reporting Service bi-m.
● International Conference on Education. Proceedings/Conference International de l'Education. Proceedings. a. until 33rd, 1971; thereafter biennial. ISSN 0074-3275

**Unesco. International Copyright Information Center**
7-9 Place de Fontenoy, 75700 Paris, France.
● International Copyright Information Centre. Information Bulletin. irreg. ISSN 0336-3686

**Unesco. International Institute for Educational Planning**
see **International Institute for Educational Planning**

**Unesco Press**
see also **Unesco**

**Unesco Press**
7 Place de Fontenoy, F-75700 Paris, France (Dist. in U.S. by: Unipub, Box 433, Murray Hill Station, New York, NY 10016)
● Bibliographical Services Throughout the World. quinquennial, 1972, no. 4.
● Documentation, Libraries and Archives: Bibliographies and Reference Works. irreg.
● Documentation, Libraries and Archives: Studies and Research. irreg.
● International Oceanographic Tables. ISSN 0538-8880
● Race Question in Modern Science. irreg. ISSN 0501-3615
● Selected List of Catalogues for Short Films and Filmstrips. irreg. ISSN 0503-440X
● Studies and Documents on Cultural Policies. irreg. ISSN 0586-6898
● Unesco Asian Fiction Series. irreg. ISSN 0566-6201
● Unesco Source Books on Curricula and Methods. irreg. ISSN 0502-9554
● World Index of Social Science Institutions/Repertoire Mondiale des Institutions de Sciences Sociales. q.

**Unesco. Regional Cultural Bureau for Latin America and the Caribbean**
Calzada 551, esq. a D, Vedado, Apdo. 1358, Havana, Cuba.
● Unesco. Centro de Documentacion, Havana. Informaciones Trimestriales. q. ISSN 0049-5204

**Unesco. Regional Office for Culture and Book Development in Asia**
21-A, Block 6, P.E.C.H.S., Karachi 2905, Pakistan.
● Unesco. Regional Office for Culture and Book Development in Asia. Newsletter. q.

**Unesco. Regional Office for Education in Asia**
Darakarn Bldg., Box 1425, Bangkok 11, Thailand.
● Asian Periodicals: a Selected List of Titles Received and Their Contents. bi-m. ISSN 0044-9210
● Education in Asia: Reviews, Reports and Notes. approx. 2 per yr. (Dist. in U.S. by: Unipub, Box 433, Murray Hill Station, New York, NY 10016)
● Educational Building Digest. irreg. (5-6 per yr)
● Population Education in Asia Newsletter. irreg. (prep. by its Population Education Programme)
● Unesco. Regional Office for Education in Asia. Bulletin. a.; biennial to 1973. ISSN 0503-4450

**Unesco. Regional Office for Education in Latin America and the Caribbean**
Enrique Delpiano 2058, Casilla 3187, Santiago, Chile.
● Unesco. Oficina Regional de Educacion para America Latina y le Caribe. Boletin de Educacion. s-a. ISSN 0041-5251

**Unesco. Regional Office of Science and Technology for Africa**
c/o Unesco Field Science Office for Africa, P.O. Box 30592, Nairobi, Kenya.
● Unesco. Regional Office of Science and Technolgy for Africa. Bulletin. q. ISSN 0503-4434

**Unesco. Regional Office of Science and Technology for Latin America and the Caribbean**
1320 Bulevar Artigas, Apartado de Correas 859, Montevideo, Uruguay.
● Unesco. Regional Office for Science and Technology for Latin American and the Caribbean. Boletin. 2 per yr.

**Unicef**
866 United Nations Plaza, 6th Floor, New York, NY 10017
(or Distribution and Sales Section, Palais des Nations, CH-1211 Geneva 10, Switzerland)
● Unicef Information Bulletin. 4 per yr. ISSN 0049-4984

**Unicef Canada**
443 Mt. Pleasant Rd., Toronto, Ontario M4S 2L8, Canada.
● Unicef News. 4 per yr. ISSN 0041-5340

**Unicef. European Office**
Palais des Nations, Case Postale 11, 1211 Geneva 10, Switzerland.
● Carnets de l'Enfance/Assignment Children; a journal concerned with children, women and youth in development. q. ISSN 0004-5128

**Union Internationale des Telecommunications**
see **International Telecommunication Union**

**Union Postale Universelle**
see **Universal Postal Union**

**Unipub**
Exclusive national distributor for indicated agencies, it also supplies publications of the United Nations and other UN system agencies as well as their titles published or copublished by commercial or institutional presses. Orders to: Box 433, Murray Hill Station, New York, NY 10016

**United Nations**
Priced publications of the United Nations are available from United Nations Publications, Room LX-2300, New York, NY 10017; or Distribution and Sales Section, Palais des Nations, 1200 Geneva 10, Switzerland. Free publications should be requested from the issuing agency.

**United Nations**
New York, NY 10017.
● Environment and Social Sciences/Environnement et Sciences Sociales. (pub. by Editions Mouton et Cie FR)
● United Nations. Social Development Division. Social Development Newsletter. 2 per yr.

**United Nations Central American Hydrometeorological Project**
San Jose, Costa Rica.
● Anuario Meteorologico del Istmo Centroamericano. a.

**United Nations Central American Hydrometeorological Project. Regional Committee for Water Resources**
Apdo. 4328, Managua, Nicaragua.
● Anuario Hidrologico del Istmo Centroamericano. a.

**United Nations. Centre for Economic and Social Information**
Palais des Nations, CH-1200 Geneva 10, Switzerland.
● Development Forum. m.

**United Nations. Centre for Housing, Building and Planning**
United Nations Headquarters, New York, NY 10017.
● Human Settlements. q. ISSN 0046-8231 (prep. by its Department of Economic and Social Affairs)

**United Nations. Centre for Natural Resources, Energy and Transport**
● Natural Resources Forum. (pub. by D. Reidel Publishing Co. NE)

**United Nations Centre for Regional Development**
Marunouchi 2-4-7, Naka-ku, Nagoya 460, Japan.
● Asian Development Dialogue. irreg. ISSN 0300-5003

**United Nations. Centro Latinoamericano de Demografia**
J. M. Infante 9, Casilla 91, Santiago, Chile.
● Centro Latinoamericano de Demografia. Boletin Demografico. s-a (with supplements) ISSN 0045-6136
● Centro Latinoamericano de Demografia. Notas de Poblacion; revista latinoamericana de demografia. 3 per yr.
● Centro Latinoamericano de Demografia. Publicaciones P I S P A L. irreg. (prep. by its Programa de Investigaciones Sociales Sobre Problemas de Poblacion Relevantes para Politicas de Poblacion en America Latina)
● Centro Latinoamericano de Demografia. Textos de Divulgacion. irreg.
● United Nations. Regional Centre for Demographic Training and Research in Latin America. Serie A/Centro Latinoamericano de Demografia. Serie A: Informes sobre Investigaciones Realizadas. irreg. ISSN 0503-3934
● United Nations. Regional Centre for Demographic Training and Research in Latin America. Serie C/Centro Latinoamericano de Demografia. Serie C: Informes sobre Investigaciones Realizadas Por los Alumnos del Centro. irreg. ISSN 0503-3942
● United Nations. Regional Centre for Demographic Training and Research in Latin America. Serie D. irreg. ISSN 0503-3950
● United Nations. Regional Centre for Demographic Training and Research in Latin America. Serie I. Recopilacion de Trabajos sobre Paises. irreg.

**United Nations Children's Fund**
see **Unicef**

**United Nations. Commission on International Trade Law**
United Nations Publications, Room LX-2300, New York, NY 10017
(or Distribution and Sales Section, Palais des Nations, CH-1211 Geneva 10, Switzerland)
● United Nations. Commission on International Trade Law. Report on the Work of Its Session. a; latest issue, 1974.
● United Nations. Commission on International Trade Law. Yearbook. a.; vol. 4, 1974.

**United Nations Conference on Trade and Development**
Distribution and Sales Section, Palais des Nations, CH-1211 Geneva 10, Switzerland
- Review of Maritime Transport. a.; latest issue, 1974. ISSN 0085-560X (Or United Nations Publications, Room LX-2300 New York, NY 10017)
- Tungsten Statistics. q. ISSN 0049-4828 (Or United Nations Publications, Room LX-2300 New York, NY 10017)
- U N C T A D Guide to Publications. a. ISSN 0041-5227

**United Nations. Department of Economic and Social Affairs**
Secretariat, New York, NY 10017.
(Dist. by: United Nations Publications, Room LX-2300, New York, NY 10017; or Distribution and Sales Section, Palais des Nations, CH-1211 Geneva 10, Switzerland)
- Demographic Yearbook. a. ISSN 0082-8041
- International Review of Criminal Policy. a.; no. 31, 1974. ISSN 0074-7688
- International Social Development Review. ISSN 0041-7386
- Population Studies. (pub. by United Nations Publications)
- Public Administration and Finance Newsletter. irreg.
- United Nations. Population and Vital Statistics Report. q. ISSN 0041-7416
- World Energy Supplies. triennial; latest issue, 1969-72. ISSN 0084-1749

**United Nations Development Programme**
Information Division, 345 E. 46th St., Rm. CN-315, New York, NY 10017
(Free Upon Request to United Nations Centre for Economic and Social Information, Ch-1211 Geneva 10, Switzerland)
- Action U N D P. bi-m.
- U N D P Business Bulletin. m.

**United Nations Disarmament Commission**
- United Nations. Disarmament Commission. Official Records. (pub. by United Nations Publications)

**United Nations. Division of Human Rights**
Palais des Nations, 1211 Geneva 10, Switzerland.
- Human Rights Bulletin. 2 per yr. ISSN 0046-8193

**United Nations. Division of Narcotic Drugs**
Palais des Nations, CH-1211 Geneva 10, Switzerland.
- United Nations. Division of Narcotic Drugs. Information Letter. m. ISSN 0085-7491

**United Nations Economic and Social Commission for Asia and the Far East**
*see* United Nations Economic and Social Commission for Asia and the Pacific

**United Nations Economic and Social Commission for Asia and the Pacific**
Sala Santitham, Bangkok 2, Thailand.
- Asian Bibliography. s-a.
- Asian Industrial Development News. a. ISSN 0572-4171 (prep. by its Division of Industry, Housing and Technology)
- Asian Population Programme News. irreg.; 3-4 issues per yr. ISSN 0084-6821 (prep. by its Population Division)
- Asian Population Studies Series. irreg.; no. 6, 1972. ISSN 0066-8451 (Dist. by: United Nations Publications, Room LX-2300, New York, NY 10017; or Distribution and Sales Section, Palais des Nations, CH-1 211 Geneva 10, Switzerland)
- E S C A P Country Monograph Series. irreg. (prep. by its Population Division) (Dist. by: United Nations Publications, Room LX-2300, New York, NY 10017; or Distribution and Sales Section, Palais des Nations, CH-1211 Geneva 10, Switzerland)
- Economic and Social Survey of Asia and the Pacific. irreg. (Dist. by: United Nations Publications, Room LX-2300, New York, NY 10017; or Distribution and Sales Section, Palais des Nations, CH-1211 Geneva 10, Switzerland)

- Economic Bulletin for Asia and the Pacific. (Dist. by: United Nations Publications, Room LX-2300, New York, NY 10017; or Distribution and Sales Section, Palais des Nations, CH-1211 Geneva 10, Switzerland)
- Mekong Bulletin. 4 per yr. (prep. by its Mekong Committee)
- Quarterly Bulletin of Statistics for Asia and the Pacific. q. (Dist. by: United Nations Publications, Room LX-2300, New York, NY 10017; or Distribution and Sales Section, Palais des Nations, CH-1211 Geneva 10, Switzerland)
- Regional Conference on Water Resources Development in Asia and the Far East. Proceedings. irreg., 10th, Manila, 1972 (pub. 1974) ISSN 0080-0589 (Dist. by: United Nations Publications, Room LX-2300, New York, NY 10017; or Distribution and Sales Section, Palais des Nations, CH-1211 Geneva 10, Switzerland)
- Sample Surveys in the ESCAP Region. a.
- Small Industry Bulletin for Asia and the Pacific. irreg. ISSN 0071-741X (Dist. by: United Nations Publications, Room LX-2300, New York, NY 10017; or Distribution and Sales Section, Palais des Nations, CH-1211 Geneva 10, Switzerland)
- Statistical Indicators in ESCAP Countries. q.
- Statistical Yearbook for Asia and the Pacific/ Annuaire Statistique pour l'Asie et le Pacifique. a. (Dist. by United Nations Publications, Room LX-2300, New York, NY 10017; or Distribution and Sales Section, Palais des Nations, CH-1211 Geneva 10, Switzerland)
- Transport & Communications Bulletin for Asia & the Far East. s-a. ISSN 0041-1396 (Dist. by: United Nations Publications, Room LX-2300, New York, NY 10017; or Distribution and Sales Section, Palais des Nations, CH-1211 Geneva 10, Switzerland)
- United Nations Economic and Social Commission for Asia and the Pacific. Development Programming Techniques Series. irreg; no. 9, vol. 3, 1973. ISSN 0082-8106 (Dist. by: United Nations Publications, Room LX-2300, New York, NY 10017; or Distribution and Sales Section, Palais des Nations, CH-1211 Geneva 10, Switzerland)
- United Nations Economic and Social Commission for Asia and the Pacific. Mineral Resources Development Series. irreg.; no. 41, vols. 1-3, 1973. ISSN 0082-8114 (Dist. by: United Nations Publications, Room LX-2300, New York, NY 10017; or Distribution and Sales Section, Palais des Nations, CH-1211 Geneva 10, Switzerland)
- United Nations Economic and Social Commission for Asia and the Pacific. Regional Economic Cooperation Series. irreg; no. 9, 1974. ISSN 0082-8122 (Dist. by: United Nations Publications, Room LX-2300, New York, NY 10017; or Distribution and Sales Section, Palais des Nations, CH-1211 Geneva 10, Switzerland)
- United Nations Economic and Social Commission for Asia and the Pacific. Social Development Division. Social Work Training and Teaching Materials Newsletter. irreg. ISSN 0085-7513 (prep. by its Social Development Division)
- United Nations Economic and Social Commission for Asia and the Pacific. Statistical Newsletter. q. (Dist. by: United Nations Publications, Room LX-2300, New York, NY 10017; or Distribution and Sales Section, Palais des Nations, CH-1211 Geneva 10, Switzerland)
- Water Resources Development Series. irreg; no. 45, 1974. ISSN 0082-8130 (Dist. by: United Nations Publications, Room LX-2300, New York, NY 10017; or Distribution and Sales Section, Palais des Nations, CH-1211 Geneva 10, Switzerland)

**United Nations Economic and Social Commission for Asia and the Pacific. Asian Development Institute**
Sri Ayudhya Rd., Box 2-136, Bangkok, Thailand.
- A D I Quarterly News Letter. q.

**United Nations Economic and Social Council**
- United Nations. Economic and Social Council. Index to Proceedings. (pub. by United Nations Publications)
- United Nations. Economic and Social Council. Official Records. (pub. by United Nations Publications)

**United Nations Economic Commission for Africa**
Box 3001, Addis Ababa, Ethopia.
- Africa Index; selected articles on socio-economic development. 3 per yr.
- African Target/Objectifs Africains. q. ISSN 0002-0230

- African Tax Systems. (pub. by International Bureau of Fiscal Documentation NE)
- African Trade/Commerce Africain. q.
- Agricultural Economics Bulletin for Africa. irreg., no. 15, 1975. ISSN 0065-4434 (Dist. by: United Nations Publications, Room LX-2300, New York, NY 10017; or Distribution and Sales Section, Palais des Nations, CH-1211 Geneva 10, Switzerland)
- Economic Bulletin for Africa. s-a. ISSN 0041-736X (Dist. by: United Nations Publications, Room LX-2300, New York, NY 10017; or Distribution and Sales Section, Palais des Nations, CH-1211 Geneva 10, Switzerland)
- Foreign Trade Statistics of Africa. Series A: Direction of Trade. irreg.; no. 22, 1974. ISSN 0071-7398 (Dist. by: United Nations Publications, Room LX-2300, New York, NY 10017; or Distribution and Sales Section, Palais des Nations, CH-1211 Geneva 10, Switzerland)
- Foreign Trade Statistics of Africa. Series B: Trade by Commodity. irreg.; no. 25, 1974. ISSN 0071-7401 (Dist. by: United Nations Publications, Room LX-2300, New York, NY 10017; or Distribution and Sales Section, Palais des Nations, CH-1211 Geneva 10, Switzerland)
- Investment Africa. q.
- New Aquisitions in the U N E C A Library. bi-m.
- Quarterly Statistical Bulletin for Africa. q. ISSN 0048-6191 (prep. by its Statistics Division)
- Tourism in Africa. Annual Bulletin. a. (Dist. by: United Nations Publications, Room LX-2300, New York, NY 10017; or Distribution and Sales Section, Palais des Nations, CH-1211 Geneva 10, Switzerland)

**United Nations Economic Commission for Europe**
Palais des Nations, 1200 Geneva 10, Switzerland (or United Nations Publications, Room LX-2300, New York, NY 10017)
- Annual Bulletin of Coal Statistics for Europe. a.; vol. 8, 1974. ISSN 0066-3808
- Annual Bulletin of Electric Energy Statistics for Europe. a.; vol. 19, 1973 (pub. 1974) ISSN 0066-3816
- Annual Bulletin of Gas Statistics for Europe/ Bulletin Annuel de Statistiques de Gaz pour l'Europe. a.; vol. 19, 1973. ISSN 0066-3824
- Annual Bulletin of General Energy Statistics for Europe. a.; vol. 7, 1973.
- Annual Bulletin of Transport Statistics for Europe. a.; latest 1974. ISSN 0066-3859
- Economic Bulletin for Europe. s-a. ISSN 0041-638X
- Economic Survey of Europe. a.; latest, 1974 (pub. 1974) ISSN 0070-8712
- Half-Yearly Bulletin of Electric Energy Statistics for Europe. 2 per yr. ISSN 0503-3772
- Quarterly Bulletin of Steel Statistics for Europe/ Bulletin Trimestriel de Statistiques de l'Acier pour l'Europe. q. ISSN 0041-7378
- Statistics of Road Traffic Accidents in Europe. a.; latest 1973. ISSN 0081-5160
- Supplementary Bulletin of Gas Statistics for Europe/Bulletin Supplementaire de Statistiques du Gaz pour l'Europe. quinquennial. ISSN 0503-3810
- Timber Bulletin for Europe. s-a. ISSN 0040-7747 (prep. by its Timber Committee) (Co-Sponsor: Food and Agriculture Organization)
- U. N. Quarterly Housing Construction Summary for Europe. q. ISSN 0041-7424
- United Nations Economic Commission for Europe. Census of Traffic on Main International Arteries. a. ISSN 0566-7631

**United Nations Economic Commission for Latin America**
Casilla 179-D, Santiago, Chile
- Economic Bulletin for Latin America. 2 per yr. ISSN 0041-6398 (Or United Nations Publications, Room LX-2300, New York, NY 10017; or Distribution and Sales Section, Palais des Nations, CH-1211 Geneva 10, Switzerland)
- Economic Survey of Latin America. (pub. by United Nations Publications)
- Notas Sobre la Economia y el Desarrollo de America Latina. fortn. ISSN 0029-3881
- Statistical Bulletin for Latin America/Boletin Estadistico de America Latina. 2 per yr. ISSN 0041-6401 (Or United Nations Publications, Room LX-2300, New York, NY 10017; or Distribution and Sales Section, Palais des Nations, CH-1211 Geneva 10, Switzerland)

**United Nations Economic Commission for Western Asia**
United Nations Building, Box 4656, Bir Hassan, Beirut, Lebanon
• Studies on Selected Development Problems in Various Countries in the Middle East. a.; latest 1973. ISSN 0085-6908 (Dist. by: Distribution and Sales Section, Palais des Nations, CH-1211 Geneva 10, Switzerland)
• United Nations Economic Commission for Western Asia. Population Bulletin. s-a.

**United Nations Educational, Scientific and Cultural Organization**
*see* Unesco

**United Nations Environment Programme**
Division of Communication, P.O. 30552, Nairobi, Kenya.
• Uniterra. m.

**United Nations Fund for Population Activities**
485 Lexington Ave., 20th Floor, New York, NY 10017.
• Population Newsletter. 4 per yr. ISSN 0048-4849

**United Nations. General Assembly**
• Resolutions of the General Assembly of the United Nations. (pub. by United Nations Publications)

**United Nations High Commissioner for Refugees**
Palais des Nations, CH-1211 Geneva 10, Switzerland.
• U N H C R. bi-m.
• U N H C R Report. irreg. ISSN 0041-5308 (Or United Nations Publications, Room LX-2300 New York, NY 10017)

**United Nations Industrial Development Organization**
Lerchenfelderstrasse 1, Box 707, A-1011 Vienna, Austria
(Orders from Europe, Africa and Middle East to: Distribution and Sales Section, Palais des Nations, 1211 Geneva 10, Switzerland. Orders from Asia, the Pacific and North and South America to: United Nations Publications, Room LX-2300, New York, NY 10017)
• Fertilizer Industry Series. irreg.; no. 8, 1976. ISSN 0071-4615
• Food Industry Studies. irreg. ISSN 0071-7193
• Industrial Development Abstracts; U N I D O industrial information system (I N D I S) 5 per yr.
• Industrial Planning and Programming Series. irreg.; no. 6, vol. 3, 1971. ISSN 0073-7577
• Industrial Research and Development News. q.
• Industrialization and Productivity Bulletin. irreg.; no. 21, 1974. ISSN 0073-7690
• New Perspectives in Management Development. irreg.
• Small-Scale Manufacturing Studies. irreg. ISSN 0587-016X
• U N I D O Documents Checklist. m. ISSN 0049-5379
• U N I D O Newsletter. m. ISSN 0049-5387
• United Nations Industrial Development Organization. Guides to Information Sources. irreg.; no. 20, 1976.

**United Nations Institute for Training and Research**
Publications Office, 801 United Nations Plaza, New York, NY 10017
• U N I T A R Conference Reports. irreg. (Order from: United Nations Publications, Room LX-2300, New York, NY 10017; or Distribution and Sales Section, Palais des Nations, CH 1211 Geneva 10, Switzerland)
• U N I T A R News. irreg. ISSN 0049-5395
• U N I T A R-P S Series. (Peaceful Settlement) irreg; latest issue, 1974. (Order from: United Nations Publications, Room LX-2300, New York, NY 10017; or Distribution and Sales Section, Palais des Nations, CH 1211 Geneva 10, Switzerland)
• U N I T A R Regional Studies. irreg. (Order from: United Nations Publications, Room LX-2300, New York, NY 10017; or Distribution and Sales Section, Palais des Nations, CH 1211 Geneva 10, Switzerland)
• United Nations Institute for Training and Research. Report of the Executive Director. a.; latest, 1974. (Order from: United Nations Publications, Room LX-2300, New York, NY 10017; or Distribution and Sales Section, Palais des Nations, CH 1211 Geneva 10, Switzerland)

**United Nations. Institute of Nutrition of Central American and Panama**
Carretera Roosevelt, Zona 11, Aptdo Postal 11-88, Guatemala City, Guatemala.
• Instituto de Nutricion de Centro America y Panama. Informe Anual. a. ISSN 0533-4179

**United Nations International Children's Emergency Fund**
*see* Unicef

**United Nations International Law Commission**
• Gilberto Amado Memorial Lecture. (pub. by United Nations International Law Seminar)
• United Nations. International Law Commission. Yearbook. (pub. by United Nations Publications)

**United Nations International Law Seminar**
Secretary, Palais des Nations, CH-1211 Geneva 10, Switzerland.
• Gilberto Amado Memorial Lecture. a. (United Nations International Law Commission)

**United Nations Library**
• United Nations Library. Monthly List of Selected Articles/Nations Unies. Bibliotheque. List Mensuelle d'Articles Selectionnes. (pub. by United Nations Publications)

**United Nations Library, Geneva**
• United Nations Library. Geneva. Monthly List of Books Catalogued in the Library of the United Nations/Nations Unies. Bibliotheque Geneva. Liste Mensuelle d'Ouvrages Catalognes a la Bibliotheque des Nations Unies. (pub. by United Nations Publications)

**United Nations. Protocol Section, Geneva Office**
Bureau 143, Palais des Nations, CH-1211 Geneva 10, Switzerland.
• Permanent Missions to the United Nations/ Missions Permanentes Aupres des Nations Unies a Geneve et Orga Principaux des Nations Unies. s-a.

**United Nations Publications**
Room LX-2300, New York, NY 10017
(or Distribution and Sales Section, Palais des Nations, CH-1211 Geneva 10, Switzerland)
• Basic Facts about the United Nations. irreg. ISSN 0067-4419
• Bulletin on Narcotics. q. ISSN 0007-523X
• Commodity Trade Statistics; according to the Standard International Trade Classification. 39 per yr. ISSN 0010-3233
• Delegations to the United Nations. biennial; 29th session, General Assembly; 1974. ISSN 0070-3303
• Economic Survey of Latin America. approx. a.; latest issue, 1974. ISSN 0070-8720 (United Nations Economic Commission for Latin America)
• Everyman's United Nations. quinquennial. ISSN 0071-3244
• Journal of Development Planning. irreg. ISSN 0085-2392
• Objective: Justice. q. ISSN 0029-7593
• Population Studies. irreg., no. 56, 1974. ISSN 0082-805X (United Nations. Department of Economic and Social Affairs)
• Progress in Land Reform. irreg.; 5th 1970. ISSN 0085-5197
• Resolutions of the General Assembly of the United Nations. irreg. ISSN 0082-8211 (United Nations. General Assembly)
• Statistics of World Trade in Steel. a.; latest 1973. ISSN 0081-5195
• U N D E X. (United Nations Documents Index) m. except Jul. and Aug. ISSN 0041-7351
• U N Monthly Chronicle. m. ISSN 0041-5367
• United Nations. Current Bibliographical Information. s-m. (22 per yr.) ISSN 0041-7343
• United Nations. Disarmament Commission. Official Records. irreg. ISSN 0082-8076
• United Nations. Economic and Social Council. Index to Proceedings. a.; 29th session, 1974. ISSN 0082-8084
• United Nations. Economic and Social Council. Official Records. irreg. ISSN 0082-8092

• United Nations. General Assembly. Index to Proceedings. a.; 29th session, 1974. ISSN 0082-8157
• United Nations. International Law Commission. Yearbook. a. ISSN 0082-8289
• United Nations. Multilateral Treaties in Respect of Which the Secretary-General Performs Depositary Functions. irreg.; annex., suppl. no. 6-31 Dec., 1974. ISSN 0082-8319
• United Nations. Security Council. Index to Proceedings. a.; 29th yr., 1974 (pub. 1975) ISSN 0082-8408 (United Nations Security Council)
• United Nations. Security Council. Official Records. irreg. ISSN 0082-8416
• United Nations. Statistical Yearbook. a. ISSN 0082-8459 (United Nations Statistical Office)
• United Nations. Trusteeship Council. Index to Proceedings. a.; 41st session, 1974. ISSN 0082-8491
• United Nations. Trusteeship Council. Official Records. irreg.; 39th session, 1972. ISSN 0082-8505
• United Nations. Trusteeship Council. Official Records. Supplements. irreg. ISSN 0082-8513
• United Nations. Yearbook. a. ISSN 0082-8521
• United Nations and What You Should Know about It. irreg. ISSN 0082-8009
• United Nations Congress on the Prevention of Crime and the Treatment of Offenders. Report. irreg.; no. 4, 1971. ISSN 0082-8025
• United Nations Juridical Yearbook. a. ISSN 0082-8297
• United Nations Legislative Series. irreg.; vol. 16, 1974. ISSN 0082-8300
• United Nations Library. Monthly List of Selected Articles/Nations Unies. Bibliotheque. List Mensuelle d'Articles Selectionnes. m. ISSN 0041-7408
• United Nations Library. Geneva. Monthly List of Books Catalogued in the Library of the United Nations/Nations Unies. Bibliotheque Geneva. Liste Mensuelle d'Ouvrages Catalognes a la Bibliotheque des Nations Unies. m. ISSN 0041-7394
• United Nations Regional Cartographic Conference for Asia and the Far East. Proceedings of the Conference and Technical Papers. irreg.; 6th, vol. 2, 1972. ISSN 0082-836X
• United Nations Statistical Office. Monthly Bulletin of Statistcs. m. ISSN 0041-7432
• World Cartography. irreg.; vol 12, 1972. ISSN 0084-1471
• World Economic Survey. a. ISSN 0084-1714
• Yearbook of International Trade Statistics. a. ISSN 0084-3822 (United Nations Statistical Office)
• Yearbook of National Accounts Statistics. a. ISSN 0084-3881
• Yearbook on Human Rights. irreg. ISSN 0084-4098
• Your United Nations. irreg. ISSN 0084-4322

**United Nations. Regional Center for Demographic Training and Research in Latin America**
*see* United Nations. Centro Latinoamericano de Demografia

**United Nations Relief and Works Agency for Palestine Refugees in the Near East**
Museitbeh Quarter, Beirut, Lebanon
(In U.S., Request from United States Committee for Refugees, 20 W. 40th St., New York,. NY 10018)
• Palestine Refugees Today. q. ISSN 0031-0336

**United Nations Research Institute for Social Development**
Reference Centre, Palais des Nations, CH-1211 Geneva 10, Switzerland.
• Regional Planning. (pub. by Editions Mouton et Cie FR)
• United Nations Research Institute for Social Development. Report. irreg. (numbered within the year)
• United Nations Research Institute for Social Development. Research Notes. irreg.; latest issue 1974.

**United Nations Security Council**
• United Nations. Security Council. Index to Proceedings. (pub. by United Nations Publications)
• United Nations. Security Council. Official Records. (pub. by United Nations Publications)

**United Nations Social Defense Research Institute**
Via Giulia 52, 00186 Rome, Italy.
• United Nations Social Defense Research Institute. Publication. irreg.

**United Nations Statistical Office**
- United Nations. Statistical Yearbook. (pub. by United Nations Publications)
- United Nations Statistical Office. Monthly Bulletin of Statistcs. (pub. by United Nations Publications)
- World Trade Annual. (pub. by Walker & Co. US)
- World Trade Annual Supplement. (pub. by Walker & Co. US)
- Yearbook of International Trade Statistics. (pub. by United Nations Publications)

**United Nations Trade and Development Board**
Palais des Nations, 1211 Geneva 10, Switzerland (or United Nations Publications, Room LX-2300, New York, NY 10017)
- United Nations. Trade and Development Board. Official Records. irreg., 11th session, 1971. ISSN 0082-8475
- United Nations. Trade and Development Board. Official Records. Supplements. irreg. ISSN 0082-8483

**United Nations Trustee Council**
- United Nations. Trusteeship Council. Index to Proceedings. (pub. by United Nations Publications)
- United Nations. Trusteeship Council. Official Records. (pub. by United Nations Publications)
- United Nations. Trusteeship Council. Official Records. Supplements. (pub. by United Nations Publications)

**Universal Postal Union**
Welpoststrasse 4, CH-3000 Berne 15, Switzerland.
- Union Postal Universelle. Documents du Congres. irreg.; 17th, Lausanne, 1974. ISSN 0083-3878
- Union Postale. bi-m. ISSN 0041-7009
- Union Postale Universelle. Statistique des Services Postaux. a.; latest 1975. ISSN 0085-7602

**W H O**
see World Health Organization

**W I P O**
see World Intellectual Property Organization

**W M O**
see World Meteorological Organization

**World Bank**
see International Bank for Reconstruction and Development

**World Health Organization**
Distribution and Sales Service, 20 Avenue Appia, CH-1211 Geneva 27, Switzerland.
- Chronique O M S. (Organisation Mondiale de la Sante) m.
- Health Literature Topics. (Documentation en Matiere de Sante) q. (prep. by its Office of Library and Health Literature Services)
- International Digest of Health Legislation. q. ISSN 0020-6563
- International Histological Classification of Tumours. irreg. ISSN 0538-7736
- Pharmacopoeia Internationalis/International Pharmacopoeia. irreg., 2nd, 1967. ISSN 0553-9382
- Public Health Papers. irreg.; no. 65, 1976. ISSN 0555-6015
- Report on the World Health Situation. quadrennial. ISSN 0085-5529
- Vaccination Certificate Requirements for International Travel/Certificats de Vaccination Exiges dans les Voyages Internationaux. a. ISSN 0512-3011
- W H O Chronicle. m. ISSN 0042-9694
- W H O Technical Report Series. irreg.; no. 603, 1977. ISSN 0512-3054
- Weekly Epidemiological Record. w. ISSN 0049-8114
- World Directory of Dental Schools. irreg. ISSN 0512-2732
- World Directory of Medical Schools/Repertoire Mondial des Ecoles de Medecine. irreg. ISSN 0512-2759
- World Directory of Post-Basic and Post-Graduate Schools of Nursing. irreg. ISSN 0512-2767
- World Directory of Schools of Pharmacy. irreg. ISSN 0512-2775
- World Directory of Schools of Public Health. irreg. ISSN 0512-2783
- World Directory of Veterinary Schools. irreg. ISSN 0512-2791
- World Health. m. ISSN 0043-8502
- World Health Organization. Bulletin. m. ISSN 0042-9686

- World Health Organization. Expert Committee on Filariasis. Report. irreg.
- World Health Organization. Monograph Series. irreg. ISSN 0512-3038
- World Health Organization. Work of WHO; annual report of the director-general to the World Health Assembly and to the United Nations. a. ISSN 0085-8285
- World Health Organization. World Health Assembly and the Executive Board. Handbook of Resolutions and Decisions. a.
- World Health Statistics Annual. a.
- World Health Statistics Report. q. ISSN 0043-8510

**World Health Organization. Centro Pan Americano de Febre Aftosa**
Pan American Health Organization. Centro Pan Americano de Febre Aftosa, Rio de Janeiro, Brazil.
- Centro Pan-Americano de Febre Aftosa. Boletin. q. ISSN 0009-0131

**World Health Organization. International Agency for Research on Cancer**
see International Agency for Research on Cancer

**World Health Organization. Pan American Health Organization**
Pan American Sanitary Bureau, 525 23rd. St., N.W., Washington, DC 20037.
- Dengue Newsletter for the Americas.
- Educacion Medica y Salud. q. ISSN 0013-1091
- Oficina Sanitaria Panamericana. Boletin. 12 issues in 2 vols. ISSN 0030-0632
- Pan American Health. q.
- Pan American Health Organization. Bulletin. q.
- Pan American Sanitary Bureau. Bulletin. q. ISSN 0085-4638

**World Health Organization. Pan American Health Organization. Caribbean Food and Nutrition Institute**
Box 140, Mona, Kingston 7, Jamaica, W.Indies.
- Cajanus. bi-m.

**World Health Organization. Pan American Health Organization. Institute of Nutrition of Central America and Panama**
see United Nations. Institute of Nutrition of Central America and Panama

**World Health Organization. Regional Office for Africa**
B.P. No.6, Brazzaville, People's Republic of the Congo.
- A F R O Technical Papers. irreg.; 2-4 per yr.
- World Health Organization. Regional Office for Africa. Report of the Regional Committee. Minutes of the Plenary Session. a. ISSN 0512-3070
- World Health Organization. Regional Office for Africa. Report of the Regional Director. a. ISSN 0510-8837

**World Health Organization. Regional Office for Europe**
Scherfigsvej 8, 2100 Copenhagen 0, Denmark.
- Glossary of Health Care Terminology. a.

**World Health Organization. Regional Office for South-East Asia**
Indraprastha Estate, Ring Road, New Delhi, India.
- Bibliography on Human Reproduction, Family Planning, and Population Dynamics. biennial (with quarterly supplements) (prep. by its Regional Centre for Documentation on Human Reproduction, Family Planning, and Populaton Dynamics)

**World Health Organization. Regional Office for the Americas**
see World Health Organization. Pan American Health Organization

**World Health Organization. Regional Office for the Eastern Mediterranean**
P.O. Box 1517, Alexandria, Egypt.
- World Health Organization. Regional Office for the Eastern Mediterranean. Annual Report of the Regional Director. a.; latest 1973-1974. ISSN 0512-3089

**World Health Organization. Regional Office for the Western Pacific**
P.O. Box 2932, Manila, Philippines.
- World Health Organization. Regional Office for the Western Pacific. Annual Report of the Regional Director to the Regional Committee for the Western Pacific. a. ISSN 0512-4921
- World Health Organization. Regional Office for the Western Pacific. Report on the Regional Seminar on the Role of the Hospital in the Public Health Programme. irreg. ISSN 0510-8845

**World Health Organization. Research and Training Centre on Human Reproduction**
Karolinska Institutet, Fack, S-104 01 Stockholm, Sweden.
- Prostaglandins in Fertility Control. a.

**World Intellectual Property Organization (WIPO)**
Publication Section, 32 Chemin des Colombettes, 1211 Geneva 20, Switzerland.
- Copyright. m. ISSN 0010-8626
- Dessins et Modeles Internationaux. m. ISSN 0011-9520
- Droit d'Auteur. m. ISSN 0012-6365
- Industrial Property. m. ISSN 0019-8625
- Industrial Property, Statistics/Propriete Industrielle, Statistiques. irreg.
- Marques Internationales. m. ISSN 0025-3936
- Propiedad Intelectual. q. ISSN 0033-1376
- Propriete Industrielle. m.

**World Meteorological Organization**
41 Ave. Giuseppe Motta, CH-1211 Geneva 20, Switzerland
(Dist. in U.S. by: Unipub, Box 433, Murray Hill Station)
- Composition of the W M O. q.
- Global Atmospheric Research Program. Publication Series. irreg. ISSN 0084-1978
- Global Atmospheric Research Programme. G A R P Special Reports. irreg. ISSN 0084-1986
- Marine Science Affairs. irreg. ISSN 0076-4507
- Operational Hydrology Reports. irreg.
- W M O Bulletin. q. ISSN 0042-9767
- Weather Reporting. irreg. ISSN 0083-7784
- World Meteorological Association. Regional Associations. Abridged Final Reports. irreg. ISSN 0084-1900
- World Meteorological Association. Technical Commissions Abridged Final Reports. irreg. ISSN 0084-1919
- World Meteorological Congress. Abridged Report with Resolutions. irreg. ISSN 0084-1927
- World Meteorological Congress. Proceedings. irreg. ISSN 0084-1935
- World Meteorological Organization. Annual Report. a. ISSN 0084-1994
- World Meteorological Organization. Basic Documents, Records and Reports. irreg. ISSN 0084-1943
- World Meteorological Organization. Executive Committee Sessions: Abridged Reports with Resolutions. irreg. ISSN 0084-196X
- World Meteorological Organization. Report on Marine Science Affairs. irreg., 1973, no. 9. ISSN 0084-2001
- World Meteorological Organization. Special Environmental Report. irreg.
- World Meteorological Organization. Technical Notes. irreg. ISSN 0084-201X
- World Weather Watch Planning Reports. irreg. ISSN 0084-2451

# UNITED STATES

**A A A Motor Club of N.E. Pennsylvania**
1035 N. Washington Ave., Scranton, PA 18509.
- A A A Motorist of Northeastern Pennsylvania. bi-m.

**A A Grapevine, Inc.**
468 Park Ave., New York, NY 10022.
- Box 1980. m. ISSN 0362-2584

**A B C-CLIO**
see American Bibliographic Center-Clio Press

**A B C Directory**
4126 College Ave., Des Moines, IA 50311.
- A B C Directory. a. ISSN 0065-0021

**A B C Leisure Magazines, Inc.**
Great Barrington, MA 01230.
- Buyer's Guide to the World of Tape. a. ISSN 0090-9033
- High Fidelity. m. ISSN 0018-1455
- High Fidelity/Musical America. m. (plus Dec. directory issue) ISSN 0018-1463
- High Fidelity's Test Reports. a. ISSN 0090-3981
- Modern Photography. m. ISSN 0026-8240
- Musical America International Directory of the Performing Arts. a.
- Stereo. q.
- Wolfman Report on the Photographic Industry in the United States. a. ISSN 0084-103X

**A B C Schwann Publications, Inc.**
137 Newbury Rd., Boston, MA 02116.
- Schwann Artists Catalog. triennial. ISSN 0582-1487
- Schwann Children's Record & Tape Guide. a.
- Schwann-1, Records, Tapes. m. ISSN 0098-356X
- Schwann-2, Records & Tapes. s-a. ISSN 0099-0167

**A B W A Co., Inc.**
9100 Ward Parkway, Kansas City, MO 64114.
- Women in Business. 9 per yr. ISSN 0043-7441 (American Business Women's Association)

**A.C. and E. Publishing Co.**
4820 Pleasant Ave., Minneapolis, MN 55409.
- Architects, Contractors & Engineers Guide to Construction Costs. a. ISSN 0066-6157
- Metro Building Industry Directory. a. ISSN 0076-700X

**A.C.T.-Action Press**
c/o Sr. Shirley Mae Burghard, Ross Towers Apt. B-1104, 710 Lodi St., Syracuse, NY 13203.
- Constructive Action for Good Health. m. (American Conference of Therapeutic Self Help, Self Health, Social Clubs A.C.T.)

**A D F Publishing, Inc.**
P. O. Box 1096, Alton, IL 62002.
- Art Dealer & Framer. m. ISSN 0091-9780

**A. D. Publications, Inc.**
1840 Interchurch Center, 475 Riverside Dr., New York, NY 10027.
- A.D. the Magazine for the United Church of Christ Family. m. (United Church of Christ)
- A.D. the Magazine for the United Presbyterian Family. m. (United Presbyterian Church in the U.S.A.)

**A.F.I.**
c/o Desi K. Bogner, Ed., 295 N. Fulton, Box 8, Mt. Vernon, NY 10552.
- Eastern European Biographies and Studies Series. irreg, 1976, vol. 4. ISSN 0070-8216

**A F L-C I O**
815 16th St. N.W., Washington, DC 20006.
- A F L-C I O American Federationist. m.
- A F L-C I O Free Trade Union News. m. ISSN 0001-1177
- A F L - C I O Library Acquisition List. m. ISSN 0001-1150
- A F L-C I O News. w. ISSN 0001-1185
- Correio Operario Norteamericano. s-m. ISSN 0300-7634
- Maritime. m. ISSN 0025-3391 (prep. by its Maritime Trades Department)
- Metaletter. m. ISSN 0047-6870 (prep. by its Metal Trades Department)
- Noticiero Obrero Norteamericano. s-m. ISSN 0300-6743

**A F L-C I O. Committee on Political Education**
815 16th St. N.W., Washington, DC 20006.
- Memo from C O P E. fortn. ISSN 0032-3160

**A F L-C I O. Industrial Union Department**
2457 E. Washington St., Indianapolis, IN 46201.
- Viewpoint (Indianapolis) q. ISSN 0042-5869

**A.F.L.-C.I.O Labor Organizations**
- Labor World. (pub. by Labor World Inc.)

**A F T A C Enterprises**
4902 La Barranca, San Antonio, TX 78233.
- Income Tax Guide for Military Personnel. irreg. ISSN 0098-1729

**A G A Corporation**
550 County Ave., Secaucus, NJ 07094.
- Infrared Information Exchange. Proceedings. biennial.

**A I D**
*see* U.S. Agency for International Development

**A I M Report**
777 14th St., N. W., Suite 427, Washington, DC 20005.
- A I M Report. m.

**A la Votre**
c/o Ed. Serena Jutkovitz, Box 157, San Francisco, CA 94101.
- A la Votre. bi-m.

**A M R International, Inc.**
1370 Ave. of the Americas, New York, NY 10019.
- Current Developments in Financial Reporting. m.

**A M S Press, Inc.**
56 E. 13th St., New York, NY 10003.
- Crime and Justice. irreg.
- Educating the Disadvantaged. irreg. ISSN 0531-8327
- Housing. irreg.
- Police and Law Enforcement. irreg.

**A N N Y Publications Inc.**
230 Park Ave., New York, NY 10017.
- A N N Y/Advertising News of New York. w. ISSN 0001-2041

**A P B A Journal**
c/o Leonard Gaydos, 29 S. Kingston St., San Mateo, CA 94401.
- A P B A Journal. m.

**A P S**
Box 777, New York, NY 10003.
- Alternative Media. bi-m.

**A P S Publications**
150 Fifth Ave., New York, NY 10011.
- American Journal of Psychoanalysis. q. ISSN 0002-9548 (Association for the Advancement of Psychoanalysis)
- Children's Literature in Education. 4 per yr. ISSN 0045-6713
- Research in Higher Education. 8 per yr.
- Urban Review. q. ISSN 0042-0972

**A Press Ltd.**
P.O. Box 311, Laguna, NM 87026.
- A: a Journal of Contemporary Literature. a.

**A-R Editions, Inc.**
315 W. Gorham, Madison, WI 53703.
- Collegium Musicum: Yale University. s-a. ISSN 0588-3024 (Yale University. Department of Music)
- Recent Researches in American Music. q. ISSN 0147-0078
- Recent Researches in the Music of the Baroque Era. q. ISSN 0484-0828
- Recent Researches in the Music of the Classical Era. q. ISSN 0147-0086
- Recent Researches in the Music of the Middle Ages and Early Renaissance. q. ISSN 0362-3572
- Recent Researches in the Music of the Renaissance. q. ISSN 0486-123X

**A R G Publishing Co.**
1 Windsor Pl., Melville, NY 11746.
- American Record Guide. m. ISSN 0003-0716

**A.S. Barnes and Co., Inc.**
- International Photography Yearbook. (pub. by Thomas Yoseloff, Inc.)

**A S C U**
Box 5488, Madison, WI 53705.
- First Friday. m. ISSN 0094-0240

**A S G Industries, Inc.**
Box 929, Kingsport, TN 37662.
- Creative Ideas in Glass. q.

**A S M P-Society of Photographers in Communications**
60 E. 42nd Street, New York, NY 10017.
- American Society of Magazine Photographers. Bulletin.

**A S U C L A Communications Board**
308 Westwood Plaza, Los Angeles, CA 90024.
- Ha'am. 6 per yr. (University of California, Los Angeles. Jewish Students)

**Aaron Burr Association**
Tremont, Inca Road, Linden, VA 22642.
- Aaron Burr Association. Chronicle. q. ISSN 0001-3048

**Abba**
Box 8516, Austin, TX 78712.
- Abba; a journal of prayer. irreg. ISSN 0361-686X

**Abbey Garden Press**
Box 3010, Santa Barbara, CA 93105.
- Cactus and Succulent Journal. bi-m. ISSN 0007-9367
- Repertorium Plantarum Succulentarum. a. ISSN 0486-4271 (International Organization for Succulent Plant Study)

**Abbey Press**
St. Meinrad, IN 47577.
- Christian Family Catalog. 5 per yr.
- Marriage and Family Living. m. (St. Meinrad Archabbey)

**Abbott, Langer & Associates**
Box 275, Park Forest, IL 60466.
- Abbott, Langer & Associates. College Recruiting Report. a. ISSN 0361-5057

**Abel News Agencies**
300 W. 17th St., New York, NY 10011.
- Abel; panem et circenses/bread and circuses. m. ISSN 0001-3153

**Abelard-Schuman**
(Subsidiary of: T.Y. Crowell Co., Inc.)
666 Fifth Ave., New York, NY 10019.
- Abelard Poets. irreg.

**Aberdeen-Angus Association**
808 Des Moines St., Webster City, IA 50595.
- Aberdeen-Angus Journal. m. ISSN 0001-3161

**Ernest H. Abernethy Publishing Co., Inc.**
75 Third St. N.W., Atlanta, GA 30308.
- Southern Advertising/Markets. m.
- Southern Garment Manufacturer. m. ISSN 0038-4151
- Southern Jeweler. m. ISSN 0038-4232
- Southern Pulp and Paper Manufacturer. m.(s-m.Oct) ISSN 0038-4488
- Southern Stationer and Office Outfitter. m. ISSN 0038-4593

**Ernest H. Abernethy Publishing Co., Inc. (Olean)**
P.O. Box 117, Olean, NY 14760.
- American International Travel. m. ISSN 0002-9017

**Abilene Christian University**
c/o Charles H. Marler, Communications Dept., Box 8174, ACU Sta., Abilene, TX 79601.
- Optimist. w. ISSN 0030-4069

**Abingdon**
201 Eighth Ave. S., Nashville, TN 37202.
- Bible in Literature Courses. irreg.
- Handbook of Denominations in the U.S. quinquennial. ISSN 0072-9787
- International Lesson Annual; commentary and teaching suggestions on the International Sunday School lessons. a. ISSN 0074-6770
- Religion in Life; a Christian quarterly of opinion and discussion. q. ISSN 0034-3986
- Studies in Christian Ethics Series. irreg.
- Yearbook of American and Canadian Churches. a. ISSN 0084-3644

**Abner Schram Enterprises, Ltd.**
1860 Broadway, New York, NY 10023.
- Image of Woman. irreg.

**Abortion Trends**
Box 261, Lakewood, CA 90714.
- Abortion Trends; a monthly report of news & opinion. m.

**Harry N. Abrams, Inc.**
110 E. 59 St., New York, NY 10022.
- Annual of New Art and Artists. a.
- Contemporary Artists. irreg.
- Modern Artists. irreg.

**Arnold Abramson**
235 E. 45th St., New York, NY 10017.
- Galaxy. bi-m. ISSN 0016-4003

**Abrasive Engineering Society**
1049 So. Main Street, Plymouth, MI 48170.
- Abrasive Engineering Society. Abrasive Usage Conference. Proceedings. a.
- Abrasive Technology. bi-m.

**Abraxas**
c/o Warren Woessner, Ed., 2322 Rugby Row, Madison, WI 53705.
- Abraxas. 2 per yr.

**Editora Abril**
444 Madison Ave, New York, NY 10022.
- Recreio. fortn.

**Absolute Sound, Ltd.**
Box 115, Sea Cliff, NY 11579
(Subscr. to 211 Bay Ave., Northport, NY 11768)
- Absolute Sound. q. ISSN 0097-1138

**Abyss Publications**
Box C, Somerville, MA 02143.
- Abyss. q. ISSN 0001-3722

**Acacia Mutual Life Insurance Co.**
51 Louisiana Ave. N.W., Washington, DC 20001.
- Acacia Clarion. q. ISSN 0001-3730

**Academia de Nueva Raza**
P.O. Box 31, Dixon, NM 87527.
- Academia de Nueva Raza. Cuaderno; de vez en cuando. q.

**Academia Norteamericana de la Lengua Espanola**
Box 7, F.D.R. Post Office, New York, NY 10022.
- Academia Norteamericana de la Lengua Espanola. Boletin. irreg. (Subscr. to: Odon Betanzos, 125 Queen St., Staten Island, N.Y. 10314)

**Academic Consortia for Higher Education**
- Acquainter. (pub. by American Association for Higher Education)

**Academic Press, Inc.**
111 Fifth Ave., New York, NY 10003
(and Berkeley Square House, London W.1, England)
- A C M Monograph Series. irreg. (Association for Computing Machinery)
- Academic Press Series in Cognition and Perception. irreg.
- Advances in Activation Analysis. irreg., 1972, vol. 2. ISSN 0065-2091
- Advances in Agronomy. irreg., 1972, vol. 24. ISSN 0065-2113
- Advances in Alicyclic Chemistry. irreg., 1971, vol. 3. ISSN 0065-2121
- Advances in Alicyclic Chemistry. Supplement. irreg. ISSN 0065-213X
- Advances in Applied Mechanics. irreg., 1973, vol. 13. ISSN 0065-2156
- Advances in Applied Microbiology. irreg., 1972, vol. 15. ISSN 0065-2164
- Advances in Applied Microbiology. Supplement. irreg. ISSN 0065-2172
- Advances in Atomic and Molecular Physics. irreg., 1972, vol. 8. ISSN 0065-2199
- Advances in Biological and Medical Physics. irreg., 1973, vol. 14. ISSN 0065-2245
- Advances in Cancer Research. irreg., 1972, vol. 16. ISSN 0065-230X
- Advances in Carbohydrate Chemistry and Biochemistry. irreg., 1972, vol. 27. ISSN 0065-2318
- Advances in Catalysis and Related Subjects. irreg., 1972, vol. 23. ISSN 0065-2342
- Advances in Cell and Molecular Biology. irreg., 1973, vol. 3. ISSN 0065-2350
- Advances in Chemical Engineering. irreg., 1970, vol. 8. ISSN 0065-2377
- Advances in Child Development and Behavior. irreg., 1972, vol. 7. ISSN 0065-2407
- Advances in Clinical Chemistry. a. ISSN 0065-2423
- Advances in Communication Systems. irreg., 1968, vol. 3. ISSN 0065-2431
- Advances in Comparative Physiology and Biochemistry. irreg., 1971, vol. 4. ISSN 0065-244X
- Advances in Computers. irreg., 1972, vol. 12. ISSN 0065-2458
- Advances in Electronics and Electron Physics. irreg., 1972, vol. 33, part A & B. ISSN 0065-2539
- Advances in Electronics and Electron Physics. Supplement. irreg., 1970, no. 7. ISSN 0065-2547

- Advances in Experimental Social Psychology. irreg., 1972, vol. 6. ISSN 0065-2601
- Advances in Food Research. irreg., 1971, vol. 19. ISSN 0065-2628
- Advances in Food Research. Supplement. irreg., 1972, no. 3. ISSN 0065-2636
- Advances in Genetics. irreg., vol. 18, 1976. ISSN 0065-2660
- Advances in Genetics. Supplement. irreg. ISSN 0065-2679
- Advances in Geophysics. irreg., 1971, vol. 15. ISSN 0065-2687
- Advances in Geophysics. Supplement. irreg. ISSN 0065-2695
- Advances in Gerontological Research. irreg., 1972, vol. 4. ISSN 0065-2709
- Advances in Heat Transfer. irreg., 1973, vol. 9. ISSN 0065-2717
- Advances in Heterocyclic Chemistry. irreg., vol. 19, 1976. ISSN 0065-2725
- Advances in High Temperature Chemistry. irreg., 1972, vol. 4. ISSN 0065-2741
- Advances in Hydroscience. irreg., 1973, vol. 9. ISSN 0065-2768
- Advances in Image Pickup and Display. irreg. ISSN 0094-7032
- Advances in Image Pickup and Display. Supplements. irreg.
- Advances in Immunology. irreg., 1973, vol. 16. ISSN 0065-2776
- Advances in Inorganic Chemistry and Radiochemistry. irreg., 1972, vol. 15. ISSN 0065-2792
- Advances in Librarianship. irreg., vol. 5, 1975. ISSN 0065-2830
- Advances in Lipid Research. irreg., 1972, vol. 10. ISSN 0065-2849
- Advances in Liquid Crystals. irreg.
- Advances in Macromolecular Chemistry. irreg., 1970, vol. 2. ISSN 0065-2865
- Advances in Magnetic Resonance. irreg., 1971, vol. 5. ISSN 0065-2873
- Advances in Mathematics. bi-m. ISSN 0001-8708
- Advances in Metabolic Disorders. irreg., 1972, vol. 6. ISSN 0065-2903
- Advances in Metabolic Disorders. Supplements. irreg, vol. 2, 1973. ISSN 0587-4394
- Advances in Microbial Physiology. irreg., 1972, vol. 8. ISSN 0065-2911
- Advances in Microbiology of the Sea. irreg. ISSN 0065-292X
- Advances in Microwaves. irreg., 1971, vol. 7. ISSN 0065-2946
- Advances in Microwaves. Supplements. irreg.
- Advances in Nuclear Science and Technology. irreg., 1973, vol. 7. ISSN 0065-2989
- Advances in Oral Biology. irreg., 1970, vol. 4. ISSN 0065-3020
- Advances in Organometalic Chemistry. irreg., 1973, vol. 11. ISSN 0065-3055
- Advances in Pharmaceutical Sciences. irreg., 1971, vol. 3. ISSN 0065-3136
- Advances in Pharmacology and Chemotherapy. a. ISSN 0065-3144
- Advances in Protein Chemistry. a. ISSN 0065-3233
- Advances in Quantum Chemistry. irreg., 1972, vol. 7. ISSN 0065-3276
- Advances in Quantum Electronics. a. ISSN 0065-3284
- Advances in Radiation Biology. irreg., vol. 6, 1976. ISSN 0065-3292
- Advances in Space Science and Technology. irreg., 1972, vol. 11. ISSN 0065-3365
- Advances in Space Science and Technology. Supplement. irreg., 1965, no. 2. ISSN 0065-3373
- Advances in Steroid Biochemistry and Pharmacology. irreg., 1972, vol. 3. ISSN 0065-339X
- Advances in the Study of Behavior. irreg., 1972, vol. 4. ISSN 0065-3454
- Advances in Theoretical Chemistry. Supplements. irreg.
- Advances in Theoretical Physics. irreg., 1968, vol. 2. ISSN 0065-3470
- Advances in Veterinary Science and Comparative Medicine. irreg., 1972, vol. 16. ISSN 0065-3519
- Advances in Virus Research. irreg., 1972, vol. 17. ISSN 0065-3527
- Alkaloids: Chemistry and Physiology. irreg.
- Analysis of Organic Materials: an International Series of Monographs. irreg., 1970, vol.5.
- Analytical Biochemistry. 13 per yr. ISSN 0003-2697
- Analytical Methods for Pesticides and Plant Growth. irreg.
- Analytical Microbiology. irreg., vol. 2, 1972. ISSN 0090-2284

- Analytical Profiles of Drug Substances. a.
- Ann Arbor Graph Theory Conference. Proceedings. irreg., 3rd, 1973.
- Annals of Biomedical Engineering. q. ISSN 0090-6964
- Annals of Physics. m (s-m during May) ISSN 0003-4916
- Annual Reports in Inorganic and General Syntheses. a. ISSN 0092-1335
- Annual Reports in Medicinal Chemistry. irreg. ISSN 0065-7743 (American Chemical Society.. Division of Medicinal Chemistry)
- Annual Reports in Organic Synthesis. a. ISSN 0066-409X
- Annual Reports on N M R Spectroscopy. a. ISSN 0066-4103
- Antimicrobial Chemotherapy. bi-m.
- Applied Mathematics and Mechanics; An international series of monographs. irreg., vol. 13, 1970. ISSN 0066-5479
- Applied Solid State Science. irreg., 1972, vol. 3. ISSN 0066-5533
- Archives of Biochemistry and Biophysics. 14 per yr. ISSN 0003-9861
- Asian-Pacific Congress of Cardiology. Proceedings. quadrennial, 1968, 4th, Jerusalem and Tel Aviv. ISSN 0066-8427
- Asian Pacific Congress of Cardiology. Symposia. irreg. ISSN 0587-5471
- Atomic and Nuclear Data Reprints. irreg.
- Atomic Data and Nuclear Data Tables; a journal devoted to compilations of experimental and theoretical results in atomic physics. m.
- Attention and Performance. Proceedings. irreg.
- Automatic Programming Information Centre Studies in Data Processing. irreg., no. 11, 1974. ISSN 0067-2483
- Behavior of Nonhuman Primates: Modern Research Trends. irreg. ISSN 0090-8592
- Behavior Therapy. 5 per yr. ISSN 0005-7894
- Behavioral Biology. m. ISSN 0091-6773
- Biochemical Actions of Hormones. irreg., v. 3, 1975.
- Biochemical and Biophysical Perspectives in Marine Biology. irreg., vol. 3, 1976.
- Biochemical and Biophysical Research Communications. s-m. ISSN 0006-291X
- Biochemical Medicine. bi-m. ISSN 0006-2944
- Bioorganic Chemistry. q. ISSN 0045-2068
- Birth Defects Institute. Symposia. a.
- Brain & Language. q.
- Carnegie Institution of Washington. Year Book. a. ISSN 0069-066X
- Cell Biology; a series of monographs. irreg.
- Cellular Immunology. 14 per yr. ISSN 0008-8749
- Clinical Engineering Series. irreg.
- Clinical Immunobiology. irreg.
- Clinical Immunology & Immunopathology. 6 per yr. ISSN 0090-1229
- Cognitive Psychology. bi-m. ISSN 0010-0285
- Commonwealth Space-Flight Symposium. Proceedings. irreg. ISSN 0573-0872
- Computer Graphics & Image Processing. 6 per yr.
- Computer Science and Applied Mathematics. irreg.
- Computers and Biomedical Research. 6 per yr. ISSN 0010-4809
- Computers in Chemical and Biochemical Research. irreg.
- Conference on Catalysis in Organic Syntheses. (Proceedings) irreg.
- Contemporary Educational Psychology. q. ISSN 0361-476X
- Contributions to Sensory Physiology. irreg., 1971, vol. 5. ISSN 0069-9705
- Control and Dynamic Systems: Advances in Theory and Applications. a. ISSN 0090-5267
- Current Chemical Concepts. irreg.
- Current Topics in Bioenergetics. irreg., 1971, vol. 4. ISSN 0070-2129
- Current Topics in Cellular Regulation. irreg., 1972, vol. 6. ISSN 0070-2137
- Current Topics in Clinical and Community Psychology. irreg., 1971, vol. 2. ISSN 0070-2145
- Current Topics in Comparative Pathobiology. irreg.
- Current Topics in Developmental Biology. irreg., 1972, vol. 7. ISSN 0070-2153
- Current Topics in Experimental Endocrinology. irreg., vol. 2, 1974.
- Current Topics in Membranes and Transport. irreg., vol. 8, 1976. ISSN 0070-2161
- Current Topics in Surgical Research. irreg., 1971, vol. 3. ISSN 0070-2196
- Developmental Biology. m. ISSN 0012-1606

- Eldridge Reeves Johnson Foundation for Medical Physics. Colloquium. Proceedings. irreg., 1969, 5th (pub. 1971) ISSN 0070-959X (University of Pennsylvania)
- Environmental Quality and Safety. irreg.
- Environmental Research. 6 per yr. ISSN 0013-9351
- Essays in Chemistry. a. ISSN 0071-1373
- Essays in Physics. irreg., 1972, vol. 4. ISSN 0071-1438
- Essays in Toxicology. irreg., 1973, vol. 4. ISSN 0071-1446
- Estuarine and Coastal Marine Science. 6 per yr. ISSN 0302-3524
- Ethnicity; an interdisciplinary journal of the study of ethnic relations. q. ISSN 0095-6139
- European Monographs in Social Psychology. irreg., vol. 5, 1975. (European Association of Experimental Social Psychology)
- Excited States. irreg. ISSN 0093-1713
- Exercise and Sport Sciences Reviews. irreg. ISSN 0091-6331
- Experimental & Molecular Pathology. 6 per yr. ISSN 0014-4800
- Experimental Botany; An International Series of Monographs. irreg., 1972, vol. 5. ISSN 0071-3392
- Experimental Cell Research. 14 per yr. ISSN 0014-4827 (International Society for Cell Biology)
- Experimental Neurology. m. ISSN 0014-4886
- Experimental Parasitology. bi-m. ISSN 0014-4894
- Explorations in Economic History. q. ISSN 0014-4983
- General and Comparative Endocrinology; an international journal. m. ISSN 0016-6480
- Gynecologic Oncology. q. ISSN 0090-8258
- Harvey Lectures. irreg., 1972, series 66. ISSN 0073-0874
- Hormonal Proteins and Peptides. irreg.
- Hormones and Behavior. 6 per yr. ISSN 0018-506X
- I C N -U C L A Symposium on Molecular Biology Proceedings. irreg., 1st, Squaw Valley, CA, 1972. (International Chemical and Nuclear Corp) (Co-Sponsor: University of California at Los Angeles, Molecular Biology Institute)
- Icarus; international journal of solar system studies. m. ISSN 0019-1035
- Immunology: an International Series of Monographs and Treatises. irreg.
- Information and Control. m. ISSN 0019-9958
- Instrumentation in Nuclear Medicine. irreg. ISSN 0074-0543
- International Bibliographical and Library Series. irreg., vol. 3, 1973.
- International Bryozoology Association. Proceedings of the Conference. irreg., 3rd, 1973.
- International Clean Air Congress. Proceedings. irreg., 1970, 2nd, Washington, D.C. ISSN 0085-2090 (International Union of Air Pollution Prevention Associations)
- International Colloquium on Rapid Mixing and Sampling Techniques Applicable to the Study of Biochemical Reactions. Proceedings. irreg. ISSN 0538-5644
- International Committee for Standardization in Hematology. Symposia. irreg., 13th, 1972.
- International Congress of Radiation Research. Proceedings. irreg. ISSN 0538-6586
- International Geophysics Series. irreg., vol. 19, 1975. ISSN 0074-6142
- International Journal of Criminology and Penology. q.
- International Journal of Man-Machine Studies. 6 per yr. ISSN 0020-7373
- International Journal of Nautical Archaeology and Underwater Research. q.
- International Library Review. q. ISSN 0020-7837
- International Review of Connective Tissue Research. irreg., 1973, vol. 6. ISSN 0074-767X
- International Review of Cytology. irreg., vol. 45, 1976. ISSN 0074-7696
- International Review of Cytology. Supplement. irreg., no. 4, 1974. ISSN 0074-770X
- International Review of Experimental Pathology. irreg., vol. 16, 1976. ISSN 0074-7718
- International Review of General and Experimental Zoology. irreg., 1970, vol. 4. ISSN 0074-7734
- International Review of Neurobiology. irreg., 1972, vol. 15. ISSN 0074-7742
- International Review of Research in Mental Retardation. irreg., 1973, vol. 6. ISSN 0074-7750
- International Review of Tropical Medicine. irreg., 1971, vol. 4. ISSN 0074-7777
- International School of Physics "Enrico Fermi." Proceedings. irreg. ISSN 0074-784X (Societa Italiana di Fisica IT)
- International School of Physics "Ettore Majorana," Erice, Italy. Proceedings. a. ISSN 0074-7858

- International Symposium on Adsorption-Desorption Phenomena. Proceedings. irreg., Florence, 1971.
- International Symposium on Comparative Endocrinology. Proceedings. a. ISSN 0539-0559
- International Thyroid Conference. Proceedings. irreg., 1965, 5th, Rome. ISSN 0074-9095
- International Union of Biochemistry/International Union of Biological Sciences. I U B/I U B S International Symposium. Proceedings. irreg. ISSN 0445-1333
- Journal of Algebra. m. ISSN 0021-8693
- Journal of Approximation Theory. m. ISSN 0021-9045
- Journal of Biological Standardization. 4 per yr. ISSN 0092-1157
- Journal of Catalysis. m. ISSN 0021-9517
- Journal of Chemical Thermodynamics. m. ISSN 0021-9614
- Journal of Colloid and Interface Science. m. (5 vols. per yr.) ISSN 0021-9797
- Journal of Combinatorial Theory. bi-m. ISSN 0021-9800
- Journal of Computational Physics. m. ISSN 0021-9991
- Journal of Computer and System Sciences. m. ISSN 0022-0000
- Journal of Differential Equations. m. ISSN 0022-0396
- Journal of Economic Theory. bi-m. ISSN 0022-0531
- Journal of Environmental Economics and Management. q. ISSN 0095-0696
- Journal of Environmental Management. 4 per yr. ISSN 0301-4797
- Journal of Experimental Child Psychology. bi-m. ISSN 0022-0965
- Journal of Experimental Social Psychology. bi-m. ISSN 0022-1031
- Journal of Fish Biology. m. ISSN 0022-1112
- Journal of Functional Analysis. m. ISSN 0022-1236
- Journal of Invertebrate Pathology; devoted to the pathology and microbiology of insects and other invertebrates. bi-m. ISSN 0022-2011
- Journal of Magnetic Resonance. m. ISSN 0022-2364
- Journal of Mathematical Analysis and Applications. m. ISSN 0022-247X
- Journal of Mathematical Psychology. 6 per yr. ISSN 0022-2496
- Journal of Molecular and Cellular Cardiology. m. ISSN 0022-2828
- Journal of Molecular Spectroscopy. 13 per yr. ISSN 0022-2852
- Journal of Multivariate Analysis; an international journal. q. ISSN 0047-259X
- Journal of Number Theory. q. ISSN 0022-314X
- Journal of Phonetics. q. ISSN 0095-4470
- Journal of Research in Personality. 4 per yr.
- Journal of Solid State Chemistry. m. ISSN 0022-4596
- Journal of Surgical Research; Clinical and Laboratory Investigation. m. ISSN 0022-4804
- Journal of Ultrastructure Research. m. ISSN 0022-5320
- Journal of Ultrastructure Research. Supplement. irreg., 1973, no. 12. ISSN 0075-4404
- Journal of Urban Economics. q. ISSN 0094-1190
- Journal of Verbal Learning and Verbal Behavior. bi-m. ISSN 0022-5371
- Journal of Vocational Behavior. 6 per yr. ISSN 0001-8791
- Laser Applications. irreg.
- Learning & Motivation. q. ISSN 0023-9690
- Linnean Society. Biological Journal. 4 per yr. ISSN 0024-4066 (Linnean Society of London UK)
- Linnean Society. Botanical Journal. 8 per yr. ISSN 0024-4074 (Linnean Society of London UK)
- Linnean Society. Zoological Journal. 8 per yr. ISSN 0024-4082 (Linnean Society of London UK)
- London Mathematical Society. Monographs. irreg., 1972, no. 2. ISSN 0076-0560
- Mathematics in Science and Engineering; series of monographs and textbooks. irreg., vol. 122, 1976. ISSN 0076-5392
- Medical Physics Series. irreg. ISSN 0076-5953
- Medicinal Chemistry; series of monographs. irreg., vol. 12, 1974. ISSN 0076-6054
- Methods in Cancer Research. irreg., 1973, vol. 8. ISSN 0076-6852
- Methods in Cell Biology. irreg. ISSN 0091-679X
- Methods in Computational Physics: Advances in Research and Applications. irreg., 1972, vol. 12. ISSN 0076-6860

- Methods in Enzymology. irreg., 1973, vol. 28, pt. B. ISSN 0076-6879
- Methods in Immunology and Immunochemistry. irreg, 1971, vol.3. ISSN 0076-6917
- Methods in Virology. irreg., 1971, vol. 5. ISSN 0076-6933
- Methods of Experimental Physics. irreg., vol. 13, pt.A, 1976. ISSN 0076-695X
- Microchemical Journal; devoted to the application of microtechniques to all branches of science. q. ISSN 0026-265X
- Microvascular Research. bi-m. ISSN 0026-2862
- Modern Materials. Advances in Development and Applications. irreg., 1970, vol. 7. ISSN 0077-0000
- Molecular Pharmacology. 6 per yr. ISSN 0026-895X
- Monographs for Students of Medicine. irreg., vol. 3, 1975.
- Monographs on Immunology. irreg. ISSN 0077-1023
- Monographs on Industrial Hygiene. irreg.
- Neuroscience Research. a. ISSN 0077-7846
- Non-Metallic Solids; a series of monographs. irreg. ISSN 0078-0995
- Nuclear Data Sheets. m. ISSN 0090-3752
- Organic Chemistry; a series of monographs. irreg., vol. 31, 1975. ISSN 0078-611X
- Organizational Behavior and Human Performance; a journal of fundamental research and theory in applied psychology. bi-m. ISSN 0030-5073
- Personality and Psychopathology; a series of texts, monographs and treatises. irreg., vol. 15, 1975. ISSN 0079-0931
- Perspectives in Immunology.
- Perspectives in Virology. irreg., 1973, vol. 8. ISSN 0072-9086
- Pesticide Biochemistry and Physiology; an international journal. 6 per yr. ISSN 0048-3575
- Pharmacological Research Communications. 10 per yr. ISSN 0031-6989
- Photographic Techniques in Scientific Research. irreg. ISSN 0302-4210
- Physical Acoustics: Principles and Methods. irreg., 1972, vol. 9. ISSN 0079-1873
- Physical Chemistry; a series of monographs. irreg., vol. 34, 1974. ISSN 0079-1881
- Physics of Thin Films; Advances in Research and Development. irreg., 1971, vol. 6. ISSN 0079-1970
- Preventive Medicine. q. ISSN 0091-7435 (American Health Foundation)
- Probability and Mathematical Statistics; A series of monographs and textbooks. irreg., vol. 25, 1974. ISSN 0079-5607
- Progress in Behavior Modification. a. ISSN 0099-037X
- Progress in Chemical Toxicology. irreg, 1969, vol. 4. ISSN 0079-6158
- Progress in Control Engineering. irreg., 1964, vol. 2. ISSN 0079-6212
- Progress in Cryogenics. irreg., 1964, vol. 4. ISSN 0079-6220
- Progress in Experimental Personality Research. irreg., 1971, vol. 6. ISSN 0079-6255
- Progress in Nucleic Acid Research and Molecular Biology. irreg., 1973, vol. 13. ISSN 0079-6603
- Progress in Surface and Membrane Science. irreg.
- Progress in Theoretical Biology. irreg., 1972, vol. 2. ISSN 0079-6859
- Psychobiology and Physiological Psychology. irreg.
- Psychology of Learning and Motivation: Advances in Research and Theory. irreg., 1972, vol. 6. ISSN 0079-7421
- Pure and Applied Mathematics; A series of mongraphs and textbooks. irreg., vol. 62, 1975. ISSN 0079-8169
- Pure and Applied Physics; a series of monographs and textbooks. irreg., vol. 41, 1975. ISSN 0079-8193
- Quality Control in the Pharmaceutical Industry. irreg.
- Quaternary Research; an interdisciplinary journal. 6 per yr. ISSN 0033-5894
- Radiation Research. m. ISSN 0033-7587
- Recent Progress in Hormone Research. Proceedings of the Laurentian Hormone Conference. irreg., 1972, vol. 28. ISSN 0079-9963
- Recent Progress in Surface Science. irreg., 1970, vol. 3. ISSN 0079-9971
- Refractory Materials; a series of monographs. irreg., 1971, vol. 7. ISSN 0080-049X
- Reviews of Modern Physics Monographs. irreg.
- Semiconductors and Semimetals. irreg., 1972, vol. 9. ISSN 0080-8784
- Sensory Processes. q.

- Social Science Research; a quarterly journal of social science methodology and quantitative research. q. ISSN 0049-089X
- Society for Developmental Biology. Symposium. irreg. ISSN 0583-9009
- Society for Experimental Biology. Symposia. irreg., 1972, vol. 26. ISSN 0081-1386
- Solid State Physics; Advances in Research and Applications. irreg., 1972, vol. 27. ISSN 0081-1947
- Solid State Physics; Advances in Research and Applications. Supplement. irreg., 1972, suppl. 13. ISSN 0081-1955
- Studies in Anthropology. irreg.
- Studies in Language. irreg.
- Studies in Population. irreg.
- Studies in Social Discontinuity. irreg.
- Studies on the Development of Behavior and the Nervous System. irreg.
- Survey of Biological Progress. irreg., 1962, vol. 4. ISSN 0081-9697
- Survey of Progress in Chemistry. irreg., 1969, vol. 5. ISSN 0081-976X
- Symposia Mathematica. irreg., 1972, vol. 9. ISSN 0082-0725 (Italian National Institute of Higher Mathematics Conventions IT)
- Symposium on Special Ceramics, Stoke-On-Trent, England. Special Ceramics, Proceedings. irreg. ISSN 0082-0954 (British Ceramic Research Association UK)
- Synopses of the British Fauna. irreg., 1972, no. 3. ISSN 0082-1101 (Linnean Society of London UK)
- Syntax and Semantics. irreg.
- Theoretical and Experimental Biology; an international series of monographs. irreg., 1967, vol. 6. ISSN 0082-3945
- Theoretical Chemistry; a series of monographs. irreg., vol. 3, 1974. ISSN 0082-3961
- Theoretical Chemistry: Advances and Perspectives. irreg. ISSN 0361-0551
- Theoretical Population Biology. 6 per yr. ISSN 0040-5809
- Toxicology and Applied Pharmacology; for those working in the fields of toxicology, pharmacology, biochemistry, nutrition, veterinary medicine. m. ISSN 0041-008X
- Treatise on Materials Science & Technology. irreg (approx 1 per yr)
- University of Wisconsin. Institute for Research on Poverty. Monograph Series. irreg. (University of Wisconsin-Madison. Institute for Research on Poverty)
- Virology. 14 per yr. ISSN 0042-6822
- Vitamins and Hormones: Advances in Research and Applications. irreg., 1972, vol. 30. ISSN 0083-6729
- Water Pollution: a Series of Monographs. irreg.
- Yeshiva University, New York. Belfer Graduate School of Science. Annual Science Conference Proceedings. a. ISSN 0084-4187

**Academic Publications**
7500 W. Camp Wisdom Rd., Dallas, TX 75211.
- Notes on Literacy. q. (Summer Institute of Linguistics)
- Notes on Translation. q. (Wycliffe Bible Translators, Inc.) (Co-sponsor: Summer Institute of Linguistics)
- S I L Publications in Linguistics and Related Fields. irreg; no. 52, 1976. ISSN 0079-7669 (Summer Institute of Linguistics)
- Summer Institute of Linguistics. Language Data. African Series. irreg; no. 7, 1976.
- Summer Institute of Linguistics. Language Data. Amerindian Series. irreg; no. 5, 1975.
- Summer Institute of Linguistics. Language Data. Asian-Pacific Series. irreg; no. 11, 1976.
- Summer Institute of Linguistics. Publications Catalog. a.

**Academic Therapy Publications, Inc.**
1539 Fourth St., Box 899, San Rafael, CA 94901.
- Academic Therapy; an interdisciplinary quarterly directed to an international audience of teachers and specialists working with capable but underachieving children and youth. 5 per yr. ISSN 0001-396X
- Directory of Facilities for the Learning Disabled. irreg., latest issue 1976. ISSN 0092-3257

**Academy for Educational Development**
680 Fifth Ave., New York, NY 10019.
- Academy for Educational Development. Academy Papers. irreg., 1973, no. 6; nos. 1 and 2 out of print. ISSN 0065-0625
- Development Communication Report. (pub. by Clearinghouse on Development Communication)

**Academy for Educational Development. Management Division**
1414 22nd St., N.W., Washington, DC 20037.
- Guide to Professional Development Opportunities for College and University Administrators: Seminars, Workshops, Conferences, and Internships. irreg. ISSN 0098-9835 (Co-sponsor: American Council on Education. Office of Leadership Development in Higher Education)

**Academy Journal Publishing Co.**
320 Broadway, Cincinnati, OH 45202.
- Cincinnati Journal of Medicine. m. ISSN 0009-6873 (Academy of Medicine of Cincinnati)

**Academy News Bulletins, Inc.**
275 Madison Ave., New York, NY 10016.
- Anesthesiology Review. m. ISSN 0093-4437 (Co-Publisher: McNamara Publishing Co.)

**Academy of American Franciscan History**
Box 34440, 9901 Carmelita Dr., Washington, DC 20034.
- Academy of American Franciscan History. Documentary Series. irreg., latest, vol. 10. ISSN 0065-0633
- Academy of American Franciscan History. Monograph Series. irreg., latest, vol. 11. ISSN 0065-0641
- Academy of American Franciscan History. Propaganda Fide Series. irreg., latest, vol. 7. ISSN 0065-065X
- The Americas; a quarterly review of Inter-American cultural history. q. ISSN 0003-1615
- Franciscan Historical Classics. irreg., 1964, no. 2. ISSN 0071-9161

**Academy of American Poets**
1078 Madison Ave., New York, NY 10028.
- Academy of American Poets. Lamont Poetry Selections. a. ISSN 0515-2003
- Envoy. 2 per yr.

**Academy of Educational Disciplines**
107-20 125th St., Richmond Hill, NY 11419.
- Journal for Special Educators of the Mentally Retarded. 3 per yr. ISSN 0012-2807

**Academy of General Dentistry**
211 E. Chicago Ave., Chicago, IL 60611.
- General Dentistry. bi-m.

**Academy of General Practice of Pharmacy**
2215 Constitution Ave. N.W., Washington, DC 20037.
- Pharmacy Practice. m.

**Academy of International Business**
- Journal of International Business Studies. (pub. by Rutgers University. Graduate School of Business Administration)

**Academy of Management**
c/o Dennis F. Ray, Box KZ, Mississippi State, MS 39762.
- Academy of Management. Journal. q. ISSN 0001-4273
- Academy of Management. Proceedings. a. ISSN 0065-0668
- Academy of Management Review. q.

**Academy of Marketing Science**
- Academy of Marketing Science. Journal. (pub. by Long Island University. School of Business Administration)

**Academy of Medicine of Brooklyn**
1313 Bedford Ave., Brooklyn, NY 11216.
- Medical Society of the County of Kings and Academy of Medicine of Brooklyn. Bulletin. m. ISSN 0025-7532 (Co-Publisher: Medical Society of the County of Kings)

**Academy of Medicine of Cincinnati**
- Cincinnati Journal of Medicine. (pub. by Academy Journal Publishing Co.)

**Academy of Medicine of Cleveland**
- Cleveland Physician. (pub. by Academy Services, Inc.)

**Academy of Medicine of Toledo and Lucas County**
4428 Secor Rd., Toledo, OH 43623.
- Academy of Medicine of Toledo and Lucas County. Bulletin. m.(except July & Aug) ISSN 0001-4303

**Academy of Natural Sciences of Philadelphia**
19th St. and the Parkway, Philadelphia, PA 19103.
- Academy of Natural Sciences of Philadelphia. Monographs. irreg.
- Academy of Natural Sciences of Philadelphia. Proceedings. a.
- Academy of Natural Sciences of Philadelphia. Special Publications. irreg.
- Bartonia. a.
- Frontiers; a magazine of natural history. 4 per yr (Sept.-June) ISSN 0016-2159
- Malacologia. irreg., vol. 14, no. 1-2, 1974. ISSN 0076-2997 (Co-Sponsor: Institute of Malacology)
- Notulae Naturae. irreg., latest issue, 1974. ISSN 0029-4608

**Academy of Political Science**
2852 Broadway, New York, NY 10025.
- Academy of Political Science. Proceedings. irreg. ISSN 0065-0684
- Political Science Quarterly. q. ISSN 0032-3195

**Academy of the Arts and Sciences of the Americas**
3551 Main Highway, Coconut Grove, Miami, FL 33133.
- Academy of the Arts and Sciences of the Americas. Monographs. irreg.

**Academy Services, Inc.**
2059 E. 105th St., Cleveland, OH 44106.
- Cleveland Physician. m. (Academy of Medicine of Cleveland)

**Acadiana Profile, Inc.**
Box 52247 Oil Center Sta., Lafayette, LA 70505.
- Acadiana Profile. q. ISSN 0001-4397

**Accent Organization Inc.**
208 Ionia N. W., Grand Rapids, MI 49503.
- Accent/Grand Rapids. 10 per yr.

**Accent Publishing Co.**
1418 Lake St., Evanston, IL 60204.
- Accent. 5 per yr.

**Access-Indian Project**
Box 106, Pala, CA 92059.
- Indian Newsletter. m.

**Access to Energy**
Box 2298, Boulder, CO 80306.
- Access to Energy; pro-science,pro-technology,pro-free enterprise monthly newsletter. m.

**Accounting Corporation of America**
1927-1929 First Ave., P.O. Box 1471, San Diego, CA 92112.
- International Congress of Accountants. Proceedings. every five years.

**Ace Books**
1120 Avenue of the Americas, New York, NY 10036.
- Best Science Fiction. irreg. ISSN 0091-9217

**Achievement Disabled Action Group, Inc.**
8585 Sunset Dr., Suite 65, Miami, FL 33143
- Achievement; the national voice of the disabled. m. (Editorial Office:, 925 N. E. 122 St., North Miami, FL 33161)

**Acme Boot Co., Inc.**
1002 Stafford St., Box 749, Clarksville, TN 37040.
- Roundup. bi-m.

**Acme Newspapers Inc.**
18 W. Chelten Ave., Philadelphia, PA 19144.
- Germantown Courier. w. ISSN 0016-8920
- Main Line Times. w.
- News of Delaware County. w.

**Acorn Press**
9 Front St., Rockville Centre, NY 11570.
- New York State Dental Society of Anesthesiology. Newsletter. s-a.

**Acoustic Corporation of America**
145 Tremont St., Boston, MA 02111.
- A.C.A. Industry Guide to Hearing Aids. International Edition. a. ISSN 0095-3474

**Acoustical and Board Products Association**
205 W. Touhy Ave., Park Ridge, IL 60068.
- Acoustical and Board Products. Bulletin; performance data acoustical materials. a.

**Acoustical Publications, Inc.**
27101 E. Oviatt Rd., Bay Village, OH 44140.
● Sound and Vibration. m. ISSN 0038-1810

**Acoustical Society of America**
● Acoustical Society of America. Journal. (pub. by American Institute of Physics)

**Acquire Publishing Co., Inc.**
170 5th Ave., New York, NY 10010.
● Collector Editions Quarterly. q.

**Acres, Inc.**
1802 Chapman Rd., Huntertown, IN 46748.
● Acres Quarterly. q. ISSN 0001-5016

**Acropolis Books**
Colortone Building, 2400 17th St., N.W., Washington, DC 20009.
● International Business Classics Library Series. irreg.

**ACTION**
see U. S. ACTION

**Action for Children's Television**
46 Austin St., Newtonville, MA 02160.
● A C T News. q.

**Action Publishers, Inc.**
4222 Campus Dr., Newport Beach, CA 92660 (Subscr. to: Box 2880, Newport Beach, CA 92663)
● Motorcycle Weekly. w.
● Motorsport Weekly. w.

**Activa Publishing Ltd.**
250 W. 57 St., New York, NY 10019.
● New York Womens Week. w.

**Actors Equity Association**
1500 Broadway, New York, NY 10036.
● Equity News. 9 per yr. ISSN 0013-9890

**Acts 29**
R.R. 2, Box 218, Harmony, PA 16037.
● Harmony (Harmony); contemporary Christian music magazine. m. ISSN 0099-0604

**Actual Size Press**
Common Ground of the Arts, 4229 Cass Ave., Detroit, MI 48201.
● Actual Size. 3 per yr. ISSN 0044-6122

**Acupuncture Letter**
c/o Arlene L. Boas, 1570 Grand Ave. No. 18, Baldwin, NY 11510.
● Acupuncture Letter. m.

**Ad Arts Associates**
c/o Thomas D. Mottin, Ed, 124 Adelle Ave., St. Louis, MO 63135.
● Adapt Reports; a quarterly digest of retail advertising & promotion ideas. q. ISSN 0001-8058

**Ad East Enterprises**
● Ad East. (pub. by Carl B.E. Shedd)

**Ad Search: the National Want Ad Newspaper**
Box 2083, Milwaukee, WI 53201.
● Ad Search: the National Want Ad Newspaper. w.

**Alger L. Adams, Ed. & Pub.**
61 Pinecrest Dr., Hastings-on-Hudson, NY 10706.
● Fairfield County Press. w. ISSN 0014-6978
● Westchester County Press. w. ISSN 0043-3373

**Adcraft Club of Detroit**
2630 Book Tower, Detroit, MI 48226.
● Adcrafter. w. ISSN 0001-8066

**Lloyd Addison, Ed. & Pub.**
P.O. Box 409, New York, NY 10035.
● Beau-Cocoa. irreg. ISSN 0067-4737

**Addison-Wesley Publishing Co. Advanced Book Program**
Reading, MA 01867.
● Horizons in Biochemistry and Biophysics. irreg., vol. 3, 1977. ISSN 0096-2708
● Physics of Quantum Electronics; proceedings of summer schools. irreg., vol. 4, 1976.

**Adelphi University**
Garden City, Long Island, NY 11530.
● Entre Nosotros. 2-3 per yr.

**Adelphi University School of Social Research**
Garden City, NY 11530.
● Perspectives in Social Work. irreg. ISSN 0079-1040

**Adept Publications**
Box 52927, Houston, TX 77052.
● Adept Quarterly. q. ISSN 0001-818X

**Adirondack Life**
Box 137, Keene, NY 12942.
● Adirondack Life. bi-m. ISSN 0001-8252

**Adirondack Mountain Club, Inc.**
172 Ridge St., Glen Falls, NY 12801.
● Adirondac. bi-m. ISSN 0001-8236

**Adlai Stevenson Institute**
5757 S. Woodlawn, Chicago, IL 60637.
● Adlai Stevenson Institute of International Affairs. Annual Report. a. ISSN 0065-194X

**Administration in Mental Health**
Box 2088, Rockville, MD 20852.
● Administration in Mental Health. s-a. ISSN 0090-1180

**Administrative Management Society**
Maryland Rd., Willow Grove, PA 19001.
● A M S Directory of Office Salaries. a.
● A M S Guide to Management Compensation. a.
● A M S Yearbook. a.
● Generalist. m. (prep. by its Management Information Center)
● Management World; devoted to disseminating technical knowledge of the profession of scientific office and administrative management. m. ISSN 0090-3825

**Adobe News, Inc.**
P.O. Box 702, Los Lunas, NM 87031.
● Adobe News. bi-m.

**Adoptees' Liberty Movement Association**
Box 154, Washington Bridge Station, New York, NY 10033.
● A L M A Searchlight. 3 per yr.

**Adrenal Metabolic Research Society**
Hypoglycemia Foundation, Inc., 1 Park Lane, Box 98, Fleetwood, Mt. Vernon, NY 10552.
● Homeostasis Quarterly. q.

**Adult Education Association in Massachusetts, Inc.**
32 Whites Ave., No. 34, Watertown, MA 02172.
● A E A-M Newsletter/Journal. bi-m. ISSN 0001-1002

**Adult Education Association of the United States of America**
810 18th St. N.W., Washington, DC 20006.
● A E A Dateline. 10 per yr.
● Adult Education. q. ISSN 0001-8481
● Handbook of Adult Education in the United States. irreg., latest ed. 1970.
● Lifelong Learning: the Adult Years. m.(Sept-June)
● Register of Research and Investigation in Adult Education. irreg., latest 1971. ISSN 0080-147X (Co-Sponsor: ERIC Clearinghouse)

**Advance Yoeman Press**
Wicklife, KY 42074.
● Dawn; the Murray State nose. 18-30 per yr. ISSN 0011-7064

**Advanced Institute for Analytic Psychotherapy**
178-10 Wexford Terrace, Jamaica Estates, NY 11432.
● Treatment Monographs on Analytic Psychotherapy. irreg; no. 5, 1974.

**Advanced Management Research**
1370 Ave. of the Americas, New York, NY 10019.
● Jack Anderson's Washington Report. fortn.

**Advanced Research Projects Agency**
● Materials Research in Science and Engineering at Purdue University. Progress Report. (pub. by Purdue University. Materials Research Business Office)

**Advanced Technology Publications, Inc.**
385 Elliot St., Newton, MA 02164.
● Energy Research Reports. bi-m.
● Laser Focus; the magazine of lasers and related technologies. m. ISSN 0023-8589
● Laser Focus Buyers' Guide. a. ISSN 0075-8027

● Laser Report; the market outlook in lasers and opto-electronics. m. ISSN 0023-8600

**Advancement and Placement Institute**
169 N. 9th St., Box 99, Greenpoint Sta., Brooklyn, NY 11222.
● Crusade for Education; a non-fee placement journal describing verified professional openings in the United States and abroad for teachers, librarians, administrators and scientists. 6 per yr. ISSN 0011-2135
● World-Wide Summer Placement Directory. a. ISSN 0512-3879

**Adventure Guides, Inc.**
36 E. 57 St., New York, NY 10022.
● Adventure Trip Guide. biennial. ISSN 0084-5965

**Adventurers**
● Pioneer. (pub. by Paldor Publications)

**Adventures in Poetry**
c/o Larry Fagin, Ed., 437 E. 12th St., New York, NY 10009.
● Adventures in Poetry. 1-2 per yr.

**Adventuresses of Sherlock Holmes**
c/o K. Karlson, Ed., 151 W. 16th St., No. 3-E, New York, NY 10011
● Serpentine Muse. q. (Subscr. to: M. E. Couchon, 52 W. 56th St., New York, NY 10019)

**Advertising Checking Bureau, Inc.**
434 S. Wabash Ave., Chicago, IL 60605.
● Scan. m.

**Advertising Research Foundation**
3 East 54th St., New York, NY 10022.
● Advertising Research Foundation. Conference Proceedings. irreg., 19th, 1973. ISSN 0568-0352
● Journal of Advertising Research. bi-m. ISSN 0021-8499

**Advertising Specialty Institute**
NBS Bldg., Second and Clearview Ave., Trevose, PA 19047.
● Advertising Specialty Register: Product Research and Source Data. a.
● Counselor. m. ISSN 0011-0027

**Advertising Trade Publications, Inc.**
19 W. 44th St., New York, NY 10036.
● Advertising Techniques. m. ISSN 0001-0235
● Art Direction; the magazine of visual communication, serves the field of advertising art, photography, typography and related graphic arts field. m. ISSN 0004-3109
● Creativity. a. (Art Direction Magazine)
● Graphic Arts Buyer. bi-m. ISSN 0017-3304

**Advisory Enterprises, Inc.**
20 Haarlem, White Plains, NY 10603.
● Contact Lens Forum; exclusively for contact lens practitioners. m.
● Optical Management; for dispensing opticians, processing labs and optical manufacturers. m. ISSN 0090-0834
● Optometric Management; the national business magazine for optometrists. m. ISSN 0030-4085

**Advisory Information Services Ltd**
30 East 42 St, New York, NY 10017.
● London Gold Report. fortn.

**Advocate (New York)**
15 Park Row, New York, NY 10038.
● Advocate (New York). w. ISSN 0001-9003

**Advocate (Providence)**
160 Chace Ave., Providence, RI 02906.
● Advocate (Providence). m.

**Advocate (San Mateo)**
2121 S. El Camino Real, Suite 307, San Mateo, CA 94403.
● Advocate (San Mateo) 26 per yr.

**Advocate House**
Advocate House, 21 South St., Cambridge, MA 02138.
● Harvard Advocate. 6 per yr. ISSN 0017-8004

**Aegir Corp.**
Box 1764, Newport Beach, CA 92660.
● Journal of Marine Education. q.

**Aeolian Press**
6762 Cibola Rd., San Diego, CA 92120
(Subscr. to: Linda Pluth, 24 Colmar Rd., Cherry
Hill, NJ 08002)
• Virginia Woolf Quarterly. q. ISSN 0090-4546

**Aerial Phenomena Research Organization**
3910 E. Kleindale Rd., Tucson, AZ 85712.
• A P R O Bulletin. m.

**Aero Publishers, Inc.**
329 Aviation Rd., Fallbrook, CA 92028.
• Aviation and Space Dictionary. irreg., 5th, 1974.
• Federal Aviation Regulations for Pilots. a. ISSN
0533-0963

**Aero West Magazine Inc.**
Post Office Box 326, Broomfield, CO 80020.
• Aero West. m. ISSN 0568-0530 (Colorado Pilots
Association, Inc.)

**Aeronautica & Air Label Collectors Club**
Box 145, Brookfield, IL 60513.
• Aeronautica and Air Label Collector. q.

**Aerophile**
4014 Belle Grove, San Antonio, TX 78230.
• Aerophile. bi-m.

**Aeroquip Corp.**
300 S. East Ave., Jackson, MI 49203.
• Flying A. 4 per yr. ISSN 0015-4814

**Aerosol Techniques, Inc.**
Old Gate Lane, Milford, CT 06460.
• Pressure Gauge. irreg.; latest issue, 1975. ISSN
0079-5054

**Aerospace Industries Association of America, Inc.**
1725 De Sales St., N.W., Washington, DC 20036.
• Aerospace. q. ISSN 0001-9321

**Aerospace Medical Association**
Washington National Airport, Washington, DC
20001.
• Aerospace Medical Association. Annual Scientific
Meeting; Preprints. a. ISSN 0065-3764
• Aviation, Space, and Environmental Medicine. m.
ISSN 0095-6562

**Aetherius Society**
6202 Afton Place, Los Angeles, CA 90028.
• Aetherius Society Newsletter. s-m.

**Aetna Life and Casualty**
151 Farmington Ave., Hartford, CT 06115.
• Aetna-Izer. m. ISSN 0001-9585

**Affiliate Artists, Inc.**
155 W. 68th St., New York, NY 10023.
• Catalyst. q.

**Afram Associates**
68-72 East 131 St., New York, NY 10037.
• Afram Drum. m.

**Africa Inland Mission**
P.O. Box 178, Pearl River, NY 10965.
• Inland Africa. bi-m. ISSN 0020-1464

**Africa Investors & Placement Services, Inc.**
114 E. 32nd St., New York, NY 10016.
• African Progress. m. ISSN 0044-6599

**Africa News Service Inc.**
Box 3851, Durham, NC 27702.
• Africa News. w.

**Africa Today Associates**
c/o University of Denver, Graduate School of
International Studies, Denver, CO 80208.
• Africa Today. q. ISSN 0001-9887

**African-American Chamber of Commerce**
65 Liberty St., New York, NY 10005.
• African-American Chamber of Commerce. News.
q.

**African American Institute**
• Africa Report. (pub. by Transaction Periodicals
Consortium)

**African-American Labor Center**
345 E. 46th St., New York, NY 10017.
• A A L C Reporter. m. ISSN 0001-009X

**African American Teachers Association**
1064 Fulton St., Brooklyn, NY 11238.
• African-American Teachers Forum. q. ISSN 0001-
9917

**African Bibliographic Center**
P.O. Box 13096, Washington, DC 20009.
• A M A: Women in African and American Worlds.
bi-m.
• African Bibliographic Center, Washington, D.C.
Current Reading List Series. irreg., latest 1976,
vol. 12. ISSN 0065-3926
• African Bibliographic Center, Washington, D.C.
Special Bibliographic Series. (pub. by Greenwood
Press)
• Current Bibliography on African Affairs. (pub. by
Baywood Publishing Co., Inc.)

**African Law Association in America, Inc.**
• African Law Studies. (pub. by Fred B. Rothman &
Co.)

**African Literature Association**
c/o Thomas A. Hale, Ed., Department of French,
Pennsylvania State University, University Park, PA
16802.
• African Literature Association Newsletter. q.

**African Methodist Episcopal Church**
468 Lincoln Drive, N. W., Atlanta, GA 30318.
• A. M. E. Church Review. q.

**African Methodist Episcopal Church (New York)**
475 Riverside Dr. Room 1926, New York, NY
10027.
• Voice of Missions. m.(Sept-June) ISSN 0042-8175

**African Methodist Episcopal Church. Division of
Christian Education**
414 Eighth Ave.,S., Nashville, TN 37203.
• Journal of Religious Education. q. ISSN 0022-
4219

**African Methodist Episcopal Zion Church**
Box 1047, Charlotte, NC 28202.
• Star of Zion. w. ISSN 0038-9870

**African Methodist Episcopal Zion Church. Church
Board of Publications**
Box 146, Bedford, PA 15522.
• A.M.E. Zion Quarterly Review. q. ISSN 0360-
3717

**African Peoples Party**
P.O. Box 61213, Los Angeles, CA 90055.
• Soulbook. q. (Co-Sponsor: Council for Black
Survival)

**African People's Socialist Party**
Box 12792, St. Petersburg, FL 32604.
• Burning Spear. m. ISSN 0045-3552

**African Picture & Information Service**
244 Lenox Ave., New York, NY 10027.
• African Opinion; journal of independent thoughts
and expression. bi-m. ISSN 0002-0095

**African Studies Association**
Brandeis University, Shiffman Center 218, Waltham,
MA 02154.
• African Studies Newsletter. 6 per yr. ISSN 0002-
0214
• African Studies Review. a. ISSN 0002-0206
• Directory of African Studies in the United States.
irreg. (prep. by its Research Liaison Committee)
• History in Africa. s-a.
• Issue; a quarterly journal of opinion. q. ISSN
0047-1607

**African Studies Association. Archives-Libraries
Committee**
• Africana Libraries Newsletter. (pub. by Boston
University. African Studies Library)

**African Violet Society of America, Inc.**
Box 1326, Knoxville, TN 37901.
• African Violet Magazine. 5 per yr. ISSN 0002-
0265

**African Wildlife Leadership Foundation**
1717 Massachusetts Ave., N.W., Washington, DC
20036.
• African Wildlife News. irreg. (3 per year) 1970,
vol. 5. ISSN 0065-4086

**African Youth Movement for Liberation & Unity**
Department of Sociology, State University of New
York, Binghamton, NY 13901.
• African Youth. bi-m.

**Africana Publishing Co.**
(Subsidiary of: Holmes & Meier Publishers, Inc.)
101 Fifth Ave., New York, NY 10003.
• African Bibliography Series. irreg.
• African Literature Today. a. ISSN 0065-4000
(University of Sierra Leone. Fourah Bay College
SL) (And Heinemann Educational Books, 48
Charles St., London, England W1X 8AH)
• Africana Journal; a bibliographic and review
quarterly. q. ISSN 0095-1080
• International Journal of African Historical Studies.
q. ISSN 0361-7882 (Boston University. African
Studies Center)

**Afro-Am Publishing Co., Inc.**
1727 Indiana Ave., Chicago, IL 60616.
• Afro-Am Portfolios. irreg., no. 9 latest issue. ISSN
0065-4175

**Afro-American Co. (Richmond)**
301 E. Clay St., Richmond, VA 23219.
• Richmond Afro-American; and the Richmond
Planet. w.

**Afro-American Historical Association of the Niagara
Frontier**
Box 1663, Hertel Sta., Buffalo, NY 14216.
• Afro-Americans in New York Life and History. s-
a. ISSN 0364-2437

**Afro-American Museum of Detroit**
1553 W. Grand Blvd., Detroit, MI 48208.
• Afro-American Museum of Detroit. Newsletter. q.

**Afro-American Music Opportunities Association**
Box 662, 2909 Wayzata Blvd., Minneapolis, MN
55440.
• A A M O A Reports. bi-m.
• Afro-American Music Opportunities Association.
Resource Papers. irreg.

**Afro-American Newspapers**
628 N. Eutaw St., Baltimore, MD 21201.
• Baltimore Afro-American. s-w.
• Dawn; a new day for Black Americans.
• Washington Afro-American. s-w. ISSN 0043-0447

**Afro-American Patrolmen's League**
7126 S. Jeffery Blvd., Chicago, IL 60649.
• Grapevine. q.

**Ag Publishing Co.**
8330 Burnet Rd., Box 9279, Austin, TX 78766.
• Ag Trucking News & Irregular Route Carrier. bi-
m.

**Against the Wall**
Box 444, Westfield, NJ 07091.
• Against the Wall. q.

**Agatherin'**
Box 175, Wynantskil, NY 12198.
• Post Script; a postal history journal. q.

**Age of Achievement, Inc.**
c/o Barbara Krohn, 835 Securities Bldg., Seattle,
WA 98101.
• Age of Achievement; independent Northwest
magazine for the older citizen. m. ISSN 0002-
0745

**Agel Publishing Co. Inc.**
75 E. 55th St., New York, NY 10022.
• Books. m. ISSN 0006-7423
• Keep in Touch. w.

**Agency for Instructional Television**
Box A, Bloomington, IN 47401.
• A I T Newsletter. q.

**AgImpact**
420 E. Main St., Batavia, NY 14020.
• AgImpact. m. (Co-sponsors: Cooperative
Extension Associations of Genesee, Monroe,
Niagara, and Orleans Counties)

**Agni Review**
222 Concord Ave., Cambridge, MA 02138.
• Agni Review. 2 per yr.

**Agri Business Publications, Inc.**
Division of Century Communications, Inc., 5520
Touhy Ave, Suite G, Skokie, IL 60076.
- Agri Finance. 7 per yr. ISSN 0002-1164
- Agri Marketing. m. ISSN 0002-1180

**Agribusiness Publications**
560 N. Trout Lake Dr., Sanger, CA 73657.
- Agribusiness Fieldman. m.
- Agribusiness News. m.

**Agricultural Development Council, Inc.**
1290 Ave. of the Americas, New York, NY 10019.
- A D C Newsletter. 4 per yr. ISSN 0001-088X
- A. D. C. Reprints. irreg.
- A.D.C. Staff Papers. irreg.
- Agricultural Development Council. Related
Training Network A. D. C. - R. T. N. irreg.

**Agricultural Education Magazine, Inc.**
R.D.2, Box 639, Halifax, PA 17032.
- Agricultural Education. m. ISSN 0002-144X

**Agricultural History Society**
- Agricultural History. (pub. by University of
California Press)

**Agricultural Missions, Inc.**
475 Riverside Dr., New York, NY 10027.
- Rural Missions. irreg. ISSN 0036-0082

**Agricultural Relations Council**
18 S. Michigan Ave., Chicago, IL 60603.
- Directory of Communicators in Agriculture. irreg.;
latest issue, 1973-74. ISSN 0419-2400 (United
Dairy Industry Association) (With: American
Dairy Assn.; National Dairy Council; Dairy
Research, Inc.)

**Agricultural Research Center, Inc.**
1305 East Main Street, Lakeland, FL 33801.
- Agricultural Research Center. Annual Report. a.

**Agriculture Teachers Directory and Handbook**
3042 Overlook, Montgomery, AL 36109.
- Agriculture Teachers Directory and Handbook. a.
ISSN 0515-7420

**Agro-Info**
8215 Donset Dr., Springfield, VA 22152.
- Washington Agricultural Proceedings. w.

**Agudas Neshei Ubnos Chabad**
770 Eastern Parkway, Brooklyn, NY 11213.
- Yiddishe Heim/Jewish Home. q. ISSN 0044-0418

**Agudath Israel of America**
5 Beekman St., New York, NY 10038.
- Jewish Observer. m(Sept.-June) ISSN 0021-6615

**Agway Inc.**
Box 1333, Syracuse, NY 13201.
- Agway Cooperator. m. ISSN 0002-2012

**Ahsahta**
Boise State University, Boise, ID 83725.
- Ahsahta. 3 per yr.

**Aid Association for Lutherans**
Appleton, WI 54919.
- Correspondent. q.

**Aid for Retarded Children**
1362 9th Ave., San Francisco, CA 94103.
- Aid to Retarded Children. Independent Living
Rehabilitation Program. Report. a.

**Air Age Inc.**
1 No. Broadway, White Plains, NY 10601.
- Model Airplane News. m. ISSN 0026-7295

**Air California**
Box 707, South Laguna, CA 92677.
- Air California. m.

**Air Cargo, Inc**
1730 Rhode Island Ave., N.W., Washington, DC
20036.
- Air Freight Directory. irreg. ISSN 0092-2870

**Air Cargo News, Inc.**
Box 32243, Jamaica, NY 11431.
- Air Cargo News. m.

**Air-Conditioning and Refrigeration Institute**
1815 N. Fort Myer Drive, Arlington, VA 22209.
- Koldfax. m.

**Air Force Association**
1750 Pennsylvania Ave.N.W., Suite 400,
Washington, DC 20006.
- Air Force Magazine. m.

**Air Force Historical Foundation**
- Aerospace Historian. (pub. by Robin Higham, Ed.
& Pub.)

**Air Force Sergeants Association**
4235 28th Ave., Suite 707, Marlow Heights, MD
20031.
- Sergeants. m. ISSN 0360-7364

**Air Line Employees Association**
5600 S. Central, Chicago, IL 60638.
- Air Line Employee. bi-m. ISSN 0002-2411

**Air Line Pilots Association International (AFL-CIO)**
1625 Massachusetts Ave., N.W., Washington, DC
20036.
- Air Line Pilot. m. ISSN 0002-242X
- Air Safety Forum. a.; latest issue, 1973. ISSN
0065-4841 (prep. by its Engineering and Air
Safety Division)

**Air Pollution Control Association**
4400 Fifth Ave., Pittsburgh, PA 15213.
- A.P.C.A. Proceedings Digest. a.
- Air Pollution Control Association. Journal. m.
ISSN 0002-2470
- Directory of Governmental Air Pollution
Agencies. a.

**Air Power Museum**
- A P M Bulletin. (pub. by Antique Airplane
Association)

**Air Service Directory, Inc.**
1 Bank St., Stamford, CT 06901.
- A. B. D. (Aviation Business Directory); aircraft
and missile buyers' guide. q. ISSN 0001-0502

**Air Traffic Control Association**
525 School St. S.W., Washington, DC 20024.
- Journal of Air Traffic Control. q. ISSN 0021-8650

**Air Transport Association of America**
1000 Connecticut Ave., N.W., Washington, DC
20036.
- Air Transport. a.

**Air Travel Bargains Worldwide Guidebook**
Box 897, Coconut Grove, Miami, FL 33133
- Air Travel Bargains. a. ISSN 0065-4868 (Dist. by
Simon & Schuster)

**Air University**
*see under* U.S. Air Force

**Aircraft Owners and Pilots Association**
Box 5800, Washington DC 20014.
- A O P A Pilot. m. ISSN 0001-2084
- A O P A's Airports U.S.A. a.

**Aires Publishing Co., Inc.**
5428 Macarthur Blvd. N.W., Washington, DC
20016.
- This Week in the Nations' Capital. w. ISSN 0040-
6317

**Airline Handbook**
c/o Paul K. Martin, Box 3694, Cramston, RI 02910.
- Airline Handbook. a. ISSN 0095-4683

**Airline Inflight Food Service Association**
- Airline Food & Flight Service. (pub. by
International Publishing Co. of America)

**Airline Marketing, Inc.**
9800 S. Sepulveda Blvd., Suite 520, Los Angeles,
CA 90045.
- Airfair Interline; official interline magazine. m.
ISSN 0044-7005

**Airline Passengers Association**
- A P A Holiday. (pub. by Curtis Publishing Co.)

**Airline Services Unlimited**
1335 Columbus Ave., San Francisco, CA 94133.
- A S U Travel Guide; the interliner's discount
directory. q.

**Airport Operators Council International**
1700 K St. N.W., Washington, DC 20006.
- Airport Highlights. w.

**Airstream**
Div. of Beatrice Foods, North Dixie Highway,
Sidney, OH 45365.
- Caravanner. bi-m. ISSN 0008-6193

**Airtrails, Inc.**
4124 Nellie Custis Drive, Arlington, VA 22207.
- Aviation Quarterly. q. ISSN 0045-1215

**Ajax Electric Co.**
60 Tomlinson Rd., Huntingdon Valley, PA 19006.
- Salt Bath Tips and Trends. s-a.

**Akron Dental Society**
157 W. Cedar, Akron, OH 44320.
- Akron Dental Society. Bulletin. 8 per yr. ISSN
0002-3701

**Akron-Summit County Public Library**
55 S. Main St., Akron, OH 44326.
- Owlet. m. ISSN 0030-7602

**Alabama. Commission on Higher Education**
Montgomery, AL 36104.
- Alabama. Commission on Higher Education.
Biennial Report to the Governor and the
Legislature. biennial. ISSN 0095-1285
- Fact Book. Alabama Institutions of Higher
Education, Universities and Colleges. irreg. ISSN
0095-0637

**Alabama. Department of Archives and History**
624 Washington Ave., Montgomery, AL 36104.
- Alabama Historical Quarterly. q. ISSN 0002-4236

**Alabama. Department of Conservation and Natural
Resources**
Union St., Administration Bldg, Montgomery, AL
36130.
- Alabama Conservation. bi-m. ISSN 0002-4171

**Alabama. Department of Conservation and Natural
Resources. Marine Resources Div.**
Box 188, Dauphin Island, AL 36528.
- Alabama Marine Resources Bulletin. irreg., no. 11,
1976. ISSN 0090-8843

**Alabama. Department of Education**
Montgomery, AL 36104.
- Alabama Department of Education. Library Media
Output.

**Alabama. Department of Industrial Relations**
Montgomery, AL 36100.
- Alabama. Department of Industrial Relations.
Annual Manpower Planning Report. a. ISSN
0361-297X

**Alabama. Department of Pensions and Security**
64 N. Union St., Montgomery, AL 36130.
- Alabama Social Welfare. 10 per yr. ISSN 0002-
4368

**Alabama. Department of Public Health**
206 State Office Bldg, Montgomery, AL 36130.
- Alabama's Health. q.

**Alabama. Development Office**
State Capitol, Montgomery, AL 36130.
- Alabama County Data Book. a.
- Alabama Development News. m.
- Alabama World Trade Directory. a. ISSN 0095-
1269
- New and Expanding Industries Report for
Alabama. a.

**Alabama. Division of Vital Statistics**
Montgomery, AL 36104.
- Alabama's Vital Events. a. ISSN 0095-3431

**Alabama. Division of Vocation Education and
Community Colleges**
c/o State Dept. of Education, Montgomery, AL
36104.
- Select Data on Students, Alabama Institutions of
Higher Learning. irreg. ISSN 0091-5246

**Alabama. Law Enforcement Planning Agency**
501 Adams Ave., Montgomery, AL 36104.
- Law Enforcement Newsletter. q.

**Alabama. Public Library Service**
155 Administrative Bldg., Montgomery, AL 36104.
- Alabama. Public Library Service. Basic State Plan
  and Annual Program. a. ISSN 0095-361X

**Alabama Academy of Science**
Auburn Univ., Ralph Brown Draughon Library,
Auburn, AL 36830.
- Alabama Academy of Science. Journal. q. ISSN
  0002-4112

**Alabama Archaeological Society**
Box 66, Moundville, AL 35474.
- Alabama Archaeological Society. Special
  Publication. irreg.
- Journal of Alabama Archaeology. s-a.
- Stones and Bones Newsletter. m.

**Alabama Association of Secondary School Principals**
c/o Ed Richardson, Ed., Andalusia High School,
Andalusia, AL 36420.
- Alabama Association of Secondary School
  Principals. Bulletin. 3 per yr. ISSN 0002-4139

**Alabama Baptist Historical Society**
c/o F. W. Helmbold, Ed., Samford Univ.,
Birmingham, AL 35209.
- Alabama Baptist Historian. s-a. ISSN 0002-4147

**Alabama Chamber of Commerce**
P.O. Box 76, Montgomery, AL 36101.
- Industrial Alabama. a. ISSN 0073-7321

**Alabama Dental Association**
1729 Springhill Ave, Mobile, AL 36604.
- Alabama Dental Association. Journal. q. ISSN
  0002-4198

**Alabama Education Association**
422 Dexter Ave., Box 4177, Montgomery, AL
36104.
- Alabama School Journal. bi-m. ISSN 0002-435X

**Alabama Farm Bureau Federation**
2108 East So. Blvd, P.O. Box 11000, Montgomery,
AL 36111.
- Alabama Farm Bureau News. m.
- Neighbors. q.

**Alabama Food Council**
Box 9208, Montgomery, AL 36108.
- Alabama Food Merchants Journal. bi-m. ISSN
  0002-421X

**Alabama Forestry Association**
Associations Bldg., 660 Adams Ave., Montgomery,
AL 36104.
- Alabama Forest Products. m. ISSN 0002-4228

**Alabama Geological Society**
P.O.B. 6184, University, AL 35486.
- Alabama Geological Society. Guidebook for the
  Annual Field Trip. a.(two books appeared in
  1964) ISSN 0065-5635

**Alabama Historical Association**
c/o Malcolm C. McMillan, Ed., Auburn Univ.,
History Dept., Auburn, AL 36830.
- Alabama Review; a journal of Alabama history. q.
  ISSN 0002-4341

**Alabama Junior College Library Association**
c/o Lucinda May, Ed., John C. Calhoun State
Junior College, Decatur, AL 35602.
- Alabama Junior College Library Association
  Newsletter. 4 per yr.

**Alabama League of Municipalities**
535 Adams Ave., Montgomery, AL 36104.
- Alabama Municipal Journal. m. ISSN 0002-4309

**Alabama Library Association, Inc.**
Box 6242, University, AL 35486.
- Alabama Librarian. bi-m. ISSN 0002-4295

**Alabama Personnel and Guidance Association**
- Alabama Personnel and Guidance Journal. (pub.
  by Auburn University Press)

**Alabama Solar Energy Association**
University of Alabama, Environmental and Energy
Studies, Box 1247, Huntsville, AL 35807.
- Sun-Clipse. m.
- Sunspot. q.

**Alabama State Bar Association**
Lock Box 4156, Montgomery, AL 36101.
- Alabama Lawyer. q. ISSN 0002-4287

**Alabama State Council on the Arts and Humanities**
322 Alabama St., Montgomery, AL 36104.
- Biennial Report of the Arts Activities in Alabama.
  biennial.

**Alabama State Nurses Association**
504 N. E. Blvd., Montgomery, AL 36109.
- A S N A Reporter. m.

**Alabama Trucking Association**
660 Adams, Montgomery, AL 36104.
- Alabama Trucker. m. ISSN 0002-4384

**Alameda- Contra Costa Medical Association**
6230 Claremont Ave., Oakland, CA 94618.
- Alameda-Contra Costa Medical Association.
  Bulletin. m. ISSN 0002-4414

**Alameda-Contra Costa Transit District**
508 16th St., Oakland, CA 94612.
- Transit-Times. m. ISSN 0049-4410

**Alamo Area Council of Governments**
118 Broadway, 400 Three Americas Building, San
Antonio, TX 78205.
- A A C O G Region. m.

**Alaska. Board of Registration for Architects,
Engineers and Land Surveyors**
Box 469, Juneau, AK 99801.
- Alaska. State Board of Registration for Architects,
  Engineers and Land Surveyors. Directory of
  Architects, Engineers and Land Surveyors. irreg.
  ISSN 0094-1786

**Alaska. Criminal Investigation Bureau**
Box 6188, Anchorage, AK 99502.
- Alaska. Criminal Investigation Bureau. Annual
  Report. a. ISSN 0362-7284

**Alaska. Department of Agriculture. Statistical
Reporting Service**
P.O. Box 799, Palmer, AK 99645.
- Alaska Agricultural Statistics. irreg., latest issue,
  1973. ISSN 0065-5694

**Alaska. Department of Economic Development.
Division of Economic Enterprise**
Pouch EE, Juneau, AK 99801.
- Directory of Alaska Commercial Establishments.
  irreg.
- Performance Report of the Alaskan Economy.
  irreg.

**Alaska. Department of Fish and Game**
Subport Bldg., Juneau, AK 99801.
- A. D. F. &. G. Technical Data Report. irreg. ISSN
  0095-4632
- Alaska. Department of Fish and Game. Annual
  Report. a. ISSN 0065-5708
- Alaska. Department of Fish and Game.
  Commercial Operators. a.
- Alaska. Department of Fish and Game. Wildlife
  Booklet Series. irreg. ISSN 0084-0130

**Alaska. Department of Fish and Game. Auke Bay**
Auke Bay, AK 99821.
- Northeast Pacific Pink Salmon Workshop.
  Proceedings. biennial. ISSN 0094-128X

**Alaska. Department of Fish and Game. Game Division**
Subport Bldg., Juneau, AK 99801.
- Alaska. Department of Fish and Game. Game
  Technical Bulletin Series. irreg.
- Alaska. Division of Game. Annual Report of
  Survey-Inventory Activities. a. ISSN 0362-6962

**Alaska. Department of Health and Social Services**
Pouch H, Juneau, AK 99811.
- Alaska. Department of Health and Social Services.
  Quarterly. 4 per yr.
- Alaska State Plan for the Construction of
  Hospitals and Medical Facilities. a. ISSN 0065-
  583X

**Alaska. Department of Health and Social Services.
Division of Medical Assistance**
Juneau, AK 99801.
- Alaska Medicaid Status Report. a. ISSN 0095-
  4667

**Alaska. Department of Health and Social Services.
Office of Alcoholism**
Juneau, AK 99801.
- Alaska. Office of Alcoholism. Report. a. ISSN
  0095-3318

**Alaska. Department of Labor. Employment Security
Division**
Research and Analysis Section, Box 3-7000, Juneau,
AK 99801.
- Alaska. Employment Security Division. Labor
  Force Estimates by Industry and Area. a.
- Alaska Economic Trends. m. ISSN 0002-4481

**Alaska. Department of Natural Resources. Division of
Geological and Geophysical Surveys**
Box 80007, College, AK 99701.
- Alaska. Division of Geological and Geophysical
  Surveys. Annual Report. a. ISSN 0065-5724
- Alaska. Division of Geological and Geophysical
  Surveys. Geochemical Report. irreg, no. 27, 1973.
  ISSN 0065-5732
- Alaska. Division of Geological and Geophysical
  Surveys. Information Circular. irreg. ISSN 0065-
  5759
- Alaska. Division of Geological and Geophysical
  Surveys. Laboratory Note. irreg. ISSN 0065-5767
- Alaska. Division of Geological and Geophysical
  Surveys. Laboratory Report. irreg. ISSN 0065-
  5775
- Alaska. Division of Geological and Geophysical
  Surveys. Mines and Geology Bulletin. q.
- Alaska. Division of Geological and Geophysical
  Surveys. Miscellaneous Paper. irreg. ISSN 0065-
  5783
- Alaska. Division of Geological and Geophysical
  Surveys. Special Report. irreg. ISSN 0065-5791

**Alaska. Department of Natural Resources. Division of
Lands**
323 E. Fourth Ave., Anchorage, AK 99501.
- Alaska Land Lines. m. ISSN 0002-4511

**Alaska. Department of Natural Resources. Division of
Oil and Gas**
3001 Porcupine Dr., Anchorage, AK 99501.
- Alaska. Division of Oil and Gas. Statistical
  Report. a. ISSN 0360-5558

**Alaska. Department of Public Safety. Planning and
Research**
State Capitol, 120 4th St., Juneau, AK 99801.
- Alaska Accident Statistics. a. ISSN 0360-9154

**Alaska. Department of Revenue**
Pouch SA, Juneau, AK 99801.
- Alaska. Department of Revenue. Revenue
  Sources. a. (prep. by its Research Section)
- Alaska. Department of Revenue. State Investment
  Portfolio. a. ISSN 0092-6736

**Alaska. Division of Family and Children Services**
Juneau, AK 99801.
- Alaska. Division of Family and Children Services.
  Annual Report. a. ISSN 0094-1174

**Alaska. Division of Public Health**
Juneau, AK 99801.
- Alaska. Division of Public Health. Annual Report.
  a. ISSN 0095-3407

**Alaska. Division of State Libraries**
Pouch G, State Capitol, Juneau, AK 99801.
- Alaska. State Library, Juneau. Historical
  Monographs. irreg. ISSN 0084-6139
- Alaska. State Library, Juneau. State and Local
  Publications Received-Alaska. a. ISSN 0568-8442
- Alaska Blue Book. biennial. ISSN 0092-1858
- Annual Report of the Public Libraries of Alaska.
  a. ISSN 0065-5821
- Library Development in Alaska: Long Range
  Program. a.
- Northern Libraries Bulletin. q. ISSN 0048-0789

**Alaska. Legislative Budget and Audit Committee**
Juneau, AK 99801.
- Alaska. Legislature. Budget and Audit Committee.
  Annual Report. a. ISSN 0095-3865

**Alaska. Office of Ombudsman**
Juneau, AK 99801.
- Alaska. Office of Ombudsman. Report of the
  Ombudsman. a. ISSN 0363-5376

**Alaska. Office of the Governor**
Juneau, AK 99801.
- Alaska. Office of the Governor. Governor's
  Manpower Plan. a. ISSN 0091-9535

**Alaska. State Council on the Arts**
619 Warehouse Ave., Suite 220, Anchorage, AK
99501.
- Arts in Alaska. 6 per yr. ISSN 0094-3568

**Alaska. Violent Crimes Compensation Board**
Juneau, AK 99801.
- Alaska. Violent Crimes Compensation Board.
Annual Report. a. ISSN 0095-3415

**Alaska Bar Association**
Box 279, Anchorage, AK 99510.
- Alaska Bar Brief. m.

**Alaska Conservation Society**
Box 80192, College, AK 99708.
- Alaska Conservation Review. q. ISSN 0002-4465

**Alaska Construction News, Inc.**
109 W. Mercer, Seattle, WA 98119.
- Alaska Construction and Oil. m.

**Alaska Directory Corp.**
409 W. Northern Lights Blvd., Anchorage, AK
99503.
- Alaska Petroleum and Industrial Directory. a.
ISSN 0065-5813

**Alaska Education Association**
207 Seward Bldg., Juneau, AK 99801.
- Alaska Teacher. 8 per yr. ISSN 0002-4589

**Alaska Geographic Society**
- Alaska Geographic. (pub. by Alaska Northwest
Publishing Co.)

**Alaska Information & Research Service**
Box 10184, Anchorage, AK 99509.
- Alaska Economic Report. bi-w.

**Alaska Library Association**
State Library, Pouch G, Juneau, AK 99801.
- Alaska Libraries and Library Personnel Directory.
irreg.
- Sourdough. q. ISSN 0002-4570 (Or c/o Alan
Edward Schorr, Rasmuson Library, University of
Alaska, Fairbanks, AK 99701)

**Alaska Methodist University Press**
Anchorage, AK 99504.
- A M U Press Alaskana Series. irreg., nos. 27-35,
1976. ISSN 0002-4554

**Alaska Native Medical Center**
Box 7-741, Anchorage, AK 99510.
- Alaska Native Medical Center. Annual Report. a.
ISSN 0362-6849

**Alaska Northwest Publishing Co.**
Box 4-EEE, Anchorage, AK 99509
(Circ. Office: 130 Second Ave. S., Edmonds, WA
98020)
- Alaska; magazine of life on the last frontier. m.
ISSN 0002-4562
- Alaska Fishing Guide; by the editors of Alaska
magazine. a. ISSN 0361-3984
- Alaska Geographic. q. ISSN 0361-1353 (Alaska
Geographic Society)
- Alaska Hunting Guide; by the editors of Alaska
magazine. a. ISSN 0095-5760
- Alaska Journal; history and arts of the North
quarterly. q. ISSN 0002-4503
- Facts About Alaska. irreg. ISSN 0361-7823
- Milepost; all-the-north-travel-guide. a. ISSN 0361-
1361
- Selected Alaska Hunting & Fishing Tales. irreg.,
vol. 4, 1976. ISSN 0361-137X

**Alaska Travel Guide**
P.O. Box 21038, Salt Lake City, UT 84121.
- Alaska Travel Guide. a. ISSN 0065-5848

**Alaska Women's Resource Center**
621 W. Fifth, Suite E, Anchorage, AK 99501.
- Sourceline; newspaper for Alaskan women. m.

**Albanian American Islamic Center New York- New
Jersey**
Box 68, Massapequa Park, NY 11762.
- Perpjekja e Jone/Our Effort. s-a.

**Albanian Orthodox Diocese of America**
Bishop Mark, 54 Burroughs St., Jamaica Plain, MA
02130.
- Drita e Vertete/True Light. m.

**Albanians of Yugoslavia, Union of the Kossovars**
189-10 33rd Ave, Flushing, NY 11358.
- Struggle of the Kossovars Bulletin. q.

**Albany Law School**
80 New Scotland Ave., Albany, NY 12208.
- Albany Law Review. 4 per yr. ISSN 0002-4678

**Albany Medical College**
47 New Scotland Ave., Albany, NY 12208.
- Albany Regional Medical Program. Report. q.
ISSN 0002-4686

**Albany Medical College. Department of
Ophthalmology**
Division of Information Services, Albany, NY
12208.
- Current Citations on Strabismus, Amblyopia, and
Other Diseases of Ocular Motility. q.

**Albee-Campbell, Inc.**
578-580 Penn Ave., Sinking Spring, PA 19608.
- Rep World; quarterly marketing newsletter. q.

**Albemarle County Historical Society**
C/O Manuscripts Department, University of
Virginia Library, Charlottesville, VA 22901.
- Magazine of Albemarle County History. a or
biennial. ISSN 0076-2342

**Albuquerque Archaeological Society**
Box 4029, Albuquerque, NM 87106.
- Albuquerque Archaeological Society Newsletter.
m. ISSN 0002-4953
- Pottery Southwest; news, queries & views on
archaeological ceramics by Southwesternists. q.

**Albuquerque Bar Association**
Rm. 507 Sandia Savings Bldg., 400 Gold Ave. S.W.,
Albuquerque, NM 87102.
- Albuquerque Bar Journal. q. ISSN 0516-5504

**Alcoholics Anonymous World Services, Inc.**
Box 459, Grand Central Sta., New York, NY 10017
(or 468 Park Ave. So., New York, NY 10016)
- International A. A. Directory. ISSN 0361-7459
- Western United States A. A. Directory. irreg.
ISSN 0362-1359

**Aldebaran**
Roger Williams College, Bristol, RI 02809.
- Aldebaran. s-a.

**Aldine Publishing Co.**
529 S. Wabash Ave., Chicago, IL 60605.
- Aldine Crime and Justice Annual. a. ISSN 0094-
7040
- Aldine Treatises in Modern Economics. irreg.
- Aldine Treatises in Social Psychology. irreg.
- Atherton Controversies. irreg.
- Behavior Change. a.
- Benefit-Cost and Policy Analysis; an Aldine
annual on forecasting, decision-making and
evaluation. a. ISSN 0091-3227
- Biofeedback and Self-Control; an Aldine annual
on the regulation of bodily processes and
consciousness. a. ISSN 0067-8708
- Current Concerns in Clinical Psychology. irreg.,
1969, no. 3. ISSN 0070-1904
- Lewis Henry Morgan Lectures. irreg., 1970, no. 5.
ISSN 0075-8922 (University of Rochester.
Department of Anthropology)
- Modern Applications of Psychology. irreg.
- Modern Applications of Social Work. irreg.
- N O R C Monographs in Social Reserach. irreg.,
1969, no. 15. ISSN 0077-5258 (National Opinion
Research Center)
- Perspectives on Personality. irreg.
- Perspectives on the Biology of Man. irreg.
- Viking Fund Publications in Anthropology. irreg.,
1968, no. 47. ISSN 0083-6249
- Worlds of Man; studies in cultural ecology. irreg.,
latest 1975.

**Aldrich Chemical Company, Inc.**
940 W. St. Paul Ave., Milwaukee, WI 53233.
- Aldrichimica Acta. q. ISSN 0002-5100

**Aldrich Entomology Club**
- Aldrich Entomology Club. Newsletter. (pub. by
University of Idaho. Department of Entomology)

**Aleph Ltd.**
7319 Willow Ave, Takoma Park, MD 20012.
- Aleph. 2-3 per yr.

**Alexander Graham Bell Association for the Deaf, Inc.**
3417 Volta Place, N.W., Washington, DC 20007.
- Volta Review. 7 per yr. ISSN 0042-8639

**Alexander Hamilton Institute**
235 E. 42nd St, New York, NY 10017.
- Modern Business Reports.
- Money Strategies.
- Personal Compass.
- Taxes Interpreted; a biweekly newsletter of
interpretive and informative material, covering
current and forthcoming developments in the field
of taxation. fortn. ISSN 0040-0203

**Alexander Research and Communications, Inc.
Downtown Research & Development Center**
270 Madison Ave., Suite 1505, New York, NY
10016.
- Downtown Idea Exchange. s-m. ISSN 0012-5822
- Downtown Mall Annual & Urban Design Report.
a. ISSN 0364-586X
- Downtown Promotion Reporter. m. ISSN 0363-
2830

**Alexandrian Society**
c/o History Department, Virginia Commonwealth
University, 926 Park Ave., Richmond, VA 23284.
- Point of Reference. a.

**Alfa Romeo Owners Club**
Box 331, Northbrook, IL 60062.
- Alfa Owner. m.

**Alfa Romeo Owners Club. Capital Chapter**
- Alfantics. (pub. by Evan Wilson Associates, Inc.)

**Alfred P. Sloan Foundation**
630 Fifth Ave., New York, NY 10020.
- Alfred P. Sloan Foundation. Report. a. ISSN
0065-6216

**Alian Publications Inc.**
507 Fifth Ave., New York, NY 10017.
- Casting & Jewelry Craft. bi-m. ISSN 0363-5767

**Alianza de Pueblos Libres**
1010 3rd St. N.W., Albuquerque, NM 87101.
- Alianza Federal de Pueblos Libres. Vox de la
Alianza. s-m. ISSN 0044-7277

**Alice James Poetry Cooperative**
138 Mt. Auburn Street, Cambridge, MA 02130.
- Alice James Books Series. irreg. (5-6 per yr.)

**Alice Lloyd College**
Box 132, Pippa Passes, KY 41844.
- Appalachian Heritage; a magazine of southern
Appalachian life and culture. q.

**Alive & Kicking**
c/o Selma Sklar, Ed., 35-50 85th St., Jackson
Heights, NY 11372.
- Alive & Kicking. 2 per yr.

**Alkebu-Lan Books**
209 W. 125th St., Room 218, New York, NY
10027.
- African-American Heritage Series. irreg.

**All-American Conference to Combat Communism**
917 15th St., N. W., Washington, DC 20005.
- Freedom's Facts Against Communism. irreg.

**All Americas Publishers Service, Inc. Canterbury
Export Group**
222 W. Adams St., 9 S. Clinton St., Chicago, IL
60606.
- Bebidas. bi-m. ISSN 0005-7533
- Beverages. bi-m. ISSN 0006-0399

**All-Church Press Newspapers**
c/o Lambuth Tomlinson, Box 1159, Fort Worth, TX
76101.
- All-Church Press Newspapers. w. ISSN 0002-5542

**All This & Less Publishers**
Regents 509, NMSU, Las Cruces, NM 88003.
- Star-Web Paper. q. ISSN 0146-2105

**Allan Hancock Foundation**
University of Southern California, Los Angeles, CA
90007.
- Allan Hancock Monographs in Marine Biology.
irreg., 1974 no. 8. ISSN 0065-6364

**Allegany Mountain Press**
111 North Tenth Street, Olean, NY 14760.
- Uroboros. 3 per yr.

**Allegheny Continental and Ozark Airlines**
- Flightime. (pub. by East-West Network, Inc.)

**Allegheny County Bar Association**
920 City-County Bldg, Pittsburgh, PA 15219.
- Pittsburgh Legal Journal. m. ISSN 0032-0331

**Allegheny County Medical Society**
713 Ridge Avenue, Pittsburgh, PA 15212.
- Allegheny County Medical Society. Bulletin. s-m (except Jul. and Aug.)

**Allegheny County Pharmaceutical Association**
111 Two Parkway Center, Pittsburgh, PA 15220.
- Allegheny County Pharmacist. m. ISSN 0002-5690

**Allegheny Ludlum Steel Corp.**
Oliver Bldg., Pittsburgh, PA 15222.
- Allegheny Ludlum Horizons. q.

**George A. Allen, Jr., Ed. & Pub.**
1155 East 4785 South, Salt Lake City, UT 84117.
- Game Bird Breeders, Aviculturists, Zoologists, & Conservationists Gazette. m.

**Paul C. Allen, Ed. & Pub.**
84 Charlton Rd., Rochester, NY 14617.
- Barsoomian. irreg., 1969, no. 15. ISSN 0067-4249

**Allen County Historical Society**
620 West Market St., Lima, OH 45801.
- Allen County Reporter. q

**Howard Allen Enterprises**
Box 76, Cape Canaveral, FL 32931.
- Instauration. m.

**Allen-Pacific Co.**
41 Sutter St., San Francisco, CA 94105.
- Pacific Goldsmith. m.
- Pacific Stationer & Office Outfitter. m.

**Allen Press Inc.**
Box 368, Lawrence, KS 66044.
- American Journal of Tropical Medicine and Hygiene. bi-m. ISSN 0002-9637 (American Society of Tropical Medicine and Hygiene)
- American Microscopical Society. Transactions. q. ISSN 0003-0023
- International Journal of Fertility. q. ISSN 0020-725X (International Foundation for Studies in Reproduction, Inc.)
- Journal of Mammalogy. q. ISSN 0022-2372 (American Society of Mammalogists)
- Journal of Parasitology. bi-m. ISSN 0022-3395 (American Society of Parasitologists) (Editorial address:, Department of Microbiology, S.U.N.Y. Upstate Medical Center, 766 Irving Ave., Syracuse, NY 13210)
- Scandinavian Studies. q. ISSN 0036-5637 (Society for the Advancement of Scandinavian Study)
- Systematic Zoology. 4 per yr. ISSN 0039-7989 (Society of Systematic Zoology)

**Allerton Press, Inc.**
150 Fifth Ave., New York, NY 10011.
- Academy of Sciences of the U S S R. Bulletin. Physical Series. m. (Akademiya Nauk S.S.S.R.)
- Applied Solar Energy. bi-m. ISSN 0003-701X
- Automatic Control and Computer Sciences. bi-m.
- Automatic Documentation and Mathematical Linguistics. q. ISSN 0005-1055
- Cytology and Genetics. bi-m. ISSN 0095-4527
- Mechanics of Solids. bi-m. ISSN 0025-6544
- Mendeleev Chemistry Journal. bi-m. ISSN 0025-925X
- Moscow University Biological Sciences Bulletin. bi-m.
- Moscow University Chemistry Bulletin. bi-m. ISSN 0027-1314
- Moscow University Geology Bulletin. bi-m.
- Moscow University Mathematics Bulletin. bi-m. ISSN 0027-1322
- Moscow University Mechanics Bulletin. bi-m. ISSN 0027-1330 (Moskovskii Universitet UR)
- Moscow University Physics Bulletin. bi-m. ISSN 0027-1349
- Moscow University Soil Science. bi-m. (Moskovskii Universitet UR)
- Power Engineering. bi-m. (Akademiya Nauk S.S.S.R. UR)
- Scientific and Technical Information Processing. q.
- Solid Fuel Chemistry. bi-m. (Akademiya Nauk S.S.S.R.)
- Soviet Aeronautics. q. ISSN 0038-5255
- Soviet Agricultural Sciences. m. (Vsesoyuznaya Akademiya Sel'skokhozyaistvennykh Nauk)
- Soviet Electrical Engineering. m. ISSN 0038-5379
- Soviet Geology and Geophysics. m.
- Soviet Mathematics. m. (U.S.S.R. Ministerstvo Visshego i Srednego Spetsialnogo Obrazovaniya UR)
- Soviet Meteorology and Hydrology. m.
- Soviet Physics-Collection. bi-m.
- Soviet Physics-Lebedev Institute Reports. m. (Akademiia Nauk S.S.S.R.. Institut Fiziki im. P. N. Lebedeva UR)
- Soviet Progress in Chemistry. m. ISSN 0038-5743
- Soviet Science. m.

**Alliance College. Department of English**
Cambridge Springs, PA 16403.
- Studies in Contemporary Satire. s-a.

**Alliance of American Insurers**
20 N. Wacker Dr., Chicago, IL 60606.
- Journal of American Insurance. q. ISSN 0021-874X

**Allied Artists of America**
1083 Fifth Ave, New York, NY 10028.
- Allied Artists of America. Annual Exhibition (Bulletin) a; 1974, no. 60.
- Allied Artists of America. Exhibition Catalog. a. ISSN 0065-6410

**Allied Business Consultants, Inc.**
Box 9005, Washington, DC 20003.
- Washington International Arts Letter. 10 per yr. ISSN 0043-0609

**Allied Gasoline Retailers Association of Florida, Inc.**
Box 14064, Orlando, FL 32807.
- A G R A News. m. ISSN 0001-1355

**Allied Graphic Arts**
475 Fifth Ave., New York, NY 10017.
- Modern Needlecraft. q. ISSN 0026-816X

**Allied Industrial Workers of America**
(AFL-CIO), 3520 W. Oklahoma Ave., Milwaukee, WI 53215.
- Allied Industrial Worker. m. ISSN 0002-6107

**Allis-Chalmers Corp.**
Box 512, Milwaukee, WI 53201.
- Allis-Chalmers Engineering Review. irreg. ISSN 0002-6123

**Allsport Publishing Corp.**
51 Atlantic Ave., Floral Park, NY 11001.
- Fishing World. bi-m. ISSN 0015-3079 (Fishing Club of America)

**Allstate Enterprises, Inc.**
Allstate Plaza, Northbrook, IL 60062.
- Discovery (Northbrook) q. ISSN 0012-3641

**Alltech Publishing Co.**
212 Cooper Center, North Park Dr. & Browning Rd., Pennsauken, NJ 08109.
- A P C Tablet. m.
- Business Automation Reference Service. Computer Edition. 2vols. & 12 m. supplements.
- Business Automation Reference Service. Computer Software. m. (2 base vols. with suppls.)
- Business Automation Reference Service. Office Equipment. m. (2 base vols. with suppls.)
- Business Automation Reference Service. Peripherals Edition.

**Allured Publishing Corp.**
Box 318, Wheaton, IL 60187.
- Cosmetic Formulary. biennial. ISSN 0070-0533
- Cosmetics and Toiletries. m.
- Perfumer & Flavorist. bi-m.

**Allyn and Bacon, Inc.**
470 Atlantic Ave., Boston, MA 02210.
- Allyn & Bacon Series in Advanced Mathematics. irreg.
- Allyn and Bacon Series in Creative Teaching in the Elementary School. irreg. ISSN 0569-0757
- Allyn & Bacon Series in Electrical Engineering. irreg.
- Bible, Life, and Worship Series. irreg. ISSN 0067-6519

**Almanac Co.**
515 W. Jackson, Woodstock, IL 60098.
- Ford Almanac; for farm and home. a.

**Alpha Beta Alpha, National Library Science Fraternity**
Milner Library, Illinois State University, Normal, IL 61761.
- Alphabet. 2-3 per yr. ISSN 0002-6433

**Alpha Beta Company**
777 S. Harbor Blvd., La Habra, CA 90631.
- Vanguard (La Habra) m.

**Alpha Delta Kappa, Honorary Sorority for Women Educators**
1615 W. 92nd St., Kansas City, MO 64114.
- Kappan. s-a. ISSN 0002-6387

**Alpha Delta Sigma**
- Linage. (pub. by Gamma Alpha Chi National Office)

**Alpha Epsilon Delta**
7 Brookside Circle, Bronxville, NY 10708.
- Scalpel. q.

**Alpha Epsilon Rho. Alpha Omega Chapter**
Dillingham Center, Ithaca College, Ithaca, NY 14850.
- Playback. m.

**Alpha Kappa Alpha Sorority**
5211 South Greenwood Ave., Chicago, IL 60615.
- Ivy Leaf. q. ISSN 0021-3276

**Alpha Kappa Delta - National Sociology Honor Society**
c/o Prof. Harry M. Johnson, 326 Lincoln Hall, University of Illinois, Urbana-Champaign, IL 61801.
- Sociological Inquiry. q. ISSN 0038-0245

**Alpha Omega Alpha Honor Medical Society**
2 Palo Alto Sq., Palo Alto, CA 94304.
- Pharos. q. ISSN 0031-7179

**Alpha Pi Mu, Industrial Engineering Honor Society**
Box 27265, Tempe, AZ 85282.
- Cogwheel. a. ISSN 0010-0293

**Alpha Psi Omega National Theatre Honorary**
Eastern Illinois University, Charleston, IL 61920.
- Alpha Psi Omega: Playbill. a.

**Alphaville Books**
Box 3424, Charlottesville, VA 22903.
- Aieee. irreg.

**Harry Alter, Ed. & Pub.**
Box 777, Youngstown, OH 44501.
- Youngstown Jewish Times. fortn. ISSN 0044-0973

**Alternative Press Centre, Inc.**
Box 7229, Baltimore, MD 21218.
- Alternative Press Index. q. ISSN 0002-662X

**Alternative Press Syndicate**
Box 777, Cooper Sta., New York, NY 10003.
- Alternative Journalism Review. bi-m.
- Alternative Press Revue. bi-m.

**Alternative Sources of Energy**
Rt. 2, Box 90-A, Milaca, MN 56353.
- Alternative Sources of Energy. 6 per yr.

**Alternatives**
701 N. Eugene St., Box 20626, Greensboro, NC 27420.
- Alternate Celebrations Catalogue. a.

**Aluminum Association**
750 Third Ave, New York, NY 10017.
- Aluminum Standards and Data. biennial. ISSN 0065-6658

**Aluminum Association. Statistical & Commercial Research Policy Committee**
750 Third Ave, New York, NY 10017.
- Aluminum Statistical Review. a. ISSN 0065-6666

**Aluminum Workers International Union**
Paul Brown Bldg., 818 Olive St., Suite 338, St. Louis, MO 63101
(Subscr. Address: 810 Rhode Island Ave., N.E., Washington, D.C. 20018)
- Aluminum Light. m. ISSN 0401-5576

**Robert S. Alvarez, Ed. & Pub.**
Box 993, S. San Francisco, CA 94080.
- Administrator's Digest. m.(except Aug) ISSN 0001-8422

- Business Information from Your Public Library. 3 per yr.

**Alyeska Reports**
Alyeska Pipeline Service Co., 1835 South Bragaw, Anchorage, AK 99504.
- Alyeska Reports. q.

**AMACOM**
*see* American Management Associations

**Amalgamated Clothing Textile Workers Union**
15 Union Square, New York, NY 10003.
- A C T W U Labor. m.

**Amalgamated Clothing Workers of America**
15 Union Square, New York, NY 10003.
- Advance (New York) m. ISSN 0001-8597

**Amalgamated Jewelry, Diamond and Watchcase Worker's Union. Local No. 1**
133 W. 44th St., New York, NY 10036.
- Jewelry Workers' Bulletin. s-m. ISSN 0021-6291

**Amalgamated Transit Union**
5025 Wisconsin Ave., N.W., Washington, DC 20016.
- In Transit. m. ISSN 0019-3291

**Amateur Astronomers Association**
212 W. 79 St., New York, NY 10024.
- Asterisks. a. ISSN 0066-9911

**Amateur Athletic Union of the United States**
3400 W. 86th St., Indianapolis, IN 46268.
- A A U Baton Twirling Rules and Regulations. irreg. ISSN 0361-221X
- A A U Junior Olympic Handbook. irreg. ISSN 0361-4654
- A A U News and Amateur Athlete. m.
- A A U Official Boxing Rules and Guide. a.
- A A U Official Track and Field Handbook, Rules and Records. biennial.
- A A U Official Weightlifting Rules and Guide. a.
- Amateur Athletic Union of the United States. Athletic Library. Official Rules for Competitive Swimming. a. ISSN 0091-3413
- Amateur Athletic Union of the United States. Official A A U Basketball Handbook. biennial. ISSN 0090-4414
- Amateur Athletic Union of the United States. Official Handbook of the A A U Code. a. ISSN 0091-3405
- Amateur Athletic Union of the United States. Official Rules for Water Polo. a. ISSN 0093-5786
- Officail A A U Trampoline and Tumbling Handbook. irreg. ISSN 0361-2899
- Official A A U Diving Rules. a.
- Official A A U Judo Rules. biennial.
- Official A A U Synchronized Swimming Handbook. a.
- Official A A U Wrestling Handbook. a.

**Amateur Chamber Music Players, Inc.**
Box 66A, Vienna, VA 22180.
- Amateur Chamber Music Players. Directory. a. ISSN 0065-6704

**Amateur Fencers League of America**
601 Curtis St., Albany, CA 94706
(or 249 Eaton Pl., Westfield, NJ 07090)
- American Fencing. bi-m. ISSN 0002-8436
- Fencing Rules for Competitions. irreg.

**Amateur Skating Union of the United States**
4423 W. Deming Place, Chicago, IL 60639.
- Amateur Skating Union of the United States. Offical Handbook. biennial. ISSN 0516-866X

**Amateur Softball Association of America**
P.O. Box 11437, Oklahoma City, OK 73111.
- Amateur Softball Association of America. Official Guide and Rule Book. a. ISSN 0065-6739
- Balls & Strikes. m.

**Amateur Trapshooting Association**
Vendalia, OH 45377.
- Amateur Trapshooting Association. Official Trapshooting Rules. a. ISSN 0065-6747

**Frank Amato Publications**
Box 02112, Portland, OR 97202.
- Salmon-Trout Steelheader. bi-m. ISSN 0029-3431

**AMAX Specialty Metals Corp.**
P.O. Box 32, Akron, NY 14001.
- Zirconium/Hafnium Newsletter. q.

**Amazing Life Games Inc.**
P.O. 506, Sausalito, CA 94965.
- Help. 5 per yr.

**Amazon Collective**
2211 E. Kenwood Blvd., Milwaukee, WI 53211.
- Amazon; a feminist journal. q.

**Amazon Press**
395 60th St., Oakland, CA 94618.
- Lesbian Reader. q. ISSN 0361-5928

**Ambassador College. School of Theology**
300 West Green, Pasadena, CA 91105.
- Good News of Tomorrow's World. irreg. ISSN 0093-5026

**Ambassador International Cultural Foundation**
1133 Ave. of the Americas, New York, NY 10036.
- Quest. m.

**Ambassador Publishing Co.**
Box 111, 300 W. Green St., Pasadena, CA 91123.
- Plain Truth (Pasadena) m. ISSN 0032-0420
- Pura Verdad; noticiario de comprension. m.
- Pure Verite. m. ISSN 0033-4588

**Ambitious Amazons**
Box 811, E. Lansing, MI 48823.
- Lesbian Connection. bi-m. (Helen Diner Memorial Womens Center)

**Ambulance and Medical Service Association of America**
Box 14178, Hartford, CT 06114.
- Aid Newsletter. m. ISSN 0002-2063

**Ambulatory Pediatric Association**
701 Grove Road, Greenville, SC 29602.
- Ambulatory Pediatric Association. Newsletter. 3 per yr. ISSN 0002-7006

**America**
191-Hill St., Colma, CA 94014.
- America. s-m. ISSN 0002-7030

**America-Israel Cultural Foundation**
4 East 54th St., New York, NY 10022.
- Culture/Tarbut. s-a.

**America Latina Connection Corporation of Florida**
2745 Ponce de Leon Blvd., Coral Gables, FL 33134.
- Directorio Industrial U.S.A; guia industrial para America Latina. irreg. ISSN 0094-5595

**America Press**
106 W. 56th St., New York, NY 10019.
- America; national Catholic weekly review. w. ISSN 0002-7049
- Catholic Mind. m. ISSN 0008-8242

**Editorial America, S.A.**
7240 N.E. 4th Ave., Miami, FL 33138.
- Cosmopolitan en Espanol. m.
- Mecanica Popular. m. ISSN 0025-6420

**America Water Ski Association**
Box 191, Winter Haven, FL 33880.
- Water Skier. 7 per yr. ISSN 0049-7002

**American Academic Association for Peace in the Middle East**
- Middle East Review. (pub. by Transaction Periodicals Consortium)

**American Academy and Institute of Arts and Letters**
633 W. 155 St., New York, NY 10032.
- American Academy and Institute of Arts and Letters. Exhibition Catalogues. irreg., (3-4 per year) 1966, no. 235.

**American Academy for Jewish Research**
3080 Broadway, New York, NY 10027
(Dist. by Kraus Reprint Corp., 16 E. 46 St., New York, N.Y. 10017)
- American Academy for Jewish Research. Proceedings of the AAJR. a. ISSN 0065-6798

**American Academy of Allergy**
- American Academy of Allergy. Pollen and Mold Committee. Statistical Report. (pub. by Ross Laboratories)
- Journal of Allergy and Clinical Immunology. (pub. by C. V. Mosby Co.)

**American Academy of Arts and Letters**
633 W. 155 St., New York, NY 10032.
- American Academy and Institute of Arts and Letters. Proceedings. a.

**American Academy of Arts and Sciences**
165 Allendale St., Jamaica Plain Sta., Boston, MA 02130.
- American Academy of Arts and Sciences. Bulletin. 8 per yr. ISSN 0002-712X
- American Academy of Arts and Sciences. Records of the Academy. a. ISSN 0065-6844
- Daedalus. q. ISSN 0011-5266
- Daedalus Library. irreg., 1968, vol. 12. ISSN 0070-2536

**American Academy of Child Psychiatry**
- American Academy of Child Psychiatry. Journal. (pub. by Yale University Press)
- American Academy of Child Psychiatry. Journal. Monograph. (pub. by International Universities Press, Inc.)

**American Academy of Environmental Engineers**
Box 1278, Rockville, MD 20850.
- American Academy of Environmental Engineers. Diplomate Newsletter. q.
- American Academy of Environmental Engineers. Roster. a. ISSN 0065-6860

**American Academy of Family Physicians**
1740 W. 92nd St., Kansas City, MO 64114.
- American Family Physician. m. ISSN 0002-838X

**American Academy of Family Physicians. Kentucky Chapter**
*see* Kentucky Academy of Family Physicians

**American Academy of Forensic Sciences**
11424 Cedar Ave., Cleveland, OH 44106.
- What's New in Forensic Sciences. a. ISSN 0511-8662

**American Academy of Implant Dentistry**
469 Washington St., Abington, MA 02351.
- Oral Implantology. q. ISSN 0048-2064

**American Academy of Mechanics**
212 Talbot Laboratory, Urbana, IL 61801.
- Mechanics. m.

**American Academy of Medical Administration**
6 Beacon St., Boston, MA 02108.
- A A M A Executive. q. ISSN 0065-6879

**American Academy of Neurology**
- Neurology. (pub. by Lancet Publications, Inc.)

**American Academy of Ophthalmology and Otolaryngology**
15 Second St., S. W., Rochester, MN 55901.
- American Academy of Ophthalmology and Otolaryngology. Transactions-Ophthalmology. bi-m.
- American Academy of Ophthalmology and Otolaryngology. Transactions-Otolaryngology. bi-m.
- American Orthoptic Journal. a. ISSN 0065-955X

**American Academy of Optometry**
- American Journal of Optometry and Physiological Optics. (pub. by Williams & Wilkins Co.)

**American Academy of Oral Medicine**
1225 S. Meramec Ave., St. Louis, MO 63105.
- Journal of Oral Medicine. q. ISSN 0022-3247

**American Academy of Oral Pathology**
- Oral Surgery, Oral Medicine and Oral Pathology. (pub. by C. V. Mosby Co.)

**American Academy of Orthopaedic Surgeons**
430 N. Michigan Ave., Chicago, IL 60611
(or 10 Shattuck St., Boston, MA 02115)
- American Academy of Orthopaedic Surgeons. Committee on Instructional Courses. Instructional Course Lectures. (pub. by C. V. Mosby Co.)
- American Academy of Orthopaedic Surgeons. Directory. a. ISSN 0516-8856
- Journal of Bone and Joint Surgery. Amer.ed. 8 per yr., British ed. 4 per yr. ISSN 0021-9355 (British address: At the Royal College of Surgeons, 35-43 Lincoln's Inn Fields, London WC2A 3PN, England)

**American Academy of Osteopathy**
2630 Airport Rd., Colorado Springs, CO 80910.
- American Academy of Osteopathy Yearbook; of selected osteopathic papers. a.

**American Academy of Pediatrics**
Box 1034, Evanston, IL 60204.
- Pediatrics. m. ISSN 0031-4005

**American Academy of Pediatrics. Committee on Fetus and Newborn**
Box 1034, Evanston, IL 60204.
- Standards and Recommendations for Hospital Care of Newborn Infants. irreg., 5th, 1971.

**American Academy of Pediatrics. Committee on Infectious Diseases**
1801 Hinman Ave., Evanston, IL 60204.
- American Academy of Pediatrics. Committee on Infectious Diseases. Report. irreg., 1974, 17th ed. ISSN 0065-6909

**American Academy of Pediatrics. Surgical Section**
- Journal of Pediatric Surgery. (pub. by Grune & Stratton, Inc.)

**American Academy of Periodontology**
211 East Chicago Ave., Chicago, IL 60611.
- Journal of Periodontology. m. ISSN 0022-3492

**American Academy of Physicians' Assistants**
- P. A. Journal. (pub. by Williams & Wilkins Co.)

**American Academy of Podiatry Administration**
602 National Bank Bldg., Lima, OH 45801
(Subscr. to: Dr. Leonard Light, 614 Central Ave., Dunkirk, NY 14048)
- American Academy of Podiatry Administration News-Letter. 3 per yr.

**American Academy of Political and Social Sciences**
3937 Chestnut St., Philadelphia, PA 19104.
- American Academy of Political and Social Science. Annals. bi-m. ISSN 0002-7162
- American Academy of Political and Social Science. Monographs. irreg., no. 17, 1973. ISSN 0065-6917

**American Academy of Psychiatry and Neurology**
17 Kingston Rd., Scarsdale, NY 10583.
- American Academy of Psychiatry and Neurology. Journal. q. ISSN 0362-9333

**American Academy of Psychiatry & the Law**
- American Academy of Psychiatry and the Law. Bulletin. (pub. by University of Pittsburgh. School of Law)

**American Academy of Psychoanalysis**
- American Academy of Psychoanalysis. Journal. (pub. by Wiley-Interscience)

**American Academy of Psychotherapists**
1040 Woodcock, Orlando, FL 32803.
- American Academy of Psychotherapists. Directory. a.
- Voices; the art and science of psychotherapy. q. ISSN 0042-8272

**American Academy of Religion**
Florida State University, Department of Religion, Tallahassee, 7Fl 32306.
- A A R Dissertation Series. irreg.
- A A R Studies in Religion. irreg. ISSN 0084-6287
- American Academy of Religion. Journal. (pub. by Scholars Press)
- Religion and the Arts. irreg. (Co-sponsor: Society of Biblical Literature)
- Studies in Religious Ethics. irreg.

**American Academy of the History of Dentistry**
216 E. Main St., Batavia, NY 14020.
- Bulletin of the History of Dentistry. s-a. ISSN 0007-5132

**American Accounting Association**
Paul L. Gerhardt, Admin. Secy., 653 S. Orange Ave., Sarasota, FL 33577.
- Accounting Review. q. ISSN 0001-4826
- American Accounting Association. Southeast Regional Group. Collected Papers of the Annual Meeting. a. ISSN 0360-8840
- Studies in Accounting Research. irreg. ISSN 0586-5050

**American Advent Mission Society**
Box 23152, Charlotte, NC 28212.
- Advent Christian Missions. m. ISSN 0001-8759

**American-African Affairs Association**
303 Fifth Ave., New York, NY 10016.
- Spotlight on Africa. irreg. ISSN 0584-9365

**American Agricultural Economics Association**
Dept. of Agricultural Economics, Univ. of Kentucky, Lexington, KY 40506.
- American Agricultural Economics Association. Handbook. quinquennial.
- American Journal of Agricultural Economics. 5 per yr. ISSN 0002-9092

**American Agricultural Editors Association**
20 N. Wacker Drive, Room 1865, Chicago, IL 60606.
- A. A. E. A. Newsletter. m.(10 per yr.) ISSN 0001-0073

**American Agriculturalist, Inc.**
Box 370, DeWitt Bldg., Ithaca, NY 14850.
- American Agriculturist and Rural New Yorker. m. ISSN 0002-7219

**American Air Filter Co., Inc.**
Box 1100, Louisville, KY 40207.
- American Air Facts (Customer Edition) q.

**American Air Mail Society**
102 Arbor Rd., Cinnaminson, NJ 08077.
- Airpost Journal. m.

**American Airlines**
Box 965 Radio City Sta., New York, NY 10019.
- Insights. q.

**American Airmail Society**
Arbor Rd., Cinnaminson, NJ 08077.
- Aero Philatelist Annals. a.

**American Alliance for Health, Physical Education, and Recreation**
1201 16th St. N.W., Washington, DC 20036.
- A A H P E R Update. m.
- American Alliance for Health, Physical Education, and Recreation. Research Quarterly. q. ISSN 0034-5377
- American Alliance for Health, Physical Education and Recreation. Research Quarterly. Reference Index. every 10 years.
- Athletic Director. 5 per yr. ISSN 0004-6647 (National Council of Secondary School Athletic Directors)
- Dance Directory; programs of professional preparation in American colleges and universities. irreg., 9th ed., 1976. ISSN 0070-2676
- Focus on Dance. irreg., no. 8, 1977. ISSN 0071-6294
- Health Education. bi-m. ISSN 0097-0050
- Journal of Physical Education and Recreation. m.(Sept-June) ISSN 0097-1170

**American Alliance for Health, Physical Education and Recreation. National Association for Girls and Women in Sport**
1201 16th St., N.W., Washington, DC 20036.
- A I A W Handbook of Policies and Operating Procedures. a. ISSN 0090-9106 (Association for Intercollegiate Athletics for Women)
- Aquatics Guide. biennial. ISSN 0401-636X
- Archery-Golf Guide. biennial.
- Basketball Guide. a. ISSN 0065-7018
- Bowling-Fencing Guide. biennial. ISSN 0099-0051
- Field Hockey-Lacrosse Guide. biennial. ISSN 0065-7026
- Gymnastics Guide. biennial.
- Soccer-Speedball-Flag Football Guide. biennial.
- Softball Guide. biennial.
- Tennis-Badminton-Squash Guide. biennial. ISSN 0065-7042
- Track and Field Guide. biennial.
- Volleyball Guide. biennial. ISSN 0065-7050

**American Alliance for Health, Physical Education and Recreation. National Council for School Nurses**
1201 16 St., N.W., Washington, DC 20036.
- School Nursing Monographs. irreg. ISSN 0569-230X

**American Alpine Club**
113 E. 90 St., New York, NY 10028.
- Accidents in North American Mountaineering. a. ISSN 0065-082X
- American Alpine Journal. a. ISSN 0065-6925
- American Alpine News. 4 per yr.

**American Amateur Baseball Congress Inc.**
212 Plaza Bldg., 2855 W. Market St., Akron, OH 44313.
- Amateur Baseball News. 8 per yr. ISSN 0002-6816

**American Analgesia Society**
- American Analgesia Society. Journal. (pub. by Charles C. Morchand Co., Inc.)

**American Animal Hospital Association**
3612 Jefferson Blvd., South Bend, IN 46615.
- American Animal Hospital Association. Scientific Presentations and Seminar Synopses of the Annual Meeting. a.
- American Animal Hospital Association Journal. bi-m. ISSN 0587-2871

**American Anthropological Association**
1703 New Hampshire Ave., N.W., Washington, DC 20009.
- American Anthropological Association. Abstracts of Meetings. a.
- American Anthropological Association. Annual Report and Directory. a. ISSN 0065-6933
- American Anthropologist. q. ISSN 0002-7294
- American Anthropologist. Special Publication. irreg. ISSN 0065-6941
- American Ethnologist. q. ISSN 0094-0496
- Anthropological Studies. irreg., no. 8, 1971. ISSN 0570-2976
- Anthropology Newsletter. 10 per yr(except July & Aug.) ISSN 0098-1605
- Studies in the Anthropology of Visual Communications. 2 per yr.

**American Anti-Vivisection Society**
1903 Chestnut St., Philadelphia, PA 19103.
- A-V. m.(except Aug) ISSN 0001-2831

**American Antiquarian Booksellers**
Box 239 W.O.B., Box 56, Town Center, West Orange, NJ 07052.
- Library Bookseller. w. ISSN 0024-2217

**American Antiquarian Society**
185 Salisbury St., Worcester, MA 01609.
- American Antiquarian Society. News-Letter. s-a. ISSN 0569-2229
- American Antiquarian Society. Proceedings. s-a. ISSN 0044-751X
- American Antiquarian Society. Reports for the Year. a.

**American Apparel Manufacturers Association**
Suite 800, 1611 No. Kent St., Arlington, VA 22209.
- Apparel Plant Wages and Personal Policies. a. ISSN 0084-6678
- Focus, an Economic Profile of the Apparel Industry. biennial.

**American-Arab Association for Commerce & Industry, Inc.**
342 Madison Ave., New York, NY 10017.
- American-Arab Association for Commerce & Industry. Bulletin. 10 per yr. ISSN 0044-7528

**American Arbitration Association**
140 W. 51st St, New York, NY 10020.
- Arbitration in the Schools. m. ISSN 0003-7885
- Arbitration Journal. q. ISSN 0003-7893
- Labor Arbitration in Government. m. ISSN 0047-3839
- Lawyers' Arbitration Letter and the Digest of Court Decisions. q.
- Summary of Labor Arbitration Awards. m. ISSN 0039-5005

**American Art Therapy Association**
- American Journal of Art Therapy. (pub. by Elinor Ulman, Ed. & Pub.)

**American Artist Magazine**
(Subsidiary of: Billboard Publications)
1515 Broadway, New York, NY 10036
(Subscr. address: 2160 Patterson St., Cincinnati, OH 45214)
- American Artist. m. ISSN 0002-7375
- American Artist Business Letter. 10 per yr (m. except Jul & Aug) ISSN 0093-1861

**American Artist Reprints**
1515 Broadway, New York, NY 10036.
- American Artist Directory of Art Schools & Workshops. a.
- Product Directory; a guide to art materials and equipment. a.

**American-Asian Educational Exchange, Inc.**
Suite 2-L, 88 Morningside Dr., New York, NY
10027.
● Asian Affairs: an American Review. bi-m.

**American Assembly**
Columbia University, 116th & Broadway, New
York, NY 10027.
● American Assembly. Report. 2 per yr. ISSN 0569-
2245

**American Assembly of Collegiate Schools of Business**
760 Office Parkway, Suite 50, St. Louis, MO 63141.
● A A C S B Bulletin. 4 per yr. ISSN 0001-0057
● A A C S B Newsline. 3 per yr.
● American Assembly of Collegiate Schools of
Business. Membership Directory. a.
● International Directory of Programs in Business
and Commerce. irreg. ISSN 0074-4611

**American Assembly of Collegiate Schools of Business (Washington)**
1755 Massachusetts Ave. N. W., Washington, DC
20036.
● International Dimension. 3 per yr.

**American Association for Automotive Medicine**
Box 222, Morton Grove, IL 60053.
● A A A M Quarterly. q. ISSN 0001-0022
● American Association for Automotive Medicine.
Proceedings. a. ISSN 0401-6351

**American Association for Cancer Research**
● Cancer Research. (pub. by Williams & Wilkins
Co.)

**American Association for Clinical Chemistry**
Box 5218, Winston-Salem, NC 27106.
● Clinical Chemistry. m. ISSN 0009-9147

**American Association for Comprehensive Health Planning**
801 N. Fairfax St., Alexandria, VA 22314.
● American Journal of Health Planning. q. ISSN
0363-7719

**American Association for Conservation Information**
c/o Jay Kaffka, Arkansas Game & Fish
Commission, Little Rock, Cheyenne, AR 72201.
● American Association for Conservation
Information. Yearbook. a.; latest issue, 1973.
ISSN 0065-6984

**American Association for Higher Education**
One Dupont Circle, Washington, DC 20036.
● A. A. H. E. College and University Bulletin. m.
except Jul.-Aug. ISSN 0001-2971
● Acquainter. 10 per yr. (Academic Consortia for
Higher Education)
● College and University Bulletin. m. ISSN 0010-
0897
● Consortium Directory. a. ISSN 0091-701X
● Current Issues in Higher Education. (pub. by
Jossey-Bass, Inc. Publishers)
● Journal of Higher Education. (pub. by Ohio State
University Press)

**American Association for Jewish Education**
114 Fifth Ave., New York, NY 10011.
● Pedagogic Reporter. 3 per yr. ISSN 0031-3793

**American Association for Laboratory Animal Science**
2317 W. Jefferson St. Suite 208, Joliet, IL 60435.
● A A L A S Bulletin. 6 per yr.
● Laboratory Animal Science. bi-m. ISSN 0023-
6764

**American Association for Public Opinion Research**
● Public Opinion Quarterly. (pub. by Columbia
University)

**American Association for Rehabilitation Therapy, Inc.**
Box 93, North Little Rock, AR 72115.
● American Archives of Rehabilitation Therapy. q.
ISSN 0002-7324

**American Association for Respiratory Therapy**
● R C. Respiratory Care. (pub. by J. B. Lippincott
Co.)

**American Association for Social Psychiatry**
● Social Psychiatry. (pub. by Grune & Stratton, Inc.)

**American Association for State and Local History**
1400 Eighth Ave. S., Nashville, TN 37203.
● American Heritage. (pub. by American Heritage
Publishing Co., Inc.)

● Directory of Historical Societies and Agencies in
the United States and Canada. triennial. ISSN
0070-5659
● History News. m.

**American Association for Textile Technology**
● American Association for Textile Technology.
Technical Review and Register. (pub. by Rayon
Publishing Corp.)

**American Association for the Advancement of Science**
1515 Massachusetts Ave., N.W., Washington, DC
20005.
● American Association for the Advancement of
Science. Handbook; Officers, Organization,
Activities. a.
● American Association for the Advancement of
Science. Meeting Program. a. ISSN 0361-1833
● Audiotapes Reprints Publications. irreg. ISSN
0363-2547
● Science. w. (4 vol. per year) ISSN 0036-8075
● Science Books & Films. q. ISSN 0098-342X
● Science Education News. 6 per yr. ISSN 0036-
8334
● Science for Society, a Bibliography. a.
● Science Guide to Scientific Instruments. a.

**American Association for the Advancement of Science. Alaska Division**
P. O. Box 80271, Fairbanks, AK 99701.
● Alaska Science Conference. Proceedings. a. ISSN
0084-6120

**American Association for the Advancement of Science. Committee on Desert and Arid Zone Research**
1515 Massachusetts Ave., N.W., Washington, DC
20005.
● American Association for the Advancement of
Science. Committee on Desert and Arid Zone
Research. Contributions. irreg. ISSN 0569-2393

**American Association for the Advancement of Slavic Studies**
190 W. 19 Ave., Rm. 254, Ohio State University,
Columbus, OH 43210.
● American Association for the Advancement of
Slavic Studies. Directory of Members. irreg. ISSN
0516-9240
● American Association for the Advancement of
Slavic Studies. Newsletter. 8 per yr. ISSN 0002-
7405
● American Bibliography of Slavic and East
European Studies. a. ISSN 0569-3497
● Current Digest of the Soviet Press. w. ISSN 0011-
3425
● Index to Pravda. m. ISSN 0099-0876
● Slavic Review; American quarterly of Soviet and
East European studies. q. ISSN 0037-6779

**American Association for the Comparative Study of Law**
School of Law (Boalt Hall), Univ. of Calif.,
Berkeley, CA 94720.
● American Journal of Comparative Law. q. ISSN
0002-919X

**American Association for the History of Medicine**
● Bulletin of the History of Medicine. (pub. by
Johns Hopkins University Press)

**American Association for the Study of Headache**
621 New Ballas Rd., St. Louis, MO 63141.
● Headache. q. ISSN 0017-8748

**American Association for the Surgery of Trauma**
● Journal of Trauma. (pub. by Williams & Wilkins
Co.)

**American Association for Thoracic Surgery**
● Journal of Thoracic and Cardiovascular Surgery.
(pub. by C. V. Mosby Co.)

**American Association for World Health**
777 United Nations Plaza, New York, NY 10017.
● American Association for World Health News. q.
● American Review of World Health. irreg. ISSN
0003-0813

**American Association of Airport Executives**
2029 K St., N.W., Washington, DC 20006.
● A M J/Airport Management Journal. q. ISSN
0362-5001
● Airport Report. s-m. ISSN 0044-7021

**American Association of Anatomists**
● Anatomical Record. (pub. by Wistar Institute
Press)

**American Association of Avian Pathologists**
Texas A & M University, Dept. of Veterinary
Microbiology, College Station, TX 77843.
● Avian Diseases. q. ISSN 0005-2086

**American Association of Bible Colleges**
Box 543, Wheaton, IL 60187.
● A A B C Newsletter. q. ISSN 0094-260X

**American Association of Bioanalysts**
Suite 805, 411 North 7th St., St. Louis, MO 63101.
● A A B Bulletin. bi-m.
● American Association of Bioanalysts. Proficiency
Testing Service. Test of the Month. 6 per yr.

**American Association of Blood Banks**
● Transfusion. (pub. by J. B. Lippincott Co.)

**American Association of Botanical Gardens and Arboreta, Inc.**
Department of Horticulture, New Mexico State
University, Las Cruces, NM 88003.
● Arboretum and Botanical Garden Bulletin. q

**American Association of Cereal Chemists, Inc.**
3340 Pilot Knob Road, St. Paul, MN 55121.
● American Association of Cereal Chemists.
Monograph Series. irreg., no. 4 latest issue. ISSN
0065-7107
● Cereal Chemistry. bi-m. ISSN 0009-0352
● Cereal Foods World. m.

**American Association of Chinese Studies**
Sun Yat Sen Hall, St. John's University, Jamaica,
NY 11439.
● American Association for Chinese Studies
Newsletter. s-a.

**American Association of Colleges for Teacher Education**
One Dupont Circle, N.W., Suite 610, Washington,
DC 20036.
● A A C T E Publication Service. m. ISSN 0001-
0065
● A A C T E Yearbook. a. ISSN 0065-7123
● American Association of Colleges for Teacher
Education. Bulletin. 12 per yr(approx) ISSN
0002-7413
● American Association of Colleges for Teacher
Education. Directory. a. ISSN 0516-9313
● Charles W. Hunt Lecture. irreg. ISSN 0069-2751

**American Association of Colleges of Pharmacy**
4630 Montgomery Ave., Bethesda, MD 20014.
● A A C P. News. m.
● American Journal of Pharmaceutical Education.
(pub. by University of the Pacific. School of
Pharmacy)

**American Association of Collegiate Registrars and Admissions Officers**
One Dupont Circle N.W., Suite 330, Washington,
DC 20036.
● College and University. q. ISSN 0010-0889
● Report on the Credit Given by Educational
Institutions. irreg. ISSN 0569-2482

**American Association of Commodity Traders**
10 Park St., Concord, NH 03301.
● Commodity Journal. bi-m. ISSN 0092-7864

**American Association of Community and Junior Colleges**
One Dupont Circle N.W., Washington, DC 20036.
● American Association of Community and Junior
Colleges. Governmental Affairs Special. irreg.
ISSN 0065-7239
● Community and Junior College Journal. m. (Sep.-
May); b-m. (Dec.-Jan.)
● Community, Junior, and Technical College
Directory. a.

**American Association of Correctional Psychologists**
● Criminal Justice & Behavior. (pub. by Sage
Publications Inc.)

**American Association of Cost Engineers**
308 Monongahela Bldg., Morgantown, WV 26505.
● A A C E Bulletin. bi-m. ISSN 0001-0049
● American Association of Cost Engineers.
Transactions of the Annual Meeting. a. ISSN
0065-7158

**American Association of Criminology**
Box 1115, North Marshfield, MA 02059.
● American Criminologist. m. ISSN 0002-8126

**American Association of Critical-Care Nurses**
- Heart and Lung. (pub. by C. V. Mosby Co.)

**American Association of Dental Examiners**
211 East Chicago Ave., Rm. 948, Chicago, IL 60611.
- American Association of Dental Examiners. Board Bulletin. m. ISSN 0002-7421

**American Association of Dental Schools**
1625 Massachusetts Ave, N.W., Washington, DC 20036.
- Admission Requirements of U.S. and Canadian Dental Schools. a.
- Bulletin of Dental Education. m. ISSN 0007-4837
- Dental Student News. 3-4 per yr. ISSN 0045-995X
- Directory of Dental Educators. irreg. ISSN 0090-0141
- Guidebook of U.S. & Canadian Postdoctoral Dental Programs. irreg. ISSN 0361-9273
- Journal of Dental Education. m. ISSN 0022-0337

**American Association of Doctor's Nurses**
9600 Colesville Rd., Silver Spring, MD 20901.
- Doctor's Nurse Bulletin. q. ISSN 0012-4451

**American Association of Endodontists**
- Journal of Endodontics. (pub. by American Dental Association)

**American Association of Equine Practitioners**
Route 5, 14 Hillcrest Circle, Golden, CO 80401.
- American Association of Equine Practitioners. Proceedings of the Annual Convention. a. ISSN 0065-7182

**American Association of Feed Microscopists**
c/o Mrs. Wilma J. Hill, Secy-Treas, P.O. Box 301, Keystone, SD 57751.
- A A F M Proceedings of Annual Meeting. a. ISSN 0569-2628

**American Association of Foot Specialists, Inc.**
P.O. Box 54, 1801 Vauxhall Rd., Union, NJ 02083.
- American Association of Foot Specialists. Program Journal. a. ISSN 0065-7190

**American Association of Fund-Raising Counsel, Inc.**
500 Fifth Ave., New York, NY 10036.
- Giving U.S.A. Annual Report; a compilation of facts and trends on American philanthropy for the year. a.
- Giving U.S.A. Bulletin; a compilation of facts and trends on American philanthropy. m. (11 per yr) ISSN 0436-0257

**American Association of Genito-Urinary Surgeons**
22 W. Greene St., Baltimore, MD 21201.
- American Association of Genito-Urinary Surgeons. Transactions. a. ISSN 0065-7204

**American Association of Hospital Consultants**
1700 K St., N.W., Washington, DC 20006.
- American Association of Hospital Consultants. Membership Brochure. a. ISSN 0065-7212

**American Association of Hospital Dentists**
Catholic Medical Center of Brooklyn and Queens, Inc., 88-25 153rd St., Jamica, NY 11432.
- Journal of Hospital Dental Practice. q. ISSN 0022-1600

**American Association of Immunologists**
- Journal of Immunology. (pub. by Williams and Wilkins Co.)

**American Association of Law Libraries**
53 W. Jackson Blvd., Chicago, IL 60604.
- A A L L Publications Series. (pub. by Fred B. Rothman & Co.)
- American Association of Law Libraries. Newsletter. q. ISSN 0572-4953
- Checklist of Basic American Legal Publications. (pub. by Fred B. Rothman & Co.)
- Current Publications in Legal and Related Fields. (pub. by Fred B. Rothman & Co.)
- Directory of Law Libraries. biennial.
- Index to Foreign Legal Periodicals. (pub. by Institute of Advanced Legal Studies UK)
- Law Library Journal. q. ISSN 0023-9283 (And Office of Librarian, Southern Methodist University School of Law, Dallas, TX 75275)

**American Association of Marriage and Family Counselors**
225 Yale Ave., Claremont, CA 91711.
- Journal of Marriage and Family Counseling. q.

**American Association of Maternal and Child Health**
- American Baby. (pub. by American Baby Inc.)

**American Association of Medical Assistants**
One E. Wacker Dr., Chicago, IL 60601.
- Professional Medical Assistant. bi-m. ISSN 0033-0140

**American Association of Medical Milk Commissions, Inc.**
Box 554, Alpharetta, GA 30201.
- American Association of Medical Milk Commissions. Methods and Standards for the Production of Certified Milk. a. ISSN 0065-7263

**American Association of Motor Vehicle Administrators**
1201 Connecticut Ave. N.W., Suite 910, Washington, DC 20036.
- A A M V A Bulletin. m. ISSN 0001-0154
- American Association of Motor Vehicle Administrators. Annual Conference. Proceedings. a. ISSN 0065-7271

**American Association of Museums**
1055 Thomas Jefferson St. N.W., Washington, DC 20007.
- Aviso. m.
- Museum News. bi-m. ISSN 0027-4089
- Official Museum Directory. (pub. by National Register Publishing Co. Inc.)

**American Association of Museums. Midwest Museums Conference**
- Midwest Museums Conference, American Association of Museums. Quarterly. (pub. by Conner Prairie Pioneer Settlement)

**American Association of Museums, Northeast Conference**
- Museologist. (pub. by Buffalo and Erie County Historical Society)

**American Association of Museums. Regional Conference**
9401 Oak Glen Road, Beaumont, CA 92223.
- American Association of Museums. Regional Conference Newsletter. q.

**American Association of Neurological Surgeons**
Dartmouth Medical School, Hanover, NH 03755.
- Journal of Neurosurgery. m. ISSN 0022-3085

**American Association of Neurosurgical Nurses**
27 W 581 Ridgeview St., W. Chicago, IL 60185
- Journal of Neurosurgical Nursing. 2 per yr. ISSN 0047-2603 (Dist. by: Williams & Wilkins, 428 E. Preston St., Baltimore, MD 21202)

**American Association of Nurse Anesthetists**
Suite 929, 111 E. Wacker Dr., Chicago, IL 60601.
- A A N A Journal. bi-m. ISSN 0094-6354

**American Association of Nurserymen**
230 Southern Bldg., 15th & H St. N.W., DC 20005.
- A L I. (Allied Landscape Industry); an allied landscape industry service produced by the American Association of Nurserymen. q.
- Allied Landscape Industry Member Directory. a. ISSN 0098-793X

**American Association of Obstetricians and Gynecologists**
- American Association of Obstetricians and Gynecologists. Transactions. (pub. by C. V. Mosby Co.)

**American Association of Occupational Health Nurses, Inc.**
- Occupational Health Nursing. (pub. by Charles B. Slack, Inc.)

**American Association of Ophthalmology**
1100 17th St. N. W., Washington, DC 20036.
- Ophthalmologist. bi-m. ISSN 0030-3763

**American Association of Orthodontists**
7477 Delmar Blvd., St. Louis, MO 63130.
- American Journal of Orthodontics. (pub. by C. V. Mosby Co.)
- Orthodontic Bulletin. q.

**American Association of Pathologists**
- American Journal of Pathology. (pub. by Harper & Row Publishers, Inc. Medical Department)

**American Association of Petroleum Geologists**
Box 979, Tulsa, OK 74101.
- American Association of Petroleum Geologists. Bulletin. m. ISSN 0002-7464
- American Association of Petroleum Geologists. Memoir. irreg., no. 24, 1976. ISSN 0065-731X

**American Association of Physical Anthropologists**
1703 New Hampshire Ave., NW., Washington, DC 20009.
- American Journal of Physical Anthropology. (pub. by Wistar Institute Press)
- Yearbook of Physical Anthropology. a.

**American Association of Physicists in Medicine**
- Medical Physics. (pub. by American Institute of Physics)
- Physics in Medicine and Biology. (pub. by Institute of Physics UK)

**American Association of Physics Teachers**
Graduate Physics Bldg., State University of New York at Stony Brook, Stony Brook, NY 11790.
- A A P T Announcer. q.
- American Journal of Physics. (pub. by American Institute of Physics)

**American Association of Psychiatric Services for Children**
1701 18th St., Washington N.W., DC 20009.
- American Association of Psychiatric Services for Children. Newsletter. q. ISSN 0093-0237

**American Association of Public Health Dentists**
c/o Mary G. Kulash, Box 2091, Raleigh, NC 27602.
- Journal of Public Health Dentistry. q. ISSN 0022-4006

**American Association of Retired Persons (Long Beach)**
215 Long Beach Blvd., Long Beach, CA 90802.
- Modern Maturity. bi-m. ISSN 0026-8046

**American Association of Retired Persons (Washington)**
1909 K St. N.W., Washington, DC 20006.
- A A R P News Bulletin. m. ISSN 0001-0200
- Dynamic Maturity. bi-m. ISSN 0012-7388

**American Association of School Administrators**
1801 N. Moore St., Arlington, VA 22209.
- American Association of School Administrators. Annotated Bibliographies on Crucial Issues. irreg.
- School Administrator. m. ISSN 0036-6439

**American Association of School Librarians**
- School Media Quarterly. (pub. by American Library Association)

**American Association of Sex Educators and Counselors for Professionals in Health, Social Welfare and Educational Organizations**
Suite 304, 5010 Wisconsin Ave., N.W., Washington, DC 20016.
- Journal of Sex Education and Therapy. s-a.

**American Association of Special Educators**
107-20 125th St., Richmond Hill, NY 11419.
- Special Children. 3 per yr.

**American Association of State Colleges and Universities**
One Dupont Circle, N.W., Suite 700, Washington, DC 20036.
- A A S C U Studies. irreg. ISSN 0065-7344
- American Association of State Colleges and Universities. Memo: to the President. m. ISSN 0047-6692
- American Association of State Colleges and Universities. Proceedings. a.

**American Association of State Highway and Transportation Officials**
341 National Press Bldg., Washington, DC 20045.
- A A S H T O Quarterly. q.
- American Association of State Highway and Transportation Officials. Proceedings. a.
- American Association of State Highway and Transportation Officials. Sub-Committee on Computer Technology. Proceedings. National Conference. a. ISSN 0091-5122
- Reference Book of Highway Personnel. a. ISSN 0516-9445
- Standard Specifications for Highway Bridges. a.

**American Association of State Libraries**
- American Association of State Libraries. President's Newsletter. (pub. by American Library Association)

**American Association of Stratigraphic Palynologists**
c/o Mobil R & D Corp. Field Research Laboratory, Box 900, Dallas, TX 75221.
- American Association of Stratigraphic Palynologists. Abstracts of Papers Presented at the Annual Meetings. a.
- American Association of Stratigraphic Palynologists. Contributions Series. irreg.
- American Association of Stratigraphic Palynologists. Newsletter. q.
- Palynology. a.

**American Association of Suicidology**
- Suicide and Life Threatening Behavior. (pub. by Human Sciences Press)

**American Association of Teacher Educators in Agriculture**
c/o Jasper Lee, Ed., Agricultural and Extension Education Program, Mississippi State University, Mississippi State, MS 39762.
- American Association of Teacher Educators in Agriculture. Journal. 3 per yr. ISSN 0002-7480

**American Association of Teachers of Arabic**
c/o Ed. Salih Altoma, Near Eastern Languages, Indiana University, Bloomington, OH 43210.
- Al-Arabiyya. s-a.

**American Association of Teachers of Esperanto**
c/o Ed. Mrs. Roy E. Holland, 5140 San Lorenzo Drive, Santa Barbara, CA 93111.
- American Association of Teachers of Esperanto Quarterly Bulletin/Amerika Asocio de Instruistoj de Esperanto Kvaronjara Bulteno. q. ISSN 0002-7499

**American Association of Teachers of French**
57 E. Armory, Champaign, IL 61820.
- French Review. 6 per yr. ISSN 0016-111X

**American Association of Teachers of German, Inc.**
339 Walnut St., Philadelphia, PA 19106.
- A A T G Newsletter. 4 per yr. ISSN 0001-0243
- German Quarterly. 4 per yr. ISSN 0016-8831
- Unterrichtspraxis. s-a. ISSN 0042-062X

**American Association of Teachers of Italian**
Dept. of Romance Languages, Rutgers University, New Brunswick, NJ 08903.
- American Association of Teachers of Italian. Directory. a.
- Italica. q. ISSN 0021-3020

**American Association of Teachers of Slavic and East European Languages**
c/o Gary L. Harris, Ed., Foreign Languages Dept., West Virginia Univ., Morgantown, WV 26506 (Orders to Joe Malik Jr., Sec.-Tr., Dept. of Russian & Slavic Studies, Univ. of Arizona, Tucson AZ 85721)
- A A T S E E L Newsletter. 6 per yr. ISSN 0001-0251
- Slavic and East European Journal. q.

**American Association of Teachers of Spanish and Portuguese**
c/o Richard B. Klein, Department of Modern Languages, Holy Cross College, Worcester, MA 01610.
- Hispania; a journal devoted to the interests of the teaching of Spanish and Portuguese. q. ISSN 0018-2133

**American Association of Textile Chemists and Colorists**
Box 12215, Research Triangle Pk., NC 27709.
- American Association of Textile Chemists and Colorists. Monographs. irreg.
- American Association of Textile Chemists and Colorists. Products: Buyer's Guide. a. ISSN 0065-7352
- Textile Chemist and Colorist. m. ISSN 0040-490X

**American Association of University Professors**
One Dupont Circle, Washington, DC 20036.
- A A U P Bulletin. 4 per yr. ISSN 0001-026X
- Academe. q. ISSN 0001-3749

**American Association of University Women**
2401 Virginia Ave. N.W., Washington, DC 20037.
- A A U W Journal. 6 per yr. ISSN 0001-0278

**American Association of University Women Consumer Bureau**
2401 Virginia Ave. N. W., Washington, DC 20037.
- Your Dollars Worth; consumer service bureau newsletter. m. ISSN 0049-8408

**American Association of University Women. New York Division**
111 E. 37, New York, NY 10016.
- A A U W. New York Division. Newsletter. s-a. ISSN 0001-0286

**American Association of Variable Star Observers**
187 Concord Ave., Cambridge, MA 02138.
- A A V S O Bulletin. a. ISSN 0516-9518
- A A V S O Report. irreg; 1975, no. 30.

**American Association of Veterinary Laboratory Diagnosticians**
6101 Mineral Point Rd., Madison, WI 53705.
- American Association of Veterinary Laboratory Diagnosticians. Proceedings of Annual Meeting. a. ISSN 0098-3543

**American Association of Workers for the Blind, Inc.**
1511 K St. N.W., Washington, DC 20005.
- American Association of Workers for the Blind. News and Views. bi-m. ISSN 0002-7510
- American Association of Workers for the Blind. Proceedings. a. ISSN 0065-7395
- Blindness. a. ISSN 0067-9186

**American Association of Zoo Veterinarians**
c/o C. W. Gray, Secy-Treas., National Zoo, Washington, DC 20009.
- Journal of Zoo Animal Medicine. q. ISSN 0093-4526

**American Association of Zoological Parks and Aquariums**
Oglebay Park, Wheeling, WV 26003.
- A A Z P A Newsletter. m. ISSN 0001-0308
- American Association of Zoological Parks and Aquariums. Proceedings. Annual A A Z P A Conference. a. ISSN 0090-4473
- Zoos & Aquariums in the Americas. biennial. ISSN 0090-1628

**American Association on Mental Deficiency**
5201 Connecticut Avenue, N.W., Washington, DC 20015.
- American Association on Mental Deficiency. Directory of Members. irreg. ISSN 0065-7409
- American Journal of Mental Deficiency. bi-m. ISSN 0002-9351
- International Research Seminar on Vocational Rehabilitation of the Mentally Retarded. Special Publications Series. irreg.
- Mental Retardation. bi-m. ISSN 0047-6765

**American Astronautical Society, Inc.**
6060 Duke St., Alexandria, VA 22304 (Publications Office: Box 746, Tarzana, CA 91356)
- A A S Goddard Memorial Symposium. Proceedings. a.
- A A S Microfiche Series. irreg. (approx. 5 vols. yrly.); vol. 22, 1975. ISSN 0065-7417
- A A S Newsletter. bi-m. ISSN 0001-0227
- Advances in the Astronautical Sciences. irreg. (2-3 per yr.), vol. 31, 1975. ISSN 0065-3438
- American Astronautical Society. Proceedings of the Annual Meeting. a. ISSN 0516-9593
- Journal of Astronautical Sciences. q. ISSN 0021-9142
- Science and Technology. irreg.; vol. 36, 1975. ISSN 0080-7451

**American Astronomical Society**
231 Space Sciences Bldg., University of Florida, Gainesville, FL 32611.
- A A S Photo-Bulletin. irreg. ISSN 0065-7433
- American Astronomical Society. Bulletin. (pub. by American Institute of Physics)
- Astronomical Journal. (pub. by American Institute of Physics)
- Astrophysical Journal. (pub. by University of Chicago Press)
- Astrophysical Journal. Supplement Series. (pub. by University of Chicago Press)

**American Atheists**
Box 2117, Austin, TX 78767.
- American Atheist Insider Newsletter. m. (Society of Separationists)

**American Austin-Bantam Club**
516 W. Washington, Washington, IA 52353.
- American Austin Bantam Club News. bi-m.

**American Automobile Association**
8111 Gatehouse Road, Falls Church, VA 22042.
- American Automobile Association. Digest of Motor Laws. a. ISSN 0093-4062
- American Motorist. bi-m.
- British Isles and Ireland Travel Guide. a. ISSN 0095-1579
- Central Europe and Scandinavia Travel Guide. irreg. ISSN 0094-3657
- Eastern Europe Travel Guide. irreg. ISSN 0094-8632
- Florida Tour Book. irreg. ISSN 0516-9674
- Great Lakes Camping. a.
- Northeastern Camping and Trailering: Including Location Maps. a.
- Northeastern Tour Book. a. ISSN 0468-6853
- Northwestern Camping & Trailering: Including Location Maps. a.
- Northwestern Tour Book. a. ISSN 0094-078X
- Southern Europe Travel Guide. irreg. ISSN 0094-3614 (prep. by its World Wide Travel Department)
- Tour Book: Alabama, Louisiana, Mississippi. a. ISSN 0361-4948
- Tour Book: Arizona, New Mexico. a. ISSN 0362-3599
- Tour Book: Atlantic Provinces and Quebec. a. ISSN 0363-1788 (Co-sponsor: Canadian Automobile Association)
- Tour Book: Georgia, North Carolina, South Carolina. a. ISSN 0361-4956
- Tour Book: Kentucky-Tennessee. a. ISSN 0361-4964
- Tour Book: Western Canada and Alaska. a. ISSN 0362-3602

**American Automobile Association. East Florida Division**
4300 Biscayne Blvd., Miami, FL 33137.
- Florida A A A Motorist. 8 per yr. ISSN 0015-3842

**American Automobile Association. Texas Division**
Box 1986, Houston, TX 77001.
- Texas Motorist. m. ISSN 0040-4497

**American Automobile Association. Wisconsin Division**
433 W. Washington Ave., Madison, WI 53703.
- Wisconsin A A A Motor News. m. ISSN 0043-6348

**American Baby Inc.**
575 Lexington Ave., New York, NY 10022.
- American Baby; for expectant and new parents. m. ISSN 0044-7544 (American Association of Maternal and Child Health)

**American Bandmasters Association**
- Journal of Band Research. (pub. by Troy State University Press)

**American Banker, Inc.**
525 W. 42 St, New York, NY 10036.
- American Banker. d.(5 times a week) ISSN 0002-7561
- American Banker Index. m. plus a. cum.

**American Bankers Association**
1120 Connecticut Ave., N. W., Washington, DC 20036.
- A B A Bank Card Letter. m. (prep. by its Bank Card Division)
- Agricultural Banker. m. (prep. by its Agricultural Bankers Division)
- Agricultural Banking Developments. a. (prep. by its Agricultural Committee)
- American Bankers Association. National Operations & Automation Conference. Proceedings. a. ISSN 0065-7441 (prep. by its Operations and Automation Division)
- American Bankers Association. Operations and Automation Division. Results of the National Operations & Automation Survey. triennial. ISSN 0363-2539
- Bank Management Committee Studies. irreg. (prep. by its Bank Card Division)
- Bank Personnel News. m. (prep. by its Bank Personnel Division)
- Bank Protection Bulletin. m. ISSN 0091-0392
- Banking. (pub. by Simmons-Boardman Publishing Corporation)
- Banking Legislation in the Congress. irreg. ISSN 0094-7555
- Capital. w.
- Directory of Bankers Schools. a. ISSN 0084-9855
- Directory of Banking Instructors. irreg. ISSN 0092-4717

- International Banking Summer School. Lectures and Proceedings. a.
- Thruput. m. (prep. by its Operations and Automation Division)
- Trust Letter. 18 per yr. (prep. by its Trust Division)

**American Bantam Association**
Box 610, North Amherst, MA 01059.
- American Bantam Association. Yearbook. a. ISSN 0065-745X
- Book of Bantams. irreg.(quadrennial or quinquennial) ISSN 0068-0117

**American Baptist Churches in the U.S.A.**
Valley Forge, PA 19481.
- American Baptist. m except Aug. ISSN 0002-757X
- American Baptist Churches in the U.S.A. Directory. a. ISSN 0091-9381
- American Baptist Churches in the U. S. A. Yearbook. a. ISSN 0092-3478
- Baptist Leader. m. ISSN 0005-5727
- Rainbow. m.
- Secret Place. q. ISSN 0037-0606
- Senior High Class. q.
- Wow. m.

**American Baptist Historical Society**
1106 S. Goodman St., Rochester, NY 14620.
- Foundations; a Baptist journal of history and theology. q. ISSN 0015-8992

**American Bar Association**
1155 E. 60th St., Chicago, IL 60637.
- American Bar Association Journal. m. ISSN 0002-7596
- Directory of Lawyer Referral Services, Legal Aid and Defender Offices and Legal Assistance Offices of the Armed Forces. a. ISSN 0070-5756 (Co-sponsor: National Legal Aid and Defender Association)
- Judges Journal; a quarterly for the American Judiciary. q. ISSN 0047-2972 (National College of the State Judiciary)

**American Bar Association. Commission on Correctional Facilities & Services**
15th Floor Hoge Bldg., Seattle, WA 98104.
- Prison Law Reporter. q. ISSN 0048-5365 (Co-Sponsor: American Bar Association. Young Lawyers Section)

**American Bar Association. Consortium on Legal Services & the Public**
1155 East 60th St., Chicago, IL 60637.
- Alternatives; legal services & the public. bi-m. ISSN 0098-8855

**American Bar Association. Department of Professional Standards**
1155 E. 60th St., Chicago, IL 60637.
- Unauthorized Practice News. 2 per yr. ISSN 0041-6452

**American Bar Association. Law Student Division**
1155 E. 60th St., Chicago, IL 60637.
- Federal Government Legal Career Opportunities. a. ISSN 0065-7476
- Student Lawyer. 9 per yr. ISSN 0039-274X

**American Bar Association. Ombudsman Committee**
c/o Ed. Bernard Frank, 832 Hamilton Mall, Box 419, Allentown, PA 18105.
- Ombudsman Survey. a. (Co-Sponsor: International Bar Association)

**American Bar Association. Section of Administrative Law**
1155 E. 60th St., Chicago, IL 60637.
- Administrative Law Review. q. ISSN 0001-8368
- American Bar Association. Section of Administrative Law. Annual Reports of Committees. a.

**American Bar Association. Section of Antitrust Law**
1155 E. 60th St., Chicago, IL 60637.
- Antitrust Law Journal. 3 per yr. ISSN 0003-6056

**American Bar Association. Section of Bar Activities**
1155 E. 60th St., Chicago, IL 60637.
- Bar Leader. bi-m. ISSN 0099-1031

**American Bar Association. Section of Corporation, Banking and Business Law**
1155 E.60th St., Chicago, IL 60637.
- Business Lawyer. q. ISSN 0007-6899

**American Bar Association. Section of Criminal Justice**
1155 E. 60th St., Chicago, IL 60637.
- American Criminal Law Review. q.
- Criminal Justice (Chicago) q. ISSN 0092-2498

**American Bar Association. Section of Economics of Law Practice**
1155 E. 60th St., Chicago, IL 60637.
- Legal Economics. q. ISSN 0360-1439

**American Bar Association. Section of Family Law**
1155 E. 60th St., Chicago, IL 60637.
- Family Law Quarterly. q. ISSN 0014-729X

**American Bar Association. Section of General Practice**
1155 E. 60th Street, Chicago, IL 60637.
- Law Notes. q. ISSN 0023-9305

**American Bar Association. Section of Individual Rights and Responsibilities**
- Human Rights. (pub. by Southern Methodist University. Printing Department)

**American Bar Association. Section of Insurance, Negligence and Compensation Law**
1155 E. 60th St., Chicago, IL 60637.
- Forum (Chicago, 1965) q. ISSN 0015-8356

**American Bar Association. Section of International and Comparative Law**
1155 E. 60th St., Chicago, IL 60637.
- International Law News. q. ISSN 0047-0813
- International Lawyer. q. ISSN 0020-7810

**American Bar Association. Section of Labor Relations Law**
1155 E. 60 St., Chicago, IL 60637.
- American Bar Association. Section of Labor Relations Law. Committee Reports. a.
- American Bar Association. Section of Labor Relations Law. Proceedings. a.

**American Bar Association. Section of Legal Education and Admissions to the Bar**
1155 E. 60th St., Chicago, IL 60637.
- Learning and the Law. q. ISSN 0093-8696

**American Bar Association. Section of Litigation**
1155 E. 60th St., Chicago, IL 60637.
- Litigation. q. ISSN 0097-9813

**American Bar Association. Section of Local Government Law**
1155 E. 60th, Chicago, IL 60637.
- American Bar Association. Section of Local Government Law. Committee Reports. a. ISSN 0587-2936
- Urban Lawyer; the national quarterly on urban law. q. ISSN 0042-0905

**American Bar Association. Section of Natural Resources Law**
1155 East 60th St., Chicag, IL 60637.
- Natural Resources Law Newsletter. q. ISSN 0077-6084
- Natural Resources Lawyer. q. ISSN 0028-0747

**American Bar Association. Section of Public Contract Law**
Section of Public Contract Law, 1155 E. 60th St., Chicago, IL 60637.
- Public Contract Law Journal. s-a. ISSN 0033-3441

**American Bar Association. Section of Real Property, Probate and Trust Law**
1155 E. 60th St., Chicago, IL 60637.
- Real Property, Probate and Trust Journal. q. ISSN 0034-0855

**American Bar Association. Section of Science and Technology**
1155 E. 60th St., Chicago, IL 60637.
- Jurimetrics Journal. q. ISSN 0022-6793

**American Bar Association. Section of Taxation**
1800 M St. N.W., 2nd Fl., So. Lobby, Washington, DC 20036.
- Tax Lawyer. q. ISSN 0040-005X

**American Bar Association. Special Committee on Environmental Law**
1155 E. 60th St., Chicago, IL 60637.
- American Bar Association. Special Committee on Environmental Law. Quarterly Newsletter. q. ISSN 0093-7797

**American Bar Association. Standing Committee on Lawyers' Title Guaranty Funds**
1155 East 60th St., Chicago, IL 60637.
- A B A Lawyers' Title Guaranty Funds Newsletter. irreg. ISSN 0361-3763

**American Bar Association. Standing Committee on Legal Assistance for Military Personnel**
1155 E. 60 St., Chicago, IL 60637.
- L A M P Occasional Newsletter. irreg, no. 6, 1974.

**American Bar Association. Young Lawyers Section**
1155 E. 60th St., Chicago, IL 60637.
- Barrister. q. ISSN 0094-5277

**American Bar Foundation**
1155 E. 60th St., Chicago, IL 60637.
- A B F Research Reporter. 3 per yr. ISSN 0084-6317
- American Bar Foundation. Research Contributions. irreg. ISSN 0065-7549
- American Bar Foundation. Research Journal. q. ISSN 0361-9486
- Lawyers in the United States. Distribution and Income. irreg.

**American Bard**
1154 No. Ogden Drive, Hollywood, CA 90046.
- American Bard. q. ISSN 0002-7618

**American Beekeeping Federation**
RFD 1, Box 68, Cannon Falls, MN 55009.
- American Beekeeping Federation. Newsletter. bi-m. ISSN 0014-9438

**American Begonia Society, Inc.**
8302 Kittyhawk Ave., Los Angeles, CA 90045.
- Begonian; devoted to the sheltered garden. m.

**American Bell Association**
Route 1, Box 286, Natrona Heights, PA 15065.
- American Bell Association. Directory. a. (some vols. accompanied by supplemental directory) ISSN 0093-1330
- Bell Tower. 9 per yr. ISSN 0092-8666

**American Benedictine Review, Inc.**
Division St. & 2nd, Atchison, KS 66002.
- American Benedictine Review. 4 per yr. ISSN 0002-7650

**American Berkshire Association**
601 W. Monroe St., Springfield, IL 62704.
- Berkshire News; devoted to the Berkshire breed of swine. m. (except Apr. & Jun.) ISSN 0005-9196

**American Better Health Publications**
Box 68, Duncannon, PA 17020.
- American Vegetarian-Hygienist. bi-m. ISSN 0003-147X (American Vegetarian Union) (Co-Sponsor: Natural Living Foundation Internationale)

**American Bible Society**
1865 Broadway, New York, NY 10023.
- American Bible Society Record. m. ISSN 0006-0o01

**American Bibliographic Service**
Darien, CT 06820.
- International Guide to Classical Studies; a continuous index to periodical literature. 4nos. per vol. ISSN 0020-6849
- International Guide to Medieval Studies; a continuous index to periodical literature. 4 nos. per vol. ISSN 0020-6865
- Quarterly Check-List of Classical Studies; international index of current books, monographs, brochures and separates. q. ISSN 0033-5363
- Quarterly Check-List of Linguistics; international index of current books, monographs, brochures and separates. q. ISSN 0033-538X
- Quarterly Check-List of Medievalia; international index of current books, monographs, brochures and separates. q. ISSN 0033-5401
- Quarterly Check-List of Musicology; international index of current books, monographs, brochures and separates. q. ISSN 0033-541X
- Quarterly Check-List of Oriental Studies; international index of current books, monographs, brochures and separates. q. ISSN 0033-5428
- Quarterly Check-List of Psychology; an international index of current books, monographs, brochures and separates. q. ISSN 0033-5436

**American Bibliographical Center-Clio Press**
Riviera Campus, Box 4397, 2040 Alameda Padre
Serra, Santa Barbara, CA 93103.
- A B C Pol Sci. (Advance Bibliography of
  Contents: Political Science and Government) 6
  per yr. (including indexes) ISSN 0001-0456
- All-Cal Index to Law Reviews and Legal
  Periodicals. base vol. with q. supplements.
- America: History and Life. Part A: Article
  Abstracts and Citation. 7 per yr. ISSN 0002-7065
- America: History and Life. Part B: Index to Book
  Reviews. 7 per yr.
- America: History and Life. Part C: American
  History Bibliography. 7 per yr.
- Austrian Historical Bibliography/Oesterreichische
  Historische Bibliographie. a. ISSN 0067-236X
- Clio Bibliography Series. irreg.
- Historical Abstracts. Part A: Modern History
  Abstracts, 1450-1914; bibliography of the world's
  periodical literature. q. ISSN 0363-2717
- Historical Abstracts. Part B: Twentieth Century
  Abstracts, 1914 to the Present; bibliography of
  the world's periodical literature. q. ISSN 0018-
  2435
- Studies in Comparative Politics Series. irreg.
- War Peace Bibliography Series. irreg. (California
  State University, Los Angeles. Center for the
  Study of Armament and Disarmanent)
- World Bibliography Series. irreg.
- World Treaty Index. irreg (supplements)

**American Bicentennial Communications Inc.**
1800 North Ave., Hollywood, CA 90028.
- American Bicentennial Observer. q. ISSN 0364-
  0051

**American Biographical Institute**
205 W. Martin St., P.O.B. 226, Raleigh, NC 27602.
- Community Leaders and Noteworthy Americans.
  a.

**American Birding Association**
Box 4335, Austin, TX 78765.
- Birding. bi-m.

**American Blake Foundation, Inc.**
Dept. of English, Memphis State University,
Memphis, TN 38152.
- Blake Studies. s-a. ISSN 0006-4548
- Materials for the Study of William Blake. s-a.

**American Board for Certification in Orthotics and
Prosthetics**
1444 N. St., N.W., Washington, DC 20005.
- Registry of Accredited Facilities and Certified
  Individuals in Orthotics and Prosthetics. a. ISSN
  0080-0686

**American Board of Missions to the Jews**
- Shepherd of Israel. (pub. by Beth Sar Shalom)

**American Board of Professional Psychology**
185 Broad St. E., Rochester, NY 14604.
- American Board of Professional Psychology.
  Policies and Procedures for the Creation of
  Diplomates in Professional Psychology. a.

**American Boccaccio Association**
Box 1375, 299 Sea Cliff Ave, Sea Cliff, NY 11579.
- Boccaccio Newsletter. q.

**American Booksellers Association**
800 Second Ave., New York, NY 10017.
- A B A Newswire. w.

**American Bowling Congress, Inc.**
5301 S.76th St., Greendale, WI 53129.
- Bowling Magazine. m. ISSN 0006-842X

**American Boxwood Society**
Blandy Experimental Farm, Boyce, VA 22620.
- Boxwood Bulletin. q. ISSN 0006-8535

**American Brewer Publishing Corp.**
c/o Ed. & Pub. Ely S. Rubin, Box 267, Kearny, NJ
07032.
- American Brewer. bi-m. ISSN 0002-7723

**American Broncho-Esophagological Association**
c/o James B. Snow, Jr., M.D., 3400 Spruce St.,
Philadelphia, PA 19140.
- American Broncho-Esophagological Association.
  Transactions. a. ISSN 0065-7603

**American Bryological & Lichenological Society**
c/o Dale M. J. Mueller, Ed., Dept. of Biology,
Texas A & M Univ., College Sta., TX 77843.
- Bryologist. q. ISSN 0007-2745

**American Bureau for Medical Aid to China**
1790 Broadway, New York, NY 10019.
- A B M A C Bulletin. bi-m. ISSN 0001-0529

**American Bureau of Metal Statistics Inc.**
420 Lexington Ave., New York, NY 10017.
- Non-Ferrous Metal Data. a. ISSN 0360-9553

**American Bureau of Shipping**
45 Broad St., New York, NY 10004.
- American Bureau of Shipping. Bulletin. m. ISSN
  0002-7758
- American Bureau of Shipping. Record. a. (with s-
  m supplements)
- Surveyor. q. ISSN 0039-629X

**American Business Communication Association**
317-B David Kinley Hall, University of Illinois,
Urbana, IL 61801.
- A B C A Bulletin. 4 per yr. ISSN 0001-0383
- Journal of Business Communication. q. ISSN
  0021-9436
- Organizational Communications Abstracts. a. (Co-
  sponsor: International Communication
  Association, Austin, Texas.)

**American Business Law Association**
c/o Wharton School, University of Pennsylvania,
Philadelphia, PA 19174.
- American Business Law Journal. 3 per yr. ISSN
  0002-7766

**American Business Men's Research Foundation**
Suite 705, Stoddard Building, Lansing, MI 48933.
- Bottom Line. bi-m.

**American Business Press, Inc.**
205 E. 42nd St, New York, NY 10017.
- Leading Advertisers in Business Publications. a.
  ISSN 0075-8310

**American Business Women's Association**
- Women in Business. (pub. by A B W A Co., Inc.)

**American Camellia Society**
Box 212, Fort Valley, GA 31030.
- American Camellia Yearbook. a. ISSN 0065-762X
- Camellia Journal. 4 per yr.(plus Yearbook) ISSN
  0008-204X

**American Camping Association**
Bradford Woods, Martinsville, IN 46151.
- Camping. m.(Jan.-June); bi-m.(Sept.-Dec) ISSN
  0008-2376
- Directory of Accredited Camps for Boys and
  Girls. a. ISSN 0070-5047

**American-Canadian Publishers, Inc.**
Drawer 2078, Portales, NM 88130.
- Archives of Post-Modern Literature Series. irreg.

**American Cancer Society, Inc.**
777 Third Ave., New York, NY 10017.
- Ca-A Cancer Journal for Clinicians. bi-m. ISSN
  0007-9235
- Cancer. (pub. by J. B. Lippincott Co.)
- Cancer Facts and Figures. a. ISSN 0069-0147
- Cancer News. s-a. ISSN 0008-5464

**American Cancer Society, Inc. Connecticut Division**
270 Amity Road, Woodbridge, CT 06525.
- MEDI-Scope. irreg.

**American Cancer Society, Inc. Louisiana Division**
333 St. Charles Ave., New Orleans, LA 70130.
- Louisiana Cancer Reporter. bi-m. ISSN 0459-
  889X

**American Cancer Society, Inc. Minnesota Division**
2750 Park Ave., Minneapolis, MN 55407.
- Herald of Hope. bi-m.

**American Canoe Association**
- Canoe. (pub. by Webb Co.)

**American Carbon Committee**
- Carbon. (pub. by Pergamon Press Inc)

**American Carpatho-Russian Orthodox Greek Catholic
Diocese**
312 Garfield St., Johnstown, PA 15906.
- Church Messenger/Cerkovnyj Vistnik. bi-w.

**American Cat Fanciers Association**
P.O. Box 203, Point Lookout, MO 65726.
- A C F A Bulletin. m.

**American Catholic Historical Association**
- Catholic Historical Review. (pub. by Catholic
  University of America Press)

**American Catholic Historical Society of Philadelphia**
Box 84, Philadelphia, PA 19105.
- American Catholic Historical Society of
  Philadelphia. Records. q. ISSN 0002-7790

**American Catholic Philosophical Association**
The Catholic University of America, Washington,
DC 20064.
- American Catholic Philosophical Association.
  Proceedings. a. ISSN 0065-7638
- New Scholasticism. q. ISSN 0028-6621

**American Cemetery Association**
250 Broad St., Columbus, OH 43215.
- International Cemetery Directory. triennial. ISSN
  0074-2155

**American Ceramic Society, Inc.**
65 Ceramic Dr., Columbus, OH 43214.
- American Ceramic Society. Bulletin. bi-m. ISSN
  0002-7812
- American Ceramic Society. Journal. bi-m. ISSN
  0002-7820
- American Ceramic Society. Special Publications.
  irreg. ISSN 0065-7654
- Ceramic Abstracts. bi-m.
- Ceramic Data Book. (pub. by Cahners Publishing
  Co. Inc.)
- Ceramic-Metal Systems Bibliography and
  Abstracts. a.

**American Chain & Cable Co. Inc.**
Box 430, 929 Connecticut Ave., Bridgeport, CT
06602.
- Accomation. q.

**American Challenge**
1149 14th Place, S.W., Birmingham, AL 35211.
- American Challenge. s-m. ISSN 0300-7219

**American Chamber of Commerce Researchers
Association**
c/o Chicago Assn. of Commerce & Industry, 130 S.
Michigan, Chicago, IL 60603
(Subscr. to: Greater Des Moines Chamber of
Commerce, 8th & High Sts., Des Moines, IA 50309)
- Cost of Living Indicators: Inter-City Index
  Report. q.
- Cost of Living Indicators: Price Report. q.

**American Checker Federation**
3475 Belmont Ave., Baton Rouge, LA 70808.
- A C F Bulletin. bi-m.

**American Chemical Society**
1155 16th St. N.W., Washington, DC 20036.
- A C S Laboratory Guide; to instruments,
  equipment and chemicals. a. ISSN 0065-7700
- A C S Monographs. (pub. by D. Van Nostrand
  Books)
- A C S Single Article Announcement. s-m. ISSN
  0044-7587
- A C S Symposium Series. irreg. ISSN 0097-6156
- Accounts of Chemical Research. m. ISSN 0001-
  4842
- Advances in Chemistry Series. irreg. ISSN 0065-
  2393
- American Chemical Society. Abstracts of Papers
  (at the National Meeting) biannual. ISSN 0065-
  7727
- American Chemical Society. Abstracts of Papers
  (at the Regional Meetings) irreg.; latest issue,
  1974. ISSN 0065-7735
- American Chemical Society. Directory of
  Graduate Research. irreg. (prep. by its Committee
  on Professional Training)
- American Chemical Society. Journal. fortn. ISSN
  0002-7863
- Analytical Chemistry. m. ISSN 0003-2700
- Annual Reports in Medicinal Chemistry. (pub. by
  Academic Press, Inc.)
- Biochemistry. fortn. ISSN 0006-2960
- Chemical Abstracts. (pub. by Chemical Abstracts
  Service)
- Chemical Abstracts - Applied Chemistry and
  Chemical Engineering Sections. (pub. by
  Chemical Abstracts Service)
- Chemical Abstracts - Biochemical Sections. (pub.
  by Chemical Abstracts Service)
- Chemical Abstracts - Macromolecular Sections.
  (pub. by Chemical Abstracts Service)
- Chemical Abstracts - Organic Chemistry Sections.
  (pub. by Chemical Abstracts Service)

- Chemical Abstracts - Physical and Analytical Chemistry Sections. (pub. by Chemical Abstracts Service)
- Chemical Abstracts Service Source Index. (pub. by Chemical Abstracts Service)
- Chemical and Engineering News. w. ISSN 0009-2347
- Chemical-Biological Activities(CBAC) (pub. by Chemical Abstracts Service)
- Chemical Industry Notes. (pub. by Chemical Abstracts Service)
- Chemical Reviews. bi-m. ISSN 0009-2665
- Chemical Technology. m. ISSN 0009-2703
- Chemical Titles. (pub. by Chemical Abstracts Service)
- Chemistry. 10 per yr. ISSN 0009-305X
- Coatings and Plastics Preprints. irreg. ISSN 0099-0701 (prep. by its Division of Organic Coatings and Plastics Chemistry)
- Environmental Science & Technology. m. ISSN 0013-936X
- Industrial & Engineering Chemistry Fundamentals. q. ISSN 0019-7874
- Industrial & Engineering Chemistry Process Design and Development. q. ISSN 0019-7882
- Industrial & Engineering Chemistry Product Research and Development. q. ISSN 0019-7890
- Inorganic Chemistry. m. ISSN 0020-1669
- Journal of Agricultural and Food Chemistry. bi-m. ISSN 0021-8561
- Journal of Chemical and Engineering Data. q. ISSN 0021-9568
- Journal of Chemical Information and Computer Sciences. q. ISSN 0095-2338
- Journal of Medicinal Chemistry. m. ISSN 0022-2623
- Journal of Organic Chemistry. fortn. ISSN 0022-3263
- Journal of Physical Chemistry. m. ISSN 0022-3654
- Laboratory Guide to Instruments, Equipment and Chemicals. a. ISSN 0458-595X
- Macromolecules. bi-m. ISSN 0024-9297
- Polymer Preprints. s-a. ISSN 0032-3934 (prep. by its Division of Polymer Chemistry)
- Polymer Science & Technology Post. (pub. by Chemical Abstracts Service)
- Reagent Chemicals. irreg. (prep. by its Committee on Analytical Reagents)
- Reports of Research Supported by the Petroleum Research Fund. a.
- Ring Index: A List of Ring Systems Used in Organic Chemistry. Supplement. (pub. by Chemical Abstracts Service)

**American Chemical Society. Chicago Section**
86 E. Randolph St., Chicago, IL 60601.
- Chemical Bulletin. m.(Sept-June) ISSN 0009-2401

**American Chemical Society. Cleveland Section**
c/o Dwight W. Chasar, Ed., 9921 Brecksville Rd., Brecksville, OH 44141.
- Isotopics. m. Sept.-May. ISSN 0021-1931

**American Chemical Society. Delaware Section**
Box 47, Wilmington, DE 19899.
- Del-Chem Bulletin. 10 per yr.

**American Chemical Society. Division of Chemical Education**
119 W. 24th St., New York, NY 10011.
- Journal of Chemical Education. m. ISSN 0021-9584

**American Chemical Society. Division of Environmental Chemistry**
4400 Fifth Ave., Pittsburgh, PA 15213.
- American Chemical Society. Division of Environmental Chemistry. Preprints of Papers. 2 per yr. ISSN 0093-3066

**American Chemical Society, Florida Section**
c/o Dr. Malcolm H. Filson, Ed., 442 Ave. A N.E., Winter Haven, FL 33880.
- F L A C S. m.(except July, Aug. & Sept) ISSN 0014-5920

**American Chemical Society. Indiana Section**
Box 1291, Indianapolis, IN 46206.
- Accelerator. m(Oct.-May) ISSN 0001-4478

**American Chemical Society. Lehigh Valley Section**
45 Charles Ave., Nazareth, PA 18064.
- Octagon. m.(Sept-May) ISSN 0029-8271

**American Chemical Society. Minnesota Section**
3631 Georgia Ave. N., Minneapolis, MN 55427.
- Minnesota Chemist. m. ISSN 0026-5411

**American Chemical Society. New Jersey Section & New York Section**
Box 802, Ridgewood, NJ 07451.
- Indicator. m.(Sept-June) ISSN 0019-6924

**American Chemical Society. Philadelphia Section**
Univ. of Pennsylvania, Dept. of Chemistry, 236 Spruce St. Wing, Philadelphia, PA 19174.
- Catalyst (Philadelphia) m.(Sept-June) ISSN 0008-767X

**American Chemical Society. Pittsburgh Section**
4400 Fifth Ave., Pittsburgh, PA 15213.
- Crucible. m. except Jul.-Aug. ISSN 0011-2119

**American Chemical Society. Rochester Section**
Box 7571, Rochester, NY 14615.
- Genesee Valley Chemunications. 6 per yr. ISSN 0016-6642

**American Chemical Society. Rubber Division**
University of Akron, Akron, OH 44325.
- Bibliography of Rubber Literature Including Patents. a.
- Rubber Chemistry and Technology. 5 per yr. ISSN 0035-9475

**American Chemical Society. St. Louis Section**
c/o Messenger Printing Co., 125 W. Argonne Dr., St. Louis, MO 63122.
- Chemical Bond. m. 8 per yr. ISSN 0009-2398

**American Chemical Society. Southern California Section**
1540 N. Hudson Ave., Suite 2, Hollywood, CA 90028.
- S C A L A C S. m. except Jul.-Aug. ISSN 0044-7595

**American Chemical Society. Syracuse Section**
Bristol Labs, Box 657, Syracuse, NY 13201.
- Syracuse Chemist. m.(Oct-June) ISSN 0039-792X

**American Chemical Society. Virginia Section**
Box 18, Richmond, VA 23201.
- American Chemical Society. Virginia Section. Bulletin. 3 per yr. ISSN 0002-7871

**American Chiropractic Association, Inc.**
2200 Grand Ave., Des Moines, IA 50312.
- A C A Journal of Chiropractic. m. ISSN 0044-7609
- Healthways; magazine digest. 6 per yr. ISSN 0017-9159

**American Choral Directors Association**
Box 17736, Tampa, FL 33682.
- Choral Journal. m.(Sept.-May) ISSN 0009-5028

**American Choral Foundation, Inc.**
130 W. 56th St., New York, NY 10019.
- American Choral Foundation. Research Memorandum Series. 6 per yr. ISSN 0002-788X (Association of Choral Conductors)
- American Choral Review. q. ISSN 0002-7898 (Association of Choral Conductors)

**American Church Union Inc.**
6013 Lawton Ave., Oakland, CA 94618.
- New Oxford Review. m.(except July & Aug.)

**American Cinema Editors, Inc.**
422 South Western Ave., Los Angeles, CA 90020.
- American Cinemeditor. q. ISSN 0044-7625

**American Citizen**
1134 N. 17th St., Box 944 DTS, Omaha, NE 61801.
- American Citizen. s-m.

**American Citizen's Band Radio Association**
Box 1702, Columbia, MO 65201.
- C Bers' News. m.

**American Civil Defense Association**
Box 910, Starke, FL 32091.
- Journal of Civil Defense. bi-m.

**American Civil Liberties Union**
22 E. 40 St., New York, NY 10016.
- Civil Liberties. bi-m. ISSN 0009-790X
- Civil Liberties Review. bi-m. ISSN 0093-6383
- Privacy Report. m. except Jul.

**American Civil Liberties Union of New Jersey**
45 Academy St., Newark, NJ 07102.
- Civil Liberties Reporter. m.(except June,July & Aug.) ISSN 0009-7934

**American Civil Liberties Union of Southern California**
633 S. Shatto Place, Los Angeles, CA 90005.
- Open Forum. m. ISSN 0030-3429

**American Civil Liberties Union of Washington**
2101 Smith Tower, Seattle, WA 98104.
- Civil Liberties. bi-m. ISSN 0045-7051

**American Classical College. Institute for Economic and Financial Research**
Box 4526, Albuquerque, NM 87106.
- Cylinder Theory Reports. s-m. ISSN 0011-443X
- Institute for Economic & Financial Research. Economic Reports. fortn.

**American Classical College. Institute for Economic & Political World Strategic Studies**
Box 4526, Albuquerque, NM 87106.
- Revue of International Affairs. m. (International Foundation for Theoretical Research)

**American Classical College. Research Center for Economic Psychology**
Box 4526, Albuquerque, NM 87106.
- American Review of Management & Inventiveness Report. m. (International Foundation for Theoretical Research)

**American Classical League**
Miami Univ., Oxford, OH 45056.
- American Classical League. Newsletter. q.
- Classical Outlook. m.(Sept.-June) ISSN 0009-8361

**American Cleft Palate Association**
c/o Betty Jane McWilliams, Ed., University of Pittsburgh, 331 Salk Hall, Administrative Office, Pittsburgh, PA 15261.
- Cleft Palate Journal. q. ISSN 0009-8701

**American Clinical and Climatological Association**
Eighth and Spruce St., Philadelphia, PA 19107.
- American Clinical and Climatological Association. Transactions. a. ISSN 0065-7778

**American Coin Club**
- Coin Bulletin. (pub. by Coin Arts, Inc.)

**American Collectors Association, Inc.**
4040 W. 70th St., Minneapolis, MN 55435.
- Collector. m. ISSN 0010-082X
- Directory of Bonded Collectors. a. ISSN 0070-5144

**American College Health Association**
2807 Central St., Evanston, IL 60201.
- A C H Action. (American College Health) 10 per yr. ISSN 0002-7952
- American College Health Association. Journal. 6 per yr. ISSN 0002-7944

**American College of Allergists**
2117 W. River Rd. N., Minneapolis, MN 55411.
- Annals of Allergy. m. ISSN 0003-4738

**American College of Apothecaries**
874 Union Ave., Memphis, Silver Spring, TN 38103.
- American College of Apothecaries. Proceedings. a. ISSN 0065-7786

**American College of Cardiology**
9650 Rockville Pike, Bethesda, MD 20014.
- A C C E L; audio cassette journal of clinical cardiology. m.
- American Journal of Cardiology. (pub. by Dun-Donnelley Publishing Corp.)

**American College of Chest Physicians**
911 Busse Hwy., Park Ridge, IL 60068.
- Cardiopulmonary Medicine. 3 per yr.
- Chest. m. ISSN 0012-3692

**American College of Clinical Pharmacology**
- Journal of Clinical Pharmacology. (pub. by Hall Associates)

**American College of Dentists**
7316 Wisconsin Ave., Bethesda, MD 20014.
- American College of Dentists. Journal. q. ISSN 0002-7979

**American College of Emergency Medical Technicians**
- Emergency Review. (pub. by Productions, Ltd.)

**American College of Emergency Physicians**
3900 Capital City Blvd., Lansing, MI 48906.
- American College of Emergency Physicians. Journal. m.

- Emergency Medicine Residency Newsletter.

**American College of Foot Orthopedists**
c/o Dr. David M. Davidson, 388 Evans St., Buffalo,
NY 14203.
- American College of Foot Orthopedists
Newsletter. q. ISSN 0002-7987

**American College of Gastroenterology**
299 Broadway, New York, NY 10007.
- American Journal of Gastroenterology. m. ISSN
0002-9270

**American College of General Practioners in
Osteopathic Medicine and Surgery**
- Osteopathic Medicine. (pub. by A. Retlaw &
Associates)

**American College of Hospital Administrators**
840 N. Lake Shore Dr., Chicago, IL 60611.
- A C H A News. m. ISSN 0001-0707
- American College of Hospital Administrators.
Directory. biennial. ISSN 0065-7794
- Hospital & Health Services Administration. q.

**American College of Legal Medicine**
- Journal of Legal Medicine. (pub. by G M T
Medical Information Systems, Inc.)

**American College of Life Underwriters**
- Insurance Literature. (pub. by Special Libraries
Association. Insurance Division)

**American College of Neuropsychiatrists**
- American College of Neuropsychiatrists. Bulletin.
(pub. by Oswego Press)

**American College of Nurse-Midwives**
1000 Vermont Ave., N.W., Washington, DC 20005.
- Journal of Nurse-Midwifery. q. ISSN 0091-2182

**American College of Nursing Home Administrators**
8641 Colesville Rd., Silver Spring, MD 20910.
- Nursing Homes. bi-m. ISSN 0029-649X

**American College of Obstetricians and Gynecologists**
One East Wacker Drive, Chicago, IL 60601.
- A C O G Newsletter. m. ISSN 0400-048X
- A C O G Technical Bulletin. q. ISSN 0569-3950
- Obstetrics and Gynecology. (pub. by Harper &
Row Publishers, Inc. Medical Department)

**American College of Orgonomy**
- Journal of Orgonomy. (pub. by Orgonomic
Publications Inc.)

**American College of Osteopathic Surgeons**
Ponce American Building, Suite 21, 4601 Ponce de
Leon Boulevard, Coral Gables, FL 33146.
- A C O S News. m. ISSN 0001-0790

**American College of Physicians**
4200 Pine St., Philadelphia, PA 19104.
- American College of Physicians. Bulletin. m. ISSN
0002-8010
- American College of Physicians. Directory.
biennial.
- Annals of Internal Medicine. m. ISSN 0003-4819

**American College of Preventive Medicine**
801 Old Lancaster Rd., Bryn Mawr, PA 19010.
- American College of Preventive Medicine
Newsletter. q. ISSN 0002-8029

**American College of Probate Counsel**
10964 West Pico Boulevard, Los Angeles, CA
90064.
- Probate Lawyer. ISSN 0094-999X
- Probate Notes. q. ISSN 0098-2229

**American College of Psychiatrists**
- American College of Psychiatrists. Papers
Presented at the Annual Meeting. (pub. by
Brunner-Mazel, Inc.)

**American College of Radiology**
c/o Ed. Charles Honaker, 20 N. Wacker Drive,
Chicago, IL 60606.
- American College of Radiology Bulletin. m. ISSN
0002-8037

**American College of Sports Medicine**
1440 Monroe St., Madison, WI 53706.
- Medicine and Science in Sports. q. ISSN 0025-
7990

**American College of Surgeons**
55 East Erie St., Chicago, IL 60611.
- American College of Surgeons. Bulletin. m. ISSN
0002-8045
- Forum on Fundamental Surgical Problems. a.
ISSN 0071-8041
- Surgery, Gynecology & Obstetrics. (pub. by
Franklin H. Martin Memorial Foundation)

**American College of Veterinary Pathologists**
c/o N.F. Chevelle, Treas., NADL Box 70, Ames,
IA 50010.
- Veterinary Pathology. bi-m. ISSN 0300-9858

**American College of Veterinary Toxicologists**
Comparative Toxicology Laboratory, Kansas State
University, Manhattan, KS 66506.
- Veterinary and Human Toxicology. q.

**American College Testing Program**
Box 168, Iowa City, IA 52240.
- A C T Monograph Series. irreg., no. 15, 1974.
ISSN 0065-7832
- A C T Research Report Series. irreg., approx. 6
per yr.
- ACTivity. q. ISSN 0001-7620
- American College Testing Program. Annual
Report. a. ISSN 0517-0680
- American College Testing Program. Handbook for
Financial Aid Administrators. a. ISSN 0094-2227

**American Collegiate Employment Institute. Summer
Employment Division**
3223 Ernst St., Franklin Park, IL 60131.
- Collegiate Summer Employment Guide. a.

**American Committee on Italian Migration**
9 E. 35 St., New York, NY 10016.
- A C I M Dispatch. 4 per yr.

**American Communications Network**
308 N. Washington St., Knightstown, IN 46148.
- Brian Bex Report. 2 per mo. ISSN 0045-2793

**American Comparative Literature Association**
Dept. of Comparative Literature, State Univ. of
New York at Binghamton, Binghamton, NY 13901.
- American Comparative Literature Association
Newsletter. s-a. ISSN 0002-8053

**American Concrete Institute**
Box 19150, Redford Station, Detroit, MI 48219.
- A C I Bibliography. irreg., no. 11, 1977. ISSN
0084-6325
- A C I Directory. irreg.
- A C I Manual of Concrete Practice. irreg., latest
1977. ISSN 0065-7875
- A C I Monograph. (pub. by Iowa State University
Press)
- A C I Supplemental Index. irreg., latest 1970 for
1959-68.
- American Concrete Institute. Compilation. irreg.
ISSN 0517-0745
- American Concrete Institute. Journal. m. ISSN
0002-8061
- American Concrete Institute. Proceedings. a.
- American Concrete Institute. Special Publication.
irreg, latest 1976. ISSN 0065-7891
- Concrete Abstracts. bi-m.

**American Conference of Academic Deans**
c/o Frederic D. Ogden, Ed., Eastern Kentucky
University, Richmond, KY 40475.
- American Conference of Academic Deans.
Proceedings. a. ISSN 0065-7905

**American Conference of Governmental Industrial
Hygienists**
P.O. Box 1937, Cincinnati, OH 45201.
- American Conference of Governmental Industrial
Hygienists. Transactions of the Annual Meeting.
a.

**American Conference of Governmental Industrial
Hygienists. Committee on Industrial Ventilation**
Box 16153, Lansing, MI 48901.
- Industrial Ventilation; a Manual of Recommended
Practice. biennial. ISSN 0569-4043

**American Conference of Therapeutic Self Help, Self
Health, Social Clubs A.C.T.**
- Constructive Action for Good Health. (pub. by
A.C.T.-Action Press)

**American Congregational Association**
- Congregational Library. Bulletin. (pub. by
Congregational Library)

**American Congress of Rehabilitation Medicine**
30 N. Michigan Ave., Chicago, IL 60602.
- Archives of Physical Medicine and Rehabilitation.
m. ISSN 0003-9993 (Co-Sponsor: American
Academy of Physical Medicine and
Rehabilitation)

**American Congress on Surveying & Mapping**
430 Woodward Bldg., 733 15th St. N.W.,
Washington, DC 20005.
- American Cartographer. s-a. ISSN 0094-1689
- American Congress on Surveying and Mapping.
Papers from the Annual Meetings. a. ISSN 0065-
7913
- American Congress on Surveying and Mapping.
Technical Monographs. irreg. ISSN 0065-7921
- Surveying and Mapping; devoted to the
advancement of the sciences of surveying and
mapping. q. ISSN 0039-6273

**American Congress on Surveying and Mapping.
Arizona Section**
- Arizona Land Surveyors Conference. Proceedings.
(pub. by University of Arizona. Civil Engineering
Department)

**American Consulting Engineers Council**
1155 15th St., N.W., Washingto, DC 20005.
- International Engineering Directory. biennial.
ISSN 0074-5774
- Last Word. m.

**American Contract Bridge League, Inc.**
2200 Democrat Rd., Memphis, TN 38116.
- Contract Bridge Bulletin. m. ISSN 0010-7840

**American Coptic Association**
Box 9119, G. L. S., Jersey City, NJ 07304.
- Copts. irreg. ISSN 0360-649X

**American Correctional Association**
4321 Hartwick Rd., L208, College Park, MD 20740.
- American Correctional Association. Annual
Congress of Correction. Proceedings. a. ISSN
0065-7948
- American Correctional Association. Resource
Document. irreg, no. 7, 1976.
- American Journal of Correction. bi-m. ISSN 0002-
9203
- Directory - Juvenile and Adult Correctional
Departments, Institutions, Agencies, and Paroling
Authorities of the United States and Canada. a.

**American Corrective Therapy Association**
c/o Ed. Alton Hodges, 4910 Bayou Vista, Houston,
TX 77091.
- American Corrective Therapy Journal. bi-m. ISSN
0002-8088

**American Council for Curricular Evaluation**
829 Woodruff Drive, Ballwin, MO 63011.
- A. C. C. E. Reporter. 10 per yr. ISSN 0001-0618

**American Council for Judaism**
309 Fifth Ave., New York, NY 10016.
- American Council for Judaism. Special Interest
Report. m.
- Brief. q. ISSN 0006-9922

**American Council for Nationalities Service**
20 W. 40th St., New York, NY 10018.
- Ethnic Press in the United States; lists of foreign
language, nationality and ethnic newspapers and
periodicals in the U. S. irreg.
- Interpreter Releases; an information service on
immigration, naturalization and related problems.
w. ISSN 0020-9686

**American Council of Independent Laboratories Inc.**
1725 K St., N.W., Washington, DC 20006.
- A C I L Bulletin. q. ISSN 0001-0723
- American Council of Independent Laboratories.
Directory. biennial. ISSN 0065-7964

**American Council of Industrial Arts Teacher
Educators**
- Industrial Arts for the Elementary School.
Yearbook. (pub. by McKnight Publishing
Company)

**American Council of Learned Societies**
345 E. 46th St., New York, NY 10017.
- A C L S Newsletter. q. ISSN 0001-074X
- American Council of Learned Societies. Report. a.
ISSN 0065-7972
- Directory of American Scholars. (pub. by R. R.
Bowker Company. Jaques Cattell Press)

**American Council of Life Insurance**
1850 K St. N.W., Washington, DC 20006.
- Family Security Features. q. ISSN 0014-7400
- Family Security Newsletter. q.
- Institute of Life Insurance. Trend Analysis Program. Trend Report. s-a.
- Life Insurance Fact Book. a. ISSN 0075-9406
- Teaching Topics. q. (Co-sponsor: Health Insurance Institute)

**American Council of Polish Cultural Clubs**
6300 Lakeview Drive, Falls Church, VA 22041.
- Quarterly Review of Polish Heritage. q.

**American Council of Teachers of Uncommonly Taught Asian Languages**
c/o D. W. Dellinger, 4403 Midstone Lane, Fairfax, VA 22030.
- A C T U A L. Newsletter. s-a.

**American Council of the Blind**
National Office, 1211 Connecticut Ave. N.W. Suite 506, Washington, DC 20036.
- Braille Forum. m. ISSN 0006-8772

**American Council of Voluntary Agencies for Foreign Service, Inc**
- T A I C H Category Report: Development Assistance Programs of U.S. Non-Profit Organizations Abroad. (pub. by Technical Assistance Information Clearing House)
- T A I C H Country Report: Development Assistance Programs of U.S. Non-Profit Organizations. (pub. by Technical Assistance Information Clearing House)
- T A I C H News. (pub. by Technical Assistance Information Clearing House)

**American Council on Consumer Interests**
c/o Karen Stein, Exec. Dir., 162 Stanley Hall, University of Missouri, Columbia, MO 65201.
- American Council on Consumer Interests.Newsletter. 9 per yr.(Sept.-May) ISSN 0010-9975
- American Council on Consumer Interests. Proceedings of the Annual Conference. a.
- Consumer Education Forum. 3 per yr. ISSN 0010-7158
- Journal of Consumer Affairs. s-a. ISSN 0022-0078

**American Council on Education**
One Dupont Circle, N.W., Washington, DC 20036.
- Accredited Institutions of Post Secondary Education. a.
- American Council on Education. Annual Report. a.
- American Council on Education. Brief Statement of Programs and Activities. a.
- American Council on Education. Meeting. Papers. a.
- American Council on Education. Office on Educational Credit. Newsletter. s-a.
- American Council on Education. Policy Analyses Service Reports. irreg.
- American Council on Education. President's Letter. q.
- American Junior Colleges. quadrennial. ISSN 0065-9029
- American Universities and Colleges. quadrennial. ISSN 0066-0922
- Educational Record. q. ISSN 0013-1873
- Fact Book on Higher Education. 4 per yr. ISSN 0014-6501
- Higher Education and National Affairs. 40 per yr. ISSN 0018-1579
- International Interaction. m. (prep. by its International Education Project)
- O L C Information Sheet. (Overseas Liaison Committee) m.
- R D N Bulletin. (Rural Development Network) q. (prep. by its Overseas Liaison Committee)

**American Council on Education for Journalism**
c/o Sec.-Treas. Milton Gross, University of Missouri, School of Journalism, Columbia, MO 65201.
- Education for a Journalism Career. a.

**American Council on Industrial Arts Teacher Education**
- American Council on Industrial Arts Teacher Education. Yearbook. (pub. by McKnight Publishing Company)

**American Council on Pharmaceutical Education**
77 W. Washington St., Chicago, IL 60602.
- Accredited Colleges of Pharmacy. a. ISSN 0065-7980

**American Council on the Teaching of Foreign Languages**
2 Park Ave., New York, NY 10016.
- A C T F L Annual Review of Foreign Language Education. (pub. by National Textbook Co.)
- Foreign Language Annals. 6 per yr. ISSN 0015-718X

**American Country Life Association, Inc.**
2118 S. Summit Ave., Sioux Falls, SD 57105.
- American Country Life Association. Proceedings of the Annual Conference. a. ISSN 0065-7999

**American Crafts Council**
44 W. 53 St., New York, NY 10019.
- A C C Directory of Craft Courses. a. (prep. by its Research and Education Department)
- Contemporary Crafts Market Place. (pub. by R.R. Bowker Company)
- Craft Horizons. bi-m. ISSN 0011-0744

**American Crafts Council. Northeast Regional Assembly**
60 Glendale Rd., Glenbrook, CT 06906.
- Northeast Gazette. q.

**American Cryptogram Association**
9504 Forest Rd., Bethesda, MD 20014.
- Cryptogram. bi-m. ISSN 0045-9151

**American Crystallographic Association**
335 East 45th St., New York, NY 10017
(Subscr. to: Polycrystal Book Service, P.O. Box 11567, Pittsburgh, Pa 15238)
- American Crystallographic Association. Monographs. irreg.; latest issue, 1971. ISSN 0514-8863
- American Crystallographic Association. Transactions. (pub. by Polycrystal Book Service)

**American Cultured Dairy Products Institute**
c/o Dr. James H. Martin, South Dakota State University, Dept. of Dairy Science, Brookings, SD 57006.
- Cultured Dairy Products Journal. q. ISSN 0045-9259

**American Cyanamid Co. Organic Chemical Division**
Bound Brook, NJ 08805.
- O. C. D. Diamond. m.

**American Cyanamid Co. Polymer & Chemicals Department**
Bound Brook, NJ 08805.
- Rubber Chem Lines. bi-m. ISSN 0035-9467

**American Daffodil Society, Inc.**
89 Chichester Road, New Canaan, CT 06840.
- Daffodil Journal. q. ISSN 0011-5290

**American Dahlia Society**
c/o Irene B. Owen, 345 Merritt Ave., Bergenfield, NJ 07621.
- American Dahlia Society. Bulletin. q. ISSN 0002-8150

**American Dairy Science Association**
113 N. Neil St., Champaign, IL 61820.
- Journal of Dairy Science. m. ISSN 0022-0302

**American Dance Guild, Inc.**
1619 Broadway, Rm. 603, New York, NY 10019.
- American Dance Guild Newsletter. 9 per yr. ISSN 0300-7448
- Dance Scope. s-a. ISSN 0011-6041

**American Dance Therapy Association, Inc.**
2000 Century Plaza, Suite 230, Columbia, MD 21044.
- A. D. T. A. Newsletter. 6 per yr.

**American Data Processing, Inc.**
22929 Industrial Dr. E., St. Clair Shores, MI 48080.
- Computer Yearbook. biennial. ISSN 0069-8180
- Who's Who in Data Processing. irreg. ISSN 0511-8956

**American Defense Preparedness Association**
819 Union Trust Bld., Washington, DC 20005.
- American Defense Preparedness Association. Annual Directory. a.
- National Defense; science - technology - management. bi-m. ISSN 0092-1491

**American Dental Assistants Association**
211 E. Chicago Ave. Suite 1224, Chicago, IL 60611.
- Dental Assistant. m. ISSN 0011-8508

**American Dental Association**
211 E. Chicago Ave., Chicago, IL 60611.
- A D A Leadership Bulletin. fortn.
- A D A News. s-m. ISSN 0001-0855
- Accepted Dental Therapeutics. biennial. ISSN 0065-079X
- American Dental Association. Annual Reports and Resolutions. a.
- American Dental Association. Council on Dental Education. Requirements and Registration Data: State Dental Examining Boards. a. ISSN 0065-8057
- American Dental Association. Journal. m. ISSN 0002-8177
- American Dental Directory. a. ISSN 0065-8073
- American Fund for Dental Health. (pub. by American Fund for Dental Education)
- Annual Report on Advanced Dental Education. a.
- Annual Report on Dental Auxiliary Education. a. ISSN 0084-6554 (prep. by its Division of Educational Measurements)
- Annual Report on Dental Education. a. ISSN 0065-8030 (prep. by its Division of Educational Measurements)
- Dental Abstracts. m. ISSN 0011-8486
- Dental Admission Testing Program. a. (prep. by its Division of Educational Measurements)
- Fluoridation Reporter. s-a. ISSN 0015-4717
- Guide to Dental Materials and Devices. biennial. ISSN 0093-9706
- Index to Dental Literature; an alphabetical author and subject index to dental literature. q (annual cumulation) ISSN 0019-3992 (prep. by its Bureau of Library Services)
- Journal of Dental Research. (pub. by Professional Publication Producers)
- Journal of Endodontics. m. (American Association of Endodontists)
- Journal of Oral Surgery. m. ISSN 0022-3255
- Oral Research Abstracts. m. ISSN 0030-4212
- Update in Oral Surgery. a.
- Update in Orthodontics. a.
- Update in Periodontics. a.

**American Dental Hygienists Association**
c/o Wilma Motley, Ed., 11 E. Chicago Ave., Chicago, IL 60611.
- Dental Hygiene. m. ISSN 0091-3979

**American Dental Society of Anesthesiology**
c/o Dr. Norman Trieger, Ed., Montefiore Hospital & Medical Center, 111 E. 210th St., Bronx, NY 10467.
- Anesthesia Progress. 6 per yr. ISSN 0003-3006

**American Dexter Cattle Association**
707 W. Water St., Decorah, IA 52101.
- American Dexter Cattle Association. Herd Book. irreg., 1966, vol. iv. ISSN 0065-8081

**American Diabetes Association, Inc.**
600 Fifth Ave., New York, NY 10020.
- Diabetes. m. ISSN 0012-1797
- Diabetes Forecast. bi-m.

**American Dialect Society**
- American Speech. (pub. by Columbia University Press)

**American Dietetic Association**
430 N. Michigan Ave., Chicago, IL 60611.
- American Dietetic Association. Annual Report and Proceedings. a.
- American Dietetic Association. Journal. m. ISSN 0002-8223

**American Directory of Obstetricians and Gynecologists**
7217 Kingston Pike, Knoxville, TN 37919.
- American Directory of Obstetricians and Gynecologists. biennial. ISSN 0517-1113

**American District Telegraph Co.**
155 Sixth Ave., New York, NY 10013.
- A D T Transmitter. q. ISSN 0001-0960

**American Dove Association**
c/o Richard Johnson, Ed., 309 E. Broadway, Salem, NJ 08079.
- American Dove Association. Monthly Bulletin. m.

**American Economic Association**
1313 21st Ave. So., Nashville, TN 37212.
- American Economic Association. Directory of Members. irreg.
- American Economic Review. q. ISSN 0002-8282

- Index of Economic Articles in Journals and Collective Volumes. irreg; no. 11, 1972. (Order from: Richard D. Irwin, Inc., 1818 Ridge Rd., Homewood, Il 60430)
- Job Openings for Economists. bi-m.
- Journal of Economic Literature. q. ISSN 0022-0515

**American Education Finance Association**
- Journal of Education Finance. (pub. by Institute for Educational Finance)

**American Educational and Historical Film Center**
St. Davids, PA 19087.
- American Film Review. a. ISSN 0065-8308

**American Educational Research Association**
1126 Sixteenth St., N.W., Washington, DC 20036.
- American Educational Research Association. Annual Meeting Paper and Symposia Abstracts. a. ISSN 0084-6341
- American Educational Research Journal. 4 per yr. ISSN 0002-8312
- Educational Researcher. m. ISSN 0013-189X
- Journal of Educational Statistics. (pub. by University of Iowa, Lindquist Center for Measurement)
- Review of Educational Research. q. ISSN 0034-6543
- Review of Research in Education. (pub. by F. E. Peacock Publishers)

**American Educational Research Association. Socialization to Adulthood**
c/o Edward Wynne, Editor, College of Education, University of Illinois, Chicago, IL 60680.
- Socializer. 5 per yr.

**American Educational Studies Association**
107 Quadrangle, Iowa State University, Ames, IA 50011.
- Educational Studies; a journal in the foundations of education. q. ISSN 0013-1946

**American Electrolysis Association**
- Electrolysis Digest. (pub. by Gordon Blackwell)

**American Electroplaters Society, Inc.**
1201 Louisiana Ave., Winter Park, FL 32789.
- Plating and Surface Finishing; electroplating, finishing of metals, organic finishing. m. ISSN 0360-3164

**American Elsevier Publishing Co.**
*see* Elsevier North-Holland, Inc., New York

**American Enka Co.**
Enka, NC 28728.
- Enka Voice. m.

**American Enterprise Institute for Public Policy Research**
1150 - 17th St. N.W., Washington, DC 20036.
- A E I Hoover Policy Studies. irreg. (Co-sponsor: Hoover Institution on War, Revolution and Peace)
- American Enterprise Institute for Public Policy Research. A E I Forums. irreg.
- American Enterprise Institute for Public Policy Research. A E I Studies. irreg.
- American Enterprise Institute for Public Policy Research. Legislative Analyses. irreg. (approx. 30 per yr.)
- American Enterprise Institute for Public Policy Research. Memorandum. q.
- American Enterprise Institute for Public Policy Research. Reprints. irreg.
- American Enterprise Institute for Public Policy Research. Review, Session of the Congress and Index of A E I Publications. a. ISSN 0360-165X

**American Entomological Institute**
5950 Warren Rd., Ann Arbor, MI 48105.
- American Entomological Institute. Contributions. irreg. (approx. 8 nos. per yr.)
- American Entomological Institute. Memoirs. irreg. ISSN 0065-8162

**American Entomological Society**
1900 Race St., Philadelphia, PA 19103.
- American Entomological Society. Memoirs. irreg. ISSN 0065-8170
- American Entomological Society. Transactions. q. ISSN 0002-8320
- Entomological News. m. ISSN 0013-872X

**American Ethical Union**
2 W. 64 St., New York, NY 10023.
- A E U Reports. q. ISSN 0001-1118
- Weis Ecology Center Bulletin. bi-m.

**American Ethnological Society**
- American Ethnological Society. Monographs. (pub. by West Publishing Co.)
- American Ethnological Society. Proceedings of Spring Meeting. (pub. by West Publishing Co.)

**American Express Co.**
65 Broadway, New York, NY 10006.
- Going Places. q.

**American Express International**
- Glimpse of London with American Express. (pub. by Warner Publicity Ltd. UK)

**American Express Publishing Corp.**
1350 Ave. of the Americas, New York, NY 10019.
- Travel & Leisure. m. ISSN 0041-2007

**American Farm Building Services, Inc.**
733 N. Van Buren, Milwaukee, WI 53202.
- Farm Building News. bi-m. ISSN 0014-7869

**American Farm Bureau Federation**
225 W. Touhy Ave., Park Ridge, IL 60068.
- Farm Bureau News. w.

**American Farm Youth Publishing Co.**
113 W. Main, Danville, IL 61832.
- American Farm Youth; the magazine for young farmers. m.(Sept-May) ISSN 0002-8401

**American Federation for Clinical Research**
- Clinical Research. (pub. by Charles B. Slack, Inc.)

**American Federation of Arts**
41 E. 65th St., New York, NY 10021.
- American Art Directory. (pub. by R. R. Bowker Company. Jaques Cattell Press)
- American Federation of Arts Program Catalogue. a.
- Who's Who in American Art. (pub. by R. R. Bowker Company. Jaques Cattell Press)

**American Federation of Astrologers**
6535 S. Rural Rd., Box 22040, Tempe, AZ 85282.
- American Federation of Astrologers Bulletin; today's astrologer. m.

**American Federation of Film Societies**
144 Bleecker St., New York, NY 10012.
- Film Society Bulletin. 9 per yr.

**American Federation of Government Employees, (AFL-CIO)**
1325 Mass. Ave., N.W., Washington, DC 20005.
- Government Standard. m. ISSN 0017-2669

**American Federation of Information Processing Societies**
210 Summit Ave., Montvale, NJ 07645.
- National Computer Conference and Exposition. (Proceedings) irreg. ISSN 0095-6880
- Summer Computer Simulation Conference. Proceedings; simulation of continuous systems. a. (Society for Computer Simulation)
- U S A-Japan Computer Conference. Proceedings. a. (Co-sponsor: Information Processing Society of Japan)

**American Federation of Jewish Fighters, Camp Inmates and Nazi Victims, Inc.**
505 Fifth Avenue, New York, NY 10017.
- Martyrdom and Freedom. bi-m.

**American Federation of Jews from Central Europe, Inc.**
1241 Broadway, New York, NY 10001.
- American Federation of Jews from Central Europe. Proceedings. a.

**American Federation of Musicians Local 47**
A F L-C I O, 817 N. Vine St., Los Angeles, CA 90038.
- Overture. m. ISSN 0030-7556

**American Federation of Musicians Local 325**
A F L-C I O, 1717 Morena Blvd., San Diego, CA 92110.
- American Federation of Musicans Local 325. m. ISSN 0036-407X

**American Federation of Musicians of the United States and Canada**
1500 Broadway, New York, NY 10036.
- International Musician. m. ISSN 0020-8051

**American Federation of State, County & Municipal Employees, AFL-CIO**
Publications Department, 1625 L St., N.W., Suite 1115, Washington, DC 20036.
- Public Employee. m.

**American Federation of State County and Municipal Employees, AFL-CIO. District Council 37**
140 Park Place, New York, NY 10007.
- Public Employee Press. s-m (m. Jul-Aug.) ISSN 0033-345X

**American Federation of Teachers**
11 Dupont Circle N.W., Washington, DC 20036.
- A F T-in-Action. w.
- A F T in the News. m.
- A F T Issues Bulletin. irreg.
- American Educator. 4 per yr.
- American Federation of Teachers. Convention Proceedings (Abridged) a.
- American Teacher. 9 per yr. ISSN 0003-1380
- Changing Education. m. Sept.-Jun. ISSN 0009-1413

**American Federation of Teachers. Colleges and Universities Department**
11 Dupont Circle N.W., Washington, DC 20036.
- On Campus.

**American Federation of Teachers. University of California Council**
2527 Dwight Way, Berkeley, CA 94704.
- University Guardian. 4 per yr.

**American Federation of Teachers. Workers Education Local 189**
c/o Lee Balliet, Treas., Rt. 1, Box 146, Independence, WV 26374.
- Directory of Labor Education. a.
- Labor Education News. q. ISSN 0023-6535
- Labor Education Viewpoints. q. ISSN 0023-6543

**American Federation of Technical Engineers. Local 195**
c/o Robert R. Turner, 76 Highfield Lane, Nutley, NJ 07110.
- Traveler. q. ISSN 0041-2112

**American Federation of Television and Radio Artists**
1350 Avenue of the Americas, New York, NY 10019.
- American Federation of Television and Radio Artists. A F T R A. q. ISSN 0044-7676

**American Fern Society**
Botany Dept., N H B No. 166, Smithsonian Institution, Washington, DC 20560.
- American Fern Journal. q. ISSN 0002-8444

**American Fertility Society**
1608 13th Ave. S.E., Ste. 101, Birmingham, AL 35205.
- Fertility and Sterility. m. ISSN 0015-0282

**American Field Publishing Co.**
222 W.Adams St., Chicago, IL 60606.
- American Field; the sportsman's newspaper of America. w. ISSN 0002-8452

**American Film Institute**
John F. Kennedy Center for Performing Arts, Washington, DC 20566.
- American Film; a journal of the film and television arts. m. ISSN 0361-4751
- American Film Institute Theater Brochure. m.
- Guide to College Courses in Film and Television. biennial from 1970 per 71. ISSN 0072-8284

**American Finance Association**
c/o Robert A. Kavesh, Graduate School of Business Admin., New York Univ., 100 Trinity Pl., New York, NY 10006.
- Journal of Finance. 5 per yr. ISSN 0022-1082

**American First Day Cover Society**
Box 23, Elberon, NJ 07740.
- First Days. bi-m.

**American Fisheries Society**
5410 Grosvenor Lane, Bethesda, MD 20014.
- American Fisheries Society. Special Publications. irreg.

- American Fisheries Society. Transactions. q. ISSN 0002-8487
- Fisheries. bi-m.

**American Flint Glass Workers' Union of North America, AFL-CIO**
Albert Vottery, 1440 S. Byrne Rd., Toledo, OH 43614.
- American Flint. m. ISSN 0002-8525

**American Folklife Society**
R.D. 2, Oley, PA 19547.
- American Folklife. m. (exc. Jun. - Sep.) ISSN 0092-5519

**American Folklore Society, Inc.**
1703 New Hampshire Ave., N.W., Washington, DC 20009.
- Journal of American Folklore. q. ISSN 0021-8715

**American Footwear Industries Association**
Suite 900, 1611 N. Kent St., Arlington, VA 22209.
- Footwear Manual. a.

**American Forage and Grassland Council**
121 Dantzler Court, Lexington, KY 40503.
- American Forage and Grassland Council. Proceedings of the Research Industry Conference. a.
- Forage and Grassland Progress. q. ISSN 0015-6906

**American Forces Press Service**
Office of Information for the Armed Forces, 1117 N. 19th St., Arlington, VA 22209
(Subscriptions to: Supt. of Documents, Washington, DC 20402)
- Commanders Digest. w. ISSN 0010-2482 (U.S. Department of Defense)

**American Foreign Law Association**
Lewis University, College of Law, Glen Ellyn, IL 60137.
- American Foreign Law Association. Newsletter. m.(except Jul-Aug)

**American Foreign Service Association**
2101 E. St., N.W., Washington, DC 20037.
- Foreign Service Journal. m. ISSN 0015-7279

**American Forensic Association**
c/o Larry K. Hannah, Dept. of Speech, Eastern Montana College, Billings, MT 59101.
- American Forensic Association. Journal. q. ISSN 0002-8533

**American Forest Institute**
1619 Massachusetts Ave. N.W., Washington, DC 20036.
- GreenAmerica. q. ISSN 0090-8088 (Forest Industries Council)
- Midwestern Tree Farm News. q.
- Southern Tree Farm News. q.
- Tree Farm News. q.
- Western Tree Farm News. q.

**American Forestry Association**
1319-18th St., N.W., Washington, DC 20036.
- American Forests. m. ISSN 0002-8541

**American Foundation for the Blind, Inc.**
15 W. 16 St, New York, NY 10011.
- American Foundation for the Blind. Annual Report. a. ISSN 0065-8359
- American Foundation for the Blind Newsletter. q. ISSN 0002-855X
- Directory of Agencies Serving the Visually Handicapped in the U.S. biennial.
- Journal of Visual Impairment and Blindness. m.(Sept-June) ISSN 0145-482X
- Washington Report. bi-m. ISSN 0043-0722

**American Foundation for the Blind, Inc. International Research Information Service**
15 W. 16th St., New York, NY 10011.
- American Foundation for the Blind. International Research Information Service. Index of Publications Issued by I R I S. a.

**American Foundation for the Study of Man**
- American Foundation for the Study of Man. Publications. (pub. by Johns Hopkins University Press)

**American Foundrymen's Society, Inc**
Golf & Wolf Rds, Des Plaines, IL 60016.
- American Foundrymen's Society. Transactions. a. ISSN 0065-8375

- International Cast Metals Journal. q. ISSN 0008-7467
- Modern Casting. m. ISSN 0026-7562

**American Fraternal Union**
111 S. 4th Ave. E., Ely, MN 55731.
- New Era/Nova Doba. m. ISSN 0028-5021

**American Freedom from Hunger Foundation**
1625 Eye St., N. W., Suite 719, Washington, DC 20006.
- American Freedom from Hunger Foundation. Bulletin. m.

**American Friends of Brazil**
Box 2279 Sta. A, Berkeley, Ca 94702.
- Brazilian Information Bulletin. q.

**American Friends of the Alliance Israelite Universelle Inc.**
61 Broadway, New York, NY 10006.
- Alliance Review. ISSN 0002-6093

**American Friends Service Committee, Inc.**
1501 Cherry St., Philadelphia, PA 19102.
- American Friends Service Committee. Annual Report. a. ISSN 0071-9617
- People's Yellow Pages. (pub. by Vocations for Social Change, Inc.)
- Quaker Service Bulletin. 3 per yr. ISSN 0033-5096

**American Friends Service Committee, Inc. New England Regional Office**
2161 Massachusetts Ave., Cambridge, MA 02140.
- Peacework; New England peace movement newsletter. 11 per yr.

**American Friends Service Committee, Inc. Pennsylvania Pretrial Justice Program**
1300 Fifth Ave., Pittsburgh, PA 15219.
- Pretrial Justice Quarterly. q. ISSN 0093-111X

**American Frozen Food Institute**
919 - 18th Street N.W., Washington, D.C.
- American Frozen Food Institute. Membership Directory. a. ISSN 0084-635X
- American Frozen Food Institute. Weekly Report. w.(48 per yr.)
- Frozen Food Report. m.

**American Fund for Dental Education**
211 E. Chicago Ave., Chicago, IL 60611.
- American Fund for Dental Health. a. (American Dental Association) (Co-sponsors: American Association for Dental Schools; American Dental Trade Association)

**American G I Forum of the United States**
44 N. Jackson Ave. F-23, San Jose, CA 95116.
- Forumeer. m. ISSN 0015-8577

**American Gas Association**
1515 Wilson Blvd., Arlington, VA 22209.
- American Gas Association. Operating Section. Proceedings. a. ISSN 0362-4994
- American Gas Association Monthly. 11 per yr. ISSN 0002-8584
- Liquified Natural Gas. (pub. by U.S. National Bureau of Standards. Cryogenic Data Center)
- Synthetic Pipeline Gas Symposium. Proceedings. irreg. (Co-sponsors: U.S. Energy Research & Development Administration; International Gas Union)

**American Gas Association. Department of Research & Engineering**
1515 Wilson Blvd., Arlington, VA 22209.
- American Gas Association. Research and Development. a. ISSN 0091-2786

**American Gas Association. Statistics Directorate**
1515 Wilson Blvd., Arlington, VA 22209.
- American Gas Association Rate Service. m.
- Gas Facts. a.
- Gas Utility and Pipeline Industry Projections. irreg. ISSN 0065-8391
- Historical Statistics of the Gas Industry. irreg. ISSN 0073-2656

**American Gastroenterological Association**
- Gastroenterology. (pub. by Williams & Wilkins Co.)

**American Gear Manufacturers Association**
1330 Massachusetts Ave. N.W., Washington, DC 20005.
- A. G. M. A. Directory. irreg. ISSN 0572-502X

**American Gem Society**
3142 Wilshire Blvd., Los Angeles, CA 90010.
- American Gem Society. Member Suppliers. a. ISSN 0065-8405

**American Genetic Association**
1028 Connecticut Ave., N.W., Washington, DC 20036.
- Journal of Heredity. bi-m. ISSN 0022-1503

**American Geographical Society**
Broadway at 156 St., New York, NY 10032.
- American Geographical Society of New York. Occasional Publication. irreg., 1969, no. 4. ISSN 0065-8413
- American Geographical Society of New York. Research Series. irreg. ISSN 0065-8421
- American Geographical Society of New York. Special Publication. irreg. ISSN 0065-843X
- Current Geographical Publications; additions to the research catalog of the American Geographical Society. m. ISSN 0011-3514
- Focus (New York, 1950) bi-m. ISSN 0015-5004
- Geographical Review. q. ISSN 0016-7428
- Icefield Ranges Research Project Scientific Results. irreg. ISSN 0073-4373 (Co-Sponsor: Arctic Institute of North America)
- Soviet Geography: Review and Translation. (pub. by Scripta Publishing Co.)
- Studies in Urban Geography. irreg. ISSN 0586-5107

**American Geological Institute**
5205 Leesburg Pike, Falls Church, VA 22041.
- American Geological Institute. Student Enrollment in Geoscience Departments. irreg. ISSN 0362-5990
- Geoscience Information Society. Proceedings. a. ISSN 0072-1409 (Geoscience Information Society)
- Geotimes; news of the earth sciences. 12 per yr. ISSN 0016-8556
- International Geology Review. m. ISSN 0020-6814

**American Geophysical Union**
1909 K St., N.W., Washington, DC 20006.
- Academy of Sciences of the U S S R. Izvestiya. Atmospheric and Oceanic Physics. m. ISSN 0001-4338 (Co-publisher: American Meteorological Society)
- Academy of Sciences of the U S S R. Izvestiya. Physics of the Solid Earth. m. ISSN 0001-4354 (Co-publisher: Geological Society of America)
- Academy of Sciences of the U S S R. Oceanology. bi-m. ISSN 0001-4370
- American Geophysical Union. Geophysical Monograph Series. irreg., no. 19, 1974. ISSN 0065-8448
- Antarctic Research Series. irreg., no. 22, 1974. ISSN 0066-4634
- Eos. m.
- Geodesy, Mapping and Photogrammetry. 4 per yr. (Co-publishers: American Congress of Surveying and Mapping; American Society of Photogrammetry)
- Geomagnetism and Aeronomy. bi-m. ISSN 0016-7932
- Geophysical Research Letters. m. ISSN 0094-8276
- Geotectonics. bi-m. ISSN 0016-8521 (Co-publisher: Geological Society of America)
- Journal of Geophysical Research. m. ISSN 0022-1406
- Radio Science. bi-m. ISSN 0048-6604
- Reviews of Geophysics & Space Physics. 4 per yr. ISSN 0034-6853
- Soviet Hydrology: Selected Papers. q. ISSN 0038-5425
- Water Resources Monographs. irreg., no. 4, 1977.
- Water Resources Research. bi-m. ISSN 0043-1397

**American Geriatrics Society**
10 Columbus Circle, New York, NY 10019.
- American Geriatrics Society. Journal. m. ISSN 0002-8614
- Geriatrics. (pub. by Lancet Publications, Inc.)

**American Goat Society, Inc.**
1606 Colorado St., Manhattan, KS 66502.
- American Goat Society. Year Book. a. ISSN 0065-8456
- Voice of A G S. bi-m. ISSN 0042-8078

**American Gold News**
c/o Cecil Helms, Ed., Box 457, Ione (Amador Cy.), CA 95640.
- American Gold News. m. ISSN 0002-8657

**American Group Practice Association**
20 S. Quaker Lane, Alexandria, VA 22314.
- American Group Practice Association Directory.
  a. ISSN 0098-2377
- Group Practice. bi-m. ISSN 0017-4726

**American Group Psychotherapy Association**
- International Journal of Group Psychotherapy.
  (pub. by International Universities Press, Inc.)

**American Guernsey Cattle Club**
70 Main St., Peterborough, NH 03458.
- Guernsey Breeders' Journal. m. ISSN 0017-5110

**American Guild of Musical Artists**
1841 Broadway, New York, NY 10023.
- Agmazine. q. ISSN 0002-0990

**American Guild of Organists**
630 Fifth Ave., Suite 2010, New York, NY.10020.
- Music; the AGO and RCCO magazine. m. ISSN
  0027-4208 (Co-sponsor: Royal Canadian College
  of Organists)

**American Guild of Organists. New York City Chapter**
456 W. 23d St., New York, NY 10011.
- A G O Times. q. ISSN 0362-5907

**American Guild of Variety Artists**
1540 Broadway, New York, NY 10036.
- A G V A Newsletter. irreg.

**American Gynecological Society**
c/o Dept. Ob/Gyn., Center for the Health Sciences,
U.C.L.A. School of Medicine, Los Angeles, CA
90024.
- American Gynecological Society. Transactions of
  the A G S. a. ISSN 0065-8480
- American Journal of Obstetrics and Gynecology.
  (pub. by C. V. Mosby Co.)

**American Hackney Horse Society**
- Hackney Journal. (pub. by Hackney Publications
  Inc.)

**American Handicap**
558 E. 8th St, Sheridan, WY 82801.
- American Handicap. q.

**American Harp Society, Inc.**
3210 56th St., Lubbock, TX 79413.
- American Harp Journal. s-a. ISSN 0002-869X

**American Health Care Association**
1200 15th St., N. W., Washington, DC 20005.
- A H C A Weekly Notes. w.
- American Health Care Association. Journal. bi-m.
  ISSN 0360-4969
- Bedside Care. q.
- Sharing and Caring. bi-m.

**American Health Foundation**
- Preventive Medicine. (pub. by Academic Press,
  Inc.)

**American Heart Association. Committee on Scientific
Sessions Program**
44 E. 23 St., New York, NY 10010.
- American Heart Association. Scientific Sessions.
  Abstracts. a. ISSN 0065-8502

**American Heart Association. Council on
Cardiovascular Surgery**
44 E. 23 St., New York, NY 10010.
- Cardiovascular Surgery. a. ISSN 0069-0406

**American Heart Association, Inc.**
7320 Greenville Ave., Dallas, TX 75231.
- American Heart Association. Monographs. irreg.,
  no. 44, 1974. ISSN 0065-8499
- Cardiovascular Nursing. bi-m. ISSN 0008-6355
- Circulation. m. ISSN 0009-7322
- Circulation. Supplement. irreg. ISSN 0069-4193
- Circulation Research. m. ISSN 0009-7330
- Circulation Research. Supplement. irreg. ISSN
  0069-4185
- Hypertension Series. a. ISSN 0073-425X
- Modern Concepts of Cardiovascular Disease. m.
  ISSN 0026-7600
- Recurring Bibliography of Hypertension. bi-m.
  ISSN 0090-1326 (Co-sponsor: U.S. National
  Library of Medicine)
- Stroke: a Journal of Cerebral Circulation. bi-m.
  ISSN 0039-2499

**American Heart Association, Inc. New York State
Affiliate**
3 West 29th St., New York, NY 10001.
- Cardiac Rehabilitation. q. ISSN 0045-5741

**American Helicopter Society, Inc**
1325 18th St., N.W., Washington, NY 10017.
- American Helicopter Society. Journal. q. ISSN
  0002-8711
- American Helicopter Society. National Forum.
  Proceedings. a. ISSN 0065-8510
- Vertiflite. bi-m. ISSN 0042-4455

**American Hellenic Educational Progressive
Associations**
- A H E P A N. (pub. by Order of Ahepa)

**American Helvetia Philatelic Society**
c/o Robert C. Ross, Ed., 28 Kenmore Pl., Glen
Rock, NJ 07452.
- Tell. m. except Jul.-Aug.

**American Hemerocallis Society**
Signal Mountain, TN 37377.
- Hemerocallis Journal; daylily gardener's magazine.
  q. ISSN 0018-0297

**American Heraldic Challenger-Informer**
Rte.1, Box 124A, Crockett, TX 75835.
- American Heraldic Challenger-Informer. irreg.

**American Hereford Association**
- American Hereford Journal. (pub. by Hereford
  Publications, Inc.)

**American Heritage Publishing Co., Inc.**
(Subsidiary of: McGraw-Hill, Inc.)
1221 Avenue of Americas, New York, NY 10020.
- American Heritage; the magazine of history. bi-m.
  ISSN 0002-8738 (American Association for State
  and Local History) (Co-Sponsor: Society of
  American Historians)
- American Heritage Biographies. irreg.
- American Heritage Index. a.
- Americana. bi-m. ISSN 0090-9114 (American
  Heritage Society)
- Horizon. q. ISSN 0018-4977

**American Heritage Society**
- Americana. (pub. by American Heritage
  Publishing Co., Inc.)

**American Histadrut Cultural Exchange Institute**
33 E. 67th St., New York, NY 10021.
- American Histadrut Cultural Exchange Institute.
  Annual Arden House Conference. Proceedings. a.
  ISSN 0065-8545
- American Histadrut Cultural Exchange Institute.
  Bulletin. 2 per yr. ISSN 0002-8754
- American Histadrut Cultural Exchange Institute.
  Round Table Pamphlet Series. irreg., 1972, no. 8.
  ISSN 0065-8553

**American Historical Association**
400 A St., S. E., Washington, DC 20003.
- A. H. A. Newsletter. m. ISSN 0001-138X
- American Historical Association. Annual Report.
  a. ISSN 0065-8561
- American Historical Review. 5 per yr. ISSN 0002-
  8762
- Discussions on Teaching. irreg.
- Recent Published Articles. 3 per yr.

**American Historical Association. Conference Group
for Central European History**
- Central European History. (pub. by Emory
  University)

**American Historical Association. Conference on Latin
American History**
- Hispanic American Historical Review. (pub. by
  Duke University Press)

**American Historical Association. Pacific Coast
Branch**
- Pacific Historical Review. (pub. by University of
  California Press)

**American Historical Society of Germans from Russia.**
615 D St., Lincoln, NE 68502.
- American Historical Society of Germans from
  Russia. Work Paper. 3 per yr.

**American Hoist & Derrick Co.**
63 S. Robert St., St. Paul, MN 55107.
- American Crosby Clipper. bi-m. ISSN 0002-8134

**American Home Economics Association**
2010 Massachusetts Ave. N.W., Washington, Dc
20036.
- A H E A Action. bi-m.
- American Home Economics Association.
  Institution Administration. a.
- American Home Economics Association. Textiles
  and Clothing Section. Textile Handbook. irreg.
  ISSN 0065-8588
- Handbook of Food Preparation. irreg., 7th, 1975.
- Home Economics in Institutions Granting
  Bachelors or Higher Degrees. biennial. ISSN
  0073-3105
- Home Economics Research Abstracts. a. ISSN
  0018-4020
- Home Economics Research Journal. q. ISSN
  0046-7774
- Journal of Home Economics. bi-m. ISSN 0022-
  1570
- Titles of Dissertations and Theses Completed in
  Home Economics. a. ISSN 0082-4534

**American Home Publishing Co., Inc.**
641 Lexington Ave., New York, NY 10022.
- American Home. m. ISSN 0002-8789

**American Horticultural Society**
Mt. Vernon, VA 22121.
- American Horticultural Society News and Views.
  6 per yr. ISSN 0002-8819
- American Horticulturist. bi-m.
- Directory of American Horticulture. irreg. ISSN
  0417-5522
- National Junior Horticultural Association.
  Newsletter. (pub. by National Junior Horticultural
  Association)

**American Hospital Association**
840 N. Lake Shore Dr., Chicago, IL 60611.
- American Hospital Association. Guide to the
  Health Care Field. a. ISSN 0094-8969
- American Hospital Association. House of
  Delegates. Proceedings. s-a.
- Cross-Reference. bi-m. ISSN 0045-9100
- Hospital Literature Index. q. ISSN 0018-5736
- Hospital Statistics; Data from American Hospital
  Association Annual Survey. a. ISSN 0090-6662
- Hospitals. s-m. ISSN 0018-5973
- Trustee. m. ISSN 0041-3674
- Volunteer Leader. q. ISSN 0005-1861
- Washington Developments; a report from the
  Washington Office of the American Hospital
  Association. fortn.

**American Hotel and Motel Association**
888 Seventh Ave., New York, NY 10019.
- American Hotel and Motel Association. Buyers
  Guide for Hotels & Motels. a.
- Directory of Hotel and Motel Systems. a.
- Hotel and Motel Red Book. (pub. by American
  Hotel Association Directory Corp.)

**American Hotel Association Directory Corp.**
888 Seventh Ave, New York, NY 10019.
- Hotel and Motel Red Book; hotels and motels
  which are members of the American Hotel and
  Motel Association; also many foreign hotels. a.
  ISSN 0073-3490 (American Hotel and Motel
  Association)
- Lodging. m. ISSN 0360-9235

**American Hotel Register Co.**
226 W. Ontario St., Chicago, IL 60610.
- Leahy's Hotel-Motel Guide and Travel Atlas. a.
  ISSN 0075-8329

**American Humane Association**
5351 S. Roslyn, Englewood, CO 80110.
- American Humane Association Annual Report. a.,
  1974.
- American Humane Magazine. m.

**American Humane Association. National Symposium
on Child Abuse**
Box 1266, Denver, CO 80201.
- American Humane Association. National
  Symposium on Child Abuse. Interdisciplinary
  Papers. irreg., no. 4, 1973.

**American Humanist Association**
602 Third St., San Francisco, CA 94107.
- Free Mind. bi-m.
- Humanist. bi-m. ISSN 0018-7399

**American Humor Studies Association**
Department of English, Virginia Commonwealth
Univ., Richmond, VA 23284.
- American Humor; an interdisciplinary newsletter.
s-a.

**American Hungarian Advertising Inc.**
Box 441 Gracie Station, New York, NY 10028.
- Magyar Holnap/Hungarian Tomorrow. m.

**American Hungarian Foundation**
Box 1084, New Brunswick, NJ 08903.
- Hungarian Studies Newsletter. 3 per yr.

**American Hungarian Word Inc.**
130 East 16th St., New York, NY 10003.
- Amerikai Magyar Szu. w.

**American Immigration and Citizenship Conference**
20 W. 40th St., New York, NY 10018.
- A I C C News. bi-m. ISSN 0001-1517

**American Independent Movement**
441 Chapel St., New Haven, CT 06511.
- Modern Times. fortn. ISSN 0001-1614

**American Indian Culture and Research Journal**
3220 Campbell Hall, University of California at Los
Angeles, Los Angeles, CA 90024.
- American Indian Culture and Research Journal. q.

**American Indian Historical Society, Inc.**
1451 Masonic Ave., San Francisco, CA 94117.
- Index to Literature on the American Indian. (pub.
by Indian Historian Press)
- Indian Historian. q. ISSN 0019-4840
- Wassaja; national newspaper of Indian America.
m.
- Weewish Tree. 7 per yr. ISSN 0049-7088

**American Indian Law Center**
Univ. of New Mexico School of Law, Albuquerque,
NM 87106.
- American Indian Law Newsletter. fortn. ISSN
0002-8886

**American Indian Lawyer Training Program, Inc.**
1000 Wisconsin Ave., N.W., Washington, DC
20007.
- Indian Law Reporter. m. ISSN 0097-1154

**American Indian Leadership Council**
Rt.3, Box 9, Rapid City, SD 57701.
- Indian. m.

**American Indian Press Association**
408 Zook Bldg., 431 W. Colfax Ave., Denver, CO
80204.
- American Indian Media Directory. a. ISSN 0093-
2094

**American Industrial Arts Association, Inc.**
N E A Headquarters Bldg., 1201 16th St. N.W.,
Washington, DC 20036.
- American Industrial Arts Association. Addresses
and Proceedings of the Annual Convention. a.
ISSN 0065-8618
- American Industrial Arts Association. Focus
Series. irreg.
- American Industrial Arts Association. Monograph
Series. irreg. ISSN 0517-2306
- Man/Society/Technology. 8 per yr. ISSN 0022-
1813

**American Industrial Development Council**
215 W. Pershing Rd., Suite 707, Kansas City, MO
64108.
- A I D C Journal; the professional voice of
industrial development. q. ISSN 0001-155X
- American Industrial Development Council.
Conference Notes. a.
- American Industrial Development Council
Newsletter. bi-m.

**American Industrial Hygiene Association**
66 South Miller Rd., Akron, OH 44313.
- American Industrial Hygiene Association.
Conference Proceedings. a.
- American Industrial Hygiene Association Journal.
m. ISSN 0002-8894

**American Industrial Real Estate Association**
5670 Wilshire Blvd., Los Angeles, CA 90036.
- American Industrial Real Estate Association.
Journal. a. ISSN 0065-8642

**American Institute Counselors, Inc.**
Great Barrington, MA 01230.
- Investment Bulletin. s-m. ISSN 0021-0072

**American Institute for Conservation**
c/o Peter G. Sparks, Ed., 219 McDowell Hall, Art
Conservation Department, University of Delaware,
Newark, DE 19711.
- American Institute for Conservation. Journal. s-a.

**American Institute for Decision Sciences**
University Plaza, 33 Gilmer St. S.E., Atlanta, GA
30303.
- Decision Line. q.
- Decision Sciences. q. ISSN 0011-7315

**American Institute for Decision Sciences. Southeast
Section**
Department of Management, Auburn University,
Auburn, AL 36830.
- American Institute for Decision Sciences.
Southeast Section. Proceedings. a.

**American Institute for Economic Research**
Great Barrington, MA 01230.
- American Institute for Economic Research.
Research Reports. w. ISSN 0034-5407
- Economic Education Bulletin. m. ISSN 0424-2769
- How to Avoid Financial Tangles: Section A.
Elementary Property Problems and Financial
Relationships. irreg., 1976, vol. 16, no. 12. ISSN
0085-1620
- How to Avoid Financial Tangles: Section B. Wills
and Trusts, Taxes, and Help for the Widow.
irreg., 1977, vol. 17, no. 1. ISSN 0085-1639

**American Institute for Exploration**
- American Institute for Exploration. Expedition
Field Reports. (pub. by Quest Productions)
- American Institute for Exploration. Occasional
Contributions. (pub. by Quest Productions)
- American Institute for Exploration. Reprint Series.
(pub. by Quest Productions)
- Mariah. (pub. by Mariah Publications)
- World Explorations. (pub. by Quest Productions)

**American Institute for Free Labor Development**
Education Dept., 1925 K St. N. W., Suite 406,
Washington, DC 20006.
- A I F L D Review/I A D S L. Revista. q. ISSN
0001-1576

**American Institute for Marxist Studies**
20 E. 30th St., New York, NY 10016.
- A I M S Newsletter. 6 per yr. ISSN 0001-1622
- American Institute for Marxist Studies.
Bibliographic Series. irreg. ISSN 0065-8650
- American Institute for Marxist Studies. Historical
Series. (pub. by Humanities Press, Inc.)
- American Institute for Marxist Studies.
Monograph Series. (pub. by Humanities Press,
Inc.)
- American Institute for Marxist Studies. Occasional
Paper. irreg., no. 20, 1976. ISSN 0084-6368

**American Institute for Performing & Fine Arts
Management, Inc.**
- Performing Arts Review. (pub. by Law-Arts
Publishers Inc.)

**American Institute for Verdi Studies**
- Verdi Newsletter. (pub. by New York University.
Department of Music)

**American Institute of Aeronautics & Astronautics**
1290 Ave. of the Americas, New York, NY 10019.
- A I A A/A S M E/S A E Structures, Structural
Dynamics, and Materials Conference.
Proceedings. irreg.
- A I A A Communications Satellite Systems
Conference. Technical Papers. (pub. by M I T
Press)
- A I A A Journal; devoted to aerospace research
and development. m. ISSN 0001-1452
- A I A A Roster. biennial. ISSN 0065-8693
- A I A A Student Journal. 4 per yr. ISSN 0001-
1460
- American Institute of Aeronautics and
Astronautics. Paper. irreg.(according to meeting
schedules) ISSN 0065-8707
- American Institute of Aeronautics and
Astronautics. Selected Reprint Series. irreg., latest
vol. 19. ISSN 0065-8715
- Astronautics & Aeronautics. m. 11 per yr. ISSN
0004-6213
- Journal of Aircraft; devoted to aeronautical
science and technology. m. ISSN 0021-8669

- Journal of Energy; bi-m.
- Journal of Hydronautics. q. ISSN 0022-1716
- Journal of Spacecraft and Rockets; devoted to
science and technology of space flight. m. ISSN
0022-4650
- Progress in Astronautics and Aeronautics Series.
(pub. by M.I.T. Press)

**American Institute of Aeronautics and Astronautics.
Technical Information Service**
750 Third Ave., New York, NY 10017.
- International Aerospace Abstracts. s-m. ISSN
0020-5842
- International Congress of the Aeronautical
Sciences. Proceedings. irreg., 9th. Haifa, 1975.
ISSN 0065-2105 (International Council of the
Aeronautical Sciences)

**American Institute of Architects**
1735 New York Ave., N.W., Washington, DC
20006.
- A I A Board of Directors. Annual Report. a.
ISSN 0517-2446
- A I A Building Construction Legal Citator.
Supplement; citations of judicial decisions relating
to the standard documents of the American
Institute of Architects. biennial. ISSN 0065-8723
- A I A Emerging Techniques. irreg. ISSN 0569-
5341
- A I A Energy Notebook. a.
- A I A Journal. m. ISSN 0001-1479
- A I A Membership List. a.
- A I A Memo. m. ISSN 0001-1487
- American Architects Directory. (pub. by R. R.
Bowker Company. Jaques Cattell Press)
- Architect's Handbook of Professional Practice.
irreg., with supplements. ISSN 0066-6173
- Journal of Architectural Research. (pub. by R I B
A Publications Ltd. UK)

**American Institute of Architects. Association of
Student Chapters**
- A S. (pub. by Ferachi & Associates)

**American Institute of Architects. Florida Association**
7100 N. Kendall Dr., Miami, FL 33156.
- Florida Architect. bi-m. ISSN 0015-3907

**American Institute of Architects. Iowa Chapter**
621 Savings and Loan Bldg., Des Moines, IA
50309.
- Iowa Architect; the face of architecture in Iowa.
q. ISSN 0021-0439

**American Institute of Architects. North Carolina
Chapter**
115 W. Morgan St., Raleigh, NC 27601.
- North Carolina Architect. bi-m. ISSN 0029-2427

**American Institute of Banking**
1120 Connecticut Ave., N.W., Washington, DC
20036.
- American Institute of Banking. Leaders Letter. 8
per yr.

**American Institute of Biological Sciences**
1401 Wilson Blvd., Arlington, VA 22209.
- A I B S Education Review. q.
- BioScience. m. ISSN 0006-3568
- Developments in Industrial Microbiology. irreg.,
1977, vol 18. ISSN 0070-4563
- Marine Biology; Proceedings of the
Interdisciplinary Conference. (pub. by Gordon &
Breach Science Publishers)

**American Institute of Biological Sciences. Biological
Sciences Curriculum Study**
1401 Wilson Blvd., Arlington, VA 22209.
- Research Problems in Biology. irreg. ISSN 0569-
5376

**American Institute of Certified Public Accountants**
1211 Avenue of the Americas, New York, NY
10036.
- A I C P A Professional Standards. (pub. by
Commerce Clearing House, Inc.)
- A I C P A Washington Report. w.
- Accountants International Studies. irreg.
- Accounting Articles Digest. q.
- American Institute of Certified Public
Accountants. Management Advisory Services.
Guideline Series. irreg.; no. 3, 1975. ISSN 0065-
8766
- C P A Letter. s-m.
- Journal of Accountancy. m. ISSN 0021-8448
- S E C Quarterly. q.
- Studies in Federal Taxation. Tax Study. irreg.
ISSN 0081-7929

- Tax Adviser. m. ISSN 0039-9957
- Tax Highlights Quarterly. q.

**American Institute of Certified Public Accountants. Division of Federal Taxation**
1211 Avenue of the Americas, New York, NY 10036.
- American Institute of Certified Public Accountants. Division of Federal Taxation. Statements on Responsibilities in Tax Practice. irreg. ISSN 0065-874X

**American Institute of Certified Public Accountants. Management Advisory Services Executive Committee**
1211 Ave. of the Americas, New York, NY 10036.
- Management Advisory Services Technical Study. irreg; 1973, no. 9. ISSN 0076-3667

**American Institute of Chemical Engineers**
345 E. 47 St., New York, NY 10017.
- A I Ch E Continuing Education Series. irreg., no. 5, 1971. ISSN 0065-8790
- A I Ch E Equipment Testing Procedures. a. ISSN 0569-5473 (prep. by its Equipment Testing Procedures Committee)
- A I Ch E Journal. bi-m. ISSN 0001-1541
- A I Ch E Symposium Series. irreg. ISSN 0065-8812
- Ammonia Plant Safety Series. a.
- Chemical Engineering Faculties of Canada and the United States. a. (prep. by its Chemical Engineering Education Projects Committee)
- Chemical Engineering Progress. (C E P) m. ISSN 0009-2495
- Chemical Engineering Progress. Reprint Manuals. irreg. ISSN 0069-2921
- Chemical Engineering Progress. Technical Manuals. irreg. ISSN 0069-2956
- International Chemical Engineering; a quarterly journal of translations from Russia, Eastern Europe, Asia and Japan. q. ISSN 0020-6318
- National Conference on Complete Water Use. Proceedings. a. (Co-sponsor: U.S. Environmental Protection Agency)
- Nuclear Engineering. irreg., approx. a. ISSN 0078-2599
- Water. irreg., latest 1975. ISSN 0083-7636

**American Institute of Chemical Engineers. Dayton & Ohio Valley Sections**
- National Conference on Energy and the Environment. Proceedings. (pub. by Wright State University)

**American Institute of Chemists, Inc.**
7315 Wisconsin Ave., Washington, DC 20014.
- American Institute of Chemists. Membership Directory. irreg. ISSN 0084-6376
- Chemist. m. ISSN 0009-3025

**American Institute of Cooperation**
1129 20th St. N.W., Rm. 505, Washington, DC 20036.
- American Cooperation Yearbook. a. ISSN 0065-793X
- American Institute of Cooperation. Newsletter. m. ISSN 0002-8924

**American Institute of Family Relations**
5287 Sunset Blvd., Los Angeles, CA 90027.
- Techniques of Marriage and Family Counseling. a. ISSN 0091-8385

**American Institute of Food Distribution, Inc.**
28-06 Broadway, Box 523, Fair Lawn, NJ 07410.
- American Institute of Food Distribution. Weekly Digest. w. ISSN 0002-8959
- Report on Food Markets. w. ISSN 0002-8940
- Washington Food Report. w. ISSN 0002-8932

**American Institute of Graphic Arts**
1059 Third Ave., New York, NY 10021.
- A I G A Children's Books Show. biennial. ISSN 0084-6384
- A I G A Packaging. a.
- Communication Graphics. a.
- Covers. biennial.
- Fifty Books of the Year. a.

**American Institute of Hypnosis**
7188 Sunset Blvd., Los Angeles, CA 90046.
- American Institute of Hypnosis. Journal. q. ISSN 0002-8975

**American Institute of Indian Studies**
1130 E. 59th St., Chicago, IL 60637.
- A I I S Annual Report. a.

**American Institute of Industrial Engineers Inc**
25 Technology Park, Norcross, GA 30071.
- A I I E Transactions; industrial engineering research and development. q. ISSN 0569-5554
- American Institute of Industrial Engineers. Proceedings of the Spring Annual Conference. a.
- Compensation of Industrial Engineers. biennial.
- Industrial Engineering. m. ISSN 0019-8234

**American Institute of Industrial Engineers, Inc. Industrial and Labor Relations Division**
25 Technology Park, Norcross, GA 30071.
- A I I E. Industrial and Labor Relations Monograph Series. irreg.

**American Institute of Islamic Studies**
Box 10191, Denver, CO 80210.
- American Institute of Islamic Studies. Bibliographic Series. irreg. ISSN 0065-8847
- Islam in Paperback. irreg. ISSN 0075-0921
- Islamic Studies. irreg. ISSN 0362-1480

**American Institute of Landscape Architects**
6810 N. 2nd Pl., Phoenix, AZ 85012.
- American Institute of Landscape Architects. Journal. q. ISSN 0002-8983

**American Institute of Maintenance**
- Cleaning Management. (pub. by Harris Communications)

**American Institute of Management**
125 E. 38 St., New York, NY 10018.
- Manual of Excellent Management. irreg., 11th, 1970. ISSN 0461-0040

**American Institute of Mining, Metallurgical and Petroleum Engineers, Inc.**
345 E. 47 St., New York, NY 10017.
- Nuclear Metallurgy Symposium. irreg.

**American Institute of Mining, Metallurgical and Petroleum Engineers, Inc. Council of Economics**
345 E. 47 St., New York, NY 10017.
- American Institute of Mining, Metallurgical and Petroleum Engineers. Council of Economics. Proceedings of the Annual Meeting. a.

**American Institute of Mining, Metallurgical and Petroleum Engineers, Inc. Iron and Steel Society**
345 E. 47th St., New York, NY 10017.
- I & S M. (Iron and Steel Maker) m.

**American Institute of Mining, Metallurgical and Petroleum Engineers, Inc. Metallurgical Society**
345 E. 47th St., New York, NY 10017.
- Journal of Metals. m. ISSN 0022-2674

**American Institute of Mining, Metallurgical and Petroleum Engineers, Inc. National Open Hearth Steel Committee**
345 E. 47 St., New York, NY 10017.
- American Institute of Mining, Metallurgical and Petroleum Engineers. National Open Hearth Steel Committee. Proceedings of the Conferene. a.

**American Institute of Mining, Metallurgical and Petroleum Engineers, Inc. Society of Mining Engineers**
540 Arapeen Drive, Box 8800, Salt Lake City, UT 84108.
- Mining Engineering. m. ISSN 0026-5187
- Society of Mining Engineers of A I M E. Transactions. q. ISSN 0037-9964

**American Institute of Mining, Metallurgical and Petroleum Engineers, Inc. Society of Petroleum Engineers**
6200 N. Central Expressway, Dallas, TX 75206.
- Journal of Petroleum Technology. m. ISSN 0022-3522
- Society of Petroleum Engineers Journal. bi-m. ISSN 0037-9999
- Society of Petroleum Engineers of American Institute of Mining, Metallurgical and Petroleum Engineers. Petroleum Transactions Reprint Series. irreg. ISSN 0081-1688
- Society of Petroleum Engineers of American Institute of Mining, Metallurgical and Petroleum Engineers. Transactions. a. ISSN 0081-1696

**American Institute of Musicology**
- American Institute of Musicology. Miscellanea. (pub. by Haenssler-Verlag GW)
- Corpus Mensurabilis Musicae. (pub. by Haenssler-Verlag GW)
- Corpus Scriptorum de Musica. (pub. by Haenssler-Verlag GW)

- Musica Disciplina. (pub. by Haenssler-Verlag GW)
- Musicological Studies and Documents. (pub. by Haenssler-Verlag GW)
- Renaissance Manuscript Studies. (pub. by Haenssler-Verlag GW)

**American Institute of Nutrition**
9650 Rockville Pike, Bethesda, MD 20014.
- American Journal of Clinical Nutrition; a journal reporting the practical application of our world-wide knowledge of nutrition. m. ISSN 0002-9165 (American Society of Clinical Nutrition, Inc.)
- Journal of Nutrition. m. ISSN 0022-3166

**American Institute of Parliamentarians**
Suite 206 Liberty Bldg., Des Moines, IA 50309.
- Parliamentary Journal. q. ISSN 0048-2994

**American Institute of Physics**
335 E. 45th St., New York, NY 10017.
- A I P Conference Proceedings. irreg., no. 35, 1977. ISSN 0094-243X
- Acoustical Society of America. Journal. m. plus 3 supplements. ISSN 0001-4966
- American Astronomical Society. Bulletin. q. ISSN 0002-7537
- American Journal of Physics. m. ISSN 0002-9505 (Subscr. to: American Association of Physics Teachers, Graduate Physics Bldg., State University of New York, Stony Brook, NY 11790)
- American Physical Society. Bulletin. 13 per yr. ISSN 0003-0503 (American Physical Society)
- Applied Optics. Supplement. irreg., 1969, no.3. ISSN 0066-5495 (Optical Society of America, Inc.)
- Applied Physics Letters. s-m. ISSN 0003-6951
- Astronomical Journal. m. ISSN 0004-6256 (American Astronomical Society)
- Current Physics Index. q. ISSN 0098-9819
- Current Physics Microform. m. ISSN 0045-9348
- Directory of Physics & Astronomy Staff Members. a. ISSN 0361-2228
- Graduate Programs: Physics, Astronomy, and Related Fields. a.
- International Conference on Experimental Meson Spectroscopy. Proceedings. irreg., 4th Boston, 1974.
- International Cyclotron Conference. Proceedings. irreg., 6th, 1972.
- J E T P Letters. s-m. ISSN 0021-3640
- Journal of Applied Physics. m. ISSN 0021-8979
- Journal of Chemical Physics. s-m. ISSN 0021-9606
- Journal of Mathematical Physics. m. ISSN 0022-2488
- Journal of Physical and Chemical Reference Data. q. ISSN 0047-2689 (Co-sponsors: American Chemical Society; U.S. National Bureau of Standards) (Subscr. to: American Chemical Society, Chemical Abstracts Service, Ohio State University, Columbus, OH 43210)
- Journal of Vacuum Science and Technology. bi-m. ISSN 0022-5355 (American Vacuum Society)
- Medical Physics. bi-m. ISSN 0094-2405 (American Association of Physicists in Medicine)
- Optical Society of America. Journal. m. ISSN 0030-3941
- Optics and Spectroscopy. m. ISSN 0030-400X (Optical Society of America, Inc.)
- Optics and Spectroscopy. Supplement. irreg., 1970, no. 4. ISSN 0078-5504 (Optical Society of America, Inc.)
- Optics News. q. ISSN 0098-907X (Optical Society of America, Inc.)
- Physical Review A (General Physics) m. ISSN 0556-2791 (American Physical Society)
- Physical Review B (Solid State) s-m. ISSN 0556-2805 (American Physical Society)
- Physical Review C (Nuclear Physics) m. ISSN 0556-2813 (American Physical Society)
- Physical Review D (Particles and Fields) s-m. ISSN 0556-2821 (American Physical Society)
- Physical Review Abstracts. s-m. ISSN 0048-4024 (American Physical Society)
- Physical Review Index. s-a. ISSN 0094-0003
- Physical Review Letters. w. ISSN 0031-9007 (American Physical Society)
- Physics. a. ISSN 0092-8437
- Physics Manpower - Education and Employment Studies. triennial.
- Physics of Fluids. m. ISSN 0031-9171
- Physics Teacher. 9 per yr. ISSN 0031-921X (Subscr. to: American Association of Physics Teachers, Graduate Physics Building, State University of New York, Stony Brook, NY 11790)
- Physics Today. m. ISSN 0031-9228

- Review of Scientific Instruments. m. ISSN 0034-6748
- Reviews of Modern Physics. q. ISSN 0034-6861 (American Physical Society)
- Rheology Bulletin. irreg. ISSN 0035-4538 (Society of Rheology)
- Searchable Physics Information Notices. m.
- Soviet Astronomy. bi-m.
- Soviet Astronomy Letters. bi-m. ISSN 0360-0327
- Soviet Journal of Low Temperature Physics. m. ISSN 0360-0335
- Soviet Journal of Nuclear Physics. m. ISSN 0038-5506
- Soviet Journal of Optical Technology. m. ISSN 0038-5514
- Soviet Journal of Particles and Nuclei. bi-m. ISSN 0090-4759
- Soviet Journal of Plasma Physics. bi-m. ISSN 0360-0343
- Soviet Journal of Quantum Electronics. m. ISSN 0049-1748
- Soviet Physics - Acoustics. bi-m. ISSN 0038-562X
- Soviet Physics - Crystallography. bi-m. ISSN 0038-5638
- Soviet Physics-Doklady. m. ISSN 0038-5689
- Soviet Physics - J E T P. m. ISSN 0038-5646
- Soviet Physics-Semiconductors. m. ISSN 0038-5700
- Soviet Physics - Solid State. m. ISSN 0038-5654
- Soviet Physics - Technical Physics. m. ISSN 0038-5662
- Soviet Physics- Uspekhi. m. ISSN 0038-5670
- Soviet Technical Physics Letters. m. ISSN 0360-120X

**American Institute of Physics. Center for History of Physics**
335 E. 45th St., New York, NY 10017.
- Center for History of Physics. Newsletter. irreg.

**American Institute of Planners**
1776 Massachusetts Ave., N.W., Washington, DC 20036.
- A I P Newsletter. m. ISSN 0001-1665
- American Institute of Planners. Journal. q. ISSN 0002-8991
- Practicing Planner. q.

**American Institute of Plant Engineers**
1021 Delta Ave., Cincinnati, OH 45208.
- A I P E Newsletter. m.
- American Institute of Plant Engineers. Journal. q.

**American Institute of Public Opinion**
53 Bank St., Princeton, NJ 08540.
- Gallup Opinion Index. m. ISSN 0016-4194

**American Institute of Real Estate Appraisers**
National Assn. of Realtors, 430 N. Michigan, Chicago, IL 60611.
- Appraisal Journal. q. ISSN 0003-7087
- Appraiser. m. (except July & Aug.) ISSN 0003-7095

**American Institute of Steel Construction, Inc.**
1221 Ave. of the Americas, New York, NY 10020.
- Engineering Journal. q. ISSN 0013-8029
- Modern Steel Construction. q. ISSN 0026-8445

**American Institute of the History of Pharmacy**
Pharmacy Bldg., Madison, WI 53706.
- Pharmacy in History. q. ISSN 0031-7047

**American Institute of Ultrasound in Medicine**
Executive Office, 6161 N. May Ave., Suite 45W, Oklahoma City, OK 73112.
- American Institute of Ultrasound in Medicine. Annual Scientific Conference. Program. a. ISSN 0065-8871
- American Institute of Ultrasound in Medicine. Proceedings of Annual Meeting. (pub. by Plenum Publishing Corp.)
- Reflections. q. ISSN 0098-9223

**American Institutes for Research**
Box 1113, Palo Alto, CA 94302.
- Innovations; highlights of evolving mental health services.

**American Institutes for Research (Pittsburgh)**
Chatham Center, Pittsburgh, PA 15219.
- American Institutes for Research. Seminar Series. irreg. ISSN 0065-891X

**American Instructors of the Deaf**
Kansas School for the Deaf, Olathe, KS 66061.
- American Instructors of the Deaf. Proceedings. biennial.

**American Instrument Co. Inc.**
8030 Georgia Ave., Silver Spring, MD 20910.
- Aminco Laboratory News. bi-m. ISSN 0003-1763
- Fluorescence News. q. ISSN 0015-4709

**American Insurance Association**
85 John St., New York, NY 10030.
- American Insurance Association. Engineering and Safety Service. Special Interest Bulletin. irreg., no. 55, 1974.

**American-International Charolais Association**
- Charolais Banner. (pub. by Banner Publishing Inc.)

**American International Investment Corporation**
351 California St., San Francisco, CA 94104.
- World Currency Charts. irreg. ISSN 0090-2810

**American Investment Co.**
8251 Maryland Ave., St. Louis, MO 63105.
- Banner. bi-m.

**American Iron and Steel Institute**
1000 16 St., N.W., Washington, DC 20036.
- American Iron and Steel Institute. Annual Statistical Report. a.
- Directory of Iron and Steel Works of the United States and Canada. triennial.
- Steel...(Year) q.
- Steel Can Recycling. m. (prep. by its Committee of Tin Mill Products Producers)

**American-Israel Chamber of Commerce and Industry, Inc.**
500 Fifth Ave., Suite 5416, New York, NY 10036.
- American-Israel Economic Horizons. bi-m. ISSN 0002-9033

**American Israel Ventures Corp.**
557 Beach 129th St., Belle Harbor, NY 11694.
- Israel Securities Review Monthly Magazine. 6 per yr.

**American Italian Historical Association**
209 Flagg Pl., Staten Island, NY 10304.
- American Italian Historical Association. Proceedings. a.

**American Jersey Cattle Club**
2105-J S. Hamilton Rd., Columbus, OH 43227.
- Jersey Journal. m. ISSN 0021-5953

**American Jewish Alternatives to Zionism, Inc.**
c/o Elmer Berger, Ed., 133 E. 73 St., No. 404, New York, NY 10021.
- American Jewish Alternatives to Zionism. Report. q.

**American Jewish Committee**
165 E. 56th St., New York, NY 10022.
- American Jewish Yearbook. (pub. by Jewish Publication Society of America)
- Commentary; journal of significant thought and opinion on contemporary issues. m. ISSN 0010-2601
- Foreign Affairs Bulletin. bi-m.
- Present Tense. q. ISSN 0092-4091

**American Jewish Committee. Institute of Human Relations**
165 E. 56th St., New York, NY 10022.
- American Jewish Committee. Institute of Human Relations. Paperback Series. irreg., 1974.

**American Jewish Committee. National Labor Service**
165 E. 56 Street, New York, NY 10022.
- Let's Be Human. bi-m.

**American Jewish Congress**
15 E. 84th St., New York, NY 10028.
- American Jewish Congress. Congress Monthly; a journal of opinion and Jewish affairs. m. (Sept.-Jun.)
- American Jewish Congress. News. (pub. by Stephen Wise Congress House)
- Judaism; a quarterly journal of Jewish life and thought. q. ISSN 0022-5762

**American Jewish Congress. Commission on Law and Social Actions**
15 E. 84 St., New York, NY 10028.
- Civil Rights and Civil Liberties Decisions of the U.S. Supreme Court. irreg. ISSN 0569-6003

**American Jewish Historical Society**
2 Thornton Rd., Waltham, MA 02154.
- American Jewish Communal History. irreg., 1969, no. 5. ISSN 0065-8936
- American Jewish Historical Quarterly. q. ISSN 0002-9068
- American Jewish Historical Society. Report. irreg.
- Studies in American Jewish History. irreg., 1968, no.5. ISSN 0081-7511

**American Jewish Life**
701 South Broad St., Trenton, NJ 08611.
- American Jewish Life. fortn.

**American Jewish Times-Outlook**
Box 10674, Charlotte, NC 28234.
- American Jewish Times-Outlook. m. ISSN 0002-9076

**American Journal of Acupuncture**
1400 Lost Acre Drive, Felton, CA 95018.
- American Journal of Acupuncture. q. ISSN 0091-3960

**American Journal of Ancient History**
Robinson Hall, Harvard University, Cambridge, MA 02138.
- American Journal of Ancient History. 3 per yr. ISSN 0362-8914

**American Journal of Economics & Sociology, Inc.**
50 E. 69th St., New York, NY 10021.
- American Journal of Economics and Sociology. q. ISSN 0002-9246 (Robert Schalkenbach Foundation) (Co-sponsor: Francis Neilson Fund)

**American Journal of Nursing Co.**
10 Columbus Circle, New York, NY 10019.
- American Journal of Nursing. m. ISSN 0002-936X (American Nurses' Association)
- Contemporary Nursing Series. irreg., vol. 7, 1973. (American Nurses Association)
- International Nursing Index. q. ISSN 0020-8124 (American Nurses' Association. National League for Nursing)
- M C N: American Journal of Maternal Child Nursing. bi-m.
- Nursing Outlook. m. ISSN 0029-6554 (American Nurses' Association. National League for Nursing)
- Nursing Research. bi-m. ISSN 0029-6562 (American Nurses' Association. National League for Nursing)

**American Journal of Science**
Box 2161, Yale Sta., New Haven, CT 06520.
- Radiocarbon. 3 per yr. ISSN 0033-8222

**American Judges Association**
Box 1399, Holyoke, MA 01040.
- Court Review. bi-m. ISSN 0011-0647

**American Judicature Society**
1155 East 60th St., Chicago, IL 60637.
- A J S Information Report Series. irreg. ISSN 0065-9010
- A J S Joint Enterprise. irreg. ISSN 0362-1057
- Judicature. m. ISSN 0022-5800

**American Junior Bowling Congress**
5301 S. 76th Street, Greendale, WI 53129.
- Junior Bowler. m.(Nov.-Apr.)

**American Kennel Club, Inc.**
51 Madison Ave., New York, NY 10010.
- Pure-Bred Dogs, American Kennel Gazette. m. ISSN 0033-4561

**American Kidney Fund**
Box 975, Washington, DC 20044.
- Torchbearer. q.

**American Labor Conference on International Affairs, Inc.**
212 Fifth Ave., New York, NY 10010.
- New Leader; a bi-weekly of news and opinion. fortn. ISSN 0028-6044

**American Lancia Club**
c/o R.E. Buckingham, 12 El Dorado Beach Club Dr., Mercer Island, WA 98040
(Subscr. to: Yale Braunstein, 110 Bleeker St., Apt. 8-E, New York, NY 10012)
- Lanciana. bi-m. ISSN 0023-7515

**American Land Development Association**
1000 16 St., N.W., Washington, DC 20036.
- American Land. bi-m.

**American Land Title Association**
1828 L St. N.W., Washington, DC 20036.
• Title News. m. ISSN 0040-8190

**American Landrace Association**
• American Landrace. (pub. by Culver Press)

**American Laryngological Association**
80 Barre St., Charleston, SC 29401.
• American Laryngological Association.
Transactions. a.

**American Laryngological Rhinological and Otological Society**
c/o Ann R. Holm, 2954 Dorman Road, Broomall, PA 19008.
• American Laryngological, Rhinological and Otological Society. Transactions. a. ISSN 0065-9037
• Laryngoscope. (pub. by Laryngoscope Co.)

**American Latvian Association in the U. S., Inc.**
P.O. Box 432, Rockville, MD 20850.
• A L A Zurnals. 3 per yr. ISSN 0044-7757

**American Law Enforcement Officers Association**
4005 Plaza Towers, New Orleans, LA 70113.
• Police Times. m. ISSN 0032-2601

**American Law Institute**
4025 Chestnut St., Philadelphia, PA 19104.
• American Law Institute. Annual Meeting. Proceedings. a. ISSN 0065-9045
• Restatement in the Courts. Supplements. irreg.

**American Law Institute-American Bar Association Committee on Continuing Professional Education**
4025 Chestnut St., Philadelpha, PA 19104.
• A L I-A B A C L E Review. w. ISSN 0044-7560
• A. L. I.-A. B. A. Course Materials Journal. bi-m.
• Practical Lawyer. 8 per yr. ISSN 0032-6429
• Practical Lawyer's Law Office Management Manual. irreg. ISSN 0092-248X
• Preview of United States Supreme Court Cases. 6 per mo. (Sep.-May) (Co-sponsor: Association of American Law Schools)

**American Lawn Bowls Association**
10337 Cheryl Dr., Sun City, AZ 85351
• A. L. B. A. Bowls. q. ISSN 0001-1754 (Or c/o Cresslyn L. Tilley, 70 Covina Ave., Long Beach, CA 90803)
• Official Lawn Bowls Handbook. every 3-4 years; 1974, 4th ed. ISSN 0065-9053

**American Leather Chemists Association**
Campus Station, Cincinnati, OH 45221.
• American Leather Chemists Association. Journal. m. ISSN 0002-9726

**American Lebanese Serian Associated Charities**
St. Jude Children's Research Hospital, 539 Lane Ave., Memphis, TN 38105.
• A L S A C News. q. ISSN 0001-1770

**American Legion**
Dept. S, Box 1055, Indianapolis, IN 46206.
• Need a Lift? a. ISSN 0548-1384

**American Legion. Department of Colorado**
3003 Tejon, Denver, CO 80211.
• Colorado Legionnaire. m.

**American Legion. Department of Indiana**
777 N. Meridian St., Indianapolis, IN 46204.
• Hoosier Legionnaire. m.(10 per yr.) ISSN 0018-4772

**American Legion. Department of Iowa**
720 Lyon, Des Moines, IA 50316.
• Iowa Legionnaire. m. ISSN 0021-0560

**American Legion, Department of Mississippi**
• Mississippi Legion-Aire. (pub. by Rankin County News)

**American Legion. Department of Missouri**
Box 179, Jefferson City, MO 65101.
• Show-Me Missouri Legionnaire. m. ISSN 0037-4334
**American Legion. Department of Montana**
Veterans & Pioneers Memorial Bldg., Helena, MT 59601.
• Montana Legionnaire. m. ISSN 0026-9999

**American Legion. Department of Nebraska**
Box 5205, Sta. C, Lincoln, NE 68505.
• Nebraska Legionnaire. m. ISSN 0028-1875

**American Legion. Department of South Dakota**
14 1st Ave, S.E., Watertown, SD 57201.
• South Dakota Legion News. m.

**American Legion. Department of Texas**
Box 789, Austin, TX 78767.
• Texas Legion News. bi-m.

**American Legion. Department of Virginia**
• Virginia Legionnaire. (pub. by Wing Publications)

**American Legion. Department of West Virginia**
• West Virginia Legionnaire. (pub. by Republican Delta)

**American Legion Auxiliary**
777 N. Meridian Street, Indianapolis, IN 46204.
• American Legion Auxiliary. National News. 7 per yr.

**American Legion Magazine**
1608 K St. N.W., Washington, DC 20006.
• American Legion Magazine. m. ISSN 0002-9734

**American Legion Press Association**
Box 1055, 700 N. Penn, Indianapolis, IN 46206.
• American Legion Press Association News-Letter. bi-m. ISSN 0002-9742

**American Library Association**
50 East Huron St., Chicago, IL 60611.
• A L A Studies in Librarianship. irreg., 1971, no. 2. ISSN 0065-907X
• A L A Yearbook; a review of library events. a.
• A S L A President's Newsletter. q. ISSN 0044-9660 (Association of State Library Agencies)
• American Association of State Libraries. President's Newsletter. 3 per yr. ISSN 0002-7472
• American Libraries. m. 11 per yr. ISSN 0002-9769
• American Library Association. Librarians, Censorship, and Intellectual Freedom; an annual annotated bibliography. irreg. ISSN 0075-8973
• American Library Association. Membership Directory. a.
• American Library Laws. irreg., 4th, 1973.
• Booklist. s-m. ISSN 0006-7385
• Guide to Reference Books. irreg., latest 9th ed. ISSN 0072-8624
• Library Technology Reports; evaluative information on library systems, equipment and supplies. bi-m. ISSN 0024-2586
• Public Library Trustee. q. ISSN 0033-3581 (American Library Trustee Association)
• School Media Quarterly. 4 per yr. (American Association of School Librarians)
• Top of the News. q. ISSN 0040-9286 (prep. by its Children's Services Division and Young Adult Services Division)

**American Library Association. Advisory Committee for Liaison with Japanese Libraries**
• U S-Japan Library Newsletter. (pub. by University of Hawaii. Graduate School of Library Studies)

**American Library Association. Conference Arrangements Office**
50 E. Huron St., Chicago, IL 60611.
• American Library Association. Annual Conference Program. a.

**American Library Association. Education Division**
50 E. Huron St., Chicago, IL 60611.
• Financial Assistance for Library Education. a. ISSN 0569-6275

**American Library Association. Government Documents Round Table**
50 E. Huron St., Chicago, IL 60611.
• Documents to the People. irreg.

**American Library Association. Health and Rehabilitative Library Services Division**
50 East Huron St., Chicago, IL 60611.
• American Library Association. Health and Rehabilitative Library Services Division. Newsletter. m.

**American Library Association. Information Science and Automation Division**
50 East Huron St, Chicago, IL 60611.
• Journal of Library Automation. q. ISSN 0022-2240

**American Library Association. Intellectual Freedom Committee**
50 E. Huron St., Chicago, IL 60611.
• Newsletter on Intellectual Freedom. bi-m. ISSN 0028-9485

**American Library Association. International Relations Round Table**
50 East Huron St., Chicago, IL 60611.
• Leads: a Fact Sheet. q. ISSN 0458-8983

**American Library Association. Junior Members Round Table**
50 E. Huron St., Chicago, IL 60611.
• Footnotes. q.

**American Library Association. Library Administration Division**
50 East Huron St., Chicago, IL 60611.
• L A D Newsletter. q.

**American Library Association. Library Education Division**
50 E. Huron, Chicago, IL 60611.
• American Library Association. Library Education Division. Newsletter. q. ISSN 0002-9785

**American Library Association. Library Technology Program**
50 E. Huron St., Chicago, IL 60611.
• Conservation of Library Materials. irreg. ISSN 0069-9136
• L T P Publications. irreg. ISSN 0065-9088

**American Library Association. Reference & Adult Services Division**
50 East Huron St., Chicago, IL 60611.
• Notable Books. a. (prep. by its Notable Books Council)
• R Q. q. ISSN 0033-7072

**American Library Association. Reference and Subscription Books Review Committee**
50 E. Huron St., Chicago, IL 60611.
• Reference and Subscription Books Reviews. a. ISSN 0080-0430

**American Library Association. Resources and Technical Services Division**
50 E. Huron St., Chicago, IL 60611.
• Library Resources & Technical Services. q. ISSN 0024-2527
• R T S D Newsletter. q. ISSN 0360-5906

**American Library Association. Social Responsibilities Round Table**
50 E. Huron St., Chicago, IL 60611.
• A L A Social Responsibilities Round Table Newsletter. bi-m. ISSN 0065-9096
• Alternatives in Print. (pub. by Glide Publications)

**American Library Association. Staff Organization Round Table**
50 E. Huron St., Chicago, IL 60611.
• S O R T Bulletin. q.

**American Library Association. Washington Office**
110 Maryland Ave., N.E., Washington, DC 20002.
• A L A Washington Newsletter. irreg. ISSN 0001-1746

**American Library Trustee Association**
• Public Library Trustee. (pub. by American Library Association)

**American Life Foundation**
Box 349, Watkins Glen, NY 14891.
• American Life Collector's Annual. a. ISSN 0065-9118

**American Life Insurance Association**
1730 Pennsylvania Ave., Washington, DC 20006.
• American Life Insurance Association. Economic and Investment Report. a. ISSN 0459-3650
• American Life Insurance Association. Proceedings of the Annual Meeting. irreg. ISSN 0095-3938

**American-Lithuanian Medical Association**
2751 W. 51st St., Chicago, IL 60632.
• Lithuanian Medical Bulletin. q. ISSN 0024-4945

**American Lithuanian Press Radio Association**
6116 St. Clair Ave., Cleveland, OH 44103.
• Dirva. w.

**American-Lithuanian R.C. Women's Alliance**
9428 S. Harding Av., Evergreen Park, IL 60642
(Subscr. to: 3005 N. 124th St., Brookfield, Wis.
53005)
• Moteru Dirva/Women's Field. bi-m.

**American Littoral Society**
Sandy Hook, Highlands, NJ 07732.
• American Littoral Society. Special Publications.
irreg. ISSN 0065-9150
• Underwater Naturalist. q. ISSN 0041-6606

**American Logistics Association**
1000 Connecticut Ave. N. W., Washington, DC
20036.
• American Logistics Association Review. bi-m.
ISSN 0034-6322

**American Lung Association**
1740 Broadway, New York, NY 10019.
• Air Conservation Newsletter. bi-m.
• American Lung Association. Bulletin. m.(except
July and Feb) ISSN 0092-5659

**American Lung Association of New York State**
8 Mountain View Ave., Albany, NY 11205.
• Life & Lung. q.

**American Lutheran Church**
• American Lutheran Church. Yearbook. (pub. by
Augsburg Publishing House)
• Lutheran Standard. (pub. by Augsburg Publishing
House)

**American Lutheran Church and Lutheran Church in
America**
• A L C-L C A Augsburg Adult Bible Studies. (pub.
by Augsburg Publishing House)
• A L C-L C A Augsburg Adult Bible Studies.
Teacher's Guide. (pub. by Augsburg Publishing
House)
• A L C-L C A Augsburg Home Bible Studies.
(pub. by Augsburg Publishing House)

**American Lutheran Church. Commission on
Evangelism**
• Christ in Our Home. (pub. by Augsburg
Publishing House)

**American Lutheran Church Women**
• Scope (Minneapolis) (pub. by Augsburg Publishing
House)

**American Lutheran Publicity Bureau**
155 E. 22nd. St., New York, NY 10010.
• Lutheran Forum; an independent journal. q. ISSN
0024-7456
• Lutheran Forum. Forum Letter. m. ISSN 0046-
4732

**American Malacological Union, Inc.**
c/o Constance E. Boone, Recording Secretary, 3706
Rice Boulevard, Houston, TX 77005.
• American Malacological Union. Bulletin. a. ISSN
0065-9169

**American Management Associations**
135 W. 50th St., New York, NY 10020
(Subscr. to: Box 319, Saranac Lake, N.Y. 12983)
• A M A Management Briefings. irreg., approx. 12
per yr.
• A M A Survey Reports. irreg., approx. 3 per yr.
• American Management Association. Research
Studies. irreg. ISSN 0065-9185
• American Management Association. Seminar
Program. irreg. ISSN 0065-9193
• Compensation Review. q. ISSN 0010-4248
• CompFlash; news of developments in employee
compensation and benefits. m.
• Health Services Manager. m.
• Management Development Guide. s-a.
• Management Review. m. ISSN 0025-1895
• Organizational Dynamics; a quarterly review of
industrial applications of the behavioral sciences.
q. ISSN 0090-2616
• Personnel. bi-m. ISSN 0031-5702
• Supervisory Management. m. ISSN 0039-5919

**American Management Associations. Executive
Compensation Service**
135 W. 50th St., New York, NY 10020
(Subscr. to: Box 319, Saranac Lake, N.Y. 12983)
• Current Compensation References. m. ISSN 0011-
3360
• Executive Compensation Service. Reports on
International Compensation. Argentina. a. ISSN
0095-4144

• Executive Compensation Service. Reports on
International Compensation. Brazil. irreg.
• Executive Compensation Service. Reports on
International Compensation. Puerto Rico. irreg.
ISSN 0090-9971
• Executive Compensation Service. Technician
Report. a.

**American Marine Register**
Box 5468, North Little Rock, AR 72119.
• American Marine Register. a. with q. supplements.
ISSN 0091-5491

**American Maritime Cases, Inc.**
28 E. 21st St., Baltimore, MD 21218.
• American Maritime Cases. m.(except Aug) ISSN
0002-9874

**American Marketing Association**
222 S. Riverside Plaza, Chicago, IL 60606.
• American Marketing Association. Bibliographies
Series. irreg. ISSN 0065-9223
• American Marketing Association. Directory of
Marketing Services and Membership Roster. a.
• American Marketing Association. Proceedings. a.
ISSN 0065-9231
• Educational Workshop Series. irreg.
• Journal of Consumer Research. q. ISSN 0093-
5301
• Journal of Marketing. q. ISSN 0022-2429
• Journal of Marketing Research. q. ISSN 0022-
2437
• Marketing News; reporting on marketing and its
association. bi-w. ISSN 0025-3790
• Paul D. Converse Symposium. Proceedings. irreg.

**American Marketing Association. Committee on
Attitude Research**
222 S. Riverside Plaza, Chicago, IL 60606.
• American Marketing Association. Committee on
Attitude Research. Papers Presented at the
Annual Conference. a.

**American Marketing Association. New York Chapter**
60 E. 42nd St., New York, NY 10017.
• International Directory of Marketing Research
Houses and Services. a. ISSN 0074-459X

**American Mathematical Society**
Box 6248, Providence, RI 02940.
• American Journal of Mathematics. (pub. by Johns
Hopkins University Press)
• American Mathematical Society. Bulletin. bi-m.
ISSN 0002-9904
• American Mathematical Society. Colloquium
Publications. irreg. ISSN 0065-9258
• American Mathematical Society. Memoirs. bi-m.
ISSN 0065-9266
• American Mathematical Society. Notices. 8 per
yr. ISSN 0002-9920
• American Mathematical Society. Proceedings. m.
ISSN 0002-9939
• American Mathematical Society. Transactions. m.
ISSN 0002-9947
• American Mathematical Society. Translations.
Series 2. irreg., latest issue 1977. ISSN 0065-9290
• Current Mathematical Publications. fortn. ISSN
0361-4794
• Directory of Women Mathematicians. irreg. ISSN
0091-7583
• Index of Mathematical Papers. s-a. ISSN 0019-
3917
• Lectures in Applied Mathematics. irreg., 1971,
vol. 14. ISSN 0075-8485
• Lectures on Mathematics in the Life Sciences.
irreg. ISSN 0075-8523
• Mathematical Reviews; a reviewing journal
covering the world literature of mathematical
research. m. ISSN 0025-5629
• Mathematical Surveys. irreg., 1973, no. 12. ISSN
0076-5376
• Mathematics of Computation. q. ISSN 0025-5718
• Mathematics of the U S S R-Izvestija. bi-m. ISSN
0025-5726
• Mathematics of the U S S R - Sbornik. m. ISSN
0025-5734
• Moscow Mathematical Society. Transactions.
irreg., latest issue, 1974. ISSN 0077-1554 (Co-
Sponsor: London Mathematical Society)
• Quarterly of Applied Mathematics. q. ISSN 0033-
569X
• S I A M - A M S Proceedings. irreg.(approx. a.)
ISSN 0080-5084 (Society for Industrial and
Applied Mathematics)
• Selected Tables in Mathematical Statistics. irreg.
ISSN 0094-8837

• Selected Translations in Mathematical Statistics
and Probability. irreg. ISSN 0065-9274 (Institute
of Mathematical Statistics)
• Soviet Mathematics-Doklady. bi-m. ISSN 0038-
5573
• Steklov Institute of Mathematics. Proceedings.
irreg., latest issue 1977. ISSN 0081-5438
• Theory of Probability and Mathematical Statistics.
q. ISSN 0094-9000 (Kievskii Universitet UR)
• Translations of Mathematical Monographs. irreg.
ISSN 0065-9282

**American Matthay Association**
63 W. Water St., Gettysburg, PA 17325.
• Matthay News. 3 per yr. ISSN 0360-8484

**American Medical Association**
535 N. Dearborn Street, Chicago, IL 60610.
• A M A Drug Evaluations. (pub. by Publishing
Sciences Group, Inc.)
• A M A Newsletter. w.
• A M A Update. bi-m. ISSN 0044-7765
• Allied Medical Education Directory. a.
• American Journal of Diseases of Children. m.
ISSN 0002-922X
• American Medical Association. Directory of
Approved Residencies. biennial.
• American Medical Association. Directory of
Officials and Staff. a. with supplements. ISSN
0569-6534
• American Medical Association. Journal. w. ISSN
0002-9955
• American Medical Directory. irreg., 26th ed.,
1973. ISSN 0065-9339
• American Medical News; the newspaper of
American medicine. w. ISSN 0001-1843
• Archives of Dermatology. m. ISSN 0003-987X
• Archives of Environmental Health. (pub. by
Heldref Publications)
• Archives of General Psychiatry. m. ISSN 0003-
990X
• Archives of Internal Medicine. m. ISSN 0003-
9926
• Archives of Neurology. m. ISSN 0003-9942
• Archives of Ophthalmology. m. ISSN 0003-9950
• Archives of Otolaryngology. m. ISSN 0003-9977
(Co-Sponsors: American Academy of Facial,
Plastic & Reconstructive Surgery; American
Society for Head & Neck Surgery)
• Archives of Pathology and Laboratory Medicine.
m.
• Archives of Surgery. m. ISSN 0004-0010
• C P T. (Physicians' Current Procedural
Terminology) irreg., 1973, 3rd ed. ISSN 0590-
4129
• Citation; current legal developments relating to
medicine and allied professions. s-m. ISSN 0009-
7446
• Computers and Medicine. bi-m.
• Current Medical Information and Terminology.
irreg., 4th ed., 1971. ISSN 0070-2005
• Directory of Blood Banking and Transfusion
Facilities and Services. irreg. ISSN 0419-2206
• Directory of Health Sciences Libraries. irreg. (Co-
sponsors: Medical Library Association; American
Hospital Association)
• Directory of National Voluntary Health
Organizations. irreg.
• Directory of Self-Assessment Programs for
Physicians. irreg.
• Directory of Women Physicians in the U.S. ISSN
0094-5471 (Co-Sponsor: American Medical
Women's Association)
• Distribution of Physicians. a.
• Legislative Roundup; a weekly report on national
medical legislation. w. ISSN 0024-0494
• Medical and Surgical Motion Pictures; a catalog
of selected films. a. ISSN 0065-9320
• Medical Socioeconomic Research Sources. q.,
cumulated annually. ISSN 0025-7540
• Medical Staff in Action. 6 per yr. ISSN 0025-
7559
• National Medico-Legal Symposium. irreg. (Co-
sponsor: American Bar Association)
• Perspectives-In Long Term Care. bi-m. ISSN
0018-4195
• Standard Nomenclature of Athletic Injuries. irreg.
ISSN 0081-427X (prep. by its Committee on
Sports Injuries)

**American Medical Association Auxiliary, Inc.**
535 N. Dearborn St., Chicago, IL 60610.
• M. D.'s Wife. q. ISSN 0024-807X

**American Medical Association. Center for Health
Services Research and Development**
535 N. Dearborn St., Chicago, IL 60610.
• Reference Data on Profile of Medical Practice. a.

● Reference Data on Socioeconomic Issues of Health. a. ISSN 0092-8836

**American Medical Association. Council on Foods and Nutrition**
535 N. Dearborn St., Chicago, IL 60610.
● Western Hemisphere Nutrition Congress. Proceedings. triennial. (Co-sponsor: American Institute of Nutrition; Nutrition Society of Canada; Sociedad Latinoameric de Nutricion)

**American Medical Association. Council on Medical Education**
535 N. Dearborn St., Chicago, IL 60610.
● Medical Licensure Statistics. a.

**American Medical Electroencephalographic Association**
720 N. Michigan Ave., Room 620, Chicago, IL 60611.
● Clinical Electroencephalography. q. ISSN 0009-9155

**American Medical Record Association**
875 N. Michigan Ave., Chicago, IL 60611.
● Medical Record News. bi-m. ISSN 0025-7486

**American Medical Student Association**
1177 Tower Rd., Schaumburg, IL 60905.
● New Physician. m. ISSN 0028-6451

**American Medical Technologists**
710 Higgins Rd., Park Ridge, IL 60068.
● American Medical Technologists. Journal. bi-m. ISSN 0002-9963

**American Medical Women's Association, Inc**
1740 Broadway, New York, NY 10019.
● American Medical Women's Association. Journal. m. ISSN 0091-7427

**American Medical Writers Association**
5272 River Rd., Suite 290, Bethesda, MD 20016.
● Medical Communications. q.

**American Mensa Ltd.**
1701 W. 3rd St., Suite 1-R, Brooklyn, NY 11223.
● Mensa Bulletin. 10 per yr. ISSN 0025-9543

**American Merchant Marine Library Association**
1 Broadway, New York, NY 10004.
● American Merchant Marine Library Association. Report. a. ISSN 0065-938X

**American Metal Climax, Inc.**
1270 Ave. of the Americas, New York, NY 10020.
● A M A X Journal. q. ISSN 0001-1851

**American Metal Stamping Association**
27027 Chardon Rd., Richmond Hts., OH 44143.
● Metal Stamping. m. ISSN 0026-069X
● Metal Stamping Buyer's Guide. a.

**American Meteorological Society**
45 Beacon St., Boston, MA 02108.
● American Meteorological Society. Bulletin. m. ISSN 0003-0007
● American Meteorological Society. Meteorological Monographs. irreg., no. 36 (vol. 14) 1973. ISSN 0065-9401
● Conference on Aerospace and Aeronautical Meteorology. Preprints. irreg., 7th, 1976.
● Conference on Probability and Statistics in Atmospheric Sciences. Preprints. irreg.
● Conference on Radar Meteorology. Preprints. biennial. ISSN 0069-8636
● Conference on Severe Local Storms. Preprints. irreg., 10th, 1977. ISSN 0069-8679
● Conference on Weather Modification. Preprints. irreg., 4th, 1974.
● Curricula in the Atmospheric and Oceanographic Sciences. biennial.
● Journal of Applied Meteorology. m. ISSN 0021-8952
● Journal of Physical Oceanography. bi-m. ISSN 0022-3670
● Journal of the Atmospheric Sciences. m. ISSN 0022-4928
● Meteorological and Geoastrophysical Abstracts. m. ISSN 0026-1130
● Monthly Weather Review. m.

**American Metric Journal Publishing Co.**
Box 847, Tarzana, CA 91356.
● A M J-S I Metricpac. bi-m. (Polymetric Services Inc.)

**American Microscopical Society**
● American Microscopical Society. Transactions. (pub. by Allen Press, Inc.)

**American Military Institute**
● Military Affairs. (pub. by Robin Higham, Ed. & Pub.)

**American Milking Shorthorn Society**
313 S. Glenstone Ave., Springfield, MO 65802.
● Journal of the Milking Shorthorn and Illawarra Breeds. m. (Co-sponsor: International Illawarra Association)

**American Mining Congress**
1100 Ring Bldg., Washington, DC 20036.
● Mining Congress Journal. m. ISSN 0026-5160

**American Montessori Society**
150 Fifth Ave., New York, NY 10011.
● A M S. Proceedings of the National Seminar. irreg. ISSN 0517-3833
● A M S Bulletin. q.
● A M S News. q.
● Constructive Triangle. 2 per yr. ISSN 0010-700X

**American Morgan Horse Association, Inc.**
Box 1, Westmoreland, NY 13490.
● Morgan Horse. m.(Feb-Dec) ISSN 0027-1098

**American Mosaic Literary Publications**
Box 9182, Lansing, Mi 48909.
● American Mosaic. q.
● Twist; quarterly chapbook of fun and poems. q.

**American Mosquito Control Association**
c/o Thomas D. Mulhern, Exec. Dir., 5545 E. Shields Ave., Fresno, CA 93727.
● Mosquito News. q. ISSN 0027-142X

**American Motor Carrier**
104 Hemlock Dr., Marietta, GA 30064.
● American Motor Carrier. bi-m. ISSN 0003-0066

**American Motorcyclist Association**
Box 141, Westerville, OH 43081.
● A M A News. m. ISSN 0003-0074

**American Mountaineering and Rockclimbing Magazine**
Box E, Aspen, CO 81611.
● Climbing. 6 per yr. ISSN 0045-7159 (Climbing, Ltd.)

**American Movement for World Government, Inc.**
● World Peace News. (pub. by World Peace News)

**American Museum of Natural History**
Central Park West at 79th St, New York, NY 10024.
● American Museum Novitates. irreg. ISSN 0003-0082
● American Museum of Natural History. Annual Report. a.
● American Museum of Natural History. Anthropological Papers. irreg. ISSN 0065-9452
● American Museum of Natural History. Bulletin. irreg. ISSN 0003-0090
● American Museum Sourcebooks in Anthropology. (pub. by Natural History Press)
● Anthropological Handbook. (pub. by McGraw Hill Inc.)
● Curator. q. ISSN 0011-3069
● H I S S News-Journal. ISSN 0090-9203 (Herpetological Information Search Systems)
● H I S S Titles and Review. 5 per yr. ISSN 0092-2307 (Herpetological Information Search Systems)
● Natural History. m.(Oct-May); bi-m.(June-Sept) ISSN 0028-0712
● New Explorers. irreg.
● Yearbook of Herpetology. a. ISSN 0098-2644 (Herpetological Information Search Systems)

**American Music Center**
250 W. 57th St., Suite 626-7, New York, NY 10019.
● American Music Center. Newsletter. q. ISSN 0003-0104

**American Musicological Society**
University of Pennsylvania, Philadelphia, PA 19104.
● American Musicological Society. Journal. 3 per yr. ISSN 0003-0139
● American Musicological Society. Studies and Documents. (pub. by Galaxy Music Corp)

**American Musicological Society. Greater New York Chapter**
City University of New York Graduate Center, 535 E. 80 St., New York, NY 10021.
● American Musicological Society. Greater New York Chapter. Publications. irreg. ISSN 0569-6666

**American Mutual Life Association**
6401 St. Clair Ave., Cleveland, OH 44103.
● Our Voice. s-m.

**American Name Society**
State University of New York at Potsdam, Potsdam, NY 13676.
● Names. q. ISSN 0027-7738

**American National Heritage Association**
● Quinto Lingo. (pub. by Language Learning Systems Inc)

**American National Metric Council**
1625 Massachusetts Ave., N.W., Washington, DC 20036.
● American National Metric Council. Annual Report. a. ISSN 0363-5260
● Metric Reporter. bi-w.

**American National Red Cross**
17 and D Sts. N.W., Washington, DC 20006.
● American National Red Cross. Annual Report. a. ISSN 0080-0384
● Good Neighbor. m.

**American National Standards Institute**
1430 Broadway, New York, NY 10018.
● A N S I Reporter. fortn. ISSN 0038-9676
● Standards Action. fortn. ISSN 0038-9633

**American National Standards Institute. Committee Z-39**
School of Library Science, Manning Hall 026 A, University of North Carolina, Chapel Hill, NC 27514.
● News About Z-39. q. ISSN 0028-8942

**American Nature Study Society**
c/o John Gustafson, Ed., R. D. 1, Homer, NY 13077.
● Nature Study. q. ISSN 0028-0860

**American Navion Society**
Box 1175, Municipal Airport, Banning, CA 92220.
● Navioneer. m. ISSN 0028-1581

**American Near East Refugee Aid, Inc.**
900 Woodward Building, 733 15 St. N.W., Washington, DC 20005.
● A N E R A Newsletter. q.

**American Newspaper Boy Press**
915 Carolina Ave., N.W., Winston-Salem, NC 27101.
● American Newspaper Boy. m. ISSN 0003-0163

**American Newspaper Markets, Inc.**
Box 182, Northfield, IL 60093.
● American Newspaper Markets Circulation. a.

**American Newspaper Publishers Association. Research Institute**
Box 598, Easton, PA 18042.
● American Newspaper Publishers Association. Research Institute. R. I. Bulletins. 30 per yr. ISSN 0001-205X

**American Nuclear Society**
555 N. Kensington Ave., La Grange Park, IL 60525.
● American Nuclear Society Transactions. s-a. ISSN 0003-018X
● Conference on Remote Systems Technology. Proceedings. a. ISSN 0069-8644
● Directory: Who's Who in Nuclear Energy. irreg. ISSN 0092-8518
● Nuclear News. m. ISSN 0029-5574
● Nuclear News Buyers Guide. a. ISSN 0078-2610
● Nuclear Science and Engineering. m. ISSN 0029-5639
● Nuclear Science Technology Monograph Series. irreg. (Co-sponsor: U.S. Energy Research & Development Administration)
● Nuclear Standards News. m. ISSN 0029-5655 (prep. by its Information Center on Nuclear Standards)

- Nuclear Technology; applications for nuclear science, nuclear engineering and related arts. m. plus mid-Apr., mid-Aug., mid-Dec. ISSN 0029-5450

**American Numismatic Association**
Box 2366, Colorado Springs, CO 80901.
- A. N. A. Club Bulletin. bi-m. ISSN 0001-1991
- Numismatist. m. ISSN 0029-6090

**American Numismatic Association, Junior Members**
P.O. Box 2366, Colorado Springs, CO 80901.
- Young Numismatist. q.

**American Numismatic Society**
Broadway between 155 & 156 Sts., New York, NY 10038.
- American Numismatic Society. Annual Report. a.
- Greek Coins in North American Collections. irreg. ISSN 0072-744X
- Numismatic Literature. s-a. ISSN 0029-6031
- Numismatic Literature. Supplement. irreg. ISSN 0078-270X
- Numismatic Notes and Monographs. irreg., 1970, no. 160. ISSN 0078-2718
- Numismatic Studies. irreg. ISSN 0517-404X
- Seaby's Coin and Medal Bulletin. (pub. by B. A. Seaby Ltd. UK)

**American Nurses Association**
2420 Pershing Rd., Kansas City, MO 64108.
- A N A Clinical Sessions. biennial (alternates with ANA Clinical Conferences) ISSN 0065-9495
- American Journal of Nursing. (pub. by American Journal of Nursing Co.)
- American Nurse. m.
- American Nurses' Association. House of Delegates. Reports. biennial. ISSN 0065-9517
- American Nurses' Association. House of Delegates. Summary Proceedings. irreg. ISSN 0361-0772
- American Nurses Association. Proceedings of the Convention. biennial.
- Contemporary Nursing Series. (pub. by American Journal of Nursing Co.)

**American Nurses Association. Council for State Boards of Nursing**
2420 Pershing Rd., Kansas City, MO 64108.
- American Nurses' Association. Conference for Members and Professional Employees of State Boards of Nursing and A N A Advisory Council. Proceedings. a. ISSN 0065-9509

**American Nurses' Association. National League for Nursing**
- International Nursing Index. (pub. by American Journal of Nursing Co.)
- Nursing Outlook. (pub. by American Journal of Nursing Co.)
- Nursing Research. (pub. by American Journal of Nursing Co.)

**American Nurses Association. Statistics Department**
2420 Pershing Rd., Kansas City, MO 64108.
- Facts about Nursing; a statistical summary. a. ISSN 0071-3651

**American Nurses' Foundation, Inc.**
2420 Pershing Rd., Kansas City, MO 64108.
- International Directory of Nurses with Doctoral Degrees. irreg., latest 1973. ISSN 0091-9462
- Nursing Research Report. q. ISSN 0044-7781

**American Occupational Medical Association**
150 N. Wacker Drive, Chicago, IL 60606.
- American Occupational Medical Association. Membership Directory. biennial.
- Journal of Occupational Medicine. m. ISSN 0022-3212

**American Occupational Therapy Association, Inc.**
6000 Executive Blvd., Rockville, MD 20852.
- American Journal of Occupational Therapy. 10 per yr. ISSN 0002-9386
- American Occupational Therapy Association. Registry and Directory. a.
- Occupational Therapy. m.

**American Oil Chemists' Society**
508 S. Sixth St., Chicago, IL 61820.
- American Oil Chemists' Society. Journal. m. ISSN 0003-021X
- Lipids. m. ISSN 0024-4201

**American Old Time Fiddlers Association**
6141 Morrill Ave., Lincoln, NE 68507.
- American Fiddlers News. q.

**American Ophthalmological Society**
- American Ophthalmological Society. Transactions. (pub. by Whiting Press, Inc.)

**American Optical Corp.**
14 Mechanic St., P.O. Box 1, Southbridge, MA 01550.
- A O News. m.

**American Optometric Association**
7000 Chippewa St., St. Louis, MO 63119.
- American Optometric Association. Journal. m. ISSN 0003-0244
- American Optometric Association News. s-m. ISSN 0094-9620

**American Orchid Society Inc.**
- American Orchid Society Bulletin. (pub. by Harvard University. Botanical Museum)

**American Orff Schulwerk Association**
Box 18495, Cleveland Heights, OH 44118.
- Orff Echo. 3 per yr.

**American Oriental Society**
329 Sterling Memorial Library, Yale Station, New Haven, CT 06520.
- American Oriental Series. irreg. ISSN 0065-9541
- American Oriental Society. Journal. q. ISSN 0003-0279

**American Ornithologists Union**
Dept. of Zoology, Oregon State University, Corvallis, OR 97331
(or National Museum of Natural History, Smithsonian Institution, Washington, DC 20560)
- American Ornithologists' Union. Publications. irreg.
- Ornithological Monographs. irreg. ISSN 0078-6594

**American Ornithologists' Union (Chicago)**
c/o University of Illinois at the Medical Center, Department of Anatomy, Box 6998, Chicago, IL 60680.
- Auk; a journal of ornithology. q. ISSN 0004-8038

**American Orthopaedic Society for Sports Medicine**
- American Journal of Sports Medicine. (pub. by Sports and Medicine Publications)

**American Orthopsychiatric Association**
1775 Broadway, New York, NY 10019.
- American Journal of Orthopsychiatry; a journal of human behavior. q. ISSN 0002-9432
- American Orthopsychiatric Association. Papers Presented at the Annual Convention. (pub. by Wayne State University Press)

**American Orthotic and Prosthetic Association**
1444 N. St. N.W., Washington, DC 20005.
- Orthotics and Prosthetics. q. ISSN 0030-5928

**American Osteopathic Academy of Orthopedics**
211 Glendale, Suite 215, Highland Park, MI 48203.
- Orthopod. q. ISSN 0030-591X

**American Osteopathic Association**
212 E. Ohio St., Chicago, IL 60611.
- A O A Newsbriefs. m. ISSN 0091-6269
- American Osteopathic Association. Journal. m. ISSN 0003-0287
- D. O; a publication for osteopathic physicians and surgeons. m. ISSN 0011-5088
- Health; an osteopathic publication. bi-m. ISSN 0017-8853
- Yearbook and Directory of Osteopathic Physicians. a. ISSN 0084-358X

**American Osteopathic College of Radiology**
2515 E. Jefferson Blvd., South Bend, IN 46615.
- Viewbox. 4 per yr.

**American Osteopathic Hospital Association**
930 Busse Highway, Park Ridge, IL 60068.
- Osteopathic Hospitals. m. ISSN 0048-2293

**American Otological Society**
1100 E. Genesee St., Syracuse, NY 13210.
- American Otological Society. Transactions. a.

**American Paint Journal Co.**
2911 Washington Ave., St. Louis, MO 63103.
- American Paint & Coatings Journal. w. ISSN 0098-5430
- American Paint & Coatings Journal Convention Daily. 5 per yr. ISSN 0097-4749
- American Paint and Wallcoverings Dealer. m.

- American Painting Contractor. m. ISSN 0003-0325

**American Paper Institute, Inc.**
260 Madison Ave., New York, NY 10016.
- American Paper Institute. Monthly Statistical Summary. m. ISSN 0003-0341

**American Patent Law Association**
Suite 203, 2001 Jefferson Davis Highway, Arlington, VA 22202.
- A P L A Quarterly Journal. q. ISSN 0091-0538

**American Peace Society**
4000 Albemarle St., N.W., Washington, DC 20016.
- World Affairs. q. ISSN 0043-8200

**American Peanut Research and Education Association**
1204 West Point Dr., Suffolk, VA 23434.
- Peanut Science. s-a. ISSN 0095-36/9

**American Pedestrian Association**
Box 624, Forest Hills Sta., Forest Hills, NY 11375.
- Pedestrian Research. q.

**American Pediatric Directory**
7217 Kingston Pk., Knoxville, TN 37919.
- American Pediatric Directory. biennial.

**American Personnel and Guidance Association**
1607 New Hampshire Ave, N.W., Washington, DC 20009.
- A P G A Directory of Members. a. ISSN 0569-6836
- A P G A Guidance and Counseling Series. irreg. ISSN 0065-9592
- A P G A Inquiry Studies. irreg. ISSN 0065-9606
- A P G A Reprint Series. irreg. ISSN 0065-9614
- American Personnel and Guidance Association. Convention Abstracts. a. ISSN 0065-9622
- Career Resource Bibliography.
- Contemporary Thought in Guidance and Counseling. irreg. ISSN 0069-9500
- Counseling and Values. q. (Co-Sponsor National Catholic Guidance Conference)
- Counselor Education and Supervision. q. ISSN 0011-0035
- Elementary School Guidance & Counseling. 4 per yr. ISSN 0013-5976
- Financial Aid for Personnel and Guidance Graduate Study. a. ISSN 0071-500X
- Guidepost. 18 per yr. ISSN 0017-5323
- Humanist Educator. q. (Association for Humanistic Education and Development)
- Inform. 10 per yr.
- Journal of College Student Personnel. bi-m. ISSN 0021-9789
- Journal of Employment Counseling. q. ISSN 0022-0787
- Journal of Non-White Concerns in Personnel and Guidance. q. ISSN 0090-5461 (Association for Non-White Concerns in Personnel and Guidance)
- Measurement and Evaluation in Guidance. q. ISSN 0025-6307
- Personnel and Guidance Journal. m.(Sept-June) ISSN 0031-5737
- Rehabilitation Counseling Bulletin. q. ISSN 0034-3552
- School Counselor. 5 per yr. ISSN 0036-6536

**American Petroleum Institute**
1801 K St., N.W., Washington, DC 20006.
- American Petroleum Institute. Research Project 44. Selected Values of Properties of Hydrocarbons and Related Compounds. Category A: Tables of Selected Values of Physical and Thermodynamic Properties of Hydrocarbons. (pub. by Thermodynamics Research Center)
- American Petroleum Institute. Research Project 44. Selected Values of Properties of Hydrocarbons and Related Compounds. Category B: Selected Infrared Spectral Data. (pub. by Thermodynamics Research Center)
- American Petroleum Institute. Research Project 44. Selected Values of Properties of Hydrocarbons and Related Compounds. Category C: Selected Ultraviolet Spectral Data. (pub. by Thermodynamics Research Center)
- American Petroleum Institute. Research Project 44. Selected Values of Properties of Hydrocarbons and Related Compounds. Category D: Selected Raman Spectral Data. (pub. by Thermodynamics Research Center)
- American Petroleum Institute. Research Project 44. Selected Values of Properties of Hydrocarbons and Related Compounds. Category E: Selected Mass Spectral Data. (pub. by Thermodynamics Research Center)

- American Petroleum Institute. Research Project 44. Selected Values of Properties of Hydrocarbons and Related Compounds. Category F: Selected Nuclear Magnetic Resonance Data. (pub. by Thermodynamics Research Center)
- American Petroleum Institute. Research Project 44. Selected Values of Properties of Hydrocarbons and Related Compounds. Category G: Selected 13C Nuclear Magnetic Resonance Spectral Data. (pub. by Thermodynamics Research Center)
- Comprehensive Index of the A P I44-T R C Selected Data on Thermodynamics and Spectroscopy. (pub. by Thermodynamics Research Center)
- Conference on Prevention and Control of Oil Spills. Proceedings. biennial. (Co-sponsors: Environmental Protection Agency; U.S. Coast Guard)
- Liquefied Petroleum Gas Report. m. ISSN 0024-421X

**American Petroleum Institute. Central Abstracting and Indexing Service**
275 Madison Ave., New York, NY 10016.
- A P I Patent Alert. w.
- Abstracts of Petroleum Substitutes Literature. m.
- Abstracts of Refining Literature and Petrochemicals Literature. w.
- Abstracts of Transportation and Storage Literature. m.
- American Petroleum Institute. Central Abstracting and Indexing Service. Thesaurus. a.
- Petroleum/Energy Business News Index. m.

**American Petroleum Institute. Committee for Air and Water Conservation**
1801 K St., N.W., Washington, DC 20006.
- Air Quality Monograph Series. irreg. ISSN 0568-3653

**American Petroleum Institute. Committee on Medicine and Environmental Health**
1801 K St., N.W., Washington, 7Dc 20006.
- American Petroleum Institute. Committee on Medicine and Environmental Health. Medical Research Reports. irreg.

**American Petroleum Institute. Division of Refining**
1801 K St., N.W., Washington, DC 20006.
- American Petroleum Institute. Division of Refining. Proceedings. a. ISSN 0569-6909

**American Petroleum Institute. Division of Statistics and Economics**
2101 L St. N. W., Washington, DC 20037.
- American Petroleum Institute. Division of Statistics & Economics. Weekly Statistical Bulletin. w. ISSN 0003-0457
- Quarterly Review of Drilling Statistics. q. ISSN 0033-5789

**American Petroleum Institute. Editorial Department**
2101 L St. N.W., Washington, DC 20037.
- Petroleum Today. q. ISSN 0031-6555

**American Petroleum Institute. Statistical Publications Section**
2101 L St. N.W., Washington, DC 20037.
- Basic Petroleum Data Book. q.

**American Pharmaceutical Association**
2215 Constitution Ave., N.W., Washington, DC 20037.
- American Pharmaceutical Association. Journal. m. ISSN 0003-0465
- APhArmacy Weekly. w.
- Evaluations of Drug Interactions. a.
- Evaluations of Drug Interactions. Supplement. a.
- Handbook of Non Prescription Drugs. biennial.
- Journal of Pharmaceutical Sciences. m. ISSN 0022-3549
- Pharmaceutical Directory. a. ISSN 0569-6917

**American Philatelic Congress**
Box 3646, Wilmington, NC 28401.
- American Philatelic Congress. Congress Book. a.

**American Philatelic Research Library**
Box 338, State College, PA 16801.
- Philatelic Literature Review; a guide to intelligent stamp collecting. q.

**American Philatelic Society, Inc.**
Box 800, State College, PA 16801.
- American Philatelist. m. ISSN 0003-0473

**American Philatelic Society. Writers Unit No. 30**
Box 22308, Memphis, TN 38122
(Subscr. address: C. C. Cratsenberg, 9928 Lancaster Dr., Sun City, AZ 85351)
- A.P.S. Writers Unit Number Thirty News Bulletin. q.

**American Philological Association**
431-432 N. Burrowes, Pennsylvania State University, University Park, PA 16802.
- American Philological Association. Directory of Members. irreg. (approx. biennial) ISSN 0044-779X
- American Philological Association. Special Publications. irreg. ISSN 0065-9703
- American Philological Association. Transactions. a.
- Philological Monographs. irreg., 1973, no. 31. ISSN 0079-1628

**American Philosophical Association**
University of Delaware, Newark, DE 19711.
- American Philosophical Association. Proceedings and Addresses. a. ISSN 0065-972X
- Paul Carus Lectures. (pub. by Open Court Publishing Co.)

**American Philosophical Society**
104 S. Fifth St, Philadelphia, PA 19106.
- American Philosophical Society. Memoirs. irreg. ISSN 0065-9738
- American Philosophical Society. Proceedings. 6 per yr. ISSN 0003-049X
- American Philosophical Society. Transactions. 1 vol. per yr. containing 1-10 parts published irregularly. ISSN 0065-9746
- American Philosophical Society. Yearbook. a. ISSN 0065-9762

**American Philosophical Society. Library**
5Th & Chestnut, Philadelphia, PA 19106.
- American Philosophical Society. Library Publications. irreg.; 1977, no. 7. ISSN 0084-6430
- Mendel Newsletter; archival resources for the history of genetics & allied sciences. 2 per yr. ISSN 0025-9241

**American Philosophical Society. Survey of Sources for the History of Biochemistry and Molecular Biology**
105 S. Fifth St., Philadelphia, PA 19106.
- Survey of Sources Newsletter. irreg. (Co-sponsor: American Academy of Arts and Sciences)

**American Physical Society**
- American Physical Society. Bulletin. (pub. by American Institute of Physics)
- Physical Review A (General Physics) (pub. by American Institute of Physics)
- Physical Review B (Solid State) (pub. by American Institute of Physics)
- Physical Review C (Nuclear Physics) (pub. by American Institute of Physics)
- Physical Review D (Particles and Fields) (pub. by American Institute of Physics)
- Physical Review Abstracts. (pub. by American Institute of Physics)
- Physical Review Letters. (pub. by American Institute of Physics)
- Reviews of Modern Physics. (pub. by American Institute of Physics)

**American Physical Therapy Association**
1156 15th St, N.W., Washington, DC 20005.
- Physical Therapy. m. ISSN 0031-9023

**American Physiological Society**
9650 Rockville Pike, Bethesda, MD 20014.
- American Journal of Physiology. m. ISSN 0002-9513
- American Journal of Physiology: Cell Physiology. q. ISSN 0363-6143
- American Journal of Physiology: Endocrinology, Metabolism and Gastrointestinal Physiology. m. ISSN 0363-6100
- American Journal of Physiology: Heart and Circulatory Physiology. m. ISSN 0363-6135
- American Journal of Physiology: Regulatory, Integrative and Comparative Physiology. q. ISSN 0363-6119
- American Journal of Physiology: Renal, Fluid and Electrolyte Physiology. m. ISSN 0363-6127
- Handbook of Physiology. (pub. by Williams & Wilkins Co.)
- Journal of Applied Physiology: Respiratory, Environmental and Exercise Physiology. m. (2 vols. per yr.)

- Journal of Neurophysiology. bi-m. ISSN 0022-3077
- Physiological Reviews. q. ISSN 0031-9333
- Physiologist. bi-m. ISSN 0031-9376
- Physiology Teacher. 5 per yr. ISSN 0048-4075

**American Phytopathological Society**
3340 Pilot Knob Rd., St. Paul, MN 55121.
- American Phytopathological Society. Monographs. irreg., no. 10, 1976. ISSN 0569-6992
- American Phytopathological Society. Proceedings. a.
- Fungicide and Nematicde Tests. a. (Orders to: E. I. Zehr, c/o Department of Plant Pathology and Physiology, Clemson University, Clemson, SC 29631)
- Phytopathology; an international journal. m. ISSN 0031-949X
- Phytopathology News. m. ISSN 0031-9503

**American Pigeon Journal Co.**
Warrenton, MO 63383.
- American Pigeon Journal; devoted to all branches of pigeon raising-fancy, utility and racing. m. ISSN 0003-0511

**American Plant Life Society**
Box 150, La Jolla, CA 92034.
- Plant Life. a. ISSN 0032-0846

**American Podiatry Association**
20 Chevy Chase Circle, N.W., Washington, DC 20015.
- American Podiatry Association. Desk Reference and Directory with Catalogue of Audio-Visual, Informational and Educational Materials and Standard Podiatric Nomenclature. a. ISSN 0065-9770
- American Podiatry Association. Journal. m. ISSN 0003-0538

**American Poetry and Poetics**
Box 348, 218 S. Egan Ave., Madison, SD 57042.
- American Poetry and Poetics. q.

**American Poets Fellowship Society**
c/o Ed. Mrs. Stella C. Tremble, 902 Tenth St., Charleston, IL 61920.
- American Poet; voice of the American Poets Fellowship Society. q. ISSN 0003-0546

**American Polar Society**
c/o A. Howard, 98-20 62nd Drive (Apt. 7H), Rego Park, NY 11374.
- Polar Times. s-a. ISSN 0032-2482

**American Political Research Corp.**
4720 Montgomery Lane, Bethesda, MD 20014.
- American Political Report. bi-w.

**American Political Science Association**
1527 New Hampshire Ave, N.W., Washington, DC 20036.
- A P S A Biographical Directory. irreg., 6th, 1973.
- A P S A Departmental Services Program Survey of Departments. a.
- A.P.S.A. Directory of Department Chairpersons. a.
- American Political Science Review. q. ISSN 0003-0554
- Guide to Graduate Study in Political Science. a. ISSN 0091-9632
- P S. q. ISSN 0030-8269

**American Polled Hereford Association**
- Polled Hereford World. (pub. by American Polled Hereford Publications, Inc.)

**American Polled Hereford Publications, Inc.**
4700 E. 63rd St., Kansas City, MO 64130.
- Polled Hereford World. m. ISSN 0032-3608 (American Polled Hereford Association)

**American Polygraph Association**
P.O. Box 74, Linthicum Heights, MD 21090.
- American Polygraph Association Newsletter. m.
- Polygraph. q.

**American Pomological Society**
c/o Dr. Loren D. Tukey, Bus. Mgr., 103 Tyson Bldg., University Park, PA 16802.
- Fruit Varieties Journal. q. ISSN 0091-3642

**American-Portuguese Overseas Information Organization**
206 Fifth Ave., New York, NY 10010.
- A P O I O. s-m.

**American Portuguese Society**
88 Morningside Dr., New York, NY 10027.
- American Portuguese Society. Journal. 2 per yr.
ISSN 0098-4981

**American Postal Workers Union - AFL-CIO**
817 14th St. N.W., Washington, DC 20005.
- American Postal Worker. m. ISSN 0044-7811

**American Postcard Journal**
Box 562, West Haven, CT 06516.
- American Postcard Journal. bi-m.

**American Powder Metallurgy Institute**
Box 2054, Princeton, NJ 08540.
- International Journal of Powder Metallurgy &
Powder Technology. q.
- P-M Literature Reference Guide. irreg. ISSN
0097-7241 (Co-sponsor: Metal Powder Industries
Federation)
- P/M Technology Newsletter. (Powder Metallurgy)
m.
- Who's Who in P-M. irreg. ISSN 0361-6304

**American Power Boat Association**
22811 Greater Mack, St. Clair Shores, MI 48080.
- American Power Boat Association. A P B A Rule
Book. a. ISSN 0065-9797

**American Power Conference**
Illinois Institute of Technology, Chicago, IL 60616.
- American Power Conference. Proceedings. a.

**American Press**
Route B North, Columbia, MO 65201.
- Community Development Society. Journal. s-a.
ISSN 0010-3829

**American Primrose Society**
c/o Mrs. John Genheimer, 7100 S.W. 209th,
Beaverton, OR 97005.
- American Primrose Society. Quarterly. q. ISSN
0003-0619

**American Printing History Association**
c/o Stuart Dobson, 215 Harriman Rd., Irvington,
NY 10533.
- A P H A Letter. bi-m.

**American Printing House for the Blind**
1839 Frankfort Ave., Louisville, KY 40206.
- Ellery Queen's Mystery Magazine. Braille Edition.
m. ISSN 0013-631X
- Negro Braille Magazine. q. ISSN 0028-2502
- Reader's Digest (Braille Edition) m,

**American Printing House for the Blind. Department
of Educational Research**
P.O. Box 6085, Louisville, KY 40206.
- American Printing House for the Blind, Louisville,
Kentucky. Department of Educational Research.
Annual Report. a. ISSN 0065-9800

**American Proctologic Society**
- Diseases of the Colon and Rectum. (pub. by J. B.
Lippincott Co.)

**American Production and Inventory Control Society,
Inc.**
Watergate Bldg., Suite 504, 2600 Virginia Ave.,
N.W., Washington, DC 20037.
- A P I C S Annual Conference Proceedings. a.
ISSN 0065-9819
- A P I C S News. m.
- Production and Inventory Management. q. ISSN
0032-9843

**American Professors for Peace in the Middle East**
69 Bank St., New York, NY 10014.
- American Professors for Peace in the Middle East.
Bulletin. 5 per yr.

**American Protestant Defense League**
354 W. 26th St., New York, NY 10001.
- American Protest. q.

**American Protestant Hospital Association**
840 N. Lake Shore Dr., Chicago, IL 60611.
- American Protestant Hospital Association.
Bulletin. q. ISSN 0003-0635

**American Psychiatric Association**
1700 18th St., N.W., Washington, DC 20009.
- American Journal of Psychiatry. m. ISSN 0002-
953X
- American Psychiatric Association. Biographical
Directory. (pub. by R. R. Bowker Company.
Jaques Cattell Press)

- American Psychiatric Association. Membership
Directory. irreg.
- American Psychiatric Association. Scientific
Proceedings in Summary Form. a.
- American Psychiatric Association. Task Force
Reports. irreg., no. 6, 1973.
- Hospital and Community Psychiatry. m. ISSN
0022-1597
- National Directory of Providers of Psychiatric
Services to Religious Institutions. irreg. ISSN
0090-4074 (prep. by its Task Force on Religion
and Psychiatry)
- Psychiatric News. fortn. ISSN 0033-2704

**American Psychiatric Association Gay Caucus**
c/o R. Pillard, Ed., 700 Harrison Ave., Boston, MA
02118.
- American Psychiatric Association Gay Caucus.
Newsletter. q.

**American Psychoanalytic Association**
1 E. 57th St., New York, NY 10027.
- American Psychoanalytic Association. Journal.
(pub. by International Universities Press, Inc.)
- American Psychoanalytic Association. Journal.
Monograph. (pub. by International Universities
Press, Inc.)
- American Psychoanalytic Association. Roster.
biennial with annual supplement.

**American Psychological Association**
1200 17th St. N.W., Washington, DC 20036.
- A P A Monitor. m. ISSN 0001-2114
- American Psychological Association. Employment
Bulletin. m. ISSN 0065-9851
- American Psychological Association. Membership
Register. biennial. ISSN 0569-714X
- American Psychological Association Biographical
Directory. biennial. ISSN 0090-9076
- American Psychologist. m. ISSN 0003-066X
- Catalog of Selected Documents in Psychology; a
publication of the Journal Supplement Abstract
Service. q. ISSN 0045-5938
- Contemporary Psychology; a journal of reviews.
m. ISSN 0010-7549 (Editorial Office: A P A,
Department of Psychology, University of Texas,
Austin, TX 78712)
- Developmental Psychology. bi-m. ISSN 0012-1649
- Journal of Abnormal Psychology. bi-m.(2 vol. per
yr.) ISSN 0021-843X
- Journal of Applied Psychology. bi-m. ISSN 0021-
9010
- Journal of Comparative and Physiological
Psychology. bi-m. ISSN 0021-9940
- Journal of Consulting and Clinical Psychology. bi-
m. ISSN 0022-006X
- Journal of Counseling Psychology; for
psychologists and personnel workers concerned
with the counseling of clients, students and
employees. bi-m. ISSN 0022-0167
- Journal of Educational Psychology. bi-m. ISSN
0022-0663
- Journal of Experimental Psychology: Animal
Behavior Processes (JEP: ABP) q. ISSN 0097-
7403
- Journal of Experimental Psychology: General
(JEP: GEN) q. ISSN 0096-3445
- Journal of Experimental Psychology: Human
Learning and Memory (JEP: HLM) bi-m. ISSN
0096-1515
- Journal of Experimental Psychology: Human
Perception and Performance (JEP: HPP) q. ISSN
0096-1523
- Journal of Personality and Social Psychology. m.
(4 vols.per yr.) ISSN 0022-3514
- Professional Psychology. q. ISSN 0033-0175
- Psychological Abstracts. m. ISSN 0033-2887
- Psychological Bulletin. bi-m. ISSN 0033-2909
- Psychological Review. bi-m. ISSN 0033-295X
- Psychology of Women Quarterly. (pub. by Human
Sciences Press)

**American Psychological Association. Division of
Clinical Psychology**
c/o Jerome H. Resnick, Psychology Dept., Temple
Univ., Philadelphia, PA 19122.
- Clinical Psychologist. q. ISSN 0009-9244

**American Psychological Association. Division of
Educational Psychology**
1200 17th St. N.W., Washington, DC 20036.
- Educational Psychologist. 3 per yr. ISSN 0046-
1520

**American Psychological Association. Division Two**
c/o Robert S. Daniel, Ed., McAlester Hall,
University of Missouri, Columbia, MO 65201.
- Teaching of Psychology. q.

**American Psychological Association. Educational
Affairs Office**
1200 Seventeenth St. N.W., Washington, DC
20036.
- Graduate Study in Psychology. a. ISSN 0072-
5277
- Population Psychology Newsletter. q.

**American Psychological Association. Section on
Clinical Child Psychology**
Child Study Center, 1100 N.E. 13th St., Oklahoma
City, OK 73117.
- Journal of Clinical Child Psychology. 3 per yr.
ISSN 0047-228X

**American Psychopathological Association**
- American Psychopathological Association.
Proceedings of the Annual Meeting. (pub. by
Johns Hopkins University Press)
- American Psychopathological Association.
Publications. (pub. by Grune and Stratton, Inc.)
- Comprehensive Psychiatry. (pub. by Grune &
Stratton, Inc.)

**American Psychosomatic Society**
- Psychosomatic Medicine. (pub. by Elsevier North-
Holland, Inc., New York)

**American Public Gas Association**
2600 Virginia Ave. N.W., Washington, DC 20037.
- American Public Gas Association. Newsletter.
irreg. approx. every 3 wks.
- Directory of Municipal Natural Gas Systems.
irreg., 1977, 7th edt.

**American Public Health Association**
1015 18th St. N.W., Washington, DC 20036.
- American Journal of Public Health. m. ISSN
0090-0036
- Health Laboratory Science. q. ISSN 0017-9035
- Medical Care. (pub. by J. B. Lippincott Co.)
- Nation's Health. m. ISSN 0028-0496
- Vital and Health Statistics Monographs. irreg.
(Dist. by: Harvard University Press, 79 Garden
St., Cambridge, MA 02138)

**American Public Power Association**
Suite 212, 2600 Virginia Ave., N.W., Washington,
DC 20037.
- Public Power. bi-m. ISSN 0033-3654

**American Public Transit Association**
1100 17th St. N.W., Washington, DC 20036.
- Passenger Transport. w.
- Transit Journal. q.

**American Public Welfare Association**
1155 16th Street N.W., Suite 201, Washington, DC
20036.
- Public Welfare. q. ISSN 0033-3816
- Public Welfare Directory. a.

**American Public Works Association**
1313 E. 60th St., Chicago, IL 60637.
- A P W A Reporter. m. ISSN 0001-2270
- American Public Works Association. Directory. a.
- American Public Works Association. Research
Foundation. Special Reports. irreg.; latest issue.
1977. ISSN 0065-9932

**American Quarter Horse Association**
3014 W. Tenth, Amarillo, TX 79102.
- Quarter Horse Journal. m.

**American Rabbit Journal**
12902 N. Meridian St., Carmel, IN 46032.
- American Rabbit Journal. m.

**American Radio Association**
270 Madison Ave, New York, NY 10016.
- A R A Log. 2 per yr. ISSN 0001-2289

**American Radio Relay League, Inc.**
225 Main St., Newington, CT 06111.
- A R R L Antenna Book. irreg.
- Q S T; devoted entirely to amateur radio. m.
ISSN 0033-4812 (International Amateur Radio
Union)
- Radio Amateur's Handbook. a. ISSN 0079-9440
- Radio Amateur's License Manual. irreg., 76th,
1977.

**American Railway Bridge and Building Association**
Cary Bldg., 18154 Harwood Ave., Homewood, IL
60430.
- American Railway Bridge and Building
Association. Proceedings. a. 1969, vol. 74. ISSN
0065-9940

**American Railway Engineering Association**
59 E. Van Buren St., Chicago, IL 60605.
- American Railway Engineering Association. Bulletin. 5 per yr. ISSN 0003-0694
- American Railway Engineering Association. Proceedings. a.

**American Real Estate and Urban Economics Association**
- American Real Estate and Urban Economics Association. Journal. (pub. by Rutgers University. Center for Urban Policy Research)

**American Record**
G.P.O. Box 1100, 271 Cadman Plaza East, Brooklyn, NY 11202.
- American Record. m.

**American Recorder Society Inc.**
141 W. 20th St., New York, NY 10011.
- American Recorder. q. ISSN 0003-0724

**American Recorder Society. Metropolitan New York Chapter**
c/o Barbara Filner, 372 Central Park West, New York, NY 10025.
- New York Recorder Guild. Newsletter. m.

**American Register**
S. John Cousins, 90 W. Broadway, New York, NY 10007.
- American Register of Exporters and Importers. a. ISSN 0065-9967

**American Research Center in Egypt**
- American Research Center in Egypt. Journal. (pub. by J. J. Augustin, Inc.)

**American Revenue Association**
1010 S. Fifth Ave., Arcadia, CA 91006.
- American Revenuer. 10 per yr.

**American Rheumatism Association**
- Index of Rheumatology. (pub. by Arthritis Foundation. American Rheumatism Association Section)

**American Rhododendron Society**
c/o Ed. Molly Grothaus, 12373 SW Boones Ferry Rd., Lake Oswego, OR 97034.
- American Rhododendron Society. Quarterly Bulletin. q. ISSN 0003-0821

**American Risk and Insurance Association**
One State Farm Plaza, Bloomington, IL 61701.
- Journal of Risk and Insurance. q. ISSN 0022-4367

**American Road and Transportation Builders Association**
525 School St., S.W., Washington, DC 20024.
- American Transportation Builder. m.
- Officials and Engineers Directory of Transportation Agency Personnel. a.

**American Road Builders Association**
ARBA Bldg., 525 School St., S.W., Washington, DC 20024.
- American Road Builders Association. Technical Bulletins. irreg.

**American Rock Garden Society**
c/o W. T. Hirsch, Sec., 3 Salisbury Land, Malvern, PA 19355.
- American Rock Garden Society Bulletin. q. ISSN 0003-0864

**American Roentgen Ray Society**
- American Journal of Roentgenology. (pub. by Charles C. Thomas, Publisher)

**American Rose Society, Inc.**
P.O. Box 30,000, Shreveport, LA 71130.
- American Rose Annual. a. ISSN 0066-0000
- American Rose Magazine. m. ISSN 0003-0899

**American Sabbath Tract Society**
510 Watchung Ave., Plainfield, NJ 07061.
- Sabbath Recorder. m. ISSN 0036-214X

**American Safe Deposit Association**
Box Q, Clarence, NY 14031.
- Access. q.

**American-Scandinavian Foundation**
127 E. 73th St., New York, NY 10021.
- Library of Scandinavian Literature. (pub. by Twayne Publishers, Inc.)
- Scan. m. ISSN 0036-5467

- Scandinavian Review. q. ISSN 0098-857X

**American School Counselor Association**
1607 New Hampshire Ave., N.W., Washington, DC 20009.
- A S C A Newsletter. bi-m. ISSN 0001-2416

**American School Food Service Association**
4101 E. Iliff Ave., Denver, CO 80222.
- School Foodservice Journal. m.(10 per yr.)

**American School Health Association**
Box 708, Kent, OH 44240.
- Directory of National Organizations Concerned with School Health. biennial.
- Journal of School Health. m.(Sept-June) ISSN 0022-4391

**American School of Classical Studies at Athens**
c/o Institute for Advanced Study, Princeton, NJ 08540.
- Hesperia. q. ISSN 0018-098X

**American Schools of Oriental Research**
126 Inman St., Cambridge, MA 02139
- American Schools of Oriental Research. Annual. irreg., latest issue 1975. ISSN 0066-0035
- American Schools of Oriental Research. Bulletin. q. ISSN 0003-097X (Subscr. to: Scholars Press, University of Montana, Missoula, MT 59812)
- American Schools of Oriental Research. Newsletter. 10 per yr.
- Biblical Archeologist. q. ISSN 0006-0895 (Subscr. to: Scholars Press, University of Montana, Missoula MT 59801)
- Journal of Cuneiform Studies. q. ISSN 0022-0256 (Subscr. to: Scholars Press, University of Montana, Missoula MT 59801)

**American Scientific Affiliation**
5 Douglas Ave., Elgin, IL 60120.
- American Scientific Affiliation. Journal. q. ISSN 0003-0988

**American Scientific Glassblowers Society**
309 Georgetown Ave., Gwinhurst, Wilmington, DE 19809.
- Fusion. q. ISSN 0016-3155
- Symposium on the Art of Glassblowing Proceedings. a. ISSN 0569-7468

**American Security Council**
- American Security Council Washington Report. (pub. by American Security Council Press)

**American Security Council Press**
Boston, VA 22713.
- American Security Council Washington Report. m. ISSN 0003-1011

**American Servicemen's Union**
46w. 21st St., New York, NY 10010.
- Bond; voice of Vets & GI's. m. ISSN 0006-7032
- Potemkin. m. ISSN 0032-5597

**American Shih Tzu Club**
Box 1016, Tryon, NC 28782.
- Shih Tzu Bulletin. irreg.

**American Shore and Beach Preservation Association**
10 Rickenbacker Causeway, Miami, FL 33149.
- Shore and Beach. s-a. ISSN 0037-4237

**American Simmental Association**
- Simmental Shield. (pub. by Shield Publishing Co.)

**American Social Health Association**
260 Sheridan Ave., Palo Alto, CA 94306.
- V D News. q.

**American Society for Adolescent Psychiatry**
- Adolescent Psychiatry. (pub. by Basic Books Inc.)
- American Society for Adolescent Psychiatry. Newsletter. (pub. by ANRO Inc.)

**American Society for Aesthetics**
- Journal of Aesthetics and Art Criticism. (pub. by Temple University)

**American Society for Artificial Internal Organs**
c/o Dr. George E. Schreiner, Department of Medicine, Georgetown University Hospital, Washington, DC 20007.
- American Society for Artificial Internal Organs. Transactions. a. ISSN 0066-0078

**American Society for Cell Biology**
- Journal of Cell Biology. (pub. by Rockefeller University Press)

**American Society for Church Architecture**
Box 42834, Chicago, IL 60642.
- American Society for Church Architecture. Journal. irreg.

**American Society for Clinical Investigation**
- Journal of Clinical Investigation. (pub. by Rockefeller University Press)

**American Society for Conservation Archaeology**
c/o Alexander J. Lindsay, Jr., Treas., Rt. 4, Box 720, Flagstaff, AZ 86001.
- American Society for Conservation Archaeology Newsletter. q.

**American Society for Cybernetics**
1025 Connecticut Ave. N.W., Suite 914, Washington, DC 20036.
- A S C Cybernetics Forum. q.
- American Society for Cybernetics. Proceedings of the Annual Symposium. a. ISSN 0066-0086
- Journal of Cybernetics and Information Science. (pub. by Western Periodicals Co.)

**American Society for Eastern Arts**
2640 College Ave., Berkeley, CA 94704.
- A S E A Newsletter. irreg. ISSN 0044-7854

**American Society for Eighteenth-Century Studies**
c/o Paul J. Korshin, Exec. Sec., Department of English, University of Pennsylvania, Philadelphia, PA 19104.
- Eighteenth-Century Studies. q. ISSN 0013-2586

**American Society for Engineering Education**
Suite 400, One Dupont Circle, N. W., Washington, DC 20036.
- A S E E Profile. a.
- Engineering College Research and Graduate Study. a.
- Engineering Education. 8 per yr. ISSN 0022-0809

**American Society for Engineering Education. Chemical Engineering Division**
Dept. of Chemical Engineering, University of Florida, Gainesville, FL 32611.
- Chemical Engineering Education. q. ISSN 0009-2479

**American Society for Engineering Education. Computers in Education Division**
P.O. Box 308, W. Long Branch, NJ 07764.
- A S E E Computers in Education Division. CoED Transactions. m.
- American Society for Engineering Education. Computers in Education Division. Application Notes. bi-m.
- American Society for Engineering Education. Computers in Education Division. Newsletter. bi-m.

**American Society for Engineering Education. Continuing Engineering Studies Division**
1 Dupont Circle, Suite 400, Washington, DC 20036.
- Continuing Engineering Studies Series. a. ISSN 0069-956X

**American Society for Engineering Education. Engineering Design Graphics Division**
c/o Garland K. Hilliard, Jr., Circ. Mgr., 239 Riddick Hall, North Carolina State University, Raleigh, NC 27607.
- Engineering Design Graphics Journal. 3 per yr. ISSN 0046-2012

**American Society for Engineering Education. Engineering Economy Division**
- Engineering Economist. (pub. by University of Texas at Dallas)

**American Society for Environmental History**
Duquesne University, College Hall, Pittsburgh, PA 15219.
- E R. (Environmental Review) 3 per yr.
- Environmental History Newsletter. s-a.

**American Society for Ethnohistory**
c/o James E. Ayres, Sec.-Treas., University of Arizona, Arizona State Museum, Tucson, AZ 85721.
- Ethnohistory; devoted to original research in the documentary history of the culture and movements of primitive peoples and related problems of broader scope. q. ISSN 0014-1801

**American Society for Gastrointestinal Endoscopy**
c/o William S. Haubrich, Scripp Clinic and
Research Foundation, 10666 N. Torrey Pines Rd.,
La Jolla, CA 92037.
- Gastrointestinal Endoscopy. q. ISSN 0016-5107

**American Society for Horticultural Science**
914 Main, Box 109, St. Joseph, MI 49085.
- American Society for Horticultural Science.
Journal. bi-m. ISSN 0003-1062
- Hortscience. q. ISSN 0018-5345
- Plant Analysis and Fertilizer Problems. irreg.

**American Society for Indian Arts and Culture**
Ed. Sri Tam Bakshi, Department of Theatre, State
University College, Brockport, NY 14420.
- Vision of India. s-a. ISSN 0042-6970

**American Society for Industrial Security**
2000 K St. N.W., Suite 651, Washington, DC
20006.
- Security Management. bi-m. ISSN 0145-9406

**American Society for Information Science**
1155 16th St., N.W., Suite 210, Washington, DC
20036.
- American Society for Information Science.
Bulletin. bi-m. ISSN 0095-4403
- American Society for Information Science.
Handbook and Directory. a. ISSN 0066-0124
- American Society for Information Science.
Journal. (J A S I S) bi-m. ISSN 0002-8231
- American Society for Information Science.
Proceedings of the Annual Meeting. a. ISSN
0044-7870
- Annual Review of Information Science and
Technology. a. ISSN 0066-4200
- Information Science Abstracts. (pub. by
Documentation Abstracts, Inc.)

**American Society for Information Science, Pacific
Northwest Chapter**
c/o Darlene Myers-Johnson, Ed., Computing
Information Center, FC-10, University of
Washington, Seattle, WA 98195.
- Points Northwest. 4-6 per yr.

**American Society for Information Science. Special
Interest Group on Education for Information
Science**
1155 16th St. N.W., Suite 210, Washington, DC
20036.
- S I G Newsletter. irreg.

**American Society for Information Science. Special
Interest Group on Information Analysis Centers**
c/o Betty McGill, Ed., Radiation Shielding
Information Center, Oak Ridge National
Laboratory, Box X, Oak Ridge, TN 37830.
- S I G/I A C Newsletter. q?

**American Society for International Law**
2223 Massachusetts Ave. N.W., Washington, DC
20008.
- American Society for International Law
Newsletter. m.

**American Society for Legal History**
- American Journal of Legal History. (pub. by
Temple University School of Law)
- Studies in Legal History. (pub. by Harvard
University Press)

**American Society for Medical Technology**
555 W. Loop, Suite 200, Bellaire, TX 77401.
- A S M T News. m. ISSN 0001-2564
- American Journal of Medical Technology. m.
ISSN 0002-9335

**American Society for Metals**
Metals Park, OH 44073.
- A S M. Bibliography Series. a. (61 topics avail.)
ISSN 0001-2556
- A S M News. 10 per yr. ISSN 0044-7889
- Alloys Index. m. ISSN 0094-8233 (Co-Sponsor:
Metals Society, London)
- Cleaning-Finishing-Coating Digest. m.
- Heat Processing Digest. m.
- International Metals Reviews. q. (Co-sponsor:
Metals Society, London)
- Metal Progress. m. ISSN 0026-0665
- Metal Progress West. q. ISSN 0362-935X
- Metallurgical Transactions A-Physical Metallurgy
and Materials Science. m. (Co-sponsor: American
Institute of Mining, Metallurgical and Petroleum
Engineers, Inc.)
- Metallurgist. (pub. by Consultants Bureau)

- Metallurgy-Materials Education Yearbook. irreg.
ISSN 0094-5447
- Metals Abstracts. m. ISSN 0026-0924 (And
Metals Society, 1 Carlton House Terrace, London
SW1Y 5DB)
- Metals Abstracts Index. m. ISSN 0026-0932 (And
Metals Society, 1 Carlton House Terrace, London
SW1Y 5DB)
- Refractories. (pub. by Consultants Bureau)
- Welding & Joining Digest. m.

**American Society for Metals. Metals Information**
Metals Park, OH 44073.
- Metalert. m.

**American Society for Microbiology**
1913 I St. N.W., Washington, DC 20006.
- A S M News. m. ISSN 0044-7897
- American Society for Microbiology. Abstracts of
the Annual Meeting. a. ISSN 0067-2777
- Antimicrobial Agents and Chemotherapy. m.
ISSN 0066-4804
- Applied and Environmental Microbiology. m.
ISSN 0099-2240
- Infection and Immunity. m. (4vols. per yr.) ISSN
0019-9567
- International Journal of Systematic Bacteriology.
q. ISSN 0020-7713 (International Association of
Microbiological Societies. International
Committee on Systematic Bacteriology)
- Journal of Bacteriology. m. ISSN 0021-9193
- Journal of Clinical Microbiology. m. ISSN 0095-
1137
- Journal of Virology. m. ISSN 0022-538X
- Microbiological Reviews. q.
- Spores. every 3 yrs.; next edt. 1978. ISSN 0584-
9144

**American Society for Neurochemistry**
c/o Dr. Claude Baxter, Chief, Neurochemical Labs
(151 F), V. A. Hospital, Sepulveda, CA 91343.
- American Society for Neurochemistry.
Transactions. a. ISSN 0066-0132

**American Society for Nondestructive Testing. South
Texas Section**
- Symposium on Nondestructive Evaluation of
Components and Materials in Aerospace,
Weapons Systems and Nuclear Applications. (pub.
by Western Periodicals Co.)

**American Society for Personnel Administration**
19 Church St., Berea, OH 44017.
- American Society for Personnel Administration.
Personnel and Industrial Relations Colleges. irreg.
ISSN 0095-2826
- Personnel Administrator. 9 per yr. ISSN 0031-
5729

**American Society for Pharmacology and Experimental
Therapeutics**
9650 Rockville Pike, Bethesda, MD 20014.
- Clinical Pharmacology and Therapeutics. (pub. by
C. V. Mosby Co.)
- Drug Metabolism and Disposition. (pub. by
Williams & Wilkins Co.)
- Pharmacological Reviews. (pub. by Williams &
Wilkins Co.)
- Pharmacologist. s-a. ISSN 0031-7004
- Rational Drug Therapy. (pub. by W. B. Saunders
Co.)
- Schools of Pharmacy in the United States and
Canada Offering Graduate Education in
Pharmacology. a.

**American Society for Photobiology**
- Photochemistry and Photobiology. (pub. by
Pergamon Press, Inc.)

**American Society for Political and Legal Philosophy**
- Nomos. (pub. by Lieber-Atherton, Inc.)

**American Society for Psychical Research, Inc.**
5 West 73rd St., New York, NY 10023.
- A S P R Newsletter. q. ISSN 0044-7919
- American Society for Psychical Research. Journal.
q. ISSN 0003-1070
- American Society for Psychical Research.
Proceedings. irreg., vol. 31, 1974.

**American Society for Psychoprophylaxis in Obstetrics
(Berkeley)**
Box 5042, Elmwood Station, Berkeley, CA 94705.
- A.S.P.O. Newsletter. q.

**American Society for Psychoprophylaxis in Obstetrics
Inc.**
1523 L St., N.W., Washington, DC 20005.
- Childbirth Education. q. ISSN 0009-403X

**American Society for Public Administration**
1225 Connecticut Ave. N.W., Washington, DC
20036.
- Public Administration News and Views. m. ISSN
0033-3328
- Public Administration Review. bi-m. ISSN 0033-
3352

**American Society for Public Administration. Section
on International and Comparative Administration**
1225 Connecticut Ave. N. W., Washington, DC
20036.
- American Society for Public Administration.
Section on International and Comparative
Administration. Occasional Papers. irreg.

**American Society for Public Instruction. National
Capital Area Chapter**
1225 Connecticut Ave., N.W., Washington, DC
20036.
- Bureaucrat. q. ISSN 0045-3544 (Co-sponsor:
Federal Executive Institute Alumni Assn.)

**American Society for Quality Control**
161 W. Wisconsin Ave, Milwaukee, WI 53203.
- American Society for Quality Control
Transactions of Annual Technical Conferences. a.
ISSN 0066-0159
- Journal of Quality Technology. q. ISSN 0022-
4065
- Quality Progress. m. ISSN 0033-524X

**American Society for Quality Control. Food, Drug
and Cosmetic Division**
161 West Wisconsin Ave., Milwaukee, WI 53203
(Subscr. c/o Department of Food Science and
Human Nutrition, Michigan State University, E.
Lansing, MI 48823)
- F D C Control. (Food, Drug, and Cosmetics
Control) q.

**American Society for Quality Control. Los Angeles
Section**
- West Coast Reliability Symposium. (pub. by
Western Periodicals Co.)

**American Society for Reformation Research**
6477 San Bonita, St. Louis, MO 63105.
- American Society for Reformation Research.
Literature Review/Literaturbericht. a.
- American Society for Reformation Research.
Newsletter. a. ISSN 0066-0167
- Archive for Reformation History. a.

**American Society for Surgery of the Hand**
c/o Gail M. Gorman, Three Parker Pl., Suite 233,
260 S. Parker Rd., Aurora, CO 80220
(Orders to Lee W. Milford, M.D., 869 Madison
Ave., Memphis, Tenn. 38104)
- Bibliography of Surgery of the Hand. irreg. ISSN
0067-7264

**American Society for Testing & Materials**
1916 Race St., Philadelphia, PA 19103.
- A S T M Journal of Testing and Evaluation. bi-m.
- A S T M Proceedings. a. ISSN 0066-0515
- A S T M Standardization News. m. ISSN 0090-
1210
- American Society for Testing and Materials. Data
Series Publications. irreg. ISSN 0066-0531
- American Society for Testing and Materials. Five-
Year Index to A S T M Technical Papers and
Reports. quinquennial. ISSN 0066-054X
- American Society for Testing and Materials.
Special Technical Publications. irreg., 1970, no.
494. ISSN 0066-0558
- Annual Book of A S T M Standards. Part 1. Steel
Piping, Tubing, and Fittings. a. ISSN 0066-0183
- Annual Book of A S T M Standards. Part 2.
Ferrous Castings, Ferro-Alloys. a. ISSN 0066-
0191
- Annual Book of A S T M Standards. Part 3. Steel
Plate, Sheet, Strip and Wire; Metallic Coated
Products. a.
- Annual Book of A S T M Standards. Part 4.
Structural Steel; Concrete Reinforcing Steel;
Pressure Vessel Plate; Steel Rails, Wheels, and
Tires. a.
- Annual Book of A S T M Standards. Part 5. Steel
Bars, Chain, and Springs; Bearing Steel; Steel
Forgings. a.

- Annual Book of a S T M Standards. Part 6. Copper and Copper Alloys (Including Electrical Conductors) a. ISSN 0066-0221
- Annual Book of A S T M Standards. Part 7. die-Cast Metals; Light Metal and Alloys (Including Electrical Conductors) a. ISSN 0066-023X
- Annual Book of A S T M Standards. Part 8. Nonferrous Metals--Nickel, Lead, and Tin Alloys, Precious Metals, Primary Metals; Reactive Metals. a.
- Annual Book of A S T M Standards. Part 9. Electrodeposited Metallic Coatings; Metal Powders, Sintered P/M Structural Parts. a.
- Annual Book of A S T M Standards. Part 10. Metals - Mechanical, Fracture, and Corrosion Testing; Fatigue; Erosion; Effect of Temperature. a.
- Annual Book of A S T M Standards. Part 11. Metallography; Nondestructive Tests. a.
- Annual Book of A S T M Standards. Part 12. Chemical Analysis of Metals; Sampling and Analysis of Metal Bearing Ores. a. ISSN 0066-0485
- Annual Book of A S T M Standards. Part 13. Cement; Lime; Ceilings and Walls (Including Manual of Cement Testing) a.
- Annual Book of A S T M Standards. Part 14. Concrete and Mineral Aggregates (Including Manual of Concrete Testing) a. ISSN 0066-0264
- Annual Book of A S T M Standards. Part 15. Bituminous Materials for Highway Construction, Waterproofing and Roofing, and Pipe; Skid Resistance. a.
- Annual Book of A S T M Standards. Part 16. Chemical-Resistant Nonmetallic Materials; Clay and Concrete Pipe and Tile; Masonry Mortars and Units; Asbestos-Cement Products. a.
- Annual Book of A S T M Standards. Part 17. Refractories, Glass and Ceramic Materials; Manufactured Carbon and Graphite Products. a. ISSN 0066-0299
- Annual Book of A S T M Standards. Part 18. Thermal and Cryogenic Insulating Materials; Building Joint Sealants; Fire Tests; Buliding Constructions; Environmental Acoustics. a. ISSN 0066-0302
- Annual Book of A S T M Standards. Part 19. Natural Building Stones; Soil and Rock; Peats, Mosses, and Humus. a.
- Annual Book of A S T M Standards. Part 20. Paper; Packaging; Business Copy Products. a.
- Annual Book of A S T M Standards. Part 21. Cellulose; Leather; Flexible Barrier Materials. a.
- Annual Book of A S T M Standards. Part 22. Wood; Adhesives. a. ISSN 0066-0329
- Annual Book of A S T M Standards. Part 23. Petroleum Products and Lubricants (1) a.
- Annual Book of A S T M Standards. Part 24. Petroleum Products and Lubricants (2) a.
- Annual Book of A S T M Standards. Part 25. Petroleum Products and Lubricants (3); Aerospace Materials. a.
- Annual Book of A S T M Standards. Part 26. Gaseous Fuels; Coal and Coke. a. ISSN 0066-0353
- Annual Book of A S T M Standards. Part 27. Paint - Tests for Formulated Products and Applied Coatings. a. ISSN 0066-037X
- Annual Book of A S T M Standards. Part 28. Paint - Pigments, Resins and Polymers. a.
- Annual Book of A S T M Standards. Part 29. Paint - Fatty Oils and Acids, Solvents, Miscellaneous; Aromatic Hydrocarbons; Naval Stores. a.
- Annual Book of A S T M Standards. Part 30. Soap; Engine Coolants; Polishes; Halogenated Organic Solvents; Activated Carbon; Industrial Chemicals. a. ISSN 0066-0388
- Annual Book of A S T M Standards. Part 31. Water. a.
- Annual Book of A S T M Standards. Part 32. Textile Materials - Yarns, Fabrics, and General Methods. a. ISSN 0066-040X
- Annual Book of A S T M Standards. Part 33. Textile Materials - Fibers, Zippers; High Modulus Fibers. a. ISSN 0066-0418
- Annual Book of A S T M Standards. Part 34. Plastic Pipe. a.
- Annual Book of A S T M Standards. Part 35. Plastics - General Test Methods; Nomenclature. a. ISSN 0066-0434
- Annual Book of A S T M Standards. Part 36. Plastics - Materials, Film, Reinforced and Cellular Plastics; Fiber Composites. a.
- Annual Book of A S T M Standards. Part 37. Rubber - Test Methods.

- Annual Book of A S T M Standards. Part 38. Rubber - Specifications; Carbon Black; Gaskets; Tires. a.
- Annual Book of A S T M Standards. Part 39. Electrical Insulating Materials - Test Methods. a. ISSN 0066-0450
- Annual Book of A S T M Standards. Part 40. Electrical Insulating Materials - Specifications; Electrical Insulating Liquids and Gases.
- Annual Book of A S T M Standards. Part 41. General Test Methods (Nonmetal); Statistical Methods; Space Simulation; Particle Size Measurement; Deterioration of Nonmetallic Materials. a. ISSN 0066-0469
- Annual Book of A S T M Standards. Part 42. Emission, Molecular, and Mass Spectroscopy; Chromatography; Resinography; Microscopy.
- Annual Book of A S T M Standards. Part 43. Electronics.
- Annual Book of A S T M Standards. Part 44. Magnetic Properties; Metallic Materials for Thermostats and for Electrical Resistance, Heating, and Contacts; Temperature Measurement. a.
- Annual Book of A S T M Standards. Part 45. Nuclear Standards.
- Annual Book of A S T M Standards. Part 46. End Use Products - Aerosols and Closures, Surgical Implants, Resilient Floor Coverings, Appearance of Materials Sensory Evaluation; Forensic Sciences.
- Annual Book of A S T M Standards. Part 47. Test Methods for Motor, Rating Motor, Diesel, and Aviation Fuels.
- Annual Book of A S T M Standards. Part 48. Index. a. ISSN 0066-0493
- Journal of Forensic Sciences. q. ISSN 0022-1198
- Tire Science and Technology. q. ISSN 0090-8657

**American Society for the Prevention of Cruelty to Animals**
441 E. 92nd St., New York, NY 10028.
- A S P C A Yellow Pages. irreg.
- Animal Protection. s-a. ISSN 0003-357X
- Traveling with Your Pet. biennial.

**American Society for Theatre Research**
C.W. Post College, Dept. of English, Greenvale, NY 11548.
- A S T R Newsletter. 2 per yr. ISSN 0044-7927
- Theatre Survey. s-a. ISSN 0040-5574

**American Society for Training and Development**
Box 5307, Madison, WI 53705.
- A S T D Journal. m.
- Cassette Library for Professional Training and Development. (pub. by C R E D R Corp.)
- National Report. 20 per yr.
- Training Resources; buyer's guide & consultant directory. a. ISSN 0098-5619
- Who's Who in Training and Development. a. ISSN 0092-4598

**American Society of Abdominal Surgeons**
675 Main St., Melrose, MA 02176.
- Abdominal Surgery. m.
- Journal of Abdominal Surgery. m. ISSN 0021-8421

**American Society of Agricultural Engineers**
2950 Niles Rd., Box 410, St. Joseph, MI 49085.
- A S A E Transactions. q. ISSN 0001-2351
- Agricultural Engineering. m. ISSN 0002-1458
- Agricultural Engineers Yearbook. a. ISSN 0065-4477

**American Society of Agronomy, Inc.**
677 South Segoe Rd., Madison, WI 53711.
- Agronomy: a Series of Monographs. irreg., 1972, nos. 15 & 16, 1976, no. 17. ISSN 0065-4663
- Agronomy Abstracts. a. ISSN 0065-4671
- Agronomy Journal. bi-m. ISSN 0002-1962
- Agronomy News. 6 per yr.
- American Society of Agronomy. A S A Special Publication. irreg. ISSN 0066-0566
- Crops & Soils. m.(bi-m. April-Sept.) ISSN 0011-1864
- Journal of Agronomic Education. a. ISSN 0094-2391
- Journal of Environmental Quality. q. ISSN 0047-2425

**American Society of Allied Health Professions**
One Dupont Circle, Ste. 300, Washington, DC 20036.
- Allied Health Trends. m.
- Journal of Allied Health. (pub. by Charles B. Slack, Inc.)

**American Society of Anesthesiologists**
- A S A Refresher Courses in Anesthesiology. (pub. by J. B. Lippincott Co.)
- Anesthesiology. (pub. by J. B. Lippincott Co.)

**American Society of Animal Science**
311 Illinois Bldg., 113 N. Neil St., Champaign, IL 61820.
- Journal of Animal Science. m. ISSN 0021-8812
- Journal of Animal Science. Supplement. irreg., latest issue 1974. ISSN 0075-4129

**American Society of Animal Science. Western Section**
49 Sheridan Ave., Albany, NY 12210.
- American Society of Animal Science. Western Section Proceedings. a. ISSN 0569-7832

**American Society of Appraisers**
Dulles International Airport, Box 17265, Washington, DC 20041.
- A S A Monograph. irreg., no. 7, 1976. ISSN 0569-7840
- American Society of Appraisers. Appraisal and Valuation Manual. irreg. ISSN 0569-7859
- Bibliography of Appraisal Literature. supplements every 2 yrs.
- Valuation Magazine. s-a. ISSN 0042-238X

**American Society of Arms Collectors**
4823 Ellenberg Dr., Dallas, TX 75234.
- American Society of Arms Collectors. Bulletin. irreg. ISSN 0362-9457

**American Society of Association Executives**
1101 16th St., N.W., Washington, DC 20036.
- Association Management. m. ISSN 0004-5578
- Who's Who in Association Management Membership Directory. a.

**American Society of Bakery Engineers**
Riverside Plaza Bldg., Room 1921, 2 North Riverside Plaza, Chicago, IL 60606.
- A. S. B. E. Letter. q. ISSN 0001-2394
- American Society of Bakery Engineers. Proceedings of the Annual Meeting. a. ISSN 0066-0582

**American Society of Bariatric Physicians**
333 West Hampden Ave., Suite 500, Englewood, CO 80110.
- Obesity & Bariatric Medicine. bi-m.

**American Society of Biological Chemists**
9650 Rockville Pike, Bethesda, MD 20014.
- Journal of Biological Chemistry. s-m. ISSN 0021-9258

**American Society of Bookplate Collectors and Designers**
429 North Daisy Avenue, Pasadena, CA 91107.
- American Society of Bookplate Collectors and Designers. Year Book. irreg.
- Bookplates in the News. q. ISSN 0045-2521

**American Society of Brewing Chemists**
3340 Pilot Knob Rd., St. Paul, MN 55121.
- American Society of Brewing Chemists. Journal. q.

**American Society of Cartographers**
Box 1493, Louisville, KY 40201.
- American Society of Cartographers. Bulletin. q. ISSN 0044-7943

**American Society of Certified Engineering Technicians**
2029 K St., N.W., Washington, DC 20036.
- Certified Engineering Technician. bi-m.

**American Society of Chartered Life Underwriters**
270 Bryn Mawr Ave., Box 59, Bryn Mawr, PA 19010.
- C L U Forum Report. a. ISSN 0066-0590
- C L U Journal. (Chartered Life Underwriters) q. ISSN 0007-8573
- Query. m. ISSN 0033-6270
- Society Page. bi-m. ISSN 0038-0075

**American Society of Church History**
305 E. Country Club Lane, Wallingford, PA 19086.
- Church History. q. ISSN 0009-6407

**American Society of Cinematographers Corporation**
1782 N. Orange Drive, Los Angeles, CA 90028.
- American Cinematographer; international journal of motion picture photography and production techniques. m. ISSN 0002-7928

**American Society of Civil Engineers**
345 E. 47th St., New York, NY 10017.
- A S C E Publications Abstract. m. ISSN 0001-2432
- American Society of Civil Engineers. Construction Division. Journal. q. ISSN 0569-7948
- American Society of Civil Engineers. Engineering Mechanics Division. Newsletter. bi-m. ISSN 0003-1100
- American Society of Civil Engineers. Engineering Mechanics Division. Journal. bi-m. ISSN 0044-7951
- American Society of Civil Engineers. Environmental Engineering Division. Journal. bi-m. ISSN 0090-3914
- American Society of Civil Engineers. Geotechnical Engineering Division. Journal. m. ISSN 0093-6405
- American Society of Civil Engineers. Hydraulics Division. Journal. m. ISSN 0044-796X
- American Society of Civil Engineers. Irrigation and Drainage Division. Journal. q. ISSN 0044-7978
- American Society of Civil Engineers. Power Division. Journal. irreg. (2-3 per yr) ISSN 0569-8030
- American Society of Civil Engineers. Proceedings. m. ISSN 0003-1119
- American Society of Civil Engineers. Structural Division. Journal. m. ISSN 0044-8001
- American Society of Civil Engineers. Structural Division. Newsletter. bi-m. ISSN 0003-1135
- American Society of Civil Engineers. Surveying & Mapping Division. Newsletter. bi-m. ISSN 0003-1143
- American Society of Civil Engineers. Surveying and Mapping Division. Journal. irreg. (2-3 per yr.) ISSN 0569-8073
- American Society of Civil Engineers. Transactions. a. ISSN 0066-0604
- American Society of Civil Engineers. Urban Planning and Development Division. Journal. irreg. (1-3 per yr.) ISSN 0569-8081
- American Society of Civil Engineers. Urban Water Resources Research Program. Technical Memorandum. irreg. ISSN 0066-0612
- American Society of Civil Engineers. Waterway, Port, Coastal and Ocean Division. Journal. q.
- American Society of Civil Engineers. Waterways & Harbors Division. Newsletter. q. ISSN 0003-1151
- Civil Engineering; environmental design/ engineered construction. m. ISSN 0009-7853
- Engineering Issues; journal of professional activities. q. ISSN 0093-8343
- Hydrotechnical Construction/Gidrotekhnicheskoe Stroitel'stvo. m. ISSN 0018-8220
- Manuals and Reports on Engineering Practice. irreg., no. 56, 1976.
- Transportation Engineering Journal. bi-m.

**American Society of Civil Engineers. Boston Society of Civil Engineers Section**
230 Boylston St., Boston, MA 02116.
- American Society of Civil Engineers. Boston Society of Civil Engineers Section. Journal. 4 per yr. ISSN 0361-087X

**American Society of Civil Engineers. Texas Section**
Univ. of Houston, Houston, TX 77004.
- Texas Civil Engineer. 10 per yr. ISSN 0040-4292

**American Society of Clinical Hypnosis**
401 Peachtree St. N.E., Suite 804, Atlanta, GA 30308.
- American Journal of Clinical Hypnosis. q. ISSN 0002-9157
- American Society of Clinical Hypnosis. Directory. irreg. ISSN 0517-5178

**American Society of Clinical Nutrition, Inc.**
- American Journal of Clinical Nutrition. (pub. by American Institute of Nutrition)

**American Society of Clinical Pathologists**
2100 W. Harrison St., Chicago, IL 60612.
- American Journal of Clinical Pathology. (pub. by J. B. Lippincott Co.)
- American Society of Clinical Pathologists. Proceedings of the Annual Symposium. a.
- Clinical Pathology Seminar. Proceedings. a.
- Laboratory Medicine. (pub. by J. B. Lippincott Co.)

**American Society of Clinical Pathologists. Commission on Continuing Education**
2100 W. Harrison St., Chicago, IL 60612
(Orders to: Box 8013, Chicago, IL 60680)
- American Society of Clinical Pathologists. Summary Report. m. ISSN 0517-5208
- American Society of Clinical Pathologists. Technical Improvement Service. q.

**American Society of Composers, Authors and Publishers**
1 Lincoln Plaza, New York, NY 10023.
- A S C A P Biographical Dictionary. irreg.
- A S C A P Symphonic Catalog. (pub. by R. R. Bowker Company)
- A S C A P Today. q. ISSN 0001-2424
- Copyright Law Symposium. (pub. by Columbia University Press)

**American Society of Consultant Pharmacists**
2300 Ninth St. So., Arlington, VA 22204.
- A S C P Update. m.

**American Society of Contemporary Medicine and Surgery**
- Comprehensive Therapy. (pub. by Book Associates, Inc.)

**American Society of Contemporary Ophthalmology**
- Annals of Ophthalmology. (pub. by Woodbine Publishers Inc.)

**American Society of Criminology**
- Criminology. (pub. by Sage Publications, Inc.)

**American Society of Dentistry for Children**
211 E. Chicago Ave., Room 920 A. D. A. Bldg., Chicago, IL 60611.
- Journal of Dentistry for Children. bi-m. ISSN 0022-0353

**American Society of Dowsers**
Danville, VT 05828.
- American Dowser. q.

**American Society of Electroencephalographic Technologists**
- American Journal of E E G Technology. (pub. by Raven Press)

**American Society of Enologists**
Box 411, Davis, CA 95616.
- American Journal of Enology and Viticulture. q. ISSN 0002-9254

**American Society of Farm Managers and Rural Appraisers**
Box 6857, Denver, CO 80206.
- American Society of Farm Managers and Rural Appraisers. Journal. s-a. ISSN 0003-116X

**American Society of Group Psychotherapy and Psychodrama**
- Group Psychotherapy, Psychodrama & Sociometry. (pub. by Beacon House Inc.)

**American Society of Heating, Refrigerating and Air-Conditioning Engineers, Inc.**
345 E. 47 St., New York, NY 10017.
- A S H R A E Handbook & Product Directory. 4 vols, each vol. revised every 4 yrs. ISSN 0066-0620
- A S H R A E Journal; heating, refrigeration, air-conditioning, ventilation. m. ISSN 0001-2491
- A S H R A E Transactions. s-a. ISSN 0001-2505

**American Society of Hospital Pharmacists**
4630 Montgomery Ave., Washington, DC 20014.
- A S H P Newsletter. m. ISSN 0001-2483
- American Hospital Formulary Service. 2 base vols. plus 4-6 supplements per yr.
- American Journal of Hospital Pharmacy. m. ISSN 0002-9289
- International Pharmaceutical Abstracts; key to the world's literature of pharmacy. s-m. ISSN 0020-8264
- Voices... (Year) (pub. by Teach'em, Inc.)

**American Society of Human Genetics**
- American Journal of Human Genetics. (pub. by University of Chicago Press)

**American Society of Ichthyologists and Herpetologists**
Division of Reptiles and Amphibians, U.S. National Museum, Washington, DC 20560.
- Copeia. 4 per yr. ISSN 0045-8511

**American Society of Internal Medicine**
535 Central Tower Bldg., 703 Market Street, San Francisco, CA 94103.
- Internist. 10 per yr. ISSN 0020-9546

**American Society of International Law**
2223 Massachusetts Ave., N.W., Washington, DC 20008.
- American Journal of International Law. 4 per yr. ISSN 0002-9300
- American Society of International Law. Newsletter. q. ISSN 0066-0639
- American Society of International Law. Proceedings. a. ISSN 0066-0647
- International Legal Materials. bi-m. ISSN 0020-7829
- Studies in Transnational Legal Policy. irreg.

**American Society of Landscape Architects**
1750 Old Meadow Rd., McLean, VA 22101.
- Land; landscape architectural news digest. m. ISSN 0023-754X
- Landscape Architecture. q. ISSN 0023-8031

**American Society of Law & Medicine, Inc.**
454 Brookline Avenue, Boston, MA 02215.
- American Journal of Law and Medicine. (pub. by M I T Press)
- Medicolegal News. q. ISSN 0097-0085

**American Society of Limnology and Oceanography**
c/o Zoology Dept., University of Wisconsin-Milwaukee, Milwaukee, WI 53201.
- Limnology and Oceanography. bi-m. ISSN 0024-3590

**American Society of Lubrication Engineers**
838 Busse Highway, Park Ridge, IL 60068.
- A S L E Transactions. 4 per yr.
- International Conference on Solid Lubrication. Proceedings. irreg.
- Lubrication Engineering. m. ISSN 0024-7154

**American Society of Mammalogists**
c/o Carnegie Museum, 4400 Forbes Ave., Pittsburgh, PA 15213.
- American Society of Mammalogists. Special Publications. irreg. ISSN 0569-8219
- Journal of Mammalogy. (pub. by Allen Press, Inc.)
- Mammalian Species. irreg. ISSN 0076-3519

**American Society of Mechanical Engineers**
345 E. 47th St., New York, NY 10017.
- Advances in Bioengineering. a. ISSN 0360-9960
- Applied Mechanics Reviews; a critical review of the world literature in applied mechanics and related engineering science. m. ISSN 0003-6900
- Cavitation and Polyphase Flow Forum. a.
- Interamerican Conference on Materials Technology. (Proceedings) irreg., 1970, 2nd, Mexico City. ISSN 0074-1086 (Southwest Research Institute)
- Journal of Applied Mechanics. q. ISSN 0021-8936
- Journal of Biomechanical Enginering. q.
- Journal of Dynamic Systems, Measurement and Control. q. ISSN 0022-0434
- Journal of Engineering for Industry. q. ISSN 0022-0817
- Journal of Engineering for Power. q. ISSN 0022-0825
- Journal of Engineering Materials and Technology. q. ISSN 0094-4289
- Journal of Fluids Engineering. q. ISSN 0098-2202
- Journal of Heat Transfer. q. ISSN 0022-1481
- Journal of Lubrication Technology. q. ISSN 0022-2305
- Journal of Pressure Vessel Technology. q. ISSN 0094-9930
- Mechanical Engineering. m. ISSN 0025-6501
- Reports on Diesel and Gas Engines Power Costs. biennial. ISSN 0569-8243

**American Society of Mechanical Engineers. Heat Transfer Division**
345 E. 47 St., New York, NY 10017.
- Symposium on Thermophysical Properties. Proceedings. irreg., 1973, 6th. ISSN 0082-0989 (prep. by its Standing Committee on Thermophysical Properties)

**American Society of Mechanical Engineers. Incinerator Division**
345 E. 47th St., New York, NY 10017.
- National Incinerator Conference. Proceedings; with discussions. biennial. ISSN 0085-3763

**American Society of Mechanical Engineers. Machine Design Division**
345 E. 47 St., New York, NY 10017.
- American Society of Mechanical Engineers. Machine Design Division. Papers. irreg. ISSN 0517-5356

**American Society of Mechanical Engineers. Pressure Vessel Division**
345 E. 47th St., New York, NY 10017.
- International Conference on Pressure Vessel Technology. Papers. irreg., 1973, 2nd, San Antonio.

**American Society of Mechanical Engineers. Rail Transportation Division**
United Engineering Center, 345 E. 47th St., New York, NY 10017.
- Rail Transportation Proceedings. a.

**American Society of Mechanical Engineers. Research Committee on Fluid Meters**
345 E. 47 St., New York, NY 10017.
- Fluid Meters: Their Theory and Application. irreg., 6th, 1971.

**American Society of Medical Technologists**
Suite 200, 5555 West Loop South, Bellaire, TX 77401.
- Clinical Laboratory Review. m.

**American Society of Military Comptrollers**
Box 91, Mt. Vernon, VA 22121.
- Armed Forces Comptroller. q. ISSN 0004-2188

**American Society of Military Insignia Collectors**
17 General Pulaski Drive, Salem, NH 03079 (or 744 Warfield Ave., Oakland, CA 94610)
- A. S. M. I. C. Newsletter. bi-m.
- Trading Post. q. ISSN 0041-0586

**American Society of Missiology**
William Carey Library, 533 Hermosa St., S. Pasadena, CA 91030.
- Missiology; an international review. q. ISSN 0091-8296

**American Society of Naturalists**
- American Naturalist. (pub. by University of Chicago Press)

**American Society of Naval Engineers, Inc.**
1012 14th St. N.W., Suite 807, Washington, DC 20005.
- Naval Engineers Journal. bi-m. ISSN 0028-1425

**American Society of Newspaper Editors**
Box 551, 1350 Sullivan Trail, Easton, PA 18042.
- American Society of Newspaper Editors. Bulletin. 9 per yr. ISSN 0003-1178
- Problems of Journalism. a.

**American Society of Notaries**
810-18th St., N.W., Washington, DC 20006.
- American Notary. bi-m. ISSN 0044-7773

**American Society of Ocularists**
- American Society of Ocularists. Selected Papers and Discussions from the Annual Meeting. (pub. by Intercontinental Medical Book Corporation)

**American Society of Ophthalmologic and Otolaryngologic Allergy**
c/o Dr. David A. Dolowitz, Ed., 2000 S. Ninth East, Salt Lake City, UT 84105.
- American Society of Ophthalmologic and Otolaryngologic Allergy. Transactions. a. ISSN 0066-0655

**American Society of Parasitologists**
- Journal of Parasitology. (pub. by Allen Press, Inc.)

**American Society of Pension Actuaries**
1112 Sinclair Bldg., Fort Worth, TX 76102.
- American Society of Pension Actuaries. Transcribings. Annual Conference. a. ISSN 0094-422X

**American Society of Pharmacognosy**
- Lloydia. (pub. by Lloyd Library and Museum)

**American Society of Pharmacology and Experimental Therapeutics, Inc**
- Journal of Pharmacology and Experimental Therapeutics. (pub. by Williams and Wilkins Co.)

**American Society of Photogrammetry**
105 N. Virginia Ave., Falls Church, VA 22046.
- American Society of Photogrammetry. Technical Papers from the Annual Meeting. a. ISSN 0066-0663
- Photogrammetric Engineering and Remote Sensing. 12 per yr. ISSN 0099-1112

**American Society of Photogrammetry. Cartography Division**
105 North Virginia Ave., Falls Chruch, VA 22046.
- Orthophoto Workshop. Papers. irreg.

**American Society of Planning Officials**
1313 East 60th St., Chicago, IL 60637.
- A S P O Planning Advisory Service. m. ISSN 0044-8044
- Land Use Law and Zoning Digest. irreg.(10-12 issues per year)
- Planning. m. ISSN 0001-2610
- Planning Advisory Service Reports. 12 per yr. ISSN 0048-430X
- Profiles of State Planning Associations in the United States. biennial.
- Tab; jobs in planning. s-m. ISSN 0362-2827

**American Society of Plant Physiologists**
9650 Rockville Pike, Bethesda, MD 20014.
- Plant Physiology. m. ISSN 0032-0889
- Plant Physiology. Supplement. a. ISSN 0079-2241

**American Society of Plant Taxonomists**
- Brittonia. (pub. by New York Botanical Garden)
- Systematic Botany. (pub. by Florida State University. Department of Biological Sciences)

**American Society of Plastic & Reconstructive Surgeons**
- Plastic and Reconstructive Surgery. (pub. by Williams & Wilkins Co.)

**American Society of Plastic and Reconstructive Surgery. Educational Foundation**
29 E. Madison St., Suite 807, Chicago, IL 60602.
- Current Bibliography of Plastic & Reconstructive Surgery. bi-m. ISSN 0360-1722

**American Society of Plumbing Engineers**
- Plumbing Engineer. (pub. by Miramar Publishing Co.)

**American Society of Polar Philatelists**
c/o Russell Ott, Sec., 3541 Calle del Sol, Irving, TX 75062.
- Ice Cap News. bi-m. ISSN 0019-1051

**American Society of Psychosomatic Dentistry and Medicine**
2802 Mermaid Ave., Brooklyn, NY 11224.
- American Society of Psychosomatic Dentistry and Medicine. Journal. q. ISSN 0003-1194

**American Society of Radiologic Technologists**
- Radiologic Technology. (pub. by Williams and Wilkins Co.)

**American Society of Safety Engineers**
850 Busse Highway, Park Ridge, IL 60068.
- American Society of Safety Engineers. Proceedings. Professional Conference. a.
- Professional Safety. m. ISSN 0099-0027

**American Society of Sanitary Engineering**
960 Illuminating Bldg., Cleveland, OH 44113.
- American Society of Sanitary Engineering. Year Book. a. ISSN 0066-068X

**American Society of Sephardic Studies**
- Sephardic Scholar. (pub. by Yeshiva University. Sephardic Studies Program)

**American Society of Sugar Beet Technologists**
Box 1546, Fort Collins, CO 80521.
- American Society of Sugar Beet Technologists. Journal. q. ISSN 0003-1216

**American Society of the French Legion of Honor, Inc.**
Mayfair House, 610 Park Ave., New York, NY 10021.
- American Society Legion of Honor Magazine; devoted to the art, history, literature, music, sciences and to all other forms of culture of France and the United States. 3 per yr. ISSN 0003-1097

**American Society of Traffic and Transportation, Inc.**
547 W. Jackson Blvd., Chicago, IL 60606.
- Transportation Journal. q. ISSN 0041-1612

**American Society of Travel Agents**
711 Fifth Ave., New York, NY 10022.
- A S T A Notes. w.
- A S T A Travel News. (pub by Travel Communications, Inc.)

**American Society of Tropical Medicine and Hygiene**
3307 Harrell St., Wheaton, MD 20906.
- American Journal of Tropical Medicine and Hygiene. (pub. by Allen Press Inc.)
- Tropical Medicine and Hygiene News. bi-m. ISSN 0041-3275

**American Society of University Composers**
250 W. 57 St., Rm. 626-7, New York, NY 10019.
- A S U C Journal of Music Scores. (pub. by Joseph Boonin, Inc.)
- American Society of University Composers. Proceedings. biennial. ISSN 0066-0701
- American Society of University Composers Newsletter. 3 per yr.

**American Society of Veterinary Clinical Pathologists**
c/o Robert L. Michel, Department of Pathobiology, University of Tennessee, Box 1071, Knoxville, TN 37901.
- American Society of Veterinary Clinical Pathologists. Bulletin. q.

**American Society of Zoologists**
c/o Mary Wiley, Box 2739, California Lutheran College, Thousand Oaks, CA 91380.
- American Zoologist. q. ISSN 0003-1569

**American Sociological Association**
1722 N St., N.W., Washington, DC 20036.
- A S A Directory. a. ISSN 0569-8545
- A S A Footnotes. 9 per yr.
- American Sociological Association. Proceedings of Annual Meeting. a.
- American Sociological Review. bi-m. ISSN 0003-1224
- American Sociologist. q. ISSN 0003-1232
- Contemporary Sociology; a journal of reviews. bi-m. ISSN 0094-3061
- Guide to Graduate Departments of Sociology. a.
- Journal of Health and Social Behavior. q. ISSN 0022-1465
- Sociological Methodology. (pub. by Jossey-Bass Inc., Publishers)
- Sociology of Education. q. ISSN 0038-0407
- Sociometry; a journal of research in social psychology. q. ISSN 0038-0431

**American Sokol Organization**
6426 W. Cermak Rd., Berwyn, IL 60402.
- American Sokol. m.(Sept-June); bi-m.(July-Aug) ISSN 0003-1259

**American Soybean Association**
Box 158, Hudson, IA 50643.
- Soybean Digest. 13 per yr. ISSN 0038-6014
- Soybean Digest Blue Book. a. ISSN 0081-3222
- Soybean Profits. 32 per yr. ISSN 0003-1275

**American Speech and Hearing Association**
9030 Old Georgetown Rd., Washington, DC 20014.
- A S H A. m. ISSN 0001-2475
- A S H A Directory. a. ISSN 0569-8561
- A S H A Monographs. irreg. ISSN 0066-071X
- A S H A Reports. irreg., no. 9, 1974. ISSN 0569-8553
- D S H Abstracts. (pub. by Deafness, Speech and Hearing Publications,Inc.)
- Journal of Speech and Hearing Disorders. q. ISSN 0022-4677
- Journal of Speech and Hearing Research. q. ISSN 0022-4685
- Language, Speech and Hearing Services in Schools. q.

**American Spelean History Association**
c/o Jack H. Speece, 711 E. Atlantic Ave., Altoona, PA 16602.
- Journal of Spelean History. q. ISSN 0022-4693

**American Square Dance Society**
c/o Bob Osgood, Ed., 462 N. Robertson, Los Angeles, CA 90048.
- Square Dancing. m. ISSN 0037-2889

**American Stamp Dealers' Association, Inc.**
595 Madison Ave., New York, NY 10021.
- A. S. D. A. Bulletin. m.

**American Statistical Association**
806 15th St., N.W., Suite 640, Washington, DC
20005.
- American Statistical Association. Business and
  Economic Statistics Section. Proceedings. a. ISSN
  0066-0736
- American Statistical Association. Journal. q. ISSN
  0003-1291
- American Statistical Association. Social Statistics
  Section. Proceedings. a. ISSN 0066-0752
- American Statistical Association. Statistical
  Computing Section. Proceedings (of the Annual
  Meeting) a.
- American Statistical Association. Statistical
  Section. Proceedings. a.
- American Statistician. q. ISSN 0003-1305
- AMSTAT News. 10 per yr.
- Current Index to Statistics; applications-methods-
  theory. a. ISSN 0364-1228
- Statisticians and Others in Allied Professions.
  triennial. ISSN 0081-508X
- Technometrics; a journal of statistics for the
  physical, chemical and engineering sciences. q.
  ISSN 0040-1706 (Co-sponsor: American Society
  for Quality Control)

**American Stock Exchange, Inc**
86 Trinity Place, New York, NY 10006.
- American Stock Exchange. AMEX Databook.
  irreg., latest issue 1976. ISSN 0066-0760
- American Stock Exchange. Annual Report. a.
  ISSN 0066-0779
- American Stock Exchange Weekly Bulletin. w.

**American String Teachers Association**
c/o G. Jean Smith, Ed., 130 Bluebird Dr., Terre
Haute, IN 47803.
- American String Teacher. q. ISSN 0003-1313

**American Student Dental Association**
211 E. Chicago Ave., Chicago, IL 60611.
- A S D A News. m. during school year.

**American Studies Association**
Box 30, Bennett Hall, Univ. of Pennsylvania,
Philadelphia, PA 19104.
- American Quarterly. (pub. by University of
  Pennsylvania)
- American Studies Association. National
  Convention Proceedings. biennial.
- American Studies International. (pub. by George
  Washington University. American Studies
  Program)

**American Studies Association. Kentucky-Tennessee
Chapter**
- Border States. (pub. by Northern Kentucky State
  College)

**American Suffolk Sheep Society**
52 N. First St., E. Logan, UT 84321.
- American Suffolk Sheep Society. Breeders List. a.
  ISSN 0066-0825

**American Sugar Cane League of the U. S. A.**
416 Whitney Bank Bldg., 228 St. Charles St., New
Orleans, LA 70130.
- Sugar Bulletin. s-m. ISSN 0039-4726

**American Surgical Association**
- American Surgical Association. Transactions. (pub.
  by J. B. Lippincott Co.)
- Annals of Surgery. (pub. by J. B. Lippincott Co.)

**American Surgical Trade Association**
- Medical Products Salesman. (pub. by McKnight
  Medical Communications, Inc.)

**American Swedish Institute**
2600 Park Ave., Minneapolis, MN 55407.
- Happenings. m.

**American-Swiss Association Inc.**
60 E. 42nd St., New York, NY 10017.
- American Swiss Memo. q.

**American Symphony Orchestra League**
Box 66, Vienna, VA 22180.
- American Symphony Orchestra League. Women's
  Council. Women's Association Reports. irreg.
- Symphony News. bi-m. ISSN 0090-5380

**American Technical Education Association, Inc.**
North Dakota State School of Science, Wahpeton,
ND 58075.
- A T E A Journal. 6 per yr.

**American Technical Society**
848 E. 58th St., Chicago, IL 60637.
- American Vocational Association. Trade and
  Industrial Division. Yearbook. a. ISSN 0066-1163

**American Telephone & Telegraph Company**
195 Broadway, New York, NY 10007.
- Bell Journal of Economics. s-a. ISSN 0361-915X
- Bell System Technical Journal; devoted to the
  scientific and engineering aspects of electrical
  communication. 10 per yr. ISSN 0005-8580
- Bell Telephone Magazine. bi-m.

**American Telephone and Telegraph Company. Long
Lines Department**
Overseas Administration, 5 World Trade Center,
New York, NY 10048.
- Calling the World. a. ISSN 0360-3539

**American Theatre Association**
1029 Vermont Avenue, N.W., Washington, DC
20005.
- A T A Placement Service Bulletin. m.
- American Theatre Association. Annual Directory
  of Members. a. ISSN 0065-8138
- Course Guide for High School Theatre. irreg.,
  1968, no. 2. ISSN 0070-136X (Secondary School
  Theatre Conference)
- Directory of American College Theatre. irreg.
  ISSN 0070-5063
- Educational Theatre Journal. q. ISSN 0013-1989
- Educational Theatre Journal. Supplement. irreg.
  ISSN 0070-9360
- Summer Theatre Directory. a. ISSN 0081-9387
- Theatre News. m. ISSN 0563-4040

**American Theatre Association. Childrens Theatre
Association of America**
1029 Vermont Ave., N. W., Washington, DC
20005.
- Children's Theatre Review. q. ISSN 0009-4196

**American Theatre Organ Society**
Box 1002, Middleburg, VA 22117.
- Theatre Organ. bi-m. ISSN 0040-5531

**American Theological Library Association**
Divinity School Library, Duke Univ., Durham, NC
27706
(Subscr. to: 7301 Germantown Ave., Philadelphia,
PA 19119)
- A T L A Bibliography Series. (pub. by Scarecrow
  Press, Inc.)
- A T L A Monograph Series. (pub. by Scarecrow
  Press, Inc.)
- American Theological Library Association.
  Conference. Summary of Proceedings. a. ISSN
  0066-0868
- American Theological Library Association.
  Newsletter. q. ISSN 0003-1399
- Index to Religious Periodical Literature. s-a. ISSN
  0019-4107

**American Thoracic Society**
Medical section of the American Lung Association,
1740 Broadway, New York, NY 10019.
- American Review of Respiratory Disease; clinical
  and laboratory studies of tuberculosis and
  respiratory diseases. m. ISSN 0003-0805
- Basics of RD. 5 per yr.
- Clinical Notes on Respiratory Diseases. q. ISSN
  0009-9198

**American Tool, Die & Stamping News Co.**
P.O. Box 81, 8086 Halfway, Brighton, MI 48116.
- American Tool, Die & Stamping News. bi-m.

**American Topical Association, Inc.**
c/o Ruth Hellard, Leggs Mills Rd., Lake Katrine,
NY 12449
(Subscr. Address: T. Range, Box 543 Church St.
Sta., New York NY 10008)
- Astrophile. bi-m. (Co-Sponsor: American
  Philatelic Society)
- Topical New Issues. a. ISSN 0090-7286
- Topical Stamp Handbooks. irreg., no. 91, 1977.
  ISSN 0049-4135
- Topical Time. bi-m. ISSN 0040-9332

**American Topical Association, Inc. Biology Unit**
c/o Gustavs E. Eglajs Ed., 5385 California Ave.,
Bethel Park, PA 15102
(Subscr. to: Mrs. Dona Jaquet, 309 Park Ave., East
Peoria, IL 61611)
- Bio-Philately; official journal of the Biology Unit
  of the American Topical Association. q.

**American Topical Association, Inc. Casey Jones
Railroad Unit**
75 Pine St., Paisley, FL 32767.
- Dispatcher. q.

**American Topical Association, Inc. Geology Study
Unit**
c/o Robert A. Fisher, Box 306, Oaks, PA 19456.
- Geo-Philatelist. 4 per yr.

**American Topical Association, Inc. Ships on Stamps
Unit**
c/o Ed. William A. Coffey, 3613 Kanawha Ave.
S.E., Charlestown, WV 25304.
- Watercraft Philately. bi-m.

**American Trade Magazines, Inc.**
500 N. Dearborn St., Chicago, IL 60610.
- American Clean Car. bi-m.
- American Coin-Op; the magazine for coin-
  operated laundry and drycleaning businessmen. m.
  ISSN 0092-2811
- American Drycleaner. m. ISSN 0002-8258
- American Laundry Digest. m. ISSN 0002-9718

**American Train Dispatchers Association**
Box 875, Ottumwa, IA 52501.
- Train Dispatcher. 8 per yr. ISSN 0041-0837

**American Transcendental Quarterly**
c/o Editors, English Department, University of
Rhode Island, Kingston, RI 02881.
- American Transcendental Quarterly; journal of
  New England writers. q. ISSN 0003-1410

**American Translators Association**
Box 129, Croton-on-Hudson, NY 10520.
- A T A Professional Services Directory. irreg.
  ISSN 0567-4263

**American Traveler, Inc.**
2 W. 46th St., New York, NY 10036.
- Travel Agent. s-w. ISSN 0041-199X
- Travel Industry Personnel Directory. a. ISSN
  0082-6146

**American Trial Lawyers Association**
20 Garden St., Cambridge, MA 02138.
- American Trial Lawyers Association. Convention
  Proceedings. irreg.

**American Trucking Associations**
1616 P St. N.W., Washington, DC 20036.
- American Motor Carrier Directory: Illinois-
  Missouri Edition. (pub. by Guide Services, Inc.)
- American Motor Carrier Directory: Middle
  Atlantic Edition. (pub. by Guide Services, Inc.)
- American Motor Carrier Directory: National
  Edition. (pub. by Guide Services, Inc.)
- American Motor Carrier Directory: New England
  Edition. (pub. by Guide Services, Inc.)
- American Motor Carrier Directory: Pacific States
  Edition. (pub. by Guide Services, Inc.)
- American Motor Carrier Directory: Southeastern
  Edition. (pub. by Guide Services, Inc.)
- American Motor Carrier Directory: Specialized
  Services Edition. (pub. by Guide Services, Inc.)
- American Trucking Trends. Statistical Report. a.
  (prep. by its Department of Economics)
- F & O S/Financial & Operating Statistics; results
  of operations class I & II motor carriers of
  property; regulated by the Interstate Commerce
  Commission. q. ISSN 0098-2245
- Financial Analysis of the Motor Carrier Industry.
  a. ISSN 0099-2445
- Transport Topics; the national newspaper of the
  motor freight carriers. w. ISSN 0041-1558

**American Type Culture Association**
12301 Parklawn Dr., Rockville, MD 20852.
- American Type Culture Collection. Catalogue of
  Strains Algae, Bacteria, Bacteriophages, Fungi and
  Protozoa. biennial.
- American Type Culture Collection. Catalogue of
  Viruses, Rickettsiae, Chlamydiae. irreg.

**American Underwriter**
12 S. 12th St., Philadelphia, PA 19107.
- New York Insurance Brokers Directory. a.

**American Universal Artforms Corp.**
Box 2242, Austin, TX 78767
- Texas Optometry. m. (Texas Optometric
  Association) (Subscr. to: Texas Optometric
  Association, 505 International Life Bldg., Austin,
  TX 78701)

**American Universities Field Staff, Inc.**
P.O. Box 150, Hanover, NH 03755.
- American Universities Field Staff. Annual Report of the Executive Director. a. ISSN 0066-1082
- American Universities Field Staff. List of Publications. a. ISSN 0066-1104
- American Universities Field Staff. Population: Perspective. (pub. by Freeman, Cooper & Co.)
- Common Ground (Hanover) q. ISSN 0099-0868
- Fieldstaff Reports. East Asia Series. irreg., 4 in 1976.
- Fieldstaff Reports. East Coast South America. irreg., 1 no. in 1976.
- Fieldstaff Reports. Northeast Africa Series. irreg., 10 nos in 1976.
- Fieldstaff Reports. South Asia Series. irreg., 14 nos. in 1976.
- Fieldstaff Reports. Southeast Asia Series. irreg., 9 nos. in 1976.
- Fieldstaff Reports. Southwest Asia Series. irreg., 1 no. in 1976.
- Fieldstaff Reports. West Coast South America. irreg., 2 nos. in 1976.
- Fieldstaff Reports. West Europe Series. irreg., 8 nos. in 1976.

**American University**
Massachusetts & Nebraska Aves. N.W., Washington, DC 20016.
- Eagle (Washington) w. ISSN 0012-8082

**American University. Center for the Study of Private Enterprise**
Washington, DC 20016.
- American University Lectures in Business Government Relations. a. ISSN 0066-1120

**American University. Jewish Studies Program**
Washington, DC 20016.
- Jewish Pickle. irreg.

**American University. Office of University Development**
Washington, DC 20016.
- American University Report. bi-m. ISSN 0300-7421

**American University. School of Business Administration**
Washington, DC 20016.
- American University. Energy Institute. Proceedings. irreg. ISSN 0071-027X

**American University. School of Education**
Washington, DC 20016.
- Journal of Classroom Interaction. s-a.

**American University. Washington College of Law**
Massachusetts and Nebraska Aves., Washington, DC 20016.
- American University Law Review. 4 per yr. ISSN 0003-1453

**American Urological Association**
- Journal of Urology. (pub. by Williams and Wilkins Co.)

**American Vacuum Society**
- Journal of Vacuum Science and Technology. (pub. by American Institute of Physics)
- Vacuum. (pub. by Pergamon Press, Inc.)
- Vacuum Metallurgy Conference. Proceedings. (pub. by Van Nostrand Reinhold Co.)

**American Vecturist Association**
Box 1204, Boston, MA 02104.
- Fare Box. m. ISSN 0014-7745

**American Vegetarian Union**
- American Vegetarian-Hygienist. (pub. by American Better Health Publications)

**American Venereal Disease Association**
- Sexually Transmitted Diseases. (pub. by J. B. Lippincott Co.)

**American Veterans Committee, Inc.**
1333 Connecticut Ave. N.W., Washington, DC 20036.
- A V C Bulletin. q. ISSN 0001-2874

**American Veterans of World War II, Korea and Viet Nam (AMVETS)**
National Headquarters, 1710 Rhode Island Ave. N.W., Washington, DC 20036.
- National AMMVET. bi-m. ISSN 0027-853X

**American Veterinary Medical Association**
930 N. Meacham Rd., Schaumburg, IL 60172.
- American Journal of Veterinary Research. m. ISSN 0002-9645
- American Veterinary Medical Association. Directory. biennial. ISSN 0066-1147
- American Veterinary Medical Association. Journal. s-m. ISSN 0003-1488

**American Veterinary Medical Association. Student Chapter**
College of Veterinary Medicine, Texas A & M Univ., College Sta., TX 77843.
- Southwestern Veterinarian. 3 per yr. ISSN 0038-495X

**American Veterinary Publications, Inc.**
P.O. Drawer KK, Santa Barbara, CA 93102.
- Modern Veterinary Practice. 13 per yr. ISSN 0026-8542
- Update Veterinary Reference Service. m.

**American Veterinary Radiology Society**
1800 Pickwick Ave., Glenview, IL 60025.
- American Veterinary Radiology Society. Journal. 6 per yr. ISSN 0066-1155

**American Vocational Association**
1510 H St. N.W., Washington, DC 20005.
- A V A Member-Gram. q. ISSN 0001-2866
- American Vocational Association. Yearbook. a.
- American Vocational Journal. m.(Sept-May) ISSN 0003-1496

**American Vocational Association. Trade and Industrial Division**
- American Vocational Association. Trade and Industrial Division. Yearbook. (pub. by American Technical Society)

**American Vocational Education Research Association**
c/o Joel Magisos, Center for Vocational Education, Ohio State University, 1960 Kenny Rd., Columbus, OH 43210.
- Journal of Vocational Education Research. q.

**American Water Resources Association**
St. Anthony Falls Hydraulic Laboratory, Mississippi River at Third Ave., S. E., Minneapolis, MN 55414.
- American Water Resources Conferences. Annual Proceedings. a. ISSN 0066-1171
- Hydata; water resources index. m. ISSN 0018-8115
- Water Resources Abstracts. m. ISSN 0043-1362
- Water Resources Bulletin; a journal of water resources research, planning, development and management. bi-m. ISSN 0043-1370

**American Water Works Association**
6666 W. Quincy Ave., Denver, CO 80235.
- American Water Works Association. Journal. m. ISSN 0003-150X
- American Water Works Association. Proceedings, A W W A Annual Conference. a. ISSN 0360-814X
- Willing Water. m.

**American Water Works Association. Southwest and Texas Sections**
306 E. Adams Ave., Temple, TX 76501.
- Southwest Water Works Journal. m. ISSN 0038-4720

**American Watercolor Society**
1083 Fifth Ave., New York, NY 10028.
- American Watercolor Society Newsletter. s-a.

**American Way Publications**
633 Third Ave., New York, NY 10017.
- American Way. m. ISSN 0003-1518

**American Welding Society**
2501 N.W. 7th St., Miami, FL 33125.
- Index of Welding Standards from 21 Nations. irreg.
- Welding Journal. m. ISSN 0043-2296

**American West Center**
- Publications in the American West. (pub. by University of Utah Press)

**American Whitewater Affiliation**
Box 1584, San Bruno, CA 94066.
- American White Water. bi-m. ISSN 0300-7626 (Subscr. to:, Box 51, Wallingford, CT 06492)

**American Woman's Society of Certified Public Accountants**
Box 389, Marysville, OH 43040.
- Woman C P A. q. ISSN 0043-7271 (Co-sponsor: American Society of Women Accountants)

**American Wood Preservers Association**
1625 Eye St, Washington, DC 20006.
- American Wood Preservers' Association. Proceedings of the Annual Meetings. a.

**American Wood Preservers Institute**
1651 Old Meadow Road, Suite 135, McLean, VA 22101.
- A/E Concepts in Wood Design. bi-m.

**American Yorkshire Club, Inc.**
1001 South St., Lafayette, IN 47902.
- Yorkshire Journal. 10 per yr. ISSN 0044-0612

**American Youth Hostels, Inc.**
National Campus, Delaplane, VA 22025.
- American Youth Hostels Guide and Handbook. a. ISSN 0066-1201

**American Youth Hostels, Inc. Metropolitan New York Council**
132 Spring St., New York, NY 10012.
- Hosteling Holidays. a.

**American Zionist Federation**
515 Park Ave., New York, NY 10022.
- American Zionist Federation. News and Views. m. ISSN 0044-8079

**American Zionist Youth Foundation**
515 Park Ave., NY 10022.
- Hora. q. (Israel Folk Dance Institute)
- Zionist Comments. bi-m. (prep. by its University Department)

**Americana Annual**
501 E. Lange St., Mundelein, IL 60060.
- Americana Annual. a.

**Americans for Constitutional Action**
955 l'Enfant Plaza North, S.W., Washington, DC 20024.
- A C A Index; analysis of voting records of members of U. S. Congress. a. ISSN 0066-1228
- Americans for Constitutional Action. Report. a. ISSN 0066-1236
- Congressional Record Digest and Tally of Roll Call Votes. 8-9 per yr. ISSN 0069-892X

**Americans for Democratic Action**
1411 K St. N.W., Washington, DC 20005.
- A D A Legislative Newsletter. s-m. when Congress is in session.
- A D A World. 6 per yr. ISSN 0001-0871

**Americans for Effective Law Enforcement**
960 State National Bank Plaza, Evanston, IL 60201.
- A.E.L.E. Law Enforcement Legal Defense Manual. bi-m. ISSN 0092-2552
- A E L E Legal Liability Reporter. m.

**Americans for Middle East Understanding, Inc.**
Room 771, 475 Riverside Dr., New York, NY 10027.
- Link. bi-m. ISSN 0024-4007

**Americans United for Separation of Church and State**
8120 Fenton St., Silver Spring, MD 20910.
- Church and State; a monthly review. m.(Sept-July) ISSN 0009-6334

**Americas Future Inc**
542 Main St, New Rochelle, NY 10802.
- America's Future; a fortnightly review of news, books and public affairs. fortn. ISSN 0003-1593

**Amerikai Magyar Szo**
130 E. 16th St., New York, NY 10003.
- Magyar Naptar (New York) irreg. ISSN 0094-1484

**Amerikas Latviesu Apvieniba**
c/o Margers Grins, 3270 Parmalee Dr., Seven Hills, OH 44131.
- Latvju Maksla. irreg. ISSN 0362-7047

**Amerikas Latvietis**
Box 23, Roxbury, Boston, MA 02119.
- Amerikas Latvietis. m. ISSN 0003-1631

**Ameron, Inc.**
4700 Ramona Blvd., Monterey Park, CA 91754.
- Ameron News. q.

**Amerpub Co.**
505 Eighth Ave., New York, NY 10018.
- American Turf Monthly. m. ISSN 0003-1445

**Ames Company**
Division Miles Laboratories, Inc., 1127 Myrtle St.,
Elkhart, IN 46514.
- Diabetes in the News. q. ISSN 0012-1800
- Diagnostica. 4 per yr. ISSN 0012-1916

**Ames Publishing Co.**
1 W. Olney Ave., Philadelphia, PA 19120.
- Industrial Distributor News. m. ISSN 0019-8161
- Industrial Maintenance & Plant Operation. m.
  ISSN 0019-8463
- Safety Products News; industrial safety products
  and security equipment. m. ISSN 0036-2530

**Amfetex Inc.**
Box 213, Arlington, MA 02174.
- Amfetex Journal of Japanese Electronics and
  Power Engineering; abstracts from Japanese
  journals. m.
- Tokyo Electronics Weekly; the most
  comprehensive newsletter on Japanese electronics
  industry. w.

**Amherst College. Alumni Council**
Box 37, Amherst, MA 01002.
- Amherst. q.

**Amish Mennonite Publishing Association**
c/o Enos H. Miller, Route 2, Box 119, Kalona, IA
52247.
- Herold der Wahrheit. m. ISSN 0300-8851

**Ammark Publishing Co., Inc.**
P.O. Box 245, Joliet, IL 60431.
- School Musician Director and Teacher. m. (Sept.-
  June) ISSN 0036-6676

**Ammon Hennacy House of Hospitality**
- Catholic Agitator. (pub. by Los Angeles Catholic
  Worker)

**Amnesty International of the U. S. A.**
200 W. 72nd St., Suite 64, New York, NY 10023.
- Amnesty Action. m. ISSN 0003-1933

**Amoco Enterprises, Inc.**
Amoco Motor Club, 200 E. Randolph Drive,
Chicago, IL 60604.
- Adventure Road. q. ISSN 0001-8805

**Amordian Press, Inc.**
Box 1882, 1320 Pearl St., Boulder, CO 80306.
- Music America. m.

**Amos Press, Inc.**
Box 150, Sidney, OH 45365.
- Coin World. w. ISSN 0010-0447
- Coin World Almanac. irreg. ISSN 0361-0845
- Gun Week. w. ISSN 0017-5633
- Linn's Stamp News. w.

**Amphoto**
750 Zeckendorf Blvd., Garden City, NY 11530.
- Amphoto Facsimile Books. irreg.

**Amterre Development Inc.**
2 Bala Cynwyd Plaza, Bala Cynwyd, PA 19004.
- Amterre Reporter. bi-m.

**Amundsen Publications, Inc.**
Box 39092, Washington, DC 20016.
- World Ports/American Seaport. 8 per yr.

**An Claidheamh Soluis, Inc.**
553 W. 51 St., New York, NY 10019.
- Ais-Eiri; the magazine of Irish-America. irreg.
  ISSN 0360-5388

**Anahata Nada**
150-30 86th Ave, Jamaica, NY 11432.
- Anahata Nada/Soundless Sound. m.

**Analog Sounds**
c/o Jacob Meyerowitz, Ed., 12 W. 17th St., New
York, NY 10011.
- Analog Sounds; directions for the new music. q.

**Analytical Psychology Club of New York, Inc.**
Suite 306, 130 E. 39th St., New York, NY 10016.
- Spring; an annual of archetypal psychology and
  Jungian thought. a.

**Anametrics, Inc.**
30 Rockefeller Plaza, New York, NY 10020.
- Findings and Forecasts. s-m.

**Ananda Marga Society**
1644 Park Rd. N.W., Washington, DC 20010.
- Sadvipra. m.

**Anchor Society**
2398 Pine St., San Francisco, CA 94115.
- New Life. m. 10 per yr. (Protestant Episcopal
  Church in the U.S.A.)

**Ancram Restoration., Inc.**
c/o Ed. John Peter Hayden, Ancram, NY 12502.
- Ancram Standard. m.

**Walter G. Anderson, Ed. & Pub.**
Box 243, Lenox Hill Station, New York, NY 10021.
- Editor's Newsletter; new trends and techniques in
  business communications. m. ISSN 0046-127X

**W. H. Anderson Co.**
Box 1576, 646 Main St., Cincinnati, OH 45201.
- American School Law Series. irreg.
- Criminal Justice Text Series. irreg.
- Directory of Law Enforcement Professors. irreg.
  ISSN 0420-0632
- Science in Law Enforcement Series. irreg.

**Anderson College**
1100 E. 5th St., Anderson, IN 46011.
- Anderson College News. bi-m. ISSN 0003-293X

**Anderson Group, Inc.**
Box 508, Madison, NJ 07940.
- Management Service Alert & The Administrative
  Officer. bi-w.

**Anderson, M.D., Hospital and Tumor Institute**
*see under* **University of Texas**

**The Anderson Ranch Arts Foundation**
Box 5645, West Village, CO 81615.
- T A R A News. q.

**Andover Newton Theological School**
Newton Centre, MA 02159.
- Andover Newton Quarterly. q. ISSN 0003-2972

**Andrew W. Mellon Foundation**
140 E. 62nd St., New York, NY 10021.
- Andrew W. Mellon Foundation. Report. a. ISSN
  0066-1694

**Andrews Paper & Chemical Co. Inc.**
1 Channel Drive, Box 509, Port Washington, NY
10050.
- Reproduction Bulletin. q.

**Andrews University Press**
Berrien Springs, MI 49104.
- Andrews University. Monographs. irreg., 1973,
  vol. 7. ISSN 0066-1708
- Andrews University Seminary Studies. s-a. ISSN
  0003-2980

**Andrews University. Student Association**
Berrien Springs, MI 49104.
- Student Movement. w.

**Angiology Research Foundation**
286 Northern Blvd., Great Neck, NY 11021.
- Angiology. m. except Aug. ISSN 0003-3197 (Co-
  sponsors: American College of Angiology;
  International College of Angiology)

**Angle Orthodontists Research & Education
Foundation, Inc.**
103 W. College Ave., Appleton, WI 54911.
- Angle Orthodontist. q. ISSN 0003-3219

**Anglican Theological Review, Inc.**
600 Haven St., Evanston, IL 60201.
- Anglican Theological Review. q. ISSN 0003-3286

**Anglo-American Associates**
President's Office, Bowdoin College, Brunswick,
ME 04011.
- British Studies Monitor. 3 per yr. ISSN 0007-1846

**Anglo-Lat**
c/o Robert Montero, Ed., 9141 Ronda Ave., San
Diego, CA 92123.
- Anglo-Lat. q.

**Angus Publishers**
131 South Barrington Place, Los Angeles, CA
90049.
- All About Snowmobiles. s-a.

**Animal Health Foundation**
8338 Rosemead Blvd., Pico Rivera, CA 90660.
- Today's Animal Health. bi-m.

**Animal Protection Institute of America**
Box 22505, Sacramento, CA 95822.
- Mainstream. q.

**Animal Rescue League of Boston**
Box 265, Boston, MA 02117.
- Our Fourfooted Friends. q. ISSN 0030-6851

**Animal Welfare Institute**
Box 3650, Washington, DC 20007.
- Animal Welfare Institute. Information Report. q.
  ISSN 0003-3596

**Ankho International Inc.**
Box 65, Phoenix, NY 13135.
- Brain Research Bulletin. bi-m.
- Pharmacology, Biochemistry and Behavior. bi-m.
  ISSN 0091-3057

**Ann Arbor Publishers**
P.O. Box 388, Worthington, OH 43085.
- Problems in Education and Nation Building. irreg.
  ISSN 0556-3100 (University of Michigan)

**Ann Arbor Review Press**
Ann Arbor, MI 48106.
- Ann Arbor Review. 3 per yr. (Washtenaw
  Community College)

**Ann Arbor Science Publishers, Inc.**
Box 1425, Ann Arbor, MI 48106.
- Man, His Community and Natural Resources
  Series. irreg.
- Pollution Control Conference. Proceedings. irreg.
- Progress in Thin-Layer Chromatography and
  Related Methods. irreg., 1972, vol. 3. ISSN 0079-
  6867

**Annals Publishing Co.**
4949 Forest Park, St. Louis, MO 63108.
- Annals of Otology, Rhinology and Laryngology.
  bi-m. ISSN 0003-4894

**Annenberg School Press**
P.O. Box 13358, Philadelphia, PA 19101.
- Journal of Communication. q. ISSN 0021-9916
  (International Communication Association)

**Annotated Bibliography of Bibliographies on Selected
Government Publications & Supplementary Guides
to the Superintendent of Documents Classification
System. Supplement**
c/o Alexander C. Body, 925 Westfall Ave.,
Kalamazoo, MI 49007.
- Annotated Bibliography of Bibliographies on
  Selected Government Publications &
  Supplementary Guides to the Superintendent of
  Documents Classification System. Supplement.
  biennial.

**Annual Reviews Inc.**
4139 El Camino Way, Palo Alto, CA 94306.
- Annual Review of Anthropology. a. ISSN 0084-
  6570
- Annual Review of Astronomy and Astrophysics.
  a. ISSN 0066-4146
- Annual Review of Biochemistry. a. ISSN 0066-
  4154
- Annual Review of Biophysics and Bioengineering.
  a. ISSN 0084-6589
- Annual Review of Earth and Planetary Sciences.
  a. ISSN 0084-6597
- Annual Review of Ecology and Systematics. a.
  ISSN 0066-4162
- Annual Review of Energy. a.
- Annual Review of Entomology. a. ISSN 0066-
  4170
- Annual Review of Fluid Mechanics. a. ISSN
  0066-4189
- Annual Review of Genetics. a. ISSN 0066-4197
- Annual Review of Materials Science. a. ISSN
  0084-6600
- Annual Review of Medicine: Selected Topics in
  the Clinical Sciences. a.

- Annual Review of Microbiology. a. ISSN 0066-4227
- Annual Review of Nuclear Science. a. ISSN 0066-4243
- Annual Review of Pharmacology and Toxicology. a.
- Annual Review of Physical Chemistry. a. ISSN 0066-426X
- Annual Review of Physiology. a. ISSN 0066-4278
- Annual Review of Phytopathology. a. ISSN 0066-4286
- Annual Review of Plant Physiology. a. ISSN 0066-4294
- Annual Review of Psychology. a. ISSN 0066-4308
- Annual Review of Sociology. a. ISSN 0360-0572

**Peter Annunziata**
551 Summit Ave., Jersey City, NJ 07306.
- Hat Life Year Book; directory of men's hat and cap industry. a. ISSN 0073-0904

**Another Mother for Peace**
407 North Maple, Beverly Hills, CA 90210.
- Another Mother for Peace. 4 per yr. ISSN 0003-5181

**ANRO Inc.**
222 Lancaster Ave., Devon, PA 19333.
- American Society for Adolescent Psychiatry. Newsletter. 4 per yr.

**Anthelion Press, Ltd.**
Box 614, Corte Madera, CA 94925.
- Anthelion. bi-m.
- Campus News. fortn.

**Anthroposophical Society in America**
211 Madison Ave., New York, NY 10016.
- Journal for Anthroposophy. s-a. ISSN 0021-8235

**Anti-Defamation League of B'nai B'rith**
315 Lexington Ave., New York, NY 10016.
- A D L Bulletin. m. ISSN 0001-0936
- Face to Face; an interreligious bulletin. q.
- Law. 3-4 per yr. ISSN 0023-916X

**Anti-Friction Bearing Manufacturers Association, Inc.**
60 E. 42 St., Rm. 764, New York, NY 10017.
- Anti-Friction Bearing Manufacturers Association. Standards for Ball and Roller Bearings and Balls. irreg. ISSN 0066-474X

**Anti-Stalinism Study Group**
Box 8724, Emeryville, CA 94608.
- Tsushin. irreg.

**Antilles Publications, Inc.**
1245 Park Ave., New York, NY 10028.
- Carib-America. q.

**Antioch College**
Publications Office, Yellow Springs, OH 45387.
- Antioch College Reports. ISSN 0003-5742

**Antioch Review, Inc.**
Box 148, Yellow Springs, OH 45387.
- Antioch Review. q. ISSN 0003-5769

**Antipode: A Radical Journal of Geography**
P.O. Box 225, West Side Station, Worcester, MA 01602.
- Antipode: A Radical Journal of Geography. irreg. (approx. 3 per yr.) ISSN 0066-4812

**Antiquarian and Landmarks Society of Connecticut, Inc.**
394 Main St., Hartford, CT 06106.
- Connecticut Antiquarian. s-a. ISSN 0010-6054

**Antiquarian Bookman**
Box AB, Clifton, NJ 07015.
- A B Bookman's Weekly; the specialist book trade weekly. w. ISSN 0001-0340
- A B Bookman's Yearbook; specialist book trade annual. a. ISSN 0065-0005
- A B C of Book Trade. quinquennial. ISSN 0065-0048
- O. P. Market. a. ISSN 0078-2882

**Antique Airplane Association**
Box H, Ottumwa, IA 52501.
- A P M Bulletin. q. ISSN 0048-2358 (Air Power Museum)
- Antique Airplane Association News. ISSN 0003-5823
- International Antique Airplane News.

**Antique Automobile Club of America**
501 W. Governor Rd., Hershey, PA 17033.
- Antique Automobile. bi-m. ISSN 0003-5831
- Northern Lights. 8 per yr. ISSN 0029-3148

**Antique Wireless Association Inc**
c/o Bruce Kelley, Ed., Main St., Holcomb, NY 14469.
- Old Timers' Bulletin. q. ISSN 0030-204X

**Antiquer**
318 Highland Ave., Syracuse, NY 13203.
- Antiquer. m.

**Antitrust Law and Economics Review, Inc.**
P.O. Box 6134, Washington, DC 20044.
- Antitrust Law and Economics Review. q. ISSN 0003-6048
- Wage-Price Law & Economics Review. q. ISSN 0361-6665

**Antwerp Bee-Argus**
154 N. Main, Antwerp, OH 45813.
- Antwerp Bee-Argus; Paulding County Eagle. w. ISSN 0003-617X

**Anvil Press**
Box 37, Millville, MN 55957.
- North Country Anvil. bi-m.

**Any-All Printers**
507 W. Main St., Walla Walla, WA 99362.
- Middle .R. a. ISSN 0076-8545

**Apalachee Correctional Institution**
Box 127, Chattahochee, FL 32324.
- Apalachee Diary. q. ISSN 0003-634X

**Apartment Association of Orange County**
- Orange County Apartment News. (pub. by Ed Mee Publications, Inc.)

**Apartment News Publications, Inc.**
4120 Atlantic Ave., Long Beach, CA 90807.
- Apartment Owner-Builder. m.

**Apartment Owners and Managers Association of America**
65 Cherry Ave., Watertown, CT 06795.
- A O M A Newsletter; profile of the industry. m.

**Apartment Owners Publishing Co.**
2868 E. Oakland Park Blvd., Fort Lauderdale, FL 33306.
- Apartment Owners News. m. ISSN 0003-6374 (Florida Co-Operative Apartment Owners Association Inc)

**Apartments for Rent, Inc.**
Box 62, Planetarium Sta., New York, NY 10024.
- Apartments for Rent. w.

**Aperture**
c/o Michael E. Hoffman, Elm St., Millerton, NY 12546.
- Aperture. q. ISSN 0003-6420

**Aphra**
Box 893, Ansonia Station, New York, NY 10023.
- Aphra; the feminist literary magazine. q. ISSN 0003-6447

**Apostolate, Inc.**
805 N. Franklin St., Philadelphia, PA 19123.
- Shlach/Way; Ukrainian Catholic weekly. w. (Ukrainian Catholic Church. Archdiocese of Philadelphia)
- Way. w. ISSN 0043-1583 (Ukrainian Catholic Church. Archdiocese of Philadelphia)

**Apostolic Lutheran Church of America**
New York Mills, MN 56567.
- Christian Monthly. m. ISSN 0009-5494

**Appalachian Associates, Inc.**
Box 5, Pipestem, WV 25979.
- Appalachian South. q. ISSN 0003-6633

**Appalachian Mountain Club**
5 Joy St., Boston, MA 02108.
- A M C Times. 10 per yr.
- Appalachia Bulletin. q.
- Appalachia Journal. s-a. ISSN 0003-6587

**Appalachian Regional Commission**
see U. S. Appalachian Regional Commission

**Appalachian State University**
Boone, NC 28608.
- Appalachian Journal. q. ISSN 0090-3779
- North Carolina Folklore Journal. irreg. ISSN 0029-246X (North Carolina Folklore Society)

**Appalachian State University. Department of History**
Boone, NC 28608.
- Albion. q. (Conference on British Studies)

**Appalachian Trail Conference**
Box 236, Harpers Ferry, WV 25425.
- Appalachian Trailway News. 5 per yr. ISSN 0003-6641

**Appaloosa Horse Club Inc.**
Box 8403, Moscow, ID 83843.
- Appaloosa Horse; Stud Book and Registry. irreg., v. 15, 1973.
- Appaloosa News. m. ISSN 0003-665X

**Appalshop Inc.**
Box 743, Whitesburg, KY 41858.
- Mountain Review. q.

**Apple River Journal**
Box 6, Star Prairie, WI 54026.
- Apple River Journal. w.

**Apple Tree Press**
Box 1012, Flint, MI 48501.
- Chases' Calendar of Annual Events; special days, weeks and months in the year. a. ISSN 0577-5728

**Appleton-Century-Crofts**
(Subsidiary of: Prentice-Hall)
292 Madison Ave., New York, NY 10017.
- Appleton Century Crofts Sociology Series. irreg.
- Appleton Century Mathematics Series. irreg.
- Appleton Century Statistics Series. irreg.
- Appleton Psychiatry Series. irreg.
- Century Philosophy Series. irreg.
- Century Psychology Series. irreg.
- Contemporary Problems in Philosophy. irreg.
- Journal of Family Practice. q. ISSN 0094-3509
- Legal Medicine Annual. a. ISSN 0075-8590
- Modern Trends in Medical Virology. irreg. ISSN 0544-6856
- Modern Trends in Neurology. irreg. ISSN 0544-6872
- Modern Trends in Vascular Surgery. irreg.
- National Medical Association. Journal. m. ISSN 0027-9684
- Obstetrics and Gynecology Annual. a.
- Pathobiology Annual. a.
- Pathology Annual. a. ISSN 0079-0184
- Recent Advances in Phytochemistry. a. ISSN 0079-9920

**Applied Computer Research**
Box 9280, Phoenix, AZ 85068.
- Directory of Top Computer Executives. 2 per yr.
- E D P Performance Review; monthly report on computer performance inprovement. m. ISSN 0091-7206
- Quarterly Bibliography of Computers and Data Processing; a subject/author index to computer literature. q. (plus annual cumulation) ISSN 0048-6132

**Applied Forestry Research Institute**
State University College of Forestry, Syracuse University, Syracuse, NY 13210.
- A F R I Miscellaneous Report. irreg., 1970, no. 3. ISSN 0066-5436
- A F R I Research Note. irreg., 1971, no. 3. ISSN 0077-9113
- Applied Forestry Research Institute. Research Report. irreg., 1970, Mar., no. 2. ISSN 0066-5444

**Applied Library Resources**
2430 Pennsylvania Ave., N.W., Washington, DC 20037.
- Applied Library Reference Series. irreg.

**Applied Mathematics Group, MIT**
- Studies in Applied Mathematics. (pub. by Elsevier North-Holland, Inc., New York)

**Applied Parking Techniques, Inc.**
Box 707, Reston, VA 22070.
- Transportation Terminal Techniques. irreg. ISSN 0362-3122

**Applied Science Center for Archaeology**
Univ. of Pennsylvania, University Museum, 33rd & Spruce Sts., Philadelphia, PA 19104.
- M A S C A Newsletter. 1-2 per yr. ISSN 0024-791X

**Approach 13-30 Corp.**
1005 Maryville Pike S.W., Knoxville, TN 37920.
- Eighteen Almanac; a handbook for leaving high school. a.
- Graduate; a handbook for leaving school. a.
- Nutshell; a handbook for college. a.

**Aqua-Field Publications**
342 Madison Ave., New York, NY 10017.
- Colt American Handgunning Annual. a.
- Daisy Shooting Annual. a.
- Daiwa Sportfishing Annual. a.
- Ithacagun Hunting & Shooting Annual. a. ISSN 0361-4999

**Aquarian Advertising Associates**
1020 Park Ave., New York, NY 10028.
- Country Property News. m.

**Aquarian Publishing Co.**
One The Crescent, Montclair, NJ 07042.
- Aquarian. s-m.

**Aquatic Research Institute**
21393 Curtis St., Haywood, CA 94545.
- Aquatica. irreg., 1963, no. 3. ISSN 0066-5592

**Arab Information Center**
1875 Connecticut Avenue, N.W., Suite 1110, Washington, DC 20009.
- Arab Report. bi-w.
- Palestine Digest. bi-m. ISSN 0300-6484

**Aralabs Inc.**
80 Republic Drive, North Haven, CT 06473.
- Aralabs. Research News. q.

**Aramtek Corporation**
122 E. 42nd St., New York, NY 10017.
- Aramtek Mideast Monthly. m.

**Archaeological Institute of America**
260 W. Broadway, New York, NY 10013.
- American Journal of Archaeology. q. ISSN 0002-9114
- Archaeology; an official publication of the Archaeological Institute of America. bi-m. ISSN 0003-8113
- Monographs on Archeology and Fine Arts. irreg. ISSN 0077-0981

**Archaeological Research Associates**
Box 277, Mound St. Monument, Moundville, AL 35474.
- Contributions to California Archaeology. irreg., no. 7, 1970. ISSN 0573-8547

**Archaeological Society of Central New York**
- Archaeological Society of Central New York. Bulletin. (pub. by Cayuga Museum of History and Art)

**Archaeological Society of Connecticut**
c/o Douglas F. Jordan, University of Connecticut, Storrs, CT 06268.
- Connecticut News. q.

**Archaeological Society of Delaware**
Box 301, Wilmington, DE 19899.
- Archaeological Society of Delaware. Bulletin. ISSN 0003-8067
- Archaeological Society of Delaware. Monograph. irreg.
- Inksherds. 5 per yr.

**Archaeological Society of New Jersey**
Humanities Bldg, Seton Hall, University of South Orange, NJ 07079.
- Archaeological Society of New Jersey Bulletin. s-a.

**Archaeological Society of New Mexico**
- Awanyu. (pub. by COAS Publishing and Research)

**Archaeological Society of North Carolina**
Univ. of North Carolina, Box 561, Chapel Hill, NC 27514.
- Southern Indian Studies. a. ISSN 0085-6525

**Archaeological Society of Ohio**
199 Converse Dr., Plain City, OH 43064.
- Ohio Archaeologist. q. ISSN 0048-153X

**Archconfraternity of Christian Mothers**
220 37th St., Pittsburgh, PA 15201.
- Christian Mother. q.

**Archdiocese of Chicago**
- New World. (pub. by New World Publishing Co., Inc.)

**Archdiocese of New York**
c/o Victor L. Ridder, 68 W. Broad St., Mt. Vernon, NY 10552.
- Catholic News. w. ISSN 0008-8250

**Archdiocese of San Francisco**
c/o Archbishop Joseph T. McGucken, 441 Church St., San Francisco, CA 94114.
- Monitor. w. ISSN 0026-9743

**Archimedia, Inc.**
1900 Chestnut St., Philadelphia, PA 19103.
- Charette. bi-m.

**Architect & Contractor**
c/o W. A. Ullner, Ed., 721 Santa Clara Ave, Alameda, CA 94501.
- Architect & Contractor. m. ISSN 0003-8423

**Architectural Index**
Box 1168, Boulder, CO 80302.
- Architectural Index. a. ISSN 0570-6483

**Architectural Metals**
c/o William N. Wilson, 1033 South Blvd., Oak Park, IL 60302.
- Architectural Metals; the voice of the architectural metals industry. bi-m. ISSN 0003-8563

**Architectural Register of America**
6 Frost St., Box 639, Springfield, MA 01101.
- American Registered Architect. bi-m. ISSN 0003-0759

**Archive of Social Innovation**
- Prometheus. (pub. by Social Innovation Information Service)
- Social Innovation. (pub. by Social Innovation Information Service)

**Archives for the Performing Arts**
3150 Sacramento St., San Francisco, CA 94115.
- Archives News. m?

**Archives of American Art**
*see under* **Smithsonian Institution**

**Archon Books**
(Subsidiary of: Shoe String Press)
995 Sherman Ave., Hamden, CT 06514.
- Connecticut Academy of Arts and Sciences. Memoirs. irreg., 1969, vol. 18. ISSN 0069-8970
- Connecticut Academy of Arts and Sciences. Transactions. irreg., 1976, vol. 46. ISSN 0069-8989
- Elizabethan Theatre. irreg.; 5th edt., 1975. ISSN 0071-0032
- Studies in British History and Culture. irreg., 1970, no. 3. ISSN 0081-7619 (Conference on British Studies) (Co-sponsor: Wittenberg University)
- World Education Series (Archon) irreg.

**Arco Corp.**
1000 16th St. N.W., Washington, DC 20036.
- F X O Report. w.

**Arco Publishing Co. Inc.**
219 Park Ave. S., New York, NY 10003.
- Internal Revenue Guide to Your Federal Income Tax. a. ISSN 0074-1205 (U.S. Internal Revenue Service)

**Arctic Publications & Productions**
Box 4-2684, Anchorage, AK 99509.
- Alaska Business & Development. bi-m.

**Arctinurus Co.**
Box G, Bellmawr, NJ 08030.
- Arctinurus Newsletter. irreg.

**Ardis Publishers**
2901 Heatherway Dr., Ann Arbor, MI 48108.
- Ardis New Poets Series. irreg., no. 7, 1977.

- Russian Literature Triquarterly. 3 per yr. ISSN 0048-881X

**Area Auto Racing News, Inc.**
2829 S. Broad St., Trenton, NJ 08610.
- Area Auto Racing News. w.

**Areito**
Box 1124, Peter Stuyvesant Sta., New York, NY 10009.
- Areito. q.

**Arena Magazine Co.**
23745 Elmira Ave., St. Clair Shores, MI 48082.
- Goldmine; the record collector's marketplace. bi-m.

**Arens Corp.**
395 S. High St., Covington, OH 45318.
- Country Living. m. ISSN 0011-0205

**Arete (San Francisco)**
830 Hyde St., No. 6B, San Francisco, CA 94109.
- Arete (San Francisco) q.

**Arete Activities, Inc.**
239 E. Second St., New York, NY 10009.
- New York Good News; a journal for optimists.

**Argus Publishers Corp.**
Box 49659, Los Angeles, CA 90049.
- Off Road. m.
- Popular Cycling. m.
- Popular Hot Rodding. m. ISSN 0032-4523
- Super Chevy. bi-m.
- Volkswagen Greats. bi-m. ISSN 0049-6723
- 1001 Custom & Rod Ideas. bi-m. ISSN 0030-2546
- 1001 Truck & Van Ideas. m.

**P. C. Argyle-Stuart, Ed. & Pub.**
Box 1192, Colorado Springs, CO 80901.
- High I.Q. Bulletin. m.

**Aries Corp.**
Box 992, Champaign, IL 61820.
- Confinement. 10 per yr.

**Arion's Dolphin**
Box 313, Cambridge, MA 02138.
- Arion's Dolphin; a quarterly of poetry. q.

**Arizona. Advisory Commission on Arizona Environment**
206 S. 17th Ave., Phoenix, AZ 85007.
- Arizona. Advisory Commission on Arizona Environment. Annual Report. a. ISSN 0097-9953

**Arizona. Advisory Council for Vocational Education**
P. O. Box 6694, 1810 W. Adams St., Phoenix, AZ 85005.
- Arizona. State Advisory Council for Vocational Education. Annual Report. a. ISSN 0091-8792

**Arizona. Commission on the Arts and Humanities**
6330 N. 7th St., Phoenix, AZ 85014.
- Arizona Commission on the Arts & Humanities. Report to the Governor. a. ISSN 0098-7387

**Arizona. Department of Administration. Finance Division**
Phoenix, AZ 85007.
- Federal Programs, State of Arizona. a. ISSN 0363-7166

**Arizona. Department of Administration. Personnel Division**
1831 West Jefferson, Phoenix, AZ 85007.
- Joint Governmental Salary Survey : Arizona. a.

**Arizona. Department of Economic Security**
1717 W. Jefferson, Box 6123, Phoenix, AZ 85005.
- Arizona. Department of Economic Security. Annual Report. a. ISSN 0094-0712
- Arizona Labor Market Newsletter. m.
- Arizona Manpower Review. s-a.
- Arizona Mining and Manufacturing. a.

**Arizona. Department of Economic Security. Office of Planning**
Box 6123, Phoenix, AZ 85005.
- Arizona Economic Indicators. q. ISSN 0004-1467
- Population Estimates of Arizona. a. ISSN 0079-3906

**Arizona. Department of Education**
Education Bldg., 1535 W. Jefferson, Phoenix, AZ 85007.
- Alert (Phoenix) m.

- Arizona. Department of Education. Annual
Report of the Superintendent of Public
Instruction. a. ISSN 0095-5310
- Arizona State Plan for the Education of Migratory
Children. irreg., latest issue, 1974.

**Arizona. Department of Health Services**
1740 W. Adams St., Phoenix, AZ 85007.
- Arizona. Department of Health Services. Annual
Report. a. ISSN 0362-1421

**Arizona. Department of Health Services. Bureau of
Air Quality Control**
1740 W. Adams St., Phoenix, AZ 85007.
- Air Quality Data for Arizona. a.; latest issue 1974.
- Pollution Control Newsletter. 8 per yr.

**Arizona. Department of Public Safety**
P.O. Box 6638, Phoenix, AZ 85005.
- Arizona. Department of Public Safety. Annual
Report. a. ISSN 0066-7382

**Arizona. Department of Transportation**
1655 W. Jackson, 1739 W. Jackson, Phoenix, AZ
85007.
- Safety Sad-Istics. q.

**Arizona. Office of Economic Planning and
Development**
1645 West Jefferson, Rm 428, Phoenix, AZ 85007.
- Arizona Directions. m.
- Arizona Directory of State Regulatory Agencies
for Businesses and Occupations. a.

**Arizona. Office of the Post Auditor**
Phoenix, AZ 85007.
- Arizona. Office of the Post Auditor. Federal
Grant-in-Aid Programs. a. ISSN 0093-8300

**Arizona. Oil & Gas Conservation Commission**
8686 N. Central Ave., Suite 106, Phoenix, AZ
85020.
- Arizona. Oil & Gas Conservation Commission.
Oil, Gas & Helium Production. m. ISSN 0570-
9520
- Arizona Oil and Gas Conservation Commission.
Report of Investigation. irreg., no. 4, 1974.

**Arizona. State Dental Board**
Phoenix, AZ 85007.
- Arizona. State Dental Board. Report. a. ISSN
0098-6828

**Arizona. State Land Department. Division of Forestry**
Box 387, 3650 Lake Mead Rd., Flagstaff, AZ
86001.
- Arizona Landmarks. a.

**Arizona. Supreme Court**
- Report of Cases Argued and Determined in the
Supreme Court of the State of Arizona. (pub. by
West Publishing Co.)

**Arizona. Water Commission**
U.S. Geological Survey, 222 N. Central Ave, Suite
800, Phoenix, AZ 85004.
- Annual Report on Ground Water in Arizona. a.

**Arizona Academy of Science**
Membership Secretary, A-324 Physical Science
Center, Arizona State Univ., Tempe, AZ 85281.
- Arizona Academy of Science Journal. 3 per yr.
ISSN 0004-1378

**Arizona Archaeological and Historical Society**
Univ. of Arizona, Tucson, Tucson, AZ 85721.
- Kiva. q. ISSN 0023-1940

**Arizona Association for Supervision and Curriculum
Development**
Dr. James John Jelinek, Ed., c/o College of
Education, Arizona State University, Tempe, AZ
85281.
- Yearbook in Education. a.

**Arizona Automobile Association**
748 East McDowell Road, Phoenix, AZ 85006.
- Arizona AAA Highroads. bi-m.

**Arizona Bank**
101 N. First Ave., Phoenix, AZ 85002.
- Arizona Bank News. m.

**Arizona Blue Book: a Guide to the State of Arizona**
P.O. Box 3305, Tucson, AZ 85722.
- Arizona Blue Book: a Guide to the State of
Arizona. biennial.

**Arizona Cactus & Native Flora Society**
- Saguaroland Bulletin. (pub. by Desert Botanical
Garden)

**Arizona Education Association**
2102 W. Indian School Rd., Phoenix, AZ 85015.
- Arizona Educator Advocate. 15 per yr.

**Arizona English Teachers Association**
c/o Dr. Sharon Crowley, English Dept., Northern
Arizona University, Flagstaff, AZ 86001.
- Arizona English Bulletin. 3 per yr.(Sept.-June)
ISSN 0004-1483

**Arizona Federation of Stamp Clubs, Inc.**
Box 10337, Phoenix, AZ 85106.
- Arizona Philatelists. m.

**Arizona Geological Society**
P.O. Box 4503, University Station, Tucson, AZ
85717.
- Arizona Geological Society. Digest. irreg. ISSN
0066-7412

**Arizona Grocers Publishing Co. Inc**
604 E. Pierce, Phoenix, AZ 85004.
- Arizona Grocer. m. ISSN 0004-1505 (Retail
Grocers Association of Arizona)

**Arizona Highways**
2039 W. Lewis Ave., Phoenix, AZ 85009.
- Arizona Highways. m. ISSN 0004-1521

**Arizona Historical Society**
949 E. Second St., Tucson, AZ 85719.
- Arizona Historical Society. Historical
Monographs. irreg., no. 5, 1976.
- Arizona Historical Society. Museum Monograph
Series. irreg., no. 7, 1976.
- Journal of Arizona History. q. ISSN 0021-9053
- Reata. q.

**Arizona Jim Co-Op**
Old Hope Schoolhouse, Cottage Grove, WI 53527.
- Velvet Light Trap. q.

**Arizona Library Extension Service. Division of
Library Archives and Public Records**
333 N. Black Canyon, Phoenix, AZ 85009.
- Arizona Public Libraries Statistical Report and
Directory. a.

**Arizona Medical Association**
810 W. Bethany Home Rd., Phoenix, AZ 85013.
- Arizona Medicine. m. ISSN 0004-1556

**Arizona Motor Transport Association**
- Arizona Roadrunner. (pub. by Donald D. Clark &
Associates, Inc.)

**Arizona Nurses Association**
4525 N. 12th St., Phoenix, AZ 85014.
- Arizona Nurse. 5 per yr. ISSN 0004-1599

**Arizona Pharmaceutical Association**
2202 N. Seventh St., Phoenix, AZ 85006.
- Arizona Pharmacist. m. ISSN 0004-1602

**Arizona Small Mine Operators Association**
P.O. Drawer 48, Bisbee, AZ 85603.
- Pay Dirt. m.

**Arizona Society of Mental Health Technology**
2500 E. Van Buren St., Phoenix, AZ 85002.
- Journal of Mental Health Technology. s-a.

**Arizona Society of Professional Engineers**
- Arizona Professional Engineer. (pub. by Donald
D. Clark & Associates, Inc.)

**Arizona-Sonora Desert Museum, Inc.**
Tucson Mountain Park, Box 5607, Tucson, AZ
85703.
- A S D M Newsletter. q. ISSN 0044-8850
- Arizona-Sonora Desert Museum. Annual Report.
a.
- Desert Speaks; the story of the Arizona-Sonora
Desert Museum. irreg.

**Arizona Speech & Hearing Association**
c/o J. A. Schall, Ed., 1640 E. Alameda Dr., Tempe,
AZ 85282.
- A R S H A Bulletin. q. ISSN 0001-2327

**Arizona State Dental Association**
3800 N. Central, Phoenix, AZ 85012.
- Arizona Dental Journal. 2 per yr. ISSN 0004-1459
- Copper State Bulletin. q.

**Arizona State University**
Center for the Study of Higher Education, Tempe,
AZ 85281.
- Monographs in Higher Education. s-a.

**Arizona State University. Bureau of Publishing**
Tempe, AZ 85281.
- Meteoritics. q. ISSN 0026-1114 (Meteoritical
Society)

**Arizona State University. Center for Asian Studies**
Tempe, AZ 85281.
- Arizona State University. Center for Asian
Studies. Occasional Papers. irreg.

**Arizona State University. Center for Latin American
Studies**
Tempe, AZ 85281.
- Arizona State University. Center for Latin
American Studies. Special Studies Series. irreg.
- Directory of ASU Latin Americanists. a.
- Hispanic American Periodical Index; an author-
subject index to periodicals and other serials at
Arizona State University. q. ISSN 0361-5502
- Latin American Digest. q. ISSN 0023-8767

**Arizona State University. Center for Public Affairs**
Tempe, AZ 85281.
- Arizona State University. Center for Public
Affairs. Monograph. irreg., latest issue 1977.
- Papers in Public Administration. irreg., no. 33,
1977. ISSN 0078-9151

**Arizona State University. College of Business
Administration**
Tempe, AZ 85281.
- Arizona Business. m.(bi-m.during summer) ISSN
0093-0717 (prep. by its Bureau of Business and
Economic Research)

**Arizona State University. College of Education**
Tempe, AZ 85281.
- Arizona State University. Bureau of Educational
Research and Services. Educational Services
Bulletin. irreg.; latest issue, no. 49. ISSN 0066-
7455
- Arizona State University. Bureau of Educational
Research and Services. Research and Services
Bulletin. irreg.; latest issue, no. 34. ISSN 0066-
7463
- Journal of American Indian Education. 3 per
yr.(Oct, Jan. & May) ISSN 0021-8731 (prep. by
its Bureau of Educational Research and Services)

**Arizona State University. College of Law**
Tempe, AZ 85281.
- Arizona State Law Journal. q.

**Arizona State University. Department of
Anthropology**
Tempe, AZ 85281.
- Newsletter of Computer Archaeology. q. ISSN
0028-9450

**Arizona State University. Faculty of Industrial
Engineering**
Tempe, AZ 85281.
- Arizona State University. Faculty of Industrial
Engineering. Industrial Engineering Research
Bulletin. a. ISSN 0570-9601

**Arizona State University. Music Department**
Tempe, AZ 85281.
- International Percussion Reference Library.
Catalog. biennial. ISSN 0085-218X

**Arizona Trailer Publications**
4110 E. Van Buren St., Phoenix, AZ 85008.
- Arizona Mobile Citizen. w. ISSN 0004-1564
- Arizona Mobile Home & Recreational Vehicle
Park Guide. a.

**Ark Ozark Publishing Co. Inc.**
Box 109, Eureka Springs, AR 72632.
- Ark/Ozark. q. ISSN 0004-170X

**Arkansas. Bureau of Vital Statistics**
Little Rock, AR 72201.
- Arkansas. Bureau of Vital Statistics. Annual
Report of Births, Deaths, Marriages and Divorces
as Reported to the Bureau of Vital Statistics. a.
ISSN 0094-3576

**Arkansas. Commission on Crime and Law
Enforcement**
Little Rock, AR 72201.
- Arkansas. Commission on Crime and Law
Enforcement. Annual Report. a. ISSN 0093-8459

**Arkansas. Department of Education**
Education Bldg., Capitol Mall, Little Rock, AR 72207.
- Arkansas Department of Education. Library Bulletin. q.
- Arkansas Department of Education Newsmagazine. 4 per yr. ISSN 0004-1777

**Arkansas. Department of Mental Retardation**
Conway, AR 72032.
- Arkansas. Department of Mental Retardation. Annual Report. a. ISSN 0093-7452

**Arkansas. Department of Parks and Tourism. Travel Division**
149 State Capitol, Little Rock, AR 72201.
- Tourism in Arkansas; Activity Report. irreg.

**Arkansas. Department of Planning. Environmental Preservation Commission**
400 Train Station Sq., Little Rock, AR 72201.
- Arkansas. Environmental Preservation Commission. Annual Report. a. ISSN 0095-2206

**Arkansas. Division of Health Statistics**
4815 W. Markham St., Little Rock, AR 72201.
- Arkansas Vital Statistics. biennial. ISSN 0364-0728

**Arkansas. Division of Human Services**
Little Rock, AR 72201.
- Action (Little Rock) m. ISSN 0363-4337

**Arkansas. Division of Rehabilitation Services**
Little Rock, AR 72201.
- Arkansas. Division of Rehabilitation Services. Annual Report. a.

**Arkansas. Employment Security Division. Research and Statistics**
Little Rock, AR 72201.
- Arkansas Average Covered Employment and Earnings by County and Industry. irreg. ISSN 0092-2889

**Arkansas. Game and Fish Commission**
2 Capitol Mall, Little Rock, AR 72201.
- Arkansas Game & Fish. q. ISSN 0004-1807

**Arkansas. Geological Commission**
Little Rock, AR 72201.
- Water Resources Summary. irreg.; latest issue, 1973. ISSN 0518-6374

**Arkansas. Industrial Development Commission**
205 State Capitol, Little Rock, AR 72201.
- Inside Arkansas. m.

**Arkansas. Judicial Department**
Justice Bldg., State Capitol Grounds, Little Rock, AR 72201.
- Amicus Curiae. 3 per yr.

**Arkansas. Manpower Council**
3 C Executive Bldg., Little Rock, AR 72205.
- Arkansas Comprehensive Manpower Plan. irreg. ISSN 0094-1166

**Arkansas. Securties Department**
Plaza West Bldg., McKinley and Lee Sts., Little Rock, AR 72205.
- Arkansas. Securities Department. Monthly Bulletin. m.

**Arkansas. State Board of Nursing**
9107 Rodney Parham Road, Little Rock, AR 72205.
- Arkansas State Board of Nursing. Statistical Report. biennial.

**Arkansas. State Highway Department**
Box 2261, Little Rock, AR 72203.
- Arkansas Highways. q. ISSN 0403-1792

**Arkansas Almanac**
Box 3652, 114th & 2nd Sts., Little Rock, AR 72201.
- Arkansas Almanac. a. ISSN 0571-0456

**Arkansas Archeological Society**
c/o University of Arkansas Museum, Central Office, Fayetteville, AR 72701.
- Arkansas Archeological Society. Field Notes. m. ISSN 0015-0711
- Arkansas Archeologist. q. ISSN 0004-1718

**Arkansas Archeological Survey**
Univ. of Arkansas Museum, Coordinating Office, Fayetteville, AR 72701.
- Arkansas Archeological Survey. Publications on Archeology. Popular Series. irreg. ISSN 0587-3533
- Arkansas Archeological Survey. Publications on Archeology. Research Series. irreg.

**Arkansas Bankers Association**
Suite 1027, Pyramid Bldg., Little Rock, AR 72201.
- Arkansas Banker. m. ISSN 0004-1726

**Arkansas-Best Freight System, Inc.**
301 S. 11th St., Ft. Smith, AR 72901.
- A B F By-Lines. m.

**Arkansas Cattlemen's Association**
318 Wallace Bldg., Little Rock, AR 72201.
- Arkansas Cattle Business. m. ISSN 0004-1750

**Arkansas Community Organizations for Reform Now (ACORN)**
523 W. 15th St., Little Rock, AR 72202
(Subscr. to: 1501 S. Arch St., Little Rock, AR 72202)
- Arkansas Advocate. m.

**Arkansas Education Association**
1500 W. 4th St., Little Rock, AR 72201.
- Arkansas Educator. m. except Jun. & Aug.

**Arkansas Electric Cooperatives**
P.O. Box 510, Little Rock, AR 72203.
- Rural Arkansas. m. ISSN 0048-878X

**Arkansas Free Enterprise Association**
Plaza Towers, Suite 8-0, Little Rock, AR 72205.
- Free Enterpriser. s-a.

**Arkansas Grocer Publishing Co.**
Box 7806, Pine Bluff, AR 71601.
- Arkansas Grocer. bi-m. ISSN 0004-1815

**Arkansas Historical Association**
Univ. of Arkansas, Dept. of History, Fayetteville, AR 72701.
- Arkansas Historical Quarterly. q. ISSN 0004-1823

**Arkansas Industrial Development Foundation**
Box 1784, Little Rock, AR 72203.
- Directory of Manufacturers in Arkansas. irreg. ISSN 0361-2996

**Arkansas Library Association**
c/o Katherine Stanick, 701 North McAdoo St., Little Rock, AR 72205.
- Arkansas Libraries. q. ISSN 0004-184X

**Arkansas LP Gas Association, Inc.**
421 Danaghey Bldg., Little Rock, AR 72201.
- Arkansas LP News. bi-m. ISSN 0044-8893

**Arkansas Medical Society**
Box 1208, Fort Smith, AR 72902.
- Arkansas Medical Society. Journal. m. ISSN 0004-1858

**Arkansas Municipal League**
Box 38, North Little Rock, AR 72115.
- Arkansas Municipalities. m. ISSN 0004-1866

**Arkansas Oil & Gas Commission**
314 East Oak, El Dorado, AR 71730.
- Arkansas Oil and Gas Statistical Bulletin. m. ISSN 0004-1874

**Arkansas Poultry Federation**
P.O. Box 1446, Little Rock, AR 72203.
- Arkansas Poultry Times. w. ISSN 0044-8907

**Arkansas Rehabilitation Research and Training Center**
Little Rock, AR 72201.
- Arkansas Rehabilitation Research and Training Center. Annual Progress Report. a. ISSN 0094-3762
- Rehabilitation Research and Practice Review. q. ISSN 0093-5131

**Arkansas State Dental Association**
Box 337, Arkadelphia, AR 71923.
- Arkansas Dental Journal. q. ISSN 0004-1769

**Arkansas State University. Division of English, Philosophy and Languages**
Box 143, State University, AR 72467.
- Mid-South Folklore. 3 per yr. ISSN 0099-2356

**Arkansas Survey**
P.O. Box 1153, Harrison, AR 72601.
- Arkansas Cave Survey. Newsletter. irreg. ISSN 0066-7633

**Arkansas Tech University**
Russellville, AR 72801.
- Arka-Tech. w. ISSN 0004-1882

**Arkansas Valley Journal, Inc**
Box 1130, 7 W. Fifth St, La Junta, CO 81050.
- Arkansas Valley Journal. w. ISSN 0004-1890 (Southern Colorado Horseman's Association)

**Arlington Historical Society, Inc.**
P.O. Box 402, Arlington, VA 22210.
- Arlington Historical Magazine. a. ISSN 0066-7684

**Arlington Publishing Co**
2 N. Riverside Plaza, Chicago, IL 60606.
- Food Product Development. 10 per yr. ISSN 0015-654X

**Armadillo Press**
P.O. Box 8131, University of Texas Station, Austin, TX 78712.
- Applications of Library Science. irreg., vol. 5, 1975.

**Armchair Press**
Dept. of English, Bowling Green State University, Bowling Green, OH 43403.
- Broadside. 24 per yr.

**Armco Steel Corporation**
7000 Roberts St., Kansas City, MO 64125.
- Fence Rider. q.

**Armco Steel Corporation. Metal Products Division**
Middletown, OH 45042.
- Construction Products. q. ISSN 0010-6887

**Armed Forces Communications and Electronics**
5205 Leesburg Pike Suite 301, Falls Church, VA 22041.
- Signal (Falls Church) m. ISSN 0037-4938

**Armed Forces Journal International**
1414 22nd St., N.W., Washington, DC 20037.
- Armed Forces Journal International. m.

**Armenian Democratic Liberal Organization**
- Nor Or. (pub. by Nor Or Publishing Co.)

**Armenian General Benevolent Union of America, Inc.**
628 2nd Ave., New York, NY 10016.
- Ararat. q. ISSN 0003-7583
- Hoosharar. m. ISSN 0018-4721

**Armenian Literary Society-New York, Inc.**
114 1st St., Yonkers, NY 10704.
- Kir-Ou-Kirk. s-a. ISSN 0017-6613

**Armenian Missionary Association of America**
12 Birch Close, N. Tarrytown, NY 10591.
- Armenian-American Outlook. q. ISSN 0004-2307 (Co-Sponsor: Armenian Evangelical Union of North America)

**Armenian Relief Society, Inc.**
212 Stuart St., Boston, MA 02116.
- A. R. S. Hai Sird. 4 per yr. ISSN 0001-2335

**Armenian Reporter, Inc.**
Box 488, Flushing, NY 11355.
- Armenian Reporter; New York's independent Armenian newsweekly. w. ISSN 0004-2358

**Armenian Welfare Association of New York, Inc.**
137-41 45th Ave., Flushing, NY 11355.
- Armenian Welfare Association of New York News. q. ISSN 0004-2382

**Armitage Press, Inc.**
1430 Massachusetts Ave., Cambridge, MA 02138.
- Women's Almanac & City Handbook. s-a.

**Armstrong Cork Co.**
Press Services, Lancaster, PA 17604.
- Armstrong Logic. m. ISSN 0044-8974

**Army Aviation Association of America, Inc.**
Westport, CT 06880.
- Army Aviation. m. ISSN 0004-248X

**Army Times Publishing Co.**
475 School St. S.W., Washington, DC 20024.
- Air Force Times. w. ISSN 0002-2403

- Army Times. w. ISSN 0004-2595
- Federal Times. w. ISSN 0014-9233
- Military Market. m. ISSN 0026-4067
- Navy Times; Marine Corps, Navy, Coast Guard. w. ISSN 0028-1697
- Times Magazine; magazine of Army-Navy-Air Force times. bi-m.

**Arnell Publications, Inc.**
4500 Campus Dr.-692, Newport Beach, CA 92660.
- Western Landscaping News; the newsmagazine of the Western Landscape industry. m. ISSN 0043-3861

**Arner Publications, Inc.**
Box 307, Westmoreland, NY 13490.
- Off-Lead; the national dog training monthly. m. ISSN 0094-0186

**Arnhem Advertising. International Patent Developers, Inc.**
812-14 N. Highland, Los Angeles, CA 90038.
- Patent Pending & Marketing. bi-m.

**Arno Press**
(Subsidiary of: New York Times Co.)
3 Park Ave., New York, NY 10016.
- Compact New York Times Magazine. m. ISSN 0362-1251
- New York Times Biographical Service. m. ISSN 0048-0088

**Arnold Air Society**
National Publications Headquarters, Texas Technological College, Air Force R.O.T.C., Lubbock, TX 79409.
- Arnold Air Letter. q. ISSN 0004-2617

**Arnold Arboretum**
Harvard Univ., 22 Divinity Ave., Cambridge, MA 02138.
- Arnold Arboretum. Journal. q. ISSN 0004-2625
- Arnoldia. 6 per yr. ISSN 0004-2633

**Arnold Bennett Newsletter**
c/o Anita Miller, Ed., 334 Hawthorn, Glencoe, IL 60022.
- Arnold Bennett Newsletter. 3 per yr.

**Arnold Select Publishing Co.**
Box 889, Camden, NJ 08101.
- Select. bi-m.

**Jason Aronson, Inc.**
59 Fourth Ave., New York, NY 10003.
- International Journal of Psychoanalytic Psychotherapy. q. ISSN 0091-0600
- Psychotherapy and Social Science Review; a journal of book reviews. m.

**Ars Moriendi**
- Omega. (pub. by Baywood Publishing Co., Inc.)

**Art and Artists of the Monterey Peninsula**
Box 1310, Monterey, CA 93940.
- Art and Artists of the Monterey Peninsula. irreg., 1970 2nd issue. ISSN 0066-7927

**Art and Nature**
10 Harborside Park, Dennisport, MA 02639.
- Cinema Studies. irreg., 1970, no. 3. ISSN 0069-4150

**Art Digest, Inc.**
23 E. 26th St., New York, NY 10010.
- Arts Magazine. 10 per yr. ISSN 0004-4059

**Art Direction Magazine**
- Creativity. (pub. by Advertising Trade Publications, Inc.)

**Art Directions Book Co.**
19 W. 44th St., New York, NY 10036.
- Advertising Directions. a.

**Art Directors Club of New York**
- Annual of Advertising, Editorial & Television Art & Design with the Annual Copy Awards. (pub. by Watson-Guptill Publications, Inc.)

**Art in America, Inc.**
(Subsidiary of: Whitney Communications Corporation)
150 E. 58th St., New York, NY 10022
(Subscr. to: 542 Pacific Ave., Marion, OH 43302)
- Art in America. bi-m. ISSN 0004-3214
- International Art Market; a monthly survey of art auction prices. m. ISSN 0020-5931

**Art Institute of Chicago**
Michigan Ave. and Adams St., Chicago, IL 60603.
- Art Institute of Chicago. Museum Studies. a.; latest issue, vol. 7. ISSN 0069-3235

**Art Instruction Schools**
500 S. Fourth St., Minneapolis, MN 55415.
- Illustrator. q. ISSN 0019-2465

**Art Libraries Society of North America**
P.O. Box 3692, Glendale, CA 91201.
- A R L I S /N A Newsletter. bi-m. ISSN 0090-3515

**Art Students League of New York**
215 W. 57th St., New York, NY 10019.
- Art Students League News. 8 per yr.

**Art Voices, Inc.**
23 E. 26th St., New York, NY 10010.
- Art Voices; an independent art magazine voicing news, views and opinions on art. q. ISSN 0004-3346

**Artforum, Inc.**
667 Madison Ave, New York, NY 10021.
- Artforum. m. except Jul. - Aug. ISSN 0004-3532

**Arthritis Foundation**
221 Park Ave. S., New York, NY 10003.
- Arthritis Foundation. Conference Series. irreg., no. 15, 1971. ISSN 0518-794X
- Bulletin on Rheumatic Diseases. m.(Sept-May) ISSN 0007-5248
- Rheumatism Review. biennial. ISSN 0080-2700

**Arthritis Foundation. American Rheumatism Association Section**
3400 Peachtree Road, N.E., Atlanta, GA 30326.
- American Rheumatism Association. Directory. biennial.
- Arthritis and Rheumatism. 8 per yr. ISSN 0004-3591
- Index of Rheumatology. a. ISSN 0019-3933 (American Rheumatism Association)

**Arthritis Foundation. Michigan Chapter**
27308 Southfield Rd., Lathrup Village, MI 48076.
- Arthritis Newsletter. q. ISSN 0044-9083

**Arthur Machen Society**
Wittenberg University, Thomas Library, Springfield, OH 45501.
- A M S Occasional. biennial.

**Artists - U S A: Guide to Contemporary American Art**
1315 Walnut St., Philadelphia, PA 19107.
- Artists - U S A: Guide to Contemporary American Art. biennial.

**Artman's Press**
1511 McGee Ave., Berkeley, CA 94703.
- Bebop Drawing Club Book. irreg.

**Artnews**
750 3rd Ave., New York, NY 10017.
- Art News. m.(Sept-May); q.(June-Aug) ISSN 0004-3273
- Artnewsletter. bi-w.

**Arts Alliance Corp.**
9220 Sunset Blvd, Los Angeles, CA 90069.
- Designers West. m.
- Designers West Resource Directory. s-a.

**Arts Reporting Service**
9214 Three Oaks Drive, Silver Spring, MD 20901.
- Arts Reporting Service. fortn.

**Artsake Studios**
45 Park Ave., Ellicott City, MD 21043.
- T K. m. (Maryland Motor Truck Association, Inc.)

**Artweek, Inc.**
1305 Franklin St., Oakland, CA 94612.
- Artweek; West Coast art news. w(Sept.-May); fortn(June, July & Aug.) ISSN 0004-4121

**Arusha-Konakri Institute (UFOMI) Inc.**
Box 17509, Chicago, IL 60617.
- Afrika Must Unite: an International Journal of Current Afrikan Affairs. m.

**Asbarez Publishing Co.**
1501 Venice Blvd., Los Angeles, CA 90006.
- Asbarez. s-w. ISSN 0004-4229

**Asbestos Textile Institute**
Box 471, 131 North York Rd., Willow Grove, PA 19090.
- Handbook of Asbestos Textiles. irreg., 1967, 3rd ed. ISSN 0066-8214

**Asbury Theological Seminary**
Wilmore, KY 40390.
- Asbury Seminarian. q. ISSN 0004-4253

**Ascot Publishing Enterprises, Inc**
22 Ascot Ridge, Great Neck, NY 11021.
- Thought Starters for Management. m.

**Asheville Area Chamber of Commerce**
Box 1011, Asheville, NC 28802.
- Asheville Area Chamber of Commerce. Report. m.

**Ashford Press**
Warrenville, CT 06278.
- Sarcophagus. irreg.

**Ashland Oil, Inc.**
P.O. Box 391, Ashland, KY 41101.
- Ashland News. m.

**Ashlee Publishing Co., Inc.**
15 E. 40th St., New York, NY 10016.
- Glass Digest; merchandising magazine of the flat glass, architectural metal and allied products industry. m. ISSN 0017-1018
- International Glass/Metal Catalog. a.

**Ashleys of America, Inc.**
68 Spring Hill Ave., Bridgewater, MA 02324.
- Ashleys of America Quarterly. s-a. ISSN 0096-1469

**Asia Foundation**
Box 3223, San Francisco, CA 94119.
- Asia Foundation. President's Review. a. ISSN 0587-3606
- Asia Foundation Program Quarterly. q. ISSN 0004-4458
- Asia Foundation Review. bi-m.
- Asian Student. bi-w. ISSN 0004-4660

**Asia Publishing House, Inc.**
440 Park Ave. S., New York, NY 10016.
- Aligarh Muslim University, Aligarh, India. Department of History. Publication. irreg. ISSN 0065-6259 (Aligarh Muslim University. Department of History II)
- Calcutta Research Series. irreg., 1967, no. 10. ISSN 0068-5364 (Institute of Public Administration, New York)
- Medieval India; a Miscellany. irreg., 1975, vol. 3. ISSN 0076-6119 (Aligarh Muslim University. Center for Advanced Study II)
- Ranganathan Series in Library Science. irreg., no. 25, 1975. ISSN 0079-967X (Sharada Ranganathan Endowment for Library Science)
- Sarojini Naidu Memorial Lecture Series. irreg., latest vol. 1977.

**Asia Society**
112 East 64 St., New York, NY 10021.
- Archives of Asian Art. a. ISSN 0066-6637 (Friends of Asia House Gallery)
- Asia. bi-m. ISSN 0004-4407
- Asia Society. Annual Report. a. ISSN 0098-1214

**Asia Society. Performing Arts Program**
133 E. 58th St., New York, NY 10022.
- Monographs on Music, Dance and Theater in Asia. a.

**Asia Society. South East Asia Development Advisory Group**
505 Park Avenue, New York, NY 10022.
- S E A D A G Reports. irreg.

**Asian Family Affair, Inc.**
Box 3445 International Branch, Seattle, WA 98114.
- Asian Family Affair. m.

**Asian Music Publications**
c/o School of Music, University of Washington, Seattle, WA 98195.
- Asian Music Publications. Series A: Bibliographic and Research Aids. irreg.; latest issue, 1974. ISSN 0081-1319 (Society for Asian Music)
- Asian Music Publications. Series B. Translations. irreg. ISSN 0081-1327 (Society for Asian Music)
- Asian Music Publications. Series C: Reprints. irreg. ISSN 0081-1335 (Society for Asian Music)

- Asian Music Publications. Series D: Monographs. irreg.,latest issue 1977. ISSN 0081-1343 (Society for Asian Music)

**Asian-Pacific Society of Cardiology**
- Asian-Pacific Congress of Cardiology. Proceedings. (pub. by Academic Press, Inc.)

**Asociacion International de Galdosianos**
University of Texas at Austin, Dept. of Spanish & Portuguese, Austin, TX 78712.
- Anales Galdosianos. a.

**Aspen Institute for Humanistic Studies**
717 Fifth Ave., New York, NY 10022.
- Aspen Institute Chronicle. a.

**Aspen Leaves Literary Foundation**
- Aspen Anthology. (pub. by Aspen Magazine, Inc.)

**Aspen Magazine, Inc.**
Box 3185, Aspen, CO 81611.
- Aspen Anthology; a literary magazine. s-a. ISSN 0362-9554 (Aspen Leaves Literary Foundation)

**Aspen Systems Corp.**
Germantown, MD 20767.
- Health Care Management Review. q. ISSN 0361-6274
- Hospital Law Manual & Quarterly Service. q. ISSN 0018-5728
- Topics in Health Care Financing. q. ISSN 0095-3814

**Assemblies of God**
1445 Boonville Ave., Springfield, MO 65802.
- Good News Crusades. bi-m. ISSN 0017-2162 (prep. by its Division of Foreign Missions)
- Sunday School Counselor. m. ISSN 0039-5285 (prep. by its Sunday School Department)

**Assemblies of Yahweh**
Bethel, PA 19507.
- Sacred Name Broadcaster. m.

**Assembling Press**
Box 1967, Brooklyn, NY 11202.
- Assembling; a collection of otherwise unpublishable creative work. a. (Participation Projects Foundation)

**Associated Builders & Contractors, Inc.**
444 N. Capitol St. N.W., Washington, DC 20001.
- Merit Shop Contractor. m.

**Associated Building Industry of California**
- California Builder. (pub. by Fellom Publications)

**Associated Business Publications, Inc.**
101 Park Ave., Suite 1838, New York, NY 10017.
- Convenience Store Merchandiser; the national magazine for convenience food stores and their suppliers. m. ISSN 0095-7151

**Associated Church Press**
326 W. State St., Media, PA 19063.
- Associated Church Press. Directory. biennial. ISSN 0066-8710

**Associated Colleges of Illinois**
343 S. Dearborn St., Chicago, IL 60604.
- Associated Colleges of Illinois. Report. a. ISSN 0066-8729

**Associated Committee of Friends on Indian Affairs**
c/o Mrs. Dora O. Hollingsworth, 341 E. Chicago Ave., Hinsdale, IL 60521.
- Indian Progress. 3 per yr. ISSN 0019-6193

**Associated Councils of the Arts**
570 Seventh Ave., New York, NY 10018.
- A C A Reports; news highlights of the arts evolving. bi-m. ISSN 0044-9393
- A C A Word from Washington. m. ISSN 0300-7065

**Associated Credit Bureaus, Inc.**
6767 Southwest Freeway, Houston, TX 77036.
- A C B Management. bi-m. ISSN 0001-0596

**Associated Editorial Consultants**
Box 2017, La Jolla, CA 92038.
- In Black and White; biweekly guide for those who write, report and edit for publications. bi-w.

**Associated Equipment Distributors**
615 W. 22nd St., Oak Brook, IL 60521.
- Construction Equipment Distribution. m. ISSN 0010-6755
- Rental Compilation; nationally averaged rental rates and model reference data for construction equipment. a.

**Associated General Contractors of America**
1957 E Street N.W., Washington, DC 20006.
- Constructor; the management magazine of the construction industry. m.

**Associated General Contractors of America. N.Y. State Chapter**
1900 Western Ave., Albany, NY 12203.
- Low Bidder. m. ISSN 0024-7030

**Associated General Contractors of Iowa**
- Central Constructor. (pub. by Central Constructor Corp.)

**Associated General Contractors of Missouri**
Box 94, 111 Madison St., Jefferson City, MO 65101.
- Construction Advisor. m. ISSN 0010-6712

**Associated Grocers of Colorado Inc.**
5151 Bannock St., Denver, CO 80217.
- A G News. m.

**Associated Industries of Massachusetts**
4005 Prudential Tower, Boston, MA 02199.
- Industry. m. ISSN 0019-9435

**Associated Industries of New York State, Inc.**
150 State St., Albany, NY 12207.
- Monitor; the voice of industry in New York State. irreg. ISSN 0077-040X

**Associated Male Choruses of America, Inc.**
1338 Oakcrest Dr., Appleton, WI 54911.
- A M C of A Newsletter. m. ISSN 0001-1894

**Associated Maritime Officers A F L-C I O**
650 Fourth Ave., Brooklyn, NY 11232.
- American Maritime Officer. m. ISSN 0002-9882 (Marine Engineers Beneficial Association)

**Associated Mennonite Biblical Seminaries**
- Institute of Mennonite Studies Series. (pub. by Faith and Life Press)

**Associated Milk Producers, Inc.**
Box 32287, San Antonio, TX 78216
- Dairymen's Digest: Southern Region Edition. m. (Subscr. to: Box 809, Arlington, TX 76010)

**Associated Motor Carriers of Oklahoma, Inc.**
Box 14607, Oklahoma City, OK 73114.
- Oklahoma Motor Carrier. q.

**Associated Music Publishers, Inc.**
866 Third Ave., New York, NY 10022.
- New York Pro Musica Instrumental Series. irreg., 1970, no. 6. ISSN 0085-4042

**Associated Musicians of Greater New York**
Local 802, A.F. of M., 261 W. 52ndSt., New York, NY 10019.
- Allegro. m. (11 per yr.) ISSN 0002-5704

**Associated Pennsylvania Constructors**
800 N. Third St., Harrisburg, PA 17102.
- Highway Builder. m. ISSN 0018-1692

**Associated Plumbing & Heating Contractors of Washington, Inc.**
- Washington Plumbing and Heating Contractor. (pub. by Ballard Printing & Publishing Co.)

**Associated Plumbing & Mechanical Contractors of Florida**
- Florida Contractor. (pub. by Frank D. Wesley)

**Associated Plumbing Contractors of Maryland, Inc.**
5910 Falls Rd., Baltimore, MD 21209.
- Maryland Master Plumber. m.

**Associated Plumbing, Heating & Cooling Contractors of Alabama**
2231 S. 20th Ave., Birmingham, AL 35223.
- Alabama Contractor. m. ISSN 0002-418X

**Associated Press**
- Official Associated Press Almanac. (pub. by Hammond Almanac, Inc.)

**Associated Public-Safety Communications Officers Inc.**
105-1/2 Canal St., P.O. Box 669, New Smyrna Beach, FL 32069.
- A P C O Bulletin. m.

**Associated Public School Systems**
- A P S S Know How. (pub. by Columbia University. Teachers College)
- Associated Public Schools Systems. Yearbook. (pub. by Columbia University. Teachers College)

**Associated Publications, Inc.**
825 Van Brunt Blvd., Kansas City, MO 64124.
- Boxoffice; the national film weekly. w. ISSN 0006-8527

**Associated Publishers, Inc.**
Box 7000, Dallas, TX 75209.
- Drilling-D C W. (Drilling Completion, Well Servicing); the wellsite publication. 13 per yr. ISSN 0012-6241

**Associated Publishing Co.**
Box 519, Brownwood, TX 76801.
- County Progress; the business magazine for county officials. m. ISSN 0011-0353 (County Judges and Commissioners Association of Texas)

**Associated Release Service, Inc.**
173 W. Madison St., Chicago, IL 60602.
- Hathorn's Suburban Press Directory; the Nation's guide to suburban newspaper market. biennial.

**Associated Retail Bakers of America**
731-735 W. Sheridan Rd., Chicago, IL 60613.
- A R B A Fresh Baked. m.

**Associated School Boards of South Dakota**
Box 1211, Pierre, SD 57501.
- A S B S D Bulletin. w. ISSN 0001-2408

**Associated Students of Linfield College**
Box 395 Linfieled Sta., McMinnville, OR 97128.
- Linews. 24 nos. per school yr.

**Associated Students of Loma Linda University**
- Criterion. (pub. by Riverside County Publishing Co.)

**Associated Students of the California Institute of Technology, Inc.**
California Institute of Technology, Caltech 105-51, Pasadena, CA 91125.
- California Tech. w. ISSN 0008-1582

**Associated Students of the University of California. Committee on Publications**
Univ. of California, Berkely, Pelican Bldg., Berkely, CA 94720.
- California Pelican. q (Oct.-May) ISSN 0008-1361

**Associated Technical Services, Inc.**
855 Bloomfield Ave., Glen Ridge, NJ 07028.
- Russian Oil and Gas Bulletin. bi-m. ISSN 0036-0309

**Associated Western Universities, Inc.**
136 E. So. Temple, Suite 1005, Salt Lake City, UT 34111.
- Associated Western Universities. Biennial Report. biennial.

**Association Canado-Americaine**
52 Concord St., Manchester, NH 03101.
- Canado-Americain. q.

**Association for Applied Psychoanalysis**
- American Imago. (pub. by Wayne State University Press)

**Association for Asian Studies, Inc.**
University of Michigan, 1 Lane Hall, Ann Arbor, MI 48109.
- Association for Asian Studies. Enduring Scholarship. Reference Series. irreg.
- Association for Asian Studies. Monographs and Papers. (pub. by University of Arizona Press)
- Association for Asian Studies. Newsletter. q. ISSN 0004-5403
- Bibliography of Asian Studies. a. ISSN 0067-7159
- Focus on Asian Studies. (pub. by Ohio State University. Service Center for Teachers of Asian Studies)
- Journal of Asian Studies. 4 per yr. ISSN 0021-9118
- Ming Studies Newsletter. (pub. by University of Minnesota. History Department)

**Association for Asian Studies, Inc. Committee on East Asian Libraries**
c/o Richard Howard, Ed., Library of Congress, Washington, DC 20540.
- Association for Asian Studies. Committee on East Asian Libraries. Bulletin. 3 per yr.

**Association for Asian Studies, Inc. Committee on Research Materials**
Univ. of Michigan, Lane Hall, Ann Arbor, MI 48109.
- Cormosea Bulletin. s-a.

**Association for Canadian Studies in the United States**
c/o Rufus Z. Smith-VPS, 1776 Massachusetts Ave. N.W., 2nd Fl., Washington, DC 20036.
- American Review of Canadian Studies. s-a.

**Association for Childhood Education International**
3615 Wisconsin Ave., N.W., Washington, DC 20770.
- A C E I Branch Exchange. 6 per yr.
- Association for Childhood Education International. Bulletin. irreg.
- Association for Childhood Education International. Yearbook. a. ISSN 0066-9075
- Bibliography: Books for Children. triennial.
- Childhood Education; a journal for teachers, administrators, church-school workers, librarians, pediatricians. 6 per yr. ISSN 0009-4056
- Good and Inexpensive Books for Children. triennial; 1978 ed. in prep.

**Association for Children with Learning Disabilities**
5225 Grace St., Pittsburgh, PA 15236.
- Directory of Organizations Concerned with Learning Disabilities. irreg.

**Association for Clinical Pastoral Education**
475 Riverside Dr., New York, NY 10027.
- Journal of Pastoral Care. q. ISSN 0022-3409

**Association for Communication Administration**
5205 Leesburg Pike, Falls Church, VA 22041.
- A C A Bulletin. irreg. ISSN 0360-0939

**Association for Comparative Economic Studies**
c/o Elizabeth Clayton, University of Missouri, Dept. of Economics, St. Louis, MO 63121.
- A C E S Bulletin. 3 per yr.

**Association for Computational Linguistics**
c/o Dr. Donald E. Walker, Sec.-Treas., Stanford Research Institute, Menlo Park, CA 94025.
- American Journal of Computational Linguistics. q.

**Association for Computing Machinery**
1133 Ave. of the Americas, New York, NY 10036.
- A C M. Communications. m. ISSN 0001-0782
- A C M Monograph Series. (pub. by Academic Press, Inc.)
- A C M Symposium on Operating Systems Principles. Proceedings. irreg, 4th, 1973.
- A C M Transaction on Mathematical Software. q.
- A C M Transactions on Data Base Systems. q. ISSN 0362-5915
- Association for Computing Machinery. Journal. q. ISSN 0004-5411
- Association for Computing Machinery. Proceedings of National Conference. a. ISSN 0066-9091
- Bibliography and Subject Index of Current Computing Literature. a.
- Computing Reviews. m. ISSN 0010-4884
- Computing Surveys; the survey and tutorial journal of the A C M. q. ISSN 0010-4892
- Graduate Assistant Directory in Computer Sciences. a. ISSN 0072-5234
- International Conference on Computer Communication. Computer Communications: Impacts and Implications. irreg.

**Association for Computing Machinery. Programming Language Committee**
Order Dept., 1133 Avenue of the Americas, New York, NY 10036
(and British Computer Society, 29 Portland Pl., London WIN 4AP, England)
- Conference on Data Systems Languages. Data Base Task Group. Report. irreg.; latest issue, 1971. ISSN 0090-7383

**Association for Computing Machinery. San Francisco Bay Area Chapters**
Box 60355, Sunnyvale, CA 94086.
- Bit Dropper. m.

**Association for Computing Machinery. Special Interest Group on Applications of Computer Technology**
1133 Ave. of the Americas, New York, NY 10036.
- S I G A C T News. q.

**Association for Computing Machinery. Special Interest Group on Automata and Compatability Theory**
1133 Ave. of the Americas, New York, NY 10036.
- A C M Symposium on the Theory of Computing. a.

**Association for Computing Machinery. Special Interest Group on Business Data Processing**
1133 Ave. of the Americas, New York, NY 10036.
- Data Base. q. ISSN 0095-0033

**Association for Computing Machinery. Special Interest Group on Computer Uses in Education**
1133 Avenue of the Americas, New York, NY 10036.
- S I G C U E Bulletin. q.

**Association for Computing Machinery. Special Interest Group on Graphics**
1133 Ave. of Americas, New York, NY 10036.
- Computer Graphics. q.

**Association for Computing Machinery. Special Interest Group on Language Analysis and Studies in the Humanities**
1133 Ave. of the Americas, New York, NY 10036.
- S I G L A S H Newsletter. 5 per yr.

**Association for Computing Machinery. Special Interest Group on Microprogramming**
1133 Ave of the Americas, New York, NY 10036.
- A C M Annual Workshop on Microprogramming. Conference Record. a.
- Micro Proceedings. a. ISSN 0361-2163 (prep. by its Workshop on Microprogramming)

**Association for Computing Machinery. Special Interest Group on Numerical Analysis**
1133 Ave. of the Americas, New York, NY 10036.
- S I G N U M Newsletter. q.

**Association for Computing Machinery. Special Interest Group on Operating Systems**
1133 Ave. of the Americas, New York, NY 10036.
- Operating Systems Review. q.

**Association for Computing Machinery. Special Interest Group on Programming Languages**
1133 Ave. of the Americas, New York, NY 10036.
- S I G P L A N Notices. m.

**Association for Continuing Higher Education**
c/o Howell W. McGee, University of Oklahoma, 1700 Asp Ave., Norman, OK 73069.
- Association for Continuing Higher Education. Membership Directory. a.
- Association for Continuing Higher Education. Proceedings. a.
- Continuing Higher Education. q.

**Association for Education in Journalism**
University of Minnesota, c/o Harold W. Wilson, Bus. Mgr. of Publications, 201 Murphy Hall, University of Minnesota, Minneapolis, MN 55455.
- Journalism Abstracts; M.A., M.S., and Ph.D. theses in journalism and mass communications. a. ISSN 0075-4412
- Journalism Educator. q. ISSN 0022-5517
- Journalism Monographs. 4 per yr. ISSN 0022-5525
- Journalism Quarterly; devoted to research in journalism and mass communications. q. ISSN 0022-5533

**Association for Education in Journalism. International Division**
c/o Ed. L. John Martin, University of Maryland, College of Journalism, College Park, MD 20742.
- I C B. (International Communications Bulletin) q. ISSN 0018-8824

**Association for Education in Journalism. Mass Communications and Society Division**
Department of Journalism, School of Communications and Theater, Temple University, Philadelphia, PA 19122.
- Mass Comm Review. 3 per yr.

**Association for Education of the Visually Handicapped, Inc.**
919 Walnut St., 4th Fl., Philadelphia, PA 19109.
- Association for Education of the Visually Handicapped. Selected Papers from A E V H Biennial Conferences. biennial. ISSN 0066-9105
- Education of the Visually Handicapped; a magazine for teachers and parents of visually handicapped children. 4 per yr. ISSN 0013-1458
- Fountainhead. 4 per yr. ISSN 0015-9069

**Association for Educational Communications and Technology**
1126 16th St. N.W., Washington, DC 20036.
- A V Communication Review. q. ISSN 0001-2890
- Association for Educational Communications and Technology. Membership Directory & Data Book. a.
- Association for Educational Communications and Technology. Monographs. irreg., no. 4, 1970.
- Audiovisual Instruction. m.(Sept-June) ISSN 0004-7635

**Association for Educational Data Systems**
1126 16th St. N.W., Washington, DC 20036.
- A E D S Bulletin. q.
- A E D S Journal. q. ISSN 0001-1037
- A E D S Monitor. m. ISSN 0001-1045
- Association for Educational Data Systems. Handbook and Directory. (pub. by National Computer Systems)

**Association for Evolutionary Economics**
509 Business Administration Bldg., Pennsylvania State University, University Park, PA 16802.
- J E I. (Journal of Economic Issues) q. ISSN 0021-3624

**Association for Field Archaeology**
- Journal of Field Archaeology. (pub. by Boston University Scholarly Publications)

**Association for Field Services in Teacher Education**
c/o John J. Dlabal, Jr., Northern Illinois University, DeKalb, IL 60115.
- New Campus. a. ISSN 0077-8168

**Association for Hospital Medical Education**
1911 Jefferson Davis Highway, Suite 1003, Arlington, VA 22202.
- A H M E Journal. q. ISSN 0090-7782

**Association for Humanistic Education and Development**
- Humanist Educator. (pub. by American Personnel and Guidance Association)

**Association for Humanistic Psychology**
Box6-T, 2 Washington Square Village, New York, NY 10012.
- A P Eastern Region Newsletter. irreg.
- Journal of Humanistic Psychology. q. ISSN 0022-1678

**Association for Institutional Research**
Claremont Colleges, Harper 106, Claremont, CA 91711.
- Association for Institutional Research. Annual Forum on Institutional Research. Proceedings. a. ISSN 0587-1948
- New Directions for Institutional Research. (pub. by Jossey-Bass, Inc. Publishers)

**Association for Intercollegiate Athletics for Women**
- A I A W Handbook of Policies and Operating Procedures. (pub. by American Alliance for Health, Physical Education and Recreation. National Association for Girls and Women in Sport)

**Association for International Medical Study, Inc.**
1040 E. McDonald St., Lakeland, FL 33801.
- International Medical Congress. Year Book. q. ISSN 0074-6932
- Journal of Continuing Medical Education International. q.

**Association for Jewish Studies**
Harvard Univ., Widener Library, Cambridge, MA 02138.
- Association for Jewish Studies Newsletter. 3 per yr.

**Association for Non-White Concerns in Personnel and Guidance**
- Journal of Non-White Concerns in Personnel and Guidance. (pub. by American Personnel and Guidance Association)

**Association for Professional Education for Ministry**
Bethany Theological Seminary, Box 408, Oak Brook, IL 60521.
- Association for Professional Education for Ministry. Report of the Biennial Meeting. biennial.

**Association for Recorded Sound Collections**
c/o James B. Wright, Exec. Sec, Fine Arts Library, University of New Mexico, Albuquerque, NM 87131.
- Association for Recorded Sound Collections Journal. 3 per yr. ISSN 0004-5438

**Association for Research and Enlightenment**
Box 595, Virginia Beach, VA 23451.
- A R E Journal. bi-m. ISSN 0571-5644
- Sundance Community Dream Journal. s-a. (Atlantic University)

**Association for Research in Growth Relationships**
c/o Thomas P. Nally, University of Rhode Island, Dept. of Education, Kingston, RI 02881.
- A R G R Journal. s-a. ISSN 0001-2300

**Association for Research in Nervous and Mental Disease**
- Association for Research in Nervous and Mental Disease. Proceedings of the Association. (pub. by Raven Press)
- Association for Research in Nervous and Mental Disease. Research Publications. (pub. by Raven Press)

**Association for Research in Vision and Ophthalmology**
- Investigative Ophthalmology and Visual Science. (pub. by C. V. Mosby Co.)

**Association for School, College and University Staffing**
Box 2151, Madison, WI 53701.
- A S C U S Annual-Teaching Opportunities for You. a. ISSN 0066-9156
- A S C U S Directory of Membership and Subject Field Index. a. ISSN 0066-9164
- Directory of Public Schools in the U.S. a.
- Journal of Educational Staffing. s-a.

**Association for Self Management**
Box 802, Ithaca, NY 14850.
- Association for Self Management Newsletter. m.

**Association for Social Anthropology in Oceania**
- Association for Social Anthropology in Oceania. Monograph Series. (pub. by University Press of Hawaii)

**Association for Social Economics**
c/o William R. Waters, De Paul University, 2323 N. Seminary Ave., Chicago, IL 60614.
- Review of Social Economy. s-a. ISSN 0034-6764

**Association for Supervision and Curriculum Development**
Suite 1100, 1701 K St., N.W., Washington, DC 20006.
- Association for Supervision and Curriculum Development. Curriculum Materials. a., latest issue 1974. ISSN 0084-6864
- Association for Supervision and Curriculum Development. Yearbook. a. ISSN 0066-9199
- Educational Leadership. m.(Oct-May) ISSN 0013-1784

**Association for Symbolic Logic, Inc**
Box 6248, Providence, RI 02940.
- Journal of Symbolic Logic. q. ISSN 0022-4812

**Association for Systems Management**
24587 Bagley Rd., Cleveland, OH 44138.
- A S M Bookshelf Series. irreg.
- Ideas for Management; proceedings of the annual conference. a. ISSN 0073-4624
- Journal of Systems Management. 12 per yr. ISSN 0022-4839

**Association for the Advancement of Baltic Studies**
366 86th St., Brooklyn, NY 11209.
- A A B S Newsletter. q.
- Association for the Advancement of Baltic Studies. Publications. irreg. ISSN 0572-4287

**Association for the Advancement of Behavior Therapy**
420 Lexington Ave., New York, NY 10017.
- Association for the Advancement of Behavior Therapy. Newsletter. bi-m.

**Association for the Advancement of Medical Instrumentation**
1901 N. Ft. Myer Dr., Suite 602, Arlington, VA 22209.
- Clinical Engineering News. bi-m. ISSN 0094-7245
- Medical Instrumentation Journal/J A A M I. bi-m.

**Association for the Advancement of Psychoanalysis**
- American Journal of Psychoanalysis. (pub. by A P S Publications)

**Association for the Advancement of Psychotherapy**
114 E. 78th Street, New York, NY 10021.
- American Journal of Psychotherapy. q. ISSN 0002-9564

**Association for the Coordination of University Religious Affairs**
c/o Ed. R. Ronald Burgess, Office of Religious Affairs, Memphis State Universtiy, Memphis, TN 38152.
- Dialogue on Campus. 3 per yr. ISSN 0012-2289

**Association for the Development of Computer-Based Instructional Systems**
8120 Penn Ave. S., Bloomington, MN 55431.
- Journal of Computer-Based Instruction. q. ISSN 0098-597X

**Association for the Development of Religious Information Systems**
c/o Rev. Richard F. Smith, S.J., Ed., Loyola University of Chicago, Dept. of Theology, Chicago, IL 60626.
- A D R I S Newsletter. q. ISSN 0300-7022

**Association for the Help of Retarded Children. New York City Chapter**
200 Park Ave. So., New York, NY 10003.
- A. H. R. C. Chronicle. 3-4 per yr. ISSN 0001-1436

**Association for the Preservation of Virginia Antiquities**
2705 Park Ave., Richmond, VA 23220.
- Discovery (Richmond) 2 per yr. ISSN 0300-7316

**Association for the Sociological Study of Jewry**
- Contemporary Jewry. (pub. by Transaction Periodicals Consortium)

**Association for the Sociology of Religion**
c/o Executive Secretary, Robert McNamara, Loyola University of Chicago, 6525 N. Sheridan Rd., Chicago, IL 60626.
- Sociological Analysis; a journal in the sociology of religion. q. ISSN 0038-0210

**Association for the Study of Afro-American Life and History, Inc**
1401 14th St. N.W., Washington, DC 20005.
- Journal of Negro History. q. ISSN 0022-2992
- Negro History Bulletin. bi-mi. ISSN 0028-2529

**Association for the Study of Dada & Surrealism**
- Dada/Surrealism. (pub. by Queens College Press)

**Association for the Study of Man-Environment Relations**
Box 57, Orangeburg, NY 10962.
- Environmental Design Perspectives; viewpoints on the profession, education and research.
- International Directory of Behavior and Design Research. biennial.
- Man-Environment Systems. bi-m. ISSN 0025-1550
- Man-Environment Systems/Focus Series.

**Association for the Study of Nationalities (U.S.S.R. and East Europe), Inc.**
c/o Stephen M. Horak, Ed., Dept. of History, Eastern Illinois University, Charleston, IL 61920
(Subscr. to Andris Skreija, Sec.-Treas., Dept. of Sociology, Univ. of Nebraska at Omaha, Box 688, Omaha, NB 68101)
- Nationalities Papers. s-a. ISSN 0090-5992

**Association for the Study of Perception**
Box 744, Dekalb, IL 60115.
- Association for the Study of Perception. Journal. s-a. ISSN 0004-5454

**Association for the Study of Religion**
3646 East 3580 South, Salt Lake City, UT 84109.
- Measuring Mormonism. a. ISSN 0094-5633

**Association for the Understanding of Man**
P.O. Box 5310, Austin, TX 78763.
- Association for the Understanding of Man. Journal. q.
- Project Starlight International Journal of Instrumented UFO Research. irreg.

**Association for Union Democracy**
215 Park Ave. So., New York, NY 10003.
- Union Democracy Review. irreg., approx. q.

**Association for University Business and Economic Research**
- Bibliography of Publications of University Bureaus of Business and Economic Research. (pub. by West Virginia University. Bureau of Business Research)

**Association for Voluntary Sterilization, Inc.**
708 Third Ave., New York, NY 10017.
- A V S News. q. ISSN 0001-2904

**Association for Women in Science**
1346 Connecticut Ave. N.W., Rm. 1122, Washington, DC 20036.
- Association for Women in Science. Newsletter. bi-m.

**Association for World Education**
3 Harbor Hill Drive, Huntington, NY 11743.
- Journal of World Education. q. ISSN 0092-2382

**Association of American Chambers of Commerce in Latin America**
- A A C C L A Report. (pub. by Chamber of Commerce of the U. S.)

**Association of American Colleges**
1818 R St., N.W., Washington, DC 20009.
- Liberal Education. 4 per yr. ISSN 0024-1822

**Association of American Editorial Cartoonists**
- Best Editorial Cartoons of the Year. (pub. by Pelican Publishing Co., Inc.)

**Association of American Feed Control Officials**
Box 16390-A, Baton Rouge, LA 70808.
- Association of American Feed Control Officials. Official Publication. a.

**Association of American Geographers**
1710 16th St. N.W., Washington, DC 20009.
- Assocation of American Geographers. Proceedings. a. ISSN 0572-4295
- Association of American Geographers. Annals. q. ISSN 0004-5608
- Association of American Geographers. Committee on College Geography. Resource Papers. 4 per yr. ISSN 0066-9369
- Association of American Geographers. Handbook - Directory. irreg. ISSN 0571-5962
- Association of American Geographers. Monograph Series. irreg., no. 8, 1976. ISSN 0066-9393
- Association of American Geographers Newsletter. m.
- Cuide to Graduate Departments of Geography in the United States and Canada. a. ISSN 0072-8497
- Professional Geographer. q. ISSN 0033-0124

**Association of American Geographers. Southeastern Division**
University of Tennessee, Department of Geography, Knoxville, TN 37916.
- Southeastern Geographer. s-a. ISSN 0038-366X

**Association of American Law Schools**
One Dupont Circle, Suite 370, Washington, DC 20036.
- Association of American Law Schools. Newsletter. q.
- Association of American Law Schools. Proceedings. a. ISSN 0066-9407
- Directory of Law Teachers. (pub. by West Publishing Co.)
- Journal of Legal Education. q. ISSN 0022-2208 (And University of Pittsburgh, School of Law, Pittsburgh PA 15260)

**Association of American Law Schools. Committee on Libraries**
One Dupont Circle, Suite 370, Washington, DC 20036.
- A A L S Library Statistics. a.

**Association of American Law Schools. Law School Admission Council**
Suite 370, 1 Dupont Circle, N.W., Washington, DC 20036
(Dist. by: Educational Testing Service, Law School Admission Council, Princeton, Nj 08540)
- Pre-Law Handbook. Official Law School Guide. a. ISSN 0075-8264

**Association of American Law Schools. Section on Foreign Exchanges of Law Teachers and Students**
Suite 370, One Dupont Circle, N.W., Washington, DC 20036.
- International Legal Education Newsletter. q.

**Association of American Library Schools**
471 Park Lane, State College, PA 16801.
- Association of American Library Schools. Directory. a.
- Journal of Education for Librarianship. q. ISSN 0022-0604

**Association of American Medical Colleges**
One Dupont Circle, N.W., Washington, DC 20036.
- A. A. M. C. Curriculum Directory. a. ISSN 0092-0371
- A A M C Education News. 5 per yr. (National Fund for Medical Education)
- Directory of American Medical Education. a.
- Journal of Medical Education. m. ISSN 0022-2577
- Medical School Admission Requirements, U. S. A. and Canada. a. ISSN 0066-9423

**Association of American Medical Colleges. Division of Educational Measurement and Research**
One Dupont Circle, N.W., Washington, DC 23036.
- Association of American Medical Colleges. Division of Educational Measurement and Research. D E M R Report. q.

**Association of American Pesticide Control Officials, Inc.**
Iowa Department of Agriculture, State Capitol, Des Moines, IA 50319.
- Association of American Pesticide Control Officials. Official Publication. a. ISSN 0066-9431

**Association of American Physicians**
- Association of American Physicians. Transactions. (pub. by William J. Dornan, Inc.)

**Association of American Physicians & Surgeons, Inc.**
2111 Enco Dr, Suite N, Oak Brook, IL 60521.
- A A P S News Letter. m. ISSN 0001-0170

**Association of American Plant Food Control Officials**
Department of Biochemistry, Purdue University, Lafayette, IN 47907.
- Association of American Plant Food Control Officials. Official Publication. a.

**Association of American Publishers**
One Park Ave., New York, NY 10016.
- Association of American Publishers. Exhibits Directory. a.

**Association of American Railroads**
American Railroads Bldg., 1920 L St., N.W., Washington, DC 20036.
- Association of American Railroads. Data Systems Division. Papers. a.
- Railway Accounting Rules. irreg.
- Railway Statistical Manual. irreg.
- Yearbook of Railroad Facts. a. ISSN 0084-3997 (prep. by its Economics and Finance Department)

**Association of American Rhodes Scholars**
c/o Bus. Mgr. J. B. Justice, 1100 Philadelphia National Bank Building, Philadelphia, PA 19107.
- American Oxonian. 4 per yr. ISSN 0003-0295

**Association of American State Geologists**
c/o E. A. Noble, Ed., North Dakota Geological Survey, University Station, Grand Forks, ND 58202.
- State Geologists Journal. a. ISSN 0039-0089

**Association of American Veterinary Medical Colleges**
University of Tennessee, Box 1071, Knoxville, TN 37901.
- Journal of Veterinary Medical Education. s-a.

**Association of American Women Dentists**
435 N. Michigan Ave., 17th Fl., Chicago, IL 60611.
- Association of American Women Dentists. Newsletter. irreg. (approx. 3 per yr.)

**Association of Americans and Canadians for Aliyah**
515 Park Ave., New York, NY 10022.
- Aliyon. m.

**Association of Aroostook Indians, Inc.**
Box 223, Houlton, ME 04730.
- Aroostook Indian. m.

**Association of Artists' Run Galleries**
178 Prince St., New York, NY 10012.
- Artists Review Art. q.

**Association of Asian-American Chambers of Commerce**
- Asian American Trade Directory. (pub. by Kayward Publications)
- Journal of Asian American Commerce. (pub. by Kayward Publications)

**Association of Asphalt Paving Technologists**
155 Experimental Engineering Bldg, University of Minnesota, Minneapolis, MN 55455.
- Association of Asphalt Paving Technologists. Proceedings. a. ISSN 0066-9466

**Association of Balloon and Airship Constructors**
Box 7, Rosemead, CA 91770.
- Aerostation. q.

**Association of Baptist Professors of Religion**
c/o R.H. Taylor, Chowan College, Murfreesboro, NC 27855.
- Perspectives in Religious Studies. 3 per yr. ISSN 0093-531X

**Association of Bay Area Governments**
Hotel Claremont, Berkeley, CA 94705.
- Bay View. m. ISSN 0300-7235

**Association of California School Administrators**
1575 Old Bayshore Highway, Burlingame, CA 94010.
- Thrust; for educational leadership. 5 per yr.

**Association of California Water Agencies**
1127 11th St. Suite 305, Sacramento, CA 95814.
- Western Water News. bi-m. ISSN 0043-4272

**Association of Child Psychology and Psychiatry**
- Journal of Child Psychology and Psychiatry. (pub. by Pergamon Press, Inc.)

**Association of Choral Conductors**
- American Choral Foundation. Research Memorandum Series. (pub. by American Choral Foundation, Inc.)
- American Choral Review. (pub. by American Choral Foundation, Inc.)

**Association of Clinical Scientists**
- Annals of Clinical Laboratory Science. (pub. by Institute for Clinical Science)

**Association of College and Research Libraries**
50 E. Huron St., Chicago, IL 60611.
- Choice. (pub. by Choice)
- College and Research Libraries/C R L. bi-m(technical journal); m.(except Aug.)(news issues) ISSN 0010-0870

**Association of College and University Auditors**
Northwestern University, c/o Auditing Dept., 633 Clark St., Evanston, IL 60201.
- Association of College and University Auditors. Proceedings: Annual Conference. a.

**Association of College and University Housing Officers**
c/o William M. Klepper, Ed., Trenton State College, Trenton, NJ 08625.
- Journal of College and University Student Housing; A C U H O journal. s-a.

**Association of College Honor Societies**
c/o Donald B. Hoffman, Sec'y- Treas., 2812 Livingston St., Allentown, PA 18104.
- Association of College Honor Societies, Booklet of Information. biennial, latest issue 1974.

**Association of College Unions-International**
Box 7286, Stanford, CA 94305.
- Association of College Unions-International. Bulletin. 6 per yr. ISSN 0004-5659
- Association of College Unions-International. Directory. a.
- Association of College Unions-International. Proceedings of the Annual Conference. a.

- Association of College Unions International. Union Wire. 8 per yr. ISSN 0004-5667

**Association of College, University and Community Arts Administrators, Inc.**
Box 2137, Madison, WI 53701.
- Association of College, University and Community Arts Administrators. Bulletin. m.

**Association of Collegiate Schools of Architecture, Inc.**
1735 New York Avenue, N.W., Washington, DC 20006.
- A C S A News. 6 per yr.
- Architecture Schools in North America. irreg., latest edt. 1977. ISSN 0092-7856 (And Peterson's Guides, Inc., 228 Alexander St., Princeton, NJ 08540)
- Journal of Architectural Education. q. ISSN 0047-2239

**Association of Collegiate Schools of Planning**
School of Urban Planning, Michigan State University, East Lansing, MI 48824.
- Association of Collegiate Schools of Planning. Bulletin. q. ISSN 0004-5675

**Association of Computer Programmers and Analysts**
P.O. Box 95, Kensington, MD 20795.
- Association of Computer Programmers and Analysts. Proceedings of the Founders Conference. a.

**Association of Consulting Foresters**
Box 6, Wake, VA 23176.
- Consultant (Wake) q. ISSN 0010-7085

**Association of Data Processing Service Organizations**
210 Summit Ave., Montvale, NJ 07645.
- A D A P S O Directory. a.
- Annual A.D.A.P.S.O. Industry Report. (pub. by Quantum Science Corp.)
- Annual Industry Survey of Computer Services Industry. (pub. by Quantum Science Corp.)

**Association of Departments of English**
62 Fifth Ave., New York, NY 10011.
- A D E Bulletin. q. ISSN 0001-0898

**Association of Departments of Foreign Languages**
62 Fifth Ave., New York, NY 10011.
- A D F L Bulletin. q. ISSN 0044-9571

**Association of Engineering Geologists**
c/o F.T. Johnson, 8310 San Fernando Way, Dallas, TX 75218.
- A E G Newsletter. q. ISSN 0514-9142
- Association of Engineering Geologists. Bulletin. s-a. ISSN 0004-5691
- Association of Engineering Geologists. Special Publications. irreg.

**Association of Evangelicals for Italian Missions**
314 Richfield Rd., Upper Darby, PA 19082.
- New Aurora. m.(except July & Aug.) ISSN 0028-4254

**Association of Existential Psychology and Psychiatry**
4002 Avenue I., Brooklyn, NY 11210.
- Review of Existential Psychology and Psychiatry. 3 per yr. ISSN 0034-656X

**Association of Exploration Geologists**
c/o Prof. H. Bloom, Colorado School of Mines, Golden, CO 80401.
- Association of Exploration Geochemists. Speical Publications. irreg.

**Association of Feminist Consultants**
222 Rawson Rd., Brookline, MA 02146.
- Association of Feminist Consultants. Directory of Members. irreg. ISSN 0362-2908

**Association of Food and Drug Officials of the United States**
Box 2240, Littleton, CO 80161.
- Association of Food and Drug Officials. Quarterly Bulletin. q.

**Association of Governing Boards of Universities and Colleges**
One Dupont Circle, Suite 720, Washington, DC 20036.
- A G B News Notes. m.
- A G B Reports. bi-m. ISSN 0044-961X

**Association of Government Accountants**
James A. Robbins, 727 S. 23rd St., Suite 120,
Arlington, VA 22202.
● Government Accountant's Journal. q.

**Association of Highway Officials of the North
Atlantic States**
1035 Parkway Ave., Trenton, NJ 08618.
● Association of Highway Officials of the North
Atlantic States. Proceedings. a.

**Association of Idaho Cities**
3314 Grace St., Boise, ID 83707.
● Idaho Cities. m.

**Association of Illinois Electric Cooperatives**
P.O. Box 3787, Springfield, IL 62708.
● Illinois Rural Electric News. m.

**Association of Immigration and Nationality Lawyers**
Committee on Publications, 50 Court St., Brooklyn,
NY 11201.
● Immigration Bar Bulletin. q. ISSN 0019-2775

**Association of Independent Colleges and Schools**
1730 M St. N.W., Washington, DC 20036.
● Compass (Washington) m. ISSN 0010-4205

**Association of Independent Colleges and Schools.
Accrediting Commission**
1730 M St. N.W., Washington, DC 20036.
● Directory of Accredited Institutions. a.

**Association of Independent Copy Machine Dealers
and Manufacturers**
● Copier/Duplicator Dealer Report. (pub. by J.
Tutching)

**Association of Industrial Accident Boards and
Commissions**
Box 3016, Des Moines, IA 50316.
● Association of Industrial Accident Boards and
Commissions.Convention Proceedings of IAIABC.
a.

**Association of Institutional Distributors**
1750 Old Meadow Rd., McLean, VA 22101.
● Association of Institutional Distributors.
Washington Desk Hotline. m.

**Association of Interstate Commerce Commission
Practitioners**
1112 ICC Bldg., Washington, DC 20423.
● I C C Practitioners' Journal. bi-m. ISSN 0018-
8859

**Association of Iron and Steel Engineers**
Suite 2350, Three Gateway Center, Pittsburgh, PA
15222.
● A I S E Yearbook. a.
● Directory Iron and Steel Plants. a. ISSN 0070-
5039
● Iron and Steel Engineer. m. ISSN 0021-1559

**Association of Jewish Libraries**
c/o National Foundation for Jewish Culture, 122 E.
42nd St., Rm. 1512, New York, NY 10017
● A J L Bulletin. 2-3 per yr. (Subscr to: Mildred
Kurland, 808 69th Ave., Philadelphia, PA. 19126)
● Association of Jewish Libraries. Proceedings of
the Annual Convention. a.

**Association of Junior Leagues, Inc.**
825 3rd Ave., New York, NY 10022.
● Junior League Review. 4 per yr.

**Association of Libertarian Feminists**
206 Mercer St., New York, NY 10012.
● A L F Newsletter. 6 per yr.

**Association of Life Insurance Medical Directors**
200 Berkley St., Boston, MA 02117.
● Association of Life Insurance Medical Directors
of America. Transactions. a. ISSN 0066-9598

**Association of Lithuanian Foresters in Exile**
2740 W. 43 St., Chicago, IL 60632.
● Girios Aidas/Echo of the Forest. biennial. ISSN
0072-4556

**Association of Lithuanian Workers**
104-07 102 St., Ozone Park, NY 11417.
● Tiesa. m. ISSN 0040-7372

**Association of Lunar and Planetary Observers**
Box 3 AZ University Park, Las Cruces, NM 88003.
● Association of Lunar and Planetary Observers.
Journal. bi-m.

**Association of Marian Helpers**
Stockbridge, MA 01262.
● Marian Helpers Bulletin. (pub. by Congregation of
Marians)
● Roze Maryi. m.

**Association of Marshall Scholars and Alumni**
Dr. Lloyd Berry, Graduate School, University of
Missouri, Columbia, MO 65201.
● Association of Marshall Scholars and Alumni
Newsletter. s-a. ISSN 0004-573X

**Association of Medical Group Psychoanalysts**
c/o David Weisselberger, M.D., Ed., 185 E. 85 St.,
New York, NY 10028.
● Groups: a Journal of Group Dynamics and
Psychotherapy. a.

**Association of Medical Rehabilitation Directors &
Coordinators, Inc.**
175 Raintree Court, Athens, GA 30601.
● A. M. R. D. & C. Quarterly Bulletin. q.

**Association of Mental Health Administrators**
2901 Lafayette Ave., Lansing, MI 48906.
● Association of Mental Health Administrators.
Newsletter. bi-m.
● Journal of Mental Health Administration. q. ISSN
0092-8623

**Association of Midwest Fish and Wildlife
Commissioners**
Gary Boushelle, Secretary, Dept. of Natural
Resources, 408 Kalamazoo Plaza, Lansing, MI
48914.
● Association of Midwest Fish and Wildlife
Commissioners. Proceedings. a.

**Association of Military Surgeons of the U. S.**
Box 104, Kensington, MD 20795.
● Military Medicine. m. ISSN 0026-4075

**Association of Missouri Electric Cooperatives, Inc.**
2722 E. McCarty St., Jefferson City, MO 65101.
● Rural Electric Missourian. m. ISSN 0048-8801

**Association of Muslim Scientists and Engineers of
North America**
Box 264, Plainfield, IN 46148.
● Muslim Scientist. 3 per yr.

**Association of National Advertisers, Inc.**
155 E. 44th St., New York, NY 10017.
● Magazine Circulation and Rate Trends. biennial.

**Association of New Jersey Environmental
Commissions**
Box 157, Mendham, NJ 07945.
● Association of New Jersey Environmental
Commissions Newsletter. q.

**Association of Official Analytical Chemists**
Box 540, Benjamin Franklin Station, Washington,
DC 20044.
● Association of Official Analytical Chemists.
Journal. bi-m. ISSN 0004-5756
● Association of Official Analytical Chemists.
Official Methods of Analysis. quinquennial; 1975,
12th ed. ISSN 0066-961X

**Association of Official Seed Analysts**
Ohio Department of Agriculture Laboratory,
Reynoldsburg, OH 43068.
● Association of Official Seed Analysts. News
Letter. q. ISSN 0004-5764
● Journal of Seed Technology. a.

**Association of Oilwell Servicing Contractors**
Box 1168, Grand Prairie, TX 77050.
● Well Servicing. bi-m.

**Association of Old Crows**
● Electronic Warfare. (pub. by E W
Communications, Inc.)

**Association of Operating Room Nurses, Inc.**
c/o Philip Patterson, 10170 E. Mississippi Ave.,
Denver, CO 80231.
● A O R N Journal. m. ISSN 0001-2092

**Association of Operating Room Technicians, Inc.**
Suite 201, 1100 W. Littleton Blvd., Littleton, CO
80120.
● O R Tech. (Operating Room) bi-m.

**Association of Orthodox Jewish Scientists**
116 E. 27th St., New York, NY 10016.
● Intercom (New York) s-a.

**Association of Pacific Coast Geographers**
● Association of Pacific Coast Geographers.
Yearbook. (pub. by Oregon State University
Press)

**Association of Private Camps**
55 W. 42nd St., New York, NY 10036.
● Association of Private Camps. Buyers Guide and
Camp Directory. irreg. ISSN 0519-1505

**Association of Professional Directors of YMCA's**
40 W. Long St., Columbus, OH 43215.
● Perspectives (Columbus) 8 per yr.

**Association of Professors of Missions**
c/o Ed. John T. Boberg, 5401 S. Cornell Ave.,
Chicago, IL 60615.
● Association of Professors of Missions. Biennial
Meeting. Proceedings. biennial. ISSN 0519-153X

**Association of Registered Bank Holding Companies**
730 15th St. N.W., Washington, DC 20005.
● Bank Holding Company Facts. irreg. ISSN 0519-
1572

**Association of Rehabilitation Nurses**
1132 Waukegan Rd., Glenview, IL 60025.
● A R N Journal. bi-m. ISSN 0362-3505

**Association of Research Libraries**
1527 New Hampshire Ave., N.W., Washington, DC
20036.
● A R L Minutes. s-a. ISSN 0044-9652
● A R L Newsletter. irreg. ISSN 0066-9652
● A R L Statistics. a.
● American Doctoral Dissertations. (pub. by
University Microfilms International)
● Association of Research Libraries. University
Library Management Studies Office. Management
Supplement. q. (prep. by its Office of University
Library Management Studies)
● Association of Research Libraries. University
Library Management Studies Office. Occasional
Paper. irreg. ISSN 0091-4479
● Foreign Acquisitions Newsletter. s-a. ISSN 0014-
8512

**Association of Research Libraries. Center for Chinese
Research Materials**
1527 New Hampshire Ave., N.W., Washington, DC
20036.
● Center for Chinese Research Materials.
Bibliographical Series. irreg. ISSN 0084-6902
● Center for Chinese Research Materials.
Newsletter. 3 per yr. ISSN 0008-9044

**Association of Research Libraries. Systems and
Procedures Exchange Center**
Office of University Library Management Studies,
1527 New Hampshire Ave. N.W., Washington, DC
20036.
● S P E C Flyer. 10 per yr.

**Association of Russian-American Scholars in U.S.A.**
85-20 114 St., Richmond Hill, NY 11418.
● Association of the Russian-American Scholars in
U.S.A. Zapiski Russkoi Akademicheskoi Gruppy v
S. Sh. A. Transactions. a. ISSN 0066-9717

**Association of School Business Officials of the United
States and Canada**
2424 W. Lawrence Ave., Chicago, IL 60625.
● Association of School Business Officials.
Proceedings, Addresses and Research Papers. a.
● School Business Affairs. m. ISSN 0036-651X

**Association of Southeastern Biologists, Inc.**
c/o Dr. R. O. Flagg, Carolina Biological Supply,
Burlington, NC 27215.
● A. S. B. Bulletin. q. ISSN 0001-2386

**Association of State Library Agencies**
● A S L A President's Newsletter. (pub. by
American Library Association)

**Association of Systematics Collections**
c/o Museum of Natural History, University of
Kansas, Lawrence, KS 66045.
● A S C Newsletter. bi-m.

**Association of Teacher Educators**
1701 K Street, N.W., Suite 1201, Washington, DC
20006.
● A T E Newsletter. bi-m. ISSN 0001-2718
● Association of Teacher Educators. Publications. 3
per yr. (unnumbered)

**Association of Teachers of Japanese**
University of Chicago, Department of Far Eastern
Languages and Civilizations, 5736 Woodlawn Ave.,
Chicago, IL 60637.
- Association of Teachers of Japanese. Journal. 3
per yr.

**Association of Teachers of Mathematics of New York
City**
434 W. 120th St., New York, NY 10027.
- Association of Teachers of Mathematics of New
York City. Summation. q. ISSN 0044-9679

**Association of Teachers of Preventive Medicine and
Community Health**
- Journal of Community Health. (pub. by Human
Sciences Press)

**Association of Teachers of Social Studies in the City
of New York**
c/o Richard Kobliner, Pres., Hillcrest High School,
160-05 Highland Ave., Jamaica, NY 11432.
- Association of Teachers of Social Studies. A. T. S.
S. Bulletin. 5-6 per yr. ISSN 0044-9687

**Association of Texas Electric Cooperatives**
8140 Burnet Rd., Box 9589, Austin, TX 78766.
- Texas Co-Op Power. m.

**Association of the Bar of the City of New York**
42 W. 44th St., New York, NY 10036.
- Association of the Bar of the City of New York.
Record. m. (Oct.-Jun.) ISSN 0004-5837

**Association of the Teachers of Mathematics in New
England**
c/o T. C. Armstrong, Box 476, Foxborough, MA
02035.
- A T M N E Journal. a. ISSN 0001-2742

**Association of the United States Army**
1529 18th St., N.W., Washington, DC 20036.
- Army. m. ISSN 0004-2455

**Association of Theological Schools**
Box 130, Vandalia, OH 45377.
- Association of Theological Schools in the United
States and Canada. Bulletin. biennial. ISSN 0362-
1472
- Association of Theological Schools in the United
States and Canada. Directory. a.
- Fact Book on Theological Education. a.
- Theological Education. 2 per yr. ISSN 0040-5620

**Association of Track and Field Statisticians**
- Association of Track and Field Statsticians.
Annual. (pub. by Tafnews Press)

**Association of Trial Lawyers of America**
20 Garden St., Cambridge, MA 02138.
- A T L A Law Reporter. 10 per yr. ISSN 0364-
8125
- Association of Trial Lawyers of America. Law
Journal. biennial.
- National Legal Magazine. bi-m. ISSN 0027-9625
- Trial; the only national news magazine for
lawyers. bi-m. ISSN 0041-2538

**Association of Universities for Research in Astronomy**
Library, Kitt Peak National Observatory, 950 N.
Cherry Ave., Box 26732, Tucson, AZ 85726.
- Cerro Tololo Interamerican Observatory (La
Serena, Chile). Contributions. irreg. ISSN 0582-
7094
- Kitt Peak National Observatory. Contributions.
(pub. by Kitt Peak National Observatory)

**Association of University Architects**
Ed. Howard Krassnoff, Temple University, 10th &
Montgomery, Philadelphia, PA 19122.
- A U A Newsletter. q. ISSN 0044-9695

**Association of University Radiologists**
- Investigative Radiology. (pub. by J. B. Lippincott
Co.)

**Association of University Summer Sessions**
Office of Summer Sessions, Indiana University,
Bloomington, IN 47401.
- Association of University Summer Sessions.
Summary Report. a. ISSN 0066-975X

**Association of Urban and Community Symphony
Orchestras**
Box 1164, Evanston, IL 60201.
- Symphony Magazine. 9 per yr.

**Association of Urban Universities**
Jacksonville University, Jacksonville, FL 32211.
- Association of Urban Universities. Proceedings. a.
- Association of Urban Universities Newsletter. q.
ISSN 0004-5853

**Association of Voluntary Action Scholars**
Box G-55, Boston College, Chestnut Hill, MA
02167.
- Journal of Voluntary Action Research. q. ISSN
0094-0607

**Association of Working Press, Inc.**
6037 N. Monticello, Chicago, IL 60659.
- Cable Report; exclusive investigation & analysis of
cable TV industry. 11 per yr.

**Association of Yeshivah-Day School Principals of
General Studies**
- Principal. (pub. by Board of Jewish Education of
Greater New York)

**Association on American Indian Affairs**
432 Park Ave., S., New York, NY 10016.
- Association on American Indian Affairs.
Proceedings. irreg.
- Indian Affairs. q. ISSN 0046-8967
- Indian Family Defense. q.

**Association-Sterling Films**
866 Third Ave., New York, NY 10022.
- Association-Sterling Films. Free Loan Films. a.
ISSN 0093-0881

**Associations Publications, Inc.**
726 Mt. Moriah, Suite 106, Box 17965, Memphis,
TN 38117.
- Shelter. 7 per yr. (National Sash & Door Jobbers
Association)

**Assyrian-American Federation**
- Assyrian Star. (pub. by Assyrian Star Inc.)

**Assyrian Star Inc.**
740 Van Buren St., Gary, IN 46402.
- Assyrian Star. bi-m. ISSN 0004-6051 (Assyrian-
American Federation)

**Asthma Publications Society**
Editorial Office, Rm. 310, 133 E. 58 St., New York,
NY 10022.
- Journal of Asthma Research. 2 per yr. ISSN 0021-
9134 (Co-Sponsor: Asthmatic Children's
Foundation)

**Astro-Gator Astronomy Club**
1025 Gulf Life Drive, Jacksonville, FL 32207
(Subscr. to: 4238 Springwood Rd., Jacksonville, FL
32207)
- Meteor News. 5 per yr. (Jacksonville Children's
Museum)

**Astro Media Corp**
411 E. Mason St., 6th Floor, Milwaukee, WI 53202.
- Astronomy. m. ISSN 0091-6358

**Astrology Services International, Inc.**
New York Astrology Center, 127 Madison Ave.,
New York, NY 10016.
- Astrology-the New Aquarian Agent; for the
contemporary astrologer. q.

**Astronomical Endeavours Publishing Co.**
18 Fairhaven Drive, Buffalo, NY 14225.
- Modern Astronomy. bi-m. ISSN 0047-7664

**Astronomical Society of New York**
Dudley Observatory, 100 Fuller Rd., Albany, NY
12205.
- Astronomical Society of New York. Newsletter.
irreg.

**Astronomical Society of the Pacific**
c/o Richard Reis, 1244 Noriega St., San Francisco,
CA 94122.
- Astronomical Society of the Pacific. Publications.
bi-m. ISSN 0004-6280
- Mercury. bi-m. ISSN 0047-6773

**At Rise**
9838 Jersey Ave., Santa Fe Springs, CA 90670.
- At Rise; a magazine in four acts. q.

**Atalanta Press**
Box 5688, University Sta., Seattle, WA 98105.
- Windhaven; a matriarchal fanzine. irreg. (4-6 per
yr)

**Atchison, Topeka and Santa Fe Railway Co.**
Railway Exchange, 80 E. Jackson Blvd., Chicago,
IL 60604.
- Santa Fe Magazine. m. ISSN 0036-4541

**ATCOM, Inc.**
2315 Broadway, New York, NY 10024.
- Car Dealer Insider Newsletter. w.
- Car Rental & Leasing Insider Newsletter. w. ISSN
0008-6053
- Journal of Psychohistory. q.
- Leisure Beverage Insider Newsletter. w.
- Motel/Hotel Insider Newsletter. w. ISSN 0027-
1489
- Real Estate Insider Newsletter. w. ISSN 0034-
0715
- Truck Insider Newsletter. w. ISSN 0041-3399

**Athanor Press**
P. O. Box 582, Clarkson, NY 14430.
- Athanor. 2 per yr. ISSN 0044-9857

**Atheneum Publishers**
122 E. 42nd St., New York, NY 10017.
- Studies in American Negro Life. irreg., latest no.
35, 1975.

**Athens International Film Festival**
Box 388, Athens, OH 45701.
- Wide Angle. q.

**Athletic Journal Publishing Co.**
1719 Howard St., Evanston, IL 60202.
- Athletic Journal. m.(Sept-June) ISSN 0004-6655

**Athletic Publishing Co.**
Box 3401, Montgomery, AL 36109.
- Directory of High School Coaches. a. ISSN 0417-
5956

**Atlanta Chamber of Commerce**
Publications Department, Atlanta, GA 30303.
- Atlanta. m. ISSN 0004-6701
- Forward Atlanta. bi-m. ISSN 0046-4759

**Atlanta Gazette, Inc.**
1189 Virginia Ave. N.E., Atlanta, GA 30306.
- Atlanta Gazette. w.

**Atlanta Regional Commission**
100 Peachtree St., Atlanta, GA 30303.
- Atlanta Regional Commission Action. m.

**Atlanta University**
Office of Public Relations, Rooms 316-17 Harkness
Hall, 223 Chestnut St. S. W., Atlanta, GA 30314.
- Atlanta University Bulletin. s-a.
- Phylon; the Atlanta University review of race and
culture. q. ISSN 0031-8906

**Atlanta Voice**
633 Pryor St., S.W., Atlanta, GA 30312.
- Atlanta Voice. w.

**Atlanta Workshop on Nonviolence**
Box 7477, Atlanta, GA 30309.
- A W I N Newsletter. m. ISSN 0001-2939

**Atlantic Advertising**
Adams, MA 01220.
- Directory of Magazine Editorial Shopping
Sections. a. ISSN 0070-5780

**Atlantic Automobile Adventure Club, Inc.**
Broad & Spruce Sts., Philadelphia, PA 19101.
- Automobile Adventures. q. ISSN 0005-1365

**Atlantic Coast District Dental Society**
2455 E. Sunrise Boulevard, Ft. Lauderdale, FL
33304.
- Explorer. bi-m.

**Atlantic Council of the United States, Inc.**
1616 H St. N.W., Washington, DC 20006.
- Atlantic Community News. m.
- Atlantic Community Quarterly. q. ISSN 0004-
6760
- Correspondents World Wide. (pub. by Atlantic
Information Centre for Teachers)
- Crisis Papers. (pub. by Atlantic Information
Centre for Teachers)

**Atlantic Economic Society**
Southern Illinois University, Edwardsville, IL 62026.
- Atlantic Economic Journal. s-a.

**Atlantic Information Centre for Teachers**
1616 H St. N.W., Washington, DC 20006.
- Correspondents World Wide. 3 per yr. (Atlantic Council of the United States Inc.)
- Crisis Papers. 7 per yr. ISSN 0571-7760 (Atlantic Council of the United States, Inc.)

**Atlantic Monthly Co.**
8 Arlington St., Boston, MA 02116.
- Atlantic Monthly. m. ISSN 0004-6795

**Atlantic Richfield Hanford Co.**
P. O. Box 250, Richland, WA 99352.
- Hanford News. m.

**Atlantic States Marine Fisheries Commission**
1717 Massachusetts Ave., N.W., Washington, DC 20036.
- Marine Resources of the Atlantic Coast. irreg. ISSN 0542-7029

**Atlantic University**
- Sundance Community Dream Journal. (pub. by Association for Research and Enlightenment)

**Helen V. Atlas, Ed. & Pub.**
119 W. 57th St., New York, NY 10019.
- Dance News. m.(Sept-June) ISSN 0011-6017

**Atlas Information Services, Inc.**
230 Park Ave., New York, NY 10017.
- Atlas World Press Review. m.

**Atlas Publishing Co.**
507 Fifth Ave., New York, NY 10017.
- Who's Who in Steel and Metals. irreg. ISSN 0511-9049

**Atlas Supply Co.**
11 Diamond Rd., Springfield, NJ 07081.
- Atlas Bulletin. m.

**Atlatl Press**
P.O. Box 1848, Durango, CO 81301.
- Rocky Mountain Review. 3 per yr.

**Atomic Industrial Forum Inc.**
1747 Pennsylvania Ave., N.W., Suite 1150, Washington, DC 20006.
- Inforum: Environmental Report Data System. bi-m. ISSN 0360-4985
- Nuclear Industry. m. ISSN 0029-5531
- Nuclear Info. m.

**Atomic Industrial Forum Inc. National Environmental Studies Project**
1747 Pennsylvania N.W., Suite 1150, Washington, DC 20006.
- N E S P. bi-m.

**Attaboy**
3874 N. Broadway No. 8, Boulder, CO 80302.
- Attaboy. irreg.

**Attakapas Historical Association**
- Attakapas Gazette. (pub. by University of Southwestern Louisiana. Center for Louisiana Studies)

**Attica Brigade of Richmond College**
Stuyvesant Pl., Staten Island, NY 10301.
- Fight Back. m.

**Attorneys' National Clearing House Co.**
3539 Hennepin Ave., Minneapolis, MN 55408.
- Birk's. irreg. ISSN 0091-4002

**Alvin B. Aubert, Ed. & Pub.**
10 Georges Place, Fredonia, NY 14063
- Obsidian: Black Literature in Review. 3 per yr. (Subscr. to: State Univ. College, English Dept., Fredonia, NY 14063)

**Auburn University**
9088 Haley Center, Auburn, AL 36830.
- Southern Humanities Review. q. ISSN 0038-4186

**Auburn University. Agricultural Experiment Station**
110 Comer Hall, Auburn, AL 36830.
- Highlights of Agricultural Research. q. ISSN 0018-1668

**Auburn University. Cooperative Extension Service**
119 Extension Hall, Auburn, AL 36830.
- Auburn Forestry Forum. a., 1972, no. 11. ISSN 0067-0421

**Auburn University Press**
Auburn University, 2006 Haley Center, Auburn, AL 36830.
- Alabama Personnel and Guidance Journal. s-a. (Alabama Personnel and Guidance Association)

**Auburn University. Project Themis**
- Auburn University. Project Themis Research. Annual Report. (pub. by Management Information Service)

**Auburn University. School of Pharmacy**
Auburn, AL 36830.
- Auburn Pharmacist. q. ISSN 0004-7414

**Auburn University. School of Veterinary Medicine**
Auburn, AL 36830.
- Auburn Veterinarian. q.

**Auburn University. Water Resources Research Institute**
205 Samford Hall, Auburn, AL 36830.
- Auburn University. Water Resources Research Institute. Annual Report. a. ISSN 0067-043X
- Auburn University. Water Resources Research Institute. W R R I News Report. q. ISSN 0044-9970

**Audio-Digest Foundation**
1577 E. Chevy Chase Dr., Glendale, CA 91206.
- Audio-Digest Anesthesiology. s-m. ISSN 0571-8600
- Audio-Digest Family Practice. w. & s-m. ISSN 0046-3221
- Audio-Digest Internal Medicine. s-m. ISSN 0047-052X
- Audio-Digest Obstetrics-Gynecology. s-m. ISSN 0571-8635
- Audio-Digest Ophthalmology. s-m. ISSN 0048-1963
- Audio-Digest Otorhinolaryngology. s-m. ISSN 0030-6673
- Audio-Digest Pediatrics. s-m. ISSN 0571-8643
- Audio-Digest Psychiatry. s-m.
- Audio-Digest Surgery. s-m. ISSN 0571-8651

**Audio Engineering Society**
60 E. 42nd St., New York, NY 10017.
- Audio Engineering Society. Journal. m. ISSN 0004-7554

**Audio Journal of Safety**
c/o Joel Charles, Park City West, 3900 Ford Road, Philadelphia, PA 19131.
- Audio Journal of Safety. 4 per yr.

**Audio-Visual Associates**
180 East California Blvd., Pasadena, CA 91105.
- International Index to Multi Media Information. q. ISSN 0094-6818

**Audio Visual Research Institute**
1346 Broadway, Detroit, MI 48226.
- Audio-Visual Index. irreg.

**Audiology & Hearing Education, Inc.**
15300 Ventura Blvd., Sherman Oaks, CA 91403.
- Audiology & Hearing Education; the journal of evaluation, instruction and rehabilitation. bi-m.

**Audit Bureau of Circulations**
123 North Wacker Drive, Chicago, IL 60606.
- A B C Factbook. a.
- A B C News Bulletin. 4 per yr. ISSN 0001-0448

**Audit, Inc.**
18 Allenhurst Rd., Buffalo, NY 14214.
- Audit-Poetry. s-a. ISSN 0004-7643

**Audit Investment Research, Inc.**
230 Park Ave., New York, NY 10017.
- Real Estate Disclosure Digest. s-m.
- Realty Trust Review; news analysis of securities of real estate investment trusts. s-m.

**Audits & Surveys, Inc.**
One Park Ave., New York, NY 10016.
- B R S Monthly Index. (Behavioral Research Studies) m. ISSN 0045-1673 (Behavioral Research Survey Center)

**Audubon Society of New Hampshire**
3 Silk Farm Road, Concord, NH 03301.
- New Hampshire Audubon News. m.(except June & Aug.) ISSN 0028-520X
- New Hampshire Audubon Quarterly. q.

**Auerbach Publishers, Inc.**
121 N. Broad St., Philadelphia, PA 19107.
- Auerbach Computer Science Series. irreg.
- Auerbach Data Communications Reports. 3 base vols. updated monthly. ISSN 0004-7724
- Auerbach Minicomputer Reports. m. ISSN 0004-7759
- Auerbach Software Reports. 2 base vols. updated monthly. ISSN 0004-7775
- Auerbach Standard E D P Reports. m. ISSN 0004-7783
- Auerbach Time Sharing Reports. bi-m. updates to base vol. ISSN 0004-7791
- Computer Technology State of the Art Series. irreg.

**Augsburg College**
731 21st Ave. S., Minneapolis, MN 55454.
- Augsburg College Now. 17 per yr. ISSN 0300-6964
- Augsburg Echo. 25 per yr. ISSN 0004-7945

**Augsburg Publishing House**
426 S. Fifth St., Minneapolis, MN 55415.
- A L C-L C A Augsburg Adult Bible Studies. q. (American Lutheran Church and Lutheran Church in America)
- A L C-L C A Augsburg Adult Bible Studies. Teacher's Guide. q. (American Lutheran Church and Lutheran Church in America)
- A L C-L C A Augsburg Home Bible Studies. q. (American Lutheran Church and Lutheran Church in America)
- American Lutheran Church. Yearbook. a. ISSN 0569-6348
- Augsburg Audiovisual Newsletter. q.
- Book News Letter. bi-m. ISSN 0006-7296
- Christ in Our Home; daily devotions. q. ISSN 0412-2968 (American Lutheran Church. Commission on Evangelism)
- Christmas: An American Annual of Christmas Literature and Art. a. ISSN 0069-3928
- Lutheran Standard. s-m. ISSN 0024-7545 (American Lutheran Church)
- Lutheran World Federation. Proceedings of the Assembly. irreg., 1970, 5th, Evian-Les-Bains, France. ISSN 0076-1540
- Scope (Minneapolis) m. ISSN 0036-8997 (American Lutheran Church Women)

**Augusta Chamber of Commerce**
c/o Robert C. Maccarthy, Ed. & Pub., Box 1645, Augusta, GA 30903.
- Augusta Magazine. q. ISSN 0004-797X

**Augustan Society, Inc.**
1617 W. 261 St., Harbor City, VA 90710.
- Augustan. q. ISSN 0004-7988
- Colonial Genealogist. q.
- Germanic Genealogical Helper. q. ISSN 0361-3062
- Irish Genealogical Helper. q. ISSN 0360-4519
- Plymouth Colony Genealogical Helper. 4 no. a year. ISSN 0360-2230
- Scottish Genealogical Helper. q.
- Spanish Genealogical Helper. q.

**Augustana College**
Rock Island, IL 61201.
- Augustana College Bulletin. 3 per yr. ISSN 0004-7996

**Augustana College. Library**
Rock Island, IL 61201.
- Augustana College Library Publications. biennial. ISSN 0067-057X

**Augustana Historical Society**
c/o Augustana College, Rock Island, IL 61201.
- Augustana Historical Society, Rock Island, Illinois. Publications. biennial, no. 24, 1974. ISSN 0067-0588

**J.J. Augustin, Inc.**
Locust Valley, NY 11560.
- Aegyptologische Forschungen. irreg. vol. 1-25, 1973.
- American Research Center in Egypt. Journal. a. ISSN 0065-9991
- Dumbarton Oaks Papers. irreg. ISSN 0070-7546 (Dumbarton Oaks Center for Byzantine Studies)
- Dumbarton Oaks Studies. irreg. ISSN 0070-7554 (Dumbarton Oaks Center for Byzantine Studies)
- Dumbarton Oaks Texts. irreg. ISSN 0070-7562 (Dumbarton Oaks Center for Byzantine Studies)
- Excavations at Dura-Europos. irreg. ISSN 0071-3287 (Yale University) (Co-Sponsor: French Academy of Inscriptions and Letter)

- Texts from Cuneiform Sources. irreg. ISSN 0082-3759
- Walter W. S. Cook Alumni Lecture. irreg. ISSN 0083-7148 (New York University. Institute of Fine Arts)

**Augustinian Order**
c/o Rev. Russell J. Desimone, Augustinian Institute, Villanova University, PA 19085.
- Augustinian Studies. a.

**Aullwood Audubon Center**
Aullwood Audubon Farm, 9101 Frederick Rd., Dayton, OH 45414.
- Aullwood Notes. q.

**Aum Temple of Universal Truth**
45837 Deva Lane, Newberry Springs, CA 92365.
- Aum, the Cosmic Light. m.

**Aurea Publications**
Allenhurst, NJ 07711.
- Seeker's Guide; a directory of unusual organizations. irreg; latest edt., 1970. ISSN 0080-8512
- World Wide Register of Adult Education; directory of home study schools. irreg.; latest issues, 1973. ISSN 0084-2486

**Aurora Book Companions**
Box 5852, Denver, CO 80217.
- Health Books Catalog. s-a.

**Austin Chamber of Commerce**
Box 1967, Austin, TX 78767.
- Austin. m.

**Austin District Dental Society**
4407 Manchaca Rd., Austin, TX 78745.
- Austin Dental News. m. ISSN 0004-8267

**Australian Information Service**
636 Fifth Ave, New York, NY 10020.
- Australia Bulletin. w.
- Australia Now. q. ISSN 0045-0197

**Australian Terrier Club of America**
c/o Mrs. Milton Fox, 1411 Dorsett Dock Rd., Pt. Pleasant, NJ 08742.
- Australian Terrier Club of America Newsletter. q.

**Austrian Information Service**
31 East 69th St., New York, NY 10021.
- Austrian Information. 8-12 per yr. ISSN 0005-0520

**Auto World, Inc.**
701 N. Keyser Ave., Scranton, PA 18508.
- Aurora AFX Road Racing Handbook. a.

**Automated Education Center**
Box 2658, Detroit, MI 48231.
- Automated Education Letter. m. ISSN 0005-1020

**Automatic Musical Instrument Collectors' Association**
c/o Tom Beckett, 6817 Cliffbrook, Dallas, TX 75240
- A M I C A Bulletin. m. (Orders to: A. N. Johnson, Membership Sec., Box 666, Grand Junction, CO 81501)

**Automatic Totalisators Inc.**
100 Bellevue Rd., Newark, DE 19713.
- Lottery World. irreg. ISSN 0098-9177

**AutoMedia**
Box 520, Lafayette, CA 94549.
- Wheel. m. (Sports Car Club of America. San Francisco Region)

**Automobile Club of Hartford**
815 Farmington Ave., West Hartford, CT 06119.
- Automobiler. m.

**Automobile Club of Maryland**
1401 Mt. Royal Ave., Baltimore, MD 21217.
- Maryland Motorist. bi-m.

**Automobile Club of Michigan**
Auto Club Drive, Dearborn, MI 48126.
- Motor News. m. ISSN 0027-1934

**Automobile Club of Missouri**
201 Progress Parkway, Box 1116, Maryland Heights, MO 63043.
- Midwest Motorist. bi-m. ISSN 0026-3435

**Automobile Club of New York, Inc.**
28 E. 78th St., New York, NY 10021.
- New York Motorist. m. ISSN 0028-7385

**Automobile Club of Southern California**
Box 2890, Terminal Annex, Los Angeles, CA 90054.
- Auto Club News Pictorial. bi-m. ISSN 0005-0725
- Westways. m. ISSN 0043-4434

**Automobile Club of Washington**
330 6th Ave. N., Seattle, WA 98109.
- Washington Motorist. m. ISSN 0043-0641

**Automobile Club of Western New York**
976 Delaware Ave., Buffalo, NY 14240.
- Western New York Motorist. m. ISSN 0043-3977

**Automobile Club Publications**
8 East Long St., Columbus, OH 43215.
- Motor Travel. bi-m. ISSN 0027-2086

**Automobile International**
386 Park Ave. South, New York, NY 10016.
- World Automotive Market. a.

**Automobile Legal Association. Auto & Travel Club**
888 Worcester St., Wellesley, MA 02181.
- A L A Sights to See Book. a. ISSN 0090-8614
- Away. q.

**Automobile Quarterly, Inc.**
221 Nassau St., Princeton, NJ 08540.
- Automobile Quarterly. 4 per yr. ISSN 0005-1438

**Automobile Quarterly Quatrefoil**
245 W. Main St., Kutztown, PA 19530.
- Automobile Quarterly Quatrefoil; a connoiseur's serendipity of select readings and sundries for the automobile enthusiast. q.

**Automotive Age Publications**
6931 Van Nuys Blvd., Van Nuys, CA 91405.
- Automotive Age/Kelley Blue Book Reporter; the news magazine of automotive sales & management. m.

**Automotive Auction Publishing, Inc.**
1101 Fulton Bldg., Pittsburgh, PA 15222.
- Automotive Market Report and Auto Week. w. ISSN 0005-1543

**Automotive Publishers, Inc.**
3001 Red Hill Ave., Bldg. 5, Costa Mesa, CA 92626.
- Automotive Independent. m. (Automotive Service Council of California)

**Automotive Publishing Co.**
2900 W. Peterson Ave., Chicago, IL 60659.
- Midwest Automotive News. m. ISSN 0026-3338
- Pacific Automotive News. bi-m.

**Automotive Service Council of California**
- Automotive Independent. (pub. by Automotive Publishers, Inc.)

**Availabilities**
18 E. 48th St., New York, NY 10017.
- Availabilities. w.

**Avalon Hill Game Co.**
4517 Harford Rd., Baltimore, MD 21214.
- Avalon Hill General. bi-m.

**Avalon Poets**
c/o Vernon Payne, 212 W. First St., San Angelo, TX 76901.
- Avalon Dispatch. irreg.
- Cyclo-Flame. biennial. ISSN 0011-4359

**Avant-Garde Media, Inc.**
- Avant Garde. (pub. by Ralph Ginzburg)

**Avco Financial Services**
620 Newport Center Dr., Newport Beach, CA 92660.
- Money Tree. m.

**Ave Maria Institute Press**
Washington, NJ 07882.
- Soul. bi-m. ISSN 0038-1756 (Blue Army of Our Lady of Fatima in U.S. and Canada)

**Ave Maria Press**
Notre Dame, IN 46556.
- Spiritual Book News. 8 per yr. ISSN 0038-7606

**Avenue Victor Hugo Publishing**
339 Newbury Street, Boston, MA 02115.
- Galileo. q.

**Aviation Maintenance Foundation, Inc.**
- International Aviation Mechanics Journal. (pub. by Aviation Maintenance Publishers, Inc.)

**Aviation Maintenance Publishers, Inc.**
Box 750, Basin, WY 82410.
- International Aviation Mechanics Journal. m. ISSN 0045-1193 (Aviation Maintenance Foundation, Inc.)

**Aviation Resources Corp.**
Administration Building, 217 Lakefront Airport, New Orleans, LA 70126.
- A/C Flyer. m.

**Aviation-Space Writers Association**
Cliffwood Rd., Chester, NJ 07930.
- Aviation/Space Writers Association Manual. a.
- Aviation/Space Writers Association News. 10 per yr.

**Aviator's Journal**
Subscription Dept., 610-Guaranty Bank Bldg., Cedar Rapids, IA 52401.
- Iowa Airport Directory. a. ISSN 0578-6541

**Ayd Medical Communications, Ltd.**
912 W. Lake Ave., Baltimore, MD 21210.
- International Drug Therapy Newsletter. m. ISSN 0020-6571

**Ayer Press**
W. Washington Sq., Philadelphia, PA 19106.
- Ayer Directory of Publications. a.

**Ayrshire Breeders' Association**
1 Union St., Brandon, VT 05733.
- Ayrshire Digest. m. ISSN 0005-2450

**Azu Magazine**
146 W. 29th St., NY 10009.
- Azu; bilingual poetry review. bi-m.

**B.A. Law List Co.**
238 W. Wisconsin Ave., Milwaukee, WI 53203.
- B. A. Law List. a. ISSN 0067-2726

**B B D O, Inc.**
383 Madison Ave., New York, NY 10017.
- B B D O Audience Coverage and Cost Guide. a. ISSN 0522-4837

**B C P R Communications**
Box 693, Los Angeles, CA 90019.
- Black Community Progress Review. m.

**B F L Communications Inc.**
1 Dupont St., Plainview, NY 11803.
- Short Story Index Reprint Series. irreg.

**B-J Paperback Books Suggestion Guide**
1701 Waterloo Road, Cedar Falls, IA 50613.
- B-J Paperback Books Suggestion Guide. (Blow-Juhl) q.

**B M T Publications, Inc.**
254 W. 31st. St., New York, NY 10001.
- Convenience Store News; the newspaper for the industry. fortn. ISSN 0045-8422
- Smokeshop. m.
- United States Tobacco Journal. w. ISSN 0041-8137

**B O A P W Ltd.**
Box 136, Rochester, NY 14601.
- Different Drummer; the magazine for jazz listeners. m.

**B P I Publishing Co.**
21 Charles St, Box 429, Saugatuck Station, Westport, CT 06880.
- Book Production Industry. bi-m. ISSN 0006-7318

**B U C International Corp.**
1881 N. E. 26th St., Fort Lauderdale, FL 33305.
- Used Boat Directory. s-a.

**Babbling Bookworm**
935 Private Rd., Winnetka, IL 60093.
- Babbling Bookworm; newsletter dedicated to bringing children and books together. m.

**Babcox Publications, Inc.**
Babcox Bldg., 11 S. Forge St., Akron, OH 41304.
- Automotive Chain Store. m. ISSN 0005-1489
- Automotive Rebuilder. m. ISSN 0567-2317
- Brake and Front End. m.
- Speed & Custom Dealer. m. ISSN 0038-7193
- Tire Review. m. ISSN 0040-8085
- Warehouse Distributor News. m. ISSN 0511-1145

**Babka Publishing Co.**
Box 1050, 100 Bryant St., Dubuque, IA 52001.
- Antique Trader. w. ISSN 0005-5912
- Antique Trader. Price Guide to Antiques and Collectors' Items. q. ISSN 0556-5367
- Antiques Journal. m. ISSN 0003-5963

**Babson College**
Babson Park, MA 02157.
- Babson Bulletin. 4 per yr.

**Babson's Reports Inc.**
370 Washington St., Wellesley Hills, MA 02181.
- Babson's Washington Service. w.

**Baby John**
5406 Latona Ave NE, Seattle, WA 98105.
- Baby John. irreg (1-2 per yr.)

**Back Door**
Box 481, Athens, OH 45701.
- Back Door. s-a.

**Backpacker**
c/o William Kemsley, 28 W. 44 St., New York, NY 10036.
- Backpacker. q.

**Backstage Publications, Inc.**
165 W. 46th St., New York, NY 10036.
- Back Stage. w. ISSN 0005-3635
- Backstage TV Film/Tape & Syndication Directory. a.
- Film and TV Festival Directory. ISSN 0085-0535

**Badlands Natural History Association**
Box 72, Interior, SD 57750.
- Badlands Natural History Association. Bulletin. irreg. ISSN 0067-2866

**Baikar Association, Inc.**
755 Mt. Auburn St., Watertown, MA 02172.
- Armenian Mirror - Spectator. w. ISSN 0004-234X

**J. H. Baird Publishing Co.**
2916 Sidco Dr., Nashville, TN 37204.
- Southern Lumberman. s-m. ISSN 0038-4313

**Baker & Bowden**
- Impact (Chicago) (pub. by Impact Publications (Chicago))

**Baker and Taylor Companies**
1515 N. Broadway, New York, NY 10036.
- Directions: a Journal for Academic Libraries. m. ISSN 0360-473X
- Forecast. 8 per yr.

**Bakery and Confectionery Workers' International Union of America, AFL-CIO-CLC**
1828 L St. N.W., Washington, DC 20036.
- B & C News. 10 per yr. ISSN 0001-043X

**Balance, Inc.**
c/o Walther Memorial Church, 4040 West Fond du Lac Ave., Milwaukee, WI 53216.
- Affirm. m. ISSN 0044-6467

**Balboa Park Information Center. Master Calendar**
House of Hospitality, San Diego, CA 92101.
- Ethnic Technology Notes. irreg., 1969, no. 4. ISSN 0071-1799

**Bale Publications**
Box 2727, New Orleans, LA 70176.
- COINfidential Report. m.(except Jul. & Aug.)

**Baleen Press**
Box 13448, Phoenix, AZ 85002.
- Inscape. irreg. ISSN 0020-1774

**Ball State University**
Publications Office, Muncie, IN 47306.
- Ball State Monographs. irreg. ISSN 0073-6821
- Ball State University Forum. q. ISSN 0005-433X
- Counselor Education Directory: Personnel and Programs. irreg., 2nd, 1974.

**Ball State University. College of Business**
Muncie, IN 47306.
- Ball State Business Review. s-a. (prep. by its Bureau of Business Research)
- Ball State Journal for Business Educators. s-a. (prep. by its Department of Business Education and Office Administration)

**Ball State University. Department of Geography and Geology**
Muncie, IN 47306.
- Geographical Survey; a quarterly journal of research and commentary. q.

**Ball State University. Department of History**
Muncie, IN 47306.
- Conspectus of History. a.
- Indiana Social Studies Quarterly. 3 per yr. ISSN 0019-6746

**Ball State University. Teachers College**
Muncie, IN 47306.
- Teacher Educator. 4 per yr.

**Ballantine Books**
201 E. 50th St., New York, NY 10022.
- Ballantine's Illustrated History of World War Two. irreg.
- Best Science Fiction of the Year. a. ISSN 0095-7119

**Ballard Printing & Publishing Co.**
5410 Ballard Ave., N. W., Seattle, WA 98107.
- Washington Plumbing and Heating Contractor. m. ISSN 0043-0692 (Associated Plumbing & Heating Contractors of Washington, Inc.)

**Ballena Press**
Box 1366, Socorro, NM 87801.
- Ballena Press Anthropological Papers. irreg.
- Ballena Press Publications in Archaeology, Ethnology and History. irreg.
- Ballena Press Studies in Mesoamerican Art, Archaeology and Ethnohistory. irreg.

**Ballet Dancer**
1170 Broadway, New York, NY 10001.
- Ballet Dancer. bi-m.

**Ballinger Publishing Co.**
17 Dunster St., Harvard Sq., Cambridge, MA 02138.
- Ballinger Studies in Environment and Urban Economy. irreg.
- Concepts in Agribusiness Management. irreg.

**Balloon Federation of America**
806 15th St. N.W., Washington, DC 20005.
- Ballooning. q.

**Balshon Printing Co.**
c/o N. Siegalovsky, Ed., 34-50 24th St., Long Island City, NY 11106.
- Our Own Word/Undzer Aygn Vort. q.

**Baltimore. Health Department. Bureau of Health Information**
Room A-200, 111 N. Calvert St., Baltimore, MD 21202.
- Perspectives (Baltimore) q.

**Baltimore City Public Schools. Division of Publications and Public Information**
1401 E. Oliver St., Baltimore, MD 21213.
- Baltimore City Public Schools Staff Newsletter. s-m.

**Baltimore College of Dental Surgery**
*see under* University of Maryland

**Baltimore County Public Library**
320 York Road, Towson, MD 21204.
- Branching Out. m.

**Baltimore Jewish Times**
2104 N. Charles St., Baltimore, MD 21218.
- Baltimore Jewish Times. w. ISSN 0005-450X

**Baltimore Women's Liberation Center**
101 East 25th Street, B-2, Baltimore, MD 21218.
- Cold Day in August. m.

**Banana Productions**
1183 Church St., San Francisco, CA 94114.
- Banana Rag. a.
- Vile. s-a.

**Bancroft-Parkman, Inc.**
121 E. 78 St., New York, NY 10021.
- American Book Prices Current. a. ISSN 0091-9357
- American Book Prices Current. Five Year Index. quinquennial.

**Bancroft-Whitney Company**
301 Brannan Street, San Francisco, CA 94107.
- California Official Reports; official advance sheets of the Supreme Court, Courts of Appeal, and Appellate Departments of the Superior Court. 36 per yr.

**Banjo Newsletter**
1310 Hawkins Lane, Annapolis, MD 21401.
- Banjo Newsletter. m.

**Bank Administration Institute**
303 S. Northwest Hwy., Park Ridge, IL 60068.
- B A I Index of Bank Performance. irreg. ISSN 0363-910X
- Bank Administration Institute. Accounting Bulletins. irreg. ISSN 0067-3501
- Bank Administration Institute. Annual Report. a. ISSN 0067-351X
- Bank Administration Institute. Security Bulletins. irreg. ISSN 0067-3544
- Journal of Bank Research. q. ISSN 0021-9215
- Magazine of Bank Administration. m. ISSN 0024-9823

**Bank Administration Institute. Personnel Administration Commission**
303 S. Northwest Hwy., Box 500, Park Ridge, IL 60068.
- Bank Administration Institute. Personnel Administration Commission. Biennial Survey of Bank Officer Salaries. ISSN 0525-4620
- Bank Administration Institute. Personnel Policies and Practices. biennial. ISSN 0067-3536

**Bank Marketing Association**
309 W. Washington St., Chicago, IL 60606.
- Bank Marketing. m.

**Bank News Inc.**
912 Baltimore Ave., Kansas City, MO 64105.
- Bank News. m. ISSN 0005-5123

**Bank of America**
Box 37000, San Francisco, CA 94137.
- BankAmerican. m.
- BankAmerican World. bi-m.
- Bibliography of Corporate Social Responsibility. a.
- Small Business Reporter. 10 per yr.

**Bank of Hawaii. Department of Business Research**
Box 2900, Honolulu, HI 96846.
- Bank of Hawaii Monthly Review; business developments in Hawaii and the Pacific Islands. m. ISSN 0005-5204
- Construction in Hawaii. a. ISSN 0069-9187
- Hawaii Annual Economic Review. a. ISSN 0067-3633

**Bank of New York**
48 Wall St., New York, NY 10015.
- Bank of New York Economic Comments. m. (prep. by its Economics Department)
- Bank One. m. ISSN 0005-5387

**Bank of San Antonio**
Suite 208, One Romana Plaza, San Antonio, TX 78205.
- Almanzar's Coins of the World. a.

**Bank Street College of Education**
610 W. 112 St., New York, NY 10025.
- Inside Outside Bankstreet. 1-2 per yr.
- Report from Bank Street. q.

**Bankers Digest, Inc.**
1208 Mercantile Securities Bldg., Dallas, TX 75201.
- Bankers Digest; a weekly newspaper devoted to Texas bank news. w. ISSN 0005-5425
- Texas Banking Red Book. a.

**Bankers Trust Company. Economics Division**
P.O. Box 318, New York, NY 10015.
- Credit and Capital Markets; sources and uses of funds. a.
- Current Business Picture. 3 per yr. ISSN 0522-2958

**Banks-Baldwin Law Publishing Co.**
University Center, Cleveland, OH 44106.
● Baldwin's Ohio Legislative Service. 9-10 per yr.
ISSN 0092-0959

**Banner Publishing Inc.**
Box 308, Shawnee Mission, KS 66201.
● Charolais Banner. m. ISSN 0009-1847 (American-International Charolais Association)

**George Banta Co., Inc.**
Curtis Reed Plaza, Menasha, WI 54952
● Pan Pipes of Sigma Alpha Iota. 4 per yr. ISSN
0031-0611 (Sigma Alpha Iota, International Music
Fraternity for Women) (Subscr. to: Executive
Office of Sigma Alpha Iota, 4119 Rollins Ave.,
Des Moines, IA 50312)

**Bantam Books, Inc.**
666 Fifth Ave., New York, NY 10019.
● World Almanac Guide to Pro Hockey. irreg. ISSN
0095-7240

**Bapi Services**
880 Boston Rd., Billerica, MA 01866.
● American Franchise & Business Opportunity
Directory. irreg. ISSN 0098-7328

**Baptist Children's Homes of North Carolina, Inc.**
515 Watson Ave., Box 338, Thomasville, NC
27360.
● Charity and Children; the voice of child care. 26
per yr. ISSN 0009-1723

**Baptist Convention of Maryland**
1313 York Rd., Lutherville, MD 21093.
● Maryland Baptist. w. ISSN 0025-4169

**Baptist Fellowship**
4161 N. Powers Dr., Orlando, FL 32808.
● Fundamentalist. m. ISSN 0016-2744

**Baptist General Conference**
● Standard (Evanston) (pub. by Harvest Publications
(Evanston))

**Baptist Medical Centers**
3201 Fourth Ave. S., Birmingham, AL 35222.
● B M C News. fortn.

**Baptist Missionary Association of America**
● Baptist Missionary Association of America.
Directory and Handbook. (pub. by Baptist News
Service)

**Baptist Missionary Association of Louisiana**
Box 1126, Denham Springs, LA 70726.
● Louisiana Baptist Builder. m. ISSN 0024-6743

**Baptist Missionary Association of Texas**
Box 4205, Dallas, TX 75208.
● Baptist Progress. w. ISSN 0005-5751

**Baptist News Service**
P.O. Box 97, Jacksonville, TX 75766.
● Baptist Missionary Association of America.
Directory and Handbook. a. ISSN 0091-2743

**Baptist Public Relations Association**
460 James Robertson Parkway, Nashville, TN
37219.
● Baptist Public Relations Association Newsletter.
m.

**Baptist World Alliance**
1628 16th St., N.W., Washington, DC 20009.
● Baptist World. m. (11 per yr.) ISSN 0005-5808
● Baptist World Alliance. Congress Reports.
quinquennial; 13th, Stockholm, 1975 (published in
1976) ISSN 0067-4095

**Bar Association of San Francisco**
220 Bush St., San Francisco, CA 94104.
● Directory of San Francisco Attorneys. a. ISSN
0092-9174
● In Re; news and reports of the Bar Association of
San Francisco. 10 per yr. ISSN 0046-8754

**Bar Association of Washoe County**
c/o Edward E. Hale, 90 Court St., Reno, NV
89504.
● Washoe County Bar Association Newsletter.
m(Sept-June) ISSN 0043-0919

**Harry Barba, Ed. & Pub.**
47 Hyde Blvd., Ballston Spa, NY 12020.
● Harian Press; one world is better than none. 3 per
yr. ISSN 0017-7776

**Barbers, Beauticians and Allied Industries
International Association**
7050 W. Washington St., Indianapolis, IN 46241.
● Journeyman Barber and Beauty Culture. m.

**Barclay Press**
600 E. Third St, Box 232, Newberg, OR 97132.
● Evangelical Friend. m. except Aug. ISSN 0014-
3340 (Evangelical Friends Alliance)
● Fruit of the Vine; friends daily devotional
readings. q. ISSN 0016-2264 (Friends Church,
Northwest Yearly Meeting)

**Bard Papers, Inc.**
Box 39096, 6090 Liberty Rd., Solon, OH 44139.
● Valley Views. q. ISSN 0042-2339

**Bards of Grand Rapids**
c/o Clarence L. Weaver, Ed., 1036 Emerald Ave.,
Grand Rapids, MI 49503.
● Bardic Echoes. q. ISSN 0005-5948

**Bargain Buster, Inc.**
41 1/2 Merchants Row, Rutland, VT 05701.
● Rutland Area Shopper. w.

**Barks Publications, Inc.**
400 N. Michigan Ave., Chicago, IL 60611.
● Electrical Apparatus with Electric Heat; magazine
of electromechanical operation and maintenance.
m.
● Electromechanical Bench Reference. a.

**Barnard College**
3001 Broadway, New York, NY 10027.
● Barnard College Bulletin. w. ISSN 0005-6014

**Barnard College. Macintosh Center**
Rm. 106, New York, NY 10027.
● Emanon. q. ISSN 0013-6514

**Barnard College. Women's Center**
3009 Broadway, New York, NY 10027.
● Women's Work and Women's Studies; an annual
interdisciplinary bibliography. a.

**Barnes and Noble**
10 East 53rd St., New York, NY 10022.
● Progress in Construction Science and Technology.
irreg., no. 2, 1973.
● Sources for Social and Economic History. irreg.

**Barnett Banks of Florida, Inc.**
100 Laura St., Jacksonville, FL 32202.
● Barnett Action. q.

**Richard Baron, Inc.**
(Subsidiary of: E.P. Dutton & Co., Inc.)
201 Park Ave. S., New York, NY 10003.
● American Civil Liberties Union Handbook Series.
irreg.

**Baron Publishing Company**
Box 820, La Puente, CA 91747.
● A F V-G2; a magazine for military vehicle
enthusiasts. bi-m. ISSN 0001-124X
● Fusilier (La Puente); a quarterly for military
historians. q. ISSN 0092-5322

**Baron von Kannon**
P.O. Box 877, Bloomington, IN 47401.
● Alternative: an American Spectator. 10 per yr.

**Baronet Publishing Co.**
509 Madison Ave., New York, NY 10022.
● Bijou: the Magazine of the Movies. bi-m.
● Cosmos; science fiction and fantasy. bi-m.

**Barrett Institute**
P.O. Box P, Burlington, MA 01803.
● Barrett Reports. m.
● Barrett Reports on Warrants. irreg.

**Barristers of the Los Angeles County Bar Association**
● Barrister Bulletin. (pub. by Los Angeles County
Bar Association)

**Barrister's Press, Inc**
Box 4252, St. Paul, MN 55104.
● Law Review Digest. bi-m. ISSN 0047-4193

**Allan P. Barron Enterprise**
31 E. 28th St., New York, NY 10016.
● Black Sports. m. ISSN 0045-2254
● Discovery (New York); the magazine for today's
black college students. q.

**Barron's Educational Series, Inc.**
113 Crossways Park Drive, Woodbury, NY 11797.
● Barron's How to Prepare for the Law School
Admission Test. biennial.
● Barron's Profiles of American Colleges. Vol. 1:
Descriptions of the Colleges. a.
● Barron's Profiles of American Colleges. Vol. 2:
Index to Major Areas of Study; index to major
areas of study. a. ISSN 0533-1072

**Barrows Co. Inc.**
P.O. Box 1591 Grand Central Sta., New York, NY
10017.
● Asia & Australasia Oil Laws & Concession
Contracts. q.
● Central American & Carribbean Oil Laws &
Concession Contracts. q.
● Europe Basic Oil Law & Concession Contracts. q.
● Middle East Basic Oil Laws & Concession
Contracts. q.
● North Africa Basic Oil Laws & Concession
Contracts. q.
● Offshore Petroleum Industry. q.
● Petroleum Taxation/Legislation Report. m.
● South America Basic Oil Laws & Concession
Contracts. q.
● South & Central Africa Basic Oil Laws &
Concession Contracts. q.

**Bart Publications, Inc.**
919 Third Ave., New York, NY 10022.
● Floor Covering Weekly. w. ISSN 0015-3761

**Bartholomew's Cobble**
19 Howland Rd., West Hartford, CT 06107.
● Bartholomew's Cobble. 3-5 per yr.

**Bernard Baruch College**
see under City University of New York

**Baseball Bulletin**
286 Penobscot Bldg, Detroit, MI 48226.
● Baseball Bulletin. m.

**Baseball-for-Fans Publications**
11860 Kiowa Ave., Box 49213, Los Angeles, CA
90049.
● Book on the World Series. a.
● Insiders Baseball Fact Book. a.
● Pitcher Performance Handbook. a.

**Basenji**
935 42nd Avenue North, St. Petersburg, FL 33703.
● Basenji. m. ISSN 0094-9744

**Basic Books Inc.**
10 E. 53 St., New York, NY 10022.
● Adolescent Psychiatry. irreg., vol. 3, 1974. ISSN
0065-2008 (American Society for Adolescent
Psychiatry)

**Basketball News**
Box 1894, Coral Gables, FL 83134.
● Basketball News. m.

**Bass Anglers Sportsman Society**
Box 3044, Montgomery, AL 36117.
● Bassmaster Magazine. bi-m.
● Southern Outdoors. bi-m.

**Bastion Enterprises**
c/o Leatha Braden, 6436 Mullen Rd., Olympia, WA
98503.
● Northern Dog News. 8 per yr. ISSN 0546-5559

**Bates College Publishing Association**
Harthorn Hall, Lewiston, ME 04240.
● Bates Student. w.(Sept.-June) ISSN 0005-6243

**Baton Rouge Chamber of Commerce**
Box 1868, Baton Rouge, LA 70821.
● Baton Rouge. m. ISSN 0005-6324

**Battelle Memorial Institute**
505 King Avenue, Columbus, OH 43201.
● Battelle Memorial Institute. Published Papers and
Articles. a. ISSN 0084-7712
● Battelle Today. q. ISSN 0145-8477
● Energy Perspectives. s-a.

**Battelle Memorial Institute. Columbus Laboratories**
505 King Ave, Columbus, OH 43201
- Battelle Memorial Institute. Columbus
  Laboratories. Report on National Survey of
  Compensation Paid Scientists and Engineers
  Engaged in Research and Development Activities.
  a. ISSN 0093-4267 (Order from: Supt. of
  Documents, U.S. Govt. Printing Office,
  Washington, DC 20402)
- Probable Levels of R & D Expenditures: Forecast
  and Analysis. a.

**Franklin P. Baugh, Ed. & Pub.**
400 Elwell Ave., Bldg. 176, Herndon Ave., Orlando,
FL 32803.
- Florida Aviation Journal. m.

**Bausch & Lomb Inc.**
One Lincoln First Sq., Rochester, NY 14601.
- Educational Focus. s-a.

**Baxter Brothers**
1030 East Putnam Ave., Greenwich, CT 06830
(Subscr. to: Route 25, Mattituck, NY 11952)
- Baxter; a world economic service (that anticipates
  price trends and business movements) w.

**Baxter County Historical Society**
c/o D. Garvin Carroll, Box 309, Mountain Home,
AR 72653.
- Baxter County History. q.

**Bay Area Air Pollution Control District**
939 Ellis St., San Francisco, CA 94109.
- Air Currents. m. ISSN 0400-8510

**Bay Area International Monthly**
Box 2929, San Francisco, CA 94126.
- Bay Area International Monthly; and activity
  guide. m. ISSN 0005-6901

**Bay Area Review Course, Inc.**
5900 Wilshire Blvd., Los Angeles, CA 90036.
- Bay Area Review Course. Civil Procedure. a.
  ISSN 0099-1244
- Bay Area Review Course. Community Property. a.
- Bay Area Review Course. Conflicts of Law. a.
  ISSN 0099-0418
- Bay Area Review Course. Constitutional Law. a.
  ISSN 0098-7638
- Bay Area Review Course. Contracts. a. ISSN
  0098-762X
- Bay Area Review Course. Corporations. a. ISSN
  0099-1236
- Bay Area Review Course. Criminal Law. a. ISSN
  0098-8049
- Bay Area Review Course. Evidence. a.
- Bay Area Review Course. Legal Ethics. irreg.
  ISSN 0098-7980
- Bay Area Review Course. Real Property. a.
- Bay Area Review Course. Remedies. irreg. ISSN
  0098-7999
- Bay Area Review Course. Torts. a. ISSN 0098-
  7611
- Bay Area Review Course. Trusts. a.
- Bay Area Review Course. Wills. a.
- National Bar Examination Digest. irreg. ISSN
  0098-2857

**Bay County Genealogical Society**
Box 27, Essexville, MI 48732.
- Chips and Ships. q. ISSN 0591-1281

**Bay Guardian Co.**
Guardian Building, 2700 19th St., San Francisco,
CA 94110.
- San Francisco Bay Guardian. w. ISSN 0036-4096

**Bay State Business World**
c/o Andrew M. Monahan Ed., P.O. Box 128,
Norwood, MA 02062.
- Bay State Business World. w.

**Bayard Publications, Inc.**
300 Broad St., Stamford, CT 06901.
- Insurance. m. ISSN 0020-4560
- Insurance Conference Planner. 4 per yr.

**Bayer AG**
- Verfahrenstechnische Berichte/Chemical and
  Process Engineering Abstracts. (pub. by Verlag
  Chemie International, Inc.)

**Bayland Publishing, Inc.**
3133 Buffalo Speedway, Box 66469, Houston, TX
77098.
- Houston Home & Garden. m. ISSN 0360-2087

**Baylor College of Dentistry. Alumni and Public
Information Office**
3302 Gaston Ave., Dallas, TX 75226.
- Baylor Dental Journal. s-a. ISSN 0005-7258

**Baylor College of Medicine. Cardiovascular Research
Center**
1200 Moursund Blvd., Houston, TX 77030.
- Cardiovascular Research Center Bulletin. q. ISSN
  0008-6371

**Baylor University. Armstrong Browning Library**
Waco, TX 76706.
- Studies in Browning and His Circle. s-a. ISSN
  0095-4489

**Baylor University. Department of Geology**
- Baylor Geological Studies Bulletin. (pub. by
  Baylor University Press)

**Baylor University. Hankamer School of Business**
Waco, TX 76706.
- Baylor Business Studies. q. ISSN 0005-724X

**Baylor University. J.M. Dawson Studies in Church
and State**
Box 380, Waco, TX 76703.
- Journal of Church and State. 3 per yr. ISSN 0021-
  969X

**Baylor University. Law School**
Waco. TX 76706.
- Baylor Law Review. q. ISSN 0005-7274

**Baylor University Medical Center**
3500 Gaston Ave., Dallas, TX 75246.
- Baylor Progress. m.

**Baylor University Press**
Baylor Univ., Waco, TX 76703.
- Baylor Geological Studies Bulletin. s-a. ISSN
  0005-7266 (Baylor University. Department of
  Geology)

**Baymer Publications, Inc.**
606 N. Larchmont, Los Angeles, CA 90004.
- Western Material Handling/Packaging/Shipping.
  bi-m. ISSN 0510-243X

**Baywood Publishing Co., Inc.**
120 Marine St., Farmingdale, NY 11735.
- Abstracts in Anthropology. q. ISSN 0001-3455
- Current Bibliography on African Affairs. q. ISSN
  0011-3255 (African Bibliographic Center)
- Drug Forum; the journal of human issues. q. ISSN
  0046-0753
- Health Issues; the journal of total health
  education. s-a.
- International Journal of Aging & Human
  Development. q. ISSN 0091-4150
- International Journal of Health Services. q. ISSN
  0020-7314
- International Journal of Instructional Media. q.
  ISSN 0092-1815
- International Journal of Psychiatry in Medicine;
  an international journal of medical psychology
  and psychiatry in the general hospital. q. ISSN
  0033-278X
- Journal of Altered States of Consciousness. q.
  (Institute for the Study of Drug Addiction)
- Journal of Collective Negotiations in the Public
  Sector. q. ISSN 0047-2301
- Journal of Drug Education. q. ISSN 0047-2379
- Journal of Educational Technology Systems. q.
  ISSN 0047-2395 (Society for Applied Learning
  Technology)
- Journal of Environmental Systems. q. ISSN 0047-
  2433
- Journal of Living, Growing and Dying. s-a.
- Journal of Recreational Mathematics. q. ISSN
  0022-412X
- Journal of Technical Writing and Communication.
  q. ISSN 0047-2816
- Omega; journal of death and dying. q. ISSN 0030-
  2228 (Ars Moriendi)

**Beacon House Inc.**
259 Wolcott Ave., Box 311, Beacon, NY 12508.
- Group Psychotherapy, Psychodrama &
  Sociometry. q. (American Society of Group
  Psychotherapy and Psychodrama)

**Beacon Press**
25 Beacon St., Boston, MA 02108.
- Source; an organizing tool. irreg.

**Bead Journal**
Box 24 C 47, Los Angeles, CA 90024.
- Bead Journal; a quarterly publication of ancient,
  ethnic and contemporary jewelry. q. ISSN 0094-
  2448

**Bean Improvement Cooperative**
- Bean Improvement Cooperative. Annual Report.
  (pub. by University of Nebraska-Lincoln.
  Department of Horticulture and Forestry)

**Bear Flag Productions, Inc.**
110 Sutter St., San Francisco, CA 94104.
- Bear Flag Republic. m.

**Bear Tribe Medicine Society**
Box 1961, Klamath Falls, OR 97601.
- Many Smokes. q. ISSN 0025-2670

**Beardsley Publishing Corp.**
Box 242, North Salem, NY 10560.
- Ski Area Management. q. ISSN 0037-6175

**Beauty Fashion, Inc.**
48 E. 43 St., New York, NY 10017.
- Beauty Fashion. 10 per yr.

**Beauty World, Inc.**
1170 Broadway, New York, NY 10001.
- Beauty & Barber Dealers World. m. ISSN 0405-
  1157
- Beauty School World. m. ISSN 0405-119X
- Beauty World.

**Beaver Dan Michigan Enterprises Ltd.**
705 Olive, Suite 309, St. Louis, MO 63101.
- Brand X International. s-a. ISSN 0098-2369

**Fitzgerald Beaver, Ed. & Pub.**
2803 E. Cherry, Seattle, WA 98122.
- Facts. w. ISSN 0427-8879

**Beckman Instruments, Inc. Spinco Div.**
1117 California Ave., Palo Alto, CA 94304.
- Ultracentrifuge Applications; a continuing
  bibliography. biennial. ISSN 0082-738X

**Bedford Stuyvesant Youth in Action, Inc.**
Bedford Stuyvesant Youth in Action, Inc., 1121
Bedford Ave., 4th Fl., Brooklyn, NY 11216.
- Bedford Stuyvesant Youth in Action Monthly
  Newsletter. m. ISSN 0005-7576

**Beecham Society**
*see* Sir Thomas Beecham Society

**Beefmaster Breeders Universal**
350 G.P. M. South Tower, 800 N. W. Loop 410,
San Antonio, TX 78216.
- Beefmaster Cowman. m.

**Beer Wholesaler Publishing Co.**
76 S.E. Fifth Ave., Delray Beach, FL 33444.
- Beer Wholesaler. q. ISSN 0005-7770

**Behavioral Neuropsychiatry Medical Publishers, Inc.**
61 East 86th St., New York, NY 10028.
- Behavioral Neuropsychiatry. bi-m. ISSN 0005-
  7932

**Behavioral Publications, Inc.**
72 Fifth Ave., New York, NY 10010.
- Management and Training Series. irreg.

**Behavioral Research Laboratories**
Ladera Professional Center, Box 577, Palo Alto, CA
94302.
- P I /L T; Occasional Papers on Programmed
  Instruction and Language Teaching. irreg. ISSN
  0078-7388

**Behavioral Research Survey Center**
- B R S Monthly Index. (pub. by Audits & Surveys,
  Inc.)

**Behn-Miller Publishers, Inc.**
16001 Ventura Blvd., Encino, CA 91436.
- Coinage. m. ISSN 0010-0455
- Popular Bridge. bi-m. ISSN 0032-4450
- Rock & Gem. m. ISSN 0048-8453

**Jerome D. Belager, Ed. & Pub.**
Rt. 1 Box 239, Waterloo, WI 53594.
- Countryside. m.

**Belaruskaja Vydaveckaja Siabrynia**
3006 Logan Blvd., Chicago, IL 60647.
- Belaruskaja Carkva. s-a. ISSN 0005-8327

**Belgian American Chamber of Commerce in the U.S.**
50 Rockefeller Plaza, New York, NY 10020.
● Belgian American Trade Review. m.

**Belgian Consulate General. Industrial Section**
50 Rockefeller Plaza, New York, NY 10020.
● Business Memo from Belgium. bi-m. ISSN 0007-6945

**Bell & Howell Co. Newspaper Indexing Center, Microphoto Division**
Old Mansfield Rd., Wooster, OH 44691.
● Chicago Tribune. Newspaper Index. m. with annual cumulation. ISSN 0098-1176
● Christian Science Monitor. Cumulated Index. a. ISSN 0578-0152
● Detroit News. Newspaper Index. m. with annual cumulation. ISSN 0361-6983
● Houston Post. Newspaper Index. m. with annual cumulation. ISSN 0363-7824
● Index to the Christian Science Monitor. m. with annual cumulation. ISSN 0098-1184
● Los Angeles Times. Newspaper Index. irreg. ISSN 0098-1192
● Los Angeles Times. Newspaper Index. m. with annual cumulation. ISSN 0098-1192
● New Orleans Times-Picayune. Newspaper Index. m. with annual cumulation. ISSN 0098-1206
● San Francisco Chronicle. Newspaper Index. m. with annual cumulation. ISSN 0363-7816
● Transdex Index. m. with annual cumulation. ISSN 0041-1116
● Washington Post. Newspaper Index. m. with annual cumulation. ISSN 0097-8167

**Bell-Arm Corp.**
630 Flowerree St., Box 582, Helena, MT 59601.
● Montana Masonic News. 11 per yr. ISSN 0027-0008 (Grand Lodge of Montana, Ancient Free & Accepted Masons) (Co-sponsor: Algeria Shrine Temple)

**Bell Directory Publishers Inc.**
2112 Broadway, New York, NY 10023.
● Eastern Manufacturers & Industrial Classified Directory and Buyers Guide. a.

**Bell Publications**
2403 Champa St., Denver, CO 80205.
● Alaska Beverage Analyst. m. ISSN 0002-4457
● American Horologist and Jeweler. m. ISSN 0002-8797
● Colorado Beverage Analyst. m. ISSN 0010-1516
● Idaho Beverage Analyst. m.
● Montana Beverage Analyst. m.
● Nebraska Beverage Analyst. m. ISSN 0028-1808
● Oregon Beverage Analyst. m. ISSN 0030-462X
● Utah Beverage Analyst. m.
● Washington Beverage Analyst. m.
● Wyoming Beverage Analyst. m. ISSN 0043-9673

**Bell Telephone Laboratories, Inc.**
600 Mountain Ave., Murray Hill, NJ 07974.
● Bell Laboratories Record; devoted to research development in the field of communications. m. ISSN 0005-8564

**Bell Telephone Laboratories, Inc. Libraries and Information Systems Center**
Rm. 3B-202, Holmdel, NJ 07733.
● Bell Laboratories Talks and Papers. a. ISSN 0067-5679

**Bellman Publishing Co.**
Box 164, Arlington, MA 02174.
● Scholarships, Fellowships, Loans News Service. q. ISSN 0036-6366

**Belmont Education Association**
Payson Park School, 71 Payson Rd., Belmont, MA 02178.
● Beacon. m.

**A.H. Belo Corp.**
Communications Center, Dallas, TX 75222.
● Texas Almanac and State Industrial Guide. biennial.

**Beloit Poetry Journal**
Box 2, Beloit, WI 53511.
● Beloit Poetry Journal. q. ISSN 0005-8661
● Beloit Poetry Journal. Chapbook. irreg., approx. biennial, 1975 no. 13. ISSN 0067-5695

**Beltone Corp.**
4201 W. Victoria St., Chicago, IL 60646.
● Between Friends; the Beltone magazine. q.

**Beltone Institute for Hearing Research**
4201 West Victoria St, Chicago, IL 60646.
● Beltone Institute for Hearing Research. Translations. 1-2 per yr. ISSN 0005-8688

**Bench Advisors**
34 Mackay Drive, Tenafly, NJ 07670.
● Bench Computer Reports; Bench selected recommendations report. m.

**Matthew Bender & Co., Inc.**
235 E. 45 St, New York, NY 10017.
● Annual Conference on Labor at New York University. Proceedings. a. (New York University. Institute of Labor Relations)
● Collier Bankruptcy Cases. irreg. ISSN 0099-1848
● Oil and Gas Tax Quarterly. q. ISSN 0030-1396
● Patent Law Annual-Southwestern Legal Foundation. a. ISSN 0553-3864
● Private Investors Abroad; problems and solutions in international business. irreg. (Southwestern Legal Foundation. International and Comparative Law Center)
● U S Tax Week. w. ISSN 0041-8129
● University of Miami, Coral Gables. Law Center. Annual Institute on Estate Planning. a.

**Bender Publications**
Box 3631, 4077 W. Pico Blvd., Los Angeles, CA 90019.
● Northern California Electronics News. bi-w.
● Southern California Electronics News. bi-w.

**Benedict Lust Publications**
490 Easy St., Box 777, Simi Valley, CA 93065.
● Nature's Path. q. ISSN 0028-0909

**Benedictine Sisters of Perpetual Adoration**
Clyde, MO 64432.
● Spirit & Life. 6 per yr. ISSN 0038-7592

**Benevolent and Protective Order of Elks of the United States of America**
425 Diversey Parkway, Chicago, IL 60614.
● Elks Magazine. m. ISSN 0013-6263

**Benjamin Company**
485 Madison Ave., New York, NY 10022.
● Benco Report; news of business-building book programs. irreg.

**Benjamin Franklin Stamp Club**
Box 746, Washington, DC 20044.
● Stamp Fun. bi-m.

**W. A. Benjamin Inc.**
(Subsidiary of: Addison-Wesley)
Reading, MA 01867.
● Biology Teaching Monograph Series. irreg.
● Computer Programs for Chemistry. irreg., vol. 4, 1972. ISSN 0588-9405
● Frontiers in Chemistry. irreg.
● Frontiers in Physics. irreg. ISSN 0429-7725

**B. M. Bennani, Ed. & Pub.**
Comparative Literature, State University of New York, Binghamton, NY 13901.
● Paintbrush; a journal of poetry, translations and letters. s-a. ISSN 0094-1964

**Frank P. Bennett & Co, Inc.**
286 Congress St., Boston, MA 02210.
● United States Investor/Eastern Banker. bi-w.

**Bennett-Scott Publishing Corp.**
99 E. Mill St., Springfield, MA 01101.
● Jewish Weekly News. w. ISSN 0021-6860

**Bennington College**
Bennington, VT 05201.
● Silo. a. ISSN 0037-5306

**Benwill Publishing Corp.**
167 Corey Rd., Brookline, MA 02146.
● Circuits Manufacturing. m. ISSN 0009-7306
● Digital Design. m.
● Minicomputer News. fortn.
● Personal Computing. bi-m.

**Berea Board of Education**
390 Fair St., Berea, OH 44017.
● Your Schools. 6 per yr. ISSN 0044-1120

**Berea College Alumni Association**
Berea, KY 40404.
● Berea Alumnus. bi-m. ISSN 0005-8874

**Berea College Appalachian Center**
CPO 2336, Berea, KY 40403.
● Berea College Appalachian Center Newsletter. q.

**Berean Bible Society**
7609 W. Belmont Ave., Chicago, IL 60635.
● Berean Searchlight. m. ISSN 0005-8890

**Bergen County (New Jersey) Historical Society**
River Edge, NJ 07661.
● Bergen County History. a. ISSN 0094-7989

**Bergman Publishers, Inc.**
224 W. 20th St., New York, NY 10011.
● Negro in the Congressional Record. irreg., 1971, vol. 10. ISSN 0077-6483
● Studies in Historical and Political Science. Extra Volumes. irreg., 1968, vol. 15. ISSN 0081-7996 (Johns Hopkins University)

**Berkeley Enterprises, Inc.**
815 Washington St., Newtonville, MA 02160.
● Computer Directory and Buyer's Guide. a.
● Computer Graphics and Art. q.
● Computers and People. m. ISSN 0361-1442
● People and the Pursuit of Truth. m. (Co-sponsor: Assassination Information Bureau)

**Berkeley Poets' Workshop and Press**
Box 459, Berkeley, CA 94701.
● Berkeley Poets Cooperative. s-a.

**Berkley Publishing Corp.**
200 Madison Ave., New York, NY 10016.
● Insiders' Guide to the Colleges. biennial.

**Bill Berkson, Ed. & Pub.**
Box 389, Bolinas, CA 94924.
● Big Sky. q.

**Gustav Berle**
Box 546189, Surfside, FL 33154.
● Florida Contractor and Builder. m. ISSN 0015-3982

**Clayton G. Berling**
P.O. Box 9393, Berkeley, CA 94709.
● Soccer America. w.

**Bermont Books**
815 15 St., N.W., Washington, DC 20005.
● Directory of Defense Electronic Products and Services: United States Suppliers. a. (Electronic Industries Association)

**Bernan Associates, Inc.**
4701 Willard Ave., Washington, DC 20015.
● Checklist of Congressional Hearings. 40 per yr. ISSN 0009-2096

**Judy Berner Publishing Co.**
10060 W. Roosevelt Rd., Westchester, IL 60153.
● Dog World. m. ISSN 0012-4893

**Arnold Bernhard & Co., Inc.**
5 E. 44th St, New York, NY 10017.
● Value Line Investment Survey. w. ISSN 0042-2401
● Value Line Option & Convertible Survey. 4 per mo.

**Bernice Pauahi Bishop Museum**
● Bernice Pauahi Bishop Museum, Honolulu. Occasional Papers. (pub. by Bishop Museum Press)
● Bernice Pauahi Bishop Museum, Honolulu. Special Publications. (pub. by Bishop Museum Press)

**Bernice Pauahi Bishop Museum. Department of Anthropology**
● Pacific Anthropological Records. (pub. by Bishop Museum Press)

**Bernice Pauahi Bishop Museum. Department of Entomology**
Box 6037, Honolulu, HI 96818.
● Journal of Medical Entomology. bi-m. ISSN 0022-2585
● Pacific Insects Monographs. irreg. ISSN 0078-7515

**Bernporter Books**
Box 209, Belfast, ME 04915.
● Bernporter International. w. (Institute of Advanced Thinking)

**Berryhill**
Box 3687, Missoula, MT 59801.
- Berryhill News. bi-m.

**William Berssen, Ed. & Pub.**
Box Q, Ventura, CA 93001.
- Sea Boating Almanac. Northern California & Nevada. a. ISSN 0363-7700
- Sea Boating Almanac. Pacific Northwest & Alaska. a. ISSN 0363-7999
- Sea Boating Almanac. Southern California, Arizona, Baja. a. ISSN 0363-6712

**Bertelsen Publishing Co.**
36 Conti Parkway, Elmwood Park, IL 60635.
- Danske Pioneer/Danish Pioneer. fortn.

**Bessire & Company, Inc.**
7999 Knue Rd., Box 50806, Indianapolis, IN 46250.
- Besco News. bi-m. ISSN 0005-9579

**A. M. Best Co.**
Oldwick, NJ 08858.
- Best's Agents Guide to Life Insurance Companies. a.
- Best's Insurance News Digest: Life-Health Edition. 70.
- Best's Insurance News Digest: Property-Casualty Edition. w.
- Best's Insurance Report: Life-Health.
- Best's Insurance Report: Property-Casualty. a.
- Best's Insurance Securities Research Service. irreg. ISSN 0362-8701
- Best's Recommended Independent Insurance Adjusters. a. ISSN 0091-830X
- Best's Review. Life/Health Insurance Edition. m. ISSN 0005-9706
- Best's Review. Property-Casualty Insurance Edition. m.
- Best's Safety Directory; safety-industrial hygiene-security. a.

**Best Friends**
329 Montclaire N.E., Albuquerque, NM 87108.
- Best Friends. a.

**Bet Midrash le-Torah ve-Hora Ah**
145 East Broadway, New York, NY 10002.
- Le-Torah ve-Hora Ah. ISSN 0094-5625

**Beta Beta Beta National Biological Society**
- B I O S. (pub. by Laurance Press Co)

**Beta Phi Mu, International Honor Society**
c/o University of Pittsburgh, Graduate School of Library and Information Sciences, Pittsburgh, PA 15260.
- Beta Phi Mu Chapbook. irreg., no. 10, 1974. ISSN 0067-6357

**Beth Sar Shalom**
Box 1331, Englewood Cliffs, NJ 07632.
- Shepherd of Israel. m. (American Board of Missions to the Jews)

**Bethel College**
North Newton, KS 67117.
- Bethel College Bulletin. m(except Jan,July & Aug) ISSN 0005-982X
- Mennonite Life. q. ISSN 0025-9365

**Bethune Jones**
321 Sunset Ave., Asbury Park, NJ 07712.
- From the State Capitals. Agriculture and Food Products. w. ISSN 0016-1632
- From the State Capitals. Airport Construction and Financing. 12 per yr. ISSN 0016-1640
- From the State Capitals. Civil Defense. 12 per yr. ISSN 0016-1659
- From the State Capitals. Drug Abuse Control. 12 per yr.
- From the State Capitals. Federal Action Affecting the States. 20 per yr. ISSN 0016-1667
- From the State Capitals. Fire Administration. 12 per yr. ISSN 0016-1675
- From the State Capitals. Fish and Game Regulation. 12 per yr. ISSN 0016-1683
- From the State Capitals. General Bulletin. 24 per yr. ISSN 0016-1691
- From the State Capitals. Highway Financing and Construction. w. ISSN 0016-1705
- From the State Capitals. Housing and Redevelopment. 12 per yr. ISSN 0016-1713
- From the State Capitals. Industrial Development. 12 per yr. ISSN 0016-1721
- From the State Capitals. Institutional Building. 12 per yr. ISSN 0016-173X

- From the State Capitals. Insurance Regulation. w. ISSN 0016-1748
- From the State Capitals. Judicial Administration. w. ISSN 0016-1756
- From the State Capitals. Juvenile Delinquency and Family Relations. 12 per yr. ISSN 0016-1764
- From the State Capitals. Labor Relations. 12 per yr. ISSN 0016-1772
- From the State Capitals. Liquor Control. w. ISSN 0016-1780
- From the State Capitals. Merchandising. w. ISSN 0016-1799
- From the State Capitals. Milk Control. 12 per yr. ISSN 0016-1802
- From the State Capitals. Motor Vehicle Regulation. w. ISSN 0016-1810
- From the State Capitals. Off-Street Parking. 12 per yr. ISSN 0016-1829
- From the State Capitals. Parks and Recreation Trends. 12 per yr. ISSN 0016-1837
- From the State Capitals. Personnel Management. 12 per yr. ISSN 0016-1845
- From the State Capitals. Police Administration. 12 per yr. ISSN 0016-1853
- From the State Capitals. Public Assistance and Welfare Trends. 12 per yr. ISSN 0016-1861
- From the State Capitals. Public Health. 12 per yr. ISSN 0016-187X
- From the State Capitals. Public Utilities. w. ISSN 0016-1888
- From the State Capitals. Racial Relations. 12 per yr. ISSN 0016-1896
- From the State Capitals. School Construction. 12 per yr. ISSN 0016-190X
- From the State Capitals. School Financing. 12 per yr.
- From the State Capitals. Sewage and Waste Disposal. 12 per yr. ISSN 0016-1926
- From the State Capitals. Small Loans, Sales Finance, Banking. 12 per yr. ISSN 0016-1934
- From the State Capitals. Taxes - Local Non-Property. 12 per yr. ISSN 0016-1942
- From the State Capitals. Taxes-Property. 12 per yr. ISSN 0046-516X
- From the State Capitals. Tourist Business Promotion. 12 per yr. ISSN 0016-1950
- From the State Capitals. Unemployment Compensation. 12 per yr. ISSN 0016-1969
- From the State Capitals. Urban Transit and Bus Transportation. 12 per yr. ISSN 0016-1977
- From the State Capitals. Wage-Hour Regulation. 12 per yr. ISSN 0016-1985
- From the State Capitals. Water Supply. 12 per yr. ISSN 0016-1993
- From the State Capitals. Workmen's Compensation. 12 per yr. ISSN 0016-2000

**Better America**
Box 1228, Coolidge, AZ 85228.
- Better America; newsletter. 12 per yr. ISSN 0006-0038

**Better Business Bureau of Eastern Massachusetts, Inc.**
150 Tremont St., Boston, MA 02111.
- B B B Tribune. m. ISSN 0005-2809 (Consumer Affairs Foundation)

**Better Business Bureau of Metropolitan New York Inc.**
110 Fifth Ave., New York, NY 10011.
- Report to Business and Consumer Information. bi-m.

**Better Education**
c/o E. G. Nilsson, Box P455, Bay Shore, NY 11706.
- Better Education. q. ISSN 0006-0127

**Better Healthkeeping, Inc.**
1841 Broadway, New York, NY 10023.
- Healthkeeping. bi-m.

**Better Homes and Gardens Idea Publications**
(Subsidiary of: Meredith Corporation)
1716 Locust St., Des Moines, IA 50336.
- Better Homes and Gardens Building Ideas. q. ISSN 0093-0938
- Better Homes and Gardens Hundreds of Do-It-Yourself Ideas. s-a.
- Better Homes and Gardens Hundreds of Ideas. s-a. ISSN 0090-6433
- Better Homes and Gardens Kitchen & Bath Ideas. irreg.

**Beverage Journal Inc.**
2 West 25th Street, Baltimore, MD 21218.
- Maryland-Washington-Delaware Beverage Journal. m. ISSN 0037-0045

**Beverage Media Ltd.**
251 Park Ave. S., New York, NY 10010.
- Beverage Media. m. ISSN 0006-0372

**Beverage News Inc.**
Box 1677, 150 N. Rock Island, Wichita, KS 67201.
- Kansas Beverage News. m. ISSN 0022-8494
- Oklahoma Beverage News. m. ISSN 0030-1663

**Beverage Publications, Inc.**
2529 Whitney Ave., Hamden, CT 06518.
- Connecticut Beverage Journal. m.

**Beverage Publishing Co. of Rhode Island, Inc.**
603 Hope St., Providence, RI 02906.
- Rhode Island Beverage Journal. m. ISSN 0035-4562

**Beverage Retailer Weekly**
250 W. 57th St., New York, NY 10019.
- Beverage Retailer Weekly. w.

**Beverly Hills Bar Association**
300 S. Beverly Dr., Suite 201, Beverly Hills, CA 90212.
- Beverly Hills Bar Association. Journal. bi-m. ISSN 0045-1827

**Beverly Review**
9925 Wood St., Chicago, IL 60643.
- Beverly Review. w. ISSN 0006-0410

**Beyond Baroque Foundation**
1639 W. Washington Blvd., Venice, CA 90291.
- Beyond Baroque (1976) irreg., 8-10 per yr.

**Beyond Our Control**
c/o Bob Richert, Ed., 526 N. Grant St., Bloomington, IN 47401.
- Beyond Our Control. irreg.

**Beyond Reality Magazine, Inc.**
303 W. 42nd St., New York, NY 10036.
- Beyond Reality; the latest discoveries in ESP, the occult & psychic phenomena. bi-m.

**Paul E. Bezanker, Ed. & Pub.**
180 Benton St., Box 14241, Hartford, CT 06114.
- Paul's Record Magazine. bi-m. ISSN 0360-2109

**Bhaktivedanta Book Trust**
3764 Watseka Ave, Los Angeles, CA 90034.
- Back to Godhead. 11 per yr. ISSN 0005-3643 (International Society for Krishna Consciousness)

**John Bialas, Ed. & Pub.**
221 Venetian Ave., Gulfport, MI 39501.
- Boogie; Gulf Coast's rock quarterly. q.

**Bible Advocate Press**
Box 33677, Denver, CO 80233.
- Bible Advocate. m. (General Conference of the Church of God)

**Bible Sabbath Association International**
Fairview, OK 73737.
- Sabbath Sentinel. m.

**Bible Science Association**
Box 1016, Caldwell, ID 83605.
- Bible Science Newsletter. m.

**Biblical Archaeology Society**
1737 H St. N.W., Washington, DC 20006.
- Biblical Archaeology Review. q. ISSN 0098-9444

**Biblical Evangelism Press**
11 Blvd. Motif, Brownsburg, IN 46112.
- Biblical Evangelist. m.

**Biblical Theology Bulletin**
40 North Main Ave, Albany, New York, NY 12203.
- Biblical Theology Bulletin. 3 per yr. ISSN 0045-1843

**Bibliographic Information Center for the Study of Political Science**
- Bibliographic Information Center for the Study of Political Science. Occasional Papers. (pub. by Blitz)

**Bibliographical Society of America**
Box 397, Grand Central Station, New York, NY 10017.
- Bibliographical Society of America. Papers. q. ISSN 0006-128X

**Bibliographical Society of the University of Virginia**
- Studies in Bibliography. (pub. by University Press of Virginia)

**Bibliography Newsletter**
c/o Terry Belanger, Ed., 21 Claremont Ave, New York, NY 10027.
- Bibliography Newsletter. m. ISSN 0145-3084

**Bibliography of Literature Relating to the Assassination of President John F. Kennedy**
c/o W. C. Thompson, 731 Riverside Drive, San Antonio, TX 78223.
- Bibliography of Literature Relating to the Assassination of President John F. Kennedy. irreg.

**Bibliotheca Islamica Booksellers**
Box 1536, Chicago, Minneapolis, IL 60690.
- Studies in Middle Eastern History. irreg., latest no. 3.
- Studies in Middle Eastern Literatures. irreg., no. 8, 1977.

**Biblos: Ukrainian Bibliography**
238 E. Sixth St., New York, NY 10003.
- Biblos: Ukrainian Bibliography. q.

**Bicentennial Publishing Corp.**
108 W. 39th St., 4th Fl., New York, NY 10018.
- New Horizon-Polish American Review. m.

**Bicycle Bibliography**
c/o David J. Luebberg, 507 South Fourth, Columbia, MO 65201.
- Bicycle Bibliography. a. ISSN 0098-1230

**Bien**
c/o Barbara R. Stribolt, 435 Duboce Ave., San Francisco, CA 94117.
- Bien; the only Danish weekly in the United States. w.

**Big Deal**
c/o Barbara Baracks, Ed., Box 830, Peter Stuyvesant Sta., New York, NY 10009.
- Big Deal. s-a.

**Big Deal Press**
709 So. Sycamore, North Platte, NE 69101.
- Chernozem. q.

**Big Farmer, Inc.**
131 Lincoln Hwy., Frankfort, IL 60423.
- Big Farmer. 10 per yr. ISSN 0006-2189

**Big Mama Rag**
1724 Gaylord, Denver, CO 80206.
- Big Mama Rag. m.

**Bigfoot Information Center**
777 Hood River, Hood River, OR 97031.
- Bigfoot News. m.

**Bill Communications, Inc.**
*see also* Hartman Communications, Inc. Rubber World

**Bill Communications Inc.**
633 Third Ave., New York, NY 10017.
- Incentive Marketing. m. ISSN 0019-3364
- Plastics Technology; machinery/materials systems for maximum productivity. m. ISSN 0032-1257
- Plastics Technology. Plastics Manufacturing Handbook and Buyers Guide. a.
- S M/Successful Meetings. m.
- Sales & Marketing Management. 16 per yr. ISSN 0361-2570
- Survey of Buying Power. a.

**Bill Communications Inc. Automotive Division**
77 N. Miller Rd., Box 5417, Akron, OH 44313
(Subscr. to: 144 E. 44th St., New York, NY 10017)
- Modern Tire Dealer; covering tire sales and car service. m. ISSN 0026-8496
- Modern Tire Dealer Products Catalog. a.

**Billboard Directories**
2160 Patterson Street, Cincinnati, OH 45214.
- Billboard International Tape Directory. a. ISSN 0090-645X

- Billboard's International Buyer's Guide of the Music, Record and Tape Industry. a. ISSN 0067-8600 (And 9000 Sunset Blvd., Los Angeles, CA 90069)
- Billboard's on Tour. a. ISSN 0361-5383 (And 9000 Sunset Blvd., Los Angeles, CA 90069)
- Billboard's Talent in Action. a. (And 9000 Sunset Blvd., Los Angeles, CA 90069)
- Campus Attractions; survey of college music industry. a. ISSN 0067-8597 (And 9000 Sunset Blvd., Los Angeles, CA 90069)
- International Studio and Equipment Directory. a. (And 9000 Sunset Blvd., Los Angeles, CA 90069)
- Protect. irreg. ISSN 0093-2256
- World of Country Music. a. ISSN 0084-2109 (And 9000 Sunset Blvd., Los Angeles, CA 90069)

**Billboard Publications Inc.**
9000 Sunset Blvd., Los Angeles, CA 90069.
- Billboard. w. ISSN 0006-2510
- Gift & Tableware Reporter. m. ISSN 0016-9846
- Gift and Tableware Reporter. Gift Guide; a buyers' guide. a. (And 1515 Broadway, 39th Floor, Astor Plaza, New York, NY 10036)
- World Radio & T.V. Handbook. a.

**Billboard Publications, Inc. Amusement Business Division**
1717 West End Ave., Nashville, TN 37203.
- Activity Programmers Sourcebook. a. ISSN 0362-5923 (National Entertainment Conference)
- Amusement Business; newsweekly for mass entertainment facility managers. w. ISSN 0003-2344
- Audarena Stadium Guide and International Directory. a. ISSN 0067-0537
- Buyers' Guide for the Mass Entertainment Industry. irreg. ISSN 0362-6180
- Carnival & Circus Booking Guide. a. ISSN 0090-2985
- Cavalcade and Directory of Acts & Attractions. a. ISSN 0090-2993
- Country Music Booking Guide. a.
- Directory of North American Fairs and Expositions. a. ISSN 0361-4255
- Funspot Directory. a. ISSN 0071-9951
- Ice Rink Directory & Hockey Buyer's Guide. a. ISSN 0084-1846
- Mass Entertainment Industry Buyers Guide. a.

**Billboard Publications, Inc. (New York)**
1515 Broadway, New York, NY 10036.
- Contract Interiors. m.
- Industrial Design; designing for industry. 6 per yr. ISSN 0019-8110
- Merchandising. m. (Circulation Department, Box 2157, Radnor PA 19089)
- Photo Information Almanac. irreg.
- Photo Weekly. w. ISSN 0031-8647
- Residential Interiors. bi-m.

**Billiard Congress of America**
1509 S. Prospect, Park Ridge, IL 60068.
- Billiard Congress of America. Bulletin. q.

**Billy Graham Evangelistic Association**
1300 Harmon Place, Minneapolis, MN 55403.
- Decision. m. ISSN 0011-7307

**Bio-Dynamic Farming and Gardening Association, Inc.**
c/o Ed. Heinz Grotzke, Bio-Dynamic Literature, Box 253, Wyoming, RI 02898.
- Bio-Dynamics; a periodical furthering soil conservation and increased fertility in order to improve nutrition and health. q. ISSN 0006-2863

**Bio-Feedback Technology Inc.**
1804 E. Ocean Blvd., Long Beach, CA 90802.
- Journal of Bio-Feedback. irreg. ISSN 0093-3597

**Biodynamica**
3837 Monona Drive, Madison, WI 53714.
- Biodynamica. irreg.2-3 per yr. ISSN 0006-3010

**Biofeedback Research Society**
4200 E. 9th Ave., Denver, CO 80220.
- Biofeedback Research Society. Proceedings of the Annual Meeting. a.

**Biological Photographic Association, Inc.**
Exec. Secy. Stanley J. McComb, Box 1057, Rochester, MN 55901.
- Biological Photographic Association. Journal; dedicated to the science, techniques and applications pertaining to the photography of all things which live or have lived. q. ISSN 0006-3215

**Biological Sciences Curriculum Study**
University of Colorado, Box 930, Boulder, CO 80306.
- B S C S Newsletter. 4 per yr. ISSN 0005-3295

**Biological Society of Nevada**
Box 167, Verdi, NV 89439.
- Biological Society of Nevada. Occasional Papers and Memoirs. irreg. ISSN 0084-7895

**Biological Society of Washington**
United States National Museum, Washington, DC 20560.
- Biological Society of Washington. Proceedings. irreg.(approx. 3 per yr.) ISSN 0006-324X

**Biological Stain Commission**
- Stain Technology. (pub. by Williams & Wilkins Co.)

**Biomedical Information Corp.**
919 Third Ave., New York, NY 10022.
- Drug Therapy. m. ISSN 0001-7094
- Drug Therapy (Hospital Edition) m.

**Biometric Society**
c/o Dr. Larry Nelson, Box 5962, Raleigh, NC 27607.
- Biometrics. q. ISSN 0006-341X

**Biophysical Society**
c/o Dr. Margaret O. Dayhoff, National Biomedical Research Foundation, Georgetown University Medical Center, 3900 Reservoir Rd. N.W., Washington, DC 20007.
- Biophysical Journal. (pub. by Rockefeller University Press)
- Biophysical Society. Abstracts. (pub. by Rockefeller University Press)
- Biophysical Society. Symposium Proceedings. irreg. ISSN 0520-1985

**BioSciences Information Service of Biological Abstracts**
2100 Arch St., Philadelphia, PA 19103.
- Abstracts of Entomology; all abstracts and references covering pure and applied studies involving insects and arachnids from Biological Abstracts and Bio Research Index. m. ISSN 0001-3579
- Abstracts of Mycology; all abstracts and references pertaining to fungi and lichens from Biological Abstracts and BioResearch Index. m. ISSN 0001-3617
- Abstracts on Health Effects of Environmental Pollutants. m. ISSN 0044-5819
- Annual Cumulative Index to Bioresearch Index. a.
- Biological Abstracts; references, abstracts, and indexes to the world's life sciences research literature. s-m. ISSN 0006-3169
- Bioresearch Index; references and indexes to the world's life sciences research literature. m. ISSN 0006-3541
- Bioresearch Today: Addiction. m.
- Bioresearch Today: Bio-Engineering & Instrumentation. m.
- Bioresearch Today: Birth Defects. m.
- Bioresearch Today: Cancer A-Cancerogenesis. m.
- Bioresearch Today: Cancer B-Anticancer Agents. m.
- Bioresearch Today: Cancer C-Immunology. m.
- Bioresearch Today: Food Additives & Residues. m.
- Bioresearch Today: Food Microbiology. m.
- Bioresearch Today: Human & Animal Aging. m.
- Bioresearch Today: Human and Animal Parasitology. m.
- Bioresearch Today: Human Ecology. m.
- Bioresearch Today: Industrial Health & Toxicology. m.
- Bioresearch Today: Pesticides. m.
- Bioresearch Today: Population, Fertility & Birth Control. m.
- Biosis: List of Serials. a. ISSN 0067-8937
- Guide to the Vocabulary of Biological Literature. a. ISSN 0090-5941

**Bird Effort Press**
25 Mudford Ave., Easthampton, NY 11937.
- Bird Effort. s-a.

**Birmingham Area Chamber of Commerce**
1914 Sixth Ave. N., Birmingham, AL 35203
(Subscr. address: Box 10127, Birmingham AL 35202)
- Birmingham. m. ISSN 0006-369X

**Birmingham Art Association**
2000 Eighth Ave., Birmingham, AL 35203.
- Birmingham Art Association. Newsletter. q.

**Birmingham Bar Association**
900 Jefferson County Court House, Birmingham, AL 35203.
- Birmingham Bar Association. Bulletin. m. ISSN 0006-3711

**Birmingham Education Association**
Robert E. Lee School, 630 18th St. S.W., Birmingham, AL 35211.
- B. E. A. Bulletin. m.(Sept.-June) ISSN 0005-3015

**Birmingham Publishing Co.**
130 S. 19th St., Birmingham, AL 35209.
- Cumberland Law Review. 3 per yr. ISSN 0360-8298 (Samford University)

**Birmingham World**
312 N. 17th St, Birmingham, AL 35203.
- Birmingham World. w. ISSN 0006-3754

**Birth and the Family Journal**
110 El Camino Real, Berkeley, CA 94705.
- Birth and the Family Journal. q. (Co-sponsors: American Society for Psychoprophylaxis in Obstetrics; International Childbirth Education Association)

**Bishop Museum**
*see* Bernice Pauahi Bishop Museum

**Bishop Museum Press**
Box 6037, Honolulu, HI 96818.
- Bernice P. Bishop Museum Bulletin. irreg. ISSN 0005-9439
- Bernice Pauahi Bishop Museum, Honolulu. Occasional Papers. irreg. ISSN 0067-6160
- Bernice Pauahi Bishop Museum, Honolulu. Special Publications. irreg. ISSN 0067-6179
- Insects of Micronesia. irreg. ISSN 0073-8115
- Pacific Anthropological Records. irreg. ISSN 0078-740X (Bernice Pauahi Bishop Museum. Department of Anthropology)

**Bits and Pieces**
c/o Mabel E. Brown, Box 746, Newcastle, WY 82701.
- Bits and Pieces. 4 per yr. ISSN 0006-3894

**Bitter Oleander Press**
310 Bradford Parkway, Syracuse, NY 13224.
- Bitter Oleander. 3 per yr.

**Bittersweet, Inc.**
Lebanon, MO 65536.
- Bittersweet. q.

**Bituminous Coal Research, Inc.**
350 Hochberg Rd., Monroeville, PA 15146.
- Mine Drainage Abstracts. a Bibliography. Supplement. a.
- Symposium on Coal Mine Drainage Research. Papers. biennial. ISSN 0085-7068 (Coal Industry Advisory Committee to the Ohio River Valley Water Sanitation Commission)

**Bitzaron, Inc.**
1141 Broadway, New York, NY 10001.
- Bitzaron; the Hebrew monthly of America. m. ISSN 0006-3932 (Hebrew Literary Foundation)

**Bix Beiderbecke Memorial Society**
2225 West 17th St., Davenport, IA 52804.
- Bixiana. irreg.

**Black Affairs**
Suite 1121, National Press Bldg., Washington, DC 20045.
- Black Affairs. bi-w.

**Black American Law Student Association**
P.O. Box 217, St. Louis, MO 63166.
- B A L S A Reports. q.

**Black Art**
137-55 Southgate St., Jamaica, NY 11413.
- Black Art; an international quarterly. q.

**Black Ascensions**
Room H-10-Circulation, 2900 Community College Ave., Cleveland, OH 44115.
- Black Ascensions. q.

**Black Book**
c/o J. Garmhousen, Ed., Department of English, Bowling Green State University, Bowling Green, OH 43403.
- Black Book. q.

**Black Box**
Box 4174, Washington, DC 20015.
- Black Box; an American magazine of poetry and its analogs. 6 per yr. (Watershed Foundation)

**Black Business Digest**
3133 N. Broad St., Philadelphia, PA 19132.
- Black Business Digest. m. ISSN 0006-4114

**Black Child Development Institute**
1463 Rhode Island Ave. N.W., Washington, DC 20005.
- Black Child Advocates. 10 per yr.

**Black Collegiate Services, Inc.**
3217 Melpomene Ave., New Orleans, LA 70125.
- Black Collegian; a magazine of black college students. bi-m. (during school year) ISSN 0045-2122

**Black Cultural Center of Trenton, Inc.**
194 Brunswick Ave., P.O. Box 1265, Trenton, NJ 08618.
- Thoughts on Blackness. a. ISSN 0082-4259

**Black Diamond Co., Inc.**
343 S. Dearborn St., Chicago, IL 60604.
- Black Diamond. m. ISSN 0006-4149

**Black Economic Research Center**
112 W. 120th St., New York, NY 10027.
- Black Economic Research Center. Occasional Paper. irreg.
- Review of Black Political Economy. (pub. by Transaction Periodicals Consortium)

**Black Ecumenical Commission of Massachusetts**
14 Beacon St., Boston, MA 02108.
- Black Church. q. ISSN 0360-3741

**Black Employees of the Library of Congress**
Christ Child Settlement House, 608 Massachusetts Ave. N.E., Washington, DC 20002.
- F. R. E. E. D. Newsletter. (Fighting Racism to End Evil Discrimination) bi-m.

**Black Forum Magazine**
Box 1090, Bronx, NY 10451.
- Black Forum. 4 per yr.

**Black Graphics International**
Ed. Aaron Ibn Pori Pitts, Box 732, Detroit, MI 48206.
- Black Graphics International; a journal of revolutionary literature & art. q. ISSN 0045-2165

**Black Hills Genealogy Club**
Box 372, Rapid City, SD 57701.
- Dakota Territory. q. ISSN 0045-9518

**Black Hills State College. Journalism Graphics Department**
1200 University Ave, Spearfish, SD 57783.
- Black Hills State TODAY. s-m.

**Black History Museum**
P.O. Box 15057, Philadelphia, PA 19130.
- Black History Museum. Newsletter. a.

**Black Jack**
c/o Art Cuelho, Ed., Box 214, Big Timber, MT 59011.
- Black Jack. irreg., no. 5, 1977.

**Black-Jewish Information Center. Media Project**
16 E. 85th St., New York, NY 10028.
- Black-Jewish Information Center. Media Project. (Release) w.

**Black List**
Box 3552, New York City, NY 10017.
- Black List; the concise and comprehensive reference guide to black journalism, radio and television, educational and cultural organizations in the USA, Africa and the Caribbean. a.

**Black Maria Collective, Inc.**
815 W. Wrightwood Ave., Chicago, IL 60614.
- Black Maria. 4 per yr. ISSN 0045-222X

**Black News**
10 Claver Place, Brooklyn, NY 11238.
- Black News. m. ISSN 0006-4203

**Black Panther Party**
8507 E. 14th St., Oakland, CA 94621.
- Black Panther. w.

**Black Photographers Annual Inc.**
55 Hicks St., Brooklyn, NY 11201
(Subscr. to: Light Impressions Corp., P.O. Box 3012, Rochester, NY 14614)
- Black Photographers Annual. a. ISSN 0090-7197

**Black Powder Times**
Box 842, Mt. Vernon, WA 98273.
- Black Powder Times. m.

**Black Secretariat Archdiocese of Detroit**
305 Michigan Ave, Detroit, MI 48226.
- For My People. m.

**Black Silent Majority Committee**
53 D Street S.E., Washington, DC 20003.
- National Crusades Monthly.

**Black Sparrow Press**
Box 3993, Santa Barbara, CA 93105.
- Sparrow. m.

**Black Stone Press**
190 S. Third West, Missoula, MT 59801.
- Montana Gothic. 3 per yr.

**Black Times Publishing Corp.**
Box 1609, Palo Alto, CA 94302.
- Black Times: Voices of the National Community. m. ISSN 0006-4289

**Black Warrior Review**
Box 2936, University, AL 35486.
- Black Warrior Review. s-a. (University of Alabama)

**Black Women's Community Development Foundation**
1028 Connecticut Ave. N.W., Washington, DC 20036.
- Binding-Ties. irreg.

**Black World Foundation**
Box 908, Sausalito, CA 94965.
- Black Scholar; journal of black studies and research. 10 per yr. ISSN 0006-4246

**Blackberry**
Box 186, Brunswick, ME 04011.
- Blackberry. 2-3 per yr.

**Blackberry (Albuquerque)**
Box 4757, Albuquerque, NM 87106.
- Blackberry (Albuquerque) 3 per yr.

**Blackbird Press**
1933 Riverside Dr., Sidney, OH 45365.
- Blackbird Circle. irreg.

**Black's Guide to the Office Space Market**
Box 266, Monmouth Beach, NJ 07750.
- Black's Guide to the Office Space Market. a.

**Blackwent Publishing Co.**
1605 Cahuenga Blvd., Los Angeles, CA 90028.
- I. F. T. Journal. bi-m. ISSN 0095-1021 (International Foundation for Telemetering)

**Blaisdell Family National Association**
c/o Ed. Sarah Yates Bird, 24 Parkway Lane, Bradford, PA 16701.
- Blaisdell Papers. s-a. ISSN 0006-4521

**Blaisdell Institute for Advanced Study of World Cultures and Religions**
143 E. Tenth St., Claremont, CA 91711.
- Blaisdell Institute. Journal. s-a.

**Blake Enterprises, Inc.**
4213 Princess Place Drive, Wilmington, NC 28401.
- Graphic Antiquarian; the magazine for collectors of photographica. q. ISSN 0017-3274

**William F. Bland Co.**
Box 1421, Stamford, CT 06904.
- International Oil News; weekly news service covering the international oil and gas industry-production, exploration, transportation, processing, marketing. w. ISSN 0043-8855

• PetroChemical News; a weekly news service devoted to the petrochemical industry. w. ISSN 0031-6342

**Bleb Press**
Box 322, Times Square Sta., New York, NY 10036.
• Bleb. 2 per yr. ISSN 0006-467X

**Blessed Sacrament Fathers**
194 E. 76th St., New York, NY 10021.
• Emmanuel. m.(Sept.-June); bi-m.(July-Aug.) ISSN 0013-6719 (Priests' Eucharistic League)
• Eucharist; the magazine of the Blessed Sacrament Fathers and Brothers. bi-m. ISSN 0014-2271

**Blest Co.**
6306 Clayton Rd., St. Louis, MO 63117.
• St. Louisan. m.

**Blewett Co., Inc.**
P.O. Box 84, Columbus, MS 39701.
• Alabama Genealogical Register. q.

**Blinded Veterans Association**
1735 DeSales St., N.W., Washington, DC 20036.
• B V A Bulletin. 6 per yr. ISSN 0005-3430

**Bliss & Laughlin Industries**
122 W. 22nd St., Oak Brook, IL 60521.
• Top Drawer. q.

**Blitz**
15 Second North, Seattle, WA 98109.
• Bibliographic Information Center for the Study of Political Science. Occasional Papers. irreg.

**Blonder-Tongue Labs, Inc.**
1 Jake Brown Rd., Old Bridge, NJ 08857.
• Amplifier; new approaches in television problem solving from Blonder-Tongue. bi-m.

**Blood Information Service**
508 Getzville Rd., Buffalo, NY 14226.
• Current Literature of Blood. w. ISSN 0001-7108
• Overview of Blood. irreg., approx. biennial.

**Bloom & Co., Inc.**
1020 Broad St., Newark, NJ 07102.
• American Jewish Ledger. m.

**Bloomfield Public Library**
90 Broad Street, Bloomfield, NJ 07003.
• Bloomfield Public Library Highlights. bi-m.

**Bloomington Independent Publishing Co.**
Box 29, Bloomington, IN 47401.
• Common Sense. s-m. ISSN 0010-3306

**Blue Anchor, Inc.**
730 Howe Ave., Box 15498, Sacramento, CA 95813.
• Blue Anchor. q. ISSN 0006-5021

**Blue Army of Our Lady of Fatima in U.S. and Canada**
• Soul. (pub. by Ave Maria Institute Press)

**Blue Cross Association**
840 N. Lake Shore Dr., Chicago, IL 60611.
• Blue Cross Association. Research Series; review of research and statistics in the health field. irreg., 1974, vol. 12.
• Blue Print for Health. a.
• Inquiry; a journal of medical care organization, provision and financing. q. ISSN 0046-9580
• Selected Studies in Medical Care and Medical Economics; annual. a. ISSN 0361-3046 (Co-Sponsor: National Association of Blue Shield Plans)

**Blue Cross of Wisconsin**
4115 N. Teutonia Ave., Milwaukee, WI 53201.
• Spotlight (Milwaukee) m.

**Blue-J, Inc.**
Box 5377, Ft. Wayne, IN 46805.
• Bowhunter. bi-m.

**Blue Pig**
c/o David Ball, Ed., 108 South St., Northampton, MA 01060.
• Blue Pig. irreg.

**Blue Rose Ministry**
Box 622, Joshua Tree, CA 92252.
• Solar Space-Letter; solar scan, rose garden. m.

**Blue Sky**
Box 1773, Boulder, CO 80302.
• Blue Sky. bi-m.

**Blueberry Hill Publishing Co.**
Box 24170, St. Louis, MO 63130.
• Top Tens and Trivia of Rock and Roll and Rhythm and Blues. Annual Supplement. a.

**Bluebonnets and Silver Shoes of Texas**
Rte. 5, Box 20, Brownwood, TX 76801.
• Bluebonnets and Silver Shoes of Texas. bi-m.

**Bluegrass Unlimited Inc.**
Box 111, Broad Run, VA 22014.
• Bluegrass Unlimited. m. ISSN 0006-5137

**B'nai B'rith**
1640 Rhode Island Ave., N.W., Washington, DC 20036.
• National Jewish Monthly. m. ISSN 0027-9552

**B'nai B'rith. Career and Counseling Services**
1640 Rhode Island Ave., N.W., Washington, DC 20036.
• Counselor's Information Service. q. ISSN 0011-0043

**B'nai B'rith Hillel Foundation**
1521 University Ave. S.E., Minneapolis, MN 55414.
• Nivim; University of Minnesota journal of unlimited Jewish expression. irreg.

**B'nai B'rith Hillel Foundation at Brooklyn College**
2901 Campus Rd., Brooklyn, NY 11210.
• Hillel Gate. m.(during school year) ISSN 0018-1862

**Bnai B'rith Messenger, Inc.**
2510 W. 7th St., Los Angeles, CA 90057.
• B'nai B'rith Messenger. w. ISSN 0006-5277

**B'nai B'rith. Metropolitan Conference**
315 Lexington Ave., New York, NY 10016.
• Metropolitan Star. m. ISSN 0026-1580

**B'nai B'rith Women**
1640 Rhode Island Ave. N.W., Washington, DC 20036.
• Women's World. 6 per yr. ISSN 0043-759X

**B'nai B'rith Youth Commission**
1640 Rhode Island Ave. N.W., Washington, DC 20009.
• Shofar. 8 per yr.

**Board of Jewish Education, Inc.**
426 W. 58th St., New York, NY 10019.
• Up-to-Date with B J E. m(except July & Aug.)
• World Over. bi-w. ISSN 0043-8820

**Board of Jewish Education of Greater New York**
426 W. 58th St., New York, NY 10019.
• Principal. m (10 per yr) (Association of Yeshivah-Day School Principals of General Studies)

**Board of Jewish Education of Greater New York. Department of Art**
426 W. 58th St, New York, NY 10019.
• Brush and Color. irreg. (2-3 per yr.)

**Boardroom Reports, Inc.**
11 W. 42nd St., New York, NY 10036.
• Boardroom Reports. s-m. ISSN 0045-2300

**Boardwalk Publications**
509 N. Fairfax, Suite 212, Los Angeles, CA 90036.
• Coast. m.

**Boast**
R.R. 4, 1142 S. 96th Ave., Zeeland, MI 49464.
• Boast. 17 per yr.

**Boat Owners Association of the United States**
880 S. Pickett St., Alexandria, VA 22304.
• Boat: U S Reports; at your service. m.

**Boating Industry Association**
401 North Michigan, Chicago, IL 60611.
• B I A Certification Handbook. a. ISSN 0067-9402

**Boating Publications, Inc.**
320 Springbrook, Adrian, MI 48107.
• Lakeland Boating; Mid-America's freshwater yachting magazine. m. ISSN 0023-7345

**Boats & Harbors**
Crossville, TN 38555.
• Boats & Harbors. 36 per yr.

**Bob Jones University**
Greenville, SC 29614.
• Biblical Viewpoint. s-a. ISSN 0006-0925
• Faith for the Family. 10 per yr.

**Bobbin Publications, Inc.**
Box 527, Columbia, SC 29202.
• Bobbin. m. ISSN 0006-5412
• Bobina. bi-m.

**Bobbs-Merrill Co., Inc.**
4300 West 62 St., Indianapolis, IN 46206.
• Advanced Study in Political Science. irreg.
• American History Landmarks. irreg.
• Bobbs-Merrill Philosophy Texts and Commentary Series. irreg.
• Bobbs-Merrill Policy Analysis Series. irreg.
• Bobbs-Merrill Series in Composition and Rhetoric. irreg.
• Bobbs-Merrill Series in Speech Communication. irreg. ISSN 0523-7874
• Bobbs-Merrill Shakespeare Series. irreg.
• Bobbs-Merrill Shaw Series. irreg.
• Bobbs-Merrill Studies in Communicative Disorders. irreg.
• Bobbs-Merrill Studies in Sociology. irreg.
• Contemporary Legal Education Series. irreg.
• Journal of Popular Culture. q. ISSN 0022-3840 (Modern Language Association of America, Popular Literature Section)
• Political Science Annual; an international review. a. ISSN 0079-3043

**Bobit Publishing Co.**
1155 Waukegan Rd, Glenview, IL 60025.
• Automotive Fleet. m. ISSN 0005-1519
• Career Education News. s-m.
• Curriculum Product Review. m.(7 per yr.)
• Metro (Glenview) bi-m.
• School Bus Fleet. bi-m. ISSN 0036-6501
• Truck Stop Management. bi-m.

**Boca Raton Historical Society**
P.O. Box 1113, Boca Raton, FL 33432.
• Spanish River Papers. s-a.

**Boccherini's Minuet**
P.O. Box 1064, Quincy, IL 62301.
• Boccherini's Minuet. q.

**Bodine Electric Co.**
2500 W. Bradley Place, Chicago, IL 60618.
• Bodine Motorgram. bi-m. ISSN 0006-5498

**Henning C. Boe, Ed. & Pub.**
2040 N.W. Market St., Seattle, WA 98107.
• Western Viking. w.

**Alfred G. Boerger, Ed. & Pub.**
P.O. Box 23822, Ft. Lauderdale, FL 33307.
• Handbook on U. S. Luminescent Stamps. irreg.(approx. every 2-3 years) ISSN 0072-9981

**Bogden and Quigley, Inc.**
18 Davis Dr., Belmont, CA 94002.
• B & Q General Chemistry Separates. irreg.

**Bohemian Freethinking School Society**
Box 87, Berwyn, IL 60402.
• Svobodna Skola/Free Thinking School. bi-m.

**Bohman Industrial Traffic Consultants, Inc. 335 E. Broadway**
Gardner, MA 01440.
• Furniture Transporter. m.

**Boian News Service**
300 E. 91st St., New York, NY 10028.
• Boian News Service; Romanian news and world report. w. ISSN 0045-2351

**Boink**
Ed. Dean Faulwell, 2403 Milvia, Berkeley, CA 94704.
• Boink. q.

**Boise State University. Department of English**
1910 College Blvd., Boise, ID 83707.
• Cold-Drill. a. ISSN 0084-8816
• Western Writers Series. 2-5 per yr.

**Bombay Duck**
3035 Fillmore, San Francisco, CA 94123.
• Bombay Duck. irreg.

**Bombshelter Press**
1092 Loma Dr., Hermosa Beach, CA 90254.
- Alley Cat Readings. 4 per yr.

**Bon Appetit**
Box 2428, Boulder, CO 80302.
- Bon Appetit. m.

**Bon Appetit (Kansas City)**
4700 Belleview, Kansas City, MO 64112.
- Bon Appetit (Kansas City) bi-m. ISSN 0006-6990

**Bond Buyer**
1 State St. Plaza, New York, NY 10004.
- Bond Buyer. d. (5 per wk) & w.
- Directory of Municipal Bond Dealers of the United States. s-a.
- Money Manager. w.

**Bond Wheelwright Co.**
Porter's Landing, Freeport, ME 04032.
- Maine Heritage Series. irreg. ISSN 0076-2652 (Maine State Museum)

**Bonnell Publications, Inc.**
437 E. Fifth St., Plainfield, NJ 07060.
- Packing and Shipping; the industrial packaging digest in packing, handling and distribution by air, land and sea. m. ISSN 0030-9176

**Howard T. Bonnett, Ed. and Pub.**
314 E. Glenwood Road, Lake Forest, IL 60045.
- Bonnet-t-e's and Kin. q.

**Bonsai Press--Jama Press**
341 South Marina, No. 1, Prescott, AZ 86301.
- Bonsai; a quarterly of Haiku. q.

**Bonsai Society of Greater New York, Inc.**
P.O. Box 343, New Hyde Park, NY 11040.
- Bonsai Bulletin. q. ISSN 0006-7180

**Book Associates, Inc.**
Box 837, Acton, MA 01720.
- Comprehensive Therapy. m. ISSN 0098-8243 (American Society of Contemporary Medicine and Surgery)

**Book Club of California**
545 Sutter St., San Francisco, CA 94102.
- Book Club of California Quarterly News Letter. q. ISSN 0006-7202

**Book Collectors of America**
- Book Shopper Newsletter. (pub. by River City Enterprises, Inc.)

**Book Digest Company, Inc.**
730 Fifth Ave., New York, NY 10019.
- Book Digest. m.

**Book News, Inc.**
303 W. 10th St., New York, NY 10014.
- Judaica Book News. s-a. ISSN 0022-5754

**Book-Of-The-Month Club**
280 Park Ave., New York, NY 10017.
- Book-Of-The-Month Club News. 15 per yr. ISSN 0006-730X
- Dolphin; book club news. m. ISSN 0012-5261

**Booklegger Press**
555 29th St, San Francisco, CA 94131.
- Booklegger. q. ISSN 0092-7686

**Booklet Pane Society**
P.O. Box 222, Forest Hills, NY 11375.
- Booklet. 3-4 per yr.

**Books About Birds**
c/o Jessie Kitching, Ed., Box 106, Kew Gardens, Jamaica, NY 11415.
- Books About Birds. 10 per yr.

**Books & Friends**
Box 292, Riverdale, MD 20840.
- Sounds Fine; the rock collector's market place. m.

**Books for Libraries, Inc.**
1 Dupont St., Plainview, NY 11803.
- Select Bibliographies Reprint Series. irreg.

**Books International of DH-TE International, Inc.**
P.O. Box 14487, St. Louis, MO 63178
(and P.O. Box 7403, Washington, D.C. 20044)
- Nonaligned Third World Annual; the politics of ideas. a. with irregular supplements. ISSN 0078-1002

**Bookswest Magazine**
2073 Outpost Dr., Hollywood, CA 90068.
- Bookswest. m.

**Bookworm**
7 West St., Box 76, Rockport, ME 04856.
- Bookworm. m. ISSN 0018-294X

**Boone, Inc**
Drawer 2, Tuscaloosa, AL 35401.
- Antique Monthly; the nation's antique newspaper. m. ISSN 0003-5882
- Gray Letter; the every-week "insider's" report serving the fine antiques community. w.

**Joseph Boonin, Inc.**
Box 2124, South Hackensack, NJ 07606.
- A S U C Journal of Music Scores. 2-3 per yr. (American Society of University Composers)
- Music Indexes and Bibliographies. irreg., no. 11, 1974. ISSN 0077-2429

**Boosey and Hawkes, Inc.**
30 W. 57th St., New York, NY 10019.
- Boosey and Hawkes. Newsletter. 3 per yr. ISSN 0006-7598

**Boot and Shoe Workers' Union(AFL-CIO)**
1265 Boylston St., Boston, MA 02215.
- Shoe Workers' Journal. bi-m. ISSN 0037-4075

**Border-Mountain Press**
Box 1296, Benson, AZ 85602.
- Quester. q.

**Borneo Research Council**
Dept. of Anthropology, College of William & Mary, Williamsburg, VA 23185.
- Borneo Research Bulletin. s-a. ISSN 0006-7806

**Ed Bosin, Jr., Ed. & Pub.**
Box 6132, Cherry Creek Sta., Denver, CO 80206.
- Thoroughbred Mid-America. m. ISSN 0027-2531

**Boston. School Department**
15 Beacon St., Boston, MA 02108.
- Boston Public Schools Review. 3-5 per yr. ISSN 0006-8004

**Boston & Maine Railroad**
Box 302, Reading, MA 01867.
- B & M Bulletin. q.

**Boston Architectural Center**
320 Newberry, Boston, MA 02116.
- Boston Architectural Center Conference. Proceedings. irreg.

**Boston Board of Fire Underwriters, Inc.**
89 Broad St., Boston, MA 02110.
- Along the Boardwalk. m. ISSN 0002-6328

**Boston Children's Medical Center**
- Boston Children's Medical Center. Publications for Parents. (pub. by Delacorte Press)

**Boston City Record**
Room 623, City Hall, Boston, MA 02201.
- Boston City Record. w. ISSN 0006-7946

**Boston College**
McElroy 116, Chestnut Hill, MA 02167.
- Aquila. (pub. by Martinus Nijhoff NE)
- Boston College Studies in Philosophy. (pub. by Martinus Nijhoff NE)
- Stylus (Chestnut Hill) q. ISSN 0039-4270

**Boston College. Graduate School of Social Work**
Chestnut Hill, MA 02167.
- Urban and Social Change Review. s-a. ISSN 0042-0832

**Boston College. Law School**
885 Centre St., Newton Centre, MA 02159.
- Annual Survey of Massachusetts Law. a. ISSN 0570-2674
- Boston College Industrial and Commercial Law Review. 6 per yr. ISSN 0006-7954
- Environmental Affairs. q. ISSN 0046-2225

**Boston College. Peripatology Program**
Boston, MA 02167.
- Long Cane News Letter. 3 per yr. ISSN 0024-6220 (Co-Sponsor: Western Michigan University Department of Blind Rehabilitation)

**Boston Critic Inc.**
77 Sacramento St., Somerville, MA 02143.
- New Boston Review. q.

**Boston Daughters of Bilitis**
O C B C, 1151 Massachusetts, Cambridge, MA 02138.
- Focus (Boston); a journal for gay women. m.

**Boston Eagle**
c/o Lee Harwood, Ed., Box 257, Peter Stuyvesant Sta., New York, NY 10003.
- Boston Eagle. 2-3 per yr.

**Boston Marine Guide Publishing, Inc.**
88 Broad St., Boston, MA 02110.
- Boston Marine Guide. w.

**Boston Museum of Fine Arts**
Huntington Ave., Boston, MA 02115.
- Boston Museum Bulletin. s-a. ISSN 0006-7997
- Boston Museum of Fine Arts. Museum Year. Annual Reports. (pub. by New York Graphic Society)

**Boston Phoenix**
c/o Stephen M. Mindich, 1100 Massachusetts Ave., Boston, MA 02115.
- Boston Phoenix. w.

**Boston Society for Gerontologic Psychiatry, Inc.**
- Boston Society for Gerontologic Psychiatry. Scientific Meetings, Proceedings. (pub. by International Universities Press Inc.)
- Journal of Geriatric Psychiatry. (pub. by International Universities Press Inc)

**Boston Street Railway Association**
Box 102, Cambridge, MA 02138.
- Roll Sign. 6 per yr. ISSN 0035-7898

**Boston Symphony Orchestra**
Program Office, Symphony Hall, Boston, MA 02115.
- Boston Symphony Orchestra Monthly Magazine. m.

**Boston Technical Publishers, Inc.**
728 Dedham St., Newton, MA 02159.
- Instant Information. m.

**Boston University**
765 Commonwealth Ave., Boston, MA 02215.
- Alcheringa. (pub. by Boston University Scholarly Publications)
- Arion. (pub. by Boston University Scholarly Publications)
- Boston University Journal. (pub. by Boston University Scholarly Publications)
- Journal of Education. q. ISSN 0022-0574
- Studies in Romanticism. (pub. by Boston University Scholarly Publications)

**Boston University. African Studies Center**
- International Journal of African Historical Studies. (pub. by Africana Publishing Co.)

**Boston University. African Studies Library**
771 Commonwealth Ave., Boston, MA 02215.
- Africana Libraries Newsletter. bi-m. (African Studies Association. Archives-Libraries Committee)

**Boston University. College of Basic Studies**
Commonwealth Ave., Boston, MA 02215.
- Perspectives. 3 per yr. ISSN 0031-5958

**Boston University Medical Center**
- P S R O Update. (pub. by United Media International, Inc.)

**Boston University Scholarly Publications**
775 Commonwealth Ave., Boston, MA 02215.
- Alcheringa; ethnopoetics. s-a. ISSN 0044-7218 (Boston University)
- Arion; a journal of humanities and the classics. q. ISSN 0004-1351 (Boston University)
- Boston University Journal; triquarterly of public affairs, literature, and the arts. 3 per yr. ISSN 0006-8039
- Journal of Field Archaeology. q. ISSN 0093-4690 (Association for Field Archaeology)
- Studies in Romanticism. q. ISSN 0039-3762 (Boston University)

**Boston University School of Law**
765 Commonwealth Ave., Boston, MA 02215.
• Boston University Law Review. 5 per yr. ISSN 0006-8047

**Boston University. School of Public Communication**
128 Bay State Rd., Boston, MA 02215.
• C R C Report Series. (Communication Research Center) irreg.

**Boston Wesleyan Association**
581 Boylston St., Boston, MA 02116.
• Zion's Herald (1976); New England United Methodist newspaper. 10 per yr.

**Boston Women's Collective, Inc.**
490 Beacon St., Boston, MA 02115.
• Women's Yellow Pages; original sourcebook for women. a., 2nd 1974.

**Bostonian Society**
Old State House, 206 Washington Street, Boston, MA 02109.
• Bostonian Society. Proceedings. a.

**Bostwick Press**
University of Richmond, Box 15, Richmond, VA 23173.
• Bostwick Paper. irreg., 1972, no. 2. ISSN 0068-0354

**Botanical Society of America, Inc.**
c/o New York Botanical Garden, Bronx, NY 10458
• American Journal of Botany; devoted to all branches of plant sciences. 10 per yr.(May-June and Nov-Dec issues combined) ISSN 0002-9122 (Orders: c/o Richard A. Popham, Department of Botany, Ohio State University, 1735 Neil Ave., Columbus, OH 43210)
• Botanical Society of America. Yearbook. biennial. ISSN 0068-0400
• Botany as a Profession. irreg.; latest issue, 1972. ISSN 0068-0397
• Guide to Graduate Study in Botany for the United States and Canada. irreg., latest edt. 1976. ISSN 0072-8500
• Plant Science Bulletin. q. ISSN 0032-0919 (Orders: c/o Richard M. Klein, Ed., University of Vermont, Burlington, VT 05401)

**Robert M. Bottorff, Ed. & Pub.**
Box 739, Camden, NJ 08102.
• Popular Periodical Index. s-a. ISSN 0092-9727

**Boulder Valley Education Association**
5595 Arapahoe, Boulder, CO 80303.
• B V E A Reporter. m. ISSN 0005-3449

**Boulevard Publications**
1755 Northwest Blvd., Columbus, OH 43212.
• Ideas for Better Living. m.

**Boumi Temple A.A.O.N.M.S. Oasis of Baltimore**
4900 Charles St., Baltimore, MD 21210.
• Boumi Temple News. m. ISSN 0006-8306

**Bowdoin College. Hawthorne-Longfellow Library**
Brunswick, ME 04011.
• Nathaniel Hawthorne Society. Newsletter. s-a.

**Bowdoin College. Museum of Art**
Brunswick, ME 04011.
• Bowdoin College. Museum of Art. Occasional Papers. a. ISSN 0084-7992

**Bowers and Ruddy Galleries, Inc.**
6922 Hollywood Blvd., Los Angeles, CA 90028.
• Rare Coin Review. q.

**R. R. Bowker Company**
1180 Ave. of the Americas, New York, NY 10036
(Orders to: Box 1807, Ann Arbor, MI 48106)
• A S C A P Symphonic Catalog. irreg., 3rd edt. 1977. ISSN 0145-5265 (American Society of Composers, Authors and Publishers)
• American Book Publishing Record/B P R; arranged by subject according to the Dewey Decimal Classification and indexed by author and title. m. ISSN 0002-7707 (Orders to: Subscription Service Dept., Box 67, Whitinsville, MA 01588)
• Audiovisual Market Place; A Multimedia Guide. a. since 1976; previously biennial. ISSN 0067-0553
• Books for Secondary School Libraries. irreg., 5th edt. 1976. ISSN 0068-0184
• Books in Print. a. ISSN 0068-0214

• Books in Series in the United States; original, reprinted, in-print, and out-of-print books, published or distributed in the U.S., in popular, scholarly, and professional series. biennial, with supplements in alternate years. ISSN 0000-0515
• Bookviews. m.
• Bowker Annual; of library and book trade information. a. ISSN 0068-0540
• Bowker Series in Problem-Centered Approaches to Librarianship. irreg.
• Bowker's Medical Books in Print. a. ISSN 0076-5929
• Business Books and Serials in Print. irreg., 3rd edt. 1977. ISSN 0146-5953
• Children's Books in Print. a. ISSN 0069-3480
• Contemporary Crafts Market Place. irreg. ISSN 0095-2710 (American Crafts Council)
• Directory of Library Consultants. irreg.
• Early Childhood Education Directory. irreg. ISSN 0070-7848
• Educational Media Yearbook. a. ISSN 0000-037X
• El Hi Textbooks in Print; including related teaching materials. a. ISSN 0070-9565
• Encyclopedia Buying Guide. biennial. ISSN 0361-1094
• Feature Films on 8mm and 16mm. irreg., 5th edt., 1977. ISSN 0071-4100
• Foreign Affairs Bibliography. irreg., 1976 covers 1962-1972. ISSN 0071-7290
• Forthcoming Books. bi-m.(issues cumulate) ISSN 0015-8119 (Orders to: Subscription Service Dept., Box 67, Whitinsville, MA 01588)
• International Literary Market Place. a. ISSN 0074-6827
• Irregular Serials and Annuals: An International Directory. biennial. ISSN 0000-0043
• L J/S L J Hot Line. (Library Journal/School Library Journal) w.(except during summer) ISSN 0000-0078 (Orders to: Subscription Service Dept., Box 67, Whitinsville, MA 01588)
• L J Special Report. irreg. ISSN 0362-448X
• Library Journal. s-m.(Sept-June); m.(July-Aug) ISSN 0000-0027 (Orders to: Subscription Service Dept., Box 67, Whitinsville, MA 01588)
• Library Journal Book Review. irreg., latest issue 1976. ISSN 0075-9082
• Library Trustee; a Practical Guide. irreg.
• Libros en Venta. irreg., 2nd edt. 1974. ISSN 0075-918X
• Libros en Venta. Supplement. irreg., latest edt. 1976 for 1974. ISSN 0075-9198
• Literary and Library Prizes. triennial. ISSN 0075-9880
• Literary Market Place; with names and numbers. a. ISSN 0075-9899
• North American Film and Video Directory; a guide to media collections and services. every 2-3 yrs. ISSN 0362-7802
• Paperbound Book Guide for Colleges. a. ISSN 0078-902X
• Paperbound Books in Print. base vol. plus two supplements annually. ISSN 0031-1235 (Orders to: Subscription Service Dept., Box 67, Whitinsville, MA 01588)
• Photography Market Place. irreg. ISSN 0095-439X
• Previews; news and reviews of non-print media. m. (Sept.-May) ISSN 0000-0051 (Orders to: Subscription Service Dept., Box 67, Whitinsville, MA 01588)
• Publishers' Trade List Annual. a. ISSN 0079-7855
• Publishers Weekly; the book industry journal. w. ISSN 0000-0019 (Orders to: Subscription Service Dept., Box 67, Whitinsville, MA 01588)
• School Library Journal; the magazine for children's, young adult and school librarians. m.(Sept-May) ISSN 0000-0035 (Orders to: Subscription Service Dept., Box 67, Whitinsville, MA 01588)
• Scientific and Technical Books in Print. a. ISSN 0000-0248
• Subject Collections; a guide to special book collections and subject emphasis in libraries. irreg., 5th edt. 1975. ISSN 0000-0140
• Subject Guide to Books in Print. a. ISSN 0000-0159
• Subject Guide to Children's Books in Print. a. ISSN 0000-0167
• Subject Guide to Forthcoming Books; a bi-monthly subject forecast of books to come. bi-m.(issues cumulate) ISSN 0000-0264 (Orders to: Subscription Service Dept., Box 67, Whitinsville, MA 01588)
• Ulrich's International Periodicals Directory. biennial. ISSN 0000-0175
• Ulrich's Quarterly. q. ISSN 0000-0507

• Weekly Record (New York) w. ISSN 0094-257X (Orders to: Subscription Service Department, Box 67, Whitinsville, MA 01588)

**R. R. Bowker Company. Jaques Cattell Press**
Box 25001, Tempe, AZ 85282
(Orders to: Box 1807, Ann Arbor, MI 48106)
• American Architects Directory. irreg., 3rd edt. 1970. ISSN 0065-695X (American Institute of Architects)
• American Art Directory. triennial. ISSN 0065-6968 (American Federation of Arts)
• American Book Trade Directory. biennial. ISSN 0065-759X
• American Library Directory. biennial. ISSN 0065-910X
• American Library Directory Updating Service. bi-m. ISSN 0002-9793
• American Men and Women of Science. Agricultural, Animal and Veterinary Sciences. irreg. ISSN 0094-5110
• American Men and Women of Science. Economics. irreg. ISSN 0094-5315
• American Men and Women of Science. Medical and Health Sciences. irreg.
• American Men and Women of Science. Physical and Biological Sciences. irreg., 13th edt. 1977. ISSN 0065-9347
• American Men and Women of Science. Social and Behavioral Sciences. irreg., 13th edt. 1977. ISSN 0065-9363
• American Psychiatric Association. Biographical Directory. irreg., 7th edt. 1977. ISSN 0065-9827
• Directory of American Scholars. irreg., 6th edt. 1974. ISSN 0070-5101 (American Council of Learned Societies)
• Industrial Research Laboratories of the U. S. irreg., 15th edt., 1977. ISSN 0073-7623
• Leaders in Education. irreg., 5th edt. 1974. ISSN 0075-8299
• Who's Who in American Art. triennial. ISSN 0000-0191 (American Federation of Arts)
• Who's Who in American Politics. biennial. ISSN 0000-0205

**Bowling Green Popular Press**
Bowling Green State University, 101 University Hall, Bowling Green, OH 43403.
• Journal of Popular Film. q. ISSN 0047-2719 (Center for the Study of Popular Culture)

**Bowling Green State University. Center for Communications Research**
322 South Hall, Bowling Green, OH 43403.
• Empirical Research in Theatre. a. (Co-Sponsor: Speech Communication Association, Theatre Division)

**Bowling Green State University. Creative Writing Program**
Bowling Green, OH 43403.
• Green Horse for Poetry. tri-q.

**Bowling Green State University. Department of English**
Bowling Green, OH 43403.
• Penny Dreadful. 3 per yr.

**Bowling Green State University. Department of Geography**
Bowling Green, OH 43403.
• East Lakes Geographer. a. ISSN 0070-8127 (Co-sponsor: Association of American Geographers, East Lakes Division)

**Bowling Green State University. Department of Sociology**
Bowling Green, OH 43403.
• Popular Music & Society. q. ISSN 0300-7766

**Bowling Green State University. Environmental Studies Center**
Bowling Green, OH 43403.
• Bird Control Seminar. Proceedings. biennial. ISSN 0067-8945 (Co-sponsors: U.S. Fish & Wildlife Service; National Pest Control Association)
• Ecocentric; for environmentally concerned educators. bi-m.

**Bowling Green State University. Library**
University Archives, Bowling Green, OH 43402.
• Bowling Green State University. University Archives, Faculty Publications. irreg; (approx. triennial) ISSN 0475-0012

**Bowling Green State University. Office of Experimental Studies**
Bowling Green, OH 43403.
- N D T. (New Directions in Teaching); a non-journal committed to the improvement of undergraduate teaching. irreg., 2-3 issues per year. ISSN 0077-8206

**Bowling Green State University. Philosophy Documentation Center**
Bowling Green, OH 43402.
- Bibliographies of Famous Philosophers. irreg.
- Philosopher's Index; an international index to philosophical periodicals and the philosophy research archives. q. ISSN 0031-7993
- Philosophy Research Archives; a bilingual microfilm journal of philosophy. a. (Co-sponsor: American Philosophical Association; Canadian Philosophical Association)

**Bowling Proprietors' Association of America, Inc.**
P. O. Box 5802, Arlington, TX 76011.
- Bowling Proprietor. m.(July & Aug.combined) ISSN 0006-8446

**Boy Scouts of America**
U.S. Highway No. 1, North Brunswick, NJ 08902.
- Boys' Life (Braille Edition) m.
- Boys' Life (Inkprint Edition) m. ISSN 0006-8608
- Exploring. 6 per yr. ISSN 0014-5033
- Scouting Magazine. bi-m. ISSN 0036-9500

**Boyce Thompson Institute for Plant Research**
1086 North Broadway, Yonkers, NY 10701.
- Boyce Thompson Institute for Plant Research. Annual Report. a.

**William H. Boyer, Ed. & Pub.**
7525 S. E. Lake Road, Suite 12, Milwaukie, OR 97215.
- Automotive News of the Pacific Northwest. m. ISSN 0005-156X

**Boynton & Associates**
8001 Forbes Place, Suite 210D, Springfield, VA 22151.
- Model Railroad Buyers Guide. irreg.
- Model Retailer. m.
- Radio Control Buyers Guide. a. ISSN 0098-9215

**Boys' Clubs of America**
771 First Ave., New York, NY 10017.
- Boys' Club Bulletin. 3 per yr. ISSN 0006-8586
- Keynote. q. ISSN 0047-3413

**Boys' Outfitter Co., Inc.**
71 W. 35 St., New York, NY 10001.
- Teens' and Boys' Magazine. m.

**W. B. Bradbury Co., Inc.**
6 E. 43rd St., New York, NY 10017.
- Military Life. bi-m. ISSN 0026-4059
- US Magazine; for the military family in Europe. bi-m. ISSN 0362-4587

**Braddock Publications**
1028 Connecticut Ave., N.W., Suite 905, Washington, DC 22036.
- Braddock's Federal-State-Local Government Directory. s-a. ISSN 0363-6275

**Bradford County Historical Society**
Towanda, PA 18848.
- Settler. q.

**Bradford's Directory**
P.O. Box 276, Dept. E, Fairfax, VA 22030.
- Bradford's Directory of Marketing Research Agencies and Management Consultants in the United States and the World. biennial. ISSN 0068-063X

**Bradley Pulverizer Co.**
123 S. Third St., Allentown, PA 18105.
- American Cement Directory; directory of companies and personnel, North, Central, and South America. a. ISSN 0065-7646

**Bradley University. Evening College**
Peoria, IL 61606.
- Association of University Evening Colleges. Newsletter. 4 per yr. ISSN 0004-5845

**Brador Publications**
Livonia, NY 14487.
- Science Teachers Bulletin. s-a. ISSN 0036-8563 (Science Teachers Association of New York State)

**Bragg Briefs**
Box 437, Spring Lake, NC 28390.
- Bragg Briefs. irreg. ISSN 0006-8713

**Braille Institute of America, Inc.**
741 N. Vermont Ave., Los Angeles, CA 90029.
- Braille Mirror; a current topic magazine. m. ISSN 0006-8810 (Co-Sponsor: Library of Congress, Division for the Blind and Physically Handicapped)
- Expectations. a.

**Brain Information Service-Brain Research Institute**
University of California, Los Angeles, Center for the Health Sciences, Los Angeles, CA 90024.
- B I S Conference Report. 3-4 per yr. ISSN 0092-4334 (Co-sponsor: National Institute of Neurological and Communicative Diseases and Stroke)
- Bibliography of Electrical Recordings in the CNS and Related Literature. a. ISSN 0084-7879 (Co-sponsor: National Institute of Neurological and Communicative Diseases and Stroke)
- Bibliography on the Hypothalamic-Pituitary-Gonadal System. a. ISSN 0084-7887
- Biogenic Amines and Transmitters in the Nervous System. s-m. ISSN 0006-3037 (Co-sponsor: National Institute of Neurological and Communicative Diseases and Stroke)
- Biogenic Amines in the Central Nervous System; a bibliography. a. (Co-sponsor: National Institute of Neurological and Communicative Diseases and Stroke)
- Cerebral Evoked Potentials. q.
- Developmental Neurobiology; current alerting bulletin. m. (Co-sponsor: National Institute of Neurological and Communicative Diseases and Stroke)
- Memo of Current Books in the Brain Sciences. m. ISSN 0085-3291
- Memory and Learning - Research in the Nervous System.
- Neuroendocrine Control Mechanism; the hypothalamic-pituitary-gonadal system. s-m. ISSN 0028-3827
- Neuroimmunology. q.
- Proteins in the Brain. q.
- Sleep Bulletin Including Sleep Reviews. m. (Co-sponsor: National Institute of Neurological and Communicative Diseases & Stroke)
- Sleep Research. a.
- Society for Neuroscience. Annual Meeting. Conference Report. a.

**Brainchild**
c/o Janet DiGirolamo, 1440 N. Fourth, Springfield, IL 62702.
- Brainchild. irreg.

**Brakeley, John Price Jones Inc.**
6 E. 43rd St., New York, NY 10017.
- News from New York. q.
- Philanthropic Digest. every 3 weeks. ISSN 0480-2853

**Bramson Publishing Co.**
Box 101, Bloomfield Hills, MI 48013.
- Production; the magazine of manufacturing. m. ISSN 0032-9819
- Production's Manufacturing Planbook. a.

**Brandeis University. English Department**
Box 2227, Waltham, MA 02154.
- Folio (Waltham); Brandeis literary & arts magazine. s-a. ISSN 0015-5780

**Brandeis University. Office of Public Affairs**
Waltham, MA 02154.
- Brandeis University Bulletin. m. during academic year. ISSN 0006-9043

**Brandeis University Press**
Waltham, MA 02154.
- Brandeis University. Society of Bibliophiles. Publications. irreg., 1968, no. 3. ISSN 0068-0672

**Brandeis University. Research Liaison Committee**
205 Shiffman Center, Waltham, MA 02154.
- Directory of African Studies in the United States. irreg.

**Herbert A. Brandon**
One World Trade Center, Suite 3169, New York, NY 10048.
- Brandon's Shipper & Forwarder. w. ISSN 0006-9086 (New York Foreign Freight Forwarders and Brokers Association, Inc.)

**Brandon House, Inc.**
555 Riverdale Station, New York, NY 10471 (Subscription address: Box 240, Bronx, NY 10471)
- Journal of Mental Imagery. s-a. ISSN 0364-5541

**Louis E. Brandt**
19 E. Main St., Chilton, WI 53014.
- Badger Sportsman. m. ISSN 0005-3775

**Braniff International**
Rm. 707, Exchange Park, Dallas, TX 75235.
- B I B-Liner. m. ISSN 0005-3082

**Brantwood Publications, Inc.**
P.O. Box 77, Elm Grove, WI 53122.
- Irrigation Journal. bi-m. ISSN 0047-1518
- Landscape Industry. bi-m. ISSN 0023-804X
- Nursery Business. 7 per yr. ISSN 0029-6406
- Southern Golf. q.
- Turf-Grass Times; journal of the Turf-Grass Industry. bi-m.

**John C. Brasfield Publishing Corp.**
5900 Wilshire Blvd., Los Angeles, CA 90036.
- Architectural Digest; the international magazine of fine interior design. 9 per yr. ISSN 0003-8520

**Brass Press**
148 Eighth Ave. North, Nashville, TN 37203.
- T.U.B.A. Series. irreg. (Tubists Universal Brotherhood Association)

**Bravado Feature Service**
c/o Marc Rangel de Algeciras, 37-40 75 St., Jackson Heights, NY 11372.
- Second Republic Newsletter. q. ISSN 0146-2547

**Brazilian-American Chamber of Commerce, Inc.**
22 W. 48th St., Rm. 603, New York, NY 10036.
- Brazilian American Chamber of Commerce News Bulletin. s-m.

**Brazilian Embassy**
3006 Massachusetts Avenue, N.W., Washington, DC 20008.
- Brazil Today. bi-m.
- Brazilian Embassy. Boletim Especial. bi-m.

**Brazilian Government Trade Bureau**
551 Fifth Ave., New York, NY 10017.
- Brazilian Bulletin. m. ISSN 0006-9485

**George Braziller, Inc.**
1 Park Ave., New York, NY 10016.
- American Culture. irreg., 1970, no. 6. ISSN 0065-8014
- Braziller Series of Poetry. irreg.
- Coffee Intelligence. m.

**Brentwood Publishing Corp.**
825 S. Barrington Ave., Los Angeles, CA 90049.
- Applied Radiology and Nuclear Medicine; the journal of medical imaging. bi-m.
- Association and Society Manager. bi-m. ISSN 0004-5292
- C V P. (Journal of Cardiovascular and Pulmonary Technology) bi-m.
- Convention Sales Leads/Incentive Travel. bi-w.
- Educational Broadcasting. bi-m. ISSN 0046-1474
- Incentive Travel Manager. bi-m. ISSN 0092-1920
- Respiratory Therapy; the journal of inhalation technology. bi-m. ISSN 0048-7392
- Respiratory Therapy Buyers Guide and Ordering Catalog. a. ISSN 0085-5561

**Robert D. Breth Organization**
7445 Andrews Ave., Philadelphia, PA 19138.
- Quotes Ending; trends in communications policy and practice. bi-m. ISSN 0033-6688

**Brethren Journal Association**
Box 408, Oak Brook, IL 60521.
- Brethren Life and Thought; a quarterly journal published in the interest of the Church of the Brethren. q. ISSN 0006-9663 (Co-Sponsor Bethamy Theological Seminary)

**Brethren Missionary Herald Co.**
Box 544, Winona Lake, IN 46590.
- Brethren Missionary Herald. s-m. (National Fellowship of Brethren Churches)

**C. Brewer & Co. Ltd.**
Box 1826, Honolulu, HI 96805.
- C. Brewer Today. m.

**George W. Bricker, Ed. & Pub.**
Box 265, South Chatham, MA 02659.
- Bricker's International Directory of University-Sponsored Executive Development Programs. a. ISSN 0361-1108

**Arthur Brickman Associates**
411 15th St., Miami Beach, FL 33139.
- Science Book Finder. m. ISSN 0025-7052

**Bridge Magazine**
199 Lafayette St., 7th Fl., New York, NY 10012.
- Bridge Magazine. 24 per yr.

**Bridge World Magazine Inc.**
39 W. 94th St., New York, NY 10025.
- Bridge World. m. ISSN 0006-9876

**Bridgeport Hospital**
267 Grant St., Bridgeport, CT 06602.
- Bridgeport Hospital News. 10 per yr. ISSN 0006-9884

**Bridgeport News Inc.**
3506 S. Halsted St., Chicago, IL 60609.
- Bridgeport News. w. ISSN 0006-9892

**Rose Mary Bridger**
Box 47, Grand Marais, MI 49839.
- People and Places; Great Lakes tales & photos, old tyme & new. w.

**Brigade in Action**
220 East 7 St., New York, NY 10009.
- Fourth Street I. irreg.

**Brigham Young University**
126-C BRMB, Provo, UT 84601.
- Eagle's Eye. m. ISSN 0046-0915 (Tribe of Many Feathers (Indian Club))

**Brigham Young University. Asian Studies Program**
270 MSRB, Provo, UT 84602.
- Newsletter of Research on Japanese Politics. a.

**Brigham Young University. Center for Thermochemical Studies**
- Brigham Young University. Center for Thermochemical Studies. Contributions (pub. by Marcel Dekker, Inc.)

**Brigham Young University. College of Engineering Sciences and Technology**
c/o Symposium Committee, Provo, UT 84602.
- Brigham Young University. College of Engineering Sciences and Technology. Annual Engineering Symposium. a. ISSN 0068-1008

**Brigham Young University. College of Family Living**
- Family Perspective. (pub. by Brigham Young University Press)

**Brigham Young University. Department of Anthropology and Archaeology**
140 Maeser Bldg., BYU, Provo, UT 84602.
- S E H A Newsletter and Proceedings. 6 per yr. ISSN 0036-1275 (Co-Sponsor: Society for Early Historic Archaeology)

**Brigham Young University. Department of Geology**
Provo, UT 84602.
- Brigham Young University. Department of Geology. Geology Studies. biennial. ISSN 0068-1016

**Brigham Young University. J. Reuben Clark Law School**
Provo, UT 84602.
- Brigham Young University Law Review. ISSN 0360-151X

**Brigham Young University. Law Library**
Provo, UT 84602.
- Abstracts of Book Reviews in Current Legal Periodicals. s-m. ISSN 0362-1065 (prep. by its Serials Section)

**Brigham Young University. Library**
Provo, UT 84601.
- Mormon Americana. fortn. ISSN 0027-111X (Utah Library Association)

**Brigham Young University. New World Archaeological Foundation**
- New World Archaeological Foundation. Papers. (pub. by Brigham Young University Press)

**Brigham Young University Press**
268 UPB, Provo, UT 84602.
- Annual Review of English Books on Asia. a. ISSN 0098-7379
- Brigham Young University Studies. q. ISSN 0007-0106
- Charles E. Merrill Monograph Series in the Humanities and Social Sciences. irreg., vol. 3, no. 1, 1973. ISSN 0069-2727
- Charles Redd Monographs in Western History. irreg (1-2 per yr.) (Charles Redd Center for Western Studies)
- Family Perspective. q. ISSN 0014-7311 (Brigham Young University. College of Family Living)
- Great Basin Naturalist. 4 per yr. ISSN 0017-3614
- New World Archaeological Foundation. Papers. irreg., 1973, no. 32. ISSN 0077-8915 (Brigham Young University. New World Archaeological Foundation)

**Bright Lights**
c/o Gary Morris, Ed., Box 26081, Los Angeles, CA 90026.
- Bright Lights. irreg.

**Brighton Park Life**
2949 W. 43rd St., Chicago, IL 60632.
- Brighton Park Life. w. ISSN 0007-0149

**Alice Briley**
1121 Major Ave., Albuquerque, NM 87107.
- Encore: a Quarterly of Verse & Poetic Arts. q. ISSN 0013-7057

**Brilliant Corners**
c/o Art Lange, Ed., 1372 W. Estes, No. 2N, Chicago, IL 60626.
- Brilliant Corners; a magazine of the arts. m.

**Russ Brinkley, Ed. & Pub.**
Box 1228, Harrisburg, PA 17108.
- Aero Graphic. m. ISSN 0001-9151

**British Book Centre**
(Subsidiary of: Pergamon Press Inc.)
Maxwell House, Fairview Park, Elmsford, NY 10523
(and Headington Hill Hall, Oxford OX3 0BW, England)
- Writers & Their Work. 6 per yr. (British Council)

**British Caribbean Philatelic Study Group**
c/o Elaine R. Durnin, Ed., Box 354, Sidney, OH 45365.
- British Caribbean Philatelic Journal. bi-m. ISSN 0045-2890

**British Council**
- Writers & Their Work. (pub. by British Book Centre)

**British Information Services. Policy and Reference Division**
845 Third Ave., New York, NY 10022.
- British Record; a review of British affairs. s-m. ISSN 0007-1722

**British Publications, Inc.**
11-03 46th Ave., Long Island City, NY 11101.
- Pins and Needles. m. ISSN 0031-9929

**Bro- Dart Publishing Co.**
1609 Memorial Ave., Williamsport, PA 17701.
- New York (State) Foreign Area Materials Center. Occasional Publication. irreg., no. 21, 1976. ISSN 0077-9261
- Tartan Book Sales Catalog. 12 per yr.

**Broadband Information Services, Inc.**
295 Madison Ave., New York, NY 10017.
- B M/E. (Broadcast Management/Engineering) m. ISSN 0005-3201

**Broadcast Education Association**
1771 N. St. N.W., Washington, DC 20036.
- Broadcast Monographs. irreg.
- Journal of Broadcasting. q. ISSN 0021-938X

**Broadcast Information Bureau Inc.**
30 East 42 St., Suite 1211, New York, NY 10017.
- Facts, Figures and Film; monthly newsletter for television executives. m. ISSN 0046-3124
- T V Feature Film Source Book. a. ISSN 0082-1357
- T V Film Source Book. Series, Serials and Packages. a. ISSN 0082-1373
- T V "Free" Film Source Book. a. ISSN 0082-1381

**Broadcast Music Inc.**
40 W. 57th St., New York, NY 10019.
- B M I: the Many Worlds of Music. 5 per yr. ISSN 0045-317X

**Broadcasting Publications, Inc.**
1735 DeSales St. N.W., Washington, DC 20036.
- Broadcasting; the newsweekly of broadcasting and allied arts. w. ISSN 0007-2028
- Broadcasting Cable Sourcebook. a.
- Broadcasting Yearbook. a. ISSN 0068-2713

**Broadman Press**
127 Ninth Ave. N., Nashville, TN 37234.
- Broadman Comments; International Sunday School Lessons. a. ISSN 0068-2721
- Ministers Tape Plan. a.
- Points for Emphasis; International Sunday School Lessons in Pocket Size. a. ISSN 0079-2543

**Broadside Press**
12651 Old Mill Pl., Detroit, MI 48238.
- Black Position. irreg.; no. 3, 1974. ISSN 0084-7909
- Broadside Critics Series. irreg.
- Broadside Series. m. ISSN 0007-2125

**Broadsider**
234 West Ave., Ocean City, NJ 08226.
- Broadsider; Ocean City's magazine. 22 per yr.

**Bob Broedel Ed. & Pub.**
Box 20049, Tallahassee, FL 32304.
- People's Bookseller; a newsletter for progressive booksellers. s-a.

**Bromeliad Society**
Box 3279, Santa Monica, CA 90403.
- Bromeliad Society Journal. bi-m. ISSN 0090-8738

**Bronx Board of Realtors**
- Bronx Real Estate and Building News. (pub. by Bronx Real Estate and Building News, Inc.)

**Bronx Chamber of Commerce, Inc.**
226 E. Fordham Rd., Bronx, NY 10458.
- Bronxboro. s-a. ISSN 0007-2273

**Bronx Community College. Evening Student Association**
University Ave. & W. 181st St., New York, NY 10458.
- B C C Evening Reporter. q.

**Bronx Council on the Arts Inc.**
57 East 184th St., Bronx, NY 10468.
- Bronx Banner. m.

**Bronx County Dental Society**
1020 Grand Concourse, Bronx, NY 10451.
- Bronx County Dental Society. Bulletin. 6 per yr. ISSN 0068-2764

**Bronx County Historical Society**
3266 Bainbridge Ave., Bronx, NY 10467.
- Bronx County Historical Society. Journal. s-a. ISSN 0007-2249

**Bronx County Medical Society**
2455 Sedgwick Ave., Bronx, NY 10468.
- Bronx Medicine. 11 per yr.

**Bronx Real Estate and Building News, Inc.**
29 E. Fordham Rd., Bronx, NY 10468.
- Bronx Real Estate and Building News. q. ISSN 0007-2265 (Bronx Board of Realtors)

**Bronxville Women's Club, Inc.**
135 Midland Ave., Bronxville, NY 10708.
- Villager. m.(Oct-June) ISSN 0042-6199

**Brookdale Hospital Medical Center**
Brookdale Plaza, Brooklyn, NY 11212.
- Brookdale Hospital Medical Center News-Scope. q.

**Brookhaven National Laboratory**
Upton, NY 11973
(Orders to: National Technical Information Service, 5285 Port Royal Rd., Springfield, VA 22151)
- Brookhaven Highlights. biennial. ISSN 0092-1548
- Brookhaven Symposia in Biology. irreg., no. 27, 1975. ISSN 0068-2799

**Brookings Institution**
1775 Massachusetts Ave. N.W., Washington, DC 20036.
- Brookings Bulletin. q. ISSN 0007-229X

- Brookings Papers on Economic Activity. 3 per yr. ISSN 0007-2303
- Studies in Defense Policy. irreg., no. 15, 1975.
- Studies in Presidential Selection. irreg., no. 7, 1976.
- Studies in Social Economics. irreg., no, 13-14, 1977.
- Studies in Social Experimentation. irreg., no. 4, 1975.
- Studies in the Regulation of Economic Activity. irreg., no. 13, 1975.
- Studies in Wage-Price Policy. irreg., no. 4, 1975.
- Studies of Government Finance: Second Series. irreg., no. 6, 1977.

**Brooklyn Arts and Cultural Association**
Brooklyn Institute of Arts & Sciences, 200 Eastern Parkway, Brooklyn, NY 11238.
- B.A.C.A. Calendar of Cultural Events. a. ISSN 0045-3242

**Brooklyn Bar Association**
123 Remsen St., Brooklyn, NY 11201.
- Brooklyn Barrister. 7 per yr. ISSN 0007-232X

**Brooklyn Botanic Garden**
Brooklyn, NY 11225.
- Plants & Gardens. q. ISSN 0032-101X

**Brooklyn College of the City University of New York**
see under City University of New York

**Brooklyn Engineers Club**
117 Remsen St., Brooklyn, NY 11201.
- Brooklyn Engineer; of greater New York. 10 per yr. ISSN 0007-2338

**Brooklyn Heights Periodicals Inc.**
141 Montague St., Brooklyn, NY 11201.
- Brooklyn Heights Press and Cobble Hill News. w. ISSN 0007-2346

**Brooklyn Insurance Brokers Association**
1860 Flatbush Ave., Brooklyn, NY 11210.
- Brooklyn Insurance Brokers Association. Bulletin. 10 per yr. ISSN 0007-2354

**Brooklyn Law School**
250 Joralemon, Brooklyn, NY 11201.
- Brooklyn Journal of International Law. irreg.

**Brooklyn Museum**
Eastern Parkway, Brooklyn, NY 11238.
- American Graphic Artists of the Twentieth Century. irreg. ISSN 0065-8472
- Wilbour Monographs. irreg.

**Brooklyn Polytechnic Institute**
- Applied Polymer Symposium. Papers. (pub. by Wiley Interscience)

**Brooklyn Polytechnic Institute. Microwave Institute Symposium Committee**
333 Jay St., Brooklyn, NY 11201
- Brooklyn Polytechnic Institute. Microwave Research Institute Symposia. irreg., vol. 23, 1975. ISSN 0068-2845 (Dist. by: John Wiley & Sons, Inc., 605 Third Ave., New York, NY 10016)

**Brooklyn Public Library**
Grand Army Plaza, Brooklyn, NY 11238.
- Brooklyn Public Library Bulletin. bi-m. ISSN 0007-2397
- Service to Business and Industry-BPL. m. (Sept.-June) ISSN 0049-0229

**Brooklyn Tuberculosis and Respiratory Disease Association Inc.**
293 Schermerhorn St., Brooklyn, NY 11217.
- In-Short. m. ISSN 0046-8762

**Brooks Bird Club**
c/o Albert R. Buckelew, Jr., Ed., Box J, Bethany, WV 26032.
- Redstart. q. ISSN 0034-2165

**Brooks-Cole Publishing Co.**
555 Abrego St., Monterey, CA 93940.
- Basic Concepts in Educational Psychology Series. irreg.
- Basic Concepts in Psychology Series. irreg.

**Brooks Memorial Art Gallery**
Overton Park, Memphis, TN 38112.
- Brooks Memorial Art Gallery. Newsletter. bi-m.

**Broom and Broom Corn News**
c/o John L. File, Ed., Box 504, Arcola, IL 61910.
- Broom and Broom Corn News. w. ISSN 0007-2400

**Brophy Preparatory School**
4701 North Central Avenue, Phoenix, AZ 85012.
- Latin: Let's Defend It. s-a.

**Brother**
Box 4387, Berkeley, CA 94704.
- Brother; a forum for men against sexism. q.

**Brotherhood of Locomotive Engineers**
1365 Ontario St., Cleveland, OH 44114.
- Locomotive Engineer. w. ISSN 0024-5747

**Brotherhood of Maintenance of Way Employes**
12050 Woodward Ave., Detroit, MI 48203.
- B M W E Railway Journal. m.

**Brotherhood of Railroad Signalmen**
601 W. Golf Rd., Mt. Prospect, IL 60056.
- Signalman's Journal. m. ISSN 0037-5020

**Brotherhood of Railway, Airline, Steamship Clerks, Freight Handlers, Express and Station Employes**
6300 River Road, Rosemont, IL 60018.
- Railway Clerk/Interchange. m.(10 per yr.) ISSN 0033-8869

**Brotherhood of Railway Carmen of America**
4929 Main St., Kansas City, MO 64112.
- Railway Carmen's Journal. m. ISSN 0033-8850

**Brotherhood of St. Herman of Alaska**
Platina, CA 96076.
- Orthodox Word. bi-m. ISSN 0030-5839

**Brothers of the Holy Eucharist**
Box 178, Cottonport, LA 71327.
- Grain and Fire. q. ISSN 0017-3045

**Wm. C. Brown Company Publishers**
2460 Kerper Blvd., Dubuque, IA 52001.
- Biology Series (Dubuque) irreg.
- College Instrumental Technique Series. irreg.
- Concepts of Biology Series. irreg.
- Contemporary Topics in Health Science Series. irreg.
- Fundamentals of Psychology Series. irreg.

**Brown Gold Publications**
Woodworth, WI 53194.
- Brown Gold. m. ISSN 0007-2494 (New Tribes Mission)

**Brown Swiss Cattle Breeders Association**
Box 1038, Beloit, WI 53511.
- Brown Swiss Bulletin. m. ISSN 0007-2516

**Brown University**
Providence, RI 02912
- Ishmael. s-a. (Co-sponsor: Rhode Island School of Design) (Subscr. to:, Box 28, SAO)
- Novel: A Forum on Fiction. 3 per yr. ISSN 0029-5132 (Subscr. to:, Box 1984)

**Brown University. Afro-American Studies**
Churchill House, Providence, RI 02912.
- B.O.P. (Blacks on Paper); journal of black writing & music. s-a.

**Brown University. Alumni Association**
Providence, RI 02912.
- Brown Alumni Monthly. m.(9 per yr) ISSN 0007-2478

**Brown University Library. Friends of the Library**
Box A, Providence, RI 02912.
- Books at Brown. irreg.

**Brown University Press**
Box 1881, Providence, RI 02912.
- Brown University. Slavic Reprint Series. irreg., no. 10, 1974. ISSN 0068-287X

**Brown University. Psychology Department**
Providence, RI 02912.
- Laboratory Primate Newsletter. q. ISSN 0023-6861

**Browning Institute, Inc.**
Box 2983, Grand Central Sta., New York, NY 10017.
- Browning Institute Studies. a. ISSN 0092-4725
- Through Casa Guidi Windows; the bulletin of the Browning Institute. irreg.

**Michael Bruce Associates**
P.O. Box 396, Powell, OH 43065.
- Corvette, the Sensuous American. 3 per yr. ISSN 0362-3777

**Bruckner Society of America Inc.**
Box 2570, Iowa City, IA 52240.
- Chord and Discord. irreg. (every 2-3 years) ISSN 0069-3758

**Brunner-Mazel, Inc.**
19 Union Sq. W., New York, NY 10003.
- American College of Psychiatrists. Papers Presented at the Annual Meeting. a.
- Annual Progress in Child Psychiatry and Child Development. a. ISSN 0066-4030
- Annual Review of Behavior Therapy Theory & Practice. a. ISSN 0091-6595
- Annual Review of the Schizophrenic Syndrome. a. ISSN 0090-287X
- Exceptional Infant. irreg., vol. 3, 1975. ISSN 0071-3295
- Mental Retardation and Developmental Disabilities. a. ISSN 0091-6315
- Modern Perspectives in Psychiatry. irreg. ISSN 0077-0043
- Progress in Community Mental Health. a.
- Progress in Psychiatric Drug Treatment. a.

**Brunswick Publishing Co.**
Industry Rd., Brunswick, ME 04011.
- Maine Medical Association. Journal. m. ISSN 0025-0694

**Bryan Publications, Inc.**
72 Fifth Ave., New York, NY 10011.
- Villager. w. ISSN 0042-6202

**Bryn Mawr College and Haverford College. Haverford Student Council**
Bryn Mawr, PA 19010.
- Bryn Mawr-Haverford Review. irreg., latest 1976. ISSN 0068-3035 (prep. by its Student Government Association)

**Bryn Mawr College. Career Planning Office**
Summer Internship Research Project, Bryn Mawr, PA 19019.
- National Directory of Summer Interships for Undergraduate Students. irreg. ISSN 0098-1451

**B.J. Buck**
One Yesler Way, Seattle, WA 98104.
- Pacific Banker and Business. m. ISSN 0030-8536

**Buck Investment Service**
Box 146, Cedar Ridge, CA 95924.
- Buck Investment Letter. fortn. ISSN 0007-2818

**Buckeye Association of School Administrators**
750 Brooksedge Blvd., Westerville, OH 43081.
- Administrator. q. ISSN 0044-6327

**Buckeye Review Publishing Company, Inc**
632 Belmont Ave., Box 1436, Youngstown, OH 44502.
- Buckeye Review. w. ISSN 0045-3285

**Bucknell University College of Engineering**
Dana Engineering Bldg., Lewisburg, PA 17837.
- Bucknell Engineer. q.

**Bucks County Bar Association**
135 East State Street, Doylestown, PA 18901.
- Bucks County Law Reporter. w. ISSN 0407-5501

**Bucks County Planning Commission**
Box 12, Cross Keys Office Center, 4259 Swamp Rd., Doylestown, PA 18901.
- Bucks County Planning Commission. Planning Progress. q.

**Paul C. Bucy & Associates**
Box 1457, Tryon, NC 28782.
- Surgical Neurology. m. ISSN 0090-3019

**Buddhist Bookstore**
1710 Octavia St., San Francisco, CA 94109.
- Butsumon. irreg.

**Buddhist Vihara Society**
5017 16th St. N.W., Washington, DC 20011.
- Washington Buddhist. bi-m.

**Buffalo and Erie County Historical Society**
25 Nottingham Court, Buffalo, NY 14216.
- Adventures in Western New York History. irreg. ISSN 0001-883X

- Museologist. q. ISSN 0027-397X (American Association of Museums, Northeast Conference)
- Niagara Frontier. q. ISSN 0028-9663

**Buffalo and Erie County Public Library**
Lafayette Sq., Buffalo, NY 14203.
- Buffalo and Erie County Public Library Bulletin. m.(except July-Aug.) ISSN 0020-966X

**Buffalo Area Chamber of Commerce**
238 Main St., Buffalo, NY 14202.
- Directory of Western New York Business and Civic Organizations. a.
- Western New York Buyers Guide & Roster. a.
- Western New York Magazine. m.

**Buffalo Fan**
Box 294, Buffalo, NY 14240.
- Buffalo Fan. bi-m.

**Buffalo Museum of Science**
Buffalo, NY 14211.
- Buffalo Society of Natural Sciences. Collections. 4 per yr.

**Buffalo Society of Natural Sciences**
- Buffalo Society of Natural Sciences. Collections. (pub. by Buffalo Museum of Science)

**Builders Association of Fort Worth & Tarrant County**
Box 8864, Fort Worth, TX 76112.
- Builders Association News. m.

**Building & Realty Record**
c/o Joseph H. Ball, 121 Chestnut St., Philadelphia, PA 19106.
- Building & Realty Record. m. ISSN 0007-3393

**Building for Profit**
1202 S. Park St., Madison, WI 53715.
- Building for Profit; merchandising magazine of the building industry. m.

**Building News, Inc.**
3055 Overland Ave., Los Angeles, CA 90034.
- Building News. w.

**Building Officials and Code Administrators International**
1313 E. 60th St., Chicago, IL 60637.
- B. O. C. A. Basic Fire Prevention Code. triennial.
- B O C A Basic Housing-Property Maintenance Code. triennial.
- B O C A Basic Mechanical Code. triennial. ISSN 0360-4152
- B O C A Basic Plumbing Code. triennial. ISSN 0098-1702
- Building Official and Code Administrator. m. ISSN 0007-3547

**Building Owners & Managers Association International**
1221 Massachusetts Ave., N.W., Washington, DC 20005.
- Building Owner and Manager. m.

**Building Research Advisory Board**
National Academy of Sciences, 2101 Constitution Ave., N. W., Washington, DC 20418.
- B R A B Newsletter. bi-m.

**Building Stone Institute**
420 Lexington Ave., New York, NY 10017.
- Building Stone News. m. ISSN 0007-3679

**Building Trades Employers Association of the City of New York**
711 Third Ave., New York, NY 10017.
- Building Trades Employers Association of the City of New York. News and Opinion; matters of interest to the building industry. 10 per yr.

**Bulletin of Concerned Asian Scholars**
Box W, Charlemont, MA 01339.
- Bulletin of Concerned Asian Scholars. q. ISSN 0007-4810

**Bulletin Publishing Co.**
Auburn, AL 36830.
- Campus Digest. w. (Tuskegee Institute)

**Bullinger's Guides, Inc.**
63 Woodland Ave., Box 501, Westwood, NJ 07675.
- Bullinger's Postal and Shippers Guide for the United States and Canada. a. ISSN 0068-4201

**Bunting and Lyon**
238 N. Main St., Wallingford, CT 06492.
- Private Independent Schools. a. ISSN 0079-5399

**Burdick Enterprises**
Box 788, Sandusky, OH 44870.
- American Square Dance; square dance and round dance. m. ISSN 0091-3383

**Bureau Issue Association**
c/o Esther H. Sullivan, 19 Maple St., Arlington, MA 02174.
- United States Specialist. m.

**Bureau of Business Practice**
24 Rope Ferry Rd., Waterford, CT 06385.
- Discipline and Grievances; labor arbitration case analyses, plus arbitrators' hints on safeguarding managements' positions. m. ISSN 0012-351X
- Dynamic Supervision. s-m. ISSN 0012-7396
- Employee Relations Bulletin. s-m. ISSN 0013-6816
- Executive Action Series. m.
- F E P Guidelines. (Fair Employment Practices) m. ISSN 0093-7630
- Hospital Supervisor's Bulletin. s-m. ISSN 0018-585X
- Human Side of Supervision. s-m.
- M.S. for Medical Secretaries. s-m. ISSN 0027-2906
- O.S.H.A. Compliance Letter. (Federal Occupational Safety and Health Act) s-m. ISSN 0092-5799
- Office Guide for Working Women. s-m.
- Office Supervisor's Bulletin. s-m. ISSN 0030-025X
- P. S. for Private Secretaries. s-m. ISSN 0030-8285

**Bureau of Foreign Languages**
131 Livingston St., Brooklyn, NY 11201.
- Foreign Language Lines. q.

**Bureau of National Affairs, Inc.**
1231 25th St., N. W., Washington, DC 20037.
- Antitrust & Trade Regulation Report. w. ISSN 0003-6021
- B N A Noise Regulation Reporter. fortn.
- B N A Pension Reporter. w. ISSN 0095-7100
- B N A Policy & Practice Series; for the personnel executive. w. ISSN 0005-3228
- B N A's Patent, Trademark & Copyright Journal. w.
- Collective Bargaining Negotiations & Contracts. fortn. ISSN 0010-079X
- Construction Labor Report. w. ISSN 0010-6836
- Criminal Law Reporter. w. ISSN 0011-1341
- Energy Users Report. w. ISSN 0093-0261
- Environment Reporter. w. ISSN 0013-9211
- Export Shipping Manual. w. ISSN 0014-5181
- Family Law Reporter. w.
- Federal Contracts Report. w. ISSN 0014-9063
- Government Employee Relations Report. w. ISSN 0017-260X
- Housing and Development Reporter. w. ISSN 0091-5939
- Labor Arbitration Reports. w.
- Labor Relations Reporter. w.
- Labor Relations Yearbook. a. ISSN 0075-7489
- Major Labor-Law Principles Established by the N.L.R.B. and the Courts. irreg. ISSN 0094-0313
- Manpower Information Service. fortn. ISSN 0542-5794
- Occupational Safety & Health Cases. irreg. ISSN 0095-5515
- Occupational Safety and Health Reporter. w.
- P P F Survey/Personnel Policies Forum Survey. irreg. ISSN 0361-7467
- Payroll/Compensation; pay policies. bi-w.
- Personnel Policies Forum. 4 per yr. ISSN 0031-580X
- Product Safety & Liability Reporter; a weekly review of consumer safety developments. w. ISSN 0092-7732
- Retail Services Labor Report. w.
- Securities Regulation & Law Report. w. ISSN 0037-0665
- Tax Management Executive Compensation Journal. m. ISSN 0093-6995
- U S Export Weekly. w. ISSN 0093-9633
- Union Labor Report. fortn. ISSN 0091-5459
- United States Law Week. w.
- United States Patents Quarterly. w. ISSN 0041-803X
- White Collar Report. w. ISSN 0043-4892

**Bureau of Social Science Research Inc.**
1990 M St. N.W., Washington, DC 20036.
- B S S R Newsletter. q.

**Burgess Publishing Co.**
7108 Ohms Lane, Minneapolis, MN 55435.
- Basic Concepts in Anthropology. irreg.
- Critical Issues in Political Science. irreg.

**Alan Burke Inc.**
Box 189, Boca Raton, FL 33432.
- Alan Burke Report. m.

**Edgar P. Burke**
1209 Rundle St., Scranton, PA 18504.
- Yesterday's Magazette. s-m.

**Burnham Corporation. Lord & Burnham Division**
Box 114, Irvington, NY 10533.
- Under Glass. bi-m. ISSN 0041-6460

**Burrelle's Press Clipping Service**
Box 7, Livingston, NJ 07039.
- Your Clipping Analyst. q. ISSN 0300-7669

**Burroughs Bibliophiles**
- Burroughs Bulletin. (pub. by House of Greystoke)
- Gridley Wave. (pub. by House of Greystoke)

**Burroughs Corp.**
Box 418, Detroit, MI 48232.
- Burroughs Clearing House; for bank and financial officers. m. ISSN 0007-6341

**Burroughs Wellcome Co.**
- Clinical Trends in Cardiology. (pub. by Science and Medicine Publishing Co. Inc.)
- Clinical Trends in Family Practice. (pub. by Science and Medicine Publishing Co., Inc.)
- Clinical Trends in Ophthalmology, Otolaryngology, Allergy. (pub. by Science and Medicine Publishing Co., Inc.)
- Clinical Trends in Osteopathic Medicine. (pub. by Science and Medicine Publishing Co., Inc.)
- Clinical Trends in Urology. (pub. by Science and Medicine Publishing Co., Inc.)

**Roy Douglass Burrow, Ed. & Pub.**
1400 N. Jefferson, El Dorado, AR 71730.
- Modern Images. q. ISSN 0026-7848

**Bush League**
7777 W. 91st. St., E-1144, Playa del Rey, CA 90291.
- Bush League. q.

**Business & Economics Book Guide**
70 Lincoln St., Boston, MA 02111.
- Business & Economics Book Guide. a.

**Business and Industry**
3009 Ingersoll, Des Moines, IA 50312.
- Business and Industry; the management purchasing magazine. m. ISSN 0021-0463

**Business and Professional People for the Public Interest**
109 N. Dearborn St., Suite 1001, Chicago, IL 60602.
- B P I Newsletter. q.

**Business Borrower**
1529 Walnut St., Philadelphia, PA 19102.
- Business Borrower. s-m.

**Business Committee for the Arts, Inc.**
1700 Broadway, New York, NY 10019.
- B C A News. q. ISSN 0005-2841

**Business Communications**
Box 4-AA, Anchorage, AK 99509.
- Alaska Industry. m. ISSN 0002-449X

**Business Communications Co., Inc. (Stamford)**
471 Glenbrook Rd., Stamford, CT 06906.
- E V/Battery Technology. 12 per yr.
- Energy. q.
- Washington Monitor on Energy. 50 per yr.

**Business Communications, Inc.**
(Subsidiary of: Thomas Publishing Co.)
One Penn Plaza, 250 W. 34th St., New York, NY 10001.
- Energy Systems Product News. bi-m.
- Heating/Combustion Equipment News. bi-m.

**Business Communications Review**
800 Enterprise Drive, Oak Brook, IL 60521.
- Business Communications Review. bi-m.

**Business Extension Bureau**
3057 17th St, San Francisco, CA 94110.
● Western Real Estate News. s-m. ISSN 0043-4124

**Business Guides, Inc.**
2 Park Ave., New York, NY 10016.
● Chain Store Guide Directory: Food Service Distributors. irreg. ISSN 0091-9152
● Directory: Home Centers & Hardware Chains, Auto Supply Chains. a. ISSN 0094-8667
● Directory of Discount Centers. a. ISSN 0070-5446

**Business-Industry Political Action Committee. Political Education Division**
1747 Pennsylvania Ave. N.W., Washington, DC 20006.
● Politics. bi-m. ISSN 0032-3276

**Business International Corp.**
One Dag Hammarskjold Plaza, New York, NY 10017.
● Business Asia; weekly report to managers of Asia/Pacific operations. w. ISSN 0572-7545
● Business Eastern Europe. w.
● Business Europe. w.
● Business International; weekly report to management on international trade and investment developments. w. ISSN 0007-6872
● Business International Iran Service. q. updates to base vols.
● Business International Money Report. w.
● Business Latin America; weekly report to managers of Latin American operations. w. ISSN 0007-6880
● Doing Business with Eastern Europe. 10 base vols. updated monthly.
● Financing Foreign Operations. m. ISSN 0015-2129
● Investing, Licensing & Trading Conditions Abroad. base vols. plus m. supplements. ISSN 0021-003X
● Management Monographs (New York) irreg., latest issue 1976. ISSN 0085-3054

**Business Journals, Inc.**
22 S. Smith St., E. Norwalk, CT 06855.
● Fashion Accessories. m.
● Gas Turbine International. bi-m. ISSN 0435-1312
● Luggage & Travelware. m.
● Luggage & Travelware Directory. a.
● Sawyer's Gas Turbine Catalog. a.

**Business Journals of America, Inc.**
217 Harrison Ave., Harrison, NY 10528.
● Connecticut Business Journal. w.
● Westchester Business Journal. w. ISSN 0043-3365

**Business News Publishing Co.**
Box 6000, Birmingham, MI 48012.
● Air Conditioning, Heating and Refrigeration News. w. ISSN 0002-2276

**Business Press, Inc.**
475 Kinderkamack Rd., Oradell, NJ 07649.
● Paper Age. m. ISSN 0031-1081

**Business Publications, Inc.**
212 Mid-Continent Bldg., Tulsa, OK 74103.
● Oklahoma Business. m.

**Business Publications Service**
717 E. Chelten Ave., Philadelphia, PA 19144.
● Clothesline. m. ISSN 0009-9473

**Business Publishers, Inc.**
Box 1067, Blair Sta., Silver Spring, MD 20910.
● Air/Water Pollution Report; weekly report on environmental pollution: the law, the market, the technology. w. ISSN 0002-2608
● Clean Water Report. bi-w. ISSN 0009-8620
● Ecology U S A. w. ISSN 0098-6615
● Energy Resources Report. w. ISSN 0093-4992
● Fair Employment Report. fortn. ISSN 0014-6919
● Federal Research Report. w.
● Industrial Fire & Security Report. fortn.
● Land Use Planning Reports. w. ISSN 0093-3864
● Noise Control Report. fortn.
● Public Transit Report. q.
● Sludge. m.
● Solar Energy Intelligence Report. w.
● Solid Waste Report. fortn. ISSN 0038-1128
● Toxic Materials News. w. ISSN 0093-5891
● World Environmental Directory. a. ISSN 0094-4742

**Business Science Corporation**
1200 Mt. Diablo Blvd., Suite 312, Walnut Creek, CA 94596.
● Journal of Management. bi-m. ISSN 0361-5782

**Business West Publishing Co**
Box 536, Oakland, CA 94604.
● Business West. m. ISSN 0045-365X

**Business World Inc.**
930 Clifton Avenue, Clifton, NJ 07013.
● Business World; business-building hints for small & medium-sized firms. m. ISSN 0007-7143

**Butane-Propane News, Inc.**
Box 1408, Arcadia, CA 91006.
● Butane-Propane News. m. ISSN 0007-7259

**Butcher Workman Educational and Benevolent Association, Inc.**
2800 N. Sheridan Rd., Chicago, IL 60657.
● Butcher Workman. m. ISSN 0007-7267

**Butt Press**
c/o Len Andersen, 156 Pleasant St., Arlington, MA 02174.
● Butt. q.

**Butte County Historical Society**
Box 2195, Oroville, CA 95965.
● Diggin's. q.

**Buttenheim Publishing Corp.**
Berkshire Common, Pittsfield, MA 01201.
● American City and County. m.
● Municipal Index; purchasing guide for city officials and consulting engineers. a. ISSN 0077-2151

**Butterick Fashion Marketing Co.**
Div. of American Can Co., 161 Ave. of the Americas, New York, NY 10013
(Subscr. to Vogue Patterns, Subscr. Dept., Greenwich, CT 06830)
● Vogue Patterns. bi-m.

**Butterick Fashion Marketing Co. Butterick Pattern Service**
2900 Beale Ave., Altoona, PA 16603.
● Butterick Home Catalog. q. ISSN 0007-7305

**Buttonwood Farms, Inc.**
● Journal of Special Education. (pub. by Grune and Stratton, Inc.)

**Buxom Belles International, Inc.**
326 Potawatomi, Royal Oak, MI 48073.
● Buxom Belle Courier. m. ISSN 0007-7364

**Buyer's Guide to Indian Art**
c/o Bill Bowe, Box 44, McIntosh, NM 87032.
● Buyer's Guide to Indian Art. a.

**Buyers Laboratory, Inc.**
20 Railroad Ave., Hackensack, NJ 07601.
● Buyers Laboratory Test Reports. Series 1: Test Reports on Office Products. bi-m.
● Buyers Laboratory Test Reports. Series 2: Test Reports on Plant & Maintenance Products. bi-m.

**Buyers Purchasing Digest**
918 N.E. 28th Ave., Ft Lauderdale, FL 33304.
● Buyers Purchasing Digest. m. ISSN 0007-7402

**Byelorussian American Association, Inc.**
Ed. Stanislau Stankevich, 166-34 Gothic Dr., Jamaica, NY 11432.
● Bielarus; Byelorussian newspaper in the Free World. m. ISSN 0006-209X

**Byelorussian-American Union**
104-29 Atlantic Ave., Richmond Hill, NY 11419.
● Byelorussian-American Union. Bulletin. m. ISSN 0007-7437

**Byelorussian-American Youth Organization**
Box 309, Jamaica, NY 11431.
● Byelorussian Youth. q.

**Byelorussian Institute of Arts and Sciences, Inc.**
3441 Tibbett Ave., Bronx, NY 10463.
● Belaruski Instytut Navuki Mactatstva. Zapisy/Byelorussian Institute of Arts and Sciences. Annals. a. ISSN 0510-3746

**Byelorussian Times**
Box 141, Whitestone, NY 11357.
● Byelorussian Times. m.

**Byte Publications, Inc.**
70 Main, Peterborough, NH 03458.
● Byte; the small systems journal. m. ISSN 0360-5280

**C A P News, Inc.**
149 Woodland Dr., Pittsburgh, PA 15236.
● Today's Chef-Food Service Executive. 8 per yr.

**C & P Research, Inc.**
Box 60, Fort Lee, NJ 07024.
● C & P Warrant Analysis. fortn. ISSN 0092-945X

**C B I A Service Corp.**
60 Washington St., Hartford, CT 06106.
● Connecticut Business & Industry. m. (Connecticut Business & Industry Association)

**C B S Consumer Publishing-West**
1499 Monrovia Ave., Newport Beach, CA 92663.
● Cycle World. m. ISSN 0011-4286
● Pickup, Van & 4WD. m. ISSN 0092-282X
● Road & Track. m. ISSN 0035-7189

**C B S Publications. Popular Magazine Group**
600 Third Ave., New York, NY 10016
● Basketball Yearbook. ISSN 0404-990X
● Field & Stream. m. ISSN 0015-0673
● Field & Stream Fishing Annual. ISSN 0362-6385
● Field & Stream Hunting Annual. a. ISSN 0361-3011
● Popular Gardening Indoors. q.
● Popular Sports. 5 per yr.
● Psychic World & the Occult. bi-m.
● World Tennis. m. ISSN 0043-910X

**C E Enterprises Inc.**
P.O.B. 12, Atlantic Highlands, NJ 07716.
● C E Cost Guide. a. with s-a. supplements. ISSN 0068-4716

**C.E.S. Publishing Corp.**
325 E. 75th St., New York, NY 10021.
● Communications Retailing. m.
● Consumer Electronics. m.

**C. G. Jung Foundation for Analytical Psychology, Inc.**
28 East 39th St., New York, NY 10016.
● Quadrant. s-a. ISSN 0033-5010

**C. G. Jung Institute of Los Angeles, Inc.**
10349 W. Pico Blvd., Los Angeles, CA 90064.
● Psychological Perspectives; an interpretive review. s-a. ISSN 0033-2925

**C. H. E. A. R., Inc**
International Foundation for Children's Hearing, Education and Research, 871 McLean Ave., Yonkers, NY 10704.
● Hearing Research Developments. bi-m.

**C I B-N A C M Corp.**
475 Park Ave. S., New York, NY 10016.
● F C I B Bulletin. bi-w. ISSN 0014-5718 (Foreign Credit Interchange Bureau. National Association of Credit Management)

**C M G Publications**
Box 630, Princeton, NJ 08540.
● Mort's Guide to Low-Cost Vacations & Lodgings on College Campuses. irreg. ISSN 0095-0386

**C M N Publications**
3740 Dempster St., Skokie, IL 60076.
● Automation in Housing/Systems Building News. bi-m. ISSN 0362-0395
● Automation in Housing/Systems Building News. Annual Buyers'guide. a.

**C M P Publications, Inc.**
280 Community Dr., Great Neck, NY 11021.
● Electronic Buyers' News. bi-w.
● Electronic Engineering Times. bi-w.

**C O R E Publications**
200 West 135 St., New York, NY 10030.
● CORE Magazine. q. (Congress of Racial Equality)
● Rights & Reviews; a magazine of the black power movement in America. ISSN 0035-5291 (Congress of Racial Equality)

**C O S M E P, Inc.**
Box 703, San Francisco, CA 94101.
● C O S M E P Newsletter. (Committee of Small Editors & Publishers) m. ISSN 0007-8832

**COSMIC**
University of Georgia Computer Center, Athens, GA 30601
- Directory of Computer Programs Available from C O S M I C. irreg. ISSN 0419-2427 (Subscr. to: Supt. of Documents, U. S. Government Printing Office, Washington DC 20402)

**C P C Communications, Inc.**
Box 4010, 500 W. Putnam Ave., Greenwich, CT 06830.
- Breast: Diseases of the Breast. q. ISSN 0361-3828

**C Q**
Box 5369, Los Angeles, CA 90055.
- C Q; a quarterly journal of California poetry and art. q.

**C R C Press, Inc.**
18901 Cranwood Pkwy, Cleveland, OH 44128.
- C R C Critical Reviews in Analytical Chemistry. q. ISSN 0007-8980
- C R C Critical Reviews in Biochemistry. q. ISSN 0045-6411
- C R C Critical Reviews in Bioengineering. q. ISSN 0045-642X
- C R C Critical Reviews in Clinical Laboratory Sciences. q. ISSN 0590-8191
- C R C Critical Reviews in Diagnostic Imaging. q.
- C R C Critical Reviews in Environmental Control. q. ISSN 0007-8999
- C R C Critical Reviews in Food Science and Nutrition. q. ISSN 0099-0248
- C R C Critical Reviews in Microbiology. q. ISSN 0045-6454
- C R C Critical Reviews in Solid State & Materials Sciences. q.
- C R C Critical Reviews in Toxicology. q. ISSN 0045-6446
- C R C Handbook of Biochemistry and Molecular Biology; selected data for molecular biology. irreg., 1975, 3rd ed.

**C R E D R Corp.**
3347 Motor Ave., Suite 201, Los Angeles, CA 90034
(Subscr. to: Box 49938, Los Angeles, CA 94009)
- Cassette Library for Professional Training and Development; new additions. a; 65 cassettes. (American Society for Training and Development)
- Cassette Library on New Technology in Organization Development. a; 83 cassettes.

**C R I & P Railroad Co.**
139 W. Van Buren St., Chicago, IL 60605.
- Rocket. bi-m. ISSN 0035-7480

**C S A Press**
Lakemont, GA 30552.
- Orion. bi-m. ISSN 0030-5561 (Christian Spiritual Alliance Inc.)

**C S I Press, Inc.**
P.O. Box 1703, Shreveport, LA 71166.
- Chain Saw Industry & Power Equipment Dealer. m. ISSN 0009-0948

**C S M Marketing, Inc.**
131-L Brook Ave., Deer Park, NY 11729.
- Catalog Showroom Merchandiser. m.

**C T B-McGraw Hill**
(Subsidiary of: McGraw Hill, Inc.)
Del Monte Research Park, Monterey, CA 93940.
- Criteria; CTB Newsletter on Evaluation. s-a.

**C T Corporation System**
277 Park Ave., New York, NY 10017.
- Corporation Journal. q. ISSN 0045-8597

**Cab Stand**
1453 Superior Ave., Cleveland, OH 44114.
- Cab Stand. ISSN 0007-9251

**Cabaret Co.**
Box 1117, 634 W. Burton St., Murfreesboro, TN 37130.
- Voice of the Tennessee Walking Horse; a national publication devoted exclusively to the breed. m.

**Cable Communications Corp.**
2828 N. 36th St., Phoenix, AZ 85008.
- Cable News. w.

**Cable TV World, Inc.**
505 Eighth Ave., New York, NY 10018.
- Cable TV World. fortn.

**Cablecommunications Resource Center**
1900 L St., N.W., Suite 205, Washington, DC 20036.
- Cablelines. m.

**Cactus Press**
P.O. Box 366, Bullhead City, AZ 86430.
- Berry Pickin. q.
- Digging for Davis. q.
- Jones Journeys. q.
- Smith Sagas. q.

**Caedmon Literature**
c/o R. Campbell, Box 57, Kenmore Station, Boston, MA 02215.
- Poets, Yeggs and Thirsties. q.

**Cafeteria**
Box 16191, San Diego, CA 92116.
- Cafeteria. s-a.

**Cahners Publishing Co., Inc.**
5 S. Wabash Ave., Chicago, IL 60603
(Circulation Office: 270 St. Paul St., Denver, CO 80206)
- Appliance Manufacturer. m. ISSN 0003-679X
- Brick and Clay Record. m. ISSN 0006-9760
- Building Design & Construction. m. ISSN 0007-3407
- Building Supply News. m. ISSN 0007-3695
- Ceramic Data Book. a. (American Ceramic Society, Inc.)
- Ceramic Industry. m. ISSN 0009-0220
- Construction Equipment Buyers Guide. a.
- Construction Equipment Magazine. 13 per yr. ISSN 0010-6763
- Foodservice Equipment Dealer. Buyers Guide and Product Directory; the magazine of distribution and design. a. ISSN 0363-1303
- Foodservice Equipment Specialist. m.
- I/V 400 Chain Report. w.
- Institutions/Volume Feeding; magazine of the Service World. s-m. ISSN 0094-6745
- Package Engineering. m. ISSN 0030-9044
- Professional Builder. m. ISSN 0033-0043
- Service World International; hotels, food service/catering, franchising, tourism. bi-m. ISSN 0049-0237
- Specifying Engineer. m.
- Traffic Management; devoted to freight transportation and distribution economics field. m. ISSN 0041-0691

**Cahners Publishing Co., Inc. (Boston)**
221 Columbus Ave., Boston, MA 01772.
- Design News; the design engineer's idea magazine. fortn. ISSN 0011-9407
- E D N Magazine/Electrical Design News. s-m. ISSN 0012-7515
- Electric Light & Power: Energy/Generation. m.
- Electric Light & Power: Transmission/Distribution. m.
- Electronic Business. m.
- Electronics in Industry; electronic technology for the non-electronic engineering management. m.
- M P, the Microprocessor; annual study of the market and applications for the microprocessor and microcomputers by E D N Magazine. a. ISSN 0361-5421
- Modern Materials Handling. m. ISSN 0026-8038
- Plastics World; adaptable information for the plastics managers, processor and designer. m. ISSN 0032-1273
- Purchasing; the news magazine for industrial buyers. fortn. ISSN 0033-4448

**Caim**
c/o Bernard Taylor, Ed., 1829 Colonial Rd., Baltimore, MD 21207.
- Caim. s-a.

**Cajal Club**
c/o Ed. & Pub. Glenn V. Russell, Univ. of Texas Medical Branch, Galveston, TX 77550.
- Cajal Club. Proceedings. 1973. ISSN 0092-6930

**Cal-Neva Wildlife**
Box 9098, University Sta., Reno, NV 89500.
- Cal-Neva Wildlife; Transactions. a. ISSN 0095-3601

**Calatomic**
Box 54984 Terminal Annex, Los Angeles, CA 90054.
- Nucleic Acids Literature. bi-m.

**Calavo Growers of California**
Box 3486, Los Angeles, CA 90051.
- Together: Calavo Newsletter. m.

**Caldwell Communications, Inc.**
747 Third Ave., New York, NY 10017.
- No. 1. m.
- Sunbound. q.

**Calf News, Inc.**
Suite 409, 18345 Ventura Blvd., Tarzana, CA 91356.
- C A L F News. (Concerning America's Livestock Feeders) m. ISSN 0007-7798

**Calgon Corporation**
Calgon Center, P.O. Box 1346, Pittsburgh, PA 15230.
- Calgon Air/Water Report. q.

**California. Administrative Office of the California Courts**
4200 State Bldg., San Francisco, CA 94102.
- California. Administrative Office of the California Courts. Annual Report. a. ISSN 0068-5488 (Cosponsor: Judicial Council of California)

**California. Air Resources Board**
Box 2815, Sacramento, CA 95812.
- California. Air Resources Board. Annual Report. a. ISSN 0068-5496
- California. Air Resources Board. Bulletin. m.
- California. Air Resources Board. Fact Sheets. irreg.
- California Air Basins. irreg.

**California. Attorney General's Office**
California State Bldg., 107 S. Broadway, Los Angeles, CA 90012.
- Crime Prevention Review. q. ISSN 0093-044X

**California. Commission on the Status of Women**
Documents Section, P.O. Box 20191, Sacramento, CA 95820.
- California Women. a.

**California. Department of Aging**
918 J St., Sacramento, CA 95814.
- Era. m.

**California. Department of Commerce**
1400 10th St., Sacramento, CA 95814.
- California International Business Directory. quadrennial.

**California. Department of Commerce. Division of International Trade**
1400 Tenth St., Sacramento, CA 95814.
- California International Trader. m.

**California. Department of Consumer Affairs. Contractor's State License Board**
1020 N St, Room 579, Sacramento, CA 95814.
- California Licensed Contractor. q.
- Contractors' State License Board Directory of Licensed Contractors. q.

**California. Department of Corporations**
California State Bldg., 217 W. 1st St., Los Angeles, CA 90012.
- Annual Reports for California Consumer Finance Laws. a. ISSN 0094-7938

**California. Department of Education**
721 Capitol Mall, Sacramento, CA 95814.
- California. Department of Education. Experimental Education Programs for Handicapped Children. irreg. ISSN 0362-8779
- California. State Board of Education. Report to the California State Legislature on the Progress of Area Vocational Planning. a. ISSN 0094-1077

**California. Department of Education. Bureau of Publications**
State Education Bldg., 721 Capitol Mall, Sacramento, CA 95814.
- California Private School Directory. a. ISSN 0098-5147
- California Public School Directory. a. ISSN 0068-5771
- Courses Offered by California Schools.

**California. Department of Education. Bureau of School Apportionments and Reports**
721 Capitol Mall, Sacramento, CA 95814.
- Salaries of Superintendents and Certain Other Administrative Officers in the Public Schools of California. a. ISSN 0092-1173

**California. Department of Education. Gifted and Talented Education Management Team**
721 Capitol Mall, Sacramento, CA 95814.
- Gifted Pupil; newsletter of programs for mentally gifted minors. q. ISSN 0016-9870

**California. Department of Education. Office of Program Evaluation and Research**
721 Capitol Mall, Sacramento, CA 95814.
- California. Department of Education. Office of Program Evaluation and Research. Innovative Programs for Child Care: Evaluation Report. irreg. ISSN 0362-7063

**California. Department of Fish and Game**
1416 Ninth St., Sacramento, CA 95814
- Annotated Bibliography of Research in Economically Important Species of California Fish and Game. Supplement. biennial. ISSN 0068-5526 (Order from: Marine Resources Region, 350 Golden Shore, Long Beach, CA 90802)
- California. Department of Fish and Game. Fish and Game Code. biennial with alternate supplements. (Subscr. to: Office of Procurement, Publications Section, Box 1015, North Highlands, CA 95660)
- California. Department of Fish and Game. Fish and Game Code. Supplement. biennial. (Subscr. to: Office of Procurement, Publications Section, Box 1015, North Highlands, CA 95660)
- California Fish and Game. q. ISSN 0008-1078 (Subscr. to: Office of Procurement, Publications Section, Box 1015, North Highlands, CA 95660)

**California. Department of Food and Agriculture. Division of Plant Industry**
1220 N St., Sacramento, CA 95814.
- Occasional Papers in Entomology. irreg. ISSN 0362-2622 (prep. by its Laboratory Services)

**California. Department of Forestry**
1416 Ninth St., Sacramento, CA 95814.
- California. Department of Forestry. Range Improvement Studies. irreg., 1970, no. 20. ISSN 0068-5569
- California. Department of Forestry. State Forest Notes. irreg.; no. 64, Nov. 1976. ISSN 0068-5577
- California Fire Prevention Notes. irreg.

**California. Department of Health. Bureau of Maternal and Child Health**
2151 Berkeley Way, Berkeley, CA 94704.
- Family Health Bulletin. q. ISSN 0014-7257

**California. Department of Health. Comprehensive Health Planning Program**
744 P Street, Room 576, Sacramento, CA 95814.
- California State Plan for Hospitals and Related Health Facilities. a.

**California. Department of Health. Facilities Licensing Section**
744 P St., Room 440, Sacramento, CA 95814.
- Health Facilities Directory. q. ISSN 0361-2929

**California. Department of Health. Vector and Waste Management**
2151 Berkeley Way, Berkeley, CA 94704.
- California Vector Views. m. ISSN 0008-1604

**California. Department of Housing and Community Development**
1807 13th St., Sacramento, CA 95814.
- California. Department of Housing and Community Development. Annual Report. a. ISSN 0363-4183
- Communities. irreg.

**California. Department of Industrial Relations**
Box 603, San Francisco, CA 94101.
- California. Department of Industrial Relations. Annual Report. a. ISSN 0362-4129 (prep. by its Agriculture and Services Agency)

**California. Department of Industrial Relations. Division of Apprenticeship Standards**
Box 603, San Francisco, CA 94101.
- Apprenticeship News. q. ISSN 0003-7109

**California. Department of Industrial Relations. Division of Labor Statistics and Research**
Box 603, San Francisco, CA 94101.
- California Industrial Relations Reports. 1-2 per yr. ISSN 0008-1191
- Work Injuries in California. Quarterly. q. (prep. by its Agriculture and Services Agency)

**California. Department of Justice. Bureau of Criminal Statistics**
P.O. Box 13427, Sacramento, CA 95813.
- California. Bureau of Criminal Statistics. Adult Criminal Detention. irreg.
- California. Bureau of Criminal Statistics. Adult Probation: Program Report. a.
- California. Bureau of Criminal Statistics. Adult Prosecution. a.
- California. Bureau of Criminal Statistics. Crime and Delinquency. a.
- California. Bureau of Criminal Statistics. Crimes and Arrests. a.
- California. Bureau of Criminal Statistics. Juvenile Probation. a.
- California. Bureau of Criminal Statistics. Reference Tables: Adult and Juvenile Probation. ISSN 0094-7717
- Homicide in California. irreg. ISSN 0098-8537

**California. Department of Justice. Office of the Attorney General**
800 Tishman Bldg., Los Angeles, CA 90010.
- Peace Officer Law Report. m.

**California. Department of Navigation and Ocean Development**
1416 Ninth St., Sacramento, CA 95814.
- A B C's of California Boating Law. a.

**California. Department of Parks and Recreation**
P.O. Box 2390, Sacramento, CA 95811.
- California. Department of Parks and Recreation. Archeological Report. irreg., 1969, no. 12. ISSN 0068-5550
- California Department of Parks and Recreation. a Stewardship Report. irreg. ISSN 0362-6563 (prep. by its Resources Agency)

**California. Department of the Youth Authority**
714 P St., Sacramento, CA 95814
(Orders to: Box 20191, Sacramento, CA 95820)
- California. Department of the Youth Authority. Affirmative Action Statistics; report. s-a. ISSN 0362-4110
- California Youth Authority Quarterly. q. ISSN 0008-1671
- Characteristics of the California Youth Authority Parole Caseload. irreg. ISSN 0575-2906
- Directory of California Justice Agencies Serving Juveniles and Adults. a. ISSN 0361-7327

**California. Department of Transportation**
Room 4113, 1120 N St., Sacramento, CA 95814.
- Transportation Focus. irreg. ISSN 0098-0129

**California. Department of Water Resources**
P.O. Box 388, Sacramento, CA 95802.
- California. Department of Water Resources. Bulletin. a. ISSN 0084-8263
- California. Department of Water Resources. Inventory of Waste Water Production and Waste Water Reclamation Practices in California. a. ISSN 0092-9158
- California State Water Project. a. ISSN 0090-5968

**California. Division of Mines and Geology**
1416 Ninth St., Room 1341, Sacramento, CA 95814.
- California. Division of Mines and Geology. Bulletin. 2-3 per yr. ISSN 0008-1000
- California Geology. m. ISSN 0026-4555

**California. Drug Abuse Information Project**
San Francisco, CA 94102.
- California. Drug Abuse Information Project. Annual Report to the Legislature. a. ISSN 0093-7827

**California. Employment Development Department**
800 Capitol Mall, Sacramento, CA 95814.
- California Employer. q.

**California. Employment Development Department. Employment Data and Research Division**
800 Capitol Mall, Sacramento, CA 95814.
- California. Employment Data and Research Division. Taxable and Total Wages, Regular Benefits Paid, Employer Contributions Earned, and Average Covered Employment, by Industry. irreg. ISSN 0098-8332
- California Labor Supply and Demand.

**California. Governor's Earthquake Council**
Resources Bldg., Rm 1115, 1416 9th St., Sacramento, CA 95817.
- California. Governor's Earthquake Council. Report. irreg. ISSN 0098-2717

**California. Governor's Office**
Sacramento, CA 95814.
- Comprehensive Annual Services Program Plan for the State of California. a. ISSN 0363-5600

**California. Health & Welfare Agency**
744 P St., Sacramento, CA 95814.
- California. Department of Health. Annual Evaluation Report Program Information. a. ISSN 0363-7484
- California. Health and Welfare Agency. Proposed Comprehensive Annual Services Program Plan. a.
- Public Welfare in California. a. ISSN 0362-742X (prep. by its Department of Benefit Payments)

**California. Health and Welfare Agency. Office of Alcoholism**
825 15th Street, Sacramento, CA 95814.
- California Alcoholism Review. bi-m.

**California. Heritage Preservation Commission**
State Archives, 1020 O St., Sacramento, CA 95814.
- Preservation, Organization and Display of State of California's Historic Documents: Report to the California State Legislature. biennial. ISSN 0068-5518

**California. Law Revision Commission**
Stanford Law School, Stanford University, Stanford, CA 94305
(Bound vols. and priced pamphlets avail. from: Department of General Services, Documents Section, P.O. Box 20191, Sacramento, CA 95820)
- California Law Revision Commission (Publications) irreg., 1973, vol. 11.

**California. Office of Administrative Hearings**
915 Capitol Mall, Rm. 470, Sacramento, CA 95814.
- Administrative Law Bulletin. ISSN 0575-3368

**California. Office of Criminal Justice Planning**
7171 Bowling Drive, Sacramento, CA 95823.
- California. Council on Criminal Justice. Comprehensive Plan for Criminal Justice. a. ISSN 0093-8912
- California Office of Criminal Justice Planning. Bulletin. m.

**California. Office of Procurement**
Documents Section, Box 20191, Sacramento, CA 95820.
- Outdoor California. bi-m. ISSN 0030-7025
- Roster-California State, County, City and Township Officials State Officials of the United States. a.

**California. Postsecondary Education Commission**
1020 12th St., Sacramento, CA 95814.
- California. Postsecondary Education Commission. Report. irreg.

**California. State Board of Cosmetology**
1020 N St, Sacramento, CA 95814.
- California. State Board of Cosmetology. Rules and Regulations. irreg. ISSN 0094-4327

**California. State Board of Equalization**
1020 N St., Room 130, Sacramento, CA 95814.
- California. State Board of Equalization. Annual Report. a. ISSN 0068-5801
- California Property Tax Laws Annotated, Including Regulations. s-a. ISSN 0527-0189
- Taxable Sales in California (Sales and Use Tax) q. and a. ISSN 0068-581X

**California. State Fire Marshal**
7171 Bowling Dr., Sacramento, CA 95823.
- S F M. q.

**California. State Lands Division**
1600 L St., Sacramento, CA 95814.
- Public Land Ownership in California. irreg. ISSN 0094-3541

**California. State Library**
Box 2037, Sacramento, CA 95809.
- California County Law Library Basic List. irreg. ISSN 0068-5879
- California State Publications. m (with annual cumulation) ISSN 0008-1574
- California Union List of Periodicals. irreg. ISSN 0095-8034
- News Notes of California Libraries. q. ISSN 0028-9248

**California. State Office of Narcotics and Drug Abuse**
Sacramento, CA 95814.
- Drug Abuse; a directory of training resources in California. irreg. ISSN 0364-0671

**California. State Water Resources Control Board**
Box 100, Sacramento, CA 95801.
- California. State Water Resources Control Board. Annual Program Guide. a.
- California Waterscape. bi-m.

**California. Teachers Retirement Board**
1416 Ninth St., Rm. 616, Sacramento, CA 95814.
- California. Teachers Retirement Board. State Teacher's Retirement System; Annual Report to the Governor and the Legislature. a. ISSN 0090-5593

**California Academy of Family Physicians**
9 First St., San Francisco, CA 94105.
- California G P. bi-m. ISSN 0410-2894

**California Academy of Sciences**
Golden Gate Park, San Francisco, CA 94118.
- California Academy of Sciences. Academy Newsletter. m. ISSN 0008-0829
- California Academy of Sciences. Memoirs. irreg.
- California Academy of Sciences. Occasional Papers. irreg (4-9 nos. per year) ISSN 0068-5461
- California Academy of Sciences. Proceedings. irreg. (12-15 issues per year) ISSN 0068-547X
- Pacific Discovery. bi-m. ISSN 0030-8641
- Pan-Pacific Entomologist. q. ISSN 0031-0603 (Pacific Coast Entomological Society)

**California Advisory Council on Educational Research**
University of Southern California, School of Education, University Park WPH-1101, Los Angeles, CA 90007.
- Educational Research Quarterly. m.

**California Advocate Newspaper**
c/o Lesly H. Kimber, Box 11826, Fresno, CA 93775.
- California Advocate Newspaper. w.

**California Agricultural Aircraft Association**
1107 9th St., Suite 217, Sacramento, CA 95814.
- A P W A Washington Report. 8 per yr. ISSN 0044-782X

**California Almond Grower Exchange**
P.O. Box 1768, Sacramento, CA 95808.
- Almond Facts. bi-m.

**California Alpine Club**
Pacific Bldg., 821 Market St., San Francisco, CA 94103.
- Trails. m. ISSN 0041-0810

**California Alumni Association**
Berkeley, CA 94720.
- California Monthly. 6 per yr. ISSN 0008-1302

**California Association for Neurologically Handicapped Children**
Box 4088, Los Angeles, CA 90051.
- C A N H C-Gram. m.

**California Association for Safety Education**
2784 W. Wilberta Lane, Anaheim, CA 92804.
- Journal of Traffic Safety Education. q.

**California Association of Dianetic Auditors**
Box 3065, Los Angeles, CA 90028.
- Dianetic Journal Notes. 8 per yr.

**California Association of Highway Patrolmen**
1225 8th St., Suite 150, Sacramento, CA 95814.
- California Highway Patrolman. m. ISSN 0008-1140

**California Association of Realtors**
505 Shatto Place, Los Angeles, CA 90020.
- California Real Estate Magazine. m. ISSN 0008-1450

**California Association of School Librarians**
Box 1277, Burlingame, CA 94010.
- California School Libraries. 4 per yr. ISSN 0008-1523

**California Beverage Publications**
8383 Wilshire Blvd., No. 252, Beverly Hills, CA 90211.
- Beverage Bulletin. Southern California. m. ISSN 0006-0356

**California Botanical Society, Inc.**
Dept. of Agronomy and Range Science, University of California, Davis, CA 95616.
- Madrono; a West American journal of botany. q. ISSN 0024-9637

**California Builder and Engineer, Inc.**
Box 10070, 4110 Transport, Palo Alto, CA 94303.
- California Builder and Engineer. bi-m. ISSN 0045-3900
- Timber/West. m.

**California Business News, Inc.**
1060 Crenshaw Blvd, Los Angeles, CA 90019.
- California Business. w. ISSN 0008-0926

**California Cattlemen's Association**
Box 1618, Auburn, CA 95603.
- California Cattleman. m. ISSN 0008-0942

**California Center for Research and Education in Government**
- California Government & Politics Annual. (pub. by California Journal Press)
- California Journal. (pub. by California Journal Press)

**California Chamber of Commerce**
Box 1736, Sacramento, CA 95808.
- California Chamber of Commerce Alert. w.
- Pacific Business Magazine. bi-m. ISSN 0030-8560

**California Citrograph Publishing Co. Ltd.**
5380 Poplar Blvd., Los Angeles, CA 90032.
- Citrograph; magazine of the citrus industry. m. ISSN 0009-7578

**California Classical Association. Southern Section**
c/o John Fendrick, Univ. of California, Classics Dept., Irvine, CA 92664
(Ed. Address: 13645 Riverside Dr., Sherman Oaks, CA 91432)
- Quid Novi. s-a.

**California College of Arts and Crafts**
5212 Broadway, Oakland, CA 94618.
- C C A C. 4 per yr.

**California Congressional Recognition Project, Inc.**
- Californians in Congress. (pub. by Claremont Men's College. Department of Political Science)

**California Council for Social Studies**
2203 16th St., Sacramento, CA 95818.
- Social Studies Review. q.

**California Council on the Education of Teachers**
c/o James W. Cusick, California State University-Fullerton, Fullerton, CA 92634.
- California Journal of Teacher Education. q.

**California Credit Union League**
2322 S. Garey Ave., Pomona, CA 91766.
- D Q. q.

**California Crop and Livestock Reporting Service**
Box 1258, Sacramento, CA 95814.
- California Fruit and Nut Acreage. a.
- California Livestock Statistics. a. ISSN 0361-9095

**California Dental Association**
Box 91258, Los Angeles, CA 90009.
- California Dental Association. Journal. m. ISSN 0008-0977

**California Design, Inc.**
300 E. Green St., Pasadena, CA 91101.
- California Design. triennial, 1971, no. 11. ISSN 0068-5542

**California District Exchange Clubs**
1079 Devonshire Dr., San Diego, CA 92107.
- California Exchangite. bi-m.

**California Educators for Movement Education**
777-South Esplanade St., Orange, CA 92669.
- Movement Education; newsletter in learning through movement. q.

**California English**
Box 4427, Whittier, CA 90607.
- California English. bi-m.

**California Farm Bureau Federation**
2885 Telegraph Ave, Berkeley, CA 94705.
- AG Alert. w.

**California Farmer Publishing Co.**
83 Stevenson St., San Francisco, CA 94105.
- Agrichemical Age. 9 per yr. ISSN 0044-6769
- Animal Nutrition & Health. m. ISSN 0003-3553
- California Farmer. s-m. ISSN 0008-1051

**California Fashion Publications**
1016 S. Broadway Place, Los Angeles, CA 90015.
- California Apparel News. w. ISSN 0008-0896
- Men's News. s-m.

**California Federation of Business & Professional Women's Clubs, Inc**
609 Sutter St., Room 202, San Francisco, CA 94102.
- California Woman. 5 per yr. ISSN 0008-1663

**California Federation of Chaparral Poets**
Box 5519, San Bernardino, CA 92412.
- Chaparral Poet. irreg.

**California Federation of Teachers**
414 13th St., Oakland, CA 94612
(Orders to: 2412 W. Magnolia, Burbank, CA 91406)
- California Teacher. m. ISSN 0410-3556
- Teacher Rights Newsletter. q.

**California Field Ornithologists, Inc.**
Box 369, Del Mar, CA 92014.
- Western Birds. q.

**California Folklore Society**
c/o Folklore & Mythology Group, GSM 1037, U.C.L.A., Los Angeles, CA 90024.
- From the Sourdough Crock. (pub. by California State University, Northridge. Department of Anthropology)
- Western Folklore. q. ISSN 0043-373X

**California Food Mart News**
c/o Bruce A. MacDougall, 922 N. Vine St., Los Angeles, CA 90038.
- California Food Mart News. 11 per yr. ISSN 0008-1086

**California Grain & Feed Association**
3333 Watt Ave., Rm. 114, Sacramento, CA 95821.
- Pacific Southwest Directory. a. ISSN 0555-8581

**California Grocers Association**
1941 O'Farrell St., San Mateo, CA 94403.
- California Grocers Advocate. m. ISSN 0045-3935

**California Historical Society**
2090 Jackson St., San Francisco, CA 94109.
- California Historical Courier. 7 per yr.
- California Historical Quarterly. q. ISSN 0008-1175
- Kemble Occasional. 1-2 per yr. (prep. by its Edward C. Kemble Collections on American Printing and Publishing)

**California Independent**
2900 Ventura, Fresno, CA 93701
- California Independent. m.

**California Indian Education Association, Inc.**
Box 4095, Modesto, CA 95352.
- Early American. bi-m. ISSN 0012-8139

**California Indian Legal Services**
447 15th St., Oakland, CA 94612.
- California Indian Legal Services. Newsletter. q.

**California Institute of International Studies**
766 Santa Ynez, Stanford, CA 94305.
- World Affairs Report. q. ISSN 0090-7103

**California Institute of Technology**
Pasadena, CA 91125.
- Engineering and Science. q. ISSN 0013-7812

**California Institute of Technology. Division of Engineering and Applied Science**
1201 E. California Blvd., Pasadena, CA 91109.
- California Institute of Technology, Pasadena. Division of Engineering and Applied Science. Report of Research and Other Activities. a. ISSN 0068-5658

**California Institute of Technology. Division of Geological and Planetary Sciences**
1200 E. California Blvd., Pasadena, CA 91125.
- California Institute of Technology, Pasadena. Division of Geological and Planetary Sciences. Report on Geological and Planetary Sciences for the Year. a. ISSN 0045-3943

**California Institute of Technology. Munger Africana Library**
Pasadena, CA 91109.
- Munger Africana Library Notes. bi-m. ISSN 0047-8350

**California Job Creation Program Board**
1125 10th St., Sacramento, CA 95814.
- California Job Creation Program Board. Annual Report. a.

**California Journal Press**
1617 10th St., Sacramento, CA 95814.
- California Government & Politics Annual. a. ISSN 0084-8271 (California Center for Research and Education in Government)
- California Journal; the monthly analysis of state government and politics. m. ISSN 0008-1205 (California Center for Research and Education in Government)

**California Jury Verdicts**
901 F St., Suite 120, Sacramento, CA 95823.
- Gavel; jury verdicts on civil actions in California Superior Courts. s-m. ISSN 0363-5783

**California Labor Federation, A F L-C I O**
995 Market St. Suite 310, San Francisco, CA 94103.
- California A F L - C I O News. w. ISSN 0008-0802

**California Library Association**
717 K. St., Suite 300, Sacramento, CA 95814.
- C L A Newsletter. m. ISSN 0007-8557
- California Librarian. q. ISSN 0008-123X

**California Macadamia Society**
P.O. Box 1352, Vista, CA 92083.
- California Macadamia Society. Yearbook. a. ISSN 0068-5720

**California Manufacturers Association**
- California Manufacturers Register. (pub. by Times Mirror Press)

**California Medical Association**
731 Market St., San Francisco, CA 94103.
- Western Journal of Medicine. m. ISSN 0093-0415

**California Mining Journal**
Drawer 628, Santa Cruz, CA 95601.
- California Mining Journal. m. ISSN 0008-1299

**California Mosquito Control Association**
1737 W. Houston Ave., Visalia, CA 93277.
- California Mosquito Control Association. Proceedings and Papers. a. ISSN 0091-6501 (Co-sponsor: American Mosquito Control Association)

**California Newspaper Publishers Association, Inc.**
6151 W. Century Blvd., Los Angeles, CA 90045.
- California Newspaper Publishers' Association. Newspaper Directory. a.
- California Publisher. m. ISSN 0008-1434

**California Nurses' Association**
790 Market St., San Francisco, CA 94102.
- California Nurse. m. ISSN 0008-1310

**California Optometric Association**
921-11th St., Box 2591, Sacramento, CA 95812.
- California Optometrist. m.

**California Park & Recreation Society**
1225 8th St., Suite 102, Sacramento, CA 95814.
- California Parks & Recreation. bi-m.

**California Personnel and Guidance Association**
654 Commonwealth Ave., Fullerton, CA 92631.
- California Personnel and Guidance Association Journal. q. ISSN 0008-137X

**California Pharmaceutical Association**
555 Capitol Mall, Suite 645, Sacramento, CA 95814.
- California Pharmacist. m.

**California-Polytechnic State University. Bureau of Agricultural Education**
San Luis Obispo, CA 93401.
- California Future Farmer. m. (except June-Sep., Dec., Mar.) ISSN 0008-1108 (Future Farmers of America. California Association)

**California Probation, Parole and Correctional Association**
1722 J Street, Suite 10, Sacramento, CA 95814.
- California Correctional News. m.

**California Reading Association**
c/o Dr. Jack B. Jones, Ed., 2464 Flora, San Luis Obispo, CA 93401.
- California Reader. q.

**California Research**
1024 10th St., Suite 300, Sacramento, CA 95814.
- Campaign Law Reporter; complete service covering lobbying regulations and election practices. m. ISSN 0094-1921
- Public Employment Relations Reporter. m.
- State Coastal Report. m.

**California Rural Legal Assistance**
1212 Market St., San Francisco, CA 94102.
- C R L A Noticiero. q.

**California Rural Legal Assistance. Senior Citizens Program**
1900 K St., Sacramento, CA 95814.
- Seniors in Sacramento.

**California Savings and Loan League**
9800 S. Sepulveda Blvd., Suite 500, Los Angeles, CA 90045.
- California Savings and Loan Data Book. a. ISSN 0084-828X
- California Savings and Loan Journal. m. ISSN 0008-1485

**California School Board Association, Inc.**
800 9th St, Suite 201, Sacramento, CA 95814.
- California School Boards. m. (combined Jan.-Feb. and Jul.-Aug.) ISSN 0008-1507

**California School Employees Association**
2350 Paragon Dr., P.O. Box 640, San Jose, CA 95106.
- California School Employee. m.(except Aug. & Sept) ISSN 0008-1515

**California Society of Certified Public Accountants**
1000 Welch Rd., Palo Alto, CA 94304.
- California C P A Quarterly. q. ISSN 0008-0934

**California State Automobile Association**
150 Van Ness Ave., San Francisco, CA 94101.
- Motorland. bi-m. ISSN 0027-2310

**California State College of Pennsylvania**
Box 92, California, PA 15419.
- Kappa Delta Epsilon Current. 4 per yr. ISSN 0022-894X

**California State College, Sonoma. Conference on Peace Research**
1801 E. Cotali Ave., Rohnert Park, CA 94928.
- Peace & Change; a journal of peace research. 3 per yr.

**California State College, Sonoma. Division of American Ethnic Studies**
Rohnert Park, CA 94928.
- Homegrown. irreg. ISSN 0095-6910

**California State College, Sonoma. Division of Humanities**
Rohnert Park, CA 94928.
- Open Reading. 3 per yr.

**California State Employees Association**
1108 O St., Sacramento, CA 95814.
- California State Employee. m. ISSN 0008-1566

**California State Employees Association. Psychiatric Technician Occupational Council**
1108 O St., Sacramento, CA 95814.
- In Care; for the people who care for patients in mental hospitals. s-a.

**California State Grange**
2101 Stockton Blvd., Sacramento, CA 95817.
- California Grange News. s-m. ISSN 0008-1124

**California State Numismatic Association**
c/o Charles G. Colver, 611 N. Banna Ave., Covina, CA 91724.
- Calcoin News. q. ISSN 0008-0616

**California State Old Time Fiddlers Association**
Box 1093, Oroville, CA 95965.
- Sound Post. bi-m.

**California State Poetry Society**
c/o Shirley Sims, 1811 Marnol, Ventura, CA 93003.
- California State Poetry Quarterly. q.

**California State University and Colleges. Office of the Chancellor**
5670 Wilshire Blvd., Los Angeles, CA 90036.
- Future Talk. q.

**California State University, Chico. Department of Biological Sciences**
Chico, CA 95929.
- Sociobiology. irreg. ISSN 0361-6525

**California State University, Fresno. Bureau of Business Research and Service**
Fresno, CA 93710.
- California State University, Fresno. Bureau of Business Research and Service. Study. irreg. ISSN 0094-0992

**California State University, Fullerton. Department of Biology**
Fullerton, CA 92634.
- Ascidian News. 2 per yr since 1976 no. 6; previously irreg. ISSN 0066-8222

**California State University, Fullerton. Library**
Fullerton, CA 92634.
- C H C Publication. (Collection for the History of Cartography) irreg. (prep. by its Special Collections Division)

**California State University, Long Beach. Department of English**
Long Beach, CA 90801.
- Gambit. a. ISSN 0016-4275

**California State University, Long Beach. General Honors Program**
6101 East 7th St., Long Beach, CA 90840.
- Lunar Retorno. 2-3 per yr.
- New Moon. q.

**California State University, Long Beach. Journalism Department**
Long Beach, CA 90840.
- Review of Southern California Journalism. q. ISSN 0048-7503

**California State University, Los Angeles. Center for the Study of Armament and Disarmament**
5151 State University Dr., Los Angeles, CA 90032.
- California State University, Los Angeles. Center for the Study of Armament and Disarmament. Occasional Papers Series. irreg.
- California State University, Los Angeles. Center for the Study of Armament and Disarmament. Political Issues Bibliography Series. irreg. (approx. 6-10 per yr.)
- War Peace Bibliography Series. (pub. by American Bibliographical Center-Clio Press)

**California State University, Los Angeles. John F. Kennedy Memorial Library**
5151 State University Drive, Los Angeles, CA 90032.
- California State University, Los Angeles. Library Report. a. ISSN 0068-5828

**California State University, Los Angeles. Pan-African Studies Department**
Los Angeles, CA 90032.
- Pass: a Journal of the Black Experience; a journal of the black experience and Pan-African issues. q.

**California State University, Northridge. Department of Anthropology**
Northridge, CA 91324.
- From the Sourdough Crock. q. ISSN 0532-7334 (California Folklore Society)

**California State University, Northridge. Department of Geography**
Northridge, CA 91330.
- Historical Geography Newsletter. s-a.

**California State University, Northridge. Department of Journalism**
Darby Annex 103, Northridge, CA 91324.
- Journalism History. q. ISSN 0094-7679
- Scene. q. ISSN 0048-931X

**California State University, Northridge. Library**
18111 Nordhoff St., Northridge, CA 91324.
- California State University, Northridge. Library. Annual Report. a.

**California State University, Sacramento. Department of Spanish and Portuguese**
6000 J St., Sacramento, CA 95819.
- Explicacion de Textos Literarios. s-a.

**California State University, Sacramento. Library**
6000 Jay St., Sacramento, CA 95819.
- Journals of Dissent and Social Change; a classified list of titles in the Sacramento State College library. irreg.; 1972, 3rd ed.

**California State University, San Bernardino. School of Natural Sciences**
San Bernardino, CA 92407.
- Tribolium Information Bulletin. a. ISSN 0082-6391

**California State University, San Jose. Women's Center**
177 S. 10th St., San Jose, CA 95192.
- Xanthippe; feminist literary magazine. a.

**California Taxpayers Association**
921 11th St., Suite 800, Sacramento, CA 95814.
- Cal-Tax News. s-m. ISSN 0008-0543

**California Teachers Association**
1705 Murchison Drive, Burlingame, CA 94010.
- C T A/N E A Action. s-m(during school year)
- California Professor. 8 per yr. ISSN 0008-1418

**California Thoroughbred Breeders Association**
201 Colorado Place, Arcadia, CA 91006.
- Thoroughbred of California. m. ISSN 0049-3821

**California Tomato Growers Association, Inc.**
9036 Thornton Rd., Stockton, CA 95207.
- California Tomato Grower. m., 11 per yr.

**California Tomorrow**
681 Market St., San Francisco, CA 94105.
- Cry California. q. ISSN 0011-2224

**California Trucking Association**
1240 Bayshore Hwy., Burlingame, CA 94010.
- Caltrux. w.

**California Vertebrate Pest Technical Committee. Library**
- Vertebrate Pest Conference. Proceedings. (pub. by University of California, Davis)

**California Veterinary Medical Association**
1024 Country Club Drive, Moraga, CA 94556.
- California Veterinarian. m. ISSN 0008-1612

**California Water Pollution Control Association**
127 N. Madison Ave., No. 304, Pasadena, CA 91011.
- California Water Pollution Control Association. Bulletin. q. ISSN 0008-1620

**California Western School of Law**
350 Cedar St., San Diego, CA 92101.
- California Western International Law Journal. 3 per yr.
- California Western Law Review. 3 per yr. ISSN 0008-1639

**California Women's Fashions**
8732 Sunset Blvd., Los Angeles, CA 90069.
- California Women's Fashions. m.

**California Wool Growers Association**
3382 El Camino Ave., No. 6, Sacramento, CA 95821.
- California Sheepman's Quarterly. m.

**Californianos**
Box 1632, San Francisco, CA 94133.
- Antepasados. s-a. ISSN 0044-8362

**Los Californianos, Inc.**
18200 S. Arboreal Way, Ripon, CA 95366.
- Noticias para los Californianos. bi-m.

**Las Californias Publishing Co.**
1009 S. St. Andrews Place, Los Angeles, CA 90019.
- Collective Bargaining Today. Proceedings. a. (Collective Bargaining Forum)

**Call Publications**
638 S. Federal, Chicago, IL 60605
(Orders to: Box 5597, Chicago, IL 60680)
- Call/Clarin; political newspaper of the October League. m. (October League (Marxist-Leninist))

**Callaghan & Co.**
6141 N. Cicero Ave., Chicago, IL 60646.
- Corporate Practice Commentator. q. ISSN 0010-8995
- Current Municipal Problems. q. ISSN 0011-3727
- Law Office Economics and Management Manual. q. ISSN 0023-9313
- Medical Trial Technique Quarterly. q. ISSN 0025-7591
- Trial Lawyer's Guide. ISSN 0041-2546

**Callahan Publications**
Box 3751, Washington, DC 20007.
- Military Research Letter. s-m. ISSN 0026-413X
- Missile/Ordnance Letter. s-m. ISSN 0026-5993
- New Factory Report. s-m. ISSN 0028-5072
- Renegotiation/Management Letter. s-m. ISSN 0034-4435
- Space Letter. s-m. ISSN 0038-6278
- Underwater Letter. 3 per mo. ISSN 0041-6592
- Washington Environmental Protection Report. s-m. ISSN 0014-9136

**Albert E. Callan, Ed. & Pub.**
Box 5293, Hamden, CT 06518.
- Connecticut Fireside. q. ISSN 0300-8258

**Caltex Petroleum Corp.**
380 Madison Ave., New York, NY 10017.
- Oil-Lifestream of Progress. q. ISSN 0030-1310

**Calvary Bible College**
1111 W. 39th St., Kansas City, MO 64111.
- Calvary Review. q. ISSN 0008-1779

**Calvary Temple Inc.**
3000 S. Raccoon Rd., Youngstown, OH 44515.
- Humbard Christian Report. w. ISSN 0046-8274

**Calvin Theological Seminary**
3233 Burton St. S.E., Grand Rapids, MI 49506.
- Calvin Theological Journal. s-a. ISSN 0008-1795

**Calyx**
Box 118, Route 2, Corvallis, OR 97330.
- Calyx; a northwest feminist review. 3 per yr.

**Camag Inc.**
16229 W. Ryerson Rd., New Berlin, WI 53151.
- Camag Bibliography Service. q. ISSN 0008-1833

**Cambridge Entomological Club**
16 Divinity Ave., Cambridge, MA 02138.
- Psyche; journal of entomology. q. ISSN 0033-2615

**Cambridge Scientific Abstracts, Inc.**
Suite 437, 6611 Kenilworth Ave, Riverdale, MD 20840.
- Computer and Information Systems; an abstract journal pertaining to the theory, design, fabrication and application of computer and information systems. 2 vols. per yr. (10 nos. per vol.) ISSN 0010-4507
- Electronics and Communications Abstracts Journal; an abstract journal involving the theory, design and application of electronic devices and systems. 10 per yr.
- Safety Science Abstracts. 10 per yr. ISSN 0092-542X
- Science Research Abstracts. Part A: MHD and Plasmas; Superconductivity Research; and Theoretical Physics. 10 per yr.
- Science Research Abstracts. Part B: Laser and Electro-Optic Reviews; Quantum Electronics. 10 per yr. ISSN 0092-0754
- Solid State Abstracts; an abstract journal involving the physics, metallurgy, crystallography, chemistry and device technology of solids. 10 per yr. ISSN 0038-108X

**Cambridge University Press**
For publications of this press see section for UNITED KINGDOM

**Camden County Record**
5th and Jersey Ave., Gloucester City, NJ 08030.
- Camden County Record. w. ISSN 0008-2031

**Camels Coming Newsletter**
Box 703, San Francisco, CA 94101.
- Camels Coming Newsletter. m.

**Camera Thirty-Five**
420 Lexington Ave., New York, NY 10017.
- Camera Thirty-Five. 10 per yr. ISSN 0008-2171

**Kenneth W. Cameron**
Box A, Station A, Hartford, CT 06106.
- Historiographer. q. ISSN 0018-2591 (Episcopal Diocese of Connecticut)

**Camp Fire Girls, Inc.**
1740 Broadway, 17th Floor, New York, NY 10019.
- Camp Fire Leadership; a magazine for adult members and leaders of blue birds, adventure, discovery and horizon clubs. q.
- Campsite Planning and Utilization. Guideline Series. irreg., 1972, no. 2.

**Campaign Associates**
516 Petroleum Bldg., Wichita, KS 67202.
- Campaign Insight; an overview of political techniques. s-m. ISSN 0008-2317

**Campaigner Publications, Inc.**
231 W. 29th St., New York, NY 10001.
- Campaigner. m. (National Caucus of Labor Committees)

**Alex N. Campbell, Jr.**
Box 76974, Los Angeles, CA 90005.
- Western Financial Journal. s-m. ISSN 0008-106X (Prudential Financial Corp. of Los Angeles)

**Camper's Guide to Area Campgrounds**
c/o Marilee B. Pearsall, Timber Ridge Dr., Box 68-A, Coal Valley, IL 61240.
- Camper's Guide to Area Campgrounds. irreg; latest 1973.

**Campground Marketing Associates**
P.O. Box 121, Palos Verdes Ests., CA 90274.
- Private Campgrounds & RV Parks Buying Guide. a.

**Campgrounds Unlimited**
Box 188, Longford, KS 67458.
- Campground Guide for Tent and Trailer Tourists. biennial. ISSN 0068-693X

**Campus Communications, Inc.**
Box 13266, University Station, Gainesville, FL 32604.
- Independent Florida Alligator. 5 per w.

**Campus Crusade for Christ**
Arrowhead Springs, San Bernardino, CA 92414.
- Student Action. 3 per yr. ISSN 0039-2707
- Worldwide Challenge. m.

**Campus Publications, Inc.**
Box 1128, St. Louis, MO 63130.
- Student Life. s-w. ISSN 0039-2758 (Washington University)

**Can-Am Media, Inc.**
313 W. 53rd Street, New York, NY 10019.
- Backgammon Illustrated. q.
- Human Response: the New Sexuality. bi-m.
- Oriental Combat and Self Defense. q.
- Oriental Fighting Arts. m.

**Can Manufacturers Institute**
1625 Massachusetts Ave., N.W., Washington, DC 20036.
- Can Manufacturers Institute. Annual Metal Cans Shipment Report. a. ISSN 0068-7014

**Canadian Air Mail Collectors Club**
Box 145, Brookfield, IL 60513.
- Canada Air Mail Notes. q.

**Canadian Embassy. Public Affairs Division**
1771 N Street, N.W., Washington, DC 20036.
- Canada Today/D'Aujourd'hui. 10 per yr. ISSN 0045-4257

**Canadian Enterprise Corporation**
12611 Lake Shore Blvd., Cleveland, OH 44108.
- Dempsey Canadian Newsletter. s-m. ISSN 0011-8354

**Cancer Care, Inc.**
1 Park Ave., New York, NY 10016.
- Cancer Care and the National Cancer Foundation. Report About the Services Your Contributions Support. q. ISSN 0027-8866 (Co-sponsor: National Cancer Foundation, Inc.)

**Cancer Control Society**
2043 N. Berendo, Los Angeles, CA 90027.
- Cancer Control Journal. bi-m.

**Cancer Letter**
1411 Aldenham Lane, Reston, VA 22090.
- Cancer Letter. w.

**Candar Publishing Co.**
235 Park Ave. S., New York, NY 10003.
- Daring. bi-m.
- Wildcat Special. q.

**Candidate Press**
4225 Office Pkwy., Dallas, TX 75204.
- Life Company Tax Newsletter. q. ISSN 0047-4606

**Canine Information Center**
- D I S C A R. (pub. by Professional Breeding Services Inc.)

**Canning Publications, Inc**
925 Anza Ave, Vista, CA 92083.
- E D P Analyzer. m. ISSN 0012-7523

**Canning Trade, Inc.**
2619 Maryland Ave., Baltimore, MD 21218.
- Food Production/Management; monthly publication of the canning, glass-packing and frozen food industry. m.

**Canterbury and York Society**
- Canterbury and York Series. (pub. by Oxford University Press)

**Cantorial Council of America**
c/o Yeshiva University, 500 W. 185th St., New York, NY 10033.
- Journal of Jewish Music and Liturgy. a.

**Cantwell-Conteville Family Association**
R.R. 1, Reese Rd., Clayton, NY 13624.
- Cantwell Tapestry. q. ISSN 0094-6907

**Canvas Products Association International**
600 Endicott Bldg., St. Paul, MN 55101.
- Industrial Fabric Products Review. m. ISSN 0019-8307

**Canyon Cinema Cooperative**
Room 220, Industrial Center Bldg., Sausalito, CA 94965.
- Canyon Cinemanews. bi-m. ISSN 0008-5758

**Capital Energy Letter**
1174 National Press Bldg., Washington, DC 20045
- Capital Energy Letter. w.

**Capital Ledger**
847 East Colfax Ave., Suite 305, Denver, CO 80218.
- Capital Ledger. m.

**Capital Management Publications**
119 Paul Drive, San Rafael, CA 94903.
- Bicycling. 12 per yr. ISSN 0006-2073

**Capital Publishers, Inc.**
P.O. Box 6235, 5306 Belt Rd., N.W., Washington, DC 20015.
- Know Your Congress. new edition each session.

**Capital Publishing Corporation**
10 S. La Salle St., Chicago, IL 60603.
- Guide to Venture Capital Sources. biennial.

**Capital Region Planning Commission**
333 North 19th Street, Baton Rouge, LA 70806.
- C R P C Info. m.

**Capital University Law School**
Columbus, OH 43209.
- Capital University Law Review; a journal of corrections and institutional control. irreg; v. 3, 1974.

**Capitalist Reporter Inc.**
800 Second Ave., New York, NY 10017.
- Free Enterprise. bi-m.

**Capitol District Communications**
Box 11, Schenectady, NY 12308.
- New Citizen. fortn.

**Capitol Publications, Inc.**
Suite G-12, 2430 Pennsylvania Ave., Washington, DC 20037.
- Nation's Schools Report; the magazine of better school administration. m. ISSN 0028-0526

**Capitol Publications, Inc. Education News Services Division**
Suite G-12, 2430 Pennsylvania Ave., N.W., Washington, DC 20037.
- Economic Opportunity Report. w. ISSN 0013-0206
- Education Daily. d.(5 per w.) ISSN 0013-1261
- Higher Education Daily. d.
- Manpower and Vocational Education Weekly. w. ISSN 0047-5785
- Report on Education of the Disadvantaged. fortn. ISSN 0034-4680
- Report on Education Research. bi-m. ISSN 0034-4699
- Report on Preschool Education. fortn. ISSN 0034-4702

**Capitol Publications, Inc. Health News Services Division**
Suite G-12, 2430 Pennslvania Ave. N.W., Washington, DC 20037.
- Health Daily; independent national news service for health administrators. d.
- Health Manpower Report. fortn.

**Capla Publications, Inc.**
18 Overlook Ave., Rochelle Park, NJ 07662.
- Educational Economics. m.

**Capra Press**
c/o Book People, 2940 Seventh St., Berkeley, CA 94710.
- Yes! Capra Chapbook Series. irreg.

**Capuchin Missions**
1820 Mt. Elliott Ave., Detroit, MI 48207.
- Sandal Prints. bi-m. ISSN 0036-4282 (Province of St. Joseph of the Capuchin Order)

**Car and Locomotive Cyclopedia**
350 Broadway, New York, NY 10013.
- Car and Locomotive Cyclopedia. quadrennial.

**Car Classics Publishing Co.**
P.O. Box 978, North Hollywood, CA 91603.
- Car Classics. bi-m. ISSN 0095-0556

**Cara**
Box 66661, Houston, TX 77006.
- Cara's Directory of the Occult and Psychic Sciences. s-a.

**Caravan, Inc**
- World Shopping Encyclopedia. (pub. by Wm. H. Wise & Co., Inc.)

**Card Memorabilia Association**
102 Ringgold St., Peekskill, NY 10566.
- Baseball Quarterly. q.

**Cardinal Mindszenty Foundation, Inc.**
Box 11321, St. Louis, MO 63105.
- Mindszenty Report. m. ISSN 0026-4474
- Red Line. m.

**Cardinal Publishing Co.**
1098 Harrison St., San Francisco, CA 94103.
- Western Machinery & Steel World Buyer's Directory. a.

**CARE, Inc.**
660 First Ave., New York, NY 10016.
- CARE World Report. q.

**Career Education Center**
Florida State University, 415 N. Monroe St., Tallahassee, FL 32306.
- Florida Vocational Journal. m. (Florida. Department of Education. Division of Vocational Education)

**Cargill, Inc.**
Box 9300, Minneapolis, MN 55440.
- Cargill Crop Bulletin; crop and weather conditions in the United States, Canada and the World. m. ISSN 0008-641X

**Caribbean Journal of Science and Mathematics**
Box 22, Cullowhee, NC 28723.
- Caribbean Journal of Science and Mathematics. s-a. ISSN 0008-6460

**Caribbean Review Inc.**
Editorial Office, College of Arts & Sciences, Florida International University, Miami, FL 33199.
- Caribbean Review; a books-oriented quarterly dealing with Caribbean-Latin American affairs. q. ISSN 0008-6525

**Carleton College**
Northfield, MN 55057.
- Carleton Miscellany. 2 per yr. ISSN 0008-6649

**Shirley L. Carlson, Ed. & Pub.**
86 N. Heck Hill Rd., Box 850, Saint Paris, OH 43072.
- German Shorthaired Pointer News. m.

**Carlson Publications, Inc.**
P.O. Box 208, Bethlehem, CT 06751.
- Job/Scope; the bimonthly publication for key men in contracting organizations. bi-m. ISSN 0449-0495

**Carnegie Commission on Higher Education**
2150 Shattuck Ave., Berkeley, CA 94704
- Carnegie Commission on Higher Education. Commission Reports. irreg. (Dist. by: McGraw-Hill, Inc, 1221 Ave. of the Americas, New York, NY 10020)
- Carnegie Commission on Higher Education. General Reports. irreg. (Dist. by: McGraw-Hill, Inc., 1221 Ave. of the Americas, New York, NY 10020)
- Carnegie Commission on Higher Education. Technical Reports. irreg. (Dist. by: Carnegie Council on Policy Studies in Higher Education, 2150 Shattuck Ave., Berkeley, CA 94704)

**Carnegie Corporation of New York**
437 Madison Ave., New York, NY 10022.
- Carnegie Corporation of New York. Annual Report. a. ISSN 0069-0635
- Carnegie Quarterly. q. ISSN 0576-7954

**Carnegie Endowment for International Peace**
345 E. 46th St., New York, NY 10017.
- Carnegie Endowment for International Peace. Financial Report. a. ISSN 0094-3029
- Carnegie Endowment for International Peace Report. a. ISSN 0069-0643

**Carnegie Foundation for the Advancement of Teaching**
437 Madison Ave., New York, NY 10022.
- Carnegie Foundation for the Advancement of Teaching. Report. a. ISSN 0069-0651

**Carnegie Institute**
4400 Forbes Ave., Pittsburgh, PA 15213.
- Carnegie Magazine; dedicated to literature, science, art and music. m.(Sept-June) ISSN 0008-6681

**Carnegie Institute of Technology. Department of Genetics**
Schenley Park, Pittsburgh, PA 15213.
- Carnegie Institute of Technology. Department of Genetics. Papers. irreg.

**Carnegie Institution of Washington**
- Carnegie Institution of Washington. Year Book. (pub. by Academic Press, Inc.)

**Carnegie Library of Pittsburgh**
Director's Office, 4400 Forbes Ave., Pittsburgh, PA 15213.
- Science and Technology; purchase guide for branch and public libraries. a. ISSN 0080-746X

**Carnegie-Mellon University**
- Benjamin F. Fairless Lectures. (pub. by Columbia University Press)

**Carnegie Mellon University. Department of Modern Languages**
Baker Hall, Pittsburgh, PA 15213.
- Latin American Literary Review. s-a. ISSN 0047-4134

**Carnegie Museum of Natural History**
4400 Forbes Ave., Pittsburgh, PA 15213.
- Carnegie Museum of Natural History. Annals of (the) Carnegie Museum. irreg.
- Paleontology and Geology of the Badwater Creek Area, Central Wyoming. irreg., latest issue no. 9.

**Carnivore Genetics Research Center**
Box 5, Newtonville, MA 02160
(and St. Stephens Rd. Nursery, Ealing, London
W.13, Eng)
● Carnivore Genetics Newsletter. s-a. ISSN 0008-
6711

**Carolina Biological Supply Co.**
Burlington, NC 27215.
● Carolina Tips. m. ISSN 0045-5865

**Carolina Bird Club**
R. 3, Box 114 A-A, Zebulon, NC 27597.
● Chat. q. ISSN 0009-1987

**Carolina Christian Publications, Inc.**
Box 5423, Sta. B, Greenville, SC 29606.
● Carolina Christian. m. ISSN 0008-672X

**Carolina Financial Times**
Box 5978, 2008 Hillsborough, Raleigh, NC 27607.
● Carolina Financial Times. w. ISSN 0008-6754

**Carolina Motor Club**
Box 60, Charlotte, NC 28230.
● Go (Charlotte) bi-m. ISSN 0017-1441

**Carolina Population Center**
University Square 300 A, University of North
Carolina, 113 Mallette Street, Chapel Hill, NC
27514.
● Carolina Population Center. Monograph. irreg.,
latest issue no. 21. ISSN 0069-0724

**Carolina Quarterly**
Box 1117, Chapel Hill, NC 27514.
● Carolina Quarterly. 3 per yr. ISSN 0008-6797

**Carolinas Genealogical Society**
407 S. Church St., Monroe, NC 28110.
● Carolinas Genealogical Society. Bulletin. q.

**Caroline Publishing Co.**
Preston, MD 21655.
● News and Farmer. w. ISSN 0048-0215

**Carolinian**
c/o P. R. Jervay, Ed., 518 E. Martin St., Raleigh,
NC 27601.
● Carolinian. w. ISSN 0045-5873

**Carpet and Rug Institute**
Box 2048, Dalton, GA 30720.
● Carpet and Rug Institute. Directory and Report.
a. ISSN 0069-0740
● Carpet and Rug Institute. Review: State of the
Industry. a. ISSN 0092-0495
● Carpet Specifier's Handbook. a. ISSN 0095-6457

**Carrier Pidgin**
c/o Barbara Robson, Ed., 1651 Greenbriar St.,
Arlington, VA 22205.
● Carrier Pidgin. q.

**Carrier Reports**
369 Main St., Old Saybrook, CT 06475.
● Carrier Reports. q. ISSN 0008-6924

**Carroll County Historical Society**
210 E. Main St., Westminster, MD 21157.
● Historical Society of Carroll County Newsletter. 4
per yr.

**Carson-Newman College**
Jefferson City, TN 37760.
● Carson and Newman College, Jefferson City,
Tennessee. Faculty Studies. a. ISSN 0069-0783

**Carstens Publications, Inc.**
Box 700, Newton, NJ 07860.
● Creative Crafts. 6 per yr. ISSN 0011-0884
● Creative Crafts Christmas Annual. a.
● Flying Models; the model builder's How-To-Do-It
magazine. m. ISSN 0015-4849
● Railfan. bi-m.
● Railroad Model Craftsman. m. ISSN 0033-877X

**Carte Blanche Corp.**
3460 Wilshire Blvd., Los Angeles, CA 90010.
● Carte Blanche. bi-m. ISSN 0008-7017

**Carter Chatter Quarterly**
2237 Grace St., Fort Worth, TX 76111.
● Carter Chatter Quarterly. q.

**Carthage College**
Kenosha, WI 53140.
● Arrow (Kenosha); student voice of Carthage
College. w. ISSN 0001-3056

**Cartoonist Profiles**
Box 325, Fairfield, CT 06430.
● Cartoonist Profiles. q. ISSN 0008-7068

**Casa Bautista de Publicaciones**
Box 4255, El Paso, TX 79914.
● Accion. q.
● Adelante. q.
● Ahora. q.
● ANCLA. q. (Southern Baptist Convention.
Foreign Mission Board)
● Conquistadores. q.
● Escudo. q. ISSN 0014-0392 (Southern Baptist
Convention. Foreign Mission Board)
● Estrella. q. ISSN 0014-1399 (Southern Baptist
Convention. Foreign Mission Board)
● Expositor Biblico; para maestros de intermedios,
jovenes, mayores, adultos. q. ISSN 0014-5238
● Hogar Cristiano. q. ISSN 0018-3229
● Marchemos. q.
● Nuestros Ninos. q. ISSN 0029-5809
● Obrero Cristiano. q.
● Promotor de Educacion Cristiana; revista para
lideres de iglesias. q. ISSN 0033-1139
● Rayito; edicion para consejeras. q. ISSN 0034-
0170 (Southern Baptist Convention. Foreign
Mission Board)
● Revista para Parvulos y Principiantes. q. ISSN
0035-0303
● Revista para Uniones de Primarios. q. ISSN 0035-
0346
● Ventana. q. ISSN 0042-3459 (Southern Baptist
Convention. Foreign Mission Board)

**Casa Grande Valley Newspapers, Inc.**
Drawer 679, Gila Bend, AZ 85337.
● Gila Bend Herald. w.

**Casaba**
500 40th St., Bellingham, WA 98225.
● Casaba. a.

**Paul Case**
1601 Fourth N.W., Albuquerque, NM 87103.
● New Mexico Beverage Journal. m. ISSN 0028-
6141

**Case Institute of Technology. Case Student Assembly**
Case Western Reserve University, Tomlinson Hall,
Cleveland, OH 44106.
● Engineering and Science Review. 4 per yr. ISSN
0013-7820

**Case Western Reserve University. Department of
English**
Gutenberg Annex, Cleveland, OH 44106.
● Bits. s-a.

**Case Western Reserve University. Law-Medicine
Center**
11075 East Blvd., Cleveland, OH 44106.
● Law Medicine Series. irreg. ISSN 0075-8248

**Case Western Reserve University. School of Dentistry**
2119 Abington Rd., Cleveland, OH 44106.
● Case Western Reserve University School of
Dentistry: Dental Alumni Bulletin. q. ISSN 0043-
4140

**Case Western Reserve University. School of Law**
Cleveland, OH 44106.
● Case Western Reserve Journal of International
Law. s-a. ISSN 0008-7254
● Case Western Reserve Law Review. 4 per yr.
ISSN 0008-7262

**Case Western Reserve University. Warner and
Swasey Observatory**
1975 Taylor Road, East Cleveland, OH 44112.
● Case Western Reserve University. Warner and
Swasey Observatory. Publications. irreg. 1-2 per
yr.

**Cash Box Publishing Co., Inc.**
119 W. 57th St., New York, NY 10019.
● Cash Box; the international music-record weekly.
w. ISSN 0008-7289

**Cason Family Association**
c/o Wm. R. Cason, Ed., P.O. Box 88393, Atlanta,
GA 30338.
● Cason Quarterly. q. ISSN 0092-7694

**Casper Publications**
618 Western Ave, Madison, WI 53711.
● One Shot. irreg; latest 1973-74.

**Cassak Publications Inc.**
2009 Morris Ave., Union, NJ 07083.
● Patient Aid Digest. bi-m.
● Surgical Business. m. ISSN 0039-6095
● Surgical Trade Buyers Guide. a. ISSN 0081-9654

**Cassandra Publications**
Box 447, Crystal City, TX 78839.
● Harbinger (Crystal City); a magazine of media
arts. a. ISSN 0017-761X

**Cassette Information Services**
Box 17727, Foy Sta., Los Angeles, CA 90057.
● Audio-Cassette Newsletter. q.
● Directory of Spoken-Voice Audio-Cassetts. a.

**Cast Iron Pipe Association**
1301 West 22nd Street, Suite 509, Oak Brook, IL
60521.
● Ductile Iron Pipe News. a.

**Casting Engineering**
c/o W. W. Troland, 1500 Elm St., Stratford, CT
06497.
● Casting Engineering. q. ISSN 0008-7513

**Castle Press Publications**
Box 1836, 1254 Lean Ct., Oroville, CA 95965.
● Diversifier. bi-m.

**Casualty Actuarial Society**
200 E. 42nd St., New York, NY 10017.
● Actuarial Review.
● Casualty Actuarial Society. Proceedings. a.

**Cat Fanciers Association**
P.O. Box 430, Red Bank, NJ 07701.
● Cat Fanciers Association. Year Book. a. ISSN
0069-1003

**Catalyst for Environmental Quality**
274 Madison Ave., Suite 1804, New York, NY
10016.
● Catalyst for Environmental Quality. q. ISSN
0008-7688

**Catfish Farmers of America**
Box 2451, Little Rock, AR 72203.
● Commercial Fish Farmer. bi-m. ISSN 0095-0491

**Catgut Acoustical Society**
c/o Stewart Hegeman, 176 Linden Ave., Glen
Ridge, NJ 07028.
● Catgut Acoustical Society Newsletter. s-a. ISSN
0576-9280

**Cathartic**
c/o Patrick M. Ellingham, Ed., Box 1301, Fort
Lauderdale, FL 33302.
● Cathartic. 1 per yr. or 1 double issue.

**Cathedral Foundation, Inc.**
320 Cathedral St., Baltimore, MD 21203.
● Catholic Review (Baltimore) w. ISSN 0008-8315

**Cathedral Publishers**
324 E. 4th St., Royal Oak, MN 48068.
● In Season. w.
● M S S. (Master Sermon Series) m. ISSN 0362-
0808

**Catholic Actors Guild of America**
Hotel Piccadilly, 227 W. 45th St., New York, NY
10036.
● Call Board. bi-m.(Oct-Jun) ISSN 0008-1701

**Catholic Advance**
c/o Bishop David M. Maloney, 424 N. Broadway,
Wichita, KS 67202.
● Catholic Advance. w. ISSN 0008-7904

**Catholic Albanian American League**
4221 Park Ave., Bronx, NY 10457.
● Jeta Katholike Shqiptare/Catholic Albanian Life.
q.

**Catholic Archdiocese of Kansas City**
2220 Central, Kansas City, KS 66110.
● Eastern Kansas Register. w. ISSN 0012-883X

**Catholic Archdiocese of Los Angeles**
1530 W. Ninth St., Los Angeles, CA 90015.
- Tidings; official Catholic weekly newspaper of Los Angeles. w. ISSN 0040-6791

**Catholic Archdiocese of St. Louis**
462 N. Taylor Ave., St. Louis, MO 63108.
- St. Louis Review. w. ISSN 0036-3022

**Catholic Biblical Association of America**
Catholic University of America, Washington, DC 20064.
- Catholic Bible Quarterly Monograph Series. irreg.
- Catholic Biblical Quarterly. q. ISSN 0008-7912
- Old Testament Abstracts. 3 per yr. ISSN 0364-8591
- Old Testament Abstracts. 3 per yr. ISSN 0364-8591

**Catholic Central Union of America**
3835 Westminister Place, St. Louis, MO 63108.
- Catholic Central Union of America. Proceedings. a. ISSN 0069-1216
- Catholic Woman's Journal. 10 per yr. ISSN 0008-8455 (National Catholic Women's Union)
- Social Justice Review; pioneer American journal of Catholic social action. m.(Sept-June)bi-m.(July-Aug) ISSN 0037-7767

**Catholic Church Extension Society of the United States**
c/o Rev. Edward J. Slattery, 1307 S. Wabash Ave., Chicago, IL 60605.
- Extension. 9 per yr.

**Catholic Diocese of Arlington. Diocese of Arlington**
200 N. Glebe Rd., Suite 905, Arlington, VA 22203.
- Arlington Catholic Herald. w. ISSN 0361-3712

**Catholic Diocese of Dodge City**
Box 1317, Dodge City, KS 67801.
- Southwest Kansas Register. w. ISSN 0038-4690

**Catholic Diocese of Orlando & St. Petersburg**
Box 3551, Orlando, FL 32802.
- Florida Catholic Newspaper. w. ISSN 0015-394X

**Catholic Diocese of Pittsburgh**
- Pittsburgh Catholic. (pub. by Pittsburgh Catholic Publishing Associates)

**Catholic Diocese of Spokane**
W. 1023 Riverside Ave, Box 48, Spokane, WA 99210.
- Inland Register. w. ISSN 0020-1510

**Catholic Diocese of Wheeling-Charleston**
P.O. Box 230, Wheeling, WV 26003.
- Catholic Spirit. fortn.

**Catholic Dioceses of Saginaw & Gaylord**
1520 Court St., Box 1405, Saginaw, MI 48605.
- Catholic Weekly. w. ISSN 0008-8439

**Catholic Family Life Program**
c/o Rev. John A. Furtmann, 2021 North 60th St., Milwaukee, WI 53208.
- Official Wisconsin Pastoral Handbook. a.

**Catholic Foreign Mission Society of America, Inc.**
Maryknoll Seminary, Maryknoll, NY 10545.
- Channel (Maryknoll); a Newsletter for Maryknollers. 3 per yr. ISSN 0009-1456
- Maryknoll. m. ISSN 0025-4142

**Catholic Guild for the Blind**
180 N. Michigan Ave., No. 1720, Chicago, IL 60601.
- Word for Word. 10 per yr.

**Catholic Hospital Association**
1438 S. Grand Blvd, St. Louis, MO 63104.
- Guidebook of Catholic Hospitals. a. ISSN 0090-2535
- Hospital Progress. m. ISSN 0018-5817

**Catholic Knights of America**
217 E. 8th St, Cincinnati, OH 45202.
- C. K. of A. Journal. m. ISSN 0007-8530

**Catholic Library Association**
461 W. Lancaster Ave., Haverford, PA 19041.
- Catholic Library World. m. ISSN 0008-820X
- Catholic Periodical and Literature Index. bi-m. ISSN 0008-8285

**Catholic Library Association. Northern Illinois Unit**
3800 Peterson Avenue, Chicago, River Forest, IL 60659.
- Catholic Library Association. Northern Illinois Unit. Newsletter. q. ISSN 0008-8161

**Catholic Library Association. Northern Ohio Unit**
Walsh College Library, 2020 Easton St., Canton, OH 44720.
- Catholic Library Association. Northern Ohio Unit. Newsletter. 2-3 per yr. ISSN 0008-817X

**Catholic Library Association. Parish & Community Libraries Section**
1440 Randolph Ave., No. 305, St. Paul, MN 55105.
- Parish and Community Libraries News. bi-m.

**Catholic Negro-American Mission Board**
335 Broadway, New York, NY 10013.
- Educating in Faith. m. ISSN 0030-6819

**Catholic News Publishing Co., Inc.**
68 West Broad St., Mount Vernon, NY 10552.
- School Guide. a.

**Catholic Order of Foresters**
305 W. Madison St., Chicago, IL 60606.
- Catholic Forester. bi-m. ISSN 0008-8048

**Catholic Order of the Franciscan Fathers**
- Miesiecznik Franciszkanski. (pub. by Franciscan Publishers)

**Catholic Peace Fellowship**
339 Lafayette St., New York, NY 10012.
- Catholic Peace Fellowship Bulletin. bi-m. ISSN 0008-8277

**Catholic Polls, Inc.**
86 Riverside Drive, New York, NY 10024.
- Homiletic and Pastoral Review. m. (bi-m. Aug. per Sept.) ISSN 0018-4268

**Catholic Press Association**
119 North Park Ave., Rockville Centre, NY 11570.
- Catholic Journalist. bi-m. ISSN 0008-8129
- Catholic Press Directory; official media reference guide to Catholic newspapers and magazines of the United States and Canada. a. ISSN 0008-8307
- Long Island Catholic. w. ISSN 0024-6255 (Roman Catholic Diocese of Rockville Centre) (Subscr. to: Long Island Catholic, Box 335, Rockville Centre, Long Island, NY 11571)

**Catholic Press Union, Inc.**
1027 Superior Ave. N.E., Cleveland, OH 44114.
- Catholic Chronicle. w. ISSN 0008-7971

**Catholic Publishing Co.**
1739 Mahoning Avenue, Youngstown, OH 44509
(Subscr. to: 517 S. Belle Vista Avenue, Youngstown, Ohio 44509)
- Katolikus Magyarok Vasarnapja; Catholic Hungarians' Sunday. w. (Commissariat of St. Stephen's Franciscan Province)

**Catholic Renascence Society**
Marquette Univ., Milwaukee, WI 53233.
- Renascence; essays on values in literature. q. ISSN 0034-4346

**Catholic Theological Society of America**
Mahwah, NJ 07430.
- Catholic Theological Society of America. Proceedings. a. ISSN 0069-1267

**Catholic Traditionalist Movement, Inc.**
Suite 303 E, Pan Am Bldg., 200 Park Ave., New York, NY 10017.
- Sounds of Truth and Tradition. q. ISSN 0038-187X

**Catholic Traveler**
Ed. G. Robert Hewitt, Box 786, Port Washington, NY 11050.
- Catholic Traveler; containing information regarding every major shrine of the world. q. ISSN 0008-8374

**Catholic Truth Society of Oregon, Inc.**
2816 E. Burnside St., Portland, OR 97214.
- Catholic Sentinel. w. ISSN 0008-8358

**Catholic University of America**
- Studies in Christian Antiquity. (pub. by Consortium Books)
- Studies in Medieval and Renaissance Latin. (pub. by Consortium Books)

**Catholic University of America. Alumni Association**
- Catholic University Law Review. (pub. by Catholic University of America Press)

**Catholic University of America. Department of Canon Law**
Washington, DC 20064.
- Jurist; studies in church order and ministry. q. ISSN 0022-6858

**Catholic University of America Press**
620 Michigan Ave., N.E., Washington, DC 20064.
- Anthropological Quarterly. q. ISSN 0003-5491
- Catalogus Translationem et Commentatorium; Medieval and Renaissance Latin translations. irreg.; latest issue, vol. 3. ISSN 0528-2594
- Catholic Historical Review. q. ISSN 0008-8080 (American Catholic Historical Association)
- Catholic University Law Review. q. ISSN 0008-8390 (Catholic University of America. Alumni Association)
- Fathers of the Church. q. ISSN 0014-8814
- Studies in Philosophy & the History of Philosophy. irreg., vol. 6, 1974. ISSN 0585-6965

**Catholic University School of Law. Center for National Policy Review**
Washington, DC 20017.
- Clearinghouse for Civil Rights Research. q.

**Catholic Women's Fraternal of Texas-the K.J.Z.T.**
Box 1884, Austin, TX 78767.
- K. J. Z. T. News. m.

**Catholic Worker Movement**
36 E. First St., New York, NY 10003.
- Catholic Worker. m.(bi-m; Mar.-April, July-Aug. & Oct.-Nov) ISSN 0008-8463

**Catholic Workman**
112 1/2 E. Main, New Prague, MN 56071
- Catholic Workman. m. ISSN 0008-8471 (Editorial Address: Box 56, Dodge, NE 68533)

**Cat's Pajamas Press**
423 S. Humphrey, Oak Park, IL 60302.
- Mojo Navigator(e) irreg.

**Cat's Paw Press**
Route 1, Box 47, Arthur, ND 58006.
- Cat and the Moon. s-a.

**Cavalcade Publications Inc.**
Box 367, Worcester, MA 01613.
- Cavalcade of Auto Racing. m.

**Cave Research Associates**
3842 Brookdale Blvd., Castro Valley, CA 94546.
- Cave Studies. irreg., no. 13, 1972. ISSN 0069-1313
- Caves and Karst; research in speleology. bi-m. ISSN 0008-8625

**Cayuga Museum of History and Art**
Auburn, NY 13021.
- Archaeological Society of Central New York. Bulletin. m.(Sept-June) ISSN 0003-8059

**Cedar Rock, Inc.**
c/o David C. Yates, Ed., 1121 Madeline, New Braunfels, TX 78130.
- Cedar Rock. q.

**Cedars-Sinai Medical Center**
8700 Beverly Blvd., Los Angeles, CA 90048.
- Cedars-Sinai Compass. q. ISSN 0008-8684

**Ceilings and Interior Systems Contractors Association**
1201 Waukegan Rd., Glenview, IL 60025.
- Sound Ideas. bi-m. ISSN 0038-1837

**Celanese Fibers Marketing Co. Customer Information Services**
1211 Ave. of the Americas, New York, NY 10036.
- Textile Topics. 3 per yr.

**Celebration**
c/o William J. Sullivan, Ed., 2707 Lawina Rd, Baltimore, MD 21216.
- Celebration. 2-3 per yr.

**Celebrity Publications, Ltd.**
Box 3, New York, NY 10023.
- Keen Teen. bi-m. ISSN 0022-961X
- Teenville. bi-m. ISSN 0040-2079

**Celebrity Service, Inc.**
171 W. 57 St., New York, NY 10019.
● Celebrity Service International Contact Book;
trade directory / entertainment industry. every 18
months. ISSN 0069-1372
● Weekly Theatrical Calendar. w.

**Celebrity Sports**
Box 3351, Reno, NV 89505.
● American Shotgunner. m.

**Celmer & Twente Associates**
913 W. Cullom Ave., Chicago, IL 60613.
● Book Collecting World. 48 per yr. ISSN 0006-
7229

**Celo Press**
Burnsville, NC 28714.
● Manual of Death Education and Simple Burial.
biennial. (Continental Association of Funeral and
Memorial Societies)

**Cemetery Research, Inc.**
Box 6616, San Jose, CA 95150.
● Directory of United States Cemeteries. irreg.
ISSN 0095-1862

**Cendex Corp.**
Box 1043, Provo, UT 84601.
● Census Index Series. irreg.

**Centaur & Company**
1629 K St., N.W., Suite 5097, Washington, DC
20006.
● Brushware. q. ISSN 0007-2710

**Centenary College**
Box 113, Shreveport, LA 71104.
● Centenary College Conglomerate. w. ISSN 0008-
9001

**Center for Applied Linguistics**
1611 N. Kent St., Arlington, VA 22209.
● Linguistic Reporter. 9 per yr. ISSN 0024-3906
● Papers in Applied Linguistics; an occasional paper
series. irreg.

**Center for Autonomous Social Action. General
Brotherhood of Workers**
Box 7086, Los Angeles, CA 90022.
● Sin Fronteras; vocero del trabajador mexicano. m.

**Center for Book Arts, Inc.**
15 Bleecker St., New York, NY 10012.
● Book Arts. a.

**Center for Business and Economic Research**
University of Tennessee, Cumberland Ave SW,
Knoxville, TN 37916.
● Tennessee Pocket Data Book. a. ISSN 0090-6557

**Center for California Public Affairs**
Box 30, Claremont, CA 91711.
● California Environment Yearbook & Directory.
irreg. ISSN 0092-1343
● California Environmental Law: A Guide. a. ISSN
0068-5585
● California Handbook. irreg. ISSN 0068-5615
● California News Index. q. ISSN 0045-3951

**Center for Computer-Oriented Research in Biblical
and Related Ancient Literatures**
c/o Richard E. Whitaker, Central College, Pella, IA
50219.
● Arithmoi. irreg. ISSN 0360-3636

**Center for Conflict Resolution**
731 State St., Madison, WI 53706.
● Center for Conflict Resolution. Monthly
Newsletter. m.

**Center for Consumer Education Services**
Building 871, Plainfield Ave., Edison, NJ 08817.
● Center for Consumer Education Services.
Monographs. irreg. ISSN 0084-8654

**Center for Continuing Education in Podiatric
Medicine (CCEPM)**
148 North 8th Street, Philadelphia, PA 19107.
● Audio Journal of Podiatric Medicine. m. ISSN
0093-7282

**Center for Cuban Studies**
220 East 23rd St., New York, NY 10010.
● Canto Libre; a bilingual trimester of Latin
American people's art. 3 per yr. ISSN 0098-8340
● Center for Cuban Studies. Newsletter. bi-m.

**Center for Cybernetic Systems Synergism**
Box 7345, Colorado Springs, CO 80933.
● Computing Newsletter for Community Colleges. 1
per yr. (Sep.-May) ISSN 0045-7957
● Computing Newsletter for Instructors of Data
Processing. 9 per yr. (Sep.-May) ISSN 0045-7965

**Center for Defense Information**
122 Maryland Ave. N.E., Washington, DC 20002.
● Defense Monitor. m?

**Center for Disease Control**
see U.S. Center for Disease Control

**Center for Educational Reform, Inc.**
P.O. Box 10085, Eugene, OR 97401.
● EdCentric; a journal of educational change. q.
ISSN 0046-1245

**Center for Environmental Education**
2100 M St., N.W., Washington, DC 20037.
● Environmental Education Report. 10 per yr. ISSN
0091-1712

**Center for Equal Education**
● Research Review of Equal Education. (pub. by
Northwestern University. School of Education)

**Center for Foreign Study**
216 S. State St., Ann Arbor, MI 48107.
● Academic Year Abroad in Europe-Africa-
Australia. a. ISSN 0098-6356

**Center for Global Perspectives**
218 E. 18 St., New York, NY 10003.
● Intercom. q. ISSN 0020-5273

**Center for Growth Alternatives**
1785 Massachusetts Ave., N.W., Washington, DC
20036.
● Growth Alternatives. q.

**Center for Hermeneutical Studies**
2465 Le Conte Ave., Berkeley, CA 94709.
● Center for Hermeneutical Studies in Hellenistic
and Modern Culture. Protocol Series of the
Colloquies. irreg. 3-5 per yr. (Co-Sponsors:
Graduate Theological Union; University of
California, Berkeley)

**Center for Information and Numerical Data Analysis
and Synthesis**
2595 Yeager Road, West Lafayette, IN 47906.
● Thermophysics and Electronics Newsletter. bi-m.

**Center for Information on America**
Washington, CT 06793.
● Population Profiles. irreg. (Co-sponsor: Council of
State Social Studies Specialists)
● Vital Issues. 10 per yr. ISSN 0042-739X

**Center for Inter-American Relations**
680 Park Ave., New York, NY 10021.
● Center for Inter-American Relations. Review;
Latin American fiction and poetry in translation.
3 per yr. ISSN 0069-1445

**Center for International Education and Research in
Accounting**
see under University of Illinois at Urbana-
Champaign

**Center for International Environment Information**
300 E. 42nd St., New York, NY 10017.
● World Environment Report. fortn.

**Center for Law and Education, Inc.**
Gutman Library, 6 Appian Way, Cambridge, MA
02138.
● Education Law Bulletin. every 6-8 wks.
● Inequality in Education. irreg.

**Center for Louisiana Studies**
Box 4-0831, USL, Lafayette, LA 70504.
● Revue de Louisiane/Louisiana Review. s-a.

**Center for Marketing Communications**
Box 411, 575 Ewing St., Research Park, Princeton,
NJ 08540.
● Center for Marketing Communications Reporter.
bi-m.

**Center for Migration Studies of New York, Inc.**
209 Flagg Place, Staten Island, NY 10304.
● International Migration Review; a quarterly
studying sociological, demographic, historical, and
legislative aspects of human migration movements
and ethnic group relations. 4 per yr. ISSN 0020-
7993
● Migration Today; a socio-pastoral magazine on
migrants and other marginal groups. bi-m.

**Center for New Images**
163-18 Jamaica Ave., Jamaica, NY 11432.
● Spirit; magazine of black arts and culture. m.

**Center for Personalized Instruction**
Room 29, Loyola Hall, Georgetown University,
Washington, DC 20057.
● Journal of Personalized Instruction. q.
● P S I Newsletter. (Personalized System of
Instruction) q.

**Center for Policy Analysis**
Box 4047, Falls Church, VA 22044.
● Contents of Selected Periodicals/Policy Sciences.
16 per yr. (National Council of Associations for
Policy Sciences)
● International Urban Issues/Contents of Selected
Periodicals. 16 per yr. (National Council of
Associations for Policy Sciences)

**Center for Policy Process**
1755 Massachusetts Ave., N.W. Suite 401,
Washington, DC 20036.
● Washington Energy Directory. a. ISSN 0098-9576

**Center for Population Research**
see under U.S. Center for Population Research

**Center for Process Studies**
1325 N. College Ave., Claremont, CA 91711.
● Center for Process Studies. Newsletter. q.

**Center for Productive Public Management**
445 W. 59th St., New York, NY 10019.
● Public Productivity Review. q. ISSN 0361-6681

**Center for Psychosocial Studies**
233 North Michigan Ave., Chicago, IL 60601.
● Directory of Psychosocial Investigators. irreg.
ISSN 0361-3771

**Center for Reformation Research**
6477 San Bonita, St. Louis, MO 63105.
● Center for Reformation Research. Newsletter. 5
per yr.
● Sixteenth Century Bibliography. 4 per yr.

**Center for Reformation Research. Sixteenth Century
Studies Conference**
● Sixteenth Century Journal. (pub. by Northeast
Missouri State University)

**Center for Research Libraries**
5721 Cottage Grove Ave., Chicago, IL 60637.
● Center for Research Libraries. Handbook. irreg.
● Center for Research Libraries. Newsletter. m.
ISSN 0008-9087

**Center for Science in the Public Interest**
1757 S St., N.W., Washington, DC 20009.
● Nutrition Action. m.
● People and Energy. m.

**Center for Teaching About Peace and War**
Wayne State University, 5229 Cass Ave., Room
101, Detroit, MI 48202.
● Center for Teaching About Peace and War.
Newsletter. 4 per yr. ISSN 0008-9133

**Center for the Development of Human Resources**
Wainwright House, 260 Stuyvesant Ave., Rye, NY
10580.
● Trends (Rye) q. (Laymen's Movement for a
Christian World, Inc.)

**Center for the Rights of Campus Journalists**
● C. R. C. J. Bulletin. (pub. by College Press
Service)

**Center for the Study of Armament and Disarmament**
see under California State University, Los Angeles

**Center for the Study of Democratic Institutions**
Box 4068, Santa Barbara, CA 93103.
● Center for the Study of Democratic Institutions.
Center Magazine. bi-m. ISSN 0008-9125
● Pacem in Terris. every 2-5 yrs.; latest issue, 1974.
● World Issues. bi-m.

**Center for the Study of Federalism**
Temple University, Philadelphia, PA 19122.
● Publius; the journal of federalism. s-a. ISSN 0048-5950

**Center for the Study of Instruction**
1000 Geary, San Francisco, CA 94109.
● Schools for the 70's. irreg.

**Center for the Study of Popular Culture**
● Journal of Popular Film. (pub. by Bowling Green Popular Press)

**Center for the Study of Public Policy, Inc.**
● Working Papers for a New Society. (pub. by Transaction Periodicals Consortium)

**Center for the Study of the Future**
4110 N.E. Alameda, Portland, OR 97212.
● Patterns. m.

**Center for the Study of the Presidency**
926 Fifth Ave., New York, NY 10021.
● Center for the Study of the Presidency. Proceedings. irreg., vol. 2, 1973.
● Presidential Studies Quarterly. q.

**Center for the Teaching of the Americas**
c/o Sister Mary Consuela, I.H.M., Director, Immaculata College, Immaculata, PA 19345.
● Focus on the Americas; a newsletter to promote the teaching of the Americas in the schools. q.

**Center for U F O Studies**
Box 11, Northfield, IL 60093.
● Center for U F O Studies. News Bulletin. bi-m (approx.)

**Center for Women's Studies & Services**
908 F St., San Diego, CA 92101.
● C W S S Feminist Bulletin. bi-m.
● Longest Review; news and views of progressive feminism.

**Center on Evaluation, Development and Research**
● Center on Evaluation, Development and Research. Quarterly. (pub. by Phi Delta Kappa)

**Center on International Race Relations**
● Race and Nations Series. (pub. by D.C. Heath & Company)

**Center Press**
2617 Benvenue, Berkeley, CA 94704.
● Center. s-a.

**Central Association of the Miraculous Medal**
475 E. Chelten Ave., Philadelphia, PA 19144.
● Miraculous Medal. q. ISSN 0026-5802

**Central Baptist Church**
Box 5567, Little Rock, AR 72215.
● Baptist Challenge; voice of independent Baptists. m. ISSN 0005-5697

**Central Baptist Theological Seminary of Minneapolis**
2105 Fremont Ave. N, Minneapolis, MN 55411.
● Central Bible Quarterly; a Biblical review of convicted conservative thought. q. ISSN 0008-9311

**Central Bureau for Jewish Aged**
225 Park Ave. S., New York, NY 10003.
● Aspects of Aging. 3 per yr.

**Central Committee for Conscientious Objectors**
2016 Walnut St., Philadelphia, PA 19103.
● C C C O News Notes; an agency for military and draft counseling. 5 per yr. ISSN 0008-5952
● Counter Pentagon. 5 per yr.
● News Notes. 5 per yr.

**Central Committee for Conscientious Objectors. San Francisco**
1251 2nd Ave., San Francisco, CA 94122.
● Newsletter on Military Law and Counseling. 10 per yr.

**Central Conference of American Rabbis**
790 Madison Ave., New York, NY 10021.
● C C A R Journal. q. ISSN 0007-7976
● Central Conference of American Rabbis. Yearbook. a. ISSN 0069-1607

**Central Conference of Teamsters**
8550 W. Bryn Mawr Ave., Suite 707, Chicago, IL 60631.
● Central Conference of Teamsters. Officers' Report. biennial. ISSN 0069-1615

**Central Constructor Corp.**
Box 4017, Des Moines, IA 50333.
● Central Constructor. m. ISSN 0008-9346 (Associated General Contractors of Iowa)

**Central Electric Railfans' Association**
P.O. Box 503, Chicago, IL 60690.
● Central Electric Railfans' Association. Bulletin. a. ISSN 0069-1623

**Central Flower News, Inc.**
549 W. Randolph St., Chicago, IL 60606.
● Flower News. w. ISSN 0015-4490

**Central Hall Artists Inc.**
52 Main St., Port Washington, NY 11050.
● Central Hall Artists Newsletter. q.

**Central Michigan University**
Anspach Hall, Mt. Pleasant, MI 48858.
● Central Michigan Life; the official campus newspaper. 3 per wk. ISSN 0008-9451

**Central Michigan University. Department of English**
Mount Pleasant, MI 48859.
● Michigan Linguistic Society. Papers. a.

**Central Missouri State University**
Warrensburg, MO 64093.
● Missouri Speech Journal. s-a. (Speech and Theatre Association of Missouri)

**Central Naugatuck Valley Regional Planning Agency**
20 E. Main St., Waterbury, CT 06702.
● Central Naugatuck Valley Regional Planning Agency. Annual Report. a. ISSN 0069-1674

**Central New York Academy of Medicine**
210 Clinton Rd., New Hartford, NY 13413.
● Central New York Academy of Medicine. Bulletin. m. ISSN 0008-946X (Co-sponsors: Medical Societies of the Counties of Oneida, Herkimer, Madison and Chenango)

**Central New York Genealogical Society**
Box 104, Colvin Sta., Syracuse, NY 13205.
● Tree Talks. q. ISSN 0041-2201

**Central Party**
● Second Page. (pub. by Second Page, Inc.)

**Central Society for Clinical Research**
● Journal of Laboratory and Clinical Medicine. (pub. by C. V. Mosby Co.)

**Central State University**
c/o Dr. James E. Alsbrook, Faculty Advisor, Wilberforce, OH 45384.
● Gold Torch. w.

**Central State University. Hallie Q. Brown Memorial Library**
● Index to Periodical Articles by and about Negroes. (pub. by G. K. Hall & Co.)

**Central States Archaeological Societies, Inc.**
1228 West Essex, St. Louis, MO 63122.
● Central States Archaeological Journal. q. ISSN 0008-9559

**Central States Speech Association**
c/o Gustav W. Friedrich, Executive Secretary, CSSA, Purdue University, Dept. of Communication, West Lafayette, IN 47907.
● Central States Speech Journal. q. ISSN 0008-9575

**Central Texas Genealogical Society, Inc.**
Waco-McLennan County Library, 1717 Austin Ave., Waco, TX 76701.
● Heart of Texas Records. q. ISSN 0093-9854

**Central Washington State College. Associated Students**
Samuelson Union Bldg., Rms. 217-218, Ellensburg, WA 98926.
● Campus Crier. w. ISSN 0008-2503

**Centre College of Kentucky. Publications Board**
Box 745, Danville, KY 40422.
● Cento. w. ISSN 0008-9141

**Century Communications Unlimited, Inc.**
1500 Carter Ave., Ashland, KY 41101.
● Southern Creativity Annual. a. ISSN 0095-4926

**Century Enterprises**
P.O. Box 607, Huntsville, AR 72740.
● Madison County Genealogist. q. ISSN 0090-5186

**Century Publishing Co.**
1020 Church St., Evanston, IL 60201.
● Auto Racing Digest. bi-m. ISSN 0090-8029
● Baseball Digest. m. ISSN 0005-609X
● Basketball Digest. 8 per yr. ISSN 0098-5988
● Football Digest. 10 per yr. ISSN 0015-6760
● Hockey Digest. m. (8 per yr.) ISSN 0046-7693

**Ceramic Age Publications**
Box 25555, Cleveland, OH 44125
(Subscr. to: Box 5, North Olmsted, OH 44070)
● Ceramic Age. bi-m. ISSN 0009-0182

**Ceramic Scope**
c/o Mel & Joyce Fiske, 6363 Wilshire Blvd., Los Angeles, CA 90048.
● Ceramic Scope. m. ISSN 0009-0247

**Certified Ballast Manufacturers Association**
2120 Keith Bldg., Cleveland, OH 44115.
● C B M News. q. ISSN 0007-7941

**Chalcedon Foundation**
Box 158, Vallecito, CA 95251.
● Journal of Christian Reconstruction. s-a. ISSN 0360-1420

**Challenge Publications, Inc.**
7805 Deering Ave., New York, CA 91304.
● Air Progress. m. ISSN 0002-2500

**Chamber of Commerce of Hawaii**
Dillingham Building, 735 Bishop St., Honolulu, HI 96813.
● Directory of Manufacturers, State of Hawaii. biennial.
● Voice of Business. m. ISSN 0042-8108

**Chamber of Commerce of the U. S.**
1615 H Street, N.W., Washington, DC 20006.
● A A C C L A Report. q. (Association of American Chambers of Commerce in Latin America)
● Association Taxation. bi-m.
● Chamber of Commerce of the U.S. Association Letter. m. ISSN 0009-1154 (prep. by its Association Department)
● Chamber of Commerce of the U.S. Newsletter. m. ISSN 0009-1146
● Chamber of Commerce of the United States. Employee Benefits. biennial. ISSN 0069-2433
● Chamber of Commerce of the United States. Foreign Commerce Handbook. every 4-5 years.
● Employment Abroad-Facts and Fallacies. a. (prep. by its International Group)
● Guide to Foreign Information Sources. irreg. (prep. by its International Group)
● National Chamber International Report. m. (prep. by its International Group)
● Nation's Business. m. ISSN 0028-047X
● Sources of State Information and State Industrial Directories. triennial.
● Survey of Local Chambers of Commerce. biennial. ISSN 0069-2441
● Washington Report. bi-w. ISSN 0043-0714

**Max Chambers, Ed. & Pub.**
Preston, MD 21655.
● Vegetable Growers Messenger. bi-m. ISSN 0042-3076

**Chaminade College**
St. Louis-Chaminade Education Center, 3140 Walalae Ave., Honolulu, HI 96816.
● Chaminade College Newsletter. q. ISSN 0009-1286

**Champagne d'Argent Rabbit Federation**
18432 Docksey, Northville, MI 48167.
● Champagne News. m. ISSN 0009-1294

**Champaign County Genealogical Society**
505 Park Haven Court, Champaign, IL 61820.
● Champaign County Genealogical Society. Newsletter. irreg.

**Champion Papers**
245 Park Ave., New York, NY 10017.
● Printing Salesman's Herald. 5 per yr. ISSN 0032-8677

**Champion Sports Publishing Corp.**
351 Manville Rd., Pleasentville, NY 10570.
- Boxing Illustrated. m. ISSN 0006-8500

**Champlin Petroleum Co.**
P.O. Box 9365, Fort Worth, TX 76107.
- Cycler. q.

**Chandler Publishing Inc.**
c/o Tyco Shipping Service, 788 Bloomfield Ave.,
Clifton, NJ 07012.
- Chandler Editions in Drama. irreg.
- Chandler Publications for Health Sciences. irreg.
- Chandler Publications in Anthropology and
  Sociology. irreg.
- Chandler Publications in Audio Visual
  Communications. irreg.
- Chandler Publications in Backgrounds to
  Literature. irreg.
- Chandler Publications in Educational Psychology.
  irreg.
- Chandler Publications in General and
  Experimental Psychology. irreg.
- Chandler Publications in History of Theatre. irreg.
- Chandler Publications in Language Arts
  Education. irreg.
- Chandler Publications in Philosophy. irreg.
- Chandler Publications in Political Science. irreg.
- Chandler Publications for Sociology. irreg.
- Problems of Philosophy (Chandler) irreg.

**Changes**
Box 92, Bisbee, AZ 85605.
- Changes. irreg. ISSN 0093-9064

**Changes Publications, Inc.**
Box 631, Cooper Sta., New York, NY 10003
- Changes (New York); journal of arts and
  entertainment. m. ISSN 0009-1391 (Dist. by:
  Curtis Circulation Co.)

**Changing Woman**
Box 14902, Portland, OR 97214.
- Changing Woman. m.

**Chan's Corporation**
2930 W. Valley Blvd., Alhambra, CA 91803.
- Acupuncture News. bi-m.

**Chapin Publishing Co.**
15 S. 9th St., Suite 420, Minneapolis, MN 55402.
- Construction Bulletin. w.

**Mary Lewis Chapman, Ed. & Pub.**
Box 711, Williamsburg, VA 23185.
- Literary Sketches; a magazine of interviews,
  reviews and memorabilia. m. ISSN 0024-4597

**Charger Productions, Inc.**
130 Olinda Place, Olinda Village, Richmond, CA
92621
(or 34249 Camino Capistrano, Capistrano Beach,
CA 92624)
- Bob Zwirz' Fishing Annual. a. ISSN 0363-5538
- Fishing Guide. a. ISSN 0362-5567
- Horse and Horseman. m.

**Charismatic Renewal Services, Inc.**
Box 617, Ann Arbor, MI 48107.
- New Covenant. m.
- Pastoral Renewal. m.

**Charles F. Kettering Foundation**
5335 Far Hills Ave., Dayton, OH 45429.
- Charles F. Kettering Foundation. Annual Report.
  a. ISSN 0069-2735
- New Ways; developments you might like to know
  about. q. ISSN 0047-9977

**Charles Redd Center for Western Studies**
- Charles Redd Monographs in Western History.
  (pub. by Brigham Young University Press)

**Charles River Associates Incorporated**
1050 Massachusetts Avenue, Cambridge, MA
02138.
- C R A Market Forecasts/Scrap. q.
- C R A Research Review. q.

**Charles S. Pierce Society**
State University of New York at Buffalo, c/o Peter
H. Hare, Dept. of Philosophy, Baldy Hall, Buffalo,
NY 14260.
- Charles S. Peirce Society, Transactions. 4 per yr.
  ISSN 0009-1774

**Charleson Publishing Co.**
124 E. 40th St., New York, NY 10016.
- Modern Floor Coverings. m.
- Non-Foods Merchandising; for sales and
  distribution of non-foods. m. ISSN 0029-103X
- Toy & Hobby World. m. ISSN 0041-011X

**Charlotte Chamber of Commerce**
- Charlotte. (pub. by Community Publishing Co.
  Inc.)

**Charlotte-Mecklenburg Board of Education**
Communications Dept., Box 149, Charlotte, NC
28230.
- Charlotte-Mecklenburg School Report. m. ISSN
  0009-1790

**Charlton Publications Inc.**
Charlton Bldg., Derby, CT 06418.
- Country Song Roundup. m. ISSN 0011-0248
- Hit Parader. m.
- Official Karate. bi-m. ISSN 0048-1505
- Real West. bi-m. ISSN 0034-0898
- Rock and Soul Songs. m. ISSN 0035-743X
- Song Hits. m. ISSN 0038-1365
- Your Astrology. q. ISSN 0044-0981

**Charlu Press**
c/o Lewis Sanders and Charles G. Roach, 125
Taylor, Jackson, TN 38301.
- Starwhispering. irreg.

**Chartcraft, Inc.**
1 West Ave., Larchmont, NY 10538.
- Chartcraft Weekly Service. w. ISSN 0009-1871

**Chase Manhattan Bank**
1 Chase Manhattan Plaza, New York, NY 10015.
- Business in Brief. bi-m. ISSN 0007-6821 (prep. by
  its Economics Group)
- Consumer Sense. m.

**Chase Publishing Co., Inc.**
1140 Industry Rd., Lexington, KY 40505.
- Chase; a full cry of hunting. m. ISSN 0009-1952

**Chase World Information Corporation**
1 World Trade Center, Suite 4627, New York, NY
10048.
- East-West Markets. fortn.
- Export Credit Reports. q.
- Mideast Markets. fortn. ISSN 0098-6461

**Pierre Chastain Family Association**
c/o G. Buland, 1100 E. Teresa, Sapulpa, OK 74066.
- Chestnut Tree. q.

**Chatham Publishing Co.**
1012 Oak Grove Ave., Burlingame, CA 94010.
- Pacific News; your Western news source. m. ISSN
  0030-879X

**Chattanooga Audubon Society**
P.O. 245, Chattanooga, TN 37401.
- Audubon Flyer. q.
- Flower and Feather. q. ISSN 0015-4466

**Chattanooga Coin and Stamp Co.**
109 E. Seventh St., Chattanooga, TN 37401.
- Coin Wholesaler. m. ISSN 0045-7280

**Chattanooga Science Fiction Convention**
- Maybe. (pub. by Irvin Koch, Ed. & Pub.)

**Check Collectors Round Table**
c/o Larry Adams, 969 Park Circle, Boone, CA
50036.
- Check List; devoted to the study of security
  paper. q.

**Chedwato Service**
R.D. 3 Box 120A, Middleboro, MA 02346.
- Car-del Scribe. 6 per yr. ISSN 0008-6029

**Cheese Reporter Publishing Co., Inc.**
115 W. Main St., Madison, WI 53703.
- Cheese Reporter. w. ISSN 0009-2142

**Cheever Publishing, Inc.**
Box 700, Bloomington, IL 61701.
- Accent on Living. q. ISSN 0001-4508

**Chekhov Publishing Corporation**
505 Eighth Avenue, New York, NY 10028.
- Chronicle of Human Rights in the U. S. S. R. 4
  per yr.

**Chelsea Associates, Inc.**
Box 5880 Grand Central Station, New York, NY
10017.
- Chelsea; a magazine for poetry, plays, stories and
  translations. s-a. ISSN 0009-2185

**Chemical Abstracts Service**
Box 3012, Columbus, OH 43210.
- Chemical Abstracts. w. ISSN 0009-2258
  (American Chemical Society)
- Chemical Abstracts - Applied Chemistry and
  Chemical Engineering Sections. fortn. ISSN 0009-
  2266 (American Chemical Society)
- Chemical Abstracts - Biochemical Sections. fortn.
  ISSN 0009-2304 (American Chemical Society)
- Chemical Abstracts - Macromolecular Sections.
  bi-w. ISSN 0009-2274 (American Chemical
  Society)
- Chemical Abstracts - Organic Chemistry Sections.
  fortn. ISSN 0009-2282 (American Chemical
  Society)
- Chemical Abstracts - Physical and Analytical
  Chemistry Sections. fortn. ISSN 0009-2290
  (American Chemical Society)
- Chemical Abstracts Service Source Index. base
  vol. updated with quarterly supplements. ISSN
  0001-0634 (American Chemical Society)
- Chemical-Biological Activities(CBAC); an index
  to current literature on the biological activity of
  chemical substances. fortn. ISSN 0009-238X
  (American Chemical Society)
- Chemical Industry Notes. w. ISSN 0045-639X
  (American Chemical Society)
- Chemical Titles. fortn. ISSN 0009-2711
  (American Chemical Society)
- Polymer Science & Technology Post. fortn. ISSN
  0032-3942 (American Chemical Society)
- Ring Index: A List of Ring Systems Used in
  Organic Chemistry. Supplement. irreg. ISSN
  0080-309X (American Chemical Society)
- Selenium & Tellurium Abstracts. m. ISSN 0037-
  1467 (Selenium & Tellurium Development
  Association, Inc.)

**Chemical Economic Services**
Box 468, Palmer Square P.O., Princeton, NJ 08540.
- Corporate Diagrams and Administrative Personnel
  of the Chemical Industry. irreg. ISSN 0574-1181
- Executive Directory of the U.S. Pharmaceutical
  Industry. irreg. ISSN 0071-3309

**Chemical Publishing Co.**
200 Park Ave. S., New York, NY 10003.
- Chemical Formulary. irreg.

**Chemical Spotlight Inc.**
P.O. Box 802, 203 Oak St., Ridgewood, NJ 07451.
- Chemical Spotlight. w. ISSN 0411-8871

**Verlag Chemie International, Inc.**
175 Fifth Ave., New York, NY 10010
(and Pappelallee 3, Postfach 1260, 6940 Weinheim,
W. Germany (B.R.D.))
- Angewandte Chemie. m. ISSN 0044-8249
  (Gesellschaft Deutscher Chemiker GW)
- Archiv der Pharmazie. m. ISSN 0003-8903
  (Deutsche Pharmazeutische Gesellschaft GW)
- Biologie in Unserer Zeit. bi-m. ISSN 0045-205X
- Bunsengesellschaft fuer Physikalische Chemie.
  Berichte. m. ISSN 0005-9021
- Chemie in Unserer Zeit. bi-m. ISSN 0009-2851
  (Gesellschaft Deutscher Chemiker GW)
- Chemie-Ingenieur-Technik; Zeitschrift fuer
  technische Chemie, Verfahrenstechnik und
  Apparatewesen. m. ISSN 0009-286X (Gesellschaft
  Deutscher Chemiker. GW)
- Chemische Berichte; Fortsetzung der Berichte der
  Deutschen Chemischen Gesellschaft. m. ISSN
  0009-2940 (Gesellschaft Deutscher Chemiker
  GW)
- Chemischer Informationsdienst. w. ISSN 0009-
  2975 (Gesellschaft Deutscher Chemiker GW)
- Dechema Monographien. irreg., vol. 80, 1976.
  ISSN 0070-315X (Deutsche Gesellschaft fuer
  Chemisches Apparatewesen e.V. - DECHEMA
  GW)
- European Journal of Immunology. m. ISSN 0014-
  2980
- Gewerblicher Rechtsschutz und Urheberrecht. m.
  ISSN 0016-9420 (Deutsche Vereinigung fuer
  Gewerblichen Rechtsschutz und Urheberrecht
  GW)
- I I C. (International Review of Industrial Property
  and Copyright Law.) bi-m. ISSN 0018-9855
  (Max-Planck-Institute for Foreign and
  International Patent, Copyright and Competition
  Law, Munich GW)

- Justus Liebigs Annalen der Chemie. m. ISSN 0075-4617
- Korrosion. irreg., vol. 25, 1974. ISSN 0075-6938
- Nachrichten aus Chemie, Technik und Laboratorium. m. (Gesellschaft Deutscher Chemiker GW)
- Pharmazie in Unserer Zeit. 6 per yr. ISSN 0048-3664 (Deutsche Pharmazeutische Gesellschaft GW)
- Physik in Unserer Zeit. bi-m. ISSN 0031-9252
- Physikalische Berichte; an abstracting journal covering all fields of physics. m. ISSN 0031-9260 (Deutsche Physikalische Gesellschaft)
- Physikalische Blaetter. m. ISSN 0031-9279 (Deutsche Physikalische Gesellschaft)
- Propellants and Explosives. bi-m.
- Die Staerke/Starch; Internationale Zeitschrift fuer die Erforschung, Verarbeitung und Verwendung von Kohlenhydraten und deren Derivaten. m. ISSN 0038-9056
- Transition Metal Chemistry. bi-m.
- Verfahrenstechnische Berichte/Chemical and Process Engineering Abstracts. w. ISSN 0042-3890 (Bayer AG)
- Vom Wasser; ein Fachbuch fuer Wasserchemie und Wasserreinigungstechnik. a. ISSN 0083-6915 (Gesellschaft Deutscher Chemiker. Fachgruppe Wasserchemie GW)
- Werkstoffe und Korrosion. m. ISSN 0043-2822 (Arbeitsgemeinschaft Korrosion GW)
- Zeitschrift fuer Pflanzenernaehrung und Bodenkunde/Journal of Plant Nutrition and Soil Science. 6 per yr. ISSN 0044-3263 (Deutsche Bodenkundliche Gesellschaft GW) (Co-Sponsor: Deutsche Gesellschaft fuer Pflanzenernaehrung)
- Zeitschrift fuer Werkstofftechnik, Materials Technology and Testing. m (Deutsche Gesellschaft fuer Metallkunde GW) (Co-Sponsor: Verein Deutscher Eisenhuettenleute)

**Cherokee Boys Club, Inc.**
Box 507, Cherokee, NC 28719.
- Cherokee Boys Club Newsletter. m.

**Cherokee Nation of Oklahoma**
Cherokee Communication Center, Box 119, Tahlequah, OK 74464.
- Cherokee Advocate. m.

**Cherokee Times**
Box 105, Cherokee, NC 28719.
- Cherokee Times. w. ISSN 0045-6551

**Cherry Valley Editions**
1416 W. Mt. Royal Ave., Baltimore, MD 21217.
- Coldspring Journal. irreg. ISSN 0098-7093
- Northeast Rising Sun; magazine of small press reviews. m. ISSN 0360-8816

**Chesapeake and Ohio Historical Society, Inc.**
Box 417, Alderson, WV 24910.
- Chesapeake and Ohio Historical Newsletter. m. ISSN 0009-3254

**Chesapeake Bay Communications, Inc.**
130 Severn Ave., Annapolis, MD 21403.
- Chesapeake Bay. m. ISSN 0045-656X

**Chesapeake Bay Foundation**
17 State Circle, Annapolis, MD 21404.
- Chesapeake Report: A Review of Issues and Events Affecting Chesapeake Bay. irreg. ISSN 0069-3189

**Chesopiean Archaeological Association**
7507 Pennington Rd., Norfolk, VA 23505.
- Chesopiean. bi-m. ISSN 0009-3300
- Current Biographies of Leading Archaeologists. irreg. ISSN 0361-4735

**Chess Digest**
Box 21225, Dallas, TX 75211.
- Chess Digest. m. ISSN 0009-3335

**Chester County Press**
South Third Street, Oxford, PA 19363.
- Lincolnian; a college newspaper. 12 per yr. (Oct.-Apr.) ISSN 0024-3701 (Lincoln University)

**Chester White Swine Record Association**
Box 228, Rochester, IN 46975.
- Chester White Journal. m. ISSN 0009-3386

**Chestnut Hill Community Association**
8434 Germantown Ave., Philadelphia, PA 19118.
- Chestnut Hill Local. w. ISSN 0009-3394

**Chevrolet Motor Division**
P.O. Box 5300, Detroit, MI 48211.
- Driver Education Digest. q. (prep. by its Driver Education Department)

**Chi Epsilon**
- Transit of Chi Epsilon. (pub. by University of Tennessee)

**Chicago. Chicago Transit Authority**
Box 3555, Merchandise Mart Plaza, Chicago, IL 60654.
- C T A Quarterly. q.

**Chicago. Crime Commission**
79 W. Monroe St., Chicago, IL 60603.
- Searchlight. bi-m.

**Chicago. Department of Development and Planning**
121 N. LaSalle, Chicago, IL 60602.
- Chicago. Department of Development and Planning. Plans and Progress. q.

**Chicago. Department of Environmental Control**
320 N. Clark St., Chicago, IL 60610.
- Environmental Currents. q.

**Chicago. Department of Urban Renewal**
320 North Clark, Chicago, IL 60610.
- Urban Renewal Review. q. ISSN 0042-093X

**Chicago Academy of Sciences**
2001 N. Clark St., Chicago, IL 60614.
- Chicago Academy of Sciences. Bulletin. irreg. ISSN 0009-3491

**Chicago and Illinois Restaurant Association**
110 N. Wacker Dr., Rm. 208, Chicago, IL 60606.
- CIRAscope. m.

**Chicago Area Transportation Study**
300 W. Adams St., Chicago, IL 60606.
- Chicago Area Transportation Study. Annual Report. a.

**Chicago Association of Commerce and Industry**
130 S. Michigan Ave., Chicago, IL 60603.
- Chicago Buyers' Guide. a. ISSN 0069-3243
- Chicagoland Development. m. ISSN 0045-6624 (prep. by its Industrial Development Division)
- Commerce; Chicagoland voice of commerce and industry. m. ISSN 0010-2741

**Chicago Athletic Association**
12 S. Michigan Ave., Chicago, IL 60603.
- Cherry Circle. 10 per yr. ISSN 0009-3238

**Chicago B.S.I.**
509 S. Ahrends, Lombard, IL 60148.
- Devon Country Chronicle. 5-6 per yr.

**Chicago Bowler Publishing Co.**
746 Webster Ave., Chicago, IL 60614.
- Chicago Bowler; world's greatest bowling weekly. w. ISSN 0009-3513

**Chicago Bridge and Iron Company**
800 Jorie Blvd., Oak Brook, IL 60521.
- C B I News. bi-m. (prep. by its Public Relations Department)

**Chicago Clergy and Laity Concerned**
542 S. Dearborn St., Chicago, IL 60605.
- Satygraha. m. (Co-Sponsor: Nonviolent Training and Action Center)

**Chicago Commission on Human Relations**
640 N. Lasalle St., Chicago, IL 60610.
- Human Relations News of Chicago. m. ISSN 0018-7283

**Chicago Dental Society**
30 N. Michigan Ave., Chicago, IL 60602.
- Chicago Dental Society Review. m. ISSN 0091-1666

**Chicago Federation of Labor and Industrial Union Council**
300 N. State St., Chicago, IL 60610.
- Federation News. m. ISSN 0014-942X

**Chicago Fireman's Association-Local 2**
54 W. Randolph, Chicago, IL 60601.
- Chicago Fire Fighter. q. ISSN 0009-3548

**Chicago Gay Crusader**
Box 872, Chicago, IL 60690.
- Chicago Gay Crusader. m.

**Chicago Genealogical Society**
Box 1160, Chicago, IL 60690.
- Chicago Genealogist. q. ISSN 0009-3556

**Chicago Herpetological Society**
Publications Secretary, Chicago Academy of Sciences, 2001 N. Clark St., Chicago, IL 60614.
- Chicago Herpetological Society. Bulletin. q. ISSN 0009-3564

**Chicago Historical Society**
1615 N. Clark St., Chicago, IL 60614.
- Chicago History. 4 per yr.

**Chicago Independent**
233 E. Ontario, Suite 902, Chicago, IL 60611.
- Chicago Independent. m.

**Chicago Jewish Student Press**
1740 Judson St., Evanston, IL 60201.
- Kol Bo/It's All Here; Chicago area Jewish student newspaper. m. ISSN 0047-3529

**Chicago Library System**
425 N. Michigan Ave., Chicago, IL 60611.
- Chicago Library System Communicator. bi-m.

**Chicago Linguistic Society**
Goodspeed Hall 205, 1050 E. 59th St., Chicago, IL 60637.
- Chicago Linguistic Society. Papers from the Regional Meetings. a. ISSN 0577-7240

**Chicago Medical Society**
310 S. Michigan Ave., Chicago, IL 60604.
- Chicago Medicine. fortn. ISSN 0009-3637 (Co-Sponsor: Medical Society of Cook County)

**Chicago Mercantile Exchange**
Market News Department, 444 W. Jackson Blvd., Chicago, IL 60606.
- Chicago Mercantile Exchange Yearbook. a. ISSN 0577-7259

**Chicago, Milwaukee, St. Paul and Pacific Railroad Co. (the Milwaukee Road)**
516 W. Jackson Blvd., Chicago, IL 60606 (Subscr. to: 824 Union Station Bldg., Chicago IL 60606)
- Milwaukee Road. q.

**Chicago New Art Association**
230 E. Ohio St., Rm. 207, Chicago, IL 60611.
- New Art Examiner; independent voice of the visual arts. 10 per yr.

**Chicago Public Library**
78 E. Washington St., Chicago, IL 60628.
- Staff Association of Chicago Public Library. Staff News. 4 per yr.

**Chicago Retail Druggists' Association**
222 W. Adams St., Suite 554, Chicago, IL 60606.
- Illinois Journal of Pharmacy. m.

**Chicago Shimpo, Inc.**
3744 N. Clark St., Chicago, IL 60613.
- Chicago Japanese American Directory. triennial.
- Chicago Shimpo. s-w. ISSN 0009-370X

**Chicago Society of Biblical Research**
800 W. Belden, Chicago, IL 60614.
- Biblical Research. a. ISSN 0067-6535

**Chicago State University**
95th St. at King Drive, Chicago, IL 60628.
- Illinois Schools Journal. q. ISSN 0019-2236

**Chicago Sun-Times**
401 N. Wabash Ave., Chicago, IL 60611.
- Showcase Book Week. w. ISSN 0037-4369 (Field Enterprises, Inc.)

**Chicago Unlimited, Inc.**
203 N. Wabash Ave., Suite 1020, Chicago, IL 60601.
- C U Directory. s-a. ISSN 0363-745X

**Chicago Zoological Society**
Zoological Park, Brookfield, IL 60513.
- Brookfield Bandarlog. irreg., 1969, no. 37. ISSN 0068-2780
- Brookfield Bison. 10 per yr.

**Chicano Community Newspaper**
811 No. La Cadena Dr. PO Box 827, Colton, CA 92324.
- Chicano Community Newspaper; una ventana abierta para la comunidad. w. ISSN 0009-3777

**Chicano Law Student Association**
School of Law, U.C.L.A., Los Angeles, CA 90024.
- Chicano Law Review. a.

**Chicano Times**
Box 7518, San Antonio, TX 78207.
- Chicano Times. fortn.

**Chicano Training Center, Inc.**
3520 Montrose, Suite 215, Houston, TX 77006.
- Mano a Mano. bi-m.

**Chicorel Library Publishing Corp.**
275 Central Park West, New York, NY 10024.
- Chicorel Index Series. irreg.

**Chief Engineers Association of Chicago**
4526 W. 95th St., Oaklawn, IL 60453.
- Chief Engineer. m.

**Child Evangelism Fellowship Inc.**
Box 348, Warrenton, MO 63383.
- Evangelizing Today's Child. bi-m.

**Child Study Press**
(Subsidiary of: Child Study Assn. of America/Wel-Met Inc.)
50 Madison Ave, New York, NY 10028.
- Children's Books of the Year. a. ISSN 0069-3499

**Child Welfare League of America, Inc.**
67 Irving Place, New York, NY 10003.
- Child Welfare. m.(Oct-July) ISSN 0009-4021
- Child Welfare League Newsletter. q. ISSN 0045-6659
- Child Welfare League of America. Directory of Member Agencies and Associates. a. ISSN 0529-1674

**Childbirth Without Pain Education Association**
20134 Snowden, Detroit, MI 48235.
- Childbirth without Pain Education Association. Newsletter. bi-m. ISSN 0009-4048

**Children's Aid Society**
105 East 22 St., New York, NY 10010.
- Children's Aid Society Newsletter. s-a.

**Childrens Art Foundation**
Box 83, Santa Cruz, CA 95063.
- Stone Soup. 5 per yr. ISSN 0094-579X

**Children's Book Council, Inc.**
67 Irving Pl., New York, NY 10003.
- Calendar; containing news of the chidlren's book world. s-a. ISSN 0008-0721
- Children's Book Showcase. Catalog. irreg. ISSN 0098-9371
- Children's Books: Awards and Prizes. biennial. ISSN 0069-3472

**Children's Book Review Service Inc.**
220 Berkeley Place, No. 1-D, Brooklyn, NY 11217.
- Children's Book Review Service. m (plus two supplements) ISSN 0090-7987

**Children's Foundation**
1028 Connecticut Ave. N.W., Washington, DC 20036.
- Feed the Kids: Its the Law. m.

**Children's Hospital Medical Center, Boston**
Public Relations Dept., 300 Longwood Ave., Boston, MA 02115.
- Children's World. q.

**Children's Hospital National Medical Center**
111 Michigan Ave., N.W., Washington, DC 20010.
- Children's Hospital National Medical Center. Clinical Proceedings. 11 per yr. ISSN 0092-7813

**Children's Hospital of Los Angeles. University Affiliated Program**
Box 54700, Los Angeles, CA 90054.
- International Interdisciplinary Seminar on Piagetian Theory and Its Implications for the Helping Professions. Proceedings; emphasis: the handicapped child. a. (prep. by its Piaget Conference Committee) (Co-sponsor: University of Southern California, School of Education)

**Children's Hospital of Philadelphia**
- Children's Hospital Notes. (pub. by Consolidated Drake Press)

**Children's House, Inc.**
Box 111, Caldwell, NJ 07006.
- Children's House Magazine. bi-m. ISSN 0009-4137

**Children's Science Book Review Committee**
Longfellow Hall, Appian Way, Cambridge, MA 02138.
- Appraisal; children's science books. 3 per yr. ISSN 0003-7052

**Children's Television Workshop**
1 Lincoln Plaza, New York, NY 10023.
- Electric Company Magazine. m.
- Sesame Street. m. ISSN 0049-0253

**Children's Theatre Conference**
John F. Kennedy Center for the Performing Arts, 726 Jackson Place, Washington, DC 20566.
- Children's Theatre Newsletter. q.

**Chilton Book Co.**
Chilton Way, Radnor, PA 19089.
- Best Short Plays. a. ISSN 0067-6284
- Chilton's Motor-Age Professional Automotive Service Manual. a. ISSN 0363-2393

**Chilton Co., Inc.**
Chilton Way, Radnor, PA 19089.
- Accent. m.
- American Jewelry Manufacturer. m. ISSN 0002-9041 (Manufacturing Jewelers and Silversmiths of America, Inc)
- Automotive Marketing. 5 per yr. ISSN 0045-107X
- Chilton's Automotive Industries. s-m.
- Chilton's Control Equipment Master. a.
- Chilton's Motor-Age Professional Labor Guide and Parts Manual. irreg. ISSN 0361-9397
- Commercial Car Journal; for fleet management. m. ISSN 0010-292X
- Distribution Worldwide. m. ISSN 0012-3951
- Electronic Component News; manufacture and design of circuits, systems and instruments. m. ISSN 0013-4856
- Fleet Specialist. bi-m.
- Food Engineering; for corporation and technical management. m. ISSN 0015-637X
- Golf Journal. 10 per yr. ISSN 0017-1794 (United States Golf Association)
- Hardware Age; the hardlines merchandising magazine. m. ISSN 0017-7660
- Hardware Age "Who Makes It" Buyers' Guide. a.
- Instrument and Apparatus News; instruments, scientific equipment, electronic and mechanical components. m. ISSN 0020-4293
- Instrument and Control Systems Buyers Guide. a. ISSN 0074-0497
- Instruments and Control Systems. m. ISSN 0020-4404
- International Product Digest. bi-m.
- Iron Age; the national metalworking weekly. w. ISSN 0021-1508
- Iron Age Metalworking International. m. ISSN 0021-1516 (prep. by its International Division)
- Jewelers' Circular-Keystone. m. ISSN 0021-6267
- Medical Electronics and Equipment News Buyers' Guide. a.
- Motor Age; for the automotive service industry. m. ISSN 0027-1772
- N C Management Report. m.
- Optical Journal and Review of Optometry. s-m. ISSN 0030-3925
- Owner Operator. bi-m. ISSN 0475-2112
- Product Design and Development. m. ISSN 0032-9738
- Spectator. m. ISSN 0038-6960
- Spectator Handy Guide. a.
- Spectator Life Insurance Review. a.
- Tennis U. S. A. m. ISSN 0040-3466 (United States Lawn Tennis Association)
- Your Car and Your Money. s-a.

**Chilton Co., Inc. Automotive Editorial Dept.**
Chilton Way, Radnor, PA 19089.
- Chilton's Auto Repair Manual; American cars from 1968 to 1975. a. ISSN 0069-3634
- Chilton's Import Automotive Repair Manual. irreg.
- Chilton's Truck and Van Repair Manual; gasoline and diesel engines. irreg.

**China-Burma-India Veterans Association**
- Ex-C B I Roundup. (pub. by Neil L. Maurer, Ed. & Pub.)

**China Consultants International, Ltd.**
3286 M St., N.W., Washington, DC 20007.
- Mei-Kuo Kung Yeh Tao Pao/American Industrial Report. bi-m. (Co-Sponsor: National Council for United States-China Trade)

**China Medical Board of New York**
420 Lexington Ave., New York, NY 10017.
- China Medical Board of New York. Annual Report. a. ISSN 0069-3685

**Chinese-American Cultural Association, Inc.**
8122 Mayfield Rd., Chesterland, OH 44026.
- Pamir Magazine/Pa Mi Erh ZaZhi. m.

**Chinese-English Translation Assistance Group**
9811 Connecticut Ave., Kensington, MD 20795.
- C E T A Bulletin. 2 per yr.

**Chinese for Affirmative Action**
669 Clay Street, San Francisco, CA 94111.
- Chinese for Affirmative Action Newsletter. m.

**Chinese Historical Society of America**
17 Adler Place, off 1140 Grant Ave., San Francisco, CA 94133.
- Chinese Historical Society of America. Anniversary Bulletin. a.
- Chinese Historical Society of America. Bulletin. m (10 per yr.) ISSN 0577-9065

**Chinese Information Service**
159 Lexington Ave., New York, NY 10016.
- Report on Mainland China. irreg. ISSN 0486-4328

**Chinese Language Teachers Association**
c/o Fred Fangyu Wang, Asian Studies Dept., Seton Hall University, South Orange, NJ 07079.
- Chinese Language Teachers Association. Journal. 3 per yr. ISSN 0009-4595

**Rev. Peter P. S. Ching, Ed. & Pub.**
144-25 Roosevelt Ave., Flushing, NY 11354.
- Rock Magazine. irreg. ISSN 0080-3367

**Choice**
100 Riverview Center, Middletown, CT 06457.
- Choice. 11 per yr. ISSN 0009-4978 (Association of College and Research Libraries)

**Chomo Uri**
506 Goodell Hall, University of Massachusetts, Amherst, MA 01002.
- Chomo Uri. 3 per yr.

**Choomia**
Box 107, Framingham, MA 01701.
- Choomia. 3 per yr.

**Chowder Press**
2858 Kingston Dr., Madison, WI 53713.
- Chowder Review. 2 per yr.

**Christendom Educational Corporation**
Christendom College, 18825 Fuller Heights Rd., Triangle, VA 22172.
- Faith & Reason; the journal of Christendom College. q. ISSN 0098-5449

**Christian and Missionary Alliance**
25 South Tenth St., Harrisburg, PA 17101.
- Alliance Witness. fortn.

**Christian Anti-Communism Crusade**
Box 890, 124 E. 1st St., Long Beach, CA 90801.
- Christian Anti-Communism Crusade. Newsletter. bi-w. ISSN 0009-5230

**Christian Association for Psychological Studies**
6850 S. Division Ave., Grand Rapids, MI 49508.
- Christian Association for Psychological Studies. Proceedings. a. ISSN 0092-072X

**Christian Beacon Press**
756 Haddon Ave., Collingswood, NJ 08108.
- Christian Beacon. w. ISSN 0009-5265
- Reformation Review. q. ISSN 0034-303X (International Council of Christian Churches)

**Christian Board of Publication**
Box 179, 2640 Pine Blvd., St. Louis, MO 63166.
- Alive; for young teens. m. ISSN 0002-5461 (Christian Church-Disciples of Christ)
- Bethany Guide. m. ISSN 0005-9803 (Christian Church - Disciples of Christ)
- Disciple (St. Louis) s-m. ISSN 0092-8372

**Christian Booksellers Association**
2031 W. Cheyenne Rd., Colorado Springs, CO 80906.
- Bookstore Journal. 10 per yr. ISSN 0006-7563
- Current Christian Books. Authors and Titles. a. ISSN 0098-5554
- Current Christian Books. Titles, Authors and Publishers. a. ISSN 0098-5562

**Christian Camping International**
Box 400, Somonawk, IL 60552.
- Christian Camping International Directory. biennial. ISSN 0069-3855
- Journal of Christian Camping. bi-m. ISSN 0021-9649

**Christian Century Foundation**
407 S. Dearborn St., Chicago, IL 60605.
- Christian Century; an Ecumenical weekly. w. ISSN 0009-5281
- Christian Ministry; a professional journal for clergy. bi-m. ISSN 0033-4138

**Christian Children's Fund**
Development Office, Box 26511, Richmond, VA 23261.
- C C F World News.

**Christian Chronicle Inc.**
Box 339, Nashville, TN 37201.
- Christian Woman. m(Sept-July) ISSN 0009-5702

**Christian Church-Disciples of Christ**
- Alive. (pub. by Christian Board of Publication)
- Bethany Guide. (pub. by Christian Board of Publication)

**Christian Citizens Crusade Inc.**
Box 1697, Atlanta, GA 30301.
- Militant Truth. m. ISSN 0026-3893

**Christian Echoes National Ministry**
Box 977, Tulsa, OK 74102.
- Christian Crusade Weekly; international Christian newspaper. w.

**Christian Educators Journal Association**
c/o Arie F. Doornbos, 4341 Kimball Ave. S.E., Grand Rapids, MI 49508.
- Christian Educators Journal. q.

**Christian Evidence League**
Box 173, Malverne, NY 11565.
- Creationist. q. ISSN 0011-0868

**Christian Family Movement**
1655 W. Jackson, Chicago, IL 60612.
- Act. m. (bi-m. Jan.-Feb.; Jul.-Aug.) ISSN 0001-5083

**Christian Government Movement**
800 Wood St., Pittsburgh, PA 15221.
- Christian Patriot. m (except Aug.) ISSN 0045-6829

**Christian Herald Association Inc.**
40 Overlook Drive, Chappaqua, NY 10514.
- Christian Herald. m. ISSN 0009-5354

**Christian Interfaith Media Evaluation Center, Ltd.**
432 Park Avenue South, New York, NY 10016.
- Religious Media Today; critical review of communications resources available to religious educators. q.

**Christian Labor Association**
Box 65, 9820 Gordon St., Zeeland, MI 49464.
- Christian Labor Herald. q. ISSN 0009-5400

**Christian Librarian's Fellowship, Inc.**
910 Union Rd, West Seneca, NY 14224.
- Christian Periodical Index; an index to subjects, authors and book reviews. a. ISSN 0069-3871

**Christian Life Publications, Inc.**
Gundersen Dr. & Schmale Rd., Wheaton, IL 60187.
- Christian Bookseller; the business magazine of religious retailing. m. ISSN 0009-5273
- Christian Life; the wonderful way of living. m. ISSN 0009-5427

**Christian Medical Society**
1122 Westgate, Oak Park, IL 60301.
- Christian Medical Society Journal. q. ISSN 0009-546X

**Christian Missions in Many Lands, Inc.**
Box 13, Spring Lake, NJ 07762.
- Christian Missions in Many Lands. m (11 per yr.)

**Christian Nationalist Crusade**
c/o Gerald L. K. Smith, Box 27895, Los Angeles, CA 90027.
- Cross and the Flag. m. ISSN 0011-1929

**Christian Record Braille Foundation, Inc**
4444 S. 52nd St., Lincoln, NE 68506.
- Christian Record; for adult blind. m. ISSN 0009-5575
- Christian Record Talking Magazine. bi-m. ISSN 0009-5583
- Life and Health; general health journal for the blind. m. ISSN 0024-3043
- Student. m. ISSN 0039-2677
- Young & Alive (Inkprint Edition) m.

**Christian Reformed Church**
- Banner. (pub. by Christian Reformed Publishing House)

**Christian Reformed Publishing House**
2850 Kalamazoo Ave. S.E., Grand Rapids, MI 49508.
- Banner. w. ISSN 0005-5557 (Christian Reformed Church)

**Christian Research Institute**
Box 500, San Juan Capistrano, CA 92675
- Christian Research Institute. Newsletter. q. ISSN 0045-6845 (Subscr. to; 1550 S. Anaheim Blvd., Suite C, Anaheim CA 92805)

**Christian Restoration Association**
5664 Cheviot Rd., Cincinnati, OH 45239.
- Restoration Herald. m.(except Aug.) ISSN 0034-5830

**Christian Rural Fellowship**
475 Riverside Drive, New York, NY 10027.
- Christian Rural Fellowship. Bulletin. ISSN 0009-5605

**Christian Scholar's Review**
3900 Bethel Dr., St. Paul, MN 55112
- Christian Scholar's Review; a Christian quarterly of the arts and sciences. q. ISSN 0017-2251 (Subscr. Address: R.D. 1, Box 40-I, Houghton, NY 14744)

**Christian Science Publishing Society**
1 Norway St., Boston, MA 02115
(Subscr. to: Box 353, Astor Sta., Boston, MA 02123)
- Christian Science Journal. m. ISSN 0009-5613
- Christian Science Quarterly (Inkprint Edition) q. ISSN 0009-5621
- Christian Science Quarterly Bible Lessons (Braille Edition) m. (First Church of Christ, Scientist)
- Christian Science Sentinel. w. ISSN 0009-563X
- Herald of Christian Science. ISSN 0018-0475

**Christian Service Brigade**
Box 150, 380 Schmale, Wheaton, IL 60187.
- Brigade Leader; for the man guiding boys. q. ISSN 0007-0084
- Venture; for young men. m. ISSN 0042-3513

**Christian Spiritual Alliance Inc.**
- Orion. (pub. by C S A Press)

**Christian Theological Seminary**
Box 88267, Indianapolis, IN 46208.
- Encounter. q. ISSN 0013-7081

**Christian Unity Press**
2211 Lincoln Ave., Box 527, York, NE 68467.
- Internationale Bibellektionen. q. (German Church of God in U. S. A.)

**Christian Writers Institute**
- Handbook for Christian Writers. (pub. by Creation House)

**Christianity and Crisis, Inc.**
537 W. 121st St., New York, NY 10027.
- Christianity and Crisis; a Christian journal of opinion. fortn. ISSN 0009-5745

**Christianity on Campus**
Box 5252, Stanford, CA 94305.
- Renaissance; a radically biblical campus critique. m. ISSN 0034-4281

**Christianity Today, Inc.**
1014 Washington Bldg., Washington, DC 20005
(Subscr. address: Box 3800, Greenwich, CT 06830)
- Christianity Today. s-m. ISSN 0009-5753

**Christophers, Inc.**
12 E. 48th St., New York, NY 10017.
- Christopher News Notes. 7 per yr.

**Christ's Mission**
275 State St., Hackensack, NJ 07602.
- Christian Heritage. m.(Sept-June) ISSN 0009-5362

**Chronicle Guidance Publications, Inc.**
Aurora St., Moravia, NY 13118.
- Career Index. a.
- College Charts. a. ISSN 0590-630X
- Colleges Classified; a guide for counselors, parents and students. irreg. ISSN 0588-2990
- Guide to External and Continuing Education. a.
- Guide to Four-Year College Majors. a. ISSN 0361-8927
- Guide to Graduate and Professional Study. a.
- Guide to Two-Year College Majors and Careers. a.
- Student Aid Annual. a. ISSN 0585-4555
- Washington Counseletter. m. Sep.-Apr.

**Chronicle of the Horse, Inc.**
Middleburg, VA 22117.
- Chronicle of the Horse; the thoroughbred horse in sport, flat racing, steeplechasing, horse shows, foxhunting etc. w. ISSN 0009-5990

**Nicholas N. Chuhnov, Ed. & Pub**
3544 Broadway, New York, NY 10031.
- Znamya Rossiyi/Banner of Russia; Russian Anti-Communist Magazine. m. ISSN 0044-4901

**Church and Synagogue Library Association**
Box 1130, Bryn Mawr, PA 19010.
- Church and Synagogue Libraries. bi-m. ISSN 0009-6342

**Church Center Press**
100 W. Park Ave., Myerstown, PA 17067.
- United Evangelical. fortn. ISSN 0041-7262 (Evangelical Congregational Church)

**Church Council of Greater Seattle**
4759 15 Ave. N.E. (3rd. Fl.), Seattle, WA 98105.
- Church Council of Greater Seattle. Occasional News; an ecumenical newsletter for the greater Seattle area. irreg. (10-12 per yr.) ISSN 0010-9924

**Church Extension Service, Inc.**
Box 988, Golden, CO 80401.
- Sermon Builder; preacher's professional periodical. m. ISSN 0037-248X

**Church Herald Inc.**
1324 Lake Dr. S.E., Grand Rapids, MI 49506.
- Church Herald. fortn. ISSN 0009-6393 (Reformed Church in America)

**Church Management, Inc.**
4119 Terrace Lane, Hopkins, MN 55343.
- Church Management: The Clergy Journal. 10 per yr. ISSN 0009-6431

**Church Music Association of America**
548 Lafond Ave., St. Paul, MN 55103.
- Sacred Music. q. ISSN 0036-2255

**Church of All Worlds**
Box 2953, St. Louis, MO 63130.
- Aquarian Age. 8 per yr.
- Green Egg. 8 per yr. ISSN 0046-6395 (Council of Earth Religions)
- Mythos. q.

**Church of God**
922 Montgomery Ave., Cleveland, TN 37311.
- Climb. (pub. by Warner Press, Inc.)
- Junior High New Life Literature. q.
- Junior New Life Literature. w.
- Learn. (pub. by Warner Press, Inc.)
- Senior High New Life Literature. q.
- Vital Christianity. (pub. by Warner Press, Inc.)

**Church of God of Prophecy**
- White Wing Messenger. (pub. by White Wing Publishing House)

**Church of Jesus Christ of Latter-day Saints**
50 E. North Temple St., Salt Lake City, UT 84150.
- Ensign. m. ISSN 0013-8606

- Index to Periodicals of the Church of Jesus Christ of Latter-Day Saints. Cumulative Edition. a. ISSN 0073-5981
- New Era. m.
- New Messenger (Talking Book) bi-m.

**Church of Jesus Christ of Latter-day Saints. Corporation of the First Presidency**
50 E. North Temple, Salt Lake City, UT 84150
- Friend. m. ISSN 0009-4102 (Braille ed.: Christian Record Braille Foundation, 4444 S. 52nd St., Lincoln, NE 68506)

**Church of Jesus Christ of Latter-day Saints. Manti Region**
94 W. 400 South, Manti, UT 84642.
- Saga of the Sanpitch. a.

**Church of Light**
c/o General Manager, Box 76862 Sanford Sta., Los Angeles, CA 90076.
- Church of Light Quarterly. q. ISSN 0009-6520

**Church of Scientology. Celebrity Center**
1551 N. La Brea Ave., Hollywood, CA 90028.
- Celebrity. m.

**Church of Scientology of California**
5930 Franklin Ave., Hollywood, CA 90028.
- Freedom. bi-m.

**Church of Scientology of California. New American Saint Hall Organization**
2723 West Temple St., Los Angeles, CA 90026.
- Auditor; journal of Scientology. m. ISSN 0044-9997

**Church of the Brethren. General Board**
1451 Dundee Ave., Elgin, IL 60120.
- Guide for Biblical Studies. q.
- Messenger. m. ISSN 0026-0355

**Church of the Eternal Source**
Box 7091, Burbank, CA 91510.
- Khepera. q.

**Church of the Hermetic Sciences**
Box 3341, Pasadena, CA 91103.
- Seventh Ray. q.

**Church of the Lutheran Brethren**
Box 655, Fergus Falls, MN 56537.
- Faith and Fellowship. s-m.

**Church of the Lutheran Confession**
c/o John Lau, Immanuel Lutheran College, Eau Claire, WI 54701.
- Journal of Theology. 5 per yr. ISSN 0361-1906
- Lutheran Spokesman. m. ISSN 0024-7537

**Church of the United Brethren in Christ**
- New Illustrator. (pub. by United Brethren Publications)

**Church Publications**
R-B-2, Tippecanoe, OH 44699.
- Sunlore. m. ISSN 0039-5390 (National Nudist Council)
- Sunshine & Health. bi-m. ISSN 0039-5439 (National Nudist Council)

**Church Women United**
475 Riverside Dr., New York, NY 10027.
- Church Woman. m.(Oct-May); bi-m.(June-Sept) ISSN 0009-6599

**Church World**
c/o Thomas H. Fahey, Jr., 15 Amerscogin Rd., Falmouth, ME 04105.
- Church World. w. ISSN 0009-6601

**Churches of God. General Conference**
Commission on Publications, Inc, Central Publishing House, 611 S. 17th St, Harrisburg, PA 17104.
- Church Advocate. m. ISSN 0009-630X

**Churchman Co.**
1074 23rd Ave., N., St. Petersburg, FL 33704.
- Churchman. m.; bi-m. in summer. ISSN 0009-6628

**Chutzpah Collective**
Box 60142, Chicago, IL 60660.
- Chutzpah. irreg.

**CIBA Pharmaceutical Co.**
556 Morris Ave., Summit, NJ 07901.
- CIBA Collection of Medical Illustrations. irreg., 1973, vol. 6. ISSN 0084-8786 (prep. by its Medical Education Division)
- Clinical Symposia. q. ISSN 0009-9295 (prep. by its Medical Education Division)

**Cider Press**
Box 10113, Columbus, OH 43201.
- Hard Cider; a quarterly journal of the literary and graphic arts. q.

**Cigar Association of America**
575 Madison Ave., New York, NY 10022.
- Cigar Association of America. Statistical Record. irreg; no. 78, 1974.

**Cimarron Zen Center**
2505 Cimarron St., Los Angeles, CA 90018.
- Tower Smiling. q. ISSN 0040-991X (Rinzai-Ji, Inc.)

**Cincinnati. Division of Police**
Dept. of Safety, Records Section, Cincinnati, OH 45200.
- Cincinnati. Division of Police. Annual Report. a. ISSN 0091-8806

**Cincinnati Art Museum**
Eden Park, Cincinnati, OH 45202.
- Cincinnati Art Museum. Bulletin. irreg., 1973, vol. 9, no. 4. ISSN 0069-4061

**Cincinnati Bar Association**
26 E. 6th St., Cincinnati, OH 45202.
- Cincinnati Bar Association. Journal. q. ISSN 0094-2243

**Cincinnati Dental Society**
3012 Glenmore Ave., Cincinnati, OH 45238.
- Cincinnati Dental Society Bulletin. irreg. ISSN 0069-4096

**Cincinnati Historical Society**
Eden Park, Cincinnati, OH 45202.
- Cincinnati Historical Society Bulletin. q.

**Cineaste**
333 6th Ave, New York, NY 10014.
- Cineaste. q. ISSN 0009-7004

**Cinema Sourcebook**
211 Thompson St., New York, NY 10012.
- Cinema Sourcebook. m.

**Cinemabook**
344 E. 50 St., New York, NY 10022.
- Cinemabook. q. ISSN 0363-9665

**Cinemagic**
c/o Donald M. Dohler, Box 125, Perry Hall, MD 21128.
- Cinemagic. a. ISSN 0090-3000

**Cinque Foil**
c/o J. F. Koval, 7626 Balfour St., Allen Park, MI 48101.
- Cinque Foil. 2-3 per yr. ISSN 0009-7225

**Circle Forum**
Box 176, Portland, OR 97207.
- Circle; a periodical of reversible poetry. biennial.

**Circle K International**
101 E. Erie St., Chicago, IL 60611.
- Circle K Magazine. m. except Jul.-Aug. ISSN 0578-3097

**Circulo de Cultura Panamericano**
16 Malvern Pl., Verona, NJ 07044.
- Circulo; revista de cultura. a. ISSN 0009-7349
- Circulo Poetico; cuadernos de poesia. irreg., 1-2 per yr. (Editorial Address:, 16 Clark Ave., Troy, NY 12180)

**Circus Fans Association of America**
4931 Rosslyn, Indianapolis, IN 46205.
- White Tops; devoted exclusively to the circus. bi-m. ISSN 0043-499X

**Circus Historical Society**
2515 Dorset Rd., Columbus, OH 43221.
- Bandwagon; the circusiana magazine. 6 per yr. ISSN 0005-4968

**CIStems, Inc.**
P.O. Box 92, New York, NY 10016.
- Cultural Information Service. m.(except Jul. & Aug.) ISSN 0097-952X

**Citadel Press, Inc.**
120 Enterprise Ave., Secaucus, NJ 07094.
- Citadel Film Series. irreg.

**The Citadel-the Military College of South Carolina**
Charleston, SC 29409.
- Brigadier. 20 per yr.

**Citibank**
399 Park Ave., New York, NY 10022.
- Citibank. Monthly Economic Letter. m. ISSN 0015-279X
- Consumer Views. m.
- Economic Week. w. (prep. by its Economics Department)
- Energy Memo. q. (prep. by its Petroleum Department)
- Sound of the Economy. m.

**Citibank. Foreign Information Service**
Economics Dept., 399 Park Ave., New York, NY 10022.
- Citibank Money International. m.

**Citicorp**
399 Park Ave., New York, NY 10022.
- Citicorp Report to Investors. q.
- Citilife. s-m.

**Citizen Publishing Co., Inc.**
Box 31, Chapel Hill, NC 27514.
- Triangle Pointer; the weekly good word on Raleigh-Durham-Chapel Hill. w. ISSN 0041-2619

**Citizen World Press, Inc.**
Box 159, Carlsbad, CA 92008.
- Emergency Product News. bi-m. ISSN 0098-2180

**Citizens Advisory Council to the Pennsylvania Department of Environmental Resources**
P.O. Box 1467, Harrisburg, PA 17120.
- Pennsylvania. Citizens' Advisory Council. Annual Report. a. ISSN 0092-7937

**Citizens and Scientists Concerned About Dangers in Environment**
419 S. Central, Olympia, WA 98501.
- C A S C A D E. m.

**Citizens Band Publishing Industries, Inc.**
531 N. Ann Arbor, Oklahoma City, OK 73127.
- C B Magazine. m. ISSN 0007-795X

**Citizens Committee for Protection of the Environment**
71 Pine Ave., Ossining, New York, NY 10562.
- Survivalist. m.

**Citizens Committee for the Right to Keep and Bear Arms**
1601 114th, S.E., No. 151, Bellevue, WA 98004.
- Point Blank. m.

**Citizen's Constitutional Committee**
Box 2527, Kansas City, KS 66110.
- Conservative, Anti-Communist and Patriotic Directory; directory and bibliography. biennial.

**Citizens Council, Inc.**
254 E. Griffith St., Jackson, MS 39202
(Box 1675, Jackson, MS 39205)
- Citizen (Jackson) m. ISSN 0578-3283 (Citizens Councils of America)

**Citizens Councils of America**
- Citizen (Jackson) (pub. by Citizens Council, Inc.)

**Citizens for Clean Air, Inc.**
25 Broad St., New York, NY 10004.
- Citizens for Clean Air. q.

**Citizens for Decency Through Law, Inc.**
450 Leader Bldg., Cleveland, OH 44114.
- National Decency Reporter. bi-m. ISSN 0027-9102

**Citizens for Farm Labor**
Box 1173, Berkeley, CA 94701.
- Farm Labor. m. ISSN 0014-8016

**Citizens for Local Democracy**
29 Middagh St., Brooklyn, NY 11201.
- Township. s-m. ISSN 0041-0055

**Citizens' Governmental Research Bureau**
125 East Wells St., Milwaukee, WI 53202.
- C G R B Bulletin. 8-18 per yr.

**Citizens League of Minneapolis**
530 Syndicate Bldg., 84 S. Sixth St., Minneapolis, MN 55402.
- C L News. 20 per yr. ISSN 0045-6969

**Citizen's Movement for Safe and Efficient Energy**
P.O. 1538, Washington, DC 20013.
- Critical Mass; newspaper of the safe energy movement. m.

**Citizens Public Expenditure Survey, Inc.**
100 State St., Albany, NY 12207.
- C P E S Albany Report. bi-m.
- C P E S Mini-Taxpayer. q.
- C P E S Taxpayer; for the citizens of New York State. bi-m.

**Citizens' Research Foundation**
245 Nassau St., Princeton, NJ 08540.
- C R F Listing of Contributions of National Level Political Committees to Incumbents and Candidates for Public Offices. a. ISSN 0069-4231
- C R F Listing of Political Contributiors of Five Hundred Dollars or More. a. ISSN 0069-424X
- Citizens Research Foundation. Series. irreg., no. 23, 1973.
- Studies in Money in Politics. irreg., no. 24, latest issue. ISSN 0081-8240

**Citizens Union of the City of New York**
15 Park Row, New York, NY 10038.
- Across from City Hall; citizens union news and comment on New York City. 5 per yr. ISSN 0001-5059

**Citrus Engineering Conference**
Bailey Motor Equipment Co., Box 3386, Orlando, FL 32802.
- Citrus Engineering Conference. Transactions. a. ISSN 0412-6300

**Citrus Industry**
Box 89, Bartow, FL 33830.
- Citrus Industry. m. ISSN 0009-7594

**City Club of New York**
55 E. 43 St., New York, NY 10017.
- City Club Comments. m. ISSN 0009-7721

**City College of New York**
Convent Ave. & West 135 St., New York, NY 10031.
- Circum-Spice. irreg. (3 issues per year) ISSN 0069-4215
- Source. (Subscr. to:, Finley Student Center, Rm. 341)

**City College of New York. Alumni Association**
Finley Student Center, New York, NY 10027.
- City College Alumnus. 6 per yr. ISSN 0045-6993

**City College of New York. Engineering School**
140th St. & Convent Ave., New York, NY 10031.
- Vector; C C N Y engineering magazine. q. ISSN 0042-2967

**City College of New York. Library**
Convent Ave. & 138th St., New York, NY 10031.
- City College Papers; contributions to knowledge in all fields originating in lectures, research and scholarship at the City College of New York. irreg. ISSN 0077-894X

**City College of New York. School of Education**
Klapper Hall, 135th St. & Convent Ave., New York, NY 10031.
- Graduate Research in Education and Related Disciplines. s-a. ISSN 0017-2839
- High School Behavioral Science. (pub. by Human Sciences Press)

**City College of New York. Workshop Center for Open Education**
6 Shepard Hall, Convent Ave. & 140 St., New York, NY 10031.
- Workshop Center for Open Education Notes. q.

**City Geese**
52 E. 7th St., New York, NY 10003.
- N Y C Poetry Calendar. m.

**City Lights Books**
261 Columbus Ave., San Francisco, CA 94133.
- City Lights Anthology. irreg.

- Journal for the Protection of All Beings. irreg., 1969, no. 3. ISSN 0075-4099
- Pocket Poets Series. irreg.; no. 34, 1976. ISSN 0079-2438

**City Moon**
c/o Ed Graverholz, P.O. Box 842, Canal St. Station, New York, NY 10013.
- City Moon. m.

**City News Publishing Co.**
Box 606, Southold, L.I, NY 11971.
- Vital Speeches of the Day. s-m. ISSN 0042-742X

**City of Burlington Common Council**
Burlington, NJ 08016.
- Burlington Story. q.

**City University of New York**
33 W. 42 St., New York, NY 10036
- R I L M Abstracts of Music Literature. (International Repertory of Music Literature) q. ISSN 0033-6955 (International Association of Music Libraries) (Co-sponsor: International Musicological Society) (European Subscr. to: Baerenreiter Verlag, Heinrich-Schuetz Alle 31-37, D-3500 Kassell, W. Germany (B.R.D.))

**City University of New York. Bernard M. Baruch College**
17 Lexington Ave., New York, NY 10010.
- Accounting Forum. s-a. ISSN 0001-4818
- Bibliography of Higher Education Collective Bargaining Involving Other Than Faculty Personnel. irreg. (National Center for the Study of Collective Bargaining in Higher Education)
- National Center for the Study of Collective Bargaining in Higher Education. Annual Conference Proceedings. a.
- National Center for the Study of Collective Bargaining in Higher Education. Newsletter. 5 per yr.

**City University of New York, Brooklyn College**
Bedford Ave. & Ave H, Brooklyn, NY 11210.
- Kingsman. w. ISSN 0023-1649

**City University of New York, Brooklyn College. Africana Institute**
Brooklyn, NY 11210.
- Black Prism; perspectives on the Black experience. s-a.

**City University of New York, Brooklyn College. Center for Respoasive Psychology**
Brooklyn, NY 11210.
- Social Action and the Law. 6 per yr.

**City University of New York, Brooklyn College. Graduate Student Association**
La Guardia Hall, Room 237C, Brooklyn, NY 11210.
- Junction. a.

**City University of New York. Comparative Urban Studies Center**
- Comparative Urban Research. (pub. by Transaction Periodicals Consortium)

**City University of New York, Graduate Center. Environmental Psychology Program**
33 West 42nd St., New York, NY 10036.
- Childhood City Newsletter. irreg. (4-6 per yr.)

**City University of New York. Graduate School and University Center**
33 West 42 St., New York, NY 10036.
- Centerpoint; journal of interdisciplinary studies. q.
- Comparative Politics. (pub. by Transaction Periodicals Consortium)
- Neerlandica Americana. q. ISSN 0047-9268 (prep. by its Program in Germanic Languages and Literatures)

**City University of New York, Graduate School and University Center. Center for Social Research**
9 E. 40th St., New York, NY 10016.
- Population Health Survey Research Bulletin. irreg. (at least 1 per year) ISSN 0079-3914

**City University of New York. Hunter College**
505 Park Ave., New York, NY 10022.
- Newshunter. 5 per yr. ISSN 0048-0274

**City University of New York. Queens College**
Flushing, NY 11367.
- American Classical Review. bi-m. ISSN 0044-7633

- Ha-or. m.

**City University of New York, Queens College. Center for Instructional Development**
Flushing, NY 11367.
- Portable Video Newsletter. m. (Portable Video Access)

**City University of New York, Queens College. Department of English**
- Language and Style. (pub. by Queens College Press)
- Shout in the Street. (pub. by Queens College Press)

**City University of New York, Queens College. Graduate Political Science Association**
Graduate Political Science Dept., Flushing, NY 11367.
- Contemporary Politics. s-a.

**City University of New York. Research Center for Musical Iconography**
Graduate School and University Center, 33 West 42 St., New York, NY 10036.
- R I d I M-R C M I Newsletter. irreg. ISSN 0360-8727 (Repertoire Internationale d'Iconographie Musicale. Research Center for Musical Iconography)

**Civic-Data Corp.**
404 S. Bixel St., Los Angeles, CA 90017.
- Official Southern California Ports Maritime Directory and Guide. a. ISSN 0094-8454
- Southern California Business Directory and Buyers Guide. a. ISSN 0093-3090 (Los Angeles Area Chamber of Commerce)

**Civil Affairs Association**
416 Eisner St., Silver Spring, MD 20901.
- Civil Affairs Journal & Newsletter. m. ISSN 0045-7035

**Civil Rights Court Digest**
1860 Broadway, New York, NY 10023.
- Civil Rights Court Digest. m. ISSN 0009-7950

**Civil War Round Table Associates**
Box 7388, Little Rock, AR 72207.
- Civil War Round Table Digest. m. ISSN 0009-8086

**Civil War Token Society**
c/o Doug Watson, Box 112, Iola, WI 54945.
- Civil War Token Society. Journal. q. ISSN 0009-8108

**Civitan International**
115 N. 21st St., Birmingham, AL 35203.
- Civitan. m. ISSN 0300-7413

**Civitas dei Foundation**
Box 665, Mundelein, IL 60060.
- Chicago Studies; an archdiocesan review. 3 per yr. ISSN 0009-3718

**Claitor's Publishing Division**
Box 239, Baton Rouge, LA 80821.
- Bolton Landing Conference. Proceedings. irreg.
- Electron Microscopy Society of America. Proceedings. a. ISSN 0424-8201

**Clan Casselberry-Casselbury-Castleberry-Castlebury of America**
Box 651, Washington, DC 20044.
- Gamp Tree. q.

**Clan MacNeil Association of America**
7 Windmoor Dr., Convent Station, NJ 07961.
- Clan MacNeil Association of America. Galley. irreg.

**Clan McLaren Society, U S A**
5843 Royalcrest, Dallas, TX 75230.
- Clan McLaren Society, U S A. Quarterly. q. ISSN 0009-8213

**Clancy Publications, Inc**
2505 N. Alvernon Way, Tucson, AZ 85712.
- American Astrology. m. ISSN 0002-7529
- American Astrology Digest. a. ISSN 0516-9550

**Clapper Publishing Company, Inc.**
14 Main St., Park Ridge, IL 60068.
- Crafts 'n Things. bi-m.
- Pack-O-Fun. m.(Sept-June) ISSN 0030-901X

**Claremont College**
149 Harper Hall, Claremont, CA 91711.
- Claremont Annual Lectures. a.

**Claremont Institute for Administrative Studies.
Claremont Graduate School**
Claremont, CA 91711.
- College Student Personnel Abstracts; abstracts of
periodical literature, monographs and conference
papers on college student behavior and attitudes,
college environment, student personnel services.
q. ISSN 0010-1168

**Claremont Men's College. Department of Political
Science**
Pitzer Hall, Claremont, CA 91711.
- Californians in Congress. biennial. ISSN 0068-
6530 (California Congressional Recognition
Project, Inc.)

**Claretian Publications**
221 W. Madison St., Chicago, IL 60606.
- Bringing Religion Home. m.
- Context. fortn.
- Media Mix; ideas and resources for media and
communication. m(8 per yr)
- U S Catholic. m. ISSN 0041-7548

**Clarion Call Memorial Publications**
Box 52, Aurora, NY 13026
(Circulation Office: 120 Fernpark Dr., Camillus, NY
13031)
- Yesteryears; a quarterly for New York State
historical and genealogical research. q. ISSN
0044-037X

**Clarion Press**
Rt. 2 Box 217-A, Henagar, AL 35978.
- Primitive Baptist Yearbook. irreg.; latest edt., vol.
2, Jan. 1976. ISSN 0092-4415

**Clarity Publishing, Inc.**
75 Champlain St., Albany, NY 12204.
- Crux of Prayer. m.
- Crux of the News. w. ISSN 0591-2296

**Arthur H. Clark Co.**
1264 S. Central Ave., Glendale, CA 91204.
- American Trail Series. irreg. ISSN 0066-0884
- Clark Guidebooks. irreg. ISSN 0069-4401
- Frontier Military Series. irreg. ISSN 0071-9641
- Northwest Historical Series. irreg. ISSN 0078-
1789
- Western Frontiersmen Series. irreg. ISSN 0083-
8888
- Western Lands and Waters Series. irreg. ISSN
0083-8934

**Donald D. Clark & Associates, Inc.**
61 E. Columbus, Phoenix, AZ 85012.
- Arizona Professional Engineer. m. (Arizona
Society of Professional Engineers)
- Arizona Roadrunner. m. ISSN 0004-1637
(Arizona Motor Transport Association)

**Dean M. Clark**
Board of Trade Bldg., 141 W.Jackson Blvd.,
Chicago, IL 60604.
- Grain & Farm Service Centers. m. ISSN 0091-
0198
- Grain Industries Plants. m.

**Raymond B. Clark, Jr., Ed. & Pub.**
Box 352, St. Michaels, MD 21663.
- Maryland and Delaware Genealogist. q. ISSN
0025-4150

**Clark Boardman Co., Ltd.**
435 Hudson St., New York, NY 10014.
- Cemetery Business & Legal Guide. m (10 per yr)
- Drug Abuse Law Review. a. ISSN 0070-7341
- Environment Law Review. a. ISSN 0071-0830
- Patent Law Review. a. ISSN 0079-0168
- Search and Seizure Law Report. m. ISSN 0095-
1005
- Securities Law Review. a. ISSN 0080-8474

**Clark County Board of Education**
1115 N. Limestone, Springfield, OH 45503.
- Educator. m. (Sep.-Jun.)

**Clark Publishing (Highland Park)**
Highland House, 500 Hyacinth Pl., Highland Park,
IL 60035.
- Fate. m. ISSN 0014-8776

**Clark Publishing Co.**
106 East Stone Ave., P.O. Box 88, Greenville, SC
29602.
- America's Textiles. m.
- Clark's Directory of Southern Textile Mills. a.
- Municipal South. m. ISSN 0027-3570
- Southern Hospitals. m.

**Clark University**
950 Main St., Worcester, MA 01610.
- Clark Now. 4 per yr. ISSN 0009-8272
- Economic Geography. q. ISSN 0013-0095

**Clark University. Graduate Board**
950 Main St., Worcester, MA 01610.
- Clark University (Worcester, Mass.) Dissertations
and Theses. a. ISSN 0578-4247

**Clark University Press**
Clark Univ., Worcester, MA 01610.
- Idealistic Studies; international philosophical
journal. 3 per yr. ISSN 0046-8541

**Frederick S. Clarke, Ed & Pub.**
Box 270, Oak Park, IL 60303.
- Cinefantastique. q.

**Richard Clarke Associates**
1270 Sixth Ave., Suite 2720, New York, NY 10020.
- Opportunities for the Minority College Graduate.
a.

**Classic Car Club of America**
Box 443, Madison, NJ 07940.
- Classic Car. q. ISSN 0009-8310

**Classic M G Yearbook**
c/o R. L. Knudson, 21 Franklin St., Oneonta, NY
13820.
- Classic M G Yearbook. a. ISSN 0098-2741

**Classic Partners**
- Classic. (pub. by Andre Laguerre)

**Classical Association of New England**
c/o Dept. of Foreign Languages and Classics,
Portland, ME 04103.
- Classical Association of New England. Annual
Bulletin. a.
- New England Classical Newsletter. (pub. by
University of Massachusetts. Department of
Classics)

**Classical Association of the Atlantic States**
- Classical World. (pub. by Pennsylvania State
University. Department of Classics)

**Classical Association of the Middle West and South,
Inc.**
c/o Ed. Hunter R. Rawlings III, University of
Colorado, Dept. of Classics, Boulder, CO 80302
(Subscr. to: Prof. W. W. de Grumond, Dept. of
Classics, Florida State Univ. Tallahassee, Fl. 32306)
- Classical Journal. bi-m. ISSN 0009-8353

**Classical Association of the Pacific Northwest**
c/o C. A. E. Luschnig, Ed., University of Idaho,
Moscow, ID 83843.
- Classical Association of the Pacific Northwest
Bulletin. s-a.

**Classical Association of the Southwestern United
States**
c/o Edward V. George, Dept. of Classical and
Romance Languages, Texas Tech University,
Lubbock, TX 79409.
- Helios. s-a.

**Classical Folia Associates**
Holy Cross College, Worcester, MA 01610.
- Classical Folia; studies in the Christian
perpetuation of the classics. s-a. ISSN 0009-8345
(Institute for Early Iberian Christian Studies)

**Alice Moser Claudel, Ed. & Pub.**
Box 1083, Chalmette, LA 70044.
- New Laurel Review. s-a.

**Rufus Clay**
1216 Pennsylvania Ave., Fort Worth, TX 76104.
- Performance (Fort Worth); the weekly talent
buying guide. w.

**Clay Minerais Society**
- Clays and Clay Minerals. (pub. by Pergamon
Press Inc.)

**Chris Clayton, Ed. & Pub**
Box 3573, Modesto, CA 95352.
- Variety Ad and News Bulletin. m.

**Sharon Clayton**
Box 498, Long Beach, CA 90801.
- Cycle News East. w.
- Cycle News West. w.

**Clayton Junior College**
P.O. Box 285, Morrow, GA 30260.
- Clay Tablet. a.

**Clearinghouse for Options in Children's Education**
Summer School Bldg., 17th and M Sts. N.W.,
Washington, DC 20036.
- C H O I C E Newsletter. bi-m.

**Clearinghouse for U F O News and Information**
3521 S.W. 104th, Seattle, WA 98146.
- U F O Newsclipping Service. m.

**Clearinghouse on Development Communication**
1414 Twenty-Second Street, N.W., Washington, DC
20037.
- Development Communication Report. bi-m.
(Academy for Educational Development)

**Clemson University. Clemson Architectural
Foundation**
Clemson, SC 29631.
- Clemson University College of Architecture.
Semester Review. 2 per yr. ISSN 0009-871X

**Clemson University. College of Industrial
Management and Textile Science**
Clemson, SC 29631.
- Clemson University Review of Industrial
Management and Textile Science. s-a, vol. 13,
1974. ISSN 0069-4649

**Clemson University. Cooperative Extension Service**
Department of Agricultural Economics and Rural
Sociology, Clemson, SC 29631.
- Palmetto Economics. m.

**Clemson University. Department of English**
Clemson, SC 29631.
- South Carolina Review. 2 per yr.

**Clemson University. Department of Forestry**
Clemson, SC 29631.
- Clemson University. Department of Forestry.
Forestry Bulletin. irreg; no. 15, 1974.

**Clemson University. Department of Political Science**
Clemson, SC 29631.
- Journal of Political Science (Clemson) irreg. ISSN
0098-4612 (South Carolina Political Science
Association)

**Clemson University. Poultry Science Department**
Clemson, SC 29631.
- Poultry Health and Management Short Course.
Proceedings. a. ISSN 0069-4630 (Co-Sponsor:
South Carolina Poultry Improvement Assn.)

**Clemson University. Water Resources Research
Institute**
Clemson, SC 29631.
- Clemson University. Water Resources Research
Institute. Report. irreg., no. 61, 1976. ISSN 0069-
4657

**Cleveland Advertising Club**
Cleveland Plaza, Cleveland, OH 44115.
- Ad Club News. m. ISSN 0001-7922

**Cleveland Automobile Club-AAA**
Box 6150, Cleveland, OH 44101.
- Ohio Motorist. m. ISSN 0030-0985

**Cleveland Citizen Publishing Co.**
2711 Detroit Ave., Cleveland, OH 44113.
- Cleveland Citizen. w. ISSN 0009-8779

**Cleveland Clinic Foundation**
9500 Euclid Ave., Cleveland, OH 44106.
- Cleveland Clinic Quarterly. q. ISSN 0009-8787

**Forrest F. Cleveland, Ed. & Pub.**
188 Richmond Ave., Lexington, KY 40502.
- Spectroscopia Molecular; bulletin de novas e
informacoes de interesse e valor al
spectroscopistas molecular. m. ISSN 0038-6995

**Cleveland Engineering Society**
3100 Chester Ave., Cleveland, OH 44114.
- Cleveland Engineering. w. ISSN 0009-8809

**Cleveland Food Dealers Association**
4204 Detroit Ave., Cleveland, OH 44113.
- Cleveland Food Dealer. m. ISSN 0009-8817

**Cleveland Foundation**
700 National City Bank Bldg., Cleveland, OH 44114.
- Cleveland Foundation Quarterly. q.

**Cleveland Institute of Music**
11021 E. Boulevard, Cleveland, OH 44106.
- Cleveland Institute of Music (Newsletter) m. Sep.-Jun.

**Cleveland Jewish Publication Co.**
13910 Cedar Rd., Cleveland, OH 44118.
- Cleveland Jewish News. w. ISSN 0009-8825

**Cleveland Magazine Co.**
1632 Keith Building, Cleveland, OH 44115.
- Cleveland. m.

**Cleveland Medical Library Association**
11,000 Euclid Ave., Cleveland, OH 44106.
- Cleveland Medical Library. Bulletin. q. ISSN 0009-8833

**Cleveland Museum of Art**
11150 E. Blvd., Cleveland, OH 44106.
- Cleveland Museum of Art. Bulletin. m.(Sept-June) ISSN 0009-8841

**Cleveland Museum of Natural History**
Wade Oval, University Circle, Cleveland, OH 44106.
- Explorer; a magazine of the natural sciences, conservation, and environment. q. ISSN 0014-5009
- Kirtlandia. irreg.; no. 23, 1976. ISSN 0075-6245

**Cleveland Public Library Staff Association**
325 Superior Ave., Cleveland, OH 44114.
- Cleveland Public Library Staff Association. News and Views. bi-m. ISSN 0009-885X

**Cleveland State University. College of Law**
1983 E. 24th St., Cleveland, OH 44115.
- Cleveland State Law Review. 4 per yr. ISSN 0009-8876

**Cleveland State University. Department of Philosophy**
Cleveland, OH 44115.
- Philosophy in Context. s-a.

**Cleveland State University. Department of Religion**
Cleveland, OH 44115.
- Ohio Journal of Religious Studies. s-a. ISSN 0094-5668

**Cleveland Trust Company**
Euclid & E. 9th St., Cleveland, OH 44101.
- Cleveland Trust Company. Business Bulletin. m. ISSN 0009-8884

**Cleworth Publishing Co., Inc.**
One River Rd., Cos Cob, CT 06807.
- Electrical Consultant (Cos Cob) bi-m.
- Ingenieria de Fabricas. m.
- Motrix; the Spanish-language automotive service magazine for Latin America. m. ISSN 0027-2396
- Transmission and Distribution. m. ISSN 0041-1280

**Client's Monthly Alert, Inc.**
c/o Practical Accountant Magazine, 964 Third Avenue, New York, NY 10022.
- Client's Monthly Alert; monthly roundup of significant business & tax developments. m.

**Ralph L. Clifford, Ed. & Pub.**
75 Maiden Lane, New York, NY 10038.
- East Side News. w. (New York Graphic)
- New York Downtown News. w. (New York Graphic)
- Wall Street Advisor. w. (New York Graphic)

**Cliggott Publishing Co.**
500 W. Putnam Ave., Greenwich, CT 06830.
- Psychosomatics. bi-m. ISSN 0033-3182

**Climax Molybdenum Co.**
1 Greenwich Plaza, Greenwich, CT 06830.
- Molybdenum Mosaic; the journal of molybdenum metallurgy. q.
- Tungsten News. q. ISSN 0049-481X

**Climax Molybdenum Co. Technical Information Department. AMAX Specialty Metals Corp.**
P.O. Box 32, Akron, NY 14001.
- Molysulfide Newsletter. q.

**Climbing, Ltd.**
- Climbing. (pub. by American Mountaineering and Rockclimbing Magazine)

**Clinch River Breeder Reactor Project**
- Breeder Briefs. (pub. by Project Management Corp.)

**Clinical Chiropractic Publishing Co., Inc**
4151 Broadway, New York, NY 10033.
- Journal of Clinical Chiropractic. q. ISSN 0021-9711

**Clinical Lab Products, Inc.**
148 Linden St., Wellesley, MA 02181.
- Clinical Lab Products. m.
- Clinical Lab Products Annual Guide. a.

**Clinical Psychiatry News**
c/o Jack O. Scher, 919 Third Ave., New York, NY 10022.
- Clinical Psychiatry News. m.

**Clinical Psychology Publishing Co., Inc.**
4 Conant Square, Brandon, VT 05733.
- Journal of Clinical Psychology. q. ISSN 0021-9762
- Journal of Community Psychology. q. ISSN 0090-4392
- Journal of the History of the Behavioral Sciences. q. ISSN 0022-5061
- Psychology in the Schools. q. ISSN 0033-3085

**Clinton Essex-Franklin Library System**
Box 570, Plattsburgh, NY 12901.
- C-E-F Trailblazer. bi-m.

**CLIO**
Indiana University-Purdue University, Fort Wayne, IN 46805.
- CLIO; an interdisciplinary journal of literature, history, and the philosophy of history. 3 per yr.

**CLIO Awards Enterprises, Inc.**
30 E. 60th St., New York, NY 10022.
- Clio: Devoted to Commercials; mass communications. q. ISSN 0009-9384

**Cloquet Publications, Inc.**
122 Avenue C, Cloquet, MN 55720.
- Central Skiland. 9 per yr.(Oct.-Mar.) ISSN 0008-9540

**Close, Martin, Schreiber & Co.**
4340 Stevens Creek Blvd., Suite 275, San Jose, CA 95129.
- P O S I S. (Point-of-Sale Information Service) m.
- Retail Automation Report. m.

**Cloud Chamber**
17 Second St., Geneseo, NY 14454
- Cloud Chamber. a. (Or.; 5 Main St., Apt. 7, Geneseo, N.Y. 14454)

**Clover Patch, Inc.**
c/o Jan Quackenbush, 75 Church St., Montrose, PA 18801.
- Clover Patch. s-a.

**Clovernook Printing House for Blind**
7000 Hamilton Ave., Cincinnati, OH 45231.
- Unity Daily Word. m. ISSN 0041-8188 (Unity School of Christianity)

**Clown War**
c/o Bob Heman, 153 Albermarle Ave., West Babylon, NY 11704.
- Clown War. 3 per yr. ISSN 0045-7191

**Clowns of America, Inc**
717 Beverly Rd., Baltimore, MD 21222.
- Calliope. m.

**Club Familiar, Inc.**
1650 Broadway, New York, NY 10019.
- Temas; revista ilustrada. m. ISSN 0040-2869

**Coach & Athlete, Inc.**
200 South Hull Street, Montgomery, AL 36104.
- Coach and Athlete; magazine for coaches, players, trainers, officials. m(9 per yr.) ISSN 0009-9872

**Coachella Valley Sun**
Box 1088, Coachella, CA 92236.
- Desert Rancher. m. ISSN 0046-0044

**Coal Industry Advisory Committee to the Ohio River Valley Water Sanitation Commission**
- Symposium on Coal Mine Drainage Research. Papers. (pub. by Bituminous Coal Research, Inc.)

**COAS Publishing and Research**
Box 3cP, Las Cruces, NM 88003
- Awanyu. q. (Archaeological Society of New Mexico) (Subscr. to the Society at Box 3485, Albuquerque, NM 87110)

**Coast**
c/o William E. Darby, Kings Highway at 50th Ave. N., Myrtle Beach, SC 29577.
- Coast. w. ISSN 0010-0005

**Coastal Bend Council of Governments**
International Airport, Corpus Christi, TX 78408.
- Coastal Bend Council of Governments. State of the Region. bi-m.

**Coastal Plains Center for Marine Development Services**
1518 Harbour Dr., Wilmington, NC 28401.
- Marine Newsletter. bi-m.
- Summary of Marine Activities of the Coastal Plains Region. a.

**Cockrel Corporation**
2311 Nashville Rd., Box 645, Bowling Green, KY 42101.
- Kentucky Farmer. m. ISSN 0023-0219

**Cody Publications, Inc.**
Box 1030, 410 Verona St., Kissimmee, FL 32741.
- Florida Cattleman and Livestock Journal. m. ISSN 0015-3958
- Florida Future Farmer. q. (Future Farmers of America. Florida Association)
- Graphics. m.
- Review of the Graphic Arts. bi-m. ISSN 0360-6740 (International Association of Printing House Craftsmen)

**Coe College**
Box 672, Cedar Rapids, IA 52402.
- Mwendo. q.

**Coe College Student Senate**
G.M.U. Box 328, 1220 First Ave., Cedar Rapids, IA 52402.
- Coe Review. q.

**Coe Laboratories**
3737 W. 127th St., Chicago, IL 60658.
- Cal. m. ISSN 0007-778X

**Coffee Gallery**
1353 Grant Ave., San Francisco, CA 94113.
- San Francisco Gallery. a.; latest issue, 1973.

**Coffee House; Contemporary Greek Arts and Letters**
c/o Dino Siotis, Ed., Box 14217, San Francisco, CA 94114.
- Coffee House; Contemporary Greek Arts and Letters. s-a.

**Anita Coffelt, Ed. & Pub.**
Box 918, New Providence, NJ 07974.
- Animal Lovers. q.

**Cogitations**
89 Fieldstone Dr., Londonderry, NH 03053.
- Cogitations. m.

**Cognizant Corp.**
Box 216, Croton-on-Hudson, NY 10520.
- China Trade Telegram. m.

**Gabriel M. Cohen, Ed. & Pub.**
611 N. Park Ave., Indianapolis, IN 46204.
- Jewish Post and Opinion. w. ISSN 0021-6658
- Kentucky Jewish Post and Opinion. w.

**Stanley Cohen, Ed. & Pub.**
2579 Warren Road, Indiana, PA 15701.
- Pennsylvania Police Criminal Law Bulletin. m. ISSN 0098-7174

**Coin Arts, Inc.**
Box 27, Midwood Station, Brooklyn, NY 11230.
- Coin Bulletin. m. ISSN 0590-9945 (American Coin Club)

**Coin Investment Communique**
Box 265, Carlsbad, CA 92008.
- Coin Investment Communique. m.

**Coinamatic Trade Publishing Co., Inc.**
60 E. 42nd St., New York, NY 10017.
- Coinamatic Age; the voice of the automatic laundry and drycleaning industry. m. ISSN 0010-0463

**Coker College**
Fifth St., Hartsville, SC 29550.
- Periscope. m. ISSN 0031-5427

**Colby College Library**
Waterville, ME 04901.
- Colby Library Quarterly. q. ISSN 0010-0552

**Cold Spring Harbor Laboratory**
Box 100, Publications Department, Cold Spring Harbor, NY 11724.
- Cold Spring Harbor Conferences on Cell Proliferation. a.
- Cold Spring Harbor Laboratory. Abstracts of Papers Presented at Meetings. irreg.; latest issue, 1974. ISSN 0084-8824
- Cold Spring Harbor Laboratory. Annual Report. a. ISSN 0069-5009
- Cold Spring Harbor Laboratory. Symposia on Quantitative Biology. a. ISSN 0091-7451

**Erwin Coleman, Inc.**
257 Osborne Rd., Albany, NY 12211.
- Capital District Business Review. m.

**Coleopterists Society**
c/o Charles W. O'Brien, Ed., Laboratory of Aquatic Entomology, Florida A & M University, Tallahassee, FL 32307.
- Coleopterists Newsletter. irreg. ISSN 0045-7337

**Coleopterists Society (Washington)**
c/o Donald R. Whitehead, Ed., Department of Entomology, Smithsonian Institution, Washington, DC 20560.
- Coleopterists' Bulletin. q. ISSN 0010-065X

**Colgate Alumni Corporation**
- Colgate Scene. (pub. by Colgate University)

**Colgate University**
Administration Building, Hamilton, NY 13346.
- Colgate Scene. 8 per yr. (Colgate Alumni Corporation)
- Powys Newsletter. (pub. by Colgate University Press)

**Colgate University Press**
304 Lawrence Hall, Hamilton, New York, NY 13346.
- Powys Newsletter. a. (Colgate University)

**Collectable Old Advertising**
c/o Jim Cope, Box 1417, Orange, TX 77530.
- Collectable Old Advertising. a. ISSN 0091-0473

**Collective Bargaining Forum**
- Collective Bargaining Today. Proceedings. (pub. by Las Californias Publishing Co.)

**Collective Black Arts, Inc.**
Box 94, Times Square Station, NY 10036.
- Expansions; collective black artists' newsletter. q.

**Collector Books**
Box 3009, Paducah, KY 42001.
- Flea Market Trader. irreg. ISSN 0364-023X

**Collectors Club**
22 E. 35th St., New York, NY 10016.
- Collectors Club Handbooks. irreg., 1973, no. 24. ISSN 0069-5521
- Collectors Club Philatelist. 6 per yr. ISSN 0010-0838

**Collector's Media, Inc.**
Box 1000, Kermit, TX 79745.
- Bottle News. m.
- Collector. m. (Subscr. to: Drawer C, Kermit, TX 79745)
- Plate Collector. m. (Subscr. to: Box 1041, Kermit, TX 79747)

**Collectors Quarterly**
102 Ringold St., Peekskill, NY 10565.
- Collectors Quarterly. q.

**College and University Personnel Association**
National Headquarters, Suite 650, One Dupont Circle, Washington, DC 20036.
- College and University Personnel Association. Journal. q. ISSN 0010-0935

**College Art Association of America**
16 East 52 St., New York, NY 10022.
- Art Bulletin. q. ISSN 0004-3079
- Art Journal. q. ISSN 0004-3249
- C A A Newsletter. q.
- R I L A. (International Repertory of the Literature of Art) s-a. (Subscr. c/o Sterling and Francine Clark Art Institute, Williamstown, MA 01267)

**College Athletics Publishing Service**
349 E. Thomas Rd., Phoenix, AZ 85012.
- Official National Collegiate Athletic Association Basketball Rules. a. ISSN 0094-5234 (National Collegiate Athletic Association)

**College Band Directors National Association**
c/o Robert O. Briggs, Secretary-Treas., University of California Bands, Berkeley, CA 94720.
- College Band Directors National Association. Proceedings. biennial. ISSN 0069-5564

**College Bound Journal**
51 Reeder St., Elmhurst, NY 11373.
- College Bound Journal. m.

**College English Association**
c/o Elizabeth Cowan, Ed., Dept. of English, Texas A & M University, College Station, TX 77843.
- C E A Critic. bi-m(Nov-May) ISSN 0007-8069
- C E A Forum. q. ISSN 0007-8034

**College Entrance Examination Board**
888 Seventh Ave., New York, NY 10019
(Order from: College Board Publication Orders, Box 2815, Princeton, NJ 08540)
- College Board News. q.
- College Board Review. q. ISSN 0010-0951
- College Entrance Examination Board. Advanced Placement Course Descriptions. a.
- College Entrance Examination Board. Annual Meeting Proceedings. a. ISSN 0588-277X
- College Entrance Examination Board. College Handbook. irreg. ISSN 0069-5653
- College Entrance Examination Board. College Placement and Credit by Examination. irreg.
- College Entrance Examination Board. College Scholarship Service. CSS Need Analysis; theory and computation procedures for the 1977-78 PCS and FAF including sample cases and tables. a. ISSN 0092-9883
- College Entrance Examination Board. College Scholarship Service Colloquium Volumes. irreg. ISSN 0069-5661
- College Entrance Examination Board. Research Monographs. irreg., no. 7, 1976. ISSN 0069-567X
- College Entrance Examination Board. Research Reports. irreg., no. 3, 1973.
- New York Times Guide to Continuing Education in America. irreg.

**College Entrance Examination Board. Admissions Testing Program**
65 E. Elizabeth Ave., Bethlehem, PA 18018.
- College Entrance Examination Board. Admissions Testing Program. College-Bound Seniors. irreg. ISSN 0095-3377

**College Entrance Examination Board. College Scholarship Service**
888 Seventh Ave., New York, NY 10019.
- Financial Aid News. irreg. (approx 6 per yr.) ISSN 0430-4748

**College Language Association**
Morgan State University, Baltimore, MD 21239.
- C L A Journal. q. ISSN 0007-8549

**College Music Society**
c/o State University of New York, Department of Music, Binghamton, NY 13901.
- Bibliographies in American Music. (pub. by Information Coordinators Inc.)
- College Music Symposium; Journal of the College Music Society. s-a. ISSN 0069-5696
- Directory of Music Faculties in Colleges & Universities U.S. and Canada. biennial.

**College of American Pathologists**
- Pathologist. (pub. by Interstate Printers & Publishers, Inc.)

**College of Emporia Alumni Society**
1300 W. 12th St., College of Emporia, Emporia, KS 66801.
- College of Emporia Compass. 5 per yr. ISSN 0010-1060

**College of Insurance**
123 William St., New York, NY 10038.
- College of Insurance. General Bulletin. a. ISSN 0069-5718

**College of Physicians and Surgeons**
630 W. 168th St., New York, NY 10032.
- Man and Medicine; journal of values and ethics in health care. q.

**College of Physicians of Philadelphia**
19 S. 22 St., Philadelphia, PA 19103.
- College of Physicians of Philadelphia. Transactions & Studies. q. ISSN 0010-1087

**College of St. Thomas**
St. Paul, MN 55105.
- Aquin. fortn. ISSN 0003-7354
- Catholic Digest. m. ISSN 0008-7998

**College of William and Mary**
Williamsburg, VA 23185.
- William and Mary Review. s-a. ISSN 0043-5600

**College of William and Mary. Department of Modern Languages**
Williamsburg, VA 23185.
- Chasqui. 3 per yr. ISSN 0145-8973

**College of William and Mary. School of Business Administration**
Williamsburgh, VA 23185.
- Virginia Business Report. irreg.

**College of Wooster**
Wooster, OH 44691.
- Wooster Alumni Magazine. 5 per yr.

**College Placement Council, Inc.**
Box 2263, Bethlehem, PA 18001.
- C P C Salary Survey; a study of beginning salary offers. 3 per yr.
- College Placement Annual. a. ISSN 0069-5734
- Directory of College Placement Offices. a. ISSN 0070-5284
- Journal of College Placement; the international magazine of placement and recruitment. 4 per yr. ISSN 0021-9770

**College Placement Services, Inc.**
Box 2322, Bethlehem, PA 18001.
- Handbook for Recruiting at the Traditionally Black Colleges. irreg.

**College Press Service**
1764 Gilpin St., Denver, CO 80218.
- C. R. C. J. Bulletin. q. (Center for the Rights of Campus Journalists)
- College Press Service. s-w. ISSN 0010-1125

**College-Rater, Inc.**
2121 South 12th St., Allentown, PA 18103.
- Where the Colleges Rank. irreg.

**College Reading Association**
Shippensburg State College, Shippensburg, PA 17257.
- College Reading Association. Monographs. irreg.
- Reading World. q.

**College Sports Information Directors of America**
c/o Phil Langan, Ed., Sports Information Director, Jadwin Gym, Princeton University, Princeton, NJ 08540.
- C O S I D A News Digest. 10 per yr.

**College Store Catalog**
299 Madison Ave., New York, NY 10017.
- Catalog for College Stores: General Merchandise Buyer's Guide for College Store Managers and Buyers. a; with quarterly update supplements. ISSN 0069-1011

**College Swimming Coaches Association of America**
c/o G. Robert Mowerson, Secretary-Treasurer, 111
A Cooke Hall, University of Minnesota,
Minneapolis, MN 55455.
- College Swimming Coaches Association of
America Newsletter. 5 per yr.

**College Theology Society**
c/o Villanova University, Villanova, PA 19085
- College Theology Society. Proceedings. (pub. by
Seabury Press)
- Horizons (Villanova) s-a. ISSN 0360-9669
(Subscr. to: CSR Executive Office, Wilfrid Laurier
University, Waterloo, Ont., Canada N2L 3C5)

**Collegiate Scene**
Box 848, Hattiesburg, MS 39401.
- Collegiate Scene. 4 per yr. ISSN 0010-1230

**Collier Books**
866 Third Ave., New York, NY 10022.
- African-American Library Series. irreg.
- Motor Sport Yearbook. a. ISSN 0091-8822

**Colombia Information Service**
Colombian Center, 140 E. 57th St., New York, NY
10022.
- Colombia Today. m. ISSN 0010-1397

**Colonial Heritage Publishing Co., Inc.**
Box 1776, Bound Brook, NJ 08805.
- Colonial Heritage. 8 per yr.

**Colonial Newsletter Foundation, Inc.**
Box 4411, Huntsville, AL 35802.
- C N L. (Colonial Newsletter) q. ISSN 0010-1443

**Colonial Society of Massachusetts**
87 Mount Vernon St., Boston, MA 02215.
- Colonial Society of Massachusetts. Publications.
irreg., vol. 50, 1975.

**Colonial Society of Massachusetts (Brunswick)**
c/o Herbert Brown, Ed., Hubbard Hall, Bowdoin
College, Brunswick, ME 04011.
- New England Quarterly: An Historical Review of
New England Life and Letters. q. ISSN 0028-
4866

**Colonial Williamsburg Foundation**
Williamsburg, VA 23185.
- Colonial Williamsburg Archaeological Series.
irreg.; latest issue, 1974. ISSN 0069-5971
- Williamsburg Research Studies. irreg. ISSN 0084-
0300

**Colorado. Air Pollution Control Commission**
Denver, CO 80203.
- Colorado. Air Pollution Control Commission.
Report to the Public; an annual progress report of
the Colorado State air pollution control program.
a. ISSN 0097-9996

**Colorado. Department of Education**
Denver, CO 80203.
- Consolidated Report on Elementary and
Secondary Education in Colorado. a. ISSN 0095-
5329

**Colorado. Department of Highways**
4201 East Arkansas, Denver, CO 80222.
- Colorado. Department of Highways. Traffic
Volume Study. biennial. ISSN 0069-6013

**Colorado. Department of Labor and Employment.
Division of Employment and Training**
1210 Sherman St., Denver, CO 80203.
- Colorado Manpower Review. m. ISSN 0010-1656

**Colorado. Department of Public Health**
Denver, CO 80203.
- Colorado. State Department of Public Health.
Annual Progress Report. State Migrant Plan for
Public Health Services. a. ISSN 0588-4543

**Colorado. Division of Commerce and Development**
500 Centennial Bldg., Denver, CO 80203.
- Colorado Development Digest. m.

**Colorado. Division of Mines**
1845 Sherman St., Denver, CO 80203.
- Summary of Mineral Industry Activities in
Colorado. a.

**Colorado. Division of Water Resources**
1845 Sherman St., Denver, CO 80203.
- Colorado Water News. m.

**Colorado. Division of Water Resources. Water
Conservation Board**
1845 Sherman, Denver, CO 80203.
- Colorado Water Resources Circular. irreg. ISSN
0092-2684 (Co-sponsor: U.S. Geological Survey)

**Colorado. Division of Wildlife**
6060 Broadway, Denver, CO 80216.
- Colorado. Division of Wildlife. Special Report.
irreg., no. 39, 1976. ISSN 0084-8875
- Colorado. Division of Wildlife. Technical
Publication. irreg., no. 31, 1975. ISSN 0084-8883
- Colorado Cooperative Wildlife Research Unit.
Special Scientific Reports. Technical Papers. (pub.
by Colorado State University. Cooperative
Wildlife Research Unit)
- Colorado Outdoors. bi-m. ISSN 0010-1699

**Colorado. Office of the Court Administrator**
323 State Capitol, Denver, CO 80203.
- Annual Statistical Report of the Colorado
Judiciary. a. ISSN 0094-7504

**Colorado. State Library**
1362 Lincoln St., Denver, CO 80203.
- Colorado State Library Newsletter. m. ISSN
0010-1761
- Directory of Colorado Libraries. a.

**Colorado Academy of Family Physicians**
2866 S. Broadway, Englewood, CO 80110.
- Colorado F.P. q. ISSN 0010-1605

**Colorado Archaeological Society, Inc.**
Univ. of Colorado, Dept. of Anthropology, Boulder,
CO 80302.
- Southwestern Lore. q. ISSN 0038-4844

**Colorado Artist Craftsmen**
19 Newland Court, Denver, Elizabeth, CO 80226.
- Colorado Artist Craftsmen; a craft newsletter of
the Rocky Mountain West. q.

**Colorado Association of Public Employees**
1390 Logan St., Denver, CO 80203.
- Citizen. every 3 weeks. ISSN 0009-7543

**Colorado Audiovisual Association**
7055 E. 18th Ave., Denver, CO 80220.
- T I P S. (Technology Information Professional
Services) m.

**Colorado Bankers Association**
- Mountain States Banker. (pub. by Mountain States
Publishing Co.)

**Colorado Council of Churches**
1313 Clarkson St., Denver, CO 80218.
- Colorado Councillor. q. ISSN 0010-1540

**Colorado Dental Association**
2045 Franklin St., No. 507, Denver, CO 80205.
- Colorado Dental Association. Journal. 3 per yr.
ISSN 0010-1559

**Colorado Education Association**
5200 S. Quebec St., Englewood, CO 80110.
- Colorado School Journal. 13 per yr. ISSN 0010-
1737

**Colorado Environmental Protection Association**
- Ecology Today. (pub. by Merriman Publishing
Co.)

**Colorado Express**
Box 18214, Capitol Hill Station, Denver, CO 80218.
- Colorado Express. s-a.

**Colorado Interstate Gas Company**
P.O. Box 1087, Colorado Springs, CO 80944.
- Colorado Industrial Capability Register. a. ISSN
0069-6021

**Colorado Language Arts Society**
- Statement. (pub. by Colorado State University.
English Department)

**Colorado Magazine Inc.**
c/o Merrill G. Hastings, Jr., 7190 W. 14th Ave.,
Denver, CO 80215.
- Colorado-Rocky Mountain West. bi-m. ISSN
0010-1796

**Colorado Medical Society**
1601 E. 19th Ave., Denver, CO 80218.
- Rocky Mountain Medical Journal. bi-m. ISSN
0035-760X

**Colorado Mining Association**
402 Majestic Building, 209 Sixteenth St., Denver,
CO 80202.
- Mining Yearbook. a.

**Colorado Mountain Club**
2530 W. Alameda Ave., Denver, CO 80219.
- Trail and Timberline. m. ISSN 0041-0756

**Colorado Municipal League**
4800 Wadsworth Blvd., Suite 204, Wheat Ridge,
CO 80033.
- Colorado Municipalities. bi-m. ISSN 0010-1664

**Colorado Music Educators Association**
165 Iroquois Drive, Boulder, CO 80303.
- Colorado Music Educator. q. ISSN 0010-1672

**Colorado-North Review**
University Center, University of Northern Colorado,
Greeley, CO 80639.
- Colorado-North Review. 3 per yr.

**Colorado Nurses Association**
5453 E. Evans Place, Denver, CO 80222.
- Colorado Nurse. m. ISSN 0010-1680

**Colorado Pilots Association, Inc.**
- Aero West. (pub. by Aero West Magazine Inc.)

**Colorado Press Association**
1336 Glenarm Place, Denver, CO 80204.
- Colorado Editor. m. ISSN 0010-1567

**Colorado Railroad Historical Foundation, Inc.**
- Colorado Rail Annual. (pub. by Colorado Railroad
Museum)

**Colorado Railroad Museum**
Box 10, Golden, CO 80401.
- Colorado Rail Annual. a. ISSN 0069-6048
(Colorado Railroad Historical Foundation, Inc.)

**Colorado School of Mines**
Golden, CO 80401.
- Colorado School of Mines. Mineral Industries
Bulletin. bi-m.(July-May) ISSN 0010-1745
- Colorado School of Mines. Professional
Contributions. irreg. ISSN 0069-6056
- Colorado School of Mines. Quarterly. q. ISSN
0010-1753

**Colorado School of Mines. Alumni Association**
Golden, CO 80401.
- Mines; around the world with the mineral
industries. m. (except Jul. & Aug.) ISSN 0026-
5055

**Colorado School of Mines. Graduate School and
Research Services**
Department of Publications, Golden, CO 80401.
- Colorado School of Mines. Research; annual
report of the research activities of the faculty and
graduate school. a. ISSN 0069-6064

**Colorado Springs Fine Arts Center**
30 W. Dale St., Colorado Springs, CO 80903.
- Colorado Springs Fine Arts Center. Report. a.;
latest issue, 1970. ISSN 0069-6072

**Colorado State University. College of Engineering**
Fort Collins, CO 80521.
- Colorado State University. Hydrology Papers.
irreg., no. 68, 1974. ISSN 0069-6110

**Colorado State University. Cooperative Wildlife
Research Unit**
Wildlife Management Institute, Fort Collins, CO
80523.
- Colorado Cooperative Wildlife Research Unit.
Special Scientific Reports. Technical Papers. irreg.
ISSN 0069-6005 (Colorado. Division of Wildlife)
(Co-sponsor: U.S. Fish and Wildlife Service)

**Colorado State University. Department of Agronomy**
Fort Collins, CO 80521.
- Barley Genetics Newsletter; an international
communication medium. a.

**Colorado State University. Department of
Atmospheric Science**
College of Engineering, Fort Collins, CO 80523.
- Colorado State University. Atmospheric Science
Paper. irreg. ISSN 0067-0340

**Colorado State University. Department of History**
Room B-350, Social Sciences Building, Fort Collins, CO 80523.
- Colorado State University. Department of History. Germans from Russia in Colorado Study Project. Information Bulletin. 3 per yr. (prep. by its Germans from Russia in Colorado Study Project)

**Colorado State University. English Department**
Liberal Arts Bldg., Fort Collins, CO 80521.
- Statement. 3 per yr. (Colorado Language Arts Society)

**Colorado State University Experiment Station**
Office of University Communications, Colorado State University, Fort Collins, CO 80523.
- Colorado State University Research. irreg.

**Colorado State University. Institute in Technical and Industrial Communications**
Fort Collins, CO 80521.
- Institute in Technical and Industrial Communications, Colorado State University. Proceedings. a. ISSN 0073-8956

**Colorado State University. University Library**
Fort Collins, CO 80523.
- Colorado State University Libraries. Publication. irreg., no. 6, 1974. ISSN 0084-8905

**Colorado Technical Reference Center**
- C T R C Newsletter. (pub. by University of Colorado)

**Colorado Women's College**
Montview Blvd. and Quebec, Denver, CO 80220.
- Colorado Women's College. Bulletin. q.

**Colorado-Wyoming Academy of Science.**
c/o Dept. of Environmental, Populations and Organismic Biology, University of Colorado, Boulder, CO 80302.
- Colorado-Wyoming Academy of Sciences Journal. a.

**Coloramic Magazine, Inc.**
Box 1098, St. Petersburg, FL 33731.
- Coloramic. m. ISSN 0010-177X

**Colortone Press**
Colortone Bldg., 2400 17th St., N.W., Washington, DC 20009.
- Washington Industry and Association News. q.

**Columban Fathers**
St. Columbans, NE 68056.
- Columban Mission. m. (except Jun. & Aug.) (St. Columban's Foreign Mission Society)

**Columbia-Barnard Filmmakers**
313 Ferris Booth Hall, Columbia University, New York, NY 10027.
- Filmmaker's Review. q.

**Columbia Books Inc.**
Suite 601, 734 Fifteenth St., N.W., Washington, DC 20005.
- National Trade and Professional Associations of the United States and Canada and Labor Unions. a. ISSN 0094-8284

**Columbia Coin Buy Letter**
407 S.W. Washington, Portland, OR 97204.
- Columbia Coin Buy Letter. m.

**Columbia Communications, Inc.**
370 Lexington Ave., New York, NY 10017.
- Auto Laundry News. m. ISSN 0005-0776
- Casual Living. m.
- Curtain, Drapery & Bedspread Magazine. bi-m. ISSN 0011-4065
- Curtain, Drapery and Bedspread National Buyers Guide. a. ISSN 0084-9502
- Interior Decorators' Handbook. s-a.
- Juvenile Merchandising. m. ISSN 0022-7161
- Linens/Domestics & Bath Products. bi-m. ISSN 0024-3833
- Musical Merchandise Review; pianos, musical instruments, organs, accessories. m. ISSN 0027-4615

**Columbia County Historical Society**
c/o Pearl Becker, Sec., 45 S. 21st St., St. Helens, OR 97051.
- Columbia County History (Oregon) a. ISSN 0069-6293

**Columbia Human Rights Law Review**
Columbia University School of Law, Box 54, 435 W. 116th St., New York, NY 10027.
- Columbia Human Rights Law Review. s-a. ISSN 0090-7944

**Columbia Journal of Transnational Law Association**
- Columbia Journal of Transnational Law. (pub. by Columbia University. School of Law)

**Columbia Publishing and Design**
111-C 7th and Walnut, 127 W. Yakima Ave., Yakima, WA 98907.
- Agrow-Marketer. m.

**Columbia River Water Management Group**
Corps of Engineers, 210 Custom House, Portland, OR 97209.
- Columbia River Water Management Report. a. ISSN 0360-6864

**Columbia Scholastic Press Advisers Association**
Box 11, Central Mail Room, Columbia University, New York, NY 10027.
- C. S. P. A. A. Bulletin. q. ISSN 0010-1990
- School Press Review; high school and college level. m.(Oct-May) ISSN 0036-6730

**Columbia Sheep Breeders Association of America**
Box 272, Upper Sandusky, OH 43351.
- Speaking of "Columbias". m. ISSN 0038-6626

**Columbia Union Conference of Seventh-Day Adventists**
7710 Carroll Ave., Takoma Park, MD 20012.
- Columbia Union Visitor. fortn.

**Columbia University**
New York, NY 10027
- Chemical Highlights. bi-m. ISSN 0009-255X (Orders to: Box 666, Havenmeyer)
- Columbia Daily Spectator. (pub. by Spectator Publishing Co.)
- Columbia Jester. s-a. ISSN 0010-1915 (Orders to: 303, 316 Ferris Booth Hall)
- Columbia Review. q. ISSN 0010-1982 (Orders to:, 206 Ferris Booth Hall)
- Johnsonian News Letter. q. ISSN 0021-728X (Orders to:, 610 Philosophy Hall)
- Journal of Philosophy. (pub. by Journal of Philosophy, Inc.)
- Public Opinion Quarterly. q. ISSN 0033-362X (American Association for Public Opinion Research) (Orders to: Journalism Bldg., Rm. 510)

**Columbia University. Ancient Near Eastern Society**
614 Kent Hall, New York, NY 10027.
- Columbia University. Ancient Near Eastern Society. Journal. a. ISSN 0010-2016

**Columbia University. Avery Architectural Library**
- Avery Index to Architectural Periodicals. Supplement. (pub. by G. K. Hall & Co.)

**Columbia University. Center for Advanced Research in Urban and Environmental Affairs**
New York, NY 10027
- Columbia University. Center for Advanced Research in Urban and Environmental Affairs. Working Papers. irreg. (Dist. by J. Rietman, 167 Spring St., New York, NY 10012)

**Columbia University. College of Physicians and Surgeons**
630 W. 168 St., New York, NY 10032.
- P & S Quarterly. (Physicians and Surgeons) q. ISSN 0030-7831 (prep. by its Alumni Association)

**Columbia University. Conservation of Human Resources Project**
- Columbia University. Conservation of Human Resources Project. Conservation of Human Resources Studies. (pub. by Praeger Publishers, Inc.)

**Columbia University. Department of Middle East Languages and Cultures**
- Publications in Near and Middle East Studies. Series A. (pub. by Mouton Publishers NE)
- Publications in Near and Middle East Studies. Series B. (pub. by Mouton Publishers NE)

**Columbia University. Department of Music**
New York, NY 10027.
- Current Musicology. s-a. ISSN 0011-3735

**Columbia University. Graduate School of Business**
408 Uris, New York, NY 10027.
- Columbia Journal of World Business. q. ISSN 0022-5428
- Columbia University Graduate School of Business. Dissertations Series. (pub. by Free Press)

**Columbia University. Graduate School of Journalism**
New York, NY 10027.
- Columbia Journalism Review. bi-m. ISSN 0010-194X

**Columbia University. Graduate Sociology Student Union**
116th & Broadway, New York, NY 10027.
- Human Factor (New York) irreg. ISSN 0362-9090

**Columbia University. Hispanic Institute of the United States**
612 W. 116th St., New York, NY 10027.
- Revista Hispanica Moderna; devoted to the study of the literature of Latin America, Portugal and Spain. q. ISSN 0034-9593

**Columbia University. Institute on East Central Europe**
420 W. 118th St., New York, NY 10027.
- Society for Slovene Studies Newsletter. s-a. ISSN 0145-6830 (Society for Slovene Studies)

**Columbia University Libraries**
New York, NY 10027.
- Columbia Library Columns. 3 per yr. ISSN 0010-1966 (Friends of Columbia Libraries. Butler Library)

**Columbia University Libraries. Systems Office**
535 W. 114 St., New York, NY 10027.
- Automation Efforts at the Columbia University Libraries. Progress Report. irreg.
- Columbia University. Libraries. Systems Office. Technical Note. 2 per yr.

**Columbia University. Parker School of Foreign and Comparative Law**
- Bibliography on Foreign and Comparative Law : Books and Articles in English. (pub. by Oceana Publications, Inc.)
- Bilateral Studies in Private International Law. (pub. by Oceana Publications Inc.)
- Guide to Foreign Legal Materials Series. (pub. by Oceana Publications Inc.)

**Columbia University. Presbyterian Hospital School of Nursing**
179 Fort Washington Ave., New York, NY 10032.
- Columbia University-Presbyterian Hospital School of Nursing. Alumnae Association. Magazine. irreg., usually 3 per yr. ISSN 0069-634X

**Columbia University Press**
136 S. Broadway, Irvington, NY 10533.
- American Speech; a quarterly of linguistic usage. q. ISSN 0003-1283 (American Dialect Society)
- Bampton Lectures in America. irreg., 1978, no. 20. ISSN 0067-3129
- Benjamin F. Fairless Lectures. a. ISSN 0067-5717 (Carnegie-Mellon University)
- Columbia Biological Series. irreg., 1968, no. 24. ISSN 0069-6285
- Columbia Essays on the Great Economists. irreg., 1976, no. 6. ISSN 0069-6323
- Columbia Series in Molecular Biology. irreg., latest 1973.
- Columbia Studies in Economics. irreg., 1977, no. 9. ISSN 0069-6331
- Columbia University. East Asian Institute. Studies. irreg., latest 1977.
- Columbia University. Institute on East Central Europe. East Central European Studies. irreg., latest 1968.
- Columbia University Studies in Library Service. irreg., 1967, no. 16. ISSN 0069-6374
- Contemporary American History Series. irreg., 1977, no. 10. ISSN 0069-9357
- Copyright Law Symposium. irreg., 1977, no. 22. ISSN 0069-9950 (American Society of Composers, Authors, and Publishers)
- Directory of Social and Health Agencies of New York City. biennial. ISSN 0085-0012 (Community Council of Greater New York, Inc.)
- International Conference of Social Work. Conference Proceedings. biennial, 18th San Juan, P.R., 1976. ISSN 0074-2961 (International Council on Social Welfare)
- Jacob Blaustein Lectures in International Affairs. irreg., 1971, no. 2. ISSN 0075-2142

- Lectures on the History of Religions. New Series. irreg., 1977, no. 11. ISSN 0075-8531
- Modern Middle East Series. irreg., 1970, no. 3. ISSN 0077-0027
- Music Forum. irreg., 1977, vol. 4.
- Radner Lectures. irreg., 1976, no. 7. ISSN 0079-9491
- Records of Civilization. Sources and Studies. irreg., no. 95. ISSN 0080-0287
- Social Work and Social Issues. irreg., 1977, no. 5. ISSN 0081-055X
- Studies in Consumer Credit. irreg., no. 4, 1975.
- Studies in Oriental Culture. irreg., no. 13. ISSN 0081-8321
- Woodbridge Lectures, Columbia University. irreg.

**Columbia University. Research Institute on Communist Affairs**
New York, NY 10027.
- Columbia University. Research Institute on Communist Affairs. Studies. irreg.

**Columbia University. Russian Institute**
New York, NY 10027.
- Columbia University. Russian Institute. Studies. irreg. ISSN 0588-5477

**Columbia University School of Dental & Oral Surgery. Alumni Association**
- Columni. (pub. by Meilen Press)

**Columbia University. School of Engineering & Applied Science**
510 S.W. Mudd Bldg., New York, NY 10027.
- Columbia Engineering Research. s-a.

**Columbia University. School of General Studies**
505 Lewisohn Hall, New York, NY 10027.
- Columbia University. American Language Program. Bulletin; instruction in English as a foreign language. a. (prep. by its American Language Program)

**Columbia University. School of International Affairs**
420 W. 118th St., New York, NY 10027.
- Journal of International Affairs. s-a. ISSN 0022-197X

**Columbia University. School of Law**
Box 16, 435 W. 116th St., New York, NY 10027.
- Columbia Journal of Environmental Law. s-a. ISSN 0098-4582
- Columbia Journal of Law and Social Problems. q. ISSN 0010-1923
- Columbia Journal of Transnational Law. 3 per yr. ISSN 0010-1931 (Columbia Journal of Transnational Law Association)
- Columbia Law Alumni Observer. every 6 weeks. ISSN 0093-304X
- Columbia Law Review. m.(Oct.-Jan., Mar.-Jun.) ISSN 0010-1958

**Columbia University. School of Library Service**
Box 44, Butler Library, 535 W. 114th St., New York, NY 10027.
- Library Service News. 2 per yr. ISSN 0024-2551 (prep. by its Alumni Association)

**Columbia University. Southern Asian Institute**
535 West 114th St., New York, NY 10027.
- Columbia University. Southern Asian Institute. Occasional Bibliographic Papers. irreg.

**Columbia University. Teachers College**
525 W. 120 St, New York, NY 10027.
- A P S S Know How. m. (Sep.-Jun.) ISSN 0023-2467 (Associated Public School Systems)
- Associated Public Schools Systems. Yearbook. a. ISSN 0066-8753 (Associated Public School Systems)
- H M L I Research Bulletin. (Horace Mann-Lincoln Institute)
- M S S C Exchange. m (Sept.-June) ISSN 0024-8444 (Metropolitan School Study Council)

**Columbia University Teachers College. Center for Adult Education**
New York, NY 10027.
- I. D. E. A. Review. (Innovation Dissemination for the Education of Adults) q.

**Columbia University. Teachers College Record Office**
525 W. 120th St., New York, NY 10027.
- Teachers College Record; a professional journal of ideas, research and informed opinion. q.(Sept-May) ISSN 0040-0475

**Columbia University. Trustees of Columbia University**
- Columbia Today. (pub. by Simmons-Boardman Publishing Corporation)

**Columbus Area Chamber of Commerce**
50 W. Broad St., Columbus, OH 43216.
- Columbus Business Forum. m. ISSN 0010-2059

**Columbus Education Association**
700 E. Broad St., Columbus, OH 43215.
- C E A Voice. 5-9 per yr. ISSN 0007-8107

**Columbus Free Press**
Box 3162, Columbus, OH 43210.
- Columbus Free Press. fortn.

**Combustion Institute**
986 Union Trust Bldg., Pittsburgh, PA 15219.
- Combustion and Flame. (pub. by Elsevier North-Holland, Inc., New York)
- Symposium (International) on Combustion. biennial; 15th, Tokyo, 1974. ISSN 0082-0784

**Combustion Institute. Western States Section**
c/o Ms. Rebecca C. Palmer, Preprints Chairperson, Mechanical Engineering Dept., University of California, Berkeley, CA 94720.
- Combustion Institute. Western States Section. Papers. s-a. ISSN 0010-2199

**Combustion Publishing Co., Inc.**
277 Park Ave., New York, NY 10017.
- Combustion; devoted to the advancement of steam plant design and operation. m. ISSN 0010-2172

**COMCRES, Inc.**
300 St. Paul Place, Baltimore, MD 21202.
- Consumer Month. m.

**Comediantes**
c/o Karl Gregg, University of Arizona, Dept. of Romance Languages, Tucson, AZ 85721.
- Bulletin of the Comediantes. s-a. ISSN 0007-5108

**Comedy Center, Inc.**
801 Wilmington Trust Bldg., Wilmington, DE 19810.
- Orben's Comedy Fillers. m. ISSN 0048-2099
- Orben's Current Comedy. s-m. ISSN 0048-2102

**Comic Book Price Guide**
c/o Bob Overstreet, Ed., 2905 Vista Dr. N. W., Cleveland, TN 37311
- Comic Book Price Guide. a. (Dist. by: Crown Publishers, 419 Park Ave. South, New York, N.Y. 10016)

**Cominsane Press**
Box 119, St. George, Staten Island, NY 10301.
- St. George Review. a.

**Comite de Mexico y Aztlan**
Box 12062, Oakland, CA 94604.
- COMEXAZ: News Monitoring Service. m.

**Commanders' Conference Information Exchange Program**
Governors Island, New York, NY 10004.
- Commanders' Conference Information Exchange Program. Report. a. ISSN 0091-2905

**Commerce Clearing House, Inc.**
4025 W. Peterson Ave., Chicago, IL 60646.
- A I C P A Professional Standards. (American Institute of Certified Public Accountants)
- Accounting Articles. m. ISSN 0007-7992
- Automobile Law Reports Insurance Decisions. fortn. ISSN 0005-1411
- Balance of Payments Reports. m. ISSN 0005-4224
- Bankruptcy Law Reports. fortn. ISSN 0005-5530
- British Tax Guide. m. ISSN 0007-1862
- C C H Tax Planning Review. m.
- Capital Changes Reports. w. ISSN 0008-5855
- College and University Reports. w.
- Commerce Clearing House. Compliance Guide for Plan Administrators. fortn. ISSN 0363-7476
- Commerce Clearing House. Personnel Guide. bi-w.
- Common Market Reports. w. ISSN 0572-9750
- Consumerism-New Developments for Business. w. ISSN 0045-8279
- Energy Management and Federal Energy Guidelines. w.
- Estate Planning Review. m. ISSN 0098-2873
- Executive's Tax Review. m. ISSN 0363-2407
- Federal Estate and Gift Taxes Explained, Including Estate Planning. irreg. ISSN 0092-6531

- Federal Graduated Withholding Tax Tables. a. ISSN 0071-4135
- Federal Tax Return Manual. a. ISSN 0071-4143
- Food, Drug, Cosmetic Law Journal. m. ISSN 0015-6361
- Government Contracts Guide. irreg.; latest edt. 1972. ISSN 0072-5145
- Guidebook to California Taxes. a. ISSN 0072-8837
- Guidebook to Florida Taxes. ISSN 0093-8637
- Guidebook to Illinois Taxes. a. ISSN 0072-8845
- Guidebook to Labor Relations. a. ISSN 0072-8853
- Guidebook to Massachusetts Taxes. a. ISSN 0072-8861
- Guidebook to Michigan Taxes. a. ISSN 0072-887X
- Guidebook to New Jersey Taxes. a. ISSN 0072-8888
- Guidebook to New York Taxes. a. ISSN 0072-8896
- Guidebook to North Carolina Taxes. a. ISSN 0091-1186
- Guidebook to Ohio Taxes. a. ISSN 0091-4010
- Guidebook to Pennsylvania Taxes. a. ISSN 0072-890X
- Guidebook to Wisconsin Taxes. irreg. ISSN 0093-8645
- Income, Estate and Gift Tax Provisions: Internal Revenue Code. a. ISSN 0073-5671
- Insurance Law Journal. m. ISSN 0020-4722
- Insurance Law Reports: Fire & Casualty. fortn. ISSN 0020-4730
- Insurance Law Reports: Life. m.
- Labor Arbitration Awards. w. ISSN 0023-6500
- Labor Law Journal; to promote sound thinking on labor law problems. m. ISSN 0023-6586
- Mutual Funds Guide. bi-w. ISSN 0027-5182
- Nuclear Regulation Reports. w. ISSN 0360-7690
- Occupational Safety and Health Decisions. irreg. ISSN 0092-3435
- Pollution Control Guide. w.
- Poverty Law Reports. fortn. ISSN 0032-5872
- Practical Guide to Individual Income Tax Return Preparation. a. ISSN 0098-1575
- S E C Accounting Rules. m.
- State Tax Handbook. a. ISSN 0081-4598
- State Tax Review. w.
- Stock Values and Dividends for Tax Purposes. a. ISSN 0081-5624
- Study of Federal Tax Law. Income Tax Volume: Business Enterprises. irreg. ISSN 0362-2983
- Study of Federal Tax Law. Income Tax Volume: Individuals. irreg. ISSN 0362-5230
- Tax Planning Review. m. ISSN 0363-4396
- Taxes; the tax magazine. m. ISSN 0040-0181
- U. S. Excise Tax Guide. a. ISSN 0083-0534
- U. S. Master Tax Guide. a. ISSN 0083-1700

**Commerce Law Services, Inc.**
1747 Penn. Ave. N.W., Washington, DC 20006.
- I.C.C. Supplemental Reports. m. ISSN 0094-4270 (U.S. Interstate Commerce Commission)

**Commerce Publishing Co.**
408 Olive St., St. Louis, MO 63102.
- American Agent and Broker. m. ISSN 0002-7200
- Club Management; national magazine of clubdom. m. ISSN 0009-9589
- Decor; the magazine of fine home accessories. 13 per yr. ISSN 0011-7358
- Life Insurance Selling. m. ISSN 0024-3140

**Commerce Publishing Corp.**
3003 L B J Freeway, Suite 201, Dallas, TX 75234.
- Texas Business. m.

**Commercial Law League of America**
222 W. Adams St., Chicago, IL 60606.
- Commercial Law Journal. m; bi-m, Jun.-Jul., Aug.-Sep. ISSN 0010-3055

**Commercial Publishing Co.**
740 S. Fulton Ave., Mt. Vernon, NY 10550.
- Commercial Bar; an international directory of commercial law counsel. a. ISSN 0098-4957

**Commercial West**
(Subsidiary of: Sun Newspapers, Inc.)
6601 W. 78th St., Minneapolis, MN 55435.
- Bank Directory of the Ninth Federal Reserve District. a.

**Commissariat of St. Stephen's Franciscan Province**
- Katolikus Magyarok Vasarnapja. (pub. by Catholic Publishing Co.)

**Commission on Professional and Hospital Activities**
1968 Green Road, Ann Arbor, MI 48105.
- C P H A News and Views. 6 per yr.
- P A S Reporter. (Professional Activity Study) irreg., 1970, vol. 8, no. 6. ISSN 0078-7353

**Commission on Rehabilitation Medicine**
123 E. Grant St., Minneapolis, MN 55403.
- Commission on Rehabilitation Medicine. Bulletin. irreg.

**Commission on Voluntary Service & Action**
475 Riverside Drive, New York, NY 10027.
- Invest Yourself. a.

**Committee Against Racism**
2417 Amherst Road, Middleton, WI 53562.
- C A R Wheel. s-a.

**Committee for a Free China**
1735 DeSales St., N.W., Suite 500, Washington, DC 20036.
- China Report. m. ISSN 0009-4463
- Nation's Press and Free China. m.

**Committee for Better Transit, Inc.**
Box 3106, Long Island City, NY 11103.
- Notes from Underground. m. ISSN 0029-4039

**Committee for Economic Development**
477 Madison Ave., New York, NY 10022.
- C E D Newsletter. a. ISSN 0069-682X
- Committee for Economic Development. Supplementary Paper. irreg., 1972, no. 35. ISSN 0084-8964
- World Symposium on Energy and Raw Materials. Summary of the Proceedings. irreg.

**Committee for Freedom of Choice in Cancer Therapy, Inc.**
146 Main St., No. 408, Los Altos, CA 94022.
- Choice (Los Altos) m.

**Committee for Monetary Research and Education, Inc.**
Box 1630, Greenwich, CT 06830.
- C M R E Money Tracts. irreg.

**Committee for Prisoner Humanity & Justice**
1414 Fourth St., San Rafael, CA 94901.
- Labyrinth. q.

**Committee for the Advancement of Kurdistan**
Box 13005, Washington, DC 20000.
- Kurdish Journal. irreg. ISSN 0454-6865

**Committee for the Furtherance of Torah Observance**
105 Hudson Street, New York, NY 10013.
- Jewish Homemaker. q. ISSN 0021-650X

**Committee for the Future, Inc.**
2325 Porter St. N.W., Washington, DC 20008.
- New Worlds Newsletter. irreg?

**Committee for the Support of Human Rights in South Korea**
P.O. Box 1001, Palo Alto, CA 94302.
- Korea Link. bi-m.

**Committee of Black Performing Arts**
Harmong House, Stanford Univ., Stanford, CA 94305.
- Hambone. a.

**Committee of Interns and Residents**
666 Third Ave., New York, NY 10017.
- Committee of Interns and Residents Bulletin. m.

**Committee of Southern Churchmen Inc.**
Box 936, College Station, Berea, KY 40404.
- Katallagete. 3 per yr. ISSN 0022-9288
- Southern Coalition on Jails and Prisons. (pub. by Southern Prison Ministry)

**Committee of University Industrial Relations Librarians**
- Committee of University Industrial Relations Librarians. Exchange Bibliography. (pub. by University of Chicago. A. G. Busch Library)

**Committee on Institutional Cooperation**
1603 Orrington Ave., Evanston, IL 60201.
- Committee on Institutional Cooperation. Annual Report. a. ISSN 0069-6854

**Committee on Research in Dance**
Dance Dept., Education 675D, New York University, 35 W. 4th St., New York, NY 10003.
- Dance Research Annual. a.
- Dance Research Journal. s-a.
- Dance Research Monograph. irreg. ISSN 0091-2301

**Committee to Combat Huntington's Disease, Inc.**
250 W. 57th St., New York, NY 10019.
- Committee to Combat Huntingtons Disease Newsletter. 3-4 per yr.

**Committee to End Violence Against the Next Generation**
977 Keeler Ave., Berkeley, CA 94708.
- Last Resort. bi-m.

**Commodities Magazine, Inc.**
219 Parkade, Cedar Falls, IA 50613.
- Commodities; the magazine of futures trading. m.

**Commodity Advisory Service**
850 Munras, No. 2, Monterey, CA 93940.
- Commodity Timing. fortn.

**Commodity Exchange, Inc.**
Southeast Plaza Bldg., 4 World Trade Center, New York, NY 10048.
- Comex Weekly Market Report for Copper, Silver and Gold. w.
- Gold Weekly Market Report. w.

**Commodity Futures Trading Commission**
61 Broadway, Room 2101, New York, NY 10006.
- Commodity Futures Trading Commission. Weekly Report. w.

**Commodity Research Bureau Inc.**
One Liberty Plaza, New York, NY 10006.
- Commodity Chart Service. w. ISSN 0010-3225
- Commodity Year Book. a. ISSN 0069-6862
- Commodity Yearbook Statistical Abstract Service. 3 per yr. ISSN 0010-3241
- Futures Market Service. w. ISSN 0016-3295

**Common Cause**
2030 M St., N.W., Washington, DC 20036.
- Frontline. bi-m.
- In Common; Common Cause report from Washington. m.

**Commonweal Publishing Co., Inc.**
232 Madison Ave., New York, NY 10016.
- Commonweal. bi-w. ISSN 0010-3330

**Commonwealth Club of California**
681 Market St., San Francisco, CA 94105.
- Commonwealth. w. ISSN 0010-3349

**Communication Arts Books**
10 East 40th St., New York, NY 10016.
- Studies in Media Management. irreg.
- Studies in Public Communication. irreg. ISSN 0585-7031

**Communication Channels Inc.**
461 Eighth Ave., New York, NY 10001.
- Container News. m. ISSN 0010-7360
- Directory of Trust Institutions. a. ISSN 0093-951X
- Fence Industry; the only trade journal of all fencing and erecting. m. ISSN 0014-9977
- National Real Estate Directory. a.
- National Real Estate Investor. m. ISSN 0027-9994
- Pension World. m.
- Plants, Sites & Parks. bi-m.
- Sanitation Industry Yearbook. a. ISSN 0080-6021 (Solid Waste Management Magazine)
- Shopping Center World. m. ISSN 0049-0393
- Solid Wastes Management/Refuse Removal Journal. m. ISSN 0038-1136
- Southwest Real Estate News. fortn. (And 2525 Stemmens Freeway, Dallas, TX 75207)
- Trusts and Estates. m. ISSN 0041-3682

**Communication Consultants, Inc.**
219 Parkade, Cedar Falls, IA 50613.
- Editing Systems. m.

**Communication Research and Services**
Arizona State University, Communications Research Center, Dept. of Speech and Theatre, Tempe, AR 85281.
- Communicontents. q.

**Communications Counselors. Inc**
Box 427, Newtown Square, PA 19073.
- Cockshaw's Construction Labor News & Opinion. m. ISSN 0094-0372

**Communications for Health**
c/o Seymour Stark, Box A-G, Port Jefferson, NY 11776.
- Communications for Health. m.

**Communications House**
40 Beechdale Rd., Dobbs Ferry, NY 10522.
- Travel Smart. m.

**Communications, Inc.**
Box 326, San Antonio, TX 78292.
- Health Letter. bi-m.

**Communications Marketing, Inc.**
5100 Edina Industrial Blvd., Edina, MN 55435.
- Blue Book of Fur Farming. a.
- Feed Industry Red Book; reference book and buyers' guide for the feed manufacturing industry. a. ISSN 0071-4518
- Feed Industry Review. q. ISSN 0014-9535
- Grain Age. 11 per yr. ISSN 0017-3029
- U S Fur Rancher. m. ISSN 0041-7653

**Communications Press**
1346 Connecticut Ave. N.W., Washington, DC 20036.
- Cable Handbook; a guide to cable and new communications technologies. a.

**Communications Publishing Corp.**
1900 W. Yale Ave., Englewood, CO 80110.
- Business Radio Buyers Guide. a.
- C A T V Buyer's Guide. (Community Antenna Television) irreg. ISSN 0068-4759
- C A T V Systems Directory, Map Service and Handbook. a. ISSN 0091-1984
- Communications; management journal for land mobile communications, telecommunications and data communications. m. ISSN 0010-356X
- T V Communications; professional journal of the cable television industry. m. ISSN 0039-8519
- Telephone Interconnect Journal. bi-m.
- V U E Magazine. w.

**Communications Satellite Corporation**
950 L'Enfant Plaza S.W., Washington, DC 20024.
- C O M S A T Technical Review. s-a.

**Communications Technology, Inc.**
Greenville, NH 03048.
- Ham Radio. m. ISSN 0017-6842
- Ham Radio Horizons. m.

**Communications Workers of America**
1925 K St. N.W., Washington, DC 20006.
- C W A News. m. ISSN 0007-9227

**Communications Workers of America. Local 1101**
1500 Broadway, New York, 1 Park Ave., NY 10036.
- New York Generator. m. ISSN 0028-7245

**Communist Labor Party**
Box 3774, Merchandise Mart, Chicago, IL 60654.
- People's Tribune; political paper of the Communist Labor Party. bi-m.

**Communist Party, U. S. A.**
23 W. 26th St., New York, NY 10010.
- Black Liberation Journal; national magazine of the Communist Party. USA. q.
- Jewish Affairs. bi-m. ISSN 0021-6305

**Community Action on Latin America**
731 State St., Madison, WI 53703.
- C A L A Newsletter. 6 per yr.

**Community College Journalism Association**
c/o Jan Rawson, Ed., Citrus College, Azusa, CA 91702.
- Community College Journalist. q.

**Community College Social Science Association**
Grossmont College, 8800 Grossmont College Drive, El Cajon, CA 92020.
- Community College Social Science Journal. 3 per yr.

**Community Congress of San Diego**
1172 Morena Blvd., San Diego, CA 92110.
- Journal of Alternative Human Services. q.

**Community Council of Greater New York, Inc.**
225 Park Ave. S., New York, NY 10003.
- Community Council of Greater New York.
  Budget Standard Service. Annual Price Survey
  and Family Budget Costs. a. ISSN 0069-7818
- Community Council of Greater New York.
  Trends and Forecasts. q.
- Directory of Social and Health Agencies of New
  York City. (pub. by Columbia University Press)

**Community Development Foundation**
- International Society for Community
  Development (Publication) (pub. by International
  Society for Community Development)

**Community Development Services Inc.**
399 National Press Bldg., Washington, DC 20045.
- Community Development Digest. s-m. ISSN
  0094-2324
- Housing Affairs Letter; weekly Washington report
  on housing. w. ISSN 0018-6554

**Community Development Society**
720 Clark Hall, University of Missouri, Columbia,
MO 65201.
- Community Development Society. Journal. (pub.
  by American Press)
- Directory: Community Development Education
  and Training Programs Throughout the World.
  irreg. ISSN 0362-4366

**Community Environmental Council, Inc.**
109 E. De La Guerra St., Santa Barbara, CA 93101.
- C. E. C. Members' Report. m.
- Survival Times. irreg.

**Community for Religious Research and Education,
Inc.**
Box 9164, Berkeley, CA 94709.
- Radical Religion. q. ISSN 0360-8212

**Community Management Corporation**
1831 Michael Faraday Dr., Reston, VA 22090.
- Community Management Report; a reference
  guide for association leaders. m.
- P U D Review; update of planned unit
  developments and condominiums. m.

**Community Nutrition Institute**
1910 K St. N.W., Washington, DC 20006.
- C N I Weekly Report. w.

**Community of Friends**
c/o Moses Yanes, Ed., 13850 Big Basin Way,
Boulder Creek, CA 95006.
- Community of Friends. q.

**Community Performance Publications Inc.**
Suite 12, 2038 Pennsylvania Ave., Madison, WI
53704.
- Aware; the environment magazine about the
  electric industry. m. ISSN 0045-1223

**Community Publications Cooperative**
Rt. 4, Box 426, Louisa, VA 23093.
- Communities; a Journal of Cooperative Living. bi-
  m.
- Leaves of Twin Oaks. bi-m. ISSN 0023-9836
  (Twin Oaks Community)

**Community Publishing Co. Inc.**
P. O. Box 15843, 12211 Westinghouse Blvd.,
Charlotte, NC 28210.
- Charlotte. bi-m. (Charlotte Chamber of
  Commerce)

**Community Renewal Society**
111 N.Wabash Ave., Chicago, IL 60602.
- Chicago Reporter; a monthly information service
  on racial issues in metropolitan Chicago. m. ISSN
  0300-6921

**Community Service, Inc.**
Box 243, Yellow Springs, OH 45387.
- Community Service Newsletter. bi-m.

**Community Service Society of New York**
Committee on Housing and Urban Development,
105 East 22nd St., New York, NY 10010.
- Housing and Urban Development Legislation in
  New York State. a. ISSN 0073-3652

**Community Television of Southern California**
KCET- Channel 28, 4400 Sunset Drive, Hollywood,
CA 90027.
- Gambit. m. ISSN 0009-1480

**Commuter, Inc.**
1001 W. Van Buren, Chicago, IL 60607.
- Chicago Illini. w.(Sept.-May); bi-w.(June-Aug.)
  ISSN 0009-3572

**Company of Fifers & Drummers, Inc.**
c/o H. Lawrence Carlson, 16 Winter Ave., Deep
River, CT 06417.
- Ancient Times. q. ISSN 0091-7176

**Company of Military Historians**
1849 Post Rd., Warwick, RI 02886.
- Military Collector & Historian. q. ISSN 0026-3966

**Comparative Administration Research Institute**
Department of Business, Kent State University,
Kent, OH 44242
(Distrib.: Kent State University Press, Kent, OH
44240)
- Organization & Administrative Sciences. q.

**Comparative and International Education Society**
- Comparative Education Review. (pub. by
  University of Chicago Press)

**Comparative and International Education Society.
Secretariat**
301 Rackley Bldg., Pennsylvania State University,
University Park, PA 16802.
- Comparative and International Education Society.
  Newsletter. q. ISSN 0010-4043

**Compass**
R.D. 1 Box 584, Honey Brook, PA 19344.
- Compass. s-a.

**Compass Publications, Inc. (Arlington)**
Suite 1000, 1117 N. 19th St., Arlington, VA 22209.
- Sea Technology; for design engineering and
  application of equipment and services for the
  marine environment. m. ISSN 0093-3651
- Sea Technology Handbook & Directory. a.
- Washington Letter of Oceanography. forth.

**Competition Surf**
11 Willben Lane, Plainview, Long Island, NY
11803.
- Competition Surf. q. ISSN 0010-4264

**Compleat Women's Classified, Inc.**
c/o K. Olson, 200 E. 42nd St., New York, NY
10017.
- Compleat Women's Classified Annual Directory.
  a.

**Complete Sports Publications, Inc.**
333 Johnson Ave., Brooklyn, NY 11206.
- Hockey Illustrated. 5 per yr. plus special issue.

**Composers & Choreographers Theatre, Inc.**
25 W. 19th St., New York, NY 10011.
- C C T Review. q.

**Composers, Authors and Artists of America, Inc.**
c/o Frederika Blankner, Ed., Hotel des Artistes,
One West 67th St., New York, NY 10023.
- Composers, Authors and Artists of America. q.
  ISSN 0010-4353

**Compressed Air Magazine Co.**
253 E. Washington Ave., Washington, NJ 07882.
- Compressed Air; a review of the capabilities and
  economies of air and gases. m. ISSN 0010-4426

**Compsco Publishing Co.**
663 Fifth Ave., New York, NY 10022.
- Latin American Travel Guide; including the
  complete Pan American Highway Guide. a., 5th
  edt., 1973.

**Computational Musicology Newsletter**
c/o J. Wenker, 1998 Pacific Ave. Unit 105, San
Francisco, CA 94109.
- Computational Musicology Newsletter. irreg.
  ISSN 0093-0253

**Computer Design Publishing Corp.**
11 Goldsmith St., Littleton, MA 01460.
- Computer Design; the magazine of digital
  electronics. m. ISSN 0010-4566
- Computer Design's Data Sheet Directory of
  Digital Electronics. irreg. ISSN 0095-6449

**Computer Directions Advisors, Inc.**
8750 Georgia Ave., Silver Spring, MD 20910.
- Bank Pooled Funds. m.
- Comparative Performance Statistics. q.
- Spectrum Four: Bank Portfolios. q.

- Spectrum One: Stock Holdings Survey. q. ISSN
  0091-6854
- Spectrum Three: Bank Stock Holdings Survey. q.
- Spectrum Two: Investment Company Portfolios. q.
  ISSN 0091-6862

**Computer- Gram**
431 E. Green St., Pasadena, CA 91101.
- Computer-Gram. w. ISSN 0010-4604

**Computer Merchants, Inc.**
75 S. Greeley Ave., Chappaqua, NY 10514.
- Computer Price Guide; the blue book of computer
  prices. q. ISSN 0045-7841

**Computer Newsfront**
61 Helen Drive, Marlboro, MA 01752.
- Computer Newsfront. w. ISSN 0590-8655

**Computer People for Peace**
291 Sterling Pl, Brooklyn, NY 11238.
- Interrupt. q.

**Computer Science Press, Inc.**
4566 Poe Ave., Woodland Hills, CA 91364.
- Journal of Design Automation & Fault Tolerant
  Computing. q. ISSN 0099-1708

**Computer Sciences Corporation**
9841 Airport Blvd., Los Angeles, CA 90045.
- C S C Report. q. ISSN 0045-7884

**Computerworld Inc.**
797 Washington St., Newton, MA 02160.
- Computerworld; newsweekly for the computer
  community. w. ISSN 0010-4841

**Computext Communications, Ltd.**
475 Fifth Ave., New York, NY 10017.
- Law Book Guide. m. (except Jul.-Aug) ISSN
  0000-0353

**Computing Newsletter for Schools of Business**
University of Colorado, Cragmor Rd., Colorado
Springs, CO 80907.
- Computing Newsletter for Schools of Business. 9
  per yr. (Sep.-Jun.) ISSN 0010-4868

**Con Safos, Inc.**
Box 31085, Los Angeles, CA 90031.
- Con Safos. irreg. ISSN 0010-5104

**Concept Development Co.**
12 Lakeside Pk., 607 North Ave., Wakefield, MA
01880.
- Nurse Educator. bi-m. (Nursing Digest, Inc.)

**Concepts for Living International Club**
499 Glen St., Glens Falls, NY 12801.
- C. L. I. C. Quarterly Bulletin. q.

**Conceptual Non-Press**
230 San Juan, Venice, CA 90291.
- Acceptance. s-a.

**Concerned Filipinos & Americans in Hawaii**
Box 11087, Honolulu, HI 96814.
- Pahayag. m.

**Conch Magazine Ltd.**
c/o Dr. S. O. Anozie, 102 Normal Ave., Buffalo,
NY 14213.
- Conch; a sociological journal of African cultures
  and literatures. 2 per yr.
- Conch Review of Books. q. ISSN 0092-7708
  (State University of New York, College at New
  Paltz)
- Studies in African Semiotics. irreg.

**Concilio Mujeres**
c/o D-Q University, Box 409, Davis, CA 95616.
- Razon Mestiza. a.

**Concordant Publishing Concern**
15570 Knochaven Rd., Canyon Country, CA 91351.
- Unsearchable Riches. bi-m. ISSN 0042-0476

**Concordia Historical Institute**
801 DeMun Ave., St. Louis, MO 63105.
- Concordia Historical Institute Quarterly. q. ISSN
  0010-5260 (Lutheran Church, Missouri Synod)

**Concordia Mutual Life Association**
20 N. Wacker Drive, Chicago, IL 60606.
- Concordia Torch. q. ISSN 0010-5287

**Concordia Publishing House**
3558 South Jefferson Ave., St. Louis, MO 63118.
- C P H Commentator. q. ISSN 0007-8905
- Church Music. s-a. ISSN 0009-6458
- Happy Times. m. (Lutheran Church. Missouri Synod. Board of Parish Education)
- Interaction; a magazine church school workers grow by. 10 per yr. ISSN 0020-5117 (Lutheran Church. Missouri Synod. Board for Parish Education)
- Lutheran Annual. a. (Lutheran Church-Missouri Synod)
- Lutheran Education. 5 per yr. ISSN 0024-7448
- Lutheran Witness. 16 per yr. ISSN 0024-757X (Lutheran Church. Missouri Synod)
- My Devotions. m. ISSN 0027-5387
- Portals of Prayer; daily devotions for adults. 6 per yr. ISSN 0032-4884
- Taegliche Andachten. 6 per yr. (Lutheran Church-Missouri Synod)

**Concordia Theological Seminary**
Fort Wayne, IN 46825.
- Concordia Theological Quarterly. q.

**Concrete Construction Publications, Inc.**
329 Interstate Rd., Addison, IL 60101.
- Concrete Construction. m. ISSN 0010-5333

**Concrete Industry Board, Inc.**
110 E. 42nd St., New York, NY 10017.
- Concrete Industry Bulletin. m. ISSN 0010-535X

**Conde Nast Publications, Inc.**
350 Madison Ave., New York, NY 10017.
- Analog Science Fiction-Science Fact. m.
- Brides. 6 per yr.
- Glamour. m. ISSN 0017-0747
- House & Garden. m. ISSN 0018-6406
- House & Garden Building Guide. s-a. ISSN 0441-3016
- House and Garden Color Guide. a.
- House & Garden Decorating Guide. s-a. ISSN 0439-6375
- House & Garden Guide to American Tradition. a. ISSN 0363-5880
- House and Garden Plans Guide. a. ISSN 0073-3555
- House & Garden Remodeling Guide. s-a. ISSN 0439-6383
- House & Garden Second House Guide. 2 per yr.
- Mademoiselle. m. ISSN 0024-9394
- Street & Smith's Baseball Yearbook. a. ISSN 0491-1520
- Street and Smith's College & Pro Official Basketball Yearbook. a. ISSN 0092-511X
- Street and Smith's Official Yearbook: College Football. a. ISSN 0091-9977
- Street and Smith's Official Yearbook: Pro Football. a. ISSN 0092-3214
- Vogue. m. ISSN 0042-8000
- Vogue Beauty & Health Guide. a.
- Vogue's Real Life Fashion Guide. a.

**Conditions**
c/o Jan Clausen, Ed., 610 6th St., Brooklyn, NY 11215.
- Conditions. q.

**Confectioner Publishing Co.**
3224 N. Hackett Ave., Milwaukee, WI 53211.
- Confectioner; candy technology, marketing, merchandising. bi-m. ISSN 0010-5457

**Conference Board, Inc.**
845 Third Ave., New York, NY 10022.
- Across the Board; reporting to management on business affairs. m.
- Announcements of Foreign Investment in U.S. Manufacturing Industries. q.
- Business Outlook. a. ISSN 0360-3938
- Conference Board. Announcements of Mergers and Acquisitions. m. ISSN 0003-5114
- Conference Board. Cumulative Index. a. ISSN 0069-8350
- Conference Board. Investment Statistics: Capital Investment Conditions. s-a. ISSN 0092-4210
- Conference Board. Manufacturing Investment Statistics. Capital Appropriations. q. ISSN 0361-4239
- Conference Board. Monthly Business Review. m. ISSN 0091-9918
- Conference Board. Report on Company Contributions. a. ISSN 0069-8369
- Conference Board. Utility Investment Statistics. Utility Appropriations. q. ISSN 0360-523X
- Conference Board Statistical Bulletin. m. ISSN 0010-5554

- Consumer Attitudes and Buying Plans. bi-m. ISSN 0547-7204
- Consumer Market Indicators. m. ISSN 0547-7212
- Focus (New York, 1964) m. ISSN 0015-5039
- Guide to Consumer Markets. a.
- Road Maps of Industry. s-m. ISSN 0035-7227
- Top Executive Compensation. biennial.
- World Business Perspectives. bi-m. ISSN 0084-1455

**Conference Board of the Mathematical Sciences**
2100 Pennsylvania Ave., N.W. 834, Washington, DC 20037.
- Conference Board of the Mathematical Sciences. Newsletter. 4 per yr. ISSN 0045-804X

**Conference for Secondary School English Department Chairmen**
- C S S E D C Newsletter. (pub. by National Council of Teachers of English)

**Conference Group for Social and Administrative History**
Box 1293, Oshkosh, WI 54901.
- Conference Group for Social and Administrative History. Transactions. s-a.
- Societas; a review of social history. q. ISSN 0037-8879

**Conference of Presidents of Major American Jewish Organizations**
515 Park Ave., New York, NY 10022.
- Conference of Presidents of Major American Jewish Organizations. Report. a.

**Conference of Public Health Laboratory Directors**
Box 555, Pierre, SD 57501.
- Public Health Laboratory. bi-m. ISSN 0033-3522

**Conference on Alternative State and Local Public Policies**
1901 Q St., N.W., Washington, DC 20009.
- Conference on Alternative State and Local Public Policies. Newsletter. 6 per yr.

**Conference on Biological Sonar and Diving Mammals. Proceedings**
c/o Dr. Ken Norris, University of California, Santa Cruz, Division of Natural Sciences, Applied Sciences Building, Santa Cruz, CA 95064.
- Conference on Biological Sonar and Diving Mammals. Proceedings. irreg., 1977 symposium at University of California, San Diego. ISSN 0069-8512

**Conference on British Studies**
- Albion. (pub. by Appalachian State University. Department of History)
- Journal of British Studies. (pub. by Trinity College (Hartford))
- Studies in British History and Culture. (pub. by Archon Books)

**Conference on Chinese Oral and Performing Literature**
- C H I N O P E R L Papers. (pub. by Cornell University. China-Japan Program)

**Conference on Christianity and Literature**
Dept. of English, Adrian College, Adrian, MI 49221.
- Christianity and Literature. q.

**Conference on College Composition and Communication**
- College Composition and Communication. (pub. by National Council of Teachers of English)

**Conference on Faith and History**
c/o Richard V. Pierard, Dept. of History, Indiana State University, Terre Haute, IN 47809.
- Fides et Historia. s-a.

**Conference on Jewish Social Studies**
250 W. 57th St., Room 904, New York, NY 10019.
- Jewish Social Studies. q. ISSN 0021-6704

**Conference on Latin American History**
- Conference on Latin American History Newsletter. (pub. by University of Wisconsin-Milwaukee. Center for Latin America)

**Confluence Press, Inc.**
Art Center, Lewis Clark Campus, Lewiston, ID 83501.
- Slackwater Review; northwest magazine of the arts. 3 per yr.

**Confluencia**
125 E. Santa Fe Ave., Santa Fe, NM 87501.
- Confluencia. 4 per yr.

**Confluent Education and Research Center**
P.O. Box 30128, Santa Barbara, CA 93105.
- Confluent Education. q.

**Ivan A. Conger, Ed. & Pub.**
1825 Osaukie Rd., Owosso, MI 48867.
- Curwood Collector. 3 per yr.

**Congregation of Marian Fathers**
4545 W. 63rd St., Chicago, IL 60629.
- Kristaus Karaliaus Laivas/Ship of Christ the King. s-m. ISSN 0023-477X

**Congregation of Marians**
Stockbridge, MA 01262.
- Marian Helpers Bulletin. q. (Association of Marian Helpers)

**Congregational Library**
14 Beacon St., Boston, MA 02108.
- Congregational Library. Bulletin. 3 per yr. ISSN 0010-5821 (American Congregational Association)

**Congress for Jewish Culture, Inc.**
25 E. 78th St., New York, NY 10021.
- World of Yiddish Bulletin. q.

**Congress of Afrikan People**
13 Belmont Ave, Newark, NJ 07103.
- Unity and Struggle. m.

**Congress of Astrological Organizations**
Box 75, Old Chelsea Sta., 223 West 20 St., New York, NY 10011.
- C A O Times. q.

**Congress of County Medical Societies (CCMS) Publishing Co.**
Suite 700, 5100 N. Brookline Ave., Oklahoma City, OK 73112.
- Private Practice. m. ISSN 0032-891X

**Congress of Illinois Historical Societies & Museums**
- Historically Speaking. (pub. by Illinois State Historical Library)

**Congress of Jewish Culture**
25 E. 78th St, New York, NY 10021.
- Zukunft. m. ISSN 0044-5460

**Congress of Neurological Surgeons**
- Clinical Neurosurgery; Proceedings. (pub. by Williams and Wilkins Co.)

**Congress of Organizations of the Physically Handicapped, Inc.**
7611 Oakland Ave., Minneapolis, MN 55423.
- C O P H Bulletin. q. ISSN 0007-8808

**Congress of Racial Equality**
- CORE Magazine. (pub. by C O R E Publications)
- Rights & Reviews. (pub. by C O R E Publications)

**Congressional Black Caucus**
306 House of Representatives, Annex 1, Washington, DC 20515.
- For the People. q, when Congress is in session.

**Congressional Digest Corp.**
3231 P St., N.W., Washington, DC 20007.
- Congressional Digest. 10 per yr. ISSN 0010-5899

**Congressional Information Bureau Inc.**
Colorado Bldg., Rm. 401, 1341 G St., N.W., Washington, DC 20005.
- Atomic Energy Clearinghouse. w. ISSN 0519-3389

**Congressional Information Service**
7101 Wisconsin Ave., Washington, DC 20014.
- American Statistics Index. m with q and a cumulations. ISSN 0091-1658
- C I S Annual. a.
- C I S Highlights.
- C I S Index. m with q and a cumulations. ISSN 0007-8514

**Congressional Quarterly Inc.**
1414 22nd St., N.W., Washington, DC 20037.
- America Votes; handbook of contemporary American election statistics. biennial. ISSN 0065-678X

- C Q Guide to Current American Government; a survey of recent significant developments in national government and politics. s-a. ISSN 0007-8956
- Congressional Quarterly Service. Weekly Report. w. ISSN 0010-5910
- Editorial Research Reports. 4 per mo. ISSN 0013-0958
- Historic Documents. a.
- Washington Information Directory. a.

**Congressional Staff Directory**
Box 62, Mount Vernon, VA 22121.
- Congressional Staff Directory. a. ISSN 0069-8938
- Election Index. biennial. ISSN 0095-7186

**Connecticut. Advisory Council on Vocational and Career Education.**
340 Capitol Ave., Hartford, CT 06115.
- Connecticut. Advisory Council on Vocational and Career Education. Vocational Education Evaluation Report. a. ISSN 0363-650X

**Connecticut. Auditors of Public Accounts**
Hartford, CT 06115.
- Connecticut. Auditors of Public Accounts. Report on Department of Transportation, Bureau of Rail and Motor Carrier Services. triennial. ISSN 0362-9503

**Connecticut. Commission on Human Rights and Opportunities**
90 Washington St., Hartford, CT 06115.
- Directory of Resource Organizations and Media Serving Minority Communities in Connecticut. irreg. ISSN 0362-9562
- Rights, Opportunities, Action Reporter. q. ISSN 0009-7942

**Connecticut. Commission to Study and Investigate the Problems of Deaf and Hearing-Impaired Persons**
Hartford, CT 06115.
- Connecticut. Commission to Study and Investigate the Problems of Deaf and Hearing-Impaired Persons. Annual Report. a. ISSN 0094-727X

**Connecticut. Connecticut Agricultural Experiment Station**
New Haven, CT 06504.
- Frontiers of Plant Science. s-a. ISSN 0016-2167

**Connecticut. Council on Environmental Quality**
State Office Bldg., Hartford, CT 06115.
- Connecticut. Council on Environmental Quality. Annual Report. a. ISSN 0095-4624

**Connecticut. Department of Community Affairs**
Box 786, 1179 Main St., Hartford, CT 06103.
- Housing Units in Connecticut. Annual Summary. a.

**Connecticut. Department of Corrections. Research Section**
340 Capitol Ave., Hartford, CT 06115.
- Connecticut. Department of Correction. Publications. irreg. ISSN 0090-2756

**Connecticut. Department of Environmental Protection**
Hartford, CT 06115.
- Connecticut Water Resources Bulletin. irreg. ISSN 0589-400X

**Connecticut. Department of Health**
79 Elm St., Hartford, CT 06115.
- Connecticut Health Bulletin. q. ISSN 0010-6127
- Directory of Registered Dentists and Registered Dental Hygienists in Connecticut. a. ISSN 0085-0004

**Connecticut. Department of Transportation. Bureau of Staff Services**
c/o Director of Planning, Bureau of Planning & Research, 24 Wolcott Hill Rd., Wethersfield, CT 06109.
- Connecticut Master Transportation Plan. a. ISSN 0069-9039

**Connecticut. Department on Aging**
90 Washington St., Hartford, CT 06115.
- Connecticut. Department on Aging. Report to the Governor and General Assembly. a. ISSN 0090-6077

**Connecticut. Energy Advisory Board**
Hartford, CT 06115.
- Connecticut. Energy Advisory Board. Annual Report to the Governor and General Assembly. Executive Summary. a. ISSN 0360-2257

**Connecticut. Judicial Department**
Box 1350, Hartford, CT 06101.
- Connecticut. Judicial Department. Report. irreg. ISSN 0098-8138

**Connecticut. Labor Department**
200 Folly Brook Blvd., Wethersfield, CT 06109.
- Connecticut. Labor Department. Bulletin. bi-m. ISSN 0010-6143

**Connecticut. Office of the Bank Commissioner**
State Office Building, 165 Capitol Ave., Hartford, CT 06115.
- List of Legal Investments for Savings Banks in Connecticut. ISSN 0098-0005

**Connecticut. Permanent Commission on the Status of Women**
Hartford, CT 06103.
- P C S W Annual Report. a.

**Connecticut. State Library**
231 Capitol Ave., Hartford, CT 06115.
- Provisioner; news and notes from the Connecticut State Library. irreg.

**Connecticut. Treasury Department**
Hartford, CT 06115.
- Connecticut. Treasury Department. Annual Report. a. ISSN 0099-0108

**Connecticut Academy of Arts and Sciences**
- Connecticut Academy of Arts and Sciences. Memoirs. (pub. by Archon Books)
- Connecticut Academy of Arts and Sciences. Transactions. (pub. by Archon Books)

**Connecticut Association of Boards of Education, Inc.**
410 Asylum St., Hartford, CT 06103.
- C A B E Journal. bi-w.

**Connecticut Audiovisual Education Association**
25 Elmwood Avenue, Trumbull, CT 06611.
- Connecticut Audiovisual Education Association. Bulletin. irreg., no. 28, 1975.

**Connecticut Bar Association, Inc.**
15 Lewis St., Hartford, CT 06103.
- Connecticut Bar Journal. q. ISSN 0010-6070

**Connecticut Business & Industry Association**
- Connecticut Business & Industry. (pub. by C B I A Service Corp.)

**Connecticut College**
- Connecticut College Monograph. (pub. by Shoe String Press, Inc.)

**Connecticut Conservation Association**
Northrop St., Bridgewater, CT 06752.
- Connecticut Conservation Reporter. 4 per yr. ISSN 0010-6100

**Connecticut Correctional Institution**
Cheshire, CT 06410.
- Fifty Cell. q.

**Connecticut Directory Co., Inc.**
322 Main St., Stamford, CT 06901.
- Classified Business Directory of the State of Connecticut. a. ISSN 0069-4517

**Connecticut Education Association**
21 Oak St., Hartford, CT 06106.
- C E A Advisor. m.(Sept-June) ISSN 0007-8050

**Connecticut Hospital Research and Education Foundation, Inc.**
P.O. Box 504, North Haven, CT 06473.
- Connecticut Health Services Research Series. a.

**Connecticut Junior Republic**
c/o Richard D. Roberts, Box 161, Litchfield, CT 06759.
- Junior Citizen. q.

**Connecticut Library Association**
c/o Cheshire Public Library, 104 Main St., Cheshire, CT 06410.
- Connecticut Libraries. q. ISSN 0010-616X

**Connecticut Nurses Association**
1 Prestige Dr., Meriden, CT 06050.
- Nursing News. m. ISSN 0029-652X

**Connecticut Public Expenditure Council, Inc.**
21 Lewis St., Hartford, CT 06103.
- C P E C Taxpayers News. bi-m. ISSN 0007-8891

**Connecticut River Valley Covered Bridge Society**
10 Congress St., Apt. 503, Greenfield, MA 01301.
- Connecticut River Valley Covered Bridge Society. Bulletin. q. ISSN 0090-8517

**Connecticut School Library Association**
- Connecticut School Library Association. Newsletter. (pub. by Matthew's Printing)

**Connecticut Society of Certified Public Accountants. Educational and Research Foundation**
179 Allyn St., Hartford, CT 06103.
- Connecticut C P A. q. ISSN 0010-6089

**Connecticut State Dental Association**
c/o Martin A. Rothman, Ed., 9 Spriteview Ave., Westport, CT 06880.
- Connecticut State Dental Association. Journal. q. ISSN 0010-6232

**Connecticut State Medical Society**
160 St. Ronan St., New Haven, CT 06511.
- Connecticut Medicine. m. ISSN 0010-6178

**Connecticut Writers League**
Box 78, Farmington, CT 06032.
- Harvest. a.

**Conner Prairie Pioneer Settlement**
30 Conner Lane, Noblesville, IN 46060.
- Midwest Museums Conference, American Association of Museums. Quarterly. q. ISSN 0026-3443 (American Association of Museums. Midwest Museums Conference)

**Connerly & Associates, Inc.**
921 11th St., Suite 701, Sacramento, CA 95814.
- California Digest; a monthly publication relating to community development and planning activities of California State Government. m.

**Conococheague Associates, Inc.**
1053 Wilson Ave., Chambersburg, PA 17201
- Anima; an experiential journal. s-a. (Subscr. to: Harry M. Buck, 1053 Wilson Avenue, Chambersburg PA 17201)

**Conquest**
318 Summit Ave., St. Paul, MN 55102.
- Conquest. 8 per yr.

**Consensus, Inc.**
30 W. Pershing Rd., Kansas City, MO 64108.
- Consensus; national commodity futures weekly. w.

**Conservation Committee of California Oil Producers**
417 South Hill Street, Rm. 868, Los Angeles, CA 90013.
- Annual Review of California Oil and Gas. a. ISSN 0517-9505

**Conservation Contractor's Association of Texas**
c/o Ruel McDaniel, 214 Suncrest Dr., Box 45, Port Lavaca, TX 77979.
- Conservation Contractor. bi-m. ISSN 0010-6453

**Conservation Education Association**
Box 6567, Fort Worth, TX 76115.
- Conservation Education Association Newsletter. q. ISSN 0010-6461

**Conservation Foundation**
1717 Massachusetts Ave., N.W., Washington, DC 20036.
- Conservation Foundation Letter; a report on environmental issues. m. ISSN 0091-536X

**Conservative Baptist Foreign Mission Society**
Box 5, Wheaton, IL 60187.
- Impact (Wheaton) m.(Sept.-April); q.(May-Aug.) ISSN 0019-2821

**Conservative Society of America**
1413 Texas Avenue, Alexandria, LA 71301.
- C S A. Newsletter. m.

**Consolidated Artists Inc.**
290 Riverside Dr., New York, NY 10025.
- Consolidated Artists Newsletter. m.

**Consolidated Drake Press**
5050 Parkside Ave, Philadelphia, PA 19137.
- Children's Hospital Notes. q. ISSN 0009-4110 (Children's Hospital of Philadelphia)

**Consolidated Edison Company of New York, Inc.**
4 Irving Place, New York, NY 10003.
- Con Edison Library Bulletin. m. ISSN 0010-5090

**Consolidated Marketing Services, Inc.**
507-Fifth Ave., New York, NY 10017.
- Drop Shipping Source Directory of Major Consumer Product Lines. a.

**Consolidated Press Printing Co., Inc.**
2228-First Ave., Seattle, WA 98121.
- Svenska Posten/Swedish Post. w.

**Consolidation Coal Co.**
3300 One Oliver Plaza, Pittsburgh, PA 15222.
- Consol News. bi-m. ISSN 0010-6577

**Consortium Books**
1 W. Deer Park, Gaithersburg, MD 20760.
- Studies in Christian Antiquity. irreg. (Catholic University of America)
- Studies in Medieval and Renaissance Latin. irreg. (Catholic University of America)

**Consortium for International Studies Education**
Ohio State University, Political Science Department, Columbus, OH 43210.
- Interchange (Columbus) bi-m.

**Consortium of University Film Centers**
Visual Aids Service, University of Illinois, 1325 S. Oak St., Champaign, IL 61820.
- C U F C Leader. s-a.

**Consortium on Revolutionary Europe**
- Consortium on Revolutionary Europe. Proceedings. (pub. by University Presses of Florida)

**Constitutional Rights Foundation**
6310 San Vicente Blvd., Los Angeles, CA 90048.
- Bill of Rights in Action. q.

**Construction Digest, Inc.**
Box 603, 101 E. 14 St., Indianapolis, IN 46206.
- Construction Digest. bi-w. ISSN 0010-6739

**Construction Industry Press, Inc.**
522 North State Rd., Briarcliff Manor, NY 10570.
- D E Journal. (Domestic Engineering) m. ISSN 0022-3786

**Construction News, Inc.**
715 W. Second St., Box 2421, Little Rock, AR 72203.
- Construction News. w.

**Construction Publications, Inc.**
Box 1689, Cedar Rapids, IA 52406.
- Construction Equipment Operation and Maintenance. bi-m. ISSN 0010-6771

**Construction Publishing Co. (Arlington)**
2420 Wilson Blvd., Arlington, VA 22201.
- Construction. fortn. ISSN 0010-6704

**Construction Publishing Co. Inc.**
450 W. 33rd St., New York, NY 10001.
- Building Cost File. a. ISSN 0091-3499
- Industrial Machinery and Equipment Pricing Guide. a. ISSN 0091-8377
- Real Estate Valuation Cost File. a. ISSN 0098-9568

**Construction Publishing Co., Inc. (Lexington)**
Box 49, Lexington, MA 02173.
- New England Construction. fortn. ISSN 0028-470X

**Construction Specifications Institute, Inc.**
1150 17th St., N.W., Suite 300, Washington, DC 20036.
- Construction Specifier; for better private and public construction. m. ISSN 0010-6925

**Construction Writers Association**
601 13 St. N.W., Rm. 202, Washington, DC 20005.
- Construction Writers Association. Newsletter. irreg., 1975. ISSN 0069-9217

**Consulate General of Japan**
280 Park Ave., New York, NY 10017.
- Japan Report. s-m. ISSN 0021-4604

**Consultant (Greenwich)**
c/o John M. O'Brien, 500 W. Putnam Ave., Greenwich, CT 06830.
- Consultant (Greenwich); the journal of medical consultations. m. ISSN 0010-7069

**Consultant Publications, Inc.**
3310 North 24th St., Phoenix, AZ 85016.
- After Market Investor. s-m.
- Consultant (Phoenix) w.
- Glamour-Scope. 44 per yr.

**Consultants Bureau**
227 W. 17 St., New York, NY 10011.
- Academy of Sciences of the U S S R. Biology Bulletin. irreg. ISSN 0098-2164 (Akademiya Nauk S.S.S.R. UR)
- Academy of Sciences of the U S S R. Chemistry Bulletin. m. ISSN 0568-5230 (Akademiya Nauk S.S.S.R. UR)
- Academy of Sciences of the U S S R. Mathematical Notes. bi-m. ISSN 0001-4346 (Akademiya Nauk S.S.S.R. UR)
- Algebra and Logic. bi-m. ISSN 0002-5232 (Akademiya Nauk S.S.S.R UR)
- All-Union Conference on High Temperature Chemistry of Oxides. a.
- Applied Biochemistry and Microbiology. bi-m. ISSN 0003-6838 (Akademiya Nauk S.S.S.R. UR)
- Astrophysics. q. ISSN 0004-6396 (Akademiya Nauk Armyanskoi S.S.R. UR)
- Automation and Remote Control. 24 per yr. ISSN 0005-1179 (Instrument Society of America)
- Biochemistry. s-m. ISSN 0006-2979 (Akademiya Nauk S.S.S.R. UR)
- Biomedical Engineering. bi-m. ISSN 0006-3398 (U.S.S.R. Ministerstvo Zdravookhraneniya UR)
- Bulletin of Experimental Biology and Medicine. m. ISSN 0007-4888 (Akademiya Meditsinskikh Nauk S.S.S.R. UR)
- Chemical and Petroleum Engineering. m. ISSN 0009-2355
- Chemistry and Technology of Fuels and Oils. m. ISSN 0009-3092 (Akademiya Nauk S.S.S.R. UR)
- Chemistry of Heterocyclic Compounds. m. ISSN 0009-3122 (Akademiya Nauk Latviiskoi S.S R UR)
- Chemistry of Natural Compounds. bi-m. ISSN 0009-3130 (Akademiya Nauk Uzbekskoi S.S.R. UR)
- Colloid Journal of the U S S R. bi-m. ISSN 0010-1303 (Akademiya Nauk S.S.S.R. UR)
- Combustion, Explosion and Shock Waves. bi-m. ISSN 0010-5082 (Akademiya Nauk S.S.S.R.. Sibirskoe Otdelenie UR)
- Cosmic Research. bi-m. ISSN 0010-9525 (Akademiya Nauk S.S.S.R. UR)
- Cybernetics. bi-m. ISSN 0011-4235 (Akademiya Nauk Ukrainskoi S.S.R. UR)
- Differential Equations. m. ISSN 0012-2661 (Akademiya Navuk Belarusskai S.S.R. UR)
- Doklady Biochemistry. bi-m. ISSN 0012-4958 (Akademiya Nauk S.S.S.R. UR)
- Doklady Biological Sciences. bi-m. ISSN 0012-4966 (Akademiya Nauk S.S.S.R. UR)
- Doklady Biophysics. s-a. ISSN 0012-4974 (Akademiya Nauk S.S.S.R. UR)
- Doklady Botanical Sciences. s-a. ISSN 0012-4982 (Akademiya Nauk S.S.S.R. UR)
- Doklady Chemical Technology. 6 per yr.(in 3 nos) ISSN 0012-4990 (Akademiya Nauk S.S.S.R.. Chemical Technology Section UR)
- Doklady Chemistry. m. ISSN 0012-5008 (Akademiya Nauk S.S.S.R. UR)
- Doklady Physical Chemistry. bi-m. ISSN 0012-5016 (Akademiya Nauk S.S.S.R. UR)
- Fibre Chemistry. bi-m. ISSN 0015-0541 (Akademiya Nauk S.S.S.R. UR)
- Fluid Dynamics. bi-m. ISSN 0015-4628 (Akademiya Nauk S.S.S.R. UR)
- Functional Analysis and Its Applications. q. ISSN 0016-2663 (Akademiya Nauk S.S.S.R. UR)
- Glass and Ceramics. bi-m. ISSN 0017-100X (Akademiya Nauk S.S.S.R. UR)
- Growth of Crystals. irreg., vol. 10, 1975. ISSN 0072-7814
- High Energy Chemistry. 6 per yr. ISSN 0018-1439 (Akademiya Nauk S.S.S.R. UR) (English Translation of: Khimiya Vysokikh Energii)
- High Temperature Physics. bi-m. ISSN 0018-151X (Akademiya Nauk S.S.S.R. UR)
- Human Physiology. bi-m. (Akademiya Nauk S.S.S.R. UR)
- Industrial Laboratory. m. ISSN 0019-8447 (Instrument Society of America)
- Inorganic Materials. m. ISSN 0020-1685 (Akademiya Nauk S.S.S.R. UR)
- Instruments and Experimental Techniques. m. ISSN 0020-4412 (Akademiya Nauk S.S.S.R. UR)
- Journal of Analytical Chemistry of the u S S R. 24 per yr. ISSN 0021-8766 (Akademiya Nauk S.S.S.R. UR)

- Journal of Applied Chemistry of the u S S R. 24 per yr. ISSN 0021-888X (Akademiya Nauk S.S.S.R. UR)
- Journal of Applied Mechanics and Technical Physics. bi-m. ISSN 0021-8944 (Akademiya Nauk S.S.S.R.. Sibirskoe Otdelenie UR)
- Journal of Applied Spectroscopy. m. ISSN 0021-9037
- Journal of Engineering Physics. m. ISSN 0022-0841 (Akademiya Navuk Belarusskai S.S.R. UR)
- Journal of Evolutionary Biochemistry and Physiology. bi-m. ISSN 0022-0930 (Akademiya Nauk S.S.S.R. UR)
- Journal of General Chemistry of the U S S R. 24 per yr. ISSN 0022-1279 (Akademiya Nauk S.S.S.R. UR)
- Journal of Organic Chemistry of the U S S R. 24 per yr. ISSN 0022-3271 (Akademiya Nauk S.S.S.R. UR)
- Journal of Soviet Mathematics. m. ISSN 0090-4104 (Akademiya Nauk S.S.S.R.. Institut Matematiki im. V. A.Steklova)
- Journal of Structural Chemistry. bi-m. ISSN 0022-4766 (Akademiya Nauk S.S.S.R. UR)
- Kinetics and Catalysis. m. ISSN 0023-1584 (Akademiya Nauk S.S.S.R. UR)
- Lithology and Mineral Resources. bi-m. ISSN 0024-4902 (Akademiya Nauk S.S.S.R. UR)
- Lithuanian Mathematical Transactions. q.
- Magnetohydrodynamics. q. ISSN 0024-998X (Akademiya Nauk Latviiskoi S.S.R. UR)
- Measurement Techniques. m. ISSN 0543-1972 (Instrument Society of America)
- Metal Science and Heat Treatment. m. ISSN 0026-0673 (Co-sponsors: American Institute of Mining, Metallurgical, and Petroleum Engineers; American Society for Testing & Materials)
- Metallurgist. bi-m. ISSN 0026-0894 (American Society for Metals) (Co-sponsors: American Institute of Mining, Metallurgical, and Petroleum Engineers; American Society for Testing and Materials)
- Microbiology. bi-m. ISSN 0026-2617 (Akademiya Nauk S.S.S.R. UR)
- Molecular Biology. bi-m. ISSN 0026-8933 (Akademiya Nauk S.S.S.R. UR)
- Neurophysiology. bi-m. ISSN 0090-2977
- Pharmaceutical Chemistry Journal. ISSN 0553-9196 (Akademiya Nauk S.S.S.R. UR)
- Polymer Mechanics. bi-m. ISSN 0032-390X (Akademiya Nauk Latviiskoi S.S.R. UR)
- Problems of Information Transmission. q. ISSN 0032-9460 (Akademiya Nauk S.S.S.R. UR)
- Programming and Computer Software. bi-m. (Akademiya Nauk S.S.S.R. UR)
- Radiophysics and Quantum Electronics. m. ISSN 0033-8443
- Refractories. m. ISSN 0034-3102 (American Society for Metals) (Co-sponsors: American Institute of Mining, Metallurgical, and Petroleum Engineers; American Society for Testing & Materials)
- Reviews of Plasma Physics. irreg., 1974, vol. 6. ISSN 0080-2050
- Siberian Mathematical Journal of the Academy of Sciences of the U. S. S. R., Novosibirsk. bi-m. ISSN 0037-4466 (Akademiya Nauk S.S.S.R.. Sibirskoe Otdelenie UR)
- Soil Mechanics and Foundation Engineering. bi-m. ISSN 0038-0741 (State Commerce for Construction in the USSR)
- Solar System Research. q. ISSN 0038-0946 (Akademiya Nauk S.S.S.R. UR) (Co-sponsor: Astronomical & Geodetic Society)
- Soviet Applied Mechanics. m. ISSN 0038-5298 (Akademiya Nauk Ukrainskoi S.S.R. UR)
- Soviet Atomic Energy. m. ISSN 0038-531X (Akademiya Nauk S.S.S.R. UR)
- Soviet Atomic Energy. Supplement. a., 1974, no. 35. ISSN 0081-3176 (Akademiya Nauk S.S.S.R. UR)
- Soviet Electrochemistry. m. ISSN 0038-5387 (Akademiya Nauk S.S.S.R. UR)
- Soviet Genetics. m. ISSN 0038-5409 (Akademiya Nauk S.S.S.R. UR)
- Soviet Journal of Bioorganic Chemistry. m. (Akademiya Nauk S.S.S.R. UR)
- Soviet Journal of Coordination Chemistry. m. (Akademiya Nauk S.S.S.R. UR)
- Soviet Journal of Developmental Biology. bi-m. ISSN 0049-173X (Akademiya Nauk S.S.S.R. UR)
- Soviet Journal of Ecology. bi-m.
- Soviet Journal of Glass Physics and Chemistry. bi-m. (Akademiya Nauk S.S.S.R. UR)
- Soviet Journal of Marine Biology. bi-m. (Akademiya Nauk S.S.S.R. UR)
- Soviet Materials Science. bi-m. ISSN 0038-5565 (Akademiya Nauk Ukrainskoi S.S.R. UR)

- Soviet Microelectronics. bi-m. ISSN 0098-6658 (Akademiya Nauk S.S.S.R. UR)
- Soviet Mining Science. bi-m. ISSN 0038-5581 (Akademiya Nauk S.S.S.R.. Sibirskoe Otdelenie UR)
- Soviet Physics Journal. bi-m. ISSN 0038-5697
- Soviet Plant Physiology. m. ISSN 0038-5719 (Akademiya Nauk S.S.S.R. UR)
- Soviet Powder Metallurgy and Metal Ceramics. m. ISSN 0038-5735 (Akademiya Nauk Ukrainskoi S.S.R.. Material Sciences Institute UR)
- Soviet Radiochemistry. bi-m. ISSN 0038-576X (Akademiya Nauk S.S.S.R. UR)
- Strength of Materials. m. ISSN 0039-2316 (Akademiya Nauk Ukrainskoi S.S.R. UR)
- Structure of Glass. irreg., 1973, vol. 8. ISSN 0081-6000
- Studies in Soviet Science. irreg.
- Theoretical and Experimental Chemistry. bi-m. ISSN 0040-5760
- Theoretical and Mathematical Physics. m. ISSN 0040-5779 (Akademiya Nauk S.S.S.R. UR)
- Theoretical Foundations of Chemical Engineering. bi-m. ISSN 0040-5795 (Akademiya Nauk S.S.S.R. UR)
- Ukrainian Mathematical Journal. bi-m. ISSN 0041-5995 (Akademiya Nauk Ukrainskoi S.S.R.. Institute of Mathematics UR)
- Water Resources. bi-m. ISSN 0097-8078 (Akademiya Nauk S.S.S.R. UR)

**Consultants Bureau. Special Research Report**
227 W. 17 St., New York, NY 10011.
- Atmospheric Optics. irreg., vol. 2, 1972.
- Exploration Geophysics. irreg., 1969, vol. 51. ISSN 0071-3473
- Particles and Nuclei Series. irreg., vol. 2, 1972-1973.
- Problems in Mathematical Analysis Report. irreg., 1971, vol. 2. ISSN 0079-5739
- Recent Advances in Plasma Diagnostics. irreg., 1971, vol. 3. ISSN 0079-9939
- Research in Surface Forces. irreg., 1974, vol. 4. ISSN 0080-1666
- Water in Biological Systems. irreg., 1971, vol. 3. ISSN 0083-7652

**Consultants News**
Templeton Road, Fitzwilliam, NH 03447.
- Directory of Executive Recruiters. a. ISSN 0090-6484
- International Directory of Executive Recruiters. irreg. ISSN 0092-4989

**Consultation on Church Union**
228 Alexander St., Princeton, NJ 08540.
- Consultation on Church Union. Digest. irreg.; approx. every 18 mos.; latest issue, 1976. ISSN 0589-4867
- In Common. irreg.

**Consumer Affairs Foundation**
- B B B Tribune. (pub. by Better Business Bureau of Eastern Massachusetts, Inc.)

**Consumer Age Press**
P.O. Box 279, Syracuse, NY 13214.
- Consumers' Guide to Prescription Prices. irreg.

**Consumer Commission on the Accreditation of Health Services, Inc.**
1381 Park Ave. So., New York, NY 10016.
- Consumer Commission on the Accreditation of Health Services Quarterly. q.
- Health Perspectives. 6 per yr.

**Consumer Education Research Group**
Box 336, South Orange, NJ 07079.
- Caveat Emptor; the environmental and consumer protection monthly. m. ISSN 0045-6004

**Consumer Farmer Foundation**
101 E. 15th St., New York, NY 10003.
- Consumer-Farmer Cooperator. a.

**Consumer Federation of America**
1012 14th St. N.W., Suite 901, Washington, DC 20005.
- Consumer News and Comment. m.

**Consumer Guide**
3323 W. Main St., Skokie, IL 60076.
- Consumer Guide: Cars. a. ISSN 0364-0809

**Consumer News, Inc.**
813 National Press Bldg., Washington, DC 20045.
- Consumer Newsweekly; news you can use from the nation's capital . w.

**Consumer Trends, Inc.**
(Subsidiary of: International Consumer Credit Association)
375 Jackson Ave., St. Louis, MO 63130.
- Consumer Trends; an independent newsletter on consumer credit and financial affairs. s-m.

**Consumers Digest, Inc.**
6316 N. Lincoln Ave., Chicago, IL 60659.
- Consumers Digest Guide to Discount Buying. irreg.

**Consumers Education & Protective Association International, Inc.**
6048 Ogontz Ave., Philadelphia, PA 19141.
- Consumers Voice; let the seller beware. m. ISSN 0010-7190

**Consumers' Research, Inc.**
Washington, NJ 07882.
- Consumers' Research. m.
- Consumers' Research Magazine Handbook of Buying. a. ISSN 0069-9241

**Consumers Union of U.S., Inc.**
256 Washington St., Mount Vernon, NY 10550.
- Consumer Reports. m. ISSN 0010-7174
- Consumers Union News Digest. s-m.

**Consumers Union of U.S., Inc. Education Division**
Orangeburg, NY 10962.
- Teaching Tools for Consumer Reports. 8 per yr.

**Contact Lens Association of Ophthalmologists**
8631 Delmar, St. Louis, MO 63124.
- Contact and Intraocular Lens Medical Journal. q. ISSN 0360-1358

**Contact Lens Society of America**
- Contact Lens Journal. (pub. by Woodbine Publishers, Inc.)

**Contact Publications**
11 Broadway, Suite 933, New York, NY 10004.
- Contact; poetry review. m.

**Contact Resources, Inc.**
1270 Ave. of the Americas, New York, NY 10020.
- Black Contact. q.

**Contacts Influential**
516 S.E. Morrison St., No. 1004, Portland, OR 97214.
- Contacts Influential Business Reference Directory: Denver, Colorado. a. ISSN 0573-7877
- Contacts Influential Business Reference Directory: East Bay Area. a. ISSN 0589-512X
- Contacts Influential Business Reference Directory: Kansas City, Missouri. a.
- Contacts Influential Business Reference Directory: Peninsula. a.
- Contacts Influential Business Reference Directory: Portland, Oregon. a.
- Contacts Influential Business Reference Directory: San Francisco. a.
- Contacts Influential Business Reference Directory: Seattle, Washington. a. ISSN 0573-7869
- Contacts Influential Business Reference Directory: Vancouver, British Columbia. a.

**Contamination Control Laboratories, Inc.**
13324 Farmington Rd., Livonia, MI 48150.
- Contamination Newsletter. m. ISSN 0010-7409

**Contempora**
74 Peachtree St. N.W., Box 673, Atlanta, GA 30301.
- Contempora; a literary art magazine. ISSN 0010-7433

**Contemporary Art-Southeast, Inc.**
Box 7873, Station C, Atlanta, GA 30309.
- Contemporary Art-Southeast. 4 per yr.

**Contemporary Associates**
- Reading Ideas. (pub. by Contemporary Press)

**Contemporary Historical Vehicle Association**
Box 4416, Redding, CA 96001.
- Action Era Vehicle. bi-m. ISSN 0044-6092

**Contemporary Literary Scene**
c/o Department of English, Virginia Commonwealth University, VA 23284.
- Contemporary Literary Scene. a.

**Contemporary Music Foundation**
4105 Devon Dr., Indianapolis, IN 46226.
- New Art Review. irreg.

**Contemporary Music Newsletter**
c/o Department of Music, New York University, 268 Waverly Bldg., Washington Square, New York, NY 10003.
- Contemporary Music Newsletter. 4-5 per yr. ISSN 0589-5286

**Contemporary Press**
Box 1524, San Jose, CA 95109.
- Reading Ideas. 8 per yr. (Contemporary Associates)

**Continental Association of Funeral and Memorial Societies**
- Manual of Death Education and Simple Burial. (pub. by Celo Press)

**Continental Corporation**
80 Maiden Lane, New York, NY 10038.
- Continental Bulletin. q. ISSN 0010-7697

**Continental Oil Co.**
High Ridge Park, Stamford, CT 06904.
- Conoco. 4 per yr.

**Continental Publishing Co., Inc.**
Box 27347, 210 Hillcrest Bldg., Ralston, NE 68127.
- Tractor Performance Pocket Book. a.

**Continental Publishing Co. (Los Angeles)**
5430 Van Nuys Blvd., Van Nuys, CA 91401.
- Today's Viewpoint; for today's woman. m.

**Continental Publishing Company**
1261 Broadway, New York, NY 10001.
- Directory of American Book Specialists; sources for antiquarian and out of print titles. biennial.

**Contra Costa County Library**
1750 Oak Park Blvd., Pleasant Hill, CA 94523.
- Library Link. q. ISSN 0024-2365

**Contra Costa County. Superintendent of Schools**
75 Santa Barbara Rd., Pleasant Hill, CA 94523.
- Contra Costa County School Bulletin. 9 per yr. (Sep.-Jun.) ISSN 0010-7816

**Contraband Press**
Box 4073, Station A, Portland, ME 04101.
- Contraband. s-a.

**Contractor Publishing Co.**
1629 W. Lafayette Blvd., Detroit, MI 48216.
- Michigan Contractor & Builder; engineering and construction. w.
- Michigan Investor. w.
- Michigan Plant & Equipment. m.

**Contractors Association of West Virginia**
411 Capitol St., Charleston, WV 25301.
- West Virginia Construction News. m.

**Convenience Store News**
254 W. 31st St., New York, NY 10001.
- Convenience Store Industry Report. a. ISSN 0084-9294

**Convention of American Instructors of the Deaf**
5034 Wisconsin Ave. N.W., Washington, DC 20016.
- American Annals of the Deaf. bi-m. ISSN 0002-726X (prep. by its Conference of Executives of American Schools for the Deaf)
- C A I D Newsletter. irreg. (2-3 per yr.) ISSN 0045-8430

**Convergence, Inc.**
Mercy College, Dobbs Ferry, NY 10522.
- Cross Currents. q. ISSN 0011-1953

**Conway Publications, Inc.**
Peachtree Air Terminal, 1954 Airport Rd., Atlanta, GA 30341.
- Industrial Development and Manufacturers Record. bi-m. ISSN 0019-8137 (Industrial Development Research Council)
- Site Selection Handbook. q. ISSN 0080-9810

**David C. Cook Publishing Co.**
850 N. Grove St., Elgin, IL 60120.
- Bible-in-Life Pix. w. ISSN 0039-5250
- Interlit. q. ISSN 0020-5575 (David C. Cook Foundation)
- Leader Guidebook; Christian education idea book for Sunday school leaders. q. ISSN 0023-9623
- Sunday Digest; selected reading for Christian adults. w. ISSN 0039-5188

**G. Stenger Cook**
Box 1470, Tustin, CA 92680.
- Poetry Forum. q.

**Cook, Bake & Broil Corp.**
c/o Joel Charles, Ed., Park City West 21P, 3900 Ford Road, Philadelphia, PA 19131.
- Cook, Bake & Broil. irreg.

**Cook County Highway Department**
Chicago Civic Center, Randolph and Clark, Chicago, IL 60602.
- Cook County Highway News. m. ISSN 0010-8251

**Cook Newspapers, Inc.**
Box 10630, Pittsburgh, PA 15235.
- Tri-State Food News. s-m. ISSN 0041-249X

**Cook's Crier**
c/o Betty Harvey Williams, 118 Fairview Ave., Warrensburg, MO 64093.
- Cook's Crier. q.

**Edward M. Cooney, Ed. & Pub.**
67 Pleasant St., Marion, MA 02738.
- Locke Report. 6 per yr. ISSN 0024-5690

**Cooper Ornithological Society, Inc.**
c/o Peter Stettenheim, Ed., Meriden Rd., Lebanon, NH 03766.
- Condor. q. ISSN 0010-5422

**Cooper Ornithological Society, Inc. (Los Angeles)**
Department of Biology, University of California, Los Angeles, CA 90024.
- Pacific Coast Avifauna. irreg., no. 37, 1974.

**Cooper Union for the Advancement of Science and Art**
Cooper Sq., New York, NY 10003.
- At Cooper Union. q. ISSN 0004-6434

**Cooper Union for the Advancement of Science and Art. School of Art and Architecture**
Cooper Square, New York, NY 10003.
- Critiques. a. ISSN 0090-4112

**Cooperative Education Association**
Drexel University, Philadelphia, PA 19104.
- Cooperative Education Association Membership Directory. biennial. ISSN 0069-9810
- Cooperative Education Association Newsletter. q. ISSN 0010-843X
- Directory of Cooperative Education. biennial. ISSN 0070-5357
- Journal of Cooperative Education. s-a. ISSN 0022-0132

**Cooperative Extension Association of Albany County. Agricultural Division**
Voorheesville, Albany, NY 12186.
- Extension News-Albany/Rensselaer/Saratoga/Washington Counties. m.

**Cooperative Extension Association of Allegany County. Agricultural Division**
P.O. Box 566, Belmont, NY 14813.
- Allegany County Farm & Home News. m.

**Cooperative Extension Association of Cayuga County**
Cayuga County Farm, Home and 4-H Center, 248 Grant Ave, Auburn, NY 13021.
- Cayuga County Farm and Home News. m. ISSN 0008-865X

**Cooperative Extension Association of Cayuga, Madison, Onondaga, Oswego Counties**
Agricultural Div., 12 Channing Place, Syracuse, NY 13202.
- Agricultural News. m. ISSN 0002-158X

**Cooperative Extension Association of Clinton County**
Old Court House Annex, Plattsburgh, NY 12901.
- Extension. m.

**Cooperative Extension Association of Delaware County**
Hamden Town Hall, Hamden, NY 13782.
- Delaware County Farm and Home News. m.

**Cooperative Extension Association of Livingston County. Agricultural Division**
158 South Main St., Mount Morris, NY 14510.
- Livingston County Agricultural News. m. ISSN 0024-5313

**Cooperative Extension Association of Nassau County**
300 Hempstead Tpke, West Hempstead, NY 11552.
- Nassau Living; suburban agricultural & gardening magazine. q.

**Cooperative Extension Association of Orleans County**
20 South Main St., Albion, NY 14411.
- Ag Impact. m.

**Cooperative Extension Association of Suffolk County**
246 Griffing Ave., Riverhead, L.I., NY 11901.
- Suffolk County Agricultural News. m. ISSN 0039-467X

**Cooperative Extension Association of Tioga County**
56 Main St., Owego, NY 13827.
- Country Living. m. ISSN 0011-0191

**Cooperative Extension Association of Wayne County**
Box 217, Alton, NY 14413.
- Wayne County Farm and Home News. m. ISSN 0043-1613

**Cooper's Hero-Hobby**
c/o John R. Cooper, Route 1, Box 371, Clarksburg, WV 26301.
- Cooper's Hero-Hobby. q. ISSN 0010-8537

**Coordinated Library Information Program, Inc.**
Box 1437, 3030 Darbo Drive, Madison, WI 53701.
- Tips from C.L.I.P. approx. bi-m. (Wisconsin. Department of Public Instruction. Division for Library Services)

**Coordinating Council for Senior Citizens**
c/o Senior Citizens' Memorial Center, 519 E. Main St., Durham, NC 27701.
- Senior Citizens Post. bi-m.

**Copley International Corp.**
7817 Herschel Ave., Box 1530, La Jolla, CA 92038.
- South Bay Economic Review; a quarterly summary of business & economic conditions in the South Bay area. q. ISSN 0038-3031
- Union-Tribune Index of San Diego Business Activity. m. ISSN 0041-7068

**Copp Organization, Inc.**
37 W. 38th St., New York, NY 10018.
- Law and Order; for all concerned with the business of law enforcement. m. ISSN 0023-9194

**Copyright Society of the U.S.A.**
- Copyright Society of the U.S.A. Bulletin. (pub. by Fred B. Rothman & Co.)

**Coral Publishing Co., Inc.**
Box 3404, Honolulu, HI 96801.
- Aloha; the magazine of Hawaii. q.

**Cord Communications Corp.**
25 W. 43 St., New York, NY 10036.
- Cord Sportfacts Fisherman Annual. a. ISSN 0590-8817
- Cord Sportfacts Guns Guide. irreg. ISSN 0590-6776
- Cord Sportfacts Hockey Guide. a. ISSN 0591-0374
- Cord Sportfacts: Hunting. irreg. ISSN 0092-8216
- Major League Baseball. (pub. by Simon & Schuster, Inc.)
- Pro Football. (pub. by Simon & Schuster, Inc.)

**Cordovan Corp.**
5314 Bingle Rd., Houston, TX 77092.
- Horseman; the magazine of western riding. m. ISSN 0018-5221
- Houston Business Journal. w.
- Jet Cargo News; journal of product marketing by air. m. ISSN 0021-6003
- Southwest Advertising & Marketing. m. ISSN 0038-4658
- Southwest Directory of Advertising and Public Relations Agencies. a. ISSN 0361-3593
- Texas Fisherman; voice of the lone star angler. m.
- Western Outfitter. m. ISSN 0049-7487

**Cormorant**
5453 College Ave., Oakland, CA 94618.
- Cormorant. s-a. ISSN 0045-8546

**Corn Belt Library System**
Normal Industrial Park, West Hovey Ave., Normal, IL 61761.
- Corn Belt Library System. Sum and Substance. m.

**Corn Refiners Association, Inc.**
1001 Connecticut Ave. N.W., Washington, DC 20036.
- Corn Annual. a. ISSN 0069-9993

**Cornell Engineer, Inc.**
Cornell University, One Carpenter Hall, Ithaca, NY 14853.
- Cornell Engineer. 5 per yr. ISSN 0010-8790 (Cornell Society of Engineers)

**Cornell Society of Engineers**
- Cornell Engineer. (pub. by Cornell Engineer, Inc.)

**Cornell University**
Ithaca, NY 14850.
- Cornell Plantations. q. ISSN 0010-8863 (Orders to:, 100 Judd Falls Rd.)
- Epoch; a magazine of contemporary literature. 3 per yr. ISSN 0300-7332 (Orders to:, 245 Goldwin Smith Hall)
- Urban Studies Bulletin. s-a.

**Cornell University. Agriculture Engineering Extension**
Riley-Robb Hall, Ithaca, NY 14850.
- Ag Engineers Notebook. irreg., 1970, vol. 4. ISSN 0065-0072

**Cornell University. Center for International Studies**
170 Uris Hall, Ithaca, NY 14850.
- Cornell Research Papers in International Studies. irreg. ISSN 0070-0037

**Cornell University. Center for Urban Development Research**
726 University Ave., Ithaca, NY 14853.
- Cornell University. Division of Urban Studies. Papers on Gaming Simulation.

**Cornell University. Chemicals-Pesticide Program**
Cooperative Extension, Comstock Hall, Ithaca, NY 14850.
- Cornell Newsletter, Chemicals-Pesticides Program. 12 per yr. ISSN 0010-8855

**Cornell University. China-Japan Program**
140 Uris Hall, Ithaca, NY 14888.
- C H I N O P E R L Papers. 2 per yr. (Conference on Chinese Oral and Performing Literature)

**Cornell University. College of Engineering**
Carpenter Hall, Ithaca, NY 14853.
- Cornell Biennial Electrical Engineering Conference. biennial. ISSN 0070-0002 (prep. by its School of Electrical Engineering)
- Engineering: Cornell Quarterly. q. ISSN 0013-7871

**Cornell University. College of Human Ecology**
Ithaca, NY 14853.
- Consumer Close-Ups. m. (except Jul. & Aug.) (prep. by its Dept. of Consumer Economics & Public Policy) (Co-sponsor: New York State Co-Operative Extension)

**Cornell University. Department of Agricultural Economics**
Ithaca, NY 14850.
- Cornell International Agricultural Development Series. Bulletins Reporting Research on the Economics of Asian Agriculture. irreg.
- Cornell University. Department of Agricultural Economics. Prices, Employment and Income Distribution Research Project. Occasional Papers. irreg; no. 72, 1974. (Co-sponsor: U.S. Agency for International Development)

**Cornell University. Department of Poultry Science**
Ithaca, NY 14853.
- Avian Chromosomes Newsletter. a. (prep. by its Cytogenetics Section)

**Cornell University. Department of Sociology**
Ithaca, NY 14850.
- Cornell Journal of Social Relations. s-a. ISSN 0010-8820

**Cornell University. Graduate School of Business and Public Administration**
Ithaca, NY 14853.
● Administrative Science Quarterly. q. ISSN 0001-8392

**Cornell University. Laboratory of Ornithology**
159 Sapsucker Woods Road, Ithaca, NY 14853.
● Living Bird. a. ISSN 0459-6137

**Cornell University. Law School**
Myron Taylor Hall, Ithaca, NY 14853.
● Cornell International Law Journal. s-a. ISSN 0010-8812
● Cornell Law Forum. 3 per yr. ISSN 0010-8839
● Cornell Law Review. bi-m. ISSN 0010-8847

**Cornell University. Libraries**
Ithaca, NY 14853.
● Cornell University. Libraries. Bulletin. q. ISSN 0045-8562

**Cornell University Libraries. Department of Manuscripts and University Archives**
101 Olin Library, Ithaca, NY 14853.
● Documentation Newsletter. s-a.

**Cornell University Libraries. John M. Olin Library**
Reference Dept., Ithaca, NY 14850.
● Cornell University. Libraries. Guide Series. irreg.

**Cornell University Medical College. Alumni Association, Inc.**
1300 York Ave., Rm. C-103, New York, NY 10021.
● Cornell University Medical College Alumni Quarterly. q. ISSN 0010-8898

**Cornell University. Office of International Agriculture**
102 Roberts Hall, Ithaca, NY 14850.
● Cornell International Agriculture Mimeographs. irreg.

**Cornell University Press**
124 Roberts Place, Ithaca, NY 14850.
● Africa in the Modern World. irreg.
● Aspects of Greek and Roman Life. irreg.
● Baker Series in Chemistry. irreg.
● Contemporary Philosophy Series. irreg. ISSN 0414-7790
● Documents of Revolution. irreg.
● Studies in Ancient Art and Archaeology. irreg.
● Studies in Modern Hebrew Literature. irreg.
● World Economic History. irreg.

**Cornell University. Sage School of Philosophy**
218 Goldwin Smith Hall, Ithaca, NY 14853.
● Philosophical Review. q. ISSN 0031-8108

**Cornell University. School of Hotel Administration**
Ithaca, NY 14850.
● Cornell Hotel & Restaurant Administration Quarterly. q. ISSN 0010-8804

**Cornell University. Southeast Asia Program**
120 Uris Hall, Ithaca, NY 14853.
● Cornell University. Library. Wason Collection. Southeast Asia Accessions List. m. ISSN 0589-7351
● Cornell University. Modern Indonesia Project. Interim Reports. irreg., no. 52, 1971.
● Cornell University. Modern Indonesia Project. Monographs. irreg., no. 56, 1972. ISSN 0589-7300
● Cornell University. Modern Indonesia Project. Translations. irreg., no. 55, 1972. ISSN 0574-0681
● Cornell University. Southeast Asia Program. Data Papers. irreg.; no. 97, 1974. ISSN 0070-0215
● Cornell University. Thailand Project. Interim Reports Series. irreg., 1971, no. 14. ISSN 0070-0223
● Indonesia. s-a. ISSN 0019-7289

**Cornell Veterinarian, Inc.**
Ithaca, NY 14853.
● Cornell Veterinarian. q. ISSN 0010-8901

**Cornerstone Genealogical Society**
Box 547, Waynesburg, PA 15370.
● Cornerstone Clues. q.

**Cornhusker Press**
5919 Military Ave., Omaha, NE 68104.
● Midwestern Trucker and Shipper. m. ISSN 0026-3508 (Nebraska Motor Carriers Association, Inc.)

**Corning Museum of Glass**
Corning Glass Center, Corning, NY 14830.
● Journal of Glass Studies. a. ISSN 0075-4250

**Corpcom Services, Inc.**
112 E. 31st St., New York, NY 10016.
● Corporate Communications Report. bi-m. ISSN 0010-8952

**Corporate Information Center**
Room 566, 475 Riverside Dr., New York, NY 10027.
● Corporate Examiner. m. (except Aug.) (Interfaith Center on Corporate Responsibility)

**Corporate Reorganization Reporter, Inc.**
1156 15th St., N.W., Suite 724, Washington, DC 20005.
● Bankruptcy Court Decisions. fortn. ISSN 0098-7336

**Corporate Report, Inc.**
c/o Don Larson, 7101 York Ave., Minneapolis, MN 55435.
● Corporate Report. m.
● Corporate Report Who's Who in Upper Midwest Business. a.
● Goldletter. w.

**Corporate Responsibility**
384 Strawtonn Rd., W. Nyack, NY 10994.
● Corporate Responsibility; a bimonthly newsletter.

**Corporate Shareholder, Inc.**
271 Madison Ave., New York, NY 10016.
● Corporate Shareholder; an inside report on investor relations. s-m.
● Review of the Financial Press. bi-w.

**Corporation for Public Broadcasting**
1111-16th St. N.W., Washington, DC 20036.
● C P B Report. fortn.

**Corporation Service Co.**
1105 N. Market, Box 552, Wilmington, DE 19899.
● Contents of Current Legal Periodicals. m. ISSN 0300-7391

**Corps of Engineers. Waterborne Commerce Statistics Center**
Box 61280, New Orleans, LA 70160.
● Waterborne Commerce of the United States. a. (in 5 separate parts) ISSN 0083-7725

**Correctional Association of New York**
135 E. 15th St., New York, NY 10003.
● Correctional Association of New York. Newsletter. q.

**Correctional Information Service, Inc.**
801 Second Ave., Suite 1404, New York, NY 10017.
● Corrections. q. ISSN 0095-4594

**Corrodentia Society**
516 Butler Library, Columbia University, Broadway & W. 116th St., New York, NY 10027.
● Worms. irreg.

**Corrosion and Protection Association**
● Corrosion Science. (pub. by Pergamon Press, Inc.)

**Corvallis Environmental Research Laboratory**
200 S.W. 35 St., Corvallis, OR 97330.
● Coastal Pollution Research Highlights. irreg.

**Cosmetic, Toiletry & Fragrance Association**
1133 15th St. N.W., Suite 1200, Washington, DC 20005.
● C T F A Cosmetic Journal. q. ISSN 0090-0591

**Cosmetology Accrediting Commission**
Suite 207, 25755 Southfield Rd., Southfield, MI 48075.
● Directory of Accredited Cosmetology Schools. a.

**Cosmic Circus**
c/o Regg King, Ed., 517 33rd St., No. 1, Oakland, CA 94609.
● Cosmic Circus. 1-2 per yr.

**Cosmic Information Agency**
Box 24, East Lansing, MI 48823.
● Invitation; artworks. irreg.

**Cosretic Laboratories**
Box 80883, Atlanta, GA 30366.
● Body Forum. m. 10 per yr.

**Gregg Costikyan, Ed. & Pub.**
1675 York Ave., New York, NY 10028.
● Urf Durfal, Grandson of Pouch. every 3 weeks.

**Costume Society of America**
Fifth Ave. and 82nd St., New York, NY 10028.
● Dress. a. ISSN 0361-2112

**Richard Cotten, Ed. & Pub.**
Box 17194, Dulles Int. Airport, Washington, DC 20041
(and Box 1808, Bakersfield, Calif. 93303)
● Richard Cotten's Conservative Viewpoint. m. ISSN 0035-5089

**Cotton Digest Co., Inc.**
708 Cotton Exchange Bldg., Houston, TX 77002.
● Cotton Digest. w. ISSN 0010-9797

**Cotton Gin and Oil Mill Press**
P.O. Box 18092, Dallas, TX 75218.
● International Green Book; directory of U.S. and Latin American processors of cottonseed, soybean, linseed and peanuts. a. ISSN 0074-6193

**Cottonwood Review**
Box J, Lawrence, KS 66044.
● Cottonwood Review. s-a.

**Council Bluffs Central Labor Union**
● Farmer-Labor Press. (pub. by Farmer-Labor Press Publishing Co. Inc.)

**Council for a Department of Peace**
110 Maryland Ave. N.E., Washington, DC 20002.
● Pax. s-a.

**Council for Advancement and Support of Education**
One Dupont Circle, Suite 530, Washington, DC 20036.
● C A S E Currents. m.
● Council for Advancement and Support of Education. Directory. a.
● Education Abstracts. 12 per yr. ISSN 0013-1210

**Council for Agricultural and Chemurgic Research**
350 Fifth Ave., New York, NY 10001.
● Council for Agricultural and Chemurgic Research. Proceedings of Annual Conferences. a.

**Council for Basic Education**
725 15th St., N.W., Washington, DC 20005.
● C B E Bulletin. m(Sept-June) ISSN 0007-7933
● Council for Basic Education. Occasional Papers. irreg.; latest issue no. 24. ISSN 0070-069X

**Council for European Studies**
156 Mervis Hall, University of Pittsburgh, Pittsburgh, PA 15260.
● European Studies Newsletter. bi-m. ISSN 0046-2802

**Council for Exceptional Children**
1920 Association Drive, Reston, VA 22091.
● C E C Update. q. ISSN 0007-8131
● Education & Training of the Mentally Retarded. q. ISSN 0013-1237
● Exceptional Child Education Resources. q.
● Exceptional Children. 8 per yr. ISSN 0014-4029
● Teaching Exceptional Children. q. ISSN 0040-0599

**Council for Financial Aid to Education**
6 E. 45th St., New York, NY 10017.
● Council for Financial Aid to Education. C.F.A.E. Corporation Support of Higher Education. biennial; 1971; no. 9. ISSN 0589-9087

**Council for Interdisciplinary Communication in Medicine**
500 Fifth Ave., New York, NY 10036.
● Philosophy and Technology of Drug Assessment. irreg., vol. 4, 1973.

**Council for International Exchange of Scholars. Conference Board of Associated Research Council**
2101 Constitution Ave., N.W., Washington, DC 20418.
● Directory of Visiting Scholars in the United States Awarded Grants under the Mutual Educational and Cultural Exchange Act (the Fulbright-Hays Act) a. ISSN 0070-6582

**Council for Old World Archaeology**
Boston University, 232 Bay State Rd., Boston, MA 02215.
- Council for Old World Archaeology: C O W A Surveys and Bibliographies. Area 1: British Isle. irreg., planned to become triennial. ISSN 0070-072X
- Council for Old World Archaeology: C O W A Surveys and Bibliographies. Area 2: Scandinavia. irreg., planned to become triennial. ISSN 0070-0738
- Council for Old World Archaeology: C O W A Surveys and Bibliographies. Area 3: Western Europe: Part 1. irreg., planned to become triennial. ISSN 0070-0746
- Council for Old World Archaeology: C O W A Surveys and Bibliographies. Area 3: Western Europe: Part 2. irreg., planned to become triennial. ISSN 0070-0754
- Council for Old World Archaeology: C O W A Surveys and Bibliographies. Area 4: Western Mediterranean. irreg., planned to become triennial. ISSN 0070-0762
- Council for Old World Archaeology: C O W A Surveys and Bibliographies. Area 5: Central Europe. irreg., planned to become triennial. ISSN 0070-0770
- Council for Old World Archaeology: C O W A Surveys and Bibliographies. Area 6: Balkans. irreg., planned to become triennial. ISSN 0070-0789
- Council for Old World Archaeology: C O W A Surveys and Bibliographies. Area 7: Eastern Mediterranean. irreg., planned to become triennial. ISSN 0070-0797
- Council for Old World Archaeology: C O W A Surveys and Bibliographies. Area 8: European Russia. irreg., planned to become triennial. ISSN 0070-0800
- Council for Old World Archaeology: C O W A Surveys and Bibliographies. Area 9: Northeast Africa. irreg., planned to become triennial. ISSN 0070-0819
- Council for Old World Archaeology: C O W A Surveys and Bibliographies. Area 10. Northwest Africa. irreg., planned to become triennial. ISSN 0070-0827
- Council for Old World Archaeology: C O W A Surveys and Bibliographies. Area 11. West Africa. irreg., planned to become triennial. ISSN 0070-0835
- Council for Old World Archaeology: C O W A Surveys and Bibliographies. Area 12. Equatorial Africa. irreg., planned to become triennial. ISSN 0070-0843
- Council for Old World Archaeology: C O W A Surveys and Bibliographies. Area 13. South Africa. irreg., planned to become triennial. ISSN 0070-0851
- Council for Old World Archaeology: C O W A Surveys and Bibliographies. Area 14. East Africa. irreg., planned to become triennial. ISSN 0070-086X
- Council for Old World Archaeology: C O W A Surveys and Bibliographies. Area 15. Western Asia. irreg., planned to become triennial. ISSN 0070-0878
- Council for Old World Archaeology: C O W A Surveys and Bibliographies. Area 16. Southern Asia. irreg., planned to become triennial. ISSN 0070-0886
- Council for Old World Archaeology: C O W A Surveys and Bibliographies. Area 17. Far East. irreg., planned to become triennial. ISSN 0070-0894
- Council for Old World Archaeology: C O W A Surveys and Bibliographies. Area 18. Northern Asia. irreg., planned to become triennial. ISSN 0070-0916
- Council for Old World Archaeology: C O W A Surveys and Bibliographies. Area 19. Southeast Asia. irreg., planned to become triennial. ISSN 0070-0924
- Council for Old World Archaeology: C O W A Surveys and Bibliographies. Area 20. Indonesia. irreg., planned to become triennial. ISSN 0070-0932
- Council for Old World Archaeology: C O W A Surveys and Bibliographies. Area 21. Pacific Islands. irreg., planned to become triennial. ISSN 0070-0940
- Council for Old World Archaeology: C O W A Surveys and Bibliographies. Area 22. Australia. irreg., planned to become triennial. ISSN 0070-0959

**Council for Planning & Conservation**
Box 228, Beverly Hills, CA 90213.
- Council for Planning & Conservation. Newsletter. q. ISSN 0045-8775

**Council for Tobacco Research--U.S.A. Inc.**
110 E. 59th St., New York, NY 10022.
- Council for Tobacco Research--U.S.A. Report. a. ISSN 0361-1612

**Council of Better Business Bureaus**
1150-17th St. N.W., Washington, DC 20036.
- Be a Better Buyer. m.
- Council of Better Business Bureaus. Annual Report. a.
- Council of Better Business Bureaus. Overview. bi-m.

**Council of Biological and Medical Abstracts**
- Soil Biology and Biochemistry. (pub. by Pergamon Press, Inc.)

**Council of Biology Editors**
- Council of Biology Editors. Newsletter. (pub. by Federation of American Societies for Experimental Biology)

**Council of Communication Societies**
P.O. Box 1074, Silver Spring, MD 20910.
- Communication Directory. irreg.; 2nd edt., 1973-74. ISSN 0094-2588

**Council of Earth Religions**
- Green Egg. (pub. by Church of All Worlds)

**Council of Educational Facility Planners**
29 W. Woodruff Ave., Columbus, OH 43210.
- C E F P Journal. bi-m. ISSN 0007-8220
- Guide for Planning Educational Facilities. irreg; approx. quinquennial. ISSN 0072-8101

**Council of Graduate Schools in the U.S.**
One Dupont Circle, Washington, DC 20036.
- Council of Graduate Schools in the United States. Proceedings of the Annual Meeting. a. ISSN 0070-1076

**Council of Higher Educational Institutions in New York City**
888 7th Ave., New York, NY 10019.
- Graduate Education in New York City: A Directory of Degree Programs. irreg. ISSN 0072-5242

**Council of Jewish Federations and Welfare Funds, Inc.**
575 Lexington Ave., New York, NY 10022.
- Directory of Jewish Health and Welfare Agencies. irreg. ISSN 0419-2818
- Jewish Federations, Welfare Funds and Community Councils Directory. a. ISSN 0075-3734
- Jewish Social Service Yearbook. a. ISSN 0075-3742

**Council of Michigan Foundations**
200 Mill St., Lansing, MI 48933.
- Michigan Foundation Directory. irreg. ISSN 0362-1561 (Co-Sponsor: Michigan League for Human Services)

**Council of Northern California Philatelic Societies**
900 Kern St., Richmond, CA 94805.
- Council of Northern California Philatelic Societies. Council Courier. q.

**Council of Planning Librarians**
c/o Judy Meyer, Ed., 308 S. Lincoln St., Kent, OH 44240.
- C P L Newsletter. q. ISSN 0045-8791

**Council of Planning Librarians. Exchange Bibliographies**
Box 229, Monticello, IL 61856.
- Council of Planning Librarians. Exchange Bibliographies. ISSN 0010-9959
- New Publications for Planning Libraries. irreg.

**Council of Profit Sharing Industries**
20 N. Wacker Dr., Chicago, IL 60606.
- Profit Sharing. m. ISSN 0033-0280

**Council of State Governments**
Box 11910, Iron Works Pike, Lexington, KY 40511.
- Book of the States. biennial. ISSN 0068-0125
- Briefs (Lexington) fortn. ISSN 0524-4714
- Legislative Research Checklist. bi-m. ISSN 0024-0486

- Legislative Session Sheet. m.
- N A S B O Newsletter. q. ISSN 0363-4965 (National Association of State Budget Officers)
- Newsletter & Digest of Selected Opinions of State Attorneys General. q. ISSN 0094-226X (National Association of Attorneys General)
- State Court Systems. irreg. ISSN 0081-4482
- State Government; the journal of state affairs. q. ISSN 0039-0097
- State Government News. m. ISSN 0039-0119
- State Headlines. fortn. ISSN 0589-9788
- Suggested State Legislation. a. ISSN 0070-1157

**Council of State Governments. Conference of Chief Justices**
36 West 44 Street Room 1208, New York, NY 10036.
- Conference of Chief Justices. Proceedings. a. ISSN 0069-8415

**Council of State Governments. Southern Legislative Conference**
3384 Peachtree Rd. N.E., Room 610, Atlanta, GA 30326.
- Council of State Governments. Southern Legislative Conference. Summary, Annual Meeting. a. ISSN 0099-006X

**Council of State Planning Agencies**
Iron Works Pike, Lexington, KY 40511.
- State Planning Issues. a. ISSN 0092-8488

**Council of Supervisors and Administrators of the City of New York**
Local 1, American Federation of School Administrators, AFL-CIO, 186 Joralemon St., Brooklyn, NY 11201.
- C S A Newsletter. bi-w.

**Council of the Southern Mountains, Inc.**
Drawer N, Clintwood, VA 24228.
- Mountain Life and Work; magazine of the Appalachian South. m. 11 per yr. ISSN 0027-2558

**Council on Abandoned Military Posts**
c/o Secretary, Box 171, Arlington, VA 22210.
- Council on Abandoned Military Posts. Periodical. 4 per yr. ISSN 0010-9967
- Headquarters Heliogram. m.

**Council on American Affairs**
Suite 210, 1785 Massachusetts Ave. NW, Washington, DC 20036.
- Journal of Social and Political Affairs. q.

**Council on Anthropology and Education**
1703 New Hampshire Ave. N.W., Washington, DC 20009.
- Anthropology & Education Quarterly. q.

**Council on Economic Priorities**
184 Fifth Ave., New York, NY 10011.
- C E B Reports and C E P Studies. bi-m.
- C E P Newsletter. 10-12 per yr.

**Council on Foreign Relations, Inc.**
58 East 68th St., New York, NY 10021
- American Foreign Relations-a Documentary Record. irreg.; latest edition, 1974. (Subscr. to: New York University Press, 21 W. Fourth St., New York, NY 10012)
- Council on Foreign Relations. Council Papers on International Affairs. irreg.
- Council on Foreign Relations. President's Report. a. ISSN 0093-4615
- Foreign Affairs; an American quarterly review. q. ISSN 0015-7120
- Political Handbook and Atlas of the World. a. ISSN 0079-3035 (Subscr. to: McGraw-Hill Book Co., Inc., 1221 Avenue of the Americas, New York, NY 10020)

**Council on Foundations, Inc.**
888 7th Ave., P.O. Box 783, Old Chelsea Sta., New York, NY 10019.
- Foundation News; the journal of philanthropy. bi-m. ISSN 0015-8976

**Council on International Educational Exchange**
777 United Nations Plaza, New York, NY 10017.
- Whole World Handbook: a Student Guide to Work, Study and Travel Abroad. a. ISSN 0070-1165

**Council on International Nontheatrical Events, Inc.**
1201 Sixteenth Street, N.W., Washington, DC
21136.
- Council on International Nontheatrical Events.
Yearbook; Golden Eagle film awards. a.

**Council on Interracial Books for Children, Inc.**
CIBC Resource Center, Room 300, 1841 Broadway,
New York, NY 10023.
- Interracial Books for Children. Bulletin. 8 per yr.
ISSN 0020-9708 (Co-sponsor: Foundation for
Change)

**Council on Legal Education for Professional
Responsibility, Inc.**
280 Park Ave., New York, NY 10017.
- Council on Legal Education for Professional
Responsibility. Newsletter. irreg.;vol.7,no.10,1974.
ISSN 0070-1173

**Council on Library Resources, Inc.**
One Dupont Circle, Suite 620, Washington, DC
20036.
- C L R Recent Developments. 5 per yr. ISSN
0034-1169
- Council on Library Resources Report. a. ISSN
0070-1181

**Council on Library Technical Assistants**
c/o School Management Institute, 750 Brooksedge
Blvd., Westerville, OH 43081.
- Council on Library Technical Assistants.
Newsletter. m.
- Directory of Institutions Offering or Planning
Programs for the Training of Library Technical
Assistants. triennial; latest, 1976.

**Council on Municipal Performance**
84 Fifth Ave., New York, NY 10011.
- C O M P News. m.
- C O M P Report. bi-m.
- Council on Municipal Performance. Annual
Report. a.

**Council on National Literatures**
Box 81, Whitestone, NY 11357.
- C N L/Quarterly World Report. q.
- Review of National Literatures. a. ISSN 0034-
6640

**Council on Postsecondary Accreditation**
One Dupont Circle, N.W., Washington, DC 20036.
- Accreditation. q. ISSN 0099-0256

**Council on Religion and International Affairs**
170 E. 64th St, New York, NY 10021.
- C R I A Special Studies. irreg.;latest issue, 1974.
ISSN 0070-119X
- Worldview Disarmament Newsletter. m.

**Council on Social Work Education**
345 E. 46th St., New York, NY 10017.
- Journal of Education for Social Work. 3 per yr.
ISSN 0022-0612
- Schools of Social Work with Accredited Master's
Degree Programs. a.
- Social Work Education Reporter. 3 per yr. ISSN
0037-8062
- Statistics on Social Work Education in the United
States. a. ISSN 0091-7192

**Council on the Environment of New York City**
51 Chambers St., New York, NY 10007.
- New York City Environmental Bulletin. bi-m.

**Council on the Teaching of Hebrew. Department of
Education and Culture**
515 Park Ave., New York, NY 10022.
- Council on the Teaching of Hebrew. Bulletin. a.;
latest issue, nos. 4-6, 1972. ISSN 0070-1203

**Councilor Research Fund, Inc.**
1827 Texas Ave., Shreveport, LA 71103.
- Councilor. s-m. ISSN 0010-9991

**Counseling Psychologist**
Washington University, Box 1053, St. Louis, MO
63130.
- Counseling Psychologist. q. ISSN 0011-0000

**Count Dracula Society**
Ed. & Pub. Gordon R. Guy, Gothick Gateway, 22
Canterbury Street, East Hartford, CT 06118.
- Count Dracula Society Quarterly; devoted to the
serious study of horror films & Gothic literature.
q. ISSN 0011-0051

**Countdown**
143 E. 27th St., New York, NY 10016.
- Countdown. 5 per yr. ISSN 0045-8821

**Countdown (Wichita)**
Box 8153, Munger Station, Wichita, KS 67208.
- Countdown (Wichita); faith, facts and freedom. m.
ISSN 0045-8813

**Counterforce**
4039 Cole, Suite 107, Dallas, TX 75204.
- Counterforce. m.

**Countermedia: the Alaska Journalism Review &
Supplement**
c/o Joe Larocca, Box 2299, Fairbanks, AK 99707.
- Countermedia: the Alaska Journalism Review &
Supplement. m.

**Countian Publishing Co.**
8003 Forsyth Blvd., Clayton, MO 63105.
- St. Louis Countian. d. ISSN 0036-2948

**Country Americana**
R.D. 1, Brass Castle, Washington, NJ 07882.
- Country Americana. bi-m.

**Country Club Golfer Corp.**
2171 Campus Drive, Irvine, CA 92664.
- Country Club Golfer. m.

**Country Dance and Song Society of America**
55 Christopher St., New York, NY 10014.
- Country Dance and Song. a. ISSN 0070-1262

**Country Journal Publishing Co.**
139 Main St., Brattleboro, VT 05301
- Blair & Ketchum's Country Journal. m. ISSN
0094-0526

**Country Lady's Daybook**
Box 8, Silverado Canyon, CA 92675.
- Country Lady's Daybook. bi-m.

**Country Messenger**
c/o R. Gillem, Editor, Route 2, Fort Atkinson, IA
52144.
- Country Messenger. q.

**Country Music**
475 Park Ave. South, Suite 1102, New York, NY
10022.
- Country Music. m. ISSN 0090-4007

**Country Music Association**
1511 Sigler St., Nashville, TN 37203.
- C M A Close-Up. m. ISSN 0009-9449

**Country Music Foundation**
- Journal of Country Music. (pub. by Country
Music Foundation Press)

**Country Music Foundation Press**
4 Music Square E., Nashville, TN 37203.
- Journal of Country Music. q. ISSN 0092-0517
(Country Music Foundation)

**Country Music Roundup**
c/o Blanche Trinajstick, Ed., 2730 Baltimore Ave.,
Pueblo, CO 81003.
- Country Music Roundup. q.

**Country Music Trail**
20232 106th Ave., Kent, WA 98031.
- Country Music Trail. bi-m.

**Country Press**
Box 614, Saratoga Springs, NY 12866.
- Letters. q.

**Country Publishing Co.**
Box 186, Fairfax, VA 22030.
- Countrywide Annual Year Book. a. ISSN 0092-
5454

**Country Style Publications Co.**
11058 W. Addison St., Franklin Park, IL 60103.
- Country Style. bi-m.

**Country Women Collective**
Box 51, Albion, CA 95410.
- Country Women. 5 per yr.

**Countryside Publishers**
Box 677, Minneapolis, MN 55440.
- Countryside. m. ISSN 0098-4566

**Countrywide Publications Inc.**
257 Park Ave. S., New York, NY 10003.
- American Horseman. m. ISSN 0091-4371
- Ancient Astronauts. q.
- Masters of Self Defense. bi-m.
- Rod Power. bi-m.
- Today's Hairdo. q.

**County Communications, Inc.**
Box 269, Westport, CT 06880.
- Fairfield County. m. ISSN 0046-3175

**County Engineers Association of Ohio**
1500 W. Third Ave., Columbus, OH 43212.
- Ohio County Engineers' News. q.

**County Judges and Commissioners Association of
Texas**
- County Progress. (pub. by Associated Publishing
Co.)

**County Publications, Inc.**
437 Ward Ave., Mamaroneck, NY 10543.
- Long Island. m.
- Westchester. m.

**County Supervisors Association of California**
Suite 201, 11th & L Building, Sacramento, CA
95814.
- California County Fact Book. a.

**Courier-Gazette, Inc.**
1 Park Drive, Rockland, ME 04841.
- State O'Maine Facts. irreg. ISSN 0097-1189

**Courier Publishing Co.**
2431 W. Hopkins St., Milwaukee, WI 53206.
- Milwaukee Courier. w. ISSN 0026-4350

**Courselector, Inc.**
355 Western Ave., Boston, MA 02135.
- Courselector. s-a.

**Court Practice Institute**
127 N. Dearborn St., Chicago, IL 60602.
- Court Practice Institute. Newsletter. irreg. ISSN
0098-9843

**Phoebe Courtney, Ed. & Pub.**
Box 636, Littleton, CO 80123.
- Independent American. bi-m. ISSN 0019-3666

**Covenant Press**
5101 N. Francisco Ave., Chicago, IL 60625.
- Covenant Companion. s-m. ISSN 0011-0671
(Evangelical Covenant Church of America)

**Cow Puddle Press**
c/o Jack Glover, Sunset Trading Post, Sunset, TX
76270.
- International Barbed Wire Gazette. m. ISSN
0047-0597

**James K. Cowan Press**
Cowan Clan United, 510 W. First St, Pittsburgh, KS
66762.
- Cowan Clan United. Newsletter. q. ISSN 0090-
6093

**Cowan Publishing Corp.**
14 Vanderventer Ave., Port Washington, NY 11050.
- C B Radio/S9. m.
- C Q; the radio amateurs' journal. m. ISSN 0007-
893X
- Merchandising 2-Way Radio. bi-m.
- Modern Recording. m. ISSN 0361-0004
- Solid State Technology. m. ISSN 0038-111X

**Cox Heart Institute**
3525 Southern Boulevard, Dayton, OH 45429.
- Cox Heart Institute Work-in-Progress Bulletin. a.

**Cox, Hicks, Hudson & Love**
Box 178, Temecula, CA 92390.
- High Country. q. ISSN 0018-1420

**Cox Publishing Co.**
832 S. Baldwin Ave., Arcadia, CA 91006.
- Pacific Coast Nurseryman and Garden Supply
Dealer. m. ISSN 0030-8587

**Coyne & Blanchard, Inc.**
410 Sherman Ave., Box 10300, Palo Alto, CA
94303.
- Communication Arts. bi-m. ISSN 0010-3519

**Crabapple Press**
300 North St., Meadville, PA 16335.
- Poor Joe's Pennsylvania Almanac. a. ISSN 0362-8523

**Crafts Report**
1529 E. 19th St., Brooklyn, NY 11230.
- Crafts Report. a.

**Craftsman Press, Inc.**
2117 West River Rd. North, Minneapolis, MN 55411.
- Architecture Minnesota. bi-m. (Minnesota Society of Architects)
- Northern Architecture. bi-m.
- Northwest Dentistry. bi-m. (Minnesota Dental Association) (Co-sponsors: North Dakota Dental Association, South Dakota Dental Society)
- Twin City Tool and Die Journal. m.

**Crain Automotive Group Inc.**
(Subsidiary of: Crain Communications, Inc.)
965 E. Jefferson Ave., Detroit, MI 48207.
- Automotive News; engineering, manufacturing, merchandising, servicing. w. ISSN 0005-1551
- Automotive News Market Data Book. a.

**Crain Automotive Group, Inc. (Akron)**
One Cascade Plaza, Suite 1302, Akron, OH 44308
- Rubber & Plastics News; the rubber industry's fortnightly newspaper. fortn. ISSN 0300-6123 (Subscr. to: Circulation Dept., Box 671, Hightstown, NJ 08520)

**Crain Communications Inc.**
740 Rush St., Chicago, IL 60611.
- Advertising Age; the national newspaper of marketing. w. ISSN 0001-8899
- Business Insurance. fortn. ISSN 0007-6864
- Industrial Marketing; newsmonthly of selling and advertising to business, industry and the professions. m. ISSN 0019-8498
- Pensions & Investments. fortn.

**Cranbrook Institute of Science**
Bloomfield Hills, MI 48013.
- Cranbrook Institute of Science, Bloomfield Hills, Michigan. Bulletin. irreg., 1972, no. 55. ISSN 0070-1416

**Crane, Russak & Company, Inc.**
347 Madison Ave., New York, NY 10017.
- Acoustical Imaging and Holography. q.
- Coastal Zone Management Journal; environment, resources and law. q. ISSN 0090-8339
- Energy Sources; an interdisciplinary international journal of science and technology. q. ISSN 0090-8312
- Energy Systems and Policy; an international interdisciplinary journal. q.
- Fiber and Integrated Optics; a journal stressing components, systems, and future trends. q.
- Leisure Sciences; an interdisciplinary journal. q.
- Marine Geotechnology; an international journal of seafloor science and engineering. q. ISSN 0360-8867
- Ocean Development and International Law; the journal of marine affairs. q. ISSN 0090-8320
- Planning Review; a journal for managerial decisionmakers. bi-m. ISSN 0094-064X (North American Society for Corporate Planning (N A S C P))

**Cranial Academy**
1140 W. 8th St., Meridian, ID 83642.
- Cranial Academy Newsletter. q. ISSN 0011-0825

**Crawdaddy Publishing Co., Inc.**
72 Fifth Ave., New York, NY 10011.
- Crawdaddy; magazine of rock. m. ISSN 0011-0833

**Crawford County Genealogical Society of Southeast Kansas**
211 W. Fourth St., Pittsburg, KS 66762.
- Seeker (Pittsburg) q. ISSN 0363-4590

**Creation House**
499 Gunderson Dr., Carol Stream, IL 60187.
- Handbook for Christian Writers. irreg. ISSN 0069-391X (Christian Writers Institute)

**Creation Research Society**
2717 Cranbrook Rd., Ann Arbor, MI 48104.
- Creation Research Society Quarterly. q. ISSN 0092-9166

**Creative Computing**
Box 789-M, Morristown, NJ 07412.
- Creative Computing. bi-m.

**Creative Education**
Box 227, Mankato, MN 56001.
- Insports. 4 per yr.

**Creative Education Foundation, Inc.**
State University College, 1300 Elmwood Ave, Buffalo, NY 14222.
- Journal of Creative Behavior. q. ISSN 0022-0175

**Creative Research Group, Inc.**
50 E. Palisade Ave., Englewood, NJ 07631.
- North Jersey Business Review. s-m. ISSN 0029-2842

**Creativity in Action**
29 Wren Drive, Box 272, Roslyn, NY 11576.
- Creativity in Action. m. ISSN 0093-5263

**Credences Press**
150 South Mantua St., Kent, OH 44240.
- Credences. 3 per yr.

**Credit Union Information Service**
see under **National Institute for Public Services**

**Credit Union National Association, Inc.**
Box 431, Madison, WI 53701.
- Credit Union Executive; for active leaders and managers of credit unions. q. ISSN 0011-1058 (prep. by its Communications Division)
- Credit Union Magazine; for credit union leaders, managers and employees. m. ISSN 0011-1066 (prep. by its Magazines Department)
- Credit Union National Association. Research Division. Research Bulletin. m.
- Credit Union Yearbook. a. ISSN 0074-4468

**Creem**
187 S. Woodward Ave., Birmingham, MI 48011.
- Creem. m. ISSN 0011-1147

**Creighton University**
2500 California St., Omaha, NE 68178.
- Alumnews. 8 per yr.

**Creighton University. Creighton Law School**
2400 California St., Omaha, NE 68178.
- Creighton Law Review. q. ISSN 0011-1155

**Cremation Association of North America**
15300 Ventura Blvd, Suite 305, Sherman Oaks, CA 91403.
- Cremationist of North America. q.

**Cricket**
Box 663, Newark, NJ 07101.
- Cricket. bi-m. ISSN 0011-1244

**Cricket Letter, Inc.**
Box 527, Ardmore, PA 19003.
- Cricket Letter. m.

**Crime and Justice Foundation**
31 St. James Ave., Rm. 348, Boston, MA 02116.
- Perspective. q.

**Crimmer's**
104 E. 40th St., Room 114, New York, NY 10014.
- Crimmer's. 3 per yr.

**Crisis Publishing Co.**
1790 Broadway, New York, NY 10019.
- Crisis (New York) m.(bi-m. June-July; Aug- Sept) ISSN 0011-1422 (National Association for the Advancement of Colored People)

**Criswell's Publications**
Citra, FL 32627.
- Bank Note Reporter. m.

**Criterion Press, Inc.**
2201 S. University Blvd., Denver, CO 80210.
- Iliff Review. 3 per yr. ISSN 0019-1795 (Iliff School of Theology)

**Critical Digest**
Room 918, 225 W. 34th St., New York, NY 10001.
- Critical Digest. fortn. ISSN 0045-9070

**Critique**
417 Convent Avenue, New York, NY 10031.
- Critique; a review of entertainment. q.

**Croatian Academy of America, Inc.**
Box 1767 Grand Central Station, New York, NY 10017.
- Journal of Croatian Studies; annual review of the Croatian Academy of America. a. ISSN 0075-4218

**Croatian Center Association**
- Danica. (pub. by Croatian Franciscan Press)

**Croatian Franciscan Fathers**
- Hrvatski Katolicki Glasnik. (pub. by Croatian Franciscan Press)

**Croatian Franciscan Press**
4851 Drexel Blvd., Chicago, IL 60615.
- Danica; hrvatski tjednik. w (Croatian Center Association)
- Hrvatski Katolicki Glasnik; mjesecnik za duhovnu izgradnju iseljenih Hrvata. m. ISSN 0018-6910 (Croatian Franciscan Fathers)

**Croatian Fraternal Union of America**
100 Delaney Dr., Pittsburgh, PA 15235.
- Zajednicar. w.

**Croatian Information Service**
P.O. Box 3025, Arcadia, CA 91006.
- American Croat/Americki Hrvat. (pub. by Peter Radielovic, Ed. & Pub.)
- Croatian Information Series. irreg. (2-3 per yr)

**Croatian Philatelic Society**
1512 Lancelot Rd., Borger, TX 79007.
- Trumpeter. q.

**Croft-N E I Publications**
24 Rope Ferry Road, Waterford, CT 06385.
- Curriculum Letter. m (10 per yr.)
- Custodian's Letter. m.(10 per yr.) ISSN 0011-4103
- Discipline and Control Update. m.
- Education Summary; bi-weekly analysis of new developments, trends, ideas and research in education. fortn. ISSN 0013-1520
- Educational Secretary. m.
- Learning Disabilities Guide. 9 per yr.
- Operational Briefing. m.
- Principal's Letters. m.
- Professional Reports. 9 per yr.
- Reading Letter. s-m.

**Croner Publications, Inc.**
211-05 Jamaica Ave., Queens Village, NY 11428.
- American Trade Schools Directory. m. ISSN 0517-564X
- Croner's Reference Book for World Traders. m.
- Narcotics and Drug Abuse A-Z. q. ISSN 0094-3991
- Trade Directories of the World. m. ISSN 0564-0482

**Crop Science Society of America**
American Society of Agronomy, 677 S. Segoe Rd., Madison, WI 53711.
- C S S A Special Publication. irreg., 1971, no. 2. ISSN 0070-1637
- Crop Science. bi-m. ISSN 0011-183X

**CROP, the Community Hunger Appeal of Church World Service**
Box 968, Elkhart, IN 46514.
- Service News. m.(6 per yr.) ISSN 0037-2617

**R. B. Cross Co.**
103 So. Howard St., Oxford, IN 47971
(Dist. by Grant C. Vietsch, 181 East Lake Shore Drive, Chicago Ill., 60611)
- Transportation Research Forum. Proceedings: Annual Meeting. a. ISSN 0091-2468 (Transportation Research Forum)

**Cross Country Press**
Box 21081, Woodhaven, NY 11421.
- Cross Country; magazine of Canadian-U.S. poetry. 3 per yr. ISSN 0318-6075

**Crosscut Saw Unltd.**
1806 Bonita, Berkeley, CA 94709.
- Ball Occasional. irreg.

**Crover Family**
c/o Willard R. Berry, Editor, 609 Spruce Ave., Tillamook, OR 97141.
- Crover Family. q.

**C. C. Crow Publications, Inc.**
Terminal Sales Bldg., Terminal, Sales Building, Portland, OR 97205.
- Crow's Buyer's & Seller's Guide of the Forest Products Industries. a.
- Crow's Forest Products Digest. m. ISSN 0011-2070
- Crow's Plywood Guide. a.

**Nelson R. Crow Publications**
P.O. Drawer 17F, Denver, CO 80217.
- Western Livestock Journal. m. & w. ISSN 0043-387X

**Thomas Y. Crowell Co.**
(Subsidiary of: Dun- Donnelley Publishing Corp.) 666 Fifth Ave., New York, NY 10019.
- Dun & Bradstreet's Guide to Your Investments. irreg. ISSN 0098-2466
- Minnesota Symposia on Child Psychology. a. ISSN 0076-9266 (University of Minnesota. Institute of Child Development)
- New African Literature and the Arts. irreg., vol. 3, 1973. ISSN 0077-7994
- Problem Studies in American History. irreg.
- Selected Studies in Social Problems. irreg.

**Crown-Freed Publishing Co.**
P.O. Box 2338, 6931 Van Nuys Blvd., Van Nuys, CA 91405.
- Motorcycle Product News. m.
- Motorcycle Product News Trade Directory. a.

**Crown Point Foundation**
Box 1977, New York, NY 10017.
- Crown Point Foundation News. s-a.

**Crown Point Press**
1555 San Pablo Ave., Oakland, CA 94612.
- Vision. 3 per yr.

**Crown Publishers, Inc.**
One Park Ave., New York, NY 10016.
- Art of the World Library. irreg.
- Dance World. a. ISSN 0070-2692
- John Gassner's Best American Plays. irreg.
- Screen World. a. ISSN 0080-8288
- Theatre World. a. ISSN 0082-3856

**Cruising World Publications**
524 Thames St., Newport, RI 02840.
- Cruising World. m. ISSN 0098-3519

**Crusade for Justice**
1567 Downing St., Denver, CO 80218.
- Gallo; la voz de la justicia. s-m. ISSN 0016-4151

**Cruzada Spanish Publications**
Box 650909, Miami, FL 33165.
- Spanish Today. 5 per yr. ISSN 0049-1802

**Cryonics Society of Michigan**
24041 Stratford, Oak Park, MI 48237.
- Outlook. m.

**Crystal Record Co.**
Box 65661, Los Angeles, CA 90065.
- Composium Directory of New Music. a.

**Cuba Resource Center**
Box 206, Cathedral Sta., New York, NY 10025.
- Cuba Review. 4 per yr.

**Cudahy Publishing Co.**
6141 Cicero Ave., Chicago, IL 60645.
- Insurance Buyer's Guide. m. ISSN 0020-4641

**Cue Publishing Co.**
545 Madison Ave., New York, NY 10022.
- Cue; the weekly entertainment guide to the New York area. w. ISSN 0011-2658

**Culinary Alliance, Local 681 and Bartenders, Local 686**
Box 811, Long Beach, CA 90801.
- Serving America; hotel, bar, restaurant news. bi-m. ISSN 0037-2749

**Culinary Institute of America**
North Rd., Hyde Park, New York, NY 12538.
- C I A-Taste. q.

**Culinary Reviews Inc.**
441 Lexington Ave., Suite 1007, New York, NY 10017.
- Chef Institutional. 8 per yr.

**Cultural Activist**
c/o Broms, 219 W. 81st St., New York, NY 10024.
- Cultural Activist. irreg.

**Cultural Correspondence**
c/o Dorrwar Bookstore, 224 Thayer St., Providence, RI 02906.
- Cultural Correspondence. q.

**Cultural Motivation Publications Inc.**
5906 Grove St., Oakland, CA 94607.
- Syndrome. bi-m. ISSN 0039-7806

**Culver Press**
Culver, IN 46511.
- American Landrace. bi-m. ISSN 0002-970X (American Landrace Association)

**Culver-Stockton College**
Canton, MO 63435.
- Megaphone (Canton) fortn. ISSN 0025-8687

**Cumberland and Coles Genealogical Society**
R.R. 1 Box 141, Toledo, IL 62468.
- Cumberland and Coles Genealogical Society. Quarterly. q.

**Cumberland Presbyterian Church**
Office of the General Assembly, 1978 Union Ave., Box 4149, Memphis, TN 38104.
- Cumberland Presbyterian. fortn. ISSN 0011-2976

**Cummins Publishing Co.**
21590 Greenfield Rd., Oak Park, MI 48237.
- Automotive Design & Development. m.
- Excavating Contractor. m. ISSN 0014-3995

**Cumulative Stock Profits Advisor**
Box 246, Forest Hills, NY 11375.
- Cumulative Stock Profits. fortn. ISSN 0011-3026

**Cumulus Corp.**
Box 8308, Atlanta, GA 30306.
- Southern Wings. m. ISSN 0038-464X

**Current History, Inc.**
4225 Main St., Philadelphia, PA 19127.
- Current History; the monthly magazine of world affairs. 10 per yr. ISSN 0011-3530

**Current Podiatry Publications**
Box 7156, Ocala, FL 32670.
- Current Podiatry; a digest for the podiatrist. m. ISSN 0011-3824

**Current World Leaders**
Box 2238, Pasadena, CA 91105.
- Almanac of Current World Leaders. triennially. ISSN 0002-6255
- Current World Leaders-Biography and News. m. ISSN 0002-6263
- Current World Leaders-Speeches, Reports and Position Papers. 3 per yr.

**Currents Information Systems, Inc**
Box 3861, Rochester, NY 14610.
- Dental Currents. s-m. ISSN 0045-9925
- Practical Public Relations. s-m. ISSN 0048-5098
- Staff Currents. s-m.

**Curriculum Advisory Service**
500 S. Clinton St., Chicago, IL 60607.
- Curriculum Review. 5 per yr.

**Curriculum Innovations, Inc.**
501 Lake Forest Ave., Highwood, IL 60040.
- Career World. m (during school year) ISSN 0361-8994
- Current Health. m (Sept-May)

**Currituck County Historical Society**
Jarisburg, NC 27947.
- Currituck County Historical Society. Journal. a. ISSN 0091-9640

**Curtis Guild & Co. Publishers, Inc.**
88 Broad St., Boston, MA 02110.
- Commercial Bulletin. w. ISSN 0010-2911

**Curtis International Ltd.**
1100 Waterway Blvd., Indianapolis, IN 46202.
- Demolition Age. bi-m. (National Association of Demolition Contractors)

- Design; the magazine of creative art, for teachers, artists & craftsmen. bi-m.(Sept-June) ISSN 0011-9253

**Curtis Publishing Co.**
1100 Waterway Blvd., Indianapolis, IN 46202.
- A P A Holiday. 6 per yr. (Airline Passengers Association)
- Country Gentleman. q.
- Indiana Business and Industry. m. ISSN 0019-6533
- Jack and Jill Magazine (Inkprint Edition) (pub. by Saturday Evening Post Company)

**Curwood Collector Society**
1825 Osaukie Road, Owosso, MI 48867.
- Curwood Collector. q.

**Elliott L. Cushman**
2214 N. Central, Phoenix, AZ 85004.
- Arizona Farmer-Ranchman. m. ISSN 0004-1491

**Stephen P. Cushman**
770 B St., Suite 417, San Diego, CA 92101.
- Today in Anaheim/Orange County. s-m. ISSN 0040-8409
- Today in San Diego. s-m. ISSN 0040-8433

**Cushman Foundation for Foraminiferal Research**
E501 U.S. National Museum, Washington, DC 20560.
- Cushman Foundation for Foraminiferal Research. Special Publication. irreg., no. 14, 1976. ISSN 0070-2242
- Journal of Foraminiferal Research. q.

**Custom Tailors and Designers Association of America, Inc.**
400 Madison Ave., New York, NY 10017.
- Custom Tailor. 3 per yr. ISSN 0011-412X

**Customart Press, Inc.**
525 North Barry Avenue, Mamaroneck, NY 10543.
- Personals. m.

**Cutler-Hammer, Inc.**
4201 27th St, Milwaukee, WI 53216.
- Cutler-Hammer Record. q. ISSN 0011-4170

**Cutler Publications, Inc.**
Box 2258, Colorado Springs, CO 80901.
- Leviathan and Kinnikinnik; a journal of politics and the arts. m. (Oct.-May) ISSN 0360-1765

**Cuyahoga County Regional Planning Commission**
415 the Arcade, Cleveland, OH 44114.
- R P C Data File. m.

**Cycle News, Inc.**
Box 2610, 2499 Cerritos Ave., Long Beach, CA 90801.
- Biker. bi-w.
- Cycle News-Central Edition. w.
- Cycle News-Dixie Edition. bi-w.

**Cycle World Magazine**
P.O. Box 1757, Newport Beach, CA 92663.
- Cycle World Road Test Annual. a.

**Cycling Press, Inc.**
461 8th Ave., New York, NY 10001.
- American Bicyclist & Motorcyclist. m. ISSN 0002-7677

**Cyclotron Trading Services**
Box 19295, Houston, TX 77024.
- Cyclotron Trading Services. w. ISSN 0011-4367

**Cymbidium Society of America, Inc.**
c/o James L. Burkey, Ed., 1250 Orchid Dr., Santa Barbara, CA 93111.
- Orchid Advocate. bi-m. ISSN 0097-9546

**Cystic Fibrosis Foundation**
3379 Peachtree Rd. N.E., Atlanta, GA 30326.
- Cystic Fibrosis. Quarterly Annotated References. q. ISSN 0011-4510
- Cystic Fibrosis: A Bibliography. irreg., latest issue 1975. ISSN 0070-2447
- Cystic Fibrosis Club Abstracts. a. ISSN 0070-2455
- National C F News Bulletin. (Cystic Fibrosis) q. ISSN 0047-8822

**Czechoslovak Publishing Co.**
Box 38, West, TX 76691.
- Hospodar. s-m. ISSN 0018-599X

**Czechoslovak Society of Arts and Sciences in America, Inc.**
Box 1614, Long Island City, NY 11101
- Promeny/Metamorphoses. q. ISSN 0033-1058 (Editorial Address:, 3523 Oxford Ave., Montreal, H4A 2X9, Canada)
- S V U. Zpravy. m(10 per yr) ISSN 0036-2050 (Editorial Address:, 6420 Birch Leaf Ct., Burke, VA 22015)

**D.A.T.A., Inc.**
45 U.S. Hwy. 46, Pine Brook, NJ 07050.
- D A T A Book of Discontinued Semiconductor Diodes. a.
- D.A.T.A. Book of Discontinued Thyristors. a. ISSN 0092-508X
- D A T A Book of Discontinued Transistors. a. ISSN 0070-2498
- Linear Integrated Circuit D.A.T.A. Book. s-a. ISSN 0024-3809
- Microwave Tube D.A.T.A. Book. s-a. ISSN 0026-2900
- Power Semiconductors. s-a. ISSN 0095-4225
- Relay D.A.T.A.Book. every 18 months.
- Semiconductor Application Notes D.A.T.A Book. s-a. ISSN 0090-3655
- Semiconductor Diode D.A.T.A. Book. s-a. ISSN 0091-9675
- Semiconductor Heat Sink, Socket & Associated Hardware D.A.T.A. Book. a. ISSN 0092-6302
- Thyristor D.A.T.A. Book. s-a.
- Transistor D.A.T.A. Book. s-a. ISSN 0041-1159

**D.A.Y. Association**
2 Talcott Rd., Suite 6, Park Ridge, IL 60068.
- D. A. Y./Dialysis and You. q.

**D. C. Gazette**
1739 Connecticut Ave. N.W., Washington, DC 20009.
- D. C. Gazette. m. ISSN 0011-7153

**D. H. Lawrence Review**
Box 2474, Fayetteville, AR 72701.
- D. H. Lawrence Review. 3 per yr. ISSN 0011-4936

**D. J. H., Publishers**
G.P.O. Box 2121, New York, NY 10001.
- Dasein; the quarterly review. q. ISSN 0011-6807

**D K S Publications**
Box 1778, Fargo, ND 58102.
- Coin Collector Reporter. m.

**D. L. Blair Corp.**
185 Great Neck Rd., Great Neck, L.I., NY 11021.
- National Promotion Audit. m. ISSN 0043-1907

**D M S Inc.**
100 Northfield St., Greenwich, CT 06830.
- Deadline Data on World Affairs. w. ISSN 0011-5061

**D N A-People's Legal Services, Inc.**
P.O. Box 306, Window Rock, AZ 86515.
- D N A Newsletter. bi-m.

**D S N Publications, Inc.**
P.O. Box 6, Mountain View, CA 94042.
- Daytime Serial Newsletter. m.

**Da Capo Press, Inc.**
227 W. 17 St., New York, NY 10011.
- American Constitutional and Legal History. irreg.

**Dacotah Territory - Territorial Press**
Box 775, Moorhead, MN 56560.
- Dacotah Territory; a magazine of poetry and comment. 2 per yr. ISSN 0084-9529

**Dadant & Sons, Inc.**
Hamilton, IL 62341.
- American Bee Journal. m. ISSN 0002-7626

**Dadazine**
1183 Church St., San Francisco, CA 94114.
- Dadazine. 2-3 per yr.

**Daily Variety Ltd.**
1400 N. Cahuenga Blvd., Hollywood, CA 90028.
- Daily Variety. 5 per w. ISSN 0011-5509

**Dairy Editorial Services, Inc.**
146 Mill St., Columbus, WI 53925.
- Modern Milk Hauler. m. ISSN 0026-8135

**Dairy Farmers Inc.**
Box 7775, Orlando, FL 32804.
- Southeastern Dairy Review. m. ISSN 0038-3643

**Dairy Goat Journal Publishing Corp.**
c/o Kent Leach, Ed., Box 1908, Scottsdale, AZ 85252.
- Dairy Goat Journal. m. ISSN 0011-5592

**Dairy Research Inc.**
6300 N. River Rd., Rosemont, IL 60018.
- Dairy Research Digest. m. (Co-sponsor: United Dairy Industry Association)

**Dairy Society International**
3008 McKinley St. N.W., Washington, DC 20015.
- Market Frontier News. bi-m. ISSN 0025-3553

**Dairylea Cooperative, Inc.**
One Blue Hill Plaza, Pearl River, NY 10965.
- Dairynews. s-m. ISSN 0011-5738

**Daisy Publishing Co. , Inc**
429 Boren Ave. N., Seattle, WA 98109.
- Little Black Book; annual directory of ceramic mold manufacturers in the United States. a.

**Dakota-North Plains Corp.**
1216 S. Main St, Aberdeen, SD 57401.
- Dakota Farmer. m. ISSN 0011-5789

**Dale Corporation**
36341 Gregory Drive, Sterling Heights, MI 48077.
- Georgia F O P News. q. (Georgia State Lodge Fraternal Order of Police)
- Michigan Corrections Association Report. a. ISSN 0026-2099 (Michigan Corrections Association)
- Peace Officer. q. ISSN 0031-3556 (Michigan Fraternal Order of Police)

**Dallas Chamber of Commerce**
1507 Pacific Ave., Dallas, TX 75201.
- Dallas. m. ISSN 0011-5835

**Dallas County Medical Society**
3630 Noble Ave., Dallas, TX 75204.
- Dallas Medical Journal. m. ISSN 0011-586X

**Dallas Fashion Retailer**
59421 Apparel Mart, Dallas, TX 75207.
- Dallas Fashion Retailer. 9 per yr.

**Dallas Southwest Media Corp.**
2902 Carlisle, Dallas, TX 75204.
- D Magazine. m.

**Dallas Theological Seminary**
3909 Swiss Ave., Dallas, TX 75204.
- Bibliotheca Sacra; a theological quarterly. q. ISSN 0006-1921

**Damascus Road**
c/o C. S. Hanna, 6271 Hill Dr., Wacosville, PA 18106.
- Damascus Road. irreg.

**Damon Runyon Walter Winchell Cancer Fund**
33 W. 56th St., New York, NY 10019.
- Damon Runyon-Walter Winchell Cancer Fund. Annual Report. a. ISSN 0095-6775

**Dana Chase Publications, Inc.**
York St., At Park Ave., Elmhurst, IL 60126.
- Appliance. m. ISSN 0003-6781

**Dana College**
Blair, NE 68008.
- Dana Review. 4 per yr.

**Dana Corp.**
Box 500, Hagerstown, IN 47346.
- Magic Circle. q.

**Danad Publishing Co.**
10 Columbus Circle, New York, NY 10019.
- After Dark; the magazine of entertainment. m. ISSN 0002-0702
- Dance. m. ISSN 0011-6009
- Dance Magazine Annual; catalogue of dance artists and attractions, programs, resources and services. a. ISSN 0070-2684

**Dance Films Association, Inc.**
250 W. 57th St., Rm. 2201, New York, NY 10019.
- Dance Films Association & Dance Society Newsletter. 10 per yr. ISSN 0011-5991

**Dance Herald**
Box 686, Ansonia Station, New York, NY 10023.
- Dance Herald; journal of black dance. q.

**Dance Life in New York**
Box 1236, Stuyvesant Sta., New York, NY 10009.
- Dance Life in New York. q. ISSN 0361-5685

**Danforth Foundation**
222 S. Central Ave., St. Louis, MO 63105.
- Danforth Foundation. Annual Report. a. ISSN 0070-2706
- Danforth News and Notes. 2 per yr. ISSN 0084-9553
- Directory of Fellowships for Graduate Study. biennial.

**Daniel Clark Foundation**
Box 65, Goffstown, NH 03045.
- Studio Potter. s-a. ISSN 0091-6641

**Daniels Business Services, Inc.**
15 Rankin Ave., Box 40, Asheville, NC 28802.
- This Week. w. ISSN 0040-6309

**Danish Brotherhood in America**
3717 Harney St., Box 31748, Omaha, NE 68131.
- American Dane. m.

**Danish Consulate General**
Danish Information Office, 280 Park Ave., New York, NY 10017.
- Study in Denmark. a.

**William O. Dannhausen**
333 N. Michigan Ave., Chicago, IL 60601.
- Better Roads. m. ISSN 0006-0208
- Gas Industries; the management magazine of gas energy transmission distribution. m. ISSN 0016-4933 (Co-Publisher: Paul Lady)

**Danubian Press**
Astor Park, FL 32002.
- Problems behind the Iron Curtain Series. irreg., no. 9, 1976. ISSN 0079-5704

**Daran, Inc.**
Box 315, Flagstaff, AZ 86002.
- Huerfano. 2 per yr.

**Dardanell Publications, Inc.**
610 Beatty Rd., Monroeville, PA 15146.
- Pennsylvania's Outdoor People. (Pennsylvania Federation of Sportsmen's Clubs)

**Dark Horse Poets Co-Op**
47 Stearns St., Cambridge, MA 02138.
- Dark Horse. q.

**Dark Tower**
University Center Room 7, Cleveland State University, Cleveland, OH 44115.
- Dark Tower. s-a.

**Darlex Corp.**
727 N. Milwaukee St., Milwaukee, WI 53202.
- Podium Review. m.

**Dartmouth College. Department of Classics**
Hanover, NH 03755.
- Calculi. bi-m. ISSN 0008-0632

**Dartmouth College. Department of Geography**
Hanover, NH 03755.
- Geography Publications at Dartmouth. a. ISSN 0418-3975

**Dartmouth College. Library**
Hanover, NH 03755.
- Dartmouth College Library Bulletin. s-a. ISSN 0011-6750
- Polar Notes; an occasional publication of the Stefansson Collection. a. ISSN 0079-2918

**Dartnell Corp.**
4660 Ravenswood Ave., Chicago, IL 60640.
- Dartnell Economic Review. q.
- Dartnell Office Adminstration Service. m. ISSN 0011-6769
- Dartnell Sales and Marketing Service. m. ISSN 0011-6777
- From Nine to Five; or thereabouts. s-m. ISSN 0016-1616
- Supervisor's Production Planner; monthly pocket guide to better leadership and supervision. m.

**Daskalakis Publishing**
1112 East Elm Street, Wheaton, IL 60187.
- Pilgrimage; monthly magazine for Greeks everywhere.

**Data and Research Technology Corp.**
1102 McNeilly Ave., Box 96007, Pittsburgh, PA 15216.
- Law Enforcement Expert. m.

**Data Courier, Inc.**
620 S. Fifth St., Louisville, KY 40202.
- Biology Digest. (pub. by Plexus Publishing, Inc.)
- Current Programs. m. ISSN 0300-6956 (World Meetings Information Center Inc.)
- Current Programs. Annual Index. a. (World Meetings Information Center, Inc.)
- I S M E C Bulletin. s-m.
- Oceanic Abstracts. 6 per yr. ISSN 0093-6901
- Pharmaceutical News Index. m.
- Pollution Abstracts. 6 per yr. ISSN 0032-3624

**Data Processing Digest, Inc.**
c/o Margaret Milligan, Ed., 6820 La Tijera Blvd., Los Angeles, CA 90045.
- Data Processing Digest. m. ISSN 0011-6858

**Data Processing Horizons**
P.O.B. 4123, Diamond Bar, CA 91765.
- Directory of Data Processing Education. a. ISSN 0069-8113

**Data Processing Management Association**
505 Busse Highway, Park Ridge, IL 60068.
- Data Management. m. ISSN 0022-0329
- International Data Processing Conference. Proceedings. a.

**Data Resources, Inc.**
29 Hartwell Ave., Lexington, MA 02173.
- D R I European Review. irreg. ISSN 0362-4730
- Data Resources Review. m. ISSN 0092-5462
- Data Resources U.S. Long-Term Bulletin. q. ISSN 0362-6199

**Data Use and Access Laboratories**
1601 N. Kent St., Suite 900, Arlington, VA 22209.
- Data Access News. 6-8 per yr.
- Review of Public Data Use. bi-m. ISSN 0092-2846 (Order from: National Technical Information Service, 5285 Port Royal Rd., Springfield, VA 22161)

**Dataflow Systems Inc.**
Academic Information Methods, 7758 Wisconsin Ave., Bethesda, MD 20014.
- Infact. q. ISSN 0073-5639

**Datapro Research Corp.**
1805 Underwood Blvd., Delran, NJ 08075.
- Datapro Newscom. m.
- Datapro Seventy; EDP buyers bible. m. ISSN 0045-9704

**Daughters of American Colonists, National Society. Genealogical Dept.**
2250 S. Arlington Ave., Reno, NV 89502.
- Colonial Courier. q. ISSN 0010-1435

**Daughters of Bilitis**
1005 Market, No. 404, San Francisco, CA 94103.
- Sisters. bi-m. ISSN 0049-0644

**Dauntless Books, Inc.**
1120 Ave. of the Americas, New York, NY 10036.
- Confidential Confessions. bi-m. ISSN 0010-5651
- Revealing Romances. m. ISSN 0034-6268
- Secrets. m. ISSN 0037-0649

**Vince Davella**
140 E. Marthart, Havertown, PA 19083 (Subscr. to: Box 242, Wallingford, PA 19086)
- Delaware County Pharmacist. (Delaware County Pharmaceutical Association)

**Dave's Friends**
Rt. 5, Box 236, Arcadia, FL 33821.
- Dave's Friends. m.

**Dave's Printers Publishers**
Box 1431, Sparks, NV 89431.
- Nevada Historical Review. q.

**David and Charles, Inc.**
North Pomfret, VT 05053.
- Wildlife International Series. irreg.
- World Realities Series. irreg.

**David C. Cook Foundation**
- Interlit. (pub. by David C. Cook Publishing Co.)

**Jonathan David Co., Inc.**
68-22 Eliot Ave., Middle Village, NY 11379.
- Best Jewish Sermons. biennial. ISSN 0409-2570

**David Douglas High School**
1500 S.E. 130 Ave., Portland, OR 97233.
- Crosstown Bus. ISSN 0084-9464

**Donald Davidson**
Box 24121, Speedway, IN 46224.
- Donald Davidson's Indianapolis Five Hundred Mile Race Annual. a.

**Davidson College**
Box 696, Davidson, NC 28036.
- Miscellany; a Davidson review. s-a. ISSN 0026-590X

**Robert Davies and John Gogol, Eds. & Pubs.**
Pacific University, Box 627, Forest Grove, OR 97116.
- Mr. Cogito. 3 per yr.

**Davies Publishing Co.**
645 N. Michigan Ave., Chicago, IL 60611.
- Meat Processing. m. ISSN 0025-6390

**F. A. Davis Co.**
1915 Arch St., Philadelphia, PA 19103.
- Cardiovascular Clinics. irreg., vol. 8, 1977. ISSN 0069-0384
- Clinical Anesthesia. irreg., vol. 11, no. 2, 1976. ISSN 0009-9112
- Complete Desk Reference of Veterinary Pharmaceuticals & Biologicals. a. ISSN 0098-4744
- Contemporary Neurology Series. irreg., vol. 18 in prep. ISSN 0069-9446
- Health Care Dimensions. s-a.

**Nord Davis, Jr., Ed. & Pub.**
Box 48, Holli, NH 03049.
- Pardon Me, But. irreg. ISSN 0085-4751

**Walter D. Davis**
Box 5195, Jackson, MS 39216.
- New pulpit digest. bi-m. ISSN 0033-4146

**Davis Publications, Inc.**
229 Park Ave., South, New York, NY 10003.
- Alfred Hitchcock's Mystery Magazine. m. ISSN 0002-5224
- Audio Digest. a.
- Backpacking Journal. q.
- Boat Builder. s-a.
- Budget Guide to Car Repair. a. ISSN 0360-1110
- C B Yearbook; guide to citizens band radio. a.
- Camping Journal. 8 per yr.
- Car-Puter's Autofacts. Used Car Prices. irreg. ISSN 0094-8527
- Car Repair & Maintenance Guide. a.
- Communications World. s-a. ISSN 0095-4063
- Electrical Installation & Repair Projects. a. ISSN 0095-084X
- Electronics Hobbyist. s-a. ISSN 0424-8384
- Electronics Theory Handbook. a.
- Elementary Electronics. bi-m. ISSN 0013-595X
- Ellery Queen's Anthology. s-a. ISSN 0013-6301
- Ellery Queen's Mystery Magazine. m. ISSN 0013-6328
- Hi-Fi Stereo Buyers' Guide; a consumers' publication on high fidelity/audio products. 6 per yr. ISSN 0018-1218
- How to Restore, Finish, and Build Furniture; a Science & Mechanics annual. a. ISSN 0095-0904
- Hunting Guide. a. ISSN 0073-4101
- Income Opportunities. 14 per yr. ISSN 0019-3429
- Isaac Asimov's Science Fiction Magazine. q.
- Kitchen & Bath Improvements. a.
- New Car Yearbook; a Science & Mechanics annual. a.
- One Hundred and One Electronics Projects; for under $15. a.
- One Thousand and One How-to Ideas. s-a. ISSN 0078-4613
- Today's Homes. q.
- Woodworker Projects & Techniques. a.
- 20 Wood Projects for Under 50 Dollars. a.
- 101 Home Plans. q.
- 110 Better Building Plans. q.

**Davis Publishing Co.**
250 Potrero St., Santa Cruz, CA 95060.
- Fire Protection Handbook Study Guide. irreg., latest 1976. ISSN 0071-5425
- Fire Yearbook. a. ISSN 0071-5468

- Police Yearbook. a. ISSN 0079-2950

**Davison Publishing Co.**
P.O. Box 477, Ridgewood, NJ 07451.
- Davison's Knit Goods Trade. a. ISSN 0070-2943
- Davison's Salesman's Book. a.
- Davison's Textile Blue Book. a. ISSN 0070-2951
- Davison's Textile Catalog and Buyer's Guide. a. ISSN 0070-296X

**Daw Books, Inc.**
1301 Ave. of the Americas, New York, NY 10019.
- Annual World's Best SF. a.

**Dawis**
Box 524, Northport, NY 11768.
- Dawis Investment Service. w.

**Dawn Enterprises**
Box 90913, Worldway Postal Center, Los Angeles, CA 90009.
- Free Market. every 6 wks. ISSN 0046-5003
- Libertarian Connection. every 6 wks. ISSN 0024-2012

**Dawn Publications,Inc.**
99 Park Ave., New York, NY 10016.
- New Dawn. bi-m.

**Dawson's Book Shop**
535 N. Larchmont Blvd, Los Angeles, CA 90004.
- Baja California Travel Series. irreg., vol. 35, 1974. ISSN 0067-2955

**John Day**
c/o Conklin Book Center, Inc., Box 5555, Binghamton, NY 13902.
- World of Archaeology (Binghamton) irreg., latest 1974.

**Day to Remember**
Box 15468, Lakewood, CO 80215.
- Day to Remember. q. ISSN 0011-7099

**Daynard & Van Thunen Co., Inc.**
125 Maiden Lane, New York, NY 10038.
- Trends in Adjusting. bi-m. ISSN 0041-2384

**Dayton & Montgomery County Public Library**
215 E. Third St., Dayton, OH 45402.
- B I T S/Business Industry Technology Service. m.(except July & Aug.) ISSN 0005-318X
- This Month in Your Library. m.(Sept.-June) ISSN 0040-6252

**Dayton & Montgomery County Public Library. Staff Association**
111 W. First St., Suite 200, Dayton, OH 45402.
- Dayton USA. bi-m. ISSN 0011-7137
- Dial. m.(Sept-June) ISSN 0012-1991

**Dayton Art Institute**
Box 941, Dayton, OH 45401.
- Dayton Art Institute. Annual Report. a. ISSN 0070-3028
- Dayton Art Institute Bulletin. s-a.

**De Camp Publishing Co.**
Gaffney, SC 29340.
- Grit and Steel. m. ISSN 0017-4297

**Maria-Luisa De la Casa, Ed. & Pub.**
2600 Walker Lane, Salt Lake City, UT 84117.
- Revista Iberica. irreg. (2-4 per yr.) ISSN 0482-6558

**De Paul University. College of Law**
25 E. Jackson Blvd., Chicago, IL 60604.
- Annual Survey of Illinois Law. a.
- De Paul Law Review. q. ISSN 0011-7188

**De Young Press**
748 Missouri Ave., Box 43, Mercedes, TX 78570.
- Crucible and Scientific Atheist. bi-m.

**Deafness, Speech and Hearing Publications,Inc.**
Gallaudet College, Washington, DC 20002.
- D S H Abstracts. q. ISSN 0011-5150 (American Speech and Hearing Association)

**Dean Enterprises Inc.**
5100 Edina Industrial Blvd., Edina, MN 55435.
- Seed Trade News. 40 per yr. ISSN 0037-0789

**Debell & Richardson**
20 Water St., Enfield, CT 06082.
- End-Use Markets for Plastics. m. ISSN 0013-7154

**Decalogue Society of Lawyers**
180 W. Washington St., Chicago, IL 60602.
- Decalogue Journal. q. ISSN 0011-7250

**December**
c/o Curt L. Johnson, Ed., 4343 N. Clarendon, Chicago, IL 60613.
- December; a magazine of the arts and opinion. irreg. ISSN 0070-3141

**Deciduous**
4208-1/2 Whitman Ave., Cleveland, OH 44113.
- Everyman. irreg. (approx. 1 per yr.) ISSN 0094-2367

**Dee Publishing Co.**
P.O. Box 9308, North Hollywood, CA 91609.
- Consumer Free Publicity. a.

**Deer Sportsman of America, Inc.**
Box 142, Marlinton, WV 24954.
- Deer Sportsman. bi-m. ISSN 0362-1952

**Deere & Company**
John Deere Road, Moline, IL 61265.
- Faaran; a journal of popular farm science and rural life. bi-m.
- Furrow; a journal of popular farm science and rural life. 8 per yr. ISSN 0016-3112
- Furrow (Transatlantic Edition); journal of popular farm science and rural life. bi-m.
- Sillon; a journal of popular farm science and rural life. bi-m.
- Solco; journal of popular farm science and rural life. bi-m.
- Sulco; journal of popular farm science and rural life. bi-m.
- Surco John Deere; journal of popular farm science and rural life. bi-m.
- Surco Latinoamericano; journal of popular farm science and rural life. bi-m.
- Voor; journal of popular farm science and rural life. bi-m.

**Dees Communications**
200 S. Hull St., Montgomery, AL 36104.
- Babe Ruth Baseball's Athletes of the Year. a. ISSN 0097-8124

**Defender Publishing Co., Inc.**
1400 French St., Wilmington, DE 19801.
- Defender (Wilmington) w. ISSN 0011-7498

**Defenders of the American Constitution, Inc.**
Box 1776, Annandale, VA 22003.
- Alert (Annandale) m. ISSN 0002-5194
- Task Force. bi-m. ISSN 0039-9752

**Defense Information School**
Fort Benjamin Harrison, IN 46216.
- Military Media Review. q.

**Defense Research Institute, Inc.**
1100 W. Wells St., Milwaukee, WI 53233.
- For the Defense. m.(Sept-June) ISSN 0015-6884

**Defensor-Chieftain**
202 Manzanares, Scorro, NM 87801.
- Defensor-Chieftain. s-w. ISSN 0011-7633

**Defiance College**
Defiance, OH 43512.
- Defender. w. ISSN 0011-7501

**Deitenbeck Publishing Co., Inc.**
17 S. Lake Ave., Orlando, FL 32801.
- Florida Field Report. s-m. Jan.-June; m. Jul.-Dec. ISSN 0015-4075

**Dekalb Community College**
555 Indian Creek Dr., Clarkston, GA 30021.
- Dekalb Literary Arts Journal. 4 per yr. ISSN 0011-7714

**Dekalb Community College-South. Department of Business Administration**
3251 Panthersville Road, Decatur, GA 30034.
- Dekalb Business and Economic Journal. 3 per yr.

**Dekalb Musicians Supply Co.**
115 Clairmont Ave., Decatur, GA 30030.
- Viol. 5 per yr. ISSN 0363-762X

**Marcel Dekker, Inc.**
270 Madison Ave., New York, NY 10016.
- Advances in Chromatography. irreg. ISSN 0065-2415
- Advances in Holography. irreg. ISSN 0361-2961

- Advances in Probability. irreg., 1971, vol. 3. ISSN 0065-3217
- Analytical Spectroscopy Series. irreg.
- Applied Quantum Chemistry. irreg. ISSN 0066-5525
- Biochemistry of Disease. irreg. ISSN 0067-8678
- Biological Macromolecules Series. irreg., 1970, no. 6. ISSN 0067-8775
- Biomathematics Series. irreg. ISSN 0067-8813
- Books in Library and Information Science. irreg., vol. 14, 1975.
- Books in Soils and the Environment. irreg. ISSN 0081-1890
- Brigham Young University. Center for Thermochemical Studies. Contributions. irreg., no. 66, 1975. ISSN 0572-6921
- Ceramics and Glass Series. ISSN 0069-2239
- Chelates in Analytical Chemistry: A Collection of Monographs. irreg., 1971, vol. 4. ISSN 0069-2867
- Chemistry and Biochemistry of Amino Acids, Peptides, and Proteins. irreg. ISSN 0069-3111
- Chemistry and Physics of Carbon: A Series of Advances. irreg., 1970, vol. 11. ISSN 0069-3138
- Clinical and Biochemical Analysis. irreg. vol. 2, 1975.
- Computers in Chemistry and Instrumentation.
- Electroanalytical Chemistry: A Series of Advances. irreg., 1971, vol. 8. ISSN 0070-9778
- Environmental Health Engineering Series. irreg., 1971, vol. 2. ISSN 0071-0873
- Enzymology Series. irreg.
- Fate of Drugs in the Organism; a Bibliographic Survey. irreg. ISSN 0098-2806 (Societe Francaise des Sciences et Techniques Pharmaceutiques FR)
- Fertilizer Science and Technology Series. irreg. ISSN 0071-4623
- Fiber Science Series. irreg. ISSN 0071-4682
- Food Science Series. irreg., 1971, vol. 3. ISSN 0071-7223
- Hydrogen Series. irreg.
- Ion Exchange: A Series of Advances. irreg., 1969, vol. 6. ISSN 0075-0328
- Ion Exchange and Solvent Extraction. irreg. ISSN 0092-0193
- Kinetics and Mechanisms of Polymerization. irreg., 1972, vol. 3. ISSN 0075-6067
- Lasers: A Series of Advances. irreg; 1971, vol. 3. ISSN 0075-8035
- Lecture Notes in Pure and Applied Mathematics. irreg., 1971, vol. 7. ISSN 0075-8469
- Medicinal Research: A Series of Monographs. irreg., 1968, vol. 6. ISSN 0076-6062
- Membranes: A Series of Advances. irreg. ISSN 0076-6356
- Methods in Free-Radical Chemistry. irreg., 1971, vol. 4. ISSN 0076-6887
- Methods in Neurochemistry. irreg., 1971, vol. 5. ISSN 0076-6925
- Modern Pharmacology-Toxicology. irreg. ISSN 0098-6925
- Monographs and Textbooks in Material Science. irreg. ISSN 0077-0744
- Monographs in Electroanalytical Chemistry and Electrochemistry. irreg. ISSN 0077-0833
- Monographs in Macromolecular Chemistry. irreg. ISSN 0077-0884
- Monographs on Plastics. irreg., vol. 1, pt. 2., 1973.
- Organic Photochemistry: A Series of Advances. irreg., 1971, vol. 3. ISSN 0078-6152
- Organic Substances of Natural Origin. irreg., 1969, vol.2. ISSN 0078-6187
- Organometallic Compounds of the Group IV Elements. irreg., 1971, vol. 2. ISSN 0078-6489
- Preparation and Properties of Solid State Materials. irreg. ISSN 0081-1939
- Protein Synthesis. irreg. ISSN 0079-7049
- Pure and Applied Mathematics Series. irreg., 1971, vol. 25. ISSN 0079-8177
- Solid State Surface Science. irreg. ISSN 0081-1971
- Studies in Organic Chemistry. irreg., vol. 2, 1974.
- Surfactant Science Series. irreg., 1971, vol. 6. ISSN 0081-9603
- Techniques and Applications in Organic Synthesis. irreg. ISSN 0082-2418
- Techniques and Methods of Polymer Evaluation. irreg., 1971, vol. 2. ISSN 0082-2434
- Techniques of Surface and Colloid Chemistry and Physics. irreg.
- Thermal Analysis Series. irreg. ISSN 0082-4011
- Toxicology Annual. a. ISSN 0361-3410
- Transition Metal Chemistry: A Series of Advances. irreg., 1971; vol. 7. ISSN 0082-5921
- Treatise on Coatings. irreg. ISSN 0082-6278
- Urban Problems and Urban Technology Series. irreg.

- Vibrational Spectra and Structure. irreg. ISSN 0090-1911

**Marcel Dekker Journals**
270 Madison Ave., New York, NY 10016
(Prepaid subscr. to: Box 11305, Church St. Sta., New York NY 10049)
- American Journal of Drug and Alcohol Abuse. 3 per yr. ISSN 0095-2990
- Analytical Letters. 15 per yr. ISSN 0003-2719
- Applied Spectroscopy Reviews. irreg., 2 nos. per vol., 1977 vol. 13. ISSN 0066-5541
- Ballet Review. q. ISSN 0522-0653
- Biomaterials, Medical Devices and Artificial Organs. irreg., 4 nos. per vol. ISSN 0090-5488
- Cancer Detection and Prevention. 4 per yr.
- Catalysis Reviews: Science and Engineering. s-a. ISSN 0360-2451
- Chemical Instrumentation; a journal of experimental techniques in chemistry and biochemistry. q. ISSN 0009-2592
- Clinical Toxicology. q. ISSN 0009-9309
- Communications in Algebra. irreg., 14 nos. per vol. ISSN 0092-7872
- Communications in Partial Differential Equations. 12 nos. per vol. ISSN 0360-5302
- Communications in Soil Science and Plant Analysis. bi-m., 9 nos. per vol. ISSN 0010-3624
- Communications in Statistics. Part A: Methods and Techniques. 6 per yr. ISSN 0361-0926
- Communications in Statistics. Part B: Simulation and Computation. 4 nos. per vol. ISSN 0361-0918
- Drug and Chemical Toxicity. 4 per yr.
- Drug Development and Industrial Pharmacy. 6 per yr. ISSN 0363-9045
- Drug Metabolism Reviews. 2 per yr. ISSN 0012-6594
- Endocrine Research Communications. irreg., 6 nos. per vol. ISSN 0093-6391
- Energy Communications. bi-m. ISSN 0097-8159
- Heart and Circulation. 6 per yr.
- Hemoglobin. 8 per yr. ISSN 0363-0269
- Immunological Communications. bi-m. ISSN 0090-0877 (State University of New York at Buffalo. Center for Immunology)
- In Situ. 4 per yr. ISSN 0146-2520
- International Journal of the Addictions. q. ISSN 0020-773X
- Journal of Carbohydrates-Nucleosides-Nucleotides; a forum for rapid communication. 6 per yr. ISSN 0094-0585
- Journal of Dialysis. 8 per yr.
- Journal of Macromolecular Science. Part A. Chemistry. 8 per yr. ISSN 0022-233X
- Journal of Macromolecular Science. Part B. Physics. q. ISSN 0022-2348
- Journal of Macromolecular Science, Part C. Reviews in Macromolecular Chemistry; a journal of advances. s-a. ISSN 0022-2356
- Journal of Structural Mechanics. 4 per yr. ISSN 0360-1218
- Marine Science Communications. 4 per yr. ISSN 0098-8383
- Medical Microbiology and Infectious Disease. 4 per yr.
- Molecular Photochemistry. q. ISSN 0026-8968
- Ophthalmic Seminars. 4 per yr. ISSN 0361-249X
- Polymer Plastics Technology & Engineering. s-a. ISSN 0360-2559
- Preparative Biochemistry. q. ISSN 0032-7484
- Psychopharmacology Communications. bi-m. ISSN 0098-616X
- Separation and Purification Methods. s-a. ISSN 0360-2540
- Separation Science; an interdisciplinary journal of methods and underlying processes. 6 per yr. ISSN 0037-2366
- Spectroscopy Letters. m. ISSN 0038-7010
- Synthesis and Reactivity in Inorganic and Metalorganic Chemistry. q. ISSN 0094-5714
- Synthetic Communications. 4 per yr. ISSN 0039-7911
- Transport Theory and Statistical Physics. 4 per yr. ISSN 0041-1450

**Delacorte Press**
(Subsidiary of: Dial Press)
1 Dag Hammarskjold Plaza, 245 E. 47 St., New York, NY 10017.
- Boston Children's Medical Center. Publications for Parents. irreg.

**Delano Historical Society**
1123 Cecil Ave., Delano, CA 93215.
- Plow. 4 per yr. ISSN 0032-1613

**Delap's Fantasy and Science Fiction Review**
11863 West Jefferson Blvd., Culver City, CA 90230.
- Delap's F and S F Review. m.

**Delaware. Department of Health and Social Services**
Dover, DE 19901.
- Delaware. Department of Health and Social Service. Annual Report. a. ISSN 0095-6422

**Delaware. Department of Health and Social Services. Division of Social Services**
P. O. Box 309, Wilmington, DE 19899.
- Delaware. Division of Social Services. Annual Report. a. ISSN 0090-3051

**Delaware. Department of Highways and Transportation**
P. O. Box 778, Dover, DE 19901.
- Delaware. Department of Highways and Transportation. Traffic Summary. a. ISSN 0070-329X

**Delaware. Department of Justice**
Dover, DE 19901.
- Delaware. Department of Justice. Annual Report. a. ISSN 0098-7832

**Delaware. Department of Natural Resources and Environmental Control**
Dover, DE 19901.
- Delaware. Department of Natural Resources and Environmental Control. Annual Report. a. ISSN 0084-9642
- Delaware Conservationist. q. ISSN 0045-9852

**Delaware. Department of Public Instruction**
Townsend Building, Dover, DE 19901.
- Delaware. Department of Public Instruction. Educational Personnel Directory. a. ISSN 0091-6188 (prep. by its Division of Planning, Research & Evaluation)
- Directory of Delaware Schools. irreg. ISSN 0362-5710
- Supply and Demand: Educational Personnel in Delaware. a. ISSN 0094-2308

**Delaware. Geological Survey**
University of Delaware, Newark, DE 19711.
- Delaware, Geological Survey. Geologic Map Series. irreg (approx 1 per yr)
- Delaware Geological Survey Bulletins. irreg., no. 21 1972. ISSN 0070-3273
- Delaware Geological Survey Reports of Investigations. irreg. ISSN 0011-7749

**Delaware. Office of Management, Budget & Planning**
Thomas Collins Bldg., Dover, DE 19901.
- Delaware State Planning Office. School Facilities Planning Study. a.
- Delaware Statistical Abstract. biennial.

**Delaware. Office of Minority Business Enterprises**
State House Annex-3rd Floor, Dover, DE 19901.
- Delaware State Minority Business Directory. irreg. ISSN 0098-6755

**Delaware. State Board of Education**
Townsend Building, Dover, DE 19901.
- Delaware. State Board of Education. Report of Educational Statistics. a. ISSN 0362-8787

**Delaware. State Treasurer**
Thomas Collins Building, Dover, DE 19901.
- Delaware. State Treasurer. Annual Report. a. ISSN 0084-9685

**Delaware Army National Guard Headquarters**
State Armory, 10th and Dupont Sts., Wilmington, DE 19899.
- Delaware Guardsman. bi-m. ISSN 0011-7757

**Delaware Art Museum**
2301 Kentmere Parkway, Wilmington, DE 19806.
- Delaware Art Museum. Annual Report. a.
- Delaware Art Museum Bulletin. m.

**Delaware County Pharmaceutical Association**
- Delaware County Pharmacist. (pub. by Vince Davella)

**Delaware Learning Resources Association**
1907 Beechwood Dr., Westwood Manor, Wilmington, DE 19810.
- D L R A Newsletter. q.

**Delaware Library Association, Inc.**
Box 1843, Wilmington, DE 19899.
- Delaware Library Association Bulletin. q. ISSN 0011-7773

**Delaware Museum of Natural History**
Box 3937, Greenville, DE 19807.
- Delaware Museum of Natural History. Monograph Series. irreg. ISSN 0084-9650
- Delaware Museum of Natural History. Reproduction Series. irreg. ISSN 0084-9669
- Delaware Museum of Natural History. Special Publications. irreg. ISSN 0084-9677
- Indo-Pacific Mollusca. irreg. ISSN 0073-7240
- Nemouria; Occasional Papers of the Delaware Museum of Natural History. irreg., 1972, no. 6. ISSN 0085-3887

**Delaware Nurses Association**
1003 Delaware Avenue, Wilmington, DE 19806.
- Delaware Nurses' Association Reporter. m.

**Delaware State Chamber of Commerce**
1102 West St., Wilmington, DE 19801.
- Delaware Directory of Commerce and Industry. biennial. ISSN 0070-3265

**Delaware Today, Inc.**
2401 Pennsylvania Ave., The Devon Suite 1A-1B, Wilmington, DE 19806.
- Delaware Today. m. ISSN 0011-779X

**Delaware Valley Outdoor News**
1150 York Rd., Box 136, Abington, PA 19001.
- Delaware Valley Outdoor News. m.

**Delaware Valley Regional Planning Commission**
Penn Towers Bldg., 1819 J. F. Kennedy Blvd., Philadelphia, PA 19124.
- Delaware Valley Regional Planning Commission. Biennial Report. biennial. ISSN 0098-6232

**Delbridge Publishing Co.**
Box 2989, Stanford, CA 94305.
- Fluidics Quarterly; the published forum for research and development in fluidics. q. ISSN 0015-4687

**Delegates World Bulletin**
120 Wall St., New York, NY 10005.
- Delegates World Bulletin. fortn.

**Dell Publishing Co. Inc.**
1 Dag Hammarskjold Plaza, 245 East 47 St, New York, NY 10017.
- Horoscope. m. ISSN 0018-5116
- Modern Romances. m. ISSN 0026-8399
- Modern Screen. m. ISSN 0026-8429

**Delmarva Advisory Council**
Suite 400, One Plaza E., Box 711, Salisbury, MD 21801.
- Delmarva Report. m. ISSN 0011-7927

**Delmarva Advisory Council. Technology Acquisition Unit**
One Plaza East, Suite 700, Box 711, Salisbury, MD 21801.
- T A U Report. m.

**Delta Air Lines**
- Sky. (pub. by East-West Network, Inc.)

**Delta Communications, Inc.**
1120 Chester Ave., Cleveland, OH 44114.
- Packaging Digest; packaging management, marketing, design, equipment, materials. m. ISSN 0030-9117

**Delta Distributing Co.**
131 South Barrington Place, Los Angeles, CA 90049.
- Trail Bike. q.

**Delta Farm Press, Inc.**
Box 998, Clarksdale, MS 38614.
- Delta Farm Press. w. ISSN 0011-8036

**Delta Kappa Epsilon Fraternity**
155 E. 45th St., New York, NY 10017.
- Deke Quarterly. q.

**Delta Kappa Gamma Society International**
Box 1589, Austin, TX 78767.
- Delta Kappa Gamma Bulletin. q. ISSN 0011-8044

**Delta Mu Delta National Honor Society in Business Administration**
800 Oakton, Evanston, IL 60202.
- Delta Mu Delta Newsletter. s-a. ISSN 0300-7146

**Delta Nu Alpha Transportation Fraternity**
10 Beech St., 19 Church St., Berea, OH 44017.
- Delta Nu Alphian. m. ISSN 0002-645X

**Delta Omicron International Music Fraternity**
c/o Jane Wiley Kuckuk, 1352 Redwood Ct., Columbus, OH 43229.
- Wheel of Delta Omicron. 4 per yr. ISSN 0043-4752

**Delta Pi Epsilon Graduate Business Education Fraternity**
National Office, Gustavus Adolphus College, St. Peter, MN 56082.
- Business Education Index. a. ISSN 0068-4414
- Delta Pi Epsilon. Research Bulletin. irreg. ISSN 0416-9336
- Delta Pi Epsilon Journal. q. ISSN 0011-8052

**Delta Psi Kappa**
c/o Fern G. Schroll, 6641 Lasley Shore Dr., Winneconne, WI 54986.
- Foil. s-a. ISSN 0015-5373

**Delta Scene Corporation**
Box B-3, D. S. U., Cleveland, MS 38733.
- Delta Scene. q. (Co-sponsor: Delta State University)

**Delta Sigma Delta**
c/o Dr. Kermit F. Knudtzon, Ed., Box 2225, Chapel Hill, NC 27514.
- Desmos. q. ISSN 0011-9474

**Delta Sigma Delta Fraternity. Arkansas Graduate Chapter**
c/o Dr. J. R. Luten, Jr., Ed., 6600 Baseline Rd., Little Rock, AR 72209.
- Arkansas Delta Sig. s-a.

**Delta Theta Phi Law Fraternity**
1660 L St. N.W., Washington, DC 20036.
- Paper Book. 4 per yr. ISSN 0011-8060

**Deltiologists of America**
- Deltiology. (pub. by James L. Lowe, Ed. & Pub.)

**Democratic Socialist Organizing Committee**
853 Broadway, Rm. 617, New York, NY 10003.
- Newsletter of the Democratic Left. m. (except July & Aug.)

**Demographic Publications, Inc.**
3301 New Mexico Ave., Washington, DC 20016.
- Washington Dossier. m.

**Dempa Publications, Inc**
380 Madison Ave., New York, NY 10017.
- Japan Fact Book. irreg.

**Dende Press, Inc.**
409-415 Cedar Ave., Scranton, PA 18505.
- Polish American Journal. fortn. ISSN 0032-2792

**Lou Deneumoustier, Ed. & Pub.**
Box 169, Cheswold, DE 19936.
- Disc Collector. irreg. ISSN 0070-6655

**Denison Scientific Association**
- Denison University. Journal of the Scientific Laboratories. (pub. by Denison University)

**Denison University**
Granville, OH 43023.
- Denison University. Journal of the Scientific Laboratories. s-a. ISSN 0022-5150 (Denison Scientific Association)

**Dental Laboratory Association**
220 W. 42nd St., New York, NY 10036.
- Dental Laboratory News. bi-m. ISSN 0011-8664 (New York State Association of Certified Dental Laboratories)

**Dental Society of the State of New York**
30 E. 42nd St., New York, NY 10017.
- New York State Dental Journal. m.(Oct-May); bi-m.(June-Sept) ISSN 0028-7571

**Dental Survey Publications**
(Subsidiary of: Harcourt Brace Jovanovich, Inc.)
4015 W. 65th St., Minneapolis, MN 55435.
- Dental Industry News; trends in manufacturing, marketing and merchandising. m. ISSN 0011-863X
- Dental Laboratory Buyer's Guide. a.
- Dental Laboratory Review; for operators of dental prosthetic laboratories. m. ISSN 0011-8672
- Dental Survey. m. ISSN 0011-8788

**Denver Art Museum**
100 W. 14th Ave. Parkway, Denver, CO 80204.
- Material Culture Monographs (American Indian) irreg. ISSN 0076-5139

**Denver Chamber of Commerce**
1301 Welton St., Denver, CO 80204.
- Metro Denver. m.

**Denver Field Ornithologists**
Denver Museum of Natural History, Denver, CO 80205.
- Lark Bunting; monthly report of field observations. m.

**Denver Freethinkers' Society**
Box 1621, Englewood, CO 80110.
- Directory of U.S. Freethought Groups and Publications. a.

**Denver Public Library**
1357 Broadway, Denver, CO 80203.
- Inkling. m. ISSN 0020-1405

**Denver Public Library. Fish and Wildlife Reference Service**
2100 W. Mississippi Ave., Denver, CO 80223.
- Fish and Wildlife Reference Service Newsletter. q. ISSN 0098-8170

**Denver Public Library. Young Adult Services**
1357 Broadway, Denver, CO 80202.
- Denver Tomato; teens opinions on matters and theoretical observations. q.

**Denver Research Institute**
see under University of Denver

**Denver Weekly News**
2547 Welton St., Denver, CO 80205
- Denver Weekly News. w. (Subscr. to, Box 2811, Denver, CO 80201)

**Denyse and Co. Inc.**
112 W. 9th St., Los Angeles, CA 90015.
- Apparel Industry. m.
- National Apparel Suppliers and Contractors Directory. a.

**Department Store Employees Union. Local 21**
790 Broad St, Newark, NJ 07102.
- Department Store Employees Union. Local Twenty One Guide. q. ISSN 0011-8885

**Department Store Workers' Union, Local 1- S**
Retail, Wholesale and Dept. Store Union, A F L- C I O, 140 W. 31 St., New York, NY 10001.
- Department Store Workers' Union. Local 1-S News. m. ISSN 0011-8915

**Dependable Lists, Inc.**
257 Park Avenue South, New York, NY 10010.
- Dependable's List Marketing Newsletter. 8 per yr.

**Depository Trust Company**
55 Water St., New York, NY 10041.
- Financial Industry Number Standard Directory. irreg. ISSN 0362-1405

**Depot Press**
Room 204, English Bldg., Urbana, IL 61801.
- Midwest Monographs. Series 1 (Drama) irreg. ISSN 0076-8596 (University of Illinois at Urbana-Champaign)
- Midwest Monographs. Series 2 (Poetry) irreg., 1969, no. 2. ISSN 0076-860X (University of Illinois at Urbana-Champaign)
- Midwest Monographs. Series 3 (Graphic Works) irreg., 1969, no. 2. ISSN 0076-8618 (University of Illinois at Urbana-Champaign)
- Midwest Monographs. Series 4 (Translation) irreg. ISSN 0076-8626 (University of Illinois at Urbana-Champaign)
- Midwest Monographs. Series 5 (Culture and Criticism) irreg. ISSN 0076-8634 (University of Illinois at Urbana-Champaign)

**W. H. Depperman, Ed. & Pub.**
24 Old Mill Rd., Chappaqua, NY 10514.
- Bill Depperman's Practical Public Relations. m. ISSN 0006-2480

**Derbyshire Publishing Co. Inc.**
Temple, NH 03084.
- Horse, of Course! m.

**Derivation and Tabulation Associates**
see D.A.T.A.

**DeRoche Publications**
2835 Roscomare Rd., Suite D-9, Los Angeles, CA 90024.
- Equipment Reporter. m.

**Derus Media Service**
Six West Hubbard St., Chicago, IL 60610.
- Editorial Pace. bi-m.

**Deseret News**
Box 838, Salt Lake City, UT 84110.
- Deseret News Church Almanac. a. ISSN 0093-786X (Co-Sponsor: Church of Jesus Christ of Latter-Day Saints)

**Desert**
c/o William Knyvett, Palm Desert, CA 92260.
- Desert. m. ISSN 0011-9237

**Desert Botanical Garden**
Box 5415, Phoenix, AZ 85010.
- Saguaroland Bulletin. 10 per yr. (Arizona Cactus & Native Flora Society)

**Desert First Works Press**
4948 N. La Canada Dr., Tuscon, AZ 85705.
- Desert First Works. irreg.

**Desert Horse Corp.**
Box 2264, Fort Collins, CO 80522.
- Arabian Horse News. 12 per yr. ISSN 0003-7486

**Desert Silhouette Publishing**
2500 N. Pantano Rd., Tucson, AZ 85715.
- Tucson. m.

**Design Methods Group**
University of California, School of Architecture, Berkeley, CA 94720.
- Design Methods and Theories. q.

**Designers West**
9200 Sunset Blvd., Los Angeles, CA 90069.
- Designers West Resource Directory. a. ISSN 0420-011X

**Desperado**
c/o Kell Robertson, Ed., 2429-A 24th St., San Francisco, CA 94110.
- Desperado. irreg.

**Desperate Living**
Box 7124, Baltimore, MD 21218.
- Desperate Living. q.

**Detective Publications, Inc.**
(Subsidiary of: Dell Publishing Co., Inc.)
1 Dag Hammarskjold Plaza, New York, NY 10017.
- Front Page Detective. m. ISSN 0016-2043
- Inside Detective. m. ISSN 0020-1847

**Gustav Detjen, Jr., Ed. & Pub.**
Box 150, Clinton Corners, NY 12514.
- Ferrary Society. Bulletin. m. (Ferrary Society)
- Fireside Chats. m. ISSN 0015-2714 (Franklin D. Roosevelt Philatelic Society)
- Insectocutor News. q. ISSN 0020-1820 (National Association of Insectocutor Manufacturers)
- J A P O S Bulletin. q. (J A P O S Study Group)
- Philatelic Directory; a handbook for the philatelic writer. biennial. (Society of Philaticians)
- Philatelic Journalist. bi-m. ISSN 0048-3710 (Society of Philaticians)

**Detroit Athletic Club**
241 Madison Ave., Detroit, MI 48226.
- D A C News. m. ISSN 0011-4707

**Detroit Bar Association**
600 Woodward Ave., Detroit, MI 48226.
- Detroit Lawyer. m. ISSN 0011-9652

**Detroit Board of Education**
5057 Woodward, Detroit, MI 48202.
- Detroit Public Schools Reporter. m.

**Detroit College of Law**
136 E. Elizabeth St., Detroit, MI 48201.
- Detroit College of Law Review. q. ISSN 0099-135X

**Detroit Diesel Allison**
13400 W. Outer Dr., Detroit, MI 48228.
- Power News. m.

**Detroit District Dental Society**
319 Fisher Bldg., Detroit, MI 48202.
- Detroit Dental Bulletin. m. ISSN 0011-9601

**Detroit Federation of Teachers. Local 231, AFL-CIO**
7451 Third Ave., Detroit, MI 48202.
- Detroit Teacher. s-m. ISSN 0011-9695

**Detroit Historical Society**
5401 Woodward Ave., Detroit, MI 48202.
- Detroit in Perspective; a journal of regional history. 3 per yr.

**Detroit Institute of Arts**
5200 Woodward Ave., Detroit, MI 48202.
- Detroit Institute of Arts. Bulletin. q. ISSN 0011-9636

**Detroit Publication Consultants**
18226 Mack Ave., Grosse Pointe Farms, MI 48236.
- Detroit Engineer. m. ISSN 0011-9628 (Engineering Society of Detroit)
- Grosse Pointer. bi-m. ISSN 0017-4629 (Grosse Point Yacht Club)
- Main Sheet. m. ISSN 0025-0600 (Detroit Yacht Club)
- Worldwide Yacht Charter & Boat Rental Guide. a.

**Detroit Society for Genealogical Research**
c/o Detroit Public Library, Burton Historical Collection, 5201 Woodward, Detroit, MI 48202.
- Detroit Society for Genealogical Research. Magazine. q. ISSN 0011-9687

**Detroit Sun, Inc.**
Box 1898, Detroit, MI 48231.
- Detroit Sun. fortn.

**Detroit Yacht Club**
- Main Sheet. (pub. by Detroit Publication Consultants)

**Samuel Deutsch, Ed. & Pub.**
430 Keller Ave., Elmont, NY 11003.
- Jewish Current Events. bi-w. ISSN 0021-6380

**Deutsche Haematologische Gesellschaft**
- Blut. (pub. by Springer- Verlag)

**Deutsche Physikalische Gesellschaft**
- Physikalische Berichte. (pub. by Verlag Chemie International, Inc.)
- Physikalische Blaetter. (pub. by Verlag Chemie International Inc.)

**Devastan Enterprises**
Box 962, Madison, WI 53701.
- Free for All. bi-w.

**Development West, Inc.**
311 California St., Suite 700, San Francisco, CA 94104.
- Manpower Planning. m.

**DeWitt & Co.**
Central National Bank Bldg., 2100 Travis St., Houston, TX 77002.
- Propylene Annual. a. ISSN 0095-4128

**Dewitt County Genealogical Society**
Box 329, Clinton, IL 61727.
- Dewitt County Genealogical Society. Quarterly. q.

**Dharma Publishing**
5856 Doyle St., Emeryville, CA 94704.
- Crystal Mirror. a. ISSN 0097-7209 (Tibetan Nyingma Meditation Center)
- Gesar; the magazine of Buddhism in the West. q. (Tibetan Nyingma Meditation Center)

**Di Cyan & Brown**
500 Fifth Ave., New York, NY 10036.
- Di Cyan & Brown Bulletin. q. ISSN 0012-1754

**Diabetes Outlook, Inc.**
515 Madison Ave., New York, NY 10002.
- Diabetes Outlook. 10 per yr. ISSN 0012-1835

**Diagnosis News Inc.**
12230 Wilkins Ave., Rockville, MD 20852.
• Internal Medicine News & Diagnosis News. s-m. ISSN 0012-1908

**Dialog, Inc.**
2375 Como Ave., St. Paul, MN 55108.
• Dialog; a journal of theology. q. ISSN 0012-2033

**Dialogue Foundation**
Box 1387, Arlington, VA 22210.
• Dialogue (Los Angeles); a journal of Mormon thought. q. ISSN 0012-2157

**Dialogue Publications, Inc.**
130 E. 16th St., New York, NY 10003.
• American Dialog. bi-m. ISSN 0002-8215

**Dialysis & Transplantation Inc.**
15300 Ventura Blvd., Suite 301, Sherman Oaks, CA 91403.
• Dialysis & Transplantation; the journal of renal technology. m. ISSN 0090-2934

**Gary L. Diamond, Ed. & Pub.**
4504 Excelsior Blvd., Minneapolis, MN 55416.
• Iowa Beverage Journal. m.
• Missouri Beverage Journal. m.
• Northwest Beverage Journal. m.

**Diamond Publications Inc**
3302 N. 3rd St, Phoenix, AZ 85012.
• Arizona Beverage Journal. m. ISSN 0004-1432

**Diamond Publishing Co.**
Box 52, 6011 S.W. 70th St., South Miami, FL 33143.
• Industria Turistica. m. ISSN 0019-7777

**Diamond Reo Trucks, Inc.**
1331 S. Washington Ave., Lansing, MI 48920.
• Diamond Reo News. q.

**Diamond Walnut Growers Inc.**
Box 1727, Stockton, CA 95201.
• Diamond Walnut News. bi-m. ISSN 0012-2319

**Diamondhead Corp.**
Mountainside, NJ 07092.
• Golf Annual. a. ISSN 0095-4071

**Diana's Bimonthly Press**
71 Elmgrove Ave., Providence, RI 02906.
• Diana's Bimonthly; deduction of the innocents pamphlet. bi-m. ISSN 0046-0222

**Diapason, Inc.**
434 S. Wabash, Chicago, IL 60605.
• Diapason; devoted to the organ, the harpsichord and church music. m. ISSN 0012-2378

**Dibco Press, Inc.**
2570 Sue Ave., San Jose, CA 95111.
• Basic Source Materials in Political Science. irreg.

**Dickinson School of Law**
Carlisle, PA 17013.
• Dickinson Law Review. q. ISSN 0012-2459

**Dickinson State College**
Box 282, Dickinson, ND 58601.
• Western Concept. s-m.

**Judson Dicks, Ed. & Pub.**
110 Mobrey Lane, Smithtown, NY 11787.
• Angels. s-a. ISSN 0003-3103

**Didactic, Inc.**
1603 Orrington Ave., Suite 2080, Evanston, IL 60201.
• Medical Challenge; the journal for professional self-evaluation. m. ISSN 0092-4032

**Diesel and Gas Turbine**
c/o Bruce W. Wadman, Ed., 11225 W. Bluemound Rd., Box 7406, Milwaukee, WI 53213
(Orders to: Box 138, Oshkosh, WI 54901)
• Diesel and Gas Turbine Progress. m. ISSN 0012-2602
• Diesel and Gas Turbine Progress Worldwide. 9 per yr.
• Diesel and Gas Turbine World Wide Catalog. a. ISSN 0070-4822

**Diesel Fuel Services Inc.**
330 E. 33rd St., New York, NY 10016.
• Directory of Diesel Fuel Stations Coast to Coast. irreg. ISSN 0360-9987

**Diesel Publications, Inc.**
80 Lincoln Ave., Stamford, CT 06904.
• Diesel Equipment Superintendent. m. ISSN 0012-2610

**Dietmeier-van Zevern Publications, Inc.**
350 Linden Ave., Wilmette, IL 60091.
• Boat & Motor Dealer. 13 per yr. ISSN 0006-5366

**Digest Books, Inc.**
540 Frontage Rd., Northfield, IL 60093.
• Age of Firearms. irreg. ISSN 0065-4213
• Camper's Digest. a., 1974, 2nd ed. ISSN 0068-6913
• Fishermen's Digest. a. ISSN 0430-6090
• Golfer's Digest. a. ISSN 0072-4971
• Gun Digest. a. ISSN 0072-9043
• Guns Illustrated. a. ISSN 0072-9078
• Handloader's Digest. a. ISSN 0073-0211
• Home Gunsmithing Digest. a. ISSN 0073-3121
• Rod Laver's Tennis Digest. a.

**Digest of Advices, Inc**
160 Broadway, New York, NY 10007.
• Digest of Investment Advices. m. ISSN 0012-2742

**Digital Equipment Computer Users Society**
• Decuscope. (pub. by Digital Equipment Corp.)

**Digital Equipment Corp.**
146 Main St. PK3/E55, Maynard, MA 01754.
• Decuscope. 4-6 per yr. ISSN 0011-7447 (Digital Equipment Computer Users Society)

**Dignity, Inc.**
755 Boylston, Rm. 413, Boston, MA 02116.
• Dignity. m.

**George O. Dillon, Ed. & Pub.**
Box 1302, Springfield, IL 62705.
• Mail Trade. m. ISSN 0025-0562

**Diners Club Inc.**
10 Denver Tech Center, Englewood, CO 80110.
• Signature; the Diners Club Magazine. m. ISSN 0037-5039

**James Dines & Co.**
Box 22, Belvedere, CA 94920.
• Dines Letter. w. ISSN 0012-2971

**Diocese of Fargo**
c/o Bishop of Fargo, 608 Broadway, Box 1750, Fargo, ND 58102.
• Catholic Action News. m. ISSN 0008-7890

**Diocese of Harrisburg**
• Catholic Witness. (pub. by Harrisburg Catholic Publishing Associates)

**Diocese of Reno**
Box 1211, Reno, NE 89504.
• Nevada Register. irreg.

**Diocese of Richmond**
c/o Most. Rev. Walter F. Sullivan, Bishop of Richmond, 800 Cathedral Pl., Richmond, VA 23220.
• Catholic Virginian. w. ISSN 0008-8404

**Diocese of San Angelo**
116 S. Oakes St., Box 1829, San Angelo, TX 76902.
• Texas Concho Register. s-m. ISSN 0040-425X

**Diocese of San Diego**
Box 81869, San Diego, CA 92138.
• Southern Cross. w.

**Diocese of the Armenian Church of America**
630 Second Ave., New York, NY 10016.
• Armenian Church. 4 per yr. ISSN 0004-2315
• Hayastanyaitz Yegeghetzy. 4 per yr. ISSN 0017-8667

**Diplomatic and Consular Officers, Retired.**
1718 H St. N.W., Washington, DC 20006.
• Diplomatic and Consular Officers, Retired. Membership Directory. irreg. ISSN 0092-010X

**Direct Mail-Marketing Association**
6 E. 43rd St., New York, NY 10017.
• D M M A in Depth. irreg.

**Direct Mail-Marketing Association (Washington)**
1730 K St. N.W., Washington, DC 20006.
• D M M A Government Affairs Report. m.

**Direct Selling Association**
1730 M St., N.W., Washington, DC 20036.
• Direct Selling; association membership roster listing major companies and commodities. a. ISSN 0070-4970

**Directional Advertising, Inc.**
Box 123, Bowie, MD 20715.
• Guide to Antique Shops. a. ISSN 0072-8233

**Director Publications Inc**
408 Olive St., St. Louis, MO 63102.
• Bank Board Letter. m. ISSN 0005-5042

**Directories International**
1718 Sherman Ave., Evanston, IL 60201.
• Advertising World; magazine for multi-national advertising. q.
• Media Guide International. Business Publications Edition. q. ISSN 0098-9398
• Media Guide International. Newspapers/Newsmagazines Edition. a. ISSN 0093-9447

**Directories of Industry, Inc.**
9371 Kramer, Unit 1, Westminster, CA 92683.
• E I A Guide. a. ISSN 0070-7821

**Directories Publishing Co.**
Box 422, Flemington, NJ 08822
• Chem Sources - Europe. a. (Outside U.S. and Canada Dist. by Chemical Sources Europe, Box 87846, 2508 The Hague, Netherlands)
• Chem Sources - U.S.A. a.

**Directors Art Institute**
436 E. 88th St., New York, NY 10028.
• Who's Who in Commerical Art and Photography. irreg. ISSN 0510-3983

**Directors Guild of America, Inc.**
7950 Sunset Blvd., Hollywood, CA 90046.
• Action (Hollywood) bi-m. ISSN 0001-7361
• Directors Guild of America. Directory of Members. a, 8th ed., 1974. ISSN 0419-2052

**Directory of Educational Specialists**
3200 Southgreen, Baltimore, MD 21207.
• Directory of Educational Specialists. irreg.

**Directory of Graduate Law Study**
c/o M. Wallace Gordon, 727 S.W. 27 St., Gainesville, FL 32601.
• Directory of Graduate Law Study. a. ISSN 0070-5608

**Directory of Specific Learning Disability Services**
P.O. Box 6495, Savannah, GA 31405.
• Directory of Specific Learning Disability Services. a. ISSN 0092-2455

**Disabled American Veterans and Auxiliary**
Box 14301, Cincinnati, OH 45214.
• D A V Magazine. m. ISSN 0011-474X

**Disc Collectors Newsletter**
Box 169, Cheswold, DE 19936.
• Disc Collectors Newsletter. m.

**Discalced Carmelite Fathers**
1125 Walker St., Box 26127, Oklahoma City, OK 73125.
• Little Flower. bi-m. ISSN 0024-502X

**Discalced Carmelite Fathers. Washington Province**
2131 Lincoln Rd., N.E., Washington, DC 20002.
• Spiritual Life. q. ISSN 0038-7630

**Disco Times International**
459 W. 15th St., New York, NY 10011.
• Discothekin; international discotheque industry monthly. m.

**Discographer**
250 Rennie Ave., Venice, CA 90291.
• Discographer. q. ISSN 0012-3536

**Discovery Productions**
Box 2343, Santa Clara, CA 95051.
• Microelectronics News; manager's casebook. w.

**Dissemination and Assessment Center for Bilingual Education**
6504 Tracor Lane, Austin, TX 78721.
• Cartel; annotations and analyses of bilingual multicultural materials. q.

**Dissent Publishing Co., Inc.**
509 Fifth Ave., New York, NY 10017.
- Dissent. q. ISSN 0012-3846

**Distilled Spirits Council of the United States, Inc.**
1300 Pennsylvania Bldg., Washington, DC 20004.
- Annual Statistical Review: The Distilled Spirits Industry. a. ISSN 0066-4367
- D I S C U S Facts Book. a.
- D I S C U S Newsletter. m.
- Distilled Spirits Council of the United States. Retail Outlets for the Sale of Distilled Spirits. irreg. ISSN 0416-0525
- Summary of State Laws and Regulations Relating to Distilled Spirits. biennial. ISSN 0081-931X

**Distillers Feed Research Council**
1435 Enquirer Bldg., Cincinnati, OH 45202.
- Distillers Feed Conference. Proceedings. a.

**Distribution Codes Inc.**
401 Wythe St., Alexandria, VA 22314.
- Code & Symbol; journal for the applied science of product identification. m. ISSN 0362-4455

**Distributive Education Clubs of America**
200 Park Ave., Falls Church, VA 22046.
- D E C A Distributor. 4 per yr. ISSN 0011-4847

**Distributive Workers of America**
13 Astor Place, New York, NY 10003.
- Distributive Worker. m. ISSN 0012-3986

**District of Columbia. City Council**
Room 509, City Hall, 14th & E Sts. N.W., Washington, DC 20004.
- District of Columbia. City Council. Annual Report. a. ISSN 0092-8364

**District of Columbia. Department of Environmental Services. Air and Water Monitoring Division**
801 N. Capitol St., Room 742, Washington, DC 20002.
- Washington, D.C. Air and Water Monitoring Division. Annual Report on the Quality of the Air in Washington, D.C.

**District of Columbia. Department of Manpower**
500 C St. N.W., Washington, DC 20001.
- Greater Washington Area Labor Summary. m.

**District of Columbia Dental Society**
4300 Fordham Rd., N.W., Washington, DC 20016.
- District of Columbia Dental Society. Journal. q. ISSN 0012-4060
- District of Columbia Dental Society. Newsletter. m.

**District of Columbia Library Association**
Box 14177, Benjamin Franklin Sta., Washington, DC 20044.
- Inter-Com; Washington Area Librarians. m. ISSN 0047-0414

**District of Columbia Sociological Society**
c/o Dept. of Sociology, Wilson College, Chambersburg, PA 17201.
- Sociologist. m.(Sept-May) ISSN 0038-0369

**Diversion Magazine**
P.O. Box 215, Bear Tavern Road, Titusville, NJ 08560.
- Diversion. bi-m.

**Divine Light Mission**
Box 532, Denver, CO 80201.
- And It Is Divine. q.

**Divine Science Federation International**
1819 East 14th Ave., Denver, CO 80218.
- Aspire; voice of Divine Science. m. ISSN 0004-4962

**Dixie Contractor, Inc.**
Box 280, Decatur, GA 30031.
- Dixie Contractor. fortn. ISSN 0012-4281

**Dixie Dung Beetle Press**
Box 20106, Tallahassee, FL 32304.
- Apalachee Quarterly. q.

**Dixie Publications and Arts Co.**
Box 703, Wadley, GA 30477.
- Dixie Logger and Lumberman. m. ISSN 0046-0435
- Woodchuck. m.

**Dixie Publishers**
Box 125, Richmond Hill, GA 31324.
- State Directory of Public Officials in Georgia. a. ISSN 0099-0175

**Dixon Springs Agricultural Center**
University of Illinois at Urbana-Champaign, Simpson, IL 62985.
- This Week at Dixon Springs. w.

**Do It Now Foundation**
National Media Center, Box 5115, Phoenix, AZ 85010.
- Drug Survival News. bi-m. ISSN 0361-5359

**Doane Agricultural Service, Inc**
8900 Manchester Road, St. Louis, MO 63144.
- Doane's Agricultural Report. w.

**Documentation Abstracts, Inc.**
Box 8510, Philadelphia, PA 19101.
- Information Science Abstracts. bi-m. ISSN 0020-0239 (American Society for Information Science) (Co-sponsors: Special Libraries Association; American Chemical Society, Division of Chemical Informations)

**Documentation Associates Information Services, Inc.**
11716 W. Pico Blvd., Los Angeles, CA 90064.
- Informer. m. ISSN 0364-5479

**Dodd, Mead & Co., Inc**
79 Madison Avenue, New York, NY 10016.
- Best Plays of ... (Year) a.

**Dodson Publishing Co.**
Box 3693, Arlington, VA 22203.
- Country Music World. ISSN 0094-1344

**William Dogan Publications**
Patio Bldg., 76 E. Fifth Ave., Delray Beach, FL 33444.
- Bath Products & Domestics Buyer. q.

**Alfred F. Dolbey**
282 Farmington Ave., Hartford, CT 06105.
- Computer Components News. bi-m.

**Doll Castle News**
Brass Castle, R.D. 1, Washington, NJ 07882.
- Doll Castle News. q.

**Domestic Petroleum Publishers, Inc.**
Box 287, Derby, KS 67037.
- American Oil & Gas Reporter. m.

**Dominican Fathers, Province of St. Albert the Great**
- Cross and Crown. (pub. by Dominican Fathers Publishers)

**Dominican Fathers, Province of St. Joseph**
- Thomist. (pub. by Thomist Press)

**Dominican Fathers Publishers**
Box 627, Oak Park, IL 60303.
- Cross and Crown; a quarterly of spiritual theology. q. ISSN 0011-1910 (Dominican Fathers, Province of St. Albert the Great)

**Dominican Sisters of Sinsinawa**
- Exchange. (pub. by Sinsinawa Publications)

**Dominion Press**
Box 37, San Marcos, CA 92069.
- Theologia 21. q. ISSN 0362-0085

**Donaldson, Lufkin and Jenrette, Inc**
140 Broadway, New York, NY 10005.
- Corporate Pension Fund Seminar. Proceedings. a. ISSN 0070-0290 (Co-sponsor: Alliance Capital Management Corp.)

**Eric Donne, Ed. & Pub.**
250 West 57th Street, Room 1527, New York, NY 10019.
- American Film Magazine. m.

**Reuben H. Donnelley Corp.**
1301 W. 22nd St., Oak Brook, IL 60521.
- Business on Wheels. q.
- Industrial Progress; a pictorial look at new industrial products and processes, plus features of interest to men. bi-m. ISSN 0019-8617 (Goodyear Industrial Products Division)
- O A G Pocket Flight Guide. (Official Airline Guide) m. ISSN 0029-6880

**Reuben H. Donnelley Corp. (Chicago)**
233 E. Congress Pkwy., Chicago, IL 60605.
- Travel Age Mid-America. bi-m.

**Reuben H. Donnelley Corp. (San Francisco)**
582 Market St., Rm. 603, San Francisco, CA 94104.
- Travel Age West; the weekly newspaper for the travel agency sales forces in the West. w. ISSN 0041-1973

**Reuben H. Donnelley Corp. Transportation Guides and Services**
2000 Clearwater Dr., Oak Brook, IL 60521.
- Air Cargo Guide. m.
- Air Cargo Magazine. m.
- O A G Travel Planner & Hotel/Motel Guide. (Official Airline Guide) q. ISSN 0090-0869
- O A G Worldwide Cruise & Shipline Guide. 6 per yr.
- Official Airline Guide. International Edition. m. ISSN 0097-5192
- Official Airline Guide. North American Quick Reference Edition. s-m. ISSN 0030-0276

**Reuben H. Donnelley Corp. Travel Magazines Division**
888 7th Ave., New York, NY 10019.
- Air Forwarder. q.
- Travel Age East. w. ISSN 0041-2104
- Travel Age Southeast. m.
- Travel Management Daily. d. ISSN 0041-2015
- TravelScene. m.

**Duane Doolittle, Ed. & Pub.**
Camden, ME 04843.
- Down East Magazine. 10 per yr. ISSN 0012-5776

**Door**
Box 2022, San Diego, CA 92112.
- Door. fortn. ISSN 0036-4029

**Door and Hardware Institute**
1815 N. Fort Myer Dr., Suite 412, Arlington, VA 22209.
- Doors and Hardware. m. ISSN 0361-5294

**Sandy Dorbin, Ed. & Pub.**
Box 4536, Santa Barbara, CA 93103.
- Schist; a journal of poetry and graphics. irreg. (2 per yr.) ISSN 0092-9425

**Doric Publishing Co., Inc.**
24 E. 38th St., New York, NY 10016.
- American Fabrics & Fashions. q. ISSN 0091-0864

**John Frederick Dorman, Ed. & Pub.**
Box 4883, Washington, DC 20008.
- Virginia Genealogist. q. ISSN 0300-645X

**Bill Dorn Associates, Inc.**
7101 York Avenue South, Minneapolis, MN 55435.
- Agri Dynamics; news of modern agriculture. q. ISSN 0002-1156
- Northliner Magazine; news and features for passengers of North Central Airlines. q. ISSN 0029-327X (North Central Airlines)
- Weeds Today. (Weed Science Society of America)

**William J. Dornan, Inc.**
Willows Ave., Collingdale, PA 19023.
- Association of American Physicians. Transactions. a. ISSN 0066-9458

**Doubleday & Company, Inc.**
245 Park Ave., New York, NY 10017.
- Prize Stories; The O. Henry Awards. a. ISSN 0079-5453

**Douglas County Historical Society**
Box 1550, Roseburg, OR 97470.
- Umpqua Trapper. q. ISSN 0041-6339

**Don Dover, Ed. & Pub.**
10890 Lemarie Dr., Box 41417, Cincinnati, OH 45241.
- Extra Twenty-Two Hundred South; locomotive news magazine. bi-m. ISSN 0014-1380

**Dover Publications, Inc.**
180 Varick St., New York, NY 10014.
- Sacred Books of the East. irreg. ISSN 0080-5246

**Dow Chemical Co.**
1703 S. Saginaw Rd., Midland, MI 48640.
- Flotation Index. a. ISSN 0071-6235

**Dow Jones & Co., Inc.**
22 Cortland St., New York, NY 10007.
- Asian Wall Street Journal. 5 per wk.
- Barron's; national business and financial weekly.
  w. ISSN 0005-6073
- National Observer Index. a. ISSN 0077-524X
- Wall Street Journal Index. a. and m. ISSN 0083-7075

**Dow, Jones, & Co., Inc. Dow Jones Books**
Box 300, Princeton, NJ 08540.
- Dow Jones Commodities Handbook. a. ISSN 0362-0689

**Dow Theory Forecasts, Inc.**
7412 Calumet Ave., Hammond, IN 46325.
- Dow Theory Forecasts; business and stock market.
  w. ISSN 0300-7324

**Dow Theory Letters, Inc**
Box 1759, La Jolla, CA 92038.
- Dow Theory Letters. 36 per yr.

**Dowden, Hutchinson & Ross, Inc.**
523 Sarah St., Stroudsburg, PA 18360
(Dist. by Halsted Press, Div. of John Wiley & Sons,
Inc. 605 Third Ave., New York NY 10016)
- Benchmark Papers in Acoustics. irreg., vol. 7, 1976.
- Benchmark Papers in Analytical Chemistry. irreg.
- Benchmark Papers in Electrical Engineering & Computer Science. irreg., vol. 13, 1976.
- Benchmark Papers in Genetics. irreg., vol. 5, 1976.
- Benchmark Papers in Geology. irreg., vol. 27, 1977.
- Benchmark Papers in Human Physiology. irreg., vol. 6, 1976.
- Benchmark Papers in Inorganic Chemistry. irreg., vol. 5, 1976.
- Benchmark Papers in Microbiology. irreg., vol. 10, 1976.
- Benchmark Papers in Nuclear Physics. irreg.
- Benchmark Papers in Optics. irreg., vol. 2, 1975.
- Benchmark Papers in Organic Chemistry. irreg., vol. 5, 1977.
- Benchmark Papers in Systematic and Evolutionary Biology. irreg., vol. 2, 1975.

**Downe Communications, Inc.**
641 Lexington Ave., New York, NY 10022.
- Discount Merchandiser. m. ISSN 0012-3579
- Family Weekly. w. ISSN 0014-7427
- Ladies' Home Journal (Inkprint Edition) m. ISSN 0023-7124
- Ladies' Home Journal Needle & Craft. s-a.
- Sport. m. ISSN 0038-7797

**Downey Communications, Inc.**
1800 M St. N.W., Suite 650 S., Washington, DC 20036.
- Ladycom; the magazine serving military wives around the world. 8 per yr. ISSN 0023-7183

**Downstate Medical Center**
450 Clarkson Ave., Brooklyn, NY 11203.
- New Caducean; Downstate's literary magazine. a. ISSN 0467-1872

**Downtown Athletic Club**
19 West St., New York, NY 10004.
- Downtown Athletic Club Journal. m. ISSN 0046-0656

**Downtown-Lower Manhattan Association**
120 Broadway, New York, NY 10005.
- Downtown Progress. s-a.

**Dragoco, Inc.**
Gordon Dr., Box 261, Totowa, NJ 07512.
- Dragoco Report. m.(fragrance edition); bi-m(flavor edition) ISSN 0012-5881

**Dragon Runners' Chronicle**
c/o Ann Cass, Ed., Box 444, Argo, IL 60501.
- Dragon Runners' Chronicle. bi-m.

**Dragonfly**
4102 N.E. 130th Place, Portland, OR 97230.
- Dragonfly; a quarterly of haiku. q.

**Marjorie Look Drake, Ed. & Pub.**
Box 2262, Pawtucket, RI 02861.
- Driftwood East. q.

**Drake Publishers, Inc.**
801 Second Ave., New York, NY 10017.
- History in Newspaper Front Pages. a. ISSN 0098-163X
- Woodworker Handbooks. irreg.

**Drake University. Law School**
Law Building, Des Moines, IA 50311.
- Drake Law Review. s-a. ISSN 0012-5938

**Drama Book Shop**
150 West 52nd St., New York, NY 10019.
- Annotated Bibliography of New Publications in the Performing Arts. q.

**Drama Book Specialists**
150 W. 52nd St., New York, NY 10019.
- Performing Arts Resources. a. ISSN 0360-3814 (Theatre Library Association)

**Dramatika Produce**
c/o John Pyros and Daughter, 390 Riverside Drive,
Suite 10b, New York, NY 10025.
- Dramatika; the magazine of performable pieces. s-a. ISSN 0012-5997

**Dramatists Guild, Inc.**
234 W. 44th St., New York, NY 10036.
- Dramatists Guild Quarterly. q. ISSN 0012-6004

**Draper World Population Fund**
1120 Nineteenth St., N. W., Washington, DC 20036.
- Draper World Population Fund. Report. s-a.

**Dravo Corp.**
One Oliver Plaza, Pittsburgh, PA 15222.
- Dravo Review. q. ISSN 0046-0672

**Dream Journal**
c/o Carl Levinson, Ed., 2760 Sacramento St., San
Francisco, CA 94115.
- Dream Journal. q.

**Dreams and Inner Spaces**
Box 26556, Edendale P.O., Los Angeles, CA 90026.
- Dreams and Inner Spaces. m.

**Kenneth Drew**
78-36 Parsons Blvd, Flushing, NY 11366.
- New York Voice. w.

**Walter R. Drew, Ed. & Pub.**
919 South St., Long Beach, CA 90805.
- Antique Motor News. m.
- Cable Newsletter. m.

**Drew University Theological School**
Madison, NJ 07940.
- Drew Gateway; a journal of comment and criticism. 3 per yr. ISSN 0012-6152

**Drexel University**
32nd & Chestnut Sts., Philadelphia, PA 19104.
- Drexel Research Conference. Summary Report. a. ISSN 0085-0071
- Drexel Technical Journal. 2 per yr. ISSN 0012-6179
- Drexel University Research Review. a. ISSN 0085-008X

**Drexel University. Graduate School of Library Science**
Lancaster Ave. and 33rd St., Philadelphia, PA 19104.
- Drexel Library Quarterly. q. ISSN 0012-6160

**Drivers License Guide Company**
1492 Oddstad Drive, Redwood City, CA 94063.
- Drivers License Guide; U. A. & Canadian edition. a.

**Dropsie University**
Broad and York Sts., Philadelphia, PA 19132.
- Jewish Quarterly Review. q. ISSN 0021-6682

**Drorbaugh Publications Inc**
51 E. 42nd St, New York, NY 10017.
- Sight & Sound Marketing. m. ISSN 0037-4814

**M. D. Drucker**
8760 Appian Way, Los Angeles, CA 90046
(Subscr. to: Box 446, Beverly Hills, CA 90213)
- Boxer Review. m.
- Collie-Shetland Sheepdog Review. m.

**Drug Abuse Council, Inc.**
1828 L St. N.W., Washington, DC 20036.
- Drug Abuse Council. Handbook. irreg; no. 3, 1974.
- Drug Abuse Council. Public Policy. 2-3 per yr.
- Drug Abuse Council. Special Studies. irreg.

**Drug, Chemical and Allied Trades Association**
42-40 Bell Blvd., Suite 204, Bayside, NY 11361.
- D C A T Bulletin. (Digest of Current Activities and Trends) fortn. ISSN 0300-7340

**Drug Intelligence & Clinical Pharmacy, Inc**
1806 24th St. N. W., Washington, DC 20008
(Subscr. to: 1241 Broadway, Hamilton, IL 62341)
- Drug Intelligence & Clinical Pharmacy; an interdisciplinary drug journal for physicians, pharmacists and nurses. m. ISSN 0012-6578

**Drum (Amherst)**
426 New Africa House, University of
Massachusetts, Amherst, MA 01060.
- Drum (Amherst) 3 per semester.

**Drum Corps News, Inc.**
P.O. Box 146, Revere, MA 02151.
- Drum Corps News. s-m.(June-Aug); 4 per mo.(Sept-May) ISSN 0012-6748

**Dry Mount Press**
Box 70, Arcola, PA 19420.
- Philadelphia Photo Review. 10 per yr.

**Dryad Press Inc.**
Box 1656, Washington, DC 20013.
- Dryad. 3-4 per yr. ISSN 0012-6780

**Du Pont de Nemours & Co.**
*see* E.I. Du Pont de Nemours & Co.

**Duaal Publishing Corp.**
75 E. 55th St., New York, NY 10022.
- Nursing Care. m. ISSN 0091-2379 (National Federation of Licensed Practical Nurses)

**Herbert T. Duane, Jr.**
Box 130, Hingham, MA 02043.
- Wrecking & Salvage Journal. m. ISSN 0043-9460

**Howard S. Dubin, Ed. & Pub.**
3 East Huron St., Chicago, IL 60611.
- Illinois Manufacturers Directory. a.

**Dubuque Leader**
1154 Iowa St., Dubuque, IA 52001.
- Dubuque Leader. w. ISSN 0012-6918

**Duck**
1030 Eastern, Wichita, KS 67207.
- Duck. q.

**Leonard G. Duck, Ed. & Pub.**
3040 Rio Linda Blvd., Sacramento, CA 95815.
- California Rancher. m. ISSN 0008-1442

**Ducks Unlimited, Inc.**
Box 66300, Chicago, IL 60666.
- Ducks Unlimited. bi-m. ISSN 0012-6950

**Dude Ranchers Association**
South Laramie via Tie Siding, WY 82084.
- Dude Rancher. q. ISSN 0012-6969

**Dudgeon Publications**
Box 5195, Terre Haute, IN 47805.
- Bichon Frise News. bi-m.
- Shih Tzu News. bi-m.

**Dudley Observatory**
100 Fuller Rd., Albany, NY 12205.
- Dudley Observatory, Albany. Reports. irreg., no. 8, 1972. ISSN 0070-7449

**Duke Bar Association**
- Devil's Advocate. (pub. by Duke University. School of Law)

**Duke Endowment**
30 Rockefeller Plaza, New York, NY 10020.
- Duke Endowment. Annual Report. a. ISSN 0419-8050

**Duke University. Commonwealth Studies Center**
6697 College Station, Durham, NC 27708.
- Duke University. Commonwealth-Studies Center. Publications. irreg., 1973, no. 44. ISSN 0070-7473

**Duke University. Council on Aging and Human Development**
P.O. Box 3003, Durham, NC 27710.
- Duke University. Council on Aging and Human Development. Proceedings of Seminars. every 3-4yrs. ISSN 0419-8093

**Duke University. Department of Classical Studies**
Box 4715, Duke Sta., Durham, NC 27706
(Dist. by Greek, Roman & Byzantine Studies, Box 144, Cambridge, Mass. 02138)
- Greek, Roman and Byzantine Monographs. irreg. ISSN 0072-7474
- Greek, Roman and Byzantine Studies. q. ISSN 0017-3916
- Greek, Roman and Byzantine Studies. Scholarly Aids. irreg., 1969, no. 2. ISSN 0072-7482

**Duke University. Divinity School**
Durham, NC 27706.
- Duke Divinity School Review. 3 per yr. ISSN 0012-7078

**Duke University. Geology Department**
Box 6665, College Sta., Durham, NC 27708.
- Southeastern Geology. q. ISSN 0038-3678
- Southeastern Geology. Special Publication. irreg. ISSN 0081-296X

**Duke University. Library**
Durham, NC 27706.
- Duke University Library News Letter. irreg. ISSN 0012-7108
- Library Notes. s-a. ISSN 0024-2438 (Friends of Duke University Library)

**Duke University Marine Laboratory. Cooperative Oceanographic Program**
Beaufort, NC 28516.
- Duke University. Cooperative Oceanographic Program. Progress Report. a. ISSN 0070-7481

**Duke University Medical Center Library. Library Systems and Communications Division**
Durham, NC 27710.
- Library Telecommunications Directory: Canada - United States. a.

**Duke University Press**
Box 6697, College Sta., Durham, NC 27708.
- American Literary Scholarship. a. ISSN 0065-9142
- American Literature; a journal of literary history, criticism and bibliography. q. ISSN 0002-9831
- Consortium for Comparative Legislative Studies. Publications. irreg.
- Duke Historical Publications. irreg. ISSN 0070-7465
- Duke Mathematical Journal. q. ISSN 0012-7094
- Ecological Monographs; a journal for all phases of biology. q. ISSN 0012-9615 (Ecological Society of America)
- Ecology; all forms of life in relation to environment. 6 per yr. ISSN 0012-9658 (Ecological Society of America)
- Hispanic American Historical Review. q. ISSN 0018-2168 (American Historical Association. Conference on Latin American History)
- History of Political Economy. q. ISSN 0018-2702
- Journal of Health Politics, Policy and Law; a journal focusing on the initiative, formulation, and implementation of health policy. q. ISSN 0361-6878
- Journal of Medieval and Renaissance Studies. s-a. ISSN 0047-2573
- Journal of Personality. q. ISSN 0022-3506
- Law and Contemporary Problems. q. ISSN 0023-9186 (Duke University. School of Law)
- South Atlantic Quarterly. q. ISSN 0038-2876

**Duke University. Program in Comparative Studies on Southern Asia**
Box 6697, College Station, Durham, NC 27708.
- Duke University. Program in Comparative Studies in Southern Asia. Monographs and Occasional Papers. irreg., no. 13, 1974. ISSN 0069-7923
- South Asian Book News. m. (Cosponsor: Duke University Library)

**Duke University. School of Engineering**
Durham, NC 27706.
- Duke Engineer. q. ISSN 0046-0818

**Duke University. School of Law**
Duke Law School, Durham, NC 27706.
- Devil's Advocate. w. ISSN 0012-1673 (Duke Bar Association)
- Duke Law Journal. bi-m. ISSN 0012-7086

- Law and Contemporary Problems. (pub. by Duke University Press)
- Library of Law and Contemporary Problems. (pub. by Oceana Publications Inc.)

**Duluth Area Chamber of Commerce**
Medical Arts Bldg., Duluth, MN 55802.
- Duluthian. m. ISSN 0012-7116

**Dumbarton Oaks Center for Byzantine Studies**
- Dumbarton Oaks Bibliographies. (pub. by Mansell Information - Publishing Ltd. UK)
- Dumbarton Oaks Papers. (pub. by J. J. Augustin, Inc.)
- Dumbarton Oaks Studies. (pub. by J. J. Augustin, Inc.)
- Dumbarton Oaks Texts. (pub. by J. J. Augustin, Inc.)

**Dumbarton Oaks Garden Library**
1703 32nd St. N.W., Washington, DC 20007.
- Colloquium on the History of Landscape Architecture. Papers. irreg.

**Dumbarton Oaks Research Library and Collections. Center for Pre-Columbian Studies**
Dumbarton Oaks, 1703 32nd St. N.W., Washington, DC 20007.
- Dumbarton Oaks Conference Proceedings. irreg., latest 1975.
- Studies in Pre-Columbian Art and Archaeology. irreg., no. 16, 1975. ISSN 0585-7023

**Richard H. Dummer**
Box 1219, Altamonte Springs, FL 32701.
- Mobile Home News. bi-m.

**Dun & Bradstreet, Inc.**
99 Church St., New York, NY 10007
- Australian Market Guide. biennial. ISSN 0067-1959 (And 24 Albert Rd., Melbourne South 3205, Australia)
- Dun and Bradstreet Reference Book of Corporate Managements. a. ISSN 0070-7627
- Dun & Bradstreet Standard Register. a. (And 26-32 Clifton St., London EC2P 2LY, England)
- Guide to Key British Enterprises I and II. a. (And 26-32 Clifton St., London EC2P 2LY, England)
- Reference Book - Argentina. a. ISSN 0080-0449 (And Florida 234, Buenos Aires, Argentina)
- Reference Book - Republic of South Africa. a. ISSN 0080-0457 (And 91 Kerk St., Johannesburg, South Africa)
- Sinopsis Dun - Brazil. a. ISSN 0080-9756 (And Avenida Sao Joao 473, 1st Fl., Sao Paulo, Brazil)

**Dun & Bradstreet, Inc. Business Economics Department**
99 Church St., New York, NY 10007.
- Building Permit Values. m. ISSN 0007-3563
- Businessmen's Expectations. q. ISSN 0007-7178
- Monthly Bank Clearings. m. ISSN 0027-0199
- Monthly Business Failures. m. ISSN 0027-027X
- New Business Incorporations. m. ISSN 0028-4378
- Quarterly Analysis of Failures. q. ISSN 0033-5290
- Wholesale Commodity Prices. w. ISSN 0043-504X
- Wholesale Food Prices. w. ISSN 0043-5058

**Dun and Bradstreet, Inc. Credit Services**
99 Church St., New York, NY 10007.
- Dun and Bradstreet Reports; newsletter for businessmen in economics, marketing, sales credit. bi-m.

**Dun & Bradstreet, Inc. Marketing Services Division**
99 Church St., New York, NY 10007.
- Dun and Bradstreet Metalworking Directory. a. ISSN 0070-7597
- Dun and Bradstreet Middle Market Directory. a. ISSN 0070-7600
- Dun and Bradstreet Million Dollar Directory. a. ISSN 0070-7619

**Dun & Bradstreet International**
Box 3224, Church Street Station, New York, NY 10008.
- DunsWorld Letter. q.
- Exporter's Encyclopaedia-World Marketing Guide. a. (including supplementary bi-m bulletins) ISSN 0071-3546
- Exporter's Encyclopedia-United States Marketing Guide. a. ISSN 0090-9475
- International Market Guide - Continental Europe. a. ISSN 0074-6908

- Principal International Businesses; the world marketing directory. a.
- World Marketing. s-m.

**Dun-Donnelley Publishing Corp.**
666 Fifth Ave., New York, NY 10019.
- American Journal of Cardiology. m. ISSN 0002-9149 (American College of Cardiology)
- American Journal of Medicine. m. ISSN 0002-9343
- American Journal of Surgery. m. ISSN 0002-9610
- Control Engineering; instrumentation and automatic control systems. m. ISSN 0010-8049 (And 222 S. Riverside Plaza, Chicago, IL 60606)
- Cutis; cutaneous medicine for practitioner. m. ISSN 0011-4162 (Yorke Medical Group)
- Dun's Review. m. ISSN 0012-7175
- Fire Engineering; the journal of the fire protection profession. m. ISSN 0015-2587
- Highway and Heavy Construction. m. (And 222 S. Riverside Plaza, Chicago, IL 60606)
- Industrial Research. 13 per yr. ISSN 0019-8722 (And 222 S. Riverside Plaza, Chicago, IL 60606)
- Modern Drug Encyclopedia and Therapeutic Index. biennial. ISSN 0076-9959
- Water and Wastes Engineering. m. ISSN 0043-115X
- World Construction. m. ISSN 0043-8375

**Dun-Donnelley Publishing Corp. Graphic Arts Division**
222 S. Riverside Plaza, Chicago, IL 60606.
- Furniture Design & Manufacturing. m. ISSN 0016-304X
- Graphic Arts Monthly and the Printing Industry. m. ISSN 0017-3312

**Duncan Enterprises, Inc.**
Box 8126, Fresno, CA 93727.
- Ceramics, the World's Most Fascinating Hobby. m.

**Dunn & Hargitt**
22 N. Second St., Lafayette, IN 47902.
- Dunn & Hargitt's Bank Trust Advisory. m.
- Dunn & Hargitt's Commodity Service. w. ISSN 0012-7167
- Dunn & Hargitt's Option Guide. w.
- Growing Child. m.

**Duodecimal Society of America, Inc.**
4728 Cielo Dr., Huntington Beach, CA 92649.
- Duodecimal Bulletin. s-a. ISSN 0046-0826

**T. N. Dupuy Associates**
P.O. Box 157, Dunn Loring, VA 22027.
- Almanac of World Military Power. biennial. ISSN 0065-647X

**Duquesne University. Department of Modern Languages**
Pittsburgh, PA 15219.
- Duquesne Hispanic Review. 3 per yr. ISSN 0012-7191

**Duquesne University. Institute of Man**
600 Forbes Ave., Pittsburgh, PA 15219.
- Envoy. 10 per yr. ISSN 0013-9408
- Humanitas. 3 per yr. ISSN 0018-7496

**Duquesne University Press**
600 Forbes Ave., Pittsburgh, PA 15219
(Dist. by Humanities Press, Inc., Atlantic Highlands, NJ 07716)
- Duquesne Studies. Language and Literature. irreg.
- Duquesne Studies. Philosophical Series. irreg. ISSN 0070-7708
- Duquesne Studies. Psychological Series. irreg. ISSN 0070-7716
- Duquesne Studies. Theological Series. irreg. ISSN 0070-7732
- Duquesne Studies in Phenomenological Psychology. triennial.

**Duquesne University. School of Law**
600 Forbes Ave., Pittsburgh, PA 15219.
- Duquesne University Law Review. q. ISSN 0012-7213
- Juris. s-a. ISSN 0022-6807

**Duquesne University. School of Music**
Pittsburgh, PA 15219.
- Kodaly Envoy. q.

**Dushkin Publishing Group**
Sluice Dock, Guilford, CT 06437.
- Annual Editions: Readings in American Government. irreg? ISSN 0090-547X

- Annual Editions: Readings in American History. a. ISSN 0090-4511
- Annual Editions: Readings in Anthropology. a. ISSN 0095-5582
- Annual Editions: Readings in Biology. a. ISSN 0090-4384
- Annual Editions: Readings in Business. irreg. ISSN 0090-4309
- Annual Editions: Readings in Economics. a. ISSN 0090-4430
- Annual Editions: Readings in Education. a. ISSN 0095-5787
- Annual Editions: Readings in Health. a. ISSN 0360-9766
- Annual Editions: Readings in Human Development. a. ISSN 0090-5348
- Annual Editions: Readings in Marketing. a.
- Annual Editions: Readings in Marriage and Family. a. ISSN 0095-6155
- Annual Editions: Readings in Personality and Adjustment. a. ISSN 0361-3836
- Annual Editions: Readings in Psychology. a.
- Annual Editions: Readings in Social Problems. a. ISSN 0094-9183
- Annual Editions: Readings in Sociology. a. ISSN 0090-4236
- Economics: Encyclopedia. a. ISSN 0090-4422

**Dustbooks**
P. O. Box 1056, Paradise, CA 95969.
- Directory of Small Magazine/Press Editors and Publishers. a.
- International Directory of Little Magazines and Small Presses. a.
- Small Press Record of Books in Print. a.
- Small Press Review. m. ISSN 0037-7228

**Dutchess County Genealogical Society**
Box 708, Poughkeepsie, NY 12602.
- Dutchess. q.

**E. P. Dutton & Co., Inc.**
201 Park Ave. S., New York, NY 10003.
- Best Detective Stories of the Year. a. ISSN 0067-625X
- Best Science Fiction Stories of the Year. a.
- Best Sports Stories. a. ISSN 0067-6292
- Let's Go: the Student Guide to Europe. a. ISSN 0075-8868
- Let's Go: the Student Guide to the United States and Canada. irreg. ISSN 0090-788X
- Making It: A Guide to Student Finances. irreg. (Subscr. to: Harvard Student Agencies, 4 Holyoke St., Cambridge MA 02138)

**Delamer Duverus Coordinates**
Duverus Bldg., Box 68, Seligman, MO 65745.
- Ozark Sunbeam. w.

**Dwarf Iris Society**
c/o Elsie A. Zuercher, Ed., 121 E. Union St, Portland, IN 47371.
- Dwarf Iris Society Portfolio. a. ISSN 0418-2057

**Dynastat, Inc.**
2704 Rio Grande, Austin, TX 78705.
- Dynastat Report. fortn.

**E.C. Publications, Inc.**
485 Madison Ave., New York, NY 10022.
- Mad. m.(8 per yr) ISSN 0024-9319

**E D A Corp.**
1812 Cadwell Ave., Box 2460, Cleveland, OH 44118.
- Dressage & CT; the national magazine. m.

**E D P News Services Inc.**
7620 Little River Turnpike, Annandale, VA 22003.
- Computer Age; world trade report. s-m. ISSN 0010-4477
- E D P Weekly. w. ISSN 0012-7558
- E F T S Report. (Electronic Funds Transfer Industry) m. ISSN 0360-3784
- Mini-Micro Computer Report; a monthly digest of significant trends in mini-computing and micro-processing. m. ISSN 0363-7905
- Peripherals Weekly. w. ISSN 0031-5400
- Software Digest. w. ISSN 0038-0636

**E G & G Inc.**
45 William St., Wellesley, MA 02181.
- EGGink. q.

**E G G**
Box 289, Surfside, CA 90743.
- E G G. q.

**E-Go Enterprises**
13510 Ventura Blvd., Sherman Oaks, CA 91423.
- All Man. m.
- Man's Delight. m.

**E. I. du Pont de Nemours & Co.**
Du Pont Bldg., 1007 Market St., Wilmington, DE 19898.
- Du Pont. bi-m. ISSN 0046-0834
- Du Pont Context. 3 per yr. ISSN 0300-7138

**E I P, Inc.**
Box 7158, Box 1648, Madison, WI 53707.
- Food Service Marketing. m. ISSN 0092-5845

**E K H E Advertising**
Box One, Brooklyn, NY 11231.
- Justice Weekly. w. ISSN 0022-7048

**E. Leitz, Inc.**
Rockleigh, NJ 07647.
- Leica Photography. irreg. ISSN 0024-063X

**E P I E Institute**
475 Riverside Dr., New York, NY 10027.
- E P I E Gram: Materials. (Educational Products Information Exchange) fortn.
- E P I E Report. (Educational Products Information Exchange) bi-m.

**E R I C**
Processing and Reference Facility, 4833 Rugby Ave., Suite 303, Bethesda, MD 20014
(Subscr. to Supt. of Documents, U.S. Government Printing Office, Washington, DC 20402)
- Current Index to Journals in Education. (pub. by Macmillan Information)
- Resources in Education. m. ISSN 0098-0897

**E R I C. Clearinghouse on Early Childhood Education**
University of Illinois, Urbana, IL 61801
(Orders to: Supt. of Documents, Washington, DC 20402)
- Research Relating to Children. Bulletins. s-a. ISSN 0080-1704

**E R I C Clearinghouse on Educational Management**
University of Oregon, Eugene, OR 97403.
- Directory of Organizations and Personnel in Educational Management. irreg. (approx. biennial) , no. 4, 1974. ISSN 0070-6035

**E R I C. Clearinghouse on Higher Education**
George Washington University, One Dupont Circle, Suite 630, Washington, DC 20036
(or American Association for Higher Education, One Dupont Circle, Suite 780, Washington, DC 20036)
- E R I C-A A H E Research Reports. 10 per yr. (Co-sponsor: American Association for Higher Education)
- ERIC/Higher Education Research Currents. 8 per yr.

**E R I C Clearinghouse on Urban Education**
Columbia University, Teachers College, Box 40, New York, NY 10027.
- I R C D Bulletin. 4 per yr. ISSN 0536-1966

**E S E California**
509 N. Harbor Rd., La Habra, CA 90631.
- Academy Awards Oscar Annual. a. ISSN 0092-5675

**E S P Research Associates Foundation**
Union National Plaza, Suite 1630, Little Rock, AR 72201.
- E S P Research Associates Foundation. News Letter. bi-m.

**E V A N-G**
see Committee to End Violence Against the Next Generation

**E W Communications, Inc.**
3921 E. Bayshore Road, Palo Alto, CA 94303.
- Electronic Warfare. bi-m. (Association of Old Crows)

**E Z Maid Inc.**
129 Broadway, Lynbrook, NY 11563.
- Homesewing Trade News. m. ISSN 0018-425X

**Ear Magazine-New York**
32 E. 2 St., New York, NY 10003.
- Ear (New York) m.

**Ear Press**
1824 Curtis St., Berkeley, CA 94702.
- Ear (Berkeley) m.

**Ear Research Institute**
256 Lake St., Los Angeles, CA 90057.
- Oto Review. q.

**Early American Industries Association**
Old Economy, Ambridge, PA 15003.
- Early American Industries Association. Chronicle. q. ISSN 0012-8147
- Shavings from the Chronicle of the Early American Industries Association. irreg., no. 26, 1976.

**Early American Society**
Box 1831, Harrisburg, PA 17105.
- Early American Life. bi-m. ISSN 0012-8155

**Early English Text Society**
- Early English Text Society. Publications. Extra Series. (pub. by Oxford University Press)
- Early English Text Society. Publications. Original Series. (pub. by Oxford University Press)
- Early English Text Society. Publications. Supplementary Texts. (pub. by Oxford University Press)

**Early Ford V-8 Club of America**
Box 2122, San Leandro, CA 94577.
- V-Eight Times. bi-m.

**Early Music Laboratory**
Box 2552, Hollywood, CA 90028.
- Early Music Laboratory. Bulletins and Tapes. a.

**Earnshaw Publications Inc.**
393 Seventh Ave., New York, NY 10001.
- Earnshaw's Infants' & Children's Review. m. ISSN 0012-8198
- Small World; the magazine of nursery furniture, wheel goods, toys and accessories. m. ISSN 0037-7260

**Earth Guild Inc**
Hot Springs, NC 28743.
- Earth Guild Mail Order Catalog. s-a.

**Earth Religious Supplies, Inc.**
35 W. 19th St., New York, NY 10011.
- Earth Religion News. 12 per yr.

**Earth Science Publishing Co.**
Box 1815, Colorado Spring, CO 80901.
- Earth Science. bi-m. ISSN 0012-8228

**Earth's Daughters**
944 Kensington Ave., Buffalo, NY 14215.
- Earth's Daughters; a feminist arts periodical. q.

**East Carolina University. Department of English**
Greenville, NC 27834.
- Teaching English in the Two-Year College. 3 per yr. ISSN 0098-6291

**East Carolina University. Department of History**
Greenville, NC 27834.
- East Carolina University Publications in History. irreg., 1966, vol. 3. ISSN 0070-8089

**East Carolina University. Department of Political Science**
Greenville, NC 27834.
- Politics. a. ISSN 0079-3078

**East Carolina University Poetry Forum Press**
Department of English, Greenville, NC 27834.
- Tar River Poets. 1-2 per yr. ISSN 0039-9639

**East Central Illinois Criminal Justice Commission, Inc.**
204 N. Logan Ave, Danville, IL 61832.
- East Central Illinois Criminal Justice Commission. Criminal Justice Plan Update. a.

**East End Publishers, Inc.**
10 W. 66th St., New York, NY 10023.
- Manhattan Gazette. m.

**East Side Chamber of Commerce**
237 First Ave., New York, NY 10003.
- East Side Chamber of Commerce Newsletter. bi-m. ISSN 0012-8538

**East Side Express**
148 W. 24th St., New York, NY 10011.
- East Side Express. w.

**East Tennessee Development District**
Box 15,000, Knoxville, TN 37901.
- E T D D Newsletter. m.

**East Tennessee Historical Society**
Lawson McGhee Library, Knoxville, TN 37902.
- Echoes from the East Tennessee Historical
  Society. q. ISSN 0422-2482

**East Tennessee State University. Research Advisory Council**
Johnson City, TN 37601.
- East Tennessee State University. Research
  Advisory Council. Publications. irreg.(3 per year)
  ISSN 0082-2744

**East Texas Chamber of Commerce**
Box 1592, Longview, TX 75601.
- East Texas. m. ISSN 0012-8554

**East Texas School Study Council**
East Texas State University, Commerce, TX 75428.
- Catalyst for Change. 3 per yr. (National School
  Development Council)

**East Texas State University**
Box 3036, E.T. Sta., Commerce, TX 75428.
- Ecumene. a. ISSN 0531-786X

**East-West Center**
1777 East-West Rd., Honolulu, HI 96822.
- East-West Center Magazine. q. ISSN 0012-8597
  (prep. by its Public Affairs Office)

**East-West Center. Communications Institute**
1777 East-West Road, Honolulu, HI 96822.
- East-West Communication Institute. Information,
  Education, Communication in Population. bi-m.
- I E C. (Information, Education, Communication)
  bi-m.

**East-West Center. Culture Learning Institute**
1777 East-West Rd., Honolulu, HI 96848.
- Culture and Language Learning Report. q.
- Language Planning Newsletter. q.

**East-West Center. East-West Technology and Development Institute**
1777 East-West Rd., Honolulu, HI 96822.
- Infotech; Technology and Development Institute
  newsletter. q.

**East-West Center. Population Institute**
1777 East-West Rd., Honolulu, HI 96822.
- Asian and Pacific Census Newsletter. q.

**East-West Network, Inc.**
5900 Wilshire Blvd., Suite 300, Los Angeles, CA 90036.
- California. m. (Pacific Southwest Airlines)
- Clipper. m. ISSN 0009-9406
- Eastern ReView. m. (Eastern Airlines)
- Flightime. m. (Allegheny Continental and Ozark
  Airlines)
- Holiday Inn Companion. m.
- Mainliner. m. ISSN 0025-083X (United Airlines)
- Sky. m. (Delta Air Lines)

**East-West Publishing Co.**
838 Grant Ave., Suite 307, San Francisco, CA 94108.
- East/West; the Chinese-American journal. w.
  ISSN 0012-8589

**East-West Trade Council**
1700 Pennsylvania Ave., Washington, DC 20006.
- East-West Trade Council. Newsletter. s-m.

**Easter Publishing**
P.O. Box 1244, Mobile, AL 36601.
- Azalea City News. w.

**Eastern Airlines**
- Eastern ReView. (pub. by East-West Network,
  Inc.)

**Eastern Apicultural Society**
Cornwall Bridge Rd., Sharon, CT 06069.
- Eastern Apicultural Society Newsletter. 4 per yr.

**Eastern Association of Student Financial Aid Administrators**
House of Printing, 8833 Brookville Road, Silver
Spring, MD 20910.
- Eastern Association of Student Financial Aid
  Administrators. Directory. a. ISSN 0091-7168

**Eastern Automotive Journal**
Box 373, Cedarhurst, NY 11516.
- Eastern Automotive Journal. bi-m.

**Eastern Band of Cherokee Indians. Tribal Council**
Box 501, Cherokee, NC 28719.
- Cherokee One Feather. w. ISSN 0045-6543

**Eastern Communication Association**
c/o Richard Bailey, Department of Speech
Communication, University of Rhode Island,
Kingston, RI 02881.
- Communication Quarterly. q.

**Eastern Dental Society**
c/o David I. Kratenstein D.D.S., Ed., 630 Fifth
Ave., New York, NY 10020.
- Eastern Dental Society Bulletin. m. ISSN 0012-
  8759

**Eastern Economic Association**
Department of Economics, Bloomsburg State
College, Bloomsburg, PA 17815.
- Eastern Economic Journal. q.

**Eastern Finance Association**
c/o Prof. John Clark, College of Business
Administration, Drexel University, Philadelphia, PA
19104.
- Eastern Finance Association. Proceedings of the
  Annual Meeting. a.
- Financial Review. a. ISSN 0066-5363

**Eastern Illinois University. Student Publications**
Charleston, IL 61920.
- Eastern News. d. (Mon.-Fri.) ISSN 0012-8864

**Eastern Massachusetts Regional Library System**
Boston Public Library, Copley Square, Boston, MA
02117.
- Eastern Massachusetts Regional Library System.
  Eastern Region News. 10 per yr. ISSN 0012-8899

**Eastern Michigan University. Department of English**
Ypsilanti, MI 48197.
- Journal of Narrative Technique. 3 per yr. ISSN
  0022-2925

**Eastern Milk Producers**
6567 Kinne Rd., Syracuse, NY 13214.
- Eastern Milk Producer. m.

**Eastern Montana Catholic Diocese**
P.O. Box 2107, Great Falls, MT 59403.
- Montana Catholic Register. w.

**Eastern Nebraska Genealogical Society**
Fremont, NE 68025.
- Eastern Nebraska Genealogical Society. Quarterly.
  q.

**Eastern New Mexico University. Department of Anthropology**
Portales, NM 88130.
- Eastern New Mexico University. Contributions in
  Anthropology. irreg. ISSN 0070-8232

**Eastern New Mexico University. Natural Sciences Research Institute**
Portales, NM 88130.
- Studies in Natural Sciences. 3 per yr.

**Eastern New Mexico University. Paleo-Indian Institute**
Paleo-Indian Institute, Portales, NM 88130.
- Abstracts of Doctoral Dissertations in
  Anthropology. a.

**Eastern North Carolina Genealogical Society**
Box 395, New Bern, NC 28560.
- Eastern North Carolina Genealogical Society.
  Quarterly Review. q.

**Eastern Pennsylvania Psychiatric Institute**
Henry Ave. & Abbottsford Rd., Philadelphia, PA
19129.
- Contemporary Issues of Mental Health:
  Monograph Series. q.

**Eastern Psychiatric Association**
- Diseases of the Nervous System. (pub. by
  Physicians Postgraduate Press)

**Eastern Publishing Co.**
1420 Prince St., Alexandaria, VA 22314.
- Stock Car Racing. m.
- Super Stock & Drag Illustrated. m. ISSN 0039-
  5692

**Eastern Regional Research Center**
600 East Mermaid Lane, Philadelphia, PA 19118.
- Eastern Regional Research Center. Publications
  and Patents. s-a.

**Eastern Review, Inc.**
G.P.O. Box 495, Brooklyn, NY 11201.
- Drum Corps Review. m. ISSN 0094-3649

**Eastern School Law Review**
c/o Stephen F. Roach, Box 307, Sun City, AZ
85351.
- Eastern School Law Review. m.(Sept.-June) ISSN
  0012-8910

**Eastern States Archeological Federation**
Bronson Museum, 8 N. Main St., Attleboro, MA
02703.
- Archaeology of Eastern North America. a. ISSN
  0360-1021

**Eastern Washington State College. Department of History**
Cheney, WA 99004.
- Pacific Northwest Forum. q.

**Eastern - Western Quarter Horse Journal**
P.O. Box 647, Route 28, Middleboro, MA 02346.
- Eastern - Western Quarter Horse Journal. m.

**Robert Eastman, Ed. & Pub.**
P.O. Box 368, Ithaca, NY 14850.
- No Deadline. irreg.

**Eastman Kodak Co.**
Rochester, NY 14650.
- Dental Radiography and Photography. q. ISSN
  0045-9941
- Kodak Dealer News. bi-m. ISSN 0023-2602
- Kodak Photonews. s-a.
- Medical Radiography and Photography. 3 per yr.
  ISSN 0025-746X
- Newsletter for Graphic Arts and Photography
  Instructors. 3 per yr.
- Studio Light/Commercial Camera. q. ISSN 0039-
  4122
- Visuals Are a Language. 3 per yr.

**Eastman Kodak Co. Eastman Organic Chemicals**
Rochester, NY 14650.
- Eastman Organic Chemical Bulletin. 4 per yr.
  ISSN 0012-897X

**Easy Money Refund Bulletin**
c/o Carol Comperchio, Ed., Box 1012, Jackson, MI
49204.
- Easy Money Refund Bulletin. m.

**Ebasco Services Incorporated**
100 Church St., New York, NY 10007.
- Analysis of Public Utility Financing. w., q., and a.
  ISSN 0421-9910

**Ebel-Doctorow Publications, Inc.**
1115 Clifton Ave., Clifton, NJ 07013.
- American Glass Review. m. (s-m. Feb.) ISSN
  0002-8649
- American Glass Review Glass Factory Directory
  Issue. a.
- Antiques Dealer. m. ISSN 0003-5947
- China Glass & Tableware. m. (s-m. Aug.) ISSN
  0009-4382
- China Glass and Tableware Red Book Directory.
  a. ISSN 0069-3677
- Home Lighting & Accessories. m.

**Ebenezer Society**
2523 Portland Ave., Minneapolis, MN 55404.
- Ebenezer. q.

**Ebsco Industries**
Box 1943, Birmingham, AL 35201.
- Ebsco Bulletin of Serials Changes. bi-m. ISSN
  0360-0637

**Ecco Press Ltd.**
1 W. 30 St., New York, NY 10001.
- American Poetry Series. irreg.; vol. 12, 1977.
- Antaeus. q. ISSN 0003-5319

**A. Ross Eckler, Ed. & Pub.**
Spring Valley Rd., Morristown, NJ 07960.
- Word Ways; journal of recreational linguistics. q.
  ISSN 0043-7980

**Eclectic Magazine Co.**
1208 E. Cliveden St., Philadelphia, PA 19119.
- Eclectic. q. ISSN 0012-9399

**Eco-Logos**
Box 393, Denver, CO 80201.
- Eco-Logos; a clearing house for facts, theories and fancies on the history, science and bibliography of the international language movement. q.

**Ecological Society of America**
c/o William E. Hazen, Ed., Dept. of Biology, San Diego State College, San Diego, CA 92115.
- Australian Journal of Ecology. (pub. by Blackwell Scientific Publications Ltd. UK)
- Ecological Monographs. (pub. by Duke University Press)
- Ecological Society of America. Bulletin. q. ISSN 0012-9623
- Ecology. (pub. by Duke University Press)

**Ecology Action East**
Box 344, Cooper Sta., New York, NY 10003.
- Roots; a magazine of social ecology. irreg.,approx 1 per yr. ISSN 0017-2790

**Ecology Center**
2179 Allston Way, Berkeley, CA 94704.
- Ecology Center Newsletter. m.

**Ecology Center of Ann Arbor**
417 Detroit St., Ann Arbor, MI 48104.
- Ecology Reports. m.

**Econocast Services**
225 W. 71st St., New York, NY 10023.
- Econocast World Banker. fortn.

**Econometric Society**
c/o Department of Economics, Northwestern University, Evanston, IL 60201
(Subscr. c/o Tieto Ltd., 5 Elton Rd., Clevedon, Bristol BS21 7RA England)
- Econometrica. bi-m. ISSN 0012-9682

**Economic Affairs Bureau, Inc.**
324 Somerville Ave., Somerville, ME 02143.
- Dollars & Sense; a monthly bulletin of economic affairs. 10 per yr.

**Economic Geology Publishing Co.**
c/o Dept. of Geology, Univ. of Minnesota-Duluth, Duluth, MN 55812.
- Economic Geology and the Bulletin of the Society of Economic Geologists. 8 per yr. ISSN 0013-0109

**Economic History Association**
c/o Eleutherian Mills Historical Library, Wilmington, DE 19807.
- Journal of Economic History. q. ISSN 0022-0507

**Economic News Agency Inc.**
Box 174, Princeton, NJ 08540.
- Green's Commodity Market Comments. s-m. ISSN 0017-4076

**Economic Research Center, Inc.**
32 College St., Dayton, OH 45407.
- Confrontation-Change Review. s-a.

**Economic Statistics Bureau of Washington, D.C.**
Box 10163, Washington, DC 20018.
- Handbook of Basic Economic Statistics; a manual of basic economic data on industry, commerce, labor and agriculture in the United States. m. ISSN 0017-7199

**Economical Driver**
211 Woodbine Avenue, Northport, NY 11768.
- Economical Driver. bi-m.

**Economics and Technology Inc.**
101 Tremont St., Boston, MA 02108.
- Trends in Communications Regulation. m.

**Economics Press Inc.**
12 Daniel Rd., Fairfield, NJ 07006.
- Better Letters. w. ISSN 0006-0178
- Bits & Pieces. m.
- Discipline. fortn. ISSN 0417-688X

**Economist Publishing Co.**
12 East Grand Ave., Chicago, IL 60611.
- Who's Who in the Securities Industry. a. ISSN 0090-418X

**Ecosources**
Sunset Hill School, 400 W. 51st St., Kansas City, MO 64112.
- Ecosources. m. ISSN 0046-1229

**Ecuadorian-American Association Inc.**
55 Liberty St., New York, NY 10005.
- Ecuadorian-American Association. Bulletin. m.

**Ecumenical Institute**
3444 W. Congress Parkway, Chicago, IL 60624.
- I. E. (Chicago) irreg. ISSN 0422-4108

**Ed-U Press**
760 Ostrom Ave, Syracuse, NY 13210.
- S I S I M S. (Say It So It Makes Sense) q. (Syracuse University. Family Planning and Population Information Center)

**Eddy Dance Foundation**
124 Chambers St., New York, NY 10007.
- Eddy. q (approx.)

**Morris Edelson, Ed. & Pub.**
151 E. Gilman, Madison, WI 53703.
- Quixote. 6 per yr. ISSN 0033-6629

**Eden Valley Press**
Box 328, Loveland, CO 80537.
- Emissary. m.

**Edgeworks**
c/o Peter Kaldheim, Editor, 8312 Seventh Ave., Brooklyn, NY 11228.
- Edgeworks. s-a.

**Julian I. Edison, Ed. & Pub.**
16 Dromara Rd., St. Louis, MO 63124.
- Miniature Book News. q. ISSN 0026-5128

**Edison Electric Institute**
90 Park Ave., New York, NY 10016.
- Annual Power Survey. a. (prep. by its Electric Power Survey Committee)
- E E I Statistical Releases. Electric Output. w. ISSN 0012-7612
- Edison Electric Institute. Statistical Yearbook of the Electric Utility Industry. a. (prep. by its Statistical Committee)
- Edison Electric Institute, New York. Publication. irreg.
- Electric Perspectives. bi-m.
- Year-End Summary of the Electric Power Situation in the United States. a. ISSN 0424-480X (prep. by its Electric Power Survey Committee)

**Editions Publisol**
P.O. Box 339, New York, NY 10028.
- International Auction Records. a. ISSN 0074-1922

**Editor & Printer Publishing Co.**
470 Atlantic Ave., Boston, MA 02210.
- New England Printer and Lithographer. m. ISSN 0028-484X

**Editor & Publisher Co., Inc.**
850 Third Ave., New York, NY 10022.
- Editor & Publisher International Year Book; encyclopedia of the newspaper industry. a. ISSN 0424-4923
- Editor & Publisher-the Fourth Estate; spot news and features about newspapers, advertisers & agencies. w. ISSN 0013-094X

**Editorial Projects for Education**
1717 Massachusetts Ave., N.W., Washington, DC 20036.
- Chronicle of Higher Education. w; b-w during summer. ISSN 0009-5982
- Chronicle of Higher Education: 15-Minute Report for College and University Trustees. 20 per yr.

**Editorial Services Inc.**
Box 440, St. Charles, IL 60174.
- Midwest Landscaping; the midcontinent magazine of lands, contracting and maintenance. m. ISSN 0026-3400 (Illinois Landscape Contractors Association)

**Editors and Engineers Ltd.**
4300 W. 62nd St., Indianapolis, IN 46268.
- Radio Handbook. irreg., 1972, 19th ed. ISSN 0079-9467

**Charles H. Edmonds, Ed. & Pub**
481 North First St., Suite 30, San Jose, CA 95112.
- Northern California Retailer. m.

**Glen Edmonds**
The Pagosa Springs Sun, Pagosa Springs, CO 81147.
- Jicarilla Chieftain. bi-w. ISSN 0021-695X (Jicarilla Apache Tribe)

**Edmund Publications Corp.**
295 Northern Blvd., Great Neck, NY 11021.
- Edmund's Auto-Pedia. a.
- Edmund's Car Prices. a.
- Edmund's Foreign Car Prices. s-a. ISSN 0531-7886
- Edmund's New Car Prices. 3 per yr.
- Edmund's Used Car Prices. q. ISSN 0424-5059

**Edo Western Corp.**
2645 South 300 West, Salt Lake City, UT 84115.
- Flying Fish Newsletter. 3 per yr. ISSN 0046-4244

**Education and Training Consultants Co. (ETC)**
Box 49899, Los Angeles, CA 90049.
- Systems Engineering of Education Series. irreg., 1975, no. 19 in prep. ISSN 0082-1217

**Education Commission of the States**
Suite 300, Lincoln Tower, 1860 Lincoln, Denver, CO 80203.
- Compact. bi-m. ISSN 0010-3934
- Directory of Professional Personnel: State Higher Education Executive Officers (S H E E O), Including Canadian Members, and Regional Higher Education Compact Agencies. a.
- Education Commission of the States. National Assessment of Educational Progress. Assessment Reports. irreg. (approx. 10-25 per yr.) (Subscr. to: Supt. of Documents, Govt. Printing Office, Washington, DC 20402)
- Education Commission of the States Bulletin. m. ISSN 0046-1407
- Higher Education in the States. 8-10 per yr. ISSN 0046-7375

**Education Commission of the States. Department of Postsecondary Education**
300 Lincoln Tower, 1860 Lincoln Street, Denver, CO 80203.
- Education Commission of the States. Department of Postsecondary Education. Update. irreg.

**Education Development Center**
Publications Office, 55 Chapel St., Newton, MA 02160.
- E D C News. s-a.
- Education Development Center. Annual Report. a. ISSN 0424-5407

**Education Exploration Center**
3104 16th Ave. So., Minneapolis, MN 55404.
- Education Exploration Center Journal. q.
- Education Exploration Center Newsletter. m.

**Education Funding Research Council**
752 National Press Bldg. N.W., Washington, DC 20045.
- Federal Funding Guide for Elementary and Secondary Education. a. ISSN 0095-3342

**Education Law Center**
605 Broad St., Newark, NJ 07102.
- E L C. q. ISSN 0364-118X

**Education Today Company, Inc.**
- Learning. (pub. by Thomas O. Ryder)

**Education-Training Market Report**
Box 795, Westbury, NY 11590.
- Education-Training Market Report. bi-m. ISSN 0013-1555

**Education Writers Association**
Box 281, Woodstown, NJ 08098.
- Education Reporter. 6 per yr. ISSN 0013-1512

**Educational Administration Services, Inc.**
Box 286, Beloit, KS 67420.
- Creative Teacher. m (Sept.-May) ISSN 0045-8988

**Educational & Community Counselors Associates, Inc.**
1629 K. St, NW, Suite 520, Washington, DC 20006.
- Journal of Afro-American Issues. q. ISSN 0094-1859

**Educational and Psychological Measurement**
Box 6907, College Station, Durham, NC 27708.
- Educational and Psychological Measurement; devoted to the development and application of measures of individual differences. q. ISSN 0013-1644

**Educational Arts Association**
90 Sherman St., Cambridge, MA 02140.
- Creative Arts. q.

**Educational Bureau, Inc.**
333 N. Michigan Ave., Rm. 528, Chicago, IL 60601.
- Boarding School Directory of the United States. irreg. ISSN 0523-7785

**Educational Catalyst**
Room 302, Ball Education Bldg., Memphis State University, Memphis, TN 38152.
- Educational Catalyst. irreg. ISSN 0361-5049

**Educational Change, Inc.**
N B W Tower, New Rochelle, NY 10801.
- Change. m. ISSN 0009-1383

**Educational Commission for Foreign Medical Graduates**
3624 Market St., Philadelphia, PA 19104.
- Educational Commission for Foreign Medical Graduates. Annual Report. a.

**Educational Communication Center**
Box 657, Camp Hill, PA 17011.
- Journal of Educational Communication. q.

**Educational Communications, Inc.**
3202 Doolittle Dr., Northbrook, IL 60062.
- Who's Who Among American High School Students. a.

**Educational Directories Inc.**
P.O. Box 199, Mount Prospect, IL 60056.
- Patterson's American Education. a. ISSN 0079-0230
- Patterson's Schools Classified. a. ISSN 0553-4054

**Educational Facilities Laboratories**
850 Third Ave., New York, NY 10022.
- Schoolhouse. 4-5 per yr.

**Educational Film Library Association, Inc.**
43 W. 61 St., New York, NY 10023.
- American Film Festival Guide. a.
- E F L A Evaluations. 10 per yr.
- Sightlines. 4 per yr. ISSN 0037-4830

**Educational Foundation for Nuclear Science**
Kent Chemical Laboratory, 1020-24 E. 58 St., Chicago, IL 60637.
- Bulletin of the Atomic Scientists; magazine of science and public affairs. m. (Sept.-June)

**Educational Freedom Foundation**
Research Committee, 20 Parkland, Glendale, MO 63122.
- Educational Freedom. s-a. ISSN 0013-1741

**Educational Media Council**
1346 Connecticut Ave. N.W., Washington, DC 20036.
- E M C Directory of Summer Session Courses on Educational Media. a (not published in 1974)

**Educational Networks, Inc.**
Box 237, Nokesville, VA 22123.
- Soap Box. q.

**Educational Pet Journal, Inc.**
44 Court St., Brooklyn, NY 11201.
- Pet News; educational pet journal. bi-m.

**Educational Press Association of America**
Glassboro State College, Glassboro, NJ 08028.
- America's Education Press. biennial.
- EdPress Newsletter. m. (Aug.-May) ISSN 0013-1024

**Educational Research Corp.**
85 Main St., Watertown, MA 02172.
- College Admissions Data Service. irreg.

**Educational Resources Information Center**
*see* E R I C

**Educational Reviewer, Inc.**
Box 3070, Grand Central Sta., New York, NY 10017.
- University Bookman; a quarterly review. q. ISSN 0041-9265

**Educational Screen, Inc.**
434 S. Wabash Ave., Chicago, IL 60605.
- A V Guide Newsletter. m.

**Educational Service Bureau, Inc.**
1835 K St., N.W., Washington, DC 20006.
- Educators Negotiating Service. s-m. ISSN 0046-1571

- Negotiations Management. m. ISSN 0047-9292
- Personnel News for School Systems. m. ISSN 0048-3478
- Rhodes Report; career opportunities in education. 8 per yr. ISSN 0048-8224
- Salary and Merit. m. ISSN 0048-9026

**Educational Subscription Service, Inc.**
- Educator's Newsletter. (pub. by Shrikumar Poddar)

**Educational Technology Publications, Inc.**
140 Sylvan Ave., Englewood Cliffs, NJ 07632.
- Educational Technology. m. ISSN 0013-1962
- Educational Technology Bibliography Series. irreg. ISSN 0070-9352

**Educational Testing Service**
Princeton, NJ 08540.
- E T S Developments. q. ISSN 0046-1547
- Education Recaps. m(10 per yr) ISSN 0013-1504
- Educational Testing Service Annual Report. a. ISSN 0091-8989
- Graduate & Professional School Opportunities for Minority Students. biennial. ISSN 0090-8266
- International Newsletter: Educational Evaluation and Research. irreg., usually twice a year. ISSN 0074-7130
- Test Collection Bulletin. q. ISSN 0563-1874

**Educational Theory**
University of Illinois at Urbana-Champaign, College of Education, Urbana, IL 61801.
- Educational Theory; a medium of expression for the John Dewey Society and the Philosophy of Education Society. q. ISSN 0013-2004

**Educational Users Group**
- Educational User's Group Newsletter. (pub. by Hewlett Packard Co. (Santa Clara))

**Educators Progress Service, Inc.**
Randolph, WI 53956.
- Educators Grade Guide to Free Teaching Aids. a. ISSN 0070-9387
- Educators Guide to Free Audio and Video Materials. a.
- Educators Guide to Free Films. a. ISSN 0070-9395
- Educators Guide to Free Filmstrips. a. ISSN 0070-9409
- Educators Guide to Free Guidance Materials. a. ISSN 0070-9417
- Educators Guide to Free Health, Physical Education & Recreation Materials. a. ISSN 0424-6241
- Educators Guide to Free Science Materials. a. ISSN 0070-9425
- Educators Guide to Free Social Studies Materials. a. ISSN 0070-9433
- Educators Index of Free Materials. a.
- Elementary Teachers Guide to Free Curriculum Materials. irreg. ISSN 0070-9980

**Edwards Publications, Inc.**
School Lane, Roosevelt, NJ 08555.
- Today's Child Newsmagazine. m. (Oct.-Jun.) ISSN 0040-8468

**Wm. B. Eerdmans Publishing Co.**
255 Jefferson Ave., S.E., Grand Rapids, MI 49502.
- Advance of Christianity through the Centuries. irreg. ISSN 0065-2067
- Reformed Church of America. Historical Series. irreg., 1970, no. 2. ISSN 0080-0481
- Reformed Journal; a periodical of reformed comment and opinion. 10 per yr. ISSN 0486-252X

**Effective Speech Writer's Newsletter**
Box 444, University of Richmond, VA 23173.
- Effective Speech Writer's Newsletter. bi-m.

**Arthur Efron, Ed. & Pub.**
123 Woodward Ave., Buffalo, NY 14214.
- Paunch. 2 per yr. ISSN 0031-3262

**Egret Press**
302 Menendez, St. Simons Island, GA 31522.
- 4 Elements. 3 per yr.

**Egyptian Philatelists International**
Box 3875, Torrance, Los Angeles, CA 90503.
- Egyptian Philatelic Topics. bi-m.

**Ehrenreich Photo-Optical Industries, Inc.**
623 Stewart Ave., Garden City, NY 11530.
- Nikon World. a. ISSN 0029-0513

**Roy Ehrhardt, Ed. & Pub.**
Box 9808, Kansas City, MO 64134.
- Pocket Watch Price Guide. a.

**J. P. Eichorn, Ed. & Pub.**
Box 2000, Napa, CA 94558.
- Pacific Traffic. m. ISSN 0030-8943

**Eight Northern Pueblos**
Box 927, San Juan Pueblo, NM 87566.
- Indian Forerunner. m.

**Eisenhower College. Board of Trustees**
Seneca Falls, NY 13148.
- Eisenhower College Newsletter. q. ISSN 0046-1636

**Richard Ekstract, Ed. & Pub.**
325 E. 75 St., New York, NY 10021.
- Audio Times. s-m.

**El Paso Archaeological Society, Inc.**
Box 4345, El Paso, TX 79914.
- Artifact. q. ISSN 0004-3680
- El Paso Archaeological Society. Special Reports. a. ISSN 0070-9573
- El Paso Archaeology. m. ISSN 0013-4023

**El Paso County Historical Society**
600 Gregory Way, El Paso, TX 79902.
- Password. q. ISSN 0031-2738

**El Ra-Ed Publications Corp.**
60 Hamilton Ave., Staten Island, NY 10301.
- El Ra-Ed News. m.

**Elder Churchman.**
c/o Rev. Max A. Kapp, Box 1392, Vineyard Haven, MA 02568.
- Elder Churchman; a journal for retired ministers of the Unitarian Universalist Association. 3 per yr. ISSN 0360-6120

**Aethelred Eldridge, Ed. & Pub.**
R.R. No. 1, Millfield, OH 45761.
- News from Golgonooza. s-m.

**Electric Machinery Mfg. Co.**
800 Central Ave., Minneapolis, MN 55413.
- E-M Synchronizer. 2 per yr. ISSN 0012-7795

**Electric Power Associations of Mississippi**
Box 8656, 2805 Greenway Dr., Jackson, MS 39204.
- Mississippi E P A News. m. ISSN 0026-6175

**Electric Power Research Institute**
P.O. Box 10412, Palo Alto, CA 94303.
- E P R I News. bi-m.

**Electric Railroaders' Association**
145 Greenwich Street, NY 10006.
- Headlights. m. ISSN 0091-8059
- Headlights News Journal. m. (Ed. Address:, 5079 Blacksmith Dr., Columbia, MD 21044)

**Electric Vehicle Council**
- Electric Vehicle News. (pub. by Porter Corp.)

**Electrical Consultant**
c/o Bill Payne, 629 Sherwood Rd. N.E., Atlanta, GA 30324.
- Electrical Consultant. m. ISSN 0361-4972

**Electrical Equipment Representatives Association**
P.O. Box 999, Morro Bay, CA 93442.
- Electrical Equipment Representatives Association. Directory. a. ISSN 0070-9689

**Electrical Information Publications, Inc.**
c/o D. W. Grosshandler, Box 1648, Madison, WI 53701.
- Electric Comfort Conditioning News. m.
- Modern Schools; food service, electric heat, lighting, cooling, audiovisual and electronic teaching devises. 9 per yr. ISSN 0026-8410

**The Electrification Council**
90 Park Ave, New York, NY 10016.
- T E C Report; for education in the efficient use of electrical energy, electrical products and electrical services. m. ISSN 0039-8314

**Electrochemical Society Inc.**
Box 2071, Princeton, NJ 08540.
- Electrochemical Society. Journal. m. ISSN 0013-4651
- Electrochemical Society Series. (pub. by Wiley-Interscience)

**Electrographic Corp.**
- Newspaper Requirements. (pub. by Reilly-Lake Shore Graphics)

**Electron Microscopy Society of America**
- Electron Microscopy Society of America. Proceedings. (pub. by Claitor's Publishing Division)

**Electronic Connector Study Group, Inc.**
Box 1428, Camden, NJ 08101.
- Electronic Connector Study Group. Annual Connector Symposium. Proceedings. a.

**Electronic Defense Association**
c/o Hamilton Burr Publishing Co., 2065 Martin Ave., Suite 104, Santa Clara, CA 95050.
- Electronic, Electro-Optic and Infrared Countermeasures. m.

**Electronic Industries Association**
Marketing Services Dept., 2001 Eye St., N.W., Washington, DC 20006.
- Directory of Defense Electronic Products and Services: United States Suppliers. (pub. by Bermont Books)
- E I A Electronics Multimedia Handbook. (pub. by Howard W. Sams & Co., Inc.)
- E I A International Report. m.
- Electronic Industries Association. Trade Directory and Membership List. a. ISSN 0091-9519
- Electronic Market Data Book. a. ISSN 0070-9867
- Electronic Trends. m. ISSN 0013-4996

**Electronic Periodicals, Inc**
33393 Aurora Rd., Cleveland, OH 44139.
- Electronic Distributing. m.

**Electronic Representatives Association**
233 E. Erie St., Suite 1002, Chicago, IL 60611.
- Directory of Electronic Representatives. a.
- Representor. m. ISSN 0034-4915

**Electronics of America**
Box 2305, Chapel Hill, NC 27514.
- Electronics of America; international airmail letter. w. ISSN 0046-1741
- New American Electronics Literature and Technical Data; monthly airmail letter. m. ISSN 0047-9519

**Elevator World**
Box 6523, Loop Branch, Mobile, AL 36606.
- Elevator World. m. ISSN 0013-6158

**Eleventh District Dental Society**
86-90 188th St., Jamaica, NY 11423.
- Eleventh District Dental Society. Bulletin. 7 per yr. ISSN 0013-6166

**H. Wayne Eley Associates Inc.**
Dept. S, 15 Broadway, New Haven, CT 06511.
- Paper Conservation News. 6 per yr. ISSN 0092-5497

**Eli Lilly & Co.**
General Offices and Principal Laboratories, Indianapolis, IN 46206.
- Clinical Dentistry. (pub. by Science and Medicine Publishing Co., Inc.)
- Tile and Till. q. ISSN 0040-7674

**Elisha Mitchell Scientific Society**
Univ. of North Carolina, Coker Hall 010-A, Chapel Hill, NC 27514.
- Elisha Mitchell Scientific Society. Journal. q. ISSN 0013-6220 (Co-Sponsor: North Carolina Academy of Science)

**Elite Publishing Corp.**
11-03 46th Ave., Long Island City, NY 11101.
- Economic News from Italy. w.
- Tourist News from Italy. m.

**Elizabeth Cady Stanton Publishing Co.**
see Stanton

**Ellen Glasgow Newsletter**
c/o Edgar E. MacDonald, Box 565, Ashland, VA 23005.
- Ellen Glasgow Newsletter. irreg.

**Ellen's Old Alchemical Press**
2850 3rd Ave., Sacramento, CA 95818.
- Hard Pressed. s-a.

**Elizabeth Prather Ellsberry**
Box 206, Chillicothe, MO 64601.
- Crane-Crane Bulletin. irreg.

**Elmside Echoes**
c/o Doris Gassen, Editor, 321 Elmside Blvd., Madison, WI 53704.
- Elmside Echoes. m.

**Elsevier North-Holland, Inc., New York**
52 Vanderbilt Avenue, New York, NY 10017.
- Applied Mathematics and Computation. q. ISSN 0096-3003
- Bioinorganic Chemistry; an interdisciplinary journal. q. ISSN 0006-3061
- Combustion and Flame. 9 per yr. ISSN 0010-2180 (Combustion Institute)
- Computer Design and Architecture Series. irreg.
- Computer Monographs. irreg., no. 23, 1975.
- Developments in Agricultural and Managed Forest Ecology. irreg.
- Developments in Atmospheric Science. irreg., vol. 6, 1976.
- Developments in Economic Geology. irreg. vol. 3, 1975.
- Environmental Science Series. irreg.
- European Congress on Molecular Spectroscopy. Proceedings. a.
- Fuel and Energy Science Series. irreg.
- Information Sciences; an international journal. bi-m. ISSN 0020-0255
- International Conference on Plutonium and Other Actinides. Proceedings. irreg.
- International Congress on Catalysis. Proceedings. irreg., 5th, 1973. ISSN 0538-6640
- International Transplutonium Element Symposium. Proceedings. irreg.
- Journal of Communication Disorders. q. ISSN 0021-9924
- Journal of Fluency Disorders. q.
- Linear Algebra and Its Applications. q. ISSN 0024-3795
- Linguistic Analysis. q.
- Mathematical Biosciences; an international journal. 10 per yr. ISSN 0025-5564
- Metallography; an international journal. q. ISSN 0026-0800 (International Metallographic Society Inc)
- Microstructural Science. irreg., vol. 4, 1976. ISSN 0361-1213 (International Metallographic Society, Inc.)
- Middle East Series. irreg., vol. 5, 1975.
- Modern Analytic and Computational Methods in Science and Mathematics. irreg., 1973, vol. 40. ISSN 0076-9908
- Psychosomatic Medicine. bi-m. ISSN 0033-3174 (American Psychosomatic Society)
- Remote Sensing of Environment; an interdisciplinary journal. q. ISSN 0034-4257
- Studies in Applied Mathematics. bi-m. ISSN 0022-2526 (Applied Mathematics Group, MIT)
- Technological Forecasting and Social Change. q. ISSN 0040-1625

**Elsim Co.**
Box 138, Wellesley Hills, MA 02181.
- Biblioscan H-L. m.
- Biblioscan Q-Z. m.

**Embassy of Chile. Press Office**
1736 Massachusetts Ave. N.W., Washington, DC 20036.
- Chile: Summary of Recent Events. bi-m.

**Embassy of Ghana**
2460 - 16th St. N.W., Washington, DC 20009.
- Ghana News. m. ISSN 0016-9579

**Embassy of Greece**
Press and Information Office, 2211 Massachusetts Ave. N.W., Washington, DC 20008.
- Greece; monthly bulletin of record and analysis. m.

**Embassy of Pakistan. Information Division**
2315 Massachusetts Ave., N.W., Washington, DC 20008.
- Pakistan Affairs. fortn. ISSN 0030-963X

**Embassy of Switzerland**
2900 Cathedral Ave. N.W., Washington, DC 20008.
- Embassy of Switzerland Bulletin. q. ISSN 0046-1865

**Embassy of the Federal Republic of Germany**
4645 Reservoir Rd., Washington, DC 20007.
- German Press Review. w.

**Embassy of the Khmer Republic**
Press Office, 4500 16th St. N.W., Washington, DC 20011.
- Khmer News. irreg., no. 19, 1974.

**Embassy of the Republic of Uganda**
5909 16th St. N. W., Washington, DC 20011.
- Uganda Newsletter. m.

**Embassy of the State of Qatar**
600 New Hampshire Ave., Washington, DC 20037.
- Qatar News. m.

**Embassy of the U S S R in the U S A**
1706 18th St. N.W., Washington, DC 20009.
- Soviet Life. m. ISSN 0038-5549

**Embassy of the United Republic of Tanzania**
2010 Massachusetts Ave., N. W., Washington, DC 20036.
- Mwenge. m.

**Embassy of Venezuela**
Information Service, 2437 California St., N.W., Washington, DC 20008.
- Venezuela Up-to-Date. m. ISSN 0042-3432

**Embroiderers Guild of America**
6 E. 45th St., New York, NY 10017.
- Needle Arts. q. ISSN 0047-925X

**Emerald City Press**
107 W. 7th St., Tempe, AZ 85281.
- Yellow Brick Road; magazine of poetry and fiction. 3 per yr. ISSN 0361-8552

**Emergency Care Research Institute**
5200 Butler Pike, Plymouth Meeting, PA 19462.
- Health Devices; a test, evaluation, & advisory service. m. ISSN 0046-7022

**Emergency Department Nurses Association**
Box 1566, 3900 Capital City Blvd., Lansing, MI 48906.
- J E N. (Journal of Emergency Nursing) bi-m. ISSN 0099-1767

**Emergency Medical Services, Inc.**
15300 Ventura Blvd., Sherman Oaks, CA 91403.
- Emergency Medical Services; the journal of emergency care and transportation. bi-m.

**Emerson Review**
130 Beacon St., Boston, MA 02116.
- Emerson Review. s-a.

**Emmess Press**
Box 1585, Iowa City, IA 52240.
- Spirit That Moves Us. 3 per yr. ISSN 0364-4014

**Emory University**
Atlanta, GA 30322.
- Central European History. q. ISSN 0008-9389 (American Historical Association. Conference Group for Central European History)

**Emory University. Candler School of Theology**
Bishops Hall, Atlanta, GA 30322.
- Candler Review. s-a.

**Emory University. Center for Research in Social Change**
Atlanta, GA 30322.
- Emory University. Center for Research in Social Change Report. irreg.

**Emory University Family Planning Program**
69 Butler St., S.E., Atlanta, GA 30303.
- True to Life. irreg. ISSN 0085-7408

**Emory University. Information Services**
c/o John Rozier, Ed., Atlanta, GA 30322.
- Excerpta; a summary for science and education writers. q.

**Emory University. Office of Alumni Publications**
Atlanta, GA 30322.
- Emory Magazine. q. ISSN 0013-6727

**Emory University. School of Law**
Atlanta, GA 30322.
- Emory Law Journal. q. ISSN 0094-4076

**Emphysema Anonymous, Inc**
Box 66, Ft. Myers, FL 33902.
- Batting the Breeze. bi-m. ISSN 0005-6367

**Empire City Pharmaceutical Society Inc.**
60 E. 42nd St., New York, NY 10017.
- Empire City Pharmacist. bi-m. ISSN 0013-6735

**Empire State College. Learning Resources Center**
Saratoga Springs, NY 12866.
- Innovative Graduate Programs Directory. irreg. ISSN 0363-2601

**Empire State Iris Society**
c/o Albert F. de Groat, 12 High St., Brockport, NY 14420.
- Empire State Iris Society Newsletter. 3 per yr. ISSN 0013-6786

**Empire State Numismatic Association**
Box 62, Schenectady, NY 12305.
- Stater. ISSN 0039-0283

**Empire State Railway Museum**
P.O. Box 666, Middletown, NY 10940.
- Steam Passenger Service Directory. a. ISSN 0081-542X

**Empire State Report, Inc.**
c/o Timothy B. Clark, Ed., 99 Washington Ave., Albany, NY 12210.
- Empire State Report; monthly magazine on politics and government in New York State. m.

**Employee Relocation Council**
333 N. Michigan Ave., Chicago, IL 60601.
- E R R E A C Directory; employee relocation real estate services. a. ISSN 0071-0113

**Employers Insurance of Texas**
Box 2759, Dallas, TX 75221.
- Brickbats & Bouquets. m. ISSN 0006-9779

**Emporia Kansas State College**
Division of Business and Business Education, 1200 Commercial St, Emporia, KS 66801.
- Business Education Journal. s-a. ISSN 0007-6686 (Co-Sponsor: Delta Pi Epsilon)

**Emporia Kansas State College. Alumni Association**
Emporia, KS 66801.
- Spotlight (Emporia) 7 per yr.: 3 newspaper, 4 magazine format.

**Emporia Kansas State College. Division of Biology**
1200 Commercial St., Emporia, KS 66801.
- Kansas School Naturalist. q. ISSN 0022-877X

**Emporia Kansas State College. School of Library Science**
Emporia, KS 66801.
- Library School Review Newsletter. s-a.

**Empress Chinchilla Breeders Cooperative, Inc.**
627 Osage St., Denver, CO 80204.
- Empress Chinchilla Breeder. m. ISSN 0013-6905

**Empty Boat Press**
P.O. Box 42, Brandywine Station, Schenectady, NY 12304.
- Empty Boat. irreg. (approx. 2-4)

**Empty Closet**
713 Monroe, Rochester, NY 14607.
- Empty Closet; gay newspaper for Rochester-Genesee Valley. m.

**Empty Elevator Shaft**
Box 27004, San Francisco, CA 94127.
- Empty Elevator Shaft. irreg.

**En Passant Poetry Quarterly**
1906 Brant Rd., Wilmington, DE 19810.
- En Passant Poetry Quarterly. q.

**Enablement Inc.**
8 Newbury St. 4th Flr., Boston, MA 02116.
- Enablement Information Service. m.

**Enabling Co.**
1035 Indiana St., Vallejo, CA 94590.
- Companis; a quarterly for worship and education. q.

**Encyclopaedia Britannica, Inc.**
425 N. Michigan Ave., Chicago, IL 60611.
- Britannica Atlas. a. ISSN 0068-1148
- Britannica Book of the Year. a. ISSN 0068-1156
- Compton Yearbook. a. ISSN 0069-8091
- Great Ideas Today. a. ISSN 0072-7288
- Yearbook of Science and the Future. a. ISSN 0096-3291

**The End (and Variations Thereof)**
c/o Pat Nolan, Ed., Box 798, Monte Rio, CA 95462.
- The End (and Variations Thereof) irreg.

**Endocrine Society**
- Endocrinology. (pub. by J. B. Lippincott Co.)
- Journal of Clinical Endocrinology and Metabolism. (pub. by J. B. Lippincott Co.)

**Endymion**
310 W. 94th St., Apt. 5D, New York, NY 10025.
- Endymion. a.

**Eneguess Publishing Co.**
42 Grove St., Peterborough, NH 03458.
- Home Builder News. m. ISSN 0018-3970
- Total Comfort Dealer. m. ISSN 0040-9693

**Energy Blacksouth Press**
P.O. Box 4174, Washington, DC 20015.
- Hoo-Doo. s-a.

**Energy Communications, Inc.**
Box 1589, Dallas, TX 75221.
- Energy Management Report. 13 per yr(including annual no) ISSN 0013-7537
- Offshore Technology Yearbook. biennial.

**Energy Daily**
1239 National Press Building, Washington, DC 20045.
- Energy Daily. w.

**Energy Research Corporation**
6 East Valerio St., Santa Barbara, CA 93101.
- Energy Review. bi-m. ISSN 0094-8063

**Engeldrum Publishing Corp.**
229 Laurel Road, East Northport, New York, NY 11731.
- Chevy Power. bi-m.
- Hot Cars and High Performance Stockers. q.

**Engineer of Southern California**
626 N. Garfield Ave., Alhambra, CA 91802.
- Engineer of Southern California. m. ISSN 0013-7766

**Engineering Alloys Digest, Inc.**
c/o Mrs. Norman E. Woldman, 356 N. Mountain Ave., Upper Montclair, NJ 07043.
- Alloy Digest. m. ISSN 0002-614X

**Engineering Contractors Associations**
- E C A Magazine. (pub. by Ned K. Rosenblatt, Ed. & Pub.)

**Engineering Foundation**
United Engineering Center, 345 East 47 Street, New York, NY 10017.
- Engineering Foundation Annual Report. a.

**Engineering Foundation. Column Research Council**
Fritz Engineering Laboratory No. 13, Lehigh University, Bethlehem, PA 18015.
- Engineering Foundation, New York. Column Research Council. Proceedings. a. ISSN 0071-030X
- Guide to Design Criteria for Metal Structures. irreg. (Distributed by: John Wiley & Sons, Inc., One Wiley Dr., Somerset, NJ 08873)

**Engineering Index, Inc.**
345 E. 47th St., New York, NY 10017.
- Bioengineering Abstracts. ISSN 0093-8378
- Energy Abstracts. m. ISSN 0093-8408
- Engineering Index; abstracting and indexing services covering sources of the world's engineering literature. m. plus annual cum. ISSN 0013-7960
- Engineering Index Notes & Comments. s-a. ISSN 0145-207X
- P I E. (Publications Indexed for Engineering) a. ISSN 0085-4581
- S H E. (Subject Headings for Engineering) irreg. plus annual supplements.

**Engineering News-Record**
- E N R Directory of Design Firms. (pub. by McGraw-Hill, Inc.)

**Engineering Societies of New England**
77 Summer St., Boston, MA 02110.
- Engineering Societies of New England. Journal. m. ISSN 0013-8118

**Engineering Society of Baltimore, Inc.**
11 W. Mount Vernon Place, Baltimore, MD 21201.
- Baltimore Engineer. m. ISSN 0005-4496

**Engineering Society of Detroit**
- Detroit Engineer. (pub. by Detroit Publication Consultants)

**Engineers' Club of St. Louis**
4359 Lindell Blvd., St. Louis, MO 63108.
- Engineers' Club of St. Louis. Journal. m. ISSN 0013-8150

**Engineers Joint Council**
345 E. 47 St., New York, NY 10017.
- Directory of Engineering Societies and Related Organizations. biennial. ISSN 0070-5470
- Engineers of Distinction; a who's who in engineering. triennial.
- Learning Resources; a directory for engineers, scientists and managers. 3 per yr. ISSN 0023-9712

**Engineers Joint Council. Engineering Manpower Commission**
345 E. 47 St., New York, NY 10017.
- Engineers Joint Council. Engineering Manpower Commission. Demand for Engineers. biennial.
- Engineers Joint Council. Engineering Manpower Commission. Engineering and Technology Degrees. irreg. ISSN 0071-0393
- Engineers Joint Council. Engineering Manpower Commission. Engineering and Technology Enrollments. a. ISSN 0071-0407
- Engineers Joint Council. Engineering Manpower Commission. Engineers' Salaries: Special Industry Report. biennial. ISSN 0071-0415
- Engineers Joint Council. Engineering Manpower Commission. Professional Income of Engineers. biennial. ISSN 0071-0423
- Engineers Joint Council. Engineering Manpower Commission. Prospects of Engineering and Technology Graduates. a. ISSN 0071-0431
- Engineers Joint Council. Engineering Manpower Commission. Salaries of Engineers in Education. biennial.
- Engineers Joint Council. Engineering Manpower Commission. Salaries of Engineering Technicians. biennial. ISSN 0071-0474

**Engineers' Society of Western Pennsylvania**
Wm. Penn Hotel, Pittsburgh, PA 15230.
- International Water Conference. Proceedings. a. ISSN 0074-9575

**Englander Communications, Inc.**
411 W. Putnam Ave., Box 4327, Greenwich, CT 06830
- Practical Sailor. m. (Subscr. to: 171 Terrace St., Box 139, Haworth NJ 07641)

**English Speaking Union Inc.**
16 East 69 St., New York, NY 10021.
- English around the World. s-a. ISSN 0085-025X
- English-Speaking Union News. 4 per yr. ISSN 0013-8371
- World Branches Conference of the English Speaking Unions. Principal Addresses and Summary of the Proceedings. irreg; 2nd issue forthcoming in 1976. ISSN 0510-8055

**Engravers Journal, Inc.**
Box 103, 43160 Grand River Ave., Novi, MI 48050.
- Engravers Journal. s-a. ISSN 0099-0043

**Enlightenment Essays**
Michael Morrisroe, Jr., 1126 W. Granville Ave., Chicago, IL 60660.
- Enlightenment Essays. q. ISSN 0013-8479

**Eno Foundation for Transportation**
P.O. Box 55, Saugatuck Station, Westport, CT 06880.
- Traffic Quarterly. q.

**Enoch Pratt Free Library**
400 Cathedral St., Baltimore, MD 21201.
- Enoch Pratt Free Library. Staff Reporter. s-m. ISSN 0013-8495
- Menckeniana. q. ISSN 0025-9233
- You're the Critic. 8 per yr.(Nov.-June) ISSN 0044-1139

**Enoch Pratt Free Library. Urban Services Program**
31 S. Payson St., Baltimore, MD 21223.
- Chicory. 10 per yr. ISSN 0009-3793

**Ensanian Physicochemical Institute**
Box 98, Eldred, PA 16731.
- Annual Summary of Progress in Gravitation Sciences. a.
- Ensanian Physicochemical Institute. Journal. q. ISSN 0013-8533
- Introduction to Gravitation Chemistry; experimental and theoretical reviews. 2 per yr.

**Entelek, Inc.**
142 Pleasant St., Newburyport, MA 01950.
- ENTELEK News About Computer-Assisted Instruction/Computer-Managed Instruction. bi-m.
- Programmed Instruction Guide. a. ISSN 0079-5992

**Enterprise Publications**
20 N. Wacker Drive, Chicago, IL 60606.
- Industrial Relations News. w. ISSN 0019-8714
- Investor Relations Newsletter. m.
- Passport; the newsletter for the discriminating international traveler. m. ISSN 0031-272X
- Recruiting Trends; the monthly newsletter for the recruiting executive. m. ISSN 0034-1827

**Enterprising Woman**
c/o Ava Stern, Ed., 525 West End Ave., New York, NY 10024.
- Enterprising Woman; a business monthly. 11 per yr.

**Entomological Society of America**
Box AJ, College Park, MD 20740.
- Entomological Society of America. Annals; devoted to the interest of classical entomology. bi-m. ISSN 0013-8746
- Entomological Society of America. Bulletin; entomological articles of general interest. q. ISSN 0013-8754
- Entomological Society of America. Miscellaneous Publications. irreg. ISSN 0071-0717
- Environmental Entomology. bi-m. ISSN 0046-225X
- Journal of Economic Entomology. bi-m. ISSN 0022-0493
- Pesticide Handbook-Entoma. s-a.
- Pesticide Index. irreg.

**Entomological Society of Pennsylvania**
107 Patterson Bldg., University Park, PA 16802.
- Entomological Society of Pennsylvania. Newsletter. irreg. ISSN 0071-0776
- Melsheimer Entomological Series. irreg. ISSN 0076-6321

**Entomological Society of Washington**
c/o Dept. of Entomology, United States National Museum, Washington, DC 20560.
- Entomological Society of Washington. Proceedings. q. ISSN 0013-8797

**Entr'acte Recording Society**
Box 2319, Chicago, IL 60690.
- Main Title. q. ISSN 0360-1935

**Envios**
P.O. Box M-228, Hoboken, NJ 07030.
- Envios; cuadernos de literatura. q. ISSN 0091-522X

**Environews, Inc.**
1097 National Press Bldg., Washington, DC 20045.
- Environmental Health Letter. s-m. ISSN 0013-9297
- Occupational Health & Safety Letter. s-m.

**Environment Co.**
Box 7855, Austin, TX 78712.
- Do-It-Yourself Directory of How-to-do-It Publications. a.

**Environment Information Center, Inc.**
292 Madison Ave., New York, NY 10017.
- Energy Directory Update. bi-m.
- Energy Index. a.
- Energy Information Abstracts. bi-m.
- Energy Information Locator; select guide to information centers, systems, data bases, abstracting services, directories, newsletters, binder services and journals. a.
- Energy Regulation Update. m.
- Environment Abstracts. m. ISSN 0093-3287
- Environment Film Review; a critical guide to ecology films. irreg. ISSN 0090-0486
- Environment Index; a guide to the key enviornmental literature of the year. a.
- Environment Regulation Handbook. m. updates.

- Land Use Planning Abstracts; a select guide to land and water resources information since 1970. s-a.

**Environmental Action Coalition**
156 Fifth Ave., Suite 1130, New York, NY 10010.
- Eco-News. 7 per yr.

**Environmental Action Inc.**
1346 Connecticut Ave., Rm. 731, Washington, DC 20036.
- Environmental Action. bi-w. ISSN 0013-922X

**Environmental Communications Corp.**
Box 1824, Washington, DC 20013.
- Washington Waterline. w.

**Environmental Defense Fund**
475 Park Ave. S., New York, NY 10016.
- E D F Letter. bi-m.
- Environmental Defense Fund. Annual Report. a. ISSN 0091-9837

**Environmental Design and Research Center**
940 Park Sq. Bldg., Boston, MA 02116.
- Bibliography of the Computer in Environmental Design. biennial.

**Environmental Energy Institute**
P.O. Box 1450, Portland, OR 97207.
- Environmental Energy Contents Monthly. m.

**Environmental Information Center of Florida**
935 Orange Ave., Winter Park, FL 32789.
- Enfo. irreg. (Florida Conservation Foundation)

**Environmental Law Institute**
1346 Connecticut Ave. N.W., Washington, DC 20036.
- Environmental Law Reporter. m. ISSN 0046-2284

**Environmental Management Association**
1701 Drew St., Clearwater, FL 33515.
- Professional Sanitation Management; the magazine of industrial sanitation of the work and product environments. 5 per yr. ISSN 0033-0191

**Environs Publishing Co.**
6201 W. Cermak Rd., Berwyn, IL 60402.
- Financial Planner. 10 per yr.

**Epilepsy Foundation of America**
1828 L St. N.W., Washington, DC 20036.
- National Spokesman. m. ISSN 0091-2387

**Epiphyllum Society of America**
218 E. Greystone Ave, Monrovia, CA 91016.
- Epiphyllum Bulletin. irreg (approx. 6 per yr)

**Episcopal Church**
- Episcopalian. (pub. by Episcopalian, Inc.)

**Episcopal Church. Historical Society**
Box 2247, Austin, TX 78767.
- Historical Magazine of the Protestant Episcopal Church. q. ISSN 0018-2486

**Episcopal Church in Hawaii**
Queen Emma Square, Honolulu, HI 96813.
- Hawaiian Church Chronicle. m (10 per yr.)

**Episcopal Church Publishing Co.**
Box 359, Ambler, PA 19002.
- Witness. m.

**Episcopal Diocese of Arkansas**
Box 6120, Little Rock, AR 72206.
- Arkansas Churchman. m.

**Episcopal Diocese of Chicago**
65 E. Huron St., Chicago, IL 60611.
- Advance (Chicago) m.(except Aug.) ISSN 0001-8562

**Episcopal Diocese of Connecticut**
- Historiographer. (pub. by Kenneth W. Cameron)

**Episcopal Diocese of Erie**
145 W. Sixth St., Erie, PA 16501.
- Forward in Erie. m.(Sept-June) ISSN 0015-8623

**Episcopal Diocese of Newark**
Cathedral House, 24 Rector St., Newark, NJ 07102.
- Newark Churchman. m.(except July & Aug.) ISSN 0028-8853

**Episcopal Diocese of Oregon**
Ed. Rev. Canon Laurence E. Davidson, Box 467, Lake Oswego, OR 97034.
- Oregon Episcopal Churchman. 9 per yr.

**Episcopal Diocese of Virginia**
110 West Franklin, Richmond, VA 23220.
- Virginia Churchman. m (except Aug.)

**Episcopal Diocese of Washington**
Episcopal Church House, Mount Saint Alban, N.W., Washington, DC 20016.
- Washington Diocese. m.(Sept-June) ISSN 0043-0544

**Episcopal Dioceses of Quincy and Springfield (Illinois)**
821 S. Second Street, Springfield, IL 62704.
- Illinois Churchman. m.

**Episcopal Peace Fellowship**
61 Gramercy Park North, New York, NY 10010 (and Membership Service, Fellowship of Reconciliation, Box 271, Nyack, NY 10960)
- New York Military Counselors' Clearinghouse Newsletter. m.

**Episcopal Recorder, Inc.**
Box 152, Pipersville, PA 18947.
- Episcopal Recorder. m. ISSN 0013-9610

**Episcopalian, Inc.**
1930 Chestnut St., Philadelphia, PA 19103.
- Episcopalian. m. ISSN 0013-9629 (Episcopal Church)

**Equal Opportunity Publications, Inc.**
Box 202, Centerport, NY 11721.
- Collegiate Woman's Career Magazine. s-a. ISSN 0095-0653
- Equal Opportunity; the Minority Student Magazine. 3 per yr. ISSN 0071-1039

**Equestrian Trails, Inc.**
10723 Riverside Dr., Box 2086, N. Hollywood, CA 91602.
- Equestrian Trails. m. ISSN 0013-9831

**Equifax, Inc.**
Box 4081, Atlanta, GA 30302.
- Equifax. q.

**Equine Products Co.**
Box 361, Hermosa Beach, CA 90254.
- Horseshit: the Offensive Review; a down to earth magazine. triennial. ISSN 0439-5794

**Equine Research Publications**
Box 347, Grapevine, TX 76051.
- Quarter Horse Reference. a., supplement or revision. ISSN 0090-435X

**Equipment Guide-Book Co.**
2800 W. Bayshore Rd., Box 10113, Palo Alto, CA 94303.
- Equipment Guide News. m.

**Equitable Life Assurance Society of the U.S.**
1285 Ave. of the Americas, New York, NY 10019.
- Agency News Items. w.
- Equinews. fortn. ISSN 0013-984X (prep. by its Corporate Relations Department, Corporate Communications Division)
- National Leaders Magazine. bi-m. ISSN 0027-9609 (prep. by its Personnel Department)

**Equity Media, Inc.**
7616 LBJ Freeway, Dallas, TX 75251.
- Financial Trend; the newsweekly of Southwestern industry and investments. w. ISSN 0040-4195

**Equity Publishing Corp.**
Orford, NH 03777.
- Vermont Slip Law Service; current acts and resolutions passed by the legislature. irreg. (5-6 per yr.)
- Virgin Islands Register. irreg. ISSN 0092-1270

**ERA Corp.**
1615 Polk St., San Francisco, CA 94109.
- Women at Work. m.

**Erasmus Press**
225 Culpepper, Lexington, KY 40502.
- American Notes & Queries. 10 per yr.(Sept-June) ISSN 0003-0171
- Appalachian Notes. q.
- Germanic Notes. 8 per yr. ISSN 0016-8882

**ERB-Dom**
c/o C. E. Cazedessos, Jr., Box 550, St. Francisville, LA 70775.
● ERB-Dom. 5 per yr. ISSN 0422-017X

**ERIC**
*see* E R I C

**Jerry E. Erich, Ed. & Pub**
1313 E. Julian St., San Jose, CA 95116.
● Good Packaging. m. ISSN 0017-2170

**Erie County Motor Club**
420 W. 6th St., Erie, PA 16507.
● Erie Motorist. m. ISSN 0046-2462

**Ernest Bloch Society**
171 Marguerite Ave., Mill Valley, CA 94941.
● Ernest Bloch Society. Bulletin. a. ISSN 0071-1195

**Ernst & Ernst**
925 Euclid Ave., Cleveland, OH 44115.
● Financial Reporting Trends: Fire and Casualty Insurance. irreg. ISSN 0093-5751
● Financial Reporting Trends: Life Insurance. a.
● Financial Reporting Trends: Savings and Loan. a.
● Foreign Exchange Rates and Restrictions. a. ISSN 0363-5430

**Erotic Folklore Newsletter**
c/o Frank A. Hoffmann, Ed., Dept. of English, State University College at Buffalo, 1300 Elmwood Ave., Buffalo, NY 14222.
● Erotic Folklore Newsletter. irreg.

**Error Trends Coin Magazine**
Box 158, Oceanside, NY 11572.
● Error Trends Coin Magazine. m.

**Esco Publishing Co.**
10854 Morrison, Suite 3, North Hollywood, CA 91601.
● Motorcycle Industry; news, products & trends. m.

**Escort**
c/o N.J. Fourlas, Box 513, Carlisle, PA 17013.
● Escort. m. ISSN 0014-0368

**Eskimo, Indian, Aleut Publishing Co.**
Box 1287, Fairbanks, AK 99707.
● Tundra Times. w. ISSN 0049-4801

**Esoteric Philosophy Center, Inc.**
523 Lovett Blvd., Houston, TX 77006.
● Centric. every 8 wks.

**Esperanto Association of North America, Inc.**
1837 N.E. 49th Ave., Portland, OR 97213.
● American Esperanto Magazine/Amerika Esperantisto. q. ISSN 0002-8339

**Esperanto Book Service**
Box 508, Burlingame, CA 94010.
● Current Esperanto Book List. bi-m. (Esperanto League for North America)

**Esperanto League for North America**
Box 508, Burlingame, CA 94010.
● Current Esperanto Book List. (pub. by Esperanto Book Service)
● E L N A Newsletter. bi-m. ISSN 0030-5065

**ESPress, Inc.**
Box 8606, Washington, DC 20011.
● Psychic Observer & Chimes; journal of spiritual science. bi-m. ISSN 0048-573X

**Esprit Createur**
Box 222, Lawrence, KS 66044.
● Esprit Createur; a critical quarterly of French literature. 4 per yr. ISSN 0014-0767 (University of Kansas)

**Esquire, Inc.**
488 Madison Ave., New York, NY 10022.
● Esquire; the magazine for men. m. ISSN 0014-0791
● Gentlemen's Quarterly/G Q. 8 per yr. ISSN 0016-6979

**Essandess Special Editions**
(Subsidiary of: Simon & Schuster)
630 Fifth Ave., New York, NY 10020.
● American Farm and Home Almanac. a. ISSN 0065-8278

**Essay Proof Society**
225 S. Fischer Ave., Jefferson, WI 53549.
● Essay Proof Journal; devoted to the historical and artistic background of stamps and paper money. q. ISSN 0014-0848

**Essence Communications Inc.**
1500 Broadway, New York, NY 10036.
● Essence. m. ISSN 0014-0880

**Esseno Publications, Inc.**
99 Park Ave., New York, NY 10016.
● Pub. m.

**Essential Press**
10453 Medina Road, Richmond, VA 23235.
● Civil War Collectors' Dealer Directory. a.

**Essex County Medical Society**
144 South Harrison St., East Orange, NJ 07018.
● Essex County Medical Society. Bulletin. m. ISSN 0014-0937

**Essex Editors, Inc.**
730 Waukegan Road, Suite 108, Deerfield, IL 60015.
● Newscope-High School/College Edition; a weekly news summary and teaching quiz. w. 36 per yr.
● Newscope-Middle/Intermediate/Junior High School Edition; a weekly news summary and teaching quiz. w. 36 per yr.
● Newsnames/Wordsearch; current events. w.
● Newspuzzler and Newsquestionnaire; current events materials. w.
● Science Puzzler and Science Questionnaire; science news materials. w.
● ScienceCope; a weekly science news summary and teaching quiz. w.

**Essex Institute**
132 Essex St., Salem, MA 01970.
● Essex Institute. Historical Collections. q. ISSN 0014-0953

**Estes Industries**
Penrose, CO 81240.
● Model Rocket News. 6 per yr.

**Eternity Science Fiction**
c/o Stephen Gregg, Box 193, Sandy Springs, SC 29677.
● Eternity Science Fiction. s-a.

**Ethiopian Students Union in North America**
3811 Clarke St., Oakland, CA 94609.
● Challenge. s-a.

**Ethnic American Coalition**
● Ethnic American News. (pub. by Ethnos Publishers)

**Ethnic Millions Political Action Committee**
Box 48, Bayville, NY 11709.
● E M P A C. bi-m.

**Ethnos Publishers**
203 Plaza Bldg., Pittsburgh, PA 15219.
● Ethnic American News. m. (Ethnic American Coalition)

**Blaine Ethridge-Books**
13977 Penrod, Detroit, MI 48223.
● Guide to Reviews of Books from and About Hispanic America/Guia a las Resenas de Libros de y Sobre Hispanoamerica. a.

**Ethyl Corporation. Research Laboratories**
1600 W. Eight Mile Rd., Ferndale, MI 48220.
● Trends in the International Petroleum-Refining Industry. triennial. ISSN 0082-6324
● World Trends in Passenger-Car Production and Engines. irreg., 1967, 2nd ed.

**Eugenia Dorothy Blount Lamar Lectures at Mercer University, Macon, Georgia**
● Lamar Lecture Series. (pub. by University of Georgia Press)

**Eureka Press**
Box 1215, Odessa, TX 79760.
● Treasure Hunter's Yearbook. a. ISSN 0082-6227

**Europa Study Unit**
Leggs Mills Road, Lake Katrine, NY 12449.
● Europa News. m.

**European American Bank and Trust Co.**
865 Merrick Avenue, Westbury, L.I., NY 11590.
● E A Letter; review of the Long Island economy. bi-m.

**European Association for the Study of Diabetes**
● Diabetologia. (pub. by Springer-Verlag)

**European Association of Experimental Social Psychology**
● European Monographs in Social Psychology. (pub. by Academic Press, Inc.)

**European Society of Neuroradiology**
● Neuroradiology. (pub. by Springer-Verlag)

**European Technical Coverage Inc.**
75 East Wacker Drive, Chicago 1, IL 60601.
● European Engineering. s-m. ISSN 0046-2764

**Euthanasia Educational Council**
250 W. 57th St., New York, NY 10019.
● Euthanasia Conference. Excerpts from Papers and Discussions. a.
● Euthanasia News. q.

**Evangelical Congregational Church**
● United Evangelical. (pub. by Church Center Press)

**Evangelical Covenant Church of America**
● Covenant Companion. (pub. by Covenant Press)

**Evangelical Covenant Church of America. Pacific Southwest Conference**
Box 1007, Turlock, CA 95380.
● Pacific Southwest Covenanter. m. except Jul., Sep.

**Evangelical Foundation**
1716 Spruce St., Philadelphia, PA 19103.
● Eternity. m. ISSN 0014-1682
● Evangelical Newsletter. fortn.

**Evangelical Free Church of America**
1515 E. 66th St., Minneapolis, MN 55423.
● Evangelical Beacon. fortn. ISSN 0014-3332

**Evangelical Friends Alliance**
● Evangelical Friend. (pub. by Barclay Press)

**Evangelical Lutheran Synod**
206 N. Second Ave. W, Lake Mills, IA 50450.
● Lutheran Sentinel. fortn. ISSN 0024-7510

**Evangelical Missions Information Service**
Box 794, Wheaton, IL 60187.
● Missionary News Service. s-m. ISSN 0026-6051 (Co-sponsor: Interdenominational Foreign Mission Association)

**Evangelical Teacher Training Association**
Box 327, Wheaton, IL 60187.
● Church Teacher Training Textbooks. irreg. ISSN 0069-4010

**Evangelical Theological Society**
5422 Clinton Blvd., Jackson, MS 39209.
● Evangelical Theological Society. Journal. q. ISSN 0071-3171

**M. Evans and Co., Inc.**
c/o J. B. Lippincott Co., Box 7, Philadelphia, PA 19105.
● World of the Future Series. irreg.

**Evans-Novak Political Report Company**
1750 Pennsylvania Ave., N.W., Suite 1312, Washington, DC 20006.
● Evans-Novak Political Report. fortn. ISSN 0014-3650

**Evansville Public Library**
22 S.E. Fifth St., Evansville, IN 47708.
● Evansville Public Library and Vanderburgh County Public Library. Staff News Bulletin. s-m. ISSN 0014-3669 (Co-Sponsor: Vanderburgh County Public Library)

**Evelyn Waugh Society**
Nassau Community College, Department of English, Garden City, NY 11530.
● Evelyn Waugh Newsletter. 3 per yr. ISSN 0014-3693

**Everbody's Money**
Box 431, Madison, WI 53701.
● E M Bibliography for Consumers. irreg. ISSN 0093-982X

**Everglades Publishing Co.**
Drawer Q, Everglades, FL 33929.
- Television Sponsors Directory; product cross-reference directory. q. ISSN 0049-3317

**Harry T. Everingham, Ed. & Pub**
Box 10555, Phoenix, AZ 85064
(and 2422 E. Indian School Rd. Phoenix, AZ 85016)
- American Patriot. m.
- Fact Finder. fortn. ISSN 0014-651X

**Everson Museum of Art of Syracuse and Onondaga County**
401 Harrison St., Syracuse, NY 13202.
- Everson Museum of Art Bulletin. m.

**Everton Publishers, Inc.**
Box 368, Logan, UT 84321.
- Genealogical Helper; for those who wish to do their own genealogical research. bi-m. ISSN 0016-6359

**Every Woman**
c/o Varda R. Murrell, 6516 W. 83rd St., Los Angeles, CA 90045.
- Every Woman. m. ISSN 0014-3766

**Everybodys Press Inc.**
Fame Ave., Hanover, PA 17331.
- Spinning Wheel; antiques & early crafts. 10 per yr.(Jan-Feb. & July-Aug. combined) ISSN 0038-755X

**Everything for Everybody**
West Village Branch, 406 W. 13 St., New York, NY 10004.
- Everything for Everybody. m.

**Ewell Neil Dental Society**
- Meharri-Dent. (pub. by Meharry Medical College. School of Dentistry)

**Ex Libris**
Tennessee Ave., Sewanee, TN 37375.
- Mountain Summer. a.

**Executive Business Media, Inc.**
Box 788, 211 Broadway, Lynbrook, NY 11563.
- Club & Food Service. m.
- College Store Executive. m. ISSN 0010-1141
- Exchange & Commissary News. m. ISSN 0014-4452

**Executive Communications, Inc.**
400 E. 54th St., New York, NY 10022.
- Ad Day/USA; the national newsletter of advertising & marketing. w.
- Handbook of Advertising and Marketing Services. a. with mid-year update.

**Executive Compensation Service**
see under **American Management Associations**

**Executive Council of the Episcopal Church**
815 Second Ave., New York, NY 10017.
- N C I W Newsletter. q. (National Committee on Indian Work)

**Executive Enterprises Publications Co., Inc.**
33 W. 60 St., New York, NY 10023.
- E E O Today. q.
- Employee Relations Law Journal. q. ISSN 0098-8898
- Supervisor's E E O Review. m.

**Executive Publications**
Box 589, Rancho Santa Fe, CA 92067.
- Executive Health. m.

**Executive Publications, Inc. (Washington)**
1725 K St. N.W., Washington, DC 20006.
- Government Executive. m. ISSN 0017-2626

**Executive Review Publishers**
224 S. Michigan Ave., Chicago, IL 60604.
- Executive Review. m. ISSN 0046-2896

**Executive Sciences Institute, Inc.**
Drawer M, Whippany, NJ 07981.
- Operations Research/Management Science; international literature digest service. m. ISSN 0030-3658
- Quality Control and Applied Statistics; abstract service. m. ISSN 0033-5207

**Executive Strategy Services Co.**
Box 144, Hamilton, NY 13346.
- Food Industry Futures: a Strategy Service. s-m. ISSN 0046-4414

**Executive Woman**
c/o Sandra M. Brown, 747 Third Ave, New York, NY 10017.
- Executive Woman. m (except June & July)

**Exhibitor Services, Inc**
- Market Place. (pub. by Market Place Publications)

**Eximbank**
see **Export- Import Bank of the United States**

**Expanded Shale, Clay and Slate Institute**
1041 National Press Bldg., Washington, DC 20004.
- Expanded Shale Lightweight Concrete Facts. irreg.
- Lightweight Concrete Information Sheets. irreg. ISSN 0075-9457

**Expatriate Review**
Box D, St. George Station, Staten Island, NY 10301.
- Expatriate Review. s-a. ISSN 0300-709X

**Experiment in International Living**
U.S. National Office, Brattleboro, VT 05301.
- Experiment in International Living. President's Report. a. ISSN 0071-3376
- Odyssey; experiment in international living. q.

**Experiment Press**
6565 N.E. Windermere Rd., Seattle, WA 98105.
- Experiment; an international review of new poetry. irreg. ISSN 0014-4770
- Experiment Theatre; "one minute" poetic drama. irreg.

**Experimental Aircraft Association, Inc.**
Box 229, Hales Corners, WI 53130.
- Sport Aviation. m. ISSN 0038-7835
- Vintage Airplane. m. ISSN 0091-6943 (prep. by its Antique Classic Division)

**Expertise Institute Inc.**
Box 38-1494, Miami, FL 33138.
- LawLab Journal. irreg. ISSN 0047-4215

**Explorations Institute**
Box 1254, Berkeley, CA 94701.
- Explorations. irreg. ISSN 0014-4967
- Group Leader's Workshop. m. ISSN 0017-4718
- Personal Growth. m.

**Explorers Club**
Box 1241r, Morristown, NJ 07960.
- Explorers Journal. q. ISSN 0014-5025

**Explorers Enterprises Inc,**
E. 2500 Sprague Ave., Spokane, WA 99202.
- Guide Magazine Explorer. m. ISSN 0046-6581

**Exponent Two**
Box 37, Arlington, MA 02174.
- Exponent Two. q.

**Export-Import Bank of the United States**
811 Vermont Ave., N.W., Washington, DC 20571.
- Eximbank Report. a.
- Export-Import Bank of the United States. Cumulative Records. irreg. ISSN 0098-8359
- Export-Import Bank of the United States. Summary of Operations. a. ISSN 0071-3511

**Extended Sweet's Mill**
Sweet's Mill, Auberry, CA 93602.
- Extended Sweet's Mill. q.

**Extension Journal, Inc.**
605 Extension Bldg., 432 N. Lake St., Madison, WI 53706.
- Journal of Extension. bi-m. ISSN 0022-0140

**Exxon Aviation Marketing Affiliates**
- Exxon Air World. (pub. by Exxon International Co.)
- Exxon Aviation News Digest. (pub. by Exxon International Co.)

**Exxon Chemical Co.**
Box 3272, Houston, TX 77001.
- Exxon Chemicals Magazine. q.

**Exxon Company, U.S.A.**
Division of Exxon Corp., Box 2180, Houston, TX 77001.
- Oilways. bi-m.

**Exxon Corporation**
1251 Avenue of the Americas, New York, NY 10020.
- Lamp. q. ISSN 0023-7418
- Medical Bulletin. 4 per yr.

**Exxon International Co.**
A Division of Exxon Corp., 1251 Ave. of Americas, New York, NY 10020.
- Exxon Air World. q. (Exxon Aviation Marketing Affiliates)
- Exxon Aviation News Digest. w. (Exxon Aviation Marketing Affiliates)

**F. A. Publications, Inc.**
174 Fifth Ave., New York, NY 10010.
- Fashion Accessories. m. ISSN 0014-8644

**F A S E B**
see **Federation of American Societies for Experimental Biology**

**F A T M Press**
113-B S. Parker St., Columbia, SC 29201.
- Sovereign Friends. m.

**F & F Publications**
405 Lexington Ave., Suite 6101, New York, NY 10017.
- Hospital Physician. m. ISSN 0018-5795

**F & W Publishing Corp.**
9933 Alliance Rd., Cincinnati, OH 45242.
- Writer's Digest. m. ISSN 0043-9525
- Writer's Market. a. ISSN 0084-2729 (Writer's Digest)
- Writer's Yearbook. a. ISSN 0084-2737 (Writer's Digest)

**F B G Enterprises, Inc.**
536 S. Poplar, Kermit, TX 79745.
- Medal World. m.
- Today's Coins. s-m.

**F.B.P. Publishing, Inc.**
108 Railroad Ave., Jersey City, NJ 07302.
- Penny Speculator; investment advisory service specializing in listed stocks under 20. w.

**F C X, Inc.**
125 E. Davie St., Raleigh, NC 27601.
- F C X Carolina Cooperator. m.

**F M Music Program Guide, Inc.**
20 Hampton Rd., Southampton, NY 11968.
- F M Guide. m. ISSN 0014-5971

**F. P. B. Enterprises**
310 Evesham Rd, Glendora, NJ 08029.
- Flag; the Music Scene. m. ISSN 0090-7308

**F. S. Publications**
5739 W. Wildbriar Dr., Palos Verdes Peninsula, CA 90274.
- Food & Liquor Digest. m. ISSN 0015-6299

**F. U. Research Institute, Inc.**
482 Richland Ave., Athens, OH 45701.
- Particles and Nuclei. m. ISSN 0031-2479

**Ethel H. Fabian, Ed. & Pub.**
Route 1, Gravette, AR 72736.
- National Fluoridation News; a general information medium for antifluoridation forces, national and international. q. ISSN 0027-9269

**Fabrangen**
4500 Connecticut Ave. N.W., Washington, DC 20008.
- Kesher; havurot and new halacha newsletter. bi-m.

**Fabulous Las Vegas**
1210 Stewart Av., Las Vegas, NV 89101.
- Fabulous Las Vegas. w. ISSN 0046-3043

**Facets Multimedia, Inc.**
1517 W. Fullerton Ave., Chicago, IL 60614.
- Focus: Chicago. bi-m. ISSN 0362-0905

**Factory Mutual Engineering Corp.**
1151 Boston-Providence Turnpike, Norwood, MA 02062.
- Factory Mutual Record; resource management for property conservation. bi-m. ISSN 0014-6595

**Factory Outlet Shopping Guide Publications**
Box 95, Oradell, NJ 07649.
- Factory Outlet Newsletter. 8 per yr.
- Factory Outlet Shopping Guide for New England. a.
- Factory Outlet Shopping Guide for New Jersey and Rockland County. a.
- Factory Outlet Shopping Guide for New York, Westchester and Long Island. a.
- Factory Outlet Shopping Guide for Pennsylvania. a.
- Factory Outlet Shopping Guide for Washington D.C., Maryland, Delaware, Virginia.

**Facts & Comparisons, Inc.**
1100 Oran Drive, St. Louis, MO 63137.
- Facts and Comparisons. m. ISSN 0014-6617

**Facts on File Inc.**
119 W. 57th St., New York, NY 10019.
- Editorials on File; newspaper editorial reference service with index. s-m. ISSN 0013-0966
- Facts on File. w. ISSN 0014-6641
- Latin America. a. ISSN 0094-7458

**Faculty Association of California Community Colleges**
926 J St., Suite 211, Sacramento, CA 95814.
- F A C C C Bulletin. q. ISSN 0046-3159

**Faculty Press**
5768 N. 5th St., Fresno, CA 93710.
- Russian Emigre Archives. irreg.

**Faculty Press (New York)**
152 Finley Hall, City College of N.Y., 138 St. & Convent Ave., New York, NY 10031.
- City 4. s-a.

**Fair**
1642 N. 8th St., Terre Haute, IN 47804.
- Fair. 3 per yr. ISSN 0014-6900

**Fair Lawn Education Association**
86 Watchung Ave., Upper Montclair, NJ 07043.
- Reflector. m. ISSN 0034-2955

**Fairbanks Native Association**
102 Lacey, Fairbanks, AK 99701.
- River Times. m.

**Fairchild Books**
(Subsidiary of: Fairchild Publications Inc.)
7 East 12th St., New York, NY 10003.
- Electronic News Financial Fact Book and Directory. a. ISSN 0070-9875
- Fairchild's Financial Manual of Retail Stores. a. ISSN 0071-3716
- Fairchild's Textile & Apparel Financial Directory. a.

**Fairchild Publications, Inc.**
(Subsidiary of: Capital Cities Media, Inc.)
7 E. 12th St., New York, NY 10003.
- American Metal Market. d.(Mon-Fri) ISSN 0002-9998
- Daily News Record. d.(Mon-Fri) ISSN 0011-5460
- Electronic News. w. ISSN 0013-4937
- Family Practice News. s-m. ISSN 0300-7073
- Footwear News. w. ISSN 0015-6833
- Headsheet. m.
- Home Furnishings Daily. w. ISSN 0018-4047
- Men's Wear. s-m. ISSN 0025-9527
- Metal Center News. m.
- Metal-Center News' Metal Distribution. a.
- Metal Statistics. a. ISSN 0076-6658
- Metalworking News. w. ISSN 0026-1025
- Pediatric News. m. ISSN 0031-398X
- Skin & Allergy News. m. ISSN 0037-6337
- Supermarket News; the industry's weekly newspaper. w. ISSN 0039-5803
- W. fortn.
- Women's Wear Daily; the retailer's daily newspaper. 5 per wk. ISSN 0043-7581

**Fairchild Tropical Garden**
10901 Old Cutler Rd., Miami, FL 33156.
- Fairchild Tropical Garden Bulletin. q. ISSN 0014-6943

**Fairleigh Dickinson University**
Rutherford, NJ 07070.
- Literary Review. q. ISSN 0024-4589

**Fairleigh Dickinson University. Department of English**
Teaneck, NJ 07666.
- Literature and Psychology; a quarterly journal of literary criticism as informed by depth psychology. q. ISSN 0024-4759 (Co-sponsor: National Association for Psychoanalytic Criticism)

**Fairleigh Dickinson University. Florham-Madison Campus**
285 Madison Ave., Madison, NJ 07940.
- Journal of New Jersey Poets. 3 per yr. ISSN 0363-4205 (prep. by its Department of English)

**Fairmont State College**
Locust Ave., Fairmont, WV 26554.
- Columns. w. ISSN 0010-2091

**Faith and Life Press**
724 Main St., Box 347, Newton, KS 67114.
- Christian Service Training Series. a. ISSN 0069-3898 (Mennonite Church, General Conference. Commission on Education)
- Church and Society Series. irreg. ISSN 0069-3979 (Mennonite Church. General Conference)
- Institute of Mennonite Studies Series. irreg. ISSN 0073-9456 (Associated Mennonite Biblical Seminaries)
- Mennonite History Series. irreg. ISSN 0076-6429 (Mennonite Church, General Conference. Commission on Education)
- Schowalter Memorial Lecture Series. irreg. ISSN 0080-6943 (Mennonite Church. General Conference)

**Faith for Today**
1100 Rancho Conejo Blvd., Newbury Park, CA 91320.
- Telenotes. bi-m. (Seventh-Day Adventist Church)

**Falcon Publications**
8432 Steller Dr., Culver City, CA 90230.
- Key (Los Angeles). w.

**Family Circle, Inc.**
(Subsidiary of: New York Times Company, Inc.)
488 Madison Ave., New York, NY 10022.
- Family Circle. 14 per yr. ISSN 0014-7206
- Home Decorating Guide. irreg., latest 1977. ISSN 0090-8630

**Family Health**
1271 Ave. of the Americas, New York, NY 10020.
- Family Health. m. ISSN 0014-7249

**Family Lines System**
908 W. Broadway, Louisville, KY 40201.
- Family Lines. bi-m.

**Family Media, Inc.**
149 Fifth Ave., New York, NY 10010.
- One Thousand and One Decorating Ideas. 6 per yr. ISSN 0030-2554
- Weight Watchers. m. ISSN 0043-2180 (W - W Twentyfirst Corporation)

**Family Motor Coach Association**
8291 Clough Pike, Cincinnati, OH 45244.
- Family Motor Coaching. bi-m.

**Family Pet**
c/o M. Linda Sabella, Box 22964, Tampa, FL 33622.
- Family Pet. q.

**Family Planning International Assistance**
810 Seventh Ave., New York, NY 10019.
- Family Planning International Assistance Newsletter. q.

**Family Process, Inc.**
149 E. 78th St., New York, NY 10021.
- Family Process. q. ISSN 0014-7370

**Family Service Association of America**
44 E. 23rd St., New York, NY 10010.
- Social Casework. m (except Aug. & Sept.) ISSN 0037-7678

**Family Therapy Institute of Marin**
- Family Therapy. (pub. by Libra Publishers, Inc.)

**Fan Press**
Lakemont, GA 30552.
- Is: A Magazine of Popular Literature and Popular Culture. q.

**Fan Publications, Inc.**
Box 2298, Shawnee Mission, KS 66201.
- Mid-Continent Bottler. bi-m.

**Fandom Unlimited Enterprises**
774 Vista Grande Ave., Los Altos, CA 94022.
- Cinefan. irreg.

**Fantasy Association**
Box 24560, Los Angeles, CA 90024.
- Fantasiae (Los Angeles) m. ISSN 0094-2375

**Fantasy Publishing Co., Inc.**
1855 W. Main St., Alhambra, CA 91801.
- Witchcraft and Sorcery; the modern magazine of weird tales. a.

**Far East Reporter**
c/o Maud Russell, Box 1536, New York, NY 10017.
- Far East Reporter. 4-5 per yr. ISSN 0014-7575

**FAR-MAR-Co., Inc.**
400 Wiley Building, Hutchinson, KS 67501.
- Marketer. m. ISSN 0025-3626

**Far West Publishing Co.**
Box 4383, Albuquerque, NM 87106.
- Astral Projection. q. ISSN 0004-6124

**Far West Ski Association**
1313 W. Eighth St., Los Angeles, CA 90017.
- Far West Ski News. s-m. (Sep.-Feb.); m. (Mar.-Jul.)

**Far Western Philosophy of Education Society**
c/o College of Education, Arizona State University, Tempe, AZ 85281.
- Philosophy of Education. a.

**Farall Instruments**
P.O. Box 1473, Grand Island, NE 68801.
- Behavioral Engineering. q.

**Fares Stephen**
16 W. 30th St., New York, NY 10001.
- New Al-Hoda; the new guidance. s-w. ISSN 0300-5453

**Joseph I. Farley Publishing Co., Inc.**
254 Drum Point Rd., Osbornville, NJ 08723.
- Equestrian Journal. m. ISSN 0013-9823

**Farm & Home Publications**
10 Lourdes Rd., Box 80 Westview Sta., Binghamton, NY 13905.
- Bradford-Tioga-Sullivan-Potter-Wyoming Farm & Home News. m.
- Lackawanna-Wayne-Pike-Susquehanna Farm & Home News. m. ISSN 0093-4909
- Seven County Farm and Home News. m.
- Southern Tier Town & Country Living. m.

**Farm and Ranch Vacations, Inc.**
36 E. 57 St., New York, NY 10022.
- Farm, Ranch & Countryside Guide. biennial.

**Farm Credit Banks of New Orleans**
Box 50590, New Orleans, LA 70150.
- Info III. q.

**Farm Credit Banks of Omaha**
3612 S.W. 9th St., Des Moines, IA 50315.
- Hired Dollars; a magazine of financial management for agriculture. 3 per yr.

**Farm Implement Publishing Co.**
1100 Upper Midwest Bldg., Minneapolis, MN 55401.
- Northwest Farm Equipment Journal. m. ISSN 0029-3350

**Farm Journal, Inc.**
230 W. Washington Sq., Philadelphia, PA 19106.
- Farm Journal. m. ISSN 0014-8008

**Farm Tempo U. S. A**
Box 117, Clarinda, IA 51632.
- Farm Tempo U. S. A. m. ISSN 0014-8156

**Farm Wife, Inc.**
733 N. van Buren, Milwaukee, WI 53202
(Subscr. address: 611 E. Wells, Milwaukee, WI 53202)
- Farm Wife News. m.

**Farmaceutico Publishing Co., Inc.**
Quaker Hill, Pittstown, NJ 08867.
- Farmaceutico. m. ISSN 0014-8180

**Farmer Genealogy Co.**
P. O. Box 140880, Dallas, TX 75214.
- Martin Family Quarterly. q. ISSN 0099-1864

**Farmer-Labor Press Publishing Co. Inc.**
1316 Sixth Ave., Box 246, Council Bluffs, IA
51501.
- Farmer-Labor Press; the voice of labor in the city
and on the farm. w. ISSN 0014-8377 (Council
Bluffs Central Labor Union)

**Farmer-Stockman Publishing Co.**
10111 N. Central Expressway, Dallas, TX 75231.
- Kansas Farmer-Stockman. m.
- Oklahoma Farmer-Stockman. m.
- Texas Farmer-Stockman. m.

**Farmers and Manufacturers Beet Sugar Association**
470 Plaza North, Saginaw, MI 48603.
- Sugar Beet Journal. q. ISSN 0039-4718

**Farmers Digest, Inc.**
Box 363, 2645 Maple Hill Lane, Brookfield, WI
53005.
- Farmer's Digest. 10 per yr. ISSN 0046-3337

**Farmers Educational & Cooperative Union of
America. South Dakota Division**
Box 1388, Huron, SD 57350.
- South Dakota Union Farmer. m.

**Farmers Friend and Rural Reporter**
c/o Fred Per Gande, Box 1306, Green Bay, WI
54301.
- Farmers Friend and Rural Reporter. w.

**Farmers Union Publishing Co.**
1667 N. Snelling Ave., St. Paul, MN 55165.
- Co-op Country News. s-m.

**Farmland Industries, Inc.**
Box 7305, Kansas City, MO 64116.
- Farmland News. s-m. ISSN 0093-5832

**Ibrahim Farrah, Inc.**
One Sherman Square, Suite 22f, New York, NY
10023.
- Arabesque; journal of Middle Eastern dance and
culture. bi-m.

**Farrar, Straus & Giroux, Inc.**
19 Union Square W., New York, NY 10003.
- Reader's Guide Series. irreg.

**Farrell Lines Inc.**
1 Whitehall St., New York, NY 10004.
- Trade Trends. 6 per yr. ISSN 0041-0489

**Farrell Publishing Co.**
Box 2683, Dallas, TX 75221.
- Morticians of the Southwest. m.

**Fash, New York**
- Problemen. (pub. by Ashuach IS)

**Fashion Newsletter Inc.**
743 Fifth Ave., New York, NY 10022.
- Fashion Newsletter; international forecast of
tomorrow's fashions. m. ISSN 0300-7111

**Fathar**
c/o Duncan McNaughton, Ed., Box 355, Bolinas,
CA 94924.
- Fathar. 1-2 per yr.

**Fatty Acid Producers Council**
475 Park Ave. South, 32nd St., New York, NY
10016.
- Fatty Acid News Digest. bi-m.

**Faulkner County Historical Society**
Box 731, Conway, AR 72032.
- Faulkner Facts and Findings. q. ISSN 0430-1188

**Fault**
c/o Terence Ames, Ed., 41186 Alice Ave., Fremont,
CA 94538.
- Fault. irreg.

**J. Faust & Co.**
Order Dept., Box 5616, Columbia, SC 29205.
- Editorial Quarterly. q.

**Fawcett Publications, Inc.**
1515 Broadway, New York, NY 10036.
- Mechanix Illustrated. m. ISSN 0025-6587
- Rudder. m. ISSN 0035-9653
- Woman's Day. m. ISSN 0043-7336
- Woman's Day Best Ideas for Christmas. a.
- Woman's Day Christmas Ideas for Children. a.
ISSN 0512-5901
- Woman's Day Decorating with House Plants. s-a.
- Woman's Day Granny Squares. a.
- Woman's Day Home Decorating Ideas. a. ISSN
0361-638X
- Woman's Day Needlework Ideas. s-a.
- Woman's Day 101 Gardening & Outdoor Ideas. a.
ISSN 0090-9319

**Fax Forecast**
610 Foxwood, Elnora, NY 12065.
- Fax Forecast; leading national report on new
product breakthroughs. fortn. ISSN 0014-8938

**F. W. Faxon Co., Inc.**
Publishing Division, 15 Southwest Park, Westwood,
MA 02090.
- Bulletin of Bibliography and Magazine Notes. q.
ISSN 0007-4780
- Faxon Librarians' Guide; to periodicals, annuals,
continuations GPO publications, monographic
series, newspapers, proceedings, serials,
transactions and yearbooks. a. ISSN 0092-0487
- French Periodical Index. irreg. ISSN 0362-5044
- Serials Updating Service. m. ISSN 0093-2310
- Serials Updating Service Annual. a. ISSN 0095-
2702
- Serials Updating Service Quarterly. q. ISSN 0093-
2329

**Feature Publications, Inc.**
100 E. Main St., Frankfort, KY 40601.
- Kentucky Beverage Journal. m. ISSN 0023-012X

**Federal Bar Association**
1815 H. St., N.W., Washington, DC 20006.
- Federal Bar Journal. q. ISSN 0014-9039
- Federal Bar News. m. ISSN 0014-9047

**Federal Bar Association. District of Columbia
Chapter**
1815 H Street, N.W., Washington, DC 20006.
- Forum (Washington, D.C.) 5 per yr. ISSN 0015-
8305

**Federal Correctional Institution**
Box W, Lompoc, CA 93436.
- Five Feathers News. m. ISSN 0046-4015

**Federal Deposit Insurance Corporation**
see U. S. Federal Deposit Insurance Corporation

**Federal Development Associates**
Box 427, San Anselmo, CA 94960.
- Federal Notes. s-m. ISSN 0014-911X

**Federal Employees News Digest**
P.O. Box 457, Merrifield, VA 22116.
- Federal Employees Almanac. a. ISSN 0071-4127

**Federal Home Loan Bank of Atlanta**
Atlanta, GA 30304.
- Federal Home Loan Bank of Atlanta. Annual
Report. a.

**Federal Home Loan Bank of Pittsburgh**
Gateway Center, 11 Stanwix St., Pittsburgh, PA
15222.
- Federal Home Loan Bank of Pittsburgh. Monthly
Statistical Report. m. (prep. by its Research and
Statistics Department)

**Federal Home Loan Bank of San Francisco**
600 California St., Box 7948, San Francisco, CA
94108.
- Conference on Resources for Housing.
Proceedings. a.
- Federal Home Loan Bank of San Francisco.
Annual Report. a. ISSN 0098-2830

**Federal Home Loan Mortgage Corporation**
311 First St., N.W., Washington, DC 20001.
- Federal Home Loan Mortgage Corporation.
Report. a. ISSN 0094-7156

**Federal Legal Publications, Inc.**
95 Morton St., New York, NY 10014.
- Antitrust Bulletin. q. ISSN 0003-603X
- Contemporary Drug Problems. q. ISSN 0091-4509
- Criminal Law Commentator (New York) bi-m.
ISSN 0093-4674

- Family Law Commentator (New York) bi-m.
ISSN 0093-4682
- Journal of Psychiatry and Law. q. ISSN 0093-
1853
- Journal of Reprints for Antitrust Law &
Economics. s-a. ISSN 0022-4243

**Federal Poets of Washington D.C.**
c/o Mary McGowan Slappey, 4500 Chesapeake St.,
N.W., Washington, DC 20016.
- Federal Poet. q.

**Federal Professional Association**
1302 18th St. N.W., Washington, DC 20036.
- F P A Newsletter. bi-m.

**Federal Publications, Inc.**
1725 K St., N.W., Washington, DC 20006.
- Briefing Papers. bi-m. ISSN 0007-0025
- Government Contractor. fortn. ISSN 0017-2596
- Tax Barometer. w. ISSN 0039-9981

**Federal Reserve Bank of Atlanta**
104 Marietta St. N.W., Atlanta, GA 30303.
- Caribbean Basin Economic Survey. bi-m. (prep. by
its Research Department)
- Federal Reserve Bank of Atlanta. Economic
Review. bi-m.
- Statistics on the Developing South. a. ISSN 0085-
672X

**Federal Reserve Bank of Boston**
30 Pearl St., Boston, MA 02106.
- Farm Finance News. m. ISSN 0014-7966
- Federal Reserve Bank of Boston Conference
Series. s-a.
- New England Economic Review. bi-m. ISSN
0028-4726

**Federal Reserve Bank of Chicago**
Box 834, Chicago, IL 60690.
- Agricultural Letter. w. ISSN 0002-1512 (prep. by
its Research Dept.)
- Conference on Bank Structure and Competition.
Proceedings. a. ISSN 0084-9154 (prep. by its
Research Dept.)
- Economic Perspectives. bi-m. (prep. by its
Research Dept.)
- Federal Reserve Bank of Chicago. International
Letter. w. ISSN 0046-3469 (prep. by its Research
Dept.)
- Federal Reserve Bank of Chicago. Seventh
District Statistics. irreg. ISSN 0430-1919 (prep.
by its Research Dept.)

**Federal Reserve Bank of Dallas**
Station K, Dallas, TX 75222.
- Farm and Ranch Bulletin. m. ISSN 0014-7842
- Federal Reserve Bank of Dallas. Review. m.

**Federal Reserve Bank of Kansas City**
Kansas City, MO 64198.
- Federal Reserve Bank of Kansas City. Monthly
Review. m.(bi-m.June-Sept) ISSN 0014-9152

**Federal Reserve Bank of Minneapolis**
250 Marquette Ave., Minneapolis, MN 55480.
- Federal Reserve Bank of Minneapolis. Annual
Statistical Review. a. (prep. by its Research
Department)
- Ninth District Quarterly. q. (prep. by its Research
Department)

**Federal Reserve Bank of New York**
33 Liberty St., New York, NY 10045.
- Federal Reserve Bank of New York. Quarterly
Review. q.

**Federal Reserve Bank of Philadelphia**
Philadelphia, PA 19105.
- Fed in Print; business and banking topics. q.
- Federal Reserve Bank of Philadelphia Business
Review. bi-m. ISSN 0007-7011
- Federal Reserve Bank Reviews. biennial. ISSN
0430-1943

**Federal Reserve Bank of Richmond**
Research Dept., Box 27622, Richmond, VA 23261.
- Business and Financial Indicators. bi-m. ISSN
0007-6481
- Federal Reserve Bank of Richmond. Economic
Review. bi-m. ISSN 0094-6893

**Federal Reserve Bank of St. Louis**
Box 442, St. Louis, MO 63166.
- Federal Reserve Bank of St. Louis. Review. m.
  ISSN 0014-9187

**Federal Reserve Bank of San Francisco**
Box 7702, San Francisco, CA 94120.
- Federal Reserve Bank of San Francisco. Business
  and Financial Letter. w.
- Federal Reserve Bank of San Francisco. Economic
  Review. q.
- Pacific Basin Economic Indicators. q.
- Western Economic Indicators. bi-m. ISSN 0091-
  0988

**Federal-State Market News Service**
1220 N St., Sacramento, CA 95814.
- Marketing California Dried Fruits: Prunes,
  Raisins, Dried Apricots & Peaches. irreg. ISSN
  0094-2510
- Marketing California Pears for Fresh Market. a.
  ISSN 0098-8928
- Movement of California Fruits and Vegetables by
  Rail, Truck, and Air. a. ISSN 0094-2790
- Production and Marketing California: Eggs,
  Chickens and Turkeys. a. (Co-Sponsor: California
  Crop and Livestock Reporting Service)

**Federal State Reports, Inc.**
Box 986, Court House Sta., Arlington, VA 22216.
- Dairy, Natural and Dietary Food Industry
  Newsletter. fortn. ISSN 0011-5657
- Of Consuming Interest. w. ISSN 0030-0047
- P A L. (Packaging and Labeling) w.

**Federal Statistics Users' Conference**
1030 15th St. N.W., Suite 356, Washington, DC
20005.
- Federal Statistics Users' Conference. Newsletter.
  m. ISSN 0014-9225

**Federally Employed Women Inc.**
National Press Bldg., Washington, DC 20045.
- F E W's News & Views. bi-m. ISSN 0046-3477

**Federated Garden Clubs of Michigan, Inc.**
- Thru the Garden Gate. (pub. by Hastings Press,
  Inc.)

**Federated Russian Orthodox Clubs**
10 Downs Dr. (Plaines), Wilkes-Barre, PA 18705.
- Russian Orthodox Journal. m. ISSN 0036-0317

**Federation for Community Planning**
1001 Huron Rd., Cleveland, OH 44115.
- Federation Forum. 3 per yr. ISSN 0300-6999

**Federation of American Hospitals**
Box 2451, Little Rock, AR 72203.
- Directory of Investor-Owned Hospitals and
  Hospital Management Companies. a. ISSN 0095-
  5191
- F A H Review. bi-m. ISSN 0046-3558

**Federation of American Scientists**
307 Massachusetts Ave. N.E., Washington, DC
20002.
- F A S Public Interest Report. m.

**Federation of American Societies for Experimental
Biology**
9650 Rockville Pike, Bethesda, MD 20014.
- Council of Biology Editors. Newsletter. bi-m.
  ISSN 0070-0975 (Council of Biology Editors)
- Federation of American Societies for
  Experimental Biology. Federation Proceedings. 13
  per yr. ISSN 0014-9446
- Multiple Sclerosis Indicative Abstracts. bi-m.
  (National Multiple Sclerosis Society)
- Neuroscience and Behavioral Physiology. (pub. by
  Scripta Publishing Co.)

**Federation of Biocommunication Societies**
University of North Carolina, School of Medicine,
Berryhill Hall, Chapel Hill, NC 27514.
- Journal of Biocommunication. 3 per yr. ISSN
  0094-2499 (Health Sciences Communications
  Association) (Co-sponsor: Association of Medical
  Illustrators)

**Federation of Genealogical Societies**
Box 743, Midlothian, IL 60445.
- Federation of Genealogical Societies Newsletter.
  q.

**Federation of Genealogical Societies. Chicago
Regional Office**
Box 743, Midlothian, IL 60445.
- Federation of Genealogical Societies. Monograph.
  irreg.

**Federation of Insurance Counsel**
1205 Red Rambler Rd., Jenkintown, PA 19046.
- Federation of Insurance Counsel. Quarterly. q.
  ISSN 0430-2583

**Federation of Jewish Agencies of Greater Philadelphia**
226 S. 16th St., Philadelphia, PA 19102.
- Jewish Exponent. w. ISSN 0021-6437

**Federation of Motion Picture Councils**
552 Broadview Rd., Upper Darby, PA 19082.
- Film Preview Reports. m.
- News Reel. m.

**Federation of New York State Bird Clubs,Inc**
Ed. Joseph W. Taylor, 20 Parish Rd., Honeoye
Falls, NY 14472.
- Kingbird. q. ISSN 0023-1606

**Federation of Orthodontic Associations**
- International Journal of Orthodontics. (pub. by
  International Academy of Orthodontics)

**Federation of Societies for Coatings Technology**
1315 S. Walnut St., Suite 830, Philadelphia, PA
19107.
- Journal of Coatings Technology. m.

**Federation of Southern Cooperatives**
Education Dept., Box 95, Epes, AL 35460.
- Southern Cooperator. bi-m. ISSN 0038-4003

**Federation of State Medical Boards of the United
States**
3624 Market St., Philadelphia, PA 19104.
- Federation of State Medical Boards of the United
  States. Federation Bulletin. m. ISSN 0014-9306

**Federation of Tax Administrators**
1313 E. 60th St., Chicago, IL 60637.
- Tax Administrators News. m. ISSN 0039-9949

**Federation of Worker's Singing Societies of the U.S.A**
1729 Springfield Ave., Maplewood, NJ 07040.
- Saenger-Zeitung. m. ISSN 0036-2336

**Alan Feinstein and Associates**
41 Alhambra Circle, Cranston, RI 02905.
- Alan Shawn Feinstein Insiders Report. m.

**Felician Sisters**
600 Doat St., Buffalo, NY 14211.
- Ave Maria. s-m.

**Fellom Publications**
693 Mission St., San Francisco, CA 94105.
- California Builder. m. (Associated Building
  Industry of California)
- Light Metal Age. bi-m. ISSN 0024-3345
- Pacific Factory; the plant management and
  production magazine of the West. m. ISSN 0030-
  865X

**Fellowship in Prayer, Inc.**
Room 10 E, 200 E. 36th St., New York, NY 10016.
- Fellowship in Prayer. bi-m. ISSN 0014-9837

**Fellowship of Reconciliation**
Box 271, Nyack, NY 10960.
- Fellowship. m. (except Jul.-Aug.) ISSN 0014-9810

**Fellowship of Religious Humanists**
105 W. North College St., Box 278, Yellow Springs,
OH 45387.
- Religious Humanism; a quarterly journal of
  religious and ethical humanism. q. ISSN 0034-
  4095

**Feminist Art Journal Inc.**
41 Montgomery Place, Brooklyn, NY 11215.
- Feminist Art Journal. q. ISSN 0300-7014

**Feminist Book Mart**
162-11 Ninth Ave., Whitestone, NY 11357.
- Girls & Boys Together; a bibliography/catalog of
  non-sexist children's literature. irreg. ISSN 0361-
  9729

**Feminist Bulletin, Inc.**
Box 262, Scarborough, NY 10510.
- Feminist Bulletin. m.

**Feminist Newsletter**
Box 954, Chapel Hill, NC 27514.
- Feminary. fortn.

**Feminist Press**
Box 334, Old Westbury, NY 11568.
- Female Studies. irreg., no. 10, 1975.
- Feminist Press. News/Notes. irreg.
- Who's Who and Where in Women's Studies. irreg.
- Women's Studies Newsletter. q.

**Feminist Studies, Inc.**
417 Riverside Dr., New York, NY 10025.
- Feminist Studies. 2 per yr. ISSN 0046-3663

**Feminists for Life, Inc.**
Box 12726, Tucson, AZ 85732.
- Sisterlife Journal. q.

**Fenwick**
Box 729, Westminster, CA 92683.
- Lunker Gazette. bi-m.

**Ferachi & Associates**
603 Europe St., Baton Rouge, LA 70802.
- A S. q. ISSN 0044-7722 (American Institute of
  Architects. Association of Student Chapters)

**Feraferia, Inc.**
Box 691, Altadena, CA 91001.
- Korythalia. 2-4 per yr.

**Ferdinand Roten Galleries**
123 W. Mulberry St., Baltimore, MD 21201.
- Ferdinand Roten Galleries. Catalog of Original
  Graphic Art. a. ISSN 0085-0527

**Ferguson-Florissant School District. Board of
Education**
655 January Ave., Ferguson, MO 63135.
- Ferguson-Florissant Schools. irreg. ISSN 0015-
  0037

**J. G. Ferguson Publishing Co.**
6 N. Michigan Ave., Chicago, IL 60602.
- Career Opportunities for Technicians and
  Specialists. irreg.

**Ferrary Society**
- Ferrary Society. Bulletin. (pub. by Gustav Detjen,
  Jr., Ed. & Pub.)

**Joseph L. Ferriere, Ed. & Pub.**
132 Fifth Ave., Woonsocket, RI 02895.
- Probe (Woonsocket); the controversial phenomena
  magazine. q. ISSN 0032-9207

**Ferris State College**
Big Rapids, MI 49307.
- Michigan Business Education Association. News
  Bulletin. 3 per yr. ISSN 0026-2048

**Fertilizer Institute**
1015 18th St. N.W., Washington, DC 20036.
- Fertilizer Progress. bi-m. ISSN 0002-1598

**Fiat-Allis Construction Machinery, Inc.**
Box F, 106 Wilmot Rd., Deerfield, IL 60015.
- Reporter. q. ISSN 0034-4788

**Fibonacci Association**
- Fibonacci Quarterly. (pub. by University of Santa
  Clara)

**Richard Fichter, Ed. & Pub.**
28 E. Vine, Oxford, OH 45056
(and Postfach 2803, 6 Frankfurt/Main, W. Germany
(B.R.D.))
- Equality. irreg.

**David Ficken, Ed. & Pub.**
132 Calvert Ave., West Babylon, NY 11704.
- Car Tips. m. ISSN 0045-5717

**Fiction**
c/o City College, Department of English, 138th St.
and Convent Ave., New York, NY 10031.
- Fiction. 3 per yr.

**Fiction, Inc.**
513 E. 13th St., New York, NY 10009.
- Comparative Literature in Canada/Literature
  Comparee au Canada. s-a. ISSN 0045-7795

**Fiction West**
c/o R. F. Burns, 4326 Hargrave Ave., Santa Rosa, CA 95401.
- Fiction West. q.

**Field Enterprises Educational Corporation**
510 Merchandise Mart Plaza, Chicago, IL 60654.
- Science Year; World Book Science Annual. a. ISSN 0080-7621
- World Book Year Book. a. ISSN 0084-1439

**Field Enterprises, Inc.**
- Showcase Book Week. (pub. by Chicago Sun-Times)

**Field Museum of Natural History**
Roosevelt Rd. and Lake Shore Drive, Chicago, IL 60605.
- Field Museum of Natural History Bulletin. 11 per yr. ISSN 0015-0703
- Fieldiana: Anthropology. irreg., vol. 69, 1977. ISSN 0071-4739
- Fieldiana: Botany. irreg. ISSN 0015-0746
- Fieldiana: Geology. irreg.
- Fieldiana: Zoology. irreg. ISSN 0015-0754

**Fielding Publications**
105 Madison Ave., New York, NY 10016.
- Fielding's Guide to the Caribbean Plus the Bahamas. a. ISSN 0071-4755
- Fielding's Low-Cost Europe. a.
- Fielding's Quick Currency Guide for Far, Near and Middle East Including Russia and China. irreg. ISSN 0071-4771
- Fielding's Selected Favorites: Hotels & Inns, Europe. a. ISSN 0092-9506 (Co-Publisher: William Morrow & Co., Inc.)
- Fielding's Selective Shopping Guide to Europe. a. ISSN 0071-478X
- Fielding's Travel Guide to Europe. a. ISSN 0071-4801

**Fifth Estate Inc.**
4403 Second, Detroit, MI 48201.
- Fifth Estate. fortn. ISSN 0015-0800

**Fifth Estate Publishing Co.**
Box 647, Ben Franklin Station, Washington, DC 20044.
- Counter Spy. q. (Organizing Committee for a Fifth Estate)

**Fifty-One Per Cent News**
Box 371, Lomita, CA 90717.
- Fifty-One Per Cent News; news and literary magazine for women. 8 per yr.

**Fighting Times**
Box 455, Annex Station, Providence, RI 02901.
- Fighting Times; Rhode Island's working class paper. m.

**Fighting Woman News**
9 E. 48th St., New York, NY 10017.
- Fighting Woman News. m.

**Figment**
c/o Jacob Bloom, Ed., 34 Andrew St., Newton, MA 02161.
- Figment. 2-3 per yr.

**Filipiniana Book Guild**
Manila, Philippines
(Dist. by Cellar Book Shops, 18090 Wyoming, Detroit, Mich. 48221)
- Filipiniana Book Guild. Publications. irreg., 1970, no. 16. ISSN 0071-4852

**Filipino- American Media of California**
830 Central Ave., Box 1783, Salinas, CA 93901.
- Philippines Mail. m.

**Film Bill, Inc.**
45 E. 55th St., New York, NY 10022.
- Film Bill. m.

**Film Culture**
Box 1499, G.P.O., New York, NY 10001.
- Film Culture. q. ISSN 0015-1211

**Film-English-Humanities Association**
265 Ernst Bessey Hall, Michigan State University, East Lansing, MI 48823.
- Film-English/Humanities Association. Journal. a. ISSN 0071-4887

**Film Journal**
c/o Thomas R. Atkins, Box 9602, Hollins College, VA 24020.
- Film Journal. 2-3 per yr. ISSN 0046-3787

**Film Library Information Council**
Box 348, Radio City Station, New York, NY 10019.
- Film Library Quarterly. q. ISSN 0015-1327

**Film News Co.**
250 W. 57th St., New York, NY 10019.
- Film News; the international review of AV materials and equipment. 5 per yr. ISSN 0015-1343
- Film News Omnibus. triennial.

**Film Society of Lincoln Center**
1865 Broadway, New York, NY 10023.
- Film Comment. bi-m. ISSN 0015-119X

**Filmdex, Inc.**
Box 22672, State University of New York, Albany, 1400 Washington Ave., Albany, NY 12222
(or 16 Bacon Lane, Albany, NY 12211)
- Film Literature Index. q. ISSN 0093-6758

**Filmwomen of Boston Inc.**
490 Beacon St., Boston, MA 02115.
- Workprint Newsletter. m.

**Filson Club**
118 W. Breckinridge St., Louisville, KY 40203.
- Filson Club History Quarterly. q. ISSN 0015-1874

**Filtration Engineering Catalog**
25 W. 45th St., New York, NY 10036.
- Filtration Engineering Catalog. a.

**Fimebrock Publishing, Inc.**
Box 1258, San Rafael, CA 94902.
- Travelday. m.

**Finance Publishing Corp.**
Box G, Lenox Hill Station, New York, NY 10021.
- Finance; the magazine of money. m. ISSN 0015-1912 (Information for Business Communications Ltd.)

**Financial Analysts Federation**
219 E. 42nd St., New York, NY 10017.
- Financial Analysts Journal. bi-m. ISSN 0015-198X

**Financial Executives Institute**
633 Third Ave., New York, NY 10017.
- Financial Executive. m. ISSN 0015-1998

**Financial Information, Inc.**
Box 473, Jersey City, NJ 07303
(and 170 Varick St., New York, NY 10013)
- Financial Corporate Bond Transfer Service. a. with m. supplements. ISSN 0360-5825
- Financial Stock Guide Service. Directory of Active Stocks. a (m. supplements) ISSN 0364-0752
- Financial Stock Guide Service. Directory of Obsolete Securities. biennial. ISSN 0085-0551

**Financial Management Association**
- Financial Management. (pub. by University of Wisconsin Press)

**Financial Markets Review**
Box 2430, New York, NY 10017.
- Financial Markets Review. m.

**Financial Publications, Inc.**
1221 Ave. of Americas, New York, NY 10020.
- Business Week Letter; personal financial strategies. fortn.

**Financial Publishing Co.**
82 Brookline Ave, Boston, MA 02215.
- Cost of Personal Borrowing in the United States. a. ISSN 0091-3855

**Financial Quarterly**
Box 14451, North Palm Beach, FL 33408.
- Financial Quarterly. q.

**Financial World**
590 Exchange St., Marion, OH 43302.
- Financial World. s-m. ISSN 0015-2064

**Fincom Inc.**
700 Harrison St., Topeka, KS 66636.
- Mid-America Commerce & Industry. m.
- Mid-America Insurance. m. ISSN 0026-2935
- Rocky Mountain Industries. m.

**Finders Keepers**
c/o Fran Verina, Ed., Route 2, Box 36, Kinsman, OH 44428.
- Finders Keepers. m.

**Fine Arts Fellowship**
P.O. 1269, Grand Rapids, MI 49501.
- For the Time Being. q.

**Fine Arts Philatelists**
875 West End Ave, New York, NY 10025.
- Fine Arts Philatelist Journal. 5 per yr.

**Fine Arts Society**
2314 W. Sixth St., Mishawaka, IN 46544.
- Poet; peu a peu. a.

**Finger Lakes Association, Inc.**
309 Lake Street, Penn Yan, NY 14527.
- Finger Lakes Travel Guide. a.

**Ruth Finley, Ed. & Pub.**
185 E. 85 St., NY 12212.
- Fashion Calendar. w. ISSN 0014-8660
- Fashion International. m.

**Finnish American Chamber of Commerce**
540 Madison Ave., New York, NY 10022.
- Finnish American Chamber of Commerce Newsletter. m. ISSN 0015-2439

**Finnish-American Historical Society of the West**
Box 3515, Portland, OR 97208.
- Finnam Newsletter. q.

**Finnish American League for Democracy**
- Raivaaja/Pioneer. (pub. by Raivaaja Publishing Co.)

**Finnish American Publishing Co.**
Box 334, Cliffside Park, NY 07010.
- Finnish American Annual/Amerikansuomalaisten Vuosikirja. a. ISSN 0362-2576

**Finnish Newspaper Co. Inc.**
4422-8th Ave., Brooklyn, NY 11220.
- New Yorkin Uutiset/Finnish New York News. w.

**Fiona Press, Inc.**
2 W. 45th St., New York, NY 10036.
- Club. m.

**Fire Exit**
c/o William Corbett, Ed., 9 Columbus Square, Boston, MA 02116.
- Fire Exit. irreg.

**Fire Fly Reporter**
c/o Isabelle Scarset, Ed., Box 95, Westbrook, MN 56183.
- Fire Fly Reporter. m.

**Fire Independent, Inc.**
1028 Connecticut Ave. N.W., Suite 909-A, Washington, DC 20036.
- Commerce Detector. w.
- Fire Independent. m. ISSN 0098-3276

**Fire Marshals Association of North America**
470 Atlantic Ave., Boston, MA 02210.
- Fire Marshals Association of North America. Year Book. a. ISSN 0090-5313

**Fireweed**
Box 9888, Columbus, OH 43206.
- Fireweed. q.

**First Boston Corp.**
20 Exchange Place, New York, NY 10005.
- Handbook of Securities of the United States Government and Federal Agencies and Related Money Market Instruments. biennial. ISSN 0072-9892

**First Catholic Slovak Union**
3289 East 55th St., Cleveland, OH 44127.
- Furdek. a.
- Jednota Kalendar. a. (Subscr. Address: Jednota Printery, Box 150, Middletown, PA 17057)

**First Century Fellowship**
2151 Young St., Memphis, TN 38104.
- Flaming Sword. m.

**First Church of Christ, Scientist**
- Christian Science Quarterly Bible Lessons (Braille Edition) (pub. by Christian Science Publishing Society)

**First Coinvestors Inc.**
F C I Bldg., Albertson, NY 11507.
- F C I Advisory Letter. m.

**First District Dental Society**
- New York Journal of Dentistry. (pub. by New York Journal of Dentistry, Inc.)

**First Hawaiian Bank**
Research Div., Box 3200, Honolulu, HI 96847.
- First Hawaiian Bank. Economic Indicators; a monthly report by the research division. m. ISSN 0015-2757

**First Issue**
c/o Bill Wertheim, 503 W. 122 St., New York, NY 10027.
- First Issue. 3 per yr.

**First Jersey National Bank**
2 Montgomery St., Jersey City, NJ 07303.
- First Jersey News. q.

**First National Bank of Boston**
Boston, Box 2016, Boston, MA 02106.
- New England Report. q.

**First National Bank of Chicago. Business & Economic Research Division**
One First National Plaza, Chicago, IL 60670.
- First Chicago World Report. a.

**First National City Bank (New York)**
see Citibank

**First Things First, Inc.**
P.O. Box 9041, Washington, DC 20003.
- 1St Things 1st. irreg.

**First Unitarian Church of Berkeley**
1 Lawson Rd., Berkeley, CA 94707.
- Uniquest; the search for meaning. s-a. ISSN 0360-8182 (Uniquest Foundation)

**First Unitarian Church of Harvard**
Harvard, MA 01451.
- Orb (Harvard) q. ISSN 0361-5472

**First World Foundation**
1580 Avon Ave., S.W., Atlanta, GA 30311.
- First World; an international journal of black thought. bi-m.

**Carl Fischer, Inc.**
62 Cooper Square, New York, NY 10003.
- Concert Notes; Carl Fischer Newsletter. irreg.

**Fischer Medical Publications, Inc.**
280 Madison Ave., New York, NY 10016.
- Emergency Medicine; common emergencies in daily practice. m. ISSN 0013-6654

**Jack I. Fishbein, Ed. & Pub.**
216 W. Jackson Blvd., Chicago, IL 60606.
- Sentinel. w. ISSN 0037-2331

**Fishermen's News, Inc.**
Fishermen's Terminal, C-3 Building, Rm. 110, Seattle, WA 98119.
- Fishermen's News. s-m (23 per yr.) ISSN 0015-2994

**Fishing Club of America**
- Fishing World. (pub. by Allsport Publishing Corp.)

**Fishing Gazette Publishing Corp**
461 Eighth Ave., New York, NY 10001.
- Fishing Gazette; recognized authority of the commercial fishing industry. m.(s-m Dec.) ISSN 0015-3028

**Fishing in Maryland, Inc.**
Box 1892, Baltimore, MD 21203.
- Fishing in Maryland & Virginia. irreg. ISSN 0363-8898
- Fishing in the Mid Atlantic; Maryland, New Jersey, Delaware, Pennsylvania, Virginia. irreg. ISSN 0363-552X

**Fishing Tackle Trade News, Inc.**
Box 70, Wilmette, IL 60091.
- Fishing Tackle Trade News. m. (June-July & Nov.-Dec. combined) ISSN 0015-3060

**William C. Fitt, Ed. & Pub.**
Box 286, Cadillac, MI 49601.
- Live Steam. m. ISSN 0300-7804

**Fitzgerald Communications, Inc.**
1597 Union St., Schenectady, NY 12309.
- Wilderness Camping. bi-m. ISSN 0043-5430

**Fitzgerald Publishing Co., Inc.**
527 Madison Ave., New York, NY 10022.
- Golden Legacy; illustrated history magazine series. ISSN 0046-6077

**Fitzsimons Army Medical Center**
see under U.S. Army

**Five Associated University Libraries**
106 Roney Lane, Syracuse, NY 13210.
- Five Associated University Libraries. Newsletter. bi-m. ISSN 0015-3176

**Flag Research Center**
3 Edgehill Rd., Winchester, MA 01890.
- Flag Bulletin. bi-m. ISSN 0015-3370

**Flambeaux Publishing Co.**
515 Gravier St., New Orleans, LA 70130.
- Metro New Orleans. m. ISSN 0300-7251

**Flamencos Internacional Association**
A. Sherry-Brener Enterprises, 3145 W. 63rd St., Chicago, IL 60629.
- Guitarra. bi-m. ISSN 0017-5498

**Flammability News Bulletin, Inc.**
Box 13085, Washington, DC 20009.
- Flammability News Bulletin. bi-m.

**Fleet Reserve Association**
1303 New Hampshire Ave., N.W., Washington, DC 20036.
- Naval Affairs; in the interest of the U.S. Navy and for personnel of the Navy and Marine Corps active, fleet reserve and retired. m. ISSN 0028-1409

**Max C. Fleischmann College of Agriculture**
see under University of Nevada

**Al Fleming Communications, Inc.**
24500 Southfield Rd., Southfield, MI 48075.
- Car Biz. m.

**Flexographic Technical Association**
50 Jericho Turnpike, Jericho, NY 11753.
- Flexographic Technical Association. Report of the Proceedings: Annual Meeting and Technical Forum. a. ISSN 0428-5670

**Flight Safety Foundation, Inc.**
1800 North Kent St., Arlington, VA 22209.
- Accident Prevention Bulletin. m.
- Air Taxi Commuter Safety Bulletin. bi-m.
- Airport Ground Safety Bulletin. bi-m.
- Airport Safety Bulletin. bi-m.
- Aviation Mechanics Bulletin. bi-m. ISSN 0005-2140
- Cabin Crew Safety Bulletin. bi-m.
- Design Notes. bi-m.
- Flight Safety Facts & Reports. m. ISSN 0098-7182
- Flight Safety Foundaton. Newsletter. bi-m.
- Helicopter Safety Bulletin. irreg. ISSN 0361-5405
- Human Factors Bulletin. bi-m.
- International Air Safety Seminar Proceedings. a.; 26th Lisbon, 1973. ISSN 0534-6592
- Pilot Safety Exchange. bi-m.

**Floating Island Publications**
Box 516, Point Reyes Station, CA 94956.
- Floating Island. 3 per yr.

**Florafax International, Inc.**
Box 45745, Tulsa, OK 74145.
- Florafacts. m. ISSN 0046-4082

**Florida. Bureau of Local Government Finance**
Tallahassee, FL 32301.
- Florida. Bureau of Local Government Finance. Annual Local Government Financial Report. a. ISSN 0094-8551

**Florida. Comptroller of Florida**
Room 111, Carlton Building, Tallahassee, FL 32304.
- Blue-Sky Bulletin. m. (prep. by its Division of Securities)
- Fiscal Guardian. m.
- Florida. Comptroller's Office. Taxpayer's Almanac. a.
- Florida Comptroller. Condensed Comparative Statement of Assets and Liabilities of State-Chartered Commercial Banks and Trust Companies. s-a.

**Florida. Crop and Livestock Reporting Service**
1222 Woodward St., Orlando, FL 32803.
- Florida Agricultural Statistics. a. ISSN 0085-0594

**Florida. Department of Administration**
Tallahassee, FL 32301.
- Florida. Department of Administration. Budget in Brief. a. ISSN 0095-5175

**Florida. Department of Administration. Division of Retirement**
Room 530, Carlton Building, Tallahassee, FL 32304.
- Florida's Local Retirement Systems: a Survey. a.

**Florida. Department of Administration. Division of State Planning**
660 Apalachee Pkwy., Tallahassee, FL 32304.
- Federal Grant-in-Aid Activity in Florida: a Summary Report. a. ISSN 0361-1582 (prep. by its Bureau of Intergovernmental Relations)
- Florida. Division of State Planning. Annual Report on State and Regional Planning. a.
- State of Florida Land Development Guide. irreg. (1-2 per yr) (prep. by its Bureau of Comprehensive Planning)

**Florida. Department of Agriculture and Consumer Services**
Mayo Bldg., 407 S. Calhoun St., Tallahassee, FL 32304.
- Florida Market Bulletin. s-m.

**Florida. Department of Agriculture and Consumer Services. Division of Forestry**
Tallahassee, FL 32301.
- Commodity Drain Report of Florida's Primary Forest Industries. irreg. ISSN 0362-191X

**Florida. Department of Agriculture and Consumer Services. Division of Plant Industry**
P.O. Box 1269, Gainesville, FL 32602.
- Arthropods of Florida and Neighboring Land Areas. irreg., vol. 8, 1973. ISSN 0066-8036
- Entomology Circular. m. ISSN 0013-8932
- Florida. Department of Agriculture and Consumer Service. Plant Industry News. q.
- Florida. Division of Plant Industry. Biennial Report. biennial. ISSN 0071-5948
- Plant Pathology Circular. m. ISSN 0032-0870
- Tri-Ology Technical Report. m. ISSN 0041-2481

**Florida. Department of Commerce**
Secretary of Commerce, 107 West Gaines St., Tallahassee, FL 32304.
- Florida. Department of Commerce. Annual Report. a.
- Florida Economic Indicators. q.

**Florida. Department of Commerce. Division of Economic Development**
Tallahassee, FL 32304.
- Directory: Florida Ports and Waterways. irreg. ISSN 0091-8458

**Florida. Department of Community Affairs. Division of Technical Assistance**
2571 Executive Center Circle, East, Tallahassee, FL 32301.
- Florida. Governor. Annual Report on State Housing Goals. a. ISSN 0091-9942

**Florida. Department of Education**
Knott Building, Tallahassee, FL 32304.
- Florida Education Directory. a.
- Florida Requirements for Teacher Certification. irreg. ISSN 0071-5999
- Florida Schools. q. ISSN 0015-4296

**Florida. Department of Education. Division of Elementary and Secondary Education**
Tallahassee, FL 32304.
- Florida. Bureau of Evaluation and Compensatory Education. Florida Statewide Assessment Program: Capsule Report. irreg. ISSN 0094-1468 (prep. by its Student Evaluation Section)

**Florida. Department of Education. Division of Vocational Education**
- Florida Vocational Journal. (pub. by Career Education Center)

**Florida. Department of Education. Professional Practices Council**
Tallahassee, FL 32304.
- Florida. Department of Education. Professional Practices Council. Report. a.

**Florida. Department of Health and Rehabilitative Services**
1323 Winewood Blvd., Tallahassee, FL 32301.
• Access (Tallahassee) m.

**Florida. Department of Health and Rehabilitative Services. Public Health Statistics Section**
P.O. Box 210, Jacksonville, FL 32201.
• Florida. Department of Health and Rehabilitative Services. Monthly Statistical Report. m.

**Florida. Department of Highway Safety and Motor Vehicles. Division of Motor Vehicles**
Neil Kirkman Building, Tallahassee, FL 32304.
• Florida. Division of Motor Vehicles. Tags and Revenue. a. ISSN 0092-0177

**Florida. Department of Natural Resources**
Crown Bldg. Rm 322, Tallahassee, FL 32304.
• Florida Conservation News. m. ISSN 0015-3974

**Florida. Department of Natural Resources. Division of Resource Management**
Bureau of Geology, 903 W. Tennessee St., Tallahassee, FL 32304.
• Florida. Bureau of Geology. Geological Bulletins. irreg., no. 56, 1973. ISSN 0085-0608
• Florida. Bureau of Geology. Information Circulars. irreg., no. 88, 1974. ISSN 0085-0616
• Florida. Bureau of Geology. Map Series. irreg., no. 73, 1975. ISSN 0085-0624
• Florida. Bureau of Geology. Report of Investigations. irreg., no. 82, 1975. ISSN 0085-0632
• Florida. Bureau of Geology. Special Publications. irreg., no. 20, 1974. ISSN 0085-0640

**Florida. Department of Natural Resources. Marine Research Laboratory**
100 8th Ave. S.E., St. Petersburg, FL 33701.
• Florida Marine Research Publications. irreg., approx 15 per yr. ISSN 0095-0157
• Memoirs of the Hourglass Cruises. irreg. ISSN 0085-0683

**Florida. Department of State. Bureau of Historic Sites and Properties**
The Capitol, Tallahassee, FL 32304.
• Florida. Bureau of Historic Sites and Properties. Bulletin. irreg. ISSN 0085-0659

**Florida. Department of State. Division of Archives, History and Records Management**
Capitol, Tallahassee, FL 32304.
• Florida. Department of State. Division of Archives. Archives and History News. bi-m. ISSN 0046-4139

**Florida. Department of State. Division of Elections**
The Capitol, Tallahassee, FL 32304.
• Florida Administrative Weekly. w. ISSN 0098-874X

**Florida. Department of Transportation**
Tallahassee, FL 32301.
• Florida. Department of Transportation. Annual Report. a. ISSN 0095-2060

**Florida. Division of Corrections**
Raiford, FL 32083.
• Florida. Division of Corrections. Financial Report. a. ISSN 0094-6435

**Florida. Division of Family Services**
Box 2050, Jacksonville, FL 32203.
• Florida. Division of Family Services. Annual Statistical Report. a. ISSN 0093-6715

**Florida. Division of Mental Health**
1323 Winewood Blvd., Tallahassee, FL 32301.
• Florida. Mental Health Program Office. Statistical Report of Community Mental Health Programs. a.

**Florida. Farm Labor and Rural Manpower Service**
Tallahassee, FL 32301.
• Florida. Farm Labor and Rural Manpower Service. Farm Labor and Rural Manpower Report. Florida. a. ISSN 0093-5484

**Florida. Game and Fresh Water Fish Commission**
Farris Bryant Building, 620 S. Meridian St., Tallahassee, FL 32304.
• Florida Wildlife. bi-m. ISSN 0015-4369

**Florida. Governor's Commission on the Status of Women**
Tallahassee, FL 32304.
• Status of Women in Florida: an Annual Report. a. ISSN 0093-7118

**Florida. Legislature. Joint Legislative Management Committee**
Holland Bldg., Tallahassee, FL 32304.
• Florida. Legislature. Joint Legislative Management Committee. Summary of General Legislation. a. ISSN 0090-1520

**Florida. Legislature. Senate**
Tallahassee, FL 32301.
• Florida Senate. biennial. ISSN 0093-4089

**Florida. Mental Health Program Office**
1323 Winewood Blvd., Tallahassee, FL 32301.
• Florida. Mental Health Program Office. Statistical Report of Hospitals. a. ISSN 0094-2294

**Florida. State Library**
Tallahassee, FL 32302.
• Florida Public Documents. m. with annual cum. ISSN 0430-7801
• Orange Seed. m.

**Florida. State Manpower Planning Council**
Caldwell Bldg., Tallahassee, FL 32304.
• State of Florida Comprehensive Manpower Plan. irreg. ISSN 0095-6430

**Florida A & M University**
Tallahassee, FL 32307.
• National Association of College Deans and Registrars. Proceedings. a. ISSN 0077-328X

**Florida Academy of Family Physicians**
Suite 229, 4057 Carmichael Ave., Jacksonville, FL 32207.
• Florida Family Physician. q. ISSN 0015-4067

**Florida Academy of Sciences, Inc.**
810 E. Rollins St., Orlando, FL 32803.
• Florida Scientist. q. ISSN 0098-4590

**Florida Anthropological Society, Inc.**
130 Florida State Museum, University of Florida, Gainesville, FL 32611.
• Florida Anthropological Society Publications. irreg.
• Florida Anthropologist. q. ISSN 0015-3893

**Florida Association for Media in Education**
c/o Billy Pennington, Pres., FSU Developmental Research School, West Call St., Tallahassee, FL 32306.
• Florida Media Quarterly. q.
• Florida Media Quarterly. (pub. by Florida State University. Developmental Research School)

**Florida Association of Realtors**
Box 1231, Orlando, FL 32802.
• Florida Realtor. m.

**Florida Atlantic University**
Boca Raton, FL 33441.
• Atlantic Sun. w. ISSN 0004-685X

**Florida Atlantic University-Florida International University. Joint Center for Environment and Urban Problems**
1515 W. Commercial Blvd., Fort Lauderdale, FL 33309.
• Florida Environmental and Urban Issues. bi-m.

**Florida Audubon Society**
P.O.Drawer 7, Maitland, FL 32751.
• Florida Naturalist. bi-m. ISSN 0015-4172

**Florida Bankers Association**
505 N. Mills Ave., Box 6847, Orlando, FL 32803.
• Florida Banker. 11 per yr. (Nov.-Dec. combined)

**Florida Bar**
Tallahassee, FL 32304.
• Florida Bar Journal. m. ISSN 0015-3915
• Florida Bar News. s-m. ISSN 0360-0114

**Florida Chamber of Commerce**
P.O. Box 5497, Tallahassee, FL 32301.
• Directory of Florida Industries. a.

**Florida Citrus Mutual**
Box 89, Lakeland, FL 33802.
• Triangle. w(except July) ISSN 0041-2570

**Florida Co-Operative Apartment Owners Association Inc**
• Apartment Owners News. (pub. by Apartment Owners Publishing Co.)

**Florida Confederation of Historical Societies**
Box 26547, Orlando, FL 32816.
• Florida History Newsletter. s-a.

**Florida Congress of Parents and Teachers**
1747 Orlando Central Parkway, Orlando, FL 32804.
• Florida P T A Bulletin. 8 per yr.

**Florida Conservation Foundation**
• Enfo. (pub. by Environmental Information Center of Florida)

**Florida Consumer Information Bureau, Inc.**
P.O. Drawer 7698, St. Petersburg, FL 33734.
• Thanatos. q. (Florida Funeral Directors Association)

**Florida Council of Teachers of English**
5110 San Amaro Dr., Coral Gables, FL 33146.
• Florida English Newsletter. 3 per yr.

**Florida Dental Association**
3021 Swann Ave., Tampa, FL 33609.
• F D A Intaglio. m.
• Florida Dental Journal. q. ISSN 0015-3990

**Florida Education Association**
208 W. Pensacola St., Tallahassee, FL 32304.
• United Teacher. s-m. (Aug.-May); m. (Nov.-Dec.)

**Florida Educational Research and Development Council**
126 Bi. E., College of Education, University of Florida, Gainesville, FL 32611.
• Florida Educational Research and Development Council. Research Bulletin. q. ISSN 0015-4024

**Florida Engineering Society**
1906 Lee Rd., Orlando, FL 32810.
• Florida Engineering Society. Journal. m. ISSN 0015-4032

**Florida English Journal**
5591 Southwest Third Court, Plantation, FL 33314.
• Florida English Journal. s-a.

**Florida Entomological Society**
Box 12425, University Station, Gainesville, FL 32604.
• Florida Entomologist. q. ISSN 0015-4040

**Florida F L Reporter**
801 N.E. 177 St., North Miami Beach, FL 33162.
• Florida F L Reporter; journal of language and culture in education. s-a. ISSN 0430-7690

**Florida Farm Bureau Federation**
Box 7605, Orlando, FL 32804.
• Florida Agriculture. m. except June, July & Aug. ISSN 0015-3869

**Florida Funeral Directors Association**
• Thanatos. (pub. by Florida Consumer Information Bureau, Inc.)

**Florida Group Childcare Association**
Box 2050, Jacksonville, FL 32203.
• Workshop for Child Care Staff of Florida's Child Caring Facilities. Report. a. ISSN 0091-8482

**Florida Historical Society**
Box 14045, University Sta., Gainesville, FL 32604.
• Florida Historical Quarterly. q. ISSN 0015-4113

**Florida Industrial Arts Association**
c/o Denis R. Binder, Ed., 2117 Farwell Dr., Tampa, FL 33603.
• Florida Industrial Arts Quarterly Bulletin. q. ISSN 0015-4121

**Florida Law Revision Council**
Office of the Clerk, Florida House of Representative, Room 346, Holland Building, Tallahassee, FL 32601.
• Florida Law Revision Council. Annual Report. a.

**Florida League of Cities**
Box 1757, Tallahassee, FL 32302.
• Florida Municipal Record. m. ISSN 0015-4164

**Florida Library Association**
2862 W. W. Kelly Rd., Tallahassee, FL 32301.
● Florida Libraries. bi-m. ISSN 0046-4147

**Florida Medical Association, Inc.**
Box 2411, Jacksonville, FL 32203.
● Florida Medical Association Journal. m. ISSN 0015-4148

**Florida Music Educators Association**
Drawer O, Tampa, FL 33675.
● Florida Music Director. m. (except June, July) ISSN 0046-4155

**Florida Nurses Association**
Box 6985, 1235 E. Concord St., Orlando, FL 32803.
● Florida Nurse. m. ISSN 0015-4199

**Florida Ocean Sciences Institute**
1500 S. E. 3rd Court, Suite 101, Deerfield Beach, FL 23441.
● Current Trend Review. irreg. ISSN 0362-4269

**Florida Pharmaceutical Association**
Box 960, Tallahassee, FL 32302.
● Florida Pharmaceutical Journal. m. ISSN 0015-4202

**Florida Psychological Association**
Eaton Park Professional Plaza, Route 5, Box 71, FL 33801.
● F P. q.

**Florida Restaurant Association**
The Florida Restaurateur, 46 N.E. 6th St., Miami, FL 33132.
● Florida Restaurateur & Purveyor News. bi-m. ISSN 0046-418X

**Florida Roofing, Sheet Metal & Air Conditioning Contractors Association, Inc.**
P.O. Drawer 988, Lakeland, FL 33802.
● Florida Forum. m.

**Florida Rural Electric Cooperatives Association**
Box 590, Tallahassee, FL 32302.
● Florida Electric Cooperative News. m.

**Florida School for the Deaf and the Blind**
St. Augustine, FL 32084.
● Florida School Herald. m. (Sep.-May) ISSN 0015-4288

**Florida Society of Geographers**
Florida Atlantic University, Boca Raton, FL 33431.
● Florida Geographer. q.

**Florida Speech Communication Association**
c/o K. P. Taylor, Comm. Dept., Florida Tech Univ, Orlando, FL 32816.
● Florida Speech Communication Journal. s-a. ISSN 0093-6138

**Florida Speleological Society**
Box 12581, University Station, Gainesville, FL 32601.
● Florida Speleological Society. Special Papers. irreg. ISSN 0071-6006

**Florida State Board of Independent Colleges and Universities**
Tallahassee, FL 32304.
● Florida. State Board of Independent Colleges and Universities. Report. a. ISSN 0093-1071

**Florida State Firemen's Association**
Box 968, Avon Park, FL 33825.
● Florida Fireman. m.

**Florida State Museum**
University of Florida, Museum Rd., Gainesville, FL 32611.
● Florida State Museum. Bulletin. Biological Sciences. irreg.
● Florida State Museum. Contributions. Anthropology and History. irreg., 1973, no. 18.
● International Congress for the Study of Pre-Columbian Cultures of the Lesser Antilles. Proceedings. irreg., 4th, 1973. ISSN 0538-6381

**Florida State Reading Council**
c/o Kathleen Gurucharri, Ed., Childhood Education, Florida International University, School of Education, Miami, FL 33199.
● Florida Reading Quarterly. 3 per yr. ISSN 0015-4261

**Florida State University**
415 N. Monroe St., Room 415, Tallahassee, FL 32301.
● I S I S Newsletter. s-a. (Individualized Science Instructional System)

**Florida State University. Center for Yugoslav-American Studies, Research, and Exchanges**
609 Keen Building, Tallahassee, FL 32306.
● Florida State University. Slavic Papers. a. ISSN 0430-7291

**Florida State University. College of Law**
Tallahassee, FL 32306.
● Florida State University Law Review. q.

**Florida State University. Department of Anthropology**
Tallahassee, FL 32306.
● Notes in Anthropology. irreg., 1969, vol. XIII. ISSN 0078-2041

**Florida State University. Department of Biological Sciences**
225 Conradi Building, Palmett Drive and Dewey St., Tallahassee, FL 32301.
● Systematic Botany. q. ISSN 0363-6445 (American Society of Plant Taxonomists)

**Florida State University. Department of Classics**
Tallahassee, FL 32306.
● Archaelogical News. q.

**Florida State University. Department of Education**
107 Gaines St., Tallahassee, FL 32306.
● Conference on the Economics of Education. Proceedings. irreg. ISSN 0084-9170
● Directory of Cooperative Education Activities in Florida. biennial.

**Florida State University. Department of Philosophy**
Tallahassee, FL 32306.
● Social Theory and Practice; an international and interdisciplinary journal of social philosophy. s-a. ISSN 0037-802X

**Florida State University. Developmental Research School**
Tallahassee, FL 32306.
● Florida Media Quarterly. q. (Florida Association for Media in Education)

**Florida State University. Institute for Social Research**
Bellamy Bldg., Tallahassee, FL 32306.
● Florida State University. Institute for Social Research. Governmental Research Bulletin. 4 per yr. !SSN 0015-430X

**Florida State University. Instructional Media Center**
Tallahassee, FL 32306.
● Florida State University. Instructional Media Center. Films. biennial.

**Florida State University. Office of the Provost, Graduate Studies & Research**
Tallahassee, FL 32301.
● Florida State University. Publications of the Faculty. irreg. ISSN 0428-6766

**Florida State University. School of Library Science**
Tallahassee, FL 32306.
● Journal of Library History. State Library History Bibliography Series. irreg.

**Florida State University System**
107 West Gaines Street, Tallahassee, FL 32304.
● Florida. State University System. Fact Book. a. ISSN 0093-9617

**Florida Supermarket Association**
● Florida Food & Grocery News. (pub. by Munroe Publications, Inc)

**Florida Technological University**
c/o Library, Box 25000, Orlando, FL 32876.
● William L. Bryant Foundation American Studies. Report. irreg. ISSN 0511-9715

**Florida Trucking Association, Inc.**
704 Gilmore St., Jacksonville, FL 32204.
● Florida Truck News. m. ISSN 0015-4334

**Raymond Flory, Ed. & Pub.**
1047 Elliott St., South Bend, IN 46628.
● Explorer. s-a. ISSN 0014-5017

**Flournoy & Associates**
1845 West Morse, Chicago, IL 60626.
● Industrial Hygiene News Report. m. ISSN 0537-5223

**Floyd Junior College. Humanities Division**
Box 1864, Rome, GA 30161.
● Old Red Kimono. a.

**Fluor Corporation**
2500 S. Atlantic Blvd., Los Angeles, CA 90040.
● Fluor Magazine. 3 per yr. ISSN 0015-4695

**Fly Fisherman Magazine, Inc.**
Dorset, VT 05251
(Subscr. to: Box 10002, Des Moines, IA 50340)
● Fly Fisherman; the magazine for the complete angler. 7 per yr. ISSN 0015-4741

**Flying Physician Association, Inc.**
2537 Larkin Rd., Lexington, KY 40503
(Subscr. to: F P A Business Office, 801 Green Bay Rd., Lake Bluff, IL 60044)
● Flying Physician. q. ISSN 0015-4857

**Flying Saucer News Co.**
359 W. 45th St., New York, NY 10036.
● Flying Saucer News. s-a. ISSN 0015-4873

**Focus-Midwest Publishing Co., Inc.**
928A N. McKnight, St. Louis, MO 63132.
● Focus/Midwest. bi-m. ISSN 0015-508X
● St. Louis Journalism Review. bi-m. ISSN 0036-2972

**Focus News**
c/o Barbara Louise Mion, 3320 Donnegal Ave., Kalamazoo, MI 49007
● Focus News. s-m.

**Folger Shakespeare Library**
201 E. Capitol St., Washington, DC 20003.
● Folger Library Newsletter. 5 per yr. ISSN 0015-5438
● Folger Shakespeare Library Annual Report. a. ISSN 0428-8211
● Poetry Clearinghouse. bi-m. (prep. by its Poetry Office)
● Shakespeare Quarterly. q. ISSN 0037-3222

**Folio Magazine Publishing Corp.**
125 Elm St., Box 697, New Canaan, CT 06840.
● Folio (New Canaan); the magazine for magazine management. m. ISSN 0046-4333

**Folk Dance Association**
Box 500, Midwood Station, Brooklyn, NY 11230.
● Mixed Pickles; newspaper for dancers, lorists and other folk. m (10 per yr.)

**Folk Dance Federation of California, South**
12350 Ida Ave., Los Angeles, CA 90066.
● Folk Dance Scene. m.(11 per yr.) ISSN 0430-8751

**Folk Dance Magazine**
777 Foster Ave., Brooklyn, NY 11230.
● Folk Dance Magazine. q.

**Folklore Feminists Communication**
P.O. Box 24053, LSU Station, Baton Rouge, LA 70803.
● Folklore Feminists Communication. 3 per yr. ISSN 0093-8475

**Folklore Forum, Inc.**
504 N. Fess St., Bloomington, IN 47401.
● Folklore Forum. 4-5 per yr. ISSN 0015-5926

**Folklore Society of Greater Washington**
Box 19303, 20th St. Sta., Washington, DC 20036.
● Folklore Society of Greater Washington Newsletter. 10 per yr. ISSN 0015-5950

**Folkscene Publication**
Box 64545, Los Angeles, CA 90064.
● Folkscene Publication. m.

**Follia di New York**
c/o Michele Sisca, 125 E. 95th St., New York, NY 10028.
● Follia di New York; satirico politico-letterario militare. m. ISSN 0015-6000

**Food Chemical News, Inc.**
1341 G. St. N. W., 420 Colorado Bldg., Washington, DC 20005.
● Food Chemical News. w. ISSN 0015-6337

- Food Chemical News Guide; current status of food additives and color additives. w.
- Pesticide & Toxic Chemical News. w.
- Pesticide Chemical News Guide. m.

**Food Distribution Research Society**
Box 1795, Hyattsville, MD 20788.
- Food Distribution Research Society. Newsletter. q.
- Journal of Food Distribution Research. 3 per yr. ISSN 0047-245X

**Food Industries Credit Bureau**
3540 Peterson Ave, P.O. Box 59447, Chicago, IL 60659.
- Food Credit Book; national reference of the food industry. a. ISSN 0085-0780

**Food Marketing Institute**
303 E. Ohio St., Chicago, IL 60611.
- F M I Monthly Index Service. m.
- Facts About New Super Markets. a. ISSN 0081-9522
- Super Market Industry Speaks. a. ISSN 0081-9530

**Food Processing Machinery and Supplies Association**
7758 Wisconsin Ave., Washington, DC 20014.
- F P M & S A News Bulletin. 5 per yr.
- Your Guide to the Food Processing Industry's Equipment; production, preparation, processing and packing. a.

**Food Research and Action Center**
25 West 43rd St., New York, NY 10036.
- More Than Tea and Toast. s-a.

**Food Selling Publications, Inc.**
439 S. Maple Dr., Beverly Hills, CA 90212.
- Food Selling Digest & Menu Merchandising. bi-m. ISSN 0015-6590

**Food Service Executives Association, Inc.**
508 IBM Bldg., Fort Wayne, IN 46805.
- Food Executive; the journal of food service management. bi-m. ISSN 0015-6388

**Foodland International Corp.**
2700 Cumberland Pkwy., Suite 500, Atlanta, Cleveland, GA 30339.
- Food Marketer. m. ISSN 0015-6485

**Football Forecaster**
15324 Mack Ave., Grosse Pointe Park, MI 48224.
- Football Forecaster. m.

**Football News Co.**
19830 Mack Ave., Grosse Pointe, MI 48236.
- Basketball Weekly. w.(during season) ISSN 0005-6170
- Football News. w.(during season)

**Foote Mineral Company**
Route 100, Exton, PA 19341.
- Foote Foundry Facts. q. (prep. by its Ferroalloys Division)
- Foote Prints. s-a.

**Foothills Trader**
Central Ave., New Hartford, CT 06057.
- Connecticut West. a.

**Footwear News**
7 E. 12th St., New York, NY 10003.
- Footwear News Fact Book. irreg. ISSN 0429-0208

**For Now**
c/o Donald Phelps, Ed., 694 Chauncey St., Brooklyn, NY 11207.
- For Now. 2-3 per yr.

**Forbes Inc.**
60 Fifth Ave., New York, NY 10011.
- Forbes. s-m. ISSN 0015-6914

**Ford Associates Inc.**
701 S. Federal Ave., Butler, IN 46721.
- Directory of Women Law Graduates and Attorneys in the U.S.A. biennial. ISSN 0092-1416

**Ford Foundation**
320 E. 43rd St., New York, NY 10017.
- Ford Foundation Annual Report. a. ISSN 0071-7274
- Ford Foundation Letter. bi-m(7 per yr.) ISSN 0015-699X

**Ford Motor Co.**
3000 Schaefer Rd., Dearborn, MI 48121.
- Continental Magazine. 3 per yr. ISSN 0010-7727
- Ford Times; the Ford owner's magazine. m. ISSN 0015-7015
- Ford World. m. ISSN 0046-4538

**Ford Motor Co. Ford Truck Division**
420 Lexington Ave., New York, NY 10017.
- Ford Truck Times. q. ISSN 0015-7023

**Fordham University**
John 23rd Center, Bronx, NY 10458.
- Diakonia; devoted to promoting Eastern Christianity in the West. q. ISSN 0012-1959
- Fordham University. Review. w.
- International Philosophical Quarterly. q. ISSN 0019-0365 (Foundation for International Philosophical Exchange)
- Thought. (pub. by Fordham University Press)

**Fordham University Press**
University Box L, Bronx, NY 10458.
- Baker Street Journal; a quarterly of Sherlockiana. 4 per yr. ISSN 0005-4070
- Orestes Brownson Series on Contemporary Thought and Affairs. irreg., 1973, no. 8. ISSN 0078-608X
- Pastoral Psychology Series. irreg., 1977, no. 9. ISSN 0079-0141 (Institute of Pastoral Psychology)
- Studies in Industrial Economics. irreg., 1967, no. 8. ISSN 0081-8011
- Thought; a review of culture and idea. q. ISSN 0040-6457 (Fordham University)
- Traditio; studies in ancient and medieval history, thought, and religion. a. ISSN 0362-1529

**Fordham University. School of Law**
Lincoln Center, 140 W. 62 St., New York, NY 10023.
- Fordham Law Review. 6 per yr. ISSN 0015-704X
- Fordham Urban Law Journal. 3 per yr.

**Ford's Travel Guides**
Box 505, 22151 Clarendon St., Woodland Hills, CA 91365.
- Ford's Deck Plan Guide. a. ISSN 0096-1353
- Ford's Freighter Travel Guide. s-a. ISSN 0015-7058
- Ford's International Cruise Guide. s-a. ISSN 0015-7066

**Forecaster Publishing Co.**
19623 Ventura Blvd., Tarzana, CA 91356.
- Forecaster. w. ISSN 0095-294X

**Foreign Area Materials Center**
60 E. 42nd St., New York, NY 10017.
- Intercultural Studies Information Service. 9 per yr. ISSN 0092-1866

**Foreign Credit Insurance Association**
1 World Trade Center, New York, NY 10048.
- F C I A News. 6 per yr.

**Foreign Credit Interchange Bureau. National Association of Credit Management**
- F C I B Bulletin. (pub. by C I B-N A C M Corp.)

**Foreign Language Association of the Red River**
Moorhead High School, Moorhead, MN 56560.
- F L A R R. q.

**Foreign Medical School Information Center**
One East Main Street, Bay Shore, NY 11706.
- Foreign Medical School Catalogue. a. ISSN 0085-0829

**Foreign Policy Association**
345 E. 46th St., New York, NY 10017.
- F P A Outreacher. 2-3 per yr.
- Foreign Policy Association. Headline Series. 5 per yr. ISSN 0017-8780
- Great Decisions. a. ISSN 0072-727X

**Foreign Policy Research Institute**
3508 Market St., Suite 350, Philadelphia, PA 19104.
- Foreign Policy Research Institute. Monograph Series. 4-6 issues per year.
- Orbis; a journal of world affairs. q. ISSN 0030-4387 (Co-sponsor: International Relations Graduate Group, University of Pennsylvania)

**Foreign Resources Associates**
Box 2353, Fort Collins, CO 80521.
- Photographic Technology U.S.S.R. bi-m. ISSN 0092-4709

**Foreign Student Service Council**
1623 Belmont St. N.W., Washington, DC 20009.
- F.S.S.C. Newsletter. q.

**Foreign Tax Law Association**
P.O. Box 2187, Ormond Beach, FL 32074.
- Foreign Tax Law Bi-Weekly Bulletin. fortn. ISSN 0095-7291

**Evan H. Foreman, Ed. & Pub.**
P.O. Drawer F, Mobile, AL 36601.
- International Directory of 16MM Film Collectors. irreg.(approx. biennial) ISSN 0074-462X

**Foremost Foods Company, S.F**
- Professional Nutritionist. (pub. by Bernard Tolk Co.)

**Forest Farmers Association**
Suite 380, 4 Executive Park East, N.E., Atlanta, GA 30347.
- Forest Farmer. m (10 per yr.) ISSN 0015-7406
- Forest Farmer. Manual Edition. biennial. ISSN 0071-7452

**Forest History Society**
Box 1581, Santa Cruz, CA 95061.
- Journal of Forest History. q. ISSN 0094-5080

**Forest Industries Committee on Timber Valuation and Taxation**
1250 Connecticut Ave., Washington, DC 20036
- Timber Tax Journal. a. ISSN 0563-5446 (Distr. by: International Scholarly Book Services, Inc., Box 555, Forest Grove, OR 97005)

**Forest Industries Council**
- GreenAmerica. (pub. by American Forest Institute)

**Forest Products Research Society**
2801 Marshall Ct., Madison, WI 53705.
- Forest Products Journal. m. ISSN 0015-7473
- Wood Science. q. ISSN 0043-7700

**Foreword Press, Inc.**
145 E. 69th St., New York, NY 10021.
- Foreword; the national student magazine. m(9 per yr.)

**Forging Industry Association**
55 Public Square, Cleveland, OH 44113.
- Forging Topics. q. ISSN 0099-233X

**Formula Enterprises**
2020 S. Susan, Suite L, Santa Ana, CA 92704.
- Formula. m.

**Forrest Publications Inc.**
20 Hill St., Morristown, NJ 07960.
- Ski Info; the equipment book. a.

**Fort Belknap Genealogical Association**
Murray Rte., Graham, TX 76046.
- Fort Belknap Genealogical Association. Bulletin. a. ISSN 0071-7738

**Fort Belknap Society**
- Fort Belknap Society. Yearbook. (pub. by Texas Wesleyan College)

**Fort Burgwin Research Center, Inc.**
Box 314, Ranchos de Taos, NM 87557.
- Fort Burgwin Research Center. Publications. irreg. ISSN 0071-7754

**Fort Collins Audubon Society**
Serials Section, Colorado State University Libraries, Fort Collins, CO 80521.
- Ptarmigan. m. ISSN 0048-5780

**Fort Concho Museum**
213 E. Avenue D, San Angelo, TX 76901.
- Fort Concho Report; news from the frontier fort on the Conchos. q. ISSN 0046-4651

**Fort Dodge Laboratories**
Fort Dodge, IA 50501.
- Fort Dodge Biochemic Review. q. ISSN 0015-8038

**Fort Hays Kansas State College**
Hays, KS 67601.
- Fort Hays Studies. New Series. Art. irreg. ISSN 0071-7762
- Fort Hays Studies. New Series. Bibliography. irreg. ISSN 0071-7770
- Fort Hays Studies. New Series. Economics. irreg. ISSN 0071-7789
- Fort Hays Studies. New Series. Literature. irreg. ISSN 0071-7800
- Fort Hays Studies. New Series. Music. irreg. ISSN 0071-7819
- Fort Hays Studies. New Series. Science. irreg. ISSN 0071-7827
- Improving Instruction. 3 per yr.

**Fort Lauderdale Historical Society, Inc.**
c/o Ed. August Burghard, 840 N.E. 12th Ave., Ft. Lauderdale, FL 33304.
- New River News. bi-m. ISSN 0548-6599

**Fort Peck Tribes**
- Wotanin-Wowapi. (pub. by Wotanin Press)

**Fort Smith Public Schools in Action**
Public Schools Service Center, 3205 Jenny Lind, Fort Smith, AR 72901.
- P. S. Public Schools in Action. 8 per yr. ISSN 0030-8323

**Fort Ticonderoga Association**
Ticonderoga, NY 12883.
- Fort Ticonderoga Museum. Bulletin. s-a. ISSN 0015-8070

**Fort Vancouver Historical Society**
P.O. Box 1834, Vancouver, WA 98663.
- Clark County History. a. ISSN 0090-449X

**Fort Wayne Public Library**
Reynolds Historical Genealogy Div., Fort Wayne, IN 47702.
- Family Fare; quarterly list of additions to the Reynolds Historical Genealogy Division of the Fort Wayne Public Library. q. ISSN 0427-959X

**Fort Worth Area Chamber of Commerce**
700 Throckmorton, Fort Worth, TX 76102.
- Fort Worth. m. ISSN 0015-8089

**Fort Worth Commercial Recorder**
Box 11038, Fort Worth, TX 76109.
- Fort Worth Commercial Recorder. d. (Mon.-Fri.) ISSN 0015-8097

**Fort Worth Como Monitor**
c/o William Howard Wilburn, Sr., Box 885, Fort Worth, TX 76101.
- Fort Worth Como Monitor. bi-w. ISSN 0046-466X

**Fort Worth Genealogical Society**
Box 864, Fort Worth, TX 76116.
- Footprints. q.

**Fort Worth Star Telegram**
P.O. Box 1870, Fort Worth, TX 76101.
- Your Texas Ancestors. a. ISSN 0085-8390

**Fortlett Publishing Corp.**
c/o James L. Kapsis, Ed., 242 W. 30th St., New York, NY 10001.
- New York Express. w. ISSN 0028-7202

**Fortnightly**
Box 252, Times Sq. Sta., New York, NY 10036.
- Fortnightly. fortn.

**Fortress Press**
2900 Queen Lane, Philadelphia, PA 19129.
- Journal of Church Music. m (except Jul. & Aug.) ISSN 0021-9703 (Lutheran Church in America)
- Yearbooks in Christian Education. a. ISSN 0084-4128 (Lutheran Church in America. Board of Publication)

**Fortune Society**
29 E. 22 St., New York, NY 10010.
- Fortune News. m. ISSN 0015-8275

**Forum for Behavioural Technology**
Box 4792, Overland Park, KS 66204.
- Forum for Behavioural Technology. q.

**Forum for the Advancement of Students in Science and Technology, Inc.**
1785 Massachusetts Avenue, N.W., Washington, DC 20036.
- F A S S T News. bi-m.
- F A S S T Tracks. q.

**Forum for the Advancement of Toxicology in Colleges of Pharmacy**
- Forum for the Advancement of Toxicology. (pub. by University of Tennessee. Center for the Health Sciences)

**Forum International**
300 Eshleman Hall, Univ. of California, Berkeley, CA 94720.
- Ecosphere. 6 per yr. ISSN 0046-1237

**Forum Literario**
c/o Dukardo Hinestrosa, Box 27645, Hollywood, CA 90027.
- Forum Literario; multilingue magazine. m.

**Forum Publications, Inc.**
2377 San Diego Ave., Box 80964, San Diego, CA 92138.
- San Diego Business Forum. m.

**Forward Times**
c/o Lenora Carter, 4411 Almeda Rd., Houston, TX 77004.
- Forward Times. w.

**Foseco Inc.**
P.O. Box 8728, Cleveland, OH 77135.
- Foseco Foundry Practice. bi-m. ISSN 0427-0517

**Foster Associates**
1101 17th St. N.W., Washington, DC 20036.
- Foster Natural Gas Report. w.

**Foster Wheeler Corp.**
Livingston, NJ 07039.
- Heat Engineering. bi-m. ISSN 0017-9329

**Foundation Center**
888 Seventh Ave, New York, NY 10019
- Comsearch Printouts. a. (Subscr. to: Columbia University Press, 136 South Broadway, Irvington-on-Hudson, N.Y. 10533)
- Foundation Center. Annual Report. a. ISSN 0548-7269
- Foundation Center Source Book. irreg. ISSN 0362-1170 (Dist. by Columbia University Press, 136 S. Broadway, Irvington-on-Hudson, NY 10533)
- Foundation Center Source Book Profiles. m.
- Foundation Directory. biennial. ISSN 0071-8092 (Dist. by: Columbia University Press, 136 South Broadway, Irvington-on-Hudson, N.Y. 10533)

**Foundation Church of the Millennium**
1147 First Ave., New York, NY 10021.
- Foundation; visions of the millennium. q.
- Founders. q.

**Foundation for Change**
1841 Broadway, New York, NY 10023.
- Viewpoint; minority outlook on current issues. irreg. (approx. 1-2 per yr)

**Foundation for Christian Living**
Pawling, NY 12564.
- Creative Help for Daily Living. m.

**Foundation for Cooperative Housing**
1001 15th St. N.W., Washington, DC 20005.
- F C H News Briefs/Noticiero F C H. m. ISSN 0014-570X

**Foundation for Economic Education, Inc.**
30 S. Broadway, Irvington, NY 10533.
- F E E Notes. bi-m. ISSN 0029-4012
- Freeman; a journal of ideas on liberty. m. ISSN 0016-0652

**Foundation for International Philosophical Exchange**
- International Philosophical Quarterly. (pub. by Fordham University)

**Foundation for National Progress**
607 Market St., San Francisco, CA 94105
(Subscr. to: 1255 Portland Pl., Boulder CO 80302)
- Mother Jones. m.(10 per yr.)

**Foundation for Religious Action in the Social and Civil Order**
1024 DuPont Circle Bldg., Washington, DC 20036.
- Blessings of Liberty. q. ISSN 0006-4696

**Foundation for Research in the Afro-American Creative Arts, Inc.**
Drawer I, Cambria Heights, NY 11411.
- Black Perspective in Music. s-a. ISSN 0090-7790

**Foundation for Research on the Nature of Man**
- Journal of Parapsychology. (pub. by Parapsychology Press)

**Foundation for Student Communication, Inc.**
Green Hall Annex, Princeton, NJ 08540.
- Business Today. q. ISSN 0007-7100

**Foundation for the Advancement of International Business Administration, Inc.**
64 Ferndale Dr., Hastings-on-Hudson, NY 10706.
- International Executive. 3 per yr. ISSN 0020-6652

**Foundation for the Community of Artists**
32 Union Sq. East, New York, NY 10003.
- Art Workers News. m(10 per yr.)

**Foundation for the Future**
Two Inn St., Box 2001, Newburyport, MA 01950.
- Future Report. m.

**Foundation for the Study of Cycles**
124 S. Highland Ave., Pittsburgh, PA 15206.
- Cycles. m. ISSN 0011-4294
- Foundation for the Study of Cycles. Research Bulletin. irreg. ISSN 0071-8106

**Foundation Management Inc.**
Box 52573, Houston, TX 77052.
- Facets. 2-3 per yr. ISSN 0046-3051 (Texas Fine Arts Society)

**Foundation Press, Inc.**
170 Old Country Rd., Mineola, NY 11501.
- Cases and Materials on Constitutional Law. irreg.
- Cases and Materials on Trade Regulation. irreg.

**Four Points Intertribal Council**
140 Meyer Ave., Dayton, OH 45431.
- Indian Spacemen. s-a.

**Four Seasons Foundation**
Box 159, Bolinas, CA 94924.
- Wheel Series. irreg.
- Writing. irreg., 1977, no. 36. ISSN 0084-2745

**Four Seasons Publications**
Fairwood Road, Bethany, CT 06525.
- Rock Scene. 8 per yr. ISSN 0090-3353

**Four Swords, Inc.**
116 W. 14th St., New York, NY 10011.
- Gay. s-m. ISSN 0046-5488

**Four Wheeler Publishing Co.**
Box 547, 8943 Fullbright Ave., Chatsworth, CA 91311.
- Four Wheeler; everyone's off road magazine. m. ISSN 0015-9123

**Four Zoas Press**
c/o S. R. Lavin, Box 461, Ware, MA 01082.
- Four Zoas; journal of poetry and letters. s-a.

**Fourth Class Cancellation Club**
- Postal History U.S.A. (pub. by J-B Publishing Co.)

**Fourth Estate**
Rm. M-104, 1100 14th St., Denver, CO 80202.
- Fourth Estate. w. ISSN 0046-4848 (University of Colorado Denver Campus)

**Fourth Seacoast Publishing Co. Inc.**
24145 Little Mack, St. Clair Shores, MI 48080.
- Great Lakes Red Book. a. ISSN 0072-7318
- Official Port of Detroit World Handbook. a. ISSN 0093-1799

**Foxfire Fund, Inc.**
Rabun Gap, GA 30568.
- Foxfire. q. ISSN 0015-9220

**Francis A. Countway Library of Medicine**
10 Shattuck St., Boston, MA 02115.
- Countway Library Associates Historical Publications. irreg.

**Francis I. Dupont & Co.**
1 Wall Street, New York, NY 10005.
● I V T. (Investment Values for Today) s-a.

**Franciscan Fathers**
361 Highland Blvd., Brooklyn, NY 11207.
● Aidai-Echoes; menesinis kulturos zurnalas. m.(Sept-June) ISSN 0002-208X
● Darbininkas. w. ISSN 0011-6637

**Franciscan Fathers of California, Inc.**
107 Golden Gate Ave., San Francisco, CA 94102.
● Way of St. Francis. 10 per yr.

**Franciscan Fathers of Maine**
Kennebunkport, ME 04046.
● Sv. Pranciskaus Varpelis/Bell of St. Francis. m.(10 per yr.)

**Franciscan Fathers of the Commissariat of the Most Holy Savior**
232 S. Home Ave., Pittsburgh, PA 15202.
● Listy Sv. Frantiska/Leaflets of St. Francis. m. ISSN 0024-4465

**Franciscan Friars of St. John the Baptist Province**
St. Michaels Mission, AZ 86511.
● Catholic Update. (pub. by St. Anthony Messenger Press)
● Medical Moral Newsletter. (pub. by St. Anthony Messenger Press)
● Padres' Trail. 6 per yr. ISSN 0030-9222
● St. Anthony Messenger. (pub. by St. Anthony Messenger Press)

**Franciscan Herald Press**
1434 W. 51st St., Chicago, IL 60609.
● Franciscan Herald. m. ISSN 0015-9816

**Franciscan Publishers**
Pulaski, WI 54162.
● Miesiecznik Franciszkanski. m. ISSN 0300-6158 (Catholic Order of the Franciscan Fathers)

**Franciscan Sisters of Allegany**
Allegany, NY 14706.
● Zeal. q. ISSN 0514-2482 (St. Elizabeth Mission Society)

**Franciscans, Custody of the Most Holy Savior**
232 S. Home Ave, Pittsburgh, PA 15202.
● Franciscanews. q.

**Emiliano A. Francisco, Ed. & Pub.**
508 Maynard Ave. S., Seattle, WN 98104.
● Filipino-American Herald. m. ISSN 0015-0991

**Francite**
c/o Anne-Marie de Moret, Ed., 221 Northgrand St., St. Louis, MO 63588.
● Francite. s-a.

**Burt Franklin & Co., Inc.**
235 E. 44th St., New York, NY 10017.
● Prospects; annual journal of American cultural studies. a. ISSN 0361-2333
● Reviews in European History; a journal of criticism-the Renaissance to the present. q. ISSN 0095-7232
● Shakespeare Studies; an annual gathering of research, criticism & review. a. ISSN 0582-9399
● Studies in Literature and Criticism. irreg.

**Franklin and Marshall College**
Lancaster, PA 17604.
● Pennsylvania Classical Association. Bulletin. 2 per yr.

**Franklin Broadcasting Co.**
8200 Ridge Ave., Philadelphia, PA 19128.
● W F L N Philadelphia Guide to Events and Places. m. ISSN 0042-9643

**Franklin County (Tennessee) Historical Society**
P.O. Box 130, Winchester, TN 37398.
● Franklin County Historical Review. s-a. ISSN 0046-4961
● Historical Tidings. q.

**Franklin County (Washington) Historical Society**
Box 1033, Pasco, WA 99301.
● Franklin Flyer; key to Franklin County history. q.

**Franklin D. Roosevelt Philatelic Society**
● Fireside Chats. (pub. by Gustav Detjen Jr., Ed. & Pub.)

**Franklin Institute**
● Franklin Institute. Journal. (pub. by Pergamon Press, Inc.)

**Franklin Institute Press**
Box 2266, Philadelphia, PA 19103.
● Cancer Therapy Abstracts. m. (U.S. National Cancer Institute)
● Ozone Chemistry and Technology; abstracts of current journal, book and patent literature. 24 per yr. (Franklin Institute Research Laboratories)

**Franklin Institute Research Laboratories**
Benjamin Franklin Parkway, Philadelphia, PA 19103.
● Explosives & Pyrotechnics. m. ISSN 0014-505X
● Ozone Chemistry and Technology. (pub. by Franklin Institute Press)
● Powder Metallurgy Science & Technology; abstracts of current journal, report and patent literature. m. ISSN 0048-5020 (prep. by its Science Information Services Dept.)

**Franklin Mint**
Franklin Center, PA 19091.
● Franklin Mint. Limited Editions. a.
● Franklin Mint Almanac. m. ISSN 0092-5039 (Franklin Mint Collectors Society)

**Franklin Mint Collectors Society**
● Franklin Mint Almanac. (pub. by Franklin Mint)

**Franklin Press (Baton Rouge)**
Box 1269, Baton Rouge, LA 70821.
● Louisiana Engineer. bi-m. ISSN 0024-6794 (Louisiana Engineering Society)

**Franklin Press (Denver)**
P. O. Box 10397, Denver, CO 80910.
● Ganely's Catholic Schools in America. biennial.

**Franklin Printing Company**
South Delsea Drive, Franklinville, NJ 08322.
● Franklin Township Sentinel. w. ISSN 0016-0040

**R Franks Publishing Ranch**
Box 7068, Amarillo, TX 79109.
● National Directory of College Athletics (Women) a.

**Fraser Management Associates**
Box 494, Burlington, VT 05401.
● Capital Preservation. m.
● Contrary Investor. fortn. ISSN 0010-793X
● Contrary Investor Follow-up Service. fortn. ISSN 0015-6019
● Energy Research Bureau. s-m.
● Fraser Opinion Letter. fortn.

**Fraternal Actuarial Association**
222 W. College Ave., Appleton, WI 54911.
● Fraternal Actuarial Association. Proceedings. a. ISSN 0071-9293

**Fraternal Order of Eagles**
2401 W. Wisconsin Ave., Milwaukee, WI 53233.
● Eagle (Milwaukee) m.(bi-m.Jan-Feb,Aug-Sept) ISSN 0012-8090

**Fraternal Order of Police**
740 S. Bancroft St., Indianapolis, IN 46201.
● Indiana F. O. P. Police Journal. q. ISSN 0019-6592

**Frayed Page Collective**
118 Pine Street, Burlington, VT 05401.
● Public Occurrence. irreg.

**J. Myrick Frazier, Ed. & Pub.**
Box 746, Linwood Sta., Detroit, MI 48206.
● Pool Checker Masters. m.

**Freark Brownelbeck Press**
2808 Laurel Ave., Manhattan Beach, CA 90266.
● Freark Brownelbeck Review. q. ISSN 0016-027X

**Freas-Rooke Computer Center**
Bucknell University, Lewisburg, PA 17837.
● F R C C. m. ISSN 0014-6102

**Fredette's**
3113 Benbrook, Fort Worth, TX 76109.
● Krafters' Klub. bi-m.

**Free Albania Committee**
150 Fifth Ave., New York, NY 10011.
● Free Albanian/Shqiptari i Lire. 1-2 per yr. ISSN 0488-728X

**Free-Economy Association, Inc.**
2618 E. 54th St., Huntington Park, CA 90255.
● Answer; a free-economy publication expounding the social economic conditions and its consequences in all phases of human and social life. q. ISSN 0003-5300

**Free Lance Poets and Prose Workshop, Inc.**
6005 Grand Ave., Cleveland, OH 44104.
● Free Lance; a magazine of poetry and prose. s-a. ISSN 0016-0369

**Free Library of Philadelphia. Reader Development Program**
236 N. 23 St., Philadelphia, PA 19103.
● Pivot. bi-m. ISSN 0032-0382

**Free Methodist Church of North America**
● Discovery (Winona Lake) (pub. by Light and Life Press)
● Light and Life. (pub. by Light & Life Press)
● Reachout. (pub. by Light and Life Press)

**Free Methodist Church of North America. Department of Christian Education**
901 College Ave., Winona Lake, IN 46590.
● Youth in Action. 9 per yr. ISSN 0044-1236

**Free People Inc.**
Box 13079, 1232 Laura St., Jacksonville, FL 32206.
● Both Sides Now. irreg., 6-12 per yr. ISSN 0006-8233

**Free Press**
c/o Macmillan, 866 Third Ave., New York, NY 10022.
● Columbia University Graduate School of Business. Dissertations Series. irreg. (Columbia University. Graduate School of Business)

**Free Thinkers of America**
Box 1654, New York, NY 10001.
● Free Thought Memoranda. irreg.

**Free Thought Opinion**
Box 162, Park Station, Paterson, NJ 07513.
● Free Thought Opinion. bi-m.

**Free Venice Beachhead**
P.O. 504, Venice, CA 90291.
● Beachhead. m.

**Free Voice of Labor Association**
33 Union Sq., W., Rm. 808, New York, NY 10003.
● Freie Arbeiter Stimme/Free Voice of Labor. m. ISSN 0016-0733

**Freebizak, Inc.**
Box 1825, FDR Sta., New York, NY 10022.
● Yesterday's Memories. irreg. ISSN 0098-1796

**Freed Publishing Co.**
Box 1144, FDR Station, New York, NY 10022.
● Directory of National Organizations Concerned with Land Pollution Control. a. ISSN 0084-9987
● Directory of State Agencies Concerned with Land Pollution Control. biennial.
● Environment Improvement Case History Report Service. m. ISSN 0046-2217
● Land Pollution Reporter. bi-m. ISSN 0023-7655

**Freedom Fellowship Church**
30 W. Pasadena, Phoenix, AZ 85013.
● Freedom Today. m.

**Freedom House**
20 W. 40th St., New York, NY 10018.
● Freedom at Issue; a periodical of comment and review. bi-m. ISSN 0016-0520

**Freedom Leadership Foundation Inc.**
P.O. 678, Ben Franklin Station, Washington, DC 20044.
● Rising Tide. fortn.

**Freedom News, Inc.**
Box 1087, Richmond, CA 94802.
● Freedom News. m. ISSN 0016-0563

**Freedom of Information Center**
University of Missouri, Columbia, MO 65201.
● F. O. I. Center Report. m. ISSN 0014-603X
● F O I Digest. bi-m. ISSN 0015-5349

**Freedom Press, Inc.**
Box 24836, Dallas, TX 75224.
● Voice of Freedom. m. ISSN 0042-8116

**Freedom to Read Foundation**
50 E. Huron St., Chicago, IL 60611.
• Freedom to Read Foundation News. q. ISSN 0046-5038

**Freedomways Associates**
799 Broadway, New York, NY 10003.
• Freedomways; a quarterly review of the Freedom Movement. q. ISSN 0016-061X

**Freeland Family Association**
425 Stratford Ct., Del Mar, CA 92014.
• Freeland and Allied Families. s-a.

**Freeland League for Jewish Territorial Colonization**
200 W. 72nd St., New York, NY 10023.
• Afn Shvel. q. ISSN 0030-7718

**Miller Freeman Publications, Inc.**
500 Howard St., San Francisco, CA 94105.
• Directory of the Forest Products Industry. a. ISSN 0070-6477
• Energy International. m. ISSN 0013-7529 (Or Circle House North, 69-71 Wembley Hill Rd., Wembley, Middlesex HA9 8BL, England)
• Forest Industries. m. (s-m. May) ISSN 0015-7430
• International Pulp & Paper Directory. biennial.
• International Symposium on Transport and Handling of Minerals. Minerals Transportation; Proceedings. biennial. ISSN 0094-7466
• Modern Sawmill Techniques; proceedings. a. ISSN 0094-9329 (Sawmill Clinic)
• Post's Pulp & Paper Directory. a.
• Pulp and Paper. m. (s-m. Jun. & Sep.) ISSN 0033-4081
• Pulp & Paper Buyers Guide. a.
• World Coal. m. ISSN 0361-7483 (Or Circle House North, 69-71 Wembley Hill Rd., Wembley, Middlesex HA9 8BL, England)
• World Mines Register. biennial. ISSN 0095-4322
• World Mining. m. ISSN 0043-8707
• World Wood; an international journal for loggers, foresters, manufacturers of wood products. m. (s-m. May) ISSN 0043-9258 (Or Circle House North, 69-71 Wembley Hill Rd., Middlesex HA9 8BL, England)

**Robert Freeman Publishing Corp.**
845 Chicago Ave., Evanston, IL 60202.
• Hotel & Motel Management. m. ISSN 0018-6082

**W.H. Freeman and Co.**
660 Market Street, San Francisco, CA 94104.
• Contemporary Developments in Mathematical Psychology. irreg.
• Laboratory Studies in Biology. irreg., no. 894, 1972.
• Scientific American Resource Library: Readings in Psychology. irreg. ISSN 0586-5719
• Scientific American Resource Library: Readings in the Earth Sciences. irreg. ISSN 0085-5987
• Scientific American Resource Library: Readings in the Life Sciences. irreg. ISSN 0586-5727
• Scientific American Resource Library: Readings in the Physical Sciences and Technology. irreg. ISSN 0586-5735
• Scientific American Resource Library: Readings in the Social Sciences. irreg. ISSN 0586-5743
• Series of Books in Astronomy and Astrophysics. irreg.
• Series of Books in Biology. irreg.
• Series of Books in Chemistry. irreg.
• Series of Books in Food and Nutrition. irreg.
• Series of Books in Geology. irreg.
• Series of Books in Mathematics. irreg.
• Series of Books in Physics. irreg.
• Series of Books in Psychology. irreg.
• Series of Books in the Biology of Plant Pathogens. irreg.

**Freeman, Cooper & Co.**
1736 Stockton St., San Francisco, CA 94133.
• American Universities Field Staff. Population: Perspective. irreg. ISSN 0091-5610 (Co-Sponsor: Caltech Population Program)

**Freeman Publishing Co. Inc.**
229 Largo Dr., Nashville, TN 37211.
• Southern Beef Producer. m.
• Southern Farm Equipment & Supply; the trade magazine of the dynamic south. q.
• Southern Hog Producer. 6 per yr.
• Sunbelt Dairyman. m. ISSN 0039-5145

**Freemen Institute**
Box 7060, Provo, UT 84601.
• Freemen Report. s-m.

**Freer Gallery of Art**
Smithsonian Institution, Washington, DC 20560.
• Ars Orientalis; the arts of Islam and the East. irreg., 1975, no. 10. ISSN 0571-1371 (Co-sponsor: University of Michigan)
• Freer Gallery of Art, Washington, D.C. Occasional Papers. irreg. ISSN 0071-9382
• Oriental Studies. irreg., no. 8, 1970. ISSN 0078-6551

**Freighter Travel Club of America**
Box 504, Newport, OR 97365.
• Freighter Travel News. m. ISSN 0016-089X

**Fremont Unified School District**
40775 Fremont Blvd., Fremont, CA 94538.
• Fremonitor. w. ISSN 0016-0997
• Fremont Schools. 3-4 per yr. ISSN 0016-1004

**French-American Review**
Box 30660-A, Texas Christian University, Fort Worth, TX 76129.
• French-American Review; a journal of the history of French and American literary relations. 3 per yr.

**French Chamber of Commerce of the United States Inc.**
1350 Ave. of the Americas, New York, NY 10019.
• French-American Commerce; an economic, industrial and financial review. bi-m. ISSN 0016-1039

**French Embassy. Cultural Services**
972 Fifth Ave, New York, NY 10021.
• France Education. 4-6 per yr.

**French Forum Inc.**
Box 5108, Lexington, KY 40505.
• French Forum. 3 per yr. ISSN 0098-9355

**French Institute-Alliance Francaise**
22 East 60th St., New York, NY 10022.
• French XX Bibliography; Critical and Biographical References for the Study of French Literature since 1885. ISSN 0085-0888

**Frenkel Mailing Service**
24 Rutgers St., New York, NY 10002.
• American Jewish Organizations Directory. ibiennial. ISSN 0065-8979

**Frente Obrero**
577 Columbus Ave., New York, NY 10024.
• Obrero en Marcha. m.

**Freshman English News**
c/o Gary Tate, Ed., Department of English, Texas Christian University, Fort Worth, TX 76129.
• Freshman English News. 3 per yr.

**Freshwater Biological Research Foundation**
2500 Shadywood Rd., Box 90, Navarre, MN 55392.
• Facets of Freshwater. q. ISSN 0046-306X
• Journal of Freshwater. q.
• Weather Guide Calendar Almanac. a.

**Freshwater Press, Inc**
463, The Arcade, Cleveland, OH 44114.
• Greenwood'S Guide to Great Lakes Shipping. a. ISSN 0072-7490

**Fresno County Medical Society**
3425 N. First St., Fresno, CA 93726.
• Fresno County Medical Society. Bulletin. m. ISSN 0016-1160

**Fresno Genealogical Society**
Box 2042, Fresno, CA 93718.
• Ashtree Echo. q. ISSN 0004-4377

**Fresno-Madera Dental Socety**
3425 North First St., Fresno, CA 93726.
• Thirteenth District Dental Society, Fresno, California. Bulletin. irreg.

**Fresno Teachers Association**
5330 N. Fresno St., Fresno, CA 93710.
• Chalk Talk. m. ISSN 0009-0964

**Fretted Instrument Guild of America**
2344 S. Oakley Ave., Chicago, IL 60608.
• F I G A News. bi-m. ISSN 0014-5890

**Friction Materials Standards Institute, Inc.**
53 Bond Street (Nr. Lafayette), New York, NY 10012.
• Brake Shoe Identification Catalog. a. ISSN 0068-0656

**Ira J. Friedman**
(Subsidiary of: Kennikat Press Corp.)
Port Washington, NY 11050.
• Empire State Historical Publications. irreg., 1968, no. 51. ISSN 0071-0091

**Friendly Publications**
109 E. 36th St., New York, NY 10016.
• Creative Black Book. a.

**Friends Church, Northwest Yearly Meeting**
• Fruit of the Vine. (pub. by Barclay Press)

**Friends Committee on Legislation of California**
2160 Lake St., San Francisco, CA 94121.
• F C L Action. irreg. ISSN 0071-9560
• F C L Newsletter. bi-m. ISSN 0532-7091

**Friends Committee on National Legislation**
245 Second St., N.E., Washington, DC 20002.
• F C N L Washington Newsletter. m. ISSN 0014-5734

**Friends Conference on Religion and Psychology**
3518 Bradley Lane, Washington, DC 20015.
• Inward Light. s-a. ISSN 0021-0250

**Friends Historical Association**
Publication Office, Haverford College Library, Haverford, PA 19041.
• Quaker History. s-a. ISSN 0033-5053

**Friends of Asia House Gallery**
• Archives of Asian Art. (pub. by Asia Society)

**Friends of Columbia Libraries. Butler Library**
• Columbia Library Columns. (pub. by Columbia University Libraries)

**Friends of Duke University Library**
• Library Notes. (pub. by Duke University. Library)

**Friends of Free Palestine**
Box 21096, Kalorama Sta., Washington, DC 20009.
• Free Palestine. m. ISSN 0016-0407

**Friends of Haiti**
Box 348, New York, NY 10956.
• Hati Report. q.

**Friends of Morris Library**
Southern Illinois University, Morris Library, Carbondale, IL 62901.
• ICarbS. s-a. ISSN 0360-8409

**Friends of Photography**
Box 239, Carmel, CA 93921.
• Untitled. q.

**Friends of the Bancroft Library**
• Bancroftiana. (pub. by University of California, Berkeley. Bancroft Library)

**Friends of the Detroit Public Library, Inc.**
5201 Woodward Ave., Detroit, MI 48202.
• Among Friends. q. ISSN 0003-195X

**Friends of the Earth**
124 Spear St., San Francisco, CA 94105.
• Eco. irreg.
• Not Man Apart. s-m.

**Friends of the Grosse Pointe Public Library**
• Grosse Pointe Public Library. Newsletter. (pub. by Grosse Point Public Library)

**Friends of the Lithuanian Front**
1634-49th Ave., Cicero, IL 60650.
• Laisve/Toward Freedom; Lithuanian magazine of politics. 3 per yr.

**Friends of the Milwaukee Public Museum**
• Lore. (pub. by Milwaukee Public Museum)

**Friends of the Nassau County Museum**
Muttontown Road, Syosset, NY 11791.
• Long Island Forum. m. ISSN 0024-628X

**Friends of the National Zoo**
National Zoological Park, Washington, DC 20009.
• Zoogoer. bi-m.

**Friends of the New York Academy of Medicine.**
**Friends of the Rare Book Room, Inc.**
- Academy Bookman. (pub. by New York Academy of Medicine. Library)

**Friends of the Oak Park Public Library**
834 Lake St., Oak Park, IL 60301.
- Library Log. a.

**Friends of the Princeton University Library**
- Princeton University Library Chronicle. (pub. by Princeton University. Library)

**Friends of the Rosenberg Library**
2310 Sealy Ave., Galveston, TX 77550.
- Rosenberg Library Bulletin. irreg. ISSN 0035-8312

**Friends of the University of Iowa Libraries**
University of Iowa, Iowa City, IA 52242.
- Books at Iowa. s-a. ISSN 0006-7474
- University of Iowa. Libraries. Newsletter. (pub. by University of Iowa Libraries)

**Friends of the University of Miami Library**
- Carrell. (pub. by University of Miami Library)

**Friends of the University of Pennsylvania Library**
Van Pelt Library, 3420 Walnut St., Philadelphia, PA 19104.
- Library Chronicle. s-a. ISSN 0024-2233

**Friends of the USC Libraries**
- Coranto. (pub. by University of Southern California. Library)

**Friends of the Washington Review of the Arts**
404 10th St., Washington, DC 20003.
- Undercover D C; Washington Review of the Arts guide. irreg. ISSN 0361-5731

**Friends of the World Council of Churches, Inc.**
- Ecumenical Courier. (pub. by United States Conference for the World Council of Churches)

**Friends of the Written Word**
2357 N. Buffum St., Milwaukee, WI 53212.
- Cheap & Fast. q.

**Friends of Youth, Inc.**
2500 Lake Washington Blvd. N., Renton, WA 98055.
- Friends of Youth Newsletter. 3 per yr. ISSN 0016-1349

**Friends Publishing Corp.**
152-A N. 15th St., Philadelphia, PA 19102.
- Friends Journal. s-m. ISSN 0016-1322 (Society of Friends)

**Friends Suburban Project**
Box 462, Concordville, PA 19331.
- Friendly Agitator. 4 per yr. (Philadelphia Yearly Meeting of Friends)

**Friends United Meeting (Quakers)**
- Quaker Life. (pub. by Friends United Press Board)

**Friends United Press Board**
101 Quaker Hill Dr., Richmond, IN 47374.
- Quaker Life. 11 per yr. ISSN 0033-5061 (Friends United Meeting (Quakers))

**Friendship Press**
475 Riverside Drive, New York, NY 10027.
- National Council of Churches. Division of Education and Ministry. Audio-Visual Resource Guide. biennial. ISSN 0077-4073

**Friendship Publications, Inc.**
Box 1472, Spokane, WA 99210.
- Bus Ride. bi-m.

**Robert F. Frink, Ed. & Pub.**
Stiles Lake, Leicester, MA 01524.
- Motorcyclist's Post. m.

**Fritz Reiner Society**
Box 202, Novelty, OH 44072.
- Podium. s-a.

**Fritzsche-D & O**
76 Ninth Ave, New York, NY 10011.
- Fritzsche-D & O Library Bulletin; a monthly checklist of current literature covering research on essential oils, aromatic chemicals, perfume and flavor raw materials. m. ISSN 0016-1527

**From beyond the Dark Gate**
c/o Harry O. Morris, 500 Wellesey, S.E., Albuquerque, NM 87106.
- From beyond the Dark Gate. 3 per yr.

**From the Kennels**
Box 1369, Vancouver, WA 98660.
- From the Kennels. s-m.

**Front Page Record, Inc.**
1459 S. Holly St., Denver, CO 80222.
- Rocky Mountain Journal. w.

**Frontier Airlines**
- Frontier. (pub. by In-Flight Publishing Co.)

**Frontier Nursing Service**
Wendover, KY 41775.
- Frontier Nursing Service. Quarterly Bulletin. q. ISSN 0016-2116

**Frontier Press, Inc.**
2718 Montana Ave., No. 18, Billings, MT 59101.
- Outdoor Guide. m. ISSN 0048-2420

**Frontiers International**
Douglas State Bank Bldg., 1314 N. 5th St., Kansas City, KS 66101.
- Frontiersman. q.

**Walter B. Frost & Co.**
97 Columbia St., Wakefield, RI 02883.
- Metal Fabricator. q. ISSN 0026-0568

**Frozen Food Age Publishing Corp.**
230 Park Ave, New York, NY 10017.
- Frozen Food Age; the industry magazine of marketing and merchandising. m. ISSN 0016-2191

**Frye-Williamson Press, Inc.**
901 N. MacArthur Blvd., Springfield, IL 62702.
- Illinois Principal. q. ISSN 0019-218X

**Don J. Fuelsch, Ed. & Pub.**
P.O. Box 2188, Hot Springs, AR 71901.
- Southern Angler's and Hunter's Guide. a. ISSN 0081-2986

**Fulfillment Management Association**
- F M A Bulletin. (pub. by Hearst Magazines)

**Full Circle Marketing Corp.**
Box 2527, Sarasota, FL 33581.
- Barter Communique. q.

**Fuller & Dees**
(Subsidiary of: Times Mirror, Inc.)
1120 Connecticut Avenue, N.W., Washington, DC 20036.
- Outstanding Elementary Teachers of America. a. ISSN 0090-4082
- Outstanding Secondary Educators of America. a. ISSN 0092-1025

**Fuller Theological Seminary**
c/o Ed. Gary A. Tuttle, 516 Winthrop Ave., New Haven, CT 06511.
- Studia Biblica et Theologica. ISSN 0094-2022

**Fuller Theological Seminary. Overseas Crusades**
School of World Mission, 135 N. Oakland, Pasadena, CA 91101.
- Church Growth Bulletin. bi-m. ISSN 0009-6385

**Fullerton College**
321 E. Chapman Ave., Fullerton, CA 92634.
- Hornet. w. ISSN 0018-5086

**Fulton County Historical & Genealogical Society**
45 North Park Drive, Canton, IL 61520.
- Fulton County (Illinois) Historical & Genealogical Society Newsletter. q.

**Funch Press**
1100 West Samano, Edinburg, TX 78539.
- Foss. s-a. ISSN 0015-8674
- Horbly Gnome. a.
- Pan American Review. s-a. ISSN 0031-059X

**Fund for Animals Inc.**
140 West 57 St., New York, NY 10019.
- Fund for Animals Quarterly. q.

**Fund Raising Institute**
Box 365, Plymouth Meeting, PA 19002.
- F R I Monthly Portfolio. m. ISSN 0014-6137

**Fundicator Inc.**
Box AA, Denville, NJ 07834.
- Fundicator; performance/rankings of mutual funds. m.

**Funk & Wagnalls**
666 Fifth Ave., New York, NY 10019.
- Young Students Encyclopedia Yearbook. a. ISSN 0094-9027

**William F. Funkhouser, Ed. & Pub.**
1111 E. 54th St., Indianapolis, IN 46220.
- Wholesale Drugs Magazine. bi-m.

**Funny Funny World**
c/o Martin A. Ragaway, 407 Commercial Center St., Beverly Hills, CA 90210.
- Funny Funny World. fortn.

**Fur Age Weekly**
127 W. 30th St., New York, NY 10001.
- Classified Fur Source Directory. a.

**Fur Parade**
330 7th Ave., New York, NY 10001.
- Fur Parade. q. ISSN 0016-2949

**Fur Takers of America Inc.**
3057 Nettie Drive, St. Louis, MO 63129.
- Fur Taker. q. ISSN 0016-2965

**Fur Vogue Publishing Co.**
127 W. 30th St., New York, NY 10001.
- Fur Age Weekly. w. ISSN 0016-2884

**Furman University**
Greenville, SC 29613.
- Furman Studies. s-a.

**Furniture Methods & Materials**
3116 Forest Hill Rd., Box 38281, Germantown, TN 38138.
- Furniture Methods & Materials. m.

**Furniture Today Publishing Inc.**
Box 2754, High Point, NC 27261.
- Furniture /Today; the business newspaper of the furniture industry. fortn.

**Furniture World- Furniture South**
127 E. 31st St., New York, NY 10016.
- Furniture World and Furniture Buyer and Decorator. fortn. ISSN 0016-3104

**Fusion Energy Foundation**
231 W. 29th St., Box 1943, New York, NY 10001.
- Fusion Energy Foundation Newsletter. bi-m.
- International Journal of Fusion Energy.

**Futura Communications, Inc.**
103-1/2 S. Walnut, Bloomington, IN 47401.
- Primo Times. m.

**Futura Publishing Co.**
295 Main St., Box 298, Mount Kisco, NY 10549.
- Archives of Podiatric Medicine and Foot Surgery. q. ISSN 0092-7651
- Contemporary Problems in Cardiology. irreg., vol. 3, 1976.
- Continuing Education in Nursing Home Administration. irreg., vols. 2-3 in prep.
- Industrial Pharmacology. a.
- Infectious Disease Reviews. irreg., 1976 vol. 4, 11th & 12th symposia. ISSN 0090-6549
- Principles and Techniques of Human Research and Therapeutics. irreg., vol. 15, 1977.

**Future Communications**
c/o Jalart House, Box 642, Scottsdale, AZ 85253.
- Future (Scottsdale)

**Future Farmers of America**
Box 15130, Alexandria, VA 22309.
- National Future Farmer. bi-m. ISSN 0027-9315

**Future Farmers of America. California Association**
- California Future Farmer. (pub. by California-Polytechnic State University. Bureau of Agricultural Education)

**Future Farmers of America. Florida Association**
- Florida Future Farmer. (pub. by Cody Publications, Inc.)

**Future Farmers of America. Georgia Association**
103 State Office Bldg., Atlanta, GA 30334.
- Georgia Future Farmer. bi-m. ISSN 0016-8262

**Future Farmers of America. Texas Association**
Texas Education Agency, 201 E. 11th St., Austin,
TX 78701.
- Texas Future Farmer. m. (except June & Aug.)
  ISSN 0040-4330

**Future Farmers of America. Wyoming Association**
Douglas Budget, 109 S. Third St., Douglas, WY
82633.
- Wyoming Future Farmer. s-a. ISSN 0043-9711

**Future Homemakers of America**
2010 Massachusetts Ave. N.W., Washington, DC
20036.
- Teen Times. q.

**Future Requirements Agency**
- Future Gas Consumption of the United States.
  (pub. by University of Denver. Denver Research
  Institute)

**Futuremics, Inc.**
2850 Connecticut Ave. N. W., Washington, DC
20008.
- Future - Abstracts. m.

**G.B.W. Publications, Inc.**
57 W. Court St., Doylestown, PA 18901.
- Bucks County Panorama. m. ISSN 0007-2877

**G. C. Conn, Ltd.**
616 Enterprise Dr., Oak Brook, IL 60521.
- Connchord. 2 per yr. ISSN 0010-6038

**G C N Inc.**
22 Bromfield St., Boston, MA 02108.
- G C N. (Gay Community News); gay weekly for
  the East. w.
- Gay Person's Guide to New England. a.

**G. C. Publishing Corporation**
Box 58, Rockville Centre, NY 11571.
- Inside Wrestling. m.
- Victory Sports Series. 28 per yr.
- Wrestler. m.

**G M L Corporation**
594 Marrett Rd., Lexington, MA 02173.
- Computer Display Review. 3 per yr. ISSN 0010-
  4582
- Computer Peripherals Review. 3 per yr.
- Computer Review. 3 per yr. ISSN 0093-416X
- Computer Terminals Review. 3 per yr.
- Minicomputer Review. 3 per yr. ISSN 0093-2302

**G M T Medical Information Systems, Inc.**
(Subsidiary of: M F I, Inc.)
777 Third Ave., New York, NY 10017.
- Journal of Legal Medicine. m. ISSN 0093-1748
  (American College of Legal Medicine)

**G.P.I. Corporation**
Box 615, Saratoga, CA 95070.
- Guitar Player; the magazine for professional and
  amateur guitarists. m. ISSN 0017-5463 (Guitar
  Players International)

**G. P. I. Corporation. Keyboard Players International**
P.O. Box 615, Saratoga, CA 95070
(Subscriptions to: Box 907, Saratoga, CA 95070)
- Contemporary Keyboard; the magazine for all
  keyboard players. m. ISSN 0361-5820

**G T E-Automatic Electric**
Northlake, IL 60164.
- G T E Automatic Electric Journal. (General
  Telephone & Electronics) q.

**G T E Laboratories, Inc.**
40 Sylvan Rd., Waltham, MA 02154.
- G T E Journal of Research and Development.
  (General Telephone & Electronics) q. ISSN 0097-
  7721

**Gaceta Publishing Co.**
2015 15th St., Box 5536, Tampa, FL 33605.
- Gaceta; tri-lingual newspaper. w. ISSN 0016-3724

**Gaines Dog Research Center**
250 North St., White Plains, NY 10625.
- Touring with Towser. a. ISSN 0082-5441

**Galactic Approximation Press**
2209 California, Berkeley, CA 94703.
- Aldebaran Review. 3 per yr. ISSN 0002-5089

**Galaxy Music Corp**
2121 Broadway, New York, NY 10023.
- American Musicological Society. Studies and
  Documents. irreg., no. 6, 1972.

**Galaxy Press**
Box 444, Hollis, NH 03049.
- Graphics. q.

**Gale Research Co.**
Book Tower, Detroit, MI 48226.
- Acronyms, Initialisms and Abbreviations
  Dictionary; a guide to alphabetic designations,
  contractions, acronyms, initialisms, and similar
  condensed appellations. irreg., 5th edt., 1976.
- American Studies Information Guide Series. irreg.
- Art and Architecture Information Guide Series.
  irreg., vol. 6, 1977.
- Author Biography Series. irreg.
- Authors at Auction Series. irreg.
- Authors in the News; compilation of news stories
  and feature articles from American newspapers
  and magazines, covering prominent writers in all
  fields. irreg., 1976, vol. 2.
- Awards, Honors and Prizes. irreg., 3rd ed., 1975.
- Bibliography of Bioethics. a.
- Biographical Dictionaries and Related Works; an
  international bibliography of collective
  biographies. irreg.
- Biographical Dictionaries and Related Works.
  Supplement; an international bibliography of
  collective biography. irreg.
- Biographical Dictionary Master Index. biennial.
- Book Publishers Directory. q.
- Book Review Index; indexes all reviews in 290
  periodicals. bi-m.
- Book Review Index: Annual Clothbound
  Cumulations. a. ISSN 0524-0581
- Bookman's Price Index; guide to the values of rare
  and other out-of-print books. irreg., vol. 12, 1977.
  ISSN 0068-0141
- Childhood in Poetry; a catalogue, with
  biographical and critical annotations, of the books
  of English and American poets comprising the
  Shaw Childhood in Poetry Collection, library of
  the Florida State University. irreg.
- Children's Literature Review. s-a. ISSN 0362-
  4145
- Commodity Prices. irreg.
- Consultants and Consulting Organizations
  Directory; a reference guide to concerns and
  individuals engaged in consultation for business,
  industry and government. irreg., 1976, 3rd edt.
- Consumer Sourcebook. irreg; 1977, 2nd edt.
- Contemporary Authors. irreg; 1977, vol. 65-68.
  ISSN 0010-7468
- Contemporary Literary Criticism Series; excerpts
  from criticism of the works of today's novelists,
  poets, playwrights, and other creative writers.
  irreg., vol. 7, 1977.
- Countries of the World; and their leaders. irreg.,
  3rd edt., 1977.
- Directory Information Service. 3 per yr.
- Directory of Special Libraries and Information
  Centers in the U.S. & Canada. irreg.; 1977, 4th
  edt. ISSN 0070-6361
- Economics Information Guide Series. irreg.
- Encyclopedia of Associations. irreg.; 11th edt.,
  1977. ISSN 0071-0202
- Encyclopedia of Business Information Sources.
  irreg.; 3rd edt., 1976. ISSN 0071-0210
- Encyclopedia of Governmental Advisory
  Organizations. irreg., 2nd ed, 1975. ISSN 0092-
  8380
- Ethnic Studies Information Guide. irreg.
- International Relations Information Guide Library.
  irreg.
- Library Bibliographies and Indexes. irreg.
- Library of Congress Classification Schedules: a
  Cumulation of Additions and Changes. irreg.
- Man and the Environment Information Guide
  Series. irreg.
- Management Information Guide Series. irreg.
  ISSN 0076-3632
- Modern Authors Checklist Series. irreg.
- Museum Media; a directory and index of
  publications and audiovisuals available from U.S.
  and Canadian institutions. irreg.
- National Faculty Directory. a. ISSN 0077-4472
- New Acronyms, Initialisms and Abbreviations. a.
- New Associations and Projects. q. ISSN 0028-
  4238
- New Consultants. s-a.
- New Research Centers. q. ISSN 0028-6591
- New Special Libraries. 2 per yr.
- New Trade Names. a., between vols. of Trade
  Names Dictionary.

- Pages (Detroit); the world of books, writers, and
  writing. a.
- Research Centers Directory. irreg., 5th ed., 1975.
  ISSN 0080-1518
- Reverse Acronyms, Initialisms and Abbreviations
  Dictionary. irreg., 5th edt., 1976.
- Something About the Author Series; facts and
  pictures about contemporary authors and
  illustrators of books for young people. irreg.; vol.
  11, 1977.
- Statistics Sources; a subject guide to data on
  industrial, business, social, educational, financial
  and other topics for the U.S. and selected foreign
  countries. irreg.; 5th edt., 1977. ISSN 0585-198X
- Subject Directory of Special Libraries and
  Information Centers. irreg.; 4th edt., 1977.
- Trade Names Dictionary. irreg.
- Weather Almanac. irreg.; 2nd edt. 1977.
- Who's Who in Consulting; a reference guide to
  professional personnel engaged in consultation for
  business, industry and government. irreg.; 2nd
  edt., 1973. ISSN 0083-9485

**Galesburg Trades & Labor Assembly**
- Galesburg Labor News. (pub. by Labor News
  Company)

**Gallagher Report Inc.**
230 Park Ave., New York, NY 10017.
- Gallagher Report; a confidential letter to
  marketing, sales, advertising and media
  executives. w. ISSN 0016-4070

**Gallant Publishing Co., Inc.**
Box HH, Capistreno Beach, CA 92624.
- Bow and Arrow. bi-m. ISSN 0006-8403
- Gun World. m. ISSN 0017-5641
- Gun World Hunting Guide. a. ISSN 0362-4749

**Gallaudet College. Alumni Association**
Washington, DC 20002.
- Gallaudet Almanac. irreg. ISSN 0095-5655

**Gallaudet College. Department of English**
Washington, DC 20002.
- Teaching English to the Deaf. 3 per yr. ISSN
  0093-8874

**Gallaudet College. Office of Alumni & Public
Relations**
Kendall Green, Washington, DC 20002.
- Gallaudet Today. q. ISSN 0016-4089

**Gallimaufry**
3208 N. 19th Rd., Arlington, VA 22201.
- Gallimaufry. 2 per yr.

**Gallo Publishing Corporation**
135 W. 26th St., New York, NY 10001.
- Greater Amusements and International
  Projectionist. m. ISSN 0017-3703
- Hotel-Motor Hotel Gazette. q.

**Galloway Publications**
5 Mountain Ave., North Plainfield, NJ 07060.
- Social Agency Management & Better Camp
  Management. q.

**Gambi Publications, Inc.**
333 Johnson Ave., Brooklyn, NY 11206.
- Saga. m. ISSN 0036-2565

**Gambler's Book Club**
Box 4115, Las Vegas, NV 89101.
- Systems and Methods. bi-m.

**Gamit Enterprises, Inc.**
5841 W. Montrose Ave., Chicago, IL 60634.
- Appliance Service News. m. ISSN 0003-6803

**Gamma Alpha Chi National Office**
Univ. of Oklahoma, Copeland Hall-Room 240,
Norman, OK 73069.
- Linage. q. ISSN 0024-3647 (Alpha Delta Sigma)

**Gamma Publishing Co.**
Box 206, New York, NY 10008.
- Albania Report. q. ISSN 0002-4651

**Gar Publishing Co.**
Box 4793, Austin, TX 78765.
- Gar. 5 per yr. ISSN 0046-5410

**Garden Center of Greater Cleveland**
11030 East Blvd., Cleveland, OH 44106.
- Garden Center Bulletin. m.

**Garden Club of America**
598 Madison Ave., New York, NY 10022.
- Garden Club of America. Bulletin. 5 per yr. ISSN 0016-4577

**Garden State Numismatic Association**
Box 63, Bricktown, NJ 08723.
- New Jersey Numismatic Journal. q.

**Garden State Publishing Co.**
4411 Landis, Sea Isle City, NJ 08243.
- Broiler Industry. m. ISSN 0007-2176
- Feed Management; the magazine for manufacturers of animal feed. m. ISSN 0014-956X
- Petfood Industry. bi-m. ISSN 0031-6245
- Poultry Digest. m. ISSN 0032-5724

**Garden Writers Association of America**
101 Park Ave., New York, NY 10017.
- Garden Writers Bulletin. 1-6 per yr. ISSN 0016-4631

**Gardner Publications, Inc.**
600 Main St., Cincinnati, OH 45202.
- Modern Machine Shop. m. ISSN 0026-8003
- Modern Machine Shop NC/CAM Guidebook. a.
- Products Finishing. m.(s-m.March) ISSN 0032-9940

**Garretson Graphics**
Box 3251, York, PA 17402.
- Circus Maximus; quarterly of contemporary poetry. q. ISSN 0145-5281

**Garrett County Historical Society**
c/o Walter W. Price, Ed., Box 305, Mtn. Lake Park, MD 21550.
- Glades Star. q. ISSN 0431-915X

**Garrett-Evangelical Theological Seminary**
c/o Kenneth I. Clawson, 2121 Sheridan Rd., Evanston, IL 60201.
- Explor. 3 per yr. ISSN 0362-0867

**Garrett Park Press**
Garrett Park, MD 20766.
- Directory of Special Programs for Minority Group Members; Career Information Services, Employment Skills, Banks, Financial Aid Sources. a.
- International Education: a Directory of Resource Materials on Comparative Education and Study in Another Country. irreg.

**Gary Public Library**
220 West 5th Ave., Gary, IN 46402.
- Gary Graphique. m.(10 per yr)

**Gary's Enterprises**
7502 N.E. 133rd Ave., P.O. Box 1535, Vancouver, WA 98663.
- Racing Wheels. w. 40 per yr.

**Gas**
4151 Southwest Frwy., Suite 735, Houston, TX 77027.
- Gas; the magazine of the gas industry. m. ISSN 0016-4836

**Gas Digest**
Box 35819, 5731 Arboles Dr., Houston, TX 77035.
- Gas Digest. m.

**Gas Industries Equipment and Appliance News, Inc.**
333 N. Michigan Ave., Chicago, IL 60601.
- Better Schools (Chicago) bi-m. ISSN 0363-373X

**Gas Magazines, Inc.**
1202 S. Park St., Madison, WI 53715.
- Cooking for Profit; the magazine of food ideas, methods, management. m. ISSN 0091-861X
- Flame Facts. m. ISSN 0430-6392

**Gas Processors Association**
1812 First Pl., Tulsa, OK 74103.
- Gas Processors Association. Annual Convention. Proceedings. a. ISSN 0096-8870

**Gas Turbine Publications, Inc.**
80 Lincoln Ave., Stamford, CT 06904.
- Gas Turbine Catalog. a. ISSN 0072-0267
- Gas Turbine International Magazine. bi-m. ISSN 0435-1312

**Gas Workers Public Relations Council**
Box 13678, St. Louis, MO 63130.
- Gas Future. m.

**Gasoline News Publishing Company**
100 N. Grant St., Columbus, OH 43215.
- Gasoline News. m. ISSN 0016-5042

**L. D. Gasteiger**
3225 E. 8th St., Long Beach, CA 90804.
- Cosmos; aka new cosmic star. bi-m. ISSN 0045-8724 (Universal Center)

**Gateway to the West-Ohio**
c/o Anita Short, 3471 State Route 49, Arcanum, OH 45304.
- Gateway to the West-Ohio. q.

**Jessyca Russell Gaver, Ed. & Pub.**
Box 251, Madison Square Sta., New York, NY 10010.
- Writers Newsletter. s-m. ISSN 0043-9541

**Gavin-Jobson Associates**
488 Madison Ave., New York, NY 10022.
- Wine Handbook. a.

**Reginald Gay, Ed. & Pub.**
Box 370, Madison Square Sta, New York, NY 10010.
- Boss. a. ISSN 0006-792X

**Gay Peoples Union at Stanford**
c/o G P U Women's Collective, P.O. Box 8265, Stanford.
- Lesbian Visions. m.

**Gay Sunshine Press, Inc.**
Box 40397, San Francisco, CA 94140.
- Gay Sunshine; journal of gay liberation. q. ISSN 0046-550X

**Gay Women's Advocate Office**
326 Michigan Union, Ann Arbor, MI 48104.
- Lesbian Lipservice. m.

**Gaylord Bros. Inc.**
Box 61, Syracuse, NY 13201.
- Access: the Supplementary Index to Periodicals. 3 per yr. ISSN 0095-5698
- Dictionary of Contemporary Quotations. s-a. ISSN 0360-215X

**Gaylords**
249 N. Summer St., Adam, MA 01220.
- Directory of Suppliers of Dropship Merchandise. a. with supplements. ISSN 0070-6434

**Gazette Publications**
Box 1046, Felton, CA 95018.
- Narrow Gauge and Short Line Gazette. bi-m.

**Gazette Publishing Co.**
Segundo, CO 81070.
- National Prospector's Gazette & Treasure Hunter's News. bi-m. ISSN 0027-9951

**Gazette Publishing Co., Inc.**
107 N. Sandusky St, Bellevue, OH 44811 (Subscr. to: 131 E. Main St., Bellevue, OH 44811)
- R F D News. ISSN 0481-5084

**Gebbie Press**
Box 1000, New Paltz, NY 12561.
- Gebbie Press All-in-One Directory. a. ISSN 0097-8175

**Henry L. Geddie, Ed. & Pub.**
608 Trans American Bldg., Fort Worth, TX 76102.
- Southwestern Builder. m. ISSN 0038-4755

**Geer Publishing Co. Inc.**
1440 Broadway, New York, NY 10018.
- Textile Directions. q.

**Gegenschein Press**
c/o Westen, 154-03 24th Rd., Whitestone, NY 11357.
- Gegenschein Quarterly. q.

**Richard E. Geis, Ed. & Pub.**
Box 11408, Portland, OR 97211.
- Science Fiction Review. q.

**Geisinger Medical Center**
Danville, PA 17821.
- Geisinger Medical Center. Bulletin. q. ISSN 0016-5913

**Gem Publishers Inc.**
1180 Raymond Blvd., Newark, NJ 07102.
- New Jersey Beverage Journal. m. ISSN 0028-5552

**Gemac Corp.**
Box 687, Mentone, CA 92359.
- Gems and Minerals; gems, gem cutting, minerals, silverwork, geology. m. ISSN 0016-6278

**Gemini Foundation**
- Madrona. (pub. by Gemini Press)

**Gemini Press**
502 12th Ave. East, Seattle, WA 98102.
- Madrona; a quarterly of poetry. irreg. ISSN 0047-5432 (Gemini Foundation)

**Gemological Institute of America**
1660 Stewart St., Santa Monica, CA 90404.
- Gems & Gemology. q. ISSN 0016-626X

**Genealogical Forum of Portland Oregon**
1812 Neighbors of Woodcraft Bldg., 1410 S. W. Morrison St., Portland, OR 97205.
- Genealogical Forum of Portland Oregon Bulletin. 10 per yr. and yearbook.

**Genealogical Institute of Oklahoma**
3813 Cashion Place, Oklahoma City, OK 73112.
- Dusty Trails. q.

**Genealogical Periodical Annual Index**
3800 Enterprise Rd., Mitchellville, MD 20716.
- Genealogical Periodical Annual Index. a. ISSN 0072-0593

**Genealogical Reference Builders**
Box 249, Post Falls, ID 83854.
- Allen Newsletter. 10 per yr.
- Baker Newsletter. 10 per yr.
- Coker Kin. q.
- Cowan Clan Newsletter. 4 per yr.
- Genealogical Reference Builders Newsletter. q. ISSN 0533-7275
- Harris Newsletter. 10 per yr.
- Hill Newsletter. 10 per yr.
- Johnson Newsletter. 10 per yr.
- Robinson Newsletter. irreg.
- Rogers Newsletter. 10 per yr.
- Scott Newsletter. 10 per yr.
- Turner Newsletter. 10 per yr.
- Walker Newsletter. 10 per yr.
- Young Newsletter. m. (10 per yr.)

**Genealogical Research**
322 State St., Fairborn, OH 45324.
- Our Family Heritage; a journal of genealogy and history of the Ohio 4 river valley. q. ISSN 0091-6447

**Genealogical Society of East Alabama**
Tuskegee, AL 36083.
- Tap Roots. q. ISSN 0494-6944

**Genealogical Society of Greater Miami**
1100 S.W. 2nd Ave., Miami, FL 33130.
- Genealogical Society of Greater Miami. Newsletter. irreg.

**Genealogical Society of New Jersey**
132 W. Franklin St., Bound Brook, NJ 08805.
- Genealogical Magazine of New Jersey. 3 per yr. ISSN 0016-6367

**Genealogical Society of Old Tryon County**
P.O. Box 745, Spindale, NC 28160.
- Genealogical Society of Old Tryon County. Bulletin. q. ISSN 0092-7953

**Genealogical Society of Pennsylvania**
1300 Locust St., Philadelphia, PA 19107.
- Pennsylvania Genealogical Magazine. s-a.

**Genealogical Society of Riverside**
Box 2557, Riverside, CA 92506.
- Lifeliner. q. ISSN 0047-4630

**Genealogical Society of Southwestern Pennsylvania**
Citizens Library, 55 S. College St., Washington, PA 15301.
- Keyhole. q.

**Genealogical Society of Tidewater Virginia**
c/o M. Catherine Blanton, 2109 Kecoughtan Rd., Apt. 41-C, Hampton, VA 23661.
- Virginia Tidewater Genealogy. q.

**Genealogist**
Ed. Ray Bakehorn, R.R. No 3, Kokomo, IN 46901.
- Genealogist. q.

**Genealogists, Inc.**
Box 435, Glastonbury, CT 06033.
- Connecticut Nutmegger. q. ISSN 0045-8120

**Genealogy Club of America**
Suite 1007, Medical Arts Bldg., 54 East South
Temple, Salt Lake City, UT 84111.
- Genealogy Digest. bi-m.

**General Advertising & Publishing, Inc.**
53 Orange St., New Haven, CT 06510.
- New Haven I N F O. m. ISSN 0028-5331
- Westside Shopper. bi-m.

**General Association of Regular Baptist Churches**
- Baptist Bulletin. (pub. by Regular Baptist Press)

**General Commission on Chaplains and Armed Forces
Personnel**
Suite 310, 5100 Wisconsin Ave., N.W., Washington,
DC 20016.
- Chaplain; a journal for chaplains serving the
Armed Forces, Veterans Administration and Civil
Air Patrol. q. ISSN 0009-1642

**General Conference of Seventh Day Adventists**
6840 Eastern Ave. N.W., Washington, DC 20012.
- Insight (Washington) (pub. by Review and Herald
Publishing Association)
- Journal of Adventist Education. (pub. by Review
and Herald Publishing Association)
- Ministry. m. ISSN 0026-5314

**General Conference of the Church of God**
- Bible Advocate. (pub. by Bible Advocate Press)

**General Council of the Assemblies of God**
1445 Boonville, Springfield, MO 65802.
- Advance (Springfield); a magazine for assemblies
of God ministers and church leaders. m. ISSN
0001-8589
- C A M. (Campus Ambassador Magazine) 6 per
yr. ISSN 0007-7801
- HiCall. w. ISSN 0018-120X
- Junior Trails. w. ISSN 0022-6718
- Pentecostal Evangel. w. ISSN 0031-4897
- Youth Alive. m. ISSN 0009-5826

**General Electric Co. Research and Development
Center**
Schenectady, NY 12301.
- R & D Review (Schenectady) irreg. ISSN 0361-
4689

**General Executive Services, Inc.**
72 Park St., New Canaan, CT 06840.
- Digest of Executive Opportunities. w. ISSN 0046-
0249

**General Federation of Women's Clubs**
1734 N St.,N.W., Washington, DC 20036.
- Clubwoman News. m.(Sept-May)

**General Society of Mayflower Descendants**
4 Winslow St., Box 297, Plymouth, MA 02360
(Subscr. to: Mrs. R. M. Sherman, 128 Massasoit
Dr., Warwick, RI 02888)
- Mayflower Quarterly. q.

**General Technical Services**
8794 W. Chester Pike, Upper Darby, PA 19082.
- Bioengineering Series. irreg.

**Generalist**
5 Beekman St., New York, NY 10038.
- Newsletter on the State of the Culture. m.(Sept.-
June) ISSN 0028-9523
- Scene; plays from Off-Off Broadway. irreg. ISSN
0090-5259
- Smith. 2 per yr. (with 2 supplements) ISSN 0037-
7309

**Genesis Publishing Inc.**
770 Lexington Ave., New York, NY 10021.
- Genesis. m.

**Genesis Way Inc.**
712 Greenwich St., New York, NY 10014.
- Where It's At. m.

**Genetics Clearinghouse**
247 Fort Lee Rd., Leonia, NJ 07605.
- Genetic Counseling. m.

**Genetics Society of America**
Drawer U, University Station, Austin, TX 78712.
- Genetics; a periodical record of investigations
bearing on heredity and variation. m. ISSN 0016-
6731

**Steven H. Gens, Ed. & Pub.**
24 Mary Dunn Rd., Hyannis, MA 02601.
- Cape Cod Illustrated. w (May-Sept.); s-m (Oct.-
May) ISSN 0008-5782

**Gentlemen's Quarterly**
488 Madison Ave., New York, NY 10022.
- G Q, Guide to Fashion Sources. a. ISSN 0072-
0062

**Geochron Laboratories, Inc.**
24 Blackstone St., Cambridge, MA 02139.
- Geochronicle. q. ISSN 0016-7045

**Geodex International, Inc.**
669 Broadway, P.O. Box 279, Sonoma, CA 95476.
- Geodex Retrieval System for Geotechnical
Abstracts. 3 per yr. ISSN 0046-5658
(International Society for Soil Mechanics &
Foundation Engineering)
- Geodex System/A - Retrieval System for
Architectural Literature. 3 per yr.
- Geodex System/S Structural Information Service.
3 per yr.

**Geoffrita Productions, Ltd.**
240 E. 93rd St., Rm. 17-A, New York, NY 10028.
- Resume; a guide for producers, agents, managers.
m.

**Geographic and Area Study Publications**
Tualatin, OR 97062.
- Geopub Review of Geographical Literature. m.
(10 per yr.) ISSN 0360-8492

**Geographical Research Institute**
5235 Ravenswood Ave., Chicago, IL 60640.
- Cartocraft Research Studies. irreg. ISSN 0069-
0791

**Geological Society of America**
3300 Penrose Place, Boulder, CO 80301.
- Bibliography and Index of Geology. m. ISSN
0098-2784
- Engineering Geology Case Histories. irreg. ISSN
0071-0326
- Geological Society of America. Abstracts with
Programs. 7 per yr. ISSN 0016-7592
- Geological Society of America. Bulletin. m. ISSN
0016-7606
- Geological Society of America. Memoirs. irreg.
ISSN 0072-1069
- Geological Society of America. Memorials. irreg.
ISSN 0091-5041
- Geological Society of America. Special Papers.
irreg. ISSN 0072-1077
- Geological Society of America. Yearbook. a. ISSN
0095-3547
- Geology. m. ISSN 0091-7613
- Reviews in Engineering Geology. irreg. ISSN
0080-2018

**Geological Society of the Oregon Country**
1351 S.W. Hume St., Portland, OR 97219.
- Geological Society of the Oregon Country.
Geological Newsletter. m. ISSN 0046-5739

**Geophysical Directory, Inc.**
2200 Welch Ave., Houston, TX 77019
(Subscr. to P.O. Box 13508, Houston, TX 77019)
- Geophysical Directory. a.

**Barbara George**
Box 1257, Brattleboro, VT 05301.
- Velo-News; a journal of bicycle racing. m. (s-m. in
Jun. & Jul.)

**Herbert George, Ed. & Pub.**
306 W. 100 St., Apt. 2, New York, NY 10025
- Tracks; a journal of artists' writings. 3 per yr.
(Orders to: Box 557, Old Chelsea Sta., New York
NY 10011)

**George Mason University**
4400 University Drive, Fairfax, VA 22030.
- Phoebe. q.

**George Peabody College for Teachers**
Nashville, TN 37203.
- Peabody Journal of Education. q. ISSN 0031-3432

**George Peabody College for Teachers. Alumni
Association**
Box 161, Nashville, TN 37203.
- Peabody Reflector. q. ISSN 0031-3459

**George Peabody College for Teachers. Division of
Surveys & Field Services**
Nashville, TN 37203.
- Free and Inexpensive Learning Materials. biennial.
ISSN 0071-9307

**George Peabody College for Teachers. School of
Library Science**
Nashville, TN 37203.
- C. C. Williamson Memorial Lecture. irreg. ISSN
0068-4708

**George S. May International Company**
111 S. Washington St., Park Ridge, IL 60068.
- May Trends. 3 per yr. ISSN 0025-6137

**George Washington University**
Washington, DC 20052.
- G W Times. q.
- George Washington Law Review. 5 per yr. ISSN
0016-8076

**George Washington University. American Studies
Program**
2108 G St. N.W., Washington, DC 20052.
- American Studies International. 3 per yr. ISSN
0003-1321 (American Studies Association)

**George Washington University. Government Contracts
Program**
2000 H St. N.W., Rm. 308, Washington, DC 20052.
- Government Contracts Monographs. irreg. ISSN
0072-5153

**George Washington University Hatchet**
800 21 St.N.W., Washington, DC 20006.
- Hatchet. s-w.(Sept.-May) ISSN 0017-8357

**George Washington University Medical Center.
Population Information Program**
1343 H St. N.W., Washington, DC 20005.
- George Washington University. Population
Information Program. Population Report. Series
A. Oral Contraceptives. irreg.
- George Washington University. Population
Information Program. Population Report. Series
B. Intrauterine Devices. irreg.
- George Washington University. Population
Information Program. Population Report. Series
C. Sterilization (Female) irreg.
- George Washington University. Population
Information Program. Population Report. Series
D: Sterilization (Male) irreg.
- George Washington University. Population
Information Program. Population Report. Series
E. Law and Policy. irreg.
- George Washington University. Population
Information Program. Population Report. Series F.
Pregnancy Termination. irreg.
- George Washington University. Population
Information Program. Population Report. Series
G. Prostaglandins. irreg.
- George Washington University. Population
Information Program. Population Report. Series
H. Barrier Methods. irreg.
- George Washington University. Population
Information Program. Population Report. Series I:
Periodic Abstinence. irreg. ISSN 0093-4496
- George Washington University. Population
Information Program. Population Report. Series J.
Family Planning Programs. irreg. ISSN 0093-4496
- George Washington University. Population
Information Program. Population Report. Series
K: Injectables and Implants. irreg.

**George Washington University. National Law Center**
Washington, DC 20052.
- Journal of International Law and Economics. 3
per yr. ISSN 0022-2003

**Georgeson & Co.**
100 Wall St., New York, NY 10005.
- Trends in Management-Stockholder Relations. m.
ISSN 0041-2406

**Georgetown Law Journal Association**
600 New Jersey Ave. N.W., Washington, DC 20001.
- Georgetown Law Journal. 6 per yr. ISSN 0016-8092

**Georgetown Medical Bulletin**
3800 Reservoir Rd. N.W., Washington, DC 20007.
- Georgetown Medical Bulletin. q. ISSN 0016-8106

**Georgetown University**
37th and O Sts. N.W., Washington, DC 20007.
- Hoya. w. ISSN 0018-6864

**Georgetown University. Center for Strategic and International Studies**
1800 K St. N.W., Washington, DC 20006.
- Georgetown University. Center for Strategic and International Studies. Monographs. irreg.
- Georgetown University. Center for Strategic and International Studies. Special Report Series. irreg.; 1975, no. 15. ISSN 0072-1204
- Washington Papers. (pub. by Sage Publications, Inc.)

**Georgetown University. Joseph and Rose Kennedy Institute for the Study of Human Reproduction and Bioethics**
Washington, DC 20057.
- New Titles in Bioethics. m. (prep. by its Center for Bioethics Library)

**Georgetown University Law Center**
600 New Jersey Ave., N.W., Washington, DC 20001.
- Law and Policy in International Business. 4 per yr. ISSN 0023-9208

**Georgetown University. Medical Center**
3900 Reservoir Rd., N.W., Washington, DC 20007.
- Georgetown Dental Journal. s-a. ISSN 0016-8084

**Georgetown University. School of Languages & Linguistics**
Washington, DC 20007.
- Colloquium on Spanish and Portuguese Linguistics. (Papers) a.
- Georgetown University Round Table on Languages and Linguistics. a. ISSN 0072-1212
- Georgetown University Working Papers on Languages and Linguistics. irreg.

**Georgetowner, Inc.**
1203 28th St. N.W., Washington, DC 20007.
- Georgetowner. fortn.

**Georgia. Bureau of Industry & Trade. Tourist Division**
Box 38097, Atlanta, GA 30334.
- Special Events in Georgia. s-a. ISSN 0038-6715

**Georgia. Department of Agriculture**
19 Hunter St. S.W., Atlanta, GA 30334.
- Georgia Farmers and Consumers Market Bulletin. w.

**Georgia. Department of Community Development**
Box 38097, Atlanta, GA 30334.
- Georgia Progress. q. ISSN 0016-836X
- Georgia Welcome Center. Research Report. (pub. by University of Georgia. College of Business Administration)

**Georgia. Department of Education**
State Office Bldg., Atlanta, GA 30334.
- Georgia. Department of Education. Statistical Report. a. ISSN 0094-1557
- Georgia Alert; a look at education's role today. bi-m. ISSN 0435-5261

**Georgia. Department of Human Resources. Division of Physical Health**
Biostatistics Service, 47 Trinity Ave. S.W., Atlanta, GA 30334.
- Georgia Vital and Health Statistics. a. ISSN 0362-0662 (prep. by its Health Services Research & Statistics Section)

**Georgia. Department of Natural Resources**
270 Washington St., Atlanta, GA 30334.
- Outdoors in Georgia. m.

**Georgia. Department of Natural Resources. Earth and Water Division**
19 Hunter St., Rm. 400, Atlanta, GA 30334.
- Georgia. Geological Survey. Bulletin. irreg.
- Georgia. Geological Survey. Circular 1. List of Publications. irreg.

- Georgia. Geological Survey. Circular 2. Mining Directory of Georgia. irreg. 1972, 17th ed.
- Georgia. Geological Survey. Information Circular. irreg. ISSN 0433-5473
- Georgia. Water Resources Survey. Hydrologic Report. irreg.

**Georgia. Department of Natural Resources. Environmental Protection Division**
47 Trinity Ave., S. W., Atlanta, GA 30334.
- Water Quality Monitoring Data for Georgia Streams. a. ISSN 0097-7519

**Georgia. Employment Security Agency**
501 Pulliam St., Rm. 306, Atlanta, GA 30312.
- Georgia Labor Market Trends. m.

**Georgia. Forestry Commission**
Box 819, Macon, GA 31202.
- Georgia Forestry. q.

**Georgia. State Data Center**
270 Washington St., S.W., Atlanta, GA 30334.
- Georgia. State Data Center. City Population Estimates. irreg. ISSN 0362-3904

**Georgia. State Economic Opportunity Office**
618 Ponce de Leon Ave., Atlanta, GA 30308.
- Georgia. State Economic Opportunity Office. Annual Report. a. ISSN 0091-3448

**Georgia Academy of Science.**
Georgia State University, University Plaza, Atlanta, GA 30303.
- Georgia Journal of Science. q. ISSN 0016-8114
- Index to the Bulletin and Other Publications of the Georgia Academy of Science. irreg. ISSN 0073-6058

**Georgia Association of Plumbing-Heating-Cooling Contractors**
301 Washington Ave., Marietta, Atlanta, GA 30060.
- Plumb. m.

**Georgia College**
Box 608, Milledgeville, GA 31061.
- Flannery O'Connor Bulletin. a. ISSN 0091-4924

**Georgia Congress of Parents and Teachers**
- Georgia Congress of Parents and Teachers. Annual Leadership Training Conference. Workshop for P T A Leaders. (pub. by University of Georgia. Center for Continuing Education)

**Georgia Conservancy**
3376 Peachtree Rd. N.E., Atlanta, GA 30326.
- Georgia Conservancy Newsletter. m.

**Georgia Council for the Social Sciences**
c/o Exec. Sec. Terry Northup, Box 124, Georgia State Univ., University Plaza, Atlanta, GA 30303.
- Georgia Social Science Journal. 3 per yr. ISSN 0016-8408

**Georgia Educational Improvement Council**
Room 656, Seven Hunter St. Bldg., Atlanta, GA 30334.
- Directory: a Guide to Colleges, Vocational-Technical and Diploma Schools of Nursing. biennial.

**Georgia Entomological Society**
c/o Richard B. Chalfant, Dept. Entomology and Fisheries, Coastal Plain Experiment Station, Tifton, GA 31794.
- Georgia Entomological Society Journal. q. ISSN 0016-8238

**Georgia Farm Bureau Federation**
2960 Riverside Dr., Macon, GA 31204.
- Georgia Farm Bureau News. m.

**Georgia Historical Society**
501 Whitaker St., Savannah, GA 31401.
- G. H. S. Foot-Notes. q. ISSN 0090-4368
- Georgia Historical Quarterly. q. ISSN 0016-8297

**Georgia Institute of Technology**
Box J, 225 North Ave. N.W., Atlanta, GA 30332.
- Tech Topics. 7 per yr. (Georgia Tech National Alumni Association)
- Technique; the south's liveliest college newspaper. w.

**Georgia Institute of Technology. Engineering Experiment Station**
Atlanta, GA 30332.
- Georgia Development News. m. ISSN 0016-8203

- Georgia Institute of Technology. Engineering Experiment Station. Quarterly Report. q.

**Georgia Institute of Technology. Industrial Development Division**
Atlanta, GA 30332.
- Small Industry Development Network. Quarterly Newsletter. q.

**Georgia Journal of International and Comparative Law, Inc.**
Univ. of Georgia, School of Law, Athens, GA 30602.
- Georgia Journal of International and Comparative Law. s-a. ISSN 0046-578X

**Georgia Law Review Association Inc**
- Georgia Law Review. (pub. by University of Georgia School of Law)

**Georgia Library Association**
Box 833, Tucker, GA 30084.
- Georgia Librarian. s-a. ISSN 0016-8319

**Georgia Life**
P.O. Drawer 1829, Decatur, GA 30031.
- Georgia Life. q.

**Georgia Motor Trucking Association**
500 Piedmont Ave., N.E., Atlanta, GA 30308.
- Trux. bi-m.

**Georgia Municipal Association**
10 Pryor St., Atlanta, GA 30303.
- Urban Georgia. m. ISSN 0042-0875

**Georgia Museum of Art**
see under University of Georgia

**Georgia Music Educators Association**
4045 Bouldervista Drive, Conley, GA 30027.
- Georgia Music News. q. ISSN 0046-5798

**Georgia Nurses Association**
269 Tenth St., N. E., Atlanta, GA 30309.
- Georgia Nursing. q. ISSN 0016-8335

**Georgia Ornithological Society**
c/o T. McRae Williams, Bus. Mgr., 755 Ellsworth Drive, N.W., Atlanta, GA 30318.
- Oriole. q. ISSN 0030-5553

**Georgia Peanut Commission**
c/o R. Maylon Nicholson, Ed., Box 706, Tifton, GA 31794.
- Southeastern Peanut Farmer. m (except Oct. & Dec) ISSN 0038-3694 (Co-sponsor: Alabama Peanut Producers Association)

**Georgia Political Science Association**
Georgia State University, Department of Political Science, Atlanta, GA 30322.
- G P S A Journal. s-a. ISSN 0092-9395

**Georgia Ports Authority**
Box 2406, Savannah, GA 31402.
- Georgia AnchorAge. bi-m. ISSN 0016-8149

**Georgia Press Association**
1075 Spring St. N.W., Atlanta, GA 30309.
- Editor's Forum. m.

**Georgia School Boards Association**
Sheraton Biltmore Hotel, 817 West Peachtree St. NE, Atlanta, GA 30383.
- Georgia School Boards Bulletin. m. ISSN 0016-8394

**Georgia Society of Certified Public Accountants, Inc.**
1504 Williams-Oliver Bldg., Atlanta, GA 30303.
- Georgia C. P. A. q. ISSN 0016-8181

**Georgia Society of Professional Engineers**
Suite 770, 1375 Peachtree St., N.E., Atlanta, GA 30309.
- Georgia Professional Engineer. bi-m. ISSN 0016-8351

**Georgia Southern College. English Department**
Box 8023, Statesboro, GA 30458.
- Milton and the Romantics. a.
- Notes on Teaching English. s-a. (Co-Sponsor: Georgia-South Carolina College English Assn.)

**Georgia State Lodge Fraternal Order of Police**
- Georgia F O P News. (pub. by Dale Corporation)

**Georgia State University**
University Plaza, Atlanta, GA 30303.
- Georgia State University Signal. w. ISSN 0016-8424

**Georgia State University. College of Business Administration**
Publishing Services Division, University Plaza, Atlanta, GA 30303.
- Atlanta Economic Review. bi-m. ISSN 0004-671X
- Georgia State University. College of Business Administration. Report of Publications and Research. a.

**Georgia State University. College of Urban Life**
University Plaza, Atlanta, GA 30303.
- Criminal Justice Review. s-a.

**Georgia State University. Department of English**
31 Gilmer St., Atlanta, GA 30303.
- Studies in the Literary Imagination. s-a. ISSN 0039-3819

**Georgia State University. Department of Psychology**
Georgia State University, Department of Psychology, Atlanta, GA 30303.
- International Journal of Symbology. 3 per yr. ISSN 0020-7705 (International Society for the Study of Symbols)

**Georgia State University. Foreign Language Department**
Atlanta, GA 30303.
- Foreign Language Beacon. 2-3 per yr. ISSN 0015-7198

**Georgia State University. Hospital Administration Program**
Atlanta, GA 30303.
- Georgia State University. Institute of Health Administration. Occasional Publication. irreg.

**Georgia State University. Library**
- Atlanta Constitution: a Georgia Index. (pub. by Microfilming Corporation of America)

**Georgia Tech National Alumni Association**
- Tech Topics. (pub. by Georgia Institute of Technology)

**Georgia Water & Pollution Control Association**
P.O. 1418, Atlanta, GA 30301.
- Georgia Operator. q. ISSN 0433-6054

**Georgian National Alliance**
c/o G. Djakeli, 535 E. 78th St., New York, NY 10021.
- Georgian Opinion. bi-m.

**Geoscience Information Society**
American Geological Institute, 5205 Leesburg Pike, Falls Church, VA 22041.
- Directory of Geoscience Libraries, U.S. and Canada. irreg., 2nd edt. 1974.
- Geoscience Information Society. Newsletter. bi-m. ISSN 0046-5801
- Geoscience Information Society. Proceedings. (pub. by American Geological Institute)

**Geothermal Energy Association**
18014 Sherman Way 169, Reseda, CA 91335.
- Geothermal Energy. m. ISSN 0093-5700

**Geothermal Resources Council**
Box 1033, Davis, CA 95616.
- Geothermal Resources Council. Bulletin. 9-12 per yr.

**H. E. & H. S. Gerber, Eds. & Pubs.**
Arizona State University, Department of English, Tempe, AZ 85281.
- English Literature in Transition (1880-1920) q. ISSN 0013-8339

**Ash Gerecht, Ed. & Pub.**
399 National Press Bldg., Washington, DC 20045.
- Housing Market Report. s-m. ISSN 0363-4744

**Germain Publishing Co. Inc.**
State Tower Bldg., Syracuse, NY 13202.
- Accountants Digest; presenting in compact form the substance of outstanding articles selected from leading accounting journals of the English-speaking world. q. ISSN 0001-4737

**German American Chamber of Commerce, Inc.**
666 Fifth Ave., New York, NY 10019.
- American Subsidiaries of German Firms. a.
- German American Trade News. m. ISSN 0016-8718

**German-American National Congress, Inc.**
4740 N. Western Ave., Chicago, IL 60625.
- Deutschamerikaner. m.

**German Church of God in U. S. A.**
- Internationale Bibellektionen. (pub. by Christian Unity Press)

**German Philatelic Society**
Box 563, Westminster, MD 21157.
- German Postal Specialist; a philatelic publication for stamp collectors specializing in Germany-related stamps. m. ISSN 0016-8823

**German Shepherd Dog Club of America, Inc.**
Box 1221, Lancaster, PA 17604.
- German Shepherd Dog Review. m. ISSN 0046-5852

**Gernsback Publications, Inc.**
200 Park Ave. S., New York, NY 10003.
- Radio-Electronics. m. ISSN 0033-7862

**Geron-X, Inc. Publishers**
Box 1108, Los Altos, CA 94022.
- Contraception. m. (2 vol. per yr.) ISSN 0010-7824
- Nutrition Reports International. m (2 vols per yr.) ISSN 0029-6635
- Political Methodology. q.
- Politics and Society. q. ISSN 0032-3292
- Prostaglandins. m. ISSN 0090-6980
- Theriogenology; an international journal of animal reproduction. m. ISSN 0093-691X

**Gerontological Society**
1 Dupont Circle, Suite 520, Washington, DC 20036.
- Gerontological Society Newsletter. irreg. ISSN 0433-8294
- Gerontologist. bi-m. ISSN 0016-9013
- Journal of Gerontology. bi-m. ISSN 0022-1422

**Gesture**
Box 1079, Northland Center, Southfield, MI 48075.
- Gesture; the magazine of the arts. bi-m. ISSN 0016-9196

**Getting Together**
P.O. Box 26229, San Francisco, CA 94126.
- Getting Together. fortn.

**Geyer-McAllister Publications**
51 Madison Ave., New York, NY 10010.
- Administrative Management; the systems magazine for administrative executives. m. ISSN 0001-8376
- Geyer's Dealer Topics; the office equipment and stationery dealers' magazine. m. ISSN 0016-948X
- Geyer's Who Makes It Directory. a. ISSN 0072-4327
- Gift and Decorative Accessories Buyers Directory. a. ISSN 0072-4505
- Gifts & Decorative Accessories; the international business magazine of gifts, china and glass, home accessories, greeting cards and social stationery. m. ISSN 0016-9889
- Playthings; the news magazine of toy, hobby & craft merchandising. m. ISSN 0032-1567
- Playthings Directory. a. ISSN 0079-2349
- Word Processing Report; news and technical guidance for the professional community involved with modern secretarial systems and automated text production. s-m. ISSN 0049-7967
- Word Processing World; the magazine of automated business communications. bi-m. ISSN 0093-5794

**Ghost Dance Press**
Dept. of American Thought and Language (EBH), Michigan State University, E. Lansing, MI 48823.
- Ghost Dance; the international quarterly of experimental poetry. q. ISSN 0016-9633

**Giannini Foundation of Agricultural Economics**
Univ. of California, Berkeley, 207 Giannini Hall, Berkeley, CA 94720.
- Giannini Foundation of Agricultural Economics. Research Report. irreg. ISSN 0072-4459

**D. Parke Gibson International, Inc.**
475 Fifth Ave., New York, NY 10017.
- Gibson Report. m. ISSN 0016-9684
- Race Relations and Industry. m. ISSN 0033-7315

**Gidra Inc.**
Box 18649, Los Angeles, CA 90018.
- Gidra; Asian American community monthly of Southern California. m. ISSN 0016-9692

**Gig Enterprises, Inc.**
415 Lexington Ave., New York, NY 10017.
- Music Gig; magazine for the record buying public. m.

**Thomas Giles**
Box 18351, Philadelphia, PA 19120.
- Crystal Well; a journal of the old religion. 6-8 per yr. ISSN 0045-916X

**Gilgamesh Publishing Co.**
6050 Boulevard East, 20-A, West New York, NJ 07093.
- Studia Sumiro-Hungarica. irreg., vol. 3, 1974. ISSN 0585-5578

**R. V. Gill Publishing Co.**
Box 420, Bellaire, OH 43906.
- Amateur Writer's Journal. m.
- Four Seasons. q.

**Ray Gillem, Ed. & Pub.**
Rte. 2, Ft. Atkinson, IA 52144.
- Country Messenger. q. ISSN 0145-6024
- Hobby Artist News. bi-m. ISSN 0145-6016

**H. Marvin Ginn Corporation**
625 N. Michigan Ave., Chicago, IL 60611.
- Fire Chief. m. ISSN 0015-2544

**Ralph Ginzburg**
251 W. 57th St., New York, NY 10019
- American Business. m. ISSN 0363-566X (Subscr. to:, 1775 Broadway, New York, NY 10019)
- Avant Garde. q. ISSN 0005-1918 (Avant-Garde Media, Inc.)
- Extra. m. ISSN 0145-3939 (Subscr. to:, 1775 Broadway, New York, NY 10019)
- Moneysworth. fortn. ISSN 0026-9646

**Giorno Poetry Systems Institute, Inc.**
222 Bowery, New York, NY 10012.
- Dial-a-Poem Poets. 2 per yr.

**Girard Associates Inc.**
Box 455, Mt. Arlington, NJ 07856.
- Biomedical Electronics. s-m. ISSN 0006-338X
- Computer Medicine. m. ISSN 0094-6028
- H M O Health Services Report. m.
- Instructional Technology. m.
- Marine Resources Digest/Marine Biology Digest. m. ISSN 0025-3286
- Microelectronics Digest. m. ISSN 0026-2722

**Frank Girard, Ed. & Pub.**
4568 Richmond, N.W., Grand Rapids, MI 49504.
- Collector's Exchange. bi-m. ISSN 0045-7353

**Girard Home News, Inc.**
1015 Chestnut St., Suite 405-09, Philadelphia, PA 19107.
- Girard Home News. w. ISSN 0017-0550

**Girl Scouts of the U.S.A.**
830 Third Ave., New York, NY 10022.
- American Girl (Braille Edition)
- American Girl (Inkprint Edition) m. ISSN 0002-8630
- Daisy. 9 per yr.
- Girl Scout Leader. 7 per yr. ISSN 0017-0577

**Girl Talk**
380 Madison Ave., New York, NY 10017.
- Girl Talk. m.

**Girls Clubs of America**
133 E. 62nd St., New York, NY 10021.
- Girls Club News. q.

**Girls' Rodeo Association News**
c/o Ed. Lydia Moore, 8909 N.E. 25 St., Spencer, OK 73084.
- Girls' Rodeo Association News. m.

**Glanville Publishers, Inc.**
75 Main St., Dobbs Ferry, NY 10522.
- Index to Periodical Articles Related to Law; selected journals not included in the Index to Legal Periodicals. q. ISSN 0019-4093
- Law Books in Print. irreg., revised every two-three years. ISSN 0075-8221
- Law Books in Review. q.
- Law Books Published. 3-4 per yr. ISSN 0023-9240

• Reprint Bulletin. q. ISSN 0034-4923

**Alfred B. Glaser**
Box 3232, Riverside, CA 92509.
• Newsnovel. irreg.

**Glass Art Magazine, Inc.**
Box 7527, Oakland, CA 94601.
• Glass Art Magazine. bi-m.

**Glass Containers Manufacturers Institute**
1800 K St., N.W., Washington, DC 20006.
• Glass Containers. a. ISSN 0072-4637

**Glassworks Press**
Box 163, Rosebank Station, NY 10305.
• Glassworks. 3 per yr. ISSN 0145-6792

**Gleason Publishing Co. Inc.**
Box 303, 162 Great Rd., Acton, MA 01720.
• Eastern Pennsylvania, Southern Delaware and
  Eastern Maryland Blue Book. a.
• Electrical Blue Book-Directory of New York &
  Northern New Jersey's Electrical Market. a.
• New England Electrical Blue Book. a. ISSN 0548-
  4456
• New England Electrical News. m. ISSN 0028-
  4734

**Glendale Adventist Medical Center Publications
Service**
Box 871, Glendale, CA 91209.
• Cumulative Index to Nursing & Allied Health
  Literature. bi-m. with annual cumulation. ISSN
  0011-3018

**Glenmary Home Missioners**
4119 Glenmary Trace, Fairfield, OH 45014.
• Glenmary's Challenge. q. ISSN 0017-1182

**Glenmary Sisters**
4580 Colerain Ave., Box 23072, Cincinnati, OH
45223.
• Kinship. q. ISSN 0023-1703

**Peter Glenn Publications, Inc.**
17 E. 48th St., New York, NY 10017.
• Madison Avenue Europe. a. ISSN 0076-213X
• Madison Avenue Handbook. a. ISSN 0076-2148
• National Radio Publicity Directory. a (with s-a.
  supplements)

**Glenwood State Hospital-School**
Glenwood, IA 51534.
• Hill Topic. q.

**Glide Publications**
330 Ellis St., San Francisco, CA 94102.
• Alternatives in Print; the annual catalog of social
  change publications. a. (American Library
  Association. Social Responsibilities Round Table.
  Task Force on Alternatives in Print)

**Global Dialogue Publications Inc.**
11 Fifth Ave., Box 385, Pelham, NY 10803.
• Global Dialogue. m. ISSN 0017-1190

**Global Engineering Documentation Services, Inc.**
3301 Macarthur Blvd., Santa Ana, CA 92704.
• Directory of Engineering Document Sources. a.

**Global Village**
A. E. Melton, 1807 Lincoln Park West, Chicago, IL
60614.
• Global Village. m. ISSN 0046-6026

**Glos Ludowy**
5854 Chene St., Detroit, MI 48211.
• Glos Ludowy/People's Voice. w.

**Goddard Space Flight Center**
NASA Field Installation, Greenbelt, MD 20770
• Space Science and Technology Today. irreg.
  (Orders to: Supt. of Documents, Washington, DC
  20402)

**Godfrey Memorial Library**
134 Newfield St., Middletown, CT 06457.
• New York Law Journal. w. ISSN 0028-7326
• U. S. Federal Register. w. ISSN 0042-1219

**David Godine Publisher**
306 Dartmouth Street, Boston, MA 02116.
• Contemporary Photographers Series. irreg.

**Ed. & Pub. Fay Gold**
Box 256, Times Square Sta., New York, NY 10036.
• Yorkshire Terrier Quarterly. q. ISSN 0044-0647

**Gold Coast Pictorial, Inc.**
Box 7396, Sunrise Professional Bldg., Fort
Lauderdale, FL 33304.
• Gold Coast Pictorial; the magazine of Florida's
  Gold Coast. 12 per yr.

**Gold Coin Newsletter**
c/o Sanford J. Durst, Ed., 133 E. 58 St., New York,
NY 10022.
• Gold Coin Newsletter. m.

**Gold Flower Collective**
Box 8341 Lake St. Station, Minneapolis, MN
55408.
• Goldflower; a Twin Cities newspaper for women.
  bi-m.

**Golden Gate Foundation for Group Treatment**
Box 1141, Vallejo, CA 94590.
• Encounterer. irreg.

**Golden Gate North Publishing Co.**
Box 3028, Santa Rosa, CA 95403.
• Golden Gate North. q. ISSN 0046-6069

**Golden Gate University. School of Law**
536 Mission St., San Francisco, CA 94105.
• Golden Gate University Law Review. 3 per yr.

**Goldenrod Publications**
Box 1397, Smyrna, GA 30080.
• Tattoo. q.

**Goldermood Rainbow Press**
331 W. Bonneville, Pasco, WA 99301.
• Nitty-Gritty (a Survival Tool Chest) 3 per yr.

**Gwenyth D. Goldsberry, Ed. & Pub.**
4760 E. Idaho Pl., Denver, CO 80222.
• Colorado Prospector. m. ISSN 0010-1702

**Goldsmith-Nagan, Inc.**
1120 19th St. N.W., Washington, DC 20036.
• Goldsmith-Nagan Bond and Money Market
  Letter. fortn. ISSN 0017-1697

**Goldstein Associates**
35 Whittemore Rd., Framingham, MA 01701.
• C A L L. (Current Awareness-Library Literature)
  bi-m.

**Dan Golenpaul Associates**
• Information Please Almanac. (pub. by Simon and
  Schuster, Inc.)

**Golf Course Superintendents Association of America**
1617 St. Andrews Drive, Lawrence, KS 66044.
• Golf Course Superintendents Association of
  America. Membership Directory. a. ISSN 0436-
  1474
• Golf Course Superintendents Association of
  America. Proceedings of the International
  Conference and Show. a. ISSN 0072-4947
• Golf Superintendent. m.(Sept-Oct., Nov.-Dec. nos.
  combined) ISSN 0017-1840

**Golf Digest, Inc.**
495 Westport Ave., Norwalk, CT 06058.
• Golf Digest. m. ISSN 0017-176X
• Golf Shop Operations. m. ISSN 0017-1824
• Hockey (Norwalk) 8 per yr. (Sep.-Apr.) ISSN
  0361-5847

**Golf Digest, Inc. Tennis Features, Inc.**
495 Westport Ave., Norwalk, CT 06856.
• Tennis; magazine of the racquet sports. m. ISSN
  0040-3423 (United States Professional Tennis
  Association)

**Golf World, Inc.**
Box 2000, Southern Pines, NC 28387.
• Golf World. w. ISSN 0017-1891

**Milton Golin, Ed. & Pub.**
1014 Indian Rd., Glenview, IL 60025.
• Adolescent Medicine. m. ISSN 0044-6335
  (Medallion Corp.)
• Medical Group News; and health services report.
  m. ISSN 0025-7265

**J. B. Goncharsky, Ed. & Pub.**
Box 14143, San Francisco, CA 94114.
• Book Review; an alternative. m. ISSN 0036-4177

**Gondolier Enterprises Inc.**
915 N.E. 20th Ave., Fort Lauderdale, FL 33304.
• Gondolier; Florida's boating magazine. m. ISSN
  0046-6107

**Gonzaga University**
Spokane, WA 99258.
• Charter; Gonzaga University's journal of Liberal
  Arts. a. ISSN 0069-2786
• Communio; international catholic review. q. ISSN
  0094-2065

**Gonzaga University School of Law**
Spokane, WA 99202.
• Gonzaga Law Review. 4 per yr. ISSN 0046-6115

**Good Gay Poets Collective**
P.O. Box 331, Kenmore Station, Boston, MA
02215.
• Fag Rag; a gay male newspaper. q. ISSN 0046-
  3167

**Good Gay Poets Press**
Box 277, Astor Station, Boston, MA 02123.
• Boston Gay Review; gay journal of reviews and
  critism of all aspects of gay culture and
  expression. q.

**Good News Broadcasting Association, Inc.**
Back to the Bible Broadcast, Box 82808, Lincoln,
NE 68501.
• Good News Broadcaster. m. ISSN 0017-2154
• Young Ambassador. m. ISSN 0044-071X

**Good Outdoor Manners Association**
Box 7095, Seattle, WA 98133.
• Howdy's Happenings. 4 per yr. ISSN 0018-683X

**Good Publishing Co.**
1220 Harding St., Fort Worth, TX 76102.
• Bronze Thrills. m.
• Hep. m. ISSN 0018-0432
• Soul Confessions. m.
• Soul Teen. m.

**Goodfellow**
c/o Christopher Weills, Ed., Box 4520, Berkeley,
CA 94704.
• Goodfellow Catalog of Wonderful Things. a.
• Goodfellow Review of Crafts; monthly crafts
  review. m.

**Goodheart-Willcox Co., Inc.**
123 W. Taft Dr., South Holland, IL 60473.
• Fix Your Chevrolet. a. ISSN 0071-5670
• Fix Your Ford. a. ISSN 0071-5689
• Fix Your Volkswagen. a. ISSN 0071-5697

**Goodyear Industrial Products Division**
• Industrial Progress. (pub. by Reuben H. Donnelley
  Corp.)

**Goodyear Tire & Rubber Co.**
1144 E. Market St., Akron, OH 44316.
• Big. q. ISSN 0006-2170
• Go (Akron) m.
• Stores. s-m.
• Triangle. s-m.
• Wingfoot Clan. w. ISSN 0043-5872

**Maynard M. Gordon, Ed. & Pub**
6525 Lincoln, Detroit, MI 48202.
• Gordon Reports & Autoworld. s-m.
• Motor News Analysis. m. ISSN 0027-1942

**Gordon and Breach Science Publishers**
One Park Ave. New York, NY 10016.
• Applied Analysis; an international journal. 4 per
  yr.
• Applied Systems Science. a.
• Coral Gables Conference on Fundamental
  Interactions at High Energy. (Proceedings) a.
  ISSN 0069-9977 (University of Miami. Center for
  Theoretical Studies)
• Counterplay; quarterly digest of the
  counterculture. q.
• Cours et Documents de Biologie. a. ISSN 0590-
  7225
• Cours et Documents de Chimie. a.
• Cours et Documents de Mathematiques et de
  Physique. a.
• Current Topics in Environmental and
  Toxicological Chemistry. a.
• Current Topics of Contemporary Thought. a.
• Demographic Monographs. a.
• Documents in Biology. a.
• Documents in Chemistry. a.
• Documents on Modern Physics. a.
• Ferroelectricity and Related Phenomena. a.
• Futurist Library. a.
• Handbook of Elemental Abundances in Meteorites
  Series: Extraterrestrial Chemistry. irreg.
• Information and Systems Theory. a. ISSN 0537-
  6149

- International Academy of Oral Pathology. Proceedings. irreg., 1969, 4th, Johannesburg. ISSN 0074-1256
- International Colloquium on Plant Analysis and Fertilizer Problems. Proceedings. irreg., 6th, 1971.
- International Conference on Ion Implantation in Semiconductors. Proceedings. irreg, 1st, Thousand Oaks, CA, 1970.
- International Congress of Cybernetcs and Systems. Record. triennial.
- International I U P A C Congress of Pesticide Chemistry. Proceedings. irreg., 2nd, Tel Aviv, 1971.
- International Monograph Series on Early Child Care. a.
- International Science Review Series. irreg., 1972, vol. 13. ISSN 0074-7866
- International Symposium on Animal and Plant Toxins. Proceedings. irreg., 2nd, Tel Aviv, 1970.
- Journal of Statistical Computation and Simulation. q. ISSN 0094-9655
- Library of Anthropology. a.
- Life Sciences. a. ISSN 0459-3774
- Marine Biology; Proceedings of the Interdisciplinary Conference. irreg., 1970, vol. 5. ISSN 0076-4442 (American Institute of Biological Sciences)
- Mathematics and Its Applications. a. ISSN 0543-0941
- Mathematics International. irreg. ISSN 0091-7214
- Midland Macromolecular Monographs. a.
- Molecular Biology; Proceedings of the International Conference. irreg., 1970, 7th, Chania, Crete. ISSN 0077-023X (International Center for Advanced Studies)
- Monograph Series on Metallurgy in Nuclear Technology. irreg.
- Monographs and Texts in the Behavioral Sciences. irreg., 1971, no. 2. ISSN 0077-0752
- Monographs on Rockets and Missiles. a.
- New Priorities Library. a.
- Notes on Mathematics and Its Applications. a.
- Nuclear Physics. a. ISSN 0550-3205
- Ocean Series. a.
- Plasma Physics. a.
- Pocket Mathematical Library. irreg., approx. 1 per yr.
- Polymer Monographs. a.
- Processes and Materials in Electronics. a.
- Progress in Extractive Metallurgy. irreg. ISSN 0091-6145
- Psychic Studies. a.
- Publicatons Gramma. a.
- Quantum Physics and Its Applications. a. ISSN 0481-1275
- Reimpressions G & B. a.
- Russian Monographs and Texts on the Physical Sciences. a.
- Russian Tracts on the Physical Sciences. a.
- Semiconductors and Insulators; a journal of ionic and covalent solids. q. ISSN 0309-5991 (Subscr. to: 42, William IV St., London W.C.2, England)
- Series on Extraterrestrial Chemistry. irreg.
- Social Change. a.
- Space Flight Technology. a.
- Studies in Operations Research. a.
- Studies in Radiation Effects in Solids. a.
- Symposium on Advanced Propulsion Concepts. Proceedings. irreg., 1967, 4th. ISSN 0082-0806 (U.S. Air Force. Office of Scientifc Research) (Co-Sponsor: Genral Electric Company)
- Theorie des Systemes. a. ISSN 0563-4407
- Topics in Astrophysics and Space Physics. a. ISSN 0564-6294
- U.S. Atomic Energy Commission. Monographs. a.
- World Institute Creative Findings. a.

**Gordon Blackwell**
30 E. 40 St., New York, NY 10016.
- Directory of Professional Electrologists; geographically classified guide to permanent hair removal services. a. ISSN 0417-6383
- Electrolysis Digest. 5 per yr. ISSN 0013-4708 (American Electrolysis Association)

**Gordon Publications, Inc.**
20 Community Pl., Morristown, NJ 07960.
- Biomedical Products. 3 per yr.
- Chemical Equipment. m. ISSN 0009-2525
- Heating & Plumbing Merchandiser. bi-m.
- Laboratory Equipment. m. ISSN 0023-6810
- Metalworking Digest. bi-m. ISSN 0026-1009
- Mining /Processing Equipment. bi-m.

- Solar Heating and Cooling. bi-m.

**June Gorentz**
Box 1310, 651 Cannery Row, Monterey, CA 93940.
- California Life. m.

**Rev. Daniel Gorham, Ed. & Pub.**
8 Ravenna St., Asheville, NC 28803.
- Vineyard; national independent orthodox journal. bi-w.

**Gorman Publishing Co.**
3460 John Hancock Center, Chicago, IL 60611.
- Bakery Production and Marketing; management magazine of the bakery industry. 13 per yr. ISSN 0005-4127
- Canner Packer. 12 per yr. ISSN 0008-557X
- Dairy Record; news publication of the dairy industry. m. ISSN 0011-5673
- Industrias Lacteas. bi-m. ISSN 0019-8951

**Goshen College**
1700 S. Main St., Goshen, IN 46526.
- Goshen College Bulletin. 8 per yr. ISSN 0017-2308

**Gospel Association for the Blind, Inc.**
15-16 College Point Blvd., College Point, NY 11356.
- Gospel Messenger. m. ISSN 0017-2359

**Gospel Music Association**
Box 1201, Nashville, TN 37202.
- Gospel Music Association. Annual Directory & Yearbook. a. ISSN 0362-7330

**Gospel Publishing House**
1445 Boonville Ave., Springfield, MO 65802.
- P F N A News. q. (Pentecostal Fellowship of North America)

**Gospel Tract Distributors**
Box 17406, Portland, OR 97217.
- Last Day Messenger. bi-m. ISSN 0023-8635 (Kenton Bible Hall, Inc.)

**Gothic Castle Publishing Co. Inc.**
509 Fifth Ave, New York, NY 10017.
- Castle of Frankenstein. bi-m.

**Annie Gottlieb, Ed. & Pub.**
149 West 4th St. 5D, New York, NY 10012.
- Elima; a journal of writing. s-a.

**Martin Gottschalk**
Dept. of Foreign Languages, Howard Payne University, Brownwood, TX 76801.
- Sehatzkammer. q.

**Gould's Position, Inc.**
21 E. 66th St., New York, NY 10021.
- Gould's Position. w. ISSN 0017-2545

**Gourmet Inc.**
777 Third Ave., New York, NY 10017.
- Gourmet; the magazine of good living. m. ISSN 0017-2553

**Gourmet's Notebook**
c/o D. M. Huey, 2314 Third Ave., Seattle, WA 98121.
- Gourmet's Notebook. m.

**Government Business Worldwide Reports**
- Defense Business. (pub. by J. H. Wagner, Ed. & Pub)

**Government Data Publications**
422 Washington Bldg., Washington, DC 20005.
- Directory of Government Production Prime Contractors. a. ISSN 0070-5594
- Government Contracts Directory. a. ISSN 0072-5137
- Government Primecontracts Monthly. m.
- R & D Contracts Monthly. (Research & Development); a continuously up-dated sales and R & D tool for all research organizations and manufacturers. m. ISSN 0033-6793
- Research and Development Directory. a. ISSN 0080-1461
- U S/R & D. m. ISSN 0436-2225

**Government Development Bank for Puerto Rico**
140 Broadway, New York, NY 10005.
- Puerto Rico Business Review. irreg.

**Government Information Services**
752 National Press Building, N.W., Washington, DC 20045.
- Federal Funding Guide for Local Governments. irreg. ISSN 0362-4285

**Government R and D Report**
P.O. 284, M.I.T. Station, Cambridge, MA 02139.
- Government R and D Report. s-m.

**Government Research Co.**
1730 M St. N.W., Washington, DC 20036.
- National Issues Outlook. m. ISSN 0092-9778
- National Journal (1975); the weekly on politics and government. w. ISSN 0360-4217

**Governmental Research Association, Inc.**
Box 387, Ocean Gate, NJ 08740.
- G R A Reporter. q. ISSN 0016-3619
- Governmental Research Association Directory; directory of organizations and individuals professionally engaged in governmental research and related activities. biennial. ISSN 0072-520X

**Governors State University**
Park Forest South, IL 60466.
- Review of Sport and Leisure. 2 per yr.

**Grace Hospital**
c/o Graphic Arts Dept., 4160 John R., Detroit, MI 48201.
- Grace Hospital Drug Therapy Newsletter; Grace Hospital pharmacy newsletter. bi-m.

**Gradiva**
c/o Ralph Morrison, Humanities Bldg., State University of New York at Stony Brook, NY 11794.
- Gradiva; journal of contemporary theory & practice. q.

**Graduate Business Admissions Council**
P. O. Box 966, Princeton, NJ 08540.
- Graduate Study in Management; a guide for prospective students. a.

**Grafton Publications, Inc.**
667 Madison Ave., New York, NY 10021.
- Addiction and Drug Abuse Report; a confidential monthly newsletter covering all aspects of drug abuse, its prevention, and treatment of its victims. m. ISSN 0001-8074
- Delinquency and Rehabilitation Report; inventing useful lives for those who never had them. m.
- Youth Report. m. ISSN 0049-8467

**Grain and Farm Service Centers**
2150 Board of Trade, Chicago, IL 60604.
- Agri-Business Buyers Reference. a. ISSN 0065-4396

**Grain Dealers Mutual Insurance Co.**
1752 N. Meridian St., Indianapolis, IN 46202.
- Our Paper. m. ISSN 0030-6932

**Gralla Publications**
1515 Broadway, New York, NY 10036.
- Bank Systems & Equipment; for officers in operations and systems management. m. ISSN 0005-5050
- Bank Systems & Equipment International. q.
- Catalog Showroom Business. m.
- Contract; the business magazine of commerical institutional design, planning and furnishing. m. ISSN 0010-7832
- Health Care Product News. m. ISSN 0018-5566
- Jewelry Fashion Guide. a.
- Kitchen Business; for all who design, sell and install kitchen cabinets and complete kitchens. m. ISSN 0023-1932
- Multi Housing News. m.
- National Jeweler. m. ISSN 0027-9544
- National Jeweler Annual Fashion Guide. a.
- P F M. (Professional Furniture Merchant); the business magazine for progressive furniture retailers. m. ISSN 0030-7963
- Premium/Incentive Business. m.
- Sporting Goods Business. m. ISSN 0038-8009
- Supermarketing. m. ISSN 0039-5811

**Grand Cru**
6684 North Oliphant Ave., Chicago, IL 60631.
- Grand Cru. bi-m.

**Grand Island Biological Co.**
3175 Staley Rd., Box 68, Grand Island, NY 14072.
- Tissue Culture Abstracts. bi-m. ISSN 0040-8174

**Grand Lodge Free and Accepted Masons of Indiana**
Box 58, Franklin, IN 46134.
● Indiana Freemason. m. ISSN 0019-6622

**Grand Lodge Free and Accepted Masons of the State of New York**
Committee on Publications, 71 West 23 St., New York, NY 10010.
● Empire State Mason. bi-m. ISSN 0013-6794

**Grand Lodge of Montana, Ancient Free & Accepted Masons**
● Montana Masonic News. (pub. by Bell-Arm Corp.)

**Grand Lodge of Oklahoma, Ancient Free and Accepted Masons**
524 E. College, Guthrie, OK 73044.
● Oklahoma Mason. m. ISSN 0030-1779

**Grand River Dam Authority**
Vinita, OK 74301.
● Oklahoma's Grand River Dam Authority. Annual Report. a. ISSN 0078-4508

**Grande Ronde Review**
c/o Ben L. Hiatt, Box 475, Folsom, CA 95630.
● Grande Ronde Review; a journal of contemporary literature and ideas. 2 per yr. ISSN 0017-3150

**Granite Cutters International Association of America**
AFL-CIO, 18 Federal Ave., Quincy, MA 02169.
● Granite Cutters Journal. q. ISSN 0017-3207

**Granite Publications**
Box 774, Hanover, NH 03755.
● Granite. s-a. ISSN 0046-6298

**Chapman Grant, Ed. & Pub.**
1114 Idaho St., Escondido, CA 92027.
● Scientists Forum. irreg. ISSN 0080-777X

**Grantechs**
3240 No. Webster Rd., Tucson, AZ 85715.
● Grantechs. fortn. ISSN 0145-8302

**Grantsmanship Center**
1015 W. Olympic Blvd., Los Angeles, CA 90015.
● Grantsmanship Center News. bi-m. ISSN 0364-3115

**Grapevine**
c/o M. M. Chambers, Ed., Dept. of Educational Administration, Illinois State University, Normal, IL 61761.
● Grapevine; state appropriations for higher education; state tax legislation; legislation affecting education beyond the high school. m.

**Grapevine (Saratoga)**
c/o L. Ransil, 19801 Braemar Dr., Saratoga, CA 95070.
● Grapevine (Saratoga) irreg. ISSN 0092-0592

**Graphic Arts International Union**
1900 L St. NW, Washington, DC 20036.
● Graphic Arts Unionist. bi-m. ISSN 0017-3363

**Graphic Arts International Union. Contract & Research Department**
1900 L St., Washington, DC 20036.
● G.A.I.U. Handbook of Wages, Hours and Fringe Benefits. irreg. ISSN 0094-4211

**Graphic Arts Technical Foundation**
4615 Forbes Ave., Pittsburgh, PA 15213.
● G A T F Capsule Report. m.
● G A T F Education Report. q.
● G A T F Environmental Control Report. 4 per yr. ISSN 0046-2241
● G A T F Health and Safety News. q.
● G A T F Technical Services Report. q.
● Graphic Arts Abstracts. m. ISSN 0017-3282
● Graphic Arts Technical Foundation. Research Project Report. irreg. (approx. 2-10 per yr)
● N S T F Report. s-a. (National Scholarship First Fund)

**Graphic Arts Trade Journal International Inc.**
280 Main St., Box 81, Farmingdale, Long Island, NY 11735.
● Graphic Arts USA. bi-m.

**Graphic Publications, Inc.**
261 S.W. 6th St., Miami, FL 33130.
● Go Boating. m. ISSN 0017-145X

**Graphic Publishing Corporation**
Box 573, Reading, PA 19603.
● Gazeta Readingska; the Polish newspaper. w.
● Pennsylvania Jewish Life. m. ISSN 0031-4552

**Grass Roots Publishing Co.**
617 E. Valley Blvd, San Gabriel, CA 91776.
● Grass Roots Forum; a paper for thinking people. q. ISSN 0017-3517

**Grassroots Collective**
Blake St., Berkeley, CA 94704.
● Grassroots (Berkeley) s-m.

**Gratz College**
10th St. & Tabor Road, Philadelphia, PA 19141.
● Annual of Jewish Studies. a.

**Kenneth V. Graves**
261 South St., Wrentham, MA 02093.
● Graves Family Newsletter. q.

**Earl G. Graves Publishing Co.**
295 Madison Ave., New York, NY 10017.
● Black Enterprise. m. ISSN 0006-4165

**Gravida, Ltd.**
P.O. Box 118, Bayville, NY 11709.
● Gravida; a quarterly journal of poetry. q. (Women's Poetry Collective)

**Gravure Research Institute**
22 Manhasset Avenue, Port Washington, NY 11050.
● G R I Newsletter. irreg. (approx. 3-4 per yr.) ISSN 0534-0489

**Gravure Research Institute. Environmental and O S H A Committee**
22 Manhasset Ave., Port Washington, NY 11050.
● Gravure Environmental and O S H A Newsletter. (Occupational Safety and Health Act) irreg. (approx. 3-4 yr.) ISSN 0091-5203 (Co-Sponsor: Gravure Technical Association)

**Gravure Technical Association Inc.**
c/o Warren R. Daum, 60 E. 42nd St., New York, NY 10017.
● Gravure Technical Association Bulletin. q. ISSN 0017-3576

**Gray Panther News**
3700 Chestnut St., Philadelphia, PA 19104.
● Gray Panther News. irreg.

**Graybar Electric Co.**
420 Lexington Ave., New York, NY 10017.
● Graybar Outlook. m. ISSN 0017-3592

**Graycroft Press**
145 E. Main St., Cambridge, NY 12816.
● Omega. q.

**Gray's Sporting Journal Co.**
1330 Beacon St., Brookline, MA 02146.
● Gray's Sporting Journal. 7 per yr.

**Great Blafigria-IS**
c/o John R. Boland, Box 1054, Santa Fe, NM 87501.
● Great Blafigria-IS. 3 per yr.

**Great Falls Genealogical Society**
1405 2nd Ave. N.W., Great Falls, MT 59404.
● Treasure State Lines. q.

**Great Lakes Basin Commission**
3475 Plymouth Rd., Box 999, Ann Arbor, MI 48106.
● Communicator (Ann Arbor) m. ISSN 0045-7671
● Great Lakes Basin Commission. Annual Report. a.

**Great Lakes Commission**
2200 Bonisteel Blvd., Ann Arbor, MI 48109.
● Great Lakes Commission. Report to the States. biennial. ISSN 0533-196X
● Great Lakes News Letter. bi-m. ISSN 0017-3665
● Great Lakes Research Checklist. s-a. ISSN 0072-7326

**Great Lakes Fishery Commission**
1451 Green Rd., Ann Arbor, MI 48105.
● Great Lakes Fishery Commission (United States and Canada) Annual Report. a. ISSN 0072-7296
● Great Lakes Fishery Commission (United States and Canada) Technical Report. irreg., no. 28, 1975. ISSN 0072-730X

**Great Lakes Historical Society**
480 Main St., Vermilion, OH 44089.
● Inland Seas. q. ISSN 0020-1537

**Great Lakes Maritime Institute**
Dossin Great Lakes Museum, Belle Isle, Detroit, MI 48207.
● Telescope. 6 per yr(plus supplements) ISSN 0040-2702

**Great Lakes Press**
Harbor Island, Maple City Postal Sta., MI 49664 (and 3750 Nixon Rd., Ann Arbor, MI 48106)
● Limnos. q. ISSN 0024-3604
● Seaway Review; voice of the lakes. q. ISSN 0037-0487

**Great Neck Newsmagazine Group Ltd.**
17 Barstow Rd. Suite 302, Great Neck, NY 11021.
● College & Pro Football Newsweekly. w. during season.

**Great Northwest Publications**
12221 N.E. 8th St., Bellevue, WA 98005.
● View Northwest. m.

**Great Plains National Instructional Television Library**
Box 80669, Lincoln, NE 68501.
● G P Newsletter. m. (Sep.-May)
● Great Plains National Instructional Television Library. Recorded Visual Instruction. a.

**Great Society Press**
451 Heckman St., Phillipsburg, NJ 08865.
● Press Booklets. s-a. ISSN 0032-7816

**Great Turtle Enterprises, Inc.**
Box 153-B, Kingston, NY 12401.
● Woodstock Aquarian. q. ISSN 0049-7932

**Greater Boston Diabetes Society Inc.**
1330 Beacon St., Brookline, MA 02146.
● Diabetes Newsletter. 5 per yr. ISSN 0012-1827

**Greater Cincinnati Chamber of Commerce**
120 West Fifth Street, Cincinnati, OH 45202.
● Cincinnati. m. ISSN 0009-689X

**Greater Cleveland Genealogy Society**
Box 9639, Cleveland, OH 44140.
● Certified Copy. m. (except July)

**Greater Cleveland Growth Association**
690 Union Commerce Bldg., Cleveland, OH 44115.
● Clevelander. m. ISSN 0009-8892

**Greater Detroit Building Trade Council**
10800 Puritan, Detroit, MI 48238.
● Building Tradesman. w. ISSN 0007-3717

**Greater Detroit Chamber of Commerce**
150 Michigan Ave., Detroit, MI 48226.
● Detroiter Business News. fortn.

**Greater Europe Mission**
P.O. Box 668, Wheaton, IL 60187.
● Greater Europe Report. bi-m.

**Greater Freehold Chamber of Commerce**
● Mid-Monmouth Panorama. (pub. by Panorama International Inc.)

**Greater Harrisburg Region Central Labor Council**
● Central Pennsylvania Labor News. (pub. by Pennsylvania Labor News Publishing Co.)

**Greater Hartford Council on Alcoholism. Capitol Region Drug Information Center**
179 Allyn Street, Hartford, CT 06103.
● Greater Hartford Council on Alcoholism Newsletter; Capitol Region Drug Information Center Newsletter. bi-m.

**Greater Hartford Publishing Co. Inc.**
9 Lewis St., Hartford, CT 06103.
● Greater Hartford. m. (combined issues Jul.-Aug. & Dec.-Jan.)

**Greater Kansas City Dental Society**
17 W. Gregory Blvd., Kansas City, MO 64114.
● Midwestern Dentist. m. ISSN 0026-3478

**Greater Milwaukee Dental Association**
161 W. Wisconsin Ave., Milwaukee, WI 53203.
● Greater Milwaukee Dental Bulletin. m. ISSN 0017-3754

**Greater Milwaukee Federation of Lutheran Churches-Missouri Synod**
6914 W. Appleton Ave., Milwaukee, WI 53216.
● Badger Lutheran. s-m.

**Greater Minneapolis Chamber of Commerce**
6601 West 78th St., Minneapolis, MN 55435.
● Greater Minneapolis. bi-m.

**Greater New York Bridge Association**
309 E. 87 St, New York, NY 10028.
● Post Mortem. 6 per yr. ISSN 0032-5279

**Greater New York Taxpayers Association**
770 Broadway, New York, NY 10003.
● Real Estate News. m. ISSN 0034-0766

**Greater Newark Chamber of Commerce**
50 Park Place, Newark, NJ 07102.
● Metro-Newark; the magazine of metropolitan New Jersey. bi-m.

**Greater North Dakota Association**
Box 2467, 107 Roberts Street, Fargo, ND 58102.
● North Dakota Horizons. q.

**Greater Omaha Chamber of Commerce**
1620 Dodge, 21st Floor, Omaha, NE 68102.
● Omaha Profile. s-m. ISSN 0030-221X

**Greater St. Louis Dental Society**
200 S. Bemiston St., St. Louis, MO 63105.
● Greater St. Louis Dental Society. Bulletin. irreg. ISSN 0072-7369

**Greater San Antonio Chamber of Commerce**
602 E. Commerce, San Antonio, TX 78296.
● San Antonian; voice of the chamber of commerce. bi-m. ISSN 0036-3952
● San Antonio. m. ISSN 0036-3960

**Greater San Francisco Chamber of Commerce**
465 California St., San Francisco, CA 94104.
● San Francisco Business. s-m(alternately as magazine & newsletter) ISSN 0036-410X

**Greater Yakima Chamber of Commerce**
Box 1498, Yakima, WN 98907.
● Working Together for a Greater Yakima. m.

**Greek-American Review**
360 W. 36th St., New York, NY 10018.
● Campana. s-m. ISSN 0022-8206

**Greek Archdiocese Press**
8 E. 79th St., New York, NY 10021.
● Orthodox Observer. fortn. (Greek Orthodox Archdiocese of America)

**Greek Orthodox Archdiocese of America**
● Orthodox Observer. (pub. by Greek Archdiocese Press)

**Greek Sunday News**
c/o William A. Harris, 231 Harrison Ave., Boston, MA 02111.
● Greek Sunday News/Kyriakatika Nea. w.

**Greek World Press**
2039 Broadway, New York, NY 10023.
● Greek World; the magazine for the friends of Greece. bi-m.

**F. F. Greeley, Ed. & Pub.**
Box 330, Syracuse, NY 13201.
● American Bullmastiff. q. ISSN 0002-774X

**Warren H. Green**
10 S. Brentwood Blvd., St. Louis, MO 63105.
● Affirmative Action Register; for effective equal opportunity recruitment. m.
● Modern Concepts of Allergy. 3-4 per yr.
● Modern Concepts of Cardiology. 3-4 per yr.
● Modern Concepts of Dermatology. 3-4 per yr.
● Modern Concepts of Education. 3-4 per yr.
● Modern Concepts of Industrial Medicine. 3-4 per yr.
● Modern Concepts of Medical Virology, Oncology and Cytology. irreg. ISSN 0544-6511
● Modern Concepts of Neurology. 3-4 per yr.
● Modern Concepts of Orthopedic Surgery. 3-4 per yr.
● Modern Concepts of Pathology. 3-4 per yr.
● Modern Concepts of Philosophy. 3-4 per yr.
● Modern Concepts of Pulmonary Disease. 3-4 per yr.
● Modern Concepts of Radiology, Nuclear Medicine and Ultrasound. 3-4 per yr.

● Modern Concepts of Surgery. 3-4 per yr.
● Monographs in Modern Concepts of Philosophy. irreg. ISSN 0085-3542

**Green Mountain Club, Inc.**
Box 94, Rutland, VT 05701.
● Long Trail News. q.

**Green Mountain Editions**
462 N. Main St., Oshkosh, WI 54901.
● Green Mountain Quarterly. q.

**Green Mountain Post**
Box 269, RFD 1, Montague, MA 01351.
● Green Mountain Post. irreg. ISSN 0028-4262

**Green River Community College. Associated Student Body**
12401 SE 320th St., Auburn, WA 98002.
● Green River Current. w. ISSN 0017-3991

**Green River Press, Inc.**
SVSC Box 56, University Center, MI 48710.
● Green River Review. 3 per yr. ISSN 0017-4009
● International Poetry Review. s-a.

**Green World**
P.O. Drawer LW, University Sta., Baton Rouge, LA 70803.
● Green World; a journal of verse. s-a. ISSN 0017-4025

**Percy Greene, Ed. & Pub.**
406 1/2 N Farish St., Jackson, MS 39202.
● Jackson Advocate. w. ISSN 0047-1704

**Greenfield Publishing Co.**
1025 N. WashingtonSt., Greenfield, OH 45123.
● Garden Path. q. ISSN 0016-4607 (Ohio Association of Garden Clubs)

**Greenfield Review Press**
Greenfield Center, NY 12833.
● Greenfield Review; a magazine of the arts. q. ISSN 0017-4041
● Greenfield Review Chapbook. irreg.

**Green's Magazine**
c/o David Green, Ed., Box 313, Detroit, MI 48231.
● Green's Magazine; fiction for the family. q.

**Greensboro Printing Co.**
2614 High Point Rd., Greensboro, NC 27403.
● Tarheel Principal. 3 per yr. ISSN 0039-9671 (North Carolina Education Association. Division of Principals)

**Greentree Publishing Corporation**
18 New Hempstead Rd., P.O. Box 9, New City, NY 10956.
● Caribbean Business Review. m.

**Greenwood Press**
51 Riverside Ave., Westport, CT 06880.
● African Bibliographic Center, Washington, D.C. Special Bibliographic Series. irreg. ISSN 0065-3934
● Contributions in American History. irreg. ISSN 0084-9219
● Contributions in American Studies. irreg. ISSN 0084-9227
● Contributions in Economics and Economic History. irreg. ISSN 0084-9235
● Contributions in Intercultural and Comparative Studies. irreg.
● Contributions in Librarianship and Information Science. irreg. ISSN 0084-9243
● Contributions in Military History. irreg. ISSN 0084-9251
● Contributions in Philosophy. irreg. ISSN 0084-926X
● Contributions in Sociology. irreg. ISSN 0084-9278
● Index to Current Urban Documents. q. ISSN 0046-8908
● Studies in Human Rights. irreg. ISSN 0146-3586

**William Greer, Ed. & Pub.**
142 W. Brookdale Place, Fullerton, CA 92632.
● Writer's Notes and Quotes. q. ISSN 0043-955X

**Greyhound Corporation**
Greyhound Tower, Phoenix, AZ 85077.
● Go Greyhound. q. ISSN 0017-1476

**Greystone Park Psychiatric Hospital**
Greystone Park, NJ 07950.
● Physchogram. q. ISSN 0033-2844
● Psychogram. s-a.

**Greystone Publishers, Inc.**
Box 1668, Columbia, SC 29202.
● Sandlapper; the magazine of South Carolina. m. ISSN 0036-4290

**Greyton H. Taylor Wine Museum**
Bully Hill Rd., Hammondsport, NY 14840.
● Vineyard View. q.

**W. B. Griffin**
919 N. Michigan Ave., Chicago, IL 60611.
● Modern Metals. m. ISSN 0026-8127

**Griffin Publishing Co., Inc.**
1160 Park Square Bldg., Boston, MA 02116.
● Griffin Report of New England. m. ISSN 0017-422X

**E. V. Griffith, Ed. & Pub.**
3118 K. St., Eureka, CA 95501.
● Poetry Now. bi-m.

**Griffith Observatory**
2800 E. Observatory Rd., Los Angeles, CA 90027.
● Griffith Observer. m.

**Grilled Flowers**
c/o Frank Graziano, Jr., Ed., Poetry Center, University of Arizona, Tucson, AZ 85719.
● Grilled Flowers. s-a.

**Grist Press**
195 Lakeview Avenue, Cambridge, MA 02130.
● Grist. 3 per yr.

**Denny Griswold, Ed. & Pub.**
127 E. 80th St., New York, NY 10021.
● Public Relations News. w. ISSN 0033-3697

**Grit Publishing Co.**
208 W. Third St., Williamsport, PA 17701.
● Grit. w. ISSN 0017-4289

**Grocer's Advisor**
2416 W. Whittier Blvd., Montebello, CA 90640.
● Brand Guide and Directory. irreg. ISSN 0362-9651

**Grocers Publishing Co. Inc.**
370 Lexington Ave., New York, NY 10017.
● Modern Grocer. w(English edt.); m(Spanish edt.) ISSN 0026-7805

**Grocery Distribution Magazine**
39 S. LaSalle St., Chicago, IL 60603.
● Grocery Distribution. bi-m.

**Grocery Industry Services, Inc.**
30 Frederick St., Morristown, NJ 07960.
● Grocery Industry Directory of Metropolitan New York. a. ISSN 0072-7709

**Grocery Trade Publishing Co.**
21 Ontario Rd., Bellerose, NY 11426.
● American Grocer; an independent journal and trade review. bi-m. ISSN 0002-8665

**Grolier Yearbook, Inc.**
Sherman Turnpike, Danbury, CT 06816.
● Encyclopedia Year Book. a.

**Grosse Point Public Library**
10 Kercheval Ave., Grosse Pointe, MI 48236.
● Grosse Pointe Public Library. Newsletter. irreg (2-4 per yr.) ISSN 0017-4610 (Friends of the Grosse Pointe Public Library)

**Grosse Point Yacht Club**
● Grosse Pointer. (pub. by Detroit Publication Consultants)

**Grosset & Dunlap**
51 Madison Ave., New York, NY 10010.
● Witches Almanac. a.

**Richard Grossinger, Ed. & Pub.**
R.F.D. 2 Box 135, Creamery Rd, Plainfield, VT 05667.
● Io. irreg., approx. 2 per yr. ISSN 0021-0331

**Grossman Publishers, Inc.**
625 Madison Ave., New York, NY 10022.
● Science Jackdaws. irreg.

**Grossmont Education Association**
Grossmont Union High School District, 9131 Fletcher Parkway, Suite 118, La Mesa, CA 92041.
● Grossmont Educator. m.(Sept-June) ISSN 0016-3635

**Ground Zero**
Box 91415, Cleveland, OH 44101.
● Ground Zero. irreg.

**Group for the Advancement of Psychiatry**
419 Park Ave. S., New York, NY 10016.
● Group for the Advancement of Psychiatry. Report. irreg., no. 92, 1975. ISSN 0072-775X

**Group Health Association of America, Inc.**
1717 Massachusetts Ave. N.W., Washington, DC 20036.
● Group Health News. m.

**Group Research Inc.**
Room 422, 1404 New York Ave. N.W., Washington, DC 20005.
● Group Research Report. m. ISSN 0017-4742

**Grove Press**
c/o Random House, 201 E. 50 St., New York, NY 10022.
● Writings of the Left. irreg.

**Growth Fund Guide**
Box 2109, San Clemente, CA 92672.
● Growth Fund Guide. m. ISSN 0017-4831

**Growth Industry News**
471 Glenbrook Rd., Stamford, CT 06906.
● Growth Industry News. 12 per yr.

**Growth Publishing Co. Inc.**
c/o Dr. Boris Sokoloff, Managing Ed., Southern Bio-Research Institute, Florida Southern College, Lakeland, FL 33802.
● Growth; devoted to problems of normal and abnormal growth. q. ISSN 0017-4793 (Southern Bio-Research Institute)

**Growth Stock Outlook Inc.**
4405 East West Highway, Box 9911, Bethesda, MD 20014.
● Growth Stock Outlook. s-m.
● Junior Growth Stocks. s-m.

**Fred Gruenberger**
Box 272, Calabasas, CA 91302.
● Popular Computing. m.

**Grumman Aerospace Corporation**
Bethpage, NY 11714.
● Grumman Aerospace Horizons. q. ISSN 0095-7615

**Grune & Stratton, Inc.**
(Subsidiary of: Harcourt Brace Jovanovich, Inc.) 111 5th Ave., New York, NY 10003.
● Advances in Blood Grouping. irreg., 1970, vol. 3. ISSN 0065-2288
● American Psychopathological Association. Publications. irreg., 1970, vol. 26, 59th meeting. ISSN 0065-9886
● Audio Journal Review: General Surgery. m. ISSN 0090-998X
● Audio Journal Review: Ophthalmology. m.
● Blood: the Journal of Hematology. m. ISSN 0006-4971
● Cardiovascular Diseases; Current Status and Advances. irreg.
● Cerebral Vascular Diseases. Conference. irreg., 9th, 1975. ISSN 0069-2255
● Clinical Cardiology Monographs. irreg.
● Clinical Endocrinology. irreg., 1968, vol. 2. ISSN 0069-4819
● Comprehensive Psychiatry. bi-m. ISSN 0010-440X (American Psychopathological Association)
● Contemporary Neurology Symposia. irreg. ISSN 0069-9454
● Current Psychiatric Therapies. a. ISSN 0070-2080
● Immunopathology; Symposium on Immunopathology. irreg., 1968, 5th. ISSN 0073-5531
● International Congress of the Transplantation Society. Proceedings. a., 5th, 1975, The Hague. ISSN 0074-3984
● International Symposium on Plastic and Reconstructive Surgery of the Face and Neck. Proceedings. irreg., 1st, 1972.

● Journal of Pediatric Surgery. bi-m. ISSN 0022-3468 (American Academy of Pediatrics. Surgical Section) (Co-sponsor: British Association of Pediatric Surgeons)
● Journal of Special Education. q. ISSN 0022-4669 (Buttonwood Farms, Inc.)
● Metabolism; clinical and experimental. m.
● Modern Surgical Monographs. irreg. ISSN 0540-5556
● Neuroradiology Workshop. irreg. ISSN 0077-7838
● Professional School Psychology. irreg., 1969, vol. 3. ISSN 0079-5933
● Progress in Atomic Medicine. irreg., 1971, vol.3. ISSN 0085-5189
● Progress in Cardiovascular Diseases. bi-m. ISSN 0033-0620
● Progress in Clinical Cancer. irreg. ISSN 0079-6166
● Progress in Clinical Pathology. a. ISSN 0079-6174
● Progress in Clinical Psychology. irreg., 1971, vol. IX. ISSN 0079-6182
● Progress in Gastroenterology. irreg., 1970, vol. 2. ISSN 0079-6271
● Progress in Gynecology. irreg., vol. 6, 1975. ISSN 0079-6298
● Progress in Haematology. irreg., vol. 8, 1973. ISSN 0079-6301
● Progress in Hemostasis. irreg.
● Progress in Learning Disabilities. irreg. ISSN 0079-6387
● Progress in Liver Diseases. irreg., 1969, vol.3. ISSN 0079-6409
● Progress in Neuropathology. a.
● Progress in Nuclear Medicine. irreg., vol. 4, 1974. ISSN 0079-6581
● Progress in Radiation Therapy. irreg., 1965, vol. 3. ISSN 0079-6735
● Review of Special Education. a(approx.) ISSN 0091-5580
● Seminars in Arthritis & Rheumatism. q. ISSN 0049-0172
● Seminars in Nuclear Medicine. q.
● Seminars in Oncology. q. ISSN 0093-7754
● Social Psychiatry. a. ISSN 0095-0858 (American Association for Social Psychiatry)
● Transplantation Proceedings. q. ISSN 0041-1345 (Transplantation Society)

**Gryphon House**
1333 Connecticut Ave., N.W., Washington, DC 20036.
● Critical Issues in Urban Management Series. irreg.

**Gryphon Press**
220 Montgomery St, Highland Park, NJ 08904.
● Mental Measurements Yearbook. irreg. (every 3-5 yrs.) ISSN 0076-6461 (Institute of Mental Measurements)
● Tests in Print. irreg.

**Guest Relations Association**
c/o G. W. F. Associates, 9 Ryan Road, Englishtown, NJ 07726.
● Visitor. bi-m.

**Guidance Exchange**
3310 Rochambeau Ave., Bronx, NY 10467.
● Guidance Exchange; the annual digest of current recommended guidance literature. a. ISSN 0017-520X

**Guidance Publications**
Box 641, Salem, IL 62881.
● Grover Brinkman's Back Home in Illinois. q.

**Guide Services, Inc.**
2161 Monroe Dr. N.E., P.O. Box 13446, Atlanta, GA 30324.
● American Motor Carrier Directory: Illinois-Missouri Edition. a. (American Trucking Associations)
● American Motor Carrier Directory: Middle Atlantic Edition. a. (American Trucking Associations)
● American Motor Carrier Directory: National Edition. s-a. (American Trucking Associations)
● American Motor Carrier Directory: New England Edition. a. (American Trucking Associations)
● American Motor Carrier Directory: Pacific States Edition. a. (American Trucking Associations)
● American Motor Carrier Directory: Southeastern Edition. a. (American Trucking Associations)
● American Motor Carrier Directory: Specialized Services Edition. a. (American Trucking Associations)

● National Distribution Directory. a. ISSN 0077-4219 (Local and Short Haul Carriers National Conference)

**Guide to Reprints, Inc.**
Box 249, Kent, CT 06757.
● Guide to Reprints. a. ISSN 0072-8667

**Guidelines Publications**
Box 456, Orinda, CA 94563.
● Chronolog. m.
● Guidelines Architectural Letter. m.

**Guideposts Associates, Inc.**
Carmel, NY 10512.
● Guideposts. m. ISSN 0017-5331

**Guides to Multinational Business, Inc.**
Box 92, Boston, MA 02138.
● American Executive Travel Companion. a. ISSN 0363-535X
● Multinational Executive Travel Companion. a.

**Francis A. Guido, Ed. and Pub.**
Box 668, San Mateo, CA 94401.
● Western Railroader and Western Railfan. m.

**Guild Book Service**
Box 14064, Norfolk, VA 23518.
● International Guild Guide. irreg. ISSN 0361-4220

**Guild for Religious Architecture**
1777 Church St. N.W., Washington, DC 20036.
● Faith and Form. s-a. ISSN 0014-7001

**Guild of Carillonneurs in North America**
Route No. 2, Bryan, OH 43506.
● Randschriften; A Newsletter for the Guild of Carillonneurs. s-a. ISSN 0085-5383

**Guild of Prescription Opticians of America**
1250 Connecticut Ave. N.W., Washington, DC 20036.
● Guild of Prescription Opticians of America. Reference List. a. ISSN 0072-8977

**Guild of Professional Translators**
5914 Pulaski Ave., Philadelphia, PA 19144.
● Professional Translator. bi-m. ISSN 0364-5568
● Russian-English Terms Exchange. m. ISSN 0364-555X
● Translator Referral Directory. a. ISSN 0096-3259

**Guild of Shaker Crafts**
401 West Savidge St., Spring Lake, MI 49456.
● World of Shaker. q.

**Guilford College. Department of Mathematics**
Greensboro, NC 27410.
● Journal of Undergraduate Mathematics. s-a. ISSN 0022-5339

**Guitar Players International**
● Guitar Player. (pub. by G.P.I. Corporation)

**Gulcher**
Box 635, Bloomington, IN 47401.
● Gulcher; Bloomington's musicpaper. q.

**Gulf and Caribbean Fisheries Institute**
4600 Rickenbacker Causeway, Miami, FL 33149.
● Gulf and Caribbean Fisheries Institute. Annual Proceedings. a. ISSN 0072-9019

**Gulf Coast History and Humanities Conference**
● Gulf Coast Conference Proceedings. (pub. by University of West Florida)

**Gulf Coast Lumberman**
708-9-10 Cotton Exchange Bldg., Houston, TX 77002.
● Gulf Coast Lumberman and Building Material Distributor. m. ISSN 0017-5560

**Gulf Coast News Digest**
300 So. Royal St., Mobile, AL 36602.
● Gulf Coast News Digest. w. ISSN 0017-5579

**Gulf Coast Publishing Corp.**
Box 2087, Beaumont, TX 77704.
● Gulf Coast Cattleman. m. ISSN 0017-5552

**Gulf Coast Research Laboratory**
Ocean Springs, MS 39564.
● Gulf Coast Research Laboratory. Publications of the Museum. irreg.
● Gulf Research Reports. a. ISSN 0072-9027

**Gulf General Atomic Inc.**
P.O. Box 81608, San Diego, CA 92138.
- General Atomic Company. Library. Journal of Holdings of the Library. a. ISSN 0072-0712

**Gulf Oil Corporation**
Gulf Bldg., Box 1166, Pittsburgh, PA 15230.
- Orange Disc. bi-m.

**Gulf Publishing Co.**
3301 Allen Parkway, P. O. Box 2608, Houston, TX 77001.
- Composite Catalog of Oil Field Equipment & Services. biennial.
- Hydrocarbon Processing. m. ISSN 0018-8190
- Ocean Industry. m. ISSN 0029-8026
- Pipe Line Industry; crude oil products, gas transmission and gas distribution. m. ISSN 0032-0145
- Texas A & M Oceanographic Studies. irreg. ISSN 0082-2922 (Texas A & M University)
- Topics in Ocean Engineering. irreg. ISSN 0085-7297 (Texas A & M University)
- World Oil. 14 per yr. ISSN 0043-8790

**Gulfshore Publishing Company, Inc.**
1039 Fifth Ave. North, Naples, FL 33940.
- Gulfshore Life; the delineator of community activities on the platinum coast. m (Nov.-Apr)

**Bill Gulley, Ed. & Pub.**
Box 3477, Madison, WI 53703.
- Zanzibar. 3-4 per yr.

**Guns Annual Book of Handguns**
c/o George von Rosen, 8150 N. Central Pk, Skokie, IL 60076.
- Guns Annual Book of Handguns. a.

**Guns Magazine**
8142 N. Lawndale, Skokie, IL 60076.
- Redbook of Used Gun Values. a. ISSN 0484-1689

**Gustavus Adolphus College**
Saint Peter, MN 56082.
- Minnesota English Journal. 3 per yr.

**Guthrie Foundation for Medical Research**
Sayre, PA 18840.
- Guthrie Bulletin. q. ISSN 0094-369X

**C. B. Guthrie Tariff Bureau**
Suite 300, 1334 G. Street, N.W., Washington, DC 20005.
- Official Freight Tariff Directory. m.

**Guthrie Theater Co**
- Minnesota Drama Editions. (pub. by University of Minnesota Press)

**Hubert P. Guy, Ed. & Pub.**
Box 404, La Mesa, CA 92041.
- Indian Trader. bi-m. ISSN 0046-9076

**Gwinnet Historical Society**
Box 261, Lawrenceville, GA 30245.
- Gwinnet Historical Society. Newsletter. q.

**Gypsy Table Series**
c/o Mother's Hen, Box 99592, San Francisco, CA 94109.
- Gypsy Table Series. 3-5 per yr.

**Gyst Publications**
Box 16, Pasadena, CA 91102.
- Rufus. 3 per yr.

**H. A. Lanzer Co.**
Main St., Union City, TN 38261.
- Cumberland Flag. m. ISSN 0011-2968

**H C C C Inc.**
30 E. 60th St., New York, NY 10022.
- Homosexual Counseling Journal. q. ISSN 0092-3052

**H D C Publications**
1010 Third Ave., New York, NY 10021.
- Designer. m. ISSN 0011-9431

**H I A S Inc.**
200 Park Ave. South, New York, NY 10003.
- H I A S. Statistical Abstract. q.
- H I A S Bulletin. s-a.

**H.I.C. Corporation**
Box W, Newport Beach, CA 92663.
- Heavy Duty Trucking. m. ISSN 0017-9434

**H P Publishing Co, Inc.**
575 Lexington Ave., New York, NY 10022.
- Hospital Practice. m. ISSN 0018-5809

**H. R. Industries, Inc.**
c/o Tichi Wilkerson Miles, Ed., 6715 Sunset Blvd., Hollywood, CA 90028.
- Hollywood Reporter. d. ISSN 0018-3660

**H T H Publishers**
1607-A E. Edinger, Santa Ana, CA 92705.
- Shuttle Craft Guild. Monographs. irreg; no. 28, 1969. ISSN 0080-9446

**H. W. Moore Equipment Co.**
Box 2491, Denver, CO 80201.
- Look Around. bi-m. ISSN 0024-6360

**Habari Barua**
1115 Fulton St., Brooklyn, NY 11238.
- Habari Barua. q. ISSN 0018-1250

**Habibi Publications**
726 Sutter Ave., Palo Alto, CA 94303.
- Habibi; Middle Eastern dance music, news, entertainment. m. (Subscr. to:, Box 4081, Mountain View, CA 94040)

**Habonim Labor Zionist Youth**
575 Sixth Ave., New York, NY 10011.
- Bagolah. 5 per yr. ISSN 0005-3929
- Hamaapil. q. ISSN 0017-6850

**Hacienda, Inc.**
Box 61-1197, 639 N.E. 125th St., North Miami, FL 33161.
- Anuario Latinoamericano. a. ISSN 0570-4359
- Hacienda. bi-m. ISSN 0017-6486

**Hackney Publications Inc.**
P.O. Box 630, Peekskill, NY 10566.
- Hackney Journal. bi-m. ISSN 0046-6700 (American Hackney Horse Society) (Co-sponsors: Mid-West Hackney Association; New England Hackney Society; Ohio Hackney Association; Michigan Hackney Club; Southeastern Hackney Association; Mid-America Hackney Association)

**Hadassah, the Women's Zionist Organization of America**
50 W. 58 St., New York, NY 10019.
- Hadassah Magazine. m.(Sept.-June) ISSN 0017-6516

**Hadassah Zionist Youth Commission**
817 Broadway, New York, NY 10003.
- Hamagshimim Newsletter. q.

**Hadoar Association, Inc.**
1841 Broadway, New York, NY 10023.
- Hadoar. w. ISSN 0017-6524 (Histadruth Ivrith of America)

**F. Haer & Co.**
Box 2138, Ann Arbor, MI 48106.
- Journal of Electrophysiological Techniques. q. ISSN 0361-0209

**Hafner Publishing Co., Inc.**
866 Third Ave., New York, NY 10022.
- Columbia University. Psychoanalytic Clinic for Training and Research. Proceedings of the Conference. irreg.
- Flora Neotropica. Monographs. a. ISSN 0071-5794 (Organization for Flora Neotropica)

**Hagedorn Publishing Co.**
235 Park Ave. So., New York, NY 10003.
- Real Estate Weekly. w.

**Joseph Haiek, Ed. & Pub.**
4367 Beverly Blvd., Box 74667, Los Angeles, CA 90004.
- Mideast Business Guide. a.

**Hairenik Association, Inc.**
212 Stuart St., Boston, MA 02116.
- Armenian Review. q. ISSN 0004-2366
- Armenian Weekly. w. ISSN 0004-2374
- Hairenik. d. ISSN 0017-677X

**Haitian Unity Council**
P.O. Box 707, Canal Street Station, New York, NY 10013.
- Unite; the Haitian-American paper. w.

**Halcyon Business Publications, Inc.**
432 Park Ave. S., New York, NY 10016.
- Area Development Magazine; the executive magazine of sites and facility planning. m. ISSN 0004-0908

**Halgo Publishing Inc.**
6305 Brookside Plaza, Kansas City, MO 64113.
- Heart of America Purchaser. m. ISSN 0017-9256 (Purchasing Management Association of Kansas City)
- Mid-Continent Purchaser. m. (Purchasing Management Association of Tulsa)

**G. K. Hall and Co.**
70 Lincoln Street, Boston, MA 02111.
- Africa South of the Sahara; Index to Periodical Literature. Supplements. irreg.
- Avery Index to Architectural Periodicals. Supplement. irreg. (Columbia University. Avery Architectural Library)
- Bibliographic Guide to Art and Architecture. a.
- Bibliographic Guide to Business and Economics. a. ISSN 0360-2702
- Bibliographic Guide to Conference Publications. a.
- Bibliographic Guide to Government Publications. a.
- Bibliographic Guide to Psychology. a.
- Bibliographic Guide to Technology. a.
- Index to Periodical Articles by and about Negroes. a. ISSN 0073-5973 (Central State University. Hallie Q. Brown Memorial Library) (Co-Sponsor: Schomburg Collection of Negro Literature and History)
- New York Academy of Medicine. Library. Subject Catalog of the Library. Supplement. irreg. ISSN 0099-0922

**George D. Hall Company**
20 Kilby St., Boston, MA 02109.
- New England Industrial Service Directory. irreg.

**Wilton E. Hall Publisher**
Anderson, SC 29621.
- National Stamp News. 3 per m. ISSN 0028-0232 (National Philatelic Society)
- Quote Magazine. w. ISSN 0033-667X

**Hall Associates**
Box 482, Stamford, CT 06904.
- Journal of Clinical Pharmacology. bi-m. ISSN 0091-2700 (American College of Clinical Pharmacology)

**Hall Publications**
Box H, Brewster, New York, NY 10509.
- Sunday Funday; a fun paper for boys and girls. w. ISSN 0049-2515

**Hall Radio Report**
c/o Douglas E. Hall, 30 Ten O'Clock Lane, Weston, CT 06880.
- Hall Radio Report. w.

**Eds. & Pubs. John Halmaghi & Vasile Posteuca**
215 Valley Dr., Pittsburgh, PA 15215.
- Drum; revista de cultura romaneasca. q.

**Halsted Press**
(Subsidiary of: John Wiley & Sons, Inc.)
605 Third Ave., New York, NY 10016.
- Advances in Aerosol Physics. irreg., vol. 7, 1973.
- Analytical Chemistry of the Elements Series. irreg., unnumbered, 1975 latest.
- British Political Sociology Yearbook. a.
- International Biodeterioration Symposium. Proceedings. Biodeterioration of Materials. irreg.
- International Conference on Global Impacts of Applied Microbiology. Proceedings. irreg., 1970 latest. ISSN 0074-3097
- Machine Intelligence Workshop. a. ISSN 0076-2032
- Primates; comparative anatomy and taxonomy. irreg., 1970, vol. 8. ISSN 0079-5100
- Programme for Growth Series. irreg., vol. 12, 1974.
- Shiloach Center for Middle Eastern & African Studies. Monograph Series. irreg., unnumbered, latest vol. 1973.

**Hamel Publishing Co., Inc.**
169 Pine St., Natick, MA 01760.
- Executive Mart. 5 per yr.

**Hamilton College**
Box 79, Clinton, NY 13323.
- Hamilton History and Political Science Review. s-m.

**Hamilton College. Trustees of Hamilton College**
Buttrick Hall, Clinton, NY 13323.
● Hamilton Alumni Review. q. ISSN 0017-7067

**Hamilton County Pharmaceutical Association**
320 Broadway, Cincinnati, OH 45202.
● Hamilton County Pharmacist. m. ISSN 0017-7075

**Hamline University. Midwestern School of Law**
1536 Hewitt Ave., St. Paul, MN 55104.
● Midwestern Advocate. m. during school yr. ISSN 0360-5094

**Hammer and Coffin Society**
Storke Student Pub. Bldg., Stanford University, CA 94305.
● Stanford Chaparral. 8 per yr. ISSN 0038-9757

**Hammer and Steel Newsletter**
Box 101, Mattapan, MA 02126.
● Hammer and Steel Newsletter. m. ISSN 0017-7105

**Anne M. Hammerman, Ed. & Pub.**
3160 Valerie Arms Dr., Dayton, OH 45405.
● Dayton Jewish Chronicle. w.

**Hammond Almanac, Inc.**
Maplewood, NJ 07040.
● Official Associated Press Almanac. a. ISSN 0090-208X (Associated Press)

**Hampden-Sydney Poetry Review**
Box 126, Hampden - Sydney, VA 23943.
● Hampden-Sydney Poetry Review. s-a.

**Hampshire College**
Amherst, MA 01002.
● Boxspring. s-a.

**Hampshire Swine Registry**
1111 Main St., Peoria, IL 61606.
● American Hampshire Herdsman. m. ISSN 0002-8681

**Hampton Books**
Route 1, Box 76, Newberry, SC 29108.
● C T V D: Cinema - TV - Digest; a quarterly review of the serious, foreign-language cinema-TV-press. q. ISSN 0007-9219

**Hampton Institute**
Box 6237, Stone Building, VA 23668.
● Hampton Script. s-m.

**Hampton Roads Educational Television Association, Inc.**
5200 Hampton Blvd., Norfolk, VA 23508.
● Fifth Dimension. m.

**Hampton Roads Science Fiction Association**
713 Paul St., Newport News, VA 23605.
● It Comes in the Mail. bi-m.

**Juanita Hancock, Ed. & Pub.**
1021 N. Madison, Eldorado, AR 71730.
● Webb Bulletin. q.

**Hand Book**
c/o R. Ratner, 50 Spring St., New York, NY 10012.
● Hand Book. s-a.

**Handbook of Florida Securities**
920 North Federal Highway, Box 835, Pompano Beach, FL 33061.
● Handbook of Florida Securities. a.

**Handcrafters News**
808 High Mountain Rd., Franklin Lakes, NJ 07417.
● Handcrafters News. m.

**Handweavers Guild of America, Inc.**
The Exchange, Farmington, CT 06032.
● Shuttle, Spindle & Dyepot. q. ISSN 0049-0423

**Handy and Harman**
850 Third Ave, New York, NY 10022.
● Silver Market. a. ISSN 0066-4332

**Carlton Haney Publications**
Rt. 2, Box 304, Elon College, NC 27244.
● Muleskinner News; magazine of blue grass and old time music. m. ISSN 0091-8733

**Hanging Loose Press**
231 Wyckoff St., Brooklyn, NY 11217.
● Hanging Loose. q.

**Hani Publications**
5636 E. Beverly Blvd., Los Angeles, CA 90022.
● Restaurant News. m. ISSN 0048-7406

**Hanover Insurance Co.**
440 Lincoln St., Worcester, MA 01605.
● Hanover News. q. ISSN 0017-7482

**Hansen Publishing Inc.**
6265 Forest, St. Louis, MO 63121.
● Automotive Messenger. m. ISSN 0045-1088
● St. Louis Bowling Review. s-m.

**Harbor Dental Society**
4220 Long Beach Blvd. 54200, Long Beach, CA 90807.
● Log. irreg. ISSN 0076-0447

**Harbor Lights**
1710 Oakwood Dr., Shoreview, MN 55112.
● Harbor Lights. 8 per yr.

**Harcourt Brace Jovanovich Health Care Publications**
4015 W. 65th St., Minneapolis, MN 55435.
● Hospital Formulary. m.
● Modern Medicine; journal of diagnosis and treatment. fortn. ISSN 0026-8070

**Harcourt Brace Jovanovich, Inc.**
757 Third Ave., New York, NY 10017
(Subscr. to: 1 E. First St., Duluth, MN 55802)
● Body Fashions/Intimate Apparel. m. ISSN 0360-3520
● Body Fashions-Intimate Apparel Directory. a. ISSN 0362-2452
● Brown's Directory of North American Gas Companies. a. ISSN 0068-2888
● Communications News. m. ISSN 0010-3632
● Dental Management. m. ISSN 0011-8680
● Drug and Cosmetic Industry. m. ISSN 0012-6527
● Electronic Technician/Dealer. m.
● Fast Service. m.
● Fast Service; drive-in, carry-out and family restaurants. m. ISSN 0363-5120
● Flooring; the magazine of interior surfaces. m.
● Food Management; schools, colleges, hospitals, nursing homes contract services. m. ISSN 0091-018X
● Gas Appliance Merchandising. bi-m. ISSN 0016-4879
● Hearing Instruments. m. ISSN 0092-4466
● Home and Auto. m. (with annual supplement)
● Home Horticulture. q. ISSN 0360-5639
● Hosiery and Underwear. m. ISSN 0018-5396
● Housewares. m. (s-m. in May) ISSN 0018-6538
● Kitchen Planning; for architects, consultants, designers and engineers. bi-m. ISSN 0300-7952
● L P-Gas. m. (with annual supplement) ISSN 0024-7103
● Market Maker. 7 per yr.
● Paper Sales. m. ISSN 0031-1170
● Paper Year Book. a.
● Pennsylvania Farmer. s-m. ISSN 0031-4471
● Pets/Supplies/Marketing. m.
● Physician's Management; the doctor's business journal. m. ISSN 0031-9066
● Practical Psychology for Physicians. m. ISSN 0095-0475
● Quick Frozen Foods Directory of Frozen Food Processors. a. ISSN 0079-9289
● Quick Frozen Foods Directory of Wholesale Distributors. biennial.
● Quick Frozen Foods International; food freezing, processing, distributing. q. ISSN 0033-6416
● R S I. (Roofing/Siding/Insulation) m. ISSN 0033-7129
● Rent-All Magazine. m. ISSN 0034-4516
● Selling Christmas Decorations. s-a. ISSN 0037-1602
● Snack Food. m. ISSN 0037-7406
● Telephone Engineer and Management; the telephone industry magazine. s-m. ISSN 0040-263X
● Telephone Engineer and Management Directory. a. ISSN 0082-2655
● Toys. m. ISSN 0041-0179
● Toys Directory. a.
● Toys Trade News. 6 per yr. during American Toy Fair.

**Hard Core News Printing Co-Op**
P.O. Box 66321, Houston, TX 77006.
● Hard Core News; newsletter of the Texas libertarian movement. irreg. ISSN 0085-1434

**Hard Rain, Inc.**
156 5th Ave., Rm. 601, New York, NY 10010.
● City Star. bi-w.

**Hardin-Simmons University**
Box P, H-SU Sta., Abilene, TX 79601.
● H S U Brand. s-w. ISSN 0017-6249

**A. R. Harding Publishing Co.**
2878 E. Main St., Columbus, OH 43209.
● Fur-Fish-Game. m. ISSN 0016-2922

**Hardwood Plywood Manufacturers Association**
P.O. Box 6246, Arlington, VA 22206.
● Where to Buy Hardwood Plywood and Veneer. a.

**William G. Hare, Ed. & Pub.**
Box 392, Newtown, CT 06470.
● Academic Journal; the educators' employment magazine. fortn.

**Hare Publications**
One Charles St., West Orange, NJ 07052.
● Pilot Showcase. m.

**Harian Publications**
1 Apricot St., Greenlawn, NY 11740.
● All About Arizona, the Healthful State. biennial.
● All of Mexico at Low Cost. biennial. ISSN 0533-0653
● America by Car. biennial. ISSN 0569-1966
● Bargain Paradises of the World. biennial; 1974, no. 16. ISSN 0408-568X
● Europe on a Shoe String. biennial.
● Fabulous Mexico; where everything costs less. biennial. ISSN 0429-9639
● How to Travel and Get Paid for It. biennial.
● Norman Ford's Florida. biennial. ISSN 0546-3432
● Travel Routes Around the World: Guide to Traveling Around the World by Passenger-Carrying Freighters. a. ISSN 0072-8772
● Where to Retire on a Small Income. biennial. ISSN 0511-8719

**Harley-Davidson Motor Co., Inc.**
Box 653, Milwaukee, WI 53201.
● Enthusiast. q. ISSN 0027-2167

**Harlo Press**
16721 Hamilton Ave., Detroit, MI 48203.
● Harlo's Anthology of Modern-Day Poets and Authors. a. ISSN 0090-2632

**Harness Horse, Inc.**
Telegraph Press Bldg., Box 1831, Harrisburg, PA 17105.
● Harness Horse. w. ISSN 0017-7857

**Harness Horsemen International, Inc.**
61 Cook Hill Road, Passante Professional Center, Windsor, CT 06095.
● International Trotter and Pacer. q. ISSN 0020-9023

**Harper and Row Publishers, Inc.**
10 East 53rd St., New York, NY 10022.
● Contempory Essay Series. irreg.
● Critical Issues in Education. irreg.
● Modern Perspectives in Biology Series. irreg.
● Nebula Award Stories. a. ISSN 0077-6408
● New Dimensions Science Fiction. irreg. ISSN 0099-0906
● Patterns of American Prejudice Series. irreg., 1969, no. 4. ISSN 0079-0192
● Perspectives on Marketing Series. irreg.
● Readers in Social Problems. irreg.
● Readings for Introduction to Teaching. irreg.
● Readings in Educational Psychology: Contemporary Perspectives. irreg. ISSN 0363-5953
● Series in Administration. irreg.
● Studies in Language. irreg.
● Wisdom of Tibet Series. irreg.
● World Perspectives. irreg., vol. 48, 1974. ISSN 0084-2168

**Harper & Row Publishers, Inc. Medical Department**
2350 Virginia Ave., Hagerstown, MD 21740.
● American Journal of Pathology. m. ISSN 0002-9440 (American Association of Pathologists)
● Clinical Obstetrics and Gynecology: a Quarterly Periodical. q. ISSN 0009-9201
● J O G N Nursing. (Journal of Obstetric, Gynecologic and Neonatal Nursing) bi-m. ISSN 0090-0311 (Nurses Association of the American College of Obstetricians and Gynecologists)
● Obstetrics and Gynecology. m. ISSN 0029-7844 (American College of Obstetricians and Gynecologists)
● Spine. q. ISSN 0362-2436

**Harper Hospital (Detroit) Department of Gynecology and Obstetrics**
- Harold C. Mack Symposium. Proceedings. (pub. by Charles C. Thomas, Publisher)

**Harper Square Press**
c/o Artcrest Products Co., 401 W. Ontario St., Chicago, IL 60610.
- Gallery Series: Poets. a. ISSN 0072-0097

**Harper's Magazine Co.**
2 Park Ave., New York, NY 10016.
- Harper's. m. ISSN 0017-789X

**Harpress Publications**
9212 Bishop, Detroit, MI 48224.
- Harbinger (Detroit) q. (Warren Education Association)

**Phillip Harris, Ed. & Pub.**
54 Margaret Ave., Lawrence, NY 11559.
- Library Employee Relations Newsletter. m.

**Harris Auction Galleries, Inc.**
873-875 N. Howard St., Baltimore, MD 21201.
- Harris Auction Galleries. Collectors' Auction. irreg. (approx. 5 per yr.) ISSN 0093-1047

**Harris Communications**
17915-B Sky Park Blvd., Irvine, CA 92714.
- Cleaning Management. bi-m. (American Institute of Maintenance)

**Harris Press**
250 Hudson St., New York, NY 10013.
- Who's Who in Baseball. a.

**Harris Publishing Co. (Cleveland)**
33140 Aurora Rd., Cleveland, OH 44139.
- Electronic Industry Telephone Directory. a. ISSN 0422-9053
- Electronic Representatives Directory. a.
- Harris Michigan Manufacturers Industrial Directory. a. ISSN 0363-1869
- Ohio Manufacturers Industrial Directory. a.
- Who's Who in Electronics. a. ISSN 0083-9507

**Harris Publishing, Inc. (Idaho Falls)**
P.O. Box 981, 520 Park Ave., Idaho Falls, ID 83401.
- Cutter and Chariot Racing World. 10 per yr. (World Cutter and Chariot Racing Association)
- Potato Grower of Idaho. m. (Potato Growers of Idaho, Inc.)
- Snowmobile West. 5 per yr.
- Sugar Producer. 10 per yr.

**Harrisburg Catholic Publishing Associates**
Box 2555, 2300 Market St, Harrisburg, PA 17105.
- Catholic Witness. w. ISSN 0008-8447 (Diocese of Harrisburg)

**Harrison Street Review**
4438 Harrison St., Kansas City, MO 64111.
- Harrison Street Review. irreg. (approx. a.)

**Harry Frank Guggenheim Foundation**
120 Broadway, New York, NY 10005.
- Harry Frank Guggenheim Foundation. Report. irreg.

**Harry S. Truman Library Institute**
Harry S. Truman Library, Independence, MO 64050.
- Whistle Stop; Harry S. Truman library institute newsletter. q.

**Harsh Publishing Co.**
Box 188, South Milwaukee, WI 53172.
- Lighting Systems. bi-m.

**Hart Publications, Inc. (Denver)**
Box 1917, Denver, CO 80201.
- Drill Bit; Southwestern petroleum news. m. ISSN 0012-6225
- Western Oil Reporter. m. ISSN 0043-3985

**Hart Publishing Co. (New York)**
15 West 4th St., New York, NY 10012.
- Applied Mathematics Series. irreg.

**Hartford Hospital**
c/o Medical Education, Hartford, CT 06115.
- Hartford Hospital Bulletin. q. ISSN 0017-7970

**Hartford Insurance Group**
Hartford Plaza, Hartford, CT 06115.
- Hartford Agent. 10 per yr. ISSN 0017-7962

**Hartford Seminary Foundation**
55 Elizabeth St., Hartford, CT 06015.
- Hartford Studies in Linguistics. irreg., latest issue no. 24. ISSN 0073-0432
- Muslim World; a journal devoted to the study of Islam and of Christiam-Muslim relationship in past and present. q. ISSN 0027-4909

**Hartford Steam Boiler Inspection and Insurance Co.**
56 Prospect St., Hartford, CT 06102.
- Locomotive. q.

**Hartman Communications, Inc.**
(Subsidiary of: Bill Communications, Inc.)
77 N. Miller Rd., Akron, OH 44313.
- Rubber World. m. ISSN 0035-9572

**Marion T. Hartung**
814 Constitution St., Emporia, KS 66801.
- Carnival Glass Price Guide. biennial. ISSN 0069-0708

**Hartwell Co.**
1617 W. 261 St., Harbor City, CA 90710.
- Chivalry. bi-m.
- English Genealogical Helper. q. ISSN 0361-7157
- Genealogical Library Quarterly. q.
- Heraldry. q.

**Harvard Divinity School**
45 Francis Ave., Cambridge, MA 02138.
- Harvard Divinity Bulletin. m. (Oct.-Jun.) ISSN 0017-8047

**Harvard Lampoon, Inc.**
44 Bow St., Cambridge, MA 02138.
- Harvard Lampoon. 5 per yr. ISSN 0017-8098

**Harvard Law Review Association**
Gannett House, Cambridge, MA 02138.
- Harvard Law Review. m. 8 per yr. ISSN 0017-811X

**Harvard Magazine, Inc.**
Wadsworth House, Cambridge, MA 02138.
- Harvard Magazine. bi-m.

**Harvard Public Health Alumni Association**
55 Shattuck St., Boston, MA 02215.
- Harvard Public Health Alumni Bulletin. s-a. ISSN 0017-8152

**Harvard School of Dental Medicine**
188 Longwood Ave., Boston, MA 02115.
- Harvard Dental Alumni Bulletin. 2 per yr. ISSN 0046-6891

**Harvard School of Public Health. Department of Nutrition**
665 Huntington Ave., Boston, MA 02115.
- Nutrition Reviews. m. ISSN 0029-6643 (Nutrition Foundation, Inc.)

**Harvard Ukrainian Research Institute**
1581-1583 Massachusetts Ave., Cambridge, MA 02138.
- Harvard Ukrainian Studies. (pub. by Peter de Ridder Press NE)
- Harvard Ukrainian Studies Newsletter. bi-m.
- Recenzija; a review of Soviet Ukrainian scholarly publications. s-a. ISSN 0034-1207

**Harvard University**
- Harvard Theological Review. (pub. by Scholars Press)
- Harvard Theological Studies. (pub. by Scholars Press)
- Review of Economics and Statistics. (pub. by North-Holland Publishing Co. NE)

**Harvard University. Aiken Computation Laboratory**
Cambridge, MA 02138.
- Harvard University. Computation Laboratory. Mathematical Linguistics and Automatic Translation; Report to National Science Foundation. irreg., 1970, no. 27. ISSN 0073-0769

**Harvard University. Botanical Museum**
Cambridge, MA 02138.
- American Orchid Society Bulletin. m. ISSN 0003-0252 (American Orchid Society Inc.)
- Botanical Museum Leaflets. irreg.(10 nos. to vol.) ISSN 0006-8098

**Harvard University. Center for International Affairs**
6 Divinity Ave., Cambridge, MA 02138.
- Harvard Studies in International Affairs. irreg., no. 34, 1975.

- Harvard University. Center for International Affairs. Annual Report. a. ISSN 0073-0734

**Harvard University. Center for Middle Eastern Studies**
- Harvard Middle Eastern Monographs. (pub. by Harvard University Press)
- Harvard Middle Eastern Studies. (pub. by Harvard University Press)

**Harvard University. Center for Studies in Education and Development**
Larsen Hall, 5Th Floor, Appian Way, Cambridge, MA 02138.
- Harvard University. Center for Studies in Education and Development. Annual Report. a. ISSN 0073-0742

**Harvard University. Charles Warren Center for Studies in American History**
Robinson Hall, Cambridge, MA 02138.
- Perspectives in American History. a. ISSN 0079-0990

**Harvard University Comics Society**
Box 21, Memorial Hall, Harvard University, Cambridge, MA 02138.
- Harvard Journal of Pictorial Fiction. s-a.

**Harvard University. Department of Economics**
- Quarterly Journal of Economics. (pub. by Wiley-Interscience)

**Harvard University. Department of Germanic Languages and Literatures**
- Harvard Germanic Studies. (pub. by Mouton Publishers NE)

**Harvard University. Department of History**
- Harvard Historical Monographs. (pub. by Harvard University Press)
- Harvard Historical Studies. (pub. by Harvard University Press)

**Harvard University. Department of Linguistics**
Cambridge, MA 02138.
- Formal Linguistics. irreg. ISSN 0361-0977

**Harvard University. Department of Romance Languages and Literature**
- Harvard Studies in Romance Languages. (pub. by Harvard University Press)

**Harvard University. East Asian Research Center**
- Harvard East Asian Monographs. (pub. by Harvard University Press)
- Harvard East Asian Series. (pub. by Harvard University Press)

**Harvard University. Graduate School of Business Administration**
Soldiers Field, Boston, MA 02163.
- Business History Review. q. ISSN 0007-6805
- Harvard Business Review. bi-m. ISSN 0017-8012
- Harvard Business School Bulletin. bi-m. ISSN 0017-8020
- Harvard Studies in Business History. (pub. by Harvard University Press)
- Harvard University. Graduate School of Business Administration. Program for Management Development. Publication. a. ISSN 0073-0785

**Harvard University. Graduate School of Business Administration. Baker Library**
Soldiers Field, Boston, MA 02163.
- Harvard University. Graduate School of Business Administration. Baker Library. Core Collection, an Author and Subject Guide. a.
- Harvard University. Graduate School of Business Administration. Baker Library. Current Periodical Publications in Baker Library. a.
- Harvard University. Graduate School of Business Administration. Baker Library. Kress Library of Business and Economics. Publications. irreg., 1972, no. 22. ISSN 0073-0777
- New Books in Business and Economics; recent additions to Baker Library. m.(Sept-June) ISSN 0028-4319
- Studies in Managerial Economics. irreg. ISSN 0585-6884

**Harvard University Graduate School of Design**
Gund Hall, Harvard University, 48 Quincy St., Cambridge, MA 02138.
- H G S D News. q.

**Harvard University. Graduate School of Education**
Longfellow Hall, 13 Appian Way, Cambridge, MA 02138.
- Harvard Educational Review. q. ISSN 0017-8055
- Harvard University. Graduate School of Education Association. Bulletin. 3 per yr. ISSN 0046-6905

**Harvard University. Gray Herbarium**
22 Divinity Avenue, Cambridge, MA 02138.
- Gray Herbarium. Contributions. irreg.

**Harvard University. Institute of Politics**
78 Mount Auburn St., Cambridge, MA 02138.
- Harvard Political Review. q. ISSN 0090-1032 (prep. by its Student Advisory Committee)

**Harvard University. John F. Kennedy School of Government**
- Public Policy. (pub. by John Wiley & Sons, Inc.)

**Harvard University. Laboratory for Computer Graphics and Spatial Analysis**
20 Gund Hall, Cambridge, MA 02138.
- Harvard Papers in Theoretical Geography. irreg., 1970, no. 41. ISSN 0073-0610

**Harvard University Law School**
Langdell Hall, Cambridge, MA 02138.
- Harvard Civil Rights-Civil Liberties Law Review. 3 per yr. ISSN 0017-8039
- Harvard International Law Journal. 3 per yr. ISSN 0017-8063
- Harvard Law School Bulletin. 4 per yr. ISSN 0017-8128

**Harvard University Law School. Legislative Research Bureau**
Langdell Hall, Cambridge, MA 02138.
- Harvard Journal on Legislation. 4 per yr. ISSN 0017-808X

**Harvard University. Law School Library**
Langdell Hall, Cambridge, MA 02138.
- Current Legal Bibliography; a selected list of books and articles received by the Harvard Law School Library. m.(Oct-June) ISSN 0011-3646
- Harvard University. Law School. Library. Annual Legal Bibliography. a. ISSN 0073-0793

**Harvard University. Law School Record Corp.**
23 Everett St, Cambridge, MA 02138.
- Harvard Law Record. 20 per yr. ISSN 0017-8101

**Harvard University Library**
Office of the Director, Cambridge, MA 02138.
- Harvard Librarian. irreg. ISSN 0073-0564
- Harvard Library Bulletin. (pub. by Harvard University Press)

**Harvard University Medical School. Department of Biophysics**
- Harvard Books in Biophysics. (pub. by Harvard University Press)

**Harvard University. Museum of Comparative Zoology**
Cambridge, MA 02138.
- Breviora. irreg., no. 441, 1976. ISSN 0006-9698
- Harvard University. Museum of Comparative Zoology. Bulletin. irreg., vol. 147, 1976. ISSN 0027-4100
- Harvard University. Museum of Comparative Zoology. Department of Mollusks. Occasional Papers on Mollusks. irreg. ISSN 0073-0807
- Johnsonia; monographs of the marine mollusks of the Western Atlantic. irreg. ISSN 0075-3920 (prep. by its Department of Mollusks)
- M C Z Newsletter. (Museum of Comparative Zoology) 3 per yr.

**Harvard University Peabody Museum of Archaeology and Ethnology**
*see* Peabody Museum of Archaeolgy and Ethnology

**Harvard University Press**
79 Garden St., Cambridge, MA 02163.
- American Foreign Policy Library. irreg.
- Archaeological Exploration of Sardis. Monographs. irreg., vol. 3, 1975. ISSN 0066-5975
- Carl Newell Jackson Lectures. a. ISSN 0528-1458
- Charles Eliot Norton Lectures. a.
- Documents in the History of Education. irreg.
- Harvard Armenian Texts and Studies. irreg., 1970, no. 3. ISSN 0073-0459
- Harvard Books in Biology. irreg., 1971, no. 7. ISSN 0073-0467

- Harvard Books in Biophysics. irreg., 1965, no. 1. ISSN 0073-0475 (Harvard University Medical School. Department of Biophysics)
- Harvard East Asian Monographs. irreg., 1973, no. 48. ISSN 0073-0483 (Harvard University. East Asian Research Center)
- Harvard East Asian Series. irreg., 1972, nos. 65-70. ISSN 0073-0491 (Harvard University. East Asian Research Center)
- Harvard Economic Studies. irreg., no. 144, 1974. ISSN 0073-0505
- Harvard English Studies. irreg., 1972, no. 3. ISSN 0073-0513
- Harvard Historical Monographs. irreg., 1973, no. 68. ISSN 0073-0521 (Harvard University. Department of History)
- Harvard Historical Studies. irreg., 1972, no. 88. ISSN 0073-053X (Harvard University. Department of History)
- Harvard Judaic Monographs. irreg.
- Harvard Library Bulletin. q. ISSN 0017-8136 (Harvard University Library) (Dist. by Watson Mailing Service, 2401 Revere Beach Pkwy, Everett, MA 02149)
- Harvard Middle Eastern Monographs. irreg., 1973, no. 22. ISSN 0073-0572 (Harvard University. Center for Middle Eastern Studies)
- Harvard Middle Eastern Studies. irreg., 1972, no. 16. ISSN 0073-0580 (Harvard University. Center for Middle Eastern Studies)
- Harvard Monographs in Applied Science. irreg. ISSN 0440-3452
- Harvard Monographs in the History of Science. irreg.
- Harvard Oriental Series. irreg., 1968, no. 47. ISSN 0073-0599
- Harvard Paperbacks. irreg., no. 86, 1972. ISSN 0073-0602
- Harvard Political Classics. irreg.
- Harvard Political Studies. irreg.
- Harvard Publications in Music. irreg., no. 7, 1975. ISSN 0073-0629
- Harvard Semitic Monographs. irreg., 1972, no. 3. ISSN 0073-0637
- Harvard Semitic Series. irreg., 1970, no. 21. ISSN 0073-0645
- Harvard Slavic Monographs. irreg.
- Harvard Studies in American-East Asian Relations. irreg., no. 6, 1974.
- Harvard Studies in Business History. irreg., no. 28, 1975. ISSN 0073-067X (Harvard University Graduate School of Business Administration)
- Harvard Studies in Classical Philology. a. ISSN 0073-0688
- Harvard Studies in Comparative Literature. irreg., 1972, nos. 31,32. ISSN 0073-0696
- Harvard Studies in Romance Languages. irreg., 1972, no. 32. ISSN 0073-0718 (Harvard University. Department of Romance Languages and Literature)
- Harvard Studies in Urban History. irreg.
- Harvard Studies in World Religions. irreg. ISSN 0440-3509
- Harvard University. Russian Research Center. Russian Research Center Studies. irreg., no. 74, 1974. ISSN 0073-0831
- Harvard-Yenching Institute. Monograph Series. irreg., vol. 22, 1975. ISSN 0073-084X
- Harvard-Yenching Institute. Studies. irreg., 1972, nos. 27, 28. ISSN 0073-0858
- Inglis Lecture. a. ISSN 0073-800X
- Joint Center for Urban Studies. Publications. irreg. ISSN 0075-3947 (Co-publisher: M I T Press)
- LeBaron Russell Briggs Prize Honors Essays in English. a. ISSN 0075-8396
- Loeb Classical Library. irreg.
- Martin Classical Lectures. irreg., 1970, no.24. ISSN 0076-471X (Oberlin College)
- Scripta Mongolica. irreg., 1969, no. 4. ISSN 0080-8377 (Harvard-Yenching Institute)
- Studies in Economic History. irreg.
- Studies in Legal History. irreg. (American Society for Legal History)
- Twentieth Century Legal Philosophy Series. irreg., 1970, no. 8. ISSN 0082-7088
- Wertheim Publications in Industrial Relations. irreg.
- Widener Library Shelflist. irreg., 1973, nos. 42-46. ISSN 0083-9892 (Harvard University. Widener Library)

**Harvard University. Program for Science and International Affairs**
9 Divinity Ave., Cambridge, MA 02138.
- International Security. q.

**Harvard University. Program on Information Technologies and Public Policy**
Cambridge, MA 02138.
- Harvard University. Program on Information Technologies and Public Policy. Working Paper. irreg.

**Harvard University. Program on Regional and Urban Economics**
Cambridge, MA 02138.
- Harvard University. Program on Regional and Urban Economics. Discussion Paper. irreg., no. 83, 1974. ISSN 0073-0815

**Harvard University. Widener Library**
- Widener Library Shelflist. (pub. by Harvard University Press)

**Harvard-Yenching Institute**
2 Divinity Ave., Cambridge, MA 02138.
- Harvard Journal of Asiatic Studies. a. ISSN 0073-0548
- Harvard-Yenching Institute. Monograph Series. (pub. by Harvard University Press)
- Harvard-Yenching Institute. Studies. (pub. by Harvard University Press)
- Scripta Mongolica. (pub. by Harvard University Press)

**Harvard-Yenching Library**
2 Divinity Avenue, Cambridge, MA 02138.
- Harvard-Yenching Library Bibliographical Series. irreg.

**Harvest Publications (Evanston)**
1233 Central, Evanston, IL 60201.
- Standard (Evanston) fortn. ISSN 0038-9382 (Baptist General Conference)

**Harvest Publishers (Santa Barbara)**
907 Santa Barbara St., Santa Barbara, CA 93101.
- Harvest Quarterly. q.

**Harvest Publishing Co. (Cleveland)**
9800 Detroit Ave., Cleveland, OH 44102.
- Pest Control. m. ISSN 0031-6121
- Weeds, Trees and Turf; commercial turf magazine for vegetation maintenance and control. m. ISSN 0043-1753

**Harwood & Charles Publishing Co.**
562 Fifth Ave., New York, NY 10036.
- Who's Who in Aviation. irreg. ISSN 0093-3015

**Hashomer Hatzair Zionist Youth Movement**
150 Fifth Ave., New York, NY 10011.
- Youth and Nation; magazine for radical Jewish youth. bi-m. ISSN 0044-1171

**Haskins & Sells**
1114 Ave. of the Americas, New York, NY 10036.
- H & S Reports. q. ISSN 0017-6117
- Haskins & Sells. Selected Papers. a. ISSN 0440-4122

**Hastings College of Law**
Students of the University of California, 198 McAllister St., San Francisco, CA 94102.
- Hastings Law Journal. 6 per yr. ISSN 0017-8322

**Hastings House Publishers, Inc.**
10 E. 40th St., New York, NY 10016.
- Humanistic Studies in the Communications Arts. irreg.
- Illustrators; The Annual of American Illustration. a. ISSN 0073-5477 (Society of Illustrators)
- International Poster Annual. biennial. ISSN 0074-7483

**Hastings Press, Inc.**
Hastings, MI 49058.
- Thru the Garden Gate. bi-m. ISSN 0040-6619 (Federated Garden Clubs of Michigan, Inc.)

**W. C. Hatch Publishing Co.**
15 Stonybrook Dr., Levittown, PA 19055.
- Master Shoe Rebuilder. m.

**Hatton, Brown & Co. Inc.**
Box 2268, 458 S. Lawrence St., Montgomery, AL 36103.
- Loggin' Times. m.
- Pulpwood Production; and timber harvesting. m. ISSN 0033-4154

**Haughton Publishing Co. of Texas**
Box 18092, Dallas, TX 75218.
- Cotton Gin and Oil Mill Press; the magazine of the cotton ginning and oilseed processing industries. fortn. ISSN 0010-9800

**Die Hausfrau, Inc.**
1517 W. Fullerton Ave., Chicago, IL 60614.
- Hausfrau. m. ISSN 0017-842X

**Haverford College**
Haverford, PA 19041.
- Bryn Mawr-Haverford College News. w.

**Hawaii. Agricultural Reporting Service**
P.O. Box 5425, Honolulu, HI 96814.
- Hawaii Weekly Weather & Crop Bulletin. w.

**Hawaii. Commission on Aging**
1149 Bethel St., Rm. 311, Honolulu, HI 96813.
- Hawaii. Commission on Aging. Report of Achievements of Programs for the Aging. a. ISSN 0090-2233

**Hawaii. Criminal Injuries Compensation Commission**
Box 339, Honolulu, HI 96809.
- Hawaii. Criminal Injuries Compensation Commission. Annual Report. a. ISSN 0098-5708

**Hawaii. Department of Agriculture**
Box 22159, Honolulu, HI 96822.
- Fresh Fruit and Vegetable Market News. 3 per wk.

**Hawaii. Department of Defense. Civil Defense Division**
Fort Ruger, Honolulu, HI 96816.
- Civil Defense Journal. bi-m.

**Hawaii. Department of Education**
Liluokalani Bldg., Honolulu, HI 96813.
- Hawaii. Department of Education. Educational Directory: State & District Office. irreg. ISSN 0092-1777

**Hawaii. Department of Education. Office of Business Services**
Honolulu, HI 96813.
- Hawaii. Department of Education. Office of Business Services. Report on Federally Connected Pupils: Hawaii Public Schools. a. ISSN 0090-9440
- Hawaii. Department of Education. Office of Business Services. Student Information & Records Administration Branch. Public and Private School Enrollment. a.

**Hawaii. Department of Education. Office of Instructional Services**
Honolulu, HI 96813.
- Hawaii. Office of Instructional Services. Special Programs Branch. Annual Performance Report on Adult Education. a. ISSN 0362-2940 (prep. by its Special Programs Branch)

**Hawaii. Department of Education. Office of Library Services**
P.O. Box 2360, Honolulu, HI 96804.
- Hawaii. Department of Education. Office of Library Services. Report. a. ISSN 0073-103X

**Hawaii. Department of Health**
Box 3378, Honolulu, HI 96801.
- Population Mobility in Hawaii. irreg. ISSN 0094-0348
- Psychiatric In-Patient Program, Hawaii State Hospital and Chronic Hospitals. a. ISSN 0079-7243

**Hawaii. Department of Health. Comprehensive Health Planning Office**
1250 Punchbowl St., Honolulu, HI 96813.
- Hawaii Health Planning News. irreg.

**Hawaii. Department of Health. Health Education Office**
Box 3378, Honolulu, HI 96801.
- Hawaii Health Messenger. q.

**Hawaii. Department of Health. Mental Health Division**
P.O. Box 3378, Honolulu, HI 96801.
- Hawaii. Children's Health Services Division. Crippled Children Branch. Report. a. ISSN 0073-1013
- Hawaii. Department of Health. Division of Mental Health. Children's Health Services. a.

- Hawaii. Department of Health. Mental Health Services for Children and Youth. a. ISSN 0362-6296
- Hawaii. Department of Health. Mental Health Statistical Section. Psychiatric Outpatient, Inpatient and Community Programs. a.
- Hawaii. Mental Health Register. Unduplicated Count of Mentally Retarded Patients Served Children's Health Services Division. irreg.

**Hawaii. Department of Health. Research and Statistics Office**
P.O. Box 3378, Honolulu, HI 96801.
- Hawaii. Department of Health. Research and Statistics Office. R & S Report. irreg. ISSN 0093-3481

**Hawaii. Department of Labor and Industrial Relations. Research and Statistics Office**
825 Mililani St., Honolulu, HI 96813.
- Area Manpower Review Hawaii-Honolulu. a.
- Hawaii. Department of Labor and Industrial Relations. Labor Force Statistics. a.
- Hawaii. Department of Labor and Industrial Relations. Research and Statistics Office. Annual Planning Report. a.

**Hawaii. Department of Land and Natural Resources**
Box 621, Honolulu, HI 96809.
- Aloha Aina/Love of Land. irreg. ISSN 0084-6244

**Hawaii. Department of Planning and Economic Development**
Office of Information and Public Services, Box 2359, Honolulu, HI 96804.
- Directories of Hawaii. irreg. ISSN 0094-209X
- Hawai'i. bi-m.
- Hawaii. Department of Planning and Economic Development. Annual Report. a. ISSN 0073-1072
- Hawaii's Scientific Resources Directory. a. ISSN 0070-5632
- State of Hawaii Data Book. a. ISSN 0073-1080

**Hawaii. Insurance Division**
Box 3614, Honolulu, HI 96811.
- Hawaii. Insurance Division. Report of the Insurance Commissioner of Hawaii. a. ISSN 0073-1110

**Hawaii. Judiciary Department**
Box 2560, Honolulu, HI 96804.
- Aha Ilono. m. ISSN 0098-9738

**Hawaii. Legislative Reference Bureau**
State Capitol, Honolulu, HI 96813.
- Directory of State, County , and Federal Officials. a. ISSN 0440-4947
- Guide to Government in Hawaii. irreg., 1973, 5th ed. ISSN 0072-8454
- Hawaii. Legislative Reference Bureau. Digest and Index of Laws Enacted. a. ISSN 0095-6619
- Hawaii. Legislative Reference Bureau. Report. irreg. ISSN 0073-1277

**Hawaii. Office of Information and Youth Affairs**
Honolulu, HI 96813.
- Hawaii. Office of Information and Youth Affairs. Annual Report. a. ISSN 0093-9099

**Hawaii. Office of the Auditor**
State Capitol, Honolulu, HI 96813.
- Hawaii. Legislative Auditor. Special Reports. irreg.(3-5 per yr)

**Hawaii. Office of the Lieutenant Governor**
Honolulu, Hawaii.
- Election Laws of Hawaii. biennial. ISSN 0091-9101

**Hawaii. Office of the Ombudsman**
Kana'ina Bldg., Iolani Palace Grounds, Honolulu, HI 96813.
- Hawaii. Office of the Ombudsman. Report. a. ISSN 0073-1137

**Hawaii. State Commission on the Status of Women**
Kamamalu Building, Room 510, 250 South King St., Honolulu, HI 96813.
- Hawaii. State Commission on the Status of Women. Annual Report. a. ISSN 0092-9190

**Hawaii. State Law Enforcement and Juvenile Delinquency Planning Agency**
Honolulu, HI 96813.
- Hawaii. State Law Enforcement and Juvenile Delinquency Planning Agency. Annual Action Program. a. ISSN 0095-4209

**Hawaii. State Library. Office of Library Services**
Honolulu, HI 96813.
- L.S.C.A. Annual Program, Hawaii State Library System. (Library Services and Construction Act) irreg. ISSN 0095-4721

**Hawaii Agricultural Experiment Station**
College of Tropical Agriculture, University of Hawaii, Honolulu, HI 96822.
- Hawaii Agricultural Experiment Station, Honolulu. Research Bulletin. irreg., 1969, no. 148. ISSN 0073-098X
- Hawaii Agricultural Experiment Station, Honolulu. Research Report. irreg., 1970, no. 182. ISSN 0073-0998
- Hawaii Agricultural Experiment Station, Honolulu. Technical Bulletin. irreg., 1970, no. 81. ISSN 0073-1005

**Hawaii Audubon Society**
Box 22832, Honolulu, HI 96822.
- Elepaio. m. ISSN 0013-6069

**Hawaii Beverage Guide**
305 Royal Hawaiian Ave., Honolulu, HI 96815.
- Hawaii Beverage Guide. m. ISSN 0017-8543

**Hawaii Business Publishing Corporation**
Box 913, Honolulu, HI 96808.
- Hawaii Business. m.
- Hawaii Buyers Guide. a.

**Hawaii Council**
Box 4263, Honolulu, HI 96813.
- Cultural Climate. m.

**Hawaii Dental Association**
1000 Bishop St., Suite 805, Honolulu, HI 96813.
- Hawaii Dental Association. Journal. s-a. ISSN 0017-8616
- Hawaii Dental Association. Transactions. a. ISSN 0073-1021

**Hawaii Foundation for American Freedoms, Inc.**
Center Mezzanine, Alexander Young Bldg., Honolulu, HI 96813.
- Factfinder. m. ISSN 0014-6528

**Hawaii Institute of Geophysics**
2525 Correa Rd., Honolulu, HI 96822.
- Hawaii Institute of Geophysics. Biennial Report.

**Hawaii Institute of Marine Biology**
University of Hawaii, Box 1346, Kaneohe, HI 96744.
- Hawaii Institute of Marine Biology. Technical Reports. irreg., no. 3, 1973. ISSN 0073-1331

**Hawaii Library Association**
Box 4441, Honolulu, HI 96813.
- Hawaii Library Association Journal. a. ISSN 0017-8586

**Hawaii Medical Association**
510 S. Beretania St., Honolulu, HI 96813.
- Hawaii Medical Journal. m. ISSN 0017-8594

**Hawaii National Guard Association**
Honolulu, HI 96816.
- Pupukahi. q.

**Hawaii Observer Corporation**
Box 10-0, Honolulu, HI 96816.
- Hawaii Observer. fortn. ISSN 0091-9845

**Hawaii State Federation of Labor**
AFL-CIO, 547 Halekauwila St., Suite 216, Honolulu, HI 96813.
- Hawaii AFL-CIO News. bi-m. ISSN 0017-8535

**Hawaii Tourist News, Inc.**
Box 32, Honolulu, HI 96810.
- Hawaii Tourist News. w.

**Hawaii Visitors Bureau**
Research Committee, 2270 Kalakaua Ave., Honolulu, HI 96815.
- Hawaii Vistors Bureau. Annual Research Report. a. ISSN 0066-412X

**Hawaiian Entomological Society**
1527 Keeaumoku St., Honolulu, HI 96822.
- Hawaiian Entomological Society. Proceedings. a. ISSN 0073-134X

**Hawaiian Historical Society**
560 Kawaiahao St., Honolulu, HI 96813.
- Hawaiian Journal of History; devoted to the history of Hawaii, Polynesia and the Pacific area. a. ISSN 0440-5145

**Hawaiian Malacological Society**
P. O. Box 10391, Honolulu, HI 96816.
- Hawaiian Shell News. m. ISSN 0017-8624

**Hawaiiana Almanac Publishing Co.**
1021 University Ave., Honolulu, HI 96814.
- Almanac of Hawaiiana. a. since 1970-72. ISSN 0065-6453

**Hawkins Publishing Co., Inc.**
933 North Kenmore St., Suite 220, Arlington, VA 22201.
- Federal Maritime Commission Service. a.
- National Transportation Safety Board Service. irreg. (approx. 8-10 per yr.)

**Haworth Press**
149 Fifth Ave., New York, NY 10010.
- Administration in Social Work; the quarterly journal of human services management. q.
- Aged Care & Counseling. bi-m.
- Child & Youth Services. bi-m.
- Collection Management. q.
- Community Mental Health Review; summaries, reviews & index to the world's literature in community mental health. bi-m. ISSN 0363-1605
- Journal of Divorce. q.
- Journal of Homosexuality. q. ISSN 0091-8369
- Journal of Social Service Research. q.
- Library Security Newsletter. q.
- Marriage & Family Review. bi-m.
- Offender Rehabilitation. q. ISSN 0364-3093
- Serials Librarian; the quarterly journal of serials management. q. ISSN 0361-526X
- Social Work in Health Care; quarterly journal of medical & psychiatric social work. q. ISSN 0098-1389

**Hay Associates**
1845 Walnut St., Philadelphia, PA 19103.
- Management Memo. m.

**Hayden Publishing Co. Inc.**
50 Essex St., Rochelle Park, NJ 07662.
- Computer Decisions; information systems, automated processing, problem solving. m. ISSN 0010-4558
- Electronic Design. fortn. ISSN 0013-4872
- Electronic Design's Gold Book. a.
- Microwaves. m.
- Microwaves Product Data Directory. a.

**Edward N. Hayes, Ed. & Pub.**
4229 Birch St., Newport Beach, CA 92660.
- Hayes Directory of Dental Supply Houses. a. ISSN 0073-1404
- Hayes Directory of Physician and Hospital Supply Houses. a. ISSN 0073-1412
- Hayes Druggist Directory. a. ISSN 0073-1420

**Hayes Historical Society**
- Hayes Historical Journal. (pub. by Rutherford B. Hayes Library)

**Haymarket Press**
3149 Fremont Ave. S., Minneapolis, MN 55408.
- So's Your Old Lady; lesbian feminist journal. bi-m. (Lesbian Resource Center)

**Hays County Historical and Genealogical Society**
Box 1387, San Marcos, TX 78666.
- Hays County Historical and Genealogical Society Quarterly. q.

**Haywood House**
Box 279, Fair Lawn, NJ 07410.
- Italix; the calligraphic quarterly. q. ISSN 0047-1666

**Healdsburg Tribune-Enterprise and Scimitar**
Box 518, Healdsburg, CA 95448.
- Healdsburg Tribune-Enterprise and Scimitar. w. ISSN 0017-8810

**Health Affairs Press**
P.O. Box 425, Davis, CA 95616.
- A M H T International; Automated Multiphasic Health Testing Programs Directory. a.

**Health and Welfare Council of Central Maryland, Inc.**
901 Court Square Bldg., 200 E. Lexington St., Baltimore, MD 21202.
- Directory of Community Services in Maryland. biennial. ISSN 0070-5306

**Health Insurance Association of America. Consumer and Professional Relations Division**
919 Third Ave., New York, NY 10022.
- Health Insurance Association of America. Consumer and Professional Relations Division. Extent of Growth--Private Health Insurance Coverage in the United States. a.
- Health Insurance Viewpoints. irreg. ISSN 0017-9027

**Health Insurance Institute**
277 Park Ave., New York, NY 10017.
- List of Worthwhile Life and Health Insurance Books. a. ISSN 0073-1471 (Co-sponsor: Institute of Life Insurance)
- Source Book of Health Insurance Data. a. ISSN 0073-148X

**Health Manpower Council of California. Annual Health Manpower Conference**
No. 1 Camino Sobrante, Orinda, CA 94563.
- Annual Health Manpower Conference. Proceedings. a. ISSN 0094-8942

**Health Physics Society**
c/o R. J. Burk, Jr., Exec. Secretary, 4720 Montgomery Lane, Bethesda, MD 20014.
- Health Physics. (pub. by Pergamon Press, Inc.)
- Health Physics Society. Newsletter. irreg. ISSN 0073-1498

**Health Policy Advisory Center**
17 Murray St., New York, NY 10007.
- Health-Pac. bi-m. ISSN 0017-9051

**Health Sciences Communications Association**
c/o Elmer Friman, Ed., Medical Educational Resources Program, Indiana University School of Medicine, Indianapolis, IN 46202.
- H E S C A Feedback. 6 per yr.
- Journal of Biocommunication. (pub. by Federation of Biocommunication Societies)

**Health Sciences Publishing Corp.**
451 Greenwich St., New York, NY 10013.
- Bereavement and Allied Fields. a. ISSN 0067-575X

**HealthRight, Inc., Women's Health Forum**
175 Fifth Ave., New York, NY 10010.
- HealthRight. q.

**Heard Heritage**
c/o Lynda S. Eller, Box 249, Lanett, AL 36863.
- Heard Heritage; Heard County, Georgia - a history of its people. 3 per yr.

**Hearing Aid Journal**
c/o Milton Bolstein, 323 Benson Bldg., Sioux City, IA 51101.
- Hearing Aid Journal. m. ISSN 0091-2166

**Hearst Books. Motor Book Department**
250 W. 55th St., New York, NY 10019.
- Motor Truck Repair Manual. a. ISSN 0098-3624

**Hearst Magazines**
250 W. 55th St., New York, NY 10019.
- American Druggist. m. ISSN 0002-824X
- American Druggist Blue Book. a.
- Cosmopolitan. m. ISSN 0010-9541
- F M A Bulletin. 25 per yr. (Fulfillment Management Association)
- Good Housekeeping. m. ISSN 0017-209X
- Harper's Bazaar. m. ISSN 0017-7873
- House Beautiful. m. ISSN 0018-6422
- House Beautiful's Building Manual. s-a. ISSN 0018-6430
- House Beautiful's Colonial Homes. a.
- House Beautiful's Gardening and Outdoor Living. a. ISSN 0073-3563
- House Beautiful's Home Decorating. q. ISSN 0018-6457
- House Beautiful's Home Remodeling. s-a. ISSN 0018-6465
- House Beautiful's Houses and Plans. a. ISSN 0073-3571
- Motor Boating & Sailing. m. ISSN 0027-1799
- Popular Mechanics. m. ISSN 0032-4558
- Science Digest. m. ISSN 0036-8296 (Subscr. to Box 10090, Des Moines, IA 50340)

- Sports Afield Almanac. irreg. ISSN 0092-7082
- Sports Afield Fishing Annual. a.
- Sports Afield Gun Annual. a. ISSN 0490-5326
- Sports Afield with Rod & Gun. m.
- Town and Country. m. ISSN 0040-9952

**Hearst Magazines. Book Division**
250 West 55th Street, New York, NY 10019.
- Motor Auto Repair Manual. a. ISSN 0077-1708
- Popular Mechanics Do-It-Yourself Yearbook. a. ISSN 0360-2273

**Hearthstone Press**
708 Inglewood Drive, Broderick, CA 95605.
- Attention Please. 3 per yr.
- Green Fuse. s-a.

**Heartland Publications, Ltd.**
c/o Hobbs, R.D. No. 1, Denton, MD 21629.
- Del-Mar-Va Heartland. 3 per yr.

**D.C. Heath & Company**
125 Spring St., Lexington, MA 02173.
- Civilization and Society: Studies in Social, Economic and Cultural History. irreg.
- Northeastern University Studies in Rehabilitation. irreg., 1970, no. 10. ISSN 0078-169X
- Problems in American Civilization. irreg.
- Problems in European Civilization. irreg.
- Race and Nations Series. irreg. (Center on International Race Relations)

**Heather Enterprises, Inc.**
Box 26469, Denver, CO 80226.
- Country Music Who's Who. a. ISSN 0070-1289

**Hebrew Literary Foundation**
- Bitzaron. (pub. by Bitzaron, Inc.)

**Hebrew Publications for Children Inc.**
515 Park Ave., New York, NY 10022.
- Olam Hadash. 10 per yr. ISSN 0472-8637

**Hebrew Union College. Jewish Institute of Religion**
3101 Clifton Ave., Cincinnati, OH 45220.
- American Jewish Archives; devoted to the preservation and study of American Jewish historical records. s-a. ISSN 0002-905X
- Bibliographica Judaica. irreg. ISSN 0067-6853
- Hebrew Union College Annual. a. ISSN 0360-9049

**Hebrew Union College. Jewish Institute of Religion. Library**
3101 Clifton Ave., Cincinnati, OH 45220.
- Studies in Bibliography and Booklore; devoted to research in the field of Jewish bibliography. irreg. ISSN 0039-3568

**Hebrew Union College. Jewish Institute of Religion (New York)**
1995 Broadway, New York, NY 10023.
- Hebrew Union College. Jewish Institute of Religion. Chronicle. q.

**Connie Hechter**
Box 9502, Minneapolis, MN 55440.
- Insider; the music news magazine of the upper midwest. m. ISSN 0046-9645
- Midwest Motor Sport. m. ISSN 0047-7303 (Subscr. to:, Box 506)
- Ski Gazette. 3 per yr. (Subscr. to:, Box 9575)

**Hedgpeth Newsletter**
4000 Pierce St. No. 90, Riverside, CA 92505.
- Hedgpeth Newsletter. 10 per yr.

**Hegel Society of America**
Box 3369, University Station, Charlottesville, VA 22903.
- Owl of Minerva. q. ISSN 0030-7580

**Heidelberg Graphics**
Box 3404, Chico, CA 95927.
- Phantasm. bi-m.

**The Heights Inc.**
Boston College, McElroy 113, Chestnut Hill, MA 02167.
- Heights. w. ISSN 0017-9590

**Heineman Foundation Laboratories**
Charlotte Memorial Hospital, Charlotte, NC 28201.
- Collected Works on Cardio-Pulmonary Disease. irreg.; latest issue, no. 19. ISSN 0069-5319

**James H. Heineman, Inc**
475 Park Ave., New York, NY 10022.
● Biographical Encyclopedia and Who's Who of the American Theatre. irreg.

**Heirs, Inc.**
657 Mission St., Rm. 205, San Francisco, CA 94105.
● Heirs. q. ISSN 0017-9884

**Heldref Publications**
4000 Albemarle St N.W., Washington, DC 20016.
● Archives of Environmental Health. m. ISSN 0003-9896 (American Medical Association)
● Best Sellers. m. ISSN 0005-9625
● Clearing House; a journal for modern junior and senior high school faculties. m.(Sept-May) ISSN 0009-8655 (Helen Dwight Reid Educational Foundation (HELDREF))
● Journal of Business Education. m.(Oct-May) ISSN 0021-9444
● Journal of Educational Research. 10 per yr. ISSN 0022-0671 (Helen Dwight Reid Educational Foundation (HELDREF))
● Journal of Experimental Education. q. ISSN 0022-0973
● Social Studies. bi-m. ISSN 0037-7996 (Helen Dwight Reid Educational Foundation (HELDREF))

**Helen Diner Memorial Womens Center**
● Lesbian Connection. (pub. by Ambitious Amazons)

**Helen Dwight Reid Educational Foundation (HELDREF)**
4000 Albemarle St., N.W., Washington, DC 20016.
● Clearing House. (pub. by Heldref Publications)
● Current; significant new material from all sources on the frontier problems of today. 11 per yr. ISSN 0011-3131
● ELECTIONews. m.
● Explicator. 4 per yr. ISSN 0014-4940
● History: Review of New Books. 10 per yr.
● Journal of Educational Research. (pub. by Heldref Publications)
● Journal of Environmental Education. q. ISSN 0013-9254
● Perspective (Washington); monthly reviews of books on government, politics & international affairs. m. ISSN 0048-3494
● Social Studies. (pub. by Heldref Publications)
● Sociology: Reviews of New Books. bi-m.
● Weatherwise; popular weather magazine. bi-m. ISSN 0043-1672

**Heliopolis Press**
Box 256, San Fernando, CA 91340.
● New World Haiku. a.

**Hellcoal Press**
Brown Literary Board, Brown University, Providence, RI 02912.
● Hellcoal Annual. a.

**Hellenic-American Chamber of Commerce**
25 Broadway, New York, NY 10004.
● Hellenic-American Chamber of Commerce. Newsletter. s-a. ISSN 0018-0025

**Hellenic American Society**
Box 22334, Indianapolis, IN 46222.
● Journal of the Hellenic Diaspora; critical thoughts on Greek and World issues. q.

**Hellenism**
509 N. La Salle St., Chicago, IL 60610.
● Hellenism; review on Greek life and culture. m. ISSN 0018-0106

**Hellric Publications**
39 Eliot St., Jamaica Plain, MA 02130.
● Ab Intra. irreg.

**Helmars Rudzitis**
7307 Third Ave., Brooklyn, NY 11209.
● Laiks; Latvian newspaper. s-w.

**Helminthological Society of Washington**
Box 368, Lawrence, KS 66044.
● Helminthological Society of Washington. Proceedings. s-a. ISSN 0018-0130

**Hemisphere Publishing Corporation**
1025 Vermont Ave., N.W., Washington, DC 20005.
● Community/Junior College Research Quarterly. q. ISSN 0361-6975 (Virginia Commonwealth University. Adult Education Program)
● Death Education; pedagogy-counseling-care, an international quarterly. q.
● Educational Gerontology; an international quarterly. q. ISSN 0360-1277
● Electric Machines and Electromechanics; an international quarterly. q. ISSN 0361-6967
● Heat Transfer Engineering. q.
● Heat Transfer Engineering; an international quarterly. q.
● Journal of Cybernetics. q. ISSN 0022-0280
● Journal of Toxicology and Environmental Health. bi-m. ISSN 0098-4108
● Series in Clinical and Community Psychology. irreg., unnumbered, latest 1977. ISSN 0146-0846

**Hemmings Motor News**
Subscription Dept., Box 100, Bennington, VT 05201.
● Hemmings Motor News. m.

**Henderson & Henderson**
1806 Treadwell, Box 3334, Austin, TX 78764.
● Textile Maintenance Reporter. m. ISSN 0040-5094

**Hendrickson Publishing Co., Inc.**
79 Washington St., Hempstead, NY 11550.
● World Convention Dates; conventions, conferences, banquets, expositions, trade shows. m. ISSN 0043-8383

**Hennepin County Board of Commissioners**
A301 Government Center, Minneapolis, MN 55487.
● Hennepin Reporter. 10 per yr. ISSN 0018-0386

**Hennepin County Library. Technical Services Division**
7001 York Ave. S., Edina, MN 55435.
● Hennepin County Library Cataloging Bulletin. bi-m. ISSN 0093-528X

**Hennepin County Medical Society**
2000 Medical Arts Bldg., Minneapolis, MN 55402.
● Hennepin County Medical Society. Bulletin. m. ISSN 0018-0378

**Hennessey & Ingalls, Inc.**
8321 Campion Dr., Los Angeles, CA 90045.
● Art and Architecture Bibliographies. irreg.
● Studies in Comparative Literature. irreg. ISSN 0081-7767

**Henry F. Henrichs Publications, Inc.**
Box 40, Sunshine Park, Litchfield, IL 62056.
● Good Reading for Everyone. m.
● Sunshine. m. ISSN 0039-5412

**Henry County Historicalog**
c/o Mary Walcott, 628 South 14th St., New Castle, IN 47362.
● Henry County Historicalog. s-a.

**Coulston R. Henry, Ed. & Pub.**
1612 Margaret St., Philadelphia, PA 19124.
● Bustleton-Somerton News. w.
● Frankford News Gleaner. w. ISSN 0015-9921
● Kensington News. w. ISSN 0023-0006
● Mayfair and Northeast News. w.

**Henry Ford Community College**
5101 Evergreen, Dearborn, MI 48128.
● Ford Estate. w. ISSN 0015-6981

**Henry Ford Hospital**
Publications Office, Detroit, MI 48202.
● Henry Ford Hospital Medical Journal. q. ISSN 0018-0416 (Co-Sponsor: Edsel B. Ford Institute for Medical Research)

**Henry George Institute**
55 W. 42 St., New York, NY 10036.
● Georgist Journal; an international journal serving the movement for land value taxation and free trade based on the philosophy of Henry George. q.

**Henry George School of Social Science**
50 E. 69th St., New York, NY 10021.
● Henry George News. bi-m. ISSN 0018-0424

**Herald Books**
Box 17E, Pelham, NY 10803.
● World Cars. a. ISSN 0084-1463 (Automobile Club d'Italia IT)

**Herald of Freedom**
Box 3, Zarephath, NJ 08890.
● Herald of Freedom. fortn. ISSN 0018-0483

**Herald Publishing Co. (Houston)**
c/o Joseph W. Samuels, 4003 Bellaire Blvd., Box 153, Houston, TX 77001.
● Jewish Herald-Voice. w. ISSN 0021-6488

**Herald Publishing Company**
c/o Dale Sipe, Box 877, 1818 Fourth St., Santa Rosa, CA 95402.
● Sonoma County Daily Herald-Recorder. 5 per wk.

**Herald Publishing House**
3225 S. Noland Rd., Drawer HH, Independence, MO 64055.
● Daily Bread. a. ISSN 0092-7147 (Reorganized Church of Jesus Christ of Latter Day Saints)
● Saints' Herald; family magazine of the Reorganized Church of Jesus Christ of Latter Day Saints. m. ISSN 0036-3251 (Reorganized Church of Jesus Christ of Latter Day Saints)

**Herb Grower Magazine**
c/o Philip W. Foster, Falls Village, CT 06031.
● Herb Grower Magazine. q. ISSN 0018-0572

**Herb Society of America**
300 Massachusetts Ave., Boston, MA 02115.
● Herbarist. a.
● Primer for Herb Growing. irreg.

**Hercules Inc.**
910 Market St., Wilmington, DE 19899.
● Hercules Chemist. s-a. ISSN 0018-0629

**Hereford Publications, Inc.**
715 Hereford Dr., Kansas City, MO 64105.
● American Hereford Journal. m. ISSN 0002-872X (American Hereford Association)

**Heritage Music Press**
501 E. 3 St., Dayton, OH 45401.
● Best of Popular Music. bi-m. (Lorenz Industries)

**Heritage Papers**
Danielsville, GA 30633.
● Carolina Genealogist. q. ISSN 0008-6762
● Family Puzzlers. w. ISSN 0014-7389
● Georgia Genealogist. q.

**Heritage Publishing Co.**
2130 S. Vermont Ave., Los Angeles, CA 90007.
● Heritage-Southwest Jewish Press. w. ISSN 0018-0726 (United Jewish Federation, San Diego) (Co-sponsor: Jewish Federation Council, Orange County)
● Orange County Jewish Heritage. fortn. ISSN 0030-4298

**Heritage Publishing Co. (North Little Rock)**
4Th & Poplar, North Little Rock, AR 72201.
● Arkansas State Directory. every 18 mos.

**John Herlings Labor Letter, Inc.**
411 K St. N.W., Washington, DC 2005.
● John Herling's Labor Letter. w. ISSN 0021-7190

**Amado F. Hernandez, Ed. & Pub.**
Box 811, Orlando, FL 32802.
● Adelante (Orlando); al servicio de la comunidad Latinoamericana. m. ISSN 0044-6238

**Hero Press**
Suite 1B, 153 West 80 St., New York, NY 10024.
● Witchcraft Digest. a. ISSN 0085-8250 (Witches International Craft Associaties; Witches Liberation Movement)
● Witches International Craft Associates. W I C A Newsletter. m. ISSN 0049-7754
● Witches Newsletter. q. ISSN 0028-4173

**John S. Herold, Inc.**
35 Mason St., Greenwich, CT 06830.
● Oil Industry Comparative Appraisals. m.
● Petroleum Outlook. m. ISSN 0031-6490

**Herpetological Information Search Systems**
● H I S S News-Journal. (pub. by American Museum of Natural History)
● H I S S Titles and Review. (pub. by American Museum of Natural History)

- Yearbook of Herpetology. (pub. by American Museum of Natural History)

**Herpetologists League**
San Diego Natural History Museum, P.O. Box 1390, San Diego, Columbus, CA 92112.
- Herpetologica. q. ISSN 0018-0831

**Herrick Public Library**
300 River Ave., Holland, MI 49423
- Family Ties. q. (Holland Genealogical Society) (Or: c/o Carol See, 344 Frances, Saugatuck, MI 49453)

**HeteroCorporation**
Univ. Station Box 7524, Provo, UT 84602.
- International Congress of Heterocyclic Chemistry. Abstracts. irreg.; 5th Ljubljana, Yugoslavia, 1975. (International Society of Heterocyclic Chemistry)
- Journal of Heterocyclic Chemistry; the international journal of heterocyclic chemistry. bi-m. ISSN 0022-152X
- Lectures in Heterocyclic Chemistry. biennial. ISSN 0090-2268

**Hewitt Bros.**
7320 Milwaukee Ave., Chicag, IL 60648.
- Hewitt-Donlon Catalog of United States Small Size Paper Money. a. ISSN 0070-7082

**Hewlett Packard Co. (Palo Alto)**
1501 Page Mill Rd., Palo Alto, CA 94304.
- Hewlett-Packard Journal. m. ISSN 0018-1153

**Hewlett Packard Co. (Santa Clara)**
5303 Stevens Creek Blvd., Santa Clara, CA 95050.
- Educational User's Group Newsletter. m.

**Hewlett Packard Co. (Waltham)**
175 Wyman St., Waltham, MA 02154.
- Measuring for Medicine & the Life Sciences. q. ISSN 0025-6331

**Hewlett-Woodmere Public Library**
- South Shore Record. (pub. by South Shore Publishers, Inc.)

**Hi-Rise Weekly**
75 East Wacker Drive, Suite 2300, Chicago, IL 60601.
- Hi-Rise Weekly. w.

**Hi-Torque Publications, Inc.**
16200 Ventura Blvd., Encino, CA 91436.
- Auto Reports. bi-m.
- Big Bike. m. ISSN 0045-1975
- Choppers Magazine; chopper guide. m. ISSN 0009-501X
- Dirt Bike. m.
- Dirt Bike Buyer's Guide. ISSN 0090-8185
- Motocross Action. m.
- Soccer Corner. 8 per yr.
- Van World. m.(s-m. Feb., Jun., Oct.)

**Hiaring Co.**
Ed. Philip Hiaring, 703 Market St., San Francisco, CA 94103.
- Wines and Vines. m (s-m. Dec.) ISSN 0043-583X
- Wines and Vines: Directory of the Wine Industry in North America. a.

**Hibiscus Press**
P.O. Box 22248, Sacramento, CA 95822.
- In a Nutshell. q.

**Higdon Family Newsletter**
1223 Wake Forest Rd., Raleigh, NC 27604.
- Higdon Family Newsletter. m.

**William J. Higginson, Ed. & Pub.**
Box 2702, Paterson, NJ 07509.
- Haiku. irreg.

**Higginson Press**
4508 38th St., Brentwood, MD 20722.
- Emily Dickinson Bulletin. s-a. ISSN 0046-1881
- Higginson Journal of Poetry. s-a.

**High Plains Publishers, Inc.**
Box 760, Dodge City, KS 67801.
- High Plains Journal. w. ISSN 0018-1471

**High Society Magazine, Inc.**
801 Second Ave., Room 705, New York, NY 10017.
- High Society. m.

**High Voltage Engineering Corporation**
S. Bedford St., Burlington, MA 01803.
- High Voltage Engineering Corporation Newsletter. q. ISSN 0018-1552

**Robin Higham, Ed. & Pub.**
Kansas State University, Department of History, Manhattan, KS 66506.
- Aerospace Historian. q. ISSN 0001-9364 (Air Force Historical Foundation)
- Current Research in British Studies by American and Canadian Scholars. quadrennial. ISSN 0590-417X
- Military Affairs; devoted to American and world military, naval and air history. q. ISSN 0026-3931 (American Military Institute)

**Dean Coughenour & Robin Higham, Eds. & Pubs.**
Box 1009, 1531 Yuma, Manhattan, KS 66502.
- Journal of the West; an illustrated classroom periodical. q. ISSN 0022-5169

**Highland Press, Inc.**
Rt. 1, Box 70C, Boerne, TX 78006.
- O. Henry Almanac. a. (O. Henry House)

**Highlander, Inc.**
Box 397, Barrington, IL 60010.
- Highlander; for and about Scottish activities. q.

**Highlands Press (Hampden)**
Box 131, Hampden, ME 04444.
- Northeast Horseman. m. ISSN 0029-2990

**Highlands Press (Radford)**
Radford College Sta., Radford, VA 24142.
- New River Review. s-a. ISSN 0360-1455

**Highlights for Children, Inc.**
2300 W. Fifth Ave., P.O. Box 269, Columbus, OH 43216.
- Highlights for Children. 11 per yr. ISSN 0018-165X

**Highway Loss Data Institute**
Watergate Six Hundred, Washington, DC 20037.
- Highway Loss Data Institute. Automobile Insurance Losses Collision Coverages Variations by Make and Series; models. s-a. ISSN 0093-0466

**Highway Safety Institute**
- Journal of Biomechanics. (pub. by Pergamon Press Inc.)

**Highway Users Federation**
1776 Massachusetts Ave., N.W., Washington, DC 20036.
- Highway Users Federation. Federation Reporter. m. ISSN 0046-7405

**Craig Hill, Ed. & Pub.**
220 Standish, Redwood, CA 94063.
- Modern Pervogue. s-a.
- Monochrome. q.

**Jesse Hill, Jr.**
787 Parsons St., S.W., Atlanta, GA 30314.
- Atlanta Inquirer. w.

**Hill and Wang**
19 Union Sq. W., New York, NY 10003.
- American Century Series. irreg. ISSN 0517-0400

**Hill International Publications**
P.O. Box 79, East Islip, NY 11730.
- Guide to Employment Abroad. a. ISSN 0434-8850
- Teaching Opportunities Overseas. biennial.

**Hillsdale College. Center for Constructive Alternative**
Hillsdale, MI 49242.
- Imprimis. m.

**Hilton Head Island Chamber of Commerce**
Box 5647, Hilton Head Island, SC 29928.
- Islander; of Hilton Head. m. ISSN 0021-1869

**Hine's Legal Directory, Inc.**
443 Duane St., P.O. Box 71, Glen Ellyn, IL 60131.
- Hine's Insurance Counsel. a.

**Hip Society**
- Hip. (pub. by C. V. Mosby Co.)

**Hiram College**
Hiram, OH 44234.
- Theatre Annual. a. ISSN 0082-3821

**Hiram College. English Department**
Box 162, Hiram, OH 44234.
- Hiram Poetry Review. s-a. ISSN 0018-2036

**Hirsch Organization, Inc.**
6 Deer Trail, Old Tappan, NJ 07675.
- Mutual Funds Almanac. a. ISSN 0076-4175
- Smart Money. m.
- Stock Trader's Almanac. a.

**Hispamerica**
c/o Saul Sosnowski, Ed., 1402 Erskine St., Takoma Park, MD 20012.
- Hispamerica; revista de literatura. 3 per yr.

**Hispanic Foundation**
- Handbook of Latin American Studies: A Selected and Annotated Guide to Recent Publications. (pub. by University of Florida. Center for Latin American Studies)

**Hispanic Institute of the United States**
see under Columbia University

**Hispano**
900 Park S.W., Albuquerque, NM 87102.
- Hispano; official Spanish language newspaper of the state of New Mexico. w. ISSN 0018-2184

**Histadruth Ivrith of America**
- Hadoar. (pub. by Hadoar Association, Inc.)

**Histochemical Society**
- Journal of Histochemistry and Cytochemistry. (pub. by Williams & Wilkins Co.)

**Historians Film Committee**
New Jersey Institute of Technology, Newark, NJ 07102.
- Film & History. q.

**Historic Madison, Inc.**
Box 2031, Madison, WI 53701.
- Historic Madison. Journal. a. ISSN 0361-574X

**Historic Schaefferstown Inc.**
Schaefferstown, PA 17088.
- Historic Schaefferstown Record. q.

**Historical Aircraft Decal Inc.**
11208 Ewing Ave., Minneapolis, MN 55431.
- Hisairdec News; the modeller's international aviation magazine. bi-m(Aug-July) ISSN 0018-2117

**Historical & Genealogical Society of Somerset County, Inc.**
Box 533, Somerset, PA 15501.
- Laurel Messenger. q. ISSN 0023-8988

**Historical Association of Southern Florida**
3290 S. Miami Ave., Miami, FL 33129.
- Tequesta. a.

**Historical Communications Inc.**
One Main Plaza, Suite 448, Houston, TX 77002.
- Omnis. q. ISSN 0030-2295

**Historical Evaluation and Research Organization**
Box 157, Dunn Loring, VA 22027.
- Historical Evaluation and Research Organization. Combat Data Subscription Service. q. ISSN 0098-7956
- History, Numbers and War. 4 per yr.

**Historical Society of Berks County**
940 Centre Ave., Reading, PA 19601.
- Historical Review of Berks County. q. ISSN 0018-2524

**Historical Society of Delaware**
505 Market St., Wilmington, DE 19801.
- Delaware History. s-a. ISSN 0011-7765

**Historical Society of Haddonfield**
343 King's Highway East, Haddonfield, NJ 08033.
- Historical Society of Haddonfield. Bulletin. q. ISSN 0018-2532

**Historical Society of Pennsylvania**
1300 Locust St., Philadelphia, PA 19107.
- Pennsylvania Magazine of History and Biography. q. ISSN 0031-4587

**Historical Society of Southern California**
200 East Ave. 43, Los Angeles, CA 90031.
- Southern California Quarterly. q. ISSN 0038-3929

**Historical Society of Western Pennsylvania**
4338 Bigelow Blvd., Pittsburgh, PA 15213.
● Western Pennsylvania Historical Magazine. q.
ISSN 0043-4035

**History Book Club, Inc.**
40 Guernsey St., Stamford, CT 06904.
● History Book Club Review. 13 per yr. ISSN 0018-2664

**History in Africa**
c/o Memorial Library, University of Wisconsin, Madison, WI 53706.
● History in Africa; an annual journal of method. a.

**History of Anthropology Newsletter**
c/o R. Bieder, Box 1384, Bloomington, IN 47401.
● History of Anthropology Newsletter. s-a.

**History of Education Society**
● History of Education Quarterly. (pub. by New York University)

**History of Science Society**
Washington, DC 20560.
● Isis; international review devoted to the history of science and its cultural influences. q. ISSN 0021-1753

**Histrionic Publishing Corp.**
280 Madison Ave., New York, NY 10016.
● Man to Man Yearbook. 2 per yr.

**Hitchcock Publishing Co.**
Geneva Rd., Wheaton, IL 60187.
● Assembly Engineering. m. ISSN 0004-5063
● Assembly Engineering Master Catalog. a. ISSN 0066-8702
● Industrial Finishing. m. ISSN 0019-8323
● Infosystems. m.
● Machine and Tool Blue Book; America's leading magazine for profitable manufacturing. m. ISSN 0024-9106
● Office Products; for retailers of office supplies, office machines, office furniture. s-m. ISSN 0030-0144
● Quality (Wheaton); the magazine of product assurance. m. ISSN 0360-9936
● Woodworking & Furniture Digest. m. ISSN 0043-7778

**Roy Hitchcock, Jr., Ed. & Pub.**
Box 6266, San Jose, CA 95150.
● Pacific Fruit News. w. ISSN 0030-8668

**Frank M. Hiteshew & Associates**
141 El Camino, Ste. 110, Beverly Hills, CA 90212.
● Western's World. 6 per yr. ISSN 0043-4329 (Western Airlines)

**W. D. Hoard and Sons Co.**
28 Milwaukee Ave. W., Fort Atkinson, WI 53538.
● Hoard's Dairyman; the national dairy farm magazine. s-m. ISSN 0018-2885

**Hob-Nob**
715 Dorsea Rd., Lancaster, PA 17601.
● Hob-Nob. q.

**Hobart and William Smith Colleges**
Geneva, NY 14456.
● Pulteney St. Survey. 9 per yr(Sep.-Jun.)
● Seneca Review. s-a. ISSN 0037-2145

**Hobart Brothers Co.**
Hobart Sq., Troy, OH 45373.
● Hobart Weldworld. q. ISSN 0018-2893

**Hobbies and Things**
3091 S. Lorain, North Olmstead, OH 44070.
● Hobbies and Things. bi-m.

**Hobby House Press**
Ed. Gary R. Ruddell, 4701 Queensbury Rd., Riverdale, MD 20840.
● Doll Reader; clearinghouse for information on dolls. bi-m.

**Hobby Publications, Inc.**
225 W. 34th St., New York, NY 10001.
● Craft, Model & Hobby Industry. m. ISSN 0011-0752
● Craft, Model & Hobby Industry Annual Trade Directory. a.

**Philip Hochstein, Ed. & Pub.**
3 E. 40 St., New York, NY 10016.
● Jewish Week and American Examiner. w. ISSN 0021-6852

**Hockey & Arena Biz**
2038 Pennsylvania Ave., Madison, WI 53704.
● Hockey & Arena Biz. m.

**Hod Mother Earth Tribe**
● Mount to the Stars. (pub. by Mr. Gail Sutton)

**Hoffman Printing Co.**
114 S. Fourth St., Muskogee, OK 74401.
● Legal Record. d. ISSN 0024-0370

**Hoffman Publications, Inc.**
3000 N.E. 30th Place, P.O. Box 11299, Fort Lauderdale, FL 33306.
● Swimming Pool Weekly/Age - Data and Reference Annual. a. ISSN 0082-0466
● Swimming Pool Weekly and Swimming Pool Age. s-m. ISSN 0039-7393

**Fritz S. Hofheimer, Inc.**
88 Third Avenue, Mineola, NY 11501.
● United States & Canadian Mailing Lists. biennial. ISSN 0073-2893

**Hofstra University**
Hempstead, NY 11550.
● Chronicle. w.(Sept.-May)
● Twentieth Century Literature. (pub. by Hofstra University Press)

**Hofstra University Press**
Hempstead, NY 11550.
● Twentieth Century Literature; a scholarly and critical journal. q. ISSN 0041-462X (Hofstra University)

**Hofstra University. School of Business**
Hempstead, NY 11550.
● Hofstra University Yearbook of Business. irreg. ISSN 0073-2907

**Hofstra University. School of Law**
Hempstead, NY 11550.
● Hofstra Law Review. 3 per yr. ISSN 0091-4029

**Edward J. Hogan, Ed. & Pub.**
66 Rogers Ave., Somerville, MA 02144.
● Aspect. q. ISSN/0004-4911

**Betsy Hogan Associates**
222 Rawson Road, Brookline, MA 02146.
● Womanpower; a monthly report on fair employment practices for women. m. ISSN 0300-659X

**Hoke Communications, Inc.**
224 Seventh St., Garden City, Long Island, NY 11530.
● Direct Marketing Magazine. m. ISSN 0012-3188
● Friday Report. w. ISSN 0046-5097
● Fund Raising Management. bi-m. ISSN 0016-268X
● Ideas in Sound. s-a.

**Holden Arboretum**
Sperry Road, Mentor, OH 44060.
● Holden Arboretum. Arboretum Leaves. q.

**Holden-Day, Inc.**
500 Sansome St., San Francisco, CA 94111.
● Steroids; an international journal. m. ISSN 0039-128X

**Holdsworth Natural Resource Center**
University of Massachusetts, Planning and Resource Development Program, Amherst, MA 01002.
● Massachusetts Heritage. q. ISSN 0025-4819

**Holland Genealogical Society**
● Family Ties. (pub. by Herrick Public Library)

**Holland Society of New York**
122 E. 58th St., New York, NY 10028.
● Halve Maen. q. ISSN 0017-6834

**Lee A. Holley, Ed. & Pub.**
Box 188, Bainbridge Island, WA 98110.
● F.E.D. Letter; plain talk for and about federal employment and the law. s-m.

**Harry Hollingsworth, Ed. & Pub.**
3250 W. 108th St., Inglewood, CA 90303.
● Hollingsworth Register. q. ISSN 0018-3636

**Hollins College**
Box 9538, VA 24020.
● Hollins Critic. 5 per yr. ISSN 0018-3644

**Hollow Spring Review of Poetry**
Box 76, Berkshire, MA 01224.
● Hollow Spring Review of Poetry. s-a.

**Holly Society of America, Inc.**
407 Fountain Green Rd., Bel Air, MD 21014.
● Holly Letter. 4 per yr. ISSN 0046-774X

**Hollycroft Press, Inc.**
Ivoryton, CT 06442.
● Art Gallery. bi-m. ISSN 0004-3184

**Hollywood Congregational Center for Study and Service**
7065 Hollywood Blvd., Hollywood, CA 90028.
● Congregational Journal. 3 per yr. ISSN 0361-2376

**Holm Seminar on Electrical Contacts**
● Electrical Contacts. (pub. by Illinois Institute of Technology. Department of Electrical Engineering)

**A. J. Holman Co.**
(Subsidiary of: J.B. Lippincott Co.)
Box 956, E. Washington Sq., Philadelphia, PA 19105.
● Family Album. a. ISSN 0094-5862

**Holmes & Meier Publishers, Inc.**
101 Fifth Ave., New York, NY 10003.
● Soviet Union. a.
● War and Society; a yearbook of military history. a. ISSN 0361-0373

**Michael I. Holmes, Ed. & Pub.**
12704 Barbara Road, Silver Spring, MD 20906.
● Mugwumps; the magazine of folk instruments. bi-m.

**John F. Holmes Publishing Co., Inc.**
Whiting, IA 51063.
● Salvage Locator. m. ISSN 0048-9050

**Holstein-Friesian World, Inc.**
Lacona, NY 13083.
● Holstein-Friesian World. bi-m. ISSN 0018-3695
● New York Holstein Friesian News. m. ISSN 0028-727X (New York Holstein-Friesian Association)
● Pennsylvania Holstein News. m. ISSN 0031-4536 (Pennsylvania Holstein Association)

**T. J. Holt & Co., Inc.**
277 Park Ave., New York, NY 10017.
● Holt Investment Advisory. s-m. ISSN 0018-3717
● Holt Option Selector. w.

**Holt, Rinehart and Winston, Inc.**
383 Madison Ave., New York, NY 10017.
● American Authors and Critics Series. irreg. ISSN 0516-9631
● American Problems Studies. irreg.
● Balskrishnan-Neustadt Series. irreg.
● Basic Anthropology Units. irreg.
● Basic Management Series. irreg.
● Berkshire Studies in American History. irreg.
● Berkshire Studies in European History. irreg.
● Case Studies in Cultural Anthropology. irreg.
● Case Studies in Education and Culture. irreg.
● Cases in International Politics. irreg.
● Modern Biology Series. irreg.
● Modern Comparative Politics Series. irreg.
● New Directions in Psychology. irreg. ISSN 0548-4340
● News from Holt. q.
● Rinehart Press Series in Electronic Technology. irreg.
● Studies in Anthropological Method. irreg. ISSN 0585-6523
● World Cultural Guides. irreg.

**Steven Holtzman, Ed. & Pub.**
44 Wimbleton Lane, Great Neck, NY 11023.
● Uproar. 5-6 per yr. ISSN 0042-0743

**Holy Cross Greek Orthodox School of Theology. Hellenic College**
● Greek Orthodox Theological Review. (pub. by Holy Cross Orthodox Press)

**Holy Cross Monastery**
West Park, NY 12493.
● Holy Cross. q. ISSN 0018-3725

**Holy Cross Orthodox Press**
50 Goddard Ave., Brookline, MA 02146.
- Greek Orthodox Theological Review. q. ISSN 0017-3894 (Holy Cross Greek Orthodox School of Theology. Hellenic College)

**Holy Trinity Monastery**
Jordanville, NY 13361.
- Pravoslaavnaya Zhizn/Orthodox Life. m. ISSN 0032-6992
- Pravoslavnaya Rus; tzerkovno-obshchestvennyi organ. fortn. ISSN 0032-7018

**Holyoke Community College**
Holyoke, MA 01040.
- Massachusetts Foreign Language Bulletin. s-a. (Massachusetts Foreign Languages Association)

**Home Builders Association of Alabama, Inc.**
Box 827, Montgomery, AL 36102.
- Alabama Builder. m. ISSN 0002-4155

**Home Builders Association of Maryland**
762 Fairmount Ave., Baltimore, MD 21204.
- Maryland Home & Apartment Journal. m.

**Home Economics Education Association**
National Education Association, 1201 16 St. N.W., Washington, DC 20036.
- Home Economics Education Association, Newsletter. q.

**Home Planet Publications**
P.O. Box 415, Stuyvesant Station, New York, NY 10009.
- Hyn Anthology. irreg. (1 per yr.)

**Homebuyers Journal (Westchester County Edition)**
Southport, CT 06490.
- Homebuyers Journal (Westchester County Edition) s-m.

**Homeopathic Medical Society of the State of Pennsylvania**
Neffsville, PA 17601.
- Hahnemannian. q. ISSN 0017-6621

**Homesewing Trade News**
129 Broadway, Lynbrook, NY 11563.
- Homesewing Resource Directory of Branded Line Merchandise in the Homesewing Industry. a.

**Homosexual Information Center**
6715 Hollywood Blvd., No. 210, Hollywood, CA 90028.
- Directory of Homosexual Organizations and Publications. a.
- Homosexual Information Center. Newsletter. irreg.
- Selected Bibliography of Homosexuality. biennial.

**Hong Kong Trade Development Council**
548 Fifth Ave., New York, NY 10036.
- Hong Kong Cable. m.

**Honolulu. Department of Civil Service**
City Hall, Honolulu, HI 96812.
- Honolulu Employee Journal. m.

**Honolulu. Mayor's Committee on the Status of Women**
Honolulu, HI 96813.
- Honolulu. Mayor's Committee on the Status of Women. Annual Report. a. ISSN 0091-8121

**Honolulu. Police Department**
Honolulu, HI 96813.
- Blue Light. m.

**Honolulu Publishing Co. Ltd.**
735 Bishop St., Suite 410, Honolulu, HI 96813.
- Honolulu Magazine. m. ISSN 0018-4640

**Hood's Texas Brigade Association**
Box 619, Hillsboro, TX 76645.
- Valor. biennial.

**Hoofs and Horns Publishing Co.**
7268 Willa Lane, Evergreen, CO 80437.
- Hoof and Horn. bi-m. ISSN 0018-4713 (Rodeo Cowboys Association) (Co-sponsor: National High School Rodeo Association)

**Hooker Chemicals & Plastics Corp. Durez Division**
528 Walck Rd., N. Tonawanda, NY 14120.
- Durez Molder. m. ISSN 0012-7264

**Hoosier Challenger**
c/o Claire Emerson, Ed., 8365 Wicklow Ave., Cincinnati, OH 45236.
- Hoosier Challenger. q.

**Hoosier Folklore Society**
504 N. Fess St., Bloomington, IN 47401.
- Indiana Folklore. s-a. ISSN 0019-6614

**Hoosier Motor Club**
40 W. 40th Street, Indianapolis, IN 46208.
- Hoosier Motorist. q.

**Hoosier Publications Inc.**
Box 552, Chesterton, IN 46304.
- Hoosier Outdoors. bi-m. ISSN 0018-4780

**Hoosier State Press Association, Inc.**
1542 Consolidated Building, 115 N. Pennsylvania St., Indianapolis, IN 46204.
- Indiana Publisher. m. ISSN 0019-6711

**Hoover Institution**
- History of Menshevism. (pub. by University of Chicago Press)
- Russian Review. (pub. by Russian Review, Inc.)

**Hoover Institution Press**
Publications Dept., Stanford, CA 94305.
- Hoover Institution Bibliographies Series. irreg., no. 58, 1977. ISSN 0085-1582 (Stanford University. Hoover Institution on War, Revolution and Peace)
- Hoover Institution on War, Revolution and Peace. Foreign Language Publications Series. irreg. (Stanford University. Hoover Institution on War, Revolution and Peace)
- Hoover Institution on War, Revolution and Peace. Library Surveys. irreg. ISSN 0085-1590 (Stanford University. Hoover Institution on War, Revolution and Peace)
- Hoover Institution on War, Revolution, and Peace. Publications Series. irreg., latest, no. 191. ISSN 0073-3296 (Stanford University. Hoover Institution on War, Revolution and Peace)
- Hoover Institution on War, Revolution, and Peace. Report. a. ISSN 0091-6293 (Stanford University. Hoover Institution on War, Revolution, and Peace)
- Hoover Institution Studies Series. irreg., no. 56, 1977. ISSN 0073-330X (Stanford University. Hoover Institution on War, Revolution and Peace)
- Yearbook on International Communist Affairs. a. ISSN 0084-4101 (Stanford University. Hoover Institution on War Revolution and Peace)

**Hopi Action Program**
c/o Ed. Linda L. Joseph, Winslow Mail, Winslow, AZ 86047.
- Hopi Action News. w.

**Ralph Hopkins, Jr., Ed. & Pub.**
210 S. Spring St., Los Angeles, CA 90012.
- Journal of Commerce-Review. d.

**Roland G. Hopkins, Ed. & Pub.**
57 Washington St., Norwell, MA 02018.
- New England Real Estate Journal. w. ISSN 0028-4890

**Hopkins Publications**
3620 N.W. 7 St., Miami, FL 33125.
- Pan-American Trader. m. ISSN 0300-6514

**Horace Mann-Lincoln Institute**
- H M L I Research Bulletin. (pub. by Columbia University. Teachers College)

**Horace Mann School**
231 West 246th Street, Bronx, NY 10471.
- Manuscript. 2 per yr. ISSN 0091-2697

**Horatio Alger Society**
1214 W. College Ave., 305 E. Leo St., Apt. A, Jacksonville, IL 62650.
- Newsboy. 12 per yr. ISSN 0028-9396

**Horizon House**
610 Washington St., Dedham, MA 02026.
- Microwave Journal. m. ISSN 0026-2897
- Telecommunications. m. ISSN 0040-2494

**Horn Book, Inc.**
Park Square Bldg., 31 St. James Ave., Boston, MA 02116.
- Horn Book Magazine; about children's books and reading. 6 per yr. ISSN 0018-5078

**Horn Speaker**
9820 Silver Meadow Drive, Dallas, TX 75217.
- Horn Speaker; the newspaper for the hobbyist of vintage electronics and sound. m.

**Horry County Historical Society**
1008 Fifth Avenue, Conway, SC 29526.
- Independent Republic Quarterly. q. ISSN 0046-8843

**Horse Lover's National**
Box 670, San Martin, CA 95046.
- Horse Lover's National Magazine. bi-m.

**Horsebreeder**
Box 1239, Ft. Collins, CO 80522.
- Horsebreeder. q.

**Horseless Carriage Club of America, Inc.**
9031 E. Florence Ave., Arrington Square, Downey, CA 90240.
- Horseless Carriage Gazette. bi-m. ISSN 0018-5213

**Horseman Publishing Co.**
Box 11688, Lexington, KY 40511.
- Horseman and Fair World; devoted to the trotting and pacing horse. w. ISSN 0018-523X

**Horsemen's Benevolent and Protective Association**
c/o R. Anthony Chamblin, 6000 Executive Blvd., Suite 317, Rockville, MD 20852.
- Horsemen's Journal. m. ISSN 0018-5256

**Horses**
1861 Coldwater Canyon, Beverly Hills, CA 90210
- Horses. m. (11 per yr.) ISSN 0046-7936 (Subscr. to:, Rte. 1, Box 366, Rosamond, CA 93560)

**Horsetrader, Inc.**
4131 Erie St., Willoughby, OH 44094.
- Horsetrader. m. ISSN 0018-5264

**Horticultural Data Processors**
Box 489, New York, NY 10028.
- Avant Gardener. s-m. ISSN 0005-1926

**Horton Publishing Co.**
317 Howard St., Evanston, IL 60202.
- Supply House Times. m. ISSN 0039-5935

**John F. Horty, Ed. & Pub.**
Box 4663, Pittsburgh, PA 15206.
- Action-Kit for Hospital Law. m.
- Action Kit for Hospital Trustees. bi-m.

**Hospital Association of New York State**
15 Computer Dr. W., Albany, NY 12205.
- Hospital Association of New York State. News. w. ISSN 0018-5574

**Hospital Financial Management Association**
666 N. Lake Shore Drive, Chicago, IL 60611.
- Hospital Financial Management. m. ISSN 0018-5639

**Hospital for Joint Diseases & Medical Center**
1919 Madison Ave., New York, NY 10035.
- Hospital for Joint Diseases. Bulletin. s-a. ISSN 0018-5647

**Hospital for Special Surgery**
535 E. 70th St., New York, NY 10021.
- Hospital for Special Surgery. Journal. irreg. ISSN 0362-0727 (New York Society for the Relief of the Ruptured and Crippled)

**Hospital Publications, Inc.**
609 Fifth Ave., New York, NY 10017.
- Hospital Medicine; a pictorial review of medicine. m.

**Hospital Research and Educational Trust**
840 N. Lake Shore Dr., Chicago, IL 60611.
- Health Services Research. q. ISSN 0017-9124

**Hospital Research and Testing Institute**
Wheeler Ave., Pleasantville, NY 10570.
- Hospital Bureau Market News. m. ISSN 0018-5590
- Research News. m. ISSN 0034-5342

**Hospital Topics, Inc.**
734 Siesta Key Circle, Sarasota, FL 33581.
- Hospital Topics. bi-m.

**Hospitalized Veterans Writing Project**
5920 Nall, Room 106, Mission, KS 66202
(Subscr. to: Ruth Davidson, 7205 Pennsylvania
Ave., Kansas City, MO 64114)
● Veterans' Voices. 3 per yr. ISSN 0504-0779

**Hotel and Restaurant Employee and Bartenders
International Union**
120 E. 4th Street, Cincinnati, OH 45202.
● Catering Industry Employee. m. ISSN 0008-7815

**Hotel Herald Co.**
Box 188, Gettysburg, PA 17325.
● Hotel Herald; representing hotels, motor inns and
resorts. s-m. ISSN 0018-6147 (Pennsylvania
Hotel-Motor Inn Association)

**Hotel, Motel & Club Employees Union Local 6**
AFL- CIO, 305 W. 44th St., New York, NY 10036.
● Hotel Voice. m. (Co-sponsor: New York Hotel
and Motel Trades Council)

**Hotel-Motel Greeters International, Lone Star
Charter**
● Key (Dallas) (pub. by This Month in Dallas, Inc.)

**Hotel Sales Management Association**
362 Fifth Ave., New York, NY 10001.
● H. S. M. A. Hotel-Motel Directory and Facilities
Guide. a. ISSN 0072-9167
● H S M A World. m.

**Hotel Service Inc.**
131 Clarendon St., Boston, MA 02116.
● Lodging and Food-Service News. bi-w. ISSN
0024-5755

**Hotel Tipton Enterprises**
Suite 5, Strollway Centre, 111 S. Ninth St.,
Columbia, MO 65201.
● Museum Scope; national journal of, by, and for
museums. bi-m.

**Hotline Quarterly**
Box 1052, Fort Dodge, IA 50501.
● Contractors Hot Line Quarterly. q.

**C. W. Hotze**
444 Frontage Rd., Northfield, IL 60093.
● Cardiology Digest. m. ISSN 0008-6347
● Clinical Medicine. m.
● Dermatology Digest. m. ISSN 0011-9105
● Medical Digest. m. ISSN 0025-7176
● O. R. L. Digest/Otorhinolarnygology Digest. m.
ISSN 0048-1254
● Ob/Gyn Digest. m. ISSN 0029-7429
● Ophthalmology Digest. m. ISSN 0048-1955
● Orthopedics Digest. m.
● Pediatrics Digest. m. ISSN 0031-4005
● Psychiatry Digest. ISSN 0555-5493
● Urology Digest. m. ISSN 0042-1170

**P.K. Houdek, Ed. & Pub.**
7140 Oak, Kansas City, MO 64114.
● Sex News; a monthly digest of news, views,
events, publications and resources. m.

**Houghton Mifflin Co.**
One Beacon St., Boston, MA 02107.
● Best American Short Stories. a. ISSN 0067-6233
● Concepts in Chemistry. irreg.
● Contemporary Government Series. irreg.
● Justice in America Series. irreg. (Law in American
Society Foundation)
● New Perspectives in History. irreg.
● Resources for the Study of Anthropology. irreg.
● World Wildlife Series. irreg., 1967, no.2. ISSN
0084-2494

**House of Greystoke**
6657 Locust, Kansas City, MO 64131.
● Burroughs Bulletin. irreg. ISSN 0007-6333
(Burroughs Bibliophiles)
● Gridley Wave. 8 per yr. ISSN 0017-419X
(Burroughs Bibliophiles)

**House of Love and Prayer Publications**
1456 Ninth Ave., San Francisco, CA 94122
(Orders to: P. O. Box 22043, San Francisco, CA
94122)
● Holy Beggars' Gazette; journal of Chassidic
Judaism. q.

**House of White Birches**
Box 337, Folly Mill Rd., Seabrook, NH 03874.
● Gay Nineties. q. ISSN 0363-5910
● Old Time Songs and Poems (Seabrook) q. ISSN
0363-8960

● Roaring Twenties. ISSN 0035-7375

**House of Words**
207 E. Buffalo St., No. 322, Milwaukee, WI 53202.
● Third Coast Archives. bi-m.

**Houston Chamber of Commerce**
1100 Milam Bldg., Houston, TX 77002.
● Houston. m. ISSN 0018-6678

**Houston Engineer Publishing Company**
2615 Fannin St., Houston, TX 77002.
● Houston Engineer. m. (Houston Engineering &
Scientific Society)

**Houston Engineering & Scientific Society**
● Houston Engineer. (pub. by Houston Engineer
Publishing Company)

**Houston Geological Society**
234 Esperson Bldg., Houston, TX 77002.
● Houston Geological Society. Bulletin. m.(Sept-
June) ISSN 0018-6686

**Houston Law Review Inc.**
4800 Calhoun, Houston, TX 77004.
● Houston Law Review. 5 per yr. ISSN 0018-6694
(University of Houston. College of Law)

**Houston Teachers Association**
1415 Southmore, Houston, TX 77004.
● H T A Today. m.

**Cloyde P. Howard Consultants**
Box 8277, Fountain Valley, CA 92708.
● Consultant's Report. m.

**Howard Needles Tammen and Bergendoff**
1805 Grand Ave., Kansas City, MO 64108.
● Inflow; news on environmental services and
methods. q.

**Howard Publications, Inc.**
1314 Seaboard Coast Line Bldg., Box 4728,
Jacksonville, FL 32201.
● American Shipper; ports, transportation and
industry. m. ISSN 0097-6237
● Jacksonville Port Handbook. a.
● Jacksonville Seafarer. m.
● South Florida Ports Handbook. a.

**Howard Publishing Co.**
308 Yale Circle, Seal Beach, CA 90740.
● Environmental Future. s-m.

**Howard University**
2215 4th St. N.W., Washington, DC 20059.
● Hilltop. w.

**Howard University. African Studies Department**
Washington, DC 20059.
● Howard University. African Studies Department.
Seminar Papers on African Studies. a.

**Howard University. Bureau of Educational Research**
Washington, DC 20001.
● Journal of Negro Education. q. ISSN 0022-2984

**Howard University. Department of History**
Washington, DC 20059.
● Rayford W. Logan Lecture Series. a.

**Howard University. Department of University
Relations and Publications**
Washington, DC 20059.
● New Directions. q. ISSN 0047-9616

**Howard University. Morland Spingarn Research
Center**
Washington, DC 20059.
● Howard University. Morland Spingarn Research
Center. Accessions. bi-m.

**Howard University Press**
Howard Univ., Washington, DC 20001.
● Journal of Religious Thought. s-a. ISSN 0022-
4235 (Howard University. School of Religion)

**Howard University. School of Business & Public
Administration**
2361 Sherman Ave. N.W., Washington, DC 20001.
● Profits. m. (prep. by its Institute for Minority
Business Education)

**Howard University. School of Law**
2935 Upton St. N.W., Washington, DC 20008.
● Howard Law Journal. s-a. ISSN 0018-6813

**Howard University. School of Religion**
● Journal of Religious Thought. (pub. by Howard
University Press)

**Howell Publishing Co.**
290 Fillmore St., Suite 301, Denver, CO 80206.
● Mining Record. w. ISSN 0026-5241

**Howmark Publishing Corporation, Inc.**
225 W. 34th St., New York, NY 10001.
● Army/Navy Store & Outdoor Merchandiser. m.
● Health Foods Business. m.
● Pet Dealer. m. ISSN 0553-8572

**Hub Rail, Inc.**
6076 Busch Blvd., Suite 3, Columbus, OH 43229.
● Hub Rail. q.

**Hubbard High School**
Hall Ave., Hubbard, OH 44425.
● Hubbard School System Office of Curriculum and
Instruction. Digest Newsletter. m.(9 per yr) ISSN
0018-6961

**Hubbord Industries**
Box 33, Leonidas, MI 49066.
● Artery; an international journal for rapid
communication of arterial research. bi-m. ISSN
0098-6127

**Stan Hubsher**
P.O. Box 373, Cedarhurst, NY 11516.
● Deli-Dairy Management. q.

**Huddleston Family Newsletter**
c/o Donald L. Cordell, Ed., 2932 Haddon Ave.,
Sun Valley, CA 91352.
● Huddleston Family Newsletter. q.

**Hudson County Dental Society**
837 Kennedy Blvd., Bayonne, NJ 07002.
● Hudson County Dental Society. Bulletin. m.(Oct-
May) ISSN 0018-7011

**Howard Penn Hudson & Mary E. Hudson, Eds. &
Pubs.**
2626 Pennsylvania Ave. N.W., Washington, DC
20037.
● Hudson's Washington News Media Contacts
Directory. a. ISSN 0441-389X
● Newsletter on Newsletters. m. ISSN 0028-9507
● Public Relations Quarterly. q. ISSN 0033-3700

**Hudson Family Association (South)**
Route Seven, Del Monte Place, Longview, TX
75601.
● Hudson Family Association, South. Bulletin. irreg.
ISSN 0363-8847

**Hudson Heritage House**
Summit Ave., Central Valley, NY 10917.
● Colonial Life in New York State. m.
● New York State Notebook Series. 10 per yr.

**Hudson Home Guides**
289 S. San Antonio Rd., Los Altos, CA 94306.
● Hudson Home Guides. m.

**Hudson Institute**
Croton-On-Hudson, NY 10520.
● Hudson Institute. Report to the Members. a. ISSN
0073-3776

**Hudson Publishing Co.**
Box 8087, Wichita, KS 67208.
● Wichita Times. w.

**Hudson Review, Inc.**
65 E. 55th St., New York, NY 10022.
● Hudson Review. q. ISSN 0018-702X

**Hudson River Press**
Box 126, Rhinecliff, NY 12574.
● Book Forum; an international transdisciplinary
review of books. q. ISSN 0094-9426

**Lee W. Huebner, Ed. & Pub.**
75 Rockefeller Plaza, New York, NY 10019.
● Oil Daily; daily newspaper of the Petroleum
Industry. d. ISSN 0030-1434

**Huebner Publications, Inc.**
5821 Harper Rd., Solon, OH 44139.
● Metlfax. m. ISSN 0026-1297
● Tooling & Production; the magazine of
metalworking manufacturing. m. ISSN 0040-9243

**Hueck Family Association**
413 One Office Park Bldg, Mobile, AL 36609.
• Hueck Family Association. Family Notes; a journal of the Hueck family. a.

**Huerta**
Box 27b, Lakeville, NY 14480.
• Huerta. 3 per yr.

**John R. Hughes, Ed. & Pub.**
188 W. Randolph St., Chicago, IL 60601.
• Columbian. w. ISSN 0010-2024

**Roger Hull, Ed. & Pub.**
920 Glenneyre, Laguna Beach, CA 92651.
• Road Rider; for the touring motorcyclist. m. ISSN 0035-7243

**Human Dimensions Institute Inc.**
4380 Main Street, Buffalo, NY 14226.
• Human Dimensions Magazine. q.

**Human Events, Inc.**
422 First St., S.E., Washington, DC 20003.
• Human Events. w. ISSN 0018-7194

**Human Factor: A Journal of Radical Sociology**
Room 203, 605 W. 115th St., New York, NY 10025.
• Human Factor: A Journal of Radical Sociology. irreg., latest issue, 1974.

**Human Factors Society**
Box 1369, Santa Monica, CA 90406.
• Human Factors. (pub. by Johns Hopkins University Press)
• Human Factors Society. Proceedings of the Annual Meeting. a.
• Human Factors Society Bulletin. m. ISSN 0438-1629

**Human Life Foundation, Inc.**
150 E. 35th St., New York, NY 10016.
• Human Life Review. q. ISSN 0097-9783

**Human Life Foundation, Inc. (Washington)**
1511 K St. N.W., Washington, DC 20005.
• Human Life Foundation Newsletter. q.

**Human Relations Area Files, Inc.**
Box 2054, Yale Station, New Haven, CT 06520.
• Behavior Science Research. q.

**Human Resources Research Organization**
300 North Washington St., Alexandria, VA 22314.
• Human Resources Research Organization. Bibliography of Publications. a. ISSN 0073-3865
• Human Resources Research Organization. Professional Papers. irreg. ISSN 0073-3873
• Human Resources Research Organization. Technical Report. irreg. ISSN 0073-389X

**Human Rights for Women, Inc.**
1128 National Press Building, Washington, DC 20045.
• H R W Newsletter. irreg. ISSN 0046-8207

**Human Sciences Press**
72 Fifth Ave., New York, NY 10011.
• Alternative Higher Education. q.
• Child Care; a comprehensive guide. irreg., vol. 3, 1978.
• Child Care Quarterly; a professional journal of day and residential child care practice. q. ISSN 0045-6632
• Child Psychiatry and Human Development; an international journal. q. ISSN 0009-398X
• Clinical Social Work Journal. q. ISSN 0091-1674 (National Federation of Societies for Clinical Social Work)
• Community-Clinical Psychology Series. irreg., vol. 4, 1977. ISSN 0090-693X
• Community Mental Health Journal. q. ISSN 0010-3853
• Community Mental Health Journal Monograph Series. irreg. ISSN 0069-7850
• Community Psychology Series. irreg., vol. 2, 1974.
• Day Care and Early Education; the magazine of the child-growth movement. bi-m. ISSN 0092-4199
• Developments in Human Services Series. irreg., vol. 2, 1974. ISSN 0092-5470
• Directory of Unpublished Experimental Mental Measures. irreg.
• Environmental Psychology and Nonverbal Behavior. s-a. ISSN 0361-3496

• High School Behavioral Science. s-a. ISSN 0092-6221 (City College of New York. School of Education)
• Issues in Child Mental Health; a journal of psychosocial process. s-a. (Jewish Board of Guardians)
• Journal of Community Health. q. ISSN 0094-5145 (Association of Teachers of Preventive Medicine and Community Health)
• Journal of Psychiatric Education. s-a. ISSN 0363-1907
• Journal of School Psychology. q. ISSN 0022-4405
• Journal of Sex & Marital Therapy. q. ISSN 0092-623X
• McLean Hospital Monograph Series. irreg.
• New Human Services Review. bi-m. ISSN 0094-5129
• Pastoral Psychology. q. ISSN 0031-2789 (Princeton Theological Seminary)
• Psychoanalytic Review; an American journal of psychoanalytic psychology devoted to the understanding of behavior and culture. q. ISSN 0033-2836
• Psychology of Women Quarterly. q. ISSN 0361-6843 (American Psychological Association)
• Sociological Practice. q. ISSN 0360-845X
• Suicide and Life Threatening Behavior. q. ISSN 0363-0234 (American Association of Suicidology)
• Yearbook of Drug Abuse. a. ISSN 0090-662X

**Human Service Press**
5530 Wisconsin Ave. N.W. Suite 1600, Washington, DC 20015.
• Career Development. m. ISSN 0045-5776

**Humana Press, Inc.**
Box 2148, Clifton, NJ 07015.
• High Temperature Science; an international journal. q. ISSN 0022-1538

**Humane Society of the United States**
2100 L St., N.W., Washington, DC 20037.
• Humane Society of the United States News (1977) q.

**Humanities Press, Inc.**
171 First Avenue, Atlantic Highlands, NJ 07716
• American Institute for Marxist Studies. Historical Series. irreg., no. 9, 1974. ISSN 0065-8669 (American Institute for Marxist Studies)
• American Institute for Marxist Studies. Monograph Series. irreg., no. 4, 1973. ISSN 0065-8677 (American Institute for Marxist Studies)
• Annuale Mediaevale. a. ISSN 0066-4456
• Indiana University Publications. African Series. irreg. (Indiana University)
• Journal of Phenomenological Psychology; studies in the science of human experience and behavior. 2 per yr. ISSN 0047-2662
• Research in Phenomenology. a. ISSN 0085-5553
• Studies in Philosophical Psychology. irreg.
• Tarikh. s-a. ISSN 0039-9698 (Historical Society of Nigeria NR) (and Longmans, Green & Co. Ltd., 48 Grosvenor St., London W. 1, England)
• Van Leer Jerusalem Foundation Series. irreg.
• Writing in Asia Series. irreg.

**Humboldt State University. Department of Sociology**
54 Library, Arcata, CA 95521.
• Humboldt Journal of Social Relations. s-a.

**Humor Exchange Network**
• Humor Exchange Newsletter. (pub. by George Q. Lewis, Ed. & Pub.)

**Hungarian Baptist Union of America**
748 Fordham Road, Palm Bay, FL 32905.
• Evangeliumi Hirnok; gospel messenger. s-m.

**Hungarian National Committee**
225 East 72 St., New York, NY 10021.
• Free Hungarian Information Service/Szabad Magyar Tajekoztatu. m.

**Hungarian Word**
130 E. 16 St., New York, NY 10003.
• Hungarian Word. w.

**Hal W. Hunt, Ed. & Pub.**
Box NC, Hayden Lake, ID 83835.
• National Chronicle. w. ISSN 0027-898X

**Kendall Hunt Publishing Co.**
(Subsidiary of: Wm. C. /Brown Publishing Co.)
135 S. Locust St., Dubuque, IA 52003.
• American Occupational Therapy Association. Publications. irreg.

**Edward Hunter, Ed. & Pub.**
4114 N. Fourth St., Box 3541, VA 22203.
• Tactics. m. ISSN 0039-8896

**Hunter College**
see under City University of New York

**Hunter Mountain Ski Bowl**
• Hunter Mountain News. (pub. by Shanty Hollow Corporation)

**Hunter Museum of Art**
10 Bluff View, Chattanooga, TN 37403.
• Hunter Museum Annual. a.

**Hunter Publishing Co.**
53 W. Jackson, Chicago, IL 60604.
• Jobber and Warehouse Executive. m. ISSN 0021-7042
• Motor Service. m. ISSN 0027-1977

**Hunterdon County Democrat Inc.**
Box 32, Flemington, NJ 08822.
• Hunterdon County Democrat. w. ISSN 0018-7844

**Hunterdon County Historical Society**
114 Main St., Flemington, NJ 08822.
• Hunterdon Historical Newsletter. 3 per yr. ISSN 0018-7852

**Hunter's Horn, Inc.**
Box 426, Sand Springs, OK 74063.
• Hunter's Horn. m. ISSN 0018-7860

**Hunting Dog Publishing Co., Inc.**
9714 Montgomery Road, Cincinnati, OH 45242.
• Hunting Dog. m. ISSN 0018-7879

**Huntingdon College**
Box 90, Montgomery, AL 36106.
• Gargoyle. s-m. ISSN 0016-4690

**Huntington Library, Art Gallery and Botanical Gardens**
San Marino, CA 91108.
• Huntington Library, Art Gallery and Botanical Gardens. Calendar. bi-m.
• Huntington Library Quarterly; a journal for the history and interpretation of English and American civilization. q. ISSN 0018-7895

**Huntsville Association of Folk Musicians**
P.O. Box 1444, Huntsville, AL 35807.
• Huntsville Association of Folk Musicians. Newsletter. irreg. ISSN 0091-9764

**Huntsville Literary Association**
Box 919, Huntsville, AL 35804.
• Poem. 3 per yr. ISSN 0032-1885

**Huntsville-Madison County Historical Society**
P.O. Box 666, Huntsville, AL 35804.
• Huntsville Historical Review. q.

**Huron Review**
c/o Frank Hamilton, Ed., 423 S. Franklin Ave., Flint, MI 48503.
• Huron Review. s-a.

**Huron Road Hospital**
East Cleveland, OH 44112.
• Huron Road Hospital. Scientific Bulletin. 2 per yr.

**Hurst House Inc.**
15 W. Tenth St., Kansas City, MO 64105.
• Modern Jeweler. m. ISSN 0026-7864

**Hustler**
40 W. Gay St., Columbus, OH 43215.
• Hustler. m.

**Phillips Huston, Ed. & Pub.**
Box 1036, Weston, CT 06880.
• New in Dentistry. m. ISSN 0028-5420

**Hutsul Association, Inc.**
c/o Ukrainian National Museum, 2453 W. Chicago Ave., Chicago, IL 60622.
• Hutsuliya. q.

**Hyacinths and Biscuits**
c/o Jane R. Card, Box 392, Brea, CA 92621.
• Hyacinths and Biscuits; poets, poetry and prose. bi-m.

**Hyborean Legion**
Box 8243, Philadelphia, PA 19101.
- Amra; swordplay & sorcery. 5 per yr. ISSN 0044-8168

**Harry Hyde, Jr., Ed. & Pub.**
Box 47, Bryn Mawr, PA 19010.
- Areas of Concern. m. ISSN 0044-8788

**Hydro Products**
Box 2528, San Diego, CA 92112.
- Seahorse. q. ISSN 0037-0118

**Hymn Society of America**
National Headquarters, Wittenberg University, Springfield, OH 45501.
- Hymn. q. ISSN 0018-8271

**Hype**
Box 14001, Washington, DC 20044.
- Hype. irreg. ISSN 0097-6539

**Hyperion Poetry Journal**
2311-C Woolsey, Berkeley, CA 94705.
- Hyperion Poetry Journal. 3-4 per yr.

**I- Am Publishing Corp.**
3 E. 54th St., New York, NY 10022.
- I-Am. m.

**I C I United States Inc.**
Concord Pike and Murphy Rd., Wilmington, DE 19899.
- Chemmunique. q. ISSN 0528-953X

**I C Update Master**
1287 Lawrence Station Rd., Sunnyvale, CA 94086.
- I C Update Master. 3 per yr.

**I D O C-North America Inc.**
235 E. 49th St., New York, NY 10017.
- I D O C/International Documentation. m(11 per yr)

**I I T Research Institute**
Box 4963, Chicago, IL 60616.
- Frontier. q. ISSN 0016-2086
- International Conference in Particle Technology. Proceedings. irreg.
- Scanning Electron Microscope Symposium. Proceedings. a. ISSN 0586-5581

**I M S America, Ltd.**
Ambler, PA 19002.
- N. D. T. I. Review. (National Disease and Therapeutic Index Review) s-a. ISSN 0027-917X

**I M S International Inc. (New York)**
- IMS Pharmaceutical Marketletter. (pub. by IMSWORLD Publications Ltd. UK)

**I. M. Systems**
Box 686, Montclair, NJ 07042.
- Money Masters Annual. a.

**I N R O, Inc, (International Naval Research Organization)**
726 N. Reynolds Rd., Toledo, OH 43615.
- Warship International. q. ISSN 0043-0374

**Ibid, Inc.**
125 W. Hubbard, Chicago, IL 60610.
- Ibid. 6 per yr. ISSN 0019-1000

**Ichthyophile**
13955 Coconut Palm Drive, Homestead, FL 33030.
- Ichthyophile. m.

**Iconoclast**
Box 7013, Dallas, TX 75209.
- Iconoclast; the weekly newmagazine of Dallas, Ft. Worth. w.

**Idaho. Bureau of Mines and Geology**
Moscow, ID 83843.
- Idaho. Bureau of Mines and Geology. Bulletin. irreg., 1969, no. 23. ISSN 0073-442X
- Idaho. Bureau of Mines and Geology. County Report. irreg., 1967, no. 6. ISSN 0073-4438
- Idaho. Bureau of Mines and Geology. Information Circular. irreg., 1973, no. 24. ISSN 0073-4446
- Idaho. Bureau of Mines and Geology. Mineral Resource Report. irreg., 1970, no. 11. ISSN 0073-4454
- Idaho. Bureau of Mines and Geology. Pamphlet. irreg., 1973, no. 154. ISSN 0073-4462

**Idaho. Department of Agriculture**
Boise, ID 83708.
- Idaho. Department of Agriculture. Annual Report. a. ISSN 0098-5716

**Idaho. Department of Education**
Len B. Jordan Bldg., Boise, ID 83720.
- Idaho. Department of Education. News and Reports. m.

**Idaho. Department of Employment**
Box 35, Boise, ID 83702.
- Basic Economic Data for Idaho. irreg. ISSN 0094-1115 (prep. by its Research and Analysis Section)
- Idaho. Department of Employment. Annual Rural Manpower Report. a.
- Idaho Economic Indicators. m. ISSN 0046-8487

**Idaho. Department of Fish and Game**
P.O.B. 25, Boise, ID 83707.
- Idaho. Department of Fish and Game. Annual Report. a. ISSN 0073-4500
- Idaho. Department of Fish and Game. Federal Aid Investigation Projects. Progress Reports and Publications. a. and irreg. ISSN 0073-4527
- Idaho Wildlife Review. bi-m. ISSN 0019-1248

**Idaho. Department of Health and Welfare. Bureau of Research and Statistics**
Boise, ID 83702.
- Idaho. Department of Health and Welfare. Annual Summary of Vital Statistics. a. ISSN 0362-9279
- Idaho. Department of Health and Welfare. Bureau of Research and Statistics. Research Report. irreg. ISSN 0098-8561

**Idaho. Department of Labor and Industrial Services**
317 Main St., Rm. 400, Boise, ID 83701.
- Idaho. Department of Labor and Industrial Services. Annual Report. a. ISSN 0362-3912
- Mining Industry of Idaho. Annual Report. a. (prep. by its Mine Safety Bureau)

**Idaho. Department of Parks and Recreation**
Statehouse Mall, Boise, ID 83720.
- Idaho. Department of Parks and Recreation. Biennial Report. biennial.

**Idaho. Department of Social and Rehabilitation Services**
Boise, ID 83702.
- Idaho. Department of Social and Rehabilitation Services. Biennial Report. biennial. ISSN 0094-8578

**Idaho. Department of Water Resources**
1365 N. Orchard St., Boise, ID 83720.
- Idaho. Department of Water Resources. Annual Report. a. ISSN 0362-3289
- Idaho Environmental Overview. irreg.

**Idaho. Division of Budget, Policy Planning & Coordination**
Boise, ID 83720.
- Directory of Idaho Information Sources. a.

**Idaho. Division of Tourism and Industrial Development**
Room 108, Capitol Bldg., Boise, ID 83720.
- Incredible Idaho. q. ISSN 0019-3542

**Idaho. Division of Veterans' Services**
P.O. Box 7765, 320 Collins Road, Boise, ID 83702.
- Idaho. Division of Veterans' Services. Bulletin. m.

**Idaho. Law Enforcement Planning Commission**
Boise, ID 83702.
- Idaho's Comprehensive Plan for Criminal Justice. irreg. ISSN 0093-7134

**Idaho. State Board for Vocational Education**
506 N. Fifth St., Boise, ID 83720.
- Idaho. State Board for Vocational Education. Annual Descriptive Report of Program Activities for Vocational Education. a. ISSN 0091-5882

**Idaho. State Board of Education**
413 Idaho St., Boise, ID 83702.
- Idaho. State Board of Education. Annual Report of the State Board of Education and Board of Regents of the University of Idaho. a. ISSN 0098-5724

**Idaho. State Board of Nursing**
2404 Bank Dr., Room 308, Boise, ID 83705.
- Idaho. State Board of Nursing. Report. a. ISSN 0073-4543

**Idaho. State Superintendent of Public Instruction**
Boise, ID 83702.
- Idaho. State Superintendent of Public Instruction. Annual Report. State of Idaho Johnson-O'Malley Program. irreg. ISSN 0093-7223

**Idaho. State Tax Commission**
5257 Fairview Ave., P.O. Box 36, Boise, ID 83722.
- Idaho. State Tax Commission. Annual Report of Tax Collections. a. ISSN 0091-3898

**Idaho. Statistical Reporting Service. Crop and Livestock Reporting Service**
Box 1699, Boise, ID 83701.
- Idaho Agricultural Statistics. a. ISSN 0094-1271

**Idaho. Traffic Safety Commission**
2419 W. State St., Boise, ID 83702.
- Idaho. Traffic Safety Commission. State of Idaho Annual Work Program. a. ISSN 0094-5706

**Idaho. Transportation Department**
P.O.B. 7129, Boise, ID 83707.
- Engineering Geology and Soils Engineering Symposium. Proceedings. a. ISSN 0071-0318 (prep. by its Division of Highways)
- Idaho Transportation Department. Highway Information. m. ISSN 0019-1175

**Idaho Cattlemen's Association**
Box 7774, 2230 Main, Boise, ID 83707.
- Idaho Cattleman. m.

**Idaho Education Association**
Box 2638, Boise, ID 83701.
- I E A Reporter (1976) m. (Sept.-May)
- Idaho Education Association. Proceedings. a. ISSN 0073-4497

**Idaho Heritage**
Box 9365, Boise, ID 83702.
- Idaho Heritage. bi-m.

**Idaho Library Association. Publications Committee**
University of Idaho Library, Moscow, ID 83843.
- Idaho Librarian. q. ISSN 0019-1213

**Idaho Pea & Lentil Commission**
P.O. Box 8566, Moscow, ID 83843.
- Idaho Pea and Lentil Commission. Annual Report. irreg. ISSN 0085-1701

**Idaho Personnel & Guidance Association**
c/o Tom Fairchild, College of Education, University of Idaho, Moscow, ID 83843.
- Idaho Guidance News & Views. 3 per yr.

**Idaho Potato Commission**
303 N. 5th St., Boise, ID 83702.
- Idaho Potato Commission. Report to the Governor of Idaho and the Legislature. biennial. ISSN 0097-8280

**Idaho Retailers & Food Dealers Association**
- Idaho Food Journal. (pub. by Lowell McClellan)

**Idaho School Trustees Association**
Box 2577, Boise, ID 83701.
- Idaho School Trustees Newsletter. m. ISSN 0046-8509

**Idaho State Historical Society**
610 N. Julia Davis Drive, Boise, ID 83706.
- Idaho Yesterdays. q. ISSN 0019-1264

**Idaho State Nurses Association**
2404 Bank Dr., Rm. 304, Boise, ID 83705.
- Gem State R. N. Newsletter. irreg. ISSN 0072-0569

**Idaho State Pharmaceutical Association**
241 Bank Dr., Imperial Plaza, Boise, ID 83705.
- Idaho Pharmacist. m. ISSN 0019-1221

**Idaho State University. College of Liberal Arts**
- Rendezvous. (pub. by Idaho State University Press)

**Idaho State University Museum**
Pocatello, ID 83209.
- Idaho State University Museum. Occasional Papers. irreg. ISSN 0073-4551
- Tebiwa Miscellaneous Papers. irreg.

**Idaho State University Press**
Box 8113, Pocatello, ID 83201.
- Rendezvous; Idaho State University Journal of Arts & Letters. s-a. ISSN 0034-4400 (Idaho State University. College of Liberal Arts)

**Idaho Water Resources Research Institute**
- University of Idaho. Water Resources Research Institute. Annual Report. (pub. by University of Idaho. Water Resources Research Institute)

**Idea Source Guide**
c/o Fred Davis, Ed., Box 66, Fairless Hills, PA 19030.
- Idea Source Guide. m. ISSN 0019-1310

**Idea Treasury, Inc.**
1280 Saw Mill River Rd., Yonkers, NY 10710.
- Brainstorms; the newsletter of low-cost promotion. s-m. ISSN 0006-9000
- Home Owner's Newsletter. m.

**Ideal**
c/o Alfred Fuller, Ed., 43561 Sola, Indio, CA 92201.
- Ideal. s-m. ISSN 0046-8533

**Ideal Publishing Corp.**
575 Madison Ave, New York, NY 10022.
- Intimate Story. m. ISSN 0020-9813
- Movie Life. m. ISSN 0027-2698
- Movie Life Yearbook. s-a.
- Movie Stars. m. ISSN 0027-2744
- Personal Romances. m. ISSN 0031-5613
- Screen Stories. m. ISSN 0036-9608
- T V Dawn to Dusk. m.
- T V Radio Talk. m.
- T V Star Annual. q. ISSN 0492-0716
- T V Star Parade. m. ISSN 0041-4530

**Ideals Publishing Corp.**
11315 Watertown Plank Rd., Milwaukee, WI 53226.
- Country Scene. q. ISSN 0362-7152
- Ideals. bi-m. ISSN 0019-137X

**Ideas**
1785 Massachusetts Ave. N. W., Washington, DC 20031.
- Exchange (Washington) q.

**Ideos, Inc.**
Box 867, Soquel, CA 95073.
- Journal of Educational Data Processing. q. ISSN 0022-0647

**Ikhwanul Muslimoon Inc.**
52 Herkimer Place, Brooklyn, NY 11216.
- Al-Jihadul Abar/Supreme Struggle. q.

**Iliff School of Theology**
- Iliff Review. (pub. by Criterion Press, Inc.)

**Illiana Genealogical & Historical Society**
Box 207, Danville, IL 61832.
- Illiana Genealogist. q. ISSN 0019-1809

**Illinois. Administrative Office of Illinois Courts**
Supreme Court Bldg., Springfield, IL 62706.
- Illinois. Administrative Office of Illinois Courts. Annual Report to the Supreme Court of Illinois. a. ISSN 0536-3713

**Illinois. Board of Higher Education**
4 W. Old Capitol Sq., 500 Reisch Bldg., Springfield, IL 62701.
- Illinois. Board of Higher Education. Directory of Higher Education. irreg. ISSN 0094-8322
- Illinois. Board of Higher Education. Report. a. from 1970; previously irreg. ISSN 0073-4756
- Illinois. Board of Higher Education. Statewide Space Survey. irreg. ISSN 0362-5524
- Master Plan for Postsecondary Education in Illinois. irreg.

**Illinois. Bureau of Employment Security. Research and Statistics Section**
Room 200, Chicago, IL 60606.
- Illinois. Bureau of Employment Security. Research and Statistics Section. Estimates of Employment, Hours, and Earnings in Nonagricultural Establishments: Decatur Standard Metropolitan Statistical Area. ISSN 0091-4517

**Illinois. Cities and Villages Municipal Problems Commission**
Springfield, IL 62706.
- Illinois. Cities and Villages Municipal Problems Commission. Annual Report to the Session of the General Assembly. a. ISSN 0094-5978

**Illinois. Community College Board**
544 Iles Park Place, Springfield, IL 62718.
- Illinois Community College Board. Biennial Report. biennial.

**Illinois. Department of Business and Economic Development**
222 S. College St., Springfield, IL 62706.
- Illinois Gross State Product. q.
- Illinois Horizons. bi-m.
- Illinois State and Regional Economic Data Book. a.

**Illinois. Department of Children and Family Services. Office of Community Relations**
623 E. Adams St., Springfield, IL 62706.
- Sparks. m.

**Illinois. Department of Conservation**
100 E. Washington St., Springfield, IL 62701.
- Illinois. Department of Conservation. Technical Bulletin. irreg.; latest no. 4, 1971. ISSN 0073-4810

**Illinois. Department of Corrections. Division of Research and Long Range Planning**
Box 736, Joliet, IL 60434.
- Population Analysis of the Illinois Adult Prison System. irreg. ISSN 0093-5603

**Illinois. Department of Insurance**
Springfield, IL 62767.
- Illinois Insurance. bi-m.

**Illinois. Department of Mental Health and Developmental Disabilities**
401 S. Spring St., Springfield, IL 62706.
- Illinois. Department of Mental Health and Developmental Disabilities. Annual Report. a.(biennial until 1970)
- Mental Health Statistics for Illinois. a. ISSN 0076-6453
- Reaching out. q. ISSN 0034-0324

**Illinois. Department of Mental Health and Developmental Disabilities. Drug Abuse Program**
State Office Bldg., 160 N. La Salle, Chicago, IL 60601.
- Illinois. Department of Mental Health. Drug Abuse Program. Progress Report. irreg. ISSN 0093-7819

**Illinois. Department of Public Aid**
222 So. College St., Springfield, IL 62762.
- Illinois. Department of Public Aid. Annual Report. a. ISSN 0091-6099
- Illinois Health Messenger. m. ISSN 0019-204X

**Illinois. Department of Public Health**
535 W. Jefferson, Springfield, IL 62761.
- Illinois. Department of Public Health. Division of Disease Control. Monthly Report. w.
- Illinois. Department of Public Health. Division of Health Facilities. Directory of Health Care Facilities. a.
- Illinois. Department of Public Health. Poison Control Program Report. a. ISSN 0094-6494

**Illinois. Department of Public Instruction**
Springfield, IL 62706.
- Illinois. Department of Public Instruction. Annual State of Education Message. a. ISSN 0098-0269
- Illinois. Department of Public Instruction. Educational Program Survey. a. ISSN 0093-9145
- Illinois. Department of Public Instruction. Handicapped Children Section. Financial and Statistical Report: Special Education. a.

**Illinois. Department of Public Instruction. Publications and Library Resources Section**
325 S. Fifth St., Springfield, IL 62706.
- Illinois. Department of Public Instruction. Publications Resource Manual. irreg. ISSN 0094-2987

**Illinois. Department of Transportation**
Springfield, IL 62706.
- Illinois. Department of Transportation. Annual Report. a. ISSN 0095-5019
- Illinois. Department of Transportation. Physical Research Report. irreg. ISSN 0095-6686

**Illinois. Department of Transportation. Division of Water Resource Management**
Springfield, IL 62706.
- Illinois. Division of Water Resource Management. Annual Report. a. ISSN 0095-1064

**Illinois. Division of Fire Prevention**
601 Armory Bldg., Springfield, IL 62706.
- Illinois. Division of Fire Prevention. Annual Report. a.

**Illinois. Division of Vocational and Technical Education**
1035 Outer Park Dr., Springfield, IL 62700.
- Illinois. Board of Vocational Education and Rehabilitation. Report. a.
- Illinois Career Education Journal. 4 per yr.
- State Side News. 5 per yr. (prep. by its Board of Vocational Education & Rehabilitation)

**Illinois. Energy Resources Commission**
State Capitol, Springfield, IL 62706.
- Illinois. Energy Resources Commission. Report to the General Assembly of the State of Illinois. a.

**Illinois. Environmental Protection Agency**
2200 Churchill Rd., Springfield, IL 62702.
- Illinois. Environmental Protection Agency. Semi-Annual Report. s-a.
- Illinois. Environmental Protection Agency. Water Pollution Control Plan. irreg. ISSN 0091-4541 (prep. by its Division of Water Pollution Control)
- Illinois Water Quality Network. Summary of Data. a. ISSN 0073-5450 (prep. by its Division of Water Pollution Control)
- Lake Michigan Shore and Open Water Report. irreg. ISSN 0094-6311
- Lake Michigan Water Quality Report. a. ISSN 0361-8188

**Illinois. Environmental Protection Agency. Division of Air Pollution Control**
2200 Churchill Rd., Springfield, IL 62706.
- Illinois. Division of Air Pollution Control. Semi-Annual Report. s-a.
- Illinois Air Quality Report. a. ISSN 0360-9162 (prep. by its Ambient Air Monitoring Section)

**Illinois. Environmental Protection Agency. Operator Certification Section**
2200 Churchill Rd., Springfield, IL 62706.
- Illinois. Environmental Protection Agency. Operator Certification Section. Digester; to promote optimum operation and maintenance of every waste water treatment facility in Illinois. irreg. ISSN 0362-8795

**Illinois. Fire Protection Personnel Standards and Education Commission**
628 E. Adams St., Springfield, IL 62701.
- Illinois. Fire Protection Personnel Standards and Education Commission. Annual Report. a. ISSN 0095-8247

**Illinois. Housing Development Authority**
201 N. Wells, Chicago, IL 60606.
- Illinois. Housing Development Authority. Annual Report. a.

**Illinois. Judicial Inquiry Board**
205 W. Wacker Dr., Suite 1515, Chicago, IL 60606.
- Illinois. Judicial Inquiry Board. Report. irreg. ISSN 0093-8939

**Illinois. Law Enforcement Commission**
120 S. Riverside Plaza, Chicago, IL 60606.
- Annual Criminal Justice Plan for Illinois. a.
- Illinois Law Enforcement Commission. Annual Report. a. ISSN 0073-487X

**Illinois. Legislative Investigating Commission**
300 W. Washington St., Chicago, IL 60606.
- Illinois. Legislative Investigating Commission. Annual Report. a.

**Illinois. Office of Education**
100 N. First St., Springfield, IL 62777.
- Financial Aids to Illinois Students. biennial. ISSN 0085-0543
- Illinois Education News. 9 per yr. ISSN 0046-8606

**Illinois. Office of Education. Migrant Education Section**
Springfield, IL 62777.
• Directory of Services for Migrant Families/ Directorio de Servicios para Familias Migrantes. irreg. ISSN 0362-7179

**Illinois. Secretary of State**
Springfield, IL 62700.
• Handbook of Illinois Government. irreg. ISSN 0095-2842

**Illinois. State Archives**
Archives Building, Springfield, IL 62756.
• For the Record. q.

**Illinois. State Board of Investment**
Springfield, IL 62706.
• Illinois. State Board of Investment. Investment Transactions. a. ISSN 0095-3148

**Illinois. State Geological Survey**
Natural Resources Bldg., Urbana, IL 61801.
• Illinois. State Geological Survey. Bulletins. irreg., 1975, no. 5. ISSN 0073-5051
• Illinois. State Geological Survey. Circulars. irreg., no. 497, 1976. ISSN 0073-506X
• Illinois. State Geological Survey. Educational Series. irreg., 1976, no. 11. ISSN 0073-5078
• Illinois. State Geological Survey. Environmental Geology Notes. irreg., no. 80, 1976. ISSN 0073-5086
• Illinois. State Geological Survey. Guidebook Series. irreg., 1973, no. 11. ISSN 0073-5094
• Illinois Minerals Notes. irreg., no. 65, 1976.
• Illinois Petroleum. irreg., no. 110, 1976.
• Monthly Report on Oil and Gas Drillings in Illinois. m.

**Illinois. State Library**
Centennial Bldg., Springfield, IL 62756.
• Directory of Selected Illinois State Agencies. irreg. ISSN 0094-6346 (Co-sponsor: Illinois Secretary of State)
• Illinois. State Library, Springfield. Publications of the State of Illinois. s-a.
• Illinois Libraries. m.(Sept-June) ISSN 0019-2104
• Illinois Nodes. fortn.

**Illinois Academy of Family Physicians**
1200 Harger Rd., Oak Brook, IL 60521.
• Family Physician. m. ISSN 0014-732X

**Illinois Association for Advancement of Archaeology**
102 Circle Drive, Cambridge, IL 61238
(Subscr. to: 518 E. Peru, Princeton, IL 61356)
• Illinois Association for Advancement of Archaeology. Quarterly Newsletter. q.

**Illinois Association for Health, Physical Education and Recreation**
• Illinois Journal of Health, Physical Education and Recreation. (pub. by Production Press)

**Illinois Association for Supervision and Correction**
De Garmo Hall, Illinois State University, Normal, IL 61761.
• Illinois School Research and Development. 3 per yr.

**Illinois Association of Plumbing-Heating-Cooling Contractors**
821 S. Grand Ave. West, Springfield, IL 62704.
• Illinois Master Plumber. m. ISSN 0019-2112

**Illinois Association of School Boards**
330 Iles Park Place, Springfield, IL 62718.
• Illinois School Board Journal. bi-m. ISSN 0019-221X

**Illinois Association of School Librarians**
c/o Cora Thomassen, Ed., 1825 Valley Rd., Champaign, IL 61820.
• I A S L News for You. q. ISSN 0018-8468

**Illinois Association of Teachers of English**
c/o Wilmer A. Lamar, Exec. Sec., 100 English Bldg., University of Illinois, Urbana, IL 61801.
• Illinois English Bulletin. 4 per yr. ISSN 0019-2023

**Illinois Audubon Society**
Box 441, Wayne, IL 60184.
• Illinois Audubon Bulletin. q.

**Illinois Bankers Association**
188 W. Randolph St., Chicago, IL 60601.
• Illinois Banker. m. ISSN 0019-185X

**Illinois Baptist State Assocation**
Box 3486, Springfield, IL 62708.
• Illinois Baptist. w. ISSN 0019-1868

**Illinois Bell Telephone Co.**
225 W. Randolph St., HQ 30B, Chicago, IL 60606.
• Telenews. bi-w.

**Illinois Beverage Media, Inc.**
c/o James E. O'Brien, Jr., 1 N. Lasalle St., Chicago, IL 60602.
• Illinois Beverage Journal. m. ISSN 0019-1892

**Illinois Central Gulf Railroad**
233 N. Michigan Ave., Chicago, IL 60601.
• Illinois Central Gulf News. 10 per yr.

**Illinois Contractors Trade Directory, Inc.**
220 S. State St., Chicago, IL 60604.
• Illinois Contractors Trade Directory. a.

**Illinois Country Opry Inc.**
Box 313, Petersburg, IL 62675.
• Illinois Music Country Magazine. q. ISSN 0098-3535

**Illinois Dental Hygienists Association**
8051 S. Wabash Ave., Chicago, IL 60619.
• Illinois Dental Hygienists' Association. Bulletin. 3 per yr. ISSN 0019-1965

**Illinois Education Association**
100 E. Edwards St., Springfield, IL 62704.
• Advocate (Springfield) m (10 per yr.)

**Illinois Federation of the Blind**
Box 1336, Springfield, IL 62705.
• Illinois Braille Messenger (Braille Edition) q.
• Illinois Braille Messenger (Inkprint Edition) q. ISSN 0019-1906

**Illinois Geographical Society**
c/o Ed. Albert J. Larson, Univ. of Illinois at Chicago Circle, Chicago, IL 60680.
• Illinois Geographical Society. Bulletin. s-a. ISSN 0019-2031

**Illinois Handcrafts Directory**
Box 157, Bondville, IL 61815.
• Illinois Handcrafts Directory. a. ISSN 0095-5337

**Illinois Horticultural Experiment Station**
Carbondale, IL 62901.
• Illinois. Horticultural Experiment Station. Publication Series. irreg., approx. 1 per year. ISSN 0073-4845

**Illinois Institute for Environmental Quality**
309 West Washington, Chicago, IL 60606.
• Illinois Institute for Environmental Quality. Annual Report. a. ISSN 0090-8967

**Illinois Institute of Technology**
• National Conference on Fluid Power. Proceedings. (pub. by National Conference on Fluid Power)

**Illinois Institute of Technology. Chicago-Kent College of Law**
77 S. Wacker Dr., Chicago, IL 60606.
• I I T/Chicago-Kent Review. 3 per yr.
• Police Law Quarterly. q. (prep. by its Institute for Criminal Justice)

**Illinois Institute of Technology. Department of Electrical Engineering**
Chicago, IL 60616.
• Electrical Contacts. a.

**Illinois Institute of Technology. National Conference on Power Transmission**
Chicago, IL 60616.
• National Conference on Power Transmission. Proceedings. a. ISSN 0095-6481

**Illinois Issues**
226 Capital Campus, Springfield, IL 62708.
• Illinois Issues; the magazine that makes public business your business. m. (Co-Sponsors: Ford Foundation; University of Illinois)

**Illinois Junior College Music Association**
Amundsen-Mayfair College, 4626 N. Knox, Chicago, IL 60630.
• I J C M A News. bi-m. (Oct-Jun) ISSN 0018-9928

**Illinois Labor History Society**
2800 N. Sheridan Rd., Chicago, IL 60657.
• Illinois Labor History Society Reporter. irreg., no. 12, 1974. ISSN 0085-1728

**Illinois Landscape Contractors Association**
• Midwest Landscaping. (pub. by Editorial Services Inc.)

**Illinois Library Association**
716 N. Rush St., Chicago, IL 60611.
• I L A Reporter. q. ISSN 0018-9979

**Illinois Lumber and Material Dealers Association**
400 Leland Building, Springfield, IL 62701.
• Illinois Building News. m. ISSN 0019-1914
• Illinois Dealer Directory and Buyer's Guide. a.

**Illinois Lung Association**
725 So. 26th Street, Springfield, IL 62703
(Subscr. to: Box 2576, Springfield, IL 62708)
• Focus (Springfield); on the problem. q.

**Illinois Magazine**
320 South Main St., Benton, IL 62812.
• Illinois Magazine. m.

**Illinois Metro East Industrial Development Corporation**
• Illinois Metro East Industrial Development Corporation. Resources Report. (pub. by Southern Illinois University, Edwardsville. Industrial Maps Project)

**Illinois Mining Institute**
203 Natural Resources Building, Urbana, IL 61801.
• Illinois Mining Institute. Proceedings. a.

**Illinois Municipal League**
1220 S. Seventh St., Springfield, IL 62703.
• Illinois Municipal Review; the magazine of the municipalities. m. ISSN 0019-2139

**Illinois Music Educators Association**
Southern Illinois University, Carbondale, IL 62901.
• Illinois Music Educator. 5 per yr. ISSN 0019-2147

**Illinois Natural History Survey**
Natural Resources Bldg., Urbana, IL 61801.
• Illinois. Natural History Survey. Biological Notes. irreg., no. 100, 1977. ISSN 0073-490X
• Illinois. Natural History Survey. Bulletin. irreg., vol. 31, no. 10, 1977. ISSN 0073-4918
• Illinois. Natural History Survey. Circular. irreg., no. 54, 1975. ISSN 0073-4926

**Illinois Nurses Association**
6 N. Michigan Ave., Chicago, IL 60602.
• Chart. m (10 per yr.) ISSN 0069-2778

**Illinois Nurses Association. Chicago District**
8 S. Michigan Ave., Suite 1520, Chicago, IL 60603.
• Chicago District. 10 per yr.

**Illinois Optometric Association**
211 East Chicago Ave., Suite 1201, Chicago, IL 60611.
• Illinois Optometric Association. Journal. bi-m.

**Illinois Park & Recreation Society**
600 E. Algonquin Rd., Des Planines, IL 60016.
• Illinois Parks & Recreation. bi-m. ISSN 0019-2155 (Co-Sponsor: Illinois Association of Park Districts)

**Illinois Petroleum Marketers Association**
Box 1508, Springfield, IL 62705.
• Oilcan. bi-m.

**Illinois Police Association**
920 Michigan Ave. N., Chicago, IL 60611.
• Illinois Police Association. Official Journal. bi-m. ISSN 0019-2171

**Illinois Press Association**
220 E. Cook, Springfield, IL 62704.
• Illinois Publisher. m.

**Illinois Regional Library Council**
425 N. Michigan Ave., Chicago, IL 60611.
• Multitype Library Cooperative News. m. ISSN 0094-0364

**Illinois Society for Medical Research**
5757 Drexel Ave., Chicago, IL 60637.
• I S M R Bulletin. 4-5 per yr. ISSN 0019-0667

**Illinois Society of Professional Engineers**
Assn. Bldg., 612 S. Second St., Springfield, IL
62704.
● Illinois Engineer. m. ISSN 0019-2015

**Illinois State Academy of Sciences**
Illinois State Museum, Springfield, IL 62706.
● Illinois State Academy of Science. Transactions. q.
ISSN 0019-2252

**Illinois State Bar Association**
Illinois Bar Center, Springfield, IL 62701.
● Illinois Bar Journal. m. ISSN 0019-1876
● Illinois Courts Bulletin. m. ISSN 0019-1957
● Illinois State Bar Association. Antitrust Law
Newsletter. irreg., 1970, vol. 12, no. 1. ISSN
0073-5000
● Illinois State Bar Association. Federal Tax Section
Newsletter. irreg., 1970, vol. 17, no. 2. ISSN
0073-5027
● Illinois State Bar Association. Individual Rights
and Responsibilities Newsletter. ISSN 0090-2608
● Illinois State Bar Association. Local Government
Law Newsletter. irreg., 1970, vol. 8, no. 1. ISSN
0073-5035
● Illinois State Bar Association. Patent, Trademark,
and Copyright Newsletter. irreg., 1970, vol. 11,
no. 1. ISSN 0073-5043
● Illinois State Bar Association. Tort Trends. q.
ISSN 0040-9626
● Illinois Student Lawyer. m. ISSN 0094-2235

**Illinois State Chamber of Commerce**
20 N. Wacker Dr., Chicago, IL 60606.
● Voice of Illinois Business. m.

**Illinois State Dental Society**
524 S. Fifth St., Springfield, IL 62701.
● Illinois Dental Journal. m. ISSN 0019-1973

**Illinois State Federation of Labor and Congress of
Industrial Organizations**
300 N. State St., 16th Floor, Chicago, IL 60610.
● Illinois State Federation of Labor and Congress of
Industrial Organizations. Weekly News Letter. w.
ISSN 0019-2279

**Illinois State Genealogical Society**
Box 2225, Springfield, IL 62705.
● Illinois State Genealogical Society Quarterly. q.
ISSN 0046-8622

**Illinois State Historical Library**
Old State Capitol, Springfield, IL 62706.
● Historically Speaking. q. (Congress of Illinois
Historical Societies & Museums)
● Illinois History; a magazine for young people.
m.(Oct-May) ISSN 0019-2058 (Illinois State
Historical Society)
● Illinois State Historical Society. Journal. 5 per yr.
ISSN 0019-2287

**Illinois State Historical Society**
● Illinois History. (pub. by Illinois State Historical
Library)
● Illinois State Historical Society. Journal. (pub. by
Illinois State Historical Library)

**Illinois State Medical Society**
55 E. Monroe, Chicago, IL 60603.
● Illinois Medical Journal. m. ISSN 0019-2120

**Illinois State Museum**
Spring and Edwards Sts., Springfield, IL 62706.
● Dickson Mounds Museum Anthropological
Studies. irreg. ISSN 0095-2907
● Illinois. State Museum. Reports of Investigations.
irreg., no. 32, 1975. ISSN 0360-0270
● Illinois. State Museum. Research Series. Papers in
Anthropology. irreg. ISSN 0095-2915
● Illinois. State Museum. Scientific Papers Series.
irreg., vol. 14, 1974. ISSN 0445-3395
● Living Museum. bi-m. ISSN 0024-5283

**Illinois State Poetry Society**
Box 35, Charleston, IL 61920.
● Lincoln Log Poetry Reader. q.
● Lincoln Log Quarterly Magazine. q.

**Illinois State University**
Normal, IL 61761.
● Illinois Quarterly. q. ISSN 0019-2295

**Illinois State University. Alumni Office**
Rambo House, Normal, IL 61761.
● Illinois State University Alumni News. 4 per yr.

**Illinois State University. Dept. of Educational
Administration**
Normal, IL 61761.
● Planning & Changing; a journal for school
administrators. q. ISSN 0032-0684

**Illinois State University. News and Publications
Service**
Normal, IL 61761.
● Illinois State University Life. m (except Jan, June,
July)

**Illinois Trucking Associations**
15 Spinning Wheel Road, Hinsdale, IL 60521.
● Illinois Truck News. m. ISSN 0019-2309

**Illinois Wesleyan University**
Bloomington, IL 61701.
● Argus. w. ISSN 0004-1181

**Illinois Wildlife Federation**
13005 S. Western Ave., Blue Island, IL 60406.
● Illinois Wildlife. m. ISSN 0019-2317

**Illuminating Engineering Society**
345 E. 47th St., New York, NY 10017.
● I E S Lighting Handbook. irreg. ISSN 0073-5469
● Illuminating Engineering Society. Journal. q.
● L D & A. (Lighting Design & Application) m.

**Illumination of the Morning Star**
c/o Louisa Bohnet, Ed., Box 317, Demming, NM
88030.
● Illumination of the Morning Star; the voice of
truth in action. bi-m.

**Illustrated Speedway News**
83 Grand Ave., Massapequa, NY 11758.
● Illustrated Speedway News. w.

**Immaculate Heart Missions**
● Missionhurst. (pub. by Missionhurst, Inc.)

**Immigration History Society**
c/o Minnesota Historical Society, 690 Cedar St., St.
Paul, MN 55101.
● Immigration History Newsletter. s-a. ISSN 0579-
4374

**Impact Films Inc.**
144 Bleecker St., New York, NY 10012.
● Impact Films Catalog. a.

**Impact Publications (Chicago)**
333 N. Michigan Ave., Suite 2025, Chicago, IL
60601.
● Impact (Chicago) m. ISSN 0019-283X (Baker &
Bowden)

**Impact Publications (Estes Park)**
Box 1972, Estes Park, CO 80517.
● Impact-Valves. 10 per yr.

**Impact Publishers, Inc.**
Box 1094, San Luis Obispo, CA 93406.
● Assert; newsletter of assertive behavior. bi-m.

**Arthur J. Imparato Associates**
21 East 40th Street, New York, NY 10016.
● Trade (New York) m.

**Impart Publishers**
175 West Moana Lane, Box 5212, Reno, NV 89502.
● International Turquoise Annual. a. (International
Turquoise Association)

**Imperial Embassy of Iran. Economic Section**
5530 Wisconsin Ave., Washington, DC 20015.
● Iran Economic News. m.

**In-Flight Publishing Co.**
1637 S. Oakland Court, Aurora, CO 80012.
● Frontier. q. (Frontier Airlines)

**Independent Bankers Association of America**
Box 267, Sauk Centre, MN 56378.
● Independent Banker. m. ISSN 0019-3674

**Independent Battery Manufacturers Association, Inc.**
100 Larchwood Drive, Largo, FL 33540.
● Battery Man; international journal for starting,
lighting, ignitions, & generating systems. m. ISSN
0005-6359

**Independent Board for Presbyterian Foreign Missions**
246 W. Walnut Lane, Philadelphia, PA 19144.
● Biblical Missions. 10 per yr. ISSN 0006-0909

**Independent Buyers Association Inc.**
27 Providence Rd., Millbury, MA 01527.
● Dairy World. m.

**Independent College Funds of America**
Suite 5108, Empire State Bldg., New York, NY
10001.
● Independent College Funds of America Bulletin.
q. ISSN 0019-3690

**Independent Educational Services**
80 Nassau St., Princeton, NJ 08540.
● Optimum. q.
● Tree. q.

**Independent Fundamental Churches of America**
Box 242, 1860 Mannheim Rd., Westchester, IL
60153.
● Voice. 6 per yr. ISSN 0049-6669

**Independent Grocers Alliance**
5725 East River Rd., Chicago, IL 60631.
● I G A Grocergram. m. ISSN 0018-9766

**Independent Insurance Agents Association of
California**
● California Independent Agent. (pub. by Insurance
Producers Services Corp.)

**Independent Insurance Agents Association of New
York, Inc.**
731 James St., Syracuse, NY 13203.
● Forum (Syracuse) m. ISSN 0013-6743

**Independent Insurance Agents of America, Inc.**
85 John St., New York, NY 10038.
● Independent Agent. m. ISSN 0002-7197

**Independent Insurance Agents of Wisconsin**
Box 96, Middleton, WI 53562.
● Wisconsin Insuror. m.

**Independent-Journal Newspapers**
c/o Herb Chase, 524 Santa Monica Blvd., Santa
Monica, CA 90401.
● Suburbia West Today; Marina mail. w.

**Independent Order of Odd Fellows of Oklahoma**
Oklahoma Printing Co., Guthrie, OK 73044.
● Oklahoma Odd Fellow. m. ISSN 0030-1809

**Independent Order of Svithiod**
5520 W. Lawrence Ave., Chicago, IL 60630.
● Svithiod Journal. m. ISSN 0300-6212

**Independent Petroleum Association of America**
1101 16th St. N.W., Washington, DC 20036.
● Oil Producing Industry in Your State. a.
● Petroleum Independent. bi-m.

**Independent Press**
c/o Ed. John A. Ostenburg, Box 132, Springfield,
IL 62705.
● Spokesman. w. ISSN 0049-1896

**Independent Schools Association of the Central
States**
1400 Maple Ave., Downers Grove, IL 60515.
● I S A C S Bulletin. s-a. ISSN 0019-0543

**Independent Schools Association of the Southwest**
Box 52297, Tulsa, OK 74152.
● Independent Schools Association of the
Southwest. Membership List. a. ISSN 0073-5779

**Index Inc.**
Box 35, Arvada, CO 80001.
● Veterinary Index. s-a., cumulated annually and
every 5 yrs.

**India Abroad Publications Inc.**
60 E. 42nd St., New York, NY 10017.
● India Abroad. w. ISSN 0046-8932

**India Information Service**
Embassy of India, 2107 Massachusetts Ave., N.W.,
Washington, DC 20008.
● India News. w. ISSN 0019-4212

**Indian America Publishing Co.**
1518 So. Owasso, Tulsa, OK 74152.
● Indian America. q. ISSN 0099-0361

**Indian Center, Inc.**
1127 W. Washington, Los Angeles, CA 90015.
● Talking Leaf. m. ISSN 0300-6247

**Indian Historian Press**
1451 Masonic Ave., San Francisco, CA 94117.
- Index to Literature on the American Indian. a. ISSN 0091-7346 (American Indian Historical Society, Inc.)

**Indian Life**
c/o Chief, Box 2600, Orange, CA 92669.
- Indian Life. bi-m.

**Indian Nations Press**
812 Mayo Building, Tulsa, OK 74103.
- Four States Genealogist. q. ISSN 0015-9115

**Indian Rights Association**
1505 Race St., Philadelphia, PA 19102.
- Indian Truth. s-a. ISSN 0019-6452

**Indian River Life**
c/o C. W. Mauere, Ed., 15 Royal Palm Rd., Vero Beach, FL 32960.
- Indian River Life; the magazine of the Indian River Florida area. 10 per yr.

**Indiana. Aeronautics Commission**
100 N. Senate Ave., Indianapolis, IN 46204.
- Indiana. Aeronautics Commission. Annual Report. a. ISSN 0073-6775

**Indiana. Civil Rights Commission**
319 State Office Bldg., Indianapolis, IN 46204.
- Indiana. Civil Rights Commission. Annual Report. a. ISSN 0073-6856

**Indiana. Department of Mental Health**
1315 W. 10th St., Indianapolis, IN 46202.
- Indiana. Department of Mental Health. Annual Report. a. ISSN 0098-4205

**Indiana. Department of Natural Resources**
612 State Office Bldg., Indianapolis, IN 46204.
- Outdoor Indiana. 10 per yr. ISSN 0030-7068

**Indiana. Department of Public Welfare**
Indianapolis, IN 46204.
- Indiana. Departmeent of Public Welfare. Semi-Annual Statistical Series. s-a. ISSN 0019-6576

**Indiana. Division of Fish and Wildlife**
607 State Office Bldg., Indianapolis, IN 46204.
- Indiana. Division of Fish and Wildlife. Annual Report. a. ISSN 0073-6872
- Indiana. Division of Fish and Wildlife. Management Series. irreg. ISSN 0095-1676

**Indiana. Division of Water**
Indianapolis, IN 46204.
- Indiana. Division of Water. Bulletin. irreg.

**Indiana. Employment Security Division**
Indianapolis, IN 46204.
- Labor Force Status of Indiana Residents. a. ISSN 0362-3793

**Indiana. Environmental Management Board**
1330 W. Michigan St., Indianapolis, IN 46206.
- Indiana. Environmental Management Board. Annual Report.

**Indiana. Geological Survey**
Department of Natural Resources, Indianapolis, IN 46204.
- Indiana. Geological Survey. Annual Report of the State Geologist. a. ISSN 0362-3513

**Indiana. Governor's Commission on the Status of Women in Indiana**
Indianapolis, IN 46204.
- Indiana. Governor's Commission on the Status of Women in Indiana. Annual Report. a. ISSN 0098-6747

**Indiana. State Advisory Council for Vocational Technical Education**
803 State Office Building, Indianapolis, IN 46206.
- Indiana. State Advisory Council for Vocational Technical Education. Annual Report. a. ISSN 0091-8970

**Indiana. State Board of Health**
State Board of Health Bldg., 1330 W. Michigan St., Indianapolis, IN 46206.
- Indiana State Board of Health Bulletin. m. ISSN 0019-6754

**Indiana. State Board of Vocational and Technical Education**
120 W. Market St., Indianapolis, IN 46204.
- Indiana State Plan for Vocational Education. a.

**Indiana. State Library**
140 N. Senate Ave., Indianapolis, IN 46204.
- Library Occurrent. q. ISSN 0024-2454
- Statistics of Indiana Libraries. a. ISSN 0081-5152

**Indiana. State Library. Extension Division**
140 N. Senate, Indianapolis, IN 46204.
- Indiana State Institutional Libraries. Newsletter. irreg.
- Indiana State Library. Extension Division Bulletin. q. ISSN 0019-6762

**Indiana Academy of Ophthalmology and Otolaryngology**
c/o Milton W. Erdel, M.D., 2 East White Street, Frankfort, IN 46041.
- Indiana Academy of Ophthalmology and Otolaryngology. Annual Meeting. a.

**Indiana Academy of Science**
140 N. Senate Ave., Indianapolis, IN 46204.
- Indiana Academy of Science. Monograph. irreg., 1969, no. 1. ISSN 0073-6759
- Indiana Academy of Science. Proceedings. a. ISSN 0073-6767

**Indiana Association of Junior and Senior High School Principals**
1100 West 42nd St, Indianapolis, IN 46208.
- Hoosier Schoolmaster. 3 per yr. ISSN 0018-4810

**Indiana Association of Plumbing-Heating-Cooling Contractors, Inc.**
3008 E. 56th Street, Indianapolis, IN 46220.
- Indiana Plumbing - Heating - Cooling Contractor. bi-m. ISSN 0019-6703

**Indiana Audubon Society, Inc.**
Audubon Sanctuary, R.R. No. 6, Connersville, IN 47331.
- Indiana Audubon Quarterly. q. ISSN 0019-6525

**Indiana Bankers Association**
929 Electric Bldg., Indianapolis, IN 46204.
- Hoosier Banker. m. ISSN 0018-473X

**Indiana Baptist Convention**
1350 N. Delaware St., Indianapolis, IN 46202.
- Indiana Baptist Observer. m. ISSN 0005-5735

**Indiana Beverage Life**
Atkinson Square, Suite G-1, 2511 E. 46th St., Indianapolis, IN 46205.
- Indiana Beverage Journal. m.

**Indiana Council of Teachers of English, Inc.**
Division of Extended Services, Indiana State University, Terre Haute, IN 47809.
- Indiana English Journal. q. ISSN 0019-6584

**Indiana Covered Bridge Society**
929 Lindberg Rd., West Lafayette, IN 47906.
- Indiana Covered Bridge Society. Newsletter. q. ISSN 0019-655X

**Indiana Dental Association**
c/o Ed. H. William Gilmore, 1920 E. 62nd St., Indianapolis, IN 46220.
- Indiana Dental Association. Journal. bi-m. ISSN 0019-6568

**Indiana Family Health Council, Inc.**
21 Beachway Dr., Suite B, Indianapolis, IN 46224.
- Council Notes. q.

**Indiana Farm Bureau, Inc.**
130 E. Washington St., Indianapolis, IN 46204.
- Hoosier Farmer. m. ISSN 0018-4748

**Indiana General**
405 Elm St., Valparaiso, IN 46383.
- Applied Magnetics. 2 per yr.

**Indiana Herald**
723 N. West St., Indianapolis, IN 46208.
- Indiana Herald. w. ISSN 0019-6630

**Indiana Historical Bureau**
408 State Library and Historical Bldg., 140 N. Senate Ave., Indiannapolis, IN 46204.
- Indiana Historical Collections. irreg. ISSN 0073-6880

- Indiana History Bulletin. m. ISSN 0019-6649 (Co-Sponsor: Indiana Historical Society)

**Indiana Historical Society**
315 W. Ohio St., Indianapolis, IN 46204.
- Genealogy. 8 per yr.
- Hoosier Genealogist. q. ISSN 0018-4756
- Indiana Historical Society. Prehistory Research Series. irreg. ISSN 0073-6899
- Indiana Historical Society. Publications. irreg., 1972, vol. 25, no. 1. ISSN 0073-6902

**Indiana Jewish Historical Society**
215 East Berry St., Fort Wayne, IN 46802.
- Indiana Jewish Historical Society. Newsletter. q.

**Indiana Library Association**
1100 W. 42 St., Indianapolis, IN 46202.
- Focus on Indiana Libraries. q. ISSN 0015-5152
- Indiana Library Association Membership Directory. a.

**Indiana Motor Truck Association, Inc.**
2165 S. High School Rd., Indianapolis, IN 46241.
- Fifth Wheel. m. ISSN 0015-0819

**Indiana Music Educators Association**
Ball State University, School of Music, Muncie, IN 47306.
- Indiana Musicator. 4 per yr.

**Indiana Oil Marketers Association, Inc.**
8780 Purdue Rd., Suite 4, Indianapolis, IN 46268.
- Hoosier Independent. q. ISSN 0018-4764

**Indiana Restaurant Association, Inc.**
2120 N. Meridian St., Indianapolis, IN 46202.
- Hoosier Chef. m.

**Indiana Society for Public Administration**
c/o Charles Wise, Ed., 400 E. Seventh St., Bloomington, IN 47401.
- Indiana Public Management. q. ISSN 0099-1023

**Indiana Society of Architects**
- Indiana Architect. (pub. by Western Newspaper Publishing Co.)

**Indiana Speech Association**
Department of Speech, Ball State University, Muncie, IN 47306.
- Indiana Speech Journal. q.

**Indiana State Chamber of Commerce**
Board of Trade Building, Indianapolis, IN 64204.
- Here Is Your Indiana Government. biennial.
- Indiana Industrial Directory. biennial. ISSN 0073-6910

**Indiana State Medical Association**
3935 N. Meridian St., Indianapolis, IN 46208.
- Indiana State Medical Association. Journal. m. ISSN 0019-6770
- Indiana State Medical Association. Journal: Roster and Yearbook Issue. a.

**Indiana State Teachers Association**
150 W. Market St., Indianapolis, IN 46204.
- Teacher Advocate. m(10 per yr.) ISSN 0300-6298

**Indiana State University**
120 N. Seventh St., Terre Haute, IN 47809.
- Indiana Statesman. d. ISSN 0019-6789

**Indiana State University, Evansville**
Hwy. 62 W., Evansville, IN 47712.
- Moving Finger. s-a.

**Indiana State University. Business Office**
217 N. 6th St., Terre Haute, IN 47809.
- Indiana State University. Financial Report. a.

**Indiana State University. Department of English**
Terre Haute, IN 47809.
- Dreiser Newsletter. s-a. ISSN 0012-6098
- Science-Fiction Studies. 3 per yr. ISSN 0091-7729

**Indiana State University. Dept. of Geography and Geology**
Terre Haute, IN 47809.
- Indiana State University. Department of Geography and Geology. Professional Papers. a. ISSN 0073-6937

**Indiana State University. Department of Library Science**
Terre Haute, IN 47809.
- Changing Concept Series. irreg., no. 2, 1973.

**Indiana State University. School of Education**
Terre Haute, IN 47809.
- Black American Literature Forum. q.
- Contemporary Education. q. ISSN 0010-7476
- Junior High-Middle School Bulletin. 3 per yr. ISSN 0300-8002

**Indiana Statewide Rural Electric Cooperative Inc.**
720 N. High School Road, Indianapolis, IN 46224.
- Indiana Rural News. m. ISSN 0442-8102

**Indiana University**
- Indiana University Publications. African Series. (pub. by Humanities Press, Inc.)

**Indiana University. Afro-American Arts Institute**
109 N. Jordan Ave., Bloomington, IN 47401.
- Blacks in American Journalism Series. irreg.

**Indiana University Alumni Association**
Bloomington, IN 47401.
- Indiana Alumni. m. ISSN 0019-6517

**Indiana University Art Museum**
Bloomington, IN 47401.
- Indiana University Art Museum. Publications. irreg. ISSN 0073-7038

**Indiana University. Audio-Visual Center**
Field Services, Bloomington, IN 47401.
- Preview. q. ISSN 0032-8111

**Indiana University. Ballantine Hall**
Bloomington, IN 47401.
- Victorian Studies; a journal of the humanities, arts and sciences. q. ISSN 0042-5222

**Indiana University. Bureau of Educational Studies and Testing**
Bloomington, IN 47401.
- Indiana Studies in Prediction. irreg. ISSN 0073-6945

**Indiana University. Bureau of Studies in Adult Education**
Bloomington, IN 47401.
- Indiana University Monograph Series in Adult Education. irreg. ISSN 0073-702X

**Indiana University. Coordinator for School Social Studies**
306 Memorial West, Bloomington, IN 47401.
- News and Notes on the Social Sciences. 3 per yr.

**Indiana University. Department of Anthropology**
Rawles Hall 108, Bloomington, IN 47401.
- Anthropological Linguistics. 9 per yr. ISSN 0003-5483

**Indiana University. Department of Chemistry**
Room 204, Bloomington, IN 47401.
- Current Awareness Profile on Quantum Chemistry. fortn. (prep. by its Quantum Chemistry Program Exchange)

**Indiana University. Department of Comparative Literature**
Ballantine Hall, Bloomington, IN 47401
(Vols. 1-11 (1952-62) Available from Russell and Russell, Publishers, 122 E. 42 St., New York, N.Y. 10017)
- Yearbook of Comparative and General Literature. a. ISSN 0084-3695

**Indiana University. Department of Geography**
Bloomington, IN 47401.
- Indiana University. Department of Geography. Geographic Monograph Series. irreg. ISSN 0073-6953

**Indiana University. Department of History**
Ballantine Hall 742, Bloomington, IN 47401.
- Indiana Magazine of History. q. ISSN 0019-6673 (Co-Sponsor: Indiana Historical Society)

**Indiana University. Department of Mathematics**
Swain Hall East, Bloomington, IN 47401.
- Indiana University Mathematics Journal. bi-m. ISSN 0022-2518

**Indiana University. Department of Philosophy**
Sycamore 126, Bloomington, IN 47401.
- Nous; a quarterly journal of philosophy. q. ISSN 0029-4624

**Indiana University. Department of Uralic and Altaic Studies**
Goodbody Hall, Bloomington, IN 47401.
- Permanent International Altaistic Conference (PIAC). Newsletter. 2-3 per yr. ISSN 0031-5508 (Permanent International Altaistic Conference)

**Indiana University. Dept. of Zoology**
Jordan Hall, Bloomington, IN 47401.
- Investigations of Indiana Lakes and Streams. irreg. ISSN 0075-0239 (Co-sponsor: Indiana Department of Natural Resoruces)

**Indiana University. Folklore Institute**
- Indiana University. Folklore Institute. Monograph Series. (pub. by Mouton Publishers NE)
- Journal of Folklore Studies. (pub. by Mouton Publishers NE)

**Indiana University. Graduate Library School**
Bloomington, IN 47401.
- Indiana University. Graduate Library School Alumni Newsletter. s-a. ISSN 0019-6827

**Indiana University. International Development Research Center**
1005 E. Tenth St., Bloomington, IN 47401.
- International Development Research Center. Case Studies. irreg.
- International Development Research Center. Occasional Papers. irreg.
- International Development Research Center. Related Studies by I D R C Scholars. irreg.
- International Development Research Center. Reprints. irreg.
- International Development Research Center. Working Papers. irreg.
- Studies in East European and Soviet Planning, Development and Trade. irreg.
- Studies in Human Resources and Development. irreg.
- Studies in Institutional Development and Modernization. irreg.

**Indiana University. Latin American Studies Program**
Lindley Hall 311, Bloomington, IN 47401.
- Latin American Studies Working Papers. irreg.

**Indiana University Library**
Bloomington, IN 47401.
- Indiana University Bookman. irreg. ISSN 0019-6800

**Indiana University. Research Center for the Language Sciences**
Indiana University, 516 E. 6th St, Bloomington, IN 47401.
- Indiana University. Research Center for the Language Sciences. African Series. (pub. by Mouton Publishers NE)
- Indiana University. Research Center for the Language Sciences. Uralic and Altaic Series. (pub. by Mouton Publishers NE)
- Inter-American Music Monograph Series. (pub. by Mouton Publishers NE)
- Language Science Monographs. (pub. by Mouton Publishers NE)
- Language Sciences. 5 per yr. ISSN 0023-8341

**Indiana University. Research Center in Anthropology, Folklore, and Linguistics**
- Indiana University. Research Center in Anthropology, Folklore, and Linguistics. Publications. (pub. by Mouton Publishers NE)

**Indiana University. School of Business**
Bloomington, IN 47401.
- Bibliographical Aids for Business Series. irreg. (prep. by its Division of Research)
- Business Horizons. bi-m. ISSN 0007-6813
- Business Information Bulletins. irreg., 1971, no. 60. ISSN 0068-4422 (prep. by its Division of Research)
- Indiana Business Papers. irreg., 1971, no. 18. ISSN 0073-683X (prep. by its Division of Research)
- Indiana Business Report. irreg., no. 47, 1973. ISSN 0073-6848 (prep. by its Division of Research)
- Indiana Business Review. bi-m. ISSN 0019-6541 (prep. by its Division of Research)
- Indiana University. Institute for Urban Transportation. Series. irreg., 1971, no. 1. ISSN 0073-7003 (prep. by its Division of Research)
- Indiana University. School of Business. Division of Research. Research Reports. irreg., 1969, no. 6. ISSN 0073-7100 (prep. by its Division of Research)

**Indiana University. Sesquicentennial Series on Insurance.** irreg., no. 4, 1971. ISSN 0073-7127 (prep. by its Division of Research)
- International Business Research Series. irreg. ISSN 0074-2120 (prep. by its Division of Research)

**Indiana University. School of Dentistry**
Indianapolis, IN 46202.
- Indiana University. School of Dentistry. Alumni Bulletin. s-a. ISSN 0073-7119

**Indiana University. School of Education**
Bloomington, IN 47401.
- Viewpoints; bulletin of the School of Education, Indiana University. bi-m. ISSN 0019-6835

**Indiana University. School of Law**
Law Building Annex, Bloomington, IN 47401.
- Indiana Law Journal. q. ISSN 0019-6665
- Iustitia. s-a. ISSN 0092-3524

**Indiana University. School of Law-Indianapolis**
735 W. New York St., Indianapolis, IN 46202.
- Indiana Law Review. 6 per yr. ISSN 0046-9106

**Indiana University. School of Medicine**
1100 W. Michigan St., Indianapolis, IN 46202.
- M E R P Memo. (Medical Education Resources Program) q. ISSN 0046-9122

**Indiana University. School of Music**
Bloomington, IN 47401.
- Indiana Directory of Music Teachers. a. (prep. by its Music Education Department)

**Indiana University. School of Public and Environmental Affairs**
400 E. Seventh, Bloomington, IN 47401.
- Indiana University. School of Public and Environmental Affairs. Occasional Papers. irreg., no. 4, 1975.

**Indiana University Student Broadcast Association**
Box 635, Bloomington, IN 47401.
- W I U S Tipsheet. 8 per yr.

**Indiana University, Northwest**
3400 Broadway, Gary, IN 46408.
- Revista Chicano-Requena. q.

**Indiana University of Pennsylvania. English Department**
Indiana, PA 15701.
- Studies in the Humanities. irreg. ISSN 0039-3800

**Indiana University of Pennsylvania. Department of History**
Indiana, PA 15701.
- Historical Musings. irreg. ISSN 0046-7553

**Indiana University of South Bend**
1825 Northside Blvd., South Bend, IN 46615.
- Preface. w (during academic year) ISSN 0048-5152

**Indianapolis Athletic Club**
350 North Meridian St, Indianapolis, IN 46204.
- I N D A C. m. ISSN 0019-3569

**Indianapolis Chamber of Commerce**
320 N. Meridian, Indianapolis, IN 46204.
- Indianapolis. m.

**Indianapolis-Marion County Public Library**
40 East Saint Clair St., Indianapolis, IN 46204.
- Reading in Indianapolis. s-m.

**Indianapolis Museum of Art**
1200 West 38th St., Indianapolis, IN 46208.
- Indianapolis Museum of Art. News Letter. q.

**Indianapolis Zoological Society, Inc.**
3120 E. 30th St., Indianapolis, IN 46218.
- Zoo's Letter. bi-m. ISSN 0044-5304

**Indians for Democracy**
- Indian Opinion. (pub. by Shrikumar Poddar)

**Indians into Communications Association**
P.O. Box 4322, Pioneer Square Station, Seattle, WA 98104.
- Northwest Indian News. m.

**Indicator Digest, Inc.**
Palisades Park, NJ 07650.
- Indicator Digest; a survey of all the vital market barometers. s-m. ISSN 0019-6940

**Indice**
P.O. Box 014474, Flagler Station, Miami, FL 33101.
- Indice. s-a.

**Indigena**
P.O. Box 4073, Berkeley, CA 94704.
- Indigena; news from Indian America. q.

**Individualized Science Instructional System**
- I S I S Newsletter. (pub. by Florida State University)

**Indochina Resource Center**
Box 4000-D, Berkeley, CA 94704.
- Indochina Chronicle. 8-10 per yr.

**Indoor Gardener Publishing Co., Inc.**
1800-1802 Grand Ave., Knoxville, TN 37901.
- G S N. Gesneriad Saintpaulia News. bi-m. ISSN 0016-3627

**Indprop Publishing Co., Inc.**
74 Shrewsbury Ave., Red Bank, NJ 07701.
- American Industrial Properties Report. bi-m.

**Industrial Ad-Reply: Delaware Valley Edition**
19 W. Winona Ave, Norwood, PA 19074.
- Industrial Ad-Reply: Delaware Valley Edition. bi-m. ISSN 0019-7807

**Industrial Bookshelf Inc.**
777 Mountain Ave., Murray Hill, NJ 07974.
- Business/Management Book Review. m.

**Industrial Cities News Service**
Box 592, Chicago, IL 60690.
- Industrial Cities News Service; an independent, socialist news service. irreg. ISSN 0085-1833

**Industrial College of the Armed Forces**
see U. S. Industrial College of the Armed Forces

**Industrial Communication Council**
- Communication Reports. (pub. by Tilley Associates)

**Industrial Construction**
c/o Leslie Miller, 18615 Detroit Ave., Lakewood, OH 44107.
- Industrial Construction. m.

**Industrial Development Research Council**
- Industrial Development and Manufacturers Record. (pub. by Conway Publications, Inc.)

**Industrial Directory Publishers**
Park Ave. Bldg., Detroit, MI 48226.
- Midwest Manufacturers & Industrial Classified Directory & Buyers Guide. a.

**Industrial Environmental Health**
c/o Dr. Lester V. Cralley, Chief Industrial Hygienist, Aluminum Co. of America, 1501 Alcoa Bldg., Pittsburgh, PA 15219.
- Industrial Environmental Health. irreg., 1972, vol. 2.

**Industrial Fasteners Institute**
1505 E. Ohio Bldg., 1717 E. Ninth St., Cleveland, OH 44114.
- Fastener Standards. irreg. ISSN 0071-4046

**Industrial Health Foundation, Inc.**
5231 Centre Ave., Pittsburgh, PA 15232.
- Industrial Health Foundation. Chemical-Toxicological Series. Bulletin. irreg., 1969, no. 8. ISSN 0073-7488
- Industrial Health Foundation. Engineering Series. Bulletin. irreg.; 1967, no. 7. ISSN 0073-7496
- Industrial Health Foundation. Legal Series Bulletin. irreg., 1972, no. 9. ISSN 0073-750X
- Industrial Health Foundation. Medical Series. Bulletin. irreg.; 1975, no. 19. ISSN 0073-7518
- Industrial Health Foundation. Nursing Series. Bulletins. irreg., 1971, no. 3.
- Industrial Health Foundation. Technical Bulletin. Management Series. irreg.
- Industrial Hygiene Digest. m. ISSN 0019-8382

**Industrial Home for the Blind**
57 Willoughby St., Brooklyn, NY 11201.
- I H B Reporter. 3 per yr. ISSN 0018-9812 (Braille ed. avail. from: I H B Braille Library, 329 Hempstead Tpke., W. Hempstead, NY 11552)

**Industrial Machinery News Corporation**
29516 Southfield Rd., C.S. No. 5002, Southfield, MI 48037.
- Industrial Machinery News. m. ISSN 0019-8455

**Industrial Management Society**
570 Northwest Highway, Des Plaines, IL 60016.
- Industrial Management. m. ISSN 0019-8471

**Industrial Market Place**
4257 W. Main St., Skokie, IL 60076.
- Industrial Market Place. bi-w.

**Industrial Mathematics Society**
Box 159, Roseville, MI 48066.
- Industrial Mathematics. s-a. ISSN 0019-8528

**Industrial Publishing Co.**
614 Superior Ave. West, Cleveland, OH 44113.
- Airconditioning and Refrigeration Business. m.
- Occupational Hazards' Executive Report. s-a.

**Industrial Relations Law Journal**
University of California, Berkeley, Boalt Hall, Rm. 1, Berkeley, CA 94720.
- Industrial Relations Law Journal. q.

**Industrial Relations Research Association**
Social Science Bldg., University of Wisconsin, Madison, WI 53706.
- I R R A Newsletter. q. ISSN 0019-0500

**Industrial Relations Research Institute**
- Journal of Human Resources. (pub. by University of Wisconsin Press)

**Industrial Research**
222 S. Riverside Plaza, Chicago, IL 60606.
- Electro-Technology. m. ISSN 0013-4635

**Industrial Research Institute**
100 Park Ave., New York, NY 10017.
- Research Management; international journal of research management. bi-m. ISSN 0034-5334

**Industrial Research Service, Inc.**
Masonic Bldg., Dover, NH 03820.
- Cost Engineering. q. ISSN 0010-9614

**Industrial Risk Insurers**
85 Woodland St., Hartford, CT 06102.
- Sentinel (Hartford) bi-m. ISSN 0037-2323

**Industrial Wastes**
434 S. Wabash, Chicago, IL 60605.
- Industrial Wastes. bi-m. ISSN 0046-9262

**Industrial Workers of the World**
752 West Webster, Chicago, IL 60614.
- Industrial Worker. m. ISSN 0019-8870

**Industry Media Inc.**
1129 E. 17th Ave., Denver, CO 80218.
- Plastics Design Forum. bi-m.

**Industry Publications**
703 Market St., San Francisco, CA 94103.
- Beverage Industry News. s-m. ISSN 0006-0364
- Beverage Industry News California Goldbook. a.
- Beverage Industry News Merchandiser. m.

**Industry Publications, Inc.(Cedar Grove)**
200 Commerce Rd., Cedar Grove, NJ 07009.
- Aerosol Age; the magazine of pressure packaging. m. ISSN 0001-9291
- Fueloil & Oil Heat. m. ISSN 0016-2418

**Industry Publishers, Inc.**
915 N.E. 125th St., North Miami, FL 33161.
- Golf Industry. 11 per yr.
- Tennis Industry. 10 per yr (Jan.-Oct.)

**Infectious Diseases, Inc.**
355 Lexington Ave., New York, NY 10017.
- Infectious Diseases. 12 per yr. ISSN 0090-8886

**Infinity Publications**
Box 412, South Point, OH 45680.
- New Infinity Review. q.

**Info-Media, Inc.**
Box 1911, Phoenix, AZ 85001.
- Builder Architect-Contractor Engineer. m.

**Info-Quest, Inc.**
Box 2627, Framingham, MA 01701.
- Collision. bi-m.
- Tow-Line. m.

**Infordata International Inc.**
Suite 4602, 175 East Delaware Place, Chicago, IL 60611.
- Index to U.S. Government Periodicals. q.

**INFORM**
see International Reference Organization in Forensic Medicine and Science

**Informador Publishing Co.**
1510 W. 18th St., Chicago, IL 60608.
- Informador. w. ISSN 0019-9869

**Informatics Inc.**
21050 Vanowen Street, Canoga Park, CA 91303.
- System/3 World. m.

**Information & Records Management Inc.**
250 Fulton Ave., Hempstead, NY 11550.
- I M C Journal. q. ISSN 0019-0012 (International Micrographic Congress)
- Information and Records Management. m. ISSN 0019-9966

**Information and Referral Services of L.A. County, Inc.**
621 S. Virgil Ave., Los Angeles, CA 90005.
- Psychiatric Outpatient Services in Los Angeles County. s-a. ISSN 0048-5721

**Information Coordinators Inc.**
1435-37 Randolph St., Detroit, MI 48226.
- Bibliographies in American Music. irreg. (College Music Society)
- Detroit Monographs in Musicology. irreg.
- Detroit Studies in Music Bibliography. irreg., no. 33, 1975. ISSN 0070-3885
- Music Index; a subject-author guide to over 300 current periodicals from the U.S., England, Canada & Australia and 19 non-English language countries. m.(annual cumulation) ISSN 0027-4348
- Work Related Abstracts. m.
- Work Related Abstracts Subject Heading List. a.

**Information Film Producers of America**
Box 1470, Hollywood, CA 90028.
- I F P A Communicator. irreg. ISSN 0099-1090

**Information for Business Communications Ltd.**
- Finance. (pub. by Finance Publishing Corp.)

**Information Planning Associates, Inc.**
310 Maple Dr., Rockville, MD 20850
(Subscr. address: P.O. Box 6318, 5632 Connecticut Ave. N.W., Washington, DC 20015)
- Alcoholism Digest. m. ISSN 0093-7010
- Alcoholism Digest Annual. a. ISSN 0093-3279
- Bioethics Digest. m.
- Reprographics (Rockville); a guide to plain paper copier-duplicators. bi-m. updates to base vol.

**Information Press Service**
Key Colony Beach, FL 33051.
- Afro-American. s-a. ISSN 0002-0567

**Information Resources Center for Mental Health and Family Life Education**
- I R C Newsletter. (pub. by Mental Health Materials Center)

**Information Resources Press**
2100 M St. N.W., Suite 316, Washington, DC 20037.
- E I S: Key to Environmental Impact Statements. m.
- National Directory of State Agencies. biennial.

**Information Services on Latin America**
Box 4267, Berkeley, CA 94704.
- I S L A. m. ISSN 0046-8401

**Information Synergy Inc.**
Box 992, Acton, MA 01720.
- T H E Journal. (Technological Horizons in Education) 11 per yr.

**Information Universal Corporation**
Box 48-1305, Miami, FL 33148.
- Parapsychology-Psychic Science Journal; magazine of psychic phenomena. m.
- Psychic Science Digest. m.

**Informational Research Systems**
2940 Cortland Pl. N.W., Washington, DC 20008.
- Legal Notes for Insurance. m. ISSN 0094-0623

**Informative Data Co.**
4401 Hampton Ave., St. Louis, MO 63109.
- Missouri Directory of Manufacturing and Mining.
  a. ISSN 0076-9584

**Ignace M. Ingianni, Ed. & Pub**
63 Mercury Ave., Tiburon, CA 94920.
- Simbolica. 3 per yr.(approx.) ISSN 0037-5381

**Inglewood Public Library**
101 W. Manchester Blvd., Inglewood, CA 90301.
- Inglewood Public Library Quarterly Report. q.
  ISSN 0020-1308

**Initia, Inc.**
Benedum- Trees Bldg., Pittsburgh, PA 15222.
- Engineer. bi-m. (Pennsylvania Society of
  Professional Engineers)

**Inky Trails**
Box 345, Middleton, ID 83644.
- Inky Trails. q.

**Inland Architect Corporation**
1800 S. Prairie Ave., Chicago, IL 60616.
- Inland Architect; the magazine of inland area
  building and planning. m. ISSN 0020-1472

**Inland Library System**
- Inland Messenger. (pub. by Riverside Public
  Library)

**Inland Steel Co.**
c/o Richard F. Killelea, 30 W. Monroe St., Chicago,
IL 60603.
- Inland; the magazine of the Middle West. q. ISSN
  0020-1456

**Inland Waterways Publishing Corp.**
330 Exchange Place, New Orleans, LA 70130.
- Mark Twain: Magazine of the Waterways. m.

**Inner Asia Society**
Box 1165, Bloomington, IN 47401.
- Inner Asia Society Bulletin. s-a.
- Inner Asian Studies. 3 per yr.

**Inner-City Cultural Center**
1309 So. New Hampshire Ave., Los Angeles, CA
90006.
- New World Quarterly of the Inner-City Cultural
  Center. q.

**Inorganic Syntheses, Inc.**
- Inorganic Syntheses Series. (pub. by McGraw-Hill
  Inc.)

**Inprint**
Box 329, Dobbs Ferry, NY 10522.
- Inprint. q.

**Inside Kung Fu**
7033 Sunset Blvd., Suite 301, Los Angeles, CA
90028.
- Inside Kung Fu. m.

**Inside Today's Sports**
19830 Mack Ave., Grosse Point, MI 48236.
- Inside Today's Sports. m.

**Insight Publishing Co., Inc.**
501 Madison Ave., New York, NY 10022.
- Ear, Nose & Throat Journal. m. ISSN 0145-5613
- Osteopathic Annals. m. ISSN 0092-9336
- Pediatric Annals. m. ISSN 0090-4481
- Psychiatric Annals. m. ISSN 0048-5713

**Institut des Etudes Francaises**
937 Marilyn, Lafayette, LA 70503.
- Tribune des Francophones. s-a.

**Institute for Advanced Philosophic Research**
P.O. Box 1373, Boulder, CO 80302.
- Philosophic Research and Analysis. bi-m. ISSN
  0048-3907

**Institute for American Democracy**
818 18th St. N.W., Washington, DC 20006.
- Homefront I A D. m. ISSN 0018-4179

**Institute for Business Planning, Inc.**
I B P Plaza, Englewood Cliffs, NJ 07632.
- Closely Held Corporations. m.
- Corporate Planning; formation, operation and
  management. m. ISSN 0010-8987
- Estate Planning. m. ISSN 0014-1216
- Estate Planning Checklists and Forms. m. ISSN
  0014-1224

- Estate Practice and Procedure Guide. m.
- Executives Wealth Report. fortn. ISSN 0014-4592
- Financial Planning. m.
- Forms of Business Agreements. m. ISSN 0015-
  7805
- How to Use Tax-Free and Tax-Sheltered
  Investments to Pyramid Your Capital. m.
- Life Insurance Planning. m. ISSN 0024-3132
- Pay Planning. m. ISSN 0031-3351
- Pay Planning Checklist and Forms. m. ISSN
  0031-336X
- Professional Corporations, Associations and
  Partnerships. m.
- Real Estate Investment Ideas. s-m. ISSN 0034-
  0723
- Real Estate Investment Planning. m. ISSN 0034-
  0731
- Real Estate Investment Planning Checklist and
  Forms. m. ISSN 0034-0693
- Regulation of Securities. m.
- Tax Planning. m. ISSN 0040-0084
- Tax Planning Ideas. s-m. ISSN 0040-0092

**Institute for Byzantine and Modern Greek Studies**
115 Gilbert Rd., Belmont, MA 02178.
- Modern Orthodox Saints. irreg. (annually or
  biennially)

**Institute for Clinical Science**
230 N. Broad St., Philadelphia, PA 19102
(Subscription Address: 1833 Delancey Pl.,
Philadelphia, PA 19103)
- Annals of Clinical Laboratory Science. bi-m. ISSN
  0091-7370 (Association of Clinical Scientists)
- Institute for Clinical Science. Proficiency Test
  Service. Report. a (compilation of monthly
  reports) ISSN 0073-8638

**Institute for Continuing Professional Development,
Inc.**
964 Third Ave., New York, NY 10022.
- Practical Accountant; accounting and taxes in
  everyday practice. bi-m. ISSN 0032-6321

**Institute for Cross-Cultural Research**
4000 Albermarle St. N.W., Washington, DC 20016.
- I C R Studies. irreg., 1968, no. 3. ISSN 0073-
  8646

**Institute for Defense Analyses**
400 Army - Navy Dr., Arlington, VA 22202.
- Institute for Defense Analyses. Papers. irreg. ISSN
  0073-8654
- Institute for Defense Analyses. Reports. irreg.
  ISSN 0073-8662 (Avail. from: National Technical
  Information Service, Springfield, VA 22151)
- Institute for Defense Analyses. Studies. irreg.
  ISSN 0073-8670

**Institute for Development of Educational Activities,
Inc.**
Informational Services, Box 446, Melbourne, FL
32901.
- I/D/E/A Monographs. irreg. ISSN 0073-8697
- I/D/E/A Occasional Papers. irreg. ISSN 0073-
  8700

**Institute for Early Iberian Christian Studies**
- Classical Folia. (pub. by Classical Folia
  Associates)

**Institute for Economic and Financial Research.**
see under **American Classical College**

**Institute for Educational Finance**
1212 S.W. 5th Ave., Gainesville, FL 32601.
- Journal of Education Finance. q. ISSN 0098-9495
  (American Education Finance Association)

**Institute for German-American Studies**
7204 Langerford Drive, Cleveland, OH 44129.
- German-American Genealogist; a journal of
  ancestral research. q. ISSN 0099-0590

**Institute for Graduate Dentists. Alumni Association**
140 W. 67th St., New York, NY 10023.
- Dental Concepts. q. ISSN 0011-8540

**Institute for Humane Studies**
1177 University Drive, Menlo Park, CA 94025.
- Law & Liberty; a project on the legal framework
  of a free society. q. ISSN 0094-0615
- Studies in History and Philosophy. Pamphlet
  Series. irreg.

**Institute for Inter-American Legal Studies**
- Studies in Inter-American Laws. (pub. by
  University of Miami. School of Law)

**Institute for International Research Ltd.**
30 East 42 St., New York, NY 10017.
- International Investment Advisor. fortn.
- International Tax Report. fortn. ISSN 0300-1628

**Institute for Invention and Innovation, Inc.**
Box 436, 85 Irving St., Arlington, MA 02174.
- Invention Management. m. ISSN 0363-6380

**Institute for Laser Documentation**
Box 2070, Rolling Hills, CA 90274.
- Journal of Current Laser Abstracts. m. ISSN
  0022-0264

**Institute for Local Self Reliance**
1717 18th N.W., Washington, DC 20009.
- Self Reliance. bi-m. ISSN 0362-8566

**Institute for Monetary Research**
1010 Vermont Ave. N.W., Washington, DC 20005.
- Institute for Monetary Research. Monographs.
  irreg. ISSN 0073-8778

**Institute for New Communications, Inc.**
206 Fifth Ave., New York, NY 10010.
- Seven Days. bi-w.

**Institute for Profit Planning Inc.**
280 John Knox Rd, Suite 223, Tallahassee, FL
32303.
- Entrepreneur. m.

**Institute for Psychoanalysis**
180 N. Michigan, Chicago, IL 60601.
- Chicago Psychoanalytic Literature Index. q. ISSN
  0009-3661
- Institute for Psychoanalysis. Newsletter. irreg.
  (approx. 3 per yr.)

**Institute for Rational Living**
45 E. 65th St, New York, NY 10021.
- Rational Living. s-a. ISSN 0034-0049

**Institute for Research on Land and Water Resources**
Pennsylvania State University, University Park, PA
16802.
- Institute for Research on Land and Water
  Resources. Newsletter. bi-m. ISSN 0020-2614

**Institute for Research on Poverty**
see under **University of Wisconsin-Madison**

**Institute for Responsive Education**
704 Commonwealth Avenue, Boston, MA 02215.
- Citizen Action in Education. q.

**Institute for Scientific Information**
325 Chestnut St., Philadelphia, PA 19106
(and 132 High St., Uxbridge, Middlesex, Eng)
- A N S A. (Automatic New Structure Alert) m.
- A S C A. (Automatic Subject Citation Alert) w.
- Arts & Humanities Citation Index. 3 per yr.
  including annual cum.
- Ascatopics. w.
- Chemical Substructure Index. m.(annual
  cumulation) ISSN 0009-269X
- Current Abstracts of Chemistry & Index
  Chemicus; an abstracting journal reporting on new
  organic compounds. w.(plus quarterly and annual
  cumulations of index section) ISSN 0011-3158
- Current Contents/Agriculture, Biology &
  Environmental Sciences. w. ISSN 0090-0508
- Current Contents/Clinical Practice. w.
- Current Contents/Engineering, Technology &
  Applied Sciences. w. ISSN 0011-3395
- Current Contents/Life Sciences. w. ISSN 0011-
  3409
- Current Contents/Physical & Chemical Sciences.
  w. ISSN 0011-3417
- Current Contents/Social & Behavioral Sciences. w.
- I S I Journal Citation Reports. a.
- I S I Magnetic Tapes. w.
- I S I's Who Is Publishing in Science. a.
- Index Chemicus Registry System; magnetic tape
  index of new organic compounds including
  Wiswesser line notations and bibliographic data
  appearing in Current Abstracts of Chemistry &
  Index Chemicus and Chemical Substructure
  Index. 12 monthly tapes plus annual cumulation
  tape. ISSN 0019-3828
- Index to Scientific & Technical Proceedings. m. (s-
  a. cum.)
- Index to Scientific Reviews. s-a (annual
  cumulation)
- P S I. (Permuterm Subject Index) q.(annual
  cumulation. ISSN 0031-5532
- Science Citation Index. q.(Annual cumulation)
  ISSN 0036-827X

- Social Sciences Citation Index. 3 per yr. (including annual cum.)

**Institute for Socioeconomic Studies**
Airport Rd., White Plains, NY 10604.
- Institute for Socioeconomic Studies. Journal. q. ISSN 0364-0779
- Socioeconomic Newsletter. m.

**Institute for Southern Studies**
P.O. Box 230, Chapel Hill, NC 27514.
- Southern Exposure. q.

**Institute for Studies in American Music**
City University of New York, Brooklyn College, Department of Music, School of Performing Arts, Brooklyn, NY 11210.
- Institute for Studies in American Music. Newsletter. s-a.

**Institute for the Certification of Computer Professionals**
P. O. Box 1442, Chicago, IL 60690.
- Institute for the Certification of Computer Professionals. Annual Report. a. ISSN 0098-2431

**Institute for the Certification of Engineering Technicians**
2029 K Street, N.W., Washington, DC 20006.
- I C E T Newsletter. q.

**Institute for the Comparative Study of Political Systems**
4000 Albemarle St. N.W., Washington, DC 20016.
- Operations and Policy Research. Institute for the Comparative Study of Political Systems. Election Analysis Series. irreg., 1968, no. 6. ISSN 0078-530X
- Operations and Policy Research. Institute for the Comparative Study of Political Systems. Political Study Series. irreg. ISSN 0078-5288

**Institute for the Development of Indian Law**
927 15th Street, N.W., Suite 200, Washington, DC 20005.
- American Indian Journal. m. ISSN 0145-7993

**Institute for the Study of Drug Addiction**
- Journal of Altered States of Consciousness. (pub. by Baywood Publishing Co., Inc.)

**Institute for the Study of Human Issues**
3401 Science Ctr., Philadelphia, PA 19104.
- I S H I Occasional Papers in Social Change. irreg.

**Institute for the Study of Man Inc.**
1785 Massachusetts Ave. N.W., No. 211, Montana College of Mineral Science and Technology, MT 59701.
- Journal of Indo-European Studies. q. ISSN 0092-2323
- Urban Anthropology. (pub. by Plenum Press)

**Institute for the Study of Nineteenth Century Europe**
188 Lawton Rd., Riverside, IL 60546.
- Studies in Modern European History and Culture. a. ISSN 0098-275X

**Institute for the Study of Nonviolence**
Box 1001, Palo Alto, CA 94302.
- Institute for the Study of Nonviolence Journal. bi-m. ISSN 0020-2630

**Institute of Advanced Studies of World Religions**
555 Madison Ave., New York, NY 10022.
- Buddhist Text Information. q. ISSN 0360-6112

**Institute of Advanced Thinking**
- Bernporter International. (pub. by Bernporter Books)

**Institute of Amateur Cinematographers**
31 Montrose St., Newton, MA 02146.
- A C Movie News. (Amateur Cinematographers) m.

**Institute of Andean Studies**
Box 9307, Berkeley, CA 94709.
- Nawpa Pacha. a. ISSN 0077-6297

**Institute of Certified Travel Agents**
Box 9206, Arlington, VA 22209.
- I.C.T.A. Roster. irreg. ISSN 0094-3517

**Institute of Chartered Financial Analysts**
P. O. Box 3668, Charlottesville, VA 22903.
- C F A Digest. q. ISSN 0046-9777
- C F A Monograph Series. irreg. ISSN 0073-9065

**Institute of Early American History & Culture**
Box 220, Williamsburg, VA 23185.
- Institute of Early American History and Culture. News Letter. 2 per yr. ISSN 0020-2843
- William and Mary Quarterly; a magazine of early American history. q. ISSN 0043-5597 (Co-Sponsors: College of William and Mary; Colonial Williamsburg Foundation)

**Institute of Electrical and Electronics Engineers Inc.**
445 Hoes Lane, Piscataway, NJ 08854.
- Advanced Techniques in Failure Analysis Symposium. Proceedings. irreg.
- Appliance Technical Conference. Preprints. a. ISSN 0066-5401
- Automatic Support Systems Symposium for Advanced Maintainability. Proceedings. a. until 1970; biennial thereafter. ISSN 0067-2491
- Cement Industry Technical Conference. Record. a. ISSN 0069-1402
- Circuits and Systems Society Newsletter. bi-m.
- Conference on Frontiers in Education. Digest. a. ISSN 0069-8547
- Conference on Laser Engineering and Applications. Digest. biennial. ISSN 0069-858X
- Conference on Underground Transmission and Distribution. Record. a. ISSN 0069-875X
- Control Systems Society Newsletter. q.
- Current Papers in Electrical & Electronics Engineering. m. ISSN 0011-3778
- Current Papers on Computers & Control/C P C. m. ISSN 0011-3794
- Electrical Process Heating in Industry. Technical Conference. Record. a. ISSN 0070-9719
- Electron, Ion and Laser Beam Technology Conference. Record. a. ISSN 0070-9808
- Electronic Components Conference. Record. a. ISSN 0070-9832
- Electronics and Aerospace Systems Convention. E A S C O N Record. irreg. ISSN 0531-6863
- Engineering in Medicine and Biology Conference. Record. a. ISSN 0071-0334
- Engineering Management Review. bi-m.
- I E E E International Conference on Acoustics, Speech and Signal Processing. Conference Record. a.
- I E E E International Conference on Communications. Conference Record. irreg., 1972, 8th, Philadelphia. ISSN 0536-1486
- I E E E International Convention and Exhibition. Record. a. ISSN 0073-9138
- I E E E International Convention Digest. a. ISSN 0090-7294
- I E E E International Symposium on Circuit Theory. I E E E Symposium Digest. Summaries of Papers. irreg. ISSN 0579-4234
- I E E E International Symposium on Electrical Insulation. Conference Record. a.
- I E E E International Symposium on Information Theory. Abstracts of Papers. a.
- I E E E Journal of Oceanic Engineering. q.
- I E E E Journal of Quantum Electronics. m. ISSN 0018-9197
- I E E E Journal of Solid State Circuits. bi-m. ISSN 0018-9200
- I E E E Membership Directory. a. ISSN 0073-9146
- I E E E Monitor. m.
- I E E E Power Engineering Society. Winter Meeting. Preprints. a. ISSN 0073-9154
- I E E E Power Processing and Electronics Specialists Conference. Record. irreg. ISSN 0090-2381
- I E E E Proceedings. m. ISSN 0018-9219
- I E E E Publications Bulletin. q. ISSN 0046-8371
- I E E E Region 5 Conference. Record. a. ISSN 0073-9197
- I E E E Spectrum. m. ISSN 0018-9235
- I E E E Standards. irreg. ISSN 0073-9162
- I E E E Student Papers. a. ISSN 0362-4536
- I E E E Symposium on Computer Software Reliability. Record. irreg. ISSN 0091-469X
- I E E E Transactions. Acoustics, Speech & Signal Processing. bi-m.
- I E E E Transactions. Aerospace and Electronic Systems. bi-m. ISSN 0018-9251
- I E E E Transactions. Antennas and Propagation. bi-m. ISSN 0018-926X
- I E E E Transactions. Automatic Control. bi-m. ISSN 0018-9286
- I E E E Transactions. Biomedical Engineering. bi-m. ISSN 0018-9294
- I E E E Transactions. Broadcasting. q. ISSN 0018-9316
- I E E E Transactions. Circuits and Systems. m.
- I E E E Transactions. Communications. m. ISSN 0090-6778

- I E E E Transactions. Computers. m. ISSN 0018-9340
- I E E E Transactions. Consumer Electronics. q. ISSN 0098-3063
- I E E E Transactions. Education. q. ISSN 0018-9359
- I E E E Transactions. Electrical Insulation. bi-m. ISSN 0018-9367
- I E E E Transactions. Electromagnetic Compatibility. q. ISSN 0018-9375
- I E E E Transactions. Electron Devices. m. ISSN 0018-9383
- I E E E Transactions. Engineering Management. q. ISSN 0018-9391
- I E E E Transactions. Geoscience Electronics. q. ISSN 0018-9413
- I E E E Transactions. Industrial Electronics and Control Instrumentation. q. ISSN 0018-9421
- I E E E Transactions. Industry Applications. bi-m.
- I E E E Transactions. Information Theory. bi-m. ISSN 0018-9448
- I E E E Transactions. Instrumentation and Measurement. q. ISSN 0018-9456
- I E E E Transactions. Magnetics. bi-m. ISSN 0018-9464
- I E E E Transactions. Manufacturing Technology. q. ISSN 0046-838X
- I E E E Transactions. Microwave Theory and Techniques. m. ISSN 0018-9480
- I E E E Transactions. Nuclear Science. bi-m. ISSN 0018-9499
- I E E E Transactions. Parts, Hybrids, & Packaging. q.
- I E E E Transactions. Plasma Science. q. ISSN 0093-3813
- I E E E Transactions. Power Apparatus and Systems. bi-m. ISSN 0018-9510
- I E E E Transactions. Professional Communication. q.
- I E E E Transactions. Reliability. 5 per yr. ISSN 0018-9529
- I E E E Transactions. Sonics and Ultrasonics. bi-m. ISSN 0018-9537
- I E E E Transactions. Systems, Man & Cybernetics. m. ISSN 0018-9472
- I E E E Transactions. Vehicular Technology. q. ISSN 0018-9545
- I E E E Vehicular Technology Conference. Record. irreg. ISSN 0098-3551
- I E E E Vehicular Technology Group. Proceedings of the Annual Conference. a.
- Industrial and Commercial Power Systems and Electrical Space Heating and Air Conditioning Joint Technical Conference. Record. a. ISSN 0073-733X
- Institute of Electrical and Electronics Engineers. Region 3. Technical Convention. Record. a. ISSN 0073-9170
- Institute of Electrical and Electronics Engineers. Region 6. Technical Conference. Record. a. ISSN 0073-9189
- Institute of Electrical and Electronics Engineers. Systems, Man, and Cybernetics Group. Annual Symposium Record. a.
- International Computer Technical Conference. Record. a. ISSN 0074-2848
- International Conference on Cybernetics and Society. Proceedings. irreg. ISSN 0360-8913
- International Conference on Engineering in the Ocean Environment. Digest. a. ISSN 0074-3062
- International Conference on the Theory and Applications of Differential Games. Proceedings. irreg., 1st, Amherst, 1969.
- International Electron Devices Meeting. Abstracts. a. ISSN 0074-4670
- International Magnetics Conference. Digest. a. ISSN 0074-6843
- International Microwave Symposium Digest. a. ISSN 0074-7009
- International Solid State Circuits Conference. Digest. a. ISSN 0074-8587
- International Symposium on Electromagnetic Compatibility. Record. a. ISSN 0074-8811
- International Symposium on Fault Tolerant Computing. Digest. a. ISSN 0074-882X
- Joint Automatic Control Conference. Record. a. ISSN 0075-3939
- Joint Engineering Societies Management Conference. Proceedings. a. ISSN 0075-3955
- Joint Power Generation Technical Conference. Preprint. a. ISSN 0075-398X
- Joint Railroad Technical Conference. Preprints. a. ISSN 0075-3998
- Key Abstracts: Electrical Measurement & Instrumentation. m.
- National Aerospace and Electronics Conference. Record. a. ISSN 0065-373X

- National Telecommunication Conference. Record. a. ISSN 0077-5878
- Northeast Electronics Research and Engineering Meeting. Record. a. ISSN 0078-1673
- Off-Shore Technology Conference. Record. a. ISSN 0078-3706
- Petroleum and Chemical Industry Technical Conference. Record. a. ISSN 0079-1288
- Power Industry Computer Applications Conference. Record. biennial. ISSN 0079-4430
- Pulp and Paper Industry. Technical Conference. Record. a. ISSN 0079-7944
- Reliability and Maintainability Conference. Record. a. (Co-Sponsor: American Society for Quality Control)
- Reliability Physics Symposium Abstracts. a. ISSN 0080-0821
- Rubber and Plastics Industry Technical Conference. Record. a. ISSN 0080-4762
- Switching and Automata Theory Conference. Record. a. ISSN 0082-0490
- Symposium on Applications of Walsh Functions. Record. a. ISSN 0082-0814
- Symposium on Reliability. Proceedings. a. ISSN 0082-092X
- Textile Industry Technical Conference. Record. biennial. ISSN 0082-3651
- Ultrasonics Symposium. Proceedings. a. ISSN 0090-5607

**Institute of Electrical and Electronics Engineers, Inc. Aerospace and Electronic Systems Society**
6411 Chillum Pl. N.W., Washington, DC 20012.
- S-AES Newsletter. m.

**Institute of Electrical and Electronics Engineers, Inc. Computer Society**
5855 Naples Plaza, Suite 301, Long Beach, CA 91324.
- Computer. m. ISSN 0018-9162

**Institute of Electrical and Electronics Engineers, Inc. Engineering Management Society**
345 E. 47th St., New York, NY 10017.
- Engineering Management Society. Newsletter. bi-m.

**Institute of Electrical & Electronics Engineers, Inc. Philadelphia Section**
Univ. of Pennsylvania, Moore School of Electrical Engineering, Philadelphia, PA 19104.
- I E E E Almanack. m.(Sep.-May) ISSN 0018-9154

**Institute of Electrical and Electronics Engineers, Inc. San Francisco Section**
Suite 2210, 701 Welch Rd., Palo Alto, CA 94304.
- I E E E Grid. m.(10 per yr.) ISSN 0018-9189

**Institute of Electrical and Electronics Engineers, Inc. United States Activities Committee**
445 Hoes Lane, Piscataway, NJ 08854.
- I E E E Professional News. bi-m.

**Institute of Environmental Sciences**
940 E. Northwest Hwy., Mt. Prospect, IL 60056.
- Institute of Environmental Sciences. Annual Meeting. Proceedings. a. ISSN 0073-9227
- Institute of Environmental Sciences. Tutorial Series. irreg. ISSN 0073-9251
- Journal of Environmental Sciences. bi-m. ISSN 0022-0906

**Institute of European Studies**
710 N. Rush St., Chicago, IL 60611.
- Institute of European Studies. Announcements. a (biennial from 1965-69) ISSN 0073-926X
- Institute of European Studies. Papers and Addresses of the Annual Conference and Academic Council. irreg.(usually 1 per year) ISSN 0073-9278

**Institute of Food Technologists**
221 N. LaSalle St., Chicago, IL 60601.
- Food Technology. m. ISSN 0015-6639
- I F T World Directory and Guide. a. ISSN 0073-9286
- Journal of Food Science. bi-m. ISSN 0022-1147

**Institute of Gas Technology**
3424 S. State St., Chicago, IL 60616.
- Conference on Natural Gas Research and Technology. Proceedings. irreg. (Co-sponsor: American Gas Association)
- Gas Abstracts. m. ISSN 0016-4844
- Gas Scope. q. ISSN 0016-4976
- Institute of Gas Technology. Annual Report. a.

- Institute of Gas Technology. Research Bulletins. irreg.
- Institute of Gas Technology. Technical Reports. irreg. ISSN 0529-0775
- International Conference on Liquefied Natural Gas. Papers. irreg. (Co-Sponsors: International Gas Union & International Institute of Refrigeration)
- International Gas Technology Highlights. fortn.

**Institute of General Semantics**
Lakeville, CT 06039.
- General Semantics Bulletin. a.(in two parts) ISSN 0072-0771

**Institute of Heating & Air Conditioning Industries**
c/o Sam Jaffe, Ed., 3055 Overland Ave., Los Angeles, CA 90034.
- Indoor Comfort News. m.

**Institute of Industrial and Labor Relations. College of Business and Public Administration**
- Annual Labor-Management Conference on Collective Bargaining and Labor Law. (pub. by University of Arizona College of Business and Public Administration. Division of Economic and Business Research)

**Institute of Industrial Launderers**
1730 M St., N.W., Washington, DC 20036.
- Industrial Launderer. m. ISSN 0046-9211

**Institute of Internal Auditors, Inc.**
249 Maitland Ave., Altamonte Springs, FL 32701.
- EDCOM. m.
- Internal Auditor. bi-m. ISSN 0020-5745

**Institute of International Education**
809 United Nations Plaza, New York, NY 10017.
- English Language and Orientation Programs in the United States; including a list of programs for training teachers of English as a second language. irreg., 5th ed., 1976. ISSN 0071-0601
- Guide to Foreign Medical Schools. irreg., 4th, 1975. (Co-publisher: Queens College Press)
- Handbook on International Study for U.S. Nationals. Vol. 1: Study in Europe. irreg.
- Handbook on U.S. Study for Foreign Nationals. irreg., 5th edt. 1973.
- I I E Report. 3-4 per yr. ISSN 0018-9871
- Meet the U. S. A; including a practical guide for academic visitors to the United States. irreg., 1970, 6th ed. ISSN 0076-6194
- Open Doors; report on international exchange. a. ISSN 0078-5172
- Summer Study Abroad. a. ISSN 0081-9379
- Teaching Abroad. irreg.
- U. S. College-Sponsored Programs Abroad: Academic Year. a. ISSN 0082-8602

**Institute of International Studies**
- Studies in International Affairs. (pub. by University of South Carolina Press)

**Institute of Jazz Studies**
- Journal of Jazz Studies. (pub. by Transaction Periodicals Consortium)

**Institute of Judicial Administration**
One Washington Sq. Village, New York, NY 10012.
- I J A Report. q. ISSN 0018-991X

**Institute of Judicial Administration. Juvenile Justice Standards Project**
80 Fifth Avenue, Room 1501, New York, NY 10011.
- Juvenile Law Litigation Directory. a. (Co-Sponsor: American Bar Association)

**Institute of Labor and Industrial Relations**
P.O. Box B-1, Ann Arbor, MI 48106.
- Institute of Labor and Industrial Relations. Policy Papers in Human Resources and Industrial Relations. irreg., no. 23, 1975. ISSN 0073-9421 (Co-Sponsors: University of Michigan; Wayne State University)
- Institute of Labor and Industrial Relations. Reprint Series. irreg., no. 65, 1975. ISSN 0073-943X (Co-Sponsors: University of Michigan; Wayne State University)

**Institute of Laboratory Animal Resources. Division of Prological Sciences-Assembly of Life Sciences**
National Research Council, 2101 Constitution Ave., Washington, DC 20418.
- I. L. A. R. News. q. ISSN 0018-9960

**Institute of Life Insurance**
Research & Statistical Services, 277 Park Ave., New York, NY 10017.
- Tally of Life Insurance Statistics. m. ISSN 0039-923X

**Institute of Living**
200 Retreat Ave., Hartford, CT 06106.
- Digest of Neurology & Psychiatry. 10 per yr. ISSN 0012-2769

**Institute of Management Sciences**
146 Westminster St., Providence, RI 02903.
- Institute of Management Sciences. Symposium on Planning. Proceedings. irreg., 1968, 11th. ISSN 0082-0911 (prep. by its Time Planning College)
- Interfaces. q. ISSN 0092-2102
- Management Science. m. ISSN 0025-1909
- Mathematics of Operations Research. q. (Operations Research Society of America)

**Institute of Mathematical Statistics**
c/o R. M. Elashoff, Treasurer, 3401 Investment Blvd., No. 6, Hayward, CA 94545.
- Annals of Statistics. bi-m. ISSN 0090-5364
- Institute of Mathematical Statistics. Bulletin. bi-m.
- Selected Translations in Mathematical Statistics and Probability. (pub. by American Mathematical Society)

**Institute of Medicine of Chicago**
332 South Michigan Ave., Chicago, IL 60604.
- Institute of Medicine of Chicago. Proceedings. bi-m. ISSN 0091-746X

**Institute of Medieval Canon Law**
Univ. of California, Berkeley, School of Law (Boalt Hall), Berkeley, CA 94720
(European Subscription Address: Biblioteca Apostolica Vaticana, 00120 Vatican City, Italy)
- Bulletin of Medieval Canon Law. New Series. a.
- Monumenta Iuris Canonici. irreg. ISSN 0077-1457

**Institute of Mental Measurements**
- Mental Measurements Yearbook. (pub. by Gryphon Press)

**Institute of Navigation**
Suite 832,815 15th St. N.W., Washington, DC 20005.
- Navigation. q. ISSN 0028-1522

**Institute of New Communications**
206 Fifth Ave., New York, NY 10010.
- Sevendays. w.

**Institute of Newspaper Controllers and Finance Officers, Inc.**
59 E. Main St., Moorestown, NJ 08057.
- Newspaper Controller. m. except Jul. ISSN 0028-9558

**Institute of Noise Control Engineering**
Purdue University, West Lafayette, IN 47907
(Subscr. to: Box 3202 Arlington Branch, Poughkeepsie NY 12603)
- Noise Control Engineering. bi-m. ISSN 0093-9978 (Co-Sponsor: Acoustical Society of America)

**Institute of Open Education**
133 Mount Auburn Street, Cambridge, MA 02138.
- Journal of Open Education. 3 per yr. (Co-sponsor: Antioch Graduate Center)

**Institute of Outdoor Drama**
202 Graham Memorial, 052A, Chapel Hill, NC 27514.
- Institute of Outdoor Drama Newsletter. m. ISSN 0020-3017

**Institute of Paper Chemistry**
1043 E. South River St., Appleton, WI 54911.
- Institute of Paper Chemistry. Abstract Bulletin. m. ISSN 0020-3033
- Institute of Paper Chemistry. Bibliographic Series. irreg.; no. 274, 1977. ISSN 0073-9480
- Institute of Paper Chemistry. Keyword Index to Abstract Bulletin. m. and s-a issues.

**Institute of Pastoral Psychology**
- Pastoral Psychology Series. (pub. by Fordham University Press)

**Institute of Positive Education**
7524 So. Cottage Grove Ave., Chicago, IL 60619.
- Black Books Bulletin. q. ISSN 0045-2114
- Black Pages Pamphlet Series. irreg.

**Institute of Public Administration, New York**
- Calcutta Research Series. (pub. by Asia Publishing House, Inc.)

**Institute of Real Estate Management**
- Income-Expense Analysis Apartments, Condominiums, & Cooperatives. (pub. by National Association of Realtors)
- Journal of Property Management. (pub. by National Association of Realtors)

**Institute of Scrap Iron and Steel Inc.**
1729 H Street N.W., Washington, DC 20006.
- Phoenix Quarterly. q. ISSN 0031-837X

**Institute of Society, Ethics and the Life Sciences**
Hastings Center, 360 Broadway, Hastings-on-Hudson, NY 10706.
- Bibliography of Society, Ethics and the Life Sciences. a. ISSN 0094-4831
- Hastings Center. Recent Activities. irreg. ISSN 0360-9006
- Hastings Center Report. bi-m. ISSN 0093-0334

**Institute of Surplus Dealers**
520 Broadway, New York, NY 10012.
- I S D Monthly Bulletin. m.
- Surplus Dealers Directory. a. ISSN 0081-9662

**Institute of Textile Technology**
Charlottesville, VA 22902.
- Textile Technology Digest. m. ISSN 0040-5191

**Institute of the Black World**
87 Chestnut St. S.W., Atlanta, GA 30314.
- I B W Monthly Report. m.
- Institute of the Black World. Black Paper. irreg.

**Institute of Transportation Engineers**
1815 N Fort Myer, Dr., Arlington, VA 22209.
- Institute of Transportation Engineers. Yearbook. a.
- Traffic Engineering. m. ISSN 0041-0675

**Institute of Ukrainian Culture**
13588 Sunset St., Detroit, MI 48212.
- Terem; problemy ukrainskoi kultury. irreg.

**Institute on the Church in Urban Industrial Society**
5700 S. Woodlawn Ave., Chicago, IL 60637.
- I C U I S Abstract Service. m.
- Notes on Urban-Industrial Mission, Literature and Training. 3 per yr. ISSN 0361-7092

**Institutes of Religion and Health**
3 W. 29th St., New York, NY 10001.
- Institutes of Religion and Health. Institutes Reporter. irreg. ISSN 0360-3679
- Journal of Religion and Health. q. ISSN 0022-4197

**Institutional Investor Systems, Inc.**
488 Madison Ave., New York, NY 10022.
- Corporate Financing Directory. a.
- Corporate Financing Week. w.
- Institutional Investor; the journal for professional investment managers. m. ISSN 0020-3580
- Institutional Investor International Edition. m.
- Journal of Portfolio Management. q. ISSN 0095-4918
- Options Letter. fortn.
- Wall Street Letter. w.

**Instituto Interamericano**
5133 NT, Denton, TX 76203.
- Interamerican. 6 per yr. ISSN 0020-5133

**Instituto Internacional de Literatura Iberoamericana**
1312 CL, University of Pittsburgh, Pittsburgh, PA 15260.
- Revista Iberoamericana. 4 per yr. ISSN 0034-9631

**Instructor Publications, Inc.**
7 Bank St., Dansville, NY 14437.
- Instructor. m. (Sep.-May) ISSN 0020-4285

**Instrument Society of America**
400 Stanwix St., Pittsburgh, PA 15222.
- Advances in Instrumentation. a. ISSN 0065-2814
- Advances in Test Measurement; with Instrumentation in the Aerospace Industry. a. ISSN 0568-0204 (prep. by its Test Measurement Division)
- Air Quality Instrumentation. irreg.
- Automation and Remote Control. (pub. by Consultants Bureau)
- Biomedical Sciences Instrumentation. a. since 1974. ISSN 0067-8856

- Fundamentals of Aerospace Instrumentation. a. ISSN 0094-3975
- I S A Mining and Metallurgy Instrumentation Symposium. Proceedings. irreg.
- I S A Transactions. q. ISSN 0019-0578
- I S A Transducer Compendium. irreg., 1968-1972, 2nd ed. ISSN 0074-0500
- Industrial Laboratory. (pub. by Consultants Bureau)
- Instrument Society of America. I S A Final Control Elements Symposium. Final Control Elements; Proceedings. irreg., latest 1977. ISSN 0091-7699
- Instrument Society of America. Standards and Practices for Instrumentation. irreg., 1977, 5th ed. ISSN 0074-0527
- Instrumentation in the Chemical and Petroleum Industry. a. ISSN 0074-0551
- Instrumentation in the Mining and Metallurgy Industries. a.
- Instrumentation in the Power Industry. a. ISSN 0074-056X
- Instrumentation in the Pulp and Paper Industry. a.
- Instrumentation Technology. m. ISSN 0020-4382
- Measurement Techniques. (pub. by Consultants Bureau)
- Temperature: Its Measurement and Control in Science and Industry. approx. every ten years.
- Water Quality Instrumentation. irreg.

**Instrumental Fair Inc.**
5012 Herzel Place, Beltsville, MD 20705.
- Mid-Atlantic Electronics. bi-m.

**Instrumentalist Co.**
1418 Lake Street, Evanston, IL 60204.
- Band Music Guide. irreg. ISSN 0084-7704
- Clavier; a magazine for pianists and organists. 9 per yr. ISSN 0009-854X
- Instrumentalist; a magazine for school and college band and orchestra director, teacher-training specialist in instrumental music education and instrumental teachers. m.(except July) ISSN 0020-4331

**Insurance Accounting & Statistical Association**
Mutual Plaza, Durham, NC 27701.
- Interpreter. m. ISSN 0020-9651

**Insurance Adjuster**
2322 Seattle-First National Bank Bldg., Seattle, WA 98154.
- Insurance Adjuster. m. ISSN 0020-4579

**Insurance Economics Society of America**
11 E. Adams St., Chicago, IL 60603.
- Insurance Economics Surveys. m. ISSN 0020-4668

**Insurance Field Co., Inc.**
4325 Old Shepherdsville Rd., Box 18441, KY 40218.
- Insurance Field. 3 per yr. ISSN 0020-4684

**Insurance Flash**
c/o Jack Piver, 424 N. Croft Ave., Box 2068, Van Nuys, CA 91404.
- Insurance Flash. s-w. ISSN 0020-4692

**Insurance Forum, Inc.**
P.O. Box 245, Ellettsville, IN 47429.
- Insurance Forum. m. ISSN 0095-2923

**Insurance Information Institute**
110 William St., New York, NY 10038.
- Insurance Facts. a. ISSN 0074-0713
- Journal of Insurance. bi-m. ISSN 0022-1929

**Insurance Institute for Highway Safety**
Watergate Office 600, Washington, DC 20037.
- Status Report. bi-w. ISSN 0018-988X

**Insurance News**
5050 E. Thomas Rd., Phoenix, AZ 85018.
- Insurance News. m. ISSN 0020-4781

**Insurance Producers Services Corp.**
465 California St., San Francisco, CA 94104.
- California Independent Agent. m. (Independent Insurance Agents Association of California)

**Insurance Stock Market Service**
Drawer 29, 121 De La Guerra, Santa Barbara, CA 93102.
- Life Stock Investment Report. fortn. ISSN 0020-4838

**Insurance Week, Inc.**
2322 Seattle-First National Bank Bldg., Seattle, WA 98154.
- Insurance Week. w. ISSN 0020-4846

**Insurance Workers International Union**
1017 12th St. N.W., Washington, DC 20005.
- Insurance Worker. m.

**Integrated Education Associates**
2003 Sheridan Rd., Evanston, IL 60201.
- Integrated Education. bi-m. ISSN 0020-4862 (Northwestern University. School of Education)

**Integrity**
c/o David Williams, Box 891, Oak Park, IL 60303.
- Integrity; gay episcopal forum. m.(except Aug. & Sep.) ISSN 0095-2184

**Interactive Data Services, Inc.**
22 Cortlandt St., New York, NY 10007.
- White's Tax Exempt Bond Market Ratings. a.

**Inter-American Affairs Press**
Box 181, Washington, DC 20044.
- Hanson's Latin America Letter. w. ISSN 0017-7539
- Inter-American Economic Affairs. q. ISSN 0020-4943

**Interamerican Association for Democracy and Freedom. U S Committee**
20 W. 40th St, New York, NY 10018.
- Hemispherica. m. ISSN 0018-0319

**Inter-American Bar Association**
Suite 315, 1730 K St., N.W., Washington, DC 20006.
- Inter-American Bar Association. Letter to Members. irreg. (3-4 per yr.)

**Inter-American Bibliographical and Library Association**
Box 600583, North Miami Beach, FL 33160.
- Doors to Latin America. q. ISSN 0012-5490

**Inter-American Bilingual Teacher Newsletter**
5240 N. Sheridan Rd., Chicago, IL 60640.
- Inter-American Bilingual Teacher Newsletter. q.

**Interamerican College of Radiology**
Box 693052, Miami, FL 33169.
- Revista Interamericana de Radiologia. q. ISSN 0034-9704

**Inter-American Commission of Women (C I M)**
- Inter-American Commission of Women. Informational Bulletin. (pub. by Organization of American States)
- Inter-American Commission of Women. News Bulletin. (pub. by Organization of American States)
- Inter-American Commission of Women. Noticiero. (pub. by Organization of American States)

**Inter-American Commission on Human Rights**
- Anuario Interamericano de Derechos Humanos/ Inter-American Yearbook on Human Rights. (pub. by Organization of American States)

**Inter-American Committee on Bibliography**
- Inter-American Review of Bibliography/Revista Interamericana de Bibliografia. (pub. by Organization of American States)

**Interamerican Defense College**
c/o Fort McNair, Washington, DC 20319.
- Interamerican Defense College. Library Bulletin/ Colegio Interamericano de Defensa. Boletin de la Biblioteca. q.

**Inter-American Development Bank**
808 17th St. N.W., Washington, DC 20577.
- Economic and Social Progress in Latin America; Annual Report. a. ISSN 0095-2850
- I D B News. m.
- Inter-American Development Bank. Annual Report. a. ISSN 0074-087X
- Inter-American Development Bank. Board of Governors. Anales (de la) Reunion. a. ISSN 0538-3102
- Inter-American Development Bank. Board of Governors. Proceedings of the Meeting. a. ISSN 0074-0861
- Inter-American Development Bank. Informe Anual. a. ISSN 0538-3080
- Inter-American Development Bank. Statement of Loans. a.

**Interamerican Press Association**
2911 N.W. 39th St., Miami, FL 33142.
- I A P A News. s-m. ISSN 0018-8409
- Inter-American Press Association. Committee on Freedom of the Press. Report. a. ISSN 0579-6695
- Inter-American Press Association. Minutes of the Annual Meeting. a.
- Press of the Americas. s-m. ISSN 0552-0185

**Interamerican Society of Psychology**
c/o Gerardo Marin, Department of Psychology, De Paul University, 2323 N Seminary Ave., Chicago, IL 60614.
- Revista Interamericana de Psicologia/ Interamerican Journal of Psychology. s-a. ISSN 0034-9690

**Inter-American Statistical Institute**
1725 I St. N.W., Washington, DC 20006.
- America en Cifras. (pub. by Organization of American States)
- Inter-American Statistical Institute. Committee on Improvement of National Statistics. Report. irreg; 11th, Ottawa, Can., 1973 (pub. 1975) ISSN 0538-3579
- Inter-American Statistical Institute. Monthly List of Publications Received. m.

**Inter-American Tropical Tuna Commission**
c/o Scripps Institution of Oceanography, La Jolla, CA 92307.
- Inter-American Tropical Tuna Commission. Bulletin/Comision Interamericana del Atun Tropical. Boletin. irreg., vol. 17, 1976. ISSN 0074-0993
- Inter-American Tropical Tuna Commission. Data Report. irreg.; no. 5, 1972. ISSN 0538-3609
- Inter-American Tropical Tuna Commission. Informe Anual. Annual Report. a. ISSN 0074-1000

**Interchange Foundation**
345 E. 46th St., New York, NY 10017.
- Issues Before the United Nations General Assembly. a. ISSN 0362-4404 (United Nations Association of the U.S.A.)

**Inter-Church Holiness Convention**
375 W. State St., Salem, OH 44460.
- Convention Herald. m.

**Intercollegiate Association of Women Students**
2401 Virginia Ave. N.W., Box 2, Washington, DC 20037.
- Feminine Focus. 6 per yr.

**Intercollegiate Broadcasting System, Inc.**
University of Oklahoma, Norman, OK 73069.
- Journal of College Radio. 7 per yr. ISSN 0010-1133

**Intercollegiate Case Clearing House**
Soldiers Field, Boston, MA 02163.
- Intercollegiate Bibliography. New Cases in Administration. a. ISSN 0095-490X

**Intercollegiate Studies Institute, Inc.**
14 S. Bryn Mawr Ave., Bryn Mawr, PA 19010.
- Intercollegiate Review; a journal of scholarship and opinion. q. ISSN 0020-5249
- Modern Age. q. ISSN 0026-7457
- Political Science Reviewer. a. ISSN 0091-3715

**Inter-Com, Inc.**
Box 417, 19 Church St., Berea, OH 44017.
- Printing Magazine Purchasing Guide. a. ISSN 0079-533X

**Intercom; the Newsletter for California Community College Librarians**
c/o Solano Community College, Box 246, Suisun City, CA 94585.
- Intercom; the Newsletter for California Community College Librarians. irreg. (5-10 per yr.)

**Intercommunications, Inc.**
P.O. Box 867, Wallingford, CT 06492.
- Coaching: Women's Athletics. bi-m.

**Intercontinental Medical Book Corporation**
381 Park Ave. S., New York, NY 10016.
- American Society of Ocularists. Selected Papers and Discussions from the Annual Meeting. a.
- Progress in Cardiac Rehabilitation. irreg.
- Serial Handbook of Modern Psychiatry. irreg.

**Intercontinental Press Publishing Association**
Box 116, Village Station, New York, NY 10014.
- Intercontinental Press. w. ISSN 0020-5303

**Intercontinental Publications, Inc.**
Box 5026, Westport, CT 06880.
- Desarrollo Nacional-Servicios Publicos. 9 per yr.
- Modern Government/National Development. 9 per yr. ISSN 0360-7941
- Today's Transport International. bi-m. ISSN 0040-859X
- Transporte Moderno. bi-m. ISSN 0041-1698
- Worldwide Projects. 6 per yr.

**Inter-County Publishers, Inc.**
22 George St., Dryden, NY 13053.
- I. P. I. Rural News. w. ISSN 0019-0322

**InterCulture Associates**
Box 277, Thompson, CT 06277.
- Interculture News. irreg.

**Interdenomination Foreign Mission Association of North America, Inc.**
P.O. Box 395, Wheaton, IL 60187.
- I. F. M. A. News. q. ISSN 0018-9723

**Interdenominational Theological Center**
671 Beckwith St., Atlanta, GA 30314.
- Interdenominational Theological Center, Atlanta. Journal. s-a. ISSN 0092-6558

**Interdisciplinary Communications Media Inc.**
15 Canal Rd., Pelham Manor, NY 10803.
- Theory and Practice in Psychology.

**Interdok Corp.**
173 Halstead Ave., Box 326, Harrison, NY 10528.
- Directory of Published Proceedings. Series PCE: Pollution Control & Ecology. s-a. ISSN 0093-5816
- Directory of Published Proceedings. Series SEMT-Science, Engineering, Medicine and Technology. 10 per yr. ISSN 0012-3293
- Directory of Published Proceedings. Series SSH-Social Sciences/Humanities. q. ISSN 0012-3307

**Interface Learning Collective Inc.**
P.O. Box 970, Utica, NY 13503.
- Interface Journal; alternatives in higher education. q.

**Interface Press**
Box 42211, Los Angeles, CA 90042.
- Brain/Mind Bulletin; frontiers of research, theory and practice. fortn.

**Interfaith Center on Corporate Responsibility**
- Corporate Examiner. (pub. by Corporate Information Center)

**Interfaith Observer**
c/o Blanche Dick, 1825 Riverside Dr., New York, NY 10034.
- Interfaith Observer. ISSN 0020-5451

**Interfraternity Research and Advisory Council**
c/o Conrad A. Blomquist, 833 South Wood St., Chicago, IL 60612.
- Interfraternity Research and Advisory Council. Bulletin. m.

**Interim Books**
Box 35, Village Station, New York, NY 10014.
- Magazine. irreg., no. 5, 1973. ISSN 0076-2334

**Interlibrary Users Association**
- Journal Holdings in the Washington-Baltimore Area. (pub. by Johns Hopkins University. Applied Physics Laboratory)

**Interline, Inc.**
2 W. 46th St., New York, NY 10036.
- Interline Reporter. m. ISSN 0020-5532

**Interlochen Arts Academy. National Music Camp**
Interlochen, MI 49643.
- Crescendo. 3-4 per yr. ISSN 0011-1171

**Intermed Communications Inc.**
414 Benjamin Fox Pavilion, Jenkintown, PA 19046.
- Nursing. m.

**Intermedia**
c/o Ed. Harley Land, 2431 Echo Park Ave., Los Angeles, CA 90026.
- Intermedia. q.

**Intermedia News and Feature Service**
229 Seventh Ave., New York, NY 10011.
- Intermedia News and Feature Service. 25 per yr. ISSN 0020-5583

**Intermission**
969 Third Ave., New York, NY 10022.
- Intermission.

**Intermodal World, Inc.**
One World Trade Center, Suite 1927, New York, NY 10048.
- Transport 2000. m.

**Intermountain Contractor, Inc.**
Box 1829, Salt Lake City, UT 84110.
- Intermountain Contractor; building and engineering construction news. w. ISSN 0020-5656

**Intermountain Farmers Association**
1800 South West Temple, Salt Lake City, UT 84115.
- I F A Cooperator. 6 per yr.

**Intermountain Jewish News**
1275 Sherman St., Denver, CO 80203.
- Intermountain Jewish News. w. ISSN 0047-0511

**Intermountain Logging News**
Box 271, Colville, WA 99114.
- Intermountain Logging News. m. ISSN 0300-7405

**International Academy at Santa Barbara. Environmental Studies Institute**
Riviera Campus, 2074 Alameda Padre Serra, Santa Barbara, CA 93103.
- Environmental Periodicals Bibliography: Indexed Article Titles; a current awareness bibliography featuring serial publications in the area of environmental studies. bi-m. ISSN 0046-2306

**International Academy of Cytology**
- Acta Cytologica. (pub. by Williams & Wilkins Co.)

**International Academy of Oral Pathology**
- International Academy of Oral Pathology. Proceedings. (pub. by Gordon & Breach Science Publishers)

**International Academy of Orthodontics**
6451 Whittier Blvd., Los Angeles, CA 90022.
- International Journal of Orthodontics. q. ISSN 0020-7500 (Federation of Orthodontic Associations)

**International Academy of Pathology**
c/o Dr. J. L. Edwards, Indiana Univ. School of Medicine, 1100 W. Michigan St., Indianapolis, IN 46202.
- International Pathology. 6 per yr. ISSN 0020-8205
- Laboratory Investigation. (pub. by Williams & Wilkins Co.)
- Monographs in Pathology. (pub. by Williams & Wilkins Co)

**International Academy of Proctology**
- American Journal of Proctology. (pub. by Romaine Pierson Publishers, Inc.)

**International Academy of Wood Science**
- Wood Science and Technology. (pub. by Springer-Verlag)

**International Advancement**
Box 75537, Los Angeles, CA 90075.
- American Bulletin of International Technology Transfer. bi-m.

**International Advertising Association**
475 Fifth Ave., New York, NY 10017.
- I A A World Directory of Marketing Communications Periodicals. a. ISSN 0538-4141
- World Advertising Expenditures. biennial. ISSN 0568-0301 (Dist. by Starch, Inra, Hooper, 420 Lexington Ave., New York, N.Y. 10017)

**International Alliance of Theatrical Stage Employees and Moving Picture Machine Operators of the United States and Canada**
1515 Broadway, New York, NY 10036.
- International Alliance of Theatrical Stage Employees and Moving Picture Machine Operators of the United States and Canada. Official Bulletin. q. ISSN 0020-5885

**International Alliance of Theatrical Stage Employees and Moving Picture Machine Operators of the United States and Canada. Local 659**
7715 Sunset Blvd., Hollywood, CA 90046.
● International Photographer. m. ISSN 0020-8299

**International Amateur Boat Building Society**
3183 Merrill, Royal Oak, MI 48072.
● Amateur Boat Builder. m.

**International Amateur Radio Union**
● Q S T. (pub. by American Radio Relay League, Inc.)

**International and Tri-States Oil Mill Superintendent's Association**
Box 35423, Houston, TX 77035.
● Oil Mill Gazetter. m. ISSN 0030-1442

**International Anesthesia Research Society**
3645 Warrensville Center Rd., Cleveland, OH 44122.
● Anesthesia and Analgesia; current researches. bi-m. ISSN 0003-2999

**International Armaments Press**
P.O. Box 40, Kailua, HI 96734.
● International Armaments Monthly. m. ISSN 0090-4813

**International Arthur Schnitzler Research Association**
c/o Donald G. Daviau, Ed., Department of Literatures and Languages, University of California, Riverside, CA 92521.
● Modern Austrian Literature. q. ISSN 0026-7503

**International Arthurian Society**
c/o John L. Grigsby, Box 1077 Washington University, St. Louis, MO 63130.
● International Arthurian Society. Bibliographical Bulletin. a. ISSN 0074-1388

**International Association for Advancement of Earth & Environmental Sciences**
● Environmental Resources. (pub. by Mid-Continent Scientific)

**International Association for Cross-Cultural Psychology**
● Journal of Cross Cultural Psychology. (pub. by Sage Publications, Inc.)

**International Association for Dental Research**
211 E. Chicago Ave., Chicago, IL 60611.
● International Association for Dental Research. Abstracts of the General Meeting. irreg.
● International Conference on Oral Biology. Proceedings. (pub. by Professional Publication Producers)

**International Association for Great Lakes Research**
1300 Elmwood Ave., Buffalo, NY 14222.
● Journal of Great Lakes Research. a.

**International Association for Hydrogen Energy**
● International Journal of Hydrogen Energy. (pub. by Pergamon Press, Inc.)

**International Association for Identification**
P.O. Box 139, Utica, NY 13503.
● Identification News. m. ISSN 0019-1450

**International Association for Mathematical Geology**
● Computers & Geosciences. (pub. by Pergamon Press, Inc.)

**International Association for Mathematics and Computers in Simulation**
c/o Robert Vehnevetsky, Dir., Department of Computer Science, Rutgers University, New Brunswick, NJ 08903.
● I M A C S News. q.
● Mathematics and Computers in Simulation. (pub. by North-Holland Publishing Co. NE)

**International Association for Pollution Control**
4733 Bethesda Ave., Washington, DC 20014.
● International Association for Pollution Control. Newsletter. irreg.

**International Association for Religious Freedom. North American Chapter**
c/o Unitarian Universalist Assn., 25 Beacon St., Boston, MA 02108.
● Interdependence. s-a. ISSN 0362-4668

**International Association for Research in Income and Wealth**
Box 2020, Yale Station, New Haven, CT 06520.
● Review of Income and Wealth. q. ISSN 0034-6586

**International Association for Scientific Study of Mental Deficiency**
c/o I. Ignacy Goldberg, Dept. of Special Education, Teachers College, Columbia University, New York, NY 10027.
● International Association for Scientific Study of Mental Deficiency. Proceedings of International Congress. triennial, 3rd, 1973, The Hague. ISSN 0085-2007

**International Association for the Advancement of Ethnology and Eugenics**
P.O.B. 3495, Grand Central Station, New York, NY 10017.
● I A A E E Monographs. irreg. ISSN 0074-1523
● I A A E E Reprint. irreg. ISSN 0074-1515

**International Association of Allergology**
c/o Dr. C. E. Arbesman, 50 High St, Buffalo, NY 14203.
● International Congress of Allergology. Proceedings. irreg., 1976, 9th, Buenos Aires. ISSN 0074-3453

**International Association of Asbestos Workers**
Machinists Bldg., 1300 Connecticut Ave., Washington, DC 20036.
● Asbestos Worker. q. ISSN 0004-4245

**International Association of Assessing Officers**
1313 East 60th St., Chicago, IL 60637.
● Assessment and Valuation Legal Reporter. m. ISSN 0090-6352
● Assessors Journal. q. ISSN 0004-5071
● International Assessor; current events in assessment administration. m.

**International Association of Bridge, Structural and Ornamental Iron Workers**
1750 New York Ave., N.W., Washington, DC 20006.
● Ironworker. m. ISSN 0021-163X

**International Association of Business Communicators**
870 Market Street, Suite 928, San Francisco, CA 94102.
● I A B C News. m.
● Journal of Organizational Communication. q. ISSN 0047-2646

**International Association of Cancer Victims and Friends**
Box 707, Solana Beach, CA 92075.
● Cancer News Journal. bi-m.

**International Association of Chiefs of Police, Inc.**
11 Firstfield Rd., Gaithersburg, MD 20760.
● I A C P Law Enforcement Legal Review. m.
● I A C P Legal Points. m.
● Journal of Police Science and Administration. q. ISSN 0090-9084 (Co-Sponsor: Northwestern University School of Law)
● Law Enforcement and Criminal Justice Education Directory. irreg. (prep. by its Technical Research Services Division)
● P S L R. (Public Safety Labor Reporter) m.
● Police Chief; professional voice of law enforcement. m.
● Police Labor Review. m.
● Police Law Reporter. q.

**International Association of Coroners and Medical Examiners**
2121 Adelbert Road, Cleveland, OH 44106.
● International Association of Coroners and Medical Examiners. Proceedings. a,; latest edt., 1972.

**International Association of Counseling Services, Inc.**
1607 New Hampshire Ave. N.W., Washington, DC 20009.
● Directory of Counseling Services. a. ISSN 0065-7581

**International Association of Country Music**
Box 147, Hamilton, OH 45012.
● Country Music Explorer. m. ISSN 0360-8697

**International Association of Drilling Contractors**
7400 Harwin Drive, Suite 305, Houston, TX 77036.
● Drilling Contractor. bi-m. ISSN 0046-0702

**International Association of Electrical Inspectors**
802 Busse Highway, Park Ridge, IL 60068.
● I A E I News. bi-m. ISSN 0020-5974

**International Association of Fire Chiefs, Inc.**
1329 18th St. N.W., Washington, DC 20006.
● International Fire Chief. m.

**International Association of Group Psychotherapy**
c/o Dr. Samuel B. Hadden, Pres., 946 Remiangton Rd., Wynnewood, NY 12508.
● International Congress of Group Psychotherapy. Proceedings. irreg., 1968, 4th, Vienna. ISSN 0074-3674

**International Association of Health Underwriters**
Box 276, Hartland, WI 53029.
● Health Insurance Underwriter. m.(Aug-Sep. combined) ISSN 0017-9019

**International Association of Independent Producers**
● Communication Arts International. (pub. by Kayward Publications)

**International Association of Insurance Counsel**
20 N. Wacker Dr., Suite 3007, Chicago, IL 60606.
● Insurance Counsel Journal. q. ISSN 0020-465X

**International Association of Jazz Record Collectors**
905 S. 48 St., Philadelphia, PA 19143.
● I. A. J. R. C. Journal. q.

**International Association of Laryngectomees**
c/o American Cancer Society, 777 3rd Ave., New York, NY 10017.
● I A L News. bi-m. ISSN 0300-6883

**International Association of Machinists and Aerospace Workers**
1300 Connecticut Ave. N.W., Washington, DC 20036.
● Machinist. m. ISSN 0047-5378

**International Association of Meteorology and Atmospheric Physics**
c/o Mr. S. Ruttenberg, P.O. Box 3000, Boulder, CO 80303.
● International Association of Meteorology and Atmospheric Physics. Report of Proceedings of General Assembly. every 3-4 yrs., 1967, 14th, Lucerne. ISSN 0074-1663
● International Conference on Atmospheric and Space Electricity. Proceedings. irreg., 1963, 3rd, Montreux, Switzerland. ISSN 0074-2996 (Co-sponsors; International Association of Geomagnetism and Aeronomy; International Union of Geodesy and Geophysics)

**International Association of Microbiological Societies. International Committee on Systematic Bacteriology**
● International Journal of Systematic Bacteriology. (pub. by American Society for Microbiology)

**International Association of Milk Control Agencies**
c/o R. C. Pearce, New York Dept. of Agriculture and Markets, Albany, NY 12226.
● International Association of Milk Control Agencies. Proceedings of Annual Meetings. a. ISSN 0074-1671

**International Association of Milk, Food and Environmental Sanitarians, Inc.**
P.O. 701, Ames, IA 50010.
● Journal of Food Protection. m. ISSN 0362-028X

**International Association of Music Libraries**
● R I L M Abstracts of Music Literature. (pub. by City University of New York)

**International Association of Personnel in Employment Security**
U.S. 60 W., Frankfort, KY 40601.
● International Association of Personnel in Employment Security. News. m. ISSN 0020-6008

**International Association of Plumbing and Mechanical Officials**
5032 Alhambra Ave., Los Angeles, CA 90032.
● International Association of Plumbing and Mechanical Officials. Uniform Plumbing Code. triennial.

**International Association of Printing House Craftsmen**
● Review of the Graphic Arts. (pub. by Cody Publications, Inc.)

**International Association of Pupil Personnel Workers**
1713 62nd Street, Kenosha, WI 53140.
● International Association of Pupil Personnel Workers. Journal. q. ISSN 0020-6016

**Inter-National Association of Refrigerated Warehouses**
7315 Wisconsin Avenue, Suite 700-W, Washington, DC 20014.
● Directory of Public Refrigerated Warehouses. a. ISSN 0070-6167

**International Association of School Librarianship**
Western Michigan Univ., School of Librarianship, Kalamazoo, MI 49001.
● I A S L Newsletter. q. ISSN 0085-2015

**International Association of Schools of Social Work**
345 E. 46th St., New York, NY 10017.
● I A S S W Directory; Member Schools and Associations. irreg. ISSN 0098-8278

**International Association of Space Philatelists**
Box 302, Yonkers, NY 10710.
● I A S P Explorer. m.

**International Association of Theoretical and Applied Limnology**
Kellogg Biological Station, Michigan State University, Hickory Corners, MI 49060.
● International Association of Theoretical and Applied Limnology. Communications. irreg. ISSN 0538-4680

**International Association of Torch Clubs**
Box 81890, Lincoln, NE 68501.
● Torch (Lincoln) q. ISSN 0040-9448

**International Association of Wall and Ceiling Contractors, Inc.**
1775 Church St., N.W., Washington, DC 20036.
● Construction Dimensions. m.
● Hexahedron. q. ISSN 0018-117X

**International Association of Wiping Cloth Manufacturers**
300 W. Washington, Chicago, IL 60606.
● I A W C M Bulletin. m.

**International Association of Women Ministers**
c/o LaVonne Althouse, Ed., 2900 Queen Lake, Philadelphia, PA 19129.
● Woman's Pulpit. q. ISSN 0043-7379

**International Association on Water Pollution Research**
● Advances in Water Pollution Research. (pub. by Pergamon Press Inc.)
● Progress in Water Technology. (pub. by Pergamon Press, Inc.)
● Water Research. (pub. by Pergamon Press Inc.)

**International Authority on Visual Merchandising**
● Visual Merchandising. (pub. by Signs of the Times Publishing Co.)

**International Bank for Reconstruction and Development**
For publications of this agency see section for UNITED NATIONS

**International Banker Association, Inc.**
422 Washington Bldg., Washington, DC 20005.
● Interbank; newsletter of international banking. m. ISSN 0538-3641

**International Bar Assocation**
c/o Bernard Frank, 832 Hamilton Mall, P.O. Box 419, Allentown, PA 18105.
● International Bar Association. Ombudsman Committee Newsletter. q.

**International Bio-Medical Information Service, Inc.**
Box 756, Miami, FL 33156.
● Bio-Medical Insight. fortn. ISSN 0006-2855
● Bio-Medical Scoreboard. m. ISSN 0095-0971
● Medical School Rounds. m. ISSN 0095-0998

**International Biological Programme**
● I B P Handbooks. (pub. by J. B. Lippincott Co.)

**International Black Writers Conference Inc.**
4019 S. Vincennes Ave., Chicago, IL 60653.
● Black Writers' News. q.

**International Board on Books for Young People. U.S. National Section**
Children's Book Council, 67 Irving Pl., New York, NY 10003.
● Friends of I B B Y Newsletter. s-a.

**International Bonhoeffer Archive and Research Committee. English Language Section**
c/o Clifford Green, Religion Department, Goucher College, Towson, MD 21204.
● International Bonhoeffer Archive and Research Committee. English Language Section. Newsletter. 3-4 per yr.

**International Botanical Congress**
● International Botanical Congress. Abstracts of Papers. (pub. by Stechert-Macmillan Publishing Co., Inc.)

**International Brain Research Organization**
● International Brain Research Organization. Monograph Series. (pub. by Raven Press)

**International Brangus Breeders Association**
9500 Tioga Dr., San Antonio, TX 78230.
● Brangus Journal. m. ISSN 0006-9132

**International Brotherhood of Electrical Workers (AFL-CIO)**
1125 15th St. N.W., Washington, DC 20005.
● I B E W Journal. m.

**International Brotherhood of Electrical Workers (AFL-CIO) Local Union No. 3**
158-11 Jewel Ave., Flushing, NY 11365.
● Electrical Union World. s-m. ISSN 0041-686X

**International Brotherhood of Electrical Workers (AFL-CIO) Local 1470**
2 Central Ave., Kearny, NJ 07032.
● I B E W - A F L -C I O. Local 1470 Journal. m. ISSN 0018-859X

**International Brotherhood of Magicians**
Kenton, OH 43326.
● Linking Ring. m. ISSN 0024-4023

**International Brotherhood of Painters & Allied Trades**
1750 New York Ave. N.W., Washington, DC 20006.
● Painter & Allied Trades Journal. m. ISSN 0030-9532

**International Brotherhood of Pottery and Allied Workers**
Box 988, E. Liverpool, OH 43920.
● Potters Herald. m. ISSN 0020-8353

**International Brotherhood of Teamsters, Chauffeurs, Warehousemen and Helpers of America**
25 Louisiana Ave., N. W., Washington, DC 20001.
● International Teamster. m. ISSN 0020-8892

**International Business-Government Counsellors Inc.**
1625 Eye St. N.W., Washington, DC 20006.
● Washington International Business Report. bi-w. ISSN 0049-691X

**International Business Machines Corp.**
Armonk, NY 10504.
● I B M Journal of Research and Development. bi-m. ISSN 0018-8646
● I B M Systems Journal. q. ISSN 0018-8670
● I B M Technical Disclosure Bulletin. m. ISSN 0018-8689

**International Business Machines Corp. Data Processing Division**
112 E. Post Rd., White Plains, NY 10604.
● Data Processor. q. ISSN 0011-6890
● I B M Agribusiness Symposium. Proceedings. irreg.
● I B M Medical Symposium. Proceedings. triennial, 10th, 1971. ISSN 0536-1184

**International Center for Advanced Studies**
● Molecular Biology; Proceedings of the International Conference. (pub. by Gordon & Breach Science Publishers)

**International Center for Arid and Semi-Arid Land Studies**
Texas Tech Univ., Box 4620 Tech Sta., Lubbock, TX 79409.
● I C A S A L S Newsletter. q. ISSN 0018-8808

**International Center of Medieval Art**
The Cloisters, Fort Tryon Park, New York, NY 10040.
● Gesta. s-a. ISSN 0016-920X

**International Centre for Mechanical Sciences**
● Mechanics Research Communications. (pub. by Pergamon Press, Inc.)

**International Centre for the Settlement of Investment Disputes**
1818 H St. N.W., Washington, DC 20433.
● International Centre for Settlement of Investment Disputes. Annual Report. a. ISSN 0074-2163

**International Centre of Heat and Mass Transfer**
● Letters in Heat and Mass Transfer. (pub. by Pergamon Press, Inc.)

**International Chamber of Commerce. United States Council**
1212 Ave. of the Americas, New York, NY 10036.
● International Chamber of Commerce. United States Council. Report. irreg. ISSN 0538-5466

**International Chemical and Nuclear Corp**
● I C N -U C L A Symposium on Molecular Biology Proceedings. (pub. by Academic Press, Inc.)

**International Chemical Workers Union**
International Chemical Workers Bldg., 1655 W. Market St., Akron, OH 44313.
● International Chemical Worker. m. ISSN 0020-6334

**International Childbirth Education Association**
Office of Membership, 195 Waterford Dr., Dayton, OH 45459.
● I C E A Forum; newsletter for groups. 3 per yr.
● I C E A News. q. ISSN 0445-0485
● I C E A Review. q.
● I C E A Sharing; International Childbirth Education Association's newsletter for teachers. 3 per yr.

**International Chiropractors Association**
741 Brady Street, Davenport, IA 52808.
● International Review of Chiropratic. bi-m.

**International Christian Broadcasters**
1822 Drew St., Suite 3, 3118 Gulf to Bay Blvd., Clearwater, FL 33518.
● International Christian Broadcasters Bulletin. q. ISSN 0020-6350

**International Christian Communications, Inc.**
Box 248, Ellicott Station, Buffalo, NY 14205.
● Christian Inquirer. m.

**International Church of the Foursquare Gospel**
1100 Glendale Blvd., Los Angeles, CA 90026.
● Foursquare World Advance. m. ISSN 0015-9182

**International City Management Association**
1140 Connecticut Ave. N.W., Washington, DC 20036.
● Directory of Municipal Management Assistants. a.
● I C M A Newsletter. s-m. ISSN 0047-0651
● M I S/Management Information Service. m. ISSN 0047-5262
● Municipal Year Book. a. ISSN 0077-2186
● Public Management; devoted to the conduct of local government. m. ISSN 0033-3611
● Urban Data Service Report. m. ISSN 0049-5654

**International Claim Association**
c/o Penn Life Insurance Co., Independence Square, Philadelphia, PA 19172.
● International Claim Association Proceedings. a.

**International Clarinet Society**
c/o James Schoepflin, Department of Music, Idaho State University, Pocatello, ID 83209
(Subscr to: Robert Schott, Department of Music, Kansas State College, Pittsburg, Kansas 66762)
● Clarinet. q.

**International College of Applied Nutrition**
Box 386, La Habra, CA 90631.
● Journal of Applied Nutrition. s-a. ISSN 0021-8960

**International College of Dentists**
3138 Commodore Plaza, Miami, FL 33133.
● I C D Letterette. ISSN 0018-8875
● International College of Dentists. India Section. Newsletter. a. ISSN 0074-2600

**International College of Dentists (San Mateo)**
c/o Dr. R. Gordon Agnew, Ed., 240 E. Bellevue
Ave., San Mateo, CA 94401.
- I.C.D. Scientific and Educational Journal. s-a.

**International College of Surgeons**
1516 North Lake Shore Dr., Chicago, IL 60610.
- International Surgery. 10 per yr. ISSN 0020-8868

**International Commission for the Prevention of
Alcoholism**
6830 Laurel St. N.W., Washington, DC 20012.
- I C P A Quarterly Bulletin. q. ISSN 0018-9006

**International Commission on Large Dams**
- International Commission on Large Dams.
Transactions. (pub. by United States Committee
on Large Dams)

**International Commission on Radiological Protection**
- I C R P. Annals. (pub. by Pergamon Press, Inc.)

**International Committee for Histochemistry and
Cytochemistry**
- International Congress of Histochemistry and
Cytochemistry. Proceedings. (pub. by Springer-
Verlag)

**International Committee of Food Science and
Technology**
c/o C. L. Wiley, Institute of Food Technologists,
221 N. la Salle St., Chicago, IL 60601.
- International Congress of Food Science and
Technology. Proceedings. irreg., 1970, 3rd,
Washington, D.C. ISSN 0074-3666

**International Committee of Weights and Measures**
- Metrologia. (pub. by Springer-Verlag)

**International Committee on General Relativity and
Gravitation**
- General Relativity and Gravitation. (pub. by
Plenum Press)

**International Communication Association**
Balcones Research Center, 10,100 Burnet Rd.,
Austin, TX 78758.
- Human Communication Research. (pub. by
Transaction Periodicals Consortium)
- I C A Newsletter. q. ISSN 0018-876X
- Journal of Communication. (pub. by Annenberg
School Press)

**International Computer Education Center**
1540 Halsted St., Chicago Heights, IL 60411.
- Computer Educator. m.

**International Computer Programs, Inc.**
1119 Keystone Way, Carmel, IN 46032.
- Financial Industry. q. ISSN 0362-1278
- I C P Insiders' Letter. m.
- I C P Mini; small business systems software
directory. s-a.
- I C P Software Directory; a catalog of saleable
computer software. s-a.
- Insurance Industry. q. ISSN 0362-8817
- Interface Series. q.
- Manufacturing and Engineering. q. ISSN 0362-
885X

**International Conference of Building Officials**
5360 S. Workman Mill Rd., Whittier, CA 90601.
- Building Standards; the national magazine for
building officials. bi-m.
- International Conference of Building Officials.
Accumulative Supplements to the Codes. a.
- International Conference of Building Officials.
Analysis of Revisions to the Uniform Building
Code. triennial.
- International Conference of Building Officials.
Building Department Administration. irreg.
- International Conference of Building Officials.
Dwelling Construction Under the Uniform
Building Code. triennial.
- International Conference of Building Officials.
One and Two Family Dwelling Code. irreg.
- International Conference of Building Officials.
Plan Review Manual. irreg.
- International Conference of Building Officials.
Uniform Code for the Abatement of Dangerous
Buildings. triennial.
- International Conference of Building Officials.
Uniform Fire Code. triennial.
- International Conference of Building Officials.
Uniform Housing Code. triennial. ISSN 0501-
1213
- International Conference of Building Officials.
Uniform Mechanical Code. triennial.

- Uniform Building Code. triennial. ISSN 0082-
7584

**International Conference of Police Associations**
60 E. 42nd St., Rm. 443, New York, NY 10017.
- Law Officer. bi-m. ISSN 0023-9321

**International Conference of Weekly Newspaper
Editors**
c/o School of Journalism, Southern Illinois
University, Carbondale, IL 62901.
- Grassroots (Carbondale) q. ISSN 0046-6328

**International Conference on Cybernetics and Society**
- International Conference on Cybernetics and
Society. Proceedings. (pub. by Institute of
Electrical and Electronics Engineers, Inc.)

**International Conference on Ion Implantation in
Semiconductors**
- International Conference on Ion Implantation in
Semiconductors. Proceedings. (pub. by Gordon
and Breach Science Publishers)

**International Conference on Social Welfare**
345 E. 46 St., New York, NY 10017.
- International Conference on Social Welfare.
Proceedings. biennial, 1972, 16th, The Hague.
ISSN 0074-3305

**International Congress of Pharmacology**
- Physicians' Drug Manual/P D M. (pub. by
Physicians Drug Manual, Inc.)

**International Congress on Automotive Safety**
3512 Graysby Ave., San Pedro, CA 90732.
- International Congress of Automotive Safety.
Proceedings. irreg., 2nd, 1973.

**International Construction Reporter**
Box 536, Oakland, CA 94604.
- International Construction Reporter. w. ISSN
0020-6423

**International Consumer Credit Association**
375 Jackson Ave., St. Louis, MO 63130.
- Credit World. m. ISSN 0011-1074

**International Convention Facilities Directory**
633 Third Ave, New York, NY 10017.
- International Convention Facilities Directory. a.

**International Cooperation Council, Inc.**
8570 Wilshire Blvd., Beverly Hills, CA 90211.
- Cooperator. a. ISSN 0045-849X
- International Cooperation Council. Directory;
worldwide guide of organizations fostering a new
person and civilization. a. ISSN 0074-4239

**International Correspondence Schools (ICS)**
Scranton, PA 18515.
- Training Digest. q.

**International Cosmetic Manufacturing Conference**
1031 South Blvd., Oak Park, IL 60302.
- National Cosmetics Regulations. irreg.

**International Cotton Advisory Committee**
South Agriculture Bldg., Washington, DC 20250.
- Cotton. Part 1: Monthly Review of the World
Situation. q.
- Cotton. Part 2: World Statistics. q.
- International Cotton Advisory Committee.
Country Statements Presented in Connection with
the Plenary Meetings. a.

**International Council for Educational Development**
680 Fifth Ave, New York, NY 10019.
- I C E D Conference Papers. a.
- I C E D Conference Reports. irreg.
- I C E D Newsletter. q.
- International Council for Educational
Development. Occasional Papers. irreg. ISSN
0070-9123

**International Council of Christian Churches**
- Reformation Review. (pub. by Christian Beacon
Press)

**International Council of Psychologists, Inc.**
4014 Cody Rd., Sherman Oaks, CA 91403.
- International Flash. q.
- International Psychologist. -a. ISSN 0047-116X
- International Understanding. irreg. ISSN 0535-
3505

**International Council of Scientific Unions. Inter-
Union Commission of Solar Terrestrial Physics**
C/O National Academy of Sciences, 2101
Constitution Ave. N.W., Washington, DC 20418.
- S T P Notes. irreg., approx. 2 per yr. ISSN 0085-
1965

**International Council of Shopping Centers**
445 Park Ave., New York, NY 10022.
- I C S C Newsletter. m.

**International Council of the Aeronautical Sciences**
- International Congress of the Aeronautical
Sciences. Proceedings. (pub. by American
Institute of Aeronautics and Astronautics)

**International Council on Health, Physical Education
and Recreation**
1201 16th St., N.W., Washington, DC 20036.
- International Council on Health, Physical
Education and Recreation. International Congress.
Report. a. ISSN 0074-4417

**International Council on Social Welfare**
- International Conference of Social Work.
Conference Proceedings. (pub. by Columbia
University Press)

**International Courtly Literature Society, Temple
University**
c/o Secretary-Treasurer, Dept. of English, Temple
University, Philadelphia, PA 19122.
- Encomia. irreg. ISSN 0363-4841

**International Data Corp.**
214 Third Ave., Waltham, MA 02154.
- Autotransaction Industry Report; news about
information appliances and automated transaction
services. fortn.
- E D P Industry Report. 24 per yr.

**International Defense and Aid Fund for Southern
Africa**
Box 17, Cambridge, MA 02138.
- Focus on Political Repression in South Africa. 6
per yr.

**International Development Association**
For publications of this agency see section for
UNITED NATIONS

**International Development Research Center**
*see under* **Indiana University**

**International District Heating Association**
5940 Baum Square, Pittsburgh, PA 15206.
- District Heating. q. ISSN 0012-401X
- International District Heating Association.
Proceedings. a. ISSN 0074-4638

**International Double Reed Society**
c/o Noah A. Knepper, Treas., School of Fine Arts,
Texas Christian University, Ft. Worth, TX 76129.
- To the World's Oboists. irreg. ISSN 0091-9683

**International Edsel Club**
Box 304, Bellevue, OH 44811.
- Edseletter. m. ISSN 0046-1326

**International Electrochemical Institute**
Box 285, Millburn, NJ 07041.
- International Electrochemical Progress. m.

**International English Shepherd Registry, Inc**
Rt. 1, Butler, IN 46721.
- National Stock Dog. q. ISSN 0028-0267

**International Executive Newsletters Co.**
35 W. Elm St., Littleton, NH 03561.
- Aerosol Newsletter. m. ISSN 0001-9305
- Corrugated Newsletter. m. ISSN 0010-9401
- Dairy Packaging Newsletter. m. ISSN 0011-5665
- Injection Moulding Newsletter. m. ISSN 0020-
1375
- Non-Woven Materials Newsletter. m. ISSN 0029-
1072
- Nonwoven Patents Digest. bi-m. ISSN 0029-1110
- Package Disposability Newsletter. m. ISSN 0030-
9036
- Reprography Newsletter. m. ISSN 0034-5008
- Water and Air Pollution Newsletter; for the paper
and pulp industry. m. ISSN 0043-132X

**International Eye Foundation**
Sibley Memorial Hospital, Hayes Hall, Washington,
DC 20016.
- Eyelights; International Eye Foundation
newsletter. q.

**International Fabricare Institute**
Box 940, Joliet, IL 60434.
• I F I Fabricare News. m.
• I F I Special Reporter. m.
• Textile Cleaning Technology. m. ISSN 0094-5781

**International Fabricare Institute. I F I Research Center**
Silver Spring, MD 20904.
• Fabrics-Fashions. ISSN 0097-2495

**International Federation for Automatic Control**
• Automatica. (pub. by Pergamon Press, Inc.)

**International Federation of Operational Research Societies. Airline Group**
c/o Mr. L. G. Klingen, Eastern Airlines, Miami International Airport, Miami, FL 33148.
• International Federation of Operational Research Societies. Airline Group (A G I F O R S) Proceedings. a. ISSN 0538-7442

**International Federation of Petroleum and Chemical Workers**
165 Cook St., Suite 304, Denver, CO 80206.
• Petro. bi-m.

**International Federation of Professional and Technical Engineers**
1126 16th St. N.W., Washington, DC 20036.
• Engineers Outlook. m.

**International Federation of Societies for Electroencephalography and Clinical Neurophysiology**
602 S. 44th Ave., Omaha, NE 68105.
• International Congress of Electroencephalography and Clinical Neurophysiology (Proceedings) irreg., 1969, 8th, Marseilles, France. ISSN 0074-3631

**International Federation of Surveyors**
c/o William B. Overstreet, Secretary General, P.O. Box 1503, Silver Spring, MD 20902.
• International Congress of Surveyors. Proceedings. triennial; latest issue, vol. 9, 1974. ISSN 0074-3976

**International Federation on Ageing**
1909 K St. N.W., Washington, DC 20049.
• Ageing International. q.

**International Film Importers and Distributors of America**
40 West 57th Street, New York, Ny 10019.
• IFIDA Film Directory. a.

**International Finance Corporation**
For publications of this agency see section for UNITED NATIONS

**International Flying Farmers, Inc.**
Mid-Continent Airport, Wichita, KS 67209.
• International Flying Farmer. m. ISSN 0020-675X

**International Foodservice Manufacturers Association**
1 E. Wacker Drive, Chicago, IL 60601.
• Foodservice Today. m.

**International Fortean Organization**
Box 367, Arlington, VA 22210.
• I N F O Journal. 6 per yr. ISSN 0019-0144

**International Foundation for Studies in Reproduction, Inc.**
• International Journal of Fertility. (pub. by Allen Press, Inc.)

**International Foundation for Telemetering**
• I. F. T. Journal. (pub. by Blackwent Publishing Co.)

**International Foundation for Theoretical Research**
• American Review of Management & Inventiveness Report. (pub. by American Classical College. Research Center for Economic Psychology)
• Revue of International Affairs. (pub. by American Classical College. Institute for Economic & Political World Strategic Studies)

**International Foundation of Employee Benefit Plans**
18700 W. Bluemound Rd., Box 69, Brookfield, WI 53005.
• Employee Benefits Journal. q. ISSN 0361-4050
• International Foundation of Employee Benefit Plans. Digest. m. ISSN 0146-1141
• Legal Legislative Reports. News Bulletin. m. ISSN 0458-9599

**International Foundations of Education Quarterly**
416 Lake St., Evanston, IL 60201.
• International Foundations of Education Quarterly. q. ISSN 0095-506X

**International Frozen Food Association**
919 18th St. N.W., Washington, DC 20006.
• International Frozen Food Association Letter. q.

**International Game Fish Association**
3000 E. Las Olas Blvd., Fort Lauderdale, FL 33316.
• World Record Marine Fishes. a. ISSN 0084-2214

**International General**
Box 350, New York, NY 10013.
• Marxism and the Mass Media; towards a basic bibliography. irreg. ISSN 0098-9509 (International Mass Media Research Center)

**International Geneva Association, Inc.**
121 W. 45th St., New York, NY 10036.
• Geneva Newsletter. 10 per yr. ISSN 0018-6163

**International Geranium Society**
c/o B. Tufenkian, 4610 Druid St., Los Angeles, CA 90032.
• Geraniums around the World. q. ISSN 0016-8599

**International Graphics Corp.**
218 Beech St., Bennington, VT 05201.
• Military Journal. bi-m.
• W W II Journal. irreg.

**International Graphoanalysis Society**
325 W. Jackson Blvd., Chicago, IL 60606.
• International Congress of Graphoanalysts. Proceedings. a. ISSN 0534-9044
• Journal of Graphoanalysis. m. ISSN 0022-1449

**International Grenfell Association**
• Among the Deep Sea Fishers. (pub. by Village Press)

**International Harpsichord Society**
Box 4323, Denver, CO 80204.
• Harpsichord. q. ISSN 0017-792X

**International Harvester Co.**
401 N. Michigan Ave., Chicago, IL 60611.
• I H Farm Forum. q.
• International Harvester Farm. q.
• International Trail. 6 per yr.

**International Honorary Society for High School Journalists**
• Quill and Scroll. (pub. by Quill & Scroll Society)

**International Hotel Directories Ltd.**
301 E. 48th St., Suite 4-M, New York, NY 10017.
• International Hotel Directory. s-a. ISSN 0020-6903

**International I U P A C Congress of Pesticide Chemistry**
• International I U P A C Congress of Pesticide Chemistry. Proceedings. (pub. by Gordon and Breach Science Publishers)

**International Inflammation Research Society**
• Inflammation. (pub. by Plenum Press)

**International Institute for Rural Reconstruction**
1775 Broadway, Suite 619, New York, NY 10019.
• I I R R Report. s-a.

**International Institute of Conservation**
• Art and Archaeology Technical Abstracts. (pub. by New York University. Institute of Fine Arts)

**International Institute of Ibero-American Literature**
University of Arizona, Tucson, AZ 85717.
• International Institute of Ibero-American Literature. Congress Proceedings. Memoria. biennial; 15th, Arizona, 1974. ISSN 0074-6495

**International Institute of Space Law**
• Colloquium on the Law of Outer Space. Proceedings. (pub. by University of California, Davis. School of Law)

**International Institute of Synthetic Rubber Producers**
45 Rockefeller Plaza, New York, NY 10020.
• International Institute of Synthetic Rubber Producers. Annual Meeting Proceedings. a.

**International Intertrade Index**
Box 636, Federal Sq., Newark, NJ 07101.
• International Intertrade Index; new foreign products-marketing techniques. m. ISSN 0020-7004

**International Invention Register**
c/o Dudley Rosborough, Box 547, Fallbrook, CA 92028.
• International Invention Register. irreg., 4-6 per yr.

**International Jewish Labor Bund**
25 E. 78th St., New York, NY 10021.
• Unser Tsait. 10 per yr. ISSN 0042-0506

**International Kart Federation**
444 West Foothill, Glendora, CA 91740.
• Karter News. m. ISSN 0096-3216

**International Labor Press Association**
815 16th St., N.W., Washington, DC 20006.
• I L P A Reporter. m. ISSN 0018-9995
• International Labor Press Association. Directory of Member Publications. a.

**International Ladies Garment Workers' Union**
1710 Broadway, New York, NY 10019.
• Giustizia. m.
• Justice. s-m. ISSN 0022-7013
• Justicia. m.

**International Ladies Garment Workers Union. Local 66**
232 W. 40th St., New York, NY 10018.
• Our Local Sixty Six. q. ISSN 0048-2390

**International Law Association. American Branch**
c/o James P. Beggans, Jr., 14 Wall St., New York, NY 10005.
• I L A Newsletter. bi-m.
• International Law Association. American Branch. Proceedings. biennial.

**International Law Fund**
• British International Law Cases. (pub. by Oceana Publications Inc.)

**International Law Perspective**
927 15th St. N.W., Washington, DC 20005.
• International Law Perspective. m.

**International Lead and Zinc Study Group**
United Nations Bldg., Rm. 901, New York, NY 10017.
• Lead and Zinc Statistics. m. ISSN 0023-9577

**International Lead Zinc Research Organization, Inc.**
292 Madison Ave., New York, NY 10017.
• I L Z R O Annual Research Report. a.
• I L Z R O Lead Research Digest. a. ISSN 0146-7980
• I L Z R O Zinc Research Digest. a. ISSN 0146-7999

**International League against Epilepsy**
• Epilepsia. (pub. by Raven Press)

**International League for the Rights of Man**
777 United Nations Plaza, New York, NY 10017.
• International League for the Rights of Man. Annual Report. a; latest issue, 1973.
• Rights of Man. s-a

**International League of Dermatological Societies**
• International Congress of Dermatology. Proceedings. (pub. by Springer-Verlag)

**International League of Liberal Christian Women**
c/o Carolyn C. Howlett (Pres.), Eastman Hill Rd., Center Lovell, ME 04016.
• International Union of Liberal Christian Women. Newsletter. a.

**International Leprosy Association**
Business Office, Box 1097, Bloomfield, NJ 07003 (Editorial Office: Leahi Hospital, 3675 Kilauea Ave., Honolulu, HI 96816)
• International Journal of Leprosy and Other Mycobacterial Diseases. q.
• International Leprosy Congress. Abstracts and Papers. quinquennial, 1973, 10th, Bergen. ISSN 0074-6762

**International Library-Book Publishers**
Editorial Offices, 2425 Wilson Blvd., Arlington, VA 22201.
• Advertising Law Anthology. a. ISSN 0093-1985
• Public Utilities Law Anthology. a.

**International Linguistic Association**
Dept. of English, Clark University, Worcester, MA 01610.
- International Linguistic Association. Monograph. irreg. ISSN 0074-6797
- International Linguistic Association. Special Publications. irreg. ISSN 0074-6800
- Word. 3 per yr. ISSN 0043-7956

**International Longshoremen's & Warehousemen's Union**
1188 Franklin St., San Francisco, CA 94109.
- Dispatcher. 24 per yr. ISSN 0012-3765

**International Longshoremen's Association, A F L-C I O. Local 1814**
343 Court St., Brooklyn, NY 11231.
- Brooklyn Longshoreman. m. ISSN 0007-2370

**International Lutheran Laymen's League**
2185 Hampton, St. Louis, MO 63139.
- Lutheran Layman. m. ISSN 0024-7464

**International Management Services**
215 Oak St., Natick, MA 01760.
- Minicomputer Applications Analyzer. m.
- Minicomputer Software Quarterly. q.

**International Markets Advertising Agency**
711 Third Ave., New York, NY 10017.
- Image/International Markets Advertising Newsletter. bi-m. ISSN 0046-8657

**International Mass Media Research Center**
- Marxism and the Mass Media. (pub. by International General)

**International Material Management Society**
Monroe Complex, 2520 Mosside Boulevard, Monroeville, PA 15146.
- Material Management Pacesetter. q.

**International Metallographic Society Inc**
- Metallography. (pub. by Elsevier North-Holland, Inc., New York)
- Microstructural Science. (pub. by Elsevier North-Holland, Inc., New York)

**International Metaphysical Festivals, Inc.**
Box 15668, Honolulu, HI 96815.
- Prism. m.

**International Micrographic Congress**
- I M C Journal. (pub. by Information & Records Management Inc.)

**International Mimes & Pantomimists**
192 Third Ave., New York, NY 10003.
- I M P Directory. irreg. ISSN 0095-2087

**International Mineralogical Association**
c/o Marjorie Hooker, Secretary, 2018 Luzerne Ave, Silver Spring, MD 20910.
- International Mineralogical Association. Proceedings of Meetings. biennial. ISSN 0074-7017

**International Mobile Air Conditioning**
6116 N. Central Expwy., Dallas, TX 75206.
- International Buyer's Guide of Mobile Air Conditioning. a.

**International Molders' and Allied Workers' Union**
1225 E. McMillan St., Cincinnati, OH 45206.
- International Molders' and Allied Workers' Journal. m. ISSN 0020-8019

**International Monetary Fund**
For publications of this agency see section for UNITED NATIONS

**International Multidisciplinary Research Association**
- Multidisciplinary Research. (pub. by Khalsa Publications)

**International Municipal Signal Association**
1511 K St., N.W., Washington, DC 20005.
- I. M. S. A. Signal Magazine. bi-m. ISSN 0019-0055

**International Narcotic Enforcement Officers Association**
Suite 1310, 112 State St., Albany, NY 12207.
- International Drug Report. bi-m.
- International Narcotic Conference. Report: Proceedings of Annual Conference. a. ISSN 0074-7114

**International Netsuke Collectors Society Journal**
P.O. Box 10426, Honolulu, HI 96816.
- International Netsuke Collectors Society Journal. q.

**International New Thought Alliance**
4533 Scottsdale Rd., Scottsdale, AZ 85251.
- New Thought. q.

**International News Keyus, Inc.**
Box 1247, Berkeley, CA 94701.
- Berkeley Barb. w. ISSN 0005-9161

**International Newspaper Collectors' Club**
Box 7271, Phoenix, AZ 85011.
- Newes. 2 per yr.

**International Newspaper Promotion Association**
Box 17422, Dulles International Airport, Washington, DC 20041.
- I N P A Advertising Newsletter. m. ISSN 0019-0152
- International Newspaper Promotion Association Advertising Copy Service Newsletter. m. ISSN 0019-0160

**International Nickel Co. Inc.**
1 New York Plaza, New York, NY 10004.
- Nickelife. q.

**International Nickel Co. Inc. Huntington Alloys**
Huntington, WV 25720.
- Huntington Alloys. s-a.
- P I Q (Process Industries Quarterly) q. ISSN 0030-803X

**International Nonwovens & Disposables Association**
10 E. 40 St., New York, NY 10016.
- International Directory of the Nonwoven Fabrics Industry. biennial. ISSN 0095-683X

**International Oceanographic Foundation**
3979 Rickenbacker Causeway, Virginia Key, Miami, FL 33149.
- Sea Frontiers. 6 per yr. ISSN 0036-9993
- Sea Secrets; an educational service. 6 per yr. ISSN 0037-0029

**International Oil Scouts Association**
Box 2121, Austin, TX 78767.
- International Oil Scouts Association. Official Publication. m. ISSN 0047-0864
- Texas Yearbook. a. ISSN 0092-7996

**International Order of Odd Fellows**
1019 S.W. 10th Ave., Portland, OR 97205.
- International Odd Fellow. 9 per yr. ISSN 0020-8140

**International Order of Odd Fellows. Grand Lodge of Oregon**
1019 S.W.10th Ave., Portland, OR 97205.
- Oregon Pacific Oddfellow. m.

**International Organization for Succulent Plant Study**
- Repertorium Plantarum Succulentarum. (pub. by Abbey Garden Press)

**International Organization for the Study of Group Tensions**
10 W. 66 St., New York, NY 10023.
- International Journal of Group Tensions. q. ISSN 0047-0732

**International Organization of Citrus Virologists**
- International Organization of Citrus Virologists. Proceedings of the Conference. (pub. by University Presses of Florida)

**International Pacific Halibut Commission**
P.O. Box 5009, University Station, Seattle, WA 98105.
- International Pacific Halibut Commission (U.S. and Canada). Annual Report. a. ISSN 0074-7238
- International Pacific Halibut Commission (U.S. and Canada). Scientific Reports. irreg.; no. 62, 1976. ISSN 0074-7246
- International Pacific Halibut Commission (U.S. and Canada). Technical Reports. irreg., no. 13, 1975. ISSN 0579-3920

**International Pediatric Research Foundation Inc**
- Pediatric Research. (pub. by Williams & Wilkins Co.)

**International Pentecostal Holiness Church**
Box 12609, Oklahoma City, OK 73112
- International Pentecostal Holiness Advocate. fortn. ISSN 0031-4900 (Subscr. to: Advocate Press, Box 98, Franklin Springs, GA 30639)

**International Percussion Reference Library**
- International Percussion Reference Library. Catalog. (pub. by Arizona State University. Music Department)

**International Personnel Management Association**
1313 E. 60th St., Chicago, IL 60637.
- I P M A News. m.
- Public Personnel Management. q. ISSN 0091-0260

**International Physical Index, Inc.**
1909 Park Ave., New York, NY 10035.
- Physics Express; digest of current Russian literature dealing with physics topics. 10 per yr. ISSN 0031-9139
- Power Express; new comprehensive digest of current Russian literature dealing with power topics. 10 nos. to vol. ISSN 0032-597X
- Russian Physics Quarterly; a source book in Soviet experiment and theory. q. ISSN 0036-0333

**International Planned Parenthood Federation**
111 Fourth Ave., New York, NY 10003.
- International Planned Parenthood Federation. Western Hemisphere Region. Library Bulletin. q.

**International Plant Protection Center**
Oregon State Univ., Corvallis, OR 97331.
- International Plant Protection Center. Infoletter. q. (Co-sponsor: U.S. Agency for International Development)

**International Plastic Modelers' Society**
Box 2555, Long Beach, CA 90801.
- Update (Long Beach) bi-m.

**International Plastic Modelers Society-U.S.A.**
Box 2555, Long Beach, CA 90801.
- International Plastic Modelers Society United States Quarterly Journal. q.

**International Plastic Modelers Society. U.S.A. Branch-Northern Delaware Chapter**
1017 Graylyn Rd., Wilmington, DE 19803.
- N O R D E L Modeler. q.

**International Poetry Forum**
University of Texas at Dallas, Box 688, Richardson, TX 75080.
- Mundus Artium; a journal of international literature and the arts. s-a. ISSN 0027-3406

**International Poetry Review (Greensboro)**
Box 2047, Greensboro, NC 27402.
- International Poetry Review (Greensboro) s-a. ISSN 0020-8329

**International Primatological Society**
c/o Dr. G. H. Bourne, Yerkes-Primate Center, Emory University, Atlanta, GA 30322
- International Congress of Primatology. Proceedings. biennial, 5th, 1974, Napoya, Japan. ISSN 0074-3895 (Proceedings of 5th Congress Avail. from: Japan Science Press Co., Ltd., Meiho-sha, 23 Kanda-Jimbo-cho, 2-chome, Chiyoda-ku, Tokyo 101, Japan)

**International Printing and Graphic Communications Union**
1730 Rhode Island Ave. N.W., Washington, DC 20036.
- International Printing and Graphic Communications Union. News and Views. m.

**International Prisoners' Aid Association**
McNeil Bldg., Rm. 203, University of Pennsylvania, Philadelphia, PA 19174.
- International Directory of Prisoners' Aid Agencies. irreg. ISSN 0538-7191
- International Prisoners Aid Association. Newsletter. 3 per yr. ISSN 0020-8396

**International Public Policy Institute**
156 Fifth Ave., Room 1223, New York, NY 10010.
- International and Comparative Public Policy. s-a.

**International Publications Service**
114 E. 32nd St, New York, NY 10016.
- International Publications; an annual annotated subject bibliography. a.

**International Publishing Co. of America**
665 La Villa Dr., Miami Springs, FL 33166
(Distributed by: Arco Publishing Co., 219 Park Ave. South, New York, N.Y. 10003)
- Airline Food & Flight Service. bi-m. (Airline Inflight Food Service Association)
- Airline Guide to Stewardess & Stewards Career. a. ISSN 0065-4914
- Official Guide to Airline Careers. a.
- Passenger & In-Flight Service. bi-m.

**International Radio and Television Society, Inc.**
420 Lexington Ave., New York, NY 10017.
- I R T S Gold Medal Annual. a. ISSN 0074-7564

**International Reading Association, Inc.**
800 Barksdale Rd., Newark, DE 19711.
- International Reading Association. Abstracts of the Annual Convention. a. ISSN 0074-7629
- International Reading Association. Annual Report. a. ISSN 0538-933X
- Journal of Reading. 8 per yr (Oct.-May) ISSN 0022-4103
- Perspectives in Reading. irreg. ISSN 0553-7576
- Reading Research Quarterly. q. ISSN 0034-0553
- Reading Teacher. 8 per yr.(Oct-May) ISSN 0034-0561

**International Reading Association, Inc. Indiana State Council**
318 Teachers College, Ball State Univ., Muncie, IN 47306.
- Indiana Reading Quarterly. q. ISSN 0019-672X

**International Reading Association, Inc. Ohio Council**
c/o Dr. Barbara D. Stoodt, Ed., College of Education, University of Akron, Akron, OH 44325.
- Ohio Reading Teacher; a journal of education whose objective is to improve reading instruction in Ohio schools. q. ISSN 0030-1035 (Co-sponsor: Bowling Green State University, Department of Education)

**International Reference Organization in Forensic Medicine & Sciences**
c/o Wm. G. Eckert, Laboratory, St. Francis Hospital, Wichita, KS 67214.
- Inform Quarterly Newsletter. q.
- International Bibliography of the Forensic Sciences. a.

**International Religious Liberty Association**
- Liberty. (pub. by Review and Herald Publishing Association)

**International Remote Sensing Institute**
Executive Airport, Sacramento, CA 95822.
- Journal of Remote Sensing. bi-m. ISSN 0047-2743

**International Reports, Inc.**
200 Park Ave. S., New York, NY 10003.
- Forex Service. m. ISSN 0015-7627
- International Business Intelligence. w. ISSN 0014-5297
- International Reports; international reports on finance and currencies. w. ISSN 0020-8507

**International Reprographic Blueprint Association**
10116 Franklin Ave., Franklin Park, IL 60131.
- Plan and Print; the magazine for design and reproduction management. 10 per yr. ISSN 0032-0595

**International Rescue Committee**
386 Park Avenue South, New York, NY 10016.
- International Rescue Committee Annual Report. a. ISSN 0538-9461

**International Research Center for Energy and Economic Development**
216 Economics Bldg., University of Colorado, Boulder, CO 80309.
- Journal of Energy and Development. s-a.

**International Review Service, Inc.**
15 Washington Place, New York, NY 10003.
- Energy Developments; atomic, petroleum & others. m. ISSN 0013-7502
- Trade and Economic Development. m. ISSN 0020-8639

**International Road Federation**
1023 Washington Bldg., Washington, DC 20005.
- World Highways. m. ISSN 0043-8529

**International Rodeo Association**
- Rodeo News. (pub. by Rodeo News, Inc.)

**International Scholarly Book Services Inc.**
Box 555, Forest Grove, OR 97116.
- Papers on Islamic History. irreg., 1972, no. 3. ISSN 0085-4662 (University of Pennsylvania. Near East Center) (Co-sponsor: Near Eastern History Group, Oxford)

**International Scientific Communications, Inc.**
808 Kings Highway, Fairfield, CT 06430.
- American Laboratory. m. ISSN 0044-7749
- American Laboratory Direct Information Service. s-a.
- International Laboratory. bi-m. ISSN 0010-2164
- International Laboratory Direct Information Service. q.

**International Shade Tree Conference, Inc.**
Box 71, Urbana, IL 61801.
- Journal of Arboriculture. m.

**International Skeletal Society**
- Skeletal Radiology. (pub. by Springer Verlag)

**International Socialist Publishing Co**
14131 Woodward Ave., Highland Park, MI 48203.
- Workers' Power. w. ISSN 0019-0535

**International Society for Astrological Research, Inc.**
70 Melrose Place, Montclair, NJ 07042.
- Journal of Astrological Studies. irreg. ISSN 0085-2384
- Kosmos. q. ISSN 0047-3650

**International Society for Cell Biology**
- Experimental Cell Research. (pub. by Academic Press Inc)

**International Society for Community Development**
345 East 46th St., New York, NY 10017.
- International Society for Community Development (Publication) s-a. (Community Development Foundation)

**International Society for Fluoride Research**
P.O. Box 692, Warren, MI 48090.
- Fluoride. q. ISSN 0015-4725

**International Society for General Semantics**
Box 2469, San Francisco, CA 94126.
- ETC; a review of general semantics. 4 per yr. ISSN 0014-164X

**International Society for Japanese Philately**
Murray H. Schaefer, 530 E. Indian Spring Dr., Silver Spring, MD 20901.
- I.S.J.P. Monograph. irreg. ISSN 0539-0249
- Japanese Philately. bi-m. (Subscr. to: Mrs. William Evans, Sec., P.O. Box 961, State College, Pennsylvania 16801)

**International Society for Krishna Consciousness**
- Back to Godhead. (pub. by Bhaktivedanta Book Trust)

**International Society for Labor Law and Social Security. United States National Committee**
3345 Wilshire Blvd., Los Angeles, CA 90010.
- Comparative Labor Law. q.

**International Society for Portuguese Philately**
Rural Rte. 3, Box 36, Bedford, NY 10506.
- Portu-Info. q.

**International Society for Soil Mechanics and Foundation Engineering**
- Foundation Facts. (pub. by Raymond International Inc.)
- Geodex Retrieval System for Geotechnical Abstracts. (pub. by Geodex International, Inc.)

**International Society for Stereology**
- International Congress for Stereology. Proceedings. (pub. by Springer-Verlag)

**International Society for Technology Assessment**
716 Fourth St., S.E., Washington, DC 20003.
- T A-Update Newsletter. bi-m.

**International Society for Terrain-Vehicle Systems**
711 Hudson St., Hoboken, NJ 07030.
- International Society for Terrain-Vehicle Systems. Proceedings of International Conference. irreg.; 5th, Detroit, Mich., 1975. ISSN 0074-8498
- Journal of Terramechanics. (pub. by Pergamon Press, Inc.)

**International Society for the Comparative Study of Civilization, American Branch**
Bradford College, Dept. of Sociology, Bradford, Geneseo, MA 01830.
- Comparative Civilization Bulletin. q.

**International Society for the Study of Symbols**
- International Journal of Symbology. (pub. by Georgia State University. Department of Psychology)

**International Society of Aesthetic Plastic Surgery**
- Aesthetic Plastic Surgery. (pub. by Springer-Verlag)

**International Society of Bassists**
University of Cincinnati, College-Conservatory of Music, Cincinnati, OH 45221.
- Bass World. a.
- International Society of Bassists. Newsletter. 3 per yr.

**International Society of Bible Collectors**
Box 2845, El Cajon, CA 92021.
- Bible Collector. q. ISSN 0006-0690

**International Society of Christian Endeavor**
1221 E. Broad St., P.O. Box 1110, Columbus, OH 43216.
- Christian Endeavor World; the voice of Christian Endeavor. 4 per yr. ISSN 0009-5338

**International Society of Food Service Consultants**
c/o Earl D. Triplett, Exec. Sec., Box 689, Bloomfield Hills, MI 48013.
- International Society of Food Service Consultants. Directory. ISSN 0539-0338

**International Society of Hematology**
c/o Dr. J. L. Tullis, 110 Francis St., Boston, MA 02215.
- International Congress of Hematology. Proceedings. biennial since 1958; 1974, 15th, Jerusalem. ISSN 0074-3682

**International Society of Heraldry & Family Trees**
Box 1717, Washington, DC 20013.
- Genealogy and Heraldry. q. ISSN 0016-6413

**International Society of Heterocyclic Chemistry**
- International Congress of Heterocyclic Chemistry. Abstracts. (pub. by HeteroCorporation)

**International Society of Nephrology**
- Kidney International. (pub. by Springer Verlag)

**International Society of Performing Arts Administrators**
515 John Muir Dr., Suite 605, San Francisco, CA 94132
(Subscr. to: James Bernhard, Jones Hall-615 Louisiana, Houston, TX 77002)
- Performing Arts Forum. 9 per yr.

**International Society of Planetarium Educators**
c/o Walter Tenschert, Thomas Jefferson High School, 6560 Braddock Rd., Alexandria, VA 22312.
- Planetarian. q. ISSN 0090-3213

**International Society of Reply Coupon Collectors**
c/o Dr. Allan Hauck, Box 176, Kenosha, WI 53141.
- Reply Coupon Collector. bi-m.

**International Society of Sugarcane Technologists**
c/o HSPA Experiment Station, Honolulu, Hawaii.
- International Congress of Sugarcane Technologists. Proceedings. triennial, 1974, 15th, Durban. ISSN 0074-3968

**International Society of Tropical Dermatology**
- International Journal of Dermatology. (pub. by J. B. Lippincott Co.)

**International Society of Weekly Newspaper Editors**
Northern Illinois University, Dept. of Journalism, De Kalb, IL 60115.
- Grassroots Editor. q. ISSN 0017-3541

**International Society on Metabolic Eye Disease**
- Metabolic Ophthalmology. (pub. by Pergamon Press, Inc.)

**International Society on Toxicology**
- Toxicon. (pub. by Pergamon Press, Inc.)

**International Sociological Association. Research Committee on Sociolinguistics**
- Sociolinguistics Newsletter. (pub. by Scholars Press)

**International Solar Energy Society**
- Solar Energy. (pub. by Pergamon Press, Inc.)

**International Solar Energy Society. American Section**
300 State Rd. 401, Cape Canaveral, FL 32920.
- Solar News and Views. q.

**International Star Class Yacht Racing Association**
c/o C. Stanley Ogilvy, 943 Greacen Pt. Rd., Mamaroneck, NY 10543
(and 1545 Waukegan Rd., Glenview, IL 60025)
- Log of the Star Class; official rule book. a. ISSN 0076-0455
- Starlights. m. ISSN 0038-9927

**International Studies Association**
University Center for International Studies, University of Pittsburgh, Pittsburgh, PA 15260.
- International Studies Newsletter. m.
- International Studies Notes. q.
- International Studies Quarterly. (pub. by Sage Publications Inc.)

**International Studies Association. Comparative Interdisciplinary Studies Section**
c/o Ann Baker Cottrell, Ed., Dept. of Sociology, San Diego State University, San Diego, CA 92115.
- International Studies Association. Comparative Interdisciplinary Studies Section. Bulletin. q.

**International Study Group for Research in Cardiac Metabolism**
- Recent Advances in Studies on Cardiac Structure and Metabolism. (pub. by University Park Press)

**International Sugar Research Foundation, Inc.**
7316 Wisconsin Ave., Bethesda, MD 20014.
- I S R F Bulletin. bi-m.
- International Sugar Research Symposia. irreg.

**International Symposium on Animal and Plant Toxins**
- International Symposium on Animal and Plant Toxins. Proceedings. (pub. by Gordon and Breach Science Publishers)

**International Symposium on Stochastic Hydraulics**
c/o University of Pittsburgh, School of Engineering, Pittsburgh, PA 15261.
- International Symposium on Stochastic Hydraulics. Proceedings. irreg.

**International Tape Association**
10 W. 66 St., New York, NY 10023.
- I T A News Digest. bi-m.

**International Taxicab Association**
222 Wisconsin Ave., Lake Forest, IL 60045.
- Taxicab Management. m. ISSN 0040-0246

**International Telex Corp.**
1313 Fulton National Bldg., Atlanta, GA 30303.
- International Telex Book. Americas Edition. irreg. ISSN 0094-6923

**International Theatre Institute of the United States**
245 W. 52nd St, New York, NY 10019.
- Theatre. a. ISSN 0082-3813

**International Thespian Society**
3368 Central Parkway, Box E, Cincinnati, OH 45225.
- Dramatics; devoted to the advancement of theatre arts in the secondary schools. 5 per yr. ISSN 0012-5989

**International Trade and Finance Review**
Box 436, 219 E. 70th St., New York, NY 10021.
- International Trade & Finance Review. m. ISSN 0362-4307

**International Trade News Letter**
160 Broadway, New York, NY 10038.
- International Trade News Letter. m.

**International Turquoise Association**
- International Turquoise Annual. (pub. by Impart Publishers)

**International Typeface Corp.**
216 E. 45th St., New York, NY 10017.
- U & L C. (Upper and Lower Case) q.

**International Typographical Union**
Executive Council, Box 157, Colorado Springs, CO 80901.
- I T U Review. w. ISSN 0019-0853
- International Typographical Union. Bulletin. m. ISSN 0020-904X
- Typographical Journal. m. ISSN 0041-4832

**International Union Against Cancer**
- International Union against Cancer. U I C C Monograph Series. (pub. by Springer-Verlag)

**International Union of Air Pollution Prevention Associations**
- International Clean Air Congress. Proceedings. (pub. by Academic Press, Inc.)

**International Union of Biochemistry**
c/o Dept. of Biochemistry, University of Miami, School of Medicine, Miami, FL 33152.
- International Union of Biochemistry. Information Bulletin. irreg.

**International Union of Bricklayers and Allied Craftsmen**
815 15th St. N.W., Washington, DC 20005.
- International Union of Bricklayers and Allied Craftsmen. Journal. m.

**International Union of Electrical, Radio and Machine Workers, AFL-CIO, CLC**
1126 16th St., N.W., Washington, DC 20036.
- I U E News. m. ISSN 0019-0861

**International Union of Elevator Constructors**
Philadelphia Saving Fund Bldg., 12 S. 12th St., Rm. 1515, Philadelphia, PA 19107.
- Elevator Constructor. m. ISSN 0013-614X

**International Union of Operating Engineers**
1125 17th St. N.W., Washington, DC 20036.
- International Operating Engineer. m. ISSN 0020-8159

**International Union of Petroleum & Industrial Workers**
335 California Ave., Bakersfield, CA 93304.
- I U P I W Views. m.

**International Union of Pharmacology**
- Pharmacology & Therapeutics Part A: Chemotherapy, Toxicology and Metabolic Inhibitors. (pub. by Pergamon Press, Inc.)
- Pharmacology & Therapeutics Part B: General and Systematic Pharmacology. (pub. by Pergamon Press, Inc.)
- Pharmacology & Therapeutics Part C: Clinical Pharmacology and Therapeutics. (pub. by Pergamon Press, Inc.)

**International Union of Psychological Science**
c/o Prof. Wayne H.Holtzman, Hogg Foundation for Mental Health, Univ. of Texas, Austin, TX 78712 (Inquire: Mme. H. Gratiot Alphadery, 28 rue Serpente, F-75066 Paris, France)
- International Congress of Psychology. Proceedings. quadrennial; 1976, 21st, Paris. ISSN 0085-2112 (Co-sponsor: British Psychological Society)

**International Union of Pure and Applied Chemistry**
- Pure and Applied Chemistry. (pub. by Pergamon Press, Inc.)

**International Union of Theoretical and Applied Mechanics**
- International Congress of Applied Mechanics. Proceedings. (pub. by Springer Verlag)

**International Universities Press, Inc.**
315 Fifth Ave., New York, NY 10016.
- American Academy of Child Psychiatry. Journal. Monograph. irreg. ISSN 0065-6852
- American Psychoanalytic Association. Journal. q. ISSN 0003-0651
- American Psychoanalytic Association. Journal. Monograph. irreg., 1971, no. 4. ISSN 0065-9843
- Annual of Psychoanalysis. a. ISSN 0092-5055
- Annual Survey of Psychoanalysis. irreg., 1971, no. 10. ISSN 0066-443X

**Boston Society for Gerontologic Psychiatry.**
Scientific Meetings, Proceedings. irreg. ISSN 0524-1200
- Index of Psychoanalytic Writings. irreg., 1975, no. 14. ISSN 0073-5884
- International Journal of Group Psychotherapy. q. ISSN 0020-7284 (American Group Psychotherapy Association)
- Journal of Geriatric Psychiatry. s-a. ISSN 0022-1414 (Boston Society for Gerontologic Psychiatry, Inc.)
- Monograph Series on Schizophrenia. irreg., 1969, no. 8. ISSN 0077-0620
- New York Psychoanalytic Institute. Kris Study Group. Monograph. irreg., no. 6, 1975. ISSN 0077-9008
- Psychoanalytic Study of Society. irreg., no. 6, 1974. ISSN 0079-7294
- Psychoanalytic Study of the Child. a. ISSN 0079-7308
- Psychoanalytic Study of the Child. Monograph. irreg., 1967, no. 4. ISSN 0079-7316
- Psychological Issues. 4 per yr. ISSN 0048-5748
- Psychological Issues. Monograph. irreg. ISSN 0079-7359

**International Violin and Guitar Makers Association**
403 West Maple, Jeffersonville, IN 47130.
- International Violin and Guitar Makers Association. Journal. q.

**International Water Resources Association**
Business Office, Box 6, Falls Church, VA 22046.
- Water International. m.

**International Wealth Success**
Box 186, Merrick, NY 11566.
- International Wealth Success Newsletter. m. ISSN 0047-1275

**International Wizard of Oz Club, Inc.**
220 North 11th St., Escanaba, MI 49829.
- Baum Bugle. 3 per yr. ISSN 0005-6677
- Oziana. a.

**International Wood Trade Publications, Inc.**
4077 Viscount, Box 18436, Memphis, TN 38118.
- Hardwood Purchasing Handbook. a.
- Import/Export Wood Purchasing Guide. 3rd edt., 1976.
- Imported Wood Purchasing News. bi-m.
- National Hardwood Magazine. m.

**International Woodworkers of America, AFL-CIO, CLC**
1622 N. Lombard, Portland, OR 97217.
- International Woodworker. m. ISSN 0020-9139

**International Word Processing Association**
Maryland Rd., Willow Grove, PA 19090.
- Viewpoint (Willow Grove) m.
- Words. q.

**Internews**
Box 4400, Berkeley, CA 94704.
- International Bulletin. fortn.

**Interreligious Foundation for Community Organization**
475 Riverside Dr., Room 572, New York, NY 10027.
- I F C O News. q. ISSN 0047-1305

**Intersection, Inc.**
756 Union St., San Francisco, CA 94133.
- Intersection Newsletter. 3 per yr.

**Inter-Society Color Council**
c/o Fred W. Billmeyer, Jr., Sec., Rensselaer Polytechnic Institute, Troy, NY 12181
- Inter-Society Color Council Newsletter. bi-m. ISSN 0300-7588 (Edit.Address: Dr. William Benson, NAS-NRC Committee on Vision, 2101 Constitution Ave.. Washington, DC 20418)

**Intersociety Committee on Pathology Information**
9650 Rockville Pike, Bethesda, MD 20014.
- Directory of Pathology Training Programs. a. ISSN 0070-6086

**Interstate**
Box 7068, Austin, TX 78712.
- Interstate; a magazine of creative acts. q. ISSN 0363-9991

**Interstate Commission on the Potomac River Basin**
4350 East West Hwy., Suite 814, Bethesda, MD
20014.
- Annual Potomac Report. a.
- Interstate Commission on the Potomac River
  Basin. Proceedings. s-a. ISSN 0535-4676
- Interstate Commission on the Potomac River
  Basin. Technical Bulletin. irreg. ISSN 0074-9966
- Potomac. a.
- Potomac River Water Quality Network. a. ISSN
  0539-2047

**Interstate Oil Compact Commission**
900 Northeast 23rd St., Box 53127, Oklahoma City,
OK 73105.
- Compact Comments. m.
- Interstate Oil Compact Commission. Committee
  Bulletin. s-a. ISSN 0020-9732
- Legal Report of Oil and Gas Conservation
  Activities. a. ISSN 0539-2063

**Interstate Printers & Publishers, Inc.**
19-27 N. Jackson St., Danville, IL 61832.
- Animal Agriculture Series. irreg.
- Junior High School Association of Illinois. Study.
  irreg. ISSN 0075-4560
- Lehigh University. Annual Reading Conference.
  Proceedings. a.
- Pathologist. m. ISSN 0031-3017 (College of
  American Pathologists)

**Intertec Publishing Corp.**
9221 Quivira Rd., Overland Park, KS 66212.
- Agricultura de las Americas. m. ISSN 0002-1350
- Blue Book, Official Inboard/Outdrive Boat Trade-
  in Guide. a. ISSN 0520-2949 (prep. by its Abos
  Marine Publications Division)
- Broadcast Engineering. m. ISSN 0007-1994
- Electronic Servicing. m. ISSN 0013-497X
- Grounds Maintenance. m. ISSN 0017-4688
- Implement & Tractor. s-m. ISSN 0019-2953
- Implement and Tractor Product File. a. ISSN
  0073-5566
- Implement and Tractor Red Book. a. ISSN 0073-
  5574
- Lawn & Garden Marketing; the merchandising
  magazine for lawn, garden and leisure living
  products. m. ISSN 0091-4665
- Official Motor Home Trade-in Guide. irreg. ISSN
  0093-1195 (prep. by its Technical Publications
  Division)
- Official Truck Camper Trade-in Guide. irreg.
  ISSN 0094-1131
- Radio y Television. m. ISSN 0033-8133
- Video Systems; the journal of closed-circuit
  communications. bi-m. ISSN 0361-0942
- World Farming. m. ISSN 0043-8421

**Inter-Tribal Council of California**
2969 Fulton Ave., Sacramento, CA 95821.
- Tribal Spokesman. m. ISSN 0041-2643

**Inter-Tribal Council of Nevada, Inc.**
98 Colony Rd., Reno, NV 89502.
- Native Nevadan. m. ISSN 0028-0534

**Inter-University Case Program**
Box 229, Syracuse, NY 13210.
- Inter-University Case Program. Case Study. irreg.
  ISSN 0074-106X

**Interuniversity Communications Council**
Box 364, Rosedale Road, Princeton, NJ 08540.
- E D U C O M Bulletin. 4 per yr. ISSN 0012-
  7566

**Inter-University Consortium for Political and Social
Research**
Box 1248, Ann Arbor, MI 48106.
- Inter-University Consortium for Political and
  Social Research. Guide to Resources and Services.
  biennial.
- Inter-University Consortium for Political
  Research. Report. a. ISSN 0074-1078

**Inter-University Seminar on Armed Forces & Society**
University of Chicago, Social Science Bldg., Box 46,
1126 E.59 St., Chicago, IL 60637
- Armed Forces and Society; an interdisciplinary
  journal on military institutions, civil-military
  relations, arms control and peacekeeping, and
  conflict management. q. ISSN 0095-327X (Or
  British Inter-University Seminar, University of
  Hull, 195 Cottingham Rd., Hull HU5 2EQ,
  England)
- Sage Research Progress Series on War, Revolution
  and Peacekeeping. (pub. by Sage Publications,
  Inc.)

- Sage Series on Armed Forces and Society. (pub.
  by Sage Publications, Inc.)

**Inter-Varsity Christian Fellowship**
5206 Main St., Downers Grove, IL 60515.
- His; magazine of campus Christian living. m.(Oct-
  June) ISSN 0018-2095

**Interview Enterprises, Inc.**
860 Broadway, New York, NY 10003.
- Andy Warhol's Interview. m. ISSN 0020-5109

**Intra-Science Research Foundation**
10968 Savona Rd., Bel Air, CA 90406.
- Quarterly Reports on Sulfur Chemistry. q. ISSN
  0033-5738

**Intrepid Press**
Box 1423, Buffalo, NY 14214.
- Beau Fleuve Series. irreg., no. 9, 1976.
- Intrepid. q. ISSN 0020-9864

**Intrigue Publications, Inc.**
711 South Saint Asaph St., Alexandria, VA 22314.
- Classic Collector. q. ISSN 0093-1918

**Inventors Workshop International**
121 N. Fir St., Ventura, CA 93001.
- Lightbulb. bi-m.

**Investarama Club**
1500 S. Ave. D, Portales, NM 88130.
- Investa-Report. m.

**Investment Company Institute**
1775 K St. N.W., Washington, DC 20006.
- Mutual Funds Forum. bi-m. ISSN 0047-8504

**Investment Dealers Digest (IDD) Inc.**
150 Broadway, New York, NY 10038.
- Eliot Sharp's Municipal Newsletter. 5 per w.
- Investment Dealers' Digest. w. ISSN 0021-0080
- National Security Traders Association. Traders'
  Annual. a. ISSN 0092-4679

**Investor Responsibility Research Center**
1522 K St N. W., Washington, DC 20005.
- News for Investors. 11 per yr.

**Investors' Institute, Inc.**
Box 70, Miami, OK 74354.
- Chart-Of-The-Week. fortn. ISSN 0009-1863
- Investors' Profit Guide. 22 per yr. ISSN 0021-
  0226

**Investors League Inc.**
1 the Crescent, Montclair, NJ 07042.
- Investors League Bulletin. 6 per yr. ISSN 0021-
  0218

**Invictus Publishing Co.**
180 S. Broadway, White Plains, NY 10605.
- Atomic Energy Law Journal. q. ISSN 0004-7104

**Iona College**
715 North Ave., New Rochelle, NY 10801.
- Ionian. w. ISSN 0021-0358

**Iowa. Bureau of Labor. Research and Statistics
Division**
East 7th and Court, Des Moines, IA 50319.
- Iowa. Bureau of Labor. Occupational Injuries and
  Illnesses Survey. a.
- Iowa. Bureau of Labor. Research and Statistics
  Division. Biennial Report. biennial.

**Iowa. Civil Rights Commission**
1201 East Court Ave., Des Moines, IA 50319.
- Challenger. q.
- Iowa Civil Rights Commission. Annual Report. a.

**Iowa. Department of Health. Division of Records and
Statistics**
Des Moines, IA 50319.
- Iowa Detailed Report of Vital Statistics. a. ISSN
  0362-9473

**Iowa. Department of Public Instruction**
Grimes State Office Bldg., Des Moines, IA 50319.
- D P I Dispatch. m(during school year)
- Data on Iowa's Area Schools. a. ISSN 0092-3761
- Iowa. Department of Public Instruction. Summary
  of Federal Programs. irreg. ISSN 0091-8962
- Opportunities in Iowa's Area Schools. a. ISSN
  0093-3465

**Iowa. Drug Abuse Authority**
615 East 14th St., Suite D, Des Moines, IA 50319.
- Iowa Comprehensive State Plan for Drug Abuse
  Prevention: Annual Performance Report. a. ISSN
  0363-4507

**Iowa. Employment Security Commission**
1000 East Grand Ave., Des Moines, IA 50319.
- Iowa. Employment Security Commission.
  Research and Statistics Division. Annual
  Manpower Planning Report. a. ISSN 0091-262X
- Iowa Employment Security Commission. Annual
  Report. a.

**Iowa. Geological Survey**
Des Moines, IA 50319.
- Iowa. Geological Survey. Annual Report of the
  State Geologist to the Geological Board. a. ISSN
  0361-7629

**Iowa. Higher Education Facilities Commission**
201 Jewett Building, Des Moines, IA 50309.
- State of Iowa Scholarships, Tuition Grants:
  Biennium Report. biennial. ISSN 0091-3588

**Iowa. Office for Planning and Programming**
Capitol Hill Annex, 523 E. 12 St., Des Moines, IA
50319.
- Quality of Life in Iowa; an economic and social
  report to the Governor. a. ISSN 0091-5696
- Report on Federal Funds Received in Iowa. a.
  ISSN 0091-8695

**Iowa. State Conservation Commission**
300 4th St., Des Moines, IA 50319.
- Iowa Conservationist. m. ISSN 0021-0471
- Iowa Wildlife Research Bulletin. irreg. (prep. by
  its Wildlife Section)

**Iowa. State Library Commission**
Historical Building, Des Moines, IA 50319.
- Aardvark; newsletter for the library group. bi-m.

**Iowa Academy of Science**
University of Northern Iowa, Cedar Falls, IA
50613.
- I A S Bulletin. irreg. ISSN 0075-0344
- Iowa Academy of Science. Proceedings. q. ISSN
  0085-2236
- Iowa Science Teachers Journal. q. ISSN 0021-
  0676

**Iowa Archaeological Society**
R.R.3, Indianola, IA 50125.
- Iowa Archaeological Society. Newsletter. q.

**Iowa Association for Lifelong Learning**
Bureau of Correspondence Study, Div. of Extension
and University Services, Univ. of Iowa, Iowa City,
IA 52240.
- I A L L Eye-Opener. s-a.

**Iowa Association of Electric Cooperatives**
Box AP, 323 University, Des Moines, IA 50302.
- Iowa R E C News. (Iowa Rural Electric
  Cooperative) m. ISSN 0021-0641

**Iowa Association of Plumbing, Heating, Cooling
Contractors, Inc.**
I.H.S.A.A. Bldg, Box 56, Boone, IA 50036.
- Iowa Plumbing, Heating, Cooling Contractor. m.
  ISSN 0021-0625

**Iowa Association of School Administrators**
c/o Lyle Kehm, Exec. Sec., Box 10, Boone, IA
50036.
- I A S A Newsletter. m. ISSN 0018-8433

**Iowa Association of School Boards**
707 Savings and Loan Bldg., Des Moines, IA
50309.
- Iowa School Board Dialogue. bi-m. ISSN 0021-
  0668

**Iowa Congress of Parents and Teachers**
412 Shops Bldg., Des Moines, IA 50309.
- Iowa P T A Bulletin. 8 per yr. ISSN 0021-0617

**Iowa Council of Teachers of English**
- Iowa English Bulletin: Yearbook. (pub. by Iowa
  State University. Department of English)

**Iowa Crop and Livestock Reporting Service**
c/o Agricultural Statistician, Federal Bldg., Room 855, 210 Walnut St., IA 50309.
- Iowa Crop and Livestock Reporting Service. Planting to Harvest. Weather and Field Crops. irreg. ISSN 0362-6539 (Co-sponsors: Iowa Department of Agriculture; United States Department of Agriculture)

**Iowa Dental Association**
333 Insurance Exchange Bldg., Des Moines, IA 50309.
- Iowa Dental Journal. 4 per yr. ISSN 0021-0498

**Iowa Dental Hygienists' Association**
731 Edgewater Dr., Coralville, IA 52241.
- Lavender Band. bi-m. ISSN 0023-9062

**Iowa Development Commission**
250 Jewett Bldg., Des Moines, IA 50309.
- Directory of Iowa Manufacturers. biennial. ISSN 0075-0379
- Iowa Development Commission. Digest. m. ISSN 0075-0360
- Iowa International Directory. a.

**Iowa Educational Media Association**
Instructional Resources Center, Iowa State University, Ames, IA 50010.
- Iowa Educational Media Association/Iowa Media Message/Library Lines. 4 per yr.

**Iowa Farm Bureau Federation**
- Iowa Farm Bureau Spokesman. (pub. by Spokesman Press)

**Iowa Genealogical Society**
P.O. Box 3815, Des Moines, IA 50322.
- Iowa Genealogical Society. Surname Index. irreg. ISSN 0090-905X

**Iowa Grain and Feed Association**
201 Shops Bldg., Walnut and 28th St., Des Moines, IA 50309.
- Iowa Grain & Feed Review. m.

**Iowa Library Association**
401 Securities Bldg., Des Moines, IA 50309.
- Catalyst (Des Moines) bi-m.

**Iowa Lumbermens Association**
7300 France Ave., So., Minneapolis, MN 55435.
- Northwestern-Iowa Dealer Reference Manual; retail lumber and building material dealer directory and buyers' guide. a. ISSN 0078-1800

**Iowa Medical Society**
1001 Grand Ave., West Des Moines, IA 50265.
- Iowa Medical Society. Journal. m. ISSN 0021-0587

**Iowa Motor Truck Association**
1533 Linden St, Des Moines, IA 50309.
- Lifeliner. m.

**Iowa Music Educators Association**
1800 Grand, Des Moines, IA 50307.
- Iowa Music Educator. 3 per yr. ISSN 0021-0609

**Iowa Nurses' Association**
308 Shops Bldg., Des Moines, IA 50309.
- Iowa Nurses' Association. Bulletin. irreg. ISSN 0075-0387

**Iowa Ornithologists' Union**
235 McClellan Blvd., Davenport, IA 52803.
- Iowa Bird Life. q. ISSN 0021-0455

**Iowa Poetry Association**
c/o Virginia Blanck Moore, Ed., 1724 E. 22nd St., Des Moines, IA 50317.
- Lyrical Iowa; poetry by Iowa authors. a. ISSN 0076-1699

**Iowa Regional Medical Program**
Univ. of Iowa, Oakdale Hospital, Oakdale, IA 52319.
- I R M P Impact. bi-m. ISSN 0019-0497

**Iowa Restaurant Association**
415 Shops Bldg., Des Moines, IA 50309.
- Appetizer. m.

**Iowa Retail Food Dealers Association**
702 Empire Bldg, Des Moines, IA 50309.
- Iowa Food Dealer. m. ISSN 0021-0528

**Iowa Society of Certified Public Accountants**
912 Insurance Exchange Bldg., Des Moines, IA 50309.
- Tickmark. m.

**Iowa State Education Association**
4025 Tonawanda Drive, Des Moines, IA 50312.
- I S E A Communique. m. (Aug.-May) ISSN 0019-0624

**Iowa State Historical Society. Division of Historical Museum and Archives**
Historical Bldg., E. 12 & Grand, Des Moines, IA 50319.
- Annals of Iowa. q. ISSN 0003-4827

**Iowa State Penitentiary at Fort Madison**
Box 316, Fort Madison, IA 52627.
- Presidio. bi-m.

**Iowa State Policeman's Association**
1221 W. 32nd St., Sioux City, IA 51103.
- Iowa Police Journal. q. ISSN 0021-0633

**Iowa State University**
Ames, IA 50010.
- Fire Service Information. bi-m. ISSN 0015-2668
- Iowa Agriculturist. 3 per yr.
- Iowa Engineer. q. ISSN 0021-0501

**Iowa State University. Department of English**
223 Ross Hall, Ames, IA 50010.
- Iowa English Bulletin: Yearbook. a. (Iowa Council of Teachers of English)

**Iowa State University. Engineering Research Institute**
Ames, IA 50011.
- Engineering Research Highlights. a.
- Iowa State University. Engineering Research Institute. Engineering Research Report. irreg. ISSN 0075-0433

**Iowa State University Library**
Ames, IA 50010.
- Iowa State University. Library. Annual Report. a. ISSN 0075-0425
- Iowa State University. Library. Notes for the Faculty. q.
- Iowa State University. Library. Series in Bibliography. irreg.

**Iowa State University Press**
S. State Ave., Ames, IA 50010.
- A C I Monograph. irreg. ISSN 0065-7883 (American Concrete Institute)
- Iowa State Journal of Research; a quarterly of research. q.
- Poet and Critic. 3 per yr. ISSN 0032-1958

**Iowa State University. Publications Distribution Center**
Printing and Publications Bldg., Ames, IA 50011.
- Iowa State University. Iowa Agriculture and Home Economics Experiment Station. Research Bulletin Series. irreg. ISSN 0021-0692
- Iowa State University. Iowa Agriculture and Home Economics Experiment Station. Special Report. irreg. ISSN 0578-6258 (Co-sponsor: Iowa Cooperative Extension Service in Agriculture and Home Economics)

**Iowa State University. Student Counseling Service**
101 Building H, Ames, IA 50010.
- Beyond the Age Barrier: Newsletter for Adult Students at Iowa State University. irreg. ISSN 0084-7801

**Iowa United Methodist Church**
- Hawkeye United Methodist. (pub. by Iowa United Methodist Communications)

**Iowa United Methodist Communications**
1019 Chestnut St., Des Moines, IA 50309.
- Hawkeye United Methodist. 10 per yr. ISSN 0017-8632 (Iowa United Methodist Church)

**Iran American Chamber of Commerce, Inc.**
Overhill Building, Scarsdale, NY 10583.
- Iran American Newsletter. m.

**Irish American Cultural Institute**
683 Osceola Ave., St. Paul, MN 55105.
- Eire-Ireland; journal of Irish studies. q. ISSN 0013-2683

**Irish People, Inc.**
273 East 194th St., Bronx, NY 10458.
- Irish People. w.

**Irish World**
853 Broadway, New York, NY 10003.
- Irish World and Gaelic American. w. ISSN 0021-1443

**Iron Castings Society**
Cast Metals Federation Bldg., 20611 Center Ridge Rd., Rocky River, OH 44116.
- Ironcaster. m. ISSN 0362-0425

**Iron Man Publishing Co.**
512 Black Hills Ave., Alliance, NE 69301.
- Iron Man. bi-m. ISSN 0047-1496

**Ironwood Press**
Box 49023, Mt. Lemmon, Tucson, AZ 85717.
- Ironwood. s-a. ISSN 0047-150X

**Irvine World Publishers**
Box Aa, Irvine, CA 92664.
- New Worlds. bi-m.

**Irving-Cloud Publishing Co.**
7300 N. Cicero Ave., Lincolnwood, Chicago, IL 60046.
- Dental Lab Products. bi-m.
- Dental Products Annual Report; a compilation of new equipment, supplies, and preventive dentistry aids. a. ISSN 0070-3702
- Dental Products Report. 10 per yr(July-Aug, Nov-Dec. combined) ISSN 0011-8737
- E M: Heavy Duty Equipment & Maintenance. 12 per yr. ISSN 0090-5178
- Fleet Maintenance and Specifying. 12 per yr.
- Hardware Merchandiser. m. ISSN 0017-7709
- Jobber Topics; for automotive jobbers and their salesmen. 12 per yr. ISSN 0021-7069
- Super Service Station. m. ISSN 0039-5676
- W D/Warehouse Distribution. 10 per yr. ISSN 0042-9589

**Israel Folk Dance Institute**
- Hora. (pub. by American Zionist Youth Foundation)

**Israel Horizons Association**
150 Fifth Ave., New York, NY 10011.
- Israel Horizons. m.(except Summer) ISSN 0021-2083

**Issues in Radical Therapy Collective**
Box 23544, Oakland, CA 94623.
- Issues in Radical Therapy. q.

**Isthmus**
Box 6877, San Francisco, CA 94102.
- Isthmus. 2 per yr.

**Istituto Italiano di Cultura**
686 Park Ave., New York, NY 10021.
- Istituto Italiano di Cultura. Newsletter. q. ISSN 0021-2490

**Italian-American News Inc.**
26 Court St., Brooklyn, NY 11242.
- Agenda, the Italian American News. w.

**Italian Americana**
State Univ. College at Buffalo, 1300 Elmwood Ave., Buffalo, NY 14222.
- Italian Americana. s-a. ISSN 0096-8846

**Italian Chamber of Commerce in Chicago**
327 S. La Salle St., Chicago, IL 60604.
- Italian Chamber of Commerce in Chicago. Bulletin. bi-m. ISSN 0021-2903

**Italian Embassy in the United States. Commercial Office**
Suite 200, 2600 Virginia Ave. N.W., Washington, DC 20037.
- Italian Trade Topics. m. ISSN 0021-2997
- Italy: An Economic Profile. a. ISSN 0075-1642

**Italian Heritage Newsletter**
Box 114, Rowayton, CT 06853.
- Italian Heritage Newsletter. m. ISSN 0300-810X

**Italian Historical Society of America**
111 Columbia Hts., Brooklyn, NY 11201.
- Italian American Review. 3-4 per yr.

**Italian Quarterly**
c/o Ed. Spencer Discala, Univ. of Massachusetts/
Boston, Harbor Campus, Boston, MA 02125.
● Italian Quarterly. 4 per yr. ISSN 0021-2954

**Italian Tribune Publishing Co.**
427 Bloomfield Ave., Newark, NJ 07107.
● Italian Tribune News. w.

**Italimuse Inc**
29 Ridgeway, Greenwich, CT 06830.
● Italimuse Italic News. irreg. ISSN 0021-3039

**Italo-American Times Publishing Co.**
1211 Wyatt St., New York, NY 10460.
● Italo-American Times. fortn.

**Italy-America Chamber of Commerce, Inc.**
350 Fifth Ave., New York, NY 10001.
● Trade with Italy. bi-m. ISSN 0041-0551

**Ithaca College. Dept. of Sociology**
c/o Ed. Reid T. Reynolds, Ithaca, NY 14850.
● Concerned Demography. q.

**Izaak Walton League of America**
1800 N. Kent St., Suite 806, Arlington, VA 22209.
● Outdoor America. bi-m. ISSN 0021-3314

**J A A D Publishing Co.**
4475 McKnight Rd., Pittsburgh, PA 15214.
● Technical Book Review Index. m.(Sept-June)
ISSN 0040-0890

**J A I Press**
Box 1285, 321 Greenwich Ave., Greenwich, CT
06830.
● Contemporary Studies in Economic and Financial
Analysis. irreg.
● Research in Economic History; an annual
compilation of research. a.

**J A P O S Study Group**
● J A P O S Bulletin. (pub. by Gustav Detjen Jr.,
Ed. & Pub.)

**J. & M. Associates**
Box 8118, Kansas City, MO 64112.
● Tax Tricks and Techniques; for the self-employed.
bi-m.

**J. B. Printing**
Box 39, Valley Park, MO 63088.
● Jaybee. m. ISSN 0010-7646

**J-B Publishing Co.**
430 Ivy Ave., Crete, NE 68333.
● Brown Family. q.
● Postal History U.S.A. q. (Fourth Class
Cancellation Club)
● Railroad Station Historical Society. Bulletin. bi-m.
● Railroad Station Historical Society. Railroad
Station Monograph. irreg; 1973, no. 4.
● Railway History Monograph. q.

**J F J Educational Services, Inc.**
Box 8470 Gentilly Station, New Orleans, LA
70182.
● Journal of Developmental Disabilities. q. ISSN
0097-8892

**J H M Publications**
3819 Knight St., Glenview, IL 60025.
● Southern Engineering; in plant ideas for the plant
design, operation and maintenance engineers of
the south and southwest. m. ISSN 0038-4062

**J.K. Lasser Tax Institute**
● J. K. Lasser Tax Institute. Monthly Tax Service.
(pub. by Simon and Schuster, Inc.)

**J P O Inc.**
1828 Pearl St., Boulder, CO 80302.
● Journal of Clinical Orthodontics. m.

**J. Paul Getty Museum**
17985 Pacific Coast Highway, Malibu, CA 90265.
● J. Paul Getty Museum Journal. irreg. ISSN 0362-
1979
● J. Paul Getty Museum. Publication. irreg. ISSN
0075-2096

**Jackson County Historical Society**
c/o James Logan Morgan, Ed., 314 Vine St.,
Newport, AR 72112.
● Stream of History. q.

**Jackson County Medical Society**
3036 Gilham Rd., Kansas City, MO 41080.
● Greater Kansas City Medical Bulletin. m.

**Jackson Laboratory**
Bar Harbor, ME 04609.
● Jackson Laboratory Annual Report. a.
● Jax. q. ISSN 0021-5570

**Jacksonville Area Chamber of Commerce**
604 Hogan St., Jacksonville, FL 32202.
● Jacksonville Magazine. bi-m. ISSN 0021-3861

**Jacksonville Children's Museum**
● Meteor News. (pub. by Astro-Gator Astronomy
Club)

**Jacksonville Genealogical Society**
P.O. Box 7076, Jacksonville, FL 32210.
● Jacksonville Genealogical Society Quarterly. q.

**Jacksonville State University. Board of Publications**
Jacksonville, AL 36265.
● Chanticleer. w. ISSN 0009-1561

**Jacobsen Publishing Co.**
300 W.Adams St., Chicago, IL 60606.
● Chicago Daily Hide and Tallow Bulletin; the first
daily hide market service established in America.
d. ISSN 0009-3521
● Feed Bulletin. d. ISSN 0014-9543
● Hide and Leather Bulletin; for the tanning and
shoe manufacturing industry. d. ISSN 0018-1293
● Jacobsen's Fats & Oils Bulletin. d. ISSN 0021-
387X

**Jag Inc.**
10 E. Charles, Oelwein, IA 50662.
● Jag. 9 per yr. ISSN 0021-390X

**Jalart House Inc.**
P.O. Box 642, Scottsdale, AZ 85252.
● Detective World. q.
● Detective Yearbook Quarterly. q.
● Official Police Detective. bi-m.
● Official Wrestling. bi-m.

**Jam To-Day**
Box 249, Northfield, VT 05663.
● Jam to-Day. irreg.

**Jamaica (B.W.I.) Study Group**
267 West Granby Rd., West Granby, Conn. 06090.
● Jamaica Study Group Bulletin. q.

**James Ford Bell Library**
University of Minnesota, Minneapolis, MN 55455.
● Merchant Explorer. a. ISSN 0543-5056

**James Ford Bell Technical Center**
General Mills Inc., 9200 Wayazata Blvd.,
Minneapolis, MN 55440.
● Progress Thru Research. s-a.

**James Sprunt Foundation, Inc.**
● James Sprunt Review. (pub. by James Sprunt
Press)

**James Willard Schultz Society**
Box 53, Andes, NY 13731.
● Piegan Storyteller. q.

**Janlen Enterprises**
2236 S. 77th St., West Allis, WI 53219.
● Midwestern Heritage. q.
● National Genealogical Inquirer. q.

**Anthony J. Jannetti, Inc.**
North Woodbury Rd., Pitman, NJ 08071.
● Pediatric Nursing. bi-m. ISSN 0097-9805
(National Association of Pediatric Nurse
Associates and Practitioners)

**Januz Marketing Communications**
Box 109, Lake Forest, IL 60645.
● Januz Direct Marketing Letter. m.

**Japan-America Society of Washington Inc.**
1755 Massachussetts Ave. N.W., Suite 308,
Washington, DC 20036.
● Japan-America Society of Washington. Bulletin.
m. ISSN 0021-4299

**Japan Group**
1700 Market St., Suite 2500, Philadelphia, PA
19103.
● Japan Group. Newsletter. 15 per yr.

**Japan Publications Trading Co. Ltd.**
Box 7752, Ricon Annex Howard St., San Francisco,
CA 94103.
● Crochet. q. ISSN 0011-166X

**Japanese American Citizens League**
125 Weller St., Los Angeles, CA 90012.
● Pacific Citizen. w. ISSN 0030-8579

**Japanese American News**
260 West Broadway, New York, NY 10013.
● New York Nichibei. w.

**Japanese American Philatelic Society**
Box 1049, El Cerrito, CA 94530.
● Postal Bell/Ekirei. bi-m. ISSN 0032-5325

**Japanese Cancer Association**
● Gann Monographs. (pub. by University Park
Press)

**Jay Publishing**
Box 1465, Sparks, NV 89431.
● Nevada Engineer. bi-m. ISSN 0047-9454 (Nevada
Society of Professional Engineers)
● Nevada Rancher. m. ISSN 0047-9489 (Nevada
Cattlemen's Association)

**Jaycees International**
Box 340577, Coral Gables, FL 33134.
● J C I World. q. ISSN 0021-3578

**Jayell Publishing Co.**
Box 630546, Miami, FL 33163.
● Who's Who in the Arts. biennial, 2nd 1973.

**Jazz Monographs**
P.O. Box 1382, Highland Park, NJ 08904.
● Jazz Monographs. irreg. ISSN 0075-3564

**Jazz Report**
Box 476, Ventura, CA 93001.
● Jazz Report. bi-m(approx.) ISSN 0021-5694

**Jefferson Communications, Inc.**
7777 Leesburg Pike, Falls Church, VA 22043.
● Conservative Digest. m.

**Jefferson Law Book Co.**
728 National Press Bldg., Washington, DC 20045.
● Journal of Law and Education. q.
● Journal of Maritime Law and Commerce. q. ISSN
0022-2410

**Jefferson Medical College. Alumni Association**
1020 Locust St., Philadelphia, PA 19107.
● Jefferson Medical College Alumni Bulletin. q.
ISSN 0021-5821

**Jehovah's Witnesses**
● Jehovah's Witnesses Yearbook. (pub. by
Watchtower Bible & Tract Society, Inc.)
● Watchtower. (pub. by Watchtower Bible & Tract
Society, Inc.)

**Jerome Press**
263 Summer St., Boston, MA 02210.
● Panorama (Boston); Boston's official guide
magazine. fortn. ISSN 0048-282X

**Jersey Society of Parapsychology**
Box 2071, Morristown, NJ 07960.
● Insights. 10 per yr.

**Jerusalem Quarterly**
Box 443, Fort Lee, NJ 07024.
● Jerusalem Quarterly. q.

**T. C. Jervay, Ed. & Pub.**
Box 1618, 412 S. Seventh St., Wilmington, NC
28401.
● Wilmington Journal. w. ISSN 0049-7649

**Jesuit Seminary Guild**
12 S. Calvert St., Baltimore, MD 21202.
● Jesuit. q. ISSN 0021-5988 (Society of Jesus)

**Jesus to the Communist World, Inc.**
P.O. Box 11, Glendale, CA 91209.
● Voice of the Martyrs. m.

**Jewish Art Quarterly**
Jewish Community House, 475 W. 140th St., New
York, NY 10031.
● Jewish Art Quarterly. q. ISSN 0361-7173

**Jewish Board of Guardians**
- Issues in Child Mental Health. (pub. by Human Sciences Press)

**Jewish Book Council**
see under National Jewish Welfare Board

**Jewish Boston, Inc.**
233 Bay State Road, Boston, MA 02215.
- Jewish Boston; guide to Jewish life in the greater Boston Jewish community with a Massachusetts supplement. a. ISSN 0085-2368

**Jewish Braille Institute of America, Inc.**
110 E. 30th St., New York, NY 10016.
- Jewish Braille Review. m. ISSN 0021-6321

**Jewish Currents, Inc.**
22 E. 17th St., New York, NY 10003.
- Jewish Currents. m. ISSN 0021-6399

**Jewish Defense League**
1133 Broadway, New York, NY 10010.
- Jewish Defense League Iton. m.

**Jewish Defense League. Youth Movement**
1133 Broadway, New York, NY 10010.
- Never Again.

**Jewish Digest Association**
Editorial Office, 28 W. 44 St., New York, NY 10036.
- Jewish Digest. m. ISSN 0021-6410

**Jewish Educational Ventures, Inc.**
523 W. 113th St., New York, NY 10025.
- Response; a contemporary Jewish review. q. ISSN 0034-5709

**Jewish Federation & Council of Greater Seattle**
609 Securities Bldg., Seattle, WA 98101.
- Jewish Transcript. s-m. ISSN 0021-678X

**Jewish Federation of Delaware**
701 Shipley St., Wilmington, DE 19801.
- Jewish Voice. fortn. ISSN 0021-6828

**Jewish Federation of St. Louis**
- St. Louis Jewish Light. (pub. by St. Louis Jewish Light, Inc.)

**Jewish Floridian**
Box 01-2973, Miami, FL 33101.
- Jewish Floridian. w. ISSN 0021-6445

**Jewish Labor Committee**
Atran Center, 25 East 78th St., New York, NY 10021.
- J L C News. q. ISSN 0447-2276

**Jewish Ledger**
721 Monroe Ave., Rochester, NY 14607.
- Jewish Ledger. w. ISSN 0021-6550

**Jewish Look**
979-42 St., Brooklyn, NY 11219.
- Jewish Look. m.

**Jewish Media Service**
Lown Building, 415 South St., Waltham, MA 02154.
- Medium; Jewish uses of the media. q.

**Jewish Monitor**
Box 9155, Birmingham, AL 35213.
- Jewish Monitor. m. ISSN 0021-6593

**Jewish News Publishing Co.**
17515 W. Nine Mile Rd., Suite 865, Southfield, MI 48075.
- Detroit Jewish News. w. ISSN 0011-9644

**Jewish Peace Fellowship**
Box 271, Nyack, NY 10960.
- Shalom. q. ISSN 0080-9160

**Jewish People**
110 E. 23rd St., New York, NY 10010.
- Jewish People. w.

**Jewish Publication Society of America**
1528 Walnut St., Philadelphia, PA 19102.
- American Jewish Yearbook. a. ISSN 0065-8987 (American Jewish Committee)

**Jewish Reconstructionist Foundation**
432 Park Ave. S., New York, NY 10016.
- Reconstructionist. m(Sept.-June) ISSN 0034-1495

**Jewish Record**
1537 Atlantic Ave., Atlantic City, NJ 08401.
- Jewish Record. w.

**Jewish Society of America, Inc.**
28-13 Steinway St., Long Island City, NY 11103.
- Ideas; a journal of contemporary Jewish thought. q. ISSN 0019-1388

**Jewish Spectator**
250 W. 57th St., New York, NY 10019.
- Jewish Spectator. q. ISSN 0021-6720

**Jewish Standard Co.**
40 Journal Sq., Jersey City, NJ 07306
(Or: 555 Cedar Lane, Teaneck, NJ 07666)
- Jewish Standard; New Jersey's oldest English-Jewish newspaper. w. ISSN 0021-6747

**Jewish Star**
693 Mission St. No. 305, San Francisco, CA 94105.
- Jewish Star; independent newspaper. bi-m.

**Jewish Student Projects of Greater Boston, Inc.**
- Genesis 2. (pub. by Rebirth, Inc.)

**Jewish Telegraphic Agency**
165 W. 46th St., Rm. 511, New York, NY 10036.
- J T A Community News Reporter. w.
- J T A Daily News Bulletin. d.(except sat. & sun.) ISSN 0021-3772
- J T A Weekly News Digest. w. ISSN 0021-6763

**Jewish Times**
118 Cypress St., Brookline, MA 02146.
- Jewish Times. w. ISSN 0021-6771

**Jewish War Veterans of the U.S.A.**
1712 New Hampshire Ave. N.W., Washington, DC 20009.
- J. W. V. A. Bulletin. q. ISSN 0021-3799 (prep. by its National Ladies Auxiliary)
- Jewish Veteran; the patriotic voice of American Jewry. m. ISSN 0047-2018

**Jewish Weekly Dispatch**
462 Market St., Saddle Brook, NJ 07662.
- Jewish Weekly Dispatch. fortn.

**Jewish Welfare Federation**
1036 Spitzer Bldg., Toledo, OH 43604.
- Toledo Jewish News. m. ISSN 0040-9081

**Jicarilla Apache Tribe**
- Jicarilla Chieftain. (pub. by Glen Edmonds)

**Jo-Ro Press**
Box 4146, University Sta., Tucson, AZ 85717.
- Mountain Newsreal. m.

**Jobson Publishing Corporation**
488 Madison Ave., New York, NY 10022.
- Liquor Store Magazine. m. ISSN 0024-4236
- Profitunities/Better Buys. m (11 per yr.)
- Stateways. 9 per yr.
- Twenty Twenty. bi-m.

**John Brown Book Club**
Box 22383, Seattle, WA 98122.
- Osawatomie. irreg.

**John Carroll University. School of Business**
University Heights, Cleveland, OH 44118.
- Carroll Business Bulletin. q. ISSN 0008-6932

**John Crerar Library**
35 W. 33rd St., Chicago, IL 60616.
- Leukemia Abstracts; dedicated to the task of assisting in the discovery of the cause and the cure of leukemia. m. ISSN 0024-1466 (Lenore Schwartz Leukemia Research Foundation. Research Information Service)
- Translations Register-Index. (pub. by National Translations Center)

**John Dewey Society**
- John Dewey Society. Studies in Educational Theory. (pub. by Ohio State University Press)

**John Dewey Society for the Study of Education and Culture**
Dewey Center, Southern Illinois University, Carbondale, IL 62901.
- Insights. irreg., 1969, vol. 6, no. 3. ISSN 0073-8123

**John E. Owens Memorial Foundation, Inc.**
- John E. Owens Memorial Foundation. Publications. (pub. by Southern Methodist University Press)

**John Edwards Memorial Foundation, Inc.**
Folklore and Mythological Center, University of California, Los Angeles, CA 90024.
- J E M F Quarterly. q.

**John G. Neihardt Foundation, Inc.**
Bancroft, NE 68004.
- Neihardt Foundation Newsletter. a.

**John Jay College of Criminal Justice. Newspaper Society**
City University of New York, 445 W. 59th St., New York, NY 10019.
- Lex. w. during school term. ISSN 0047-4452

**John Marshall Bar Association**
Holland Law Center, University of Florida, Gainesville, FL 32601.
- Verdict. m. ISSN 0049-593X

**John Marshall Law School**
315 S. Plymouth Ct., Chicago, IL 60604.
- John Marshall Journal of Practice and Procedure. 3 per yr. ISSN 0021-7212

**John Milton Society for the Blind**
366 Fifth Ave., New York, NY 10001.
- John Milton Talking Book. bi-m. ISSN 0021-7220

**John Steinbeck Society**
English Dept., Ball State Univ., Munci, IN 47306.
- Steinbeck Monograph Series. a. ISSN 0085-6746
- Steinbeck Quarterly. 4 per yr. ISSN 0039-100X

**Johnny Appleseed Patriotic Publications**
Box 50393, Chicago, IL 60650.
- New Patriot. m. ISSN 0047-9829

**Johns Hopkins Hospital School of Nursing**
Mt. Royal and Guilford, Baltimore, MD 21218.
- Johns Hopkins Hospital School of Nursing. Alumni Magazine. q. ISSN 0002-6700

**Johns Hopkins University**
Baltimore, MD 21218.
- Johns Hopkins Magazine. bi-m. ISSN 0021-7255
- Letters & Papers on the Social Sciences: an Undergraduate Review. ISSN 0092-718X (Subscr. to: Box 1310, Baltimore, MD 21218)
- Nocturne; literary journal. s-a. (Subscr. to: Box 1320, Baltimore, MD 21218)
- Studies in Historical and Political Science. Extra Volumes. (pub. by Bergman Publishers, Inc.)

**Johns Hopkins University. Applied Physics Laboratory**
Johns Hopkins Rd., Laurel, MD 20810.
- A P L Technical Digest. q. ISSN 0001-2211
- Journal Holdings in the Washington-Baltimore Area. biennial. (Interlibrary Users Association)

**Johns Hopkins University. Department of Earth and Planetary Sciences**
- Johns Hopkins University Studies in Geology. (pub. by Johns Hopkins University Press)

**Johns Hopkins University. Milton E. Eisenhower Library**
Baltimore, MD 21218.
- Level Talk; the Milton S. Eisenhower Library Newsletter. s-m. (with q. special issues)

**Johns Hopkins University. Office of Student Affairs**
Box 392, Baltimore, MD 21211.
- Johns Hopkins University Undergraduate Science Bulletin. s-a.

**Johns Hopkins University Press**
Baltimore, MD 21218.
- American Foundation for the Study of Man. Publications. irreg. ISSN 0569-4833
- American Journal of Mathematics. bi-m. ISSN 0002-9327 (American Mathematical Society) (Co-sponsor: Johns Hopkins University)
- American Journal of Philology. q. ISSN 0002-9475
- American Psychopathological Association. Proceedings of the Annual Meeting. a.
- Britain in the World Today. irreg. ISSN 0068-1105 (Exclusive Commonwealth edition from Chatto and Windus, 40-42 William IV St., London W. C. 2, England)

- Bulletin of the History of Medicine. q. ISSN 0007-5140 (American Association for the History of Medicine) (Co-Sponsor: Johns Hopkins Institute of the History of Medicine)
- Diacritics; a review of contemporary criticism. q. ISSN 0300-7162
- E L H. (English Literary History) q. ISSN 0013-8304
- English Institute. Selected Essays. a. ISSN 0071-0598 (Vols. before 1978 pub. by: Columbia University Press, 136 S. Broadway, Irvington-on-Hudson, NY 10533)
- Governance of Metropolitan Regions. Series. irreg. (Resources for the Future Inc.)
- Human Factors. bi-m. ISSN 0018-7208 (Human Factors Society)
- International Symposium on Molecular Biology. Proceedings. irreg., 7th, Baltimore, Maryland and Vienna, Austria, 1974.
- Johns Hopkins Medical Journal. m. ISSN 0021-7263 (Johns Hopkins University School of Medicine) (Co-Sponsors: Johns Hopkins Hospital; Johns Hopkins Medical and Surgical Assn.)
- Johns Hopkins Oceanographic Studies. irreg. 1977, no. 6. ISSN 0075-3858
- Johns Hopkins Series in Integration and Community Building in Eastern Europe. irreg. ISSN 0075-3866
- Johns Hopkins Symposia in Comparative History. irreg. ISSN 0075-3874
- Johns Hopkins University Studies in Geology. irreg., 1973, no. 21. ISSN 0075-3890 (Johns Hopkins University. Department of Earth and Planetary Sciences)
- Johns Hopkins University Studies in Historical and Political Science. irreg. ISSN 0075-3904
- M L N. (Modern Language Notes) 6 per yr. ISSN 0026-7910
- New Literary History; a journal of theory and interpretation. 3 per yr. ISSN 0028-6087
- Schouler Lectures in History and Political Science. irreg.
- Studies in International Affairs. irreg; no. 26, 1975. ISSN 0081-802X (Washington Center of Foreign Policy Research)

**Johns Hopkins University. School of Hygiene and Public Health**
615 N. Wolfe St., Baltimore, MD 21205.
- American Journal of Epidemiology. m.(2 vols. of 6 nos. each per yr.) ISSN 0002-9262 (Society for Epidemiologic Research)

**Johns Hopkins University School of Medicine**
- Johns Hopkins Medical Journal. (pub. by Johns Hopkins University Press)

**Johns-Manville Corporation**
Greenwood Plaza, Denver, CO 80217.
- J-M Future. q.

**Johnson C. Smith University**
100 Beatties Ford Rd., Charlotte, NC 28216.
- Johnson C. Smith Newsletter. q. (prep. by its Alumni Office)
- Treewell. a. ISSN 0085-7378

**Johnson Hill Press, Inc.**
1233 Janesville Ave., Ft. Atkinson, WI 53538.
- Farm Equipment. m. ISSN 0014-7958
- Feed and Grain Times. 10 per yr.

**Johnson Management Institute**
Box 757, Twin Lakes, WI 53181.
- Passwords in Preventive Dentistry. q.

**Johnson Publishing Co., Inc**
820 S. Michigan Ave., Chicago, IL 60605.
- Black Stars. m.
- Ebony. m. ISSN 0012-9011
- Ebony Jr. 10 per yr. ISSN 0091-8660
- Jet. w. ISSN 0021-5996

**Johnson Publishing Co. (Loveland)**
Box 455, Eighth & van Buren, Loveland, CO 80537.
- United States Trade Associations. irreg. ISSN 0093-6685
- World Wide Chamber of Commerce Directory. a. ISSN 0084-2478

**Johnson's Charts, Inc.**
1800 Rand Bldg., Buffalo, NY 14203.
- Johnson's Investment Company Charts. a.

**Johnston International Publishing Corporation**
386 Park Ave. South, New York, NY 10016.
- Automobile International/Automovil Internacional; an international publication serving fleet and service management in Europe, Africa, Asia and Latin America. m. ISSN 0005-1594
- Export/Exportador; for distributors & dealers of consumer hardgoods outside the U.S. and Canada. m. ISSN 0014-519X
- Industrial World en Espanol. m.
- Modern Africa; the business magazine for Africa. bi-m. (Or: Halton House 20-23, London, ECIN 2JD, England)
- Near East Business. bi-m.

**Johnstown Motor Club**
P.O. Box 186, Johnstown, PA 15907.
- Motorist. bi-m.

**Joint Center for Political Studies**
1426 H St. N.W., Suite 926, Washington, DC 20005.
- Focus (Washington, D.C.) m.
- National Roster of Black Elected Officials. a. ISSN 0092-2935

**Joint Center for Urban Studies**
53 Church St., Cambridge, MA 02138.
- Joint Center for Urban Studies. Research Report from M I T-Harvard. irreg. ISSN 0098-5244

**Joint Committee on Powder Diffraction Standards.**
1601 Park Lane, Swarthmore, PA 14081.
- Powder Diffraction File Search Manual. Alphabetical Listing. Inorganic. a. ISSN 0092-0509
- Powder Diffraction File Search Manual. Fink Method. Inorganic. a. ISSN 0092-1300
- Powder Diffraction File Search Manual. Hanawalt Method. Inorganic. a. ISSN 0092-1319
- Powder Diffraction File Search Manual. Organic. a. ISSN 0092-0576

**Joint Council of Teamsters No. 37**
1020 N. E. Third Ave, Portland, OR 97232.
- Oregon Teamster. s-m. ISSN 0030-4840

**Joint Council of Teamsters No. 42**
1616 W. Ninth St., Los Angeles, CA 90015.
- Southern California Teamster. bi-w. ISSN 0038-3953

**Joint Council on Economic Education**
1212 Ave. of the Americas, New York, NY 10036.
- College and University Newsletter. s-a.
- Economic Education Experiences of Enterprising Teachers; report developed from the entries in the International Paper Company foundation awards program for the teaching of economics. a. ISSN 0070-8534
- Economic Topics Series. irreg., approx 2 per yr. ISSN 0013-0397
- Joint Council on Economic Education. Checklist; catalog of classroom materials for the teacher and student. s-a. ISSN 0009-2088
- Journal of Economic Education. 2 per yr. ISSN 0022-0485
- Progress in Economic Education. q. ISSN 0021-7328
- School Services Curriculum Perspectives. 2 per yr. ISSN 0048-9476

**Joint Council on Educational Broadcasting Television**
1126 16th St. N.W., Washington, DC 20036.
- J C E T News. m.

**Joint Federal-State Land Use Planning Commission for Alaska**
733 West Fourth Ave., Anchorage, AK 99501.
- Alaska's Land. a.
- Joint Federal-State Land Use Planning Commission for Alaska. Annual Report. a. ISSN 0094-9515

**Joint Institute for Laboratory Astrophysics**
University of Colorado, Boulder, CO 80309.
- J I L A Information Center. Report. irreg. ISSN 0449-1343

**Joint Planning Commission, Lehigh-Northampton Counties**
ABE Airport, Lehigh Valley, PA 18103.
- J P C Newsletter. bi-m.

**Joint Reference Library. Public Administration Service**
1313 E. 60th St., Chicago, IL 60637.
- Recent Publications on Governmental Problems. s-m. ISSN 0034-1185

**Joint Strategy and Action Committee**
475 Riverside Dr., Room 1700 A, New York, NY 10027.
- J S A C Grapevine. m.

**Don Jolly & Associates**
Subscription Department, 9348 Santa Monica Blvd., Suite 101, Beverly Hills, CA 90210.
- Who's Where in Music. m. ISSN 0360-4411

**Edward L. Jones, Ed. & Pub.**
c/o Frayn Printing Co., 2518 Western Ave., Seattle, WA 98121.
- Black Studies Series. irreg.

**H. Jones, Ed. & Pub.**
P.O. Box 3063, San Francisco, CA 94119.
- Motorcycle Blue Book. ISSN 0091-3774

**Milton W. Jones**
120 Green St., San Francisco, CA 94111.
- San Francisco. m. ISSN 0036-4088

**Jones Lang Wootton**
375 Park Ave., New York, NY 10022.
- International Property Review. q.

**Jones Medical Publications**
Greenbrae, CA 94904.
- Handbook of Medical Treatment. biennial. ISSN 0072-9841

**Clyde C. Jordan, Ed. & Pub.**
1501 State St., East St. Louis, IL 62205.
- East St. Louis Monitor. w. ISSN 0046-0966

**Jordan Information Bureau**
1701 K St N.W., Washington, DC 20006.
- Jordan. q.

**Josep Communications**
Box 1286, Denver, CO 80201.
- National Panorama of American Youth. a. ISSN 0360-0815

**Joseph Jacobs Organization**
60 East 42nd Street, New York, NY 10017.
- Jewish Press in America. biennial.

**Josephite Society**
1130 N. Calvert St., Baltimore, MD 21202.
- Josephite Harvest. q. ISSN 0021-7603

**Joslin Diabetes Foundation, Inc.**
One Joslin Pl., Boston, MA 02215.
- Joslin Diabetes Foundation. Newsletter. s-a. ISSN 0021-7611

**Joslyn Art Museum**
2200 Dodge St., Omaha, NE 68102.
- Joslyn Art Museum Calendar of Events. 9 per yr.

**Jossey-Bass, Inc., Publishers**
615 Montgomery St., San Francisco, CA 94111.
- Advances in Psychological Assessment. irreg., vol. 3, 1975. ISSN 0065-325X
- Carnegie Council on Policy Studies in Higher Education. Carnegie Council Series. irreg.
- Current Issues in Higher Education. a. ISSN 0070-1971 (American Association for Higher Education)
- New Directions for Community Colleges. q.
- New Directions for Higher Education. q.
- New Directions for Institutional Research. q. (Association for Institutional Research)
- Sociological Methodology. a. ISSN 0081-1750 (American Sociological Association)

**Journal and Bulletin Agency**
Box 9471, 215 W. Harrison St., Seattle, WA 98109.
- King County Medical Society. Bulletin. m. (King County Medical Society)
- Seattle-King County Dental Society. Journal. m.(Aug.-May) ISSN 0037-0452
- W A F P Journal. (Washington Family Physician) q.

**Journal of Advertising**
c/o School of Journalism, University of Kansas, Lawrence, KS 66045.
- Journal of Advertising. q. ISSN 0091-3367

**Journal of Applied Communications Research**
Drawer NJ, Mississippi State, MS 39762.
- Journal of Applied Communications Research. s-a.
  ISSN 0090-9882

**Journal of Black Poetry**
Box 771, San Francisco, CA 94101.
- Journal of Black Poetry. irreg.

**Journal of Clinical Computing, Inc.**
166 Morris Ave., Buffalo, NY 14214.
- Journal of Clinical Computing. 6 per yr. ISSN
  0090-1091

**Journal of Commerce**
99 Wall St., New York, NY 10005.
- Import Bulletin. w. ISSN 0019-297X
- Transportation Telephone Tickler. a. ISSN 0447-
  9181

**Journal of Contemporary Poets**
Box 444, Brentwood, NY 11717.
- Journal of Contemporary Poets. 4 per yr.

**Journal of Correctional Education**
Ed. Wilson C. Bell, Box 221, Raiford, FL 32083.
- Journal of Correctional Education. q. ISSN 0022-
  0159

**Journal of Dermatologic Surgery, Inc.**
475 Park Ave. S., New York, NY 10016.
- Journal of Dermatologic Surgery and Oncology.
  bi-m.

**Journal of Drug Issues**
Box 4021, Tallahassee, FL 32303.
- Journal of Drug Issues. q. ISSN 0022-0426

**Journal of Hispanic Philology Inc.**
c/o Daniel Eisenberg, Dept. of Modern Languages,
Florida State University, Tallahassee, FL 32306.
- Journal of Hispanic Philology. 3 per yr.

**Journal of Neuropathology and Experimental
Neurology**
630 W. 168th St., New York, NY 10032.
- Journal of Neuropathology and Experimental
  Neurology. bi-m. ISSN 0022-3069

**Journal of Nursing Administration, Inc.**
12 Lakeside Park, 607 North Ave., Wakefield, MA
01880.
- Journal of Nursing Administration. m. ISSN 0002-
  0443

**Journal of Philosophy, Inc.**
720 Philosophy Hall, New York, NY 10027.
- Journal of Philosophy. m. ISSN 0022-362X
  (Columbia University)

**Journal of Reproductive Medicine, Inc.**
2 Jackalynn Ct., St. Louis, MO 63132.
- Journal of Reproductive Medicine. m. ISSN 0024-
  7758

**Journal of Southern African Affairs**
c/o Rosette S. Thompson, 4133 Art /Sociology
Bldg., University of Maryland, College Park, MD
20742.
- Journal of Southern African Affairs. q.

**Journal of Taxation, Ltd.**
Box 158, Titusville, FL 32780.
- Taxation for Accountants. m. ISSN 0040-0165
- Taxation for Lawyers. bi-m.

**Journal of the History of Medicine and Allied
Sciences, Inc.**
Owen H. Wangensteen Historical Library of Biology
and Medicine, Diehl Hall, University of Minnesota,
Minneapolis, MN 55455
(Subscr. to: Science History Publications, 156 Fifth
Ave., New York, NY 10010)
- Journal of the History of Medicine and Allied
  Sciences. q. ISSN 0022-5045

**Journal of the History of Philosophy, Inc.**
Dept. of Philosophy, Claremont Graduate School,
Harper Hall, Claremont, CA 91711.
- Journal of the History of Philosophy. q. ISSN
  0022-5053 (Co-sponsors: Claremont Colleges;
  Washington University- St. Louis; Stanford
  University; University of California)

**Journal of Undergraduate Psychological Research**
West Valley College, 14000 Fruitvale Ave.,
Saratoga, CA 95070.
- Journal of Undergraduate Psychological Research.
  ISSN 0096-1337

**Journal on Political Repression, Inc.**
297 Park Ave. South. Rm. 23, New York, NY
10010.
- Journal on Political Repression. s-a. ISSN 0362-
  8809 (National Conference of Black Political
  Scientists) (Co-sponsor: Commission for Racial
  Justice, United Church of Christ)

**Journal Press**
Box 543, 2 Commercial St., Provincetown, MA
02657.
- Genetic Psychology Monographs. q.(2 vols.per
  yr.) ISSN 0016-6677
- Journal of General Psychology; experimental,
  physiological, and comparative psychology. q.(2
  vols.per yr) ISSN 0022-1309
- Journal of Genetic Psychology; developmental and
  clinical psychology. q. (2 vols.per yr) ISSN 0022-
  1325
- Journal of Psychology; the general field of
  psychology. bi-m.(3 vols.per yr) ISSN 0022-3980
- Journal of Social Psychology. bi-m(3 vols.per yr)
  ISSN 0022-4545

**Journal Publications (Camden)**
Camden, ME 04843.
- National Fisherman. m. ISSN 0027-9250
- National Fisherman. Yearbook Issue. a. ISSN
  0077-457X

**Journal Publishers, Inc. (Ft. Collins)**
Box 2205, 6408 S. College Ave, Fort Collins, CO
80522.
- International Limousin Journal. m. (North
  American Limousin Foundation)

**Journal Publishing Affiliates**
727 De La Guerra Plaza, Santa Barbara, CA 90007.
- Journal of Motor Behavior. q. ISSN 0022-2895

**Journal Publishing Co. (Irvington)**
Box 175, Irvington, NJ 07111.
- International Journal; the news and views paper
  for the modern hobbyist. q. ISSN 0020-7039

**Journal-Record Publishing Co.**
4515 N. Santa Fe, Oklahoma City, OK 73118.
- Daily Law Journal Record. d. ISSN 0011-5452

**Journal Thirty One**
Box 2109, San Francisco, CA 94126.
- Journal Thirty One. q. ISSN 0047-2921

**Journalism Education Association, Inc.**
Box 884, Springfield, MO 65801.
- Communication: Journalism Education Today. 3
  per yr. ISSN 0010-3535

**Joy Manufacturing Co. Denver Equipment Division**
600 Broadway, Denver, CO 80217.
- Deco Trefoil. q. ISSN 0011-734X

**Helen & Felix Juda Collection**
644 South June St., Los Angeles, CA 90005.
- Newsletter on Contemporary Japanese Prints.
  irreg. ISSN 0085-4174

**Judaica Bibliography and News**
Ed. Paul Stone, 135 W. 26th St., New York, NY
10001.
- Judaica Bibliography and News; Jewish culture
  and social action. bi-m. ISSN 0047-2964

**Judo Illustrated Inc.**
3445 North Broadway, Chicago, IL 60657.
- Judo Illustrated. bi-m. ISSN 0022-5835

**Juilliard School**
Lincoln Center Plaza, New York, NY 10023.
- Juilliard News Bulletin. 6 per yr. ISSN 0022-6173

**Jump Cut**
Box 865, Berkeley, CA 94701.
- Jump Cut; a review of contemporary cinema. q.

**Junction Enterprises**
2194 Briarcliff Road, Atlanta, GA 30329.
- Entrepreneur. bi-m.

**Junior Academy of the Ohio Academy of Science**
- Ohio Academy of Science News. (pub. by Ohio
  Academy of Science)

**Junior Astronomy Club**
100 Washington Sq., E., New York, NY 10003.
- Junior Astronomy News. bi-m. ISSN 0022-6491

**Junior High School Association of Illinois**
- Junior High School Association of Illinois. Study.
  (pub. by Interstate Printers and Publishers, Inc.)

**Junior Philatelic Society of America**
RD No. 1, Boyertown, PA 19512.
- Philatelic Observer. bi-m.

**Junior Statesmen Foundation**
480 California Ave., Suite 102, Palo Alto, CA
94306.
- Junior State Report. 5 per yr.

**Juniper Editions**
Box 7, Manitou Springs, CO 80829.
- Latin American Political Guide. irreg., 16th ed.,
  1975. ISSN 0075-8124

**Juniper Press**
1310 Shorewood Drive, La Crosse, WI 54601.
- Northeast. s-a.

**Junularo Esperantista de Nord-Ameriko**
c/o Julie Tonkin, 2131 Tryon St., Philadelphia, PA
19148.
- Jen-Bulteno. 5 per yr approx. ISSN 0021-5848

**Juridical Digests Institute**
1860 Broadway, Suite 1401, New York, NY 10023.
- Administrative Court Digest. m. ISSN 0044-6297
- Corrections Court Digest. m. ISSN 0360-196X
- Ecclesiastical Court Digest. m.
- Mental Health Court Digest. m. ISSN 0025-9640
- Public Health Court Digest. m. ISSN 0033-3514
- Sex Problems Court Digest. m. ISSN 0049-0318

**Jury Verdict Research, Inc.**
5325 Naiman Parkway, Suite B, Solon, OH 44139.
- Injury Valuation Reports and Special Research
  Reports. m. ISSN 0020-1391
- Personal Injury Valuation Handbooks; injury
  valuation & special research reports. m. ISSN
  0031-5591
- Verdict Reports. w. ISSN 0092-2293

**Just Compensation, Inc.**
Box 5133, Sherman Oaks, CA 91403.
- Just Compensation. m.

**K & K Publishing Inc.**
9348 Santa Monica Blvd., Beverly Hills, CA 90210.
- Performing Arts; the music & theatre monthly. m.
  ISSN 0031-5222

**K & M Publications Inc**
2000 Frankfort Ave., Louisville, KY 40206.
- Coatings Adlibra; key to world literature serving
  the coatings & allied industries. s-m.
- Foods Adlibra; key to the world's food literature.
  fortn.

**K-Dee Publishing Co.**
1997 N.E. 150 St., Miami, FL 33181.
- Karting Digest. m.

**K. of C. Auto & Travel Club**
157 N. 15th St., Philadelphia, PA 19102.
- Ka-Se-Ac Monthly. m.

**K R C Associates**
105 Wagner Ave., Mamaroneck, NY 10543.
- K R C Letter; an exchange of information and
  ideas for fund raisers. 10 per yr.

**K T O Press**
(Subsidiary of: Kraus-Thomson Organization Ltd.)
Route 100, Millwood, NY 10546.
- Film Review Digest. q. ISSN 0098-0471
- Index to Bank Letters, Bulletins, and Reviews. q.
  with a. cum.

**Kach Nazar: Armenian Satirical Monthly**
6646 Hollywood Boulevard, Suite 219, Hollywood,
CA 90028.
- Kach Nazar: Armenian Satirical Monthly. m.

**Paul Kagan Associates, Inc.**
100 Merrick Rd., Rockville Centre, New York, NY
11570.
- Broadcast Investor; newsletter on radio-TV station
  finance. s-m.
- Cable T V Regulation; newsletter on federal-state-
  city regulation of cable television. s-m.
- Cablecast. bi-m.

- Multicast; newsletter on multipoint distribution service. s-m.
- Pay TV Newsletter; newsletter on developments in pay television. s-m.

**Kahaal Nahalot Israel**
504 Frankhauser Rd., Williamsville, NY 14221
- Buffalo Jewish Review. w. (Subscr. to: 110 Pearl St., Buffalo NY 14202)

**Kahane**
Box 1847, New York, NY 10001.
- Kahane; the magazine of the authentic Jewish idea. m.

**Kaiser Foundation Medical Care Program**
Public Affairs, 27th Floor, Ordway Building, Kaiser Center, Oakland, CA 94666.
- Kaiser Foundation Medical Care Program. Annual Report. a. ISSN 0075-4668

**Kalamazoo Review, Inc.**
Box 191, Kalamazoo, MI 49005.
- Kalamazoo Review. m.

**Kalb, Voorhis and Co.**
27 William St., New York, NY 10005.
- K V Convertible Fact Finder Service. w. ISSN 0451-243X

**Kalmbach Publishing Co.**
1027 N. 7th St., Milwaukee, WI 53233.
- Model Railroader. m. ISSN 0026-7341
- Trains; the magazine of railroading. m. ISSN 0041-0934

**Kamikaze Press**
1642 28th Ave., San Francisco, CA 94122.
- Out of Sight. bi-m. ISSN 0030-7009

**Dan Kamrow & Associates, Inc.**
Box 60085, Chicago, IL 60660.
- M H/R V Builders News; the magazine for builders of manufactured/mobile/modular/marine homes and recreational vehicles. 6 per yr.

**Frank Kane Corporation**
121-11 14th Rd., Box 213, College Point, NY 11356.
- Frank Kane's Weekly Letter; for the beverage industry. w.

**Kankakee Valley Genealogical Society**
c/o Kankakee Public Library, 304 S. Indiana Ave., Kankakee, IL 60901.
- A-Ki-Ki. q. ISSN 0091-1607

**Kansas. Advisory Council on Ecology**
Room 459 W, State Office Bldg., Topeka, KS 66612.
- Kansas. Advisory Council on Ecology. Annual Report. a.

**Kansas. Commission on Civil Rights**
535 Kansas Ave., 5Th Floor, Topeka, KS 66603.
- Docket; newsletter of the Kansas commission on civil rights. q. ISSN 0012-4427

**Kansas. Department of Economic Development**
503 Kansas Ave., Topeka, KS 66603.
- Directory of Kansas Manufacturers and Products. a. ISSN 0070-5721
- Kansas Economic Development Report. m. ISSN 0022-8532

**Kansas. Department of Health and Environment. Bureau of Health and Environmental Education**
Topeka, KS 66620.
- Post Rock. q.

**Kansas. Department of Human Resources**
401 Topeka Ave., Topeka, KS 66603.
- Kansas Job Opportunities. q. ISSN 0022-863X

**Kansas. Division of Registration and Health Statistics Services**
Topeka, KS 66600.
- Kansas Accidental Death Report. biennial.

**Kansas. Division of Vocational Rehabilitation**
Kansas City, KS 66101.
- Kansas. Division of Vocational Rehabilitation. Annual Report. a.

**Kansas. Economic Development Commission**
503 Kansas Ave., Topeka, KS 66603.
- Kansas! q. ISSN 0022-8435

**Kansas. Forestry, Fish and Game Commission. Information-Education Division**
Box 1028, Pratt, KS 67124.
- Kansas Fish and Game. bi-m. ISSN 0022-8591

**Kansas. Geological Survey**
1930 Ave. "A", Campus West, University of Kansas, Lawrence, KS 66044.
- Kansas Geological Survey. Basic Data Series. Ground-Water Releases. irreg.
- Kansas Geological Survey. Bulletin. irreg.
- Kansas Geological Survey. Chemical Quality Series. irreg.
- Kansas Geological Survey. Computer Contribution. irreg., 1970, no. 50. ISSN 0075-4927
- Kansas Geological Survey. Educational Series. irreg.
- Kansas Geological Survey. Energy Resources Series. irreg.
- Kansas Geological Survey. Geology Series. irreg.
- Kansas Geological Survey. Ground Water Series. irreg.
- Kansas Geological Survey. Short Papers in Research. a. ISSN 0075-4935
- Kansas Geological Survey. Subsurface Geology Series. irreg.

**Kansas. Legislative Research Department**
Topeka, KS 66612.
- Kansas. Legislative Research Department. Report on Kansas Legislative Interim Studies. a.

**Kansas. State Board of Agriculture**
Topeka, KS 66612.
- Kansas Agriculture. a. ISSN 0091-6900

**Kansas. State Conservation Commission**
Topeka, KS 66612.
- Conservation in Kansas. a. ISSN 0094-1670

**Kansas. State Department of Education**
Topeka, KS 66612.
- Books for Kansas Schools. a. ISSN 0363-6518
- Kansas. State Department of Education. Administration and Finance Division. Annual Statistical Report. a. ISSN 0091-9802
- Kansas. State Department of Education. Bulletin. irreg.
- Kansas Educational Directory. a. ISSN 0099-0728

**Kansas. State Department of Social Welfare**
Topeka, KS 66600.
- Juvenile Court Statistics and Adoption Petitions in Kansas. a.

**Kansas. State Highway Commission**
Topeka, KS 66612.
- Highway Highlights. m.

**Kansas Academy of Science**
Kansas Wesleyan, Dept. of Biology, c/o Dr. B. L. Owen, Salina, KS 67401.
- Kansas Academy of Science. Transactions. q. ISSN 0022-8443

**Kansas Agricultural Experiment Station**
Kansas State Univ., Manhattan, KS 66506.
- Kansas Corn Performance Tests. a.
- Kansas Grain Sorghum Performance Tests. a.

**Kansas Anthropological Association**
Box 41, Hays, KS 67601.
- Kansas Anthropological Association. Newsletter. m.(Sept-May) ISSN 0022-8451 (Co-Sponsor: Kansas State Historical Society)

**Kansas Association of School Boards**
825 Western Ave., Topeka, KS 66606.
- Kansas School Board Journal. q. ISSN 0022-8761

**Kansas Association of Teachers of English**
- Kansas English. (pub. by World Co.)

**Kansas Bankers Association**
707 Merchants National Bank Bldg., Topeka, KS 66612.
- Kansas Banker. m. ISSN 0022-8478

**Kansas Bar Association**
Box 1037, Topeka, KS 66601.
- Kansas Bar Association Journal. q. ISSN 0022-8486

**Kansas City Association of Trusts and Foundations**
406 Board of Trade Bldg., Kansas City, MO 64105.
- Comments. bi-m.

**Kansas City Jewish Chronicle**
Box 8709, Kansas City, MO 64114.
- Kansas City Jewish Chronicle. w. ISSN 0022-8524

**Kansas City Woman**
3920 W. 96 St., Shawnee Mission, KS 66207.
- Kansas City Woman. m.

**Kansas Council for Geographic Education**
c/o Dept. of Geography, Kansas State University, Manhattan, KS 66506.
- Kansas Geographer. a.

**Kansas Dietetic Association**
Univ. of Kansas Medical Center, Kansas City, Kans.
- Sunflower. 4 per yr. ISSN 0039-5382

**Kansas Electric Cooperatives, Inc.**
5709 W. 21st St., Box 4267, Gage Center Sta., Topeka, KS 66604.
- Kansas Country Living. m. ISSN 0091-9586

**Kansas Engineering Society, Inc.**
4125 Gage Center Drive, Topeka, KS 66604.
- Kansas Professional Engineer. m. ISSN 0047-3170

**Kansas Entomological Society**
Kansas State Univ., Dept. of Entomology, Manhattan, KS 66506.
- Kansas Entomological Society. Journal. q. ISSN 0022-8567 (Co-sponsor: Central States Entomological Society)

**Kansas Farm Bureau, Inc.**
2321 Anderson Ave., Manhattan, KS 66502.
- Kansas Farm Bureau News. m.(combined July-Aug.) ISSN 0022-8575

**Kansas Folklore Society**
Bethany College, Dept. of English, Speech and Drama, Lindsborg, KS 66104.
- Kansas Folklore Society. Newsletter.

**Kansas Food Dealers Association**
Box 816, A. C. Office Bldg., Arkansas City, KS 67005.
- Kansas Food Dealers Bulletin. m. ISSN 0022-8605

**Kansas Grange**
- Kansas Grange Monthly. (pub. by Linn County Publishing Co.)

**Kansas Judicial Council**
1105 Merchants Bank Bldg., Topeka, KS 66612.
- Kansas Judicial Council Bulletin. s-a. ISSN 0022-8656

**Kansas Kernels**
c/o Carol Robbins, Ed., Box 26, Valley Center, KS 67147.
- Kansas Kernels. q. ISSN 0022-8664

**Kansas Law Review, Inc.**
Green Hall, Lawrence, KS 66044.
- University of Kansas Law Review. a.(issued in 4 parts) ISSN 0083-4025

**Kansas Livestock Association**
2044 Fillmore, Topeka, KS 66604.
- Kansas Stockman. m. ISSN 0022-8826

**Kansas Medical Society**
1300 Topeka Ave., Topeka, KS 66612.
- Kansas Medical Society. Journal. m. ISSN 0022-8699

**Kansas Motor Carriers Association**
2900 S. Topeka Blvd., Box 1673, Topeka, KS 66601.
- Kansas Transporter. m. ISSN 0022-8842

**Kansas Municipal Utilities, Inc.**
Box 1225, McPherson, KS 67460.
- K M U News Report. s-m.

**Kansas Oil Marketeers Association**
439 1st National Bank Bldg., Wichita, KS 67202.
- Kansas Oil Marketer. m.

**Kansas Optometric Association**
708 Gage Blvd., Topeka, KS 66606.
- Kansas Optometric Journal. bi-m.

**Kansas Ornithological Society**
c/o Charles A. Ely, Ed., Division of Biological
Sciences, Fort Hays Kansas State College, Hays, KS
67601.
- Kansas Ornithological Society. Bulletin. q. ISSN
0022-8729

**Kansas Peace Officers Association**
Box 2592, Wichita, KS 67201.
- Kansas Peace Officer. q.

**Kansas Pharmaceutical Association**
1308 W. 10th, P. O. Box 4218, Topeka, KS 66604.
- Journal of Kansas Pharmacy. m.

**Kansas Press Association**
Box 1773, Topeka, KS 66601.
- Kansas Publisher. m. ISSN 0022-8737

**Kansas Restaurant Association**
359 South Hydraulic, Wichita, KS 67211.
- Kansas Restaurant. m. ISSN 0022-8753

**Kansas Speech and Hearing Association**
- Kansas Speech and Hearing Association Journal.
(pub. by Wichita State University. Department of
Logopedics)

**Kansas State College of Pittsburg. Reading Services
Center**
Pittsburg, KS 66762.
- Reading Quarterly. q. ISSN 0034-0545

**Kansas State Dental Association**
861 Brotherhood Bldg., Kansas City, KS 66101.
- Kansas State Dental Association. Journal. q. ISSN
0022-8796

**Kansas State Historical Society**
Memorial Bldg., 120 W. Tenth, Topeka, KS 66612.
- Kansas Historical Quarterly. q. ISSN 0022-8621

**Kansas State Nurses Association**
820 Quincy St., Topeka, KS 66612.
- Kansas Nurse. 10 per yr. ISSN 0022-8710

**Kansas State Teachers Association**
715 W. 10th St., Topeka, KS 66612.
- Kansas Teacher. m.(s-m:Feb-Mar, Sep.-Oct.) ISSN
0022-8834

**Kansas State University. Center for Energy Studies**
Manhattan, KS 66502.
- Kansas State University. Center for Energy
Studies. Report. irreg.

**Kansas State University. College of Business
Administration**
Manhattan, KS 66502.
- Management Horizons. m. ISSN 0025-1836

**Kansas State University. College of Education**
Holton Hall, Manhattan, KS 66506.
- Educational Considerations. 3 per yr.

**Kansas State University. Computing Center**
Manhattan, KS 66506.
- Kansas State University. Computing Center.
Newsletter. m. 10 per yr.

**Kansas State University. Department of Economics**
339 Waters Hall, Manhattan, KS 66506.
- Regional Science Perspectives. a. (Mid-Continent
Regional Science Association)

**Kansas State University. Department of English**
106 Denison, Manhattan, KS 66506.
- Kansas Quarterly. q. ISSN 0022-8745

**Kansas State University. Department of Modern
Languages**
Manhattan, KS 66506.
- Journal of Spanish Studies: Twentieth Century. 3
per yr. ISSN 0092-1807 (Co-sponsor: Colorado
State University;)
- Studies in Twentieth Century Literature. s-a.

**Kansas State University. Division of Biology**
Manhattan, KS 66502.
- Bird Watch. m. (prep. by its Bird Populations
Institute)

**Kansas State University. Engineering Student Council**
Seaton Hall, Manhattan, KS 66506.
- Kansas State Engineer. q. ISSN 0047-3189

**Kansas State University. Food and Feed Grain
Institute**
Manhattan, KS 66506.
- Kansas State University. Food and Feed Grain
Institute. Technical Assistance in Food Grain
Drying, Storage, Handling and Transportation.
irreg. ISSN 0071-7150 (Co-sponsor: U. S. Agency
for International Development)

**Kansas State University. Institute of Nuclear
Materials Management, Inc.**
20 Seaton Hall, Manhattan, KS 66506.
- Institute of Nuclear Materials Management.
Proceedings of Annual Meeting. a. ISSN 0073-
9472
- Nuclear Materials Management. q.

**Kansas State University Library**
Manhattan, KS 66502.
- Kansas State University. Library Bibliography
Series. irreg., 1972, no. 10. ISSN 0075-4951

**Kansas Water Resources Board**
Mills Building, 4th Fl., 109 W. Ninth, Topeka, KS
66612.
- Kansas Water News. q. ISSN 0022-8869

**Kansas Wildlife Federation, Inc.**
c/o Ted Cunningham, Ed., R.R. 1, Wamego, KS
66547.
- Kansas Sportsman. m. ISSN 0453-2805

**Kansas 4-H Foundation Inc.**
Umberger Hall, Kansas State University, Manhattan,
KS 66506.
- Kansas 4-H Journal. m.

**Kapitalistate**
Box 1292, Palo Alto, CA 94302.
- Kapitalistate. irreg., approx 1 per yr.

**Samuel R. Kaplan**
10 Cutter Mill Rd., Great Neck, NY 11021.
- Embotellador. bi-m. ISSN 0013-6603

**Kappa Delta Epsilon**
- Kappa Delta Epsilon Current. (pub. by California
State College of Pennsylvania)

**Kappa Delta Pi Honor Society in Education**
116 Ramseyer Hall, 29 W. Woodruff Ave.,
Columbus, OH 43210.
- Educational Forum. 4 per yr. ISSN 0013-1725
- Kappa Delta Pi Record. q. ISSN 0022-8958

**Kappa Mu Epsilon**
Central Michigan Univ. Dept. of Mathematics,
Mount Pleasant, MI 48858.
- Pentagon; a mathematics magazine for students. s-
a. ISSN 0031-4870

**Kappa Tau Alpha**
National Headquarters, University of Missouri,
School of Journalism, Columbia, MO 65201.
- Kappa Tau Alpha Yearbook. a. ISSN 0075-5060

**Kappi Pi International Honorary Art Fraternity**
Box 7843, Midfield, Birmingham, AL 35228.
- Sketch Book. a.

**Karamu Association**
English Department, Eastern Illinois University,
Charleston, IL 61920.
- Karamu. a. ISSN 0022-8990

**Karikazo**
c/o Judith Magyar, Ed., 257 Chestnut Ave., Bogota,
NJ 07603.
- Karikazo; Hungarian folklore newsletter. q.

**Edward J. Karnarkowski, Ed. & Pub.**
Box 323, Highlands, NJ 07732.
- Saint Thomas More Political Science Journal. 3
per yr. ISSN 0036-3197

**Kate Greenaway Society**
- Under the Window. (pub. by James L. Lowe, Ed.
& Pub.)

**Kate Smith U.S.A. Friends Club**
8 Glendale Road, Scotia, NY 12302.
- Our Kate; honoring Kate Smith, America's first
lady of song. s-a.

**Kates-Boylston Publications, Inc.**
1501 Broadway, New York, NY 10036.
- American Blue Book of Funeral Directors.
biennial. ISSN 0065-7565
- American Cemetery. m. ISSN 0002-7804
- American Funeral Director. m. ISSN 0002-8576

**Kathell**
Box 1158, Fort Lee, NJ 07024.
- Ms. Memo. m.

**Menke Katz, Ed. & Pub.**
Box 51 Blythebourne Station, Brooklyn, NY 11219.
- Bitterroot; an international quarterly magazine of
poetry. 4 per yr. ISSN 0006-3908

**Kay Publishing Co.**
Box 608, Ridgewood, NJ 07451.
- National Speed Sport News. w. ISSN 0028-0208

**Kayak Books, Inc.**
325 Ocean View Ave., Santa Cruz, CA 95062.
- Kayak. q. ISSN 0022-9555

**Kaye Publishing Corporation**
535 Fifth Ave., New York, NY 10017.
- Graphics: U.S.A. m. ISSN 0017-3428

**Kayward Publications**
(Subsidiary of: International Press Service)
Box 2801, Washington, DC 20013.
- Asian American Trade Directory. irreg.
(Association of Asian-American Chambers of
Commerce)
- Communication Arts International. q. ISSN 0010-
3500 (International Association of Independent
Producers)
- Journal of Asian American Commerce. bi-m.
(Association of Asian-American Chambers of
Commerce)

**Kearney State College**
Kearney, NE 68847.
- Platte Valley Review. irreg. ISSN 0092-4318

**Keats Publishing, Inc.**
36 Grove St., New Canaan, CT 06840.
- Health Quarterly. q.
- Inspiration Three. irreg. ISSN 0092-9018
- Nutritional Update. q. ISSN 0091-4045

**Keats-Shelley Association of America, Inc.**
The Carl H. Pforzheimer Library, Room 815, 41
East 42nd St., New York, NY 10017.
- Keats-Shelley Journal; Keats, Shelley, Byron,
Hunt, and their circles. a. ISSN 0453-4387

**George S. Keenan**
79 Albertson Ave., Albertson, NY 11507.
- Church Bulletin. m. ISSN 0009-6369

**Keep America Beautiful, Inc.**
99 Park Ave., New York, NY 10016.
- K A B Reports. 4 per yr.

**Keeping Abreast Journal**
c/o Jimmie Lynne Avery, Ed., Box 6459, Cherry
Creek Sta., Denver, CO 80206.
- Keeping Abreast Journal. q. ISSN 0146-7638

**Keeping up with Music Education**
1220 Ridge Rd., Muncie, IN 47304.
- Keeping up with Orff-Schulwerk in the Classroom.
5 per yr. ISSN 0092-797X

**Henry A. Keitel, Ed. & Pub.**
727 S. Dearborn St., Chicago, IL 60605.
- Brewers Bulletin. s-w. ISSN 0006-9701

**Thomas R. Kellaway, Ed. & Pub.**
Box 65007, Los Angeles, CA 90065.
- American Art Review. bi-m. ISSN 0092-1327

**J. J. Keller & Associates, Inc.**
145 W. Wisconsin Ave., Neenah, WI 54956.
- Metric Bulletin. m.
- Metric System Guide. Vol. 1-Metrication in the
United States. irreg.; with q. supplements.
- Metric System Guide. Vol. 2-Legislation and
Regulatory Controls. irreg. with q. supplements.
- Metric System Guide. Vol. 3-Metric Units. q.
- Metric System Guide. Vol. 4 - Metric Reference.
irreg. with supplements.
- Metric System Guide. Vols. 5 - Definitions and
Terminology. irreg. with q. supplements.
- Motor Carrier Safety Report. m. plus supplements.
- Truck Broker Directory. irreg. ISSN 0362-5737

**Keller Publishing Corporation**
10 Cutter Mill Rd., Great Neck, NY 11021.
- Beverage World; international magazine of the
beverage industry. m. ISSN 0098-2318

- International Instrumentation. bi-m.
- Reportero Industrial; new equipment, machinery and techniques for industry. m. ISSN 0034-4818
- Scope (Great Neck); news and views of the beverage world. m.
- World Industrial Reporter; new equipment, machinery and techniques for industry. m. ISSN 0043-8561

**Kelley Blue Book**
Box 7127, Long Beach, CA 90807.
- Kelley Blue Book R V Guide. irreg. ISSN 0094-8446

**Augustus M. Kelley Publishers**
300 Fairfield Rd., Fairfield, NJ 07006.
- Economic Books: Current Selections. q. ISSN 0093-2485 (University of Pittsburgh. Department of Economics) (Co-Sponsor: University of Pittsburg Libraries)

**Kellogg Co. (Battle Creek)**
235 Porter St., Battle Creek, MI 49016.
- Straight Talk. m.

**M. W. Kellogg Co. (Houston)**
1300 Three Greenway Plaza East, Houston, TX 77046.
- Kellogg World. s-a. ISSN 0453-4867

**Robert Kelly, Ed. & Pub.**
Bard College, Annandale, NY 12504.
- Matter. ISSN 0025-6005

**Keltner Statistical Service, Inc.**
1004 Baltimore Ave., Kansas City, MO 64105.
- Keltner Commodity Letter. w. ISSN 0022-9806

**P. J. Kenedy & Sons**
P.O. Box 729, New York, NY 10022.
- Official Catholic Directory; official directory of the Catholic Church in the United States and its possessions. a. ISSN 0078-3854

**Kennecott Copper Corporation**
Box 11299, Salt Lake City, UT 84147.
- Kennescope. m.

**Kennedy & Kennedy, Inc.**
Templeton Rd., Fitzwilliam, NH 03447.
- Consultants News. m. ISSN 0045-8201

**Kennedy Galleries, Inc.**
40 W. 57th St., 5th Floor, New York, NY 10019.
- American Art Journal. s-a. ISSN 0002-7359 (Co-sponsor: Israel Sack, Inc.)
- Kennedy Quarterly. q. ISSN 0453-512X

**Kent Feeds, Inc.**
Muscatine, IA 52761.
- Beef Roundup. s-a.
- Dairy Roundup. a.
- Pork Roundup. s-a.
- Rural Roundup. a. ISSN 0036-0104

**Kent State University. Center for Business and Economic Research**
Kent, OH 44242.
- Kent State University. Center for Business and Economic Research. Comparative Administration Research Institute Series. irreg., 1970, no. 2. ISSN 0078-4184
- Kent State University. Center for Business and Economic Research. Labor and Industrial Relations Series. irreg., no. 3, 1975. ISSN 0078-4192
- Kent State University. Center for Business and Economic Research. Printed Series. irreg., 1968, no. 9. ISSN 0078-4206
- Kent State University. Center for Business and Economic Research. Research Papers. irreg., 1968, no. 6. ISSN 0078-4214

**Kent State University. Department of English**
Kent, OH 44240.
- Human Issue. 3 per yr. ISSN 0018-7232

**Kent State University. Department of History**
Kent, OH 44242.
- Civil War History; a journal of the Middle Period. q. ISSN 0009-8078

**Kent State University Libraries**
Kent, OH 44242.
- Kent State University. Libraries. Occasional Paper. irreg. ISSN 0078-4222

**Kent State University Press**
Kent, OH 44242.
- Mid-Continental Journal of Archaeology. s-a.

**Kent State University. Student Publications Policy Committee**
Taylor Hall, Rm. 100, Kent, OH 44242.
- Daily Kent Stater. 4 per w. ISSN 0011-5444

**Kenton Bible Hall, Inc.**
- Last Day Messenger. (pub. by Gospel Tract Distributors)

**Kentucky. Adjutant-General's Office**
Frankfort, KY 40601.
- Kentucky. Adjutant-General's Office. Report. irreg.

**Kentucky. Crop and Livestock Reporting Service**
Frankfort, KY 40601.
- Kentucky Agricultural Statistics. irreg.

**Kentucky. Department of Child Welfare**
Frankfort, KY 40601.
- Kentucky. Department of Child Welfare. Annual Report. a.

**Kentucky. Department of Commerce**
Capital Plaza Tower, Frankfort, KY 40601.
- Kentucky Directory of Manufacturers. a. ISSN 0075-5494
- Kentucky Directory of Selected Industrial Services. irreg. ISSN 0363-5198
- Kentucky Manufacturing Developments. irreg.

**Kentucky. Department of Commerce. Division of Research and Planning**
Capitol Plaza Tower, Frankfort, KY 40601.
- Kentucky Deskbook of Economic Statistics. irreg. ISSN 0361-591X

**Kentucky. Department of Education**
Capital Plaza Tower, Frankfort, KY 40601.
- Kentucky School Directory. a. ISSN 0091-0775
- School News. m. ISSN 0036-6692

**Kentucky. Department of Education. Bureau of Administration and Finance**
Frankfort, KY 40601.
- Summary of Kentucky Education Statistics. irreg. ISSN 0362-6679

**Kentucky. Department of Fish and Wildlife**
Frankfort, KY 40601.
- Kentucky Happy Hunting Ground. bi-m. ISSN 0023-0235

**Kentucky. Department of Health**
275 E. Main St., Louisville, KY 40201.
- Kentucky. Department of Health. News and Plans. m.
- Kentucky Medical Assistance Program Briefs. q. ISSN 0023-0286

**Kentucky. Department of Health. Department for Human Resources**
State Office Building Annex, KY 40601.
- Kentucky Vital Statistics. a. ISSN 0098-6739

**Kentucky. Department of Natural Resources**
Frankfort, KY 40601.
- Kentucky. Department of Natural Resources. Annual Report. a.

**Kentucky. Office for Local Government**
Frankfort, KY 40601.
- Kentucky Local Debt Report. a. ISSN 0095-1498

**Kentucky Academy of Family Physicians**
Medical Arts Bldg., 1169 Eastern Parkway, Louisville, KY 40217.
- K A F P Journal. q. ISSN 0090-5089

**Kentucky Academy of Science**
- Kentucky Academy of Science. Transactions. (pub. by University of Louisville. Water Resources Laboratory)

**Kentucky Agricultural Experiment Station**
Frankfort, KY 40601.
- Kentucky. Agricultural Experimental Station. Report. a.

**Kentucky Association for Health, Physical Education & Recreation**
c/o Lee Gentry, Eastern Kentucky University, Richmond, KY 40475.
- K A H P E R Journal. 2 per yr. ISSN 0022-7269

**Kentucky Association of Communication Arts**
c/o Robert Valentine, Dept. of Speech & Theatre, Murray State University, Murray, KY 42071.
- Kentucky Journal of Communication Arts. s-a.

**Kentucky Association of Electric Cooperatives**
4515 Bishop Lane, Louisville, KY 40218.
- Rural Kentuckian. m. ISSN 0036-0066

**Kentucky Association of Highway Contractors**
c/o Victor E. Comley, Drawer 637, Frankfort, KY 40601.
- Scraper. bi-m. ISSN 0036-9535

**Kentucky Association of Plumbing-Heating-Cooling Contractors**
1501 Durrett Lane, Louisville, KY 40213.
- Kentucky Plumbing & Heating Index. m.

**Kentucky Association of School Librarians**
4027 St. Germaine Ct., Louisville, KY 40207.
- Kentucky Association of School Librarians. Bulletin. s-a.

**Kentucky Association on Alcohol Abuse and Alcoholism, Inc.**
628 N. Broadway, Lexington, KY 40508.
- Accent on Alcohol. bi-m.

**Kentucky Bankers Association**
425 S. Fifth St., Louisville, KY 40202.
- Kentucky Banker. m. ISSN 0023-0111

**Kentucky Baptist Convention**
10701 Shelbyville Rd., Middletown, KY 40243.
- Western Recorder. w. ISSN 0043-4132

**Kentucky Bar Association**
315 W. Main St., Frankfort, KY 40601.
- Kentucky Bench & Bar. q.

**Kentucky Civil War Round Table**
c/o Paul T. Crowdus, Ed., 3452 Belvoir Dr., Lexington, KY 40502.
- Kentucky Civil War Round Table. Bulletin. 5 per yr. ISSN 0023-0146

**Kentucky Council of Economic Advisors**
- Kentucky Council of Economic Advisors. Quarterly Report. (pub. by University of Kentucky. College of Business and Economics)

**Kentucky Council of Teachers of English**
Univ. of Kentucky, Dept. of English, Lexington, KY 40506.
- Kentucky English Bulletin. 3 per yr. ISSN 0023-0197

**Kentucky Council on Public Higher Education**
Capitol Plaza Office Tower, Frankfort, KY 40601.
- Kentucky. Council on Public Higher Education. Origin of Enrollments, Accredited Colleges and Universities. irreg. ISSN 0098-9770

**Kentucky Dental Association**
c/o Dr. Harold F. Klein, Ed., 1940 Princeton Dr., Louisville, KY 40205.
- Kentucky Dental Association. Journal. q. ISSN 0023-0162

**Kentucky Education Association**
101 W. Walnut St., Louisville, KY 40202.
- K E A. Research Publications. 7 per yr.
- K E A News. w (Sep.-May); m (June-Aug)

**Kentucky Elementary School Principal**
c/o Glen Edelen, Ed., Lowe Elementary School, 210 Oxfordshire Ln., Louisville, KY 40222.
- Kentucky Elementary School Principal. 4 per yr. ISSN 0023-0189

**Kentucky Farm Bureau Federation**
120 S. Hubbard Lane, Louisville, KY 40207.
- Kentucky Farm Bureau News. m. ISSN 0023-0200

**Kentucky Federation of the Blind**
- Braille Cardinal. (pub. by National Publishers Press)

**Kentucky Folklore Society**
Box U-169, Western Kentucky University, Bowling Green, KY 42101.
- Kentucky Folklore Record. q. ISSN 0023-0227
- Kentucky Folklore Series. irreg., no. 6, 1975. ISSN 0075-5508

**Kentucky Geological Survey**
University of Kentucky, 307 Mineral Industries
Bldg., University of Kentucky, Lexington, KY
40506.
- University of Kentucky. Geological Survey.
  Guidebook to Geological Field Trips. irreg. ISSN
  0075-5575
- University of Kentucky. Geological Survey. Series
  X. Bulletin. irreg., 1969, no. 5. ISSN 0075-5559
- University of Kentucky. Geological Survey. Series
  X. County Report. irreg., no. 5, 1973. ISSN 0075-
  5567
- University of Kentucky. Geological Survey. Series
  X. Information Circular. irreg., no. 22, 1974.
  ISSN 0075-5583
- University of Kentucky. Geological Survey. Series
  X. Report of Investigations. irreg., no. 15, 1974.
  ISSN 0075-5591
- University of Kentucky. Geological Survey. Series
  X. Reprints. irreg., no. 43, 1974. ISSN 0075-5605
- University of Kentucky. Geological Survey. Series
  X. Special Publications. irreg., no. 22, 1974. ISSN
  0075-5613
- University of Kentucky. Geological Survey. Series
  X. Thesis Series. irreg., 1970, no. 3. ISSN 0075-
  5621

**Kentucky Historical Society**
Old State House, Box H, Frankfort, KY 40601.
- Kentucky Ancestors. q. ISSN 0023-0103
- Kentucky Historical Society. Register. q. ISSN
  0023-0243

**Kentucky Law Enforcement Council**
Eastern Kentucky University, Box 608, KY 40475.
- Kentucky Law Enforcement Council. Annual
  Report. a. ISSN 0095-6384

**Kentucky Library Association**
c/o Tom Sutherland, Paducah Public Library, 555
Washington St., Paducah, KY 42001.
- K L A Bulletin. q. ISSN 0022-734X

**Kentucky Manpower Development, Inc.**
412 Executive Park, Louisville, KY 40207.
- Kentucky Manpower Development. Annual
  Report. a. ISSN 0095-5574

**Kentucky Medical Association**
3532 Ephraim McDowell Drive, Louisville, KY
40205.
- Kentucky Medical Association. Journal. m. ISSN
  0023-0294

**Kentucky Municipal League**
Suite 229, Commerce Bldg., Univ. of Kentucky,
Lexington, KY 42728.
- Kentucky City. m.

**Kentucky Music Teachers Association**
c/o Ed. Martin D. Mc Kay, P. O. Box 211,
Lancaster, KY 40444.
- Bluegrass Music News. 4 per yr. ISSN 0006-5129

**Kentucky Nurses Association**
1400 S. First St., Box 8342, Sta. E., Louisville, KY
40208.
- Kentucky Nurses Association Newsletter. q. ISSN
  0023-0316

**Kentucky Poetry Review**
1568 Cherokee Rd., Louisville, KY 40205.
- Kentucky Poetry Review. q.

**Kentucky Press Association**
63 Fountain Place, Frankfort, KY 40601.
- Kentucky Press. m. ISSN 0023-0324

**Kentucky Society of Certified Public Accountants**
310 W. Liberty, Louisville, KY 40202.
- Kentucky Accountant. m. ISSN 0023-009X

**Kentucky State AFL-CIO**
706 Broadway, Louisville, KY 40202.
- Kentucky Labor News. w. ISSN 0023-0251

**Kenyon College**
c/o Ed. Kevin Martin, Box B, Gambier, OH 43022.
- Hika. q. ISSN 0018-179X

**Kephart Communications Inc.**
410 First St. S.E., Washington, DC 20003.
- Audio-Forum Review. q.
- Inflation Survival Letter. fortn.

**Robert Kerdasha, Ed. & Pub.**
420 Lexington, Rm. 2540, New York, NY 10017.
- Eastern Tennis. q. ISSN 0012-8929

**Kern County Dental Society**
1406 Jefferson, Delano, CA 93215.
- Kern County Dental Society Newsletter. m. ISSN
  0023-0634

**Kern County Historical Society**
Box 141, Bakersfield, CA 93301.
- Historic Kern. q. ISSN 0018-2397

**Osheen Keshishian, Ed. & Pub.**
6646 Hollywood Blvd., Hollywood, CA 90028.
- Armenian Observer. w. ISSN 0044-894X

**Kettering Laboratory**
292 Madison Avenue, New York, NY 10017.
- Kettering Abstracts of Available Literature on the
  Biological and Related Aspects of Lead and Its
  Compounds. q. (Lead Industries Association, Inc.)
  (Co-Sponsor: International Lead Zinc Research
  Organization of New York)

**Key Club International**
101 E. Erie, Chicago, IL 60611.
- Keynoter. m. except summer.

**Key Dayton Scene**
c/o Jean M. Sharp, 7 Stonemill Rd., Dayton, OH
45409.
- Key Dayton Scene. m.

**Key Markets Publishing Co.**
Box 4476, Rockford, IL 61110.
- Metric News. bi-m. ISSN 0093-3708
- Weighing & Measurement. m.

**Key Organization**
- Key Magazine/Carmel & Monterey Peninsula.
  (pub. by Tri-County Publications)

**Key-This Week in Chicago**
c/o Walter L. West, Jr., 105 W. Madison St.,
Chicago, IL 60602.
- Key-This Week in Chicago. w. ISSN 0040-6279

**Keyboard World, Inc.**
Box 4399, Downey, CA 90241.
- Keyboard World. m. (National Association of
  Organ Teachers)

**Keystone Automobile Club AAA**
2040 Market St., Philadelphia, PA 19103.
- Keystone Motorist. m. ISSN 0023-0995

**Keystone Publishing Co.**
435 North Lake Ave., Pasadena, CA 91101.
- California Senior Citizen News. m. ISSN 0008-
  1531 (Senior Citizens Association of Los Angeles
  County) (Co-sponsor: Allied Senior Citizen's
  Clubs of California)

**Khalsa Publications**
Box 1020, Claremont, CA 91711.
- Multidisciplinary Research. s-a. ISSN 0098-8553
  (International Multidisciplinary Research
  Association)

**Lu Kibler, Ed. & Pub.**
43949 N. 60th St. W., Lancaster, CA 93534.
- Piggin String. m. ISSN 0031-9791

**Kilgore's Tree**
913 7th Ave. N., Clear Lake, IA 50428.
- Kilgore's Tree. q.

**Kimberly Communications Corporation**
1067 National Press Bldg., Washington, DC 20045.
- Helicopter News. fortn.

**Kimport Dolls**
Box 495, Independence, MO 64051.
- Doll Talk; a magazine in miniature for doll
  enthusiasts and collectors. every 8 weeks. ISSN
  0012-5229

**King County Library System**
300 8th Ave., North, Seattle, WA 98109.
- Etcetera. q.

**King County Medical Society**
- King County Medical Society. Bulletin. (pub. by
  Journal and Bulletin Agency)

**King Enterprises**
4136 Peak St., Toledo, OH 43612.
- Music Tempo. 4 per yr. ISSN 0027-447X

**King Publications**
Box 19332, Washington, DC 20036.
- Joint Conference; magazine of inmate writings &
  art. 3-4 per yr. ISSN 0145-8795

**Kingdom Digest**
Box 24600, Dallas, TX 75224.
- Kingdom Digest. m. ISSN 0023-1614

**The Kingdom Press**
Chestnut Hill Rd., Amherst, NH 03031
- Standard (Amherst); upholding the Standard set
  by the Master (Jesus Christ) m. ISSN 0038-9404
  (Subscr. to: Frank S. Murray, Ed., 180 Western
  Ave., Essex, MA 01929)

**King's College**
Wilkes-Barre, PA 18702.
- Dialogist. 3 per yr. ISSN 0012-2076

**Kipen Publishing Corporation**
5810 W. Oklahoma Ave., Milwaukee, WI 53219.
- Spare Time. 9 per yr. ISSN 0038-6499

**Kiplinger Washington Editors, Inc.**
1729 H St., N.W., Washington, DC 20006.
- Changing Times; the Kiplinger magazine. m. ISSN
  0009-143X
- Kiplinger Agricultural Letter. fortn. ISSN 0023-
  1746
- Kiplinger California Letter. m.
- Kiplinger Florida Letter. 15 per yr. ISSN 0023-
  1754
- Kiplinger Tax Letter. fortn. ISSN 0023-1762
- Kiplinger Washington Letter. w. ISSN 0023-1770

**Jack & Viola Kirecofe, Eds. & Pubs.**
300 Front St., Boiling Springs, PA 17007.
- Modern Game Breeding, Avicultural and
  Zoological News; published in the interests of all
  game breeders. m. ISSN 0026-7767

**Kirklanda Esperanto-Centro**
1856 Third St., Kirkland, WA 98033.
- Esperantologio. q.
- Hodiau. q.
- Juda Esperantisto. q.
- Tempo/Spaco/Vivo. q.
- Usono. q.
- Verda Papilio. q.

**Kirkley Press Inc.**
Box 200, Timonium, MD 21093.
- Better Business by Telephone. s-m.

**Kirkus Service, Inc.**
200 Park Ave. So., New York, NY 10003.
- Kirkus Reviews. s-m. ISSN 0042-6598

**Sandra D. Kirshenbaum, Ed. & Pub.**
P.O. Box 7741, San Francisco, Ca 94120.
- Fine Print; a review for the arts of the book. 4 per
  yr. ISSN 0361-3801

**Kite Books**
c/o Creative Writing Program, Boston University,
236 Bay State Rd., Boston, MA 02215.
- Boston University Fiction Series. irreg.

**Kitt Peak National Observatory**
The Library, 950 N. Cherry Ave., Box 26732,
Tucson, AZ 85726.
- Kitt Peak National Observatory. Contributions.
  irreg. ISSN 0075-6253 (Association of
  Universities for Research in Astronomy)

**M. S. Kiver Publications, Inc**
222 W. Adams St., Chicago, IL 60606.
- E P A C: Electronic Production Aids Catalog. a.
  ISSN 0424-8287
- Electro-Optical Systems Design. m.
- Electronic Packaging and Production; for the
  engineers who convert the circuit diagram into
  the finished product. m. ISSN 0013-4945
- Electronic Packaging and Production Vendor
  Selection Issue. a.

**Kiwanis International**
101 E. Erie, Chicago, IL 60611.
- Kiwanis Club International. Proceedings. a.
- Kiwanis Magazine; published for community
  leaders. m.(bi-m Dec.-Jan. & July-Aug.) ISSN
  0023-1967

**Klas Publishing Co.**
Box 66, 518 Main St., Boonton, NJ 07005.
- Lighting Supply & Design. m.

**Sholom Klass, Ed. & Pub.**
338-Third Ave., Brooklyn, NY 11215.
● Jewish Press. w. ISSN 0021-6674

**Klass Publications, Inc**
112 Broadway, Malverne, NY 11565.
● Jewish Executive. bi-m.

**Anthony C. Kleber**
66 E. 34th Street, New York, NY 10016.
● Baby Talk. m. ISSN 0005-3589

**Bernard A. Klein**
Box 4288, Pittsburgh, PA 15203.
● National Glass Budget; review of the American glass industry. s-m. ISSN 0027-9390

**B. Klein Publication, Inc.**
Box 8503, Coral Springs, FL 33065.
● Directory of College Stores. biennial. ISSN 0084-988X
● Directory of Mailing List Houses. biennial. ISSN 0419-2923
● Guide to American Directories. biennial. ISSN 0533-5248
● Mail Order Business Directory. biennial. ISSN 0085-2953

**Kleinhans Co.**
Main & Clinton Sts., Buffalo, NY 14203.
● Clarion. bi-m.

**Klevens Publications, Inc.**
6500 Kelvin Ave., Canoga Park, CA 91306.
● Camp Directors Purchasing Guide. a.
● Freighter Travel-Letter; monthly reports on new sailings, new ships, and new places throughout the world. m. ISSN 0046-5054
● Garment Manufacturer's Index. a.
● Resorts & R V Parks Purchasing Guide. a.

**Kliatt Paperback Book Guide**
425 Watertown St., Newton, MA 02158.
● Kliatt Paperback Book Guide; an annotated list of current paperback books for young adults. 3 per yr. (with 5 newsletter supplements) ISSN 0023-2114

**Charles H. Kline & Co., Inc.**
330 Passaic Ave., Fairfield, NJ 07006.
● Directory of U.S. and Canadian Marketing Surveys and Services. every 2-3 yrs.
● Kline Guide to the Chemical Industry. triennial.
● Kline Guide to the Packaging Industry. triennial.
● Kline Guide to the Paint Industry. triennial.
● Kline Guide to the Paper and Pulp Industry. triennial.

**Kline Geology Laboratory**
Yale Univ., Box 2161, Yale Sta., New Haven, CT 06520.
● American Journal of Science; devoted to the geological sciences and to related fields. m.(except July & Sept) ISSN 0002-9599

**Ralph A. Kling**
Box 156, Grundy Center, IA 50638.
● Collectors News. m. ISSN 0010-0846

**Curtis C. Klinger**
309 Bloomfield Ave., Caldwell, NJ 07006.
● Fuel Oil News; magazine of automatic oil heating. m. ISSN 0016-2396

**Knave Publications, Inc.**
120 E. 56th St., New York, NY 10022.
● Knave. m.

**Knickerbocker Club, New York**
2 E. 62nd St., New York, NY 10022.
● Knickerbocker Club. Club Book. a. ISSN 0362-5168

**Knights of Columbus**
P.O. Drawer 1670, New Haven, CT 06507.
● Columbia; America's largest Catholic family magazine. m. ISSN 0010-1869

**Knights of Columbus. Service Dept.**
Columbus Plaza, New Haven, CT 06507.
● Squires Newsletter. m.

**Knights of Lithuania**
1467 Force Dr., Mountain Side, NJ 07092.
● Vytis/Knight. 10 per yr. ISSN 0042-9384

**Alfred A. Knopf**
(Subsidiary of: Random House)
201 E. 50 St., New York, NY 10022.
● Alfred A. Knopf Books in Economics. irreg.
● Borzoi Books on Latin America. irreg. ISSN 0520-6294
● Borzoi Series in United States Constitutional History. irreg.
● Studies in World Civilization. irreg.

**Know**
Ed. N. Mezvinsky, Suite 2G, 340 E. 51st St., New York, NY 10022.
● Know. fortn. ISSN 0047-3480

**Know, Inc.**
Box 86031, Pittsburgh, PA 15221.
● Know News Service. irreg. (approx. 9 per yr.) ISSN 0300-7901

**Knowledge Industry Publications, Inc.**
2 Corporate Park Dr., White Plains, NY 10604.
● Advanced Technology Libraries. m. ISSN 0044-636X
● B. P. Report; on the business of book publishing. w.
● Educational Marketer. s-m. ISSN 0013-1806
● Knowledge Industry Report; a businessman's newsletter on the knowledge industry. q. ISSN 0023-2491
● Library Networks. biennial.
● Overseas Assignment Directory Service. m.
● Video Publisher. s-m. ISSN 0300-7057

**Donald D. Knowles, Ed. & Pub.**
1118 N. Raynor Ave., Joliet, IL 60435.
● Engineers and Engines Magazine. bi-m. ISSN 0013-8142

**Knox College**
Galesburg, IL 61401.
● Knox Now and the Knox Alumnus. 3 per yr.

**Knox County Illinois Genealogical Society**
P.O. Box 13, Galesburg, IL 61401.
● Knox County Illinois Genealogical Society. Quarterly. q.

**Knuth Beth**
1436 Brush St., Detroit, MI 48226.
● Detroiter Abend-Post. s-w.

**Irvin Koch, Ed. & Pub.**
c/o 835 Chattanooga Bank Bldg., Chattanooga, TN 37402.
● Maybe; Worlds of Fandom. s-a. (Chattanooga Science Fiction Convention)

**Allen Koenigsberg**
650 Ocean Avenue, Brooklyn, NY 11226.
● Antique Phonograph Monthly. m. ISSN 0361-2147

**Kogos International Corp.**
77 Maple Drive, Great Neck, NY 11020.
● Who's Who in Designing; america's foremost clothing designers. irreg.

**James Koller, Ed. & Pub.**
P.O. Box 629, Brunswick, ME 04011.
● Coyote's Journal. irreg. ISSN 0011-0736

**Kona Communications, Inc.**
2751 Lake Cook Rd., Deerfield, IL 60015.
● Heavy-Duty Distribution. m.

**Konglomerati Press**
5719 29th Ave. S., Gulfport, FL 33707.
● Konglomerati. irreg.

**Sipapu Konocti Books**
Route 1, Box 216, Winters, CA 95694.
● Sipapu. 2 per yr. ISSN 0037-5837

**Korea Research and Publication, Inc.**
c/o Cellar Book Shop, 18090 Wyoming, Detroit, MI 48221.
● Monograph Series on Korea. irreg., no.7, 1973. ISSN 0077-0604

**Korea Stamp Society, Inc.**
c/o Forrest W. Calkins, Secretary-Treasurer, Box 1057, Grand Junction, CO 81501.
● Korean Philately. q.

**Korea Week Publishing Co.**
757 National Press Bldg., Washington, DC 20045.
● Korea Week. bi-m. ISSN 0023-3951

**Korean Research Council**
1565 Miramar Ave., Seaside, CA 93955.
● Korean Research Bulletin. s-a.

**Korean Traders Association, Inc**
460 Park Ave., New York, NY 10022.
● Korean Trade News. w.

**Herbert Kornblitt, Ed. & Pub.**
Box 806, South Miami, FL 33143.
● Current Medicine for Attorneys; a quarterly report on the latest trends in medicine as these apply to the general practice of law, personal injury and casualty suits. q. ISSN 0011-3719

**Kosciuszko Foundation**
15 E. 65th St., New York, NY 10021.
● Kosciuszko Foundation Monthly Newsletter. m (except Jul & Aug.)

**Koss Corp.**
4129 N. Port Washington Ave., Milwaukee, WI 53212.
● Koss Sounds. bi-m.

**N. A. Kovach, Ed. & Pub.**
4801-09 Second Ave., Los Angeles, CA 90043.
● International Press Bulletin. q. ISSN 0020-8361

**Kovner Publications Inc.**
319 N. Soto St., Los Angeles, CA 90033.
● Mexican American Sun. w.

**Michael J. Krajsa**
Box 150, Middletown, PA 17057.
● Slovak American/Slovak V Amerike. w.

**Kratville Publications**
516 Farnam Building, Omaha, NE 68101.
● Railroad Car Journal. ISSN 0091-5572

**Kraus- Thomson Organization Ltd.**
see K T O Press

**Krause Publications, Inc.**
700 E. State St., Iola, WI 54945.
● Coin Prices. bi-m. ISSN 0010-0412
● Coins; the complete magazine for coin collectors. m. ISSN 0010-0471
● Numismatic News. w. ISSN 0029-604X
● Old Cars; the newspaper of the hobby. fortn. ISSN 0048-1637
● World Coin News. w.

**Krauth Memorial Library**
Lutheran Theologial Seminary, 7301 Germantown Ave., Philadelphia, PA 19119.
● Teamwork. q. (Southeastern Pennsylvania Theological Library Association)

**Kresge Art Center Gallery**
● Kresge Art Center Bulletin. (pub. by Michigan State University)

**Kresge Foundation**
Troy, MI 48084.
● Kresge Foundation. Annual Report. a. ISSN 0075-711X

**Phyllis van Kriedt, Ed. & Pub.**
Box 70, Mill Valley, CA 94941.
● Wineletter. m. ISSN 0043-5821

**Krieger Publishing Co., Inc.**
Box 542, Huntington, NY 11743.
● Airplane, Missile and Spacecraft Structure Series. irreg., 1966, latest vol. unnumbered. ISSN 0568-3866
● C I B A Lectures in Microbial Biochemistry. irreg.

**Kritika**
1737 Cambridge St., Cambridge, MA 02138.
● Kritika; a review of current Soviet books on Russian history. 3 per yr. ISSN 0023-4826

**Kroc Foundation**
● Kroc Foundation Series. (pub. by Raven Press)

**Kroeber Anthropological Society**
Dept.of Anthropology, Univ. of California, Berkeley, CA 94720.
● Kroeber Anthropological Society. Papers. irreg., approx. s-a. ISSN 0023-4869

**Barbara Krohn and Associates**
835 Securities Bldg., Seattle, WA 98101.
● Washington Education Directory. a. (Washington (State) Superintendent of Public Instruction)

**Kronos Press**
c/o Warner Sizemore, Ed., Glassboro State College,
Glassboro, NJ 08028.
- Kronos; a journal of interdisciplinary synthesis. q.
ISSN 0361-6584

**Diane Kruchkow, Ed. & Pub.**
Box 715, Newburyport, MA 01950.
- Zahir. s-a. ISSN 0049-8505

**Ktaadn**
Eds. Lionel Basney & John Leax, Box 25,
Houghton, NY 14744.
- Ktaadn. 3 per yr. ISSN 0023-4982

**Kudzu**
Box 22502, Jackson, MS 39205.
- Kudzu. every 2-4 weeks. ISSN 0023-4990

**F. William Kuethe, Jr., Ed. & Pub.**
700 Glenview Ave. , S.W., Glen Burnie, MD 21061.
- Journal of Necromantic Numismatics. a. ISSN
0022-2976
- Magic Cauldron. q. ISSN 0024-9904

**Kuhlman Electric Company**
101 Kuhlman Blvd., Versailles, KY 40383.
- Kuhlman Kurrents. q.

**Kuksu Press**
Box 980, Alleghany Star Rt., Nevada City, CA
95959.
- Kuksu; journal of backcountry writing. s-a.

**Henry Kuntz, Jr., Ed. & Pub**
1921 Walnut, No. 1, Berkeley, CA 94704.
- Bells; a newsletter of opinion, news and reviews of
improvised music. bi-m.

**George Kurian Reference Books**
Box 154, Pelham, NY 10803.
- Children's Literary Almanac. biennial. ISSN 0093-
0431
- Current Register of American Leaders; national
gazette of heads of American govern,ents and
organizations. 3 per yr. ISSN 0360-8786

**Kutztown State College. English Department**
Kutztown, PA 19344.
- Compass (Kutztown) s-a.

**Kyiw Publishing House**
4800 North 12th St., Philadelphia, PA 19141.
- Ukrainian Book/Ukrainska Knyha/Ukrainische
Buch; Ukrainian bibliographic quarterly. q.
(Shevchenko Scholastic Society) (Co-sponsor:
Association of Ukrainian Librarians in America)

**Kyle Publishing Co.**
Box 2349, Tampa, FL 33601.
- Citrus and Vegetable Magazine. m. ISSN 0009-
7586

**L B I News**
129 E. 73rd St., New York, NY 10021.
- L B I News. s-a. ISSN 0023-625X

**L. D. Pankey Alumni Association**
785 Delaware Ave., Delmar, NY 12054.
- Pankey-Gram. q.

**L.E.N., Inc.**
448 W. 56 St., New York, NY 10019.
- Law Enforcement News. m.

**L. H. Bailey Hortorium**
Cornell University, Ithaca, NY 14853.
- Baileya; a journal of horticultural taxonomy. irreg.
ISSN 0005-4003
- Gentes Herbarum; occasional papers on the kinds
of plants. irreg., 1973, vol. 11. ISSN 0072-0879

**L. H. Publishing Co.**
289 Quincy Pl., R.D. 1, Langhorne, PA 19047.
- Racing/Circuits; the bi-monthly journal of model
car racing. bi-m.

**L N S News Service, Inc.**
17 W. 17 St., New York, NY 10011.
- Liberation News Service. w. ISSN 0024-1911

**L'Officiel-U S A, Inc.**
455 Central Ave., Scarsdale, NY 10583.
- L'Officiel/U S A. bi-m.

**L.Q.C. Lamar Society of International Law**
- Journal of Space Law. (pub. by University of
Mississippi Law Center)

**L. S. B. Leakey Foundation**
20685 Foundation Center, Pasadena, CA 91125.
- L. S. B. Leakey Foundation News. q.

**L. S. W. Associates**
Box 82, Mattituck, NY 11952.
- Astronomy Through Practical Investigation.
irreg??

**L.V.A. "Ramove" Inc.**
341 Highland Blvd., Brooklyn, NY 11207.
- Karys; monthly for American-Lithuanian veterans.
m. ISSN 0022-9199

**L-5 Society**
1620 N. Park, Tucson, AZ 85719.
- L-5 News. m.

**La Leche League International, Inc**
9616 Minneapolis Ave., Franklin Park, IL 60131.
- La Leche League News; good mothering through
breastfeeding the world over. bi-m.
- Leaven. bi-m.

**La Motte Enterprises**
1236 National Press Bldg., Washington, DC 20045.
- Clyde LaMotte's Washington Energy Memo. w.
ISSN 0300-7243

**La Salette Fathers**
Twin Lakes, WI 53181.
- Our Lady's Digest. 5 per yr. ISSN 0030-6886

**La Salle College**
Philadelphia, PA 19141.
- Four Quarters. q. ISSN 0015-9107

**Labor Cooperative Educational & Publishing Society,
Inc**
400 First St. N.W., Washington, DC 20001.
- Labor; an international tri-weekly newspaper. tri-
weekly. ISSN 0023-6497

**Labor Herald Publishing Co.**
27 Orient Way, Rutherford, NJ 07070.
- New Jersey Labor Herald. m. ISSN 0028-5781

**Labor News Company**
193 N. Cherry St., Galesburg, IL 61401.
- Galesburg Labor News. w. ISSN 0016-4054
(Galesburg Trades & Labor Assembly)

**Labor Record Publishing Co., Inc.**
205 N. Joliet, Joliet, IL 60431.
- Labor Record. w. ISSN 0023-6616 (Will County
Federation of Labor)

**Labor Research Association**
80 E. 11th St., New York, NY 10003.
- Economic Notes. m. ISSN 0013-0184

**Labor Today Associates**
343 S. Dearborn St., Rm.600, Chicago, IL 60604.
- Labor Today; a monthly journal and independent
forum for organized labor. m.(Sept.-July) ISSN
0023-6640

**Labor Tribune Publishing Co.**
7777 Bonhomme, Suite 1000, St. Louis, MO 63105.
- St. Louis Labor Tribune; the offical weekly AFL-
cIo newspaper. w.
- Southern Illinois Labor Tribune. w.

**Labor World Inc.**
2002 London Rd., Room 102, Duluth, MN 55812.
- Labor World. w. ISSN 0023-6667 (A.F.L.-C.I.O
Labor Organizations)

**Labor Zionist Alliance**
- Yiddisher Kemfer. (pub. by Labor Zionist Letters,
Inc.)

**Labor Zionist Letters, Inc.**
575 Sixth Ave., New York, NY 10011.
- Jewish Frontier. m. ISSN 0021-6453
- Yiddisher Kemfer. w. ISSN 0044-0434 (Labor
Zionist Alliance)

**Laboratory of Climatology, Centerton, N.J.**
- Publications in Climatology. (pub. by C. W.
Thornwaite)

**Laborers' International Union of North America**
905 16th St., N.W., Washington, DC 20006.
- Laborer. m. ISSN 0023-6888

**Gary H. Labowitz, Ed. & Pub.**
1100 Betzwood Dr., Norristown, PA 19401.
- Canticles from Labowitz. 4 per yr. ISSN 0008-
5707

**Lackawanna Bar Association**
Court House, Scranton, PA 18503.
- Lackawanna Jurist. w. ISSN 0023-7078

**Ladue Board of Education**
9703 Conway Rd., St. Louis, MO 63124.
- Ladue Public Schools Bulletin. bi-m. ISSN 0023-
7140

**Robert E. Ladum**
Box 3499, Portland, OR 97208.
- Wall Street Coin Investor. fortn.

**Laging Una**
c/o M. M. Monosco, 3003 Future Place, Los
Angeles, CA 90065.
- Laging Una. m. ISSN 0300-7855

**Andre Laguerre**
551 Fifth Ave., New York, NY 10017.
- Classic; the magazine about horses and sport. bi-
m. (Classic Partners)

**Lahey Clinic Foundation**
605 Commonwealth Ave., Boston, MA 02215.
- Lahey Clinic Foundation Bulletin. q. ISSN 0023-
7299

**Laissez Faire Books**
206 Mercer St., New York, NY 10012.
- Laissez Faire Anarchist Catalog. a.
- Laissez Faire Libertarian Catalog. s-a.

**Lake Carriers' Association**
1411 Superior Ave. N.W., Cleveland, OH 44113.
- Lake Carriers' Association. Annual Report. a.
ISSN 0075-7748
- Lake Carriers' Association Bulletin. 3-4 per yr.
ISSN 0023-7329

**Lake Placid Education Foundation. Forest Press
Division**
85 Watervliet Ave., Albany, NY 12206.
- Dewey Decimal Classification, Additions, Notes
and Decisions. irreg., vol. 3, 1974.

**Lake Publishing Corporation**
700 Peterson Rd., Box 159, Libertyville, IL 60048.
- Insulation/Circuits; for the electrical and
electronic manufacturing industries. m. ISSN
0020-4544
- Insulation/Circuits Desk Manual; for the
electrical/electronic industries. a.
- Plastics Design & Processing. m. ISSN 0032-1176

**Lake Region Publishing Corp.**
- Citrus World. (pub. by Mike Zotti)

**Lake Shore Club**
850 Lake Shore Dr., Chicago, IL 60611.
- Discus. ISSN 0012-3676

**Lake Superior Review**
Box 724, Ironwood, MI 49938.
- Lake Superior Review; magazine of the arts. 3 per
yr.

**Lake Superior State College**
Sault Ste. Marie, MI 49783.
- Woods-Runner. 5 per yr.

**Lake Survey Center**
see under U.S. National Ocean Survey

**Lakewood Publications, Inc.**
731 Hennepin Ave., Minneapolis, MN 55403.
- Airport Services Management; the management
magazine for airports and airport-based
operations. m. ISSN 0002-2829
- Food Plant Ideas. bi-m. ISSN 0015-6515
- Potentials in Marketing. m (9 per yr) ISSN 0032-
5619
- Training; the magazine of manpower and
management development. m. ISSN 0095-5892

**Cene Lamb, Ed. & Pub.**
2403 Champa St., Denver, CO 80205.
- Western Wear & Equipment. bi-m. ISSN 0043-
4280

**Lambda Alpha Honor Society**
Wichita State University, Department of
Anthropology, Wichita, KS 67208.
- Lambda Alpha Journal of Man. s-a. ISSN 0047-3928

**Lambda Kappa Sigma International Pharmaceutical Sorority**
c/o Avon Printing Co. Inc., 401 Main St.,
Rochester, MI 48063.
- Blue and Gold Triangle of Lamba Kappa Sigma. 5 nos. every 2 years. ISSN 0006-503X

**Julia M. Lampkin-Asom, Ed. & Pub.**
P.O. Box 2115, Tuscaloosa, AL 35401.
- Malignant Intrigue. irreg. ISSN 0076-342X

**Lamplight Enterprises, Inc.**
180 Madison Ave., New York, NY 10016.
- All Time Baseball Greats. a.
- All Time Football Greats. q.
- Daily T V Serials.

**Lamplighter**
Box 2064, Springfield, IL 62705.
- Lamplighter. q.

**Lancaster County Historical Society**
230 N. President Ave., Lancaster, PA 17603.
- Lancaster County Historical Society. Journal. q. ISSN 0023-7477

**Lancaster Farming**
22 E. Main St., Lititz, PA 17543.
- Lancaster Farming. w. ISSN 0023-7485

**Lancaster Magazine**
229 East Chestnut St., Lancaster, PA 17602.
- Lancaster Magazine. m.

**Lancaster Mennonite Conference Historical Society**
2215 Millstream Rd., Lancaster, PA 17602.
- Mennonite Research Journal. q. ISSN 0025-9381
- Mirror. bi-m. (Co-sponsor: Mennonite Historical Associates)

**Lancet Publications, Inc.**
4015 W. 65th St., Minneapolis, MN 55435.
- Geriatrics; devoted to diseases and processes of aging. m. ISSN 0016-867X (American Geriatrics Society)
- Neurology. m. ISSN 0028-3878 (American Academy of Neurology)

**Land Data Corporation**
14 Executive Park Drive, Atlanta, GA 30329.
- Metro Atlanta Builder. bi-m.
- Real Estate Atlanta Magazine. m.

**Land Improvement Contractors of America**
Box 1376, Fort Dodge, IA 50501.
- Land & Water. q.

**Landers Associates**
Box 69760, Los Angeles, CA 90069.
- Landers Film Reviews. 5 per yr. ISSN 0023-785X

**Dennis Landman Publishers**
1150 18th St., Santa Monica, CA 90404.
- Inside Your Government. bi-w.

**Landscape**
Ed. Blair Boyd, Box 7177 Landscape Station,
Berkeley, CA 94707.
- Landscape. 3 per yr. ISSN 0023-8023

**Landslide (Eureka)**
c/o Thomas Collins, Ed., Box 1347, Eureka, CA 95501.
- Landslide (Eureka); the slope stability review. s-a. ISSN 0093-0679

**Lane Publishing Co.**
85 Willow Rd., Menlo Park, CA 94025.
- Sunset; the magazine of Western living. m. ISSN 0039-5404
- Sunset Christmas Ideas and Answers. a.
- Sunset Ideas for Improving Your Home. s-a. ISSN 0099-2313
- Sunset Joy of Gardening. a.

**Langdon Publishing Co.**
1609 W. Windrove, Phoenix, AZ 85029.
- Advanced Solar Energy Technology Newsletter. m.

**Lange Medical Publications**
Drawer L, Los Altos, CA 94022.
- Correlative Neuroanatomy & Functional Neurology. triennial.
- Current Medical Diagnosis and Treatment. a.
- Current Pediatric Diagnosis & Treatment. biennial.
- Current Surgical Diagnosis & Treatment. biennial.
- General Ophthalmology. triennial.
- General Urology. triennial.
- Handbook of Obstetrics and Gynecology. triennial.
- Handbook of Pediatrics. biennial. ISSN 0440-1921
- Handbook of Poisoning: Diagnosis and Treatment. triennial.
- Handbook of Psychiatry. triennial.
- Physician's Handbook. triennial. ISSN 0079-192X
- Principles of Clinical Electrocardiography. triennial. ISSN 0552-0975
- Review of Medical Microbiology. biennial. ISSN 0486-6118
- Review of Medical Pharmacology. biennial. ISSN 0557-7519
- Review of Medical Physiology. biennial.
- Review of Physiological Chemistry. biennial. ISSN 0080-1976

**Language Americas Association**
1250 National Press Bldg., Washington, DC 20004.
- Interamerican Scene. q. ISSN 0020-5141
- L A M A's Travel Digest for Latin America. bi-m. ISSN 0094-5013

**Language by Radio Interest Group**
University of Alabama in Birmingham, Sterne
Library, University Station, Birmingham, AL 35294.
- L B R I G Newsletter. s-a.

**Language Learning Systems Inc**
101 S. Whiting St., P.O. Box 9340, Alexandria, VA 22304.
- Quinto Lingo; multi-lingual magazine. m. (American National Heritage Association)

**Lapidary Journal, Inc.**
Box 80937, San Diego, CA 92138.
- Lapidary Journal. m. ISSN 0023-8457

**Large Families of America, Inc.**
54 Miller St., Fairfield, CT 06430.
- Large Family News. q.

**Larimi Communications Ltd.**
151 E. 50 St., New York, NY 10022.
- Television Contacts. a.

**Larkin Publications, Inc.**
210 Boylston St., Chestnut Hill, MA 02167.
- Boutique Fashions. 10 per yr.
- Kids Fashions. 8 per yr.
- Music Retailer; merchandising sound of the music industry. m.
- New England Fashion Retailer. m.

**William Larsen, Jr., Ed. & Pub.**
Box 36068, Los Angeles, CA 90036.
- Genii-the Conjurors' Magazine. m. ISSN 0016-6855

**Larue D. Carter Memorial Hospital**
Medical Library, 1315 W. 10th St., Indianapolis, IN 46202.
- Mnemonic; bi-monthly bulletin of the Medical Library. bi-m. ISSN 0026-7066

**Laryngoscope Co.**
222 Pine Lake Rd., Collinsville, IL 62234.
- Laryngoscope; a monthly journal on diseases of the ear, nose and throat. m. ISSN 0023-852X (American Laryngological, Rhinological and Otological Society)

**Las Vegas Israelite**
Box 10496, Las Vegas, NV 89114.
- Las Vegas Israelite. w.

**Las Vegas Voice Inc.**
616 N. H St., Las Vegas, NV 89106.
- Las Vegas Voice. w. ISSN 0023-8546

**Lasersphere**
c/o William E. Bushor, RR 3, Box 290, Michigan City, IN 46360.
- Lasersphere. m. ISSN 0047-4118

**J. K. Lasser Institute**
- J. K. Lasser's Your Income Tax. (pub. by Simon and Schuster, Inc.)

- J. K. Lasser's Your Income Tax, Professional Ed. (pub. by Simon and Schuster, Inc.)

**Latham Publications Inc.**
Box 328, Conroe, TX 77301.
- Lost Treasure. m.
- Rockhound; where and how to find gems & minerals. bi-m. ISSN 0048-847X

**Tony Lathrop**
726 Butterfield Rd., Oak Brook Terrace, Chicago, IL 60181.
- Everyday. s-a.

**Norman Lathrop Enterprises**
2342 Star Drive, Wooster, OH 44691.
- Index to How to do It Information. a. ISSN 0073-5930

**Latimer Publications**
9000 Sunset Boulevard, Suite 1510, Los Angeles, CA 90069.
- Songwriter Magazine. m. ISSN 0362-7373

**Latin American Documentation**
1312 Massachuetts Ave. N.W., Washington, DC 20005.
- L A D O C. m.
- L A D O C "Keyhole" Series. irreg.

**Latin American Index, Ltd.**
Suite 502, 1835 K St. N.W., Washington, DC 20006.
- Latin American Index. s-m. ISSN 0090-9416

**Latin American Perspectives, Inc.**
Box 792, Riverside, CA 92502.
- Latin American Perspectives; a journal of capitalism and socialism. 4 per yr. ISSN 0094-582X

**Latin American Policy Alternatives Group**
2434 Guadalupe, Austin, TX 78705.
- U R L A Newsletter. (Union of Radical Latin Americanists) q.

**Latin American Studies Association**
c/o Felicity M. Trueblood, Exec. Sec., Box 13362
University Sta., Gainesville, FL 32604
- Latin American Research Review; a journal to achieve greater and more systematic communication among individuals and institutions concerned with scholarly studies of Latin America. 3 per yr. ISSN 0023-8791 (Orders to: Latin American Research Review, Hamilton Hall, University of North Carolina, Chapel Hill, NC 27514)
- Latin American Studies Association Newsletter. q. ISSN 0023-8805

**Latin New York**
234 W. 55th St., New York, NY 10019.
- Latin New York. q.

**Latvian Literary Society Celinieks**
7012 Church St., Morton Grove, IL 60053.
- Mazputnins; Latvian children's magazine. m. ISSN 0025-6218

**Laubach Literacy Inc.**
Box 131, Syracuse, NY 13210.
- Literacy Advance. q. ISSN 0047-4142 (National Affiliation for Literacy Advance)

**Laufer Publishing Co.**
7060 Hollywood Blvd., Hollywood, CA 90028.
- Right On. m. ISSN 0048-8305
- Tiger Beat. m. ISSN 0040-7380

**Laughing Bear**
Box 14, Woodinville, WA 98072.
- Laughing Bear. 3 per yr.

**Laurance Press Co**
400 First St. S. East, Cedar Rapids, IA 52401.
- B I O S. 4 per yr. ISSN 0005-3155 (Beta Beta Beta National Biological Society)

**Laurel Press**
1605 N. Martel Ave., Los Angeles, CA 90046.
- Openspaces. irreg.

**Laventhol & Horwath**
1845 Walnut St, Philadelphia, PA 19103.
- Laventhol and Horwath Perspective; semiannual publication covering subjects of general business and financial interest. s-a.

- U. S. Lodging Industry; annual report on hotel and motor hotel operations. a.
- Worldwide Lodging Industry; annual report on international hotel operations. a. ISSN 0361-218X

**Law and Society Association**
200 W. 14th Ave., Denver, CO 80204.
- Law & Society Review. q. ISSN 0023-9216

**Law-Arts Publishers Inc.**
453 Greenwich St., New York, NY 10013.
- Performing Arts Review; the journal of management & law of the arts. q. ISSN 0031-5249 (American Institute for Performing & Fine Arts Management, Inc.)

**Law Bulletin Publishing Co.**
415 N. State St., Chicago, IL 60610.
- Chicagoland's Real Estate Advertiser. w. ISSN 0009-3769

**Moody T. Law, Ed. & Pub.**
P.O. Box 1026, Pomona, CA 91766.
- Pomona Clarion. w.

**Law in American Society Foundation**
33 North Lasalle St., Suite 1700, Chicago, IL 60602.
- Justice in America Series. (pub. by Houghton Mifflin Co.)
- Law in American Society. q. (National Center for Law-Focused Education)

**Law Publications, Inc.**
1180 S. Beverly Dr., Los Angeles, CA 90035.
- Lawyer's Newsletter. bi-m.

**Law Reprints, Inc.**
37 W. 20 St., New York, NY 10011.
- Law Reprints. Trade Regulation Series. irreg. ISSN 0075-8256

**Gary Lawless, Ed. & Pub.**
Box 186, Brunswick, Me 04079.
- Blackberry Books. irreg.
- Salted in the Shell. 6-8 per yr.

**William Lawrence Corp.**
Box 2830, Newport Beach, CA 92663.
- Bicycle Dealer Showcase. m. ISSN 0361-381X

**Lawsearch, Inc.**
Box 5508, Derwood, MD 20855.
- Recent Developments in Maryland Law. fortn. ISSN 0363-8006

**Lawyer-Pilots Bar Association**
2908 First National Tower, Portland, OR 97201.
- Legal Eagles News. m.(except July & Aug.) ISSN 0024-0354

**Lawyer to Lawyer Consultation Panel**
5325 Naiman Pkwy, Solon, OH 44139.
- Lawyer-to-Lawyer Consultation Panel. a. ISSN 0091-0430

**Lawyers Co-Operative Publishing Co.**
Aqueduct Bldg., Rochester, NY 14603.
- Case and Comment. bi-m. ISSN 0008-7238
- Lawyer's Medical Journal. q. ISSN 0023-947X

**Lawyers Title Insurance Corporation**
Box 27567, Richmond, VA 23261.
- Lawyers Title News. bi-m.

**Laymen's Home Missionary Movement**
Chester Springs, PA 19425.
- Bible Standard and Herald of Christ's Kingdom. m. ISSN 0006-081X
- Present Truth and Herald of Christ's Epiphany. bi-m. ISSN 0032-7700

**Laymen's Movement for a Christian World, Inc.**
- Trends (Rye) (pub. by Center for the Development of Human Resources)

**Lea & Febiger**
600 Washington Sq., Philadelphia, PA 19106.
- Progress in Cardiology. a. ISSN 0097-109X

**Lead Industries Association, Inc.**
292 Madison Ave., New York, NY 10017.
- Kettering Abstracts of Available Literature on the Biological and Related Aspects of Lead and Its Compounds. (pub. by Kettering Laboratory)
- Lead. s-a. ISSN 0023-9550

**Leader-Observer, Inc.**
80-34 Jamaica Ave., Woodhaven, NY 11421.
- Realty. fortn.

**Leader Publications Inc.**
11 Warren St., New York, NY 10007.
- Civil Service Leader. w. ISSN 0009-8000

**Leadership Resources (Washington)**
1750 Pennsylvania Ave., Washington, DC 20006.
- Looking into Leadership Series. irreg. ISSN 0076-0889

**Leadership Resources Inc.**
6400 Arlington Blvd., Falls Church, VA 22042.
- Management Monographs. irreg. ISSN 0076-3640

**League for Economic Democracy**
Box 1858, San Pedro, CA 90733.
- Synthesis. q.

**League for Industrial Democracy**
112 E. 19 St., New York, NY 10003.
- Looking Forward; a series of occasional papers. irreg., no. 18, 1971. ISSN 0076-0870

**League for International Food Education**
1126 16th St., N.W., Rm. 404, Washington, DC 20036.
- L.I.F.E. Newsletter. m.

**League for Socialist Reconstruction**
Box 80, Madison Square Garden, New York, NY 10010.
- Socialist Republic. 6 per yr.

**League of California Cities**
Hotel Claremont, Berkeley, CA 94705.
- Western City. m. ISSN 0043-356X

**League of Iowa Municipalities**
444 Insurance Exchange Bldg., Des Moines, IA 50309.
- Iowa Municipalities. 12 per yr. ISSN 0021-0595

**League of Kansas Municipalities**
112 W. Seventh St., Topeka, KS 66603.
- Kansas Government Journal. m. ISSN 0022-8613

**League of Minnesota Cities**
300 Hanover Building, 480 Cedar St., St. Paul, MN 55101.
- Minnesota Cities. m.

**League of Minnesota Poets**
Star Route, Box 66, Brimson, MN 55602.
- Moccasin. s-a. ISSN 0026-7244

**League of Nebraska Municipalities**
Coryell Bldg., 1320 J St., Lincoln, NE 68508.
- Nebraska Municipal Review. m. ISSN 0028-1905

**League of United Latin American Citizens (LULAC)**
- Adelante S E R. (pub. by S E R-Jobs for Progress, Inc.)

**League of Wisconsin Municipalities**
122 W. Washington Ave., Madison, WI 53703.
- Municipality. m. ISSN 0027-3597

**League of Women Voters of Massachusetts**
120 Boylston St., Boston, MA 02116.
- State House Reporter. fortn. during legislative session.

**League of Women Voters of the City of New York**
817 Broadway, New York, NY 10003.
- League of Women Voters of the City of New York. Quarterly Review. q.

**League of Women Voters of the U.S.**
1730 M St., N .W., 10th A., Washington, DC 20036.
- National Voter. 4 per yr. ISSN 0028-0372

**League of Women Voters of Washington**
1406 18th Ave., Seattle, WA 98122.
- Washington State Voter. bi-m. ISSN 0043-0846

**Learning Exchange**
P.O. Box 920, Evanston, IL 60204.
- Learning Exchange News. q.

**Learning Resources Corporation**
2817-N Dorr Avenue, Fairfax, VA 22030.
- Learning Resources Corporation. Selected Reading Services. irreg., 1969, no. 9. ISSN 0077-5908

**Leasco Corporation**
280 Park Ave., New York, NY 10017.
- Reliance Group. 3 per yr.

**Leathercraftsman, Inc.**
Box 1386, Fort Worth, TX 76101.
- Make It with Leather. bi-m.

**Lebanon Valley College Student Council**
Annville, PA 17003.
- Vie Collegienne. m. ISSN 0300-7596

**Lebhar-Friedman, Inc.**
425 Park Ave., New York, NY 10022.
- C S A Co-Ops & Voluntaries. m.
- C S A Specs Buying Guide for Store Planners. (Chain Store Age) irreg. ISSN 0098-3047
- Chain Store Age Drug Edition. m.
- Chain Store Age General Merchandise Edition. m.
- Chain Store Age Supermarket Sales Manual. a. ISSN 0069-2395
- Discount Store News. fortn. ISSN 0012-3587
- National Home Center News. bi-w.
- Nation's Restaurant News; the newspaper of the food service industry. 25 per yr. ISSN 0028-0518

**Edward T. LeBlanc, Ed. & Pub.**
87 School St., Fall River, MA 02720.
- Dime Novel Round-Up; devoted to the collecting, preservation and literature of the old time dime and nickel novels, libraries and popular story papers. m. ISSN 0012-2874

**G. Leblanc Corporation**
7019 30th Ave., Kenosha, WI 53141.
- Leblanc World of Music. irreg. ISSN 0361-5758

**LeBlanc Research Corporation**
5454 Post Rd., E. Greenwich, RI 02818.
- Plastics Flammability Patents. m.
- Textile Flammability Digest. m.

**Lederle Laboratories**
515 Madison Ave., New York, NY 10022.
- Dermatology in Practice. 6 per yr. ISSN 0046-0001

**Lee County Historical Society**
Box 58, Dixon, IL 61021.
- Lee County Historical Society. Historical Yearbook. a.

**Hubert F. Lee, Ed. & Pub.**
P.O. Box 119, Atlanta, GA 30301
(Subscr. to: 4592 Covington Hwy., Decatur, GA 30032)
- Dixie Business; the voice of Southern progress. q.

**Lee Publishing Co.**
3540 4th Ave., Sacramento, CA 95817.
- Sacramento Observer. w. ISSN 0036-2212

**Curtis E. Lees and Associates**
2704 Lyndale Lane, Box 911, Billings, MT 59103.
- Montana Beverage News. m. ISSN 0026-9913

**Lee's Mardi Gras Enterprises, Inc.**
Box 1271, New York, NY 10009.
- Drag. q.

**Lee's Philatelist**
Box St, Shrub Oak, NY 10588.
- Lee's Philatelist. m.

**Leeward Publications Inc.**
Box 12415, Charlotte, NC 28205.
- Textile Equipment. m.

**Left Curve**
1230 Grant Ave., Box 302, San Francisco, CA 94133.
- Left Curve; art & revolution. irreg.

**Legal-Medical Studies, Inc.**
Box 8219, John F. Kennedy Station, Boston, MA 02114.
- Reporter on Human Reproduction & the Law; cases, statutes and materials on law and life sciences. bi-m.

**Legal Medicine Press**
2531 Coventry Rd., Columbus, OH 43221.
- Index of Legal Medicine. q. ISSN 0046-886X

**Legal Research Institute, Inc.**
600 W. Evergreen, San Antonio, TX 78212.
- Real Estate Law Brief Case. m. ISSN 0034-0758

**Legation of Latvia**
4325-17th St. N.W., Washington, DC 20011.
- Latvian Information Bulletin. q.

**Legion for Survival of Freedom Inc.**
Box 1306, Torrance, CA 90505.
- American Mercury. q.

**Legislative Research International**
P.O. Box 1511, Washington, DC 20013.
- News from the Hill. m.

**Lehigh University**
Bethlehem, PA 18105
- Journal of Differential Geometry. q. ISSN 0022-040X (Subscr. to: American Mathematical Society, Box 6248, Providence, RI 02940)
- Lehigh University. Annual Reading Conference. Proceedings. (pub. by Interstate Printers and Publishers, Inc.)

**Lehigh Valley Labor Council and AFL-CIO Union Council of Northampton and Warren County**
809 No. 4th St., Box 206, Allentown, PA 18105.
- Lehigh Valley Labor Herald. w. ISSN 0024-0559

**Lehigh Valley Motor Club**
1020 Hamilton St., Allentown, PA 18105.
- Lehigh Valley Motor Club News. bi-m.

**Herbert Leibowitz, Ed. & Pub.**
205 West 89 Street, New York, NY 10024.
- Parnassus: Poetry in Review. s-a. ISSN 0048-3028

**Leisure Publications, Inc.**
3923 W. 6th St., Los Angeles, CA 90020.
- Pool 'n Patio. s-a. ISSN 0032-4272
- Pool News; swimming pool industry news. s-m. ISSN 0032-4280
- Pool News Directory. a.

**Leisure Time Institute**
Box 721, New Rochelle, NY 10802.
- Leisure Time. bi-m. ISSN 0024-0729

**Leisureguides, Inc.**
1515 N.W. 167 St., Miami, FL 33169.
- Leisureguide - Chicago. a.
- Leisureguide - Grand Strand (Myrtle Beach, S.C.) a.
- Leisureguide - the Florida Gold Coast. a.

**Russell G. Leiter, Ed. & Pub.**
1828 Summit St., Portsmouth, OH 45662.
- Psychological Service Center Journal. a.

**Leman Publications, Inc.**
Box 394, Wheat Ridge, CO 80033.
- Quilter's Newsletter. m.

**Alberto S. Lemos, Ed. & Pub.**
1912 Church Lane, San Pablo, CA 94806.
- Portuguese Journal/Jornal Portugues. w. ISSN 0032-5163

**Lemoyne College**
Syracuse, NY 13214.
- Oral English. q.

**Lending Law Forum, Inc.**
Box 85, Rockville Centre, New York, NY 11570.
- Lending Law Forum. 8 per yr. ISSN 0098-891X

**Lenoir Rhyne College. English Dept.**
Hickory, NC 28601.
- Graffiti. s-a.

**Lenore Schwartz Leukemia Research Foundation. Research Information Service**
- Leukemia Abstracts. (pub. by John Crerar Library)

**Lenox Hill Publishing and Distributing Corporation**
235 E. 44th St., New York, NY 10017.
- Burt Franklin American Classics in History and Social Sciences. irreg., 1973, no. 246. ISSN 0068-4287
- Burt Franklin Art History and Art Reference Series. irreg., 1973, no. 44. ISSN 0068-4295
- Burt Franklin Bibliography and Reference Series. irreg. ISSN 0068-4309
- Burt Franklin Essays in History, Economics, and Social Sciences. irreg. ISSN 0068-4317
- Burt Franklin Essays in Literature and Criticism. irreg., 1973, no. 300. ISSN 0068-4325
- Burt Franklin Research and Source Works Series. irreg. ISSN 0068-4341

- Monographs in Philosophy and Religious History. irreg. (approx. 25 per yr); 1973, no. 129. ISSN 0068-4333

**Lepidoptera Research Foundation, Inc.**
Santa Barbara Museum of Natural History, 2559 Puesta del Sol Rd., Santa Barbara, CA 93105.
- Journal of Research on the Lepidoptera. q. ISSN 0022-4324

**Lepidopterists Society**
Peabody Museum, Entomology Department, Yale Univ., New Haven, CT 06520.
- Lepidopterist's Society. Journal. q. ISSN 0024-0966
- Lepidopterists' Society. Memoirs. irreg. ISSN 0075-8795 (Orders to: Dr. Lee D. Miller, Sec., Allyn Museum of Entomology, 3701 Bay Shore Rd., Sarasota, FL 33580)

**Le'sbeinformed**
2104 Stevens Ave., Minneapolis, MN 55404.
- Le'sbeinformed. m.

**Lesbian Alliance Newsletter**
Box 4201, Tower Grove Sta., St. Louis, MO 63163.
- Lesbian Alliance Newsletter. m.

**Lesbian Feminist**
c/o L F L, 243 W. 20th St., New York, NY 10011.
- Lesbian Feminist. m.

**Lesbian Front**
Box 8342, Jackson, MS 39204.
- Lesbian Front. m.

**Lesbian Resource Center**
- So's Your Old Lady. (pub. by Haymarket Press)

**Lesbian Switchboard**
University YMCA, 306 N. Brooks St., Madison, WI 53715.
- We Got It. m.

**Lesstrang Publishing Corporation**
3750 Nixon Road, Ann Arbor, MI 48105.
- The Great Lakes Ports of North America. biennial.

**Letz Co. Inc.**
Box 2386, Fort Worth, TX 76101.
- Santa Gertrudis Journal. m. ISSN 0036-455X

**Leviathan**
c/o S I M C H A, Redwood Building, University of California, Santa Cruz, CA 95064.
- Leviathan. 3 per yr.

**Levin Publishing Co., Inc.**
651 Brannan St., San Francisco, CA 94107.
- Key: This Week in San Francisco and Northern California. w. ISSN 0023-0820

**S. Jay Levy, Ed. & Pub.**
Box 26, Chappaqua, NY 10514.
- Industry Forecast. 11 per yr. (or more)

**Lewis & Clark Law School**
Northwestern School of Law, 10015 S.W. Terwilliger Blvd., OR 97219.
- Environmental Law. 3 per yr. ISSN 0046-2276

**Lewis & Clark Trail Heritage Foundation, Inc.**
Old Courthouse, 11 N. 4th St., St. Louis, MO 63102
- We Proceeded On. q. (Inquire, Bus. Mgr.: E. G. Chuinard, 3025 N. Vancouver Ave., Portland OR 97227)

**A.F. Lewis and Co. of New York, Inc.**
c/o Harrie F. Lewis, 853 Broadway, New York, NY 10003.
- Graphic Arts Green Book. a.
- Printing Trades Blue Book. New York Edition; directory of graphic arts operating firms in metropolitan New York and New Jersey. a. ISSN 0079-5348
- Printing Trades Blue Book. Northeastern Edition; directory of graphic arts operating firms in New England and upstate New York. biennial. ISSN 0079-5356
- Printing Trades Blue Book. Southeastern Edition; directory of graphic arts operating firms from Pennsylvania south through Florida. biennial. ISSN 0079-5364

**Lewis Carroll Society of North America**
617 Rockford Rd., Silver Spring, MD 20902.
- Carroll Studies. a.

**George Q. Lewis, Ed. & Pub.**
Box 835, Grand Central Sta., New York, NY 10017.
- Humor Exchange Newsletter. m. ISSN 0018-764X (Humor Exchange Network)

**Lewis Publishing Co.**
P.O. Box 153, Lynden, WA 98264.
- Farm Review. m.

**Lewis University. Correctional Programs**
1s 101 Route 53 & Roosevelt Rd., Glen Ellyn, IL 60137.
- Candle (Chicago); correctional program news. bi-m.

**Lexington Books**
(Subsidiary of: D. C. Heath Company)
125 Spring St., Lexington, MA 02173.
- Voluntary Action Research Series. irreg.

**Lexington Library**
355 Lexington Ave., New York, NY 10017.
- In the Know. m. ISSN 0098-3055

**Lexington Philharmonic Society**
Box 838, Lexington, KY 40501.
- Lexington Philharmonic Society Newsletter. 5 per yr. ISSN 0024-161X

**Lexington School for the Deaf. Parents Association**
26-26 75th St., Jackson Heights, NY 11370.
- Sounds of Lexington. m. (11 per yr.)

**Lexington Theological Seminary**
631 S. Limestone St., Lexington, KY 40508.
- Lexington Theological Quarterly. q. ISSN 0024-1628

**Peter Li, Inc**
2451 E. River Rd., Dayton, OH 45439.
- Catechist. m. ISSN 0008-7726
- Today's Catholic Teacher. m(Sept.-May) ISSN 0040-8441

**Liberal Religious Youth, Inc.**
25 Beacon St., Boston, MA 02108.
- People Soup. 8 per yr.

**Liberation Publications (Milwaukee)**
P.O. Box 92203, Milwaukee, WI 53202.
- G. P. U. News. (Gay People's Union) m.

**Liberation Support Movement**
Box 2077, Oakland, Canada, CA 94604.
- L S M News. q. ISSN 0315-1840

**Liberator Press**
1404 Grand Ave., Fort Worth, TX 76106.
- Liberator; an independent journal of commentary on feminist issues. m.

**Libertarian Alternative Newsletter**
Box 15011, San Diego, CA 92115.
- Libertarian Alternative Newsletter. m.

**Libertarian Forum**
Box 341, Madison Sq. Station, New York, NY 10010.
- Libertarian Forum. m. ISSN 0047-4517

**Libertarian Press Service**
Box 444, Westfield, NJ 07091.
- Libertarian Press Service. m.

**Libertarian Republican Alliance**
1811 E. 34th St., Brooklyn, NY 11234.
- Limit. m.

**Libertarian Review, Inc.**
200 Park Ave. S., New York, NY 10003.
- Libertarian Review. m.

**Libertarian Scholar**
Box 394, DeKalb, IL 60115.
- Libertarian Scholar. q.

**Liberty Bell Publications**
(Subsidiary of: Raybar, Inc.)
Reedy, WV 25270.
- Liberty Bell. m.

**Liberty Library Corp.**
250 W. 57th St., New York, NY 10019.
- Liberty, Then and Now; the nostalgia magazine. q. ISSN 0360-3342

**Liberty Lowdown**
300 Independence Ave. S.E., Washington, DC 20003.
- Liberty Lowdown. m.

**Libra Publishers, Inc.**
391 Willets Rd., Roslyn Heights, L.I., NY 11577.
- Adolescence. q. ISSN 0001-8449
- Family Therapy. 3 per yr. ISSN 0091-6544 (Family Therapy Institute of Marin)

**Libraries Unlimited, Inc.**
Box 263, Littleton, CO 80160.
- American Reference Books Annual. a. ISSN 0065-9959
- Challenge to Change: Library Applications of New Concepts. irreg; no. 2, 1977.
- Government Reference Books; a biennial guide to U.S. Government publications. biennial. ISSN 0072-5188
- Guide to Reference Books for School Media Centers. irreg.
- Heritage of Librarianship Series. irreg. (1-3 per yr.)
- Research Studies in Library Science. irreg. ISSN 0080-1739

**Library Associates, Inc.**
P.O. Box 3411, Boulder, CO 80303.
- Reference Book Guides. bi-m.

**Library Associates of Brooklyn College, Inc.**
c/o Ed. Prof. Harold D. Jones, Library Dept., Brooklyn College, Brooklyn, NY 11210.
- Library Associate. irreg. ISSN 0024-2187

**Library Association of the City University of New York**
Baruch College Library, Lexington Ave. & 23rd St., New York, NY 10010.
- L A C U N Y Journal. q. ISSN 0094-615X
- L A C U N Y Occasional Papers. 3 per yr. ISSN 0094-615X

**Library Binding Institute**
50 Congress St., Boston, MA 02109.
- Library Scene. q. ISSN 0090-8746

**Library-College Associates, Inc.**
Box 956, Norman, OK 73070.
- Learning Today; an educational magazine of library-college thought. 8 per yr. (plus supplement: Omnibus) ISSN 0091-7281
- Library-College Experimenter. 3 per yr.
- Library-College Omnibus. q.

**Library of Congress**
see U. S. Library of Congress

**Library of Congress Professional Association**
Washington, DC 20540.
- Library of Congress Professional Association. Newsletter. m. ISSN 0041-4913

**Library Publicity Clippings**
Box 742, Santa Ana, CA 92702.
- Library Publicity Clippings. 10 per yr. ISSN 0024-2500

**Library Trustees Foundation of New York State**
71 W. 23rd St., Box 208, New York, NY 10010.
- Library Trustees Foundation of New York State. Newsletter. q. ISSN 0047-4541

**Licensed Beverage Journal Inc.**
c/o Ed. & Pub. Norman J. Bogart, 2917 Bruckner Blvd., Bronx, NY 10461.
- Licensed Beverage Journal. s-m. ISSN 0024-2764

**Licensed Practical Nurses of New York, Inc.**
250 W. 57th St., New York, NY 10019.
- New York L P N. q. ISSN 0028-730X

**Licensing Executives Society, Inc.**
c/o Jack Stuart Ott, Ed., 1225 Elbur Ave., Cleveland, OH 44107.
- Les Nouvelles. 4 per yr. ISSN 0047-4576

**Lick Observatory. Library**
University of California, Santa Cruz, Santa Cruz, CA 95060.
- Lick Observatory. Publications. irreg., 1967, vol. 22. ISSN 0075-9325

- Lick Observatory Bulletin. irreg.(8-9 per yr.) ISSN 0075-9317

**Lieber-Atherton, Inc.**
1841 Broadway, New York, NY 10023.
- Nomos. a. ISSN 0078-0979 (American Society for Political and Legal Philosophy)

**Life Foundation, Inc.**
Box 37, Austell, GA 30001.
- Health for Life. q. ISSN 0046-7057
- Today's Chiropractic. m.

**Life Insurance Marketing and Research Association (LIMRA)**
170 Sigourney St., Hartford, CT 06105.
- Current Practices; a summary bulletin of information. m. ISSN 0011-3832
- Life Insurance Marketing and Research Association. Proceedings of the Annual Meeting. a.
- Manager's Magazine. m. ISSN 0025-1968

**Life Insurers Conference**
1004 N. Thompson St., Box 6856, Richmond, VA 23230.
- Life Insurers Conference. Annual Proceedings. a. ISSN 0075-9414

**Life Office Management Association**
100 Park Ave., New York, NY 10017.
- L. O. M. A. Resource. bi-m.
- Life Office Management Association. Annual Conference. Proceedings of Concurrent Sessions. a.

**Life Underwriters Association of the City of New York**
500 Fifth Ave., New York, NY 10036.
- Life Underwriters' Association of the City of New York, Inc. Bulletin. m. ISSN 0024-3221

**Lifestyle Publishing Co., Inc.**
3609 Marconi Ave., Sacramento, CA 95821.
- Sacramento Valley. bi-m.

**Light**
Box 1105, New York, NY 10009.
- Light; a poetry review. q.

**Light and Life Press**
Winona Lake, IN 46590.
- Discovery (Winona Lake) w. ISSN 0039-2022 (Free Methodist Church of North America)
- Light and Life. s-m. ISSN 0024-3299 (Free Methodist Church of North America)
- Reachout. w. ISSN 0040-2036 (Free Methodist Church of North America)

**The Lighter Than Air Society**
1800 Triplett Blvd., Akron, OH 44306.
- Buoyant Flight. bi-m.

**Lightner Publishing Corporation**
1006 S. Michigan Ave., Chicago, IL 60605.
- Hobbies; the magazine for collectors. m. ISSN 0018-2907

**Kathleen Lignell, Ed. & Pub.**
861 Arlington Blvd., El Cerrito, CA 94530.
- Pro Musica Magazine. bi-m. ISSN 0363-5244

**Lilith Publications, Inc.**
500 E. 63 St., Suite 16C, New York, NY 10021.
- Lilith; exploring the world of the Jewish woman. q.

**Eli Lilly & Co.**
General Offices and Principal Laboratories, Indianapolis, IN 46206.
- N. A. C. D. S. Lilly Digest. a. ISSN 0092-8410 (National Association of Chain Drug Stores)

**Lincoln Library**
326 S. 7th St., Springfield, IL 62701.
- Lincoln Library Bulletin. m(Oct-June) ISSN 0024-3698

**Lincoln Memorial University Press**
Harrogate, TN 37752.
- Lincoln Herald; magazine of Lincolniana. q. ISSN 0024-3671

**Lincoln National Life Insurance Co.**
Fort Wayne, IN 46802.
- Reinsurance Reporter. q. ISSN 0034-3641

**Lincoln Park Zoological Society**
2045 N. Lincoln Park West, Chicago, Il 60614.
- Ark. q.

**Lincoln University**
- Lincolnian. (pub. by Chester County Press)

**Lincoln University College of Law**
281 Masonic Ave., San Francisco, CA 94118.
- Lincoln Law Review. s-a. ISSN 0024-368X

**Lindencroft Publications Inc.**
New Hope, PA 18938.
- American Antiques. m.

**Herbert Linder, Ed. & Pub.**
140 E. 28 St., New York, NY 10016.
- Filmhefte. s-a.

**H. L. Lindquist Publications, Inc.**
153 Waverly Place, New York, NY 10014.
- Stamps. w. ISSN 0038-9358

**Linear & Circular Permutations**
1817 De La Vina St., Santa Barbara, CA 93101.
- Astrologia; a journal about time, consciousness and liberation. s-a.
- Nous Letter; studies in noetics/science of the nature of consciousness and altering states. s-a.

**Linen Supply Association of America**
Box 402427, Miami Beach, FL 33140.
- Linen Supply News. m. ISSN 0024-3825

**Linguistic Society of America**
1611 North Kent St., Arlington, VA 22209.
- International Journal of American Linguistics. (pub. by University of Chicago Press)
- L S A Bulletin. q. ISSN 0023-6365
- Language. q. ISSN 0023-8260
- Language Monographs. irreg., 1967, no. 27. ISSN 0075-7950
- Linguistic Society of America. Meeting Handbooks. s-a. ISSN 0075-9600

**Linkage for Ancestral Research**
924 Solar Rd. N.W., Albuquerque, NM 87107.
- Linkage for Ancestral Research. q.

**Linley Publishing Co., Inc.**
1833 W. Eighth St., Los Angeles, CA 90057.
- Western Paint Review. m. ISSN 0043-4027

**Linn County Publishing Co.**
P.O. Box 478, Pleasanton, KS 66075.
- Kansas Grange Monthly. m. (Kansas Grange)

**Linnaean Society of New York**
American Museum of Natural History, Central Park West at 79th St., New York, NY 10024.
- Linnaean News-Letter. m.(Sept-May) ISSN 0024-4058
- Linnaean Society of New York. Proceedings. irreg. ISSN 0075-9694
- Linnaean Society of New York. Transactions. irreg. ISSN 0075-9708

**Linnett Books**
995 Sherman Ave., Hamden, CT 06514.
- Studies in Library Management. irreg. vol. 2, 1975.

**Lionhead Publishing**
3016 West Michigan St., Milwaukee, WI 53208.
- Roar; an annual journal for poetry and poetics. a.

**Lions International**
York and Cermak Roads, Oak Brook, IL 60521.
- Lion; an international magazine for service-minded men. m. ISSN 0024-4163
- Lion en Espanol. bi-m. ISSN 0024-4171

**Lipid Research, Inc.**
Federation of American Societies for Experimental Biology, 9650 Rockville Pike, Bethesda, MD 20014.
- Journal of Lipid Research. bi-m. ISSN 0022-2275

**J. B. Lippincott Co.**
E. Washington Square, Philadelphia, PA 19105.
- A S A Refresher Courses in Anesthesiology. a. (American Society of Anesthesiologists)
- American Drug Index. a. ISSN 0065-8111
- American Journal of Clinical Pathology. m. ISSN 0002-9173 (American Society of Clinical Pathologists)
- American Surgeon. m. ISSN 0003-1348 (Southeastern Surgical Congress)

- American Surgical Association. Transactions. a. ISSN 0066-0833
- Anesthesiology. m. ISSN 0003-3022 (American Society of Anesthesiologists)
- Annals of Surgery; review of surgical science and practice. m. ISSN 0003-4932 (American Surgical Association)
- Cancer. m. ISSN 0008-543X (American Cancer Society, Inc.)
- Clinical Nuclear Medicine. m.
- Clinical Orthopaedics and Related Research. 8 per yr. ISSN 0009-921X
- Clinical Pediatrics. m. ISSN 0009-9228
- Critical Periods of History Series. irreg.
- Diseases of the Colon and Rectum. 8 per yr. ISSN 0012-3706 (American Proctologic Society)
- Endocrinology. m. ISSN 0013-7227 (Endocrine Society)
- Hospital Pharmacy. m. ISSN 0018-5787
- I B P Handbooks. irreg., no. 24, 1975. ISSN 0074-2074 (International Biological Programme)
- International Journal of Dermatology. 10 per yr. ISSN 0011-9059 (International Society of Tropical Dermatology)
- Investigative Radiology. bi-m. ISSN 0020-9996 (Association of University Radiologists)
- Journal of Clinical Endocrinology and Metabolism. m. ISSN 0021-972X (Endocrine Society)
- Journal of Preventive Dentistry. bi-m.
- Journal of Preventive Dentistry. bi-m.
- Laboratory Medicine. m. ISSN 0007-5027 (American Society of Clinical Pathologists)
- Medical Care. m. ISSN 0025-7079 (American Public Health Association)
- Pavlovian Journal of Biological Science; a Pavlovian journal of research & therapy. q. ISSN 0093-2213 (Pavlovian Society of America)
- R C. Respiratory Care. m. ISSN 0098-9142 (American Association for Respiratory Therapy)
- Review of Surgery. bi-m. ISSN 0034-6780
- Sexually Transmitted Diseases. q. (American Venereal Disease Association)
- Transfusion. bi-m. ISSN 0041-1132 (American Association of Blood Banks)
- United States Dispensatory. irreg., 1973, 27th ed.

**Alan R. Liss, Inc**
150 Fifth Ave., New York, NY 10011.
- Aggressive Behavior; a multidisciplinary journal devoted to the experimentaland observational analysis of conflict in humans and animals. q.
- American Journal of Hematology. q.
- Catheterization and Cardiovascular Diagnosis. q.
- Journal of Neuroscience Research. bi-m. ISSN 0360-4012
- Journal of Supramolecular Structure. 8 per yr. ISSN 0091-7419
- Journal of Surgical Oncology. bi-m. ISSN 0022-4790
- Medical and Pediatric Oncology. q. ISSN 0098-1532
- Pharmacology and Therapeutics in Dentistry. q. ISSN 0001-4389
- Progress in Clinical and Biological Research. irreg.

**Listening**
7200 W. Division St., River Forest, IL 60305.
- Listening; journal of religion and culture. 3 per yr. ISSN 0024-4414

**Listening Library, Inc.**
1 Park Ave., Old Greenwich, CT 06870.
- Listening Library of LP Recordings. a. ISSN 0075-9864

**Lister Hill Center for Biomedical Communications**
8600 Rockville Pike, Bethesda, MD 20014.
- Lister Hill National Center for Biomedical Communications. Report to the Congress. ISSN 0095-0831

**Literary Guild**
501 Franklin Ave., Garden City, NY 11531.
- Literary Guild. m. ISSN 0024-4538
- Works in Progress. irreg. ISSN 0512-5472 (Dist. by: Doubleday and Co., Inc., 245 Park Ave., New York, NY 10017)

**Literary Publications Foundations Inc.**
221 Columbus Ave., Boston, MA 02116.
- Poet Lore; a quarterly of world literature. q. ISSN 0032-1966

**Literature Searchers**
Box 8232, Riverside, CA 92505.
- Hypoglycemia Literature. m.

**Lithuanian Alliance of America**
307 W. 30th St., New York, NY 10001.
- Tevyne. s-m. ISSN 0040-4071

**Lithuanian American Community**
708 Custis Rd., Glenside, PA 19038.
- Violations of Human Rights in Soviet Occupied Lithuania; a report. irreg. ISSN 0360-7453

**Lithuanian Cooperative Publishing Society, Inc.**
102-02 Liberty Ave., Ozone Park, New York, NY 11417.
- Laisve; the Lithuanian weekly. w. ISSN 0044-703X

**Lithuanian Historical Society, Inc.**
10425 S. Kenton, Oak Lawn, IL 60453.
- Lietuviu Tauto Praeitis/Lithuanian Historical Review. a. ISSN 0091-4347

**Lithuanian National Foundation, Inc.**
Information Service, 29 W. 57th St., New York, NY 10019.
- Elta. m. ISSN 0013-6417 (Supreme Committee for Liberation of Lithuania)

**Lithuanian National League of America**
840 W. 33rd St., Chicago, IL 60608.
- Sandara/League. m.

**Lithuanian Workers Literary Association**
102-02 Liberty Ave., Ozone Park, NY 11417.
- Sviesa/Light. q.

**Litmus**
2209 California, Berkeley, CA 94703.
- Litmus; a freek wently of the arts. 6 per yr. ISSN 0024-4953

**Littell Families of America**
1219 Katcalani Ave., Sebring, FL 33870.
- Littell's Living Age. s-a.

**Little Big Horn Associates**
c/o Mrs G. O. Harris, 6717 46 St. S.W., Seattle, WA 98116.
- Little Big Horn Associates Research Review. q.

**Little Brothers of the Good Shepherd**
Box 389, Albuquerque, NM 87103.
- Shepherd's Call. q. ISSN 0037-3605

**Little, Brown & Co.**
34 Beacon St., Boston, MA 02106.
- Annals of Thoracic Surgery. m. ISSN 0003-4975 (Society of Thoracic Surgeons) (Co-Sponsor: Southern Thoracic Surgical Association)
- Critical Issues in American History Series. irreg.
- International Anesthesiology Clinics. q. ISSN 0020-5907
- International Ophthalmology Clinics. q. ISSN 0020-8167
- Motion Picture Market Place. a.
- Perspectives on International Relations. irreg.
- Series in Laboratory Medicine. irreg. ISSN 0582-8090
- Surgical Techniques. q.

**Little Face, Inc**
909 Beacon St., Boston, MA 02215.
- Pop Top; the record buyers' guide monthly.

**Little Free Press**
c/o Larry F. Johnson, 715 E. 14th St, Minneapolis, MN 55404.
- Little Free Press. bi-m.

**Arthur D. Little, Inc.**
25 Acorn Park, Cambridge, MA 02140.
- Arthur D. Little Inc. Bulletin. bi-m.

**Little Magazine**
Box 207, Cathedral Sta., New York, NY 10025.
- Little Magazine. 3 per yr (approx.) ISSN 0033-6300

**Little People of America, Inc**
1408 Brent St., 1212 William St., Fredericksburg, VA 22401.
- L P A News. bi-m. ISSN 0023-6357

**Little Publications, Inc.**
6263 Poplar Ave., Suite 540, Memphis, TN 38138.
- Cotton Farming. m (Jan.-Aug.); bi-m (Nov.-Dec.) ISSN 0574-2323
- Custom Applicator. q. ISSN 0011-4111
- Rice Farming; and rice industry news. 6 per yr.

**Little Review Press**
Box 205, Marshall University, Huntington, WV 25701.
- Little Review. s-a. ISSN 0024-5054

**Little Rock Chamber of Commerce**
100 S. Main Street, Little Rock, AR 72201.
- Little Rock Currents. w.

**Litton Charolais Ranch, Inc.**
c/o G. P. Schoenfelder, Box 188, Chillicothe, MO 64601.
- Charolais Bull-O-Gram. bi-m.

**Litton Publication, Inc.**
550 Kinderkamack Rd., Oradell, NJ 07649.
- Drug Topics. s-m. ISSN 0012-6616

**Lituanus Foundation, Inc.**
6621 S. Troy St., Chicago, IL 60629.
- Lituanus; Lithuanian quarterly journal of arts and sciences. q. ISSN 0024-5089

**Liturgical Conference**
1221 Massachusetts Ave. N.W., Washington, DC 20005.
- Homily Service. m.
- Liturgy. bi-m. ISSN 0458-063X
- Living Worship. m. (10 per yr.) ISSN 0360-6244

**Liturgical Press**
St. John's Abbey, Collegeville, MN 56321.
- Bible Today; a periodical promoting popular appreciation of the Word of God. 6 per yr. ISSN 0006-0836

**Live Free, Inc.**
Box 743, Harvey, IL 60426.
- Live Free; tracking the modern wilderness. q.
- National Outdoor Living Directory. irreg (with annual supplements)

**Live Leads Corp.**
369 Lexington Ave., New York, NY 10017.
- Building Planned List. m.

**Livermore Research Center of California, Inc.**
P.O.Box 1041, 1805 Holmes St., Livermore, CA 94550.
- Adam Smith's Wealth Newsletter. m. ISSN 0300-6980

**Livestock Breeder Journal, Inc.**
Ed. John T. Jenkins, 567 Arlington Place, Macon, GA 31208.
- Livestock Breeder Journal. m. ISSN 0024-5178

**Livestock Market Digest, Inc**
4900 Oak St., Kansas City, MO 64112.
- Livestock Market Digest; trade journal of competitive livestock marketing. w. ISSN 0024-5208

**Livestock Service, Inc.**
2609 N. Main St., Box 4530, Fort Worth, TX 76106.
- Weekly Livestock Reporter. w. ISSN 0043-1842

**Livestock Services**
Box 796, Columbia, MO 65201.
- Sheep Breeder and Sheepman. m. ISSN 0037-3400

**Living Blues Publications**
Box 11303, Chicago, IL 60611.
- Living Blues. bi-m. ISSN 0024-5232

**Living Church Foundation, Inc.**
407 E. Michigan St., Milwaukee, WI 53202.
- Living Church; an independent weekly record ot the news of the Church and the views of Episcopalians. w. ISSN 0024-5240

**Living Hand**
525 Hawthorne Ave., Chicago, IL 60657.
- Living Hand. s-a.

**Living History Centre**
Box B, Novato, CA 94947.
- Crossroads. s-a.

**Living in the Ozarks Newsletter**
Pettigrew, AZ 72752.
- Living in the Ozarks Newsletter. m.

**Leo Livingston, Ed. & Pub.**
Star Rt. 2, Box 310, Belfair, WA 98528.
- Pacific Bakers News. m. ISSN 0030-8528

**R. W. Livingston, Ed. & Pub.**
Box 5332, North Charleston, SC 29406.
● Sports Weekly Newsletter. Football Analyst. w.
● Sports Weekly Newsletter-Baseball. w.
● Sports Weekly Newsletter-Basketball. w.

**Llano Estacado Heritage, Inc.**
P.O. Box 2446, Hobbs, NM 88240.
● Greater Llano Estacado Southwest Heritage. q.

**Llewellyn Publications**
P.O. 3383, St. Paul, MN 55165.
● Astrology Now; contemporary news of modern
astrology. bi-m. ISSN 0145-8809
● Daily Planetary Guide. a.
● Gnosis. m.
● Gnostica; esoteric knowledge for the new age. bi-
m. ISSN 0145-885X
● Llewellyn's Astrological Calendar. a. ISSN 0145-
8868
● Llewellyn's Moon Sign Book. a.
● Nature Magick Almanac. q.

**Lloyd Library and Museum**
917 Plum St., Cincinnati, OH 45202
● Lloydia; the journal of natural products. bi-m.
ISSN 0024-5461 (American Society of
Pharmacognosy) (Co-publisher: John B. Griggs)
(Subscr. to: Lloydia, c/o Spahr & Glenn Co., 225
E. Spring St., Columbus OH 43215)

**Lloyd's Hearing Aid Corp.**
P.O. Box 1645, 128 Kishwaukee St., Rockford, IL
61110.
● Lloyd's Listening Post. q.

**Lloyd's Register of Shipping**
17 Battery Pl., New York, NY 10004.
● Lloyd's Register of American Yachts. a. ISSN
0076-0226

**Loblolly Inc.**
Box 88, Gary, TX 75643.
● Loblolly. q. ISSN 0361-3577

**Local and Short Haul Carriers National Conference**
● National Distribution Directory. (pub. by Guide
Services, Inc.)

**Local Pennsylvanian, Inc.**
Local Government Center, 2941 N. Front St.,
Harrisburg, PA 17110.
● Pennsylvanian; the magazine of local government.
m. ISSN 0031-4714 (Co-sponsors: Pennsylvania
State Association of Boroughs; Pennsylvania
Municipal Authorities Association; Pennsylvania
Secretaries Association; Assessors' Association of
Pennsylvania; Pennsylvania State Association of
Township Commissioners)

**Locale Publishing Co.**
1948 Riverside Drive, Los Angeles, CA 90039.
● Monterey Bay Area Locale. q (Monterey Savings
and Loan Association)

**Lock Haven State College**
Lock Haven, PA 17745.
● Lock Haven Review. a. ISSN 0459-6730

**Lockheed-California Co.**
Burbank, CA 91520.
● Airborne ASW Log; describes development,
testing and employment of aircraft and related
equipment used for anti-submarine warfare,
including user experience by US navy and allied
forces. q.
● Lockheed Orion Service Digest. irreg., no. 32,
1976. ISSN 0024-5704

**Edward B. Lockwood, Inc.**
250 Park Ave., New York, NY 10017.
● Park Avenue Social Review. m.

**Lockwood Trade Journal Co. Inc.**
551 Fifth Ave., New York, NY 10017.
● Tobacco International. fortn. ISSN 0049-3945
● Tobacco Science Yearbook. a. ISSN 0082-4623

**Locomotive Maintenance Officers Association**
1721 Parker St, North Little Rock, AR 72114.
● Locomotive Maintenance Officers Association.
Annual Proceedings. a. ISSN 0076-0285
● Locomotive Maintenance Officers Association.
Preconvention Report; full text of all seven
technical committee reports on diesel locomotive
and M.U. train maintenance. a. ISSN 0076-0293

**Locus Publications**
34 Ridgewood Lane, Oakland CA 94611
● Locus; the newspaper of the science fiction field.
15 per yr. ISSN 0047-4959 (Subscr to:, Box 3938,
San Francisco CA 94119)

**Lodestar Press Inc.**
3855 E. Mira Loma Ave., Anaheim, CA 92803
● Photo-Image. q. ISSN 0362-4102 (Dist. by:
Haddad's Fine Arts Inc., Box 3016C, Anaheim,
CA 92803)

**Baxter Loe, Ed. & Pub.**
2521 Walnut, Amarillo, TX 79107.
● Gospel Tidings. m. ISSN 0017-2375

**Loewenthal Publications Inc.**
507 Fifth Ave., New York, NY 10017.
● Caribbean News. m. ISSN 0045-5822

**Loggers World, Inc.**
Box 1006, Chehalis, WA 98532.
● Loggers World. m. ISSN 0047-4983

**Logos International Fellowship Inc.**
201 Church St., Plainfield, NJ 07060.
● Logos Journal; the magazine of New Testament
Christianity. bi-m.

**Loma Linda University. Department of Archives and
Special Collections**
Loma Linda, CA 92354.
● Adventist Heritage; a journal of Adventist history.
s-a. ISSN 0360-389X

**Loma Linda University. Geoscience Research
Institute**
Loma Linda, CA 92354.
● Origins. s-a. ISSN 0093-7495

**Loma Linda University. School of Dentistry Alumni
Association**
Loma Linda, CA 92354.
● S D A Dentist. a. ISSN 0024-5968

**Lomond Publications**
P.O. Box 56, Mt. Airy, MD 21771.
● Information Retrieval & Library Automation. m.
● R & D Management Digest. m. ISSN 0361-753X
● Systems, Technology and Science for Law
Enforcement and Security. m.

**London Northwest**
929 South Bay Rd., Olympia, WA 98506.
● Chaney Chronical. irreg. (1-2 per yr)
● What's New About London, Jack? irreg.

**G. C. London Publishing Corp.**
Box 58, Rockville Centre, NY 11571.
● Sports Review Series. m.

**London Stage Project**
Lawrence Univeristy, Appleton, WI 54911.
● London Stage Information Bank. Newsletter.
irreg., approx. a.

**Long Island Builders Institute**
c/o Robert Frank, Ed., 425 Broad Hollow Rd.,
Melville, NY 11746.
● Long Island Builder. m. ISSN 0024-6247

**Long Island Commercial Review Inc.**
303 Sunnyside Blvd., Plainview, NY 11803.
● Long Island Business Review. w.

**Long Island Fisherman Publishing Co.**
8 West 7th St., P.O. Box 143, Deer Park, NY
11729.
● Long Island Fisherman. w.

**Long Island Historical Society**
128 Pierrepont St., Brooklyn, NY 11201.
● Journal of Long Island History. irreg., vol. 10,
1973. ISSN 0449-2722

**Long Island Institute for Mental Health**
97-29 64th Rd., Forest Hills, NY 11374.
● Journal of Contemporary Psychotherapy. s-a.
ISSN 0022-0116

**Long Island Kegler Enterprises**
Box 402, Farmingdale, NY 11735.
● Ten Pin Corner. w.

**Long Island Lighting Co.**
175 E. Old Country Rd., Hicksville, NY 11801.
● L I L C O Almanac; Trimester factbook recording
status of the Nassau and Suffolk region. 3 per yr.
ISSN 0047-5041

**Long Island Poetry Collective, Inc.**
2441 Riverside Dr., Wantagh, NY 11793.
● Long Island Poetry Collective. Newsletter. 10 per
yr.
● Xanadu. s-a. (And: 1704 Auburn Rd., Wantagh,
NY 11793)

**Long Island Police News**
Box 36, Copiague, NY 11726.
● Long Island Police News. w.

**Long Island Sportsmen's Society**
c/o Sportsmen's Enterprises Inc., 184 New York
Ave., Huntington, NY 11743.
● Long Island Sportsman. m.

**Long Island University. Brooklyn Center**
385 Flatbush Ave Extension, Brooklyn, NY 11201.
● Collegiate. 9 per yr. ISSN 0045-7396

**Long Island University. English Department**
Brooklyn, NY 11201.
● Confrontation; a literary journal of Long Island
University. s-a. ISSN 0010-5716

**Long Island University Press**
Zeckendorf Campus, Brooklyn, NY 11201.
● International Conference on Urban Affairs.
Proceedings. irreg., 7th, 1971.

**Long Island University. SALENA Library Learing
Center**
University Plaza, Brooklyn, NY 11201.
● Library Leaves. 4 per yr. ISSN 0024-2349

**Long Island University. School of Business
Administration**
C. W. Post Center, Greenvale, NY 11548.
● Academy of Marketing Science. Journal. q. ISSN
0092-0703

**Long Publishing, Inc.**
7101 York Ave. So., Edina, St. Paul, NM 55435.
● Northern Automotive Journal. m. ISSN 0029-
3059

**Long View Publishing Co., Inc.**
205 W. 19th St., New York, NY 10011.
● Daily World. d. ISSN 0011-5533

**Longwood Program**
● Longwood Program Seminars. (pub. by University
of Delaware. College of Agricultural Sciences)

**Looking Glass Publications**
119 West 57th Street, New York, NY 10010.
● Mystery Monthly. m.

**Loon**
Box 11633, Santa Rosa, CA 95406.
● Loon. s-a. ISSN 0360-5612

**Lopez Publications, Inc.**
21 West 26th St., New York, NY 10010.
● Football Roundup. a.
● Lady's Circle. m. ISSN 0023-7191
● Sports Quarterly-Football Pros. a.
● Teen Bag. m.

**Lorain County Community College. Student Activities
Office**
1005 N. Abbe Rd., Elyria, OH 44035.
● Collegian. fortn. ISSN 0010-1206

**Loras College**
1450 Alta Vista St., Dubuque, IA 52001.
● I orian. 18 per yr. ISSN 0024-6506

**Loras College. Delta Epsilon Sigma**
Dubuque, IA 52001.
● Delta Epsilon Sigma Bulletin. q. ISSN 0011-8028

**Lorenz Industries**
● Best of Popular Music. (pub. by Heritage Music
Press)

**Los Alamos Scientific Laboratory**
Box 1663, Los Alamos, NM 87544.
● Atom. 6 per yr. ISSN 0004-7023

**Los Angeles (County) Air Pollution Control District**
Special Services Division, 434 S. Pedro St., Los
Angeles, CA 90013.
- A P C D Digest. m. ISSN 0092-8593

**Los Angeles (County) Department of Regional
Planning**
320 W. Temple St., Los Angeles, CA 90012.
- Los Angeles County Department of Regional
Planning. Quarterly Bulletin; population and
dwelling units. q.

**Los Angeles (County) Public Library**
320 W. Temple St., Box 111, Los Angeles, CA
90053.
- Progress. q. ISSN 0033-0531

**Los Angeles Area Chamber of Commerce**
P.O. Box 3696, Los Angeles, CA 90051.
- Southern California Business. w. (bi-w, in Jul,
Aug, Sep)
- Southern California Business Directory and
Buyers Guide. (pub. by Civic-Data Corp.)

**Los Angeles Athletic Club**
431 W. Seventh St., Los Angeles, CA 90014.
- Mercury. m. ISSN 0025-9969

**Los Angeles Catholic Worker**
605 N. Cummings St., Los Angeles, CA 90033.
- Catholic Agitator. m. ISSN 0045-5970 (Ammon
Hennacy House of Hospitality)

**Los Angeles Cinematheque, Inc.**
Box 2509, Hollywood, CA 90028.
- Los Angeles Cinematheque. m.

**Los Angeles College of Chiropractic**
920 E. Broadway, Glendale, CA 91205.
- Chirogram; chiropractic physician. m. ISSN 0009-
4692

**Los Angeles Commercial News**
3181 Fernwood Ave., Lynwood, CA 90262.
- Los Angeles Commercial News; Southern
California's transportation and business
newspaper. w. ISSN 0047-5068

**Los Angeles County Bar Association**
606 S. Olive Street, Los Angeles, CA 90014.
- Barrister Bulletin. q. ISSN 0094-310X (Barristers
of the Los Angeles County Bar Association)
- Los Angeles Bar Journal. m.

**Los Angeles County Federation of Labor**
AFL-CIO, 2130 W. 9th St., Los Angeles, CA
90006.
- Los Angeles Citizen. w. ISSN 0024-6549

**Los Angeles County Medical Association**
P.O. Box 3465, Los Angeles, CA 90054.
- Los Angeles County Medical Association.
Bulletin. s-m. ISSN 0047-5076

**Los Angeles County Museum of Art**
5905 Wilshire Blvd., Los Angeles, CA 90036.
- Los Angeles County Museum of Art. Bulletin. a.
ISSN 0024-6557
- Los Angeles County Museum of Art. Graphic
Arts Council. Newsletter. m(except June, July
and Aug.) ISSN 0047-5084

**Los Angeles Geographical Society**
- Los Angeles Geographical Society. Publication.
(pub. by Pacific Books, Publishers)

**Los Angeles Hillel Council. Jewish Federation-
Council, los Angeles**
900 Hilgard Ave., Los Angeles, CA 90024.
- Davka; the West Coast Jewish quarterly. 4 per yr.
ISSN 0011-7048

**Los Angeles Institute of Contemporary Art**
2040 Avenue of the Stars, Los Angeles, CA 90067.
- Los Angeles Institute of Contemporary Art.
Journal. q. ISSN 0094-8985

**Los Angeles Junior Chamber of Commerce**
404 S. Bixel St., Los Angeles, CA 90051.
- Headlines. b-w. ISSN 0300-7782

**Los Angeles Valley College Library. Periodicals
Department**
5800 Fulton, Van Nuys, CA 91401.
- Periodicals Periodical. irreg.

**Lott Publishing Co.**
Box 1107, Santa Monica, CA 90406.
- American Carwash Review. 6 per yr.

**Jack Lotto, Ed. & Pub.**
265 Jericho Turnpike, Floral Park, NY 11001.
- Disclosure Record. w. ISSN 0094-2561

**Louis Harris and Associates, Inc.**
1270 Ave. of the Americas, New York, NY 10020.
- Harris Survey Column Subscription. s-w. ISSN
0046-6875
- Harris Survey Yearbook of Public Opinion; a
compendium of current American attitudes. irreg
(approx. a.) ISSN 0085-1442

**Louisburg College**
Louisburg, NC 27549.
- Louisburg College Journal of Arts and Sciences. a.

**Louisiana. Advisory Commission on Coastal and
Marine Resources**
Baton Rouge, LA 70804.
- Louisiana. Advisory Commission on Coastal and
Marine Resources. Annual Report. a.

**Louisiana. Commissioner of Securities**
315 Louisiana State Office Bldg., New Orleans, LA
70112.
- Louisiana. Commissioner of Securities. Securities
Bulletin. q.

**Louisiana. Department of Agriculture**
Box 44345, Capitol Station, Baton Rouge, LA
70804.
- Louisiana. Department of Agriculture. Analysis of
Official Pesticide Samples; Annual Report. a.
ISSN 0099-1929
- Louisiana Fairs and Festivals. a. ISSN 0093-0687

**Louisiana. Department of Agriculture. Milk Division**
5790 Florida Blvd., Suite 103, Baton Rouge, LA
70804.
- Louisiana Annual Milk Marketing Report. a. ISSN
0085-2880

**Louisiana. Department of Art, Historical and Cultural
Preservation**
Old State Capitol, Corner North Boulevard and St.
Phillip St., Baton Rouge, LA 70801.
- Louisiana. Department of Art, Historical and
Cultural Preservation. Report of Activities. a.
ISSN 0095-2230

**Louisiana. Department of Commerce and Industry**
P.O. Box 44185, Capitol Station, Baton Rouge, LA
70804.
- Louisiana Directory of Manufacturers. biennial.
ISSN 0076-1028

**Louisiana. Department of Employment Security**
P.O. Box 44094, Baton Rouge, LA 70804.
- Louisiana Annual Rural Manpower Report. a.
ISSN 0092-0673
- Louisiana Labor Market. m. ISSN 0091-4711

**Louisiana. Department of Public Safety**
Box 1791, Baton Rouge, LA 70821.
- Louisiana. Department of Public Safety. Summary
of Motor Vehicle Accident Reports. m.

**Louisiana. Department of Public Works**
P.O. Box 44155, Capitol Station, Baton Rouge, LA
70804.
- Directory of Louisiana Cities, Towns and Villages.
irreg. ISSN 0092-0614

**Louisiana. Division of Mental Health**
Box 42215, Baton Rouge, LA 70804.
- Louisiana. Division of Mental Health. Annual
Performance Report and Continuation of the
State Plan for Drug Abuse Prevention. a. ISSN
0362-7098

**Louisiana. Geological Survey**
Box G, University Station, Baton Rouge, LA 70803.
- Clay Resources Bulletin. irreg., 1969, no. 2. ISSN
0069-4592

**Louisiana. Health and Human Resources
Administration**
Baton Rouge, LA 70804.
- Louisiana. Health and Human Resources
Administration Comprehensive Annual Services
Program Plan for Social Services Under Title 20.
a. ISSN 0362-8868

**Louisiana. Health and Social and Rehabilitation
Services Administration**
New Orleans, LA 70113.
- Louisiana. Health and Social and Rehabilitation
Services Administration. Statistical Report. a.
ISSN 0098-8057

**Louisiana. State Board of Nurse Examiners**
150 Baronne St., New Orleans, LA 70112.
- Louisiana. State Board of Nurse Examiners.
Report. a. ISSN 0095-5884

**Louisiana. State Planning Office**
4528 Bennington Ave., Baton Rouge, LA 70808.
- Louisiana. State Planning Office. State Planning
Bulletin.
- Louisiana State of the State. irreg.

**Louisiana. Wild Life and Fisheries Commission**
Wild Life and Fisheries Bldg., 400 Royal St., New
Orleans, LA 70130.
- Louisiana Conservationist. bi-m. ISSN 0024-6778

**Louisiana Academy of Sciences**
c/o Dr. Bruce Boudreaux, Department of
Entomology, Louisiana State University, Baton
Rouge, LA 70803.
- Louisiana Academy of Sciences. Proceedings. a.

**Louisiana Archaeological Society**
c/o Dr. Jon L. Gibson, Ed., 120 Beta Dr.,
Lafayette, LA 70506.
- Louisiana Archaeological Society Newsletter and
Bulletin. s-a.

**Louisiana Association of Insurance Agents, Inc.**
638 Louisana National Bank Building, 451 Florida
Blvd., Baton Rouge, LA 70801.
- Louisiana Insurer. fortn. ISSN 0024-6832

**Louisiana Bankers Association**
Box 2871, Baton Rouge, LA 70821.
- Louisiana Banker. m.

**Louisiana Contractor**
c/o Joyce J. Rhodes, Box 15686, Baton Rouge, LA
70895.
- Louisiana Contractor. bi-m.

**Louisiana Council of Teachers of English**
c/o Mari Ann Pritchett, State Department of
Education, P.O. Box 44064, Baton Rouge, LA
70804.
- Louisiana English Journal. a. ISSN 0456-7463

**Louisiana Dental Association**
3100 Woodlawn, Shreveport, LA 71104.
- Louisiana Dental Association. Journal. q. ISSN
0024-6786

**Louisiana Engineering Society**
- Louisiana Engineer. (pub. by Franklin Press
(Baton Rouge))

**Louisiana Folklore Society**
c/o Department of English, LSU in New Orleans,
New Orleans, MS 70122.
- Louisiana Folklore Miscellany. ISSN 0459-8962

**Louisiana Forestry Association**
Box 5067, Alexandria, LA 71301.
- Forests & People. q. ISSN 0015-7589

**Louisiana Gridweek**
Box 51444, New Orleans, LA 70151.
- Louisiana Gridweek. 27 per yr.

**Louisiana Historical Association**
Box 4-0831, University of Southwestern Louisiana,
Lafayette, LA 70504.
- Louisiana History. q. ISSN 0024-6816

**Louisiana Indian Hobbyist Association, Inc.**
8009 Wales St., New Orleans, LA 70126.
- Whispering Wind; American Indian: past &
present. m. ISSN 0300-6565

**Louisiana Library Association**
Box 131, Baton Rouge, LA 70821.
- L L A Bulletin. q. ISSN 0024-6867

**Louisiana LP-Gas Association**
c/o Ed. & Pub. Gene B. Denmary, Box 2754,
Monroe, LA 71201.
- Louisiana L P-Gas News. bi-m. ISSN 0024-6840

**Louisiana Motor Transportation Association**
- Louisiana Motor Transport Association News. (pub. by Rhodes Publishing Co., Inc.)

**Louisiana Municipal Association**
5615 Corporate Blvd., Suite 3B, Baton Rouge, LA 70808.
- Louisiana Municipal Review. bi-m.

**Louisiana Oil Marketers Association**
Box One, Shreveport, LA 71161.
- Hose & Nozzle. q. ISSN 0018-5361
- L O M A Bulletin. w.

**Louisiana Polytechnic Institute. Agricultural Engineering Department**
Ruston, LA 71271.
- Directory of Louisiana Information Resources. irreg. ISSN 0094-4963 (Co-Sponsor: Louisiana Department of Commerce and Industy)

**Louisiana School Boards Association**
P. O. Drawer 53217, Baton Rouge, LA 70805.
- Boardman. 10 per yr. ISSN 0006-5358

**Louisiana State Medical Society**
1700 Josephine St., New Orleans, LA 70113.
- Louisiana State Medical Society. Journal. m. ISSN 0024-6921

**Louisiana State Nurses Association**
639 S. Rendon St., New Orleans, LA 70119.
- Pelican News. q. ISSN 0031-4161

**Louisiana State Pharmaceutical Association**
2337 St. Claude Ave., New Orleans, LA 70117.
- Louisiana Pharmacist. m.

**Louisiana State University**
Drawer D, University Sta., Baton Rouge, LA 70893.
- Southern Review; a literary and critical quarterly magazine. q. ISSN 0038-4534

**Louisiana State University. Agricultural Experiment Station**
Baton Rouge, LA 70803.
- Louisiana Agriculture. q. ISSN 0024-6735

**Louisiana State University. Alumni Federation**
Box 17170-A, Baton Rouge, LA 70893.
- L S U/Alumni News. 6 per yr. ISSN 0023-6403

**Louisiana State University. Animal Science Department**
Baton Rouge, LA 70803.
- Louisiana State University. Animal Science Department. Livestock Producers' Day. a. ISSN 0076-1052 (Co-Sponsors: Louisiana Agricultural Experiment Station; Louisiana Cooperative Extension Service)

**Louisiana State University. College of Business Administration**
Baton Rouge, LA 70803.
- Louisiana Business Review. m. ISSN 0024-6751 (prep. by its Division of Research)

**Louisiana State University. College of Engineering**
Rm. 29, Atkinson Hall, Baton Rouge, LA 70803.
- L S U Engineering News. 4 per yr. ISSN 0023-6411
- Louisiana State University. Division of Engineering Research. Engineering Research Bulletin. irreg., 1967, no. 92. ISSN 0076-1060

**Louisiana State University. Cooperative Wildlife Research Unit**
Baton Rouge, LA 70803.
- Louisiana Cooperative Wildlife Research Unit. Quarterly Report. q.

**Louisiana State University. Division of Business and Economic Research**
New Orleans, LA 70122.
- Statistical Abstract of Louisiana. biennial. ISSN 0081-4695

**Louisiana State University. Division of Continuing Education**
Baton Rouge, LA 70803.
- Louisiana State University. School of Forestry and Wildlife Management. Annual Forestry Symposium. Proceedings. a. ISSN 0076-1095

**Louisiana State University. Law School**
Baton Rouge, LA 70803.
- Louisiana Law Review. 4 per yr. ISSN 0024-6859

**Louisiana State University. Law School. Institute on Mineral Law. Proceedings. a. ISSN 0076-1087 (prep. by its Institute of Continuing Legal Education)**

**Louisiana State University Library**
Baton Rouge, LA 70803.
- Louisiana State University. Library. Library Lectures. irreg., 1976, no. 5. ISSN 0085-2759
- Louisiana State University. Library. Report of the Director. a.

**Louisiana State University. Museum of Geoscience**
Geology Building, Baton Rouge, LA 70803.
- Louisiana State University. Museum of Geoscience. Melanges. irreg, (approx. 4 per yr.)

**Louisiana State University. Office of Information Services**
Rm. 244, Thomas Boyd Hall, Baton Rouge, LA 70803.
- L S U Outlook. bi-m.

**Louisiana State University. Office of Sea Grant Development**
Center for Wetland Resources Bldg., Baton Rouge, LA 70803.
- Aquanotes. bi-m.
- Louisiana Coastal Law Report; coastal zone management in Louisiana.

**Louisiana State University Press**
University Station, Baton Rouge, LA 70803.
- Walter Lynwood Fleming Lectures in Southern History. irreg. ISSN 0083-7121

**Louisiana State University. School of Forestry and Wildlife Management**
Baton Rouge, LA 70803.
- L S U Wood Utilization Notes. irreg., 1971, no. 22. ISSN 0076-1109

**Louisiana State University. School of Geoscience**
Baton Rouge, LA 70803.
- Geoscience and Man. irreg., vol. 15, 1976. ISSN 0072-1395
- Louisiana State University. School of Geoscience. Miscellaneous Publications. irreg.; latest issue 1977.

**Louisiana Studies Institute**
Northwestern State University of Louisiana, Natchitoches, LA 71457.
- Southern Studies: an Interdisciplinary Journal of the South. q.

**Louisiana Teacher's Association**
1755 Nicholson Dr., Box 1906, Baton Rouge, LA 70821.
- Louisiana Schools. m.(Sept-May) ISSN 0024-6905

**Louisiana Tech University**
Box 5336, Reston, VA 71270.
- Louisiana Tech Engineer. 4 per yr (during school year) ISSN 0047-5122

**Louisiana Tech University. Division of Administration and Business Research**
Box 5796 Tech Station, Ruston, LA 71270.
- Louisiana Economy. q.
- Louisiana Tech University. Research Monograph Series. irreg.

**Louisiana Tech University. Division of Life Sciences Research**
Box 5797, Tech. Station, Ruston, LA 71270.
- Louisiana Tech University. Division of Life Science Research. Research Bulletin. irreg., approx. 4 per year. ISSN 0076-1044

**Louisiana Tech University. Prescott Library**
Ruston, LA 71270.
- Abstracts of Theses Accepted by the Graduate School of Louisiana Tech University. a.

**Louisiana Tourist Commission**
P.O. Box 44291, Baton Rouge, LA 70804.
- Louisiana. q.

**Louisiana Water Resources Research Institute**
Louisiana State University, 146 Engineering Drawing Building, Baton Rouge, LA 70803.
- Louisiana Water Resources Research Institute. Annual Report. a.

**Louisville Area Chamber of Commerce**
300 W. Liberty, Louisville, KY 40202.
- Action (Louisville) m. ISSN 0001-737X

- Louisville. m. ISSN 0024-6948

**Louisville Board of Education**
675 River City Mall, Louisville, KY 40202.
- Daybreak. m.

**Love Conspiracy**
Box 17079, San Diego, CA 92117.
- Love Conspiracy. m.

**Love Project**
Box 7601, San Diego, CA 92107.
- Seeker Newsletter. q.

**Love Publishing Co.**
6635 E. Villanova Place, Denver, CO 80222.
- Focus on Exceptional Children. m.(Sept.-May) ISSN 0015-511X
- Focus on Guidance. m.(except July & Aug.) ISSN 0015-5136

**Lovejoy's College Guide Inc.**
2 Drummond Pl., Drawer Q, Red Bank, NJ 07701.
- Lovejoy's Guidance Digest. 10 per yr. ISSN 0024-7022

**Benjamin Lowe, Ed. & Pub.**
Governors State University, College of Human Learning & Development, Park Forest South, IL 60466.
- Sport Sociology Bulletin. s-a.

**James L. Lowe, Ed. & Pub.**
3709 Gradyville Rd., Newtown Square, PA 19073.
- Deltiology; a journal for postcard collectors and dealers. bi-m. (Deltiologists of America)
- Under the Window; dedicated to the life and work of Kate Greenaway (1846-1901) q. (Kate Greenaway Society)

**Lowell Observatory**
Flagstaff, AZ 86001.
- Lowell Observatory Bulletin. irreg. ISSN 0024-7057

**Lowell Press**
115 E. 31st St., Kansas City, MO 64141.
- Trail Guide. irreg., (approx. q.) (Westerners. Kansas City Posse)

**Lowell University**
1 Textile Ave, Lowell, MA 01854.
- Text. fortn. ISSN 0040-4780

**Lower Cape Fear Historical Society**
Box 813, Wilmington, NC 28401.
- Lower Cape Fear Historical Society. Bulletin. s-a. ISSN 0458-4201

**Lowlands Review**
1305 Rosetta, Lake Charles, LA 70605.
- Lowlands Review. s-a.

**Ken Lowman Ed. & Pub.**
2606 W. Burbank Blvd., Burbank, CA 91505.
- California Bowling News. w. ISSN 0008-0918

**Lowry Enterprises**
Box 896, Fallbrook, CA 92028.
- Panzerfaust & Campaign; games of strategy-strategy of games. bi-m.

**Loyal Order of Moose**
Mooseheart, IL 60539.
- Moose. m. 10 per yr. ISSN 0027-0954

**Loyola Law School**
6363 St. Charles Ave., New Orleans, LA 70118.
- Loyola Lawyer; a journal of student opinion on selected legal topics. 3 per yr. ISSN 0361-8935

**Loyola Marymount University**
7101 W. 80th St., Los Angeles, CA 90045.
- Los Angeles Loyolan. w.

**Loyola University**
New Orleans, LA 70118.
- New Orleans Review. q. ISSN 0028-6400

**Loyola University of Chicago**
6525 Sheridan Rd., Chicago, IL 60626.
- Mid-America; an historical review. q. (3 per yr. in 1976-77) ISSN 0026-2927

**Loyola University of Chicago. Center for Research in Urban Government**
820 North Michigan Avenue, Chicago, IL 60611.
- Loyola University. Center for Research in Urban Government. Studies. irreg., 1968, no.11. ISSN 0076-1397

**Loyola University of Chicago. Department of English**
820 N. Michigan Ave., Chicago, IL 60611.
- Restoration & Eighteenth Century Theatre Research. s-a. ISSN 0034-5822

**Loyola University of Chicago. School of Dentistry**
2160 S. First Ave., Maywood, IL 60153.
- Bur. s-a. ISSN 0007-6007 (prep. by its Alumni Assn.)

**Rev. Silas Emmitt Lucas, Jr. Ed. & Pub.**
Box 738, Easley, SC 29640.
- Georgia Genealogical Magazine; a magazine of genealogical source material concerning Georgians. q. ISSN 0435-5385

**Lucille Press**
2106 1/2 Pearl St., Austin, TX 78705.
- Lucille. s-a.

**Dr. W.O. Lucin, Ed. & Pub.**
418 W. Nittany Ave., State College, PA 16801.
- Life & School/Zhyttia i Shkola; independent cultural & educational periodical. bi-m.

**Lucis Publishing Co.**
866 United Nations Plaza, Suite 566-7, New York, NY 10017
(European and British Commonwealth countries, except Canada, subscr. address: Lucis Press Ltd., 235 Finchley Rd., Hampstead, London NW3 6LS England)
- Beacon. bi-m. ISSN 0005-7339

**Luckiamute**
224 N.W. 10th St., Corvallis, OR 97330.
- Luckiamute; contemporary northwest poetry. irreg.

**Lufkin Industries, Inc.**
Box 849, Lufkin, TX 75901.
- Lufkin Line. q. ISSN 0024-7243

**Luggage and Leather Goods Manufacturers of America**
220 Fifth Ave., New York, NY 10001.
- Showcase (New York) q. ISSN 0361-3232

**Lumber Co-Operator, Inc.**
339 East Ave., Rochester, NY 14604.
- Lumber Co-Operator. m. ISSN 0024-7294 (Northeastern Retail Lumbermens Association)

**Lumbermens Credit Association, Inc.**
600 S. Michigan Ave., Chicago, IL 60605.
- Lumbermens Red Book; reference book of the Lumbermens Credit Association. s-a plus w. supplements.

**Luna Publications**
655 Orchard St., Oradell, NJ 07649.
- Luna. q.

**Lunatic Fringe**
P.O. Box 237, South Salem, New York, NY 10590.
- Lunatic Fringe. q.

**A. A. Lund Associates**
Sheffield, MA 01257.
- Shepherd and Sheep Raiser; national journal of sheep production & management. m.

**Luptonian**
c/o David Walker Lupton, 1941 Oakwood Dr., Fort Collins, CO 80521.
- Luptonian. 2 per yr. ISSN 0099-1791

**Lure of Litchfield Hills**
West Cornwall, CT 06796.
- Lure of Litchfield Hills. s-a. ISSN 0047-519X

**Sally Luscomb, Ed. & Pub.**
500 No. Main St., Sputhington, CT 06489.
- Just Buttons; especially for button collectors. m. ISSN 0022-7005

**Luso-Aericano Co., Inc.**
88 Ferry St., Newark, NJ 07105.
- Luso-Americano; Portuguese language newsweekly. w.

**Lute Society of America**
c/o Sally Newcomb, 13120 Two Farm Dr., Silver Spring, MD 20904.
- Lute Society of America. Journal. a. ISSN 0076-1524
- Lute Society of America. Newsletter. q.

**H. Lutgens, Ed. & Pub.**
111 Sutter St., San Francisco, CA 94104.
- Western Banker. m. ISSN 0043-3519

**Lutheran Academy for Scholarship**
3558 S.Jefferson Ave., St. Louis, MO 63118.
- Academy. q. ISSN 0362-708X

**Lutheran Braille Evangelism Association**
660 E. Montana Ave., St. Paul, MN 55106.
- Tract Messenger. m. ISSN 0041-0357

**Lutheran Center Association**
156 37 Harper Ave., Detroit, MI 48224.
- Detroit and Suburban Lutheran. bi-w. ISSN 0011-9660

**Lutheran Church in America**
2900 Queen Lane, Philadelphia, PA 19129.
- Journal of Church Music. (pub. by Fortress Press)
- Lutheran; news magazine of the Lutheran Church in America. s-m. ISSN 0024-743X

**Lutheran Church in America. Board of Publication**
- Yearbooks in Christian Education. (pub. by Fortress Press)

**Lutheran Church in America. Division for World Mission and Ecumenism**
2900 Queen Lane, Philadelphia, PA 19129.
- World Encounter. 4 per yr. ISSN 0043-8413

**Lutheran Church in America. Minnesota Synod**
122 W. Franklin, Minneapolis, MN 55404.
- Minnesota Synod Lutheran. 8 per yr.

**Lutheran Church in America. New Jersey Synod**
- Lutheran Times in New Jersey. (pub. by Lutheran Publications in New Jersey)

**Lutheran Church Library Association**
122 W. Franklin Ave., Minneapolis, MN 55404.
- Lutheran Libraries. q. ISSN 0024-7472

**Lutheran Church, Missouri Synod**
- Concordia Historical Institute Quarterly. (pub. by Concordia Historical Institute)
- Happy Times. (pub. by Concordia Publishing House)
- Interaction. (pub. by Concordia Publishing House)
- Lutheran Annual. (pub. by Concordia Publishing House)
- Lutheran Witness. (pub. by Concordia Publishing House)
- Taegliche Andachten. (pub. by Concordia Publishing House)

**Lutheran Church-Missouri Synod. Board of Missions for the Blind**
3558 S. Jefferson Ave., St. Louis, MO 63118.
- Lutheran Messenger for the Blind. m. ISSN 0024-7480

**Lutheran Church, Missouri Synod. Board of Youth Ministry**
500 N. Broadway, St. Louis, MO 63102.
- Resources for Youth Ministry. q. ISSN 0034-5660

**Lutheran Church-Missouri Synod. Michigan District**
3773 Geddes Rd., Ann Arbor, MI 48105.
- Michigan Lutheran. m.

**Lutheran Church Women**
2900 Queen Lane, Philadelphia, PA 19129.
- Lutheran Women. 11 per yr. ISSN 0024-7596

**Lutheran Community Services**
525 Clinton Ave., Brooklyn, NY 11238.
- Focus (Brooklyn); our 70's. bi-m.

**Lutheran Council in the U.S.A.**
Office for Governmental Affairs, Suite 2720, 475 l'Enfant Plaza SW, Washington, DC 20024.
- Focus on Governmental Affairs. m.
- Lutherans in Step. bi-m.

**Lutheran Education Association**
7400 Augusta Blvd., River Forest, IL 60305.
- L E A Yearbook. a. ISSN 0076-1532

**Lutheran General Hospital**
1775 Dempster St., Park Ridge, IL 60068.
- Human Ecology. q. ISSN 0046-8169
- Quarterly Pediatric Bulletin. q. (prep. by its Division of Pediatrics)

**Lutheran Human Relations Association**
Valparaiso Univ., Valparaiso, IN 46383.
- Vanguard (Valparaiso) 10 per yr. ISSN 0042-2568

**Lutheran News, Inc.**
Box 168, New Haven, MO 63068.
- Christian News. w. ISSN 0009-5516

**Lutheran Publications in New Jersey**
Box 30, Trenton, NJ 08601.
- Lutheran Times in New Jersey. m.(except July & Aug.) (Lutheran Church in America. New Jersey Synod) (Co-sponsor: Lutheran Church-Missouri Synod, N.J. District)

**Lutheran Society for Worship, Music and the Arts**
Valparaiso University, Valparaiso, IN 46383.
- Accent on Worship, Music, the Arts. 5 per yr. ISSN 0360-3962
- Response-In-Worship-Music-the Arts. 3 per yr. ISSN 0034-5733

**Lutheran Theological Seminary**
Gettysburg, PA 17325.
- Gettysburg Seminary Bulletin. q. ISSN 0016-9366

**Luz (Denver)**
c/o Daniel T. Valdes, 360 S. Monroe, Suite 320, Denver, CO 80209.
- Luz (Denver). m.

**Luz Magazine, Inc.**
200 Park Avenue S., New York, NY 10003.
- Luz (New York). m.

**Lykes Bros. Steamship Co. Inc.**
Lykes Center, 300 Poydras St., New Orleans, LA 70130.
- Lykes Fleet Flashes. m.

**Lyle Printing & Publishing Co.**
185-189 E. State St., Box 38, Salem, OH 44460.
- Farm and Dairy. w. ISSN 0014-7826

**Lynatrace, Inc.**
P.O. 2144, Pompano Beach, FL 33061.
- Professional Investor. s-m.

**Lynch-Bowes, Inc.**
120 Broadway, New York, NY 10005.
- Lynch International Investment Survey. s-m.

**Lynchburg Foundry**
A Mead Company, P.O. Drawer 411, Lynchburg, VA 24505.
- Iron Worker. q. ISSN 0021-1621

**Lynx House Press**
P.O. Box 800, Amherst, MA 01002.
- Lynx; a magazine of poetry and the arts. 3 per yr.

**Lyons Band**
530 Riverview, Elkhart, IN 46514.
- Lyons Teacher-News. 3 per yr. ISSN 0093-0164

**Lyric Opera of Chicago**
20 N. Wacker Dr., Chicago, IL 60606.
- Lyric Opera News. 2 per yr. ISSN 0024-7839

**M B A Communications, Inc.**
730 Third Ave., New York, NY 10017.
- Juris Doctor; magazine for the new lawyer. 11 per yr. ISSN 0047-3014
- M B A. (Masters in Business Administration) 11 per yr, ISSN 0024-7952
- Medical Dimensions. 11 per yr. ISSN 0047-648X
- New Engineer. 11 per yr. ISSN 0047-9632

**M C-B Manufacturing Chemists**
2909 Highland Ave., Norwood, OH 45212.
- Chemical Reference Manual. irreg. ISSN 0094-6249

**M C P Publications**
401 Commonwealth Ave., Boston, MA 02215.
- Apothecary. bi-m. ISSN 0003-6560 (Massachusetts College of Pharmacy)

**M. D. Anderson Hospital and Tumor Institute**
see under University of Texas

**M D Publications, Inc.**
30 E. 60th St., New York, NY 10022.
- M D en Espanol. m. ISSN 0024-8002
- M D Medical News Magazine. m. ISSN 0024-8010
- M D Pacific. m. ISSN 0024-8037

**M F C Services**
414 North St., Box 449, Jackson, MS 39205.
- M F C News. m. ISSN 0024-8134

**M. F. Enterprises Inc.**
257 Park Ave. S., New York, NY 10010.
- Best of Duke. s-a.
- Duke. 9 per yr.

**M Farmaceutico Publishing Co., Inc.**
Quaker Hill Road, Pittstown, NJ 08867.
- Veterinario y la Industria. bi-m. ISSN 0042-4838

**M-G Publications**
Box 352, Northfield, IL 60093.
- American Automatic Merchandiser. m. ISSN 0002-7545

**M I N Publishing**
150 E. 52 St., New York, NY 10022.
- Media Industry Newsletter. w. ISSN 0024-9793

**M I T Press**
28 Carleton St., Cambridge, MA 02142.
- A I A A Communications Satellite Systems Conference. Technical Papers. irreg. (American Institute of Aeronautics and Astronautics)
- American Journal of Law and Medicine. q. ISSN 0098-8588 (American Society of Law and Medicine, Inc.)
- Cell. m. ISSN 0092-8674
- Current Studies in Linguistic Series. irreg., no. 5, 1974.
- Introduction to Systematic Geomorphology Series. irreg., no. 5, 1972. ISSN 0074-9990
- Journal of Interdisciplinary History. 4 per yr. ISSN 0022-1953
- Linguistic Inquiry. q. ISSN 0024-3892
- M I T Monographs in Economics. irreg., no. 9, 1968, no. 12, 1975. ISSN 0076-5007 (Massachusetts Institute of Technology)
- M I T Press Research Monograph Series. irreg., latest issue 1971. ISSN 0076-5015 (Massachusetts Institute of Technology)
- M I T Regional Science Studies Series. irreg., no. 11, 1972. ISSN 0076-5031 (Massachusetts Institute of Technology)
- M I T Reports. irreg., no. 17, 1969; no. 25, 1973. ISSN 0076-5023 (Massachusetts Institute of Technology)
- Monographs in Modern Electrical Technology. irreg; no. 9, 1975.
- Neurosciences Research Program. Bulletin. 4 per yr. ISSN 0028-3967 (Massachusetts Institute of Technology. Neurosciences Research Program)
- Neurosciences Research Symposium Summaries. irreg., no. 8, 1977. ISSN 0077-7854
- Oppositions; a journal for ideas and criticism in architecture. q. ISSN 0094-5676
- Progress in Astronautics and Aeronautics Series. irreg; latest issue vol. 47. ISSN 0079-6050 (American Institute of Aeronautics and Astronautics)
- Selected Readings from Econometrica. irreg.
- Society for the History of Technology. Monograph Series. irreg., latest issue no. 8. ISSN 0081-1491
- Studies in International Communism. irreg; no. 21, 1975. ISSN 0081-8054 (Massachusetts Institute of Technology. Center for International Studies)
- Workshop on Alternative Energy Strategies. Technical Report. irreg.

**M.O. Publishing Company**
Box 136, Brookeville, MD 20729.
- Modus Operandi. m. ISSN 0026-8828

**M P L A Solidarity Committee**
825 West End Ave., New York, NY 10025.
- Angola Weekly News. w.

**M Press**
12315 Judson Rd., Wheaton, MD 20906.
- Gamesletter. irreg., approx. bi-m. ISSN 0016-4356 (National Fantasy Fan Federation. Games Bureau)
- Gamesman. 2-4 per yr. ISSN 0016-4364 (National Fantasy Fan Federation. Games Bureau)
- S F & F Journal. s-a. (Washington Science Fiction Association)

**M.S.S. Information Corporation**
655 Madison Ave., New York, NY 10021.
- Attitudes Toward Death.
- Recent Articles and Research in Progress. irreg.

**M. W. Prince Hall Grand Lodge**
F. & A.M. of Louisiana, Box 2974, Baton Rouge, LA 70821.
- Plumb Line. m. ISSN 0032-163X

**MAC Publications Inc.**
6565 Sunset Blvd., Los Angeles, CA 90028.
- MAC Western Advertising News. w.

**Macabre**
c/o Joseph Payne Brennan, 26 Fowler St., New Haven, CT 06515.
- Macabre. irreg. ISSN 0024-8886

**McAnally & Associates, Inc.**
Box 765, La Canada, CA 91011.
- O & A Marketing News. bi-m.

**McCall Pattern Co.**
230 Park Ave., New York, NY 10017.
- Gloria Vanderbilt Designs for Your Home. q. ISSN 0362-5419
- McCall's Needlework & Crafts. q. ISSN 0024-8924

**McCall Publishing Co.**
230 Park Ave., New York, NY 10017
- McCall's. m. ISSN 0024-8908 (Subscr. to: McCall St., Dayton, OH 45401)
- McCall's Cooking School. a. ISSN 0094-0305

**Pat McCarty**
118 W. Nakoma, San Antonio, TX 78216.
- Texas Farm & Ranch News. w. ISSN 0049-3511

**Lowell McClellan**
1665 Eastman St., Boise, ID 83702.
- Idaho Food Journal. bi-m. (Idaho Retailers & Food Dealers Association)

**George E. McCracken, Ed. & Pub**
1232 39th St., Des Moines, IA 50311.
- American Genealogist. q. ISSN 0002-8592

**Robert M. McCune**
Box 819, 14970 Chandler, Corona, CA 91720.
- Dairyman. m. ISSN 0011-572X

**McCutchan Publishing Corp.**
2526 Grove St., Berkeley, CA 94704.
- Contemporary Educational Issues. irreg.

**Ames McDaniel, Ed. & Pub.**
633 Ridgewood, Orlando, FL 32803.
- Fountain. q.

**Macdaniel Publications Ltd.**
Box 45, Port Lavaca, TX 77979.
- Wig & Hairgoods Business. m. ISSN 0043-5392

**MacDonald Publishing Co.**
35 E. Wacker Drive, Suite 240, Chicago, IL 60601.
- Chicagoland Food News. m. ISSN 0009-3742

**McDonnell Douglas Corporation**
Box 516, St. Louis, MO 63166
(and 3955 Lakewood Blvd., Long Beach, CA 90846)
- McDonnell Douglas Spirit. m. ISSN 0024-8991

**Macedonian Patriotic Organization**
542 S. Meridian St., Indianapolis, IN 46225.
- Macedonian Tribune. w. ISSN 0024-9009

**Ralph McElroy Co., Inc.**
2102 Rio Grande, Austin, TX 78705.
- Kobunshi Ronbunshu (English Edition)/Japanese Polymer Science and Technology. m.
- Melliand Textilberichte (English Edition)/International Textile Reports. m.
- Soviet Chemical Industry. m. ISSN 0038-5344
- Soviet Power Engineering. m. ISSN 0049-1756

**McElroy Family Newsletter**
c/o Kenneth V. Graves, Box 762-G, 261 South St., Wrentham, MA 02093.
- McElroy Family Newsletter. q.

**McFadden Business Publications**
6364 Warren Dr., Norcross, GA 30071.
- American Bank Directory. s-a. ISSN 0569-292X
- Southern Banker. m. ISSN 0038-383X
- World Trade Journal. bi-m.

**Macfadden Women's Media, Inc.**
205 E. 42nd St., New York, NY 10017.
- Motion Picture Magazine. m. ISSN 0027-1624
- Photoplay. m. ISSN 0031-885X
- Silver Screen. m. ISSN 0037-5365
- T V Mirror. m.
- True Confessions. m. ISSN 0041-3488
- True Love. m. ISSN 0041-3550

**Macfarland Co.**
1716 E. 2nd St., Scotch Plains, NJ 07076.
- American Potato Yearbook. a. ISSN 0065-9789

**Richard M. McGrath**
Dover Rd., Barneveld, NY 13304.
- Thruway-Interstate Highway Guide; travel directory for New York State, including Vermont, New Jersey and Ontario. a. ISSN 0082-4267

**McGrath Publishing Co.**
821 Fifteenth St., Washington, DC 20005.
- Health Organizations of the U.S., Canada and Internationally; a directory of voluntary associations, professional societies and other groups concerned with health and related fields. irreg., 1974 3rd edition. ISSN 0440-5609

**McGraw Hill Book Co.**
1221 Avenue of the Americas, New York, NY 10020.
- Cases in Practical Politics. irreg. ISSN 0528-2187
- Chemistry-Biology Interface Series. irreg.
- Cinema Two. irreg.
- Concepts in Introductory Geology Series. irreg.
- Contemporary Studies in Literature. irreg.
- McGraw-Hill Accounting Series. irreg.
- McGraw-Hill Advanced Physics Monograph Series. irreg.
- McGraw-Hill Automotive Technology Series. irreg.
- McGraw-Hill Chemical Engineering Series. irreg.
- McGraw-Hill Civil Engineering Series. irreg.
- McGraw-Hill Computer Science Series. irreg.
- McGraw-Hill Computer Usage Series. irreg.
- McGraw-Hill Electrical and Electronic Engineering Series. irreg.
- McGraw-Hill Electronic Science Series. irreg.
- McGraw-Hill European Engineering Programme. irreg.
- McGraw-Hill European Geography and Geology Series. irreg.
- McGraw-Hill European Series in Education. irreg.
- McGraw-Hill European Series in Management. irreg.
- McGraw-Hill European Technical and Industrial Programme. irreg.
- McGraw-Hill General Engineering Series. irreg.
- McGraw-Hill Insurance Series. irreg.
- McGraw-Hill International Series in the Earth and Planetary Sciences. irreg.
- McGraw-Hill Management Manuals. irreg.
- McGraw-Hill Mechanical and Production Engineering Series. irreg.
- McGraw-Hill Paperback Series in Psychopathology. irreg.
- McGraw-Hill Problems Series in Geography. irreg.
- McGraw-Hill Publications in Industrial Education. irreg.
- McGraw-Hill Publications in Psychology. irreg.
- McGraw-Hill Publications in the Agricultural Sciences. irreg.
- McGraw-Hill Series in Advanced Chemistry. irreg.
- McGraw-Hill Series in Agricultural Economics. irreg.
- McGraw-Hill Series in Bioengineering. irreg.
- McGraw-Hill Series in Construction Engineering and Management. irreg.
- McGraw-Hill Series in Continuing Education for Engineers. irreg.
- McGraw-Hill Series in Control Systems Engineering. irreg.
- McGraw-Hill Series in Education. irreg.
- McGraw-Hill Series in Electronic Systems. irreg.
- McGraw-Hill Series in Finance. irreg.
- McGraw-Hill Series in Forest Resources. irreg.
- McGraw-Hill Series in Fundamental Physics. irreg.
- McGraw-Hill Series in Geography. irreg.
- McGraw-Hill Series in Health Education, Physical Education, and Recreation. irreg.
- McGraw-Hill Series in Higher Mathematics. irreg.
- McGraw-Hill Series in Industrial Engineering and Management. irreg.
- McGraw-Hill Series in Information Processing and Computers. irreg.
- McGraw-Hill Series in International Business. irreg.

- McGraw-Hill Series in International Development. irreg.
- McGraw-Hill Series in Invertebrates. irreg.
- McGraw-Hill Series in Library Education. irreg.
- McGraw-Hill Series in Management. irreg.
- McGraw-Hill Series in Marketing and Advertising. irreg.
- McGraw-Hill Series in Materials Science and Engineering. irreg.
- McGraw-Hill Series in Mechanical Engineering. irreg.
- McGraw-Hill Series in Missile and Space Technology. irreg. ISSN 0460-3400
- McGraw-Hill Series in Modern Applied Mathematics. irreg.
- McGraw-Hill Series in Modern Structures. irreg.
- McGraw-Hill Series in Music. irreg.
- McGraw-Hill Series in Nuclear Engineering. irreg.
- McGraw-Hill Series in Organismic Biology. irreg.
- McGraw-Hill Series in Political Science. irreg.
- McGraw-Hill Series in Population Biology. irreg.
- McGraw-Hill Series in Probability and Statistics. irreg.
- McGraw-Hill Series in Sanitary Science and Water Resources Engineering. irreg.
- McGraw-Hill Series in Sociology. irreg.
- McGraw-Hill Series in Special Education. irreg.
- McGraw-Hill Series in Speech. irreg.
- McGraw-Hill Series in Systems Science. irreg.
- McGraw-Hill Series in Transportation. irreg.
- McGraw-Hill Series in Undergraduate Astronomy. irreg.
- McGraw-Hill Series in Undergraduate Chemistry. irreg.
- McGraw-Hill Series in Water Resources and Environmental Engineering. irreg.
- McGraw-Hill Social Problems Series. irreg.
- McGraw-Hill Television Series. irreg.
- Modern Artist and His World Series. irreg.

**McGraw-Hill Book Co. Gregg Division**
1221 Ave. of the Americas, New York, NY 10020.
- Business Education World. bi-m. ISSN 0007-6694
- Technical Education News. 4 per yr.
- Today's Secretary. m.(Oct-May) ISSN 0040-8565

**McGraw-Hill, Inc.**
1221 Avenue of the Americas, New York, NY 10020.
- Administration in Education Series. irreg.
- Advance Job Listings. w. (prep. by its Classified Advertising Dept.)
- American Machinist. m. ISSN 0002-9858
- Anthropological Handbook. irreg. ISSN 0517-3868 (American Museum of Natural History)
- Architectural Record. m. ISSN 0003-858X
- Aviation Week & Space Technology. w. ISSN 0005-2175
- Aviation Week and Space Technology. Marketing Directory. a. ISSN 0067-267X
- Business Week. w. ISSN 0007-7135
- Chemical Engineering. fortn. ISSN 0009-2460
- Chemical Week. w. ISSN 0009-272X
- Coal Age. m. ISSN 0009-9910
- Coal Week. w.
- Construction Methods and Equipment. m. ISSN 0010-6844
- Contemporary Ob/Gyn. m. ISSN 0090-3159
- Contemporary Surgery. m.
- Data Communications. bi-m.
- E C & M's Electrical Products Yearbook. (Electrical Construction and Maintenance) a. ISSN 0093-3236
- E/M J Mining Activity Digest. (Engineering & Minig Journal) fortn.
- E N R Directory of Contractors. (Engineering News-Record) a. ISSN 0098-6453
- E N R Directory of Design Firms. a. ISSN 0098-6305 (Engineering News-Record)
- Electric Utility Generation Planbook. a.
- Electrical Construction and Maintenance. m. ISSN 0013-4260
- Electrical Marketing Newsletter. s-m.
- Electrical Week; the electric utility industry newsletter. w. ISSN 0046-1695
- Electrical Wholesaling. m. ISSN 0013-4430
- Electrical World. s-m. ISSN 0013-4457
- Electronics. fortn. ISSN 0013-5070
- Electronics Buyers' Guide. a. ISSN 0090-5291
- Energy Legislative Service. s-m. (Platt's Oilgram News Service)
- Engineering & Mining Journal. m. (Subscr. to: Box 515, Hightstown, NJ 08540)
- Engineering News-Record. w. ISSN 0013-807X
- Fleet Owner. m. ISSN 0015-3567
- House and Home. m. ISSN 0018-6414
- Industry Mart. bi-m.

- Inorganic Syntheses Series. a., vol. 16, 1974. ISSN 0073-8077 (Inorganic Syntheses, Inc.)
- International Construction Week. w. (prep. by its Engineering News-Record)
- International Management. m. (English edition); bi-m (Spanish edition) ISSN 0020-7888 (And McGraw-Hill International Publications Ltd., McGraw-Hill House, Maidenhead, Berkshire, Eng.)
- Legal Briefs for Architects, Engineers, and Contractors. s-m.
- McGraw-Hill Yearbook of Science and Technology. a. ISSN 0076-2016
- Management Awareness Program; selections from significant new business books of all publishers. 6 per yr.
- Materials Handbook. irreg.
- Medical World News; the newsmagazine of medicine. fortn. ISSN 0025-763X
- Metals Week. w. ISSN 0026-0975
- Modern Nursing Home Directory of Nursing Homes in the United States, U.S. Possessions and Canada. irreg. (Subscr. to:, 230 W . Monroe St., Chicago IL 60606)
- Modern Plastics. m. ISSN 0026-8275
- Modern Plastics Encyclopedia. a. ISSN 0085-3518
- Modern Plastics International. m. ISSN 0026-8283 (Subscr. to: 50 Avenue de la Gare, Lausanne, Switzerland)
- N P N Bulletin; a weekly information service for important people in oil marketing. w. ISSN 0027-6901 (National Petroleum News)
- National Petroleum News. 13 per yr. ISSN 0027-9889
- Nucleonics Week. w. ISSN 0048-105X
- P S R O Letter. (Professional Standards Review Organizations) fortn. (Subscr. to: 437 National Press Bldg., Washington DC 20004)
- Physician and Sportsmedicine. m. ISSN 0091-3847
- Platt's Oilgram News Service. d.
- Platt's Oilgram Price Service. d.
- Power. m. ISSN 0032-5929
- Securities Week. w.
- Textile World. m. ISSN 0040-5213 (Subscr. to:, 1175 Peachtree St. N.E., Atlanta GA 30309)
- Textile World Buyer's Guide/Fact File; McGraw-Hill's international textile magazine. a. ISSN 0495-369X (Subscr. to: 1175 Peachtree St. N.E., Atlanta, GA 30309)
- Washington Drug & Device Letter. w. (Subscr. to:, 437 National Press Bldg., Washington DC 20004)
- Washington Report on Health Legislation. 50 per yr. ISSN 0098-2512 (Subscr. to:, 457 National Press Bldg., Washington DC 20045)
- Washington Report on Long Term Care. w. ISSN 0091-7311 (Subscr. to: 437 National Press Bldg., Washington DC 20004)
- Washington Report on Medicine & Health. w. ISSN 0043-0730 (Subscr. to:, 437 National Press Bldg., Washington DC 20004)
- 26 Plus. 4 per yr.
- 33 Magazine; McGraw-Hill's magazine of metal producing. m. ISSN 0563-4725

**McGraw-Hill Information Systems Co. Sweet's Division**
1221 Ave. of the Americas, New York, NY 10020.
- Sweet's Engineering Catalog File. Summary Edition: Mechanical, Sanitary and Related Products. a. ISSN 0361-1388
- Sweet's Industrial Construction & Renovation File with Plant Engineering Extension Market List. a. ISSN 0094-825X
- Sweet's System for the Engineering Market. a.
- Sweet's System for the Industrial Construction & Renovation Market. a.

**McGraw-Hill Publications Co**
1221 Avenue of the Americas, New York, NY 10020.
- Dodge Construction News. d. ISSN 0012-480X
- Keystone Coal Industry Manual. a.
- Modern Healthcare. m. (Subscr. to: Modern Healthcare, P.O. Box 665, Hightstown, N.J. 08520)
- Postgraduate Medicine. m. ISSN 0032-5481
- Power's Energy Management Guidebook. a.

**McHenry Publishing Co.**
Box 2296, Orange, CA 92669.
- Motor West. m. ISSN 0027-2124

**Machinery and Allied Products Institute**
1200 18th St., N.W., Washington, DC 20036.
- Capital Goods Review. q. ISSN 0008-588X

- Series on Company Approaches to Industrial Relations. irreg., no. 5, 1969. ISSN 0080-8997 (Co-Sponsor: Council for Technological Advancement)

**Machinery Dealers National Association**
- Locator. (pub. by Machinery Dealers National Information System Inc.)

**Machinery Dealers National Information System Inc.**
1110 Spring St., Silver Spring, MD 20910.
- Locator. m. ISSN 0460-1327 (Machinery Dealers National Association)

**Machlett Laboratories, Inc**
A Subsidiary of Raytheon Co, Springdale, CT 06879.
- Cathode Press. q. ISSN 0008-7882

**Don L. Macintyre, Ed. & Pub.**
666 E. Main St., Bradford, PA 16701.
- Union. m. ISSN 0041-6797

**Mack Associates**
P.O. Box 7123, Kansas City, MO 64113.
- Action in Pharmacy. irreg. ISSN 0065-1753

**David McKay Co.**
750 Third Ave., New York, NY 10017.
- Fodor's Austria. a. ISSN 0071-6340
- Fodor's Belgium and Luxembourg. biennial. ISSN 0071-6359
- Fodor's Caribbean, Bahamas and Bermuda. a. ISSN 0071-6561
- Fodor's Czechoslovakia. irreg. ISSN 0071-6367
- Fodor's France. a. ISSN 0071-6383
- Fodor's Germany. a. ISSN 0071-6391
- Fodor's Great Britain. a. ISSN 0071-6405
- Fodor's Greece. a. ISSN 0071-6413
- Fodor's Guide to Europe. a. ISSN 0071-6375
- Fodor's Hawaii. a. ISSN 0071-6421
- Fodor's Holland. biennial. ISSN 0071-643X
- Fodor's Hungary. irreg. ISSN 0071-6448
- Fodor's India. biennial. ISSN 0071-6456
- Fodor's Ireland. a. ISSN 0071-6464
- Fodor's Israel. a. ISSN 0071-6588
- Fodor's Italy. a. ISSN 0071-6472
- Fodor's Japan and Korea. a.
- Fodor's London. a. ISSN 0071-6596
- Fodor's Mexico. a. ISSN 0071-6499
- Fodor's Morocco. a. ISSN 0071-6502
- Fodor's Paris. biennial.
- Fodor's Peking. irreg.
- Fodor's Portugal. a. ISSN 0071-6510
- Fodor's Scandinavia. a. ISSN 0071-6529
- Fodor's South America. a. ISSN 0071-6537
- Fodor's Southeast Asia. biennial.
- Fodor's Soviet Union. biennial. ISSN 0095-1358
- Fodor's Spain. a. ISSN 0071-6545
- Fodor's Switzerland. a. ISSN 0071-6553
- Fodor's Tunisia. irreg.
- Fodor's Turkey. a. ISSN 0071-6618
- Fodor's Venice: A Companion Guide. irreg. ISSN 0071-6626
- Fodor's Vienna. irreg.
- Fodor's Yugoslavia. a. ISSN 0071-657X

**Mackay Publishing Corporation**
95 Madison Ave., New York, NY 10016.
- Greetings. m.
- Intimate Fashion News. fortn.

**McKeand Publications, Inc**
636 First Ave., West Haven, CT 06516.
- Petroleum Marketer. bi-m.

**McKellar Publications**
2801 W. 6th St., Suite 401, Los Angeles, CA 90057.
- Pacific Coast Builder. m.
- Western Building Design. m.

**Mackinac Island State Park Commission**
Mackinac Island, MI 49757.
- Mackinac History; an informal series of illustrated vignettes. irreg. (approx. 2-3 per yr) ISSN 0541-6507
- Reports in Mackinac History and Archaeology. irreg., approx. a.

**McKinsey & Co. Inc.**
245 Park Ave., New York, NY 10017.
- McKinsey Quarterly. q. ISSN 0047-5394

**McKnight Medical Communications, Inc.**
550 Frontage Rd., Northfield, IL 60093.
- Medical Products Salesman. m. (American Surgical Trade Association)
- Pharmaceutical Salesman. m. ISSN 0048-3621

**McKnight Publishing Company**
Bloomington, IL 61701.
- American Council on Industrial Arts Teacher Education. Yearbook. a. ISSN 0084-6333
- Industrial Arts for the Elementary School. Yearbook. a. (American Council of Industrial Arts Teacher Educators)

**McLean Guide to Kennels of America**
c/o C. D. McLean, Ed., Chester Springs, PA 19425.
- McLean Guide to Kennels of America. irreg. ISSN 0093-2531

**McLean Hospital**
Public Relations Dept., 115 Mill St., Belmont, MA 02178.
- McLean Bulletin. m. ISSN 0047-5408

**Maclean-Hunter Publishing Corporation**
300 W. Adams St., Chicago, IL 60606.
- Boxboard Containers. m. ISSN 0006-8489
- Coal Mining & Processing. m. ISSN 0009-9961
- Concrete Products. m. ISSN 0010-5368
- Inland Printer/American Lithographer. m. ISSN 0020-1502
- Rock Products; industry's recognized authority. m. ISSN 0035-7464

**Fred McMahon, Ed. & Pub.**
Darby Annex 213, California State University, Northridge, Northridge, CA 91330.
- Exetasis. q.

**McMahon Publishing Co.**
Box 325, Rowayton, CT 06853.
- American Journal of I.V. Therapy. bi-m.
- Anesthesia Staff News. bi-m.
- Surgical Team. bi-m.

**Macmillan, Inc.**
866 Third Ave., New York, NY 10022.
- Cars of the World in Color. irreg., vol. 5, 1971.
- Collier's Yearbook. a. ISSN 0069-5793
- Recent Sociology. a. ISSN 0080-0023
- Wars of the United States Series. irreg.
- Who's Who in American Education. biennial; 1967-68, vol. XXIII. ISSN 0083-9418

**Macmillan Information**
(Subsidiary of: Macmillan Publishing Co., Inc.)
866 Third Ave., New York, NY 10022.
- Call for Papers. w. ISSN 0575-6375
- Computer Programs Directory. ISSN 0069-8156
- Current Index to Journals in Education. m. ISSN 0011-3565 (E R I C)
- Occupational Education. ISSN 0360-5434

**Macmillan Professional Magazines, Inc.**
866 Third Ave., New York, NY 10022.
- Industrial Education. m.(Sept-June) ISSN 0091-8601
- Industrial Education Product Guide. 2 per yr.
- Resource Guide to Mathematics Programs & Materials. irreg.
- Resource Guide to Reading & Language Arts Programs & Materials. irreg. ISSN 0092-4423
- Teacher. m.(Sept-May)

**Macmillan Publishing Co., Inc.**
866 Third Ave., New York, NY 10022.
- American Dipolmatic History Series. irreg.
- College Blue Book. biennial. ISSN 0069-5572
- Current Concepts in Biology. irreg.
- Current Topics in Classroom Instruction Series. irreg.
- International Symposium on Submarine and Space Medicine. Proceedings. irreg. ISSN 0535-3114
- Macmillan Biology Series. irreg.
- Macmillan Core Series in Biology. irreg.
- Macmillan Decision Series. irreg.
- Macmillan Modern Mind Series. irreg.
- Macmillan Series in Applied Computer Science. irreg.
- Macmillan Series in Economics. irreg.
- Macmillan Series in Electrical Science. irreg.
- Macmillan Series in Mechanical Engineering. irreg.
- Macmillan Series in Operations Research. irreg.
- Macmillan Series in Physical Anthropology. irreg.
- Macmillan Sky and Telescope Library of Astronomy. irreg. ISSN 0583-5224
- Modern Concepts in Medical Physiology. irreg.
- Problems in Ancient History. irreg.
- Science for the Modern Mind. irreg.
- Series of Books in Applied Mathematics. irreg.
- Series on Contemporary Javanese Life. irreg. ISSN 0582-8155

- Sources in Western Political Thought. irreg. ISSN 0560-8996
- Urban Environment. a. ISSN 0083-4696

**Macmillan Science Co., Inc.**
8200 South Hoyne Ave., Chicago, IL 60620.
- Turtox News. bi-m.

**MacNair- Dorland Co., Inc.**
101 W. 31st St., New York, NY 10001.
- American Inkmaker; for manufacturers of printing inks, coatings and colors. m. ISSN 0002-8916 (National Association of Printing Ink Makers)
- Building Services Contractor. bi-m. ISSN 0007-3644
- Maintenance Supplies. m. ISSN 0025-0929
- Soap/Cosmetics/Chemical Specialties. m. ISSN 0091-1372

**McNamara Publishing Co. Inc.**
275 Madison Ave., New York, NY 10016.
- Orthopaedic Review. m. (Co-publisher: Academy News Bulletins, Inc.)

**Maco Publishing Co., Inc.**
380 Madison Ave., New York, NY 10017.
- Baseball Guidebook. a. ISSN 0408-6104
- Budget Decorating & Remodeling. bi-m. ISSN 0360-4993
- Fishing Guidebook. a. ISSN 0428-5190
- Hunter's Gun. a.
- Modern Hi-Fi & Music. 10 per yr. ISSN 0097-2533
- New Fishing. a. ISSN 0092-1734
- Sports All Stars Baseball. a.

**Macomb County Circuit Court**
- Macomb County Legal News. (pub. by Panax Newspapers, Inc.)

**MacRae's Blue Book Co.**
100 Shore Drive, Hinsdale, IL 60521.
- MacRae's Blue Book. a. ISSN 0076-2067

**William H. McRee, Ed. & Pub.**
3735 Ector St., Beaumont, TX 77705.
- Spoke Wheels. m. ISSN 0049-187X

**Macro-Comm Corp.**
8322 Beverly Blvd., Los Angeles, CA 90048.
- Private Pilot. m. ISSN 0032-8901

**McVay-McVeigh-McVey Family Archives Quarterly**
c/o Agnes McVeigh Brooks, 1301 El Finito Way, Santa Ana, CA 92705.
- McVay-McVeigh-McVey Family Archives Quarterly. q.

**Madisen Publishing Division**
Box 1936, Appleton, WI 54911.
- Park Maintenance. m. ISSN 0031-2134

**Madison Area Committee on Southern Africa**
731 State St., Madison, WI 53703.
- M A C S A News. m.

**Madison Avenue Magazine, Inc.**
750 Third Ave., New York, NY 10017.
- Madison Avenue; the magazine of New York advertising. m. ISSN 0024-9483

**Madison Metropolitan School District**
545 W. Dayton St., Madison, WI 53703.
- Learning Tree. bi-m.

**Madison Teachers Inc.**
121 South Hancock St., Madison, WI 53703.
- Reporter. bi-m.

**Madness Network News**
Box 684, San Francisco, CA 94101.
- Madness Network News. bi-m.

**Magazine Management Co. Inc.**
575 Madison Avenue, New York, NY 10022.
- Celebrity. m.
- For Men Only. m. ISSN 0426-844X
- Intimate Romance. bi-m.
- Male. m. ISSN 0464-7734
- Man's World. bi-m.
- Men. m.
- Modern Movies' Hollywood Exposed. bi-m.
- Movie World. m. ISSN 0027-2779
- Screen Stars Yearbook. a.
- Secret Story. m (8 per yr.)
- Soap Opera Serials. m.
- Stag. m.
- T V by Day. m.

**Magazine of Bibliographies**
1209 Clover Lane, Fort Worth, TX 76107.
- Magazine of Bibliographies. q.

**Magazine Publishers Association, Inc.**
575 Lexington Ave., New York, NY 10022.
- M P A Update. m.

**Magazines-Creative, Inc.**
37 W. 39th St., New York, NY 10018.
- Creative Signs & Displays. bi-m.

**Magazines for Industry, Inc.**
777 Third Ave., New York, NY 10017.
- Beverage Industry. fortn.
- Beverage Industry Annual Manual. a.
- Candy & Snack Industry; news of confectionery and baked snack manufacturing and marketing. fortn.
- Candy & Snack Industry Buying Guide. a.
- Candy Marketer. m. ISSN 0008-5545
- Dairy & Ice Cream Field. m. ISSN 0011-555X
- Dairy Industries Catalog. a. ISSN 0070-2587
- Food and Drug Packaging. bi-w. ISSN 0015-6272
- Glass Industry. m. ISSN 0017-1026
- Inside Industry. m. ISSN 0300-7049
- Official Board Markets; "the yellow sheet". w. ISSN 0030-0284
- Official Container Directory. s-a. ISSN 0030-0292
- Paperboard Packaging. m. ISSN 0031-1227

**Magic Industries**
20 E. 46th St., New York, NY 10017.
- Magic Magazine (New York) m. ISSN 0097-5176

**Magna Publishing Co.**
621 N. Sherman Ave., Madison, WI 53704.
- Collegiate Hedlines. w.
- National On-Campus Report. m. ISSN 0300-6646

**Magnum-Royal Publications Inc.**
18 E. 41st St., New York, NY 10017.
- High Performance Engines.
- Rodder and Super Stock Car Magazine. bi-m.
- Stock Cars. a. ISSN 0081-5616
- Supercycle Sports. q.
- Swank. m.

**Al Magnuson, Ed. & Pub.**
Rt. 1, Box 89 F, Eastsound, WA 98245.
- Islands' Sounder; serving all of San Juan County & Fidalgo Island. 32 per yr.

**Maher Publications, Inc.**
222 W. Adams St., Chicago, IL 60606.
- Down Beat. fortn. ISSN 0012-5768
- Music Handbook. a. ISSN 0077-2372

**William F. Mahler, Ed. & Pub.**
Southern Methodist University Herbarium, Dallas, TX 75275.
- Sida; Contributions to Botany. 2 per yr. ISSN 0080-9470

**Mahoning Mimeograph and Pamphlet Service**
Box 176, Marion Center, PA 15759.
- Indiana County Historical Series. irreg., 1964, no. 2. ISSN 0073-6864

**Mail**
311 West 90th St, New York, NY 10024.
- Mail. 3 per yr. ISSN 0025-0546

**Mailbox Club, Inc.**
404 Eager Rd., Valdosta, GA 31601.
- Teen Talk. q. ISSN 0492-5408

**Steven L. Maimes, Ed. & Pub.**
224 Judah Street 1, San Francisco, CA 94122.
- Tzaddikim; a catalogue of Chassidic, Kabbalistic and selected Judaic books. s-a.

**Main Lafrentz & Co. (Certified Public Accountants)**
280 Park Ave, New York, NY 10017.
- Main Lafrentz & Company. News Summary. m.
- Main Lafrentz & Company. Tax Newsletter. m.
- Viewpoint (New York) s-a.

**Maine. Bureau of Labor and Industry. Department of Commerce and Industry**
State Office Building, Augusta, ME 04330.
- Maine. Bureau of Labor and Industry. Occupational Wage Survey. a. ISSN 0093-7886

**Maine. Bureau of Labor and Industry. Department of Manpower Affairs**
Capitol Shopping Center, Western Avenue, Augusta, ME 04330.
- Census of Maine Manufactures. a. ISSN 0090-7111

**Maine. Bureau of Property Taxation**
Room 202, State Office Building, Augusta, ME 04330.
- Maine. Bureau of Property Taxation. Biennial Report. biennial. ISSN 0361-3550

**Maine. Commission on the Arts and the Humanities**
State House, Augusta, ME 04333.
- Update (Augusta) bi-m.

**Maine. Criminal Justice Planning & Assistance Agency**
11 Parkwood Dr., Augusta, ME 04330.
- Maine. Criminal Justice Planning & Assistance Agency. Maine Criminal Justice Internship Program; Report and Evaluation. irreg., latest 1974. ISSN 0090-9386
- Maine. Criminal Justice Planning & Assistance Agency. Progress Report. a.

**Maine. Department of Conservation**
Bureau of Forestry, Entomology Laboratory, 50 Hospital St., Augusta, ME 04330.
- Maine. Department of Conservation. Bureau of Forestry. Forest Insect and Disease Notes. a.

**Maine. Department of Environmental Protection**
Division of Information and Education, Augusta, ME 04333.
- Maine Environnews. fortn.

**Maine. Department of Health and Welfare**
State House, Augusta, ME 04330.
- C H P Communicator. (Comprehensive Health Planning) q. ISSN 0007-8379
- Maine Communicator. bi-m. ISSN 0047-553X

**Maine. Department of Inland Fisheries and Wildlife**
284 State St., Augusta, ME 04333.
- Maine Fish and Wildlife. q.

**Maine. Department of Manpower Affairs. Employment Security Commission**
Augusta, ME 04330.
- Maine. Employment Security Commission. Annual Rural Manpower Report. a. ISSN 0094-1913
- Maine Manpower. m. ISSN 0025-0686

**Maine. Department of Marine Resources**
State House Annex, Augusta, ME 04330.
- Maine. Department of Marine Resources. Fisheries Circulars, Bulletins and Contributions. irreg. ISSN 0076-2628

**Maine. Department of the Attorney General. Criminal Division**
Augusta, ME 04330.
- Maine Prosecutor Bulletin. m. ISSN 0094-5439 (prep. by its Law Enforcement Education Section)

**Maine. Department of the Attorney General. Law Enforcement Education Section**
State House, Augusta, ME 04330.
- Maine Prosecutor, Criminal Legislation Manual. irreg.

**Maine. Department of Transportation**
Augusta, ME 04330.
- Maine. Department of Transportation. Annual Report. a. ISSN 0094-5048

**Maine. Geological Survey**
Department of Conservation, Marden Building, 308 State St., Augusta, ME 04330.
- Maine Geological Survey. Bulletins. irreg.
- Maine Geological Survey. Mineral Resources Index Series. irreg. ISSN 0460-6736
- Maine Geological Survey. Miscellaneous Publications. irreg. ISSN 0076-2644
- Maine Geological Survey. Special Economic Studies Series. irreg. ISSN 0542-1136

**Maine. Higher Education Facilities Commission**
Augusta, ME 04330.
- Maine. Higher Education Facilities Commission. Enrollment and Facilities Inventory. a.

**Maine. Labor Market Evaluation and Planning Section**
Augusta, ME 04330.
- Maine. Labor Market Evaluation and Planning Section. Annual Manpower Planning Report. a. ISSN 0093-8122

**Maine. Manpower Research Division**
Augusta, ME 04330.
- Maine. Manpowr Research Division. Annual Report on State and Occupation Requirements for Vocationaal Education. a. ISSN 0095-473X

**Maine. School Administrative District 70**
c/o Lloyd R. Chase, Ed., Box 323, Houlton, ME 04730.
- Maine School Administrative District No. 70 News & Notes. 7 per yr.

**Maine. Soil and Water Conservation Commission**
State House, Augusta, ME 04333.
- Maine. Soil and Water Conservation Commission. Biennial Report. biennial. ISSN 0085-297X

**Maine. State Development Office**
Desk MMD, State House, Augusta, ME 04333.
- Maine Marketing Directory. a.

**Maine. State Library**
Cultural Bldg., Augusta, ME 04330.
- Downeast Libraries. 5 per yr. (Co-Sponsor: Maine Library Association)
- Libraries of Maine; Directory and Statistics. a. (prep. by its Department of Educational and Cultural Services)
- Maine. State Library. Special Subject Resources in Maine. irreg., latest issue 1972. ISSN 0091-0759

**Maine. State Planning Office**
189 State Street, Augusta, ME 04330.
- Maine. State Planning Office. Annual Report. a. ISSN 0091-0678

**Maine A F L-C I O**
499 Broadway, Bangor, ME 04401.
- Maine State Labor News. m. ISSN 0025-0759

**Maine Agricultural Experiment Station**
University of Maine at Orono, Orono, ME 04473.
- Research in the Life Sciences. irreg. ISSN 0034-5261

**Maine Antique Digest, Inc.**
Box 358, Waldoboro, ME 04572.
- Maine Antique Digest. m.

**Maine Digest Inc**
Box 142, Rockport, ME 04856.
- Maine Digest. q. ISSN 0025-0627

**Maine Edition**
c/o Stephen Cook, Ed., 22 Bridge St., Topsham, ME 04086.
- Maine Edition. q.

**Maine Genealogical Inquirer**
Box 253, Oakland, ME 04963.
- Maine Genealogical Inquirer. q.

**Maine Good Roads Association**
146 State St., Augusta, ME 04330.
- Maine Trail. m. ISSN 0047-5548

**Maine Guarantee Authority**
State House, Augusta, ME 04330.
- Maine Guarantee Authority. Annual Report. a.

**Maine Historical Society**
485 Congress St., Portland, ME 04111.
- Maine Historical Society. Quarterly. q.

**Maine Medical Association**
- Maine Medical Association. Journal. (pub. by Brunswick Publishing Co.)

**Maine Municipal Association**
Local Government Center, Community Drive, Augusta, ME 04330.
- Maine Townsman. m. ISSN 0025-0791

**Maine National Bank**
c/o Kenneth J. Keller, 400 Congress St., Portland, ME 04111.
- Maine Business Indicators. bi-m. ISSN 0025-0619

**Maine Nature**
Box 509, Brunswick, ME 04011.
- Maine Nature. m. ISSN 0025-0708

**Maine Organic Farmer and Gardener**
Box 187, 110 Water St., Hallowell, ME 04347.
- Maine Organic Farmer and Gardener. bi-m.

**Maine Potato Council**
Box 632, Presque Isle, ME 04769.
- Potato Councillor. m. ISSN 0032-5570

**Maine State Grocers Association**
c/o Arthur H. Charles, Ed., 320 Baxter Blvd., Portland, ME 04101.
- Maine State Grocers Bulletin. a.

**Maine State Museum**
- Maine Heritage Series. (pub. by Bond Wheelwright Co.)

**Maine Teachers' Association**
184 State St., Augusta, ME 04330.
- Maine Teacher. 20 per yr. ISSN 0025-0775

**Maine Times**
Main St., Topsham, ME 04086.
- Maine Times; Maine journal of news and opinion. w. ISSN 0025-0783

**Maine Water Utilities Association**
225 Douglass St., Portland, ME 04104.
- Maine Water Utilities Association. Journal. 6 per yr. ISSN 0025-0805

**Maine Writers' Conference**
- Maine Writers' Conference Chapbook. (pub. by Prejepscot Press)

**Maji-Maji**
c/o Coles-Sutton, Wiatt Hall, 1830 N. Parkmall, Philadelphia, PA 19122.
- Maji-Maji. 5 per yr.

**Major Magazines, Inc.**
235 Park Ave. South, New York, NY 10003.
- Cracked. m. (8 per yr.)
- True Frontier; factual stories of the old West. bi-m.

**Majority Report Co.**
74 Grove St., Sheridan Square, New York, NY 10014.
- Majority Report; feminist news for women. bi-w.

**Malayan Tin Bureau**
2000 K St., N. W., Washington, DC 20006.
- Tin News. m. ISSN 0040-7968 (Tin Industry (Research and Development) Board)

**Malaysian Rubber Bureau**
1925 K St. NW, Washington, DC 20006.
- Natural Rubber News. m. ISSN 0028-0755 (Malaysian Rubber Research and Development Board MY)

**Robert Malcomson, Ed. & Pub.**
38559 Asbury Park Drive, Mt. Clemens, MI 48043.
- Those Enduring Matinee Idols. bi-m. ISSN 0040-6422

**Maledicta Press**
331 S. Greenfield Ave., Waukesha, WI 53186.
- Maledicta Press Publications. irreg. ISSN 0363-9037
- Maledicta: the International Journal of Verbal Aggression. 3 per yr. ISSN 0363-3659

**Malki Museum, Inc.**
11-795 Fields Road, Morongo Indian Reservation, Banning, CA 92502.
- Journal of California Anthropology. s-a.

**Malpractice Lifeline, Inc.**
1240 Meadow Rd., Suite 207, Northbrook, IL 60062.
- Malpractice Lifeline; newsletter on professional liability. s-m. ISSN 0361-8412

**Malraux Society**
c/o Dr. W. Langlois, Box 3231, Univ. of Wyoming, Laramie, WY 82071.
- Melanges Malraux Miscellany. s-a. ISSN 0025-892X

**Mamelle**
Box 3123, San Francisco, CA 94119.
- Mamelle; an alternative anthology of contemporary West Coast art. q.

**Man and His Music**
1346 Chapel St., New Haven, CT 06511.
- Man and His Music. q. ISSN 0025-150X

**Man & Manager Inc.**
799 Broadway, New York, NY 10003
(Subscr. to: 87 Terminal Dr., Plainview, N.Y. 11803)
- Businessman & the Law. s-m. ISSN 0007-716X
- Employee Relations in Action. m. ISSN 0013-6824
- Manufacturing & the Law. s-m. ISSN 0025-2549
- Marketing in Action. s-m.
- O S H A Report. (Federal Occupational Safety and Health Act) m.
- Protection Management. s-m. ISSN 0048-5624
- White Collar Management. s-m. ISSN 0043-4884

**Man-Flight Systems, Inc.**
Box 872, Worcester, MA 01613.
- Skysurfer. q.

**Man in the Northeast**
Box 425, George's Mills, NH 03751.
- Occasional Publications in Northeastern Anthropology. irreg.

**Management Information Corporation**
140 Barclay Center, Cherry Hill, NJ 08034.
- Computer Personnel Management Reports. m.
- Data Entry Awareness Report Newsletter. m.
- Datacomm Awareness Report. m.
- Packaged Software Reports. m.
- Small Business Computer News. m.

**Management Information Service**
Box 5129, Detroit, MI 48326.
- Auburn University. Project Themis Research. Annual Report. irreg.

**Management Reports Inc.**
210 South St., Boston, MA 02111.
- Bank Installment Lending Newsletter. m. ISSN 0005-5069
- Securities Regulation and Transfer Report. s-m. ISSN 0037-0673

**Management Resources, Inc.**
757 Third Ave., New York, NY 10017.
- Fair Employment Compliance; a confidential letter to management. s-m.

**Management Science Publishing Inc.**
430 Park Ave., New York, NY 10022.
- A D P Newsletter/Automatic Data Processing Newsletter. fortn. ISSN 0044-5649

**Management-Scope**
c/o Lawrence Leiter and Co., 427 W. 12th St., Kansas City, MO 64105.
- Management-Scope; information of interest about all phases of management. q. ISSN 0047-5718

**Management Services Associates**
Box 3750, Austin, TX 78764.
- Tax Correspondent. 18 per yr.

**Manas Publishing Co.**
Box 32112, El Sereno Sta., Los Angeles, CA 90032.
- Manas. w. ISSN 0025-1976

**Andrew R. Mandala, Ed. & Pub.**
898 National Press Bldg., Washington, DC 20004.
- Mortgage Commentary; a weekly newsletter serving institutional mortgage investors. w.

**Mangineer Publications**
P.O. Box 403, Birmingham, MI 48012.
- Mangineer. bi-m.

**Mangum Family Bulletin**
Rt. 1 Box 378, Westview St., Scottsboro, AL 35802.
- Mangum Family Bulletin. a.

**Manhattan Arts Review, Inc.**
560 Riverside Drive, New York, NY 10027.
- New York Arts Journal. bi-m.

**Manhattan Center for Advanced Psychoanalytic Studies, Inc.**
- Modern Psychoanalysis. (pub. by Modern Psychoanalytic Publications)

**Manhattan College. Department of English and World Literature**
Bronx, NY 10471.
- Literary Research Newsletter. q.

**Manhattan College. School of Engineering**
Bronx, NY 10471.
- Manhattan College Engineer. q. ISSN 0025-2093

**Manion Forum**
St. Joseph Bank Bldg., South Bend, IN 46601.
- Manion Forum. w. ISSN 0025-2174

**Manitowoc County Historical Society**
1115 North 18th St., Manitowoc, WI 54220.
- Manitowoc County Historical Society. Mini Newsletter. irreg.

**Mankato State University**
Box 58, Mankato, MN 56001.
- Mankato State Independent. 3 per w.
- Medicine Jug. 3 per yr.

**Mankind Publishing Co.**
8060 Melrose Ave., Los Angeles, CA 90046.
- Mankind; the magazine of popular history. q. ISSN 0025-2336

**Mano Enterprises, Inc.**
Box 161, Franksville, WI 53126.
- Referee; magazine for sports officials. bi-m.

**Manomet Bird Observatory**
P.O. Box 0, Manomet, MA 02345.
- Manomet Bird Observatory Research Report. 2 per yr.

**ManRoot**
Box 982, South San Francisco, CA 94080.
- ManRoot. 1-2 per yr. ISSN 0025-2441

**Man's Magazine**
919 Third Ave., New York, NY 10022.
- Man's Magazine. m. ISSN 0025-2476

**Mansfield State College. Department of English**
Mansfield, PA 16933.
- Falcon. s-a. ISSN 0014-7079

**Manson Western Corp.**
12031 Wilshire Blvd., Los Angeles, CA 90025
(Subscr. Address: Box 2810, Boulder CO 80302)
- Human Behavior; the newsmagazine of the social sciences. m. ISSN 0046-8134

**Manufactured Housing Reporter**
Box 34475, Dallas, TX 75234.
- Manufactured Housing Reporter. m.

**Manufacturer Publishing Co.**
8543 Puritan Ave., Detroit, MI 48238.
- Directory of Michigan Manufacturers. a. ISSN 0070-5845
- Michigan Manufacturer and Financial Record. m. ISSN 0026-2277

**Manufacturers' Agent Publishing Co., Inc.**
663 Fifth Ave., New York, NY 10022.
- Manufacturers' Agents' Guide. biennial. ISSN 0076-4213
- Verified Directory of Manufacturers' Representatives. biennial. ISSN 0083-5692

**Manufacturers' Agents National Association**
3130 Wilshire Blvd., Suite 509, Los Angeles, CA 90010.
- Agency Sales /With Agent & Representative. m. ISSN 0044-6718

**Manufacturers Hanover Trust Co. International Division**
350 Park Ave., New York, NY 10022.
- Banking Guides - Asia, Australia, New Zealand with Principal Hotels and Bank Holidays. a.

**Manufacturer's News, Inc.**
3 E. Huron St., Chicago, IL 60611.
- Alabama Industrial Directory. a. ISSN 0401-149X
- Alaska Directory of Commercial Establishments. biennial.
- Arizona Directory of Manufacturers. biennial. ISSN 0571-0006
- Arkansas Directory of Industries. a.

- Chicago Zip-Coded Manufacturers Directory. biennial. ISSN 0069-3383
- Directory of South Dakota Industries. biennial. ISSN 0417-6529
- Georgia Manufacturing Directory. a. ISSN 0435-5482
- Illinois Services Directory. biennial. ISSN 0092-3818
- Scott's Ontario Industrial Directory. biennial. ISSN 0582-3072
- Scott's Quebec Industrial Directory. biennial. ISSN 0582-3080
- Scott's Western Canada Industrial Directory; includes Manitoba, Saskatchewan, Alberta, British Columbia. triennial.
- Texas Manufacturers Directory. a.
- Vermont State Industrial Directory. biennial.
- Virginia Industrial Directory. biennial.
- Washington State Manufacturers Directory. triennial.
- Wisconsin Manufacturers Directory. a.
- Wyoming Directory of Manufacturing and Mining. a. ISSN 0511-0289

**Manufacturing Chemists Association**
1825 Connecticut Ave., N.W., Washington, DC 20009.
- Chemecology. m.

**Manufacturing Confectioner Publishing Co.**
175 Rock Rd., Glen Rock, NJ 07452.
- Candy Buyers Directory. a. (prep. by its Directory Division)
- Manufacturing Confectioner. m. ISSN 0025-2573

**Manufacturing Jewelers and Silversmiths of America, Inc**
- American Jewelry Manufacturer. (pub. by Chilton Co., Inc.)

**Mapat Publications Inc.**
527 Madison Ave., New York, NY 10022.
- Models and the People Around Them. bi-m.

**Mapix**
Box 220, Roslyn, Long Island, NY 11576.
- Fantastic Creatures. bi-m.

**Maple Leaf Club**
5560 West 62nd Street, Los Angeles, CA 90056.
- Rag Times. bi-m. ISSN 0090-4570

**Maps**
c/o John Taggart, 311 E. Garfield, Shippensburg, PA 17257.
- Maps. a. ISSN 0542-626X

**Marathon Oil Co.**
Press and Publications Division, 539 S. Main St., Findlay, OH 45840.
- Marathon World. q. ISSN 0025-2743

**Marburger Publishing Co., Inc.**
Hartford, AR 72938.
- Gamecock. m. ISSN 0016-4313

**Marcom-West, Inc.**
Box 8268, Van Nuys, CA 91409.
- Food Broker; sales and marketing. a.
- Food Industry Directory. a.
- Grocery Communications; showcase of the Western food industry. m.

**Marden-Kane, Inc.**
666 Fifth Ave., New York, NY 10019.
- John Scarne's Newsletter. m.

**Margins**
Box A, Fairwater, WI 53931.
- Margins; a review of little magazines & small press books. m. ISSN 0300-7553

**Mariah Publications**
3401 W. Division St., Chicago, IL 60651
(Subscr. to: Box 2690, Boulder CO 80302)
- Mariah. q. (American Institute for Exploration)

**Marian Library**
University of Dayton, Dayton, OH 45469.
- Marian Library Studies. New Series. a. ISSN 0076-4434

**Maricopa Urban Teachers Association**
2102 W. Indian School Rd., Phoenix, AZ 85015.
- Maricopa Urban Teachers Association Newsletter. 3-4 per yr. ISSN 0025-3030

**Marie Selby Botanical Gardens**
800 S. Palm Ave., Sarasota, FL 33577.
● Selbyana. irreg. ISSN 0361-185X

**Marietta College**
Marietta, OH 45750.
● Marcolian. w. ISSN 0025-2867

**Marilyn**
150 W. Ninth St., Claremont, CA 91711.
● Marilyn; a magazine of new poetry. s-a.

**Marina News, Inc.**
27601 Little Mack, Saint Clair Shores, MI 48081.
● Marine & Recreation News. w. ISSN 0025-312X

**Marine Advisory Service**
University of Rhode Island, Narragansett, RI 02882.
● Marine Recreation Conference. Report. a.

**Marine Annuals, Inc.**
P.O. Box 1486, Annapolis, MD 21404.
● Waterway Guide; the yachtsman's Bible. a.

**Marine Aquarist Publications, Inc.**
Box 35, Marlboro, MA 01752.
● Marine Aquarist. 10 per yr. ISSN 0047-5947

**Marine Biological Laboratory**
Woods Hole, MA 02543.
● Biological Bulletin. bi-m.(2 vols. per yr.) ISSN 0006-3185

**Marine Business**
48 E. 43rd St., New York, NY 10017.
● Marine Business. 6 per yr.

**Marine Corps Association**
Box 1775, Quantico, VA 22134.
● Leatherneck; magazine of the Marines. m. ISSN 0023-981X
● Marine Corps Gazette; the professional magazine for United States Marines. m. ISSN 0025-3170

**Marine Digest Inc.**
Rm. 218, National Bldg., 1008 Western Ave., Seattle, WA 98104.
● Marine Digest. w. ISSN 0025-3197

**Marine Engineers Beneficial Association**
● American Maritime Officer. (pub. by Associated Maritime Officers A F L-C I O)

**Marine Historical Associations, Inc.**
c/o Mystic Seaport Stores, Inc., Mystic, CT 06355.
● Bibliography of Periodical Articles on Maritime and Naval History. a.

**Marine Hobbyist News**
205 Orr Drive, Normal, IL 61761.
● Marine Hobbyist News. m. ISSN 0363-2881

**Marine Publications**
c/o Ralph Wilbur, 130 Shepard St., Lawrence, MA 01843.
● Power Boat Annual; accessory directory. a. ISSN 0085-5057

**Marine Retailer**
48 E. 43rd St., New York, NY 10017.
● Marine Retailer. m.

**Marine Safety Council**
Coast Guard Headquarters, Washington, DC 20590.
● Marine Safety Council. Proceedings. m.

**Marine Technology Society**
1730 M St. N.W., Washington, DC 20036.
● Marine Technology Society. Annual Conference Proceedings. a. (Co-sponsor: Institute of Electrical and Electronics Engineers)
● Marine Technology Society Journal. 6 per yr.

**A. J. Marineau**
P.O. Box 8187, Moscow, ID 83843.
● Northwest Experience. bi-m.

**Mario Negri Institute for Pharmacological Research**
● Mario Negri Institute for Pharmacological Research. Monographs. (pub. by Raven Press)

**Maritime Activity Reports, Inc.**
107 E. 31st St., New York, NY 10016.
● Maritime Reporter and Engineering News. s-m. ISSN 0025-3448

**Maritime Association of the Port of N.Y.**
80 Broad St., New York, NY 10004.
● Maritime Association of the Port of New York. Newsletter. fortn.

**Maritime Postmark Society**
1029 Martin Road, Houston, TX 77018.
● Seaposter. bi-m. ISSN 0048-9891

**Maritime Research, Inc.**
11 Broadway, New York, NY 10004.
● Chartering Annual. a.
● Maritime Research. Weekly Newsletter. w.

**Mark-Age, Inc.**
327 N.E. 20th Terrace, Miami, FL 33137.
● M A I N. (Mark-Age Inform-Nations) 10 per yr.

**Mark Distributors**
49 Downing St., New York, NY 10014.
● Yellow Book; gay monthly review.

**J. Mark Press**
Box 2057, N. Babylon, NY 11703.
● All-Time Favorite Poetry. a. ISSN 0065-633X
● American Scenes. q.
● Best in Poetry. q.
● Best Poets of the Twentieth Century on Man and Environment. q. (Winston Paramount Books)
● Contemporary Poets. q.
● Poetry of Our Times. q. ISSN 0048-461X
● Poetry of the Year. q.
● Poets of the Twentieth Century. q.

**Mark Twain Journal**
Kirkwood, MO 63122.
● Mark Twain Journal. s-a. ISSN 0025-3499

**Mark Twain Research Foundation, Inc.**
Perry, MO 63462.
● Twainian. bi-m. ISSN 0041-4573

**Mark 40 Enterprises,Inc.**
120 Sylvan Ave., Englewood Cliffs, NJ 07632.
● 40 for Presidents. bi-m.

**Markell Publishing Co.**
Box 1200, CA 91722.
● Record Collector's Journal. m.

**Market Chronicle**
c/o Wm. B. Dana Co., 25 Park Place, New York, NY 10007.
● Market Chronicle. w.

**Market Communications Inc.**
225 E. Michigan, Milwaukee, WI 53202.
● Archery Retailer. 5 per yr.
● Archery World. bi-m. ISSN 0003-827X
● Camping Industry. 7 per yr. ISSN 0008-2430
● FarmFutures. m.
● SnoTrack. 6 per yr (during winter) ISSN 0049-0822

**Market News Publishing Corporation**
156 Fifth Ave., New York, NY 10010.
● Fibre Market News. 3 per w. ISSN 0046-3728
● Recycling Today. m.

**Market Place Publications**
Box 58421, 170 World Trade Mart, Dallas, TX 75258.
● Gift Digest. bi-m.
● Market Place. m. ISSN 0025-357X (Exhibitor Services, Inc)

**Market-Show Publications, Inc.**
Suite 1010, MONY Bldg., 1655 Peachtree St. N.E., Atlanta, GA 30309.
● Southern Office. m. ISSN 0584-455X

**Marketeer**
c/o V. B. Cook, 1602 E. Glen Ave., Peoria, IL 61614.
● Marketeer. m.

**Marketing Development**
402 Border Rd., Concord, MA 01742.
● New Product Directory of N.Y.S.E. Listed Companies. (New York Stock Exchange) a.

**Marketing Economics Institute, Ltd.**
441 Lexington Ave., New York, NY 10017.
● M E I Marketing Economics Guide. a. ISSN 0092-4857
● Marketing Economics Key Plants; guide to industrial purchasing power. biennial. ISSN 0076-4531

**Marketing Forum Magazine**
19 W. 44th St., New York, NY 10036.
● Marketing Image. bi-m. ISSN 0025-3707

**Marketing Handbooks Inc.**
31 Wallacks Lane, Stamford, CT 06902.
● Travel Market Yearbook; a world of travel facts, figures & trends. a. ISSN 0564-1632

**Marketing News, Inc.**
Box 1425, Sedalia, MO 65301.
● Marketing News Midwest; business news for appliance, home entertainment, furniture, and floor covering retailers. m.

**Marketing Programs and Services Group, Inc.**
Box 554, Gaithersburg, MD 20760.
● P B X Systems Guide. q. ISSN 0092-8828
● Telecommunications Product Review. m.

**Marketing Publications Inc.**
National Press Bldg., Washington, DC 20045.
● Customer Service Newsletter. m. ISSN 0145-8442
● Distribution /Warehouse Cost Digest. fortn. ISSN 0012-3927

**Marketing Science Institute**
14 Story St., Cambridge, MA 02138.
● Marketing Science Institute Newsletter. q.

**Marketing Services Group International**
Box 1292, San Mateo, CA 94401.
● Frontier Australasia. m.

**Marketplace Publications Inc.**
Box 696, 125 Elm St., New Canaan, CT 06840.
● C P A's Market Place. q.
● Dentist Market Place. q. ISSN 0011-8818
● Lawyers Marketplace. q. ISSN 0023-9461
● Physicians Market Place. bi-m. ISSN 0031-9074
● Travel Agents Marketplace. 6 per yr.

**Markham Publishing Co.**
3322 W. Peterson Ave., Chicago, IL 60645.
● Lectures in Advanced Mathematics. irreg., 1968, no. 3. ISSN 0075-8477

**Marking Devices Publishing Co., Inc.**
18 E. Huron St., Chicago, IL 60611.
● Marking Industry. m. ISSN 0025-3839

**Markson Science Inc.**
Box 767, Del Mar, CA 92014.
● Science Supply News. q.

**Marple's Business Roundup, Inc.**
465A Colman Bldg., Seattle, WA 98104.
● Marple's Business Newsletter. fortn.

**Marquette Engineer**
1515 W. Wisconsin Ave., Milwaukee, WI 53233.
● Marquette Engineer. q. ISSN 0025-3960

**Marquette University**
1131 W. Wisconsin Ave., Milwaukee, WI 53233.
● Marquette Journal. 4-6 per yr. ISSN 0025-3979
● Marquette Today. q.
● Marquette Tribune. s-w. ISSN 0025-3995

**Marquette University. Aristotelean Society**
● Aquinas Lecture Series. (pub. by Marquette University Press)

**Marquette University. College of Business Administration**
Milwaukee, WI 53233.
● Marquette Business Review. q. ISSN 0025-3952

**Marquette University. Law School**
1103 W. Wisconsin Ave., Milwaukee, WI 53233.
● Marquette Law Review. q. ISSN 0025-3987

**Marquette University Press**
1131 W. Wisconsin Ave, Milwaukee, WI 53233.
● Aquinas Lecture Series. a. ISSN 0066-5614 (Marquette University. Aristotelean Society)
● Marquette Slavic Studies. irreg. ISSN 0076-4671 (Marquette University. Slavic Institute)
● Mediaeval Philosophical Texts in Translation. irreg. ISSN 0076-5856

**Marquette University. School of Dentistry**
604 N. 16th St., Milwaukee, WI 53233.
● Dental Images. 3 per yr. ISSN 0070-3664

**Marquette University. Slavic Institute**
● Marquette Slavic Studies. (pub. by Marquette University Press)

**Marquis Academic Media**
(Subsidiary of: Marquis Who's Who, Inc.)
200 E. Ohio St., Chicago, IL 60611.
- Annual Register of Grant Support. a. ISSN 0066-4049
- Consumer Protection Directory. irreg.
- Directory of Publishing Opportunities. irreg., 3rd, 1975. ISSN 0070-623X
- Directory of Registered Lobbyists and Lobbyist Legislation. irreg., 2nd 1975.
- Environmental Protection Directory. irreg., 2nd 1975.
- N I H Factbook. biennial. (U.S. National Institutes of Health)
- National Aeronautics and Space Administration. N A S A Factbook. irreg. 1975 2nd ed. ISSN 0077-3085
- Standard Education Almanac. a. ISSN 0081-4237
- U. S. National Science Foundation. N S F Factbook. irreg., 2nd ed. 1975. ISSN 0083-2375
- Worldwide Directory of Computer Companies.
- Worldwide Directory of Federal Libraries. irreg.
- Yearbook of Adult and Continuing Education. a.
- Yearbook of Equal Educational Opportunities. irreg.
- Yearbook of Higher Education. a. ISSN 0084-3784
- Yearbook of Special Education. a.

**Marquis Who's Who Inc.**
200 E. Ohio St., Chicago, IL 60611
(and 4300 W. 62nd St., Indianapolis, Ind. 46268)
- Directory of Medical Specialists. biennial. ISSN 0070-5829
- Directory of Osteopathic Specialists. irreg.
- Energy: a Guide to Organizations and Information Resources in the U.S.
- International Scholars Directory.
- Who Was Who in America. irreg.
- Who's Who in America. biennial. ISSN 0083-9396
- Who's Who in Finance and Industry. biennial. ISSN 0083-9523
- Who's Who in Government. biennial, 2nd 1975.
- Who's Who in Religion. biennial.
- Who's Who in the East. biennial. ISSN 0083-9760
- Who's Who in the Midwest. biennial. ISSN 0083-9787
- Who's Who in the South and Southwest. biennial. ISSN 0083-9809
- Who's Who in the West. biennial. ISSN 0083-9817
- Who's Who in the World. biennial; 3rd edition, 1976. ISSN 0083-9825
- Who's Who of American Women. biennial. ISSN 0083-9841
- World Who's Who in Science. irreg. ISSN 0084-246X

**Marriott Corporation**
5161 River Rd., Washington, DC 20016.
- Marriott Management Newsletter. m.

**Marshall-Wythe School of Law**
Williamsburg, VA 23185.
- William & Mary Law Review. q. ISSN 0043-5589

**Marstellar Inc.**
866 Third Ave., New York, NY 10022.
- Checkout. bi-m.

**C. F. Martin and Co.**
Nazareth, PA 18064.
- 1833; the Martin magazine. q.

**Martin Center**
3561 N. College Ave., Indianapolis, IN 46205.
- Afro-American Journal. q.

**Martin Co., Inc.**
20 N. Wacker Drive, Chicago, IL 60606.
- Electrified Industry; industrial progress through wise energy use. m. ISSN 0013-4562
- Modern Stores and Offices. bi-m. ISSN 0026-8453

**Gloria A. Martin, Ed. & Pub.**
829 26th Ave., Council Bluffs, IA 51501.
- Glowing Lanterns. 3 per yr.

**Robert L. Martin, Ed. & Pub.**
Univ. of Maine, Dept. of Biology, Farmington, ME 04938.
- Bat Research News. q. ISSN 0005-6227

**Martin Luther King, Jr. Center for Social Change**
671 Beckwith St. S.W., Atlanta, GA 30314.
- Martin Luther King, Jr. Center for Social Change Newsletter. q.

**Franklin H. Martin Memorial Foundation**
55 E. Erie St., Chicago, IL 60611.
- Surgery, Gynecology & Obstetrics. m. ISSN 0039-6087 (American College of Surgeons)

**Martin Psychiatric Research Foundation**
Mid-Continent Hospital, 122 North Cooper, Olathe, KS 66061.
- Corrective and Social Psychiatry and Journal of Behavioral Technology Methods and Therapy. q.

**Martin Publications (Sacramento)**
2120 28th St., Sacramento, CA 95818.
- On the Go. m.

**Martin Publishing Co.**
Box 155, North English, IA 52316.
- Genealogy Bug. m.

**Martindale-Hubbell, Inc.**
1 Prospect St., Summit, NJ 07901.
- Martindale-Hubbell Law Directory. a.

**Marvel Comics Group**
574 Madison Ave., New York, NY 10022.
- Foom. q.

**Robert B. Marvin, Ed. & Pub.**
Box 326, Jasper, FL 32052.
- Journal of the Southern Confederacy; the magazine of the Old South. q. ISSN 0047-2859

**Mary Washington College. Department of Geography**
Fredericksburg, VA 22401.
- Virginia Geographer. 2 per yr. ISSN 0042-6512 (Virginia Geographical Society)

**Maryland. Bureau of Air Quality Control**
610 N. Howard St., Baltimore, MD 21201.
- Maryland. Bureau of Air Quality Control. State-Local Cooperative Air Sampling Program Yearly Data Report. a. ISSN 0094-4629

**Maryland. Bureau of Traffic Engineering**
Annapolis, MD 21401.
- Maryland. Bureau of Traffic Engineering. Traffic Trends. irreg. ISSN 0094-6265

**Maryland. Commission on Intergovernmental Cooperation**
Old Armory Bldg., Box 231, Annapolis, MD 21404.
- Maryland. Commission on Intergovernmental Cooperation. Annual Report. a. ISSN 0098-8766

**Maryland. Correctional Training Commission**
Room 16, 7 Church Lane, Pikesville, MD 21208.
- Maryland. Correctional Training Commission. Annual Report to the Governor, the Secretary of Public Safety and Correctional Services, and Members of the General Assembly. a. ISSN 0090-9963

**Maryland. Council for Higher Education**
2100 Guilford Ave., Baltimore, MD 21218.
- Inventory of Programs in Maryland'S Private and Public Universities and Colleges. a. ISSN 0075-0174
- Maryland. Council for Higher Education. Annual Report and Recommendations. irreg. ISSN 0361-140X
- State Directory of Higher Education Institutions and Agencies in Maryland. a. ISSN 0098-4132

**Maryland. Crime Investigating Commission**
Box 3208, Baltimore, MD 21228.
- Maryland Crime Report. 3 per yr. ISSN 0025-4207

**Maryland. Department of Economic and Community Development**
2525 Riva Rd., Annapolis, MD 21401.
- Directory of Maryland Exporters-Importers; an International Handbook. irreg. ISSN 0070-5799
- Directory of Maryland Manufacturers. biennial. ISSN 0070-5802
- Directory of Science Resources for Maryland. biennial. ISSN 0070-6256
- Maryland. q. ISSN 0025-4290
- Maryland. Department of Economic and Community Development. Annual Report. a. ISSN 0091-9810

**Maryland. Department of Economic and Community Development. Maryland Office of Tourism**
1748 Forest Dr., Annapolis, MD 21401.
- Maryland Travel Scene. q. ISSN 0300-7502

**Maryland. Department of Education**
P.O. Box 8717, Friendship International Airport, Baltimore, MD 21240.
- Facts About Maryland Public Education. a. ISSN 0092-461X

**Maryland. Department of Education. Division of Library Development and Services**
Box 8717, Friendship International Airport, Baltimore, MD 21240.
- Library Keynotes; news and views of library activities in Maryland. 2-3 per yr. ISSN 0024-2330

**Maryland. Department of Education. Division of Library Development and Services, School Media Services Section**
Baltimore, MD 21201.
- Issues in Media Management. irreg. ISSN 0098-7239

**Maryland. Department of Employment and Social Services**
Employment Security Administration, 1100 N. Eutaw St., Baltimore, MD 21201.
- Employment Report for Maryland and Metropolitan Baltimore. m.
- Maryland. Department of Employment and Social Services. Pamphlet. irreg. ISSN 0092-8720

**Maryland. Department of Fiscal Services. Division of Fiscal Research**
P.O. Box 231, Annapolis, MD 21404.
- Local Government Finances in Maryland. a. ISSN 0085-2821

**Maryland. Department of Health and Mental Hygiene**
Public Information Services, 201 W. Preston St., Baltimore, MD 21201.
- Maryland's Health. irreg. ISSN 0025-4401

**Maryland. Department of Human Resources**
Social Services Administration, 1315 St. Paul St., Baltimore, MD 21202.
- Maryland. Department of Human Resources. Information Pamphlet. irreg. ISSN 0092-9476

**Maryland. Department of Juvenile Services**
Department of Health and Mental Hygiene, 201 W. Preston St., Baltimore, MD 21201.
- Maryland. Department of Juvenile Services. Annual Statistical Report. a. ISSN 0076-4744
- Maryland. Department of Juvenile Services. Monthly Report. m.

**Maryland. Department of Legislative Reference**
16 Francis St., P.O. Box 348, Annapolis, MD 21404.
- Maryland. State Department of Legislative Reference. Snynopsis of Laws Enacted by the State of Maryland. a. ISSN 0093-0520

**Maryland. Department of Natural Resources**
Tawes State Office Building, 580 Taylor Ave., Annapolis, MD 21401.
- Maryland. Department of Natural Resources. Activities Report. a.
- Maryland Conservationist. bi-m. ISSN 0025-4193

**Maryland. Department of State Planning**
301 W. Preston St, Baltimore, MD 21201.
- Maryland. Department of State Planning. Activities Report. a. ISSN 0076-4752
- Maryland. Department of State Planning. Newsletter. bi-m.

**Maryland. Division of Correction**
920 Greenmount Ave., Baltimore, MD 21202.
- Maryland. Division of Correction. Report. a. ISSN 0362-9198

**Maryland. Division of Marketing**
College Park, MD 20740.
- Maryland. Division of Marketing. Publication. irreg.

**Maryland. Division of Social Security**
Annapolis, MD 21404.
- Maryland. Division of Social Security. Report. irreg. ISSN 0093-3007

**Maryland. Division of State Documents**
Box 802, Annapolis, MD 21404.
- Maryland Register. fortn. ISSN 0360-2834

**Maryland. Geological Survey**
Johns Hopkins University, Merryman Hall, Baltimore, MD 21218.
- Maryland. Geological Survey. Archeological Studies. irreg.
- Maryland. Geological Survey. Bulletin. irreg., 1972, no. 31. ISSN 0076-4779
- Maryland. Geological Survey. Educational Series. irreg., 1971, no. 3. ISSN 0076-4787
- Maryland. Geological Survey. Information Circular. irreg; no. 21, 1975. ISSN 0076-4795
- Maryland. Geological Survey. Report of Investigations. irreg; no. 27, 1976. ISSN 0076-4809
- Maryland. Geological Survey. Water Resources Basic Data Report. irreg., no. 8, 1976. ISSN 0076-4817

**Maryland. Governor's Commission on Law Enforcement and the Administration of Justice**
Suite 302, Executive Plaza One, Cockeysville, MD 21030.
- Maryland. Governor's Commission on Law Enforcement and the Administration of Justice. Comprehensive Plan. a.

**Maryland. Hall of Records Commission**
P.O. Box 828, Annapolis, MD 21404.
- Maryland Manual. biennial.

**Maryland. Social Services Administration**
1315 St. Paul Street, Baltimore, MD 21202.
- Maryland. Social Services Administration. Incidents of Suspected Child Abuse in Maryland. ISSN 0092-0169

**Maryland. State Board for Community Colleges**
State Treasury Bldg., Annapolis, MD 21404.
- Maryland. State Board for Community Colleges. Selected Statistical Data. irreg. ISSN 0099-2089

**Maryland Bankers Association**
Box 822, Baltimore, MD 21203.
- Maryland Banking Quarterly. m.

**Maryland Center of Public Broadcasting**
Owings Mills, MD 21117.
- Maryland Center of Public Broadcasting. Network News. m.

**Maryland Congress of Parents and Teachers Inc.**
17 Commerce St. Room 100, Baltimore, MD 21202.
- Maryland P T A Bulletin. m.(10 per yr.) ISSN 0025-4339

**Maryland-Delaware-D.C. Press Association**
9 W. Chase St., Baltimore, MD 21201.
- Maryland-Delaware-D. C. Press News. m. ISSN 0025-4215

**Maryland English Journal**
c/o Ed. Elsa R. Graser, 2735 North Charles St., Baltimore, MD 21218.
- Maryland English Journal. s-a. ISSN 0542-8343

**Maryland Genealogical Society**
c/o Ed. John J. Brinkley, 201 W. Monument St., Baltimore, MD 21201.
- Maryland Genealogical Society Bulletin. q. ISSN 0542-8351

**Maryland Herpetological Society**
2643 N. Charles St., Baltimore, MD 21218.
- Maryland Herpetological Society. Bulletin. q. ISSN 0025-4231 (Natural History Society of Maryland, Inc.)

**Maryland Historical Society**
201 W. Monument St., Baltimore, MD 21201.
- Maryland Historical Magazine. q. ISSN 0025-4258
- Maryland Historical Society. News and Notes. 6 per yr.

**Maryland Historical Trust**
2525 Riva Rd., Annapolis, MD 21401.
- Maryland Historical Trust. Annual Report. a. ISSN 0098-3403

**Maryland Horse Breeders Association**
Box 4, Timonium, MD 21093.
- Maryland Horse. m. ISSN 0025-4274

**Maryland Library Association**
115 W. Franklin St., Baltimore, MD 21201.
- Crab. bi-m.

**Maryland Media, Inc.**
Box U, College Park, MD 20742.
- Argus Magazine. w.

**Maryland Motor Truck Association, Inc.**
- T K. (pub. by Artsake Studios)

**Maryland Municipal League Inc.**
76 Maryland Ave., Annapolis, MD 21401.
- Municipal Maryland. 11 per yr.

**Maryland Nurses Association**
2315-17 St. Paul St., Baltimore, MD 21218.
- Maryland Nurse. 6 per yr. ISSN 0047-6080

**Maryland Ornithological Society, Inc.**
Cylburn Mansion, 4915 Greenspring Ave., Baltimore, MD 21209.
- Maryland Birdlife. q.

**Maryland Pharmaceutical Association**
650 W. Lombard St., Baltimore, MD 21201.
- Maryland Pharmacist. m. ISSN 0025-4347

**Maryland Police Training Commission**
7 Church Lane, Pikesville, MD 21208.
- Maryland. Police Training Commission. Annual Report to the Governor and the General Assembly. a. ISSN 0085-3135

**Maryland Port Administration**
World Trade Center Baltimore, Baltimore, MD 21202.
- Port of Baltimore Bulletin. m. ISSN 0032-4817
- Port of Baltimore Handbook. biennial since 1957. ISSN 0079-3981

**Maryland School for Blind**
3501 Taylor Ave., Baltimore, MD 21236.
- Maryland Oriole (Braille Edition) 3 per yr.
- Maryland Oriole (Inkprint Edition) 3 per yr. ISSN 0025-4320

**Maryland State Bar Association**
905 Keyser Bldg., Baltimore, MD 21202.
- Maryland Bar Journal. q. ISSN 0025-4177
- Maryland Lawyer's Manual. a. ISSN 0542-836X

**Maryland State Dental Association**
1924 Wilkens Ave., Baltimore, MD 21223.
- Maryland State Dental Association. Journal. 3 per yr. ISSN 0025-4355

**Maryland State Horticultural Society**
Univ. of Maryland Fruit Lab, Hancock, MD 21750.
- Maryland Fruit Grower. q. ISSN 0025-4223

**Maryland State Teachers Association**
344 N. Charles St., Baltimore, MD 21201.
- Action Line (Baltimore) w. ISSN 0001-7442
- Maryland Teacher. q. ISSN 0025-4371

**Maryland Writers Council**
16 W. Franklin St., Baltimore, MD 21201.
- Maryland Writers Council. Bulletin. Supplement. m.

**Mash Family Bulletin**
3755 Robinhood Rd., Houston, TX 77005.
- Mash Family Bulletin. irreg.

**Al-Mashriq**
25639 Southwood, Southfield, MI 48075.
- Al-Mashriq. w.

**George Mason**
Box 966, Fresno, CA 93721.
- California Courier. w. ISSN 0008-0950

**Phillip Mason, Ed. & Pub.**
Box 157, Front Royal, VA 22630.
- Dulcimer Players News. bi-m. ISSN 0098-3527

**Mason and Associates, Financial Consultants**
P.O. Box 9718, Marina del Rey, CA 90291.
- Annual Evaluation of U. S. Gold Coin Prices. a. ISSN 0092-3303

**Mason-Charter Publishers. Petrocelli Division**
641 Lexington Ave., New York, NY 10022.
- Auerbach Annual: Best Computer Papers. a.

**Mason Clinic**
1118 Ninth Ave., Seattle, WA 98101.
- Mason Clinic Bulletin. q. ISSN 0025-4657

**Mason Contractors Association of America, Inc.**
17W601 14th St., Oakbrook Terrace, IL 60181.
- Masonry. m(Nov. & Dec. combined) ISSN 0025-4681

**Mass Media Ministries, Inc.**
2116 N. Charles St., Baltimore, MD 21218.
- Mass Media Newsletter. fortn. ISSN 0361-865X

**Mass Retailing Institute**
570 Seventh Avenue, New York, NY 10018.
- M R I Compensation in Mass Retailing, Salaries and Incentives. biennial. ISSN 0092-5950

**Mass Transit**
c/o C. Carroll Carter, Ed., 538 National Press Bldg., Washington, DC 20045.
- Mass Transit. m.

**Massachusetts. Aeronautics Commission**
Boston-Logan Airport, East Boston, MA 02128.
- Talespinner. 2-3 per yr. ISSN 0039-9159

**Massachusetts. Board of Higher Education**
182 Tremont St., Boston, MA 02111.
- Report: Massachusetts State Scholarship Programs. irreg.

**Massachusetts. Bureau of Curriculum Services**
182 Tremont St., Boston, MA 02111.
- Kaleidoscope (Boston) ISSN 0095-5213

**Massachusetts. Bureau of Library Extension**
648 Beacon St., Boston, MA 02116.
- Mediawrite. m.

**Massachusetts. Committee on Criminal Justice**
80 Boylston St., Boston, MA 02116.
- Massachusetts. Committee on Criminal Justice. Comprehensive Criminal Justice Plan, Criminal Justice Programs. irreg. ISSN 0098-5740

**Massachusetts. Criminal History Systems Board**
80 Boylston St., Room 740, Boston, MA 02116.
- Massachusetts. Criminal History Systems Board. Annual Report. a. ISSN 0098-5112

**Massachusetts. Department of Civil Service and Registration. Board of Public Accountancy**
Leverett Saltonstall Bldg., Government Center, 100 Cambridge St., MA 02202.
- Massachusetts. Board of Public Accountancy. Annual Report. a. ISSN 0362-1898

**Massachusetts. Department of Community Affairs. Bureau of Regional Planning**
141 Milk St., Boston, MA 02109.
- Massachusetts. Bureau of Regional Planning. Regional Profiles. a. ISSN 0362-3718

**Massachusetts. Department of Correction**
Advisory Committee on Correction, 100 Cambridge St., Boston, MA 02202.
- Massachusetts. Advisory Committee on Correction. Annual Report. a. ISSN 0076-4884
- Massachusetts. Department of Correction. Commissioner of Correction. Statistical Reports. a. (Order from: Bureau of Public Documents, Room 116, State House, Boston, MA 02133)
- Massachusetts Correctional Institution, Norfolk, Norfolk Colony School. Report. a. ISSN 0085-3143 (prep. by its Massachusetts Correctional Institution) (And 43 Main St., Norfolk, MA 02056)
- Question Mark. s-m. (prep. by its Massachusetts Correctional Institution) (And 43 Main St., Norfolk, MA 02056)

**Massachusetts. Department of Education**
Boston, MA 02202.
- Massachusetts. Department of Education. Educational Revenue and Expenditure Data. irreg. ISSN 0094-3266

**Massachusetts. Department of Mental Health**
190 Portland St., Boston, MA 02114.
- Massachusetts. Department of Mental Health. Newsletter. bi-m. ISSN 0076-4906
- Massachusetts Journal of Mental Health. q. ISSN 0047-6137

**Massachusetts. Department of Public Health**
600 Washington St., Boston, MA 02111.
- Massachusetts. Department of Public Health. Annual Report. a.

**Massachusetts. Department of Public Welfare. State Advisory Board**
Boston, MA 02202.
- Massachusetts. Department of Public Welfare. State Advisory Board. Annual Report. a. ISSN 0095-4020

**Massachusetts. Division of Employment Security**
Charles F. Hurley Bldg., Government Center, Boston, MA 02114.
- Massachusetts. Division of Employment Security. Employment and Wages. a. ISSN 0076-4922
- Massachusetts. Division of Employment Security. Occupational Characteristics. Insured Unemployed. q.
- Massachusetts. Division of Employment Security. Quarterly Survey of Unfilled Job Openings - Boston. q. ISSN 0580-7727
- Massachusetts. Division of Employment Security. Research Department. Annual Manpower Planning Report. a. ISSN 0076-4930 (prep. by its Research Dept.)
- Massachusetts. Division of Employment Security. Statistical Digest. a. ISSN 0076-4949
- Massachusetts Trends in Employment and Unemployment. m. ISSN 0025-4916

**Massachusetts. Division of Fisheries and Game**
100 Cambridge St., Boston, MA 02202.
- Massachusetts. Division of Fisheries and Game. Annual Report. a. ISSN 0076-4957
- Massachusetts Wildlife. bi-m. ISSN 0025-4924

**Massachusetts. Division of Mineral Resources**
100 Cambridge St., Boston, MD 02202.
- Massachusetts. Division of Mineral Resources. Annual Report. a. ISSN 0092-3362

**Massachusetts. Governor's Highway Safety Bureau**
Boston, MA 02201.
- Massachusetts. Governor's Highway Safety Bureau. Annual Work Program. a. ISSN 0098-3152

**Massachusetts. Rehabilitation Commission**
296 Boylston St., Boston, MA 02130.
- Massachusetts. Rehabilitation Commission. Expenditures Report. irreg. ISSN 0095-8050

**Massachusetts. Security and Privacy Council**
904 Saltonstall Bldg., Boston, MA 02202.
- Massachusetts. Security and Privacy Council. Annual Report. a. ISSN 0098-5759

**Massachusetts Advocacy Center**
2 Park Square, Boston, MA 02116.
- Massachusetts Advocacy Center. Annual Report. a. ISSN 0362-1383

**Massachusetts Archaeological Society, Inc.**
Bronson Museum, 8 No. Main St., Attleboro, MA 02703.
- Massachusetts Archaeological Society Bulletin. 2 per yr.

**Massachusetts Audubon Society**
S. Great Rd., Lincoln, MA 01773.
- Curious Naturalist; the magazine for beginning naturalists. 4 per yr. ISSN 0574-7120
- Man and Nature. a.
- Massachusetts Audubon Newsletter. 10 per yr. ISSN 0076-4892

**Massachusetts Bar Association**
1 Center Plaza, Boston, MA 02108.
- Massachusetts Law Quarterly. q. ISSN 0025-4835

**Massachusetts College of Pharmacy**
179 Longwood Ave., Boston, MA 02115.
- Apothecary. (pub. by M C P Publications)
- Massachusetts College of Pharmacy. Bulletin. 5 per yr. ISSN 0025-4789

**Massachusetts Council for the Social Studies**
c/o Winchester High School, 80 Skillings Rd., Winchester, MA 01890.
- M C S S Newsletter. 5 per yr.

**Massachusetts Council on the Arts and Humanities**
14 Beacon St., Boston, MA 02108.
- Massachusetts Council on the Arts and Humanities. News. irreg, latest 1975.

**Massachusetts Dental Society**
Prudential Tower, Rm. 4318, Boston, MA 02199.
- Massachusetts Dental Society. Journal. q. ISSN 0025-4800

**Massachusetts Foreign Languages Association**
- Massachusetts Foreign Language Bulletin. (pub. by Holyoke Community College)

**Massachusetts Herpetological Society**
c/o David Taylor, Box 263, Byfield, MA 01922.
- M.H.S. Review. s-a. ISSN 0093-9560

**Massachusetts Historical Society**
1154 Boylston St., Boston, MA 02215.
- M.H.S. Miscellany. q? ISSN 0024-8185
- Massachusetts Historical Society. Proceedings. a. ISSN 0076-4981

**Massachusetts Horticultural Society**
Horticultural Hall, 300 Massachusetts Ave., Boston, MA 02115.
- Horticulture. m. ISSN 0018-5329

**Massachusetts Housing Finance Agency**
Old City Hall, 45 School St., Boston, MA 02108.
- Massachusetts Housing Finance Agency. Annual Report. a. ISSN 0076-499X

**Massachusetts Institute of Technology**
Cambridge, MA 02139.
- Ergo; the campus voice of reason. w. (except during Summer) ISSN 0046-2438 (Orders to:, W20-443)
- International Biophysics Congress. Abstracts. irreg. (Orders to:, Room 20B-221)
- M I T Monographs in Economics. (pub. by M.I.T. Press)
- M I T Press Research Monograph Series. (pub. by M.I.T. Press)
- M I T Regional Science Studies Series. (pub. by M.I.T. Press)
- M I T Reports. (pub. by M.I.T. Press)
- Sloan Management Review. 3 per yr. ISSN 0019-848X (Orders to:, 50 Memorial Dr.)
- Tech Engineering News. m.(Oct-May) ISSN 0040-084X (Orders to:, W20-453)

**Massachusetts Institute of Technology. Alumni Association**
Cambridge, MA 02139.
- Technology Review. m. (Nov-Jul) ISSN 0040-1692

**Massachusetts Institute of Technology. Center for International Studies**
- Studies in International Communism. (pub. by M.I.T. Press)

**Massachusetts Institute of Technology. Flight Transportation Laboratory**
Cambridge, MA 02139.
- Massachusetts Institute of Technology. Flight Transportation Laboratory. F T L Report. irreg.

**Massachusetts Institute of Technology. Neurosciences Research Program**
- Neurosciences Research Program. Bulletin. (pub. by M.I.T. Press)

**Massachusetts Institute of Technology. Political Science Department**
Cambridge, MA 02142.
- Public Science Newsletter. m. 10 per yr. ISSN 0091-1720 (prep. by its Science and Public Policy Program)

**Massachusetts Institute of Technology Press**
see M I T Press

**Massachusetts Institute of Technology. Research Laboratory of Electronics**
Cambridge, MA 02139.
- Massachusetts Institute of Technology. Research Laboratory of Electronics. s-a.

**Massachusetts Law Reform Institute**
2 Park Square, Boston, MA 02116.
- Legal Services Monthly. m.

**Massachusetts League of Cities and Towns**
6 Beacon St., Boston, MA 02108.
- Massachusetts Municipal Directory. irreg. ISSN 0361-2090

**Massachusetts Library Association**
Box 7, Nahant, MA 01908.
- Bay State Librarian. q. ISSN 0005-6944

**Massachusetts Medical Society**
10 Shattuck St., Boston, MA 02115.
- New England Journal of Medicine. w. ISSN 0028-4793

**Massachusetts Motor Truck Association, Inc.**
262 Washington St., Boston, MA 02108.
- Modern Trans. m. ISSN 0026-8518

**Massachusetts Music Educators Association, Inc.**
c/o J. Anthony Di Giore, Ed., P.O. Box 532, W. Springfield, MA 01089.
- Massachusetts Music News. 4 per yr.

**Massachusetts Nurses Association**
20 Ashburton Place, Boston, MA 02108.
- Massachusetts Nurse. q.

**Massachusetts Physician, Inc.**
483 Beacon St., Boston, MA 02115.
- Massachusetts Physician. m. ISSN 0025-4851

**Massachusetts Port Authority**
99 High St., Boston, MA 02110.
- Waterborne Commerce of the Port of Boston. a.

**Massachusetts Psychological Center, Inc.**
Suite 300, 25 Huntington Ave., Boston, MA 02116.
- Massachusetts Psychological Center. Bulletin. 5 per yr. ISSN 0047-6145

**Massachusetts Review, Inc.**
Univ of Massachusetts, Amherst, MA 01003.
- Massachusetts Review; literature, arts, public affairs etc. q. ISSN 0025-4878

**Massachusetts Secondary School Principals Association**
73 Tremont St., Boston, MA 02108.
- M S S P A Bugle. 9 per yr (Sept.-June) ISSN 0024-8452

**Massachusetts Society for the Prevention of Cruelty to Animals**
180 Longwood Ave., Boston, MA 02115.
- Animals. bi-m. ISSN 0030-6835

**Massachusetts Society of Certified Public Accountants, Inc.**
Three Center Plaza, Boston, MA 02108.
- Massachusetts C P A Review. 6 per yr. ISSN 0025-4770

**Massachusetts Society of Professional Engineers**
77 Summer St., Boston, MA 02110.
- Massachusetts Professional Engineer. bi-m. ISSN 0025-486X

**Massachusetts State Labor Council, AFL-CIO**
6 Beacon St., Room 720, Boston, MA 02108.
- Massachusetts State Labor Council AFL-CIO Newsletter. q. ISSN 0025-4894

**Massachusetts Taxpayers Foundation**
145 Tremont St., Boston, MA 02111.
- Massachusetts Tax Primer. irreg. ISSN 0362-868X

**Massachusetts Teachers Association**
20 Ashburton Pl., Boston, MA 02108.
- Massachusetts Teacher. m.(Sept-May) ISSN 0025-4908

**Master Brewers Association of America**
4513 Vernon Blvd., Madison, WI 53705.
- M B A A Technical Quarterly. q. ISSN 0024-7960
- Master Brewers Association of America. Communications. bi-m.

**Master Drawings Association, Inc.**
33 E. 36th St., New York, NY 10016.
- Master Drawings; devoted exclusively to the study and illustration of drawings. q. ISSN 0025-5025

**Master Indicator of the Stock Market**
Box 3024, West Palm Beach, FL 33402.
- Master Indicator of the Stock Market. 24 per yr. ISSN 0047-6188

**Master Plan Service, Inc.**
89 E. Jericho Turnpike, Mineola, NY 11501.
- Distinguished Home Plans & Products. m.

**Master Publications (Minneapolis)**
5901 Brooklyn Blvd., Suite 203, Minneapolis, MN 55429.
- Northern Hardware Trade. m.

**Master Publications, Inc.**
300 Park Ave. S., New York, NY 10010.
- Confession Time. bi-m.
- Real Experiences. bi-m.

**Master Teacher, Inc.**
Leadership Lane, Manhattan, KS 66502.
- Master Teacher. w.

**Matagiri**
Montagiri, Mt. Tremper, NY 12457.
- Collaboration. q.

**Match**
Ed. F. Woodworth, Box 3488, Tucson, AZ 85722.
- Match; an internationally circulated anarchistic publication. m. ISSN 0047-620X

**Maternity Center Association**
- Briefs. (pub. by Charles B. Slack, Inc.)

**Mathematical Association of America**
1225 Connecticut Ave., N.W., Washington, DC 20036.
- American Mathematical Monthly. 10 per yr. ISSN 0002-9890
- Carus Mathematical Monographs. irreg., 1968, vol. 15. ISSN 0069-0813
- Mathematics Magazine. bi-m.(Sept-June) ISSN 0025-570X
- Studies in Mathematics. irreg. ISSN 0081-8208 (Dist. by Prentice-Hall, Inc., Englewood Cliffs, NJ 07631)
- Two-Year College Mathematics Journal. 4 per yr. ISSN 0049-4925

**Mathematics Associations of Two-Year Colleges Journal, Inc.**
Nassau Community College, Department of Mathematics & Computer Science, Garden City, NY 11530.
- M A T Y C Journal. 3 per yr. ISSN 0300-7650

**Matilda Ziegler Publishing Co. for the Blind, Inc.**
20 W. 17th St., New York, NY 10011.
- Matilda Ziegler Magazine for the Blind. m. ISSN 0025-5955 (Matilda Ziegler Foundation for the Blind, Inc.)

**Matrix**
Box 4218, N. Hollywood, CA 91607.
- Matrix; for She of the New Aeon. irreg. ISSN 0085-3186

**Paul R. Matt**
Box 33, Temple City, CA 91780.
- Historical Aviation Album. irreg.; vol. 15, 1977. ISSN 0018-2443

**Mattachine Society of the Niagara Frontier**
Box 975 Ellicott Sta., Buffalo, NY 14205.
- Fifth Freedom. m.

**Matterhorn Sports Club**
3 West 57th St., New York, NY 10019.
- Sybarite Review. m. ISSN 0039-7563

**Matthew's Printing**
Wallingford, CT 06492.
- Connecticut School Library Association. Newsletter. 5 per yr. ISSN 0010-6224

**Mattingley Publishing Co., Inc.**
61 Monmouth Rd., Oakhurst, NJ 07755.
- Test Engineering & Management. bi-m. ISSN 0040-3954

**Maumee Valley Historical Society**
Wolcott House Museum, 1031 River Rd, Maumee, OH 43537.
- Northwest Ohio Quarterly; a journal of history and civilization. q. ISSN 0029-3407

**Neil L. Maurer, Ed. & Pub.**
Box 125, Laurens, IA 50554.
- Ex-C B I Roundup. m. except Aug.-Sep. ISSN 0014-388X (China-Burma-India Veterans Association)

**Maury County Historical Society**
c/o Mrs. William Shackelford, 210 First Ave., Mt. Pleasant, TN 38474.
- Historic Maury. q. ISSN 0018-2400

**Maverick Media, Inc.**
Box 508, Syracuse, NE 68446.
- Southeast Nebraska Agri-Business Bulletin. m.

**Maverick Publications**
Box 243, Bend, OR 97701.
- Flea Market Quarterly; official U.S. flea market directory. q.
- Old Bottle Magazine. m. ISSN 0030-1965

**Max**
141 El Camino, Beverly Hills, CA 90212.
- Max. q.

**Nigen A. Maxey, Ed. & Pub.**
Box 1047, Welch, WV 24801.
- Mail Order Selling & Small Business World. bi-m.

**Mayhill Publications, Inc.**
P.O. Box 90, Knightstown, IN 46148.
- Eastern Indiana Farmer. w. ISSN 0420-3690
- Tri-State Trader. w. ISSN 0041-2503

**Mayo Clinic**
Rm. 1042, Plummer Bldg., Rochester, MN 55901.
- Mayo Clinic Proceedings. m. ISSN 0025-6196

**Mayo Foundation. Alumni Association**
Rochester, MN 55901.
- Mayo Alumnus. q. ISSN 0300-7456

**Mazamas**
909 N.W. 19th Ave., Portland, OR 97209.
- Mazama. m(13 per yr)

**Katherine F. Meadows, Ed. & Pub.**
928 Farber Street, Glendora, CA 91740.
- Geothermal World Directory. a. ISSN 0094-9779

**Meadville-Lombard Theological School**
- Zygon. (pub. by University of Chicago Press)

**Means Co., Inc.**
100 Construction Plaza, Duxbury, MA 02332.
- Building Construction Cost Data. a. ISSN 0068-3531
- Labor Rates for the Construction Industry. a.
- Means Construction Cost Indexes. q. ISSN 0361-9591

**Measurements and Data Corp.**
2994 W. Liberty Ave., Pittsburgh, PA 15216.
- M E D. (Medical Electronics & Data) bi-m. ISSN 0024-810X (Medical Electronics and Data Society)
- Measurements and Control. bi-m.

**Meat Plant Magazine**
8678 Olive Blvd., St. Louis, MO 63132.
- Meat Plant Magazine. m.

**Mechanical Contractors Association of South Carolina**
Box 384, Columbia, SC 29202.
- Palmetto Piper. m. ISSN 0048-2781

**Med-Law Publishers, Inc.**
P.O. Box 293, Westville, NJ 08093.
- Emergency Physician Legal Bulletin. q. ISSN 0098-1524

**Med Publishers**
12 E. 41st St., New York, NY 10017.
- Practical Cardiology. m. ISSN 0361-3372

**Medallic Art Company**
Old Ridgebury Road, Danbury, CT 06810.
- Art Medalist. bi-m.

**Medallion Corp.**
1014 Indian Road, Glenview, IL 60025.
- Adolescent Medicine. (pub. by Milton Golin, Ed. & Pub.)
- C M E Today. m.
- Surgery Update. bi-m.

**Medi-Facts Publishing Co.**
2337 Lemoine Avenue, Fort Lee, NJ 17024.
- P.M.B.R. Physician's Medical Book Reference. a. ISSN 0093-2248

**Media General Financial Services**
P.O. Box 26991, Richmond, VA 23261.
- Industriscope. m. ISSN 0094-1352
- M G Financial Weekly. w.

**Media Montage Inc.**
Box 224, Topsfield, MA 01983.
- Ski East. 5 per yr.

**Media Records, Inc.**
370 Seventh Ave., New York, NY 10001.
- Media Records Report of Business Publication Advertising. s-a.

**Media Report to Women, Inc.**
3306 Ross Place, N.W., Washington, DC 20008.
- Media Report to Women; what women are doing and thinking about the communications media. m.

**Media Resources**
310 East Jackson, Harlingen, TX 78850.
- Valley Business Journal. m.

**Mediaeval Academy of America**
1430 Massachusetts Ave., Cambridge, MA 02138.
- Corpus Commentariorum in Aristotelem. Versio Anglica. irreg.
- Corpus Commentariorum in Aristotelem. Versio Arabica. irreg.
- Corpus Commentariorum in Aristotelem. Versio Hebraica. irreg.
- Corpus Commentariorum in Aristotelem. Versio Latina. irreg.
- Mediaeval Academy of America. Publications. irreg., no. 86, 1977. ISSN 0076-583X
- Speculum; a journal of mediaeval studies. q. ISSN 0038-7134

**Median Iris Society Press**
2 Warburton Lane, Westboro, MA 01581.
- Medianite. q. ISSN 0025-6927

**Mediatex Communications Corp.**
Box 1569, Austin, TX 78767.
- Texas Monthly. m.

**Medic Alert Foundation International**
Box 1009, Turlock, CA 95380.
- Medic Alert Newsletter. 6 per yr. ISSN 0300-7200

**Medica Press Inc.**
1231 Industrial Bank Bldg., Providence, RI 02903.
- Regan Report on Hospital Law. m. ISSN 0034-317X
- Regan Report on Medical Law. m. ISSN 0034-3188
- Regan Report on Nursing Law. m. ISSN 0034-3196

**Medical Age, Inc.**
5220 Travis, Houston, TX 77002.
- American Journal of Orthopedic Surgery. irreg. ISSN 0065-9002 (Texas Orthopedic Association)

**Medical and Chirurgical Faculty of the State of Maryland**
1211 Cathedral St, Baltimore, MD 21201.
- Maryland State Medical Journal. m. ISSN 0025-4363

**Medical Arts Publishing Foundation**
6723 Bertner Dr., Houston, TX 77025.
- Cancer Bulletin. bi-m. ISSN 0008-5448 (University of Texas. M.D. Anderson Hospital and Tumor Institute)

**Medical Association of Georgia**
938 Peachtree St., N.E., Atlanta, GA 30309.
- Medical Association of Georgia. Journal. m. ISSN 0025-7028

**Medical Association of the State of Alabama**
19 S. Jackson St., Montgomery, AL 36104.
- Medical Association of the State of Alabama. Journal. m. ISSN 0025-7044

**Medical Book Club, Inc.**
3100 Broadway Suite 1111, Kansas City, MO 64111.
- Continuing Education for the Family Physician. m. ISSN 0092-735X

**Medical Center Hospital of Vermont**
Colchester Ave., Burlington, VT 05401.
- Progress & Care; at the Medical Center Hospital. bi-m. ISSN 0033-0612

**Medical College of Georgia Foundation, Inc.**
AA 156, Augusta, GA 30902.
- M C G Today. q. ISSN 0047-6471

**Medical College of Virginia**
Biophysics Department, Richmond, VA 23298.
- Virginia Journal of Science. q. ISSN 0042-658X (Virginia Academy of Science)

**Medical College of Virginia. School of Medicine**
Richmond, VA 23298.
- Medical College of Virginia Quarterly. q. ISSN 0025-7141

**Medical Counterpoint, Inc.**
3 Far Hills Mall, Far Hills, NJ 07931.
- Medical Counterpoint; journal of controversial medicine. m. ISSN 0025-715X

**Medical Digest**
444 Frontage Rd., Northfield, IL 60093.
- Dermatology Digest. m.
- Pediatrics Digest. m.

**Medical Dynamics, Ltd.**
501 E. Brambleton Ave., Norfolk, VA 23501.
- Rhodes Directory of Black Dentists Registered in the United States. triennial with a. supplements. ISSN 0090-7995
- Rhodes Directory of Black Physicians in the United States. triennial.

**Medical Economics Co.**
680 Kinderkamack Rd., Oradell, NJ 07649.
- Clinical Laboratory Reference. a. (Medical Laboratory Observer)
- Current Prescribing. m.
- Drug Topics Health & Beauty Aids Directory; the pink book. biennial. ISSN 0419-764X
- Drug Topics Redbook. a. ISSN 0070-7376
- Marketing Guide. a. ISSN 0093-125X
- Medical Economics. fortn. ISSN 0025-7206
- Medical Laboratory Observer. m.
- Physicians' Desk Reference. a. ISSN 0093-4461
- R N; national magazine for nurses. m. ISSN 0033-7021

**Medical Electronics and Data Society**
- M E D. (pub. by Measurements and Data Corp.)

**Medical Examination Publishing Co., Inc.**
65-36 Fresh Meadow Lane, Flushing, NY 11365.
- Annual Review of Allergy. a. ISSN 0090-1083
- Basic Science Review Series. irreg.
- Hematology Case Studies. irreg. ISSN 0091-2336

**Medical Group Management Association**
4101 E. Louisiana Ave., Denver, CO 80222.
- Medical Group Management. bi-m. ISSN 0025-7257
- Medical Group Management Association. International Directory. biennial.

**Medical Laboratory Observer**
- Clinical Laboratory Reference. (pub. by Medical Economics Co.)

**Medical Law Publications, Inc.**
663 Fifth Ave., New York, NY 10022.
- Medical Law Letter for Physicians, Surgeons & Health Professionals. m. ISSN 0098-4833

**Medical Letter Inc.**
56 Harrison St., New Rochelle, NY 10801.
- Medical Letter on Drugs and Therapeutics. fortn. ISSN 0025-732X

**Medical Library Association**
919 North Michigan Ave., Suite 3208, Chicago, IL 60611.
- Directory of Health Sciences Libraries in the United States. irreg.
- M L A News. m. ISSN 0541-5489
- Medical Library Association. Bulletin. q. ISSN 0025-7338
- Medical Library Association. Current Catalog Proof Sheets. w. ISSN 0025-7346
- Medical Library Association. Publication. irreg. ISSN 0076-5945
- Vital Notes on Medical Periodicals. 3 per yr. ISSN 0042-7411

**Medical Library Center of New York**
17 E. 102 St., New York, NY 10029.
- Medical Library Center of New York. Union Catalog of Medical Periodicals. irreg., latest issue 1976. ISSN 0090-0672

**Medical Reader**
6605 Lincoln Dr., Philadelphia, PA 19119.
- Medical Reader. m.

**Medical Research Technology Inc.**
Reprint Department, Great Notch, NJ 07424.
- Medical Research Engineering; a practical and ethical journal in the new field of medico-engineering. 6 per yr. ISSN 0025-7508

**Medical Self-Care: Access to Medical Tools**
Box 31549, San Francisco, CA 94131.
- Medical Self-Care: Access to Medical Tools. q.

**Medical Society Magazine Group. Academy of Medicine**
2025 N. Central Ave., Phoenix, AZ 85004.
- Northern Virginia Medical Bulletin. bi-m.

**Medical Society of Delaware**
1925 Lovering Ave, Wilmington, DE 19806.
- Delaware Medical Journal. m. ISSN 0011-7781

**Medical Society of New Jersey**
Box 904, Trenton, NJ 08605.
- Medical Society of New Jersey. Journal. m. ISSN 0025-7524

**Medical Society of the County of New York**
40 W. 57th St., New York, NY 10019.
- New York County Medical Society Newsletter. m.

**Medical Society of the County of Queens**
112-25 Queens Blvd., Forest Hills, NY 11375.
- Medical Society of the County of Queens. Bulletin. 10 per yr. (Co-Sponsor: Academy of Medicine of Queens County)

**Medical Society of the State of New York**
420 Lakeville Rd., Lake Success, NY 11040.
- New York State Journal of Medicine. m, ISSN 0028-7628
- News of New York. s-m. ISSN 0028-9264
- What Goes on in Medicine. s-m; m.(July & Aug.) ISSN 0043-4507

**Medical Society of Virginia**
4205 Dover Rd, Richmond, VA 23221.
- Virginia Medical. m.

**Medical Tribune Inc.**
880 Third Ave., New York, NY 10022.
- Hospital Tribune. s-m. ISSN 0018-5876
- Medical Tribune; world news of medicine and its practice. w. ISSN 0025-7605

**Medical University of South Carolina. Alumni Association**
80 Barre St., Charleston, SC 29401.
- South Carolina. Medical University. Bulletin. q. ISSN 0049-1497

**Medical World News**
1221 Avenue of the Americas, New York, NY 10020.
- Cardiovascular Review; a Medical World News Publication. a. ISSN 0069-0392
- Psychiatry; a Medical World News Publication. a. ISSN 0079-7278

**Medicine Book Guide**
70 Lincoln St., Boston, MA 02111.
- Medicine Book Guide. a.

**Medicine Wheel**
Box 48, Rte. 62, Lander, WY 82526.
- Medicine Wheel. q.

**Medieval Association of the Pacific**
Department of French and Italian, Univ. of California, Davis, CA 95616.
- Chronica. s-a. ISSN 0009-5931

**Ed Mee Publications, Inc.**
4000 W. Chapman-Suite 101, Orange, CA 92668.
- Orange County Apartment News. m. (Apartment Association of Orange County)

**Meetings & Expositions, Inc.**
22 Pine St., Morristown, NJ 07960.
- Meetings & Expositions. bi-m.

**Mega**
9730 Hyne Rd., Brighton, MI 48116.
- A Is A; writings on freedom and individualism. irreg.
- A Is A Libertarian Directory; access to ideas. irreg (approx 1 per yr)

**Meharry Medical College. School of Dentistry**
1005 18 Ave. N., Nashville, TN 37208.
- Meharri-Dent. 3 per school year. ISSN 0025-8725 (Ewell Neil Dental Society)
- Meharry Medical College. School of Dentistry. Proceedings of an Oral Research Seminar. biennial.

**Meiklejohn Civil Liberties Institute**
1715 Francisco St., Berkeley, CA 94703.
- Human Rights Organizations & Periodicals Directory. biennial. ISSN 0098-0579
- What's Happening to the Law. m.

**Meilen Press**
445 Greenwich St., New York, NY 10013.
- Columni. q. ISSN 0010-2083 (Columbia University School of Dental & Oral Surgery. Alumni Association)

**Meister Publishing Co.**
37841 Euclid Ave., Willoughby, OH 44094.
- Agri-Fieldman. 6 per yr.
- American Cotton Grower. m. ISSN 0044-765X
- American Fruit Grower. m. ISSN 0002-8568
- American Vegetable Grower. m. ISSN 0003-1461
- Cotton International. a. ISSN 0070-0673
- Farm Chemicals. m. ISSN 0092-0053
- Farm Chemicals Handbook. a. ISSN 0430-0750
- Pesticide Dictionary. a.
- Plant Food Dictionary. a.
- Weed Control Manual and Herbicide Guide. a. ISSN 0511-411X

**Mejor Mundo**
61 Woodbine Ave., Plainfield, NJ 07060.
- Mejor Mundo. m.

**Walter C. Melichar, Ed. & Pub.**
7 N. Hartford Ave., Atlantic City, NJ 08401.
- Fruit by Telegraph. s-a. ISSN 0031-6474

**Melkite Apostolic Excharate of the U.S.**
19 Dartmouth St., P.O. Box 83, West Newton, MA 02165.
- Sophia; the review of the Melkite Church in America. q.

**Melville Society**
Dept. of English, Glassboro State College, Glassboro, NJ 08028.
- Extracts; an occasional newsletter. 4 per yr.

**Membrane Press**
P.O. Box 5431, Shorewood, Milwaukee, WI 53211.
- Stations. 3 per yr. ISSN 0090-4171

**Memorial Sloan-Kettering Cancer Center**
1275 York Ave., New York, NY 10021.
- Memorial-Sloan Kettering Cancer Center. Clinical Bulletin. q. ISSN 0047-6706

**Memphis Area Chamber of Commerce**
42 S. Second St., Box 224, Memphis, TN 38101.
- M Report. fortn. ISSN 0024-8355

**Memphis Retail Grocers Association**
410 N. McLean Blvd., Memphis, TN 38112.
- Dixie Foods. bi-m. ISSN 0012-429X

**Memphis State University. College of Business Administration**
Bureau of Business & Economic Research, Memphis, TN 38152.
- Mid-South Quarterly Business Review. q.

**Memphis State University. College of Education**
Ball Educational Bldg., Memphis, TN 38152.
- Educational Quest; a journal of educational research and services. s-a. ISSN 0422-6739

**Memphis State University College of Education. Bureau of Educational Research and Services**
Room 302, Memphis, TN 38152.
- B E R S Newsletter.

**Memphis State University. Department of Philosophy**
Memphis, TN 38152.
- Southern Journal of Philosophy. q. ISSN 0038-4283

**Memphis State University. John Willard Brister Library**
Memphis, TN 38152.
- M V C Bulletin. (Mississippi Valley Collection) irreg., 1969, no. 2. ISSN 0076-9525

**Memphis State University Press**
Southern Ave., Memphis, TN 38152.
- M.L. Seidman Memorial Town Hall Lecture Series. a. ISSN 0076-1729

**Memphis State University. School of Law**
Memphis, TN 38152.
- Memphis State University Law Review. q. ISSN 0047-6714

**Men and Women of Hawaii**
420 Ward Ave., Honolulu, HI 96814.
• Men and Women of Hawaii. every 7-10 yrs; 9th
edt. 1972. ISSN 0461-7398

**David H. Menashe & Co.**
Warner Victory Centre, Suite 304, P.O. Box 663,
Woodland Hills, CA 91365.
• Menashe Timing Service (1976) bi-w.

**Mendocino County Historical Society**
243 Bush St., Fort Bragg, CA 95437.
• Mendocino County Historical Society. Newsletter.
bi-m. ISSN 0025-9268

**Menninger Foundation**
Box 829, Topeka, KS 66601.
• Menninger Clinic. Bulletin. bi-m. ISSN 0025-9284
• Menninger Perspective. q. ISSN 0025-9292

**Mennonite Brethren Publishing House**
Hillsboro, KS 67063.
• Christian Leader. fortn. ISSN 0009-5419 (U S
Conference of Mennonite Brethren Churches)

**Mennonite Broadcasts, Inc.**
Box 472, Harrisonburg, VA 22801.
• Alive. bi-m. ISSN 0002-547X

**Mennonite Church. General Conference**
722 Main St., Box 347, Newton, KS 67114.
• Bote; ein mennonitsches familienblatt. w. ISSN
0006-8209
• Church and Society Series. (pub. by Faith and
Life Press)
• Mennonite. w. ISSN 0025-9330
• Schowalter Memorial Lecture Series. (pub. by
Faith and Life Press)

**Mennonite Church, General Conference. Commission
on Education**
• Christian Service Training Series. (pub. by Faith
and Life Press)
• Mennonite History Series. (pub. by Faith and Life
Press)

**Mennonite Church. Historical Committee**
1700 South Main, Goshen, IN 46526.
• Mennonite Historical Bulletin. q. ISSN 0025-9357

**Mennonite Historical Society**
Goshen College, Goshen, IN 46526.
• Mennonite Quarterly Review. q. ISSN 0025-9373
• Studies in Anabaptist and Mennonite History.
(pub. by Mennonite Publishing House)

**Mennonite Publishing House**
610-616 Walnut Ave., Scottdale, PA 15683.
• Christian Living; a magazine for home and
community. m. ISSN 0009-5435
• Gospel Herald. w. ISSN 0017-2340
• Mennonite Yearbook and Directory. a.
• On the Line. w. ISSN 0043-7999
• Story Friends. w. ISSN 0039-2006
• Studies in Anabaptist and Mennonite History.
irreg., no. 17, 1974. ISSN 0081-7538 (Mennonite
Historical Society)
• With; a magazine for the middle teens. m. ISSN
0043-6984

**Men's Garden Clubs of America**
5560 Merle Hay Rd, Des Moines, IA 50323.
• Gardener. bi-m. ISSN 0016-464X

**Mental Health Materials Center**
419 Park Ave. South, New York, NY 10016.
• I R C Newsletter. 5 per yr. (Information
Resources Center for Mental Health and Family
Life Education)
• Selective Guide to Materials for Mental Health
and Family Life Education. (pub. by Perennial
Education, Inc.)

**Mercer County Community College**
Box B, Trenton, NJ 08690.
• College Voice. w. ISSN 0010-1192

**Mercer University. Walter F. George School of Law**
Macon, GA 31207.
• Mercer Law Review. 4 per yr. ISSN 0025-987X

**Merchandise Mart Directory**
830 Merchandise Mart Plaza, Chicago, IL 60654.
• Merchandise Mart Directory. s-a. ISSN 0539-
3876

**Merchandiser Publishing Co. (New York)**
419 Park Ave. So., New York, NY 10016.
• Merchandiser Mass Retailer Buyers Directory.
irreg. ISSN 0581-1244

**Merchandising Publications Co.**
65 Crocker Ave., Piedmont, CA 94611.
• Chain Merchandiser; a national service &
promotion publication & program. bi-m. ISSN
0009-0921

**Merchant Magazine, Inc.**
4500 Campus Dr., Suite 476, Newport Beach, CA
92660.
• Merchant. m.

**Merchants and Manufacturers Association**
2300 Occidental Center, 1150 S. Olive St., Los
Angeles, CA 90015.
• Engineering, Scientific and Technical Salary
Survey. irreg. ISSN 0093-5735

**Merck and Co. Inc**
Rahway, NJ 07065.
• Merck Index; an Encyclopedia of Chemicals and
Drugs. irreg., 9th ed., 1976. ISSN 0076-6518
• Merck Manual; a Handbook of Diagnosis and
Therapy. irreg., 1972, 12th ed. ISSN 0076-6526
• Merck Veterinary Manual; a Handbook of
Diagnosis and Therapy for the Veterinarian.
irreg., 1973, 4th ed. ISSN 0076-6542

**Mercury Press, Inc**
Box 56, Cornwall, CT 06753.
• Magazine of Fantasy and Science Fiction. m.
ISSN 0024-984X

**Mercury Productions, Inc.**
1070 St. Charles Ave., New Orleans, LA 70130.
• Figaro. w.

**Mercyhurst College**
501 E. 38th St., Erie, PA 16501.
• Journal of Erie Studies. s-a. ISSN 0090-1938 (Co-
Sponsor: Erie County Historical Society)

**Meredith Corporation**
1716 Locust St., Des Moines, IA 50336.
• Apartment Life. m. ISSN 0092-0444
• Better Homes and Gardens. m. ISSN 0006-0151
• Better Homes and Gardens Christmas Ideas. a.
ISSN 0405-6590
• Better Homes and Gardens Furnishings and
Decorating Ideas. s-a. ISSN 0092-7961
• Better Homes and Gardens Garden Ideas and
Outdoor Living. a.
• Better Homes and Gardens Holiday Crafts. a.
• Better Homes & Gardens Remodeling Ideas. q.
• Successful Farming; for families that make farming
their business. m. ISSN 0039-4432

**Mergers & Acquisitions, Inc.**
1621 Brookside Rd., Box 36, McLean, VA 22101.
• Mergers & Acquisitions. q. ISSN 0026-0010
• Mergers & Acquisitions. a Comprehensive World
Bibliography. quinquennial.

**Merkos l'Inyonei Chinuch, Inc.**
770 Eastern Parkway, Brooklyn, NY 11213.
• Shmuessen mit Kinder Un Yugent. m. ISSN 0300-
7960
• Talks and Tales. m. ISSN 0039-9213

**Merrill Analysis Inc.**
Box 228, Chappaqua, NY 10514.
• Technical Trends. w.

**Merrill-Palmer Institute**
71 E. Ferry Ave., Detroit, MI 48202.
• Merrill-Palmer Quarterly of Behavior and
Development. q. ISSN 0026-0150

**Charles E. Merrill Publishing Co.**
1300 Alum Creek Drive, Columbus, OH 43216.
• African Afro-American Studies Series. irreg.

**Merriman Publishing Co.**
Box 2154, Boulder, CO 80306.
• Ecology Today. q. (Colorado Environmental
Protection Association)

**Mershon Center for Education in National Security**
199 West 10th Ave., c/o Ohio State University,
Columbus, OH 43201
(Orders to: 1712 Neil Ave., Columbus, Ohio 43210)
• Mershon Center for Education in National
Security. Pamphlet Series. (pub. by Ohio State
University Press)

• Mershon Center Quarterly Report. q.

**Mesquita and Silver, Inc.**
49 W. 47th St., New York, NY 10036.
• American Diamond and Jewelry Trade Directory.
a.

**Messenger Press**
Carthagena Station, Celina, OH 45822.
• Philosophy Today. q. ISSN 0031-8256

**Messenger Publishing Co. (Kansas City)**
544 Wabash, Kansas City, MO 64124.
• Messenger/Messaggero. m. ISSN 0026-0363

**Messenger Publishing House**
211 Main St., Joplin, MO 64801.
• Christian Adventurer. w. ISSN 0009-5214
• Gospel Carrier. w. ISSN 0017-2332
• Junior Life. w.
• Pentecostal Messenger. m. ISSN 0031-4919

**Messianic Jewish Alliance of America**
3841 W. Lawrence Ave., Chicago, IL 60625.
• American Messianic Jewish Quarterly. q.

**Metal Building Review**
Box 217, Edwardsburg, MI 49112.
• Metal Building Review. m. ISSN 0026-0525

**Metal Center News**
7 E. 12th St., New York, NY 10003.
• Metal Distribution. a. ISSN 0098-2210

**Metal Fabricating Institute Inc.**
724 Forbes St., Rockford, IL 61105.
• Metal Fabricating News. bi-m. ISSN 0026-055X

**Metal Polishers, Buffers, Platers and Helpers
International Union**
5578 Montgomery Rd., Cincinnati, OH 45212.
• Metal Polisher, Buffer and Plater. bi-m. ISSN
0026-0649

**Metal Powder Industries Federation**
Box 2054, Princeton, NJ 08540.
• International Powder Metallurgy Conference.
Proceedings-Modern Developments in Powder
Metallurgy. triennial since 1973; 5th, Chicago.
ISSN 0074-7513
• New Perspectives in Powder Metallurgy. irreg.,
vol. 6, 1973.
• Progress in Powder Metallurgy; P-M Technical
Conference proceedings. a. ISSN 0079-6719

**Metal Tube Packaging Council of North America**
118 E. 61st. St., New York, NY 10021.
• Tube Topics. bi-m. ISSN 0300-6190

**Metals and Ceramics Information Center**
Battelle's Columbus Laboratories, 505 King Ave.,
Columbus, OH 43201.
• Metals and Ceramics Information Center
Newsletter. m.
• Metals and Ceramics Information Center Review
of Ceramic Technology. m.
• Metals and Ceramics Information Center Review
of Metals Technology. w.

**Metals and Plastics Publications, Inc.**
One University Plaza, Hackensack, NJ 07601.
• Metal Finishing; devoted exclusively to metallic
surface treatments. m. ISSN 0026-0576
• Metal Finishing Guidebook & Directory. a.

**Metanoia**
1018- 9th St., No. 47, University Village, Albany,
CA 94710.
• Metanoia; an independent journal of radical
Lutheranism. q. ISSN 0026-105X

**Meteoritical Society**
• Meteoritics. (pub. by Arizona State University.
Bureau of Publishing)

**Methodist Board of Publication**
Box 508, Greensboro, NC 27402.
• North Carolina Christian Advocate. fortn. ISSN
0029-2435 (United Methodist Church. North
Carolina Conference and Western North Carolina
Conference)

**Methodist Federation for Social Action**
76 Clinton Ave., Staten Island, NY 10301.
• Social Questions Bulletin. bi-m. ISSN 0037-7821

**Methodist Hospital of Dallas**
Box 5999, Dallas, TX 75222.
• Dallas. Methodist Hospital. Bulletin of the Medical Staff. s-a. ISSN 0045-9550

**Methods-Time Measurement Association for Standards and Research**
9-10 Saddle River Rd, Fair Lawn, NJ 07410.
• M T M/Journal of Methods-Time Measurement. 4 per yr. ISSN 0024-8509

**Ha-Metivta**
452 E. 9th St., Brooklyn, NY 11218.
• Ha-Metivta. ISSN 0094-9701

**Metmenys Corp.**
3308 W. 62nd Place, Chicago, IL 60629.
• Metmenys; kuryba ir analize. s-a. ISSN 0543-615X

**Metric Supply International**
1906 Main Street, Cedar Falls, IA 50613.
• Bi-si Metric Instructor. 8 per yr.

**METRO**
*see* New York Metropolitan Reference & Research Library Agency

**Metro Magazine, Inc.**
Holiday Inn Scope, Suite 304, Norfolk, VA 23510.
• Metro; magazine of southeastern Virginia. m.

**Metrologic Instruments Inc.**
143 Harding Ave., Bellmawr, NJ 08030.
• Education News from Metrologic. a. ISSN 0046-144X

**Metropolitan Air Post Society**
c/o Collector's Club, 22 East 35 St., New York, NY 10016.
• Metropolitan Air Post Society Bulletin. m.

**Metropolitan Almanac**
80 E. 11 St., New York, NY 10003.
• Metropolitan Almanac. w.

**Metropolitan Area Planning Council**
44 School St., Boston, MA 02108.
• Metropolitan Area Planning Council Regional Report. m. ISSN 0047-696X

**Metropolitan Atlanta Rapid Transit Authority (M A R T A)**
100 Peachtree St. N.W., Atlanta, GA 30303.
• Third Friday. m.
• Transit Times. m.

**Metropolitan Baltimore Chamber of Commerce**
22 Light St., Baltimore, MD 21202.
• Baltimore. m. ISSN 0005-4453

**Metropolitan Church Association**
323 Broad St., Lake Geneva, WI 53147.
• Burning Bush. bi-m. ISSN 0007-6309

**Metropolitan Community Church**
Box 514, Hartford, CT 06101.
• Gay Christian. bi-m.

**Metropolitan Council of the Twin Cities Area**
Suite 300, Metro Square, 7Th & Robert, St. Paul, MN 55101.
• Perspectives (St. Paul) q.

**Metropolitan Council on Housing**
24 W. 30 St., New York, NY 10001.
• Tenant. m. ISSN 0040-3083

**Metropolitan Detroit AFL-CIO**
2310 Cass Street, Detroit, MI 48204.
• Detroit Labor News. w.

**Metropolitan Fund, Inc.**
21700 Northwestern, Suite 970, Southfield, MI 48075.
• Region. bi-m.

**Metropolitan Library Service Agency**
Griggs-Midway Bldg., 1821 University Ave., Rm. S-275, St. Paul, MN 55104.
• M E L S A Messenger. bi-m.
• Metropolitan Library Service Agency. Annual Report. a. ISSN 0076-7050

**Metropolitan Life Insurance Company**
1 Madison Ave., New York, NY 10010.
• Metropolitan Life Insurance Company. Statistical Bulletin. 11 per yr. ISSN 0026-1513

**Metropolitan Milwaukee Association of Commerce**
828 N. Broadway, Milwaukee, WI 53202.
• Metropolitan Milwaukee Association of Commerce. Urban Research & Development Division. Trends in Selected Economic Indicators. m. ISSN 0076-7069
• Metropolitan Milwaukee Economic Fact Book. a.
• Milwaukee Commerce. s-m. ISSN 0026-4342

**Metropolitan Museum of Art**
Fifth Ave. & 82nd St., New York, NY 10028.
• Metropolitan Museum Journal. a. ISSN 0077-8958
• Metropolitan Museum of Art. Bulletin. q. ISSN 0026-1521

**Metropolitan Nashville Board of Education**
2601 Bransford Ave, Nashville, TN 37204.
• Metropolitan Nashville Board of Education. News and Views; official publication of the public school of metropolitan Nashville Davidson County. m. ISSN 0026-153X

**Metropolitan New York Council**
132 Spring St., New York, NY 10012.
• Hosteling. bi-m. (Co-Sponsor: American Youth Hostels, Inc.)

**Metropolitan Opera Guild, Inc.**
1865 Broadway, New York, NY 10023.
• Opera News. m. (May-Nov.); w- (Dec.-Apr.) ISSN 0030-3607

**Metropolitan Opera National Council. Central Opera Service**
Lincoln Center, New York, NY 10023.
• Central Opera Service Bulletin. q. ISSN 0008-9508

**Metropolitan Petroleum Company**
380 Madison Ave., New York, NY 10017.
• Power from Oil. q.

**Metropolitan Pittsburgh Public Broadcasting**
4802 Fifth Ave., Pittsburgh, PA 15213.
• Pittsburgh; Pittsburgh's magazine of the arts and public affairs. m.

**Metropolitan Restaurant News, Inc.**
1225 Broadway, New York, NY 10001.
• Metropolitan Restaurant News. m. ISSN 0026-1564

**Metropolitan School Study Council**
• M S S C Exchange. (pub. by Columbia University. Teachers College)

**Metropolitan Tulsa Chamber of Commerce**
616 S. Boston Ave., Tulsa, OK 74119.
• Tulsa. m. ISSN 0041-4042

**Metropolitan Washington Board of Trade**
1129 20th St, N.W., Washington, DC 20036.
• Business Viewpoint. m.
• Manufacturers and Distributors Directory of the Washington, D.C. Area. a. ISSN 0509-8262
• Metropolitan Washington Board of Trade News. m. ISSN 0026-1599

**Metropolitan Washington Builders Association**
5100 Wisconsin Ave., Suite 310, Washington, DC 20015.
• Insight on Site. m. ISSN 0090-9238

**Metropolitan Washington Council of Governments**
Suite 201, 1225 Connecticut Ave., N.W., Washington, DC 20036.
• Cog Wheel. bi-m.
• Metropolitan Washington Council of Governments. Annual Report. a. ISSN 0076-7107
• Metropolitan Washington Council of Governments. Regional Directory. a. ISSN 0076-7115
• Metropolitan Washington Council of Governments. Regional Report. m. ISSN 0539-5429

**Metropolitan Water District of Southern California**
Box 54153, Los Angeles, CA 90054.
• Aqueduct. q. ISSN 0092-0622
• Meter. m.

**Mexican-American Legal Defense and Educational Fund**
145 Ninth St., San Francisco, CA 94103.
• M A L D E F Newsletter. q.

**Thomas Mezick**
205 W. Main St., New London, OH 44851.
• Firelands Farmer. fortn.

**Miami Magazine, Inc.**
3361 S.W. T ird Ave., Miami, FL 33145.
• Miami Magazine. m.

**Miami Malacological Society**
c/o M. Ellen Crovo, 2915 S.W. 102nd Avenue, Miami, FL 33165.
• Miami Malacological Society. Quarterly. q. ISSN 0090-323X

**Miami University**
Oxford, OH 45056.
• Old Northwest. q. ISSN 0360-5531

**Miami University-Middletown**
4200 Manchester Rd., Middletown, OH 45042.
• Kaos. fortn. ISSN 0022-8931

**Miami Valley Milk Producers Association**
135 S. Perry St., Dayton, OH 45402.
• Miami Valley Dairyman. 10 per yr. ISSN 0026-1955

**Michael Reese Hospital & Medical Center**
Public Relations Dept., 2929 S. Ellis, Chicago, IL 60616.
• Michael Reese News. fortn.
• Rounds. m.

**Michael's Thing**
200 W. 72nd St., New York, NY 10023.
• Michael's Thing. w.

**Michie Co.**
Box 7587, Charlottesville, VA 22906.
• Legal Malpractice Reporter. m. ISSN 0363-2490

**Michigan. Advisory Commission on Physician Assistants**
Lansing, MI 48914.
• Michigan. Advisory Commission on Physician Assistants. Annual Report to the Michigan Department of Public Health. a. ISSN 0095-5604

**Michigan. Advisory Council for Vocational Education**
Lansing, MI 48933.
• Michigan. Advisory Council for Vocational Education. Annual Report. a. ISSN 0093-9137

**Michigan. Aeronautics Commission**
Capital City Airport, Lansing, MI 48906.
• Michigan Aviation. m. ISSN 0539-8703

**Michigan. Bureau of Medical Assistance**
Lansing, MI 48933.
• Michigan. Bureau of Medical Assistance. Annual Report, Medical Assistance Program. a. ISSN 0098-5767

**Michigan. Center for Health Statistics**
3500 N. Logan St., Lansing, MI 98914.
• Michigan Health Statistics. a. ISSN 0539-7413

**Michigan. Department of Agriculture. Division of Plant Industry**
Lewis Cass Bldg., Lansing, MI 48926.
• Michigan. Plant Industry Division. Plant Pest Control Programs. a. ISSN 0076-8073

**Michigan. Department of Civil Rights**
125 W. Allegan St., Lansing, MI 48933.
• Michigan. Civil Rights Commission. Annual Report. a.
• Michigan Civil Rights Commission Newsletter. q. ISSN 0047-7087

**Michigan. Department of Commerce**
Lansing, MI 48913.
• Michigan. Department of Commerce. Annual Report Summary. a. ISSN 0094-3479

**Michigan. Department of Commerce. Corporation & Securities Bureau**
5511 Enterprise Drive, Lansing, MI 48913.
• Blue Sky Bulletin. m. (prep. by its Securities Division)
• Michigan Department of Commerce. Corporation & Securities Bureau. Securities Bulletin. m. ISSN 0047-7109

**Michigan. Department of Education**
Lansing, MI 48933.
• Directory of Michigan Institutions of Higher Education. irreg.

- Michigan Postsecondary Admissions & Financial Assistance Handbook. a.
- Summary of Expenditure Data for Michigan Public Shcools. a. ISSN 0094-8268

**Michigan. Department of Education. Division of Vocational Education**
P.O. Box 928, Lansing, MI 48904.
- Michigan. Division of Vocational Education. Report. a. ISSN 0076-7913
- Michigan State Plan for Vocational Education. a. ISSN 0094-1506

**Michigan. Department of Education. State Library Services**
Box 30007, Lansing, MI 48909.
- Family Trails. s-a.
- Michigan. State Library Services. Catalog of Books on Magnetic Tape. irreg., latest issue 1972. ISSN 0092-5349
- Michigan Documents. q. ISSN 0026-2110
- Michigan in Books. irreg. ISSN 0026-2218
- Michigan Library Directory & Statistics. a. ISSN 0076-8081
- Michigan Magazine Index. q. ISSN 0026-2250

**Michigan. Department of Management and Budget**
Stevens T. Mason Bldg., 2nd Fl., West Wing, Lansing, MI 48933.
- Michigan. Department of Management and Budget. Annual Report. a. ISSN 0095-733X
- Michigan State Employees' Retirement System Financial and Statistical Report. a. ISSN 0092-9212

**Michigan. Department of Mental Health**
Lewis Cass Bldg., Lansing, MI 48926.
- Link. m. ISSN 0047-4738

**Michigan. Department of Natural Resources**
Box 30034, Lansing, MI 48909.
- Michigan Natural Resources. bi-m. ISSN 0026-2358

**Michigan. Department of Natural Resources. Geology Division**
Box 30028, Lansing, MI 48909.
- Michigan. Geological Survey Division. Miscellany. irreg. ISSN 0085-3364
- Michigan Mineral Producers; Annual Directory. a. ISSN 0085-3372
- Michigan's Oil and Gas Fields; Annual Statistical Summary. a. ISSN 0085-3429
- Mineral Industry of Michigan; Annual Statistical Summary. a. ISSN 0085-3445

**Michigan. Department of Natural Resources. Institute for Fisheries Research**
Univ. Museums Annex, Ann Arbor, MI 48109.
- Michigan. Department of Natural Resources. Institute for Fisheries Research. Miscellaneous Publication. irreg. ISSN 0076-7905

**Michigan. Department of Natural Resources. Natural Resources Council**
Scientific Advisory Committee, Lansing, MI 48926.
- Michigan Natural Resources Council. Scientific Advisory Committee. Annual Report. a. ISSN 0076-8057

**Michigan. Department of Natural Resources. Office of Surveys and Statistics**
Box 30028, Lansing, MI 48909.
- Michigan. Department of Natural Resources. Surveys and Statistical Services Report. irreg. ISSN 0095-120X

**Michigan. Department of Public Health**
Lansing, MI 48914.
- Michigan's Health. m.(Oct-May) ISSN 0026-2501

**Michigan. Department of Public Health. Bureau of Industrial Health**
3500 North Logan, Lansing, MI 48914.
- Michigan's Occupational Health. q. ISSN 0026-251X

**Michigan. Department of Social Services**
Lansing, MI 48933.
- Michigan. Department of Social Services. Program Statistics. irreg. ISSN 0093-7835

**Michigan. Department of Social Services. Bureau of Quality Control and Statistical Analysis**
Lansing, MI 48933.
- Michigan. Department of Social Services. Public Assistance Statistics. irreg. ISSN 0093-6774

**Michigan. Department of State. Michigan History Division**
Lansing, MI 48918.
- Michigan History. q. ISSN 0026-2196 (Co-sponsor: Michigan Historical Commission)

**Michigan. Department of State Police**
714 S. Harrison Rd., East Lansing, MI 48823.
- Michigan. Department of State Police. Annual Report. a.
- Uniform Crime Report for the State of Michigan. a. ISSN 0360-9146

**Michigan. Employment Security Commission**
7310 Woodward Ave., Detroit, MI 48202.
- Detroit Labor Market Review. m. (prep. by its Research and Statistics Division)
- Michigan. Employment Security Commission. Annual Planning Report. a.
- Michigan Labor Market Review. m. ISSN 0098-0307 (prep. by its Research and Statistics Division)

**Michigan. Environmental Protection Branch**
Lansing, MI 48933.
- Michigan State Plan for Air Pollution Control, Water Pollution Control, Solid Waste Management. irreg. ISSN 0095-6368

**Michigan. Geological Survey**
2400 Science Parkway, Red Cedar Research Park, Okemos, MI 48864.
- Ground-Water Data for Michigan. a. ISSN 0085-6924 (Co-Sponsor: U.S. Geological Survey)

**Michigan. Manpower Commission**
Lansing, MI 48900.
- Michigan. Manpower Commission. Manpower Report of the Governor. irreg.

**Michigan. Office of Criminal Justice Programs**
Lewis Cass Building, 2d Fl., Lansing, MI 48913.
- Michigan. Office of Criminal Justice Programs. Annual Report. a. ISSN 0092-2773
- Michigan. Office of Criminal Justice Programs. Comprehensive Law Enforcement and Criminal Justice Plan. a. ISSN 0093-9390

**Michigan. Office of Highway Safety Planning**
1020 Long Blvd., Suite 14, Lansing, MI 48910.
- Michigan. Office of Highway Safety Planning. Annual Highway Safety Work Plan. a. ISSN 0094-1069

**Michigan. Office of the Court Administrator**
Lansing, MI 48933.
- Michigan. Office of the Court Administrator. Judicial Statistics. a. ISSN 0098-7875

**Michigan. State Housing Development Authority**
Plaza One, Fourth Fl., 401 S. Washington Square, Box 30044, Lansing, MI 48909.
- Michigan Housing Market Information System Monograph Series. irreg.
- Michigan State Housing Development Authority. Annual Report. a.

**Michigan A F L-C I O News, Inc.**
2310 Cass, Detroit, MI 48201.
- Michigan A F L - C I O News. w. ISSN 0026-1998

**Michigan Academy of Science, Arts and Letters**
Tuomy House, 2117 Washtenaw Ave., Ann Arbor, MI 48104.
- Michigan Academician. q. ISSN 0026-2005
- Michigan Academy of Science, Arts, and Letters. Academy Letter. m. ISSN 0047-7052

**Michigan Association for Media in Education**
401 S. Fourth St., Ann Arbor, MI 48103.
- Media Spectrum. q.

**Michigan Association for Supervision and Curriculum Development**
Box 673, East Lansing, MI 48823.
- M A S C D Newsletter. bi-m. ISSN 0300-7707

**Michigan Association of Chiefs of Police**
Leland House, 400 Bagley, Detroit, MI 48226.
- Michigan Police Journal. irreg., 1972, vol. 36. ISSN 0085-3380

**Michigan Association of Health and Physical Education**
- Michigan Association of Health and Physical Education. M.A.H.P.E.R. Journal. (pub. by Pioneer Press)

**Michigan Association of Home Builders**
8Th Floor, One Northland Plaza, Southfield, MI 48075.
- Bildor. m. ISSN 0006-2448 (Co-Sponsor: Builders Association of Southeastern Michigan)

**Michigan Association of Osteopathic Physicians and Surgeons, Inc.**
33100 Freedom Rd., Farmington, MI 48024.
- Michigan Osteopathic Journal. 10 per yr. ISSN 0026-2374

**Michigan Association of School Administrators**
421 W. Kalamazoo St., Lansing, MI 48933.
- Fortnighter. fortn.

**Michigan Association of School Boards, Inc.**
421 W. Kalamazoo, Lansing, MI 48933.
- Michigan School Board Journal. m. ISSN 0026-2439

**Michigan Association of Secondary School Principals**
401 S. Fourth St., University of Michigan, Ann Arbor, MI 48103.
- Michigan Association of Secondary School Principals' Bulletin. m.(Sept-May) ISSN 0026-2013
- Secondary Education Today. q.

**Michigan Audubon Society**
7000 N. Westnedge, Kalamazoo, MI 49001.
- Jack-Pine Warbler. q. ISSN 0021-3845

**Michigan Beverage News Inc.**
24681 Northwestern Highway, Suite 408, Southfield, MI 48075.
- Michigan Beverage News. s-m. ISSN 0026-2021

**Michigan Botanical Club**
c/o Howard Crum, Ed., Herbarium, University of Michigan, Ann Arbor, MI 48109
(Subscr. to: 1509 Kearney Rd., Ann Arbor, MI 48104)
- Michigan Botanist. q. ISSN 0026-203X

**Michigan Business Education Association**
- Michigan Business Education Association. News Bulletin. (pub. by Ferris State College)

**Michigan Christian Advocate Publishing Co.**
316 Springbrook Ave., Adrian, MI 49221.
- Michigan Christian Advocate. 46 per yr. ISSN 0026-2072 (United Methodist Church. West Michigan and Detroit Annual Conferences)

**Michigan Corrections Association**
- Michigan Corrections Association Report. (pub. by Dale Corporation)

**Michigan Dental Association**
230 N. Washington Ave., Lansing, MI 48933.
- Michigan Dental Association. Journal. fortn. ISSN 0026-2102

**Michigan Dental Hygienists Association**
305 Elm St., Ypsilanti, MI 48197.
- Michigan Dental Hygienist Association. Bulletin. q. ISSN 0047-7095

**Michigan Education Association**
Box 673, E. Lansing, MI 48823.
- Teacher's Voice. fortn. ISSN 0026-2129

**Michigan Education Association. Region Six**
5460 Arden, Warren, MI 48092.
- Region Six Sentinel. m. ISSN 0034-3315

**Michigan Engineering Society**
100 Farnsworth, Detroit, MI 48202.
- Michigan Engineer. bi-m. ISSN 0026-2137

**Michigan Entomological Society**
c/o Dept. of Entomology, Michigan State Univ., East Lansing, MI 48823.
- Great Lakes Entomologist. q. ISSN 0090-0222

**Michigan Farm Bureau**
7373 W. Saginaw Hwy., Box 30690, Lansing, MI 48909.
- Michigan Farm News. m. ISSN 0026-2161

**Michigan Food Dealers Association**
209 Seymouiz Ave., Lansing, MI 48933.
- Michigan Food News. m. ISSN 0047-7117

**Michigan Fraternal Order of Police**
- Peace Officer. (pub. by Dale Corporation)

**Michigan Hospital Association**
2213 E. Grand River Ave., Lansing, MI 48912.
• Michigan Hospitals. m. ISSN 0026-220X

**Michigan Independent Press, Inc.**
204 S. 4th Ave., Ann Arbor, MI 48108.
• Michigan Free Press. w.

**Michigan Institute of Psychosynthesis**
• World Journal of Psychosynthesis. (pub. by
Psychodiagnostic Test Co.)

**Michigan Law Review Association**
Ann Arbor, MI 48104.
• Michigan Law Review. 8 per yr. ISSN 0026-2234

**Michigan Library Association**
226 W. Washtenaw, Lansing, MI 48933.
• Michigan Librarian. 4 per yr. ISSN 0026-2242

**Michigan Linguistic Society**
• Michigan Linguistic Society. Papers. (pub. by
Central Michigan University. Department of
English)

**Michigan Milk Producers Association**
24270 W. Seven Mile Rd., Detroit, MI 48219.
• Michigan Milk Messenger. m. ISSN 0026-2315

**Michigan Municipal League**
1675 Green Rd., Box 1487, Ann Arbor, MI 48106.
• Directory of Michigan Municipal Officials. s-a.
• Michigan Municipal League. Information Bulletin.
irreg. ISSN 0076-8006
• Michigan Municipal League. Municipal Legal
Briefs. irreg. ISSN 0076-8014
• Michigan Municipal League. Ordinance Analysis.
irreg. ISSN 0076-8030
• Michigan Municipal League. Salaries, Wages and
Fringe Benefits for Michigan Villages and Cities
1000-4000 Population. a. ISSN 0077-216X
• Michigan Municipal League. Salaries, Wages, and
Fringe Benefits in Michigan Municipalities over
4,000 Population. a. ISSN 0080-5548
• Michigan Municipal League. Technical Topic.
irreg. ISSN 0076-8049
• Michigan Municipal Review. m. ISSN 0026-2331

**Michigan Museum Association**
c/o Detroit Historical Museum, 5401 Woodward
Ave., Detroit, MI 48202.
• Michigan Museums Review. s-a.

**Michigan Music Educators Association**
c/o Beatrice Mangino, Business Manager, Music
Dept., Michigan State University, E. Lansing, MI
48824.
• Michigan Music Educator. 3 per yr. ISSN 0026-
234X

**Michigan Music Theory Society**
c/o School of Music, University of Michigan, Ann
Arbor, MI 48109.
• In Theory Only. m. ISSN 0360-4365

**Michigan Nurses Association**
120 Spartan Ave., East Lansing, MI 48823.
• Michigan Nurse. q. ISSN 0026-2366
• Michigan Nurse Newsletter. 11 per yr.

**Michigan Optometric Association**
540 Stoddard Bldg., Lansing, MI 48933.
• Michigan Optometrist. m.

**Michigan Personnel & Guidance Association**
29300 11 Mile Road, Farmington, MI 48024
(Subscr. to 1420 S. Bapoor Rd., Midland, Mi.
48640)
• Michigan Personnel and Guidance Journal.

**Michigan Pharmacists Association**
Michigan National Tower, Lansing, MI 48933.
• Michigan Pharmacist. m. ISSN 0026-2404

**Michigan Plumbing & Mechanical Contractors
Association**
• Michigan Master Plumber & Mechanical
Contractor. (pub. by Wellman Press, Inc.)

**Michigan Restaurateur**
10214 E. Warren, Detroit, MI 48214.
• Michigan Restaurateur. m.

**Michigan Society for Respiratory Therapy**
Box 808, Royal Oak, MI 48067.
• Michigan Airway. q. ISSN 0047-7060

**Michigan Society of Architects**
Michigan Architectural Foundation, 28 W. Adams
St., Detroit, MI 48226.
• M S A. Monthly Bulletin. m. ISSN 0024-8363

**Michigan Speech and Hearing Association**
1500 Kendale Blvd., East Lansing, MI 48823.
• M S H A. 1-2 per yr. ISSN 0024-8398

**Michigan State Chamber of Commerce**
501 S. Capitol Ave., Lansing, MI 48933.
• Michigan Challenge. 8 per yr.

**Michigan State Florist Association**
1152 Haslett Rd., Haslett, MI 48840.
• Michigan Florist. m. ISSN 0026-217X

**Michigan State Medical Society**
120 W. Saginaw, East Lansing, MI 48823.
• Michigan Medicine. m. ISSN 0026-2293

**Michigan State University**
E. Lansing, MI 48824
• Centennial Review. q. ISSN 0008-901X (Subscr.
to:, 110 Morrill Hall)
• Consortium for the Study of Nigerian Rural
Development. C S N R D Working Paper. irreg.,
1969, no. 11. ISSN 0069-9179
• Kresge Art Center Bulletin. m.(Oct.-July) ISSN
0023-4605 (Kresge Art Center Gallery)
• University College Quarterly. q. ISSN 0041-9281
(Subscr. to:, Bessey Hall)

**Michigan State University. African Studies Center**
100 International Center, E. Lansing, MI 48823.
• African Urban Notes. 3 per yr. ISSN 0044-6629
• Consortium for the Study of Nigerian Rural
Development. irreg., 1969, no. 33. ISSN 0069-
9160
• Rural Africana; current research in social sciences.
3 per yr. ISSN 0085-5839

**Michigan State University. Agricultural Experiment
Station**
Agriculture Hall, East Lansing, MI 48824.
• Michigan Beef Cattle Day Report. a. ISSN 0076-
7824
• Michigan Science in Action. irreg. (4-12 issues per
year) ISSN 0076-809X

**Michigan State University. Agriculture and Natural
Resources Education Institute**
Agriculture Hall, E. Lansing, MI 48823.
• Michigan State University. Agriculture and
Natural Resources Education Institute. Action
Abstracts; summaries of social science research
particularly useful to Extension Service workers. 3
per yr.

**Michigan State University. Alumni Association**
c/o John R. Kinney, Union Building, East Lansing,
MI 48823.
• Michigan State University Alumni Magazine. 6
per yr. ISSN 0026-2463

**Michigan State University. Asian Studies Center**
101 International Center, East Lansing, MI 48824.
• Journal of South Asian Literature. q. ISSN 0025-
0503
• Michigan State University. Asian Studies Center.
Occasional Papers: East Asian Series. irreg., no. 5,
1974. ISSN 0076-812X
• Michigan State University. Asian Studies Center.
Occasional Papers: South Asian Series. irreg., no.
27, 1975. ISSN 0076-8138

**Michigan State University. Bureau of Business and
Economic Research**
Berkey Hall, East Lansing, MI 48824.
• M S U Business Topics. q. ISSN 0024-8460
• Michigan State Economic Record; a monthly
report on business conditions in Michigan. m.
(except July & Aug.) ISSN 0026-2455

**Michigan State University. Center for International
Programs**
East Lansing, MI 48823.
• Michigan State University. Center for
International Programs. International Report. a.
ISSN 0047-7141

**Michigan State University. Center for Rural
Manpower & Public Affairs**
Agricultural Economics Dept., 39 Agriculture Hall,
East Lansing, MI 48823.
• Michigan State University. Center for Rural
Manpower & Public Affairs. Mimeograph. irreg.

• Michigan State University. Center for Rural
Manpower & Public Affairs. Report. irreg.
• Michigan State University. Center for Rural
Manpower & Public Affairs. Special Paper. irreg.

**Michigan State University. Computer Laboratory**
User Information Center, East Lansing, MI 48824.
• Acronyms. 8 per yr.

**Michigan State University. Continuing Education
Service**
Kellogg Center for Continuing Education, East
Lansing, MI 48824.
• Conference for College and University Leaders in
Continuing Education. Proceedings. a. ISSN
0084-9138

**Michigan State University. Cooperative Extension
Service**
East Lansing, MI 48824.
• Michigan State University. Cooperative Extension
Service. Annual Report. irreg., latest issue 1967.

**Michigan State University. Department of
Agricultural Economics**
E. Lansing, MI 48824.
• Michigan State University. Agricultural
Economics Report. irreg.; (approx 20 per yr)
ISSN 0065-4442

**Michigan State University. Department of Animal
Husbandry**
105 Anthony Hall, E. Lansing, MI 48824.
• Michigan Beef Cattleman. irreg. ISSN 0085-3348

**Michigan State University. Department of English**
East Lansing, MI 48824.
• Conference in the Study of Twentieth-Century
Literature, Michigan State University.
Proceedings. irreg., 1966, no. 4. ISSN 0069-8407
• Gypsy Scholar; graduate forum for literary
criticism. 3 per yr.
• Red Cedar Review. s-a. ISSN 0034-1967

**Michigan State University. Department of
Entomology**
East Lansing, MI 48824.
• Insect Disease and Nematode Alerts. m., w in
summer.

**Michigan State University. Department of Physics**
East Lansing, MI 48824.
• Michigan State University. Department of Physics.
Cyclotron Project. irreg., 1964, no. 21. ISSN
0076-8146

**Michigan State University. Department of Secondary
Education and Curriculum**
East Lansing, MI 48824.
• Michigan State University. Agriculture and
Natural Resources Education Institute.
Newsletter. 3 per yr.

**Michigan State University. Department of Sociology**
East Lansing, MI 48824.
• Summation. s-a. ISSN 0047-7168 (prep. by its
Graduate School Collective)

**Michigan State University. Graduate School of
Business Administration**
Division of Research, Berkey Hall, East Lansing,
MI 48823.
• Michigan Statistical Abstract. biennial. ISSN
0076-8308

**Michigan State University. Institute for Community
Development and Services**
East Lansing, MI 48823.
• Michigan State University. Institute for
Community Development and Services.
Population Report. Community Development
Series. irreg. ISSN 0092-4733

**Michigan State University. Institute for International
Studies in Education**
513 Erickson Hall, E. Lansing, MI 48823.
• Michigan State University. Institute for
International Studies in Education. Publications.
irreg.

**Michigan State University. Institute of Water
Research**
334 Natural Resources Bldg., East Lansing, MI
48824.
• Michigan State University. Institute of Water
Research. Annual Report. a.

**Michigan State University. Latin American Studies Center**
200 International Center, East Lansing, MI 48824.
- Michigan State University. Latin American Studies Center. Monograph Series. irreg. ISSN 0076-8189
- Michigan State University. Latin American Studies Center. Newsletter. bi-m. ISSN 0047-715X
- Michigan State University. Latin American Studies Center. Occasional Papers. irreg. ISSN 0076-8197
- Michigan State University. Latin American Studies Center. Research Reports. irreg. ISSN 0076-8200

**Michigan State University. Learning Systems Institute**
East Lansing, MI 48823.
- Michigan State University. Learning Systems Institute. Paper. irreg. ISSN 0076-8219

**Michigan State University Libraries. International Library**
East Lansing, MI 48824.
- Michigan State University. Library. Africana: Select Recent Acquisitions. irreg. (approx. 8 per yr.) ISSN 0147-0604

**Michigan State University. Museum**
East Lansing, MI 48824.
- Michigan State University. Museum Publications. Biological Series. irreg. (approx. 2-3 per year) ISSN 0076-8227
- Michigan State University. Museum Publications. Cultural Series. irreg., 1967, vol. 1, no. 3. ISSN 0076-8235 (And Exchange Dept., MSU Library, E. Lansing MI 48824)
- Michigan State University. Museum Publications. Paleontological Series. irreg.

**Michigan State University. Outdoor Education Project**
403 Erickson Hall, East Lansing, MI 48823.
- Outdoor Education; newsletter for the exchange of ideas. 2-3 per yr. ISSN 0030-7033 (Co-Sponsor: American Alliance for Health Physical Education & Recreation, Council on Outdoor Education & Camping)

**Michigan State University. Public Administration Program**
East Lansing, MI 48823.
- Michigan State University. Public Administration Program. Research Report. irreg., 1960, no. 3. ISSN 0076-8243

**Michigan State University. Sahel Documentation Center**
W-316 University Libraries, East Lansing, MI 48824.
- Sahel Bibliographic Bullentin/Bulletin Bibliographique. q. ISSN 0145-9481

**Michigan State University. School of Labor and Industrial Relations**
East Lansing, MI 48824.
- Michigan State University. School of Labor and Industrial Relations. Newsletter. 3 per yr. ISSN 0036-6706

**Michigan State University. Special Programs**
443 Administration Bldg., East Lansing, MI 48824.
- Educational opportunity Program Notes. s-a. ISSN 0098-9827

**Michigan Technic**
3077 E. Engineering Bldg., Ann Arbor, MI 48104.
- Michigan Technic. m.(Oct-Apr) ISSN 0026-2471

**Michigan Technological University. Library**
Houghton, MI 49931.
- Michigan Technological University. Library. Library Publication. irreg., 1973, no. 7. ISSN 0076-8324
- Michigan Technological University. Library. Serial Holdings List. irreg. ISSN 0076-8316
- Theses and Dissertations Accepted in Partial Fulfillment of the Requirements for Degrees Granted by the Michigan Technological University. irreg., latest issue 1976.

**Michigan Trucking Association**
501 S. Capitol Ave., Lansing, MI 48933.
- Michigan Trucking Today. bi-m.

**Michigan United Conservation Clubs Inc**
2101 Wood St., Box 30235, Lansing, MI 48909.
- Michigan Out-Of-Doors. m. ISSN 0026-2382

**Michigan Water Pollution Control Association**
8Th Floor, Stevens T. Mason Bldg., Lansing, MI 48926.
- Wastewater Works News. q. ISSN 0043-1028

**Microcard Edition Books**
5500 S. Valentia Way, Englewood, CO 80110.
- Reader Series in Library and Information Science. irreg.

**Microcard Editions**
5500 S. Valentia Way, Englewood, CO 80110.
- Announced Reprints. 3 per yr. ISSN 0003-5106
- Fitzgerald/Hemingway Annual. a. ISSN 0071-5654
- Microcard Bulletin. irreg. ISSN 0026-2641
- Nathaniel Hawthorne Journal. a. ISSN 0073-1382

**Microcomputer Associates, Inc.**
2589 Scott Blvd., Santa Clara, CA 95050.
- Microcomputer Digest and Industry Report. m.

**Microfilm Publishing, Inc.**
P.O. Box 313, Wykagyl Station, New Rochelle, NY 10804.
- International Microfilm Source Book. a.
- Micrographics Newsletter; a twice a month report for business executives who use or market microfilm services and equipment. ISSN 0026-2749
- School Security. 10 per yr. ISSN 0362-9406

**Microfilming Corporation of America**
21 Harristown Rd., Glen Rock, NJ 07452.
- Atlanta Constitution: a Georgia Index. a. (Georgia State University. Library)
- New York Times Index Highlights. bi-m.
- New York Times School Microfilm Collection Index by Reels. irreg. ISSN 0095-5663

**Microform Review, Inc.**
520 Riverside Ave., Box 405, Saugatuck Station, Westport, CT 06880.
- Guide to Microforms in Print. a. ISSN 0017-5293
- Microform Review. q. ISSN 0002-6530
- Micrographics Equipment Review. q. ISSN 0362-1006
- Micropublishers' Trade List Annual. a. ISSN 0361-2635
- Subject Guide to Microforms in Print. a. ISSN 0090-290X

**Microforms International Marketing Corporation**
Fairview Park, Elmsford, NY 10523.
- M I M C Microforms Annual. a. ISSN 0362-4552
- Reference Guide & Comprehensive Catalog of International Serials; originals & reprints. microfilms & microfiches featuring science, technology, medicine, the humanities. irreg. ISSN 0094-0151

**Micropaleontology Press**
American Museum of Natural History, Central Park West at 79 St., New York, NY 10024.
- Bibliography and Index of Micropaleontology. m(with annual subject index) ISSN 0300-7227
- Micropaleontology. q. ISSN 0026-2803

**Mid-America Dairymen, Inc.**
800 West Tampa, Box 1837 SSS, Springfield, MO 65805.
- Mid-Am Reporter. m.

**Mid-America Lumbermens Service Corporation**
4901 Main Street, Kansas City, MO 64112.
- Retail Lumberman; in the interest of retail lumber and building material dealers. m. ISSN 0034-608X

**Mid-America Publishing Corporation**
4251 Pennsylvania, Kansas City, MO 64111.
- Flower and Garden Magazine. m. ISSN 0015-4474

**Mid-America Publishing Corporation (Shenandoah)**
Box 130, Shenandoah, IA 51601
(Or: 214 Ninth St., Des Moines, IA 50309)
- Iowan; Iowa's own magazine. q. ISSN 0021-0722

**Mid-Atlantic Regional Archives Conference**
c/o Ed. Donald Harrison, National Archives, Machine Readable Archives Division (NNR), Washington, DC 20408
(Subscr. to: Martha Slotten, Library, Dickinson College, Carlisle, PA 17013)
- Mid-Atlantic Archivist. 5 per yr.

**Mid-Continent Banker**
408 Olive St., St. Louis, MO 63102.
- Mid-Continent Banker. m. ISSN 0026-296X

**Mid-Continent Regional Science Association**
- Regional Science Perspectives. (pub. by Kansas State University. Department of Economics)

**Mid-Continent Scientific**
780 Kenilworth Ct., Des Plaines, IL 60016.
- Environmental Resources. 4 per yr. ISSN 0094-1034 (International Association for Advancement of Earth & Environmental Sciences) (Co-sponsor: Northeastern Illinois University Foundation)

**Mid-Eastern Cooperatives**
75 Amor Ave., Carlstadt, NJ 07072.
- Co-Op Highlights. 10 per yr. ISSN 0009-9740

**Mid-Hudson Genealogical Journal**
1112 Pond Rd. W., Columbia, SC 29169.
- Mid-Hudson Genealogical Journal. q.

**Mid-Hudson Library System**
103 Market St., Poughkeepsie, NY 12601.
- Mid-Hudson Library System Newsletter. b-m.

**Mid-Hudson School Study Council**
State University College, New Paltz, NY 12561.
- Channel (New Paltz) q. ISSN 0009-1464

**Mid-Ohio Regional Planning Commmission**
514 South High St., Columbus, OH 43215.
- Mid-Ohio Review. bi-m.

**Midatlantic Review**
Box 398, Baldwin Place, NY 10505.
- Midatlantic Review. q.

**Midcontinent American Studies Association**
- American Studies. (pub. by University of Kansas. American Studies Department)

**Midcontinent Farmers Association**
201 S. 7th St., Columbia, MO 65201.
- Today's Farmer. m.

**Middaugh Printers at Sugarcreek**
Sugarcreek, OH 44681.
- Coin Dealer. m. ISSN 0010-0374

**Middle East Enterprise**
635 Madison Ave., New York, NY 10022.
- Middle East Enterprise. fortn.

**Middle East Institute**
1761 N St. N.W., Washington, DC 20036.
- James Terry Duce Memorial Series. irreg., vol. 3, 1975. ISSN 0075-3009
- Middle East Institute Newsletter. irreg.
- Middle East Journal. q. ISSN 0026-3141

**Middle East Librarians Association**
c/o Janet Heineck, Regenstein Library, Rm. 560, University of Chicago, 1100 E. 57 St., Chicago, IL 60637.
- M E L A Notes. 3 per yr. ISSN 0364-2410

**Middle East Perspective, Inc.**
850 Seventh Ave., New York, NY 10019.
- Middle East Perspective; a newsletter on Eastern Mediterranean and North African affairs. m. ISSN 0026-3176

**Middle East Research & Information Project**
Box 3122, Columbia Heights Station, Washington, DC 20010.
- Middle East Research & Information Project Reports/M E R I P Reports. m. ISSN 0047-7265

**Middle East Studies Association of North America, Inc.**
New York Univ., New York, NY 10003.
- Middle East Studies Association. Bulletin. q. ISSN 0026-3184

**Middle States Association of Colleges and Secondary Schools**
Gateway One, Newark, NJ 07102.
- Middle States Association of Colleges and Secondary Schools. Proceedings. a. ISSN 0076-8561

**Middlebury College**
Forest Hall, Middlebury, VT 05753.
- Middlebury College News Letter. q.

**MidEast Report, Inc.**
60 E. 42nd St., New York, NY 10017.
- MidEast Report. s-m. ISSN 0026-3230

**Midland Cooperatives, Inc.**
2021 E. Hennepin Ave., Minneapolis, MN 55413 (Subscr. Address: 2206 Winter St., Superior, WI 54880)
- Cooperative Builder. w. ISSN 0010-8413
- Midland Cooperator. bi-w. ISSN 0047-7281

**Midland Genealogical Society**
Box 1191, Midland, TX 79701.
- Thorny Trail. s-a. ISSN 0094-0844

**Midland Lutheran College**
Fremont, NE 68025.
- Midland. w. ISSN 0026-3249

**Midland Mutual Life Insurance Co.**
250 E. Broad St., Columbus, OH 43215.
- Builder. m. ISSN 0007-3261

**Midmarch Associates**
Box 3304, Grand Central Station, New York, NY 10017.
- Women Artists Newsletter. 10 per yr. ISSN 0361-9117

**Midrex Corporation**
One NCNB Plaza, Charlotte, NC 28280.
- Direct from Midrex. 3 per yr.

**Midwest Agricultural Relations, Inc.**
Box 127, Stockyards Station, St. Joseph, MO 64488.
- Journal of Livestock and Agriculture. w. ISSN 0022-2283

**Midwest Art**
2025 E. Fernwood Ave., Box 07419, Milwaukee, WI 53207.
- Midwest Art. m.

**Midwest Association for Latin American Studies**
c/o Kenneth J. Grieb, Ed., University of Wisconsin-Oshkosh, Dept. of History, Oshkosh, WI 54901.
- M A L A S Newsletter. q.

**Midwest Beverage Publications**
2511 E. 46th St., Suite G-1, Indianapolis, IN 46205.
- Buckeye Beverage Journal; first trade journal of Ohio's beverage, restaurant and hotel industry. m. ISSN 0007-2826

**Midwest Chaparral Poets**
5508 Osage Ave., Kansas City, KS 66106.
- Midwest Chaparral. 3 per yr. ISSN 0026-3346

**Midwest Conference of Political Scientists**
- American Journal of Political Science. (pub. by Wayne State University Press)

**Midwest Genealogical Society**
2911 Rivera, Wichita, KS 67211.
- Midwest Genealogical Society. Surname Index. irreg. ISSN 0091-6439

**Midwest History of Education Society**
- Midwest History of Education Society. Journal. (pub. by University of Northern Iowa. College of Education)

**Midwest Modern Langage Association**
311 English-Philosophy Bldg., Univ. of Iowa, Iowa City, IA 52240.
- Midwest Modern Language Association Bulletin. s-a. ISSN 0026-3419

**Midwest Newsclip**
176 W. Adams, Box 1359, Chicago, IL 60690.
- Midwest Media. a.

**Midwest Oil Register, Inc.**
Drawer 7248, Tulsa, OK 74105.
- Directory of Electric Light and Power Companies. a.
- Directory of Gas Utility Companies. a.

- Directory of Geophysical and Oil Companies Who Use Geophysical Service. a. ISSN 0417-5905
- Directory of Oil Marketing and Wholesale Distributors. a. ISSN 0070-5993
- Directory of Oil Well Drilling Contractors. a. ISSN 0415-9764
- Directory of Oil Well Supply Companies. a. ISSN 0415-9772
- Oil Directory of Alaska. a. ISSN 0471-3850
- Oil Directory of Canada. a. ISSN 0474-0114
- Oil Directory of Companies Outside the U.S. and Canada. a. ISSN 0472-7711
- Oil Directory of Houston, Texas. a. ISSN 0471-3877

**Midwest Outdoors**
111 Shore Drive, Hinsdale, IL 60521.
- MidWest Outdoors. m.

**Midwest Petroleum Marketers Association**
10400 W. Higgins Rd., Suite 412, Rosemont, IL 60018.
- Marketing Trends. bi-m.

**Midwest Publishers (Ann Arbor)**
611 Church St., Ann Arbor, MI 48014.
- International Journal of Biomedical Engineering. q.

**Midwest Publishing Co., Inc. (Skokie)**
8328 N. Lincoln Ave., Skokie, IL 60076.
- P V. (Printing Views); for the Midwest printer and publisher. m. ISSN 0030-8439

**Mid-West Publishing Company, Inc. (Topeka)**
1101 Topeka Ave., Topeka, KS 66612.
- Mid-West Truckman. bi-m. ISSN 0026-3052

**Midwest Racing News, Inc.**
6646 W. Fairview Ave., Milwaukee, WI 53213.
- Midwest Racing News. w. (May-Sep.), m. (Apr., Oct., Dec.) ISSN 0047-732X

**Mid-West Records Inc**
Box 766, 2537 Madison Ave, Kansas City, MO 64141.
- Mid-West Contractor. fortn. ISSN 0026-3044

**Midwest Research Institute**
425 Volker Blvd., Kansas City, MO 64110.
- M R I Quarterly. irreg. ISSN 0024-8347

**Midwest Review of Public Administration, Inc.**
Park College, Parkville, MO 64152.
- Midwest Review of Public Administration. q. ISSN 0026-346X

**Midwest Sociological Society**
Department of Sociology, Southern Illinois University, Carbondale, IL 62901.
- Sociological Quarterly. q. ISSN 0038-0253

**Mid-West Tennessee Genealogical Society**
Box 3343, Jackson, TN 38301.
- Family Findings. q. ISSN 0533-0939

**Midwest Traders Ltd.**
Box 2737, Carbondale, IL 62901.
- Fuel Savers International Newsletter. m.

**Midwest Wool Marketing Cooperative**
125 East 10th Avenue, South Hutchinson, KS 67505.
- Midwest Wool Growers News. 7 per yr.

**Midwest World**
P.O. 6644, Bexley, OH 43209.
- Midwest World. m.

**Midwestern Association of Graduate Schools**
Loyola University, 802 N. Michigan Ave., Chicago, IL 60611.
- Midwestern Association of Graduate Schools. Proceedings of the Annual Meeting. a.

**Mid-Western Banker**
161 W. Wisconsin Ave., Milwaukee, WI 53203.
- Mid-Western Banker. m. ISSN 0026-3060

**Migrant Legal Action Program**
1910 K St. N.W., Washington, DC 20006.
- Earth Bond. m. ISSN 0098-9479

**Mike Causey's Federal Employe Newsletter**
Box 716, Glen Echo, MD 20768.
- Mike Causey's Federal Employe Newsletter. fortn.

**Milady Publishing Corporation**
3839 White Plains Rd., Bronx, NY 10467.
- National Beauty School Journal. m. ISSN 0027-8769
- New Dimensions for Teaching Personal Development. (Personality Improvement) bi-m.

**Milbank Memorial Fund**
- Milbank Memorial Fund Quarterly/Health and Society. (pub. by Neale Watson Academic Publications, Inc.)

**Miles Laboratories Inc.**
Research Products Division, Elkhart, IN 46514.
- International Symposium on Molecular Biology. Publications. irreg., 3rd, New York, 1969.

**Milestone Car Society Inc.**
Box 1166, Pacific Palisades, CA 90272.
- Mile Post. bi-m.
- Milestone Car. (pub. by Taylor-Constantine)

**Militant Publishing Association**
14 Charles Lane, New York, NY 10014.
- Militant; published in the interests of the working people. w. ISSN 0026-3885

**Military Chaplains Association of the United States of America**
7758 Wisconsin Ave. Suite 401, Washington, Washington, DC 20014.
- Military Chaplain. bi-m. ISSN 0026-3958

**Military Collectors News**
P.O. Box 7582, Tulsa, OK 74105.
- Military Collectors News. m. ISSN 0047-7370

**Military Communications**
275 Madison Ave., New York, NY 10016.
- Stateside Family. m.

**Military History Associates, Inc.**
P.O. Box 5248, Austin, TX 78763.
- Military History of Texas and the Southwest. q. ISSN 0047-7389

**Military Law Project**
108 Washington Blvd., Laurel, MD 20810.
- Military Law Project News - Notes. irreg.

**Military Order of the World Wars**
1100 17th St. N.W., Suite 1000, Washington, DC 20036.
- Officer Review. 10 per yr.

**Milk, Inc.**
8413 Lake Ave., Cleveland, OH 44102.
- Milk Reporter. m.

**Milk Industry Foundation**
910 17th St., N.W., Washington, DC 20006.
- Milk Facts.

**Milky Way Press (San Francisco)**
130 Eureka, San Francisco, CA 94114.
- Kosmos; milky way journal. s-a.

**Milky Way Productions Inc.**
Box 432, Old Chelsea Sta., New York, NY 10011.
- Screw; the sex review. w. ISSN 0036-9624

**Mill Hollow Corp.**
156 E. 52nd St., New York, NY 10022.
- Laundry News. m.

**Mill Trade Journal**
c/o M. D. Oberman, 6311 Gross Point Rd., Niles, IL 60648.
- Mill Trade Journal. w. ISSN 0047-7427

**Miller & Fink Corp.**
16 Thorndal Circle, Darien, CT 06820.
- Patient Care. 21 per yr. ISSN 0031-305X

**William J. Miller Associates, Inc.**
145 E. 49th St, New York, NY 10017.
- New Practitioner's Action Guide. bi-m.

**Miss Lee Miller, Ed. & Pub.**
190 E. 21st St., Brooklyn, NY 11226.
- Bulletin Board. bi-m.

**Miller Electric Manufacturing Co.**
718 South Bounds St., Appleton, WI 54911.
- M E M C O News. q.

**Miller Index**
c/o Bette Miller Radewald, Ed., 639 Sandalwood
Court, Riverside, CA 92507.
- Miller Index. a, with irregular supplement:
Misplaced Millers.

**Miller Publishing Co.**
2501 Wayzata Blvd., Minneapolis, MN 55440.
- Dairy Herd Management; the business magazine
for top dairy farmers. m. ISSN 0011-5614
- Farm Store Merchandising; for farm supply
dealers & distributors interested in better selling.
m. ISSN 0014-8121
- Feed Additive Compendium. a.(with 11
supplements) ISSN 0071-450X
- Feedlot Management; a national farm business
magazine for cattle and lamb feeders. m.
- Feedstuffs; the weekly newspaper for agribusiness.
w. ISSN 0014-9624
- Hog Farm Management; the national farm
business magazine for major hog producers. m.
ISSN 0018-3180
- Home and Garden Supply Merchandiser;
merchandising and management magazine for
garden centers and distributors. m. ISSN 0018-
3954
- Home & Garden Supply Merchandiser Green
Book. a.
- Tack 'n Togs Book. a.
- Tack 'n Togs Merchandising. m.

**Millimeter Magazine Inc.**
c/o William Blake & Peter Jablow, 12 E. 46th St.,
New York, NY 10017.
- Millimeter; the magazine for film and videotape
people. m.

**Millinery Research Corporation**
22 E. 42nd St., New York, NY 10017.
- Wigs, Hats and Accessories; the voice of the
millinery and wig industries. bi-w.

**Million Dollar Round Table**
Continental Office Plaza, 2340 River Road, Des
Plaines, IL 60016.
- Round the Table. q.

**Millionaires of Today or Tomorrow**
888 7th Ave., Suite 400, New York, NY 10019.
- Finders Keepers. w.

**Mills College. Associated Students**
Oakland, CA 94613.
- Mills Stream. w. ISSN 0026-430X

**Milton College Student Senate**
c/o Stoughton Courier Hub, Stoughton, WI 56536.
- Milton College Blue and Gold. w. ISSN 0026-
4318

**Milton Helpern Library of Legal Medicine**
- International Microform Journal of Legal
Medicine. (pub. by University Microfilms
International)

**Milton Society of America**
c/o Michael Lieb, Dept of English, University of
Illinois, Chicago Circle, Chicago, IL 60680.
- Milton Society of America. Proceedings. a. ISSN
0540-0961
- Seventeenth-Century News. (pub. by Pennsylvania
State University. Department of English)

**Milwaukee. Bureau of Budget and Management
Analysis**
Milwaukee, WI 53202.
- Milwaukee. Bureau of Budget and Management
Analysis. Budget Summary. a. ISSN 0092-1513

**Milwaukee County News**
4124 S. Austin St., Milwaukee, WI 53207.
- Milwaukee County News. w.

**Milwaukee District Nurses' Association**
611 East Wells St., Milwaukee, WI 53202.
- Milwaukee Professional Nurse. 4 per yr. ISSN
0026-4369

**Milwaukee Fire Department Athletic Association**
711 W. Wells St., Milwaukee, WI 53233.
- M. F. D. Register. (Milwaukee Fire Department)
m.

**Milwaukee Public Library**
814 W. Wisconsin Ave., Milwaukee, WI 53233.
- Booktruck. m.
- Milwaukee Reader. w. ISSN 0026-4377

**Milwaukee Public Museum**
c/o Robert Gorski, 800 N. Wells St., Milwaukee,
WI 53233.
- Lore. q. ISSN 0024-6492 (Friends of the
Milwaukee Public Museum)

**Milwaukee Public Schools**
Board of School Directors, P. O. Drawer 10K,
Milwaukee, WI 53201.
- Milwaukee Public Schools Staff Bulletin. w.(Sept.-
June)

**Mineral Digest, Ltd.**
Box 341, Murray Hill Station, New York, NY
10016.
- Mineral Digest. q.

**Mineralogical Record, Inc.**
Box 783, Bowie, MD 20715.
- Mineralogical Record. bi-m. ISSN 0026-4628

**Mineralogical Society of America**
1909 K St., N.W., Washington, DC 20006.
- American Mineralogist. bi-m. ISSN 0003-004X
- Mineralogical Abstracts. (pub. by Mineralogical
Society UK)

**Mini-Micro Systems**
5 Kane Industrial Drive, Hudson, MA 01741.
- Mini-Micro Systems. m.

**Mining Equipment News**
Box 225, Clarendon Hills, IL 60514.
- Mining Equipment News. m. ISSN 0026-5195

**Ministerial Sisterhood Unitarian Universalist**
c/o Rev. Marjorie N. Leaming, 438 View Dr., Santa
Paula, CA 93060.
- M S U U Newsletter. irreg. ISSN 0360-7046

**Ministers Life Resources, Inc.**
3100 West Lake St., Minneapolis, MN 55416.
- Church and Clergy Finance. bi-w. ISSN 0045-
6861
- Clergy Tax Tips. q.

**Ministry of Christ Church**
Box 423, Glendale, CA 91209.
- Identity. q.

**Minkus Publications Inc.**
116 W. 32 St., New York, NY 10001.
- American Stamp Catalog. a.
- Minkus New American Stamp Catalog. a. ISSN
0076-9061
- Minkus New World Wide Stamp Catalog. a. ISSN
0076-907X
- Minkus Stamp Journal. q. ISSN 0026-5357

**Minneapolis Athletic Club**
615 Second Ave. S., Minneapolis, MN 55402.
- M. A. C. Gopher. m. ISSN 0024-7898

**Minneapolis District Dental Journal**
805 Physician & Surgeons' Bldg., 63 S. 9th St.,
Minneapolis, MN 55402.
- Minneapolis District Dental Journal. q. ISSN
0026-5365

**Minneapolis Medical Research Foundation, Inc.**
501 Park Avenue South, Minneapolis, MN 55415.
- Evaluation. irreg. ISSN 0090-4449 (Co-sponsors:
National Institute of Mental Health, Program
Evaluation Resource Center)

**Minneapolis Society of Fine Arts**
2400 Third Ave. South, Minneapolis, MN 55404.
- Minneapolis Institute of Arts. Annual Report. a.
ISSN 0076-9096
- Minneapolis Institute of Arts. Bulletin. a. ISSN
0076-910X

**Minnesota. Criminal Justice Information Section**
St. Paul, MN 55101.
- Minnesota Crime Information. a. ISSN 0093-2345

**Minnesota. Department of Administration**
5Th Floor, Centennial Bldg., 194 Centennial Bldg.,
St. Paul, MN 55155.
- Insight (St. Paul); information systems newsletter.
m. ISSN 0046-9653

**Minnesota. Department of Agriculture**
140 Centennial Office Bldg., St. Paul, MN 55155.
- Minnesota Dairy Plants. a.

**Minnesota. Department of Corrections**
430 Metro Square Bldg., State Office Bldg., St. Paul,
MN 55101.
- Minnesota. Department. of Corrections.
Characteristics on Institutional Populations. a.

**Minnesota. Department of Economic Development**
480 Cedar St., St. Paul, MN 55101.
- Camping Guide. a.
- Directory of Manufacturers-Minnesota. biennial.
- Guide to Skiing in Minnesota. a.
- International Trade & Investment News. m.
- Minnesota Export Survey Summary. biennial.
- Minnesota Exporter's Assistance Guide. a.
- Minnesota Industrial Development News. irreg.
- Minnesota International Trade Directory. biennial.
- Minnesota New & Expanding Industry. a.
- Minnesota Profile. a.
- Minnesota's Role in International Trade. irreg.
- Tourism News. m.

**Minnesota. Department of Education**
550 Cedar, Capitol Square Bldg., St. Paul, MN
55101.
- Education Update. m.(during school year)
- Mathematics Flyer. 3 per yr. ISSN 0025-5696
- Minnesota. Department of Education. Biennial
Report. biennial. ISSN 0093-870X
- Minnesota. Department of Education. Public
Library Newsletter. m. ISSN 0026-5438

**Minnesota. Department of Education. Office of Public
Libraries and Interlibrary Cooperation**
301 Hanover Bldg., 480 Cedar St., St. Paul, MN
55101.
- Minnesota Libraries. q. ISSN 0026-5551

**Minnesota. Department of Employment Services**
390 N. Robert St., St. Paul, MN 55101.
- Current Minnesota Labor Conditions. q.
- Minnesota. Department of Employment Services.
Annual Report. a.

**Minnesota. Department of Health**
Health Education and Information, 717 S.E.
Delaware St., Minneapolis, MN 55440.
- Minnesota's Health. q.

**Minnesota. Department of Human Rights**
200 Capitol Square Bldg., St. Paul, MN 55101.
- Minnesota. Department of Human Rights. Annual
Report. a. ISSN 0076-9118

**Minnesota. Department of Natural Resources**
350 Centennial Office Bldg., St. Paul, MN 55155.
- Minnesota. Department of Natural Resources.
Biennial Report. biennial.
- Minnesota. Department of Natural Resources.
Proposed Program Budget, Detailed Estimates.
biennial.
- Minnesota Volunteer. 6 per yr.

**Minnesota. Department of Natural Resources.
Division of Fish and Wildlife**
St. Paul, MN 55155.
- Minnesota. Division of Fish and Wildlife,
Environment Section. Special Publication. irreg.
ISSN 0363-5341
- Minnesota. Division of Fish & Wildlife. Technical
Bulletin. irreg., 1969, no. 10.
- Minnesota Fisheries Investigations. irreg., 1969,
no. 5. ISSN 0076-9150

**Minnesota. Department of Public Safety**
210 State Highway Bldg., St. Paul, MN 55155.
- Minnesota Alcohol Programs for Highway Safety;
an overview with statistics. irreg. ISSN 0093-2558
(Co-Sponsor: U.S. National Highway Traffic
Safety Administration)

**Minnesota. Department of Public Welfare**
Centennial Bldg., St. Paul, MN 55155.
- People. Biennial Report. biennial.

**Minnesota. Department of Public Welfare. Public
Information, Education Section**
658 Cedar St., St. Paul, MN 55155.
- Directory of Minnesota's Area Mental Health,
Mental Retardation, Inebriety Programs. irreg.
ISSN 0095-4888

**Minnesota. Department of Revenue**
Centennial Office Bldg., St. Paul, MN 55145.
- Minnesota. Department of Revenue. Biennial
Report. biennial. ISSN 0095-0645
- Minnesota. Department of Revenue. Petroleum
Division. Annual Report. a. ISSN 0095-3024
(prep. by its Petroleum Division)

- Minnesota Sales and Use Tax Quarterly Report Bulletin. q.

**Minnesota. Geological Survey**
University of Minnesota, 1633 Eustis St., St. Paul, MN 55108.
- Minnesota. Geological Survey. Bulletin. irreg. ISSN 0076-9169
- Minnesota. Geological Survey. Special Publication Series. irreg., no. 13, 1970. ISSN 0076-9185

**Minnesota. Governor's Commission on Crime Prevention and Control**
St. Paul, MN 55155.
- Minnesota.Governor's Commission on Crime Prevention and Control. Comprehensive Plan. a. ISSN 0094-2073

**Minnesota. Health Statistics Section**
717 Delaware St. S. E., Minneapolis, MN 55440.
- Minnesota Health Statistics. a. ISSN 0094-5641

**Minnesota. Office of Ombudsman for Corrections**
St. Paul, MN 55155.
- Minnesota. Office of Ombudsman for Corrections. Annual Report. a. ISSN 0094-1409

**Minnesota. Office of Revisor of Statutes**
St. Paul, MN 55155.
- Minnesota Statutes. Supplement. irreg. ISSN 0094-1727

**Minnesota. Pollution Control Agency**
1935 West County Rd., Roseville, MN 55113.
- Air Quality in Minnesota. a. ISSN 0361-5650

**Minnesota. State Board of Health**
717 Delaware St. S.E., Minneapolis, MN 55440.
- Minnesota. State Board of Health. Biennial Report. biennial.

**Minnesota. State Manpower Council**
St. Paul, MN 55155.
- Minnesota. State Manpower Council. Report to the Governor. irreg. ISSN 0099-2119

**Minnesota. State Planning Agency. Development Planning Division**
St. Paul, MN 55155.
- Minnesota Pocket Data Book. irreg. ISSN 0094-3983

**Minnesota. State Planning Agency. Environmental Planning Section**
Capitol Square Building, 550 Cedar St., St. Paul, MN 55155.
- Minnesota. Governor. Annual Report on the Quality of the Environment. a. ISSN 0094-1697
- Minnesota. State Planning Agency. Environmental Planning Division. Land Use Planning Report. irreg.

**Minnesota Academy of Science**
3100 38th Ave. S., Minneapolis, MN 55406.
- Minnesota Academy of Science. Journal. s-a. ISSN 0026-539X

**Minnesota Association of Plumbing-Heating-Cooling Contractors Inc.**
100 E. 14th St., Minneapolis, MN 55403.
- Minnesota Plumbing Heating Cooling Contractor. m.

**Minnesota Center for Philosophy of Science**
- Minnesota Studies in the Philosophy of Science. (pub. by University of Minnesota Press)

**Minnesota Congress of Parents, Teachers and Students**
55 Sherburne Ave., St. Paul, MN 55103.
- Minnesota P T S A News. m.

**Minnesota Dental Association**
- Northwest Dentistry. (pub. by Craftsman Press, Inc.)

**Minnesota Education Association**
41 Sherburne Ave., St. Paul, MN 55103.
- M E Advocate. 20 per yr.

**Minnesota Education Association. Northern Division**
1414 Bixby, Bemidji, MN 56601.
- Northern Minnesota Educator. q. ISSN 0029-3172

**Minnesota Federated Women's Clubs**
Box 24, Pine River, MN 56474
(Subscr. to: 912 Upper Midwest Bldg., 425 Hennepin Ave., Minneapolis, Minnesota 55401)
- Minnesota Clubwoman. 4 per yr.

**Minnesota Food Retailers Association**
555 Wabasha St., Suite 215, Saint Paul, MN 55102.
- Minnesota Food Guide. m. ISSN 0026-5489

**Minnesota Geographic Society**
1501 S. Fourth St., Minneapolis, MN 55406.
- Earth Journal. q.

**Minnesota Great Lakes Commission**
St. Paul, MN 55155.
- Report of the Minnesota Great Lakes Commission. biennial. ISSN 0360-1803

**Minnesota Historical Society**
690 Cedar St., St. Paul, MN 55101.
- Historic Fort Snelling Chronicles; a leaflet series. irreg.
- Minnesota Historic Sites Pamphlet Series. irreg., no. 14, 1977. ISSN 0544-3571
- Minnesota Historical Archaeology Series. irreg., no. 3, 1975. ISSN 0076-9193
- Minnesota History. q. ISSN 0026-5497
- Minnesota History News. bi-m. ISSN 0544-358X
- Minnesota Prehistoric Archaeology Series. irreg., no. 10, 1973; no. 11, 1974.
- Roots; the Minnesota history magazine for elementary students. 3 per yr.

**Minnesota Law Review Foundation**
- Minnesota Law Review. (pub. by University of Minnesota. Law School)

**Minnesota Leader**
2314 Elliot Ave. S., Minneapolis, MN 55104.
- Minnesota Leader. s-m.

**Minnesota League for Nursing**
Box 35, Rosemount, MN 55068.
- M L N Bulletin. 6 per yr. ISSN 0047-7508

**Minnesota Motor Transport Association**
- Midwest Motor Transport News. (pub. by Northland Publishing Corporation)

**Minnesota Music Educators Association**
- Gopher Music Notes. (pub. by Park Region Publishing Co.)

**Minnesota Newspaper Association**
84 S. Sixth St., Minneapolis, MN 55402.
- Minnesota Press. m. ISSN 0026-5632

**Minnesota Nurses Association**
1821 University Ave., Rm. 152, St. Paul, MN 55104.
- Minnesota Nursing Accent. 4 per yr. ISSN 0026-5586

**Minnesota Optometric Association**
Grigg-Midway Bldg., St. Paul, MN 55104.
- Minnesota Optometrist. bi-m. ISSN 0026-5594

**Minnesota Ornithologist's Union**
James Ford Bell, Museum of Natural History, University of Minnesota, Minneapolis, MN 55455.
- Loon. q. ISSN 0024-645X

**Minnesota Police & Peace Officers Association**
- Minnesota Police Journal. (pub. by Police Press Inc.)

**Minnesota Private College Fund**
906 Northwestern Bank Bldg., Minneapolis, MN 55402.
- Minnesota Private College Fund. Report. a. ISSN 0076-9223

**Minnesota Review**
Box 5416, Milwaukee, WI 53211.
- Minnesota Review. s-a. ISSN 0026-5667

**Minnesota Sentinel Publishing Co.**
84 S. 6th St., Suite 501, Minneapolis, MN 55402.
- Twin Cities Courier. w. ISSN 0300-6603

**Minnesota Society of Architects**
- Architecture Minnesota. (pub. by Craftsman Press, Inc.)

**Minnesota Speech and Hearing Association**
319 - 15th Ave. S. E., Rm. 30, Minneapolis, MN 55455
(Subscr. to: Mary e Ambroe, 8446 Humboldt Ave. S., Bloomington MN 55431)
- Minnesota Speech and Hearing Association. Newsletter. s-a.

**Minnesota State Automobile Association**
7 Travelers Trail, Burnsville, MN 55331.
- Minnesota A. A. A. Motorist. m. ISSN 0026-5381

**Minnesota State Horticultural Society**
Univ. of Minnesota, St. Paul Campus, St. Paul, MN 55101.
- Minnesota Horticulturist. 9 per yr. ISSN 0026-5500

**Minnesota State Medical Association**
101 E. Fifth St., N. 900, St. Paul, MN 55101.
- Minnesota Medicine. m. ISSN 0026-556X

**Minnesota State Pharmaceutical Association**
- Minnesota Pharmacist. (pub. by State Pharmaceutical Editorial Association)

**Minnesota State Sheriffs Association**
- Minnesota Sheriff. (pub. by Ramco Publishing Co)

**Minnesota Turkey Growers Association**
2387 University Ave. W., St. Paul, MN 55114.
- Gobbles. m. ISSN 0017-1506

**Minnesota Vocational Association**
1609 9th Ave. S.E., St. Cloud, MN 56301.
- M V A Viewpoints. 4 per yr.

**Minnesota Women's Center**
306 Walter Library, University of Minnesota, Minneapolis, MN 55455.
- Women's Advocate. 8 per yr. ISSN 0300-6611 (Co-Sponsor: Univ. of Minnesota Women's Studies Program)

**R. B. Minogue**
8824 Tuckerman Lane, Potomac, MD 20854.
- New Settler's Guide for Washington, D.C. and Communities in Nearby Maryland and Virginia. a. ISSN 0097-8213

**Minority Business Information Institute**
295 Madison Ave., New York, NY 10017.
- M B I I Newsletter. q.

**Minority Report**
Box 252, Dayton, OH 45401.
- Minority Report. fortn. ISSN 0026-5713

**Minority Research Center**
117 R Street, N.E., Washington, DC 20002.
- Directory of Black Literary Magazines. irreg.,

**Minot State College. Publications Board**
Minot, ND 58701.
- Red and Green. fortn. ISSN 0034-1959

**Minotaur Press**
2923 B Rose St., Anchorage, AK 99504.
- Minotaur. q.

**Minutemen**
Box57, Independence, MO 64051.
- On Target. m. ISSN 0030-2341

**Mirage**
P.O. 391172, Miami Beach, FL 33139.
- Mirage; voice of transsexual consciousness.

**Mirage Press (Baltimore)**
5111 Liberty Heights Ave., Baltimore, MD 21207.
- Voyager Series. irreg.

**Miramar Publishing Co.**
2048 Cotner Ave., Los Angeles, CA 90025.
- Plumbing Engineer. bi-m. (American Society of Plumbing Engineers)
- Reeves Journal; plumbing, heating & cooling. m. ISSN 0048-7066
- Rental Equipment Register. m. ISSN 0034-4524

**Mirror Northwest**
c/o English Dept., Bellevue Community College, Bellevue, WA 98007.
- Mirror Northwest. a.

**Karlo Mirth, Ed. & Pub.**
Box 1767, Grand Central, New York, NY 10017.
● Croatia Press; review and news bulletin. q. ISSN 0011-1627

**Mise-en-Scene**
c/o Louis Gianetti, 4080 Crawford Hall, Case Western Reserve University, Cleveland, OH 44106.
● Mise-en-Scene. irreg.

**Miss Black America**
245 W. Chelten Ave, Philadelphia, PA 19144.
● Miss Black America. bi-m. ISSN 0017-9825

**Mission Aviation Fellowship**
3519 W. Commonwealth Ave., Box 2828, Fullerton, CA 92633.
● Mission Aviation. q.

**Mission Journal, Inc.**
1710 West Airport Freeway, Irving, TX 75062.
● Mission. m. ISSN 0026-6027

**Mission of the State of Kuwait to the United Nations**
235 E. 42nd St., New York, NY 10017.
● Kuwait. m. ISSN 0023-5784

**Missionary Society of St. Paul the Apostle in the State of New York**
● New Catholic World. (pub. by Paulist Press)

**Missionary Society of the Oblate Fathers of Texas**
907 Pasadena St., P.O. Box 96, San Antonio, TX 78291.
● Oblate World and Voice of Hope; southern Province edition. bi-m.

**Missionhurst, Inc.**
4651 N. 25th St., Arlington, VA 22250.
● Missionhurst. 6 per yr. ISSN 0026-6086 (Immaculate Heart Missions)

**Missions Advanced Research & Communication Center**
919 W. Huntington Drive, Monrovia, CA 91016.
● M A R C Newsletter. bi-m.
● Mission Handbook: North American Protestant Ministries Overseas. triennial. ISSN 0093-8130

**Missions Education**
Box 2337, Anderson, IN 46011.
● Church of God Missions. m (except Aug.) ISSN 0009-6504

**Mississippi. Agricultural & Industrial Board**
Sillers Office Bldg., Jackson, MS 39205.
● Mississippi Magic. s-a. ISSN 0026-6310

**Mississippi. Board of Architecture**
P.O. Box 2473, Jackson, MS 39205.
● Mississippi. State Board of Architecture. Annual Report. a.

**Mississippi. Department of Education**
Box 771, Jackson, MS 39205.
● Education in Mississippi. bi-m.
● Educational Directory of Mississippi Schools. irreg. ISSN 0363-874X
● Mississippi Teachers Directory. irreg.

**Mississippi. Game and Fish Commission**
Box 451, Jackson, MS 39205.
● Mississippi. State Game and Fish Commission. Annual Report to the Regular Session of the Mississippi Legislature. a. ISSN 0098-7840
● Mississippi Game and Fish. bi-m. ISSN 0026-6256

**Mississippi. Governor's Office of Human Resources**
MS 39200.
● Mississippi. Governor's Office of Human Resources. Annual Report. a.

**Mississippi. Library Commission**
P.O. Box 3260, Jackson, MS 39207.
● Packet; newsletter of the Mississippi Library Commission. m.

**Mississippi Agricultural and Forestry Experiment Station**
Mississippi State, MS 39762.
● M A F E S Research Highlights. m. ISSN 0091-4460

**Mississippi Arts Commission**
● Arts in Mississippi. (pub. by University of Mississippi)

**Mississippi Association of Educators**
119 E. Pearl, Drawer 22529, Jackson, MS 39205.
● Mississippi Educator. 5 per yr.

**Mississippi Band of Choctaw Indians**
Route 7, Box 21, Philadelphia, MS 39350.
● Choctaw Community News. m.

**Mississippi Bankers Association**
Box 37, Jackson, MS 39205.
● Mississippi Banker. m. ISSN 0026-6159

**Mississippi Baptist Convention Board**
Box 530, Jackson, MS 39205.
● Baptist Record. w. ISSN 0005-5778

**Mississippi Board of Trustees of State Institutions of Higher Learning**
P.O. Box 2336, Jackson, MS 39205.
● Mississippi. Board of Trustees of State Institutions of Higher Learning. Annual Report. a.

**Mississippi Cattlemen's Association**
121 North Jefferson St., Jackson, MS 39202.
● Cattle Business. bi-m.

**Mississippi Congress of Parents and Teachers**
401 First Federal Bldg., P.O. Box 1946, Jackson, MS 39201.
● Mississippi Congress of Parents and Teachers. Proceedings. a. ISSN 0076-9460
● Mississippi Congress of Parents and Teachers. Yearbook. a. ISSN 0076-9479

**Mississippi Council for Geographic Education**
● Mississippi Geographer. (pub. by University of Southern Mississippi)

**Mississippi Dental Association**
Box 748, Tupelo, MS 38801.
● Mississippi Dental Association. Journal. 4 per yr. ISSN 0047-7532

**Mississippi Farm Bureau Federation**
Box 1570, 429 Mississippi St., Jackson, MS 39205.
● Mississippi Farm Bureau News. m. ISSN 0026-6205

**Mississippi Folklore Society**
c/o O. S. Vickers, East Central Jr. College, Decatur, MS 39327.
● Mississippi Folklore Register. q. ISSN 0026-6248

**Mississippi Hereford Association**
● Mississippi Valley Stockman-Farmer. (pub. by Mississippi Valley Publishing Co.)

**Mississippi Historical Society**
Box 571, Jackson, MS 39205.
● Journal of Mississippi History. q. ISSN 0022-2771 (Co-Sponsor: Mississippi Department of Archives and History)

**Mississippi Library Association**
Clinton, MS 39056.
● Mississippi Library News. q. ISSN 0026-6302 (Co-Sponsor: Mississippi Library Commission)

**Mississippi Marine Resources Council**
Box 497, Long Beach, MS 39560.
● Mississippi Marine Resources Council. Annual Report. a. ISSN 0095-6783

**Mississippi Modern Language Association**
Univ. of Mississippi, Modern Languages Dept., University, MS 38677.
● Mississippi Language Crusader. 3 per yr. ISSN 0026-6272

**Mississippi Mud**
3125 S.E. Van Water, Portland, OR 97202.
● Mississippi Mud. q.

**Mississippi Municipal Association**
230 Barefield Complex, Jackson, MS 39202.
● Mississippi Municipalities. m. ISSN 0026-6337

**Mississippi Music Educators Association**
Box 5284, Southern Station, Hattiesburg, MS 39401.
● Mississippi Music Educator. 4 per yr.

**Mississippi Nurses' Association**
135 Bounds St., Jackson, MS 39206.
● Mississippi R N. q. ISSN 0026-6388

**Mississippi Rag, Inc.**
P.O. Box 19068, Minneapolis, MN 55419.
● Mississippi Rag. m.

**Mississippi Research and Development Center**
3825 Ridgewood Rd., Drawer 2470, Jackson, MS 39205.
● Directory of Economic Research in Mississippi. a.
● Mississippi Manufacturing Atlas. irreg.
● Plastics Manufacturing Capabilities in Mississippi. biennial. ISSN 0099-0450
● R & D Economic Comment. q.
● R & D Report. 6 per yr.

**Mississippi Retail Grocers Association**
1631 Pinevale, Jackson, MS 39211.
● Mississippi Grocers' Guide. m. ISSN 0026-6264

**Mississippi State Medical Association**
735 Riverside Dr., Box 5229, Jackson, MS 39216.
● Mississippi State Medical Association. Journal. m. ISSN 0026-6396

**Mississippi State University. Christian Student Center**
Mississippi State, MS 39762.
● Mississippi State University. Christian Student Center. Annual Lectureship. a. ISSN 0076-9517

**Mississippi State University. College of Arts and Sciences**
Mississippi State, MS 39762
● Mississippi Quarterly; the journal of southern culture. q. ISSN 0026-637X (Subscr. to:, Box 23, Mississippi State, MS39762)
● Mississippii State University. College of Arts and Sciences. Department of Anthropology. Occasional Papers in Anthropology. irreg. (Subscr. to:, Department of Sociology and Anthropology)

**Mississippi State University. College of Business & Industry**
Mississippi State, MS 39762.
● Mississippi Business Review. m. ISSN 0026-6167 (prep. by its Division of Research)

**Mississippi State University. Forest Products Utilization Laboratory**
Mississippi State, MS 39762.
● Mississippi State University. Forest Products Utilization Laboratory. Information Series. irreg. ISSN 0076-9509
● Mississippi State University. Forest Products Utilization Laboratory. Research Report. irreg. ISSN 0026-640X

**Mississippi State University. Graduate School**
c/o Mitchell Memorial Library, P.O. Box 5408, State College, MS 39762.
● Mississippi State University Abstracts of Theses. biennial. ISSN 0540-3847

**Mississippi State University. Mitchell Memorial Library**
Mississippi State, MS 39762.
● Books and Library Notes. m. ISSN 0006-7466

**Mississippi State University. Water Resources Research Institute**
State College, MS 39762.
● Mississippi Water Resources Conference. Proceedings. a. ISSN 0076-9533

**Mississippi Valley Publishing Co.**
Drawer 89, Raymond, MS 38154.
● Mississippi Valley Stockman-Farmer. m. ISSN 0026-6434 (Mississippi Hereford Association) (Co-sponsor: Mississippi Polled Hereford Association)

**Missouri. Air Conservation Commission**
117 Commerce Dr., Box 1062, Jefferson City, MO 65101.
● Missouri. Air Conservation Commission. Annual Report. a. ISSN 0093-9102

**Missouri. Center for Health Statistics**
Broadway State Office Bldg., Jefferson City, MO 65101.
● Missouri Vital Statistics. irreg. ISSN 0098-1974

**Missouri. Department of Community Affairs**
505 Missouri Boulevard, Jefferson City, MO 65101.
● Directory of Missouri's Regional Planning System. ISSN 0090-7812

**Missouri. Department of Conservation**
Box 180, Jefferson City, MO 65101.
● Missouri. Department of Conservation. Annual Report. a. ISSN 0085-3496
● Missouri Conservationist. m. ISSN 0026-6515

**Missouri. Department of Elementary and Secondary Education**
Box 480, Jefferson Bldg., Jefferson City, MO 65101.
● Missouri Schools. m. (Sep-May)

**Missouri. Department of Higher Education**
600 Clark Ave., Jefferson City, MO 65101.
● Directory of Institutions of Higher Education in Missouri. a. ISSN 0070-5675
● Geographic Origin and Distribution of Students, Missouri Institutions of Higher Education. irreg. ISSN 0362-594X

**Missouri. Department of Mental Health. Division of Alcoholism and Drug Abuse**
2002 Missouri Blvd, Jefferson City, MO 65101.
● Drug Dependencies. bi-m.

**Missouri. Department of Natural Resources**
Box 176, 1014 Madison St., Jefferson City, MO 65101.
● Missouri's Environment. m.

**Missouri. Department of Natural Resources. Division of Geology and Land Survey**
Box 250, Rolla, MO 65401.
● Bibliography of the Geology of Missouri. a. ISSN 0067-7272
● Contribution to Precambrian Geology. irreg., no. 6, 1976.
● Missouri. Division of Geological Survey and Water Resources. Engineering Geology Series. irreg., 1973, no. 5. ISSN 0076-9606
● Missouri. Division of Geological Survey and Water Resources. Water Resources Report. irreg., no. 30, 1974. ISSN 0076-9614

**Missouri. Department of Public Health and Welfare. Division of Mental Health**
722 Jefferson, Jefferson City, MO 65101.
● Missouri. Division of Mental Health. Annual Report. a. ISSN 0091-231X

**Missouri. Department of Revenue**
Jefferson City, MO 65101.
● Missouri. Department of Revenue. Annual Combined Financial Report. a. (Co-Sponsor: Missouri State Treasurer)

**Missouri. Department of Social Services. Division of Health**
Box 570, Jefferson City, MO 65101.
● Missouri Monthly Vital Statistics. m. (prep. by its Center for Health Services)

**Missouri. Disaster Planning and Operations Office**
1717 Industrial Drive, Jefferson City, MO 65101.
● Missouri Disaster Planning and Operations Newsletter. bi-m. ISSN 0026-6531

**Missouri. Division of Commerce and Industrial Development**
P.O. Box 118, Jefferson City, MO 65101.
● Missouri's New and Expanding Industries. a. ISSN 0540-4193

**Missouri. Division of Fisheries**
Columbia, MO 65201.
● Missouri. Division of Fisheries. Abstracts of Fishery Research Reports. a. ISSN 0094-3630

**Missouri. Division of Highway Safety**
2634 Industrial Drive, Jefferson City, MO 65101.
● Missouri Annual Highway Safety Work Program. a. ISSN 0091-1097

**Missouri. Division of Insurance**
Jefferson Bldg., 11th Floor, Jefferson City, MO 65101.
● Missouri. Division of Insurance. Annual Report and Statistical Data. a.

**Missouri. Division of Youth Services**
402 Dix Rd., Box 447, Jefferson City, MO 65101.
● Missouri. State Division of Youth Services. Annual Report. a. ISSN 0098-0110

**Missouri. Public Service Commission**
Jefferson City, MO 65101.
● Missouri. Public Service Commission. Regulated Electric Study. a. ISSN 0093-0741

**Missouri. State Library**
308 E. High St., Jefferson City, MO 65101.
● Directory of Missouri Libraries; public, college & university libraries. a. ISSN 0092-4067
● Missouri State Government Publications. m. ISSN 0091-6633

● Show-Me Libraries. m. ISSN 0037-4326

**Missouri Academy of General Practice**
● Missouri Family Doctor. (pub. by Trail Press Inc.)

**Missouri Archaeological Society**
P.O. Box 958, Columbia, MO 65201.
● Missouri Archaeological Society. Memoir Series. irreg. ISSN 0076-9541
● Missouri Archaeological Society. Newsletter. m. except Jul.-Aug. ISSN 0076-955X
● Missouri Archaeological Society. Research Series. irreg. ISSN 0076-9568
● Missouri Archaeologist. a. ISSN 0076-9576

**Missouri Area Bluegrass Committee**
R.R. 1, Hamburg, IL 62045.
● M A B C Bluegrass Ramblin's. m.

**Missouri Association of Osteopathic Physicians and Surgeons**
● Cooperation. (pub. by State Osteopathic Journal Group)

**Missouri Association of Teachers of English**
English Department, Northwest Missouri, Kirksville, MO 63501
(Subscr. to: Peter Hasselriis, 216 Education Bldg., Univ. of Missouri, Columbia MO 65201)
● Missouri English Bulletin. 8 per yr.

**Missouri Association of Trial Attorneys**
823 Walnut St., Kansas City, MO 64106.
● M. A. T. A. Newsletter. irreg. ISSN 0094-2995

**Missouri Baptist Convention**
Missouri Baptist Building, Jefferson City, MO 65101.
● Word and Way. w. ISSN 0049-7959

**Missouri Bar**
326 Monroe St, Jefferson City, MO 65101.
● Missouri Bar. Journal. 8 per yr. ISSN 0026-6485

**Missouri Beef Cattleman, Inc.**
P.O. Box 16050, Kansas City, MO 64112.
● Missouri Beef Cattleman. m.

**Missouri Botanical Garden**
2315 Tower Grove Ave., St. Louis, MO 63110
● Missouri Botanical Garden. Annals. 3 per yr. ISSN 0026-6493 (Subscr. to: Allen Press, 1041 New Hampshire, Lawrence KS 66044)
● Missouri Botanical Garden Bulletin. m. ISSN 0026-6507

**Missouri Congress of Parents and Teachers Associations**
State Office, Box 962, 402 S. 5th, Columbia, MO 65201.
● Missouri Parent-Teacher. m. (Sep-May)

**Missouri Council of Architects, Inc.**
c/o Wendell Locke, 308 E. High St., Box 401, Jefferson City, MO 65101.
● Missouri Architect. q. ISSN 0026-6477

**Missouri Dental Association**
101 West McCarty St., Jefferson City, MO 65101.
● Missouri Dental Association. Journal. m. ISSN 0026-6523

**Missouri Farm Bureau Federation**
Box 658, Jefferson City, MO 65101.
● Missouri Farm Bureau News. m. ISSN 0026-6574

**Missouri Historical Society**
Jefferson Memorial Bldg., St. Louis, MO 63112.
● Missouri Historical Society. Bulletin. q. ISSN 0026-6590

**Missouri L P Gas Association**
705 Jefferson St, Jefferson City, MO 65101.
● Missouri LP-Gas Talks. m. ISSN 0026-6612

**Missouri Library Association**
403 S. Sixth St., Columbia, MO 65201.
● M L A Newsletter. 6 per yr. ISSN 0024-8223

**Missouri Life, Inc.**
1209 Elmerine Ave., Jefferson City, MO 65101.
● Missouri Life. bi-m. ISSN 0090-760X

**Missouri Municipal League**
1913 William St., Jefferson City, MO 65101.
● Missouri Municipal Review. m. ISSN 0026-6647

**Missouri Music Educators Association**
c/o Lewis B. Hilton, Ed., Dept. of Music, Washington Univ., St. Louis, MO 63130.
● Missouri Journal of Research in Music Education. a. ISSN 0085-350X
● Missouri School Music. (pub. by Northeast Missouri State University)

**Missouri Nurses Association**
206 E. Dunklin, Jefferson City, MO 65101.
● Missouri Nurse. bi-m. ISSN 0026-6655

**Missouri Oil Jobbers Association**
235 E. High St., Jefferson City, MO 65101.
● Missouri Oil Jobber. m.

**Missouri Pacific Railroad Co.**
210 N. 13th St., St. Louis, MO 63103.
● Mopac News. m. ISSN 0027-0989

**Missouri Pharmaceutical Association**
410 Madison St., Jefferson City, MO 65101.
● Missouri Pharmacist. m. ISSN 0026-6663

**Missouri Police Chiefs Association**
Central Missouri State Univ., Suite 400A, Humphrey's Bldg, Warrensburg, MO 64093.
● Missouri Police Chiefs Journal. m.

**Missouri Political Science Association**
University of Missouri, 118 Middlebush Hall, Columbia, MO 65201.
● M P S A Newsletter. s-a. ISSN 0464-1973
● Missouri Political Science Association. Proceedings of the Annual Meeting. a.

**Missouri Power & Light Co.**
101 Madison St., Jefferson City, MO 65101.
● MoPoLiCo News. m.

**Missouri Press Association**
Eighth and Locust, Columbia, MO 65201.
● Missouri Press News. m. ISSN 0026-6671

**Missouri Province Educational Institute**
4511 W. Pine Blvd., St. Louis, MO 63108.
● Jesuit Bulletin. q.

**Missouri Regional Medical Program**
Lewis Hall, 406 Turner, Columbia, MO 65201.
● Liaison. bi-m. ISSN 0024-1695

**Missouri River Basin Commission**
Suite 403, 10050 Regency Circle, Omaha, MO 68114.
● Coordination Directory of State and Federal Agency Water and Land Resources Officials. irreg. ISSN 0363-8170
● Missouri River Basin Commission. Annual Report. a. ISSN 0092-7945

**Missouri School Boards Association**
206 Hill Hall, Univ. of Missouri, Columbia, MO 65201.
● Missouri School Board. m.(except July & Aug.) ISSN 0026-6698
● Missouri School Boards Association. School Law Letter. q.

**Missouri Society of Professional Engineers**
Box 365, Jefferson City, MO 65101.
● Missouri Engineer. m. ISSN 0026-6558

**Missouri Speleological Society**
c/o Kenneth C. Thompson, Ed., Southwest Missouri State University, Dept. of Geography and Geology, Springfield, MO 65802.
● M.S.S. Liaison. m.

**Missouri Speleological Survey, Inc.**
c/o Ed. Kenneth J. Thomson, Dept. of Geography & Geology, Southwest Missouri State Univ., Springfield, MO 65802.
● Missouri Speleology. q. ISSN 0026-671X

**Missouri State Medical Association**
113 Madison St., Jefferson City, MO 65101.
● Missouri Medicine. m. ISSN 0026-6620

**Missouri State Teachers Association**
P. O. Box 458, Columbia, MO 65201.
● School and Community. m.(Sept-May) ISSN 0036-6447

**Missouri Training Center for Men**
Box 7, Moberly, MO 65270.
● Inmate Free Press. m.

**Missouri Valley Adult Education Association**
1411 66th St., Des Moines, IA 50311.
- Missouri Valley Adult Education Association. Journal. s-a. ISSN 0026-6736
- Missouri Valley Adult Education Association. Newsletter. ISSN 0026-6744

**Missouri Valley Economic Association**
Edwardsville, IL 62025.
- Journal of Economics. a. ISSN 0361-6576

**Missouri Veterinary Medical Association**
c/o C. M. Kroeck, Ed., 113-B W. High, Suite 3, Jefferson City, MO 65101.
- Show Me Veterinarian. a. ISSN 0080-942X

**Dwight Emerson Mitchell, Ed. & Pub.**
520 Lowell Ave., Palo Alto, CA 94301.
- D E Mly. s-m. ISSN 0011-8184

**Gary D. Mitchell, Ed. & Pub.**
Box 735, Huntsville, AL 35801.
- Chasm. irreg.

**Mitchell Manuals, Inc.**
Box 80427, San Diego, CA 92138.
- National Service Data; Domestic. irreg.

**Seymour Mittlemark Organization Inc.**
Lincoln Bldg., Suite 631, 60 E. 42nd St., New York, NY 10017.
- Bagvertising Weekly. w. ISSN 0005-3937
- Coatvertising Weekly. w.
- Dressvertising Weekly. w. ISSN 0012-6128
- Footwear Fashions. w. ISSN 0015-6817
- Foundation Fashions in Review. w.
- Hatvertising Weekly. w. ISSN 0017-8381
- Knitwear Fashions. w.
- Lingerie Ad Clip Review. w.
- Men's & Boy's Wear Scene. w.
- Sportswear on Parade. w. ISSN 0038-8297
- Tot 'n Teen Fashions. w. ISSN 0040-9677

**Mizrachi Women's Organization of America**
817 Broadway, New York, NY 10003.
- Mizrachi Woman. 8 per yr. ISSN 0026-7007

**Mo-Kan Bi-State Planning Commission**
St. Joseph, MO 64501.
- Mo-Kan Bi-State Planning Commission. Annual Report. a. ISSN 0092-2412

**Mobay Chemical Corporation. Chemagro Agricultural Division**
P.O. Box 4913, Hawthorn Rd., Kansas City, MO 64120
(Main Office: Bayer Pflanzenschutz, Leverkusen, W. Germany (B.R.D.))
- Chemagro Courier. irreg., latest issue, 1975.

**Mobile Area Chamber of Commerce**
Box 2187, Mobile, AL 36601.
- Who's Who in the Mobile Area. a.

**Mobile Genealogical Society**
Box 6224, Mobile, AL 36606.
- Deep South Genealogical Quarterly. q.

**Mobile Post Office Society**
163 Old Farm Road, Pleasantville, NY 10570.
- Transit Postmark Collector. 3 per yr. ISSN 0041-1175

**Mockingbird Press**
Box 7, Alpine, TX 79830.
- Creative Guitar International. 3 per yr. ISSN 0092-8887

**Model T Ford Club of America**
Box 711, Oceanside, CA 92054.
- Vintage Ford. bi-m. ISSN 0042-6350

**Modern Brewery Age Publishing Co.**
80 Lincoln Ave., Stamford, CT 06904.
- Modern Brewery Age. w. ISSN 0026-7538
- Modern Brewery Age Blue Book. a. ISSN 0076-9932

**Modern Cycle Publishing Co. Inc.**
7950 Deering Ave., Canoga Park, CA 91304.
- Treasure. m. ISSN 0049-4593

**Modern Data Services, Inc.**
c/o S. Henry Sacks, 5 Kane Industrial Dr., MA 01749.
- Minimicro News. m.

**Modern Day Periodicals, Inc.**
257 Park Ave. S., New York, NY 10010.
- Hairdo Originals. q.
- Hall of Fame Series. q.

**Modern Greek Society: a Newsletter.**
Box 102, New Hampton, NY 10958.
- Modern Greek Society: a Newsletter. s-a.

**Modern Greek Studies Association**
Box 337, Harvard Sq. Branch, Cambridge, MA 02138.
- Modern Greek Studies Association Bulletin. s-a. ISSN 0047-7702

**Modern Handcraft, Inc.**
4251 Pennsylvania Ave., Kansas City, MO 64111.
- Workbasket. m. ISSN 0043-8049
- Workbench. bi-m. ISSN 0043-8057

**Modern Housing Inc.**
4043 Irving Place, Culver City, CA 90230.
- Western Mobile News. w. ISSN 0043-3942

**Modern Keyboard Review**
c/o William Irwin, 436 via Media, Palos Verdes Estates, CA 90274.
- Modern Keyboard Review; the magazine for modern, contemporary, popular organists and pianists. bi-m. ISSN 0023-0960

**Modern Language Association. English X Group**
- Victorian Newsletter. (pub. by New York University)

**Modern Language Association of America**
62 Fifth Ave., New York, NY 10011.
- M L A Abstracts of Articles in Scholarly Journals. 3 vols per yr.
- M L A International Bibliography of Books and Articles on the Modern Languages and Literatures. 3 vols. per yr. ISSN 0024-8215
- M L A Newsletter. 4 per yr.
- P M L A. 6 per yr. ISSN 0030-8129

**Modern Language Association of America. Center for Editions of American Authors**
Univ. of South Carolina, Dept. of English, Columbia, SC 29208.
- C E A A Newsletter. irreg., 1973, no. 6.

**Modern Language Association of America. Comparative Romance Linguistics Section**
c/o Margaret W. Epro, Ed., University of Pennsylvania, Dept. of Romance Languages, Philadelphia, PA 19174.
- Comparative Romance Linguistics Newsletter. 1-2 per yr. ISSN 0010-4167

**Modern Language Association of America Conference**
c/o Ed W. R. Elton, City University of New York, 33 W. 42nd St., New York, NY 10036.
- Shakespeare Research and Opportunities; Report of the Modern Language Association of America Conference. a. ISSN 0080-9144

**Modern Language Association of America. Conference on Research Opportunities in Renaissance Drama**
c/o David M. Bergeron, Ed., Department of English, University of New Orleans, New Orleans, LA 70122.
- Research Opportunities in Renaissance Drama. a. ISSN 0098-647X

**Modern Language Association of America. Early American Literature Group**
University of Massachusetts, Bartlett Hall, Amherst, MA 01002.
- Early American Literature. 3 per yr. ISSN 0012-8163

**Modern Language Association of America, Old English Group**
Ohio State Univ., 320 Main Library, 1858 Neil Ave., Columbus, OH 43210.
- Old English Newsletter. s-a. ISSN 0030-1973

**Modern Language Association of America. Oriental-Western Literary Relations Group**
Roy E. Teele, Box 8107, University Station, Austin, TX 78712.
- Literature East & West. q. ISSN 0024-4767

**Modern Language Association of America, Popular Literature Section**
- Journal of Popular Culture. (pub. by Bobbs-Merrill Co., Inc.)

**Modern Language Association of America. Southern Conference on Language Teaching**
62 Fifth Ave., New York, NY 10011.
- Dimension: Languages; proceedings of the Southern Conference on Language Teaching. a. ISSN 0070-4881

**Modern Language Association of America. Spanish I Section**
c/o S. D. Kirby, Dept. of Foreign Languages & Literatures, Purdue University, West Lafayette, IN 47907.
- Coronica. s-a.

**Modern Language Association. Seminar on Science-Fiction**
c/o Thomas D. Clareson, Ed., College of Wooster, Box 3186, Wooster, OH 44691.
- EXtrapolation; journal of science fiction and fantasy. s-a. ISSN 0014-5483

**Modern Microfilm Co.**
1350 South West Temple St., Salt Lake, UT 84115
(Subscr. to: P.O. Box 1884, Salt Lake City, UT 84110)
- Salt Lake City Messenger. irreg. (approx. 2-4 per yr.) ISSN 0586-7282

**Modern People Productions**
11058 Addison St., Franklin Park, IL 60131.
- Modern People; America's fastest growing family newspaper. w.

**Modern Photography**
One Astor Plaza, New York, NY 10036.
- Modern Photography Annual. a. ISSN 0580-8162

**Modern Poetry Association**
1228 N. Dearborn Pkwy., Chicago, IL 60610.
- Poetry. m. ISSN 0032-2032

**Modern Poetry Studies**
147 Capen Blvd., Buffalo, NY 14226.
- Modern Poetry Studies. 2-3 per yr. ISSN 0026-8305

**Modern Psychoanalytic Publications**
16 West 10th St., New York, NY 10011.
- Modern Psychoanalysis. s-a. ISSN 0361-5227 (Manhattan Center for Advanced Psychoanalytic Studies, Inc.)

**Modernage**
319 E. 44th St., New York, NY 10017.
- Photo Reporter. m. ISSN 0048-3982

**Modine Gunch Press**
507 Wisconsin Union, Madison, WI 52706.
- Modine Gunch. 3 per yr. ISSN 0026-8763 (University of Wisconsin. Department of English) (Co-Sponsor: Wisconsin Union)

**Mohawk Nation. Program in American Studies**
Rooseveltown, NY 13683.
- Akwesasne Notes. 5 per yr. ISSN 0002-3949

**Mohegan Fine Arts Committee**
c/o James Coleman, Ed., Mohegan Community College, Norwich, CT 06360.
- Red Fox Review. s-a.

**Mojo Navigator(e)**
c/o John Jacob, 102 S. Austin, Oak Park, IL 60304.
- Mojo Navigator(e) irreg. ISSN 0026-8909

**H. N. & A. L. Moldenke, Eds. & Pubs.**
303 Parkside Rd., Plainfield, NJ 07060.
- Phytologia; designed to expedite botanical publication. irreg. ISSN 0031-9430

**Moment Magazine Associates**
150 Fifth Ave., New York, NY 10011.
- Moment; new magazine for America's Jews. 10 per yr. ISSN 0099-0280

**Momentum Press**
c/o Century City Educational Arts Project, 10508 W. Pico Blvd., Los Angeles, CA 90064.
- Momentum. 3 per yr.

**Momo's Press**
Box 14061, San Francisco, CA 94114.
- Shocks. 3 per yr. ISSN 0360-912X

**Monday Morning Press**
2912 N. Hackett, Milwaukee, WI 53211.
- Wisconsin Poets' Series. irreg.

**Monex International Ltd.**
4910 Birch, Newport Beach, CA 90807.
● Gold and Silver Newsletter. m.

**Money Digest Press, Inc.**
175 Fifth Ave., New York, NY 10010.
● Money Digest. m. ISSN 0364-2429

**Money Making Reporter**
Box 3573, Modesto, CA 95352.
● Money Making Reporter. m.

**Money Market Directories, Inc.**
370 Lexington Ave., New York, NY 10016.
● Money Market Directory. a. ISSN 0077-0388

**Money Market Investor, Inc.**
Box 67433, Los Angeles, CA 90067.
● Money Market Investor. m.

**Mongolia Society**
Box 606, Bloomington, IN 47401.
● Mongolia Society. Occasional Papers. irreg. ISSN 0077-0396
● Mongolian Studies. s-a.

**Monitor Book Co. Inc.**
195 So. Beverly Dr., Beverly Hills, CA 90212.
● What They Said. a. ISSN 0512-5804

**Monitor Publications (Miami)**
P.O. Box 1055, Miami, FL 33133.
● Florida Bank Monitor; selected financial data for Florida banks. a.

**Monitor Publishing (Washington)**
1120 19th St. N.W., Washington, DC 20036.
● International Drug Regulatory Monitor. m.

**Monitor Trade Publications Inc.**
150 W. 28th St., New York, NY 10001.
● International Insurance Monitor. m. ISSN 0020-6997

**Monks of St. John's Abbey**
Collegeville, MN 56321.
● Worship; concerned with the problems of liturgical renewal. 6 per yr. ISSN 0043-941X

**Monmouth College**
Editorial Office, Cedar Ave., West Long Branch, NJ 07664.
● Monmouth Reviews; Journal of the Literary Arts. a. ISSN 0085-3534

**Monmouth County Education Association**
268 Norwood Ave., West Long Branch, NJ 07764 (Subscr. to: Box 56, Long Branch NJ 07740)
● Monmouth Educator; M C E A monitor. 10 per yr. ISSN 0026-9808

**Monmouth-Ocean Development Council**
622 Mattison Ave, Asbury Park, NJ 07712.
● Compass (Asbury Park) q. ISSN 0010-4191

**Monster Times Publishing Co., Inc.**
11 W. 17th St., New York, NY 10011.
● Inside Comics. q.
● Monster Times. m. ISSN 0047-7915

**Montag Publications**
1120 Connecticut Avenue, N. W., Washington, DC 20036.
● Woman's Guide to Washington, D. C. a. ISSN 0090-080X

**Montana. Advisory Council for Vocational Education**
Helena, MT 59601.
● Montana Advisory Council for Vocational Education. Annual Report. a. ISSN 0093-6472

**Montana. Bureau of Mines and Geology**
Montana College of Mineral Science and Technology, Room 203-B, Main Hall, Butte, MT 59701.
● Current Geological and Geophysical Studies in Montana. a. ISSN 0092-9565
● Montana. Bureau of Mines and Geology. Bulletin. irreg; B101, 1977. ISSN 0077-1090
● Montana. Bureau of Mines and Geology. Directory of Mining Enterprises. a. ISSN 0077-1104
● Montana. Bureau of Mines and Geology. Ground Water Reports. irreg. ISSN 0077-1112
● Montana. Bureau of Mines and Geology. Memoir. irreg., M43, 1973. ISSN 0077-1120
● Montana. Bureau of Mines and Geology. Special Publications. irreg; SP 74, 1976. ISSN 0077-1139

● Progress Report on Clays and Shales of Montana. irreg. (approx. biennial) ISSN 0079-6913

**Montana. Criminal Justice Data Center**
Helena, MT 59601.
● Montana Arrests, Offenses. a. ISSN 0361-414X

**Montana. Department of Business Regulation**
805 N. Main, Helena, MT 59601.
● Montana. Department of Business Regulation. Annual Report. a. ISSN 0093-8246
● Report of Milk Utilization in Montana. ISSN 0080-1267 (prep. by its Milk Control Division)

**Montana. Department of Health and Environmental Services**
Cogswell Building, Helena, MT 59601.
● Montana State Plan for Alcohol Abuse and Alcoholism Prevention, Treatment and Rehabilitation. a. ISSN 0090-3809
● Montana Vital Statistics. a. ISSN 0077-1198

**Montana. Department of Livestock. Animal Health Division**
Helena, MT 59601.
● Montana. Animal Health Division. Statistical Summary. a.

**Montana. Department of Military Affairs**
State Armory Building, 1100 North Main St., Helena, MT 59601.
● Montana. Department of Military Affairs. Annual Report. a. ISSN 0091-0368

**Montana. Department of Natural Resources and Conservation**
32 S. Ewing St., Helena, MT 59601.
● Montana. Water Resources Board. Inventory Series. irreg. ISSN 0077-1201

**Montana. Department of Public Instruction**
Helena, MO 59601.
● Montana. Department of Public Instruction. Descriptive Report of Program Activities for Vocational Education. a. ISSN 0090-6743

**Montana. Department of Social and Rehabilitation Services**
P.O. Box 1723, Helena, MT 59601.
● Montana. Department of Social and Rehabilitation Services. Annual Report. a. ISSN 0091-0996
● Montana. Department of Social and Rehabilitation Services. Statistical Report. m.
● S R S News; let older Americans be of service. m.

**Montana. Division of Planning and Economic Development**
Helena, MT 59601.
● Montana Federal Grants-in-Aid Report. a. ISSN 0095-585X (prep. by its Information Systems Bureau)
● Montana Manual of State and Local Government. irreg. ISSN 0093-7142 (Co-Sponsor; Montana Governor's State-Local Coordinator's Office)

**Montana. Environmental Quality Council**
Helena, MT 59601.
● Montana. Environmental Quality Council. Annual Report. a.

**Montana. Office of Budget & Program Planning**
Capitol Building, Helena, MT 59601.
● Montana. Governor's Annual Report. a. ISSN 0085-3550

**Montana. Office of Public Instruction**
State Capitol, Helena, MT 59601.
● Montana Schools. 8 per yr.

**Montana. Office of the Legislative Auditor**
Department of Institutions Reimbursements Program, State Capitol, Helena, MT 59601.
● Montana. Office of the Legislative Auditor. Department of Institutions Reimbursements Program; Report on Audit. a. ISSN 0090-4325
● Montana. Office of the Legislative Auditor. State of Montana Board of Investments. Report on Examination of Financial Statements. a. ISSN 0090-9912

**Montana. State Library**
930 East Lyndale Avenue, Helena, MT 59601.
● Montana. State Library, Helena. State Documents in the Montana State Library. a. ISSN 0091-2735
● Montana Library Directory, with Statistics of Montana Public Libraries. irreg. ISSN 0094-873X
● Montana Newsletter. irreg.

**Montana. Water Resources Division**
Sam W. Mitchell Bldg., Helena, MT 59601.
● Montana. Water Resources Division Progress Report of the Montana State Water Plan. biennial.

**Montana Archaeological Society**
Dept. of Sociology, Montana State Univ., Bozeman, MT 59715.
● Archaeology in Montana. 3 per yr. ISSN 0044-8591

**Montana Associated Utilities**
Box 1641, Great Falls, MT 59401.
● Montana Rural Electric News. m. ISSN 0047-7974

**Montana Education Association**
1232 E. Sixth Ave., Helena, MT 59601.
● M.E.A. Today. m.

**Montana Farm Bureau Federation**
Box 1207, Bozeman, MT 59715.
● Montana Agriculture. m. ISSN 0026-9905

**Montana Food Distributors Association**
Box 7038, Missoula, MT 59807.
● Montana Food Distributor. m. ISSN 0047-7931

**Montana Forest and Conservation Experiment Station**
University of Montana, Missoula, MT 59801.
● Western Wildlands; natural resources journal. q.

**Montana Grain Growers Association**
Box 6699, Great Falls, MT 59406.
● Wheat Scoop. 8 per yr. ISSN 0043-4728

**Montana Historical Society**
225 No. Roberts St., Helena, MT 59601.
● Montana; the magazine of western history. q. ISSN 0026-9891
● Montana Post. q. ISSN 0047-7958

**Montana Law Enforcement Academy**
● Montana Law Enforcement Academy. Annual Report to the Governor of Montana. (pub. by Montana State University)

**Montana League of Cities & Towns**
Box 1704, Helena, MT 59602.
● Montana League of Cities & Towns. Newsletter. ISSN 0026-9980

**Montana Motor Transport Association, Inc.**
● Roadwise. (pub. by Motor Carrier Service Inc.)

**Montana Music Educators Association**
Montana State University Music Dept, Bozeman, MT 59715.
● Cadenza. 4 per yr. ISSN 0007-9405

**Montana Oil Journal, Inc.**
Box 20255, Billings, MT 59104.
● Montana Oil Journal. w. ISSN 0047-794X

**Montana Press Association**
P.O. Box 1186, Helena, MT 59601.
● Montana Fourth Estate. m.

**Montana Reconnaissance Project**
224 N. Higgins, Missoula, MT 59801.
● Borrowed Times; alternative news for Montanans. 20 per yr.

**Montana State University**
Bozeman, MT 59715
● Montana Law Enforcement Academy. Annual Report to the Governor of Montana. a. ISSN 0093-9048 (Subscr. to:, Room 400, Colter Hall)

**Montana State University. Associated Students**
Bozeman, MT 59715.
● Exponent. s-w. ISSN 0014-5076

**Montana State University. Cooperative Extension Service**
Bozeman, MT 59715.
● Now. q. ISSN 0029-5353 (Co-publisher: Agricultural Experiment Station)

**Montana State University. Mathematics Department**
Bozeman, MT 59715.
● M S U Mathematics Letter. s-a. ISSN 0024-8479

**Montana Stockgrowers Association**
Box 1679, Helena, MI 59601.
● Montana Stockgrower. m. ISSN 0047-7990

**Montana University Joint Water Resources Research Center**
Montana State University, Bozeman, MT 59715.
- Montana University Joint Water Resources Research Center. Annual Report. a.
- Montana University Joint Water Resources Research Center. Technical Reports. 10 per yr.

**Montana Wool Growers Association**
Box 1693, Helena, MT 59601.
- Montana Wool Grower. bi-m. ISSN 0027-0024

**Montcalm Publishing Corp.**
99 Park Ave., New York, NY 10016.
- Gallery. m.

**Montclair Art Museum**
South Mountain and Bloomfield Aves., Montclair, NJ 07042.
- Montclair, N.J. Art Museum. Bulletin. bi-m. ISSN 0027-0059

**Montclair Board of Education**
22 Valley Road, Montclair, NJ 07042.
- Montclair Schools. q. ISSN 0027-0075

**Montclair State College. Center for Economic Education**
Upper Montclair, NJ 07043.
- Economic Education Bulletin. q. ISSN 0013-0087

**Montclair State College. Department of Adult Continuing Education**
Upper Montclair, NJ 07043.
- A E C Newsletter. (Adult Education Clearing House) m.

**Montebello Teachers Association**
901 W. Whittier Blvd., Montebello, CA 90640.
- M T A News. m.(Sept.-June) ISSN 0024-8487

**Montemora Foundation Inc.**
Box 336, Cooper Station, New York, NY 10003.
- Montemora. s-a.

**Monterey Savings and Loan Association**
- Monterey Bay Area Locale. (pub. by Locale Publishing Co.)

**Montfort Missionaries**
- Queen. (pub. by Queen of All Hearts)

**Montgomery-Bucks County Dental Society**
368 High St., Pottstown, PA 19464.
- Montgomery-Bucks Dental Society. Bulletin. 7 per yr. ISSN 0027-0156

**Monthly Review, Inc.**
62 W. 14th St., New York, NY 10011.
- Monthly Review; an independent socialist magazine. m.(bi-m.July-Aug) ISSN 0027-0520

**Monthly Review of Management Research**
Box 4, Dolton, IL 60419.
- Monthly Review of Management Research. m. ISSN 0025-1887

**Monument Builders of North America**
1612 Central St., Evanston, IL 60201.
- M. B. News. m.

**Monument Press**
4508 Mexico Gravel Rd., Columbia, MO 65201.
- Monument in Cantos and Essays. a. ISSN 0027-0733

**Moody Bible Institute of Chicago**
820 N. la Salle St., Chicago, IL 60610.
- Moody Monthly; the Christian magazine for all the family. m. ISSN 0027-0806

**Moody's Investors Service, Inc.**
99 Church St., NewYork, NY 10007.
- Moody's Banks and Finance. s-w. ISSN 0027-0814
- Moody's Handbook of Common Stocks. 4 per yr. ISSN 0027-0830
- Moody's Industrial Manual. a. ISSN 0545-0217
- Moody's Industrials. s-w. ISSN 0027-0849
- Moody's Municipal & Government Manual. a. ISSN 0545-0233
- Moody's Municipals and Governments. s-w. ISSN 0027-0857
- Moody's O T C Industrials. w. ISSN 0027-0865
- Moody's Public Utilities. s-w. ISSN 0027-0873
- Moody's Stock Survey. w. ISSN 0027-0881

- Moody's Transportation; railroads, airlines, shipping, traction, bus and truck lines. s-w. ISSN 0027-089X

**Moonbeam Publications**
1321 Swallow Lane, Memphis, TN 38116.
- Moondance. s-a.

**K. E. Moore, Ed. & Pub.**
Box 386, Brownwood, TX 76801.
- Pigeon News. m.(except combined July-Aug. issue) ISSN 0031-9783

**Moorhead State College**
Box 267, Moorhead, MN 56560.
- Aegis. s-a.

**Moorpack College**
7075 Campus Road, Moorpack, CA 93021.
- Pacific Journal of the Arts in Two-Year Colleges. s-a.

**Moral Education Forum**
Hunter College, 695 Park Ave., New York, NY 10021
- Moral Education Forum. 5 per yr.

**Morality in Media, Inc.**
487 Park Ave., New York, NY 10028.
- Morality in Media Newsletter. m. ISSN 0027-1004

**Donald Norman Moran, Ed. & Pub.**
7741 Fair Ave. C552sun Valley, Bixby Station, CA 91352.
- Searcher. q. ISSN 0037-0401 (Southern California Genealogical Society Inc.)

**Moravian Church in America-North and South**
Publications Commission, 5 W. Market St., Bethlehem, PA 18018.
- North American Moravian. m (except Jul.-Aug. combined) ISSN 0027-1012

**Moravian Music Foundation**
Salem Sta., Winston-Salem, NC 27108.
- Moravian Music Foundation Bulletin. s-a. ISSN 0027-1020

**Charles C. Morchand Co., Inc.**
421 Hudson St., New York, NY 10016.
- American Analgesia Society. Journal. s-a. ISSN 0002-7243 (American Analgesia Society)

**Morehead State University**
Box 681, Morehead, KY 40351.
- Bulletin of Applied Linguistics. w.(36 per yr.) ISSN 0007-4756

**Morehouse-Barlow Co.**
14 E. 41st St., New York, NY 10017.
- Episcopal Church Annual. a. ISSN 0071-1012

**Morehouse College**
223 Chestnut St. S.W., Atlanta, GA 30314.
- Maroon Tiger. m.

**Morehouse College. Public Relations and Alumni Affairs Office**
Atlanta, GA 30314.
- Morehouse College Bulletin; the alumnus. q. ISSN 0027-1047

**Moreland School District**
4710, Campbell Ave., San Jose, CA 95130.
- Moreland News and Views. bi-w. ISSN 0027-1055

**Robert Morey Associates**
Box 98, Dana Point, CA 92629.
- Advanced Battery Technology. m. ISSN 0001-8627
- Energy Info; a monthly executive summary of events occurring in the fields of power generation and research. m. ISSN 0013-7510

**Morgan & Morgan, Inc.**
145 Palisade St., Dobbs Ferry, NY 10522.
- Leica Manual. irreg. ISSN 0093-9374
- Photo-Lab Index; cumulative formulary of standard recommended photographic procedures. a (q.updates)

**G. Russell Morgan, Ed. & Pub.**
Route 2, Box 1580, Camas, WA 98607.
- Goodly Co. 3 per yr.

**Morgan- Grampian, Inc.**
205 E. 42 St., New York, NY 10017.
- Factory. m.
- Industrial Bulletin. m. ISSN 0019-8021
- Industrial Distribution; for industrial distributors and their sales personnel. m. ISSN 0019-8153
- Mart; magazine of appliance and TV retailing. s-w. ISSN 0025-4061 (Subscr. to:, Berkshire Common, Pittsfield MA 01201)
- Modern Packaging. m. ISSN 0026-8224
- Modern Packaging Encyclopedia. a. ISSN 0077-0035 (Orders to: G. Barney, 60 Harding Ave., Dover NJ 07801)
- Product Engineering. m. ISSN 0032-9754

**Morgan Guaranty Trust Co. of New York**
23 Wall St., New York, NY 10015.
- Morgan Guaranty Survey. m. ISSN 0027-108X

**Morgan Guaranty Trust Co. of New York. Trust and Investment Division**
9 W. 57th St., New York, NY 10019.
- Morgan Guaranty Trust Company of New York. Trust and Investment Division. Report. a.

**Morgan Press**
1819 N. Oakland Ave., Milwaukee, WI 53202.
- Hey Lady. 10 per yr. ISSN 0018-1188

**Kay Titus Mormino, Ed. & Pub.**
260 Vista Marina, San Clemente, CA 92672.
- Modern Haiku. 4 per yr. ISSN 0026-7821

**Mormon History Association**
1302 Edvalson St., Ogden, UT 84403.
- Journal of Mormon History. a. ISSN 0094-7342

**Morning Star Press**
West Whately, Via RFD Haydenville, MA 01039.
- Phoenix; a radical humanitarian literary magazine. q. ISSN 0031-8310

**Sydney Morrell & Co. Inc.**
152 East 78th St., New York, NY 10021.
- Australia Newsletter. m. ISSN 0004-8615 (Victoria Promotion Committee, Melbourne AT)

**Morris Arboretum**
Univ. of Pennsylvania, 9414 Meadowbrook Ave., Philadelphia, PA 19118.
- Morris Arboretum Bulletin. a. ISSN 0027-1187

**Robert Morris Associates**
1432 Philadelphia National Bank Bldg., Philadelphia, PA 19107.
- Domestic and International Commercial Loan Charge-Offs. a.
- Journal of Commercial Bank Lending. m. ISSN 0021-986X
- Robert Morris Associates. Annual Statement Studies. a. ISSN 0080-3340

**Morris Harvey College Publications**
Charleston, WV 25304.
- Stories from the Hills. a. ISSN 0081-5861
- Yearbook of Works re Appalachia. a.

**A. B. Morse Co.**
200 James St., Barrington, IL 60010.
- Water Supply Management. m. ISSN 0012-6233

**Mortgage Bankers Association of America**
1125 15th St. N.W., Washington, DC 20005.
- Mortgage Banker. m. ISSN 0027-1241
- Mortgage Banking: Financial Statements and Operating Ratios. a. ISSN 0077-1546 (prep. by its Economics and Research Department)
- Mortgage Banking: Loans Closed and Servicing Volume. a. (prep. by its Economics and Research Department)
- Mortgage Banking: Survey of Single-Family Loan Operations (Cost Study) irreg.

**Morton Arboretum**
Lisle, IL 60532.
- Morton Arboretum Quarterly. q. ISSN 0027-125X

**C. V. Mosby Co.**
11830 Westline Industrial Dr., St. Louis, MO 63141.
- American Academy of Ophthalmology and Otolaryngology. Selected Proceedings. a.
- American Academy of Orthopaedic Surgeons. Committee on Instructional Courses. Instructional Course Lectures. a. ISSN 0065-6895 (American Academy of Orthopaedic Surgeons)

- American Association of Obstetricians and Gynecologists. Transactions. a. ISSN 0065-728X (American Association of Obstetricians and Gynecologists)
- American Heart Journal; an international publication for the study of the circulation. m. ISSN 0002-8703
- American Journal of Obstetrics and Gynecology. s-m. ISSN 0002-9378 (American Gynecological Society)
- American Journal of Orthodontics. m. (American Association of Orthodontists)
- American Society of Plastic and Reconstructive Surgeons. Proceedings. irreg., vol. 7, 1973.
- Atlas of External Diseases of the Eye. biennial; vol. 4, 1973. ISSN 0067-0308
- Clinical Pharmacology and Therapeutics. m. ISSN 0009-9236 (American Society for Pharmacology and Experimental Therapeutics) (Co-Sponsor: American Society for Clinical Pharmacology and Therapeutics)
- Current Concepts in Clinical Nursing. biennial. ISSN 0070-1890
- Current Concepts in Ophthalmology. irreg. ISSN 0097-8353
- Current Concepts in Radiology. irreg.
- Current Practice in Orthopaedic Surgery. irreg., vol. 6, 1975. ISSN 0070-203X
- Current Therapy in Dentistry. biennial. ISSN 0070-2110
- Drugs of Choice. biennial. ISSN 0070-7406
- Handbook of Ocular Therapeutics and Pharmacology. irreg.; 4th edt., 1973. ISSN 0072-985X
- Heart and Lung; journal of critical care. bi-m. (American Association of Critical-Care Nurses)
- Hip; proceedings of the Open Scientific Meeting of the Hip Society. a. ISSN 0095-7216 (Hip Society)
- Investigative Ophthalmology and Visual Science. m. (Association for Research in Vision and Ophthalmology)
- Journal of Allergy and Clinical Immunology. m. ISSN 0091-6749 (American Academy of Allergy)
- Journal of Laboratory and Clinical Medicine. m. ISSN 0022-2143 (Central Society for Clinical Research)
- Journal of Pediatrics; devoted to the problems and diseases of infancy and childhood. m. ISSN 0022-3476
- Journal of Prosthetic Dentistry. m. ISSN 0022-3913
- Journal of Thoracic and Cardiovascular Surgery. m. ISSN 0022-5223 (American Association for Thoracic Surgery)
- Neuro-Ophthalmology. irreg., vol. 8, 1975. ISSN 0077-7803
- New Orleans Academy of Ophthamology. Transactions. a. ISSN 0077-8605
- Oral Surgery, Oral Medicine and Oral Pathology. m. ISSN 0030-4220 (American Academy of Oral Pathology)
- Pacific Coast Obstetrical and Gynecological Society. Transactions. a. ISSN 0078-7442 (Pacific Coast Obstetrical and Gynecological Society)
- Surgery; devoted to the art and science of surgery. m. ISSN 0039-6060
- Surgical Pathology. irreg., 1968, 4th ed. ISSN 0081-9646
- William Mackenzie Memorial Symposium. Proceedings. triennial.

**Mother Cabrini League**
Missionary Sisters of the Sacred Heart of Jesus, 2520 Lakeview Ave., Chicago, IL 60614.
- Mother Cabrini Messenger. bi-m. ISSN 0027-1527

**Mother Earth News, Inc.**
Box 70, Hendersonville, NC 28739.
- Mother Earth News; it tells you how. bi-m. ISSN 0027-1535

**Mothers' Manual Inc.**
420 Lexington Ave., New York, NY 10017 (Ed. Offices: 176 Cleveland Dr., Croton-on-Hudson NY 10520)
- Mothers' Manual. bi-m. ISSN 0027-1551

**Motion Picture Editor's Federal Credit Union**
1600 Broadway, Room 313, New York, NY 10019.
- Sync Points Newsletter. m.

**Motor Cargo, Inc.**
Box 4169, 1509 Madison Ave., Memphis, TN 38104.
- Southern Motor Cargo. m. ISSN 0038-4372

**Motor Carrier Service Inc.**
1727 11th Ave., Helena, MT 59601.
- Roadwise. bi-m. (Montana Motor Transport Association, Inc.)

**Motor Club of America**
c/o Robert A. Green, Ed., 484 Central Ave., Newark, NJ 07107.
- Motor Club News. q. ISSN 0463-6457

**Motor Publications**
(Subsidiary of: Hearst Magazines)
250 W. 55th St., New York, NY 10019.
- Motor; the automotive business magazine. m. ISSN 0027-1748
- Motor Handbook. a. ISSN 0094-1514
- Motor Imported Car Crash Estimating Guide. irreg.
- Motor Parts and Time Guide. a. ISSN 0077-1716

**Motor Transport Association of Connecticut**
508 Tolland St., East Hartford, CT 06108.
- Connecticut Motor Transport News. q.

**Motor Transportation Association of South Carolina, Inc.**
2425 Devine St, Columbia, SC 29205.
- Motor Transportation Hi-Lights. m. ISSN 0027-2078

**Motor Vehicle Manufacturers Association of the U.S. Inc.**
320 New Center Bldg., Detroit, MI 48202.
- M V M A Motor Vehicle Facts and Figures. a. ISSN 0146-048X
- World Motor Vehicle Data. a. ISSN 0085-8307

**Motorboat, Inc**
38 Commercial Wharf, Boston, MA 02110 (Subscr. address: 126 Blaine Ave., Marion, OH 43302)
- Motorboat. m. from 1975. ISSN 0093-6782
- Motorboat & Equipment Directory. a.

**Mount Alverno Press**
P.O. Box 5143, Santa Monica, CA 90405.
- Sunset Palms Hotel. 3 per yr.

**Mount Desert Island Biological Laboratory**
Salsbury Cove, ME 04672.
- Mount Desert Island Biological Laboratory. Bulletin. a.

**Mount Holyoke College. Alumnae Association**
College St., South Hadley, MA 01075.
- Mount Holyoke Alumnae Quarterly. q. ISSN 0027-2493

**Mount Saint Mary's College**
Emmitsburg, MD 21727.
- Mount Saint Mary's College. Interdisciplinary Essays. s-a. ISSN 0047-8245

**Mount St. Scholastica Convent**
Atchison, KS 66002.
- Benedictines. s-a. ISSN 0005-8726

**Mount Saviour Monastery**
Pine City, NY 14871.
- Monastic Studies. irreg. ISSN 0026-9190

**Mount Sinai Hospital**
19 E. 98th St., New York, NY 10029.
- Mount Sinai Journal of Medicine. bi-m. ISSN 0027-2507

**Mount Washington Observatory Inc.**
Gorham, NH 03581.
- Mount Washington Observatory News Bulletin. q. ISSN 0027-2523

**Mountain Business Publishing**
8585 W. 14th Ave., Denver, CO 80215.
- Colorado Business. bi-m. ISSN 0092-5071

**Mountain Call, Inc.**
Box 611, Kermit, WV 25674.
- Mountain Call; for the mountains, their people, their culture. m.

**Mountain Club of Maryland**
5128 S. Rolling Rd., Baltimore, MD 21227.
- M C M Newsletter. bi-m. ISSN 0024-7987

**Mountain Empire Publishing, Inc.**
231 Detroit St., Denver, CO 80206.
- Shale Country. m. ISSN 0097-5222

**Mountain Plains Adult Education Association**
c/o Editors, Journal of Adult Education, University of Wyoming, Box 3274 University Station, Laramie, WY 82071.
- M P A E A Newsletter. q.
- Mountain Plains Journal of Adult Education. s-a. ISSN 0090-4244

**Mountain-Plains Library Association**
c/o University of South Dakota Libraries, Vermillion, SD 57069.
- M P L A Newsletter. bi-m. ISSN 0145-6180

**Mountain Press**
1 Ridge Rd., Box 9, Gatlinburg, TN 37738.
- Mountain Visitor. w. ISSN 0027-2612

**Mountain Publishing Co Inc**
2201 Stout St, Denver, CO 80205.
- Rocky Mountain Construction. fortn. ISSN 0035-7561

**Mountain Safety Research**
631-X S. 96th St., Seattle, WA 98108.
- Mountain Safety Research Newsletter. s-a.

**Mountain States Publishing Co.**
1150 First National Bank Bldg., Denver, CO 80293.
- Mountain States Banker. m. ISSN 0027-2590 (Colorado Bankers Association)

**Mountaineers**
719 Pike St., Seattle, WA 98101.
- Mountaineer. m.(s-m. June & July) ISSN 0027-2620

**Mountainside Publishing, Inc**
P.O. Box 3496, Boulder, CO 80307.
- Journal of Academic Librarianship. bi-m. ISSN 0099-1333

**Mouth**
106 Jewett Ave., Buffalo, NY 14214.
- Mouth. q.

**Mouth of the Dragon**
Box 107, Cooper Sta., New York, NY 10003.
- Mouth of the Dragon; poetry journal of male love. q.

**Movement for Economic Justice**
1735 T St. N.W., Washington, DC 20009.
- Just Economics. m.

**Movement Shorthand Society**
Box 4949, Irvine, CA 92716.
- Notation News. s-a.

**Moving On**
434 26th St, Santa Monica, CA 90402.
- Moving On. q. ISSN 0027-2825

**Moving Out**
4866 Third, Rm. 207, Wayne State University, Detroit, MI 48202.
- Moving Out; feminist literary & arts journal. s-a. ISSN 0047-830X

**Mr. Cogito**
Box 627, Pacific University, Forest Grove, OR 97116.
- Mr. Cogito. 3 per yr.

**Ms. Atlas Press**
53 W. San Fernando, San Jose, CA 95113.
- Lesbian Voices. q.

**Ms Magazine Corporation**
370 Lexington Ave., New York, NY 10017.
- Ms; the new magazine for women. m. ISSN 0047-8318

**Mu Alpha Theta**
University of Oklahoma, Dept. of Mathematics, Norman, OK 73019.
- Mathematical Log. 3 per yr. ISSN 0025-5580

**Mu Beta Psi National Honorary Musical Fraternity**
3401 Hickory Crest Dr., Marietta, GA 30064.
- Clef. s-a. ISSN 0045-7132

**Mu Phi Epsilon International Music Sorority**
1097 Arnott Way, Campbell, CA 95008.
- Triangle of Mu Phi Epsilon. q. ISSN 0041-2600

**Mueller Electric Co**
1583 E. 31st St, Cleveland, OH 44114.
- Mueller Clipper. q. ISSN 0027-2965

**Mugwumps' Instrument**
12704 Barbara Rd., Silver Spring, MD 20906.
- Mugwumps' Instrument Herald. Catalog Reprint Series. irreg.

**Muhammads Mosque No. 2**
2548 S. Federal St., Chicago, IL 60616.
- Bilalian News. w.

**Mullen Publications, Inc.**
Box 1569, Charlotte, NC 28232.
- Southern Textile News. w. ISSN 0038-4607

**Arthur W. Muller, Ed. & Pub.**
414 N. Braddock St., Winchester, VA 22601.
- Pendulum of Time and the Arts. bi-m(except July-Aug.) ISSN 0031-4269

**Multi-Communication Ministries, Inc.**
Box 1775, Clinton, MS 39056.
- Sword & Trowel. m. ISSN 0039-7539

**Multidex Computing Co.**
7 Clinton Place, Suffern, NY 10901.
- Auto Index. q.

**Multimedia Education Inc.**
747 Third Ave., New York, NY 10017.
- I P I Newsletter. (Individually Prescribed Instructions) 7 per yr. ISSN 0019-0306
- P E N/Preschool Education Newsletter. m(Oct-May) ISSN 0030-7939

**Multnomah County Medical Society**
2188 S.W. Park Place, Portland, OR 97205.
- Portland Physician. m. ISSN 0032-4930

**Munford Publications, Inc.**
3636 N. First St., Suite 150, Fresno, CA 93726.
- California and Western States Grape Grower. m. ISSN 0092-2145
- California-Arizona Cotton. m. ISSN 0008-090X
- Western Hay & Grain Grower - Northern Edition. q.
- Western Hay & Grain Grower-Southern Edition. m.

**Municipal Bond News Inc.**
Box 690, Federal Square, Newark, NJ 07101.
- New Jersey Municipal Bond News; vital bond market information for the professional finance officer. m. ISSN 0097-8434

**Municipal Clerks Association of N.J. Inc.**
177 Colonial Road, Summit, NJ 07901.
- Quill. q. ISSN 0033-6483

**Municipal Engineers of the City of New York**
51 Chambers St., New York, NY 10007.
- Municipal Engineers Journal. q. ISSN 0027-3465

**Municipal Finance Officers Association**
1313 E. 60th St., Chicago, IL 60637.
- Governmental Finance. q. ISSN 0091-4835
- M F O A Newsletter. s-m.
- M F O A Study. irreg.

**Municipal Law Reports, Inc.**
Box 417, Plano, TX 75074.
- Zoning Reporter. m. ISSN 0360-9561

**Municipal League of Seattle & King County**
725 Central Bldg, Seattle, WA 98104.
- Municipal League of Seattle. Municipal News. m. ISSN 0027-352X

**Municipal Publications, Inc. (Boston)**
1050 Park Square Bldg., Boston, MA 02116.
- Boston. m. ISSN 0006-7989

**Municipal Publications, Inc. (Philadelphia)**
1500 Walnut St., Philadelphia, PA 19102.
- Philadelphia. m. ISSN 0031-7233

**Municipal Reference Library**
Room 1004, City Hall, Chicago, IL 60602.
- Chicago. Municipal Reference Library. Checklist of Publications Issued by the City of Chicago. q. ISSN 0300-712X
- Chicago. Municipal Reference Library. Recent Additions. m. ISSN 0300-7081

**Municipal Research and Services Center of Washington**
4719 Brooklyn Ave., N.E., Seattle, WA 98105.
- Municipal Research and Services Center of Washington. Information Bulletins. a.

**Munroe Publications, Inc**
Drawer 7, Indian Rocks Beach, FL 33535.
- Florida Food & Grocery News. m. ISSN 0015-4083 (Florida Supermarket Association)
- Food Promotions. m. ISSN 0015-6558
- Housewares Promotions. bi-m. ISSN 0018-652X

**Munson-Williams-Proctor Institute**
310 Genesse St., Utica, NY 13502.
- Munson-Williams-Proctor Institute. Bulletin. m. ISSN 0027-3627

**Murphy-Richter Publishing Company**
20 N. Wacker Drive, Chicago, IL 60606.
- Progressive Railroading. bi-m. ISSN 0033-0817

**Murray Hill News Corp.**
237 Madison Ave, New York, NY 10016.
- Murray Hill News. m. ISSN 0027-3686

**Murray Publishing Co.**
104 W. Roy St., Seattle, WA 98119.
- Masonic Tribune. w. ISSN 0025-4673

**Murray State University. College of Business and Public Affairs**
School of Business, Murray, KY 42071.
- Business and Public Affairs. s-a.

**Muscle Man Inc.**
1665 Utica Ave., Brooklyn, NY 11234.
- Muscle Training Illustrated. bi-m. ISSN 0047-8407

**Muscular Dystrophy Association, Inc.**
810 Seventh Ave., New York, NY 10019.
- M D A News. bi-m.

**Muse Publishing Co., Inc.**
154 W. 57th St., New York, NY 10019.
- Intermezzo; the magazine of Carnegie Hall. m. 9 per yr.

**Museo del Barrio**
1945 Third Ave., New York, NY 10029.
- Quimbamba. q.

**Museum of American Folk Art**
49 W. 53rd St., New York, NY 10019.
- Clarion; folk art newsletter. irreg. (approx. 2-4 per yr.)

**Museum of Fine Arts, Houston**
Box 6826, 1001 Bissonnet, Houston, TX 77005.
- Houston, Texas. Museum of Fine Arts Bulletin. q. ISSN 0018-6708

**Museum of Fine Arts, St. Petersburg**
255 Beach Drive N., St. Petersburg, FL 33701.
- Mosaic. bi-m.
- Pharos. q. ISSN 0031-7160

**Museum of New Mexico Press**
Box 2087, Santa Fe, NM 87501.
- Palacio. q. ISSN 0031-0158
- Papers in Anthropology. irreg., no. 15, 1966, no. 17, 1974. ISSN 0078-9054

**Museum of Northern Arizona**
Route 4, Box 720, Flagstaff, AZ 86001.
- Museum of Northern Arizona Ceramic Series. irreg. ISSN 0430-635X
- Museum of Northern Arizona Glen Canyon Series. irreg. ISSN 0428-5387
- Museum of Northern Arizona Technical Series. irreg. ISSN 0428-5395

**Museum of the City of New York**
Fifth Ave. and 103 St., NY 10029.
- New York (City). Museum of the City of New York. Bulletin. q.

**Museum of the Confederacy**
1201 E. Clay St., Richmond, VA 23219.
- Confederate Studies. a.
- Museum of the Confederacy. Newsletter. q.

**Museum of the Fur Trade**
Route 2, Box 18, Chadron, NE 69337.
- Museum of the Fur Trade Quarterly. q. ISSN 0027-4135

**Museum of the Great Plains**
Box 68, Lawton, OK 73502.
- Great Plains Journal. s-a. ISSN 0017-3673

**Music Article Guide**
Box 12216, Philadelphia, PA 19144.
- Music Article Guide. q. ISSN 0027-4240

**Music Business Reference, Inc.**
21 Homeside Lane, White Plains, NY 10605.
- New on the Charts. m.

**Music City News Publishing Co., Inc.**
Box 22975, 1302 Division St., Nashville, TN 37202.
- Music City News. m. ISSN 0027-4291

**Music Educators National Conference**
Center for Educational Associations, 1902 Association Drive, Reston, VA 22091.
- Music Educators Journal. 9 per yr. ISSN 0027-4321
- Music Educators National Conference. Selective Music List: Vocal Solos and Ensembles. irreg. ISSN 0077-2402
- Music Educators National Conference. Selective Music Lists: Band, Orchestra, and String Orchestra. irreg.
- Music Educators National Conference. Selective Music Lists: Instrumental Solos and Ensembles. irreg.
- Music Power. q.
- Original Manuscript Music for Wind and Percussion Instruments. irreg. ISSN 0078-6586

**Music Journal Inc.**
20 Hampton Rd., Southampton, NY 11968.
- Music and Artists Annual Directory. a. ISSN 0077-2380
- Music Journal; educational music magazine. m.(Sept-June) ISSN 0027-4364
- Music Journal Anthology. a. ISSN 0077-2437

**Music Library Association**
343 S. Main, Room 205, Ann Arbor, MI 48108.
- Music Cataloging Bulletin. m. ISSN 0027-4283
- Music Library Association. Index and Bibliography Series. irreg.
- Music Library Association. Newsletter. q. ISSN 0580-289X
- Music Library Association. Technical Reports; information for music media specialists. irreg.
- Music Library Association, Notes. q. ISSN 0027-4380

**Music Notes (Chicago)**
3037 W. Jarvis, Chicago, IL 60645.
- Music Notes (Chicago) q.

**Music Teachers Association**
408 Carew Tower, Cincinnati, OH 45202.
- American Music Teacher. bi-m. ISSN 0003-0112

**Music Trades Corporation**
Box 432, 80 West St., Englewood, NJ 07631.
- Music Trades. m. ISSN 0027-4488
- Purchaser's Guide to the Music Industries. a.

**Musica**
1668 Great Highway, San Francisco, CA 94122.
- Musica; women in music and the music in women. bi-m.

**Musical Box Society International**
19 Colony Drive, Summit, NJ 07901.
- Musical Box Society International. Bulletin. 3 per yr.

**Musical Newsletter, Inc.**
654 Madison Ave., Suite 1703, New York, NY 10021.
- Musical Newsletter. q. ISSN 0047-8466

**Musicana Collector**
2219 E. Belmont Ave., Fresno, CA 93701.
- Musicana Collector. q.

**Musicdata, Inc.**
18 W. Chelten Ave., Philadelphia, PA 19144.
- Choral Music in Print. a.
- Organ Music in Print. a.

**Musician's Guide Publications**
739 Boylston St., Boston, MA 02116.
- Musician's Guide. m.

**Mutual Beneficial Association of Rail Transportation Employees, Inc.**
Amtrak Station-30th St., Rm. 359, Philadelphia, PA 19104.
- Mutual Beneficial Association of Rail Transportation Employees. Mutual Magazine. m. ISSN 0027-5190

**Mutual Benefit Life Insurance Co.**
520 Broad St., Newark, NJ 07101.
- Mutual Benefit Estate and Tax Letter. bi-m. ISSN 0027-5158
- Pelican. m. ISSN 0031-4153

**Mutual Funds Scoreboard**
6 Deer Trail, Old Tappan, NJ 07675.
- Mutual Funds Scoreboard. q.

**Mutual Of New York Life Insurance Co. Public Relations Department**
1740 Broadway, New York, NY 10019.
- M O N Y News; for its employers and field force. fortn. ISSN 0024-8282

**Mutual U F O Network, Inc.**
c/o Walter H. Andrus, Jr., 103 Oldtowne Road, Seguin, TX 78155.
- Mufon U F O Journal. m.

**My Little Salesman, Inc,**
P.O. Box 2328, Eugene, OR 97402.
- My Little Salesman. m.

**Myasthenia Gravis Foundation Inc.**
230 Park Ave., New York, NY 10017.
- International Symposium on Myasthenia Gravis. Proceedings. (pub. by New York Academy of Sciences)
- M G Conquest. q. ISSN 0024-8169

**Mycological Society of America**
- Mycologia. (pub. by New York Botanical Garden)

**Mycotaxon, Ltd.**
Box 264, Ithaca, NY 14850.
- Mycotaxon. q. ISSN 0093-4666

**John Bernard Myers, Ed. & Pub.**
59 E. 73rd St., New York, NY 10021.
- Parenthese: a Magazine of Words and Pictures. q.

**Myers Publishing Co., Inc.**
381 Park Ave., S., New York, NY 10016.
- Chemical Purchasing; for buyers in the chemical process industries. m. (plus annual Chemicals Directory) ISSN 0009-2657
- Chemical Purchasing Chemicals Directory. a.

**Myrianyn - the Layman**
1219 North Avers Ave., Chicago, IL 60651.
- Myrianyn - the Layman. bi-m.

**Myrin Institute for Adult Education**
521 Park Ave., NY 10021.
- Myrin Institute for Adult Education Proceedings. irreg.

**Myrjon Press**
Box 86, New Gretna, NJ 08224.
- Iconoclast; a library quarterly. q. ISSN 0019-1132

**Mystery & Detection Annual.**
c/o Donald K. Adams, Ed. & Pub., Department of English, Occidental College, Los Angeles, CA 90041.
- Mystery & Detection Annual. a. ISSN 0000-0302

**Mystery Writers of America, Inc.**
105 E. 19th St., New York, NY 10003.
- Third Degree. m. ISSN 0040-6139

**Mystic Seaport, Inc.**
Mystic, CT 06355.
- American Maritime Library. (pub. by Wesleyan University Press)
- Log of Mystic Seaport. q. ISSN 0024-5828
- Wind Rose. m. ISSN 0049-7657

**Mystic Seaport, Inc. G.W. Blunt White Library**
Mystic, CT 06355.
- Mystic Seaport Manuscripts Inventory. irreg., 1966, no. 5. ISSN 0077-2615

**Mythopoeic Society**
Box 4671, Whittier, CA 90607.
- Mythlore. q.
- Mythprint. m.
- Mythril. irreg.

- Parma Eldalamberon. irreg.

**N A A C P**
*see* **National Association for the Advancement of Colored People**

**N.A.D.A.**
*see* **National Automobile Dealers Association**

**N A S A**
*see* **U. S. National Aeronautics and Space Administration**

**N B Enterprises, Inc.**
274 Madison Avenue, New York, NY 10016.
- C & S. (Casket and Sunnyside) m. ISSN 0008-7327

**N C A A Publishing Service**
Box 1906, Shawnee Mission, KS 66222.
- Official National Collegiate Athletic Association Football Rules Interpretations. a. ISSN 0094-5226 (National Collegiate Athletic Association)

**N C R Corporation**
Dayton, OH 45479.
- N C R World. q.

**N E G M Publishing Co.**
67 Federal Ave., Quincy, MA 02169.
- New England Grocery Merchandiser. m. ISSN 0028-4769

**N I M M Educational Media Service, Inc.**
Box 1345, Gary, IN 46807.
- N I M M. (New in Mass Media); what's new in mass media. 4 per yr.

**N J M Associates**
Box 993, Farmingdale, NY 11737.
- New Jersey Monthly. m.

**N L S P, Inc.**
*see* **National Live Stock Publishing**

**N O K Publishers, Ltd.**
150 Fifth Ave., New York, NY 10011.
- Studies in East African Society and History. irreg.

**N T L Institute for Applied Behavioral Science**
1501 Wilson Blvd., Arlington, VA 22209.
- Journal of Applied Behavioral Science. q. ISSN 0021-8863
- Social Change; ideas and applications. 4 per yr.

**N.Y.M. Company of California**
9665 Wilshire Blvd., Beverly Hills, CA 90212.
- New West. bi-w.

**N Y M Corporation**
755 Second Ave., New York, NY 10017.
- New York. w. ISSN 0028-7369

**N Y R E V, Inc.**
250 W. 57th St., New York, NY 10019
- New York Review of Books. 22 per yr. ISSN 0028-7504 (Subscr. to: New York Review, Box 940, Farmingdale NY 11737)

**Names of Distinction, Inc.**
925 S. Limestone St., Suite 2, Lexington, KY 40503.
- Who's Who in North Carolina. irreg. ISSN 0093-4178

**Nanogens International**
Box 487, Freedom, CA 95019.
- Nanogen Index. irreg. with periodic updating service.

**Nantucket Maria Mitchell Association**
1 Vestal Street, Nantucket, MA 02554.
- Nantucket Maria Mitchell Association. Annual Report. a.

**Nantucket Review**
P.O. Box 1444, Nantucket, MA 02554.
- Nantucket Review. 3 per yr. ISSN 0094-4114

**Napa-Solano Dental Society**
301 Alamo Dr., Vacaville, CA 95688.
- Oracle. m.

**Narcotics Education, Inc.**
6840 Eastern Ave. N.W., Washington, DC 20012.
- Listen. (pub. by Pacific Press Publishing Association)
- Winner. 9 per yr. ISSN 0043-5937

**Naropa Institute**
1441 Broadway, Boulder, CO 80302.
- Loka. irreg.

**NASA**
*see* **U.S. National Aeronautics and Space Administration**

**Jay R. Nash, Ed. & Pub.**
Box 4327, Chicago, IL 60680.
- Literary Times. m. ISSN 0024-4619

**Nashotah House**
Nashotah, WI 53058.
- Nashotah Review. q. ISSN 0047-8660

**Nassau Community College**
State University of New York, Garden City, NY 11530.
- Nassau Review. a. ISSN 0077-2879

**Nassau County. Department of Recreation and Parks**
Eisenhower Park, East Meadow, NY 11554.
- Senior Citizens Gazette. m.

**Nassau County Bar Association**
15 and West Sts., Mineola, NY 11501.
- Nassau Lawyer. 9 per yr. ISSN 0047-8695

**Nassau County Medical Center**
2201 Hempstead Turnpike, East Meadow, NY 11554.
- Nassau County Medical Center. Proceedings. q. ISSN 0094-7202

**Nassau Herald**
379 Central Ave, Lawrence, NY 11559.
- Nassau Herald. w.

**Nassau Library System**
Public Relations Office, Lower Concourse, Roosevelt Field, Garden City, NY 11530.
- Library Lines. m. ISSN 0024-2357

**Nassau-Suffolk Regional Planning Board**
Veterans Memorial Highway, Hauppauge, NY 11787.
- Long Island Economic Trends. m.

**Stella Nathan**
Box 543, Cotati, CA 94928.
- Back Roads; a semi-annual magazine of literature and art. s-a.

**Nathaniel Hawthorne Society**
- Nathaniel Hawthorne Society. Newsletter. (pub. by Bowdoin College. Hawthorne-Longfellow Library)

**Nation Co. Inc.**
333 Sixth Ave., New York, NY 10014.
- Nation. w. ISSN 0027-8378

**National Academy of Code Administration**
3900 Washington Ave. N.W., Suite 100 N, Washington, DC 20016.
- Code Administration Review. q. ISSN 0091-6609

**National Academy of Sciences**
National Academy of Sciences, 2101 Constitution Ave. N.W., Washington, DC 20418.
- M R I S Abstracts. s-a. (U. S. Maritime Administration)
- M R I S Current Awareness Service. (Maritime Research Information Service) m. (U.S. Maritime Administration)
- National Academy of Sciences. Annual Report. a. ISSN 0077-2925
- National Academy of Sciences. Biographical Memoirs. irreg. ISSN 0077-2933
- National Academy of Sciences. National Academy of Engineering. National Research Council. Institute of Medicine. News Report. m. ISSN 0027-8432 (Co-sponsors: National Academy of Engineering; National Research Council; Institute of Medicine)
- National Academy of Sciences. Proceedings. m. ISSN 0027-8424
- Scientific, Technical and Related Societies of the United States. irreg. ISSN 0085-5995

**National Academy of Sciences. Committee on Fire Research**
2101 Constitution Ave., Washington, DC 20418.
- Directory of Fire Research in the United States. biennial. ISSN 0419-2648

- Fire Research Abstracts and Reviews. 3 per yr.
  ISSN 0015-265X (Subscr to: National Technical
  Information Service, Springfield VA 22151)

**National Academy of Sciences. Committee on
Scholarly Communication with the Peoples
Republic of China**
2101 Constitution Ave., N.W., Washington, DC
20418.
- China Exchange Newsletter. bi-m.

**National Academy of Sciences. Conference on
Electrical Insulation and Dielectric Phenomena**
2101 Constitution Ave., N.W., Washington, DC
20418.
- Conference on Electrical Insulation and Dielectric
  Phenomena. Annual Report. a. ISSN 0084-9162
- Digest of Literature on Dielectrics. a. ISSN 0070-
  4865

**National Academy of Sciences. Institute of
Laboratory Animal Resources**
2101 Constitution Ave., N.W., Washington, DC
20418.
- Animals for Research. biennial. ISSN 0547-8626

**National Academy of Sciences. National Committee
on Tunneling Technology**
2101 Constitution Ave. N.W., Washington, DC
20418.
- Tunneling Technology Newsletter. q.

**National Academy of Sciences. Ocean Affairs Board**
2101 Constitution Ave., Washington, DC 20018.
- Directory of Marine Scientists in the United
  States. irreg., 1964, no. 4.

**National Academy of Sciences Transportation
Research Board**
2101 Constitution Ave. N.W., Washington, DC
20418.
- H R I S Abstracts. (Highway Research
  Information Service) q. ISSN 0017-6222
- National Cooperative Highway Research Program
  Reports. irreg. ISSN 0077-5614
- Transportation Research Board Special Report.
  irreg.
- Transportation Research News. q.
- Transportation Research Record. 1rreg.

**National Accreditation Council for Agencies Serving
the Blind and Visually Handicapped**
79 Madison Ave, New York, NY 10016.
- Standard-Bearer. 3 per yr. ISSN 0049-206X

**National Acupuncture Association**
1033 Gayley Ave., Suite 200, Los Angeles, CA
90024.
- Acupuncture; a selected bibliography. irreg. ISSN
  0092-5047

**National Advertising Co-Op**
2111 Taliesen Lane, Rockford, IL 61107.
- Truckers Action Catalog. 4 per yr.

**National Advisory Council on Supplementary Centers
and Services**
425 13th St. N.W., Suite 529, Washington, DC
20004.
- Title Three Quarterly. q.

**National Aeronautic Association of the U.S.A.**
Shoreham Bldg., 806 15th St., NW, Washington,
DC 20005.
- Journal of Aerospace Education. m.

**National Aeronautics and Space Administration**
see U.S. National Aeronautics and Space
Administration

**National Aerospace Association**
Middle Tennessee State University, Murfreesboro,
TN 37132.
- Skylights. m.(Sept-May) ISSN 0037-6620

**National Affairs**
Box 542, Old Chelsea Post Office, New York, NY
10011.
- Public Interest. q. ISSN 0033-3557

**National Affairs Inc.**
345 E. 46th St., New York, NY 10017
(Subscr. to: 155 Allen Blvd., Farmingdale, NY
11735)
- Foreign Policy. q. ISSN 0015-7228

**National Affiliation for Literacy Advance**
- Literacy Advance. (pub. by Laubach Literacy Inc.)

**National Agricultural Institute**
1625 Eye N. W., Washington, DC 20006.
- Background Washington. m.

**National Agricultural Library**
see U.S. National Agricultural Library

**National Alliance for Family Life**
- International Journal of Family Counseling. (pub.
  by Transaction Periodicals Consortium)
- Journal of Family Counseling. (pub. by New York
  Family Counselors Institute)

**National Alliance of Postal and Federal Employees**
1644 Eleventh Street, N.W., Washington, DC
20001.
- National Alliance. m. ISSN 0027-8513

**National Alliance Television and Electronic Service
Associations**
5908 S. Troy St., Chicago, IL 60629.
- N A T E S A Scope. m. ISSN 0027-6030

**National Amateur Press Association**
c/o Virginia Baker, 1326 W. 400 South, Salt Lake
City, UT 84104.
- National Amateur. q. ISSN 0027-8521

**National American Studies Connections Collective**
c/o Doris Friedersohn, Exec. Sec'y, 209 Hillcrest
Ave., Leonia, NJ 07605.
- Connections Two. irreg.

**National-American Wholesale Grocer's Association,
Inc.**
51 Madison Ave., New York, NY 10010.
- N A W G A Management and Controller's
  Bulletin. bi-m. ISSN 0027-6103

**National Americanism Commission**
American Legion, Box 1055, Indianapolis, IN
46206.
- Firing Line. m. ISSN 0015-2722

**National Appliance and Radio-Electronic Dealers
Association**
2 North Riverside Plaza, Chicago, IL 60606.
- N A R D A News. m. ISSN 0047-8717

**National Architectural Accrediting Board, Inc.**
1735 New York Ave. N. W., Washington, DC
20006.
- Accredited Programs in Architecture. a.

**National Archives and Records Service**
see U.S. National Archives and Records Service

**National Art Education Association**
1916 Association Drive, Reston, VA 22091.
- Art Education. 8 per yr (Sept.-Apr.) ISSN 0004-
  3125
- Art Teacher. 3 per yr.
- National Art Education Association. Research
  Monograph. irreg., 1972, no. 5. ISSN 0077-3174
- Studies in Art Education; a journal of issues and
  research in art education. 3 per yr. ISSN 0039-
  3541

**National Art Material Trade Association**
- Art Material Trade News. (pub. by Syndicate
  Magazines Inc.)

**National Asphalt Pavement Association**
6811 Kenilworth Ave., Riverdale, MD 20840.
- National Asphalt Pavement Association. Paving
  Forum. q. ISSN 0048-3079

**National Assembly of Religious Brothers**
100 Monastery Ave, West Springfield, MA 01089.
- Brothers Newsletter. q. ISSN 0007-2451

**National Assembly of Women Religious (N.A.W.R.)**
1307 S. Wabash, Chicago, IL 60605.
- Probe (Chicago); the American sister today. m.

**National Assessment of Educational Progress.
Education Commission of the States**
700 Lincoln Tower, 1860 Lincoln, Denver, CO
80295.
- N A E P Newsletter. 6 per yr. ISSN 0094-0208

**National Association for Better Broadcasting**
Box 43640, Los Angeles, CA 90043.
- Better Radio and Television. q. ISSN 0006-0194
- Television for the Family; comprehensive guide to
  family viewing. a. ISSN 0082-2698

**National Association for Business Teacher Education**
1906 Association Drive, Reston, VA 22091.
- N A B T E Review. a.

**National Association for Community Development**
1424 Sixteenth St. N.W., Washington, DC 20036.
- N A C D News. m.
- N A C D Newsletter. q.

**National Association for Core Curriculum, Inc.**
407D R.I. White Hall, Kent State Univ., Kent, OH
44242.
- Core Teacher. q. ISSN 0045-8538

**National Association for Creative Children and Adults**
8080 Spring Valley Dr., Cincinnati, OH 45236.
- Creative Child and Adult Quarterly. q. ISSN
  0098-7565
- It's Happening. irreg.

**National Association for Environmental Education**
5940 S. W. 73rd St., Miami, FL 33143.
- N. A. E. E. Newsletter. m.

**National Association for Foreign Student Affairs**
1860 19 St. N.W., Washington, DC 20009.
- N A F S A Directory. a. ISSN 0077-3190
- N A F S A Newsletter. m.(Oct.-June) ISSN 0027-
  5824

**National Association for Girls and Women in Sport**
1201-16th St., N.W., Washington, DC 20036.
- N.A.G.W.S. Guide, Aquatics. irreg. ISSN 0361-
  719X
- N.A.G.W.S. Guide, Basketball. irreg. ISSN 0362-
  3254

**National Association for Hearing and Speech Action**
814 Thayer Ave., Silver Spring, MD 20910.
- Hearing & Speech Action. bi-m.

**National Association for Humanities Education**
P. O. Box 370, Tempe, AZ 85281.
- Humanities Journal. 3 per yr. ISSN 0046-8266

**National Association for Mental Health**
1800 N. Kent St., Rosslyn, VA 22209.
- Catalog of Selected Films for Mental Health
  Education. a. ISSN 0069-1038
- M H. (Mental Hygiene) q. ISSN 0025-9683

**National Association for Music Therapy, Inc.**
Box 610, Lawrence, KS 66044.
- Journal of Music Therapy. q. ISSN 0022-2917

**National Association for Non-Parents**
8 Sudbrook Lane, Baltimore, MD 21208.
- N O N Newsletter. bi-m.

**National Association for Physical Education of
College Women**
c/o Jean K. Marsh, 6140 Sinbad Pl., School of
Physical Education, MD 21045.
- Quest (Columbia) s-a. ISSN 0033-6297 (Co-
  Sponsor: National College Physical Education
  Assn. for Men)

**National Association for Practical Nurse Education
and Service, Inc.**
122 E. 42nd St., New York, NY 10017.
- Journal of Practical Nursing. m. ISSN 0022-3867

**National Association for Public Continuing and Adult
Education**
1201 16th St. N.W., Washington, DC 20036.
- Administrator's Swap Shop Newsletter. bi-m.
- Public Continuing and Adult Education Almanac.
  a. ISSN 0079-7545
- Pulse of Public Continuing & Adult Education.
  m.(Oct.-May) ISSN 0033-4219
- Techniques for Teachers of Adults. m.(Oct.-May)
  ISSN 0040-1358

**National Association for Regional Ballet**
1860 Broadway, New York, NY 10023.
- Dance /America. q. ISSN 0045-9577

**National Association for Research in Science
Teaching**
- Journal of Research in Science Teaching. (pub. by
  Wiley Interscience)

**National Association for Retarded Citizens**
2709 Ave. E, East Arlington, TX 76011.
- Mental Retardation News. a. ISSN 0009-4072

**National Association for Stock Car Auto Racing, Inc.**
1801 Volusia Ave., Daytona Beach, FL 32015.
- N A S C A R Newsletter. s-m. ISSN 0027-5999

**National Association for the Advancement of Colored People**
1790 Broadway, New York, NY 10019.
- Crisis (New York) (pub. by Crisis Publishing Co.)
- N A A C P Annual Report. a. ISSN 0077-3212

**National Association for the Education of Young Children**
1834 Connecticut Ave., N.W., Washington, DC 20009.
- Young Children. 6 per yr. ISSN 0044-0728

**National Association for Uniformed Services**
956 N. Monroe St., Arlington, VA 22201.
- N A U S Newsletter. bi-m.

**National Association for Women Deans, Administrators and Counselors**
1028 Connecticut Ave., N.W., Suite 922, Washington, DC 20036.
- National Association for Women Deans, Administrators and Counselors. Journal. q.

**National Association of Accountants**
919 Third Ave., New York, NY 10022.
- M A P Newsletter. (Management Accounting Practices) bi-m.
- Management Accounting. m. ISSN 0025-1690

**National Association of Amateur Oarsmen**
4 Boat House Row, Philadelphia, PA 19130
(Edit. Address: 60 Boylston St., Cambridge MA 02138)
- Oarsman. 5 per yr.

**National Association of American Balloon Corps Veterans**
634 Wagner Road, Lafayette Hill, PA 19444.
- Haul Down and Ease Off. q.

**National Association of Animal Breeders**
401 Bernadette St., Box 1033, Columbia, MO 65201.
- Advanced Animal Breeder. 9 per yr.
- Conference on Artificial Insemination of Beef Cattle. Proceedings. a. ISSN 0084-9146
- National Association of Animal Breeders Annual Proceedings. a. ISSN 0077-3255

**National Association of Attorneys General**
- Newsletter & Digest of Selected Opinions of State Attorneys General. (pub. by Council of State Governments)

**National Association of Auto Trim Shops**
129 Broadway, Lynbrook, NY 11563.
- Auto Trim News; devoted to needs of the auto trim industry, replacement, maintenance and repair of auto upholstery, etc. m. ISSN 0005-0865

**National Association of Bank Women**
111 E. Wacker Dr., Chicago, IL 60601.
- N A B W Journal. bi-m.

**National Association of Bedding Manufacturers**
1150 17th St. N.W., Washington, DC 20036.
- Bedding. m. ISSN 0005-7568

**National Association of Biology Teachers**
11250 Roger Bacon Drive, Reston, VA 22090.
- American Biology Teacher. m.(Jan-May & Sept-Dec) ISSN 0002-7685

**National Association of Black Psychologists**
104 Administration Bldg., Univ. of Cincinnati, Cincinnati, OH 45221.
- Journal of Black Psychology. s-a. ISSN 0095-7984

**National Association of Blackfeet Indians**
Blackfeet Indian Reservation, Browning, MT 59417.
- Browning Sentinel; home of the Blackfeet Indians, gateway to Glacier National Park. m. ISSN 0007-2540

**National Association of Blue Shield Plans**
211 E. Chicago Ave., Chicago, IL 60611.
- Blue Shield (Chicago) m. ISSN 0523-7688

**National Association of Broadcast Employees and Technicians**
AFL-CIO, 80 E. Jackson Blvd., Chicago, IL 60604.
- N A B E T News. bi-m. ISSN 0027-5697

**National Association of Broadcasters**
1771 N St. N.W., Washington, DC 20036.
- N A B Highlights. w.

**National Association of Business and Educational Radio**
1330 New Hampshire Ave. N.W., Washington, DC 20036.
- Business Radio/Action. m. ISSN 0093-0245

**National Association of Business Law Teachers, Inc.**
West Virginia University, Armstrong Hall, Morgantown, WV 26506.
- Business Law Review. s-a.

**National Association of Chain Drug Stores**
- N. A. C. D. S. Lilly Digest. (pub. by Eli Lilly & Co.)

**National Association of Christian Schools**
Box 550, Wheaton, IL 60187.
- Christian Teacher. bi-m. ISSN 0009-5672

**National Association of College Admissions Counselors**
9933 Lawler Ave., Skokie, IL 60076.
- National Association of College Admissions Counselors. Journal. 3 per yr.
- National Association of College Admissions Counselors. Membership Directory. biennial. ISSN 0090-3965
- National Association of College Admissions Counselors. Newsletter. irreg. ISSN 0027-8416

**National Association of College and University Attorneys**
One Dupont Circle, Suite 510, Washington, DC 20036.
- College Law Digest. bi-m. ISSN 0045-737X
- Journal of College and University Law. q. ISSN 0093-8688 (Subscr. to: Fred B. Rothman & Co., 57 Leuning St., South Hackensack, NJ 07606)

**National Association of College and University Business Officers**
Suite 510, One Dupont Circle, Washington, DC 20036.
- College and University Business Officer. m. ISSN 0010-0919
- National Association of College & University Business Officers. Professional File. 8 per yr.

**National Association of College Deans and Registrars**
- National Association of College Deans and Registrars. Proceedings. (pub. by Florida A & M University)

**National Association of College Stores, Inc.**
528 E. Lorain St., Oberlin, OH 44074.
- College Store Journal. 6 per yr. ISSN 0010-115X

**National Association of College-University Food Services**
Grant Towers, Northern Illinois University, De Kalb, IL 60115.
- N A C U F S Technical Bulletin. s-a. ISSN 0027-5751

**National Association of College Wind & Percussion Instructors**
- N A C W P I Journal. (pub. by Simpson Publishing Co.)

**National Association of Colleges and Teachers of Agriculture**
608 W. Vermont, Urbana, IL 61801.
- N A C T A Journal. q. ISSN 0027-8602

**National Association of Collegiate Directors of Athletics**
- Athletic Administration. (pub. by Spencer Marketing Services)

**National Association of Congregational Christian Churches**
801 Bushnell, Beloit, WI 53511.
- Congregationalist. m. ISSN 0010-5856

**National Association of Conservation Districts**
Box 855, League City, TX 77573.
- National Association of Conservation Districts. Tuesday Letter. w. ISSN 0047-8733

**National Association of Corrosion Engineers**
Box 1499, Houston, TX 77001.
- Corrosion; scientific data on corrosion and control. m. ISSN 0010-9312

- Corrosion Abstracts; abstracts of the world's literature on corrosion and corrosion mitigation. bi-m. ISSN 0010-9339
- Materials Performance; applicatory information on protecting materials. m. ISSN 0094-1492
- Materials Performance Buyer's Guide; the corrosion control products/services purchasing directory. irreg. ISSN 0095-7976

**National Association of Counties**
1735 New York Ave. N.W., Washington, DC 20006.
- County News. w.
- County Year Book. a. ISSN 0099-1015

**National Association of Counties. Research Foundation**
1735 New York Ave. N.W., Washington, DC 20006.
- County Manpower Report. bi-m.

**National Association of Credit Management**
475 Park Ave. So., New York, NY 10016.
- Credit and Financial Management. m. ISSN 0011-0973
- Credit and Financial Newsletter. m. ISSN 0011-0981
- Credit Manual of Commercial Laws. a. ISSN 0070-1467

**National Association of Demolition Contractors**
- Demolition Age. (pub. by Curtis International Ltd.)

**National Association of Dental Laboratories**
3801 Mt. Vernon Ave., Alexandria, VA 22305.
- N A D L Journal. m.

**National Association of Dramatic and Speech Arts**
Shaw University, Box 124, Raleigh, NC 27602
(Dist. by Joseph Adkins, NADSA, Fort Valley State College, Fort Valley, Ga. 31030)
- Encore. a. ISSN 0071-0164

**National Association of Educational Broadcasters**
1346 Connecticut Ave. N.W., Suite 1101, Washington, DC 20036.
- N A E B Letter. m.
- Public Telecommunications Review (PTR) bi-m. ISSN 0093-8149

**National Association of Educational Buyers**
111 Cantiague Rock Rd., Westbury, NY 11590.
- N A E B. Bulletin. m.

**National Association of Educational Negotiators**
1835 K St.N.W., Suite 908, Washington, DC 20006.
- N A E N Bulletin. m.

**National Association of Educational Secretaries**
1801 N. Moore St., Arlington, VA 22209.
- National Educational Secretary. 4 per yr. ISSN 0027-9196

**National Association of Electric Companies**
1140 Connecticut Ave., Washington, DC 20036.
- N A E C Weekly Newsletter. w.

**National Association of Electrical Distributors**
111 Prospect St., Stamford, CT 06901.
- Electrical Distributor. m. ISSN 0422-8707

**National Association of Elementary School Principals**
1801 N. Moore St., Arlington, VA 22209.
- National Elementary Principal. 6 per yr. ISSN 0027-920X

**National Association of Evangelicals**
Box 28, Wheaton, IL 60187.
- United Evangelical Action. q. ISSN 0041-7270

**National Association of Federally Licensed Firearms Dealers**
c/o Andrew Molchan, Ed., 7001 N. Clark St., Chicago, IL 60626.
- American Firearms Industry. m.

**National Association of Fire Investigators**
53 W. Jackson, Chicago, IL 60604.
- N A F I Newsletter. q.

**National Association of Fleet Administrators, Inc.**
c/o Robert Berke, 295 Madison Ave., New York, NY 10017.
- N A F A Bulletin. m.
- N A F A Conference Brochure & Reference Book. a. ISSN 0550-8843

**National Association of Flight Instructors**
Box 20204, Columbus, OH 43220.
• N A F I Newsletter. bi-m.

**National Association of Geology Teachers**
Business Office, Box 368, Lawrence, KS 66044.
• Journal of Geological Education. 5 per yr. ISSN 0022-1368

**National Association of Glove Manufacturers**
52 S. Main St., Gloversville, NY 12078.
• Glove News. irreg. ISSN 0072-4777

**National Association of Health Services Executives**
551 Fifth Ave, New York, NY 10017.
• N A H S E 's Resume. q.

**National Association of Home Builders of the United States**
15th & M Sts. N.W., Washington, DC 20005.
• N A H B. Journal-Scope. w.

**National Association of Hosiery Manufacturers**
516 Charlottetown Mall, Box 4314, Charlotte, NC 28204.
• Hosiery Newsletter. fortn. ISSN 0018-540X
• Hosiery Statistics. a.

**National Association of Housing and Redevelopment Officials**
Watergate Bldg., Suite 404, 2600 Virginia Ave. N.W., Washington, DC 20037.
• Journal of Housing. 11 per yr. ISSN 0022-1635
• N A H R O Letter; weekly dispatch for N A H R O agency members. w. ISSN 0300-6409

**National Association of Housing Cooperatives**
1828 L. St. N. W., Washington, DC 20036.
• Cooperative Housing Bulletin. m. ISSN 0097-9759
• Cooperative Housing Journal. 3 per yr. ISSN 0589-6355
• Directory of Housing Cooperatives in the United States. irreg.

**National Association of Human Rights Workers**
527 West 39th St., Kansas City, MO 64111.
• Journal of Intergroup Relations. q. ISSN 0047-2492

**National Association of Independent Insurance Adjusters**
175 W. Jackson Blvd., Chicago, IL 60604.
• Independent Adjuster. q. ISSN 0019-3658

**National Association of Independent Insurers**
2600 River Rd., Des Plaines, IL 60018.
• N A I I News Memo. irreg. ISSN 0027-5859
• N A I I Press Samplings. irreg. ISSN 0027-5867

**National Association of Independent Schools**
4 Liberty Square, Boston, MA 02109.
• Independent School. q.
• National Association of Independent Schools. Annual Report. a. ISSN 0550-7421

**National Association of Industrial and Technical Teacher Educators**
Purdue Univ., c/o School of Technology, Lafayette, IN 47907.
• Journal of Industrial Teacher Education. 4 per yr. ISSN 0022-1864

**National Association of Insectocutor Manufacturers**
• Insectocutor News. (pub. by Gustav Detjen Jr., Ed. & Pub.)

**National Association of Installment Companies**
38 W. 32nd St., New York, NY 10001.
• Installment Retailing. 3 per yr. ISSN 0020-2126

**National Association of Institutional Laundry Managers**
c/o Robert J. Conard, Ed., 1524 Rankin St., Appleton, WI 54911.
• N. A. I. L. M Bulletin; of practical answers to practical questions. irreg.
• N. A. I. L. M News. m. ISSN 0027-5875

**National Association of Insurance Brokers, Inc.**
111 John St., Suite 2700, New York, NY 10038.
• Friday Flash. w. ISSN 0016-1233

**National Association of Insurance Commissioners**
633 W. Wisconsin Ave., Suite 1015, Milwaukee, WI 53203.
• N A I C Malpractice Claims. q.
• National Association of Insurance Commissioners. Proceedings. s-a.

**National Association of Intercollegiate Athletics**
1205 Baltimore St., Kansas City, MO 64105.
• N A I A Handbook. biennial. ISSN 0077-3336
• N A I A News. q.
• N A I A Official Record Book. a. ISSN 0077-3344

**National Association of Interdisciplinary Ethnic Studies**
• National Association of Interdisciplinary Ethnic Studies. Newsletter. (pub. by University of Wisconsin-La Crosse. Institute for Minority Studies)

**National Association of Investment Clubs**
1515 E. Eleven Mile Rd., Royal Oak, MI 48067.
• Better Investing. m. ISSN 0006-016X

**National Association of Jazz Educators**
Box 724, Manhattan, KS 66502.
• N A J E Educator. 4 per yr. ISSN 0047-8741

**National Association of Jewish Center Workers**
15 E. 26 St, New York, NY 10010.
• National Association of Jewish Center Workers. Conference Papers. a. ISSN 0077-3352

**National Association of Jewish Homes for the Aged**
2525 Centerville Rd., Dallas, TX 75228.
• National Association of Jewish Homes for the Aged. Progress Report. q.

**National Association of Laboratory Schools**
University of Northern Colorado, Bishop-Lehr, Greeley, CO 80631.
• National Association of Laboratory Schools. Journal. q.

**National Association of Language Laboratory Directors**
Middlebury College, Sunderland Hall, Middlebury, VT 05753.
• N A L L D Journal. q. ISSN 0027-5905

**National Association of Letter Carriers (A.F.L.-C.I.O.)**
100 Indiana Ave., N.W., Washington, DC 20001.
• Postal Record. m. ISSN 0032-5376

**National Association of Letter Carriers. N Y L C Branch 36**
261 W. 43rd St., New York, NY 10036.
• New York Letter Carriers' Outlook. m. ISSN 0028-7342

**National Association of Life Underwriters**
1922 F St., N.W., Washington, DC 20006.
• Life Agency Management Program Brochure. a. ISSN 0072-0607 (prep. by its General Agents and Managers Conference)
• Life Association News. m. ISSN 0024-3078

**National Association of Manufacturers**
1776 F St., N.W., Washington, DC 20006.
• Enterprise. m.
• Service for Company Communicators. m.

**National Association of Manufacturers. Fiscal & Economic Policy Department**
1776 F St. N.W., Washington, DC 20006.
• National Association of Manufacturers. Fiscal & Economic Policy Department. Taxation Report. irreg.

**National Association of Metal Finishers**
22 S. Park St., Montclair, NJ 07042.
• Directory of the Leading Firms in the Job Plating and Enameling Industry Who Are Members of the National Association of the Metal Finishers, Inc. irreg. ISSN 0092-6418
• Finishers' Management. m. ISSN 0015-2358
• N A M F Accounting Manual; a uniform accounting system for metal finishers. irreg. ISSN 0077-3360
• N A M F Management Manual. irreg. ISSN 0077-3379

**National Association of Minority C.P.A. Firms**
1625 I St., N.W., Suite 325-A, Washington, DC 20006.
• Pen & Ledger. s-m.

**National Association of Music Merchants Inc.**
35 E. Wacker Drive, Chicago, IL 60601.
• N A M M Music Retailer News. m. ISSN 0027-5913

**National Association of Mutual Insurance Companies**
2511 E. 46th St., Suite H, Indianapolis, IN 46205.
• Mutual Insurance Bulletin. m.

**National Association of Mutual Savings Banks**
200 Park Ave., New York, NY 10017.
• Directory of the Mutual Savings Banks of the United States. a. ISSN 0092-6132
• Savings Bank Journal. m. ISSN 0036-5130

**National Association of Naturopathic Physicians**
c/o Mrs. John W. Noble, 1920 N. Kilpatrick, Portland, OR 97217.
• Natural Health World. m.

**National Association of Organ Teachers**
7938 Bertram Ave., Hammond, IN 46324.
• Keyboard World. (pub. by Keyboard World, Inc.)
• Organ Teacher. bi-m(except July & Aug)

**National Association of Pattern Manufacturers**
21010 Center Ridge Road, Cleveland, OH 44116.
• Industrial Models & Patterns. bi-m. ISSN 0019-8552

**National Association of Pediatric Nurse Associates and Practitioners**
• Pediatric Nursing. (pub. by Anthony J. Jannetti, Inc.)

**National Association of Postal Supervisors**
Box 23456, Washington, DC 20024.
• Postal Supervisor. m. ISSN 0032-5384

**National Association of Postmasters of the United States**
490 l'Enfant Plaza East, S.W., Box 23550, Suite 4200, Washington, DC 20024.
• Postmasters Gazette. m.(bi-m.Nov-Dec) ISSN 0032-552X

**National Association of Power Engineers, Inc.**
176 W. Adams St., Chicago, IL 60603.
• National Engineer. m. ISSN 0027-9218

**National Association of Printing Ink Makers**
• American Inkmaker. (pub. by MacNair- Dorland Co., Inc.)

**National Association of Private Psychiatric Hospitals**
1701 K St. N.W., Suite 1205, Washington, DC 20006.
• National Association of Private Psychiatric Hospitals. Journal. q. ISSN 0027-8629
• National Association of Private Psychiatric Hospitals. News Letter. bi-m. ISSN 0027-8637

**National Association of Professors of Hebrew**
University of Louisville, Social Science Bldg., Louisville, KY 40208.
• Hebrew Studies. a.

**National Association of Public Insurance Adjusters**
1613 Munsey Bldg., Baltimore, MD 21202.
• N A P I A Bulletin. m. ISSN 0027-5964

**National Association of Purchasing Agents**
11 Park Place, New York, NY 10007.
• Journal of Purchasing & Materials Management. q.

**National Association of Radiotelephone Systems**
• Communicator (Washington) (pub. by Smith Bucklin and Associates)

**National Association of Real Estate Investment Trusts**
1101 17th St., N.W., Washington, DC 20036.
• R.E.I.T. Fact Book. a. ISSN 0095-1374
• R E I T Handbook of Member Trusts. a. ISSN 0092-4865

**National Association of Realtors**
155 E. Superior St., Chicago, IL 60611.
• Income-Expense Analysis Apartments, Condominiums, & Cooperatives; statistical compilation and analysis of actual (yr.) income and expenses experienced in apartment building operation. a. (Institute of Real Estate Management)
• Journal of Property Management. bi-m. ISSN 0022-3905 (Institute of Real Estate Management)
• National Roster of Realtors. (pub. by Stamats Publishing Co.)
• Real Estate Today. m.(except June & Dec.) ISSN 0034-0804

**National Association of Regional Councils**
1700 K St. N.W., Washington, DC 20006.
- Directory of Regional Councils. a. ISSN 0070-6205
- National Association of Regional Councils. from a Regional Perspective. 10-12 per yr.
- National Association of Regional Councils. Washington Report. bi-m.

**National Association of Regulatory Utility Commissioners**
1102 Interstate Commerce Commission Bldg., Box 684, Washington, DC 20044.
- National Association of Regulatory Utility Commissioners. Annual Report on Utility and Carrier Regulation. a.
- National Association of Regulatory Utility Commissioners. Bulletin. w. ISSN 0027-8645
- National Association of Regulatory Utility Commissioners. Proceedings. a. ISSN 0077-3387

**National Association of Relay Manufacturers**
Box 1649, Scottsdale, AZ 85252.
- National Relay Conference. Proceedings; Relay Conference Papers. a. ISSN 0077-5401

**National Association of Retail Druggists**
c/o Willard B. Simmons, 1E. Wacker Dr., Chicago, IL 60601.
- N A R D Alamanac. a.
- N. A. R. D. Journal. s-m. ISSN 0027-5972

**National Association of Retired Federal Employees**
1533 New Hampshire Ave., N.W., Washington, NH 20036.
- Retirement Life. m. ISSN 0034-6179

**National Association of School Psychologists**
c/o Dr. John Guidubaldi, 300 Education Bldg., Kent State Univ., Kent, OH 44242.
- School Psychology Digest. q.

**National Association of Schools of Art**
11250 Roger Bacon Dr., No. 5, Reston, VA 22090.
- Careers in Art and a Guide to Art Studies. irreg. (approx 1 per yr.)

**National Association of Schools of Music**
11250 Roger Bacon Dr., No. 5, Reston, VA 22090.
- Monographs on Music in Higher Education. irreg., no. 2, 1974. ISSN 0093-6642
- Music in Higher Education. a. ISSN 0077-2410
- National Association of Schools of Music. Directory. a. ISSN 0547-4175
- National Association of Schools of Music. Proceeding of the Annual Meeting. a. ISSN 0077-3409

**National Association of Schools of Public Affairs and Administration**
1225 Connecticut Ave., N.W., Suite 300, Washington, DC 20036.
- Graduate School Programs in Public Affairs and Public Administration. irreg. ISSN 0094-6648

**National Association of Science Writers Inc.**
Box H, Sea Cliff, NY 11579.
- Clipsheet. q. ISSN 0009-9414

**National Association of Secondary School Principals**
1904 Association Dr., Reston, VA 22091.
- Legal Memorandum. bi-m.
- N.A.S.S.P. Newsletter. m (Sept.-June)
- National Association of Secondary-School Principals. Bulletin. m.(Sept-May) ISSN 0027-8653
- National Association of Secondary School Principals. Curriculum Report. bi-m.
- Practitioner. q. (prep. by its Research Department)
- Student Advocate. m(Sept-May) ISSN 0094-0836

**National Association of Securities Dealers Inc.**
1735 K St. N.W., Washington, DC 20006.
- N A S D News. q.

**National Association of Small Business Investment Companies**
512 Washington Bldg., Washington, DC 20005.
- N A S B I C News. s-m. ISSN 0469-323X

**National Association of Social Workers**
Publication Sales, 1425 H Street, N.W., Washington, DC 20005.
- Encyclopedia of Social Work. irreg., (approx. every 3-5 yrs.); 1977, no. 17, 2 vols. ISSN 0071-0237
- Health and Social Work. q. ISSN 0360-7283

- N A S W News. m (except Aug.) ISSN 0027-6022
- Social Work. 6 per yr. ISSN 0037-8046 (And Box 504, Murray Hill Station, New York, NY 10016)
- Social Work Research and Abstracts. q.

**National Association of State Budget Officers**
- N A S B O Newsletter. (pub. by Council of State Governments)

**National Association of State Universities and Land-Grant Colleges**
Suite 710, One Dupont Circle, N.W., Washington, DC 20036.
- F Y I. (For Your Information) m. ISSN 0046-3019 (prep. by its Office of Research and Information)
- National Association of State Universities and Land-Grant Colleges. Appropriations of State Tax Funds for Higher Education. a. ISSN 0077-3425
- National Association of State Universities and Land-Grant Colleges. Proceedings. a. ISSN 0077-3433

**National Association of Student Personnel Administrators**
c/o Channing M. Briggs, NASPA Central Office, Portland State Univ., Box 751, Portland, OR 97207.
- N A S P A Journal. q. ISSN 0027-6014

**National Association of Suggestion Systems**
435 N. Michigan, Chicago, IL 60611.
- National Association of Suggestion Systems. Statistical Report. a. ISSN 0077-3441

**National Association of Teachers' Agencies**
1825 K St. N.W., Washington, DC 20006.
- National Association of Teachers' Agencies. List of the Accredited Members. a. ISSN 0077-345X

**National Association of Teachers of Singing, Inc.**
2930 Sheridan Rd., Chicago, IL 60657.
- N A T S Bulletin. q. ISSN 0027-6073

**National Association of Temple Educators**
358 S. Gramercy Place, Los Angeles, CA 90020.
- N A T E News. q. ISSN 0300-6689

**National Association of the Deaf**
5125 Radnor Road, Indianapolis, IN 46226 (Subscr. to: 814 Thayer Ave., Silver Spring MD 20910)
- Deaf American; the national magazine for all the deaf. m(Sept-June); bi-m(July-Aug.) ISSN 0011-720X

**National Association of the Partners of the Alliance**
*see* Partners of the Americas

**National Association of Tobacco Distributors, Inc.**
58 E. 79 St., New York, NY 10021.
- Coordinator. a. ISSN 0077-3468

**National Association of Trade and Technical Schools**
2021 L St. N.W., Washington, DC 20036.
- N A T T S News. m. ISSN 0027-6081

**National Association of Trailer Owners, Inc.**
1323 Main St., Box 1418, Sarasota, FL 33578.
- Mobile Living. bi-m. ISSN 0026-7198

**National Association of Training Schools and Juvenile Agencies**
5256 N. Central Ave., Indianapolis, IN 46220.
- National Association of Training Schools and Juvenile Agencies. Proceedings. a. ISSN 0077-3476

**National Association of Underwater Instructors**
22809 Barton Rd., Colton, CA 92324.
- N A U I News. m.

**National Association of Watch and Clock Collectors**
Box 33, Columbia, PA 17512.
- National Association of Watch and Clock Collectors. Bulletin. 6 per yr. ISSN 0027-8688

**National Association of Wholesaler-Distributors**
1725 K St., NW, Washington, DC 20006.
- Channels (Washington) m.

**National Association of Women Artists**
156 Fifth Ave., New York, NY 10010.
- National Association of Women Artists. Annual Exhibition Catalog. a

**National Association of Women Lawyers**
American Bar Center, 1155 E. 60th St., Chicago, IL 60637.
- Women Lawyers Journal. q. ISSN 0043-7468

**National Association of Womens & Childrens Apparel Salesmen**
1819 Peachtree Rd. N.E., Suite 515, Atlanta, GA 30309.
- N A W C A S Guild News. fortn.

**National Association to Keep and Bear Arms Inc.**
Box 3688, Redding, CA 96001.
- Armed Citizen News. m. ISSN 0044-8931

**National Asthma Center**
1999 Julian St., Denver, CO 80204.
- National Asthma Center News. q.

**National Astrological Society**
127 Madison Ave, New York, NY 10016.
- N A S O Journal. 1-3 per yr.

**National Athletic Trainers Association**
3315 South St., Lafayette, IN 47904.
- Athletic Training. q.

**National Auctioneers Association**
135 Lakewood Drive, Lincoln, NE 68510.
- Auctioneer. m. ISSN 0004-7465

**National Audio-Visual Association, Inc.**
3150 Spring Street, Fairfax, VA 22030.
- Audio-Visual Equipment Directory. a. ISSN 0571-8759
- N A V A Membership Directory. a.
- N A V A News. fortn. ISSN 0027-609X

**National Audiovisual Center**
*see* U.S. National Audiovisual Center

**National Audubon Society**
950 Third Ave., New York, NY 10022.
- American Birds; devoted to reporting the distribution, migration and abundance of North American birds. bi-m. ISSN 0004-7686
- Audubon Leader. s-m. ISSN 0045-0014
- Audubon Magazine. bi-m. ISSN 0004-7694
- National Audubon Society. Nature Center News. q.
- New York City Audubon Newsletter. q.

**National Audubon Society. Nature Center Planning Division**
1130 Fifth Ave., New York, NY 10028.
- Directory of Nature Centers and Related Environmental Education Facilities. irreg., 1971, 3rd ed. ISSN 0070-5497

**National Auto Auction Association**
135 Lakewood Dr., Lincoln, NE 68510.
- Auto Auction. irreg., latest edt. 1974. ISSN 0067-2394

**National Automobile Association**
Box 29037, Atlanta, GA 30329.
- N A A Where to Stay Book. irreg. ISSN 0099-0205

**National Automobile Club**
65 Battery St., San Francisco, CA 94111.
- National Motorist. bi-m.

**National Automobile Dealers Association**
2000 K St., N.W., Washington, DC 20006.
- Automotive Executive.
- Cars and Trucks; the management magazine of the automotive retailing industry. m. ISSN 0027-5778
- N.A.D.A. Recreation Vehicle Appraisal Guide. 3 per yr. ISSN 0092-4601 (Recreational Vehicle Dealers of America)

**National Automobile Dealers Association. Appraisal Guides**
Box 1407, Covina, CA 91722.
- N.A.D.A. Boat Appraisal Guide. s-a.
- N.A.D.A. Mobile Home Appraisal Guide. s-a. ISSN 0095-6538
- N.A.D.A. Motorcycles Appraisal Guide. 3 per yr.
- N.A.D.A. Official Car and Truck Appraisal Guide. fortn.
- N. A. D. A. Official Used Car Guide. m. ISSN 0027-5794

**National Automotive Radiator Service Association**
319 Courtland St., Box 567, Lansdale, PA 19446.
- Automotive Cooling Journal. m. ISSN 0005-1497

**National Baseball Congress**
Box 1420, Wichita, KS 67201.
- National Baseball Congress. Official Baseball Annual. a. ISSN 0077-3549

**National Beta Club**
Box 730, Spartanburg, SC 29304.
- College Facts Chart. a. ISSN 0069-5688
- National Beta Club Journal. s-m.

**National Bible Knowledge Association**
1501 Farragut St. N.W., Washington, DC 20011.
- Capital Voice. m. ISSN 0008-5898

**National Bilingual Education Association**
9332 Vista Bonita, Cypress, CA 90630.
- Journal of Comparative Cultures. q.

**National Black Gazette**
Suite 1000, 1100 17th St. N.W., Washington, DC 20036.
- National Black Gazette. q.

**National Blue Books, Inc.**
20929-3 Roscoe Blvd., Canoga Park, CA 91304.
- National Metalworking Blue Book. irreg. ISSN 0363-1737

**National Bluegrass Association**
Rte 3, Box 364, Claremore, OK 74017.
- National Bluegrass News. m. ISSN 0099-0035

**National Board of Medical Examiners**
3930 Chestnut St., Philadelphia, PA 19104.
- National Board Examiner. 8 per yr (Oct.-May) ISSN 0027-8785

**National Board of Review of Motion Pictures, Inc.**
210 East 68th St., New York, NY 10021.
- Films in Review. m. ISSN 0015-1688

**National Book Critics Circle Inc.**
Box 1409, Federal Station, Worcester, MA 01601.
- National Book Critics Circle Journal. q.

**National Braille Association**
85 Godwin Ave., Midland, NJ 07432.
- National Braille Association. Bulletin. 4 per yr. ISSN 0550-5666
- National Braille Association. National Conference. Proceedings. biennial; 14th National Conference, 1977.

**National Braille Press Inc.**
88 St. Stephen St., Boston, MA 02115.
- Our Special; magazine devoted to matters of interest to blind women. m. ISSN 0030-6959

**National Bureau of Economic Research**
261 Madison Ave., New York, NY 10016.
- Annals of Economic and Social Measurement; journal of computers, information retrieval, and research methodology. q. ISSN 0044-832X
- Conference on Research in Income and Wealth. irreg., no. 41, 1976. ISSN 0069-8652
- Explorations in Economic Research; occasional papers of the National Bureau of Economic Research. q. ISSN 0094-0852
- National Bureau of Economic Research. Annual Report. a. ISSN 0077-3611
- National Bureau of Economic Research. Fiscal Studies. irreg., 1971, no. 14. ISSN 0071-5484
- National Bureau of Economic Research. General Series. irreg., no. 101, 1974. ISSN 0077-3638 (Since 1964 Dist. by: Columbia University Press, 136 South Broadway, Irvington-on-Hudson, N.Y. 10533)
- National Bureau of Economic Research, Urban and Regional Studies. irreg., no. 4, 1976.
- Studies in Business Cycles. irreg., no. 23, 1974. ISSN 0081-7643 (Since 1965 Dist. by: Columbia University Press, 136 South Broadway, Irvington-on-Hudson, N.Y. 10533)
- Studies in Capital Formation and Financing. irreg., 1973, no. 13. ISSN 0081-766X
- Studies in Consumer Instalment Financing. irreg., 1967, no. 13. ISSN 0081-7791
- Studies in Corporate Bond Financing. irreg., 1967, no. 4. ISSN 0081-7805
- Studies in International Economic Relations. irreg., no. 8, 1974. ISSN 0081-8062 (Since 1968 Dist. by: Columbia University Press, 136 South Broadway, Irvington-on-Hudson, N.Y. 10533)
- Universities-National Bureau Conference Series. irreg., no. 28, 1976. ISSN 0083-3940

**National Bureau of Standards**
see U.S. National Bureau of Standards

**National Burglar & Fire Alarm Association**
- N B F A A Signal. (pub. by Smith Bucklin and Associates)

**National Business Education Association**
1906 Association Drive, Reston, VA 22091.
- Business Education Forum. m.(Oct-May) ISSN 0007-6678
- National Business Education Yearbook. a. ISSN 0547-4728

**National Business Forms Association**
433 E. Monroe Ave., Alexandria, VA 22301.
- Form; the voice of the independent business forms distributor. m.

**National Button Society**
c/o Jeanne H. Talbert, Secy., Box 39, Eastwood, KY 40018.
- National Button Bulletin; devoted to the promotion of the hobby of button collecting. bi-m. ISSN 0027-884X

**National Cable Television Institute**
P.O. Box 1475, Englewood, CO 80110.
- Cable Tech. bi-m. ISSN 0090-4376

**National Cancer Conference**
219 E. 42 St., New York, NY 10017.
- National Cancer Conference. Proceedings; addresses and panel discussions sponsored by the American Cancer Society and the National Cancer Institute. irreg. ISSN 0077-3670

**National Cancer Institute**
see U.S. National Cancer Institute

**National Candy Wholesalers Association, Inc.**
1430 K St. N.W., Washington, DC 20005.
- National Candy Wholesaler; the magazine for candy and tobacco distributors. m. ISSN 0027-8882

**National Canners Association**
1133 20th St. N.W., 113 20 St. N.W., Washington, DC 20036.
- Canned Food Pack Statistics. a. ISSN 0069-018X

**National Capital Planning Commission**
see U. S. National Capital Planning Commission

**National Cartographic Information Center**
see U. S. National Cartographic Information Center

**National Catholic Cemetery Conference**
710 N. River Rd., Des Plaines, IL 60016.
- Catholic Cemetery. m.

**National Catholic Educational Association**
One Dupont Circle, Suite 350, Washington, DC 20036.
- Catholic Schools in the United States. a. ISSN 0091-9527 (prep. by its Research Department)
- National Catholic Educational Association. Calendar of Meetings of National and Regional Educational Associations. irreg. ISSN 0547-485X
- National Catholic Educational Association. Momentum. 4 per yr. ISSN 0026-914X

**National Catholic Educational Association. Special Education Department**
4472 Lindell Blvd., St. Louis, MO 63108.
- Special Education Newsletter. 3 per yr. ISSN 0049-1837

**National Catholic News Service**
1312 Massachusetts Ave. N.W., Washington, DC 20005.
- Origins, N C Documentary Service. 48 per yr. ISSN 0093-609X

**National Catholic Reporter Publishing Co., Inc.**
115 E. Armour Blvd., Box 281, Kansas City, MO 64141.
- Celebration: a Creative Worship Service. m. ISSN 0094-2421
- National Catholic Reporter. w. ISSN 0027-8939
- Successful Marriage Newsletter. 10 per yr.

**National Catholic Rural Life Conference**
3801 Grand Ave., Des Moines, IA 50312.
- Catholic Rural Life. m. ISSN 0008-8331

**National Catholic Women's Union**
3835 Westminster Pl., St. Louis, MO 63108.
- Catholic Woman's Journal. (pub. by Catholic Central Union of America)
- National Catholic Women's Union. Proceedings. a.

**National Caucus of Labor Committees**
- Campaigner. (pub. by Campaigner Publications, Inc.)

**National Center for Atmospheric Research**
Boulder, CO 80302.
- Atmospheric Technology. s-a. ISSN 0091-2026 (University Corporation for Atmospheric Research)

**National Center for Audio Tapes**
University of Colorado, Stadium Bldg. 348, Boulder, CO 80302.
- National Center for Audio Tapes. Catalog. triennial. ISSN 0077-3719

**National Center for Community Action**
1711 Connecticut Ave. N.W., Washington, DC 20009.
- National Center Reporter. m.

**National Center for Education Communications**
see U. S. National Center for Education Communications

**National Center for Education Statistics**
see U.S. National Center for Education Statistics

**National Center for Educational Brokering**
405 Oak St., Syracuse, NY 13203.
- National Center for Educational Brokering. Bulletin. m.

**National Center for Health Statistics**
see U.S. National Center for Health Statistics

**National Center for Law-Focused Education**
- Law in American Society. (pub. by Law in American Society Foundation)

**National Center for Resource Recovery, Inc.**
1211 Connecticut Ave., N.W., Washington, DC 20036.
- N C R R Bulletin. q.
- N C R R Update. m.

**National Center for Social Statistics**
see U. S. National Center for Social Statistics

**National Center for State Courts**
1660 Lincoln St., Suite 200, Denver, CO 80264.
- National Center for State Courts. Publications. irreg.
- National Center for State Courts. Report. m.
- State Court Journal. q.
- Survey of Judicial Salaries in State Court Systems. q.

**National Center for the Study of Collective Bargaining in Higher Education**
- Bibliography of Higher Education Collective Bargaining Involving Other Than Faculty Personnel. (pub. by City University of New York. Bernard M. Baruch College)
- National Center for the Study of Collective Bargaining in Higher Education. Annual Conference Proceedings. (pub. by City University of New York. Bernard M. Baruch College)
- National Center for the Study of Collective Bargaining in Higher Education. Newsletter. (pub. by City University of New York. Bernard M. Baruch College)

**National Center for Voluntary Action**
1785 Massachusetts Ave., N.W., Washington, DC 20036.
- Voluntary Action Leadership. bi-m.

**National Center on Educational Media and Materials for the Handicapped**
Ohio State University, Columbus, OH 43210.
- Apropos. irreg. (2-3 per yr)

**National Cheerleaders Association**
Box 30674, Dallas, TX 75230.
- Megaphone (Dallas) 4 per yr(during school year) ISSN 0025-8695

**National Child Labor Committee**
145 E. 32nd St., New York, NY 10016.
- New Generation. q. ISSN 0028-5102 (Co-Sponsor: National Committee on Employment of Youth)

**National Christian Association**
850 W. Madison St., Chicago, IL 60607.
- Christian Cynosure. q. ISSN 0009-5311

**National Christian News**
Box 1739, Ocala, FL 32670.
- National Christian News. m. ISSN 0027-8971

**National Christmas Tree Association**
611 East Wells St., Milwaukee, WI 53202.
- American Christmas Tree Journal. q. ISSN 0002-7901

**National Civic League, Inc.**
Box 248, Arlington, VA 22210.
- Civic Forum. q. ISSN 0009-7780

**National Civil Service League**
917 15th St., N.W., Washington, DC 20005.
- Good Government. q. ISSN 0017-2065
- N C S L Exchange. m. (prep. by its Center for Public Personnel Management)
- National Civil Service League. Annual Report. a. ISSN 0077-3735

**National Classification Management Society**
P.O. Box 7453, Alexandria, VA 22307.
- Classification Management. a. ISSN 0009-8434

**National Clearinghouse for Alcohol Information**
*see* U. S. National Clearinghouse for Alcohol Information

**National Clearinghouse for Drug Abuse Information**
*see* U. S. National Clearinghouse for Drug Abuse Information

**National Clearinghouse for Legal Services, Inc.**
500 N. Michigan Ave., Suite 2220, Chicago, IL 60611.
- Clearinghouse Review. m. ISSN 0009-868X

**National Clearinghouse for Poison Control Centers**
*see* U. S. National Clearinghouse for Poison Control Centers

**National Clearinghouse for Smoking and Health**
*see* U. S. National Clearinghouse for Smoking and Health

**National Clearinghouse on Offender Employment Restrictions**
1705 DeSales St., Washington, DC 20036.
- Offender Employment Review. irreg. ISSN 0094-6699

**National Climatic Center**
*see* U.S. National Climatic Center

**National Coal Association**
Coal Bldg., 1130 17 St. N.W., Washington, DC 20036.
- Coal Data. a.
- Coal Facts. biennial.
- Coal Traffic Annual. a. ISSN 0069-4916
- International Coal. a.
- Steam- Electric Fuels. a.

**National Coffee Association of U.S.A. Inc.**
120 Wall St., New York, NY 10005.
- National Coffee Association of U.S.A., Inc. Newsletter. w.

**National College of Criminal Defense Lawyers and Public Defenders**
c/o College of Law, University of Houston, TX 77004.
- Criminal Defense. bi-m. ISSN 0093-8610
- National Journal of Criminal Defense. s-a. ISSN 0098-9533

**National College of the State Judiciary**
- Judges Journal. (pub. by American Bar Association)
- National College of the State Judiciary. (pub. by University of Nevada)

**National College Physical Education Association for Men**
108 Cooke Hall, University of Minnesota, Minneapolis, MN 55455.
- N C P E A M Proceedings. a.

**National Collegiate Athletic Association**
Box 1906, U.S. Highway 50 and Nall Ave., Shawnee Mission, KS 66222.
- N.C.A.A. Football Records. a.
- N C A A News. m. ISSN 0027-6170
- National Collegiate Athletic Association. Annual Reports. a. ISSN 0077-3794
- National Collegiate Athletic Association. Convention Proceedings. a. ISSN 0077-3808
- National Collegiate Athletic Association. Manual. a. ISSN 0077-3816
- National Collegiate Athletic Association. Proceedings of the Special Convention. irreg. ISSN 0094-4459
- National Collegiate Championships. a. ISSN 0077-3824
- Official National Collegiate Athletic Association Basketball Rules. (pub. by College Athletics Publishing Service)
- Official National Collegiate Athletic Association Football Rules Interpretations. (pub. by N C A A Publishing Service)

**National Collegiate Players**
Northern Illinois Univ., University Theatre, Dekalb, IL 60115.
- Players Magazine; the magazine of American theatre. bi-m.(Oct-Aug) ISSN 0032-1486

**National Commercial Finance Conference Inc.**
One Penn Plaza, New York, NY 10001.
- Commercial Financing. bi-m. ISSN 0010-2962

**National Commission on Human Life, Reproduction and Rhythm**
Box 508 Oak Park, IL 60303.
- Child and Family; a quarterly survey of family centered child care. q. ISSN 0009-3882

**National Commission on Resources for Youth**
36 West 44 St., New York, NY 10036.
- Resources for Youth. q.

**National Committee Against Discrimination, Inc.**
1425 H. Street, N.W., Suite 410, Washington, DC 20005.
- Trends in Housing. bi-m. ISSN 0300-6026

**National Committee Against Repressive Legislation**
1250 Wilshire Blvd., Suite 501, Los Angeles, CA 90017.
- Abolition News. 2-3 per yr. ISSN 0001-3234

**National Committee for Labor Israel Inc.**
33 East 67th St, New York, NY 10021.
- Histadrut Foto News. bi-m.

**National Committee for Monetary Reform**
1524 Hillary St., New Orleans, LA 70118.
- Gold Newsletter. m.
- International Harry Schultz Letter. m.

**National Committee for Prevention of Child Abuse**
111 Wacker Drive East, Chicago, IL 60601.
- Caring. q.

**National Committee on Indian Work**
- N C I W Newsletter. (pub. by Executive Council of the Episcopal Church)

**National Committee on the Emeriti Inc.**
Box 24451, Los Angeles, CA 90024.
- Emeriti for Employment.

**National Committee on U.S.-China Relations**
777 U. N. Plaza, New York, NY 10017.
- National Committee on U. S. China Relations. Highlights of Notes. q.

**National Committee on Uniform Traffic Laws and Ordinances**
1776 Massachusetts Avenue, N.W., Washington, DC 20036.
- Traffic Laws Commentary. irreg., latest issue 1975. ISSN 0082-5859

**National Computer Program Abstract Service**
P.O. 3783, Washington, DC 20007.
- Computer Program Index Newsletter. q.

**National Computer Systems**
1201 16th St., N. W., Washington, DC 20036.
- Association for Educational Data Systems. Handbook and Directory. irreg., latest issue 1973. ISSN 0092-6280

**National Concrete Masonry Association**
Box 135, McLean, VA 22101.
- C/M Newsletter. m.

**National Condominium Owners Association (N C O A)**
4120 Atlantic Ave., Long Beach, CA 90807.
- Condominium Living. bi-m.

**National Conference of Bankruptcy Judges**
Box 1109, Bangor, ME 04401.
- American Bankruptcy Law Journal. q. ISSN 0027-9048

**National Conference of Bar Examiners**
Suite 1025, 333 N. Michigan Ave., Chicago, IL 60601.
- Bar Examiner. 3-6 per yr. ISSN 0005-5824

**National Conference of Black Political Scientists**
- Journal on Political Repression. (pub. by Journal on Political Repression, Inc.)

**National Conference of Catholic Charities**
1346 Connecticut Ave N.W., Washington, DC 20036.
- Charities U S A. m. (except Jul. & Aug.)
- Directory. Diocesan Agencies of Catholic Charities. United States, Puerto Rico and Canada. a. ISSN 0091-1003
- Social Thought. q. ISSN 0099-183X (Co-Sponsor: Catholic University of America, National Catholic School of Social Service)

**National Conference of Commissioners on Uniform State Laws**
645 N. Michigan Ave., Suite 510, Chicago, IL 60611.
- National Conference of Commissioners on Uniform State Laws. Handbook and Proceedings. a.

**National Conference of Editorial Writers**
1725 N St., N.W., Washington, DC 20036.
- Masthead. q. ISSN 0025-5122

**National Conference of Jewish Communal Service**
15 E. 26 St., New York, NY 10010.
- Journal of Jewish Communal Service. q. ISSN 0022-2089

**National Conference of Standards Laboratories**
- National Conference of Standards Laboratories. Proceedings. (pub. by U.S. National Bureau of Standards)
- National Conference of Standards Laboratories Newsletter. (pub. by U.S. National Bureau of Standards)

**National Conference of State Legislatures**
1405 Curtis St., 23rd Floor, Denver, CO 80202.
- State Legislatures. bi-m.

**National Conference of State Social Security Administrators**
P.O. Box 2543, Madison, WI 53701.
- National Conference of State Social Security Administrators. Proceedings. a.

**National Conference of Synagogue Youth**
116 East 27th St., New York, NY 10016.
- Keeping Posted with N C S Y. m. ISSN 0022-9644 (Union of Orthodox Jewish Congregations of America)

**National Conference on Fluid Power**
10 West 33rd St., Chicago, IL 60616.
- National Conference on Fluid Power. Proceedings. a. (Illinois Institute of Technology)

**National Conference on Social Welfare**
22 W. Gay St., Columbus, OH 43215.
- National Conference on Social Welfare. Conference Bulletin. q. ISSN 0027-9056
- Social Welfare Forum. Papers. a. ISSN 0081-0525

**National Conference on Soviet Jewry**
11 W. 42 St., Rm. 1075, New York, NY 10036.
- National Conference on Soviet Jewry. News Bulletin. w.

**National Conference on Weights and Measures**
- National Conference on Weights and Measures. Report. (pub. by U.S. National Bureau of Standards)

**National Congress of American Indians**
1346 Connecticut Ave. N.W., Suite 312, Washington, DC 20036.
- National Congress of American Indians. Bulletin. m. ISSN 0047-8784
- Sentinel (Washington, D.C.) m.

**National Congress of Parents and Teachers**
700 N. Rush St., Chicago, IL 60611.
- National Congress of Parents and Teachers. Convention Digest. a.
- P.T.A. Handbook. irreg. ISSN 0361-266X

**National Consumer Finance Association**
1000 16th St., N.W., Washington, DC 20036.
- Credit. m.
- Finance Facts; a monthly publication on consumer financial behavior. m. ISSN 0015-1963 (prep. by its Educational Services Division)
- Human Relations - Tips & Trends. q. ISSN 0018-7275
- N. C. F. A. Office Manual. a. ISSN 0094-1522
- Selected and Annotated Bibliography of Reference Materials in Consumer Credit. irreg. ISSN 0077-4014

**National Consumers League**
1785 Massachusetts Ave. N.W., Washington, DC 20036.
- National Consumers League Bulletin. bi-m.

**National Contest**
Box 2547, Laguna Hills, CA 92653.
- National Contest. m.

**National Contract Management Association**
675 East Wardlow Rd., Long Beach, CA 90807.
- N C M A Newsletter. m. ISSN 0027-6332
- National Contract Management. Journal. s-a. ISSN 0027-9064

**National Coordinating Council on Drug Education**
1601 Connecticut Ave., N.W., Suite 301, Washington, DC 20009.
- National Drug Reporter. m. ISSN 0091-2395

**National Cottonseed Products Association**
P.O. Box 12023, Memphis, TN 38112.
- National Cottonseed Products Association. Trading Rules. a. ISSN 0077-4022

**National Council for Community Services to International Visitors**
Meridian House International, 1630 Crescent Place N. W., Washington, DC 20009.
- C O S E R V Newsletter. q. ISSN 0547-5619

**National Council for Critical Analysis**
Jersey City State College, 2039 Kennedy Memorial Blvd., Jersey City, NJ 07305.
- Journal of Critical Analysis. q. ISSN 0022-0213

**National Council for Geographic Education**
115 N. Marion St., Oak Park, IL 60301
- Journal of Geography. 7 per yr. ISSN 0022-1341 (Subscr. to: c/o Dr. Ronald E. Nelson, Ed., Western Illinois University, Dept. of Geography, Macomb, IL 61455)
- National Council for Geographic Education. Do It This Way. irreg., no. 10, 1974. ISSN 0469-9130
- National Council for Geographic Education. Geographic Education Series. irreg., no. 7, 1967.
- National Council for Geographic Education. Instructional Activities Series. irreg.
- National Council for Geographic Education. Miscellaneous Papers. irreg., latest issue no. 25.
- National Council for Geographic Education. Pacesetter Series. a. (Order from: Geopub Books, Tualatin, OR 97062)
- National Council for Geographic Education. Special Publications. irreg., no. 16, 1970. ISSN 0547-5643
- National Council for Geographic Education. Topics in Geography. irreg., no. 5, 1970.
- Perspective. irreg. during school year.

**National Council for Homemaker Home Health Aide Services, Inc.**
67 Irving Place, New York, NY 10003.
- National Council for Homemaker-Home Health Aide Services. News. q.

**National Council for Jewish Education**
114 Fifth Ave., New York, NY 10011.
- Jewish Education. q. ISSN 0021-6429
- Sheviley Hahinuch. q. ISSN 0037-3656

**National Council for the Social Studies**
1515 Wilson Blvd., Arlington, VA 22209.
- National Council for the Social Studies. Bulletins. irreg. ISSN 0077-4049
- National Council for the Social Studies. Crisis Series. irreg. ISSN 0085-3704
- National Council for the Social Studies. Curriculum Series. irreg. ISSN 0085-3690
- National Council for the Social Studies. How to do It Series. irreg. ISSN 0085-3712
- National Council for the Social Studies. Social Studies Readings. irreg. ISSN 0077-4057
- National Council for the Social Studies. Yearbook. a. ISSN 0085-3720
- Social Education. 7 per yr. ISSN 0037-7724 (Subscr.: c/o Daniel Roselle, Ed., 1201 16th St. N.W., Washington, DC 20036)
- Social Studies Professional. q. ISSN 0586-6235

**National Council for the Traditional Arts, Inc.**
1346 Connecticut Ave. N. W., Washington, DC 20036.
- Calendar of Folk Festivals and Related Events. a. (Co-Sponsor: Library of Congress, Archive of Folk Song)
- Tradition. q.

**National Council for U.S.-China Trade**
Suite 350, 1050 17 St. N.W., Washington, DC 20036.
- China Business Review. bi-m.

**National Council for Universal & Unconditional Amnesty**
339 Lafayette St., New York, NY 10012.
- Amnesty Update; the national amnesty newsletter. bi-m.

**National Council of Administrative Women in Education**
1815 Fort Myer Dr. N., Arlington, VA 22209.
- N C A W E News. q. ISSN 0027-6227

**National Council of Architectural Registration Boards**
1735 New York Ave. N.W., Suite 700, Washington, DC 20006.
- N C A R B Bulletin. s-a. ISSN 0027-6197

**National Council of Associations for Policy Sciences**
- Contents of Selected Periodicals/Policy Sciences. (pub. by Center for Policy Analysis)
- International Urban Issues/Contents of Selected Periodicals. (pub. by Center for Policy Analysis)

**National Council of Churches. Division of Education and Ministry**
- National Council of Churches. Division of Education and Ministry. Audio-Visual Resource Guide. (pub. by Friendship Press)

**National Council of College Publications Advisers**
TMU-300, Indiana State Univ., Terre Haute, IN 47809.
- College Press Review. q. ISSN 0010-1117
- Directory of the College Student Press in America. (pub. by Oxbridge Communications, Inc.)
- N C C P A Newsletter. bi-m. ISSN 0027-6251

**National Council of Engineering Examiners**
Box 5000, Seneca, SC 29678.
- N C E E Registration Bulletin. q.
- National Council of Engineering Examiners. Proceedings. a. ISSN 0077-4081

**National Council of Farmer Cooperatives**
1129 20th St. N.W., Washington, DC 20036.
- Directory of Farmer Cooperatives. irreg.

**National Council of Jewish Women. Tulsa Section**
2205 E. 51st St., Tulsa, OK 74105.
- Tulsa Jewish Review. m.

**National Council of Juvenile Court Judges**
P.O. Box 8978, University of Nevada, Reno, NV 89507.
- Juvenile Court Digest. m. ISSN 0085-2430
- Juvenile Justice. q. ISSN 0093-7231

**National Council of La Raza**
1725 I St. N.W., Suite 210, Washington, DC 20006.
- Agenda. q.

**National Council of Negro Women, Inc.**
1346 Connecticut Ave. N.W., Washington, DC 20036.
- Black Women's Voice. q.

**National Council of Physical Distribution Management**
222 W. Adams St., Chicago, IL 60606.
- National Council of Physical Distribution Management. Annual Meeting. Proceedings. a.

**National Council of Secondary School Athletic Directors**
- Athletic Director. (pub. by American Alliance for Health, Physical Education and Recreation)

**National Council of Small Business Management Development**
- Journal of Small Business Management. (pub. by West Virginia University. Bureau of Business Research)

**National Council of State Garden Clubs, Inc.**
4401 Magnolia Ave., St. Louis, MO 63110.
- National Gardener. 6 per yr. ISSN 0027-9331

**National Council of Teachers of English**
Ex. Secy., Robert F. Hogan, 1111 Kenyon Rd., Urbana, IL 61801.
- Abstracts of English Studies. 10 per yr.(Sept-June) ISSN 0001-3560
- C S S E D C Newsletter. 4 per yr. (Conference for Secondary School English Department Chairmen)
- Classroom Practices in Teaching English. a. ISSN 0550-5755
- College Composition and Communication. 4 per yr. ISSN 0010-096X (Conference on College Composition and Communication)
- College English. 8 per yr (Oct-May) ISSN 0010-0994
- Council-Grams. 5 per yr.
- English Education. 4 per yr. ISSN 0007-8204 (prep. by its Conference on English Education)
- English Journal. 9 per yr(Sept-May) ISSN 0013-8274
- Language Arts. 8 per yr. (Sept.-Nov. & Jan.-May) ISSN 0360-9170 (prep. by its Elementary Section)
- N C T E Guide to Teaching Materials for English; Grades 7-12. irreg.
- Research in the Teaching of English. 3 per yr. ISSN 0034-527X

**National Council of Teachers of Mathematics**
1906 Association Dr., Reston, VA 22091.
- Arithmetic Teacher. m(Oct-May) ISSN 0004-136X
- Journal for Research in Mathematics Education. 5 per yr. ISSN 0021-8251
- Mathematics Student. 4 per yr.
- Mathematics Teacher. m (Sept.-May) ISSN 0025-5769
- National Council of Teachers of Mathematics. Yearbook. a. ISSN 0077-4103

**National Council of the Churches of Christ in the U.S.A.**
475 Riverside Drive, New York, NY 10027.
- Chronicles. 3 per yr.
- Church World Service Planned Parenthood Program Newsletter. q.
- Film Information. m. ISSN 0015-1297 (prep. by its Communication Commission) (Subscr. to:, Box 500, Manhattanville Sta., N.Y., N.Y. 10027)
- National Council of the Churches of Christ in the United States of America. Church World Service. Annual Report. a. ISSN 0077-4111
- Occasional Bulletin of Missionary Research. 8 per yr. (prep. by its Missionary Research Library) (Co-Sponsor: Union Theological Seminary)

**National Council of the Churches of Christ in the U.S.A. Division of Overseas Ministries**
Rm. 616, 475 Riverside Dr., New York, NY 10027.
- China Notes. q. ISSN 0009-4412 (prep. by its East Asia and the Pacific Committee, China Program)
- National Council of the Churches of Christ in the United States of America. Division of Overseas Ministries. Overseas Ministries. triennial. ISSN 0077-412X

**National Council of the Knights of Peter Claver**
1821 Orleans Ave., New Orleans, LA 70116.
- Claverite. bi-m. ISSN 0009-8531

**National Council of the Paper Industry for Air and Stream Improvement, Inc.**
260 Madison Ave., New York, NY 10016.
- Atmospheric Quality Improvement Technical Bulletin. irreg. ISSN 0360-8778
- National Council of the Paper Industry for Air and Stream Improvement. Report to Members. a. ISSN 0077-4146
- Stream Improvement Technical Bulletin. irreg. ISSN 0360-8751

**National Council of United States Magistrates**
c/o Ralph J. Geffen, Ed., U.S. Courthouse, Los Angeles, CA 90012.
- National Council of United States Magistrates. Bulletin. q.

**National Council of Y M C As**
291 Broadway, New York, NY 10007.
- Y M C A Yearbook and Official Roster. a. ISSN 0084-4292

**National Council of Young Israel**
3 West 16th St, New York, NY 10011.
- Young Israel Viewpoint. m (except Jul. & Aug.) ISSN 0044-0809

**National Council on Alcoholism**
730 Fifth Ave., New York, NY 10019.
- Labor-Management Alcoholism Journal. bi-m.
- N C A Bulletin. q.
- National Council on Alcoholism. Friday Letter. m (8 per yr.) ISSN 0047-8806

**National Council on Black Aging, Inc.**
Box 8522, Durham, NC 27707.
- Black Aging. bi-m.

**National Council on Crime and Delinquency**
Continental Plaza, 411 Hackensack Ave., Hackensack, NJ 07601.
- Crime & Delinquency. q. ISSN 0011-1287
- Criminal Justice Abstracts. q.
- Criminal Justice Newsletter. fortn. ISSN 0045-9038

**National Council on Crime and Delinquency. Research Center**
Brinley Terrace, 609 2nd St., Davis, CA 95616.
- Journal of Research in Crime and Delinquency. s-a. ISSN 0022-4278

**National Council on Drug Abuse**
8 South Michigan Ave., Suite 310, Chicago, IL 60603.
- N C D A Drug/Health Alert! m.

**National Council on Educational Materials**
- Index to Free Periodicals. (pub. by Pierian Press)

**National Council on Family Relations**
1219 University Ave. S.E., Minneapolis, MN 55414.
- Family Coordinator; journal of education, counseling and services. q. ISSN 0014-7214
- Journal of Family History; studies in family, kinship and demography. q. ISSN 0363-1990
- Journal of Marriage and the Family. q. ISSN 0022-2445
- National Council on Family Relations. Annual Meeting Proceedings. a. ISSN 0077-4162
- National Council on Family Relations Newsletter. q.

**National Council on Measurement in Education**
c/o Irvin J. Lehmann, Office of Evaluation Services, Michigan State University, East Lansing, MI 48824.
- Journal of Educational Measurement. q. ISSN 0022-0655
- Measurement in Education. q. ISSN 0047-6323
- National Council on Measurement in Education. Measurement News. q. ISSN 0025-6315

**National Council on Radiation Protection and Measurements**
7910 Woodmont Ave., Suite 1016, Washington, DC 20014.
- N C R P News. 3 per yr.
- N C R P Report. irreg.; no. 53, 1977. ISSN 0083-209X
- N C R P Statements. irreg.

**National Council on the Aging**
1828 L St. N.W., Suite 504, Washington, DC 20036.
- Current Literature on Aging. q. ISSN 0011-3662
- Industrial Gerontology. q. ISSN 0019-8358
- National Council on the Aging. Memo. m.
- Perspective on Aging. bi-m.

**National Cowboy Hall of Fame and Western Heritage Center**
1700 N.E. 63rd St., Oklahoma City, OK 73111.
- Persimmon Hill. q.
- Wild Bunch. q. (Rodeo Historical Society)

**National Credit Office**
1290 Avenue of the Americas, New York, NY 10019.
- Electronic Marketing Directory. a. ISSN 0070-7589

**National Credit Union Administration**
see U.S. National Credit Union Administration

**National Criminal Justice Information and Statistics Service**
see U. S. National Criminal Justice Information and Statistics Service

**National Crushed Stone Association**
1415 Elliot Place N.W., Washington, DC 20007.
- Research Engineering Technical Services Digest. q. ISSN 0048-7295

**National Cutting Horse Association**
P.O. Box 12155, Fort Worth, TX 76116.
- National Cutting Horse Association. Rule Book. a.

**National CYO Federation**
United States Catholic Conference, 1312 Massachusetts Ave., N.W., Washington, DC 20005.
- Emmaus Letter. q.

**National Dairy Council**
6300 N. River Rd., Rosemont, IL 60018.
- Dairy Council Digest; an interpretive review of recent nutrition research. bi-m. ISSN 0011-5568 (prep. by its Nutrition Research Division & Library)
- Food News; for boys and girls. a.
- Nutrition Education Materials. a.
- Nutrition News. q.

**National Decorating Products Association**
9334 Dielman Industrial Dr., St. Louis, MO 63132.
- Decorating Retailer. m. ISSN 0011-7404

**National Defense Transportation Association**
1612 K St., N. W., Washington, DC 20006.
- Defense Transportation Journal; magazine of international defense transportation. bi-m. ISSN 0011-7625

**National Democratic Forum**
1621 Connecticut Ave., N.W., Washington, DC 20009.
- Democratic Forum - Review. bi-m.

**National Dental Association**
5344 Highlight Place, Los Angeles, CA 90016.
- N. D. A. Quarterly. (National Dental Association) q. ISSN 0027-9129

**National Directory Service, Inc.**
252 Ludlow Ave., Cincinnati, OH 45220.
- Summer Employment Directory of the United States. a. ISSN 0081-9352

**National District Attorneys Association**
211 E. Chicago Ave., Chicago, IL 60611.
- Economic Crime Digest. bi-m. (Subscr. to:, 1900 L St. N.W., Suite 607, Washington, DC 20036)
- National District Attorneys Association. Economic Crime Project. Annual Report. a. (Subscr. to:, 1900 L St., N.W., Suite 607, Washington, DC 20036)
- Prosecutor. bi-m. ISSN 0027-6383

**National Earthquake Information Center**
see under U. S. Geological Survey

**National Easter Seal Society for Crippled Children & Adults**
2023W. Ogden Ave., Chicago, IL 60612.
- Easter Seal Communicator. 8 per yr.
- Rehabilitation Literature; for use by professional personnel and students in all disciplines concerned with rehabilitation of the handicapped. m. ISSN 0034-3579

**National Education Association**
1201 16th St. N.W., Washington, DC 20036.
- N E A Advocate. m.
- N E A Reporter. m. ISSN 0027-6405

- National Education Association of the United States. Addresses and Proceedings. a. ISSN 0077-4243 (Order from: N E A Order Dept., Academic Bldg., Saw Mill Rd., West Haven CT 06516)
- National Education Association of the United States. Annual Summative Evaluation Report. a. ISSN 0092-5691
- School Nurse. q. ISSN 0048-945X (prep. by its Department of School Nurses)
- Today's Education. bi-m (Sep.-May) ISSN 0040-8484
- What Research Says to the Teacher Series. irreg. ISSN 0083-9116 (Order from: N E A Order Dept., Academic Bldg., Saw Mill Rd., West Haven, CT 06516)

**National Education Program**
c/o Dr. George S. Benson, Pres., Harding College Campus, 900 E. Center, Searcy, AR 72143.
- National Program Letter. m. ISSN 0027-9943

**National Educational Film Center**
Route 2, Finksburg, MD 21048.
- Media Digest. 4 per yr.

**National Educator**
c/o James H. Townsend, Ed., 1110 S. Pomona Ave., Fullerton, CA 92632.
- National Educator. m.

**National Electrical Contractors Association**
7315 Wisconsin Ave., Washington, DC 20014.
- Electrical Contractor. m. ISSN 0033-5118

**National Electrical Manufacturers Association**
2101 L St. N.W., Washington, DC 20037.
- Electrical Electronics Insulation Conference. Record. biennial. ISSN 0070-9697 (Co-Sponsor: Institute of Electrical and Electronic Engineers)
- N E M A Bulletin. m.

**National Electronic Distributors Association, Inc.**
3525 W. Peterson Ave., Chicago, IL 60659.
- Electronic Merchandising. m.

**National Electronic Injury Surveillance System**
see U.Snational Electronic Injury Surveillance System

**National Electronic Service Dealers Association**
1715 Expo Lane, Indianapolis, IN 46224.
- Service Shop. m.

**National Electronics Conference**
1211 W. 22nd St., Oak Brook, IL 60521.
- National Electronics Conference. Proceedings. a. ISSN 0077-4413
- National Electronics Conference. Record. a. ISSN 0077-4421

**National Emergency Civil Liberties Committee**
25 East 26th St., Suite 916, New York, NY 10010.
- Rights. bi-m. ISSN 0035-5283

**National Employers Directory Service**
2506 Ralph St., Houston, TX 77006.
- Directory of Summer Employment Opportunities. a. ISSN 0419-3652

**National Employment Association**
c/o Ed. Kenneth A. Fisher, 1835 K St., N.W., Suite 910, Washington, DC 20006.
- Placement Age. bi-m.

**National Endowment for the Arts**
see U. S. National Endowment for the Arts

**National Endowment for the Humanities**
see U. S. National Endowment for the Humanities

**National Energy Information Center**
see entry for U.S. Federal Energy Administration

**National Enquirer, Inc.**
600 S.E. Coast Ave., Lantana, FL 33462.
- National Enquirer. w.

**National Entertainment and Campus Activities Association**
Box 11489, Columbia, SC 29211.
- Student Activities Programming. 8 per yr. ISSN 0098-1664

**National Entertainment Conference**
- Activity Programmers Sourcebook. (pub. by Billboard Publications, Inc. Amusement Business Division)

**National Environmental Health Association**
1200 Lincoln St., Suite 704, Denver, CO 80203.
- Journal of Environmental Health. bi-m. ISSN 0022-0892

**National Environmental Research Center**
Cincinnati, OH 45268.
- National Environmental Research Center. Annual Report. a. ISSN 0093-9021

**National Environmental Research Center (Research Triangle Park)**
Research Triangle Park, NC 27711.
- National Environmental Research Center, Research Triangle Park, N. C. Annual Report. a. ISSN 0098-5341

**National Epilepsy League, Inc.**
6 N. Michigan Ave., Chicago, IL 60602.
- Horizon. m. ISSN 0437-8768

**National Exchange Club**
3050 Central Ave., Toledo, OH 43606.
- Exchangite; an educational publication for Exchange Club members. m. ISSN 0014-4487

**National Eye Institute**
see U.S. National Eye Institute

**National Eye Research Foundation**
18 S. Michigan Ave., Chicago, IL 60603.
- Contacto; international contact lens journal. bi-m. ISSN 0045-8317

**National Fantasy Fan Federation. Games Bureau**
- Gamesletter. (pub. by M Press)
- Gamesman. (pub. by M Press)

**National Farm and Power Services, Inc.**
10877 Watson Rd., St. Louis, MD 63127.
- Farm & Power Equipment. m. ISSN 0014-7834

**National Farm-City Council, Inc.**
101 E. Erie St., Chicago, IL 60611.
- Farm City Week Newsletter. fortn. ISSN 0014-7893

**National Farmers Union**
12025 E. 45th Ave., Box 39251, Denver, CO 80239.
- National Farmers Union's Washington Newsletter. w. ISSN 0027-9226

**National Features Syndicate, Inc**
1066 National Press Building, Washington, DC 20045.
- Medicare Report. s-m. ISSN 0025-7672

**National Federation of Abstracting and Indexing Services**
3401 Market St., Philadelphia, PA 19104.
- N F A I S Newsletter. bi-m. ISSN 0090-0893
- National Federation of Abstracting and Indexing Services. Report. irreg. ISSN 0077-4502

**National Federation of Business and Professional Women's Clubs, Inc.**
2012 Massachusetts Ave., N.W., Washington, DC 20036.
- National Business Woman. 11 per yr. ISSN 0027-8831

**National Federation of Catholic Physicians Guild**
850 Elm Grove Road, Elm Grove, WI 53122.
- Linacre Quarterly; a journal of the philosophy and ethics of medical practice. q. ISSN 0024-3639

**National Federation of Independent Business**
San Mateo, CA 94402.
- National Federation of Independent Business. Quarterly Economics Report. q. ISSN 0094-7695

**National Federation of Jewish Men's Clubs Inc.**
9706 Foster Ave., Chicago, IL 60656.
- Torch (Chicago) q. ISSN 0049-416X

**National Federation of Licensed Practical Nurses**
- Nursing Care. (pub. by Duaal Publishing Corp.)

**National Federation of Modern Language Teachers Associations**
c/o Richard S. Thill, Bus. Mgr., Box 688, Omaha, NE 68101.
- Modern Language Journal. bi-m(Sept-April) ISSN 0026-7902

**National Federation of Music Clubs**
310 S. Michigan Ave., Suite 1936, Chicago, IL 60604.
- Junior Keynotes. 4 per yr. ISSN 0022-6629

**National Federation of Press Women, Inc.**
c/o Ed. Lois Lauer Wolfe, 1105 Main St., Box 99, Blue Springs, MO 64015.
- Press Woman. m. ISSN 0032-7824

**National Federation of Republican Women**
310 First St. S.E., Washington, DC 20003.
- Challenge (Washington) m. ISSN 0045-6233

**National Federation of Settlements and Neighborhood Centers**
232 Madison Ave., New York, NY 10016.
- National Federation of Settlements and Neighborhood Centers News & Round Table. bi-m.

**National Federation of Societies for Clinical Social Work**
- Clinical Social Work Journal. (pub. by Human Sciences Press)

**National Federation of State High School Associations**
Federation Place, Box 98, Elgin, IL 60120.
- Baseball Case Book. a.
- Baseball Rules. a.
- Baseball Umpires Manual. a.
- Basketball Case Book. a. ISSN 0525-4663
- Basketball Handbook. biennial.
- Basketball Officials Manual. biennial.
- Basketball Rules. a.
- Basketball Rules - Simplified and Illustrated. a.
- Boys Gymnastics Rules. a.
- Football Case Book. a.
- Football Handbook. a.
- Football Officials Handbook. a.
- Football Rules. a.
- Football Rules - Simplified and Illustrated. a.
- Girls Gymnastics Manual. biennial.
- Girls Gymnastics Rules. a.
- Soccer Rules. a.
- Swimming & Diving Case Book. a.
- Swimming Rules. a.
- Track and Field Rules and Records. a.
- Volleyball Rules. a.
- Wrestling Officials Manual. a.
- Wrestling Rules. a.

**National Federation of State Poetry Societies Inc.**
c/o A. Briley, 1121 Major Ave N.W., Albuquerque, NM 87107.
- Strophes. q.

**National Federation of Temple Brotherhoods**
838 Fifth Ave., New York, NY 10021.
- Brotherhood. q. ISSN 0007-2435

**National Federation of the Blind**
218 Randolph Hotel Bldg., Des Moines, IA 50309.
- Braille Monitor (Inkprint Edition) m. ISSN 0006-8829

**National Fellowship of Brethren Churches**
- Brethren Missionary Herald. (pub. by Brethren Missionary Herald Co.)

**National Fertilizer Development Center**
see under U. S. Tennessee Valley Authority

**National Fertilizer Solutions Association**
1701 W. Detweiller, Peoria, IL 61614.
- Fertilizer Solutions. bi-m. ISSN 0015-0312

**National Field Archery Association**
Rt. 2, Box 514, Redlands, CA 92373.
- Archery; a sportsman's magazine devoted to hunting and field archery. m. ISSN 0003-8253

**National Fire Prevention and Control Administration**
see U.S. National Fire Prevention and Control Administration

**National Fire Protection Association**
470 Atlantic Ave., Boston, MA 02210.
- Fire Command. m. ISSN 0015-2560
- Fire Journal. bi-m. ISSN 0015-2617
- Fire News. 10 per yr. ISSN 0015-2625
- Fire Protection Handbook. quintennial. ISSN 0071-5417
- Fire Protection Reference Directory. a.
- Fire Technology. q. ISSN 0015-2684
- N F P A Technical Committee. Report. s-a. ISSN 0077-4553

- National Fire Protection Association. National Fire Codes. a. ISSN 0077-4545
- National Fire Protection Association. Yearbook and Committee List. a. ISSN 0077-4561

**National Food Distributors Association**
111 E. Wacker Drive, Chicago, IL 60601.
- Food Distributors News. bi-m. ISSN 0015-6353

**National Food Engineering Conference**
c/o Purdue Univ., Lafayette, IN 46207.
- National Food Engineering Conference. Proceedings. a.

**National Football League**
410 Park Ave., New York, NY 10022.
- National Football League. Official Guide. a. ISSN 0091-0821
- National Football League. Record Manual. ISSN 0077-4588

**National Foreign Trade Council**
10 Rockefeller Plaza, New York, NY 10020.
- Breve; weekly digest of European reports. w. ISSN 0520-9404
- National Foreign Trade Council. Middle East Notes. m.
- Noticias; weekly digest of hemisphere reports. w. ISSN 0029-4152
- Pacific Asia Report. bi-w.

**National Foremen's Institute**
24 Rope Ferry Rd., Waterford, CT 06386.
- Construction Foreman's & Supervisor's Letter. s-m. ISSN 0010-678X
- Foreman's Letter. s-m. ISSN 0015-7333
- Security Management-Plant and Property Protection. s-m.
- Supervisor's Bulletin. s-m. ISSN 0039-5889
- Utility Supervision. s-m. ISSN 0042-1596

**National Forest Products Association**
1619 Massachusetts Ave. N.W., Washington, DC 20036.
- Forest Products Industry Fingertip Facts and Figures. m. ISSN 0015-7465

**National Forum for Philosophical Reasoning in the Schools**
c/o College of Education, University of Nebraska at Omaha, Box 688, Omaha, NE 68101.
- National Forum for Philosophical Reasoning in the Schools. Newsletter. q.

**National Foundation for Consumer Credit**
1819 H St. N.W., Washington, DC 20006.
- N F C C Members' Bulletin. q.

**National Foundation for Jewish Culture**
122 E. 42nd St., New York, NY 10017.
- Association of Jewish Studies. Review. q.
- Jewish Cultural News. q.

**National Foundation-March of Dimes**
1275 Mamaroneck Ave., White Plains, NY 10605.
- Birth Defects: Original Article Series. irreg., vol. 11, 1975.
- N F News. 9 per yr.
- Syndrome Identification. (Junior College) irreg. ISSN 0091-1747

**National Foundation on the Arts and the Humanities**
see listings for U. S. National Endowment for the Arts, U. S. National Endowment for the Humanities

**National Fraternal Club**
100 E. Ohio, Suite 418, Chicago, IL 60610.
- National Fraternal Club News. m. ISSN 0027-9307

**National Fraternity of the Performing Arts**
c/o Ed. Richard P. Pheneger, 446 Hollister St., C-24, Stratford, CT 06497.
- Cue of Theta Alpha Phi. 3 per yr. ISSN 0011-2666

**National Free Lance Photographers Association**
4 E. State St., Doylestown, PA 18901.
- Freelance Photography. bi-m.

**National Frozen Food Association, Inc.**
One Chocolate Ave., Hershey, PA 17033.
- Frozen Food Factbook and Directory. a. ISSN 0071-9684

**National Fund for Medical Education**
- A A M C Education News. (pub. by Association of American Medical Colleges)

**National Furniture Warehousemens Association**
222 W. Adams St., Chicago, IL 60606.
- Direction. m. ISSN 0092-7449

**National Gallery of Art**
Washington, DC 20565.
- National Gallery of Art. Annual Report. a.
- Studies in the History of Art. a. ISSN 0091-7338

**National Genealogical Society**
1921 Sunderland Place, N.W., Washington, DC 20036.
- National Genealogical Society Quarterly. q. ISSN 0027-934X

**National Geographic Society**
17th & M Sts. N.W., Washington, DC 20036.
- Books for Young Explorers Series. a.
- National Geographic. m. ISSN 0027-9358
- National Geographic Books. Second Series. 4 per yr. ISSN 0077-4618
- National Geographic Society, Washington, D.C. Research Reports; abstracts and reviews of research and exploration authorized under grants from the National Geographic Society. irreg., no. 9, 1976. ISSN 0077-4626
- National Geographic World. m.

**National Geophysical and Solar-Terrestrial Data Center**
see U.S. National Geophysical and Solar Terrestrial Data Center

**National Glass Dealers Association**
1000 Connecticut Ave., Washington, DC 20036.
- Glass Dealer. m. ISSN 0094-3746

**National Governors' Conference**
Iron Works Pike, Lexington, KY 40511.
- National Governors' Conference. Proceedings. a. ISSN 0077-4634

**National Grain and Feed Association**
c/o Avlin E. Oliver, 500 Folger Bldg., 725 15 St. N.W., Washington, DC 20005.
- Feed and Feeding Digest. m.

**National Greyhound Association**
Box 543, Abilene, KS 67410.
- Greyhound Review. m.

**National Guard Association of the United States**
1 Massachusetts Ave., N.W., Washington, DC 20001.
- National Guardsman. m except Aug. ISSN 0027-9412

**National Guild of Piano Teachers**
Box 1807, Austin, TX 78716.
- National Guild of Piano Teachers. Guild Syllabus. a. ISSN 0077-4642
- Piano Guild Notes. bi-m. ISSN 0031-9546

**National Hardwood Lumber Association**
332 S. Michigan Ave., Chicago, IL 60604.
- National Hardwood Lumber Association Yearbook. a.

**National Hardwood Magazine**
4077 Viscount Ave., Memphis, TN 38118.
- National Hardwood Magazine. m.

**National Health Council**
1740 Broadway, New York, NY 10019.
- National Health Council. Annual Report. a. ISSN 0085-3755

**National Health Federation**
Box 688, Monrovia, CA 91016.
- National Health Federation. Bulletin. m. ISSN 0027-9420

**National Health Lawyers Association**
552 21st St. N.W., Suite 708, Washington, DC 20006.
- Health Lawyers News Report. m.

**National Hearing Aid Society**
20361 Middlebelt, Livonia, MI 48152.
- Audecibel. q. ISSN 0004-7473

**National Heart and Lung Institute**
see U.S. National Heart and Lung Institute

**National Highway Traffic Safety Administration**
see U.S. National Highway Traffic Safety Administration

**National Historical Publications and Records Commission**
see U. S. National Historical Publications and Records Commission

**National Historical Society**
Box 1831, Telegraph Press Bldg., Harrisburg, PA 17105.
- American History Illustrated. m.(except Mar & Sept) ISSN 0002-8770
- Civil War Times Illustrated; a magazine for persons interested in American History, particularly in the Civil War period. 10 per yr. ISSN 0009-8094

**National Home Furnishings Association**
405 Merchandise Mart Plaza, Chicago, IL 60654.
- N H F A Reports. m. ISSN 0027-6944

**National Home Study Council**
1601 18 St. N.W., Washington, DC 20009.
- Directory of Accredited Home Study Schools. irreg.
- N H S C News. m. ISSN 0027-6596

**National Horseman**
Box 4067, Baxter Station, Louisville, KY 40204.
- National Horseman. m. ISSN 0027-9455

**National Hot Rod Association**
10639 Riverside Drive, N. Hollywood, CA 91602.
- National Dragster. w.

**National Housing and Economic Development Law Project**
2313 Warring St., Berkeley, CA 94704.
- Law Project Bulletin. m. (University of California, Berkeley)

**National Housing Publications, Inc.**
803 National Press Bldg., Washington, DC 20045.
- Housing and Urban Affairs Daily. d. ISSN 0018-6600

**National Huguenot Society**
2606 Coolidge Ave., Wichita, KS 67204.
- Cross of Languedoc. s-a. ISSN 0011-1961

**National Independent Meat Packers Association**
- Meat Science Institute. Proceedings. (pub. by University of Georgia. Center for Continuing Education)

**National Indian Youth Council**
201 Hermosa N.E., Albuquerque, NM 87108.
- Americans Before Columbus. irreg.(approx. m.) ISSN 0066-121X

**National Industrial Recreation Association**
20 N. Wacker Dr., Chicago, IL 60606.
- Recreation Management; the national magazine of recreation in business and industry. 10 per yr. ISSN 0034-1770

**National Industrial Television Association**
Communications Office, 15 Madison Ave, Summit, NJ 07901
(Ed. Address: Box 1676, San Mateo, CA 94401)
- Industrial Television News. m. ISSN 0300-7685

**National Information Bureau, Inc.**
419 Park Ave. South, New York, NY 10016.
- Wise Giving Bulletin; a reporting and advisory service for contributors. a.

**National Information Center for Educational Media**
University of Southern California, University Park, Los Angeles, CA 90007.
- Index to Psychology-Multimedia. biennial.
- Index to Vocational and Technical Education-Multimedia. biennial.

**National Information Center for the Handicapped**
see U.S. National Information Center for the Handicapped

**National Informer**
11058 W. Addison St., Franklin Park, IL 60131.
- National Informer. w.

**National Injury Information Clearinghouse**
see U.S. National Injury Information Clearinghouse

**National Institute for Architectural Education**
20 W. 40th St., New York, NY 10018.
- National Institute for Architectural Education. Yearbook. a. ISSN 0077-474X

**National Institute for Burn Medicine**
200 North Ingalls St., Ann Arbor, MI 48104.
- International Bibliography on Burns. Supplement. a. ISSN 0360-1196

**National Institute for Campus Ministries**
885 Centre St., Newton Centre, MA 02159.
- N I C M Journal for Jews and Christians in Higher Education. q. ISSN 0362-0794
- National Institute for Campus Ministries. National Newsletter. q. ISSN 0362-4633

**National Institute for Occupational Safety and Health**
see U. S. National Institute for Occupational Safety and Health

**National Institute for Public Services. Credit Union Information Service**
7315 Wisconsin Ave., Suite 210-W, Washington, DC 20014.
- C U I S Documentary Service. irreg.
- C U I S Newsletter. bi-w.
- C U I S Resources. m.
- C U I S Special Reports. (Credit Union Information Service) m.
- Credit Union Directory and Buyers' Guide. a. ISSN 0092-4954

**National Institute of Arthritis Metabolism and Digestive Diseases**
see U.S. National Institute of Arthritis, Metabolism, and Digestive Diseases

**National Institute of Child Health and Human Development**
see U.S. National Institute of Child Health and Human Development

**National Institute of Dental Research**
see U. S. National Institute of Dental Research

**National Institute of Education**
see U. S. National Institute of Education

**National Institute of Environmental Health Sciences**
see U.S. National Institute of Environmental Health Sciences

**National Institute of Mental Health**
see U. S. National Institute of Mental Health

**National Institute of Municipal Law Officers**
839 17th St. N.W., Washington, DC 20006.
- Municipal Attorney. m. ISSN 0027-3449
- Municipal Law Court Decisions. m. ISSN 0027-3503
- Municipal Ordinance Review. m. ISSN 0027-3538
- N I M L O Municipal Law Review. a.

**National Institute of Neurological and Communicative Disorders and Stroke**
see U.S. National Institute of Neurological and Communicative Disorders and Stroke

**National Institute of Packaging, Handling and Logistics Engineers**
Box 2765, Arlington, VA 22202.
- P H L Bulletin. (Packaging, Handling, Logistics) bi-m.

**National Institute on Alcohol Abuse and Alcoholism**
see U. S. National Institute on Alcohol Abuse and Alcoholism

**National Institute on Drug Abuse**
see U. S. National Institute on Drug Abuse

**National Institutes of Health**
see U.S. National Institutes of Health

**National Insulation Contractors Association**
1120 19th Street, N.W., Suite 405, Washington, DC 20036.
- N I C A Outlook. m. ISSN 0047-8881

**National Interagency Council on Smoking and Health**
419 Park Ave. S., New York, NY 10016.
- Smoking and Health Newsletter. q.

**National Interreligious Service Board for Conscientious Objectors**
550 Washington Bldg., 15th St. & New York Ave., N.W., Washington, DC 20005.
- Reporter for Conscience' Sake. m. ISSN 0034-4796

**National Intervenors**
153 E St. S.E., Washington, DC 20003.
- National Intervenors Newsletter. m.

**National Investigations Committee on Aerial Phenomena**
3535 University Bldg., Kensington, MD 20795.
- U F O Investigator; facts about unidentified flying objects. m. ISSN 0041-5073

**National Investment Publishing Co.**
Box 7212, Main P.O., Chicago, IL 60680.
- National Coin Reporter Hard Asset & Currency Review. m.
- National Hard Asset Reporter. m.
- National Portfolio Reporter. fortn.

**National Investor Relations Institute**
1629 K St., N.W., Washington, DC 20006.
- National Investor Relations Institute. Proceedings of the Annual National Conference. a. ISSN 0094-1204

**National Jewish Welfare Board**
15 E. 26th St., New York, NY 10010.
- J W B Circle. 7 per yr. ISSN 0021-3780
- Jewish Community Center Program Aids. q. ISSN 0021-6372
- National Jewish Welfare Board. Yearbook. a. ISSN 0077-507X

**National Jewish Welfare Board. Jewish Book Council**
15 E. 26th St., New York, NY 10010.
- Jewish Book Annual. a. ISSN 0075-3726
- Jewish Bookland. 7 per yr.

**National Jogging Association**
1910 K St. N.W., Suite 202, Washington, DC 20006.
- Bibliography on Jogging. biennial.
- Jogger. m.

**National Josep Publishing Co.**
P.O. Box 1495, Pueblo, CO 81002.
- Who's Who in National High School Football. a. ISSN 0091-6935

**National Junior Classical League**
c/o Joan Myers, American Classical League, Miami University, Oxford, OH 45056.
- Torch: U.S. 3 per yr. ISSN 0493-5284

**National Junior College Athletic Association**
Box 1586, Hutchinson, KS 67501.
- Juco Review. 9 per yr. ISSN 0047-2956

**National Junior Horticultural Association**
Mount Vernon, VA 22121.
- National Junior Horticultural Association. Newsletter. irreg. ISSN 0077-5088 (American Horticultural Society)

**National Kappa Kappa Iota**
1875 E. 15, Tulsa, OK 74104.
- Kappa Kappa Iota Bulletin. s-a.

**National Keyboard Arts Associates**
741 Alexander Road, University Park, Princeton, NJ 08540.
- Keyboard Arts. 3 per yr. ISSN 0090-3361

**National Kidney Foundation**
116 E. 27th St., New York, NY 10016.
- Kidney. bi-m. ISSN 0023-1304
- National Kidney Foundation. Annual Report. a. ISSN 0077-5096

**National Knitted Outerwear Association**
51 Madison Ave., New York, NY 10010.
- Knitting Times. w. ISSN 0023-2300
- Knitting Times Buyers' Guide Directory. a.
- Knitting Times Yearbook. ISSN 0085-2562

**National L P-Gas Association**
1301 W. 22nd St., Oak Brook, IL 60521
- Annual Symposium on Thermal Agriculture. Proceedings. a. ISSN 0066-4448 (And Gas Processors Association, 1812 First Place, Tulsa, OK 74103)
- L P-Gas Market Facts; statistical handbook of the LP-gas industry. a. ISSN 0075-9759

**National Labor Relations Board**
see U.S. National Labor Relations Board

**National Lawyers Guild**
Box 673, Berkeley, CA 94701.
- Guild Practitioner. q. ISSN 0017-5390

**National Lawyers Guild (New York)**
853 Broadway, Room 1705, New York, NY 10003.
- National Lawyers Guild. Guild Notes. bi-m.

**National Lawyers Guild (Seattle)**
411 Smith Tower, Seattle, WA 98104.
- Contempt. bi-m.

**National Laymen's Council, Church League of America**
422 North Prospect St., Wheaton, IL 60187.
- National Laymen's Council Church League of America. News and Views. m.

**National League for Nursing**
10 Columbus Circle, New York, NY 10019.
- Baccalaureate Education in Nursing: Key to a Professional Career in Nursing. a. ISSN 0069-5602
- Education for Nursing: The Diploma Way. a. ISSN 0070-9166
- Masters Education: Route to Opportunities in Modern Nursing. a. ISSN 0076-5104
- N L N News. m. ISSN 0027-6804
- National League for Nursing. Associate Degree Education for Nursing. a. ISSN 0077-5118
- National League for Nursing. Baccalaureate Programs Accredited for Public Health Nursing Preparation. irreg. (prep. by its Council of Baccalaureate and Higher Degree Programs)
- National League for Nursing. Directory of Career Mobility Programs in Nursing Education. irreg., 2nd edt., 1975-1976.
- National League for Nursing. League Exchange. irreg., no. 107, 1975. ISSN 0077-5134
- National League for Nursing. Nurse-Faculty Census. biennial. ISSN 0077-5142
- National League for Nursing. Yearly Review. a. (prep. by its Department of Home Health Agencies and Community Health Services)
- Some Statistics on Baccalaureate and Higher Degree Programs in Nursing. a. ISSN 0081-203X
- State-Approved Schools of Nursing - L. P. N./L. V. N. a. ISSN 0081-4423
- State-Approved Schools of Nursing - R. N. a. ISSN 0081-4431

**National League of American Pen Women, Inc.**
Pen-Arts Bldg., 1300 17th St., N.W., Washington, DC 20036.
- Pen Woman. m.(Oct-June) ISSN 0031-4242

**National League of Cities**
1620 Eye St. N.W., Washington, DC 20006.
- N L C Washington Report to the Nations Cities. fortn.
- National Municipal Policy. a.
- Nation's Cities. m. ISSN 0028-0488
- Urban Affairs Abstracts. w. with s-a. and a. cumulations. ISSN 0300-6859 (Co-Sponsor: U.S. Conference of Mayors)

**National League of Families of American Prisoners and Missing in Action in Southeast Asia**
1608 K St., Washington, DC 20006.
- National League of Families of American Prisoners and Missing in Action in Southeast Asia Newsletter. bi-m.

**National League of Postmasters**
955 l'Enfant Plaza, Suite 4400, Washington, DC 20024.
- Postmasters Advocate. q. ISSN 0032-5511

**National Learning Corp.**
20 Dupont St., Plainview, NY 11803.
- Functional Series; Teacher's License Examination Series. irreg.

**National Legal Aid and Defender Association**
1155 E. 60th St., Chicago, IL 60637.
- Legal Aid Briefcase. q. ISSN 0024-0338

**National Librarians Association**
Monteith Library, Alma College, Alma, MI 48801.
- N L A Newsletter. q.

**National Library Literary Review**
1515 W. 10th, Topeka, KS 66604.
- National Library Literary Review. s-a.

**National Library of Medicine**
see U.S. National Library of Medicine

**National Life Insurance Company of Vermont**
Montpelier, VT 05602.
- National Messenger. m. ISSN 0027-9714

**National Live Stock and Meat Board**
444 N. Michigan Ave., Chicago, IL 60611.
- American Meat Science Association. Reciprocal Meat Conference. Proceedings. a.
- Food & Nutrition News. 5 per yr. ISSN 0015-6310
- Meat Board Reports. s-m. ISSN 0025-6358

**National Live Stock Publishing**
733 N. Van Buren, Milwaukee, WI 53202.
- National Live Stock Producer. 10 per yr. ISSN 0027-9668

**National Livestock Feeders Association, Inc.**
309 Livestock Exchange Bldg., Omaha, NE 68107.
- N L F A Feed-Lines. s-m. ISSN 0047-8938

**National Lubricating Grease Institute**
4635 Wyandotte St., Kansas City, MO 64112.
- N L G I Spokesman. m. ISSN 0027-6782

**National Macaroni Manufacturers Association**
Box 336, Palatine, IL 60067.
- Macaroni Journal. m. ISSN 0024-8894

**National Machine Tool Builders' Association**
7901 Westpark Drive, McLean, VA 22101.
- Directory of Machine Tools and Related Products; built by members of the National Machine Tool Builders' Assn. a. ISSN 0070-5772
- Economic Handbook of the Machine Tool Industry. a. ISSN 0070-8550

**National Management Association**
2210 Arbor Blvd., Dayton, OH 45439.
- Manage. bi-m. ISSN 0025-1623

**National Maple Syrup Digest**
c/o Lloyd H. Sipple, R. D. No. 2, Bainbridge, NY 13733.
- National Maple Syrup Digest. q.

**National Marine Electronics Association**
49 Delwood Lane, Tinton Falls, NJ 07724.
- N.M.E.A. News. bi-m.

**National Marine Engineers Beneficial Association**
AFL-CIO, Rm. 1930, 17 Battery Place, New York, NY 10004.
- American Marine Engineer. m. ISSN 0002-9866

**National Marine Fisheries Service**
see U.S. National Marine Fisheries Service

**National Maritime Union of America. A F L - C I O**
346 W. 17th St., New York, NY 10011.
- N M U Pilot. m. ISSN 0027-6855

**National Mediation Board**
see U.S. National Mediation Board

**National Medical Association**
- National Medical Association. Journal. (pub. by Appleton- Century- Crofts)

**National Medical Audiovisual Center**
see U.S. National Medical Audiovisual Center

**National Medical Fellowships Inc.**
250 W. 57th Street, New York, NY 10019.
- National Medical Fellowships Newsletter. q.

**National Merit Scholarship Corporation**
990 Grove St., Evanston, IL 60201.
- Guide to the National Merit Scholarship Program. a. ISSN 0072-8721
- National Merit Scholarship Corporation. Student Bulletin. a.

**National Meteorological Center**
see U.S. National Meteorological Center

**National Microfilm Association**
Suite 1101, 8728 Colesville Rd., Silver Spring, MD 20910.
- N M A Annual Report. a.

**National Microfilm Association. Metropolitan New York Chapter**
P.O. Box 506, Radio City Station, New York, NY 10010.
- New York Micro-Times. m.

**National Micrographics Association**
8728 Colesville Road, Suite 1101, Silver Spring, MD 20910.
- Buyer's Guide to Micrographic Equipment, Products, and Services. a.
- Guide to Micrograpic Equipment. triennial. ISSN 0360-8654
- Journal of Micrographics. bi-m. ISSN 0022-2712
- Micrographics Today. bi-m.
- National Micrographics Association. Proceedings of the Annual Conference. a.

**National Middle School Association**
P.O. Box 968, Fairborn, OH 45324.
- Middle School Journal. q. ISSN 0094-0771

**National Milk Producers Federation**
30 F Street, N.W., Washington, DC 20001.
- Dairy Producer Highlights. a.

**National Minority Business Campaign**
1016 Plymouth Ave., Minneapolis, MN 55411.
- Guide to Minority Business Directories. irreg. ISSN 0362-3459
- National Minority Business Directory. a. ISSN 0077-5231

**National Mirror Inc.**
257 Park Ave. So., New York, NY 10017.
- Uncensored. bi-m.

**National Model Railroad Association**
Box 2186, Indianapolis, IN 46206.
- National Model Railroad Association. Bulletin. m. ISSN 0027-9722

**National Multiple Sclerosis Society**
205 E. 42nd St., New York, NY 10017.
- M S Briefs. (Multiple Sclerosis) 10 per yr. ISSN 0024-838X
- M S Keynotes. (Multiple Sclerosis) q. ISSN 0024-841X
- M S Patient Service News. (Multiple Sclerosis) 3 per yr. ISSN 0024-8436
- Multiple Sclerosis Indicative Abstracts. (pub. by Federation of American Societies for Experimental Biology)

**National Municipal League**
47 E. 68th St., New York, NY 10021.
- National Civic Review. m.(Sept-July) ISSN 0027-9013

**National Music Council**
250 West 57th Street, New York, NY 10019.
- National Music Council Bulletin. s-a. ISSN 0027-9749

**National Muzzle Loading Rifle Association**
Box 67, Friendship, IN 47021.
- Muzzle Blasts. m. ISSN 0027-5360

**National Neighbors**
119 N. 18th St., Philadelphia, PA 19103.
- Neighbors - Interracial Living. bi-m. ISSN 0047-9314

**National News Service, Inc.**
110 Wall St., New York, NY 10005.
- Bank and Quotation Record. m. ISSN 0005-5026
- Commercial & Financial Chronicle. w. ISSN 0010-2903

**National Newspaper Association**
491 National Press Bldg., Washington, DC 20045.
- N N A National Directory of Weekly Newspapers. a.
- Publishers Auxiliary. w. ISSN 0048-5942

**National Newspaper Publishers Association**
770 National Press Building, Washington, DC 20045.
- Black Press Information Handbook. biennial.

**National Notary Association**
23012 Ventura Blvd., Woodland Hill, CA 91364.
- Customs and Practices of Notaries Public and Digest of Notary Laws in the U.S. biennial. ISSN 0070-2269
- National Notary. bi-m.
- Notary Viewpoint. q.

**National Nudist Council**
- Sunlore. (pub. by Church Publications)
- Sunshine & Health. (pub. by Church Publications)

**National Nutritional Foods Association**
- Health Foods Retailing. (pub. by Syndicate Magazines, Inc.)

**National Ocean Survey**
see U.S. National Ocean Survey

**National Oceanographic Data Center**
see U.S. National Oceanographic Data Center

**National Oceanographic Instrumentation Center**
see U.S. National Oceanographic Instrumentation Center

**National Office for Black Catholics**
1234 Massachusetts Ave., N.W., Washington, DC 20005.
- Freeing the Spirit. q.
- Impact (Washington) m?

**National Office Machine Dealers Association**
1510 Jarvis Ave., Elk Grove Village, IL 60007.
- N O M D A Spokesman. q. ISSN 0027-6871

**National Office Products Association**
1500 Wilson Blvd., Arlington, VA 22209.
- Office Products Industry Report. bi-w.
- Special Report to Office Products Industry. q.

**National Opera Association, Inc.**
c/o Constance Eberhart, Hotel Wellington, 7Th Ave. at 55th St., New York, NY 10019.
- National Opera Association. Membership Directory. a. ISSN 0085-381X
- Opera Journal. (pub. by University of Mississippi)

**National Opinion Research Center**
6030 S. Ellis, Chicago, IL 60637.
- N O R C Monographs in Social Reserach. (pub. by Aldine Publishing Co.)
- National Opinion Research Center. Newsletter. irreg., no. 9, 1974. ISSN 0077-5266
- National Opinion Research Center. Report. irreg., no. 126, 1974. ISSN 0077-5274

**National Organization for Women. Atlanta Chapter**
P.O. Box 54045, Atlanta, GA 30308.
- N O W Notes-Atlanta Chapter. m.

**National Organization for Women. Central New Jersey Chapter**
The Woman's Place, 14 1/2 Witherspoon St., Princeton, NJ 08540.
- N O W Newsletter, Central New Jersey. 11 per yr.

**National Organization for Women. Eastern Massachusetts Chapter**
45 Newbury St., Boston, MA 02116.
- National Organization for Women. Boston N O W. m.

**National Organization for Women. Houston, Texas Chapter**
3602 Milan, Houston, TX 77047.
- Broadside (Houston) m.

**National Organization for Women. Madison Chapter**
P.O. Box 2512, Madison, WI 53701.
- Equality NOW! m.

**National Organization for Women. Metropolitan Detroit Chapter**
Box 1455, Detroit, MI 48231.
- As We See It Now. m.

**National Organization for Women. Pennsylvania Chapter**
132 Sunridge Drive, Pittsburgh, PA 15234.
- Pennsylvania N O W; western report. m.

**National Organization for Women. San Diego County Chapter**
P.O. Box 80292, San Diego, CA 92138.
- N O W San Diego News. m.

**National Organization for Women. San Francisco Chapter**
P.O. Box 1267, San Francisco, CA 94101.
- N O W Newsletter, San Francisco. m.

**National Organization for Women. San Joaquin Chapter**
P.O. Box 4073, Stockton, CA 95204.
- San Joaquin N O W Newsletter. m.

**National Organization for Women. Washington, D.C. Chapter**
1424 16th St., N.W. ( 104), Washington, DC 20036.
- Vocal Majority. m.

**National Organization on Legal Problems of Education**
5401 S.W. 7th, Topeka, KS 66606.
- N O L P E Notes. m. ISSN 0047-8997
- N O L P E School Law Journal. s-a. ISSN 0047-8989
- N O L P E School Law Reporter. bi-m.

**National Ornamental and Miscellaneous Metals Association**
Suite 106, 443 E. Paces Ferry Rd. , NE, Atlanta, GA 30305.
- Ornamental Metal Fabricator. bi-m.

**National Paint and Coatings Association**
Technical Library, 1500 Rhode Island Ave., N.W., Washington, DC 20005.
- Abstract Review. m. ISSN 0001-3390
- National Paint and Coatings Association. Annual Report. a. ISSN 0095-2729

**National Park Service**
see U.S. National Park Service

**National Parking Association**
1101 17th St., N.W., Washington, DC 20036.
- Parking. q. ISSN 0031-2193
- Parking World. m.

**National Parks and Conservation Association**
1701 18th St. N.W., Washington, DC 20009.
- National Parks & Conservation Magazine; the environmental journal. m. ISSN 0027-9870

**National Particleboard Association**
2306 Perkins Place, Silver Spring, MD 20910.
- National Particleboard Association. Technical Bulletin. irreg.

**National Peach Council**
Box 1085, Martinsburg, WV 25401.
- National Peach Council. Annual Proceedings. a.
- Peach-Times. 12 per yr. ISSN 0031-3610

**National Periodical Library**
Box 47, Flint, MI 48501.
- Guide to Social Science and Religion in Periodical Literature. q.(cumulated annually & triennially) ISSN 0017-5307

**National Petroleum News**
- N P N Bulletin. (pub. by McGraw-Hill Inc.)

**National Pharmaceutical Association, Inc.**
Howard Univ., College of Pharmacy, Washington, DC 20001.
- National Pharmaceutical Association. Journal. q. ISSN 0027-9897

**National Philatelic Society**
- National Stamp News. (pub. by Wilton E. Hall Publisher)

**National Pilots Association**
805 15th St. N.W., Washington, DC 20005.
- National Pilots Association News. m.

**National Planning Association**
1606 New Hampshire Ave., N.W., Washington, DC 20009.
- Looking Ahead and Projection Highlights. m.
- National Planning Association Reports. irreg.
- New International Realities. 3 per yr.

**National Poetry Foundation, Inc.**
- Paideuma. (pub. by University of Maine at Orono Press)

**National Poetry Press**
3210 Selby Ave., Los Angeles, CA 90034.
- Creative Writing. bi-m. ISSN 0011-0930

**National Police Chiefs & Sheriffs Information Bureau**
828 N. Broadway, Milwaukee, WI 53202.
- National Directory of Law Enforcement Administrators and Correctional Agencies. a. ISSN 0547-6224

**National Police Officers Association of America, Inc.**
Police Hall of Fame Bldg, Venice, FL 33595.
● Enforcement Journal. 4 per yr. ISSN 0042-2347

**National Pontius Association**
Route 1, Downey, ID 83234.
● Bridge Builder. s-a.

**National Prep Sports Network, Inc.**
4707 N. 12th St., Phoenix, AZ 85014.
● Joe Namath's National Prep Sports Magazine. bi-m.

**National Press Club**
National Press Bldg., Washington, DC 20045.
● National Press Club Record. 48 per yr. ISSN 0027-9927

**National Press Photographers Association**
Box 1146, Durham, NC 27702.
● News Photographer; dedicated to the service and advancement of news photography. m.

**National Prisoners' Reform Association**
Box 8273, Cranston, RI 02920.
● National Prisoners' Reform Association. News. m.

**National Property Law Digests, Inc.**
8401 Connecticut Ave., N.W., Washington, DC 20015.
● National Property Law Digests. m. ISSN 0363-8340

**National Provisioner, Inc.**
15 W. Huron St., Chicago, IL 60610.
● National Provisioner. w. ISSN 0027-996X

**National Psychological Association for Psychoanalysis, Inc.**
150 W. 13 St, New York, NY 10011.
● National Psychological Association for Psychoanalysis. Bulletin. a. ISSN 0077-5339

**National Publishers Press**
517 Ottawa Ave., N.W., Grand Rapids, MI 49502.
● Braille Cardinal. s-a. ISSN 0006-8748 (Kentucky Federation of the Blind)

**National Publishing Corporation**
3150 Des Plaines Ave., Des Plaines, IL 60018.
● Chicago, Cook County and Illinois Industrial Directory. a. ISSN 0069-3251

**National Racquetball Club, Inc.**
4101 Dempster St., Skokie, IL 60076.
● National Racquetball. bi-m. (U S Racquetball Association)

**National Radio Institute**
3939 Wisconsin, Washington, DC 20016.
● N R I Journal. bi-m. ISSN 0027-6952

**National Railway Historical Society. Pacific Northwest Chapter**
Room 1, Union Station, Portland, OR 97209.
● Trainmaster. 9 per yr. ISSN 0041-0926

**National Railway Historical Society. Tacoma Chapter**
Box 340, Tacoma, WA 98401.
● Train Sheet. m.(except July & Aug.) ISSN 0041-0845

**National Railway Publication Co.**
424 West 33 St, New York, NY 10001.
● Official Intermodal Equipment Register. q.
● Official Railway Equipment Register. q. ISSN 0030-0373
● Official Railway Guide. North American Freight Service Edition. bi-m.
● Official Railway Guide. North American Passenger Travel Edition. 10 per yr. ISSN 0094-5218
● Pocket List of Railroad Officials; contains listing of over 20,000 officials of railroads, private car companies, etc. q. ISSN 0032-1826

**National Reading Conference, Inc.**
Clemson Univ., Clemson, SC 29631.
● Journal of Reading Behavior. q. ISSN 0022-4111

**National Ready Mixed Concrete Association**
900 Spring St., Silver Spring, MD 20910.
● N R M C A Publication. irreg., 1973, no. 144. ISSN 0077-5355

**National Recreation and Park Association**
1601 North Kent St., Arlington, VA 22209.
● Congress for Recreation and Parks. Proceedings. a. ISSN 0069-8903
● Design. q. (prep. by its Park Practice Program)
● Grist. bi-m. ISSN 0031-2150 (prep. by its Park Practice Program)
● Journal of Leisure Research. q. ISSN 0022-2216 (Co-sponsor: U.S. Department of the Interior, Bureau of Outdoor Recreation)
● N R P A. Washington Action Report. fortn.
● Parks and Recreation; journal of park and recreation management. m. ISSN 0031-2215
● Therapeutic Recreation Journal. q. ISSN 0040-5914 (National Therapeutic Recreation Society)
● Trends. q. (prep. by its Park Practice Program)

**National Reform Association**
45 S. Bryant Ave., Pittsburgh, PA 15202.
● Christian Statesman. bi-m. ISSN 0009-5664

**National Register of Prominent Americans**
Drawer 656, Venice, FL 33595.
● National Register of Prominent Americans and International Notables. biennial. ISSN 0077-5371

**National Register Publishing Co., Inc.**
(Subsidiary of: Standard Rate and Data Service)
5201 Old Orchard Rd., Skokie, IL 60076.
● Ad Change. w. ISSN 0001-7914
● Chicago Metro Book. a.
● Consumer's Register of American Business. a. ISSN 0098-7344
● Corporate Action. 5 per yr.
● Directory of Corporate Affiliations. a. ISSN 0070-5365
● Official Museum Directory. biennial. ISSN 0090-6700 (American Association of Museums)
● Standard Directory of Advertisers. a. ISSN 0081-4229
● Standard Directory of Advertising Agencies; the agency red book. 3 per yr. ISSN 0085-6614

**National Rehabilitation Association**
1522 K Street, N.W., Washington, DC 20005.
● Journal of Applied Rehabilitation Counseling. q. ISSN 0047-2220
● Journal of Rehabilitation. bi-m. ISSN 0022-4154

**National Religious Broadcasters, Inc**
Box 2254R, Morristown, NJ 07960.
● Religious Broadcasting. bi-m. ISSN 0034-4079

**National Remodelers Association**
c/o Joseph M. Nahay, 50 E. 42nd St., New York, NY 10017.
● Remodeling Contractor. m. ISSN 0034-4249

**National Renaissance Party**
Box 10, New York, NY 10024.
● National Renaissance Bulletin. bi-m. ISSN 0028-0003

**National Renderers Association**
3150 Des Plaines Ave., Des Plaines, IL 60018.
● N R A Newsletter. m. ISSN 0027-691X
● Spectrum. a.

**National Research Bureau Inc.**
424 N. Third St., Burlington, IA 52601.
● American Salesman; the national magazine for sales professionals. m. ISSN 0003-0902
● Cooperative Advertising Plans Directory. irreg. ISSN 0069-9802
● Directory of Shopping Centers. a. ISSN 0419-3512
● Gebbie House Magazine Directory. a. ISSN 0072-0526
● Shopping Center Newsletter. m. ISSN 0559-9091
● Supervision; the magazine of industrial relations and operating management. m. ISSN 0039-5854
● Working Press of the Nation. a. ISSN 0084-1323

**National Research Council. Commission on Human Resources**
2101 Constitution Ave., Washington, DC 20418.
● Doctoral Scientists and Engineers in the United States. Profile. biennial.

**National Research Council. Committee on Polar Research**
National Academy of Sciences, 2101 Constitution Ave., Washington, DC 20418.
● National Research Council. Committee on Polar Research. Report on United States Antarctic Research Activities. a. ISSN 0361-2279

**National Research Council. Division of Biological Science**
2101 Constitution Ave., Washington, DC 20418.
● International Congress of Zoology. Proceedings. a.

**National Research Council. Highway Research Board**
2101 Constitution Ave., N.W., Washington, DC 20418.
● Transportation Noise Bulletin. irreg. ISSN 0094-0682

**National Research Council. Transportation Research Board**
2101 Constitution Ave, Washington, DC 20418.
● National Research Council. Transportation Research Board. Special Reports.

**National Restaurant Association**
One IBM Plaza - Suite 2600, Chicago, IL 60611.
● N R A News. m. ISSN 0465-7004
● National Restaurant Association. Washington Report. w.
● Tableservice Restaurant Operations Report. a.

**National Retail Hardware Association**
964 N. Pennsylvania St., Indianapolis, IN 46204.
● Hardware Retailing. m.

**National Retail Merchants Association**
100 W. 31st St., New York, NY 10001.
● Creditalk. m. ISSN 0045-9011 (prep. by its Credit Management Division)
● E D P Conference for Retailers. irreg., 1966, 8th. ISSN 0070-7805
● National Retail Merchants Association. Specifications A. Standards for the Retail Industry; voluntary standards for the retail industry. biennial.
● Promotion Exchange. m.
● Retail Broadcaster-Radio Edition. m.
● Retail Broadcaster-Television Edition. m.
● Retail Operations News Bulletin. q. ISSN 0048-7422
● Stores. m. ISSN 0039-1867
● Traffic Topics. 10 per yr.

**National Retail Merchants Association. Financial Executives Division**
100 W 31st St., New York, NY 10001.
● Financial and Operating Results of Department and Specialty Stores. a. ISSN 0547-8804
● Merchandise & Operating Results of Department and Speciality Stores. a.
● Retail Control. m. (bi-m Apr.-May & Jun. Jul.) ISSN 0034-6047

**National Retired Teachers Association**
701 N. Montgomery St., Ojai, CA 93023.
● N R T A Journal. bi-m. ISSN 0027-6979
● N R T A News Bulletin. m. ISSN 0027-6987

**National Review, Inc.**
150 E. 35th St., New York, NY 10016.
● National Review; a journal of fact and opinion. fortn. ISSN 0028-0038
● National Review Bulletin. fortn. ISSN 0028-0046

**National Rifle Association of America**
1600 Rhode Island Ave. N. W., Washington, DC 20036.
● American Hunter. m. ISSN 0092-1068
● American Rifleman. m. ISSN 0003-083X
● N R A Conservation Yearbook. a. ISSN 0069-9098
● N R A Hunting Annual; register of North American guides, outfitters and hunting camps. a.
● N R A Unified Sportsmen of America. Reports from Washington. fortn.
● Uniform Hunter Casualty Report. a. ISSN 0082-7606

**National Right to Work Committee**
8316 Arlington Blvd., Fairfax, VA 22030.
● National Right to Work Newsletter. m.

**National Rural Electric Cooperative Association**
2000 Florida Ave. N.W., Washington, DC 20009.
● Management Quarterly; a guide to better management. q. ISSN 0025-1860 (prep. by its Management Services Department)
● N R E C A-A P P A Legal Reporting Service. m. ISSN 0362-8833 (prep. by its Management Services Department) (Co-sponsor: American Public Power Association)
● National Rural Electric Cooperative Association. Government Relations Department. Research Division. Research Papers and Circulars. irreg. ISSN 0077-5657

- R E Magazine. (Rural Electrification) m.

**National Rural Letter Carriers Association**
1750 Pennsylvania Ave., N.W., Suite 1204,
Washington, DC 20006.
- National Rural Letter Carrier. 4 per m. ISSN
0028-0089

**National Safety Council**
444 N. Michigan Ave., Chicago, IL 60611.
- Accident Facts. a.
- Campus Safety. bi-m. (prep. by its College and
University Section)
- College and University Safety Newsletter. 5 per
yr.(Sept-June) ISSN 0010-0943 (prep. by its
College and University Section)
- Driver Trainer Newsletter. m.
- Family Safety. q. ISSN 0014-7397
- Farm Safety Review. bi-m. ISSN 0014-8105 (prep.
by its Farm Department)
- Fleet Safety Newsletter - Motor Transportation.
m. ISSN 0547-888X
- Guide to Occupational Safety Literature. a. ISSN
0099-0612
- Industrial Supervisor. m. ISSN 0019-879X
- Journal of Safety Research. q. ISSN 0022-4375
- Labor Organization Newsletter. bi-m.
- Motorcycle Facts. a. ISSN 0091-5793 (prep. by its
Statistics Division)
- National Safety Council. Product Safety UP TO
Date. m. ISSN 0091-8954
- National Safety News. m. ISSN 0028-0100
- Recreational Safety Newsletter. m.
- Safe Driver. m. ISSN 0486-8323
- Safe Worker. m.
- Traffic Safety. m. ISSN 0041-0721

**National Safety Council. Lehigh Valley Chapter**
452 Main St, Bethlehem, PA 18018.
- Lehigh Valley Safety News. m. ISSN 0024-0567

**National Sales Development Institute**
24 Rope Ferry Rd., Waterford, CT 06386.
- It's Good Psychology. s-m. ISSN 0021-3217
- Sales Manager's Bulletin. s-m. ISSN 0036-3421

**National Salesmen's Organizations, Inc.**
127 John St., New York, NY 10038.
- National Voice of Salesmen. 4 per yr. ISSN 0028-
0364

**National Sand and Gravel Association**
900 Spring St., Silver Spring, MD 20910.
- N S G A Circular. irreg., 1973, no. 120. ISSN
0077-5673

**National Sash & Door Jobbers Association**
- Shelter. (pub. by Associations Publications, Inc.)

**National Savings and Loan League**
1101 15th St. N.W., Washington, DC 20005.
- National Savings and Loan League. Legal Bulletin.
ISSN 0547-7794
- National Savings and Loan League Journal. m.
ISSN 0095-781X

**National Scholarship First Fund**
- N S T F Report. (pub. by Graphic Arts Technical
Foundation)

**National Scholarship Service and Fund for Negro
Students**
1776 Broadway, New York, NY 10019.
- N S S F N S News. q. ISSN 0047-908X

**National Scholastic Press Association**
c/o Judy Schell, Ed., 720 Washington Ave., S.E.,
Suite 205, Univ. of Minnesota, Minneapolis, MN
55414.
- Scholastic Editor. m.(Sept-May; Dec & Jan issues
combined) (Co-sponsor: Associated College Press)

**National School Boards Association**
1055 Thomas Jefferson St. N.W., Washington, DC
20007.
- American School Board Journal. m. ISSN 0003-
0953
- National School Boards Association. Yearbook. a.
ISSN 0077-569X

**National School Development Council**
- Catalyst for Change. (pub. by East Texas School
Study Council)

**National School Public Relations Association**
1801 N. Moore St., Arlington, VA 22209.
- Education U. S. A. w. ISSN 0013-1571

- It Starts in the Classroom; the public relations
newsletter for classroom teachers. m.(Sept-May)
ISSN 0021-2717
- Paragraphs. m.(except Aug-Dec) ISSN 0031-1669

**National School Volunteer Program, Inc.**
300 N. Washington St., Alexandria, VT 22314.
- School Volunteer. bi-m.

**National School Yearbook-Newspaper Association**
Box 4080, Texas Tech University, Lubbock, TX
79409.
- Photolith. m.(during school year) ISSN 0031-8825

**National Science Foundation**
*see* U.S. National Science Foundation

**National Science Teachers Association**
1742 Connecticut Ave. N.W., Washington, DC
20009.
- Bibliography of Science Courses of Study and
Textbooks for Grades K-12. irreg.
- Journal of College Science Teaching. 5 per yr.
ISSN 0047-231X
- Science and Children. m. ISSN 0036-8148
- Science Teacher. 9 per yr. ISSN 0036-8555

**National Sculpture Society**
777 Third Ave., New York, NY 10017.
- National Sculpture Review. q. ISSN 0028-0127
- National Sculpture Society, New York. Annual
Exhibition. a. ISSN 0098-4817

**National Sea Grant Depository**
Pell Library Building, University of Rhode Island,
Narragansett Bay Campus, Narragansett, RI 02882.
- Sea Grant Publications Index. a.

**National Secretaries Association (International)**
2440 Pershing Rd., Suite G-10, Kansas City, MO
64108.
- Secretary. 10 per yr. ISSN 0037-0622

**National Securities & Research Corp.**
605 Third Ave., New York, NY 10016.
- National Securities and Research Corporation.
Annual Forecast. a. ISSN 0077-5703

**National Security Traders Association**
- National Security Traders Association. Traders'
Annual. (pub. by Investment Dealers' Digest
(IDD) Inc.)

**National Service Secretariat, Inc.**
5140 Sherrier Pl., N.W., Washington, DC 20016.
- National Service Newsletter. q.

**National Sharecroppers Fund & Rural Advancement
Fund**
2128 Commomwealth Ave., Charlotte, NC 28205.
- Condition of Farmworkers and Small Farmers. a.

**National Shellfisheries Association**
Biological Laboratory, Oxford, MD 21654.
- National Shellfisheries Association. Proceedings. a.
ISSN 0077-5711

**National Sheriffs' Association**
1250 Connecticut Ave., Washington, DC 20036.
- National Sheriff. bi-m. ISSN 0028-016X

**National Shoe Retailers Association**
200 Madison Ave., New York, NY 10016.
- Footwear Focus. 4 per yr.

**National Shorthand Reporters Association**
2361 S. Jefferson Davis Highway, Arlington, VA
22202.
- National Shorthand Reporter. m.(Oct-July) ISSN
0028-0178
- National Shorthand Reporters Association.
Proceedings of the Annual Convention. a. ISSN
0077-572X

**National Skeet Shooting Association**
Box 28188, San Antonio, TX 78228.
- National Skeet Shooting Association. Records
Annual. a. ISSN 0077-5738
- Skeet Shooting Review; covering the sport of
skeet shooting world wide. m. ISSN 0037-6140

**National Ski Areas Association**
P.O. Box 83, West Hartford, CT 06107.
- N S A A Newsletter. s-m. ISSN 0300-6670

**National Slovak Society of U.S.A.**
516 Court Place, Pittsburgh, PA 15219.
- Narodne Noviny. s-m. ISSN 0027-7940

**National Small Business Association**
1225 19th St., Washington, DC 20036.
- Voice of Small Business. m. ISSN 0037-7198

**National Socialist White People's Party**
Box 5505, Arlington, VA 22205.
- White Power; the revolutionary voice of national
socialism. m. ISSN 0043-4957

**National Society for Autistic Children**
169 Tampa Ave., Albany, NY 12208.
- N S A C Newsletter. q. ISSN 0047-9101

**National Society for Hebrew Day Schools**
229-Park Ave. S., New York, NY 10003.
- Olomeinu/Our World. m(8 per yr) ISSN 0030-
2139
- Torah Umesorah Report. q. ISSN 0040-9405

**National Society for Medical Research**
1000 Vermont Ave., N.W., Suite 1100, Washington,
DC 20005.
- National Society for Medical Research. Bulletin.
m. ISSN 0028-0186

**National Society for Performance and Instruction**
Box 266, Charles Town, WV 25414.
- Improving Human Performance Quarterly. 4 per
yr.
- N S P I Journal. m. (10 per yr) ISSN 0027-7002

**National Society for Preservation of Covered Bridges
Inc.**
130 Westfield Drive, Holliston, MA 01746.
- Covered Bridge Topics. q. ISSN 0011-071X

**National Society for the Prevention of Blindness, Inc.**
79 Madison Ave., New York, NY 10016.
- Prevention of Blindness News. q. ISSN 0032-8014
- Sight-Saving Review. q. ISSN 0037-4822
- Wise Owl News. 4 per yr. ISSN 0043-6755

**National Society for the Study of Education**
- National Society for the Study of Education.
Yearbook. (pub. by University of Chicago Press)

**National Society of Accountants for Cooperatives**
Virginia Commonwealth University, 1015 Floyd
Avenue, Richmond, VA 23284.
- Cooperative Accountant; accounting management
for agricultural cooperatives. q. ISSN 0010-8391

**National Society of Professional Engineers**
2029 K St., N.W., Washington, DC 20006.
- Professional Engineer. m. ISSN 0033-0051

**National Society of Public Accountants**
1717 Pennsylvania Ave. N.W., Washington, DC
20006.
- N S P A Washington Reporter. m.
- National Public Accountant. m. ISSN 0027-9978
- National Society of Public Accountants.
Proceedings of the Annual Professional Institute.
a. ISSN 0077-5770

**National Society of Scabbard and Blade**
Box 1021, Stillwater, OK 74074.
- Scabbard and Blade Journal. 4 per yr. ISSN 0036-
5408

**National Society of the Daughters of the American
Revolution**
1776 D St., N.W., Washington, DC 20006.
- Daughters of the American Revolution. m(except
July & Aug.) ISSN 0011-7013

**National Society of the Sons of the American
Revolution**
2412 Massachusetts Ave., N.W., Washington, DC
20008.
- Sons of the American Revolution Magazine. q.
ISSN 0038-1470

**National Solid Wastes Management Association**
1730 Rhode Island Ave. N.W., Suite 800,
Washington, DC 20036.
- International Waste Equipment and Technology
Exposition. Official Proceedings. a.

**National Soybean Processors Association**
1133 15th St. N.W., Washington, DC 20005.
- National Soybean Processors Association.
Yearbook. a. ISSN 0077-5789

**National Speleological Society. Cascade Grotto**
Chas. Coughlin, 6433 S. 127 Pl., Seattle, WA 98178.
- Cascade Caver. 10 per yr. ISSN 0008-7211

**National Speleological Society. Huntsville Grotto**
P.O. Box 1702, Huntsville, AL 35807.
- Huntsville Grotto Newsletter. m.

**National Speleological Society, Inc.**
Cave Ave., Huntsville, AL 35810.
- N S S Bulletin. q. ISSN 0028-0216
- N S S News. m. ISSN 0027-7010

**National Spiritual Assembly of the Baha'is of the United States**
112 Linden Ave., Wilmette, IL 60091.
- World Order; a Baha'i magazine. q. ISSN 0043-8804

**National Spiritualist Association of Churches**
P.O. 128, Cassadaga, FL 32706.
- National Spiritualist. m.

**National Sporting Goods Association**
717 N. Michigan Ave., Chicago, IL 60611.
- Selling Sporting Goods. m. ISSN 0037-1610

**National Spotlight**
300 Independence Ave. S.E., Washington, DC 20003.
- National Spotlight. m.

**National Spotted Swine Record, Inc.**
Bainbridge, IN 46105.
- Spotted News. 10 per yr. ISSN 0038-8432

**National Standards Association, Inc.**
1321 14th St. N.W., Washington, DC 20005.
- Standards and Specifications Information Bulletin. w. ISSN 0038-9641

**National States Rights Party**
- Thunderbolt. (pub. by Thunderbolt, Inc.)

**National Story League**
5835 Martel Ave., Dallas, TX 75206.
- Story Art; a magazine for storytellers. bi-m. ISSN 0039-1999

**National Strategy Information Center**
111 E. 58th St., New York, NY 10022.
- National Strategy Information Center. Strategy Papers. irreg. (2-3 per yr.)

**National Student Nurses' Association**
10 Columbus Circle, New York, NY 10019.
- Imprint. 4 per yr. ISSN 0019-3062

**National Student Volunteer Program**
see U. S. National Student Volunteer Program

**National Supply Distributors Association Inc.**
37 Landsdowne St., Boston, MA 02215.
- National Supply Distributors Association Bulletin. w.

**National Survey**
Chester, VT 05143.
- Vermont Yearbook. a. ISSN 0083-5781

**National Tank Truck Carriers, Inc.**
1616 P St. N.W., Washington, DC 20036.
- National Tank Truck Carrier Directory. a. ISSN 0077-586X

**National Tatler**
2717 North Pulaski Road, Chicago, IL 60639.
- National Tatler.

**National Tax Association-Tax Institute of America**
21 E. State St., Columbus, OH 43215.
- National Tax Association-Tax Institute of America. Proceedings of the Annual Conference. a. ISSN 0069-8687
- National Tax Journal. q. ISSN 0028-0283

**National Technical Information Service**
see U.S. National Technical Information Service

**National Technical Information Service**
Springfield, VA 22161.
- Reports of N R L Progress. m. ISSN 0027-6960

**National Telephone Cooperative Association**
2100 M. St. 100, Washington, DC 20037.
- Phone Call. m.

**National Terrazo and Mosaic Association, Inc.**
2-A W. Loudon St., Leesburg, VA 22075.
- Terrazzo Topics. 10 per yr. ISSN 0040-3806

**National Textbook Co.**
8259 Niles Center Rd., Skokie, IL 60076
- A C T F L Annual Review of Foreign Language Education. a. ISSN 0068-1180 (American Council on the Teaching of Foreign Languages) (And M L A Publications Center, 62 Fifth Ave., New York, NY 10011)
- Luz (Skokie) 8 per yr. (Oct.-May) ISSN 0024-7707
- Vie. m. (Oct.-May) ISSN 0042-5575

**National Therapeutic Recreation Society**
- Therapeutic Recreation Journal. (pub. by National Recreation and Park Association)

**National Tire Dealers and Retreaders Association**
1343 L St., N. W., Washington, DC 20005.
- N T D R A Dealer News. w. ISSN 0027-7045
- N T D R A Tire Dealers Survey. a. ISSN 0077-5886

**National Tool Die and Precision Machining Association**
9300 Livingston Rd., Washington, DC 20022.
- National Tool, Die and Precision Machining Association. Buyers Guide. a.

**National Traffic Law News**
c/o Robert I. Jacquith, Box 157, Warrensburg, MO 64093.
- National Traffic Law News. m. ISSN 0094-1875

**National Training Center of Lie Detection, Inc.**
57W. 57th St., New York, NY 10019.
- Journal of Polygraph Science. bi-m.

**National Transit Newsletter**
953 West University, Madison Heights, MI 48071.
- National Transit Newsletter. fortn.

**National Translations Center**
35 W 33rd St., Chicago, IL 60616.
- Translations Register-Index. m. ISSN 0041-1256 (John Crerar Library)

**National Treasury Employees Union**
Suite 1101, 1730 K St., N.W., Washington, DC 20006.
- National Treasury Employees Union. Bulletin. fortn. ISSN 0095-4748

**National Trust for Historic Preservation**
740-748 Jackson Place N.W., Washington, DC 20006.
- Historic Preservation. q. ISSN 0018-2419
- Preservation News. m. ISSN 0032-7735

**National Underwriter Co.**
420 E. Fourth St., Cincinnati, OH 45202
- Agent's and Buyer's Guide. a. ISSN 0065-4272
- Argus F. C. & S. Chart. (Fire Casualty & Surety) a. ISSN 0360-8921 (prep. by its Statistical Department)
- Insurance Exchange Magazine; insurance news of Illinois. m. ISSN 0020-4676 (Ed. Address: 175 W. Jackson Blvd., Chicago IL 60604)
- Interest-Adjusted Index; life insurance payment and cost comparisons. a. ISSN 0095-5221
- Life Rates & Data. a.
- National Underwriter. Life & Health Insurance Edition. w. ISSN 0028-033X
- National Underwriter. Property & Casualty Insurance Edition. w.
- State Underwriter; insurance news of Ohio. m. ISSN 0039-0178
- Who Writes What. a.

**National Union of Christian Schools**
865 28th St., S.E., Grand Rapids, MI 49508.
- Christian Home & School. 10 per yr. ISSN 0009-5389
- Christian School Directory. a. ISSN 0069-388X

**National Union of Hospital and Health Care Employees**
310 W. 43rd St., New York, NY 10036.
- Eleven Ninety Nine News. m. ISSN 0012-6535

**National University Extension Association**
Suite 360, One Dupont Circle, Washington, DC 20036.
- Guide to Independent Study Through Correspondence Instruction. biennial. ISSN 0072-8322
- N U E A Newsletter. bi-w.
- N U E A Spectator. q. ISSN 0027-7096
- National University Extension Association. Handbook and Directory. a.
- On- Campus/Off- Campus Degree Programs for Part Time Students. biennial.

**National Urban Coalition**
2100 M St. N.W., Washington, DC 20037.
- Network/Urban Coalition. m. ISSN 0047-9373

**National Urban League**
500 E. 62nd St., New York, NY 10021.
- National Urban League Progress Report. a. ISSN 0098-7735
- Urban League News. m.
- Urban League Review. (pub. by Transaction Periodicals Consortium)

**National Urban League. Council of Executive Directors**
105-14th Ave., Seattle, WA 98122.
- New Frontiers (Seattle) s-a. ISSN 0095-5248

**National Vocational Guidance Association**
1607 New Hampshire Ave. N.W., Washington, DC 20009.
- Vocational Guidance Quarterly. q. ISSN 0042-7764

**National Water Supply Improvement Association**
10500 Ellis Avenue, P.O. 8300, Fountain Valley, CA 92708.
- N W S I A Newsletter. m.
- W S I A Journal. s-a.

**National Waterways Conference, Inc.**
1130 17th St., N.W., Washington, DC 20036.
- National Waterways Conference Newsletter. fortn. ISSN 0028-0380

**National Weather Service**
see U.S. National Weather Service

**National Wildlife Federation, Inc.**
1412 16th St. N.W., Washington, DC 20036.
- Conservation Directory; a listing of organizations, agencies and officials concerned with natural resource use and management. a. ISSN 0069-911X
- Conservation News. s-m. ISSN 0010-647X
- Conservation Report. w. ISSN 0010-6488
- International Wildlife; dedicated to the wise use of the world's natural resources. bi-m. ISSN 0020-9112
- National Wildlife; dedicated to the wise use of our natural resources. bi-m. ISSN 0028-0402
- Ranger Rick's Nature Magazine. 12 per yr. ISSN 0033-9229

**National Woman's Christian Temperance Union**
1730 Chicago Ave., Evanston, IL 60201.
- Union Signal. m. ISSN 0041-7033

**National Wool Growers Association**
600 Crandall Bldg., Salt Lake City, UT 84101.
- National Wool Grower. m. ISSN 0028-0410

**National Writers Club**
1365 Logan St., Denver, CO 80203.
- Authorship. bi-m. ISSN 0005-0660
- National Writers Club. Bulletin for Professional Members. s-a. ISSN 0028-0429

**National Young Judea**
817 Broadway, New York, NY 10003.
- Kol Ha T'nuah/Voice of the Movement. m.
- Young Judaean. m.(Nov-June) ISSN 0044-0817

**National Youth Alternatives Project**
1346 Connecticut Ave., N.W., Washington, DC 20036.
- Youth Alternatives. m.

**National 4-H Council**
150 N. Wacker Drive, Chicago, IL 60606.
- National 4-H News. m. ISSN 0027-9285

**Nationwide Papers**
5735 East River Rd., Chicago, IL 60631.
- Forum (Chicago, 1974) q.

**Native American Rights Fund**
1506 Broadway, Boulder, CO 80302.
- National Indian Law Library. Catalogue; an index to Indian legal materials and resources. a.
- Native American Rights Fund. Announcements. q.

**Native American Student Alliance**
Rt 1, Box 2170, Davis, CA 95616.
- Coyote. irreg. ISSN 0084-9421

**Native American Training Associates Institute**
Box 1505, Sacramento, CA 95807.
- Stealing of California. q.

**Natural Hazards Research and Applications Information Center**
Institute of Behavioral Science 6, University of Colorado, Boulder, CO 80309.
- Natural Hazards Observer. q.

**Natural Health World**
c/o Mrs. John W. Noble, 1920 N. Kilpatrick, Portland, OR 97217.
- Natural Health World. m. ISSN 0028-0704

**Natural High**
830 Mission Street, Santa Cruz, CA 95060.
- Natural High. bi-m.

**Natural History Museum Alliance of Los Angeles County**
900 Exposition Blvd., Los Angeles, CA 90007.
- Terra. q.

**Natural History Museum of Los Angeles County**
900 Exposition Blvd., Los Angeles, CA 90007.
- Natural History Museum of Los Angeles County. Contributions in History. irreg. ISSN 0076-0927
- Natural History Museum of Los Angeles County. Contributions in Science. irreg. ISSN 0076-0900
- Natural History Museum of Los Angeles County. Science Bulletin. irreg., no. 27, 1976. ISSN 0076-0935
- Natural History Museum of Los Angeles County. Science Series. irreg., no. 28, 1976. ISSN 0076-0943

**Natural History Press**
c/o: Doubleday and Co., 501 Franklin Ave., Garden City, NY 11530.
- American Museum Sourcebooks in Anthropology. irreg., latest issue 1972. ISSN 0065-9460 (American Museum of Natural History)

**Natural History Society of Maryland, Inc.**
- Maryland Herpetological Society. Bulletin. (pub. by Maryland Herpetological Society)

**Natural Resources Council of Maine**
20 Willow St., Augusta, ME 04330.
- Maine Environment. m.

**Natural Resources Defense Council Inc.**
15 West 44th St., New York, NY 10036.
- N R D C Newsletter. bi-m.

**Natural Science for Youth Foundation**
763 Silvermine Rd., New Canaan, CT 06840.
- Directory of Natural Science Centers. biennial.
- Natural Science Centers Conference. Proceedings.

**Natural Science Research**
Box 545, Winona Lake, IN 46590.
- Natural Science News. irreg.

**Nature Conservancy**
1800 N. Kent St., Suite 800, Arlington, VA 22209.
- Nature Conservancy News. q. ISSN 0028-0852

**Nature Society**
Griggsville, IL 62340.
- Purple Martin News; North America's backyard journal. m.

**Naturegraph Publishers**
Box 1075, Happy Camp, CA 96039.
- American Wildlife Region Series. irreg. ISSN 0569-9096
- Naturegraph Ocean Guidebooks. irreg., latest issue 1974. ISSN 0077-6106

**Nausea**
c/o Leo Mailman, Ed., Box 4261, Long Beach, CA 90804.
- Nausea. s-a.

**Nautilus**
11 Chelten Rd., Havertown, PA 19083.
- Nautilus; the Pilsbry quarterly devoted to the interests of conchologists. q. ISSN 0028-1344

**Nautilus Press, Inc.**
1056 National Press Bldg., Washington, DC 20045.
- Coastal Zone Management; newsletter of coastal resource development, conservation & enhancement. w. ISSN 0045-723X
- Marine Fish Management. m.
- Marine Mammal News. m.
- Ocean Science News. w. ISSN 0029-8069

**Navajo Community College**
Tsaile, AZ 86556.
- Navajo Community College. President's Newsletter. m.

**Navajo Linguistic Society**
c/o Paul Platero, Ed., 11100 Pecos, S.W., Albuquerque, NM 87105.
- Dine Bizaad Manil'iih/Navajo Language Review. q.

**Navajo Museum and Research Department**
Navajo Tribal Museum, Drawer K, Window Rock, AZ 86515.
- Navajo Historical Publications. Biographical Series. irreg., no. 3, 1970. ISSN 0091-6684
- Navajo Historical Publications. Cultural Series. irreg.
- Navajo Historical Publications. Documentary Series. irreg.
- Navajo Historical Publications. Historical Series. irreg.

**Naval Institute Press**
Annapolis, MD 21402.
- Ships and Aircraft of the United States Fleet. irreg., 1975, 10th ed. ISSN 0080-9292
- U. S. Naval Institute. Naval Review; annual review of world seapower. a. ISSN 0077-6238
- U. S. Naval Institute. Proceedings. m. ISSN 0041-798X

**Naval Stores Review and Terpene Chemicals**
6613 Schouest St., Metairie, LA 70003.
- Naval Stores Review and Terpene Chemicals. bi-m. ISSN 0028-1468

**Naval Surface Weapons Center**
Public Affairs Office, Silver Spring, MD 20910.
- Oak Leaf. bi-m. ISSN 0029-7356

**Joseph Peter Navarro, Ed. & Pub.**
Box 13861 (UCSB), Santa Barbara, CA 93107.
- Journal of Mexican American History. irreg. ISSN 0047-2581

**Navigators**
Colorado Springs, CO 80901.
- Navlog. bi-m.

**Navillus Publishing Corporation**
1074 Hope St., Box 4790, Stamford, CT 06907.
- Health Media Buyer's Guide. s-a.
- Medical Marketing & Media; the monthly intercom of the medical marketplace. m. ISSN 0025-7354

**Naya Daur**
1065 Shady Hill Drive, Columbus, OH 43221.
- Naya Daur. q.

**Near East Foundation**
54 E. 64 St., New York, NY 10021.
- Near East Foundation. Annual Report. a., publication suspended between 1950 and 1960. ISSN 0077-6319
- Near East Foundation News. 1-3 nos.per year. ISSN 0028-1751

**Near East Research, Inc.**
444 N. Capitol St. N.W., Suite 412, Washington, DC 20001.
- Near East Report; a Washington newsletter on American policy in the Near East. w. ISSN 0028-176X

**Near North News, Inc.**
26 E. Huron St., Chicago, IL 60611.
- Near North News. w. ISSN 0028-1778

**Kenneth Nebenzahl, Inc.**
333 N. Michigan Ave., Chicago, IL 60601.
- Rare Americana; Catalogue. irreg. ISSN 0098-485X

**Nebraska. Bureau of Vital Statistics**
Lincoln, NE 68500.
- Nebraska Statistical Report of Abortions. irreg. ISSN 0095-3105

**Nebraska. Commission on Law Enforcement and Criminal Justice**
Box 94946, Lincoln, NE 68509.
- Nebraska. Commission on Law Enforcement and Criminal Justice. Criminal Justice Action Plan. irreg. ISSN 0091-9195
- Nebraska. Commission on Law Enforcement and Criminal Justice. Criminal Justice Comprehensive Plan. irreg. ISSN 0091-9128
- State of Nebraska Uniform Crime Report. a. ISSN 0090-3221

**Nebraska. Department of Economic Development**
Box 94666, State Capitol, Lincoln, NE 68509.
- Directory of Nebraska Manufacturers. biennial. ISSN 0070-5926
- Nebraska. Department of Economic Development. Annual Economic Report. irreg. ISSN 0362-1138 (prep. by its Division of Research)
- Nebraska Now. m.
- Nebraska on the March. q. ISSN 0028-193X
- Nebraska Statistical Handbook. irreg. ISSN 0097-9325 (prep. by its Division of Research)

**Nebraska. Department of Education. Division of Administrative Services**
Lincoln, NE 68508.
- Statistics & Facts About Nebraska Schools. a. ISSN 0561-9440 (prep. by its Statistical Services Section)

**Nebraska. Department of Education. Division of Vocational Education**
233 South 10th St., Lincoln, NE 68508.
- Nebraska. Manpower Development and Training Section. Annual Review. a. ISSN 0091-2239

**Nebraska. Department of Public Institutions**
Box 94728, Lincoln, NE 68509.
- D.P.I. Yellow Pages. a. ISSN 0360-4357
- Nebraska. Department of Public Institutions. Mental Health and Mental Retardation Services Annual Statistical Report. a.

**Nebraska. Department of Public Welfare**
P.O. Box 95026, 301 Centennial Mall So., Lincoln, NE 68509.
- Nebraska. Department of Public Welfare. Annual Report. a.

**Nebraska. Department of Roads**
So. Jct. N-2 & U.S. 77, Box 94759, Lincoln, NE 68509.
- Nebraska. Department of Roads. Focus on Nebraska Highways; one and six-year program. a.
- Nebraska. Department of Roads. Traffic Analysis Unit. Continuous Traffic Count Data and Traffic Characteristics on Nebraska Streets and Highways. a. ISSN 0091-844X
- Nebraska Highway Statistics: State and Local Construction Mileage. irreg. ISSN 0099-0442 (prep. by its Highway Statistical Unit)

**Nebraska. Division of Community Affairs**
Lincoln, NE 68509.
- Nebraska Community Improvement Program. a. (Co-Sponsor: University of Nebraska Extension Division)

**Nebraska. Equal Opportunity Commission**
1620 M St., Lincoln, NE 68508.
- Nebraska. Equal Opportunity Commission. Annual Report. a. ISSN 0077-636X

**Nebraska. Game and Parks Commission**
Lincoln, NE 68509.
- Nebraska. Fisheries Production Division. Annual Report. a. ISSN 0092-1696 (prep. by its Fisheries Division)
- Nebraska Afield and Afloat. m.
- Nebraskaland. m. ISSN 0028-1964

**Nebraska. Governor's Conference on Human Resource Development**
Lincoln, NE 68509.
- Nebraska. Governor's Conference on Human Resource Development Report. a. ISSN 0098-826X

**Nebraska. Indian Commission**
Lincoln, NE 68508.
- Nebraska. Indian Commission. Report. irreg. ISSN 0360-683X

**Nebraska. Library Commission**
1420 P St, Lincoln, NE 68508.
- Nebraska Library Commission. Annual Report. a. ISSN 0099-0299
- Nebraska State Publications Checklist. (pub. by Nebraska Publications Clearinghouse)
- Overtones from the Underground. s-m.

**Nebraska. Natural Resources Commission**
Box 94725, Statehouse Station, Lincoln, NE 68509.
- Nebraska. Natural Resources Commission. State Water Plan Publication (Lincoln) irreg. ISSN 0092-6442
- Nebraska Resources. q. ISSN 0047-9217

**Nebraska. Office of Athletic Commissioner**
Lincoln, NE 68508.
- Nebraska. Office of Athletic Commissioner. Report. a. ISSN 0091-942X

**Nebraska. Office of Mental Retardation**
State House Station, Box 94728, Lincoln, NE 68509.
- Nebraska. Office of Mental Retardation. Directory of Community-Based Mental Retardation Services. irreg. ISSN 0096-3054

**Nebraska. State Accounting Division**
Lincoln, NE 68509.
- Nebraska. Accounting Division. Annual Report of Receipts and Disbursements State of Nebraska. a. ISSN 0090-628X

**Nebraska. State Patrol**
State House, Box 94637, Lincoln, NE 68509.
- Nebraska. State Patrol. Annual Report. a. ISSN 0094-1247

**Nebraska. State Personnel Department**
Box 94905, Lincoln, NE 68509.
- Statehouse Observer. m. ISSN 0091-1402

**Nebraska Academy of Sciences**
306 Morrill Hall, 14th & U Sts., Lincoln, NE 68508.
- Nebraska Academy of Sciences. Proceedings. a. ISSN 0077-6343
- Nebraska Academy of Sciences. Transactions. a., 1973, vol. 2. ISSN 0077-6351

**Nebraska & Omaha Food Retailers Association**
4563 Cuming St., Omaha, NE 68132.
- Nebraska Retailer. m. ISSN 0028-1948

**Nebraska Art Association**
- Nebraska Art Association Quarterly. (pub. by Sheldon Memorial Art Gallery)

**Nebraska Baptist State Convention**
6404 Maple St., Omaha, NE 68104.
- Nebraska Baptist Messenger. m (10 per yr.)

**Nebraska Democratic State Central Committee**
2635 O Street, Lincoln, NE 68510.
- Nebraska Democrat. 6 per yr.

**Nebraska Dental Association**
134 S. 13th St., Lincoln, NE 68508.
- Nebraska Dental Association. Journal. q. ISSN 0028-1832

**Nebraska Farm Bureau Federation**
P.O. Box 80299, Lincoln, NE 68501.
- Nebraska Agriculture. s-m(m. July-Aug.)

**Nebraska Farmer Co.**
5601 O St., Lincoln, NE 68501.
- Colorado Rancher and Farmer. m. ISSN 0010-1729
- Nebraska Farmer. s-m.

**Nebraska Law Enforcement Training Center**
Rt. 3, Box 50, Grand Island, NE 68801.
- Report on Law Enforcement Training in Nebraska. a. ISSN 0092-7198

**Nebraska Library Association**
3420 S. 37th St., Lincoln, NE 68506.
- Nebraska Library Association Quarterly. q. ISSN 0028-1883

**Nebraska Lumber Merchants Association**
1026 Terminal Bldg., Lincoln, NE 68508.
- Lumber Merchant. m. ISSN 0024-7308

**Nebraska Medical Association**
1902 First National Bank Bldg., Lincoln, NE 68508.
- Nebraska Medical Journal. m. ISSN 0091-6730

**Nebraska Motor Carriers Association Inc.**
521 South 14th St., Rm. 101, Lincoln, NE 68508.
- Midwestern Trucker and Shipper. (pub. by Cornhusker Press)
- Nebraska Trucker. m.

**Nebraska Nurses' Association**
Suite 26, 10730 Pacific Street, Omaha, NE 68114.
- Nebraska Nurse. q. ISSN 0028-1921

**Nebraska Optometric Association**
9Th and Minn., Hastings, NE 68901.
- Nebraska Optometric Association. Journal. bi-m. ISSN 0470-5661

**Nebraska Ornithologists' Union, Inc.**
5109 Underwood Ave., Omaha, NE 68132.
- Nebraska Bird Review; a magazine of the ornithology of the Nebraska region. q. ISSN 0028-1816

**Nebraska Pharmaceutical Association**
1001 Anderson Bldg., Lincoln, NE 68508.
- Nebraska Mortar and Pestle. m. ISSN 0028-1891

**Nebraska Poultry Industries, Inc.**
Poultry Science Building, University of Nebraska, Lincoln, NE 68503.
- Nebraska Poultry Industries. Bulletin. irreg.

**Nebraska Press Association**
Suite 723, Sharp Building, Tenth & O Sts., Lincoln, NE 68508.
- Nebraska Newspaper. m. ISSN 0028-1913

**Nebraska Public Power District**
P.O. Box 499, Columbus, NE 68601.
- Spotlighting Nebraska. q.

**Nebraska Publications Clearinghouse**
1420 P St., NE, Lincoln, NE 68508.
- Guide to Nebraska State Agencies. a. ISSN 0091-0716
- Nebraska State Publications Checklist. bi-m. ISSN 0091-0406 (Nebraska. Library Commission)

**Nebraska Rural Electric Association**
1320 N St., Lincoln, NE 68501.
- Rural Electric Nebraskan. m.

**Nebraska State Education Association**
94846 Statehouse, Lincoln, NE 68509.
- Nebraska Ed News. w.(Sept-May)

**Nebraska State Historical Society**
1500 R St., Lincoln, NE 68508.
- Nebraska History. q. ISSN 0028-1859
- Nebraska State Historical Society Historical Newsletter. m.

**Nebraska Water Resources Research Institute**
University of Nebraska, Lincoln, NE 68503.
- Nebraska Water Resources Research Institute, University of Nebraska. Annual Report of Activities. a. ISSN 0077-6394

**Nedelni Hlasatel**
1545 West 18th St., Chicago, IL 60608.
- Nedelni Hlasatel. w.

**Needle and Bobbin Club**
c/o Mrs. P. Guth, 955 Fifth Ave., New York, NY 10021.
- Needle and Bobbin Club Bulletin. s-a.

**Needlepoint, Inc.**
50 South U.S. 1, Suite 200, Jupiter, FL 33458.
- Needlepoint Bulletin. bi-m.

**Needlework Guild of America**
1736 Pine St., Philadelphia, PA 19103.
- Needlework Guild of America. Annual Report. a. ISSN 0360-1102

**NEF Publishing Co.**
Box 148, Lincoln Center, MA 01773.
- Winged Purposes. s-a.

**Negro Airmen International, Inc.**
Box 38166, Detroit, MI 48238
(Subscr. to: Box 723, Westbury, NY 11590)
- Negro Airmen International Newsletter. q.

**Negro Educational Review, Inc.**
Box 2895, West Bay Annex, Jacksonville, FL 32216.
- Negro Educational Review. q.

**Negro Lawmaker Journal**
Box 1615, South Carolina State College, Orangeburg, SC 29115.
- Negro Lawmaker Journal. q. ISSN 0047-9306

**Negro Universities Press**
51 Riverside Ave., Westport, CT 06880.
- Contributions in Afro-American and African Studies. irreg. ISSN 0069-9624

**Thomas Nelson and Sons**
405 Seventh Ave. South, Nashville, TN 37203.
- Applications of Mathematics Series.

**A. Verner Nelson Associates**
1282 Old Skokie Road, Highland Park, IL 60035.
- Evaluation Engineering. bi-m. ISSN 0014-3316
- Modern Applications News for Design and Manufacturing. bi-m. ISSN 0026-7473

**Nelson Gallery-Atkins Museum**
4525 Oak St., Kansas City, MO 64111.
- Nelson Gallery and Atkins Museum. Bulletin. irreg., 3 issues annually. ISSN 0077-6513
- Nelson Gallery and Atkins Museum. Gallery Events. m. ISSN 0047-9322

**Nelson-Hall Publishing Co.**
325 W. Jackson Blvd., Chicago, IL 60606.
- Practical Knowledge. m. ISSN 0032-6410

**Neo-American Church**
Box 948, Montpelier, VT 05602
- Divine Toad Sweat. m. ISSN 0046-0427 (Subscr. to:, 7941-C Milton, Whittier, CA 90602)

**Neptune Productions**
Box 360, Belmar, NJ 07719.
- Female Impersonator. q.
- Shemale. q. (United Transvestite Transexual Society)

**Netherlands Chamber of Commerce in U.S.**
1 Rockefeller Plaza, New York, NY 10020
- Netherlands-American Trade. 11 per yr. ISSN 0028-2855 (And, Spui 3, Box 10, the Hague, Netherlands)

**Netherlands Consulate General. Economic Information Service**
One Rockefeller Plaza, New York, NY 10020.
- Netherlands Economic Bulletin for the Foreign Press. s-m. ISSN 0028-2901

**Nettennis, Inc.**
168-20 127th Ave., Box 484, Rochdale Village, Jamaica, NY 11434.
- Nettennis. q.

**Neturei Karta of U.S.A.-Guardians of the Holy City**
P.O. 2143, Brooklyn, New York, NY 11202.
- Jewish Guardian. bi-m.

**Neue Zeitung**
9471 Hidden Valley Place, Beverly Hills, CA 90210.
- Neue Zeitung; American - European weekly serving the entire German speaking community of California. w.

**Neuroelectric Society, Inc.**
c/o Anthony Sances, Medical College of Wisconsin, 8700 W. Wisconsin Ave., Milwaukee, WI 53226.
- Neuroelectric News. 3 per yr. ISSN 0047-942X

**Neurotics Anonymous International Liaison, Inc.**
Rm. 426, Colorado Bldg., 1341 G. St. N.W., Washington, DC 20005.
- Journal of Mental Health. m. ISSN 0022-2658

**Nevada. Advisory Council for Manpower Training and Career Education**
Carson City, NV 89701.
- Nevada. Advisory Council for Manpower Training and Career Education. Annual Evaluation Report. a. ISSN 0093-9595

**Nevada. Bureau of Mines and Geology**
- Nevada. Bureau of Mines and Geology. Report. (pub. by University of Nevada. Mackay School of Mines)

**Nevada. Commission on Crime, Delinquency, and Corrections**
Carson City, NV 89701.
- Nevada. Commission on Crime, Delinquency and Corrections. Comprehensive Law Enforcement Plan. irreg. ISSN 0092-1084

- State of Nevada Comprehensive Criminal Justice
Plan. irreg.

**Nevada. Department of Economic Development**
Capitol Complex, Carson City, NV 89710.
- Nevada. q.

**Nevada. Department of Education**
400 West King St., Carson City, NV 89701.
- Survey of Adult and Continuing Education
Programs in Nevada. s-a.

**Nevada. Department of Highways**
1263 S. Stewart St., Carson City, NV 89712.
- Nevada. Department of Highways. Planning
Survey Division. Status of Road Systems. a. ISSN
0077-7870

**Nevada. Division of Personnel**
Carson City, NV 89701.
- Nevada. Division of Personnel. Biennial Report.
biennial. ISSN 0077-7889

**Nevada. Employment Security Department**
500 E. Third St., Carson City, NV 89713.
- State of Nevada Wage Report. a. ISSN 0081-4563

**Nevada. Gaming Control Board. Economic Research
Unit**
515 E. Musser St., Carson City, NV 89701.
- Direct Levies on Gaming in Nevada; analysis of
the rates and structure by all levels of
government. a. ISSN 0093-8823

**Nevada. Office of Legislative Auditor**
Carson City, NV 89701.
- Nevada. Office of Legislative Auditor. Biennial
Report. a.

**Nevada. Public Works Board**
Legislative Bldg, Carson City, NV 89701.
- Nevada. State Public Works Board.
Recommended Capital Improvement Program.
biennial. ISSN 0091-0694

**Nevada. Research and Education Planning Center**
University of Nevada, College of Education,
Research Coordination Unit, Rm. 201, Reno, NV
89507.
- R C U Report. (Research Coordinating Unit) m.
ISSN 0047-9497

**Nevada. State Board for Vocational Education**
Carson City, NV 89701.
- Nevada State Plan for Vocational Education. a.
ISSN 0094-1123

**Nevada. State Library**
Capitol Complex, Carson City, NV 89710.
- Nevada Library Directory and Statistics. a.
- Nevada State Library. Official Nevada
Publications. m. ISSN 0028-4106

**Nevada. State Planning Coordinators Office**
Capital Building, Room 306, Carson City, NV
89701.
- Nevada Planner. q. ISSN 0300-8908

**Nevada. Tax Commission**
Capital Plaza, 1100 E Williams St., Carson City,
NV 89701.
- Nevada Tax Commission. Local Government Red
Book; ad valoren tax rates & budget summaries. a.

**Nevada Cattlemen's Association**
- Nevada Rancher. (pub. by Jay Publishing)

**Nevada Farm Bureau Federation**
- Nevada Livestock and Agriculture Journal. (pub.
by Western Printing & Publishing Co.)

**Nevada Historical Society**
1650 N. Virginia St., Reno, NV 89502.
- Nevada Historical Society Quarterly. q. ISSN
0047-9462

**Nevada League of Cities**
Box 2307, Carson City, NV 89701.
- Nevada Government Today. q. ISSN 0360-9731

**Nevada Library Association**
c/o State Library, Carson City, NV 89710.
- Nevada Libraries Highroller. q.

**Nevada Music Educators Association**
1100 Forson Drive, Reno, NV 89502.
- Nevada Notes. q. ISSN 0028-4076

**Nevada Publishing Co.**
300 E. 1st St., Rm. 4, Box 99, Reno, NV 89504.
- Nevada Beverage Index. m.

**Nevada Society of Professional Engineers**
- Nevada Engineer. (pub. by Jay Publishing)

**Nevada State Education Association**
151 Park St., Carson City, NV 89701.
- Nevada Education Journal. q. ISSN 0028-4033

**Nevada State Medical Association**
3660 Baker Lane, Reno, NV 89509.
- Nevada State Medical Association. Bulletin. bi-m.

**Nevada State Museum**
Carson City, NV 89701.
- Nevada. State Museum, Carson City.
Anthropological Papers. irreg., no. 16, 1975. ISSN
0077-7897
- Nevada. State Museum, Carson City. Natural
History Publications. irreg., 1969, no. 2. ISSN
0077-7900
- Nevada. State Museum, Carson City. Occasional
Papers. irreg. ISSN 0077-7919
- Nevada. State Museum, Carson City. Popular
Series. irreg., 1972, no. 4. ISSN 0077-7927

**Nevil Interagency Referral Service**
919 Walnut St. Rm. 400, Philadelphia, PA 19107.
- Blindness, Visual Impairment, Deaf-Blindness;
listing of current literature. s-a. ISSN 0363-7689

**New Age Communications Inc.**
32 Station St., Brookline Village, MA 02146
- New Age. q. (Subscr. to:, Box 4921, Manchester
NH 03105)

**New Age Teachings**
37 Maple St., Brookfield, MA 01506.
- New Age Teachings. m.

**New Alaskan Publishing Co.**
Rt. 1-Box 677, Ketchikan, AK 99901.
- New Alaskan. m. (10 per yr.) ISSN 0300-8959

**New Alchemy Institute - West**
Box 376, Tescadero, CA 94060.
- New Alchemy Institute - West. Newsletter. q.

**New American Library**
Box 999, Bergenfield, NJ 07621.
- Complete Handbook of Soccer. a. ISSN 0363-
6046

**New American Library (New York)**
1301 Ave. of the Americas, New York, NY 10019.
- Complete Handbook of Pro Football. irreg. ISSN
0361-2988

**New American Movement**
6025 Shattuck Ave., Oakland, CA 94609.
- New American Movement. m.

**New Atlantean Research Society**
4280 68 Ave. N., Pinellas Park, FL 33565.
- New Atlanteans Journal. q.

**New Awareness Publishing Co., Inc.**
2274 Como Ave., St. Paul, MN 55108.
- O T J /Occult Trade Journal; new awareness
booknews. 10 per yr. (Occult Communications
Corporation)

**New Banner Institute, Inc.**
c/o W. Robert Black, Box 1972, Columbia, SC
29202.
- New Banner. s-m. ISSN 0047-9527

**New Books**
R.D.3, Trumansburg, NY 14886.
- New American & Canadian Poetry. 3 per yr.
ISSN 0028-4203

**New Broom**
P.O. 1646, Dallas, TX 75221.
- New Broom; journal of witchcraft. q.

**New Collage Press**
5700 N. Trail, Sarasota, FL 33580.
- New Collage. 3 per yr. ISSN 0028-4467

**New Daily Cardinal Corporation**
821 University Ave., Madison, WI 53706.
- Daily Cardinal. d. ISSN 0011-5398

**New Day Publishing Co.**
1600 W. Oxford St., Philadelphia, PA 19121.
- New Day. w. ISSN 0028-453X

**New Detroit, Inc.**
719 Griswold, 1010 Commonwealth Bldg., Detroit,
MI 48226.
- New Detroit Now. q.

**New Dimensions**
Box 11106, San Francisco, CA 94101.
- New Dimensions. 10 per yr.

**New Dimensions in Education, Inc.**
83 Keeler Ave., Norwalk, CT 06854.
- Alpha News. irreg.

**New Directions for Women, Inc.**
223 Old Hool Rd., Westwood, NJ 07675.
- New Directions for Women; feminist news
quarterly. q.

**New Earth Books**
58 St. Marks Place, New York, NY 10003.
- New Earth Review. q.

**New East, Inc.**
223 W. 10th St., Greenville, NC 27834.
- New East; the family magazine of North Carolina.
bi-m.

**New England Association of Teachers of English**
Box 234, Lexington, MA 02173.
- Leaflet. q. ISSN 0023-964X

**New England Beverage Publications, Inc.**
Bodwell St., Avon, MA 02322.
- Maine, New Hampshire, Vermont Beverage
Journal. m. ISSN 0025-0716
- Massachusetts Beverage Journal. m.

**New England Board of Higher Education**
40 Grove St., Wellesley, MA 02181.
- Channel (Wellesley) bi-m. ISSN 0045-6330 (New
England Library Information Network)
- Facts about New England Colleges, Universities
and Institutes. a. ISSN 0071-3643
- New England Board of Higher Education. New
England Regional Student Program: Graduate
Level. a.
- New England Board of Higher Education. New
England Regional Student Program:
Undergraduate Level. a.

**New England Botanical Club, Inc.**
Botanical Museum, Oxford St., Cambridge, MA
02138.
- Rhodora. q. ISSN 0035-4902

**New England Bride**
Box 397, Sudbury, MA 01776.
- New England Bride. q. ISSN 0028-4688

**New England Caller, Inc.**
80 Central St., Norwell, MA 02061.
- New England Square Dance Caller. m. ISSN
0028-4920

**New England Council of Optometrists**
101 Tremont St., Boston, MA 02108.
- New England Journal of Optometry. m. (Sept-
June) ISSN 0028-4807

**New England Crop and Livestock Reporting Service**
Massachusetts Department of Agriculture, 100
Cambridge St., Boston, MA 02202.
- Massachusetts Agricultural Statistics. a. ISSN
0092-9794

**New England Fuel Institute**
390 Commonwealth Ave., Boston, MA 02215.
- Yankee Oilman. m. ISSN 0044-0205

**New England Furniture News**
2 Knowlton St., Box 378, Beverly, MA 01915.
- New England Furniture News. bi-m. ISSN 0028-
4742

**New England Gardening**
14 Presbrey Court, Taunton, MA 02780.
- New England Gardening. m.

**New England Genealogical Society. Committee on
Heraldry**
101 Newbury St., Boston, MA 02116.
- Roll of Arms. irreg.

**New England Hardware Publications**
13 Main Street, Hingham, MA 02043.
- New England Hardware. m. ISSN 0028-4777

**New England Historic Genealogical Society**
101 Newbury St, Boston, MA 02116.
- New England Historical and Genealogical Register. q. ISSN 0028-4785

**New England History Teachers Association**
Home Office, Bentley College, Waltham, MA 02154.
- New England Social Studies Bulletin. s-a. ISSN 0028-4912

**New England Interstate Water Pollution Control Commission**
607 Boylston St., Boston, MA 02116.
- N E I W P C C Aqua News. q.

**New England Library Board**
231 Capitol Ave., Hartford, CT 06115.
- N E L B Link. 5 per yr. ISSN 0362-1618

**New England Library Information Network**
- Channel (Wellesley) (pub. by New England Board of Higher Education)

**New England Prisoner's Association**
Franconia College, Franconia, NH 03580.
- N E P A News. m.

**New England Program in Teacher Education**
Pettee Brook Offices, Durham, NH 03824.
- Common. 10 per yr.

**New England Railroad Club**
Box 550, Pembroke, MA 02359.
- New England Railroad Club. Official Proceedings. 4 per yr.(approx.) ISSN 0028-4874

**New England Reading Association**
University of Rhode Island, Kingston, RI 02881.
- New England Reading Association. Journal. 3 per yr. ISSN 0028-4882

**New England River Basins Commission**
55 Court St., Boston, MA 02108.
- New England River Basins Commission. Regional Report. bi-m.
- New England River Basins Commission. Report. a. ISSN 0077-8265

**New England Road Builders Association**
20 Kilby St., Boston, MA 02109.
- C I M Construction Journal. w.
- N E R B A Annual Directory; a directory and catalog of highway and heavy construction in New England. a. ISSN 0077-8281

**New England School Development Council**
55 Chapel St., Newton, MA 02160.
- N E S D E C Exchange. m.

**New England School of Law**
126 Newbury St., Boston, MA 02116.
- New England Journal on Prison Law. s-a. ISSN 0095-7364
- New England Law Review. s-a. ISSN 0028-4823

**New England Science Fiction Association Inc.**
Box G., MIT Branch P.O., Cambridge, MA 02139.
- N.E.S.F.A. Index: Science Fiction Magazines and Anthologies. irreg.

**New England Telephone Co.**
99 High St., Boston, MA 02110.
- Topics. bi-m. ISSN 0040-9367

**New England Water Works Association**
990 Washington St., Dedham, MA 02026.
- New England Water Works Association. Journal. q. ISSN 0028-4939

**New Environment Association**
c/o Harry Schwarzlander, Ed., 270 Fenway Drive, Syracuse, NY 13224.
- New Environment Bulletin. m.

**New Era Educational Society, Inc.**
245 N. Fifth St., Reading, PA 19601.
- New Era. w. ISSN 0028-503X (United Labor Council of Reading and Berks County)

**New Era Magazine**
c/o Vernon L. Frye, 22031 Bushard, Huntington Beach, CA 92646.
- New Era Laundry & Cleaning Lines. m. ISSN 0028-5056

**New Gay Life**
Box 13420, Philadelphia, PA 19101.
- New Gay Life. m.

**New Gospel Treasure Publishing Co**
201 Grizzard R-12, Nashville, TN 37207.
- New Gospel Treasure Select-a-Song; gospel sheet music locator catalog. a. ISSN 0362-7357

**New Hampshire. Bureau of Vital Statistics**
Concord, NH 03301.
- New Hampshire Vital Statistics. ISSN 0095-5523

**New Hampshire. Commission on Crime and Delinquency**
Concord, NH 03301.
- New Hampshire Comprehensive Law Enforcement Plan. irreg. ISSN 0094-7628

**New Hampshire. Council on Aging**
71 So. Main St., Box 786, Concord, NH 03301.
- Directory of Resources for Older People in New Hampshire. irreg. ISSN 0094-1441

**New Hampshire. Department of Agriculture. Bureau of Markets**
State House Annex, Concord, NH 03301.
- Weekly Market Bulletin. w. ISSN 0043-1850

**New Hampshire. Department of Education**
64 No. Main St., Concord, NH 03301.
- New Hampshire. Department of Education. Division of Administration. Education Directory. a. ISSN 0362-6709
- New Hampshire Polyglot. q. ISSN 0028-5293 (Co-sponsor: New Hampshire Association for Teaching of Foreign Languages)

**New Hampshire. Department of Education. Food and Nutrition Service**
State House Annex, Concord, NH 03301.
- Tiffin Topics Newsletter. bi-m.

**New Hampshire. Department of Employment Security**
Concord, NH 03301.
- New Hampshire Occupational Outlook. irreg. ISSN 0095-1102

**New Hampshire. Division of Public Health. Program on Alcohol & Drug Abuse**
66 South St., Concord, NH 03301.
- New Hampshire Program on Alcohol & Drug Abuse Bulletin. bi-m.

**New Hampshire. Employment Service Bureau**
Concord, NH 03301.
- New Hampshire Annual Rural Manpower Report. a. ISSN 0094-7687

**New Hampshire. Fish and Game Department**
34 Bridge St., Concord, NH 03301.
- New Hampshire. Fish and Game Department. Biennial Report. biennial. ISSN 0077-8362
- New Hampshire Natural Resources. q. ISSN 0028-5285

**New Hampshire. Fish and Game Department. Game Management and Research Division**
34 Bridge St., Concord, NH 03301.
- New Hampshire. Fish and Game Department. Management and Research. Biological Survey Bulletin. irreg., 1968, no. 10. ISSN 0077-8397
- New Hampshire. Fish and Game Department. Management and Research Division. Biological Survey Series. irreg., 1970, no. 9. ISSN 0077-8370
- New Hampshire. Fish and Game Department. Management and Research. Technical Circular Series. irreg., 1968, no. 22a. ISSN 0077-8389

**New Hampshire. State Library**
20 Park St., Concord, NH 03301.
- Granite State Libraries. bi-m. ISSN 0046-6301

**New Hampshire Archeological Society Inc.**
Averill Rd., Brookline, NH 03033.
- New Hampshire Archeologist. a. ISSN 0077-8346

**New Hampshire Archeological Society, Inc. (Manchester)**
129 Amherst St., Manchester, NH 03104.
- New Hampshire Archaeological Society Newsletter. s-a.

**New Hampshire Association of Conservation Commissions**
5 S. State St., Concord, NH 03301.
- N. H. Conservation Commission News. q. ISSN 0027-6537

**New Hampshire Campground Owners Association**
- New Hampshire Camping Guide. (pub. by Stephen W. Winship and Co.)

**New Hampshire Dental Society**
23 School St., Concord, NH 03301.
- N H D S Newsletter. bi-m. ISSN 0027-6545

**New Hampshire Education Association**
103 N. State St., Concord, NH 03301.
- New Hampshire Educator. 10 per yr. ISSN 0028-5234

**New Hampshire Historical Society**
30 Park St., Concord, NH 03301.
- Historical New Hampshire. q. ISSN 0018-2508

**New Hampshire Library Association**
Bedford, NH 03102.
- New Hampshire Library Association. Newsletter. 3 per yr. ISSN 0028-5269

**New Hampshire Music Educators Association**
Ed. Douglas L. Osborne, RFD 5 Water St., Penacook, NH 03301.
- New Hampshire Quarter Notes. 4 per yr. ISSN 0028-5315

**New Hampshire Nurses Association**
48 West St., Concord, NH 03301.
- New Hampshire Nursing News. q. ISSN 0029-6538

**New Hampshire School Administrators Association**
4 Myrtle Swamp, Hillsboro, NH 03244.
- N H S A A. m. ISSN 0027-6588

**New Hampshire School Boards Association**
Morrill Hall, Durham, NH 03824.
- N. H. School Boards Association Newsletter. bi-m. ISSN 0027-660X

**New Hampshire Social Welfare Council**
52-A Pleasant St., Concord, NH 03301.
- Human Services. bi-m.

**New Hampshire Truck Owners Association**
Box 665, Manchester, NH 03105.
- New Hampshire Motor Transport. m. ISSN 0028-5277

**New Horizons Communications Group Press**
Box 914, Culver City, CA 90230.
- Coastline Magazine. irreg.

**New Horse Play**
Box 247, 50-B Ridge Rd., Greenbelt, MD 20770.
- New Horse Play. m.

**New Internationalist Publications Ltd.**
113 Atlantic Ave., Brooklyn, NY 11201.
- New Internationalist. m.

**New Jersey. Advisory Commission on the Status of Women**
363 West State St., Trenton, NJ 08625.
- New Jersey. Advisory Commission on the Status of Women. Newsletter. bi-m.

**New Jersey. Bureau of Community Mental Health Services**
Trenton, NJ 08625.
- New Jersey. Bureau of Community Mental Health Services. Community Mental Health Projects Summary Statistics. irreg. ISSN 0098-6399

**New Jersey. Bureau of Geology and Topography**
Box 2809, Trenton, NJ 08625.
- New Jersey. Bureau of Geology and Topography. Annual Report. a. ISSN 0362-2649
- New Jersey. Bureau of Geology and Topography. Bulletin. irreg., no. 74, 1975.
- New Jersey. Bureau of Geology and Topography. Geologic Report Series. irreg., latest no. 11.

**New Jersey. Bureau of Statistical Analysis and Social Research**
Trenton, NJ 08625.
- New Jersey. Bureau of Statistical Analysis and Social Research. Schools for the Mentally Retarded. a. ISSN 0548-5150

**New Jersey. Department of Agriculture**
P.O. Box 1888, Trenton, NJ 08625.
- New Jersey. Department of Agriculture. Highlights of the Annual Report. a. ISSN 0077-846X
- New Jersey Equine Industry News. q. ISSN 0028-5706

**New Jersey. Department of Community Affairs. Division of Local Government Services**
363 W. State St., Box 2768, Trenton, NJ 08625.
- Local Planner. q. (prep. by its Local Planning Assistance Unit)

**New Jersey. Department of Corrections**
Box 7387, Trenton, NJ 08625.
- New Jersey Correction News. 5 per yr. ISSN 0028-5595

**New Jersey. Department of Education**
225 West State St., Trenton, NJ 08625.
- D. H. E. Data Briefs. bi-m. (prep. by its Division of Higher Education)
- New Jersey. Department of Education. Educational Assessment Program State Report. irreg. ISSN 0362-5958 (prep. by its Division of Research, Planning and Evaluation)
- New Jersey Historical Commission Newsletter. (pub. by New Jersey Historical Commission)
- New Jersey Interact. 9 per yr.
- Perspective. irreg., no. 7, 1974. ISSN 0091-2875 (prep. by its Division of Research, Planning and Evaluation)

**New Jersey. Department of Education. Division of Curriculum and Instruction**
107 W. State St., Trenton, NJ 08625.
- Bureau Briefs. 3-4 per yr. ISSN 0007-6066 (prep. by its Branch of Special Education and Pupil Services)
- Migrant Education/Educacion Migrantes. q. (prep. by its Office of Migrant Education)

**New Jersey. Department of Education. Division of Vocational Education**
225 West State Street, Trenton, NJ 08625.
- Directory of Private Trade, Technical and Art Schools. s-a. ISSN 0092-4202
- Feedback for Improving Vocational-Technical and Career Education. q.
- New Jersey State Plan for Vocational Education. a.

**New Jersey. Department of Environmental Protection**
John Fitch Plaza, Trenton, NJ 08625.
- New Jersey. Department of Environmental Protection. Annual Report. a. ISSN 0092-3311
- New Jersey Department of Environmental Protection D. E. P. Decisions. m.
- New Jersey Outdoors. bi-m.

**New Jersey. Department of Environmental Protection. Division of Water Resources**
Trenton, NJ 08625
(Order from: Bureau of Geology and Topography, Box 2809, Trenton NJ 08625)
- New Jersey. Division of Water Resources. Special Report. irreg., no. 38, 1974. ISSN 0092-1602
- New Jersey. Division of Water Resources. Water Resources Circulars. irreg, latest issue no. 23. ISSN 0545-2252

**New Jersey. Department of Environmental Protection. New Jersey Clean Air Council**
John Fitch Plaza, Trenton, NJ 08625.
- New Jersey Clean Air Council. Report. a. ISSN 0077-8451

**New Jersey. Department of Human Services. Division of Youth and Family Services**
One South Montgomery St, Trenton, NJ 08625.
- Family. m.

**New Jersey. Department of Labor and Industry**
Trenton, NJ 08625.
- New Jersey Job Guide. irreg., no. 24, 1974. ISSN 0548-5762

**New Jersey. Department of Labor and Industry. Division of Planning and Research.**
Box 359, Trenton, NJ 08625.
- New Jersey. Department of Labor and Industry. Division of Planning and Research. Commercial and Industrial Construction Plans Approved; Annual Summary. a. ISSN 0098-0285
- New Jersey. Department of Labor and Industry. Employment in Nonagricultural Establishments. a.
- New Jersey. Department of Labor and Industry. Hours and Earnings of Production Workers. a.
- New Jersey. Department of Labor and Industry. Production Workers in Manufacturing Establishments by Two-Digit Industry. a.
- New Jersey Covered Employment Trends by Geographical Areas of the State. a. ISSN 0092-1459

**New Jersey. Department of Labor and Industry. Office of Business Economics**
Box 845, Trenton, NJ 08625.
- New Jersey. Office of Business Economics. Population Estimates for New Jersey. a. ISSN 0091-9187

**New Jersey. Department of Law and Public Safety. Division of Civil Defense-Disaster Control**
Eggert Crossing Rd., Box 979, Trenton, NJ 08625.
- Siren. 2 per yr. ISSN 0037-5853

**New Jersey. Department of the Treasury. Division of Taxation**
W. State & Willow Sts., Trenton, NJ 08625.
- New Jersey. Department of the Treasury. Local Property and Public Utility Branch News. 6 per yr plus annual report. (prep. by its Local Property and Public Utility Branch)
- State Tax News. bi-m.

**New Jersey. Department of Transportation**
1035 Parkway Ave., Trenton, NJ 08625.
- New Jersey. Department of Transportation. Report of Operations. a. ISSN 0085-3921
- New Jersey Airport Directory. a. ISSN 0091-6978

**New Jersey. Developmental Disabilities Council**
169 West Hanover St, Trenton, NJ 08625.
- Interface. bi-m.
- New Jersey. Developmental Disabilities Council. Annual Report. a. ISSN 0090-077X

**New Jersey. Division of Administrative Procedure**
10 N. Stockton St., Trenton, NJ 08608.
- New Jersey Register. m. ISSN 0300-6069

**New Jersey. Division of Banking**
Trenton, NJ 08625.
- New Jersey. Division of Banking Annual Report. a. ISSN 0098-7409

**New Jersey. Division of Criminal Justice. Appellate Section**
7 Glenwood Ave., East Orange, NJ 07017.
- Criminal Justice Quarterly. q. ISSN 0092-3907

**New Jersey. Highway Authority. Garden State Parkway**
Traffic Division, Woodbridge, NJ 07095.
- Garden State Parkway Traffic Report. m.

**New Jersey. Office of Economic Policy**
134 W. State St., Trenton, NJ 08625.
- New Jersey. Economic Policy Council. Annual Report of Economic Policy Council and Office of Economic Policy. a. ISSN 0077-8478

**New Jersey. Office of International Trade**
Room 508, 1100 Raymond Blvd., Newark, NJ 07102.
- International Report. m.

**New Jersey. State Health Benefits Commission**
Trenton, NJ 08625.
- State Health Benefits Program of New Jersey. Annual Report. a. ISSN 0099-2100

**New Jersey. State Law Enforcement Planning Agency**
447 Bellevue Ave., Trenton, NJ 08618.
- Criminal Justice Plan for New Jersey. irreg. ISSN 0092-4652

**New Jersey. State Legislature. Office of Fiscal Affairs**
Trenton, NJ 08625.
- New Jersey. Legislature. Office of Fiscal Affairs. Annual Report. a. ISSN 0093-9986

**New Jersey. State Library**
185 West State Street, Trenton, NJ 08625.
- Checklist of Official New Jersey Publications. bi-m.
- New Jersey. State Library. Union List of Serials. irreg. ISSN 0094-890X
- New Jersey Area Library Directory. irreg. ISSN 0362-2967
- New Jersey Days; a calendar of notable events and personalities in New Jersey history. m. ISSN 0028-5633 (prep. by its Archives and History Bureau)
- New Jersey Public Libraries. Statistics. a.

**New Jersey. State Office on Aging**
Dept. of Community Affairs, Box 2768, Trenton, NJ 08625.
- Added Years. m.

**New Jersey. Violent Crimes Compensation Board**
1100 Raymond Blvd., Newark, NJ 07102.
- New Jersey. Violent Crimes Compensation Board. Annual Report. a. ISSN 0092-3079

**New Jersey Academy of Science**
Exec. Sec. M. Lelyn Branin, Box B, Rutgers University, New Brunswick, NJ 08903.
- New Jersey Academy of Science. Bulletin. s-a. ISSN 0028-5455
- New Jersey Academy of Science. Newsletter. irreg. ISSN 0028-5463

**New Jersey Association for Health, Physical Education and Recreation**
Fullerton St, Montclair, NJ 07042.
- New Jersey Association for Health, Physical Education and Recreation Reporter. q. ISSN 0034-477X

**New Jersey Association of Certified Dental Laboratories, Inc.**
857 Main Ave., Passaic, NJ 07055.
- New Jersey Association of Certified Dental Laboratories, Inc. Bulletin. ISSN 0028-5501

**New Jersey Association of Certified Dental Laboratories, Inc. (Springfield)**
118 Henshaw Ave., Springfield, NJ 07081.
- New Jersey Dental Laboratory Industry. Bulletin. 10 per yr. ISSN 0028-565X

**New Jersey Association of Osteopathic Physicians & Surgeons**
1212 Stuyvesant Ave., Trenton, NJ 08618.
- New Jersey Association of Osteopathic Physicians & Surgeons. Journal. m. ISSN 0028-5528

**New Jersey Association of Realtors**
Box 2098, 46 Parsonage Rd., Edison, NJ 08817.
- New Jersey Realtor. m. ISSN 0028-5919

**New Jersey Audubon Society**
790 Ewing Ave., Franklin Lakes, NJ 07417.
- New Jersey Audubon. m.

**New Jersey Bankers Association**
Box 573, Princeton, NJ 08540.
- New Jersey Banker. 3 per yr. ISSN 0028-5536

**New Jersey Bell Telephone Co**
Room 1705, 540 Broad St., Newark, NJ 07101.
- Communication. q.
- New Jersey Bell. q. ISSN 0028-5544

**New Jersey Civil Service Association**
- Shield. (pub. by New Jersey Shield Publishing Co., Inc.)

**New Jersey Classical Association**
Box 68, Lawrenceville, NJ 08648.
- New Jersey Classical Association. Bulletin. 3 per yr.

**New Jersey Committee for the Humanities**
137 Church St., New Brunswick, NJ 08903.
- New Jersey Committee for the Humanities Newsletter. bi-m.

**New Jersey Comprehensive Health Planning Agency**
John Fitch Plaza, Box 1540, Trenton, NJ 08625.
- Comprehensive Health Plan for New Jersey. a. ISSN 0094-1336

**New Jersey Congress of Parents and Teachers**
900 Berkeley Ave., Trenton, NJ 08607.
- New Jersey Parent Teacher. m.(Sept-June) ISSN 0028-5897

**New Jersey Cooperative Extension Service**
● Solid Waste Management. (pub. by Rutgers University. Cook College)

**New Jersey Council of School Administrators**
407 W. State St., Trenton, NJ 08608.
● Adminstrator Quarterly. q. ISSN 0001-8414

**New Jersey Council on Alcohol Problems**
100 South Willow Street, Trenton, NJ 08608.
● New Jersey Council News. bi-m. ISSN 0028-5609

**New Jersey Crop Reporting Service**
Trenton, NJ 08625.
● New Jersey Orchard and Vineyard Survey. irreg. ISSN 0098-9541

**New Jersey Dental Association**
Box 1715, North Brunswick, NJ 08902.
● New Jersey Dental Association. Journal. q. ISSN 0093-7347

**New Jersey Division of Savings and Loan Associations**
Trenton, NJ 08625.
● New Jersey. Divisions of Savings and Loan Associations. Annual Report. a. ISSN 0098-8073

**New Jersey Federation of Business & Professional Woman's Clubs, Inc.**
c/o Mrs. Eleanor Steger, 1108 Hollywood Blvd., Pt. Pleasant, NJ 08742.
● New Jersey Business Woman. bi-m. ISSN 0028-5579

**New Jersey Federation of Planning Officials**
1308 Wood Valley Road, Mountainside, NJ 07092.
● New Jersey Federation of Planning Officials. Federation Planner. bi-m. ISSN 0028-5714
● New Jersey Federation of Planning Officials. Federation Planning Information Reports. 4-5 per yr. ISSN 0028-5722

**New Jersey Federation of Shade Tree Commissions**
Cook College, Rutgers University, New Brunswick, NJ 08903.
● Shade Tree. 10 per yr. ISSN 0037-3133

**New Jersey Genesis Quarterly**
151 E. 81st St., New York, NY 10028.
● New Jersey Genesis Quarterly. q. ISSN 0028-5730

**New Jersey Historical Commission**
State Library, 185 W. State St., Trenton, NJ 08625.
● New Jersey Historical Commission Newsletter. m (10 per yr.) ISSN 0047-9772 (New Jersey. Department of Education)

**New Jersey Historical Society**
230 Broadway, Newark, NJ 07104.
● Cockpit. 4 per yr. ISSN 0010-0102
● Crossroads; a regular bulletin for New Jersey students. m. (Oct.-May) ISSN 0011-2046
● New Jersey History; a magazine of New Jersey history. q. ISSN 0028-5757
● New Jersey Messenger. 3 per yr. ISSN 0028-582X

**New Jersey Institute of Technology**
323 High St., Newark, NJ 07102.
● Nexus. q.

**New Jersey Jazz Society**
c/o Helen Dorn, 504 Vanderveer Rd., Bridgewater, NJ 08807.
● Jersey Jazz. m.

**New Jersey Law Journal Publishing Co.**
240 Mulberry St., Newark, NJ 07101.
● New Jersey Law Journal. w. ISSN 0028-5803

**New Jersey Library Association**
221 Blvd., Passaic, NJ 07055
● Evil John's Almanac. 5 per yr. (Subsc.: c/o Bloomfield Public Library, 90 Broad St., Bloomfield, NJ 07003)
● New Jersey Libraries; a news and opinion letter. m. ISSN 0028-5811

**New Jersey Manufacturers Association**
50 Park Place, Newark, NJ 07101.
● New Jersey Business; the magazine of industry and business. m. ISSN 0028-5560

**New Jersey Mortgage Finance Agency**
Trenton, NJ 08608.
● New Jersey Mortgage Finance Agency. Annual Report. a. ISSN 0362-1375

**New Jersey Mosquito Control Association, Inc**
c/o Henry R. Rupp, Ed., 1440 Mohawk Rd., North Brunswick, NJ 08902.
● New Jersey Mosquito Control Association. Proceedings. a.

**New Jersey Motor Truck Association**
Box 160, East Brunswick, NJ 08816.
● New Jersey Motor Truck Association. Bulletin. s-m. ISSN 0028-5838

**New Jersey Music and Arts**
c/o Louis A. de Furia, 572 Main St., Chatham, NJ 07928.
● New Jersey Music and Arts. 10 per yr. ISSN 0028-5854

**New Jersey Optometric Association**
514 Greenwood Ave., Trenton, NJ 08609.
● New Jersey Journal of Optometry. bi-m. ISSN 0028-5765

**New Jersey Pharmaceutical Association**
118 W. State St., Trenton, NJ 08608.
● New Jersey Journal of Pharmacy. m. ISSN 0028-5773

**New Jersey Poetry Society**
P.O. Box 217, Wharton, NJ 07885.
● Poetidings. m.

**New Jersey Postal History Society**
c/o E. E. Fricks, Ed., Box 663, Bound Brook, NJ 08805.
● New Jersey Postal History Society. Journal. bi-m.

**New Jersey Press Association**
Winants Hall, Rutgers Univ., New Brunswick, NJ 08903.
● Jersey Publisher. m. ISSN 0021-5961

**New Jersey Real Estate Commission**
Dept. of Insurance, 201 E. State St., Trenton, NJ 08625.
● New Jersey Advisor. q.

**New Jersey Savings League**
50 Park Place, Room 1530, Newark, NJ 07102.
● New Jersey Savings League News. q.

**New Jersey School Boards Association**
383 W. State St., Box 909, Trenton, NJ 08605.
● New Jersey School Boards Association. Legislative Bulletin. 4-5 per yr. ISSN 0024-046X
● New Jersey School Boards Association. Negotiations News and School Law Reporter. irreg., (7-13 per yr.)
● New Jersey School Leader. 6 per yr.
● School Boards Newsletter. m. ISSN 0036-648X

**New Jersey School Development Council**
Rutgers University, Graduate School of Education, New Brunswick, NJ 08903.
● N. J. S. D. C. Research Bulletin; council schools at work. q. ISSN 0028-5927

**New Jersey Shield Publishing Co., Inc.**
40 N. Van Brunt St., Englewood, NJ 07631.
● Shield; Civil Service news. w. ISSN 0037-3672 (New Jersey Civil Service Association)

**New Jersey Shore Builders Association**
2807 Bridge Ave., Point Pleasant, NJ 08742.
● New Jersey Shore Builders Association Bulletin Board; voice of the building industry at the Jersey shore. m.

**New Jersey Society of Architects**
110 Halsted St., East Orange, NJ 07018.
● Architecture New Jersey. q. ISSN 0003-8733

**New Jersey Society of Professional Engineers, Inc.**
495 W. State St., Trenton, NJ 08618.
● New Jersey Professional Engineer. q. ISSN 0028-5900

**New Jersey Speech and Hearing Association**
40 Oxford St., Montclair, NJ 07042.
● New Jersey Speech and Hearing Association. Journal. s-a. ISSN 0028-5935

**New Jersey Speech and Hearing Association (Rocky Hill)**
2 Lemore Circle, Rocky Hill, NJ 08553.
● New Jersey Speech and Hearing Association. Newsletter. 3-6 per yr. ISSN 0077-8516

**New Jersey State Agency for Social Security**
20 W. Front St., Trenton, NJ 08625.
● New Jersey. State Agency for Social Security. Annual Report. a.

**New Jersey State Bar Association**
172 W. State St., Trenton, NJ 08608.
● New Jersey State Bar Journal. q. ISSN 0028-5951

**New Jersey State Federation of Women's Clubs**
55 Clifton Ave., New Brunswick, NJ 08901.
● New Jersey Club Woman and Even'tide. 6 per yr. ISSN 0028-5587

**New Jersey State League of Municipalities**
433 Bellevue Ave., Trenton, NJ 08618.
● New Jersey Municipalities. m.(Oct.-June) ISSN 0028-5846

**New Jersey State Museum**
205 W. State St., Trenton, NJ 08625.
● New Jersey State Museum, Trenton. Bulletin. irreg., 1973, no. 14. ISSN 0077-8524
● Science Notes. irreg.

**New Jersey State Nurses' Association**
60 So. Fullerton Ave., Montclair, NJ 07042.
● N J S N A Newsletter. q. ISSN 0028-5870

**New Jersey State Patrolmen's Benevolent Association**
40 Main St., Butler, NJ 07405.
● New Jersey's Finest. m. ISSN 0028-5994

**New Jersey State Safety Council**
50 Park Place, Newark, NJ 07102.
● Safety Briefs. 7 per yr. ISSN 0036-245X

**New Journal at Yale, Inc.**
3432 Yale Sta., New Haven, CT 06520.
● New Journal. fortn. ISSN 0028-6001

**New Korea**
1368 W. Jefferson Blvd., Los Angeles, CA 90007.
● New Korea. w.

**New Magazine, Inc.**
867 River Rd., Piermont, NY 10968.
● New Magazine; people, places and ideas. . in Rockland County. 10 per yr. ISSN 0028-6109

**New Mexico. Bureau of Mines and Mineral Resources**
Socorro, NM 87801.
● New Mexico. Bureau of Mines and Mineral Resources. Bulletin. irreg., no. 107, 1976.
● New Mexico. Bureau of Mines and Mineral Resources. Circular. irreg., no. 154, 1976.
● New Mexico. Bureau of Mines and Mineral Resources. Hydrologic Report. irreg., no. 4, 1976.
● New Mexico. Bureau of Mines and Mineral Resources. Memoir. irreg., no. 30, 1975. ISSN 0548-5975
● New Mexico. Bureau of Mines and Mineral Resources. Progress Report. irreg., no. 8, 1973. ISSN 0098-7077

**New Mexico. Department of Agriculture**
P.O. Box 3189, Las Cruces, NM 88001.
● New Mexico Agricultural Statistics. a. ISSN 0077-8540 (Co-Sponsor: U.S. Department of Agriculture)

**New Mexico. Department of Development**
113 Washington Ave., Santa Fe, NM 87503.
● Directory of New Mexico Manufacturing and Mining. biennial. ISSN 0070-5934
● New Mexico Magazine. m. ISSN 0028-6249

**New Mexico. Department of Education. Veterans Approval Division**
200 West de Vargas, Santa Fe, NM 87501.
● Directory of Educational Institutions in New Mexico Approved for the Education of Veterans, War Orphans and Other Eligible Persons. a. ISSN 0084-991X

**New Mexico. Department of Game and Fish**
State Capitol, Sante Fe, NM 87501.
● New Mexico Wildlife. bi-m. ISSN 0028-6338

**New Mexico. Department of State Forestry**
Box 2167, Santa Fe, NM 87501.
● New Mexico Forest Products Directory. irreg. ISSN 0094-2782

New Mexico. Employment Security Commission
505 Marguette, N.W., P.O. Box 1928, Albuquerque, NM 87103.
- New Mexico. Employment Security Commission. Annual Rural Manpower Service Report. a. ISSN 0077-8559
- New Mexico Manpower Review. m. (prep. by its Research and Statistics Section)

New Mexico. Governor's Council on Criminal Justice Planning
Santa Fe, NM 87501.
- New Mexico. Governor's Council on Criminal Justice Planning. New Mexico Comprehensive Plan. a.

New Mexico. Secretary of State
Legislative-Executive Building, Santa Fe, NM 87501.
- New Mexico Blue Book. biennial.

New Mexico. State Planning Office
Santa Fe, NM 87501.
- New Mexico. State Planning Office. Annual Report. a.

New Mexico. State Records Center and Archives. Publications Management Division
404 Montezuma, Santa Fe, NM 87501.
- New Mexico. State Records Center & Archives. Publications and Rules Filed. m.

New Mexico. Supreme Court
- Report of Cases Determined in the Supreme Court and Court of Appeals of the State of New Mexico. (pub. by West Publishing Co.)

New Mexico. Veterans' Service Commission
Villagra Bldg., 408 Galisteo St., Santa Fe, NM 87501.
- New Mexico. Veterans' Service Commission. Report. biennial. ISSN 0094-7326

New Mexico Association of Elementary School Principals
2100 Morris N.E., Albuquerque, NM 87112.
- Nuevo Mexico Elementary Principal. s-a.

New Mexico Book League
8632 Horacio Pl, N. E., Albuquerque, NM 87111.
- Book Talk. bi-m.

New Mexico Cattle Growers Association
c/o Bill Hunt, Pub., 2231 Rio Grande Blvd. N.W., Box 7127, Albuquerque, NM 87104.
- New Mexico Stockman. m. (Co-sponsors: New Mexico Wool Growers; New Mexico Horse Council)

New Mexico Committee on Children and Youth
Box 6223, Albuquerque, NM 87107.
- New Mexico. Committee on Children and Youth. Annual Report. a. ISSN 0092-329X

New Mexico Educational Association
Box 729, Santa Fe, NM 87501.
- New Mexico School Review. q.(academic year) ISSN 0028-6303

New Mexico Farm & Ranch, Inc.
421 North Water St., Las Cruces, NM 88001.
- New Mexico Farm & Ranch. m. ISSN 0028-6192

New Mexico Geological Society
Campus Station, Socorro, NM 87801.
- New Mexico Geological Society. Guidebook, Field Conference. a. ISSN 0077-8567

New Mexico Motor Carriers' Association, Inc.
Box 25266, 1500 Indian School Rd. N.E., Albuquerque, NM 87125.
- New Mexico Transporter. m. ISSN 0047-9810

New Mexico Municipal League
1229 Paseo de Peralta, Box 846, Santa Fe, NM 87501.
- Directory of Municipal Officials of New Mexico. a. ISSN 0070-5888
- New Mexico Municipal League. Municipal Reporter. m. ISSN 0028-6257

New Mexico Music Educators Association
Ed. Melvin A. Hill, Music Dept., New Mexico Highlands Univ., Las Vegas, NM 87701.
- New Mexico Musician. 3 per yr. ISSN 0028-6265

New Mexico Pharmaceutical Association
4800 Zuni S.E., Albuquerque, NM 87108.
- Boticario. m. ISSN 0006-825X

New Mexico Review and Legislative Journal
Box 2328, Santa Fe, NM 87501.
- New Mexico Review and Legislative Journal. m. ISSN 0028-629X

New Mexico Rural Electrification Cooperative Association
614 Don Gaspar, Box 416, Santa Fe, NM 87501.
- Enchantment. m. ISSN 0046-1946

New Mexico Society of Professional Engineers
1615 University N.E., Albuquerque, NM 87102.
- New Mexico Professional Engineer. m. ISSN 0028-6281

New Mexico Solar Energy Association
Box 20004, Santa Fe, NM 87501.
- N M S E A Bulletin. m.

New Mexico State University Press
Las Cruces, NM 88001.
- Western Society for French History. Proceedings of the Annual Meeting. a. ISSN 0099-0329

New Mexico State University. Rio Grande Historical Collections Library
Box 3475, Las Cruces, NM 88003.
- Rio Grande History. s-a.

New Mexico State University. Writing Center
Box 3E, Las Cruces, NM 88003.
- Puerto del Sol. s-a.

New Moon Communications
Box 3488, Ridgeway Station, Stamford, CT 06905.
- Monthly Extract. irreg.

New Orleans Academy of Ophthalmology
- New Orleans Academy of Ophthalmology. Transactions. (pub. by C. V. Mosby Co.)

New Orleans Jazz Club
833 Conti St., New Orleans, LA 70112.
- Second Line. q. ISSN 0037-0576

New Orleans Jazz Club of California
Box 1225, Kerrville, TX 78028.
- Jazzologist. 6-9 per yr.

New Orleans Jazz Club of Southern California
Box No. 6192, Buena Park, CA 90620.
- Intermission. m.

New Orleans Public Library
219 Loyola Ave., New Orleans, LA 70140.
- Keynotes. w.

New Orleans Retail Grocers Association
Clyde de la Houssaye, Exec, Dir., 613 Cotton Exchange Bldg., New Orleans, LA 70130.
- Louisiana Grocer. m.

New Orleans Socialist Union
Box 53393, New Orleans, LA 70153.
- Louisiana Worker. 8 per yr.

New Politics Publishing Co.
507 Fifth Ave., New York, NY 10017.
- New Politics; a journal of socialist thought. q. ISSN 0028-6494

New Readers' Press
(Subsidiary of: Laubach Literacy, Inc.)
Box 131, Syracuse, NY 13210.
- News for You; weekly newspaper for adults with low reading skill. w. ISSN 0028-9051

New Renaissance
c/o Louise T. Reynolds, Ed., 9 Heath Rd., Arlington, MA 02174.
- New Renaissance; a magazine of ideas and opinions, emphasizing literature & the arts. irreg. ISSN 0028-6575

New Republic
1244 19th St., N.W., Washington, DC 20036.
- New Republic; a journal of opinion. w. ISSN 0028-6583

New Review Inc.
2700 Broadway, New York, NY 10025.
- Novyj Zhurnal/New Review. q. ISSN 0029-5337

New Scholar
Third World Studies Q-015, University of California, San Diego, La Jolla, CA 92093.
- New Scholar; studies, essays and reviews. s-a. ISSN 0028-6613

New School for Social Research
65 Fifth Ave., Rm. 351, New York, NY 10003.
- Social Research; an international journal of political and social science. q. ISSN 0037-783X

New School for Social Research. Center for New York City Affairs
66 Fifth Ave., New York, NY 10011.
- City Almanac. bi-m. ISSN 0009-7683
- New York City's Population: Socioeconomic Characteristics from the Current Population Survey. a.

New Schools Exchange
Pettigrew, AR 72752.
- New Schools Exchange Newsletter. 10 per yr. ISSN 0028-6656

New Sense
c/o Sidmel Estes, 2131 Ridge Ave., Evanston, IL 60201.
- New Sense. q.

New Skete Monastery
c/o Brother Job, Cambridge, NY 12816.
- Gleanings. q.

New Social Perspectives, Inc.
186 Hampshire St., Cambridge, MA 02139.
- Liberation. 10 per yr. ISSN 0024-189X

New South Press
Box 15060, New Orleans, LA 70175.
- Barataria. irreg.

New Times Communications Corp.
One Park Ave., New York, NY 10016.
- New Times (New York); the feature news magazine. fortn.

New Times, Inc.
1000 21st St., Rock Island, IL 61201.
- New Times (Rock Island); the quad-cities alternative newspaper. m.

New Times, Inc. (Tempe)
P.O. Box J, Tempe, AZ 85281.
- New Times (Tempe) w. ISSN 0047-9942

New Tribes Mission
- Brown Gold. (pub. by Brown Gold Publications)

New Unity
Box 891, Springfield, MA 01101.
- New Unity. m. ISSN 0047-9950

New Venture Publishing
c/o Stephen Fahnestalk, Ed., N. W. 440 Windus St., Pullman, WA 99163.
- New Venture. q.

New Viewpoints
c/o Franklin Watts, Inc., 730 Fifth Ave, 8th Floor, New York, NY 10019.
- Modern Scholarship on European History. irreg.
- Studies in Contemporary Politics. irreg.

New Voices
c/o Don Fried, Ed., 102 Butterville, New Paltz, NY 12561.
- New Voices. a.

New Way Enterprises, Ltd.
5850 Hollywood Blvd., Los Angeles, CA 90028.
- Los Angeles Free Press. w. ISSN 0024-6573

New Woman, Inc.
Box 24202, Ft. Lauderdale, FL 33307.
- New Woman; a digest for the woman of the Seventies. bi-m. ISSN 0028-6974

New World Arts Workshop
Rm. 414 Ohio Union, 1739 N. High St., Ohio State University, Columbus, OH 43210.
- Proud Black Images. a. ISSN 0048-5640

New World Club, Inc.
2121 Broadway, New York, NY 10023.
- Aufbau/Reconstruction. w. ISSN 0004-7813

**New World Forum, Inc.**
Box 5047, F.D.R. Station, New York, NY 10022.
● Unified World. 6 per yr. ISSN 0363-0994

**New World Haiku**
Box 256, San Fernando, CA 91340.
● New World Haiku. a.

**New World Press**
P.O. Box 15347-H, Tampa, FL 33684.
● New World Action; fiction quarterly. q.

**New World Publishing Co., Inc.**
109 N. Dearborn St., Chicago, IL 60602.
● New World. w. ISSN 0028-7016 (Archdiocese of Chicago)

**New World Review Publications, Inc.**
156 Fifth Ave., New York, NY 10010.
● New World Review. bi-m. ISSN 0028-7067

**New York (City) Addiction Services Agency**
65 Worth St., New York, NY 10013.
● New York (City). Comprehensive Plan for Drug Abuse Prevention and Treatment. a.; latest issue, 1972.

**New York (City) Board of Education**
110 Livingston St., Brooklyn, NY 11201.
● English Teacher. (pub. by New York Association of Teachers of English)
● High Points; in the New York City public schools. irreg. ISSN 0018-148X
● Instructional Resources. 4 per yr. (prep. by its Bureau of Audio Visual Instruction)
● Learning in New York. 5 per yr.
● Reading Intercom. 3 per yr. (prep. by its Funded High School Reading Program)

**New York (City) Bureau of the Budget**
Municipal Bldg., New York, NY 10007.
● New York (City) Capital Budget. a.

**New York (City) Comptrollers Office**
Municipal Building, New York, NY 10007.
● New York (City) Comptrollers Office. Report. m.

**New York (City) Department for the Aging**
250 Broadway, New York, NY 10007.
● Options: News for Older New Yorkers. m.

**New York (City) Department of Health**
125 Worth Street, New York, NY 10013.
● Spotlight on Health. m.

**New York (City) Department of Public Works. Bureau of Gas & Electricity**
Municipal Bldg., New York, NY 10007.
● Currents; items of interest to the electrical industry. bi-m.

**New York (City) Department of Social Services. Human Resources Administration**
Dept. of Social Services, 250 Church St., New York, NY 10013.
● Checkmate. m.

**New York (City) Fire Department**
110 Church St., New York, NY 10007.
● W N Y F. (With New York Firemen) q. ISSN 0042-9775

**New York (City) Health Systems Agency of New York City**
111 Broadway, New York, NY 10006.
● F Y I. (For Your Information) 10 per yr.

**New York (City) Housing Authority**
250 Broadway, New York, NY 10007.
● Housing Authority Journal. bi-m. ISSN 0018-6627

**New York (City) Metropolitan Transportation Authority**
1700 Broadway, New York, NY 10019.
● M T A News. m.

**New York (City) Office of Labor Relations**
250 Broadway, New York, NY 10007.
● New York (City). Office of Labor Relations. Interpretive Memorandum. irreg.

**New York (City) Office of the Mayor**
City Hall, New York, NY 10007.
● New York (City) Mayor. Schedules Supporting the Executive Budget. irreg. ISSN 0094-7547

**New York (City) Police Department**
51 Chambers St., New York, NY 10007.
● Spring Thirty-One Hundred; the magazine for policemen by policemen. 10 per yr. ISSN 0038-8572

**New York (City) Post Office**
Room 3509, G.P.O., New York, NY 10001.
● Postscript; voice of the New York Post Office. m.

**New York (City) Transit Authority**
370 Jay St., Brooklyn, NY 11201.
● Transit Record. m. ISSN 0041-1183

**New York (State) Consumer Protection Board**
Albany, NY 12207.
● New York (State) Consumer Protection Board. Annual Report. a. ISSN 0095-5590

**New York (State) Crime Victims Compensation Board**
875 Central Ave., Albany, NY 12206.
● New York (State) Crime Victims Compensation Board. Report. a. ISSN 0077-9148

**New York (State) Department of Audit and Control**
State Office Building, Albany, NY 12225.
● New York (State). Department of Audit and Control. Index to the Public Schools. irreg. ISSN 0091-3251
● New York (State) Department of Audit and Control. Municipal Affairs Review. m. ISSN 0467-6297 (prep. by its Municipal Affairs Administration Office)

**New York (State) Department of Commerce**
99 Washington Ave., Albany, NY 12245.
● Annual Summary of Business Statistics, New York State. a. ISSN 0066-4375
● Business Trends in New York State. m. ISSN 0007-7127
● New York (State) Department of Commerce. Exports of New York Manufactures. irreg., latest issue 1975.
● New York State Business Fact Book. Part 1: Business and Manufacturing. approx. every 5 years. ISSN 0077-9083
● New York State Business Fact Book. Part 2: Population and Housing. every 10 years. ISSN 0077-9091
● New York State Business Fact Book. Supplement. a. ISSN 0077-9105
● Personal Income in Counties of New York State. a. ISSN 0079-0907
● Quarterly Summary of Business Statistics, New York State. q.(annual cumulation) ISSN 0033-5851 (prep. by its Division of Economic Research and Statistics)

**New York (State) Department of Environmental Conservation**
50 Wolf Rd., Albany, NY 12233.
● Conservationist. bi-m. ISSN 0010-650X
● New York (State). Department of Environmental Conservation. Annual Report. a.
● New York (State). Environmental Quality Research and Development Unit. Technical Paper. irreg. ISSN 0362-6210 (prep. by its Environmental Quality Research and Development Unit)
● New York Fish and Game Journal. s-a. ISSN 0028-7210
● New York State Environment. m. ISSN 0048-0053

**New York (State) Department of Labor. Division of Research and Statistics**
Two World Trade Center (68th Fl.), New York, NY 10047
● Collective Bargaining Settlements in New York State. m plus annual report. ISSN 0045-7345 (Dist. by: Office of Public Information, State Campus, Albany, N.Y. 12240)
● Employment Review. m. ISSN 0013-6883 (Dist. by: Office of Public Information, State Campus, Albany, N.Y. 12240)
● New York (State) Department of Labor. Division of Research and Statistics. Employment Statistics. a; 1973, vol. 10. ISSN 0091-0767 (Dist. by: Office of Public Information, State Campus, Albany, N.Y. 12240)
● New York (State) Department of Labor. Division of Research and Statistics. Labor Research Report. irreg. ISSN 0093-5034 (Dist. by: Office of Public Information, State Campus, Albany, N.Y. 12240)

● New York (State) Department of Labor. Division of Research and Statistics. Statistics on Minorities and Women. a. (Dist. by: Office of Publications, State Campus, Albany, N.Y. 12240)
● New York (State) Department of Labor. Labor News Management. bi-w. (Dist. by: Office of Public Information, State Campus, Albany, N.Y. 12240)
● New York (State) Department of Labor. Legislative Digest. (Dist. by: Office of Public Information, State Campus, Albany, N.Y. 12240)
● New York (State) Department of Labor. Operations/Employment Service and Unemployment Insurance. m.
● New York (State). Department of Labor. Statistics on Operations. a. ISSN 0550-6638 (Dist. by: Office of Public Information, State Campus, Albany, N.Y. 12240)
● Statistics on Work Stoppages, New York State. a.

**New York (State) Department of Labor. Labor Staff Academy Library**
2 World Trade Center, New York, NY 10047.
● New York (State) Department of Labor. Manpower Services Division. Staff Academy Library. Selected Additions List. m.

**New York (State) Department of Law**
Office of the Attorney General, Justice Bldg, Empire State Plaza, Albany, NY 12224.
● New York (State) Opinions of the Attorney General. a.

**New York (State) Department of Law. Environmental Protection Bureau**
2 World Trade Center, Rm. 4772, New York, NY 10047.
● Environews. bi-m.

**New York (State) Department of Mental Hygiene**
44 Holland Ave., Albany, NY 11208.
● Mental Health Newsletter. q.
● Mental Hygiene News. s-m. ISSN 0047-6757

**New York (State) Department of Social Services**
1450 Western Ave., Albany, NY 12243.
● New York (State) Department of Social Services. Bureau of Research. Program Analysis Report. irreg., latest no. 54, 1974.
● New York (State) Department of Social Services. Bureau of Research. Program Brief. irreg., latest issue Nov. 1974. ISSN 0092-0878

**New York (State) Department of State**
162 Washington Ave, Albany, NY 12231.
● New York (State) Department of State. Manual for the Use of the Legislature of the State of New York; New York State Legislative manual. biennial.
● New York State Bulletin. bi-w. ISSN 0028-7555

**New York (State) Department of Taxation and Finance**
Sales Tax Bureau, State Campus, Albany, NY 12227.
● Sales Tax Newsletter. s-a.

**New York (State) Division of Criminal Justice Services**
Executive Park Tower, Stuyvesant Plaza, Albany, NY 12203.
● New York (State). Division of Criminal Justice Service. Annual Report. a. ISSN 0095-4047
● New York (State) Division of Criminal Justice Services. Felony Processing Quarterly Report. q.

**New York (State) Division of the Budget. Office of Statistical Coordination**
State Capitol, Albany, NY 12224.
● New York (State) Division of the Budget. New York State Statistical Yearbook. a. ISSN 0077-9334

**New York (State) Drug Abuse Control Commission**
Executive Park South, Albany, NY 12203.
● Attack; on narcotic addiction and drug abuse. q. ISSN 0571-8597
● D A C C Attack. q.

**New York (State) Education Department**
Albany, NY 12234.
● Inside Education. m.(Sept-June) ISSN 0020-1855
● Naho. (pub. by New York State Museum and Science Service)
● P S. (Post-Secondary Education in New York State) bi-m.
● Right to Read Forum & Exchange. q.

**New York (State) Education Department. Bureau of Educational Finance Research**
University of the State of New York, Albany, NY 12224.
- New York (State) University. Bureau of Educational Finance Research. Analysis of School Finances, New York State School Districts. a. ISSN 0077-9342
- State University of New York. Bureau of Educational Finance Research. Understanding Financial Support of Public Schools. irreg. ISSN 0362-3610 (Co-sponsor: State University of New York)

**New York (State) Education Department. Division of Education Management Services**
Albany, NY 12224.
- School Business Management Handbook. irreg. ISSN 0548-7900

**New York (State) Education Department. Information Center on Education**
Albany, NY 12234.
- College and University Admissions and Enrollment, New York State. a.
- College and University Degrees Conferred, New York State. a. ISSN 0077-9172
- Distribution of High School Graduates and College Going Rate in New York State. a. ISSN 0077-9210
- Education Statistics New York State. a.
- Employees in Colleges and Universities, New York State. a. (Co-Sponsor: State University of New York)
- New York (State) Education Department. Public School Professional Personnel Report. a. ISSN 0077-9229
- New York (State) Education Department. Survey of Enrollment, Staff and Schoolhousing. a. ISSN 0077-9245
- New York (State) Information Center on Education. Annual Educational Summary. a. ISSN 0085-4077
- Nonpublic Schools Enrollment and Staff, New York State. a. ISSN 0077-9253
- Racial/Ethnic Distribution of Public School Students and Staff in New York State. a. ISSN 0085-4093

**New York (State) Education Department. Office of Health, Pupil and Non-Pupil Public School Service**
University of the State of New York, Albany, NY 12235.
- Pupil Personnel Serivces. m (during school year)
- School Health Digest. bi-m.

**New York (State) Education Department. Office of Occupational Education**
Albany, NY 12224.
- Directory of Occupational Education Programs in New York State. irreg. ISSN 0098-096X

**New York (State) Education Department. Office of State History**
99 Washington Ave., Albany, NY 12210.
- Research and Publications in New York State History. a. ISSN 0080-1488

**New York (State) Energy Research and Development Authority**
230 Park Ave., New York, NY 10017.
- New York (State) Energy Research and Development Authority. Annual Report. a. ISSN 0361-2058

**New York (State) Foreign Area Materials Center**
- New York (State) Foreign Area Materials Center. Occasional Publication. (pub. by Bro- Dart Publishing Co.)

**New York (State) Geological Survey**
- Empire State Geogram. (pub. by New York State Museum and Science Service)

**New York (State) Health and Mental Hygiene Facilities Improvement Corporation**
44 Holland Ave., Albany, NY 12208.
- New York (State) Health and Mental Hygiene Facilities Improvement Corporation. Annual Report of Architectural and Construction Program. a. ISSN 0550-9556

**New York (State) Insurance Department**
Empire State Plaza, Agency Bldg. No. 1, Albany, NY 12223.
- Directory of Insurance Companies Licensed in New York State. irreg. ISSN 0070-5691

- New York (State) Insurance Department. Annual Report of the Superintendent of Insurance to the New York Legislature. a.
- New York (State) Insurance Department. Fees and Taxes Charged Insurance Companies Under the Laws of New York Together with Abstracts of Fees, Taxes and Other Requirements of Other States. a.
- New York (State) Insurance Department. Loss and Expense Ratios. a.
- New York (State) Insurance Department. Statistical Tables from Annual Statements. a.

**New York (State) Interdepartmental Committee on Indian Affairs**
1450 Western Ave., Albany, NY 12203.
- New York. State Interdepartmental Committee on Indian Affairs. Report. a. ISSN 0077-927X

**New York (State) Medical Care Facilities Finance Agency**
1250 Broadway, New York, NY 10001.
- New York State Medical Care Facilities Finance Agency. Annual Report. a. ISSN 0361-4018

**New York (State) Office for the Aging**
Empire State Plaza, Albany, NY 12223.
- New York State Office for the Aging. Newsletter. m.

**New York (State) Office of Parks and Recreation**
Albany, NY 12224.
- New York (State) Office of Parks and Recreation. Biannual Report. biennial. ISSN 0098-6712

**New York (State) Office of Planning Services**
488 Broadway, Albany, NY 12207.
- New York (State). Office of Planning Services. Annual Report. a.

**New York (State) Office of Welfare Inspector General**
655 Madison Ave., New York, NY 10021.
- New York (State), Office of Welfare Inspector General. Annual Report. a.

**New York (State) Public Employment Relations Board**
50 Wolf Rd., Albany, NY 12205.
- P E R B News. m.

**New York (State) State Library**
Albany, NY 12224.
- Bookmark; news about library services. bi-m. ISSN 0006-7407
- New York. State Library, Albany. Checklist of Official Publications of the State of New York. m., cumulated every year, every 5 years, every 15 years. ISSN 0077-9296 (prep. by its Gift and Exchange Section)

**New York (State) State Library. Division of Library Development**
Albany, NY 12224.
- Directory of College and University Libraries in New York State. a. ISSN 0070-5276
- Directory of Medical Libraries in New York State. irreg. ISSN 0070-5810
- Directory of New York State Public Library Systems. a. ISSN 0070-5950
- Directory of Reference and Research Library Resources Systems in New York State. a. ISSN 0070-6183
- New York. State Library, Albany. Division of Library Development. Excerpts from New York State Education Law, Rules of the Board of Regents, and Regulations of the Commissioner of Education Pertaining to Public and Free Association Libraries, Library Systems, Trustees and Librarians. a. ISSN 0077-930X
- New York. State Library, Albany. Division of Library Development. Institution Libraries Statistics. irreg. ISSN 0077-9318
- New York. State Library, Albany. Division of Library Development. Public and Association Libraries Statistics. a. ISSN 0077-9326

**New York (State) State Police**
Public Security Building, State Campus, Albany, NY 12226.
- Trooper. m. ISSN 0564-3287

**New York (State) Urban Development Corporation**
1345 Ave. of the Americas, New York, NY 10019.
- New York State Urban Development Corporation. Annual Report. a. ISSN 0077-9423

**New York (State) Workmen's Compensation Board**
Two World Trade Center, New York, NY 10047.
- New York (State) Workmen's Compensation Board. Summary of Activities. a.

**New York Academy of Dentistry**
Room 1102, 30 East 42nd St, Brooklyn, NY 10017.
- Annals of Dentistry. q. ISSN 0003-4770

**New York Academy of Medicine**
2 E. 103rd St., New York, NY 10029.
- New York Academy of Medicine. Bulletin. 10 per yr. ISSN 0028-7091
- New York Academy of Medicine. News Notes. 3 per yr. ISSN 0028-7105

**New York Academy of Medicine. Library**
Charles C. Morchand, Secy, 2 East 103rd St., New York, NY 10029.
- Academy Bookman. s-a. ISSN 0001-4249 (Friends of the New York Academy of Medicine. Friends of the Rare Book Room, Inc.)
- New York Academy of Medicine. Library. Subject Catalog of the Library. Supplement. (pub. by G. K. Hall & Co.)

**New York Academy of Sciences**
2 East 63rd St., New York, NY 10021.
- International Symposium on Myasthenia Gravis. Proceedings. quinquennial, 1970, 4th, New York. ISSN 0074-8870 (Myasthenia Gravis Foundation Inc.)
- New York Academy of Sciences. Annals. irreg.
- Sciences. m. ISSN 0036-861X

**New York Association of Teachers of English**
School of Education, Brooklyn College-C. U. N. Y., Brooklyn, NY 11210.
- English Teacher. s-a. (New York (City) Board of Education)

**New York Athletic Club**
180 Central Park South, New York, NY 10019.
- Winged Foot. m. ISSN 0043-5856

**New York Botanical Garden**
Bronx, NY 10458.
- Botanical Review; interpreting botanical progress. q. ISSN 0006-8101
- Brittonia. q. ISSN 0007-196X (American Society of Plant Taxonomists)
- Economic Botany; devoted to applied botany and plant utilization. q. ISSN 0013-0001 (Society for Economic Botany)
- Mycologia. bi-m. ISSN 0027-5514 (Mycological Society of America)
- New York Botanical Garden. Memoirs. irreg. ISSN 0077-8931
- New York Botanical Garden Newsletter. m. ISSN 0550-6565
- North American Flora. irreg. ISSN 0078-1312

**New York C.S. Lewis Society**
32 Park Drive, Ossining, NY 10562.
- C S L Bulletin. (C.S. Lewis Society) m.

**New York Cactus & Succulent Society, Inc.**
600 Lafayette Ave., Brooklyn, NY 11216.
- Cactus Comments. m. ISSN 0007-9383

**New York Chamber of Commerce and Industry**
65 Liberty St., New York, NY 10005.
- C C I Action. w.
- Real Estate Bulletin. s-m.
- World Trade Bulletin. fortn. ISSN 0043-9150

**New York City Central Labor Council. AFL-CIO**
386 Park Ave. S., New York, NY 10016.
- Labor Chronicle. 10 per yr. ISSN 0023-6519
- New York City Trade Union Handbook. irreg., 1975 latest edt. ISSN 0545-6061

**New York City Community College**
300 Jay St, Brooklyn, NY 11201.
- Arts and Sciences. bi-w. ISSN 0004-394X
- Concord. 2-3 per yr. ISSN 0010-5244

**New York City Elementary School Principals Association**
c/o Thomas J. Hiler, Public School 48, 6015 18th Ave., Brooklyn, NY 11204.
- New York Supervisor. s-a.

**New York City Housing Patrolmen's Benevolent Association, Inc.**
299 Broadway, New York, NY 10007.
- On the Beat. m.

**New York City Regional Center for Life-Long Learning**
Pace Plaza, New York, NY 10038.
- Directory of Continuing Education Opportunities in New York City. irreg. ISSN 0094-095X

**New York Civil Liberties Union**
84 Fifth Ave., New York, NY 10011.
- N. Y. Civil Liberties. bi-m.

**New York Civil Service Employees Publishing Co., Inc.**
150 Nassau St., New York, NY 10038.
- Chief. w. ISSN 0009-3807

**New York Clearing House**
100 Broad St., New York, NY 10004.
- Metropolis. q.

**New York College of Podiatric Medicine**
52 E. 124th St., New York, NY 10035.
- Alumnus. q.

**New York Conference of Mayors and Municipal Officials**
6 Elk St., Albany, NY 12207.
- Across the Table. m.
- New York Conference of Mayors and Municipal Officials. Legal Bulletin. m.

**New York Construction News, Inc.**
101 Park Avenue, New York, NY 10017.
- New York Construction News; serving the entire construction industry in Metropolitan New York and in Northern New Jersey. w. ISSN 0028-7164

**New York Convention & Visitors Bureau, Inc.**
90 East 42nd St., New York, NY 10017.
- New York Convention & Visitors Bureau. Quarterly Calendar of Events. q. ISSN 0028-7288

**New York County Lawyers' Association**
14 Vesey St., New York, NY 10007.
- Vesey Street Letter. 6 per yr. ISSN 0049-6030

**New York Credit & Financial Management Association**
71 W. 23rd St., New York, NY 10010.
- Credit Executive. bi-m. ISSN 0011-1007

**New York Crop Reporting Service**
c/o Dept. of Agriculture and Markets, State Campus, Albany, NY 12235.
- New York Agricultural Statistics. a. ISSN 0077-8966
- New York Dairy Statistics. a.

**New York Culture Review**
128 E. Fourth St., New York, NY 10003.
- East River Poetry Review. 4 per yr.
- New York Culture Review. 12 per yr. ISSN 0094-0194

**New York Dairy Herd Improvement Cooperative, Inc.**
Box 368, Ithaca, NY 14850.
- Northeast Improver. bi-m.

**New York Educators Association**
50 Wolf Rd., Albany, NY 12205.
- N Y E A Advocate. w.

**New York Entomological Society**
c/o Waksman Institute of Microbiology, Rutgers Univ., New Brunswick, NJ 08903.
- New York Entomological Society. Journal; devoted to entomology in general. q. ISSN 0028-7199

**New York Eye Publishing Co. Inc.**
Box 335, Lawrence, NY 11559.
- New York Antique Almanac. m.

**New York Family Counselors Institute**
Rutgers University, New Brunswick, NJ 08903.
- Journal of Family Counseling; official publication of the National Alliance for Family Life. s-a. ISSN 0093-3171 (National Alliance for Family Life)

**New York Folklore Society**
c/o Betty Morris, Cooperstown, NY 13326.
- New York Folklore. q. ISSN 0361-204X

**New York Foreign Freight Forwarders and Brokers Association, Inc.**
- Brandon's Shipper & Forwarder. (pub. by Herbert A. Brandon)

**New York Friends of the Earth**
72 Jane St., New York, NY 10014.
- N Y F O E. q.

**New York Genealogical and Biographical Society**
122 E. 58th St., New York, NY 10022.
- New York Genealogical and Biographical Record. q. ISSN 0028-7237

**New York Graphic**
- East Side News. (pub. by Ralph L. Clifford, Ed. & Pub.)
- New York Downtown News. (pub. by Ralph L. Clifford, Ed. & Pub.)
- Wall Street Advisor. (pub. by Ralph L. Clifford, Ed. & Pub.)

**New York Graphic Society**
140 Greenwich Ave., Greenwich, CT 06830.
- Boston Museum of Fine Arts. Museum Year. Annual Reports. a. (Boston Museum of Fine Arts)

**New York Historical Society**
170 Central Park West, New York, NY 10024.
- New-York Historical Society Quarterly. s-a. ISSN 0028-7253

**New York Holstein-Friesian Association**
- New York Holstein Friesian News. (pub. by Holstein-Friesian World, Inc.)

**New York Industrial Arts Association**
P. O. Box 34, Orangeburg, NY 10962.
- Spokesman. q. ISSN 0049-1888
- Spokesman Newsletter. m.

**New York Institute for Child Development Inc.**
36 E. 36th St., New York, NY 10016.
- Reaching Children. q.

**New York International Bible Society**
5 E.48th St., New York, NY 10017.
- BibleWorld; a quarterly review of the work of the New York Bible Society. q.

**New York Jets**
595 Madison Ave, New York, NY 10022.
- New York Jets Official Yearbook. a.

**New York Jewish Labor Committee. Educators Chapter**
25 East 78 Street, New York, NY 10021.
- J. L. C. Educator. 9 per yr.

**New York Journal of Dentistry, Inc.**
295 Madison Ave., New York, NY 10017.
- New York Journal of Dentistry. m.(Oct-May); bi-m.(June-Sept) ISSN 0028-7296 (First District Dental Society)

**New York Knickerbockers Basketball Club**
4 Pennsylvania Plaza, New York, NY 10001.
- New York Knicks Yearbook; official guide and record book. a.

**New York Law School Law Review**
57 Worth St., New York, NY 10013.
- New York Law School Law Review. 4 per yr.

**New York League for the Hard of Hearing**
71 W. 23rd St., New York, NY 10010.
- Hearing Rehabilitation Quarterly. q.
- New York League for the Hard of Hearing. Highlights. q. ISSN 0028-7334

**New York Library Association**
60 East 42 St., Suite 1242, New York, NY 10017.
- N. Y. L. A. Bulletin. m (Sep.-Jun.) ISSN 0027-7134

**New York Library Club**
6 Murray St., New York, NY 10007.
- New York Library Club Bulletin. irreg. (2-3 per yr.) ISSN 0028-7350

**New York Life Insurance Co.**
Marketing Dept. for the Field Representatives, 51 Madison Ave., New York, NY 10010.
- N Y L I C Review. m. ISSN 0027-7142

**New York Mercantile Exchange**
6 Harrison, New York, NY 10013.
- New York Mercantile Exchange Statistical Yearbook. a. ISSN 0090-8991

**New York Metro Area Postal Union**
461 Eighth Ave., New York, NY 10001.
- New York Metro Area Postal Union. Union Mail. m. (Nov.-Jun.); bi-m. (Jul.-Oct)

**New York Metropolitan Reference & Research Library Agency**
11 W. 40th St., New York, NY 10018.
- For Reference. m. ISSN 0015-685X
- METRO C.A.P. Catalog; a dictionary catalog of materials purchased through the Cooperative Acquisitions Program. a. ISSN 0363-1257
- METRO; New York Metropolitan Reference and Research Library Agency. METRO Miscellaneous Publications Series. irreg., no. 6, 1970, no. 7, 1974. ISSN 0076-7018
- New York Metropolitan Reference & Research Library Agency. Directory of Members. every 2-3 yrs. ISSN 0362-8744

**New York-New Jersey Trail Conference, Inc.**
Box 2250, New York, NY 10001.
- Trail Walker; news of hiking and conservation. bi-m.

**New York Paleontological Society**
127 W. 83d St., Box 287, Planetarium Station, New York, NY 10024.
- New York Paleontological Society. Notes. irreg.

**New York Personnel Management Association**
358 Fifth Ave., New York, NY 10001.
- N Y P M A Bulletin. 10 per yr. ISSN 0027-7150

**New York Planning Federation**
301 S. Allen St., Albany, NY 12208.
- New York State Planning News. bi-m. ISSN 0028-7679

**New York Psychoanalytic Institute. Kris Study Group**
- New York Psychoanalytic Institute. Kris Study Group. Monograph. (pub. by International Universities Press, Inc.)

**New York Public Library**
Fifth Ave. & 42nd St., New York, NY 10018.
- B N Y P L. Bulletin. 4 per yr. ISSN 0028-7466 (Subscr. to: Readex Books, 101 Fifth Ave., New York NY 10003)

**New York Public Library. Office of Adult Services**
8 E. 40th St., New York, NY 10016.
- Borinquen; a bilingual list of books, films and records on the Puerto Rican experience. irreg., 3rd edt. 1974.
- No Crystal Stair: a Bibliography of Black Literature. irreg. ISSN 0077-6491

**New York Public Library. Office of Branch Libraries**
8 E. 40 St., New York, NY 10016.
- Black Experience in Children's Books. irreg., latest issue 1974. ISSN 0067-9070
- Children's Books and Recordings: Suggested as Holiday Gifts. a.
- New York Public Library. Films; a catalogue of the film collection. irreg. ISSN 0077-9016

**New York Public Library. Office of Young Adult Services**
8 East 40th St., New York, NY 10016.
- Books for the Teen Age. a. ISSN 0068-0192

**New York Public Library. Schomburg Center for Research in Black Culture**
103 W. 135 St., New York, NY 10036.
- New York Public Library. Schomburg Center for Research in Black Culture. Journal. q.

**New York Public Library. Science and Technology Research Center**
Fifth Ave., and 42nd St., New York, NY 10018.
- New Technical Books; a selective list with descriptive annotations. m (except Aug. and Sept.) ISSN 0028-6869

**New York Publicity Outlets**
Box 327, Washington Depot, CT 06794.
- New York Publicity Outlets. a. ISSN 0077-9024

**New York Quarterly Poetry Review Foundation Inc.**
Box 2415, Grand Central Station, New York, NY 10017.
- New York Quarterly. irreg. ISSN 0028-7482

**New York Radical Feminists' Association**
75 Perry St., New York, NY 10014.
- N Y R F Newsletter. m.

**New York Rangers Hockey Club**
Madison Square Garden, 4 Pennsylvania Plaza, New York, NY 10001.
- New York Rangers Yearbook; official guide and records. a.

**New York School Counselor Association**
c/o Karen Ziff, Ed., Deer Park High School, Deer Park, NY 11729.
- New York School Counselor Association. Newsletter. q.

**New York Shavians, Inc.**
14 Washington Place, New York, NY 10003.
- Independent Shavian. 3 per yr. ISSN 0019-3763

**New York Society for the Relief of the Ruptured and Crippled**
- Hospital for Special Surgery. Journal. (pub. by Hospital for Special Surgery)

**New York State Academy of Family Physicians**
84 Main St., Binghamton, NY 13905.
- New York Family Physician. bi-m.

**New York State Archeological Association**
Ed. Louis A. Brennan, c/o Rochester Museum & Science Center, Rochester, NY 14607.
- New York State Archeological Association. Bulletin. 3 per yr. ISSN 0028-7512
- New York State Archeological Association. Occasional Papers. irreg., 1963, no. 4. ISSN 0077-9059
- New York State Archeological Association. Researches and Transactions. irreg., 1967, vol. 16. ISSN 0077-9067

**New York State Association for Retarded Children, Inc.**
175 Fifth Ave., New York, NY 10010.
- Our Children's Voice. q.

**New York State Association for Supervision and Curriculum Development**
c/o Peter Incalcaterra, 44 Ridgewood Ave. RD5, Kingston, NY 12401.
- Impact on Instructional Improvement. q.

**New York State Association of Certified Dental Laboratories**
- Dental Laboratory News. (pub. by Dental Laboratory Association)

**New York State Association of Teachers of Mentally Retarded**
65 Court St., 8th Fl., Brooklyn, NY 11201.
- Special Teacher. s-a.

**New York State Bankers Association**
485 Lexington Ave., New York, NY 10017.
- New York State Banker. fortn. ISSN 0028-7539

**New York State Bar Association**
1 Elk St., Albany, NY 12207.
- New York State Bar Journal. 8 per yr. ISSN 0028-7547
- New York State Law Digest. s-m (m. Jul, Oct, Nov & Dec.) ISSN 0028-7636

**New York State College of Agriculture and Life Sciences**
Cornell University, Ithaca, NY 14853.
- Cornell Agricultural Waste Management Conference. Proceedings. ISSN 0065-4604 (Co-Sponsors: U.S. Environmental Protection Agency, National Waste Treatment Research Program; National Canners Association)
- Cornell Countryman. m.(Oct-May) ISSN 0010-8782
- Cornell University. International Agricultural Development Bulletin. 3 per yr. ISSN 0010-888X (prep. by its International Agriculture Program)
- Cornell University. New York State College of Agriculture and Life Sciences. Biometrics Unit. Annual Report. a.
- Environmental Leaders Forum. Proceedings. irreg.
- New York's Food and Life Sciences Quarterly. q. ISSN 0028-7938
- Tree Fruit Production Recommendations. a. ISSN 0070-0118
- Vegetable Production Recommendations. a.

**New York State College of Ceramics at Alfred University**
Library, Alfred, NY 14802.
- Alfred Union List of Serials. irreg., latest issue 1975. (Co-Sponsors: Alfred University; State University of New York, Agricultural and Technical College at Alfred)

**New York State College of Human Ecology**
Cornell University, Ithaca, NY 14853.
- Human Ecology Forum. q. ISSN 0018-7178

**New York State Conference of Mayors and Other Municipal Officials**
6 Elk St., Albany, NY 12207.
- New York State Conference of Mayors and Other Municipal Officials. Legal Bulletin. m. ISSN 0028-7563

**New York State Congress of Parents and Teachers, Inc.**
11 N. Pearl St., Albany, NY 12207.
- New York Parent-Teacher. m.

**New York State Council for the Social Studies**
State University College, Buffalo, 1300 Elmwood, Buffalo, NY 14222.
- Social Science Record. 3 per yr. ISSN 0037-7872

**New York State Council on Alcohol Problems**
1690 1/2 Western Ave., Albany, NY 12203.
- Action (Albany) bi-m. ISSN 0001-7396

**New York State Craftsmen, Inc.**
27 W. 53rd St., New York, NY 10019.
- Crafts Bulletin. m.

**New York State Dental Society of Anesthesiology**
- New York State Dental Society of Anesthesiology. Newsletter. (pub. by Acorn Press)

**New York State English Council (Geneseo)**
State University College, Geneseo, NY 14454.
- English Record. q. ISSN 0013-8363

**New York State English Council (Oswego)**
c/o State University of New York at Oswego, Department of English, Oswego, NY 13126.
- New York State English Council. Monograph Series. irreg. ISSN 0548-9040

**New York State Food Merchants Association**
280 N. Central Ave., Hartsdale, NY 10530.
- Food Merchants Advocate. m. ISSN 0015-6493

**New York State Historical Association**
Cooperstown, NY 13326.
- New York History. q. ISSN 0028-7261
- New York State Historical Association. Newsletter. s-a.
- Yorker (1976) q.

**New York State Horticultural Society**
900 Jefferson Rd., Rochester, NY 14623.
- New York State Horticultural Society Newsletter. 7 per yr.

**New York State Hotel & Motel Association, Inc.**
141 W. 51st St., New York, NY 10019.
- Fire Prevention Bulletin. bi-m. ISSN 0015-2633

**New York State Motor Truck Association**
257 Park Ave. South, Rm. 1505, New York, NY 10010.
- Truck News. m.

**New York State Museum and Science Service**
Education Bldg. Annex, Hawk St., Albany, NY 12234.
- Empire State Geogram. 3 per yr. ISSN 0013-676X (New York (State) Geological Survey)
- Naho. q. ISSN 0027-7681 (New York (State) Education Department) (Co-sponsor: State University of New York)

**New York State Nurses Association**
Executive Park East, Stuyvesant Plaza, Albany, NY 12203.
- N Y S N A Legislative Bulletin. fortn.(during New York State legislative session)
- New York State Nurses Association. Journal. 4 per yr. ISSN 0028-7644
- New York State Nurses Association. Report. m. ISSN 0028-7652

**New York State Occupational Education Association**
Box 390, Monroe, New York, NY 10950.
- New York State Occupational Education Association. Newsletter. q.

**New York State Probation and Parole Officers Association**
Box 408, Madison Square Station, New York, NY 10010.
- Probation and Parole. a. ISSN 0079-5615

**New York State Psychological Association, Inc.**
250w. 57th Street, New York, NY 10019.
- New York State Psychologist. bi-m. ISSN 0028-7687

**New York State Safe Deposit Association**
521 Fifth Ave., New York, NY 10017.
- Safe Deposit Bulletin. m. ISSN 0036-2379

**New York State School Boards Association, Inc.**
111 Washington Ave., Albany, NY 12210.
- New York State School Boards Association. Legislative Bulletin. w.
- New York State School Boards Association Journal. m. ISSN 0028-7709

**New York State School Music Association**
Box 2620, Schenectady, NY 12309.
- School Music News. m.(Sept-May) ISSN 0036-6668

**New York State School Nurse-Teachers Association**
3 Computer Drive, Room 105, Albany, NY 12205.
- N Y S S N T A Journal. 4 per yr.

**New York State School of Industrial and Labor Relations**
Cornell University, Ithaca, NY 14853.
- Cornell International Industrial and Labor Relations Reports. irreg.; no. 9, 1977. ISSN 0070-0029
- Cornell Studies in Industrial and Labor Relations. irreg.; no. 19, 1977. ISSN 0070-0053
- Cornell University. New York State School of Industrial and Labor Relations. Key Issues Series. irreg.; no. 22, 1977. ISSN 0070-0185
- Cornell University. New York State School of Industrial and Labor Relations. Technical Monograph Series. irreg.; latest issue, 1969. ISSN 0070-0207
- I L R Paperbacks. irreg.; no. 16, 1977. ISSN 0070-0177
- Industrial and Labor Relations Bibliography Series. irreg.; no. 14, 1976. ISSN 0070-0142
- Industrial and Labor Relations Forum. q. ISSN 0019-7912
- Industrial and Labor Relations Report. q. ISSN 0019-7920
- Industrial and Labor Relations Review. q. ISSN 0019-7939
- New York State School of Industrial and Labor Relations. Bulletin. irreg.; no. 65, 1976. ISSN 0070-0134

**New York State Sea Grant Program**
- New York State Sea Grant Program. Annual Report. (pub. by State University of New York)

**New York State Society of Anesthesiologists, Inc.**
30 E. 42nd St., New York, NY 10017.
- N Y S S A Sphere. bi-m. ISSN 0095-2273

**New York State Society of Dentistry for Children**
27 E. 95th St., New York, NY 10028.
- New York State Society of Dentistry for Children. Bulletin. s-a. ISSN 0028-7741

**New York State Society of Dispensing Opticians, Inc.**
c/o Patrick E. Roche, Box 161, Williamsville, NY 14221.
- Ophthalmic Dispenser. m. (except Jul. & Aug.)

**New York State Society of Real Estate Appraisers**
Executive Tower, Stuyvesant Plaza, Albany, NY 12203.
- Appraisal Digest. q. ISSN 0003-7060

**New York State Speech Association**
c/o Brian P. Holleran, State Univ., Oneonta, NY 13820.
- New York State Speech Association. Reports. 3 per yr. ISSN 0028-775X

**New York State Teachers Association**
143 Washington Ave., Albany, NY 12210.
- Challenger. 35 per yr. ISSN 0045-6268

**New York State Education.** m.(Oct-May) ISSN 0028-7598

**New York State Trial Lawyers Association**
132 Nassau St. Suite 200, New York, NY 10038.
• Trial Lawyers Quarterly. q. ISSN 0041-2554

**New York State United Teachers**
260 Park Ave., S., New York, NY 10010.
• New York Teacher. w.

**New York State Young Americans for Freedom**
25 Jane St., New York, NY 10014.
• Conservative Journal. q. ISSN 0589-4522

**New York Stock Exchange**
11 Wall St., New York, NY 10005.
• New York Stock Exchange. Exchange Report. 10 per yr.
• New York Stock Exchange Monthly Review. m. ISSN 0548-7390

**New York Teamsters Joint Council. Carpenters District Council**
• Trade Union Courier. (pub. by Socio-Economic Publications, Inc.)

**New York Telephone Co.**
Room 2111, 140 West St., New York, NY 10007.
• New York City News. m.

**New York Theological Seminary**
235 E. 49th St., New York, NY 10017.
• New York Theological Seminary Bulletin. q. ISSN 0028-7792

**New York Times Co.**
229 W. 43rd St., New York, NY 10036.
• New York Times Book Review. w. ISSN 0028-7806
• New York Times Film Reviews. biennial. ISSN 0362-3688
• New York Times Large Type Weekly. w. ISSN 0028-7814
• New York Times School Weekly. w.(during school year) ISSN 0028-7830

**New York Times Company**
488 Madison Ave., New York, NY 10022.
• Us. bi-w.

**New York Typographical Union Number Six**
817 Broadway, New York, NY 10003.
• New York Typographical Union Number Six. Bulletin. m. ISSN 0049-4968

**New York University**
Washington Sq., New York, NY 10003.
• History of Education Quarterly. q. ISSN 0018-2680 (History of Education Society)
• Victorian Newsletter. s-a. ISSN 0042-5192 (Modern Language Association. English X Group)

**New York University. Bobst Library**
Division of Special Collections, Washington Square South, New York, NY 10012.
• New York University. Libraries. Bibliographical Series. irreg., latest issue 1971. ISSN 0077-9482

**New York University. Center for the Study of Financial Institutions**
90 Trinity Pl., New York, NY 10006.
• New York University Bulletin - Monograph. irreg., no. 93-99, 1974.

**New York University. Courant Institute of Mathematical Sciences**
• Communications on Pure and Applied Mathematics. (pub. by Wiley-Interscience)

**New York University. Criminal Law Education and Research Center**
40 Washington Square So., Room 434, New York, NY 10012
(Dist. by Fred B. Rothman, 57 Leuning St., S. Hackensack, N.J. 07606)
• American Series of Foreign Penal Codes. irreg., no. 21, 1977. ISSN 0066-0051
• New York University. Comparative Criminal Law Project. Publications. irreg., no. 6, 1968. ISSN 0077-944X
• New York University. Criminal Law Education and Research Center. Monograph Series. irreg., no. 9, 1969. ISSN 0077-9458

**New York University. Department of Music**
24 Waverly Place, New York, NY 10003.
• Verdi Newsletter. s-a. (American Institute for Verdi Studies)

**New York University. Institute of Fine Arts**
1 E. 78 St., New York, NY 10021
(Dist. by J. J. Augustin, Inc., Locust Valley, N.Y. 11560)
• Art and Archaeology Technical Abstracts; abstracts of the technical literature on archaeology and the fine arts. s-a. ISSN 0004-2994 (International Institute of Conservation)
• Artibus Asiae. (pub. by Artibus Asiae Publishers SZ)
• Marsyas. biennial. ISSN 0076-4701
• Walter W. S. Cook Alumni Lecture. (pub. by J. J. Augustin, Inc.)

**New York University. Institute of Labor Relations**
• Annual Conference on Labor at New York University. Proceedings. (pub. by Matthew Bender & Co., Inc.)

**New York University. Institute of Retail Management**
Tisch Bldg., Washington Sq., New York, NY 10003.
• Journal of Retailing. q. ISSN 0022-4359

**New York University. Law Publications**
249 Sullivan St., New York, NY 10012
• Annual Survey of American Law. 4 per yr. ISSN 0066-4413 (Or, 40 Washington Square South, N.Y., NY 10012)
• New York University Journal of International Law and Politics. 3 per yr. ISSN 0028-7873
• New York University Law Review. 6 per yr. ISSN 0028-7881
• Review of Law & Social Change. s-a. ISSN 0048-7481
• Tax Law Review. (pub. by Warren, Gorham and Lamont, Inc.)

**New York University Medical Center**
550 First Ave, New York, NY 10016.
• New York University Medical Center News. m.(except summer) ISSN 0028-789X
• New York University Medical Quarterly. q. ISSN 0028-7903
• Symposium on Ethical Issues in Human Experimentation. Proceedings. irreg. (prep. by its Urban Health Affairs Program)

**New York University Post-Graduate Medical School**
317 E 34th St., New York, NY 10016.
• New York University Post-Graduate Medical School. Inter-Clinic Information Bulletin. bi-m. ISSN 0028-7911

**New York University Press**
21 W. Fourth St., New York, NY 10012.
• Anson G. Phelps Lectureship on Early American History. irreg. ISSN 0066-4618
• Anthology Film Archives Series. irreg.
• Charles C. Moskowitz Lectures. a. ISSN 0084-8727 (New York University. School of Commerce)
• Deems Lectureship. irreg. ISSN 0070-3222
• New York University Studies in Comparative Literature. irreg. ISSN 0077-9504
• Studies in Contemporary Philosophy. irreg., vol. 2, 1973.
• Studies in Near Eastern Civilization. irreg. ISSN 0081-8291

**New York University. Public Relations Department**
21 Washington Place, New York, NY 10003.
• New York University Report. fortn. (Oct.-May); m. (June.-Sep.)

**New York University. School of Commerce**
• Charles C. Moskowitz Lectures. (pub. by New York University Press)

**New York University. School of Education, Health, Nursing and Arts Profession**
239 Greene St., New York, NY 10003.
• New York University Education Quarterly. q. ISSN 0550-5054

**New York University. School of the Arts**
51 W. 4th St., Rm. 300, New York, NY 10012.
• Drama Review. (T D R); international journal documenting historical and contemporary trends in the performing arts. q. ISSN 0012-5962

**New York University. Tamiment Institute**
New York University, Bobst Library, 7th Floor, 70 Washington Sq. South, NY 10012.
• Labor History. 4 per yr. ISSN 0023-656X

**New York University. Tamiment Library**
70 Washington Sq. So., New York, NY 10012.
• New York University. Libraries. Bulletin of the Tamiment Library. irreg., no. 49, 1974. ISSN 0077-9490

**New York Urban League. Brooklyn Branch**
1251 Dean St., Brooklyn, NY 11216.
• Brooklyn Urban League Herald. q.

**New York Workers' News & Perspective**
Box 240, Van Brunt Sta., Brooklyn, NY 11215.
• New York Workers' News & Perspective; a newspaper by, for, and about working people. s-m.

**New York Yearly Meeting of the Religious Society of Friends**
15 Rutherford Place, New York, NY 10003.
• Spark. 5 per yr. ISSN 0024-0591

**New York Zoological Society**
Zoological Park, Bronx, NY 10460.
• Animal Kingdom. bi-m. ISSN 0003-3537

**New Yorker Magazine, Inc.**
25 W. 43rd St., New York, NY 10036.
• New Yorker. w. ISSN 0028-792X

**New Yorkers for Abortion Law Repeal**
P.O. Box 240, Planetarium Station, New York, NY 10024.
• New Yorkers for Abortion Law Repeal. Newsletter. 10 per yr. ISSN 0300-7790

**New Yorski Tjednik Inc.**
101 Fifth Avenue, New York, NY 10003.
• Hrvatski Preporod/Croatian Rebirth. m.

**Newark Museum Association**
43-49 Washington St., Newark, NJ 07101.
• Newark Museum. News Notes. m.(Sept-June) ISSN 0028-9256
• Newark Museum Quarterly. q. ISSN 0098-3373

**Newark Public Library**
5 Washington St., Newark, NJ 07101.
• Criminology, Corrections and Police Science. m. (prep. by its Social Science and Labor Division)
• Labor in Print. q. ISSN 0023-6578 (prep. by its Lending and Reference Department)

**Newberry College**
Newberry, SC 29108.
• Studies in Short Fiction. q. ISSN 0039-3789

**Newberry Library**
60 W. Walton St., Chicago, IL 60610.
• Newberry Library Bulletin. irreg.
• Newberry Newsletter. 3 per yr.

**Newberry Library. Hermon Dunlap Smith Center for the History of Cartography**
60 W. Walton St., Chicago, IL 60610.
• Mapline. q.

**Newbury House, Publishers, Inc.**
68 Middle Road, Rowley, MA 01969.
• Studies in Bilingual Education. irreg.

**Newedi Press**
Dept. of English, Bowling Green University, Bowling Green, OH 43403.
• Betelgeuse Chapbook Series-Newedi Fiction Series. 4 per yr.

**Newhall Co.**
P.O. Box 9187, Berkeley, CA 94709.
• Stamp Auction Directory. a. ISSN 0081-4199

**Newkirk Associates**
3500 De Pauw Blvd. 1040, Box 1727, Indianapolis, IN 46206.
• Fraternal Monitor. m. ISSN 0016-0105 (Research and Review Service of America, Inc.)
• Handbook of Servicemen's and Veterans Benefits. irreg. ISSN 0072-9914 (Research and Review Service of America, Inc.)

**Newkirk Products, Inc.**
1092 Madison Ave, Albany, NY 12208.
• Monthly Digest of Tax Articles. m. ISSN 0027-0385

**Newlaw Media Inc.**
230 Park Ave., New York, NY 10017.
- New York Lawyer. m.

**Newport Historical Society**
82 Touro St., Newport, RI 02840.
- Newport History. q. ISSN 0028-8918

**Newport News Shipbuilding**
Newport News, VA 23607.
- Shipyard Bulletin. m.

**News & Letters Committees**
1900 E. Jefferson, Detroit, MI 48207.
- News & Letters. 10 per yr. ISSN 0028-8969

**News Bank, Inc.**
P.O. 645, Greenwich, CT 06830.
- Index to the F.B.I.S. Daily Report: Peoples Republic of China. q.
- Index to the F.B.I.S. Daily Report: Soviet Union. q.

**News Circle**
c/o Joseph Haiek, Box 74637, Los Angeles, CA 90004.
- American Arabic Speaking Community Almanac. a. ISSN 0094-8543
- Mideast Business Exchange. m.
- Mideast Business Guide. a.
- News Circle. m.

**News Leader, Inc.**
c/o J. K. Land, Box 1921, Baton Rouge, LA 70821.
- Monroe News Leader. w. ISSN 0026-9840

**Newscribes Group**
110 W 40 St., New York, NY 10018.
- Newscribes. irreg.

**Newsletters, Inc.**
300 E. 40 St., New York, NY 10016.
- Photo Industry Newsletter. s-m. ISSN 0300-7723
- Sporting Goods Newsletter. s-m.
- Travel Marketing Newsletter; group sales leads, publicity & promotion, travel data, travel marketing. s-m. ISSN 0041-2023

**Newsletters International**
2600 South Gessner Rd., Houston, TX 77063.
- Business & Acquisition Newsletter. m.
- Jewelery Newsletter International. m.

**Newspaper Advertising Bureau, Inc.**
485 Lexington Ave., New York, NY 10017.
- Expenditures of National Advertisers in Newspapers. a.; latest issue, 1974. ISSN 0071-3325

**Newspaper and Mail Deliverers' Union**
41-18 27th St., Long Island City, NY 11101.
- Newspaper and Mail Deliverers' Union Bulletin. m.

**Newspaper Enterprise Association, Inc.**
230 Park Ave., New York, NY 10017.
- World Almanac and Book of Facts. a. ISSN 0084-1382 (prep. by its World Almanac Division)

**Newspaper Fund, Inc.**
P.O. Box 300, Princeton, NJ 08540.
- Journalism Scholarship Guide; and directory of college journalism programs. a. ISSN 0449-3362
- Newspaper Fund Newsletter. m.

**Newspaper Guild**
A F L-C I O, 1125 15th St. N.W., Washington, DC 20005.
- Guild Reporter. s-m. ISSN 0017-5404
- Newspaper Guild. Annual T.N.G. Convention Officers' Report. a. ISSN 0090-2209

**Newspaper Guild of New York**
133 W. 44th St., New York, NY 10036.
- Frontpage. m. ISSN 0016-2183

**Newsprint Information Committee**
633 Third Ave., New York, NY 10017.
- Newsprint Facts. 5 per yr.

**Newsweb**
3503 N. Ashland, Chicago, IL 60657.
- Chicago Maroon. s-w. ISSN 0009-3610 (University of Chicago)

**Newsweek Books**
444 Madison Ave., New York, NY 10022.
- Milestones of History. irreg.

**Newsweek, Inc.**
444 Madison Ave., New York, NY 10022.
- Newsweek. w. ISSN 0028-9604

**Next**
c/o Andrew Reinbach, Editor, 49 W. 11th St., New York, NY 10011.
- Next. s-a.

**Niagara Frontier Transportation Authority.**
1600 Statler Hilton Hotel, Buffalo, NY 14202.
- Metro Newsletter. m.

**Niagara Magazine**
369 Pennsylvania St., Buffalo, NY 14201.
- Niagara Magazine. 3 per yr.

**Nichiren Shoshu Academy**
- N.S.A. Photo Album. (pub. by World Tribune Press)
- N.S.A. Quarterly. (pub. by World Tribune Press)
- World Tribune. (pub. by World Tribune Press)

**Nichols College**
Dudley, MA 01570.
- Nichols Alumnus. 5 per yr. ISSN 0300-6778 (prep. by its Alumni Association)

**Nickelodeon Graphics Arts Service**
1131 White, Kansas City, MO 64126.
- Nickelodeon. q.

**Nickerson & Collins Co.**
1800 Oakton, Des Plaines, IL 60018.
- Locksmith Ledger. m.
- Locksmith Ledger/Security Guide & Directory. a.
- Refrigeration Service and Contracting. m. ISSN 0034-3145

**Lewis Nicolas Co.,Inc.**
351 W. 22nd St., New York, NY 10011.
- Ningas-Cogon; newsmagazine for Filipinos. 10 per yr.

**Niekas Publications**
Belknap College, Center Harbor, NH 03226.
- Niekas. a. ISSN 0028-9809

**A.C. Nielsen Co.**
Nielsen Plaza, Northbrook, IL 60062.
- Nielsen Newscast. q. ISSN 0468-1835
- Nielsen Researcher. bi-m.
- Preview. w.

**Nieman Foundation**
48 Trowbridge, Cambridge, MA 02138.
- Nieman Reports. q. ISSN 0028-9817

**Nigerian Consulate General**
575 Lexington Ave., New York, NY 10022.
- Nigeria Trade Journal. q. ISSN 0029-0041

**Nightwings Press**
Box 244, Moorpark, CA 93021.
- Silver. irreg. ISSN 0090-5682

**Nitewriter Newsletter**
Box 263, 40-03 164th St., Flushing, NY 11358.
- Nitewriter Newsletter. 10 per yr.

**No Eyed Monster**
Ed. Norman Masters, 720 Bald Eagle Lake Rd., Ortonville, MI 48462.
- No Eyed Monster. q. ISSN 0029-0807

**No More Fun and Games**
c/o Cell 16, 14A Eliot St., Cambridge, MA 01238.
- No More Fun and Games; a journal of female liberation. irreg. ISSN 0029-0815

**No-Till Farmer, Inc.**
733 N. Van Buren, Milwaukee, WI 53202.
- No-Till Farmer. m. ISSN 0091-9993

**Noble and Most Singular Order of the Blue Carbuncle (N.M.S.O.B.C.)**
c/o Victor Hale, Ed., 11911 N.E. Halsey, Portland, OR 97220.
- Feathers from the Nest. q.

**Gilbert W. Noble, Ed. & Pub.**
Box 931, Winter Park, FL 32789.
- Noble Official Catalog of Canada Precancels. irreg., 10th ed., 1975. ISSN 0078-091X
- Noble Official Catalog of United States Bureau Precancels. a. ISSN 0078-0928

**Jason A. Nogee, Ed. & Pub.**
1434 S. Yale Ave., Arlington Heights, IL 60005.
- American Book Collector. bi-m. ISSN 0002-7693
- Health Data Index. q. ISSN 0017-8942

**Noise**
c/o Don McClelland, Ed., 278 Carl St., San Francisco, CA 94117.
- Noise. 4 per yr.

**Noise Control Foundation**
Box 1758, Poughkeepsie, NY 12603.
- Noise/News. bi-m.

**Nomis Publications Inc.**
Box 5122, Youngstown, OH 44514.
- Yellow Book of Funeral Directors & Services. National Yellow Book of Funeral Directors & Suppliers. a. ISSN 0098-3322

**Non-Intervention in Chile (NICH)**
Box 800, Berkeley, CA 94701.
- Chile Newsletter. bi-m.

**Non-Profit Organization Tax Letter**
Box 9902, Washington, DC 20015.
- Non-Profit Organization Tax Letter. s-m. ISSN 0550-8401

**Nor Or Publishing Co.**
7466 Beverly Blvd., Los Angeles, CA 90036.
- Nor Or. s-w. ISSN 0029-1161 (Armenian Democratic Liberal Organization)

**Nor-Shor Mgc.**
959 W. Drayton, Ferndale, MI 48220.
- Old Time Radio News. q.

**Norco Publications, Inc.**
12505 Lake City Way N.E., Seattle, WA 98125.
- Government Lands Digest. m.

**Norda Inc.**
475 Tenth Ave., New York, NY 10018.
- Norda Briefs. m. ISSN 0090-1903

**Nordco Pub. Inc.**
15917 Strathern St., Van Nuys, CA 91406.
- Powerboat. m. ISSN 0032-6089

**Norden Laboratories**
601 W. Cornhusker Hwy., P.O. Box 80809, Lincoln, NE 68521.
- Norden News. q.

**Norfolk and Western Railway Co.**
8 North Jefferson St., Roanoke, VA 24011.
- Norfolk and Western. 11 per yr. ISSN 0029-1633

**Norfolk Botanical Garden Society**
Airport Rd., Norfolk, VA 23518.
- Norfolk Botanical Garden Society Bulletin. m. ISSN 0029-1641

**Norfolk Chamber of Commerce**
Box 327, Norfolk, VA 23501.
- New Norfolk. m. ISSN 0028-6389

**Norman Glenn Publications, Inc.**
342 Madison Ave., New York, NY 10017.
- Decisions. m.

**Norman Publishing Corp.**
3090 N. Lincoln Ave., Box 1811, Altadena, CA 91001.
- Correspondence Education. bi-m.

**James Normington, Ed. & Pub.**
4724 Marlborough Way, Carmichael, CA 95608.
- Alcaeus Review. s-a.

**Luther Norris**
3844 Watseka Ave., Culver City, CA 90230
- Pontine Dossier. a. (Outside U.S. Dist. by: G. Ken Chapman Ltd., 2, Ross Rd., London, S.E. 25, Eng.)

**Harold Norse, Ed. & Pub.**
P.O. Box 3449, San Francisco, CA 94119.
- Bastard Angel. irreg. (approx. 1-2 per yr.)

**North American Association of Summer Sessions**
School for Summer & Continuing Education, Georgetown University, Washington, DC 20007.
- North American Association of Summer Sessions. Newsletter. q.

**North American Baptist Conference**
1 S. 210 Summit Ave., Oakbrook Terrace, IL
60181.
- Baptist Herald. m. ISSN 0005-5700

**North American Benefit Association**
1338 Military St., Port Huron, MI 48060.
- N. A. B. A. Review. bi-m. ISSN 0027-5689

**North American Bird Bander**
84-55 Daniels St., Jamaica, NY 11435
- North American Bird Bander. q. (Co-sponsors:
Eastern Bird Banding Association & Western Bird
Banding Association)

**North American Congress on Latin America, Inc.**
Box 226, Berkely, CA 94701
(and Box 57 Cathedral Sta., New York, NY 10025)
- N A C L A's Latin America & Empire Report. m
(10 per yr.)

**North American Council on Adoptable Children
(NACAC)**
c/o Ed. Joan McNamara, 6 Madison Ave.,
Ossining, NY 10562.
- National Adoptalk. q. ISSN 0027-8459

**North American Dostoevsky Society**
c/o Nadine Natov, George Washington University,
Dept. of Slavic Languages and Literatures,
Washington, DC 20006.
- International Dostoevsky Society Bulletin. s-a.
ISSN 0047-0686

**North American Fireman's Association**
6830 26th St."N. E., Seattle, WA 98115.
- Fire Station Digest. m. ISSN 0015-2676

**North American Game Breeders and Shooting
Preserve Operators Association**
Rt. 1, Box 28, Goose Lake, IA 52750.
- Wildlife Harvest. m.

**North American Gladiolus Council**
Box 857, Edgewood, MD 21040.
- North American Gladiolus Council Bulletin. q.
ISSN 0029-2370

**North American Gladiolus Council. Commercial
Growers Division**
5007 60th St. E., Bradenton, FL 33505.
- Gladio Grams. q.

**North American Jewish Students Network**
15 E. 26th St., Suite 1350, New York, NY 10010.
- Network; a monthly forum of the Jewish student
movement. m. ISSN 0085-3909

**North American Limousin Foundation**
- International Limousin Journal. (pub. by Journal
Publishers, Inc. (Ft. Collins))

**North American Mycological Association**
4245 Redinger Rd., Portsmouth, OH 45662.
- Mycophile. 6 per yr. ISSN 0027-5549

**North American Patristics Society**
c/o M. P. McHugh, Box U-57, University of
Connecticut, Storrs, CT 06268.
- Patristics. s-a. ISSN 0360-652X

**North American Pizza Association, Inc.**
23 N. Washington St., Suite 201, Ypsilanti, MI
48197.
- Slice of Pizza. bi-m. ISSN 0049-0733

**North American Publishing Co.**
401 N. Broad St., Philadelphia, PA 19108.
- American Import and Export Bulletin. m.
- American School & University. m. ISSN 0003-
0945
- Arte Tipografico. bi-m. ISSN 0004-346X
- Audio. m. ISSN 0004-752X
- Bestsellers. m. ISSN 0005-9730
- Business Forms Reporter. m. ISSN 0007-6767
- Computer Digest. m. ISSN 0010-4574
- Custom House Guide. a. ISSN 0070-2250
- Data Processing for Education. m. ISSN 0011-
6866
- Executive Housekeeper; the magazine of
institutional housekeeping. m. ISSN 0014-455X
- Food Trade News. bi-w. ISSN 0015-6663
- Institutional Management. m.
- Lab World. Annual Reference Guide. a.
- Media & Methods; exploration in education.
m.(Sept-May) ISSN 0025-6897
- Optical Scanning News. every 3 weeks. ISSN
0030-3933

- Package Printing & Diecutting. m. ISSN 0098-
7778
- Packascope-U S A; your Monday morning briefing
on latest developments in the packaging industry.
w.
- Printing Impressions. m. ISSN 0032-860X
- Reproductions Review and Methods. m.
- What's New in Home Economics. 15 per yr. ISSN
0043-4590

**North American Review**
c/o Ed. Robley Wilson, University of Northern
Iowa, Cedar Falls, IA 50613.
- North American Review. q. ISSN 0029-2397

**North American Saxophone Alliance**
c/o Richard Kennell, 1126 S. Wilke Rd., Arlington
Heights, IL 60005.
- Saxophone Symposium. q.

**North American Securities Administrators
Association, Inc.**
Plaza West, Suite 590, McKinley & Lee St., Little
Rock, AR 72205.
- Blue Sky News. bi-m.

**North American Simulation and Gaming Association**
- Simulation/Gaming. (pub. by Simulation-Gaming-
News, Inc.)

**North American Society for Corporate Planning (N A
S C P)**
- Planning Review. (pub. by Crane Russak &
Company, Inc.)

**North American Society for Sport History**
101 White Building, Pennsylvania State University,
University Park, PA 16802.
- Journal of Sport History. s-a. ISSN 0094-1700
- North American Society for Sport History.
Proceedings. a.
- North American Society for Sport History
Newsletter. q.

**North American Student Cooperative Organization
(N.A.S.C.O.)**
Box 130, Ann Arbor, MI 48106.
- Monthly News of Co-Op Communities. 9 per yr.
- New Harbinger; a journal of the cooperative
movement. q.

**North American Vegetarian Society**
501 Old Harding Highway, Malaga, NJ 08328.
- Vegetarian Voice. bi-m.

**North Cal-Neva Resource Conservation and
Development Project**
Cedarville, CA 96104.
- North Cal-Neva Resource Conservationan and
Development Project. Annual Work Plan. a. ISSN
0097-7268

**North California State Dental Hygienists Association**
220 Montgomery St., San Francisco, CA 94104.
- Dental Hygienist. bi-m. ISSN 0045-9933

**North Carolina. Commission on Higher Education
Facilities**
P.O. Box 2147, Raleigh, NC 27602.
- North Carolina. State Commission on Higher
Education Facilities. Facilities Inventory and
Utilization Study, for the State of North Carolina.
a. ISSN 0078-141X

**North Carolina. Council on State Goals and Policy**
Dept. of Administration, 116 W. Jones St., Raleigh,
NC 27603.
- North Carolina. Council on State Goals and
Policy. Annual Report. a. ISSN 0093-9730

**North Carolina. Criminal Justice Training and
Standards Council**
Box 149, Raleigh, NC 27602.
- North Carolina. Criminal Justice Training and
Standards Council. Annual Report. a. ISSN 0095-
179X

**North Carolina. Department of Agriculture**
Raleigh, NC 27611.
- North Carolina Seed Law. irreg.

**North Carolina. Department of Community Colleges**
114 W. Edenton St., Rm. 177, Education Bldg.,
Raleigh, NC 27611.
- For Adults Only. q. ISSN 0046-4473 (prep. by its
Division of Adult Services)
- Open Door. q. ISSN 0030-3410

**North Carolina. Department of Cultural Resources**
109 E. Jones Street, Raleigh, NC 27611.
- Library Reporter. q. (prep. by its State Library)

**North Carolina. Department of Human Resources**
325 N. Salisbury St., Raleigh, NC 27611.
- North Carolina. Department of Human Resources.
Annual Plan of Work. a. ISSN 0095-4942

**North Carolina. Department of Human Resources.
Division of Health Services**
P. O. Box 2091, Raleigh, NC 27602.
- North Carolina. Division of Health Services.
Public Health Statistics Branch. North Carolina
Vital Statistics. a. ISSN 0078-1371
- North Carolina Communicable Disease Morbidity
Statistics. a. ISSN 0085-428X
- North Carolina Reported Abortions. biennial.
(prep. by its Public Health Statistics Branch)

**North Carolina. Department of Human Resources.
Division of Social Services**
Raleigh, NC 27611.
- North Carolina. Division of Social Services. Social
Services Personnel in North Carolina Countries.
a. ISSN 0092-3613
- North Carolina. Division of Social Services.
Statistical Journal. q. ISSN 0098-051X

**North Carolina. Department of Natural and Economic
Resources. Division of Economic Development**
Raleigh, NC 27611.
- North Carolina Report. q. ISSN 0029-2605

**North Carolina. Department of Natural and Economic
Resources. Geology and Mineral Resources Section**
Box 27687, Raleigh, NC 27611.
- North Carolina. Geology and Mineral Resources
Section. Bulletin. irreg., no. 85, 1977.
- North Carolina. Geology and Mineral Resources
Section. Economic Paper. irreg., no. 68, 1970.
- North Carolina. Geology and Mineral Resources
Section. Information Circular. irreg., no. 21, 1972.
- North Carolina. Geology and Mineral Resources
Section. Special Publication. irreg., no. 6, 1977.

**North Carolina. Department of Natural and Economic
Resources. Groundwater Section**
Raleigh, NC 27611.
- Groundwater Bulletin. irreg. ISSN 0468-5067

**North Carolina. Department of Revenue**
Raleigh, NC 27611.
- North Carolina. Department of Revenue.
Franchise Tax and Corporate Income Tax
Bulletins for Taxable Years. biennial. ISSN 0078-
138X

**North Carolina. Division of Archives and History**
Raleigh, NC 27611.
- North Carolina. Division of Archives and History.
Archives Information Circular. irreg. ISSN 0093-
9056
- North Carolina Historical Review. q. ISSN 0029-
2494

**North Carolina. Division of Commerce and Industry.
Research and Statistics Section**
Box 27687, Raleigh, NC 27611.
- Industrial Contact List for North Carolina
Communities. a. ISSN 0095-1870

**North Carolina. Governor's Highway Safety Program**
N.C. Dept. of Transportation and Highway Safety,
Raleigh, NC 27600.
- North Carolina. Governor's Highway Safety
Program. Summary of Activities. irreg. ISSN
0361-2295

**North Carolina. Human Relations Council**
Box 19204, Raleigh, NC 27609.
- North Carolina. Human Relations Council.
Biennial Report. biennial.

**North Carolina. Office of Intergovernmental
Relations**
116 W. Jones St., Raleigh, NC 27603.
- North Carolina Environmental Bulletin. q.

**North Carolina. Secretary of State**
Administration Bldg., Raleigh, NC 27603.
- North Carolina. Secretary of State. North
Carolina Elections. irreg. ISSN 0092-1726
- North Carolina Manual. biennial.

**North Carolina. State Bar**
Justice Building, Raleigh, NC 27611.
- North Carolina Bar. q. ISSN 0048-0657

**North Carolina. Wildlife Resources Commission**
Albemarle Bldg., 325 N. Salisbury St., Raleigh, NC 27611.
• Wildlife in North Carolina. m. ISSN 0043-549X

**North Carolina Association of Educators**
111 W. Morgan St., Box 27347, Raleigh, NC 27611.
• N C A E News Bulletin. 9 per yr. ISSN 0027-6189
• North Carolina Education. m. ISSN 0029-2451

**North Carolina Association of Plumbing-Heating-Cooling Contractors, Inc.**
611 Tucker St., Suite 208, Raleigh, NC 27603.
• North Carolina Plumbing-Heating-Cooling Forum. m.

**North Carolina Bankers Association**
Box 30609, 3707 National Drive, Raleigh, NC 27612.
• Tarheel Banker. m. ISSN 0039-9663

**North Carolina Central University**
Durham, NC 27707.
• Ex-Umbra; magazine of the arts. q. ISSN 0014-3944 (Co-Sponsor: North Carolina Arts Council)
• Varia. a. ISSN 0083-5242 (prep. by its Faculty Research Committee)

**North Carolina Citizens Association, Inc.**
P.O. Box 2508, Raleigh, NC 27602.
• We the People of North Carolina. m.

**North Carolina Education Association. Division of Principals**
• Tarheel Principal. (pub. by Greensboro Printing Co.)

**North Carolina Electric Membership Corp.**
Box 27306, Raleigh, NC 27611.
• Carolina Country. m. ISSN 0008-6746

**North Carolina English Teachers Association**
• North Carolina English Teacher. (pub. by Wake Forest University)

**North Carolina Folklore Society**
• North Carolina Folklore Journal. (pub. by Appalachian State University)

**North Carolina Genealogical Society**
Box 1492, Raleigh, NC 27602.
• North Carolina Genealogical Society Journal. q. ISSN 0360-1056

**North Carolina Independent Publishing Co. Inc.**
Box 1148, Durham, NC 27702.
• North Carolina Anvil; a weekly newspaper of politics and the arts. w. ISSN 0029-2419

**North Carolina Law Enforcement Officers Association**
Box 2581, Charlotte, NC 28201.
• North Carolina Law Enforcement Journal. bi-m. ISSN 0029-2516

**North Carolina League for Nursing**
Box 687, Chapel Hill, NC 27514.
• North Carolina League for Nursing News. q. ISSN 0029-2532

**North Carolina League of Municipalities**
1010 Raleigh Bldg., 5 W. Hargett St., Box 3069, Raleigh, NC 27602.
• Directory of North Carolina Municipal Officials. biennial.
• Southern City. m.

**North Carolina Library Association**
Box 212, Appalachian State University, Boone, NC 28608.
• North Carolina Libraries. q. ISSN 0029-2540

**North Carolina Medical Society**
222 N. Person St., Raleigh, NC 27611
• North Carolina Medical Journal. m. ISSN 0029-2559 (Subscr. to:, Box 27167, Raleigh, NC 27611)
• North Carolina Medical Society. Transactions. a. ISSN 0361-5537

**North Carolina Motor Carriers Association, Inc.**
219 W. Martin St., Box 2977, Raleigh, NC 27602.
• Tarheel Wheels. m. ISSN 0039-968X

**North Carolina Museum of Art**
Raleigh, NC 27611.
• North Carolina Museum of Art. Bulletin. irreg. ISSN 0029-2567

• North Carolina Museum of Art. Calendar of Art Events. 10-11 per yr. ISSN 0029-2575

**North Carolina Music Teachers Association**
Department of Music, University of North Carolina, Chapel Hill, NC 27514.
• North Carolina Music Teacher. s-a. ISSN 0546-4854

**North Carolina Nurses Association**
Box 12025, Raleigh, NC 27605.
• Tar Heel Nurse. 10 per yr. ISSN 0039-9620

**North Carolina School Boards Association**
Box 2476, Raleigh, NC 27602.
• North Carolina School Boards Association Bulletin. m. ISSN 0029-2613

**North Carolina Speech and Drama Association**
c/o Dr. Terry W. Cole, Dept. of Speech, Appalachian State Univ., Boone, NC 28608.
• North Carolina Journal of Speech and Drama. q.

**North Carolina State University**
Raleigh, NC 27607
• Southern Engineer. 4 per yr. ISSN 0038-4054 (Order from: Print Shop, 400-B Daniels Hall, Raleigh, N C 27607)
• William D. Carmichael Jr. Lecture Series. irreg. ISSN 0512-4859 (Order from: Box 5067, Raleigh, N. C. 27607)

**North Carolina State University. Agricultural Experiment Station**
Raleigh, NC 27607.
• Research and Farming. s-a. ISSN 0034-5121

**North Carolina State University. D.H. Hill Library**
P.O. Box 5007, Raleigh, NC 27607.
• D.H. Hill Library Focus. irreg.
• D.H. Hill Library Serials Catalog; on microfiche. m.

**North Carolina State University. Department of Adult and Community College Education**
Raleigh, NC 27607.
• Community College Review. q. ISSN 0091-5521

**North Carolina State University. Department of Computer Science**
Raleigh, NC 27600.
• Southeastern Symposium on System Theory. Proceedings. a. ISSN 0094-2898

**North Carolina State University. Department of Crop Science**
Raleigh, NC 27607.
• North Carolina State University. Department of Crop Science. Research Report. irreg., no. 50, 1974. ISSN 0078-1517

**North Carolina State University. Department of Economics and Business**
Raleigh, NC 27607.
• Tar Heel Economist. m. ISSN 0039-9612

**North Carolina State University. Department of English**
Raleigh, NC 27607.
• Southern Poetry Review. s-a. ISSN 0038-447X

**North Carolina State University. Department of Foreign Languages and Literatures**
c/o Ed. C. Russell Reynolds, Box 5156, Raleigh, NC 27607.
• North Carolina Foreign Language Review. 2-3 per yr.

**North Carolina State University. Development Council**
12 Holiday Hall, Raleigh, NC 27607.
• North Carolina State University. Development Council. Report. a. ISSN 0078-1428

**North Carolina State University. Engineering Research Services Division**
School of Engineering, Raleigh, NC 27607.
• Engineering Research News. q. ISSN 0013-810X

**North Carolina State University. Industrial Extension Service**
Box 5506, Raleigh, NC 27607.
• North Carolina State University. Industrial Extension Service. Newsletter.

**North Carolina State University. Minerals Research Laboratory**
180 Coxe Ave., Asheville, NC 28801.
• Minerals Research Laboratory Newsletter. q.

**North Carolina State University. School of Agriculture-Life Sciences**
Box 5125, Raleigh, NC 27607.
• Agricultural Chemical Manual. a. ISSN 0065-4418

**North Carolina State University. School of Design**
Raleigh, NC 27607.
• North Carolina State University. School of Design. (Student Publication) irreg; vol. 25, 1977. ISSN 0078-1444

**North Carolina State University. School of Forest Resources**
Raleigh, NC 27607.
• North Carolina State University. School of Forest Resources. Technical Report. 3-4 per yr. ISSN 0090-0664

**North Carolina State University. Water Resources Research Institute**
124 Riddick Building, Raleigh, NC 27607.
• North Carolina State University. Water Resources Research Insitute. Report. irreg., no. 102, 1974. ISSN 0078-1525

**North Carolina Veterinary Medical Association**
112 Johnston St., Smithfield, NC 27577.
• North Carolina Veterinarian. bi-m. ISSN 0029-263X

**North Carolina Wildlife Federation, Inc.**
Box 10626, Raleigh, NC 27605.
• Friend O'Wildlife. bi-m. ISSN 0016-1284

**North Central Airlines**
• Northliner Magazine. (pub. by Bill Dorn Associates, Inc.)

**North Central Association of Colleges and Schools**
1221 University Ave., Boulder, CO 80302.
• N C A Today. q. ISSN 0027-6219
• North Central Association Quarterly. q. ISSN 0029-2648

**North Central Reading Association**
190 Coffey Hall, University of Minnesota, St. Paul, MN 55101.
• College and Adult Reading; Yearbook of the North Central Reading Association. irreg., vol. 7, 1974. ISSN 0069-553X

**North Central Sociological Association**
c/o Margaret M. Poloma, Ed., Univ. of Akron, Dept. of Sociology, Akron, OH 44325.
• Sociological Focus. q. ISSN 0038-0237

**North Central Texas Council of Governments**
P.O. Drawer COG, Arlington, TX 76011.
• Your Region. m.

**North Central Wool Marketing Corp.**
Box 328, Brookings, SD 57006.
• Wool Sack. m. ISSN 0043-7840

**North Coast Poetry Cooperative of Washington County**
P.O. Box 56, East Machias, ME 04636.
• North Coast Poetry. 2-3 per yr; no. 8, 1976.

**North Conway Institute, Inc.**
14 Beacon St., Boston, MA 02108.
• N C I Catalyst; interfaith action on alcohol and other drug problems. 2-3 per yr. ISSN 0048-0673

**North Country Publications Inc.**
c/o Richard S. Dexter, Ed. & Pub., St. A, Portland, ME 04101.
• North Country; an independent bi-monthly of news, analysis, and opinion. fortn. ISSN 0029-2672

**North Country Reference & Research Resources Council**
73 Park St., Canton, NY 13617.
• North Country Reference & Research Resources Council. Newsletter. bi-m. ISSN 0029-2699

**North Dakota. Business and Industrial Development Department**
523 E. Bismark Ave., Bismarck, ND 58505.
• Directory of North Dakota Manufacturers. biennial. ISSN 0090-5577

- North Dakota BIDD for Progress. bi-m. ISSN 0029-2729
- North Dakota Growth Indicators. irreg. ISSN 0549-8368

**North Dakota. Commissioner of Securities**
Capitol Bldg., Bismarck, ND 58505.
- North Dakota Securities Bulletin. m. ISSN 0549-8333

**North Dakota. Consumer Credit Division**
Bismarck, ND 58501.
- North Dakota. Consumer Credit Division. Consolidated Annual Report of Licensees. a. ISSN 0091-2093

**North Dakota. Department of Agriculture**
Bismarck, ND 58501.
- North Dakota. Department of Agriculture. Annual Report. irreg. ISSN 0093-8203

**North Dakota. Department of Health**
Bismarck, ND 58501.
- North Dakota. State Department of Health. Report. irreg. ISSN 0094-1816

**North Dakota. Department of Health. Division of Alcoholism and Drug Abuse**
320 Avenue B East, Bismarck, ND 58501.
- Alcohol in Our Society. irreg.
- North Dakota Monitor. q.

**North Dakota. Department of Public Instruction**
Bismarck, ND 58501.
- North Dakota. Department of Public Instruction. Special Annual Report of the Superintendent of Public Instruction. a. ISSN 0094-8357

**North Dakota. Division of Comprehensive Health Planning**
Bismarck, ND 58501.
- Comprehensive Health Plan for the State of North Dakota. irreg. ISSN 0095-3091

**North Dakota. Division of Vocational Rehabilitation**
Administrative Office, 1025 N. Third St., Bismarck, ND 58501.
- North Dakota State Plan for Rehabilitation Facilities and Workshops; annual modification. a. ISSN 0093-7843

**North Dakota. Employment Security Bureau**
Box 1537, 1000 E. Divide Ave., Bismarck, ND 58505.
- North Dakota. Employment Security Bureau. Annual Report. a. ISSN 0078-155X
- North Dakota. Employment Security Bureau. Biennial Report to the Governor. biennial. ISSN 0078-1568
- North Dakota Employment Trends. m. ISSN 0029-2702 (Co-sponsor: U. S. Dept. of Labor)

**North Dakota. Game and Fish Department**
1121 Lovett Ave., Bismarck, ND 58505.
- North Dakota Outdoors. m. ISSN 0029-2761

**North Dakota. Geological Survey**
Grand Forks, ND 58202.
- North Dakota. Geological Survey. Educational Series. irreg., no. 10, 1975. ISSN 0091-9004 (Co-sponsor: North Dakota Department of Public Instruction)
- North Dakota. Geological Survey. Miscellaneous Series. irreg., no. 55, 1975. ISSN 0078-1576
- North Dakota. Geological Survey. Oil and Gas Production Statistics. s-a. ISSN 0363-2512

**North Dakota. Highway Department**
Traffic Safety Programs Division, Capitol Grounds, Bismarck, ND 58501.
- North Dakota's Comprehensive Annual Highway Safety Work Program. quinquennial.

**North Dakota. Social Service Board**
State Capitol, Bismarck, ND 58501.
- Case & Counsel; North Dakota social service report. m. ISSN 0008-7246
- North Dakota. Social Service Board. Area Social Service Centers. a. ISSN 0095-6333
- North Dakota. Social Service Board. Report. irreg. ISSN 0095-6325
- North Dakota. Social Service Board. Research and Statistics. Statistics Juvenile Court and State Youth Authority. irreg. ISSN 0098-8782
- Social Services in North Dakota; annual report. a. ISSN 0094-1220

**North Dakota. State Advisory Council for Vocational Education**
Bismarck, ND 58501.
- North Dakota. State Advisory Council for Vocational Education. Annual Evaluation Report. a. ISSN 0094-8306

**North Dakota. State Aeronautics Commission**
Box U, Bismarck, ND 58501.
- North Dakota Aviation Newsletter. bi-m.

**North Dakota. State Bar Board**
State Capitol, Bismarck, ND 58501.
- Directory of North Dakota Lawyers. a.

**North Dakota. State Library Commission**
Bismarck, ND 58501.
- Flickertale Newsletter. m.
- North Dakota Academic Library Statistics. a. ISSN 0094-5455
- North Dakota Library Notes. m. ISSN 0024-2446

**North Dakota. State Wheat Commission**
1305 E. Central Ave., Bismarck, ND 58501.
- North Dakota. State Wheat Commission. Annual Report. a. ISSN 0098-5295

**North Dakota Academy of Science**
- North Dakota Academy of Science. Proceedings. (pub. by University of North Dakota Press)

**North Dakota Agricultural Experiment Station**
State University Station, Fargo, ND 58102.
- North Dakota Farm Research. bi-m.

**North Dakota Association of Rural Electric Cooperatives**
Box 727, Mandan, ND 58554.
- North Dakota Rural Electric Magazine. m. ISSN 0029-2788

**North Dakota Crop and Livestock Reporting Service**
Box 3166, Fargo, ND 58102.
- North Dakota Crop and Livestock Statistics. a. ISSN 0078-1541

**North Dakota Education Association**
Box J., Bismarck, ND 58501.
- North Dakota Education News. 6 per yr. ISSN 0048-0681
- North Dakota Journal of Education. 4 per yr. ISSN 0029-2737

**North Dakota Historical Society of Germans from Russia**
Box 1671, 107-1/2 N. Fourth St., Bismarck, ND 58501.
- Heritage Review. 3 per yr.
- Stammbaum. a.

**North Dakota Judicial Council**
Bismarck, ND 58501.
- North Dakota Judicial Council Statistical Compilation and Report. s-a. ISSN 0095-6120

**North Dakota League of Cities**
Box 2235, Bismarck, ND 58501.
- Directory: North Dakota City Officials. biennial. ISSN 0090-1989
- North Dakota League of Cities Bulletin. m.

**North Dakota Library Association**
c/o Grand Forks Public Library, 2110 Library Circle, Grand Forks, ND 58201.
- Good Stuff. q.

**North Dakota Milk Stabilization Board**
2061/2 North 6th St., Room 5, Bismarck, ND 58501.
- North Dakota. Milk Stabilization Board. Annual Report of Administrative Activities. a. ISSN 0091-9446

**North Dakota Motor Carriers Association**
Box 874, Bismarck, ND 58501.
- Rolling Along. m. ISSN 0048-8542

**North Dakota Music Educator's Association**
Box 783, Mayville, ND 58257.
- North Dakota Music Educator. q. ISSN 0029-2753

**North Dakota Natural Science Society**
Univ. of North Dakota, Institute for Ecological Studies, Grand Forks, ND 58202.
- Prairie Naturalist. q. ISSN 0091-0376

**North Dakota Newspaper Association**
c/o E. G. Carr, Box 8137, University Sta., Grand Forks, ND 58201.
- North Dakota Publisher. m. ISSN 0300-6832

**North Dakota Society for Medical Technology**
Dept. of Pathology, University of North Dakota, Grand Forks, ND 58201.
- North Dakota Society of Medical Technologists. Newsletter. q. ISSN 0048-069X

**North Dakota State Nurses Association**
219 N. 7th, Bismarck, ND 58501.
- Prairie Rose. q. ISSN 0032-6666

**North Jersey Highlands Historical Society**
Box 1, Newfoundland, NJ 07435.
- North Jersey Highlander. q. ISSN 0029-2850

**North Loop News Corp.**
c/o Bud R. Albanese, Ed., 800 N. Clark St., Chicago, IL 60610.
- North Loop News. w. ISSN 0029-2877

**North Pacific Fur Seal Commision**
National Marine Fisheries Service, Washington, DC 20235.
- North Pacific Fur Seal Commission. Proceedings of the Annual Meeting. a. ISSN 0078-1622

**North Penn Y.M.C.A. Chess Club**
608 E. Main, Lansdale, PA 19486.
- Overboard. q.

**North Shore Examiner**
2311 Main St., Evanston, IL 60202.
- North Shore Examiner; the newspaper with a social conscience. s-m.

**North Shore Feminists**
c/o Ed. Pub. Pat Watson, 68 Granite St., Rockport, MA 01966.
- Essecondsex; a newsletter for North Shore feminists. bi-m. ISSN 0300-7103

**North Star Sled Dog Club**
c/o Anita Hartigan, Rte. 1, Big Lake, MN 55309.
- Tug Line. m.

**North Stone Review**
University Station, Box 14098, Minneapolis, MN 55414.
- North Stone Review. s-a.

**North Texas State University**
Denton, TX 76203
- Studies in the Novel. q. ISSN 0039-3827 (Subscr. to:, Box 13706, North Texas Sta., Denton, TX 76203)

**North Texas State University. School of Library and Information Sciences**
NT Box 13796, Denton, TX 76203.
- Call Number. 3 per yr. ISSN 0008-1744

**North Wind-Skagway's Newspaper**
c/o Cyril A. Coyne, Ed., Box 395, Skagway, AK 99840.
- North Wind-Skagway's Newspaper. m. ISSN 0029-294X

**North Woods Call, Inc.**
Rt. 2, Box 195, Charlevoix, MI 49720.
- North Woods Call. fortn. ISSN 0029-2958

**Northampton County Motor Club**
Hecktown and Country Club Rds., Box 284, Easton, PA 18042.
- Motorist. bi-m.

**Northcenter Press**
3919 Lincoln Ave., Chicago, IL 60613.
- Northcenter News. w. ISSN 0029-2966

**Northeast Colorado Antique Bottle and Collectors Club**
227 W. Beam Ave., Fort Morgan, CO 80701.
- Northeast Colorado Antique Bottle and Collectors Club. m.

**Northeast Conference on the Teaching of Foreign Languages**
Box 623, Middlebury, VT 05753.
- Northeast Conference on the Teaching of Foreign Languages. Reports of the Working Committees. a. ISSN 0078-1665

**Northeast Dairy Cooperative Federation Inc**
Box 1344, Syracuse, NY 13201.
- N E D C O Today. m.

**Northeast Folklore Society**
South Stevens Hall, University of Maine, Orono,
ME 04473.
- Northeast Folklore. a. ISSN 0078-1681
- Northeast Folklore Society Newsletter. q. ISSN
0546-5370

**Northeast Missouri State University**
Kirksville, MO 63501.
- Baldwin Lectures in Teacher Education. a. ISSN
0067-303X
- Missouri School Music. 4 per yr. ISSN 0026-6701
(Missouri Music Educators Association)
- Sixteenth Century Journal; an interdisciplinary
journal for Renaissance and Reformation students
and scholars. s-a. ISSN 0361-0160 (Center for
Reformation Research. Sixteenth Century Studies
Conference)

**Northeast Missouri State University. Division of
Language and Literature**
Kirksville, MO 63501.
- Chariton Review. s-a. ISSN 0098-9452

**North East Modern Language Association**
English Dept., University of Rhode Island,
Kingston, RI 02881.
- Modern Language Studies. s-a. ISSN 0047-7729

**Northeast Ohio Areawide Coordinating Agency**
400 The Arcade, Cleveland, OH 44114.
- N O A C A News. m.

**Northeast Philadelphia Chamber of Commerce**
1528 Overington St., Philadelphia, PA 19124.
- Northeast Business. m. ISSN 0029-2982

**Northeast Texas Genealogical Society**
Box 458, Mineola, TX 75773.
- Northeast Texas Genealogical Society Quarterly.
q.

**Northeastern Agricultural Economics Council**
- Northeastern Agricultural Economics Council.
Journal. (pub. by University of Massachusetts.
Division of Resource Management)

**Northeastern Bird Banding Association**
c/o Robert H. Shaw, Treas., 631 Main St., Concord,
MA 01742.
- Bird-Banding; journal of ornithological
investigation. q. ISSN 0006-3630

**Northeastern Forest Fire Protection Commission**
66 Buckley Highway, Stafford Springs, CT 06076.
- Northeastern Forest Fire Protection Commission.
Compact News. q. ISSN 0546-5427

**Northeastern Illinois Planning Commision**
400 W. Madison St., Chicago, IL 60606.
- Planning in Northeastern Illinois. q. ISSN 0048-
4318

**Northeastern Illinois University. College of Arts and
Sciences**
Chicago, IL 60625.
- Great Lakes Review-Journal of Midwest Culture.
s-a. (prep. by its Depts. of English and History)

**Northeastern Industrial World**
2 Penn Plaza, New York, NY 10001.
- Northeastern Industrial World. m.

**Northeastern Loggers' Association, Inc.**
Old Forge, NY 13420.
- Northern Logger and Timber Processer. m. ISSN
0029-3156

**Northeastern Nevada Historical Society**
Northeastern Nevada Museum, P.O. Box 503, Elko,
NV 89801.
- Northeastern Nevada Historical Society Quarterly.
q.

**Northeastern Oklahoma State University**
Tahlequa, OK 74464.
- Northeastern Oklahoma State University. Faculty
Research, Publications, In-Service Activities. a.

**Northeastern Political Science Association**
- Polity. (pub. by University of Massachusetts)

**Northeastern Poultry Producers Council**
322 Oxford Valley Rd., Fairless Hills, PA 19030.
- N E P P C O News. m. ISSN 0027-6456

**Northeastern Publishing Corp.**
157 E. 86th St., New York, NY 10028.
- Manhattan East. w. ISSN 0025-2107

**Northeastern Retail Lumbermens Association**
- Lumber Co-Operator. (pub. by Lumber Co-
Operator, Inc.)

**Northeastern University**
360 Huntington Ave., Boston, MA 02115.
- Northeastern News. w. ISSN 0029-3032

**Northeastern University. Department of English**
Boston, MA 02115.
- Studies in American Fiction. 2 per yr. ISSN 0091-
8083

**Northeastern Weed Science Society**
c/o J.V. Parochetti, Sec.-Treas., University of
Maryland, Agronomy Department, College Park,
MD 20742.
- Northeastern Weed Science Society. Proceedings.
a. ISSN 0078-1703

**Northern Arizona Society of Science and Art**
Rt. 4, Box 720, Flagstaff, AZ 86001.
- Plateau. q. ISSN 0032-1346

**Northern Arizona University. School of Forestry**
Box 4098, Flagstaff, AZ 86001.
- Arizona Forestry Notes. irreg., no. 12, 1974. ISSN
0066-7404

**Northern California Alliance**
2811 Mission St., San Francisco, CA 94110.
- Common Sense. 12 per yr.

**Northern California Golf Association**
Box 1157, Pebble Beach, CA 93953.
- Northern California Golf Association. Blue Book.
a.

**Northern District Dental Society**
100 Northcreek-Ste. 310, 3715 Northside Pkwy.
N.W., Atlanta, GA 30327.
- Northern District Dental Society. Dental Mirror.
9 per yr. ISSN 0029-3075

**Northern Illinois University. Center for Southeast
Asian Studies**
DeKalb, IL 60115.
- Northern Illinois University. Center for Southeast
Asian Studies. Occasional Papers Series. irreg.,
no., 4, 1974.
- Northern Illinois University. Center for Southeast
Asian Studies. Special Report Series. irreg., no.
14, 1977. ISSN 0073-4934 (Dist. by: Cellar Book
Shop, 18090 Wyoming, Detroit, MI 48221)

**Northern Illinois University. Department of History**
Dekalb, IL 60115.
- Third Republic/Troisieme Republique. s-a.

**Northern Illinois University. Department of Outdoor
Teacher Education**
Taft Field Campus, Box 299, Oregon, IL 61061.
- Journal of Outdoor Education. 2 per yr. ISSN
0022-3336

**Northern Illinois University. Department of
Sociology**
De Kalb, IL 60115.
- Heuristics; the journal of innovative sociology. s-a.
ISSN 0018-1145
- Journal of Political and Military Sociology. (pub.
by Transaction Periodicals Consortium)

**Northern Illinois University Press**
515 Garden Road, Dekalb, IL 60115.
- Annotated Secondary Bibliography Series on
English Literature in Transition, 1880-1920. irreg.
- Perspectives in Geography. irreg.

**Northern Indiana Historical Society**
112 South Lafayette Blvd., South Bend, IN 46601.
- Old Courthouse News. q. (St. Joseph County's
Official Museum)

**Northern Kentucky Independent Food Dealers
Association**
505 Scott St., Covington, KY 41011.
- Individual Grocer. m. ISSN 0300-855X

**Northern Kentucky State College**
Highland Heights, KY 41076.
- Border States. a. ISSN 0092-4571 (American
Studies Association. Kentucky-Tennessee
Chapter)

**Northern Kentucky University. Salmon P. Chase
College of Law**
Covington, KY 41011.
- Northern Kentucky Law Review. s-a.

**Northern Michigan University**
Marquette, MI 49855.
- North Wind. w.

**Northern Natural Gas Co.**
2223 Dodge St., Omaha, NE 68102.
- Transmission. q.

**Northern New England Review**
Box 825, Franklin Pierce College, Rindge, NH
03461.
- Northern New England Review. 2 per yr.

**Northern New York Publishing Co.**
212 Greene St., Ogdensberg, NY 13669.
- Racquette. w. ISSN 0033-7447 (Student
Government Association, SUC at Potsdam)

**Northern Nut Growers Association**
4518 Holston Hills Road, Knoxville, TN 37914.
- Northern Nut Growers Association. Annual
Report. a.

**Northern State College**
Aberdeen, SD 57401.
- South Dakota Musician. q. ISSN 0038-3341

**Northern Trust Co.**
50 S. La Salle St., Chicago, IL 60690.
- Business Comment. m. ISSN 0007-6554
- Northerner. q. ISSN 0029-3245 (prep. by its
Advertising and Public Relations Department)

**Northern Virginia Planning District Commission**
7309 Arlington Boulevard, Falls Church, VA 22042.
- Northern Virginia Planning District Commission.
Annual Report. a. ISSN 0078-1770

**Northland Diocese Association**
1200 Memorial Dr., Crookston, MN 56716.
- Our Northland Diocese. m. ISSN 0030-6924

**Northland Public Library Writers Workshop**
120 Three Degree Road, Pittsburgh, PA 15237.
- Write on. s-a.

**Northland Publishing Corporation**
6215 Brooklyn Drive, Minneapolis, MN 55430
- Midwest Motor Transport News. m. ISSN 0026-
3427 (Minnesota Motor Transport Association)
(Subscrip. to: Midwest Motor Transport News,
1821 University Ave., St. Paul, MN 55104)
- Motor North. m. ISSN 0300-6301

**Northrop Corp.**
3901 W. Broadway, Hawthorne, CA 90250.
- F-5 Technical Digest. m.

**Northwest Arkansas Genealogical Society**
Box 362, Rogers, AR 72756.
- Backtracker. q. ISSN 0094-6915

**Northwest Arts**
c/o Maxine Cushing Gray, Ed. & Pub., Box 15601,
Seattle, WA 98115
- Northwest Arts; fortnightly journal of news and
opinion. bi-w. (Editorial Address:, 538 N.E. 98
St., Seattle WA 98115)

**Northwest Association of Schools and Colleges**
3700-B University Way N.E., Seattle, WA 98105.
- Northwest Association of Schools and Colleges.
Proceedings. a.
- Northwest Association of Schools and Colleges,
Committee on Research and Service. Newsletter.
s-a.

**Northwest Community College**
Powell, WY 82435.
- Cthulhu Calls. q.

**Northwest Community Hospital**
800 W. Central, Arlington Heights, IL 60005.
- Northwest Community Hospital Medical Bulletin.
3 per yr. ISSN 0029-3334

**Northwest Furniture Retailers' Association**
121 Boren Ave. N., Seattle, WA 98109.
- Pacific Marketer; the Northwest's only home furnishings magazine. bi-m. ISSN 0048-2633

**North West Georgia Historical and Genealogical Society**
Box 2484, Rome, GA 30161.
- North West Georgia Historical and Genealogical Society. Quarterly. q.

**Northwest Institute of Ethics and Life Sciences**
6241 31st Ave., N.E., Seattle, WA 98115.
- Bioethics Northwest. q. ISSN 0362-0824

**Northwest Missouri State University**
Maryville, MO 64468.
- Northwest Missouri State University Bulletin. q. ISSN 0091-7540

**Northwest Missouri State University. Department of Sociology**
Maryville, MO 64468.
- Northwest Missouri State University. Studies. q. ISSN 0091-3782

**Northwest Motor**
83 Columbia St., Seattle, WA 98104.
- Northwest Motor; journal for the automotive industry. m. ISSN 0029-3393

**Northwest Passage**
1000 Harris Ave., Box 105, Bellingham, WA 98225.
- Northwest Passage; the Pacific Northwest journal of ecology, politics & the arts. fortn. ISSN 0029-3415

**Northwest Regional Foundation Inc.**
Box 5296, Spokane, WA 99205.
- Futures Conditonal. 6 per yr.

**Northwest Scientific Association**
- Northwest Science. (pub. by Washington State University Press)

**Northwest Unit Farm Magazines**
(Subsidiary of: Cowles Publishing Co.)
Review Bldg, Spokane, WA 99210
- Idaho Farmer-Stockman. s-m. (Subscr. to: 413 W. Idaho St., Suite 101, Boise ID 83702)
- Montana Farmer-Stockman. s-m. (Subscr. to: Professional Bldg., Great Falls MT 59401)
- Oregon Farmer-Stockman. s-m. (Subscr. to: Terminal Sales Bldg., Portland OR 97205)
- Utah Farmer-Stockman. s-m. (Subscr. to: 610 Crandall Bldg., Salt Lake City UT 84101)
- Washington Farmer-Stockman. s-m.

**Northwestern Banker Co.**
306 15th St., Des Moines, IA 50309.
- Northwestern Banker. m.

**Northwestern Bell Telephone Co.**
100 S. 19th St., Omaha, NE 68102.
- Channels (Omaha); of business communication. q. ISSN 0009-1502

**Northwestern College**
1300 Western Ave., Watertown, WI 53094.
- Black and Red. m.

**Northwestern Lumbermen, Inc.**
7300 France Ave., S., Minneapolis, MN 55435.
- Northwestern Lumberman. m. ISSN 0092-0681

**Northwestern Mutual Life Insurance Co.**
720 E. Wisconsin, Milwaukee, WI 53202.
- Field Notes. bi-m. ISSN 0015-072X

**Northwestern Publishing Co.**
1011 Upper Midwest Bldg., Hennpin Ave. at Fifth St., Minneapolis, MN 55401.
- Northwest Insurance. m. ISSN 0029-3377

**Northwestern Publishing House**
3624 W. North Ave., Milwaukee, WI 53208.
- Northwestern Lutheran. fortn. ISSN 0029-3512 (Wisconsin Evangelical Lutheran Synod)

**Northwestern Technological Institute**
Evanston, IL 60201.
- Northwestern Engineer. q. ISSN 0029-3482

**Northwestern University**
2530 Ridge Ave., Evanston, IL 62205.
- Northwestern Report. q. ISSN 0029-3563

**Northwestern University Alumni Association. Medical Division**
Medical Division, 303 E. Chicago Ave., Chicago, IL 60611.
- Northwestern University Medical Center Magazine. 3 per yr.

**Northwestern University Cancer Center**
Ward Memorial Bldg., 303 E. Chicago Ave., Chicago, IL 60611.
- Cancer Focus. q.

**Northwestern University. Dental School Library**
311 E. Chicago Ave, Chicago, IL 60611.
- Northwestern University. Dental School Library Acquisitions Lists. bi-m.
- Northwestern University. Dental School Library. Current Subscriptions List. a.

**Northwestern University. Department of English**
Evanston, IL 60201.
- Analyst. irreg. ISSN 0066-152X

**Northwestern University. Library**
Evanston, IL 60201.
- Joint Acquisitions List of Africana. bi-m. ISSN 0021-731X (prep. by its African Department)
- Lantern's Core. s-m. ISSN 0047-4053 (prep. by its Staff Association)
- Women's Collection Newsletter. s-a. (prep. by its Special Collections Department)

**Northwestern University. Materials Research Center**
2145 Sheridan Rd., Evanston, IL 60201.
- Northwestern University. Materials Research Center. Annual Technical Report. a.

**Northwestern University. Music Library**
1810 Hinman Ave., Evanston, IL 60201.
- Eighteen-Ten Overture. irreg. ISSN 0093-0288

**Northwestern University Press**
1735 Benson Ave., Evanston, IL 60201.
- African Urban Studies. irreg.
- International Congress on Marine Corrosion and Fouling. Proceedings. irreg., 3rd, 1974.
- Studies in Jungian Thought. irreg.

**Northwestern University. Program of African Studies**
630 Dartmouth Place, Evanston, IL 60201.
- Pan Africanist. s-a.

**Northwestern University. School of Education**
2003 Sheridan Rd., Evanston, IL 60201.
- Integrated Education. (pub. by Integrated Education Associates)
- Research Review of Equal Education. q. (Center for Equal Education)

**Northwestern University. School of Law**
357 E. Chicago Ave., Chicago, IL 60611.
- Journal of Criminal Law & Criminology. (pub. by Williams & Wilkins Co.)
- Northwestern University Law Review. bi-m. ISSN 0029-3571

**Northwestern University. Speech Annex**
Evanston, IL 60201.
- Film Reader. a. ISSN 0361-722X

**Northwestern University. Transportation Center**
Leverone Hall, 2001 Sheridan Rd., Evanston, IL 60201.
- Containerization: A Bibliography. irreg. ISSN 0069-9314
- Current Literature in Traffic and Transportation. m. ISSN 0011-3654
- Doctoral Dissertations on Transportation. irreg. ISSN 0070-6809 (prep. by its Library)

**Northwood Institute**
2 Shell Plaza, Suite 2197, Houston, TX 77002.
- Answers to Economic Problems. m.

**Northwoods Press, Inc.**
R. D. 1, Meadows of Dan, VA 24120.
- Northwoods Journal; a magazine for writers. 8 per yr.

**Northwoods Publishing**
Box 609, Menomonee Falls, WI 53051.
- Fishing Facts. m.

**W. W. Norton & Company, Inc.**
500 Fifth Ave., New York, NY 10036.
- Ancient Culture and Societies. irreg.
- Motor Racing Year. a. ISSN 0090-2144
- Problems of the Modern Economy Series. irreg.

- World Naturalist Series. irreg., latest 1973.
- Yearbook of Astronomy. a. ISSN 0084-3660

**Norton International, Inc.**
1 New Bond St., Worcester, MA 01606.
- Grits and Grinds; a technical magazine featuring information on the latest abrasive tools and methods for better grinding and surface finishing. 4 per yr. ISSN 0017-4319

**Jeffrey Norton Publishers Inc.**
145 E. 49th St., New York, NY 10017.
- Audio Catalog. a.

**Norwegian American Chamber of Commerce, Inc.**
800 Third Ave., New York, NY 10022
(Norwegian headquarters: Drammensveien 40, Oslo 2, Norway)
- Norwegian American Commerce. q. ISSN 0029-3644

**Norwegian-American Historical Association**
St. Olaf College, Northfield, MN 55057.
- Norwegian-American Historical Association. Newsletter. irreg. ISSN 0078-1967
- Norwegian-American Historical Association. Topical Studies. irreg. ISSN 0085-4352
- Norwegian-American Historical Association. Travel and Description Series. irreg., vol. 8, 1973. ISSN 0078-1975
- Norwegian-American Studies. irreg.; vol. 27, 1976. ISSN 0078-1983

**Norwegian Information Service**
825 Third Ave., New York, NY 10022.
- News of Norway. fortn. ISSN 0028-9272

**Norwegian Singers Association of America, Inc.**
3316 Xenwood Avenue South, Minneapolis, MN 55416.
- Sanger-Hilsen/Singers Greetings. bi-m.

**Nor'westing Inc.**
Box 375, Edmonds, WA 98020.
- Nor'westing. m.

**Nosferatu Press**
c/o Eds. Richard Pflum & David Wade, 420 N. Washington, Bloomington, IN 47401.
- Stoney Lonesome. a.

**Nostalgia News**
Box 34305, Dallas, TX 75234.
- Nostalgia News. bi-m. ISSN 0048-0851

**Notebook Press**
Box 180, Birmingham, MI 48012.
- Notebook and Other Reviews.

**Notes and Sketches**
McCondy, MS 38854.
- Notes and Sketches. m.

**Notes on Contemporary Literature**
c/o William S. Doxey & Ben W. Griffith, 550 N. White St., Carrollton, GA 30117.
- Notes on Contemporary Literature. q. ISSN 0029-4047

**Notes on Modern American Literature**
c/o St. John's University, Department of English, Jamaica, NY 11439.
- Notes on Modern American Literature. s-a.

**Notre Dame English Association**
- Notre Dame English Journal. (pub. by University of Notre Dame. Department of English)

**Robert Novak, Ed. & Pub.**
c/o English Dept., Indiana University, Fort Wayne, IN 46805.
- Windless Orchard; a quarterly magazine of photography and contemporary poetry. q. ISSN 0043-5716

**Now Voyager**
193 Beacon St., Boston, MA 02116.
- Now Voyager. q.

**Noyes Data Corporation**
Noyes Bldg., Park Ridge, NJ 07656.
- Chemical Technology Review. irreg; no. 83, 1977.
- Energy Technology Review. irreg; no. 11, 1977.
- Food Technology Review. irreg; no. 39, 1977. ISSN 0071-7215
- Pollution Technology Review. irreg; no. 31, 1977. ISSN 0079-3116

**Nu?**
c/o Hillel, Univ. of Massachusetts, Amherst, MA 01002.
- Nu; five college Jewish Community monthly. m.

**Nuclear Assurance Corporation**
24 Executive Park West, Atlanta, GA 30329.
- Nuclear Fuel Status and Forecast. q. ISSN 0092-993X
- Nuclear Industry Status. q. ISSN 0092-9751
- Nuclear Powerplant Performance. q. ISSN 0092-9948
- Status of the Market Nuclear Fuel Fabrication. a. ISSN 0094-7482

**Numeridex, Inc**
241 Holbrook Dr., Wheeling, IL 60090.
- N/C Commline. bi-m.

**Numismatic Association of Southern California**
P.O. Box 1765, Santa Monica, CA 90406.
- N. A. S. C. Quarterly. q. ISSN 0027-6006

**Numismatic Fine Arts, Inc.**
16661 Ventura Blvd., Encino, CA 91316.
- Journal of Numismatic Fine Arts. q. ISSN 0047-2611

**Nurses Association of the American College of Obstetricians and Gynecologists**
- J O G N Nursing. (pub. by Harper & Row Publishers, Inc. Medical Department)

**Nurses Association of the Counties of Long Island**
1 Hanson Place, Brooklyn, NY 11243.
- Nursing News. 5 per yr. ISSN 0029-6546

**Nursing Digest, Inc.**
12 Lakeside Park, 607 North Avenue, Wakefield, MA 01880.
- Nurse Educator. (pub. by Concept Development Co.)
- Nursing Digest. q. ISSN 0091-4215

**Nursing Home Report**
Box 2346, Rockville, MD 20852.
- Nursing Home Report. s-m.

**Nursing Publications, Inc.**
c/o Alice R. Clarke, Ed., Box 218, Hillsdale, NJ 07642.
- Nursing Forum. q. ISSN 0029-6473
- Perspectives in Psychiatric Care. q. ISSN 0031-5990

**Nutrition Foundation, Inc.**
- Nutrition Reviews. (pub. by Harvard School of Public Health. Department of Nutrition)

**Nutrition Today, Inc.**
101 Ridgely Ave., Box 465, Annapolis, MD 21404.
- Nutrition Today. bi-m. ISSN 0029-666X

**Nuttall Ornithological Club**
c/o Museum of Comparative Zoology, Harvard Univ., Cambridge, MA 02138.
- Nuttall Ornithological Club. Publications. irreg., no. 15, 1974. ISSN 0550-4082

**Nye Family of America Association**
East Sandwich, MA 02537.
- Nye Family Newsletter. irreg.

**Gerald Nygaard, Ed. & Pub.**
Box 513, Vermillion, SD 57069.
- Jerry Nygaard's Great Lakes of the Dakota Tabloid. m. (w. May-Aug.)

**Nystrom Publishing Co., Inc.**
207 S. Manitola Ave., Wayzata, WA 55391.
- Sports and Recreation. bi-m.

**O. Henry House**
- O. Henry Almanac. (pub. by Highland Press, Inc.)

**O M I Farm News**
1514 West Bancroft, Toledo, OH 43606.
- O M I Farm News. (Ohio, Michigan & Indiana) m. ISSN 0029-716X

**O. P. Publications Corp.**
733 Third Ave., New York, NY 10017.
- Osteopathic Physician. m. ISSN 0030-6371

**O S I Publications**
411 Hackensack Ave., Hackensack, NJ 07601.
- TeleSystems Journal. bi-m. ISSN 0360-1862

**Oahu Development Conference**
119 Merchant St., Honolulu, HI 96813.
- O D C Planning Issues. irreg.

**Oak Publications**
33 W. 60 St., New York, NY 10023.
- American Folk Music Occasional. irreg. ISSN 0065-8316
- Studies in Ethnomusicology. irreg., 1965, no. 2. ISSN 0081-7902

**Oak Ridge Associated Universities, Inc.**
P.O. Box 117, Oak Ridge, TN 37830.
- Oak Ridge Associated Universities. Medical Division. Research Report. a. ISSN 0078-2890 (prep. by its Information Services Department)
- Oak Ridge Associated Universities. Newsletter. m. ISSN 0029-7372
- Oak Ridge Associated Universities. Report. a. ISSN 0078-2904

**Oak Ridge National Laboratory**
P.O. Box X, Oak Ridge, TN 37830.
- Oak Ridge National Laboratory Review. q. ISSN 0048-1262

**Oakland Public Library**
125 14th St., Oakland, CA 94612.
- Oak Leaves. m. ISSN 0029-7364

**Oan Vap Press**
R.R. 1, Norfolk, NE 68701.
- Amateur Archaeology. q.

**O'Bannon Genealogist**
65 Airlane Dr., Clearfield, UT 84015.
- O'Bannon Genealogist. q.

**Obedinenie Pervopokhodnikov**
c/o Th. Puchalsky, 1315 Chelton Way, South Pasadena, CA 91030.
- Pervopokhodnik; letopis Beloi borby. bi-m.

**Oberlin College**
Rice Hall, Oberlin, OH 44074.
- Field. s-a. ISSN 0015-0657
- Martin Classical Lectures. (pub. by Harvard University Press)
- Oberlin Review. (pub. by Press of the Times)

**Oberlin College. Allen Memorial Art Museum**
Oberlin, OH 44074.
- Allen Memorial Art Museum. Bulletin. 2 per yr. ISSN 0002-5739

**Oberlin College. Alumni Association**
Bosworth Hall, Oberlin, OH 44074.
- Oberlin Alumni Magazine. bi-m. ISSN 0029-7518

**Oberlin Political Caucus**
Box 32, Wilder Hall, Oberlin College, Oberlin, OH 44074.
- Alternatives; a Forum for Activism in the Seventies. 3 per yr.

**O'Brien and O'Brien**
Box 271, Buffalo, NY 14221.
- National Faculty Placement Bureau Bulletin. 4 per yr.

**Observations from the Treadmill**
R. F. D. 1, Union, ME 04862.
- Observations from the Treadmill. q. (approx.) ISSN 0048-1335

**Observer Press, Inc.**
Box 85, Bard College, Annandale on Hudson, NY 12504.
- Observer; an alternative newsmedia project. w. ISSN 0005-593X

**Obsidian**
c/o Alvin Aubert, State University of New York at Fredonia, Department of English, Fredonia, NY 14063.
- Obsidian; black literature in review. 3 per yr. ISSN 0360-6724

**O'Casey Studies**
Box 333, Holbrook, NY 11741.
- Sean O'Casey Review. s-a. ISSN 0363-2245

**Occidental College. Jeffers Committee**
c/o Ed. Tyrus G. Harmsen, College Librarian, 1600 Campus Rd., Los Angeles, CA 90041.
- Robinson Jeffers Newsletter. q. ISSN 0300-7936

**Occidental Petroleum Corporation**
10889 Wilshire Blvd., Los Angeles, CA 90024.
- Occidental Petroleum Corporation. Annual Report. a. ISSN 0085-4425

**Occidental Publishing Co.**
1200 S. Central Ave., Glendale, CA 91204.
- Optometric World. m. ISSN 0030-4107

**Occult Americana**
Box 667, Painesville, OH 44007.
- Occult Americana. bi-m.

**Occult Communications Corporation**
2274 Como Ave., St. Paul, MN 55108.
- New Awareness Magazine. 6 per yr.
- O T J /Occult Trade Journal. (pub. by New Awareness Publishing Co., Inc.)

**Occum Press**
Box 68, South Willington, CT 06265.
- Occum Ridge Review. s-a.

**Occurrence**
928 Pine St., Apt. 12-B, Philadelphia, PA 19107.
- Occurrence. irreg.

**Ocean Engineering Information Service**
P.O. Box 989, La Jolla, CA 92037.
- Ocean Engineering Information Series. irreg., 1972, vol. 6. ISSN 0078-3137

**Ocean Living**
Box 17463, Los Angeles, CA 90017.
- Ocean Living. irreg. ISSN 0029-8034

**Ocean Science Services International Inc.**
663 Fifth Ave., New York, NY 10022.
- Ocean Law Letter. m.

**Oceana Publications Inc.**
Dobbs Ferry, NY 10522.
- African Law Reports; Commercial Law Series. irreg., 1973, vol. 13. ISSN 0065-3993
- American Cities Chronologies Series. irreg.
- Annual Review of United Nations Affairs. a. ISSN 0066-4340
- Bibliography on Foreign and Comparative Law : Books and Articles in English. quinquennial. ISSN 0067-7329 (Columbia University. Parker School of Foreign and Comparative Law)
- Bilateral Studies in Private International Law. irreg., no. 17, 1968. ISSN 0067-8562 (Columbia University. Parker School of Foreign and Comparative Law)
- British International Law Cases. irreg., 1973, no. 9. ISSN 0068-2195 (International Law Fund) (Co-sponsor: British Institute of Foreign and Comparative Law)
- Business Almanac Series. irreg., 1973, no. 22. ISSN 0068-4384
- Chronologies and Documentary Handbooks of the States Series. irreg., 1973, no. 10.
- Digest of Commercial Laws of the World. irreg. ISSN 0419-1285
- Digest of Legal Activities of International Organizations and Other Institutions. a. ISSN 0070-4857 (Unidroit (International Institute for the Unification of Private Law))
- East African Law Journal. a. ISSN 0070-797X
- Ethnic Chronology Series. irreg., latest issue 1975. ISSN 0071-1780
- Guide to Foreign Legal Materials Series. irreg., 1968, no. 3. ISSN 0072-842X (Columbia University. Parker School of Foreign and Comparative Law)
- International Commercial Arbitration. irreg. (British Institute of International and Comparative Law UK)
- International Financing and Investment. irreg. ISSN 0074-607X (World Community Association)
- Investment Laws of the World. irreg.
- Israel. Supreme Court. Selected Judgments. a. (Supreme Court of the State of Israel)
- Legal Almanac Series. irreg., no. 78, 1975. ISSN 0075-8582
- Library of Law and Contemporary Problems. irreg., no. 19, 1974. ISSN 0075-9120 (Duke University. School of Law)
- Malawi Law Reports. irreg., 1971, no. 5. ISSN 0076-3187
- Oceana Docket Classics. irreg., 1966, no. 2. ISSN 0078-3161
- Presidential Chronology Series. irreg.
- Sierra Leone Law Reports. irreg. ISSN 0080-9543
- Studies in Comparative Law. irreg.

- Uniform Law Review. s-a. (Unidroit (International Institute for the Unification of Private Law))
- World Chronologies Series. irreg.

**Oceania, Inc.**
1720 NE 177th, Seattle, WA 98155.
- Postmarked OCENIA. m.

**Oceanic Society**
- Oceans. (pub. by Oceans Magazine Co.)

**Oceanic Society. Long Island Sound Chapter**
Stamford Marine Center, Magee Ave., Stamford, CT 06902.
- Taffrail. s-a.

**Oceanography Newsletter**
c/o Ed. Benson Miller, Drawer 629, Solana Beach, CA 92075.
- Oceanography Newsletter; news of mining, drilling, farming & populating the sea floor. s-m.

**Oceans Magazine Co.**
240 Fort Mason, San Francisco, CA 94123.
- Oceans. 6 per yr. ISSN 0029-8174 (Oceanic Society)

**Francis V. O'Connor, Ed. & Pub.**
250 E. 73rd St., Apt. 11c, New York, NY 10021.
- Federal Art Patronage Notes. irreg.

**October**
c/o Jaap Reitman, 157 Spring St., New York, NY 10012.
- October. q.

**October League (Marxist-Leninist)**
- Call/Clarin. (pub. by Call Publications)

**Ocular Publishing**
1549 Platte St., Denver, CO 80202.
- Ocular; the directory of information and opportunities for the visual arts. q.

**Oculist Witnesses**
c/o Alan Davies, Editor, 68 Downer Ave., Dorchester, MA 02125.
- Oculist Witnesses. s-a.

**Odontological Society of Western Pennsylvania**
206 Jenkins Bldg., Pittsburgh, PA 15222.
- Odontological Bulletin. m.(Sept-June) ISSN 0029-8433

**J. R. O'Dwyer Co., Inc.**
271 Madison Ave., New York, NY 10016.
- Jack O'Dwyer's PR Newsletter. w.
- O'Dwyers Directory of Public Relations Firms. a. ISSN 0078-3374

**Odysseus**
65 N.W. Sleret Ave., Gresham, OR 97030.
- Odysseus; magazine of the arts. bi-m.

**Odyssey Press**
Wayne Warehousing Corp., 150 Paris Drive, Wayne, NJ 07470.
- Perspectives on American Literature. irreg.

**Of Sea & Shore Publications**
Box 33, Port Gamble, WA 98364.
- Catalog of Dealers' Prices for Marine Shells. biennial. ISSN 0084-862X
- Of Sea and Shore. q. ISSN 0030-0055
- Sheller's Directory of Clubs, Books, Periodicals and Dealers. biennial. ISSN 0085-607X

**Off-Beat Digest**
James W. Lee, 5905 York Blvd., Los Angeles, CA 90042.
- Off-Beat Digest. q.

**Off Off Broadway Alliance**
162 W. 56 St., New York, NY 10019.
- O.O.B.A. Guidebook of Theatres. irreg. ISSN 0361-6606

**Off Our Backs Inc.**
1724 20th St. N.W., Washington, DC 20009.
- Off Our Backs; a woman's news-journal. m. ISSN 0030-0071

**Office and Professional Employees International Union**
AFL-CIO, CLC, Room 610, 265 W. 14th St., New York, NY 10011.
- White Collar. m. ISSN 0043-4876

**Office Education Association**
1120 Norse Rd., Columbus, OH 43229.
- O E A Communique. q.

**Office Publications, Inc.**
1200 Summer St., Stamford, CT 06904.
- International Business Equipment. 11 per yr. ISSN 0020-6288
- Office; magazine of management, equipment, automation. m. ISSN 0030-0128
- Office Equipment Exporter. ISSN 0471-1424
- Oficina; Revista de Equipos para Oficinas. a. ISSN 0085-445X

**Office Research Institute**
Box 55-7536, Miami, FL 33155.
- Energy Activists Directory; who's who in energy. a.

**Official Meeting Facilities Guide**
Box 606, Neptune, NJ 07753.
- Official Meeting Facilities Guide. s-a.

**Official Motor Carrier Directory, Inc.**
1130 S. Canal St., Chicago, IL 60607.
- Official Motor Carrier Directory. s-a.

**Official Motor Freight Guide, Inc.**
1130 S. Canal St., Chicago, IL 60607.
- Official Motor Freight Guide. s-a. ISSN 0030-0357
- Official Shippers Guide-Chicago Motor Freight Directory. s-a.
- Official Shippers Guide-New York Motor Express Guide. s-a.
- Official Shippers Guide-St. Louis Motor Freight Directory. s-a.

**Official Organ Blue Book**
c/o Zeb Billings, Sight & Sound International, Inc., 6055 W. Fond du Lac Ave., Milwaukee, WI 53218.
- Official Organ Blue Book; international used organ valuation guide. a. ISSN 0048-1513

**Ohio. Administration of Justice Division**
Columbus, OH 43215.
- Ohio's Comprehensive Criminal Justice Plan. a. ISSN 0094-0984

**Ohio. Advisory Council for Vocational Education**
5900 Sharon Woods Blvd., Columbus, OH 43229.
- Ohio. Advisory Council for Vocational Education. Annual Report. a. ISSN 0098-5139

**Ohio. Attorney General's Office**
State House Annex, Columbus, OH 43215.
- Ohio. Attorney General's Office. Report. irreg. ISSN 0098-8820

**Ohio. Board of Regents**
88 E. Broad St., Rm. 770, Columbus, OH 43215.
- Ohio Higher Education. Basic Data Series. irreg. ISSN 0094-6109

**Ohio. Bureau of Employment Services**
Columbus, OH 43215.
- Ohio. Bureau of Employment Service. Biennial Report. biennial. ISSN 0093-6723

**Ohio. Commission on Aging**
34 N. High St., Columbus, OH 43215.
- Ohio. Commission on Aging. Annual Report. a. ISSN 0363-9207

**Ohio. Department of Economic and Community Development**
Box 1001, Columbus, OH 43216.
- Ohio. Department of Economic and Community Development. Review and Outlook. United States and Ohio Economy. irreg. ISSN 0094-7873

**Ohio. Department of Economic and Community Development. Bureau of Business Research**
65 South Front St., Columbus, OH 43215.
- Ohio Inventory of Business and Industrial Change. irreg. ISSN 0362-9716

**Ohio. Department of Education. Division of Special Education**
Columbus, OH 43215.
- Special Education Directory. irreg. ISSN 0364-0035

**Ohio. Department of Health**
Box 118, Columbus, OH 43216.
- Ohio's Health. 12 per yr. ISSN 0030-1256

**Ohio. Department of Industrial Relations. Division of Mines**
2323 W. Fifth Ave, Columbus, OH 43216.
- Ohio. Division of Mines. Report; with coal and industrial mineral directories of reporting firms. a. ISSN 0078-401X

**Ohio. Department of Mental Health and Mental Retardation**
Ohio Departments Building, Room 1104, 65 S. Front St., Columbus, OH 43215.
- Motive. q. ISSN 0580-0420
- Ohio. Department of Mental Health and Mental Retardation. Annual Financial and Statistical Report. a. ISSN 0094-6508
- Ohio Juvenile Court Statistics. a. ISSN 0094-2677 (prep. by its Bureau of Statistics)

**Ohio. Department of Mental Health and Mental Retardation. Office of Developmental Disabilities**
2929 Kenny Rd., B104A, Columbus, OH 43221.
- Ohio. Department of Mental Health and Mental Retardation. State Plan, Developmental Disabilities Services and Facilities Construction Act of 1970. a.

**Ohio. Department of Natural Resources. Division of Geological Survey**
Columbus, OH 43215.
- Ohio. Division of Geological Survey. Guidebook. irreg. ISSN 0097-9473
- Ohio. Division of Geological Survey. Miscellaneous Report. irreg. ISSN 0361-0519

**Ohio. Department of Natural Resources. Division of Wildlife**
8689 Horseshoe Rd., Ashley, OH 43003.
- Ohio Fish and Wildlife Report. irreg., 1972, no. 3. ISSN 0085-4468

**Ohio. Department of State Personnel**
Ohio Dept. Bldg., Columbus, OH 43215.
- Ohio. Department of State Personnel. Report. a. ISSN 0078-4001

**Ohio. Division of Safety and Hygiene**
2325w. Fifth Ave., Columbus, OH 43204.
- Monitor. m. ISSN 0026-9751

**Ohio. State Library**
65 S. Front St., Columbus, OH 43215.
- Ohio. State Library. State Library Review. a.
- Ohio Documents. q.
- Round-up - Children's Services. m. (10 per yr.) ISSN 0035-8541

**Ohio Academy of Family Physicians**
4075 N. High St., Columbus, OH 43214.
- Ohio Family Physician News. m. ISSN 0030-0888

**Ohio Academy of Science**
445 King Ave., Columbus, OH 43201.
- Ohio Academy of Science News. s-a. ISSN 0030-0764 (Junior Academy of the Ohio Academy of Science)
- Ohio Journal of Science. bi-m. ISSN 0030-0950

**Ohio AFL-CIO**
271 E. State St., Columbus, OH 43215.
- Focus (Columbus, 1967) m (except Jun, Jul. & Dec.) ISSN 0015-5047
- Ohio AFL-CIO News and Views. 3 per m (except July) ISSN 0030-0772

**Ohio Agricultural Research and Development Center**
Wooster, OH 44691.
- Ohio Agricultural Research and Development Center, Wooster. Library. List of References: Maize Virus Diseases and Corn Stunt. a. (prep. by its Library)
- Ohio Agricultural Research and Development Center, Wooster. Research Bulletin. irreg. ISSN 0078-3951
- Ohio Agricultural Research and Development Center, Wooster. Research Circular. irreg. ISSN 0078-396X
- Ohio Report on Research and Development in Agriculture, Home Economics, and Natural Resources. bi-m.

**Ohio Arts Council**
50 W. Broad St., Suite 2840, Columbus, OH 43215.
- Apollo's Diary; Ohio Arts Council poetry newsletter. 5 per yr.
- Ohio Arts Council. Annual Report. a.
- Viewpoint (Columbus) q. ISSN 0361-2678

**Ohio Association of Garden Clubs**
- Garden Path. (pub. by Greenfield Publishing Co.)

**Ohio Association of Secondary School Administrators**
750 Brooksedge Blvd., Westerville, OH 43081.
- American Secondary Education. q. ISSN 0003-1003

**Ohio Bankers Association**
33 North High St., Columbus, OH 43215.
- Ohio Banker. m. ISSN 0030-0802

**Ohio Biological Survey**
- Ohio Biological Survey. Biological Notes. (pub. by Ohio State University)
- Ohio Biological Survey. Bulletin. New Series. (pub. by Ohio State University)
- Ohio Biological Survey. Informative Circular. (pub. by Ohio State University)
- Surveyor. (pub. by Ohio State University)

**Ohio Brass Co**
380 N. Main St, Mansfield, OH 44902.
- Hi-Tension News. m. ISSN 0018-1242

**Ohio College Library Center**
1125 Kinnear Rd., Columbus, OH 43212.
- O C L C Newsletter. m.
- Ohio College Library Center. Annual Report. a. ISSN 0090-8673

**Ohio Congress of Parents & Teachers, Inc.**
427 E. Town St., Columbus, OH 43215.
- Ohio Parent Teacher. 6 per yr. ISSN 0030-1019

**Ohio Contractors Association**
1375 W. Lane Ave., Columbus, OH 43221.
- Ohio Contractor. m. ISSN 0030-0861

**Ohio Cooperative Wildlife Research Unit**
- O C W R U Quarterly Report. (pub. by Ohio State University)

**Ohio Council on Economic Education**
Copeland Hall, Ohio University, Athens, OH 45701.
- Ohio Council on Economic Education. Newsletter. s-a.

**Ohio Education Association**
225e. Broad St., Box 2550, Columbus, OH 43216.
- Ohio Schools. s-m. (Sep.-May); m. (Dec.) ISSN 0030-1086

**Ohio Educational Library Media Association**
236 E. Clearview, Worthington, OH 43085.
- Ohio Media Spectrum. q.

**Ohio Farm Bureau Federation and Affiliated Co-Operatives**
245 N. High St., Columbus, OH 43216.
- Buckeye Farm News. m. ISSN 0007-2834

**Ohio Florists Association**
2001 Fyffe Court, Columbus, OH 43210.
- Ohio Florists Association. Bulletin. m. ISSN 0030-090X

**Ohio Forestry Association, Inc.**
Suite 205, 665 E. Dublin Granville Rd., Columbus, OH 43229.
- Ohio Forestry Association. Bulletin. m. ISSN 0030-0918
- Ohio Woodlands/Conservation in Action. q. ISSN 0030-123X
- Sanlog. m.

**Ohio Genealogical Society**
Edwards Brothers, 2500 S. State St., Ann Arbor, MI 48106.
- Ohio Records & Pioneer Families; the cross road of our nation. q.

**Ohio Historical Society**
Ohio Historical Center, Columbus, OH 43211.
- Echoes. m. ISSN 0012-933X
- Ohio History. q. ISSN 0030-0934

**Ohio Jersey Breeders Association Inc.**
Box 532, Prospect, OH 43342.
- Ohio Jersey News. m. ISSN 0048-1556

**Ohio Journal**
c/o William Allen, Ed., Ohio State University, 164 W. 17th Ave., Columbus, OH 43210.
- Ohio Journal; magazine of literature and visual arts. q.

**Ohio Library Association**
40 S. Third St., Suite 409, Columbus, OH 43215.
- O L A Bulletin. q. ISSN 0029-7135
- Ohio Library Newsletter. 8 per yr.

**Ohio Library Trustees Association**
40 S. Third St., Columbus, OH 43215.
- Ohio Library Trustee. q. ISSN 0030-0977

**Ohio Municipal League**
The Neil House, Suite 105, 41 S. High St., Columbus, OH 43215.
- Cities and Villages. m. ISSN 0009-7535

**Ohio Music Education Association**
c/o Melvin C. Platt, Ed., School of Music, Kent State University, Kent, OH 44242.
- Contributions to Music Education. a.

**Ohio Music Education Association (Akron)**
c/o Wallace Nolin, Ed., Department of Music, University of Akron, Akron, OH 44325.
- Triad. 6 per yr. ISSN 0041-2511

**Ohio Northern University**
Ada, OH 45810.
- Ohio Northern University Law Review. q. ISSN 0094-534X

**Ohio Nurses Association**
4000 E. Main St., Columbus, OH 43213.
- Ohio Nurses Review. 10 per yr. ISSN 0030-0993

**Ohio Osteopathic Association of Physicians and Surgeons**
- Buckeye Osteopathic Physician. (pub. by State Osteopathic Journal Group)

**Ohio School Boards Association**
700 Brooksedge Blvd., Westerville, OH 43081.
- Ohio School Boards Journal. m. ISSN 0030-1078

**Ohio Society of Certified Public Accountants**
Box 617, Worthington, OH 43085.
- Ohio C P A. q.

**Ohio Society of Professional Engineers**
431 Ohio Bldg. B, 191 S. Main St., Akron, OH 44308
(Subscr. 445 King Ave., Columbus, Oh 43201)
- Ohio-en Engineering News. m.

**Ohio State Bar Association**
33 W. 11th Ave., Columbus, OH 43201.
- Ohio State Bar Association Report. w. ISSN 0030-1094

**Ohio State Grange**
1031 E. Broad St., Columbus, OH 43205.
- Ohio Grange; a leader in rural-urban affairs. m. ISSN 0030-0926

**Ohio State Medical Association**
600 S. High St., Columbus, OH 43215.
- Ohio State Medical Journal. m. ISSN 0030-1124

**Ohio State Pharmaceutical Association**
41 S. High St., Suite 0-62, Columbus, OH 43215.
- Ohio Pharmacist. m. ISSN 0030-1027

**Ohio State University**
1735 Neil Ave., Columbus, OH 43210.
- O C W R U Quarterly Report. q. ISSN 0473-9787 (Ohio Cooperative Wildlife Research Unit) (Co-sponsors: U.S. Fish and Wildlife Service; Ohio Division of Wildlife)

**Ohio State University**
484 W. 12th Ave., Columbus, OH 43210.
- Ohio Biological Survey. Biological Notes. irreg., no. 9, 1975. ISSN 0078-3986
- Ohio Biological Survey. Bulletin. New Series. irreg., vol. 5, 1974. ISSN 0078-3994
- Ohio Biological Survey. Informative Circular. irreg., no. 8, 1975.
- Surveyor. irreg.

**Ohio State University. Alumni Association**
2400 Olentangy River Rd., Columbus, OH 43210.
- Ohio State University Monthly. m.(exc. Aug.) ISSN 0030-1167

**Ohio State University. Center for Business and Economic Research**
1775 S. College Rd., Columbus, OH 43201.
- Bulletin of Business Research. m. ISSN 0007-4799

**Ohio State University. Center for Vocational Education**
1960 Kenny Rd., Columbus, OH 43210.
- Resources in Vocational Education. bi-m.

**Ohio State University. College of Administrative Science**
417 Hagerty Hall, 1775 S. College Rd., Columbus, OH 43210.
- Ohio State University. College of Administrative Science. Monograph. irreg. ISSN 0078-4087

**Ohio State University. College of Biological Sciences**
484 W. 12th Ave., Columbus, OH 43210.
- Microbial Genetics Bulletin. a.

**Ohio State University. College of Education**
149 Arps, 1945 N. High St., Columbus, OH 43210.
- Theory Into Practice. 5 per yr. ISSN 0040-5841

**Ohio State University. College of Engineering**
2070 Neil Ave., Columbus, OH 43210.
- Ohio State Engineer. 6 per yr.

**Ohio State University. College of Law**
1659 North High St., Columbus, OH 43210.
- Ohio State Law Journal. q. ISSN 0048-1572
- Ohio State University. College of Law. Law Forum Series. (pub. by Ohio State University Press)

**Ohio State University. Disaster Research Center**
Derby Hall, Columbus, OH 43210.
- Ohio State University. Disaster Research Center. D R C - T R. irreg. ISSN 0078-4109
- Ohio State University. Disaster Research Center. Report Series. irreg. ISSN 0078-4133
- Unscheduled Events. q. ISSN 0042-0468

**Ohio State University. Engineering Experiment Station**
2070 Neil Ave., Columbus, OH 43210.
- News in Engineering. bi-m. ISSN 0028-9205

**Ohio State University. Extension Entomologists**
1735 Neil Ave., Columbus, OH 43210.
- Ohio Insect Information. 10-25 per yr. ISSN 0048-1548

**Ohio State University. Graduate Institute for World Affairs**
- Ohio State University. Graduate Institute for World Affairs. Publications. (pub. by Ohio State University Press)

**Ohio State University Hospitals. Department of Communications and Public Affairs**
Starling Leving Hall, Columbus, OH 43210.
- Outreach. m.

**Ohio State University. Institute of Polar Studies**
i25 S. Oval Dr., Columbus, OH 43210.
- Ohio State University. Institute of Polar Studies. Report Series. irreg., no. 49, 1973. ISSN 0078-415X

**Ohio State University Libraries**
1858 Neil Ave., Columbus, OH 43210.
- Ohio State University. Libraries. Report of the Director. a. ISSN 0078-4176
- Under the Sign of Pisces: Anais Nin and Her Circle. q. ISSN 0041-6479

**Ohio State University Marion Campus**
1465 Mt. Vernon Ave., Marion, OH 43302.
- Cornfield Review; an annual of the creative arts. a. ISSN 0363-4574

**Ohio State University. Medical Administration Center**
370 W. Ninth Ave., Columbus, OH 43210.
- Ohio State University. College of Medicine. Journal. q. ISSN 0030-1132

**Ohio State University Press**
2070 Neil Ave., Columbus, OH 43210.
- Geographical Analysis; an international journal of theoretical geography. q. ISSN 0016-7363
- John Dewey Society. Studies in Educational Theory. irreg., no. 8, 1971. ISSN 0075-3831
- Journal of Higher Education. bi-m. ISSN 0022-1546 (American Association for Higher Education)
- Journal of Money, Credit & Banking. q. ISSN 0022-2879 (prep. by its Journals Department)
- Mershon Center for Education in National Security. Pamphlet Series. irreg., 1967, no. 6. ISSN 0076-6593

- Modern America. irreg., no. 4, 1975. ISSN 0076-9894
- Ohio State University. College of Law. Law Forum Series. irreg., no. 9, 1974. ISSN 0078-4095
- Ohio State University. Graduate Institute for World Affairs. Publications. irreg., 1966, no. 6. ISSN 0078-4141
- Vascular Flora of Ohio. irreg. ISSN 0083-5269

**Ohio State University. Project on Linguistic Analysis**
- Monographs on Linguistic Analysis. (pub. by Mouton Publishers NE)

**Ohio State University. School of Allied Medical Professions**
1583 Perry St., Columbus, OH 43210.
- Recurring Bibliography, Education in the Allied Health Professions. a. ISSN 0080-0341

**Ohio State University. School of Journalism**
c/o Dr. W. E. Hall, 242 W. 18th Ave., Columbus, OH 43210.
- Ohio State Lantern. d. ISSN 0030-1116

**Ohio State University. School of Music**
Div. of Music Education, Columbus, OH 43210.
- Current Issues in Music Education. irreg., 1970, no. 5. ISSN 0070-198X

**Ohio State University. Service Center for Teachers of Asian Studies**
29 W. Woodruff Ave., Columbus, OH 43210.
- Focus on Asian Studies. 3 per yr. ISSN 0046-4295 (Association for Asian Studies, Inc.)

**Ohio State University. Slavic Languages Department**
Columbus, OH 43210.
- Ohio Slavic and East European Newsletter. s-m.

**Ohio State University. Theatre Research**
309 Thompson Library, 1858 Neil Ave., Columbus, OH 43210.
- Theatre Studies. a.

**Ohio State University. Water Resources Center**
1791 Neil Ave., Columbus, OH 43210.
- Symposium on Water Resources Research. Proceedings. a. ISSN 0082-1012

**Ohio Testing Services**
65 S. Front St., State Dept. of Education, 751 Northwest Blvd., Columbus, OH 43212.
- Ohio Higher Education Notebook. biennial. ISSN 0085-4476

**Ohio Trucking Association**
Neil House Hotel, Columbus, OH 43215.
- Ohio Truck Times. m.

**Ohio University**
Ellis Hall, Athens, OH 45701.
- Ohio Review. 3 per yr.

**Ohio University. Center for Educational Research & Service**
Athens, OH 45701.
- Ohio University. Center for Educational Research and Service. Pupil Services Series. irreg. ISSN 0078-4230

**Ohio University. Center for International Studies**
- Papers in International Studies: Africa Series. (pub. by Ohio University Press)
- Papers in International Studies: Southeast Asia Series. (pub. by Ohio University Press)

**Ohio University. Department of English**
Athens, OH 45701.
- Milton Quarterly. q. ISSN 0026-4326

**Ohio University Press**
56 E. Union St., Athens, OH 45701.
- Papers in International Studies: Africa Series. irreg. (4-5 per yr.), no. 30, 1976. ISSN 0078-9100 (Ohio University. Center for International Studies)
- Papers in International Studies: Southeast Asia Series. irreg. (4-5 per yr.), no. 43, 1977. ISSN 0078-9119 (Ohio University. Center for International Studies)

**Ohio University Press Administrative Annex**
Athens, OH 45701
(and MacLaren & Sons, Ltd., London, England)
- Who's Who of British Engineers. irreg. ISSN 0083-985X

**Ohio University. Student Publications Board**
Baker Center, Athens, OH 45701.
- Post. d.

**Ohio Valley Area Libraries**
8 S. Ohio Ave., Wellston, OH 45692.
- O V A L Ideas. bi-m.
- O V A L Observations. m.

**Ohio Valley Philosophy of Education Society**
Indiana State University Print Shop, Terre Haute, IN 47809.
- Ohio Valley Philosophy of Education Society. Proceedings of the Annual Meeting. a. ISSN 0078-4044

**Ohio Valley Retailer**
c/o John W. Hargy, 163 Brocdorf Dr., Cincinnati, OH 45215.
- Ohio Valley Retailer. m.

**Ohio Veterinary Medical Association**
1350 W. Fifth Ave., Columbus, OH 43212.
- Ohio Veterinary Medical Association. Newsletter. m.

**Ohio Wesleyan University**
Delaware, OH 43015.
- Ohio Wesleyan Magazine. q. ISSN 0030-1221

**Ohioana Library Association**
c/o Martha Kinney Cooper Ohioana Library, 1105 Ohio Departments Bldg., 65 S. Front St., Columbus, OH 43215.
- Ohioana Quarterly. q. ISSN 0030-1248

**Oil Buyers Guide**
Box 998, Lakewood, NJ 08701.
- Oil Buyers Guide. w.

**Oil, Chemical and Atomic Workers International Union**
AFL-CIO, CLC, 1636 Champa St., Denver, CO 80202.
- Oil, Chemical and Atomic Workers International Union. Union News. m. ISSN 0030-1426

**Oil Information, Inc.**
380 Madison Ave., New York, NY 10019.
- Oil Information. m.

**Oil Men's Association of America**
c/o Hank Seale, Ed., 1606 South Jackson St., Amarillo, TX 79102.
- Hank Seale Oil Directory: Central United States. a. ISSN 0073-0238
- Hank Seale Oil Directory: Eastern United States. a. ISSN 0073-0246
- Hank Seale Oil Directory: Louisiana, Mississippi, Arkansas, Texas Gulf Coast and East Texas. a. ISSN 0073-0254
- Hank Seale Oil Directory: Texas Including Southeast New Mexico. a. ISSN 0073-0262

**Oil Review Publishing Co.**
P.O. Box 145, Jackson, MS 39205.
- Southeastern Oil Review. w.

**Oildom Publishing Co.**
3314 Mercer St., Box 22267, Houston, TX 77027.
- Pipe Line Annual Directory of Pipelines. a.
- Pipeline. 7 per yr.
- Pipeline & Underground Utilities Construction. s-m. ISSN 0032-0196

**Okeechobee Waterway Association**
Box 1255, Fort Myers, FL 33902.
- Southern Waterways. m. ISSN 0038-4631

**Oklahoma. Aeronautics Commission**
424 United Founders Tower Bldg., Oklahoma City, OK 73112.
- Directory of Oklahoma Airports. biennial. ISSN 0094-5390
- Oklahoma. Aeronautics Commission. Annual Report. a. ISSN 0092-9980

**Oklahoma. Attorney General's Office**
Rm 112, State Capitol, Oklahoma City, OK 73105.
- Digest of Opinions of the Attorney General. m. ISSN 0012-2777
- Oklahoma. Attorney General's Office. Opinions of the Attorney General. a. ISSN 0475-0926

**Oklahoma. Board of Medicolegal Investigations. Office of the Chief Medical Examiner**
Box 26901, 800 Northeast 13th St., Oklahoma City, OK 73190.
- Oklahoma Journal of Forensic Medicine. irreg. ISSN 0363-2679

**Oklahoma. Conservation Commission**
Oklahoma City, OK 73105.
- Oklahoma. Conservation Commission. Biennial Report. biennial. ISSN 0095-442X

**Oklahoma. Department of Education. Curriculum Improvement Commission**
Oliver Hodge Education Bldg., Suite 220, Oklahoma City, OK 73105.
- Successful Ventures in Contemporary Education in Oklahoma. a. ISSN 0090-4023

**Oklahoma. Department of Health**
N. E. Tenth and Stonewall, P.O. 53551, Oklahoma City, OK 73105.
- Oklahoma. Department of Health. Monthly Vital Statistics Report. m.
- Oklahoma Health Statistics. a. ISSN 0098-5651 (prep. by its Public Health Statistics Division)

**Oklahoma. Department of Highways. Planning Division**
Oklahoma City, OK 73105.
- Oklahoma. Department of Highways. Sufficiency Rating Report and Needs Study: Oklahoma State Highways. biennial. ISSN 0094-6230

**Oklahoma. Department of Industrial Development**
500 Will Rogers Bldg., Oklahoma City, OK 73105.
- Oklahoma P E P. (Program for Economic Prosperity). m.

**Oklahoma. Department of Institutions Social and Rehabilitative Services**
P.O. Box 25352, Oklahoma City, OK 73125.
- Medical Assistance. q. ISSN 0047-6455

**Oklahoma. Department of Libraries**
200 N. E. 18th St., Oklahoma City, OK 73105.
- Annual Report and Directory of Libraries in Oklahoma. a. ISSN 0066-4065
- Library Services Branch Newsletter. s-m.
- Oklahoma. Department of Libraries. Annual Report and Directory of Libraries in Oklahoma. a.
- Oklahoma Gazette. s-m. ISSN 0030-1728 (prep. by its Legislative Reference Division)

**Oklahoma. Department of Mental Health**
Biometrics Division, P.O. Box 53277, Oklahoma City, OK 73105.
- Oklahoma. Department of Mental Health. Statistical Report for Private Non-Profit Mental Health Facilities. a.

**Oklahoma. Department of Public Welfare**
P.O. Box 25352, Oklahoma City, OK 73125.
- Oklahoma. Department of Public Welfare. Annual Report. a. ISSN 0078-4362

**Oklahoma. Department of Wildlife Conservation**
1801 N. Lincoln, Oklahoma City, OK 73105.
- Oklahoma. Fishery Research Laboratory, Norman. Bulletin. (pub. by Oklahoma Fishery Research Laboratory)
- Outdoor Oklahoma. m. ISSN 0030-7106

**Oklahoma. Division of Maternal and Child Health**
Oklahoma City, OK 73105.
- Family Planning Programs in Oklahoma; annual statistical report. a. ISSN 0095-3121

**Oklahoma. Drug Abuse Division**
Oklahoma City, OK 73105.
- Oklahoma. Drug Abuse Division. Annual Report. a.

**Oklahoma. Employment Security Commission. Actuarial Division**
Will Rogers Bldg., Oklahoma City, OK 73105.
- Oklahoma. Employment Security Commission. Actuarial Division. Handbook of Employment Security Program Statistics; data for: v.i. program & financial rates & ratios, state v.i., employ. serv. activities, fed. employees benefits, vets. benefit activities, m.d.t., extended benefits. a.

**Oklahoma. Employment Security Commission. Research & Planning Division**
Will Rogers Bldg., Oklahoma City, OK 73105.
- Handbook of Labor Force Data for Selected Areas of Oklahoma. a.

- Handbook of Oklahoma Employment Statistics. a.
- Oklahoma. Employment Security Commission. Research and Planning Division. Annual Report to the Governor. a.
- Oklahoma. Employment Security Commission. Research and Planning Division. County Employment and Wage Data. a.
- Oklahoma Economic Indicators. m. ISSN 0474-070X
- Oklahoma Employment Security Review. m. ISSN 0471-492X
- Oklahoma Labor Market. m. ISSN 0030-1744
- Oklahoma Population Estimates. a.

**Oklahoma. Geological Survey**
The University of Oklahoma, 830 Van Vleet Oval, Room 163, Norman, OK 73019.
- Oklahoma. Geological Survey. Bulletin. irreg., no. 122, 1977. ISSN 0078-4389
- Oklahoma. Geological Survey. Circular. irreg; no. 77, 1976. ISSN 0078-4397
- Oklahoma. Geological Survey. Guide Book. irreg; no. 17, 1969. ISSN 0078-4400
- Oklahoma Geology Notes. bi.-m. ISSN 0030-1736

**Oklahoma. Indian Affairs Commission**
4901 N. Lincoln Blvd., Oklahoma City, OK 73105.
- Oklahoma, Indian Affairs Commission. Biennial Report. biennial. ISSN 0360-7518

**Oklahoma. Industrial Development Department**
500 Will Rogers Bldg., Oklahoma City, OK 73105.
- Oklahoma Directory of Manufacturers and Products. biennial.

**Oklahoma. Office of Community Affairs and Planning**
4901 N. Lincoln, Oklahoma City, OK 73105.
- Directory. Sub-State Planning Districts in Oklahoma. irreg. ISSN 0094-5994

**Oklahoma. State Board of Public Accountancy**
265 West Court, 4545 Lincoln Boulevard, Oklahoma City, OK 73105.
- Directory of Certified Public Accountants and Public Accountants of Oklahoma Registered in Accordance with Oklahoma Statutes and Rules of the Oklahoma State Board of Public Accountancy. irreg. ISSN 0361-4115

**Oklahoma. Tax Commission. Ad Valorem Division**
2501 Lincoln Blvd., Oklahoma City, OK 73194.
- Oklahoma. Ad Valorem Tax Division. Progress Report to the Legislature on Property Revaluation. a.

**Oklahoma. Turnpike Authority**
3500 North Eastern, P.O. Box 11357, Oklahoma City, OK 73111.
- Oklahoma Turnpike Authority. Annual Report to the Governor. a.

**Oklahoma. Water Resources Board**
Dialex Bldg., 2241 N.W. 40th St., Oklahoma City, OK 73112.
- Oklahoma. Water Resources Board. Annual Report. irreg. ISSN 0099-1635

**Oklahoma Academy of Science**
c/o Jim Lovell, S-300, State St., Southwestern Oklahoma State Univ., Weatherford, OK 73096.
- Oklahoma Academy of Science. Annals. a. ISSN 0078-4311
- Oklahoma Academy of Science. Proceedings. a. ISSN 0078-4303

**Oklahoma Agricultural Experiment Station**
Stillwater, OK 74074.
- Oklahoma Current Farm Economics. q. ISSN 0030-1701

**Oklahoma Anthropological Society**
University of Oklahoma, Norman, OK 73069.
- Oklahoma Anthropological Society. Bulletin. a. ISSN 0078-432X
- Oklahoma Anthropological Society. Memoir. irreg. ISSN 0474-0696
- Oklahoma Anthropological Society. Newsletter. irreg. ISSN 0078-4338
- Oklahoma Anthropological Society. Special Bulletin. irreg. ISSN 0078-4346

**Oklahoma Art Center**
3113 Pershing Blvd., Oklahoma City, OK 73107.
- Oklahoma Art Center. Annual Eight State Exhibition of Painting and Sculpture Catalog. a. ISSN 0085-4484 (Co-Sponsor: State Fair of Oklahoma)

**Oklahoma Association of Electric Cooperatives**
P.O. Box 11047, Oklahoma City, OK 73111.
- Oklahoma Rural News. m. ISSN 0048-1610

**Oklahoma Bankers Association**
643 N.E. 41st St., Oklahoma City, OK 73105.
- Oklahoma Banker. m. ISSN 0030-1647

**Oklahoma Bar Association**
Oklahoma Bar Center, Box 53036, Oklahoma City, OK 73105.
- Oklahoma Bar Association. Journal. w. (m. during recess of Supreme Court) ISSN 0030-1655

**Oklahoma Bluegrass Club Inc.**
419 N. Beard, Shawnee, OK 74801.
- Oklahoma Bluegrass Gazette. m.

**Oklahoma Cattlemen's Association**
2500 Exchange Ave., Oklahoma City, OK 73108.
- Oklahoma Cowman. m. ISSN 0030-1698

**Oklahoma City Chamber of Commerce**
One Santa Fe Plaza, Oklahoma City, OK 73102.
- Oklahoma. s-m. ISSN 0030-1639

**Oklahoma City Geological Society**
1020 Cravens Bldg., Oklahoma City, OK 73102.
- Shale Shaker. m.(Sept-June) ISSN 0037-3257

**Oklahoma Congress of Parents and Teachers**
555 E. Constitution St., Norman, OK 73069.
- Oklahoma Parent-Teacher. q. ISSN 0030-1817

**Oklahoma Council on Economic Education**
Oklahoma State Univ., Rm. 112 Business Bldg., Stillwater, OK 74074.
- Oklahoma Council on Economic Education Newsletter. a.

**Oklahoma County Libraries**
Public Information Office, 131 N.W. 3, Oklahoma City, OK 73102.
- Ad Libs. w. ISSN 0001-7957

**Oklahoma Dental Association**
629 N.W. Expressway, Oklahoma City, OK 73118.
- Your Oklahoma Dental Association. Journal. q.

**Oklahoma Education Association**
323 E. Madison, Oklahoma City, OK 73105.
- Oklahoma Teacher. m.(Sept-May) ISSN 0030-1884

**Oklahoma Farm Bureau**
2501 N. Stiles, Oklahoma City, OK 73105.
- Oklahoma Farm Bureau Farmer. m. ISSN 0048-1599

**Oklahoma Farmers Union**
1141 West Sheridan, Oklahoma City, OK 73106.
- Oklahoma Union Farmer. m. ISSN 0030-1620

**Oklahoma Fishery Research Laboratory**
1416 Planck St., Norman, OK 73069.
- Oklahoma. Fishery Research Laboratory, Norman. Bulletin. irreg., 1968, no.8. ISSN 0078-4370 (Oklahoma. Department of Wildlife Conservation) (Co-Sponsor: University of Oklahoma Biological Survey)

**Oklahoma Historical Society**
Historical Bldg., 2100 N. Lincoln, Oklahoma City, OK 73105.
- Chronicles of Oklahoma. q. ISSN 0009-6024
- Oklahoma Series. irreg.

**Oklahoma Library Association**
University of Oklahoma, 401 W. Brooks, Rm. 149, Norman, OK 73019.
- Oklahoma Librarian. q. ISSN 0030-1760

**Oklahoma LP-Gas Association**
2910 N. Walnut, Suite 114-A, Oklahoma City, OK 73105.
- Sooner L P G Times. m. ISSN 0038-1500

**Oklahoma Oil Marketers Association**
1140 N.W. 63rd Street, Oklahoma City, OK 73118.
- Oklahoma Oil Marketer. m.

**Oklahoma Ornithological Society**
c/o Jack D. Tyler, Ed., Dept. of Biology, Cameron University, Lawton, OK 73501.
- Oklahoma Ornithological Society. Bulletin. q. ISSN 0474-0750

**Oklahoma Reading Council**
College of Behavioral Sciences, Northeastern Oklahoma State University, Tahlequah, OK 74464.
- Oklahoma Reader. q. ISSN 0030-1833

**Oklahoma Restaurant Association**
2207 N. Broadway, Oklahoma City, OK 73103.
- Midsouthwest Restaurant. m.

**Oklahoma Retail Grocers Association**
25 N.E. 52, Box 18716, Oklahoma City, OK 73118.
- Oklahoma Food Journal. m.

**Oklahoma Retailer Publishing Co.**
4500 N. Sewell, Oklahoma City, OK 73118.
- Oklahoma Retailer. m. ISSN 0030-1841

**Oklahoma River Basin Survey**
University of Oklahoma, 1808 Newton Dr., Norman, OK 73069.
- Oklahoma River Basin Survey. Archaeology Site Report. irreg., no. 32, 1977.
- Oklahoma River Basin Survey. General Survey Report. irreg., no. 16, 1976.

**Oklahoma Society of Professional Engineers Inc.**
Suite 426, East Bldg., 2000 Classen Center, OK 73106.
- Oklahoma Professional Engineer. m. (except June, July, Aug.)

**Oklahoma State Medical Association**
601 N.W. Expressway, Oklahoma City, OK 73118.
- Oklahoma State Medical Association. Journal. m. ISSN 0030-1876

**Oklahoma State Nurses Association**
4400 N. Lincoln Blvd., Suite 153, Oklahoma City, OK 73105.
- Oklahoma Nurse. 10 per yr. ISSN 0030-1787

**Oklahoma State University. College of Arts and Sciences**
203 B Morrill Hall, Stillwater, OK 74074.
- Cimarron Review. q. ISSN 0009-6849

**Oklahoma State University. College of Business Administration**
Stillwater, OK 74074.
- Oklahoma State University. College of Business Administration. Working Papers. irreg.

**Oklahoma State University. College of Engineering**
Engineering and Industrial Extension, Stillwater, OK 74074.
- Advanced Water Conference. Proceedings. irreg, 3rd, 1971.
- Frontiers of Power Technology Conference. Proceedings. irreg.

**Oklahoma Today**
Will Rogers Memorial Bldg., Oklahoma City, OK 73105.
- Oklahoma Today. q. ISSN 0030-1892

**Oklahoma University College of Law**
630 Parrington Oval, Norman, OK 73069.
- American Indian Law Review. a. ISSN 0094-002X

**Oklahoma Water Resources Research Institute**
Stillwater, OK 74074.
- Oklahoma Water Resources Research Institute. Annual Report. a. ISSN 0092-2528

**Oklahomans for Indian Opportunity**
555 Constitution, Norman, OK 73069.
- Oklahomans for Indian Opportunity Newsletter. m.

**Okra Press**
306 W. Drew, Houston, TX 77006.
- Okra Press. 4 per yr. ISSN 0030-1930

**Old Car Value Guide**
910 Tony Lama St., El Paso, TX 79915.
- Old Car Value Guide. s-a. ISSN 0475-1876

**Old Dartmouth Historical Society**
Whaling Museum, 18 Johnny Cake Hill, New Bedford, MA 02740.
- Bulletin from Johnny Cake Hill. q.

**Old Dominion University. Conference on Scottish Studies**
Arts and Letters Building, Norfolk, VA 23508.
- Conference on Scottish Studies. Proceedings. a.

**Old Fort Genealogical Society of Southeastern Kansas**
802 S. Eddy, Fort Scott, KS 66701
(or Fort Scott Community College, 2108 Horton)
- Old Fort Log. q. ISSN 0098-4760

**Old Friends**
P.O. Box 24, The Plains, VA 22171.
- Old Friends; a new arts review. q.

**Old-House Journal Corporation**
199 Berkeley Place, Brooklyn, NY 11217.
- Old-House Journal. m. ISSN 0094-0178
- Old-House Journal Buyers' Guide; a catalog of sources for products, materials and services for the restoration and decoration of vintage homes. a.

**Old Lyme Investment Co.**
Old Lyme, CT 06371.
- Bacchus Journal. q. ISSN 0005-3597

**Old Marble Press**
Box 1701, East Lansing, MI 48823.
- Local Tenderness. q.

**Old Salem, Inc.**
Drawer F, Salem Station, Winston-Salem, NC 27108.
- Old Salem Gleaner. irreg. ISSN 0078-4540

**Old Soldiers of Baker Street of the Two Saults**
909 Prospect, Sault Ste. Marie, MI 49783.
- Commonplace Book. s-a. ISSN 0010-3314

**Old Sturbridge Village**
Sturbridge, MA 01566.
- New-England Galaxy. q. ISSN 0028-4750
- Old Sturbridge Village Booklet Series. irreg., no. 29, 1972. ISSN 0078-4559

**Oleander Press**
210 Fifth Ave., New York, NY 10010
(Outside U.S. and Canada: 17 Stansgate Ave., Cambridge CB2 2QZ, Eng.)
- Books on Libya Series.
- Language and Literature Series.
- Oleander Dramascripts Series.
- Oleander Modern Poets Series. irreg.
- Portrait of a City Series.

**Olivant Press**
Box 1409, Homestead, FL 33030.
- Weid: the Sensibility Revue. 3 per yr. ISSN 0145-983X

**Michael Oliver**
Box 485, Carson City, NV 89701.
- M. Oliver Newsletter. irreg. ISSN 0085-2929

**C. Dalley Oliver, Ed. & Pub.**
P.O. Box 25, Rowayton, CT 06853.
- Under Twenty-Five Newsletter; the newsletter concerning youth as a market and force to be reckoned with. m. ISSN 0300-6077

**Oliver Press**
1400 Ryan Creek Rd., Willits, CA 95490.
- Monthly List of Government Publications Selected for High School and Public Libraries. m.

**Olmstead's Genealogy Recorded**
c/o Walt Steesy, RD1-Box 150, Interlaken, NY 14847.
- Olmstead's Genealogy Recorded. q.

**Humphrey A. Olsen, Ed. & Pub.**
205 S. Ninth St., Williamsburg, KY 40769.
- Snowy Egret. s-a. ISSN 0037-7473

**David E. Olson, Ed. & Pub.**
RFD 1, Liberty, ME 04949.
- Maine Life. m. ISSN 0025-0678

**Olympic Club**
524 Post St., San Francisco, CA 94102.
- Olympian. m. ISSN 0030-2163

**Olympic Genealogical Society**
c/o Roseann Mitchell, Rt. 5, Box 747F, Bremerton, WA 98310.
- Family Backtracking. q.

**Olympic Media Information**
71 W. 23rd St., New York, NY 10010.
- Educational Media Catalogs on Microfiche. a. with q. updates.
- Educational Media Talent and Marketing Profiles. a.

- Hospital/Health Care Training Media Profiles. bi-m. ISSN 0095-0580
- Training Film Profiles. bi-m.

**Om**
c/o Melvin L. Yosso, Ed., Village Box 104, New York, NY 10014.
- Om. q.

**Omaha-Council Bluffs Metropolitan Area Planning Agency**
7000 West Center Rd., Suite 200, Omaha, NE 68106.
- M A P A Capsule. q.

**Omaha District Dental Society**
727 Medical Arts Bldg., 17th & Dodge St., Omaha, NE 68102.
- Omaha District Dental Society. Chronicle. m (10 per yr.) ISSN 0030-2201

**Omaha Jewish Federation**
333 S. 132nd St., Omaha, NE 68154.
- Jewish Press. w. ISSN 0021-6666

**Omaha Westerners**
514 Barker Bldg., Omaha, NE 68102.
- Droppings. q. (Westerners International)

**Oman Publishing Co.**
Keystone Bldg., Box 72, Mill Valley, CA 94941.
- Meat Industry. m. ISSN 0099-2011

**Omega Epsilon Phi Fraternity**
c/o Dr. Norbert Kastner, Ed., Box 152, Iselin, NJ 08830.
- Optist. 3 per yr.

**Omega Group Ltd.**
Box 693, Boulder, CO 80306.
- Soldier of Fortune; the journal of professional adventurers. bi-m.

**Omen Press Inc.**
Box 12457, Tucson, AZ 85711.
- Omen. m(9 per yr.) ISSN 0030-2236

**Omicron Delta Epsilon Fraternity**
c/o Ed. Michael Szenberg, Long Island Universtiy, Dept. of Economics, Brooklyn, NY 11201.
- American Economist. s-a. ISSN 0002-8290

**Omicron Nu Home Economics Honor Society**
Human Ecology Bldg., Michigan State University, East Lansing, MI 48824.
- Omicron Nu Newsletter. 4 per yr.

**Ommation Press**
c/o Effie Mihopoulos, Ed., 5548 N. Sawyer, Chicago, IL 60625.
- Mati: a Poetry Magazine. q.

**Omni Industries, Inc.**
6033 Melody Lane, Dallas, TX 75231.
- T V Host. w.

**Omni Publications Bulletin**
Box 216, Hawthorne, CA 90250.
- Omni Publications Bulletin; the meaning and importance of the money question.

**One Parent Community**
Box 5877, Santa Monica, CA 90405.
- Single Parent News. bi-m.

**One-Size-Fits-All Press**
Box 371, Brooklyn, NY 11230.
- Blank Tape. 3 per yr.

**Jerome H. O'Neil**
1886 Osage Dr., Okemos, MI 48864.
- Michigan Banking & Business News. m.

**William O'Neil & Co., Inc.**
Box 24933, Los Angeles, CA 90024.
- Daily Graphs. American Stock Exchange. w.
- Daily Graphs. Stock Option Guide. w.
- Daily Graphs-N.Y.S.E./O.T.C. w.

**Online, Inc.**
11 Tannery Lane, Weston, CT 06883.
- Online. q. ISSN 0146-5422

**Open Court Publishing Co.**
Box 599, La Salle, IL 61301.
- Cricket; the magazine for children. m. ISSN 0090-6034

- Library of Living Philosophers. irreg., vol. 14, 1974. ISSN 0075-9139
- Monist. q. ISSN 0026-9662
- Open Court Newsletter. 5 per yr. (Sept.-May) ISSN 0048-1912
- Paul Carus Lectures. irreg., no. 14, 1973. ISSN 0079-0257 (American Philosophical Association)

**Open Road Publishing Co.**
1015 Florence St., Fort Worth, TX 76102.
- Open Road and the Professional Driver. m. ISSN 0030-3437

**Open Window Society, Inc.**
301 Hicks St., Brooklyn, NY 11201.
- Voyeur. m.

**Operations Research Society of America**
428 E. Preston St., Baltimore, MD 21202.
- Mathematics of Operations Research. (pub. by Institute of Management Sciences)
- Operations Research. bi-m. ISSN 0030-364X
- Operations Research Society of America. Bulletin. s-a. ISSN 0030-3666
- Transportation Science. q. ISSN 0041-1655

**Operative Plasterers' and Cement Masons' International Association of the United States and Canada**
1125 17th St., N.W., Washington, DC 20036.
- Plasterer and Cement Mason. m. ISSN 0032-1036

**Ophthalmic Publishing Co.**
233 East Ontario St., Suite 1401, Chicago, IL 60611.
- American Journal of Ophthalmology. m. ISSN 0002-9394

**Opinion Publications**
c/o Dr. James E. Kurtz, Ed., Box 1885, Rockford, IL 61110.
- Opinion; a journal of thought. m.

**Opinion Publications, Inc.**
c/o Noah Gordon, 82 Cochituate Rd., Framingham, MA 01701.
- Journal of Human Stress. 4 per yr.
- Psychiatric Opinion. 6 per yr. ISSN 0033-2712

**Opportunities Press, Inc.**
300 E. 42 St., New York, NY 10017.
- Home Office Report; a monthly roundup of news, ideas, time & money saving hints to help you work at home more successfully. m. ISSN 0018-411X

**Opportunities Unlimited Publications**
301 N. Orchard Ave., Farmington, NM 87401.
- Energy Forecasts to 1990. irreg.

**Opportunity Publishing Co.**
1460 John Hancock Center, Chicago, IL 60611.
- Salesman's Opportunity Magazine. m. ISSN 0036-3510

**Optical Publishing Co., Inc**
Box 1146, Berkshire Common, Pittsfield, MA 01201.
- Optical Industry and Systems Directory. a. ISSN 0078-5474
- Optical Spectra. m. ISSN 0030-395X

**Optical Society of America, Inc.**
2000 L St. N.W., Washington, DC 20036.
- Applied Optics. m. ISSN 0003-6935 (Subscr. to: American Institute of Physics, 335 E. 45th St., New York, NY 10017)
- Applied Optics. Supplement. (pub. by American Institute of Physics)
- Optical Society of America. Journal. (pub. by American Institute of Physics)
- Optics and Spectroscopy. (pub. by American Institute of Physics)
- Optics and Spectroscopy. Supplement. (pub. by American Institute of Physics)
- Optics News. (pub. by American Institute of Physics)

**Opticians Association of America**
1250 Connecticut Ave., N.W., Ed. James H. McCormick, DC 20036.
- Dispensing Optician. m.

**Option Weekly**
Box 124, Annandale, VA 22003.
- Option Weekly. w.

**Options Publishing Co.**
Box 311, Wayne, NJ 07470.
● Options; the Jewish resources newsletter. m. ISSN 0362-2770

**Optosonic Press**
Box 883, Ansonia Post Office, New York, NY 10023.
● State of the Art Review Series. irreg., 1973, vol. 7. ISSN 0081-458X

**O'Quinn Studios, Inc.**
180 Madison Ave., New York, NY 10016.
● Starlog. q.

**Oracle of Maat Publishing Company**
Box 281, Bronx, NY 10462.
● Oracle of Maat. m.

**Oral History Association**
Box 13734, North Texas State University, Denton, TX 76203.
● Oral History Association. Newsletter. q.
● Oral History Review. a.

**Oral Roberts Evangelistic Association Inc.**
Box 2187, Tulsa, OK 74102.
● Daily Blessing. q. ISSN 0011-538X

**Orange County Bar Association**
17291 Irvine Blvd., Suite 309, Tustin, CA 92680.
● Orange County Bar Journal. q. ISSN 0096-3143

**Orange County Califonia Geneaological Society**
Box 1587, Orange, CA 92668.
● Orange County California Genealogical Society Quarterly. q.

**Orange County Cooperative Extension**
Agricultural Division, 239-283 Wisner Ave., Middletown, NY 10940.
● Orange County Farm News. m. ISSN 0030-4271

**Orange County Illustrated, Inc.**
Box 1816, Newport Beach, CA 92663.
● Orange County Business; quarterly journal of commerce & industry. bi-m. ISSN 0030-4255
● Orange County Illustrated. m. ISSN 0030-428X

**Orange Press**
226 West 104 St., New York, NY 10025.
● Verse Gazette. irreg.

**Orangeburg Historical and Genealogical Society**
Route 1, Box 1069-C, Orangeburg, SC 29115.
● Orangeburg Historical and Genealogical Record. q. ISSN 0030-431X

**Orbe Publications Inc.**
705 N. Windsor Blvd., Hollywood, CA 90038.
● Grafica. bi-m. ISSN 0017-2898

**Order of Ahepa**
1422 K St. N.W., Washington, DC 20005.
● A H E P A N. bi-m. (American Hellenic Educational Progressive Associations)

**Order of Demolay. International Supreme Council**
201 E. Armour Blvd, Kansas City, MO 64111.
● International DeMolay Cordon. m. ISSN 0020-6520

**Order of Friars Minor**
Butler, NJ 07405.
● Friar Magazine. m. ISSN 0016-1225

**Order of Runeberg**
100 Park Place Bldg, Seattle, WA 98101.
● Leading Star/Ledstjaernan. m.

**Order of the Sons of Italy in America. Grand Lodge of California**
5051 Mission St., San Francisco, CA 94112.
● Leone; giornale ufficiale della grande loggia di California dell'ordine figli d'Italia in America. m. ISSN 0024-0958

**Order of the Sons of Italy in America. Grand Lodge of Massachusetts**
126 Cambridge St., Boston, MA 02114.
● Sons of Italy News. m. ISSN 0038-1446

**Order of United Commercial Travelers of America**
632 N. Park St., Columbus, OH 43215.
● Sample Case. q. ISSN 0036-3898

**Orders and Medals Society of America**
3444 S. Home, Berwyn, IL 60402.
● Medal Collector. m. ISSN 0025-6633

**Oregon. Department of Agriculture**
Salem, OR 97310.
● Consumer Newsletter; consumer protection. m.
● Oregon Agri-Record. q. ISSN 0030-4603

**Oregon. Department of Economic Development**
317 S.W. Alder St., Ninth Fl., Portland, OR 97204.
● Directory of Oregon Manufacturers. biennial.
● Doing Business in Oregon. biennial.
● Financing New and Expanding Businesses in Oregon. irreg.
● Oregon, an Economic Profile. biennial.
● Oregon County Economic Indicators. a.
● Oregon Progress Newsletter. bi-m.
● Oregon, the Solid State. irreg.
● Sources of International Trade Information. a.

**Oregon. Department of Education**
942 Lancaster Drive NE, Salem, OR 97310.
● Oregon. Department of Education. Racial and Ethnic Survey. a. ISSN 0090-1059
● Oregon School Directory. a. ISSN 0078-5679

**Oregon. Department of Fish and Wildlife**
Box 3503, 1634 S. E. Alder St., Portland, OR 97208.
● Oregon. Department of Fish and Wildlife. Environmental Management Section. Special Report. irreg.
● Oregon. State Game Commission. Bulletin. m. ISSN 0030-4824 (prep. by its State Game Commission)
● Oregon Wildlife. m.

**Oregon. Department of Forestry**
2600 State St., Salem, Salem, OR 97310.
● Forest Log. m. ISSN 0015-7449

**Oregon. Department of Geology and Mineral Industries**
1069 State Office Bldg., Portland, OR 97201.
● Ore Bin. m.
● Oregon. State Department of Geology and Mineral Industries. Bulletin. irreg., no. 90, 1976. ISSN 0078-5709
● Oregon. State Department of Geology and Mineral Industries. G M I Short Papers. irreg., no. 25, 1976. ISSN 0078-5717
● Oregon. State Department of Geology and Mineral Industries. Miscellaneous Publications. irreg., latest issue, 1975. ISSN 0078-5733
● Oregon. State Department of Geology and Mineral Industries. Miscellaneous Papers. irreg., no. 18, 1975. ISSN 0078-5725
● Oregon. State Department of Geology and Mineral Industries. Oil and Gas Investigations. irreg., no. 5, 1976. ISSN 0078-5741

**Oregon. Department of Revenue**
State Office Bldg., Salem, OR 97310.
● Oregon. Department of Revenue. Sales Ratio Study. a.
● Oregon Property Tax Statistics. a.
● Personal Income Tax Analysis. a.

**Oregon. Department of Transportation. Mass Transit Division**
Highway Building, Salem, OR 97310.
● Oregon. Mass Transit Division. Annual Report. a. ISSN 0090-3906

**Oregon. Department of Transportation. Motor Vehicles Division**
Salem, OR 97310.
● Oregon. Motor Vehicles Division. Oregon Motorcycle Accidents. irreg. ISSN 0092-9913
● Oregon Log Truck Accidents. a.
● Oregon Truck Accidents. a.
● Oregon's Driving Population. irreg. ISSN 0091-5769

**Oregon. Department of Transportation. State Parks and Recreation Branch**
Salem, OR 97310.
● Oregon Recreation Briefs. m. ISSN 0474-4616

**Oregon. Educational Coordinating Commission**
495 State St., Salem, OR 97310.
● Oregon. Educational Coordinating Council. Annual Program Amendment for Title I, Higher Education Act of 1965; program impact. a.
● Oregon. Educational Coordinating Council. Degrees and Awards Offered and Granted in Oregon's Post- Secondary Institutions. a.

**Oregon. Fish Commission**
307 State Office Bldg., Portland, OR 97201.
● Oregon Fish Commission. Research Reports. irreg. ISSN 0078-5636

**Oregon. Governor's Commission on Youth**
775 Court St. N.E., Salem, OR 97310.
● Oregon. Governor's Commission on Youth. End-of-the-Month Clearance. m.

**Oregon. Governor's Steering Committee for Management Selection and Development**
240 Cottage St. S.E., Salem, OR 97310.
● Oregon. Governor's Steering Committee for Management Selection and Development. Management Selection and Development, Annual Status Report. a.

**Oregon. Office of Community Health Services**
Box 231, Portland, OR 97207.
● Oregon. Office of Community Health Services. Local Health Services Annual Summary. a. ISSN 0092-3060

**Oregon. Public Utility Commissioner**
Labor & Industries Bldg., Salem, OR 97310.
● Oregon. Public Utility Commissioner. Statistics of Electric, Gas, Steam Heat, Telephone, Telegraph and Water Companies. a. ISSN 0091-0546

**Oregon. Public Welfare Division**
304 Public Service Bldg., Salem, OR 97310.
● Public Welfare in Oregon. q. ISSN 0474-4039

**Oregon. Secretary of State**
121 State Capitol, Salem, OR 97310.
● Oregon Blue Book. biennial.

**Oregon. State Advisory Council for Career and Vocational Education**
4263 Commercial St. S.E., Salem, OR 97310.
● Oregon. State Advisory Council for Career and Vocational Education. Annual Evaluation Report. a. ISSN 0364-0027

**Oregon. State Board of Accountancy**
Labor & Industreis Bldg., 4th Fl., Salem, OR 97310.
● Oregon. State Board of Accountancy. Certified Public Accountants, Public Accountants, Professional Corporations, and Accountants Authorized to Conduct Municipal Audits in Oregon. a. ISSN 0090-6735

**Oregon. State Employment Division. Research & Statistics**
875 Union St., N.E., Salem, OR 97310.
● Oregon Unemployment Insurance Tax Rates; tax rate comparisons for rate years. irreg. (every 2-3 yrs.)

**Oregon. State Health Division**
Box 231, Portland, OR 97207.
● Oregon Health Bulletin. m. ISSN 0030-4700
● Oregon Public Health Statistics Report. a.

**Oregon. State Health Division. Office of Health Planning Services**
Suite 213, 2111 Front St. N.E., Salem, OR 97310.
● Oregon State Plan for the Construction and Modernization of Hospitals, Public Health Centers and Medical Facilities. a. ISSN 0078-575X

**Oregon. State Library**
Salem, OR 97310.
● Checklist of Official Publications of the State of Oregon. q.
● Watermark. m.

**Oregon. Workmen's Compensation Board. Accident Prevention Division**
Labor & Industries Bldg., Salem, OR 97310.
● Industrial Fatalities. 7-9 per yr.
● Safer Oregon. 6 per yr. ISSN 0036-2425

**Oregon Archaeological Society**
Box 13293, Portland, OR 97213.
● Screenings. m. ISSN 0048-9832

**Oregon Association for Supervision and Curriculum Development**
Box 421, Salem, OR 97308.
● Oregon A S C D Curriculum Bulletin. q. ISSN 0048-2137

**Oregon Association of Nurserymen**
222 S.W. Harrison, Suite GA-7, Portland, OR
97201.
- O.A.N. Digger. bi-m.

**Oregon Cattlemen's Association, Inc.**
Box 2027, Wenatchee, WA 98801.
- Oregon Cattleman. m. ISSN 0471-9174

**Oregon College of Education. Humanities Department**
Monmouth, OR 97361.
- O C E Poetry Anthology. a.

**Oregon Daily Emerald Publishing Co., Inc.**
300 E M U, Eugene, OR 97403.
- Oregon Daily Emerald. d. ISSN 0030-4662

**Oregon Dental Association**
620 S.W. 5th Ave., Suite 810, Portland, OR 97204.
- Oregon Dental Association. Journal. 4 per yr.
(journal) 8 per yr (newsletter) ISSN 0030-4670

**Oregon Education Association**
1 Plaza Southwest, 6900 S.W. Haines Rd., Tigard,
OR 97223.
- Oregon Education. s-m (Sept.-May), m (Dec.)
ISSN 0030-4689

**Oregon Educational Media Association**
631 N.E. Clackamas St., Portland, OR 97208.
- Interchange (Portland) q. ISSN 0047-0457

**Oregon Environmental Council**
2637 S.W. Water Ave., Portland, OR 97201.
- Earthwatch Oregon. m.

**Oregon Farm Bureau Federation**
1730 Commercial, S. E., Box 2209, Salem, OR
97308.
- Oregon Agriculture. m. ISSN 0030-4611

**Oregon Feed, Seed & Supplies Association**
1812 N.W. Kearney St., Portland, OR 97209.
- Oregon Feed, Seed and Suppliers Association.
Commercial Review. w. ISSN 0010-3101

**Oregon Historical Society**
1230 S.W. Park Ave., Portland, OR 97205.
- Oregon Historical Quarterly. q. ISSN 0030-4727
- Oregon Historical Society. News. bi-m. ISSN
0474-4535

**Oregon Library Association**
Catalog Dept., Univ. of Oregon Library, Eugene,
OR 97403.
- Oregon Library News. 6 per yr. ISSN 0030-4735

**Oregon Licensee, Inc.**
c/o Western Printing, Inc., 3850 Portland Rd. N.E.,
Salem, OR 97303.
- Host. m.

**Oregon Music Educator**
337 W. Riverside Dr., Roseburg, OR 97310.
- Oregon Music Educator. 5 per yr. ISSN 0030-
4743

**Oregon Nurses Association**
1212 Failing Bldg., 618 S.W. Fifth, Portland, OR
97204.
- Oregon Nurse. q. ISSN 0030-4751

**Oregon Optometric Association**
Ed. William J. Baker, P. O. Box 298, McMinnville,
OR 97128.
- Oregon Optometrist. q. ISSN 0030-476X (Co-
Sponsor: Pacific Univ. Optometric Alumni Assn.)

**Oregon Outdoors Publishing Co.**
c/o Dennis M. Hunt, Ed., Box 1376, Eugene, OR
97401.
- Oregon Sportsman and Conservationist. fortn.
ISSN 0030-4808

**Oregon Psychological Association**
P.O. Box 3196, Eugene, OR 97407.
- Oregon Psychological Association. Newsletter. 5
per yr. ISSN 0471-9336

**Oregon Regional Medical Program**
3181 S. W. San Jackson Park Rd., Portland, OR
97201.
- O R M P Newsletter. 3-4 per yr. ISSN 0029-7216

**Oregon Regional Primate Research Center**
505 N.W. 185th Ave., Beaverton, OR 97005.
- Primate News. m. ISSN 0032-8324

**Oregon Research Institute**
Box 3196, Eugene, OR 97403.
- Oregon Research Institute. Occasional Papers in
Applied Policy Research. irreg.
- Oregon Research Institute. Research Bulletins.
irreg., latest issue 1975. ISSN 0078-5644
- Oregon Research Institute. Research Monographs.
irreg., latest issue 1975. ISSN 0078-5652

**Oregon Rural Electrical Cooperative Association**
- Ruralite. (pub. by Ruralite Services, Inc.)

**Oregon School Study Council**
124 College of Education, University of Oregon,
Eugene, OR 97403.
- O.S.S.C. Bulletin. irreg. ISSN 0095-6694

**Oregon Science Teachers Association**
c/o Bill Marker, 6900 S.W. Haines Rd., Tigard, OR
97223.
- Oregon Science Teacher. m (Sept-May) ISSN
0030-4794

**Oregon State Association of Plumbing-Heating-
Cooling Contractors, Inc.**
301 Equitable Bldg., Salem, OR 97301.
- Oregon Plumbing-Heating-Cooling Contractor. m.

**Oregon State Bar**
1776 S.W. Madison St., Portland, OR 97205.
- Oregon State Bar Bulletin. m. ISSN 0030-4816

**Oregon State Grange**
1313 S. E. 12th Ave, Portland, OR 97214.
- Oregon Grange Bulletin. s-m. ISSN 0030-4697

**Oregon State System of Higher Education**
Office of High School Relations, P.O. Box 3175,
Eugene, OR 97403.
- Counseling for College. irreg. ISSN 0070-122X

**Oregon State University. Air Resources Center**
Corvallis, OR 97331.
- Oregon State University Air Resources Center.
Air Research Summary. biennial. ISSN 0094-8160

**Oregon State University. Department of Horticulture**
Corvallis, OR 97331.
- Ornamentals Northwest. m. (prep. by its Oregon
Agricultural Experiment Station) (Co-sponsors:
Washington State University; University of Idaho)

**Oregon State University. Environmental Health
Sciences Center**
Corvallis, OR 97331.
- Environmental Health Sciences Series. irreg. ISSN
0071-0881

**Oregon State University. Forest Research Laboratory**
Corvallis, OR 97331.
- Oregon State University. Forest Research
Laboratory. Annual Report. a. ISSN 0078-5865
- Oregon State University. Forest Research
Laboratory. Research Bulletin. irreg., no. 19,
1976. ISSN 0078-5903
- Oregon State University. Forest Research
Laboratory. Research Note. irreg., no. 59, 1977.
ISSN 0078-5911
- Oregon State University. Forest Research
Laboratory. Research Paper. irreg., latest issue no.
36. ISSN 0078-592X

**Oregon State University. Genetics Insitute**
- Genetics Lectures. (pub. by Oregon State
University Press)

**Oregon State University. Marine Advisory Program**
Extension Service, Corvallis, OR 97331.
- Oregon Commercial Fisheries. 4 per yr.

**Oregon State University Press**
101 Waldo Hall-Box 689, Corvallis, OR 97330.
- Association of Pacific Coast Geographers.
Yearbook. a. ISSN 0066-9628
- Atlas of the Pacific Northwest. every 4-5 yrs.
- Genetics Lectures. irreg., vol. 4, 1975. ISSN 0072-
081X (Oregon State University. Genetics Insitute)
- Improving College and University Teaching;
international quarterly journal. q. ISSN 0019-3089
- Improving College and University Teaching
Yearbook. a. ISSN 0363-2598
- Oregon State Monographs. Bibliographic Series.
irreg. ISSN 0078-5768
- Oregon State Monographs. Studies in Botany.
irreg. ISSN 0078-5776
- Oregon State Monographs. Studies in Economics.
irreg. ISSN 0078-5784

- Oregon State Monographs. Studies in Education
and Guidance. irreg., latest issue 1973. ISSN
0078-5792
- Oregon State Monographs. Studies in
Entomology. irreg., 1966, no. 4. ISSN 0078-5806
- Oregon State Monographs. Studies in Geology.
irreg., 1971, no. 10. ISSN 0078-5814
- Oregon State Monographs. Studies in History.
irreg., no. 6, 1975. ISSN 0078-5822
- Oregon State Monographs. Studies in Zoology.
irreg., 1968, no. 12. ISSN 0078-5830
- Oregon State University. Annual Biology
Colloquium. Proceedings. a. ISSN 0078-5857
- Pacific Northwest Conference on Higher
Education. Proceedings. a. ISSN 0078-7620

**Oregon State University. School of Engineering**
Corvallis, OR 97331.
- Engineering Focus. s-a.
- Oregon State University. School of Engineering.
Graduate Research and Education. irreg., 1970,
Jan., no. 39. ISSN 0078-5938
- Oregon State University. School of Engineering.
Research Activities. biennial. ISSN 0078-5946
- University Engineer. 3 per yr. ISSN 0041-929X
(prep. by its Engineering Student Council)

**Oregon State University. School of Forestry**
Corvallis, OR 97331.
- Forestry Update. m.

**Oregon State University. Sea Grant College Program**
Corvallis, OR 97331.
- Currents. bi-m.
- Technical Conference on Estuaries of the Pacific
Northwest. Proceedings. a. ISSN 0085-7122
(prep. by its School of Engineering)

**Oregon State University. Water Resources Research
Institute**
Corvallis, OR 97330.
- Oregon State University. Water Resources
Research Institute. Water Research Summary.
biennial. ISSN 0078-5849
- Publications in Water Research at Oregon State
University. a. ISSN 0079-7766

**Oregon Voter Digest**
c/o C. R. Hillyer, Ed., 108 N. W. 9th, Portland,
OR 97209.
- Oregon Voter Digest. s-m. ISSN 0030-4859

**Organ Historical Society, Inc.**
Box 209, Wilmington, OH 45177.
- Organ Historical Society. National Convention
(Proceedings) irreg.
- Tracker. q. ISSN 0041-0330

**Organic Preparations and Procedures, Inc.**
Box 9, Newton Highlands, MA 02161.
- Organic Preparations and Procedures
International; the new journal for organic
synthesis. bi-m. ISSN 0030-4948

**Organization for Defense of Four Freedoms for
Ukraine Inc.**
Box 304, Cooper Sta., New York, NY 10003.
- Visnyk/Herald; suspil'no-politychnyi misiachnyk.
m. ISSN 0042-7004

**Organization for Flora Neotropica**
- Flora Neotropica. Monographs. (pub. by Hafner
Publishing Co., Inc.)

**Organization for the Rebirth of Ukraine**
2315 W. Chicago Ave., Chicago, IL 60622.
- Samostiina Ukrayina/Independent Ukraine. bi-m.
ISSN 0036-3847

**Organization of American Historians**
Indiana Univ., Ballantine Hall, Bloomington, IN
47401.
- Journal of American History. q. ISSN 0021-8723

**Organization of American Kodaly Educators**
c/o Christine Kunko, Duquesne University School
of Music., Pittsburgh, PA 15219.
- Kodaly Envoy. irreg.

**Organization of American States**
General Secretariat, Department of Publications,
17th & Constitution Ave. N.W., Washington, DC
20006.
- America en Cifras. biennial; 8th edt., 1974. ISSN
0065-6771 (Inter-American Statistical Institute)
- Americas. m. ISSN 0003-1577

- Anuario del Desarrollo de la Educacion, la Ciencia y la Cultura en America Latina. a. ISSN 0570-4200
- Anuario Interamericano de Derechos Humanos/ Inter-American Yearbook on Human Rights. biennial. (Inter-American Commission on Human Rights)
- Chiefs of State and Cabinet Ministers of the American Republics. q. ISSN 0475-5529
- Ciencia Interamericana. 4 per yr. ISSN 0009-675X
- Composers of the Americas/Compositores de America. a. ISSN 0069-8016
- Estadistica. q. ISSN 0014-1135
- Inter-American Bulletin on Taxation. irreg. (prep. by its Tax Program)
- Inter-American Commission of Women. Informational Bulletin. irreg. (Inter-American Commission of Women (C I M))
- Inter-American Commission of Women. News Bulletin. 3 per yr. ISSN 0538-2912 (Inter-American Commission of Women (C I M))
- Inter-American Commission of Women. Noticiero. irreg. ISSN 0538-2920 (Inter-American Commission of Women (C I M))
- Inter-American Commission of Women. Special Assembly. Final Act/Comision Interamericana de Mujeres. Asamblea Extraordinaria. Acta Final. irreg., 1968, 5th. ISSN 0074-0764
- Inter-American Commission on Human Rights. Report on the Work Accomplished During Its Special Sessions. s-a; latest issue, 1970. ISSN 0074-0780
- Inter-American Council for Education, Science, and Culture. Final Report. a. ISSN 0074-0829
- Inter-American Economic and Social Council. Final Report of the Annual Meeting at the Ministerial Level. a. ISSN 0074-0918
- Inter-American Nuclear Energy Commission. Final Report. a. ISSN 0074-0942
- Inter-American Review of Bibliography/Revista Interamericana de Bibliografia. q. ISSN 0020-4994 (Inter-American Committee on Bibliography)
- O A S. General Secretariat. Annual Report. a. ISSN 0078-6403
- O A S Chronicle. m. ISSN 0029-6910
- Organization of American States. Department of Cultural Affairs. Estudios Bibliotecarios. irreg.; vol. 8, nos. 1-2, 1972. ISSN 0078-6373
- Organization of American States. Department of Cultural Affairs Manuales del Bibliotecario. irreg. ISSN 0078-6381
- Organization of American States. Department of Scientific Affairs. Newsletter. q.
- Organization of American States. Department of Scientific Affairs. Report of Activities. irreg.
- Organization of American States. Department of Scientific Affairs. Serie de Biologia: Monografias. irreg.; latest issue, no. 14. ISSN 0553-0342
- Organization of American States. Department of Scientific Affairs. Serie de Fisica: Monografias. irreg., no. 12, 1976. ISSN 0078-6322
- Organization of American States. Department of Scientific Affairs. Serie de Matematica: Monografias. irreg., no. 17, 1976. ISSN 0078-6330
- Organization of American States. Department of Scientific Affairs. Serie de Quimica: Monografias. irreg., latest issue no. 17. ISSN 0553-0377
- Organization of American States. Development Financing/Financimiento del Desarrollo. q.
- Organization of American States. Directory. m.
- Organization of American States. General Assembly. Actas y Documentos. irreg.
- Organization of American States. Official Records. Indice y Lista General. irreg. ISSN 0078-642X
- Organization of American States. Permanent Council. Decisions Taken at Meetings (Cumulated Edition) a. ISSN 0078-6438
- Organization of American States. Regional Scientific and Technological Program. Newsletter. m. (prep. by its Department of Scientific Affairs)
- Pan American Associations in the United States; A Directory with Supplementary Lists of Other Associations. Inter-American and General. irreg. ISSN 0553-0326
- Pan American Union. Department of Social Affairs. Studies and Monographs. irreg. ISSN 0553-0407
- Revista Interamericana de Ciencias Sociales. irreg. ISSN 0556-6703
- Statistical Compendium of the Americas. irreg. ISSN 0585-1432
- Studies in Export Promotion. irreg. ISSN 0553-0237

- Work Accomplished by the Inter-American Juridicical Committee During Its Meeting. a. ISSN 0074-0837

**Organization of Black American Culture, Writers' Workshop**
77 E. 35th St., Chicago, IL 60616.
- Nommo. q. ISSN 0029-1005

**Organization of Historical Studies**
American University, Dept. of History, Washington, DC 20016.
- Journal of Historical Studies (Washington) s-a. ISSN 0361-7246

**Organization of North American Indian Students**
140 University Center, Northern Michigan University, Marquette, MI 49855.
- Nishnawbe News. m.

**Organizing Committee for a Fifth Estate**
- Counter Spy. (pub. by Fifth Estate Publishing Co.)

**Orgonomic Publications Inc.**
Box 565, Ansonia Sta., New York, NY 10023.
- Journal of Orgonomy. s-a. ISSN 0022-3298 (American College of Orgonomy)

**Oriental Rug Importers Association of America**
295 Fifth Ave., New York, NY 10016.
- Oriental Rug. m. ISSN 0030-5332

**Orion**
12108 Drake St., Minneapolis, MN 55433.
- Orion. 4 per yr (approx.)

**Orion Press**
Box 366, Willows, CA 95988.
- Eureka Review. 2-3 per yr.

**Orleans Parish Medical Society**
1430 Tulane Ave., New Orleans, LA 70112.
- Orleans Parish Medical Society. Bulletin. m. ISSN 0030-5669

**Orr-Flanagan Co.**
100 N. Grant St., Columbus, OH 43215.
- Ohio Tavern News. s-m. ISSN 0030-1183

**Orthodox Church in America**
Box 675, Syosset, NY 11791.
- Avtokefalnaia Amerikanskaia Pravoslavnaia Tserkov. Ezhegodnik Pravoslavnoi Tserkvi V Amerike. a.
- Orthodox Church. m.(except July & August) ISSN 0048-2269 (prep. by its Metropolitan Council)
- Orthodox Church in America. Yearbook and Church Directory. a.

**Orthodox Lore Of the Gospel of Our Savior Mission**
Box 5333, St. Louis, MO 63115.
- O L O G O S. bi-m. ISSN 0029-7143

**Orthodox Reformed Publishing Society**
3268 Chestnut, S.W., Grandville, MI 49418.
- Reformed Scope. m.

**Orthopedic Nurses Association**
- Orthopedic Nurses Association. Journal. (pub. by Charles B. Slack, Inc.)

**Orton Society, Inc.**
8415 Bellona Lane, Towson, MD 21204.
- Orton Society. Bulletin. a. ISSN 0078-6624

**Oryx Press**
3930 E. Camelback Rd., Suite 206, Phoenix, AZ 85018.
- Bibliography of Agriculture. m. ISSN 0006-1530 (U.S. National Agricultural Library)
- Grant Information System. m. ISSN 0099-0213
- T V Season. a. ISSN 0363-9487
- World Directory of Environmental Research Centers. triennial. (State University of New York, College at Fredonia. Lake Erie Environmental Studies) (Distributor: R. R. Bowker Co., Box 1807, Ann Arbor, MI 48106)

**Osiris**
Box 297, Deerfield, MA 01342.
- Osiris; an international journal. s-a. ISSN 0095-019X

**Osterhus Publishing House, Inc.**
4500 W. Broadway, Minneapolis, MN 55422.
- Bible Friend; monthly magazine of biblical faith & Christ's teaching. m. ISSN 0006-0739

**Oswego County Historical Society**
Richardson-Bates House, 135 E. 3rd St., Oswego, NY 13126.
- Oswego County Historical Society. Journal. a. ISSN 0092-9549

**Oswego Press**
Oswego, NY 13126.
- American College of Neuropsychiatrists. Bulletin. 2-3 per yr. ISSN 0002-7995 (American College of Neuropsychiatrists)

**Othello Outlook**
Drawer O, Othello, WA 99344.
- Columbia Basin Farmer. m. ISSN 0010-1877

**Other Side**
Box 158, Savannah, OH 44874.
- Other Side. bi-m.

**Otterbein College**
Westerville, OH 43081.
- Otterbein Miscellany. a.

**Otto Rank Association**
35 W. State St., Doylestown, PA 18901.
- Otto Rank Association. Journal. s-a. ISSN 0030-6711

**Our American Heritage Committee News Bulletin**
Box 12312, Oklahoma City, OK 73112.
- Our American Heritage Committee News Bulletin. m. ISSN 0030-6770

**Our People's Underworld**
Box 310, Shelbyville, IN 46176.
- Snafu; a journal of conspiracy. m. ISSN 0037-7422

**Our Sunday Visitor, Inc.**
Noll Plaza, Huntington, IN 46750.
- Catholic Almanac. a. ISSN 0069-1208
- Our Sunday Visitor. w. ISSN 0030-6967
- Pope Speaks; The Church Documents Quarterly. q. ISSN 0032-4353
- Priest. m. ISSN 0032-8200

**Our Town**
1550 York Ave., New York, NY 10028.
- Our Town. w. ISSN 0048-2404

**Out There**
8334 Ridgeway, Skokie, IL 60076.
- Out There. 4 per yr.

**Outdoor Eduquip**
Wilderness Leadership Center, Box 770, North Fork, CA 93643.
- Come out to the Beautiful Life; magazine of wilderness and country living. q.

**Outdoor Empire Publishing, Inc.**
511 Eastlake Ave. E., Box C 19000, Seattle, WA 98109.
- Fishing and Hunting News. w. ISSN 0015-301X
- Hunter Safety News. bi-m.

**Outdoor Times**
c/o M. L. Harrell, 4515 Prentice, Dallas, TX 75206.
- Outdoor Times. w. ISSN 0048-2439

**Outdoor Writers Association of America, Inc.**
4141 W. Bradley Rd., Milwaukee, WI 53209.
- Outdoors Unlimited. m. ISSN 0030-7181

**Outdoorsman Publishing Co.**
Box 3, Banks, ID 83602.
- Outdoorsman. m. ISSN 0048-2455

**Outfitters Professional Society, Inc.**
45 Trappers Lake Road, Meeker, CO 81641.
- Colorado Outfitter; covering professional outfitting: big game, fishing, outdoor recreation. 10 per yr (except Oct.-nov.)

**Outlook Publications**
2111 Jefferson Davis Highway No. 4225, Arlington, VA 22202.
- Outlook in Alcohol & Drug Abuse. s-m.
- Outlook in Education. m.

**Outlook Publications, Inc.**
7317 Cahill Rd., Edina, MN 55435.
- Lutheran Journal. q.

**Outlook Publishers, Inc.**
512 E. Main St., Richmond, VA 23219.
- Going-To-College Handbook. a. ISSN 0072-4904
- Presbyterian Outlook. w. ISSN 0032-7565

**Outside the Net**
P.O. Box 184, Lansing, MI 48901.
- Outside the Net; a magazine in radical education. q. ISSN 0048-248X

**Outworlds**
c/o William L. Bowers, Box 2521, North Canton, OH 44720.
- Outworlds. q.

**Over-The-Counter Securities Review**
Box 110, Jenkintown, PA 19046.
- Over-The-Counter Securities Review. m. ISSN 0030-736X

**Over the Garden Fence, Inc.**
3960 Cobblestone Dr., Dallas, TX 75229.
- Over the Garden Fence; natural living in North Texas. 10 per yr.

**Overbrook School for the Blind**
54th and Malvern Ave., Philadelphia, PA 19151.
- Towers. 3 per yr. ISSN 0040-9928

**Overseas Crusades, Inc.**
3033 Scott Blvd., Santa Clara, CA 95050.
- Cable. q. ISSN 0007-9286

**Overseas Development Council**
1717 Massachusetts Avenue, Washington, DC 20036.
- Overseas Development Council. Annual Report. a. ISSN 0092-7643
- Overseas Development Council. Communique. irreg., no. 26, 1974.
- Overseas Development Council. Development Papers. irreg., no. 18, 1975.
- Overseas Development Council. Monograph Series. irreg., no. 18, 1973. ISSN 0078-7108
- Overseas Development Council. Occasional Papers. irreg., no. 7, 1973.
- U S and the Developing World: Agenda for Action. a.

**Overseas Missionary Fellowship**
404 S. Church St., Robesonia, PA 19551.
- East Asia Millions. bi-m. ISSN 0012-8406

**Overseas Press Club of America, Inc.**
55 E. 43rd St., New York, NY 10017.
- Overseas Press Bulletin. s-m. ISSN 0048-2544

**Owens Valley Indian Education Center**
Box 1648, Bishop, CA 93514.
- Owens Valley Indian Education Center Monthly Newsletter. m. ISSN 0300-6719

**Ox Head Press**
414 N. Sixth St., Marshall, MN 56258.
- Ox Head. irreg. ISSN 0030-7629

**Oxbridge Communications, Inc.**
1345 Ave. of the Americas, New York, NY 10019.
- Directory of the College Student Press in America. biennial. ISSN 0085-0020 (National Council of College Publications Advisers)
- Standard Periodical Directory. biennial. ISSN 0085-6630

**Oxford Industries, Inc.**
444 N. Larchmont Blvd., Los Angeles, CA 90004.
- Let's Live. m. ISSN 0024-1288

**Oxford University Press**
For publications of this press see also section for UNITED KINGDOM

**Oxford University Press**
200 Madison Ave., New York, NY 10016 (and Ely House, 37 Dover St., London W1X 4AH, England)
- Appreciation of the Arts. irreg., 1973, no. 8. ISSN 0066-5568
- Baroque Operatic Arias. irreg.
- British Year Book of International Law. irreg., 1971, vol. 45. ISSN 0068-2691 (Royal Institute of International Affairs UK)
- Canada in World Affairs. irreg. ISSN 0068-7685 (Canadian Institute of International Affairs)

- Canterbury and York Series. irreg. (Canterbury and York Society)
- Clarendon Aristotle Series. irreg.
- Clarendon English Series. irreg.
- Clarendon French Series. irreg.
- Clarendon German Series. irreg.
- Clarendon Law Series. irreg.
- Clarendon Library of Logic and Philosophy. irreg.
- Clarendon Mediaeval and Tudor Series. irreg. ISSN 0529-8784
- Discoveries in the Judaean Desert of Jordan. irreg., 1968, vol. 5. ISSN 0070-668X
- Documents on International Affairs. irreg.
- Early English Text Society. Publications. Extra Series. irreg., latest issue no. 124. ISSN 0070-7864
- Early English Text Society. Publications. Original Series. irreg., no. 270, 1974. ISSN 0070-7872
- Early English Text Society. Publications. Supplementary Texts. irreg., 1971, no. 2. ISSN 0070-7880
- English Historical Documents. irreg. ISSN 0071-058X
- English Studies Series. irreg, 1971, no.8. ISSN 0071-0644
- Freud in America.
- Home University Library. irreg. ISSN 0073-3148
- International African Seminar. Studies Presented and Discussed. a, 13th, 1975. ISSN 0534-655X
- Middle Eastern Monographs. irreg., no. 11, 1973. ISSN 0076-8537 (Royal Institute of International Affairs UK)
- Monographs in Electrical and Electronic Engineering. irreg.
- Monographs on Physical Biochemistry. irreg.
- Monographs on Plastic Surgery. irreg.
- Monographs on the Physics and Chemistry of Materials. irreg.
- New Zealand Fiction. irreg., 1970, no. 2. ISSN 0077-9970
- Oxford Applied Mathematics and Computing Science Series. irreg.
- Oxford Chemistry Series. irreg. ISSN 0302-4199
- Oxford English Memoirs and Travels. irreg.
- Oxford English Monographs. irreg.
- Oxford Forestry Memoirs. irreg.
- Oxford Handbook for Medical Auxiliaries. irreg.
- Oxford Historical Series. irreg., 1969, no. 16. ISSN 0078-7205
- Oxford History of English Literature. irreg., 1963, vol. 12. ISSN 0078-7221
- Oxford History of Modern Europe. irreg.
- Oxford in Asia; College Texts. irreg.
- Oxford in Asia; Current Affairs. irreg.
- Oxford in Asia; Historical Reprints. irreg.
- Oxford in Asia; Modern Authors. irreg.
- Oxford Library of East Asian Literatures. irreg.
- Oxford Library of Far Eastern Classics. irreg.
- Oxford Library of Italian Classics. irreg.
- Oxford Library of the Physical Sciences. irreg. ISSN 0472-3325
- Oxford Mathematical Handbooks. irreg.
- Oxford Medical Publications. irreg.
- Oxford Monographs on Classical Archaeology. irreg.
- Oxford Monographs on Medical Genetics. irreg.
- Oxford Monographs on Meteorology. irreg.
- Oxford Monographs on Social Anthropology. irreg.
- Oxford Neurological Monographs. irreg.
- Oxford Paleographical Handbooks. irreg.
- Oxford Paperback English Texts. irreg.
- Oxford Paperbacks University Series. irreg., no. 69, 1974. ISSN 0078-723X
- Oxford Physics Series. irreg., vol. 10, 1975.
- Oxford Readings in Philosophy. irreg.
- Oxford Readings in Social Studies. irreg.
- Oxford Regional Economic Atlases. irreg.
- Oxford Research Studies in Geography. irreg.
- Oxford Russian Readers. irreg. ISSN 0474-9774
- Oxford Science Research Papers. irreg., latest vol. 1974. ISSN 0078-7248
- Oxford Standard Authors. irreg.
- Oxford Studies of Composers. irreg., no. 11, 1974. ISSN 0078-7264
- Oxford Theological Monographs. irreg. ISSN 0078-7272
- Oxford Tropical Handbooks. irreg.
- Oxford University. Pitt Rivers Museum. Occasional Papers on Technology. irreg., vol. 10, 1970.
- Oxford University Almanack. a.
- Oxford University Calendar. a.
- Oxford University Handbook. irreg.
- Problems in European History. irreg.
- Reconstruction of Society Series. irreg.
- Science and Engineering Policy Series. irreg.
- Select Bibliographical Guides. irreg.

- Series of Short Biographies of Distinguished Black Americans and Black Africans. irreg.
- Series of Studies in Tudor and Stuart Literature. irreg.
- Series on World Poverty. irreg.
- Short Oxford History of the Modern World. irreg., latest vol., 1973. ISSN 0080-939X
- Studies in African Economics. irreg., 1969, no. 2. ISSN 0081-7473
- Studies in Behavioral Political Science. irreg.
- Studies in Mathematics. irreg., 1973, no. 6. ISSN 0081-8216 (Tata Institute of Fundamental Research. Bombay II)
- Survey of International Affairs. irreg.
- Sylloge of Coins of the British Isles. irreg. ISSN 0082-0628
- Times Literary Supplement. T.L.S; Essays and Reviews. irreg., vol. 12, 1974. ISSN 0082-4410
- Whidden Lectures. a. ISSN 0083-9248 (McMaster University CN)

**Oz Publications**
447 E. 15th, Eugene, OR 97401.
- 10 Point 5; magazine of the arts. q.

**Ozarks Mountaineer**
Branson, MO 65616.
- Ozarks Mountaineer. 11 per yr. ISSN 0030-7769

**Jerome S. Ozer Publisher Inc.**
475 Fifth Ave., New York, NY 10017.
- Major Issues in American History. irreg.

**P A I A Electronics, Inc.**
1020 West Wilshire Boulevard, Oklahoma City, OK 73116.
- Polyphony. q.

**P C A Inc.**
676 N. Lasalle St., Chicago, IL 60610.
- Faces. bi-m.

**P E A L**
Box 4134, Pittsburgh, PA 15202.
- Publishing, Entertainment and Advertising and Allied Fields Law Quarterly. q. ISSN 0555-6392

**P. E. N. American Center**
156 Fifth Ave., New York, NY 10010.
- Grants and Awards Available to American Writers. a.
- Grants and Awards Available to Foreign Writers. a. ISSN 0093-3163
- PENewsletter. 8 per yr.

**P-EN Publications Inc.**
1506 Gardena Ave., Box 1809, Glendale, CA 91209.
- Print-Equip News. m. ISSN 0048-5314

**P.G. Sports Service Inc.**
Box 465, Main Post Office, Niagara Falls, NY 14302.
- P.G. Football Newsletter. 14 per yr. ISSN 0048-3613

**P-H-C Information Services**
7315 Wisconsin Ave., Washington, DC 20014.
- Medvin P-H-C Tradeletter. s-m.

**P.I.M.E. Missionaries**
9800 Oakland Ave., Detroit, MI 48211.
- Catholic Life. m.(except July & Aug.) ISSN 0008-8218

**P J D Publications**
Box 966, Westbury, NY 11590.
- Journal of Medicine (Clinical, Experimental and Theoretical) bi-m.
- Research Communications in Chemical Pathology and Pharmacology. m. ISSN 0034-5164
- Research Communications in Psychology, Psychiatry and Behavior. q.

**P J S Publications, Inc.**
News Plaza, Peoria, IL 61601.
- Profitable Craft Merchandising. m.
- Rotor & Wing. m. ISSN 0035-8452
- Shooting Times. m. ISSN 0038-8084

**P.M. Inc.**
7060 Hollywood Blvd., Suite 726, Hollywood, CA 90028.
- Nutrition & the M.D. m.

**P M S Publishing Co. Inc.**
3161 Fillmore St., San Francisco, CA 94123
- Super-8 Filmaker. 8 per yr. ISSN 0049-2574
  (Subscr. to:, Box 10052, Palo Alto CA 94303)

**P N Y X Publishing Co.**
Box 67, Glenview, IL 60025.
- Chicago P N Y X. s-m. ISSN 0009-3645

**P P A Publications, Inc.**
1090 Executive Way, Oak Leaf Commons, Des
Plaines, IL 60018.
- Directory of Professional Photography. a. ISSN
  0070-6140 (Professional Photographers of
  America)
- Professional Photographer. m. ISSN 0033-0167
  (Professional Photographers of America)

**P P G Industries, Inc.**
One Gateway Center, Pittsburgh, PA 15222.
- P P G Products. q. ISSN 0030-820X
- Plans & Specs. q.

**P R, Inc. (Partisan Review)**
522 Fifth Ave., New York, NY 10036.
- Partisan Review. q. ISSN 0031-2525 (Rutgers
  University)

**P R Publishing Co., Inc.**
Box 600, Dudley House, Exeter, NH 03833.
- P R Reporter; weekly newsletter of public
  relations, public affairs & communication. w. ISSN
  0048-2609
- Who's Who in Public Relations (International)
  irreg. ISSN 0511-9022

**P S C Publications Committee**
P.O. Box 891, Red Bank, NJ 07701.
- Power Sources Symposium. Proceedings. biennial.
  ISSN 0079-4457 (U.S. Army Electronics
  Command)

**P S Communications, Inc.**
1929 Royce Ave., Beloit, WI 53511.
- Auto and Flat Glass Journal. m. ISSN 0005-0717

**P.T.J. Publishing, Inc.**
Box 397, Park Forest, IL 60466.
- Passenger Train Annual. a.
- Passenger Train Journal. m.

**P T N Publishing Corp.**
250 Fulton Ave., Hempstead, NY 11550.
- Functional Photography. 6 per yr.
- Microfilm Techniques; the magazine for
  operational microfilm personnel. bi-m. ISSN
  0047-7184
- Photographic Processing. 6 per yr. ISSN 0031-
  8744
- Photographic Trade News. fortn. ISSN 0031-8779
- Photographic Trade News Master Buying Guide.
  a.
- Professional Film Production. bi-m.
- Professional Photographic Equipment Directory
  and Buying Guide. a.
- Security Industry and Product News. bi-m.
- Studio Photography. m.
- Technical Photography. m. ISSN 0040-0971
- Today's Film Maker. bi-m.

**P W Communications**
488 Madison Ave., New York, NY 10022.
- Female Patient; practical advice for better care. m.
  ISSN 0364-1198
- Primary Cardiology; cardiovascular medicine for
  the primary care physician. m. ISSN 0363-5104

**P. W. Publishing Co. Inc.**
1949 E. 105th St., Cleveland, OH 44101.
- Call and Post. w. ISSN 0045-4036

**Pace Publications**
1324 Carolina St., Greensboro, NC 27401.
- Pace. bi-m.

**Pacific Area Travel Association**
274 Brannan St., San Francisco, CA 94107.
- Pacific Area Destination Handbook. a. ISSN
  0363-4817
- Pacific Hotel Directory & Travel Guide. s-a. ISSN
  0479-0790
- Pacific Travel News. (pub. by Western Business
  Publications)

**Pacific Basin Reports**
Custom House, Box 26581, San Francisco, CA
94126.
- Pacific Basin Report Service. s-m.

**Pacific Books, Publishers**
P. O. Box 558, Palo Alto, CA 94302.
- Borestone Mountain Poetry Awards. a. ISSN
  0067-6276
- Los Angeles Geographical Society. Publication.
  irreg. ISSN 0076-096X

**Pacific Coast Archaeological Society, Inc.**
Box 926, Costa Mesa, CA 92627.
- Pacific Coast Archaeological Society Quarterly. q.
  ISSN 0552-7252

**Pacific Coast Aviation Directory**
c/o E. A. Brennan & Co., 15111 E. Whittier Blvd.,
Whittier, CA 94305.
- Pacific Coast Aviation Directory. a.

**Pacific Coast Council on Latin American Studies**
- Pacific Coast Council on Latin American Studies.
  Proceedings. (pub. by San Diego State University
  Press)

**Pacific Coast Electrical Association, Inc.**
1545 Wilshire Blvd., Los Angeles, CA 90017.
- P C E A Annual Engineering & Operating
  Conference. a.

**Pacific Coast Entomological Society**
- Pan-Pacific Entomologist. (pub. by California
  Academy of Sciences)

**Pacific Coast Obstetrical and Gynecological Society**
- Pacific Coast Obstetrical and Gynecological
  Society. Transactions. (pub. by C. V. Mosby Co.)

**Pacific Coast Renderers Association**
18260 Gentian Ave., Riverside, CA 92054.
- Render; the magazine of rendering. 6 per yr.

**Pacific Coast Slavic Baptist Association, Inc.**
Box 866, Bryte, CA 95605.
- Our Days/Nashi Dni. w.

**Pacific Coast Society of Orthodontists**
2021 Ygnacio Valley Rd., Walnut Creek, CA 94598.
- Pacific Coast Society of Orthodontists. Bulletin. q.
  ISSN 0030-8617

**Pacific County Historical Society Inc.**
Box 384, Raymond, WA 98577.
- Sou'wester. q. ISSN 0038-4984

**Pacific Horticultural Foundation**
Hall of Flowers, Box 22609, San Francisco, CA
94122.
- Pacific Horticulture. q.

**Pacific Hotel-Motel News**
P.O. Box 2296, Orange, CA 92669.
- Pacific Hotel-Motel News. m. ISSN 0030-8706

**Pacific Inter-Club Yacht Association of Northern
California**
Publication Office, 1050 Sansome St., San
Francisco, CA 94111.
- Yachting Year Book of Northern California. a.
  ISSN 0094-8136

**Pacific Islands Studies and Notes**
c/o N.L.H. Krauss, 2437 Parker Place, Honolulu,
HI 96822.
- Pacific Islands Studies and Notes. irreg. ISSN
  0085-459X

**Pacific Journal of Mathematics**
103 Highland Blvd., Berkeley, CA 94708.
- Pacific Journal of Mathematics. m. ISSN 0030-
  8730

**Pacific Lutheran Theological Seminary**
2770 Marin Avenue, Berkeley, CA 94708.
- Lutheran Quarterly. q. ISSN 0024-7499

**Pacific Marine Fisheries Commission**
342 State Office Bldg., 1400 S.W. Fifth Ave.,
Portland, OR 97201.
- Pacific Marine Fisheries Commission. Annual
  Report. a. ISSN 0078-7574
- Pacific Marine Fisheries Commission. Bulletin.
  irreg., no. 8, 1972. ISSN 0078-7582
- Pacific Marine Fisheries Commission. Newsletter.
  irreg., no. 26, 1976. ISSN 0078-7590

**Pacific Mutual Life Insurance Co.**
700 Newport Center Dr., Newport Beach, CA
92663.
- Soundings. q.

**Pacific Northwest Aviation Historical Foundation**
400 Broad St., Seattle, WA 98109.
- P N A H F Journal. a.

**Pacific Northwest Bird and Mammal Society**
Univ. of Puget Sound, Tacoma, WA 98416.
- Murrelet. 3 per yr. ISSN 0027-3716

**Pacific Northwest Conference on Foreign Languages**
c/o H. Reinert, Secy.-Treas., Edmonds School Dist.,
3800-196th S.W., Lynnwood, WA 98036.
- Pacific Northwest Conference on Foreign
  Languages. Proceedings. a. ISSN 0078-7612

**Pacific Northwest Library Association**
University of Washington FM-30, Seattle, WA
98195.
- P N L A Quarterly. q. ISSN 0030-8188

**Pacific Northwest River Basins Commission**
1 Columbia River, Box 908, Vancouver, WA 98660.
- Nor'wester. s-a.

**Pacific Northwest Ski Association**
- Northwest Skier. (pub. by Western Ski
  Promotions, Inc.)

**Pacific Orchid Society of Hawaii**
3860 Manoa Rd., Honolulu, HI 96822.
- Na Okika O Hawaii/Hawaii Orchid Journal. q.
  (Co-Sponsor: Honolulu Orchid Society)

**Pacific Perceptions, Inc.**
1906 Parnell Ave., Los Angeles, CA 90025.
- Stonecloud. a.

**Pacific Press, Inc.**
G.P.O. Box 2044, New York, NY 10001.
- Physiological Chemistry and Physics. bi-m. ISSN
  0031-9325

**Pacific Press Publishing Association**
1350 Villa St., Mountain View, CA 94042.
- Centinela/Watchman. m. (Seventh-Day
  Adventists)
- Listen; journal of better living. m. ISSN 0024-
  435X (Narcotics Education, Inc.)
- Our Little Friend. w. ISSN 0030-6894 (Seventh-
  Day Adventists)
- Primary Treasure. w. ISSN 0032-8316 (Seventh-
  Day Adventists)
- Signs of the Times. m. ISSN 0037-5047 (Seventh-
  Day Adventists)

**Pacific Publications**
Box 57218, Los Angeles, CA 90057.
- Multihull Sailing. bi-m. ISSN 0027-3163

**Pacific Publishing Foundation Inc.**
1819 Tenth St., Berkeley, CA 94710.
- People's World. w. ISSN 0031-5044

**Pacific Railroad Society Inc.**
Box 8726, San Marino, CA 91108.
- Wheel Clicks. m. ISSN 0043-4744

**Pacific Science Association**
Box 6037, Honolulu, HI 96818.
- Pacific Science Association. Congress Proceedings.
  quadrennial; 13th, Vancouver, 1975. ISSN 0078-
  7647
- Pacific Science Association. Information Bulletin.
  6 per yr. ISSN 0030-8889

**Pacific Scientific Information Center**
Bernice P. Bishop Museum, Box 6037, Honolulu, HI
96818.
- Pacific Entomologists. irreg. ISSN 0078-7485

**Pacific Search**
715 Harrison St., Seattle, WA 98109.
- Pacific Search; about nature in the Pacific
  Northwest. m. except Jan. & Aug. ISSN 0030-
  8897

**Pacific Shippers, Inc.**
1050 Sansome St., San Francisco, CA 94111.
- Coast Marine and Transportation Directory. a.

**Pacific Sociological Association**
- Pacific Sociological Review. (pub. by Sage
  Publications, Inc.)

**Pacific Southwest Airlines**
- California. (pub. by East-West Network, Inc.)

**Pacific Studies Center**
867 W. Dana St., no. 204, Mountain View, CA 94041.
- Pacific Research and World Empire Telegrams. bi-m. ISSN 0030-8854

**Pacific Sun Publishing Co. Inc.**
21 Corte Madera Ave., Mill Valley, CA 94941.
- Pacific Sun. w. ISSN 0048-2641

**Pacific Tropical Botanical Garden**
Box 340, Lawai, HI 96765.
- Allertonia; a series of occasional papers. irreg.
- Pacific Tropical Botanical Garden. Bulletin. q. ISSN 0093-3996

**Pacific Western Agricultural Publications**
Box 1877, Salinas, CA 93901.
- Vegetable Crop Management. m. ISSN 0042-3068
- Western Fruit Grower. m. ISSN 0043-3764

**Pacific Wilderness Journal**
Box 22272, Portland, OR 97222.
- Pacific Wilderness Journal. bi-m.

**Pacifica Foundation WBAI**
359 E. 62 St., New York, NY 10021.
- W B A I Folio. irreg. ISSN 0042-9554

**Packaging Machinery Manufacturers Institute**
2000 K Street N.W., Washington, DC 20006.
- P M M I Pack-Age. q.
- Packaging Machinery Manufacturers Institute. Official Packaging Machinery Directory. biennial. ISSN 0078-7698

**Packard Automobile Classics**
Box 2808, Oakland, CA 94618
- Cormorant News Bulletin. bi-m (news bulletin ) q (magazine) ISSN 0045-8554 (Editorial Address:, 306 N. Plum St., Northfield, MN 55057)

**Padan Aram**
52 Dunster St., Harvard University, Cambridge, MA 02138.
- Padan Aram; Harvard-Radcliffe poetry magazine. 4 per yr.

**Ralph Page, Ed. & Pub.**
117 Washington St., Keene, NH 03431.
- Northern Junket. bi-m. ISSN 0029-313X

**Tony Page, Ed. & Pub.**
Meacham Field, Fort Worth, TX 76106.
- Cross Country News. every 3 weeks. ISSN 0011-1945

**C. A. Page Publishing Co**
3181 Fernwood Ave., Lynwood, CA 90262.
- Commercial News. w.

**Paideia Press**
c/o J. Fang, Ed., Philosophy Department, Old Dominion University, Norfolk, VA 23508.
- Philosophia Mathematica. s-a. ISSN 0031-8019

**Painted Bride Quarterly, Inc.**
527 South St., Philadelphia, PA 19147.
- Painted Bride Quarterly. q.

**Painters District Council Nine of New York City**
45 W. 14th St., New York, NY 10011.
- District Council Nine Newsletter. m. ISSN 0012-3994

**Painting and Decorating Contractors of America**
7223 Lee Highway, Falls Church, VA 22046.
- Painting and Decorating Craftsman Manual and Textbook. irreg., 5th edt., 1975.
- Professional Decorating & Coating Action. m. ISSN 0099-0310

**Paisano Publications Inc.**
Box 52, Malibu, CA 90265.
- Easyriders. every 6 wks. ISSN 0046-0990

**Pajarito Publications**
2633 Granite N.W., Albuquerque, NM 87104.
- De Colores; journal of emerging Raza philosophies. q.

**Pakistan Perspective**
78-01 34th Ave., A51, Jackson Heights, NY 11372.
- Pakistan Perspective. m. ISSN 0048-2730

**Palabra**
Box 500, Steilacom, WA 98388.
- Palabra. q. ISSN 0048-2765

**Palatines to America**
157 N. State St., Salt Lake City, UT 84103.
- Palatine Immigrant. q.

**Paldor Publications**
225 E. Utah, Fairfield, CA 94533.
- Pioneer. irreg. (Adventurers)

**Paleontological Research Institution**
1259 Trumansburg Rd., Ithaca, NY 14850.
- Bulletins of American Paleontology. 2 vols. per yr. ISSN 0007-5779
- Palaeontographica Americana. irreg; latest issue no. 50. ISSN 0078-8546

**Paleontological Society**
Department of Geology and Minerology, Ohio State University, 125 S. Oval Mall, Columbus, OH 43210.
- Paleobiology. q. ISSN 0094-8373
- Paleontological Society. Memoir. irreg. ISSN 0078-8597

**Palestine Solidarity Committee**
Box 1757, Manhattanville Sta., New York, NY 10027.
- Palestine! m.

**Palm Beach County Genealogy Society**
Box 1746, West Palm Beach, FL 33402.
- Ancestry. q.

**Palm Beach Newspapers, Inc.**
265 Royal Poinciana Way, Box 1176, Palm Beach, FL 33480.
- Palm Beach Life; America's oldest society journal. m. ISSN 0031-0417

**Palm Society, Inc.**
1320 S. Venetian Way, Miami, FL 33139.
- Principes. q. ISSN 0032-8480

**Palm Springs Life**
250 E. Palm Canyon Drive, Palm Springs, CA 92262.
- Palm Springs Life. m. ISSN 0031-0425

**Palmer Publications**
25 W. 45th St., New York, NY 10036.
- Sugar y Azucar. m. ISSN 0039-4742
- Sugar y Azucar Yearbook. ISSN 0081-9212

**Palmer Publications Inc.**
510 Main St., Amherst, WI 54406.
- Ray Palmer's Forum. q. ISSN 0034-0162
- Search-Flying Saucers. q.
- Space World. m. ISSN 0038-6332

**Palmerton Publishing Co., Inc.**
461-8th Ave., New York, NY 10001.
- Adhesives Age; manufacture, application, technology and sale. m. ISSN 0001-821X
- Adhesives Red Book. a. ISSN 0065-1931
- Elastomerics. m.
- Modern Paint and Coatings. m.
- Paint Red Book; directory of the paint and coatings industry. a. ISSN 0090-5402
- Rubber Red Book; directory of the rubber industry. a.

**Palomino Horse Breeders of America**
Box 249, Mineral Wells, TX 76067.
- Palomino Horses. m. ISSN 0031-045X

**Pan-African Institute**
- Pan-African Journal. (pub. by East African Literature Bureau KE)

**Pan American Cancer Cytology Society**
170 W. Spanish River Blvd., Boca Raton, FL 33432.
- Cancer Cytology. s-a.

**Pan-American Coffee Bureau**
1350 Ave. of the Americas, New York, NY 10019.
- Annual Coffee Statistics. a; latest issue, 1974. ISSN 0066-3875
- Coffee Drinking in the United States. a.(except 1952) ISSN 0069-4967
- How do Americans Drink Their Coffee? irreg.
- Pan-American Coffee Bureau. Boletin Mensual/ Oficina Panamericana del Cafe. Boletin Mensual. m. ISSN 0048-1521
- Pan-American Coffee Bureau. Carta Semanal - Mercado del Cafe. w.

**Pan American Development Foundation**
1625 I St. N.W., Room 622, Washington, DC 20006.
- P A D F News. q.

- Pan American Development Foundation. Annual Report. a. ISSN 0552-9913

**Pan American Health Organization**
For publications of this agency see section for UNITED NATIONS

**Pan American Institute of Comparative Law**
3001 Ponce de Leon Blvd., Coral Gable, FL 33134.
- Comparative Juridical Review. a. ISSN 0069-7893 (Rainforth Foundation)

**Pan American Medical Women's Alliance**
Ed. & Pub. Ruth Knubloch, M.D., 203 Court St., Little Valley, NY 14755.
- Pan American Medical Women's Alliance. Newsletter. irreg. ISSN 0078-8864

**Pan American University**
Education Bldg. No. 143, Edinburg, TX 78539.
- Pan American University. Inter-American Affairs Newsletter. 9 per yr.

**Pan American World Airways**
Pan Am Bldg., New York, NY 10017.
- Pan Am's World Guide; encyclopedia of travel. a., latest issue 23rd ed. ISSN 0553-0601
- Worldwide Marketing Horizons; a Pan Am publication about world trade. bi-m. ISSN 0043-9371

**Pan Pacific Centers**
845 via de la Paz, Pacific Palisades, CA 90272.
- Asia Calling. q. ISSN 0004-4431

**Panache**
Box 2214, Princeton, NJ 08540.
- Panache. s-a. ISSN 0031-062X

**Panax Newspapers, Inc.**
Box 707, Mt. Clemens, MI 48043.
- Macomb County Legal News. w. ISSN 0024-9289 (Macomb County Circuit Court)

**Pandora Press**
Box 5094, Seattle, WA 98105.
- Pandora: a Washington Women's News Journal. m.

**Panel Publishers**
14 Plaza Rd., Greenvale, NY 11548
- Community Property Journal. q. (Orders to:, 232 N. Canon Dr., Beverly Hills, CA 90210)
- Journal of Pension Planning and Compliance. bi-m.

**Panel Publishers. Cantor Fitzgerald Group Ltd.**
14 Plaza Rd., Greenvale, NY 11548.
- International Tax Journal. bi-m. ISSN 0097-7314

**Panhandle Eastern Pipe Line Co.**
3000 Bissonnet Ave., Box 1642, Houston, TX 77001.
- Panhandle. q. ISSN 0031-076X

**Panjandrum Press**
99 Sanchez St., San Francisco, CA 94114.
- Panjandrum Poetry Journal. a. ISSN 0092-5535

**Panorama International Inc.**
Box 679, Colonial News Bldg., Freehold, NJ 07728.
- Mid-Monmouth Panorama. bi-m. ISSN 0026-3028 (Greater Freehold Chamber of Commerce)

**Panorama of Las Vegas, Inc.**
Box 14830, Las Vegas, NE 89114.
- Las Vegas Panorama. w.

**Pantheon Books, Inc.**
c/o Random House, 201 E. 50th St., New York, NY 10022.
- World of Man. irreg., latest, 1973.

**Pantheon Press- General Enterprises**
Box 1566, Fontana, CA 92335.
- Cosmopolitan Contact. q. ISSN 0010-955X (Planetary Legion for Peace - PLP)

**Paon Press**
Box 12304, Dallas, TX 75225.
- Argus Poets. irreg., v. 3, 1973.

**Papa Bach Paperbacks**
11317 Santa Monica Blvd., West Los Angeles, CA 90025.
- Bachy. s-a. ISSN 0091-1488

**Paper and Twine Journal**
1860 Broadway, New York, NY 10023.
- Paper and Twine Journal; the national magazine for merchants and salesmen. m. ISSN 0031-1103

**Paper Bag Institute**
41 East 42nd Street, New York, NY 10017.
- Paper Bag Institute, New York. Grocers Bags and Grocers Sacks; a Graphic and Tabular Review. irreg. ISSN 0553-1454

**Paper House, Inc.**
1801 York St., Denver, CO 80206.
- Ski Racing Redbook. a. ISSN 0091-1461

**Paper Industry Management Association**
2570 Devon Ave., Des Plaines, IL 60018.
- Paper Industry. m.

**Paper Makers Advertising Association**
90 Elm St., Westfield, MA 01085.
- D/A. q. ISSN 0011-4693

**Parabola**
Box 505, Lenox Hill Sta., 166 E. 61 St., New York, NY 10021.
- Parabola. q.

**Paragon Publications, Inc.**
Box 552, Mt. Ayr, IA 50854.
- Herald of Health. m. ISSN 0018-0505

**Paralyzed Veterans of America, Inc.**
935 Coastline Drive, Seal Beach, CA 90740.
- Paraplegia News. m. ISSN 0031-1766

**Parapsychological Association**
- Research in Parapsychology. (pub. by Scarecrow Press, Inc.)

**Parapsychology Foundation**
29 W. 57th St., New York, NY 10019.
- Parapsychological Monographs. irreg., latest edt. 1975. ISSN 0078-9437
- Parapsychology Review. bi-m. ISSN 0031-1804

**Parapsychology Press**
Box 6847 College Station, Durham, NC 27708.
- Journal of Parapsychology; a scientific quarterly dealing with extrasensory perception, the psychokinetic effect and related topics. q. ISSN 0022-3387 (Foundation for Research on the Nature of Man)

**Parent Cooperative Preschools International**
9111 Alton Parkway, Silver Spring, MD 20910.
- Parent Cooperative Preschools International Journal. 3 per yr. ISSN 0048-2978

**Parent-Teacher Association of Connecticut, Inc.**
282 Farmington Ave., Hartford, CT 06105.
- Connecticut Parent-Teacher. m. ISSN 0010-6186

**Parenteral Drug Association, Inc.**
Western Savings Bank Bldg., Broad & Chestnut Sts., Philadelphia, PA 19107.
- Parenteral Drug Association. Bulletin. 6 per yr. ISSN 0048-2986

**Parents Magazine Enterprises, Inc.**
52 Vanderbilt Ave., New York, NY 10017.
- Baby Care. q. ISSN 0005-3570
- Children's Digest. m. (except June & Aug.) ISSN 0009-4099
- Children's Playcraft. m(except Jun-Aug)
- Expecting. q. ISSN 0014-472X
- Humpty Dumpty's Magazine; magazine for little children (3-7) m.(except June & Aug.) ISSN 0018-7666
- Parents' Magazine and Better Homemaking; On Rearing Children From Crib To College. m.
- Young Miss. m.(except June & August) ISSN 0044-0833

**Parents' Theosophical Research Group**
336 S. Pueblo Ave., Ojai, CA 93023.
- Parents' Bulletin. q. ISSN 0031-188X (Theosophical Society in America)

**Parents Without Partners Inc.**
7910 Woodmont Ave., Washington, DC 20014.
- Single Parent. m. ISSN 0037-5748

**Marjorie Parham**
c/o News Ed. Ray Paul, 863 Lincoln Ave., Cincinnati, OH 45206.
- Cincinnati Herald. w.

**PariPassu**
c/o S. K. de Lobo, Suite 705, 516 5th Ave., New York, NY 10036.
- PariPassu. m.

**Paris Publications, Inc.**
2 Haven Ave., Port Washington, NY 11050.
- Catalogue de l'Edition Francaise/French Books in Print. a. ISSN 0069-1089

**Paris Review, Inc.**
45-39 171 Place, Flushing, NY 11358.
- Paris Review. 4 per yr. ISSN 0031-2037

**Parish Visitors of Mary Immaculate**
Box 658, Monroe, NY 10950.
- Parish Visitor. q.

**Park College**
Governmental Research Bureau, Kansas City, MO 64152.
- East Europe in German Books; a bulletin listing new books on East Europe published in the German language. irreg., vol. 5, 1977. ISSN 0070-8097
- East Europe Monographs. irreg., no. 4, 1974. ISSN 0070-8100 (Studiengesellschaft fuer Fragen Mittel - und Osteuropaeischer Partnerschaft GW)

**Park East News Inc.**
341 E. 79th St., New York, NY 10021.
- Park East. 10 per yr. ISSN 0031-2126

**Park Region Publishing Co.**
Alexandria, MN 56308.
- Gopher Music Notes. q. ISSN 0017-2235 (Minnesota Music Educators Association)

**Parker and Son Publications, Inc.**
6500 Flotilla St., Los Angeles, CA 90022.
- Parker Directory of Attorneys. a. ISSN 0079-0044

**Parker Publishing Co. Inc.**
Rte. 59A at Brookhill Drive, West Nyack, NY 10994.
- Basketball Clinic. 10 per yr. ISSN 0146-5007
- Career Education Workshop. 10 per yr.
- Elementary Teacher's Ideas and Materials Workshop. m(10 per yr.) ISSN 0013-5992
- Guidance Clinic. 10 per yr. ISSN 0146-1168
- K-3 Bulletin of Teaching Ideas and Materials. m (10 per yr.) ISSN 0047-3065
- Natural Health Bulletin. fortn. ISSN 0047-9152
- Slow Learner Workshop. m. ISSN 0146-1184
- Teacher's Arts & Crafts Workshop. 10 per yr. ISSN 0496-9944

**Parker School of Foreign and Comparative Law**
*see under* Columbia University

**Parnassos, Greek Cultural Society of New York**
2928 Grand Central Station, New York, NY 10017.
- Charioteer; an annual review of modern Greek culture. a. ISSN 0577-5574

**Parola del Popolo Publishing Association**
6740 W. Diversey, Chicago, IL 60635.
- Parola del Popolo. bi-m. ISSN 0031-2363

**Parousia Press**
Box 500, Storrs, CT 06268.
- Children's Literature (Storrs); the great excluded. a. ISSN 0092-8208 (University of Connecticut. English Department)

**Russell O. Parta**
Box 158, New York Mills, MN 56567.
- Amerikan Uutiset. s-w.

**Participation Projects Foundation**
- Assembling. (pub. by Assembling Press)

**Partners of the Americas**
2001 S. St., N.W., Washington, DC 20009.
- Partners. q. ISSN 0031-2568

**Pasadena City College**
1570 E. Colorado Blvd., Pasadena, CA 91106.
- Inscape. a. ISSN 0094-2715

**Pasaules Brivo Latviesu Apvieniba**
400 Hurley Ave., Box 16, Rockville, MD 20850.
- Latvija Sodien. a. ISSN 0093-8920

**Pascack Historical Society**
Box 285, Park Ridge, NJ 07656.
- Relics. bi-m. ISSN 0034-3897

**Paseo del Rio Association of San Antonio**
c/o Claire Regnier, Ed., 306 N. Presa, Suite 8, San Antonio, TX 78205.
- Paseo del Rio Showboat; about San Antonio, one of America's four unique cities. m. ISSN 0031-2592

**Passaic County Dental Society**
c/o Dr. A. Rand, 1000 Clifton Ave., Clifton, NJ 07013.
- Passaic County Dental Society. Bulletin. irreg. ISSN 0079-0125

**Passaic County Historical Society**
Box 1729, Paterson, NJ 07509.
- Castlelite. q.
- Passaic County Historical Society. Bulletin. 3 per yr. ISSN 0031-2665

**Passaic County Medical Society**
642 Broad St, Clifton, NJ 07013.
- Passaic County Medical Society. Bulletin. m. ISSN 0031-2673

**Passaic County Technical and Vocational High School**
45 Reinhardt Rd., Wayne, NJ 07470.
- County Voc- Tec News. w.

**Passionist Missions, Inc.**
Monastery Place, Union City, NJ 07087.
- Sign. 10 per yr. ISSN 0037-4873

**Marvin Patchen, Inc.**
2241 N.W. 40th St., Oklahoma City, OK 73112.
- Aero. m. ISSN 0001-9097

**Patent Publications, Inc.**
20 Nassau St., Princeton, NJ 08540.
- U S Chemical Patent Index. irreg. ISSN 0362-4358

**Patent Searching Service**
422 Washington Bldg., Washington, DC 20005.
- Trade-Mark Register of the United States. a. ISSN 0082-5786

**Paterson Redevelopment Division**
52 Church St., Paterson, NJ 07505.
- Operation Comeback. q.

**George Gordon Paton & Co.**
182 Front St., New York, NY 10030.
- Coffee Annual. a.

**Patriarchal Parishes of the Russian Orthodox Church in the U.S.A.**
15 East 97th St., New York, NY 10029
- One Church/Yedinaya Tserkov. bi-m. ISSN 0030-2503 (Subscr. to: One Church, 158 Stiles St., Elizabeth NJ 07208)

**Patrolmen's Benevolent Association of New York City**
250 Broadway, New York, NY 10007.
- Front and Center. m. ISSN 0046-5186

**Patten Co., Inc.**
161 W. Wisconsin Ave., Milwaukee, WI 53203.
- Exclusively Yours, Wisconsin. 15 per yr.

**Pattern Makers' League of North America**
1000 Connecticut Ave., N.W., Washington, DC 20036.
- Pattern Makers' Journal. bi-m. ISSN 0031-319X

**Pattern Recognition Society**
- Pattern Recognition. (pub. by Pergamon Press, Inc.)

**Patterson Publishing Co.**
2606 N. Stirling, Peoria, IL 61604.
- Ideas That Made Millions. bi-m.

**Patterson Smith Publishing Corporation**
23 Prospect Terrace, Montclair, NJ 07042.
- Patterson Smith Series in Criminology, Law Enforcement and Social Problems. irreg. ISSN 0079-0222

**Paulist Press**
545 Island Rd., Ramsey, NJ 07446.
- Ancient Christian Writers: The Works of the Fathers in Translation. irreg., 1970, no. 37. ISSN 0066-1597
- Ecumenist; a journal for promoting Christian unity. bi-m. ISSN 0013-080X
- New Catholic World. bi-m. (Missionary Society of St. Paul the Apostle in the State of New York)

- Popes through History. irreg., 1968, vol. 3. ISSN 0079-3833
- Woodstock Papers: Occasional Essays for Theology. irreg., 1967, no. 8. ISSN 0084-117X

**Pavlovian Society of America**
- Pavlovian Journal of Biological Science. (pub. by J. B. Lippincott Co.)

**Payment Systems, Incorporated**
90 Park Ave., New York, NY 10016.
- Payment Systems Newsletter. m. ISSN 0300-7715

**Josephine Payne, Ed. & Pub.**
2205AA Echols St., Bryan, TX 77801.
- Texas Traveler. s-a.

**Alexander Pazandak**
Box 251, Orange, NJ 07051.
- New Voices. q. ISSN 0028-694X

**Pea River Historical and Genealogical Society**
Box 628, Enterprise, AL 36330.
- Pea River Trails. s-a.

**Pea Vine Music Co.**
18632 Nordhoff St., Northridge, CA 91324.
- R and B Magazine.

**Peabody Institute. Conservatory of Music**
1 E. Mt. Vernon Place, Baltimore, MD 21202.
- Peabody Notes. m.(Oct-June) ISSN 0031-3440

**Peabody Museum of Archaeology and Ethnology**
Harvard University, 11 Divinity Ave., Cambridge, MA 02138.
- American School of Prehistoric Research. Bulletin. irreg. ISSN 0066-0027
- Peabody Museum of Archaeology and Ethnology. Memoir. irreg. ISSN 0079-029X
- Peabody Museum of Archaeology and Ethnology. Monographs. irreg.
- Peabody Museum of Archaeology and Ethnology. Paper. irreg. ISSN 0079-0303

**Peabody Museum of Natural History**
Yale University, New Haven, CT 06520.
- Discovery (New Haven) s-a. ISSN 0012-3625
- Peabody Museum of Natural History. Bulletin. irreg., no. 40, 1975. ISSN 0079-032X
- Peabody Museum of Natural History. Special Publication. irreg., no. 14, 1974. ISSN 0079-0338
- Postilla. irreg., no. 171, 1977. ISSN 0079-4295

**Peabody Museum of Salem**
East India Marine Hall, Salem, MA 01970.
- American Neptune; a quarterly journal of maritime history. q. ISSN 0003-0155

**H. L. Peace Publications**
Box 607, Mandeville, LA 70448.
- Fish Boat/Sea Food Merchandising; the national magazine of the commercial fishing industry. 12 per yr. ISSN 0015-2900
- Work Boat. m. ISSN 0043-8014

**Peace Publishers & Co.**
P.O. 8757, Phoenix, AZ 85066.
- Bnai Shalom. q.

**Peace Research Laboratory**
Character Research Association, 6251 San Bonita, St. Louis, MO 63105.
- Peace Research Laboratory. Annual Report. irreg. ISSN 0085-4808

**Peace Science Society (International)**
McNeil Bldg. (C R), 3718 Locust Walk, Univ. of Pennsylvania, Philadelphia, PA 19174.
- Journal of Peace Science. a. ISSN 0094-3738
- Peace Science Society (International). Papers. s-a. ISSN 0094-8055

**Peacemaker Movement**
Box 4793, Arcata, CA 95521.
- Peacemaker. every 3 weeks. ISSN 0031-3602

**Peacock Business Press, Inc.**
200 S. Prospect Ave., Park Ridge, IL 60068.
- Home Improvement Contractor. m. ISSN 0018-4063
- Paper, Film and Foil Converter. m. ISSN 0031-1138
- Sources of Supply/Buyers Guide. a. ISSN 0081-2129

**F. E. Peacock Publishers**
401 W. Irving Park Rd., Itasca, IL 60143.
- Review of Research in Education. a. ISSN 0091-732X (American Educational Research Association)

**Peanut Journal Publishing Co.**
Box 347, Suffolk, VA 23434.
- Peanut Journal and Nut World. m. ISSN 0031-3661 (Virginia-Carolina Peanut Association) (00-sponsor: National Peanut Council, Inc.)

**Pearl**
16728 Daisy Ave., Fountain Valley, CA 92708.
- Pearl. s-a.

**Peat, Marwick, Mitchell & Co.**
345 Park Ave., New York, NY 10022.
- Management Controls. 6 per yr. ISSN 0025-1739

**Melvin A. Peavey, Ed. & Pub.**
Box 588, Lexington, KY 40501.
- Horse World. m.(except Jan.) ISSN 0018-5191

**Pebble**
118 South Boswell, Crete, NE 68333.
- Pebble; a magazine of poetry. 2-3 per yr. ISSN 0031-3696

**Creighton Peden**
Augusta College, Augusta, GA 30904.
- Journal of Social Philosophy. 3 per yr. ISSN 0047-2786

**Pedestrian Press**
552 25th Ave., San Francisco, CA 94121.
- Out There. irreg.

**Pediatric Portfolio**
3800 Reservoir Rd., N.W., Washington, DC 20007.
- Pediatric Portfolio. s-m. ISSN 0048-3141

**Pegasus**
c/o Bobbs-Merrill, 4300 W. 62nd St., Indianapolis, IN 46268.
- Biological Sciences Curriculum Study Books. irreg.
- Studies in Contemporary American Politics. irreg.

**Matthew W. Pelczynski, Ed. & Pub.**
1335 E. Delavan Ave., Buffalo, NY 14215.
- Am-Pol Eagle. w.

**Pelican Publishing Co., Inc.**
c/o Milburn Calhoun, Pub., 630 Burmaster St., Gretna, LA 70058.
- Best Editorial Cartoons of the Year. a. ISSN 0091-2220 (Association of American Editorial Cartoonists)

**Pembroke State University**
P.O. Box 60, Pembroke, NC 28372.
- Pembroke Magazine. a. (Co-Sponsor: North Carolina Arts Council)

**Pen & Pencil Set**
Box 2000, Vacaville, CA 95688.
- Pathways. q. ISSN 0031-3033

**Pendle Hill, a Quaker Center for Study and Contemplation**
- Pendle Hill Pamphlets. (pub. by Pendle Hill Publications)

**Pendle Hill Publications**
338 Plush Mill Road, Wallingford, PA 19086.
- Pendle Hill Pamphlets. 6 per yr. ISSN 0031-4250 (Pendle Hill, a Quaker Center for Study and Contemplation)

**Pendleton Publications**
1718 Lynwood, Champaign, IL 61820.
- Leisure Information Newsletter. q.

**Penfer**
Box 1122, Rockville, MD 20850.
- Spots. a. ISSN 0095-7461

**Penguin Books, Inc.**
625 Madison Ave., New York, NY 10022.
- Architect and Society. irreg.
- Pelican Classics. irreg.
- Pelican Guide to Modern Theology. irreg., latest issue, vol. 3. ISSN 0079-0427
- Penguin Classics. irreg.
- Penguin Companion to Literature. irreg.
- Penguin Handbooks. irreg.
- Penguin Modern Economics Reading. irreg.
- Penguin Modern Economics Texts. irreg.

- Penguin Modern Playwrights. irreg.
- Penguin Modern Poets. irreg. ISSN 0553-4917
- Penguin Modern Psychology. irreg.
- Penguin Modern Psychology Readings. irreg.

**Peninsula Bulletin Publishing Co.**
2332 University Ave., E. Palo Alto, CA 94303.
- Peninsula Bulletin. w.

**Peninsula Electronics News**
748 Bryant St., Palo Alto, CA 94301.
- Peninsula Electronics News. fortn.

**Peninsula Hospital Center**
Far Rockaway, NY 11691.
- Hospital Chronicle. m.

**Peninsula Motor Club**
1515 N. West Shore Blvd., Box 22087, Tampa, FL 33607.
- Florida Explorer. m. ISSN 0015-4059

**Peninsula Newspapers, Inc.**
Box 300, Palo Alto, CA 94302.
- Peninsula Living. w. ISSN 0031-4293

**Peninsula Publishing Co.**
2306 South Hubert Ave., Tampa, FL 33609.
- Florida Builder; the magazine of Florida construction. m. ISSN 0015-3923

**Peninsular State Philatelic Society**
Box 51, East Lansing, MI 48823.
- Peninsular Philatelist. q.

**Penjerdel Corporation**
1528 Walnut St., Philadelphia, PA 19102.
- Delaware Valley Business Fortnight. fortn. ISSN 0017-3762

**Penman Publishing Co.**
Box 758, Elmhurst, IL 60126.
- R T L Proxy. 3 per yr.

**Penn Central Transportation Co.**
6 Penn Center Plaza, Philadelphia, PA 90204.
- Penn Central Post. m. ISSN 0031-4323

**Penn Valley Community College**
3201 Southwest Trafficway, Kansas City, MO 64111.
- Entrelineas. irreg. ISSN 0013-9017

**Pennant Publishing Co. Inc**
2630 Avon Drive, Newport Beach, CA 92660.
- Pacific Skipper. m.

**Betty L. Pennington, Ed. & Pub.**
6059 Emery St., Riverside, CA 92509.
- Fisher Facts. q.

**Pennmarva Dairymen's Cooperative Federation**
1717 Gwynn Oak Ave., Baltimore, MD 21207.
- Pennmarva. m.

**Pennsylvania. Board of Probation and Parole. Research and Statistical Division**
Harrisburg, PA 17120.
- Pennsylvania Board of Probation and Parole. Monthly Statistical Report. m. ISSN 0031-4366

**Pennsylvania. Bureau of Aviation**
Capital City Airport, New Cumberland, PA 17070.
- Pennsylvania Aircraft Accident and Violation Analysis. a.

**Pennsylvania. Civil Service Commission. Bureau of Examinations**
Box 569, Harrisburg, PA 17120.
- S W A P. (Sharing with a Purpose) bi-m. (prep. by its Division of Research and Special Projects)

**Pennsylvania. Commonwealth Child Development Committee**
700 State St. Bldg., Harrisburg, PA 17101.
- In the Best Interest of Chldren. bi-m.
- Pennsylvania. Commonwealth Child Development Committee. Child Development State Plan. irreg. ISSN 0093-8009

**Pennsylvania. Crime Commission**
523 E. Lancaster Ave., St. Davids, PA 19087.
- Pennsylvania. Crime Commission. Report. a.

**Pennsylvania. Crop Reporting Service**
2301 N. Cameron St., Harrisburg, PA 17120.
- Pennsylvania Crop and Livestock Annual Summary. a. ISSN 0079-046X

**Pennsylvania. Department of Commerce**
415 South Office Bldg., Harrisburg, PA 17120.
• Commerce Reporter. bi-m.

**Pennsylvania. Department of Commerce. Bureau of International Commerce**
Harrisburg, PA 17120.
• Pennsylvania International Trademark. m.

**Pennsylvania. Department of Commerce. Bureau of Statistics, Research & Planning**
630B Health and Welfare Bldg., Harrisburg, PA 17120.
• Exports by Pennsylvania Manufacturers. a.
• Pennsylvania. Department of Commerce. Bureau of Statistics, Research and Planning. Statistics for Manufacturing Industries. a. ISSN 0556-3615
• Pennsylvania. Department of Commerce. Bureau of Statistics. Statistics by Industry and Size of Establishment. a. ISSN 0556-3593
• Pennsylvania Exporters Directory. a. ISSN 0360-8859
• Statistics for Electric Utilities in Pennsylvania. a.
• Statistics for Gas Utilities in Pennsylvania. a.
• Statistics for Water Utilities Including Water Authorities in Pennsylvania. a. ISSN 0094-4335

**Pennsylvania. Department of Commerce. Bureau of Travel Development**
431 S. Office Bldg., 402 S. Office Bldg., Harrisburg, PA 17120.
• Pennsylvania Calendar of Events. a.

**Pennsylvania. Department of Community Affairs**
108 South Office Bldg., Harrisburg, PA 17120.
• Pennsylvania. Department of Community Affairs. D C A Reports. m.

**Pennsylvania. Department of Education**
Box 911, Harrisburg, PA 17126.
• Directory Listing Curriculums Offered in the Community Colleges of Pennsylvania. irreg. ISSN 0092-8526
• Inventory of Continuing Education Activities in the Public School Districts of Pennsylvania. (pub. by University of Pennsylvania. Department of Planning Studies in Continuing Education)
• Pennsylvania. Department of Education. Special Education Programs-Services. irreg. ISSN 0099-0302
• School Food Services Bulletin. m. ISSN 0036-6552

**Pennsylvania. Department of Education. Bureau of Educational Statistics**
Box 911, Harrisburg, PA 17126.
• Pennsylvania. Department of Education. Our Colleges and Universities Today. a. ISSN 0085-4816

**Pennsylvania. Department of Education. Bureau of Information and Publications**
Box 911, Harrisburg, PA 17126.
• Pennsylvania Education. fortn. (Sep.-Jun.) ISSN 0031-4455

**Pennsylvania. Department of Education. Bureau of Vocational, Technical and Continuing Education**
Box 911, Harrisburg, PA 17126.
• Pennsylvania State Plan for the Administration of Vocational-Technical Education Programs. irreg. ISSN 0091-5114

**Pennsylvania. Department of Environmental Resources**
Harrisburg, PA 17120.
• Pennsylvania. Office of Mines and Land Protection. Annual Report. a.
• Pennsylvania Econotes. m.

**Pennsylvania. Department of Environmental Resources. Bureau of Topographic and Geologic Survey**
Harrisburg, PA 17120.
• Pennsylvania Geology. bi-m. ISSN 0048-3214

**Pennsylvania. Department of Justice. Bureau of Criminal Justice Statistics**
Harrisburg, PA 17120.
• Pennsylvania. Bureau of Criminal Justice Statistics. Monthly Summary of Pennsylvania Criminal Justice Statistics. m. ISSN 0031-4447
• Summary of Pennsylvania Criminal Justice Statistics. a. ISSN 0091-8504

**Pennsylvania. Department of Public Health. Air Management Services**
801 Arch St., Philadelphia, PA 19107.
• Air Pollution Control Progress. q.

**Pennsylvania. Department of Public Welfare**
Harrisburg, PA 17120.
• Pennsylvania. Department of Public Welfare. Public Welfare Annual Statistics. a. ISSN 0098-8510

**Pennsylvania. Fish Commission**
Box 1673, Harrisburg, PA 17120.
• Pennsylvania Angler. m. ISSN 0031-434X

**Pennsylvania. Game Commission**
Game News Section, South Office Bldg., Harrisburg, PA 17120.
• Pennsylvania Game News. m. ISSN 0031-451X

**Pennsylvania. Historical and Museum Commission**
Box 1026, Harrisburg, PA 17120.
• Pennsylvania. Historical and Museum Commission. Anthropological Series. irreg., latest issue no.
• Pennsylvania Heritage. q.

**Pennsylvania. Human Relations Commission**
100 N. Cameron, Harrisburg, PA 17101.
• Pennsylvania Human Relations Report. q. ISSN 0031-4544

**Pennsylvania. Labor Relations Board**
1617 Labor & Industry Bldg., 7Th & Forster Sts., Harrisburg, PA 17120.
• Pennsylvania. Labor Relations Board. Report. a.

**Pennsylvania. Office of the Budget**
Main Capitol Bldg., Harrisburg, PA 17120.
• Pennsylvania. Office of the Budget. Program Budget. a. ISSN 0085-4824

**Pennsylvania. State Advisory Council for Vocational Education**
Suite 611/612 Executive House, Second and Chestnut Sts., Harrisburg, PA 17101.
• Pennsylvania. State Advisory Council for Vocational Education Annual Report. a. ISSN 0093-9129

**Pennsylvania. State Board of Vocational Rehabilitation**
Bureau of Vocational Rehabilitation, Labor and Industry Bldg., Harrisburg, PA 17120.
• Success. bi-m.

**Pennsylvania Academy of Ophthalmology and Otolaryngology**
232 N. 5th St., Reading, PA 19604.
• Pennsylvania Academy of Ophthalmology and Otolaryngology. Transactions. s-a. ISSN 0048-3206

**Pennsylvania Association for Retarded Citizens, Inc.**
1500 N. Second St., Harrisburg, PA 17102.
• Pennsylvania Message. bi-m. ISSN 0031-4609

**Pennsylvania Association for the Blind**
2843 N. Front St., Harrisburg, PA 17110.
• Seer(Inkprint Edition); a quarterly bulletin for the prevention and conquest of blindness. q. ISSN 0037-0851

**Pennsylvania Association of Plumbing Contractors, Inc.**
219 Pine St., Harrisburg, PA 17101.
• Pennsylvania Contractor; plumbing-heating-cooling. m. ISSN 0031-4412

**Pennsylvania Association of Secondary School Principals**
Box 953, Easton, PA 18042.
• Pennsylvania Schoolmaster. q.

**Pennsylvania Automotive Association**
1925 N. Front St., Harrisburg, PA 17102
(Orders to: Box 2955, Harrisburg, PA 17105)
• Pennsylvania Automotive Dealer. m.

**Pennsylvania Chamber of Commerce**
222 N. Third St., Harrisburg, PA 17101.
• Pennsylvania Chamber of Commerce. Directory of State, Regional and Commercial Organizations. irreg. ISSN 0098-5368

**Pennsylvania Chiefs of Police Association**
• Pennsylvania Chiefs of Police Association Bulletin. (pub. by Strawhecker Printing Co.)

**Pennsylvania Classical Association**
• Pennsylvania Classical Association. Bulletin. (pub. by Franklin and Marshall College)

**Pennsylvania Commission for Women**
512 Finance Building, Harrisburg, PA 17120.
• Pennsylvania Commission for Women News. bi-m.

**Pennsylvania Council of Teachers of English**
Williamsport Area Community College, Williamsport, PA 17701.
• P C T E Bulletin. s-a.
• P C T E Newsletter. bi-m. ISSN 0476-1960

**Pennsylvania Dental Association**
Box 3341, Harrisburg, PA 17105.
• Pennsylvania Dental Journal. 8 per yr. ISSN 0031-4439

**Pennsylvania Economy League**
P.O.B. 105, Harrisburg, PA 17108.
• P. E. L. State Bulletin; a report to League members on significant government developments. irreg., 1969, vol. XII, no. 2. ISSN 0079-0486

**Pennsylvania Economy League. Eastern Division**
215 South Broad Street, Philadelphia, PA 19107.
• Citizen's Business. irreg. ISSN 0009-756X

**Pennsylvania Federation of Sportsmen's Clubs**
• Pennsylvania's Outdoor People. (pub. by Dardanell Publications, Inc.)

**Pennsylvania Fish Culturists Association**
1823 Dudley St., Philadelphia, PA 19145.
• Fish Culturist. m. ISSN 0015-2919

**Pennsylvania Flower Growers**
Box 384, Bloomsburg, PA 17815.
• Pennsylvania Flower Growers. Bulletin. m. ISSN 0031-448X

**Pennsylvania Folklife Society**
Box 1053, Lancaster, PA 17604.
• Pennsylvania Folklife. q. ISSN 0031-4498

**Pennsylvania Folklore Society**
University of Pennsylvania, Rm. 411 Logan Hall CN, Philadelphia, PA 19174.
• Keystone Folklore. 4 per yr.

**Pennsylvania Forestry Association**
5221 E. Simpson St., Mechanicsburg, PA 17055.
• Pennsylvania Forests. q. ISSN 0031-4501

**Pennsylvania German Society**
Rd 1, Box 469, Breinigsville, PA 18031.
• Reggeboge. q. ISSN 0034-3269

**Pennsylvania Grocers Association**
3701 N. Broad Street, Philadelphia, PA 19140.
• Pennsylvania Grocer. m.

**Pennsylvania Historical Association**
806 Liberal Arts Bldg., University Park, PA 16802.
• Pennsylvania History. q. ISSN 0031-4528

**Pennsylvania Holstein Association**
• Pennsylvania Holstein News. (pub. by Holstein-Friesian World Inc.)

**Pennsylvania Home Rule Association**
300 Ruskin Drive, Altoona, PA 16602.
• Pennsylvania Road Builder. m. ISSN 0048-3257

**Pennsylvania Hotel-Motor Inn Association**
• Hotel Herald. (pub. by Hotel Herald Co.)

**Pennsylvania Illustrated**
Box 246, Camp Hill, PA 17011.
• Pennsylvania Illustrated. bi-m. ISSN 0363-194X

**Pennsylvania Institute of Certified Public Accountants**
1100 Lewis Tower Bldg., Philadelphia, PA 19102.
• Pennsylvania C P A Spokesman. 5 per yr. ISSN 0031-4390

**Pennsylvania Labor News Publishing Co.**
313 Dauphin Bldg., Harrisburg, PA 17101.
• Central Pennsylvania Labor News. w. ISSN 0008-9524 (Greater Harrisburg Region Central Labor Council)

**Pennsylvania Library Association**
100 Woodland Rd., Pittsburgh, PA 15232.
• Pennsylvania Library Association. Bulletin. bi-m. ISSN 0031-4579

**Pennsylvania Manufactured Housing Association**
Box 248, New Cumberland, PA 17070.
- Pennsylvania News. bi-m. ISSN 0048-3230

**Pennsylvania Medical Society**
20 Erford Rd., Lemoyne, PA 17043.
- Pennsylvania Medicine. m. ISSN 0031-4595

**Pennsylvania Music Educators Association, Inc.**
Swope Hall, West Chester State College, West Chester, PA 19380.
- Bulletin of Research in Music Education. a.
- P M E A News. 4 per yr. ISSN 0030-8102

**Pennsylvania Newspaper Publishers Association**
2717 N. Front St., Harrisburg, PA 17110.
- P N P A Press. 10 per yr. ISSN 0030-8196

**Pennsylvania Nurses Association**
2515 N. Front St., Harrisburg, PA 17110.
- Pennsylvania Nurse. 12 per yr. ISSN 0031-4617

**Pennsylvania P T A**
4804 Derry St., Harrisburg, PA 17701.
- Pennsylvania Parent Teacher Bulletin. m.

**Pennsylvania Pharmaceutical Association**
508 N. Third St., Harrisburg, PA 17101.
- Pennsylvania Pharmacist. m. ISSN 0031-4633

**Pennsylvania Prison Society**
311 S. Juniper St., Philadelphia, PA 19107.
- Prison Journal. s-a. ISSN 0032-8855

**Pennsylvania Restaurant Association**
c/o Lester Benson, 1121 N. Second St., Harrisburg, PA 17102.
- Pennsylvania Restaurant Journal. m.

**Pennsylvania S.P.C.A.**
350 E. Erie Ave., Philadelphia, PA 19134.
- Animaldom. m.(except Aug) ISSN 0003-360X

**Pennsylvania School Boards Association**
412 N. Second St., Harrisburg, PA 17101.
- P S B A Bulletin. bi-m. ISSN 0031-4668

**Pennsylvania School Study Council**
327 Cedar Bldg., Pennsylvania State University, University Park, PA 16802.
- Pennsylvania School Study Council. Reports. irreg. (20-25 per year) ISSN 0079-0508

**Pennsylvania Society of Professional Engineers**
- Engineer. (pub. by Initia, Inc.)

**Pennsylvania State Association for Health, Physical Education and Recreation**
105 White Bldg., University Park, PA 16802.
- Pennsylvania Journal of Health, Physical Education and Recreation. q.

**Pennsylvania State Association of Township Supervisors**
3001 Gettysburg Rd., P.O. Box 158, Camp Hill, PA 17011.
- Pennsylvania Township News. m. ISSN 0048-3265

**Pennsylvania State Education Association**
400 N. Third St., Box 1724, Harrisburg, PA 17105.
- Pennsylvania School Journal. q. ISSN 0031-4676

**Pennsylvania State Grange**
Box 1084, 1604 N. Second St., Harrisburg, PA 17108.
- Pennsylvania Grange News. m (10 per yr)

**Pennsylvania State Modern Language Association**
- Pennsylvania State Modern Language Association. Bulletin. (pub. by Temple University)

**Pennsylvania State University. Audio-Visual Services**
University Park, PA 16802.
- Films: the Visualization of Anthropology. every 2-3 years.
- Psychological Cinema Register; films in the behavioral sciences.

**Pennsylvania State University. Center for Air Environment Studies**
226 Fenske Laboratory, University Park, PA 16802.
- Air Pollution Titles. bi-m. ISSN 0002-2497

**Pennsylvania State University. Coal Research Section**
Deike 517, College of Earth & Mineral Sciences, Univ. Park, PA 16802.
- Catalog of Fossil Spores and Pollen. irreg.(3 per yr)

**Pennsylvania State University. College of Agriculture**
229 Agricultural Administration Bldg., 444 Ag. Adm. Bldg., University Park, PA 16802.
- Science in Agriculture. q. ISSN 0048-9670

**Pennsylvania State University. College of Business Administration**
Center for Research, 801 Business Administration Building, University Park, PA 16802.
- Pennsylvania Business Survey. m. ISSN 0031-4382
- Pennsylvania State University. College of Business Administration. Center for Research. Occasional Papers. irreg. ISSN 0079-0540

**Pennsylvania State University. College of Earth & Mineral Sciences, Earth & Mineral Sciences Continuing Education**
110 Mineral Sciences Bldg., University Park, PA 16802.
- Earth & Mineral Sciences. m.(Oct.-June) ISSN 0026-4539

**Pennsylvania State University. College of Earth and Mineral Sciences**
Earth and Mineral Sciences Experiment Sta., 416 Environmental Science Bldg., University Park, PA 16802.
- Pennsylvania State University. Earth and Mineral Sciences Experiment Station. Bulletin. irreg. ISSN 0079-0591
- Pennsylvania State University. Earth and Mineral Sciences Experiment Station. Bulletin. Mineral Conservation Series. Paper. irreg. ISSN 0079-0605
- Pennsylvania State University. Earth and Mineral Sciences Experiment Station. Circular. irreg. ISSN 0079-0613

**Pennsylvania State University. Cooperative Extension Service**
323 Agricultural Administration Bldg., University Park, PA 16802.
- Farm Economics. m. ISSN 0014-7923

**Pennsylvania State University. Dept. of Anthropology**
University Park, PA 16802.
- Occasional Papers in Anthropology. irreg., 1973, no. 10. ISSN 0078-3005

**Pennsylvania State University. Department of Classics**
University Park, PA 16802.
- Classical World. m.(Sept.-May) ISSN 0009-8418 (Classical Association of the Atlantic States)

**Pennsylvania State University. Department of English**
University Park, PA 16802.
- Seventeenth-Century News. q. ISSN 0037-3028 (Milton Society of America)

**Pennsylvania State University. Department of French**
S 401 Burrowes, University Park, PA 16802.
- Bonnes Feuilles. s-a. ISSN 0090-7820
- Cahiers Cesairiens. a.

**Pennsylvania State University. Engineering Publications**
Hammond Bldg., University Park, PA 16802.
- Pennsylvania State University. College of Engineering. Engineering Research Bulletin. irreg. ISSN 0079-0567

**Pennsylvania State University. Institute for Research on Land and Water Resources**
University Park, PA 16802.
- Pennsylvania State University. Institute for Research on Land and Water Resources. Information Reports. irreg; no. 80, 1976. ISSN 0079-0621
- Pennsylvania State University. Institute for Research on Land and Water Resources. Research Publication. irreg; no. 96, 1976. ISSN 0079-063X

**Pennsylvania State University Press**
215 Wagner Bldg., University Park, PA 16802.
- Chaucer Review; only quarterly journal in America focusing on medieval studies and literary criticism. q. ISSN 0009-2002
- Corpus Palladianum. irreg. ISSN 0070-038X

- General Linguistics; covering the field of linguistics, psycholinguistics and sociolinguistics. q. ISSN 0016-6553
- J G E/Journal of General Education. q. ISSN 0021-3667
- Penn State Studies. irreg. ISSN 0079-0451
- Philosophy and Rhetoric. q. ISSN 0031-8213
- Shaw Review. 3 per yr. ISSN 0037-3354
- Yearbook of Comparative Criticism. a. ISSN 0084-3709

**Pennsylvania State University. University Libraries**
University Park, PA 16802.
- Pennsylvania State University. Libraries. Bibliographic Series. irreg., no. 6, 1974. ISSN 0079-0656

**Pennsylvania State University. Vice President for Research and Graduate Studies**
207 Old Main Building, University Park, PA 16802.
- Intercollege Research. biennial.
- Pennsylvania State University. Research in the College of Science. biennial.
- Pennsylvania State University. Research Publications and Professional Activities. a.

**Penny Pincher**
Box 7113, Rochester, NY 14616.
- Penny Pincher. m.

**Penny Press**
2949 Alder Dr., Camino, CA 95709.
- Penny Stock Handbook. a. ISSN 0090-9327

**Pennzoil Co.**
900 Southwest Tower, Houston, TX 77002.
- Resources. q. ISSN 0095-2966

**Pension Trends**
5563 Lansbury Road, Lyndhurst, OH 44124.
- Pension Trends. w.

**Pentecostal Fellowship of North America**
- P F N A News. (pub. by Gospel Publishing House)

**Penthouse Photo World Ltd.**
909 Third Ave., New York, NY 10022.
- Penthouse Photo World. bi-m.

**Penthouse Poster Press**
(Subsidiary of: Penthouse-Viva International)
909 Third Ave., New York, NY 10022
(Orders to: 155 Allen Blvd., Farmingdale, NY 11735)
- Rock Superstars.
- Superstars of Soul. m.

**Penton-IPC**
614 Superior Ave., Cleveland, OH 44113
(or Penton Plaza, 1111 Chester Ave., Cleveland, OH 44114)
- Fluid Power Handbook & Directory. biennial. ISSN 0428-7738
- Foundry Catalog File. biennial.
- Foundry Management & Technology. m. ISSN 0360-8999
- Government Product News. m.
- Handling & Shipping. m. ISSN 0017-7385
- Handling & Shipping. Presidential Issue. a.
- Hospitality Lodging. m.
- Hydraulics and Pneumatics. m. ISSN 0018-814X
- Industry Week; the magazine for management. fortn. ISSN 0039-0895
- Machine Design. 28 per yr. ISSN 0024-9114
- Machine Design Reference Issues. a.
- Management Time & Leisure. m.
- Material Handling Engineering; technical magazine for material handling, packaging and shipping specialists. m. ISSN 0025-5262
- Modern Office Procedures. m. ISSN 0026-8208
- New Equipment Digest; equipment, materials, processes, designs, literature. m. ISSN 0028-4963
- Occupational Hazards; industrial safety/security management. m. ISSN 0029-7909
- Power Transmission Design. m. ISSN 0032-6070
- Power Transmission Design Handbook. biennial.
- Precision Metal. m. ISSN 0032-714X
- Production Engineering. m. ISSN 0146-1737
- Restaurant Hospitality. m.
- Roundtable Report. m. ISSN 0300-6085
- School Product News. m. ISSN 0036-6749
- Today's Manager. m.
- Welding Data Book. biennial. ISSN 0511-4365
- Welding Design and Fabrication. m. ISSN 0043-2253

**People Against Racism in Education**
49 West 75th St., New York, NY 10023.
- P. A. R. E. Paper. q.

**People of the Living God**
2101 Prytania St., New Orleans, LA 70130.
- Marturion. m. ISSN 0047-6064

**People-to-People Health Foundation**
2233 Wisconsin Ave., N.W., Washington, DC 20007.
- HOPE News. q.

**People-To-People International**
No. 3 Crown Center, Suite G30, Kansas City, MO 64108.
- People (Kansas City) bi-m. ISSN 0031-501X

**People United to Save Humanity. P.U.S.H.- Operation Push**
Box 5432, Chicago, IL 60680.
- People United to Save Humanity. P.U.S.H.- Operation Push. m. ISSN 0048-332X

**Peoples Business Commission**
1346 Connecticut Ave., N.W., Washington, DC 20036.
- Peoples Business. bi-m.

**Peoples Christian Coalition**
1029 Vermont Ave. N.W., Washington, DC 20005.
- Sojourners. m.

**Peoples Church of Chicago**
941 Lawrence Ave., Chicago, IL 60640.
- Liberalist. m. (Sep.-May) ISSN 0360-6953

**People's Computer Co.**
Box E, Menlo Park, CA 94025.
- Computer Music Journal. bi-m.
- Dr. Dobb's Journal of Computer Calisthenics & Orthodontia. 10 per yr.
- People's Computer Company. 6 per yr.

**People's Party**
1404 M St. N.W., Washington, DC 20005.
- Grass Roots. m.

**People's Publishing Co., Inc.**
1440 W. Walnut St., Compton, CA 90220.
- Car Prices. a.
- Western & Eastern Treasures. m.

**Peoplesmedia Inc.**
1380 Howard St., San Francisco, CA 94103.
- Peoples Media Digest. bi-m.
- Rama; the peoplesmedia anthology. bi-m.

**Peoria Academy of Science**
Lakeview Center for the Arts and Sciences, 1125 W. Lake Ave., Peoria, IL 61614
(and 677 E. High Pt. Terrace, Peoria IL 61614)
- Peoria Academy of Science. Proceedings. a. ISSN 0079-0745

**Peoria Labor News**
400 N. Jefferson, Peoria, IL 61603.
- Peoria Labor News; official weekly publication of organized labor in central Illinois. w. ISSN 0031-5052

**Pepperdine University. School of Law**
1520 South Anaheim Blvd., Anaheim, CA 92803.
- Pepperdine Law Review. 3 per yr. ISSN 0092-430X

**Pequot Press**
Old Chester Rd., Chester, CT 06412.
- Guide to the Recommended Country Inns of New England. irreg. ISSN 0093-4585

**Pequot Publishing, Inc.**
Box 494, Southport, CT 06490.
- Gas Turbine World. bi-m.

**Per Jacobsson Foundation**
International Monetary Fund Bldg., Washington, DC 20431.
- Per Jacobsson Foundation. Proceedings. a. ISSN 0079-0761

**Perceptual and Motor Skills**
Box 9229, Missoula, MT 59807.
- Perceptual and Motor Skills. bi-m.(2 vols.per yr) ISSN 0031-5125

**Percussive Arts Society, Inc.**
130 Carol Drive, Terre Haute, IN 47805.
- Percussionist and Percussive Notes. 6 per yr. ISSN 0031-5168

**Perennial Education, Inc.**
1825 Willow Road, Northfield, IL 60093.
- Selective Guide to Materials for Mental Health and Family Life Education. biennial. (Mental Health Materials Center)

**Henry Perez**
P.O. Box 5802, Riverside, CA 92507.
- Chicano Education Digest. m.

**Perfins Club**
c/o Floyd A. Walker, Box 82, Grandview, MO 64030.
- Perfins Bulletin. m.

**Performance Guide Publications, Inc**
P.O. Box 2604, Palos Verdes Peninsula, CA 90274.
- Performance Guide Publications. Mutual Funds and Timing. m.(plus special issues) ISSN 0300-7693

**Performance Publications**
Box 269, Lorton, VA 22079.
- Motor Vehicle Industry Report. fortn.

**Performing Arts Journal**
Box 858, Peter Stuyvesant Station, New York, NY 10009.
- Performing Arts Journal. 3 per yr.

**Performing Arts Social Society, Inc.**
Box 1174, San Francisco, CA 94101.
- Storefront Classroom. bi-m.
- Utopian Eyes; journal of utopian thought. q.

**Pergamon Press, Inc.**
Maxwell House, Fairview Park, Elmsford, NY 10523
(U.K. office: Pergamon Press Ltd., Headington Hill Hall, Oxford OX3 OBW, England)
- Accident Analysis & Prevention. q. ISSN 0001-4575
- Accounting, Organizations and Society; a new international journal devoted to the behavioural organizational & social aspects of accounting. q.
- Acta Astronautica. m. ISSN 0094-5765
- Acta Metallurgica; an international journal for the science of materials. m. ISSN 0001-6160
- Acupuncture and Electro-Therapeutics Research; the international journal. q.
- Addictive Behaviors; an international journal. q.
- Advances in Behavior Research and Therapy. 4 per yr.
- Advances in Brain Research. q.
- Advances in Enzyme Regulation. a. ISSN 0065-2571
- Advances in Machine Tool Design and Research. irreg., 1971, vol. 9. ISSN 0065-2857
- Advances in Manufacturing Systems, Research and Development. irreg.
- Advances in Water Pollution Research. irreg., 1970, 5th. ISSN 0065-3535 (International Association on Water Pollution Research)
- Annals of Nuclear Energy. m.
- Annals of Occupational Hygiene. q. ISSN 0003-4878 (British Occupational Hygiene Society UK)
- Archives of Oral Biology. m. ISSN 0003-9969
- Art Psychotherapy; an international journal. q. ISSN 0090-9092
- Astronautical Research. irreg., 21st, 1970.
- Atmospheric Environment; an international journal. m. ISSN 0004-6981
- Automatica; the international journal on automatic control and automation. bi-m. ISSN 0005-1098 (International Federation for Automatic Control)
- Automobile Electronic Equipment. irreg. ISSN 0587-5919
- Behaviour Research and Therapy. bi-m. ISSN 0005-7967
- Biochemical Pharmacology. 24 per yr. ISSN 0006-2952
- Biochemical Systematics and Ecology. q. ISSN 0305-1978
- Biophysics. bi-m. ISSN 0006-3509
- Biorheology; an international journal. bi-m. ISSN 0006-355X
- Building and Environment. q.
- Bulletin of Mathematical Biology. bi-m. ISSN 0092-8240
- Carbon. bi-m. ISSN 0008-6223 (American Carbon Committee)
- Cement and Concrete Research. bi-m. ISSN 0008-8846
- Chemical Engineering Science/Journal International de Genie Chimique. m. ISSN 0009-2509
- Chemosphere. bi-m. ISSN 0045-6535
- Chinese Astronomy. s-a.
- Chromatographia; international journal of chromatography & related techniques. m. ISSN 0009-5893
- Clays and Clay Minerals. bi-m. ISSN 0009-8604 (Clay Minerals Society)
- Communications in Psychopharmacology. bi-m.
- Comparative Biochemistry and Physiology. Part A: Comparative Physiology. m. ISSN 0300-9629
- Comparative Biochemistry and Physiology. Part B: Comparative Biochemistry. m. ISSN 0305-0491
- Comparative Biochemistry and Physiology. Part C: Comparative Pharmacology. bi-m. ISSN 0306-4492
- Computer Coupling of Phase Diagrams and Thermochemistry. q.
- Computer Languages. q. ISSN 0096-0551
- Computerized Tomography. q.
- Computers & Chemical Engineering. q.
- Computers & Chemistry. q.
- Computers and Education; an international journal. q.
- Computers and Electrical Engineering. q. ISSN 0045-7906
- Computers and Fluids. q. ISSN 0045-7930
- Computers & Geosciences; an international journal. q. (International Association for Mathematical Geology)
- Computers and Graphics. q. ISSN 0361-4913
- Computers & Industrial Engineering; an international journal. q.
- Computers & Mathematics with Applications. q. ISSN 0097-4943
- Computers & Operations Research. q. ISSN 0305-0548
- Computers & Structures. bi-m. ISSN 0045-7949
- Computers and the Humanities. bi-m. ISSN 0010-4817
- Computers in Biology and Medicine. q. ISSN 0010-4825
- Conservation and Recycling. q.
- Corporate Planner's Yearbook. a. (Society for Long Range Planning)
- Corrosion Science. m. ISSN 0010-938X (Corrosion and Protection Association)
- Current Advances in Ecological Sciences. m. ISSN 0306-3291
- Current Advances in Genetics. m.
- Current Advances in Plant Science. m.
- Current Clinical Chemistry. m.
- Current Titles in Immunology Transplantation and Allergy. 26 per yr.
- Deep-Sea Research. 18 per yr.
- Design Abstracts International. q.
- Disasters; the international journal of disaster studies and practice. q.
- Electric Technology U. S. S. R. q. ISSN 0013-4155
- Electrochimica Acta. m. ISSN 0013-4686
- Endeavor. q.
- Energy Conversion. q. ISSN 0013-7480
- Energy, the International Journal; technologies, resources, reserves, demands, impact, conservation, management and policy. q.
- Engineering Fracture Mechanics. q. ISSN 0013-7944
- Environmental and Experimental Botany; an international journal devoted to plant radiobiology and closely related fields. q.
- Ethics in Science & Medicine. q. ISSN 0306-4581
- European Polymer Journal. m. ISSN 0014-3057
- Evaluation and Program Planning. q.
- Evaluation in Education-International Progress. 4 per yr.
- Experimental Gerontology. bi-m. ISSN 0531-5565
- Food and Cosmetics Toxicology. bi-m. ISSN 0015-6264 (British Industrial Biological Research Association UK)
- Franklin Institute. Journal. m. ISSN 0016-0032
- General Pharmacology. bi-m.
- Geochimica et Cosmochimica Acta. m. ISSN 0016-7037
- Geoforum; the international multi-disciplinary journal of physical, human and regional geosciences. bi-m. ISSN 0016-7185
- Geothermics; international journal of geothermal research. q. (International Institute for Geothermal Research, Pisa, Italy IT)
- Government Publications Review; an international journal. q. ISSN 0093-061X
- Habitat; the international journal on all aspects of human settlements both urban and rural. bi-m.
- Health Physics. m (2 vols per year) ISSN 0017-9078 (Health Physics Society)

- I C R P. Annals. q. (International Commission on Radiological Protection)
- Immunochemistry. m. ISSN 0019-2791
- Information Processing and Management. bi-m. ISSN 0306-4573
- Information Systems. q.
- Information Technology and Human Concern. q.
- Infrared Physics. bi-m. ISSN 0020-0891
- Inorganic and Nuclear Chemistry Letters. m. ISSN 0020-1650
- Insect Biochemistry. bi-m.
- International Abstracts of Biological Sciences; a comprehensive survey of the world literature. m. ISSN 0020-5818
- International Catecholamine Symposium. Proceedings. irreg.
- International Commission on Radiological Protection. Report. irreg., vol. 23, 1975. ISSN 0074-2759
- International Conference of Printing Research Institutes. Proceedings. irreg., 10th, 1971.
- International Conference on Photoconductivity. Proceedings. irreg., 3rd, 1971.
- International Conference on Water Pollution Research. Proceedings. irreg.
- International Encyclopedia of Physical Chemistry and Chemical Physics. Topic 1. Mathematical Techniques. irreg., 1968, vol. 1, ISSN 0074-5626
- International Encyclopedia of Physical Chemistry and Chemical Physics. Topic 2. Classical and Quantum Mechanics. irreg. ISSN 0074-5669
- International Encyclopedia of Physical Chemistry and Chemical Physics. Topic 3. Electronic Structure of Atoms. irreg. ISSN 0074-5707
- International Encyclopedia of Physical Chemistry and Chemical Physics. Topic 4. Electronic Structure of Molecules. irreg.
- International Encyclopedia of Physical Chemistry and Chemical Physics. Topic 6. Kinetic Theory of Gases. irreg.
- International Encyclopedia of Physical Chemistry and Chemical Physics. Topic 8. Statistical Mechanics. irreg. ISSN 0074-574X
- International Encyclopedia of Physical Chemistry and Chemical Physics. Topic 9. Transport Phenomena. irreg. ISSN 0074-5758
- International Encyclopedia of Physical Chemistry and Chemical Physics. Topic 10. the Fluid State. irreg. ISSN 0074-5650
- International Encyclopedia of Physical Chemistry and Chemical Physics. Topic 11. Ideal Crystalline State. irreg. ISSN 0074-5596
- International Encyclopedia of Physical Chemistry and Chemical Physics. Topic 13. Mixtures, Solutions, Chemical and Phase Equilibria. irreg. ISSN 0074-560X
- International Encyclopedia of Physical Chemistry and Chemical Physics. Topic 14. Properties of Interfaces. irreg. ISSN 0074-5634
- International Encyclopedia of Physical Chemistry and Chemical Physics. Topic 15. Equilibrium Properties of Electrolyte Solutions. irreg. ISSN 0074-5561
- International Encyclopedia of Physical Chemistry and Chemical Physics. Topic 16. Transport Properties of Electrolytes. irreg., 1965, vol. 3. ISSN 0074-5642
- International Encyclopedia of Physical Chemistry and Chemical Physics. Topic 17. Macromolecules. irreg. ISSN 0074-5618
- International Encyclopedia of Physical Chemistry and Chemical Physics. Topic 19. Gas Kinetics. irreg. ISSN 0074-557X
- International Encyclopedia of Physical Chemistry and Chemical Physics. Topic 20. Solution Kinetics. irreg. ISSN 0074-5693
- International Encyclopedia of Physical Chemistry and Chemical Physics. Topic 21. Solid and Surface Kinetics. irreg. ISSN 0074-5685
- International Journal for Parasitology. bi-m. ISSN 0020-7519 (Australian Society for Parasitology AT)
- International Journal of Applied Radiation and Isotopes. m. ISSN 0020-708X
- International Journal of Biochemistry. m. ISSN 0020-711X
- International Journal of Engineering Science. m. ISSN 0020-7225
- International Journal of Heat and Mass Transfer. m. ISSN 0017-9310
- International Journal of Housing Science and its Applications.
- International Journal of Hydrogen Energy. q. (International Association for Hydrogen Energy)
- International Journal of Insect Morphology and Embryology. bi-m. ISSN 0020-7322
- International Journal of Machine Tool Design and Research. q. ISSN 0020-7357

- International Journal of Mechanical Sciences. m. ISSN 0020-7403
- International Journal of Multiphase Flow. bi-m. ISSN 0301-9322
- International Journal of Non-Linear Mechanics. bi-m. ISSN 0020-7462
- International Journal of Nuclear Medicine and Biology. q. ISSN 0047-0740
- International Journal of Nursing Studies. q. ISSN 0020-7489
- International Journal of Radiation: Oncology - Biology - Physics. m.
- International Journal of Rock Mechanics and Mining Sciences and Geomechanics Abstracts. bi-m.
- International Journal of Solids and Structures. m. ISSN 0020-7683
- International Journal on Child Abuse and Neglect. q.
- International Series in Aeronautics and Astronautics. Division 1. Solid and Structural Mechanics. irreg.
- International Series in Aeronautics and Astronautics. Division 2. Aerodynamics and Astronautics. irreg., 1969, vol. 7.
- International Series in Aeronautics and Astronautics. Division 3. Propulsion Systems Including Fuels. irreg., 1970, vol. 6.
- International Series in Aeronautics and Astronautics. Division 4. Avionics. irreg.
- International Series in Aeronautics and Astronautics. Division 5. Aviation and Space Medicine. irreg.
- International Series in Aeronautics and Astronautics. Division 7. Astronautics. irreg., 1964, vol. 5.
- International Series in Aeronautics and Astronautics. Division 9. Symposia. irreg., 1969, vol. 20.
- International Series in Infrared Sciences and Technology. irreg., vol. 2, 1967. ISSN 0538-9917
- International Series in Interdisciplinary and Advanced Topics in Science and Engineering. irreg., 1970, vol. 3. ISSN 0074-817X
- International Series in Library and Information Sciences. irreg., 1972, vol. 15. ISSN 0074-820X
- International Series in Natural Philosophy. irreg., vol. 86, 1976. ISSN 0074-8064
- International Series in Pure and Applied Mathematics. irreg., vol. 105, 1976. ISSN 0539-0125
- International Series in Solid State Physics. irreg., 1970, vol. 7. ISSN 0539-0133
- International Series on Analytical Chemistry. irreg., vol. 58, 1975. ISSN 0074-8099
- International Series on Automation and Automatic Control. irreg., 1965, vol. 7. ISSN 0074-8080
- International Series on Cerebrovisceral and Behavioral Psychology and Conditioned Reflexes. irreg., vol. 3, 1974. ISSN 0538-9968
- International Series on Chemical Engineering. irreg., vol. 13, 1973. ISSN 0074-8021
- International Series on Civil Engineering. irreg., 1972, vol. 5. ISSN 0538-9887
- International Series on Earth Sciences. irreg., vol. 33, 1971. ISSN 0538-9984
- International Series on Electromagnetic Waves. irreg., 1973, vol. 17. ISSN 0538-9992
- International Series on Electronics and Instrumentation. irreg., vol. 24, 1964. ISSN 0074-8129
- International Series on Heating, Ventilation and Refrigeration. irreg., vol. 11, 1975. ISSN 0538-9895
- International Series on Oral Biology. irreg., 1964, vol. 3. ISSN 0074-8234
- International Series on Organic Chemistry. irreg., vol. 9, 1968. ISSN 0074-8242
- International Series on Pure and Applied Biology. Biochemistry Division. irreg., 1971, vol. 6.
- International Series on Pure and Applied Biology. Botany Division. irreg.
- International Series on Pure and Applied Biology. Modern Trends in Physiological Science Division. irreg., vol. 38, 1973.
- International Series on Pure and Applied Biology. Plant Physiology Division. irreg.
- International Series on Pure and Applied Biology. Zoology Division. irreg., vol. 52, 1973.
- International Series on Semiconductors. irreg., 1970, vol. 10. ISSN 0074-8315
- International Union of Biochemistry. I.U.B. Symposium Series. irreg. ISSN 0074-9354
- Iranian Journal of Agricultural Research. s-a. (Pahlavi University. Faculty of Agriculture IR)
- Iranian Journal of Science and Technology. q. (Pahlavi University. Faculty of Engineering IR)
- Journal of Aerosol Science. bi-m. ISSN 0021-8502

- Journal of Applied Mathematics and Mechanics. bi-m. ISSN 0021-8928
- Journal of Atmospheric and Terrestrial Physics. m. ISSN 0021-9169
- Journal of Behavior Therapy and Experimental Psychiatry. q. ISSN 0005-7916
- Journal of Bioengineering. bi-m.
- Journal of Biomechanics. m. ISSN 0021-9290 (Highway Safety Institute)
- Journal of Child Psychology and Psychiatry. q. ISSN 0021-9630 (Association of Child Psychology and Psychiatry)
- Journal of Chronic Diseases; devoted to the problems and management of chronic illness in all age groups. m. ISSN 0021-9681
- Journal of Criminal Justice. q. ISSN 0047-2352
- Journal of Developmental and Comparative Immunology. q.
- Journal of Enterprise Management. 3 per yr.
- Journal of Inorganic and Nuclear Chemistry. m. ISSN 0022-1902
- Journal of Insect Physiology. m.
- Journal of Libertarian Studies. q.
- Journal of Neurochemistry. m. ISSN 0022-3042
- Journal of Physics and Chemistry of Solids. m. ISSN 0022-3697
- Journal of Products Liability. q. ISSN 0363-0404
- Journal of Psychiatric Research. q. ISSN 0022-3956
- Journal of Psychosomatic Research. bi-m. ISSN 0022-3999
- Journal of Quantitative Spectroscopy and Radiative Transfer. m. ISSN 0022-4073
- Journal of Steroid Biochemistry. m. ISSN 0022-4731
- Journal of Stored Products Research. q. ISSN 0022-474X
- Journal of Terramechanics. q. ISSN 0022-4898 (International Society for Terrain Vehicle Systems)
- Journal of the Mechanics and Physics of Solids. bi-m. ISSN 0022-5096
- Journal of Thermal Biology. q.
- Leonardo: Art Science and Technology; international journal of the contemporary artist/revue internationale de l'artiste contemporain. q. ISSN 0024-094X
- Letters in Applied and Engineering Sciences. bi-m. ISSN 0090-6913
- Letters in Heat and Mass Transfer. bi-m. ISSN 0094-4548 (International Centre of Heat and Mass Transfer)
- Leukemia Research. q.
- Library Acquisitions: Practice and Theory. q.
- Life Sciences. s-m. ISSN 0300-9653
- Long Range Planning. bi-m. ISSN 0024-6301 (Society for Long Range Planning)
- Marine Pollution Bulletin. m. ISSN 0025-326X
- Materials and Society. bi-m.
- Materials Research Bulletin. m. ISSN 0025-5408
- Mathematical Table Series. irreg., 1966, vol. 40. ISSN 0076-5384
- Mazingira. q.
- Meccanica. q. ISSN 0025-6455
- Mechanics Research Communications. bi-m. ISSN 0093-6413 (International Centre for Mechanical Sciences)
- Mechanics Today. a.
- Mechanisms and Machine Theory. bi-m. ISSN 0094-114X
- Metabolic Ophthalmology; international journal of basic research and clinical applications. q. (International Society on Metabolic Eye Disease)
- Metabolic Ophthalmology. q.
- Microelectronics and Reliability. bi-m. ISSN 0026-2714
- Micron; the international journal of electron microscopy, electron probe micro-analysis & associated techniques. q. ISSN 0047-7206
- Molecular Aspects of Medicine; an interdisciplinary review journal. bi-m.
- Neuropharmacology. m. ISSN 0028-3908
- Neuropsychologia; an international journal. bi-m. ISSN 0028-3932
- Neuroscience; an international journal. bi-m.
- Non-Linear Analysis. bi-m.
- Nuclear Track Detection. q.
- Ocean Engineering; an international journal. bi-m. ISSN 0029-8018
- Oceanographic Abstracts and Bibliography. bi-m.
- Operational Research Quarterly. 8 per yr. ISSN 0030-3623 (Operational Research Society UK)
- Pattern Recognition. q. ISSN 0031-3203 (Pattern Recognition Society)
- Pergamon Bio-Medical Sciences Series. irreg.
- Pergamon Biological Sciences Series. irreg.
- Pergamon Frontiers in Anthropology Series. irreg., vol. 2, 1974.

- Pergamon Management and Business Series. irreg., v. 3, 1974.
- Pergamon Series in Dentistry. irreg., 1969, vol. 7. ISSN 0079-0850
- Pergamon Studies in the Life Sciences. irreg.
- Petroleum Chemistry(USSR) q. ISSN 0031-6458
- Pharmacology & Therapeutics Part A: Chemotherapy, Toxicology and Metabolic Inhibitors; international journal of the encyclopedia of pharmacology and therapeutics. q. (International Union of Pharmacology)
- Pharmacology & Therapeutics Part B: General and Systematic Pharmacology; international journal of the encyclopedia of pharmacology and therapeutics. q. ISSN 0306-039X (International Union of Pharmacology)
- Pharmacology & Therapeutics Part C: Clinical Pharmacology and Therapeutics; international journal of the encyclopedia of pharmacology and therapeutics. q. (International Union of Pharmacology)
- Photochemistry and Photobiology; an international journal. m.(2 vols. per yr.) ISSN 0031-8655 (American Society for Photobiology)
- Physics and Chemistry of the Earth. 6 per yr. ISSN 0079-1946
- Physics of Metals and Metallography. m.(2 vols. per yr.) ISSN 0031-918X
- Physiology and Behavior. m.(2 vols. per yr.) ISSN 0031-9384
- Phytochemistry; an international journal of plant biochemistry. m. ISSN 0031-9422
- Planetary & Space Science. m. ISSN 0032-0633
- Plasma Physics. m. ISSN 0032-1028
- Polymer Science, U. S. S. R. m. ISSN 0032-3950
- Popular Lectures in Mathematics Series. irreg; 1965, vol. 16. ISSN 0079-3841
- Population and Environment; a review journal in social demography, ethnic relations and human ecology. q.
- Practical Table Series. irreg., 1966, vol. 7. ISSN 0079-4821
- Problems and Progress in Development. irreg.
- Progress in Aerospace Sciences. 4 per yr.
- Progress in Biophysics and Molecular Biology. bi-m. ISSN 0079-6107
- Progress in Chemical Engineering Science. q.
- Progress in Crystal Growth. 4 per yr.
- Progress in Energy and Combustion Science. q.
- Progress in Information Science & Technology. q.
- Progress in Materials Science. 6 per yr. ISSN 0079-6425
- Progress in Neuro-Psychopharmacology. 4 per yr.
- Progress in Nuclear Energy. Series 3: Process Chemistry. q. ISSN 0079-6514
- Progress in Nuclear Energy. Series 9: Analytical Chemistry. q. ISSN 0079-6530
- Progress in Nuclear Energy. Series 12: Health Physics. irreg., 1969, vol. 2. ISSN 0079-6557
- Progress in Nuclear Magnetic Resonance Spectroscopy of Cyclopentadienyl Compounds. q.
- Progress in Oceanography. q. ISSN 0079-6611
- Progress in Particle and Nuclear Physics. q.
- Progress in Polymer Science. q. ISSN 0079-6700
- Progress in Psychiatric Research. q.
- Progress in Reaction Kinetics. q. ISSN 0079-6743
- Progress in Solid State Chemistry. q. ISSN 0079-6786
- Progress in the Chemistry of Fats and Other Lipids. 4 per yr. ISSN 0079-6832
- Progress in the Science and Technology of the Rare Earths. q. ISSN 0079-6840
- Progress in Water Technology. bi-m. (International Association on Water Pollution Research)
- Protides of the Biological Fluids. a. ISSN 0079-7065
- Psychoneuroendocrinology. q.
- Pure and Applied Chemistry. m. (International Union of Pure and Applied Chemistry)
- Radiation Physics and Chemistry. m.
- Regional Studies. bi-m. ISSN 0034-3404 (Regional Studies Association)
- Reports on Mathematical Physics. bi-m.
- Rheology Abstracts; a survey of world literature. q. ISSN 0035-452X (British Society of Rheology UK)
- Scripta Metallurgica. m. ISSN 0036-9748
- Sculpture International. s-a.
- Social Science & Medicine; an international journal. 18 per yr. ISSN 0037-7856
- Socio-Economic Planning Sciences. bi-m. ISSN 0038-0121
- Sociotechnology; an international journal. q.
- Soil Biology and Biochemistry. bi-m. ISSN 0038-0717 (Council of Biological and Medical Abstracts)

- Solar Energy; the journal of solar energy science and engineering. bi-m. ISSN 0038-092X (International Solar Energy Society)
- Solid State Communications; an international journal. 48 per yr. ISSN 0038-1098
- Solid-State Electronics; an international journal. m. ISSN 0038-1101
- Spectrochimica Acta. Part A: Molecular Spectroscopy. m. ISSN 0584-8539
- Spectrochimica Acta. Part B: Atomic Spectroscopy. m. ISSN 0584-8547
- Studies in History and Philosophy of Science. q. ISSN 0039-3681
- Talanta; an international journal of analytical chemistry. m. ISSN 0039-9140
- Tetrahedron. 24 per yr.
- Tetrahedron Letters; the international organ for the rapid publication of preliminary communications in organic chemistry. w. ISSN 0040-4039
- Thermal Engineering. m. ISSN 0040-6015 (Akademiya Nauk S.S.S.R. UR)
- Thrombosis Research; an international journal on vascular obstruction, hemorrhage and hemostasis. m. (2 vols. per yr.) ISSN 0049-3848
- Topology; an international journal of mathematics. q. ISSN 0040-9383
- Toxicon. bi-m. ISSN 0041-0101 (International Society on Toxicology)
- Trade Associations and Professional Bodies of the United Kingdom. irreg., 6th edt. 1976. ISSN 0082-5689
- Transportation Research. bi-m. ISSN 0041-1647
- U S S R Computational Mathematics and Mathematic Physics. bi-m. ISSN 0041-5553
- Ultrasound in Medicine & Biology. q. ISSN 0301-5629
- Underground Space. q.
- Urban Systems. q.
- Vacuum; the international journal and abstracting service for vacuum science and technology. bi-m. ISSN 0042-207X (American Vacuum Society)
- Vertica; the international journal of rotorcraft and powered lift aircraft. q.
- Vistas in Astronomy. q. ISSN 0083-6656
- Water Research. m. ISSN 0043-1354 (International Association on Water Pollution Research)
- Wenner Gren Center International Symposium Series. irreg., 1973, vol. 20. ISSN 0083-7989
- Westminster Series. irreg., 1968, vol. 8. ISSN 0083-906X
- World Development. m. ISSN 0305-750X

**Perkin-Elmer Corp.**
Main Ave., Norwalk, CT 06856.
- Atomic Absorption Newsletter. bi-m. ISSN 0044-9954
- Chromatography Newsletter. irreg.

**Perkin-Elmer Corp. Instrument Division**
Main Ave., Norwalk, CT 06856.
- N M R Quarterly. (Nuclear Magnetic Resonance) q.

**Perkins School for the Blind**
Watertown, MA 02172.
- Lantern. 3 per yr. ISSN 0023-8414

**Permanent International Altaistic Conference**
- Permanent International Altaistic Conference (PIAC). Newsletter. (pub. by Indiana University. Department of Uralic and Altaic Studies)

**Permanent Mission of Oman to the U.N.**
605 Third Ave., New York, NY 10016.
- Oman News. m.

**Permanent Press**
P.O. Box 8434, Lake St. Station, Minneapolis, MN 55408.
- Moons and Lion Tailes; a midwestern journal of poetry and comment. 3 per yr.

**Permian Basin District Dental Society**
20009 W. Ohio, Midland, TX 79701.
- Consultant (Midland) bi-m. ISSN 0010-7077

**Perpetual Help Center**
294 East 150th St., Bronx, NY 10451.
- Perpetual Help World. q. ISSN 0048-3427 (Redemptorist Fathers of New York)

**Perry Publications**
Box 8357, Knoxville, TN 37916.
- Broadcasting & the Law. fortn.

**Perry Rhodan Science Fiction Magazine**
2495 Glendower Ave., Hollywood, CA 90027.
- Perry Rhodan Science Fiction Magazine. m.

**Personnel Journal, Inc.**
Box 1520, Santa Monica, CA 90406.
- Assignments in Management; a guide to supervisory action. m. ISSN 0004-5136
- Personnel Journal; the magazine of industrial relations and personnel management. m. ISSN 0031-5745

**Personnel Psychology, Inc.**
Box 6965, College Station, Durham, NC 27708.
- Personnel Psychology. q. ISSN 0031-5826

**Perspecta**
Yale University, Box 2121, Yale Station, New Haven, CT 06520.
- Perspecta; The Yale Architectural Journal. a. ISSN 0079-0958

**Perspectives, Inc.**
700 7th St. S.W., Washington, DC 20024.
- Perspectives (Washington); a Polish-American educational and cultural quarterly. bi-m. ISSN 0048-3508

**Perspectives of New Music, Inc.**
Bard College, Annandale-on-Hudson, NY 12504.
- Perspectives of New Music. s-a. ISSN 0031-6016

**Editorial Pesca y Marina S.A.**
c/o Fernando Flores, Box 38038, Los Angeles, CA 90038.
- Pesca y Marina. bi-m. ISSN 0031-6083

**Pescara Enterprises**
300 W. 49th St., New York, NY 10019.
- American Review of Art and Science. q. ISSN 0569-7344

**Peter Publications**
947 Elliott Sq. Bldg, Buffalo, NY 14203.
- Buffalo Volksfreund. w.

**F.E. Peters Co.**
Box 21587, Fort Lauderdale, FL 33316.
- Headmaster U.S.A. s-a. ISSN 0363-1877

**C. F. Peters Corporation**
373 Park Ave. So., New York, NY 10016.
- Peters Notes; the newsletter of C.F. Peters, Music Publishers since 1800. q.

**Eric C. Peters, Ed. & Pub.**
1521 Old Black Horse Pike, Blackwood, NJ 08012.
- Old Fashioned Prophecy. 3 per yr. ISSN 0030-1981

**Peters Publishing Co. of Texas**
P.O. Box 28351, Dallas, TX 75228.
- Texas Contractor. s-m.

**Petersen Publishing Co.**
8490 Sunset Blvd., Los Angeles, CA 90069.
- Basic Auto Repair Manual. a. ISSN 0067-4338
- Basic Bodywork and Painting. irreg., 1973, no. 3. ISSN 0067-4362
- Basic Cams, Valves and Exhaust Systems. irreg., 1971, no. 2. ISSN 0067-4370
- Basic Carburetion and Fuel Systems. irreg., 1973, no. 4. ISSN 0067-4389
- Basic Chassis, Suspension and Brakes. irreg., 1971, no. 2. ISSN 0067-4397
- Basic Clutches and Transmissions. irreg., 1971, no. 2. ISSN 0067-4400
- Basic Ignition and Electrical Systems. irreg., 1973, no. 3. ISSN 0067-4427
- Car Craft. m. ISSN 0008-6010
- Complete Chevrolet Book. irreg., no. 4, 1975. ISSN 0069-7982
- Complete Ford Book. irreg., 1973, no. 3. ISSN 0069-7990
- Complete Volkswagen Book. irreg., 1971, no. 2. ISSN 0069-8008
- Guns & Ammo. m. ISSN 0017-5684
- Guns and Ammo Annual. a. ISSN 0072-906X
- Hot Rod. m. ISSN 0018-6031
- Hot Rod Industry News; voice of the automotive high performance and custom industry. m. ISSN 0018-6023
- Hot Rod Yearbook. a. ISSN 0073-3482
- Import Car Buyer's Guide. irreg. ISSN 0073-5582
- Motor Trend. m. ISSN 0027-2094
- Motorcycle Buyer's Guide. a. ISSN 0077-1678
- Motorcyclist. m. ISSN 0027-2205

- Petersen's Photographic Magazine. m. ISSN 0048-3583
- Peterson's Hunting. m.
- Pro Football. a. ISSN 0079-5526
- Skin Diver Magazine; devoted to the underwater world. m. ISSN 0037-6345
- Teen. m. ISSN 0040-2001 (Orders to:, 5900 Hollywood Blvd., los Angeles, CA 90028)
- True; for today's man. m. ISSN 0041-3461

**Fred. L. Peterson, Ed. & Pub.**
North 2012 Ruby St., Spokane, WA 99207.
- Outdoor Press. w.

**George Peterson, Inc.**
907 North Elm Office Park, Hinsdale, IL 60521.
- Heat Treating. m. ISSN 0017-9345

**Peterson's Guides Inc.**
Box 2123, Princeton, NJ 08540.
- Peterson's Annual Guide to Undergraduate Study. a. ISSN 0079-1253
- Peterson's Guides. Annual Guides to Graduate and Undergraduate Study. Book 3: Biological and Health Sciences. a. ISSN 0079-1180
- Peterson's Guides. Annual Guides to Graduate and Undergraduate Study. Book 4: Physical Sciences. a. ISSN 0079-1237
- Peterson's Guides. Annual Guides to Graduate and Undergraduate Study. Book 5: Engineering and Applied Sciences. a. ISSN 0079-1229
- Peterson's Guides. Annual Guides to Graduate Study. Book 1; Graduate Institutions of the U.S. and Canada-an Overview. a. ISSN 0079-1164
- Peterson's Guides. Annual Guides to Graduate Study. Book 2: Humanities and Social Sciences. a.

**A. J. Petrando**
3449-51 N. Western Ave., Chicago, IL 60618.
- American Cage-Bird Magazine. m. ISSN 0002-7782

**Petrocelli Books**
(Subsidiary of: Mason /Charter Publishers)
641 Lexington Ave., New York, NY 10022.
- Management and Communications Series. irreg.
- Systems and Management Annual. ISSN 0094-6842

**Petroleum Geology: a Digest of Russian Literature on Petroleum Geology**
Box 171, McLean, VA 22101.
- Petroleum Geology: a Digest of Russian Literature on Petroleum Geology. m.

**Petroleum Information Corp.**
P.O. Box 2612, Denver, CO 80201.
- Energy Information. w.

**Petroleum Intelligence Weekly**
c/o Wanda Jablonski, 48 W. 48th St., New York, NY 10036.
- Petroleum Intelligence Weekly. w. ISSN 0480-2160

**Petroleum Legislation**
Box 1591, New York, NY 10017.
- Europe: Basic Oil Laws and Concession Contracts; original texts. supplement. irreg. ISSN 0093-5018

**Petroleum Publishers Inc.**
222 South Brea Blvd., Brea, CA 92621.
- Pacific Oil World. m. ISSN 0008-1329

**Petroleum Publishing Co.**
Box 1260, Tulsa, OK 74101.
- Eastern Hemisphere Petroleum Directory. a. ISSN 0070-8224
- International Petroleum Encyclopedia. a.
- Latin American Petroleum Directory. a. ISSN 0075-8116
- Offshore. m. ISSN 0030-0608
- Oil and Gas Journal. w. ISSN 0030-1388
- Oil, Gas & Petrochem Equipment. m. ISSN 0030-1353
- Petroleo Internacional. m. ISSN 0093-7851
- U S A Oil Industry Directory. a. ISSN 0082-8599
- Worldwide Offshore Contractors Directory. a. ISSN 0084-2575
- Worldwide Petrochemical Directory. a. ISSN 0084-2583
- Worldwide Refining and Gas Processing. a. ISSN 0084-2591

**Petroleum Publishing Co. Dental Economics Division**
Box 1260, Tulsa, OK 74101.
- Dental Economics. m. ISSN 0011-8583

- Proofs; the magazine of dental sales. m. ISSN 0033-1236

**Petroleum Publishing Co. (Houston)**
Box 1941, Houston, TX 77001.
- Ocean Oil Weekly Report. w. ISSN 0029-8042

**Petty Papers**
1211 West 400 South, Salt Lake City, UT 84104.
- Petty Papers; a genealogical research quarterly newsletter. q.

**Pewter Collectors' Club of America**
c/o Webster Goodwin, 730 Commonwealth Ave., Warwick, RI 02886.
- Pewter Collectors' Club of America. Bulletin. s-a. ISSN 0031-6644

**Phaedrus, Inc.**
Box 1166, Marblehead, MA 01945.
- Phaedrus; international journal of children's literature research. s-a. ISSN 0098-3365

**Phaeton Press, Inc.**
85 Tompkins St., Staten Island, NY 10304.
- Studies in Hispanic Literatures. irreg.

**Phantasmicom Press**
1339 Welden Ave., Baltimore, MD 21211.
- Khatru. irreg.

**Pharmaceutical Manufacturers Association**
1155-15th St. N.W., Washington, DC 20005.
- P M A Newsletter. w. ISSN 0030-8099

**Pharmaceutical Society of the State of New York**
117 E. 69th St., NewYork, NY 10021.
- New York State Pharmacist. m. ISSN 0028-7660

**Pharmaco-Medical Documentation, Inc.**
Box 401, 205 Main St., Chatham, NJ 07928.
- Unlisted Drugs. m. ISSN 0042-0441
- Unlisted Drugs on Cards. m. ISSN 0042-045X

**Pharmacy Reports, Inc.**
Rm. 1152, National Press Bldg., Washington, DC 20045.
- Drug Research Reports - "Blue Sheet". w. ISSN 0012-6608
- Weekly Pharmacy Reports; the green sheet. w. ISSN 0043-1893

**PharmChem Research Foundation**
1844 Bay Road, Palo Alto, CA 94303.
- PharmChem Newsletter. 10 per yr.

**Phi Alpha Theta. Beta Alpha Chapter**
Department of History, University of Texas, Austin, TX 20012.
- Paisano. a. ISSN 0078-7841

**Phi Alpha Theta International Honor Society in History**
c/o Dr. D. B. Hoffman, 2812 Livingston St., Allentown, PA 18104.
- Historian; a journal of history. q. ISSN 0018-2370

**Phi Beta Kappa**
*see* United Chapters of Phi Beta Kappa

**Phi Chi Theta**
National Fraternity for Women in Business and Economica, 718 Judah St., San Francisco, CA 94122.
- Iris. q. ISSN 0021-1001

**Phi Delta Epsilon**
145 E. 52nd St., New York, NY 10022.
- Phi Delta Epsilon News & Scientific Journal. q. ISSN 0031-7209

**Phi Delta Kappa**
International Headquarters, Eighth St. & Union Ave., Box 789, Bloomington, IN 47401.
- Center on Evaluation, Development and Research. Quarterly. q.
- News, Notes, and Quotes. bi-m. ISSN 0028-923X
- Phi Delta Kappan. m(Sept-June) ISSN 0031-7217

**Phi Delta Kappa at Western Illinois University**
- Timely Issues in Education. (pub. by Western Illinois University. College of Education)

**Phi Delta Kappa Educational Foundation**
Eighth St. and Union Ave., Box 789, Bloomington, IN 47401.
- Phi Delta Kappa Fastbacks. irreg.

**Phi Delta Theta Fraternity**
2 So. Campus, Oxford, OH 45056.
- Scroll of Phi Delta Theta. q. ISSN 0036-9799

**Phi Epsilon Kappa Fraternity**
9030 Log Run Drive N., Indianapolis, IN 46234.
- Physical Education around the World. Monograph. irreg., no. 7, 1976. ISSN 0079-189X
- Physical Educator; a magazine for the profession. 4 per yr. ISSN 0031-8981

**Phi Kappa Phi**
3001 Plymouth Rd., Box 650, Ann Arbor, MI 48105.
- Phi Kappa Phi Journal. q.
- Phi Kappa Phi Newsletter. bi-m.

**Phi Kappa Tau Fraternity**
15 North Campus Ave., Oxford, OH 45056.
- Laurel of Phi Kappa Tau. q. ISSN 0023-8996

**Phi Lambda Upsilon, Honorary Chemical Society**
Washburn Univ, Dept. of Chemistry, Topeka, KS 66621.
- Washburn University. Department of Chemistry. Register. s-a. ISSN 0041-9664

**Phi Mu Alpha Sinfonia Fraternity of America, Inc.**
10600 Old State Rd., Evansville, IN 47711.
- Sinfonian Newsletter. 5 per yr. ISSN 0037-5594

**Phi Rho Sigma Medical Society**
Box 10886, Pittsburgh, PA 15236.
- Journal of Phi Rho Sigma. q. ISSN 0022-3581

**Phi Sigma Iota Honor Society**
Boston University, Boston, MA 02215.
- Phi Sigma Iota Forum. s-a.

**Phi Sigma Society**
c/o Lowell L. Getz, Ed., Vivarium Bldg., Wright & Healey Sts., Champaign, IL 61820.
- Biologist; a journal promoting research interest in the biological sciences. q. ISSN 0006-3339

**Phi Sigma Tau**
Dept. of Philosophy, Marquette University, Milwaukee, WI 53233.
- Dialogue (Milwaukee) 3 per yr. ISSN 0012-2246

**Phi Upsilon Omicron**
6500 Pioneers Blvd., Lincoln, NB 68506.
- Candle (Lincoln) s-a. ISSN 0008-5510

**Philadelphia Art Alliance**
251 S. 18th St., Philadelphia, PA 19103.
- Art Alliance Bulletin. 8 per yr. ISSN 0004-296X

**Philadelphia Association for Psychoanalysis**
15 St. Asaph's Rd., Bala Cynwyd, Philadelphia, PA 19004.
- Philadelphia Association for Psychoanalysis. Journal. q. ISSN 0094-1476

**Philadelphia Association of Retail Druggists**
2017 Spring Garden St., Philadelphia, PA 19130.
- P A R D Bulletin. bi-m. ISSN 0030-7815

**Philadelphia Bar Association**
423 City Hall Annex, Philadelphia, PA 19107.
- Shingle. m.(Oct-June) ISSN 0037-377X

**Philadelphia College of Pharmacy and Science**
43rd St. & Kingsessing Mall, Philadelphia, PA 19104.
- American Journal of Pharmacy and the Sciences Supporting Public Health. bi-m. ISSN 0002-9467
- Philadelphia College of Pharmacy and Science Bulletin. m. ISSN 0031-725X

**Philadelphia College of Textiles and Science. Alumni Association**
School House Lane & Henry Ave, Philadelphia, PA 19144.
- Ramifications. q.

**Philadelphia County Dental Society**
225 E. Washington Square, Philadelphia, PA 19106.
- Philadelphia County Dental Society. Bulletin. m. (Oct.-May) ISSN 0031-7268

**Philadelphia County Medical Society**
2100 Spring Garden St., Philadelphia, PA 19130.
- Philadelphia Medicine. m. ISSN 0031-7306

**Philadelphia Dental Laboratory Association**
Medical Arts Bldg., 16th & Walnut Sts.,
Philadelphia, PA 19102.
- Philadelphia Dental Laboratory Association
Journal. bi-m. ISSN 0031-7276

**Philadelphia Gas Works**
1800 N. 9th St., Philadelphia, PA 19122.
- P G W News. m.

**Philadelphia Jewish Times**
1530 Spruce St., Philadelphia, PA 19102.
- Philadelphia Jewish Times. w. ISSN 0031-7292

**Philadelphia Museum of Art**
Box 7646, Philadelphia, PA 19101.
- Philadelphia Museum of Art. Bulletin. q. ISSN
0031-7314

**Philadelphia Port Corporation**
940 Public Ledger Bldg., Independence Square,
Philadelphia, PA 19106.
- Destination: Philadelphia. bi-m. ISSN 0090-3833

**Philadelphia Society of Clinical Psychologists**
Box 4021, Philadelphia, PA 19118.
- P S C P Times. m.

**Philadelphia Task Force on Women in Religion**
Box 24005, Philadelphia, PA 19139.
- Genesis III. m.

**Philadelphia Tribune**
520-26 S. 16th St., Philadelphia, PA 19146.
- Philadelphia Tribune. s-w. ISSN 0048-3702

**Philadelphia Yearly Meeting of Friends**
- Friendly Agitator. (pub. by Friends Suburban
Project)

**Philatelic Guild**
Box 798, Lakewood, NJ 08701.
- Philatelic Guild's Investment Newsletter. m.

**Philips Electronic Instruments, Inc.**
750 S. Fulton St., Mount Vernon, NY 10550.
- Norelco Reporter. q. ISSN 0029-1625

**Philips Roxane Laboratories, Inc.**
330 Oak St., Columbus, OH 43216.
- White Sheet. m.

**Phillie Newsletter**
Box 29, Columbia, PA 17512.
- Phillie Newsletter. m.

**Phillips Academy**
Andover, MA 01810.
- Andover Review; journal for secondary education.
s-a. ISSN 0362-6075

**Phillips Exeter Academy**
Jeremiah Smith Hall, Exeter, NH 03833.
- Phillips Exeter Bulletin; the bulletin of the Phillips
Exeter Academy. 6 per yr. ISSN 0031-7942

**Phillips Petroleum Company**
Public Affairs, 4 A-3 PB, Bartlesville, OK 74004.
- Phillips Shield. q.
- Philnews. m.

**Phillips Publishing, Inc.**
8401 Connecticut Ave., Washington, DC 20015.
- Joyer Travel Report. m.
- Pink Sheet on the Left; America's authoratative
report on left-wing activities. bi-w. ISSN 0048-
4180
- Retirement Letter; the money newsletter for
mature people. m. ISSN 0093-5352

**Phillips University**
Enid, OK 73701.
- Oklahoma English Bulletin. s-a.

**Philo Institute**
Circulation Manager, 800 West Belden Avenue,
Chicago, IL 60614.
- Studia Philonica. a. ISSN 0093-5808

**Philological Association of the Pacific Coast**
c/o R. S. Meyerstein, Sec.-Treas., Department of
Foreign Languages and Literatures, California State
University, Northridge, CA 91324.
- Pacific Coast Philology. a. ISSN 0078-7469

**Philomathean Society**
University of Pennsylvania, Philadelphia, PA 19104.
- Era; a Pennsylvania magazine of commentary and
literature. a. ISSN 0013-9920

**Philosophic Society for the Study of Sport**
217 Cooke Hall, University of Minnesota,
Minneapolis, MN 55455.
- Journal of the Philosophy of Sport. a. ISSN 0094-
8705

**Philosophical Forum, Inc.**
Box 247, Boston University Sta., Boston, MA
02215.
- Philosophical Forum. q. ISSN 0031-806X

**Philosophical Research Society Inc.**
3910 Los Feliz Blvd., Los Angeles, CA 90027.
- P. R. S. Journal. q. ISSN 0030-8250

**Philosophy Documentation Center**
Bowling Green University, Bowling Green, OH
43403.
- Directory of American Philosophers. biennial.
ISSN 0070-508X
- International Directory of Philosophy and
Philosophers. biennial until 1974; quadrennial
from 1978. ISSN 0074-4603

**Philosophy Education Society, Inc.**
Catholic Univ of America, Washington, DC 20017.
- Review of Metaphysics; a philosophical quarterly.
q. ISSN 0034-6632

**Philosophy of Education Society**
Dr. Francis T. Villemain, Southern Illinois
University, College of Education, Edwardsville, IL
62025.
- Philosophy of Education Society. Proceedings of
the Annual Meetings. a. ISSN 0079-1733

**Philosophy of Science Association**
18 Morrill Hall, Dept. of Philosophy, Michigan
State Univ., East Lansing, MI 48824.
- Philosophy of Science. q. ISSN 0031-8248

**Phoenix-Capital**
Route 2 & 200 W., Box 116, Albion, IN 46701.
- American Business Trend Synopsis. s-m.

**Phoenix Jewish News, Inc.**
1530 W. Thomas Rd., Phoenix, AZ 85015.
- Phoenix Jewish News. fortn. ISSN 0031-8353

**Phonemic Spelling Council**
Ed. Newell W. Tune, 5848 Alcove Ave., N.
Hollywood, CA 91607.
- Spelling Progress Bulletin. q. ISSN 0038-7339

**Phono-Log Publishing**
Division of Trade Service Publications, 2720
Beverly Blvd., Los Angeles, CA 90057.
- List-O-Tapes; loose-leaf tape catalog covering all
tape releases, open reel, cartridge and cassette.
serviced with weekly revised replacement sheets.
ISSN 0024-4309

**Photo Gallery**
335 Hicksville Rd., Far Rockaway, NY 11691.
- Photo Gallery. bi-m. ISSN 0048-3958

**Photo Marketing Association**
603 Lansing Ave., Jackson, MI 49202.
- Photo Marketing. m. ISSN 0031-8531

**Photo News Publishers, Inc**
803 25th St., Box 1583, W. Palm Beach, FL 33402.
- Photo News. w. ISSN 0031-854X

**Photo Pictorialists of Milwaukee, Inc.**
c/o Ed. Ronald M. Buege, 2909 S. 101st, West
Allis, WI 53227.
- Pictorialist. m.

**Photographic Historical Society of New York**
Box 1839, Radio City Sta., New York, NY 10019.
- Photographic Historical Society of New York.
Membership Directory. irreg. ISSN 0093-254X
- Photographica. 10 per yr. ISSN 0090-2063

**Photographic Society of America, Inc.**
4707-F N. Paulina St., Chicago, IL 60640.
- P S A Journal. m. ISSN 0030-8277

**Photon**
c/o Mark Frank, Ed., 801 Ave. C, Brooklyn, NY
11218.
- Photon. 1-2 per yr. ISSN 0031-8833

**Phycological Society of America**
c/o Dr. Janet R. Stein, Ed., Ohio State Univ., Dept.
of Botany, Columbus, OH 43210.
- Journal of Phycology. q. ISSN 0022-3646

**Phycological Society of America**
c/o Dr. Carole A. Lembi, Ed., Purdue Univ., W.
Lafayette, IN 47907.
- Phycological Newsletter. 3 per yr. ISSN 0045-
3072

**Physical Biological Sciences, Ltd.**
Publishing Division, Blacksburg, VA 24060.
- Industrial Organization Review. (pub. by
University Publications)
- Journal of Biological Physics. (pub. by University
Publications)
- Monographs in Quantitative Biophysics. irreg.

**Physical Education Publications**
Box 8, Old Saybrook, CT 06475.
- Physical Education Newsletter. s-m. ISSN 0031-
8973

**Physical Education Society of the YMCA'S of North
America**
c/o Douglas P. Boyea, 105 Black Rock Ave., New
Britain, CT 06052.
- Journal of Physical Education. bi-m. ISSN 0022-
3662

**Physicians Drug Manual, Inc.**
61 East 86th St., New York, NY 10028.
- Physicians' Drug Manual/P D M. bi-m. ISSN
0031-9058 (International Congress of
Pharmacology)

**Physicians International Press, Inc.**
12230 Wilkins Ave., Rockville, MD 20852.
- Ob. Gyn. News. s-m. ISSN 0029-7437

**Physicians Postgraduate Press**
Box 38293, Memphis, TN 38138.
- Diseases of the Nervous System. m. ISSN 0012-
3714 (Eastern Psychiatric Association) (Co-
Sponsor: Titus Harris Society)

**Physician's Record Co.**
3000 S. Ridgeland Ave., Berwyn, IL 60402.
- Hospital Abstract Service. m. ISSN 0018-5493
- Medical Abstract Service. m. ISSN 0025-6943

**Physicians World, Inc.**
488 Madison Ave., New York, NY 10022.
- Physician's World; physician and patient in a
changing environment. m. ISSN 0091-200X

**Pi Gamma Mu, National Social Science Honor
Society**
Toledo University, Toledo, OH 43606.
- Social Science. q. ISSN 0037-7848

**Pi Kappa Delta**
- Forensic. (pub. by William Jewell College)

**Pi Lambda Theta**
4101 E. Third St., Box A-850, Bloomington, IN
47401.
- Educational Horizons. q. ISSN 0013-175X

**Pi Mu Epsilon**
601 Elm Ave. Room 423, University of Oklahoma,
Norman, OK 73069.
- Pi Mu Epsilon Journal. s-a. ISSN 0031-952X

**Piano Quarterly, Inc.**
Box 815, Wilmington, VT 05363.
- Piano Quarterly. q. ISSN 0031-9554

**Piano Technicians Guild, Inc.**
Box 1813, Seattle, WA 98111.
- Piano Technician's Journal. m. ISSN 0031-9562

**Piano Trade Publishing Co.**
434 S. Wabash Ave., Chicago, IL 60605.
- P T M; the world of music magazine. m. ISSN
0030-8358

**Pick Publishing Corp.**
21 West St., New York, NY 10006.
- Pick's Currency Yearbook. a. ISSN 0079-2063
- Pick's World Currency Report. m. ISSN 0048-
4113

**Pickaway County Historical Society**
120 Montclair Ave., Circleville, OH 43113.
- Pickaway Quarterly. q.

**Pick'n' and Sing'n' Gather'n', Inc.**
8 Lindbergh Dr., Latham, NY 12110.
- Pick'n and Sing'n Gather'n' . Newsletter. m. ISSN 0031-9627

**Pictures Publishing Co.**
30 E. 60th St., New York, NY 10022.
- Pictures on Exhibit; world wide reviews of the art shows. bi-m. ISSN 0031-9686

**Piedmont CB Directory**
Rt. 10, Box 453, Statesville, NC 28677.
- C. B. Voice; the big picture of the C B Radio. m.

**Pierce-Arrow Society, Inc.**
135 Edgerton St., Rochester, NY 14607.
- Arrow (Rochester) q.
- Pierce-Arrow Service Bulletin. 6 per yr.

**Pierian Press**
5000 Washtenaw Ave., Ann Arbor, MI 48104.
- Book Review Index to Social Science Periodicals. a.
- Consumers Index. q plus annual cumulation.
- Consumers Index to Product Evaluations and Information Sources. q. with annual cum.
- Index to Free Periodicals. s-a. (National Council on Educational Materials)
- Media Review Digest; the only complete guide to reviews of non-book media. q. with annual cum.
- R S R (Reference Services Review) q. ISSN 0090-7324
- Reference Book Review Index. triennial.
- Serials Review. q. ISSN 0098-7913

**Pierre Fauchard Academy**
4015 W. 65th St., Minneapolis, MN 55435.
- Dental World. q. ISSN 0011-880X

**Pierson Printing Co.**
331 S. East St., Indianapolis, IN 46204.
- Dental Student Newsletter. q. ISSN 0011-8761

**Romaine Pierson Publishers, Inc.**
80 Shore Rd., Port Washington, NY 11050.
- American Journal of Proctology; journal of proctology, gastroenterology and allied subjects. bi-m. ISSN 0002-9521 (International Academy of Proctology)
- Medical Times; journal for the family physician. m. ISSN 0025-7583
- Pharmacy Times; devoted to professional pharmacy, pharmacy economics, and prescription practice. m. ISSN 0003-0627
- Resident and Staff Physician. m. ISSN 0034-5555

**Pigiron Press**
P.O.Box 237, Youngstown, OH 44501.
- Pig Iron. irreg. ISSN 0362-5214

**Pikes Peak Area Council of Governments**
27 E. Vermijo St., Colorado Springs, CO 80903.
- Regionews. bi-m.

**Pikeville College. Appalachian Studies Center**
Pikeville, KY 41501.
- Twigs. s-a. ISSN 0041-4646

**Pilgrim Publishers**
R-55 Summer St., Box J, Kingston, MA 02364.
- Cranberries; the national cranberry magazine. m. ISSN 0011-0787

**Pilgrim Society**
75 Court St., Plymouth, MA 20901.
- Pilgrim Society Notes. irreg. ISSN 0031-9813

**Pilot Books**
347 Fifth Ave., New York, NY 10016.
- Directory of Franchising Organizations. a. ISSN 0070-556X
- Directory of State and Federal Funds Available for Business Development. irreg., latest edt. 1977. ISSN 0070-640X

**Pimienta Publishing Corp.**
6360 N.E. 4th Court, Miami, FL 33138.
- Pimienta. m.

**Pinecrest State School**
Box 191, Pineville, LA 71360.
- Pine Cone. m. ISSN 0031-9856

**Pinto Horse Association of America Inc.**
Box 3984, San Diego, CA 92103.
- Pinto Horse. m. ISSN 0031-9937

**Pioneer America (Louisiana State University)**
Box 22230, Baton Rouge, LA 70893.
- Pioneer America; the journal of American historic material culture. s-a. ISSN 0032-0005

**Pioneer America Society**
626 S. Washington Ave., Falls Church, VA 22046.
- Echoes of History. bi-m. ISSN 0046-1091

**Pioneer Girls, Inc.**
27 W. 130 St. Charles Rd., Box 788, Wheaton, IL 60187.
- Perspective. q.
- Reflection. bi-m.
- Trails. bi-m.

**Pioneer Press**
502 N. State St., Big Rapids, MI 49307.
- Michigan Association of Health and Physical Education. M.A.H.P.E.R. Journal. q. ISSN 0047-7079

**Pioneer Women- The Women's Labor Zionist Organization of America**
315 Fifth Ave., New York, NY 10016.
- Pioneer Woman. m. ISSN 0032-0021

**Pirquet Society of Clinical Medicine, Inc.**
310 E. 14th St., New York, NY 10003.
- Pirquet Bulletin of Clinical Medicine. m.(Oct-June) ISSN 0032-0250

**Pisces Publishing Corp.**
Box 805, Belden Station, Norwalk, CA 06852.
- Today's Aquarist. q.

**Pit and Quarry Publications, Inc.**
105 West Adams St., Chicago, IL 60603.
- Concrete Industries Yearbook. a. ISSN 0069-827X
- Modern Concrete. m. ISSN 0026-7619
- Pit & Quarry. m. ISSN 0032-0293
- Pit & Quarry Handbook and Buyers Guide; equipment and technical reference manual for nonmetallic industry. a.

**Pittsburg State University**
Pittsburg, KS 66762.
- Collegio. w. ISSN 0010-1249
- Midwest Quarterly; a journal of contemporary thought. 4 per yr. ISSN 0026-3451

**Pittsburgh Athletic Association**
4215 Fifth Ave., Pittsburgh, PA 15213.
- Winged Head. m. ISSN 0043-5864

**Pittsburgh Catholic Publishing Associates**
110 Third Ave., Pittsburgh, PA 15222.
- Pittsburgh Catholic. w. ISSN 0032-0323 (Catholic Diocese of Pittsburgh)

**Pittsburgh History and Landmarks Foundation**
Old Post Office Museum, Pittsburgh, PA 15212.
- Stones of Pittsburgh. irreg. ISSN 0081-5799

**Pittsburgh Musical Society**
Local No.60, A.F.M., 709 Forbes Ave., Pittsburgh, PA 15219.
- Pittsburgh Musician. bi-m. ISSN 0032-034X

**Pittsburgh Regional Library Center**
Chatham College, Beatty Hall, Pittsburgh, PA 15232.
- Pittsburgh Regional Union List of Periodicals. irreg., 2nd edt. 1972. ISSN 0092-1998

**Pittsburgh Symphony Society**
Heinz Hall, 600 Penn Ave., Pittsburgh, PA 15222.
- Pittsburgh Symphony Orchestra Program. w. (Sep.-May) ISSN 0032-0358

**Pittsburgh Teachers Education Association**
1410 Union Bank Bldg., Pittsburgh, PA 15222.
- Pittsburgh Teachers Education Association Newsletter. m.(Sept-June) ISSN 0032-0366

**Pitysmont Post**
c/o Owens Hand Browne, E.D., 3214 Wade Avenue, Raleigh, NC 27607.
- Pitysmont Post. m.

**Pizza and Pasta Publishing Co.**
23 N. Washington, Suite 201, Ypsilanti, MI 48197.
- Pizza and Pasta. q.

**Place of Herons Press**
101G W. Milton, Austin, TX 78704.
- Wood Ibis; a journal of contemporary shamanism. s-a.

**Plain Dirt**
Box 86, Cobham, VA 22929.
- Plain Dirt. m.

**Plain Rapper**
424 Lytton Ave., Palo Alto, CA 94301.
- Plain Rapper. m. ISSN 0032-0412

**Plain Truth**
Box 2148 Station A, Champaign, IL 61820.
- Plain Truth; serving the North End. m. ISSN 0032-0439

**Plains Conference**
c/o Elizabeth A. Morris, Ed., Dept. of Anthropology, Colorado State Univ., Ft. Collins, CO 80523.
- Plains Anthropologist; a medium for the anthropological interpretation of the Plains area in the United States. q. ISSN 0032-0447

**Plainsong**
c/o James D. Thueson, Box 14174 University Station, Minneapolis, MN 55414.
- Plainsong. ISSN 0032-0455

**Planarian Research Group**
Box 644, Ann Arbor, MI 48107.
- Journal of Biological Psychology /Worm Runner's Digest. s-a. ISSN 0021-9274

**Planet-Drum Foundation**
Box 31251, San Francisco, CA 94131.
- Planet/Drum. q.

**Planetary Legion for Peace - PLP**
- Cosmopolitan Contact. (pub. by Pantheon Press-General Enterprises)

**Planned Parenthood Federation of America, Inc. The Alan Guttmacher Institute**
515 Madison Ave., New York, NY 10022.
- Family Planning Perspectives. bi-m. ISSN 0014-7354 (prep. by its Research and Development Division)
- Family Planning/Population Reporter. bi-m. ISSN 0090-0923 (prep. by its Research and Development Division)
- International Family Planning Digest. q. (prep. by its Research and Development Division)
- Planned Parenthood- World Population. Washington Memo. 20 per yr. (prep. by its Research and Development Division)

**Planned Parenthood League of Connecticut, Inc.**
406 Orange St., New Haven, CT 06511.
- P P L C News. q.

**Planned Parenthood-World Population**
Katherine Dexter McCormick Library, 810 Seventh Ave., New York, NY 10019.
- Current Literature in Family Planning. m.

**Planning Executives Institute**
Box 70, Oxford, OH 45056.
- Managerial Planning. bi-m. ISSN 0025-1941

**Planning Transport Associates, Inc.**
Box 4824, Duke Sta., Durham, NC 27706.
- High Speed Ground Transportation Journal. 3 per yr. ISSN 0018-1501

**Plants Inc.**
5509 1st Ave S., Seattle, WA 98108.
- Plants Alive. m.

**Plastics Focus Publishing Co., Inc.**
509 Fifth Ave., New York, NY 10017.
- Plastics Focus. w.

**Platt Saco Lowell**
Drawer 2327, Greenville, SC 29602.
- Mill Report. irreg.

**Platt Saco Lowell. Replacement Parts Center**
Box 327, Greenville, SC 29602.
- Platt Saco Lowell Replacement Parts News. irreg.

**Plattdeutsche Post**
91 New Dorp Plaza, Staten Island, NY 10306.
- Plattdeutsche Post. w. ISSN 0032-1419

**Platte Publishing Co.**
Box 18195, Denver, CO 80218.
- Current Education Law. 9 per yr.

**Platt's Oilgram News Service**
- Energy Legislative Service. (pub. by McGraw-Hill, Inc.)

**Play Meter**
Box 24170, New Orleans, LA 70184.
- Play Meter. m.

**Play Schools Association**
120 W. 57th St., New York, NY 10019.
- Play Schools Newsletter. a. ISSN 0032-1443

**Playbill Inc**
151 E. 50th St., New York, NY 10022.
- Playbill; the magazine for theatre goers. m. ISSN 0032-146X

**Playboy Enterprises Inc.**
919 N. Michigan Ave, Chicago, IL 60611.
- Playboy. m. ISSN 0032-1478

**Playboy Publications Inc.**
919 N. Michigan Ave., Chicago, IL 60611.
- Oui; for the man of the world. m. ISSN 0090-2047

**Players International Publications**
8060 Melrose Ave., Los Angeles, CA 90046.
- Players. m.

**Plays, Inc.**
8 Arlington St., Boston, MA 02116.
- Plays; the drama magazine for young people. m.(Oct-May) ISSN 0032-1540

**Plenum Press**
227 W. 17th St., New York, NY 10011
(and 4A Lower John St., London W.1, England)
- A.L.Z.A. Conference Series. irreg., vol. 2, 1973.
- Acoustical Holography. irreg., vol. 6, 1975. ISSN 0065-0870
- Advances in Biology of Skin. irreg., vol. 12, 1972. ISSN 0065-2253
- Advances in Corrosion Science and Technology. irreg., 1974, vol. 4. ISSN 0065-2474
- Advances in Cryogenic Engineering. irreg., vol. 20, 1975. ISSN 0065-2482
- Advances in Experimental Medicine and Biology. irreg., vol. 64, 1975. ISSN 0065-2598
- Advances in Human Genetics. a. ISSN 0065-275X
- Advances in Information Systems Science. a. ISSN 0065-2784
- Advances in Molten Salt Chemistry. irreg., vol. 3, 1975. ISSN 0065-2954
- Advances in Neurochemistry. irreg. ISSN 0098-6089
- Advances in Nuclear Physics. irreg., vol. 8, 1975. ISSN 0065-2970
- Advances in the Study of Communication and Affect. irreg., vol. 2, 1975.
- Advances in X-Ray Analysis. a. ISSN 0069-8490 (University of Denver. Denver Research Institute)
- Analytical Calorimetry. irreg., vol. 3, 1974. ISSN 0066-1538
- Archives of Sexual Behavior. 6 per yr. ISSN 0004-0002
- Atomic Physics. irreg., no.4, 1975. ISSN 0090-6360
- Basic Life Sciences. irreg., vol. 7, 1976. ISSN 0090-5542
- Battelle Institute Materials Science Colloquia. irreg.
- Behavior Genetics; an international journal devoted to research in the inheritance of behavior in animals and man. q. ISSN 0001-8244
- Biochemical Genetics; reports of original research in the biochemical genetics of diploid organisms. m. ISSN 0006-2928
- Biofeedback & Self Regulation. q.
- Biological Psychiatry. bi-m. ISSN 0006-3223 (Society of Biological Psychiatry)
- Biology of Brain Dysfunction. irreg. ISSN 0090-1652
- Biomembranes. irreg., vol. 8, 1976. ISSN 0067-8864
- Boron; Proceedings of the Conferences on Boron. irreg., 1966, vol. 2. ISSN 0068-0311
- Computer Applications in the Earth Sciences. irreg.
- Contemporary Topics in Immunobiology. irreg., vol. 4, 1974. ISSN 0093-4054
- Contemporary Topics in Molecular Immunology. irreg., vol. 4, 1975. ISSN 0090-8800
- Current Topics in Molecular Endocrinology. irreg., vol. 2, 1975.
- Current Topics in Neurobiology. irreg.
- General Motors Symposia Series. irreg.

- General Relativity and Gravitation. m. ISSN 0001-7701 (International Committee on General Relativity and Gravitation)
- Human Ecology; an interdisciplinary journal. q. ISSN 0300-7839
- Human Relations; a journal of studies towards the integration of the social sciences. m. ISSN 0018-7267 (Tavistock Institute of Human Relations UK)
- I B M Research Symposia Series. irreg. ISSN 0085-2082
- Inflammation. q. ISSN 0360-3997 (International Inflammation Research Society)
- International Association for Mathematical Geology. Journal. 6 per yr. ISSN 0020-5958
- International Cryogenics Monograph Series. irreg. ISSN 0538-7051
- International Journal of Computer and Information Science. q. ISSN 0091-7036
- International Journal of Theoretical Physics. 12 per yr. ISSN 0020-7748
- Journal of Abnormal Child Psychology. q. ISSN 0091-0627
- Journal of Autism and Childhood Schizophrenia. q. ISSN 0021-9185
- Journal of Chemical Ecology. q. ISSN 0098-0331
- Journal of Electronic Materials. 6 per yr.
- Journal of Low Temperature Physics. 24 per yr. ISSN 0022-2291
- Journal of Optimization Theory and Applications. m. ISSN 0022-3239
- Journal of Pharmacokinetics and Biopharmaceutics. bi-m. ISSN 0090-466X
- Journal of Psycholinguistical Research. q. ISSN 0090-6905
- Journal of Solid-Phase Biochemistry. q.
- Journal of Solution Chemistry. m.
- Journal of Statistical Physics. m. ISSN 0022-4715
- Journal of Youth and Adolescence; multidisciplinary research publication. q. ISSN 0047-2891
- Materials Science Research. irreg., vol. 10, 1975. ISSN 0076-5201
- Methods in Membrane Biology. irreg., vol. 6, 1976. ISSN 0093-4771
- Modern Aspects of Electrochemistry. irreg., no. 11, 1975. ISSN 0076-9924
- Monographs in Geoscience. irreg.
- Monographs in Inorganic Chemistry. irreg.
- Monographs in Lipid Research. irreg.
- Monographs in Low Temperature Physics. irreg.
- Monographs in Semiconductor Physics. irreg., vol. 6, 1970. ISSN 0544-8417
- Neurochemical Research. bi-m.
- Ocean Technology. irreg., second 1970. ISSN 0078-3153
- Optical Physics and Engineering. irreg. ISSN 0078-5482
- Oxidation of Metals; an international journal of the science of gas-solid reactions. 6 per yr. ISSN 0030-770X
- Progress in Analytical Chemistry. irreg., vol. 7, 1974. ISSN 0079-6042
- Progress in Medicinal Chemistry. biennial, 1969, vol. 6. ISSN 0079-6468
- Progress in Stereochemistry. irreg., vol. 4, 1969. ISSN 0079-6808
- Research Methods in Neurochemistry. s-a.
- Sex Roles: a Journal of Research. q. ISSN 0360-0025
- Somatic Cell Genetics. 6 per yr. ISSN 0098-0366
- Studies in the Natural Sciences. irreg., vol. 8, 1975. (University of Miami. Center for Theoretical Studies)
- Sub-Cellular Biochemistry. a.
- Underwater Acoustics. irreg, 1967, vol.2. ISSN 0082-7444
- Urban Anthropology. q. (Institute for the Study of Man, Inc.)

**Plenum Publishing Corp.**
see also **Consultants Bureau**

**Plenum Publishing Corp.**
227 W. 17th St., New York, NY 10011.
- American Institute of Ultrasound in Medicine. Proceedings of Annual Meeting. a. ISSN 0065-888X
- American Journal of Digestive Diseases. m.
- Canadian Society for Chemical Engineering Symposium Series. a.
- Computer and Information Sciences Symposium. Proceedings. irreg.
- Consciousness and Self-Regulation: Advances in Research. a.
- Evolutionary Biology. irreg., vol. 8, 1975. ISSN 0071-3260

- Monographs in Psychology: an International Series. irreg.

**Plenum Publishing Corp. I.F.I.--Plenum Data Co.**
227 W. 17th St., New York, NY 10011.
- Guide to Fluorescence Literature. irreg., 1974, vol. 3. ISSN 0072-8403
- Guide to Gas Chromatography Literature. irreg., 1974, vol. 3. ISSN 0072-8446
- Handbook of Electronic Materials. irreg., 1972, vol. 9. ISSN 0072-9795
- Solid State Physics Literature Guides. irreg., vol. 7, 1975. ISSN 0081-1963

**Plexus**
2600 Dwight Way, no. 209, Berkeley, CA 94704.
- Plexus. m.

**Plexus Publishing, Inc.**
Box 32305, Louisville, KY 40232.
- Biology Digest. m (Sep.-May) ISSN 0095-2958 (Data Courier, Inc.)

**Ploughshares, Inc.**
Box 529, Cambridge, MA 02139.
- Ploughshares; a journal of the arts. 3 per yr. ISSN 0048-4474 (Co-sponsors: Massachusetts Council on the Arts, Coordinating Council of Literary Magazines)

**Plug Press**
3565 Hunters Glen Rd., Abilene, TX 79605.
- English Plug. q. ISSN 0013-8347

**Plumbing & Mechanical Contractors Council of Harris County, Inc.**
812 Wakefield, Houston, TX 77018.
- Gulf Coast Plumbing-Heating-Cooling News. m. ISSN 0046-659X

**Plus Media, Inc.**
238 Nashville House, One Vantage Way, Nashville, TN 37228.
- Nashville! m.

**Plus Publications**
2626 Pennsylvania Ave. N.W., Washington, DC 20037.
- Access Reports; newsletter on freedom of information and privacy. bi-w.

**Plus Publications, Inc.**
2814 Pennsylvania Ave. N.W., Washington, DC 20007
- Behavior Today; the weekly newsletter. w. ISSN 0005-7924 (Subscriptions to: Box 17029, Baltimore, MD 21203)
- Day Care and Child Development Reports. fortn.

**Plymouth Four and Six Cylinder Owners Club**
44 Glasco Turnpike, Woodstock, NY 12498.
- Plymouth Bulletin. bi-m. ISSN 0032-1737

**L. Wilson Poarch, Jr., Ed. & Pub.**
2965 Freeman Avenue, Sarasota, FL 33580.
- Southern Sawdust. q. ISSN 0038-4542

**Editorial Pocho che**
P.O. Box 1959, San Francisco, CA 94101.
- Tin Tan; revista cosmica. q.

**Pocket Pal**
Box 433, R.F.D.3, Rochester, NH 03867.
- Pocket Pal. 3 per yr.

**Podiatry Record Publishing Co., Inc.**
130 S. Oak Park Ave., Oak Park, IL 60302.
- Journal of Podiatric Medicine. q. ISSN 0022-3794

**Podiatry Society of the State of New York**
Statler Hilton Hotel, 33rd St. & 7th Ave., New York, NY 10001.
- New York Podiatrist. bi-m. ISSN 0028-7431

**Poema Convidado**
c/o Teresinka Pereira, Ed., Department of Spanish and Portuguese, University of Colorado, Boulder, CO 80301.
- Poema Convidado. 3 per yr.

**Poetry Eastwest Publications**
Box 391, Sumter, SC 29150.
- Creative Moment; a biannual of creative writing and criticism. s-a. ISSN 0045-897X
- Poetry Eastwest. a. ISSN 0079-2519

**Poetry Miscellany**
Box 175, Williamstown, MA 01267.
• Poetry Miscellany. s-a. ISSN 0048-4601

**Poetry Project**
St. Marks Church In-The-Bowery, 10th St & Second Ave., New York, NY 10003.
• World. 4-5 per yr. ISSN 0043-8154

**Poetry Society of America**
15 Gramercy Park, New York, NY 10003.
• Poetry Society of America. Bulletin. m. ISSN 0032-2172

**Poetry Society of Michigan**
1207 Walsh St., Lansing, MI 48912.
• Peninsula Poets. q. ISSN 0031-4307

**Poets & Writers, Inc.**
201 W. 54 St., New York, NY 10019.
• Coda; poets & writers newsletter. 5 per yr. ISSN 0091-5645
• Directory of American Fiction Writers. a. (Dist. by: Publishing Center for Cultural Resources, 27 W. 53rd St., New York, NY 10019)
• Directory of American Poets. a (approx.)

**Poets' Guild**
Helen Woods, 317 6th St., Idaho Falls, ID 83401.
• Poets' Guild. q. ISSN 0048-4628

**Poet's League of Greater Cleveland**
Box 6055, Cleveland, OH 44101.
• P L G C Newsletter. m.

**Henry A. Pohs, Ed. & Pub.**
4537 Quitman St., Denver, CO 80212.
• Underground Lamp Post. 2 per yr. ISSN 0049-5174

**Point Blanc Press**
2830 Napier Ave., Macon, GA 31204.
• Gray Day. s-a.

**Point Foundation**
Box 428, Sausalito, CA 94965.
• Co-Evolution Quarterly. q.

**Point Loma Publications, Inc.**
Box 9966, San Diego, CA 92109.
• Eclectic Theosophist. bi-m. ISSN 0046-1105

**Point of View**
2150 Rexwood Rd., Cleveland, OH 44118.
• Point of View. fortn. ISSN 0032-2318

**Pointblank Times**
Box 14643, Houston, TX 77021.
• Pointblank Times. m.

**Poison Pen Press**
627 East 8th St., Brooklyn, NY 11218.
• Masiform D. irreg.

**Rev. Jerome Pokorny, Ed. & Pub**
Valparaiso, NE 68065.
• Catholic Quote; instant inspiration. m.

**Poland China Record Association**
1058 E. Losey St., Drawer 71, Galesburg, IL 61401.
• Poland China World. 10 per yr. ISSN 0032-2466

**Police Officers Journal Inc.**
Box 4291, Long Island City, NY 11104.
• Police Officers Journal. m.

**Police Press Inc.**
2468 Louisiana Ave. N., Minneapolis, MN 55427.
• Minnesota Police Journal. bi-m. ISSN 0026-5624 (Minnesota Police & Peace Officers Association)

**Policy Studies Organization**
University of Illinois at Urbana-Champaign, 361 Lincoln Hall, Urbana, IL 61801.
• Policy Studies Directory. irreg. ISSN 0362-6016 (Co-Sponsor: Institute of Government and Public Affairs)
• Policy Studies Journal. q. (and special issues)
• Political Science Utilization Directory. irreg. ISSN 0362-4765

**Polish American Historical Association**
984 Milwaukee Ave., Chicago, IL 60622.
• P A H A Bulletin. q.
• Polish American Studies; a journal devoted to Polish American life and history. s-a. ISSN 0032-2806 (Polish Museum of America)

**Polish Army Veterans Association of America, Inc.**
17 Irving Place, New York, NY 10003.
• Veteran. m. ISSN 0042-4765

**Polish Falcons of America**
97 S. 18th St., Pittsburgh, PA 15203.
• Sokol Polski/Polish Falcon. s-m. ISSN 0038-0822

**Polish Institute of Arts and Sciences in America**
59 E. 66th St., New York, NY 10021.
• Polish Review. q. ISSN 0032-2970
• Studies in Polish Civilization. quadrennial. ISSN 0085-6886

**Polish Museum of America**
984 Milwaukee Ave., Chicago, IL 60622.
• Polish American Studies. (pub. by Polish American Historical Association)
• Polish Museum of America Quarterly. q.

**Polish National Alliance**
6100 N. Cicero Ave., Chicago, OH 60646.
• Zgoda; fraternal, cultural, sports and general news. s-m.

**Polish National Alliance of Brooklyn**
155 Noble St., Brooklyn, NY 11222.
• Pol-Am Journal. m.

**Polish National Alliance. Sports Youth Commission**
1514-20 W. Division St., Chicago, IL 60632.
• Promien. q. ISSN 0033-1090

**Polish National Union of America**
1002 Pittston Ave., Scranton, PA 18505.
• Straz/Guard. w.

**Polish Roman Catholic Union of America**
984 Milwaukee Ave., Chicago, IL 60622.
• Narod Polski. s-m. ISSN 0027-7894

**Polish Star Publishing Co. Inc.**
3022 Richmond St., Philadelphia, PA 19134.
• Gwiazda/Polish Star. w.

**Polish Tatra Mountaineers Alliance**
c/o J. W. Gromada, 264 Palsa Ave., Elmwood Park, NJ 07407.
• Tatrzanski Orzel/Tatra Eagle. q. ISSN 0039-9914

**Polish Western Association of America**
1130 N. Ashland Ave., Chicago, IL 60622.
• Polish Western Association of America. Quarterly. q. ISSN 0032-3047

**Polish Women's Alliance of America**
1309 N. Ashland Ave., Chicago, IL 60622.
• Glos Polek/Polish Womens' Voice. fortn.

**Political Affairs Publishers, Inc.**
235 W. 23rd St., New York, NY 10011.
• Political Affairs; theoretical journal of the Communist Party, U.S.A. m. ISSN 0032-3128

**Political Research, Inc.**
Fifth Fl., Continental Bldg., 1500 Jackson St., Dallas, TX 75201.
• Clements' Encyclopedia of World Governments. biennial.
• Clements' International Report. m.
• Taylor's Encyclopedia of Government Officials. Federal and State. biennial. ISSN 0082-2183
• World of Politics. m. ISSN 0094-2316

**R.L. Polk & Co.**
2001 Elm Hill Pike, Box 1340, Nashville, TN 37202.
• Polk's World Bank Directory. International Edition. a. ISSN 0085-4999
• Polk's World Bank Directory. North American Edition. 2 per yr.

**Polk County Medical Society**
606 Equitable Bldg, Des Moines, IA 50309.
• Polk County Medical Society. Bulletin. m. ISSN 0032-3586

**Pollution Equipment News**
8550 Babcock Blvd, Pittsburgh, PA 15237.
• Pollution Equipment News. bi-m. ISSN 0032-3659

**Polycrystal Book Service**
P.O. Box 11567, Pittsburgh, PA 15238.
• American Crystallographic Association. Transactions. a. ISSN 0065-8006

**Polymetric Services Inc.**
• A M J-S I Metricpac. (pub. by American Metric Journal Publishing Co.)

**Polytechnic Institute of New York**
333 Jay St., Brooklyn, NY 11201.
• Polytechnic Engineer. 4 per yr. ISSN 0032-406X

**Polytechnic Institute of New York. Libraries**
333 Jay St, Brooklyn, NY 11201.
• Stacks. irreg. ISSN 0038-8890

**Pomona College**
Claremont, CA 91711.
• Pomona Today. 4 per yr. ISSN 0032-4183

**Pontifical College Josephinum**
Worthington, OH 43085.
• Josephinum. s-a. ISSN 0021-759X

**Pontifical Association of the Holy Childhood**
National Office-U.S., 800 Allegheny Ave., Pittsburgh, PA 15233.
• It's Our World; mission news from the Holy Childhood Association. q.

**Pontotoc County Historical and Genealogical Society**
221 W. 16th St., Ada, OK 74820.
• Oklahoma Pontotoc County Quarterly. q. ISSN 0091-1054

**Pony Baseball, Inc.**
Box 225, Washington, PA 15301.
• Pony Baseball. Blue Book. triennial.
• Pony Baseball Newsletter. q.

**Pony Express**
c/o Therese S. Jose, Box 326, Sonora, CA 95370.
• Pony Express; stories of pioneers and old trails. m. ISSN 0032-4264

**Pony of the Americas Club Inc.**
c/o G. B. LaLonde, Box 1447, Mason City, IA 50401.
• Pony of the Americas. m. except Jan.

**Poodle Review**
26 Commerce St., New York, NY 10014.
• Poodle Review. 11 per yr.

**Poole Publications**
Box 6697, Burbank, CA 91510.
• Trailer Boats. m. ISSN 0300-6557

**Poor Farm Productions**
c/o Kenneth Cutter, Ed., 63 Lyndale Ave., Methuen, MA 01844.
• Poor Farm. m.

**Poor Richard Club**
1319 Locust St., Philadelphia, PA 19107.
• Poor Richard's Almanack. q. ISSN 0032-4302

**Pope Families Association**
c/o Wiley R. Pope, Ed., 718 Sims Ave., St. Paul, MN 55106.
• Pope Family Register. q. ISSN 0360-9421

**Poppy Press Inc.**
17 W. 60th St., New York, NY 10023.
• Words & Music. m.

**Popular Astronomy**
Box 2740, Boulder, CO 80302.
• Popular Astronomy. m.

**Popular Ceramics Publications, Inc.**
6011 Santa Monica Blvd., Los Angeles, CA 90038.
• Popular Ceramics. m. ISSN 0032-4477

**Popular Culture Association**
University Hall 101, Bowling Green University, Bowling Green, OH 43403.
• Popular Culture Association Newsletter. 3 per yr. ISSN 0048-4822

**Popular Handicraft and Hobbies**
Box 428, Seabrook, NH 03874.
• Popular Handicraft and Hobbies. bi-m.

**Popular Press**
Bowling Green State University, Department of Popular Culture, Bowling Green, OH 43403.
• Abstracts of Popular Culture. q

**Popular Publications, Inc.**
420 Lexington Ave., New York, NY 10017.
• Argosy. m.

- Cars. m.
- Club Tennis; the international magazine for tennis people anywhere. 6 per yr.
- Railroad Magazine. m. ISSN 0033-8761

**Popular Rotorcraft Association**
Box 570, Stanton, CA 90680.
- Popular Rotorcraft Flying. bi-m. ISSN 0032-4620

**Popular Science Publishing Co.**
- Homeowners How to Handbook. (pub. by Times Mirror Magazines, Inc.)
- Motorcamping Handbook. (pub. by Times-Mirror Magazines, Inc.)
- Ski. (pub. by Times-Mirror Magazines, Inc.)

**Population Association of America**
Box 14182, Benjamin Franklin Station, Washington, DC 20044.
- Demography. q. ISSN 0070-3370
- P A A Affairs. q. ISSN 0300-6816

**Population Association of America. Office of Population Research**
21 Prospect Ave., Princeton, NJ 08540.
- Population Index. q. ISSN 0032-4701

**Population Council**
One Dag Hammarskjold Plaza, New York, NY 10017.
- International Conference on Intra-Uterine Contraception. Proceedings. (pub. by Excerpta Medica NE)
- Population and Development Review. q. ISSN 0098-7921
- Population Council, New York. Country Profiles. irreg. ISSN 0079-3876
- Studies in Family Planning. m. ISSN 0039-3665

**Population Crisis Committee**
1835 K St., Washington, DC 20006.
- Population; briefing papers on issues of national and international importance in the population field. irreg.

**Population Institute. Organization Liaison Division**
110 Maryland Ave. N.E., Washington, DC 20002.
- Population Issues. m.

**Population Reference Bureau, Inc.**
1337 Conn. Ave., N.W., Washington, DC 20036.
- Interchange (Washington); population education newsletter. 5 per yr. ISSN 0047-0465
- Intercom (Washington) m. ISSN 0092-444X
- P R B Report. irreg. ISSN 0146-7646
- Population Bulletin. 6 per yr. ISSN 0032-468X
- World Population Data Sheet. a. ISSN 0085-8315

**Port Authority of New York & New Jersey**
One World Trade Center-63S, New York, NY 10048.
- Via Port of New York. m. ISSN 0042-5001

**Port Authority of New York and New Jersey. Police Division**
J.S.T.C.-One Path Plaza, Jersey City, NJ 07306.
- Signal 8-2. q. ISSN 0037-5012

**Port of Houston Authority**
Box 2562, Houston, TX 77001.
- Port of Houston. m. ISSN 0032-4825

**Port of New Orleans**
2 Canal St., Box 60046, New Orleans, LA 70160.
- New Orleans Port Record. m. ISSN 0028-6397
- Port of New Orleans Annual Directory. a. ISSN 0085-5030

**Port of Portland**
Box 3529, Portland, OR 97208.
- Portside. q. ISSN 0048-489X

**Port of Seattle**
Box 1209, Seattle, WA 98111.
- Port of Seattle Reporter. m.

**Port of Stockton**
- Tideways. (pub. by Shirl Olympius)

**Port Publications, Inc.**
125 E. Main St., Port Washington, WI 53074.
- Sailing; the beauty of sail. m. ISSN 0036-2719

**Portable Video Access**
- Portable Video Newsletter. (pub. by City University of New York, Queens College. Center for Instructional Development)

**Portage County Historical Society**
Univ. of Wisconsin, Stevens Point, WI 54481.
- Pinery. q.

**Porter Corp.**
Box 533, Westport, CT 06880.
- Electric Vehicle News; the magazine committed to better transportation. q. (Electric Vehicle Council)

**Andrew Porter, Ed. & Pub.**
Box 4175, New York, NY 10017.
- Algol; the magazine about science fiction. 3 per yr. ISSN 0002-5364

**Portland Art Association**
S.W. Park & Madison, Portland, OR 97205.
- Portland Art Museum Calendar. m (except Jul & Aug)

**Portland Cement Association**
Reinforced Concrete Research Council, c/o Dr. W.G. Corley, Secretary, 5420 Old Orchard Road, Skokie, IL 60076.
- Reinforced Concrete Research Council. Bulletins. irreg. ISSN 0569-8057

**Portland Chamber of Commerce**
824 W. Fifth Ave., Portland, OR 97204.
- Portland. m.

**Portola Institute**
330 Ellis St., San Francisco, CA 94102.
- Briarpatch Review; a journal of right livelihood and simple living. 4 per yr.

**Portsmouth Chamber of Commerce**
Box 70, 524 Middle St., Portsmouth, VA 23705.
- Portsmouth Chamber of Commerce. Newsletter. m. ISSN 0032-5023

**Portuguese Times, Inc.**
61 West Rodney, French Blvd., New Bedford, MA 02744.
- Portuguese Times. w.

**Thomas W. Poskropski, Ed. & Pub.**
3100 Grand Blvd., Baldwin, NY 11510.
- Polish American World. w.

**Jack Posner, Ed. & Pub**
1220 Madison Ave., New York, NY 10016.
- Capitol Comedy. w.

**Post Card Collector's Magazine**
Box 27, Somerdale, NJ 08083.
- Post Card Collector's Magazine. irreg.

**Post Library Association**
Long Island Univ., C.W. Post Center, Greenvale, NY 11548.
- P L A Report. 4 per yr.

**Post Publishing Co. Inc.**
800 Van Houten Ave., Clifton, NJ 07013.
- Post Eagle; America's leading independent American-Polish weekly. w. ISSN 0300-6786

**Postal History Society, Inc.**
Box 20, Bayside, NY 11361.
- Postal History Journal. 3 per yr. ISSN 0032-5341

**Postal World**
7315 Wisconsin Ave., Washington, DC 20014.
- Postal World. w.

**Postgraduate Center for Mental Health**
124 E. 28th St., New York, NY 10016.
- Transnational Mental Health Research Newsletter. q.

**Potash Institute**
1649 Tullie Circle, N.E., Atlanta, GA 30329.
- Better Crops with Plant Food. q. ISSN 0006-0089

**Potato Association of America**
Univ. of Maine, Orono, ME 04473.
- American Potato Journal. m. ISSN 0003-0589

**Potato Growers of Idaho, Inc.**
- Potato Grower of Idaho. (pub. by Harris Publishing, Inc. (Idaho Falls))

**Potomac Appalachian Trail Club**
1718 N St., N.W., Washington, DC 20036.
- Potomac Appalachian. m.

**Potomac Aviation Publications**
733-15th St., N.W., Washington, DC 20005.
- Sport Modeler. bi-m.

**Potomac Books, Inc.**
Box 40604, Washington, DC 20016.
- State Information Book. biennial.
- Washington; a comprehensive directory of the Nations Capital. biennial. ISSN 0083-7393

**Potomac Lung Association**
9735 Main St., Box 277, Fairfax, VA 22030.
- Potomac View; on the prevention and control of lung diseases. m.(except July & Aug.) ISSN 0032-5643

**Potomac Press**
Box 111, Herndon, VA 22070.
- Campground Directory, Mid Atlantic. irreg. ISSN 0098-5236

**Potomac Research, Inc**
Box 427, Rockville, MD 20856.
- P R I Investment Letter. m.

**Potomac Review, Inc.**
435 Marvin Center, George Washington Univ., Washington, DC 20052.
- Potomac Review; graduate studies in the social studies. s-a. ISSN 0091-2573 (Washington Consortium of Universities)

**Potomac State College**
Journalism Dept., Keyser, WV 26726.
- Pasquino. 10-11 per yr. ISSN 0031-2657

**Pottery Collectors Newsletter**
Box 446, Asheville, NC 28802.
- Pottery Collectors Newsletter. m.

**Pottstown Automobile Club**
135 High St, Pottstown, PA 19464.
- Pottstown Motorist. bi-m.

**Poultry & Egg News, Inc.**
Box 1338, Gainesville, GA 30501.
- Poultry and Eggs Marketing. fortn. ISSN 0032-5716

**Poultry Press**
Box 947, York, PA 17405.
- Poultry Press. m. ISSN 0032-5783

**Poultry Science Association**
113 N. Neil St., Champaign, IL 61820.
- Poultry Science. bi-m. ISSN 0032-5791

**Powell-Savory Corp.**
2340 8th Ave., New York, NY 10027.
- New York Amsterdam News. w. ISSN 0028-7121

**Power Curbers Inc.**
Box 1639, Salisbury, NC 28144.
- News from the Gutter. 2-4 per yr. ISSN 0028-9159

**Power Publishers, Inc.**
60 Vose Ave., So. Orange, NJ 07079.
- Hypnosis Quarterly; hypnotism in all its phases. q. ISSN 0018-8344

**Powercom, Inc.**
Box 2445, Oxnard, CA 93034.
- Solid State Power Conversion. bi-m.

**Powhatan Press**
Box 764, Davis, CA 95616.
- Attan-Akamik; voice of the Powhatan-Renapoak people. irreg (1-3 per yr)

**Practising Law Institute. Public Defenders' Workshop**
1133 Ave. of the Americas, New York, NY 10036.
- Annual Public Defenders' Workshop. Handbook. a. ISSN 0093-8653

**Prads, Inc.**
380 Madison Ave., New York, NY 10017.
- Clothes. 2 per mo. ISSN 0009-9465

**Praeger Publishers, Inc.**
111 4th Ave., New York, NY 10003.
- American Art and Artists. irreg.
- American Decorative Arts Series. irreg.
- Arts and Civilization of Indian America. irreg.
- Aspen Notebooks. irreg.
- Aspen Series on Communication and Society. irreg.
- Basic Concepts in Political Science. irreg.

- Columbia University. Conservation of Human Resources Project. Conservation of Human Resources Studies. irreg.
- Contemporary Soviet Union Series; Institutions and Problems. irreg.
- Man, State, and Society. irreg.
- Modern Arts in Finland Series. irreg., vol. 4, 1970.
- New Directions in Management and Economics. irreg.
- New Perspectives in American History (Praeger) irreg.
- Phaidon Guides. irreg.
- Praeger Country Profile Series. irreg.
- Praeger Film Books. irreg.
- Praeger Film Library. irreg.
- Praeger Handbooks to the Modern World. irreg.
- Praeger History of Civilization. irreg.
- Praeger History of Music Series. irreg.
- Praeger Introductory Geographies. irreg.
- Praeger Library of African Affairs. irreg.
- Praeger Library of Chinese Affairs. irreg.
- Praeger Library of U.S. Government Departments and Agencies. irreg.
- Praeger Monographs in Geography. irreg.
- Praeger Special Studies: Design-Environmental Planning Series. irreg.
- Praeger Special Studies in International Economics and Development. irreg.
- Praeger Special Studies in International Politics and Government. irreg.
- Praeger Special Studies in U.S. Economic, Social and Political Issues. irreg.
- Praeger Special Studies on Urban Affairs. irreg.
- Praeger Surveys in Economic Geography. irreg.
- Source Books and Studies in Chinese History. irreg.
- Source Books and Studies in Russian and Soviet History. irreg.
- Source Books and Studies on Inner Asia. irreg.
- Source Books and Studies on Latin America. irreg.
- Source Books and Studies on the Pacific Area. irreg.
- Studies in International Order. irreg.
- Voices from the Nations. irreg.
- World of Art Series. irreg., latest 1975.

**Pragmatist in Art**
63 Livingston Ave., Dobbs Ferry, NY 10522.
- Pragmatist in Art. s-a. ISSN 0032-6577

**Prairie Club**
6 E. Monroe St., Room 1507, Chicago, IL 60603.
- Prairie Club Bulletin; organized for the promotion of outdoor recreation in the form of walks, outings, camping and canoeing. m(Sept-June) ISSN 0032-6607

**Prairie Farmer Publishing Co.**
2001 Spring Rd., Oak Brook, IL 60521.
- Prairie Farmer; a farm progress publication. s-m. ISSN 0032-6615

**Prairie Press East**
206 Clarke St., Syracuse, NY 13210.
- International Craft Swap. a.

**Prairie School Press**
12509 S. 89th Ave., Palos Park, IL 60464.
- Prairie School Review. q. ISSN 0032-6674

**Prakken Publications, Inc.**
416 Longshore Dr., Ann Arbor, MI 48107.
- Education Digest. m.(Sept-May) ISSN 0013-127X
- School Shop; for industrial education teachers. m.(Sept-June) ISSN 0036-682X
- Technician Education Yearbook. biennial. ISSN 0082-2353

**Prather Bulletin**
c/o Elizabeth P. Ellsberry, Box 206, Chillicothe, MO 64601.
- Prather Bulletin. bi-m.

**Pratt Graphics Center**
160 Lexington Ave., New York, NY 10016.
- Print Review. s-a. ISSN 0091-3731

**Pratt Institute. Office of Public Affairs**
215 Ryerson St., Brooklyn, NY 11205.
- Pratt Reports. 5 per yr.

**Pre-Han Newsletter**
c/o David N. Keightley, Department of History, University of California, Berkeley, CA 94720.
- Pre-Han Newsletter. biennial.

**Precision Shooting Inc.**
Box 6, Athens, PA 18810.
- Precision Shooting. m. ISSN 0048-5144

**Predicament, Inc.**
1311 Yewell Street, Iowa City, IA 52240.
- Predicament. 10 per yr.

**Predicasts Inc.**
200 University Circle Research Center, 11001 Cedar Ave., Cleveland, OH 44106.
- Chemical Market Abstracts. m. ISSN 0009-2606
- Electronic Trends. q.
- Electronics & Equipment Market Abstracts. q. ISSN 0095-7275
- Equipment Market Abstracts. m.
- F & S Index International; industries, countries, companies. m. (quarterly cum) ISSN 0014-5661
- F & S Index International Annual. a.
- F & S Index of Corporate Change. q.
- F & S Index of Corporations and Industries. w(m. & q. cumulations) ISSN 0014-567X
- F & S Index of Corporations and Industries. Annual. a.
- Federal Index; covering the Congressional Record, Federal Register, Presidential Documents, Commerce Business Daily, Washington Post. m.
- Paper Trends. q. ISSN 0031-1200
- Plastics Trends. q. ISSN 0032-1265
- Predi-Briefs. m. ISSN 0551-9276
- Predicasts. q. ISSN 0032-7166
- Predicasts. Basebook. a. ISSN 0093-8025
- Predicasts. Source Directory. a. ISSN 0092-7767
- Technical Survey; a world report on advances in technology. w. ISSN 0040-1005
- World-Product-Casts. a. ISSN 0043-8898
- World-Regional-Casts. a. ISSN 0043-8936

**Al Preiss Ltd.**
P.O.B. 2430, Hollywood, CA 90028.
- Pay Television. bi-m.

**Prejepscot Press**
10 Mason St., Brunswick, ME 04011.
- Maine Writers' Conference Chapbook. a. ISSN 0076-2717

**Premiere**
Winter St., Lincoln, MA 01773.
- Premiere. 2-3 per yr. ISSN 0032-7395

**Prentice-Hall, Inc.**
Englewood Cliffs, NJ 07632.
- Almanac of Business and Industrial Financial Ratios. a.
- Artists in Perspective Series. irreg.
- Central Issues in Philosophy Series. irreg.

**Prentice-Hall, Inc. General Book Mktg. Div.**
Box 500, Englewood Cliffs, NJ 07632.
- Prentice-Hall Contemporary Comparative Politics Series. irreg.
- Prentice-Hall Contemporary Perspectives in Music Education Series. irreg.
- Prentice-Hall Foundations of Modern Psychology Series. irreg.
- Prentice-Hall History of Music Series. irreg.
- Prentice-Hall History of the American People Series. irreg.
- Prentice-Hall Series in Social Policy. irreg.

**Presbyterian Church in the United States**
341 Ponce de Leon Ave., N. E., Atlanta, GA 30308.
- Presbyterian Survey. m. ISSN 0032-759X

**Presbyterian Church U.S. Synod of Red River**
Box 1098, Denton, TX 76201.
- Presbyterian. m. (Co-sponsor: United Presbyterian Church, U.S.A. Synod of the Sun)

**Presbyterian Guardian Publishing Corp.**
7401 Old York Rd., Philadelphia, PA 19126.
- Presbyterian Guardian. 10 per yr. ISSN 0032-7522

**Presbyterian Historical Society**
425 Lombard St., Philadelphia, PA 19147.
- Journal of Presbyterian History. q. ISSN 0022-3883

**Presbyterian Lay Committee**
1729 Delancey Place, Philadelphia, PA 19103.
- Presbyterian Layman. m. ISSN 0555-0572

**Preservation Society of Charleston**
Box 521, Charleston, SC 29402.
- Preservation Progress. q. ISSN 0478-1392

**Presgraves Reunion**
10804 Rock Run Drive, Potomac, MD 20854.
- Presgraves Reunion. q. ISSN 0032-7743

**President, Inc.**
(Subsidiary of: Time Inc.)
c/o Time, Inc., Time- Life Bldg., Rockefeller Center, New York, NY 10020
(and 1-2-3 Aoyama Bldg. Kita-Aoyama Minato-Ku Tokyo, Japan)
- President. m. ISSN 0032-7751
- President Directory. a.

**President Publications**
Drawer AG, Beverly Hills, CA 90213.
- Gambling Illustrated. m. ISSN 0016-4291

**President's Committee on Employment of the Handicapped**
Washington, DC 20210.
- Performance (Washington) m. ISSN 0031-5214

**Press of the Times**
60 S. Pleasant St., Oberlin, OH 44074.
- Oberlin Review. s-w. ISSN 0029-7526 (Oberlin College)

**Press-Tech, Inc.**
2211 Fordem Ave., Madison, WI 53701.
- Software Age. m. ISSN 0038-061X

**Pressure Technology Corporation of America**
Boalsburg, PA 16827.
- Pressure Research Notes. 6 per yr. ISSN 0556-1442

**Preston Publications, Inc.**
6366 Gross Point Rd., Box 312, Niles, IL 60648.
- Gas Chromatography Literature-Abstracts & Index. m. ISSN 0016-4895
- Journal of Analytical Toxicology. bi-m.
- Journal of Chromatographic Science. m. ISSN 0021-9665
- Liquid Chromatography Literature- Abstracts and Index. bi-m.
- Nuclear Magnetic Resonance Literature-Abstracts & Index. m.

**Prestressed Concrete Institute**
c/o Ed. George D. Nasser, 20 N. Wacker Dr., Chicago, IL 60606.
- Prestressed Concrete Institute. Journal. bi-m. ISSN 0032-793X

**Renan Prevost, Ed. & Pub.**
Box 126, 7920 Imperial Ave., Lemon Grove, CA 92045.
- Southern California Rancher. bi-m. ISSN 0038-3937

**Robert C. Price, Ed. & Pub.**
Box 2283, Arlington, VA 22202.
- Astrograph. bi-m. ISSN 0094-1417

**Price Guide Publishers**
525 Kenmore Station, Kenmore, WA 98028.
- Used Book Price Guide. quinquennial. ISSN 0083-4807

**Price Waterhouse & Co.**
60 Broad St., New York, NY 10004.
- Price Waterhouse Review. q. ISSN 0032-8170

**Pride Publications**
33 E. Upsal St., Philadelphia, PA 19119.
- Pride. bi-m. ISSN 0032-8197

**Pride Publications, Inc.**
Box 13, Wakefield, MA 01880.
- New England Journeys. 10 per yr. ISSN 0028-4815

**Priests' Eucharistic League**
- Emmanuel. (pub. by Blessed Sacrament Fathers)

**Priests of Holy Cross. Indiana Province**
Ave Maria, Notre Dame, IN 46556.
- A. D. Correspondence. fortn. ISSN 0005-1942

**Priests of the Sacred Heart**
6889 S. Lovers Lane, Hales Corners, WI 53130.
- Reign of the Sacred Heart. m. ISSN 0048-7155

**Primal Institute**
620 N. Almont Drive, Los Angeles, CA 90069.
- Journal of Primal Therapy. q.

**Primary Sources**
11 Bleecker St., New York, NY 10012.
- Soviet Journal of Non-Ferrous Metals. m. ISSN 0038-5484

**Prince George's County Genealogical Society**
Box 819, Bowie, MD 20715.
- Prince George's County Genealogical Society. Bulletin. 10 per yr.

**Prince George's County Memorial Library System**
6532 Adelphi Rd., Hyattsville, MD 20782.
- For Better Communities; wherever they are and better informed people who care. 5 per yr.

**Princeton Arts Journal**
200 W. 72 St., New York, NY 10023.
- Princeton Arts Journal. 10 per yr.

**Princeton Theological Seminary**
Box 29, Princeton, NJ 08540.
- Pastoral Psychology. (pub. by Human Sciences Press)
- Theology Today. q. ISSN 0040-5736

**Princeton University**
Princeton, NJ 08540.
- University; a Princeton quarterly. q. ISSN 0041-9249

**Princeton University. Art Museum**
Princeton, NJ 08540.
- Princeton University. Art Museum. Record. s-a. ISSN 0032-843X

**Princeton University. Center of International Studies**
Corwin Hall, Princeton, NJ 08540.
- Princeton University. Center of International Studies. Occasional Papers. irreg., no. 4, 1976.
- Princeton University. Center of International Studies Policy Memorandum. irreg., no. 39, 1974. ISSN 0079-5267
- Princeton University. Center of International Studies. Research Monograph Series. irreg., no. 43, 1974. ISSN 0555-1501
- World Politics. (pub. by Princeton University Press)

**Princeton University. Department of Electrical Engineering**
Princeton, NJ 08540.
- Princeton University. Computer Sciences Laboratory. Technical Report. irreg. ISSN 0079-5283 (prep. by its Computer Sciences Laboratory)

**Princeton University. Department of Psychology**
Green Hall, Princeton, NJ 08540.
- Princeton University Cutaneous Research Project Reports. s-a. ISSN 0032-8448

**Princeton University. Econometric Research Program**
207 Dickinson Hall, Princeton, NJ 08540.
- Princeton University. Econometric Research Program. Research Memorandum. irreg., no. 199, 1976. ISSN 0079-5291

**Princeton University. Graduate School**
Princeton, NJ 08540.
- Association of Graduate Schools in Association of American Universities. Journal of Proceedings and Addresses. a. ISSN 0066-9563

**Princeton University. Industrial Relations Section**
Box 248, Princeton, NJ 08540.
- Princeton University. Industrial Relations Section. Research Report. irreg., 1969, no. 113. ISSN 0079-5305
- Princeton University. Industrial Relations Sections Selected References. 5 per yr. ISSN 0037-1351

**Princeton University. International Finance Section**
Box 644, Princeton, NJ 08540.
- Essays in International Finance. irreg., no. 120, 1977. ISSN 0071-142X
- Reprints in International Finance. irreg., no. 18, 1975. ISSN 0080-1380
- Special Papers in International Economics. irreg. no. 12, 1977. ISSN 0081-3559
- Studies in International Finance. irreg., no. 40, 1977. ISSN 0081-8070

**Princeton University. Library**
Princeton, NJ 08540.
- Princeton University Library Chronicle. 3 per yr. ISSN 0032-8456 (Friends of the Princeton University Library)

**Princeton University. Library Staff Association**
Princeton University Library, Princeton, NJ 08540.
- Green Pyne Leaf. m. (during school year) ISSN 0017-3975

**Princeton University Press**
Princeton, NJ 08540.
(and University of Tokyo Press, Tokyo, Japan)
- A. W. Mellon Lectures in the Fine Arts. irreg., latest issue no. 22. ISSN 0065-0129
- Annals of Mathematics. bi-m. ISSN 0003-486X (Co-Sponsor: Institute for Advanced Study)
- Annals of Mathematics Studies. irreg., no. 88, 1974.
- Monographs in Geology and Paleontology. irreg., 1967, no. 1. ISSN 0077-085X
- Monographs in Population Biology. irreg., latest issue no. 10. ISSN 0077-0930
- Papers of Woodrow Wilson. s-a. ISSN 0031-1286 (Woodrow Wilson Foundation) (Co-sponsor: Princeton University)
- Philosophy and Public Affairs. q. ISSN 0048-3915
- Princeton Essays in Literature. irreg., latest issue no. 20. ISSN 0079-5186
- Princeton Essays on the Arts. irreg.
- Princeton Mathematical Series. irreg., 1971, no. 32. ISSN 0079-5194
- Princeton Monographs in Art and Archaeology. irreg., latest, no. 41. ISSN 0079-5208
- Princeton Series in Physics. irreg., latest issue no. 6. ISSN 0079-5216
- Princeton Studies in Mathematical Economics. irreg., latest issue no. 6. ISSN 0079-5240
- Princeton Studies in Music. irreg., 1973, no. 6. ISSN 0079-5259
- Studies in Manuscript Illumination. irreg., 1970, no. 6. ISSN 0081-8178
- Virginia and Richard Stewart Memorial Lectures. irreg.
- World Politics; a quarterly journal of international relations. q. ISSN 0043-8871 (Princeton University. Center of International Studies)

**Princeton University. School of Engineering and Applied Science**
Princeton, NJ 08540.
- Princeton Engineer. q. ISSN 0032-8405

**Prindle Weber and Schmidt Inc.**
20 Newbury St., Boston, MA 02116.
- Prindle, Weber and Schmidt Complementary Series in Mathematics. irreg., 1967, no. 6. ISSN 0079-5313

**Print Collector's Newsletter Inc.**
205 E. 78th St. 1-D, New York, NY 10021.
- Print Collector's Newsletter. bi-m. ISSN 0032-8537

**Print Media Services, Ltd.**
222 S. Prospect Ave., Park Ridge, IL 60068.
- Wheelers Recreational Vehicle Resort and Campground Guide: North American Edition. a.
- Wheelers Recreational Vehicle Resort and Campground Guide: Northeasterner Edition. a.
- Wheelers Recreational Vehicle Resort and Campground Guide: Southeasterner Edition. a.
- Wheelers Recreational Vehicle Resort and Campground Guide: Westerner Edition. a.

**Printable Arts Society, Inc.**
- Box 749. (pub. by Seven Square Press)

**Printer**
Ghost Town Museum Park, Rural Route Four, Findlay, OH 45840.
- Printer. m.

**Printing Craftsmen, Inc.**
Pocono Pines, PA 18350.
- This Week in the Poconos. 24 per yr.

**Printing News, Inc.**
468 Park Ave., S., New York, NY 10016.
- Printing News. w. ISSN 0032-8626

**Printing Platemakers Association, Inc.**
415 E. Hitt St., Mount Morris, IL 61054.
- Printing Plates. m. ISSN 0032-8634

**Printway, Inc.**
100 Subscription Processing Center, South Milwaukee, WI 53172.
- World News of the Week. 36 per yr. ISSN 0043-874X

**Priory Press**
1111 N. Richmond St, Chicago, IL 60612.
- Institute of Spirituality. Special Lectures. a. ISSN 0073-974X

**Prison Action Group**
121 N. Fitzhugh St., Rochester, NY 14614.
- Prison Action Group. Newsletter. m.

**Prisoners Union**
1315 18th St., San Francisco, CA 94107.
- Outlaw. bi-m.

**Pritchard Publications**
P.O. Box 2079, Sarasota, FL 33578.
- Furniture Forum. a. ISSN 0071-9994

**Pritchard Publishing Co.**
44 Putnam Park Road, Redding, CT 06896.
- Utility Purchasing & Stores. m. ISSN 0042-1588
- Utility Specifier Engineer. bi-m.

**Privacy Journal**
Box 8844, Washington, DC 20003.
- Privacy Journal; an independent monthly on privacy in a computer age. m. ISSN 0145-7659

**Private Carrier Conference, Inc.**
American Trucking Assns., 1616 P St. N. W., Washington, DC 20036.
- Private Carrier. m. ISSN 0032-8871

**Private Police Publishers**
422 Vine Court, Wilmette, IL 60091.
- Private Police Publishers Newsletter. m.

**E. L. Prizer, Ed. & Pub.**
Box 2207, Orlando, FL 32802.
- Orlando-Land. m.

**Pro Ecclesia Foundation**
663 Fifth Ave., New York, NY 10022.
- Pro Ecclesia. m.
- Talks of Pope Paul VI. s-m.

**Pro Football Weekly, Inc.**
5606 N. Western Ave., Chicago, IL 60659.
- Pro Football Weekly. w. ISSN 0032-9053

**Pro Se Collective**
400 Huntington Ave., Boston, MA 02115.
- Pro Se; the National Law Women's Newsletter. 4 per yr. ISSN 0093-8858

**Probe (Santa Barbara)**
Box 13390 UCSB, Santa Barbara, CA 93107.
- Probe (Santa Barbara) irreg. ISSN 0032-9177

**Probe, Inc.**
78 Randall Ave., Rockville Centre, NY 11570.
- Probe (Rockville Centre) s-m. ISSN 0032-9193

**Proceedings in Print, Inc.**
Box 247, Mattapan, MA 02126.
- Proceedings in Print. bi-m. ISSN 0032-9568

**Procrastinators' Club of America**
1111 Board, Locust Bldg., Philadelphia, PA 19102.
- Last Month's Newsletter. irreg.

**Walter T. Proctor, Ed. & Pub.**
Box 3627, Urbandale Br., Des Moines, IA 50322.
- American Host. m. ISSN 0002-8827

**Produce Marketing Association**
700 Barksdale Rd., Suite 6, Newark, DE 19711.
- Directory of Research Reports Relating to Produce Packaging and Marketing. irreg. ISSN 0070-6213
- Produce Marketing Association. Yearbook. a. ISSN 0079-5860

**Producers' Council, Inc.**
1717 Massachusetts Ave. N.W., Washington, DC 20036.
- Guide to Quality Construction Products. a.

**Producers Guild of America**
8201 Beverly Blvd., Los Angeles, CA 90048.
- Producers Guild of America. Journal. q. ISSN 0032-9703

**Production Press**
307 E. Morgan, Jacksonville, IL 62650
(Subscr. Address: H P E D, McCormick Hall,
Illinois State University, Normal, Ill. 61676)
● Illinois Journal of Health, Physical Education and
Recreation. s-a. ISSN 0019-2074 (Illinois
Association for Health, Physical Education and
Recreation)

**Production Publishing Co.**
804 Church St., Nashville, TN 37203.
● Furniture Production. m. ISSN 0532-8942

**Productions, Ltd.**
Route 80, Box 175, North Branford, CT 06471.
● Emergency Review. bi-m. (American College of
Emergency Medical Technicians)

**Professional Breeding Services Inc.**
Box 176, Rte. 209, Hurley, NY 12443.
● D I S C A R. (Dog Information Storage Control
and Retrieval) q. ISSN 0145-9066 (Canine
Information Center)

**Professional Communications Associates**
625 North Michigan Ave., Chicago, IL 60611.
● Current Concepts in Gastroenterology. q. ISSN
0363-6526
● Current Concepts in Psychiatry. q. ISSN 0360-
7569

**Professional Development Associates**
Box 4303, Austin, TX 78765.
● Professional Development Associates. Staff
Development Newsletter. 10 per yr.

**Professional Exchange**
350 Madison Ave., Cresskill, NJ 07626.
● Nutrition in Medicine. m.

**Professional Golfers' Association of America**
Box 12458, Lake Park, FL 33403.
● Professional Golfer. m. ISSN 0033-0132

**Professional Grounds Management Society**
19 Hawthorne Ave., Pikesville, MD 21208.
● Manager's Memo. m.

**Professional Information Sources, Inc.**
Box 533, Englewood, NJ 07631.
● Medical Education Sources. a.

**Professional Installer**
521 N. LaCienega Blvd., Suite 210, Los Angeles,
CA 90048.
● Professional Installer. 6 per yr.

**Professional Insurance Agents**
Investment Bldg., Washington, DC 20005.
● Professional Agent. m.

**Professional Liability Reporter**
Suite 600, 126 Post St., San Francisco, CA 94108.
● Professional Liability Reporter. m.

**Professional Medical Services Co.**
Box 643, Ridgewood, NJ 07451.
● Urology. m. ISSN 0090-4295

**Professional Photographers of America**
● Directory of Professional Photography. (pub. by P
P A Publications, Inc.)
● Professional Photographer. (pub. by P P A
Publications, Inc.)

**Professional Photographers of California, Inc.**
319 Pacific Ave., San Francisco, CA 94111.
● California Professional Photographer. bi-m.

**Professional Press, Inc.**
101 E. Ontario St., Chicago, IL 60611.
● Blue Book of Optometrists. biennial. ISSN 0067-
9283
● International Contact Lens Clinic. bi-m. ISSN
0094-1840
● Journal of Learning Disabilities. m. ISSN 0022-
2194
● Optical Index. m.
● Optometric Weekly. w. ISSN 0030-4093
● Red Book of Ophthalmology. biennial.

**Professional Productivity Associates**
Box 2662, Carbondale, IL 62901.
● Specialia. 2 per yr.(approx.) ISSN 0038-6847
(Southern Illinois University, Latin American
Institute)

**Professional Publication Producers**
Box 25027, Houston, TX 77005.
● International Conference on Oral Biology.
Proceedings. irreg.; latest issue, 1974. ISSN 0074-
3216 (International Association for Dental
Research)
● Journal of Dental Research. bi-m. ISSN 0022-
0345 (American Dental Association)

**Professional Publications, Inc.**
Box 80543, Atlanta, GA 30366.
● Georgia Commercial Post. fortn.

**Professional Publications, Inc. (Atlanta)**
Box 80097, Atlanta, GA 30341.
● Your School and the Law. m. ISSN 0094-0399

**Professional Publications, Inc. (Columbus)**
Box 12448, 1609 Northwest Blvd., Columbus, OH
43212.
● Ceramics Monthly. m. ISSN 0009-0328

**Professional Publishing Corp.**
P.O. Box 4187, San Rafael, CA 94903.
● Realty Bluebook. a. ISSN 0090-399X

**Professional Rehabilitation Workers with the Adult
Deaf, Inc.**
814 Thayer Ave., Silver Spring, MD 20910.
● Deafness Annual. a.
● Journal of Rehabilitation of the Deaf. q. ISSN
0022-4170

**Professional Rodeo Cowboys Association**
2929 W. 19th Ave., Denver, CO 80204.
● Rodeo Sports News. s-m. ISSN 0035-7758

**Professional Staff Congress - City University of New
York**
25 W. 43 St., New York, NY 10036.
● P S C Clarion. 9 per yr.

**Profiles Publishing Corp.**
2 Reservoir Rd., Hanover, NH 03755.
● New Hampshire Profiles. m. ISSN 0028-5307

**Profit Press, Inc.**
400 E. 89 St., New York, NY 10028.
● Food Industry Newsletter. fortn.

**Progress-Register**
200 Upper Midwest Bldg., Minneapolis, MN 55401.
● Minnesota Legal Register; opinions of the
Minnesota Attorney General. m. & a. ISSN 0026-
5543

**Progressive Farmer Co.**
Box 2581, Birmingham, AL 35202.
● Progressive Farmer. m. ISSN 0033-0760
● Southern Living. m. ISSN 0038-4305
● Southern Supermarketing. bi-m.

**Progressive Grocer Publishing Co.**
708 Third Ave., New York, NY 10017.
● Progressive Grocer; the magazine of
supermarketing. m. ISSN 0033-0787
● Progressive Grocer/Convenience Stores Bi-
Monthly. bi-m.
● Progressive Grocer's Annual Report of the
Grocery Trade. a.
● Progressive Grocer's Market Scope. a.
● Progressive Grocer's Marketing Guidebook. a.
ISSN 0079-6921

**Progressive, Inc.**
408 W. Gorham, Madison, WI 53703.
● Progressive. m. ISSN 0033-0736

**Progressive Labor Party**
220 E. 23 St., New York, NY 10010.
● Challenge (New York); the Revolutionary
newspaper. w. ISSN 0009-1049
● Progressive Labor. 4 per yr. ISSN 0033-0795

**Progressive Publishing Co.**
2678 Heury St., Augusta, GA 30904.
● Progressive Teacher. m.(Sept-June) ISSN 0033-
0825

**Project Concern, Inc.**
3802 Houston St., San Diego, CA 92110.
● Project Concern News. m. ISSN 0033-0906

**Project - Guidelines to Equal Opportunity**
Box 8214, Philadelphia, PA 19101.
● Project - Guidelines to Equal Opportunity. bi-m.
ISSN 0033-0892

**Project House Foundation, Inc.**
2513-B Ashwood Ave., Nashville, TN 37212.
● Barbeque Planet. q.

**Project Innovation**
1362 Santa Cruz Ct., Chula Vista, CA 92010.
● College Student Journal; a journal pertaining to
college students. q.
● Education. q. ISSN 0013-1172
● Reading Improvement; a journal for the
improvement of reading teaching. q. ISSN 0034-
0510

**Project Magazine Inc.**
P.O. Box 8214, Philadelphia, PA 19101.
● Black Careers. bi-m. ISSN 0006-4122
● Minority Supplies Report & Directory; industrial
reference guide of minority businesses in the U.S.
a.

**Project Management Corp.**
617 Walnut St., Knoxville, TN 37902.
● Breeder Briefs. m. (Clinch River Breeder Reactor
Project)

**Project on Linguistic Analysis**
2222 Piedmont Ave., Berkeley, CA 94720.
● Journal of Chinese Linguistics. s-a. ISSN 0091-
3723

**Prol Publishing Co.**
561 Riford Rd., Glen Ellyn, IL 60137.
● Best Sermons; an interdenominational magazine.
bi-m. ISSN 0005-9633

**Promenade Magazines, Inc.**
c/o James White, Ed., 45 E. 45 St., New York, NY
10017.
● Promenade. s-a.

**Proof**
Box 5252, Grosse Pointe Farms, MI 48236.
● Proof. m. ISSN 0033-121X

**Proofreaders Club of New York**
38-15 149 St, Flushing, NY 11354.
● First to Final. irreg. ISSN 0015-2803

**Propeller Club of the United States**
1730 M St., N.W., Suite 413, Washington, DC
20036.
● American Merchant Marine Conference.
Proceedings. a.
● Propeller Club Quarterly. q. ISSN 0048-5551

**Properties**
4900 Euclid Ave., Cleveland, OH 44103.
● Properties. m. ISSN 0033-1287

**Proprietary Association**
1700 Pennsylvania Ave. N.W., Washington, DC
20006.
● Proprietary Association. Committee on Scientific
Development. Annual Research and Scientific
Development Conference. Proceedings. a. ISSN
0079-7006

**Proscenium Press**
P.O. Box 361, Newark, DE 19711.
● Adaptations Series. irreg., no. 3, 1977. ISSN
0065-1877
● Contemporary Drama Series. irreg., no. 2, 1974.
ISSN 0069-9381
● Irish Play Series. irreg., no. 10, 1975. ISSN 0075-
0816
● Journal of Irish Literature. 3 per yr. ISSN 0047-
2514
● Lost Play Series. irreg., no. 12, 1977. ISSN 0076-
1001
● Short Play Series. irreg., no. 6, 1974. ISSN 0080-
9403

**Proscenium Publications**
4 Park Ave., New York, NY 10016.
● New York Theatre Critics' Reviews. 22-30 per yr.
ISSN 0028-7784
● Theatre Information Bulletin. w. ISSN 0040-5515

**Prospector Research Services, Inc.**
751 Main St., Waltham, MA 02154.
● Commercial Expansion Reporter. 15 per mo.
ISSN 0010-2954
● Sales Prospector. 15 per mo. ISSN 0036-3456

**Prospectors' Club International**
Box 1057, Anderson, IN 46015.
● Prospector. q. ISSN 0033-152X

**Prostaglandin Information Center**
Worcester Foundation, 222 Maple Ave.,
Shrewsbury, MA 01545.
- Research in Prostaglandins. bi-m. ISSN 0048-7309

**Protestant Episcopal Cathedral Foundation**
Mt. St. Alban, Washington, DC 20016.
- Cathedral Age; an international magazine devoted
  to cathedral interests throughout the world. q.
  ISSN 0008-7874

**Protestant Episcopal Church in the U.S.A.**
- New Life. (pub. by Anchor Society)

**Proteus Press**
1004 N. Jefferson St., Arlington, VA 22205.
- Proteus. q. ISSN 0090-2071

**Proust Research Association**
Dept. of French and Italian, Univ. of Kansas,
Lawrence, KS 66045.
- Proust Research Association Newsletter. s-a. ISSN
  0048-5659

**Providence Hospital**
16001 Nine Mile Rd., Southfield, MI 48075.
- Providence Hospital of Southfield. Medical
  Bulletin. s-a. ISSN 0033-1864

**Province of St. Joseph of the Capuchin Order**
- Sandal Prints. (pub. by Capuchin Missions)

**Prudential Financial Corp. of Los Angeles**
- Western Financial Journal. (pub. by Alex N.
  Campbell, Jr.)

**Prudential Insurance Co. of America**
Public Relations & Advertising Dept., 5 Plaza,
Newark, NJ 07101.
- Real Estate Investment Department Quarterly. q.

**Pruitt- Scott Publications**
P.O. Box 228, Kingsbridge Station, New York, NY
10463.
- Disc and That. m. ISSN 0092-0436

**Psi Chi National Office**
APA Bldg., 1200 17th St. N.W., Washington, DC
20036.
- Psi Chi Newsletter. q. ISSN 0033-2569

**Psi Omega Fraternity**
1030 Lincoln Ave., Prospect Park, PA 19076.
- Frater of Psi Omega. irreg. ISSN 0071-9285

**Psy-Ed Corp.**
Rm. 708, Statler Office Bldg., 20 Providence St.,
Boston, MA 02116.
- Exceptional Parent; children with disabilities/
  practical guidance. 6 per yr. ISSN 0046-9157

**Psychiatric Institute Foundation. Center for Group
Studies**
Michigan Ave. and Franklin St., N.W., Washington,
DC 20017.
- Group Studies Journal. irreg. ISSN 0363-714X

**Psychiatry Digest**
c/o W. Hotze, 444 Frontage Rd., Northfield, IL
60093.
- Psychiatry Digest; a summary of the world's
  psychiatric literature. m. ISSN 0033-2771

**Psychic Magazine, Inc.**
680 Beach St., Suite 408, San Francisco, CA 94109
(Subscr. Address: Box 26289, Custom House, San
Francisco, Calif. 94126)
- New Realities. bi-m.

**Psychical Research Foundation, Inc.**
Duke Station, Durham, NC 27706.
- Theta; a journal for research on the problem of
  survival after bodily death. q. ISSN 0040-6066

**Psychoanalytic Quarterly, Inc**
57 W. 57th St, New York, NY 10019.
- Psychoanalytic Quarterly. q. ISSN 0033-2828

**Psychodiagnostic Test Co.**
Box 859, E. Lansing, MI 48823.
- World Journal of Psychosynthesis. bi-m. ISSN
  0043-860X (Michigan Institute of
  Psychosynthesis)

**Psychological Record**
Kenyon College, Gambier, OH 43022.
- Psychological Record; a quarterly journal in
  theoretical and experimental psychology. q. ISSN
  0033-2933

**Psychological Reports**
Box 9229, Missoula, MT 59807.
- Psychological Reports. bi-m.(2 vols.per yr.) ISSN
  0033-2941

**Psychologists for Social Action**
Box 173, New York, NY 10003.
- Social Action. bi-m.

**Psychology**
Box 6495, Station C, Savannah, GA 31405.
- Psychology; a journal of human behavior. q. ISSN
  0033-3077

**Psychometric Society**
c/o Howard Wainer, Department of Psychology,
Univ. of Chicago, Chicago, IL 60637.
- Psychometrika; a journal devoted to the
  development of psychology as a quantitative
  rational science. q. ISSN 0033-3123

**Psychonomic Society, Inc.**
1108 W. 34th, Austin, TX 78705.
- Animal Learning & Behavior. q. ISSN 0090-4996
- Behavior Research Methods and Instrumentation.
  bi-m. ISSN 0005-7878
- Memory and Cognition. bi-m. ISSN 0090-502X
- Perception & Psychophysics. m. ISSN 0031-5117
- Physiological Psychology. q. ISSN 0090-5046
- Psychonomic Society. Bulletin. m. ISSN 0090-
  5054

**Psychosynthesis Institute**
3352 Sacramento St., San Francisco, CA 94118.
- Psychosynthesis Program Brochure. 4 per yr.

**Public Affairs Council**
1601 Eighteenth Street, N.W., Washington, DC
20009.
- Directory of Corporate Urban Affairs Officers.
  irreg., latest issue 1972. ISSN 0090-4066

**Public Affairs Information Service, Inc.**
11 W. 40th St., New York, NY 10018.
- Public Affairs Information Service. Bulletin. 44
  per yr. (cumulated 5 per yr.) ISSN 0033-3409
- Public Affairs Information Service Foreign
  Language Index. q. ISSN 0048-5810

**Public Affairs Research Council of Louisiana**
Box 3118, 300 Louisiana Ave., Baton Rouge, LA
70821.
- P. A. R. Analysis. 8 per yr. ISSN 0030-7807

**Public Choice Society**
- Public Choice. (pub. by Virginia Polytechnic
  Institute and State University. Center for Study of
  Public Choice)

**Public Citizen**
1346 Connecticut Ave N.W., Washington, DC
20036.
- Public Citizen. irreg.

**Public Citizen Platform**
Box 19404, Washington, DC 20036.
- Public Citizen Platform.

**Public Citizen's Tax Reform Research Group**
Box 14198, Ben Franklin Station, Washington, DC
20044.
- People and Taxes. m.

**Public Education Association Information Service**
20 West 40 St., New York, NY 10018.
- P E A Reports. m.

**Public Interest Briefs**
c/o Ed. John Phillips, 10203 Santa Monica Blvd.,
Los Angeles, CA 90067.
- Public Interest Briefs.

**Public Interest Economics Foundation**
1714 Massachusetts Ave. N.W., Washington, DC
20036.
- P I E Newsletter. bi-m.
- Public Interest Economics Review. bi-m.

**Public Issues Research Bureau, Inc.**
290 Madison Ave., New York, NY 10017.
- Editorial Opinion Reports. m.

**Public Law Education Institute**
Suite 610, 1346 Connecticut Ave. N.W.,
Washington, DC 20036.
- Military Law Reporter. 6 per yr.

**Public Library Association**
A Division of the American Library Assn., 50 E.
Huron St., Chicago, IL 60611.
- P L A Newsletter. 4 per yr. ISSN 0022-6998
- Public Library Reporter. irreg. ISSN 0555-6031

**Public Library of Cincinnati and Hamilton County**
800 Vine St., Cincinnati, OH 45202.
- Guide Post. 10 per yr. ISSN 0017-5269

**Public Library of Des Moines**
100 Locust St., Des Moines, IA 50309.
- Des Moines. Public Library. Monthly Memo; a
  timely report to you about business. m. ISSN
  0011-9156

**Public Library of Newark**
Business Library, 34 Commerce St., Newark, NJ
07102.
- Business Literature. 10 per yr., Sep.-Jun. ISSN
  0007-6902

**Public Library of Youngstown and Mahoning County**
305 Wick Ave., Youngstown, OH 44503.
- Public Library of Youngstown and Mahoning
  County. Staff Bulletin. m. ISSN 0033-3573

**Public Relations Aids, Inc.**
221 Park Ave. S., New York, NY 10003.
- P R Aids' Party Line; a weekly roundup of what
  editors in all media need in the way of feature
  and story material. w. ISSN 0030-8226
- Publicist. bi-m.

**Public Relations Board Inc.**
150 East Huron St., Chicago, IL 60611.
- U S /Japan Outlook; digest of American views of
  Japan. s-a. ISSN 0091-407X

**Public Relations Plus, Inc.**
Box 327, Washington Depot, CT 06794.
- T V Publicity Outlets-Nationwide. q. ISSN 0041-
  4514

**Public Relations Society of America, Inc.**
845 Third Ave., New York, NY 10022.
- Channels (New York) m. ISSN 0009-1510
- Public Relations Journal; a journal of opinion in
  the field of public relations practice. m. ISSN
  0033-3670
- Public Relations Register. a; 1972, 23rd ed.

**Public Safety Personnel Research Institute, Inc.**
960 State National Bank Plaza, Evanston, IL 60201.
- Fire Department Personnel Reporter. m.

**Public Service Magazine, Inc.**
1935 County Rd. B-2, Roseville, South Minneapolis,
MN 55113.
- Public Service Magazine. m. ISSN 0033-3778

**Public Service Materials Center**
355 Lexington Ave., New York, NY 10017.
- Where America's Large Foundations Make Their
  Grants; who gets them and how much each
  receives. irreg. ISSN 0083-9167

**Public Services Laboratory**
Georgetown University, Washington, DC 20007.
- Planning, Programming, Budgeting for City, State,
  County Objectives. P P B Note Series. irreg.,
  1971-1972 notes, 12, 13, 14. ISSN 0079-2217

**Public Utilities Reports, Inc**
Suite 502, 1828 L. St, N.W., Washington, DC
20036.
- P. U. R. Executive Information Service. w. ISSN
  0030-8420
- Public Utilities Fortnightly. fortn. ISSN 0033-3808

**Public Works Journal Corporation**
200 South Broad St., Ridgewood, NJ 07451.
- Environmental Wastes Control Manual. a. ISSN
  0071-0946
- Public Works; city, country and state. m. ISSN
  0033-3840
- Street and Highway Manual. a. ISSN 0081-5977
- Water Works Manual. a. ISSN 0083-7717

**Publican**
R.R. 2, Box 49, Brunswick, MO 65236.
- Publican. m.

**Publication House, Inc.**
75 Rockefeller Plaza, New York, NY 10020.
- T V Picture Life. m. ISSN 0039-856X

**Publications for Industry**
21 Russell Woods Rd, Great Neck, NY 11021.
- American Industry. m. ISSN 0002-8908
- Industrial Purchasing Agent. m. ISSN 0019-8641

**Publications Image**
Box B, Seaside Park, NJ 08752.
- Publications Image. q.

**Publications International Ltd.**
3841 W. Oakton, Skokie, IL 60076.
- Consumer Guide Magazine. 36-42 per yr.
- Consumer Guide Magazine: Auto. 6 per yr. ISSN 0097-8337
- Consumer Guide Magazine: Stereo & Tape Equipment Test Reports. q. ISSN 0097-8957
- Consumer Guide Photo Annual. a.

**Publications Planning**
176 Alexander St., Princeton, NJ 08540.
- Dairy Industry News. fortn. ISSN 0011-5649

**Publications South, Inc.**
500 Plasamour Drive N.E., Box 13449, Atlanta, GA 30324.
- Pecan South. 6 per yr.

**Publicity Club of Boston**
Box 445, Prudential Center Station, Boston, MA 02199.
- Bell Ringer. 10 per yr. ISSN 0005-8572

**Publishers Advertising Co.**
220 S. State St., Chicago, IL 60604.
- Graphic Arts Trade Directory and Register. a. ISSN 0072-5498

**Publishers Development Corp.**
8150 N. Central Park, Skokie, IL 60076.
- American Handgunner. bi-m.
- Arts and Activities; creative activities for the classroom. m.(Sept-June) ISSN 0004-3931
- Guns; finest in the firearms field. m. ISSN 0017-5676
- Shooting Industry. m. ISSN 0037-4148

**Publisher's Inc.**
243 12th St., Drawer P, Del Mar, CA 92014.
- Armchair Detective; a quarterly journal devoted to the appreciation of mystery, detective and suspense fiction. q. ISSN 0004-217X

**Publishers' Information Bureau Inc.**
575 Lexington Ave., New York, NY 10022.
- P I B Monthly Service/Leading National Advertisers Monthly Service; magazine advertising expenditures. m. ISSN 0030-7998

**Publishers Printing House, Inc.**
P.O. Box 109, Berne, IN 46711.
- United States Volleyball Association. Official Volleyball Guide and Rule Book. a. ISSN 0083-3592

**Publishers Professional Services**
109 W. Mercer St., Seattle, WA 98119.
- Northwest Construction News Daily. d.
- Northwest Construction News Weekly. w.
- Pacific Builder and Engineer. s-m. ISSN 0030-8544
- Seattle Business. bi-m. ISSN 0037-0444 (Seattle Chamber of Commerce)

**Publishers Service Inc.**
8060 Melrose Ave., Los Angeles, CA 90046.
- Adam; the man's home companion. m. ISSN 0001-8007
- Knight; the magazine for the adult male. bi-m. ISSN 0023-2262

**Publishing Associates**
10169 Sherman Rd., Chardon, OH 44024.
- Quest (Chardon); a publication for collectors who like adventure and exploration with their collecting. m. ISSN 0033-6319

**Publishing Center for Cultural Resources**
27 W. 53 St., New York, NY 10019.
- Crafts Annual. a.

**Publishing Center, Inc.**
560 Cook Rd., Detroit, MI 48236.
- Book Review Magazine. bi-w.
- Book Review Newsletter. m.

- Quarterly Review of Biography. q.
- Quarterly Review of European Books. q.

**Publishing Dynamics, Inc.**
209 Dunn Ave., Stamford, CT 06905.
- Industrial Gas. m. ISSN 0019-834X
- Industrial Gas Energy Newsletter. fortn.

**Publishing Sciences Group, Inc.**
162 Great Rd., Acton, MA 07120.
- A M A Drug Evaluations. irreg. ISSN 0065-9304 (American Medical Association)
- Critical Issues Series. irreg. (Washington Journalism Center)

**Pubsun Corp.**
1251 Ave. of the Americas, New York, NY 10020.
- Independent Film Journal; trade paper for exhibitors of motion pictures. fortn. ISSN 0019-3712

**Pueblo Education Association, Inc.**
Suite G, 710 W. Fourth St., Pueblo, CO 81003.
- This & That. fortn.

**Pueblo of Zuni**
Box 338, Zuni, NM 87327.
- Zuni Newsletter. bi-w.

**Puerto Rican Solidarity Community**
P.O. Box 319, Cooper Station, New York, NY 10003.
- Puerto Rico Libre. m.

**Fred C. Pugarelli, Ed. & Pub.**
436 Pau St., Suite 6, Honolulu, HI 96815.
- Waikiki News. m.

**Puget Sound Maritime Historical Society**
2161 E. Hamlin St., Seattle, WA 98102.
- Sea Chest. q.

**Pullen Walker Publishing Co.**
8206 South Cottage Grove Avenue, Chicago, IL 60619.
- Mstique; magazine of the new generation black female. m.

**Pullman Standard**
200 S. Michigan Ave., Chicago, IL 60604.
- Carbuilder. q.

**Pulp**
720 Greenwich St. Apt. 4H, New York, NY 10028.
- Pulp. q.

**Pulp Era Press**
413 Ottokee St., Wauseon, OH 43567.
- First Fandom Magazine. 2 per yr.
- Pulp Era. irreg. ISSN 0033-4111

**Punk Publications, Inc.**
Box 675, New York, NY 10009.
- Punk. m.

**Punto de Contacto-Point of Contact, Inc.**
110 Bleeker St., 16B, New York, NY 10012
- Point of Contact/Punto de Contacto. q. (Subscr. Address: Ibero-American Language and Area Center (N.Y.U.), 566 Waverly, New York, N. Y. 10003)

**Puppeteers of America**
c/o Don Avery, Ed., 2015 Novem Dr., Fenton, MO 63026.
- Puppetry Journal. 6 per yr. ISSN 0033-443X

**Purchasing Agents Association of Rochester**
1070 Sibley Tower, Rochester, NY 14604.
- Purchasing Professional. m.

**Purchasing and Management Personnel**
- Southern Purchasor. (pub. by Purchasing Management Association of Carolinas-Virginia, Inc.)

**Purchasing Management Association**
412 W. 6th St., Los Angeles, CA 90014.
- Golden West Purchasor. m. ISSN 0017-162X

**Purchasing Management Association of Alabama**
930 N. 6th Ave., Birmingham, AL 35203.
- Alabama Purchasor. m. ISSN 0002-4325

**Purchasing Management Association of Arizona**
4019 W. Las Palmaritas Dr., Phoenix, AZ 85021.
- Arizona Purchasor. m.

**Purchasing Management Association of Boston, Inc.**
185 Devonshire St., Boston, MA 02110.
- New England Purchaser/Connecticut Purchaser. m.

**Purchasing Management Association of Buffalo, Inc.**
c/o Donald W. Boyd, Jr., 802 Kenmore Ave., Buffalo, NY 14216.
- Niagara Frontier Purchaser. m. ISSN 0048-0320

**Purchasing Management Association of Carolinas-Virginia, Inc.**
102 N. Elm St., Suite 914, Greensboro, NC 27401.
- Southern Purchasor. bi-m. ISSN 0049-1624 (Purchasing and Management Personnel)

**Purchasing Management Association of Chicago**
201 N. Wells, Chicago, IL 60606.
- Chicago Purchasor. m. ISSN 0009-367X

**Purchasing Management Association of Cincinnati, Inc.**
1631 Central Ave., Cincinnati, OH 45214.
- Cincinnati Purchasor. m. ISSN 0009-6903

**Purchasing Management Association of Cleveland, Inc.**
1501 Euclid Ave., Cleveland, OH 44115.
- Midwest Purchasing. m. ISSN 0047-7311

**Purchasing Management Association of Florida, Inc.**
Box 1858, Jacksonville, FL 32201.
- Florida Purchaser. m. ISSN 0015-4245

**Purchasing Management Association of Indianapolis, Inc.**
527 Glendale Bldg., 6100 N. Keystone Ave., Indianapolis, IN 46220.
- Hoosier Purchasor. m. ISSN 0018-4799

**Purchasing Management Association of Kansas City**
- Heart of America Purchaser. (pub. by Halgo Publishing Inc.)

**Purchasing Management Association of Louisville**
3415 Bardstown Rd., Box 18204, Louisville, KY 40218.
- Kentuckiana Purchasor. m. ISSN 0023-0073

**Purchasing Management Association of Northern California, Inc.**
9 First St., San Francisco, CA 94105.
- Pacific Purchasor. m. ISSN 0030-8846

**Purchasing Management Association of Oregon**
519 S.W. 3rd Ave., Portland, OR 97204.
- Oregon Purchasor. m. ISSN 0030-4786

**Purchasing Management Association of Philadelphia, Inc.**
1518 Walnut St., Philadelphia, PA 19102.
- Philadelphia Purchasor. m. ISSN 0031-7322

**Purchasing Management Association of Syracuse and Central New York**
1106 Burnett Ave., Syracuse, NY 13203.
- Purchasor. m. ISSN 0033-4499

**Purchasing Management Association of Tulsa**
- Mid-Continent Purchaser. (pub. by Halgo Publishing Inc.)

**Purchasing Management Association of Washington, Inc.**
Box 9038, Seattle, WA 98109.
- Washington Purchaser. m. ISSN 0043-0706

**Purchasing Management Associations of New York and New Jersey**
510 Adeline St., Trenton, NJ 08611.
- Metropolitan Purchaser. m.

**Purchasing Management Associations of Texas, Louisiana and New Mexico**
- Southwest Business. (pub. by Southwestern Purchaser, Inc.)

**Purdue Alumni Association**
Memorial Union Bldg, West Lafayette, IN 47907.
- Purdue Alumnus. 9 per yr. (Sep.-Jul.) ISSN 0033-4502

**Purdue Musical Organizations**
Edward C. Elliott Hall of Music, Purdue Univ., W. Lafayette, IN 47907.
- P. M. O. Notes. bi-m. ISSN 0030-8153

**Purdue Opinion Panel**
Measurement & Research Center, Purdue University
AGA 1, Lafayette, IN 47907.
- Purdue Opinion Panel, Lafayette, Indiana. Report.
irreg., vol. 33, 1974. ISSN 0079-807X

**Purdue University. Agricultural Experiment Station**
West Lafayette, IN 47907.
- Indiana. Agricultural Experiment Station.
Inspection Report. irreg. ISSN 0073-6783
- Indiana. Agricultural Experiment Station.
Research Bulletin. irreg., 12-15 per yr. ISSN
0073-6791
- Purdue Agriculture Reports. q. (prep. by its
Cooperative Extension Service)

**Purdue University. Department of Agricultural
Economics**
Krannert Bldg., West Lafayette, IN 47907.
- Keeping Track, Current News from the
Department of Agricultural Economics at Purdue.
a. ISSN 0075-5303

**Purdue University. Dept. of English**
West Lafayette, IN 47907.
- Modern Fiction Studies; a critical quarterly
devoted to criticism, scholarship and bibliography
of American, English and European fiction since
about 1880. 4 per yr. ISSN 0026-7724

**Purdue University Libraries and Audio Visual Center**
West Lafayette, IN 47907.
- Pulse (Lafayette) 6 per yr. ISSN 0033-4170

**Purdue University. Materials Research Business
Office**
West Lafayette, IN 47907.
- Materials Research in Science and Engineering at
Purdue University. Progress Report. a. ISSN
0079-8126 (Advanced Research Projects Agency)

**Purdue University. Office of Manpower Studies**
West Lafayette, IN 47907.
- Purdue University. Office of Manpower Studies.
Manpower Report. irreg., no. 74-3, 1974. ISSN
0079-8134

**Purdue University. School of Civil Engineering**
West Lafayette, IN 47907.
- Conference on Land Surveying, Purdue
University. Proceedings. a. ISSN 0069-8571
- Environmental Engineering Newsletter. m.
- Industrial Waste Conference, Purdue University,
Lafayette, Indiana. Proceedings. a. ISSN 0073-
7682 (Distr. by: Ann Arbor Science Publishers,
Inc., Ann Arbor, MI 48106)
- Purdue Air Quality Conference. Proceedings. a.
- Purdue University. Civil Engineering Reprints.
irreg., no. 303, 1976. ISSN 0079-8096
- Purdue University. Engineering Experiment
Station. Joint Highway Research Project.
Research Reports. irreg., no. 36, 1976. ISSN
0079-810X (prep. by its Joint Highway Research
Project) (Co-Sponsor: Indiana State Highway
Commission)
- Purdue University. Road School. Proceedings of
Annual Road School. a. ISSN 0079-8142

**Purdue University. School of Electrical Engineering**
West Lafayette, IN 47907.
- Purdue University. School of Electrical
Engineering. Annual Research Summary. a. ISSN
0033-4537

**Purdue University. School of Pharmacy**
W. Lafayette, IN 47907.
- Purdue Pharmacist. 4 per yr.(Sept-June) ISSN
0033-4529

**Purdue University. Undergraduates of the University**
Box 651, Stewart Center, West Lafayette, IN 47907.
- Purdue Engineer. 6 per yr. ISSN 0033-4510

**Put Money in the Bank Refunders Bulletin**
Box 260a, R.R. 3, Bellefronte, PA 16823.
- Put Money in the Bank Refunders Bulletin. m.

**Putman Publishing Co.**
430 N. Michigan Ave., Chicago, IL 60611.
- Baking Industry. m. ISSN 0005-416X
- Chemical Processing. m. ISSN 0009-2630
- Food Equipment. q.
- Food Processing. m. ISSN 0015-6523
- What's New in Chemical Processing Equipment.
q. ISSN 0511-8654

**Putman Publishing Company**
111 East Delaware, Chicago, IL 60611.
- New Perspectives on Black America. irreg.

**G. P. Putnam's Sons**
200 Madison Ave., New York, NY 10016.
- Book Collectors' Handbook of Values. irreg.

**Pyramid Books**
757 Third Ave., New York.
- Analog Annual. a. ISSN 0362-7403

**Pyramid Publications, Inc.**
(Subsidiary of: Harcourt, Brace, Jovanovich)
757 Third Ave., New York, NY 10017.
- Basketball Stars. a. ISSN 0585-0258
- Hockey Stars. a. ISSN 0073-2869
- New Ideas for Hair Styling. bi-m.
- Sports Stars. 6 per yr. ISSN 0038-8246

**Pyro Press Publications**
Box 12010, Lexington, KY 40511.
- American Pyrotechnist Fireworks News. m.

**Quad Publications**
159 W. 33rd St., Room 1010, New York, NY
10001.
- Caribbeat; the magazine of reggae, calypso,
steelpan and spooze. m.

**Quaker Oats. Corporate Affairs Department**
Chicago, IL 60654.
- Interim. bi-m.

**Quaker Theological Discussion Group**
Route 1, Alburtis, PA 18011.
- Quaker Religious Thought. irreg. ISSN 0033-5088

**Quaker Yeomen**
Box 1791, Portland, OR 97207.
- Quaker Yeomen. q.

**Qualified Remodeler, Inc.**
333 N. Michigan Ave., Suite 2714, Chicago, IL
60601.
- Qualified Remodeler. 9 per yr. ISSN 0098-9207

**Quantum Science Corp.**
245 Park Ave., New York, NY 10017.
- Annual A.D.A.P.S.O. Industry Report. a. ISSN
0098-8324 (Association of Data Processing
Service Organizations)
- Annual Industry Survey of Computer Services
Industry. a. ISSN 0066-3999 (Association of Data
Processing Service Organizations)
- Remote Computing Directory. irreg. ISSN 0098-
0722

**Quapaw Quarter Association**
Box 1104, Little Rock, AR 72203.
- Quapaw Quarter Chronicle. bi-m.

**Quarter Century Wireless Association, Inc.**
1409 Cooper Drive, Irving, TX 75061.
- Q C W A News. q.
- Quarter Century Wireless Association Year-Book;
amateur radio. biennial.

**Quarter Racing Publishers, Inc.**
Box 2473, Fort Worth, TX 76101.
- Quarter Racing Record; the magazine of Quarter
Horse Racing. m. ISSN 0091-7516

**Quarter Racing World, Inc.**
Box 1000, Norman, OK 73070.
- Speedhorse. m.

**Quarterly Review of Literature**
26 Haslet Ave., Princeton, NJ 08540.
- Quarterly Review of Literature. 2 per yr. ISSN
0033-5819

**Quartet**
1119 Neal Pickett Dr., College Station, TX 77840.
- Quartet; a magazine of the arts. q. ISSN 0033-
586X

**Queen of All Hearts**
40 So. Saxon Ave., Bay Shore, NY 11706.
- Queen. bi-m. ISSN 0033-6017 (Montfort
Missionaries)

**Queens Borough Public Library**
89-11 Merrick Blvd., Jamaica, NY 11432.
- Queens Borough Public Library News. irreg.

**Queens Botanical Garden Society Inc**
43-50 Main St., Flushing, NY 11355.
- Gardens on Parade. q. ISSN 0016-4666

**Queens Chamber of Commerce**
24-16 Bridge Plaza S., Long Island City, NY 11101.
- Queensborough. m. ISSN 0033-6068

**Queens College**
see under **City University of New York**

**Queens College Press**
Flushing, NY 11367.
- Dada/Surrealism. a. ISSN 0084-9537 (Association
for the Study of Dada & Surrealism)
- Interpretation; a journal of political philosophy. 3
per yr. ISSN 0020-9635
- Language and Style; an international journal. q.
ISSN 0023-8317 (City University of New York,
Queens College. Department of English)
- Shout in the Street; journal of literary and visual
art. 3 per yr. ISSN 0363-079X (City University of
New York, Queens College. Department of
English)
- Yiddish. q.

**Queens Council on the Arts. Literary Arts Division**
161-04 Jamaica Ave., Jamaica, NY 11432.
- Source. s-a.

**Queens County Bar Association**
90-35 148 St., Jamaica, NY 11435.
- Queens County Bar Association. Queens Bar
Bulletin. 8 per yr. ISSN 0048-6302

**Quest (Washington, D.C.)**
P.O. Box 8843, Washington, DC 20003.
- Quest (Washington, D.C.); a feminist quarterly. q.

**Quest Productions**
1809 Nichols Rd., Kalamazoo, MI 49007.
- American Institute for Exploration. Expedition
Field Reports. a. (Co-Sponsors: American
Heritage Research (California), Exploration Club
of Hokkaido University (Japan))
- American Institute for Exploration. Occasional
Contributions. irreg. (approx. 1-2 per yr.)
- American Institute for Exploration. Reprint Series.
irreg. (approx. 1-2 per yr.)
- World Explorations. irreg.; (approx. 1 per yr.)
(American Institute for Exploration) (Co Sponsor:
World Explorations Program of Richard Williams)

**Quest Publication**
Box 1988, Ann Arbor, MI 48106.
- Michigan Adventures. q.

**Quest Publishing**
853 Williamson St., Madison, WI 53703.
- Beyond Mars. irreg.

**Quest Publishing Co.**
Box 4141, Diamond Bar, CA 91765.
- Guide to Biomedical Standards. a. ISSN 0085-
1353
- Newsletter of Biomedical Safety & Standards. m.
ISSN 0048-0282

**Quick Books**
Box 4434, Boulder, CO 80306.
- Look Quick. irreg.

**Quickenings in Trillum Land**
4344 S.W. Concord, West Seattle, WA 98136.
- Quickenings in Trillum Land. q.

**Quiet Birdmen**
19 Church St., Berea, OH 44017.
- Q B Beam. m. ISSN 0033-4774

**Quigley Publishing Co.**
159 W. 53 St., New York, NY 10019.
- International Motion Picture Almanac; reference
tool of the film industry. a. ISSN 0074-7084
- International Television Almanac. a. ISSN 0539-
0761
- Motion Picture Product Digest. fortn.

**Quill & Scroll Society**
School of Journalism, Univ. of Iowa, Iowa City, IA
52242.
- Quill and Scroll. 4 per yr. ISSN 0033-6505
(International Honorary Society for High School
Journalists)

**Quiltmakers Time**
Ed. Sally Goodspeed, 521 Orkney Rd., Baltimore, MD 21212.
● Quiltmakers Time. irreg.

**Quincy College**
Quincy College, Quincy, IL 62301.
● Quincy College Bulletin. 5 per yr. ISSN 0033-6556

**Quinlan Publishing Co. Inc.**
88 Broad St., Boston, MA 02110
(and 191 High St., Boston, MA 02110)
● Narcotics Law Bulletin. m.
● School Law Bulletin. m.
● Search and Seizure Bulletin. m. ISSN 0037-0193
● Zoning Bulletin. m.

**Quinn Publications, Inc. (Compton)**
Box 6040, Compton, CA 90224
(Subscr. address: Box 267, Mt. Morris, IL 61054)
● Custom Bike. m.
● Cycle Guide. m. ISSN 0011-4278
● Cycle Guide Road Test Annual. a. ISSN 0590-4641

**Quinn Publications, Inc. (Ft. Worth)**
3339 W. Freeway, Ft. Worth, TX 76107.
● Bicycle Journal. m. ISSN 0006-2065
● Outdoor Power Equipment. m.

**Quirk's Reviews**
74 Charles St., New York, NY 10014.
● Quirk's Reviews. s-m.

**Quiz-Set Publishing Co.**
Box 8084, Chicago, IL 60680.
● American Black Directory. a. ISSN 0364-0833

**R A Productions, Inc.**
Box 9100, Boston, MA 02114.
● Boston Bruins Official Yearbook. a. ISSN 0361-6398

**R. & B Enterprises**
P.O. Box 328, Plymouth Meeting, PA 19462.
● I T E M. (Interference Technology Engineers Master) a. (Robar Industries, Inc.)

**R & D Press**
Box 1226, 885 North San Antonio Rd, Los Altos, CA 94022.
● Information Access Series. irreg.

**R. & W. Management Co. Inc.**
1028 Connecticut Ave. N.W., Washington, DC 20036.
● Club Executive. m. ISSN 0009-9554

**R C A**
*see* Radio Corporation of America

**R-C Modeler Corp.**
171 W. Sierra Madre Blvd., Sierra Madre, CA 91024.
● R-C Modeler. m. ISSN 0033-6866

**R C P Publications, Inc.**
P.O. Box 3486, Merchandise Mart, Chicago, IL 60654.
● Revolution. m.

**R C Publications, Inc.**
6400 Goldsboro Road, N.W., Washington, DC 20034.
● Best in Advertising Campaigns. a. ISSN 0360-8263
● Best in Annual Reports. a. ISSN 0360-8743
● Best in Covers. a. ISSN 0361-2066
● Best in Environmental Graphics. a. ISSN 0360-8271
● Best in Packaging. a. ISSN 0360-8689
● Best in Posters. a. ISSN 0360-8085
● 37 Design & Environment Projects. a. ISSN 0363-9525

**R. C. Publications, Inc. (New York)**
355 Lexington Ave., New York, NY 10017.
● Print; American's graphic design magazine. bi-m. ISSN 0032-8510
● Urban Design; the interprofessional magazine for architects, engineers, city planners, landscape architects, designers. q.

**R D Communications**
Box 683, Ridgefield, CT 06877.
● Plastics in Building Construction. m.

**R F D**
4525 Wolf Creek Rd., Wolf Creek, OR 97497.
● R F D. q.

**R G H Publishing Corp.**
235 Park Ave. S., New York, NY 10003.
● Master Detective. m. ISSN 0025-5017
● Official Detective Stories. m. ISSN 0030-0306
● True Detective. m. ISSN 0041-350X

**R. H. M Associates Inc.**
840 Willis Ave., Albertson, NY 11507.
● R H M Warrant and Stock Survey Plus Stocks Under Ten. w.

**R L D Group, Inc.**
2602 Gross Point Rd., Evanston, IL 60201.
● Mobile Home Merchandiser. m.

**R N Publications**
(Subsidiary of: Medical Economics Co.)
550 Kinderkamack Rd., Oradell, NJ 07649.
● Nursing Opportunities. a.

**R P C Publications**
P.O.B. 296, Godfrey, IL 62035.
● Railway Passenger Car Annual. a.

**R.S.H. Publications**
710 Roeder Rd. 1005, Silver Spring, MD 20910.
● C S Journal. m.

**R S H Publications Worldwide**
818 Roeder Rd., Suite 302, Silver Spring, MD 20910.
● C S Journal; the Christian magazine people bank on. m. ISSN 0360-4055

**R S T Corp.**
501 S. Fairfax Ave. No. 204, Los Angeles, CA 90036.
● Southern California Guide; the current directory of restaurants, hotels, motels, entertainment, sightseeing, tourist attractions. m. ISSN 0038-3902

**R T S Music Gazette**
711 W. 17th St., Building G-1, Costa Mesa, CA 92627.
● R T S Music Gazette. m.

**R T T Y Journal**
Box 837, Royal Oaks, MI 48068.
● R T T Y Journal. m. ISSN 0033-7161

**R.V.K. Publishing Co**
Box 264, Menomonee Falls, WI 53051.
● Poetry: People. irreg. (1-2 per yr)

**R. W. Beck and Associates**
200 Tower Bldg, Seattle, WA 98101.
● R.W. Beck and Associates' Newsletter; engineers and consultants. q. ISSN 0033-7188

**R X Golf and Travel, Inc.**
447 S. Main, Hillsboro, IL 62049.
● R X Sports and Travel; the recreation and leisure magazine for physicians. bi-m. ISSN 0033-720X

**Rabbi Isaac Elchanan Theological Seminary**
Student Organization of Yeshiva, 2540 Amsterdam Ave., New York, NY 10033.
● Gesher. irreg. (1-2 per yr.) ISSN 0016-9145

**Rabbinical Alliance of America**
156 Fifth Ave., New York, NY 10010.
● Perspective (New York); journal of Torah Hashkafah. s-a.

**Rabbinical Assembly**
3080 Broadway, New York, NY 10027.
● Conservative Judaism. s-a. ISSN 0010-6542 (Co-sponsor: Jewish Theological Seminary of America)
● Rabbinical Assembly, New York. Proceedings. a. (suspended 1970-1973) ISSN 0079-936X

**Rabbinical Council of America**
220 Park Ave. S., New York, NY 10003.
● Hadorom. s-a. ISSN 0017-6532
● Tradition; a journal of orthodox Jewish thought. q. ISSN 0041-0608

**Racing Pictorial Magazine**
Ed. Ray Mann, Box 500 B, Indianapolis, IN 46206.
● Racing Pictorial Magazine. q.

**Racquet and Paddle Publications, Inc.**
370 Seventh Ave., New York, NY 10001.
● Paddle World; the magazine for platform tennis players. 5 per yr.

**Radcap Inc.**
Box 96, Wall St. Sta., New York, NY 10005.
● Professional Tape Reader. m.

**Radcliffe College. Alumnae Association**
10 Garden St., Cambridge, MA 02138.
● Radcliffe Quarterly. q. ISSN 0033-7528

**Radiation Shielding Information Center**
Oak Ridge National Laboratory, Box X, Oak Ridge, IN 37830.
● R S I C Newsletter. m.

**Radical America**
Box B, Cambridge, MA 02140.
● Radical America. bi-m.

**Radical Education Project**
Box 561a, Detroit, MI 48232.
● Something Else. bi-m(5 per yr) ISSN 0038-1330

**Radical Jewish Union**
300 Eshleman Hall, University of Calif., Berkeley, CA 94720.
● Jewish Radical. 4 per yr. ISSN 0047-200X

**Radical Therapist, Inc.**
Box 89, W. Somerville, MA 02144.
● R T: a Journal of Radical Therapy. irreg.(approx. 6 per yr.)

**Radicals Against Poverty**
Box 736, New York, NY 10009.
● R A P. m. ISSN 0033-6742

**Peter Radielovic, Ed. & Pub.**
Box 3025, Arcadia, CA 91006.
● American Croat/Americki Hrvat. q. (Croatian Information Service)

**Radio Amateur Callbook, Inc.**
925 Sherwood Drive, Lake Bluff, IL 60044.
● Foreign Radio Amateur Callbook Magazine. a. ISSN 0015-7260
● Radio Amateur Callbook Magazine; United States listings. a. ISSN 0033-7706

**Radio and Television Weekly**
254 W. 31st St., New York, NY 10001.
● Radio and Television Weekly; electronic parts, accessories. w. ISSN 0033-7765

**Radio Club of America, Inc.**
Box 2112, Grand Central Station, New York, NY 10017.
● Radio Club of America. Proceedings. irreg. ISSN 0033-779X

**Radio Corporation of America Broadcast Systems**
Bldg. 2-2A, Camden, NJ 08102.
● R C A Broadcast News. q.

**Radio Corporation of America. Corporate Engineering Services**
2-8 Camden, Camden, NJ 08110.
● R C A Engineer. bi-m. ISSN 0048-6574

**Radio Corporation of America Laboratories**
Princeton, NJ 08540.
● R C A Review. q. ISSN 0033-6831

**Radio Corporation of America. Technical Services Training**
600 North Sherman Drive, Indianapolis, IN 46201.
● R C A Plain Talk and Technical Tips. irreg. ISSN 0048-6582

**Radio Technical Commission for Aeronautics**
Suite 655, 1717 H St., N.W., Washington, DC 20006.
● Radio Technical Commission for Aeronautics. Proceedings of the Annual Assembly Meeting. a.

**Radio Television News Directors Association**
1735 DeSales St. N.W., Washington, DC 20036.
● R T N D A Communicator. m. ISSN 0033-7153

**Radiological Society of North America, Inc.**
One MONY Plaza, Syracuse, NY 13202.
● Radiology; a monthly journal devoted to clinical radiology and allied sciences. m. ISSN 0033-8419

**Radius Group Inc.**
408 W. 57th St., New York, NY 10019.
- Arts Management. 5 per yr. ISSN 0004-4067

**Radix (Berkeley)**
Box 4307, Berkeley, CA 94704.
- Radix (Berkeley) 10 per yr.

**Rag Collective**
2330 Guadalupe, Austin, TX 78705.
- Rag. fortn. ISSN 0033-8621

**Lawrence Ragan Communications, Inc.**
South Dearborn St., Chicago, IL 60605.
- Ragan Report; a weekly survey of ideas and methods for communication executives. w.

**Rags**
46 Grand St., New York, NY 10013.
- Rags. m.

**Norman W. Raies**
3435 N.E. Broadway, Portland, OR 97232.
- Chain Saw Age. m. ISSN 0009-093X

**Rail-Europe**
Box 3255, Alexandria, VA 22302.
- Baxter's Eurailpass Travel Guide. a.
- Baxter's U.S.A. Bus Travel Guide. a.
- Baxter's U.S.A. Train Travel Guide. a.

**Rail Travel News**
Box 9007, Berkeley, CA 94709.
- Rail Travel News. s-m.

**Railroad Enthusiasts, New York Division, Inc.**
Box 1318 Grand Central Sta., New York, NY 10017.
- Railroad Enthusiasts. New York Division. Bulletin. m.

**Railroad Research Information Service**
2101 Constitution Ave., N.W., Washington, DC 20418.
- Railroad Research Bulletin. s-a. ISSN 0097-0042

**Railroad Station Historical Society**
- Railroad Station Historical Society. Bulletin. (pub. by J-B Publishing Co.)
- Railroad Station Historical Society. Railroad Station Monograph. (pub. by J-B Publishing Co.)

**Railroad Yardmasters of America**
1411 Peterson Ave., Park Ridge, IL 60068.
- Railroad Yardmaster. 8 per yr. ISSN 0033-8796

**Railway and Locomotive Historical Society**
c/o John H. White, Ed., Smithsonian Institution, Div. of Transportation, Washington, DC 20560
- Railroad History. s-a. ISSN 0090-7847 (Subscr.to: Samuel J. Gilfix, 11 Burbank Rd., Medford, MA 02155)

**Railway Equipment and Publication Co.**
424 W. 33rd St., New York, NY 10001.
- Sound Approach to the Railroad Market. a. ISSN 0362-8213

**Railway Fuel and Operating Officers Association**
10414 S. Wood St, Chicago, IL 60643.
- Modern Locomotive Handbook. irreg.
- Railway Fuel and Operating Officers Association. Proceedings. a. ISSN 0079-9521

**Railway Tie Association**
314 N. Broadway, St. Louis, MO 63102.
- Cross Ties. m.

**Rain Umbrella, Inc.**
2270 N.W. Irving, Portland, OR 97210.
- Rain; journal of appropriate technology. m.

**Rainbow Press**
1332 Riverside Drive, New York, NY 10033.
- Mysterious Barricades. s-a.

**Rainforth Foundation**
- Comparative Juridical Review. (pub. by Pan American Institute of Comparative Law)

**Raivaaja Publishing Co.**
811 Main St., Fitchburg, MA 01420.
- Raivaaja/Pioneer. w. (Finnish American League for Democracy)

**Rajo Publications, Inc.**
P.O. Box 1014, Grass Valley, CA 95945.
- Family Food Garden. 10 per yr.

**Ramco Publishing Co**
287 E. Sixth St, St. Paul, MN 55101.
- Minnesota Sheriff. q. ISSN 0026-5683 (Minnesota State Sheriffs Association)

**Ramcon, Inc.**
223 Scott St., Memphis, TN 38112.
- Environmental Control News for Southern Industry. m. ISSN 0013-9238

**Rancho Santa Ana Botanic Garden**
Claremont, CA 91711.
- Aliso. a. ISSN 0065-6275

**Rand Corporation**
1700 Main St., Santa Monica, CA 90406.
- Rand Report Series. irreg.
- Selected Rand Abstracts; to provide a timely and comprehensive index-guide to the Rand Corporation unclassified publications. q. ISSN 0037-1343

**Rand McNally & Co.**
8225 N. Central Pk., Skokie, IL 60076
(Orders to: Box 7600, Chicago, IL 60680)
- Guide to Canada. a.
- Key to American Bankers Association Routing Numbers. a.
- Rand McNally Campground and Trailer Park Guide. a. ISSN 0079-9610
- Rand McNally Commercial Atlas and Marketing Guide. a.
- Rand McNally Discover Historic America. a. ISSN 0079-9637
- Rand McNally National Park Guide. a. ISSN 0079-9629
- South American Handbook. a. ISSN 0081-2579

**Randall Publishing Co.**
Box 2029, Tuscaloosa, AL 35401.
- Who's Who Among Music Students in American High Schools; a biographical dictionary of outstanding music students in American high schools. irreg. ISSN 0362-3750
- Who's Who Among Students in American Universities and Colleges. a., 41st 1975.
- Who's Who Among Students in American Vocational and Technical Schools. a. ISSN 0360-5248

**Randolph-Macon College**
Ashland, VA 23005.
- Randolph-Macon College. Bulletin. 7 per yr.

**Random House**
201 East 50th St., New York, NY 10022.
- Book Angles. q. ISSN 0045-2505
- China Reader. irreg.
- Contemporary Jewish Civilization Series. irreg.
- Studies in Modern Societies. irreg.

**Random Lengths Publications, Inc.**
Box 867, Eugene, OR 97401.
- Random Lengths; a weekly report on lumber and plywood markets. w.
- Random Lengths Export Market Report; a bi-weekly report on export markets for forest products. fortn.
- Random Lengths Yearbook. a. ISSN 0485-9960

**Rangefinder Publishing Co.**
3511 Centinela Ave., Los Angeles, CA 90066.
- Rangefinder. m. ISSN 0033-9202

**Rankin County News**
Brandon, MS 39042.
- Mississippi Legion-Aire. m. ISSN 0026-6299 (American Legion, Department of Mississippi)

**William E. Rapfogel, Ed. & Pub.**
110 East 23rd St., New York, NY 10010.
- Jewish People. w.

**Rapistan, Inc.**
Grand Rapids, MI 49505.
- Rapid Handler. every 8 weeks. ISSN 0033-9261

**Rapport Publishing Co., Inc.**
6311 Yucca St., Hollywood, CA 90028.
- West Coast Review of Books. bi-m.

**Rare-Earth Information Center**
Iowa State University, Ames, IA 50011.
- R I C News. q. (prep. by its Energy and Mineral Resources Research Institute)

**Rare Journeys, Inc.**
Box 8088, Richmond, VA 23223.
- Rare Journeys. bi-m.

**Rational Transportation**
4215-37th St. N.W., Washington, DC 20008.
- Rational Transportation. m.

**Rationalist Association, Inc.**
Box 994, St. Louis, MO 63188.
- American Rationalist. bi-m. ISSN 0003-0708

**Raunchy Rock Publishing**
Box 254, Totowa, NJ 07511.
- Raunchy Rock. m.

**Raven Press**
1140 Ave. of the Americas, New York, NY 10036.
- Advances in Biochemical Psychopharmacology. irreg; vol. 15, 1976. ISSN 0065-2229
- Advances in Cyclic Nucleotide Research. irreg; vol. 7, 1976. ISSN 0084-5930
- Advances in Cytopharmacology. irreg; vol. 2, 1974. ISSN 0084-5949
- Advances in Neurology. irreg; vol. 16, 1977. ISSN 0091-3952
- Advances in Pain Research and Therapy. irreg.
- Advances in Prostaglandin and Thromboxane Research. irreg; vol. 2, 1976.
- Aging. irreg; vol. 3, 1976.
- American Journal of E E G Technology. q. ISSN 0002-9238 (American Society of Electroencephalographic Technologists)
- Association for Research in Nervous and Mental Disease. Proceedings of the Association. a.
- Association for Research in Nervous and Mental Disease. Research Publications. a.
- Atherosclerosis Reviews. a.
- Carcinogenesis. irreg.
- Clinical Neuropharmacology. irreg.
- Epilepsia. q. ISSN 0013-9580 (International League against Epilepsy)
- European Organization for Research on Treatment of Cancer. Monograph Series. irreg; vol. 2, 1976.
- Frontiers in Neuroendocrinology. irreg; vol. 4, 1976. ISSN 0532-7466
- International Brain Research Organization. Monograph Series. irreg; vol. 2, 1976.
- Journal of Computer Assisted Tomography; a radiological journal dedicated to the basic and clinical aspects of transmission and emission reconstructive tomography. q. ISSN 0363-8715
- Journal of Cyclic Nucleotide Research. m. ISSN 0095-1544
- Kroc Foundation Series. irreg; vol. 7, 1977.
- Mario Negri Institute for Pharmacological Research. Monographs. irreg., no. 8, 1975. ISSN 0085-3100
- Miles International Symposium Series. irreg; no. 9, 1976.
- Nutrition and the Brain. irreg; vol. 2, 1977.
- Princeton Conference on Cerebrovascular Diseases. irreg; no. 10, 1976.
- Progress in Cancer Research and Therapy. irreg; vol. 3, 1977.
- Progress in Chemical Fibrinolysis and Thrombolysis. irreg; vol. 2, 1976.
- Progress in Prostaglandin Research. irreg.
- Reviews of Neuroscience. irreg; vol. 2, 1976.
- Society of General Physiologists Series. a.

**Ravenswood Post**
640 Roble Ave., Menlo Park, CA 94025.
- Ravenswood Post. w.

**Ravenswood Publishing Co**
166 N. 87th, Wauwatosa, WI 53226.
- Yesterday; when life was simpler and happier. bi-m. ISSN 0049-8297

**Allen Raymond, Inc.**
11 Hale Lane, Darien, CT 06820
(Subscription Address: Box 1069, Skokie, IL 60076)
- Early Years; a magazine for teachers of preschool through grade three. m (9 per yr.) ISSN 0094-6532
- Early Years Parent. q. in 1976, m. from 1977.

**Raymond International Inc.**
Box 22718, Houston, TX 77027.
- Foundation Facts. 2 per yr. ISSN 0015-8933 (International Society for Soil Mechanics and Foundation Engineering)

**Raymond Lee Organization, Inc.**
230 Park Avenue, New York, NY 10017.
- Innovation World. q. ISSN 0046-9564

**Rayon Publishing Corp.**
303 Fifth Ave., New York, NY 10016.
● American Association for Textile Technology.
  Technical Review and Register. a. ISSN 0065-
  7069
● Modern Knitting Management. bi-m. ISSN 0026-
  7899
● Modern Textiles Magazine. m. ISSN 0026-8488

**Raytheon Co.**
Lexington, MA 02173.
● Electronic Progress. q. ISSN 0013-4961

**La Raza Associates**
Ed. Raul Ruiz, Box 31004, Los Angeles, CA 90031.
● Raza. m. ISSN 0034-0219

**Reader**
Box 80803, San Diego, CA 92138.
● Reader; San Diego's weekly. w.

**Readers Digest Association, Inc.**
Pleasantville, NY 10570
● Reader's Digest. m. ISSN 0034-0375 (Braille &
  Talking Book Editions:, American Printing House
  for the Blind, 1839 Frankfort Ave., Louisville, KY
  40206)
● Reader's Digest Almanac and Yearbook. a. ISSN
  0079-9831

**Readex Microprint Corp.**
101 Fifth Ave., New York, NY 10003.
● Readex Microprint Publications. a. ISSN 0079-
  984X

**Reading Reform Foundation**
7054 E. Indian School Rd., Scottsdale, AZ 85253.
● Reading Informer. irreg. (4-5 per yr.)

**Real Estate Forum, Inc.**
30 E. 42nd St., New York, NY 10017.
● Real Estate Forum. m. ISSN 0034-0707
● Realty Roundup. w.

**Real Estate News Inc.**
720 S. Dearborn St., Chicago, IL 60605.
● Real Estate News. w.

**Real Estate Success Secrets**
c/o Bob Barriskill, Box 4939, Walnut Creek, CA
94596.
● Real Estate Success Secrets. m.

**Real Property Inventory of Metropolitan Cleveland**
608 the Arcade, Cleveland, OH 44114.
● Sheet-A-Week. w. ISSN 0037-3427

**Real Resources Group**
13920 McClellan Blvd., Box A, Reno, NV 89506.
● American Boating. m.
● American Collector. m.
● Autoweek/Competition Press. w. ISSN 0005-1802

**Real World**
29 West 10 St., New York, NY 10011.
● Real World. q.

**Realist**
595 Broadway, New York, NY 10012.
● Realist. 6 per yr. ISSN 0034-091X

**Realities Library**
Box 33512, San Diego, CA 92103.
● Seven Stars Poetry. 6 per yr.

**Realities Series**
Box 453, Marina, CA 93933.
● Realities Series. irreg.

**Reality Evangelism**
Box 979, Washington, DC 20044.
● Reality Magazine. m. ISSN 0034-0987

**Reason Enterprises**
Box 40105, Santa Barbara, CA 93103.
● Reason. m. ISSN 0048-6906

**Rebirth, Inc.**
233 Bay State Rd., Boston, MA 02215.
● Genesis 2. m. ISSN 0016-6669 (Jewish Student
  Projects of Greater Boston, Inc.)

**Reblooming Iris Reporter**
1 Fairview Ave., Staten Island, NY 10314.
● Reblooming Iris Reporter. s-a. ISSN 0034-1134

**Record Handbook**
P. O. Box 1382, Highland Park, NJ 08904.
● Record Handbook. irreg. ISSN 0080-0279

**Record Publishing Co.**
750 Old Main St., Rocky Hill, CT 06067.
● Commercial Record. w. ISSN 0010-3098

**Record Publishing Co. (Dallas)**
c/o Mrs. John C. Leslie, Drawer 5770, Dallas, TX
75222.
● Insurance Record. fortn. ISSN 0020-4803

**Record Publishing, Inc.**
Box 11788, Lexington, KY 40512.
● Thoroughbred Record and the Racing Calendar.
  w. ISSN 0040-6414

**Record Research**
65 Grand Ave., Brooklyn, NY 11205.
● Blues Research. irreg., no. 17, 1975.
● Record Research; the magazine of record statistics
  and information. bi-m (approx.) ISSN 0034-1592

**Record Stockman Inc.**
105 Livestock Exchange Bldg., Denver, CO 80216.
● Record Stockman. w. ISSN 0034-1614

**Record World Publishing Co. Inc.**
1700 Broadway, New York, NY 10019.
● Record World. w. ISSN 0034-1622

**Recorded Sound Research**
1506 W. Barker, Peoria, IL 61606.
● Record Collector's Source Book. irreg.

**Recorder Group Publications, Inc.**
340 Main Street, Worcester, MA 01608.
● Worcester Recorder and Labor News. w.

**Recorder Review**
A. Nitka, 166 W. 48th St., New York, NY 10036.
● Recorder Review. irreg. ISSN 0361-5855

**Recording and Broadcasting Publications**
1850 N. Whitley Ave., Suite 220, Box 2449,
Hollywood, CA 90028.
● Broadcast Programming and Production. bi-m.

**Recording Engineer-Producer**
Box 2449, 1850 Whitley, No. 220, Hollywood, CA
90068.
● Recording Engineer-Producer. bi-m. ISSN 0034-
  1673

**Recording for the Blind**
215 East 58th St., New York, NY 10028.
● Recording for the Blind. Catalog of Recorded
  Books. biennial. ISSN 0484-1506

**Recordkeeper Tax Publications, Inc.**
48 West 21st. St., New York, NY 10010.
● Automatic Taxfinder and Tax Preparer's
  Handbook. irreg. ISSN 0092-6876

**Recreation Consultants**
Box 842, Seattle, WA 98111.
● Bicycle Paper. m. (April-Sept.); plus winter issue.

**Recreational Vehicle Dealers of America**
● N.A.D.A. Recreation Vehicle Appraisal Guide.
  (pub. by National Automobile Dealers
  Association)

**Red Angus Association of America**
Box 776, Denton, TX 76201.
● American Red Angus. m.

**Red Cloud Indian School, Inc.**
Pine Ridge, SD 57770.
● Red Cloud Country. q. ISSN 0300-6344

**Red Dust Inc.**
218 East 81st St., New York, NY 10028.
● Red Dust; new writing. a.

**Red Hill Press**
6 San Gabriel Drive, Fairfax, CA 94930.
● Invisible City. 3-4 per yr.

**Red Poll Cattle Club of America**
3275 Holdrege St., Lincoln, NE 68503.
● Red Poll News. s-a. ISSN 0034-2033

**Red River Valley Historical Association**
c/o Museum and Archives of the Red River Valley,
601 N. 16th St., Durant, OK 74701.
● Red River Valley Historical Journal of World
  History. q. ISSN 0362-6547
● Red River Valley Historical Review. q.

**Red Weather**
Box 1104, Eau Claire, WI 54701.
● Red Weather; poems, translations, essays, reviews.
  3 per yr.

**Redbook Publishing Co.**
230 Park Ave., New York, NY 10017.
● Redbook. m. ISSN 0034-2106
● Redbook's Be Beautiful. s-a.
● Redbook's Easy Decorating. s-a.
● Redbook's Young Mother. 3 per yr.

**Redemptorist Fathers**
Liguori, MO 63057.
● Liguorian. m. ISSN 0024-3450

**Redemptorist Fathers of New York**
● Perpetual Help World. (pub. by Perpetual Help
  Center)

**Redgrave Information Resources**
Sylvan Rd., Westport, CT 06880.
● Contributions in the History of Science. irreg.
  ISSN 0084-9286

**Redgrave Publishing Co.**
(Subsidiary of: Docent Corp.)
430 Manville Rd., Pleasantville, NY 10570.
● Medical Anthropology (Pleasantville); cross-
  cultural studies in health and illness. q.
● Psychocultural Review; interpretations in the
  psychology of art, literature and society. q.
● Quarterly Review of Film Studies. q.
● Review of Education. bi-m. ISSN 0098-5597
● Reviews in Anthropology. bi-m. ISSN 0093-8157
● Wall Street Review of Books; a quarterly review.
  q. ISSN 0091-1526
● Yale Italian Studies. q.

**Reds Alert**
Box 525, Shelbyville, KY 40065.
● Reds Alert. w.

**Redwood Empire Dental News**
3920 Princeton Dr., Santa Rosa, CA 95405.
● Redwood Empire Dental News. m. ISSN 0034-
  2173

**Stanley Foster Reed, Ed. & Pub.**
Box 36, McLean, VA 22101.
● Directors & Boards; journal of corporate action. q.

**Thomas Reed, Ed. & Pub.**
Box 207, Purdin, MO 64674.
● Musical Six-Six Newsletter. s-a.

**Reed Printing and Publishing Co.**
Box 83, R.No.1, Carlos, IN 47329.
● Doll Collector. m. ISSN 0012-5210

**Reese Publishers**
Box 614, Albertville, AL 35950.
● Alabama's Distinguished. biennial.

**Reese Publishing Co. Inc.**
235 Park Ave. S., New York, NY 10003.
● Pro-Sports. q. ISSN 0032-9126
● Sport World. bi-m. ISSN 0038-7940
● Super Sports. 6 per yr. ISSN 0039-5684
● Teen Pin-Ups. q. ISSN 0040-201X
● Woman. bi-mo. ISSN 0043-7239

**Reference & Index Services**
1935 N. Capitol Ave., Indianapolis, IN 46202.
● Keyword Index in Internal Medicine. s-a. ISSN
  0097-0220

**Reformed Church in America**
● Church Herald. (pub. by Church Herald Inc.)

**Reformed Ecumenical Synod**
1677 Gentian Drive SE, Grand Rapids, MI 49508.
● R E S News Exchange. m. ISSN 0033-6904
● R E S Theological Forum. q.
● R E S World Diaconal Bulletin. q.

**Regiment Publications**
Gallery Three Enterprises, P. O. Box 247, Grand
Central Station, New York, NY 10017.
● Gay Scene. m. ISSN 0016-5298

**Regional Institute of Social Welfare Research**
- Regional Institute of Social Welfare Research. Annual Report. (pub. by University of Georgia. School of Social Work)

**Regional Plan Association, Inc.**
235 East 45th St., New York, NY 10017.
- Regional Plan Association Library Acquisitions. bi-m. ISSN 0300-6441
- Regional Plan News. ISSN 0034-3374
- Region's Agenda. m. ISSN 0034-3420

**Regional Science Association**
3718 Locust Walk, University of Pennsylvania, PA 19174.
- Regional Science Association. Newsletter. 3 per yr.
- Regional Science Association. Papers. s-a. ISSN 0486-2902

**Regional Science Research Institute**
Box 8776, Philadelphia, PA 19101.
- Journal of Regional Science. 3 per yr. ISSN 0022-4146
- Regional Science Research Institute, Philadelphia. Bibliography Series. irreg. ISSN 0080-0619
- Regional Science Research Institute, Philadelphia. Discussion Paper Series. irreg. ISSN 0485-8255
- Regional Science Research Institute, Philadelphia. Monograph Series. irreg. ISSN 0080-0627

**Regional Studies Association**
- Regional Studies. (pub. by Pergamon Press Inc.)

**Regional Training Directors Association**
170 Sigourney St., Hartford, CT 06105.
- Training Directors Newsletter. m. ISSN 0041-0888

**Regular Baptist Press**
1300 North Meacham Rd., Box 95500, Schaumburg, IL 60195.
- Baptist Bulletin. m. ISSN 0005-5689 (General Association of Regular Baptist Churches)

**Regular Common Carrier Conference**
ATA 1616 P St., N.W., Washington, DC 20036.
- Highway Common Carrier Newsletter. fortn. ISSN 0018-1706

**Rehabilitation Institute of Oregon**
Div. of Good Samaritan Hospital & Medical Center, 2010 N.W. Kearney, Portland, OR 97209.
- R I O Newsletter. q. ISSN 0033-6963

**Rehabilitation International**
432 Park Avenue South, New York, NY 10016.
- International Rehabilitation Review. q. ISSN 0020-8477
- International Seminar on Special Education. Proceedings. irreg.; latest issue, Australia, 1972. ISSN 0074-7939 (Dist. by: Rehabilitation International Information Service, Box 101 409, 6900 Heidelberg 1, B.R.D., W. Germany)

**Rehabilitation International USA**
20 West 40th St., New York, NY 10018.
- Rehabilitation/World; U.S. journal of international news and information. q. ISSN 0360-0726

**Rehabilitation Psychology**
Box 26034, Tempe, AZ 85282.
- Rehabilitation Psychology. q.

**Reilly-Lake Shore Graphics**
812 W. Van Buren St., Chicago, IL 60607.
- Newspaper Requirements. irreg., 1973, 19th ed. (Electrographic Corp.)

**Reilly Publishing Co.**
216 W. Higgins Rd., Park Ridge, IL 60068.
- Medical Electronics and Equipment News. 6 per yr.

**Reinhardt-Keymer Publishing Co., Inc.**
60 E. 42nd St., Suite 1026, New York, NY 10017.
- Health Care Education. q.
- Sales Training; management/marketing/supervision. bi-m.

**Reinhold Publishing Co., Inc.**
(Subsidiary of: Penton-IPC)
600 Summer St., Stamford, CT 06904.
- Air Transport World. m. ISSN 0002-2543
- Chemical Engineering Catalog. a.
- H P A C Info-Dex. (Heating/Piping/Air Conditioning Mechanical Systems Information Index) a.
- Heating, Piping & Air Conditioning. m. ISSN 0017-940X
- Materials Engineering. m. ISSN 0025-5319
- Materials Selector. a. ISSN 0465-2886
- Progressive Architecture. m. ISSN 0033-0752
- Used Equipment Directory. m.

**J. Reisinger, Ed. & Pub.**
1020 Central Ave., Sparta, WI 54656.
- Lost in Canada; Canadian-American query exchange. q. ISSN 0362-4293

**Otto F. Reiss Co.**
243 E. 39th St., New York, NY 10016.
- Art and Archaeology Newsletter. q. ISSN 0004-2986

**Release the World for Christ Foundation**
Suite 1509, 600 Jefferson, Houston, TX 77002.
- Far East Reporter (Houston)

**Releim Publishing Corp.**
161 E. Erie St., Chicago, IL 60611.
- Fling. bi-m.

**Relief for Africans in Need in the Sahel**
475 Riverside Drive, Room 560, New York, NY 10027.
- R A I N S Newsletter. m.

**Religion and Society Inc.**
P.O. Box 244, Stillwater, MN 55082.
- St. Croix Review. bi-m. ISSN 0093-2582

**Religion Newswriters Association**
140 Meisner Ave., Staten Island, NY 10306.
- R N A Newsletter. bi-m. ISSN 0034-4109

**Religious & Theological Abstracts Inc.**
Myerstown, PA 17067.
- Religious & Theological Abstracts. q. ISSN 0034-4044

**Religious Book Review Press, Inc.**
19 Franklin St., Williston Park, NY 11596.
- Religious Book Review. q. ISSN 0008-7939

**Religious Education Association**
409 Prospect St., New Haven, CT 06510.
- Religious Education; a platform for the free discussion of issues in the field of religion and their bearing on education. bi-m. ISSN 0034-4087

**Religious Liberty Publishing Association**
1151 Xenia St., Denver, CO 80220.
- Sabbath Watchman. m. ISSN 0098-9517

**Religious Publishing Co.**
198 Allendale Rd., King of Prussia, PA 19406.
- Your Church. bi-m. ISSN 0049-8394

**Religious Research Association**
Box 228, Cathedral Sta., New York, NY 10025.
- Review of Religious Research. 3 per yr. ISSN 0034-673X

**Relim Publishing Company, Inc.**
1485 Bayshore Blvd., Box 400, San Francisco, CA 94124.
- Macho. bi-m.

**Remember When**
Box 34305, Dallas, TX 75234.
- Remember When. m.

**Remington Review, Inc.**
505 Westfield Ave., Elizabeth, NJ 07208.
- Remington Review. s-a.

**Renacimiento, Inc.**
915 N. Washington Ave, Lansing, MI 48902.
- Renacimiento; el periodico hispano mas grande de Michigan. bi-m.

**Renaissance House**
Box 292, Village Station, New York, NY 10014.
- Gayellow Pages; classified directory of gay U. S. A. organizations and businesses. s-a. ISSN 0363-826X

**Renaissance Society of America**
1161 Amsterdam Ave., New York, NY 10027.
- Renaissance Quarterly. q. ISSN 0034-4338

**Renfro Valley Press**
Renfro Valley, KY 40473.
- Renfro Valley Bugle. m. ISSN 0034-4451

**Renown Publications Inc.**
Box 69150, Los Angeles, CA 90069.
- Mike Shayne Mystery Magazine. m. ISSN 0026-3621

**Rensselaer Polytechnic Institute**
Troy, NY 12181.
- At Rensselaer. 5 per yr.
- Polytechnic. w. ISSN 0032-4051
- Rensselaer Engineer; technical journal of the Students of the Rensselaer Polytechnic Institute. q. ISSN 0034-4508

**Rensselaer Polytechnic Institute. Center for Urban and Environmental Studies**
Troy, NY 12181.
- Intersections; a journal of urban and environmental studies. s-a. ISSN 0095-6945

**Rensselaerville Historical Society**
Box 8, Rensselaerville, NY 12147.
- Rural Folio. q.

**Reorganized Church of Jesus Christ of Latter Day Saints**
- Daily Bread. (pub. by Herald Publishing House)
- Saints' Herald. (pub. by Herald Publishing House)

**Reparation Society of the Immaculate Heart of Mary, Inc.**
Fatima House, 100 E. 20th St., Baltimore, MD 21218.
- Fatima Findings; the smallest newspaper on earth for the greatest cause in heaven. m. ISSN 0014-8830

**Repartee**
c/o Milbish Pute, Box 3232-a, Birmingham, AL 35205.
- Repartee. irreg.

**Repertoire Internationale d'Iconographie Musicale. Research Center for Musical Iconography**
- R I d I M-R C M I Newsletter. (pub. by City University of New York. Research Center for Musical Iconography)

**Replay Publishing**
23065 Leonora Dr., Woodland Hills, CA 91364.
- Replay; a professional publication for the music/amusement industry. m. ISSN 0360-7348

**Reporter Publishing Co. (San Francisco)**
1366 Turk St., San Francisco, CA 94115.
- California Voice. w.
- Sun Reporter. w.

**Reporters Committee for Freedom of the Press**
Rm. 1211, 1750 Pennsylvania Ave., N.W., Washington, DC 20006.
- Press Censorship Newsletter. 9 per yr.

**Reporting on Governments, Inc.**
2 Fifth Ave., New York, NY 10011.
- Reporting on Governments; weekly analysis of highest-grade bond and money markets, monetary and fiscal policies, the economic outlook and interest rate trends. w. ISSN 0034-4834

**Reports Corp.**
1 Bond St., Chatham, NJ 07928.
- Constructioneer; news-photo coverage of construction in New York, Pennsylvania, New Jersey, Delaware. fortn. ISSN 0010-6968
- Constructioneer Directory. a.

**Reports, Inc.**
Kent, CT 06757.
- Report on Credit Unions. m.

**Republic National Life Insurance Co.**
3988 N. Central Expressway, Dallas, TX 75204.
- What's News in Reinsurance. ISSN 0043-4612

**Republican Delta**
P.O. Box 550, Buckhannon, WV 26201
(Subscr. to: P.O. Box 3191, Charleston, WV 26201)
- West Virginia Legionnaire. m. (American Legion. Department of West Virginia)

**Republican Journal**
66 High St., Belfast, ME 04915.
- Republican Journal. w. ISSN 0034-5075

**Republican National Committee**
310 First St., S.E., Washington, DC 20003.
- First Monday. m.

- Republican Almanac. irreg. ISSN 0363-9290 (prep. by its Political/Research Division)

**Research and Development Associates for Military Food & Packaging Systems Inc.**
Rm. 1315, 90 Church St., New York, NY 10007.
- Research & Development Associates for Military Food and Packaging Systems. Activities Report. s-a.

**Research & Documentation Corp.**
14 Plaza Rd., Greenvale, NY 11548.
- Monthly Digest of Legal Articles. m. ISSN 0027-0350

**Research and Review Service of America, Inc.**
3500 Depauw Blvd., Box1727, Indianapolis, IN 46206.
- Fraternal Monitor. (pub. by Newkirk Associates)
- Handbook of Servicemen's and Veterans Benefits. (pub. by Newkirk Associates)
- R and R Magazine. m. ISSN 0033-6823
- Social Security Handbook. irreg. ISSN 0081-0495

**Research Center for Religion & Human Rights in Closed Societies**
475 Riverside Dr., New York, NY 10027.
- R C D A-Religion in Communist Dominated Areas. bi-m. ISSN 0034-3978

**Research Company of America**
654 Madison Ave., New York, NY 10021.
- Brewing Industry Survey. a. ISSN 0068-0958

**Research Corporation**
405 Lexington Ave., New York, NY 10017.
- Research Corporation Quarterly Bulletin. q. ISSN 0486-4867

**Research Group, Inc.**
Box 7187, Charlottesville, VA 22906.
- Maryland Researcher; an analysis and digest of recent Maryland case law. m. ISSN 0047-6099
- Massachusetts Researcher; an analysis and digest of recent Massachusetts case law. m. ISSN 0047-6153
- Michigan Researcher; an analysis and digest of recent Michigan case law. m. ISSN 0047-7133
- North Carolina Researcher; an analysis and digest of recent North Carolina case law. m. ISSN 0048-0665
- Pennsylvania Researcher; an analysis and digest of recent Pennsylvania case law. m. ISSN 0048-3249
- Personal Injury Researcher; a digest of recent state and federal case law. m. ISSN 0048-3435
- Supreme Court Researcher; an analysis and digest of recent supreme court case law. m. ISSN 0049-2612
- Tennessee Legislative Researcher. s-m.
- Virginia Researcher; an analysis and digest of recent Virginia case law. m. ISSN 0049-6499

**Research in Electrocardiology, Inc.**
Box 923B, San Diego, CA 92109.
- Journal of Electrocardiology. q. ISSN 0022-0736

**Research in Psychotherapy**
c/o Ernst G. Beier, Department of Psychology, University of Utah, Salt Lake City, UT 84112.
- Research in Psychotherapy. irreg. ISSN 0486-4999

**Research Institute of America**
111 Radio Circle, Mt. Kisco, NY 10549.
- Marketing for Sales Executives. m. ISSN 0047-6013

**Research Institute of America, Inc.**
Research Institute Bldg., 589 Fifth Ave., New York, NY 10017.
- Personal Report for the Executive. fortn. ISSN 0048-3443
- Personal Report for the Professional Secretary. fortn.
- R I A Tax Guide Developments. fortn.
- Research Institute of America. Research Institute Recommendations. w. ISSN 0048-7317
- Tax Coordinator. w. ISSN 0039-999X
- Your Business and the Law; simplified guide to your common legal problems. fortn. ISSN 0093-3503

**Research Press Co.**
2612 N. Mattis Ave., Champaign, IL 61820.
- Law and Behavior. q.

**Research Publications**
Box 92, Cedar Falls, IA 50613.
- Master's Theses in Education. a. ISSN 0076-5112

**Researched News and Commentary**
Box 9461, Roslyn Station, Arlington, VA 22209.
- Researched News and Commentary. fortn.

**Reserve Forces Benefit Association**
Chamber of Commerce Bldg., Baltimore, MD 21202.
- Reservist. q.

**Reserve Officers Association of U.S.**
1 Constitution Ave. N.E., Washington, DC 20002.
- Officer. m. ISSN 0030-0268

**Reserve Research, Ltd.**
63 Wall St., New York, NY 10005.
- Powell Monetary Analyst. fortn.

**Resist**
763 Massachusetts Ave., Room 4, Cambridge, MA 02139.
- Resist Newsletter. m. ISSN 0034-558X

**Herbert Resnick**
P.O. Box 52, Farmington, CT 06032.
- Connecticut Construction. q.

**Resophonic Echoes**
R.R.1, Madill, OK 73446.
- Resophonic Echoes. bi-m.

**Resort Management, Inc.**
Box 4169, Memphis, TN 38104.
- Resort Management; the national magazine for resort operators. m. ISSN 0034-5636

**Resource Publications**
Box444, Saratoga, CA 95070.
- Modern Liturgy. 8 per yr.

**Resources for the Future, Inc.**
1755 Massachusetts Ave. N.W., Washington, DC 20036.
- Governance of Metropolitan Regions. Series. (pub. by Johns Hopkins University Press)
- Resources. 3 per yr. ISSN 0048-7376

**Restaurant Association of Metro Washington**
Suite 1295, 5454 Wisconsin Ave., Washington, DC 20015.
- Restaurateur. m.

**Restaurant Association of the State of Washington**
722 Securities Bldg., Seattle, WA 98101.
- Restaurant News and Hotel Magazine of Washington State. m. ISSN 0034-5776

**Restaurant Business Inc.**
633 Third Ave., New York, NY 10017.
- Institutional Distribution. m. ISSN 0020-3572
- Restaurant Business. m. ISSN 0097-8043

**Reston Publishing Company, Inc.**
11480 Sunset Hills Rd., Reston, VA 22090.
- Reston Series in Construction Technology. irreg.

**Resumen**
613 S.W. 4 St., Miami, FL 33130.
- Resumen; bimestral de arte y cultura. bi-m. ISSN 0034-5865

**Retail Clerks International Association**
Suffridge Bldg., Washington, DC 20006.
- Retail Clerks Advocate. bi-m. ISSN 0034-6039

**Retail Directions, Inc.**
48 E. 43 St., New York, NY 10017.
- Department Store Economist. 8 per yr.

**Retail Gasoline Dealers Association of Monroe, Wayne, Ontario & Livingston Counties**
c/o Julian S. Underhill, Ed., 1315 East Ridge Road, Rochester, NY 14621.
- R G D A News. m.

**Retail Grocers Association**
2812 W. 47 St, Suite D, Kansas City, MO 66103.
- Kansas City Grocer. m. ISSN 0022-8516
- Kansas City Grocer Annual Food Industry Directory. a.

**Retail Grocers Association of Arizona**
- Arizona Grocer. (pub. by Arizona Grocers Publishing Co. Inc)

**Retail Reporting Bureau**
101 Fifth Ave., New York, NY 10003.
- Costume Jewelry Review. s-m.
- Executive Mens Advertising Service; men's wear advertising mat service. s-a.
- Men's Art Service. q. ISSN 0025-942X
- Menswear Advertising. s-m.
- Plan Ahead. 4 per yr. ISSN 0032-0587
- Retail Advertising Week. w. ISSN 0034-5997
- Shoes on Parade. w. ISSN 0037-4083
- Store Planning Service. m. ISSN 0039-1859
- Views & Reviews. w. ISSN 0042-5915

**Retail Wholesale and Department Store Union**
AFL-CIO, 101 W. 31st St., New York, NY 10001.
- R W D S U Record. m. ISSN 0033-7196

**Retail Wholesale, Chain Store Food Employees Union. Local 338**
1790 Broadway, New York, NY 10019.
- Three Hundred Thirty-Eight News; labor monthly of the food service industry. bi-m. ISSN 0040-6546

**Retailer and Marketing News**
c/o Michael J. Anderson, Ed., Box 57194, Dallas, TX 75207.
- Retailer and Marketing News. m.

**Reticuloendothelial Society**
c/o Ed. Quentin N. Myrvik, Dept. of Microbiology, Bowman-Gray School of Medicine, Winston-Salem, NC 27103.
- Reticuloendothelial Society. Journal. m (2 vols. per year) ISSN 0033-6890

**Retired Officers' Association**
1625 Eye St., N.W., Washington, DC 20006.
- Retired Officer. m. ISSN 0034-6160

**Retirement Living Publishing Co.**
150 E. 58th St., New York, NY 10022.
- Retirement Living. m. ISSN 0090-4910

**A. Retlaw & Associates**
1633 Orrington Ave., Suite 2080, Evanston, IL 60201.
- Osteopathic Medicine. m. ISSN 0363-7360 (American College of General Practioners in Osteopathic Medicine and Surgery)

**Retreading Consultant Services, Inc.**
Box 17203, Louisville, KY 40217.
- Retreader's Journal; a technical digest for tire retreaders. m. ISSN 0557-644X

**Fleming H. Revell Co.**
Old Tappan, NJ 07675.
- Tarbell's Teacher's Guide; to the International Bible Lessons for Christian teaching of the uniform course. a. ISSN 0082-1713

**Revenue Sharing Advisory Service**
2120 L St., N.W., Suite 210, Washington, DC 20037.
- Revenue Sharing Bulletin. m.

**Revere Publishing, Inc.**
Box 344, West Nyack, NY 10994.
- Sports Car. m. ISSN 0300-6387 (Sports Car Club of America)

**Reverend Oblate Fathers**
1749 Grand Ave, Carthage, MO 64836.
- Roses and Gold from Our Lady of the Ozarks. m. ISSN 0035-8320

**Review and Herald Publishing Association**
6856 Eastern Ave., N.W., Washington, DC 20012.
- Advent Review and Sabbath Herald; general church paper of the Seventh-Day Adventists. w.
- Insight (Washington); a magazine of Christian understanding for young Adventists. w. ISSN 0020-1944 (General Conference of Seventh-Day Adventists)
- Journal of Adventist Education. 5 per yr. ISSN 0021-8480 (General Conference of Seventh Day Adventists)
- Liberty; a magazine of religious freedom. bi-m. ISSN 0024-2055 (International Religious Liberty Association)
- Life and Health. m. ISSN 0024-3035

**Review for Religious**
612 Humboldt Bldg., St. Louis, St. Louis, MO 63103.
- Review for Religious. bi-m. ISSN 0034-639X

**Review la Bouche**
615 Paris Court, Columbia, MO 65201.
• Review la Bouche. s-a.

**Review of the News Inc.**
395 Concord Ave., Belmont, MA 02178.
• Review of the News. w. ISSN 0034-6802

**Review Publishing Co., Inc**
Travelers Bldg, Box 100, Richmond, VA 23201.
• Virginia Municipal Review; the municipal officials magazine. m. ISSN 0042-6660

**Rexair Inc,**
Box 287, Detroit, MI 43231.
• Rexevents. m. ISSN 0035-4422

**Rexall Drug Co.**
3901 N. Kingshighway, St. Louis, MO 63115.
• Rexall Reporter. q. ISSN 0035-4414

**Reynolds Publishing Co., Inc.**
Box 578, Glen Echo, MD 20768.
• Public Works News. w.
• Washington Atomic Energy Report. s-m.

**Rhea, Greiner & Co., Inc.**
Box 1061, Colorado Springs, CO 80901.
• Dow Theory Comment. fortn. ISSN 0012-575X

**Rho Pi Phi International Pharmaceutical Fraternity**
c/o Murray Wolfe, Santa Pharmaceuticals, 3435 Bailey Ave., Buffalo, NY 14215.
• Rope News. q. ISSN 0035-824X

**Rhode Island. Department of Economic Development**
One Weybosset Hill, Providence, RI 02903.
• Rhode Island Directory of Manufacturers.
• This Is Rhode Island. biennial.

**Rhode Island. Department of Education**
199 Promenade St., Providence, RI 02908.
• Education in Rhode Island. m.
• Rhode Island. Department of Education. Statistical Table. a.

**Rhode Island. Department of Employment Security**
24 Mason St., Providence, RI 02903.
• Rhode Island. Departments of Labor & Employment Security. Employment Bulletin. m. ISSN 0035-4600

**Rhode Island. Department of Health**
101 Health Bldg., Davis St., Providence, RI 02908.
• Rhode Island. Department of Health. Vital Statistics. a.

**Rhode Island. Department of Mental Health, Retardation and Hospitals**
Aime J. Forand Bldgs., 600 New London Ave., Cranston, RI 02920.
• Rhode Island. Department of Mental Health, Retardation and Hospitals. Mental Health, Retardation and Hospitals. a. ISSN 0094-291X

**Rhode Island. Department of State Library Services**
95 Davis St., Providence, RI 02908.
• Rhode Island. Department of State Library Services. Newsletter. m. ISSN 0035-4597

**Rhode Island. Manpower Planning Council**
Providence, RI 02900.
• Rhode Island Comprehensive Manpower Plan. irreg. ISSN 0095-2745

**Rhode Island. State Library**
State House, Documents Division, Providence, RI 02903.
• Rhode Island. State Library. Check-List of Publications of State Agencies. biennial.

**Rhode Island Agricultural Experiment Station**
Woodward Hall, Kingston, RI 02881.
• Rhode Island Resources. q. ISSN 0035-4635 (University of Rhode Island. Cooperative Extension Service)

**Rhode Island Bar Association**
17 Exchange St., Providence, RI 02903.
• Rhode Island Bar Journal. m. Oct.-Jun.

**Rhode Island College**
Providence, RI 02908.
• Folio (Providence) q.

**Rhode Island College Alumni Association**
600 Mt. Pleasant Ave., Providence, RI 02908.
• Rhode Island College Alumni Association. Alumni Review. q.

**Rhode Island Education Association**
300 Hennessey Ave., North Providence, RI 02911.
• Rhode Island Education Association. Journal. a. ISSN 0080-2751

**Rhode Island Historical Society**
52 Power St., Providence, RI 02906.
• Rhode Island History. q. ISSN 0035-4619

**Rhode Island Jewish Historical Association**
130 Sessions St., Providence, RI 02906.
• Rhode Island Jewish Historical Notes. a. (approx.) ISSN 0556-8609

**Rhode Island Library Association**
13 Summer St., Pawtucket, RI 02860.
• Rhode Island Library Association. Bulletin. m. (except Aug.)

**Rhode Island Medical Society**
106 Francis St., Providence, RI 02903.
• Rhode Island Medical Journal. m. ISSN 0035-4627

**Rhode Island School of Design**
Museum of Art, Providence, RI 02903.
• Museum Notes. a. ISSN 0027-4097

**Rhode Island School of Design. Student Board**
Box F-7, RISD, 2 College Street, Providence, RI 02903.
• R I S D Press. w.

**Rhode Island State Council on the Arts**
4365 Post Rd., E. Greenwich, RI 02818.
• Rhode Island State Council on the Arts. Report. a. ISSN 0363-8774

**Rhode Island State Dental Society**
c/o 565 Hope Street, Bristol, RI 02809.
• Rhode Island State Dental Society. Journal. q. ISSN 0035-4643

**Rhode Island Statewide Planning Program**
Room 201, 265 Melrose St., Providence, RI 02907.
• Rhode Island Statewide Planning Program Monthly Progress Report. m. ISSN 0300-6468

**Rhode Island Yearbook Foundation, Inc.**
1 Peck Ave, Riverside, RI 02915.
• Rhode Island Yearbook. a. ISSN 0080-2816

**Rhodes Publishing Co., Inc.**
1724 Dallas Dr., Suite 7, Box 15686, Baton Rouge, LA 70895.
• Louisiana Motor Transport Association News. m. ISSN 0024-6883

**Rhodesian Information Office**
2852 McGill Terrace N.W., Washington, DC 20008.
• Rhodesian Viewpoint. s-m. ISSN 0035-4899

**Rhythm**
859 1/2 Hunter St. N.W, Atlanta, GA 30314.
• Rhythm. q. ISSN 0048-8240

**Milton Riback, Inc.**
20 E. 35th St., New York, NY 10016.
• Plus-Profit Publicity; the public relations viewsletter. 10 per yr. ISSN 0300-7731

**Rican Journal Inc.**
Box 11039, Chicago, IL 60611.
• Rican; a journal of contemporary Puerto Rican thought. q. ISSN 0048-8259

**Rice Journal Enterprises**
Box 14260, Washington, DC 20003.
• Rice Journal. m. ISSN 0035-4961

**Rice University**
Houston, TX 77001.
• Austrian History Yearbook. a. ISSN 0067-2378 (Co-Sponsor: Conference Group for Central European History)
• Studies in English Literature 1500-1900. q. ISSN 0039-3657

**Rice University. History Department**
Fondren Library, Box 1892, Houston, TX 77001.
• Rice University Studies; writings in all scholarly disciplines. q. ISSN 0035-4996

**Rice University. Program of Development Studies**
121 Sewall Hall, Houston, TX 77001.
• Rice University. Program of Development Studies. Discussion Papers. irreg. (approx 12-16 per yr)

**Rich Publishing, Inc.**
Box 555, Temecula, CA 92390.
• Horse & Rider. m. ISSN 0018-5159
• Horse & Rider All-Western Yearbook. a.

**Richard and Co.**
Drawer 999, New Bus Terminal Bldg., Middlesboro, KY 40965.
• Independent Coal Operator. m. ISSN 0019-3682

**Richards Industries, Inc.**
Affiliate of Richards Industries, Inc., 407 Blade St., Cincinnati, OH 45216.
• Tennis for Travelers. a. ISSN 0082-2825

**Richards, Lawrence & Co.**
Box 2311, Van Nuys, CA 91404.
• Foreign Projects Newsletter; a biweekly advance summary of significant capital expansion projects and economic development programs outside u.s.a. fortn. ISSN 0015-7244

**Richards Rosen Press**
29 E. 21 St., New York, NY 10010.
• Careers in Depth. irreg. ISSN 0069-0449
• Enjoying the Arts. irreg.
• Military Research Series. irreg. ISSN 0076-8774
• Science Student Explores. irreg.
• Social Studies Student Investigates. irreg.
• Student Journalist Guide Series. irreg. ISSN 0081-6078
• Theatre Student Series. irreg. ISSN 0082-3848

**Richardson Heritage Society**
Box 123, 944 South G. St., Broken Bow, NE 68822.
• Richardson Family Researcher and Historical News. q.

**Paul Richmond and Co.**
1100 Glendon Avenue, Los Angeles, CA 90024.
• South Pacific Travel Digest. a. (Co-sponsors: Australian Tourist Commission; New Zealand Government Tourist Office, Fiji Visitors Bureau, New Caledonia Tourist Bureau)

**Richmond Chamber of Commerce**
201 E. Franklin St., Richmond, VA 23219.
• Greater Richmond Chamber of Commerce. Research Bulletin. m. ISSN 0035-5100

**Richmond County Historical Society**
c/o Augusta College Library, 2500 Walton Way, Augusta, GA 30904.
• Richmond County History. s-a. ISSN 0035-5119

**Richmond Heights General Hospital**
27100 Chardon Rd., Cleveland, OH 44143.
• Vital Signs. m. ISSN 0300-6654

**Richmond Historian**
130 Stuyvesant Pl., Staten Island, NY 10301.
• Richmond Historian. s-a. ISSN 0360-1978

**Rickard Publishing Co.**
20 N. Wacker Dr., Rm. 1709, Chicago, IL 60606.
• Eastern Electrical Buyers' Guide. s-a.
• Midwest Electrical Buyers' Guide. s-a. ISSN 0076-8588
• Midwest Electrical News; a news magazine of the electrical construction industry. bi-m. ISSN 0026-3362
• Southern Electrical Buyers' Guide. s-a.
• Western Electrical Buyers' Guide. s-a.

**Rickenbacker Report Corp.**
Box 1000, Briarcliff Manor, NY 10510.
• Rickenbacker Report. fortn. ISSN 0300-791X

**Rickey de Montrond**
8962 Bainford Drive, Huntington Beach, CA 92646.
• Vapor Trail's Boating News and Manufacturing Report. m.
• Vapor Trail's Yachting and Cruiser News. m.

**Ridge Association of Retarded Citizens**
Ridge State Home and Training School, 10285 Ridge Rd., Wheat Ridge, CO 80033.
• Ridge News. q. ISSN 0035-5143

**Ridge Runners**
c/o William A. Yates, Ed., Box 1687, Rifle, CO 81650.
• Ridge Runners. q. ISSN 0093-6987

**Ridgewood Pentecostal Church**
457 Harmon St., Brooklyn, NY 11237.
- Bread of Life. m. (except Aug. & Sep.) ISSN 0006-9515

**Riemenschneider Bach Institute**
Baldwin-Wallace College, Berea, OH 44017.
- Bach. q. ISSN 0005-3600

**H. K. Rigg, Ed. & Pub.**
Second St. at Spa Creek, Annapolis, MD 21404.
- Skipper. m. ISSN 0037-6353

**Ted Riggs, Ed. & Pub.**
805 Bridgewater Rd., Knoxville, TN 37919.
- Film Collectors Registry. bi-m. ISSN 0015-1181

**Ben Rinaldo Co.**
P.O. Box 1280, Studio City, CA 91604.
- Skier. 10 per yr.

**Ring, Inc.**
120 W. 31st St., New York, NY 10003.
- Ring; world's official boxing magazine. m. ISSN 0035-5410

**Ringling Museum of Art**
Box 1838, Sarasota, FL 33578.
- Ringling Museums Newsletter. q. ISSN 0035-5461

**Rinzai-Ji, Inc.**
- Tower Smiling. (pub. by Cimarron Zen Center)

**Rio Grande Educational Association**
P.O. Box 2241, Santa Fe, NM 87501.
- Rio Grande Educational Association Newsletter. q.

**Rio Grande Writers Association**
Box 40126, Albuquerque, NM 87106.
- Rio Grande Writers Newsletter.

**Ripon College**
Ripon, WI 54971.
- Ripon College Magazine. 5 per yr. ISSN 0300-7928

**Ripon Society, Inc. (Charlestown)**
Box 226, Charlestown, MA 02129.
- Ripon Forum. m. ISSN 0035-5526

**Rising Sign: the Astrology Newspaper**
P.O. Box 4868, No. Hollywood, CA 91607.
- Rising Sign: the Astrology Newspaper. m.

**Risk and Insurance Management Society, Inc.**
205 E. 42nd Street, New York, NY 10017.
- Risk Management. 12 per yr. ISSN 0035-5593

**Ritchie County Historical Society**
616 E. Main St., Harrisville, WV 26362.
- Ritchie County Historical Society Newsletter. bi-m.

**Ritenour Consolidated School District**
2420 Woodson Rd., Overland, MO 63114.
- Intercom (Overland) w.(during school year) ISSN 0035-564X
- Ritenour School District News. 6 per yr. ISSN 0035-5631

**River Bend Library System**
Box 125, Coal Valley, IL 61240.
- River Bend Library System. Report of the Director. a. ISSN 0080-3227

**River Bottom**
c/o R. C. Halla, 1212 W. Fourth Ave., Oshkosh, WI 54901.
- River Bottom. a.

**River City Enterprises, Inc.**
Box 7401, 9 Lefever Lane, Little Rock, AR 72207.
- Book Shopper Newsletter. bi-m. ISSN 0006-7350 (Book Collectors of America)

**River City Press**
Old Flatiron Bldg., 2148 N. Broadway, Wichita, KS 67214.
- River City. s-a. ISSN 0360-4381

**Riverside County Farm Bureau Inc.**
Box 5138, Riverside, CA 92517.
- Riverside County Farm & Agricultural Business News. m. ISSN 0035-5690

**Riverside County Publishing Co.**
4745 Hiers, Riverside, CA 92505.
- Criterion. w. (Associated Students of Loma Linda University)

**Riverside Public Library**
404 N. Sierra Way, San Bernardino, CA 92415.
- Inland Messenger. bi-m. (Inland Library System)

**Riverside Quarterly**
Box 14451 University Sta., Gainesville, FL 32604.
- Riverside Quarterly. q. ISSN 0035-5704

**Road Apple Press**
159 Annonen Rd., Winlock, WA 98596.
- Alternate Sounds Newsletter. q.

**Road King Magazine**
Box 319, Park Forest, Chicago, IL 60466.
- Road King; the magazine for the professional driver. q. (Union Oil of California)

**Road Runner Press**
3263 Shorewood Dr., Oshkosh, WI 54901.
- Road Apple Review. q. ISSN 0035-7200

**Roadcap and Associates**
327 S. Lasalle St, Chicago, IL 60604.
- World Airline Record. irreg., 7th edt. 1972, with q. supplements. ISSN 0084-1374

**Roadmasters and Maintenance of Way Association of America**
18154 Harwood Ave., Homewood, IL 60430.
- Roadmasters and Maintenance of Way Association of America. Proceedings. a. ISSN 0080-3316

**Roanoke College**
Salem, VA 24153.
- Brackety - Ack. w. ISSN 0006-8667
- Roanoke Review. s-a. ISSN 0035-7367

**Roanoke Tribune**
P.O. Box 6021, Roanoke, VA 24017.
- Roanoke Tribune. w.

**Roanoke Valley Chamber of Commerce**
Box 20, Roanoke, VA 24001.
- New Directions. m. ISSN 0028-4629

**Roanoke Valley Historical Society**
Box 1904, Roanoke, VA 24008.
- Roanoke Valley Historical Society Journal. a.

**Roband Publications**
185 Madison Ave., New York, NY 10016.
- After Noon TV. 6 per yr.

**Robar Industries, Inc.**
- I T E M. (pub. by R. & B Enterprises)

**Robert Dumm Piano Review**
144 Fleetwood Terrace, Silver Spring, MD 20910.
- Robert Dumm Piano Review. s-a. ISSN 0035-7383

**Robert Kahn and Associates**
P.O. Box 343, Lafayette, CA 94549.
- Retailing Today. m.

**Robert Schalkenbach Foundation**
- American Journal of Economics and Sociology. (pub. by American Journal of Economics & Sociology, Inc.)

**Robert Wood Johnson Foundation**
Forrestal Center, Box 2316, Princeton, NJ 08540.
- Robert Wood Johnson Foundation. Annual Report. a. ISSN 0091-3472

**Martin Roberts & Associates, Inc.**
Box 5254x, Beverly Hills, CA 90210.
- Videocassette & CATV Newsletter; the systems, the market, the future. m.

**F. M. Roberts Enterprises**
Box 608, Dana Point, CA 92629.
- Underwater Photographer. q. ISSN 0091-1887

**Roberts Publishing Corp.**
45 John St., New York, NY 10038.
- Insurance Advocate. w. ISSN 0020-4587

**Ruby A. Roberts**
Bremo Bluff, VA 23022.
- Lyric. q. ISSN 0024-7820

**Sanford and Patricia Roberts**
c/o Sanford Roberts, Ed., 15011 Oak Creek Rd., El Cajon, CA 92021.
- American Dachshund. bi-m. ISSN 0002-8142

**Robertson Publishing Co.**
Box 164, Lafayette Hill, PA 19444.
- Home Finders Directory. m. ISSN 0018-4039

**Robertson Review**
Box 85, Camberwell, Vic. 3124, Australia.
- Robertson Review. m.

**R. L. Robinson**
P.O. Box 161, Mt. Laguna, CA 92048.
- Folk Harp Journal. q. ISSN 0094-8934 (Society of Folk Harpists and Craftsmen)

**Shepard D. Robinson, Ed. & Pub.**
410 Grove Ave., Barrington, IL 60010.
- Manufactured Housing Newsletter. s-m.

**Roche Laboratories Inc.**
12230 Wilkins Ave., Rockville, MD 20852.
- Urology News. m.

**Rochester Chamber of Commerce**
55 St. Paul St., Rochester, NY 14604.
- Greater Rochester Commerce. m. ISSN 0017-3797

**Rochester Engineering Society, Inc.**
55 St. Paul St., Rochester, NY 14604.
- Rochester Engineer. m. ISSN 0035-7405

**Rochester Institute of Technology**
One Lomb Memorial Dr., Rochester, NY 14623.
- R I T Reporter. w.

**Rochester Institute of Technology. Department of Mechanical Engineering**
One Lomb Memorial Dr., Rochester, NY 14623.
- Mechanical Engineering News. q. ISSN 0025-651X

**Rochester Institute of Technology. Evening Student Association**
One Lomb Dr., Rochester, NY 14623.
- Image (Rochester) q.

**Rochester Institute of Technology. Graphic Arts Research Center**
One Lomb Memorial Drive, Rochester, NY 14623.
- G A R C Newsletter. m.
- Graphic Arts Literature Abstracts; an expansion of the Graphic Arts index. m.
- Graphic Arts Patent Abstracts. m. ISSN 0017-3320

**Rochester Institute of Technology. Photographic Science and Instrumentation Division**
c/o Dr. Ronald Francis, 1 Lomb Memorial Drive, Rochester, NY 14623.
- Photo Scientist. q. (Co-sponsor: Society of Photographic Scientists and Engineers)

**Rochester Public Library**
115 South Ave., Rochester, NY 14604.
- Rochester History. q. ISSN 0035-7413

**Rock**
166 Lexington Ave., New York, NY 10016.
- Rock. fortn. ISSN 0092-0401

**Rock and Dirt**
Crossville, Tn 38555.
- Rock and Dirt. 36 per yr.

**Rockbridge Historical Society**
101 E. Washington St., Lexington, VA 24450.
- Rockbridge Historical Society, Lexington, Virginia. Proceedings. irreg., vol. 8, 1975. ISSN 0080-3383

**Rockefeller Foundation**
1133 Ave. of Americas, New York, NY 10036.
- R F Illustrated. q.
- Rockefeller Foundation. Annual Report. a. ISSN 0080-3391

**Rockefeller University**
- Rockefeller University, New York. Annual Report. (pub. by Rockefeller University Press)

**Rockefeller University Press**
1230 York Ave., New York, NY 10021.
- Biology and Behavior Series. irreg. ISSN 0572-6557

**Biophysical Journal.** m (4 vols. of 3 nos. per year) ISSN 0006-3495 (Biophysical Society)
- Biophysical Society. Abstracts. a. ISSN 0067-8910
- Journal of Cell Biology. m.(4 vols. of 3 nos.per yr.) ISSN 0021-9525 (American Society for Cell Biology)
- Journal of Clinical Investigation. m (2 vols. of 6 nos. per year) ISSN 0021-9738 (American Society for Clinical Investigation)
- Journal of Experimental Medicine. m (2 vols. of 6 nos. per year) ISSN 0022-1007
- Journal of General Physiology. m (2 vols. of 6 nos. per year) ISSN 0022-1295 (Society of General Physiologists)
- Rockefeller University, New York. Annual Report. a. ISSN 0080-3405

**Rocket-Jet Flying Magazine**
c/o Dr. Constantin Paul Lent, 108-02-72nd Ave., Room 1d, Forest Hills, NY 11375.
- Rocket-Jet Flying Magazine. q. ISSN 0035-7499

**Rockford Catholic Diocese**
1260 N. Church St., Rockford, IL 61101.
- Observer. w. ISSN 0029-7739

**Rockhurst College**
Kansas City, MO 64110.
- Rockhurst Hawk. fortn. ISSN 0035-7510

**Rockland County Feminists**
24 Debaun Ave., Suffern, NY 10901.
- Aurora: Prism of Feminism. q.

**Rocks and Minerals**
Box 29, Peekskill, NY 10566.
- Rocks and Minerals; mineralogy, geology, lapidary. m. ISSN 0035-7529

**Rockwell International**
400 N. Lexington Ave., Pittsburgh, PA 15208.
- Flow Line; magazine of flow measurement and control. q. ISSN 0015-4458 (prep. by its Flow Control Division)
- Rockwell Water Journal; devoted to the operation and management of water works and sewage treatment plants. q. ISSN 0035-7553

**Rockwell International. Corporate Offices**
600 Grant St., Pittsburgh, PA 15219.
- Skyline. q. ISSN 0037-6639

**Rockwell International. Rocky Flats Plant**
P. O. Box 464, Golden, CO 80401.
- Rockwell News. s-m.

**Rocky Mountain Analgesia Society**
c/o Dr. Jerome Y. Greene, 7060 E. Hampden Ave., Denver, CO 80222.
- Rocky Mountain Analgesia Society. Journal. q. ISSN 0048-8488

**Rocky Mountain Association of Genealogists**
505 Colorado Bldg., Denver, CO 80202.
- Mountain Geologist. q. ISSN 0027-254X

**Rocky Mountain Creative Arts Journal**
Box 3185, Casper, WY 82601.
- Rocky Mountain Creative Arts Journal. s-a.

**Rocky Mountain Farmers Union**
12025 E. 45th Ave, Denver, CO 80201 (Subscr. Address: Box 628, Denver, Colo. 80201)
- Rocky Mountain Union Farmer. m. ISSN 0035-7650

**Rocky Mountain Food Dealers Association**
1711 Pennsylvania St., Denver, CO 80203.
- Rocky Mountain Food Dealer. m. ISSN 0035-7588

**Rocky Mountain Mathematics Consortium**
Arizona State University, Department of Mathematics, Tempe, AZ 85281.
- Rocky Mountain Journal of Mathematics. q. ISSN 0035-7596

**Rocky Mountain Mineral Law Foundation**
Univ. of Colorado, Fleming Law Bldg., Boulder, CO 80302.
- Public Land & Resources Law Digest. s-a.
- Rocky Mountain Mineral Law Newsletter. m.
- Water Law Newsletter. 3-4 per yr. ISSN 0043-1249 (Co-sponsor: University of Wyoming Land and Water Center)

**Rocky Mountain Modern Language Association**
2056 Annex, Univ. of Utah, Salt Lake City, UT 84112.
- Rocky Mountain Review of Language and Literature. q.

**Rod Action**
Box 688, Evanston, IL 60204.
- Rod Action. m.

**Rodale Press, Inc.**
33 E. Minor St., Emmaus, PA 18049.
- Compost Science. bi-m. ISSN 0010-4388
- Executive Fitness Newsletter. fortn. ISSN 0014-4525
- Organic Classroom. irreg.
- Organic Directory. irreg. ISSN 0078-6128
- Organic Gardening and Farming. m. ISSN 0030-4913
- Prevention; the magazine for better health. m. ISSN 0032-8006
- Rodale's Environment Action Bulletin. bi-w. ISSN 0048-850X
- Theatre Crafts. bi-m. ISSN 0040-5469

**Rode Publishing Company**
300 Bassett Building, Box 412, Summit, NJ 07901.
- Chemicals Today. m.

**Rodeo Cowboys Association**
- Hoof and Horn. (pub. by Hoofs and Horns Publishing Co.)

**Rodeo Historical Society**
- Wild Bunch. (pub. by National Cowboy Hall of Fame and Western Heritage Center)

**Rodeo News, Inc.**
Box 587, Pauls Valley, OK 73075.
- Rodeo News; the voice of professional rodeo. m. (International Rodeo Association)

**Rodman Publications, Inc.**
Box 555, 26 Lake St., Ramsey, NJ 07446.
- Carpet & Rug Industry. m.
- Formed Fabrics Industry; the international magazine for the nonwoven fabrics and disposable soft goods industry. m.

**Rodniye Dali**
1117 N. Berendo St., Los Angeles, CA 90029.
- Rodniye Dali; Russian language bulletin. m. ISSN 0300-6476

**Rogers Publishing Co., Inc.**
(Subsidiary of: Cahners Publishing Co., Inc.)
270 St. Paul St., Denver, CO 80206.
- Design News Specifier's Annual Directory. a.
- Plastics World Information Cards. s-a. ISSN 0032-1281

**Rogue Valley Genealogical Society**
Box 628, Ashland, OR 97520.
- Rogue Digger. q. ISSN 0048-8534

**Rohm and Haas Co.**
Independence Mall West, Philadelphia, PA 19105.
- Amber-Hi-Lites. q. ISSN 0002-693X
- Resin Review. q. ISSN 0034-5571
- Rohm and Haas Reporter. q. ISSN 0035-7847

**Rohmer Review**
4 Forest Ave., Salem, MA 01970.
- Rohmer Review. irreg.

**Rohrich Corp.**
903 Tallmadge Ave., Akron, OH 44310.
- Akron Law Review. 4 per yr. ISSN 0002-371X (University of Akron. School of Law)
- Blue Book of College Athletics. a.
- Blue Book of Junior College Athletics. a. ISSN 0520-2973

**Roll Call**
c/o Sidney L. Yudain, Ed., 428 8th St. S.E., Washington, DC 20003.
- Roll Call; the newspaper of Capitol Hill. w. ISSN 0035-788X

**Roller Skating Rink Operators Association**
7700 "A" St., Lincoln, NE 68510.
- Skate. q. ISSN 0037-6124

**Rollins College Student Association**
Rollins College, Box 2742, Winter Park, FL 32789.
- Rollins Sandspur. w. ISSN 0035-7936

**Rolls-Royce Owners' Club, Inc.**
Box 725, Morrisville, VT 05661.
- Flying Lady. bi-m. ISSN 0015-4830
- Rolls-Royce Owners' Club, Directory and Register. biennial. ISSN 0485-3695

**Roman Catholic Bishop of Honolulu**
c/o Rev. John J. Scanlan, 1184 Bishop St., Honolulu, HI 96813.
- Hawaii Catholic Herald. w.

**Roman Catholic Bishop of Worcester**
247 Mill St., Worcester, MA 01602.
- Catholic Free Press. w. ISSN 0008-8056

**Roman Catholic Diocese of Amarillo**
1800 N. Spring St., Amarillo, TX 79107.
- West Texas Catholic. w.

**Roman Catholic Diocese of Bismarck**
Box 1575, Bismarck, ND 58501.
- Dakota Catholic Action. 10 per yr. ISSN 0011-5770

**Roman Catholic Diocese of Brooklyn**
- Tablet. (pub. by Tablet Publishing Co.)

**Roman Catholic Diocese of Davenport**
Suite 500, First National Bldg., Box 939, Davenport, IA 52805.
- Catholic Messenger. w. ISSN 0008-8234

**Roman Catholic Diocese of Rockville Centre**
- Long Island Catholic. (pub. by Catholic Press Association)

**Roman Reports**
c/o A. Roman, Ed., 14605 Brunswick, Maple Heights, OH 44137.
- Roman Reports. q.

**Romanian Library**
200 E. 38st., New York, NY 10016.
- Romanian Bulletin. m. ISSN 0035-8053

**Romanian Orthodox Episcopate of America**
2522 Grey Tower Rd., Jackson, MI 49201.
- Solia; the Herald. m. ISSN 0038-1039

**Matthew F. Romano, Ed. & Pub.**
P.O. Box 11685, Philadelphia, PA 19116.
- Hybrid Microelectronics Review; the industry scanner. m.

**Rook Society, Inc.**
805 West First Avenue, Derry, PA 15627.
- John Berryman Studies. q. ISSN 0098-2199
- Thistle. 3 per yr.

**Roosevelt University**
430 S. Michigan Ave., Chicago, IL 60605.
- Oyez Review. s-a.

**Roosevelt University. Walter E. Heller College of Business Administration**
430 S. Michigan Ave., Chicago, IL 60605.
- Business and Society; a journal of interdisciplinary exploration. s-a. ISSN 0007-6503

**A. I. Root Co.**
Medina, OH 44256.
- Gleanings in Bee Culture. m. ISSN 0017-114X

**Roper Public Opinion Research Center**
Williams College, Williamstown, MA 01267.
- Current Opinion. m.

**Roq Press**
834 E. College Ave., State College, PA 16801.
- Aguila. s-a.

**Rosary College**
7900 W. Division, River Forest, IL 60305.
- Ego. irreg.

**Rose Publishing Co. Inc.**
76 W.St. John St., San Jose, CA 95113.
- San Jose Post-Record; daily legal, real estate & financial news. d. ISSN 0036-4185

**Rosebud Associates Inc.**
750 Third Ave., Grand Central Sta., New York, NY 10017.
- MORE; a journalism review. m. ISSN 0047-8091

**Roseburg Lumber Co.**
c/o Hugh Dwight Advertising, Inc., Or 97205, Portland, OR 97470.
- Roseburg Woodsman. m. ISSN 0035-8304

**Rosemead Graduate School of Psychology**
Box 6000, Rosemead, CA 91770.
- Journal of Psychology and Theology. q. ISSN 0091-6471

**Ned K. Rosenblatt, Ed. & Pub**
9836 Jersey St., Drawer 2887, Santa Fe Springs, CA 90670.
- Aerial Applicator; farm, forest and fire. 9 per yr. ISSN 0001-9070
- E C A Magazine. m. (Engineering Contractors Associations)
- S C H C. (Southern California Heavy Construction) 9 per yr.

**Rosenstiel School of Marine and Atmospheric Science**
4600 Rickenbacker Causeway, Miami, FL 33149
- Bulletin of Marine Science. 4 per yr. ISSN 0007-4977 (Subscr. to: Bulletin of Marine Science, Box 368, Lawrence, KS 66044)
- Studies in Tropical Oceanography. irreg., no. 12, 1974. ISSN 0081-8720

**Rosicrucian Fellowship**
Box 713, Oceanside, CA 92054.
- Rays from the Rose Cross. m.

**Rosicrucian Order, AMORC**
Rosicrucian Park, San Jose, CA 95191.
- Rosicrucian Digest. m. ISSN 0035-8339

**Ross Laboratories**
625 Cleveland Ave., Columbus, OH 43216.
- American Academy of Allergy. Pollen and Mold Committee. Statistical Report. a.

**Rossica Society of Russian Philately**
c/o N. Epstein, 33 Crooke Ave, Brooklyn, NY 11226.
- Rossica Society of Russian Philately Journal. s-a. ISSN 0035-8363

**Rostam Publishing Inc.**
Box 1374, New York, NY 10022.
- Action Sports Hockey. 7 per yr.

**Rotary International**
1600 Ridge Ave., Evanston, IL 60201.
- Revista Rotaria; una publicacion internacional. bi-m. ISSN 0035-0443
- Rotarian. m. ISSN 0035-838X

**Gerald Rothberg, Ed. & Pub.**
747 3rd Ave., New York, NY 10017.
- Circus. bi-w. ISSN 0009-7365

**Fred B. Rothman & Co.**
57 Leuning St., South Hackensack, NJ 07606.
- A A L L Publications Series. irreg., no. 13, 1977. ISSN 0065-7255 (American Association of Law Libraries)
- African Law Studies. 2 per yr. ISSN 0002-0060 (African Law Association in America, Inc.)
- Checklist of Basic American Legal Publications. irreg. (American Association of Law Libraries)
- Copyright Society of the U.S.A. Bulletin. 6 per yr. ISSN 0010-8642
- Current Publications in Legal and Related Fields. m.(except June, July & Sept.) plus annual cumulative no. ISSN 0011-3859 (American Association of Law Libraries)
- International Institute of Space Law. Colloquium. Proceedings. a., 19th, Anaheim, Calif., 1977.

**Rough Notes Co., Inc.**
1200 No. Meridian St., Indianapolis, IN 46206.
- Insurance Market Place; the agents and brokers guide to non-standard & specialty lines, aviation, marine & international insurance. a. ISSN 0538-2629
- Insurance Salesman. m. ISSN 0020-482X
- Rough Notes; property, casualty, surety. m. ISSN 0035-8525
- Sales/Slants. irreg. ISSN 0036-3464
- What It Costs to Run an Agency. biennial, 15th 1973.

**Rough Rock Demonstration School**
Rough Rock, AZ 86503.
- Rough Rock News. fortn. (during school year)

**Rountree Publishing Co. Inc.**
117 Brixton Rd., Garden City, NY 11530.
- Rountree Report; devoted to new products, new processes, new developments. fortn. ISSN 0048-8674

**Routledge & Kegan Paul**
9 Park St., Boston, MA 02108.
- Arguments of the Philosophers. irreg.
- Birth of Modern Britain Series. irreg.
- Journal of Mithraic Studies. s-a.
- Year Book of Social Policy in Britain. a.

**Rowman and Littlefield**
81 Adams Drive, Totowa, NJ 07512.
- Besterman World Bibliographies. irreg.
- European Parliament Digest. irreg. ISSN 0095-7607
- National Agricultural Library Catalog. m. ISSN 0027-8505

**Royal Arch Masons, General Grand Chapter**
- Royal Arch Mason. (pub. by York Rite Publishing Co.)

**Royal Globe Insurance Co.**
Corporate Communications Dept., 150 William St., New York, NY 10038.
- Red Shield News. fortn.

**Royal Neighbors of America**
230 16th St., Rock Island, IL 61201.
- Royal Neighbor; a home magazine. m. ISSN 0035-905X

**Royal United Services Institute**
- R. U. S. I. and Brassey's Defence Yearbook. (pub. by Westview Press)

**Royalton College Press**
South Royalton, VT 05068.
- Royalton Review. q.

**Rubber Manufacturers Association**
1901 Pennsylvania Ave. N.W., Washington, DC 20006.
- Rubber Manufacturers Association. Statistical Report. m.

**S. M. Rubel & Co.**
10 S. La Salle St., Chicago, IL 60603.
- Venture Capital; only financial analyst of small business investment companies and Venture Capital companies. m.

**Samuel K. Rubin, Ed. & Pub.**
734 Philadelphia St., Indiana, PA 15701.
- Classic Film Collector. q. ISSN 0009-8329

**Ruder and Finn Inc.**
110 E. 59th St., New York, NY 10022.
- Japan Trade Center Information Service. Monthly Economic Report. m.

**Rudinger Foundation**
Firelands Campus, Huron, OH 44839.
- Firelands Arts Review. a. ISSN 0094-8012

**Rudolf Virchow Medical Society**
- Rudolf Virchow Medical Society in the City of New York. Proceedings. (pub. by Verlag Ferdinand Berger AU)

**Ruffin Publications, Inc.**
Box 1218, 845 Minnesota Ave., Kansas City, KS 66117.
- Everybody; Afro-American news. m.

**Rumford Publishing Co.**
Box 5370, Chicago, IL 60680.
- Previews of Heat and Mass Transfer. q.

**Rumpf Publishing Division**
(Subsidiary of: Nickerson & Collins Co.)
1800 Oakton St., Des Plaines, IL 60018.
- Chain Shoe Stores and Leased Shoe Department Operators. a. ISSN 0069-2387
- Leather and Shoes. m. ISSN 0023-9747
- Leather Buyers Guide and Leather Trade Marks. a. ISSN 0075-8345

**Runestone**
c/o Stephen A. McNallen, Ed., 2021 Channing Way, no. 8, Berkeley, A P O, CA 94704.
- Runestone. q.

**Rural Advancement Fund of the National Sharecroppers Fund**
2128 Commonwealth Ave., Charlotte, CA 28205.
- Rural Advance. irreg. ISSN 0557-8183

**Rural Education Association**
515 Education Center, Univ. of Northern Iowa, Cedar Falls, IA 50613.
- Rural Education News. bi-m. ISSN 0036-0023

**Rural Gravure Service Inc.**
2564 Branch St., Middleton, WI 53562.
- Midwest Roto. m.

**Rural Housing Alliance**
1346 Connecticut Ave., N.W., Washington, DC 20036.
- R H Reporter. m.

**Rural Sociological Society (Auburn)**
306-A Comer Hall, Auburn University, Auburn, AL 36830.
- Directory of Universities Offering Graduate Degrees in Rural Sociology. irreg.

**Rural Sociological Society (College Point)**
317 Agriculture Bldg., Texas A & M University, College Station, TX 77840.
- Rural Sociology; devoted to scientific study of rural and small-town life. q. ISSN 0036-0112

**Ruralite Services, Inc.**
Box 557, Forest Grove, OR 97116.
- Ruralite. m. (Oregon Rural Electrical Cooperative Association)

**Ruritan National, Inc.**
Ed. Russell Burgess, Box 487, Dublin, VA 24084.
- Ruritan. m. ISSN 0036-0147

**Rush-Presbyterian-St. Luke's Medical Center and Its Alumni Foundation**
1753 W. Congress Parkway, Chicago, IL 60612.
- Rush-Presbyterian-St. Luke's Medical Bulletin. q. ISSN 0032-7581

**Rush Publishing Co., Inc.**
Box 1, Rush, NY 14543.
- Women Studies Abstracts. q. ISSN 0049-7835

**Russell's Guides, Inc.**
817 Second Ave., S.E., Cedar Rapids, IA 52406.
- Russell's Official National Motor Coach Guide; official publication of bus lines in the United States, Alaska, Canada and Mexico. m. ISSN 0036-0171

**Russian Brotherhood Organization of the U. S.**
1733 Spring Garden St., Philadelphia, PA 19130.
- Truth. m. ISSN 0041-3690

**Russian Life, Inc.**
2460 Sutter St., San Francisco, CA 94115.
- Russian Life Daily. d.

**Russian Orthodox Catholic Mutual Aid Society**
100 Hazle St., Wilkes-Barre, PA 18701.
- Svit/Light. s-m. ISSN 0039-7156

**Russian Review, Inc.**
Stanford, CA 94305.
- Russian Review; an American quarterly devoted to Russia past and present. q. ISSN 0036-0341 (Hoover Institution)

**Russky Golos Publishing Corp.**
130 E. 16th St., New York, NY 10003.
- Russky Golos/Russian Voice. w. ISSN 0036-0406

**Rutgers Center of Alcohol Studies. Publications Division**
New Brunswick, NJ 08903.
- Classified Abstract Archive of the Alcohol Literature. q. ISSN 0009-8450
- International Bibliography of Studies on Alcohol. irreg., vols. 3 and 4 in prep. ISSN 0074-204X
- Journal of Studies on Alcohol. m.
- Journal of Studies on Alcohol. Supplement. irreg., 1972, no. 6.
- N.I.A.A.A.-R.U.C.A.S. Alcoholism Treatment Monographs. irreg.
- Rutgers University. Center of Alcohol Studies. Monograph. irreg; no. 11, 1976. ISSN 0080-4983

**Rutgers University**
Camden, NJ 08102.
- Partisan Review. (pub. by P R, Inc. (Partisan Review))

- Rutgers Gleaner. w.(Sept.-June)
- Soil Science. (pub. by Williams & Wilkins Co.)

**Rutgers University. Bureau of Biological Research**
- Rutgers University. Bureau of Biological Research. Research Conference. Research Conferences of the Bureau of Biological Research (Proceedings) (pub. by Rutgers University Press)

**Rutgers University. Center for Urban Policy Research**
Building 4051, Kilmer Campus, New Brunswick, NJ 08903.
- American Real Estate and Urban Economics Association. Journal. q. ISSN 0092-914X

**Rutgers University. College of Engineering**
Bureau of Engineering Research, New Brunswick, NJ 08903.
- Rutgers University.Bureau of Engineering Research. Annual Report. a. ISSN 0080-4975

**Rutgers University. Cook College**
Box 231, New Brunswick, NJ 08903.
- Environmental Spectrum. bi-m. ISSN 0013-9386
- Solid Waste Management. bi-m. (New Jersey Cooperative Extension Service)

**Rutgers University. Department of Alumni Relations**
New Brunswick, NJ 08903.
- Rutgers Alumni Magazine. 5 per yr. ISSN 0036-0457

**Rutgers University. Department of Botany**
New Brunswick, NJ 08903.
- William L. Hutcheson Memorial Forest. Bulletin. irreg. ISSN 0511-9723

**Rutgers University. Graduate School of Business Administration**
92 New St., Newark, NJ 07104.
- Journal of International Business Studies. s-a. ISSN 0047-2506 (Academy of International Business)

**Rutgers University. Graduate School of Library Science**
Bureau of Library and Information Science Research, 189 College Ave., New Brunswick, NJ 08903.
- Issues in the Library and Information Sciences. irreg., no. 2, 1975.
- Jobs in Print. 21 per yr.
- Rutgers University. Graduate School of Library Service. Occasional Papers. 5 per yr.

**Rutgers University. Institute of Management and Labor Relations**
New Brunswick, NJ 08903.
- New Jersey Public Employer-Employee Relations. irreg., 1971, no. 7. ISSN 0077-8508

**Rutgers University Library. Associated Friends of the Library**
New Brunswick, NJ 08903.
- Rutgers University Library. Journal. s-a. ISSN 0036-0473

**Rutgers University Press**
30 College Ave., New Brunswick, NJ 08903.
- Brown and Haley Lecture Series. irreg., latest issue 1975. ISSN 0068-2861
- Rutgers Banking Series. irreg. ISSN 0080-4924
- Rutgers Byzantine Series. irreg., 1970, no. 7.
- Rutgers Series on Systems for the Intellectual Organization of Information. irreg. ISSN 0080-4940
- Rutgers University. Bureau of Biological Research. Research Conference. Research Conferences of the Bureau of Biological Research (Proceedings) irreg., proceedings of some conferences not published. ISSN 0080-4967
- World History of the Jewish People. irreg., 1972, vol. 11. ISSN 0084-1838

**Rutgers University. School of Law**
180 University Ave., Newark, NJ 07102.
- Rutgers Journal of Computers and the Law. s-a. ISSN 0048-8844
- Rutgers Law Review. 5 per yr. ISSN 0036-0465

**Rutgers University. School of Law (Camden)**
5Th and Penn Sts., Camden, NJ 08102.
- Rutgers - Camden Law Journal. 4 per yr. ISSN 0036-0449

**Rutherford B. Hayes Library**
1337 Hayes Ave., Fremont, OH 43420.
- Hayes Historical Journal. s-a. (Hayes Historical Society)

**Rutland Historical Society**
101 Center St., Rutland, VT 05701.
- Rutland Historical Society Quarterly. q.

**Rutward Mail Order Publications**
Box 471, Georgetown, CT 06829.
- Drop Ship Buyers Guide. biennial.

**Thomas O. Ryder**
530 University Ave, Palo Alto, CA 94301.
- Learning; magazine for creative teaching. 9 per yr (Sept-May) ISSN 0090-3167 (Education Today Company, Inc.)

**Ryukyu Philatelic Specialist Society**
Box 4092, Berkeley, CA 94704.
- From the Dragon's Den. 4 per yr.

**S A F International, Inc.**
630 Third Ave., New York, NY 10010.
- American Dyestuff Reporter; devoted to textile wet-processing, dyeing, finishing, bleaching, etc., new product information, news of the industry. m. ISSN 0002-8266
- Knitting Industry; for manufacturers of hosiery, outerwear, underwear, fabric and all knit products. m. ISSN 0023-2335

**S. A. M., Inc.**
16 West Erie St., Chicago, IL 60610.
- S A M/Serving Advertising in the Midwest. w. ISSN 0036-083X

**S B R, Inc.**
Box 35441, Houston, TX 77035.
- South Texas Retailer. m.

**S E R-Jobs for Progress, Inc.**
9841 Airport Blvd., Suite 1020, Los Angeles, CA 90045.
- Adelante S E R. (Service, Employment, Redevelopment) bi-m. (League of United Latin American Citizens (LULAC)) (Co-Sponsor: Incorporated Mexican American Government Employees (IMAGE))

**S F Booklog**
Rt.2, Box 42, Union, MS 39365.
- S F Booklog. bi-m.

**S. F. Camera Publishing Co. Inc.**
84 Vandewater St., San Francisco, CA 94133.
- San Francisco Camera. q. ISSN 0036-4118

**S Gaugian**
c/o Donald J. Heimburger, Ed., 504 Walnut St., Tolono, IL 61880.
- S Gaugian. bi-m.

**S.I.C. Publishing Corp.**
8705 N. Port Washington Rd., Milwaukee, WI 53217.
- Wisconsin Industrial Product News. 10 per yr.

**S-N Publications, Inc.**
18 S. Michigan Ave., Chicago, IL 60603.
- Supervisor Nurse. m. ISSN 0039-5870

**S. O. D. Publishing, Inc.**
420 Lexington Avenue, New York, NY 10017.
- Soap Opera Digest. m.

**S. O. S. U. S. A., Ship of State**
18 Boardman St., Salem, MA 01970.
- S. O. S. U. S. A., Ship of State. m. ISSN 0036-1801

**S P Books**
(Subsidiary of: Spectrum Publications, Inc.)
86-19 Sancho St., Holliswood, NY 11423.
- Current Developments in Psychopharmacology.

**S P E A K, Inc.**
Hillspeak, Eureka Springs, AR 72632.
- Anglican Digest. (Society for Promoting and Encouraging Arts and Knowledge, Inc.) q. ISSN 0003-3278

**S P R Charter**
Olema, CA 94950.
- Man on Earth. ISSN 0025-1593

**S X O Corp.**
200 Park Ave S., New York, NY 10003.
- Together. m.

**Sabin's Discount Records**
3212 Penn. Ave., S.E., Washington, DC 20020.
- Radio Free Jazz. m. ISSN 0093-0490

**Sacramento Area Central Labor Council. Building Trades Council, Printing Trades Council**
2525 Stockton Blvd., Sacramento, CA 95817.
- Sacramento Valley Union Labor Bulletin. w. ISSN 0036-2247

**Sacramento City Teachers Association**
2564 21st St., Sacramento, CA 95818.
- Sacramento Teacher. 6 per yr. ISSN 0036-2239

**Sacramento Metropolitan Chamber of Commerce**
917 Seventh St, Sacramento, CA 95814.
- Sacramento Business. m. ISSN 0036-2204

**Sacramento State College**
Forum Free Press, 6000 J St., Sacramento, CA 95819.
- Student (Sacramento) 6 per yr. ISSN 0039-2650

**Sacred Heart University**
Bridgeport, CT 06604.
- Connecticut English Journal. s-a.

**Saddle and Bridle**
c/o William H. Thompson, 2333 Brentwood, St. Louis, MO 63144.
- Saddle and Bridle. m.(Feb-Dec) ISSN 0036-2271

**Sadie's Chatter**
Box 2061, Tulsa, OK 74101.
- Sadie's Chatter. m.

**Safeco Insurance Companies**
Safeco Plaza, Seattle, WA 98185.
- Safeco Agent. bi-m. ISSN 0036-2409

**Safety Electronics, Inc.**
1058 W. Club Blvd., Office Suite 210, Durham, NC 27701.
- Product Safety News. m.

**Sagamore Publishing Company, Inc.**
1120 Old Country Rd, Plainview, NY 11803.
- Db, the Sound Engineering Magazine. m. ISSN 0011-7145

**Sage Publications, Inc.**
275 South Beverly Drive, Beverly Hills, CA 90212 (and Sage Publications, Ltd., St. George's House, 44 Hatton Garden, London EC1N 8ER, England)
- Administration and Society. q.
- American Behavioral Scientist. bi-m. ISSN 0002-7642
- American Politics Quarterly. q. ISSN 0044-7803
- Behavior Modification. q. ISSN 0145-4455
- Centre for Environmental Studies Series. irreg., vol. 3, 1974.
- Communication Research. q. ISSN 0093-6502
- Comparative Political Studies. q. ISSN 0010-4140
- Criminal Justice & Behavior; an international journal of correctional psychology. q. ISSN 0093-8548 (American Association of Correctional Psychologists)
- Criminology; an interdisciplinary journal. q. ISSN 0011-1384 (American Society of Criminology)
- Education and Urban Society. q. ISSN 0013-1245
- Environment and Behavior. q. ISSN 0013-9165
- Evaluation Quarterly; a journal of applied social research. q. ISSN 0145-4692
- Evaluation Studies Review Annual. a.
- German Political Studies. a.
- Human Resources Abstracts; an international information service. q. ISSN 0099-2453 (University of Michigan-Wayne State University. Institute of Labor & Industrial Relations)
- International Studies Quarterly. q. ISSN 0020-8833 (International Studies Association)
- Interpersonal Development; international journal for humanistic approaches to group psychotherapy, sensitivity training and organizational development. q. ISSN 0047-1283
- Journal of Black Studies. q. ISSN 0021-9347
- Journal of Conflict Resolution; research on war and peace between and within nations. q. ISSN 0022-0027
- Journal of Cross Cultural Psychology. q. ISSN 0022-0221 (International Association for Cross-Cultural Psychology)

- Journal of Interamerican Studies and World Affairs. q. ISSN 0022-1937 (University of Miami. Center for Advanced International Studies)
- Journal of Urban History. q. ISSN 0096-1442
- Latin American Urban Research. a. ISSN 0075-8167
- Modern China; an international quarterly. q. ISSN 0097-7004
- Pacific Sociological Review. q. ISSN 0030-8919 (Pacific Sociological Association)
- Political Theory; an international journal of political philosophy. q. ISSN 0090-5917
- Primary Socialization, Language, and Education. irreg. ISSN 0079-5089
- Public Finance Quarterly. q. ISSN 0048-5853
- Quantitative Applications in the Social Sciences. irreg.
- Sage Annual Reviews of Communication Research. a.
- Sage Criminal Justice Systems Annual. irreg.
- Sage Professional Papers in Administrative and Policy Studies.
- Sage Professional Papers in American Politics. 8 per yr.
- Sage Professional Papers in Comparative Politics. 8 per yr. ISSN 0080-5343
- Sage Professional Papers in Contemporary Political Sociology. 8 per yr.
- Sage Professional Papers in International Studies. 8 per yr. ISSN 0048-8976
- Sage Public Administration Abstracts. q. ISSN 0094-6958
- Sage Research Papers in the Social Sciences. 8 per yr.
- Sage Research Progress Series on War, Revolution and Peacekeeping. a. ISSN 0080-536X (Inter-University Seminar on Armed Forces and Society)
- Sage Series on Armed Forces and Society. irreg., vol. 10, 1977. ISSN 0080-5378 (Inter-University Seminar on Armed Forces and Society)
- Sage Series on Politics and the Legal Order. irreg., vol. 5, 1976. ISSN 0080-5386
- Sage Urban Studies Abstracts. q. ISSN 0090-5747
- Simulation & Games. q. ISSN 0037-5500
- Small Group Behavior; an international journal of therapy, counseling and training. q. ISSN 0090-5526
- Social Service Delivery Systems; an international annual. a.
- Social Studies of Science. q. ISSN 0306-3127
- Sociological Methods & Research. q. ISSN 0049-1241
- Sociology of Work and Occupations; an international journal. q. ISSN 0093-9285
- Teaching Political Science. q. ISSN 0092-2013
- Teaching Sociology. q.
- Urban Affairs Annual Reviews. biennial. ISSN 0083-4688
- Urban Affairs Quarterly. q. ISSN 0042-0816
- Urban Education. q. ISSN 0042-0859
- Urban Life; a journal of ethnographic research. q. ISSN 0098-3039
- Urban Research News. fortn. ISSN 0042-0964
- Us; an international review of research in the social dimensions. q.
- Washington Papers. 10 per yr. (Georgetown University. Center for Strategic and International Studies)
- Youth & Society. q. ISSN 0044-118X

**Sage School of Philosophy**
*see under* **Cornell University**

**Sailing the Road Clear**
c/o Jane Creighton, Box 238, Old Mystic, CT 06372.
- Sailing the Road Clear. irreg.

**St. Andrews Presbyterian College**
Laurinburg, NC 28352.
- St. Andrews Review. s-a. ISSN 0036-2751

**St. Anthony Messenger Press**
1615 Republic St., Cincinnati, OH 45210.
- Catholic Update. m. (Franciscan Friars of St. John the Baptist Province)
- Homily Helps. 62 per yr.
- Medical Moral Newsletter. 10 per yr. ISSN 0025-7397 (Franciscan Friars of St. John the Baptist Province)
- St. Anthony Messenger. m. ISSN 0036-276X (Franciscan Friars of St. John the Baptist Province)

**St. Augustine Historical Society**
271 Charlotte St., St. Augustine, FL 32084.
- Escriban. a. ISSN 0014-0376

**St. Augustine's Center for American Indians**
4512 North Sheridan Rd., Chicago, IL 60640.
- Cross and the Calumet. 2 per yr.

**Saint Augustine's College**
Raleigh, NC 27602.
- Saint Augustine's College. Faculty Research Journal. s-a. ISSN 0014-6781

**St. Bonaventure University**
St. Bonaventure, NY 14778.
- Cithara; essays in Judaeo-Christian tradition. s-a. ISSN 0009-7527
- Saint Bonaventure University. Science Studies. a. ISSN 0080-5467

**St. Bonaventure University. Franciscan Institute**
St. Bonaventure, NY 14478.
- Cord. m. ISSN 0010-8685
- Saint Bonaventure University. Franciscan Institute. Philosophy Series. irreg., no. 16, 1972. ISSN 0080-5432
- Saint Bonaventure University. Franciscan Institute. Text Series. irreg., no. 16, 1972. ISSN 0080-5440
- Saint Bonaventure University. Franciscan Studies. a. ISSN 0080-5459

**St. Charles Seminary**
Overbrook, Philadelphia, PA 19151.
- Dimension: Journal of Pastoral Concern. 3 per yr. ISSN 0012-2890

**St. Clair County Historical Society**
701 E. Washington, Belleville, IL 62221.
- St. Clair County Historical Society. Journal. irreg. ISSN 0095-3911

**St. Cloud State College**
St. Cloud, MN 56301.
- Master's Thesis Abstracts Bulletin. irreg. ISSN 0025-5114
- Sinclair Lewis Newsletter. a. ISSN 0080-9608 (prep. by its School of Arts and Sciences)

**St. Columban's Foreign Mission Society**
- Columban Mission. (pub. by Columban Fathers)

**St. Edwards University**
c/o Publication Office, St. Edward's University, Austin, TX 78704.
- St. Edwards Univ. students. w. ISSN 0018-1870

**St. Elizabeth Mission Society**
- Zeal. (pub. by Franciscan Sisters of Allegany)

**St. George Association of the U.S.A.**
83 Christopher St., New York, NY 10014.
- St. George Association Newsletter. q.

**St. James Armenian Apostolic Church**
465 Mt. Auburn St, Watertown, MA 02172.
- Looys. m(10 per yr.) ISSN 0024-6476

**St. John Medical Center**
1923 So. Utica, Tulsa, OK 74104.
- Pulse (Tulsa) m. ISSN 0033-4197

**Saint John's Abbey**
Collegeville, MN 56321.
- Sisters Today. m. ISSN 0037-590X

**St. John's College. Office of College Relations**
College Ave., Annapolis, MD 21404.
- College. q. ISSN 0010-0862

**St. John's University. Business Research Institute**
Room 103, Grand Central & Utopia Parkway, Jamaica, NY 11439.
- Review of Business. m. ISSN 0034-6454

**St. John's University. Hill Monastic Manuscript Library**
Collegeville, MN 56321.
- Medieval and Renaissance Studies. irreg; no. 7, 1974.

**St. John's University Press**
Grand Central and Utopia Parkways, Jamaica, NY 11439.
- Asia in the Modern World Series. irreg., 1974, no. 13. ISSN 0084-6805
- Asian Institute Translations. irreg., 1972, no. 4. ISSN 0084-6813
- Asian Philosophical Studies. irreg; 1972, no. 5. ISSN 0066-8443
- Vincentian Studies. irreg. ISSN 0083-6281

**St. John's University. School of Law**
Grand Central and Utopia Parkways, Jamaica, NY 11439.
- Catholic Lawyer. q. ISSN 0008-8137
- St. John's Law Review. q. ISSN 0036-2905

**St. Joseph County's Official Museum**
- Old Courthouse News. (pub. by Northern Indiana Historical Society)

**St. Joseph Light & Power Co.**
520 Francis, St. Joseph, MO 64502.
- Contact. q.

**St. Joseph Museum**
11th and Charles Sts., St. Joseph, MO 64501.
- Museum Graphic. irreg. ISSN 0027-4046

**Saint Joseph's College (Collegeville)**
Box 772, Collegeville, IN 47978.
- Stuff. w. ISSN 0039-4181

**Saint Joseph's College (Philadelphia)**
c/o Humanistic Research Office, Philadelphia, PA 19131.
- Hephaistos. q. ISSN 0018-0440

**St. Joseph's Hospital**
523 North Third St., Brainerd, MN 56401.
- Heartbeat of St. Joseph's Hospital. q. ISSN 0017-9272

**St. Labre Indian School**
Ashland, MT 59003.
- Arrow (Ashland) m.
- Morning Star People. q. ISSN 0047-8121

**Saint Lawrence Seaway Development Corporation**
*see* **U.S. Saint Lawrence Seaway Development Corporation**

**St. Lawrence University**
Canton, NY 13617.
- St. Lawrence University. Conference on the Adirondack Park (Proceedings) a.

**St. Lawrence University. Department of English**
c/o Joe David Bellamy, Ed., Canton, NY 13617.
- Fiction International. s-a. ISSN 0092-1912

**St. Lazarus Trust**
c/o D. R. Puller, Ed., 32 Blue Spruce Circle, Weston, CT 06880.
- International Lazarite. q.

**St. Louis. Board of Police Commissioners**
Metropolitan Police Dept., 1200 Clark Ave., St. Louis, MO 63103.
- Saint Louis Police Journal. 6-10 per yr.

**St. Louis (County) Health Department. Conference of Local Environmental Health Administrators**
504 East 2nd St., Duluth, MN 55805.
- Conference of Local Environmental Health Administrators. Newsletter. q. ISSN 0010-5562

**St. Louis Art Museum**
Forest Park, St. Louis, MO 63110.
- St. Louis Art Museum. Annual Report. a.
- St. Louis Art Museum. Bulletin. bi-m.

**St. Louis College of Pharmacy**
4588 Parkview Pl., St. Louis, MO 63110.
- Pharmaceutical Trends; continuing education for pharmacists and physicians. m.

**St. Louis Genealogical Society**
Suite 203, 1695 S. Brentwood Blvd., St. Louis, MO 63144.
- St. Louis Genealogical Society. News and Notes. m.
- St. Louis Genealogical Society Quarterly. q. ISSN 0036-2956

**St. Louis Jewish Light, Inc.**
Room 1300, Railway Exchange Bldg., 611 Olive St., St. Louis, MO 63101.
- St. Louis Jewish Light; the newspaper of the Jewish community of Greater St. Louis. fortn. ISSN 0036-2964 (Jewish Federation of St. Louis)

**St. Louis Park Medical Center**
5000 W. 39th St, Minneapolis, MN 55416.
- St. Louis Park Medical Center. Bulletin. q. ISSN 0036-2980

**St. Louis Pharmacists' Association**
100 St. Francois St., Suite 209, Florissant, MO 63031.
- St. Louis Pharmacists' Association Magazine. ISSN 0036-2999

**St. Louis Public Library**
1301 Olive St., St. Louis, MO 63103.
- Index to St. Louis Newspapers. m.

**St. Louis Regional Commerce and Growth Association**
10 Broadway, St. Louis, MO 63102.
- St. Louis Commerce. m. ISSN 0036-293X

**St. Louis University**
St. Louis, MO 63103.
- Classical Bulletin. m.(Nov-Apr) ISSN 0009-8337

**St. Louis University. College of Philosophy and Letters**
3700 W. Pine Blvd., St. Louis, MO 63108.
- Modern Schoolman; a quarterly of philosophy. q. ISSN 0026-8402 (Co-sponsor: St. Louis University. Department of Philosophy)

**St. Louis University. Pius XII Memorial Library**
3655 W. Pine St., St. Louis, MO 63108.
- Afro-American Research Bibliography. irreg., no. 6, 1972. ISSN 0065-4183
- Manuscripta; a journal devoted to manuscript studies. 3 per yr. ISSN 0025-2603
- St. Louis University. Pius XII Library. Publications. irreg. ISSN 0080-5483

**St. Louis University. School of Divinity**
St. Louis, MO 63108.
- Theology Digest. q. ISSN 0040-5728

**St. Louis University School of Law**
3642 Lindell Blvd., St Louis, MO 63108.
- Saint Louis University Law Journal. q. ISSN 0036-3030

**St. Louis Westerners**
227 Hyacinth Court, St. Louis, MO 63122.
- Westward. s-a.

**St. Luke's Hospital Medical Staff**
130 E. Bannock Street, Boise, ID 83702.
- St. Luke's Hospital. Medical Staff Journal. 3 per yr.

**St. Martin's Press**
175 Fifth Ave., New York, NY 10010.
- Biological Sciences. irreg.
- Documents of Modern History. irreg.
- Grants Register. biennial. ISSN 0072-5471 (And St. James Press, 3 Percy St., London W1P 9FA, England)
- International Index to Film Periodicals. irreg. ISSN 0000-0388
- Macmillan New Studies in Ethics Series. irreg.
- Making of the Twentieth Century. irreg.
- Surveys of Applied Economics. irreg.
- West and the World: Studies in History. irreg.

**Saint Mary's College**
Notre Dame, IN 46556.
- Chimes. q. ISSN 0009-4285

**St. Mary's University School of Law**
One Camino Santa Maria, San Antonio, TX 78284.
- St. Mary's Law Journal. 4 per yr.

**St. Mawr Jazz Poetry Project**
St. Mawr, Box 615, Middlebury, VT 05753.
- Veins. q.

**St. Meinrad Archabbey**
- Marriage and Family Living. (pub. by Abbey Press)

**St. Olaf College**
Northfield, MN 55057.
- Viking. irreg. ISSN 0095-5744

**St. Patrick's Parish House**
14 E. 51st St., New York, NY 10022.
- Alive and Well and Living in New York City Saint Patrick's Cathedral. m.

**St. Paul. Metropolitan Transit Commission**
Metro Square Bldg., St. Paul, MN 55101 (Dist. by Natl. Technical Information Service, Springfield, Va. 22151)
- St. Paul, Minnesota. Metropolitan Transit Commission. Annual Report. a. ISSN 0082-710X

**Saint Paul. St. Paul**
801 American Center, St. Paul, MN 55101.
- Transit News. q. ISSN 0049-4402

**St. Paul Area Chamber of Commerce**
Suite 300, The Osborn Building, St. Paul, MN 55102.
- Saint Paul Area Chamber of Commerce Action. m. ISSN 0036-3146
- Saint Paul Area Chamber of Commerce Dialogue. 3 per m.

**St. Paul Athletic Club**
340 Cedar St., St. Paul, MN 55101.
- Ace. m. ISSN 0044-5932

**St. Paul Companies Inc.**
385 Washington St., St. Paul, MN 55102.
- St. Paul News. fortn. ISSN 0036-3154

**St. Paul Public Library**
90 W. Fourth St., St. Paul, MN 55102.
- St. Paul Dispatch & Pioneer Press Newspaper Index. m. (plus cumulative nos. 2 per yr.) ISSN 0048-900X
- Your Library Presents. m. ISSN 0044-1058

**St. Paul's Abbey**
Box 7, Newton, NJ 07860.
- Pax. q.

**St. Paul's Indian Mission**
Marty, SD 57361.
- Little Bronzed Angel. bi-m. ISSN 0024-5011

**St. Regis Paper Co.**
150 E. 42nd St., New York, NY 10017.
- St. Regis News. m.

**St. Regis Publications, Inc.**
6 E. 43 St., New York, NY 10017.
- Consumer Electronics Product News. m.
- Engineering Graphics. m.
- High Fidelity Trade News. m. ISSN 0046-7367
- Personal Communications Show Daily. d.

**St. Rita School for the Deaf**
1720 Glendale-Milford Rd., Cincinnati, OH 45215.
- Silent Advocate. bi-m. ISSN 0037-5187

**St. Stephens Mission**
St. Stephens, WY 82524.
- Wind River Rendezvous. bi-m.

**St. Vladimir's Orthodox Theological Seminary**
575 Scarsdale Rd., Crestwood, Tuckahoe, NY 10707.
- St. Vladimir's Theological Quarterly. q. ISSN 0036-3227

**St. Xavier College**
c/o Dr. Harry A. Marmion, 103 Aud Central Park Ave., Chicago, IL 60655.
- Continuum. q. ISSN 0010-7786

**Frank Salantrie, Ed. & Pub.**
Box 1641, Chicago, IL 60690.
- The Original Art Report (TOAR); committed to the preservation, comprehension, and progress of art and artists. m. ISSN 0030-5529

**Salart House Inc.**
P.O. Box 642, Scottsdale, AZ 85252.
- Boxing Guide. irreg.

**Salem County Historical Society**
79-83 Market St., Salem, NJ 08079.
- Salem County Historical Society Newsletter. q. ISSN 0036-3383

**Salem State College. Student Government Association**
SGA Office, Student Union, Lafayette St., Salem, MA 01970.
- Gone Soft. s-a.

**Sales and Marketing Executives International, Inc.**
380 Lexington Ave., New York, NY 10017.
- Marketing Times; journal of continuing education. bi-m.

**Sales Association of the Chemical Industry, Inc.**
79 Madison Ave., New York, NY 10016.
- Chemical Peddler. a. ISSN 0069-2999

**Sales Executives Club of New York**
Hotel Roosevelt, Madison Ave. & 45th St., New York, NY 10017.
- Sales Executive. w.(except Aug.) ISSN 0036-3405

**Salesian Missions**
Box 30-148 Main St., New Rochelle, NY 10802.
- Salesian. q. ISSN 0036-3480

**Salesman's Guide, Inc.**
1140 Broadway, New York, NY 10001.
- Directory of Buying Offices and Accounts. a. ISSN 0070-5195
- Directory of Premium, Incentive and Travel Buyers. a. with quarterly supplements.
- Infants to Teens Wear Buyers. s-a. ISSN 0019-9559
- Men's and Boys' Wear Buyers. s-a. ISSN 0025-9411
- Nationwide Directory of Men's and Boys Wear Buyers (Exclusive of New York Metropolitan Area) a.(with quarterly supplements) ISSN 0077-5983
- Nationwide Directory of Women's and Children's Wear Buyers (Exclusive of New York Metropolitan Area) a.(with quarterly supplements) ISSN 0077-5991
- Nationwide Major Mass Market Merchandisers (Exclusive of New York Metropolitan Area) a. ISSN 0077-6009
- Women's Accessories Directory; New York Metropolitan Area. a. ISSN 0084-1056
- Women's Coats and Suits Directory; New York Metropolitan Area. a. ISSN 0084-1064
- Women's Intimate Apparel Buyers. s-a. ISSN 0043-7549
- Women's, Misses & Jr. Dress Buyers. s-a.
- Women's, Misses & Jr. Sportswear Buyers. s-a.

**Salisbury State College**
Salisbury, MD 21801.
- Literature/Film Quarterly. q. ISSN 0090-4260

**Salisbury Times, Inc.**
Salisbury, MD 21801.
- Delmarva Poultry & Farm. w. ISSN 0011-7919

**Salk Institute for Biological Studies**
Box 1809, San Diego, CA 92112.
- Salk Institute for Biological Studies. Occasional Papers. irreg. ISSN 0080-5653

**Salome**
5548 N. Sawyer Ave., Chicago, IL 60625.
- Salome. q.

**Salon Ltd.**
111 S. Pine St., Norborne, MO 64668.
- Controversy (Norborne) s-m.

**Salt Lake Area Chamber of Commerce**
19 E. 2nd South St., Salt Lake City, UT 84111.
- Salt Lake Business Comminique. m.

**Salt Lick Press**
Box 1064, Quincy, IL 62301.
- Salt Lick. irreg. ISSN 0036-360X

**Salt Water Sportsman, Inc.**
10 High St., Boston, MA 02110.
- Salt Water Sportsman. m. ISSN 0036-3618

**Salted Feathers**
932 S. E. 40th, Portland, OR 97214.
- Salted Feathers. irreg. ISSN 0036-3626

**Saltzman Companies**
27540 Pacific Coast Highway, Malibu, CA 90265.
- Eurail Guide; how to travel Europe by train. a. ISSN 0085-0330

**Salvage Bids**
Box 5, Laconia, NH 03246.
- Salvage Bids. fortn. ISSN 0036-3669

**Salvation Army**
545 Avenue of the Americas, New York, NY 10011.
- War Cry. w. ISSN 0043-0234

**Sam Houston State University. English Department**
Huntsville, TX 77340.
- Sam Houston Literary Review. irreg.

**Sam Houston State University. Institute of Contemporary Corrections and the Behavioral Sciences**
Huntsville, TX 77340.
- Sam Houston State University. Institute of Contemporary Corrections and the Behavioral Sciences. Proceedings Interagency Workshop. a.

**Sam Lusky**
Suite 811 First National Bank, Denver, CO 80202.
- Sportscope. m.

**Samford University**
- Cumberland Law Review. (pub. by Birmingham Publishing Co.)

**Samisdat**
Box 1534, San Jose, CA 95109.
- Samisdat. q.

**Howard W. Sams & Co., Inc.**
4300 W. 62nd St., Indianapolis, IN 46268.
- E I A Electronics Multimedia Handbook. irreg. ISSN 0360-1757 (Electronic Industries Association)
- Forest H. Belt's Yearbook of Consumer Electronics. a. ISSN 0093-3155
- North American Radio-T V Guide. a. ISSN 0078-1347
- Photofact Annual Index. a. ISSN 0556-5006
- Refernce Data for Radio Engineers. irreg.
- Rocket and Space Science Series. irreg. ISSN 0080-3413
- Sams Modular Hi-Fi Components. m.
- Sams Transistor Radio. m.

**San Antonio Development Agency**
418 South Laredo, San Antonio, TX 78207.
- Project. m.

**San Antonio District Dental Society**
935 Eventide, San Antonio, TX 78209.
- San Antonio District Dental Society. Journal. m. ISSN 0036-3979

**San Bernardino County Library**
104 W. 4th St., San Bernardino, CA 92415.
- Friends of the San Bernardino County Library. News Letter. bi-m. ISSN 0016-1330
- San Bernardino County Library Newsletter. m. ISSN 0036-3995

**San Bernardino County Museum Association**
2024 Orange Tree Lane, Redlands, CA 92373.
- San Bernardino County Museum Association. Newsletter. m. ISSN 0048-9077
- San Bernardino County Museum Association. Quarterly. q.

**San Diego (City) City Planning Department**
202 C St., San Diego, CA 92101.
- San Diego Population and Land Use Bulletin. q.

**San Diego (County) County Planning Department**
1600 Pacific Highway, San Diego, CA 92101.
- San Diego County Planning Department. Planning Data. irreg.

**San Diego (County) Department of Education**
Superintendent of Schools, 6401 Linda Vista Rd., San Diego, CA 92111.
- Education San Diego County. m.(10 per yr.)

**San Diego (County) Integrated Planning Office**
1600 Pacific Highway, San Diego, CA 92101.
- San Diego County Integrated Planning Office Population and Housing. s-a.

**San Diego Applause Magazine, Inc.**
2461 Fifth Ave., San Diego, CA 92101.
- Applause; San Diego magazine of the arts. m.

**San Diego Biomedical Symposium. Proceedings**
Box 965, San Diego, CA 92112.
- San Diego Biomedical Symposium. Proceedings. a. ISSN 0095-5876

**San Diego Chamber of Commerce**
233 A St., Suite 300, San Diego, CA 92101.
- San Diego Business Survey. a. ISSN 0080-5882

**San Diego County Dental Society**
306 Walnut, Suite 31, San Diego, CA 92103.
- San Diego County Dental Society. News. m.

**San Diego County Labor Council**
2232 el Cajon Blvd., San Diego, CA 92104.
- Labor Leader. s-m. ISSN 0023-6594

**San Diego County Medical Society**
3702 Ruffin Rd., Box 23015, San Diego, CA 92103.
- San Diego Physician. m. ISSN 0036-4061

**San Diego Floral Association**
Balboa Park, San Diego, CA 92101.
- California Garden. bi-m. ISSN 0008-1116

**San Diego Genealogical Society**
Studio 30, Spanish Village, Balboa Park, San Diego, CA 92101.
- San Diego Leaves and Saplings. q.

**San Diego Historical Society**
Serra Museum Library & Tower Gallery, Presidio Park, Box 81825, San Diego, CA 92138.
- Journal of San Diego History. q. ISSN 0022-4383

**San Diego Law Review Association**
- San Diego Law Review. (pub. by University of San Diego. School of Law)

**San Diego Magazine Publishing Co.**
3254 Rosecrans, San Diego, CA 92110.
- San Diego. m. ISSN 0036-4045

**San Diego Museum of Man**
Balboa Park, San Diego, CA 92101.
- San Diego. Museum of Man. Ethnic Technology Notes. irreg., 1973, no. 11. ISSN 0080-5890
- San Diego. Museum of Man. Papers. irreg., 1969, no. 6. ISSN 0080-5904

**San Diego Numismatic Society Inc.**
611 Oakwood Way, El Cajon, CA 92021.
- San Diego Numismatic Society. Bulletin. m. ISSN 0036-4053

**San Diego Society of Natural History**
Balboa Park, Box 1390, San Diego, CA 92112.
- San Diego Society of Natural History. Memoirs. irreg. ISSN 0080-5920
- San Diego Society of Natural History. Occasional Papers. irreg. ISSN 0080-5939
- San Diego Society of Natural History. Transactions. irreg. ISSN 0080-5947

**San Diego State University. Bureau of Business and Economic Research**
School of Business Administration, San Diego, CA 92182.
- San Diego State University. Bureau of Business and Economic Research. Monographs. irreg. ISSN 0068-5836
- San Diego State University. Bureau of Business and Economic Research. Research Studies and Position Papers. irreg., 1968, no. 18. ISSN 0068-5844

**San Diego State University Press**
San Diego, CA 92182.
- Pacific Coast Council on Latin American Studies. Proceedings. a.

**San Francisco Aquarium Society Inc.**
California Academy of Sciences, Golden Gate Park, San Francisco, CA 94118.
- Golden Gate Aquarist. m.

**San Francisco Bay Area Dance Coalition**
1412 Van Ness Ave., San Francisco, CA 94109.
- West Coast Dance Calendar. 12 per yr.

**San Francisco Bay Area Rapid Transit District**
800 Madison St., Oakland, CA 94607.
- San Francisco Bay Area Rapid Transit District. Annual Report. a. ISSN 0362-2800

**San Francisco Bay Conservation and Development Commission**
30 Van Ness Ave., San Francisco, CA 94102.
- San Francisco Bay Conservation and Development Commission. Annual Report. a. ISSN 0085-5898

**San Francisco Labor Council, AFL-CIO**
- Northern California Labor. (pub. by San Francisco Labor Council Newspaper Association)

**San Francisco Labor Council Newspaper Association**
3068-16th St., San Francisco, CA 94103.
- Northern California Labor. m. (San Francisco Labor Council, AFL-CIO) (Co-Sponsor: Santa Clara County Central Labor Council)

**San Francisco Maritime Museum**
Foot of Polk St., San Francisco, CA 94109.
- Sea Letter. q. ISSN 0037-0010

**San Francisco Medical Society**
250 Masonic Ave., San Francisco, CA 94118.
- San Francisco Medicine. m.

**San Francisco Phoenix**
Box 15081, 79 Beaver St., San Francisco, CA 94115.
- San Francisco Phoenix. fortn.

**San Francisco Planning and Urban Renewal Association**
126 Post St., San Francisco, CA 94108.
- S.P.U.R. Report. m. ISSN 0361-6444

**San Francisco Publishing Co.**
84 Vandewater, San Francisco, CA 94133.
- San Francisco Reel; cinemagazine. bi-m. ISSN 0036-4150

**San Francisco Review of Books**
2140 Vallejo St., San Francisco, CA 94123.
- San Francisco Review of Books. m.

**San Francisco Society for the Prevention of Cruelty to Animals**
2500 16th St., San Francisco, CA 94103.
- Our Animals. bi-m. ISSN 0030-6789

**San Francisco State University. Adan E. Treganza Anthropology Museum**
1600 Holloway Ave., San Francisco, CA 94132.
- Adan E. Treganza Anthropology Museum. Papers. irreg, nos. 9-15, 1975. ISSN 0065-1850

**San Francisco State University. Alumni Association**
1600 Holloway, San Francisco, CA 94132.
- Franciscan. q. ISSN 0015-9808

**San Francisco State University. Audio Visual Center**
1600 Holloway, San Francisco, CA 94132.
- San Francisco State University. Audio-Visual Center. Media Catalog. irreg. ISSN 0068-5860

**San Francisco State University. Journalism Department**
1600 Holloway, San Francisco, CA 94132.
- Feed/back; the journalism report and review for Northern California. q.

**San Francisco Sunday Examiner & Chronicle**
925 Mission St., San Francisco, CA 94103.
- California Living. w.

**San Francisco Theological Seminary**
San Anselmo, CA 94960.
- Pacific Theological Review. 3 per yr.

**San Francisco Unified School District**
135 Van Ness Ave., San Francisco, CA 94102.
- San Francisco Unified School District Newsletter. bi-m. ISSN 0036-4169

**San Gabriel Valley Dental Society**
2360 Huntington Drive, Suite 301, San Marino, CA 91108.
- San Gabriel Valley Dental Society. Bulletin. m. ISSN 0048-9093

**San Jose State University**
San Jose, CA 95192.
- San Jose Studies. 3 per yr.

**San Jose State University. School of Business**
San Jose, CA 95192.
- Journal of Financial Education. a. ISSN 0093-3961

**San Jose Teachers Association**
2476-A Almaden Expressway, San Jose, CA 95125.
- S J T A News. bi-m. ISSN 0036-1577

**San Luis Obispo County Historical Society**
696 Monterey St., San Luis Obispo, CA 93401.
- Vista/View. s-a. ISSN 0042-708X

**San Luis Valley Historical Society, Inc.**
Box 982, Alamosa, CO 81101.
- San Luis Valley Historian. q. ISSN 0036-4215

**San Mateo County Dental Society**
1941 O'Farrel St., San Mateo, CA 94403.
- San Mateo County, California. Dental Society. Bulletin. irreg. ISSN 0080-598X

**Sanborn Map Company, Inc.**
12 E. 41st St., New York, NY 10017.
- Real Estate Directory of Manhattan. a. ISSN 0098-8936
- Real Estate Record and Builder's Guide. w. ISSN 0034-0774

**Sanders Worldwide, Inc.**
Box 44428, Panorama City, CA 91402.
• Marijuana Monthly. m.

**T. K. Sanderson Organization**
200 E. 25 St., Baltimore, MD 21218.
• Directory of American Savings and Loan
Associations. a. ISSN 0070-5098
• Directory of Central Atlantic States
Manufacturers. Maryland, Delaware, Virginia,
West Virginia, North Carolina, South Carolina. a.
ISSN 0070-5241

**Sandoz Pharmaceuticals. Drug Information
Association**
East Hanover, NJ 07936.
• Drug Information Journal. 2-4 per yr. ISSN 0092-
8615

**SANE: A Citizens' Organization for a Sane World**
318 Massachusetts Ave. N. E., Washington, DC
20002.
• SANE World. m. ISSN 0036-4304

**Sangamon State University**
Springfield, IL 62708.
• Community College Frontiers. q. (Co-Sponsor:
Governors State Univ.)

**Sangamon State University. Illinois Legislative
Studies Center**
Springfield, IL 62709.
• Illinois Issues Annual. a.

**Sangre de Cristo Press**
1325 Cabrillo Ave., No.12, Venice, CA 90291.
• Janus & S C T H. (Sonnet, Cinquain, Tanka and
Haiku) q. ISSN 0021-4272

**Sanitary Maintenance**
407 E. Michigan St., Milwaukee, WI 53201.
• Sanitary Maintenance; the journal of the sanitary
supply industry. m. ISSN 0036-4436

**Sanity Now**
Box 261, La Puente, CA 91747.
• Sanity Now. m.

**Santa Barbara Museum of Natural History**
2559 Puesta del Sol Road, Santa Barbara, CA
93105.
• Santa Barbara Museum of Natural History.
Museum Bulletin. bi-m.

**Santa Clara (County) County Planning Department**
70 W. Hedding St., San Jose, CA 95110.
• Info. 3 per yr.
• Santa Clara Valley Plans. 3 per yr.

**Santa Clara County Historical and Genealogical
Society**
City Library, 2635 Homestead Rd., Santa Clara, CA
95051.
• Santa Clara County Historical & Genealogical
Quarterly. q. ISSN 0036-4517

**Sarah Lawrence College**
Bronxville, NY 10708.
• Sarah Lawrence Literary Review. a. ISSN 0036-
4746

**Sarasota Publishing Corp.**
Box 3555, Sarasota, FL 33578.
• Sarasota Town & County Magazine. bi-m.

**Porter Sargent Publishers, Inc.**
11 Beacon St., Boston, MA 02108.
• Directory for Exceptional Children; educational
and training facilities. biennial; 8th ed., 1978.
ISSN 0070-5012
• Guide to Summer Camps and Summer Schools.
biennial; 20th ed., 1977. ISSN 0072-8705
• Handbook of Private Schools. a. ISSN 0072-9884
• Schools Abroad. irreg., 3rd. edt. 1975. ISSN 0080-
6900

**Sasquatch Publishing, Inc.**
85 South Washington St., Seattle, WA 98104.
• Weekly of Metropolitan Seattle. w.

**Joel Sater, Ed. & Pub.**
Box B, 225 E. Market, Marietta, PA 17547.
• Antiques and Auction News. fortn.

**Saturday Evening Post Company**
1100 Waterway Blvd., P.O. Box 567B, Indianapolis,
IN 46206.
• Child Life; mystery and science-fiction magazine.
m.(Sept-June); bi-m.(June-Sept) ISSN 0009-3971
• Children's Playmate. m. (bi-m. Jun-July; Aug-Sep)
ISSN 0009-4161
• Jack and Jill Magazine (Inkprint Edition) m (Oct.-
May); bi-m (Jun.-Sept.) ISSN 0021-3829 (Curtis
Publishing Co.)
• Plywood & Panel. m. ISSN 0032-177X
• Post Scripts. m.
• Saturday Evening Post. m (except Jan. , Jun.,
Aug.) ISSN 0048-9239
• Trap & Field. m. ISSN 0041-1760
• Young World. m.

**Saturday Review Book Club**
59 Fourth Ave., New York, NY 10003.
• Saturday Review Book Club News. m.

**Saturday Review Inc.**
488 Madison Ave., New York, NY 10022.
• Saturday Review; a review of ideas, creative arts
and human condition. w.

**W. B. Saunders Co.**
West Washington Square, Philadelphia, PA 19105.
• Clinics in Perinatology. s-a. ISSN 0095-5108
• Clinics in Plastic Surgery. q. ISSN 0094-1298
• Dental Clinics of North America. 4 per yr. ISSN
0011-8532
• Human Pathology. bi-m. ISSN 0046-8177
• Medical Clinics of North America. bi-m. ISSN
0025-7125
• Nursing Clinics of North America. q. ISSN 0029-
6465
• Orthopedic Clinics of North America. q. ISSN
0030-5898
• Otolaryngologic Clinics of North America. 3 per
yr. ISSN 0030-6665
• Pediatric Clinics of North America. q. ISSN
0031-3955
• Pediatric Conferences with Sydney Gellis. bi-m.
ISSN 0091-004X
• Primary Care: Clinics in Office Practice. q. ISSN
0095-4543
• Radiologic Clinics of North America. 3 per yr.
ISSN 0033-8389
• Rational Drug Therapy. m. ISSN 0031-7020
(American Society for Pharmacology &
Experimental Therapeutics)
• Surgical Clinics of North America. bi-m. ISSN
0039-6109
• Today's Surgery. bi-m.
• Urologic Clinics of North America. 3 per yr.
ISSN 0094-0143
• Veterinary Clinics of North America. q. ISSN
0091-0279

**Savage**
1049 West Taylor St., Chicago, IL 60607.
• Savage; a Chicano magazine. s-a.

**Savannah Magazine, Inc.**
101 East 36 St, Savannah, GA 31401.
• Savannah. m.

**Savannah State College**
State College Branch, c/o Office of Public
Relations, Savannah, GA 31404.
• Savannah State College Bulletin. a. ISSN 0036-
5076

**Save on Shopping Directory**
Box 96, Dearborn, MI 48121.
• S.O.S. Directory. (Save on Shopping, Shop Outlet
Stores) a. ISSN 0092-8003

**Savings Association League of New York State**
700 White Plains Rd., Scarsdale, NY 10583.
• Savings Association League of New York State.
Legislative Bulletin. w.
• Savings Association News. m. ISSN 0036-5122

**Savings Bank Association of New York State**
200 Park Ave., New York, NY 10017.
• It's Your Money. m.

**Savings Banks Association of Massachusetts**
50 Congress St., Boston, MA 02109.
• Savings Banker. m.

**Sawmill Clinic**
• Modern Sawmill Techniques. (pub. by Miller
Freeman Publications, Inc.)

**Scandalous Bohemians of New Jersey**
c/o Norman Nolan, 68 Crest Rd., Middletown, NJ
07748.
• Scandal Sheet. irreg.

**Scandinavian American Bulletin**
6005 Eighth Ave., Brooklyn, NY 11220.
• Scandinavian American Bulletin. m. ISSN 0048-
9263

**Scandinavian Philatelic Services Corp.**
Box 175, Ben Franklin Sta., Washington, DC 20044.
• Scandinavian Scribe. m.

**Scarborough Publishing Co.**
Box 225, Briarcliff Manor, NY 10510.
• Package Development & Systems; the magazine
for packaging professionals. bi-m.

**Scarecrow Books**
1050 Magnolia, No. 2, Millbrae, CA 94030.
• Crow's Nest. a.
• West Conscious Review. s-a.

**Scarecrow Press, Inc.**
52 Liberty St., Box 656, Metuchen, NJ 08840.
• A T L A Bibliography Series. irreg. (American
Theological Library Association)
• A T L A Monograph Series. irreg. (American
Theological Library Association)
• African Historical Dictionaries. irreg; no. 12,
1977.
• Annual Index to Popular Music Record Reviews.
a. ISSN 0092-3486
• Author Bibliographies Series. irreg.
• Bookman's Guide to Americana. irreg; 7th ed.,
1977. ISSN 0068-0133
• Catalog of Reprints in Series. Supplements. a,
21st., 1972.
• Index of American Periodical Verse. a. ISSN
0090-9130
• Index to Book Reviews in Historical Periodicals.
irreg. ISSN 0362-8671
• Library Lit. a. ISSN 0085-2767
• Popular Music Periodicals Index. a. ISSN 0095-
4101
• Research in Parapsychology. a. ISSN 0094-7172
(Parapsychological Association)
• Scarecrow Author Bibliographies. irreg; no. 33,
1977.
• Scarecrow Concordances. irreg.
• Speech Index; an index to 259 collections of
orations and speeches for various occasions. irreg.,
1966, 4th ed. ISSN 0081-3656
• Titles in Series; a handbook for librarians and
students. irreg. ISSN 0082-4526

**Sidney Schafer**
2200 Welch Ave., Houston, TX 77019.
• Oil & Gas Directory. a. ISSN 0471-380X

**R. & M. Scharfenberg Literature Searchers**
P.O. Box 8232, Riverside, CA 92505.
• C I P H E R Literature Searchers. (Current Index
to Physical Education and Recreation) m.
• Hypnosis Literature. m.

**Meyer Schattner**
246 W. 44 St., New York, NY 10036.
• Stubs; the seating plan guide for Western theatres,
music halls, sports stadia. irreg. ISSN 0081-6051
(Stubs Publications)

**Schechter Report-Labs**
c/o Mal Schechter, 1230 National Press Bldg.,
Washington, DC 20045.
• Schechter Report-Labs. 22 per yr.

**Schenkman Publishing Company, Inc.**
250 James Street, Morristown, NJ 07960.
• Schenkman Social Stratification Series. irreg.

**Schiffli Lace and Embroidery Manufacturers
Association**
512 23 St., Union City, NJ 07087.
• Embroidery Directory. a. ISSN 0080-6811

**Victor O. Schinnerer & Co.**
5028 Wisconsin Ave., N.W., Washington, DC
20016.
• A. E. Legal Newsletter. (Architects and
Engineers) m. ISSN 0090-2411
• Guidelines for Improving Practice. Architects and
Engineers Professional Liability. irreg., latest issue
1975. ISSN 0091-8245

**G. Schirmer, Inc.**
866 Third Ave., New York, NY 10022.
• Musical Quarterly. 4 per yr. ISSN 0027-4631

**Charles Schlacks, Jr., Ed. & Pub.**
c/o G-6 Mervis Hall, University of Pittsburgh,
Pittsburgh , PA 15260.
• Byzantine Studies. 2-4 per yr.
• Canadian-American Slavic Studies/Revue
Canadienne-Americaine d'Etudes Slaves. q. ISSN
0090-8290 (Co-Sponsor: Temple Univ.)
• East Central Europe/Europe du Centre Est. 2-4
per yr. ISSN 0094-3037
• Russian History/Histoire Russe. q. ISSN 0094-
288X
• Southeastern Europe. 2-4 per yr. ISSN 0094-4467
• Soviet Union/Union Sovietique. irreg. ISSN 0094-
2863

**Phyllis Schlafly**
Box 618, Alton, IL 62002.
• Phyllis Schlafly Report. m. ISSN 0556-0152

**Schlumberger Well Services**
5000 Gulf Freeway, Houston, TX 77023.
• Schlumberger Sonde Off. bi-m.

**Schnell Publishing Co.**
100 Church St., New York, NY 10007.
• Chemical Marketing Reporter. w. ISSN 0090-
0907

**Schocken Books, Inc.**
200 Madison Ave., New York, NY 10016.
• Studies in the Life of Women. irreg.

**Arnold Schoenberg Institute**
c/o University of Southern California, University
Park, Los Angeles, CA 90007.
• Arnold Schoenberg Institute. Journal. 3 per yr.

**Schoharie County Historical Society**
Schoharie, NY 12157.
• Schoharie County Historical Review. s-a. ISSN
0361-8528

**Scholarly Resources, Inc.**
1508 Pennsylvania Ave., Wilmington, DE 19806.
• Diplomatic History. q. (Society for Historians of
American Foreign Relations (S.H.A.F.R.))

**Scholars Press**
Univ. of Montana, Missoula, MT 59812.
• American Academy of Religion. Journal. q. ISSN
0002-7189 (American Academy of Religion)
• Harvard Theological Review. q. ISSN 0017-8160
(Harvard University)
• Harvard Theological Studies. irreg., 1970, no. 25.
ISSN 0073-0726 (Harvard University)
• Journal of Biblical Literature. q. ISSN 0021-9231
(Society of Biblical Literature)
• Journal of Religious Ethics. s-a.
• Masoretic Studies. irreg. (Society of Biblical
Literature) (Co-sponsor: International
Organization for Masoretic Studies)
• Semeia; an experimental journal for biblical
criticism. 3 per yr. (Society of Biblical Literature)
• Society of Biblical Literature. Texts and
Translations. irreg. (Society of Biblical Literature)
• Sociolinguistics Newsletter. q. ISSN 0049-1217
(International Sociological Association. Research
Committee on Sociolinguistics)

**Scholastic Magazines, Inc.**
50 W. 44th St., New York, NY 10036
(Subscr. to: 900 Sylvan Ave., Englewood Cliffs, NJ
07632)
• Art and Man. m.(6 per yr.) ISSN 0004-3052
• Bonjour.
• Ca Va. m. (Oct.-Jun.) ISSN 0007-9243
• Chez Nous. m. ISSN 0009-3424
• Co-Ed. m. ISSN 0009-9724
• Rad. m (Oct.-Jun.) ISSN 0033-7455
• Roller. m (Oct.-Jun.) ISSN 0035-7901
• Dynamite. m.
• Sol. m (Oct.-Jun.) ISSN 0038-0849
• Forecast for Home Economics. 9 per yr. ISSN
0015-7090
• Hoy Dia. m. (Oct.-Jun.) ISSN 0018-6856
• Junior Scholastic; a national magazine for junior
high school and upper elementary grades. w.(24
per yr.) ISSN 0022-6688
• Let's Find Out. m.(Oct-May) ISSN 0024-1261
• Literary Cavalcade. m.(8 per yr) ISSN 0024-4511
• News Citizen. w.(28 per yr.)
• News Explorer. w.(28 per yr.) ISSN 0028-9019
• News Trails; a weekly classroom periodical for
third graders. 28 per yr. ISSN 0028-9361

• Newstime; a Scholastic magazine. w.(Sept-May)
ISSN 0028-9590
• Que Tal. m.(during school year) ISSN 0033-5940
• Scholastic Action.
• Scholastic Coach. m. ISSN 0036-6382
• Scholastic News Pilot. w.(28 per yr.) ISSN 0028-
9329
• Scholastic News Ranger. w.(28 per yr.) ISSN
0036-6404
• Scholastic Scope. 24 per yr. ISSN 0036-6412
• Scholastic Search. fortn.(18 per yr.)
• Scholastic Voice. fortn.(18 per yr.) ISSN 0032-
6380
• Schuss. m.(Oct.-Jun.) ISSN 0048-9492
• Science World. w.(18 per yr.) ISSN 0036-8601
• Senior Scholastic. fortn.(18 per yr.) ISSN 0037-
2242
• Sprint. fortn.

**School Administration Publications**
Box 8492, Asheville, NC 28804.
• School Student and the Courts. q. ISSN 0098-
8952

**School Arts Magazine**
50 Portland St., Worcester, MA 01608.
• School Arts Magazine; the art education magazine
for teachers. 10 per yr.(Sept-June) ISSN 0036-
6463

**School Law Digest Corporation**
1611 Borel Pl., Suite 251, San Mateo, CA 94402
(Subscr. to: Box 6220, San Mateo CA 94403)
• California School Law Digest. m. ISSN 0094-2057
• Central School Law Digest. m.
• Western School Law Digest. m.

**School Law Review**
Box 307, Sun City, AZ 85351.
• North Central School Law Review. m.(Sept-June)
ISSN 0029-2664

**School Management Study Group**
860-18th Ave., Salt Lake City, UT 84103.
• S M S G Newsletter. 8 per yr. ISSN 0048-9441

**School Management Study Group (Fremont)**
4674 Richmond Ave, Fremont, CA 94536.
• Directory of Educational Consultants. a.

**School of Living**
Box 3233, York, PA 17402.
• Green Revolution. 10 per yr. ISSN 0017-3983

**School of Modern Photography**
1500 Cardinal Drive, Little Falls, NJ 07424.
• S M P Photo Market Newsletter. m.

**School of Natural Science Life in Action**
25355 Spanish Ranch Road, Los Gatos, CA 95030.
• Life in Action Magazine. bi-m.

**School of Ozarks Troglophiles**
Box 15, Point Lookout, MO 65726.
• Underground Leader. q.

**School Science and Mathematics Association, Inc.**
Box 1614, Indiana Univ. of Pa., Indiana, PA 15701.
• School Science and Mathematics; journal for all
science and mathematical teachers. m. (Oct-May)
ISSN 0036-6803

**School Sisters of Notre Dame. Mequon Province**
Notre Dame of the Lake, Mequon, WI 53092.
• School Sister of Notre Dame. q. ISSN 0487-6830

**School Vocational Center (Marion County)**
Jackson St., Fairmont, WV 26554.
• C E A - C T A News. m. ISSN 0007-8042

**Schoonmaker Associates**
Drawer M, Coram, NY 11727.
• Mainly Marketing; the Schoonmaker report to
technical managements. m. ISSN 0464-591X

**Simon Schuchat, Ed. and Pub.**
Box 1030, Peter Stuyvesant Sta., New York, NY
10009.
• 432 Review; a literary magazine. irreg.

**Schuyler County Historical Museum**
Corner Congress and Madison St., Rushville, IL
62681.
• Schuylerite. q.

**Schuyler County Historical Society**
Watkins Glen, NY 14801.
• Schuyler County Historical Society. Journal. q.

**Schwenkfelder Church. General Conference**
1 Seminary St., Pennsburg, PA 18073.
• Schwenkfeldian. q. ISSN 0036-8032

**Science Activities Publishing Co.**
8150 N. Central Park Ave, Skokie, IL 60076.
• Science Activities. m. ISSN 0036-8121

**Science & Behavior Books, Inc.**
Box 11457, Palo Alto, CA 94306.
• Clinical Approaches to the Problems of
Childhood: The Langley Porter Child Psychiatry
Series. irreg., vol. 5, 1971. ISSN 0069-4797

**Science and Government Report Inc.**
Box 6226, Washington, DC 20015.
• Science and Government Report. s-m. ISSN 0048-
9581

**Science & Medicine Publications**
3 W. 57th St., New York, NY 10019.
• Searle Review of Obstetrics & Gynecologic
Literature. a.

**Science and Medicine Publishing Co., Inc.**
515 Madison Ave., New York, NY 10022.
• Clinical Dentistry. bi-m. ISSN 0093-8769 (Eli
Lilly & Co.)
• Clinical Trends in Anesthesiology. bi-m. ISSN
0045-7175
• Clinical Trends in Cardiology. 8 per yr.
(Burroughs Wellcome Co.)
• Clinical Trends in Family Practice. 8 per yr.
(Burroughs Wellcome Co.)
• Clinical Trends in Ophthalmology,
Otolaryngology, Allergy. 8 per yr. ISSN 0529-
9675 (Burroughs Wellcome Co.)
• Clinical Trends in Osteopathic Medicine. 8 per yr.
(Burroughs Wellcome Co.)
• Clinical Trends in Rheumatology. bi-m. ISSN
0009-9317
• Clinical Trends in Urology. 8 per yr. (Burroughs
Wellcome Co.)
• Ob-Gyn Observer; the newsmagazine of obstetrics
and gynecology. 6 per yr. ISSN 0029-7445

**Science and Society, Inc.**
Room 4331, John Jay College C.U.N.Y., 445 W.
59th St., New York, NY 10003.
• Science and Society. q. ISSN 0036-8237

**Science and Technology**
48 E. 43rd St., 4th Fl., New York, NY 10017.
• Science and Technology; an interdisciplinary
monthly magazine for professional scientists and
engineers. m. ISSN 0036-8245

**Science Associates International Inc.**
1841 Broadway, New York, NY 10023.
• Computer Programs in Science and Technology.
q. ISSN 0045-7868
• Directory of Computerized Information in Science
and Technology. irreg. ISSN 0070-5330
• Information Hotline. 11 per yr.
• Information Reports and Bibliographies. 6 per yr.
• Readers Advisory Service. q.

**Science Editors, Inc.**
149 Thierman Lane, P.O. Box 7185, Louisville, KY
40207.
• Clin-Alert. 24 per yr. ISSN 0069-4770

**Science Fiction Book Review Index**
c/o Ed. Hal Hall, 3608 Meadow Oaks Lane, Bryan,
TX 77801.
• Science Fiction Book Review Index. a. ISSN
0085-5979

**Science Fiction Research Association**
3415 W. Pratt, Lincolnwood, IL 60645.
• Science Fiction Research Association Newsletter.
m. ISSN 0048-9646

**Science Fiction Review Monthly**
56 Eighth Ave., New York, NY 10014.
• Science Fiction Review Monthly. m.

**Science Fiction Writers of America**
c/o Thomas F. Monteleone, 7954 Lakecrest Drive,
Greenbelt, MD 20770.
• S F W A Bulletin. bi-m. ISSN 0036-1364

**Science for the People**
16 Union Square, Somerville, MA 02143.
• Science and Society Series. irreg.

**Science House Publishers**
59 Fourth Ave., New York, NY 10003.
- Current Issues in Psychiatry. irreg. ISSN 0590-3955

**Science Museum of Minnesota**
30 E. 10th St., St. Paul, MN 55101.
- Science Museum of Minnesota. Monograph. irreg.
- Science Museum of Minnesota. Scientific Publications, New Series. irreg.

**Science of Man**
c/o Joseph E. Vincent, 10421 Lampson Ave., Garden Grove, CA 92640.
- Science of Man. bi-m. ISSN 0048-9689

**Science of Mind Publications**
3251 W. Sixth St., Los Angeles, CA 90020.
- Science of Mind. m. ISSN 0036-8458

**Science Research Associates**
259 East Erie Street, Chicago, IL 60611.
- S R A Computer Science Series. irreg.
- Science Research Associates. Handbook of Job Facts. irreg. (prep. by its Guidance Publications and Service Department)

**Science Service, Inc. (Marion)**
231 W. Center St., Marion, OH 43302.
- Things of Science. m.

**Science Service, Inc. (Washington)**
1719 N St., N. W., Washington, DC 20036.
- Science News; the weekly summary of current science. w. ISSN 0036-8423

**Science Teachers Association of New York State**
- Science Teachers Bulletin. (pub. by Brador Publications)

**Scientific American Inc.**
415 Madison Ave., New York, NY 10017.
- Scientific American. m. ISSN 0036-8733

**Scientific Manpower Commission**
1776 Massachusetts Avenue, N.W., Washington, DC 20036.
- Salaries of Scientists, Engineers and Technicians; a summary of salary surveys. biennial.
- Science & Engineering Careers - a Bibliography. irreg.
- Scientific, Engineering, Technical Manpower Comments. m. ISSN 0036-8768
- Test Yourself for Science. irreg. ISSN 0420-0942

**Scientific Meetings Publications**
16336 Orchard Bend Road, Poway, CA 92064.
- Scientific Meetings. q. ISSN 0036-8806

**Scientific Newsletters, Inc.**
Box 4546, Anaheim, CA 92803.
- Radioassay News. m. ISSN 0098-0889
- Rx: R I A for Physicians. 10 per yr. ISSN 0362-5451

**Scientists Institute for Public Information (New York)**
49 East 53rd Street, New York, NY 10022.
- Scientists' Institute for Public Information Workbooks. irreg.

**Scientists Institute for Public Information (St. Louis)**
560 Trinity Ave., St. Louis, MO 63130
- Environment. 10 per yr. ISSN 0013-9157 (Subscr. to:, Box 3066, St. Louis, MO 63130)

**Scope Enterprises, Inc.**
2228 El Cajon Blvd., San Diego, CA 92104.
- Navy News. m. ISSN 0028-1662

**Scope Publications Inc.**
1132 National Press Bldg., Washington, DC 20004.
- Alcoholism and Alcohol Education Newsletter. m. ISSN 0044-7226
- Drugs and Drug Abuse Education. m. ISSN 0012-6675
- Energy Digest. s-m. ISSN 0012-317X
- Mental Health Scope. s-m. ISSN 0025-9675

**Scotia Publications**
71 Vanderbilt Ave., Box 3194, Grand Central Annex, New York, NY 10017.
- Scotia News. 10 per yr.

**E. P. Scott**
Box 446, Sudan, TX 79371.
- Parrott Talk. q. ISSN 0093-9811

**Scott Advertising & Publishing Co.**
30595 W. 8 Mile Rd., Livonia, MI 48152.
- Ceramic Arts & Crafts. m. ISSN 0009-0190
- Ceramic Teaching Projects and Trade News. q.

**Scott Air Force Base**
Headquarters, Belleville, IL 62225.
- Air Weather Service Observer. m. ISSN 0002-2616

**O. M. Scott & Sons**
Marysville, OH 43040.
- Lawn Care. 3 per yr. ISSN 0023-9402

**Scott Periodicals Corp.**
110 N. York Rd., Elmhurst, IL 60126.
- Ground Water Age. m. ISSN 0046-645X
- Wholesaler. m. ISSN 0032-1680
- Wholesaler Product Directory; the who-what-where of the plumbing, heating, piping, air-conditioning & refrigeration industry. a.

**Scott Publishing Company**
530 Fifth Ave., New York, NY 10036.
- Scott's Monthly Stamp Journal. m.
- Scott's Specialized Catalogue of U.S. Stamps. a.
- Scott's Standard Postage Stamp Catalogue. a.

**Scout Memorabilia**
1000 Golfview Rd., Glenview, IL 60025.
- Scout Memorabilia. 5 per yr.

**Scowrers & Molly Maguires of San Francisco**
4712 17th St., San Francisco, CA 94117.
- Vermissa Herald; a journal of Sherlockian affairs. q. ISSN 0042-4129

**Scrambling Press**
104 West Montgomery Ave., Apt. D, Ardmore, PA 19003.
- House Plants and Porch Gardens. bi-m.

**Scranton Publishing Co.**
434 S. Wabash Ave., Chicago, IL 60605.
- Rural & Urban Roads. m. ISSN 0035-9998
- Water and Sewage Works. m. ISSN 0043-1125
- Water and Wastes Digest. bi-m. ISSN 0043-1141

**Scree**
c/o Kirk Robertson, Box 761, Fallon, NV 89406.
- Scree. 3-4 per yr. ISSN 0360-2672

**Screen Actors Guild**
7750 Sunset Blvd., Hollywood, CA 90046.
- Screen Actor. q. ISSN 0036-956X

**Screen Actors Guild. New York Branch**
551 Fifth Ave., New York, NY 10017.
- Reel. s-a. ISSN 0034-2238

**Screw Machine Publishing Co., Inc.**
65 Broad St., Rochester, NY 14614.
- Automatic Machining. m. ISSN 0005-1071

**Scribe**
Box 96, Brookville, OH 45309.
- Scribe. q.

**Charles Scribner's Sons**
597 Fifth Ave., New York, NY 10017.
- Studies in Cultural History. irreg.

**Scripps Clinic and Research Foundation**
10666 N. Torrey Pines Rd., La Jolla, CA 92037.
- Scripps Clinic and Research Foundation. Annual Report. a. ISSN 0080-830X
- Scripps Clinic and Research Foundation. Scientific Report. irreg. ISSN 0361-3054

**Scripps Institution of Oceanography**
La Jolla, CA 92037.
- S I O: a Report on the Work and Programs of Scripps Institution of Oceanography. a. ISSN 0091-1518
- Scripps Institution of Oceanography. Bulletin. (pub. by University of California Press)
- Scripps Institution of Oceanography. Contributions. a. ISSN 0080-8326
- Scripps Institution of Oceanography. Deep Sea Drilling Project. Initial Reports. irreg. ISSN 0080-8334 (Dist. by: Supt. of Documents, Washington, DC 20402)

**Scripta Mathematica**
Amsterdam Ave. & 186th St., New York, NY 10033.
- Scripta Mathematica; devoted to the philosophy, history and expository treatment of mathematics. q. ISSN 0036-9713

**Scripta Publishing Co.**
1511 K St., N.W., Washington, DC 20005.
- Electrical Engineering in Japan; scripta electronica Japonica I. bi-m. ISSN 0036-9691 (Institute of Electrical Engineers of Japan JA)
- Electronics and Communications in Japan; scripta electronica Japonica II. m. ISSN 0036-9683 (Institute of Electronics and Communication Engineers of Japan JA)
- Engineering Cybernetics. bi-m. ISSN 0013-788X (Akademiya Nauk S.S.S.R. UR)
- Entomological Review. q. ISSN 0013-8738 (Akademiya Nauk S.S.S.R. UR) (Co-Publisher: Entomological Society of America)
- Heat Transfer- Japanese Research. q. (Society of Chemical Engineers of Japan) (Co-sponsor: A S M E Heat Transfer Division)
- Hydrobiological Journal. bi-m. ISSN 0018-8166 (Ukrainian Academy of Sciences) (Co-Publisher: American Fisheries Society)
- Journal of Ichthyology/Problemy Ikhtiologii. bi-m. ISSN 0032-9452 (Akademiya Nauk S.S.S.R. UR) (Co-Publisher: American Fisheries Society)
- Neuroscience and Behavioral Physiology. q. (Federation of American Societies for Experimental Biology)
- Radio Engineering and Electronic Physics. m. ISSN 0033-7889 (Akademiya Nauk S.S.S.R. UR)
- Soviet Automatic Control. bi-m. ISSN 0038-5328 (Akademiya Nauk Ukrainskoi S.S.R.. Institut Kibernetiki UR)
- Soviet Geography: Review and Translation; designed to make available in English, reports of current Soviet research in geography. m.(Sept-June) ISSN 0038-5417 (American Geographical Society)
- Soviet Soil Science. bi-m. ISSN 0038-5832 (Akademiya Nauk S.S.S.R. UR)
- Systems-Computers-Controls; scripta electronica japonica III. bi-m. ISSN 0036-9705
- Telecommunications and Radio Engineering. m. ISSN 0040-2508

**Scripta Technica, Inc.**
1511 K St. N.W., Washington, DC 20005.
- Doklady - Earth Science Sections. bi-m. ISSN 0012-494X
- Geochemistry International. bi-m. ISSN 0016-7029
- Paleontological Journal. q. ISSN 0031-0301 (Akademiya Nauk S.S.S.R. UR)

**Scripture Press Publications, Inc.**
1825 College Ave., Wheaton, IL 60187.
- Bible-Time. q. ISSN 0006-0828
- Counselor. q. ISSN 0011-0019
- Freeway; a power/line paper. q.
- Power for Living. q. ISSN 0032-6003
- Primary Days; makes Bible truths live. q. ISSN 0032-8278
- Teen Power; a power/line paper. q.

**Sculpture in the Environment**
60 Greene St., New York, NY 10012.
- On S I T E. a. (Site, Inc.)

**Sdruzenia Slovenskych Katolikyo**
605 Ninth Ave, Munhall, PA 15120.
- Dobry Pastier. m.

**Sea Turtle Inc.**
c/o Robert D. Sloane, Pres., Box 15610, Ft. Lauderdale, FL 33318.
- Sloane Travel Agency Reports. bi-m.

**Seaboard Subscription Agency**
Box 1482, Allentown, PA 18105.
- Comprehensive Listing of Recommended Periodicals for Catholic Secondary School Libraries. a.

**Seabury Press**
815 Second Ave., New York, NY 10017.
- College Theology Society. Annual Publication. a.
- College Theology Society. Proceedings. a. ISSN 0069-5750 (College Theology Society)
- New Review of Books and Religion. m. (except Aug. & Dec.)

**Seafarers' International Union of North America**
AFL-CIO, 675 Fourth Ave., Brooklyn, NY 11232.
• Seafarers Log. m. ISSN 0037-0096

**Seal Club Chatter**
1605 E. 24th St., Des Moines, IA 50317.
• Seal Club Chatter. bi-m.

**Seamen's Church Institute of New York**
15 State St., New York, NY 10004.
• Lookout. 10 per yr. ISSN 0024-6425

**Seaport Publishing Co.**
c/o Ed. Clifford M. Montague, 843 Delray Ave.,
Grand Rapids, MI 49506.
• Yachtsman's Guide to the Caribbean. irreg., latest
issue 1975. ISSN 0084-3261
• Yachtsman's Guide to the Great Lakes. a. ISSN
0084-327X

**Search Group Inc.**
1620 35th Ave., Suite 200, Sacramento, CA 95822.
• Interface (Sacramento) q.
• Search Group. Technical Memorandum. irreg. (3-4
per yr)
• Search Group. Technical Report. irreg. (1-2 per
yr)

**G. D. Searle and Co.**
Box 1045, Skokie, IL 60076.
• Clinician. q.

**G.D. Searle & Co. Management Information Services**
P.O. Box 1054, Skokie, IL 60076.
• Management Contents. fortn. ISSN 0360-2400

**Sears Foundation for Marine Research**
Box 2161, Yale Station, New Haven, CT 06520.
• Journal of Marine Research. 4 per yr. ISSN 0022-
2402

**Seaside Topics**
Box 132, Westerly, RI 02891.
• Seaside Topics. w. Jun.-Sep.

**Seattle Audubon Society**
714 Joshua Green Bldg., Seattle, WA 98040.
• Seattle Audubon Society Notes. m. ISSN 0037-
0436

**Seattle Chamber of Commerce**
• Seattle Business. (pub. by Publishers Professional
Services)

**Seattle Film Society**
5236 18th Ave. N.E., Seattle, WA 98105.
• Movietone News. 10 per yr.

**Seattle-First National Bank**
Box 3586, Seattle, WA 98124.
• Summary of Pacific Northwest Industries. q. ISSN
0039-5013

**Seattle Folklore Society**
424 35th Ave., Seattle, WA 98122.
• Seattle Folklore Society Newsletter. q. ISSN
0037-0460

**Seattle Genealogical Society**
Box 549, Seattle, WA 98111.
• Seattle Genealogical Society Bulletin. q.

**Seattle-King County Dental Society**
• Seattle-King County Dental Society. Journal. (pub.
by Journal and Bulletin Agency)

**Seattle Opportunities Industrialization Center**
2332 E. Madison, Seattle, WA 98112.
• Adherent. s-a. ISSN 0360-9588 (Co-Sponsors:
Opportunities Industrialization Center of America;
Executive Directors Association)

**Seattle Professional Engineering Employees
Association**
5019 Barton Place South, Seattle, WA 98118.
• Aerospace Structures Design Conference. Papers.
irreg, 2nd, 1970.
• Spotlite. m. (except Jun, Jul, Aug.)

**Seattle Public Library**
1000 4th Ave., Seattle, WA 98104.
• Flash. m. ISSN 0015-3508

**Seattle Repertory Theatre**
c/o Bruce Bailey, P.O. Box B, Queen Anne Station,
Seattle, WA 98109.
• Seattle Centerstage. irreg. ISSN 0048-9948

**Seattle Teachers Association**
720 Nob Hill Ave. N., Seattle, WA 98109.
• S T A News. s-m. ISSN 0036-195X

**Seattle University**
Seattle, WA 98122.
• Seattle University Spectator. s-w. ISSN 0037-0479

**Seattle University. Department of English**
900 Broadway, Seattle, WA 98122.
• Fragments; a literary magazine. a. ISSN 0015-
9344

**Second Coming Press**
Box 31246, San Francisco, CA 94131.
• Second Coming. 2-3 per yr. ISSN 0048-9956

**Second Foundation**
Box 4183, Portland, OR 97208.
• Fountain. m.

**Second Page, Inc.**
P.O. Box 14145, San Francisco, CA 94114.
• Second Page. irreg. (approx 3 per yr.) (Central
Party)

**Second Wave**
Box 344 Cambridge A, Cambridge, MA 02139.
• Second Wave; a magazine of new feminism. q.
ISSN 0048-9980

**Secondary School Theatre Conference**
• Course Guide for High School Theatre. (pub. by
American Theatre Association)

**Secular Subjects**
Box 2931, St. Louis, MO 63130.
• Secular Subjects. m.

**Securities Industry Association, Inc.**
20 Broad St., New York, NY 10005.
• I B A Municipal Statistical Bulletin. q. ISSN
0018-8522
• I B A Occasional Paper. irreg. ISSN 0075-0255
• I B A Statistical Bulletin; a summary of new
security issues. s-a. ISSN 0018-8549
• Municipal Markets Developments. m.

**Securities Industry Association, Inc. (Washington)**
490 L'Enfant Plaza East S.W., Washington, DC
20024.
• Compliance and Legal Seminar. Proceedings. a.
ISSN 0093-7800
• Securities Industry Association. State and Local
Pension Funds. biennial. ISSN 0075-0263

**Securities Investor Protection Corp.**
900 17th St. N.W., Suite 800, Washington, DC
20006.
• Securities Investor Protection Corporation. Annual
Report. a. ISSN 0094-467X

**Security Letter, Inc.**
475 Fifth Ave., New York, NY 10017.
• Security Letter. fortn.

**Security Pacific National Bank**
Research Dept. H8-3, Box 2097, Terminal Annex,
Los Angeles, CA 90051.
• Monthly Summary of Business Conditions in
Southern California. m. ISSN 0027-058X

**Security World Publishing Co., Inc.**
2639 S. La Cienega Blvd., Los Angeles, CA 90034.
• S.C.A., State & County Administrator. irreg. ISSN
0363-9401
• Security Distributing & Marketing. m. ISSN 0049-
0016
• Security World; the magazine of professional
security administration and practice. m. ISSN
0037-0703

**Sedona Life**
Box 1748, Sedona, AZ 86336.
• Sedona Life; red rock country. m.

**See Magazines**
333 Sixth Ave., New York, NY 10019.
• Caper. bi-m.

**Karl Seebacher, Ed. & Pub.**
G.P.O. Box 1201, New York, NY 10001.
• Quality Rock Reader. q. ISSN 0360-4071

**Seed World**
434 South Wabash Ave., Chicago, IL 60605.
• Seed Trade Buyer's Guide. a. ISSN 0080-8504
• Seed World. 12 per yr. ISSN 0037-0797

**Seeing Eye Inc.**
Morristown, NJ 07960.
• Seeing Eye Annual Report. a.
• Seeing Eye Guide. q. ISSN 0037-0819

**Seely Genealogical Society**
c/o Esther H. Houtz, Box 131, Allenspark, CO
80510.
• Seeley Genealogical Society (Newsletter) irreg.

**Seems**
c/o Jerome Klinkowitz, Ed., Department of English,
University of Northern Iowa, Cedar Falls, IA
50613.
• Seems. q.

**Seer Ox**
Box 42923, Los Angeles, CA 90050.
• Seer Ox; American senryu magazine. q.

**Seer's Catalogue Inc.**
4207 San Isidro, N.W., Albuquerque, NM 87107.
• Seer's Catalogue. fortn.

**Seismological Society of America**
Box 826, Berkeley, CA 94701.
• Seismological Society of America. Bulletin. bi-m.
ISSN 0037-1106

**Seismological Society of America. Eastern Section**
U.S. Geological Survey, Denver Federal Center, D2,
Bldg. 25, Denver, CO 80225.
• Earthquake Notes. q. ISSN 0012-8287

**Selby Botanical Gardens**
see **Marie Selby Botanical Gardens**

**Select Information Exchange**
2095 Broadway, New York, NY 10023.
• Investment Sources & Ideas. irreg. ISSN 0085-
6355
• S I E Guide to Business and Investment Books.
irreg.(approx. every 4-5 years) ISSN 0072-8276
• Sophisticated Investor. s-a.

**Select Publishing Co.**
c/o Gertrude Struck, 114 N. Carroll St., Madison,
WI 53703.
• Madison Select; Madison review of fashion, travel,
arts and society. m. ISSN 0024-9513

**Selected Bibliography of Gerbil Research Publications**
c/o Robert H. Yager, Institute of Laboratory
Animal Resources, 2101 Constitution Ave.,
Washington, DC 20418.
• Selected Bibliography of Gerbil Research
Publications; cumulative index on Meriones
unguiculatus and other gerbillinae. s-a.

**Selenium & Tellurium Development Association, Inc.**
• Selenium & Tellurium Abstracts. (pub. by
Chemical Abstracts Service)

**Self-Realization Fellowship, Inc.**
3880 San Rafael Ave, Los Angeles, CA 90065.
• Gemeinschaft der Selbst-Verwirklichung.
Jahresheft. a. ISSN 0072-0577
• Self-Realization. q. ISSN 0037-1564

**Self Reliance Association of American Ukrainians**
98 Second Ave., New York, NY 10003.
• Nash Swit/Our World; the bi-monthly magazine
journal of economic-cooperative and community
thought. bi-m. ISSN 0027-8246

**Selmer Company**
Box 310, Elkhart, IN 46514.
• Selmer Bandwagon. 4 per yr. ISSN 0037-1637

**Seminar on the Acquisition of Latin American Library
Materials**
c/o Benson Latin American Collection, University
of Texas at Austin, Austin, TX 78712.
• S A L A L M Newsletter. q. ISSN 0098-6275
• Seminar on the Acquisition of Latin American
Library Materials. Final Report and Working
Papers. a. ISSN 0080-8849
• Seminar on the Acquisition of Latin American
Library Materials. Microfilming Projects
Newsletter. a. ISSN 0080-8857

**Seminex**
607 N. Grand, St. Louis, MO 63103.
• Currents in Theology and Mission. bi-m.

**Seminole Junior College. Student Government Association**
Sanford, FL 32771.
- Doors; Seminole Junior College literary magazine. s-a.

**Semiotext (e), Inc.**
522 Philosophy Hall, Columbia University, New York, NY 10027.
- Semiotext(e) 3 per yr. ISSN 0093-9579

**Semplex of U.S.A.**
4805 Lyndale Ave. North, Minneapolis, MN 55430 (Subscr. address: P.O. Box 12276, Minneapolis, MN 55412)
- Catalog of Supplies for the Amateur Winemaker. s-a.

**David Senahi, Ed. & Pub.**
335 W. Fayette St., Syracuse, NY 13202.
- Central New Yorker. m. ISSN 0008-9486

**Senior Citizen News**
10175 S.W. Barbur Blvd., Room 109B, Portland, OR 97219.
- Senior Citizen News. m.

**Senior Citizens Association of Los Angeles County**
- California Senior Citizen News. (pub. by Keystone Publishing Co.)

**Senior Citizens Today**
2530 J St., Suite 302, Sacramento, CA 95816.
- Senior Citizens Today. m. ISSN 0049-0199

**Senior Golf Publications Co.**
Box 4716, Clearwater, FL 33518.
- Senior Golfer. bi-m. ISSN 0037-2218

**Senior World Publications**
4425 Cass St., San Diego, CA 92101 (Subscr. to: Box 9534 San Diego CA 92109)
- Senior World. m.

**Sentinal Publishing Co.**
1777 Wynkoop St., Suite 1, Denver, CO 80202.
- Arabian Horse. m. ISSN 0097-9503

**Sentry Books Inc.**
10718 White Oak Ave., Granada Hills, CA 91344.
- Airpower; the story of combat aviation. bi-m.

**Sepher-Hermon Press, Inc.**
175 Fifth Ave., New York, NY 10010.
- Journal of Jewish Art. a. (Spertus College of Judaica)
- Studies in Jewish Jurisprudence. irreg. ISSN 0085-686X

**Sequoia Institute at Claremont**
Box 30, Claremont, CA 91711.
- World Directory of Environmental Organizations/ Annuaire Mondiale des Organismes de l'Environnement. irreg., 2nd edt. 1976. ISSN 0092-0908 (Sierra Club International Program)

**Serbian Literary Association**
448 Barry Ave., Chicago, IL 60657.
- Serbian Struggle/Srpska Borba. w.

**Serina Press**
70 Kennedy St., Alexandria, VA 22305.
- Current Statistical Profile of the Fifty States. a.
- Guide to Free Loan Films About Foreign Lands. irreg., latest issue 1975.
- Guide to Free-Loan Training Films (16 MM) irreg. ISSN 0072-8438
- Guide to Government Loan Film. irreg.
- Guide to Government-Loan Films Volume 1: the Civilian Agencies. irreg., 4th edt. 1976. ISSN 0072-8462

**Service Employees International Union**
AFL-CIO, CLC, 2020 K St., N.W., Ste. 200, Washington, DC 20006.
- Service Employee. m. ISSN 0037-2609

**Service Publications, Inc.**
100 Park Ave., New York, NY 10017.
- American Hairdresser/Salon Owner. m.
- Confidential Beauty & Barber Buying Guide. a.
- Men's Hairstylist and Barber's Journal. m. ISSN 0025-9500
- Professional Men's Hairstylists. m.

**Service Publishing Co.**
Washington Building 639, 15th and New York Ave. N.W., Washington, DC 20005.
- A D C A; American Directory Collections Agencies. a. ISSN 0084-5833

**Seton Hall University**
South Orange, NJ 07079.
- Spirit; a magazine of poetry. s-a. ISSN 0038-7584

**Seton Hall University. School of Business Administration**
Bureau of Business Research, South Orange, NJ 07079.
- Journal of Business. s-a. ISSN 0021-9401

**Seton Hall University. Student Center**
South Orange, NJ 07079.
- Chimaera; undergraduate literary magazine. irreg (3-4 per yr)

**Seven**
211/2 N. Harvey (Terminal Arcade), Oklahoma City, OK 73102.
- Seven. irreg.

**Seven Arts Press, Inc.**
6605 Hollywood Blvd., Suite 215, Hollywood, CA 90028.
- Entertainment Industry Series. irreg. ISSN 0071-0695

**Seven Square Press**
Box 749, Old Chelsea Station, New York, NY 10011.
- Box 749. 1-2 per yr. (Printable Arts Society, Inc.)

**Seventh-Day Adventist Church**
6840 Eastern Avenue, N.W., Washington, DC 20012.
- Guide. w. ISSN 0017-5226
- Telenotes. (pub. by Faith for Today)
- These Times. (pub. by Southern Publishing Association)

**Seventh-Day Adventist Reform Movement**
Box 20234, Sacramento, CA 95820.
- Standard Bearer. q. ISSN 0038-9447

**Seventh-Day Adventists**
1350 Villa St., Mt. View, CA 94042.
- Centinela/Watchman. (pub. by Pacific Press Publishing Association)
- Israelite. q.
- Our Little Friend. (pub. by Pacific Press Publishing Association)
- Primary Treasure. (pub. by Pacific Press Publishing Association)
- Signs of the Times. (pub. by Pacific Press Publishing Association)

**Seventies Press**
Odin House, Madison, MN 56256.
- Seventies; a magazine of poetry and opinion. irreg. ISSN 0037-5969

**Severn-Wylie Jewett Co.**
Box 1660, Portland, ME 04104.
- Mekeel's Stamp News. w. ISSN 0025-8857

**Sex Information and Education Council of the U.S.**
137 N. Franklin St., Hempstead, NY 11550.
- S I E C U S Report. bi-m. ISSN 0091-3995

**Sexual Law Reporter**
c/o Thomas Coleman, 1800 N. Highland Ave., Suite 106, Los Angeles, CA 90028.
- Sexual Law Reporter. bi-m.

**Seybold Publications, Inc.**
Box 644, Media, PA 19063.
- Seybold Report. s-m.

**Sha-Sim Enterprises, Inc.**
Box 1087, Maitland, FL 32751.
- Florida Horseman; all breed newspaper throughout Florida. m.

**Shaded Room Press**
365 Avenue E, Pittsburgh, PA 15221.
- Shaded Room. s-a. ISSN 0037-3141

**Shakespeare Newsletter**
c/o Louis Marder, Ed., University of Illinois at Chicago Circle, Dept. of English, Chicago, IL 60680.
- Shakespeare Newsletter. 6 per yr.(Sept-May) ISSN 0037-3214

**Shaman, Inc.**
47 Fletcher St., Keunebunk, ME 04043.
- Shaman. s-a.

**Shambhala Publications Inc.**
1123 Spruce St., Boulder, CO 80302.
- Clear Light Series. irreg.
- Maitreya. s-a. ISSN 0025-1011
- Shambhala Review of Books & Ideas. bi-m.

**Shameless Hussy Press**
Box 424, San Lorenzo, CA 94580.
- Shameless Hussy Review. a.

**Shamie Publishing Co.**
22725 Mack Ave., St. Clair Shores, MI 48080.
- Grocers' Spotlight. m. ISSN 0017-4394

**Shankpainter**
c/o Lyle Fox, Ed., Box 565, Provincetown, MA 02657.
- Shankpainter. 1-2 per yr.

**Shannon County Historical Society**
c/o Dr. Robert Jacquot Lee, Eminence, MO 65466.
- Ozarker. m. ISSN 0030-7750

**Shantih**
Box 125, Bay Ridge Station, Brooklyn, NY 11220.
- Shantih; new international writings. irreg. ISSN 0037-329X

**Shanty Hollow Corporation**
Hunter, NY 12442.
- Hunter Mountain News. 10 per yr. (Hunter Mountain Ski Bowl)

**M. E. Shapre, Inc.**
901 North Broadway, White Plains, NY 10603.
- Soviet Anthropology and Archaeology; a journal of translations from Soviet sources. q. ISSN 0038-528X

**Sharada Ranganathan Endowment for Library Science**
- Ranganathan Series in Library Science. (pub. by Asia Publishing House, Inc.)

**Sharing**
c/o Gayle Rawlings, 29 Library Lane, Bayville, NY 11709.
- Sharing. q.

**Sharing: a Journal of Community**
3354 Biscayne Boulevard, Arnold, MO 63010.
- Sharing: a Journal of Community. q.

**M. E. Sharpe, Inc.**
901 North Broadway, White Plains, NY 10603.
- Challenge (White Plains); journal of economic affairs. 6 per yr.
- Chinese Economic Studies; a journal of translations. q. ISSN 0009-4552
- Chinese Education; a journal of translations containing articles published in mainland China and other sources. q. ISSN 0009-4560
- Chinese Law and Government; a journal of translations. q. ISSN 0009-4609
- Chinese Sociology and Anthropology; a journal of translations containing articles published in mainland China and other sources. q. ISSN 0009-4625
- Chinese Studies in History; English translations of articles that have appeared in mainland China and other sources. q. ISSN 0009-4633
- Chinese Studies in Philosophy; English translations of articles that have appeared in mainland China and other sources. q. ISSN 0023-8627
- Eastern European Economics; a journal of translations from Bulgaria, Czechoslovakia, East Germany, Hungary, Poland, Rumania and Yugoslavia. q. ISSN 0012-8775
- International Journal of Management and Organization. q.
- International Journal of Mental Health. q. ISSN 0020-7411
- International Journal of Politics; a journal of translations. q. ISSN 0012-8783
- International Journal of Sociology. q. ISSN 0020-7659
- Japanese Economic Studies. q. ISSN 0021-4841
- Matekon; translations of Russian and East European mathematical economics. q. ISSN 0025-1127
- Problems of Economics; selected articles from Soviet economic journals in English translation. m. ISSN 0032-9436

- Soviet and Eastern European Foreign Trade; a journal of translations. q. ISSN 0038-5263
- Soviet Education; selected articles from Soviet education journals in English translation. m. ISSN 0038-5360
- Soviet Law and Government; a journal of translations. q. ISSN 0038-5530
- Soviet Neurology and Psychiatry. q. ISSN 0038-559X
- Soviet Psychology; a journal of translations. q. ISSN 0038-5751
- Soviet Review; a journal of translations. q. ISSN 0038-5794
- Soviet Sociology; a journal of translations from scholarly Soviet sources. q. ISSN 0038-5824
- Soviet Statutes and Decisions; a journal of translations. q. ISSN 0038-5840
- Soviet Studies in History; a journal of translations. q. ISSN 0038-5867
- Soviet Studies in Literature; a journal of translations. q. ISSN 0038-5875
- Soviet Studies in Philosophy; a journal of translations from Soviet scholarly sources. q. ISSN 0038-5883
- Western European Education; a journal of translations. q. ISSN 0043-3675

**Shasta Historical Society**
P.O. Box 277, Redding, CA 96001.
- Covered Wagon. irreg. ISSN 0574-3680

**Dennis Shattuck**
P.O. Box 9261, Encinitas, CA 92024.
- Western Aviation-Airport News. m.

**Shaw Society of California**
1933 S. Broadway, Los Angeles, CA 90007.
- California Shavian. bi-m. ISSN 0008-154X

**Shawnee Nation**
c/o Tukemas, Ed., P.O. Box 609, Xenia, OH 45385.
- Tosan; American Indian people's inter-tribal news. irreg. (5-7 per yr)

**William K. Shearer, Ed. & Pub.**
8158 Palm Street, Lemon Grove, CA 92045.
- American Independent. m.
- California Statesman. m.
- California Statesman's Foreign Policy Review. m.
- California Statesman's Legislative Survey. m.

**Carl B.E. Shedd**
360 Park Square Bldg., Boston, MA 02116.
- Ad East. m. (Ad East Enterprises)

**Sheet Metal Workers' International Association**
1750 New York Ave. N.W., Washington, DC 20006.
- Sheet Metal Workers' Journal. m. ISSN 0037-3451

**Sheffer Co.**
Box 19247, Houston, TX 77024.
- Ocean Construction Report. w.
- Offshore Rig Newsletter. m.

**Shelby Publishing Co. Inc.**
P.O. Box 49367, Atlanta, GA 30329.
- Shelby Report of the Southeast. m.

**Shelby Publishing Corporation**
Wellesley Office Park, Wellesley Hills, MA 02181.
- John Liner Letter. m. ISSN 0021-7204

**Sheldon Memorial Art Gallery**
12th & R Sts., University of Nebraska, Lincoln, NE 68508.
- Nebraska Art Association Quarterly. q. ISSN 0047-9195

**Shell**
362 Waban Ave., Waban, MA 02168.
- Shell. q.

**Shell Oil Co.**
Box 2463, Houston, TX 77001.
- Shell News. bi-m.

**Shelter Publications, Inc.**
915 Burlington St., Downers Grove, IL 60515.
- American Roofer and Building Improvement Contractor; devoted to roofing, siding, insulating, waterproofing. m. ISSN 0003-0880

**Herbert M. Shelton, Ed. & Pub.**
Box 1277, San Antonio, TX 78295.
- Dr. Shelton's Hygienic Review. m. ISSN 0012-5849

**Shepard's Citations, Inc.**
(Subsidiary of: McGraw-Hill, Inc.)
420 N. Cascade Ave., Colorado Springs, CO 80903
(Orders to: Box 1235, Colorado Springs, CO 80901)
- Shepard's Acts and Cases by Popular Names, Federal and State. irreg., with annual supplement. ISSN 0080-9233
- Shepard's Federal Law Citations in Selected Law Reviews. q. ISSN 0094-9531

**Sheperd College**
Shepherdstown, WV 25443.
- Shepherd College Picket. w.

**Sheriff & Police Reporter**
1526 N.W. Ballard Way, Seattle, WA 98107.
- Sheriff & Police Reporter. q.

**Sheriffs' Association of Texas**
Box 4488, N. Austin Sta., Austin, TX 78765.
- Texas Lawman; dedicated to all Texas peace officers. m. ISSN 0040-442X

**Dean Sherman, Inc.**
213 S.W. Ash St., Portland, OR 97204.
- Dean Sherman's Forest Industry Affairs Letter; information for decision. s-m. ISSN 0011-7234

**Sherwood Anderson Society**
University of Richmond, Richmond, VA 23173.
- Winesburg Eagle. s-a.

**Shevchenko Scholastic Society**
- Ukrainian Book/Ukrainska Knyha/Ukrainische Buch. (pub. by Kyiw Publishing House)

**Shevchenko Scientific Society**
302 W. 13th St., New York, NY 10014.
- Shevchenko Scientific Society. Proceedings of the Section of Chemistry, Biology and Medicine. irreg.
- Shevchenko Scientific Society. Proceedings of the Section of Mathematics and Physics. irreg.
- Ukrainian Archives. irreg.
- Ukrainian Literary Library. irreg.
- Ukrainian Studies. irreg.

**Shield Publishing Co.**
c/o Chester Petersen, Jr., Ed., Box 511, Lindborg, KS 67456.
- Simmental Shield. m. (American Simmental Association)

**C. W. Shilling Auditory Research Center, Inc.**
Box N, Groton, CT 06340.
- Journal of Auditory Research; for all workers seriously interested in the scientific study of hearing. q. ISSN 0021-9177

**Shimer College**
Mt. Carroll, IL 61053.
- Uzzano. 3 per yr.

**Shining Waters Press**
P.O. Box 52, Ann Arbor, MI 48107.
- Ripples; the poetry and fiction newsletter. q. with a. cumulation.

**Shipbuilders Council of America**
Watergate 600, Washington, DC 20037.
- Shipyard Weekly. w.

**Shipping Digest Inc.**
25 Broadway, New York, NY 10004.
- Shipping Digest; for export and transportation executives. w. ISSN 0037-3893

**Shirl Olympius**
Box 182, Stockton, CA 95201.
- Tideways. bi-m. (Port of Stockton)

**Shiryoku Inc.**
Box 188, Wellesley, MA 02181.
- Fox. bi-m.

**Sh'ma Inc.**
Box 567, Port Washington, NY 11050.
- Sh'ma; a journal of Jewish responsibility. fortn. ISSN 0049-0385

**Shoe Service Institute of America**
222 W.Adams St., Chicago, IL 60606.
- Shoe Service and Shoe Service Wholesaler. m. ISSN 0037-4067

**Shoe String Press Inc.**
995 Sherman Ave., Hamden, CT 06514.
- Case Studies in Library Science. irreg., 1972, no. 5. ISSN 0069-0848
- Connecticut College Monograph. irreg.; latest issue, no. 10. ISSN 0069-9012 (Connecticut College)
- Contributions to Library Literature. irreg., latest issue 1975. ISSN 0069-9683
- Essential Articles. irreg; no. 8, 1977. ISSN 0071-1470
- Foreign Area Studies Series. irreg., no. 15, 1975. ISSN 0071-7312

**Shoe-the Coast Shoe Reporter**
c/o Daniel W. Tennant, 1016 S. Broadway Pl., Los Angeles, CA 90015.
- Shoe-the Coast Shoe Reporter. m. ISSN 0010-0013

**Shoe Trades Publishing Co.**
15 East St., Boston, MA 02111.
- American Shoemaking. w. ISSN 0003-1038
- Leather Manufacturer. m. ISSN 0023-9763

**Shopping Center Digest**
c/o Murray Shor, Ed., Box 2, Suffern, NY 10901.
- Shopping Center Digest; the locations newsletter. s-m.

**Shore Publishing Co.**
2931 S. 57th St., Milwaukee, WI 53219.
- Shore Review. 4 per yr. ISSN 0049-0407

**Show Reporter Publishing Co., Inc.**
10 High St., Boston, MA 02110.
- Show Reporter. 14 per yr.

**Showcase Publishing Co., Inc.**
3729 Apparel Mart, Dallas, TX 75207.
- Fashion Showcase. m.

**Shreveport Chamber of Commerce**
Box 74, Shreveport, LA 71120.
- Shreveport Magazine. m. ISSN 0037-4385

**Shreveport Sun, Inc.**
P.O. Box 1742, Shreveport, LA 71166.
- Shreveport Sun. w.

**Shrikumar Poddar**
South Point Plaza, Lansing, MI 48910.
- Educator's Newsletter. fortn. (Educational Subscription Service, Inc.)
- Indian Opinion. fortn. (Indians for Democracy)
- Washington Watch. w.

**Leo Shull Publications**
136 W. 44th St., New York, NY 10036.
- Show Business; the entertainment weekly. w. ISSN 0037-4318
- Who's Where; who's where in show business. biennial. ISSN 0508-6795

**Shuttle Craft Guild**
- Shuttle Craft Guild. Monographs. (pub. by H T H Publishers)

**Paul Shuttleworth, Ed. & Pub.**
2526-42nd Ave., San Francisco, CA 94116.
- Aisling; a quarterly of Irish and American poetry. q.

**Siberian Husky Club of America, Inc.**
3 Crestview Rd., Terryville, CT 06786.
- Siberian Husky Club of America Newsletter. bi-m. ISSN 0583-1776

**Sibyl-Child Press, Inc.**
c/o Candyce Stapen, Ed., 6906 West Park Dr., Hyattsville, MD 20783.
- Sibyl-Child; a women's arts and culture quarterly. 3 per yr.

**Siebel Publishing Co.**
4049 W. Peterson Ave., Chicago, IL 60646.
- Bakers Digest. bi-m. ISSN 0005-4089
- Brewers Digest. m. ISSN 0006-971X
- Brewers Digest Annual Buyers Guide and Brewery Directory. a.

**Siempre Inc.**
Box 4329, New Orleans, LA 70178.
- Siempre. bi-m. ISSN 0037-4717

**Siena College**
Department of English, Loudonville, NY 12211.
● Greyfriar/Siena Studies in Literature. a. ISSN 0533-2869

**Sierra Club**
530 Bush St., San Francisco, CA 94108.
● Sierra Club. National News Report. w. ISSN 0049-044X
● Sierra Club Bulletin. m. ISSN 0037-4725
● Sierra Club Exhibit Format Series. irreg., 1968, vol. 25. ISSN 0080-9519

**Sierra Club. Atlantic Chapter**
50 W. 40 St, New York, NY 10018.
● Sierra Atlantic. q.

**Sierra Club International Program**
● World Directory of Environmental Organizations/ Annuaire Mondiale des Organismes de l'Environnement. (pub. by Sequoia Institute at Claremont)

**Sierra Club. New York City Group**
50 W. 40th St., New York, NY 10018.
● Subway Sierran. irreg. (4 per yr.)

**Sierra Club. Oklahoma Chapter**
5604 N.W. 82, Oklahoma City, OK 73132.
● Oklahoma Sierran. m.

**Sierra Economic Services**
800 Welch Road, Palo Alto, CA 94304.
● Sierra Sourcebook: Electronics Industry Market Data. a. ISSN 0092-7120

**Sigma Alpha Iota, International Music Fraternity for Women**
● Pan Pipes of Sigma Alpha Iota. (pub. by George Banta Co., Inc.)

**Sigma Delta Kappa**
Arlington Executive Bldg., 2009 N. 14th St., Arlington, VA 22201.
● Si-De-Ka Magazine. q. ISSN 0037-444X

**Sigma Gamma Epsilon**
c/o Charles J. Mankin, University of Oklahoma, 830 Van Vleet Oval, Room 163, Norman, OK 73019.
● Compass; an honorary scientific society magazine devoted to the Earth Sciences. 4 per yr. ISSN 0010-4213

**Sigma Nu Phi Fraternity (Legal)**
9700 Fernwood Rd., W. Bethesda Branch, Washington, DC 20034.
● Adelphia. q.

**Sigma Theta Tau National Honor Society of Nursing**
1100 W. Michigan St., Indianapolis, IN 46202.
● Image (Indianapolis) 3 per yr.

**Sigma Xi, Scientific Research Society of North America**
345 Whitney Ave., New Haven, CT 06511.
● American Scientist; published in the interest of scientific research. bi-m. ISSN 0003-0996

**Sigma Zeta**
1100 E. Fifth St., Anderson, IN 46011.
● Sigma Zetan. a. ISSN 0080-9578

**Signalert Corporation**
Box 1227, Old Village Station, Great Neck, NY 11023.
● Systems and Forecasts. fortn.

**Significant Advances in Science**
c/o Ed. Royal M. Frye, Box 65, Royalston, MA 01368.
● Significant Advances in Science. s-m.

**Signpost Press**
Box 2314, Bellingham, WA 98225.
● Bellingham Review. q.

**Signpost Publications**
16812 36th Ave. W., Lynnwood, WA 98036.
● Signpost. 16 per yr. ISSN 0583-2594

**Signs of the Times Publishing Co.**
407 Gilbert Ave., Cincinnati, OH 45202.
● Screen Printing. m. ISSN 0036-9594
● Signs of the Times; the national journal of advertising displays. m. ISSN 0037-5063
● Visual Merchandising. m. ISSN 0094-4610 (International Authority on Visual Merchandising)

**Sikorsky Aircraft**
Stratford, CT 06602.
● Sikorsky News. m. ISSN 0037-5152

**Silent Majority V.O.I.C.E.**
Box 6068, Seattle, WA 98168.
● Silent Majority V.O.I.C.E; Voter's Objective Information about Current Events. m.

**Silent Press Inc.**
2 Pennsylvania Plaza, Suite 1500, New York, NY 10001.
● Silent News; America's most popular newspaper for the deaf. m. ISSN 0049-0490

**Silky Terrier Club of America, Inc.**
Box 3521, San Francisco, CA 94119.
● Silky Terrier Club of America Newsletter. m.

**Silver and Gold Report**
16 Shamrock Lane, Norwalk, CT 06850.
● Silver and Gold Report. fortn.

**Silver Institute**
Suite 1138, 1001 Connecticut Ave. N.W., Washington, DC 20036.
● New Silver Technology; silver abstracts from the current world literature. q. ISSN 0095-9286

**Silver Publishing Co. Inc.**
1619-a S. W. Jefferson St., Portland, OR 97201.
● Silver. bi-m. ISSN 0037-5357

**Silver Scarab Press**
500 Wellesley, S.E., Albuquerque, NM 87106.
● Nyctalops. s-a.

**Simian Society of America, Inc.**
Box 343, Wakefield, MA 01880.
● Simian. m. ISSN 0037-539X

**Simmental Journal, Inc.**
Box 410, Cody, WY 82414.
● Simmental Journal. s-m.

**Simmons-Boardman Publishing Corporation**
350 Broadway, New York, NY 10013.
● Banking. m. ISSN 0005-5492 (American Bankers Association)
● Columbia Today. q. (Columbia University. Trustees of Columbia University)
● International Railway Journal. m. ISSN 0020-8450
● Marine Catalog. a. ISSN 0076-4450
● Marine Catalog Buyers Guide. a.
● Marine Engineering/Log. m. ISSN 0025-3219
● Marine Engineering/Log Annual Maritime Review and Yearbook Issue. a. ISSN 0076-4469
● Plant Location; the industrial & economic development workbook. a. ISSN 0554-2731
● Railway Age. s-m. ISSN 0079-9505
● Railway Track and Structures. m. ISSN 0033-9016

**Simmons College. Alumnae Association**
300 the Fenway, Boston, MA 02115.
● Simmons Review. q. ISSN 0049-0512

**Simmons College. School of Library Science**
Alumni Association, 300 The Fenway, Boston, MA 02115.
● Simmons Librarian. s-a. ISSN 0037-5438

**Simmons Kinfolk**
c/o Marcia Eisenberg, 15 Edgewood Parkway, Fayetteville, NY 13066.
● Simmons Kinfolk. q.

**Q. K. Simms**
c/o Kent B. Newell, Box 628, San Anselmo, CA 94960.
● Q. K. Simms' American Almanack; American hand-made goods, natural foods, outdoor supplies. a.

**Simon and Schuster, Inc.**
630 Fifth Ave., New York, NY 10020
● Information Please Almanac. a. ISSN 0073-7860 (Dan Golenpaul Associates) (Orders from: 1 W. 39th St., New York, N.Y. 10018)
● International Commercial Law of Nations. irreg.
● J. K. Lasser Tax Institute. Monthly Tax Service. m. (10 per yr.) (Orders from:, 1 W. 39 St., New York, NY 10018)
● J. K. Lasser's Your Income Tax. a. ISSN 0084-4314 (J. K. Lasser Institute) (Orders from: 1 W. 39th St., New York, N.Y. 10018)
● J. K. Lasser's Your Income Tax, Professional Ed. a. ISSN 0075-2061 (J. K. Lasser Institute)

● Lovejoy's Career and Vocational School Guide. irreg., latest issue 1975. ISSN 0076-1346
● Lovejoy's College Guide. irreg., latest issue 1974. ISSN 0076-132X
● Lovejoy's Prep School Guide. irreg., 4th edt. 1974. ISSN 0459-925X
● Major League Baseball. a. ISSN 0076-2849 (Cord Communications Corp.)
● Modern Film Scripts. irreg. (Orders from: 1 W. 39th St., New York, N.Y. 10018)
● Pro Football. a. ISSN 0079-5534 (Cord Communications Corp.)
● Problems of American Society. irreg. (Orders from: 1 W. 39th St., New York, N.Y. 10018)
● World of Tennis; a BP and commercial union yearbook. a.

**H.K. Simon Co., Inc.**
1280 Saw Mill River Rd., Yonkers, NY 10710.
● Profit Seminar/Absentee Business Newsletter. s-m.
● Real Estate Brainstorms Newsletter. s-m.
● Table Topics Newsletter. s-m.

**Simon Public Relations, Inc.**
11661 San Vicente Blvd., Los Angeles, CA 90049.
● Editorial Offices in the West. biennial. ISSN 0070-9107

**Simplicity Pattern Co., Inc.**
200 Madison Ave., New York, NY 10016.
● Simplicity Home Catalog. 3 per yr. ISSN 0364-1732
● Simplicity School Catalog. s-a. ISSN 0488-8812

**Simpson Publishing Co.**
Kirksville, MO 63501.
● N A C W P I Journal. q. ISSN 0027-576X (National Association of College Wind & Percussion Instructors)

**Sims Printing Co., Inc.**
1726 N. 22 Ave., Phoenix, AZ 85009.
● Arizona Political Almanac. biennial. ISSN 0571-0111

**Simulation Councils, Inc.**
Box 2228, La Jolla, CA 92038.
● Simulation; technical journal of the Society for Computer Simulation. m. ISSN 0037-5497 (Society for Computer Simulation)
● Simulation Councils Proceedings. s-a. ISSN 0037-5519 (Society for Computer Simulation)
● Simulation Today. a. (Society for Computer Simulation)

**Simulation-Gaming-News, Inc.**
Box 3039, University Station, Moscow, ID 83843.
● Simulation/Gaming. 6 per yr. (North American Simulation and Gaming Association)

**Simulations Publications, Inc.**
44 E. 23d St., New York, NY 10010.
● Strategy and Tactics; the magazine of conflict simulation. bi-m. ISSN 0049-2310

**Sinai Hospital of Detroit**
6767 W. Outer Drive, Detroit, MI 48235.
● Sinai Hospital of Detroit. Bulletin. q. ISSN 0037-5535

**David Sinclair Publications**
3831 West 12th Street, Erie, PA 16505.
● Mini-Auto International; the magazine for the adult collector of fine miniature vehicles. irreg., no. 4, 1977?

**Sing out, Inc.**
270 Lafayette St., New York, NY 10012.
● Sing Out. bi-m. ISSN 0037-5624

**Singer Company. Kearfott Division**
1150 McBride Ave., Little Falls, NJ 07424.
● Tech Notes. irreg.

**Raman K. Singh, Ed. & Pub.**
Box 3425, Fredericksburg, VA 22401.
● Studies in Black Literature. 3 per yr. ISSN 0039-3576

**Singing News**
2611 W. Cervantes, P.O. Box 5188, Pensacola, FL 32505.
● Singing News; the printed voice of gospel music. m.

**Single Parent Resource Center**
3896 24th St., San Francisco, CA 94114.
- One Parent Family; a magazine for single parents. irreg.

**Single Service Institute**
250 Park Ave. So., New York, NY 10017.
- Environment News Digest. bi-m.

**Singles-Mingles, Inc.**
Box 284, Yonkers, NY 10702.
- Singles-Mingles. m. ISSN 0049-0555

**Singles World Corporation**
121 Cedar Lane, Teaneck, NJ 07666.
- Singles World. m.

**Sinister Wisdom**
311 Country Club Dr., Charlotte, NC 28205.
- Sinister Wisdom. 3 per yr.

**Sino-American Buddhist Association**
Gold Mountain Monastery, 1731 15th St., San Francisco, CA 94103.
- Vajra Bodhi Sea. m. ISSN 0507-6986

**Sinsinawa Publications**
Sinsinawa, WI 53824.
- Exchange. q. ISSN 0014-4444 (Dominican Sisters of Sinsinawa)

**Sioux City Magazine**
c/o Jerry Parden, Ed., 1320 Pierce St., Sioux City, IA 51105.
- Sioux City Magazine. s-m.

**Sioux City Newspapers, Inc.**
Box 118, Sioux City, IA 51102.
- Farm Weekly. w.
- Sioux City Journal Farm Weekly. w. ISSN 0037-5829

**Sioux Falls College Student Association**
1501 South Prarie, Sioux Falls, SD 57101.
- Stylus (Sioux Falls) s-m. ISSN 0039-4297

**Sir Thomas Beecham Society (Cleveland)**
c/o Thomas E. Patronite, Ed., Box 6361, Cleveland, OH 44101.
- Grand Baton. q. ISSN 0434-3336

**Sir Thomas Beecham Society (Redondo Beach)**
664 South Irena Ave., Redondo Beach, CA 93401.
- Beecham Society Bulletin. irreg. ISSN 0084-7763

**Siskiyou County Historical Society**
910 S. Main St., Yreka, CA 96097.
- Siskiyou Pioneer and Yearbook. a. ISSN 0583-4449

**Sister Cities International**
1612 K St., N.W., Washington, DC 20006.
- Sister City News. bi-m.

**Sister Courage**
Box 296, Allston, MA 02134.
- Sister Courage. m.

**Sisterhood**
The Women's Liberation Organization of Ilinois, 2140 N. Magnolia St., Chicago, IL 60614.
- Link. m.

**Sisters of Mercy**
2301 Grandview, Cincinnati, OH 45206.
- Mercy Profile. q. ISSN 0025-9977

**Sisters of St. Joseph of Peace**
St. Joseph's Home, Box 288, Jersey City, NJ 07303.
- St. Joseph's Messenger and Advocate of the Blind. q.

**Site, Inc.**
- On S I T E. (pub. by Sculpture in the Environment)

**Six Thirteen**
Box 168, Brooklyn, NY 11223.
- Six Thirteen. 10 per yr.

**Sixpack, Inc.**
Box 158, Lake Toxaway, NC 28747
(and Pierre Joris, 19 Deal Rd., London SW17, England)
- Sixpack. q.

**Sixteen & Vine Church of Christ**
1610 Vine St., Abilene, TX 79602.
- Glad Tidings of Good Things. q. ISSN 0017-0739

**Sixteen Magazines, Inc.**
157 W. 57 St., New York, NY 10019.
- Sixteen. m.

**Skarien & Associates**
1910 W. Olmos Drive, San Antonio, TX 78201.
- Seedsmen's Digest. m. ISSN 0037-0800

**Skeptic Magazine, Inc.**
Presidio Ave., Santa Barbara, CA 93101
(Subscr. to: 1255 Portland Place, Boulder, CO 80302)
- Skeptic. bi-m. ISSN 0093-5050

**Ski America Enterprises**
Tyringham, MA 01264.
- Ski America. q.

**Ski Club News, Inc.**
Box 7192, The Capitol, Albany, NY 12224.
- Winter Sports. 5 per yr.

**Ski Racing, Inc.**
180 Cook, Denver, CO 80206.
- Ski Racing. 27 per yr. ISSN 0037-6213

**Skidmore College**
Saratoga Springs, NY 12866.
- Salmagundi; a quarterly of the humanities & social sciences. q. ISSN 0036-3529

**Skil Corporation**
5033 N. Elston, Chicago, IL 60630.
- Skil Chips. s-a. ISSN 0037-6302

**Skillings' Mining Review**
c/o David N. Skillings, Jr., Ed., 210 Sellwood Bldg., Duluth, MN 55802.
- Skillings' Mining Review. w. ISSN 0037-6329

**Anthony F. Skirius**
4364 Sunset Blvd., Los Angeles, CA 90029.
- Lietuviu Dienos/Lithuanian Days. m. ISSN 0024-2950

**Skisport**
c/o Joseph van Zandt, Ed., Box 258, Antioch, IL 60002.
- Skisport. 6 per yr.

**Sky Diver**
Box 1024, La Habra, CA 90631.
- Sky Diver. m. ISSN 0037-6612

**Sky Publishing Corporation**
49 Bay State Rd., Cambridge, MA 02138.
- Sky and Telescope. m. ISSN 0037-6604

**Skyline Publishers, Inc.**
Box 1029 Federal Sta., Portland, OR 97207.
- Pharmindex. s-m. ISSN 0031-7152

**Skywriter Press**
c/o Dolores C. Warner, Ed., Box 32391, Jamaica, NY 11431.
- Skywriter Journal of Psychiatry. q.

**Skywriting**
511 Campbell St., Kalamazoo, MI 49007.
- Skywriting. 2 per yr.

**Charles B. Slack, Inc.**
6900 Grove Rd, Thorofare, NJ 08086.
- American Journal of the Medical Sciences. bi-m. ISSN 0002-9629
- Briefs. 10 per yr. ISSN 0007-0068 (Maternity Center Association)
- Clinical Research. 5 per yr. ISSN 0009-9279 (American Federation for Clinical Research)
- Health Education Monographs. q.
- Journal of Allied Health. q. ISSN 0090-7421 (American Society of Allied Health Professions)
- Journal of Continuing Education in Nursing. bi-m. ISSN 0022-0124
- Journal of Gerontological Nursing. bi-m. ISSN 0098-9134
- Journal of Nursing Education. 9 per yr. ISSN 0022-3158
- Journal of Pediatric Ophthalmology. q. ISSN 0022-345X
- Journal of Psychiatric Nursing and Mental Health Services. m.

- Occupational Health Nursing. m. ISSN 0029-7933 (American Association of Occupational Health Nurses, Inc.)
- Ophthalmic Surgery. bi-m. ISSN 0022-023X
- Orthopedic Nurses Association. Journal. m.

**George O. Slankard, Ed. & Pub.**
114-120 Franklin Ave., Sesser, IL 62884.
- American Cooner. m. ISSN 0002-807X
- Cars & Parts. m. ISSN 0008-6975

**Slate Services**
Box 8796, Fountain Valley, CA 92708.
- D A I R S and Systems for Instruction Newsletter. 6 per yr. ISSN 0012-2009

**Slavic Gospel Association**
2434 N. Kedzie Blvd., Chicago, IL 60647.
- Slavic Gospel News. 3-4 per yr. ISSN 0049-0709

**Slit Wrist Magazine**
435 E. 76th St., No. 4-B, New York, NY 10021.
- Slit Wrist Magazine. 3 per yr.

**Sloan-Kettering Institute for Cancer Research**
410 E. 68 St., New York, NY 10021.
- Sloan-Kettering Institute for Cancer Research. Progress Report. irreg., 1968, no. 18. ISSN 0081-0045

**Slovak-American Cultural Center**
Box 291, New York, NY 10008.
- Slovak Press Digest. irreg. ISSN 0037-6914

**Slovak Institute**
2900 East Blvd., Cleveland, OH 44104.
- Most; stvrtocnik pre slovensku kulturu/a quarterly for Slovak culture. q. ISSN 0027-1438

**Slovak League of America**
313 Ridge Ave., Middletown, PA 17057.
- Slovakia. a. ISSN 0583-5623

**Slovak V Amerike Weekly Newspaper**
Box 150, Middletown, PA 17057.
- Literarny Almanach Slovaka V Amerike. irreg., latest 1974. ISSN 0489-1376

**Slovenian Women's Union of America**
2032 W. Cermak Rd., Chicago, IL 60608.
- Zarja/Dawn. m. ISSN 0044-1848

**Slovenskeho Katolickeho Sokola**
205 Madison St, Passaic, NJ 07055.
- Katolicky Sokol. q.

**Slovenskych Otcov Benediktinov**
2900 East Blvd., Cleveland, OH 44104.
- Ave Maria. m.

**Small Businessman's Clinic**
c/o Austin M. Elliott, Ed., 113 Vista del Lago, Scotts Valley, CA 95066.
- Small Businessman's Clinic. m. ISSN 0094-2464

**Small Farm Press**
P.O. Box 563, Jefferson City, TN 37760.
- Small Farm. s-a.

**Small Pond**
10 Overland Dr., Stratford, CT 06497.
- Small Pond; journal of poetry, short fiction and opinion. 3 per yr. ISSN 0037-721X

**Small Towns Institute**
P.O. Box 517, Ellensburg, WA 98926.
- Small Town. m.

**Smaller Manufacturers Council**
339 Blvd. of the Allies, Pittsburgh, PA 15222.
- Smaller Manufacturer. 11 per yr.

**Al Smith, Ed. & Pub.**
2241 Cedar Crest Blvd., Dallas, TX 75203.
- Key News. w.

**Raymond D. Smith**
Box 557, Washington, PA 15301.
- Cats Magazine. m. ISSN 0008-8544

**Richard Arlen Smith, Ed. & Pub.**
Box 35-K, Tracey's Landing, MD 20869.
- Water Desalination Report. w. ISSN 0043-1206

**Gladys Smith & Associates**
P.O. Box 5062, Sherman Oaks, CA 91413.
- Singles Critique. m.

**Wilbur Smith and Associates**
4500 Jackson Boulevard, Columbia, SC 29202.
- Puerto Rico Highway Improvement Program. a. ISSN 0092-8941

**Smith Bucklin and Associates**
1730 Pennsylvania Ave. N.W., Washington, DC 20006.
- Communicator (Washington) m. (National Association of Radiotelephone Systems)
- N B F A A Signal. q. ISSN 0049-0474 (National Burglar & Fire Alarm Association)

**H. Royer Smith Co.**
2019 Walnut St., Philadelphia, PA 19103.
- New Records. m. ISSN 0028-6559

**Allen Smith Co., Inc.**
1435 N. Meridian St., Indianapolis, IN 46202.
- Defense Law Journal. bi-m. ISSN 0011-7587

**Smith College**
Northampton, MA 01060.
- Grecourt Review. 2 per yr. ISSN 0017-3827
- Katherine Asher Engel Lectures. a. ISSN 0075-5265
- Smith College Studies in History. irreg. ISSN 0081-0193

**Smith College. School for Social Work**
Northampton, MA 01060.
- Smith College Studies in Social Work. 3 per yr. ISSN 0037-7317

**Smith Publications, Inc.**
4358 Charlemagne Ave., Box 7765, Long Beach, CA 90808.
- Dive Business. bi-m.

**W.R.C. Smith Publishing Co.**
1760 Peachtree Rd., N.W., Atlanta, GA 30357.
- American Building Supplies. 12 per yr. ISSN 0002-7731
- Fiber Producer. s-a. ISSN 0361-4921
- National Automotive Directory. a. ISSN 0469-8029
- Southern Automotive Journal; covering automotive sales and service. m. ISSN 0038-3821
- Southern Hardware. m. ISSN 0038-416X
- Southern Wholesalers' Guide. a. ISSN 0586-8491
- Sports Merchandiser. m. ISSN 0049-1985
- Textile Industries. m. ISSN 0040-4985
- Textile Industries Buyers Guide. a.
- Textile Panamericanos; revista para la industria textile. m. ISSN 0040-5140

**Smithsonian Institution**
Washington, DC 20560
(Inquiries Are to Be directed to the attention of the Assn's Secretary-Treasurer, c/o Anthropology-MNH 368, Smithsonian Institution, Washington, DC 20560)
- Biotropica. 4 per yr. ISSN 0006-3606
- Smithsonian. m. ISSN 0037-7333
- Smithsonian Institution. Interdisciplinary Communications Program. Annotated Bibliography. s-a.
- Smithsonian Opportunities for Research and Study in History Art Science. irreg. ISSN 0081-0339
- Smithsonian Research Reports. q. (prep. by its Office of Public Affairs)
- Smithsonian Torch. m. ISSN 0037-7341

**Smithsonian Institution. Archives of American Art**
41 East 65th St., New York, NY 10021.
- Archives of American Art. Journal. q. ISSN 0003-9853

**Smithsonian Institution Astrophysical Observatory**
60 Garden St., Cambridge, MA 02138.
- Smithsonian Institution. Astrophysical Observatory. Central Bureau for Astronomical Telegrams. Circular. irreg., 1973, no. 2530. ISSN 0081-0304 (Co-sponsor: International Astronomical Union)
- Smithsonian Institution. Astrophysical Observatory. S A O Special Report. irreg. ISSN 0081-0320

**Smithsonian Institution. Center for Short Lived Phenomena**
60 Garden St., Cambridge, MA 02138
- Smithsonian Institution. Center for Short Lived Phenomena. Annual Report. a. ISSN 0085-6142 (Subscr. to: Unipub, Box 433, Murray Hill Station, New York, NY 10016)

**Smithsonian Institution. History of Science Society**
- ISIS Cumulative Bibliography. (pub. by Mansell Information - Publishing Ltd. UK)

**Smithsonian Institution. Information Systems Division**
Washington, DC 20560.
- Procedures in Computer Sciences. irreg. ISSN 0095-1951

**Smithsonian Institution. Museum of History and Technology**
Washington, DC 20560.
- Living Historical Farms Bulletin. q. ISSN 0047-4851 (Co-sponsors: Association for Living Historical Farms and Historical Museums; Museums of History and Technology)

**Smithsonian Institution Press**
Washington, DC 20560.
- Atoll Research Bulletin. irreg. ISSN 0077-5630
- Smithsonian Contributions to Anthropology. irreg. ISSN 0081-0223
- Smithsonian Contributions to Astrophysics. irreg., no. 17, 1974. ISSN 0081-0231
- Smithsonian Contributions to Botany. irreg. ISSN 0081-024X
- Smithsonian Contributions to Paleobiology. irreg. ISSN 0081-0266
- Smithsonian Contributions to the Earth Sciences. irreg. ISSN 0081-0274
- Smithsonian Contributions to Zoology. irreg. ISSN 0081-0282
- Smithsonian Institution. Annual Symposia Publications. a. ISSN 0489-2313 (Subscr. to: Publications Distribution Center, 1111 N. Capitol St., Washington DC 20002)
- Smithsonian Studies in History and Technology. irreg. ISSN 0081-0258

**Smithsonian Science Information Exchange**
Room 300, 1730 M Street, N.W., Washington, DC 20036.
- S S I E Science Newsletter. 10 per yr. ISSN 0094-7024

**Smoke-Eater Publications**
Box 118, Pierce, NE 68767.
- Minnesota Smoke-Eater. m.
- Nebraska Smoke-Eater. m.

**Smudge on the Window**
c/o Douglas Mumm, 33069 Grennada, Livonia, MI 48154.
- Smudge on the Window. q.

**Ray Smutek, Ed. & Pub.**
15630 S.E. 124th St., Renton, WA 98055.
- Off Belay. bi-m.

**Foster D. Snell, Inc.**
Hanover Rd., Florham Park, NJ 07932.
- Chemical Digest. irreg. ISSN 0009-2428

**Snell Publishing Co. Inc.**
Hastings, NE 68901.
- Shotgun News; trading post for anything that shoots. s-m. ISSN 0049-0415

**Snibbe Publications, Inc.**
523 Lakeview Rd., Clearwater, FL 33516.
- All About Christmas.
- Auto Racing Guide. a. ISSN 0067-2408
- Baseball Guide. a. ISSN 0067-4273
- Boating Guide. a. ISSN 0067-9399
- Bowling Guide. a. ISSN 0068-0567
- Bridge Bidding Guide. a.
- Brown Thumber's Handbook of House Plants. a.
- Camping Guide. a. ISSN 0068-6964
- Football Guide. a. ISSN 0069-5548
- Four Things Every Woman Should Know. a. ISSN 0073-3156
- Fresh Water Fishing Guide. a. ISSN 0071-5611
- Golf Guide. a. ISSN 0072-4955
- Great Black Athletes. a. ISSN 0072-5579
- Horse Racing Guide. a.
- Old Glory; the story of our flag. a.
- Pro Basketball Guide. a. ISSN 0079-5518
- Pro Hockey Guide. a. ISSN 0079-5577
- Pro Soccer Guide. a.
- Skier's Guide. a. ISSN 0080-9918
- Tennis Guide. a. ISSN 0082-2833

**Snips Magazine, Inc.**
407 Mannheim Rd., Bellwood, IL 60104.
- Snips. m. ISSN 0037-7457

**Snow Goer**
1999 Shepard Rd., St. Paul, MN 55116.
- Snow Goer. m. (Sep.-Jan.)

**Snowmobiler's Race & Rally Magazine**
c/o James E. Beilke, Ed., Box 182, Alexandria, MN 56308.
- Snowmobiler's Race & Rally Magazine. 3 per yr.

**Snowsports Publications, Inc.**
1500 E. 79th St., Minneapolis, MN 55420.
- Snow Sports Magazine for Snowmobile Families. 3 per yr. ISSN 0049-0830
- Snowsports Dealer News. m.
- SnowSports Invitation to Snowmobiling Annual. a.

**Arlis M. Snyder, Ed. & Pub.**
1226 W. Talmage, Springfield, MO 65803.
- Quoin. q. ISSN 0033-6653

**Thelma H. Snyder, Ed. & Pub.**
2421 Old Arch Rd., Norristown, PA 19401.
- American Racing Pigeon News. m.(Sept-July) ISSN 0003-0686

**Soap and Detergent Association**
475 Park Ave. S., New York, NY 10016.
- Water in the News. q. ISSN 0043-1222

**Soaring Society of America, Inc.**
Box 66071, Los Angeles, CA 90066.
- Soaring. m. ISSN 0037-7503

**Soccer Associates, Inc.**
Box 634, New Rochelle, NY 10802.
- Soccer News. m. ISSN 0037-7538

**Soccer Life Publishing Co.**
2660 San Benito Dr., Walnut Creek, CA 94598.
- Soccer Life. 10 per yr.

**Social Concern, Inc.**
Box 215, Rochdale Village Station, Jamaica, NY 11434.
- Forum. q.

**Social Democrats, U.S.A.**
275 7th Ave., New York, NY 10001.
- New America. m. ISSN 0028-419X

**Social Innovation Information Service**
1211 Connecticut Ave., Suite 604, Washington, DC 20036.
- Prometheus; a review of the literature of social development and institutional change. q. ISSN 0048-5535 (Archive of Social Innovation)
- Social Innovation. q. (Archive of Social Innovation)

**Social Legislation Information Service**
1346 Connecticut Ave. N.W., Washington, DC 20036.
- Washington Social Legislation Bulletin. s-m.

**Social Psychiatry Research Institute**
150 E. 69th St., New York, NY 10021.
- Social Psychiatry Newsletter. irreg. ISSN 0049-0873

**Social Science Education Consortium**
855 Broadway, Boulder, CO 80302.
- Social Studies Curriculum Materials Data Book Supplement. s-a.

**Social Science History Association**
- Social Science History. (pub. by University of Pittsburgh. University Center for International Studies)

**Social Science Research Council**
1755 Massachusetts Ave. N.W., Washington, DC 20036.
- Social Indicators Newsletter. irreg.

**Social Service Board of North Dakota**
Bismarck, ND 58501.
- North Dakota. Social Service Board. Statistics. a. ISSN 0095-1633

**Social Service Employees Union. Local 371**
817 Broadway, New York, NY 10003.
- Unionist; a publication of the Social Service Employees Union Local 371. District Council 37, AFSCME, AFL-CIO. bi-w. ISSN 0041-7092

**Social Service Publications**
211-05 Jamaica Ave., Queens Village, NY 11428.
- National Directory of Private Agencies. m.

**Socialist Forum**
G.P.O. 1948, New York, NY 10001.
- Perspective (New York); monthly newsletter of socialist political commentary. m.
- Socialist Forum. irreg. ISSN 0037-8194

**Socialist Labor Party**
914 Industrial Ave., Palo Alto, CA 94303.
- Weekly People. w. ISSN 0043-1885

**Sociedad de la Raza**
Box 40040, San Francisco, CA 94110.
- Basta Ya. m. ISSN 0005-6200

**Sociedad Honoraria Hispanica for Secondary Schools**
c/o Frederick N. Raile, William Workman High School, 16303 E. Temple Ave., City of Industry, CA 91744
(Orders to: Dr. Frank M. Figueroa, Collegium of Comparative Cultures, Eckerd College, St. Petersburg, FL 33733)
- Albricias. q.

**Sociedades Hispanas Confederados de los Estados Unidos de America**
231 W. 18th St., New York, NY 10011.
- Espana Libre. m. ISSN 0014-0511

**Societe des Professeurs Francais en Amerique**
c/o Michel Coclet, 22 E. 60th St., New York, NY 10022.
- Societe des Professeurs Francais en Amerique. Bulletin Annuel. a. ISSN 0081-0916

**Societe pour l'Etude de la Numismatique Francaise**
435 Cleveland Ave. North, Canton, OH 44701.
- S A E N F. s-a.

**Society for a Classical America**
10-41 51 Ave., Long Island City, NY 11101.
- Classical America. 2 per yr.

**Society for Academic Achievement**
W.C.U. Bldg., Quincy, IL 62301.
- Academic Achievement. 3 per yr. ISSN 0001-3951

**Society for Advancement of Continuing Education for Ministry**
855 Locust St., Collegeville, PA 19426.
- S A C E M Newsletter. 6 per yr.

**Society for Advancement of Management**
135 West 50th St., New York, NY 10020
(Subscr. to: Box 319, Saranac Lake, N.Y. 12983)
- Advanced Management Journal. q. ISSN 0036-0805
- S.A.M. News International. bi-m. ISSN 0049-1144

**Society for American Archaeology**
1703 New Hampshire Ave., N.W., Washington, DC 20009.
- American Antiquity. q. ISSN 0002-7316
- Society for American Archaeology. Memoirs. irreg. ISSN 0081-1300

**Society for American Indian Studies**
P.O. Box 443, Hurst, TX 76053.
- American Indian Quarterly. q. ISSN 0095-182X (Fort Worth Museum of Science and History)

**Society for Ancient Numismatics**
c/o Beate Rauch, Box 60321, Terminal Annex, Los Angeles, CA 60321.
- Society for Ancient Numismatics. S A N Journal. q. ISSN 0049-1152

**Society for Animal Rights, Inc.**
421 South State St., Clarks Summit, PA 18411.
- S A R Report. 6 per yr.

**Society for Applied Learning Technology**
- Journal of Educational Technology Systems. (pub. by Baywood Publishing Co., Inc.)

**Society for Applied Spectroscopy**
428 E. Preston St., Baltimore, MD 21202.
- Applied Spectroscopy. bi-m. ISSN 0003-7028

**Society for Asian Music**
- Asian Music Publications. Series A: Bibliographic and Research Aids. (pub. by Asian Music Publications)
- Asian Music Publications. Series B. Translations. (pub. by Asian Music Publications)
- Asian Music Publications. Series C: Reprints. (pub. by Asian Music Publications)

- Asian Music Publications. Series D: Monographs. (pub. by Asian Music Publications)

**Society for Asian Music (New York)**
112 E. 64 St., New York, NY 10021.
- Asian Music. 2 per yr. ISSN 0044-9202

**Society for Cinema Studies**
c/o Jack C. Ellis, Ed., Dept. Radio-TV-Film, Northwestern University, Evanston, IL 60201.
- Cinema Journal. s-a. ISSN 0009-7101

**Society for Clinical and Experimental Hypnosis**
129A Kings Park Dr., Liverpool, NY 13088
- International Journal of Clinical and Experimental Hypnosis. q. ISSN 0020-7144 (Subscr. to:, 111 N. 49 St., Phila. PA 19139)
- S C E H Newsletter. q. ISSN 0583-8975

**Society for College and University Planning**
3 Washington Square Village, New York, NY 10012.
- Planning for Higher Education. bi-m.

**Society for Computer Simulation**
- Simulation. (pub. by Simulation Councils, Inc.)
- Simulation Councils Proceedings. (pub. by Simulation Councils, Inc.)
- Simulation Today. (pub. by Simulation Councils, Inc.)
- Summer Computer Simulation Conference. Proceedings. (pub. by American Federation of Information Processing Societies)

**Society for Czechoslovak Philately, Inc.**
2936 Rosemoor Lane, Fairfax, VA 22030.
- Czechoslovak Specialist. 10 per yr.

**Society for Democracy in Greece**
c/o K. Mantis, 2352 Buford Ave., St. Paul, MN 55108.
- Greece in Chains. m. ISSN 0046-6360

**Society for Economic Botany**
- Economic Botany. (pub. by New York Botanical Garden)

**Society for Education in Laissez-Faire**
2861-37th Ave., Sacramento, CA 95824.
- S.E.L.F. Report. irreg.

**Society for Epidemiologic Research**
- American Journal of Epidemiology. (pub. by Johns Hopkins University. School of Hygiene and Public Health)

**Society for Ethnomusicology**
201 S. Main St., Room 513, Ann Arbor, MI 48108.
- Ethnomusicology. 3 per yr. ISSN 0014-1836
- S E M Newsletter. bi-m. ISSN 0036-1291

**Society for Experimental and Descriptive Malacology**
P.O. Box 801, Whitmore Lake, MI 48189.
- Malacological Review. a. ISSN 0076-3004

**Society for Experimental Biology and Medicine**
630 W. 168th St., New York, NY 10032.
- Society for Experimental Biology and Medicine. Proceedings. 11 per yr. ISSN 0037-9727

**Society for Experimental Stress Analysis**
21 Bridge Sq., Westport, CT 06880.
- Experimental Mechanics. m. ISSN 0014-4851
- Experimental Mechanics; Proceedings. irreg., 1965, 2nd, Washington D.C. ISSN 0071-3422
- S E S A Proceedings. s-a. ISSN 0036-1313

**Society for French - American Affairs**
Box 551 Cathedral Station, New York, NY 10025.
- Today in France. bi-m. ISSN 0040-8417

**Society for French Historical Studies**
Ohio State University, Department of History, Dulles Hall, 230 17th Ave, Columbus, OH 43210.
- French Historical Studies. s-a. ISSN 0016-1071

**Society for General Systems Research**
P. O. Box 1055, Louisville, KY 40201.
- Behavioral Science. bi-m. ISSN 0005-7940 (Co-sponsor: Institute of Management Sciences)
- General Systems. Yearbook. a. ISSN 0072-0798

**Society for Geology Applied to Mineral Deposits**
- Mineralium Deposita. (pub. by Springer-Verlag)

**Society for German-American Studies**
7204 Langerford Dr., Cleveland, OH 44129
- Journal of German-American Studies. a. (OR 21010 Mastick Rd., Cleveland, OH 44126)

**Society for Health and Human Values**
- Journal of Medicine and Philosophy. (pub. by University of Chicago Press)

**Society for Historians of American Foreign Relations (S.H.A.F.R.)**
c/o Tennessee Technological University, Department of History, Cookeville.
- Diplomatic History. (pub. by Scholarly Resources, Inc.)
- Society for Historians of American Foreign Relations. Newsletter. q.

**Society for Historical Archaeology**
c/o Roderick Sprague, University of Idaho, Department of Anthropology, Moscow, ID 83843.
- Historical Archaeology. a. ISSN 0440-9213
- Society for Historical Archaeology. Newsletter. q. ISSN 0037-9735
- Society for Historical Archaeology. Special Publication Series. irreg.

**Society for History Education**
California State University, Long Beach, CA 90840.
- History Teacher. q. ISSN 0018-2745

**Society for Individual Liberty**
400 Bonifant Rd., Silver Spring, MD 20904.
- Individualist. m. ISSN 0034-0030

**Society for Individual Liberty (Warminster)**
Box 1147, Warminster, PA 18947.
- Individual Liberty. m.

**Society for Industrial and Applied Mathematics**
33 South 17th Street, Philadelphia, PA 19103.
- Conference Board of the Mathematical Sciences. Regional Conference Series in Applied Mathematics. 4 per yr.
- S I A M - A M S Proceedings. (pub. by American Mathematical Society)
- S I A M Journal on Applied Mathematics. 8 per yr. ISSN 0036-1399
- S I A M Journal on Computing. q.
- S I A M Journal on Control and Optimization. 6 per yr.
- S I A M Journal on Mathematical Analysis. 6 per yr. ISSN 0036-1410
- S I A M Journal on Numerical Analysis. 6 per yr. ISSN 0036-1429
- S I A M News. bi-m.
- S I A M Review. q. ISSN 0036-1445
- Theory of Probability and Its Applications. q. ISSN 0040-585X

**Society for Industrial Archeology**
Room 5020, National Museum of History and Technology, Smithsonian Institution, Washington, DC 20560.
- Society for Industrial Archeology Newsletter. bi-m.

**Society for Information Display**
654 North Sepulveda Blvd., Los Angeles, CA 90049.
- S I D International Symposium. Digest of Technical Papers. a. ISSN 0082-0830
- S. I. D. Proceedings. q. ISSN 0036-1496

**Society for International Development**
1346 Connecticut Ave. N.W., Washington, DC 20036.
- Comentarios Sobre el Desarrollo Internacional. bi-m.
- Focus: Technical Cooperation. q.
- International Development Review/Revista de Desarrollo Internacional/Revue du Developpement Internationale. q. ISSN 0020-6555
- Society for International Development. World Conference Proceedings. irreg. (approx. 18 mos. to 2 yrs.) ISSN 0081-1416
- Survey of International Development. bi-m. ISSN 0039-6230

**Society for International Education, Training and Research**
- International Journal of Intercultural Relations. (pub. by Transaction Periodicals Consortium)

**Society for International Numismatics**
Box 943, Santa Monica, CA 90406.
- Sinformation. bi-m. ISSN 0037-5616

**Society for Investigative Dermatology**
- Journal of Investigative Dermatology. (pub. by Williams & Wilkins Co.)

**Society for Iranian Studies**
Box K-154, Boston College, Chestnut Hill, MA 02167.
- Iranian Studies. q. ISSN 0021-0862

**Society for Italian Historical Studies**
Center for Italian Studies, University of Connecticut, Storrs, CT 06268.
- Society for Italian Historical Studies. Newsletter. a. ISSN 0081-1424

**Society for Japanese Studies**
Thomson Hall, Dr-05, University of Washington, Seattle, WA 98195.
- Journal of Japanese Studies. s-a. ISSN 0095-6848

**Society for Long Range Planning**
- Corporate Planner's Yearbook. (pub. by Pergamon Press, Inc.)
- Long Range Planning. (pub. by Pergamon Press Inc.)

**Society for Louisiana Irises**
Box 4-0175, U.S.L., Lafayette, LA 70504.
- Society for Louisiana Irises. Special Publications. irreg.
- Society for Louisiana Irises Newsletter. q.

**Society for Medical Anthropology**
1703 New Hampshire Ave., N.W., Washington, DC 20009.
- Medical Anthropology. q.

**Society for Neuroscience**
9650 Rockville Pike, Bethesda, MD 20014.
- Society for Neuroscience. Annual Meeting. Conference Report. (pub. by Brain Information Service-Brain Research Institute)
- Society for Neuroscience. Directory of Members. irreg. ISSN 0098-9460

**Society for Nutrition Education**
2140 Shattuck Ave., 1110, Berkeley, CA 94704.
- Journal of Nutrition Education. q. ISSN 0022-3182

**Society for Pennsylvania Archaeology**
Vincent R. Mrozoski, Secy, Box 368, Aliquippa, PA 15001.
- Pennsylvania Archaeologist. 3 per yr. ISSN 0031-4358

**Society for Personality and Social Psychology**
1200 17th Street,N.W., Washington, DC 20036.
- Personality and Social Psychology Bulletin. q.

**Society for Personality Assessment, Inc.**
7840 S. W. 51st St., Portland, OR 97219.
- Journal of Personality Assessment. bi-m. ISSN 0022-3891

**Society for Photographic Education**
Box 1651, F. D. R. Post Office, New York, NY 10022.
- Exposure. q. ISSN 0098-8863

**Society for Psychophysiological Research**
2380 Lisa Lane, Rte 2, Madison, WI 53711.
- Psychophysiology. bi-m. ISSN 0048-5772

**Society for Range Management**
2760 W. Fifth Ave., Denver, CO 80204.
- Journal of Range Management; covering the study, management, and use of rangeland ecosystems and range resources. bi-m. ISSN 0022-409X
- Rangeman's Journal. bi-m. ISSN 0095-6236

**Society for Research in Child Development, Inc.**
- Child Development. (pub. by University of Chicago Press)
- Child Development Abstracts and Bibliography. (pub. by University of Chicago Press)
- Review of Child Development Research. (pub. by University of Chicago Press)

**Society for Slovene Studies**
420 W. 118 St., New York, NY 10027.
- Society for Slovene Studies. Documentation Series. irreg.
- Society for Slovene Studies Newsletter. (pub. by Columbia University. Institute on East Central Europe)

**Society for South India Studies**
Williams College, Department of Religion, Williamstown, MA 01267.
- Society for South India Studies. Newsletter. 3 per yr.

**Society for Spanish and Portuguese Historical Studies**
Department of History, College of the City of New York, NY 10031.
- Spanish and Portuguese Historical Studies. Newsletter. 3 per yr.

**Society for Technical Communication**
Suite 421, 1010 N.W. Vermont Ave, Washington, DC 20005.
- Technical Communication. q. ISSN 0049-3155

**Society for the Advancement of Education**
1860 Broadway, New York, NY 10023.
- Intellect. m.

**Society for the Advancement of Food Service Research**
2710 N. Salisbury St., West Lafayette, IN 47906.
- Society for the Advancement of Food Service Research. Proceedings. a. ISSN 0081-1483

**Society for the Advancement of Material and Process Engineering**
Box 613, Azusa, CA 91702.
- S A M P E Quarterly; a journal for the science of advanced materials and processes. q. ISSN 0036-0821
- Science of Advanced Material and Process Engineering. a. ISSN 0080-7559
- Society for the Advancement of Material and Process Engineering. National S A M P E Technical Conference. N S T C Preprint Series. a. ISSN 0081-1556

**Society for the Advancement of Scandinavian Study**
- Scandinavian Studies. (pub. by Allen Press, Inc.)

**Society for the Experimental Analysis of Behavior, Inc.**
Indiana Univ., Dept. of Psychology, Bloomington, IN 47401.
- Journal of the Experimental Analysis of Behavior. 6 per yr. ISSN 0022-5002

**Society for the Experimental Analysis of Behavior, Inc. (Lawrence)**
Department of Human Development, University of Kansas, Lawrence, KS 66044.
- J A B A Monograph Series. (Journal of Applied Behavior Analysis) irreg. ISSN 0021-8855
- Journal of Applied Behavior Analysis. q. ISSN 0021-8855

**Society for the History of Discoveries**
5404 Thunder Hill Road, Columbia, MD 21043.
- Society for the History of Discoveries. Annual Report. a.
- Studies in the History of Discoveries. (pub. by University of Chicago Press)

**Society for the History of Technology**
- Technology and Culture. (pub. by University of Chicago Press)

**Society for the Investigation of the Unexplained**
Columbia, NJ 07832.
- Pursuit; the journal of the Society for the Investigation of the Unexplained. q. ISSN 0033-4685

**Society for the Preservation and Encouragement of Barber Shop Quartet Singing in America, Inc.**
6315 Third Ave., Kenosha, WI 53141.
- Harmonizer. 6 times a year. ISSN 0017-7849

**Society for the Preservation of Birds of Prey**
Pacific Palisades, CA 90272.
- Raptor Report. 3 per yr.

**Society for the Preservation of Long Island Antiquities**
93 North Country Rd., Setauket, NY 11733.
- Society for the Preservation of Long Island Antiquities. Newsletter. a. ISSN 0583-9181

**Society for the Preservation of New England Antiquities**
141 Cambridge St, Boston, MA 02114.
- Old-Time New England; devoted to the ancient buildings, household furnishings, domestic arts, manners and customs, and minor antiquities of the New England people. q. ISSN 0030-2031

**Society for the Propagation of the Faith**
366 Fifth Avenue, New York, NY 10001.
- World Mission. q.

**Society for the Protection of New Hampshire Forests**
5 South State St., Concord, NH 03301.
- Forest Notes; New Hampshire's conservation magazine. q. ISSN 0015-7457

**Society for the Psychological Study of Social Issues**
Box 1248, Ann Arbor, MI 48106.
- Journal of Social Issues. q. ISSN 0022-4537

**Society for the Rehabilitation of the Facially Disfigured, Inc.**
550 First Ave., New York, NY 10016.
- S F D News. irreg., 1971 latest issue.

**Society for the Scientific Study of Sex**
138 E. 94th St., New York, NY 10028.
- Journal of Sex Research. 4 per yr. ISSN 0022-4499

**Society for the Study of Amphibians and Reptiles**
Ohio University, Department of Zoology, Athens, OH 45701.
- Herpetological Review. q. ISSN 0018-084X
- Journal of Herpetology. q. ISSN 0022-1511

**Society for the Study of Early China**
c/o University of California, Department of History, Berkeley, CA 94720.
- Early China. a.

**Society for the Study of Evolution**
Dr. R.E. Beer, University of Kansas, Entomology Department, Lawrence, KS 66045.
- Evolution; international journal of organic evolution. q. ISSN 0014-3820

**Society for the Study of Midwestern Literature**
240 Ernst Bassey Hall, Michigan State University, East Lansing, MI 48824.
- Midamerica. a.
- Society for the Study of Midwestern Literature. Newsletter. 3 per yr. ISSN 0085-6304

**Society for the Study of Reproduction**
311 Illinois Bldg., 113 N. Neil St., Champaign, IL 61820.
- Biology of Reproduction. 10 per yr. ISSN 0006-3363

**Society for the Study of Social Biology**
1180 Observatory Dr. Rm. 5440, Madison, WI 53706.
- Social Biology. q. ISSN 0037-766X

**Society for the Study of Social Problems**
114 Rockwell Hall, State University College at Buffalo, 1300 Elmwood Ave., Buffalo, NY 14222.
- Social Problems. 5 per yr. ISSN 0037-7791

**Society of Actuaries**
208 S. La Salle St., Chicago, IL 60604.
- Actuary. m. ISSN 0001-7825
- Society of Actuaries. Transactions. a. ISSN 0037-9794

**Society of Airway Pioneers**
Box 1720, San Diego, CA 92117.
- Airway Pioneer. q. ISSN 0002-2861
- Airway Pioneer; Yearbook of the Society of Airway Pioneers. a. ISSN 0065-4930

**Society of Alabama Geographers**
c/o Dr. Walter F. Koch, P.O. Box 1945, University, AL 35486.
- Alabama Geographer; a newsletter for Alabama's geographers. q.

**Society of Allied Weight Engineers**
Box 60024, Terminal Annex, Los Angeles, CA 90060.
- S.A.W.E. Journal. irreg. ISSN 0583-9270

**Society of American Archivists**
c/o Library, Box 8198, University of Illinois at Chicago Circle, Chicago, IL 60680.
- American Archivist. q. ISSN 0002-7332

**Society of American Florists. Ornamental Horticulturists**
901 N. Washington St., Alexandria, VA 22314.
- Who's Who in Floriculture. irreg. ISSN 0511-8964

**Society of American Foresters**
1010 16th St., N. W., Washington, DC 20036.
- Forest Science; a journal of research and technical progress. q. ISSN 0015-749X
- Forest Science Monographs. irreg., 1969, no. 16. ISSN 0071-7568
- Journal of Forestry; a journal reporting on the science, practice and profession of forestry. m. ISSN 0022-1201
- Multilingual Forestry Terminology Series. irreg. ISSN 0077-2046

**Society of American Magicians**
c/o Herbert B. Donns, National Sec., 66 Marked Tree Road, Needham, MA 02192.
- M U M. (Magic, Unity, Might) m. ISSN 0047-5300

**Society of American Travel Writers**
1120 Connecticut Ave. N.W. (Rm. 940), Washington, DC 20036.
- Society of American Travel Writers. Roster of Members. a. ISSN 0091-4991

**Society of Animal Artists**
151 Carroll St., City Island, Bronx, NY 10464.
- Society of Animal Artists Newsletter. 4 per yr.

**Society of Architectural Historians**
c/o Rosann S. Berry, Exec. Secy., 1700 Walnut St., Rm. 716, Philadelphia, PA 19103.
- Society of Architectural Historians. Journal. 4 per yr. ISSN 0037-9808
- Society of Architectural Historians Newsletter. 6 per yr. ISSN 0049-1195

**Society of Audio Consultants**
49 East 34th St., New York, NY 10016.
- Audio Digest & Personal Communications. q.

**Society of Automotive Engineers**
400 Commonwealth Dr., Warrendale, PA 15096.
- Advances in Engineering. irreg. ISSN 0065-2555
- Automotive Engineering. m. ISSN 0098-2571
- Convergence; International Colloquium on Automotive Electronic Technology. irreg. (Co-sponsor: Institute of Electrical and Electronics Engineers;)
- Engineering Know-How in Engine Design. a. ISSN 0489-5606
- Reliability and Maintainability. a. ISSN 0080-0813
- S A E Handbook. a.
- S A E Quarterly Abstracts. q.
- S A E Transactions. a.
- Stapp Car Crash Conference Proceedings. a. ISSN 0585-086X

**Society of Biblical Literature**
- Journal of Biblical Literature. (pub. by Scholars Press)
- Masoretic Studies. (pub. by Scholars Press)
- Semeia. (pub. by Scholars' Press)
- Society of Biblical Literature. Texts and Translations. (pub. by Scholars Press)

**Society of Biological Psychiatry**
- Biological Psychiatry. (pub. by Plenum Press)

**Society of Cable Television Engineers**
- Communications/Engineering Digest. (pub. by Titsch Publishing Co.)

**Society of Carbide and Tool Engineers**
International Headquarters, Box 437, Bridgeville, PA 15017.
- Carbide Journal. bi-m. ISSN 0045-5733

**Society of Catholic Medical Missionaries, Inc.**
8400 Pine Rd., Philadelphia, PA 19111.
- Medical Mission Sisters News. bi-m.

**Society of Certified Consumer Credit Executives**
7405 University Drive, St Louis, MO 63130.
- Journal of Consumer Credit Management. q. ISSN 0022-0086

**Society of Chartered Property & Casualty Underwriters**
P.O. Box 566, Media, PA 19063.
- C P C U Annals. q.
- C P C U News. m (except Jul. & Dec) ISSN 0007-8883
- Society of Chartered Property and Casualty Underwriters. Annals. q. ISSN 0037-9824

**Society of Chemical Engineers of Japan**
- Heat Transfer- Japanese Research. (pub. by Scripta Publishing Co.)

**Society of Christ for Polish Emigrants**
127 Starview Way, San Francisco, CA 94131.
- Migrant Echo. q. ISSN 0047-7338

**Society of Colonial Wars**
122 East 58th St., New York, NY 10022.
- Society of Colonial Wars. Bulletin. q.

**Society of Cosmetic Chemists**
50 E. 41st St., New York, NY 10017.
- Society of Cosmetic Chemists. Journal. 13 nos.per yr. ISSN 0037-9832

**Society of Critical Care Medicine**
- Critical Care Medicine. (pub. by Williams & Wilkins Co.)

**Society of Cryobiology**
New York Blood Center, 310 East 67th St., New York, NY 10021.
- Cryobiology. bi-m. ISSN 0011-2240

**Society of Data Educators**
516 Mark Ave., Truth or Consequences, NM 87901.
- Journal of Data Education. m(Oct-May) ISSN 0022-0310

**Society of Die Casting Engineers, Inc.**
16007 West 8 Mile Rd., Detroit, MI 48235.
- Die Casting Engineer. bi-m. ISSN 0012-253X
- S D C E International Die Casting Congress. Transactions. biennial. ISSN 0074-4557

**Society of Economic Paleontologists and Mineralogists**
Box 4756, Tulsa, OK 74104.
- Journal of Paleontology. bi-m. ISSN 0022-3360

**Society of Exploration Geophysicists**
Box 3098, Tulsa, OK 74101.
- Geophysics. bi-m. ISSN 0016-8033
- Society of Exploration Geophysicists. Special Publications (Symposia) Series. irreg.

**Society of Federal Linguists, Inc.**
Box 7765, Washington, DC 20044.
- Federal Linguist. s-a. ISSN 0046-3434
- Society of Federal Linguists. Newsletter. m (10 per yr.)

**Society of Flight Test Engineers**
Box 1821, Lancaster, CA 93534.
- Society of Flight Test Engineers. Annual Symposium Proceedings. a.

**Society of Folk Harpists and Craftsmen**
- Folk Harp Journal. (pub. by R. L. Robinson)

**Society of Friends**
- Friends Journal. (pub. by Friends Publishing Corp.)

**Society of General Physiologists**
- Journal of General Physiology. (pub. by Rockefeller University Press)
- Society of General Physiologists Series. (pub. by Raven Press)

**Society of Georgia Archivists**
Georgia State Univ., University Plaza, Atlanta, GA 30303.
- Georgia Archive. s-a.

**Society of Glass Decorators**
207 Grant St., Port Jefferson, NY 11777.
- Society of Glass Decorators. Papers Presented at Annual Seminar. a. ISSN 0081-1602

**Society of Harvard Engineers and Scientists**
Harvard Univ., Room G12B, Pierce Hall, Cambridge, MA 02138.
- H. E. S. Bulletin. s-a.

**Society of Illustrators**
- Illustrators; The Annual of American Illustration. (pub. by Hastings House Publishers, Inc.)

**Society of Independent Professional Earth Scientists**
Box 3370, Midland, TX 79701.
- Society of Independent Professional Earth Scientists. Newsletter. bi-m. ISSN 0037-9913

**Society of Irreproducible Research**
Box 234, Chicago Heights, IL 60411.
- Journal of Irreproducible Results. 4 per yr. ISSN 0022-2038

**Society of Jesus**
- Jesuit. (pub. by Jesuit Seminary Guild)

**Society of Jewish Science**
825 Round Swamp Road, Old Bethpage, NY 11804.
- Jewish Science Interpreter. 8 per yr.

**Society of Logistics Engineers**
3322 South Memorial Parkway, Suite 65, Huntsville, AL 35801.
- Logistics Spectrum. q. ISSN 0024-5852
- Society of Logistics Engineers. Proceedings. a. ISSN 0081-1629

**Society of Manufacturing Engineers**
20501 Ford Rd., Dearborn, MI 48128.
- Manufacturing Engineering. m. ISSN 0361-0853
- Manufacturing Engineering Transactions. a.
- Manufacturing Management Series. irreg., 1970, vol. 3. ISSN 0076-4256
- North American Metalworking Research Conference. Proceedings. irreg.
- Powder Coating Conference. irreg., latest issue 1975. ISSN 0092-0479
- Society of Manufacturing Engineers. Collected Papers and Technical Papers Presented at Southeastern Engineering and Tool Exposition. irreg., latest issue 1975. ISSN 0081-1637
- Society of Manufacturing Engineers. Collected Papers and Technical Papers Presented at Western Metal and Tool Exposition and Conference. irreg., latest issue 1975. ISSN 0081-1645
- Society of Manufacturing Engineers. Technical Digest; technical papers on microfiche and hard copy. q. ISSN 0049-1209
- Society of Manufacturing Engineers. Technical Papers. a. ISSN 0081-1653

**Society of Maritime Arbitrators**
26 Broadway, Suite 1200, New York, NY 10004.
- Society of Maritime Arbitrators. Award Service. 3 per yr.

**Society of Medalists**
West Branch Rd., Weston, CT 06880.
- Society of Medalists. News Bulletin. a. ISSN 0037-9948

**Society of Medical Friends of Wine**
Box 218, Sausalito, CA 94965.
- Society of Medical Friends of Wine. Bulletin. s-a. ISSN 0037-9956

**Society of Motion Picture and Television Engineers**
862 Scarsdale Ave., Scarsdale, NY 10583.
- S M P T E Journal. m. ISSN 0036-1682

**Society of Multivariate Experimental Psychology**
- Multivariate Behavioral Research. (pub. by Texas Christian University Press)

**Society of Naval Architects and Marine Engineers**
One World Trade Center, Suite 1369, New York, NY 10048.
- Journal of Ship Research. q. ISSN 0022-4502
- Marine Technology. q. ISSN 0025-3316
- Society of Naval Architects and Marine Engineers. Transactions. a. ISSN 0081-1661

**Society of Nematologists**
c/o J. M. Ferris, Dept. of Entomology, Purdue University, West Lafayette, IN 47907.
- Journal of Nematology. q. ISSN 0022-300X
- Society of Nematologists. Membership Directory. irreg. ISSN 0586-8300

**Society of Nuclear Medicine**
475 Park Ave. S., New York, NY 10016.
- Journal of Nuclear Medicine. m. ISSN 0022-3123
- Journal of Nuclear Medicine Technology. q. ISSN 0091-4916
- S N M Newsline. 6 per yr.

**Society of Ohio Archivists**
c/o Stephen C. Morton, University Archives, BGSU Library, Bowling Green, OH 43403.
- Ohio Archivist. s-a. ISSN 0030-0780

**Society of Paper Money Collectors, Inc.**
Box 858, Anderson, SC 29621.
- Paper Money; devoted to the world of currency and its collectors. bi-m. ISSN 0031-1162

**Society of Pharmacological and Environmental Pathologists**
Box 143, Mount Zion, IL 62549
- Society of Pharmacological and Environmental Pathologists. Bulletin. q. ISSN 0094-1824 (Subscr. To. C. Hans Keysser, M.D., Squibb Institute for Medical Research, New Brunswick NJ 08903)

**Society of Philatelic Americans**
11713 Chapel Rd., Clifton, VA 22024.
- S. P. A. Journal. m. ISSN 0036-181X

**Society of Philaticians**
- Philatelic Directory. (pub. by Gustav Detjen Jr., Ed. & Pub.)
- Philatelic Journalist. (pub. by Gustav Detjen Jr., Ed. & Pub.)

**Society of Photo-Optical Instrumentation Engineers**
405 Fieldston Rd., Box 10, Bellingham, WA 98225.
- Optical Engineering. bi-m.
- Society of Photo-Optical Instrumentation Engineers. Seminar Proceedings. 30 per yr. ISSN 0583-9572

**Society of Photographic Scientists and Engineers**
1411 K St. N.W., Suite 930, Washington, DC 20005.
- Journal of Applied Photographic Engineering. q. ISSN 0098-7298
- Photographic Science and Engineering. bi-m. ISSN 0031-8760
- Society of Photographic Scientists and Engineers. Proceedings of the Annual Fall Symposium. a.

**Society of Plastics Engineers**
656 W. Putnam Ave., Greenwich, CT 06830.
- Plastics Engineering. m. ISSN 0091-9578
- Polymer Engineering and Science. m. ISSN 0032-3888

**Society of Professional Investigators**
Box 1197, Church St. Sta., New York, NY 10008.
- Society of Professional Investigators. Bulletin. a. ISSN 0038-0008

**Society of Professional Journalists, Sigma Delta Chi**
35 E. Wacker Dr., Chicago, IL 60601.
- Quill; a magazine for journalists. m. ISSN 0033-6475

**Society of Professional Well Log Analysts**
13507 Tosca Lane, Houston, TX 77079.
- Log Analyst. bi-m. ISSN 0024-581X
- Society of Professional Well Logging Analysts. S P W L A Annual Logging Symposium Transactions. a. ISSN 0081-1718

**Society of Professors of Education**
c/o Roberta E. Bayles, Atlanta University, Atlanta, GA 30314.
- S P E Annual Monography. a.
- Society of Professors of Education. Quarterly Review. 3 per yr. ISSN 0028-0194

**Society of Protozoologists**
Box 368, Lawrence, KS 66044.
- Journal of Protozoology. 4 per yr. ISSN 0022-3921

**Society of Real Estate Appraisers**
7 South Dearborn St, Chicago, IL 60603.
- Appraisal Briefs. w.
- Real Estate Appraiser. bi-m. ISSN 0034-0677

**Society of Research Administrators**
2855 East Coast Hwy., Ste. 225, Corona del Mar, CA 92625.
- Society of Research Administrators. Journal. q. ISSN 0038-0024

**Society of Rheology**
- Rheology Bulletin. (pub. by American Institute of Physics)
- Society of Rheology. Transactions. (pub. by John Wiley & Sons, Inc.)

**Society of St. Edmund**
St. Edmund's Novitiate, Enders Island, Mystic, CT 06355.
- Edmundite. m. ISSN 0013-1016
- Your Edmundite Missions News Letter. (pub. by Southern Missions, Inc.)

**Society of St. Paul**
323 Scenic Ave., Box 1000, Sandy, OR 97055.
- St Paul's Printer. q. ISSN 0038-8815

**Society of St. Paul (Canfield)**
Canfield, OH 44406.
- Pastoral Life; the magazine for today's ministry. m. ISSN 0031-2762

**Society of Separationists**
Box 2117, Austin, TX 78768.
- American Atheist. m.
- American Atheist Insider Newsletter. (pub. by American Atheists)

**Society of Systematic Zoology**
- Systematic Zoology. (pub. by Allen Press, Inc.)

**Society of the Classic Guitar**
409 East 50th St., New York, NY 10022.
- Guitar Review. irreg.(approx 3 per yr) ISSN 0017-5471

**Society of the Divine Word**
Province of St. Augustine, Bay Saint Louis, MS 39520.
- Divine Word Messenger. q. ISSN 0012-4214

**Society of the Plastics Industry**
- Structural Foam Conference. Proceedings. (pub. by Technomic Publishing Co. Inc.)

**Society of Thoracic Surgeons**
- Annals of Thoracic Surgery. (pub. by Little, Brown & Co.)

**Society of Vertebrate Paleontology**
Texas Memorial Museum, Balcones Res. Ctr., 10100 Burnet Rd., Austin, TX 78758.
- Society of Vertebrate Paleontology. News Bulletin. 3 per yr.

**Society of Wireless Pioneers**
Box 530, Santa Rosa, CA 95402.
- Ports O'Call. q. ISSN 0032-5015
- Society of Wireless Pioneers. Yearbook. biennial. ISSN 0098-5910
- Sparks. a.
- Sparks Journal Quarterly. q.

**Society of Women Engineers**
One Emerson Place, Boston, MA 02114.
- Society of Women Engineers. Newsletter. 5 per yr. ISSN 0038-0067

**Society of Wood Science and Technology**
Box 5062, Madison, WI 53705.
- Wood and Fiber. q. ISSN 0043-7654

**Society of World War 1 Aero Historians**
10443 S. Memphis Ave., Whittier, CA 90604.
- Cross & Cockade Journal. q. ISSN 0011-1902

**Socio-Economic Publications, Inc.**
156 Fifth Ave., New York, NY 10010.
- Trade Union Courier. m. ISSN 0041-0497 (New York Teamsters Joint Council. Carpenters District Council)

**Sociological Abstracts, Inc.**
Box 22206, San Diego, CA 92122.
- Community Development Abstracts.
- L L B A. (Language and Language Behavior Abstracts) q. ISSN 0023-8295
- Sociological Abstracts. 6 per yr. ISSN 0038-0202

**Sociologists for Women in Society**
c/o Dawn Day, Ed., Brooklyn College/CUNY, Sociology Dept., Brooklyn, NY 11210.
- Sociologists for Women in Society Newsletter. q.

**A. W. Sockwell**
4313 N. Central Expy., Dallas, TX 75205.
- Furniture News Journal. q. ISSN 0046-533X

**Sod House Society of America**
Sod House Survey, Colby, KS 67701.
- Sons and Daughters of the Soddies. Reports; sod houses and dugouts in North America. irreg. (1-2 per yr.)

**Softball**
c/o Seifert, 938 S. Grove Rd., Ypsilanti, MI 48197.
- Softball. q. ISSN 0049-1268

**Soho Weekly News, Inc.**
111 Spring Street, New York, NY 10012.
- Soho Weekly News. w.

**Soil Conservation Society of America**
7515 Northeast Ankeny Rd., Ankeny, IA 50021.
- Journal of Soil and Water Conservation. bi-m. ISSN 0022-4561
- Soil Conservation Society of America. Proceedings of the Annual Meeting. a. ISSN 0081-1882

**Soil Science Society of America**
677 S. Segoe Rd., Madison, WI 53711.
- North American Forest Soils Conference. Proceedings. quinquennial. ISSN 0078-1320 (Co-Sponsors: Soil Science Society of Canada; Canadian Institute of Forestry; Society of American Foresters)
- S S S A Special Publication Series. irreg., 1970, no. 4. ISSN 0081-1904
- Soil Science Society of America. Journal. bi-m.

**Solar Energy Digest**
Box 17776, San Diego, CA 92117.
- Solar Energy Digest. m.

**Solar Engineering Publishers, Inc.**
8433 N. Stemmons, Suite 880, Dallas, TX 75247
- Solar Engineering. m. (Or: Solar Energy Industries Association, 8433 N. Stemmons, Suite 880, Dallas TX 75247)

**Solar Vision, Inc.**
200 E. Main St., Box z, Port Jervis, NY 12771.
- Solar Age; a magazine of the sun. m.

**Soldier Shop**
1013 Madison Ave., New York, NY 10021.
- Soldier Shop Annual. a.

**Solid Waste Management Magazine**
- Sanitation Industry Yearbook. (pub. by Communication Channels, Inc.)

**Solo Press**
1209 Drake Circle, San Luis Obispo, CA 93401.
- Cafe Solo. s-a. ISSN 0007-9537

**Solomon Schechter Day School Association**
- B'kitzur/Briefs. (pub. by United Synagogue of America. Commission on Jewish Education)

**Solvay Institute of Chemistry**
- Solvay Conference Proceedings - Chemistry. (pub. by Wiley-Interscience)

**Solvay Institute of Physics**
- Solvay Conference Proceedings - Physics. (pub. by Wiley-Interscience)

**Some**
309 W. 104 St., Apt. 9d, New York, NY 10025.
- Some. s-a.

**Some Friends**
c/o Terry J. Cooper, Ed., Box 3395, Tyler, TX 75701.
- Some Friends. 2-4 per yr.

**Some Hard-to-Locate Sources of Information**
762 Ave. "N" S.E., Winter Haven, FL 33880.
- Some Hard-to-Locate Sources of Information. irreg.

**Somerset Newspapers Inc.**
334 W. Main St., Somerset, PA 15501.
- Somerset Daily American. d.

**Somerville Poetry Conspiracy**
Box 306, 102 Charles St., Boston, MA 02114.
- Toy Sun. q.

**Something for Everybody Ad Bulletin**
Box 3573, Modesto, CA 95352.
- Something for Everybody Ad Bulletin. m.

**Somick Publishing Co.**
P.O. Box 12356, Cincinnati, OH 45212.
- Pest Control Technology. m.

**Song**
c/o Richard Behm, Ed., 222 Georgia Ave., Bowling Green, OH 43402.
- Song; magazine of poetry and essay. s-a.

**Songwriter's Review**
1697 Broadway, New York, NY 10019.
- Songwriter's Review; the guiding light to Tin Pan Alley. bi-m. ISSN 0038-1373

**Alexander Sonnenschein**
6717 Olive Blvd, St. Louis, MO 63130.
- Claytonian-Tribune.

**Sons of Norway**
1455 W. Lake St., Minneapolis, MN 55408.
- Sons of Norway Viking. m. ISSN 0038-1462

**Sons of the American Revolution. Massachusetts Society**
Box 1776, Weymouth, MA 02188.
- Sons of the American Revolution. Massachusetts Society. President's Newsletter. s-a.

**Sons of the Desert**
- Pratfall. (pub. by Way Out West Tent)

**Soon**
129 W. 85th St., New York, NY 10024.
- Soon. s-a.

**Sorghum Producers Association**
1708-a 15th St., Lubbock, TX 79401.
- Grain Sorghum News. m.

**Soroptimist International of the Americas**
1616 Walnut St., Philadelphia, PA 19103.
- Soroptimist of the Americas. 8 per yr. ISSN 0097-9562

**Sosland Publishing Co.**
173 W. Madison St., Chicago, IL 60602
(Subscr. address: 4800 Main St., Kansas City, MO 64112)
- Milling & Baking News. w. ISSN 0091-4843
- Milling & Grain Directory; plants and managers. biennial.
- Retail Baking Today; retail bakers' own magazine, including in-store bakeries & donut shops. m.

**Sotheby Parke Bernet Inc.**
980 Madison Ave., New York, NY 10021.
- Art at Auction; the Year at Sotheby's and Parke-Bernet. a. ISSN 0084-6783

**Soul and Jazz Record**
1680 Vine St., Suite 1017, Hollywood, CA 90028.
- Soul and Jazz Record. m. ISSN 0361-2619

**Soul in Review Publications**
572 W. 125 St., New York, NY 10027.
- Soul in Review. irreg. ISSN 0098-0730

**Soul Publications, Inc.**
8271 Melrose Ave., Suite 208, Los Angeles, CA 90046.
- Soul. bi-w.

**Sound Image**
Box 472, Amherst, MA 01002.
- Sound Image; a magazine of aural and visual art. a. ISSN 0362-3955

**Sound Publications Co.**
Box 593, Hialeah, FL 33011.
- Hi-Fi Newsletter. q. ISSN 0046-7340

**Sound Publishing Co., Inc.**
150 E. 37th St., New York, NY 10016.
- Musical Product News & Musical Electronics. 10 per yr.
- Sound & Communications. m. ISSN 0038-1845

**Sounds Fine**
Box 292, Riverdale, MD 20840.
- Sounds Fine; rock collector's marketplace. m.

**Source**
2101 22nd St., Sacramento, CA 95818.
- Source; music of the avant garde. s-a. ISSN 0038-1888

**South African Consulate General. Consul (Commercial)**
225 Baronne Street, New Orleans, LA 70112.
- South African Economic Newsletter and Trade Inquiries. q.

**South African Information Service**
655 Madison Ave., New York, NY 10021.
- South African Scope. m. ISSN 0038-2663

**South and West, Inc.**
6804 Cloverdale Drive, Little Rock, AR 72209.
- Voices International; a South and West publication. q. ISSN 0042-8280

**South Atlantic Modern Language Association**
Box 638, Chapel Hill, NC 27514.
- South Atlantic Bulletin. 4 per yr. ISSN 0038-2868

**South Carolina. Board of Engineering Examiners**
SCN Center, Suite 1020, Main & Landy Sts., Columbia, SC 29201.
- Directory of Engineers and Land Surveyors Registered in South Carolina. a. ISSN 0420-2155

**South Carolina. Board of Health**
Columbia, SC 29201.
- Update. q.

**South Carolina. Budget and Control Board**
Division of Research and Statistical Services, P.O. Box 11038, Columbia, SC 29211.
- South Carolina Statistical Abstract. irreg.

**South Carolina. Commission on Alcoholism and Drug Abuse**
1205 Pendelton St., Columbia, SC 29201.
- South Carolina. Commission on Alcoholism and Drug Abuse. Annual Report. a.

**South Carolina. Department of Archives & History**
Box 11669, Capitol Station, 1430 Senate St., Columbia, SC 29211.
- New South Carolina State Gazette. q. (Co-Sponsor: Confederation of S.C. Local Historical Societies)
- South Carolina. Department of Archives and History. Annual Report. a.
- South Carolina Historic Preservation Plan: Annual Preservation Program. a. ISSN 0361-1639

**South Carolina. Department of Education**
1208 Rutledge Bldg., 1429 Senate St., Columbia, SC 29201.
- South Carolina School Directory. irreg. ISSN 0363-9495 (prep. by its Planning and Dissemination Office)
- South Carolina Schools. m. ISSN 0038-3171

**South Carolina. Department of Health and Environmental Control. Bureau of Health Facilities and Services**
J. Marion Sims Bldg., 2600 Bull St., Columbia, SC 29201.
- South Carolina State Plan for Franchising, Construction and Modernization of Hospital and Related Medical Facilities. a. ISSN 0081-2692

**South Carolina. Department of Highways and Public Transportation**
Box 191, Columbia, SC 29202.
- Carolina Highways. m. ISSN 0008-6789

**South Carolina. Department of Labor**
Box 11329, 3600 Forest Dr., Columbia, SC 29211.
- South Carolina. Department of Labor. Annual Report. a.

**South Carolina. Department of Mental Health. William S. Hall Psychiatric Institute**
Box 119, Columbia, SC 29202.
- Psychiatric Forum. s-a. ISSN 0033-2690

**South Carolina. Division of Vital Records**
2600 Bull St., Columbia, SC 29201.
- South Carolina Vital and Morbidity Statistics. a. ISSN 0094-6338

**South Carolina. Employment Security Commission**
Box 995, Columbia, SC 29202.
- South Carolina Economic Indicators. m. ISSN 0038-304X
- South Carolina's Manpower in Industry; labor force estimates and nonagricultural wage and salary employment by major industry division and selected industry groups; annual averages. ISSN 0095-4799 (prep. by its Research and Statistics Section)

**South Carolina. State Board for Technical and Comprehensive Education**
1429 Senate St., Columbia, SC 29201.
- Impact (Columbia); technical education in South Carolina. q. ISSN 0019-2856

**South Carolina. State Development Board**
Box 927, Columbia, SC 29202.
- Geologic Notes. q. ISSN 0016-7541 (prep. by its Division of Geology)
- Industrial Directory of South Carolina. a. ISSN 0085-6444

**South Carolina Metalworking Directory. irreg.**
ISSN 0363-5090 (prep. by its Industrial Services Division)

**South Carolina. State Library**
P.O. Box 11469, 1500 Senate St., Columbia, SC 29211.
- Checklist of South Carolina State Publications. a.
- News for South Carolina Libraries. m.
- South Carolina State Library. Annual Report. a.

**South Carolina. Wildlife Resources Department**
Box 167, Columbia, SC 29202.
- South Carolina Wildlife. bi-m. ISSN 0038-3198

**South Carolina Arts Commission**
Columbia, SC 29201.
- South Carolina Arts Commission. Annual Report. a. ISSN 0081-2684

**South Carolina Associations of Young Farmers and Future Farmers**
Box 417, Winnsboro, SC 29180.
- South Carolina Young Farmer and Future Farmer. q. ISSN 0038-3201

**South Carolina Dental Journal**
1506 Gregg St., Columbia, SC 29201.
- South Carolina Dental Journal. m. ISSN 0049-1489

**South Carolina Education Association**
421 Zimalcrest Drive, Columbia, SC 29210.
- South Carolina Education News Emphasis. 12 per yr. ISSN 0038-3066

**South Carolina Electric Cooperative Association**
P.O. Box 145, Cayce, SC 29033.
- Living in South Carolina. m. ISSN 0047-486X

**South Carolina Historical Society**
Fireproof Bldg., Charleston, SC 29401.
- South Carolina Historical Magazine. q. ISSN 0038-3082

**South Carolina Labor News, Inc.**
Box 1032, Columbia, SC 29202.
- South Carolina Labor News. q.

**South Carolina Library Association**
c/o Laurance R. Mitlin, Ed., Dacus Library, Winthrop College, SC 29733.
- South Carolina Librarian. s-a. ISSN 0038-3112

**South Carolina Magazine Corporation**
Box 89, Columbia, SC 29202.
- South Carolina Magazine. m. ISSN 0038-3120

**South Carolina Medical Association**
P.O. Box 11188, Columbia, SC 29211.
- South Carolina Medical Association. Journal. m. ISSN 0038-3139

**South Carolina Political Science Association**
- Journal of Political Science (Clemson) (pub. by Clemson University. Department of Political Science)

**South Carolina State College**
Orangeburg, SC 29115.
- Explorations in Education. a. ISSN 0071-3481

**South Carolina State Ports Authority**
Box 817, Charleston, SC 29402.
- South Carolina Port News. m.

**South Central Modern Language Association**
Department of English, University of Houston, Houston, TX 77004.
- South Central Bulletin. 4 per yr. ISSN 0038-321X

**South Central Research Library Council**
DeWitt Bldg., Office 6-A, 215 N. Cayuga St., Ithaca, NY 14850.
- South Central Research Library Council. Library Directory. a. ISSN 0081-2722
- South Central Research Library Council. Pamphlet Series. irreg., latest issue 1975. ISSN 0081-2730

**South Dakota. Department of Agriculture. Crop & Livestock Reporting Service**
312 South Minnesota Avenue, Sioux Falls, SD 57101.
- South Dakota Agriculture. a.

**South Dakota. Department of Economic and Tourism Development. Industrial Development Division**
620 South Cliff, Sioux Falls, SD 57103.
- South Dakota. q. ISSN 0038-3236
- South Dakota Manufacturers & Processors Directory. irreg. ISSN 0094-2758

**South Dakota. Department of Game, Fish and Parks**
Pierre, SD 57501.
- South Dakota Conservation Digest. bi-m. ISSN 0038-3279

**South Dakota. Department of Health**
Pierre, SD 57501.
- South Dakota Vital Statistics Annual Report. a. ISSN 0095-4802

**South Dakota. Department of Labor**
Box 1730, Aberdeen, SD 57401.
- Manpower Bulletin. m.

**South Dakota. Department of Revenue. Division of Property Tax**
Capitol Lake Plaza Bldg., Peirre, SD 57501.
- South Dakota. Department of Revenue. Annual Statistical Report. a. ISSN 0085-6460

**South Dakota. Division of Highway Safety**
Pierre, SD 57501.
- South Dakota Highway Safety Work Program. irreg. ISSN 0361-3461

**South Dakota. Economic Opportunity Office**
Capitol Building, 120 E. Capitol, Pierre, SD 57501.
- Poverty in South Dakota. a.

**South Dakota. Employment Security Division**
Box 730, Aberdeen, SD 57401.
- South Dakota. Employment Security Division. Research and Statistics. Annual Report on State and Area Occupational Requirements for Vocational Education. a. ISSN 0094-2200

**South Dakota. Geological Survey**
Science Center University, Vermillion, SD 57069.
- South Dakota Geological Survey. Bulletin. irreg., latest issue 1975. ISSN 0085-6479
- South Dakota Geological Survey. Circular. irreg., latest issue 1972. ISSN 0085-6487
- South Dakota Geological Survey. Guidebook. irreg. ISSN 0081-2765
- South Dakota Geological Survey. Reports of Investigation. irreg., latest issue 1974. ISSN 0085-6495

**South Dakota. Rural Manpower Service**
Pierre, SD 57501.
- South Dakota. Rural Manpower Service. Rural Manpower Report. a. ISSN 0093-9455

**South Dakota. State Legislative Research Council**
Pierre, SD 57501.
- Facts About South Dakota. biennial. ISSN 0094-4262

**South Dakota. State Library**
322 South Fort St., Pierre, SD 57501.
- South Dakota State Library Newsletter. bi-m. ISSN 0361-8560

**South Dakota Academy of Science**
University of South Dakota, Dept. of Biology, Vermillion, SD 57069.
- South Dakota Academy of Science. Proceedings. a.

**South Dakota Association of County Commissioners**
- South Dakota Journal of County Government. (pub. by University of South Dakota. Center for Continuing Education)

**South Dakota Dental Association**
Box 1194, 222 E. Capitol, Pierre, SD 57501.
- South Dakota Dental Association. Newsletter. fortn. ISSN 0038-3287

**South Dakota Education Association**
Box 939, 411 E. Capitol Ave., Pierre, SD 57501.
- South Dakota Education Association. Educators' Advocate. 16 per yr. ISSN 0013-2047

**South Dakota Indian Recipients of Social Welfare**
Capitol Lake Plaza, Pierre, SD 57501.
- South Dakota Indian Recipients of Social Welfare. irreg. ISSN 0094-372X

**South Dakota Library Association**
Karl E. Mundt Library, Dakota State College, Madison, SD 57042.
- Catalyst (Madison) 6 per yr. ISSN 0045-5954

**South Dakota Motor Carriers Association**
c/o Lyon County Reporter, 310 First Ave., Rock Rapids, IA 51246.
- South Dakota Motor Carrier. m. ISSN 0038-3333

**South Dakota Municipal League**
214 E. Capitol, Pierre, SD 57501.
- South Dakota Municipalities. m. ISSN 0300-6182

**South Dakota Ornithologists' Union**
Highmore, SD 57345.
- South Dakota Bird Notes. q. ISSN 0038-3252

**South Dakota Rural Electric Association**
222 W. Pleasant Drive, Pierre, SD 57501.
- South Dakota High Liner. m. ISSN 0038-3309

**South Dakota School of Mines and Technology. Geology, Mining & Metallurgy Depts.**
Rapid City, SD 57701.
- Mineral Industries Newsletter. s-a. ISSN 0026-4547

**South Dakota State Historical Society**
Memorial Bldg., Capitol Ave., Pierre, SD 57501.
- South Dakota. Department of History. Historical Collections. biennial.
- South Dakota History. q.
- South Dakota State Historical Society. Collections. biennial. ISSN 0081-2773

**South Dakota State Medical Association**
608 West Ave., N., Sioux Falls, SD 57104.
- South Dakota Journal of Medicine. m. ISSN 0038-3317

**South Dakota State Poetry Society**
c/o Dorothy I. Davie, Ed., 801 S. West Ave., Sioux Falls, SD 57104.
- Pasque Petals. 10 per yr. ISSN 0031-2649

**South Dakota State University. Agricultural Experiment Station**
Brookings, SD 57006.
- Farm & Home Research; agricultural experiment station quarterly. q. ISSN 0038-3295

**South Dakota State University. Alumni Association**
Brookings, SD 57006.
- South Dakota State University Alumnus. q.

**South Dakota Stock Growers Association**
426 St. Joe St., Rapid City, SD 57701.
- South Dakota Stockgrower. m. ISSN 0038-3384

**South Georgia College**
Douglas, GA 31533.
- South Georgian. every 3 weeks.

**South Georgia Conference Commission on Archives and History of the United Methodist Church**
Epworth-by-the-Sea, St. Simons Island, GA 31522.
- Historical Highlights. s-a.

**South Penn Motor Club**
230 Lincoln Way E, Chambersburg, PA 17201.
- South Penn Motorist. m. ISSN 0038-3503

**South Publishing Co.**
1129 Ingraham Bldg., Miami, FL 33131.
- Florida Supplement; opinions of Florida trial courts and Florida Public Service Commission. s-a. ISSN 0015-4318

**South Shore Publishers, Inc.**
Hewlett Plaza, Hewlett, NY 11557.
- South Shore Record. w. ISSN 0038-352X (Hewlett-Woodmere Public Library)

**South Street Seaport Museum**
16 Fulton St., New York, NY 10038.
- South Street Reporter. q. ISSN 0038-3538

**South Suburban Genealogical and Historical Society**
Box 96, South Holland, IL 60473.
- Where the Trails Cross. q. ISSN 0092-4164

**South Texas College of Law**
1303 San Jacinto, Houston, TX 77002.
- South Texas Law Journal. 3 per yr. ISSN 0038-3546

**South Trade Publications, Co.**
Box 9377, Greensboro, NC 27408.
- Southern Plumbing, Heating, Cooling. m. ISSN 0038-4461

**Southeast Farm Press Inc.**
Box 1147, Intersection Highways 61-N and 6, Clarksdale, MS 38614.
- Southeast Farm Press. w.

**Southeast Georgian, Inc.**
Box 1059, Kingsland, GA 31548.
- Southeast Georgian. w.

**Southeast Louisiana Historical Association**
Box 1937, Hammond, LA 70401.
- Southeast Louisiana Historical Association. Papers. irreg. ISSN 0098-9193

**Southeast Michigan Council of Governments**
800 Book Bldg., Detroit, MI 48226.
- Population and Occupied Dwelling Units in Southeast Michigan. a. ISSN 0362-5079
- Southeast Michigan Council of Governments. Annual Report. a. ISSN 0362-3475

**Southeast Missouri State College. Department of English**
Cape Girardeau, MO 63701.
- Cape Rock; a journal of poetry. s-a.

**Southeast Missouri State University**
Academic Hall, Cape Girardeau, MO 63701.
- Capaha Arrow. w. ISSN 0008-5774

**Southeast Retail Furniture Association**
1631 Pinevale St., Jackson, MS 39211.
- Southeast Furniture & Appliance News. bi-m. ISSN 0038-3627

**Southeastern Association of Game and Fish Commissioners**
c/o Arnold L. Mitchell, Capital Plaza Tower, 4th Fl., Frankfort, KY 40601.
- Southeastern Association of Game and Fish Commissioners. Proceedings of the Annual Conference. a. ISSN 0081-2943

**Southeastern Baptist Theological Seminary**
Wake Forest, NC 27587.
- Outlook. 6 per yr. ISSN 0030-7238

**Southeastern Composers' League**
c/o Arthur Jannery, Radford College, Radford, VA 24141.
- Music Now. 3 per yr. ISSN 0027-4437

**Southeastern Conference on Latin American Studies**
c/o Ed. Eugene R. Huck, Kennesaw Junior College, Marietta, GA 30061.
- S E C O L A S Annals. a. ISSN 0081-2951

**Southeastern Conference on Latin American Studies (University)**
Dept. of History, University of Alabama, University, AL 35486.
- South Eastern Latin Americanist. q. ISSN 0049-1527

**Southeastern Library Association**
c/o Ann W. Morton, Box 987, Tucker, GA 30084.
- Southeastern Librarian. q. ISSN 0038-3686

**Southeastern Library Network**
615 Peachtree St. N. E. Suite 820, Atlanta, GA 30308.
- Southeastern Library Network. Annual Report. a. ISSN 0099-085X

**Southeastern Pennsylvania Theological Library Association**
- Teamwork. (pub. by Krauth Memorial Library)

**Southeastern Poultry and Egg Association**
345 Green St. N.W., Box 1338, Gainesville, GA 30501.
- Poultry Times. w. ISSN 0048-4989

**Southeastern Press, Inc.**
P.O. Box 3, Columbia, SC 29202.
- All South Carolina Football Annual. a.

**Southeastern Professional Photographers Association, Inc.**
Box 1428, Selma, AL 36701.
- Southern Exposure. q. ISSN 0038-4070

**Southeastern Renaissance Conference**
Duke University, Editorial Office, 402 Allen Bldg., Durham, NC 27706.
- Renaissance Papers. a. ISSN 0584-4207

**Southeastern School of Alcohol Studies**
- Southeastern School of Alcohol Studies. Proceedings. (pub. by University of Georgia. Center for Continuing Education)

**Southeastern Surgical Congress**
- American Surgeon. (pub. by J. B. Lippincott Co.)

**Southern Adirondack Library System**
22 Whitney Place, Saratoga Springs, NY 12866.
- Proof Sheet. q. ISSN 0033-1228

**Southern Africa Committee**
244 W. 27th St., New York, NY 10001.
- Southern Africa. m. ISSN 0038-3775

**Southern Agricultural Economics Association**
c/o John W. Nixon, Ed., Agricultural Economics Dept., University of Georgia, Athens, GA 30602 (or Department of Economics and Business, North Carolina State University, Raleigh, NC 27607)
- Southern Journal of Agricultural Economics. s-a. ISSN 0081-3052

**Southern & Southwestern Railway Club**
Box 1744, Roanoke, VA 24008.
- Southern and Southwestern Railway Club. Proceedings. q. ISSN 0038-3805

**Southern Anthropological Society**
- Southern Anthropological Society. Proceedings. (pub. by University of Georgia Press)

**Southern Association of Colleges and Schools**
795 Peachtree St., N.E. Atlanta, GA 30308.
- Southern Association of Colleges and Schools. Proceedings. 8 per yr. ISSN 0038-3813

**Southern Baptist Convention**
460 James Robertson Parkway, Nashville, TN 37219.
- Baptist Program. m. ISSN 0005-5743
- Southern Baptist Convention. Annual. a. ISSN 0081-3001
- Southern Baptist Educator. bi-m. ISSN 0038-3848

**Southern Baptist Convention. Brotherhood Commission**
1548 Poplar Ave., Memphis, TN 38104.
- Crusader. m. ISSN 0011-2151
- Probe (Memphis) m. ISSN 0032-9215
- World Mission Journal. m.

**Southern Baptist Convention. Foreign Mission Board**
3806 Monument Ave., Richmond, VA 23230.
- ANCLA. (pub. by Casa Bautista de Publicaciones)
- Commission; Southern Baptist Foreign Missions journal. m. ISSN 0010-3179
- Escudo. (pub. by Casa Bautista de Publicaciones)
- Estrella. (pub. by Casa Bautista de Publicaciones)
- Rayito. (pub. by Casa Bautista de Publicaciones)
- Ventana. (pub. by Casa Bautista de Publicaciones)

**Southern Baptist Convention. Historical Commission**
127 Ninth Ave. N., Nashville, TN 37234.
- Baptist History and Heritage. q. ISSN 0005-5719
- Index of Graduate Theses in Baptist Theological Seminaries. triennial. ISSN 0073-5825
- Southern Baptist Convention. Historical Commission. Microfilm Catalogue. a. ISSN 0081-301X
- Southern Baptist Periodical Index. a. ISSN 0081-3028

**Southern Baptist Convention. Home Mission Board**
1350 Spring St., N.W., Atlanta, GA 30309.
- Home Missions. m. ISSN 0018-408X

**Southern Baptist Convention. Sunday School Board**
127 Ninth Avenue, North, Nashville, TN 37234.
- Bible Discoverers: Teacher. q.
- Bible Searchers. q. ISSN 0006-078X
- Bible Searchers: Teacher. q. ISSN 0006-0798
- Children's Leadership; administrative magazine for all Sunday school workers with children. q.
- Choral Overtones. q. ISSN 0360-2443
- Choral Tones. q. ISSN 0360-2524
- Church Musician. m. ISSN 0009-6466
- Deacon. q. ISSN 0045-9771
- Event. m. ISSN 0014-374X
- Facts and Trends. m. ISSN 0014-6625
- Home Life; a Christian family magazine. m. ISSN 0018-4071

- Media: Library Services Journal. q. ISSN 0009-6423
- Music Leader. q. ISSN 0027-4372 (prep. by its Church Music Dept)
- On the Wing. q.
- Proclaim; the pastor's journal for biblical preaching. q.
- Search (Nashville) q. ISSN 0048-9913
- Southern Baptist Convention. Sunday School Board, Quarterly Review; a survey of Southern Baptist progress. q.
- Student (Nashville) m.(Oct-June) ISSN 0039-2685
- Sunday School Adults. q.
- Sunday School Senior Adults. q. ISSN 0585-9328
- Teaching Pictures for Bible Searchers. q. ISSN 0040-0645
- Young Adult Bible Study. q.
- Young Adults in Training. q.
- Young Musicians. q. ISSN 0044-0841

**Southern Baptist Convention. Woman's Missionary Union**
600 N. 20th St., Birmingham, AL 35203.
- Royal Service. m. ISSN 0035-9084

**Southern Baptist General Convention of California**
678 E. Shaw Ave., Fresno, CA 93755.
- California Southern Baptist. w. ISSN 0008-1558

**Southern Baptist Radio and Television Commission**
6350 W. Freeway, Fort Worth, TX 76116.
- Beam International; newsletter serving broadcasters around the world. m. except combined March-April issue.

**Southern Baptist Theological Seminary**
Louisville, KY 40206.
- Review and Expositor. q. ISSN 0034-6373
- Tie. m(except Feb., May, Aug & Nov.) ISSN 0040-7232

**Southern Bell Telephone Co.**
Atlanta, GA 30311.
- Southern Bell Views. 7-10 per yr. ISSN 0038-3856

**Southern Beverage Journal, Inc.**
Box 561107, 13225 S.W. 88th Ave., Miami, FL 33156.
- Southern Beverage Journal. m.

**Southern Bio-Research Institute**
- Growth. (pub. by Growth Publishing Co. Inc.)

**Southern Boating and Yachting Inc.**
615 S. W. 2 Ave., Miami, FL 33130.
- Southern Boating. m.

**Southern Building Code Congress**
- Southern Building. (pub. by Southern Building Code Publishing Co., Inc.)

**Southern Building Code Publishing Co., Inc.**
3617 Eighth Ave. S., Birmingham, AL 35222.
- Southern Building. bi-m. ISSN 0038-3864 (Southern Building Code Congress)

**Southern California Academy of Sciences**
c/o James Dale Smith, Ed., California State Univ., Dept. of Biology, Fullerton, CA 92634.
- Southern California Academy of Sciences. Bulletin. 3 per yr. ISSN 0038-3872

**Southern California Association of Governments**
1600 S. Commonwealth Ave., Suite 1000, Los Angeles, CA 90005.
- S C A G Annual Report. a.

**Southern California Dental Hygienists' Association**
8530 Wilshire Blvd., Suite 313, Beverly Hills, CA 90211.
- Southern California Dental Hygienists' Association. Journal. q. ISSN 0038-3899

**Southern California Dental Laboratory Association**
3333 Glendale Blvd., Suite 4, Los Angeles, CA 90039.
- Southern California Dental Laboratory Association. Bulletin. m. ISSN 0038-3945

**Southern California Educational Theatre Association**
9811 Pounds Ave., Whittier, CA 90603.
- Educational Theatre News. 6 per yr. ISSN 0013-1997

**Southern California Genealogical Society Inc.**
- Searcher. (pub. by Donald Norman Moran, Ed. & Pub.)

**Southern California Golf Association**
3740 Cahuenga Blvd., North Hollywood, CA 91604.
- Fore. q. ISSN 0300-8509

**Southern California Grocers Association**
1636 W. 8th St., Los Angeles, CA 90017.
- Grocers' Journal. m.

**Southern California Jewish Historical Society**
2429 23rd St., Santa Monica, CA 90405.
- Western States Jewish Historical Quarterly. q. ISSN 0043-4221

**Southern California Local History Council**
Box 909, Anaheim, CA 92805.
- Biblio-Cal Notes. a. ISSN 0045-1851

**Southern California Psychiatric Society**
9713 Santa Monica Blvd., Beverly Hills, CA 90210.
- Southern California Psychiatric Society News. m. (except Jul. & Aug.) ISSN 0049-1586

**Southern California Rapid Transit District**
1060 S. Broadway, Los Angeles, CA 90015.
- Southern California Rapid Transit District. Annual Report. a. ISSN 0362-2843

**Southern California Retailer**
440 S. Anaheim Bldg., Anaheim, CA 92805.
- Southern California Retailer. m.

**Southern California School of Theology**
1325 N. College Ave., Claremont, CA 91711.
- School of Theology at Claremont. Perspective. 7 per yr. ISSN 0036-6722

**Southern Center for Studies in Public Policy**
Clark College, Atlanta, GA 30314.
- Georgia Legislative Review. irreg. ISSN 0362-5931
- Public Policy Studies in the South; a selected research guide. a.

**Southern Christian Advocate, Inc.**
Box 11589, Columiba, SC 29211.
- South Carolina Methodist Advocate. w. ISSN 0038-3147 (United Methodist Church. South Carolina Conference)

**Southern Christian Leadership Conference**
334 Auburn Ave. N.E., Atlanta, GA 30303.
- Soul Force. m. ISSN 0038-1764

**Southern Colorado Horseman's Association**
- Arkansas Valley Journal. (pub. by Arkansas Valley Journal, Inc)

**Southern Colorado State College**
Dept. of English, Pueblo, CO 81005.
- Poetry Bag; an annual journal of poems. a. ISSN 0032-2067

**Southern Comparative Literature Association**
c/o Dept. of English, North Carolina State Univ., Box 5308, Raleigh, NC 27607.
- S L A Newsletter. q.

**Southern Conference Educational Fund**
3210 W. Broadway, Louisville, KY 40211.
- Southern Struggle. bi-m.

**Southern Council of Optometrists**
Box 18617, Atlanta, GA 30326.
- Southern Journal of Optometry. m. ISSN 0038-4275

**Southern Dairy Products Journal**
5265 Antelope Lane, Stone Mountain, GA 30083.
- Southern Dairy Products Journal. m. ISSN 0038-402X

**Southern Economic Association**
- Southern Economic Journal. (pub. by University of North Carolina at Chapel Hill)

**Southern Feminists: the Feminist Newsletter**
Box 954, Chapel Hill, NC 27514.
- Southern Feminists: the Feminist Newsletter. fortn.

**Southern Florist and Nurseryman**
120 St. Louis St., Fort Worth, TX 76104.
- Southern Florist and Nurseryman. w. ISSN 0038-4119

**Southern Furniture, Inc.**
Southern Furniture Exposition Bldg., High Point, NC 27260.
• Furniture South. m. ISSN 0016-3074

**Southern Historical Association**
B. H. Wall, Sec.-Treas., Tulane Univ., New Orleans, LA 70118
• Journal of Southern History. q. ISSN 0022-4642 (Co-Sponsor: Rice University) (Ed. Address: Rice University, Box 1892, Houston, TX 77001)

**Southern Host Publishing Corporation**
Box 10168, Wilton Manors, FL 33305.
• Southern Host. fortn.

**Southern Humanities Conference**
Box 4715, Tech Sta., Ruston, LA 71270.
• Humanities in the South; newsletter of the Southern Humanities Conference. s-a. ISSN 0018-7577

**Southern Illinois University, Carbondale**
Outdoor Laboratory, Carbondale, IL 62901.
• I C R H Newsletter. m. ISSN 0018-9022

**Southern Illinois University, Carbondale. Business Research Bureau**
Carbondale, IL 62901.
• Business Science Monographs. irreg. ISSN 0068-449X
• Southern Illinois University, Carbondale. Business Research Bureau. Regional Studies in Business and Economics. Monographs. irreg. ISSN 0073-4942

**Southern Illinois University, Carbondale. Center for Dewey Studies**
Carbondale, IL 62901.
• Dewey Newsletter. s-a. ISSN 0012-172X

**Southern Illinois University, Carbondale. Center for Soviet & East-European Studies**
Carbondale, IL 62901.
• Center for Soviet and East-European Studies in the Performing Arts. Bulletin. 4 per yr. ISSN 0008-9095

**Southern Illinois University, Carbondale. Center for Vietnamese Studies**
Carbondale, IL 62901.
• Southeast Asia; an international quarterly. q. ISSN 0049-1551

**Southern Illinois University, Carbondale. Department of Anthropology**
c/o Philip C. Dark, Ed., Carbondale, Il 62901.
• Pacific Art Newsletter. s-a.

**Southern Illinois University, Carbondale. Department of Foreign Languages**
Carbondale, IL 62901.
• Jack London Newsletter. 3 per yr. ISSN 0021-3837

**Southern Illinois University, Carbondale. Department of Geography**
Carbondale, IL 62901.
• Southern Illinois Universiity, Carbondaale. Occasional Paper Series in Geography. irreg. ISSN 0073-4969
• Southern Illinois University, Carbondale. Department of Georgraphy. Discussion Paper. irreg., 1972, no. 4. ISSN 0073-4950

**Southern Illinois University, Carbondale. Department of Philosophy**
Carbondale, IL 62901.
• Kinesis; graduate journal in philosophy. s-a. ISSN 0023-1568

**Southern Illinois University, Carbondale. Morris Library**
Carbondale, IL 62901.
• Southern Exposure Library Staff Bulletin. m.(except Sept.) ISSN 0038-4089
• Southern Illinois University, Carbondale. University Libraries. Bibliographic Contributions. irreg., 1973, no. 8. ISSN 0073-4977

**Southern Illinois University, Carbondale. University Museum**
Carbondale, IL 62901.
• Mesoamerican Studies. irreg., no. 10, 1977. ISSN 0076-6607
• Southern Illinois Studies. irreg., no. 17, 1977. ISSN 0081-3044

• Southern Illinois University. University Museum Studies. irreg., no. 11, 1977. ISSN 0073-4985

**Southern Illinois University, Edwardsville**
Edwardsville, IL 62025.
• Papers on Language and Literature; a quarterly journal. q. ISSN 0031-1294
• Sou'wester; literary magazine. 3 per yr. ISSN 0038-4976 (prep. by its Board of Trustees)

**Southern Illinois University, Edwardsville. Center for Urban and Environmental Research and Services**
Edwardsville, IL 62025.
• Southern Illinois University, Edwardsville. Center for Urban and Environmental Research and Services. C U E R S. Report. irreg. ISSN 0073-4993

**Southern Illinois University, Edwardsville. Industrial Maps Project**
Edwardsville, IL 62025.
• Illinois Metro East Industrial Development Corporation. Resources Report. irreg. ISSN 0073-4896

**Southern Illinois University, Edwardsville. University Graphics and Publications**
Edwardsville, IL 62025.
• Southern Illinois University, Edwardsville. Asian Studies. Occasional Paper Series. irreg.

**Southern Illinois University, Latin American Institute**
• Specialia. (pub. by Professional Productivity Associates)

**Southern Illinois University Press**
P. O. Box 3697, Carbondale, IL 62901.
• Perspectives in Sociology. irreg.

**Southern Jewish Weekly, Inc.**
Box 3297, Jacksonville, FL 32206.
• Southern Jewish Weekly. w. ISSN 0038-4240

**Southern Literary Messenger**
c/o William Shirley, University of South Alabama, Mobile, AL 36688.
• Southern Literary Messenger. q.

**Southern Market Preview & Shopping Planner**
Box 828, 209 S. Main St., High Point, NC 27261.
• Southern Market Preview & Shopping Planner. s-a.

**Southern Medical Association**
2601 Highland Ave., Birmingham, AL 35205.
• Southern Medical Journal. m. ISSN 0038-4348
• Southern Medicine. bi-m.

**Southern Methodist University. Department of Anthropology**
Southern Methodist University, Dallas, TX 75275.
• Contributions in Anthropology. irreg., no. 12, 1974. ISSN 0069-9632

**Southern Methodist University. Industrial Information Services**
Science Information Center, Dallas, TX 75275.
• Southern Methodist University. Industrial Information Services. Newsletter. irreg. ISSN 0038-4364

**Southern Methodist University. Institute for the Study of Earth and Man**
c/o Heroy Science Hall, 3225 Daniel Street, Dallas, TX 75203.
• Institute for the Study of Earth and Man Newsletter. q.

**Southern Methodist University. Perkins School of Theology**
Dallas, TX 75222.
• Perkins School of Theology Journal. s-a. ISSN 0031-5451

**Southern Methodist University Press**
Southern Methodist University, Dallas, TX 75275.
• John E. Owens Memorial Foundation. Publications. irreg. ISSN 0075-384X
• Southwest Review. q. ISSN 0038-4712

**Southern Methodist University. Printing Department**
Box 475, Dallas, TX 75275.
• Human Rights. 3 per yr. ISSN 0046-8185 (American Bar Association. Section of Individual Rights and Responsibilities)

**Southern Methodist University School of Law**
University Park, Dallas, TX 75275.
• Brief of the School of Law. 4 per yr. ISSN 0006-9965
• Journal of Air Law and Commerce. q. ISSN 0021-8642
• Southwestern Law Journal. 5 per yr. ISSN 0038-4836

**Southern Missions, Inc.**
1428 Broad St., Selma, AL 36701.
• Your Edmundite Missions News Letter. bi-m. ISSN 0044-1015 (Society of Saint Edmund)

**Southern Motorsports Journal**
c/o Bob Hoffman, Ed., Drawer 637, Opp, AL 36467.
• Southern Motorsports Journal. 40 per yr.

**Southern Newspaper Enterprises**
390 Courtland St. N.E., Atlanta, GA 30303.
• Southern Israelite. w. ISSN 0038-4224

**Southern Oregon College. English Department**
c/o Lawson Inada, Ashland, OR 97520.
• Rogue River Gorge. q.

**Southern Pacific Transportation Co.**
One Market St. Room 975, San Francisco, CA 94105.
• Southern Pacific Bulletin. 10 per yr.

**Southern Political Science Associaiation**
University of Florida, Gainesville, FL 32611.
• Journal of Politics. q. ISSN 0022-3816

**Southern Presbyterian Journal Co., Inc.**
Weaverville, NC 28787.
• Presbyterian Journal. w. ISSN 0032-7549

**Southern Preservation Society, Inc.**
P.O. Box 26, High Point, NC 27261.
• Preservation Spectator. q.

**Southern Printer & Lithographer**
75 3rd St. N.W., Atlanta, GA 30308.
• Southern Printer and Lithographer. m.

**Southern Prison Ministry**
Box 12044, Nashville, TN 37212.
• Southern Coalition on Jails and Prisons. bi-m. (Committee of Southern Churchmen, Inc.)

**Southern Publishers, Inc.**
614 Holly, Columbia, SC 29205.
• Contracting in the Carolinas. m. ISSN 0010-7875

**Southern Publishing Association**
1900 Elm Hill Pike, Nashville, TN 37202.
• Message. bi-m. ISSN 0026-0231
• These Times. m. ISSN 0040-6058 (Seventh Day Adventist Church)

**Southern Publishing Co.**
Box 1228, Pensacola, FL 32502.
• Florida Restaurant, Hotel & Motel Journal. bi-m. ISSN 0015-427X

**Southern Region School Boards Research and Training Center, Inc.**
520 First Federal Bldg., Tuscaloosa, AL 35401.
• Southern School Law Digest. m. ISSN 0361-0861

**Southern Regional Education Board**
130 Sixth St., N.W., Atlanta, GA 30313.
• Fact Book on Higher Education in the South. biennial.
• Financing Higher Education. irreg; no. 27, 1976.
• Issues in Higher Education. irreg; no. 9, 1975.
• Regional Action. q. ISSN 0034-3323
• Regional Spotlight; news of higher education in the South. 4 per yr. ISSN 0034-3390
• S R E B Educational Board. Annual Report. a. ISSN 0081-3060
• S R E B Research Monograph Series. irreg., no. 20, 1974. ISSN 0081-3079
• Southern Regional Education Board. State and Local Revenue Potential. a. ISSN 0090-8649
• Southern Regional Education Board. State Legislation Affecting Higher Education in the South. irreg. ISSN 0081-3087

**Southern Regional Science Association**
• Review of Regional Studies. (pub. by University of Alabama in Birmingham. School of Business)

**Southern Research Institute**
2000 Ninth Ave., S., Birmingham, AL 35205.
- Southern Research Institute Bulletin. q. ISSN 0038-4518

**Southern Sociological Society**
Dept. of Sociology, Virginia Polytechnic Institute and State Univ., Blacksburg, VA 24061.
- Southern Sociologist. q. ISSN 0038-4577

**Southern Speech Communication Association**
- Southern Speech Communication Journal. (pub. by University of Tennessee)

**Southern States Cooperative, Inc.**
Box 1656, Richmond, VA 23213.
- Cooperative Farmer; a farm paper published by farmers for farmers. m. ISSN 0010-8448

**Southern Tier Library System**
Civic Center Plaza, Corning, NY 14830.
- Topics; southern tier library system newsletter. m.

**Southern Trade Publications Co.**
Box 9377, Greensboro, NC 27408.
- Restaurant South. m.
- Southern Industrial Supplier. m. ISSN 0038-4208
- Southern Tobacco Journal. m. ISSN 0300-6239

**Southern University Law Review**
Southern Branch P.O., Baton Rouge, LA 70813.
- Southern University Law Review. s-a.

**Southern Utah News**
Ed. Marlin B. Brown, Box 90, Kanab, UT 84741.
- Southern Utah News. w. ISSN 0049-1659

**Southern Veterinarian, Inc.**
Route 1, Box 241, Springville, AL 35146.
- Southern Veterinarian. m. ISSN 0038-4623

**Southern Weed Science Society**
c/o Ed. James F. Miller, University of Georgia, Extension Agronomy Department, Athens, GA 30602.
- Southern Weed Science Society. Proceedings. a.

**Southland Publishing Co.**
2805 Crescent Ave., Birmingham, AL 35223.
- Southlander; magazine of the historic south. q.

**Southwest Art Magazine**
P.O. Box 13037, Houston, TX 77019.
- Southwest Art Magazine. m. (except July) ISSN 0091-8830

**Southwest Bluegrass Club**
2704 Haley Ave., Ft. Worth, TX 76117.
- Bluegrass Reflections. m. ISSN 0361-5774

**Southwest College Student Government**
7500 S. Pulaski, Chicago, IL 60652.
- Inditer. q. ISSN 0019-7122

**Southwest Conference on Asian Studies**
c/o Virgil Medlin, Editor, 308 Gold Star Bldg., Oklahoma University, Oklahoma City, OK 73106.
- Southwest Conference on Asian Studies. Newsletter. s-a.

**Southwest Homefurnishings Association**
Box 64667, Dallas, TX 75206.
- Southwest Homefurnishings News. 4 per yr.

**Southwest Jewish Chronicle**
324 N. Robinson St., Suite 313, Oklahoma City, OK 73102.
- Southwest Jewish Chronicle. q. ISSN 0038-4674

**Southwest Minnesota State College**
Marshall, MN 56258.
- Crazy Horse. q. ISSN 0011-0841
- Journal of English Teaching Techniques. q. ISSN 0022-0884

**Southwest Museum**
Highland Park, Los Angeles, CA 90042.
- Masterkey; for Indian lore and history. q. ISSN 0025-5084
- Southwest Museum. Frederick Webb Hodge Anniversary Publication Fund. Publications. irreg., 1969, vol. 10. ISSN 0076-0986
- Southwest Museum. Papers. irreg., no. 24, 1974. ISSN 0076-0994

**Southwest New Mexico Council of Governments**
211 1/2 N. Bullard, Box 1211, Silver City, NM 88061.
- Southwest New Mexico Council of Governments. Annual Work Program. a. ISSN 0095-4810

**Southwest Radio Church**
Box 1144, Oklahoma City, OK 73101.
- Gospel Truth. m. ISSN 0017-2383

**Southwest Research and Information Center**
P.O. Box 4524, Albuquerque, NM 87106.
- New Mexico; an Annotated Directory of Information Sources. irreg.
- Workbook. 10 per yr.

**Southwest Research Institute**
8500 Culebra, San Antonio, TX 78284.
- Interamerican Conference on Materials Technology. (Proceedings) (pub. by American Society of Mechanical Engineers)
- Symposium on Nondestructive Evaluation. Proceedings. s-a. (prep. by its Nondestructive Testing Data Support Center)
- Tomorrow through Research. q. ISSN 0040-9146

**Southwest Society of Periodontists**
310 Medical Park Tower, Austin, TX 78705.
- Periodontology Today. s-a. ISSN 0031-5397

**Southwest Texas State University. Department of English**
San Marcos, TX 78666.
- Studies in American Humor. 3 per yr. (Co-Sponsor: American Humor Studies Assn.)

**Southwestern American Literature**
Box 13646, N.T. Station, Denton, TX 76203.
- Southwestern American Literature. 3 per yr. ISSN 0049-1675 (Co-Sponsor: North Texas State University)

**Southwestern Art, Inc.**
Box 1763, Austin, TX 78767.
- Southwestern Art; a journal devoted to recognition of the arts in the West and Southwest. q. ISSN 0038-4739

**Southwestern Association Inc.**
Box 700-Denison, TX 75020.
- All Outdoors. m. ISSN 0002-5607

**Southwestern Association of Naturalists. Division of Biology**
Dept. Wildlife & Fisheries Sciences, Emporia Kansas State College, Emporia, KS 66801.
- Southwestern Naturalist. 4 per yr. ISSN 0038-4909

**Southwestern Association on Indian Affairs**
Box 1964, Santa Fe, NM 87501.
- Southwestern Association on Indian Affairs. Inc. Quarterly. q. ISSN 0038-4747

**Southwestern at Memphis**
2000 North Parkway, Memphis, TN 38112.
- Ginger. q. ISSN 0017-0058

**Southwestern Baptist Theological Seminary**
Faculty, School of Theology, Box 22000 2E, Fort Worth, TX 76122.
- Southwestern Journal of Theology. s-a. ISSN 0038-4828
- Southwestern News. m.(Sept-July) ISSN 0038-4917

**Southwestern Baptist Theological Seminary. Fleming Library**
Box 22,000-2E, Fort Worth, TX 76122.
- Book Reviews of the Month; an index to reviews appearing in selected theological journals. m. ISSN 0006-7342

**Southwestern Institute of Forensic Sciences**
Box 35728, Dallas, TX 75235
(and 41-42 William IV St., London WC2, Eng)
- Forensic Science Gazette. 4 per yr. ISSN 0046-4570

**Southwestern Journal of Philosophy**
Eds. Robert W. Shahan & A. E. Keaton, Rm. 605 Dale Hall Tower, 455 W. Lindsey, Norman, OK 73069.
- Southwestern Journal of Philosophy. 3 per yr. ISSN 0038-481X

**Southwestern Legal Foundation. International and Comparative Law Center**
- Private Investors Abroad. (pub. by Matthew Bender & Co., Inc.)

**Southwestern Library Association**
7371 Paldao Drive, Dallas, TX 75240.
- Cassette Journal. bi-m.
- S. W. L. A. Newsletter. bi-m. ISSN 0036-2085

**Southwestern Mission Research Center**
Arizona State Museum, University of Arizona, Tucson, AZ 85721.
- S M R C Newsletter. q.

**Southwestern Oklahoma Historical Society**
916 1/2 B Ave., Lawton, OK 73501.
- Prairie Lore. q. ISSN 0032-6631

**Southwestern Pennsylvania Regional Planning Commission**
564 Forbes Ave., Pittsburgh, PA 15219.
- S P R P C Reports. q. ISSN 0049-1691

**Southwestern Philosophical Society**
c/o Ted E. Klein, Department of Philosophy, Texas Christian University, Fort Worth, TX 76129.
- Southwestern Philosophical Society. Newsletter. s-a. ISSN 0038-4925

**South Western Publishing Co.**
5101 Madison Rd., Cincinnati, OH 45227.
- Balance Sheet; a magazine on business and economic education. m(Sept-April) ISSN 0005-4232
- Century 21 Reporter. s-a.
- Collegiate News and Views. 3 per yr. ISSN 0010-1222

**Southwestern Purchaser, Inc.**
L.T.V. Tower, TX 75201.
- Southwest Business. m. (Purchasing Management Associations of Texas, Louisiana and New Mexico)

**Southwestern Retailer**
c/o Carle Jobe, Box 10975, Dallas, TX 75207.
- Southwestern Retailer. 7 per yr. ISSN 0038-4933

**Southwestern Social Science Association**
- Social Science Quarterly. (pub. by University of Texas Press)

**Southwestern University**
Students Association, Box 48, S.U. Sta, Georgetown, TX 78626.
- Megaphone (Georgetown) w. ISSN 0025-8709
- Southwestern. q. ISSN 0038-4852

**Souvenirs and Novelties Publishers, Inc.**
327 Wagaraw Rd., Hawthorne, NJ 07506.
- Campground Merchandising. 3 per yr.
- Souvenirs and Novelties; for the souvenir, novelty, post card and gift field. bi-m. ISSN 0038-4968
- Tourist Attractions and Parks. s-a.

**Soviet Business and Trade. Porter International**
Suite 600, 1776 K St. N.W., Washington, DC 20006.
- East-West Technology Digest. m.

**Space Age Market Research**
1968 Halekoa Dr, Honolulu, HI 96821.
- Space Age Market Research. m. ISSN 0038-6235

**Space Age Translations**
F. Martinez c/o J. R. Longland, 490 West End Ave., 2-D, New York, NY 10024.
- Space Age News; publication on linguistics.

**Space and Time**
c/o Gordon Linzer, Editor, 138 W. 70 St., New York, NY 10023.
- Space and Time. bi-m.

**Space Propulsion Reports, Inc.**
1067 National Press Bldg., Washington, DC 20004.
- Aerospace Propulsion. s-m.

**Space Publications Inc.**
1341 G St. N.W., Washington, DC 20005.
- Defense/Business Space Daily. d.
- Soviet Aerospace. w. ISSN 0092-105X
- Space Business Week. w. ISSN 0038-6251
- Who's Who in Space; international edition. a. ISSN 0083-9728

**Spaceview Magazine**
Suite 103, Goodhue Bldg., Beaumont, TX 77701.
- Spaceview Magazine. bi-m.

**Spafaswap**
c/o Lois J. Long, Ed., 1070 Ahern Dr., La Puente, CA 91746.
- Spafaswap; some poetry, a few anecdotes, some wisdom and philosophy. 6 per yr. ISSN 0038-6367

**Spain-U.S. Chamber of Commerce Inc.**
500 Fifth Ave., New York, NY 10036.
- Spain-U.S. Trade Bulletin. bi-m. ISSN 0561-5313

**Spangler, Jennings, Spangler & Dougherty**
250 North Main Street, Crown Point, IN 46307.
- Transportation and Products Legal Directory. a. ISSN 0092-6175

**Spanish American News Inc.**
505 5th Ave., New York, NY 10017.
- Noticias de New York. s-m.

**Spanish Institute, Inc.**
684 Park Ave., New York, NY 10021.
- Spanish Institute. Annual Report. a. ISSN 0081-3516

**Sparrow Press**
103 Waldron St., West Lafayette, IN 47906.
- Sparrow. 2 per yr. ISSN 0038-6588

**Spartacist League**
Box 1377, G.P.O., New York, NY 10001.
- Spartacist. q. ISSN 0038-6596
- Workers Vanguard. fortn.

**Spartacus Press**
Box 71, South Dartmouth, MA 02748.
- Social Science Reports. irreg.

**Spartacus Youth Publishing Co.**
Box 825, Canal Street, New York, NY 10013.
- Young Spartacus. m.

**Speakout Publications**
Box 6165, Albany, NY 12206.
- Speakout; a feminist journal. m.

**Spec Tech Publications, Inc.**
2323 Roosevelt Blvd., Oxnard, CA 93030
(Subscr. to: P.O. Box 2035, Oxnard, CA 93034)
- Finishing Highlights; painting & chemical coatings, plating & anodic treatments, polishing & surface preparation. bi-m(plus 2 special show issues.) ISSN 0046-3922
- Powder Finishing World. q.

**Special Child Publications**
(Subsidiary of: Bernie Straub Publishing Co., Inc.)
4535 Union Bay Place N.E., Seattle, WA 98105.
- Educational Therapy; educational programs. irreg. ISSN 0070-9379
- Learning Disorders. irreg. ISSN 0075-8337

**Special Education Instructional Materials Center**
400 First Ave., New York, NY 10010.
- At Your Service.

**Special Interest Publications**
Box 196, Bennington, VT 05201.
- Special-Interest Autos. bi-m. ISSN 0049-1845

**Special Interest Publications (Des Moines)**
1716 Locust St., Des Moines, IA 50336.
- Window & Wall Decorating Ideas. irreg. ISSN 0363-5406

**Special Libraries Association**
235 Park Ave. S., New York, NY 10003.
- Sci-Tech News. q. ISSN 0036-8059 (prep. by its Science-Technology Division)
- Special Libraries. m. ISSN 0038-6723

**Special Libraries Association. Advertising and Marketing Division**
c/o Ruth Fromkes, Foote, Cone & Belding, 200 Park Ave., New York, NY 10017.
- What's New in Advertising and Marketing. 10 per yr. ISSN 0043-4558

**Special Libraries Association. Cleveland Chapter**
26010 Lakeland Blvd., Cleveland, OH 44132.
- S L A Cleveland Chapter Bulletin. q. ISSN 0036-1593

**Special Libraries Association. Food Librarians Division**
c/o McCormick and Co., 204 Wright Ave., Baltimore, MD 21031.
- Food for Thought. bi-m.

**Special Libraries Association. Geography and Map Division**
19927 Edward Ave., Bethesda, MD 20014.
- Special Libraries Association. Geography and Map Division. Bulletin. q. ISSN 0036-1607

**Special Libraries Association. Indiana Chapter**
c/o Lilly Endowment. Library, 2801 N. Meridian St., Indianapolis, IN 46208.
- Indiana Slant. 4 per yr. ISSN 0019-6738

**Special Libraries Association. Insurance Division**
235 Park Ave. S., New York, NY 10003
- Insurance Literature. m.(10 per yr.) ISSN 0020-4765 (American College of Life Underwriters) (Subscr. to: c/o Marjorie Fletcher, Ed., American College of Life Underwriters, Bryn Mawr, PA 19010)
- Insurance Periodicals Index. a. ISSN 0074-073X (Subscr. to: c/o Robert L. Enequist, Ed., College of Insurance, 123 William St., New York, NY 10038)

**Special Libraries Association. Metals-Materials Division**
Ed. Arleen N. Somerville, Science Librarian, University of Rochester Libraries, Rochester, NY 14627.
- Special Libraries Association. Metals/Materials Division News. q. ISSN 0038-6766

**Special Libraries Association. New York Chapter**
235 Park Ave. South, New York, NY 10003.
- Special Libraries Directory of Greater New York. biennial.

**Special Libraries Association. Pacific Northwest Chapter**
815 East Howe St., Seattle, WA 98102.
- Interface (Seattle) q. ISSN 0020-5435

**Special Libraries Association. Upstate New York Chapter**
c/o Barbara Mann, Science and Engineering Library, State University of New York at Buffalo, Buffalo, NY 14214.
- Special Libraries Association. Upstate New York Chapter. Bulletin. 3 per yr.

**Special Libraries Association, Virginia Chapter**
c/o Reynolds Metals Co., Exec. Office Library, 6601 W. Broad St., Richmond, VA 23261.
- V A S L A. 4 per yr. ISSN 0042-1723

**Special Libraries Association. Washington D.C. Chapter**
P.O. Box 287, Benjamin Franklin Station, Washington, DC 20044.
- Special Libraries Association. Washington D.C. Chapter. Publication. irreg. ISSN 0081-3540

**Special Reports, Inc.**
Box 727, McLean, VA 22101.
- Exclusive; digest and analysis of Washington intelligence for limited distribution. w. ISSN 0046-2888

**Specialist Publications, Inc.**
17835 Ventura Blvd., Suite 312, Encino, CA 91316.
- Installation Specialist. m. ISSN 0446-3161

**Specialized Agricultural Publications, Inc.**
559 Jones Franklin Rd., Suite 150, Raleigh, NC 27606.
- Flue Cured Tobacco Farmer. m.(Nov.-June) ISSN 0015-4512
- Peanut Farmer. m. ISSN 0031-3653

**Specialty Bakery Owners of America**
299 Broadway, New York, NY 10007.
- Specialty Baker's Voice. bi-m. ISSN 0038-688X

**Specialty Publications, Inc.**
7033 Sunset Blvd., No. 222, Los Angeles, CA 90028.
- Official Talent & Booking Directory. a. ISSN 0078-3889

**Specialty Salesman Magazine, Inc.**
307 N. Michigan Ave, Chicago, IL 60601.
- Specialty Salesman and Business Opportunities. m. ISSN 0038-6901

**Specom, Inc.**
22543 Ventura Blvd., Woodland Hills, CA 91364.
- Industry's Product News. bi-m.

**Spectator International Inc.**
9667 Wilshire Blvd., Beverly Hills, CA 90212.
- Cinema. 3 per yr. ISSN 0009-7047

**Spectator Publishing Co.**
318 Ferris Booth Hall, New York, NY 10027.
- Columbia Daily Spectator; the official newspaper of the students of Columbia University. 5 per week. ISSN 0010-1893 (Columbia University)

**Spectrum Publications, Inc.**
175-20 Wexford Terrace, Jamaica, NY 11432.
- Addictive Diseases; an international journal. q. ISSN 0094-0267
- Advances in Sleep Research. a.
- Child Behavior and Development. irreg.
- Health Systems Management. irreg., no. 10, 1977.
- Monographs in Modern Neurobiology. irreg., no. 5, 1977.
- Monographs in Pharmacology and Physiology. irreg.
- Sociomedical Sciences Series. irreg.

**Speech and Hearing Association of Virginia**
- Speech and Hearing Association of Virginia. Journal. (pub. by Wayside Press)

**Speech and Theatre Association of Missouri**
- Missouri Speech Journal. (pub. by Central Missouri State University)

**Speech Communication Association**
5205 Leesburg Pike, Falls Church, VA 22041.
- Bibliographic Annual in Speech Communication. a. ISSN 0067-6837
- Communication Education. 4 per yr.
- Communication Monographs. 4 per yr.
- Directory of Graduate Programs in the Speech Communication Arts and Sciences. biennial. ISSN 0070-5616
- Free Speech. 3 per yr.
- Quarterly Journal of Speech. 4 per yr. ISSN 0033-5630
- S C A Free Speech Yearbook. a.
- Spectra. bi-m.
- Speech Communication Association. Directory. a.

**Speech Communication Association of Ohio**
c/o Dr. Trent, Ed., Speech Department, Miami University, Oxford, OH 45056.
- Ohio Speech Journal. a. ISSN 0078-4052

**J. B. Speed Art Museum**
2035 S. Third St., Louisville, KY 40208.
- J. B. Speed Art Museum Bulletin. 3-4 per yr. ISSN 0021-356X

**J. R. Spencer**
2921 Axtell St., Clovis, NM 88101.
- New Mexico Almanac. a. ISSN 0360-1048

**Charles D. Spencer & Associates, Inc.**
222 W. Adams St., Chicago, IL 60606.
- E B P R Research Reports; weekly news digest. w.
- Employee Benefit Plan Review. m. ISSN 0013-6808
- I B I S. (International Benefits Information Service) m. ISSN 0018-8611

**Spencer Marketing Services**
370 Lexington Ave., New York, NY 10017.
- Athletic Administration. q. ISSN 0044-9873 (National Association of Collegiate Directors of Athletics)

**Sperry New Holland**
Division of Sperry Rand Corporation, Franklin and Roberts Sts., New Holland, PA 17557.
- Sperry New Holland News. 10 per yr.

**Sperry Rand Corporation**
Library Bureau Div., 801 Park Ave., Herkimer, NY 13350.
- Pioneer. q. ISSN 0031-9996

**Spertus College of Judaica**
- Journal of Jewish Art. (pub. by Sepher-Hermon Press, Inc.)

**Spertus College of Judaica Press**
618 S. Michigan Avenue, Chicago, IL 60605.
- Perspectives in Jewish Learning. a. ISSN 0079-1016

**Spex Industries Inc.**
Box 798, Metuchen, NJ 08840.
- Spex Speaken. bi-m. ISSN 0490-4176

**Spiegel Grove**
1337 Hayes Ave., Fremont, OH 43420.
- Hayes Historical Journal. s-a.

**Spiritual Community Publications**
Box 1080, San Rafael, CA 94902.
- New Spiritual Community Guide for North America. irreg.
- Pilgrim's Guide to Planet Earth. irreg.
- Sat Nam Series. irreg., vol. 2, 1973.
- Spiritual Community Guide. irreg; no. 4, 1978 per 79.

**Spiritual Life Institute of America**
Sedona, AZ 86336.
- Desert Call. q. ISSN 0011-9229

**Spokane. Mayor and City Council of Spokane, Washington**
City Clerk, Rm. 651 City Hall, North 221 Wall St., Spokane, WA 99201.
- Spokane, Washington Official Gazette. w. ISSN 0038-7711

**Spokane Chamber of Commerce**
W. 1020 Riverside Ave. Box 2147, Spokane, WA 99210.
- Spokane Affairs. bi-w. ISSN 0038-7681

**Spokane Public Schools**
825 Trent Ave.W, Spokane, WA 99201.
- Spokane Schools. 2-4 per yr. ISSN 0038-7703

**Spokane Tribe of Indians Tribal Council**
- Rawhide Press. (pub. by Times Publishing Co.)

**Spokane Westerners Corral**
Box 1717, Spokane, WA 99210.
- Pacific Northwesterner. q. ISSN 0030-882X

**Spokesman Press**
Box 155, Grundy Center, IA 50638.
- Iowa Farm Bureau Spokesman. w. ISSN 0021-051X (Iowa Farm Bureau Federation)

**Spoon River Poetry Press**
Dept. of English, Bradley University, Peoria, IL 61625.
- Spoon River Quarterly. q.

**Sport Fishing Institute**
608 13 St. N.W., Washington, DC 20005.
- S F I Bulletin. 10 per yr. ISSN 0085-6592

**Sport Hobbyist**
Box 3731, Detroit, MI 48215.
- Sport Hobbyist. bi-m.

**Sporting News Publishing Co.**
1212 N. Lindbergh Blvd., St. Louis, MO 63166
(Orders to: Box 56, St. Louis, MO 63166)
- Batting and Pitching Averages at a Glance. irreg.
- Football Register. a. ISSN 0071-7258
- Hockey Register. a. ISSN 0090-2292
- How to Score. irreg.
- Knotty Problems of Baseball. irreg. ISSN 0075-6385
- Official American and National League Baseball Schedules and Records. a.
- Official Baseball Dope Book. a. ISSN 0067-4265
- Official Baseball Guide. a. ISSN 0078-3838
- Official Baseball Record Book. a. ISSN 0078-4605
- Official Baseball Register. a. ISSN 0067-4281
- Official Baseball Rules. a. ISSN 0078-3846
- Official N B A and College Basketball Schedules. a.
- Official N F L and Collegiate Football Schedules and Records. a.
- Official National Basketball Association Guide. a. ISSN 0078-3862
- Official World Series Records. a. ISSN 0078-3900
- Pro and Amateur Hockey Guide. a. ISSN 0079-550X
- Sporting Goods Dealer; national magazine of the sporting goods trade. m. ISSN 0038-8017
- Sporting News; the nation's oldest and finest sports publication. w. ISSN 0038-805X

**Sports and Medicine Publications**
(Subsidiary of: Williams & Wilkins Co.)
428 E. Preston St., Baltimore, MD 21202.
- American Journal of Sports Medicine. bi-m. (American Orthopaedic Society for Sports Medicine)

**Sports Car Club of America**
- Sports Car. (pub. by Revere Publishing, Inc.)

**Sports Car Club of America. San Francisco Region**
- Wheel. (pub. by AutoMedia)

**Sports Communications, Inc.**
P.O. Box 95, Waco, TX 76703.
- Dallas Cowboys Outlook. a.
- Texas Football Newsmagazines. 6 per season.

**Sports Eye, Inc.**
343 Great Neck Rd., Great Neck, NY 11021.
- Football Action. s-a.

**Sports Philatelists International**
P.O. Box 159, Berwyn, IL 60402
(Subs. Address: Leonard K. Eichorn, 4331 Baintree Rd., University Hgts, OH 44118)
- Journal of Sports Philately. bi-m.

**Sportshelf**
P.O. Box 634, New Rochelle, NY 10802.
- Official Rules of Sports and Games. biennial.
- Sportshelf News; the sport, hobby and recreation publication. 4 per yr. ISSN 0038-8270

**Sportwatch Inc.**
134 Linden Ave., Westbury, NY 11590.
- Play Ball New York; New York's baseball weekly. w. ISSN 0048-4407

**Spotlight Publishing Co. Ltd.**
180 Madison Ave., New York, NY 10016.
- T V Showpeople. m.

**Spree Publishing Co.**
4511 Harlem Rd., Buffalo, NY 14226.
- Buffalo Spree. q. ISSN 0300-7499

**Spring Arbor College**
Spring Arbor, MI 49283.
- Spring Arbor College Update. m.

**Spring Manufacturers Institute**
Box 959, Bristol, CT 06010.
- Springs. s-a. ISSN 0584-9667

**Spring Rain**
Box 15319, Seattle, WA 98115.
- Spring Rain. 2-4 per yr.

**Springer Publishing Co., Inc.**
200 Park Ave. S., New York, NY 10003.
- American Neurological Association. Transactions. a. ISSN 0065-9479
- Drugs in Current Use and New Drugs. a. ISSN 0070-7392

**Springer-Verlag**
175 Fifth Ave., New York, NY 10010
(and Heidelberger Platz 3, 1000 Berlin 33, W. Germany (B.R.D.); Neuheimer Landstr. 28-30, 6900 Heidelberg, W. Germany (B.R.D.); Moelkerbastei 5, Postfach 367, 1011 Vienna, Austria)
- Acta Informatica. 2 vols. per yr., 4 nos. per vol. ISSN 0001-5903
- Acta Mechanica. 3 vols. per yr., 4 nos. per vol. ISSN 0001-5970
- Acta Neurochirurgica. 2 vols. per yr., 4 nos. per vol. ISSN 0001-6268
- Acta Neuropathologica. 4 vols. per yr., 4 nos. per vol. ISSN 0001-6322
- Acta Neuropathologica. Supplement. irreg., no. 6, 1975. ISSN 0065-1435
- Acta Physica Austriaca. 2 vols per yr(4 nos. per vol) ISSN 0001-6713
- Acta Physica Austriaca. Supplement. irreg., no. 15, 1977. ISSN 0065-1559
- Advances in Anatomy, Embryology and Cell Biology. irreg., no. 53, 1977. ISSN 0071-1098
- Advances in Biochemical Engineering. irreg., no. 5, 1977. ISSN 0065-2210
- Advances in Neurosurgery. irreg., vol. 4, 1977. ISSN 0302-2366
- Advances in Polymer Science/Fortschritte der Hochpolymeren-Forschung. irreg., vol. 24, 1977. ISSN 0065-3195
- Aesthetic Plastic Surgery. ISSN 0364-216X (International Society of Aesthetic Plastic Surgery)
- Akademie der Wissenschaften, Vienna. Mathematisch-Naturwissenschaftliche Klasse. Anzeiger. irreg. ISSN 0065-535X
- Anaesthesiology and Resuscitation/ Anaesthesiologie und Wiederbelebung/ Anesthesiologie et Reanimation. irreg., vol. 107, 1977. ISSN 0066-1341
- Anaesthesist. m. ISSN 0003-2417 (Deutsche Gesellschaft fuer Anaesthesie und Wiederbelebung GW) (Co-sponsor: Oesterreichische und Schweizerische Gesellschaft fuer Anaesthesiologie und Reanimation)
- Anatomy and Embryology. 2 vols. per yr. (3 nos. per vol.) ISSN 0340-2061
- Anleitung fuer die Chemische Laboratoriumspraxis. irreg., vol. 15, 1976. ISSN 0066-1910
- Annals of Life Insurance Medicine. irreg., no. 5, 1974. ISSN 0066-2305 (Swiss Reinsurance Co.)
- Anorganische und Allgemeine Chemie in Einzeldarstellungen. irreg., no. 10, 1969. ISSN 0066-4553
- Antibiotics. irreg., vol. 3, 1975.
- Applied Mathematical Sciences. irreg., vol. 22, 1977. ISSN 0066-5452
- Applied Mathematics and Optimization; an international journal. 1 vol. per yr. (4 nos. per vol.) ISSN 0095-4616
- Applied Minerology. Technische Minerologie. irreg., vol. 11, 1977. ISSN 0066-5487
- Applied Physics. 3 vols. per yr. (4 nos. per vol.) ISSN 0340-3793 (Deutsche Physikalische Gesellschaft GW)
- Applied Physics and Engineering. irreg., 1976, no. 12. ISSN 0066-5509
- Archiv fuer Elektrotechnik. 1 vol. per yr.(6 nos. per vol.) ISSN 0003-9039 (Verband Deutscher Elektrotechniker e.V. GW)
- Archiv fuer Gynaekologie. 3 vols. per yr., 4 nos. per vol. ISSN 0003-9128 (Deutsche Gesellschaft fuer Gynaekologie GW)
- Archiv fuer Meteorologie, Geophysik und Bioklimatologie. Series A. Meteorology and Geophysics. 4 per yr. ISSN 0066-6416
- Archiv fuer Meteorologie, Geophysik und Bioklimatologie. Series A. Meteorology and Geophysics. Supplement. irreg. ISSN 0066-6394
- Archiv fuer Meteorologie, Geophysik und Bioklimatologie. Series B. Climatology, Environmental Meteorology and Radiation Research. 4 per yr. ISSN 0066-6424
- Archiv fuer Orthopaedische und Unfall-Chirurgie. 4 vols. per yr., 3 nos. per vol. ISSN 0003-9330 (Deutsche Gesellschaft fuer Unfallheilkunde, Versicherungs-, Versorgungs- und Verkehrsmedizin GW)
- Archiv fuer Psychiatrie und Nervenkrankheiten. 2 vols. per yr.(4 nos. per vol.) ISSN 0003-9373 (Gesamtverband Deutscher Nervenaerzte GW)
- Archive for History of Exact Sciences. 2 vols. per yr., 4 nos. per vol. ISSN 0003-9519
- Archive for Rational Mechanics and Analysis. 4 vols. per yr., 4 nos. per vol. ISSN 0003-9527
- Archives for Dermatological Research/Archiv fuer Dermatologische Forschung. 3 vols. per yr., 3 nos. per vol. ISSN 0003-9187 (Deutsche Dermatologische Gesellschaft GW)
- Archives of Environmental Contamination & Toxicology. 4 per yr. ISSN 0090-4341
- Archives of Microbiology. 4 vols. per year (3-4 nos. per vol.) ISSN 0302-8933
- Archives of Oto-Rhino-Laryngology. 2 vols. per yr. (4 nos. per vol.) ISSN 0302-9530 (Deutsche Gesellschaft fuer Hals-, Nasen-, Ohrenheilkunde, Kopf- und Halschirurgie GW)
- Archives of Toxicology/Archiv fuer Toxikologie. 2 vols. per yr., 4 nos. per vol. ISSN 0003-9446 (Deutsche Pharmakologische Gesellschaft GW) (Co-sponsor: Deutsche Gesellschaft fuer Rechtsmedizin)
- Archives of Virology. 3 vols. per yr. (4 nos. per vol.) ISSN 0304-8608
- Astronomy and Astrophysics; a European journal. 8 vols. per yr., 2-3 nos. per vol. ISSN 0004-6361 (European Southern Observatory GW)
- Astronomy and Astrophysics Abstracts. irreg., vol. 17, 1977. ISSN 0067-0022
- Atlas of Mammalian Chromosomes. irreg., vol. 9, 1975. ISSN 0073-3768
- Background to Migraine Symposia. irreg., 1970, 3rd. ISSN 0067-2769
- Bauingenieur; Zeitschrift fuer das gesamte Bauwesen. 1 vol. per yr.(12 nos. per vol.) ISSN 0005-6650
- Bayer-Symposien. irreg., vol. 6, 1977. ISSN 0067-4672 (Bayer AG GW)
- Behavioral Ecology and Sociobiology. 4 per yr. ISSN 0340-5443
- Beilsteins Handbuch der Organischen Chemie. Fourth Supplement. irreg., vol. 19, 1977. ISSN 0067-4915
- Berg- und Huettenmaennische Monatshefte. m. ISSN 0005-8912
- Berg- und Huettenmaennische Monatshefte. Supplement. irreg., 1970, no. 2. ISSN 0067-5768

- Berichte Biochemie und Biologie/Biochemistry-Biology. 18 vols. per yr., 6 nos. per vol. ISSN 0005-9013
- Berichte Physiologie, Physiologische Chemie und Pharmakologie. 7 vols. per yr., 6 nos. per vol. ISSN 0005-9048
- Berichte ueber Die Allgemeine und Spezielle Pathologie. 2 vols. per yr., 6 nos. per vol. ISSN 0005-9056
- Berichte ueber Die Gesamte Gynaekologie und Geburtshilfe Sowie Deren Grenzgebiete. 6 per yr. ISSN 0005-9064
- Biological Cybernetics; transmission, processing of information and control processes in organisms and automata. 4 vols. per yr., 4 nos. per vol. ISSN 0340-1200
- Biomathematics. irreg., vol. 7, 1977. ISSN 0067-8821
- Biophysics of Structure and Mechanism. 1 vol. per yr. (4 nos. per vol.) ISSN 0340-1057
- Blaetter fuer Technikgeschichte. irreg., vol. 34, 1972. ISSN 0067-9127 (Technisches Museum fuer Industrie und Gewerbe, Vienna AU)
- Blood Cells. 3 per yr. ISSN 0340-4684
- Blut; zeitschrift fuer die gesamte Blutforschung. m. ISSN 0006-5242 (Deutsche Haematologische Gesellschaft) (Co-sponsor: Deutsche Gesellschaft fuer Bluttransfusion)
- Bulletin of Environmental Contamination and Toxicology. 2 vols. per yr.(6 nos. per vol.) ISSN 0007-4861
- Calcified Tissue Research. 2vols. per yr., 3 nos. per vol. ISSN 0008-0594
- Cancer Immunology and Immunotherapy. ISSN 0340-7004
- Cancer Teaching Symposium. Proceedings. biennial.
- Carlsberg Research Communications. irreg(approx. 10 per yr.) (Carlsberg Laboratorium DK)
- Cell and Tissue Research. 9vols. per yr., 4 nos. per vol. ISSN 0302-766X
- Chemie, Physik und Technologie der Kunststoffe in Einzeldarstellungen. irreg., vol. 15, 1970. ISSN 0069-3073
- Chirurg; Zeitschrift fuer alle Gebiete der operativen Medizin. m(1 vol. per yr) ISSN 0009-4722 (Berufsverband der Deutschen Chirurgen, e-V. GW)
- Chirurgia Plastica. 1 vol. per yr. (4 nos. per vol.) ISSN 0009-4803
- Chromosoma. 5 vols. per yr., 4 nos. per vol. ISSN 0009-5915
- Chromosome Atlas: Fish, Amphibians, Reptiles and Birds. irreg., vol. 3, 1975. ISSN 0084-876X
- Communication and Cybernetics. irreg., vol. 17, 1976. ISSN 0340-0034
- Communications in Mathematical Physics. 6vols. per yr., 3 nos. per vol. ISSN 0010-3616
- Comprehensive Manuals of Surgical Specialties. irreg.
- Computing; archiv fuer informatik und numerik/archives for informatics and numerical computation. 2 vols. per yr., 4 nos. per vol. ISSN 0010-485X
- Contributions to Mineralogy and Petrology/Beitraege zur Mineralogie und Petrographie. 5 vols. per yr., 4 nos. per yr. ISSN 0010-7999
- Current Topics in Microbiology and Immunology. irreg., vol. 76, 1977. ISSN 0070-217X
- Current Topics in Pathology. irreg., vol. 64, 1977. ISSN 0070-2188
- Deutsche Gesellschaft fuer Endokrinologie. Symposium. irreg., 17th, 1971. ISSN 0070-4059
- Deutsche Gesellschaft fuer Urologie. Verhandlungsbericht. irreg., 26th session, 1975. ISSN 0070-413X
- Deutsche Ophthalmologische Gesellschaft. Zusammenkunft. Bericht. irreg., 73rd, 1975. ISSN 0070-427X
- Diabetologia. 1 vol. per yr.(6 nos. per vol.) ISSN 0012-186X (European Association for the Study of Diabetes)
- E und M/Elektrotechnik und Maschinenbau. 12 per yr. ISSN 0012-8058
- Ecological Studies; Analysis and Synthesis. irreg., vol. 22, 1977. ISSN 0070-8356
- Encyclopedia of Plant Physiology. New Series. irreg., vol. 5, 1977.
- Engineering in Medicine. irreg., vol. 2, 1976.
- Environmental Management (New York) 6 per yr.? ISSN 0364-152X
- Enzyklopaedie der Rechts- und Staatswissenschaft. New Series. Staatswissenschaft. irreg. ISSN 0085-0276
- Ergebnisse der Inneren Medizin und Kinderheilkunde. New Series/Advances in Internal Medicine and Pediatrics. irreg., vol. 39, 1977. ISSN 0071-111X

- Ergebnisse der Mathematik und Ihrer Grenzgebiete. irreg., no. 93, 1977. ISSN 0071-1136
- European Journal of Applied Microbiology. q. ISSN 0340-2118
- European Journal of Applied Physiology and Occupational Physiology. i vols. per yr., 4 nos. per vol. ISSN 0301-5548
- European Journal of Biochemistry. 10 vols. per yr. (2-3 nos. per vol.) ISSN 0014-2956 (Federation of European Biochemical Societies NE)
- European Journal of Clinical Pharmacology. (Pharmacologia Clinica) 2 vols. per yr., 6 nos. per vol. ISSN 0031-6970
- European Journal of Nuclear Medicine. ISSN 0340-6997
- European Journal of Pediatrics. 3 vols. per yr. (4 nos. per vol.) ISSN 0340-6997
- Experimental Brain Research/Experimentation Cerebrale/Experimentelle Hirnforschung. 3 vols. per yr (5, nos. per vol.) ISSN 0014-4819
- Experimentelle Medizin, Pathologie und Klinik. irreg., 1972, vol. 36. ISSN 0071-3430
- Fertigung und Betrieb. irreg., vol. 8, 1976.
- Forschungen aus Staat und Recht. irreg., vol. 40, 1977. ISSN 0071-7657
- Fortschritte der Chemie Organischer Naturstoffe/Progress in the Chemistry of Organic Natural Products. irreg., vol. 34, 1977. ISSN 0071-7886
- Fortschritte der Praktischen Dermatologie und Venerologie. irreg., vol. 8, 1976. ISSN 0071-7932
- Fresenius' Zeitschrift fuer Analytische Chemie; labor- und betriebsverfahren. 5 vols. per yr.(5 nos. per vol.) ISSN 0016-1152 (Gesellschaft Deutscher Chemiker. Fachgruppe Analytische Chemie GW)
- Gastrointestinal Radiology. 4 per yr. ISSN 0364-2356
- Germany (Federal Republic, 1949- ) Bundesgesundheitsamt. Abhandlungen. irreg., vol. 9, 1970. ISSN 0072-1530
- Gesellschaft fuer Biologische Chemie, Mosbach. Colloquium. irreg., no. 26, 1976.
- Graduate Texts in Mathematics. irreg., vol. 55, 1977. ISSN 0072-5285
- Grundlehren der Mathematischen Wissenschaften in Einzeldarstellungen. irreg., no. 229, 1977. ISSN 0072-7830
- Gynaekologe. 1 vol. per yr.(4 nos. per vol.) ISSN 0017-5994
- H N O. (Hals-, Nasen-, Ohren-Heilkunde) m.(1 vol per yr.) ISSN 0017-6192
- Hafenbautechnische Gesellschaft. Jahrbuch. irreg., no. 34, 1975. ISSN 0072-9264
- Handbook of Geochemistry. irreg., no. 2, pt. 4, 1970. ISSN 0072-9817
- Handbook of Sensory Physiology. irreg. ISSN 0072-9906
- Handbuch der Analytischen Chemie. Part 2: Qualitative Nachweisverfahren. irreg. ISSN 0073-0009
- Handbuch der Analytischen Chemie. Part 3: Quantitative Bestimmungs- und Trennungsmethoden. irreg. ISSN 0073-0017
- Handbuch der Experimentellen Pharmakologie/Handbook of Experimental Pharmacology. irreg., vol. 48, 1977. ISSN 0073-0033
- Handbuch der Mikroskopischen Anatomie des Menschen. irreg. ISSN 0073-0114
- Handbuch der Physik/Encyclopedia of Physics. irreg., latest issue 1977. ISSN 0085-140X
- Hautarzt; Zeitschrift fuer Dermatologie, Venerologie und verwandte Gebiete. 1 vol. per yr.(12 nos. per vol.) ISSN 0017-8470
- Hefte zur Unfallheilkunde. irreg., no. 129, 1977. ISSN 0085-1469
- Heidelberg Science Library. irreg., no. 27, 1977. ISSN 0073-1595
- Heidelberger Akademie der Wissenschaften. Mathematisch-Naturwissenschaftliche Klasse. Sitzungsberichte. irreg. ISSN 0073-1625
- Heidelberger Arbeitsbuecher. irreg., no. 10, 1976. ISSN 0073-1633
- Heidelberger Jahrbuecher. a. ISSN 0073-1641
- Heidelberger Taschenbuecher. irreg., no. 188, 1977. ISSN 0073-1684
- Histochemistry. 4 vols. per yr. (4 nos. per vol.)
- Holz als Roh- und Werkstoff. 1 vol. per yr.(12 nos. per vol.) ISSN 0018-3768 (Deutsche Gesellschaft fuer Holzforschung GW)
- Human Genetics. 4 vols. per yr., 3 nos. per vol. ISSN 0340-6717
- Immunogenetics. 1 vol. per yr. (6 nos. per vol.) ISSN 0093-7711
- Ingenieur-Archiv. 1 vol. per yr.(6 nos. per vol.) ISSN 0020-1154 (Gesellschaft fuer angewandte Mathematik und Mechanik GW)
- Ingenieurwissenschaftliche Bibliothek/Engineering Science Library. irreg.

- Institut fuer Staedtebau, Raumplanung und Raumordnung. Schriftenreihe. irreg., no. 19, 1972. ISSN 0082-2582 (Institut fuer Staedtebau, Raumplanung und Raumordnung GW)
- Intensive Care Medicine. ISSN 0340-0964
- International Archives of Occupational and Environmental Health/Internationales Archiv fuer Arbeits- und Umweltmedizin. 2 vols. per yr. (4 nos. per vol.)
- International Conference on Internal Friction and Ultrasonic Attenuation in Crystalline Solids. Proceedings. irreg.
- International Congress for Stereology. Proceedings. irreg., 1967, 2nd, Chicago. ISSN 0074-3437 (International Society for Stereology)
- International Congress of Applied Mechanics. Proceedings. irreg., 1968, 12th, Stanford, Calif. ISSN 0074-350X (International Union of Theoretical and Applied Mechanics)
- International Congress of Dermatology. Proceedings. quinquennial; 1967, 13th, Munich. ISSN 0074-3623 (International League of Dermatological Societies)
- International Congress of Histochemistry and Cytochemistry. Proceedings. quadrennial; 1964, 2nd, Frankfurt am Main. ISSN 0074-3690 (International Committee for Histochemistry and Cytochemistry)
- International Orthopaedics. 4 per yr. (International Society of Orthopaedic Surgery and Traumatology BE)
- International Society for the Study of Time. Conference. Proceedings; the study of time. irreg., 2nd, Oberwolfach, 1976.
- International Symposium on Neurosecretion. (Proceedings) irreg., 6th, 1973, publ. 1974. ISSN 0074-8889
- International Symposium on X-Ray Optics and X-Ray Microanalysis. Proceedings. triennial, 1968, 5th, Tuebingen. ISSN 0074-8943
- International Union against Cancer. U I C C Monograph Series. irreg., 1969, no. 12. ISSN 0074-9214
- Internationale Universitaetswochen fuer Kernphysic der Karl-Franzenus-Universitaet Graz. Proceedings. ISSN 0539-1695 (Germany, Federal Republic. Bundesministerium fuer Unterricht GW)
- Internist. 1 vol. per yr.(12 nos. per vol.) ISSN 0020-9554 (Berufsverband Deutscher Internisten GW)
- Inventiones mathematicae. 5 vols. per yr., 3 nos. per vol. ISSN 0020-9910
- Jahresberichte ueber Holzschutz/Annual Report on Wood Protection. irreg., vol. 1961 per 62, 1971. ISSN 0075-2878
- Journal of Comparative Physiology. A: Sensory, Neural, and Behavioral Physiology. 8 vols. per yr., 3 nos. per vol. ISSN 0340-7594
- Journal of Geophysics. bi-m. ISSN 0044-2801
- Journal of Mathematical Biology. 1 vol. per yr. (4 nos. per vol.) ISSN 0303-6812
- Journal of Membrane Biology; an international journal for studies on the structure, function and genesis of biomembranes. 5 vols. per yr., 4 nos. per vol. ISSN 0022-2631
- Journal of Molecular Evolution. 3 vols. per yr., 4 nos. per vol. ISSN 0022-2844
- Journal of Neural Transmission; a multidisciplinary journal for the study of the autonomic nervous system and of neuroendocrinology. 4 per yr. ISSN 0300-9564
- Journal of Neural Transmission. Supplement. irreg., no. 11, 1974. ISSN 0303-6995
- Journal of Neurology. 3 vols. per yr., 4 nos. per vol. ISSN 0340-5354 (Deutsche Gesellschaft fuer Neurologie GW) (Co-sponsor: Deutsche Gesellschaft fuer Neurochirurgie)
- Juristische Blaetter. 24 per yr. ISSN 0022-6912
- Kampf dem Laerm. bi-m. ISSN 0022-8249 (Deutscher Arbeitsring fuer Laermbekaempfung e.V. GW)
- Kidney International. 2 vol. per yr., 6 nos. per vol. ISSN 0085-2538 (International Society of Nephrology)
- Klinische Wochenschrift. 1 vol. per yr.(24 nos. per vol.) ISSN 0023-2173 (Gesellschaft Deutscher Naturforscher und Aerzte GW)
- Kongresszentralblatt fuer die Gesamte Innere Medizin. 2 vols per yr. ISSN 0024-9998 (Deutsche Gesellschaft fuer Innere Medizin GW)
- Konstruktion im Maschinen-, Apparate-und Geraetebau. 1 vol. per yr.(12 nos. per vol.) ISSN 0023-3625 (Verein Deutscher Ingenieure. Gesellschaft Konstruktion und Entwicklung GW) (Co-Sponsor: V D I/A W F-Fachgruppe Getriebetechnik)
- Konstruktionsbuecher. irreg., vol. 30, 1972. ISSN 0075-6768

- Kriminologische Abhandlungen. irreg., no. 11, 1975. ISSN 0075-7152
- Landolt-Boernstein, Zahlenwerte und Funktionen aus Naturwissenschaften und Technik. Neue Serie. Group 1: Nuclear Physics/Landolt-Boernstein Numerical Data and Functional Relationships in Science and Technology. New Series. irreg., vol. 8, 1973. ISSN 0075-7888
- Landolt-Boernstein, Zahlenwerte und Funktionen aus Naturwissenschaften und Technik. Neue Serie. Group 2: Atomic Physics. irreg., vol. 7, 1976. ISSN 0075-7918
- Landolt-Boernstein, Zahlenwerte und Funktionen aus Naturwissenschaften und Technik. Neue Serie. Group 3: Crystal Physics. irreg., vol. 9, 1975. ISSN 0075-787X
- Landolt-Boernstein, Zahlenwerte und Funktionen aus Naturwissenschaften und Technik. Neue Serie. Group 4: Macroscopic and Technical Properties of Matter. irreg. ISSN 0075-7926
- Landolt-Boernstein, Zahlenwerte und Funktionen aus Naturwissenschaften und Technik. Neue Serie. Group 5: Geophysics. irreg. ISSN 0075-790X
- Landolt-Boernstein, Zahlenwerte und Funktionen aus Naturwissenschaften und Technik. Neue Serie. Group 6: Astronomy. irreg. ISSN 0075-7896
- Langenbecks Archiv fuer Chirurgie Vereinigt mit Bruns Beitraege fuer Klinische Chirurgie. 3 vols. per yr., 4 nos. per vol. ISSN 0023-8236 (Deutsche Gesellschaft fuer Chirurgie GW)
- Lecture Notes in Economics and Mathematical Systems; Operations Research, Computer Science, Social Science. irreg., vol. 145, 1977. ISSN 0075-8442
- Lecture Notes in Mathematics. irreg., vol. 388, 1977. ISSN 0075-8434
- Lecture Notes in Physics. irreg., no. 63, 1977. ISSN 0075-8450
- Library of Exact Philosophy. irreg., no. 11, 1974. ISSN 0075-9104
- Linzer Hochschulschriften. irreg., no. 7, 1974. ISSN 0075-9724
- Lung. 1 vol. per yr. (4 nos. per vol.) (Deutsche Gesellschaft fuer Lungen- und Atmungsforschung GW)
- Lung. Supplement. irreg. (Deutsche Gesellschaft fuer Lungen- und Atmungsforschung GW)
- Manuscripta Mathematica. 3 vols. per yr.(4 nos. per vol.) ISSN 0025-2611
- Mathematical Systems Theory. 1 vol. per yr. (4 nos. per vol.) ISSN 0025-5661
- Mathematische Annalen. 6vols. per yr., 3 nos. per vol. ISSN 0025-5831
- Mathematische Zeitschrift. 6 vols. per yr., 3 nos. per vol. ISSN 0025-5874
- Max-Planck-Institut fuer Aeronomie. Mitteilungen. irreg. ISSN 0076-5643
- Medical Microbiology and Immunology; Zeitschrift fuer medizinische Mikrobiologie und Immunologie. 1 vol. per yr. (4 nos. per vol.) ISSN 0300-8584
- Medical Progress through Technology. 1 vol. per yr.(4 nos. per vol.) ISSN 0047-6552
- Medizinische Laenderkunde. Geomedical Monograph Series. irreg., 1968, no. 4. ISSN 0076-6151
- Metrologia; international journal of scientific metrology. q.(1 vol. per yr.) ISSN 0026-1394 (International Committee of Weights and Measures)
- Microbial Ecology. 1 vol. per yr. (4 nos. per vol.) ISSN 0095-3628
- Mikrochimica Acta. 2 per vol. per yr. (6 nos. per vol.) ISSN 0026-3672
- Mikrochimica Acta. Supplement. irreg., no. 7, 1977. ISSN 0076-8642
- Mineralium Deposita; international journal for Geology, Mineralogy, and Geochemistry of Mineral Deposits. 3 per yr. ISSN 0026-4598 (Society for Geology Applied to Mineral Deposits)
- Minerals and Rocks; monograph series of theoretical and experimental studies. irreg., vol. 12, 1977.
- Moderne Methoden der Pflanzenanalyse/Modern Methods of Plant Analysis. irreg., 1964, no. 7. ISSN 0077-0183
- Molecular & General Genetics; an international journal. 6 vols. per yr., 3 nos. per vol. ISSN 0026-8925
- Molecular Biology, Biochemistry and Biophysics. irreg., no. 24, 1977. ISSN 0077-0221
- Monatshefte fuer Chemie. 6 per yr. ISSN 0026-9247
- Monatshefte fuer Mathematik. 8 per yr. ISSN 0026-9255

- Monatsschrift fuer Kinderheilkunde. 1 vol. per yr. (12 nos. per vol.) ISSN 0026-9298 (Deutsche Gesellschaft fuer Kinderheilkunde GW)
- Monographien aus dem Gesamtgebiete der Psychiatrie - Psychiatry Series. irreg., no. 13, 1977. ISSN 0077-0671
- Monographs on Endocrinology. irreg., vol. 10, 1977. ISSN 0077-1015
- Monographs on Theoretical and Applied Genetics. irreg., vol. 3, 1977.
- N M R. (Nuclear Magnetic Resonance); basic principles and progress. irreg., vol. 13, 1976. ISSN 0078-088X
- Naturwissenschaften. m.(1 vol.per yr.) ISSN 0028-1042 (Max-Planck-Gesellschaft zur Foerderung der Wissenschaften GW) (Co-sponsor: Gesellschaft Deutscher Naturforscher und Aertze)
- Naunyn-Schmiedeberg's Archives of Pharmacology. 4 vols. per yr. (3 nos. per vol.) ISSN 0028-1298 (Deutsche Pharmakologische Gesellschaft GW)
- Nervenarzt; Monatsschrift fuer alle Gebiete nervenaerztlicher Forschung und Praxis. 1 vol. per yr.(12 nos. per vol.) ISSN 0028-2804 (Deutsche Gesellschaft fuer Psychiatrie und Nervenheilkunde GW)
- Neuroradiology. 2 vols. per yr. (5 nos. per vol.) ISSN 0028-3940 (European Society of Neuroradiology)
- News/Previews. m. ISSN 0095-2680
- News/Previews (International Edition) s-a.
- Numerische Mathematik. 2 vols. per yr. (4 nos. per vol.) ISSN 0029-599X
- O Z E/Oesterreichische Zeitschrift fuer Elektrizitaetswirtschaft. 12 per yr. ISSN 0029-9618
- Oecologia. 4vols. per yr. (4 nos. per vol.) ISSN 0029-8549 (International Association for Ecology NE)
- Oekonometrie und Unternehmensforschung/ Econometrics and Operations Research. irreg., no. 21, 1976. ISSN 0078-3390
- Oesterreichische Gesellschaft fuer Raumforschung und Raumplanung. Schriftenreihe. irreg., no. 17, 1972. ISSN 0078-3498
- Oesterreichische Ingenieur Zeitschrift; Zeitschrift des Oesterreichischen Ingenieur- und Architekten-Vereines. 12 per yr. ISSN 0029-9219
- Oesterreichische Wasserwirtschaft; Zeitschrift fuer alle wissenschaftlichen, technischen, rechtlichen und wirtschaftlichen Fragen des gesamten Wasserwesens. 12 per yr. ISSN 0029-9588
- Oesterreichische Zeitschrift fuer Oeffentliches Recht. Supplement. irreg., no. 3, 1974. ISSN 0078-3552
- Oesterreichische Zeitschrift fuer Oeffentliches Recht und Voelkerrecht. 4 per yr.
- Organische Chemie in Einzeldarstellungen. irreg., no. 15, 1974. ISSN 0078-6225
- Orthopaede. 1 vol. per yr. (4 nos. per vol.) ISSN 0085-4530
- Osram-Gesellschaft. Technisch-Wissenschaftliche Abhandlungen. irreg., no. 11, 1973. ISSN 0078-6799
- Paediatrie und Paedologie. 4 per yr. ISSN 0030-9338
- Pediatric Radiology. q. ISSN 0301-0449
- Perspectives in Mathematical Logic. irreg.
- Pfluegers Archiv; European journal of physiology. 6 vols. per yr. (3 nos. per vol.) ISSN 0031-6768
- Physics and Chemistry in Space. irreg., no. 9, 1977. ISSN 0079-1938
- Planta; an international journal of plant biology. 5 vols. per yr. (3 nos. per vol.) ISSN 0032-0935
- Praxis der Psychotherapie. bi-m. ISSN 0032-7077
- Progress in Botany. a. ISSN 0340-4773
- Progress in Molecular and Subcellular Biology. biennial. ISSN 0079-6484
- Progress in Toxicology/Special Topics. irreg.
- Protoplasma. 4 vols. per yr. (4 nos. per vol.) ISSN 0033-183X
- Protoplasmatologia; Handbuch der Protoplasmaforschung. irreg ISSN 0079-7073
- Psychological Research; an international journal of perception, learning and communications. 1 vol. per yr. (4 nos. per vol.) ISSN 0340-0727
- Psychopharmacology. 5 vols. per yr. (3 nos. per vol.) ISSN 0033-3158
- Public International Law. 1 vol. per yr. (2 nos. per vol.) ISSN 0340-7349
- Radiation and Environmental Biophysics. 1 vol. per yr.(4 nos. per vol.) ISSN 0301-634X
- Radiologe. 1 vol. per yr. (12 nos. per vol.) ISSN 0033-832X
- Recent Results in Cancer Research/Fortschritte der Krebsforschung. irreg., vol. ISSN 0080-0015
- Rechts- und Staatswissenschaften. irreg., vol. 23, 1971. ISSN 0080-0163

- Reine und Angewandte Metallkunde in Einzeldarstellungen. irreg., vol. 25, 1975. ISSN 0080-0791
- Research in Experimental Medicine. 2 vols. per yr. (3 nos. per vol.) ISSN 0300-9130
- Residue Reviews. irreg., no. 68, 1977. ISSN 0080-181X
- Results and Problems in Cell Differentiation. irreg., no. 7, 1975. ISSN 0080-1844
- Reviews of Physiology, Biochemistry and Experimental Pharmacology. irreg., vol. 78, 1977. ISSN 0080-2042
- Rock Mechanics/Fels Mechanik/Mecanique des Roches. 4 per yr. ISSN 0035-7448
- Rock Mechanics/Felsmechanik/Mechanique des Roches. Supplement. irreg., no. 5, 1977. ISSN 0080-3375
- Roux' Archives of Developmental Biology. 2 vols. per yr. (4 nos. per vol.) ISSN 0340-0794
- Schiffbautechnische Gesellschaft. Jahrbuch. a. ISSN 0080-6803
- Schriftenreihe Neurologie/Neurology Series. irreg., vol. 19, 1977. ISSN 0080-715X
- Semigroup Forum. 2 vols. per yr. (4 nos. per vol.) ISSN 0037-1912
- Siemens Forschungs- und Entwicklungsberichte/ Siemens Research and Development Report. bi-m. ISSN 0080-9497 (Siemens Aktiengesellschaft GW)
- Skeletal Radiology. irreg., 4 nos. per vol. ISSN 0364-2348 (International Skeletal Society)
- Social Psychiatry/Psychiatrie Sociale/ Sozialpsychiatrie. q.(1 vol. per yr.) ISSN 0037-7813
- Sonnblick-Verein. Jahresberichte. irreg., nos. 68-69, 1973. ISSN 0081-2064
- Sources in the History of Mathematics and Physical Sciences. irreg.
- Spezielle Pathologische Anatomie. irreg., vol. 9, 1975. ISSN 0081-3699
- Springer Advanced Texts in Life Sciences. irreg.
- Springer Series in Optical Sciences. irreg., 1977, vol. 5.
- Springer Tracts in Modern Physics. irreg., 1977, vol. 80. ISSN 0081-3869
- Springer Tracts in Natural Philosophy. irreg., 1977, no. 29. ISSN 0081-3877
- Steirische Beitraege zur Hydrogeologie. a. ISSN 0085-6754
- Structure and Bonding. irreg., vol. 33, 1977. ISSN 0081-5993
- Struktur und Eigenschaften der Materie in Einzeldarstellungen. irreg. ISSN 0081-6035
- Studies in the Foundations, Methodology and Philosophy of Science. irreg., 1971, no. 4. ISSN 0081-8577
- Studies in the History of Mathematics and Physical Sciences. irreg.
- T M P M/Tschermaks Mineralogische und Petrographische Mitteilungen. 4 per yr. ISSN 0041-3763
- Die Talsperren Oesterreichs. irreg., vol. 21, 1974. ISSN 0082-1551
- Technische Physik in Einzeldarstellungen. irreg., vol. 18, 1973. ISSN 0082-2590
- Texts and Monographs in Physics. irreg.
- Theoretica Chimica Acta/Theoretical Chemistry. 3 vols. per yr. (4 nos. per vol.) ISSN 0040-5744
- Theoretical and Applied Genetics; internationale Zeitschrift fuer theoretische und angewandte Genetik. 2 vol. per yr. (6 nos. per vol.) ISSN 0040-5752
- Topics in Applied Physics. irreg.
- Topics in Current Chemistry. irreg., vol. 69, 1977.
- Topics in Infectious Diseases. irreg.
- Tuberkulose-Jahrbuch. irreg., 1970, 1966-67 issue. ISSN 0082-6669
- Tuberkulose und ihre Grenzgebiete in Einzel-Arstellungen. irreg., vol. 19, 1967. ISSN 0082-6677
- Unfallheilkunde/Traumatology. 1 vol. per yr. (12 nos. per vol.) (Deutsche Gesellschaft fuer Unfallheilkunde, Versicherungs-, Versorgungs- und Verkehrsmedizin GW)
- Universitaet Stuttgart. Institut fuer Steuerungstechnik der Werkzeugmaschinen und Fertigungseinrichtungen. i S W Berichte. irreg., 1972, vol. 3. ISSN 0085-6916
- Universite de Strasbourg. Seminaire de Probabilities. a.
- Urologe - Ausgabe A; Zeitschrift fuer Klinische und Praktische Urologie. 1 vol. per yr. (6 nos. per vol.) ISSN 0042-1103
- Urologe-Ausgabe B. 1 vol. per yr. (6 nos. per vol.) ISSN 0042-1111 (Berufsverband der Deutschen Urologen GW)
- Urological Research. 1 vol. per yr. (4 nos. per vol.) ISSN 0300-5623

- Verstaendliche Wissenschaft. irreg., vol. 114, 1977. ISSN 0083-5846
- Virchows Archiv. A: Pathological Anatomy and History. 4 vols. per yr. (4 nos. per vol.) ISSN 0340-1227
- Virchows Archiv. Abteilung B; Cell Pathology. 2 vols. per yr. (4 nos. per vol.) ISSN 0042-6431
- Virology Monographs/Virusforschung in Einzeldarstellungen. irreg., vol. 16, 1977. ISSN 0083-6591
- Von Graefes Archiv fuer Klinische und Experimentelle Ophthalmologie/Von Graefe's Archive for Clinical and Experimental Ophtalmology. 4 vols. per yr. (3 nos. per vol.) ISSN 0017-2847
- Waerme- und Stoffuebertragung/Thermo- and Fluid Dynamics. 1 vol. per yr. (4 nos per vol.) ISSN 0042-9929
- Werke der Kunst in Heidelberg. irreg., 1969, no. 3. ISSN 0083-8039
- Werkstattstechnik; wt-Zeitschrift fuer industrielle Fertigung. m.(1 vol. per yr.) ISSN 0043-2806 (Verein Deutscher Ingenieure. Fachgruppe Betriebstechnik GW)
- Wiener Klinische Wochenschrift. w. (24 per yr.) ISSN 0043-5325
- Wiener Zeitschrift fuer Nervenheilkunde und deren Grenzgebiete. Supplement. irreg., 1969, no. 2. ISSN 0084-0092
- Wissenschaftliche Normung. irreg., 1965, no. 7. ISSN 0084-0947
- Wissenschaftliche und Angewandte Photographie. irreg. ISSN 0084-0998
- Wood Science and Technology; journal for wood and pulp. 1 vol. per yr. (4 nos. per vol.) ISSN 0043-7719 (International Academy of Wood Science)
- World Journal of Surgery. 6 per yr. (International Society of Surgery BE)
- Zeitschrift fuer Krebsforschung und Klinische Onkologie/Cancer Research and Clinical Oncology. 4 vols. per yr. (3 nos. per vol.) ISSN 0084-5353 (Deutsche Krebsgesellschaft GW)
- Zeitschrift fuer Lebensmittel-Untersuchung und Forschung. 3 vols per yr (6 nos. per vol.) ISSN 0044-3026
- Zeitschrift fuer Nationaloekonomie/Journal of Economics. 4 per yr. ISSN 0044-3158
- Zeitschrift fuer Parasitenkunde. 3 vols. per yr. (3 nos. per vol.) ISSN 0044-3255 (Deutsche Gesellschaft fuer Parasitologie GW)
- Zeitschrift fuer Physik. Section A: Atoms and Nuclei. 4 vols. per yr. (4 nos. per vol.) ISSN 0340-2193 (Deutsche Physikalische Gesellschaft GW)
- Zeitschrift fuer Physik. Section B: Quanta and Matter. 3 vols. per yr. (4nos. per vol.) ISSN 0340-224X
- Zeitschrift fuer Rechtsmedizin/Journal of Legal Medicine. 2 vols. per year (4 nos. per vol.) ISSN 0044-3433 (Deutsche Gesellschaft fuer Rechtsmedizin GW)
- Zeitschrift fuer Wahrscheinlichkeitstheorie und Verwandte Gebiete. 4vols. per yr. (4 nos. per vol.) ISSN 0044-3719
- Zentralblatt fuer Die Gesamte Kinderheilkunde. 2 vols. per yr. (6 nos. per vol.) ISSN 0044-4111 (Deutsche Gesellschaft fuer Kinderheilkunde GW)
- Zentralblatt fuer Die Gesamte Neurologie und Psychiatrie/Neurology-Psychiatry. 3 vols. per yr. (6 nos. per vol.) ISSN 0044-412X (Archiv fuer Psychiatrie und Nervenkrankheiten GW) (Co-sponsor: Gesamtverbande Deutscher Nervenaerzte)
- Zentralblatt fuer Die Gesamte Ophthalmologie und ihre Grenzgebiete/Ophthalmology. 2 vols. per yr. (6 nos. per vol.) ISSN 0044-4138
- Zentralblatt fuer Die Gesamte Radiologie/ Radiology. 2 vols. per yr. (6 nos. per yr.) ISSN 0044-4146 (Deutsche Roentgengesellschaft GW)
- Zentralblatt fuer Die Gesamte Rechtsmedizin und ihre Grenzgebiete/Legal Medicine. 2 vols. per yr. (5 nos. per vol.) ISSN 0044-4154 (Deutsche Gesellschaft fuer Rechtsmedizin GW)
- Zentralblatt fuer Hals-, Nasen- und Ohrenheilkunde- Plastische Chirurgie an Kopf und Hals. 3 vols. per yr. (6 nos. per vol.) ISSN 0340-5214 (Deutsche Gesellschaft fuer Hals-, Nasen-, Ohrenheilkunde, Kopf- und Halschirurgie GW)
- Zentralblatt fuer Haut- und Geschlechtskrankheiten Sowie Deren Grenzgebiete/Dermatology. 2 vols. per yr. (9 nos. per vol.) ISSN 0044-4219 (Deutsche Dermatologische Gesellschaft GW) (Co-sponsor: Vereinigung Deutschsprachiger Dermatologen)

- Zentralblatt fuer Mathematik und ihre Grenzgebiete; mathematics abstracts. 23 vols. per yr. (1 no. per vol.) ISSN 0044-4235 (Deutsche Akademie der Wissenschaften zu Berlin GW) (Co-sponsor: Heidelberger Akademie der Wissenschaften)
- Zentralorgan fuer Die Gesamte Chirurgie und ihre Grenzgebiete. 2 vols. per yr. (6 nos. per vol.) ISSN 0044-4308 (Deutsche Gesellschaft fuer Chirurgie GW)
- Zoomorphologie. 3 vols. per yr. (3 nos. per vol.) ISSN 0340-6725
- Zoophysiology and Ecology. irreg. ISSN 0084-5663

**Springfield Library and Museums Association**
220 State St., Springfield, MA 01103.
- Springfield, Massachusetts. City Library Bulletin. bi-m. ISSN 0038-8599

**Springfield Public Schools**
940 N. Jefferson, Springfield, MO 65802.
- Springfield Public Schools. News and Views. m (during school yr.) ISSN 0038-8602

**James Sprunt Press**
Box 353, Kenansville, NC 28349.
- James Sprunt Review. s-a. (James Sprunt Foundation, Inc.)

**Spudman**
Ed. Dan Crawford, Box 476, Tulelake, CA 96134.
- Spudman; voice of the potato industry. 6 per yr. ISSN 0038-8661

**Spur Inc.**
Delaplane, VA 22025.
- Spur. bi-m. ISSN 0098-5422

**Squadron Shop**
23500 John Rd., Hazel Park, MI 48030.
- Squadron. q. ISSN 0049-2027

**Square Dance Federation of Minnesota**
330 Lilac Lane, St Paul, MN 55112.
- New Roundup. m.

**E.R. Squibb & Sons, Inc.**
Box 4000, Princeton, NJ 08540.
- Transient Equilibrium; Squibb nuclear alumni newsletter. q.

**Sri Chinmoy Centre, Inc.**
85-45 149th St., Jamaica Hills, New York, NY 11435.
- Aum: the Message of Sri Chinmoy; a monthly journal containing the spiritual writings of the Hindu philosopher, poet and spiritual master, Sri Chinmoy. m.

**Srpske Narodne Odrane u Americi**
3909 W. North Ave., Chicago, IL 60647.
- Sloboda/Liberty. w. ISSN 0037-6868

**SS. Cyril & Methodias Seminary**
Box 5175, Orchard Lake, MI 48033.
- Sodalis-Polonia. m (Oct.-June)

**Ed. & Pub. Olga Stacevich**
P.O. Box 6128, San Mateo, CA 94403.
- Samizdat Bulletin. m.

**Stackpole Books**
Cameron and Kelker Sts., Harrisburg, PA 17105.
- Air Officer's Guide. a. ISSN 0065-4825
- Officer's Guide. biennial. ISSN 0078-3811

**Stained Glass Association of America**
1125 Wilmington Ave., St. Louis, MO 63111.
- Stained Glass; devoted to the craft of painted and stained glass. q. ISSN 0038-9161

**Stained Glass Club**
Box 244, Norwood, NJ 07648.
- Glass Workshop. bi-m. ISSN 0017-1077

**Albert & Rita Stainton, Eds. & Pubs.**
Box 332, Machias, ME 04654.
- Bartleby's Review. s-a.

**Stamats Publishing Co.**
c/o Pub. Ray J. Walther, 427 Sixth Ave., S.E., Cedar Rapids, IA 52401.
- Buildings; the construction and building management journal. m. ISSN 0007-3725
- National Roster of Realtors. a. ISSN 0090-1741 (National Association of Realtors)
- Perfect Home. m. ISSN 0031-5184

**Lazar Stambovsky, Ed. & Pub.**
333 Bridge St., Springfield, MA 01103.
- Western Massachusetts Commercial News. w.

**Stamler Publishing Co.**
297 Main St., Box 367, S.C. Station, Branford, CT 06405.
- Highway & Vehicle/Safety Report. fortn.

**Stamp Shows,Inc.**
Box 284, Larchmont, NY 10538.
- Stamp Show News. m.

**Stamp Wholesaler**
Box 529, Burlington, VT 05402.
- Stamp Wholesaler; world's largest stamp trade journal. 21 per yr. ISSN 0038-9315

**Stamper**
Box 489, Rock Falls, IL 61071.
- Stamper. m.

**Stan Kenton's Creative World**
1012 S. Robertson Blvd., Box 35216, Los Angeles, CA 90035.
- Creative World. q.

**Standard Abstract Corp.**
132 Nassau St., New York, NY 10038.
- Manhattan Directory of Commercial & Industrial Properties. irreg. ISSN 0095-0688

**Standard & Poor's Corporation**
345 Hudson St., New York, NY 10014.
- American Bankers Association. Committee on Uniform Security Identification Procedures. C U S I P Directory. a. ISSN 0569-2954
- American Bankers Association. Committee on Uniform Security Identification Procedures. C U S I P Directory: Corporate Directory. a. ISSN 0091-3804
- American Stock Exchange Stock Reports. s-w. ISSN 0002-8347
- Analysts Handbook. a.
- Fixed Income Investor. w. ISSN 0091-8415
- New York Stock Exchange Stock Reports. d.
- O - T - C and Regional Exchange Stock Reports. 3 per wk.
- O T C Chart Manual. bi-m. ISSN 0029-7291
- Poor's Register of Corporations, Directors and Executives. a. with 3 supplements. ISSN 0079-3825
- Standard & Poor's Bond Guide. m.
- Standard & Poor's Called Bond Record. s-w.
- Standard & Poor's Commercial Paper Reports Service. w.
- Standard and Poor's Corporation. Industry Surveys. w.
- Standard & Poor's Corporation Records. d.
- Standard & Poor's Daily Stock Price Record. American Exchange. q.
- Standard & Poor's Daily Stock Price Record. New York Stock Exchange. q.
- Standard & Poor's Daily Stock Price Record. over the Counter Exchange. q.
- Standard and Poor's Directory of Bond Agents. irreg.
- Standard & Poor's Dividend Record (Daily) d.
- Standard & Poor's Dividend Record (Quarterly) q.
- Standard & Poor's Dividend Record (Weekly) w.
- Standard & Poor's Earnings Forecaster. w.
- Standard & Poor's International Stock Report. m. ISSN 0020-8795
- Standard & Poor's Municipal Bond Selector. bi-m.
- Standard & Poor's Outlook. w. ISSN 0030-7246
- Standard & Poor's Registered Bond Interest Record. w.
- Standard & Poor's Review of Securities Regulation; an analysis of current laws, regulations and court decisions affecting the securities industry. s-m(m. July & Aug.) ISSN 0034-6756
- Standard & Poor's Statistical Service. m.
- Standard & Poor's Stock Guide. m.
- Standard & Poor's Stock Summary. m. ISSN 0038-9420
- Standard & Poor's Transportation Securities. w.
- Standard & Poor's Trendline's Current Market Perspectives. m. ISSN 0041-2333
- Trendline Daily Basis Stock Charts. w.

**Standard Educational Corporation**
130 N. Wells St., Chicago, IL 60606.
- World Progress; the standard quarterly review, an alphabetically arranged quarterly covering current events. q. ISSN 0043-8901

**Standard Oil Company (Indiana)**
200 E. Randolph Dr., Chicago, IL 60601.
- Span. q. ISSN 0584-8016

**Standard Oil Company (Ohio) Government and Public Affairs Department**
1775 Guildhall, Cleveland, OH 44115.
- Sohioan. bi-m.

**Standard Oil Company of California**
225 Bush St., San Francisco, CA 94104.
- Standard Oil Company of California Bulletin. q.

**Standard Press**
364 Somerset St., New Brunswick, NJ 08901.
- Otagu Sip; magyar fulyoirat. q.

**Standard Publishing**
8121 Hamilton Ave., Cincinnati, OH 45231.
- Christian Standard. w. ISSN 0009-5656
- Discovering Together. w.
- Four and Five. w. ISSN 0015-9077
- Jet Cadet. w. ISSN 0022-6645
- Key to Christian Education. q. ISSN 0023-0839
- Now. w.
- Seek. q (in weekly parts)
- Standard Lesson Commentary; International Sunday School lessons. a. ISSN 0081-4245
- Today's Christian Parent. q.
- Weekly Bible Reader. w.

**Standard Publishing (Boston)**
89 Broad St., Boston, MA 02110.
- Standard (Boston) w. ISSN 0038-9390

**Standard Rate and Data Service, Inc.**
5201 Old Orchard Rd., Skokie, IL 60076.
- Contractor. s-m. ISSN 0010-7891
- Standard Rate and Data Service. British Rate and Data. m. ISSN 0038-9471 (And: 30 Old Burlington St., London W1X 2AE, England)
- Standard Rate and Data Service. Business Publication Rates and Data. m. ISSN 0038-948X
- Standard Rate and Data Service. Canadian Advertising Rates and Data. m. ISSN 0038-9498
- Standard Rate and Data Service. Consumer Magazine and Farm Publication Rates and Data. m. ISSN 0038-9595
- Standard Rate and Data Service. Dati e Tariffe. 6 per yr. ISSN 0038-9501 (And: Giovanni B. Carta, Via Meraviglia 3, Milan, Italy)
- Standard Rate and Data Service. Direct Mail List Rates and Data. s-a. ISSN 0038-9463
- Standard Rate and Data Service. Media Daten. 6 per yr. ISSN 0038-951X
- Standard Rate and Data Service. Medios Publicitarios Mexicanos. q. ISSN 0038-9528 (And: Morelos 58, 1001 y 1002, Apdo. Postal 215, Mexico 1, D.F. Mexico)
- Standard Rate and Data Service. Network Rates and Data. bi-m. ISSN 0038-9536
- Standard Rate and Data Service. Newspaper Rates and Data. m. ISSN 0038-9544
- Standard Rate and Data Service. Print Media Production Data. m. ISSN 0038-9455
- Standard Rate and Data Service. Spot Radio Rates and Data. m. ISSN 0038-9560
- Standard Rate and Data Service. Spot Television Rates and Data. m. ISSN 0038-9552
- Standard Rate and Data Service. Tariff Media. q. ISSN 0038-9579
- Standard Rate and Data Service. Transit Advertising Rates and Data. q. ISSN 0038-9609
- Standard Rate and Data Service. Weekly Newspaper Ratees and Data. s-a. ISSN 0038-9587

**Standard Research Consultants**
Standard & Poor's Bldg., 345 Hudson St., New York, NY 10014.
- S R C Quarterly Reports. q.

**Standards Engineers Society**
6700 Penn Ave. S., Minneapolis, MN 55423.
- Standards Engineering. bi-m. ISSN 0038-9668
- Standards Engineers Society. Proceedings of Annual Meeting. a. ISSN 0081-430X

**Stanford Museum. Committee for Art at Stanford**
Stanford, CA 94305.
- Stanford Museum. a. ISSN 0085-6665

**Stanford Research Institute**
333 Ravenswood Ave., Menlo Park, CA 94025.
- Investments in Tomorrow. q.
- S R I International. irreg., 1970, no. 15. ISSN 0080-5114

**Stanford Research Institute. Chemical Information Services Department**
Menlo Park, CA 94025.
- Benzene-Toluene-Xylenes and Derivatives. a, with semi-annual supplements.
- Chemical Economics Newsletter. bi-m.
- C4 Hydrocarbons and Derivatives. a, with semi-annual supplements.
- Directory of Chemical Producers. a, with semi-annual supplements. ISSN 0012-3277
- Ethylene and Derivatives. a, with semi-annual supplements.
- Propylene and Derivatives. a, with semi-annual supplements.

**Stanford University**
Stanford, CA 94305.
- Stanford Observer. m.(Oct-June) ISSN 0038-979X
- Stanford University. University Relations Office. Campus Report. w. (fortn. during summer term) ISSN 0049-2108

**Stanford University. Associated Students**
ASSU Office, Tressidder Memorial Union, Stanford, CA 94305.
- Sequoia. 3 per yr. ISSN 0037-2420

**Stanford University. Committee on Linguistics**
Stanford, CA 94305
(Available from: E R I C, National Institute of Education, U.S. Dept. of H.E.W., Washington DC 20208)
- Papers and Reports on Child Language Development. irreg.
- Stanford Occasional Papers in Linguistics. irreg. ISSN 0085-6673

**Stanford University. Department of English**
Stanford, CA 94305.
- Virginia Woolf Miscellany. s-a.

**Stanford University. Department of Spanish and Portuguese**
Stanford, CA 94305.
- Vortice; literatura y critica. 3 per yr.

**Stanford University. Food Research Institute**
Stanford, CA 94305.
- Food Research Institute Studies. 3 per yr.

**Stanford University. Graduate School of Business**
Stanford, CA 94305.
- Teaching of Organization Behavior; a journal of teaching theory and technique. q.

**Stanford University. Hoover Institution on War, Revolution and Peace**
- Hoover Institution Bibliographies Series. (pub. by Hoover Institution Press)
- Hoover Institution on War, Revolution and Peace. Foreign Language Publications Series. (pub. by Hoover Institution Press)
- Hoover Institution on War, Revolution and Peace. Library Surveys. (pub. by Hoover Institution Press)
- Hoover Institution on War, Revolution, and Peace. Publications Series. (pub. by Hoover Institution Press)
- Hoover Institution on War, Revolution, and Peace. Report. (pub. by Hoover Institution Press)
- Hoover Institution Studies Series. (pub. by Hoover Institution Press)
- Yearbook on International Communist Affairs. (pub. by Hoover Institution Press)

**Stanford University. Library**
Stanford, CA 94305.
- Stanford University. Libraries. Annual Report. a.

**Stanford University. School of Earth Sciences**
Stanford, CA 94305.
- Stanford University. Publications. Geological Sciences. irreg., vol. 13, 1973. ISSN 0081-4350

**Stanford University. Stanford Alumni Association**
Bowman Alumni House, Stanford, CA 94305.
- Stanford Alumni Almanac. 4 per yr. ISSN 0038-9749

**Stanford University. Stanford Business School Alumni Association**
Stanford, CA 94305.
- Stanford Business School Alumni Bulletin. q.

**Stanford University. Stanford Center for Research and Development in Teaching**
Stanford, CA 94305.
- Teaching. irreg., no. 4, 1974. ISSN 0082-223X

**Stanford University. Stanford Law School**
Stanford, CA 94305.
- Stanford Journal of International Studies. a. ISSN 0081-4326
- Stanford Law Review. 6 per yr. ISSN 0038-9765
- Stanford Law School Journal. m. ISSN 0049-2086

**Stanford University. Stanford Medical Alumni Association**
School of Medicine, Stanford, CA 94305.
- Stanford M. D. q. ISSN 0038-9781

**Stewart Stanley, Ed. & Pub.**
1806 Main St., Joplin, MO 64801.
- Times Observer. s-m.

**Stanley Foundation**
Stanley Bldg., Muscatine, IA 52761.
- Conference on the United Nations of the Next Decade. Report. a. ISSN 0069-8733
- Conference on United Nations Procedures. Report. a. ISSN 0069-8601
- Stanley Foundation. Occasional Paper. irreg; no. 13, 1977.
- Strategy for Peace Conference. Report. a. ISSN 0081-5942
- Vantage Conference Report. irreg; no. 5, 1975.

**Stanley Publications, Inc.**
261 Fifth Ave., New York, NY 10016.
- Guns & Game. bi-m.

**Stanley Publishing Co.**
300 W. Lake St., Chicago, IL 60606.
- Automotive Body Repair News. m.

**Elizabeth Cady Stanton Publishing Co.**
5857 Marbury Rd., Bethesda, MD 20034.
- Women's Rights Almanac. a.

**Staple Cotton Cooperative Association**
210-214 W. Market St., Greenwood, MS 38930.
- Staple Cotton Review. m. ISSN 0038-9838

**Staples Area Vocational Technical Institute**
Staples, MN 56479.
- Farm Business Management Program for Northeastern Minnesota. Annual Report. a. ISSN 0070-7538

**Star**
U.S. Public Health Service Hospital, Box 325, Carville, LA 70721.
- Star; radiating the light of truth on Hansen's disease. bi-m. ISSN 0049-2116

**Star Guidance, Inc.**
75 Rockefeller Plaza, New York, NY 10019.
- Astrology Guide. (pub. by Sterling's Magazines, Inc.)
- Movie and TV Gossip. m.
- Movie TV Family Album. q.
- T V Radio Show. m. ISSN 0039-8594

**Star Publishing Company**
505 Eighth Ave., New York, NY 10018.
- Racing Star Weekly. w. ISSN 0033-7439

**Star West Publications**
Box 731, Sausalito, CA 94965.
- Larvae du Golden Gate. irreg. ISSN 0023-8511
- Star West; a multi-lingual literary newspaper. s-a. ISSN 0038-9900

**Stark Jewish News**
c/o David F. Leopold, Box 9112, Canton, OH 44711.
- Stark Jewish News. m.

**Starrucca Valley Publications**
Lanesboro Road, Starrucca, PA 18462.
- Railroading Series. s-a.

**Stash**
118 South Bedford, Madison, WI 53703.
- Grassroots (Madison) m. ISSN 0361-1515
- Journal of Psychedelic Drugs. q. ISSN 0022-393X (Student Association for the Study of Hallucinogens)

**State**
c/o W. B. Wright, Box 2169, Raleigh, NC 27602.
- State; down home in North Carolina. m. ISSN 0038-9994

**State Bar Association of North Dakota**
- North Dakota Law Review. (pub. by University of North Dakota)

**State Bar of Arizona**
234 N. Central Ave., Phoenix, AZ 85004.
- Arizona Bar Journal. 6 per yr. ISSN 0004-1424
- State Bar of Arizona. Newsletter. irreg. ISSN 0099-1058

**State Bar of California**
1230 W. Third St., Los Angeles, CA 90017.
- California State Bar Journal. bi-m. ISSN 0039-002X

**State Bar of California and Conference of California Judges**
601 McAllister St., San Francisco, CA 94102.
- Public Affairs Manual for the Bench and Bar of California. a. ISSN 0079-7642

**State Bar of Georgia**
1510 Fulton Nat. Bank Bldg, Atlanta, GA 30303.
- Georgia State Bar Journal. q. ISSN 0016-8416

**State Bar of Michigan**
306 Townsend, Lansing, MI 48933.
- Michigan State Bar Journal. m. ISSN 0026-2447

**State Bar of Nevada**
328 California Ave., Reno, NV 89505.
- Nevada State Bar Journal. q. ISSN 0028-4092

**State Bar of New Mexico**
1117 Stanford, N.E., Albuquerque, NM 87131.
- State Bar of New Mexico. Bulletin and Advance Opinions. w. ISSN 0039-0038

**State Bar of Texas**
Box 12487, Capitol Sta., Austin, TX 78711.
- Bar. m. ISSN 0092-3877
- Texas Bar Journal. m.(Aug-June) ISSN 0040-4187
- Texas Lawyers' Weekly Digest. w. ISSN 0098-8987

**State Bar of Utah**
564 Kennecott Building, Salt Lake City, UT 84111.
- Utah Bar Journal. irreg. ISSN 0091-9691

**State Bar of Wisconsin**
402 W. Wilson St., Madison, WI 53703.
- Wisconsin Bar Bulletin. bi-m. ISSN 0043-6380

**State Commerce for Construction in the USSR**
- Soil Mechanics and Foundation Engineering. (pub. by Consultants Bureau)

**State Communities Aid Association**
105 E. 22nd St., New York, NY 10010.
- Albany Bulletin on Health and Welfare Legislation. w.
- State Communities Aid Association Annual Report. a. ISSN 0585-1149

**State Education Journal Index**
Box 244, Westminster, CO 80030.
- State Education Journal Index; an annotated index to materials in the field of education. s-a. ISSN 0039-0046

**State Education Publications**
131 S. 31st St., Kenilworth, NJ 07033.
- Hawaii Teacher Advocate. 10 per yr.
- Maryland Action Line. 10 per yr.
- Michigan Teacher's Voice. m.

**State Farm Insurance Companies**
Agency Communications Dept., One State Farm Plaza, Bloomington, IL 61701.
- Reflector. m. ISSN 0034-2939

**State Historical Society of Colorado**
Colorado Heritage Center, 1300 Broadway, Denver, CO 80203.
- Colorado Magazine. q. ISSN 0010-1648
- Mountain & Plain History Notes. m. ISSN 0047-8261

**State Historical Society of Iowa**
Iowa City, IA 52240.
- Palimpsest. bi-m. ISSN 0031-0360
- State Historical Society of Iowa. News for Members. q.

**State Historical Society of Missouri**
Columbia, MO 65201.
- Missouri Historical Review. q. ISSN 0026-6582

**State Historical Society of North Dakota**
Liberty Memorial Bldg., Bismarck, ND 58501.
- North Dakota History; journal of the northern plains. q. ISSN 0029-2710

**State Historical Society of Wisconsin**
816 Wisconsin St., Madison, WI 53706.
- Guides to Historical Resources. irreg.
- Wisconsin Magazine of History. q. ISSN 0043-6534
- Wisconsin Public Documents. m.(plus annual cumulation)
- Wisconsin Then and Now. m. ISSN 0043-6739

**State Industrial Directories, Inc.**
2 Penn Plaza, New York, NY 10001.
- Connecticut State Industrial Directory. a.
- Maine State Industrial Direcotry. biennial.
- New Hampshire State Industrial Directory. biennial.
- New Jersey State Industrial Directory. a.
- New York State Industrial Directory. a. ISSN 0548-9067
- Pennsylvania State Industrial Directory. a. ISSN 0553-6065
- Vermont State Industrial Directory. biennial.

**State Medical Society of Wisconsin**
Ed. Dr. V. S. Falk, 330 E. Lakeside St., Madison, WI 53701.
- Wisconsin Medical Journal. m. ISSN 0043-6542

**State Osteopathic Journal Group**
c/o William McCausland Associates, Box 101, Pitman, NJ 08071.
- Buckeye Osteopathic Physician. m. (Ohio Osteopathic Association of Physicians and Surgeons)
- Cooperation. bi-m. (Missouri Association of Osteopathic Physicians and Surgeons)

**State Pharmaceutical Editorial Association**
222 W. Adams St., Rm. 546, Chicago, IL 60606.
- Indiana Pharmacist. m.
- Iowa Pharmacist. m.
- Kentucky Pharmacist. m.
- Minnesota Pharmacist. m. ISSN 0026-5616 (Minnesota State Pharmaceutical Association)
- Mississippi Pharmacist. m.
- Palmetto Pharmacist. m.
- Texas Pharmacy. m.

**State Principals Association**
15 Western Ave, Augusta, ME 04330.
- State Principals Association. Bulletin. m.(10 per yr.) ISSN 0039-0143

**State Revenue Society**
3919 Enola Ct., Fort Wayne, IN 46804.
- State Revenue Newsletter. bi-m.

**State Review Publishing Co.**
1613 E. Kalamazoo St., Box 13038, Lansing, MI 48901.
- Michigan Roads and Construction. w.

**State University of New York**
99 Washington Ave., Albany, NY 12210.
- New York State Sea Grant Program. Annual Report. a. ISSN 0360-3326
- Union List of Serials of the Libraries of the State University of New York. irreg., 1972, 4th ed. ISSN 0082-769X

**State University of New York, Agricultural and Technical College at Farmingdale. Social Science Department**
c/o Paul Lovizio, Farmingdale, NY 11735.
- American Italian Historical Association. Newsletter. 3 per yr. ISSN 0569-5961

**State University of New York at Albany**
1400 Washington Ave, Albany, NY 12203.
- Professional Communications: Libraries. bi-m. ISSN 0091-763X

**State University of New York at Albany. Department of Art**
Albany, NY 12203.
- Observation. a. ISSN 0078-2971

**State University of New York at Albany. Department of Philosophy**
- Metaphilosophy. (pub. by Basil Blackwell & Mott Ltd. UK)

**State University of New York at Albany. Faculty Senate**
8 Thurlow Terrace, Albany, NY 12201.
- State University of New York at Albany. Faculty Senate. Annual Faculty Assembly Proceedings. a. ISSN 0077-9350

**State University of New York at Albany. Graduate School of Public Affairs**
Mohawk Tower, Washington Ave., Albany, NY 12202.
- Helderberg Review. s-a. ISSN 0046-7197

**State University of New York at Albany. School of Library and Information Science**
1400 Washington Ave., Albany, NY 12222.
- State University of New York at Albany. School of Library and Information Science. Bulletin. biennial.

**State University of New York at Binghamton**
Box Z, Binghamton, NY 13901.
- Choice (Binghamton); a magazine of poetry and graphics. a.
- Nachalah. s-a.
- Pipe Dream. s-w. ISSN 0048-4210

**State University of New York at Binghamton. English Department**
Binghamton, NY 13901.
- Boundary 2; a journal of postmodern literature. 3 per yr.

**State University of New York at Binghamton. Max Reinhardt Archive**
Binghamton, NY 13901.
- Modern International Drama; magazine of comtemporary international drama in translation. s-a. ISSN 0026-7856

**State University of New York at Binghamton. Medieval Center**
Binghamton, NY 13901.
- Mediaevalia. a. ISSN 0361-946X

**State University of New York at Binghamton. School of Management**
Binghamton, NY 13901.
- Northeast Regional Science Review. a.

**State University of New York at Buffalo**
Buffalo, NY 14214.
- Philosophy and Phenomenological Research. q. ISSN 0031-8205
- Red Buffalo; a radical journal of American studies. ISSN 0048-699X
- Studies in Psychotherapy and Behavioral Change. irreg.

**State University of New York at Buffalo. Center for Immunology**
- Immunological Communications. (pub. by Marcel Dekker Journals)

**State University of New York at Buffalo. Center for Theoretical Biology**
4248 Ridge Lea Road, Amherst, NY 14226.
- Quarterly Bulletin of Theoretical Biology. irreg. (approx. 2-3 per yr.)

**State University of New York at Buffalo. Child Study Center**
1300 Elmwood Ave, Buffalo, NY 14222.
- Child Study Journal. q. ISSN 0009-4005

**State University of New York at Buffalo. Department of Classics**
Buffalo, NY 14261.
- Arethusa. s-a. ISSN 0004-0975

**State University of New York at Buffalo. Department of Foundational Studies**
1300 Elmwood Ave., Buffalo, NY 14222.
- Paideia; journal of foundational studies in education. a.

**State University of New York at Buffalo. Department of German and Slavic**
Ellicott Complex, Amherst Campus, 240 Crosby Hall, Buffalo, NY 14214.
- Lyrik und Prosa. q.

**State University of New York at Buffalo. Department of Italian, Spanish and Portuguese**
Buffalo, NY 14214.
- F I/Forum Italicum. q. ISSN 0014-5858

**State University of New York at Buffalo. Faculty of Law and Jurisprudence**
John Lord O'brian Hall, Amherst Campus, Buffalo, NY 14260.
- Buffalo Law Review. 4 per yr. ISSN 0023-9356

**State University of New York at Buffalo. Law Library**
Buffalo, NY 14214.
- State University of New York at Buffalo. Law Library. Law Library Periodicals. irreg. ISSN 0095-392X

**State University of New York at Buffalo. Program in East European and Slavic Studies**
c/o J. M. Ertavy-Barath, Ed., 1041 Stephenson Rd., Lithonia, GA 30058.
- State University of New York at Buffalo. Program in East European and Slavic Studies. Publications. irreg.

**State University of New York at Stony Brook**
230 Humanities Building, Stony Brook, NY 11790
- Gradiva; a journal of contemporary theory and practice. q. ISSN 0363-8057 (European Subscriptions to: Buri (Gradiva), Cassetta Postale 311, 30100-Venezia, Italy)

**State University of New York at Stony Brook. Department of Hispanic Languages and Literatures**
Stony Brook, NY 11790.
- Tlaloc. a.

**State University of New York, College at Brockport**
Brockport, NY 14420
- Literary Research Newsletter. q. ISSN 0362-1294 (Dist. by: M. A. O'Donnell, Department of English, Manhattan College, Bronx, NY 10471)

**State University of New York, College at Brockport. Department of Foreign Languages and Literatures**
Brockport, Ny 14420.
- Garcia Lorca Review. a.
- Literary Onomastics Studies. a.

**State University of New York, College at Buffalo. United Students Government, Inc.**
1300 Elmwood Ave., Buffalo, NY 14222.
- State University of New York. College at Buffalo. Record. s-w. ISSN 0039-0186

**State University of New York, College at Cortland. Department of Sociology and Anthropology**
Cortland, NY 13045.
- Third World Review. s-a.

**State University of New York, College at Fredonia. Department of Foreign Languages**
Fredonia, NY 14063.
- Nineteenth Century French Studies. q.

**State University of New York, College at Fredonia. Lake Erie Environmental Studies**
- World Directory of Environmental Research Centers. (pub. by Oryx Press)

**State University of New York, College at Fredonia. Office of College Relations**
Fredonia, NY 14063.
- Fredonia Statement. 8 per yr. ISSN 0046-4988

**State University of New York, College at Geneseo. School of Library and Information Science**
Geneseo, NY 14454
- Geneseo Studies in Library and Information Science. irreg. ISSN 0072-0801 (Order from: College Bookstore, SUNY at Geneseo, NY, 14454)
- Mary C. Richardson Lecture. a. ISSN 0076-4728
- State University College of Arts & Science at Geneseo. School of Library and Information Science. Newsletter. 3 per yr.

**State University of New York, College at New Paltz**
- Conch Review of Books. (pub. by Conch Magazine, Ltd.)

**State University of New York, College at Oneonta. Department of Political Science**
Oneonta, NY 13820.
- Asian Thought & Society: an International Review. 3 per yr. ISSN 0361-3968

**State University of New York, College at Plattsburgh. English Department**
Plattsburgh, NY 12901.
- Genre. q. ISSN 0016-6928

**State University of New York, College at Potsdam. Department of English**
Potsdam, NY 13676.
- Perspectives. irreg.

**State University of New York, College at Potsdam. Philosophy Department**
Potsdam, NY 13676.
- Agora. s-a. ISSN 0002-1016

**State University of New York. Downstate Medical Center**
450 Clarkson Ave., Brooklyn, NY 11203.
- Downstate Reporter. 3 per yr. ISSN 0012-5814
- State University of New York. Downstate Medical Center. Faculty Briefs. bi-m. ISSN 0039-0208
- What's News. fortn.

**State University of New York. Foundations of Education Association**
1300 Elmwood Ave., Buffalo, NY 14222.
- Foundational Studies. 2 per yr.

**State University of New York Librarians Association**
University Library, State University of New York, 1400 Washington Ave., Albany, NY 12222.
- S U N Y L A Newsletter. bi-m.

**State University of New York Press**
99 Washington Ave., Albany, NY 12246.
- Dante Studies; with the Annual Report of the Dante Society. a. ISSN 0070-2862
- Studies in Islamic Philosophy and Science. irreg.

**State University of New York. Research Foundation**
Box 9, Albany, NY 12201.
- Chronica. 5 per yr. ISSN 0009-594X
- Search at the State University of New York. q. ISSN 0360-8476

**State University of New York, Upstate Medical Center**
Library, 766 Irving Ave., Syracuse, NY 13210.
- New York (State) Upstate Medical Center, Syracuse. Library. Faculty Bibliography. irreg., latest issue 1969. ISSN 0077-9407
- New York (State) Upstate Medical Center, Syracuse. Library. Library Guide. biennial. ISSN 0077-9415
- State University of New York. Upstate Medical Center. Library Bulletin. m. ISSN 0024-2225

**Staten Island Community College**
715 Ocean Terrace, Staten Island, NY 10301.
- Dolphin. w. ISSN 0046-0516

**Staten Island Community College. Department of English**
715 Ocean Terrace, Staten Island, NY 10301.
- Outerbridge. s-a.

**Staten Island Historical Society**
Richmondtown, Staten Island, NY 10306.
- Staten Island Historian. q. ISSN 0039-0232

**Staten Island Institute of Arts and Sciences**
75 Stuyvesant Place, Staten Island, NY 10301.
- Staten Island Institute of Arts & Sciences. Proceedings. 3 per yr. ISSN 0039-0240

**Staten Island Zoological Society**
Staten Island, NY 10310.
- Animaland. q. ISSN 0019-3127

**Statewide Air Pollution Research Center**
University of California, Riverside, CA 92521.
- California Air Environment. 3 per yr. ISSN 0008-0861

**Statewide Homeowners Association**
953 Eighth Ave., San Diego, CA 92101.
- California Homeowner. q. ISSN 0008-1183

**Harry J. Stathos, Ed. & Pub.**
1345 Third Ave., New York, NY 10021.
- Hellenic Times. w.

**Stauffer Communications, Inc.**
616 Jefferson, Topeka, KS 66607.
- Capper's Weekly. fortn. ISSN 0008-5936

**Steamship Historical Society of America, Inc.**
c/o Mrs. Alice S. Wilson, Secy., 414 Pelton Ave., Staten Island, NY 10310.
- Steamboat Bill; relating primarily to steam and other power vessels, past and present. q. ISSN 0039-0844

**George R. Stearns, Ed. & Pub.**
12 E. Grand Ave., Chicago, IL 60611.
- Realty and Building. w. ISSN 0034-1045

**Peter N. Stearns, Ed. & Pub.**
Dept. of History, Carnegie Mellon University, Pittsburgh, PA 15213.
- Journal of Social History. q. ISSN 0022-4529

**Stechert-Macmillan Publishing Co., Inc.**
(Subsidiary of: Macmillan, Inc.)
866 Third Ave., New York, NY 10022.
- International Botanical Congress. Abstracts of Papers. irreg., 1970, vol. 11. ISSN 0074-2090
- International Botanical Congress. Proceedings. every five years, 11th, 1970.
- International Congress of Philosophy. Proceedings. irreg., 14th, 1971.

**Steel Founders' Society of America**
20611 Center Ridge Rd., Rocky River, OH 44116.
- Casteel. s-a. ISSN 0008-7483
- Directory of Steel Foundries in the United States, Canada and Mexico. biennial. ISSN 0070-6426
- Journal of Steel Castings Research. q. ISSN 0022-4723
- Steel Founders' Society of America. Research Report. irreg.

**Steel Structures Painting Council**
4400 Fifth Ave., Pittsburgh, PA 15213.
- Steel Structures Painting Bulletin. biennial.

**Stein and Day Publishers**
Scarbourough House, Briarcliff Manor, NY 10510.
- Blues Series. irreg.
- New Aspects of Archaeology. irreg.

**Stein Collectors International**
c/o J. Thomas Maccleland, 115 Haven Ct, Sacremento, CA 95831.
- Prosit; a quarterly bulletin for collectors of antique beer steins. q. ISSN 0016-6316

**John A. Stein, Ed. & Pub.**
1050 Sansome St., San Francisco, CA 94111.
- Pacific Shipper. w. ISSN 0030-8900

**Jerry Steinman, Ed. & Pub.**
55 Virginia Ave., W. Nyack, NY 10994.
- Beer Marketer's Insights. s-m. ISSN 0300-7480

**Steinway and Sons**
Steinway Place, Long Island City, NY 11105.
- Steinway News. q.

**Sten-O-Press**
Box 207, 1862 23rd St., San Pablo, CA 94806.
- Cal-O S H A Reporter. (California Occupational Safety and Health Act) w.

**Stephen F. Austin State University. School of Forestry**
Nacogdoches, TX 75961.
- Stephen F. Austin State University. School of Forestry. Bulletin. irreg., 1972, no. 25. ISSN 0082-318X
- Texas Forestry Papers. irreg., no. 16, 1972. ISSN 0082-304X

**Stephen F. Austin State University. School of Liberal Arts**
Nacogdoches, TX 75962.
- Re: Artes Liberales. s-a.

**Stephen Wise Congress House**
15 E. 84th St., New York, NY 10028.
- American Jewish Congress. News. m.

**Stephens College. Department of English**
Box 2085, Columbia, MO 65201.
- Open Places; a magazine of poetry, fiction and reviews. s-a.

**Steppenwolf**
P.O. Box 55045, Omaha, NE 68155.
- Steppenwolf; a journal of poetry and opinion. a. ISSN 0081-5462

**Steranko Supergraphics Publications**
Box 445, Wyomissing, PA 19610.
- Media Scene. bi-m.

**Beverly M. Stercula, Ed. & Pub.**
20602 107th St. E., Sumner, WA 98390.
- Thompson Family Magazine. q. ISSN 0040-6333

**Stereophile, Inc.**
Box 49, Elwyn, PA 19063.
- Stereophile; for the high-fidelity stereo perfectionist. q. ISSN 0585-2544

**Stereopus**
P.O. Box 269, Fort Walton Beach, FL 32548.
• Stereopus. q.

**A.M. Sterk, Ed. & Pub.**
P.O. Box 187, Milwaukee, WI 53201.
• Wisconsin Poetry. irreg.

**Sterling Group, Inc.**
315 Park Ave. S., New York, NY 10010.
• Who's Who in Movies. a. ISSN 0083-9639

**Sterling Publishing Co., Inc.**
419 Park Ave. S., New York, NY 10016.
• Book of Baseball Records. a.

**Sterling's Magazines, Inc.**
355 Lexington Ave., New York, NY 10017.
• Astrology Guide. m. ISSN 0004-6191 (Star
Guidance, Inc.)
• Daytime T V. m. ISSN 0011-7129
• Modern Love Confessions. m.
• Movie Mirror. m. ISSN 0027-271X
• Nightime T V. m.
• Photo Screen. m. ISSN 0031-8566
• Real Confessions. m. ISSN 0034-0642
• T V and Movie Screen. m. ISSN 0041-4492
• Your Personal Astrology Magazine. q. ISSN 0044-
1082

**Stern Brothers & Co.**
Box 13486, Kansas City, MO 64199.
• In Brief. m. ISSN 0019-3135

**Stern College for Women**
245 Lexington Ave., New York, NY 10016.
• Stern College for Women. Observer. fortn. (Sep.-
Jun.) ISSN 0029-7747

**Irving Stettner, Ed. & Pub.**
129 Second Ave, New York, NY 10003.
• Stroker; a poem-prose-art review. q.

**Stevens Alumni Association**
Castle Point Sta., Hoboken, NJ 07030.
• Stevens Indicator. q. ISSN 0039-1328

**Stevens Publishing**
8000 E. Girard, Denver, CO 80231.
• Denver. m.

**Stevens Publishing Corporation**
4901 Bosque Blvd., Box 7573, Waco, TX 76710.
• Dental Student; a journal for students and recent
graduates of dentistry. m.(Oct-June) ISSN 0011-
877X
• Occupational Health & Safety. bi-m.

**Steward Anthropological Society**
Department of Anthropology, University of Illinois,
Urbana, IL 61801.
• Steward Anthropological Society. Journal. s-a.
ISSN 0039-1344

**Stile Press**
c/o Dennis Ray, Ed., 667 Stony Hill Rd., Hinckley,
OH 44233.
• Stile. s-a.

**Stinktree Press**
Box 14762, Memphis, TN 38114.
• Stinktree. s-a. ISSN 0049-2264

**Stock Information Reporting Service (SIRS) Inc.**
Box 299, Edwardsburg, MI 49112.
• Growth Stock Digest. q. ISSN 0017-484X
• Stock Market Journal. m.

**Stock Research Corporation**
55 Liberty Street, New York, NY 10005.
• Weekly Insider Report. w.

**Stockbroker's Observer, Inc.**
4311 Wilshire Blvd., Suite 219, Los Angeles, CA
90010.
• Stockbroker's Observer; voice of Western finance.
q.

**Stockton-San Joaquin County Library**
605 N. El Dorado St., Stockton, CA 95202.
• Stockton-San Joaquin County Public Library
Newsletter. bi-m. ISSN 0039-1662

**Stockton Teachers Association**
Box 8465, Stockton, CA 95204.
• S T A Educator. irreg. ISSN 0036-1941

**Stoller Research Co. Inc.**
Box 1071, Santa Cruz, CA 95060.
• Science and Practice of Mushroom Growing. q.
ISSN 0036-8210

**Roy A. Stone**
Box 509, Crossville, TN 38555.
• Trade-A-Plane. 3 per mo. ISSN 0041-0365

**Stone Country Press**
20 Lorraine Rd., Madison, NJ 07940.
• Stone Country; a magazine of poetry, art, and
letters. 3 per yr.

**Stone County Historical Society**
Mountain View, AR 72560.
• Heritage of Stone. q.

**Lee Stone, Ed. & Pub.**
704 Taylor, Topeka, KS 66603.
• Write-In, USA. m.(except Aug.) ISSN 0049-819X

**Stone Magazine**
1324 Euclid, Boulder, CO 80302.
• Stone. s-a. ISSN 0039-176X

**Stone Press**
5399 1/2 Bryant, Oakland, CA 94618.
• J. w.

**Stone Press (Okemos)**
1790 Grand River, Okemos, MI 48864.
• Happiness Holding Tank. 4 per yr. ISSN 0046-
6832

**Stone Soup Society, Inc.**
Stone Soup Gallery, 313 Cambridge St., Boston,
MA 02114.
• Stone Soup Poetry. bi-m.

**Stony Brook Foundation, Inc.**
State Univ. of New York, Stony Brook, NY 11794.
• Quarterly Review of Biology. q. ISSN 0033-5770

**Stony Brook- Millstone Watersheds Association, Inc.**
Box 171, Pennington, NJ 08534.
• Watershed News. 6 per yr. ISSN 0043-1494

**Stoody Co.**
16425 Gale Ave., Industry, CA 91745.
• Fusion Facts. q. ISSN 0016-3171

**Everett L. Storey, Ed. & Pub.**
Suite 703, First National Bank Bldg., Las Vegas,
NV 89101.
• West. q. ISSN 0043-2938

**Storm & Associates**
P.O. Box 367, Urbana, IL 61801.
• Water Equipment News. m.

**Storrs Agricultural Experiment Station**
University of Connecticut, Storrs, CT 06268.
• Storrs Agricultural Experiment Station. Research
Report. irreg., 1967, no. 20. ISSN 0069-8997

**James Stout, Ed. & Pub.**
1325 Rimrock Dr., San Jose, CA 95120.
• Light Song. 4 per yr.

**Stover Publishing Co.**
Box 471, 131 N. York Road, Willow Grove, PA
19090.
• Asbestos. m. ISSN 0004-4237

**Stover Quarterly**
c/o Sheila Spencer Stover, 1279 Union St., Bangor,
ME 04401.
• Stover Quarterly. q.

**Straight Arrow Publishers**
745 Fifth Ave., New York, NY 10022.
• Rolling Stone. s-m. ISSN 0035-791X

**Straight Creek Publishing Co.**
2051 York, Denver, CO 80205.
• Straight Creek Journal. w.

**Straight Enterprises**
551 Fifth Ave., New York, NY 10017.
• Antiques. m. ISSN 0003-5939

**Straight to Hell**
Box 982, Radio City, New York, NY 10019.
• Straight to Hell. m.

**Strange Faeces**
c/o Bruce Hutchinson, 122 New Wickham Dr.,
Penfield, NY 14625.
• Strange Faeces. 3-4 per yr.

**Strato Publishing Co.**
209 East 56th St., New York, NY 10022.
• Revista Aerea Latinoamericana; la revista de
aviacion para las Americas. m. ISSN 0034-6934

**Stratton Intercontinental Medical Book Corporation**
381 Park Avenue South, New York, NY 10016.
• Advances in Pathobiology. irreg, vol. 1, 1975.
• Pediatric Nephrology. irreg. ISSN 0097-5257
• Seminars in Hematology. q. ISSN 0037-1963
• Seminars in Roentgenology. q. ISSN 0037-198X
• Seminars in Thrombosis and Hemostasis. q. ISSN
0094-6176

**Straub Clinic & Hospital, Inc.**
888 S. King St., Honolulu, HI 96813.
• Straub Clinic Proceedings. q. ISSN 0039-2251

**Straw Enterprises, Inc.**
312 Franklin St., Clarksville, TN 37040.
• Business Opportunities Digest; clearing house of
business opportunities information. m. ISSN 0007-
6953

**Strawbridge & Clothier**
801 Market St., Philadelphia, PA 19105.
• Store Chat. m.(10 per yr) ISSN 0039-1840

**Strawhecker Printing Co.**
1447 Regina St., Harrisburg, PA 17103.
• Pennsylvania Chiefs of Police Association
Bulletin. q. ISSN 0031-4404 (Pennsylvania Chiefs
of Police Association)

**Street**
1 Somerset Ave., Mastic, NY 11950.
• Street. 4 per yr.

**Street Cries**
Box 210, Old Westbury, NY 11568.
• Street Cries. s-a.

**Street Fiction Press**
201 E. Liberty St., Ann Arbor, MI 48108.
• Anon Nine. irreg.
• Periodical Lunch. bi-m.

**Strength and Health Publishing Co.**
Box 1707, York, PA 17405.
• Muscular Development. bi-m. ISSN 0047-8415
• Strength & Health Magazine. bi-m. ISSN 0039-
2308 (York Barbell Co)

**Strike It Rich Publications**
Suite 211 F, Bank of Kendall Bldg., 8603 S. Dixie
Highway, Miami, FL 33143.
• Whats and Whens. m.

**Strout Realty**
Plaza Towers, Springfield, MO 65804.
• Strout World. m. ISSN 0039-2545

**Stryker-Post Publications Inc.**
888 Seventeenth St., N.W., Washington, DC 20006.
• World Today Series: Africa. a. ISSN 0084-2281
• World Today Series: Far East and Southwest
Pacific. a. ISSN 0084-229X
• World Today Series: Latin America. a. ISSN
0084-2303
• World Today Series: Middle East and South Asia.
a. ISSN 0084-2311
• World Today Series: Soviet Union and Eastern
Europe. a. ISSN 0084-232X
• World Today Series: Western Europe. a. ISSN
0084-2338

**Stubs Publications**
• Stubs. (pub. by Meyer Schattner)

**Studebaker Family National Association**
781 West Drive, Woodruff Place, Indianapolis, IN
46201.
• Studebaker Story. q. ISSN 0300-8703

**Student American Pharmaceutical Association**
2215 Constitution Ave. N.W., Washington, DC
20037.
• S A P H A News. bi-m.

**Student American Pharmaceutical Association. Ohio Northern University Chapter**
Ohio Northern Univ. College of Pharmacy, Ada, OH 45810.
- Ampul. q. ISSN 0003-2042

**Student Association for the Study of Hallucinogens**
- Journal of Psychedelic Drugs. (pub. by Stash)

**Student Conservation Association**
P.O. Box 573-A, Olympic View Drive, Rte. 1, Vashon, WA 98070.
- Conversational Conservation. irreg.

**Student Government Association, SUC at Potsdam**
- Racquette. (pub. by Northern New York Publishing Co.)

**Student National Education Association**
1201 16th St. N.W., Washington, DC 20036.
- Impact: Forum of the Student National Education Association. 4 per yr'

**Student National Medical Association**
2109 E Street, N. W., Suite 400, Washington, DC 20037.
- Black Bag. q.

**Student Non-Violent Coordinating Committee**
360 Nelson St. S.W., Atlanta, GA 30313.
- S N C C Newsletter. m. ISSN 0036-1712

**Student Struggle for Soviet Jewry**
200 W. 72nd St. Suites 30-31, New York, NY 10023.
- S. O. S. Soviet Jewry. 4 per yr. ISSN 0036-1798
- Soviet Jewry Action Newsletter. fortn. ISSN 0038-5468

**Student Zionist Organization**
4 E. 34th St., New York, NY 10016.
- Zionist Collegiate. 5 per yr. ISSN 0044-4766

**Students of Boston University**
Box 371 Boston Univ. Sta., Boston, MA 02215.
- Free Press. fortn. ISSN 0016-0415

**Students of Holy Cross College**
Worcester, MA 01610.
- Holy Cross Purple. s-a. ISSN 0018-3733

**Students of Mercer University**
Box 1210, Macon, GA 31207.
- Mercer Cluster; pacesetter of the seventies. w. ISSN 0025-9853

**Students of Southern University**
Box 10215-Southern Branch P.O., Baton Rouge, LA 70813.
- Southern Digest. w.

**Students of the Brooklyn Law School**
250 Joralemon St., Brooklyn, NY 11201.
- Brooklyn Law Review. 4 per yr. ISSN 0007-2362

**Students Ski Association**
c/o Kim Chaffee, 233 N. Pleasant St., Amherst, MA 01002.
- Student Skier. 4 per yr (Sep.-Jun.)

**Studia Slovenica**
Box 232, New York, NY 10032
(and Box 4531, Washington, DC 20017)
- Studia Slovenica. irreg., no. 9, 1974. ISSN 0585-5543
- Studia Slovenica. Special Series. irreg., 1971, no. 2. ISSN 0081-6922

**Studies in Philosophy and Education Inc.**
Southern Illinois Univ., Edwardsville, IL 62025.
- Studies in Philosophy and Education. q. ISSN 0039-3746 (Co-Sponsor: Philosophy of Education Society)

**Studio Museum in Harlem**
2033 Fifth Ave, New York, NY 10035.
- Studio Museum in Harlem. q.

**Stump**
c/o Douglas Knapp, Box 1049, Athens, OH 45701.
- Stump. s-a.

**Stylus (Brockport)**
College Center, Brockport, NY 14420.
- Stylus (Brockport) w. ISSN 0039-4289

**Subdued Publications Ltd.**
Box 12486, Milwaukee, WI 53212.
- Milwaukee Bugle. 36 per yr. ISSN 0045-3366

**Subject Index to Children's Magazines**
2223 Chamberlain Ave., Madison, WI 53705.
- Subject Index to Children's Magazines. m. (semi-annual cumulations in Feb. & Aug) ISSN 0039-4351

**Subterrranean Sociological Association**
Dept. of Sociology, Eastern Michigan University, Ypsilanti, MI 48197.
- Subterranean Sociology Newsletter. 2 per yr. ISSN 0039-4394

**Suburban Action Institute**
257 Park Ave. So., New York, NY 10010.
- Regional Equity. 4-5 per yr.

**Suburban Home Buys**
Hunting Ridge Mall, Bedford Village, NY 10506.
- Suburban Home Buys. fortn.

**Suburban Homes Guide**
Hunting Ridge Mall, Bedford Village, NY 10506.
- Suburban Homes Guide. s-a.

**Suburban Newspapers, Inc.**
6601 West 78th St., Minneapolis, MN 55435.
- Commercial West. w. ISSN 0010-3144

**Suburban Publishing Co.**
Main St., Pleasant Valley, NY 12569.
- Hudson Valley Magazine. m.

**Success Publications, Inc.**
3121 Maple Dr. N.E., Suite 1, Atlanta, GA 30305.
- Success Orientation; the management newsletter for supervisors, salesmen, and personal development. m.

**Success Publishing Co. Inc.**
13263 Ventura Blvd., Studio City, CA 91604.
- Money Making Opportunities. 8 per yr.

**Success Unlimited, Inc.**
Arcade Bldg., 6355 Broadway, Chicago, IL 60660.
- Success Unlimited. m. ISSN 0039-4424

**Successful Meetings. Directory Department**
633 Third Ave., New York, NY 10017.
- Directory of Conventions. a. plus supplement. ISSN 0417-5751

**Suction**
c/o Darrell Gray, Ed., 197 14th St., San Francisco, CA 94103.
- Suction. irreg.

**Suffolk County Community College. English Department**
Selden, NY 11784.
- Long Pond Review. s-a.

**Suffolk County Dental Society**
130 W. Sixth St., Deer Park, NY 11729.
- Suffolk County Dental Society. Bulletin. 6 per yr. ISSN 0039-4688

**Suffolk County Library Association**
Data Editor, Box 188, Bellport, NY 11713.
- S C L A Data. s-a. ISSN 0036-1143

**Suffolk University Law School**
41 Temple St., Boston, MA 02114.
- Suffolk University Law Review. 5 per yr. ISSN 0039-4696

**Sugar Journal**
c/o Wm. Flanagan, 107 Camp St., New Orleans, LA 70130.
- Sugar Journal. m. ISSN 0039-4734

**Sugar Publications**
503 Broadway, Fargo, ND 58102.
- Sugarbeet Grower. 6 per yr. ISSN 0039-4750

**Sulphur Institute**
1725 K St. N.W., Washington, DC 20006.
- Sulphur Institute. Technical Bulletin. irreg., no. 22, 1977. ISSN 0081-9255

**Summer Institute of Linguistics**
see also under **Peru Instituto Linguistico de Verano**

**Summer Institute of Linguistics**
- Notes on Literacy. (pub. by Academic Publications)
- S I L Publications in Linguistics and Related Fields. (pub. by Academic Publications)
- Summer Institute of Linguistics. Language Data. African Series. (pub. by Academic Publications)
- Summer Institute of Linguistics. Language Data. Amerindian Series. (pub. by Academic Publications)
- Summer Institute of Linguistics. Language Data. Asian-Pacific Series. (pub. by Academic Publications)
- Summer Institute of Linguistics. Publications Catalog. (pub. by Academic Publications)

**Murray Summers, Ed. & Pub.**
Orlean, VA 22128.
- Filmograph. q. ISSN 0015-1629

**Summit**
44 Mill Creek Rd., Big Bear Lake, CA 92315.
- Summit; a mountaineering magazine. bi-m. ISSN 0039-5056

**Summit County Labor News**
969 Grant St., Akron, OH 44311.
- Summit County Labor News. w. ISSN 0039-5064

**Summit Publishing Co.**
6836 San Pedro Ave., Suite 116, San Antonio, TX 78216.
- Southwest Airlines. m.

**Sun**
456 Riverside Drive-5B, New York, NY 10027.
- Sun. s-a. ISSN 0039-5374

**Sun and Moon**
4330 Hartwick Rd., College Park, MD 20740.
- Sun and Moon; a quarterly of literature and art. q.

**Sun Co., Inc.**
Box 790, Espanola, NM 87532.
- Rio Grande Sun. w.

**Sun Oil Co.**
1608 Walnut St., Philadelphia, PA 19103.
- Our Sun. 3 per yr.

**Sun Oil Company**
Economics and Industry Affairs, 240 Radnor-Chester Road, St. Davids, PA 19087.
- Analysis of World Tank Ship Fleet. a.

**Sun Publishing Co.**
81 Division St., New York, NY 10014.
- Novi Napriamy/New Directions. q.

**Sun Valley Co.**
Sun Valley, ID 83353.
- Sun Valley. m.

**Sunburst Anthology**
c/o Clarence Poulin, Ed., 87 High St., Penacook, NH 03301.
- Sunburst Anthology. a.

**Sunbury**
Box 528, Planetarium Station, New York, NY 10024.
- Sunbury; a poetry magazine. 3 per yr.

**Sunbury Press**
Box 274, Jerome Station, Bronx, NY 10468.
- Sunbury Poetry Chapbooks. irreg.
- Sunbury Women Chapbooks. irreg.

**Suncat Enterprises**
1471 Second Ave., Apt. 19, New York, NY 10021.
- Crossroads Quarterly. q.

**Suncraft International Corp.**
Box 115, Ward Hill, MA 01830.
- Filmmakers' Newsletter. m. ISSN 0015-1610

**Sunday Publications Inc.**
3003 S. Congress Avenue, Palm Springs, FL 33461.
- Nova et Vetera. 10 per yr.

**Sundby Sports Inc.**
410 Broadway, Santa Monica, CA 90401.
- International Gymnast. m.

**Sunrise**
Box 271, Macomb, IL 61455.
- Sunrise. m.

**Sunstone Press**
P.O. Box 2321, Santa Fe, NM 87501.
- Sunstone Review. q. ISSN 0049-2558

**Suomi College**
601 Quincy St., Hancock, MI 49930.
- Suomi-Opiston Viesti. q. ISSN 0300-7820

**Superior Stamp and Coin Co. Inc.**
9301 Wilshire Blvd., Beverly Hills, CA 90210.
- Money Talks. 10 per yr.

**Supreme Committee for Liberation of Lithuania**
- Elta. (pub. by Lithuanian National Foundation, Inc.)

**Supreme Court Historical Society**
1629 K St., Washington, DC 20006.
- Supreme Court Historical Society. Yearbook. a. ISSN 0362-5249

**Supreme Court of the State of Israel**
- Israel. Supreme Court. Selected Judgments. (pub. by Oceana Publications Inc.)

**Supreme Grand Lodge of AMORC, Inc.**
Rosicrucian Park, San Jose, CA 95191.
- Rosacruz. bi-m. ISSN 0035-8266

**Supreme Lodge of the Ancient Order of the United Workmen**
P.O. Box 98830, Seattle, WA 98188.
- Ancient Order of United Workmen. Supreme Lodge. Report of Officers and Proceedings. biennial. ISSN 0090-8010

**Surfer Publications**
Box 1028, Dana Point, CA 92629.
- Powder. 5 per yr.
- Skateboarder. bi-m.
- Surfer; the international surfing magazine. bi-m. ISSN 0039-6036

**Surfside Poetry Review**
P.O. Box 289, Surfside, CA 90743.
- Surfside Poetry Review. q.

**Surplus Record, Inc.**
20 N. Wacker Dr., Chicago, IL 60606.
- Surplus Record; index of available capital equipment. m. ISSN 0039-615X

**Survey of Ophthalmology, Inc.**
80 Boylston St., Suite 825, Boston, MA 02116.
- Survey of Ophthalmology. bi-m. ISSN 0039-6257

**Survival Magazine**
2247 Prince St., Berkeley, CA 94705.
- Survival Magazine. q. ISSN 0039-6346

**Survival of American Indians Association**
Box 719, Tacoma, WA 98401.
- Renegade. irreg.

**Surviving in America**
c/o H. Samuel Hamod, 1612 Euclid Ave., Flint, MI 48503.
- Surviving in America. 2 per yr.

**Susquehanna Classicists Association**
Franklin and Marshall College, Lancaster, PA 17604.
- Susquehanna Newsletter. s-a.

**Susquehanna River Basin Commission**
Mechanicsburg, PA 17055.
- Susquehanna River Basin Commission. Annual Report. a. ISSN 0094-6427

**Susquehanna University Alumni Association**
Susquehanna University, Selinsgrove, PA 17870.
- Susquehanna Alumnus. q.

**Susquehanna Valley Regional Medical Program**
Box 541, Camp Hill, PA 17011.
- S V R M P Newsletter. irreg. ISSN 0036-2042

**Susquehannock Trail Club**
c/o Mrs. Wilbur Ahn, R.D. 6, Ulysses, PA 16948.
- Susquehannock Hiker. a.

**Sutherland Publications, Inc.**
4801 Montgomery Lane, Washington, DC 20014.
- Modern Bulk Transporter. m. ISSN 0031-6431

**Mr. Gail Sutton**
218 Walnut Place, Oracle, AZ 85623.
- Mount to the Stars. s-a. ISSN 0027-2515 (Hod Mother Earth Tribe)

**Sutton Place Publications**
13132 W. Dixie Highway, Miami, FL 33161.
- Franchising Investments Around the World. 10 per yr.

**Sutton Publishing Co. Inc.**
172 S. Broadway, White Plains, NY 10605.
- Contractors' Electrical Equipment. m. ISSN 0010-7913
- Electrical Equipment. m. ISSN 0013-4325

**Suzuki Association of the Americas**
Box 164, Mendham, NJ 07945.
- American Suzuki Journal. q.

**Swap**
Box 1048, Adler Center, Champaign, IL 61820.
- Swap. q.

**Swarthmore College. Swarthmore College Student Council**
Swarthmore, PA 19081.
- Phoenix. s-w.

**Swedenborg Foundation**
139 E. 23 St., New York, NY 10010.
- Swedenborg Foundation Newsletter. s-a.

**Swedenborg Scientific Association**
Bryn Athyn, PA 19009.
- New Philosophy. q. ISSN 0028-6443

**Swedenborgian Church**
Department of Publication, 48 Sargent St., Newton, MA 02158.
- New Church Messenger. m. ISSN 0028-4424

**Swedish Information Service**
825 Third Avenue, New York, NY 10022.
- News from Sweden. m.

**Swedish Pioneer Historical Society, Inc.**
5125 N. Spaulding Ave., Chicago, IL 60625.
- Swedish Pioneer Historical Quarterly. 4 per yr. ISSN 0039-7326

**Sweet Briar Alumnae Association**
Sweet Briar College, Sweet Briar, VA 24595.
- Sweet Briar College. Alumnae Magazine. q. ISSN 0039-7342

**Sweet Home Central School District-Towns of Amherst and Tonawanda**
1901 Sweet Home Rd., Buffalo, NY 14221.
- Your Schools. 10 per yr. ISSN 0044-1112

**Sweet Publishing Co.**
Box 4055, Austin, TX 78765.
- Living Word Commentary. irreg., latest issue no. 14. ISSN 0076-0080

**Swift & Co.**
115 W. Jackson Blvd., Chicago, IL 60604.
- Mark. q.

**Swift-Dorr Publications**
17 Suncrest Terrace, Oneonta, NY 13820.
- Woodwind World-Brass & Percussion. 6 per yr. ISSN 0098-4574

**Swimming World, Inc.**
8622 Bellanca, Los Angeles, CA 90045.
- Swimming Technique. q. ISSN 0039-7415
- Swimming World. m. ISSN 0039-7431

**Swiss American Historical Society**
Old Dominion University, Norfolk, VA 23508.
- S A H S Newsletter. 3 per yr. ISSN 0036-0740

**Swiss Publishing Co., Inc.**
548 Columbus Ave., San Francisco, CA 94133.
- Swiss Journal/Schweizer Journal. w. ISSN 0039-7474

**Swiss Reinsurance Co.**
- Annals of Life Insurance Medicine. (pub. by Springer-Verlag)

**Swizzle Stick Enterprises**
Box 370, 1204 Chimes Terrace, Vineland, NJ 08360.
- Swizzle Stick; magazine of fine wines, beers, liquors. bi-m. ISSN 0090-9009

**Sword of the Lord Publishers**
Box 1099, 224 Bridge Ave., Murfreesboro, TN 37130.
- Sword of the Lord. w. ISSN 0039-7547

**Swordsman Publishing Co.**
2961 W. Eighth St., Los Angeles, Calif.
- Swordsman Review. q. ISSN 0039-7555

**Symcon Marine Corp**
- World Dredging & Marine Construction. (pub. by Symcon Publishing Co.)

**Symcon Publishing Co.**
444 W. Ocean Bl., Long Beach, CA 90802
(Mailing Address: Box 31, Long Beach CA 90801)
- Marine Equipment News. bi-m. ISSN 0025-3332
- World Dredging & Marine Construction. m. ISSN 0043-8405 (Symcon Marine Corp)

**Symphonette Press**
6 Commercial St., Hicksville, NY 11803.
- Crimes and Punishment Encyclopedia. m.

**Synagogue Council of America. Institute for Jewish Policy Planning and Research**
432 Park Ave. South, New York, NY 10016
- Analysis. m(10 per yr.) (And 1776 Massachusetts Ave. N. W., Washington, DC 20036)

**Synapse Inc.**
4307 Locust St., Philadelphia, PA 19104.
- Whole City Catalog; a directory of human resources in the Delaware Valley. a.

**Syndicate Inc.**
Box 242, Lewisville, TX 75067.
- Nostalgia Journal. fortn.

**Syndicate Magazines Inc.**
6 E. 43 St., New York, NY 10017.
- Art Material Trade News; the journal of all art & craft supplies. m. ISSN 0004-3265 (National Art Material Trade Association)
- Art Material Trade News Directory of Art & Craft Materials. a.
- Better Nutrition. m. ISSN 0405-668X
- Graphics Today. bi-m.
- Health Foods Retailing. m. ISSN 0017-8977 (National Nutritional Foods Association)
- Today's Art. m. ISSN 0493-3656
- Today's Living. m.

**Synerjy**
Box 4790, Grand Central Sta., New York, NY 10017.
- Synerjy; a directory of energy alternatives. s-a.

**Syntex Laboratories Inc.**
3401 Hillview Ave., Palo Alto, CA 94304.
- Family Planner. bi-m.

**Synthesis Communications, Inc.**
125 West 69 St., New York, NY 10023.
- Computer Technology & Biomedicine. bi-m.

**Synthesis Journal**
830 Woodside Rd., Ste. 5, Redwood City, CA 94061.
- Synthesis: the Realization of the Self. 3 per yr.

**Synthetic Organic Chemical Manufacturers Association**
1075 Central Park Ave., Scarsdale, NY 10583.
- S O C M A Newsletter. m.

**Syracuse Peace Council**
924 Burnet Ave., Syracuse, NY 13203.
- Peace Newsletter; central NY's antiwar /social justice paper. m.

**Syracuse University**
c/o Hendricks Chapel, Syracuse, NY 13210.
- Haotz/Thorn. s-a.

**Syracuse University. Center on Human Policy**
216 Ostrum Ave., Syracuse, NY 13210.
- Center on Human Policy. Notes from the Center. irreg.

**Syracuse University College of Law**
c/o John Zappe, Ed., E. I. White Hall, Syracuse, NY 13210.
- Judge. w. ISSN 0022-5789
- Syracuse Journal of International Law & Commerce. s-a. ISSN 0093-0709
- Syracuse Law Review. q. ISSN 0039-7938

**Syracuse University. Continuing Education Center for the Public Service**
610 E. Fayette St., Syracuse, NY 13202.
- Metropinion; a journal of public affairs. q.

**Syracuse University. Department of English**
Syracuse, NY 13210.
- Thoth. 3 per yr. ISSN 0040-6430

**Syracuse University. Department of Geography**
- Syracuse Geographical Series. (pub. by Syracuse University Press)

**Syracuse University. Department of Religion**
Syracuse, NY 13210.
- B. G. Rudolph Lectures in Judaic Studies. a. ISSN 0067-2742

**Syracuse University. Department of Romance Languages**
- Symposium. (pub. by Syracuse University Press)

**Syracuse University. Family Planning and Population Information Center**
- S I S I M S. (pub. by Ed-U Press)

**Syracuse University. Libraries**
Syracuse, NY 13210.
- Syracuse University. Libraries. Annual Report. a. ISSN 0094-5900

**Syracuse University Library Associates**
661 Bird Library, Syracuse Univ., Syracuse, NY 13210.
- Courier (Syracuse) q. ISSN 0011-0418

**Syracuse University. Maxwell Graduate Student Association**
Maxwell Graduate School of Citizenship & Public Affairs, Syracuse, NY 13210.
- Maxwell Review. s-a. ISSN 0025-6110

**Syracuse University Press**
1011 E. Water St., Syracuse, NY 13210.
- Education in Large Cities Series. irreg., no. 4, 1972. ISSN 0070-9239
- Procedural Aspects of International Law Series. irreg; vol. 11, 1972. ISSN 0079-5828 (Or: University Press of Virginia, Box 3608 University Sta., Charlottesville, VA 22903)
- Special Education and Rehabilitation Monograph Series. irreg; no. 12, 1977. ISSN 0081-3532
- Symposium; a quarterly journal in modern foreign literatures. q. ISSN 0039-7709 (Syracuse University. Department of Romance Languages)
- Syracuse Geographical Series. irreg; no. 4, 1975. ISSN 0082-1160 (Syracuse University. Department of Geography)

**Syracuse University. Program of East African Studies**
119 College Pl., Syracuse, NY 13210.
- Syracuse University. Program of East African Studies. East African Bibliographic Series. irreg., no. 3 latest issue. ISSN 0586-3414
- Syracuse University. Program of East African Studies. Eastern African Studies. irreg., vol. 18, 1975.
- Syracuse University. Program of East African Studies. Occasional Bibliographies. irreg., no. 24, 1974. ISSN 0586-3422
- Syracuse University. Program of East African Studies. Occasional Papers. irreg., no. 57, 1970. ISSN 0586-3430
- Syracuse University. Program of East African Studies. Special Publications. irreg., no. 3, 1971.

**Syracuse University. Publications in Continuing Education**
224 Huntington Hall, 150 Marshall St., Syracuse, NY 13210.
- Syracuse University Publications in Continuing Education. Landmark and New Horizons Series. irreg.
- Syracuse University Publications in Continuing Education. Notes and Essays. irreg.
- Syracuse University Publications in Continuing Education. Occasional Papers. irreg., no. 46, 1976. ISSN 0082-1179

**Syracuse University. School of Education**
Syracuse, NY 13210.
- Resources for Educators of Adults. irreg.

**Syracuse University School of Information Studies. Subject Access Project**
113 Euclid Ave., Syracuse, NY 13210.
- Syracuse University. School of Information Studies. Subject Access Project. Occasional Newsletter. irreg.

**Systemation, Inc.**
Box 730, Colorado Springs, CO 80901.
- Systemation Service. m. ISSN 0039-8004

**T A W Publishing Co.**
9731 Riverside Dr., Greenville, MI 48838.
- Trails-a-Way. 10 per yr.

**T-E Publications, Inc.**
522 Briar Oak Lane, San Antonio, TX 78216.
- Total Energy. m. ISSN 0040-9707

**T.F.H. Publications, Inc.**
211 W. Sylvania Ave., Neptune City, NJ 07753.
- Tropical Fish Hobbyist. m. ISSN 0041-3259

**T.I.L.L.**
67 E. Shore Rd., Huntington, NY 11743.
- Individualized Learning Letter. 13 per yr.

**T R**
424 Commercial Square, Cincinnati, OH 45202.
- T R. (Tobacco Reporter); devoted to all segments of the international tobacco trade. m. ISSN 0361-5693

**T R A Publishing Co.**
P.O. Box 40909, San Francisco, CA 94140.
- T R A. (Toward Revolutionary Art) q.

**T R M Publications Inc.**
1132 N. Brookhurst St., Anaheim, CA 92801.
- Street Chopper. m. ISSN 0049-2329
- Street Rodder. m.
- Truckin' m.

**T R Report**
225 S. 15th St., Philadelphia, PA 19102.
- Travelore Report. m.

**T R W. Systems Application Center**
1 Space Park, Redondo Beach, CA 90278.
- T R W Space Log. a. ISSN 0082-1349

**T V Digest, Inc.**
520 University Ave, St. Paul, MN 55103.
- T V Digest. w. ISSN 0041-4506

**T V News Company, Inc.**
Box 20226, 6330 Ferguson St., Indianapolis, IN 46220.
- T V News. w.

**T. V. Sports, Inc.**
Box 58, Rockville Centre, NY 11571.
- International Boxing. bi-m.
- World Boxing. bi-m.

**Tablet Publishing Co.**
1 Hanson Place, Brooklyn, NY 11243.
- Tablet. w. ISSN 0039-8845 (Roman Catholic Diocese of Brooklyn)

**Tacoma Area Chamber of Commerce**
Box 1933, Tacoma, WA 98401.
- Tacoma Area Progress. m.

**Tafnews Press**
Box 296, Los Altos, CA 94022.
- Association of Track and Field Statsticians. Annual. a. ISSN 0361-8048

**Taft Corporation**
1000 Vermont Ave., N.W., Washington, DC 20005.
- News Monitor of Philanthropy; a supplement to the "Taft information system". m.

**Taggart Publishing Co.**
Box 50361, Dallas, TX 75250.
- Psychic World. bi-m.

**Take Over**
Box 706, Madison, WI 53701.
- Take Over. fortn. ISSN 0049-2868

**Talcott Communications Corp.**
1111 E. Touhy Ave., Des Plaines, IL 60018.
- Giftware News; the national magazine for gifts, china and glass, stationery and home accessories. bi-m.

**Tales Publishing Co.**
Box 24226, St. Louis, Missouri.
- Tales. q.

**Talisman**
c/o Blythe Ayne, Ed., Box 80713, Lincoln, NE 68501.
- Talisman. 4 per yr.

**Talisman Co.**
Box 948, Chicago, IL 60690.
- Popular Talisman Bulletin; bi-monthly publication for cultivating practical creativity. bi-m. ISSN 0032-4655

**Talladega College**
Talladega, Alabama.
- Talladegan. 5 per yr.

**Tallahassee Tall Timbers Research Station**
Route 1, Box 160, Tallahassee, FL 32303.
- Tall Timbers Conference on Ecological Animal Control by Habitat Management. Proceedings. irreg. ISSN 0070-833X
- Tall Timbers Fire Ecology Conference. Proceedings. a. ISSN 0082-1527

**Tamalpais Union High School District**
Larkspur, CA 94939.
- Tamalpais Union High School District. District Doings. m. ISSN 0012-4001

**Tamarind Institute**
108 Cornell Ave., S.E., Albuquerque, NM 87106.
- Tamarind Institute Report. q.
- Tamarind Technical Papers. s-a.

**Tams-Witmark Music Library, Inc.**
757 Third Ave., New York, NY 10017.
- Musical Show; devoted to the amateur presentation of Broadway musical shows on the stage. 6 per yr. ISSN 0027-4658

**Tamworth Swine Association**
R. 2 Box 126-A, Hillsboro, OH 45133.
- Tamworth Annual. irreg. ISSN 0082-1608

**Tan King Publications, Inc**
9712 Robin Hill Lane, Dallas, TX 75238.
- Let's Gossip; the daytime soap opera review. m.

**Tandy Corp.**
c/o Pub. John Ratliff, 1303 Foch St., Fort Worth, TX 76107.
- Decorating & Craft Ideas. m.(except Jan. & July)

**Tangent (Estuary Press)**
9075 River Styx Rd., Wadsworth, OH 44281.
- Tangent. q. ISSN 0039-9388

**Tankian Publishing Corp.**
G.P.O. Box 638, New York, NY 10001.
- Arab Digest. m.
- Armenian Digest. m. ISSN 0004-2323

**Tanner Publications Co., Inc.**
515 Madison Ave., New York, NY 10022.
- Encore American & Worldwide News. fortn. ISSN 0046-1954

**Tanners' Council of America, Inc.**
411 Fifth Ave., New York, NY 10016.
- Tanners' Council of America, Inc. Council News. w. ISSN 0010-9932

**Tansy**
1144 1/2 Indiana, Lawrence, KS 66044.
- Tansy. s-a.

**Tao-Tao Industries**
Box 2342, Palo Alto, CA 94305.
- China Medical Reporter. m (Sept.-June) ISSN 0090-5003

**Tapco Ltd.**
Box 307, Pemberton, NJ 08068.
- Burlington County Times Advertiser. w. ISSN 0007-6279

**Tape Deck Quarterly**
Box 1592, 20 Hampton Rd., Southhampton, NY 11968.
- Tape Deck Quarterly. q.

**Taplinger Publishing Co.**
200 Park Ave. S., New York, NY 10003.
- Who's Who in Literature Series. irreg.

**Target Communications Corp.**
Box 106, Northfield, IL 60093.
- Construction Machinery Maintenance. bi-m.

**Target Publishers**
Box 172, 1451 Danville Blvd., Alamo, CA 94507.
- Ruff Times. s-m.

**Tariffs and Trade**
P.O. Box 307, Ansonia Station, New York, NY 10023.
- Tariffs and Trade. bi-m. ISSN 0494-7088

**Tarrant County Hospital District**
1500 S. Main, Fort Worth, TX 76104.
- Perspective (Ft. Worth) bi-m.

**Tarter Communications, Inc.**
29 Park Ave., Manhasset, NY 11030.
- Specialty Food Merchandising. m.

**Tasco Publishing Corp.**
305 E. 53rd St., New York, NY 10022.
- Impact: the American Wine Market Review and Forecast. a.
- Impact: Wine and Spirits Newsletter. s-m.

**Tasmania Press, Inc.**
4375 Beverly Blvd., Los Angeles, CA 90004.
- Spectator. irreg. (2-5 per yr)

**Tau Beta Pi Association Inc.**
Box 8840, University Station, Knoxville, TN 37916.
- Bent of Tau Beta Pi. q. ISSN 0005-884X

**Tau Epsilon Rho Law Fraternity**
7907 Ogontz Ave., Philadelphia, PA 19150.
- Summons. q. ISSN 0039-5072

**Taunton Press**
Box 355, Newtown, CT 06470.
- Fine Woodworking. q. ISSN 0361-3453

**Tax Executives Institute**
425 13th St. N.W., Washington, DC 20004.
- Tax Executive. q. ISSN 0040-0025

**Tax Foundation, Inc.**
50 Rockefeller Plaza, New York, NY 10020.
- Facts and Figures on Government Finance. biennial. ISSN 0071-3678
- Federal Budget: Focus and Perspectives. irreg. ISSN 0363-5422
- Government Finance Brief. New Series. irreg., 1972, no. 22. ISSN 0072-5161
- Monthly Tax Features. m. ISSN 0047-8040
- Source References for Facts and Figures on Government Finance. biennial. ISSN 0494-8203
- Tax Foundation, New York. Research Publications. New Series. irreg., 1973, no. 28. ISSN 0082-2159
- Tax Foundation's Research Bibliography. irreg. ISSN 0496-974X
- Tax Review. m. ISSN 0040-0114

**Tax Foundation of Hawaii**
680 Alexander Young Bldg, Honolulu, HI 96813.
- Government in Hawaii. a. ISSN 0072-517X

**Tax Institute of America**
*see* National Tax Association-Tax Institute of America

**Tax Management Inc.**
1231 25th St., N.W., Washington, DC 20037.
- Executive Compensation Journal. m. ISSN 0094-789X
- Tax Management International Journal. m. ISSN 0090-4600

**Tax Research Group, Ltd.**
2825 S. Washington Ave., Titusville, FL 32780.
- Journal of Taxation; a National journal of current news and comment for professional tax men. m. ISSN 0022-4863

**Tax Shelter Monitor**
c/o Berne Clark, Ed., Box 512, Grand Central Sta., New York, NY 10017.
- Tax Shelter Monitor. m.

**Tax Strike News**
Box 1089, Porterville, CA 93257.
- National Tax Strike News. m.

**Taxation with Representation**
2369 N Taylor St., Arlington, VA 22207.
- Taxation with Representation. Newsletter; public interest taxpayers' lobby. 8-9 per yr.

**Taxation with Representation (Pembroke)**
107 North Vance St., Pembroke, NC 28372.
- T A S Bulletin. m.

**Taxes and Estates**
Munsey Bldg., Baltimore, MD 21202.
- Taxes and Estates. m. ISSN 0040-019X

**Taxi News Digest**
420 Statler Office Bldg., Boston, MA 02116.
- Taxi News Digest; voice of the New England taxi industry. m. ISSN 0040-0211

**Taxpayers Association of New Mexico**
Box 697, Santa Fe, NM 87501.
- New Mexico Tax Bulletin. q. ISSN 0028-632X

**Sally Taylor & Friends**
756 Kansas St., San Francisco, CA 94107.
- Redwood Rancher. m. ISSN 0034-2181

**Taylor-Constantine**
Hopewell, NJ 08525.
- Milestone Car. q. (Milestone Car Society Inc.)

**Taylor County Historical Society**
P.O. Box 14, Campbellsville, KY 42718.
- Central Kentucky Researcher. m. ISSN 0095-1439

**Taylor Publishing Co.**
1550 W. Mockingbird Lane, Dallas, TX 75221.
- Taylor Talk. bi-m. ISSN 0492-3901

**Tea and Coffee Trade Journal Co.**
Box 71, Whitestone, NY 11357.
- Tea and Coffee Trade Journal. m. ISSN 0040-0343

**Teach'em, Inc.**
625 N. Michigan Ave., Chicago, IL 60611.
- Voices... (Year) m. (American Society of Hospital Pharmacists)

**Teacher Information Center**
61 Surrey Lane, Sudbury, MA 01776.
- T. I. C. Newsletter. m.

**Teacher Travel**
P.O. Box 4087, Long Island City, NY 11104.
- Teacher Travel. m(except July & Aug.) ISSN 0049-3120

**Teachers and Writers Collaborative**
186 West 4 St., New York, NY 10014.
- Teachers & Writers Magazine. 3 per yr. ISSN 0146-3381

**Teachers Association of Long Beach, Inc.**
4362 Atlantic Ave., Long Beach, CA 90807.
- T A L B Talks. 5 per yr. ISSN 0039-8225

**Teachers College Press**
Teachers College, Columbia University, 1234 Amsterdam Ave., New York, NY 10027.
- Anthropolgy and Education Series. irreg.
- Classics in Education. irreg., no. 50, 1974. ISSN 0069-4495
- Columbia University. Center for Education in Africa. Publications. irreg.
- Columbia University. Center for Education in Asia. Publications. irreg.
- Columbia University. Center for Education in Latin America. Publications. irreg.
- Foresight Books in Psychology. irreg.
- New Aims in Children's Literature Series. irreg.
- New Humanistic Research Series. irreg.
- Nursing Education Monographs. irreg. ISSN 0078-2831
- Practical Suggestions for Teaching. irreg.
- Series in Guidance and Student Personnel Administration. irreg.
- Studies in Culture and Communication. irreg.
- Studies in International Education. irreg.
- Studies in Science Education. irreg.
- Teachers College Series in Special Education. irreg.
- Teachers College Studies in Education. irreg.

**Teachers Guide to Television**
P.O. 564, Lenox Hill Station, New York, NY 10021.
- Teachers Guide to Television. s-a.

**Teachers of English to Speakers of Other Languages**
c/o James E. Alatis, School of Languages & Linguistics, Georgetown Univ., Washington, DC 20007.
- T. E. S. O. L. Quarterly. q. ISSN 0039-8322

**Teaching Philosophy**
Location 047, University of Cincinnati, Cincinnati, OH 45221.
- Teaching Philosophy. s-a.

**Teamsters Joint Council 13**
300 S. Grand, St. Louis, MO 63103.
- Missouri Teamster. m. ISSN 0026-6728

**Techni Research Associates**
Professional Center Bldg., Willow Grove, PA 19090.
- World Technology. bi-m.

**Technical Assistance Information Clearing House**
200 Park Ave. S., New York, NY 10003.
- T A I C H Category Report: Development Assistance Programs of U.S. Non-Profit Organizations Abroad. irreg. (American Council of Voluntary Agencies for Foreign Service, Inc)
- T A I C H Country Report: Development Assistance Programs of U.S. Non-Profit Organizations. irreg. (American Council of Voluntary Agencies for Foreign Service, Inc.)
- T A I C H News. 4 per yr. ISSN 0039-8209 (American Council of Voluntary Agencies for Foreign Service, Inc.)

**Technical Association of the Graphic Arts**
P.O. Box 3064, Federal Sta., Rochester, NY 14614.
- T A G A Newsletter. s-a.
- T A G A Proceedings; technical papers presented at annual meeting. a. ISSN 0082-2299

**Technical Association of the Pulp & Paper Industry**
Dunwoody Park, Atlanta, GA 30341.
- T A P P I. m. ISSN 0039-8241
- T A P P I Monographs. irreg.
- T A P P I Standards and Provisional Methods. s-a.
- Technical Association of the Pulp and Paper Industry. Directory. a. ISSN 0091-7737

**Technical Economics Associates**
Box 1110, Estes Park, CO 80517.
- Cryogenic Information Report. 10 per yr. ISSN 0011-2259

**Technical Economics, Inc.**
Box 9033, 573 The Alameda, Berkeley, CA 94707.
- Journal of Biomedical Systems. q. ISSN 0021-9312
- Logistics Review. 6 per yr. ISSN 0024-5844

**Technical Information Service (Washington)**
1030 Woodward Building, Washington, DC 20005.
- Alpha-Numerical Index with Correlations: Index to U. S. Government Research Reports. irreg., 1970, vol. 4. ISSN 0065-6550

**Technical Insights, Inc.**
Box 1304, Fort Lee, NJ 07024.
- Inside R & D; a weekly news report for technical managers. w. ISSN 0300-757X

**Technical Publications**
(Subsidiary of: Interec Publishing Corp.)
1014 Wyandotte St., Kansas City, MO 64105.
- Blue Book Official Lawn Equipment Trade-in Guide. irreg. ISSN 0094-4955

**Technical Publishing Co.**
1301 S. Grove Ave., Barrington, IL 60610.
- Consulting Engineer. m. ISSN 0010-7107
- Plant Engineering. fortn. ISSN 0032-082X
- Plant Engineering Directory & Specifications Catalog. a. ISSN 0554-2693
- Pollution Engineering; magazine of total environmental control. m. ISSN 0032-3640
- Power Engineering. m. ISSN 0032-5961 (Agency for All Foreign Subscriptions: J. B. Tratsart, Ltd., 154a, Greenford Rd., Harrow, Middlesex HA13QT, Eng)
- Research/Development. m. ISSN 0034-5199
- Vacuum Technology Directory & Buyers Guide. a.

**Technical Publishing Co. (Greenwich)**
35 Mason St., Greenwich, CT 06833.
- Purchasing World. w. ISSN 0093-1659

**Technical Publishing Co. (los Angeles)**
1801 S. La Cienega Blvd., Los Angeles, CA 90035.
- Datamation. m. ISSN 0011-6963

**Technical Reporting Corp.**
c/o Earl Palmer, Box 745, 1098 S. Milwaukee Rd.,
South Wheeling, IL 60090.
- Service Reporter; bulletin board of the industry.
m.

**Technicraft**
Box 3994, Anaheim, CA 92803.
- TechniCraft Trader. w.

**Technifax Publications, Inc**
120 N. Hale, Box 937, Wheaton, IL 60187.
- Cutting Tool Engineering. bi-m. ISSN 0011-4189

**Technocracy, Inc**
7513 Greenwood Ave., N., Seattle, WA 98103.
- Northwest Technocrat. q. ISSN 0029-3474
- Technocrat. q. ISSN 0040-1595
- Technocratic Trendevents; Technocratic analysis
of trends and events in the news. m. ISSN 0040-
1617

**Technology Clearing House, Inc.**
Suite 80, 1105 Market St., Wilmington, DE 19801.
- New Technology Index. 6 per yr.

**Technology Marketing Corp.**
642 Westover Road, Stamford, CT 06902.
- High Solids Coatings. q.
- Journal of Radiation Curing. q.
- Materials Digest. q. ISSN 0047-6226
- Radiation Curing. q.

**Technology News Center Inc.**
P.O. Box 2549, Palo Verdes, PA 90274.
- Technology Transfer Action. 12 per yr.

**Technology Organization Inc.**
1 Emerson Pl., Boston, MA 02114.
- Technology & Conservation. q.

**Technomic Publishing Co. Inc.**
265 Post Rd. W., Westport, CT 06880.
- Advances in Fire Retardants. a. ISSN 0094-3932
- Advances in Urethane Science and Technology. a.
ISSN 0044-6378
- Environmental Impact News. m.
- Handbook of Environmental Management Series.
irreg. ISSN 0046-6786
- Journal of Cellular Plastics. bi-m. ISSN 0021-
955X
- Journal of Coated Fabrics. q. ISSN 0093-4658
- Journal of Combustion Toxicology. q.
- Journal of Composite Materials. q. ISSN 0021-
9983
- Journal of Consumer Product Flammability. q.
- Journal of Elastomers and Plastics. q.
- Journal of Fire & Flammability. q. ISSN 0022-
1104
- Journal of Fire Retardant Chemistry. q.
- Journal of Thermal Insulation. q.
- Northeastern Regional Antipollution Conference.
Proceedings. a. ISSN 0048-0746 (University of
Rhode Island)
- Progress in Fire Retardancy. irreg. ISSN 0048-
5497
- Reuse/Recycle. m. ISSN 0048-7457
- Soviet Progress in Polyurethanes. irreg., latest
issue 1975. ISSN 0049-1764
- Stack Sampling News. m.
- Structural Foam Conference. Proceedings. irreg.
(Society of the Plastics Industry)
- United States Foamed Plastic Markets and
Directory. a. ISSN 0083-0968
- Urethane Plastics and Products. m. ISSN 0049-
5700

**Peter Teichmann**
315 W. 6th St., Los Angeles, CA 90014.
- California Staats-Zeitung. w.

**Tejidos**
Box 7383, Austin, TX 78712.
- Tejidos. q.

**Tektronix, Inc.**
P.O. Box 500, Beaverton, OR 97077.
- Tekscope. bi-m.

**Telberg Book Corp.**
Box N, Sag Harbor, NY 11963.
- Who's Who in Soviet Science and Technology.
irreg.(approx. every 2-3 years) ISSN 0083-9701
- Who's Who in Soviet Social Sciences, Humanities,
Art and Government. irreg. ISSN 0083-971X

**Telecommunications Reports**
1204 National Press Bldg., Washington, DC 20045.
- Telecommunications Reports. w.

**Teleflora, Inc.**
c/o Robert Harker, Ed., 2400 Compton Blvd.,
Redondo Beach, CA 90278.
- Teleflora Spirit; the magazine of professional
flower shop management. m. ISSN 0040-2532

**Telefood Magazine**
35 East Wacker Dr., Chicago, IL 60601.
- Telefood Magazine; serving the fancy food and
beverage trade. m. ISSN 0040-2540

**Telegraphic Cable & Radio Registrations, Inc.**
1600 Harrison Ave., Mamaroneck, NY 10543.
- Marconi's International Register; international
cable address directory. a. ISSN 0076-4418

**Telephone**
c/o Maureen Owen, Ed., Box 672, Old Chelsea
Sta., New York, NY 10011.
- Telephone. 2 per yr.

**Telephone Report**
c/o Ed. Jerry W. Finefrock, 3705 California Ave.,
Long Beach, CA 90807.
- Telephone Report. m.

**Telephony Publishing Corp.**
53 W. Jackson Blvd., Chicago, IL 60604.
- Communications Management and Engineering. q.
- Telephony; journal of the telephone industry. w.
ISSN 0040-2656
- Telephony's Directory of the Telephone Industry.
a. ISSN 0082-2671

**Television Bureau of Advertising**
1345 Avenue of the Americas, New York, NY
10019.
- T V Basics. a.

**Television Digest, Inc.**
1836 Jefferson Place, N.W., Washington, DC
20036.
- C A T V and Station Coverage Atlas and 35-Mile
Zone Maps. a. ISSN 0068-4694
- Television Digest. w. ISSN 0497-1507
- Television Factbook. a. ISSN 0082-268X

**Television Editorial Corp.**
666 Fifth Ave., New York, NY 10019.
- Television/Radio Age. fortn. ISSN 0040-277X

**Television Index, Inc.**
150 Fifth Ave., New York, NY 10011.
- Media News Keys; leads and contacts in all fields.
w. ISSN 0033-3913
- Network Futures. w.
- Ross Reports Television; New York casting -
national script contacts. m. ISSN 0035-8355
- T V Pro-Log; television programs and production
news. w.
- Television Index; television network program and
production reporting service. w.
- Television Network Movies. q.

**Television International Magazine**
P.O. Box 2430, Hollywood, CA 90028.
- Television International Magazine. bi-m.

**Maurice Telleen, Ed. & Pub.**
Route 3, Waverly, IA 50677.
- Draft Horse Journal. q. ISSN 0012-5865

**Telltale Compass**
18418 South Old River Drive, Lake Oswego, OR
97034.
- Telltale Compass. m.

**Telluride Association**
217 W. Ave., Ithaca, NY 14850.
- Telluride Newsletter. q.

**Telos Press**
c/o Sociology Dept., Washington Univ., MO 63130.
- Telos. q. ISSN 0040-2842

**Temko Enterprises Inc.**
500 Monterey Pass Rd., Monterey Pk., CA 91754.
- Pacific Printers Pilot; the graphic arts journal for
the West. m.

**Tempest Publications, Inc.**
257 Park Ave. S., New York, NY 10010.
- Brut. 9 per yr.
- Sports Special. q.
- True Sex Crimes. bi-m.

**Templar Press**
Box 98, FDR Station, New York, NY 10022.
- Double-F; a magazine of effeminism. 6 per yr.

**Temple of Truth**
P.O. Box 3125, Pasadena, CA 91103.
- White Light. q.

**Temple University**
Philadelphia, PA 19122.
- Journal of Aesthetics and Art Criticism. q. ISSN
0021-8529 (American Society for Aesthetics)
- Journal of Ecumenical Studies. 4 per yr. ISSN
0022-0558
- Journal of Modern Literature. 4 per yr. ISSN
0022-281X
- Journal of the History of Ideas; a quarterly
devoted to cultural and intellectual history. q.
ISSN 0022-5037
- Pennsylvania State Modern Language Association.
Bulletin. s-a. ISSN 0031-4684
- Temple University Alumni Review. q.

**Temple University. Center for the Study of
Communal Societies**
Gladfelter Hall, Rm. 222, Philadelphia, PA 19111.
- Communal Studies Newsletter. s-a.

**Temple University. Center for the Study of
Federalism**
Philadelphia, PA 19122.
- Temple University. Center for the Study of
Federalism. Center Report. irreg.

**Temple University. Department of English**
Philadelphia, PA 19122.
- Poetry Newsletter. q.
- Scriblerian and Kit-Cats; a newsjournal devoted to
Pope, Swift, and their circle, the Kit-Cats and
Dryden. s-a. (Co-Sponsor: Northeastern
University)

**Temple University. Department of History**
Philadelphia, PA 19122.
- Sung Studies Newsletter. s-a. ISSN 0049-254X

**Temple University. Department of Radio-TV-Film**
Philadelphia, PA 19122.
- Mass Media Booknotes. m.

**Temple University. Laboratory of Anthropology**
c/o Miss Muriel Kirkpatrick, Coordinator,
Laboratory of Anthropology, Temple University,
Philadelphia, PA 19122.
- Ceramica de Cultura Maya. irreg. ISSN 0577-
3334

**Temple University Press**
General Services Bldg., Broad and Oxford Sts.,
Philadelphia, PA 19122.
- Children's Literature. a.
- International and Comparative Broadcasting. irreg.

**Temple University. School of Business Administration**
Philadelphia, PA 19122.
- Journal of Economics and Business. 3 per yr.

**Temple University School of Law**
N. Broad St. & Montgomery Ave., Philadelphia, PA
19122.
- American Journal of Legal History. q. ISSN 0002-
9319 (American Society for Legal History)
- Temple Law Quarterly. q. ISSN 0040-2974

**Temple University School of Pharmacy. Pharmacy
Alumni Association**
3307 N. Broad St., Philadelphia, PA 19140.
- Temple Apothecary. 4 per yr. ISSN 0040-2958

**Tenneco Inc.**
Box 2511, Houston, TX 77001.
- Tenneco. q. ISSN 0040-3121

**Tennessee. Advisory Council on Vocational Education**
909 Mountcastle St., Knoxville, TN 37916.
- Tennessee. State Advisory Council on Vocational Education. Annual Evaluation Report. a. ISSN 0093-0903

**Tennessee. Department of Agriculture. Division of Plant Industries**
Tennessee Department of Agriculture, Box 40627, Melrose Station, Nashville, TN 37204.
- Tennessee Cooperative Economic Insect Survey Report: Annual Summary. a. (prep. by its Insect Survey Comm)

**Tennessee. Department of Conservation**
2611 West End Ave., Nashville, TN 37203.
- Tennessee Conservationist. bi-m. ISSN 0040-3202

**Tennessee. Department of Economic and Community Development**
10th Floor, Andrew Jackson Bldg., Nashville, TN 37219.
- Industrial Growth in Tennessee, Annual Report. a. ISSN 0099-1872
- Tennessee Manufacturers Directory. a. since 1975. ISSN 0360-5477
- Tennessee Thrusts. q. ISSN 0092-3427

**Tennessee. Department of Employment Security**
Research and Statistics Section, 519 Cordell Hull Building, Nashville, TN 37219.
- Tennessee Annual Average Labor Force Estimates. a.
- Tennessee Labor Market in Nashville. m.

**Tennessee. Department of Human Services**
State Office Bldg., Nashville, TN 37219.
- Record (Nashville) bi-m.

**Tennessee. Department of Revenue. Sales and Use Tax Division**
Nashville, TN 37219.
- Retailing in Tennessee. irreg. ISSN 0361-0020

**Tennessee. Department of Safety**
Andrew Jackson State Office Bldg., Nashville, TN 37219.
- Tennessee. Department of Safety. Annual Report. a. ISSN 0095-1994

**Tennessee. Division of Veterans Affairs**
215 Eighth Ave., Nashville, TN 37203.
- Tennessee Division of Veterans Affairs. Monthly Bulletin. m. ISSN 0040-3210

**Tennessee. Division of Water Quality Control**
621 Cordell Hull Bldg., Nashville, TN 37219.
- Tennessee. Division of Water Quality Control. Annual Report. a.

**Tennessee. Division of Water Resources**
6213 Charlotte Ave., Nashville, TN 37209.
- Summary of Ground Water Data for Tennessee. a. ISSN 0093-0539

**Tennessee. Higher Education Commission**
908 Andrew Jackson State Office Bldg., Nashville, TN 37219.
- Tennessee. Higher Education Commission. Biennial Report. biennial.

**Tennessee. State Board for Vocational Education**
Nashville, TN 37219.
- Tennessee. State Board for Vocational Education. Information Series. irreg. ISSN 0093-9889

**Tennessee. State Library and Archives. Public Libraries Section**
Nashville, TN 37219.
- Tennessee Public Library Statistics. a. ISSN 0363-7158

**Tennessee. State Planning Office**
660 Capitol Hill Bldg., Nashville, TN 37219.
- Local Planning News. m.
- Tennessee. State Planning Office. State Planning Office Publication. irreg. ISSN 0082-2752
- Tennessee Planner. q. ISSN 0040-3350

**Tennessee. State Planning Office. Middle Tennessee Section**
6213 Charlotte Ave., Nashville, TN 37209.
- Tennessee. State Planning Office. Middle Tennessee Section. Publication. irreg.

**Tennessee. Wildlife Resources Agency**
Nashville, TN 37219.
- Tennessee. Wildlife Resources Agency. Annual Report. a. ISSN 0363-4191

**Tennessee Academy of Science**
Ed. Gus Tomlinson, Box 153, George Peabody College, Nashville, TN 37203.
- Tennessee Academy of Science. Journal. q. ISSN 0040-313X

**Tennessee Association of Plumbing-Heating-Cooling Contractors, Inc.**
c/o Gladys E. Kiss, Ed., 1410 Walton Road, Memphis, TN 38117.
- Tennessee Plumbing, Heating, Cooling Contractor. a.

**Tennessee Association of Realtors**
11th Floor, 3rd National Bank Bldg., Nashville, TN 37219.
- Tennessee Realtor. bi-m.

**Tennessee Bankers Association**
21st Floor, Life & Casualty Tower, Nashville, TN 37219.
- Tennessee Banker. m. ISSN 0040-3199

**Tennessee Congress of Parents and Teachers**
1905 Acklen Ave., Nashville, TN 37212.
- Tennessee Parent-Teacher. 10 per yr. (Aug-May) ISSN 0049-3392

**Tennessee Dental Association**
2104 Sunset Place, Nashville, TN 37212.
- Tennessee Dental Association. Journal. q. ISSN 0040-3385

**Tennessee Education Association**
598 James Robertson Parkway, Nashville, TN 37219.
- T E A News. m. ISSN 0039-8292
- Tennessee Teacher. m. ISSN 0040-3407

**Tennessee Electric Cooperative Association**
710 Spence Lane, Nashville, TN 37217.
- Tennessee Magazine. m. ISSN 0492-746X

**Tennessee Farm Bureau Federation**
Box 313, Columbia, TN 38401.
- Tennessee Farm Bureau News. m. ISSN 0040-3237

**Tennessee Fine Arts Center and Botanical Gardens**
Cheek Road, Nashville, TN 37205.
- Cheekwood Mirror. m.

**Tennessee Folklore Society**
Box 234, Murfreesboro, TN 37130.
- Tennessee Folklore Society Bulletin. 4 per yr. ISSN 0040-3253

**Tennessee Genealogical Society**
Box 12124, Memphis, TN 38112.
- "Ansearchin" News. q. ISSN 0003-5246

**Tennessee Historical Commission**
170 Second Avenue, Nashville, TN 37201.
- Courier (Nashville) q. ISSN 0590-0174
- Tennessee Historical Commission. Biennial Report. biennial.

**Tennessee Historical Society**
Nashville, TN 37219.
- Tennessee Historical Quarterly. q. ISSN 0040-3261

**Tennessee Law Enforcement Officers Association**
309 Volunteer Bldg., Chattanooga, TN 37401.
- Tennessee Law Enforcement Journal. bi-m. ISSN 0040-327X

**Tennessee Law Review Association, Inc.**
1505 W. Cumberland Ave., Knoxville, TN 37916.
- Tennessee Law Review. q. ISSN 0040-3288

**Tennessee Library Association**
Box 12085, Nashville, TN 37212.
- Tennessee Librarian. q. ISSN 0040-3296

**Tennessee Livestock Association**
P.O. Box 67, Trenton, TN 38382.
- Tennessee Stockman. m.

**Tennessee Medical Association**
112 Louise Ave., Nashville, TN 37203.
- Tennessee Medical Association. Journal. m. ISSN 0040-3318

**Tennessee Municipal League**
226 Capitol Blvd., Nashville, TN 37219.
- Tennessee Town and City. m. ISSN 0040-3415

**Tennessee Music Educators Association**
Memphis City Schools, 2597 Avery Ave., Memphis, TN 38112.
- Tennessee Musician. q. ISSN 0040-3334

**Tennessee Nurses Association**
1720 West End Bldg., Nashville, TN 37203.
- Tennessee Nurses Association. Bulletin. bi-m. ISSN 0040-3342

**Tennessee Ornithological Society**
c/o Dr. Gary O. Wallace, Ed., Route 7, Sunrise Dr., Box 338, Elizabethton, TN 37643.
- Migrant. q. ISSN 0026-3575

**Tennessee Research Coordinating Unit for Vocational Education**
909 Mountcastle St., Knoxville, TN 37916.
- Tennessee Research Coordinating Unit for Vocational Education. Research Series. irreg.

**Tennessee School Boards Association**
323 McLemore St. Suite A, Nashville, TN 37203.
- Tennessee School Board Bulletin. m. ISSN 0049-3406

**Tennessee School for the Blind**
115 Stewarts Ferry, Donelson, TN 37214.
- Tennessee Mockingbird. s-a. ISSN 0040-3326

**Tennessee State University. Department of Public Relations**
Box 130, 3500 Centennial Blvd., Nashville, TN 37203.
- Tennessee State University. Faculty Journal; journal of research, creative writing & literary criticism. s-a.

**Tennessee Technological University**
Cookeville, TN 38501.
- Tennessee Tech Journal. a. ISSN 0082-2779

**Tennessee Valley Authority**
see U.S. Tennessee Valley Authority

**Tennessee Valley Historical Society**
University of North Alabama, Florence, AL 35630.
- Journal of Muscle Shoals History. a.

**Tennessee Valley Old Time Fiddlers Association**
Route 4, Box 634, Madison, AL 35758.
- Devil's Box. q. ISSN 0092-0789

**Tennis Gazette, Inc.**
c/o Steven Lewitt, 16 Tennis Place, Flushing, NY 11375.
- Tennis Gazette. bi-m.

**Tennis News, Inc.**
P. O. Box 1706, F.D.R. Station, New York, NY 10022.
- Tennis Week. w.

**Tenniswoman**
50 72 St., New York, NY 10023.
- Tenniswoman. m.

**Tentagel, Inc.**
Box 2008, Menlo Park, CA 94025.
- Horse. bi-m.
- Setter. bi-m.
- Sheltie Special. bi-m. ISSN 0559-7692
- Shetland Sheepdog. bi-m.
- World of Collies. bi-m.

**Tenth District Dental Society Headquarters**
165 N. Village Ave., Rockville Centre, NY 11570.
- Tenth District Dental Society of the State of New York. Bulletin. m. May-Oct. ISSN 0070-3729

**Tenth Muse**
2942 W. 5th St., Brooklyn, NY 11224.
- Tenth Muse. s-a. ISSN 0094-162X

**Tenth Presbyterian Church**
1700 Spruce St., Philadelphia, PA 19103.
- Tenth; an Evangelical quarterly. q. ISSN 0049-3430

**C. S. Tepfer Publishing Co., Inc.**
607 Main St., Box 565, Ridgefield, CT 06877.
- CableLibraries. 12 per yr.

- E T V Newsletter; biweekly news report of educational & instructional television. ISSN 0012-8023
- Educational & Industrial Television. m. ISSN 0046-1466
- Video Trade News. m.
- Videoplay Program Source Guide. a.
- Videoplay Report. fortn.

**Teratology Society**
- Teratology. (pub. by Wistar Institute Press)

**Terminal Publications, Inc.**
c/o James Seton Kingston, Ed, 6543 North 2nd Street, Philadelphia, PA 19126.
- Food Industry Journal; the food industry advocate. m.

**Terminus Media**
1819 Peachtree Rd. N.W., Atlanta, GA 30309.
- Media Fax. 3 per yr.
- Terminus Business Directory. a.

**Territorial Imperative, Inc.**
Box 5327, Madison, WI 53705.
- Assets Protection. bi-m. ISSN 0098-9169

**Teton**
Box 1903, Jackson's Hole, WY 83001.
- Teton. a. ISSN 0049-3481

**Tevai Jezuitai Cikagoje**
2345 West 56th Street, Chicago, IL 60636.
- Musu Zinios. fortn.

**Texaco, Inc.**
135 E. 42nd St., New York, NY 10017.
- Lubrication; a technical publication devoted to the selection and use of lubricants. q. ISSN 0024-7146
- Texaco Star. q.

**Texas. Advisory Council for Technical-Vocational Education**
201 East 11th St., Box 1886, Austin, TX 78767.
- Texas. Advisory Council for Technical-Vocational Education. Annual Report. a. ISSN 0090-2799

**Texas. Crop and Livestock Reporting Service**
P. O. Box 70, Austin, TX 78767.
- Texas Livestock Statistics. a. ISSN 0091-1550
- Texas Small Grains Statistics. a. ISSN 0091-4673

**Texas. Department of Agriculture**
P.O. Box 12847, Austin, TX 78711.
- Texas Field Crop Statistics. a. ISSN 0092-153X

**Texas. Department of Community Affairs. Office of Early Childhood Development**
P.O. Box 13166, Austin, TX 78701.
- Early Childhood Development in Texas. biennial.

**Texas. Department of Corrections**
Box 32, Huntsville, TX 77340.
- Echo. m. ISSN 0046-1059
- Texas. Department of Corrections. Research and Development Division. Research Report. irreg. ISSN 0095-1900 (prep. by its Research and Development Division)

**Texas. Department of Health Resources**
Austin, TX 78700.
- Texas Vital Statistics. irreg. ISSN 0495-257X

**Texas. Department of Highways and Public Transportation**
Austin, TX 78701.
- Texas Highways. m. ISSN 0040-4349

**Texas. Employment Commission**
Manpower Data Analysis and Research Dept., TEC Bldg., Austin, TX 78778.
- Texas Manpower Trends. m. ISSN 0040-4462

**Texas. Farm Bureau**
Box 489, 7420 Fish Pond Rd., Waco, TX 76710.
- Texas Agriculture. m. ISSN 0040-4152

**Texas. Forest Service**
- Texas. Forest Service. Cooperative Forest Tree Improvement Program. Progress Report. (pub. by Texas A & M University)

**Texas. Forest Service. Forest Products Laboratory**
P.O. Box 310, Lufkin, TX 75910.
- Forest Products Notes. q.

**Texas. Governor's Committee on Aging**
Box 12786, Capitol Station, Austin, TX 78711.
- Texas. Governor's Committee on Aging. Biennial Report. biennial. ISSN 0082-3058

**Texas. Industrial Commission**
Austin, TX 78700.
- Texas. Industrial Commission. Annual Report. a. ISSN 0361-2597

**Texas. Legislative Reference Library**
P.O. Box 12488-Capitol Station, Austin, TX 78711.
- Texas. Legislative Reference Library. Chief Elected and Administrative Officials. biennial.

**Texas. Office of Economic Opportunity**
611 So Congress Ave., Box 13166, Capitol Stat., Austin, TX 78711.
- Poverty in Texas. a. ISSN 0097-7950

**Texas. Office of Minority Business Enterprises**
Information Office, 1711 San Antonio St., Austin, TX 78701.
- Directory of Minority Owned Businesses in Texas. irreg. ISSN 0094-8004

**Texas. Office of the Governor**
Division of Planning Coordination, Box 12428, Capitol Station, San Antonio, TX 78711.
- Governor's Workshop on Intergovernmental Relations and Regional Planning. Proceedings. a. ISSN 0092-8445

**Texas. Parks and Wildlife Department**
John H. Reagan State Office Bldg., Austin, TX 78701.
- Texas Parks and Wildlife Magazine. m. ISSN 0040-4586

**Texas. Railroad Commission**
Capitol Station, P.O. Drawer 12967, Austin, TX 78711.
- Summary of Texas Natural Gas. m. ISSN 0094-2766

**Texas. Railroad Commission. Oil and Gas Division**
State Office Bldg., Colorado and 10th Sts., Austin, TX 78701.
- Monthly Summary of Texas Natural Gas. m.
- Texas. Railroad Commission. Oil and Gas Division. Inactive Oil and Gas Fields. irreg. ISSN 0360-6236

**Texas. Secretary of State**
Box 819, Texas Commondore Bldg., Office of the Secretary of State, Austin, TX 78701.
- Texas Register. s-w. ISSN 0362-4781

**Texas. State Library**
Austin, TX 78701.
- Texas Special Libraries Directory. biennial. ISSN 0082-3163

**Texas. State Library. Department of Library Development**
Box 12927, Capitol Station, Austin, TX 78711.
- Library Developments. bi-m.
- Texas Public Library Statistics. a. ISSN 0082-3120

**Texas. State Securities Board**
709 Lyndon B. Johnson Bldg., Austin, TX 78711.
- Texas Monthly Securities Bulletin. m.

**Texas. Water Development Board**
P.O. Box 13087, Capitol Station, Austin, TX 78711.
- Texas. Water Development Board. Biennial Report. biennial. ISSN 0082-3554
- Texas. Water Development Board. Report. irreg. ISSN 0082-3562
- Water for Texas. m.

**Texas. Water Quality Board**
Box 13246, Capitol Station, Austin, TX 78711.
- Texas. Water Quality Board. Agency Publication. irreg. ISSN 0091-0848
- Texas. Water Quality Board. Biennial Report. biennial. ISSN 0082-3570

**Texas A & I University**
Box 2228, Kingsville, TX 78363.
- T A I U S. (Texas A & I University Studies) a. ISSN 0564-7169

**Texas A & M University**
College Station, TX 77843.
- Texas. Forest Service. Cooperative Forest Tree Improvement Program. Progress Report. a. ISSN 0082-3031 (Texas. Forest Service)

- Texas A & M Oceanographic Studies. (pub. by Gulf Publishing Co.)
- Texas Water Resources Institute. Technical Report. irreg.
- Topics in Ocean Engineering. (pub. by Gulf Publishing Co.)

**Texas A & M University. Association of Former Students**
Box 7368, College Station, TX 77840.
- Texas Aggie. 8 per yr.

**Texas A & M University. Center for Dredging Studies**
College Station, TX 77843.
- Dredging Seminar. Proceedings. irreg.

**Texas A & M University. Center for Energy and Mineral Resources**
College Station, TX 77843.
- Texas Energy and Mineral Resources. m (except combined June-July and Aug.-Sep. issues)

**Texas A & M University. College of Business Administration**
College Station, TX 77843.
- Texas Business Executive. 3 per yr. (prep. by its Executive Development Programs)

**Texas A & M University. Department of Agricultural Communications**
College Station, TX 77843.
- Food and Fiber Economics. m. (Texas Agricultural Extension Service)
- Texas Agricultural Progress. q. ISSN 0049-349X (Texas Agricultural Extension Service) (Co-sponsor: Texas Agricultural Experiment Station)

**Texas A & M University. Department of Oceanography**
College Station, TX 77840.
- Texas A & M University. Department of Oceanography. Contributions in Oceanography. a. ISSN 0069-9640

**Texas A & M University Libraries**
College Sta., TX 77843.
- Texas A & M University Library Notes. bi-m. ISSN 0040-4136

**Texas A & M University. Sea Grant Program Office**
College Station, TX 77843.
- Sea Grant Seventies. m. ISSN 0048-9875 (U.S. National Oceanic and Atmospheric Administration)

**Texas Academy of Family Physicians**
1905 N. Lamar, Austin, TX 78705.
- Texas Family Physician. bi-m. ISSN 0098-1052

**Texas Academy of Science**
Box 10979, San Angelo, TX 76901.
- Texas Academy of Science. Newsletter. (pub. by Texas Tech University. Department of Biology)
- Texas Journal of Science. q. ISSN 0040-4403

**Texas Agricultural Extension Service**
- Food and Fiber Economics. (pub. by Texas A & M University. Department of Agricultural Communications)
- Texas Agricultural Progress. (pub. by Texas A & M University. Department of Agricultural Communications)

**Texas and Southwestern Cattle Raisers Association Inc.**
410 E. Weatherford St., Fort Worth, TX 76102.
- Cattleman. m. ISSN 0008-8552

**Texas Archeological Society**
Box 161, Dallas, TX 75275.
- Texas Archeological Society. Bulletin. a. ISSN 0082-2930
- Texas Archeology; the newsletter of the Texas Archeological Society. irreg., 1970, vol. 14, no. 4. ISSN 0082-2949

**Texas Association of Business**
1212 Main St., Houston, TX 77002.
- T. A. B. Quarterly. q.

**Texas Association of Secondary School Principals**
316 W. 12th St., Austin, TX 78701.
- T A S S P News Hilites. 4 per yr. ISSN 0039-825X
- Texas Study of Secondary Education Research Bulletin. s-a. ISSN 0040-4705

**Texas Beverage News**
Box 71, Fort Worth, TX 76101.
- Texas Beverage News. s-m.

**Texas Bluegrass Association**
6544 Balcer Blvd, Fort Worth, TX 76118.
- Texas Bluegrass Association. Newsletter. m.

**Texas Books in Review**
3503 Monclair, Odessa, TX 79762.
- Texas Books in Review. a.

**Texas Certified Seed Directory**
Austin, TX 78700.
- Texas Certified Seed Directory. a. ISSN 0095-1927

**Texas Christian University. Department of English**
Fort Worth, TX 76129.
- Descant. 4 per yr. ISSN 0011-9210

**Texas Christian University Press**
Fort Worth, TX 76129.
- Multivariate Behavioral Research. q. ISSN 0027-3171 (Society of Multivariate Experimental Psychology)
- Texas Christian University Monographs in History and Culture. irreg., no. 11, 1975. ISSN 0082-2973

**Texas Classroom Teachers Association**
Box 1489, Austin, TX 78767.
- T C T A News. m. ISSN 0039-8284

**Texas College and University System**
LBJ Building, Box 12788, Austin, TX 78711.
- C B Report; monthly notes from the Coordination Board. m.
- Texas. Coordinating Board. Texas College and University System. C B Annual Report. a. ISSN 0082-2981
- Texas. Coordinating Board. Texas College and University System. C B Policy Paper. irreg., 1973, no. 9. ISSN 0082-299X
- Texas. Coordinating Board. Texas College and University System. C B Study Paper. irreg; no. 25, 1975. ISSN 0082-3007

**Texas Congress of Parents and Teachers**
408 W. 11, Austin, TX 78701.
- Texas P T A Communicator. 9 per yr.

**Texas Cooperative Ginners Association**
708 Brown Building, Austin, TX 78701.
- Texas Cooperative News. bi-m. ISSN 0040-4268

**Texas Council for Social Studies**
North Texas State Univ., Box 5427, Denton, TX 76203.
- Southwestern Journal of Social Education. s-a. ISSN 0049-1683

**Texas Criminal Defense Lawyers Association**
1632 American Bank Tower, Austin, TX 78701.
- Voice for the Defense. q.

**Texas Dental Assistants Association**
6110 Tyne, Houston, TX 77007.
- Texas Dental Assistants Association. Bulletin. q. ISSN 0049-3503

**Texas Dental Association**
4920 N. Interregional, Austin, TX 78751.
- Texas Dental Journal. m. ISSN 0040-4284

**Texas Dental Hygienists Association**
1218 Columbus, Houston, TX 77019
(Subscr. Address: 5722 Capello, Houston, Tex. 77035)
- Texas Dental Hygienists' Association. Journal. q. ISSN 0040-4276

**Texas Education Agency**
201 E. 11th St., Austin, TX 78701.
- Texas Child Migrant Program. Annual Report. a. (prep. by its Division of Evaluation)
- Texas Public School Law Bulletin. irreg. ISSN 0362-6334

**Texas Elementary Principals and Supervisors Association**
316 W. 12th St., Austin, TX 78701.
- T E P S A Journal. s-a. ISSN 0300-6433

**Texas Fine Arts Society**
- Facets. (pub. by Foundation Management Inc.)

**Texas Folklore Society**
Box 3007 SFA Sta., Nacogdoches, TX 75962.
- Texas Folklore Society. Paisano Series. irreg., latest issue 1970. ISSN 0082-3015
- Texas Folklore Society. Publications. a. ISSN 0082-3023

**Texas Heart Institute**
P.O. Box 20269, Houston, TX 77025.
- Cardiovascular Diseases. q. ISSN 0093-3546

**Texas High School Coaches Association**
P.O. Drawer 14627, Suite 11, Austin, TX 78761.
- Texas Coach. m ( except Jun., Jul. & Dec.) ISSN 0040-4241

**Texas Hospital Association**
Box 4553, Austin, TX 78765.
- Texas Hospitals. m. ISSN 0040-4357

**Texas Hotel & Motel Association**
8602 Crownhill Blvd., San Antonio, TX 78209.
- Texas and Southwest Hotel-Motel Review. m. ISSN 0040-4160

**Texas Independent Producers & Royalty Owners Association**
1770 Austin National Bank Bldg., Austin, TX 78701.
- T I P R O Reporter. q. ISSN 0039-8403

**Texas Institute for Educational Development**
c/o Cecilio Garcia-Camarillo, 1511 Culebra, San Antonio, TX 78201.
- Caracol. 12 per yr.

**Texas International Airlines, Houston, Texas**
- Texas Flyer. (pub. by Texas Parade, Inc.)

**Texas International Law Journal**
2500 Red River, Austin, TX 78705.
- Texas International Law Journal. s-a.

**Texas Jewish Post**
Box 742, Fort Worth, TX 76101
- Texas Jewish Post. w. ISSN 0040-439X

**Texas Joint Council of Teachers of English**
East Texas Station, Commerce, TX 75428.
- English in Texas. q. (Co-Sponsor: University of Houston)

**Texas Law Review Publications, Inc.**
2500 Red River, Austin, TX 78705.
- Texas Law Review. 8 per yr. ISSN 0040-4411

**Texas Library and Historical Commission**
Box 12927, Capitol Sta., Austin, TX 78711.
- Texas Libraries. q. ISSN 0040-4438

**Texas Library Association**
8989 Westheimer, Suite 108, Houston, TX 77063.
- Texas Library Journal. q. ISSN 0040-4446

**Texas LP-Gas Association**
Box 9925, Austin, TX 78757.
- Texas LP-Gas News. m. ISSN 0040-4454

**Texas Medical Association**
1801 N. Lamar Blvd., Austin, TX 78701.
- Texas Medicine. m. ISSN 0040-4470

**Texas Memorial Museum**
24th & Trinity Sts., Austin, TX 78705.
- Mustang. bi-m.
- Pearce Sellards Series. irreg; no. 26, 1977. ISSN 0079-0354
- Texas Memorial Museum. Bulletin. irreg; no. 24, 1974. ISSN 0082-3074
- Texas Memorial Museum. Information Circulars. a. (University of Texas at Austin)
- Texas Memorial Museum. Miscellaneous Papers. irreg; no. 5, 1977. ISSN 0082-3082

**Texas Metropolitan Publications**
Box 5566, Arlington, TX 76001.
- Texas Metro; magazine of Texas living. m. ISSN 0049-352X

**Texas Motor Transportation Association**
Box 1669, 406 E. 11th, Austin, TX 78767.
- Steering Wheel. m. ISSN 0039-1298

**Texas Municipal League**
1020 Southwest Tower, Austin, TX 78701.
- Texas Town & City. m. ISSN 0040-473X

**Texas Music Educators Association**
Box 9908, Houston, TX 77015.
- Southwestern Musician. m.(Aug-May) ISSN 0038-4895

**Texas Numismatic Association**
Box 74, Weslaco, TX 78596.
- T N A News. m. ISSN 0039-842X

**Texas Nurses Association**
314 Highland Park Blvd., Suite 504, Austin, TX 78752.
- Texas Nursing. m.

**Texas Observer Publishing Co.**
600 W. Seventh, Austin, TX 78701.
- Texas Observer; a journal of free voices. fortn. ISSN 0040-4519

**Texas Oil Journal**
c/o Margaret V. Estes, Box 1792, Longview, TX 75601.
- Texas Oil Journal. m. ISSN 0040-4535

**Texas Oil Marketers Association**
Box 1424, 701 W. 15th, Austin, TX 78767.
- Texas Oil Marketer. m.

**Texas Optometric Association**
- Texas Optometry. (pub. by American Universal Artforms Corp.)

**Texas Ornithological Society**
Dept. of Biology, Texas Tech University, Lubbock, TX 79409.
- Texas Ornithological Society. Bulletin. a. ISSN 0040-4543

**Texas Orthopedic Association**
- American Journal of Orthopedic Surgery. (pub. by Medical Age, Inc.)

**Texas Outdoor Guide, Inc.**
Box 55573, Houston, TX 77055.
- Texas Outdoor Guide. q.

**Texas Parade, Inc.**
Box 12037, Capitol Station, Austin, TX 78711.
- Texas Flyer. m. (Texas International Airlines, Houston, Texas)
- Texas Parade. m. ISSN 0040-456X

**Texas Pecan Growers Association**
Drawer CC, College Station, TX 77840.
- Pecan Quarterly. q. ISSN 0048-3117

**Texas Personnel and Guidance Association**
University of Texas at Austin, College of Education (EDB 262C), Austin, TX 78712.
- T P G A Journal. s-a.

**Texas Press Association**
718 W. 5th St., Austin, TX 78701.
- Texas Press Messenger. m. ISSN 0040-4624

**Texas Public Employees Association**
Drawer 12217, Capitol Sta., Austin, TX 78711.
- Texas Public Employee. every 3 weeks. ISSN 0040-4640

**Texas Research Foundation, Renner**
- Texas Research Foundation, Renner. Contributions. (pub. by University of Texas at Dallas)

**Texas Restaurant Association**
Box 1429, Austin, TX 78767.
- Chuck Wagon. m(10 per yr.) ISSN 0009-6210

**Texas Retail Grocers' Association**
1701 Lasalle Ave, Waco, TX 76706.
- Texas Food Merchant. m. ISSN 0040-4322

**Texas School Directory**
201 E. 11 St., Austin, TX 78701.
- Texas School Directory. irreg. ISSN 0363-4566

**Texas Sheep and Goat Raisers' Association**
San Angelo, TX 76901.
- Sheep and Goat Raiser; the ranch magazine. m. ISSN 0037-3397

**Texas Slough**
Box 5303, Ravensdasle, Austin, TX 78723.
- Texas Slough. 3 per yr.

**Texas Society of Architects**
2121 Austin National Bank Bldg., Austin, TX 78701.
- Texas Architect. bi-m. ISSN 0040-4179

**Texas Society of Certified Public Accountants.**
200 Corrigan Tower, Dallas, TX 75201.
- Texas C P A News. (Texas Certified Public Accountant) m.

**Texas Society of Professional Engineers**
Box 2145, Austin, TX 78767.
- Texas Professional Engineer. m. ISSN 0040-4632

**Texas Southern University. School of Law**
3201 Wheeler St., Houston, TX 77004.
- Texas Southern University Law Review. 3 per yr. ISSN 0092-3559

**Texas Spectator Magazines, Inc.**
3818 Garrott, Houston, TX 77006.
- Enjoy Houston. m. ISSN 0013-8452
- Entre Nous Houston. m. ISSN 0013-9009
- Key Houston. m. ISSN 0023-0782

**Texas Speech Communication Association**
University of Texas, Dept. of Speech Communication, Austin, TX 78712.
- Texas Speech Communication Journal. a. ISSN 0363-8782

**Texas Speleological Association**
5315 Laurel Lake, Waco, TX 76710.
- Texas Caver. m. ISSN 0040-4233

**Texas State Board of Landscape Architects**
320 Sam Houston Bldg., Austin, TX 78701.
- Texas. State Board of Landscape Architects. Annual Roster. a. ISSN 0092-3745

**Texas State Historical Association**
Richardson Hall 2-306, Univ. Station, Austin, TX 78712.
- Southwestern Historical Quarterly. q. ISSN 0038-478X
- Texas Historian. 5 per yr(Sept-May) ISSN 0022-6602

**Texas State Teachers Association**
316 W. 12th St., Austin, TX 78701.
- T S T A Texas Schools. bi-m.
- Texas Outlook. m. ISSN 0040-4551

**Texas Student Publications**
Box D, Austin, TX 78712.
- Daily Texan. d (5 per wk.) (University of Texas at Austin)

**Texas Tech University**
Lubbock, TX 79409.
- Conradiana. 3 per yr. ISSN 0010-6356 (Orders to:, Box 4530)
- Studies in Burke and His Time. 3 per yr. ISSN 0039-3584
- Texas Tech Journal of Education. 3 per yr. ISSN 0360-5590
- Texas Tech University. Graduate Studies. irreg. ISSN 0082-3198 (Orders to:, Gift and Exchange Dept., Texas Tech University Library)
- Water Resources Report Series. irreg. (Orders to:, Box 4630)

**Texas Tech University. College of Home Economics**
Box 4170, Lubbock, TX 79409.
- Tips and Topics in Home Economics. q. ISSN 0040-8042

**Texas Tech University. Department of Biology**
Lubbock, TX 79409.
- Texas Academy of Science. Newsletter. q. ISSN 0040-4144

**Texas Tech University. Ex-Students Association**
Box 4009, Lubbock, TX 79409.
- Texas Techsan. 7 per yr. ISSN 0040-4721

**Texas Tech University. Friends of the University Library**
Lubbock, TX 79409.
- Ex Libris. s-a. ISSN 0014-3901

**Texas Tech University. Institute for Studies in Pragmaticism**
Texas Tech University, Box 4530, Lubbock, TX 79409.
- Charles S. Peirce Newsletter. s-a.

**Texas Tech University. Interdepartmental Committee on Comparative Literature**
Box 4079, Lubbock, TX 79409
(Subscr. to: Gift and Exchange Dept., Tex. Tech U. Library, Box 4079, Lubbock, TX 79409)
- Texas Tech University. Interdepartmental Committee on Comparative Literature. Proceedings of the Comparative Literature Symposium. a. ISSN 0084-9103

**Texas Transportation Institute**
Texas A & M Univ., College Sta., TX 77843.
- Texas Transportation Researcher. q. ISSN 0040-4748

**Texas Veterinary Medical Association**
513 Scarbrough Bldg., Austin, TX 78701.
- Texas Veterinary Medical Journal. bi-m. ISSN 0040-4756

**Texas Watchmakers Association**
Box 3960, Dallas, TX 75208.
- Independent Jeweler. m. ISSN 0038-4798 (Co-sponsors: Oklahoma Horological Association; Louisiana Retail Jewelers' Association)

**Texas Water Resources Institute**
- Texas Water Resources Institute. Technical Report. (pub. by Texas A & M University)

**Texas Wesleyan College**
Fort Worth, TX 76105.
- Fort Belknap Society. Yearbook. a. ISSN 0071-7746

**Texas Western Press**
University of Texas at El Paso, El Paso, TX 79968.
- Southwestern Studies. Monographs. q. ISSN 0081-315X (University of Texas at El Paso)
- Studies in Language and Linguistics. biennial. ISSN 0586-6928

**Texian Press**
P. O. Box 1684, Waco, TX 76703.
- Texana. q. ISSN 0040-411X

**Textile Economics Bureau, Inc.**
489 Fifth Ave., New York, NY 10017.
- Textile Organon; featuring man-made fibers. m. ISSN 0040-5132

**Textile Information Sources**
1587 Third Ave., New York, NY 10028.
- Textile Information Sources and Resources. 8 per yr. ISSN 0584-1739

**Textile Museum**
2320 S. St. N.W., Washington, DC 20008.
- Textile Museum Journal. a. ISSN 0083-7407

**Textile Research Institute**
Box 625, Princeton, NJ 08540.
- Textile Research Journal. m. ISSN 0040-5175

**Textile Workers Union of America**
AFL-CIO, CLC., 99 University Place, New York, NY 10003.
- Textile Labor. m.(except July) ISSN 0040-5027

**Textile World**
330 W. 42d St., New York, NY 10036.
- Directory of Textile Plant Processes. irreg. ISSN 0419-9154

**Thackrey Publishing Co., Inc.**
225 Park Ave., S., New York, NY 10003.
- Better Times; the health and welfare weekly newspaper. w. ISSN 0006-0224

**That New Magazine Inc.**
60 W. 13 St., New York, NY 10011.
- Christopher Street. m.

**The**
c/o Jack Collom, Ed., 1704 Grove, Boulder, CO 80302.
- The. 1-2 per yr.

**Theater Sources, Inc.**
c/o Michael R. Firth, Ed., 104 N. St. Mary, Dallas, TX 75214.
- Prolog. q.
- Theater Across America. 5 per yr.

**Theatre Arts Books**
333 Sixth Ave., New York, NY 10014.
- Bhaisajaguru Series. irreg.

**Theatre Communications Group**
355 Lexington Ave., New York, NY 10017.
- T C G National Working Conference. Proceedings. irreg.
- T C G Newsletter. 12 per yr.
- Theatre Profiles; an informational handbook of nonprofit professional theatres in the United States. biennial. ISSN 0361-7947

**Theatre, Drama and Speech Information Center**
1 Erin Court, Pleasant Hill, CA 94523.
- Theatre/Drama Abstracts. 3 per yr (plus annual cumulation)

**Theatre Historical Society**
Box 101, Notre Dame, IN 46556.
- Marquee. q. (plus annual no.) ISSN 0025-3928

**Theatre Library Association**
111 Amsterdam Ave., New York, NY 10023.
- Broadside (New York, 1940) q. ISSN 0068-2748
- Performing Arts Resources. (pub. by Drama Book Specialists)

**Theatre Scene**
1015 Norman Dr., Annapolis, MD 21403.
- Theatre Scene; theatre news of Annapolis and area drama groups. m.

**Theodor Herzl Institute**
515 Park Ave, New York, NY 10022.
- Herzl Institute Bulletin. w. (Oct.-May)
- Midstream; a monthly Jewish review. m. ISSN 0026-332X (Co-Sponsor: World Zionist Organization)

**Theodore Roosevelt Association**
Box 720, Oyster Bay, NY 11771.
- Theodore Roosevelt Association Journal. q.

**Theological Studies, Inc.**
3520 Prospect St., NW, Rm. 401, Washington, DC 20007.
- Theological Studies. q. ISSN 0040-5639

**Theosophical Book Association for the Blind, Inc.**
Krotona 54, Ojai, CA 93023.
- Braille Star Theosophist. bi-m. ISSN 0006-8918

**Theosophical Society in America**
Box 270, Wheaton, IL 60187.
- American Theosophist. m.(10 per yr.) plus 2 special semi-annual issues. ISSN 0003-1402
- Parents' Bulletin. (pub. by Parents' Theosophical Research Group)

**Theosophy Co.**
245 W. 33rd St., Los Angeles, CA 90007.
- Theosophy; devoted to the theosophical movement and the brotherhood of humanity, the study of occult science and philosophy and Aryan literature. m. ISSN 0040-5906

**Therapeutic Research Press, Inc.**
163 Stonehurst Drive, Tenafly, NJ 07670.
- Current Therapeutic Research; clinical and experimental. m.

**Thermodynamics Research Center**
Texas A & M University, College Station, TX 77843.
- American Petroleum Institute. Research Project 44. Selected Values of Properties of Hydrocarbons and Related Compounds. Category A: Tables of Selected Values of Physical and Thermodynamic Properties of Hydrocarbons. irreg; supplement A-74, 1977. ISSN 0065-9630
- American Petroleum Institute. Research Project 44. Selected Values of Properties of Hydrocarbons and Related Compounds. Category B: Selected Infrared Spectral Data. irreg; supplement B-78, 1976. ISSN 0065-9649
- American Petroleum Institute. Research Project 44. Selected Values of Properties of Hydrocarbons and Related Compounds. Category C: Selected Ultraviolet Spectral Data. irreg; supplement C-45, 1970. ISSN 0065-9657
- American Petroleum Institute. Research Project 44. Selected Values of Properties of Hydrocarbons and Related Compounds. Category D: Selected Raman Spectral Data. irreg; supplement D-21, 1977. ISSN 0065-9665
- American Petroleum Institute. Research Project 44. Selected Values of Properties of Hydrocarbons and Related Compounds. Category E: Selected Mass Spectral Data. irreg; supplement E-53, 1977. ISSN 0065-9673

- American Petroleum Institute. Research Project 44. Selected Values of Properties of Hydrocarbons and Related Compounds. Category F: Selected Nuclear Magnetic Resonance Data. irreg; supplement F-23, 1977. ISSN 0065-9681
- American Petroleum Institute. Research Project 44. Selected Values of Properties of Hydrocarbons and Related Compounds. Category G: Selected 13C Nuclear Magnetic Resonance Spectral Data. irreg; supplement G-6, 1977.
- Comprehensive Index of the A P I44-T R C Selected Data on Thermodynamics and Spectroscopy. irreg., 2nd edt. 1974. ISSN 0069-8059 (American Petroleum Institute)
- T R C Current Data News. bi-m.
- Thermodynamics Research Center. International Data Series. Selected Data on Mixtures. Series A. Thermodynamic Properties of Non-reacting Binary Systems of Organic Substances. irreg.
- Thermodynamics Research Center Data Project. Selected Values of Properties of Chemical Compounds. Category A. Tables of Selected Values of Physical and Thermodynamic Properties of Chemical Compounds. irreg; supplement A-37, 1976. ISSN 0082-4046
- Thermodynamics Research Center Data Project. Selected Values of Properties of Chemical Compounds. Category B. Selected Infrared Spectral Data. irreg; supplement B-19, 1976. ISSN 0082-402X
- Thermodynamics Research Center Data Project. Selected Values of Properties of Chemical Compounds. Category C. Selected Ultraviolet Spectral Data. irreg; supplement C-7, 1975. ISSN 0082-4054
- Thermodynamics Research Center Data Project. Selected Values of Properties of Chemical Compounds. Category D. Selected Raman Spectral Data. irreg., supplement D-3, 1974. ISSN 0082-4038
- Thermodynamics Research Center Data Project. Selected Values of Properties of Chemical Compounds. Category E. Selected Mass Spectral Data. irreg; supplement E-14, 1976. ISSN 0082-4062
- Thermodynamics Research Center Data Project. Selected Values of Properties of Chemical Compounds. Category F. Selected Nuclear Magnetic Resonance Spectral Data. irreg; supplement F-24, 1976. ISSN 0082-4070

**Things to Watch & Watch For**
84 Rand St., Rochester, NY 14615.
- Things to Watch & Watch For. s-m. ISSN 0040-6104

**Thiokol Corp.**
Bristol, PA 19007.
- Aerospace Facts. q. ISSN 0001-9356

**Third Federal Savings & Loan Association of Cleveland,Ohio**
7007 Broadway, Cleveland, OH 44105.
- Third Federal Savings & Loan Association of Cleveland, Ohio. News. s-a. ISSN 0040-6147

**Third Millenia Inc.**
465-a Woodland Hills, Philadelphia, MS 39350.
- Battle Flag. m.

**Third Press**
444 Central Park West, New York, NY 10025.
- Third Press Review. bi-m.

**Third Rail**
Box 79, Babylon, NY 11702.
- Third Rail; the magazine of rapid transit. bi-m.

**Third World Reader Service**
1500 Farragut St. N. W., Washington, DC 20011.
- Third World Reader Service. m.

**Thirty Inc.**
P.O. Box 543, Toledo, OH 43693.
- Roll "n" Wheels. q.

**This**
235 Missouri St., San Francisco, CA 94107.
- This. 1-2 per yr.

**This Month in Dallas, Inc.**
3225 Lemmon Ave., West, Suite 301, Dallas, TX 75204.
- Key (Dallas) m. (Hotel-Motel Greeters International, Lone Star Charter)

**This Week in Richmond**
4915 Caskie St., Richmond, VA 23226.
- This Week in Richmond. w.

**Thomas Gilcrease Institute of American History and Art**
R.R. No. 6, Tulsa, OK 74106.
- American Scene; a Gilcrease quarterly. q. ISSN 0003-0929

**Thomas Jefferson Center for Political Economy**
University of Virginia, Rouss Hall, Charlottesville, VA 22901.
- Statistical Abstract of Virginia. irreg., vol. 2, 1970. ISSN 0081-475X
- Thomas Jefferson Center for Political Economy. Research Monographs. irreg. ISSN 0082-4178

**Thomas More Association**
180 N. Wabash Ave., Chicago, IL 60601.
- Critic; a Catholic review of books and the arts. 4 per yr. ISSN 0011-149X
- Keys; for a richer understanding of the bible. 22 per yr.
- Overview; a continuing interpretation of Catholic trends and opinions. m. ISSN 0030-7564
- Sola; a newsletter for the single Catholic woman. 22 per yr.

**Charles C. Thomas, Publisher**
301-327 E. Lawrence Ave., Springfield, IL 62717.
- American Journal of Roentgenology. m. (American Roentgen Ray Society) (Co-Sponsor: American Radium Society)
- American Lectures in Allergy and Immunology. irreg.
- American Lectures in Anatomy. irreg.
- American Lectures in Anesthesiology. irreg.
- American Lectures in Behavioral Science and Law. irreg.
- American Lectures in Cerebral Palsy. irreg.
- American Lectures in Clinical Microbiology. irreg.
- American Lectures in Clinical Psychiatry. irreg.
- American Lectures in Dentistry. irreg.
- American Lectures in Dermatology. irreg.
- American Lectures in Environmental Studies. irreg.
- American Lectures in Epidemiology. irreg.
- American Lectures in Geriatrics. irreg.
- American Lectures in Gynecology and Obstetrics. irreg.
- American Lectures in Hematology. irreg.
- American Lectures in Living Chemistry. irreg.
- American Lectures in Medical Writing and Communication. irreg.
- American Lectures in Nuclear Medicine. irreg.
- American Lectures in Objective Psychiatry. irreg.
- American Lectures in Orthopaedic Surgery. irreg.
- American Lectures in Pharmacology. irreg.
- American Lectures in Philosophy. irreg.
- American Lectures in Psychology. irreg.
- American Lectures in Public Protection. irreg.
- American Lectures in Radiation Therapy. irreg.
- American Lectures in Roentgen Diagnosis. irreg.
- American Lectures in Social and Rehabilitation Psychology. irreg.
- American Lectures in Special Education. irreg.
- American Lectures in Speech and Hearing. irreg.
- American Lectures in Sportsmedicine, Physical Education and Recreation. irreg.
- American Lectures in the History of Medicine and Science. irreg.
- Cerebral Function Symposium. Proceedings. irreg., 2nd, 1972.
- Harold C. Mack Symposium. Proceedings. irreg., latest issue, 1972. (Harper Hospital (Detroit). Department of Gynecology and Obstetrics) (Co-sponsor: Wayne State University)
- John Alexander Monograph Series on Various Phases of Thoracic Surgery. irreg. ISSN 0075-3815

**Thomas Publishing Co.**
One Penn Plaza, New York, NY 10001.
- Industrial Equipment News; what's new in equipment parts, materials and literature and catalogs. m. ISSN 0019-8285
- Technology Mart. bi-m. ISSN 0049-3198
- Thomas Grocery Register. a. ISSN 0082-4151
- Thomas Register of American Manufacturers. a. ISSN 0082-4216

**Thomist Press**
487 Michigan Ave., N.E., Washington, DC 20017.
- Thomist; a speculative quarterly review of theology and philosophy. q. ISSN 0040-6325 (Dominican Fathers, Province of St. Joseph)

**Thompson Bureau**
5395 S. Miller St., Littleton, CO 80123.
- Cat World. bi-m.
- Topicator; classified article guide to the advertising/communications/marketing periodical press. m. ISSN 0040-9340

**Allan Thompson, Ed. & Pub.**
1041 E. Green St., Pasadena, CA 91106.
- Architectural Design, Cost & Data. m. ISSN 0003-8512

**Phillip Thomson, Ed. & Pub.**
836 Georgia St., Williamston, MI 48895.
- Index to Book Reviews in the Humanities. a. ISSN 0073-5892

**Thomson Tattler**
c/o University of Washington, Institute for Comparative and Foreign Area Studies, Seattle, WA 98195.
- Thomson Tattler. m.

**Thoreau Fellowship, Inc.**
Box 551, Old Town, ME 04468.
- Thoreau Journal Quarterly. q. ISSN 0040-6392

**Thoreau Lyceum**
156 Belknap St., Concord, MA 01742.
- Concord Saunterer. q.

**Thoreau Society, Inc.**
State University College, Geneseo, NY 14454.
- Thoreau Society Booklets. irreg.
- Thoreau Society Bulletin; devoted to the life and writings of Henry David Thoreau. q. ISSN 0040-6406

**Thorndyke File**
c/o Philip T. Asdell, Ed., R.R. 5, Box 355, Frederick, MD 21701.
- Thorndyke File. s-a.

**C. W. Thornwaite**
Rt. 1, Centerton, Elmer, NJ 08318.
- Publications in Climatology. irreg., vol. 27, 1974. (Laboratory of Climatology, Centerton, N.J.)

**Thoroughbred Owners & Breeders Association**
Box 4038, Lexington, KY 40504.
- Blood-Horse. w. ISSN 0006-4998

**Thoroughbred Racing Associations**
522 Fifth Ave., New York, NY 10036.
- Thoroughbred Racing Associations. Directory and Record Book. a. ISSN 0082-4240

**Thorp Springs Press**
2311-C Woolsey, Berkeley, CA 94705
- Hyperion; a poetry journal. q. ISSN 0018-8328 (Order: c/o Judy Hogan, Chase Park 2D, Chapel Hill NC 27514)
- Tawte; a Journal of Texas Culture; Texas artists, writers and thinkers in exile. s-a.

**Thought and the Spark**
139 West Valley Stream Blvd., Valley Stream, N.Y.
- Thought and the Spark. q. ISSN 0040-6473

**Thread Institute, Inc.**
1133 Avenue of the Americas, Suite 3122, New York, NY 10036.
- Register of Thread Trademarks in the U.S.A. every 3 to 5 years.

**Three Continents Press**
1346 Connecticut Ave. N.W., Suite 1121, Washington, DC 20036.
- Critical Perspectives. irreg.

**Three H O Foundation**
1620 Preuss Rd., Los Angeles, CA 90035.
- Beads of Truth. q.

**Three Mountains Press**
P.O. Box 50, Cooper Station, New York, NY 10003.
- Book Collector's Market; the book collector's little magazine.

**Three Rivers Press**
P.O. Box 21, Carnegie-Mellon University, Pittsburgh, PA 15213.
- Three Rivers Poetry Journal. s-a.

**Three Sons Publishing Co.**
6311 Gross Point Rd., Niles, IL 60648.
- Scrap Age. m. ISSN 0036-9527

- Waste Age. m. ISSN 0043-1001

**Thresholds in Education Foundation**
329 Graham Hall, Northern Illinois University, Dekalb, IL 60115.
- Thresholds in Secondary Education. q.

**Through to Victory**
731 N. Sanders, Ridgecrest, CA 93555.
- Through to Victory. 11 per yr. ISSN 0040-6600

**Thrum's All About Hawaii**
P.O. Box 100, Honolulu, HI 96810.
- Thrum's All About Hawaii. a.

**Thunderbird American Indian Dancers**
c/o Margaret D. Meizner, 5 Tudor City Place, New York, NY 10017.
- American Indian News. m. ISSN 0300-7278

**Thunderbolt, Inc.**
Box 1211, Marietta, GA 30061.
- Thunderbolt. s-m. ISSN 0040-6643 (National States Rights Party)

**Tibet Society**
Indiana University, Goodbody Hall 101, Bloomington, IN 47401.
- Tibet Society Bulletin. irreg. (approx. 1-2 per yr.)
- Tibet Society Newsletter. s-a.

**Tibetan Nyingma Meditation Center**
- Crystal Mirror. (pub. by Dharma Publishing)
- Gesar. (pub. by Dharma Publishing)

**Ticker Publishing Co.**
70 Seventh St., Garden City, NY 10022.
- Magazine of Wall Street. fortn. ISSN 0024-9858

**Ticonium Company**
Division of CMP Industries, Inc., Box 407, North Chatham, NY 12132.
- Tic; a magazine for dentists, dental assistants and dental hygienists. m. ISSN 0040-6716

**Tide Collective**
373 No. Western, Room 202, Los Angeles, CA 90004.
- Tide; voice of the lesbian feminist community. m.

**Tidewater Automobile Association**
c/o J. T. Timmons, 739 Bousn St., Norfolk, VA 23510.
- Tidewater Motorists. s-m. ISSN 0040-6783

**Tile Contractors' Association of America, Inc**
c/o Pub. J. R. Wilson, 3421 Ocean View Blvd., Glendale, CA 91208.
- Tile & Architectural Ceramics. m. ISSN 0040-7666

**Tilley Associates**
617 Cliffside Drive, Akron, OH 44313.
- Communication Reports. m. ISSN 0010-3543 (Industrial Communication Council)

**Time Barrier Enterprises, Inc.**
Box 1109, White Plains, NY 10602.
- Time Barrier Express; into the roots of rock & roll. 8 per yr. ISSN 0099-0396

**Time Inc.**
Time & Life Bldg., New York, NY 10020.
(Subscr. to: Time, Inc., 591 N. Fairbanks Ct., Chicago, IL 60611)
- Fortune. m. ISSN 0015-8259
- Money. m.
- People (New York) w. ISSN 0093-7673
- Sports Illustrated. w. ISSN 0038-822X
- Time; the weekly newsmagazine. w. ISSN 0040-781X

**Time, Inc. Fortune Division**
Time & Life Bldg., Rm. 1828, Rockefeller Center, New York, NY 10020.
- Fortune Double 500 Directory. a.
- Fortune World Business Directory; the 500 largest industrials and the 50 largest banks outside the U.S. a.

**Time-Life Books, Inc.**
(Subsidiary of: Time, Inc.)
777 Duke Street, Alexandria, VA 22314.
- Nature/Science Annual. a. ISSN 0085-3860
- Photography Year. a. ISSN 0090-4406

**Times-Mirror Magazines, Inc.**
380 Madison Ave., New York, NY 10017.
- Golf. m. ISSN 0017-1808
- Homeowners How to Handbook. bi-m. (Popular Science Publishing Co.)
- Motorcamping Handbook. s-a. (Popular Science Publishing Co.)
- Outboard Boating Handbook. a. ISSN 0094-8101
- Outdoor Life. m. ISSN 0030-7076
- Popular Science; the what's new magazine. m. ISSN 0032-4647
- Ski. 7 per yr. ISSN 0037-6159 (Popular Science Publishing Co.)
- Ski Business. m. ISSN 0037-6191
- Ski Magazine's Guide to Cross Country Skiing. a.

**Times Mirror Press**
1115 S. Boyle Ave., Los Angeles, CA 90023.
- California Manufacturers Register. a. ISSN 0068-5739 (California Manufacturers Association)

**Times of Havana Publishing Co., Inc.**
830 Woodward Building, Washington, DC 20005.
- Times of the Americas. fortn. ISSN 0040-7917

**Times Publishing Co.**
Box 373, Wellpinit, WA 99040.
- Rawhide Press. m. ISSN 0300-6328 (Spokane Tribe of Indians Tribal Council)

**Timken Co.**
1835 Dueber Ave. S.W., Canton, OH 44706.
- Timken. 6 per yr. ISSN 0040-7925

**Tin Container Collectors Association**
1496 S. Macon St., Aurora, CO 80010.
- Tin Type. m.

**Tin Industry (Research and Development) Board**
- Tin News. (pub. by Malayan Tin Bureau)

**Tire and Rim Association, Inc.**
3200 W. Market St., Akron, OH 44313.
- Tire and Rim Association. Standards Year Book. a. ISSN 0082-4496

**Tissue Culture Association, Inc.**
12111 Parklawn Dr., Rockville, MD 20852.
- Index of Tissue Culture Literature; a guide to literature in the field. a.

**Titanic Historical Society, Inc.**
P.O. Box 53, Indian Orchard, MA 01051.
- Titanic Commutator. q. ISSN 0040-8182

**Title Guarantee - New York**
120 Broadway, New York, NY 10005.
- Summary of Recent Decisions Relating to the Law of Real Property. q.

**Title Varies**
Box 704, Chapel Hill, NC 27514.
- Title Varies. bi-m. ISSN 0092-6108

**Titsch Publishing Co.**
1139 Delaware Plaza, Box 4305, Denver, CO 80204.
- Cable File. a. ISSN 0363-1915
- Cablevision. bi-w. ISSN 0361-8374
- Communications/Engineering Digest. m. (Society of Cable Television Engineers)
- Two-Way Radio Dealer. m.

**Toastmasters International**
2200 N. Grand Ave., Santa Ana, CA 92711.
- Toastmaster; for better listening, thinking, speaking. m. ISSN 0040-8263

**Tobacco Associates**
1101 17 St. N.W., Washington, DC 20036.
- Tobacco Associates. Annual Report. a. ISSN 0082-4593

**Tobacco Literature Service**
2314 D. H. Hill Library, North Carolina State University, Raleigh, NC 27607.
- Tobacco Abstracts; world literature on nicotiana. m. ISSN 0040-8298
- Tobacco Reprint Series. irreg.

**Tobacco Merchants Association of the United States**
Statler Hilton, 7Th Ave. & 33rd St., New York, NY 10001.
- B I T S. (Bi-Weekly Index of the Tobacco Scene)
- T M A Guide to Tobacco Taxes; summaries of key provisions of tobacco tax laws, all tobacco products, all states. q.
- T M A Leaf Bulletin. w. (approx.)

- Tobacco Barometer: Cigarettes, Cigars. m.
- Tobacco Barometer: Smoking, Chewing, Snuff. q.
- Tobacco Trade Barometer. m. ISSN 0495-6753
- Tobacco Update. q.

**Tobey Publishing Co.**
Box 428, New Canaan, CT 06840.
- Easy Magazine. m.

**Today Publications and News Service, Inc.**
621 National Press Building, Washington, DC 20045.
- Adult & Community Education Organizations & Leaders Directory. a.
- Adult & Continuing Education Today. fortn. ISSN 0001-8473
- Journal of Reprints Affecting Women's Rights & Opportunities. q. ISSN 0362-062X
- Law & Women Series. irreg.
- Official Registry of C B Operators. a.
- Women Today. fortn. ISSN 0043-7506
- Women's Organizations & Leaders Directory. a. ISSN 0092-6639

**Todd Publications**
Box 535, Rye, NY 10580.
- Guide to American Educational Directories. irreg. ISSN 0072-8225
- Guide to American Scientific and Technical Directories. biennial; 3rd edt., 1978. ISSN 0094-4505
- Reference Encyclopedia of the American Indian. triennial; 3rd edt., 1977.

**Token and Medal Society**
Ed. Virginia Culver, Box 96, Thiensville, WI 53092.
- T A M S Journal. bi-m. ISSN 0039-8233

**Tolar Creek Syndicate**
1901 S. 7th, Tucumcari, NM 88401.
- Tolar Creek Syndicate. irreg. ISSN 0040-9030

**Toledo Area Chamber of Commerce**
Chamber of Commerce Bldg., 218 Huron St., Toledo, OH 43604.
- Toledo Business News. m. ISSN 0040-9057

**Toledo Commission of Publicity and Efficiency**
618 Michigan St., Toledo, OH 43624.
- Toledo City Journal. w. ISSN 0040-9065

**Toledo Dental Society**
c/o Mrs. Kathy Bender, 515 Madison Ave., Suite 505, Toledo, OH 43604.
- Toledo Dental Society. Bulletin. m. ISSN 0040-9073

**Toledo Federation of Art Societies, Inc**
- Toledo Area Artists Exhibition. (pub. by Toledo Museum of Art)

**Toledo-Lucas County Port Authority**
241 Superior St., Toledo, OH 43604.
- Port of Toledo News. q. ISSN 0032-4868

**Toledo Museum of Art**
Box 1013, Toledo, OH 43697.
- Toledo Area Artists Exhibition. a. ISSN 0082-4852 (Toledo Federation of Art Societies, Inc)
- Toledo Museum News. q. ISSN 0049-4062

**Toledo Organization of Psychic Sciences (T O P S)**
Mulberry St., Toledo, OH 43604.
- Psychic Eye. m.

**Bernard Tolk Co.**
2226 Clay St., San Francisco, CA 94115.
- Professional Nutritionist. q. ISSN 0033-0159 (Foremost Foods Company, S.F)

**Tolkien Society of America**
Belknap College, Center Harbor, NH 03226.
- Tolkien Journal. q. ISSN 0040-909X

**Tolkien Society. University of Wisconsin**
c/o Ed. Richard C. West, 1922 Madison St., Madison, WI 53711.
- Orcrist; a journal of fantasy in the arts. a. (approx.) ISSN 0474-3369

**Toll Free Digest Co.**
Box 800, Claverack, NY 12513.
- Toll Free Digest; a directory of toll free telephone numbers. a. ISSN 0363-2962

**Tolphus Books**
P.O. 248, Edgewater, NJ 07020.
- Third Thing. s-a.

**Tombstone Epitaph**
Box 1880, Tombstone, AZ 85638.
- Tombstone Epitaph; the historical journal of the old West. m.

**Francis J. Tominey**
470 Atlantic Ave., Boston, MA 02210.
- New England Advertising Week. w. ISSN 0028-4653

**Tonatiuh International, Inc.**
2150 Shattuck Ave., Berkeley, CA 94704.
- Grito del Sol; a Chicano quarterly. q.

**Tonto Publishing Co.**
1309 E. McDowell Rd., Phoenix, AZ 85006.
- Car Model. m.

**Tooth of Time Review**
c/o John Brandi, Ed., Box 356, Guadalupita, NM 87722.
- Tooth of Time Review. 4-6 per yr.

**Toothpaste Press**
Box 546, West Branch, IA 52358.
- Dental Floss. s-a.

**Toothpick, Lisbon & the Orcas Islands Press**
922 E. Alder, Seattle, WA 98122.
- Declassified. q.
- Toothpick, Lisbon & the Orcas Islands. irreg.

**Topeka Public Library**
1515 W. 10th St., Topeka, KS 66604.
- Tall Windows. 4 per yr. ISSN 0085-7084

**Michael Torf**
115 2nd Ave., Waltham, MA 02154.
- Dealerscope. m. ISSN 0011-7218

**Torrey Botanical Club**
c/o H. David Hammond, Ed., Dept. of Biological Sciences, S.U.C. at Brockport, Brockport, NY 14420.
- Torrey Botanical Club. Bulletin. q. ISSN 0040-9618

**Torrington Co.**
Bearings Division, Torrington, CT 06790.
- Bearing Engineer. bi-m. ISSN 0005-7428

**Carlos Tort International, Inc.**
4753 Broadway, Chicago, IL 60640.
- Hospital. bi-m.
- Panadero Latinoamericano/Latin American Baker. bi-m. ISSN 0031-0638

**Totalworld Services of Provincetown, Inc.**
596A Commercial St., Provincetown, MA 02657.
- Provincetown Poets. q. ISSN 0362-8396

**Tottel's**
c/o Ron Silliman, Ed., 3028 California, San Francisco, CA 94115.
- Tottel's. 2-5 per yr.

**Touchdown Publications Inc.**
One Embarcadero Center, San Francisco, CA 94111.
- Touchdown Illustrated. 45 per yr.

**Touche Ross & Co.**
Box 919, Radio City Station, New York, NY 10019.
- Tempo. q. ISSN 0040-3016

**Tour Arrangements, Inc.**
82 Washington St., Marblehead, MA 01945.
- Everyday Gourmet. bi-w.

**Tourist Court Journal Co.**
306 E. Adams Ave., Temple, TX 76501.
- Motel/Motor Inn Journal. m. ISSN 0040-9790

**Tovarystvo Ukrayins'kykh Inzheneriv Ameryki**
- Visti Ukrayins'kykh Inzheneriv/Ukrainian Engineering News. (pub. by Ukrainian Engineers' Society of America)

**Toward Freedom, Inc.**
343 S. Dearborn St., Chicago, IL 60604.
- Toward Freedom; a newsletter on new nations. m. ISSN 0040-9898

**Tower International TechnoMedical Institute, Inc.**
Box 4594, Philadelphia, PA 19131.
- T. I. T. Journal of Life Sciences. q. ISSN 0039-8160

**Tower Press, Inc.**
Box 428, Seabrook, NH 03874.
- Aunt Jane's Sewing Circle. q.
- Good Old Days. 14 per yr. ISSN 0046-6158
- Good Old Days Christmas Annual. a.
- Good Old Days Specials. q.
- Looking Back to Those Wonderful Days Gone by. q. since 1975. ISSN 0360-5108
- Olde Time Needlework, Patterns and Design. bi-m.
- Popular Needlework and Craft. bi-m.
- Quilt World. s-a.
- Singles Circle. bi-m.
- Stitch 'n Sew. bi-m.
- Women's Circle Homeworker. bi-m.
- Women's Comfort. m. ISSN 0510-7350
- Women's Household. m. ISSN 0510-7385

**Town & Village Inc.**
235 Park Ave., New York, NY 10003.
- Town and Village. w. ISSN 0040-9979

**Township Officials of Illinois**
411 1/2 S. Fifth, Springfield, IL 62701.
- Illinois County and Township Official. m. ISSN 0019-1949 (Co-Sponsor: Illinois Assn. of County Officials)

**Towson State College. International Studies Department**
Box 1951, Baltimore, MD 21204.
- Towson State Journal of International Affairs. s-a. ISSN 0041-0063

**Track & Field News, Inc.**
Box 296, Los Altos, CA 94022.
- Track & Field News. m. ISSN 0041-0284
- Track Newsletter. 20 per yr. ISSN 0041-0306
- Track Technique; the quarterly journal of track & field athletics. q. ISSN 0041-0314

**Tracommunications**
21121 Richmond Circle, Huntington Beach, CA 92646.
- Compleat Review. m.

**Trade Activities, Inc.**
435 Hudson St., New York, NY 10014.
- Patent and Trademark Review. m.(bi-m.July-Aug) ISSN 0031-2835

**Trade Periodicals Inc.**
434 S. Wabash, Chicago, IL 60605.
- A V Guide: the Learning Media Magazine. m.

**Trade Press Publishing Co.**
407 E. Michigan St., Milwaukee, WI 53202.
- Building Operating Management; the national magazine for commercial, industrial and institutional buildings. m. ISSN 0007-3490
- Hot Line. 3 per yr.

**Trade Publications, Inc.**
Box 5857, Baltimore, MD 21208.
- Food World. m.

**Trade Publications, Inc. (Miami)**
1301 S.W. First St., Miami, FL 33135.
- Florida Grocer. m.

**Trade Publishing Co. Ltd.**
287 Mokauea St., Honolulu, Hawaii, HI 96819.
- Builders Report Pacific. w. ISSN 0007-3296

**Trader Speaks**
c/o Dan Dischley, Ed., 3 Pleasant Dr., Lake Ronkonkoma, NY 11779.
- Trader Speaks. m.

**Trades Publishing Co.**
Washington & Main St., Albert Lea, MN 56007.
- Northwestern Jeweler. m. ISSN 0029-3490

**Trades Unionist Inc. A F L-C I O**
1126 16th St., N.W. Room 317, Washington, DC 20036.
- Trades Unionist. w. ISSN 0041-0578 (Co-Sponsor: Greater Washington Central Labor Council AFL-CIO)

**Tradeshow Week, Inc.**
1605 Cahuenga Blvd., Los Angeles, CA 90028.
- Tradeshow Week; the management newsletter of the tradeshow industry. 48 per yr.

**Traffic Analysis Service**
Box 942, Duncan, OK 73533.
- Carrier Case Reports; analysis and annotations of current decisions of the Federal courts and the Interstate Commerce Commission. m. ISSN 0362-2916

**Traffic Service Corp.**
815 Washington Bldg., Washington, DC 20005.
- Daily Traffic World; a complete daily report of all traffic and transportation news. d.
- Traffic Bulletin. w. ISSN 0041-0659
- Traffic World; a working tool for traffic and transportation executives. w. ISSN 0041-073X

**George L. Trager, Ed. & Pub.**
Box 85, Taos, NM 87571.
- Studies in Linguistics. Occasional Paper. irreg., no. 13, 1975. ISSN 0081-816X

**Trail Blazer's Publishing Co.**
206 W. Fourth St., Kewanee, IL 61443.
- Trail Blazer's Almanac. a.

**Trail Press Inc.**
Fayette, MO 65248.
- Missouri Family Doctor. m. ISSN 0026-6566 (Missouri Academy of General Practice)

**Trailbeau Publications Inc.**
2823 N. 48 St., Phoenix, AZ 85008.
- Arizona Business and Industry. m.

**Trailer Dealer Publishing Co.**
6229 Northwest Highway, Chicago, IL 60631.
- Mobile Home Park Management & Developer. bi-m.
- Mobile-Modular Housing Dealer. m.
- R V Dealer. m.

**Trailer Life Publishing Co. Inc.**
23945 Craftsman Rd., Calabasas, CA 91302.
- Motorhome Life & Camper Coachman. bi-m. ISSN 0361-1043
- Recreational Vehicle Retailer; the RV dealer magazine that knows the RV buying public. m. ISSN 0300-628X
- Rider; motorcycle touring & commuting. q. ISSN 0095-1625
- Trailer Life. m. ISSN 0041-0780
- Trailer Life's Recreational Vehicle Campground and Services Directory. a.

**Train Collectors Association**
501 Kissel Hill Rd., Lititz, PA 17543.
- Train Collectors Quarterly. q. ISSN 0041-0829

**Trans-High Corp.**
Drawer 919 Madison Square Sta., New York, NY 10010.
- Dealer. m.

**Trans-High Corporation**
Box 386, Cooper Station, New York, NY 10003.
- High Times; the magazine of high society. q.

**Trans-Media Publishing Co.**
Dobbs Ferry, NY 10522.
- Economics Working Papers. m. ISSN 0094-6451
- Economics Working Papers: Bibliography. s-a.

**Trans Mediterranean Airways**
155-04 New York Blvd., Jamaica, NY 11434.
- T M A Expertise. m.

**Trans Pacific Stamp Co.**
Box 48715, Los Angeles, CA 90048.
- Hebert's Catalogue of Used Plate Number Singles. irreg. ISSN 0098-2326

**Trans Tech Publications**
411 Long Beach Pkwy., Bay Village, OH 44140.
- Diffusion and Defect Data; a continuous compilation of new reference data on solid and liquid state diffusion and the defect solid state. 2 per yr.
- Mechanical Properties. s-a. ISSN 0361-2821
- Series on Bulk Materials Engineering. irreg. (3-5 per yr.)
- Series on Rock and Soil Mechanics. irreg (4-6 per yr) ISSN 0080-9004

**Trans World Airlines**
- T W A Ambassador. (pub. by Webb Co.)

**Transaction Periodicals Consortium**
Rutgers University, New Brunswick, NJ 08903.
- Africa Report. bi-m. ISSN 0001-9836 (African American Institute)
- Comparative Politics. q. ISSN 0010-4159 (City University of New York. Graduate School and University Center. Political Science Ph. D. Program)
- Comparative Urban Research. 3 per yr. ISSN 0090-3892 (City University of New York. Comparative Urban Studies Center)
- Contemporary Jewry; a journal of sociological inquiry. s-a. ISSN 0147-1694 (Association for the Sociological Study of Jewry)
- Human Communication Research. q. ISSN 0360-3989 (International Communication Association)
- International Journal of Critical Sociology. s-a.
- International Journal of Family Counseling. s-a. ISSN 0147-1775 (National Alliance for Family Life)
- International Journal of Intercultural Relations. q. ISSN 0147-1767 (Society for International Education, Training and Research)
- Journal of Jazz Studies. s-a. ISSN 0093-3686 (Institute of Jazz Studies)
- Journal of Political and Military Sociology. s-a. ISSN 0047-2697 (Northern Illinois University. Department of Sociology)
- Middle East Review. q. ISSN 0097-9791 (American Academic Association for Peace in the Middle East)
- Review of Black Political Economy. q. ISSN 0034-6446 (Black Economic Research Center)
- Society; social science & modern society. bi-m.
- Studies in Comparative International Development. 3 per yr. ISSN 0039-3606
- Urban League Review. s-a. ISSN 0147-1740 (National Urban League. Research Department)
- Washington Review of Strategic and International Studies. q. ISSN 0147-1465
- Women & Literature; a journal of women writers and the literary treatment of women. s-a. ISSN 0147-1759
- Working Papers for a New Society. q. ISSN 0091-1615 (Center for the Study of Public Policy, Inc.)

**Transamerican Press, Inc.**
1532 N. Cahuenga Blvd., Los Angeles, CA 90028.
- Overdrive. m. ISSN 0030-7394

**Transatlantic Arts, Inc.**
North Village Green, Levittown, NY 11756
(and Thames & Hudson, London, Eng.)
- Walter Neurath Memorial Lectures. a. ISSN 0085-7874

**Transatlantik Publishing Corp.**
601 W. 26th St., New York, NY 10001.
- Kontinent. m. ISSN 0023-3706

**Transcommunications International Inc.**
Box 191, Back Bay Annex, Boston, MA 02117.
- International New Product Newsletter. s-m.

**Transient Press**
Box 4662, Albuquerque, NM 87106.
- Transient. irreg.

**Transit Research Foundation of Los Angeles Inc.**
Box 3542, Terminal Annex Station, Los Angeles, CA 90051.
- City and Suburban Travel. m. ISSN 0045-6985

**Translation Company of America**
500 Fifth Ave., New York, NY 10036.
- Translation Talk. 2-4 per yr. ISSN 0041-123X

**Transmedia**
9811 Edgelake Rd., La Mesa, CA 92041.
- Surfboard Builders' Yearbook. a. ISSN 0081-9611

**Transnational Family Research Institute**
8307 Whitman Dr., Bethesda, MD 20034.
- Abortion Research Notes. 3 per yr.

**Transnational News Co. Inc.**
160 E. 88th St., New York, NY 10028
(Subscr. Address: Sheffer Co., Box 19247, Houston, TX 77024)
- Who's Who in Ecology. biennial. ISSN 0091-3154

**TransPacific**
c/o Nicholas Crome, Ed., Yellow Springs, OH 45387.
- TransPacific. irreg. ISSN 0041-1299

**Transpersonal Institute**
345 California Ave., Palo Alto, CA 94303.
- Journal of Transpersonal Psychology. s-a. ISSN 0022-524X

**Transpharma, Inc.**
Box 170, Huntington Station, NY 11746.
- Pharmascope; new products & investigational drugs. m. ISSN 0048-3648

**Transplantation Society**
- International Congress of the Transplantation Society. Proceedings. (pub. by Grune and Stratton, Inc.)
- Transplantation. (pub. by Williams & Wilkins Co.)
- Transplantation Proceedings. (pub. by Grune & Stratton, Inc.)

**Transport Workers Union of America**
1980 Broadway, New York, NY 10023.
- T W U Express. m. ISSN 0039-8659

**Transportation Alternatives**
20 Exchange Place, Rm. 5500, New York, NY 10005.
- City Cyclist. 5-6 per yr.

**Transportation Engineer**
911 W. Big Beaver Road, Troy, MI 48084.
- Transportation Engineer. m. ISSN 0041-1604

**Transportation Guides, Inc.**
299 Madison Ave., New York, NY 10017.
- Official Steamship Guide. m. ISSN 0030-0381

**Transportation Research Forum**
- Transportation Research Forum. Proceedings: Annual Meeting. (pub. by R. B. Cross Co.)

**Transportation Research Information Service**
Room 9411, 400 7th St. S.W., Washington, DC 20590.
- Trisnet News. m.

**Travel Communications, Inc.**
488 Madison Ave., New York, NY 10022.
- A S T A Travel News. m. ISSN 0001-2637 (American Society of Travel Agents)

**Travel Magazine, Inc.**
Travel Bldg., Floral Park, NY 11001.
- Holiday. m. ISSN 0018-3520
- Travel. m. ISSN 0041-1965

**Travel Master**
645 Stewart Ave., Garden City, NY 11530.
- Travel Master. s-a from 1977.

**Travel Publications, Inc.**
Box 610, Alta Loma, CA 91701.
- Runaway. q.

**Travel Rates and Places**
11 Park Ave., New York, NY 10006.
- Trip. m.

**Travel Research Association**
- Journal of Travel Research. (pub. by University of Colorado. Graduate School of Business Administration)

**Travel Trade Publishing Co.**
605 Fifth Ave., New York, NY 10017.
- Travel Trade; the business paper of the travel industry. m. ISSN 0041-2066

**Travelcade Publications, Inc.**
2195 Lantern Lane, Lafayette Hill, PA 19444.
- Travelcade. m.

**Travelers Insurance Companies**
1 Tower Sq., Hartford, CT 06115.
- Protection. m. ISSN 0033-1708

**Travelers Protective Association of America**
3755 Lindell Blvd., St. Louis, MO 36108.
- T. P. A. Travelers. q. ISSN 0039-8454

**Travelers' Research Publishing Co., Inc.**
8034 S. Prairie Ave., Chicago, IL 60619.
- Negro Traveler & Conventioneer. bi-m. ISSN 0028-2537

**Travelog Publications**
Westchester House, Suite 814, 554 S. Summit, Fort Worth, TX 76104.
- Travelog. a.

**Traveltips**
Box 11061, Oakland, CA 94611.
- Sav-on-Hotels. a. ISSN 0098-4507

**TravLtips Inc.**
40-21 Bell Blvd., Bayside, NY 11361.
- TravLtips Freighter Bulletin; budget travel news. bi-m. ISSN 0049-4585

**O. Traylor Mercer Publications, Inc.**
Box 2491, Honolulu, HI 96804.
- Honolulu Weekly Snooper. w. ISSN 0018-4659

**Treasure Hunting Unlimited**
406 Broadway St., Truth or Consequences, NM 87901.
- Treasure Hunting Unlimited. q.

**Treasure Search**
P.O. Box 175, Thousand Oaks, CA 91360.
- Treasure Search. bi-m.

**Tree Books**
Box 9005, Berkeley, CA 94709.
- Tree. s-a. ISSN 0041-2171

**Tree-Ring Society**
- Tree-Ring Bulletin. (pub. by University of Arizona. Laboratory of Tree-Ring Research)

**Trees**
7621 Lewis Rd., Olmsted Falls, OH 44138.
- Trees; journal of American arboriculture. q. ISSN 0041-2228

**Trellis Press Association**
Box 656, Morgantown, WV 26505.
- Trellis. irreg.
- Trellis Supplement. irreg.

**Tremco News**
10701 Shaker Blvd., Cleveland, OH 44104.
- Tremco News. bi-m.

**Trend Publications Inc.**
Box 2350, Tampa, FL 33601.
- Florida Trend; magazine of Florida business and finance. m. ISSN 0015-4326
- South; the journal of southern business. bi-m.

**Trendline**
345 Hudson St., New York, NY 10014.
- Trendline's Current Market Perspectives. m.

**Trends Publishing, Inc.**
National Press Bldg., Washington, DC 20045.
- Energy Today. s-m. ISSN 0093-500X
- Environment Report. s-m. ISSN 0013-9203
- Radioisotope Report. bi-m. ISSN 0033-829X
- Science Trends. w. ISSN 0043-0749
- Scientific Information Notes. q. ISSN 0036-8784

**Trendway Advisory Service, Inc.**
Box 7184, Louisville, KY 40207.
- Trendway Advisory Service. w. ISSN 0041-2430

**Trenton-Mercer County Chamber of Commerce**
Trenton, NJ 08608.
- Trenton. m. ISSN 0041-2449

**Trenton State College. Department of Geography**
Trenton, NJ 08625.
- Directions. q. ISSN 0012-3234

**Tri-County Dental Society**
31 Dehart St., Morristown, NJ 07960.
- Tri-County Dental Society. Bulletin. 7 per yr. ISSN 0041-2465

**Tri County Newspapers Inc.**
1413 Dorset Lane, Philadelphia, PA 19151.
- Key (Philadelphia) w. ISSN 0023-0766
- Overbrook Adviser. w. ISSN 0030-7386
- Tri County News. w. ISSN 0041-2473

**Tri-County Publications**
P.O. Box 2123, Carmel, CA 93921.
- Key Magazine/Carmel & Monterey Peninsula. m. (Key Organization)

**Tri-State Regional Planning Commission**
One World Trade Center, New York, NY 10048.
- Tri-State Regional Planning Commission. Annual Regional Report. a. ISSN 0092-2358
- Tri-State Regional Planning Commission. Regional Profile. irreg., vol. 2, 1973.

**Tri-State Transportation Commission**
One World Trade Center, New York, NY 10048.
- Tri-State Transportation Commission. Public Transport Services to Non C/B/D Employment Concentrations; Progress Report. irreg. ISSN 0082-6359

**Tri-State United Way**
99 Park Ave., New York, NY 10016.
- Together (New York) q.

**Triangle**
Ed. Herbert F. Scobie, 2114 Central St., Evanston, IL 60201.
- Triangle Review. q. ISSN 0041-2627

**Triangle Communications Inc.**
850 3rd Ave., New York, NY 10022.
- Seventeen. m. ISSN 0037-301X

**Triangle Publications**
250 King of Prussia St., Radnor, PA 19088.
- T V Guide. w. ISSN 0039-8543
- Tape Recording. bi-m.

**Triangle Publications Inc.**
731 Plymouth Court, Chicago, IL 60605.
- Daily Racing Form Chart Book. m.

**Tribal Press**
c/o Howard McCord, Ed., 149 S. Prospect, Bowling Green, OH 43402.
- Measure. s-a.

**Tribe of Many Feathers (Indian Club)**
- Eagle's Eye. (pub. by Brigham Young University)

**Tribuna de New Jersey**
70 Kossuth Street, Newark, NJ 07105.
- Tribuna. s-m.

**Tribune Publishing Co.**
4614 Dodge St., Omaha, NE 68103.
- Milwaukee Herald. w.
- Sonntagspost. w.
- Volkszeitung Tribune. w.
- Welt Post und Staatsanzeiger. w.

**Trilateral Commission**
345 East 46 St., New York, NY 10017.
- Trialogue; bulletin of North American-European-Japanese affairs. 3 per yr.

**Trinc Transportation Consultants**
485 L'Enfant Plaza, S. W., Suite 4200, Washington, DC 20024.
- Dun & Bradstreet Reference Book of Transportation. irreg. ISSN 0093-9528
- Trinc's Blue Book of the Trucking Industry. a. ISSN 0082-6499

**Trinity College (Hartford)**
Hartford, CT 06106.
- Journal of British Studies. s-a. ISSN 0021-9371 (Conference on British Studies)

**Trinity College (Washington)**
Washington, DC 20017.
- Trinity College Record. q. ISSN 0041-3054

**Trinity Evangelical Divinity School**
2045 Half Day Road, Deerfield, IL 60015.
- Trinity Journal. a. ISSN 0360-3032

**Trinity Lutheran Hospital**
31 St. & Wyandotte St., Kansas City, MO 64108.
- Trinity Report. q.

**Trinity University. Department of Religion**
715 Stadium Dr., San Antonio, TX 78284.
- Trinity University Studies in Religion; papers by members of Trinity University Studies in Religion Seminar. irreg. (every 2-3 yrs), 1971, vol. 9. ISSN 0082-6596

**Trinity University Press**
Trinity University, 715 Stadium Dr., San Antonio, TX 78284.
- Checklists in the Humanities and Education. irreg. ISSN 0069-2824
- Trinity University Monograph Series in Religion. irreg. (approx every 18 mos.)

**Trio Publications**
127 Powelton Ave., Woodlynne, NJ 08107.
- Singles News. m.

**TriQuarterly**
Northwestern Univeristy, University Hall 101, Evanston, IL 60201.
- TriQuarterly. 3 per yr. ISSN 0041-3097

**Abner L. Tritt**
Box 15500, New Orleans, LA 70115.
- Jewish Civic Press. m. ISSN 0021-6348

**Triumph Magazine, Inc.**
278 Broadview Ave., Warrenton, VA 22186.
- Catholic Currents. s-m. ISSN 0008-798X
- Triumph. m.(except July-Aug) ISSN 0041-3127

**Trocadero Publishing Co., Inc.**
1111 Lexington Ave., New York, NY 10021.
- France-Amerique. w.

**Harlan Trott, Ed. & Pub.**
681 Market St., San Francisco, CA 94105.
- Business Digest. m. ISSN 0007-6651

**Trouser Press**
732 S. Forest St. No. 5, Ann Arbor, MI 48104.
- Anaesthesia Review. s-a.

**Trout Unlimited**
4260 E. Evans Ave., Denver, CO 80222.
- Trout. q. ISSN 0041-3364

**Troy Enterprises Co.**
Box 53371, Oklahoma City, OK 73105.
- Oklahoma Observer. s-m. ISSN 0030-1795

**Troy State University Press**
Troy, AL 36081.
- Journal of Band Research. s-a. ISSN 0021-9207 (American Bandmasters Association) (Co-Sponsors: College Band Directors National Assn.; National Band Assn.; American School Band Directors Assn.)

**Truck Press**
c/o David Wilk, Ed., 1141 James Ave., St. Paul, MN 55105.
- Truck. 2-3 per yr.

**Truck Tracks Inc.**
Box 1575, Lake Grove, OR 97034.
- Truck Tracks. m.

**Truck Trends**
Ed. Melvin W. Morgan, 3950 Lake Shore Dr., Chicago, IL 60613.
- Truck Trends. m. ISSN 0049-478X

**Trucking Activities, Inc.**
1240 Bayshore Hwy., Burlingame, CA 94010.
- Go (Burlingame); Transport Times of the West. m. ISSN 0017-1433

**Truly Fine Press**
525 12th Street, Bemidji, MN 56601.
- Letters to F. A. q.

**Estelle Trust, Ed. & Pub.**
166 Albany Ave., Shreveport, LA 71105.
- Quintessence. q. ISSN 0033-6564

**Truth Seeker Co., Inc.**
Box 2832, San Diego, CA 92112.
- Atheist. irreg.
- Truth Seeker. m. ISSN 0041-3712

**Try It, You'll like It**
c/o Joyce Kline, Editor, 4031 Greenwood Rd., New Kensington, PA 15068.
- Try It, You'll like It.

**John Tsitrian, Ed. & Pub.**
8626 Santa Margarita Lane, La Palma, CA 90623.
- American Collective. bi-m.

**Tubists Universal Brotherhood Association**
- T.U.B.A. Series. (pub. by Brass Press)

**Tucson Educational Association**
4625 E. Second St., Tucson, AZ 85711.
- T E A Newsletter; a professional journal for a united teaching profession. w. ISSN 0039-8306

**Tuesday Publications, Inc.**
625 N. Michigan Ave., Chicago, IL 60611.
- Tuesday. m. ISSN 0041-3933

**Tufts Kinsmen Association**
Box 571, Dedham, MA 02026.
- Tufts Kinsmen. q.

**Tufts New England Medical Center**
Office of Public Relations, 173 Harrison Ave. Box 442, Boston, MA 02111.
- Tufts Health Science Review. q. ISSN 0041-395X

**Tufts University Theater**
Medford, MA 02155.
- Prologue (Medford) 3-4 per yr. ISSN 0033-1007

**Tufty Communications, Inc.**
986 National Press Bldg, Washington, DC 20004.
- Value Engineering and Management Digest/Defence Contract Guide. m.

**Tulane Institute of Comparative Law**
6823 St. Charles Ave., New Orleans, LA 70118.
- Inter-American Law Review/Revista Juridica Inter-Americana. s-a. ISSN 0020-4951

**Tulane Law Review Association**
Tulane University Station, New Orleans, LA 70118.
- Tulane Law Review. 4 per yr. ISSN 0041-3992

**Tulane Medical Center. Alumni Association**
1430 Tulane Ave., New Orleans, LA 70112.
- Tulane Medicine: Faculty and Alumni. q. ISSN 0041-400X

**Tulane University. Department of Biology**
New Orleans, LA 70118.
- Tulane Studies in Zoology and Botany. irreg., 1969, vol. 16, no. 2. ISSN 0082-6782

**Tulane University. Department of English**
New Orleans, LA 70118.
- Tulane Studies in English. a. ISSN 0082-6758

**Tulane University. Department of Geology**
New Orleans, LA 70118.
- Tulane Studies in Geology and Paleontology. q. ISSN 0041-4018

**Tulane University. Department of Mechanical Engineering**
Tulane, LA 70118.
- Southeastern Seminar on Thermal Sciences. Proceedings. irreg.

**Tulane University. Department of Philosophy**
- Tulane Studies in Philosophy. (pub. by Martinus Nijhoff NE)

**Tulane University. Department of Political Science**
New Orleans, LA 70118.
- Tulane Studies in Political Science. a. ISSN 0082-6774

**Tulane University. Department of Sociology and Anthropology**
New Orleans, LA 70118.
- Human Mosaic. s-a. ISSN 0018-7240

**Tulane University. Division of Alumni Activities**
6319 Willow St., New Orleans, LA 70118.
- Tulanian. q. ISSN 0041-4026

**Tulane University. Library**
New Orleans, LA 70118.
- Howard-Tilton Memorial Library. Report. a. ISSN 0082-6790

**Tulane University School of Law**
New Orleans, LA 70118.
- Tulane Civil Law Forum. q.

**Tulsa City-County Library System**
Business and Technology Dept., 400 Civic Center, Tulsa, OK 74103.
- I N F O. m. ISSN 0019-0136

**Tulsa County Bar Association**
822 Beacon Bldg., Tulsa, OK 74103.
- Tulsa Lawyer. q. ISSN 0041-4069

**Tunnell Publications, Inc.**
1602 Harold St, Houston, TX 77006.
- Refrigerated Transporter. m. ISSN 0034-3129
- Trailer-Body Builders. m. ISSN 0041-0772

**Turf and Sport International, Ltd.**
511 Oakland Ave., Baltimore, MD 21212.
- Turf and Sport Digest. q. ISSN 0041-4158

**Turkish Embassy**
1606 23rd St., N.W., Washington, DC 20008.
- Turkey Today. m. ISSN 0494-2884

**John D. Turrel, Ed. & Pub.**
R. 2, Mt. Vernon, IL 62864.
- Electric Letter; covering the power-supplier/public interface. bi-w.

**Turtle Bay Association**
224 E. 47th St., New York, NY 10017.
- Turtle Bay Gazette. q. ISSN 0049-4879

**Turtle Island Foundation**
2845 Buena Vista Way, Berkeley, CA 94708.
- New World Journal. a.

**Tuskegee Institute**
- Campus Digest. (pub. by Bulletin Publishing Co.)

**J. Tutching**
Box 121, Saugatuck, CT 06880.
- Business Equipment Marketing. m.
- Copier/Duplicator Dealer Report. m. (Association of Independent Copy Machine Dealers and Manufacturers)
- Copier-Duplicator World. m.

**Tuvoti Books**
Box 439, California, PA 15419.
- Tuvoti Books. a.

**Twain Associates**
Box 1179, Lowell, MA 01853.
- Massachusetts Apartment and Condominium Living. m.

**Twayne Publishers, Inc.**
(Subsidiary of: G.K. Hall, Inc.)
70 Lincoln St., Boston, MA 02111.
- Immigrant Heritage of America Series. irreg.
- Library of Scandinavian Literature. irreg. ISSN 0075-9155 (American-Scandinavian Foundation)
- Twayne's English Authors Series. 16-20 per yr. ISSN 0564-559X
- Twayne's United States Authors Series. 16-20 per yr. ISSN 0496-6015
- Twayne's World Leaders Series. irreg.

**Twentieth Century Fund**
41 E. 70th St., New York, NY 10021.
- Twentieth Century Fund. Newsletter. 3 per yr.(approx.) ISSN 0041-4611

**Twentieth Century Publications, Inc.**
Box 978, 6226 Vineland Ave., North Hollywood, CA 91603.
- Custom Vans. m.
- Minicycle. m.

**Twenty-Third Publications**
Box 180, West Mystic, CT 06388.
- Religion Teacher's Journal. m. ISSN 0034-401X
- Today's Parish. m. ISSN 0040-8549

**Twilight**
Box 853, G. P. O. Bronx, NY 10451.
- Twilight. w. ISSN 0049-4909

**Twin Circle Publishing Co.**
Box 25986, Los Angeles, CA 90025.
- National Catholic Register. w. ISSN 0027-8920
- Twin Circle; the National Catholic Press. w. ISSN 0041-4654

**Twin Cities Media Project Inc.**
Box 17113, St. Paul, MN 55117.
- Twin Cities Journalism Review. bi-m.

**Twin City Purchasing Management Association**
c/o Robert R. Burns, 2617 E. Hennepin Ave., Minneapolis, MN 55413.
- Purchasing Management. m.

**Twin Coast Newspapers, Inc.**
99 Wall St., New York, NY 10005.
- Directory of United States Importers. a. ISSN 0070-6531
- Journal of Commerce. 5 per w. ISSN 0021-9827

**Twin Oaks Community**
- Leaves of Twin Oaks. (pub. by Community Publications Cooperative)

**Two Feet of Poetry**
c/o Barry Targan, Ed., 46 Burgoyne St., Sschuylerville, NY 12871.
- Two Feet of Poetry. irreg.

**Two Hands News**
1125 W. Webster, Chicago, IL 60614.
- Two Hands News. m. except Jul.-Aug.

**Typewriter**
Box 409, Iowa City, IA 52240.
- Typewriter. 1-2 per yr.

**U.A.W. & A.F.L.-C.I.O. Local Unions. Capital Area Community Action Program**
342 Clare St., Lansing, MI 48917.
- Lansing Labor News. fortn. ISSN 0023-8384

**U.F.W., A.F.L.-C.I.O.**
Box 62, Keene, CA 93531.
- Malcriado/Voice of the Farm Worker. fortn. ISSN 0025-1356

**U H A Publishing**
Drawer 690, Middleboro, MA 02346.
- United Horsemen. q. (United Horsemen Association)

**U S A-C I O Local Union 1010**
3703 Euclid Ave., East Chicago, IN 46312.
- Local 1010 Steelworker; at Inland Steel Company. m. ISSN 0041-5448

**U S A-C I O. Local 1104**
2501 Broadway, Lorain, OH 44052.
- Lorain Labor Leader. w. ISSN 0024-6484

**U S A Publishing Co., Inc.**
530 E. 72nd St., New York, NY 10021.
- U S A. m. ISSN 0041-7483

**U S - Austrian Chamber of Commerce**
165 W. 46th St., New York, NY 10036.
- Austrian Business. bi-m.

**U S Capitol Historical Society**
200 Maryland Ave. N.E., Washington, DC 20515.
- Capitol Studies. s-a. ISSN 0045-5687

**U S-China Friendship Association**
50 Oak St., San Francisco, CA 94102.
- U S-China Friendship Association. Bulletin. q.

**U S-China Peoples Friendship Association**
41 Union Square W., New York, NY 10003.
- New China. 4 per yr.

**U S Conference of Mennonite Brethren Churches**
- Christian Leader. (pub. by Mennonite Brethren Publishing House)

**U S Directory Service**
Box 1832, Kansas City, MO 64141.
- Guide to the American Left; directory and bibliography. a. ISSN 0017-5315

**U S Directory Service (Miami)**
121 S. E. 1st St., Box 1565, Miami, FL 33101.
- U S Medical Directory. irreg. ISSN 0091-8393

**U..S. Employment and Training Administration**
601 D St. N.W., Washington, DC 20213.
- Conference of State Employment Security Personnel Officers. Report. a. ISSN 0093-1942

**U S Glass Publications, Inc.**
2158 Union Ave., Suite 401, Memphis, TN 38104.
- Architects' Guide to Glass, Metal & Glazing. a.
- U S Glass, Metal & Glazing. bi-m. ISSN 0041-7661

**U S Handball Association**
4101 Dempster St., Skokie, IL 60076.
- Handball. bi-m. ISSN 0046-6778

**U S Hang Gliding Association**
Box 66306, Los Angeles, CA 90066.
- Hang Gliding. m.

**U S Institute for Theatre Technology, Inc.**
1501 Broadway, New York, NY 10036.
- Theatre Design and Technology; news on the construction of theatres, new technical developments, stage design. lighting, sound, administration. q. ISSN 0040-5477
- U S I T T Newsletter. 5 per yr. ISSN 0565-6311

**U S Jaycees**
Box 7, Tulsa, OK 74102.
- Future. bi-m. ISSN 0016-3260

**U S L A Justice Committee**
853 Broadway, New York, NY 10003.
- U S L A Reporter. 2 per yr.

**U. S. M. M. A.**
Kings Point, NY 11024.
- Hear This; Kings Points monthly newspaper. m. ISSN 0017-9175

**U S Medicine, Inc.**
1601 18th St., N.W., Washington, DC 20009.
- U S Medicine. s-m. ISSN 0042-1227

**U S Metric Association, Inc.**
Sugarloaf Star Route, Boulder, CO 80302.
- U S Metric Association Newsletter. q.

**U S Microfilm Sales Corp.**
235 Montgomery St., San Francisco, CA 94104.
- Micro-Topics. 3 per yr.

**U S Naval Academy Alumni Association, Inc.**
Annapolis, MD 21402.
- Shipmate. 10 per yr. ISSN 0037-3869
- U.S. Naval Academy Alumni Association. Register of Alumni. a.

**U S News and World Report, Inc.**
2300 N. St., N.W., Washington, DC 20037.
- U S News and World Report. w. ISSN 0041-5537
- U S Newsletter. w.

**U S News and World Report, Inc. (New York)**
45 Rockefeller Plaza, Suite 2300, New York, NY 10020.
- Wine and Spirits Marketing Bulletin. bi-m.

**U S Park Police**
1100 Ohio Drive S.W., Washington, DC 20242.
- U.S. Park Police. Annual Report. a.

**U S Philatelic Classics Society Inc.**
Box 2424, Arlington, VA 22202.
- Chronicle of U.S. Classic Postal Issues. q. ISSN 0009-6008

**U S Pipe and Foundry Co.**
3300 1st Ave., North, Birmingham, AL 35204.
- U S Piper. q. ISSN 0041-8048

**U S Racquetball Association**
- National Racquetball. (pub. by National Racquetball Club, Inc.)

**U S Servas Committee, Inc.**
Box 790, Old Chelsea Station P.O., New York, NY 10011.
- United States SERVAS Committee. Newsletter. a. ISSN 0083-324X

**U S Ski Association. Eastern Division**
22 High St., Brattleboro, VT 05301.
- Ski Competition East. 11 per yr. ISSN 0145-918X
- Skier (Brattleboro) 8 per yr. ISSN 0037-6248

**U S Transportation, Inc.**
1601 18th St., N. W., Washington, DC 20009.
- U S Transport. m. ISSN 0041-8145

**U S Travel Data Center**
1100 Connecticut Ave. N.W., Washington, DC 20036.
- Travel Printout; research news from the U.S. Travel Data Center. m.

**U S Yugoslav Economic Council, Inc.**
51 East 42nd St., New York, NY 10017.
- U S Y E C Business News. bi-m.

**U S 1 Poets' Cooperative**
78 Dempsey Ave., Princeton, NJ 08540.
- U S 1 Worksheets. 2-4 per yr.

**Ukrainian Academy of Sciences**
- Hydrobiological Journal. (pub. by Scripta Publishing Co.)

**Ukrainian Artist's Association in U.S.A. Philadelphia Branch**
1022 N. Lawrence St., Philadelphia, PA 19123.
- Ukrainian Art Digest/Notatki z Mistetstba. m? ISSN 0550-0850

**Ukrainian Catholic Church. Archdiocese of Philadelphia**
- Shlach/Way. (pub. by Apostolate, Inc.)
- Way. (pub. by Apostolate Inc.)

**Ukrainian Congress Committee of America**
203 Second Ave., New York, NY 10009.
- Ukrainian Quarterly; journal of East European and Asian affairs. q. ISSN 0041-6010

**Ukrainian Engineers' Society of America**
2 E. 79th St., New York, NY 10021.
- Visti Ukrayins'kykh Inzheneriv/Ukrainian Engineering News. q. ISSN 0042-7136 (Tovarystvo Ukrayins'kykh Inzheneriv Ameryki) (Co-Sponsor: Ukrayins'ke Tekhnichne Toyarystvo V Kanadi)

**Ukrainian Evangelical Alliance of North America**
5610 Trowbridge Dr., Dunwoody, GA 30338.
- Yevanhelskyj Ranok/Evangelical Morning. q. ISSN 0044-0388

**Ukrainian Evangelical Baptist Convention**
1042 North Damien Avenue, Chicago, IL 60622.
- Messenger of Truth. bi-m.

**Ukrainian Historian**
Box 312, Kent, OH 44240
(European Subscr. Adress: Ukrainian Historian, Ayingerstr. 17/12, 28, Munich 80, W. Germany)
- Ukrains'kyi Istoryk/Ukrainian Historian; zhurnal ukrainskoho istorychnoho towarystwa. q. ISSN 0041-6061 (Ukrainian Historical Association)

**Ukrainian Historical Association**
- Ukrains'kyi Istoryk/Ukrainian Historian. (pub. by Ukrainian Historian)

**Ukrainian Medical Association of North America**
2 E. 79th St., New York, NY 10027.
- Ukrainian Medical Association of North America. Journal. m. ISSN 0041-607X

**Ukrainian Museum-Archives, Inc.**
3425 Broadview Rd., Cleveland, OH 44109.
- Bibliohrafichnyi Pokazhczyk Ukrains'koi Presy Poza Mezhamy Ukrainy/Bibliographical Index of the Ukrainian Press Outside Ukraine. a. ISSN 0067-737X

**Ukrainian National Aid Association of America**
Box 1948, 527 Second Ave., Pittsburgh, PA 15219.
- Ukrainian National Word/Ukrainske Narodne Slovo. s-m.

**Ukrainian National Association, Inc.**
81-83 Grand St., Jersey City, NJ 07303.
- Rainbow/Veselka. m. ISSN 0300-6379

**Ukrainian National Women's League**
108 Second Ave., New York, NY 10003.
- Our Life. m.

**Ukrainian Orthodox Church of the U.S.A.**
P. O. Box 495, So. Bound Brook, NJ 08880.
- Ukrainian Orthodox Word. English Edition. m.

**Ukrainian Philatelic and Numismatic Society**
Box C, Southfields, NY 10975.
- Ukrains'kyi Filatelist/Ukrainian Philatelist. q.

**Ukrainian Publishing Co.**
4933 Larkins, Detroit, MI 48210.
- Lys Mykyta/Fox. m. ISSN 0024-7863

**Ukrainian Student Organization of Michnowsky, T.U.S.M.**
Box 113, Riverton, NJ 08077.
- Phoenix; journal of cultural and social thought. irreg. ISSN 0079-1776

**Ukrainian Workingmen's Association**
440 Wyoming Ave., Scranton, PA.
- Forum (Scranton); a Ukrainian review. q. ISSN 0015-8399

**Elinor Ulman, Ed. & Pub.**
Box 4918, Washington, DC 20008.
- American Journal of Art Therapy; art in education, rehabilitation and psychotherapy. q. ISSN 0007-4764 (American Art Therapy Association)

**Ulster County Extension Association**
74 John St., Kingston, NY 12401.
- Ulster County, New York Agricultural News. m.

**Ulster County Genealogical Society**
Box 84, Stone Ridge, NY 12484.
- Ulster Genie. irreg.

**Umbra**
c/o David Henderson, Ed., Box 4338 Sathergate Sta., Berkeley, CA 94704.
- Umbra. a.

**Unabashed Librarian**
Box 2631, New York, NY 10001.
- Unabashed Librarian; the "how I run my library good" letter. q. ISSN 0049-514X

**Unda-International Catholic Association for Radio & T V**
1229 S. Santee St., Los Angeles, CA 90015.
- Unda-U S A Newsletter. bi-m.

**Undena Publications**
Box 97, Malibu, CA 90265.
- Afroasiatic Dialects. irreg.
- Afroasiatic Linguistics. irreg., 7-10 per yr.
- Monographs on the Ancient Near East. irreg.

**Underground Engineering Contractors' Association**
8615 Florence Ave., Suite 205, Downey, CA 90240.
- U E C A Publication. m. ISSN 0049-5166

**Underground Teacher**
2277 Homecrest Ave., 277 Homecrest Ave., Brooklyn, NY 11229.
- Underground Teacher. q.

**Undersea Medical Society, Inc.**
9650 Rockville Pike, Bethesda, MD 20014.
- Pressure. bi-m.
- Undersea Biomedical Research. q. ISSN 0093-5387

**Understanding, Inc.**
Star Route Box 588-F, Tonopah, AZ 85354.
- Understanding. 10 per yr. ISSN 0041-655X

**Underwriter Printing and Publishing Co.**
291 South Van Brunt St., Englewood, NJ 07631.
- Insurance Almanac; Who, What, When and Where in Insurance. a. ISSN 0074-0675
- Insurance Casebook. a. ISSN 0074-0683
- Telephone Tickler for Insurance Men and Women. a.
- Weekly Underwriter. w. ISSN 0043-1966
- Who's Who in Insurance. a. ISSN 0083-9574
- Who's Who in Risk Management. a.

**Underwriters Laboratories, Inc.**
207 E. Ohio St., Chicago, IL 60611.
- Lab Data. q. (prep. by its Public Information Office)
- Underwriters' Laboratories. Annual Product Directories. Quarterly Supplement. q.

**Underwriters' Report**
667 Mission St., San Francisco, CA 94105.
- Underwriters' Report of California. w. ISSN 0041-6622

**Underwriters Review**
c/o Malcolm Freeland, 700 Harrison St., Topeka, KS 66633.
- Underwriters Review. m. ISSN 0041-6630

**Unesco**
For publications of this agency see section for UNITED NATIONS

**Frederick Ungar Publishing Co., Inc.**
250 Park Ave. S., New York, NY 10003.
- World Dramatists. irreg.

**Unicef**
For publications of this agency see section for UNITED NATIONS

**Unicorn**
1153 E. 26th St., Brooklyn, NY 11210.
- Unicorn; a miscellaneous journal. 3 per yr. ISSN 0041-6673

**Unicorn Press**
18 Karen Drive, Cherry Hill, NJ 08003.
- Aussiecon Flyer. m. (World Science Fiction Association)

**Unicorn Systems Company**
Information Services Division, 3807 Wilshire Blvd., Suite 1102, Los Angeles, CA 90010.
- California Publicity Outlets. a.

**Unidroit (International Institute for the Unification of Private Law)**
- Digest of Legal Activities of International Organizations and Other Institutions. (pub. by Oceana Publications Inc.)
- Uniform Law Review. (pub. by Oceana Publications, Inc.)

**Unified Science and Mathematics for Elementary Schools**
Education Development Center, Newton, MA 02160.
- Real Problem Solving in Education. s-a.

**Uniformed Fire Officers Association. Local 854 I.A.F.F.-AFL-CIO**
255 Broadway, New York, NY 10007.
- Trumpet. s-a.

**Uniformed Firefighters Association of Greater New York. Local 94**
225 Broadway, New York, NY 10007.
- Fire Lines. m.

**Uniformed Sanitationmen's Association**
23-25 Cliff St., New York, NY 10038.
- U S A Record. m. ISSN 0041-5464

**Uniformed Services Almanac, Inc.**
Box 76, Washington, DC 20044
- Reserve Forces Almanac. a. ISSN 0363-860X (Subscr. to:, Dept. R)
- Uniformed Services Almanac. a. ISSN 0503-1982 (Subscr. to:, Dept. A)

**Uniforms and Accessories Review**
15 W. 44th St., New York, NY 10036.
- Uniforms and Accessories Review. q. ISSN 0041-6738

**Union Carbide Corp.**
270 Park Ave., New York, NY 10017.
- Molecular Sieve Abstracts. 2 per yr. ISSN 0047-7826

**Union College**
1033 Springfield Ave., Cranford, NJ 07016.
- Union (Cranford). irreg. ISSN 0098-9525

**Union College (Lincoln) Associated Student Body**
3800 S. 48th St., Lincoln, NE 68506.
- Clock Tower. w. ISSN 0009-9430

**Union College (Schenectady)**
Lamont House, Schenectady, NY 12308.
- Union College. 6 per yr.

**Union College (Schenectady) Character Research Project**
207 State St., Schenectady, NY 12305.
- Character Potential; a record of research. irreg. ISSN 0009-1669
- Union College. Character Research Project. Newsletter. irreg.

**Union Labor Life Insurance Co.**
850 Third Ave., New York, NY 10022.
- U L L I C O Bulletin. m. ISSN 0041-5189

**Union of American Hebrew Congregations**
838 Fifth Ave., New York, NY 10021.
- Adventures in Living Judaism. irreg.
- Keeping Posted. m.(Oct.-May) ISSN 0022-9636
- Reform Judaism. m. (Sept.-May)
- Union of American Hebrew Congregations. State of Our Union. biennial. ISSN 0363-3810

**Union of Orthodox Jewish Congregations of America**
116 East 27 Street, New York, NY 10016.
- Jewish Action. 5 per yr.
- Jewish Life. q. ISSN 0021-6577
- Keeping Posted with N C S Y. (pub. by National Conference of Synagogue Youth)

**Union of Telephone Workers**
307 Fifth Ave., Room 900, New York, NY 10016.
- Message. m. ISSN 0047-679X

**Union Oil Co.**
Box 7600, Los Angeles, CA 90051.
- Seventy Six. bi-m.

**Union Oil of California**
- Road King. (pub. by Road King Magazine)

**Union Saint-Jean-Baptiste**
1, Social St., Woonsocket, RI 02895.
- Union. q.

**Union Special Corp.**
404 N. Franklin St., Chicago, IL 60610.
- Needle's Eye. bi-m. ISSN 0028-2359

**Union Theological Seminary**
3041 Broadway, New York, NY 10027.
- Union Seminary Quarterly Review. 4 per yr. ISSN 0041-7025

**Union Theological Seminary in Virginia**
3401 Brook Road, Richmond, VA 23227.
- Affirmation. 2 per yr. ISSN 0001-9674
- As I See It Today. m (except Jul. & Aug.)
- Interpretation; a journal of bible and theology. q. ISSN 0020-9643
- Scholars' Choice; significant current theological literature from abroad. s-a. ISSN 0036-6358

**Union Trust Co.**
Stamford, CT 06904.
- Fairfield County Economy. bi-m. ISSN 0014-696X

**Union Women's Alliance to Gain Equality**
P.O. Box 462, Berkeley, CA 94701.
- Union W.A.G.E. bi-m. ISSN 0300-6336

**Unipub**
650 First Ave., New York, NY 10016
(Subscr. to: Box 433, Murray Hill Sta., New York NY 10016)
- I B I D. (International Bibliography, Information, Documentation) q. ISSN 0000-0329

**Unique Periodicals Co.**
1811 Prosser Ave., Los Angeles, CA 90025.
- Single People's Directory. m.

**Uniquest Foundation**
- Uniquest. (pub. by First Unitarian Church of Berkeley)

**Unitarian Historical Society**
c/o Conrad Wright, Harvard Divinity School, Andover Hall, Cambridge, MA 02138.
- Unitarian Historical Society. Proceedings. a. ISSN 0082-7819

**Unitarian Universalist Association**
25 Beacon St., Boston, MA 02108.
- Unitarian Universalist Directory. a. ISSN 0082-7827
- Unitarian Universalist World. s-m (m. Jan., June, July, Aug. & Sept.) ISSN 0041-7122

**Unitarian Universalist Association. New Hampshire-Vermont District**
23 School St., Concord, NH 03301.
- Progress (Concord) bi-m. ISSN 0360-8239

**United Airlines**
- Mainliner. (pub. by East-West Network, Inc.)

**United Association of Journeymen and Apprentices of the Plumbing and Pipe Fitting Industry of the United States and Canada**
901 Massachusetts Ave., N.W., Washington, DC 20001.
- United Association Journal. m. ISSN 0041-7181

**United Automobile Aerospace and Agricultural Implement Workers of America**
8000 E. Jefferson, Detroit, MI 48214.
- U A W Washington Report. w. ISSN 0041-4980

**United Black Artist Guild**
Literary Arts Section, P.O. Box 22246, Seattle, WA 98122.
- Dark Waters. q.

**United Board for Christian Higher Education in Asia**
475 Riverside Drive, New York, NY 10027.
- New Horizons. 3 per yr. ISSN 0028-5374

**United Brethren Publications**
302 Lake St., Box 650, Huntington, IN 46750.
- Adult Bible Studies. q.
- New Illustrator; a quarterly for adult and youth teachers in the Sunday school. q. ISSN 0028-5412 (Church of the United Brethren in Christ) (Co-Sponsor: Evangelical Congregational Church)

**United Brotherhood of Carpenters and Joiners of America**
101 Constitution Ave., N.W., Washington, DC 20001.
- Carpenter. m. ISSN 0008-6843

**United Business Publications, Inc.**
750 Third Ave., New York, NY 10017.
- Audio-Visual Communications. 12 per yr. ISSN 0004-7562

- Biomedical Communications. bi-m. ISSN 0092-8607
- Government Data Systems. bi-m. ISSN 0046-6212
- In-Plant Printer. m.(combined issues Jan.-Feb. & Jul.-Aug.) ISSN 0019-3232
- Industrial Photography; the magazine that advances the ideas, techniques and uses of applied photography. m. ISSN 0019-8595
- Lab Animal. bi-m. ISSN 0093-7355
- Laboratory Management. m. ISSN 0023-6845
- Laboratory Management /Europe. s-a.
- Law Enforcement Communications. bi-m.
- Medical Lab. m. ISSN 0025-7311
- Medical Meetings. 8 per yr. ISSN 0093-1314
- Physician Assistant. bi-m.
- Reprographics. bi-m. ISSN 0034-4982
- Videography. m.

**United Business Service Company**
210 Newbury St., Boston, MA 02116.
- United Business & Investment Report. w. ISSN 0360-8662
- United Graphic Guide. a. ISSN 0082-7916

**United California Bank**
Research and Planning Division, P. O. Box 3666, Los Angeles, CA 90051.
- Forecast. a. ISSN 0071-7282

**United Cement, Lime and Gypsum Workers International Union**
7830 W. Lawrence Ave., Chicago, IL 60656.
- Voice of the Cement, Lime, Gypsum and Allied Workers. m. ISSN 0042-8191

**United Cerebral Palsy of New York City, Inc.**
122 E. 23rd St., New York, NY 10010.
- Dental Guidance Council on the Handicapped. Journal. 2 per yr.
- Polling. irreg? (Co-sponsor: Epilepsy Foundation of America)

**United Chapters of Phi Beta Kappa**
1811 Q St., N.W., Washington, DC 20009.
- American Scholar. q. ISSN 0003-0937
- Key Reporter. q. ISSN 0023-0804

**United Church Board for Homeland Ministries**
c/o Theodore H. Erickson, 287 Park Ave., New York, NY 10010.
- New Conversations. s-a. ISSN 0360-0181
- Youth. (pub. by United Church Press)

**United Church of Christ**
287 Park Ave., New York, NY 10010.
- A.D. The Magazine for the United Church of Christ Family. (pub. by A. D. Publications, Inc.)
- United Church of Christ. Pension Boards. a. ISSN 0360-9782

**United Church of Christ. Massachusetts Conference**
14 Beacon St., Boston, MA 02108.
- Pilgrim State News. m.

**United Church of Christ. United Church Board for Homeland Ministries**
Todd Hill Rd., Lakeside, CT 06758
(Subscr. to: 119 West 24th St. New York, N.Y. 10011)
- Journal of Current Social Issues. q. ISSN 0041-7211

**United Church Press**
1505 Race St., Philadelphia, PA 19102.
- Youth; a pocket magazine for high school youth. m. ISSN 0044-1147 (United Church Board for Homeland Ministries)

**United Consumer Service Corp.**
466 Lexington Ave., New York, NY 10017.
- Consumer Gazette. bi-m.

**United Dairy Industry Association**
- Directory of Communicators in Agriculture. (pub. by Agricultural Relations Council)

**United Duroc Swine Registry**
1803 W. Detweiller Dr., Peoria, IL 61614.
- Duroc News. m. ISSN 0012-7299

**United Electrical, Radio & Machine Workers of America**
11 E. 51st St., New York, NY 10022.
- U E News. fortn. ISSN 0041-5065

**United Farm Agency, Inc.**
612 West 47th St., Kansas City, MO 64112.
- United Land. m.

**United Flathead Racers Association**
23748 1/2 Lyons Ave., Newhall, CA 91321.
- United Flathead Racers Association Newsletter. m.

**United Furniture Workers of America, AFL-CIO**
700 Broadway, New York, NY 10003.
- Furniture Workers Press. m. ISSN 0016-3090

**United Garment Workers of America**
200 Park Ave. So., New York, NY 10003.
- Garment Worker. m. ISSN 0016-4712

**United Glass and Ceramic Workers of North America, AFL-CIO**
556 E. TownSt., Columbus, OH 43215.
- Glass Workers News. bi-m. ISSN 0017-1069

**United Horsemen Association**
- United Horsemen. (pub. by U H A Publishing)

**United Hospital Fund of New York**
New York.
- Health Careers; a directory of career information and training for New York State. irreg. ISSN 0362-8337

**United Hospitals of Newark. Babies Hospital Unit**
15-19 Roseville Ave, Newark, NJ 07107.
- Pediatric Conferences. q. ISSN 0031-3963

**United Housing Foundation**
465 Grand St., New York, NY 10002.
- Cooperator. 5 per yr. ISSN 0010-8472

**United Jewish Federation, San Diego**
- Heritage-Southwest Jewish Press. (pub. by Heritage Publishing Co.)

**United Kennel Club, Inc.**
321 W. Cedar St., Kalamazoo, MI 49006.
- Bloodlines. bi-m.

**United Labor Council of Reading and Berks County**
- New Era. (pub. by New Era Educational Society, Inc.)

**United Lutheran Society**
223 E. Main St., Ligonier, PA 15658.
- United Lutheran. m. ISSN 0041-7300

**United Marine Publishing, Inc.**
38 Commercial Wharf, Boston, MA 02110.
- Sail. m. ISSN 0036-2700
- Sailboat & Sailboat Equipment Directory. a.

**United Media International, Inc.**
306 Dartmouth St., Boston, MA 02116.
- Aviation Monthly; monthly aviation safety summary and report.
- Business Digest. m. ISSN 0095-0084
- Business Monthly; composite of effective business techniques. m. ISSN 0095-0092
- Commonwealth Letter. m.
- Homegrown. m. ISSN 0095-0165
- Money Management Digest; a guide to personal money management. q. ISSN 0145-1030
- P S R O Update. m. (Boston University Medical Center)
- Potting Shed. m.
- Real Estate Investor. m. ISSN 0095-0211
- Real Estate Investor Letter. m.

**United Methodist Church**
- Accent on Youth. (pub. by United Methodist Publishing House. Graded Press)
- Music Ministry. (pub. by United Methodist Publishing House. Graded Press)
- Nursery Days. (pub. by United Methodist Publishing House. Graded Press)
- United Methodist Periodical Index. (pub. by United Methodist Publishing House)
- Vine. (pub. by United Methodist Publishing House)

**United Methodist Church. Arkansas Area**
Box 3547, Little Rock, AR 72203.
- Arkansas Methodist. w.

**United Methodist Church. Board of Church and Society**
100 Maryland Ave. N.E., Washington, DC 20002.
- Engage/Social Action. m. ISSN 0090-3485 (Co-Sponsor: United Church of Christ, Center for Social Action)

**United Methodist Church. Board of Discipleship**
1908 Grand Ave., Nashville, TN 37203.
- Aposento Alto. bi-m. ISSN 0003-6552
- Christian Home. (pub. by United Methodist Publishing House. Graded Press)
- Face-To-Face. q. ISSN 0014-6277 (prep. by its Section on Curriculum Resources)
- Upper Room; daily devotional guide, interdenominational, international. bi-m. ISSN 0042-0735

**United Methodist Church. Board of Global Ministries**
475 Riverside Dr., New York, NY 10027.
- New World Outlook; missions and ecumenical relationships. m. ISSN 0043-8812

**United Methodist Church. Commission on Archives and History**
Box 488, Lake Junaluska, NC 28745.
- Methodist History. q. ISSN 0026-1238

**United Methodist Church. Division of Education**
475 Riverside Drive, Room 1323, New York, NY 10027.
- Response. m (except July-August) ISSN 0034-5717

**United Methodist Church. Division of Education. Department of Adult Publications**
Dept. of Adult Publications, 201 Eighth Ave. S., Nashville, TN 37203.
- United Methodist Church (United States) Division of Education. Adult Planbook. a. ISSN 0082-7983

**United Methodist Church. Historical Society**
Box 2050, Bloomington, IL 61701.
- Historical Messenger. q. (prep. by its Central Illinois Conference)

**United Methodist Church. North Carolina Conference and Western North Carolina Conference**
- North Carolina Christian Advocate. (pub. by Methodist Board of Publication)

**United Methodist Church. North Mississippi and Mississippi Conference**
Box 1093, Jackson, MS 39205.
- Mississippi Methodist Advocate. s-w. ISSN 0026-6329

**United Methodist Church. Section of Records and Statistics**
1200 Davis St., Evanston, IL 60201.
- United Methodist Church. General Minutes of the Annual Conferences. a. ISSN 0503-3551

**United Methodist Church. South Carolina Conference**
- South Carolina Methodist Advocate. (pub. by Southern Christian Advocate, Inc.)

**United Methodist Church. Virginia Conference**
4016 W. Broad St., Richmond, VA 23230.
- Virginia Advocate. w. ISSN 0042-6458

**United Methodist Church. West Michigan and Detroit Annual Conferences**
- Michigan Christian Advocate. (pub. by Michigan Christian Advocate Publishing Co.)

**United Methodist Communications**
601 Riverview Ave., Dayton, OH 45406.
- Interpreter. m. ISSN 0020-9678

**United Methodist Communications Council**
Newspaper Division, Box 1076, TX 75221.
- Texas Methodist/United Methodist Reporter. w.

**United Methodist Homes of New Jersey**
71 Clark Ave., Ocean Grove, NJ 07756.
- Horizon. q.

**United Methodist Publishing House**
201 Eighth Ave., S., Nashville, TN 37203.
- Beehive. w.
- Cross-Talk. q. ISSN 0090-3949
- Mature Years. q. ISSN 0025-6021
- One/Two. w. ISSN 0030-2562
- United Methodist Directory. irreg. ISSN 0503-356X
- United Methodist Periodical Index; an author and subject index to selected United Methodist periodicals. q. ISSN 0041-7319 (United Methodist Church)
- Vine. w. (United Methodist Church)

**United Methodist Publishing House. Graded Press**
201 Eighth Ave. S., Nashville, TN 37203.
- Accent on Youth. m. ISSN 0001-4516 (United Methodist Church)
- Christian Home. m. ISSN 0009-5370 (United Methodist Church. Board of Discipleship)
- Kindergartner. m. ISSN 0023-1517
- Music Ministry; for all with music responsibilities in church and church school. m. ISSN 0027-4402 (United Methodist Church)
- Nursery Days. m. ISSN 0029-6414 (United Methodist Church)

**United Mine Workers**
900 Fifteenth Street, N.W., Washington, DC 20005.
- United Mine Workers Journal. s-m. ISSN 0041-7327

**United Missionaries in Higher Education**
UMHE Communication Office, 3 West 29th St. Rm. 708, New York, NY 10001.
- Connexion. 5 per yr.

**United Nations Association of the U.S.A.**
345 E. 46th St., New York, NY 10017.
- Inter Dependent. m(10 per yr.)
- Issues Before the United Nations General Assembly. (pub. by Interchange Foundation)
- Making Your U.N. Day Count: Ideas for Action. a.

**United Nations Fund for Population Activities**
For publications of this agency see section for UNITED NATIONS

**United Nations Institute for Training and Research**
For publications of this agency see section for UNITED NATIONS

**United Nations Trade and Development Board**
For publications of this agency see section for UNITED NATIONS

**United Native Americans, Inc.**
Box 26149, San Francisco, CA 94126.
- Warpath. m.

**United Neighborhood Houses of New York**
101 E. 15th St., New York, NY 10003.
- United Neighborhood Houses. News. q. ISSN 0041-7440

**United Order of True Sisters**
150 West 85th St., New York, NY 10024.
- Echo. q. ISSN 0046-1067

**United Ostomy Association, Inc.**
1111 Wilshire Blvd., Los Angeles, CA 90017.
- Ostomy Quarterly. q. ISSN 0030-6517

**United Paperworkers International Union**
Box 7 - Fresh Meadow Station, Flushing, NY 11365.
- Paperworker. m.

**United Parents Associations of New York City**
15 E. 26th St., New York, NY 10010.
- School Parent. bi-m.
- United Parents Association of New York City Newsletter. m during school year.

**United Presbyterian Church in the U.S.A.**
Room 1244, 475 Riverside Dr., New York, NY 10027.
- A.D. the Magazine for the United Presbyterian Family. (pub. by A. D. Publications, Inc.)
- Church and Society. bi-m. ISSN 0037-7805
- New World Outlook.
- United Presbyterian Church in the United States of America. Minutes of the General Assembly. a. ISSN 0082-8548

**United Presbyterian Church in the U. S. A. United Presbyterian Women**
475 Riverside Dr., New York, NY 10027.
- Concern Magazine/Newsfold. 14 per yr.

**United Presbyterian Health, Education and Welfare Association**
475 Riverside Dr., Room 1268, New York, NY 10027.
- Survival Bulletin. q.

**United Prospectors Inc.**
31217 Tower Rd., Visalia, CA 93277.
- Locating Gold; the prospector's guide. bi-m. ISSN 0024-5658

**United Publications, Inc.**
5001 W. 80th St., Bloomington, MN 55437.
- Mainstreet. q.

**United Publishing Corp.**
2728 Euclid Ave., Cleveland, OH 44115.
- Veterinary Economics; the Veterinarian's business magazine. m. ISSN 0042-4862

**United Rubber, Cork, Linoleum and Plastic Workers of America**
AFL-CIO, CLC, 87 S. High St., Akron, OH 44308.
- United Rubber Worker. m. ISSN 0041-7475

**United Russian Orthodox Brotherhood of America**
333 Blvd. of Allies, Pittsburgh, PA 15222.
- Russian Messenger/Russkij Vistnik. bi-m. ISSN 0036-0287

**United Secularists of America**
377 Vernon St., Oakland, CA 94610.
- Progressive World. m. ISSN 0033-085X

**United Service Organizations, Inc.**
237 E. 52 St, New York, NY 10022.
- U S O Annual Report. a. ISSN 0082-8556
- Wherever They Go. bi-m.

**United Sisters**
c/o Ginger Daire-Reber, 4213 West Bay Ave., Tampa, FL 33616.
- United Sisters. q.

**United Slate, Tile and Composition Roofers, Damp and Waterproof Workers' Association**
1125 17th St., Washington, DC 20036.
- Journeyman Roofer and Waterproofer. m. ISSN 0022-5673

**U. S. ACTION. National Student Volunteer Program**
see U. S. National Student Volunteer Program

**U. S. ACTION. Peace Corps**
see U. S. Peace Corps

**U.S. Administration on Aging**
U.S. Office of Human Development, U.S. Dept. of Health, Education and Welfare, Washington, DC 20201
- Aging. 10 per yr. ISSN 0002-0966 (Orders to: U.S. Supt. of Documents, Washington, DC 20204)
- U.S. Administration on Aging. Annual Report. a. ISSN 0098-8405

**U.S. Administrative Office of the United States Courts**
Supreme Court Bldg., Washington, DC 20544.
- Federal Probation; a journal of correctional philosophy and practice. q. ISSN 0014-9128
- U.S. Administrative Office of the United States Courts. Report on Applications for Orders Authorizing or Approving the Interception of Wire or Oral Communications. irreg. ISSN 0097-7977
- U.S. Judicial Conference of the United States. Report of the Proceedings. a. (Orders to: Supt. Documents, Washington DC 20402)

**U. S. Advisory Commission on Intergovernmental Relations**
726 Jackson Place N.W., Washington, DC 20575.
- U. S. Advisory Commission on Intergovernmental Relations. Annual Report. a. ISSN 0082-8610
- U.S. Advisory Commission on Intergovernmental Relations. Intergovernmental Perspective. q.

**U. S. Advisory Commission on International Educational and Cultural Affairs**
U. S. Dept. of State, Washington, DC 20520
- International Educational and Cultural Exchange. q. ISSN 0020-6601 (Orders to: Superintendent of Documents, Washington, DC 20402)

**U.S. Advisory Council on Historic Preservation**
1522 K St. N.W.,Suite 430, Washington, DC 20005
- U. S. Advisory Council on Historic Preservation. Report. 8 per yr. ISSN 0098-4035 (Orders to: Supt. Doc., Washington, DC 20402)

**U. S. Agency for International Development**
320 Twenty-First St. N.W., Washington,
DC 20523.
- A I D Research and Development Abstracts. q.
ISSN 0096-1507 (prep. by its Technical
Assistance Bureau)
- Development Digest. q. ISSN 0012-1576 (Orders
to: Supt. of Documents, Washington, DC 20402)
- U.S. Agency for International Development.
Office of Financial Management. Status of
Foreign Currency Funds Administered by the
Agency for International Development. q. ISSN
0094-968X
- U. S. Agency for International Development.
Projects: by Field of Activity and Country. a.
ISSN 0082-8629
- U. S. Agency for International Development.
Proposed Foreign Aid Program, Summary
Presentation to Congress. a. ISSN 0082-8637
(Orders to: Supt. Doc., Washington, DC 20402)
- War on Hunger. m. ISSN 0043-0269

**U.S. Agricultural Marketing Service**
U.S. Department of Agriculture, Washington, DC
20250.
- Fresh Fruit and Vegetable Market News; weekly
summary, shipments-unloads. w. ISSN 0094-4858
(prep. by its Fruit and Vegetable Division)
- Honey Market News. m. (prep. by its Fruit and
Vegetable Division)
- Peanut Market News. w. ISSN 0093-4429 (prep.
by its Fruit and Vegetable Division)
- Tobacco Stocks. q. (prep. by its Tobacco Division)
- U.S. Agricultural Marketing Service. Annual
Report on Tobacco Statistics. a. (Orders to: Supt.
Doc., Washington, DC 20402)
- U.S. Agricultural Marketing Service. Dairy
Division. Federal Milk Order Market Statistics.
m. ISSN 0498-2002

**U.S. Agricultural Marketing Service. Cotton Division**
4841 Summer Ave., Box 17723, Memphis, TN
38117.
- Monthly Cotton Linters Review. m. ISSN 0027-
0318
- United States: Cotton Quality Reports for
Ginnings. m. ISSN 0041-7580

**U.S. Agricultural Marketing Service. Grain and Seed Division**
Grain Market News Service, 301 W. Lexington
Ave., Independence, MO 64050.
- Feed Market News. w. ISSN 0364-2046
- Grain Market News; weekly summary and
statistics. w. ISSN 0364-099X

**U.S. Agricultural Research Service**
U.S. Department of Agriculture, 6505 Belcrest
Road, Hyattsville, MD 20782
- Agricultural Research. m. ISSN 0002-161X
(Orders to: Supt. of Documents, Washington, DC
20402)
- Family Economics Review. q. (prep. by its
Consumer and Food Economics Institute)
- Plant Disease Reporter. m. ISSN 0032-0811 (prep.
by its Agricultural Research Center) (Orders to:
Supt. of Documents, Washington, DC 20402)

**U.S. Agricultural Research Service. Animal Improvement Programs Laboratory**
Building 263, BARC-East, Beltsville, MD 20705.
- Dairy Herd Improvement. irreg, vol. 50, 1974.
ISSN 0085-7580 (Co-sponsors: National
Cooperative Dairy Herd Improvement Program;
Animal Physiology and Genetics Institute)
- Egg Production Tests: United States and Canada.
a.
- Hatcheries and Dealers Participating in the
National Poultry Improvement Plan. a. ISSN
0082-9722 (prep. by its Animal Physiology and
Genetics Institute)
- Tables on Hatchery and Flock Participation in the
National Poultry Improvement Plan. a. ISSN
0082-8661
- U S D A-D H I A Cow Performance Index List.
a. ISSN 0501-4697 (Co-sponsor: Dairy Herd
Improvement Association)
- U S D A-D H I A Sire Summary List. a. (Co-
Sponsor: Dairy Herd Improvement Associations)

**U. S. Agricultural Research Service. North Central Region**
2000 W. Pioneer Parkway, Peoria, IL 61614.
- U. S. Agricultural Research Service. A R S-N C.
irreg., no. 20, 1975. ISSN 0092-1785

**U.S. Agricultural Research Service. Plum Island Animal Disease Center**
*see* U. S. Plum Island Animal Disease Center

**U.S. Agricultural Research Service. Southern Region**
P. O. Box 53326, New Orleans, LA 70153.
- U. S. Agricultural Research Service. A R S-S.
irreg. ISSN 0092-1939
- U.S. Agricultural Research Service. Southern
Regional Research Center. Publications and
Patents. s-a. ISSN 0038-4615

**U.S. Agricultural Research Service. Western Regional Research Center**
2850 Telegraph Hill, Berkeley, CA 94705.
- U.S. Agricultural Research Service. Western
Regional Research Center. List of Publications
and Patents with Abstracts. s-a.

**U.S. Air Force**
The Pentagon, Washington, DC 20330
(Subscriptions to: Supt. of Documents, Washington,
DC 20402)
- Air Force Comptroller. q. ISSN 0002-2365 (prep.
by its Comptroller) (Subscriptions to: Supt. of
Documents, Washington, DC 20402)
- Air Force Policy Letter for Commanders. s-m.
ISSN 0002-2381
- Air Reservist Magazine. 10 per yr. ISSN 0002-
2535
- Airman. m. ISSN 0002-2756
- Security Police Digest. 3 per yr. ISSN 0037-0681
(prep. by its Chief of Security Police)
- U.S.A.F. Fighter Weapons Review. q.
- United States Air Force Medical Service Digest.
m. ISSN 0041-7491 (prep. by its Office of the
Surgeon General. Air Force Medical Service)
(Subscriptions to: Supt. of Documents,
Washington, DC 20402)

**United States Air Force Academy**
Colorado Springs, CO 80840.
- Harmon Memorial Lectures in Military History. a.
ISSN 0073-0394 (prep. by its Dept. of History)
- Talon. m.(Oct-June) ISSN 0039-9248
- U.S. Air Force Academy Assembly. Proceedings.
a. ISSN 0082-8688 (prep. by its Dept. of Political
Science) (Co-Sponsor: Columbia University
American Assembly Program) (Orders to:
National Technical Information Service,
Springfield, VA 22151)
- U. S. Air Force Academy Library. Special
Bibliography Series. irreg. ISSN 0082-8696

**U.S. Air Force Accounting and Finance Center**
3800 York St., Denver, CO 80205.
- Air Force Accounting and Finance Technical
Digest. fortn. ISSN 0002-2330

**U.S. Air Force. Air Training Command**
Bldg. 3875, Mather Air Force Base, CA 95655
(Orders to: Supt. of Documents, Washington, DC
20402)
- Navigator. 3 per yr. ISSN 0028-1557

**U.S. Air Force. Air University**
Maxwell Air Force Base, AL 36112.
- Air University Review. bi-m. ISSN 0002-2594

**U.S. Air Force. Air University Library**
Maxwell Air Force Base, AL 36112.
- Air University Library Index to Military
Periodicals. q., cumulated annually. ISSN 0002-
2586

**U.S. Air Force Association**
- Aerospace International. (pub. by Moench
Verlagsgesellschaft mbH GW)

**U. S. Air Force Cambridge Research Laboratories**
Hanscom Field, Bedford, MA 01730
- U. S. Air Force Cambridge Research Laboratories,
Bedford, Massachusetts. A F C R L (Series) irreg.
ISSN 0082-870X (Order from: National Technical
Information Service, Springfield, VA 22161)

**U.S. Air Force. Civil Air Patrol**
Headquarters, Maxwell Air Force Base, AL 36112.
- Civil Air Patrol News. bi-m. ISSN 0009-7810

**U.S. Air Force Inspection and Safety Center**
Norton Air Force Base, CA 92409
(Orders to: Supt. of Documents, Washington, DC
20402)
- Aerospace Safety. m. ISSN 0001-9429

- Driver; traffic safety magazine for military drivers.
m. (Issued in cooperation with: U.S. Navy and
U.S. Army Departments)
- Maintenance. m. ISSN 0364-7145

**U.S. Air Force Institute of Technology. Civil Engineering School**
Wright-Patterson A F B, OH 45433
- Air Force Engineering & Services Quarterly. q.
(Order from: Superintendent of Documents,
Government Printing Office, Washington DC
20402)

**U.S. Air Force. Judge Advocate General's School**
LMDC/5A, Maxwell AFB, AL 36112.
- Air Force Law Review. q. ISSN 0094-8381

**U.S. Air Force. Military Airlift Command**
Scott Air Force Base, IL 62225
(Orders to: Supt. of Documents, Washington, DC
20402)
- M A C Flyer. m. ISSN 0024-788X

**U.S. Air Force Office of Scientific Research**
- Chapel Hill Conference on Combinatorial
Mathematics and Its Applications. Proceedings.
(pub. by University of North Carolina at Chapel
Hill. Department of Statistics)
- Symposium on Advanced Propulsion Concepts.
Proceedings. (pub. by Gordon and Breach Science
Publishers)

**U.S. Air Force. School of Aerospace Medicine**
Aeromedical Library (SUL-2), Brooks Air Force
Base, TX 78235.
- Aeromedical Reviews. irreg., ISSN 0065-3683

**U.S. Air Force Strategic Air Command**
Offutt Air Force Base, Omaha, NE 68113.
- Combat Crew. m. ISSN 0010-213X

**U.S. Air Force Systems Command**
AFSC/OII, Andrews Air Force Base, Washington,
DC 20331.
- A F S C Newsreview. m. ISSN 0002-239X

**U. S. Alcohol, Drug Abuse, and Mental Health Administration. National Institute on Drug Abuse**
*see* U. S. National Institute on Drug Abuse

**U. S. Alcohol, Drug Abuse, and Mental Health Administration. National Institute of Mental Health**
*see* U. S. National Institute of Mental Health

**U.S. Animal and Plant Health Inspection Service**
U. S. Department of Agriculture, 6505 Belcrest Rd.,
Federal Bldg., No. 1, Hyattsville, MD 20782.
- C P P R. (Cooperative Plant Pest Report) w.; (m.
Jan., Nov., Dec.) (prep. by its New Pest
Detection and Survey Staff, Plant Protection and
Quarantine Programs)
- U.S. Department of Agriculture. Animal and Plant
Health Inspection Service. Cooperative State-
Federal Brucellosis Eradication Program:
Statistical Tables. a.
- U.S. Department of Agriculture. Animal and Plant
Health Inspection Service. Cooperative State-
Federal Tuberculosis Eradication Program:
Statistical Tables. a.
- U.S. Department of Agriculture. Animal and Plant
Health Inspection Service. Reported Arthropod-
Borne Encephalitides in Horses and Other
Equidae. a.

**U.S. Appalachian Regional Commission**
1666 Connecticut Ave. N.W., Washington, DC
20235.
- Appalachia. bi-m. ISSN 0003-6595
- Appalachian Regional Commission. Annual
Report. a. ISSN 0503-5422
- Appalachian Regional Commission. Study A R C.
irreg.

**U. S. Archives of American Art**
*see under* Smithsonian Institution

**U.S. Arms Control and Disarmament Agency**
Dept. of State Bldg., Washington, DC 20451
- U. S. Arms Control and Disarmament Agency.
Annual Report to Congress. a. ISSN 0082-8769
- World Military Expenditures. a.

**U.S. Army**
Washington, DC 20301
(Orders to: Supt. of Documents, Washington, DC 20402)
- Soldiers. m. ISSN 0093-8440

**U. S. Army Administration Center**
Fort Benjamin Harrison, IN 46216.
- Army Administrator. bi-m. ISSN 0361-7300

**U.S. Army Air Defense School**
Fort Bliss, TX 79916.
- Air Defense Magazine. 4 per yr.

**U. S. Army Armor School**
Box O, Fort Knox, KY 40121.
- Armor; the magazine of mobile warfare. bi-m. ISSN 0004-2420

**U.S. Army Aviation School**
Fort Rucker, AL 36362
- United States Army Aviation Digest. m. ISSN 0004-2471 (Orders to: Supt. of Documents, Washington, DC 20402)

**U.S. Army. Center of Military History**
Washington, DC 20315.
- Army Museum Newsletter. 2-4 per yr. ISSN 0004-2536

**U. S. Army Coastal Engineering Research Center**
see U. S. Coastal Engineering Research Center

**U.S. Army Cold Regions Research and Engineering Laboratory**
P.O. Box 282, Hanover, NH 03755
- Bibliography on Cold Regions Science and Technology. a. (Orders to: National Technical Information Service, Springfield, VA 22151)

**U.S. Army Command and General Staff College**
Fort Leavenworth, KS 66027.
- Military Review. m. ISSN 0026-4148

**U.S. Army. Corps of Engineers.**
Washington, DC 20310
- U.S. Army. Corps of Engineers. Port Series. irreg. ISSN 0083-0305 (Orders to: Supt. Doc., Washington, DC 20402)
- U.S. Army. Corps of Engineers. Technical Reports, T R (Series) irreg. ISSN 0083-0313 (Order from: National Technical Information Service, 5285 Port Royal Rd., Springfield, VA 22151)

**U. S. Army Corps of Engineers, Buffalo District**
1776 Niagara St., Buffalo, NY 14207.
- Lake Erie Water Quality Newsletter. q. (prep. by its Lake Erie Study)

**U.S. Army. Corps of Engineers, Detroit District**
Box 1027, Detroit, MI 48231.
- Great Lakes and Connecting Channels Water Levels and Depths. bi-m.
- U.S. Army. Corps of Engineers. Detroit District. Monthly Bulletin of Lake Levels for the Great Lakes. m.

**U.S. Army Electronics Command**
- Power Sources Symposium. Proceedings. (pub. by P S C Publications Committee)

**U.S. Army. Fitzsimons Army Medical Center**
Denver, CO 80200.
- Annual Symposium on Pulmonary Diseases. a. ISSN 0361-5006

**U.S. Army Infantry School**
P.O.B. 2005, Fort Benning, GA 31905
- U. S. Army Infantry Center. History; Annual Supplement. a. ISSN 0091-2271 (No subscriptions, free copies to qualified military agencies)
- U.S. Army Infantry School; the professional magazine for infantrymen. bi-m. ISSN 0019-9532

**U.S.Army. Judge Advocate General's School**
Charlottesville, VA 22901.
- Army Lawyer. ISSN 0364-1287
- Military Law Review. q. ISSN 0026-4040 (Orders to: Supt. of Documents, Washington, DC 20402)

**U.S. Army Legal Services Agency**
Defense Appellate Division, HQDA (JAAJ-DD), NASSIF Bldg., Falls Church, VA 22041.
- Advocate. bi-m.

**U.S. Army Logistics Management Center**
Ft. Lee, VA 23801
(Subscr. to: Supt. of Documents, U.S. Gov't. Printing Office, Washington, D.C. 20402)
- Army Logistician; the official magazine of the United States Army logistics. bi-m. ISSN 0004-2528

**U.S. Army Materiel Development and Readiness Command**
Washington, DC 20301
(Orders to: Supt. of Documents, Washington, DC 20402)
- Army Research and Development. bi-m. ISSN 0004-2560 (Published in coordination with DARCOM Information Office, Office of Chief of Engineers. Office of Surgeon General's Medical R & D Command, and Office of Deputy Chief of Staff for Research, Development and Acquisition. HQ. Dept. of the Army)

**U.S. Army Medical Department**
Dept. of Defense, The Pentagon, DC 20301
- U.S. Army Medical Department Medical Science Publications. irreg. ISSN 0082-8807 (Orders to: Supt. Doc., Washington, DC 20402)

**U.S. Army Medical Research Institute of Infectious Diseases**
Fort Detrick, Frederick, MD 21701.
- U.S. Army Medical Research Institute of Infectious Diseases. Annual Progress Report. a.

**U.S. Army Military Police School**
Fort McClellan, AL 36201.
- Military Police Law Enforcement Journal. q.

**U.S. Army. Military Traffic Management Command**
Washington, DC 20315
- Translog; journal of military transportation management. m. ISSN 0041-1639 (Orders to: Supt. of Documents, Washington, DC 20402)

**U.S. Army Personnel Information Activity**
Fort Benjamin Harrison, IN 46249
(Subscr. to: Supt. of Documents, U.S. Gov't Printing Office, Washington, D.C. 20402)
- Tips; the army personnel magazine. q. ISSN 0049-3937

**U.S. Army Recruiting Command**
USARCCS-PA, Ft. Sheridan, IL 60037.
- U.S. Army Recruiting and Career Counseling Journal. m. ISSN 0041-7513 (prep. by its Public Affairs Office)

**U.S. Army Reserve. Office of the Chief Army Reserve**
Washington, DC 20310.
- Army Reserve Magazine. bi-m. ISSN 0004-2579

**U.S. Army Russian Institute**
APO, NY 09053.
- Soviet Affairs Symposium. a. ISSN 0085-6533

**U.S. Army Security Agency**
Arlington Hall Station, Arlington, VA 22212.
- Hallmark. m. ISSN 0440-1352

**U. S. Army War College**
Carlisle Barracks, PA 17013.
- Parameters. q. ISSN 0031-1723

**U.S. Army Warrant Officers Assn.**
Box 3765, Washington, DC 20007.
- U. S. Army Warrant Officers Association Newsletter. m.

**U.S. Board of Geographic Names**
U.S. Geological Survey, National Center, 12201 Sunrise Valley Drive, Reston, VA 22092.
- U.S. Board of Geographic Names. Decisions of Geographic Names in the United States. q. ISSN 0363-6828

**U.S. Bureau of Community Health Service**
Room 12-A-33, 5600 Fishers Lane, Rockville, MD 20852.
- Family Planning Memorandum. bi-m. (Prepared by the Alan Guttmacher Institute, the Research and Development Division of Planned Parenthood-World Population)

**U. S. Bureau of Domestic Commerce**
see under U. S. Domestic and International Business Administration

**U. S. Bureau of East- West Trade**
see under U. S. Domestic and International Business Administration

**U.S. Bureau of Economic Analysis**
U.S. Dept. of Commerce, Washington, DC 20230
(Subscriptions to: Supt. of Documents, Washington, DC 20402)
- Business Conditions Digest. m. ISSN 0007-6597 (prep. by its Statistical Indicators Division)
- Current Population Reports, P-91: International Population Reports. irreg. ISSN 0082-9498
- Defense Indicators. m. ISSN 0418-5013
- Survey of Current Business. m. with weekly supplements. ISSN 0039-6222 (Orders to: Supt. of Documents)

**U.S. Bureau of Health Planning and Resources Development. Division of Nursing**
U.S. Health Resources Administration, Bethesda, MD 20014.
- U.S. Bureau of Health Resources Development. Division of Nursing. Special Project Grants and Contracts Awarded for Improvement in Nurse Training. a. ISSN 0095-2141

**U. S. Bureau of Indian Affairs**
1951 Constitution Ave., N.W., Washington, DC 20245.
- Downdraft. irreg. ISSN 0070-7171

**U.S. Bureau of Indian Affairs. Area Office, Albuquerque**
5301 Central Ave. N.E., Albuquerque, NM 87108.
- Native American Scholar. bi-m.

**U. S. Bureau of International Commerce**
see under U. S. Domestic and International Business Administration

**U. S. Bureau of International Economic Policy and Research**
see under U. S. Domestic and International Business Administration

**U.S. Bureau of Labor Statistics**
411 G St. N.W., Washington, DC 20212
- Directory of National Unions and Employee Associations. irreg. ISSN 0090-4163 (Orders to Supt. of Documents, Government Printing Office, Washington, DC 20402)
- Employment and Earnings: United States. a. (Order from: Supt. of Documents, Washington, DC 20402)
- North American Conference on Labor Statistics. Selected Papers. irreg., latest issue, 1973. ISSN 0074-9974
- U. S. Bureau of Labor Statistics. Analysis of Work Stoppages. m. and a. ISSN 0082-9013 (Order from: Supt. of Documents, Washington, DC 20402;)
- U.S. Bureau of Labor Statistics. Area Wage Surveys. irreg. throughout the year for individual areas. (Order from: Supt. of Documents, Washington, DC 20402;)
- U. S. Bureau of Labor Statistics. B L S Staff Paper. irreg. ISSN 0082-903X (Orders to: Supt. of Documents, Washington, DC 20402)
- U. S. Bureau of Labor Statistics. Bulletins. irreg. ISSN 0082-9021 (Order from: Supt. of Documents, Washington, DC 20402;)
- U.S. Bureau of Labor Statistics. Chartbook on Prices, Wages, and Productivity. m. ISSN 0095-4837 (Orders to: Supt. of Documents, Washington, DC 20402)
- U.S. Bureau of Labor Statistics. CPI Detailed Report. m. ISSN 0095-926X (Order from: Supt. of Documents, Washington, DC 20402;)
- U.S. Bureau of Labor Statistics. Current Wage Developments. m. ISSN 0011-3972 (Orders to: . Supt. of Documents, Washington, DC 20402)
- U.S. Bureau of Labor Statistics. Digest of Selected Pension Plans. irreg., approx. 2 supplements per yr. (Orders to Supt. of Documents, Government Printing Office, Washington, DC 20402)
- U.S. Bureau of Labor Statistics. Employee Compensation in the Private Nonfarm Economy. a. (Orders to: Supt. of Documents, Washington, DC 20402)
- U.S. Bureau of Labor Statistics. Employment and Earnings. m. ISSN 0013-6840 (Orders to: Supt. of Documents, Washington, DC 20402)
- U. S. Bureau of Labor Statistics. Employment and Earnings: States and Areas. a. (Orders from: Supt. of Documents, Washington, DC 20402)
- U.S. Bureau of Labor Statistics. Employment and Wages. q. ISSN 0091-9403

- U. S. Bureau of Labor Statistics. Handbook of Labor Statistics. a. ISSN 0082-9056 (Order from: Supt. of Documents, Washington, DC 20402;)
- U. S. Bureau of Labor Statistics. Industry Wage Surveys. issued irreg. throughout the year by regional offices. ISSN 0082-9064 (Orders to: Supt. of Documents, Washington, DC 20402)
- U. S. Bureau of Labor Statistics. Major Programs. a.
- U.S. Bureau of Labor Statistics. Monthly Labor Review. m. ISSN 0027-044X (Subscriptions to: Monthly Labor Review, Box 353, La Plata, MD 20646)
- U.S. Bureau of Labor Statistics. National Survey of Professional, Administrative, Technical and Clerical Pay. a. ISSN 0501-7041 (Order from Supt. of Documents, Washington, D.C 20402;)
- U.S. Bureau of Labor Statistics. Occupational Outlook Handbook. biennial. (Order from: Supt. of Documents, Washington, DC 20402;)
- U.S. Bureau of Labor Statistics. Occupational Outlook Quarterly. q.(Sept-June) ISSN 0029-7968 (Orders to: Supt. of Documents, Washington, DC 20402)
- U.S. Bureau of Labor Statistics. Productivity Indexes for Selected Industries. a. (Order from: Supt. of Documents, Washington, DC 20402;)
- U. S. Bureau of Labor Statistics. Publications. s-a.
- U.S. Bureau of Labor Statistics. Union Wages and Hours Surveys. issued irreg. throughout the year by regional offices; ISSN 0082-9099 (Order from: Supt. of Documents, Washington, DC 20402;)
- U.S. Bureau of Labor Statistics. Wage Chronologies. irreg. ISSN 0082-9102 (Orders to: Supt. of Documents, Washington, DC 20402)

**U.S. Bureau of Land Management**
U.S. Dept. of the Interior, Washington, DC 20240.
- Our Public Lands. q. ISSN 0030-6940 (Orders to: Supt. of Documents, Washington, DC 20402)
- U. S. Bureau of Land Management. Public Land Statistics. a. ISSN 0082-9110 (prep. by its Division of Record Systems)

**U. S. Bureau of Mines**
Dept. of the Interior, Washington, DC 20240.
- Analyses of Natural Gases of the United States. irreg. ISSN 0066-149X
- International Coal Trade. m. ISSN 0364-054X
- International Petroleum Annual. a. ISSN 0074-7319
- Motor Gasolines. s-a. (Orders to: 4800 Forbes Ave., Pittsburgh, PA 15213)
- U. S. Bureau of Mines. Bulletin. irreg. ISSN 0082-9129
- U. S. Bureau of Mines. Commodity Data Summaries. a. ISSN 0082-9137
- U.S. Bureau of Mines. Mineral Industry Surveys. a. ISSN 0498-7845 (Orders to: 4800 Forbes Ave., Pittsburgh, PA 15213)
- U.S. Bureau of Mines. Minerals Yearbook. a. ISSN 0076-8952 (Orders to: Supt. Doc., Washington, DC 20402)
- U.S. Bureau of Mines. Research and Technologic Work on Explosives, Explosions, and Flames. a. ISSN 0080-1496
- U. S. Bureau of Mines. Technical Progress Report. irreg.

**U. S. Bureau of Outdoor Recreation**
U.S. Dept. of the Interior, Washington, DC 20240 (Orders to: Supt. of Documents, Washington, DC 20402)
- Outdoor Recreation Action. q. ISSN 0030-7130
- U.S. Bureau of Outdoor Recreation. Recreation Grants-in-Aid Manual. irreg.

**U.S. Bureau of Outdoor Recreation. Northeast Regional Office**
600 Arch St., Philadelphia, PA 19106.
- Northeast Outdoor Memo. m.

**U.S. Bureau of Radiological Health**
Rockville, MD 20850.
- Progress in Radiation Protection. a. ISSN 0094-8470

**U.S. Bureau of Reclamation**
Washington, DC 20240
- Reclamation Era; water review quarterly. q. ISSN 0034-141X (Orders to: Supt. of Documents, Washington, DC 20402)
- U.S. Bureau of Land Reclamation. Federal Reclamation Projects: Water & Land Resource Accomplishments. annual report of the Commissioner, issued as summary report with 3 statistical appendices.

**U.S. Bureau of Reclamation. Engineering and Research Center**
Bldg. 67, Box 25007, Denver Federal Center, Denver, CO 80225.
- Project Skywater. Annual Report. a. ISSN 0079-6956 (prep. by its Office of Design and Construction)
- Reclamation Safety News. q. ISSN 0034-1436
- U. S. Bureau of Reclamation. Bibliography. irreg. ISSN 0082-9269 (prep. by its Office of Design and Construction)

**U. S. Bureau of Reclamation. Mid-Pacific Region**
Federal Office Bldg., 2800 Cottage Way, Sacramento, CA 95825.
- Central Valley Project (California) Annual Report. a. ISSN 0084-8662

**U.S. Bureau of the Census**
Subscriber Services Section, Washington, DC 20233
- Cotton Ginnings in the United States. a. ISSN 0070-0681
- Current Business Reports. (Subscriptions to Monthly Retail and Wholesale Trade Reports to: Supt. of Documents, Washington, DC 20402, Other reports in the series available from Bureau's Subscriber Services Section)
- Current Business Reports: Canned Food; stocks, pack, shipments. 5 per yr.
- Current Business Reports: Green Coffee Inventories and Roastings. q.
- Current Business Reports: Monthly Department Store Sales for Selected Areas. m. ISSN 0565-1034
- Current Business Reports: Monthly Retail Trade. m. ISSN 0565-0909 (Subscriptions to: Supt. of Documents, Washington, DC 20402)
- Current Business Reports: Monthly Selected Services Receipts. m. ISSN 0092-038X
- Current Business Reports: Monthly Wholesale Trade; sales and inventories. m. (Orders to: Supt. of Documents, Washington, DC 20402)
- Current Construction Reports. (Subscriptions to series C-20, C-30, C-40 to: Supt. of Documents, Washington, DC 20402, Other reports in the series available from Bureau's Subscriber Services Section)
- Current Construction Reports, C-20: Housing Starts. m. ISSN 0498-8442 (Subscriptions to: Supt. of Documents, Washington, DC 20402)
- Current Construction Reports, C-25: New One Family Homes Sold and for Sale. m.(plus annual numbers)
- Current Construction Reports, C-30: Value of New Construction Put in Place. m. (Orders to: Supt. of Documents, Washington, DC 20402)
- Current Construction Reports, C-40: Housing Authorized by Building Permits and Public Contracts; states and selected standard metropolitan statistical areas. m. ISSN 0091-4762 (Subscriptions to: Supt. of Documents, Washington, DC 20402)
- Current Construction Reports, C-45: Housing Units Authorized for Demolition in Permit-Issuing Places. a.
- Current Governments Reports. quarterly and annual. (Series GE, GF, GR, GT available from Bureau's Subscriber Services Section, Other series available from: Supt. of Documents, Washington, DC 20402)
- Current Governments Reports, GE-Government Employment. annual.
- Current Governments Reports, GE-1: Public Employment. a.
- Current Governments Reports, GE-2: City Employment. a. ISSN 0091-9209
- Current Governments Reports, GE-3: Local Government in Selected Metropolitan and Large Counties. a.
- Current Governments Reports, GE-4: County Employment. a.
- Current Governments Reports, GF - Government Finance. a.
- Current Governments Reports, GF-1: State Tax Collections. annual.
- Current Governments Reports, GF-2: Finances of Employee Retirement Systems of State and Local Governments. annual.
- Current Governments Reports, GF-3: State Government Finances. a. ISSN 0090-5895
- Current Governments Reports, GF-4: City Government Finances. a. irreg. ISSN 0082-9439
- Current Governments Reports, GF-5: Governmental Finances. annual.

- Current Governments Reports, GF-6: Local Government Finances in Selected Metropolitan Areas and Large Counties. annual.
- Current Governments Reports, GF-7: Chart Book on Government Data: Organization, Finances, and Employment. a. ISSN 0360-2508
- Current Governments Reports, GF-8: County Government Finances. annual.
- Current Governments Reports, GR Finances of Selected Public Employee Retirement Systems. q.
- Current Governments Reports, GSS State and Local Government Special Studies. irreg. (Orders to: Supt. Doc., Washington, D.C. 20402)
- Current Governments Reports, GT Quarterly Summary of State and Local Tax Revenue. q.
- Current Housing Reports. (Combined subscription for H-111 and H-121 available from: Supt. of Documents, Washington, DC 20402, Other reports in the series available from Bureau's Subscriber Services Section)
- Current Housing Reports, H-111: Housing Vacancies. quarterly and annual. ISSN 0498-8469 (Subscriptions to: Supt. of Documents, Washington, DC 20402)
- Current Housing Reports, H-121: Housing Characteristics. irreg. ISSN 0498-8450 (Subsctiptions to: Supt. of Documents, Washington, DC 20402)
- Current Housing Reports, H-130: Market Absorption of Apartments. q. (Issued jointly with: U.S. Department of Housing and Urban Development)
- Current Industrial Reports. m.,q., and annual reports. ISSN 0498-8477 (Request complete listing of titles in the series from the Bureau's Subscriber Services Section)
- Current Population Reports. irreg. ISSN 0082-9471 (Orders to: Supt. of Documents, Washington, DC 20402)
- Current Population Reports, P-20: Population Characteristics. irreg. ISSN 0363-6836 (Subscriptions to: Supt. of Documents, Washington, DC 20402)
- Current Population Reports, P-20: Population Characteristics. Geographic Mobility. a. (Orders to: Supt. of Documents, Washington, DC 20402)
- Current Population Reports; P-20: Population Characteristics. Household and Family Characteristics. a. ISSN 0082-948X (Orders to: Supt. of Documents, Washington, DC 20402)
- Current Population Reports, P-20: Population Characteristics. Marital Status and Living Arrangements. a. (Orders to: Supt. of Documents, Washington, DC 20402)
- Current Population Reports, P-20: Population Characteristics. School Enrollment: Social and Economic Characteristics of Students. a. (Orders to: Supt. of Documents, Washington, DC 20402)
- Current Population Reports, P-20: Population Characteristics. Social and Economic Characteristics of the Black Population. a. (Orders to: Supt. of Documents, Washington, DC 20402)
- Current Population Reports, P-23 Special Studies. irreg. ISSN 0498-8485 (Orders to: Supt. of Documents, Washington, DC 20402)
- Current Population Reports, P-25: Population Estimates and Projections. m. (Orders to: Supt. of Documents, Washington, DC 20402)
- Current Population Reports, P-25: Population Estimates and Projections. Estimates of the Population of the United States and Components of Population Change. a. ISSN 0071-1616 (Orders to: Supt. of Documents, Washington, DC 20402)
- Current Population Reports, P-25: Population Estimates and Projections. Estimates of the Population of the United States by Age, Sex, and Race. a. (Orders to: Supt. of Documents, Washington, DC 20402)
- Current Population Reports, P-26: Federal-State Cooperative Program for Population Estimates. irreg. (Orders to: Supt. of Documents, Washington, DC 20402)
- Current Population Reports, P-27: Farm Population. irreg. (Orders to: Supt. of Documents, Washington, DC 20402)
- Current Population Reports, P-28: Special Censuses. irreg. (Biannual summaries available from: Supt. of Documents, Washington, DC 20402, Other P-28 reports available from Bureau's Subscriber Services Section)
- Current Population Reports, P-60: Consumer Income. irreg. (Orders to: Supt. of Documents, Washington, DC 20402)
- Current Population Reports, P-60: Consumer Income. Income in (Year) of Families and Persons in the United States. a. (Orders to: Supt. of Documents, Washington, DC 20402)

- Current Population Reports, P-60: Consumer Income. Money Income (in Year) of Families and Persons in the United States. a. (Orders to: Supt. of Documents, Washington, DC 20402)
- Current Population Reports, P-65: Consumer Buying Intentions. irreg. (Orders to: Supt. of Documents, Washington, DC 20402)
- Foreign Trade Reports. (Subscriptions for Series FT 135, 410, 800, 990 to: Supt. of Documents, Washington, DC 20402, Other reports in the series available from the Bureau's Subscriber Services Section)
- Foreign Trade Reports, FT-130: General Imports of Cotton Manufactures. m.
- Foreign Trade Reports, FT-135: U.S. General Imports - Schedule a - Commodity by Country. m. (Subscriptions to: Supt. of Documents, Washington, DC 20402)
- Foreign Trade Reports, FT-410: U.S. Exports - Schedule B - Commodity by Country. m. (Subscriptions to: Supt. of Documents, Washington, DC 20402)
- Foreign Trade Reports, FT-800: U.S. Trade with Puerto Rico and U.S. Possessions. m. (Subscriptions to: Supt. of Documents, Washington, DC 20402)
- Foreign Trade Reports, FT-810: Bunker Fuels. monthly and annual.
- Foreign Trade Reports, FT-900: Summary of U.S. Export and Import Merchandise Trade. m.
- Foreign Trade Reports, FT-975: Vessel Entrances and Clearances. a.
- Foreign Trade Reports, FT-985: U.S. Waterborne Exports and General Imports; trade area, district, port, type service and U.S. flag. monthly and annual. ISSN 0095-0890
- Foreign Trade Reports, FT-986: U.S. Airborne Exports and General Imports. m.
- Foreign Trade Reports, FT-990: Highlights of U.S. Exports and Imports. m. (Subscriptions to: Supt. of Documents, Washington, DC 20402)
- Historical Statistics of the United States. irreg. ISSN 0073-2664 (Orders to: Supt. of Documents, Washington, DC 20402)
- Households with Television Sets in the United States. irreg. ISSN 0073-3601 (Orders to: Supt. Doc., Washington, DC 20402)
- Pocket Data Book, USA. biennial. ISSN 0079-2403 (Orders to: Supt. of Documents, Washington, DC 20402)
- Statistical Abstract of the United States. a. ISSN 0081-4741 (Orders to: Supt. of Documents, Washington, DC 20402)
- Status; a monthly chartbook of social and economic trends. m.
- U.S. Bureau of the Census. Annual Survey of Manufactures. a; exemption for the years covered by Census of Manufactures. ISSN 0082-9307
- U.S. Bureau of the Census. Bureau of the Census Catalog. quarterly cumulative issues (plus monthly supplements) ISSN 0007-618X (Orders to: Supt. of Documents, Washington, DC 20402)
- U.S. Bureau of the Census. Census Bureau Methodological Research. irreg. ISSN 0565-0828 (Orders to: Supt. of Documents, Washington, DC 20402)
- U. S. Bureau of the Census. Census of Agriculture. quinquennial. ISSN 0082-9315 (Orders to: Supt. of Documents, Washington, DC 20402)
- U. S. Bureau of the Census. Census of Construction Industries. quinquennial; irreg. until 1967. ISSN 0082-934X (Orders to: Supt. of Documents, Washington DC 20402)
- U. S. Bureau of the Census. Census of Governments. quinquennial since 1957. ISSN 0082-9358 (Orders to: Supt. of Documents, Washington, DC 20402)
- U. S. Bureau of the Census. Census of Housing. decennial. ISSN 0082-9366 (Orders to: Supt. of Documents, Washington, DC 20402)
- U. S. Bureau of the Census. Census of Manufactures. quinquennial; 1972 census reports issued periodically. ISSN 0082-9374 (Order forms and announcements available from the Bureau; publication orders to: Supt. of Documents, Washington, DC 20402)
- U. S. Bureau of the Census. Census of Mineral Industries. quinquennial. ISSN 0082-9382 (Orders to: Supt. Doc., Washington, DC 20402)
- U. S. Bureau of the Census. Census of Population. decennial. ISSN 0082-9390 (Orders to: Supt. of Documents, Washington, DC 20402)
- U.S. Bureau of the Census. Census of Retail Trade, Wholesale Trade and Selected Service Industries. quinquennial. (Orders to: Supt. Doc., Washington, DC 20402)

- U. S. Bureau of the Census. Census of Transportation. quinquennial. ISSN 0082-9404 (Orders to: Supt. of Documents, Washington, DC 20402)
- U. S. Bureau of the Census. Census Tract Manual. irreg. ISSN 0082-9412 (Orders to: Supt. Doc., Washington, DC 20402)
- U. S. Bureau of the Census. Congressional District Data Book. irreg. ISSN 0082-9447 (Orders to: Supt. of Documents, Washington, DC 20402)
- U. S. Bureau of the Census. County and City Data Book. irreg. ISSN 0082-9455 (Orders to: Supt. of Documents, Washington, DC 20402)
- U. S. Bureau of the Census. County Business Patterns. a. ISSN 0082-9463 (Orders to: Supt. Doc., Washington, DC 20402)
- U.S. Bureau of the Census. Data User News. m. ISSN 0096-9877
- U. S. Bureau of the Census. Guide to Foreign Trade Statistics. irreg. ISSN 0565-0933 (prep. by its Foreign Trade Division) (Orders to: Supt. of Documents, Washington, DC 20402)
- U.S. Bureau of the Census. Research Document Series. irreg. (prep. by its International Demographic Statistics Center)
- U. S. Bureau of the Census. Technical Notes. irreg. ISSN 0082-9536
- U. S. Bureau of the Census. Technical Paper. irreg. ISSN 0082-9544
- U. S. Bureau of the Census. Working Papers. irreg. ISSN 0082-9552
- United States Import Duties Annotated. irreg. ISSN 0083-1263 (Orders to: Supt. of Documents, Washington, DC 20402)

**U.S. Center for Disease Control**
1600 Clifton Rd., N.E., Atlanta, GA 30333.
- U.S. Center for Disease Control. Abortion Surveillance. Annual Summary. a. ISSN 0094-0933
- U.S. Center for Disease Control. Abortion Surveillance Report. q. ISSN 0300-6972
- U.S. Center for Disease Control. Brucellosis Surveillance: Annual Summary. a. ISSN 0090-1156
- U.S. Center for Disease Control. Congenital Malformations Surveillance. ISSN 0092-5594
- U. S. Center for Disease Control. Diphtheria Surveillance Report. irreg.
- U.S. Center for Disease Control. Family Planning Services: Annual Summary. a. ISSN 0094-4424
- U.S. Center for Disease Control. Foodborne & Waterborne Disease Outbreaks. Annual Summary. a. ISSN 0098-6623
- U.S. Center for Disease Control. Leprosy Surveillance Report. irreg, no. 2, 1972.
- U.S. Center for Disease Control. Listeriosis Surveillance Report. irreg.
- U.S. Center for Disease Control. Malaria Surveillance Report. a. ISSN 0501-8390
- U.S. Center for Disease Control. Morbidity and Mortality Weekly Report. w. ISSN 0091-0031
- U.S. Center for Disease Control. Neurotropic Viral Diseases Surveillance: Aseptic Meningitis. a.
- U.S. Center for Disease Control. Neurotropic Viral Diseases Surveillance: Encephalitis. a.
- U.S. Center for Disease Control. Neurotropic Viral Diseases Surveillance: Enterovirus. a.
- U.S. Center for Disease Control. Neurotropic Viral Diseases Surveillance: Poliomyelitis. a.
- U.S. Center for Disease Control. Salmonella Surveillance. Annual Summary. a. (prep. by its Bureau of Epidemiology. Bacterial Disease Division)
- U.S. Center for Disease Control. Tetanus Surveillance; Report. irreg. ISSN 0094-6605 (prep. by its Bureau of Epidemiology)
- V.D. Fact Sheet. ISSN 0095-6937
- Weekly Summary of Countries with Areas Infected with Quarantinable Diseases. w. (prep. by its Bureau of Epidemiology. Quarantine Division)

**U. S. Center for Disease Control. National Clearinghouse for Smoking and Health**
see U. S. National Clearinghouse for Smoking and Health

**U. S. Center for Disease Control. National Institute for Occupational Safety and Health**
see U. S. National Institute for Occupational Safety and Health

**U.S. Center for Disease Control. Tuberculosis Control Division**
1600 Clifton Rd. N.E., Atlanta, GA 30333.
- U.S. Center for Disease Control. Reported Tuberculosis Data. a.

- U.S. Center for Disease Control. Tuberculosis Program Reports. a.
- U.S. Center for Disease Control. Tuberculosis: States and Cities. a.

**U.S. Center for Population Research**
U.S. National Institute of Child Health and Human Development, Bethesda, MD 20014
- Population Sciences: Index of Biomedical Research. m. ISSN 0093-7398 (Prepared from MEDLARS (Medical Literature Analysis and Retrieval System) Tapes of the National Library of Medicine) (Orders to: Supt. of Documents, Washington, DC 20402)
- U.S. Center for Population Research. Inventory of Federal Population Research. a.
- U.S. Center for Population Research. Reports from Population Research Centers and Program Projects. ISSN 0095-6295

**U.S. Central Intelligence Agency**
Washington, DC 20505
- Directory of Polish Officials. irreg. ISSN 0090-9955
- International Oil Developments; Statistical Survey. s-m. (prep. by its Office of Economic Research)
- U.S. Central Intelligence Agency. Appearances of Soviet Leaders. s-a.

**U.S. Children's Bureau**
Office of Child Development, U.S. Department of Health, Education and Welfare, Washington, DC 20201
- Children Today; an interdisciplinary journal for the professions serving children. bi-m. ISSN 0361-4336 (Subscriptions to: Supt. of Documents, Washington, DC 20402)

**U.S. Citizens' Advisory Council on the Status of Women**
- Women (Washington) (pub. by U.S. Employment Standards Administration. Women's Bureau)

**U.S. Civil Aeronautics Board**
1825 Connecticut Ave. N.W., Washington, DC 20428.
- Air Carrier Financial Statistics. q. ISSN 0002-2225 (prep. by its Bureau of Accounts and Statistics)
- Air Carrier Traffic Statistics. m. ISSN 0002-2233 (prep. by its Bureau of Accounts and Statistics)
- Commuter Air Carrier Traffic Statistics. biennial. (prep. by its Bureau of Operating Rights)
- List of United States Air Carriers. irreg.
- U. S. Civil Aeronautics Board. Aircraft Operating Cost and Performance Report. a. ISSN 0082-9609 (Orders to: Supt. Doc., Washington, DC 20402)

**U.S. Civil Defense Council**
P.O. Box 370, Portsmouth, VA 23705.
- U. S. Civil Defense Council Bulletin. m.

**U.S. Civil Service Commission**
1900 E St. N.W., DC 20415
- Civil Service Journal. q. ISSN 0009-7985 (Orders to: Supt. of Documents, Washington, DC 20402)
- E E O Spotlight. bi-m. (prep. by its Office of Assistant Executive Director)
- Federal Labor-Management Consultant. bi-w. ISSN 0046-3418 (prep. by its Office of Labor-Management Relations)
- Personnel Literature. m. ISSN 0031-5753 (prep. by its Library) (Orders to: Supt. of Documents, Washington, DC 20402)
- U. S. Civil Service Commission. m.
- U.S. Civil Service Commission. Bureau of Personnel Management Evaluation. Evaluation Methods Series. irreg. ISSN 0361-6797
- U. S. Civil Service Commission. Personnel Research and Development Center. Technical Study. irreg. ISSN 0093-366X

**U. S. Civil Service Commission. Bureau of Manpower Information Systems. Manpower Statistics Division**
see U. S. Civil Service Commission. Manpower Statistics Division

**U. S. Civil Service Commission. Manpower Statistics Division**
Bureau of Manpower Information Systems, 1900 E St. N.W., DC 20415.
- U. S. Civil Service Commission. Manpower Statistics Division. Annual Report of Federal Civilian Employment by Geographic Area. a. ISSN 0090-6263
- U.S. Civil Service Commission. Manpower Statistics Division. Federal Civilian Work Force Statistics; Monthly Release. m.
- U.S. Civil Service Commission. Manpower Statistics Division. Occupations of Federal Blue-Collar Workers. biennial. (Orders to Supt. of Documents, Washington, DC 20402)
- U.S. Civil Service Commission. Manpower Statistics Division. Occupations of Federal White-Collar Workers. a. (Subscr. to Supt. of Docs., Washington, DC 20402)
- U.S. Civil Service Commission. Manpower Statistics Division. Pay Structure of the Federal Civil Service. a. (Subcr. to Supt. Docs., Govt. Printing Off., Washington, DC 20402)
- U.S. Civil Service Commission. Manpower Statistics Division. Study of Employment of Women in the Federal Government. a. ISSN 0097-7764 (Subscr. to Supt. of Docs., Washington, DC 20402)
- U.S. Civil Service Commission. Manpower Statistics Division. Study of Minority Group Employment in the Federal Government. s-a. (Subscr. to Supt. of Docs., Govt. Printing Off., Washington, DC 20402)

**U.S. Civil Service Commission. Office of Public Affairs**
Washington, DC 20415.
- Civil Service News Releases. ISSN 0009-8019
- Federal News Clipsheet. m.
- U.S. Civil Service Commission. Annual Report. a. (Orders to Supt. of Documents, Government Printing Office, Washington, DC 20402)

**U.S. Coast Guard**
Washington, 400 Seventh St. S.W., DC 20590.
- Boating Safety Newsletter. q. ISSN 0145-109X (prep. by its Office of Boating Safety)
- Coast Guard Engineer's Digest. q. ISSN 0013-8177
- Merchant Vessels of the United States. a. ISSN 0076-650X (Orders to: Supt. of Documents, Washington, DC 20402)
- On Scene. q. ISSN 0093-2124 (prep. by its Search and Rescue Coordinator)
- U.S. Coast Guard. Environmental Protection Newsletter. q. (prep. by its Commandant G-WEP-4)
- U. S. Coast Guard. Oceanographic Reports (CG-373 Series) irreg. ISSN 0082-9625 (prep. by its Oceanographic Unit)
- U.S. Coast Guard. Polluting Incidents in and Around U.S. Waters. irreg. ISSN 0092-0320
- U.S. Coast Guard Boating Statistics. a. ISSN 0565-1530 (prep. by its Commandant G-BD-2)
- U.S. Coast Guard Marine Safety Council. Proceedings. m. ISSN 0364-0981

**U. S. Coast Guard. Public Information Office**
1520 Market St., St. Louis, MO 63103.
- River Currents. m. ISSN 0145-0689

**U.S. Coastal Engineering Research Center**
Kingman Building, Fort Belvoir, VA 22060
(Subscr to: National Technical Information Service, Operations Division, 5285 Port Royal Rd., Springfield, Va 22151)
- U.S. Coastal Engineering Research Center. Bulletin and Progress Reports. a. ISSN 0565-1603

**U.S. Commission for Education and Cultural Affairs. Board of Foreign Scholarships**
Washington, DC 20036.
- Exchange. q.

**U.S. Commission on Civil Rights**
1121 Vermont Ave., Washington, DC 20425.
- Civil Rights Digest. q. ISSN 0009-7969
- U.S. Commission on Civil Rights. Clearinghouse Publications. irreg. ISSN 0082-9641 (Orders to: Supt. of Documents, Washington, DC 20402;, or up to 50 copies available Free from U.S. Commission on Civil Rights)

**U.S. Community Services Administration**
1200 Nineteenth St., N.W., Washington, DC 20506
- U. S. Community Services Administration. Federal Outlays in Summary. a. ISSN 0091-3553 (Orders to: National Technical Information Service, Springfield, VA 22151)

**U.S. Congress**
- U.S. Congress. Congressional Directory. (pub. by U.S. Government Printing Office)
- U.S. Congress. Congressional Record. (pub. by U.S. Government Printing Office)

**U.S. Consumer Information Center**
see under U.S. General Services Administration

**U.S. Consumer Product Safety Commission. National Injury Information Clearinghouse**
see U.S. National Injury Information Clearinghouse

**United States Court of Claims**
717 Madison Place N.W., Washington, DC 20005.
- Cases Decided in the Court of Claims of the United States. irreg. ISSN 0069-0872

**U.S. Crop Reporting Board**
U.S. Dept. of Agriculture Statistical Reporting Service, 14th and Independence Ave. S.W., Washington, DC 20250.
- U.S. Crop Reporting Board. Agricultural Prices. m. with annual summary. ISSN 0002-1601
- U.S. Crop Reporting Board. Crop Production. m. with annual summary. ISSN 0363-8561
- U.S. Crop Reporting Board. Reports. periodic reports on specific crops, livestock and related topics. (Crop Reporting Board Catalog, available on request, describes contents of each report)

**U. S. Customs Service**
1301 Constitution Ave. N.W., Washington, DC 20229
(Orders to: Supt. of Documents, Washington, DC 20402)
- Customs Bulletin; regulations, rulings, decisions, and notices concerning customs and related matters and decisions of Court of Customs and Patent Appeals and Customs Court. w. ISSN 0011-4146

**U.S. Defense Civil Preparedness Agency**
U.S. Dept. of Defense, The Pentagon, Washington, DC 20301.
- Foresight (Washington) q. ISSN 0093-6049

**U. S. Defense Property Disposal Service**
Washington, DC 20305.
- United States. Defense Property Disposal Service. Annual Historical Summary. a. ISSN 0098-4027

**U. S. Department of Agriculture**
14th and Independence Ave. S.W., Washington, DC 20250.
- Agriculture Decisions. m. ISSN 0002-1741 (prep. by its Office of Information)
- Guidelines for the Use of Insecticides to Control Insects Affecting Crops, Livestock, Households, Stored Products, Forest & Forest Products. a. (Prepared Jointly by: U.S. Agricultural Research Service and U.S. Forest Service)
- Service; USDA's report to consumers. m. ISSN 0037-2544
- U.S. Department of Agriculture. Agricultural Economics Report. irreg. ISSN 0083-0445
- U.S. Department of Agriculture. Agricultural Statistics. a. ISSN 0082-9714 (Orders to: Supt. of Documents, Washington, DC 20402)
- U.S. Department of Agriculture. Agriculture Handbook. irreg. ISSN 0065-4612
- U.S. Department of Agriculture. Agriculture Information Bulletin. irreg. ISSN 0065-4639
- U.S. Department of Agriculture. Bimonthly List of Publications and Visuals. bi-m. ISSN 0092-5896 (prep. by its Office of Communication)
- U.S. Department of Agriculture. Food and Home Notes. w. ISSN 0090-9688
- U.S. Department of Agriculture. Home and Garden Bulletin. irreg. ISSN 0073-3075
- U.S. Department of Agriculture. Home Economics Research Report. irreg. ISSN 0073-3113
- U.S. Department of Agriculture. Marketing Bulletins. irreg.
- U.S. Department of Agriculture. Marketing Research Report. irreg. ISSN 0082-9781
- U.S. Department of Agriculture. Production Research Reports. irreg. ISSN 0082-979X
- U. S. Department of Agriculture. Report of the Secretary of Agriculture. a. ISSN 0082-9803

- U.S. Department of Agriculture. Technical Bulletin. irreg. ISSN 0082-9811
- U.S. Department of Agriculture. Yearbook of Agriculture. a. ISSN 0084-3628

**U. S. Department of Agriculture. Agricultural Marketing Service**
see U. S. Agricultural Marketing Service

**U.S. Department of Agriculture. Agricultural Research Service**
see U.S. Agricultural Research Service

**U. S. Department of Agriculture. Agricultural Stabilization and Conservation Service**
Rm. 46, West Administration Bldg., Washington, DC 20250.
- U.S. Department of Agriculture. Agricultural Stabilization and Conservation Service. Pesticide Review. a. ISSN 0079-1148 (prep. by its Emergency Preparedness Division)

**U.S. Department of Agriculture. Animal and Plant Health Inspection Service**
see U.S. Animal and Plant Health Inspection Service

**U. S. Department of Agriculture. Cooperative State Research Service**
Washington, DC 20250.
- Index of Current Equine Research. irreg., latest issue 1975. ISSN 0070-1947
- U. S. Department of Agriculture. Cooperative State Research Service. Inventory of Agricultural Research. a. ISSN 0360-5841

**U.S. Department of Agriculture. Economic Research Service**
ERS Information Division, Publications Unit, Washington, DC 20250
- Agricultural Economics Research. q. ISSN 0002-1423 (Subscriptions to: Supt. of Documents, Washington, DC 20402)
- Agricultural Situation in Africa and West Asia. a.
- Agricultural Situation in Eastern Europe. a.
- Agricultural Situation in the Far East and Oceania. a. ISSN 0566-9502
- Agricultural Situation in the People's Republic of China. a.
- Agricultural Situation in the Soviet Union. a.
- Agricultural Situation in the Western Hemisphere. a. ISSN 0501-9257
- Agricultural Situation in Western Europe. a.
- Farm Index. m. ISSN 0014-7982 (Orders to: Supt. of Documents, Gov't. Printing Office, Washington, DC 20402)
- Farm Real Estate Taxes, Recent Trends and Developments.
- Foreign Agricultural Trade of the United States. m.; two supplements annually. ISSN 0046-4546
- Outlook for U.S. Agricultural Exports. q. (Prepared with: U.S. Foreign Agricultural Service)
- U. S. Department of Agriculture. Economic Research Service. Agricultural Finance Outlook. a (in December) ISSN 0501-9117
- U. S. Department of Agriculture. Economic Research Service. Agricultural Finance Review. a. ISSN 0002-1466 (Orders to: Supt. of Documents, Washington, DC 20402)
- U. S. Department of Agriculture. Economic Research Service. Agricultural Finance Statistics. a. ISSN 0091-3502 (Orders to: Supt. of Documents, Washington, DC 20402)
- U.S. Department of Agriculture. Economic Research Service. Agricultural Outlook. m. ISSN 0099-1066 (Orders to: Supt. of Documents, Washington, DC 20402)
- U.S. Department of Agriculture. Economic Research Service. Cotton and Wool Situation. 5 per yr.
- U. S. Department of Agriculture. Economic Research Service. Cost of Storing and Handling Cotton at Public Storage Facilities. irreg. ISSN 0092-9530
- U.S. Department of Agriculture. Economic Research Service. Dairy Situation. 5 per yr. ISSN 0011-5703
- U.S. Department of Agriculture. Economic Research Service. Foreign Agricultural Economic Reports. irreg., no. 127, 1976. ISSN 0083-0453
- U.S. Department of Agriculture. Economic Research Service. Fats and Oils Situation. 5 per yr. ISSN 0014-8865
- U.S. Department of Agriculture. Economic Research Service. Feed Situation. 5 per yr. ISSN 0014-9578
- U.S. Department of Agriculture. Economic Research Service. Fruit Situation. 4 per yr.

- U.S. Department of Agriculture. Economic Research Service. Fertilizer Situation. a.
- U.S. Department of Agriculture. Economic Research Service. Livestock and Meat Situation. 6 per yr. ISSN 0024-516X
- U.S. Department of Agriculture. Economic Research Service. National Food Situation. q. ISSN 0027-9277
- U.S. Department of Agriculture. Economic Research Service. Poultry and Egg Situation. 4 per yr. ISSN 0032-5708
- U.S. Department of Agriculture. Economic Research Service. Rice Situation. s-a. ISSN 0501-915X
- U.S. Department of Agriculture. Economic Research Service. Sugar and Sweetener Report. m. ISSN 0362-9511
- U.S. Department of Agriculture. Economic Research Service. Tobacco Situation. q. ISSN 0040-8344
- U.S. Department of Agriculture. Economic Research Service. Vegetable Situation. q. ISSN 0042-3084
- U.S. Department of Agriculture. Economic Research Service. Wheat Situation. 4 per yr.
- U.S. Foreign Agricultural Trade Statistical Report, Calendar Year. a.
- U.S. Foreign Agricultural Trade Statistical Report, Fiscal Year. a.
- World Agricultural Situation. 3 per yr. (Jun, Sep, Dec); regional reports issued during Mar-May. ISSN 0084-1358
- World Economic Conditions in Relation to Agricultural Trade. s-a.

**U.S. Department of Agriculture. Extension Service**
Washington, DC 20250
(Subscriptions to: Supt. of Documents, Washington, DC 20402)
- Extension Service Review: includes pertinent information on agriculture extension programs of the United States, 4-H Club work, conservation, home demonstration. bi-m. ISSN 0014-5408

**U.S. Department of Agriculture. Farmer Cooperative Service**
*see* U.S. Farmer Cooperative Service

**U.S. Department of Agriculture. Federal Crop Insurance Corporation**
*see* U.S. Federal Crop Insurance Corporation

**U.S. Department of Agriculture. Food and Nutrition Service**
Washington, DC 20250
(Subscr. to: Supt. of Documents, Govt. Printing Office, Washington, DC 20402)
- Food and Nutrition. bi-m. ISSN 0046-4384
- U.S. Food and Nutrition Service. Food and Nutrition Programs. a. ISSN 0360-4594

**U. S. Department of Agriculture. Foreign Agricultural Service**
*see* U. S. Foreign Agricultural  Service

**U.S. Department of Agriculture. Forest Service**
*see* U.S. Forest Service

**U.S. Department of Agriculture. National Agricultural Library**
*see* U.S. National Agricultural Library

**U.S. Department of Agriculture. Rural Electrification Administration**
*see* U.S. Rural Electrification Administration

**U.S. Department of Agriculture. Soil Conservation Service**
*see* U.S. Soil Conservation Service

**U.S. Department of Agriculture. Statistical Reporting Service**
Washington, DC 20250
- Agricultural Situation; crop reporters' magazine. m. (Jan.-Feb. combined issue) ISSN 0002-1660 (Orders to: Supt. of Documents, Washington, DC 20402)

**U.S. Department of Commerce**
Fourteenth St. Between Constitution Ave. and E. St. N.W., Washington, DC 20203
(Orders to: Supt. of Documents, Washington, DC 20402)
- Business Service Checklist; a weekly guide to U.S. Dept. of Commerce publications, plus key business indicators. w. ISSN 0007-7062
- Commerce America. bi-w. ISSN 0361-0438

- Government Inventions for Licensing. w. (Order from: NTIS, Springfield, VA 22161)
- National Income and Product Accounts of the United States: Statistical Tables. irreg. ISSN 0361-3895 (prep. by its Office of Business Economics) (Orders to: Supt. Doc, Washington, Dc, 20402)
- U.S. Department of Commerce. Consumer Goods and Services Division. Franchise Opportunities Handbook. a. (Orders to Supt. of Documents, U.S. Government Printing Office, Washington, DC 20402)
- U.S. Department of Commerce. Effects of Pollution Abatement on International Trade. a. ISSN 0093-9692
- U. S. Department of Commerce. Publications; a Catalog and Index. a. ISSN 0091-9039

**U. S. Department of Commerce. Bureau of Economic Analysis**
*see* U. S. Bureau of Economic Analysis

**U.S. Department of Commerce. Bureau of the Census**
*see* U.S. Bureau of the Census

**U.S. Department of Commerce. Domestic and International Business Administration**
*see* U. S. Domestic and International Business Administration

**U.S. Department of Commerce. Economic Development Administration**
*see* U.S. Economic Development Administration

**U.S. Department of Commerce. Maritime Administration**
*see* U.S. Maritime Administration

**U.S. Department of Commerce. National Bureau of Standards**
*see* U.S. National Bureau of Standards

**U.S. Department of Commerce. National Fire Prevention and Control Administration**
*see* U.S. National Fire Prevention and Control Administration

**U.S. Department of Commerce. National Oceanic and Atmospheric Administration**
*see* U.S. National Oceanic and Atmospheric Administration

**U.S. Department of Commerce. National Technical Information Service**
*see* U.S. National Technical Information Service

**U.S. Department of Commerce. Office of Minority Business Enterprise**
*see* U.S. Office of Minority Business Enterprise

**U.S. Department of Commerce. Patent and Trademark Office**
*see* U.S. Patent and Trademark Office

**U.S. Department of Commerce. Travel Service**
*see* U.S. Travel Service

**U. S. Department of Defense**
The Pentagon, Washington, DC 20301
(Orders to: Supt. of Documents, G.P.O., Washington, D.C. 20402)
- Commanders Digest. (pub. by American Forces Press Service)
- U. S. Department of Defense. Defense Department Report; a statement by the Secretary of Defense to the Congress on the budget and defense programs. a. ISSN 0091-6919
- U. S. Department of Defense. Defense Program and Defense Budget. a. ISSN 0082-9862
- U. S. Department of Defense. Report of Secretary of Defense to the Congress. a. ISSN 0098-3888

**U. S. Department of Defense. Defense Civil Preparedness Agency**
*see* U. S. Defense Civil Preparedness Agency

**U.S. Department of Defense. Office of Assistant Secretary of Defense (Manpower, Reserve Affairs and Logistics)**
Cameron Station, Alexandria, VA 22314
- Defense Management Journal. bi-m. ISSN 0041-7599 (Available from: Supt. of Documents, Washington D.C. 20402)

**U.S. Department of Health, Education and Welfare**
Washington, DC 20202
(Orders to: Supt. of Documents, Washington, DC 20402)
- Directory of Rehabilitation Consultants. (pub. by University of Florida. Rehabilitation Research Institute)
- U.S. Department of Health, Education and Welfare. Catalog of Publications. a.
- U. S. Department of Health, Education and Welfare. Health, Education and Welfare Trends. a. ISSN 0082-9897 (Orders to: Supt. Doc., Washington, DC 20402)
- U. S. Department of Health, Education, and Welfare. Mental Retardation Activities. a. ISSN 0082-9919 (Orders to: Supt. Doc., Washington, DC 20402)
- U. S. Department of Health, Education, and Welfare. Proposed Mental Retardation Programs. a. ISSN 0082-9927

**U. S. Department of Health, Education, and Welfare. National Institute of Education**
*see* U. S. National Institute of Education

**U. S. Department of Health, Education, and Welfare. Office of Consumer Affairs**
*see* U. S. Office of Consumer Affairs

**U. S. Department of Health, Education, and Welfare. Office of Education**
*see* U. S. Office of Education

**U. S. Department of Health, Education, and Welfare. Office of Human Development**
*see* U.S. Office of Human Development

**U. S. Department of Health, Education, and Welfare. Project Share**
*see* U. S. Project Share

**U. S. Department of Health, Education, and Welfare. Public Health Service**
*see* U. S. Public Health Service

**U. S. Department of Health, Education, and Welfare. Social and Rehabilitation Service**
*see* U. S. Social and Rehabilitation Service

**U. S. Department of Health, Education, and Welfare. Social Security Administration**
*see* U. S. Social Security Administration

**U. S. Department of Housing and Urban Development**
451 Seventh St. S.W., Washington, DC 20410
- H U D Challenge Magazine. m. ISSN 0017-6303 (Orders to: Supt. of Documents, Washington, DC 20402)
- H U D Newsletter. w. ISSN 0017-6311 (Orders to: Supt. of Documents, Washington, DC 20402)
- H U D Research. q. (prep. by its Office of Policy Development and Research)
- Housing and Planning References. bi-m. ISSN 0018-6570 (Orders to: U.S. Supt. of Documents, Washington, DC 20402)
- Housing and Urban Development Trends. q. ISSN 0018-6619
- U. S. Department of Housing and Urban Development. Annual Report. a. ISSN 0565-2820 (Orders to: Supt. Doc., Washington, DC 20402)
- U.S. Department of Housing and Urban Development. Community Development Evaluation Series. irreg.
- U.S. Department of Housing and Urban Development. Office of International Affairs. Foreign Publications Accessions List. irreg., 1973, no. 32. ISSN 0364-0930
- U.S. Department of Housing and Urban Development. Urban Renewal Handbook. irreg. ISSN 0083-3525 (Orders to: Supt. Doc., Washington, DC 20402)

**U. S. Department of Housing and Urban Development. Federal Housing Administration**
*see* U. S. Federal Housing Administration

**U.S. Department of Justice.**
Constitution & 10th St. N.W., Washington, DC 20530
(Orders to: Supt of Documents, Washington, DC 20402)
- U. S. Department of Justice. Annual Report of the Attorney General of the United States. a. ISSN 0082-9943
- U. S. Department of Justice. Opinions of Attorney General. irreg. ISSN 0082-9951

**U.S. Department of Justice. Drug Enforcement Administration**
see U.S. Drug Enforcement Administration

**U.S. Department of Justice. Federal Bureau of Investigation**
see U.S. Federal Bureau of Investigation

**U.S. Department of Justice. Immigration and Naturalization Service**
see U.S. Immigration and Naturalization Service

**U.S. Department of Justice. Law Enforcement Assistance Administration**
see U.S. Law Enforcement Assistance Administration

**U. S. Department of Labor**
200 Constitution Ave. N.W., Washington, DC 20210.
- Black News Digest. w. ISSN 0045-2238 (prep. by its Office of Information)
- Women and Work; news from the Department of Labor. m. (prep. by its Office of Information)

**U. S. Department of Labor. Bureau of Labor Statistics**
see U. S. Bureau of Labor Statistics

**U.S. Department of Labor. Employment and Training Administration**
see U.S. Employment and Training Administration

**U.S. Department of Labor. Employment Standards Administration**
see U.S. Employment Standards Administration

**U.S. Department of Labor. Labor Management Services Adminstration**
see U.S. Labor Management Services Administration

**U.S. Department of Labor. Occupational Safety and Health Administration**
200 Constitution Ave. N.W., Washington, DC 20210
- Job Safety and Health. m. ISSN 0090-4589 (Orders to: Supt. of Documents, Washington, DC 20402)

**U.S. Department of State**
2201 C St. N.W., Washington, DC 20250
- Digest of the United States Practice in International Law. a. ISSN 0095-3369 (Orders to: Supt. of Documents, Washington, Dc 20402)
- U.S. Department of State. Foreign Affairs Research Documentation Center. Foreign Affairs Research Papers Available; monthly accessions list. m. (Orders to: Supt. of Documents, Washington, DC 20402)
- U.S. Department of State. Historical Studies Division. Major Publications: an Annotated Bibliography. irreg.

**U.S. Department of State. Agency for International Development**
see U.S. Agency for International Development

**U.S. Department of State. Bureau of Education and Cultural Affairs**
2201 C St,NW, Washington, DC 20520.
- Statistical Profile of the U.S. Exchange Program. irreg., latest issue, 1971. ISSN 0091-8075

**U.S. Department of State. Bureau of Intelligence and Research**
2201 C St. N.W., Washington, DC 20520
(Orders to: Supt. of Documents, Washington, DC 20402)
- F A R Horizons Newletter. (Foreign Area Research) q. ISSN 0014-7613 (prep. by its Office of External Research)
- U.S. Department of State. World Strength of the Communist Party Organizations. Annual Report; report by the President to Congress. a. ISSN 0084-2257

**U.S. Department of State. Bureau of Public Affairs**
Washington, DC 20520
(Orders to Supt. of Documents, Washington, DC 20402)
- Foreign Consular Offices in the United States. a. ISSN 0071-7320
- Foreign Relations of the United States. a. ISSN 0071-7355
- U. S. Department of State. African Series. irreg. ISSN 0083-0003
- U. S. Department of State. Biographic Register. a. ISSN 0083-0011
- U. S. Department of State. Bulletin; official record of United States foreign policy. w. ISSN 0041-7610
- U. S. Department of State. Commercial Policy Series. irreg. ISSN 0083-002X
- U. S. Department of State. Department and Foreign Service Series. irreg. ISSN 0083-0038
- U.S. Department of State. Diplomatic List. q. ISSN 0012-3099
- U. S. Department of State. East Asian and Pacific Series. irreg. ISSN 0083-0054
- U. S. Department of State. Economic Cooperation Series. irreg. ISSN 0083-0062
- U. S. Department of State. European and British Commonwealth Series. irreg. ISSN 0083-0070
- U. S. Department of State. General Foreign Policy Series. irreg. ISSN 0083-0097
- U. S. Department of State. Inter-American Series. irreg. ISSN 0083-0143
- U. S. Department of State. International Information and Cultural Series. irreg. ISSN 0083-0119
- U. S. Department of State. International Organization and Conference Series. irreg. ISSN 0083-0127
- U. S. Department of State. International Organization Series. irreg. ISSN 0083-0135
- U.S. Department of State. Key Officers in Foreign Service Posts; guide for businessmen. 3 per yr. ISSN 0023-0790
- U. S. Department of State. Near and Middle Eastern Series. irreg. ISSN 0083-0151
- U. S. Department of State. Treaties and Other International Acts Series. irreg. ISSN 0083-0186
- U. S. Department of State. Treaties in Force. a. ISSN 0083-0194
- U. S. Department of State Newsletter. m. ISSN 0041-7629
- United States Participation in the United Nations. a. ISSN 0083-0208
- United States Treaties and Other International Agreements. a. ISSN 0083-3487

**U.S. Department of the Army**
Washington, DC 20310
- U.S. Department of the Army. Projects Recommended for Deauthorization, Annual Report. a. ISSN 0361-2651 (Orders to: Supt. Doc, Washington, D.C. 20402)

**U.S. Department of the Interior.**
C St. Between Eighteenth and Nineteenth Sts. N.W., Washington, DC 20240
- U. S. Department of the Interior. Annual Report. a. ISSN 0083-0321 (Orders to: Supt. Doc., Washington, DC 20402)
- U. S. Department of the Interior. Area Redevelopment Technical Leaflets. irreg. ISSN 0083-033X (Orders to: Supt. Doc., Washington, DC 20402)
- U.S. Department of the Interior. Conservation Bulletins. irreg. ISSN 0069-9101 (Orders to: Supt. Doc., Washington, DC 20402)
- U.S. Department of the Interior. Conservation Yearbook. a. ISSN 0069-9152 (Orders to: Supt. Doc., Washington, DC 20402)
- U. S. Department of the Interior. Decisions of the Department of the Interior. m. ISSN 0011-7331 (Orders to: Supt. of Documents, Washington, D.C 20402)
- U.S. Department of the Interior. Energy Research Program. a. ISSN 0098-518X (Orders to: Supt. of Documents, Washington, DC 20402)
- U. S. Department of the Interior. Office of Personnel Management. Annual Manpower Personnel Statistics. a. ISSN 0093-3716
- U. S. Department of the Interior. Safety Conference Guides. irreg. ISSN 0083-0364
- U.S. Solicitor for the Department of the Interior. Solicitor's Review. irreg. ISSN 0361-4530

**U. S. Department of the Interior. Bureau of Indian Affairs**
see U. S. Bureau of Indian Affairs

**U.S. Department of the Interior. Bureau of Land Management**
see U.S. Bureau of Land Management

**U.S. Department of the Interior. Bureau of Mines**
see U.S. Bureau of Mines

**U.S. Department of the Interior. Bureau of Outdoor Recreation**
see U.S. Bureau of Outdoor Recreation

**U.S. Department of the Interior. Bureau of Reclamation**
see U.S. Bureau of Reclamation

**U.S. Department of the Interior. Fish and Wildlife Service**
see U.S. Fish and Wildlife Service

**U.S. Department of the Interior. Geological Survey**
see U.S. Geological Survey

**U.S. Department of the Interior. Mining Enforcement and Safety Administration**
see U.S. Mining Enforcement and Safety Administration

**U.S. Department of the Interior. National Park Service**
see U.S. National Park Service

**U.S. Department of the Interior. Office of Water Research and Technology**
see U.S. Office of Water Research and Technology

**U. S. Department of the Interior. Oil Shale Environmental Advisory Panel**
Missouri Basin Region, Denver, CO 80225.
- U.S. Department of the Interior. Oil Shale Environmental Advisory Panel. Annual Report. a. ISSN 0360-4543

**U.S. Department of the Navy. Office of Civilian Manpower Management**
Code 58, Washington, DC 20390.
- Advisor, Navy Civilian Manpower Management. q. ISSN 0364-0426

**U.S. Department of the Navy. Office of Naval Research**
Arlington, DC 22217
- Naval Research Logistics Quarterly. q. ISSN 0028-1441 (Orders to: Supt. of Documents, Washington, DC 20402)
- Naval Research Reviews. m. ISSN 0028-145X (Orders to: Supt. of Documents, Washington, DC 20402)
- Symposium on Naval Hydrodynamics. Proceedings. biennial. ISSN 0082-0849

**U.S. Department of the Navy. Office of the Judge Advocate General**
Washington, DC 20370
- J A G Journal. q. ISSN 0021-3519 (Orders to: Supt. of Documents, Washington, DC 20402)

**U.S. Department of the Treasury**
115th St. and Pennsylvania Ave. N.W., Washington, DC 20220.
- U.S. Office of the Secretary of the Treasury. Treasury Papers. m. ISSN 0364-6696
- U.S. Treasury Department. Combined Statement of Receipts; Expenditures; and Balance of the United States, Government. a. (Orders to: Supt. of Documents, Washington, DC 20402)
- U. S. Treasury Department. Treasury Bulletin. m. ISSN 0041-2155 (Orders to: Supt. of Documents, Washington, DC 20402)

**U.S. Department of the Treasury. Bureau of Alcohol, Tobacco and Firearms**
15th & Pennsylvania Ave. N.W., Washington, DC 20224
- Alcohol, Tobacco and Firearms Bulletin. m. ISSN 0098-0757 (Orders to: Supt. Doc., Washington, DC 20402)

**U. S. Department of the Treasury. Bureau of Government Financial Operations**
Washington, DC 20226.
- U. S. Treasury Department. Bureau of Government Financial Operations. Report on Foreign Currencies Held by the U. S. Government. irreg. ISSN 0098-3896

**U.S. Department of the Treasury. Bureau of Public Debt**
15th St. and Pennsylvania Ave. N.W., Washington, DC 20220
- Tables of Redemption Values for U.S. Savings Bonds, Series A-E. s-a. ISSN 0039-8829 (Subscriptions to: Supt. of Documents, Washington, DC 20402)

**U.S. Department of the Treasury. Internal Revenue Service**
see U.S. Internal Revenue Service

**U. S. Department of the Treasury. United States Savings Bond Division**
1111 20th St. N.W., Washington, DC 20226.
- Bond Teller. q.

**U. S. Department of Transportation**
400 Seventh St. S.W., Washington, DC 20590.
- Transportation. Current Literature. w. ISSN 0091-1410 (prep. by its Library Services Division)
- Transportation Topics for Consumers. q. ISSN 0364-6653
- Transportation USA. q. ISSN 0094-9922 (Subscriptions to: Supt. of Documents, Washington, DC 20402)
- U.S. Department of Transportation. Aircraft Accident Reports. m. (Orders to: National Technical Information Service, 5825 Port Royal Rd., Springfield, VA 22151)
- U. S. Department of Transportation. Annual Report on High Speed Ground Transportation Act. a. ISSN 0083-0399 (prep. by its Administrative Standards Branch)
- U. S. Department of Transportation. Annual Report on Highway Safety Improvement Programs. a. ISSN 0098-3209 (Order from: Supt. of Documents, Washington DC 20402)
- U. S. Department of Transportation. Bibliographic Lists. irreg. ISSN 0083-0380 (Order from: National Technical Information Service, 5285 Port Royal Rd., Springfield, VA 22151)
- U.S. Department of Transportation. Climatic Impact Assessment Program Office. Technical Abstract Report. m. ISSN 0091-8644
- U. S. Department of Transportation. Energy Statistics; a supplement to the summary of national transportation statistics. a. ISSN 0360-8980 (Orders to Supt. of Documents, U. S. Government Printing Office, Washington, DC 20590)
- U. S. Department of Transportation. Fiscal Year Budget in Brief. irreg. ISSN 0092-3117
- U.S. Department of Transportation. Office of Policy Review. Working Paper. irreg. ISSN 0091-7354
- U.S. Department Transportation. Office of University Research. Awards to Academic Institutions by the Department of Transportation. a. ISSN 0099-2267
- U.S. Department of Transportation. Year-End Report. irreg. ISSN 0093-9897

**U.S. Department of Transportation. Federal Highway Administration. Federal Highway Administration**
see U.S. Federal Highway Administration

**U.S. Department of Transportation. Federal Aviation Administration**
see U.S. Federal Aviation Administration

**U.S. Department of Transportation. Federal Railroad Administration**
see U.S. Federal Railroad Administration

**U.S. Department of Transportation. National Highway Traffic Safety Administration**
see U.S. National Highway Traffic Safety Administration

**U.S. Department of Transportation. Saint Lawrence Seaway Development Corporation**
see U.S. Saint Lawrence Seaway Development Corporation

**U.S. Department of Transportation. U.S. Coast Guard**
see U.S. Coast Guard

**U.S. Department of Transportation. Urban Mass Transportation Administration**
see U.S. Urban Mass Transportation Administration

**U. S. District of Columbia**
see District of Columbia

**U.S. Domestic and International Business Administration**
U.S. Dept. of Commerce, Washington, DC 20230
- Commerce Business Daily. d. (Mon.-Fri.) ISSN 0095-3423 (prep. by its Office of Field Operations) (Subscriptions to: Supt. of Documents, Washington, DC 20402)

**U.S. Domestic and International Business Administration. Bureau of Domestic Commerce**
U.S. Dept. of Commerce, Fourteenth St. Between Constitution Ave. and E St. N.W., Washington, DC 20230
(Orders to: Supt. of Documents, Washington, DC 20402)
- Construction Review. m. ISSN 0010-6917
- Containers and Packaging. q. ISSN 0010-7387
- Copper. q. with annual issue. ISSN 0097-7829
- Printing and Publishing. q. ISSN 0032-8588
- Pulp, Paper and Board. q. ISSN 0033-412X
- U.S. Bureau of Domestic and International Business Administration. Overseas Business Reports. irreg. ISSN 0082-9846
- U. S. Industrial Outlook. a. ISSN 0083-1344

**U.S. Domestic and International Business Administration. Bureau of East-West Trade**
Washington, DC 20230
(Orders to: Supt. of Documents, Washington, DC 20402)
- Summary of United States Export Control Regulations. irreg. ISSN 0081-9336
- U.S. Bureau of East-West Trade. Export Administration Regulations. a. ISSN 0094-8411
- U.S. Bureau of East-West Trade. Office of Export Administration. Export Administration Report; report on U.S. export controls to the President and Congress. s-a. ISSN 0092-3206 (Available from: Operations Division, Office of Export Administration, Room 1617, U.S. Dept. of Commerce, Washington, DC 20230)

**U.S. Domestic and International Business Administration. Bureau of International Commerce**
Washington, DC 20230.
- Commercial News for the Foreign Service. bi-m. ISSN 0363-678X (prep. by its Office of International Marketing)
- Foreign Economic Trends and Their Implications for the United States. irreg. ISSN 0090-9467 (Subscriptions to: Supt. of Documents, Washington, DC 20402)
- Index to Foreign Market Reports. m. ISSN 0094-2634 (Subscriptions to: NTIS, Springfield, VA 22161)
- U. S. Bureau of International Commerce. Annual Reports. a. ISSN 0082-8939 (Orders to: Supt. Doc., Washington, DC 20402)
- U. S. Bureau of International Commerce. Trade Lists. irreg. ISSN 0082-8963

**U.S. Domestic and International Business Administration. Bureau of International Economic Policy and Research**
U.S. Dept. of Commerce, Washington, DC 20230.
- International Economic Indicators and Competitive Trends. q. ISSN 0096-9907 (prep. by its International Trade Analysis Staff)
- Multinational Corporation: Studies on U.S. Foreign Investment. irreg., only vol. 1 issued to date. (prep. by its Office of International Investment)

**U. S. Drug Enforcement Administration**
U.S. Dept. of Justice, 1405 I St., N. W., Washington, DC 20537.
- Drug Enforcement. q. ISSN 0098-3470

**U.S. Economic Development Administration. Office of Economic Research**
Washington, DC 20230.
- U. S. Economic Development Administration. Office of Economic Research. Research Review. irreg.

**U. S. Educational Resources Information Center**
see E R I C

**U. S. Emergency Loan Guarantee Board**
U.S. Dept. of the Treasury, 15th St. and Pennsylvania Ave. N.W., Washington, DC 20220
- U.S. Emergency Loan Guarantee Board. Annual Report. a. ISSN 0090-8002 (Orders to: Supt. of Documents, G.P.O., Washington, DC 20402)

**U.S. Employment and Training Administration**
601 D St. N.W., Washington, DC 20210.
- E T A Interchange. m. ISSN 0364-2011
- Job Corps Happenings. m. ISSN 0095-0025
- U.S. Department of Labor. Employment and Training Administration. Area Trends in Employment and Unemployment. m. ISSN 0004-0916
- U.S. Department of Labor. Employment and Training Administration. Guide to Local Occupational Information. irreg., 5th edt., 1976.
- U.S. Department of Labor. Employment and Training Administration. Manpower Research and Development Projects. a.
- Worklife Magazine. m. (Dist. by: Supt. of Documents, Washington, D.C. 20402)

**U.S. Employment and Training Administration. Unemployment Insurance Service**
see U.S. Unemployment Insurance Service

**U.S. Employment Standards Administration.**
U.S. Dept. of Labor, 200 Constitution Ave. N.W., Washington, DC 20210.
- U.S. Employment Standards Administration. Labor Law Series. irreg. ISSN 0082-8998

**U.S. Employment Standards Administration. Women's Bureau**
U.S. Department of Labor, 200 Constitution Ave. N.W., Washington, DC 20210
- Handbook on Women Workers. biennial. ISSN 0083-3622 (Orders to: Supt. Doc., Washington, DC 20402)
- Women (Washington) a. ISSN 0095-1536 (U.S. Citizens' Advisory Council on the Status of Women)

**U.S. Energy Research and Development Administration. Technical Information Center**
Box 62, Oak Ridge, TN 37830
- E R D A Energy Research Abstracts. s-m. ISSN 0360-3571 (Subscriptions to: Supt. Docs, Washington DC 20402)
- Energy Abstracts for Policy Analysis. m. ISSN 0098-5104 (Subscr. to Supt. of Documents, Washington, DC 20402)
- Fossil Energy Update. m. (Subscriptions to: NTIS, Springfield, VA 22161)
- Nuclear Safety; a bimonthly technical progress review. bi-m. ISSN 0029-5604 (Orders to: Supt. of Documents, Washington, D.C. 20402)
- Power Reactor Docket Information. m. (11 issues plus annual cumulation)
- Solar Energy Update. m. (Subscriptions to: NTIS, Springfield, VA 22161)
- U.S. Energy Research and Development Administration. Directory of E R D A Information Centers. irreg.

**U.S. Environmental Data Service**
3300 Whitehaven St., Washington, DC 20235.
- International Decade of Ocean Exploration. Progress Report. a.

**U.S. Environmental Data Service. National Climatic Center**
see U.S. National Climatic Center

**U.S. Environmental Data Service. National Geophyiscal and Solar-Terrestrial Data Center**
see U.S. National Geophysical and Solar-Terrestrial Data Center

**U.S. Environmental Data Service. National Oceanographic Data Center**
see U.S. National Oceanographic Data Center

**U.S. Environmental Data Service. World Data Center A for Glaciology**
Institute of Artic and Alpine Research, University of Colorado, Boulder, CO 80309.
- Glaciological Data. q. (Co-Sponsor: National Academy of Sciences)

**U.S. Environmental Protection Agency**
Washington
(For sale by the Supt. of Docs., G.P.O., Washington, D.C. 20240)
- E P A Reports Bibliography Quarterly. q. ISSN 0360-2265 (Orders to: National Technical Information Service, Springfield, VA 22161)
- Environmental Information Systems Directory. a. ISSN 0094-3231
- Municipal Waste Facilities in the U. S. irreg. ISSN 0077-2178 (Orders to: Supt. Doc., Washington, DC 20402)
- Sewage Facilities Construction. a. ISSN 0083-050X (prep. by its Office of Water Program Operations) (Orders to: Supt. Doc., Washington, DC 20402)
- Solid Waste Management: Abstracts from the Literature. a. ISSN 0092-0541 (Orders to: Supt. Doc., Washington, DC 20402)
- Solid Waste Management; Available Information Materials. q. (prep. by its Office of Solid Waste Management Programs)
- U.S. Environmental Protection Agency. Clean Water; Report to Congress. a.
- U. S. Environmental Protection Agency. Fish Kills Caused by Pollution. a. ISSN 0071-5506 (prep. by its Office of Water Programs) (Orders to: Supt. Doc., Washington, DC 20402)
- U.S. Environmental Protection Agency. Montly Listing of Awards for Construction Grants for Waste Water Treatments - Public Law 92-500 Project Records. m. (prep. by its Grants Administration Division) (Orders to: National Technical Information Service, Springfield, VA 22161)
- U.S. Environmental Protection Agency. Office of General Counsel. a Collection of Legal Opinions. a. ISSN 0361-6673
- U. S. Environmental Protection Agency. Office of Research and Development. Indexed Bibliography. irreg.
- U. S. Environmental Protection Agency. Office of Research and Development. Selected Irrigation Return Flow Abstracts. a. ISSN 0090-6808
- U. S. Environmental Protection Agency. Pesticides Enforcement Division. Notices of Judgement under Federal Insecticide, Fungicide, and Rodenticide Act. irreg. ISSN 0083-0518 (Orders to: Supt. Doc., Washington, DC 20402)
- U.S. Environmental Protection Agency. Summaries of Foreign Government Environmental Reports. m. ISSN 0094-3142 (Orders to: National Technical Information Service, Springfield, VA 22161)
- U. S. Environmental Protection Agency. Upgrading Metal-Finishing Facilities to Reduce Pollution. irreg. ISSN 0092-9689

**U. S. Environmental Protection Agency. Arctic Environmental Research Laboratory**
College, AK 99701
- Cold Climate Research Highlights. s-a. (Orders to: EPA Office of Public Affairs, 200 S.W. 35th St., Corvallis, OR 97330)

**U. S. Environmental Protection Agency. Grosse Ile Laboratory**
9311 Groh Rd., Grosse Ile, MI 48138
- Great Lakes Research Highlights. s-a. (Subscr. to: Office of Public Affairs, 200 S.W. 35th St., Corvallis, OR 97330)

**U. S. Environmental Protection Agency. Gulf Breeze Environmental Research Laboratory**
Sabine Island, Gulf Breeze, FL 32561
- Toxic-Organics -- Pesticides Research Highlights. s-a. (Subscr. to: Office of Public Affairs, 200 S.W. 35th St., Corvallis, OR 97330)

**U. S. Environmental Protection Agency. National Marine Water Quality Laboratory**
South Ferry Rd., Narragansett, RI 02882
- Marine Ecology Research Highlights. s-a. (Subscr. to: Office of Public Affairs, 200 S.W 35th St., Corvallis, OR 97330)

**U. S. Environmental Protection Agency. National Water Quality Laboratory**
6201 Congdon Blvd., Duluth, MN 55804
- Freshwater Aquatic Life Research Highlights. s-a. (Subscr. to: Office Public Affairs, 200 S.W. 35th St., Corvallis, OR 97330)

**U.S. Environmental Protection Agency. Office of Air Quality Planning and Standards**
Air Pollution Technical Information Center, Research Triangle Park, NC 27709
(Orders to: NTIS, Springfield, VA 22161)
- National Air Quality Emissions Trends. Report. a.
- U.S. Environmental Protection Agency. Office of Air Quality Planning and Standards. State Air Pollution Implementation Plan Progress Report. a. ISSN 0094-2871

**U.S. Environmental Protection Agency. Office of Pesticides Programs**
Chamblee, GA 30341
- Pesticides Abstracts. m. ISSN 0093-3295 (Available from Supt. of Docs., Government Printing Office)
- Pesticides Monitoring Journal. q. ISSN 0031-6156 (Orders to: Supt. of Documents, Washington, DC 20402)

**U.S. Environmental Protection Agency. Office of Radiation Programs**
Montgomery, AL 36109.
- U.S. Environmental Protection Agency. Eastern Environmental Radiation Facility. Annual Report. a.

**U.S. Environmental Protection Agency. Region V**
230 S. Dearborn, Chicago, IL 60604.
- Environment Midwest. m. ISSN 0364-2151

**U.S. Environmental Protection Agency. Water Planning Division**
WH-554, Waterside Mall, East Tower, Room 815, 401 M St., S.W., Washington, DC 20460.
- U.S. Environmental Protection Agency. Water Planning Division. Water Quality Strategy Paper. a.

**U.S. Equal Employment Opportunity Commission**
2401 E. Street, N. W., Washington, DC 20037.
- E E O C Compliance Manual. w.
- U.S. Equal Employment Opportunity Commission. Annual Report. a. ISSN 0083-0526 (Orders to: Supt. Doc., Washington, DC 20402)

**U. S. Executive Office of the President**
1600 Pennsylvania Ave., N.W., Washington, DC 20500
(Orders to: Supt. of Documents, Washington, DC 20402)
- U. S. Executive Office of the President. Economic Report of the President. a.
- U.S. Executive Office of the President. International Economic Report of the President. a. ISSN 0091-2492

**U. S. Executive Office of the President. Central Intelligence Agency**
see U. S. Central Intelligence Agency

**U.S. Executive Office of the President. Council of Economic Advisers**
Executive Office Bldg., Washington, DC 20506
- Economic Indicators. m. ISSN 0013-0125 (Orders to: Supt. of Documents, Washington, DC 20402)

**U.S. Executive Office of the President. Office of Management and Budget**
see U. S. Office of Management and Budget

**U. S. Export- Import Bank**
see Export- Import Bank of the United States

**U.S. Farm Credit Administration.**
485 L'Enfant Plaza West, S.W., Washington, DC 20578
- U. S. Farm Credit Administration. Annual Report of the Farm Credit Administration on the Work of the Cooperative Farm Credit System. a. ISSN 0083-0542 (Orders to: Supt. Doc., Washington, DC 20402)

**U.S. Farmer Cooperative Service**
U.S. Department of Agriculture, Rm. 1474 South Bldg., Washington, DC 20250
- Farmer Cooperatives. m. (Subscr. to: Supt. of Documents, Washington, DC 20250)

- U. S. Department of Agriculture. Farmer Cooperative Service. Information (Series) irreg. ISSN 0082-9765
- U. S. Department of Agriculture. Farmer Cooperative Service. Statistics of Farmer Cooperatives. a. ISSN 0081-5128

**U. S. Federal Aviation Administration**
800 Independence Ave., Washington, DC 20591
- Airman's Information Manual. Part 1: Basic Flight Manual and ATC Procedures. s-a. ISSN 0002-2764 (Subscriptions to: Supt. of Documents, Washington, DC 20402)
- Airman's Information Manual. Part 2: Airport Directory. s-a. ISSN 0002-2772 (Subscriptions to: Supt. of Documents, Washington, DC 20402)
- Airman's Information Manual. Part 3: Operational Data. every 8 weeks. (Subscriptions to: Supt. of Documents, Washington, DC 20402)
- Airman's Information Manual. Part 3A: Notices to Airmen. bi-w. (Subscriptions to: Supt. of Documents, Washington, DC 20402)
- Airman's Information Manual. Part 4: Graphic Notices and Supplemental Data. q. (Subscriptions to: Supt. of Documents, Washington, DC 20402)
- Aviation Medical Education Series. irreg. ISSN 0067-2661 (prep. by its Aviation Medicine Office)
- Census of U.S. Civil Aircraft. a. ISSN 0069-1437 (Orders to: Supt. Doc., Washington, DC 20402)
- F A A General Aviation News. m. ISSN 0362-7942 (Subscriptions to: Supt. of Documents, Washington, DC 20402)
- Flight Standards Information Manual. s-a. ISSN 0565-4866
- International Notices to Airmen. w. ISSN 0364-6742 (Orders to: Supt. of Documents, Washington, DC 20402)
- Overview of the F A A Engineering & Development Programs. irreg. ISSN 0092-3591
- U.S. Federal Aviation Administration. Information and Statistics Division. Current Aviation Statistics. ISSN 0096-3364
- U. S. Federal Aviation Administration. National Aviation System Policy Summary. irreg., ISSN 0092-4555 (Orders to: Supt. of Documents, Washington, DC 20402)
- U. S. Federal Aviation Administration. Office of the General Counsel. Statistical Summary: Air Carrier Enforcement Cases. a.
- U.S. Federal Aviation Administration. Systems Research and Development. Report FAA-RD. irreg. (prep. by its Systems Research and Development Service) (Order from: National Technical Information Service, 5285 Port Royal Rd., Springfield, VA 22151)

**U. S. Federal Bureau of Investigation**
Ninth St. and Pennsylvania Ave., DC 20535.
- F B I Law Enforcement Bulletin. m. ISSN 0014-5688
- Uniform Crime Reports for the United States. each edition kept up-to-date with quarterly and annual supplements. ISSN 0082-7592
- U.S. Federal Bureau of Investigation. Bomb Summary. a. ISSN 0360-3245 (Co-sponsor: National Bomb Data Center)

**U.S. Federal Communications Commission**
1919 K St. N.W., Washington, DC 20554
- Federal Communications Commission Reports; decisions, reports, public notices, and other documents of the Federal Communications Commission of the United States. w. (Orders to: Supt. of Documents, Washington, DC 20402)
- Statistics of the Communications Industry in the United States. a. ISSN 0081-5179 (Orders to: Supt. of Documents, Washington, DC 20402)
- U. S. Federal Communications Commission. Annual Report. a. ISSN 0083-0585 (Orders to: Supt. Doc., Washington, DC 20402)
- U. S. Federal Communications Commission. I N F Bulletins. irreg., latest issue, 1976. ISSN 0083-0607
- U. S. Federal Communications Commission. Rules and Regulation. irreg. ISSN 0083-0615 (Orders to: Supt. of Documents, Washington, DC 20402)

**U.S. Federal Council for Science and Technology. Interdepartmental Committee for Atmospheric Sciences**
- U. S. Federal Council for Science and Technology. Interdepartmental Committee for Atmospheric Sciences. I C A S Reports. (pub. by U.S. National Science Foundation)

**U.S. Federal Crop Insurance Corporation.**
U.S. Dept. of Agriculture, Washington, DC 20250
- U.S. Federal Crop Insurance Corporation. Annual Report to Congress. a. ISSN 0083-064X (Orders to: Supt. Doc., Washington, DC 20402)

**U.S. Federal Deposit Insurance Corporation**
550 17th St., N.W., Washington, DC 20429.
- U. S. Federal Deposit Insurance Corporation. Annual Report. a. ISSN 0083-0658
- U.S. Federal Deposit Insurance Corporation. Assets and Liabilities - Commercial and Mutual Savings Banks and Report of Income. s-a.
- U. S. Federal Deposit Insurance Corporation. Bank Operating Statistics. a. ISSN 0083-0666
- U. S. Federal Deposit Insurance Corporation. Changes Among Operating Banks and Branches. a. ISSN 0083-0674
- U.S. Federal Deposit Insurance Corporation. Federal Deposit Insurance Act, Rules and Regulations, and Related Laws. loosleaf supplements issued bi-monthly.
- U.S. Federal Deposit Insurance Corporation. News Releases. w.
- U.S. Federal Deposit Insurance Corporation. Operating Bank Offices. a.
- U.S. Federal Deposit Insurance Corporation. Summary of Deposits in All Commercial and Mutual Savings Banks. a. ISSN 0092-8496
- U.S. Federal Deposit Insurance Corporation. Trust. Assets of Insured Commercial Banks. a.

**U.S. Federal Energy Administration**
National Energy Information Center, Washington, DC 20461
- Directory of State Government Energy-Related Agencies. irreg. ISSN 0361-3445
- Energy Reporter; Federal Energy Administration citizen newsletter. m. ISSN 0363-8820
- Monthly Energy Review. m. ISSN 0095-7356 (Orders to: NTIS, Springfield, VA 22161)
- Monthly Petroleum Product Price Report. m. (Orders to: NTIS, Springfield, VA 22161)
- Monthly Petroleum Statistics Report. m. ISSN 0364-0205 (Orders to: NTIS, Springfield, VA 22161)
- Petroleum Market Shares: Report on Sales of Refined Petroleum Products. m. (Orders to: NTIS, Springfield, VA 22161)
- Petroleum Market Shares: Report on Sales of Retail Gasoline. m. (Orders to: NtIS, Springfield, VA 22161)
- Trends in Refinery Capacity and Utilization. Petroleum Refineries in the United States. Foreign Refinery Exporting Centers. a.
- U.S. Federal Energy Administration. Report to Congress on the Economic Impact of Energy Actions. a. ISSN 0361-6126 (Orders to: NTIS, Springfield, VA 22161)

**U. S. Federal Fire Council**
National Bureau of Standards, Washington, DC 20234.
- Federal Fire Council News Letter. 4 per yr. ISSN 0014-908X
- U. S. Federal Fire Council. Federal Fire Experience for Fiscal Year. irreg. ISSN 0083-0682
- U. S. Federal Fire Council. Minutes of Annual Meeting. irreg. ISSN 0083-0690
- U. S. Federal Fire Council. Recommended Practices. irreg. ISSN 0083-0704

**U. S. Federal Highway Administration**
400 Seventh St. S.W., Washington, DC 20591.
- Highway Planning Notes. irreg. ISSN 0073-2176 (prep. by its Management Systems Branch)
- Potentially Reactive Carbonate Rocks; Progress Report. irreg. ISSN 0091-0813
- Public Roads; a journal of highway research. q. ISSN 0033-3735 (Orders to: Supt. of Documents, Washington, DC 20402)
- U.S. Federal Highway Administration. Federally Coordinated Program of Highway Research and Development. a. ISSN 0361-4204 (Orders to: Supt. Doc., Washington, D.C. 20402)
- U. S. Federal Highway Administration. Highway and Urban Mass Transportation. irreg (2-3 per yr)

- U.S. Federal Highway Administration. Highway Planning Technical Reports. irreg. ISSN 0073-2184 (Subscr. to Supt. of Documents, Government Printing Office, Washington, DC 20402)
- U.S. Federal Highway Administration. Highway Statistics. a. (prep. by its Highway Statistics Division) (Orders to: Supt. of Documents, U.S. Government Printing Office, Washington, DC 20402)
- U.S. Federal Highway Administration. Highway Transportation Research and Development Studies. irreg. ISSN 0092-3389 (Orders to: Supt. of Documents, Washington, DC 20402)
- U. S. Federal Highway Administration. Motor Vehicle Registrations by Standard Metropolitan Statistical Areas. irreg. ISSN 0091-6056
- U.S. Federal Highway Administration Research and Development Program. a. ISSN 0098-0234

**U. S. Federal Home Loan Bank Board**
320 First St. N. W., Washington, DC 20552.
- Federal Savings and Loan Insurance Corporation. List of Member Institutions. a. ISSN 0428-1365
- U.S. Federal Home Loan Bank Board. Journal. m. ISSN 0041-7645 (Subscriptions to: Supt. of Documents, Washington, DC 20402)
- U. S. Federal Home Loan Bank Board. Report. a. ISSN 0083-0720
- U. S. Federal Home Loan Bank Board. Trends in the Savings and Loan Field. a. ISSN 0083-0747

**U. S. Federal Housing Administration**
451 Seventh St., S.W., Washington, DC 20410.
- U.S. Federal Housing Administration. F H A Homes; data for states on characteristics of FHA operations under Section 203. irreg. ISSN 0091-4932

**U. S. Federal Judicial Center**
1520 H St. N.W., Washington, DC 20005.
- Third Branch; a bulletin of the federal courts. m. ISSN 0040-6120

**U.S. Federal Maritime Commission.**
1110 L St. N. W., Washington, DC 20573 (Orders to: Supt. Doc., Washington, DC 20402)
- U. S. Federal Maritime Commission. Annual Report. a. ISSN 0083-0755
- U. S. Federal Maritime Commission. Report: Decisions of the Federal Maritime Commission. a. ISSN 0083-0763

**U.S. Federal Mediation and Conciliation Service.**
2100 K St. N.W., Washington, DC 20427.
- U. S. Federal Mediation and Conciliation Service. Annual Report. a. ISSN 0083-0771

**U.S. Federal Power Commission**
825 North Capitol St. N.E., Washington, DC 20426
- Electric Power Statistics; production of energy and capacity of plants, fuel consumption of electric power plants, electric utility system loads, sales of electric energy. financial statistics of private utilities. m. ISSN 0013-4139 (Orders to: Supt. of Documents, Washington, DC 20402)
- F P C News. w. ISSN 0014-6080 (prep. by its Office of Public Information)
- Gas Supply Indicators; a quarterly report of natural gas trends in the United States. q. ISSN 0097-8671 (prep. by its Office of Policy Analysis)
- Hydroelectric Power Resources of the United States, Developed and Undeveloped. irreg. ISSN 0073-4209 (Orders to: Supt. Doc., Washington, DC 20402)
- Statistics of Privately Owned Electric Utilities in the United States. a.
- Statistics of Publicly Owned Electric Utilities in the United States. a.
- U. S. Federal Power Commission. Annual Report. a. ISSN 0083-078X (Orders to: Supt. Doc., Washington, DC 20402)
- U. S. Federal Power Commission. Hydroelectric Plant Construction Cost and Annual Production Expenses. Supplements. a. ISSN 0083-0798 (prep. by its Bureau of Power) (Orders to: Supt. Doc., Washington, DC 20402)
- U. S. Federal Power Commission. Power Series. irreg. ISSN 0083-0801 (Orders to: Supt. Doc., Washington, DC 20402)
- U. S. Federal Power Commission. Sales by Producers of Natural Gas to Natural Gas Pipeline Companies. a. ISSN 0083-081X (Orders to: Supt. Doc., Washington, DC 20402)
- U. S. Federal Power Commission. Statistical Series. irreg. ISSN 0083-0860 (Orders to: Supt. Doc., Washington, DC 20402)

- U. S. Federal Power Commission. Statistics of Interstate Natural Gas Pipeline Companies; classes A and B companies. a. (prep. by its Office of Accounting and Finance)
- U.S. Federal Power Commission. Steam-Electric Plant Air and Water Quality Control Data; summary data. a. (prep. by its Bureau of Power) (Orders to Supt. of Documents, U.S. Government Printing Office, Washington, DC 20426)
- U. S. Federal Power Commission. Steam-Electric Plant Construction Cost and Annual Production Expenses. Supplements. a. ISSN 0083-0852 (Orders to: Supt. Doc., Washington, DC 20402)
- World Power Data. a. ISSN 0084-2192 (Orders to: Supt. Doc., Washington, DC 20402)

**U. S. Federal Railroad Administration**
2100 Second St., S.W., Washington, DC 20591
- Railroad Research Bulletin. s-a. (prep. by its Office of Research, Development, and Demonstrations) (Orders to: NTIS, Springfield, VA 22151)
- U. S. Federal Railroad Administration. Rail Passenger Statistics in the Northeast Corridor. irreg. ISSN 0091-9667
- U. S. Federal Railroad Administration. Summary of Accidents Investigated by the Federal Railroad Administration. irreg. ISSN 0092-2781

**U.S. Federal Reserve System. Board of Governors**
Washington, DC 20551.
- Federal Reserve Bulletin. m. ISSN 0014-9209
- Federal Reserve Monthly Chart Book. m.
- U. S. Federal Reserve System. Annual Report. a. ISSN 0083-0887

**U.S. Federal Trade Commission.**
Pennsylvania Ave. at Sixth St. N.W., Washington, DC 20580
(Orders to: Supt. of Documents, Washington, DC 20402)
- U. S. Federal Trade Commission. Annual Report. a. ISSN 0083-0917
- U. S. Federal Trade Commission. Consumer Bulletins. irreg. ISSN 0069-9233 (Orders to: Supt. of Documents, Orders to: Supt. of Documents, Washington, DC 20402)
- U. S. Federal Trade Commission. Federal Trade Commission Decisions, Findings, Orders and Stipulations. a. ISSN 0083-0925
- U. S. Federal Trade Commission. Quarterly Financial Report for Manufacturing, Mining and Trade Corporations. q. ISSN 0098-681X
- U. S. Federal Trade Commission. Statutes and Court Decisions Pertaining to the Federal Trade Commission. Supplements. a. ISSN 0083-0933

**U. S. Fish and Wildlife Service**
U.S. Dept. of the Interior, Washington, DC 20240.
- Fish and Wildlife Facts. irreg. ISSN 0069-9128
- Fish Disease Leaflets. irreg., no. 43, 1975. ISSN 0071-5492
- Fisheries of the United States and Alaska; a Preliminary Review. a. ISSN 0071-5573
- Fishery Statistics of the United States. a. ISSN 0071-5603 (Orders to: Supt. Doc., Washington, DC 20402)
- North American Fauna. irreg. ISSN 0078-1304 (Orders to: Supt. Doc., Washington, DC 20402)
- Progressive Fish-Culturist; for fishery biologists and fish-culturists. q. ISSN 0033-0779 (Orders to: Supt. of Documents, Washington, DC 20402)
- Propagation & Distribution of Fishes from National Fish Hatcheries. a. (prep. by its Division of Fish Hatcheries)
- Sport Fishery Abstracts; an abstracting service for fishery research and management. q. ISSN 0038-786X (Orders to: U.S. Dept. of the Interior, U.S. Post Office, Narragansett, RI 02882)
- U. S. Fish and Wildlife Service. Investigations in Fish Control. irreg. ISSN 0565-0704
- U. S. Fish and Wildlife Service. Research Reports. irreg. ISSN 0083-0941 (Orders to: Supt. Doc., Washington, DC 20402)
- U.S. Fish and Wildlife Service. Selected List of Federal Laws and Treaties Relating to Sport Fish and Wildlife. irreg. ISSN 0093-4631 (Orders to: Supt. of Documents, Washington, DC 20402)
- U. S. Fish and Wildlife Service. Sport Fishery and Wildlife Research. a. ISSN 0362-0700 (Orders to: Supt. Doc., Washington, DC 20402)
- U. S. Fish and Wildlife Service. Wildlife Leaflets. irreg. ISSN 0084-0165
- Wildlife Review; an abstracting service for wild life management. q. ISSN 0043-5511 (prep. by its Patuxent Wildlife Research Center)

**U. S. Food and Drug Administration**
5600 Fisher's Lane, Rockville, MD 20852.
- F D A Clinical Experience Abstracts. m. ISSN 0429-9442
- F D A Consumer. m (July-Aug. and Dec.-Jan. issues combined) ISSN 0362-1332 (Orders to: U.S. Supt. of Documents, Washington, DC 20402)
- F D A Drug Bulletin. irreg. ISSN 0361-4344
- U.S. Food and Drug Administration. National Drug Code Directory. irreg. ISSN 0077-4235 (prep. by its Bureau of Drugs) (Orders to: Supt. Doc., Washington, DC 20402)

**U.S. Food and Drug Administration. Bureau of Radiological Health**
see U.S. Bureau of Radiological Health

**U. S. Food and Drug Administration. National Clearinghouse for Poison Control Centers**
see U. S. National Clearinghouse for Poison Control Centers

**U.S. Foreign Agricultural Service**
U.S. Department of Agriculture, Washington, DC 20250
- Foreign Agriculture. w. ISSN 0015-7163 (Orders to: Supt. of Documents, Washington, DC 20402)
- U. S. Foreign Agricultural Service. Food and Agricultural Export Directory. a.(approx.) ISSN 0083-0976
- U. S. Foreign Agricultural Service. Miscellaneous Reports. irreg. ISSN 0083-0992

**U.S. Foreign Broadcast Information Service**
- U.S. Foreign Broadcast Information Service. Daily Reports: Asia & Pacific. (pub. by U. S. National Technical Information Service)
- U.S. Foreign Broadcast Information Service. Daily Reports: Latin America. (pub. by U. S. National Technical Information Service)
- U.S. Foreign Broadcast Information Service. Daily Reports: Middle East & North Africa. (pub. by U. S. National Technical Information Service)
- U.S. Foreign Broadcast Information Service. Daily Reports: People's Republic of China. (pub. by U. S. National Technical Information Service)
- U.S. Foreign Broadcast Information Service. Daily Report: SubSaharan Africa. (pub. by U. S. National Technical Information Service)
- U.S. Foreign Broadcast Information Service. Daily Reports: Soviet Union. (pub. by U. S. National Technical Information Service)
- U.S. Foreign Broadcast Information Service. Daily Reports: Western Europe. (pub. by U. S. National Technical Information Service)

**U.S. Forest Products Laboratory**
see under U.S. Forest Service. Forest Products Laboratory

**U. S. Forest Service**
U. S. Department of Agriculture, Washington, DC 20250
- Fire Management Notes; devoted to the techniques of forest fire prevention and control. q. (Orders to: Supt. of Documents, Washington, DC 20402)
- Forest Insect and Disease Leaflets. irreg.
- Forest Insect Conditions in the United States. ISSN 0071-7487
- Forest Tree Nurseries in the United States. triennial. ISSN 0071-7576
- Report of Forest Planting, Seeding and Silvical Treatments in the United States. a.
- State Agencies Cooperating with the U.S. Department of Agriculture Forest Service in Administration of Various Forestry Programs. a. ISSN 0490-8287
- Tree Planters' Notes. q. ISSN 0564-1829
- U.S. Forest Service. Annual Fire Report for National Forests. a. ISSN 0083-1026
- U. S. Forest Service. Division of Cooperative Fire Control. Forest Fire Statistics. a. ISSN 0083-1034
- U.S. Forest Service. Forest Resource Reports. irreg. ISSN 0071-755X (Orders to: Supt. Doc., Washington, DC 20402)
- U.S. Forest Service. Forest Service Research Accomplishments. a. ISSN 0090-239X
- U. S. Forest Service. National Forest System Areas. a.
- U. S. Forest Service. Technical Equipment Reports. irreg. ISSN 0083-1077

**U.S. Forest Service. Forest Products Laboratory**
N. Walnut St., Madison, WI 53705.
- U.S. Forest Service. Forest Products Laboratory, Madison, Wisconsin. Report of Research at the Forest Products Laboratory. irreg. ISSN 0083-1018

**U. S. Forest Service. Intermountain Forest and Range Experiment Station**
507 25th St, Ogden, UT 84401.
- U.S.D.A. Forest Service General Technical Report INT. irreg. ISSN 0092-9654
- U.S. Forest Service. Intermountain Forest and Range Experiment Station. Recent Reports. q.

**U.S. Forest Service. North Central Forest Experiment Station**
Folwell Ave., St. Paul, MN 55108.
- U.S.D.A. Forest Service Research Note NC. 20 per yr.
- U.S.D.A. Forest Service Research Paper NC. 15 per yr. ISSN 0565-8721
- U.S.D.A. Forest Service Resource Bulletin NC. 3 per yr. ISSN 0565-873X
- U.S. Forest Service. North Central Forest Experiment Station. List of Publications. a.

**U.S. Forest Service. Northeastern Forest Experiment Station**
6816 Market St., Upper Darby, PA 19082.
- U.S.D.A. Forest Service General Technical Report NE. a. ISSN 0083-2480

**U.S. Forest Service. Pacific Northwest Forest and Range Experiment Station**
Box 3141, Portland, OR 97208.
- Forest Pest Conditions in the Pacific Northwest. a.
- States of Washington and Oregon Annual Cone Crop Report. a. ISSN 0094-2847
- U.S.D.A. Forest Service Resource Bulletin PNW. irreg.
- U.S. Forest Service. Pacific Northwest Forest and Range Experiment Station. Annual Report. a. ISSN 0083-2987

**U. S. Forest Service. Pacific Southwest Forest and Range Experiment Station**
P.O. Box 245, Berkeley, CA 94701.
- U.S. Forest Service. Pacific Southwest Forest and Range Experiment Station. Annual List of Publications. a.
- U.S. Forest Service. Pacific Southwest Forest and Range Experiment Station. Annual Report. a. ISSN 0083-2995

**U. S. Forest Service. Rocky Mountain Forest and Range Experiment Station**
240 W. Prospect, Fort Collins, CO 80521.
- U.S.D.A. Forest Service Research Note RM. irreg. ISSN 0502-4994
- U.S.D.A. Forest Service Research Paper RM. irreg. ISSN 0502-5001

**U.S. Forest Service. Southern Forest Experiment Station**
701 Loyola Ave., New Orleans, LA 70113.
- U.S. Forest Service. Southern Forest Experiment Station. Research Accomplished. irreg.

**U.S. General Accounting Office**
441 G. St., N.W., Washington, DC 20548
- Decisions of the Comptroller General of the United States. m. ISSN 0011-7323 (Orders to: Supt. of Documents, Washington, DC 20402)
- G A O Review. q. ISSN 0016-3414 (Orders to: Supt. of Documents, Washington, DC 20402)
- U. S. General Accounting Office. Financial Status of Selected Major Weapon Systems, Department of Defense; report to the Congress by the Comptroller General of the United States. s-a. ISSN 0092-4075
- U.S. General Accounting Office. Monthly List of GAO Reports. m. ISSN 0364-8265

**U. S. General Services Administration**
General Services Bldg., Eighteenth and F Sts. N.W., Washington, DC 20405
- U.S. General Services Administration. Management Improvement and Cost Reduction Goals. irreg. ISSN 0566-5655 (Orders to Supt. of Documents, U. S. Government Printing Office, Washington, DC 20402)
- U.S. General Services Administration. Management Report. a. ISSN 0091-6242

**U.S. General Services Administration. Consumer Information Center**
Pueblo, CO 81009.
- Consumer Information. q.

**U. S. General Services Administration. National Archives and Records Service**
see U. S. National Archives and Records Service

**U. S. General Services Administration. National Audiovisual Center**
see U. S. National Audiovisual Center

**U.S. General Services Administration. Office of Preparedness**
General Services Bldg., Eighteenth and F Sts. N.W., Washington, DC 20405.
- U.S. Office of Preparedness. Stockpile Report to the Congress. s-a.

**U.S. General Services Administration. Public Buildings Service**
General Services Bldg., Eighteenth and F Sts. N.W., Washington, DC 20405.
- U.S. Public Buildings Service. Value Engineering Program; Annual Report. a. ISSN 0092-0207

**U.S. Geological Survey**
12001 Sunrise Valley Drive, Reston, VA 22092 (Branch of distribution: 1200 South Eads St., Arlington, VA 22202)
- Earthquake Information Bulletin. bi-m. ISSN 0046-0931 (Orders to: Supt. of Documents, Washington, DC 20502)
- U. S. Geological Survey. Bulletin. irreg. ISSN 0083-1093
- U. S. Geological Survey. Circular. irreg. ISSN 0083-1107
- U. S. Geological Survey. Geological Survey Research. a. ISSN 0083-1115
- U.S. Geological Survey. Journal of Research. bi-m. ISSN 0091-374X (Subscriptions to: Superintendent of Documents, U.S. Government Printing Office, Wash., D.C. 20402)
- U.S. Geological Survey. Professional Papers. irreg. (Orders to: Supt. of Documents, Washington, DC 20402)
- U. S. Geological Survey. Water Resources Investigations. ISSN 0092-332X (Most report available only in microform from: NTIS, Springfield, VA 22161)
- U. S. Geological Survey. Water Supply Papers. irreg. ISSN 0083-1131
- Water Resources Review. m. ISSN 0043-1400 (Co-sponsor: Canada, Water Resources Branch)

**U. S. Geological Survey. National Cartographic Information Center**
see U. S. National Cartographic Information Center

**U. S. Geological Survey. National Earthquake Information Center**
Boulder, CO 80302
- U.S. National Earthquake Information Center. Preliminary Determination of Epicenters, Monthly Listing. m. ISSN 0364-7072 (Subscriptions to: Supt. of Documents, Washington, DC 20402)

**U.S. Geological Survey. Seismic Engineering Branch**
345 Middlefield Rd., Mail Stop 78, Menlo Park, CA 94025
(Requests to: U.S. Geological Survey Branch of Distribution, 1200 South Eads Street, Arlington, VA 22202)
- U. S. Geological Survey. Seismic Engineering Branch. Seismic Engineering Program Report. 3 per yr.

**U.S. Geological Survey. Water Resources Division (New York)**
1505 Kellum Place, Mineola, NY 11501.
- Long Island Water Resources Bulletin. irreg (approx. 2 per year)

**U.S. Government Printing Office**
Washington, DC 20402.
- Monthly Catalog of United States Government Publications. m. ISSN 0362-6830
- Public Documents Highlights. bi-m. ISSN 0145-062X
- Selected United States Government Publications. m. ISSN 0566-8549

- U.S. Congress. Congressional Directory. a.
- U.S. Congress. Congressional Record; proceedings and debates of the Congress. daily when Congress is in session. ISSN 0363-7239

**U.S. Health Resources Administration**
5600 Fishers Lane, Rockville, MD 20852.
- U.S. Health Resources Administration. Health Resources News. m.
- U.S. Health Resources Administration. Public Health Reports. bi-m. ISSN 0090-2918 (Orders to: Supt. of Documents, Washington, DC 20402)

**U.S. Health Resources Administration. Bureau of Health Planning and Resources Development**
see U.S. Bureau of Health Planning and Resources Development

**U. S. Health Resources Administration. National Center for Health Statistics**
see U. S. National Center for Health Statistics

**U. S. Health Services Administration. Bureau of Community Health Service**
see U. S. Bureau of Community Health Service

**U.S. Health Services Administration. Indian Health Service**
see U.S. Indian Health Service

**U.S. Immigration and Naturalization Service**
425 I St. N.W., Washington, DC 20536.
- I and N Reporter. q. ISSN 0018-8514
- U. S. Immigration and Naturalization Service. Administrative Decisions under Immigration and Nationality Laws. irreg. ISSN 0083-1220 (Orders to: Supt. of Documents, Washington, DC 20402)
- U. S. Immigration and Naturalization Service. Administrative Decisions under Immigration and Nationality Laws. Interim Decisions of the Department of Justice. irreg. ISSN 0083-1239 (Orders to: Supt. of Documents, Washington, DC 20402)
- U. S. Immigration and Naturalization Service. Annual Report. a. ISSN 0083-1247 (Orders to: Supt. of Documents, Washington, DC 20402)

**U.S. Indian Arts and Crafts Board**
Department of the Interior Building, Washington, DC 20240
- Native American Arts. irreg. ISSN 0077-6017 (Orders to: Supt. Doc., Washington, DC 20402)

**U.S. Indian Health Service**
Office of Program Statistics, 5600 Fishers La., Rockville, MD 20852.
- Indian Health Trends and Services. irreg.

**U.S. Industrial College of the Armed Forces**
Fort Lesley J. McNair, Washington, DC 20319.
- Perspectives in Defense Management. 3-4 per yr. ISSN 0048-3524
- U. S. Industrial College of the Armed Forces. Monograph Series. irreg. ISSN 0083-1328
- U. S. Industrial College of the Armed Forces. Research Project Abstracts. a. ISSN 0083-1336

**U. S. Information Agency**
1776 Pennsylvania Ave. N.W., Washington, DC 20547.
- Dialogue (Washington)/Facetas. q. ISSN 0012-2262
- Problems of Communism. bi-m. ISSN 0032-941X (Subscriptions to: Supt. of Documents, Washington, DC 20402)

**U.S. Interagency Arctic Research Coordinating Committee**
- Arctic Bulletin. (pub. by U.S. National Science Foundation)

**U. S. Interim Compliance Panel**
Room 800, 1730 K St, NW, Washington, DC 20006.
- U. S. Interim Compliance Panel. Annual Report to the Congress of the United States. a. ISSN 0093-2396

**U.S. Intermountain Forest and Range Experiment Station**
see under U.S. Forest Service

**U. S. Internal Revenue Service**
12th & Constitution Ave., Washington, DC 20025
- Internal Revenue Bulletin. w. ISSN 0020-5761 (Orders to: Supt. of Documents, Washington, DC 20402)

- Internal Revenue Guide to Your Federal Income Tax. (pub. by Arco Publishing Co. Inc.)
- U. S. Internal Revenue Service. Annual Report. a. ISSN 0083-1476 (Orders to: Supt. Doc., Washington, DC 20402)
- U. S. Internal Revenue Service. Chief Counsel: Annual Report. a. ISSN 0092-4784
- U. S. Internal Revenue Service. Tax Guide for Small Business. a. ISSN 0083-1484 (Orders to: Supt. Doc., Washington, DC 20402)
- U. S. Internal Revenue Service. Tobacco Tax Guide. irreg. ISSN 0083-1492 (Orders to: Supt. Doc., Washington, DC 20402)

**U.S. International Trade Commission**
701 E St. N.W., Washington, DC 20436
- Synthetic Organic Chemicals, United States Production and Sales. a. ISSN 0082-1144 (Orders to: Supt. Doc., Washington, DC 20402)
- Tariff Schedules of the United States Annotated. irreg. ISSN 0082-173X (Order from: U. S. Govnt. Printing Office, Washington, DC 20402)
- U.S. International Trade Commission. Annual Report. a.
- U.S. International Trade Commission. Imports of Benzenoid Chemicals and Products. a. ISSN 0083-3436
- U.S. International Trade Commission. Operation of the Trade Agreements Program. a. ISSN 0083-3444
- U.S. International Trade Commission. Quarterly Report to the Congress and the East-West Foreign Trade Board on Trade Between the United States and the Nonmarket Economy Countries. q. ISSN 0098-910X (Orders to: Supt. Doc., Washington, DC 20402)

**U.S. Interstate Commerce Commission**
Twelfth St. and Constitution Ave. N.W., Washington, DC 20423.
- I.C.C. Supplemental Reports. (pub. by Commerce Law Services, Inc.)
- Transport Economics. q. ISSN 0041-1434 (prep. by its Bureau of Economics)
- Transportation Statistics in the United States. irreg. ISSN 0082-5956 (Orders to: Supt. Doc., Washington, DC 20402)
- U. S. Interstate Commerce Commission. Advance Bulletin of Interstate Commerce Acts Annotated. bi-m. ISSN 0083-1506
- U. S. Interstate Commerce Commission. Annual Report. a. ISSN 0083-1514 (Orders to: Supt. Doc., Washington, DC 20402)
- U. S. Interstate Commerce Commission. Interstate Commerce Acts Annotated. irreg. ISSN 0083-1522 (Orders to: Supt. Doc., Washington, DC 20402)
- U. S. Interstate Commerce Commission. Interstate Commerce Commission Reports. Decisions of the Interstate Commerce Commission of the United States. irreg. ISSN 0083-1530 (Orders to: Supt. Doc., Washington, DC 20402)

**U.S. Labor Management Services Administration**
Washington, DC
- U.S. Department of Labor. Register of Reporting Labor Organization. irreg. (Orders to: Supt. of Documents, U.S. Government Printing Office, Washington, DC 20402)
- U. S. Labor-Management Services Administration. Decisions and Reports on Rulings of the Assistant Secretary of Labor for Labor-Management Relations. w. ISSN 0091-2646 (Order bound volumes from: Supt. of Documents, Washington, DC 20402)

**U.S. Law Enforcement Assistance Administration**
633 Indiana Ave., N.W., Washington, DC 20531
- U. S. Law Enforcement Assistance Administration. Annual Report. a. ISSN 0565-6567 (Orders to: Supt. of Documents, Washington, DC 20402, For sale by the Supt. of Docs., G.P.O., Washington, D.C. 20402)
- U.S. Law Enforcement Assistance Administration. Document Retrieval Index. q.

**U.S. Law Enforcement Assistance Administration. National Criminal Justice Information and Statistics Service**
see U.S. National Criminal Justice Information and Statistics Service

**U.S. Library of Congress**
10 First St. S.E., Washington, DC 20540
- Children's Books; a List of Books for Preschool through Junior High School Age. a. ISSN 0069-3464 (Orders to: Supt. of Documents, Washington, DC 20402)
- Dewey Decimal Classification Additions, Notes and Decisions. irreg. ISSN 0083-1573 (prep. by its Decimal Classification Division) (Free to Subscribers of LC Card Service, Purchasers of 18th Edition of Dewey Decimal Classification, and teachers of library science Upon request To. Forest Press, 85 Watervliet Ave., Albany, NY 12206)
- Films and Other Materials for Projection. q. (including annual and quinquennial cumulations) ISSN 0091-3294 (prep. by its Catalog Publication Division) (Subscriptions to: LC Cataloging Distribution Service, Building No. 159, Navy Yard Annex, Washington, DC 20541)
- L C Science Tracer Bullet. ISSN 0090-5232 (prep. by its Science and Technology Division)
- Library Resources Notes. irreg. ISSN 0095-4098 (prep. by its Reference Department)
- Monographic Series. q(with annual cumulation) ISSN 0093-0571 (prep. by its Catalog Publication Division) (Subscriptions to: LC Cataloging Distribution Service, Building No. 159, Navy Yard Annex, Washington, DC 20541)
- Music, Books on Music and Sound Recordings. s-a (with annual and quinquennial cumulations) ISSN 0092-2838 (prep. by its Catalog Publication Division) (Subscriptions to: LC Cataloging Distribution Service, Building No. 159, Navy Yard Annex, Washington, DC 20541)
- National Register of Microform Masters. a. ISSN 0547-8448 (prep. by its Catalog Publication Division) (Orders to: LC Cataloging Distribution Service, Building, No. 159, Navy Yard Annex, Washington DC 20541)
- National Union Catalog. 9 monthly issues, 3 quarterly cumulations, annual cumulations for 4 years and quinquennial in the fifth. ISSN 0028-0348 (prep. by its Catalog Publication Division) (Requests to: LC Cataloging Distribution Service, Building No. 159, Navy Yard Annex, Washington, DC 20541)
- National Union Catalog of Manuscript Collections. a. ISSN 0090-0044 (prep. by its Descriptive Cataloging Division) (Subscriptions to: LC Cataloging Distribution Service, Building No. 159, Navy Yard Annex, Washington, DC 20541)
- New Serial Titles; a union list of serials commencing publication after December 31, 1949. 8 monthly, 4 quarterly and cumulation issues. ISSN 0028-6680 (prep. by its Serial Record Division) (Prepared Under the sponsorship of the Joint Committee on the Union List of Serials) (Orders to: LC Cataloging Distribution Service, Building No. 159, Navy Yard Annex, Washington, DC 20541)
- New Serial Titles-Classed Subject Arrangement. m. ISSN 0028-6699 (prep. by its Serial Record Division)
- Newspapers Currently Received and Permanently Retained in the Library of Congress. irreg., 4th ed. 1974. ISSN 0083-1646 (prep. by its Serial Record Division) (Orders to: Supt. of Documents, Washington, D.C. 20402)
- Newspapers in Microform. a. (prep. by its Catalog Publication Division) (Subscriptions to: LC Cataloging Distribution Service, Building No. 159, Navy Yard Annex, Washington, DC 20541)
- U. S. Library of Congress. Annual Report of the Librarian of Congress. a. ISSN 0083-1565 (Free to libraries Upon request to LC Central Services Division; foreign libraries apply to LC Exchange and Gift Division, also available from Supt. of Documents, Washington DC 20402)
- U.S. Library of Congress. Chinese Cooperative Catalog. m. ISSN 0095-1072 (prep. by its Catalog Publication Division) (Subscriptions to: LC Cataloging Distribution Service, Building No. 159, Navy Yard Annex, Washington, DC 20541)
- U. S. Library of Congress. Congressional Research Service Digest of Public Bills and Resolutions. fortn.(during Congressional session) ISSN 0012-2785 (Subscriptions to: Supt. of Documents, Washington, DC 20402)
- U. S. Library of Congress. Hispanic Foundation. Bibliographic Series. irreg. ISSN 0083-1581 (Orders to: LC Information Office)

- U. S. Library of Congress. Information Bulletin. w. ISSN 0041-7904 (Orders to: LC Central Services Division)
- U. S. Library of Congress. L. C. Classification - Additions and Changes. q. ISSN 0041-7912 (prep. by its Subject Cataloging Division)
- U.S. Library of Congress. Library of Congress Name Headings with References. 3 quarterly issues and annual cumulation. ISSN 0093-0563 (prep. by its Catalog Publication Division) (Subscriptions to: LC Cataloging Distribution Service, Building No. 159, Washington, DC 20541)
- U. S. Library of Congress. Library of Congress Publications in Print. a. ISSN 0083-1603 (Order from LC Central Services Division)
- U. S. Library of Congress. Manuscript Division. Register of Papers. irreg. ISSN 0083-1611
- U. S. Library of Congress. Monthly Checklist of State Publications. m.(plus Separate index) ISSN 0027-0288 (prep. by its Exchange and Gift Division) (Free to U.S. agencies which send state publications to LC Exchange and Gift Division, Subscr. to: Supt. of Documents, Gov't. Printing Office, Washington, DC 20402)
- U.S. Library of Congress. Newspaper and Gazette Report. approx. 3 per yr. ISSN 0361-0152 (Requests to: LC Information Office; foreign libraries apply to LC Exchange and Gift Division)
- U.S. Library of Congress. Processing Department. Cataloging Service Bulletin. q. ISSN 0041-7890 (Requests to: LC Cataloging Distribution Service, Building No. 159, Navy Yard Annex, Washington, DC 20541)
- U. S. Library of Congress. Processing Dept. Newsletter. ISSN 0092-8429
- U. S. Library of Congress. Quarterly Journal. q. ISSN 0041-7939 (Free to libraries Upon request to LC Central Services Division; foreign libraries apply to LC Exchange and Gift Division, also Available from: Supt. of Documents, Washington, DC 20402)
- U.S. Library of Congress. Subject Catalog. q. (with annual and quinquennial cumulations) ISSN 0096-8803 (prep. by its Catalog Publication Division) (Subscriptions to: LC Cataloging Distribution Service, Building No. 159, Navy Yard Annex, Washington, DC 20541)
- U. S. Library of Congress Subject Headings Supplement. q. (Subscriptions to: LC Cataloging Service Division, Building No. 159, Navy Yard Annex, Washington, DC 20541)

**U.S. Library of Congress. Copyright Office**
The Library of Congress, Washington, DC 20559
(Orders to: Supt. of Documents, Washington, DC 20402)
- Decisions of the United States Courts Involving Copyrights. biennial. ISSN 0070-3176
- U. S. Copyright Office. Annual Report of the Register of Copyrights. a. ISSN 0082-9676
- U.S. Copyright Office. Catalog of Copyright Entries. Third Series. Part 1: Books and Pamphlets; including serials and contributions to periodicals. s-a. ISSN 0041-7815
- U.S. Copyright Office. Catalog of Copyright Entries. Third Series. Part 2: Periodicals. a. ISSN 0041-784X
- U.S. Copyright Office. Catalog of Copyright Entries. Third Series. Parts 3-4: Drama and Works Prepared for Oral Delivery. s-a. ISSN 0041-7858
- U.S. Copyright Office. Catalog of Copyright Entries. Third Series. Part 5: Music. s-a. ISSN 0041-7866
- U.S. Copyright Office. Catalog of Copyright Entries. Third Series. Part 6: Maps and Atlases. s-a. ISSN 0041-7874
- U.S. Copyright Office. Catalog of Copyright Entries. Third Series. Parts 7-11A: Works of Art; reproductions of works of art, scientific and technical drawings, photographic works, prints, and pictorial illustrations. s-a. ISSN 0041-7882
- U.S. Copyright Office. Catalog of Copyright Entries. Third Series. Part 11b Commercial Prints and Labels. a. ISSN 0041-7823
- U.S. Copyright Office. Catalog of Copyright Entries. Third Series. Parts 12-13: Motion Pictures and Filmstrips. s-a. ISSN 0041-7831
- U.S. Copyright Office. Catalog of Copyright Entries. Third Series. Part 14: Sound Recordings. s-a. ISSN 0094-3592

**U. S. Library of Congress. Division for the Blind and Physically Handicapped**
1291 Taylor Street, Washington, DC 20542.
- Braille Book Review (Inkprint Edition) bi-m. ISSN 0006-873X

- Braille Book Review and Talking Book Topics (Braille Edition) bi-m. ISSN 0093-285X
- Cassette Books. irreg., 3rd ed. 1974-1976. ISSN 0363-9029
- Directory of Library Resources for the Blind and Physically Handicapped. irreg.
- For Younger Readers, Braille and Talking Books. biennial. ISSN 0071-7266
- Musical Mainstream. bi-m. ISSN 0364-7501
- Press Braille, Adult. biennial. ISSN 0079-502X
- Talking Book Topics (Inkprint Edition) bi-m. ISSN 0039-9183
- Talking Books, Adult. a. ISSN 0082-1519

**U. S. Library of Congress. Federal Library Committee**
Washington, DC 20540.
- F L C Newsletter. 10 per yr. ISSN 0014-5939

**U.S. Library of Congress. Overseas Operations Division**
Washington, DC 20540.
- L C Foreign Acquisitions Newsletter. s-a.
- U.S. Library of Congress. Accessions List. Bangladesh. s-a. ISSN 0090-8304 (Correspondence to: Field Director, Library of Congress Office, American Embassy, New Delhi, India, U.S. orders to: Field Director, New Delhi-LOC, U.S. Dept. of State, Washington, DC 20520)
- U. S. Library of Congress. Accessions List: Brazil. bi-m. ISSN 0095-795X (Correspondence to: Field Director, LC Office, American Consulate General, Av. Presidente Wilson 147, 20000 Rio de Janeiro, Brazil, U.S. Correspondence to: LC Office, American Consulate General, APO, New York, Ny 09676)
- U. S. Library of Congress. Accessions List: Eastern Africa. bi-m. ISSN 0090-371X (U. S. Correspondence to: Field Director, Karachi-LOC, Dept. of State, Washington, DC 20520;, Correspondence from other areas to: Field Director-LOC, American Consulate General, Abdullah Haroon Rd., Karachi, Pakistan)
- U.S. Library of Congress. Accessions List: India. m. ISSN 0041-7734 (Correspondence to: Field Director, Library of Congress Office, American Embassy, New Delhi, India)
- U.S. Library of Congress. Accessions List: Middle East. m. ISSN 0041-7769 (Correspondence to: U.S. Library of Congress Office, Cairo, Egypt;)
- U.S. Library of Congress. Accessions List: Nepal. s-a. ISSN 0090-3744 (Correspondence to: Field Director, Library of Congress Office, American Embassy, New Delhi, India;, U.S.. orders to: Field Director, New Delhi-LOC, U.S. Dept. of State, Washington, DC 20520)
- U. S. Library of Congress. Accessions List: Pakistan. m. ISSN 0041-7777 (Correspondence to: Field Director, Library of Congress Office, American Consulate General, Karachi, Pakistan)
- U.S. Library of Congress. Accessions List: Southeast Asia. m. ISSN 0096-2341 (Orders originating outside of Indonesia to: Field Director, LC Office, American Consulate General, Karachi, Pakistan, Orders originating in Indonesia to: Library of Congress Office, American Embassy, Merdeka Selatan 3-5, Jakarta)
- U.S. Library of Congress. Accessions List: Sri Lanka. s-a. ISSN 0090-3736 (Correspondence to: Field Director, Library of Congress Office, American Embassy, New Delhi, India)

**U.S. Marine Corps**
Commandant of the Marine Corps, U.S. Department of the Navy, Washington, DC 20380.
- Reserve Marine. m. ISSN 0034-5547

**U.S. Marine Corps. History and Museums Division**
Headquarters, Washington, DC 20380.
- Fortitudine; newsletter of the marine corps historical program. 4 per yr.

**U.S. Maritime Administration**
GAO Bldg., 5Th & G Sts., N.W., Washington, DC 20235
(Orders to: Supt. of Documents, Washington, DC 20402)
- Domestic Waterborne Trade of the United States. a.
- M R I S Abstracts. (pub. by National Academy of Sciences)
- M R I S Current Awareness Service. (pub. by National Academy of Sciences)
- Statistical Analysis of World's Merchant Fleets Showing Age, Size, Speed and Draft by Frequency Groupings. a. since 1975; previously biennial. ISSN 0081-4768 (prep. by its Office of Subsidy Administration)

- U. S. Maritime Administration. Annual Report. a. ISSN 0083-1670
- U. S. Maritime Administration. Research and Development Progress. a. ISSN 0083-1689
- U. S. Maritime Administration. Technical Report Index, Maritime Administration Research and Development. a. ISSN 0083-1697
- Vessel Inventory Report; United States Flag dry cargo and tanker fleets 1,000 gross tons & over. s-a. (prep. by its Office of Subsidy Administration) (Available from the Administration's Division of Trade Studies and Statistics)

**U. S. Military Academy**
West Point, NY 10996.
- Pointer. m. ISSN 0032-2350 (prep. by its Corps of Cadets)
- U S M A Library Bulletin. irreg.

**U.S. Mining Enforcement and Safety Administration**
401 Wilson Blvd., Arlington, VA 22203
- MESA; the magazine of mining and safety. bi-m. ISSN 0362-370X (Dist. by: Supt. of Documents, G.P.O., Washington, D.C. 20402)
- U.S. Mining Enforcement and Safety Administration. Informational Report. irreg. ISSN 0097-9376

**U.S. National Advisory Committee on the Handicapped**
U.S. Office of Education, 400 Maryland Ave. S.W., Washington, DC 20202
(Orders to: Supt. of Documents, Washington, DC 20402)
- U.S. National Advisory Committee on the Handicapped. Annual Report. a.

**U.S. National Advisory Council on Extension and Continuing Education**
Room 710, 1325 G Street, N.W., Washington, DC 20005.
- U.S. National Advisory Council on Extension and Continuing Education. Annual Report. a. ISSN 0360-8166

**U. S. National Advisory Council on Indian Education**
Washington, DC 20202
(Orders to: U. S. Superintendent of Documents, Washington, DC 20402)
- U.S. National Advisory Council on Indian Education. Through Education: Self Determination. a.

**U.S. National Aeronautics and Space Administration**
400 Maryland Ave. S.W., Washington, DC 20546
- Energy: a Continuing Bibliography with Indexes. q. (Orders to: National Technical Information Service, Springfield, VA 22161)
- N A S A Patent Abstracts Bibliography; a Continuing Bibliography. Section 1. Abstracts. s-a. (Not available on subscription; single issues available from: NTIS, Springfield, VA 22161)
- N A S A Patent Abstracts Bibliography; a Continuing Bibliography. Section 2. Indexes. s-a. (Not Available on Subscription; Single issues available from: NTIS, Springfield, VA 22161)
- N A S A Report to Educators. q. ISSN 0092-346X (prep. by its Education Programs Division)
- N A S A-University Conference on Manual Control (Papers) a. ISSN 0077-2623 (Order from: National Technical Information Service, Springfield, VA 22161)
- National Aeronautics and Space Administration. N A S A Facts. irreg. ISSN 0077-3093 (Orders to: Supt. Doc., Washington, DC 20402)
- National Aeronautics and Space Administration. Selected Listing of N A S A Scientific and Technical Reports. a. ISSN 0077-3123 (Orders to: Supt. Doc., Washington, DC 20402)
- National Aeronautics and Space Administration. Technical Notes. irreg. ISSN 0077-3131 (Order from: National Technical Information Service, Springfield, VA 22161)
- National Aeronautics and Space Administration. Technical Reports. irreg. ISSN 0077-314X (Orders to: Supt. Doc., Washington, DC 20402)
- National Aeronautics and Space Administration. Technical Translations. irreg. ISSN 0077-3158 (Order from: National Technical Information Service, 5285 Port Royal Rd., Springfield, VA 22151)
- STAR. (Scientific and Technical Aerospace Reports) s-m. ISSN 0036-8741 (prep. by its Scientific and Technical Information Office) (Orders to: Supt. of Documents, Washington, DC 20402)

- U. S. National Aeronautics and Space
Administration. Measurement Technology. irreg.
(Orders to: National Technical Information
Service, Springfield, VA 22161)
- U.S. National Aeronautics and Space
Administration. Research and Technology
Operating Plan (RTOP) Summary. a. (Orders to:
National Technical Information Service,
Springfield, VA 22161)
- U. S. National Aeronautics and Space
Administration. Welding Technology. irreg.
(Orders to: National Technical Information
Service, Springfield, VA 22161)
- Weekly Government Abstracts. N A S A Earth
Resources Survey Program. (pub. by U.S.
National Technical Information Service)

**U. S. National Aeronautics and Space Administration.**
**Goddard Space Flight Center**
*see* **Goddard Space Flight Center**

**U.S. National Aeronautics and Space Administration.**
**Jet Propulsion Laboratory**
California Institute of Technology, CA 91109
- U.S. National Aeronautics and Space
Administration. Jet Propulsion Laboratory.
Bibliography. a. ISSN 0068-5666 (Order from:
National Technical Information Service,
Springfield, VA 22161)
- U.S. National Aeronautics and Space
Administration. Jet Propulsion Laboratory.
Report. a. ISSN 0068-5674 (Order from: National
Technical Information Service, Springfield, VA
22161)
- U.S. National Aeronautics and Space
Administration. Jet Propulsion Laboratory.
Technical Memorandum. irreg. ISSN 0068-5682
(Order from: National Technical Information
Service, Springfield, VA 22161)
- U.S. National Aeronautics and Space
Administration. Jet Propulsion Laboratory.
Technical Report. irreg. ISSN 0068-5690 (Order
from: National Technical Information Service,
Springfield, VA 22161)

**U. S. National Aeronautics and Space Administration.**
**Technology Utilization Office**
Code KT, Washington, DC 20546
- Computer Program Abstracts. q. ISSN 0045-785X
(Orders to: Supt. of Documents, Washington, DC
20402)
- N A S A Tech Briefs. q. ISSN 0145-319X

**U.S. National Agricultural Library**
10301 Baltimore Avenue, Beltsville, MD 20705.
- Agricultural Libraries Information Notes. m. ISSN
0095-2699
- Bibliography of Agriculture. (pub. by Oryx Press)
- National Agricultural Library. Food and Nutrition
Information and Educational Materials Center.
Catalog. Supplement. irreg. ISSN 0095-1307

**U. S. National Archives and Records Service**
Eighth St. and Pennsylvania Ave. N.W.,
Washington, DC 20408.
- Prologue (Washington); the journal of the
National Archives. q. ISSN 0033-1031
- U.S. National Archives and Records Service.
Catalog of National Archives Microfilm
Publications. irreg. ISSN 0094-629X
- U. S. National Archives and Records Service.
National Archives Inventories. irreg., 1970, no. 2.
ISSN 0083-1735
- U. S. National Archives and Records Service.
National Archives Reference Information Papers.
irreg. ISSN 0083-1743
- U. S. National Archives and Records Service.
Preliminary Inventories. irreg. ISSN 0083-1751
- U. S. National Archives and Records Service.
Special Lists. irreg. ISSN 0083-176X

**U. S. National Archives and Records Service.**
**National Historical Publications and Records**
**Commission**
*see* **U. S. National Historical Publications and**
**Records Commission**

**U.S. National Archives and Records Service. Office of**
**the Federal Register**
*see* **U.S. Office of the Federal Register**

**U.S. National Audiovisual Center**
General Services Administration, Washington, DC
20409.
- Directory of U. S. Government Audiovisual
Personnel. a. ISSN 0098-1109

**U.S. National Bureau of Standards**
U.S. Dept. of Commerce, Washington, DC 20234
- Dimensions N B S. m. ISSN 0093-0458 (Orders
to: Supt. of Documents, Washington, DC 20402)
- Directory of United States Standardization
Activities. irreg. ISSN 0070-6558 (Orders to: Supt
of Documents, Washington, DC 20402)
- Hydraulic Research in the United States and
Canada. a. ISSN 0094-1832 (Orders to: Supt.
Doc., Washington, DC 20402)
- N B S Publications Newsletter. bi-m. ISSN 0469-
337X (prep. by its Office of Technical
Publications)
- National Conference of Standards Laboratories.
Proceedings. irreg. ISSN 0081-4318 (Orders to:
Supt. Doc., Washington, DC 20402)
- National Conference of Standards Laboratories
Newsletter. q. (Orders to NBS, Boulder, CO
80302, atten. K. Armstrong)
- National Conference on Weights and Measures.
Report. a. ISSN 0077-3964 (Available from NBS,
Office of Weights and Measures, and Supt. of
Documents, Washington, DC 20402)
- Overlap; measurements agreement through process
evaluation. m.
- U.S. National Bureau of Standards. Annual
Report. a. (Orders to: Supt. Doc., Washington,
DC 20402)
- U.S. National Bureau of Standards. Applied
Mathematics Series. irreg. ISSN 0083-1786
(Orders to: Supt. of Documents, Washington, DC
20402)
- U. S. National Bureau of Standards. Building
Science Series. irreg. ISSN 0083-1794 (Orders to:
Supt. of Documents, Washington, DC 20402)
- U. S. National Bureau of Standards. Commercial
Standards. irreg. ISSN 0083-1808 (Orders to:
Supt. of Documents, Washington, DC 20402)
- U.S. National Bureau of Standards. Consumer
Information Series. irreg. ISSN 0069-9276
(Orders to: Supt. of Documents, Washington, DC
20402)
- U. S. National Bureau of Standards. Journal of
Research. Section A: Physics and Chemistry. bi-
m. ISSN 0022-4332 (Orders to: Supt. of
Documents, Washington, DC 20402)
- U. S. National Bureau of Standards. Journal of
Research. Section B: Mathematical Sciences. q.
ISSN 0022-4340 (Orders to: Supt. of Documents,
Washington, DC 20402)
- U. S. National Bureau of Standards. Methods of
Measurement for Semiconductor Materials,
Process Control, and Devices; Quarterly Report.
q. ISSN 0090-8541
- U.S. National Bureau of Standards. National
Standard Reference Data Series. irreg. ISSN
0083-1840 (Orders to: Supt. of Documents,
Washington, DC 20402)
- U. S. National Bureau of Standards. Product
Standards. irreg. ISSN 0083-1859 (Orders to:
Supt. Doc., Washington, DC 20402)
- U. S. National Bureau of Standards. Standards
Development Services Section. Voluntary Product
Standards: PS. irreg. (Orders to: Supt. of
Documents, Washington, DC 20402)
- U. S. National Bureau of Standards. Technical
Notes. irreg. ISSN 0083-1913 (Orders to: Supt. of
Documents, Washington, DC 20402)

**U. S. National Bureau of Standards. Cryogenic Data**
**Center**
Boulder, CO 80302.
- Biweekly Cryogenics Current Awareness Service.
bi-w. ISSN 0364-0868
- Liquified Natural Gas; a literature survey issued
quarterly. q. ISSN 0024-4228 (American Gas
Association) (Subscr. to: NTIS, Springfield, VA
22161)
- Superconducting Devices and Materials; a
literature survey. q. ISSN 0039-5714 (Co-sponsor:
U.S. Office of Naval Research) (Orders to: NTIS,
Springfield, VA 22161)

**U. S. National Bureau of Standards. Electromagnetic**
**Metrology Information Center**
Boulder, CO 80302.
- Electromagnetic Metrology Current Awareness
Service. m. ISSN 0046-1709

**U.S. National Bureau of Standards. High Pressure**
**Data Center**
5093 Lee Library, Brigham Young University,
Provo, UT 84602.
- Bibliography on High Pressure Research. 6 per yr.
ISSN 0045-1932

**U.S. National Cancer Institute**
Bethesda, MD 20014
- Cancer Therapy Abstracts. (pub. by Franklin
Institute Press)
- Cancer Treatment Reports. m. ISSN 0361-5960
(Orders to: Supt. of Documents, Washington, DC
20402)
- Carcinogenesis Abstracts. m. ISSN 0008-6258
(prep. by its Division of Cancer Cause and
Prevention) (Abstracting and indexing by:
Franklin Institute Research Laboratories, Science
Information Services, Biomedical Section)
- National Cancer Institute. Journal. m. ISSN 0027-
8874 (Orders to: Supt. of Documents,
Washington, Dc 20402)
- U.S. National Cancer Institute. Division of Cancer
Treatment. Reports. irreg (3-4 per yr.)
- U.S. National Cancer Institute. Etiology Area.
Report of the Carcinogenesis Program. a. ISSN
0090-2403 (prep. by its Office of the Associate
Director for Carcinogenesis)
- U. S. National Cancer Institute. Monograph. irreg.
ISSN 0083-1921 (Orders to: Supt. of Documents,
Washington, DC 20402)
- U. S. National Cancer Program. Report of the
National Cancer Advisory Board Submitted to the
President of the United States for Transmittal to
the Congress of the United States. a. ISSN 0092-
9468

**U.S. National Capital Planning Commission**
1325 G St., N.W., Washington, DC 20576.
- U.S. National Capital Planning Commission.
Quarterly Review of Commission Proceedings. q.
ISSN 0098-308X

**U.S. National Cartographic Information Center**
c/o U.S. Geological Survey, 507 National Center,
Reston, VA 22092.
- U.S. National Cartographic Information Center.
Newsletter. q. ISSN 0364-7064

**U.S. National Center for Education Communications**
400 Maryland Ave. S.W., Washington, DC 20202.
- Current Topics in Education. q.

**U. S. National Center for Education Statistics**
400 Maryland Ave. S. W., Washington, DC 20202
(Orders to: Supt. of Documents, Washington, DC
20402)
- Condition of Education; a statistical report on the
condition of American education. irreg. ISSN
0098-4752
- Conference on Higher Education General
Information Survey. Final Report. a. ISSN 0091-
5815
- Education Directory. a.
- Education Directory. (School Year): Colleges and
Universities. a.
- Education Directory, Public Schools. a. (Orders
to: Supt. Doc., Washington, DC 20402)
- Occupational Education Enrollments and
Programs in Noncollegiate Secondary Schools. a.
- U.S. National Center for Education Statistics.
Digest of Educational Statistics. a. ISSN 0083-
2634
- U.S. National Center for Education Statistics.
Earned Degrees Conferred. a. ISSN 0565-744X
- U.S. National Center for Education Statistics.
Higher Education, Fall Enrollment in Higher
Education. a.
- U.S. National Center for Education Statistics.
Higher Education: Students Enrolled for
Advanced Degrees, Fall (Year) a. (Orders to:
Supt. Doc., Washington, DC 20402)
- U.S. National Center for Education Statistics.
Library Statistics of Colleges and Universities.
biennial.
- U.S. National Center for Education Statistics.
Numbers of Employees in Institutions of Higher
Education. irreg. ISSN 0361-610X
- U.S. National Center for Education Statistics.
Preliminary Statistics of State School Systems.
biennial. ISSN 0083-2766
- U.S. National Center for Education Statistics.
Projects, Products and Services. a.
- U.S. National Center for Education Statistics.
Statistics of Local Public School Systems:
Finances. a.
- U.S. National Center for Education Statistics.
Statistics of Local Public School Systems: Pupils
and Staff. a.
- U.S. National Center for Education Statistics.
Statistics of Public Elementary and Secondary
Day Schools. a.

- U.S. National Center for Education Statistics. Statistics of State School Systems. biennial. ISSN 0083-2820 (Orders to: Supt. Doc., Washington, DC 20402)
- U.S. National Center for Educational Statistics. Expenditures and Revenues for Public Elementary and Secondary Education. ISSN 0090-7618
- U.S. National Center for Educational Statistics. Financial Statistics of Public Television Licensees.
- U.S. National Center for Educational Statistics. Statistics of Public Schools: Advance Report. a.

**U.S. National Center for Health Statistics**
5600 Fishers Lane, Rockville, MD 20857.
- Cooperative Health Statistics System News. q.
- Public Health Conference on Records and Statistics. Proceedings. a. ISSN 0079-7588
- U.S. National Center for Health Statistics. Current Listing and Topical Index to the Vital and Health Statistics Series. biennial.
- U. S. National Center for Health Statistics. Health Resources Statistics. a. ISSN 0083-1956
- U.S. National Center for Health Statistics. Monthly Vital Statistics Report. m.
- U.S. National Center for Health Statistics. Vital and Health Statistics. Series 1. Programs and Collection Procedures. irreg. ISSN 0083-2014
- U.S. National Center for Health Statistics. Vital and Health Statistics. Series 3. Analytical Studies. irreg. ISSN 0083-2065
- U.S. National Center for Health Statistics. Vital and Health Statistics. Series 4. Documents and Committee Report. irreg. ISSN 0083-2073
- U. S. National Center for Health Statistics. Vital and Health Statistics. Series 10. Data from the Health Interview Survey. irreg. ISSN 0083-1972
- U. S. National Center for Health Statistics. Vital and Health Statistics. Series 11. Data from the Health Examination Survey. irreg. ISSN 0083-1980
- U.S. National Center for Health Statistics. Vital and Health Statistics. Series 13. Data on Health Resources Utilization. irreg.
- U.S. National Center for Health Statistics. Vital and Health Statistics. Series 14. Data on Health Resources: Manpower and Facilities. irreg. ISSN 0083-1999
- U. S. National Center for Health Statistics. Vital and Health Statistics. Series 20. Data on Mortality. irreg. ISSN 0083-2022
- U. S. National Center for Health Statistics. Vital and Health Statistics. Series 21. Data on Natality, Marriage, and Divorce. irreg. ISSN 0083-2030
- U.S. National Center for Health Statistics. Vital and Health Statistics. Series 23: Data from the National Survey of Family Growth. irreg.
- Vital Statistics of the United States. a. ISSN 0083-6710
- Where to Write for Birth and Death Records: U.S. and Outlying Areas. irreg. (Orders to: Superintendent of Documents, U.S. Government Printing Office, Washington, DC 20402)
- Where to Write for Birth and Death Records: U.S. Citizens Who Were Born or Died Outside the United States. irreg. (Orders to: Superintendent of Documents, U.S. Government Printing Office, Washington, DC 20402)
- Where to Write for Divorce Records: U.S. and Outlying Areas. irreg. ISSN 0565-8454 (Orders to: Superintendent of Documents, U.S. Government Printing Office Washington, D.C. 20402)
- Where to Write for Marriage Records: U.S. and Outlying Areas. irreg. ISSN 0565-8462 (Orders to: Superintendent of Documents, U.S. Government Printing Office, Washington, DC 20402)

**U. S. National Center for Social Statistics**
U.S. Dept. of Health, Education, and Welfare, 330 Independence Ave., S. W., Washington, DC 20201.
- Medicaid Recipient Characteristics and Units of Selected Medical Services. a. ISSN 0098-3616
- Medicaid Statistics. a. ISSN 0091-8164
- Medicaid Statistics: Medical Assistance (Medicaid) Financed Under Title XIX of the Social Security Act. m. ISSN 0091-3103
- Social Services U.S.A. q.
- U.S. National Center for Social Statistics. Applications and Case Dispositions for Public Assistance. q. ISSN 0360-6848
- U.S. National Center for Social Statistics. Fair Hearings in Public Assistance. s-a.
- U.S. National Center for Social Statistics. Public Assistance Statistics. m. ISSN 0145-952X

**U. S. National Clearinghouse for Alcohol Information**
Box 2345, Rockville, MD 20852.
- N I A A A Information and Feature Service. 10-14 per yr. ISSN 0364-0531 (U.S. National Institute on Alcohol Abuse and Alcoholism)

**U. S. National Clearinghouse for Drug Abuse Information**
P. O. Box 1635, Rockville, MD 20850.
- D A C A S. (Drug Abuse Current Awareness System) bi-w.
- Tune In; drug abuse news for broadcasters/about broadcasting. 4 per yr.
- U. S. National Clearinghouse for Drug Abuse Information. Report Series. irreg.
- U.S. National Clearinghouse for Drug Abuse Information. Selected Reference Series. irreg.

**U.S. National Clearinghouse for Poison Control Centers**
c/o George Armstrong, 5401 Westbard Ave., Bethesda, MD 20016.
- U. S. National Clearinghouse for Poison Control Centers. Bulletin. m. ISSN 0049-5484

**U. S. National Clearinghouse for Smoking and Health**
Technical Information Center, 1600 Clifton Rd., Atlanta, GA 30333.
- Bibliography on Smoking and Health. a. ISSN 0067-7361
- Directory of On-Going Research in Smoking and Health. biennial. ISSN 0070-6000
- Health Consequences of Smoking. a. ISSN 0098-311X
- Smoking and Health Bulletin. irreg.(approx. 10 issues per year) ISSN 0081-0363

**U.S. National Climatic Center**
Federal Building, Asheville, NC 28801.
- Atmospheric Turbidity and Precipitation Chemistry Data for the World. irreg. ISSN 0094-4696 (Co-Sponsor: World Meteorological Organization)
- Climatological Data for Antarctic Stations. a.
- Climatological Data for the World. m. (Co-Sponsor: World Meteorological Organization)
- Storm Data. m. ISSN 0039-1972
- U.S. National Climatic Center. Climatolgical Data. m.(Annual cumulation) ISSN 0009-8949
- U.S. National Climatic Center. Climatological Data; National Summary. m. with annual summary. ISSN 0095-4365
- U.S. National Oceanic and Atmospheric Administration. National Climatic Center. Marine Climatological Summaries. irreg. ISSN 0091-8512 (Co-Sponsor: World Meteorological Organization)

**U.S. National Commission for Manpower Policy**
1522 K St. N.W., Suite 300, Washington, DC 20005.
- U.S. National Commission for Manpower Policy. Annual Report to the President and the Congress. a. ISSN 0361-7440

**U.S. National Credit Union Administration**
2025 M. St. N.W., Washington, DC 20456.
- Administrator's Letter; technical news for today's credit union community. bi-m.
- U.S. National Credit Union Administration. Annual Report. a.
- U.S. National Credit Union Administration. N C U A Quarterly. q. ISSN 0090-7863 (Subscriptions to: Supt. of Documents, Washington, DC 20402)
- U. S. National Credit Union Administration. Research Report. irreg., June 1976, no. 10. ISSN 0564-9498
- U.S. National Credit Union Administration. Working Papers. irreg.

**U.S. National Criminal Justice Information and Statistics Service**
U.S. Law Enforcement Assistance Administration, 633 Indiana Ave. N.W., Washington, DC 20531.
- Children in Custody. a.
- Criminal Victimization in the United States. ISSN 0095-5833

**U. S. National Earthquake Information Center**
see under U. S. Geological Survey

**U.S. National Electronic Injury Surveillance System**
- N E I S S News. (pub. by U.S. National Injury Information Clearinghouse)
- Tabulation of Data from the National Electronic Injury Surveillance System. (pub. by U.S. National Injury Information Clearinghouse)

**U.S. National Endowment for the Arts**
2401 E St. N.W., Washington, DC 20506.
- Cultural Post. bi-m.
- Federal Design Matters. q. ISSN 0363-8812 (Subscr. to: Supt. of Documents, Gov't Printing Office, Washington, DC 20402)
- National Endowment for the Arts. Guide to Programs. a. ISSN 0547-6658
- U. S. National Endowment for the Arts. Annual Report. a. ISSN 0083-2103 (Orders to: Supt. Doc., Washington, DC 20402)

**U.S. National Endowment for the Humanities**
806 Fifteenth St. N.W., Washington, DC 20506.
- Humanities. m. ISSN 0018-7526
- National Endowment for the Humanities. Annual Report. a. ISSN 0083-2111
- National Endowment for the Humanities. Occassional Papers. irreg. ISSN 0083-212X
- National Endowment for the Humanities. Program Announcement. a. ISSN 0361-1221
- U.S. National Endowment for the Humanities. Education Programs. a.

**U. S. National Energy Information Center**
see entry for U. S. Federal Energy Administration

**U. S. National Eye Institute**
National Institutes of Health, Bethesda, MD 20014
- Annual Conference of Model Reporting Area for Blindness Statistics. Proceedings. a. ISSN 0066-3883 (Orders to: Supt. Doc., Washington, DC 20402)

**U.S. National Fire Prevention and Control Administration**
U.S. Dept. of Commerce, Washington, DC 20230.
- Firework. q.

**U. S. National Foundation on the Arts and Humanities**
see listings for U.S. National Endowment for the Arts, U.S. National Endowment for the Humanities

**U.S. National Geophysical and Solar-Terrestrial Data Center**
3100 Marine Ave., Boulder, CO 80302
- Earthquake History of the United States. quinquennial. (Orders to National Technical Information Service, Springfield, VA 22161)
- Solar-Geophysical Data. Part 1-Prompt Reports. m(plus "annual descriptive text issue") (Orders to: National Climatic Center, Asheville, NC 28801)
- Solar-Geophysical Data: Part 2-Comprehensive Reports. m. (Orders to: National Climatic Center, Asheville, NC 28801)
- United States Earthquakes. a. ISSN 0091-1429 (Available from Supt. of Documents, U.S. Government Printing Office, Washington, D.C. 20402)

**U.S. National Heart and Lung Institute**
National Institutes of Health, Bethesda, MD 20014
- Hemostasis and Thrombosis; a Bibliography. m. ISSN 0360-7607 (Compiled by: National Library of Medicine) (Subscriptions to: Supt. of Documents, Washington, DC 20402)
- U. S. National Heart and Lung Advisory Council. Annual Report. a. ISSN 0095-0262
- U. S. National Heart and Lung Institute. Annual Report of the Director; national heart, blood vessel, lung, and blood program. a. ISSN 0095-0254

**U.S. National Highway Traffic Safety Administration**
N48-41, 400 7th St. Sw, Washington, DC 20590.
- Highway Safety Literature; a monthly abstract journal. m. ISSN 0300-6905 (prep. by its Technical Reference Branch)
- Highway Safety Literature Annual Cumulations. a. ISSN 0073-2214
- Highway Safety Literature Indexes. a. ISSN 0073-2222
- Motor Vehicle Safety; a report on activities under the National Traffic and Motor Vehicle Safety Act of 1966. a. (Prepared with: U.S. Federal Highway Administration)
- Traffic Safety; a report on activities under the Highway Safety Act of 1966. a. (Prepared with: U.S. Federal Highway Administration)
- U. S. National Highway Traffic Safety Administration. Motor Vehicle Safety Defect Recall Campaigns. q. ISSN 0565-7717 (Subscriptions to: Supt. of Documents, Washington, DC 20402)
- U. S. National Highway Traffic Safety Administration. Technical Report; a bibliography. a.

**U.S. National Historical Publications and Records Commission**
National Archives Bldg., Washington, DC 20408.
- Annotation. q.

**U.S. National Information Center for the Handicapped**
Box 1492, Washington, DC 20013.
- Report from Closer Look. q.

**U.S. National Injury Information Clearinghouse**
Washington, DC 20402.
- N E I S S News. m. ISSN 0364-6475 (U.S. National Electronic Injury Surveillance System)
- Tabulation of Data from the National Electronic Injury Surveillance System. a. ISSN 0360-9952

**U.S. National Institute for Occupational Safety and Health**
5600 Fishers Lane, Rockville, MD 20852.
- U. S. National Institute for Occupational Safety and Health. Toxic Substances List. a.

**U.S. National Institute of Arthritis Metabolism and Digestive Disease**
Bethesda, MD 20014
(Orders to: Supt. of Documents, Washington, DC 20402)
- Diabetes Literature Index. m. ISSN 0012-1819 (Prepared from: MEDLARS (Medical Literature Analysis and Retrieval System) Tapes of the National Library of Medicine)
- Diabetes-Related Literature Index by Authors and Key Words in the Title. a. ISSN 0070-4652
- Endocrinology Index. bi-m. ISSN 0013-7235 (Prepared from: MEDLARS (Medical Literature Analysis and Retrieval System) data of the National Library of Medicine)
- Gastroenterology Abstracts and Citations. m. ISSN 0016-5093
- Index of Dermatology. m. ISSN 0090-1245 (Prepared from MEDLARS (Medical Literature Analysis and Retrieval System) Tapes of the National Library of Medicine)
- Kidney Disease and Nephrology Index. bi-m. ISSN 0363-2369 (Prepared from: MEDLARS (Medical Literature Analysis and Retrieval System) Tapes of the National Library of Medicine)

**U.S. National Institute of Child Health and Human Development. Center for Population Research**
see U.S. Center for Population Research

**U.S. National Institute of Dental Research**
National Instiutes of Health, Bldg. W, Rm. 551, Bethesda, MD 20014.
- Dental Research in the United States and Other Countries. a.

**U.S. National Institute of Education**
1200 19th St. N.W., Washington, DC 20002.
- Annual Survey of Hearing Impaired Children and Youth. 5 per yr. (Co-sponsor Gallaudet College, Office of Demographic Studies)
- National Institute of Education. Career Education Program: Program Plan. irreg. ISSN 0361-1507
- P R E P. Reports. (Putting Research into Educational Practice) irreg; no. 29, 1974.
- Pacesetters in Innovation. a. ISSN 0078-7396
- Research in the Teaching of Science. biennial. ISSN 0080-1690

**U. S. National Institute of Education. Educational Resources Information Center**
see E R I C

**U.S. National Institute of Environmental Health Sciences**
Box 12233, Research Triangle Park, NC 27709
- E H P. (Environmental Health Perspectives) q. ISSN 0091-6765 (Subscriptions to: Supt. of Documents, Washington, DC 20240)

**U. S. National Institute of Mental Health**
5600 Fishers Lane, Rockville, MD 20852
(Orders to: Supt. of Documents, Washington, DC 20402)
- Crime and Delinquency Topics, Monograph Series. irreg. (prep. by its Center for Studies of Crime and Delinquency)
- International Directory of Investigators in Psychopharmacology. biennial
- Mental Health Directory. a.
- Psychopharmacology Abstracts. q. ISSN 0033-3166
- Psychopharmacology Bulletin. q (plus special biennial no) ISSN 0048-5764

- Schizophrenia Bulletin. q. ISSN 0586-7614

**U. S. National Institute of Mental Health. Division of Biometry and Epidemiology**
5600 Fishers Lane, Rockville, MD 20857.
- U.S. National Institute of Mental Health. Mental Health Statistical Notes. irreg. (prep. by its Survey and Reports Branch)
- U.S. National Institute of Mental Health. Report Series on Mental Health Statistics. Series A: Mental Health Facilities Report. (prep. by its Survey and Reports Branch)
- U.S. National Institute of Mental Health. Report Series on Mental Health Statistics. Series B: Analytical and Special Study Reports. (prep. by its Survey and Reports Branch)
- U.S. National Institute of Mental Health. Report Series on Mental Health Statistics. Series C: Methodology Reports. ISSN 0566-7038 (prep. by its Survey and Reports Branch)
- U.S. National Institute of Mental Health. Report Series on Mental Health Statistics. Series D: Conference or Committee Reports, and Analytical Reviews of Literature. (prep. by its Survey and Reports Branch)

**U.S. National Institute of Neurological and Communicative Disorders and Stroke**
Bethesda, MD 20014
- Cerebrovascular Bibliography; including neurological, vascular, hematological aspects. q. ISSN 0090-1407 (Prepared by: Joint Council Subcommittee on Cerebrovascular Disease, National Institute of Neurological and Communicative Disorders and Stroke, National Heart and Lung Institute; in cooperation with the National Library of Medicine) (Orders to: Supt. of Documents, Washington, DC 20402)
- Epilepsy Abstracts. m. ISSN 0013-9599 (Orders to: Excerpta Medica Foundation, Nassau Bldg., 228 Alexander St., Princeton, NJ 08540)
- Parkinson's Disease and Related Disorders. Cumulative Bibliography. a. ISSN 0079-0060
- Parkinson's Disease and Related Disorders: Citations from the Literature. m. ISSN 0079-0079 (Prepared from MEDLARS (Medical Literature Analysis and Retrieval System) Tapes of the National Library of Medicine) (Available from: NTIS, Springfield, VA 22161)
- U.S. National Institute of Neurological Diseases and Stroke. Research Program Reports. irreg. ISSN 0094-9582 (Orders to: U.S. Supt. of Documents, Washington, DC 20402)

**U.S. National Institute on Alcohol Abuse and Alcoholism**
Box 2345, Rockville, MD 20852
- Alcohol Health and Research World. q. ISSN 0090-838X (Orders to: Supt. of Documents, Washington, DC 20402)
- N I A A A Information and Feature Service. (pub. by U. S. National Clearinghouse for Alcohol Information)

**U.S. National Institute on Drug Abuse**
5600 Fishers Lane, Rockville, MD 20852.
- Marihuana and Health; Annual Report to the U.S. Congress from the Secretary of Health, Education and Welfare. a.
- National Institute on Drug Abuse Statistical Series; Quarterly Report. q. ISSN 0145-1065

**U.S. National Institutes of Health**
Room 2B-03, Bldg. 31, Bethesda, MD 20014
- Guide for Laboratory Animal Facilities and Care. irreg., 1968, 3rd. ISSN 0072-8098 (Orders to: Supt. Doc., Washington, DC 20402)
- N I H Factbook. (pub. by Marquis Academic Media)
- N I H Publications List. a. ISSN 0027-6650 (prep. by its Division of Public Information. Editorial Operations Branch)
- U. S. National Institutes of Health. Division of Research Grants. Research Grants Index. a. ISSN 0083-2189 (Orders to: Supt. Doc., Washington, DC 20402)
- U.S. National Institutes of Health. Medical and Health Related Sciences Thesaurus. a.
- U. S. National Institutes of Health. Scientific Directory and Annual Bibliography. a. ISSN 0083-2197

**U. S. National Institutes of Health. Division of Computer Research and Technology**
Computer Center, Bldg. 12, Rm. 2244, Bethesda, MD 20014.
- Interface (Bethesda) 9 per yr. ISSN 0020-5419

- U. S. National Institutes of Health. Division of Computer Research and Technology. Technical Reports. irreg. ISSN 0083-2170

**U.S. National Institutes of Health. National Cancer Institute**
see U.S. National Cancer Institute

**U.S. National Institutes of Health. National Eye Institute**
see U.S. National Eye Institute

**U.S. National Institutes of Health. National Heart and Lung Institute**
see U.S. National Heart and Lung Institute

**U.S. National Institutes of Health. National Institute of Arthritis Metabolism and Digestive Diseases**
see U.S. National Institute of Arthritis Metabolism and Digestive Diseases

**U. S. National Institutes of Health. National Institute of Child Health and Human Development. Center for Population Research**
see U. S. Center for Population Research

**U. S. National Institutes of Health. National Institute of Dental Research**
see U. S. National Institute of Dental Research

**U.S. National Institutes of Health. National Institute of Environmental Health Sciences**
see U.S. National Institute of Environmental Health Sciences

**U.S. National Institutes of Health. National Institute of Neurological and Communicative Disorders and Stroke**
see U.S. National Institute of Neurological and Communicative Disorders and Stroke

**U.S. National Institutes of Health. National Library of Medicine**
see U.S. National Library of Medicine

**U. S. National Labor Relations Board**
1717 Pennsylvania Ave. N.W., Washington, DC 20570
(Orders to: Supt. of Documents, Washington, DC 20402)
- Classified Index of National Labor Relations Board Decisions and Related Court Decisions. 5 per yr. ISSN 0092-4962
- U. S. National Labor Relations Board. Annual Report. a. ISSN 0083-2200
- U. S. National Labor Relations Board. Court Decisions Relating to the National Labor Relations Act. irreg. ISSN 0083-2219

**U.S. National Library of Medicine**
8600 Rockville Pike, Bethesda, MD 28014
(Orders to: Supt. of Documents, Washington, DC 20402)
- Abridged Index Medicus. m. ISSN 0001-3331
- Bibliography of the History of Medicine. a., quinquennial cumulation. ISSN 0067-7280
- Cumulated Abridged Index Medicus. a.
- Cumulated Index Medicus. a. ISSN 0590-3408
- Current Bibliography of Epidemiology. m. ISSN 0011-3247 (Cosponsor: American Public Health Association)
- Index Medicus. m. ISSN 0019-3879
- List of Journals Indexed in Index Medicus. a. ISSN 0093-3821
- Medical Subject Headings. a.
- Monthly Bibliography of Medical Reviews. m. ISSN 0027-0202
- National Library of Medicine. Literature Search Series. irreg. ISSN 0083-2251 (For list of available titles, write: NLM Literature Search Program, Reference Section)
- National Library of Medicine. Programs and Services. a. ISSN 0093-0393 (Available from NLM Office of Inquiries)
- National Library of Medicine Current Catalog. q. with annual cumulation. ISSN 0027-9641
- National Library of Medicine Current Catalog Proofsheets. w. (Subscriptions to: Medical Library Association, 919 N. Michigan Ave., Suite 3208, Chicago, IL 60611)
- National Library of Medicine News. m. ISSN 0027-965X (Available from NLM Office of Inquiries)
- National Medical Audiovisual Center. Catalog. irreg. ISSN 0083-2294

- Notes for Medical Catalogers. irreg. ISSN 0078-2025 (Also Distributed by: Medical Library Association, 919 N. Michigan Ave., Suite 3208, Chicago, IL 60611)
- Selected References on Environmental Quality as It Relates to Health. m. ISSN 0049-0105
- Toxicity Bibliography. q. ISSN 0041-0071

**U. S. National Marine Fisheries Service**
National Oceanic and Atmospheric Administration, Washington, DC 20235.
- Canned Fishery Products. a. (prep. by its Statistics and Market News Division)
- Fisheries of the United States. a. (Orders to: Supt. of Documents, Government Printing Office, Washington, DC 20402)
- Food Fish Market Review and Outlook. 3 per yr. ISSN 0091-8105 (prep. by its Economic & Marketing Research Division) (Subscr. to: Supt. of Documents, Government Printing Office Washington, D.C. 20402)
- Industrial Fishery Products. a. (prep. by its Statistics and Market News Division)
- Industrial Fishery Products; Market Review and Outlook. 3 per yr. ISSN 0093-8327 (prep. by its Technical Information Division)
- New Jersey Landings. a. ISSN 0028-579X
- Shellfish Market Review and Outlook. 3 per yr. ISSN 0098-8014 (prep. by its Market Research and Services Division) (Orders to: Supt. of Documents, Washington, DC 20402)
- Translated Tables of Contents of Current Foreign Fisheries, Oceanographic, and Atmospheric Publications. m. (prep. by its Language Services Division)
- U.S. National Marine Fisheries Service. Grant-in-Aid for Fisheries: Program Activities. a.
- U. S. National Marine Fisheries Service. Imports and Exports of Fishery Products. a. (prep. by its Statistics and Market News Division)
- U.S. National Marine Fisheries Service. Report. ISSN 0093-9412 (Orders to: Supt. of Documents, Washington, DC 20402)

**U.S. National Marine Fisheries Service. Scientific Publications Division**
Scientific Publications Staff, 1107 N. E. 45th St., Rm. 450, Seattle, WA 98105
- Fishery Bulletin. q. ISSN 0090-0656 (Orders to: Supt. of Documents, Washington, DC 20402)
- Fishery Facts. irreg. (Orders to: Supt. of Documents, Washington, DC 20402)
- Marine Fisheries Review. m. ISSN 0090-1830 (Orders to: Supt. of Documents, Washington, DC 20402)
- U.S. National Marine Fisheries Service. Special Scientific Report: Fisheries. irreg. ISSN 0082-8904

**U. S. National Mediation Board**
1425 K St. N.W., Washington, DC 20572.
- U. S. National Mediation Board. Annual Report. a. ISSN 0083-2286
- U. S. National Mediation Board. (Reports of Emergency Boards) 3-4 per yr. ISSN 0083-2278

**U.S. National Medical Audiovisual Center**
- National Medical Audiovisual Center. Catalog. (pub. by U.S. National Library of Medicine)

**U.S. National Meteorological Center**
U.S. National Weather Service, Washington, DC 20233
(Orders to: Supt. of Documents, Washington, DC 20402)
- U.S. National Meteorological Center. Long Range Prediction Group. Average Monthly Weather Outlook. bi-m. ISSN 0090-0613

**U.S. National Ocean Survey**
Rockville, MD 20850.
- National Ocean Survey. Collected Reprints. irreg. ISSN 0361-2805

**U.S. National Ocean Survey. Lake Survey Center**
231 W. Lafayette St., 630 Federal Bldg., Detroit, MI 48226.
- Great Lakes Water Levels. a. ISSN 0090-2187
- U. S. National Ocean Survey, Lake Survey Center. Monthly Bulletin of Lake Levels.

**U.S. National Oceanic and Atmospheric Administration**
6010 Executive Blvd., Rockville, MD 20852
- International Field Year for the Great Lakes. Bulletin. irreg. (Subscr. to: National Technical Information Service, 5825 Port Royal Rd., Springfield, VA 22151)

- N O A A. q. ISSN 0014-0821 (Orders to: Supt. of Documents, Washington, DC 20402)
- Sea Grant Seventies. (pub. by Texas A & M University. Sea Grant Program Office)
- U. S. National Oceanic and Atmospheric Administration. Manned Undersea Science and Technology Program; Report. a. ISSN 0092-8917 (Orders to: Supt. of Documents, Washington, DC 20402)
- U.S. National Oceanic and Atmospheric Administration. Report to the Congress on Ocean Dumping and Other Man-Induced Changes to Ocean Ecosystems. a. ISSN 0094-5196

**U.S. National Oceanic and Atmospheric Administration. Environmental Data Service**
see U.S. Environmental Data Service

**U.S. National Oceanic and Atmospheric Administration. Federal Coordinator for Meteorological Services and Supporting Research**
Rockville, MD 20852.
- U. S. Office of Federal Coordinator for Meteorological Services and Supporting Research. National Hurricane Operations Plan. irreg. ISSN 0092-2056

**U.S. National Oceanic and Atmospheric Administration. National Marine Fisheries Service**
see U.S. National Marine Fisheries Service

**U.S. National Oceanic and Atmospheric Administration. National Oeanographic Instrumentation Center**
see U.S. National Oceanographic Instrumentation Center

**U.S. National Oceanic and Atmospheric Administration. National Ocean Survey**
see U.S. National Ocean Survey

**U.S. National Oceanic and Atmospheric Administration. National Weather Service**
see U.S. National Weather Service

**U.S. National Oceanographic Data Center**
Page Bldg. 1, Rm. 400, D762, Washington, DC 20235.
- Mariners Weather Log; a climatic review of North Atlantic and North Pacific Ocean and Great Lake areas. bi-m. ISSN 0025-3367
- U. S. National Oceanographic Data Center. Key to Oceanographic Records Documentation. irreg. ISSN 0091-9500 (Orders to: Supt. Doc., Washington, DC 20402)

**U.S. National Oceanographic Instrumentation Center**
Rockville, MD 20852.
- U. S. National Oceanographic Instrumentation Center. Instrument Fact Sheet. irreg.
- U. S. National Oceanographic Instrumentation Center. Technical Bulletin. irreg.
- U. S. National Oceanographic Instrumentation Center. Technical Memorandum. irreg.

**U. S. National Park Service**
Interior Bldg., Washington, DC 20240
- Publications in Archaelogy. irreg. (Orders to: Supt. Doc., Washington, DC 20402)
- U. S. National Park Service. Historical Handbook Series. irreg. ISSN 0083-2316 (Orders to: Supt. Doc., Washington, DC 20402)
- U.S. National Park Service. Public Use of the National Park System; Calendar Year Report. a. ISSN 0361-9737
- U. S. National Park Service. Public Use of the National Park System; Fiscal Year Report. a. ISSN 0093-3074
- U.S. National Park Service. Research Reports by Service Personnel. 5-10 reports per year. ( order from NTIS, Springfield, VA 22161)
- U. S. National Park Service. Source Books Series. irreg. ISSN 0083-2324

**U. S. National Science Foundation**
10 First St., Washington, DC 20550.
- Antarctic Bibliography. every 18 mos. ISSN 0066-4626 (prep. by its Office of Polar Programs)
- Antarctic Journal of the United States. q. ISSN 0003-5335 (Orders to: Supt. of Documents, Washington, DC 20402)
- Arctic Bulletin. q. ISSN 0092-427X (U.S. Interagency Arctic Research Coordinating Committee)
- Current Antarctic Literature. m. (prep. by its Division of Polar Programs)

- Graduate Fellowship Awards Announced by National Science Foundation. ISSN 0072-5250 (Orders to: Supt. Doc., Washington, DC 20402)
- Mosaic. bi-m. ISSN 0027-1284 (Orders to: Supt. of Documents)
- N S F Bulletin. 10 per yr.
- National Patterns of R. & D. Resources; Funds & Manpower in the United States. irreg. ISSN 0093-8572 (Orders to: Supt. of Documents, Washington, DC 20402)
- National Science Foundation Guide to Programs. a.
- U. S. Federal Council for Science and Technology. Interdepartmental Committee for Atmospheric Sciences. I C A S Reports. a. ISSN 0083-0631
- U. S. National Science Foundation. Annual Report. a. ISSN 0083-2332 (Orders to: Supt. Doc., Washington, DC 20402)
- U.S. National Science Foundation. Course and Curriculum Improvement. irreg. (Orders to: Supt. Doc., Washington, DC 20402)
- U.S. National Science Foundation. Course and Curriculum Improvement Materials; mathematics, science, social sciences. irreg. (Orders to: Supt. of Documents, Washington, DC 20402)
- U.S. National Science Foundation. Division of Environmental Systems and Resources. Summary of Awards. a. ISSN 0094-7857 (Orders to; Supt. of Documents, Washington, DC 20402)
- U.S. National Science Foundation. Federal Funds for Research, Development, and Other Scientific Activities. a. (Orders to: Supt. Doc., Washington, DC 20402)
- U.S. National Science Foundation. Graduate Science Education Student Support and Postdoctorals. irreg. ISSN 0094-7881 (Orders to: Supt. of Documents, Washington, DC 20402)
- U. S. National Science Foundation. Research and Development in Industry. a. ISSN 0083-2383 (Orders to: Supt. Doc., Washington, DC 20402)
- U. S. National Science Foundation. Reviews of Data on Science Resources. irreg. ISSN 0080-2026 (Orders to: Supt. Doc., Washington, DC 20402)
- U. S. National Science Foundation. Scientific, Technical and Health Personnel in the Federal Government. a. ISSN 0083-2413 (Orders to: Supt. Doc., Washington, DC 20402)
- U. S. National Science Foundation. Surveys of Science Resources Series. irreg. ISSN 0083-2405 (Orders to: Supt. Doc., Washington, DC 20402)

**U.S. National Science Foundation Directory Service**
- Directory of National Science Foundation Programs. (pub. by Western Michigan University. Office of Research Services)

**U.S. National Student Volunteer Program**
806 Connecticut Ave. N.W., Washington, DC 20525.
- Synergist. 3 per yr. ISSN 0049-2752

**U.S. National Technical Information Service**
5285 Port Royal Road, Springfield, VA 22161.
- Aerospace References in Medicine & Biology. m. (Compiled by: Library of Congress, American Institute of Aeronautics and Astronautics)
- Directory of Computerized Data Files, Software and Related Technical Reports. a. ISSN 0094-0062
- Government Reports Announcements and Index. bi-w. ISSN 0097-9007
- Market Share Reports. irreg.
- Translations of People's Republic of China Press. irreg. with quarterly index. (Translations by U. S. Consulate General in Hong Kong)
- U.S. Foreign Broadcast Information Service. Daily Reports: Asia & Pacific. d.
- U.S. Foreign Broadcast Information Service. Daily Reports: Latin America. d.
- U.S. Foreign Broadcast Information Service. Daily Reports: Middle East & North Africa. d.
- U.S. Foreign Broadcast Information Service. Daily Reports: People's Republic of China. d.
- U.S. Foreign Broadcast Information Service. Daily Report: SubSaharan Africa. d.
- U.S. Foreign Broadcast Information Service. Daily Reports: Soviet Union. d. ISSN 0565-5560
- U.S. Foreign Broadcast Information Service. Daily Reports: Western Europe. d.
- Weekly Government Abstracts. Administration. w.
- Weekly Government Abstracts. Agriculture & Food. w.
- Weekly Government Abstracts. Behavior and Society. w.
- Weekly Government Abstracts. Biomedical Technology & Human Factors Engineering. w.

- Weekly Government Abstracts. Building Industry Technology. w.
- Weekly Government Abstracts. Business & Economics. w.
- Weekly Government Abstracts. Chemistry. w.
- Weekly Government Abstracts. Civil Engineering. w.
- Weekly Government Abstracts. Communication. w .
- Weekly Government Abstracts. Computers, Control & Information Theory. w.
- Weekly Government Abstracts. Electrotechnology. w.
- Weekly Government Abstracts. Energy. w.
- Weekly Government Abstracts. Environmental Pollution & Control. w.
- Weekly Government Abstracts. Government Inventions for Licensing. w.
- Weekly Government Abstracts. Health Planning. w.
- Weekly Government Abstracts. Industrial & Mechanical Engineering. w.
- Weekly Government Abstracts. Library & Information Sciences. w.
- Weekly Government Abstracts. Materials Sciences. w.
- Weekly Government Abstracts. Medicine & Biology. w.
- Weekly Government Abstracts. N A S A Earth Resources Survey Program. w. (U.S. National Aeronautics and Space Administration)
- Weekly Government Abstracts. Natural Resources & Earth Sciences. w.
- Weekly Government Abstracts. Ocean Technology & Engineering. w.
- Weekly Government Abstracts. Physics. w.
- Weekly Government Abstracts. Problem-Solving Information for State and Local Governments. w.
- Weekly Government Abstracts. Transportation. w.
- Weekly Government Abstracts. Urban and Regional Technology and Development. w.

U.S. National Weather Service
Washington, DC 20233.
- Gulfstream. m. ISSN 0565-8543
- U. S. National Weather Service. Data Acquisition Division. Marine Surface Observations. irreg. ISSN 0091-8725

U.S. Naval Academy. Department of English
Annapolis, MD 21402.
- The Arnoldian. 3 per yr.

U.S. Naval Air Systems Command
c/o Rosario Rausa, Potomac Annex, Bldg. 6, 23rd and E Sts. N.W., Washington, DC 20372
- Naval Aviation News. m. ISSN 0028-1417 (Orders to: Supt. of Documents, Washington, DC)

U.S. Naval Arctic Research Laboratory
3426 N. Washington Blvd., Arlington, VA 22201.
- U. S. Naval Arctic Research Laboratory. Proceedings. irreg.

U. S. Naval Facilities Engineering Command
Washington, Alexandria, DC 20360
- Navy Civil Engineer. q. ISSN 0009-7837 (Subscriptions to: Supt. of Documents, Washington, DC 20402)

U.S. Naval Institute
- U. S. Naval Institute. Naval Review. (pub. by Naval Institute Press)
- U. S. Naval Institute. Proceedings. (pub. by Naval Institute Press)

U.S. Naval Medical Research Unit No. 2, Taipei, Taiwan
Box 14, APO San Francisco, CA 96263.
- Namrugram. m. ISSN 0027-7762

U. S. Naval Observatory
Washington, DC 20350
- American Ephemeris and Nautical Almanac. a. ISSN 0065-8189 (Orders to: Supt. of Documents, Washington, DC 20402)
- Astronomical Phenomena. a. ISSN 0083-2421 (Orders to: Supt. of Documents, Washington, DC 20402)
- Ephemeris of the Sun, Polaris and Other Selected Stars with Companion Data and Tables. a. ISSN 0071-0962 (Orders to: Supt. of Documents, Washington, DC 20402)

- U. S. Naval Observatory. Astronomical Papers Prepared for Use of American Ephemeris and Nautical Almanac. irreg., vol. 22, 1976. ISSN 0083-243X
- U. S. Naval Observatory. Publications. Second Series. irreg. ISSN 0083-2448

U.S. Naval Research Laboratory. Shock and Vibration Information Center
Washington, DC 20375.
- Shock and Vibration Digest. m. ISSN 0583-1024

U.S. Naval Safety Center
Norfolk, VA 23511
(Subscriptions to: Supt. of Documents, Washington, DC 20402)
- Approach; Naval aviation safety review. m. ISSN 0570-4979
- Fathom; surface ship and submarine safety review. q. ISSN 0014-8822
- Mech; naval aviation maintenance safety review. q. ISSN 0025-6471
- Navy Lifeline. bi-m.

U. S. Naval War College
Newport, RI 02840.
- Naval War College Review. q. ISSN 0028-1484

U.S. Navy. Bureau of Medicine and Surgery
Washington, DC 20372
- U. S. Navy Medicine. m. (Subscription to: Supt. of Documents, Washington, DC 20402)

U.S. Navy. Bureau of Naval Personnel
Washington, DC 20370.
- Navy Chaplains Bulletin. q. ISSN 0028-1654 (prep. by its Office of the Navy Chief of Chaplains)

U.S. Navy. Military Sealift Command
Washington, DC 20390.
- Sealift. m. ISSN 0037-0134

U. S. North Central Forest Experiment Station
see under U. S. Forest Service

U. S. Northeastern Forest Experiment Station
see under U. S. Forest Service

U. S. Nuclear Regulatory Commission
1717 H St. N.W., Washington, DC 20555
- U. S. Nuclear Regulatory Commission. Construction Status of Nuclear Power Plants. a. (Orders to: National Technical Information Service, Springfield, VA 22161)
- U.S. Nuclear Regulatory Commission. News Releases. w.
- U.S. Nuclear Regulatory Commission. Operating Units Status Report. m. (Orders to: NTIS, 5285 Port Royal Road, Springfield, VA 22161)

U. S. Occupational Safety and Health Administration
see under U. S. Department of Labor

U.S. Occupational Safety and Health Review Commission
1825 K St. N.W., Washington, DC 20006
(For sale by the Supt. of Docs. G.P.O., Washington, D.C. 20402)
- U.S. Occupational Safety and Health Review Commission. Administrative Law Judge and Commission Decisions. m. ISSN 0094-7776

U. S. Office of Child Development
330 Independence Ave., S.W., Washington, DC 20201.
- U.S. Department of Health, Education and Welfare. Annual Report to the Congress of the United States on Services Provided to Handicapped Children in Project Head Start. a. ISSN 0093-3430

U. S. Office of Child Development. Children's Bureau
see U. S. Children's Bureau

U.S. Office of Child Development. Project Head Start
Box 1182, Washington, DC 20013.
- Head Start Newsletter. bi-m. ISSN 0017-8721

U. S. Office of Consumer Affairs
U.S. Dept. of Health, Education, and Welfare, Rm. 621, Reporters Bldg., Washington, DC 20201
- Consumer News. s-m. ISSN 0045-8260 (Subscriptions to: Consumer Information Center, Pueblo, CO 89001)

- U.S. Office of Consumer Affairs. Directory: Federal, State, County and City Government Consumer Offices. a. (Orders to: Supt. of Documents, Washington, DC 20402)

U.S. Office of Education
Washington, DC 20202
(Orders to: Supt. of Documents, Washington, DC 20402)
- American Education. m(Jan-Feb. & Aug-Sep. nos are combined) ISSN 0002-8304
- Directory of Education Associations. a.
- Progress of Education in the United States of America. a.
- U.S. Office of Education. Opportunities for Teachers Abroad. a.

U.S. Office of Human Development
330 Independence Ave., S.W., DC 20201
- Developmental Disabilities Abstracts. q. (prep. by its Developmental Disabilities Office) (Co-sponsor: American Association on Mental Deficiency) (Subscriptions to: Supt. of Documents, Washington, DC 20402)

U. S. Office of Human Development. Administration on Aging
see U. S. Administration on Aging

U. S. Office of Human Development. Office of Child Development
see U. S. Office of Child Development

U. S. Office of Human Development. Office of Native American Programs
see U. S. Office of Native American Programs

U. S. Office of Human Development. Office of Youth Development
see U. S. Office of Youth Development

U. S. Office of Human Development. President's Committee on Mental Retardation
see U.S. President's Committee on Mental Retardation

U.S. Office of Human Development. Rehabilitation Services Administration
see U.S. Rehabilitation Services Administration

U.S. Office of Management and Budget
DC 20503
(Orders to: Supt. of Documents, Washington, DC 20402)
- Public Management Sources. m. (Subscriptions to: NTIS, Springfield, VA 22161)
- Statistical Reporter; current developments in federal statistics. m. ISSN 0039-050X
- U. S. Office of Management and Budget. Catalog of Federal Domestic Assistance. s-a (Spring and Fall)
- U.S. Office of Management and Budget. Special Analysis: Budget of the United States Government. a.

U.S. Office of Minority Business Enterprise
U.S. Dept. of Commerce, Washington, DC 20230.
- Access (Washington) bi-m. ISSN 0091-5688
- U.S. Office of Minority Business Enterprise. Minority Enterprise Progress Report. a. ISSN 0091-4630

U.S. Office of Native American Programs
200 Independence Ave. S.W., Washington, DC 20201.
- Native American. 11 per yr.

U. S. Office of Naval Research
see under U. S. Department of the Navy

U.S. Office of Technology Assessment
119 D Street N.E., Washington, DC 20510
- U.S. Office of Technology Assessment Annual Report to the Congress. a. ISSN 0095-2109 (Avail. from Supt. of Documents, U.S. Government Printing Office, Washington, DC 20402)

U. S. Office of the Federal Register
National Archives and Records Service, Washington, DC 20408
(Orders to: Supt. of Documents, Washington, DC 20402)
- Public Papers of the Presidents of the United States. a. ISSN 0079-7626

- U. S. Office of the Federal Register. Code of Federal Regulations. revised at least once each calender year and issued quarterly. ISSN 0083-2960
- U. S. Office of the Federal Register. Federal Register. daily, cumulated annually in the Code of federal Regulations. ISSN 0097-6326
- U. S. Office of the Federal Register. Guide to Record Retention Requirements. a. ISSN 0083-2979
- U.S. Office of the Federal Register. Weekly Compilation of Presidential Documents. w. ISSN 0511-4187
- United States Government Organization Manual. a. ISSN 0083-1174
- United States Statutes at Large. a. ISSN 0083-3401

**U.S. Office of Water Research and Technology**
U.S. Department of the Interior, Washington, DC 20240
- Selected Water Resources Abstracts. s-m. ISSN 0037-136X (prep. by its Water Resources Scientific Information Center) (Available from: NTIS, Springfield, VA 22161)
- U. S. Office of Water Research and Technology. Annual Report; cooperative water research and training. a. (approx.)
- Water Resources Research Catalog. a. ISSN 0083-7695

**U.S. Office of Youth Development**
U.S. Dept. of Health, Education and Welfare, Washington, DC 20201.
- U.S. Office of Youth Development. Grants. irreg. ISSN 0094-1387
- Youth Reporter. m. except Nov. ISSN 0092-5438

**U. S. Pacific Northwest Forest and Range Experiment Station**
*see under* U. S. Forest Service

**U. S. Pacific Southwest Forest and Range Experiment Station**
*see under* U. S. Forest Service

**U.S. Patent and Trademark Office**
Washington, DC 20231
(Orders to: Supt. of Documents, Washington, DC 20402)
- Attorneys and Agents Registered to Practice Before the U. S. Patent Office. irreg. ISSN 0092-5934
- General Information Concerning Trademarks. irreg. ISSN 0083-3029
- Index of Patents Issued from the United States Patent and Trademark Office. a. ISSN 0362-0719
- Index of Trademarks Issued from the U.S. Patent and Trademark Office. a.
- Official Gazette of the United States Patent and Trademark Office. Patents. w. ISSN 0098-1133
- Official Gazette of the United States Patent and Trademark Office. Trademarks. w. ISSN 0360-5132
- U.S. Patent and Trademark Office. Annual Report of the Commissioner of Patents. a. ISSN 0083-3002
- U.S. Patent and Trademark Office. Classification Bulletins. irreg. ISSN 0083-3010
- U.S. Patent and Trademark Office. Trademark Rules of Practice of the Patent and Trademark Office with Forms and Statutes. irreg.

**U. S. Peace Corps**
ACTION, 806 Connecticut Ave., N.W., Washington, DC 20525
- U. S. Peace Corps. Annual Report. a. ISSN 0083-3088 (Orders to: Supt. Doc., Washington, DC 20402)

**U.S. Plum Island Animal Disease Center**
Box 848, Greenport, NY 11944.
- Bibliography of African Horse Sickness. irreg.
- Monthly Bibliography on Exotic Animal Diseases. m. (prep. by its Library)
- Vesicular Stomatitis Viris: A Bibliography. a.

**U. S. Postal Service**
475 l'Enfant Plaza West S.W., Washington, DC 20260
- Postage Stamps of the United States. biennial. ISSN 0079-4244 (Orders to: Supt. Doc., Washington, DC 20402)
- Postal Bulletin. bi-w. ISSN 0032-5333 (Orders to: Suptt. of Documents, Washington, DC 20402)
- Postal Life; the magazine for postal employees. bi-m. ISSN 0032-5368 (Orders to: Supt. of Documents, Washington, DC 20402)

- U. S. Postal Service. Support Group. Revenue and Cost Analysis. a. ISSN 0092-2765 (prep. by its Finance and Administration Dept.)

**U.S. President's Committee on Employment of the Handicapped**
Washington, DC 20210.
- U.S. Committee on Barrier-Free Design. Newsletter. bi-m.
- U.S. President's Committee on Employment of the Handicapped. How Federal Agencies Have Served the Handicapped. irreg. ISSN 0091-4584

**U.S. President's Committee on Mental Retardation**
Washington, DC 20201.
- P C M R Message. 4 per yr. ISSN 0030-7874
- U.S. President's Committee on Mental Retardation. Mental Retardation and the Law. q. ISSN 0098-8111

**U.S. President's Council on Physical Fitness and Sports**
Washington, DC 20201.
- Physical Fitness Research Digest. q. ISSN 0094-9108

**U. S. Project Head Start**
*see under* U.S. Office of Child Development

**U. S. Project Share**
P. O. B. 2309, Rockville, MD 20852.
- Journal of Human Services Abstracts. q. ISSN 0364-4782

**U.S. Public Health Service**
5600 Fishers Lane, Rockville, MD 20852.
- Conference of State Sanitary Engineers. Report of Proceedings. a. ISSN 0069-8474
- Environmental Health Series: Air Pollution. irreg. ISSN 0071-089X
- Environmental Health Series: Radiological Health. irreg. ISSN 0071-0911
- Public Health Monograph. irreg. ISSN 0079-7596

**U. S. Public Health Service. Center for Disease Control**
*see* U. S. Center for Disease Control

**U. S. Public Health Service. Division of Dentistry**
Prince Georges Plaza, Hiattsville, MD 20782.
- U.S. Public Health Service. Division of Dentistry. Annual Fluoridation Census Report. irreg. ISSN 0083-3126

**U. S. Public Health Service. Food and Drug Administration**
*see* U. S. Food and Drug Administration

**U. S. Public Health Service. Health Resources Administration**
*see* U. S. Health Resources Administration

**U. S. Public Health Service. Health Services Administration**
*see* U. S. Health Services Administration

**U. S. Public Health Service. National Institutes of Health**
*see* U. S. National Institutes of Health

**U. S. Public Health Service. President's Council on Physical Fitness and Sports**
*see* U. S. President's Council on Physical Fitness and Sports

**U.S. Railroad Retirement Board**
844 Rush St., Chicago, IL 60611
- U.S. Railroad Retirement Board. Annual Report. a. (Order from: Supt. of Documents, Washington, Dc 20402)
- U.S. Railroad Retirement Board. Monthly Benefit Statistics. m. ISSN 0364-7129
- U.S. Railroad Retirement Board. Quarterly Review. q. ISSN 0033-8788

**U.S. Rehabilitation Services Administration**
Mary E. Switzer Bldg., Rm. 1427, 330 C St. S.W., Washington, DC 20201
(Orders to: U.S. Supt. of Documents, Washington, DC 20402)
- American Rehabilitation. bi-m.

**U. S. Rocky Mountain Forest and Range Experiment Station**
*see under* U. S. Forest Service

**U. S. Rural Electrification Administration**
U.S. Dept. of Agriculture, Washington, DC 20250.
- U. S. Rural Electrification Administration. Annual Statistical Report. Rural Electrification Borrowers. a. ISSN 0083-3177
- U. S. Rural Electrification Administration. Annual Statistical Report. Rural Telephone Program. a. ISSN 0083-3185

- U. S. Rural Electrification Administration. Report of the Administrator of the Rural Electrification Administration. a. ISSN 0083-3193

**U.S. Saint Lawrence Seaway Development Corporation**
800 Independence Ave. S.W., Washington, DC 20591
- Traffic Report of the St. Lawrence Seaway. ISSN 0082-5867 (Co-Sponsor: Canadian St. Lawrence Seaway Authority)
- U. S. Saint Lawrence Seaway Development Corporation. Annual Report. a. ISSN 0083-3207

**U.S. Securities and Exchange Commission**
500 N. Capitol St., Washington, DC 20549.
- Broker-Dealer Directory. q. ISSN 0094-3002 (prep. by its Office of Registrations and Reports)
- Directory of Companies Filing Annual Reports with the U.S. Securities and Exchange Commission. a. (prep. by its Office of Economic Research) (Orders to: Supt. of Documents, Washington, DC 20402)
- Investment Adviser Directory. q. ISSN 0091-2328
- S E C Docket. w. ISSN 0091-4061 (Orders to: Supt. of Documents, Washington, DC 20402)
- S E C News Digest. d. ISSN 0364-6718 (Orders to: Supt. of Documents, Washington, DC 20402)
- U. S. Securities and Exchange Commission. Annual Report. a. ISSN 0083-3215 (Orders to: Supt. of Documents, Washington, DC 20402)
- U. S. Securities and Exchange Commission. Decisions and Reports. irreg. ISSN 0083-3223 (Orders to: Supt. of Documents, Washington, DC 20402)
- U. S. Securities and Exchange Commission. Judicial Decisions. irreg. ISSN 0083-3231 (Orders to: Supt. of Documents, Washington, DC 20402)
- U.S. Securities and Exchange Commission. Official Summary of Security Transactions and Holdings. m. ISSN 0364-2267 (Orders to: Supt. of Documents, Washington, DC 20402)
- U. S. Securities and Exchange Commission. Statistical Bulletin. m. ISSN 0039-0410 (Orders to: Supt. of Documents, Washington, DC 20402)

**U.S. Selective Service System**
1724 F St. N.W., Washington, DC 20435
- U. S. Director of Selective Service. Semiannual Report. s-a. (Orders to: Supt. of Documents, Washington, DC 20402)

**U. S. Small Business Administration**
1441 L St., N.W., Washington, DC 20416
- Management Aids for Small Manufacturers. irreg. ISSN 0076-3578 (Orders to: Supt. Doc., Washington, DC 20402)
- Small Business Management Series. irreg. ISSN 0081-0118 (Orders to: Supt. Doc., Washington, DC 20402)
- U. S. Small Business Administration. Annual Report. a. ISSN 0083-3274
- U.S. Small Business Administration. SBIC Digest. m. (prep. by its Investment Division)

**U.S. Social and Rehabilitation Service**
Dept. of Health, Education, and Welfare, 330 C St., S.W., Washington, DC 20201.
- U.S. Social and Rehabilitation Service. Annual Report of Welfare Programs. a. ISSN 0360-487X
- U.S. Social and Rehabilitation Service. Juvenile Court Statistics. a. ISSN 0082-9900
- U.S. Social and Rehabilitation Service. Office of Management. Quality Control, States' Corrective Action Activities. irreg. ISSN 0361-2643
- U. S. Social and Rehabilitation Service. Record. m. except Dec-Jan and Jul-Aug (combined issues) (Orders to: Supt. of Documents, Washington, DC 20402)

**U. S. Social and Rehabilitation Service. National Center for Social Statistics**
*see* National Center for Social Statistics

**U.S. Social Security Administration**
6401 Security Blvd., Baltimore, MD 21235
- Social Security Bulletin. m. ISSN 0037-7910
  (Orders to: Supt. of Documents, Washington, DC
  20402)
- Social Security Rulings on Federal Old-Age,
  Survivors, Disability and Health Insurance,
  Supplemental Security Income, and Miners
  Benefits. q. ISSN 0037-7929 (Orders to: Supt. of
  Documents, Washington, DC 20402)
- U.S. Social Security Administration. Monthly
  Benefit Statistics; old-age survivors, disability and
  health insurance and supplemental security
  income. m. ISSN 0364-040X
- U.S. Social Security Administration. Research and
  Statistics Notes. irreg (1-2 per mo) ISSN 0566-
  0327 (prep. by its Office of Research and
  Statistics)
- U.S. Social Security Administration. Research
  Report. irreg. ISSN 0566-0335 (prep. by its Office
  of Research and Statistics)

**U. S. Soil Conservation Service**
U.S. Dept. of Agriculture, Washington, DC 20250
- Soil Conservation. m. ISSN 0038-0725
  (Subscriptions to: Supt. of Documents,
  Washington, DC 20402)
- U. S. Soil Conservation Service. National
  Engineering Handbook. irreg. ISSN 0083-3304
  (Orders to: Supt. of Documents, Washington, DC
  20402)
- U. S. Soil Conservation Service. Soil Survey
  Investigation Reports. irreg. ISSN 0083-3320
  (Orders to: Supt. Doc., Washington, DC 20402)
- U. S. Soil Conservation Service. Technical
  Publications. irreg. ISSN 0083-3339

**U.S. Soil Conservation Service. Water Supply
Forecasting Unit**
111 Federal Bldg., 511 N.W. Broadway, Portland,
OR 97209.
- Basic Data Summary of Snow Survey and Soil
  Moisture Measurements for Western United
  States, Including Columbia River Drainage in
  Canada. a. ISSN 0566-0378

**U. S. Southern Forest Experiment Station**
*see under* U. S. Forest Service

**U.S. Tax Court**
400 Second St. N.W., Washington, DC 20217
(Orders to: Supt. of Documents, Washington, DC
20402)
- United States Tax Court Report. m. ISSN 0040-
  0017

**U.S. Tennessee Valley Authority**
Knoxville, TN 37902.
- Flood Damage Prevention; an Indexed
  Bibliography. irreg., 7th edt. 1973. ISSN 0071-
  5735 (prep. by its Technical Library)
- Tennessee Valley Authority. Engineering
  Laboratory. Research in the Fields of Civil
  Engineering, Mechanical Engineering,
  Instrumentation. biennial. ISSN 0071-0369 (prep.
  by its Engineering Laboratory)
- Tennessee Valley Authority. Technical
  Monographs. irreg. ISSN 0082-2809 (prep. by its
  Engineering Reports and Information Office)
- Tennessee Valley Authority. Technical Reports.
  irreg. ISSN 0082-2817 (prep. by its Engineering
  Reports and Information Office)
- Tennessee Valley Perspective. q. ISSN 0364-2615
  (prep. by its Office of Information)
- Tributary Area Development Newsletter. q.

**U.S. Tennessee Valley Authority. Division of
Environmental Planning**
Chattanooga, TN 37401.
- Tennessee Valley Authority. Division of
  Environmental Planning. Annual Report. a. ISSN
  0097-4757

**U.S. Tennessee Valley Authority. Division of
Forestry, Fisheries, and Wildlife Development**
Norris, TN 37828.
- Tennessee Valley Authority. Division of Forestry,
  Fisheries, and Wildlife Development. Annual
  Report. a. ISSN 0082-2787
- Tennessee Valley Authority. Division of Forestry,
  Fisheries, and Wildlife Development. Technical
  Note. irreg. ISSN 0096-1248

**U.S. Tennessee Valley Authority. National Fertilizer
Development Center**
Muscle Shoals, AL 35660.
- Estimated World Fertilizer Production Capacity as
  Related to Future Demand. ISSN 0094-145X
- Fertilizer Abstracts. m. ISSN 0015-0290
- Fertilizer Trends. biennial. ISSN 0071-4631
- National Fertilizer Development Center. Annual
  Report. a. ISSN 0077-4510

**U.S. Tennessee Valley Authority. Power Reports and
Information Office**
815 Power Building, Chattanooga, TN 37401.
- Industrial Development in the T.V.A. Area. a.
  ISSN 0495-145X
- Tennessee Valley Authority. Operations:
  Municipal and Cooperative Distributors of T.V.A.
  Power. a. ISSN 0362-3432
- Tennessee Valley Authority. Power Annual
  Report. a. ISSN 0082-2795

**U.S. Travel Service**
Washington, DC 20590.
- Summary and Analysis of International Travel in
  the U.S. m. ISSN 0095-3482 (prep. by its Office
  of Research and Analysis)

**U.S. Unemployment Insurance Service**
601 D St. N.W., Washington, DC 20213.
- Unemployment Insurance Statistics. m.
- U.S. Unemployment Insurance Service. Benefit
  Series Service; unemployment insurance report.
  m. ISSN 0005-8750

**U. S. Urban Mass Transportation Administration**
U.S. Department of Transportation, 400 Seventh St.
S. W., Washington, DC 20590.
- U. S. Urban Mass Transportation Administration
  Report to Congress Concerning the
  Demonstration of Fare-Free Mass Transportation.
  a. ISSN 0360-750X
- Urban Mass Transportation Abstracts. a. ISSN
  0090-8223 (Orders to: National Technical
  Information, 5285 Port Royal Rd., Springfield,
  VA 22161)

**U. S. Veterans Administration**
810 Vermont Avenue, N.W., Washington, DC
20420.
- Conference on Veterans Administration Studies in
  Mental Health and Behavioral Sciences.
  Highlights. a. ISSN 0069-8768 (prep. by its Dept.
  of Medicine and Surgery)
- Safety, Occupational Health and Fire Protection
  Bulletin. q.
- U. S. Veterans Administration. Annual Report. a.
  ISSN 0083-3533 (Orders to: Supt. Doc.,
  Washington, DC 20402)
- U.S. Veterans Administration. Annual Report on
  Relief from Administrative Error. a. ISSN 0360-
  9464 (Orders to: Supt. Doc., Washington, D.C.
  20402)
- U.S. Veterans Administration. Manpower Planning
  Data. ISSN 0094-4106
- U. S. Veteran's Administration. Spinal Cord Injury
  Conference. Conference Proceedings. biennial.
  ISSN 0083-3568
- U. S. Veterans Administration. V A Fact Sheets.
  a. ISSN 0083-3576

**U.S. Veterans Administration. Medical Research
Service**
810 Vermont Ave., N.W., Washington, DC 20420
- Medical Research in the V.A. a. ISSN 0073-2141
  (Orders to Supt. of Documents, U.S. Government
  Printing Office, Washington, DC 20402)
- U. S. Veterans Administration. Medical Research
  Program. a. ISSN 0083-355X (Orders to: Supt. of
  Documents, U. S. Government Printing Office,
  Washington, DC 20402)

**U. S. Veterans Administration. Research Center for
Prosthetics**
252 Seventh Ave., New York, NY 10001
(Subscr. to: Sup't of Documents, U.S. Gov't Printing
Office, Washington, D.C. 20402)
- Bulletin of Prosthetics Research. s-a. ISSN 0007-
  506X

**United States Animal Health Association**
1444 E. Main St., Richmond, VA 23219.
- United States Animal Health Association.
  Proceedings of the Annual Meeting. a. ISSN
  0082-8750

**United States Anti Communist Congress Inc.**
8001 MacArthur Boulevard N.W., Washington, DC
20034.
- Washington Intelligence Report. m.

**United States Auto Club**
4910 W. 16th St., Indianapolis, IN 46224.
- U S A C News. fortn.

**United States Basketball Writers Association**
Indianapolis Star, Sports Department, 307 N.
Pennsylvania St., Indianapolis, IN 46206.
- U S B W A Tip-Off. m.(Nov-April) ISSN 0041-
  5472

**United States Catholic Conference**
1011 First Ave., Suite 1300, New York, NY 10022.
- Film & Broadcasting Review. 2 per mo.

**United States Catholic Conference. Department of
Education**
1312 Massachusetts Ave., N.W., Washington, DC
20005
- Living Light; an interdisciplinary review of
  Christian education. q. ISSN 0024-5275 (Dist. by:
  Our Sunday Visitor, Inc., Noll Plaza, Huntington,
  IN 46750)

**United States Catholic Mission Council**
1302 18th St., Washington, DC 20036.
- Mission Intercom. m (10 per yr.)
- United States Catholic Mission Council.
  Handbook. biennial.

**United States Chess Federation**
186 Route 9W, New Windsor, NY 12550.
- Chess Life & Review. m. ISSN 0009-3351

**United States Coalition for Life**
Box 315, Export, PA 15632.
- Pro-Life Reporter. q.

**United States Committee for Refugees**
20 W. 40 St, New York, NY 10018.
- United States Committee for Refugees. World
  Refugee Report. a. ISSN 0082-965X
- World Refugee Survey Report. a.

**United States Committee for UNICEF**
331 E. 38th St., New York, NY 10016.
- News of the World's Children. 4 per yr. ISSN
  0028-9299

**United States Committee on Large Dams**
c/o Engineers Joint Council, 345 E. 47 St., New
York, NY 10017.
- International Commission on Large Dams.
  Transactions. triennial since 1961: 1976, 12th,
  Mexico. ISSN 0074-4115
- U S C O L D Newsletter. 3 per yr. ISSN 0041-
  5480

**United States Conference for the World Council of
Churches**
475 Riverside Drive, New York, NY 10027.
- Ecumenical Courier. q. ISSN 0013-0761 (Friends
  of the World Council of Churches, Inc.)

**United States Conference of Mayors**
1620 Eye St., N.W., Washington, DC 20006.
- Mayor. s-m.

**United States Cross-Country Coaches Association**
c/o Mel Brodt, Sec., 215 Stadium Drive, Bowling
Green, OH 43403.
- United States Cross-Country Coaches Association.
  Proceedings. a.

**United States Divorce Reform, Inc.**
Box 243, Kenwood, CA 95452.
- Divorce Chats. 3-8 per yr. ISSN 0012-4230

**United States Fidelity and Guaranty Co.**
Calvert & Redwood, Baltimore, MD 21203.
- U S F & G Bulletin. q. ISSN 0041-5499

**United States Field Hockey Association**
25 Front St., Marblehead, MA 01945.
- Official Field Hockey Rules for School Girls.
  irreg. ISSN 0362-3270

**United States Golf Association**
Far Hills, NJ 07931.
- Golf Journal. (pub. by Chilton Co., Inc.)
- U S G A Green Section Record. 6 per yr. ISSN
  0041-5502

**United States Hereditary Register, Inc.**
1346 Connecticut Ave., N.W., Suite 1024,
Washington, DC 20036.
● Herediatry Register of the United States of
America. a.

**United States Hockey League**
Box 1093, Green Bay, WI 54305.
● U.S.H.L. Yearbook. a. ISSN 0363-7050

**United States Independent Telephone Association**
1801 K. Street N.W. Suite 1201, Washington, DC
20006.
● United States Independent Telephone Association.
Annual Statistical Volume. a. ISSN 0083-1298

**United States Industrial Chemicals Co.**
99 Park Ave., New York, NY 10016.
● U. S. I. News. q.

**United States Industrial Publications, Inc.**
209 Dunn Ave., Stamford, CT 06905.
● Commercial Kitchen & Dining Room. q. ISSN
0010-3047
● Environmental Design; systems and products. q.
● Modern Plant Operation and Maintenance. q.
ISSN 0026-8259
● Supermarket Management. q. ISSN 0039-579X

**United States International University**
Publications Board, San Diego, CA 92131.
● U S I U International News. w.

**United States International University. Doctoral
Society**
8655 Pomerado Rd., San Diego, CA 92124.
● U S I U Doctoral Society Journal. s-a. ISSN
0041-5510

**United States Judicial Reporter**
P.O. Box 541, Harrisburg, PA 17108.
● United States Judicial Reporter. m. ISSN 0094-
2553

**United States Judo Association, Inc.**
6417 Manchester Ave., St. Louis, MO 63139.
● American Judoman; the voice of American judo. 6
per yr.

**United States Lawn Tennis Association**
● Tennis U. S. A. (pub. by Chilton Co., Inc.)
● United States Lawn Tennis Association. Yearbook.
(pub. by Harold O. Zimman, Inc.)

**United States League of Savings Associations**
111 E. Wacker Drive, Chicago, IL 60601.
● Savings and Loan Fact Book. a. ISSN 0581-8761
● Savings and Loan News. m. ISSN 0036-5114
● Savings Association Annals. irreg. ISSN 0098-
8944

**United States Olympic Committee**
57 Park Avenue, New York, NY 10016.
● Olympian. 10 per yr.

**United States Pharmacopeial Convention, Inc.**
12601 Twinbrook Parkway, Rockville, MD 20852.
● National Formulary. irreg., 14th ed., 1975. ISSN
0084-6414
● Pharmacopeia of the United States of America.
19th revision, 1975. ISSN 0079-1407
● U S A N and the U S P Dictionary of Drug
Names. a. ISSN 0090-6816
● U S P Comment Proof. fortn.
● U S P Guide to Select Drugs. a. ISSN 0091-3839

**United States Polo Association**
1301 W. 22nd St., Suite 706, Oak Brook, IL 60521.
● Polo Newsletter. m.
● United States Polo Association. Yearbook. a.
ISSN 0083-3118

**United States Polo Association (Middleburg)**
Box 267, Middleburg, VA 22117.
● Polo Magazine. m (except Jan.)

**United States Professional Tennis Association**
● Tennis. (pub. by Golf Digest, Inc. Tennis
Features, Inc.)

**United States Review Publishing Co.**
617 W. Ave., Jenkintown, PA 19046.
● United States Review. w. ISSN 0041-8056

**United States Ski Association**
1726 Champa St., Suite 300, Denver, CO 80202.
● United States Ski Association. Directory. a. ISSN
0083-3258

**United States Soccer Federation**
Empire State Bldg., 350 Fifth Ave., New York, NY
10001.
● Soccer Monthly. m.

**United States Squash Racquets Association**
200 E. 66 St, New York, NY 10021.
● United States Squash Raquets Association. Official
Year Book. a. ISSN 0083-3398

**United States Steel Corp.**
600 Grant St., Pittsburgh, PA 15230.
● U S Steel News. 6 per yr. ISSN 0041-8102
● U S Steel Quarterly. 3 per yr. ISSN 0041-8110

**United States Table Tennis Association**
12 Lake Ave, Merrick, NY 11566.
● Table Tennis Topics. bi-m.

**United States Tobacco Journal**
254 W. 31st St., New York, NY 10001.
● United States Tobacco Journal Supplier Directory.
a. ISSN 0083-3479

**United States Track Coaches Association**
1705 Evanston, Kalamazoo, MI 49008.
● Track and Field Quarterly Review. q. ISSN 0041-
0292

**United States Trademark Association**
6 E. 45th St., New York, NY 10017.
● Trademark Reporter. m. ISSN 0041-056X

**United States Trotting Association**
750 Michigan Ave., Columbus, OH 43215.
● Hoof Beats. m. ISSN 0018-4683
● Trotting and Pacing Guide; official handbook of
harness racing. a. ISSN 0083-3509
● U S T A Sires and Dams; the register. a.
● U S T A Year Book. a. ISSN 0083-3517

**United States Volleyball Association**
● United States Volleyball Association. Official
Volleyball Guide and Rule Book. (pub. by
Publishers Printing House, Inc.)

**United Steelworkers of America**
Five Gateway Center, Pittsburgh, PA 15222.
● Nonferrous Report; newsletter of USWA activity
in mining, smelting, refining & fabricating
operations of the nonferrous metals industry. m.
ISSN 0029-1102
● Steel Labor. m. ISSN 0039-0941

**United Synagogue of America**
3080 Broadway, New York, NY 10027.
● United Synagogue Review. q. ISSN 0041-8153

**United Synagogue of America. Commission on Jewish
Education**
155 5th Ave., New York, NY 10010.
● B'kitzur/Briefs. 2-3 per yr. (Solomon Schechter
Day School Association)
● Impact! q.
● In Your Hands. bi-m. ISSN 0019-3321
● Your Child. q. ISSN 0044-1007

**United Synagogue of America. Department of Youth
Activities**
155 Fifth Ave., New York, NY 10010.
● Achshav. q.

**United Synagogue of America. National Academy for
Adult Jewish Studies**
155 Fifth Ave., New York, NY 10010.
● Adult Jewish Education; a journal devoted to the
promotion of adult Jewish education in the
synagogue and in the general Jewish community.
irreg. ISSN 0001-8546

**United Talmudical Academy**
82 Lee Ave., Brooklyn, NY 11211.
● Yidisher Kval. w. ISSN 0044-0450

**United Teachers of Dade**
U T D Towers, 1809 Brickell Ave., Miami, FL
33129.
● U. T. D. Today. s-m(during school year)

**United Technical Publications, Inc.**
645 Stewart Ave., Garden City, NY 11530.
● Corporate Systems; casebook for corporate
executives. 6 per yr.
● E E M. (Electronic Engineers Master) a. ISSN
0423-9938
● Electronic Marketing/Management. m.
● Electronic Products Magazine. m. ISSN 0013-
4953

● Electronics Retailing. m.
● I C Update/Master Supplement. a with q.
supplements.
● Lens. bi-m. ISSN 0363-2636
● O.T.S.: off-the-Shelf Catalog of Electro Products.
irreg. ISSN 0095-7143
● Office Products News. 10 per yr. ISSN 0030-0241
● Office World News. m.

**United Technologies Corp.**
Hartford, CT 06101.
● United Technologies Quarterly. q.

**United Telegraph Workers**
10605 Concord St. Room 105, Kensington, MD
20795.
● Telegraph Worker Journal. m. ISSN 0040-2583

**United Theological Seminary of the Twin Cities**
3000 Fifth St. N.W., New Brighton, MN 55112.
● Theological Markings. irreg. ISSN 0362-0603

**United Thoroughbred Trainers of America, Inc.**
19363 James Couzens Hwy., Detroit, MI 48235.
● Backstretch. q. ISSN 0005-366X

**United Transportation Union**
14600 Detroit Ave., Cleveland, OH 44107.
● U T U News. w. ISSN 0098-5937

**United Transvestite Transexual Society**
● Shemale. (pub. by Neptune Productions)

**United Way for the Greater New Orleans Area**
211 Camp St., New Orleans, LA 70130.
● Torchlighter. q.

**United Way of America**
801 N. Fairfax, Alexandria, VA 22313.
● Community Focus. m.
● United Way of America. Information Center.
Digest of Selected Reports. 2 per yr.
● United Way of America. International Directory.
a.

**United Women's Societies of the Adoration of the
Most Blessed Sacrament**
Polish National Church of U.S. and Canada, 1004
Pittston Ave., Scranton, PA 18505.
● Polka; Polish women's quarterly magazine. q.
ISSN 0032-3594

**Unity Buying Service, Inc.**
Hicksville, NY 11802.
● Consumer Life. q.

**Unity in Diversity Centers**
8570 Wilshire Blvd., Beverly Hills, CA 90211.
● Unity in Diversity Centers Bulletin. m.

**Unity of the Brethren**
5905 Carleen Dr., Austin, TX 78731.
● Brethren Journal/Bratrske Listy. m. ISSN 0006-
9655

**Unity School of Christianity**
Unity Village, MO 64063.
● Daily Word. m. ISSN 0011-5525
● Unity. m.
● Unity Daily Word. (pub. by Clovernook Printing
House for Blind)
● Wee Wisdom (Braille Edition) m.
● Wee Wisdom (Inkprint Edition) 10 per yr. ISSN
0043-1710

**Universal Center**
● Cosmos. (pub. by L. D. Gasteiger)

**Universal Christian Publications**
8648 Oakleigh Rd., Baltimore, MD 21234.
● Interim. ISSN 0020-5478

**Universal Coterie of Pipe Smokers**
c/o Thomas Allan Dunn, Ed., 20-37 120th St.,
College Point, NY 11356.
● Pipe Smoker's Ephemeris. q. ISSN 0032-0161

**Universal Edition Sales, Inc.**
Box 2124, South Hackensack, NJ 07606
(In Association with Universal Edition, Vienna,
London, Zurich, Mainz, Milan)
● Haydn Yearbook. Haydn Jahrbuch. irreg., vol. 9,
1975. ISSN 0073-1390 (Verein Internationale
Joseph Haydn Institut, Eisenstadt AU)

**Universal Esperanto Association**
Box 105, Pharr, TX 78577
(and Nieuwe Binnenweg 176, Rotterdam 3002, Netherlands)
● Esperanto Documents. 10 per yr.

**Universal Fellowship of Metropolitan Community Churches. Board of Institutional Ministry**
● Cellmate. (pub. by Universal Fellowship Press)

**Universal Fellowship Press**
Box 5570, Los Angeles, CA 90055.
● Cellmate. bi-m. (Universal Fellowship of Metropolitan Community Churches. Board of Institutional Ministry)

**Universal Graphics Corp.**
46 Ford Rd., Denville, NJ 07834.
● Pickin' m. ISSN 0098-1761

**Universal News, Inc.**
Box 55225, Houston, TX 77055.
● Pipeline Digest. s-m.

**Universal Oil Products Co. Johnson Division**
Box 3118, St. Paul, MN 55165.
● Johnson Drillers Journal; in the interest of the well drilling and water supply industry. bi-m. ISSN 0021-7271

**Universal Publications of America**
P.O. Drawer 20238, Oklahoma City, OK 73120.
● Professional Karate. q.

**Universal Publishing and Distributing Corp.**
235 E. 45th St., New York, NY 10017.
● Family Handyman; the do-it-yourself magazine. 10 per yr. ISSN 0014-7230
● Worlds of If. bi-m. ISSN 0043-9312

**Universal Serials and Book Exchange**
3335 V St. N.E., Washington, DC 20018.
● U S B E News. m.

**Universal Services, Inc.**
1049 Northwest Blvd., Winston-Salem, NC 27101.
● Southern MotoRacing. bi-w. ISSN 0049-1616

**Universal Spiritual League in America Inc.**
938 18th St., Hermosa Beach, CA 90254.
● Awakener; a journal devoted to Meher Baba. q. ISSN 0005-2388

**Universalist Historical Society**
25 Beacon St., Boston, MA 02108.
● Universalist Historical Society. Journal. a. ISSN 0083-3886

**Universariun Foundation, Inc.**
3620 S.E. 84th Ave., Portland, OR 97266.
● Voice of Universarius. m.

**University Associates Publishers**
7596 Eads Ave., La Jolla, CA 92037.
● Annual Handbook for Group Facilitators. a. ISSN 0094-601X
● Group & Organization Studies; international journal for group facilitators. q. ISSN 0364-1082

**University Centers for Rational Alternatives**
110 W. 40th St., New York, NY 10018.
● University in Crisis. irreg.

**University City Science Center**
3624 Science Center, Philadelphia, PA 19104.
● University City Science Center. Philosophical Monographs. 4 per yr.

**University Communications, Inc.**
P.O. Box 1234, Rahway, NJ 07065.
● Directions'80. q.

**University Corporation for Atmospheric Research**
● Atmospheric Technology. (pub. by National Center for Atmospheric Research)

**University Council for Educational Administration**
29 West Woodruff Ave., Columbus, OH 43210.
● Educational Administration Abstracts. 3 per yr. ISSN 0013-1601
● Educational Administration Quarterly. 3 per yr. ISSN 0013-161X
● U C E A Case Series in Educational Administration. irreg., latest issue, 1975. ISSN 0083-3967

**University Digest Services**
Box 343, Troy, MI 48099.
● U D S Air Quality Control Digest. bi-m. ISSN 0002-2527
● U D S Energy Digest. q.
● U D S Metal Joining Digest. bi-m. ISSN 0026-0630
● U D S Surface Coatings Digest. bi-m.
● U D S Water Quality Control Digest. bi-m. ISSN 0043-1346

**University Film Association**
Dept. of Photography and Cinema, Ohio State University, 156 W. 19th Ave., Columbus, OH 43210
(or c/o Donald Staples, Exec. Officer, New York University Department of Cinema Studies, New York NY 10003)
● University Film Association. Journal. q. ISSN 0041-9311
● University Film Association. Membership Directory. irreg. ISSN 0094-3010

**University Film Study Center**
Box 275, Cambridge, MA 02138.
● University Film Study Center. Newsletter. bi-m.

**University Folklore Association**
● Folklore Annual. (pub. by University of Texas at Austin. Center for Intercultural Studies in Folklore and Oral History)

**University Microfilms International**
300 N. Zeeb Rd., Ann Arbor, MI 48106.
● American Doctoral Dissertations. a. ISSN 0065-809X (Association of Research Libraries)
● Comprehensive Dissertation Index. Supplement. a. ISSN 0361-6657
● Curriculum Materials Clearinghouse. Index and Curriculum Briefs. irreg. ISSN 0095-4977
● Dissertation Abstracts International. Section A: Humanities and Social Sciences. m.
● Dissertation Abstracts International. Section C: European Abstracts. q.
● Dissertation Abstracts International Section B: Physical Sciences and Technology. m.
● Doctoral Dissertations on Asia. s-a. ISSN 0098-4485
● International Microform Journal of Legal Medicine. q. ISSN 0020-7977 (Milton Helpern Library of Legal Medicine)
● Masters Abstracts; catalog of selected masters theses on microfilm. q. ISSN 0025-5106
● Monograph Abstracts. irreg. ISSN 0362-3831
● Research Abstracts. q.
● Serials Bulletin. bi-m. ISSN 0037-2447
● Source. irreg. ISSN 0085-6347

**University Microfilms International. Indexing Services**
300 N. Zeeb Rd., Ann Arbor, MI 48106.
● Billboard Index. irreg.
● Criminal Justice Periodical Index. 3 per yr.
● New York Index. irreg.

**University of Akron. College of Business Administration**
302 E. Buchtel Ave., Akron, OH 44325.
● Akron Business and Economic Review. q. ISSN 0044-7048

**University of Akron. Department of Geography**
Akron, OH 44325.
● Ohio Geographers: Recent Research Themes. a.

**University of Akron. School of Law**
● Akron Law Review. (pub. by Rohrich Corp.)

**University of Alabama**
● Black Warrior Review. (pub. by Black Warrior Review)

**University of Alabama. Graduate School of Business**
Box AK, University, AL 35486.
● Alabama Business. m. ISSN 0002-4163 (prep. by its Center for Business and Economic Research)
● University of Alabama. Center for Business and Economic Research Monograph Series. irreg.

**University of Alabama in Birmingham**
Box 348 N.B.S.B, University Station, Birmingham, AL 35294.
● Aura Literary Arts Review. s-a.

**University of Alabama in Birmingham. Medical Center**
Univ. Station, Birmingham, AL 35294.
● Alabama Journal of Medical Sciences. q. ISSN 0002-4252
● University of Alabama, Birmingham. Medical Center. bi-m.

**University of Alabama in Birmingham. School of Business**
Department of Economics, Birmingham, AL 35294 (Subscr. to: James C. Hite, Sec.-Treas. SRSA, 100 Long Hall, Clemson University, Clemson, SC 29631)
● Review of Regional Studies. 3 per yr. ISSN 0048-749X (Southern Regional Science Association)

**University of Alabama in Biriminigham. Center for Labor Education and Research**
University Station, Birmingham, AL 35294.
● CLEAR Report. q.

**University of Alabama Press**
Drawer 2877, University, AL 35486
(also Published by Max Hueber Verlag, Munich)
● Alabama Linguistic and Philological Series. irreg. ISSN 0084-6112
● American Dialect Society. Publications. s-a. ISSN 0002-8207
● Prague Studies in Mathematical Linguistics. irreg., 1973, vol. 4. ISSN 0079-4856 (Ceskoslovenska Akademie Ved CS)
● Revista de Estudios Hispanicos. 3 per yr. ISSN 0034-818X
● Southern Historical Publications. irreg., no. 19, 1975. ISSN 0081-3036

**University of Alabama. School of Law**
Box 1976, University, AL 35486.
● Alabama Law Review. 3 per yr. ISSN 0002-4279

**University of Alabama. School of Law and Department of Psychology**
Box 1435, University, AL 35486.
● Law and Psychology Review. a. ISSN 0098-5961

**University of Alaska**
Victor Fischer, College, AK 99701.
● Alaska Review of Business and Economic Conditions. m. ISSN 0034-6462

**University of Alaska. Cooperative Extension Service**
Fairbanks, AK 99701.
● Alaska Forest Products Newsletter. s-a.
● Quarterly Report on Alaska's Food Prices. q. (Co-sponsor: U. S. Department of Agriculture)
● University of Alaska. Cooperative Extension Service. Local Government Hi-Lites. m. (Co-sponsor: U. S. Department of Agriculture)
● What's Developing in Alaska. m?

**University of Alaska. Department of Anthropology**
● University of Alaska. Anthropological Papers. (pub. by University of Alaska Press)

**University of Alaska. Department of Journalism**
Fairbanks, AK 99701.
● Alaska Today. a.

**University of Alaska. Geophysical Institute**
Fairbanks, AK 99701.
● Northern Engineer. q. ISSN 0029-3083
● University of Alaska. Geophysical Institute. Bibliography of Publications. irreg. ISSN 0065-5856
● University of Alaska. Geophysical Institute. Report Series. irreg. ISSN 0041-9362

**University of Alaska. Institute of Agricultural Sciences**
College, AK 99701.
● Agroborealis. 2-3 per yr. ISSN 0002-1822

**University of Alaska. Institute of Marine Science**
Fairbanks, AK 99701.
● University of Alaska. Institute of Marine Science. Occasional Publication. irreg., no. 3, 1973. ISSN 0084-6147
● University of Alaska. Institute of Marine Sciences. Technical Report. irreg. ISSN 0065-5929

**University of Alaska. Institute of Social and Economic Research**
Fairbanks, AK 99701.
● I S E R Alaska Review of Business and Economic Conditions. a.
● I S E R Occasional Papers. irreg; no. 12, 1976.
● I S E R Research Notes. irreg., latest issue, 1975.

• Institute of Social and Economic Research.
Reports. irreg., no. 47, 1976.

**University of Alaska. Institute of Water Resources**
Fairbanks, AK 99701.
• University of Alaska. Institute of Water
Resources. Annual Report. a. ISSN 0065-5953

**University of Alaska. Mineral Industry Research Laboratory**
Fairbanks, AK 99701.
• University of Alaska. Mineral Industry Research
Laboratory. Report. irreg., 1973, no. 31. ISSN
0065-5961

**University of Alaska Museum**
Fairbanks, AK 99701.
• University of Alaska Museum. Annual Report. a.
ISSN 0093-7436

**University of Alaska. Office of University Relations**
Fairbanks, AK 99701.
• Now in the North. q.

**University of Alaska Press**
Box 95212, Fairbanks, AK 99701.
• University of Alaska. Anthropological Papers. s-a.
ISSN 0041-9354 (University of Alaska.
Department of Anthropology)

**University of Alaska. Registrar's Office**
Fairbanks, AK 99701.
• University of Alaska. State Wide Bulletin. irreg.
ISSN 0091-584X

**University of Alaska Sea Grant Program**
Fairbanks, AK 99701.
• Alaska Seas and Coasts. 5 per yr.

**University of Alaska. Student Orientation Services**
Fairbanks, AK 99701.
• Theata. a.

**University of Arizona**
Tucson, AZ 85721.
• Arizona Quarterly. q. ISSN 0004-1610
• Obsidian. irreg.
• Sun Trails. q.

**University of Arizona. Alumni Office**
Room 103, Alumni Bldg., Tucson, AZ 85721.
• Arizona Alumnus. q. ISSN 0004-1394

**University of Arizona. Center for Creative Photography**
• Center for Creative Photography. (pub. by
University of Arizona Library)

**University of Arizona. Civil Engineering Department**
Engineering Experiment Station, Tuscon, AZ 85721.
• Arizona Land Surveyors Conference. Proceedings.
biennial. ISSN 0066-7439 (American Congress on
Surveying and Mapping. Arizona Section)

**University of Arizona. College of Agriculture**
Tucson, AZ 85721.
• Progressive Agriculture in Arizona. q. ISSN 0033-
0744
• University of Arizona. Agricultural Experiment
Station. Technical Bulletin. 10 per yr. ISSN 0041-
9389

**University of Arizona College of Business and Public Administration. Division of Economic and Business Research**
Institute of Industrial and Labor Relations, Tucson,
AZ 85721.
• Annual Labor-Management Conference on
Collective Bargaining and Labor Law. a. (Institute
of Industrial and Labor Relations. College of
Business and Public Administration)
• Arizona Review. m. ISSN 0004-1629

**University of Arizona. College of Education**
Bureau of Educational Services, Tucson, AZ 85721.
• University of Arizona. College of Education.
Monograph Series. irreg. ISSN 0066-751X

**University of Arizona. College of Engineering**
206 Civil Engineering Bldg., Tucson, AZ 85721.
• Impact. q.

**University of Arizona. College of Law**
Tucson, AZ 85721.
• Arizona Advocate. m. ISSN 0004-1386
• Arizona Law Review. 4 per yr. ISSN 0004-153X

**University of Arizona. College of Pharmacy**
Tucson, AZ 85721.
• University of Arizona. College of Pharmacy.
Poisoning Control Information Center. News
Bulletin. irreg. ISSN 0066-7528

**University of Arizona. Department of Anthropology**
• University of Arizona. Anthropological Papers.
(pub. by University of Arizona Press)

**University of Arizona. Department of English**
Tucson, AZ 85721.
• University of Arizona. Department of English.
Graduate English Papers. a. or s-a. ISSN 0066-
7536

**University of Arizona. Engineering Experiment Station**
Tuscon, AZ 85721.
• E E S Series Report. irreg., latest issue, 1973
(issues not numbered consecutively) ISSN 0066-
7560

**Univ. of Arizona. Institute of Government Research**
Tucson, AZ 85721.
• American Government Studies. (pub. by
University of Arizona Press)
• Arizona Government Studies. (pub. by University
of Arizona Press)
• Arizona Model United Nations. a. ISSN 0066-
7447
• Comparative Government Studies. (pub. by
University of Arizona Press)
• Political Theory Studies. (pub. by University of
Arizona Press)
• University of Arizona. Institute of Government
Research. International Studies. (pub. by
University of Arizona Press)
• University of Arizona. Institute of Government
Research. Research Series. q.

**University of Arizona. Laboratory of Tree-Ring Research**
Tucson, AZ 85721.
• Tree-Ring Bulletin. a. ISSN 0041-2198 (Tree-Ring
Society)

**University of Arizona. Library**
Rm. 310, Tucson, AZ 85721.
• Arizona and the West; a journal of history. q.
ISSN 0004-1408
• Books of the Southwest; a critical checklist of
current Southwestern Americana. m. ISSN 0006-
7520
• Center for Creative Photography. irreg.
(University of Arizona. Center for Creative
Photography)
• University of Arizona Library. Bibliographic
Bulletin. s-a. ISSN 0044-8877
• University of Arizona Library. Occasional Papers.
irreg.

**University of Arizona. Optical Sciences Center**
Tucson, AZ 85721.
• University of Arizona. Optical Sciences Center.
Newsletter. irreg.(approx. 3-5 issues per year)
ISSN 0066-7609
• University of Arizona. Optical Sciences Center.
Technical Report. irreg. ISSN 0066-7617

**University of Arizona Press**
Box 3398, College Station, Tucson, AZ 85722.
• American Government Studies. irreg., 1970, no. 3.
ISSN 0065-8464 (University of Arizona. Institute
of Government Research)
• Arizona Government Studies. irreg., no. 11, 1974.
ISSN 0066-7420 (University of Arizona. Institute
of Government Research)
• Association for Asian Studies. Monographs and
Papers. irreg., 1970, no. 26. ISSN 0066-9059
• Comparative Government Studies. irreg., no. 6,
1974. ISSN 0069-7885 (University of Arizona.
Institute of Government Research)
• Contributions to Highway Salvage Archaeology in
Arizona. irreg., no. 40, 1975.
• Political Theory Studies. irreg., no. 2, 1975. ISSN
0079-306X (University of Arizona. Institute of
Government Research)
• Series of Southwest Chronicles. irreg.
• University of Arizona. Anthropological Papers.
irreg., no. 26, 1975. ISSN 0066-7501 (University
of Arizona. Department of Anthropology)
• University of Arizona. Institute of Government
Research. International Studies. irreg., no. 4,
1974. ISSN 0066-7579
• University of Arizona. Laboratory of Tree-Ring
Research. Papers. irreg., 1969, no. 3. ISSN 0066-
7587

• University of Arizona. Lunar and Planetary
Laboratory. Communications. irreg. ISSN 0066-
7595

**University of Arkansas**
434 Hawthorn St., Fayetteville, AR 72701.
• Journal of Thought. q. ISSN 0022-5231

**University of Arkansas. Agricultural Experiment Station**
Fayetteville, AR 72701.
• Arkansas Farm Research. bi-m. ISSN 0004-1785

**University of Arkansas. College of Business Administration**
Fayetteville, AR 72701.
• Arkansas Business and Economic Review. q. ISSN
0004-1742 (prep. by its Bureau of Business and
Economic Research)

**University of Arkansas. College of Engineering**
E-204, Fayetteville, AR 72701.
• Arkansas Engineer. 4 per yr.

**University of Arkansas. Department of English**
Fayetteville, AR 72701.
• Style. q. ISSN 0039-4238

**University of Arkansas. Industrial Research and Extension Center**
Box 3017, Little Rock, AR 72203.
• University of Arkansas. Industrial Research and
Extension Center. Annual Report. a. ISSN 0518-
6544
• University of Arkansas. Industrial Research and
Extension Center. Research Memorandum. irreg.

**University of Arkansas. Law School**
Fayetteville, AR 72701.
• Arkansas Law Review. q. ISSN 0004-1831

**University of Baltimore**
Baltimore, MD 21201.
• Forum. ISSN 0094-1948

**University of Baltimore. School of Business**
Charles at Mt. Royal, Baltimore, MD 21201.
• American Journal of Small Business. q. ISSN
0363-9428

**University of Baltimore School of Law**
Executive Editor, 1420 North Charles Street,
Baltimore, MD 21201.
• University of Baltimore Law Review. s-a. ISSN
0091-5440

**University of California, Berkeley**
Berkeley, CA 94720.
• California Management Review. q. ISSN 0008-
1256
• Health Sciences Journal. m.
• Law Project Bulletin. (pub. by National Housing
and Economic Development Law Project)

**University of California, Berkeley. Agricultural Experiment Station**
c/o Agricultural Publications, Berkeley, CA 94720.
• Hilgardia; a journal of agricultural science. irreg.
ISSN 0073-2230
• Information Series in Agricultural Economics.
irreg. ISSN 0073-7887 (prep. by its Cooperative
Extension Service) (Co-Sponsor: Giannini
Foundation of Agricultural Economics)

**University of California, Berkeley. Archaeological Research Facility**
Berkeley, CA 94720.
• University of California, Berkeley. Archaeological
Research Facility. Contributions. irreg., no. 22,
1974. ISSN 0068-5933

**University of California, Berkeley. Bancroft Library**
Berkeley, CA 94720.
• Bancroftiana. 3-4 per yr. ISSN 0067-3412
(Friends of the Bancroft Library)

**University of California, Berkeley. Center for Chinese Studies**
12 Barrows Hall, Berkeley, CA 94720.
• China Research Monographs. irreg; no. 12, 1976.
ISSN 0069-3693
• Studies in Chinese Terminology. irreg; no. 17,
1976.

**University of California, Berkeley. Center for Real Estate and Urban Economics**
2420 Bowditch St., Berkeley, CA 94720.
- University of California, Berkeley. Center for Real Estate and Urban Economics. Research Report. irreg., no. 37, 1972. ISSN 0068-5976
- University of California, Berkeley. Center for Real Estate and Urban Economics. Reprint Series. irreg., no. 96, 1975. ISSN 0068-5968
- University of California, Berkeley. Center for Real Estate and Urban Economics. Special Report. irreg., no. 11, 1975. ISSN 0068-5984
- University of California, Berkeley. Center for Real Estate and Urban Economics. Technical Report. irreg., 1972, no. 4. ISSN 0068-5992

**University of California, Berkeley. Center for Research and Development in Higher Education**
2150 Shattuck Ave., 5th Floor, Berkeley, CA 94704.
- California University Center for Research and Development in Higher Education. Research Reporter. q. ISSN 0034-5393

**University of California, Berkeley. Center for South and Southeast Asian Studies**
Berkeley, CA 94720.
- Tamasha/Slametan. m.
- University of California. Center for South and Southeast Asia Studies. Occasional Papers. irreg., no. 11, 1973. ISSN 0068-600X
- University of California. Center for South and Southeast Asia Studies. Research Monograph Series. irreg., no. 12, 1974. ISSN 0068-6018

**University of California, Berkeley. College of Engineering**
Sanitary Engineering Research Laboratory, Richmond Field Station, 1301 S. 46th St., Richmond, CA 94804.
- University of California. Sanitary Engineering Research Laboratory. News Quarterly. q. ISSN 0036-4428

**University of California, Berkeley. Cooperative Extension**
Berkeley, CA 94720.
- California Plant Pathology. bi-m. ISSN 0094-3800

**University of California, Berkeley. Department of Anthropology**
Berkeley, CA 94720.
- Urban Anthropology Newsletter. s-a. ISSN 0098-3675

**University of California, Berkeley. Department of Forestry and Conservation**
145 Mulford Hall, Berkeley, CA 94720.
- Horace M. Albright Conservation Lectureship. a. ISSN 0073-3369
- S. J. Hall Lectureship in Industrial Forestry. a. ISSN 0080-5092

**University of California, Berkeley. Design Methods Group**
Berkeley, CA 84720.
- D M G Occasional Papers. irreg. (approx. 1-2 per yr.)

**University of California, Berkeley. Division of Agricultural Sciences**
Berkeley, CA 94720.
- California Agriculture; reports of progress in research. m. ISSN 0008-0845

**University of California, Berkeley. Earthquake Engineering Research Center**
1301 South 46th Street, Richmond, CA 94804.
- Abstract Journal in Earthquake Engineering. a.

**University of California, Berkeley. Forest Products Library**
1301 S. 46th St., Richmond, CA 94804.
- California Forestry and Forest Products. ISSN 0008-1094

**University of California, Berkeley. Graduate Sociology Union**
410 Barrows, Berkeley, CA 94720.
- Berkeley Journal of Sociology; critical review. a. ISSN 0067-5830

**University of California, Berkeley. Institute of Business and Economic Research**
156 Barrows Hall, Berkeley, CA 94720.
- I B E R Special Publications. irreg. ISSN 0068-6069

- University of California. Institute of Business and Economic Research. Publications. (pub. by University of California Press)

**University of California, Berkeley. Institute of Governmental Studies**
109 Bernard Moses Hall, Berkeley, CA 94720.
- Public Affairs Report. bi-m. ISSN 0033-3417
- University of California. Institute of Governmental Studies Library. Accessions List. m. ISSN 0041-9443

**University of California, Berkeley. Institute of Human Development**
1203 Tolman Hall, Berkeley, CA 94720.
- University of California, Berkeley. Institute of Human Development. Annual Report. a. ISSN 0068-6085

**University of California, Berkeley. Institute of Industrial Relations**
Berkeley, CA 94720.
- C P E R. (California Public Employee Relations) q.
- Industrial Relations; a journal of economy and society. 3 per yr. ISSN 0019-8676

**University of California, Berkeley. Institute of International Studies**
Berkeley, CA 94720.
- University of California, Berkeley. Institute of International Studies. Policy Papers in International Affairs. 4-5 per yr.
- University of California, Berkeley. Institute of International Studies. Research Series. 2-3 per yr; no. 30, 1977. ISSN 0068-6093

**University of California, Berkeley. Institute of Race and Community Relations**
2543 Channing Way, Berkeley, CA 94720.
- Intergroup Relations Newsletter. m. ISSN 0024-6689

**University of California, Berkeley. Institute of Transportation and Traffic Engineering**
409 McLaughlin Hall, Berkeley, CA 94720.
- California Transportation and Public Works Conference. Proceedings. a. ISSN 0068-5887

**University of California, Berkeley. Institute of Transportation Studies Library**
412 McLaughlin, Berkeley, Richmond, CA 94720.
- University of California. Institute of Transportation Studies. Selected List of Recent Acquisitions of the Transportation Library. bi-m. ISSN 0068-6123
- University of California, Berkeley. Institute of Transportation Studies. Library References. irreg; no. 44, 1976. ISSN 0068-6115

**University of California, Berkeley. Language Behavior Research Laboratory**
2220 Piedmont Ave., Berkeley, CA 94720.
- University of California, Berkeley. Language Behavior Research Laboratory. Monograph Series. irreg.
- University of California, Berkeley, Language Behavior Research Laboratory, Working Paper Series. irreg., no. 47, 1977.

**University of California, Berkeley. Lawrence Berkeley Laboratory**
Berkeley, CA 94720
- Lawrence Berkeley Laboratory. Materials and Molecular Research Division. Annual Report. a. (Order from: National Technical Information Service, 5285 Port Royal Rd., Springfield, VA 22151)
- Lawrence Berkeley Laboratory. Research Highlights. a. ISSN 0091-9489

**University of California, Berkeley. Library**
Berkeley, CA 94720.
- University of California, Berkeley. Serials Key Word Index. 2nd edt., 1974. ISSN 0091-8113

**University of California, Berkeley. Library School Library**
Berkeley, CA 94720.
- University of California, Berkeley. Library School Library. Selected Additions to the Library School Library Collection. bi-m. ISSN 0037-1300

**University of California, Berkeley. Music Library**
Berkeley, CA 94720.
- Cum Notis Variorum. m.

**University of California, Berkeley. Office of Institutional Research**
Berkeley, CA 94720.
- University of California, Berkeley. Office of Institutional Research . Campus Statistics. irreg. ISSN 0092-0290

**University of California, Berkeley. Office of Public Information**
101 Sproul Hall, Berkeley, CA 94720.
- University of California. Office of Public Information. Monday Paper. w.

**University of California, Berkeley. School of Criminology**
101 Haviland Hall, Berkeley, CA 94720.
- Crime and Social Justice; a journal of radical criminology. s-a. ISSN 0094-7571
- University of California, Berkeley. School of Criminology. San Francisco Project. Research Report. irreg., 1969, no. 14. ISSN 0068-6174

**University of California, Berkeley. School of Law**
Boalt Hall, Berkeley, CA 94720.
- California Law Review. 6 per yr. ISSN 0008-1221
- Ecology Law Quarterly. q. ISSN 0046-1121

**University of California, Berkeley. Science Curriculum Improvement Study**
Lawrence Hall of Science, Berkeley, CA 94710.
- Science Curriculum Improvement Study Newsletter. 4 per yr. ISSN 0036-8288

**University of California, Berkeley. Seismographic Station**
Berkeley, CA 94720.
- University of California. Seismographic Stations. Bulletin. s-a. ISSN 0041-946X

**University of California, Berkeley. Student Engineers' Joint Council**
9 Northgate Hall, Berkeley, CA 94720.
- California Engineer. 4 per yr. ISSN 0008-1027

**University of California, Berkeley. University Extension**
Berkeley, CA 94720.
- Drug Abuse Papers. irreg. ISSN 0070-735X

**University of California, Berkeley. Vice-President-University Relations**
131 University Hall, Berkeley, CA 94720.
- University of California U C Clip Sheet. w.

**University of California, Berkeley. Visual Science Information Center**
Berkeley, CA 94720.
- Vision Index. q. ISSN 0049-6510

**University of California, Davis**
Davis, CA 95616.
- Vertebrate Pest Conference. Proceedings. biennial. ISSN 0507-6773 (California Vertebrate Pest Technical Committee. Library)

**University of California, Davis. Cooperative Extension**
Davis, CA 95616.
- California's Environment. bi-m.

**University of California, Davis. Department of Avian Sciences**
Davis, CA 95616.
- University of California, Davis. Game Bird Workshop. Proceedings. biennial.

**University of California, Davis. Department of English**
100 Sproul Hall, Davis, CA 95616.
- California Quarterly; journal of literature, reviews and translation. q. ISSN 0045-3978

**University of California, Davis. Food Protection and Toxicology Center**
Davis, CA 95616.
- University of California, Davis. Food Protection and Toxicology Center. Summary Report. a. ISSN 0094-7962

**University of California, Davis. Institute of Governmental Affairs**
Davis, CA 95616.
- California Government Notes. irreg. ISSN 0068-5607
- University of California, Davis. Institute of Governmental Affairs. Environmental Quality Series. irreg., no. 21, 1974. ISSN 0084-8298

**University of California, Davis. Packaging Program**
Packaging Library, Room 450, Main Library Bldg.,
Davis, CA 95616.
- Current Packaging Abstracts. s-m.

**University of California, Davis. School of Law**
Davis, CA 95616
(Dist. by Fred B. Rothman & Co., 57 Leuning St.,
S. Hackensack, N.J. 07606)
- Colloquium on the Law of Outer Space.
Proceedings. 16th, 1973, Baku, U.S.S.R. ISSN
0069-5831 (International Institute of Space Law)
(Co-sponsor: International Astronautical
Federation)

**University of California, Davis. University Library**
Library Associates, Davis, CA 95616.
- Keepsake. irreg., no. 6, 1974. ISSN 0075-5311

**University of California, Davis. Water Resources
Center**
Davis, CA 95616.
- Conference on Ground Water. Proceedings.
biennial. ISSN 0094-9671 (Co-Sponsor: California
Department of Water Resources)
- University of California, Davis. Water Resources
Center. Annual Report. a. ISSN 0068-6298
- University of California, Davis. Water Resources
Center. Contributions. irreg (5-7 nos. per yr.)
ISSN 0068-6301

**University of California, Irvine. Center for
Pathobiology**
Irvine, CA 92664.
- University of California, Irvine. Center for
Pathobiology. Miscellaneous Publications. irreg.,
1970, no. 2. ISSN 0068-6131

**University of California, Irvine. Museum of
Systematic Biology**
Irvine, CA 92664.
- University of California, Irvine. Museum of
Systematic Biology. Research Series. irreg., nos. 4
& 5, 1975. ISSN 0068-614X

**University of California, Irvine. School of Humanities**
Irvine, CA 92664.
- Irvine Humanities Review. ISSN 0091-6676

**University of California, Los Angeles**
- U C L A Forum in Medical Sciences. (pub. by
University of California Press)

**University of California, Los Angeles. African Studies
Center**
405 Hilgard Ave, Los Angeles, CA 90024.
- African Arts. q. ISSN 0001-9933
- Journal of African Studies. (pub. by University of
California Press)
- Studies in African Linguistics. 3 per yr. ISSN
0039-3533 (Co-sponsor: U.C.L.A. Department of
Linguistics)
- Ufahamu. 3 per yr. ISSN 0041-5715 (Co-sponsor:
African Activist Association)
- University of California, Los Angeles. African
Studies Center. Occasional Paper. irreg. ISSN
0068-6190

**University of California, Los Angeles. Asian American
Studies Center**
3232 Campbell Hall, Los Angeles, CA 90024.
- Amerasia Journal. s-a. ISSN 0044-7471

**University of California, Los Angeles. Biomedical
Library**
Center for the Health Sciences, Los Angeles, CA
90024.
- University of California, Los Angeles. Biomedical
Library. Serials Holdings List. biennial.

**University of California, Los Angeles, Brain
Information Service**
*see* **Brain Information Service-Brain Research
Institute**

**University of California, Los Angeles. Center for
Medieval and Renaissance Studies**
Los Angeles, CA 90024.
- Comitatus; a Journal of Medieval and Renaissance
Studies. a. ISSN 0069-6412
- University of California, Los Angeles. Center for
Medieval and Renaissance Studies. Contributions.
(pub. by University of California Press)
- University of California, Los Angeles. Center for
Medieval and Renaissance Studies. Publications.
(pub. by University of California Press)
- Viator. (pub. by University of California Press)

**University of California, Los Angeles. Center for the
Study of Comparative Folklore and Mythology**
- University of California, Los Angeles. Center for
the Study of Comparative Folklore and
Mythology. Publications. (pub. by University of
California Press)

**University of California, Los Angeles. Center for the
Study of Evaluation**
405 Hilgard Ave., 145 Moore Hall, Los Angeles,
CA 90024.
- C S E Monograph Series in Evaluation. irreg (2-6
numbers per year)
- Evaluation Comment; the journal of educational
evaluation. q.

**University of California, Los Angeles. Chicano Studies
Center**
Campbell Hall, Rm. 3122, 405 Hilgard Ave., Los
Angeles, CA 90024.
- Aztlan-International Journal of Chicano Studies
Research. 3 per yr.
- Mirlo Canta de Noticatlan. m.
- University of California, Los Angeles. Chicano
Studies Center. Creative Series. a. ISSN 0045-
3986
- University of California, Los Angeles. Chicano
Studies Center. Monographs. irreg. 1972, no. 2.
ISSN 0045-3994

**University of California, Los Angeles. Department of
Anthropology**
405 Hilgard Ave., Los Angeles, CA 90024.
- Anthropology UCLA. s-a. ISSN 0003-5564

**University of California, Los Angeles. Department of
Geography**
405 Hilgard Ave., Los Angeles, CA 90024.
- China Geographer. 3 per yr.

**University of California, Los Angeles. Department of
Linguistics**
405 Hilgard Ave., Los Angeles, CA 90024.
- Occasional Papers in Linguistics. irreg.

**University of California, Los Angeles. Department of
Music**
Los Angeles, CA 90024.
- Selected Reports in Ethnomusicology. irreg. ISSN
0361-6622

**University of California, Los Angeles. Department of
Slavic Languages**
- International Journal of Slavic Linguistics and
Poetics. (pub. by Peter de Ridder Press NE)

**University of California, Los Angeles. Graduate
School of Management**
405 Hilgard Ave., Los Angeles, CA 90024.
- Current Management Research. a.
- G S M Quarterly. q.
- Interdisciplinary Colloquium on Mathematics in
the Behavioral Sciences. a. (Western Management
Sciences Institute)
- U C L A Business Forecast for the Nation and
California. a. ISSN 0082-7126 (prep. by its
U.C.L.A. Business Forecasting Project)
- University of California, Los Angeles. Graduate
School of Management. Annual Report. a.
- University of California, Los Angeles. Graduate
School of Management. Publications. irreg.
- World Economic Outlook. a. (prep. by its UCLA
Business Forecasting Project)

**University of California, Los Angeles. Institute of
Archaeology**
405 Hilgard Ave., Los Angeles, CA 90024.
- Journal of New World Archaeology. irreg.
- Monumenta Archaeologica (Los Angeles) irreg.
ISSN 0363-7565
- University of California, Los Angeles. Institute of
Archaeology. Archaeological Survey. Special
Monograph Series. irreg., no. 4, 1974. ISSN 0068-
6204

**University of California, Los Angeles. Institute of
Government and Public Affairs**
405 Hilgard Avenue, CA 90024.
- University of California, Los Angeles. Institute of
Government and Public Affairs. Mimeographed
Report (MR) Series. irreg. (10-15 per yr)

**University of California, Los Angeles. Institute of
Industrial Relations**
Los Angeles, CA 90024.
- University of California, Los Angeles. Institute of
Industrial Relations. Monograph Series. irreg.,
1970, no. 15. ISSN 0068-6255

**University of California, Los Angeles. Jewish
Students**
- Ha'am. (pub. by A S U C L A Communications
Board)

**University of California, Los Angeles. Latin American
Center**
405 Hilgard Ave., Los Angeles, CA 90024.
- Journal of Latin American Lore. s-a. ISSN 0360-
1927
- Statistical Abstract of Latin America. a (plus
supplements) ISSN 0081-4687 (prep. by its
Documentation Section)
- University of California, Los Angeles. Latin
American Center. Latin American Activities and
Resources. a.
- University of California, Los Angeles. Latin
American Center. Latin American Studies Series.
irreg; vol. 37, 1977. ISSN 0075-8132
- University of California, Los Angeles. Latin
American Center. Monograph Series. irreg.
- University of California, Los Angeles. Latin
American Center. Reference Series. irreg; vol. 8,
1976. ISSN 0068-6263

**University of California Los Angeles Medical Center.
School of Dentistry**
Los Angeles, CA 90024.
- Operative Dentistry. q.

**University of California, Los Angeles. Musuem of
Cultural History**
Los Angeles, CA 90024.
- University of California, Los Angeles. Museum of
Cultural History. Occasional Papers. irreg. ISSN
0068-628X

**University of California, Los Angeles.
Neuropsychiatric Institute**
Center for the Health Sciences, Los Angeles, CA
90024.
- Los Angeles Neurological Societies. Bulletin. q.
ISSN 0024-659X
- M R/Child News. q. (prep. by its Mental
Retardation and Child Psychiatry Division)

**University of California, Los Angeles. School of
Dentistry**
Los Angeles, CA 90024.
- Mentalis. irreg. ISSN 0360-7232

**University of California, Los Angeles. School of
Engineering & Applied Science**
405 Hilgard Ave, Los Angeles, CA 90024.
- University of California, Los Angeles. School of
Engineering and Applied Science. Research
Development, and Public Service Activities. irreg.,
latest issue, 1973. ISSN 0084-831X

**University of California, Los Angeles. School of Law**
Los Angeles, CA 90024.
- Black Law Journal. 3 per yr. ISSN 0045-2181
(Co-sponsor: U.C.L.A. Center for Afro-American
Studies)
- U C L A-Alaska Law Review.
- U C L A Law Review. 6 per yr. ISSN 0041-5650

**University of California, Los Angeles. University
Research Library**
Reference Dept, Los Angeles, CA 90024.
- New Reference Books at U C L A; additions to
the reference collections of the University
Library. q. ISSN 0028-6567

**University of California Press**
2223 Fulton Street, Berkeley, CA 94720
(and 25 West 45th St., New York, N.Y. 10036)
- Agricultural History. q. ISSN 0002-1482
(Agricultural History Society)
- Asian Survey. m. ISSN 0004-4687
- Berkeley Symposia on Mathematical Statistics and
Probability. irreg., 6th, 1972.
- Botanical Monographs. irreg.
- California Insect Survey. Bulletin. irreg. ISSN
0068-5631
- California Natural History Guides. irreg. ISSN
0068-5755
- California Slavic Studies. irreg. ISSN 0068-5798
- California Studies in Classical Antiquity. irreg.
ISSN 0068-5895

- California Studies in the History of Art. irreg. ISSN 0068-5909
- English Monarch Series. irreg. ISSN 0071-0628
- Ernest Bloch Lectures. irreg. ISSN 0071-1187
- Ethos. q. ISSN 0091-2131
- Film Quarterly. q. ISSN 0015-1386
- Folk Literature of the Sephardic Jews. irreg.
- Fountainwell Drama Texts. irreg.
- Hermaneutics: Studies in the History of Religions. irreg.
- History of the World Economy in the Twentieth Century. irreg.
- Ibero-Americana. irreg. ISSN 0073-4349
- Islamic World. irreg. ISSN 0075-0948
- Jefferson Memorial Lecture Series. irreg. ISSN 0075-3599
- Journal of African Studies. q. (University of California, Los Angeles. African Studies Center)
- Lane Studies in Regional Government. irreg.
- New Studies in Practical Philosophy. irreg.
- Nineteenth-Century Fiction. q. ISSN 0029-0564
- Pacific Historical Review. q. ISSN 0030-8684 (American Historical Association. Pacific Coast Branch)
- Patterns of Religious Commitment. irreg. ISSN 0079-0214
- Perspectives in Criticism. irreg. ISSN 0079-1008
- Perspectives in Medicine. irreg.
- Perspectives on Southern Africa. irreg.
- Policy Analysis. q. ISSN 0098-2067
- Rabindranath Tagore Memorial Lectureship. irreg. ISSN 0079-9386
- Romance Philology. q. ISSN 0035-8002
- Russian and East European Studies. irreg. ISSN 0080-4886
- Sather Classical Lectures. irreg. ISSN 0080-6684
- Science Surveys. irreg. ISSN 0080-7613
- Scripps Institution of Oceanography. Bulletin. irreg. ISSN 0080-8318
- Studies in Ecology. irreg.
- Studies in the Logic of Science. irreg.
- Topics in Philosophy. irreg.
- U C L A Forum in Medical Sciences. irreg. ISSN 0082-7134 (University of California, Los Angeles)
- University of California. Institute of Business and Economic Research. Publications. irreg. ISSN 0068-6077
- University of California, Los Angeles. Center for Medieval and Renaissance Studies. Contributions. irreg. ISSN 0068-6239
- University of California, Los Angeles. Center for Medieval and Renaissance Studies. Publications. irreg. ISSN 0068-6220
- University of California, Los Angeles. Center for the Study of Comparative Folklore and Mythology. Publications. irreg. ISSN 0068-6247
- University of California Publications. Anthropological Records. irreg. ISSN 0068-6336
- University of California Publications. Classical Studies. irreg. ISSN 0068-6344
- University of California Publications. Folklore & Mythology Studies. irreg.
- University of California Publications. Near Eastern Studies. irreg. ISSN 0068-6514
- University of California Publications. Occasional Papers. irreg. ISSN 0068-6522
- University of California Publications in Anthropology. irreg. ISSN 0068-6379
- University of California Publications in Automatic Computation. irreg. ISSN 0068-6387
- University of California Publications in Botany. irreg. ISSN 0068-6395
- University of California Publications in Contemporary Music. irreg. ISSN 0068-6409
- University of California Publications in Culture and Society. irreg.
- University of California Publications in Education. irreg.
- University of California Publications in Egyptian Archaeology. irreg. ISSN 0068-6433
- University of California Publications in Entomology. irreg. ISSN 0068-6417
- University of California Publications in Geography. irreg. ISSN 0068-6441
- University of California Publications in Geological Sciences. irreg. ISSN 0068-645X
- University of California Publications in History. irreg. ISSN 0068-6468
- University of California Publications in Librarianship. irreg. ISSN 0068-6476
- University of California Publications in Linguistics. irreg. ISSN 0068-6484
- University of California Publications in Modern Philology. irreg. ISSN 0068-6492
- University of California Publications in Zoology. irreg. ISSN 0068-6506

- Viator; Medieval and Renaissance Studies. a. ISSN 0083-5897 (University of California, Los Angeles. Center for Medieval and Renaissance Studies)
- 19th Century Music. 3 per yr.

**University of California, Riverside. Department of Anthropology**
1334 Watkins St., Riverside, CA 92502.
- Journal of California Anthropology. s-a. ISSN 0361-7181

**University of California, Riverside. Spanish Department**
Riverside, CA 92502.
- Alaluz; revista de poesia y narracion. q. ISSN 0044-7064

**University of California, San Diego. Central University Library**
La Jolla, CA 92903.
- Archive for New Poetry Newsletter. irreg.

**University of California, San Diego. Institute of Marine Resources**
Box 1529, La Jolla, CA 92037.
- University of California, San Diego. Institute of Marine Resources. Biennial Report. biennial.

**University of California, San Francisco. Drug Abuse Information Project**
San Francisco, CA 94102.
- University of California, San Francisco. Drug Abuse Information Project. Report to the Legislature. a. ISSN 0068-6050

**University of California, San Francisco. Hastings College of the Law**
305 Golden Gate Ave., San Francisco, CA 94102.
- Hastings Constitutional Law Quarterly. q. ISSN 0094-5617

**University of California, San Francisco. Synapse Publication Board**
San Francisco, CA 94143.
- Synapse. m.

**University of California, Santa Barbara. Library**
Santa Barbara, CA 93106.
- Soundings; collections of the University Library. s-a. ISSN 0038-1853

**University of California, Santa Cruz. College 5**
Santa Cruz, CA 95064.
- Quarry West; a journal of literature & the arts. s-a.

**University of California, Santa Cruz, Lick Observatory**
*see* Lick Observatory

**University of Chicago**
Faculty Exchange, Box C, Chicago, IL 60637.
- Chicago Maroon. (pub. by Newsweb)
- Chicago Review. q. ISSN 0009-3696

**University of Chicago. A. G. Bush Library**
Industrial Relations Center, 1225 E. 60th St., Chicago, IL 60637.
- A. G. Bush Library Abstracts. m. ISSN 0001-1304
- Committee of University Industrial Relations Librarians. Exchange Bibliography. irreg.

**University of Chicago Alumni Association**
5733 University Ave., Chicago, IL 60637.
- University of Chicago Magazine. q. ISSN 0041-9508

**University of Chicago. Biology Department**
1103 E. 57th St., Chicago, IL 60657.
- Evolutionary Theory; an international journal of fact and interpretation. irreg. ISSN 0093-4755

**University of Chicago. Center for Health Administration Studies**
5720 S. Woodlawn, Chicago, IL 60637.
- University of Chicago. Center for Health Administration Studies. Research Series. irreg., 1970, no. 27. ISSN 0069-3316

**University of Chicago. Center for Studies in Criminal Justice**
Chicago, IL 60637.
- University of Chicago. Center for Studies in Criminal Justice. Annual Report. a. ISSN 0069-3332

**University of Chicago. Department of Anthropology**
1126 E. 59th St., Chicago, IL 60637.
- University of Chicago Studies in Anthropology. Series in Social, Cultural, and Linguistic Anthropology. irreg.

**University of Chicago. Department of Geography**
5828 S. University Ave., Chicago, IL 60637.
- University of Chicago. Department of Geography. Research Papers. irreg, latest issue, 1974. ISSN 0069-3340

**University of Chicago. Department of Psychology**
5848 University Ave., Chicago, IL 60637.
- Psychotherapy. q. ISSN 0090-144X

**University of Chicago. Division of Biological Sciences**
Chicago, IL 60637.
- University of Chicago. Division of Biological Sciences and Pritzker School of Medicine. Report. s-a.

**University of Chicago. Graduate School of Business**
Chicago, IL 60637.
- Journal of Accounting Research. s-a. ISSN 0021-8456 (prep. by its Institute of Professional Accounting)
- Journal of Accounting Research. Supplement. a. (prep. by its Institute of Professional Accounting)
- Studies in Business and Society. (pub. by University of Chicago Press)
- University of Chicago. Graduate School of Business. Selected Papers. irreg. ISSN 0069-3359

**University of Chicago. Ida Noyes Hall**
1212 E. 59th St., Chicago, IL 60637.
- Primavera. irreg.

**University of Chicago. Industrial Relations Center**
1225 E. 60 St., Chicago, IL 60637.
- University of Chicago. Industrial Relations Center. Occasional Papers. irreg; no. 37, 1976. ISSN 0529-0937

**University of Chicago Law School**
1111 E. 60th St., Chicago, IL 60637.
- Journal of Law and Economics. s-a. ISSN 0022-2186
- Journal of Legal Studies. s-a. ISSN 0047-2530
- University of Chicago. Law School. Law Alumni Journal. s-a. ISSN 0094-0968
- University of Chicago Law Review. q. ISSN 0041-9494

**University of Chicago. Midwest Administration Center**
5835 S. Kimbark Ave., Chicago, IL 60637.
- Administrators Notebook. 9 per yr. ISSN 0001-8430
- University of Chicago . Midwest Administration Center. Monograph Series. irreg., latest issue, 1973. ISSN 0076-857X

**University of Chicago. Oriental Institute**
- Assyriological Studies. (pub. by University of Chicago Press)
- Materials for the Assyrian Dictionary. (pub. by University of Chicago Press)
- Studies in Ancient Oriental Civilization. (pub. by University of Chicago Press)
- University of Chicago Oriental Institute. Publications. (pub. by University of Chicago Press)

**University of Chicago Press**
5801 S. Ellis Ave., Chicago, IL 60637
(Orders to: 11030 Langley Ave., Chicago, IL 60628)
- American Journal of Human Genetics; a record of research, review and bibliographic material relating to heredity in man. bi-m. ISSN 0002-9297 (American Society of Human Genetics)
- American Journal of Sociology. bi-m. ISSN 0002-9602
- American Naturalist; devoted to the advancement and correlation of the biological sciences. bi-m. ISSN 0003-0147 (American Society of Naturalists)
- Assyriological Studies. irreg., vol. 19, 1974. ISSN 0066-9903 (University of Chicago. Oriental Institute)
- Astrophysical Journal; an international review of astronomy and astronomical physics. bi-m. ISSN 0004-637X (American Astronomical Society)
- Astrophysical Journal. Supplement Series. m. ISSN 0067-0049 (American Astronomical Society)

- Botanical Gazette; a journal embracing all departments of botanical science. q. ISSN 0006-8071
- Center for Children's Books. Bulletin. m.(Sept-July) ISSN 0008-9036
- Chicago History of American Civilization. irreg., 1972, no. 28. ISSN 0069-3278
- Chicago History of American Religion. irreg.
- Chicago Lectures in Mathematics. irreg., no. 10, 1974. ISSN 0069-3286
- Chicago Lectures in Physics. irreg., vol. 6, 1973. ISSN 0069-3294
- Child Development. q. ISSN 0009-3920 (Society for Research in Child Development, Inc.)
- Child Development Abstracts and Bibliography. 3 per yr. ISSN 0009-3939 (Society for Research in Child Development, Inc.)
- Classic European Historians. irreg., vol. 13, 1975. ISSN 0069-4452
- Classical Philology; devoted to research in the languages, literatures, history and life of classical antiquity. q. ISSN 0009-837X
- Classics in Anthropology. irreg., vol. 9, 1973. ISSN 0069-4487
- Classics of British Historical Literature. irreg., no. 13, 1975. ISSN 0069-4509
- Comparative Education Review. 3 per yr. ISSN 0010-4086 (Comparative and International Education Society) (Editorial Address: c/o Andreas M. Kazamias, Ed., 206 Education Bldg., University of Wisconsin, Madison WI 53706)
- Critical Inquiry. q. ISSN 0093-1896
- Current Anthropology; world journal of the sciences of man. 4 per yr. ISSN 0011-3204
- Economic Development and Cultural Change. q. ISSN 0013-0079 (University of Chicago. Research Center in Economic Development and Cultural Change)
- Economic Research Studies. irreg., 1970, no. 10. ISSN 0070-8623
- Elementary School Journal. m (except Aug.) ISSN 0013-5984
- Ethics; an international journal of social, political and legal philosophy. q. ISSN 0014-1704
- Folktales of the World. irreg., 1970, no. 12. ISSN 0071-6804
- German Literary Classics in Translation. irreg., vol. 5, 1972.
- Germanic Review; devoted to studies dealing with the Germanic languages and literatures. q. ISSN 0016-8890 (Until 1978, Vol. 53, pub. by Columbia University Press, 136 S. Broadway, Irvington-on-Hudson, NY 10533)
- Heritage of Sociology. irreg., no. 33, 1974. ISSN 0073-1986
- History and Structure of Languages. irreg., no. 3, 1972. ISSN 0073-2710
- History of Menshevism. irreg., no. 3, 1975. ISSN 0073-2737 (Hoover Institution)
- History of Religions; an international journal for comparative historical studies. q. ISSN 0018-2710
- History of Science and Medicine. irreg. ISSN 0073-2745
- I J A L Native American Texts Series. (International Journal of American Linguistics) irreg.
- International Journal of American Linguistics. q. ISSN 0020-7071 (Linguistic Society of America) (Co-sponsor: American Anthropological Association) (Subscr. to: Mrs. Alice Zorn, Bus. Mgr., Indiana University, Bloomington, IN 47401)
- Journal of Business. q. ISSN 0021-9398
- Journal of Geology. bi-m. ISSN 0022-1376
- Journal of Infectious Diseases. m (2 vols. per yr.) ISSN 0022-1899 (Orders to: 11030 Langley Ave., Chicago, IL 60628)
- Journal of Medicine and Philosophy. q. ISSN 0360-5310 (Society for Health and Human Values)
- Journal of Modern History. q. ISSN 0022-2801
- Journal of Near Eastern Studies. q. ISSN 0022-2968
- Journal of Political Economy. bi-m. ISSN 0022-3808
- Journal of Religion. q. ISSN 0022-4189
- Library Quarterly; a journal of investigation and discussion in the field of library science. q. ISSN 0024-2519
- Materials for the Assyrian Dictionary. irreg., 1970, no. 5. ISSN 0076-518X (University of Chicago. Oriental Institute)
- Modern Philology; a journal devoted to research in medieval and modern literature. q. ISSN 0026-8232
- Monuments of Renaissance Music. irreg., vol. 6, 1975. ISSN 0077-1503

- National Society for the Study of Education. Yearbook. a. in 2 pts. ISSN 0077-5762
- Negro American Biographies and Autobiographies. irreg., no. 6, 1973. ISSN 0077-6475
- Patterns of Literary Criticism. irreg., vol. 12, 1974. ISSN 0079-0206
- Perspectives in Biology and Medicine. q. ISSN 0031-5982
- Physiological Zoology; a quarterly journal of zoological research. q. ISSN 0031-935X
- Prehistoric Archaeology and Ecology. irreg., vol. 2, 1975.
- Requirements for Certification of Teachers, Counsellors, Librarians, Administrators for Elementary Schools, Secondary Schools, Junior Colleges. irreg., no. 40, 1975. ISSN 0080-1429
- Review of Child Development Research. irreg., vol. 4, 1975. (Society for Research in Child Development, Inc.)
- Romanic Review. q. ISSN 0035-8118 (Until 1978, Vol. 69, pub. by: Columbia University Press, 136 S. Broadway, Irvington-on-Hudson, NY 10533)
- School Review; a journal for research, theory and philosophical inquiry in education and related disciplines. 4 per yr. ISSN 0036-6773
- Serial Publications in Anthropology. a.
- Signs; journal of women in culture and society. q. ISSN 0097-9740
- Social Service Review; devoted to the scientific and professional interests of social work. q. ISSN 0037-7961
- Society for Research in Child Development. Monographs. irreg. ISSN 0037-976X
- Stars and Stellar Systems. irreg., no. 9, 1975. ISSN 0081-4407
- Statistical Research Monographs. irreg., vol. 4, 1974. ISSN 0081-5020 (Co-Sponsors: Institute of Mathematical Statistics; University of Chicago)
- Studies in Ancient Oriental Civilization. irreg., no. 37, 1974. ISSN 0081-7554 (University of Chicago. Oriental Institute)
- Studies in Business and Society. irreg., no. 9, 1975. ISSN 0081-7635 (University of Chicago. Graduate School of Business)
- Studies in Crime and Justice. irreg., vol. 5, 1975.
- Studies in Imperialism. irreg.
- Studies in the History of Discoveries. irreg., vol. 4, 1975. ISSN 0081-8615 (Society for the History of Discoveries)
- Studies of Urban Society. irreg., no. 7, 1975. ISSN 0081-8801
- Supreme Court Review. a. ISSN 0081-9557
- Technology and Culture; devoted to the study of the development of technology and its relations with society and culture. q. ISSN 0040-165X (Society for the History of Technology)
- United States & the World: Foreign Perspectives. irreg.
- University of Chicago. Center for Middle Eastern Studies. Publications. irreg., vol. 9, 1973. ISSN 0069-3324
- University of Chicago Oriental Institute. Publications. irreg., vol. 99, 1974. ISSN 0069-3367
- University of Chicago Press Documents in American History. irreg.
- University of Chicago Studies in Library Science. irreg., vol. 45, 1975. ISSN 0069-3375
- Wildlife Behavior and Ecology. irreg., vol. 4, 1975. ISSN 0084-0122
- Zygon; journal of religion and science. q. ISSN 0591-2385 (Meadville-Lombard Theological School) (Co-sponsor: Institute on Religion in an Age of Science)

**University of Chicago. Pritzker School of Medicine**
1025 E. 57th Street, Chicago, IL 60637.
- University of Chicago. Pritzker School of Medicine. Alumni Association. Bulletin. 3 per yr. ISSN 0009-3734

**University of Chicago. Research Center in Economic Development and Cultural Change**
- Economic Development and Cultural Change. (pub. by University of Chicago Press)

**University of Chicago. Vice-President for Public Affairs**
5801 South Ellis Avenue, Chicago, IL 60637.
- University of Chicago Record. irreg., 6-9 per yr. ISSN 0362-4706

**University of Cincinnati**
643 Baldwin Hall, Cincinnati, OH 45221.
- Cooperative Engineer. q.

**University of Cincinnati. College of Law**
Cincinnati, OH 45221.
- Cincinnati Law Review. q. ISSN 0009-6881

**University of Cincinnati. Department of Classics**
Cincinnati, OH 45221.
- Excavations of the University of Cincinnati: Guide Book. irreg. ISSN 0069-410X

**University of Cincinnati. Department of English**
Cincinnati, OH 45221.
- Cincinnati Poetry Review. s-a.

**University of Cincinnati. Department of Romance Languages and Literature**
Cincinnati, OH 45221.
- Estreno; journal on the contemporary Spanish theater. s-a.

**University of Colorado**
Boulder, CO 80309.
- C T R C Newsletter. bi-m. ISSN 0045-7434 (Colorado Technical Reference Center) (Orders to:, 208 Norlin Library)
- Colorado Quarterly. q. ISSN 0010-1710 (Orders to:, Hellems 134)
- East European Quarterly. q. ISSN 0012-8449 (Orders to:, Regent Hall)
- English Language Notes. q. ISSN 0013-8282 (Orders to:, 125 Hellems)

**University of Colorado. Black Studies Program**
Boulder, CO 80309.
- Umoja; journal of black experience. 3 per yr.

**University of Colorado. Bureau of Governmental Research and Service**
125 Ketchum Building, Boulder, CO 80302.
- Colorado Governmental Research Newsletter. s-a.

**University of Colorado. College of Engineering**
Engineering Center OT 1-7, Boulder, CO 80309.
- Colorado Engineer. 4 per yr. ISSN 0010-1583

**University of Colorado Denver Campus**
- Fourth Estate. (pub. by Fourth Estate)

**University of Colorado. Graduate School of Business Administration**
Boulder, CO 80309.
- Colorado Business Review. m. ISSN 0010-1524
- Colorado County and City Retail Sales by Standard Industrial Classification. q. ISSN 0091-4789 (Co-Sponsor: Colorado Retail Council)
- Colorado Ski and Winter Recreation Statistics. a. ISSN 0084-8891
- Directory of Colorado Manufacturers. ISSN 0084-9898
- Journal of Travel Research. q. ISSN 0047-2875 (Travel Research Association)
- Travel Trends in the United States and Canada. irreg., latest edt., 1975.

**University of Colorado. Institute of Arctic and Alpine Research**
c/o Kathleen Salzberg, Ed., Boulder, CO 80309.
- Arctic and Alpine Research. q. ISSN 0004-0851
- University of Colorado. Institute of Arctic and Alpine Research. Occasional Papers. irreg. ISSN 0069-6145

**University of Colorado. Institute of Behavioral Science**
Boulder, CO 80302.
- Human Organization. q. ISSN 0018-7259
- Natural Hazard Research Working Papers. irreg., approx. 5 per year. ISSN 0082-5166

**University of Colorado Libraries**
Boulder, CO 80309.
- Focus on Robert Graves. 2 per yr.
- University of Colorado Libraries. Report. a. ISSN 0069-6161

**University of Colorado Libraries. Interlibrary Loan Service**
Boulder, CO 80302.
- Just B'twx Us; an Interlibrary Loan Service Newsletter. irreg., 1973, vol. 2, no. 4. ISSN 0075-4587

**University of Colorado. Mountain View Center for Environmental Education**
1511 University Ave., Boulder, CO 80302.
- Outlook. q.

**University of Colorado. Norlin Library**
Boulder, CO 80302.
• Norlin Library, University of Colorado.
Occasional Notes. q. ISSN 0048-055X

**University of Colorado. School of Law**
Fleming Law Bldg., Rm. 290, Boulder, CO 80302.
• University of Colorado Law Review. 4 per yr.
ISSN 0041-9516

**University of Colorado. School of Pharmacy**
Boulder, CO 80302.
• Colorado Journal of Pharmacy. q. ISSN 0010-163X

**University of Colorado. Women Studies Program**
Hillside Ct. 104, Boulder, CO 80309.
• Frontiers: a Journal of Women Studies. 3 per vol.

**University of Connecticut. Center for Real Estate & Urban Economic Studies**
Storrs, CT 06268.
• Real Estate Reports. irreg., no. 16, 1974. ISSN 0079-9890
• University of Connecticut. Center for Real Estate and Urban Economic Studies. General Series. irreg. ISSN 0069-9047
• University of Connecticut. Center for Real Estate and Urban Economic Studies. Working Paper. irreg.

**University of Connecticut. College of Agriculture and Natural Resources**
Box U-67, Storrs, CT 06268.
• Connecticut Greenhouse Newsletter. bi-m. (prep. by its Cooperative Extension Service)

**University of Connecticut. Department of History**
Storrs, CT 06268.
• Chinese Republican Studies Newsletter. s-a.

**University of Connecticut. English Department**
• Children's Literature (Storrs) (pub. by Parousia Press)

**University of Connecticut. Institute of Materials Science**
Storrs, CT 06268.
• I M S Bulletin. q. ISSN 0019-0063

**University of Connecticut. Institute of Public Service**
Storrs, CT 06268.
• Conference on Management Analysis in State and Local Government. Papers. irreg. ISSN 0069-8717
• Connecticut Government. q. ISSN 0010-6119
• I P S Local Government Newsletter. m. (Sept-June) ISSN 0045-8139

**University of Connecticut. Institute of Urban Research**
Storrs, CT 06268.
• Connecticut Urban Research Report. irreg., no. 23, 1973. ISSN 0069-9055

**University of Connecticut. Institute of Water Resources**
Storrs, CT 06268.
• University of Connecticut. Institute of Water Resources. Report Series. irreg; no. 26, 1976. ISSN 0069-9063
• University of Connecticut. Institute of Water Resources. Wetlands Conference. Proceedings. a.

**University of Connecticut Library. Special Collections**
c/o Ms. Joanne V. Akeroyd, Storrs, CT 06268.
• Olson; the journal of the Charles Olson Archives. s-a.

**University of Connecticut. School of Social Work**
1800 Asylum Ave., West Hartford, CT 06117.
• Journal of Sociology and Social Welfare. bi-m.

**University of Dallas**
c/o Moses M. Nagy, Univ. of Dallas Station, Irving, TX 75061.
• Claudel Studies. s-a. ISSN 0090-1237 (Co-Sponsor: Cultural Services of the French Embassy)

**University of Dayton**
300 College Park, Dayton, OH 45469.
• Fact-O-Gram. q.
• University of Dayton Review. 3 per yr. ISSN 0041-9524

**University of Dayton. Law School**
300 College Park, Dayton, OH 45469.
• University of Dayton Intramural Law Review. s-a. ISSN 0363-2148

**University of Dayton. School of Education**
Dayton, OH 45469.
• University of Dayton. School of Education. Abstracts of Research Projects. a. ISSN 0070-3044
• University of Dayton. School of Education. Workshop Proceedings. irreg., latest issue, 1971. ISSN 0070-3052

**University of Delaware. College of Agricultural Sciences**
Newark, DE 19711.
• Longwood Program Seminars. a. (Longwood Program)

**University of Delaware. Department of Anthropology**
Newark, DE 19711.
• Liberian Studies Journal. s-a. ISSN 0024-1989

**University of Delaware. Department of Civil Engineering**
John M. Clayton Hall, Newark, DE 19711.
• Mid-Atlantic Industrial Waste Conference Proceedings. irreg. ISSN 0544-0327

**University of Delaware. Water Resources Center**
Newark, DE 19711.
• University of Delaware. Water Resources Center. Annual Report. a.

**University of Denver**
Denver, CO 80210.
• Denver Quarterly; a journal of modern culture. q. ISSN 0011-8869
• University of Denver News. 5 per yr.

**University of Denver. College of Business Administration**
Div. of Research, 2020 S. Race St., Denver, CO 80210.
• University of Denver. College of Business Administration. Occasional Studies. irreg. ISSN 0070-3761
• University of Denver. College of Business Administration. Special Publication. irreg. ISSN 0070-377X

**University of Denver. College of Law**
200 W. 14th Ave., Denver, CO 80204.
• Denver Law Journal. q. ISSN 0011-8834
• Law and Society Newsletter. q. (prep. by its Law and Society Association)

**University of Denver. Denver Research Institute**
Denver, CO 80210.
• Advances in X-Ray Analysis. (pub. by Plenum Press)
• Future Gas Consumption of the United States. biennial. (Future Requirements Agency)

**University of Denver. Department of Chemical Engineering and Metallurgy**
Denver, CO 80210.
• Studies in Restoration of the Environment. irreg., 1971, no. 2. ISSN 0081-8445

**University of Denver. Graduate School of International Studies**
University Park, Denver, CO 80210.
• Monograph Series in World Affairs. 4 per yr. ISSN 0077-0582

**University of Denver. Graduate School of Librarianship**
Publications Dept., Denver, CO 80210.
• Studies in Librarianship. irreg., no. 9, 1973. ISSN 0081-8151

**University of Detroit. School of Dentistry**
Detroit, MI 48207.
• Detroit Mirror and Explorer. irreg. (4nos. per year)

**University of Detroit. School of Law**
651 E. Jefferson Ave., Detroit, MI 48226.
• Journal of Urban Law. 4 per yr. ISSN 0041-9559

**University of Florida**
Gainesville, FL 32601.
• Carleton Newsletter. q.
• Florida Quarterly. 3 per yr. ISSN 0015-4253 (Orders to: 336 Reitz Union)

• Southern Folklore Quarterly. q. ISSN 0038-4127 (Co-Sponsor: South Atlantic Modern Language Assn.) (Orders c/o Roger M. Thompson, Ed., Anderson Hall)

**University of Florida. Center for Latin American Studies**
15 N.W. 15 St., Gainesville, FL 32603.
• Handbook of Latin American Studies: A Selected and Annotated Guide to Recent Publications. a. beginning with no. 36, even numbered volumes cover humanities; odd numbered volumes cover social sciences. ISSN 0072-9833 (Hispanic Foundation)
• Latin American Monographs. (pub. by University Presses of Florida)

**University of Florida. Center for Tropical Agriculture**
2001 McCarty Hall, Gainesville, FL 32611.
• Livestock and Poultry Conference on Latin America. a. ISSN 0085-2805

**University of Florida. College of Business Administration**
Gainesville, FL 32611.
• Building Permit Activity in Florida. m. ISSN 0007-3555 (prep. by its Bureau of Economic and Business Research)
• Business and Economic Dimensions. bi-m. ISSN 0007-6457 (prep. by its Bureau of Economic and Business Research)
• Economic Leaflets. 10 per yr. ISSN 0013-0141 (prep. by its Bureau of Economic and Business Research)
• Florida Statistical Abstract. a. ISSN 0071-6022 (prep. by its Bureau of Economic and Business Research)
• University of Florida. Bureau of Economic and Business Research. Population Studies. 4 per yr. ISSN 0071-6030 (prep. by its Bureau of Economic and Business Research)

**University of Florida. College of Dentistry**
Box 202 MSB, Gainesville, FL 32610.
• Update. 2 per yr.

**University of Florida. College of Education**
Box 2456, Norman Hall, Gainesville, FL 32601.
• New Voices in Education. q.

**University of Florida College of Engineering. Engineering and Industrial Experiment Station**
Gainesville, FL 32601.
• E I E S Research Report. a. ISSN 0091-6668

**University of Florida. College of Law**
Law Center, Gainesville, FL 32611.
• University of Florida Law Review. q. ISSN 0041-9583

**University of Florida. Communication Sciences Laboratory**
Department of Speech, Gainesville, FL 32601.
• University of Florida. Communication Sciences Laboratory. Quarterly Progress Reports. 4 per yr. ISSN 0046-4198

**University of Florida. Department of Accounting**
• University of Florida. Department of Accounting. Accounting Series. (pub. by University Presses of Florida)

**University of Florida. Department of History**
Gainesville, FL 32603.
• University of Florida. Department of History. Lecture Series on American Civilization. irreg. (lecture series is annual but lectures are not always published) ISSN 0071-6073

**University of Florida. Department of Mathematics**
Gainesville, FL 32601.
• Florida Symposium on Automata and Semigroups. irreg., latest issue, 1971. ISSN 0090-1997

**University of Florida. Department of Zoology**
Gainsville, FL 32611.
• Selysia; news letter of odonatology. irreg. ISSN 0080-875X

**University of Florida. Growth Conference**
Gainesville, FL 32611.
• University of Florida. Growth Conference. Prepared Papers. a. ISSN 0094-0801

**University of Florida. Institute of Food and Agricultural Sciences**
Gainesville, FL 32601.
- Cost of Picking and Hauling Florida Citrus Fruits. ISSN 0093-6553 (prep. by its Food and Resource Economics Department)
- Florida Food and Resource Economics. bi-m. (prep. by its Food and Resource Economics Department)
- International Symposium on Canine Heartworm Disease. Proceedings. irreg., 2d, Jacksonville, 1971. (prep. by its Department of Veterinary Science)
- Sunshine State Agricultural Research Report. q. ISSN 0039-5447 (prep. by its Agricultural Experiment Station)
- University of Florida. Food and Resource Economics Department. Economics Report. irreg?
- University of Florida. Institute of Food and Agricultural Sciences. Annual Research Report. a. ISSN 0071-609X

**University of Florida. Library**
Gainesville, FL 32611.
- University of Florida. Libraries. Bibliographic Series. irreg. ISSN 0071-612X
- University of Florida. Libraries. Technical Processes Department. Caribbean Acquisitions. irreg. ISSN 0071-6138

**University of Florida Press**
*see* University Presses of Florida

**University of Florida. Rehabilitation Research Institute**
Box 208, J. Hollis Miller Health Center, Gainesville, FL 32610.
- Directory of Rehabilitation Consultants. irreg. (U. S. Department of Health Education and Welfare)

**University of Florida. School of Forest Resources & Conservation**
Gainesville, FL 32601.
- University of Florida. School of Forest Resources & Conservation. Cooperative Forest Genetics Research Program. Progress Report. irreg.

**University of Florida. University College**
Gainesville, FL 32601.
- University of Florida. University College Series. irreg. ISSN 0071-6170

**University of Georgia**
Athens, GA 30602.
- Georgia Review. q. ISSN 0016-8386

**University of Georgia Alumni Society**
Alumni House, Athens, GA 30601.
- Georgia Alumni Record. 6 per yr. ISSN 0016-8130

**University of Georgia. Anthropology Curriculum Project**
Athens, GA 30602.
- University of Georgia. Anthropology Curriculum Project. Publication. irreg. ISSN 0072-1255

**University of Georgia. Center for Continuing Education**
Athens, GA 30601.
- Georgia Congress of Parents and Teachers. Annual Leadership Training Conference. Workshop for P T A Leaders. a., 52nd edt., 1974.
- Meat Science Institute. Proceedings. a. ISSN 0090-5631 (National Independent Meat Packers Association)
- Southeastern School of Alcohol Studies. Proceedings. irreg., (approx. biennial) 10th edition, 1970. ISSN 0081-2978
- University of Georgia. School of Pharmacy. Pharmaceutical Services for Small Hospitals and Nursing Homes. irreg. ISSN 0072-1344
- University of Georgia. School of Veterinary Medicine. Annual Conference for Veterinarians. a. ISSN 0072-1352

**University of Georgia. College of Agriculture**
208 Barrow Hall, Athens, GA 30602.
- Georgia Agriculturist. q.

**University of Georgia. College of Agriculture Experiment Stations**
Athens, GA 30601.
- Georgia Agricultural Research. q. ISSN 0016-8122
- University of Georgia. College of Agriculture Experiment Stations. Bulletin. irreg. ISSN 0072-1271

- University of Georgia. College of Agriculture Experiment Stations. Research Reports. irreg., 1969, no. 43. ISSN 0072-128X

**University of Georgia. College of Business Administration**
Athens, GA 30602.
- Georgia Business. bi-m. ISSN 0016-8173 (prep. by its Division of Research)
- Georgia Economy Series. irreg., no. 3, 1972. ISSN 0085-1035 (prep. by its Division of Research)
- Georgia Statistical Abstract. biennial. ISSN 0085-1043 (prep. by its Division of Research)
- Georgia Welcome Center. Research Report. irreg. ISSN 0533-8387 (Georgia. Department of Community Development)
- Journal of Business Research. q. (Co-Sponsors: Southern Finance Assn.; Southern Management Assn.; Southern Marketing Assn.) (Orders as of Vol. 5 to: Elsevier North-Holland, Inc. New York, 52 Vanderbilt Ave., New York, NY 10017)
- University of Georgia. College of Business Administration. Research Monograph Series. irreg., 1971, no. 5. ISSN 0085-1051 (prep. by its Division of Research)
- University of Georgia. College of Business Administration. Travel Research Series. irreg.,1973,nos. 1-15. ISSN 0072-1263

**University of Georgia. College of Education**
G-3 Aderhold Bldg., Athens, Atlanta, GA 30602.
- Journal of Research and Development in Education. q. ISSN 0022-426X

**University of Georgia. College of Veterinary Medicine**
- University of Georgia. School of Veterinary Medicine. Annual Conference for Veterinarians. (pub. by University of Georgia. Center for Continuing Education)

**University of Georgia. Environmental Education Materials Center**
Athens, GA 30602.
- Georgia Environmental Education Newsletter. q.

**University of Georgia. Geography Curriculum Project**
Athens, GA 30602.
- University of Georgia. Geography Curriculum Project Publications. irreg., latest issue, 1974. ISSN 0435-5113

**University of Georgia. Georgia Museum of Art**
Athens, GA 30602.
- Georgia Museum of Art Bulletin. q.

**University of Georgia. Graduate School**
Athens, GA 30602.
- University of Georgia. Graduate School. Graduate Report. q. ISSN 0041-9591

**University of Georgia. Institute of Community and Area Development**
300 Old College, Athens, GA 30602.
- University of Georgia. Institute of Community and Area Development. Publications. irreg. ISSN 0072-1298

**University of Georgia. Institute of Ecology**
Athens, GA 30601.
- University of Georgia. Institute of Ecology. Annual Report. a. ISSN 0094-9205

**University of Georgia. Institute of Government**
Terrell Hall, Athens, GA 30602.
- State and Local Government Review. 3 per yr.
- University of Georgia. Institute of Government. Research Papers. irreg.

**University of Georgia Law School Association**
- Georgia Advocate. (pub. by University of Georgia School of Law)

**University of Georgia Libraries**
c/o Rea Christoffersson, Athens, GA 30602.
- G.R.U.B; Georgia review of unusual books. 3 per yr.
- Interface (Athens) m.
- University of Georgia Libraries. Annual Report. a. ISSN 0072-1301
- University of Georgia Libraries. Bibliographies Series. irreg; no. 8, 1976.

**University of Georgia. Marine Institute**
Sapelo Island, GA 31327.
- University of Georgia. Marine Institute. Collected Reprints. irreg., 1970 latest issue. ISSN 0072-1328

**University of Georgia Press**
Athens, GA 30602.
- Lamar Lecture Series. a. ISSN 0075-7772 (Eugenia Dorothy Blount Lamar Lectures at Mercer University, Macon, Georgia)
- Southern Anthropological Society. Proceedings. a. ISSN 0081-2994
- Wormsloe Foundation. Publications. irreg, no. 11 (vol. 3), 1972. ISSN 0084-2621

**University of Georgia School of Law**
Athens, GA 30602.
- Georgia Advocate. 3 per yr. ISSN 0435-5253 (University of Georgia Law School Association)
- Georgia Law Review. q. ISSN 0016-8300 (Georgia Law Review Association Inc)

**University of Georgia. School of Pharmacy**
- University of Georgia. School of Pharmacy. Pharmaceutical Services for Small Hospitals and Nursing Homes. (pub. by University of Georgia. Center for Continuing Education)

**University of Georgia. School of Social Work**
1260-80 S. Lumpkin St., Athens, GA 30601.
- Regional Institute of Social Welfare Research. Annual Report. a. ISSN 0091-2859

**University of Hartford**
200 Bloomfield Ave., W. Hartford, CT 06117.
- Hartford Studies in Literature; a journal of interdisciplinary criticism. 3 per yr. ISSN 0017-7989

**University of Hawaii**
1776 University Ave., Hall 208, Honolulu, HI 96822.
- Asian Perspectives. (pub. by University Press of Hawaii)
- Hawaii Free Peoples Press. q.
- Hawaii Pono Journal. q. ISSN 0046-6956
- Oceanic Linguistics. (pub. by University Press of Hawaii)
- Pacific Science. (pub. by University Press of Hawaii)
- Philosophy East and West. (pub. by University Press of Hawaii)
- Wind Engineering Research Digest. a. (Co-Sponsor: National Science Foundation)

**University of Hawaii. Asian Studies Program**
- Asian Studies at Hawaii Monograph Series. (pub. by University Press of Hawaii)

**University of Hawaii. Board of Publications**
2465 Campus Dr., Honolulu, HI 96822.
- Hawaii Review. s-a. ISSN 0093-9625

**University of Hawaii. College of Education**
1776 University Ave., Honolulu, HI 96822.
- Educational Perspectives. q. ISSN 0013-1849

**University of Hawaii. College of Tropical Agriculture**
Honolulu, HI 96822
(Order Information Available from Publications and Information Office, 2500 Dole St., Univ. of Hawaii, Honolulu, HI 96822)
- Hawaii Farm Science; agricultural progress quarterly. q. ISSN 0046-6948 (prep. by its Hawaii Agricultural Experiment Station)
- Horticulture Digest. 6-8 per yr. ISSN 0046-6964 (prep. by its Cooperative Extension Service)
- University of Hawaii. College of Tropical Agriculture. Cooperative Extension Service. Circular. irreg., no. 486, 1975. ISSN 0073-1161 (prep. by its Cooperative Extension Service)
- University of Hawaii. College of Tropical Agriculture. Cooperative Extension Service Leaflet. irreg., no. 193, 1975. ISSN 0073-117X (prep. by its Cooperative Extension Service)
- University of Hawaii. College of Tropical Agriculture. Cooperative Extension Service. Miscellaneous Publication. irreg., no. 121, 1975. ISSN 0073-1188 (prep. by its Cooperative Extension Service)

**University of Hawaii. Counseling and Testing Center**
2327 Dole St., Honolulu, HI 96822.
- University of Hawaii. Counseling and Testing Center. Report. irreg., 1969, no. 12. ISSN 0073-1196

**University of Hawaii. Department of Electrical Engineering**
- Hawaii International Conference on System Sciences. Proceedings. (pub. by Western Periodicals Co.)

**University of Hawaii. Department of European Languages & Literature**
Moore Hall 470, Honolulu, HI 96822.
- Language and Literature in Hawaii. irreg.
- Mele; international poetry letter. q. ISSN 0025-8954

**University of Hawaii. Graduate School of Library Studies**
Honolulu, HI 96822.
- U S-Japan Library Newsletter. 4 per yr. (American Library Association. Advisory Committee for Liaison with Japanese Libraries)

**University of Hawaii. Hawaii Institute of Geophysics**
535 Ward Ave., Honolulu, HI 96814.
- International Indian Ocean Expedition. Oceanographic Monographs. irreg. ISSN 0074-6347 (Co-sponsor: East-West Center)

**University of Hawaii. Industrial Relations Center**
2404 Maile Way, Honolulu, HI 96822.
- University of Hawaii. Industrial Relations Center. Occasional Publications. irreg., no. 107, 1975. ISSN 0073-1226

**University of Hawaii Library**
Hawaiian and Pacific Collection, 2550 the Mall, Honolulu, HI 96822.
- Current Hawaiiana; a quarterly bibliography. q. ISSN 0011-3522

**University of Hawaii. Office of University Relations and Development**
2444 Dole St., Honolulu, HI 96822.
- Green Sheet; University of Hawaii newsletter. 9 per yr. ISSN 0046-6409

**University of Hawaii. Sea Grant College Program**
2540 Maile Way, Spalding 253, Honolulu, HI 96822.
- Hawaii. University, Honolulu. Sea Grant College Program. Sea Grant Newsletter. m.

**University of Hawaii. Social Sciences and Linguistics Institute**
- Oceanic Linguistics. Special Publications. (pub. by University Press of Hawaii)

**University of Hawaii. Southeast Asian Studies Program**
Honolulu, HI 96844.
- Southeast Asia Working Papers. 1-2 per yr.

**University of Hawaii. Water Resources Research Center**
2540 Dole St., Honolulu, HI 96822.
- University of Hawaii. Water Resources Research Center. Collected Reprints. biennial. ISSN 0073-1293
- University of Hawaii. Water Resources Research Center. Technical Report. irreg. ISSN 0073-1307

**University of Houston. College of Law**
- Houston Law Review. (pub. by Houston Law Review Inc.)

**University of Houston. Department of English**
Cullen Blvd., Houston, TX 77004.
- Harvest. a. ISSN 0073-0866
- Hippocrene. a. ISSN 0085-1531

**University of Houston. Department of Mathematics**
3801 Cullen Blvd., Houston, TX 77004.
- Houston Journal of Mathematics. q.

**University of Houston. Friends of the Library**
Houston, TX 77004.
- Aldus. s-a. ISSN 0002-5119

**University of Houston. Graduate School and University Libraries**
Houston, TX 77004.
- University of Houston. Graduate School. Bibliography of Theses and Dissertations. irreg., 1970, 4th edition. ISSN 0073-3695

**University of Houston. University News Service and Office of Development**
3801 Cullen Blvd., Houston, TX 77004.
- Forum (Houston) 3 per yr. ISSN 0015-8410

**University of Idaho. Center for Business Development and Research**
Moscow, ID 83843.
- Idaho Business and Economic Review. s-a. ISSN 0019-1167

- Idaho Statistical Abstract. irreg.(approx. every 5 years) ISSN 0073-456X

**University of Idaho. College of Forestry, Wildlife and Range Sciences**
Moscow, ID 83843.
- Focus on Natural Renewable Resources. a.
- University of Idaho Library Additions. irreg.

**University of Idaho. College of Law**
Moscow, ID 83843.
- Idaho Law Review. s-a. ISSN 0019-1205

**University of Idaho. Cooperative Extension Service**
Moscow, ID 83843.
- Idaho Woodland Farmer. irreg. ISSN 0019-1256

**University of Idaho. Department of Entomology**
Moscow, ID 83843.
- Aldrich Entomology Club. Newsletter. irreg., 1972, vol. 10. ISSN 0065-6143

**University of Idaho. Department of Sociology-Anthropology**
Moscow, ID 83843.
- Northwest Anthropological Research Notes. s-a. ISSN 0029-3296
- University of Idaho. Department of Sociology/Anthropology. Anthropological Monographs. a.

**University of Idaho. Forest, Wildlife and Range Experiment Station**
Moscow, ID 83843.
- University of Idaho. Forest, Wildlife and Range Experiment Station, Moscow. Station Bulletin. irreg. ISSN 0073-4586
- University of Idaho. Forest, Wildlife and Range Experiment Station, Moscow. Station Note. irreg., 1970, no. 15. ISSN 0073-4594
- University of Idaho. Forest, Wildlife and Range Experiment Station, Moscow. Station Paper. irreg., 1970, no. 6. ISSN 0073-4608

**University of Idaho. Water Resources Research Institute**
Moscow, ID 83843.
- University of Idaho. Water Resources Research Institute. Annual Report. a. ISSN 0073-4616

**University of Illinois at Chicago Circle**
c/o Ed. F. P. Scioli, Jr., Chicago Circle, Chicago, IL 60680.
- Experimental Study of Politics. 3 per yr. ISSN 0046-2926

**University of Illinois at Chicago Circle. College of Urban Sciences**
P.O. Box 4348, Chicago, IL 60680.
- University of Illinois at Chicago Circle. College of Urban Sciences. Occasional Paper Series. irreg.

**University of Illinois at Urbana-Champaign**
- American Journal of Psychology. (pub. by University of Illinois Press)
- Illinois Journal of Mathematics. (pub. by University of Illinois Press)
- Journal of Aesthetic Education. (pub. by University of Illinois Press)
- Journal of English and Germanic Philology. (pub. by University of Illinois Press)
- Midwest Monographs. Series 1 (Drama) (pub. by Depot Press)
- Midwest Monographs. Series 2 (Poetry) (pub. by Depot Press)
- Midwest Monographs. Series 3 (Graphic Works) (pub. by Depot Press)
- Midwest Monographs. Series 4 (Translation) (pub. by Depot Press)
- Midwest Monographs. Series 5 (Culture and Criticism) (pub. by Depot Press)

**University of Illinois at Urbana- Champaign. Agricultural Experiment Station**
Urbana, IL 61801.
- Illinois Research. q. ISSN 0019-2201
- University of Illinois at Urbana-Champaign. Agricultural Experiment Station. Special Publication. irreg., no. 32, 1974. ISSN 0073-473X

**University of Illinois at Urbana-Champaign. Alumni Association**
University of Illinois, 227 Illini Union, Urbana, IL 61801.
- Illinois Alumni News. 8 per yr. ISSN 0019-1841

**University of Illinois at Urbana-Champaign. Bureau of Institutional Research**
409 E. Chalmers St., Champaign, IL 61820.
- Enrollment in Institutions of Higher Learning in Illinois. a.

**University of Illinois at Urbana-Champaign. Bureau of Urban and Regional Planning Research**
909 West Nevada, Urbana, IL 61801.
- Planning and Public Policy. q.

**University of Illinois at Urbana-Champaign. Center for Advanced Computation**
Dept. of Computer Science, Urbana, IL 61801.
- C.A.C. Document. irreg. ISSN 0360-1617

**University of Illinois at Urbana-Champaign. Center for International Education and Research in Accounting**
320 Commerce West, Urbana, IL 61801.
- International Journal of Accounting Education and Research. s-a. ISSN 0020-7063
- University of Illinois at Urbana-Champaign. Center for International Education and Research in Accounting. Monograph. irreg. ISSN 0073-5191

**University of Illinois at Urbana-Champaign. Classics Department**
- Illinois Classical Studies. (pub. by University of Illinois Press)

**University of Illinois at Urbana-Champaign. College of Agriculture**
Office of Agricultural Communications, Urbana, IL 61801.
- University of Illinois at Urbana-Champaign. College of Agriculture. Agricultural Communications Research Report. irreg. ISSN 0073-5299
- University of Illinois at Urbana-Champaign. College of Agriculture. Current Affairs. bi-m. ISSN 0011-3174
- University of Illinois at Urbana-Champaign. College of Agriculture. Special Publication. irreg; no. 46, 1977. ISSN 0073-5205

**University of Illinois at Urbana-Champaign. College of Commerce and Business Administration**
408 David Kinley Hall, Urbana, IL 61801.
- Illinois Business Review. m. ISSN 0019-1922 (prep. by its Bureau of Economic and Business Research)
- Quarterly Review of Economics and Business. q. (prep. by its Bureau of Economic and Business Research)

**University of Illinois at Urbana-Champaign. College of Education**
140 Education Bldg., Urbana, IL 61801.
- Illinois Education Review.

**University of Illinois at Urbana-Champaign. College of Law**
Champaign, IL 61820.
- University of Illinois Law Forum. q. ISSN 0041-963X

**University of Illinois at Urbana-Champaign. Computing Services Office**
Urbana, IL 61801.
- Off-Line. bi-w.

**University of Illinois at Urbana-Champaign. Cooperative Extension Service**
Urbana, IL 61801.
- Economic Questions for Illinois Agriculture. irreg., 1971, EQ-5. ISSN 0070-8615

**University of Illinois at Urbana-Champaign. Department of Agricultural Economics**
Urbana, IL 61801.
- Illinois Agricultural Economics. s-a. ISSN 0019-1833
- University of Illinois at Urbana-Champaign. Department of Agricultural Economics. Agricultural Finance Program Report. irreg. ISSN 0073-5213
- University of Illinois at Urbana-Champaign. Department of Agricultural Economics. Landlord and Tenant Shares. a.
- University of Illinois at Urbana-Champaign. Department of Agricultural Economics. Research Report. irreg. ISSN 0073-523X

University of Illinois at Urbana-Champaign.
**Department of Anthropology**
109 Devenport Hall, Urbana, IL 61801.
- University of Illinois at Urbana-Champaign. Department of Anthropology. Research Reports. irreg. ISSN 0073-5248

University of Illinois at Urbana-Champaign.
**Department of Art**
Fine and Applied Arts Bldg., Champaign, IL 61820.
- University of Illinois at Urbana-Champaign. Department of Art. Newsletter. a. or biennial. ISSN 0073-5256

University of Illinois at Urbana-Champaign.
**Department of Civil Engineering**
Engineering Documents Center, Urbana, IL 61801.
- University of Illinois at Urbana-Champaign. Civil Engineering Studies. Construction Research. irreg, no. 17, 1973. ISSN 0069-4266
- University of Illinois at Urbana-Champaign. Civil Engineering Studies. Structural Research Series. irreg. ISSN 0069-4274

University of Illinois at Urbana-Champaign.
**Department of Comparative Literature**
2054 Foreign Language Bldg., Urbana, IL 61801.
- Comparative Literature Studies. q. ISSN 0010-4132

University of Illinois at Urbana-Champaign.
**Department of Electrical Engineering**
Urbana, IL 61801.
- Annual Allerton Conference on Circuit and System Theory. a.
- Incremental Motion Control Systems and Devices Newsletter. s-a. (Co-sponsor: Warner Electric Brake & Clutch Co.)
- Symposium on Incremental Motion Control Systems and Devices. Proceedings. a. ISSN 0092-1661 (Co-Sponsors: Warner Electric Brake & Clutch Co., (U.S.); Westool Ltd., (England))
- University of Illinois at Urbana-Champaign. Department of Electrical Engineering. Aeronomy Laboratory. Aeronomy Report. irreg. ISSN 0568-0581

University of Illinois at Urbana-Champaign.
**Department of Linguistics**
Urbana, IL 61801.
- University of Illinois. Department of Linguistics. Working Papers. s-a. ISSN 0049-2388

University of Illinois at Urbana-Champaign.
**Department of Theoretical and Applied Mechanics**
212 Talbot Laboratory, Urbana, IL 61801.
- T & A M Report. irreg; no. 413, 1976. ISSN 0073-5264
- University of Illinois at Urbana-Champaign. Student Symposium on Engineer Mechanics. a.

University of Illinois at Urbana-Champaign. **Division of Home Economics Education**
351 Education Bldg., Urbana, IL 61801.
- Illinois Teacher of Home Economics. q. ISSN 0536-5139

University of Illinois at Urbana-Champaign.
**Engineering Experiment Station**
112 Engineering Hall, Urbana, IL 61801.
- University of Illinois at Urbana - Champaign. College of Engineering. Bulletin Series. irreg. (2-5 per yr.)
- University of Illinois at Urbana - Champaign. Engineering Experiment Station. Bulletin. irreg., 1970, no. 505. ISSN 0073-5272
- University of Illinois at Urbana-Champaign. Engineering Experiment Station. Summary of Engineering Research. a. ISSN 0073-5280

University of Illinois at Urbana-Champaign.
**Engineering Publications Office**
112 Engineering Hall, Urbana, IL 61801.
- Engineering Outlook at the University of Illinois at Urbana-Champaign. m. ISSN 0013-8088
- Public Water Supply Engineers Conference (Proceedings) a.

University of Illinois at Urbana-Champaign. **English Department**
Urbana, IL 61801.
- Ascent. 3 per yr. ISSN 0098-9363

University of Illinois at Urbana-Champaign. **Eta Kappa Nu Association**
c/o Dept. of Electrical Engineering, Urbana, IL 61801.
- Bridge of Eta Kappa Nu. q. ISSN 0006-9809

University of Illinois at Urbana-Champaign. **Graduate School of Library Science**
249 Armory Bldg., Champaign, IL 61801
- Library Trends. q. ISSN 0024-2594 (Subscr. to: University of Illinois Press, Urbana, IL 61801)
- Phineas L. Windsor Lecture in Librarianship. (pub. by University of Illinois Press)
- University of Illinois at Urbana-Champaign. Clinic on Library Applications of Data Processing. Proceedings. a. ISSN 0069-4789
- University of Illinois at Urbana-Champaign. Graduate School of Library Science. Allerton Park Institute. Papers. a. ISSN 0536-4604
- University of Illinois at Urbana-Champaign. Graduate School of Library Science. Library Research Center. Annual Report. a. ISSN 0073-5361
- University of Illinois at Urbana-Champaign. Graduate School of Library Science. Monograph Series. irreg. ISSN 0073-5302
- University of Illinois at Urbana-Champaign. Graduate School of Library Science. Occasional Papers. irreg; nos. 127-131, 1977. ISSN 0073-5310

University of Illinois at Urbana-Champaign. **Institute of Aviation**
318 Civil Engineering Bldg., Urbana, IL 61803.
- Aeronautics Bulletin. irreg. ISSN 0065-3705

University of Illinois at Urbana-Champaign. **Institute of Government & Public Affairs**
1201 W. Nevada St., Urbana, IL 61801.
- Illinois Government Research. irreg., no. 38, 1975.

University of Illinois at Urbana-Champaign. **Institute of Labor and Industrial Relations**
504 E. Armory Ave., Champaign, IL 61820.
- University of Illinois at Urbana-Champaign. Institute of Labor and Industrial Relations. Reprint Series. irreg. ISSN 0073-5353

University of Illinois at Urbana- Champaign **Library Friends**
Publication Office of the University of Illinois, Graduate School of Library Science, 249 Armory, Urbana-Champaign, IL 61820.
- Non Solus. a. ISSN 0094-8977

University of Illinois at Urbana-Champaign. **Office of Instructional Resources**
307 Engineering Hall, Urbana, IL 61801.
- University of Illinois at Urbana-Champaign. Office of Instructional Resources. Measurement and Research Division. Research Report. irreg. ISSN 0073-5388

University of Illinois at Urbana-Champaign. **School of Music**
Urbana, IL 61801.
- Council for Research in Music Education. Bulletin. q. ISSN 0010-9894

University of Illinois at Urbana-Champaign. **Small Homes Council - Building Research Council**
1 E. St. Mary's Rd., Champaign, IL 61820.
- University of Illinois. Small Homes Council. Building Research Council. Circulars. irreg. ISSN 0073-5396
- University of Illinois. Small Homes Council. Building Research Council. Research Report. irreg. ISSN 0073-540X
- University of Illinois. Small Homes Council. Building Research Council. Technical Notes. irreg., no. 11, 1975. ISSN 0073-5426

University of Illinois at Urbana-Champaign. **Visual Aids Service**
1325 S. Oak St., Champaign, IL 61820.
- Lens and Speaker. s-a. ISSN 0459-0953

University of Illinois at Urbana-Champaign. **Water Resources Center**
Urbana, IL 61801.
- University of Illinois at Urbana-Champaign. Water Resources Center. Annual Report. a. ISSN 0073-5434
- University of Illinois at Urbana-Champaign. Water Resources Center. Research Report. irreg. ISSN 0073-5442

University of Illinois Press
Urbana, IL 61801.
- American Journal of Psychology. q. ISSN 0002-9556 (University of Illinois at Urbana-Champaign)
- Blacks in the New World. irreg.
- Illinois Biological Monographs. irreg. ISSN 0073-4748

- Illinois Classical Studies. irreg. (University of Illinois at Urbana-Champaign. Classics Department)
- Illinois Journal of Mathematics. q. ISSN 0019-2082 (University of Illinois at Urbana-Champaign)
- Illinois Studies in Anthropology. irreg. ISSN 0073-5167
- Illinois Studies in Language and Literature. irreg. ISSN 0073-5175
- Illinois Studies in the Social Sciences. irreg. ISSN 0073-5183
- Journal of Aesthetic Education. q. ISSN 0021-8510 (University of Illinois at Urbana-Champaign)
- Journal of English and Germanic Philology. q. ISSN 0022-0868 (University of Illinois at Urbana-Champaign)
- National Party Platforms. Supplement. irreg., 5th edt., 1973. ISSN 0077-5282
- Phineas L. Windsor Lecture in Librarianship. irreg. ISSN 0079-1768 (University of Illinois at Urbana-Champaign. Graduate School of Library Science)

University of Indiana. **Department of Geography**
Bloomington, IN 47401.
- University of Indiana. Department of Geography. Occasional Publication. irreg. ISSN 0073-6961

University of Iowa
Dept. of Publications, Iowa City, IA 52242.
- Iowa Publications in Philosophy. (pub. by Martinus Nijhoff NE)
- Iowa State Archaeologist. Report. irreg., 1972, no. 5. ISSN 0085-2252
- Philological Quarterly; devoted to scholarly investigation of the classical and modern languages and literatures. q. ISSN 0031-7977

University of Iowa. **Associated Students of Engineering**
Iowa City, IA 52242.
- Hawkeye Engineer. m.(Sept-May)

University of Iowa. **College of Business Administration**
Center for Labor and Management, Phillips Hall, Iowa City, IA 52240.
- University of Iowa. Center for Labor and Management. Research Series. irreg. ISSN 0578-6371

University of Iowa **College of Dentistry**
Iowa City, IA 52240.
- Iowa Dental Bulletin. s-a. ISSN 0021-048X

University of Iowa. **College of Law**
Iowa City, IA 52240.
- Iowa Advocate. irreg. ISSN 0578-6533 (Co-Sponsor: Iowa Law School Foundation)
- Iowa Law Review. 5 per yr. ISSN 0021-0552
- Journal of Corporation Law. 3 per yr.

University of Iowa. **Comparative Legislative Research Center**
304 Schaeffer Hall, Iowa City, IA 52242.
- Legislative Studies Quarterly. q.

University of Iowa. **Department of Botany**
Iowa City, IA 52240.
- University of Iowa Studies in Natural History. irreg. ISSN 0041-9656

University of Iowa. **Graduate Program in Hospital and Health Administration**
Iowa City, IA 52241.
- University of Iowa. Graduate Program in Hospital and Health Administration. Health Research Series. irreg., 1973, no. 20. ISSN 0073-1439

University of Iowa. **Institute of Public Affairs**
Iowa City, IA 52242.
- Horizons in Personnel Development. 2 per yr (approx)

University of Iowa. **Laboratory for Political Research**
Iowa City, IA 52242.
- S S Data: Newsletter of Social Science Archival Acquisitions. q.

University of Iowa. **Libraries**
Iowa City, IA 52242.
- Iowa Documents. q. ISSN 0444-4566 (prep. by its Government Publications Department)
- University of Iowa. Libraries. Newsletter. 3 per yr. ISSN 0047-1402 (Friends of the University of Iowa Libraries)

**University of Iowa, Lindquist Center for Measurement**
Iowa City, IA 52240.
- Journal of Educational Statistics. q. (American Educational Research Association) (Co-sponsor: American Statistical Association)

**University of Iowa. Museum of Art**
Iowa City, IA 52242.
- University of Iowa. Museum of Art. Bulletin. q.

**University of Iowa Press**
Iowa City, IA 52242.
- Studies in Natural History. irreg. ISSN 0081-8283

**University of Iowa. Russian Department**
Gilmore Hall, Iowa City, IA 52242.
- Forum at Iowa on Russian Literature. s-a.

**University of Iowa. School of Letters**
Iowa City, IA 52242.
- Iowa Review. q. ISSN 0021-065X

**University of Iowa. School of Library Science**
Iowa City, IA 52242.
- University of Iowa. School of Library Science. Newsletter. a. ISSN 0041-9648

**University of Iowa. School of Social Work**
Iowa City, IA 52242.
- Iowa Journal of Social Work. q. ISSN 0021-0536

**University of Kansas**
Lawrence, KS 66045.
- Esprit Createur. (pub. by Esprit Createur)
- University of Kansas. Paleontological Contributions. Articles. irreg. ISSN 0075-5044
- University of Kansas. Paleontological Contributions. Papers. irreg., no. 72, 1974. ISSN 0075-5052
- University of Kansas Publications. Humanistic Studies. irreg., (approx. a.) ISSN 0085-2473

**University of Kansas. American Studies Department**
Lawrence, KS 66045.
- American Studies. s-a. ISSN 0026-3079 (Midcontinent American Studies Association)

**University of Kansas. Center for East Asian Studies**
106 Strong Hall, Lawrence, KS 66045
- University of Kansas. Center for East Asian Studies. International Studies: East Asian Series. Reference Series. irreg., no. 2, 1975. ISSN 0070-8070 (Dist. by: Paragon Book Gallery, Ltd., 14 E. 38th St., New York, NY 10016)
- University of Kansas. Center for East Asian Studies. International Studies: East Asian Series. Research Series. irreg., no. 8, 1976. ISSN 0070-8062 (Dist. by: Paragon Book Gallery, Ltd., 14 E. 38th St., New York, NY 10016)

**University of Kansas, Center for Latin American Studies**
106 Strong Hall, Lawrence, KS 66044.
- Latin American Theatre Review; a journal devoted to the theatre and drama of Spanish & Portuguese America. s-a. ISSN 0023-8813
- University of Kansas. Center for Latin American Studies. Graduate Studies on Latin America. irreg. ISSN 0075-4986

**University of Kansas College of Health Sciences and Hospital**
Kansas City, KS 66103.
- University of Kansas College of Health Sciences and Hospital. Bulletin. bi-m.

**University of Kansas. Department of Anthropology**
Lawrence, KS 66045.
- University of Kansas. Department of Anthropology. Publications in Anthropology. irreg., 1973, no. 4. ISSN 0085-2457

**University of Kansas. Department of Geology**
Lawrence, KS 66044.
- University of Kansas. Department of Geology. Special Publications. irreg., 1970, no. 4. ISSN 0075-4994

**University of Kansas. Department of Philosophy**
Lawrence, KS 66045.
- Lindley Lecture. a. ISSN 0075-9554

**University of Kansas. Department of Sociology**
Lawrence, KS 66045.
- Mid-American Review of Sociology. s-a.

**University of Kansas Libraries**
Lawrence, KS 66045.
- University of Kansas Libraries. Library Series. irreg. ISSN 0075-5001

**University of Kansas Libraries. Director of Libraries**
Lawrence, KS 66045.
- Books and Libraries at the University of Kansas. irreg., approx. 3 per yr. ISSN 0006-7458

**University of Kansas. Library Exchange & Gift Section**
Lawrence, KS 66044.
- Kansas University Science Bulletin. irreg. ISSN 0022-8850

**University of Kansas. Linguistics Department**
Lawrence, KS 66045.
- Kansas Linguistics Conference. Papers. irreg., 1971, 5th ed. ISSN 0075-4919

**University of Kansas. Museum of Art**
Lawrence, KS 66044.
- University of Kansas. Museum of Art. Miscellaneous Publications. irreg., no. 98, 1975. ISSN 0075-501X
- University of Kansas. Museum of Art. Register. (pub. by University of Kansas Press)

**University of Kansas. Museum of Natural History**
Lawrence, KS 66045.
- University of Kansas. Museum of Natural History. Miscellaneous Publications. irreg; latest no. 64, 1976. ISSN 0075-5028
- University of Kansas. Museum of Natural History. Monographs. irreg.; latest no. 5, 1976. ISSN 0085-2465
- University of Kansas. Museum of Natural History. Occasional Papers. irreg.; latest no. 66, 1977.
- University of Kansas. Museum of Natural History. Publications. irreg.

**University of Kansas. National Sculpture Center**
Lawrence, KS 66045.
- National/International Sculpture Conference. Proceedings. biennial. ISSN 0363-5937

**University of Kansas News Bureau**
Lawrence, KS 66045.
- University of Kansas Newsletter. w during school year. ISSN 0041-9680

**University of Kansas Press**
Lawrence, KS 66045.
- University of Kansas. Museum of Art. Register. s-a. ISSN 0041-9672 (University of Kansas. Museum of Art)

**University of Kansas. School of Engineering**
215 Learned Hall, Lawrence, KS 66045.
- Kansas Engineer. 4 per yr. ISSN 0022-8559

**University of Kansas. School of Law**
Rm. 5, Green Hall, Lawrence, KS 66045.
- Kansas Law Review. q. ISSN 0449-8429

**University of Kansas. School of Social Welfare**
Lawrence, KS 66045.
- Journal of Social Welfare. 3 per yr. ISSN 0094-3495

**University of Kansas Southwest Center**
222 Fulton Terrace, P.O. Box 653, Garden City, KS 67846.
- Kansas Oil Lifting Short Course Selected Papers. biennial (approx.) (Co-sponsor: Petroleum Industry Educational Steering Committee of the Southwest)

**University of Kentucky**
1139 Office Tower, Lexington, KY 40506.
- Kentucky Romance Quarterly. q. ISSN 0023-0332

**University of Kentucky. College of Agriculture**
Lexington, KY 40506.
- Kentucky Agri-Business Spotlight. m. (prep. by its Cooperative Extension Service)

**University of Kentucky. College of Business and Economics**
Lexington, KY 40506.
- Growth and Change; a journal of regional development. q. ISSN 0017-4815
- Kentucky Council of Economic Advisors. Quarterly Report. q. (Kentucky Council of Economic Advisors)

**University of Kentucky, College of Business and Economics. Center for Public Affairs**
409 Commerce Bldg., Lexington, KY 40506.
- Public Affairs Analyst. q.

**University of Kentucky. College of Engineering**
Lexington, KY 40506.
- Carnahan Conference on Electronic Crime Countermeasures. Proceedings. irreg. (prep. by its Office of Research and Engineering Services)

**University of Kentucky. College of Law**
Lexington, KY 40506.
- Kentucky Law Journal. 4 per yr. ISSN 0023-026X

**University of Kentucky. College of Library Science**
Lexington, KY 40506.
- Continuing Education in Librarianship. irreg. (prep. by its Office for Continuing Education)

**University of Kentucky. Department of Germanic and Classical Languages**
- Colloquia Germanica. (pub. by Francke Verlag SZ)

**University of Kentucky Libraries. Government Publications Department**
Lexington, KY 40506.
- Kentucky; monthly checklist of Kentucky state publications. m. ISSN 0091-5653

**University of Kentucky. Office of Development Services and Business Research**
College of Business and Economics, Lexington, KY 40506.
- Kentucky Personal Income. irreg, latest issue no. 3 (includes income studies: 1971-1972) ISSN 0075-5532

**University of Kentucky Press**
Lexington, KY 45506.
- Review of Allied Health Education. irreg. ISSN 0095-7224

**University of Kentucky. Research Foundation**
Lexington, KY 40506.
- University of Kentucky Research Foundation. Annual Report. a. ISSN 0566-8719

**University of Kentucky. Southeast Community College**
Cumberland, KY 40823.
- Southeasterner. s-m. ISSN 0038-3716

**University of Louisville**
Louisville, KY 40208.
- Perspective of Contemporary Literature. s-a. ISSN 0098-7301

**University of Louisville. Library Associates**
University of Louisville Library, Louisville, KY 40208.
- Library Review. s-a. ISSN 0041-9788

**University of Louisville. Office of Academic Publications**
Louisville, KY 40208.
- Dickens Studies Newsletter. q. ISSN 0012-2432

**University of Louisville. Perceptual Alternatives Laboratory**
Louisville, KY 40208.
- University of Louisville. Perceptual Alternatives Laboratory. Newsletter. bi-m.

**University of Louisville School of Law**
Louisville, KY 40208.
- Journal of Family Law. q. ISSN 0022-1066

**University of Louisville. Speed Scientific School**
Director of Professional Development, Louisville, KY 40208.
- University of Louisville. Speed Scientific School. Environmental Engineering and Science Conference. Proceedings. a.

**University of Louisville. Water Resources Laboratory**
Louisville, KY 40208.
- Kentucky Academy of Science. Transactions. s-a. ISSN 0023-0081

**University of Maine at Orono**
265 Stevens Hall, Orono, ME 04473.
- Maine Review. s-a.

**University of Maine at Orono. Cooperative Extension Service**
105 Nutting Hall, Orono, ME 04473.
- Maine Cooperative Extension Service. Forestry Facts. q. (Co-Sponsor: United States Department of Agriculture)

**University of Maine at Orono Press**
225 Stevens Hall, Univ. of Maine, Orono, ME 04473.
- Paideuma; a journal devoted to Ezra Pound scholarship. 3 per yr. ISSN 0090-5674 (National Poetry Foundation, Inc.)

**University of Maine at Portland-Gorham**
246 Deering Ave., Portland, ME 04102.
- Maine Law Review. s-a. ISSN 0025-0651
- Presumpscot. s-a.

**University of Maryland**
Rm 241, Center of Adult Education, College Park, MD 20742.
- Maryland. q.

**University of Maryland. Agronomy Department**
Rm 1129, H. J. Patterson Hall, College Park, MD 20742.
- Agronomist. m. ISSN 0044-6874

**University of Maryland. Baltimore College of Dental Surgery**
Baltimore, MD 21201.
- Baltimore College of Dental Surgery, Journal. irreg. ISSN 0067-3072

**University of Maryland. Center for Environmental and Estuarine Studies**
Solomons, MD 20688.
- Chesapeake Science; a regional journal of research and progress on natural resources. q. ISSN 0009-3262 (prep. by its Chesapeake Biological Laboratory)

**University of Maryland. College of Library and Information Services**
College Park, MD 20742.
- University of Maryland. College of Library and Information Services. Conference Proceedings. irreg. ISSN 0076-4833
- University of Maryland. College of Library and Information Services. Student Contribution Series. irreg., no. 8, 1976. ISSN 0076-4841

**University of Maryland. Department of Chemistry**
College Park, MD 20742.
- Regional Educators Annual Chemistry Teaching Symposium. REACTS; Proceedings. a. ISSN 0080-0597

**University of Maryland. Department of English**
College Park, MD 20740.
- Resources for American Literary Study. s-a. ISSN 0048-7384 (Co-Sponsor: Virginia Commonwealth University)

**University of Maryland. Department of Zoology**
College Park, MD 20742.
- Index Catalogue to Russian, Central & Eastern European, & Chinese Literature in Medical Entomology. irreg. ISSN 0019-381X

**University of Maryland. History Department**
College Park, MD 20742.
- Maryland Historian. s-a. ISSN 0025-424X

**University of Maryland. Institute for Fluid Dynamics and Applied Mathematics**
College Park, MD 20742.
- University of Maryland. Institute for Fluid Dynamics and Applied Mathematics. Public Lecture Series. irreg., no. 52, 1973. ISSN 0076-4825

**University of Maryland. Natural Resources Institute**
Solomons, MD 20688.
- University of Maryland. Natural Resources Institute. N. R. I. Special Report. irreg. ISSN 0090-9750

**University of Maryland School of Law**
500 W. Baltimore St., Baltimore, MD 21201.
- Maryland Law Review. q. ISSN 0025-4282

**University of Maryland School of Law. Student Bar Association**
500 West Baltimore St., Baltimore, MD 21201.
- Maryland Law Forum. 3 times during a semester.

**University of Maryland. School of Medicine**
31 S. Green St., Baltimore, MD 21201.
- Maryland University School of Medicine Bulletin. q. ISSN 0025-438X (prep. by its Faculty of Medicine and Medical Alumni Association)

**University of Massachusetts**
R.S.O. No. 102, Campus Center, Amherst, MA 01002.
- Spectrum. s-a. ISSN 0038-7061

**University of Massachusetts**
Amherst, MA 01003.
- Polity. q. ISSN 0032-3497 (Northeastern Political Science Association)

**University of Massachusetts. Agricultural Experiment Station**
Room 217, Stockbridge Hall, Amherst, MA 01002.
- Findings. bi-m.

**University of Massachusetts. Bureau of Government Research**
Amherst, MA 01002.
- Bureau of Government Research Bulletin. q. ISSN 0007-6163

**University of Massachusetts. Daily Collegian Publishing Board**
Student Union Bldg., Amherst, MA 01002.
- Massachusetts Daily Collegian. d. ISSN 0025-4797

**University of Massachusetts. Department of Anthropology**
Amherst, MA 01002.
- University of Massachusetts. Department of Anthropology. Research Reports. irreg., no. 13, 1973. ISSN 0076-5066

**University of Massachusetts. Department of Classics**
Amherst, MA 01003.
- New England Classical Newsletter. q. (Classical Association of New England)

**University of Massachusetts. Department of English**
Amherst, MA 01002.
- English Literary Renaissance. 3 per yr. ISSN 0013-8312
- Massachusetts Studies in English. s-a. ISSN 0047-6161
- Spenser Newsletter. 3 per yr. ISSN 0038-7347 (Co-Sponsor: Holyoke Community College)

**University of Massachusetts. Division of Resource Management**
c/o Mary Templeton, Morgantown, WV 26506.
- Northeastern Agricultural Economics Council. Journal. s-a.

**University of Massachusetts. Fine Arts Council**
125 Herter Hall, Amherst, MA 01002.
- University of Massachusetts. Art Acquisitions. a.

**University of Massachusetts. Labor Relations and Research Center**
Amherst, MA 01002.
- Industrial Relations Chronologies. a.

**University of Massachusetts. School of Business Administration**
Business Publication Services, Rm. 357, Amherst, MA 01002.
- Management Research. bi-m.
- Massachusetts Business and Economic Report. q. (prep. by its Center for Business and Economic Research)

**University of Massachusetts. School of Engineering**
Amherst, MA 01002.
- University of Massachusetts. School of Engineering. Annual Report. a. ISSN 0542-9307

**University of Massachusetts. Seminar on the Acquisition of Latin American Library Materials**
Amherst, MA 01002.
- Seminar on the Acquisition of Latin American Library Materials. Resolutions and Lists of Commitees. irreg. ISSN 0361-9966

**University of Miami. Center for Advanced International Studies**
- Journal of Interamerican Studies and World Affairs. (pub. by Sage Publications, Inc.)

**University of Miami. Center for Theoretical Studies**
Box 249055, Coral Gables, FL 33124.
- Coral Gables Conference on Fundamental Interactions at High Energy. (Proceedings) (pub. by Gordon and Breach Science Publishers)
- Studies in the Natural Sciences. (pub. by Plenum Press)
- University of Miami. Center for Theoretical Studies. Quarterly Bulletin. q.

**University of Miami. Clean Energy Research Institute**
Coral Gables, FL 33124.
- Ocean Thermal Energy Conversion Workshop. Workshop Proceedings. irreg.

**University of Miami. Law Center**
- University of Miami, Coral Gables. Law Center. Annual Institute on Estate Planning. (pub. by Matthew Bender & Co., Inc.)

**University of Miami Library**
Box 8214, Coral Gables, FL 33124.
- Carrell. a. since 1974. ISSN 0008-6894 (Friends of the University of Miami Library)

**University of Miami. School of Law**
Box 8087, Coral Gables, FL 33124.
- Lawyer of the Americas. 3 per yr. ISSN 0023-9445 (Co-Sponsor: Inter-American Bar Association)
- Studies in Inter-American Laws. irreg. ISSN 0585-6795 (Institute for Inter-American Legal Studies)
- University of Miami Law Review. q. ISSN 0041-9818

**University of Michigan**
2001 North University Bldg., Ann Arbor, MI 48104.
- Language Learning; journal of applied linguistics. s-a. ISSN 0023-8333
- Michigan Quarterly Review. q. ISSN 0026-2420
- Problems in Education and Nation Building. (pub. by Ann Arbor Publishers)
- Rackham Literary Studies. a.

**University of Michigan. Audio-Visual Education Center**
416 Fourth St., Ann Arbor, MI 48103.
- Educational Films. triennial (with yearly supplements)

**University of Michigan. Bentley Historical Library**
Ann Arbor, MI 48104.
- Bentley Library Annual. a. ISSN 0362-6881

**University of Michigan. Board in Control of Student Publications**
420 Maynard St., Ann Arbor, MI 48104.
- Generation; the University of Michigan inter-arts magazine. 3 per yr. ISSN 0016-6626

**University of Michigan. Burns Research Center**
Ann Arbor, MI 48104.
- International Bibliography on Burns. irreg.

**University of Michigan. Center for Chinese Studies**
Lane Hall, Ann Arbor, MI 48109.
- Michigan Abstracts of Chinese and Japanese Works on Chinese History. irreg; no. 5, 1976. ISSN 0076-7808
- Michigan Papers in Chinese Studies. irreg; no. 29, 1976. ISSN 0076-8065

**University of Michigan. Center for Japanese Studies**
- Studies in Japanese Culture. (pub. by University of Michigan Press)
- University of Michigan. Center for Japanese Studies. Bibliographical Series. (pub. by University of Michigan Press)
- University of Michigan. Center for Japanese Studies. Occasional Papers. (pub. by University of Michigan Press)

**University of Michigan. Center for Research on Learning and Teaching**
109 E. Madison, Ann Arbor, MI 48104.
- Center for Research on Learning and Teaching. Memo to the Faculty. q. ISSN 0025-911X

**University of Michigan. Center for South and Southeast Asian Studies**
130 Lane Hall, Ann Arbor, MI 48104.
- Michigan Papers on South and Southeast Asia. irreg.
- Michigan Series in South and Southeast Asian Languages and Linguistics. irreg.

**University of Michigan. Department of Chemistry**
Ann Arbor, MI 48104.
- Bulletin of Thermodynamics and Thermochemistry. a. ISSN 0068-4139

**University of Michigan. Department of Geography**
Ann Arbor, MI 48104.
- Michigan Geographical Publications. irreg., no. 13, 1974. ISSN 0076-7948

**University of Michigan. Department of German**
Ann Arbor, MI 48104.
- Michigan Germanic Studies. s-a.

**University of Michigan. Department of Psychology**
Ann Arbor, MI 48104.
- Sex Discrimination in Education Newsletter. q.

**University of Michigan. Department of Romance Languages**
MLB 4222, Ann Arbor, MI 48104.
- Dispositio: Revista Hispanica de Semiotica Literaria. 3 per yr.

**University of Michigan. Department of Slavic Languages and Literatures**
3040 Modern Language Bldg., Ann Arbor, MI 48109.
- Michigan Slavic Contributions. irreg., vol. 8, 1973. ISSN 0076-8103
- Michigan Slavic Translations. irreg., no. 2, 1973.

**University of Michigan. Division of Research Development and Administration**
Editorial Office, Ann Arbor, MI 48109.
- University of Michigan. Division of Research Development and Administration. Research News. m. ISSN 0041-9842
- University of Michigan Bibliography; scholarly and creative activities of the faculty and staff. irreg., latest issue, 1972.

**University of Michigan. English Language Institute**
Ann Arbor, MI 48104.
- E S L Video Newsletter. s-a.

**University of Michigan. Graduate School of Business Administration**
University of Michigan, Monroe and Tappan St., Ann Arbor, MI 48104.
- Dividend. 3 per yr. ISSN 0046-0400
- Industrial Relations Law Digest. q. ISSN 0019-8706
- Michigan Business and Economic Research Bibliography. irreg., latest issue. ISSN 0091-9047 (prep. by its Division of Research)
- Michigan Business Cases. irreg. ISSN 0076-7832
- Michigan Business Papers. irreg. ISSN 0076-7840
- Michigan Business Reports. irreg. ISSN 0076-7859
- Michigan Business Studies. irreg. ISSN 0076-7867
- Michigan Directory of Importers. ISSN 0091-0708
- Michigan International Business Studies. irreg. ISSN 0076-7972
- Michigan International Commerce Reports. irreg., 1970, no. 2. ISSN 0076-7980
- Michigan International Labor Studies. irreg., vol. 5, 1972. ISSN 0076-7999
- National Symposium on the State of the Black Economy. Selected Proceedings. irreg. (prep. by its Division of Research) (Co-sponsor: Chicago Economic Development Corp.)
- Personnel Management Abstracts. q. ISSN 0031-577X
- University of Michigan. Graduate School of Business Administration. Leadership Award Lecture. a. ISSN 0076-8332
- University of Michigan. Graduate School of Business Administration. Proceedings of the Annual Business Conference. irreg.
- University of Michigan Business Review. bi-m.(Nov-July)
- William K. McInally Lecture. a. ISSN 0084-0246

**University of Michigan. Great Lakes Research Division**
Ann Arbor, MI 48105.
- University of Michigan. Great Lakes Research Division. Special Report. irreg., no. 51, 1974. ISSN 0543-940X

**University of Michigan. Institute for Social Research**
Box 1248, Ann Arbor, MI 48106.
- Economic Outlook U.S.A. q. ISSN 0095-3830 (prep. by its Survey Research Center)
- Institute for Social Research. Newsletter. (I S R) q. ISSN 0020-2622
- Surveys of Consumers. a. ISSN 0085-3410

**University of Michigan. Institute of Gerontology**
543 Church St., Ann Arbor, MI 48104.
- University of Michigan. Institute of Gerontology. Occasional Papers in Gerontology. irreg.

**University of Michigan. Institute of Public Policy Studies**
1516 Rackham Bldg., Ann Arbor, MI 48104.
- Michigan Governmental Studies. irreg., 1968, no. 50. ISSN 0076-7956
- Papers in Public Administration. irreg., 1965, no. 47. ISSN 0078-916X
- Woytinsky Lectures. irreg., 1968, no. 2. ISSN 0084-263X

**University of Michigan Law School**
731 Legal Research Building, Ann Arbor, MI 48104.
- University of Michigan Journal of Law Reform. 3 per yr. ISSN 0033-1546

**University of Michigan Law School. Institute of Continuing Legal Education**
625 South State, Ann Arbor, MI 48104.
- Advocacy Institute. Proceedings. a. ISSN 0462-3134

**University of Michigan Library**
Ann Arbor, MI 48104.
- University of Michigan Librarian. fortn.

**University of Michigan Medical Center**
Ann Arbor, MI 48104.
- University of Michigan Medical Center Journal. q. ISSN 0041-9826

**University of Michigan. Mental Health Research Institute**
Ann Arbor, MI 48104.
- University of Michigan. Mental Health Research Institute. Annual Report. a.

**University of Michigan. Museum of Anthropology**
University Museums Building, Ann Arbor, MI 48104.
- University of Michigan. Museum of Anthropology. Anthropological Papers. irreg; no. 62, 1977. ISSN 0076-8367
- University of Michigan. Museum of Anthropology. Memoirs. irreg; no. 9, 1977. ISSN 0076-8375
- University of Michigan. Museum of Anthropology. Technical Reports. a.

**University of Michigan Museum of Art**
Alumni Memorial Hall, Ann Arbor, MI 48104.
- University of Michigan. Museum of Art. Bulletin. a. ISSN 0076-8391

**University of Michigan. Museum of Paleontology**
Museums Bldg., Ann Arbor, MI 48104.
- University of Michigan. Museum of Paleontology. Contributions. irreg., (approx. 20-25 per yr.) ISSN 0041-9834

**University of Michigan. Museum of Zoology**
Ann Arbor, MI 48109.
- University of Michigan. Museum of Zoology. Miscellaneous Publications. irreg., no. 148, 1976. ISSN 0076-8405
- University of Michigan. Museum of Zoology. Occasional Papers. irreg. ISSN 0076-8413

**University of Michigan. National Program for the Advancement of Pre-College Russian and East European Studies**
210 Lane Hall, Ann Arbor, MI 48104.
- University of Michigan. National Program for the Advancement of Pre-College Russian and East European Studies. National Newsletter. q.

**University of Michigan Observatories**
Department of Astronomy, Physics Astronomy Bldg., Ann Arbor, MI 48104.
- University of Michigan Observatories. Publications. irreg. ISSN 0076-8421

**University of Michigan. Office of University Relations and Development**
Ann Arbor, MI 48109.
- Michigan Today. q. ISSN 0041-9850

**University of Michigan. Population Studies Center**
Ann Arbor, MI 48104.
- University of Michigan. Population Studies Center. Annual Report. a.

**University of Michigan Press**
615 E. University, Ann Arbor, MI 48106.
- Jerome Lectures. irreg. ISSN 0075-3610
- Michigan Mathematical Journal. q. ISSN 0026-2285
- Recognition Series. irreg.
- Studies in Japanese Culture. irreg. ISSN 0081-8127 (University of Michigan. Center for Japanese Studies)
- University of Michigan. Center for Japanese Studies. Bibliographical Series. irreg. ISSN 0076-8340
- University of Michigan. Center for Japanese Studies. Occasional Papers. irreg. ISSN 0076-8359

**University of Michigan. School of Dentistry**
Ann Arbor, MI 48104.
- University of Michigan. School of Dentistry. Alumni Bulletin. a. ISSN 0076-843X

**University of Michigan. School of Education**
E. and S. University Aves., Ann Arbor, MI 48104.
- Innovator. m. ISSN 0046-9572
- Notes and Abstracts of American and International Education. q. ISSN 0029-3962
- University of Michigan. School of Education. Bulletin. biennial.

**University of Michigan. School of Public Health**
M2240, M2210 School of Public Health, Ann Arbor, MI 48109.
- Abstracts of Hospital Management Studies. q. ISSN 0001-3595 (prep. by its Cooperative Information Center for Hospital Management Studies)
- Medical Care Review. m. ISSN 0025-7087 (prep. by its Bureau of Public Health Economics)

**University of Michigan. University Herbarium**
North University Building, Ann Arbor, MI 48104.
- University of Michigan. Herbarium. Contributions. irreg. ISSN 0580-6097

**University of Michigan-Wayne State University. Institute of Labor & Industrial Relations**
- Human Resources Abstracts. (pub. by Sage Publications, Inc.)

**University of Michigan. William L. Clements Library of American History**
Ann Arbor, MI 48104.
- Quarto; issued quarterly for the Clements Library Associates. q.

**University of Michigan. Women's Studies Program**
Ann Arbor, MI 48104.
- University of Michigan Papers in Women's Studies. q.

**University of Minnesota. Agricultural Experiment Station**
Institute of Agriculture, St. Paul, MN 55101.
- Minnesota Science. q. ISSN 0026-5675

**University of Minnesota. Audio Visual Library Service**
3300 University Ave. S.E., Minneapolis, MN 55414.
- Audio Visual Journal. 3 per yr. ISSN 0004-7570
- University of Minnesota. Audio-Visual Library Service. Educational Resources Bulletin. irreg. ISSN 0076-9274

**University of Minnesota. Board of Publications**
Minneapolis, MN 55455.
- Minnesota Technolog. m.(Oct-May) ISSN 0026-5691

**University of Minnesota. Center for Advanced Studies in Language, Style, and Literary Theory**
University of Minnesota, 207 Main Engineering. Building, Minneapolis, MN 55455.
- Centrum. s-a. ISSN 0091-9144

**University of Minnesota. Center for Research in Human Learning**
205 Elliott Hall, Minneapolis, MN 55455.
- University of Minnesota. Center for Research in Human Learning. Report. a. ISSN 0076-9282

**University of Minnesota. Center for Youth Development**
325 Hacker Hall, St. Paul, MN 55108.
- University of Minnesota. Center for Youth Development and Research. Seminar Series. a.

**University of Minnesota. Cereal Rust Laboratory**
St. Paul, MN 55108.
- Cereal Rust Bulletin. irreg.

**University of Minnesota. Department of Agricultural Economics**
260 Coffey Hall, St. Paul, MN 55105.
- Minnesota Economic Data: Countries and Regions. 2-3 per yr. ISSN 0544-3512 (prep. by its Agricultural Extension Service)

**University of Minnesota. Department of Economics**
Rm. 315 Science Classroom Bldg., Minneapolis, MN 55455.
- University of Minnesota. Center for Economic Research. Discussion Papers. 10 per yr. (prep. by its Center for Economic Research)

**University of Minnesota. Graduate School Research Center**
422 Johnston Hall, Minneapolis, MN 55455.
- University of Minnesota. Graduate School Research Center. Inventory of Faculty Research. a. ISSN 0076-9290

**University of Minnesota. History Department**
Minneapolis, MN 55455.
- Ming Studies Newsletter. s-a. (Association for Asian Studies, Inc.) (Co-sponsor: China & Inner Asia Council)

**University of Minnesota. Immigration History Research Center**
826 Berry St., St. Paul, MI 55114.
- Spectrum. q.

**University of Minnesota. Industrial Relations Center**
Minneapolis, MN 55455.
- Minnesota I R C News. 2 per yr. ISSN 0026-5519

**University of Minnesota. Institute of Child Development**
- Minnesota Symposia on Child Psychology. (pub. by Thomas Y. Crowell Co.)

**University of Minnesota James Ford Bell Library**
*see* James Ford Bell Library

**University of Minnesota. Law School**
Minneapolis, MN 55455.
- Minnesota Law Review. 6 per yr. ISSN 0026-5535 (Minnesota Law Review Foundation)

**University of Minnesota. Minnesota Alumni Association**
2610 University Ave., St. Paul, MN 55114.
- University of Minnesota Alumni News. m.(Sep-June) ISSN 0041-9869

**University of Minnesota Press**
2037 University Ave. S.E., Minneapolis, MN 55455.
- Minnesota Drama Editions. irreg., no. 9, 1975. ISSN 0076-9142 (Guthrie Theater Co)
- Minnesota Monographs in the Humanities. irreg., no. 10, 1977. ISSN 0076-9215
- Minnesota Studies in the Philosophy of Science. irreg; vol. 8, 1977. ISSN 0076-9258 (Minnesota Center for Philosophy of Science)
- Wesley W. Spink Lectures on Comparative Medicine. biennial.

**University of Minnesota. University Student Telecommunications Corp.**
University/Community Video Center, 506A Rarig Center, Minneapolis, MN 55455.
- Live Wire; the Twin Cities newsletter on telecommunications. irreg.

**University of Minnesota. Water Resources Research Center**
c/o Documents Section, Centennial Office Bldg., Room 140, St. Paul, MN 55155.
- University of Minnesota. Water Resources Research Center. Regional Research Series. irreg.

**University of Minnesota, Duluth. Bureau of Business and Economic Research**
Duluth, MN 55812.
- Duluth Business Indicators and Selected Area Economic Data; a graphic summary with tables. a. (prep. by its School of Business and Economics)
- Minnesota Business Directory; a directory of the 210 largest firms headquartered or transacting at least 50% of their business in Minnesota. a.

**University of Minnesota, Duluth. Department of English**
Duluth, MN 55803.
- Steelhead. 3 per yr.

**University of Minnesota, Morris**
Morris, MN 56267.
- Midwest Studies in Philosophy. a.

**University of Mississippi**
University Extension, MS 38677.
- Arts in Mississippi. m. (Mississippi Arts Commission)
- Opera Journal. q. ISSN 0030-3585 (National Opera Association, Inc.)

**University of Mississippi. Bureau of Governmental Research**
University, MS 38677.
- Public Administration Survey. bi-m. ISSN 0033-3360

**University of Mississippi. Department of Engineering**
University, MS 38677.
- Ole Miss Engineer. q.

**University of Mississippi. Department of English**
MS 38677.
- University of Mississippi. Department of English. Studies in English. a. ISSN 0081-7880

**University of Mississippi Law Center**
University, MS 38677.
- Journal of Space Law. s-a. (L.Q.C. Lamar Society of International Law)

**University of Mississippi Law School**
Box 146, University, MS 38677.
- Mississippi Law Journal. bi-m. ISSN 0026-6280 (Co-Sponsor: Mississippi State Bar)

**University of Mississippi. School of Business Administration**
University, Lafayette Cy., MS 38677.
- Mississippi's Business. bi-m. ISSN 0026-6442 (prep. by its Bureau of Business and Economic Research)

**University of Missouri-Columbia**
Columbia, MO 65201.
- University of Missouri, Columbia. Mathematical Sciences Technical Reports. irreg. ISSN 0076-9665

**University of Missouri-Columbia. Agriculture & Engineering Department**
Columbia, MO 65201.
- Missouri Irrigation and Land Forming Newsletter. bi-m.

**University of Missouri-Columbia. College of Business and Public Administration**
Business and Public Administration Bldg., Columbia, MO 65201.
- University of Missouri. College of Business and Public Administration. Office of Research, Annual Report. a. ISSN 0076-969X

**University of Missouri-Columbia. College of Education**
Columbia, MO 65201.
- Journal of Career Education. q.

**University of Missouri-Columbia. Department of Agronomy**
117 Curtis Hall, Columbia, MO 65201.
- Stadler Genetics Symposium. Proceedings. irreg., vol. 5, 1973. ISSN 0081-4148

**University of Missouri-Columbia. Department of Psychiatry**
803 Stadium Rd., Columbia, MO 65201.
- Journal of Operational Psychiatry. s-a. ISSN 0047-2638 (Co-Sponsor: Missouri Institute of Psychiatry)

**University of Missouri-Columbia. Department of Regional & Community Affairs**
726 Clark Hill, Columbia, MO 65201.
- Community Development Focus; reports on programs in Bolivia, Guyana, Nepal, Tanzania. irreg.

**University of Missouri-Columbia. Department of Sociology and Rural Sociology**
Columbia, MO 65201.
- Review of Social Theory. s-a.

**University of Missouri-Columbia. Environmental Health Center and Extension Division**
Columbia, MO 65201.
- Conference on Trace Substances in Environmental Health. Proceedings. a. ISSN 0069-8741

**University of Missouri-Columbia. Museum of Anthropology**
Columbia, MO 65201.
- University of Missouri, Columbia. Museum of Anthropology. Museum Briefs. irreg; no. 22, 1975. ISSN 0076-9673
- University of Missouri Monographs in Anthropology. irreg.

**University of Missouri-Columbia. Museum of Art and Archaeology**
Ellis Library 4D 11, Columbia, MO 65201.
- Muse. a. ISSN 0077-2194

**University of Missouri-Columbia. School of Law**
Columbia, MO 65201.
- Missouri Law Review. q. ISSN 0026-6604

**University of Missouri-Columbia. Veterinary Medical Diagnostic Labrary**
Columbia, MO 65201.
- University of Missouri, Columbia. Veterinary Medical Diagnostic Laboratory. Annual Report. a. ISSN 0076-9711

**University of Missouri- Kansas City**
5346 Charlotte, Kansas City, MO 64110.
- New Letters. q.

**University of Missouri-Kansas City. School of Administration**
Kansas City, MO 64110.
- Business and Public Administration Student Review. s-a. ISSN 0007-649X

**University of Missouri-Kansas City. School of Law**
5100 Rockhill Rd., Kansas City, MO 64110.
- U M K C Law Review. 3 per yr. ISSN 0047-7575

**University of Missouri Press**
107 Swallow Hall, Columbia, MO 65201.
- Missouri Handbook Series. irreg., 1964, no. 5. ISSN 0076-9630
- Missouri Literary Frontiers Series. irreg. ISSN 0076-9649
- Paul Anthony Brick Lectures. irreg., 1973, no. 9. ISSN 0079-0249
- University of Missouri Studies. irreg; no. 65, 1977. ISSN 0076-9703

**University of Missouri- Rolla**
Rolla, MO 65401.
- U M R Journal. s-a. ISSN 0544-5396

**University of Missouri-Rolla. Department of Civil Engineering**
Rolla, MO 65401.
- International Specialty Conference on Cold-Formed Steel Structures. (Proceedings) irreg.

**University of Missouri- St. Louis. Center for International Studies**
St. Louis, MO 63121.
- University of Missouri, St. Louis. Center for International Studies. Monograph. irreg; no. 3, 1971. ISSN 0076-9657

**University of Montana. Associated Students**
Department of English, Missoula, MT 59812.
- Cutbank. s-a.

**University of Montana. Bureau of Business and Economic Research**
Missoula, MT 59801.
- Montana Business Quarterly. q. ISSN 0026-9921 (Co-Sponsor: Univ. of Montana, School of Business Administration)

**University of Montana. Bureau of Government Research**
Missoula, MT 59801.
- Montana Public Affairs Report. 3-4 per yr. ISSN 0047-7966

**University of Montana. Department of Anthropology**
Missoula, MT 59801.
- University of Montana. Department of Antropology. Contributions to Anthropology. irreg., no. 4, 1974. ISSN 0077-118X

**University of Montana. Department of Geology**
Missoula, MT 59801.
- Northwest Geology. a.

**University of Montana. Division of Educational Research and Services**
Missoula, MT 59801.
- University of Montana. Division of Educational Research and Services. Education Monograph. irreg.

**University of Montana. Information Services**
Missoula, MT 59801.
- Profiles. bi-m.

**University of Montana. Publications in History**
Department of History, Missoula, MT 59801.
- Montana Historian. 2 per yr.

**University of Montana. School of Education**
Missoula, MT 59801.
- Education Bulletin (Missoula) ISSN 0093-9277 (Co-Sponsor: Phi Delta Kappa, University of Montana Chapter)

**University of Montana, School of Forestry**
Montana Forest and Conservation Experiment Station, Missoula, MT 59801.
- University of Montana. Forest and Conservation Experiment Station, Missoula. Bulletin. irreg., 1970, no. 39. ISSN 0077-1155
- University of Montana. Forest and Conservation Experiment Station, Missoula. Research Notes. irreg., 1972, no. 12. ISSN 0077-1163
- University of Montana. Forest and Conservation Experiment Station, Missoula. Special Publication. irreg., 1968, no. 3. ISSN 0077-1171
- Western Wildlands. q. (prep. by its Forest Conservation and Experiment Station)

**University of Montana. School of Journalism**
Missoula, MT 59801.
- Montana Journalism Review. a. ISSN 0077-1147

**University of Montana. School of Law**
Missoula, MT 59801.
- Montana Law Forum. s-a. ISSN 0026-9964 (prep. by its Student Bar Association)
- University of Montana Law School News. 3 per yr. ISSN 0041-9877

**University of Montana. Students of School of Law**
Missoula, MT 59801.
- Montana Law Review. s-a. ISSN 0026-9972

**University of Nebraska-Lincoln**
201 Andrews Hall, Lincoln, NE 68508.
- Prairie Schooner. q. ISSN 0032-6682
- Saltillo. q.
- Western Association of Africanists. Newsletter. s-a. ISSN 0035-7642

**University of Nebraska-Lincoln. Alumni Association**
3835 Holdrege, Box 30186, Lincoln, NE 68503.
- Nebraska Alumnus. bi-m. ISSN 0028-1794

**University of Nebraska-Lincoln. Bureau of Business Research**
200 CBA Bldg., Lincoln, NE 68508.
- Business in Nebraska. m. ISSN 0007-683X

**University of Nebraska-Lincoln. College of Business Administration**
Lincoln, NE 68508.
- Business Research Bulletin. irreg. ISSN 0362-823X (prep. by its Bureau of Business Research)
- Nebraska Journal of Economics and Business. q. ISSN 0028-1867

**University of Nebraska-Lincoln. College of Engineering and Technology**
W 181 Nebr. Hall, Lincoln, NE 68503.
- Nebraska Blue Print. q.

**University of Nebraska-Lincoln. College of Law**
Lincoln, NE 68508.
- Nebraska Law Review. q. ISSN 0047-9209
- Nebraska Transcript. irreg.

**University of Nebraska- Lincoln. Department of Agricultural Education**
Lincoln, NE 68503.
- University of Nebraska. Department of Agricultural Education. Report. irreg. ISSN 0548-0906

**University of Nebraska-Lincoln. Department of Horticulture and Forestry**
c/o Ed. Dermot P. Coyne, Lincoln, NE 68503.
- Bean Improvement Cooperative. Annual Report. a. ISSN 0084-7747

**University of Nebraska- Lincoln. Department of Publications Services & Control**
209 Nebraska Hall, Lincoln, NE 68508.
- University of Nebraska. Museum Notes. s-a (Sept-March) ISSN 0041-9885 (University of Nebraska State Museum)

**University of Nebraska-Lincoln. Institute of Agriculture and Natural Resources**
Rm. 101, Agricultural Communications Bldg., Rm. 209, Information Bldg., Lincoln, NE 68583.
- Farm, Ranch and Home Quarterly. q.

**University of Nebraska-Lincoln. Libraries**
Serials Department, Lincoln, NE 68508.
- University of Nebraska Studies. New Series. irreg., latest issue, 1974. ISSN 0077-6386

**University of Nebraska-Lincoln. School of Journalism**
Lincoln, NE 68508.
- University of Nebraska. School of Journalism. Depth Report. irreg. ISSN 0077-6378

**University of Nebraska Medical Center. Clinical Neurology Information Center**
Omaha, NE 68105.
- Concise Clinical Neurology Review. s-m. ISSN 0094-9302 (Co-sponsor: National Institute of Neurological and Communicative Diseases and Stroke)

**University of Nebraska. North Platte Agricultural Experiment Station**
North Platte, NE 69101.
- Nebraska. Agricultural Experiment Station, North Platte. Fall Crops and Irrigation Field Day. a. ISSN 0085-3879

**University of Nebraska-Omaha. Center for Applied Urban Research**
Box 688, Omaha, NE 68101.
- Review of Applied Urban Research. m. ISSN 0094-1972

**University of Nebraska Press**
901 N. 17 St., Lincoln, NE 68508.
- Nebraska Symposium on Motivation (Publication) a. ISSN 0070-2099

**University of Nebraska State Museum**
Morrill Hall 212, Lincoln, NE 68508.
- University of Nebraska. Museum Notes. (pub. by University of Nebraska- Lincoln. Department of Publications Services & Control)
- University of Nebraska State Museum. Bulletin. irreg.

**University of Nevada**
Judicial College Bldg., Reno, NV 89507.
- National College of the State Judiciary. a. ISSN 0095-2028

**University of Nevada. Anthropology Department**
Las Vega, NE 89154.
- University of Nevada. Anthropology Department. Student Papers in Anthropology. irreg. ISSN 0085-3925

**University of Nevada. Basque Studies Program**
Getchell Library, Reno, NV 89557.
- University of Nevada. Basque Studies Program Newsletter. 2 per yr.

**University of Nevada. Bureau of Business and Economic Research**
College of Business Administration, Reno, NV 89557.
- Nevada Review of Business and Economics. q.
- University of Nevada. Bureau of Business and Economic Research. Research Report. irreg. ISSN 0077-7943

**University of Nevada. Bureau of Governmental Research**
Reno, NV 89507.
- Governmental Research Newsletter. 9 per yr. ISSN 0017-2677

**University of Nevada. Department of Psychology**
Reno, NV 89557.
- Behaviorism. s-a. ISSN 0090-4155

**University of Nevada. Departments of History and Political Science**
- Nevada Studies in History and Political Science. (pub. by University of Nevada Press)

**University of Nevada. Desert Research Institute**
Reno, NV 89507.
- University of Nevada. Western Studies Center. Desert Research Institute. Publications in the Social Sciences. irreg. ISSN 0077-7951
- University of Nevada. Western Studies Center. Desert Research Institute. Technical Report. irreg. ISSN 0077-796X

**University of Nevada Library. Special Collections Department**
Reno, NV 89507.
- Top Secret. s-m.

**University of Nevada. Mackay School of Mines**
Reno, NV 89501.
- Nevada. Bureau of Mines and Geology. Report. irreg. ISSN 0095-5264

**University of Nevada. Max C. Fleischmann College of Agriculture**
Reno, NV 89507.
- Max C. Fleischmann College of Agriculture. Publications. B (Series) irreg. ISSN 0076-5589
- Max C. Fleischmann College of Agriculture. Publications. C (Series) irreg. ISSN 0076-5597
- Max C. Fleischmann College of Agriculture. Publications. R (Series) irreg. ISSN 0076-5600
- Max C. Fleischmann College of Agriculture. Publications. T (Series) irreg. ISSN 0076-5619

**University of Nevada Press**
Reno, NV 89507.
- Nevada Studies in History and Political Science. irreg., no. 13, 1974. ISSN 0077-7935 (University of Nevada. Departments of History and Political Science)

**University of Nevada. Seismological Laboratory**
Reno, NV 89507.
- University of Nevada. Seismological Laboratory. Bulletin. irreg., latest issue, 1973. ISSN 0092-4288

**University of New Hampshire. Agricultural Experiment Station**
Durham, NH 03824.
- New Hampshire. Agricultural Experiment Station, Durham. Research Reports. irreg; latest issue, 1976. ISSN 0077-832X
- New Hampshire. Agricultural Experiment Station, Durham. Station Bulletins. irreg; latest issue, 1976. ISSN 0077-8338

**University of New Hampshire. Alumni Association**
Alumni House, Durham, NH 03824.
- New Hampshire Alumnus. bi-m. ISSN 0028-5196

**University of New Hampshire. Cooperative Extension Service**
Taylor Hall, Durham, NH 03824.
- University of New Hampshire. Cooperative Extension Service. Extension Publication. 1rreg., latest issue, 1974.

**University of New Hampshire. Department of Music**
Durham, NH 03824.
- International Alban Berg Society. Newsletter. irreg. ISSN 0538-4257

**University of New Hampshire. Institute of Natural and Environmental Resources**
Durham, NH 03824.
- University of New Hampshire. Institute of Natural and Environmental Resources. Research Reports. irreg., latest issue, 1974. ISSN 0077-8400

**University of New Hampshire. Publications Office**
Schofield House, Durham, NH 03824.
- U N H Magazine. bi-m. ISSN 0041-5316

**University of New Haven**
West Haven, CT 06516.
- Essays in Arts and Sciences. a.

**University of New Mexico**
Mesa Vista 1013, Albuquerque, NM 87131.
- New Mexico Historical Review. q. ISSN 0028-6206

**University of New Mexico. American Studies Program**
Alburquerque, NM 87131.
- New America: a Review. q.

**University of New Mexico. Art Museum**
Albuquerque, NM 87106.
- University of New Mexico Art Museum. Bulletin. a. ISSN 0077-8583

**University of New Mexico. Board of Student Publications**
Box 20, Albuquerque, NM 87106.
- New Mexico Lobo. 5 per wk. ISSN 0028-6230

**University of New Mexico. Bureau of Business & Economic Research**
I A R S Bldg., Albuquerque, NM 87131.
- New Mexico Business. m. ISSN 0028-6168
- New Mexico Statistical Abstract. irreg. ISSN 0077-8575
- University of New Mexico. Bureau of Business and Economic Research. Business Information Series. irreg. ISSN 0068-4430
- University of New Mexico. Bureau of Business and Economic Research. Studies in Business and Economics. irreg., 1973, no. 22. ISSN 0081-7627

**University of New Mexico. Department of Anthropology**
Albuquerque, NM 87131.
- Journal of Anthropological Research. q. ISSN 0091-7710

**University of New Mexico. Department of Civil Engineering**
Albuquerque, NM 87131.
- Paving Conference. Proceedings. a. ISSN 0079-0273

**University of New Mexico. Department of Geology**
Albuquerque, NM 87131.
- University of New Mexico. Institute of Meteoritics. Special Publication. irreg., 1976, no. 17. ISSN 0085-3968 (prep. by its Institute of Meteoritics)

**University of New Mexico. Institute for Applied Research Services**
Albuquerque, NM 87131.
- University of New Mexico. Division of Government Research. Review. 3 per yr.

**University of New Mexico. Office of Research Administration**
235 N, Scholes Hall, Albuquerque, NM 87131.
- University of New Mexico. Office of Research Administration. Research Notes. s-m.

**University of New Mexico. School of Law**
1117 Stanford N.E., Albuquerque, NM 87131.
- Natural Resources Journal. q. ISSN 0028-0739
- New Mexico Law Review. s-a. ISSN 0028-6214

**University of New Mexico. Technology Application Center**
Albuquerque, NM 87131.
- Heat Pipe Technology. q (plus annual cumulative no.) ISSN 0046-7146
- Hydrogen Energy. q.
- Quarterly Review of Remote Sensing. q. (Co-sponsor: U.S. National Aeronautics and Space Administration)
- Solar Thermal Energy Utilization. Vol. 1: Solar Thermal Power Generation. q.
- Solar Thermal Energy Utilization. Vol. 2: Solar Thermal Components. q.
- Solar Thermal Energy Utilization. Vol. 3: Solar Thermal Heating and Cooling. q.

**University of New Mexico. Women's Center**
1824 Las Lomas, N.E., Albuquerque, NM 87131.
- Joyous Struggle: A Women's Newsletter. irreg. ISSN 0085-2422

**University of New Orleans. College of Business Administration**
College of Business Administration, Lake Front, New Orleans, LA 70122.
- Review of Business and Economic Research. 3 per yr. (prep. by its Business and Economic Research Division)

**University of North Carolina at Asheville. Student Government Association**
Asheville, NC 28801.
- Images; fine arts magazine. a. ISSN 0019-2678 (Co-Sponsor: North Carolina Arts Council, Raleigh)

**University of North Carolina at Chapel Hill**
Chapel Hill, NC 27514.
- Hispanofila. 3 per yr. ISSN 0018-2206
- Southern Economic Journal. q. ISSN 0038-4038 (Southern Economic Association) (Subscr. to:, 300 Hanes Hall)

- Statistical Abstract of Higher Education in North Carolina. a. ISSN 0081-4644 (Subscr. to:, Box 2688)

**University of North Carolina at Chapel Hill. Department of English**
Chapel Hill, NC 27514.
- Southern Literary Journal. s-a. ISSN 0038-4291

**University of North Carolina at Chapel Hill. Department of Geography**
203 Saunders, Chapel Hill, NC 27514.
- Carolina Geographical Symposium. Papers. irreg.

**University of North Carolina at Chapel Hill. Department of Psychology**
Davie Hall, Chapel Hill, NC 27514.
- Representative Research in Social Psychology. s-a. ISSN 0034-4907

**University of North Carolina at Chapel Hill. Department of Romance Languages**
Dey Hall 014A, Chapel Hill, NC 27514.
- North Carolina Studies in the Romance Languages and Literatures. irreg., no. 179, 1976.
- Romance Notes. 3 per yr.

**University of North Carolina at Chapel Hill. Department of Statistics**
Chapel Hill, NC 27514.
- Chapel Hill Conference on Combinatorial Mathematics and Its Applications. Proceedings. irreg., 1970 vol. 2. ISSN 0084-8719 (U.S. Air Force Office of Scientific Research)
- University of North Carolina, Chapel Hill. Institute of Statistics. Mimeo Series. irreg (approx. 3 per mo.) ISSN 0078-1495

**University of North Carolina at Chapel Hill. Graduate School of Business Administration**
Chapel Hill, NC 27514.
- Research in Economics/Business Administration. irreg., 1975, no. 21. ISSN 0080-1631
- University of North Carolina, Chapel Hill. Graduate School of Business Administration. Technical Papers. irreg., 1968, no. 9. ISSN 0078-1452

**University of North Carolina at Chapel Hill. Highway Safety Research Center**
Publications Manager, Chapel Hill, NC 27514.
- Highway Safety Highlights. m.

**University of North Carolina at Chapel Hill. Institute for Research in Social Science**
Chapel Hill, NC 27514.
- University of North Carolina, Chapel Hill. Institute for Research in Social Science. Annual Report. a. ISSN 0078-1479
- University of North Carolina News Letter. q.

**University of North Carolina at Chapel Hill. Institute of Government**
Box 990, Chapel Hill, NC 27514.
- Health Law Bulletin. irreg.
- Local Government Law Bulletin. irreg. ISSN 0362-5729
- North Carolina. Laws, Statutes, Etc. Planning Legislation in North Carolina. biennial. ISSN 0550-7006
- Popular Government. q. ISSN 0032-4515
- Purchasing Bulletin for Local Governments. irreg. ISSN 0478-927X

**University of North Carolina at Chapel Hill. Library**
Chapel Hill, NC 27515.
- Bookmark; for the Friends of the University of North Carolina Library. irreg. ISSN 0006-7393

**University of North Carolina at Chapel Hill. School of Dentistry**
Chapel Hill, NC 27514.
- Cyberdent; newsletter of data processing in dental education. q.

**University of North Carolina at Chapel Hill. School of Law**
Chapel Hill, NC 27514.
- North Carolina Law Review. q(Dec-June) ISSN 0029-2524

**University of North Carolina at Chapel Hill. School of Library Science Alumni Association**
Chapel Hill, NC 27514.
- News from Chapel Hill. s-a.

**University of North Carolina at Chapel Hill. School of Public Health**
Chapel Hill, NC 27514.
- E S E Notes. (Environmental Sciences and Engineering) irreg (approx. 5 issues per yr.) ISSN 0546-4552 (prep. by its Department of Environmental Sciences and Engineering)
- International Program of Laboratories for Population Statistics. Occasional Publications. irreg. (prep. by its Department of Biostatistics)
- International Program of Laboratories for Population Statistics. Scientific Report Series. irreg. (prep. by its Department of Biostatistics)

**University of North Carolina at Chapel Hill. Waste Water Research Center**
School of Public Health, Dept. of Environmental Science & Engineering, Chapel Hill, NC 27514.
- University of North Carolina, Chapel Hill. Waste Water Research Center. Report. irreg. (approx. 4-5 per yr.)

**University of North Carolina at Greensboro**
Room 205, Elliott Hall, Greensboro, NC 27412.
- Coraddi. s-a.
- Greensboro Review. 2-3 per yr. ISSN 0017-4084
- University of North Carolina, Greensboro. Faculty Publications. a. ISSN 0078-1460

**University of North Carolina at Greensboro. School of Business and Economics**
Greensboro, NC 27412.
- North Carolina Review of Business and Economics. q. (prep. by its Center for Applied Research)

**University of North Carolina Press**
Box 2288, Chapel Hill, NC 27514.
- High School Journal. 8 per yr. ISSN 0018-1498
- Social Forces. 4 per yr. ISSN 0037-7732
- Studies in Comparative Literature. irreg; no. 60, 1977. ISSN 0081-7775
- Studies in Philology. 5 per yr. ISSN 0039-3738
- Studies in the Germanic Languages and Literatures. irreg; no. 86, 1976. ISSN 0081-8593

**University of North Carolina. Sea Grant College Program**
1235 Burlington Labs., Raleigh, NC 27607.
- University of North Carolina. Sea Grant College Newsletter. m.

**University of North Dakota**
Grand Forks, ND 58201.
- North Dakota Law Review. q. ISSN 0029-2745 (State Bar Association of North Dakota) (Co-Sponsor: Univ. of North Dakota School of Law)
- North Dakota Quarterly. q. ISSN 0029-277X

**University of North Dakota. Center for Teaching and Learning**
Grand Fork, ND 58202.
- Journal of Teaching and Learning. 3 per yr.

**University of North Dakota Press**
University Station, Grand Forks, ND 58201.
- North Dakota Academy of Science. Proceedings. a.

**University of Northern Colorado**
Greeley, CO 80631.
- Colorado Journal of Educational Research. q. ISSN 0045-7426

**University of Northern Colorado. Museum of Anthropology**
c/o George E. Fay, Ed., Greeley, CO 80639.
- El Dorado; a newsletter- bulletin on South American anthropology. 3 per yr. ISSN 0095-165X
- Katunob; a newsletter- bulletin on Mesoamerican anthropology. q.
- University of Northern Colorado. Museum of Anthropology. Occasional Publications in Anthropology. Archaeology Series. irreg. ISSN 0085-1221
- University of Northern Colorado. Museum of Anthropology. Occasional Publications in Anthropology. Ethnology Series. irreg. ISSN 0085-1205
- University of Northern Colorado. Museum of Anthropology. Occasional Publications in Anthropology. Linguistics Series. irreg. ISSN 0085-123X
- University of Northern Colorado. Museum of Anthropology. Occasional Publications in Anthropology. Miscellaneous Series. irreg. ISSN 0085-1213

**University of Northern Iowa**
112 Union, Cedar Falls, IA.
- Northern Iowan. s-w.

**University of Northern Iowa. College of Education**
Education Center 513, Cedar Falls, IA 50613.
- Midwest History of Education Society. Journal. a. ISSN 0092-2986

**University of Northern Iowa. Department of Geography**
Sabin 1, Cedar Falls, IA 50613.
- Geographical Perspectives. s-a. (Co-Sponsor: Iowa Council for Geographic Education)

**University of Notre Dame**
Notre Dame, IN 46556.
- American Journal of Jurisprudence. a. ISSN 0065-8995
- American Midland Naturalist. q. ISSN 0003-0031
- American Midland Naturalist Monograph Series. irreg. ISSN 0065-9436
- Notre Dame Journal of Formal Logic. q. ISSN 0029-4527
- Notre Dame Magazine. 5 per yr.
- Notre Dame Technical Review. q. ISSN 0029-4543
- Research Reports in the Social Sciences. s-a. ISSN 0034-5423
- Review of Politics. q. ISSN 0034-6705

**University of Notre Dame. Department of Economics**
IN 46556
(Rev. Mark J. Fitzgerald, Box 476, Notre Dame, Indiana 46556)
- University of Notre Dame. Department of Economics. Union-Management Conference. Proceeding. a. ISSN 0078-2076
- University of Notre Dame. Saint Mary's College. Law School. Department of Economics. Conference on Changing Factors in Collective Bargaining. Proceedings. a.

**University of Notre Dame. Department of English**
O'Shaughnessy Hall, Notre Dame, IN 46556.
- Notre Dame English Journal. s-a. ISSN 0029-4500 (Notre Dame English Association)
- Ward-Phillips Lectures in English Language and Literature. (pub. by University of Notre Dame Press)

**University of Notre Dame. Department of Information Services**
Notre Dame, IN 46556.
- Notre Dame Report. s-m.

**University of Notre Dame. Department of Theology**
- University of Notre Dame. Department of Theology. Liturgical Studies. (pub. by University of Notre Dame Press)
- University of Notre Dame. Department of Theology. Studies in Christian Democracy. (pub. by University of Notre Dame Press)

**University of Notre Dame. Lobund Laboratory**
Notre Dame, IN 46556.
- Bibliography of Germfree Research. a.

**University of Notre Dame. Mediaeval Institute**
- Texts and Studies in the History of Mediaeval Education. (pub. by University of Notre Dame Press)
- University of Notre Dame. Medieval Institute. Publications in Mediaeval Studies. (pub. by University of Notre Dame Press)

**University of Notre Dame Press**
Notre Dame, IN 46556.
- Texts and Studies in the History of Mediaeval Education. irreg., no. 4, 1974. ISSN 0082-3732
- University of Notre Dame. Department of Theology. Liturgical Studies. irreg., no. 11, 1977. ISSN 0076-003X
- University of Notre Dame. Department of Theology. Studies in Christian Democracy. irreg., 1969, vol. 3. ISSN 0081-7708
- University of Notre Dame. Medieval Institute. Publications in Mediaeval Studies. irreg., 1969, no. 21. ISSN 0079-7677
- Ward-Phillips Lectures in English Language and Literature. irreg., no. 7, 1975. ISSN 0083-7210 (University of Notre Dame. Department of English)

**University of Notre Dame. Radiation Chemistry Data Center**
Radiation Laboratory, Notre Dame, IN 46556.
- Biweekly List of Papers on Radiation Chemistry. fortn.

**University of Notre Dame. School of Law**
Box 486, Notre Dame, IN 46556.
- Notre Dame Journal of Legislation. 2 per yr.
- Notre Dame Lawyer. 5 per yr. ISSN 0029-4535

**University of Oklahoma Association**
900 Asp Ave., MZ 3, Norman, OK 73069.
- Sooner. 8 per yr. ISSN 0038-1497

**University of Oklahoma. Center for Economic and Management Research**
College of Business Administration, 307 W. Brooks St., Rm. 4, Norman, OK 73019.
- Oklahoma Business Bulletin. m. ISSN 0030-1671
- Review of Regional Economics and Business. s-a.
- Statistical Abstract of Oklahoma. a. ISSN 0078-4354
- University of Oklahoma. Center for Economic and Management Research. Monograph Series. irreg. ISSN 0078-4435

**University of Oklahoma. College of Law**
300 Timberdell Rd., Norman, OK 73019.
- American Indian Law Review. s-a.
- Oklahoma Law Review. q. ISSN 0030-1752

**University of Oklahoma. Department of Psychiatry and Behavioral Sciences**
Health Science Center, OK 73104
- Biological Psychology Bulletin. ISSN 0093-1004 (Subscriptions to: Whiteman House for Mental Health Research, 607 NE 15, Oklahoma City, OK 73104)

**University of Oklahoma. Departments of Anthropology, Geography and History**
Norman, OK 73019.
- Comparative Frontier Studies. s-a.

**University of Oklahoma. H. H. Herbert School of Journalism**
Norman, OK 73069.
- Cecil H. Brite Lecture Series in Advertising and Publications Management. irreg.
- Sooner State Press. bi-m. ISSN 0038-1519

**University of Oklahoma Press**
1005 Asp Ave., Norman, OK 73016.
- American Exploration and Travel. irreg. ISSN 0065-8219
- Centers of Civilization Series. irreg. ISSN 0069-1461
- Civilization of the American Indian. irreg. ISSN 0069-4304
- Western Frontier Library. irreg. ISSN 0083-887X
- World Literature Today; a literary quarterly of the University of Oklahoma. q.

**University of Oklahoma Research Institute**
Norman, OK 73069.
- Researcher. q. ISSN 0034-5458

**University of Oklahoma. Student Publication Board**
860 VanVleet Oval, Norman, OK 73019.
- Oklahoma Daily; a student newspaper serving the University of Oklahoma. d. ISSN 0030-171X

**University of Oregon**
Eugene, OR 97403.
- Comparative Literature. q. ISSN 0010-4124
- Northwest Review. 3 per yr. ISSN 0029-3423

**University of Oregon. Bureau of Business Research**
140 Gilbert Hall, Eugene, OR 97403.
- Oregon Economic Statistics. a. ISSN 0078-5628

**University of Oregon. Bureau of Governmental Research and Service**
Box 3177, Eugene, OR 97403.
- University of Oregon. Bureau of Governmental Research and Service. Information Bulletin. irreg;no.170,1975. ISSN 0078-5970
- University of Oregon. Bureau of Governmental Research and Service. Legal Bulletin. irreg., 1970, no. 14. ISSN 0078-5989
- University of Oregon. Bureau of Governmental Research and Service. Local Government Finance. irreg.
- University of Oregon. Bureau of Governmental Research and Service. Local Government Notes and Information: Policy and Practice Series. irreg; no. 38, 1975. ISSN 0078-5997

- University of Oregon. Bureau of Governmental Research and Service. Planning Bulletin. irreg; no. 8, 1975.

**University of Oregon. Center for Educational Policy and Management**
1472 Kincaid, Eugene, OR 97401.
- Center. s-a.
- University of Oregon. Center for Educational Policy and Management. Periodical. s-a.
- University of Oregon. Center for Educational Policy and Management. Technical Reports. irreg., 1970, no. 11. ISSN 0078-6020

**University of Oregon. Center for the Advanced Study of Educational Administration**
1472 Kincaid St., Eugene, OR 97401.
- University of Oregon. Center for the Advanced Study of Educational Administration. Monographs. irreg., 1969, no. 20. ISSN 0078-6004
- University of Oregon. Center for the Advanced Study of Educational Administration. Occasional Papers. irreg. ISSN 0078-6012
- University of Oregon. Center for the Advanced Study of Educational Administration. Research and Development Perspectives. 3 per yr. ISSN 0048-2153

**University of Oregon. College of Business Administration**
Eugene, OR 97403.
- University of Oregon. College of Business Administration. Current Issues Conference. Proceedings. a.

**University of Oregon. College of Health, Physical Education and Recreation**
Microform Publications, Eugene, OR 97403.
- Health, Physical Education and Recreation Microform Publications Bulletin. s-a. ISSN 0090-5119

**University of Oregon. Dental School Alumni Association**
611 S. W. Campus Drive, Portland, OR 97201.
- Caementum. s-a. ISSN 0007-9499

**University of Oregon. Department of Anthropology**
Eugene, OR 97403.
- University of Oregon Anthropological Papers. irreg., vol. 11, 1977. ISSN 0078-6071

**University of Oregon. Department of Biology**
c/o E. Novitski, Eugene, OR 97403.
- Drosophila Information Service. s-a. ISSN 0070-7333

**University of Oregon. Department of Sociology**
Eugene, OR 97403.
- Insurgent Sociologist. q. ISSN 0047-0384

**University of Oregon Library**
Eugene, OR 97403.
- Imprint: Oregon. s-a. ISSN 0094-0232
- University of Oregon. Library. Occasional Paper. irreg., no. 6, 1974. ISSN 0078-6039

**University of Oregon. Museum of Natural History**
Eugene, OR 97403.
- University of Oregon. Museum of Natural History. Bulletin. irreg., no. 19, 1972, no. 21, 1973. ISSN 0078-6047

**University of Oregon. School of Law**
Eugene, OR 97403.
- Oregon Law Review. q.

**University of Pennsylvania**
Logan Hall, Box 1, Philadelphia, PA 19174.
- American Quarterly. 4 nos. and 1 supplement per year. ISSN 0003-0678 (American Studies Association)

**University of Pennsylvania**
Philadelphia, PA 19104.
- Eldridge Reeves Johnson Foundation for Medical Physics. Colloquium. Proceedings. (pub. by Academic Press, Inc.)
- International Economic Review. 3 per yr. ISSN 0020-6598 (Co-Sponsor: Osaka University Institute of Social and Economic Research Association)
- Pennsylvania Gazette. m.

**University of Pennsylvania**
332 Towne Bldg., Philadelphia, PA 19104.
- Pennsylvania Triangle. 4 per yr.

**University of Pennsylvania**
3417 Spruce St., Philadelphia, PA 19174.
- Poor Richard's Record. a. ISSN 0361-9419
- Punch Bowl. q.

**University of Pennsylvania. Department of Astronomy**
Philadelphia, PA 19104.
- International Astronomical Union. Finding List for Observers of Eclipsing Variables. irreg., 1963, 4th ed. ISSN 0071-5174

**University of Pennsylvania. Department of History**
Philadelphia, PA 19104.
- Translations and Reprints from the Original Sources of European History. irreg., 1969, vol. 6, no. 2. ISSN 0082-593X

**University of Pennsylvania. Department of Linguistics**
- Papers on Formal Linguistics. (pub. by Mouton Publishers NE)

**University of Pennsylvania. Department of Planning Studies in Continuing Education**
University Park, PA 16802.
- Inventory of Continuing Education Activities in the Public School Districts of Pennsylvania. a. (Pennsylvania. Department of Education)

**University of Pennsylvania. Department of Regional Science**
3718 Locust St., Philadelphia, PA 19174.
- International Regional Science Review. s-a.

**University of Pennsylvania. Graduate School of Education**
Center for Field Studies, 3700 Walnut Street, Suite D-5, Philadelphia, PA 19104.
- Economic Aspects of Public Education in Pennsylvania. a. ISSN 0085-0144

**University of Pennsylvania. Health Affairs Division**
Room 203, 133 S. 36th St., Philadelphia, PA 19174.
- Health Affairs. q. ISSN 0092-8577

**University of Pennsylvania. Institute for Environmental Studies**
3400 Walnut St., Philadelphia, PA 19104.
- University of Pennsylvania. Institute for Environmental Studies. City Planning Series. ISSN 0079-0680
- University of Pennsylvania. Institute for Environmental Studies. Report. irreg. ISSN 0079-0699

**University of Pennsylvania Law School**
3400 Chestnut St., Philadelphia, PA 19174.
- University of Pennsylvania Law Review. 6 per yr.(Nov.-July) ISSN 0041-9907

**University of Pennsylvania. Linguistics Research Project**
Williams Hall, Philadelphia, PA 19174.
- University of Pennsylvania. Department of Linguistics. Transformations and Discourse Analysis Papers. irreg., 1971, no. 87. ISSN 0079-0672

**University of Pennsylvania. Near East Center**
- Papers on Islamic History. (pub. by International Scholarly Book Services Inc.)

**University of Pennsylvania. Population Studies Center**
3935 Locust St., Philadelphia, PA 19104.
- University of Pennsylvania. Population Studies Center. Analytical and Technical Report. irreg. ISSN 0553-5816

**University of Pennsylvania Press**
3933 Walnut St., Philadelphia, PA 19104.
- Haney Foundation Series. irreg., latest issues (2) published in 1977. ISSN 0073-022X

**University of Pennsylvania. Romance Languages Department**
Philadelphia, PA 19174.
- Hispanic Review; a quarterly journal devoted to research in the Hispanic languages and literatures. q. ISSN 0018-2176

**University of Pennsylvania. School of Dental Medicine**
Philadelphia, PA 19104.
- International Conference on Endodontics. Transactions. quinquennial, 1973, 5th, Philadelphia. ISSN 0074-3054

**University of Pennsylvania. School of Dentistry**
Philadelphia, PA 19104.
- Penn Dental Journal. 3 per yr. ISSN 0031-4331

**University of Pennsylvania. Student Planners Association**
Graduate School of Fine Arts, Philadelphia, PA 19104.
- Planning Comment. s-a. ISSN 0032-0706

**University of Pennsylvania. University Museum**
33rd & Spruce Sts., Philadelphia, PA 19104.
- Expedition. q. ISSN 0014-4738

**University of Pennsylvania. Wharton School of Finance and Commerce**
Philadelphia, PA 19104.
- Studies of Negro Employment. irreg. ISSN 0081-878X (prep. by its Industrial Research Unit)
- University of Pennsylvania. Wharton School of Finance and Commerce. Industrial Research Unit. Studies. irreg., 1969, no. 45. ISSN 0083-9094
- University of Pennsylvania. Wharton School of Finance and Commerce. Labor Relations and Public Policy Series. Reports. irreg. ISSN 0075-7470 (prep. by its Industrial Research Unit)
- University of Pennsylvania. Wharton School of Finance and Commerce. Studies in Quantitative Economics. irreg. ISSN 0081-8437 (prep. by its Economics Research Unit)
- Wharton Magazine. 4 per yr.

**University of Pittsburgh**
Pittsburgh, PA 15213.
- Black Lines: a Journal of Black Studies. q. ISSN 0045-2203

**University of Pittsburgh. College of Arts and Sciences, Book Center**
- Book Notes. (pub. by University of Pittsburgh Press)

**University of Pittsburgh. Communications Media Research Center**
c/o Patrick R. Penland, Graduate School of Library and Information Science, 135 No. Bellefield, Pittsburgh, PA 15260.
- Discourse Units in Human Communication for Librarians. irreg., no. 11, 1973. ISSN 0070-6663

**University of Pittsburgh. Department of Anthropology**
Pittsburgh, PA 15260.
- Ethnology; an international journal of cultural and social anthropology. q. ISSN 0014-1828

**University of Pittsburgh. Department of Economics**
- Economic Books: Current Selections. (pub. by Augustus M. Kelley Publishers)

**University of Pittsburgh. Department of Philosophy**
- American Philosophical Quarterly. Monograph Series. (pub. by Basil Blackwell & Mott Ltd. UK)

**University of Pittsburgh. Department of Slavic Languages & Literatures**
119 LF, Pittsburgh, PA 15260.
- University of Pittsburgh. Department of Slavic Languages and Literatures. Slavic Series. biennial.

**University of Pittsburgh. Graduate School of Business**
Pittsburgh, PA 15213.
- Pittsburgh Business Review. q. ISSN 0032-0315 (prep. by its Bureau of Business Research)

**University of Pittsburgh. Graduate School of Library and Information Sciences**
135 N. Bellefield, Pittsburgh, PA 15260.
- Beta Phi Mu Newsletter. s-a. ISSN 0005-9757
- Pittsburgh Studies in Library and Information Sciences. irreg. ISSN 0079-2144

**University of Pittsburgh Libraries**
G27 Hillman Library, Pittsburgh, PA 15260.
- Romanian Sources. s-a. ISSN 0098-6054 (Co-Sponsor: American Romanian Institute for Research, Inc.)

**University of Pittsburgh. Pediatric and Obstetrical Nursing Departments**
3505 Fifth Ave., Pittsburgh, PA 15213.
- Maternal-Child Nursing Journal. q. ISSN 0090-0702

**University of Pittsburgh Press**
127 N. Bellefield Ave., Pittsburgh, PA 15260.
- Book Notes. 4 per yr. (University of Pittsburgh. College of Arts and Sciences, Book Center) (Co-sponsor: Hillman Library)

- Contemporary Community Health Series. irreg.
- Critical Essays in Modern Literature. irreg., 1969, no. 15. ISSN 0070-153X
- Milton Studies. a. ISSN 0076-8820
- Series in the Philosophy of Science. irreg., 1970, vol.4. ISSN 0080-8970

**University of Pittsburgh. Pymatuning Laboratory of Ecology**
Pittsburgh, PA 15213.
- University of Pennsylvania. Pymatuning Laboratory of Ecology. Special Publication. irreg. ISSN 0079-8207

**University of Pittsburgh. School of Law**
Pittsburgh, PA 15260.
- American Academy of Psychiatry and the Law. Bulletin. q. ISSN 0091-634X
- University of Pittsburgh Law Review. 4 per yr. ISSN 0041-9915

**University of Pittsburgh. University Center for International Studies**
G-6 Mervis Hall, Pittsburgh, PA 15260.
- Cuban Studies/Estudios Cubanos. s-a. (prep. by its Center for Latin American Studies)
- Eighteenth Century Life. q. ISSN 0098-2601
- Historical Methods Newsletter. q. ISSN 0018-2494
- Korean Studies Forum. s-a.
- Peasant Studies Newsletter. q.
- Pennsylvania Ethnic Studies Newsletter. bi-m. (prep. by its Pennsylvania Ethnic Heritage Studies Center)
- Social Science History. q. (Social Science History Association)
- University of Pittsburgh. Center for International Studies: Latin American Studies. Occasional Papers. irreg., no. 10, 1974. ISSN 0075-8140
- University of Pittsburgh. University Center for International Studies. International Newsletter. 4 per yr.

**University of Pittsburgh. University Health Center**
12th Floor, Scaife Hall, Pittsburgh, PA 15261.
- Communique (Pittsburgh) q.

**University of Pittsburgh at Johnstown**
Johnstown, PA 15904.
- Panther. w. ISSN 0031-1006

**University of Portland**
Portland, OR 97203.
- University of Portland Review; journal of arts and sciences. s-a. ISSN 0041-9923

**University of Redlands Associated Students**
Box 1242, Redlands, CA 92373.
- Redlands Bulldog. w. ISSN 0034-2130

**University of Rhode Island**
Memorial Union, Rm. 109, Kingston, RI 02881.
- Good 5-Cent Cigar. s-w.
- Northeastern Regional Antipollution Conference. Proceedings. (pub. by Technomic Publishing Co., Inc.)

**University of Rhode Island. Association of Friends of the Library**
Kingston, RI 02881.
- University of Rhode Island. Library. Library Letter. a.

**University of Rhode Island. Bureau of Government Research**
Kingston, RI 02881.
- University of Rhode Island. Bureau of Government Research. Information Series. irreg. ISSN 0080-2778
- University of Rhode Island. Bureau of Government Research. Metropolitan Series. irreg., 2 issues published through Sept. 1974. ISSN 0080-2786
- University of Rhode Island. Bureau of Government Research. Newsletter. bi-m. ISSN 0007-6171
- University of Rhode Island. Bureau of Government Research. Research Series. irreg. ISSN 0080-2794

**University of Rhode Island. College of Business Administration**
Kingston, RI 02881.
- New England Journal of Business & Economics. s-a. (prep. by its Research Center in Business and Economics)

**University of Rhode Island. College of Pharmacy**
Kingston, RI 02881.
• Pharmacists Quarterly. q. ISSN 0031-6962

**University of Rhode Island. Cooperative Extension Service**
• Rhode Island Resources. (pub. by Rhode Island Agricultural Experiment Station)

**University of Rhode Island. Department of Political Science**
Kingston, RI 02881.
• Occasional Papers in Political Science. irreg. ISSN 0473-7490

**University of Rhode Island. Graduate School of Oceanography**
Kingston, RI 02881.
• Maritimes. q. ISSN 0025-3472
• University of Rhode Island. Graduate School of Oceanography. Collected Reprints. irreg., vol. 10, 1973.
• University of Rhode Island. Graduate School of Oceanography. Marine Technical Reports. irreg., latest issue, no. 35.
• University of Rhode Island. Narragansett Marine Laboratory. Occasional Publication. irreg., 1973, no. 5. ISSN 0077-2828

**University of Rhode Island. Marine Advisory Service**
Narragansett Bay Campus, Narragansett, RI 02882.
• Marine Affairs Journal. a. (prep. by its Marine Affairs Program)
• New England Marine Resources Information. m. ISSN 0047-9659 (prep. by its Sea Grant Program) (Co-Sponsor: U.S. Department of Commerce, National Oceanic and Atmospheric Administration, Office of Sea Grant Programs)

**University of Rhode Island. Water Resources Center**
Kingston, RI 02881.
• University of Rhode Island. Water Resources Center. Annual Report. a.

**University of Richmond. Institute for Business and Community Development**
601 N. Lombardy St., Richmond, VA 23220.
• University of Richmond. Institute for Business and Community Development. Newsletter. irreg. ISSN 0080-3006

**University of Richmond. School of Law**
Richmond, VA 23173.
• University of Richmond Law Review. s-a. ISSN 0566-2389

**University of Rochester**
Rochester, NY 14627.
• University of Rochester Library Bulletin. 2 per yr. ISSN 0041-9974 (prep. by its Rush Rhees Library)

**University of Rochester. Department of Anthropology**
• Lewis Henry Morgan Lectures. (pub. by Aldine Publishing Co.)

**University of San Diego**
San Diego, CA 92210.
• Pequod. a.

**University of San Diego. School of Law**
Alcala Park, San Diego, CA 92110.
• San Diego Law Review. 4 per yr. ISSN 0036-4037 (San Diego Law Review Association)

**University of San Fernando Valley. College of Law**
Sepulveda, CA 91343.
• University of San Fernando Valley Law Review. s-a. ISSN 0042-000X

**University of San Francisco**
San Francisco, CA 94117.
• Wasmann Journal of Biology. s-a. ISSN 0043-0927

**University of San Francisco. Labor Management School**
San Francisco, CA 94117.
• Panel. q. ISSN 0031-0735

**University of San Francisco. School of Law**
Kendrick Hall, 2130 Fulton St., San Francisco, CA 94117.
• University of San Francisco Law Review. 4 per yr. ISSN 0042-0018

**University of Santa Clara**
Santa Clara, CA 95053.
• Asilomar Conference on Circuits and Systems. Conference Record. (pub. by Western Periodicals Co.)
• Fibonacci Quarterly; a journal devoted to the study of integers with special properties. q. ISSN 0015-0517 (Fibonacci Association)

**University of Santa Clara. School of Law**
Santa Clara, CA 95053.
• Santa Clara Lawyer. 4 per yr. ISSN 0581-6106

**University of South Carolina**
Campus P.O. Box 5137, Columbia, SC 29208.
• Crucible; a literary magazine. s-a. ISSN 0045-9135
• Language of Poems. 3 per yr.

**University of South Carolina. Belle W. Baruch Institute for Marine Biology & Coastal Research**
• University of South Carolina. Belle W. Baruch Library in Marine Science and Coastal Research. Collected Papers. (pub. by University of South Carolina Press)

**University of South Carolina. Bureau of Governmental Research**
Columbia, SC 29208.
• University of South Carolina Governmental Review. q. ISSN 0042-0050

**University of South Carolina. College of Business Administration**
Bureau of Business and Economic Research, Columbia, SC 29208.
• Business and Economic Review. 6 per yr. ISSN 0007-6465
• Essays in Economics. 3 per yr. ISSN 0014-0864
• University of South Carolina. Bureau of Business and Economic Research. Occasional Studies. irreg. (prep. by its Bureau of Business and Economic Research)

**University of South Carolina. College of Education**
Columbia, SC 29208.
• University of South Carolina Education Report. m.(Oct-Dec, Feb-April) ISSN 0042-0042

**University of South Carolina. Department of English**
Columbia, SC 29208.
• Names in South Carolina. a. ISSN 0077-2690
• Proof: The Yearbook of American Bibliographical and Textual Studies. a. ISSN 0079-6980
• Stephen Crane Newsletter. q. ISSN 0039-1182
• Studies in the American Renaissance. a.

**University of South Carolina. Department of Foreign Languages and Literatures**
Columbia, SC 29208.
• Contemporary French Civilization. 3 per yr.
• French Literature Series. a.

**University of South Carolina. Graduate School of Social Work**
Columbia, SC 29208.
• Arete. s-a.

**University of South Carolina. Institute of International Studies**
Columbia, SC 29208.
• University of South Carolina. Institute of International Studies. Essay Series. irreg. ISSN 0085-6452

**University of South Carolina Libraries**
Director of Libraries, Columbia, SC 29208.
• University of South Carolina. Libraries. Report of the Director of Libraries. a. ISSN 0081-2706

**University of South Carolina Press**
Columbia, SC 29208.
• Studies in International Affairs. irreg. ISSN 0081-8046 (Institute of International Studies)
• Studies in Scottish Literature. a. ISSN 0039-3770
• University of South Carolina. Belle W. Baruch Library in Marine Science and Coastal Research. Collected Papers. irreg (approx. 2 per yr)

**University of South Carolina. School of Law**
Columbia, SC 29208.
• South Carolina Law Review. 5 per yr. ISSN 0038-3104

**University of South Dakota. Center for Continuing Education**
Vermillion, SD 57069.
• South Dakota Journal of County Government. m. (South Dakota Association of County Commissioners)

**University of South Dakota. College of Arts and Sciences**
Vermillion, SD 57069.
• South Dakota Review. 4 per yr. ISSN 0038-3368

**University of South Dakota. Governmental Research Bureau**
Vermilion, SD 57069.
• Precinct Returns for Major Elections in South Dakota. biennial. ISSN 0085-5081
• Public Affairs. q. ISSN 0555-5914

**University of South Dakota. Institute of Indian Studies**
Vermillion, SD 57069.
• University of South Dakota Bulletin. 19 per yr. ISSN 0042-0069

**University of South Dakota. School of Business**
Vermillion, SD 57069.
• South Dakota Business Review. q. ISSN 0038-3260 (prep. by its Business Research Bureau)

**University of South Dakota. School of Law**
Vermillion, SD 57069.
• South Dakota Law Review. 3 per yr. ISSN 0038-3325

**University of South Florida. College of Arts and Letters**
4202 E. Fowler Ave., Tampa, FL 33620.
• University of South Florida Language Quarterly. s-a(double issue) ISSN 0042-0077

**University of South Florida. College of Medicine**
Tampa, FL 33620.
• Cancer Seminar. a. ISSN 0069-0171

**University of South Florida. Department of English**
Tampa, FL 33620.
• Scholia Satyrica. q.

**University of Southern California**
Los Angeles, CA 90007.
• Sociology and Social Research; an international journal. q. ISSN 0038-0393

**University of Southern California. Department of History**
Los Angeles, CA 90007.
• International Labor and Working Class History. 2 per yr. (prep. by its Study Group on Labor and Working Class History)

**University of Southern California. Department of Linguistics**
Los Angeles, CA 90007.
• Papers in Japanese Linguistics. a. (prep. by its Japanese Linguistics Workshop)

**University of Southern California. Department of University Affairs**
Univ. Park, Los Angeles, CA 90007.
• Trojan Family. m. ISSN 0042-0085

**University of Southern California Law Center**
Los Angeles, CA 90007.
• Preventive Law Newsletter. a. ISSN 0555-0963
• Southern California Law Review. 5 per yr. ISSN 0038-3910

**University of Southern California. Library**
University Park, Los Angeles, CA 90007.
• Coranto. s-a. ISSN 0010-8669 (Friends of the USC Libraries)

**University of Southern California Press**
c/o Bookstore, Los Angeles, CA 90007.
• Far Eastern and Russian Research Series Monographs. irreg. ISSN 0071-3813
• U S C Annual Distinguished Lecture Series Monographs in Special Education and Rehabilitation. a. ISSN 0070-6736 (University of Southern California. School of Education)

**University of Southern California. School of Education**
• U S C Annual Distinguished Lecture Series Monographs in Special Education and Rehabilitation. (pub. by University of Southern California Press)

**University of Southern California. School of International Relations**
Los Angeles, CA 90007.
- World Studies. q.

**University of Southern California. School of Philosophy**
University Park, Los Angeles, CA 90007.
- Personalist; an international review of philosophy. q. ISSN 0031-5621

**University of Southern Mississippi**
Hattiesburg, MS 39401.
- Mississippi Geographer. a. (Mississippi Council for Geographic Education) (Orders to:, Box 468)
- Southern Quarterly; a scholarly journal in the humanities and the social sciences. q. ISSN 0038-4496
- University of Southern Mississippi, Hattiesburg. Annual Report of the President to the Board of Trustees of State Institutions of Higher Learning. a.

**University of Southern Mississippi. Alumni Association**
Box 13, Southern Sta., Hattiesburg, MS 39401.
- Southern News and Views. q. ISSN 0038-4380

**University of Southern Mississippi. Center for Writers**
Ed. Gordon Weaver, Box 37, Southern Station, Hattiesburg, MS 39401.
- Mississippi Review. 3 per yr. ISSN 0047-7559

**University of Southern Mississippi. Department of English**
Hattiesburg, MS 39401.
- Notes on Mississippi Writers. s-a. ISSN 0029-4071

**University of Southern Mississippi. School of Education and Psychology**
Box 107, Southern Sta., Hattiesburg, MS 39401.
- Southern Journal of Education Research. q. ISSN 0038-4267

**University of Southwestern Louisiana**
Box 4-0831, Lafayette, LA 70504.
- U S L History Series. s-a.

**University of Southwestern Louisiana. Center for Louisiana Studies**
Box 831 USL, Lafayette, LA 70501.
- Attakapas Gazette. q. ISSN 0571-8236 (Attakapas Historical Association)

**University of Tampa**
Tampa, FL 33606.
- U T Review. q.

**University of Tennessee**
Knoxville, TN 37916.
- Southern Speech Communication Journal. q. (Southern Speech Communication Association)
- Transit of Chi Epsilon. s-a. ISSN 0041-1167 (Chi Epsilon)
- University of Tennessee. Library Lectures. triennial.
- University of Tennessee. Report on Research and Publications. a.

**University of Tennessee. Agricultural Experiment Station**
Knoxville, TN 37901.
- Tennessee Agricultural Experiment Station. Bulletin. 15 per yr. ISSN 0040-3148
- Tennessee Farm and Home Science. q. ISSN 0040-3229

**University of Tennessee at Chattanooga**
Chattanooga, TN 37401.
- Tristania. s-a. ISSN 0360-3385

**University of Tennessee. Center for Business and Economic Research**
Knoxville, TN 37916.
- Tennessee Statistical Abstract. triennial. ISSN 0082-2760

**University of Tennessee. Center for the Health Sciences**
Memphis, TN 38103.
- Forum for the Advancement of Toxicology. q. (Forum for the Advancement of Toxicology in Colleges of Pharmacy)

**University of Tennessee. College of Dentistry**
847 Monroe Ave., Memphis, TN 38103.
- U. T. Dental Alumni News. q. ISSN 0041-5596

**University of Tennessee. College of Engineering**
124 Perkins Hall, Knoxville, TN 37916.
- Tennessee Engineer. 3 per yr.

**University of Tennessee. Department of English**
301 McClung Tower, Knoxville, TN 37916.
- Tennessee Studies in Literature. a. ISSN 0497-2384

**University of Tennessee. Drug and Toxicology Information Center**
University of Tennessee Medical Units, 800 Madison Avenue, Memphis, TN 38103.
- Drug Information Newsletter. bi-m.

**University of Tennessee. Institute for Public Service**
Knoxville, TN 37916.
- University of Tennessee. Institute for Public Service. MTAS Technical Report. irreg. (prep. by its Municipal Technical Advisory Service)

**University of Tennessee. National Alumni Association**
605 Andy Holt Tower, Knoxville, TN 37916.
- Tennessee Alumnus. 4 per yr. ISSN 0040-3156

**University of Texas at Arlington**
- Walter Prescott Webb Memorial Lectures. (pub. by University of Texas Press)

**University of Texas at Arlington. Department of English**
Arlington, TX 76019.
- American Literary Realism: 1870-1910. q. ISSN 0002-9823
- World Literature Written in English. s-a.

**University of Texas at Austin**
- Daily Texan. (pub. by Texas Student Publications)
- Texas Memorial Museum. Information Circulars. (pub. by Texas Memorial Museum)
- Texas Quarterly. (pub. by University of Texas Press)
- Texas Studies in Literature and Language. (pub. by University of Texas Press)

**University of Texas at Austin. African and Afro-American Studies and Research Center**
- Research in African Literatures. (pub. by University of Texas Press)

**University of Texas at Austin. Bureau of Business Research**
Austin, TX 78712.
- Building Construction in Texas. m. ISSN 0007-3415
- Directory of Texas Manufacturers. a. ISSN 0070-6450
- J. Anderson Fitzgerald Lecture. irreg., 1969, no. 5. ISSN 0075-2045
- Richard J. Gonzalez Lecture. irreg., no. 5, 1974. ISSN 0080-2972
- Selected Trade and Professional Associations in Texas. a. ISSN 0080-8644
- Studies in Human Resources Development. irreg. (prep. by its Center for the Study of Human Resources)
- Texas Business Review. m. ISSN 0040-4209
- Texas Economic Indicators. m.
- Texas Industrial Expansion. m. ISSN 0040-4365
- Texas Industry Series. irreg., 1968, no. 11. ISSN 0082-3066
- University of Texas, Austin. Bureau of Business Research. Area Economic Survey. irreg., no. 34, 1973. ISSN 0082-3228
- University of Texas, Austin. Bureau of Business Research. Bibliography. irreg; no. 18, 1976. ISSN 0082-3236
- University of Texas, Austin. Bureau of Business Research. Business Guide. irreg., no. 15, 1974. ISSN 0082-3244
- University of Texas, Austin. Bureau of Business Research. Publications. a. ISSN 0495-2634
- University of Texas, Austin. Bureau of Business Research. Research Monograph. irreg., no. 36, 1973. ISSN 0082-3279
- University of Texas, Austin. Bureau of Business Research. Studies in Accounting. irreg; no. 7, 1977. ISSN 0081-7465
- University of Texas, Austin. Bureau of Business Research. Studies in Banking and Finance. irreg., no. 10, 1972. ISSN 0081-7570
- University of Texas, Austin. Bureau of Business Research. Studies in Insurance and Actuarial Science. irreg., no. 3, 1973. ISSN 0085-6851

- University of Texas, Austin. Bureau of Business Research. Studies in Latin American Business. irreg; no. 16, 1975. ISSN 0081-8135
- University of Texas, Austin. Bureau of Business Research. Studies in Marketing. irreg; no. 23, 1976. ISSN 0081-8186
- University of Texas, Austin. Bureau of Business Research. Studies in Personnel and Management. irreg., no. 23, 1971. ISSN 0081-8348
- W. H. Irons Memorial Lecture Series. irreg.

**University of Texas at Austin. Bureau of Economic Geology**
Box X, University Station, Austin, TX 78712.
- Texas Mineral Producers. irreg., 1970, no. 3. ISSN 0082-3104
- University of Texas, Austin. Bureau of Economic Geology. Annual Report. a. ISSN 0082-3287
- University of Texas, Austin. Bureau of Economic Geology. Geologic Quadrangle Maps (with Text) irreg; no. 41, 1976. ISSN 0082-3317
- University of Texas, Austin. Bureau of Economic Geology. Geological Circular. irreg; no. 76-6, 1976. ISSN 0082-3309
- University of Texas, Austin. Bureau of Economic Geology. Guidebook. irreg., no. 15, 1973. ISSN 0082-3295
- University of Texas, Austin. Bureau of Economic Geology. Handbook. irreg; no. 4, 1974. ISSN 0082-3325
- University of Texas, Austin. Bureau of Economic Geology. Mineral Resource Circulars. irreg; no. 57, 1975. ISSN 0082-3333
- University of Texas, Austin. Bureau of Economic Geology. Publication Series. irreg., latest issue, 1967. ISSN 0082-3341
- University of Texas, Austin. Bureau of Economic Geology. Report of Investigations. irreg; no. 86, 1976. ISSN 0082-335X

**University of Texas at Austin. Center for Communication Research**
Austin, TX 78712.
- Communication Research Notes. irreg.?

**University of Texas at Austin. Center for Intercultural Studies in Folklore and Ethnomusicology**
SWB 306, Austin, TX 78712.
- Folklore Newsletter. s-a. ISSN 0092-0983 (Co-Sponsor: University Folklore Association)

**University of Texas at Austin. Center for Intercultural Studies in Folklore and Oral History**
S.W.B. 306, Austin, TX 78712.
- Folklore Annual. a. ISSN 0071-6782 (University Folklore Association)

**University of Texas at Austin. Center for Neo-Hellenic Studies**
Austin, TX 78712.
- Neo-Hellenika. s-a. ISSN 0077-6521
- University of Texas, Austin. Center for Neo-Hellenic Studies. Bulletin. a. ISSN 0067-0707

**University of Texas at Austin. Center for Research in Water Resources**
Balcones Research Center, 10,100 Burnet Rd., Austin, TX 78758.
- C R W R News. q. ISSN 0049-3538

**University of Texas at Austin. Department of Anthropology**
Austin, TX 78712.
- University of Texas, Austin. Department of Anthropology. Anthropology Series. irreg. ISSN 0082-3414

**Univ. of Texas at Austin. Department of Astronomy**
Physics-Math-Astronomy Bldg, Room 15.212, Austin, TX 78712.
- University of Texas Monographs in Astronomy. irreg. ISSN 0082-3546

**University of Texas at Austin. Department of English**
Austin, TX 78712.
- Direction Line; newsletter for bibliographers and textual critics. s-a.

**University of Texas at Austin. Department of Germanic Languages**
Box 7939, Austin, TX 78712.
- Dimension; contemporary German arts and letters. 3 per yr. ISSN 0012-2882

**University of Texas at Austin. Electronics Research Center**
Austin, TX 78712.
- Texas Annual of Electronics Research. a.

**University of Texas at Austin. Ex-Students Association**
Box 7278, University Sta., Austin, TX 78712.
- Alcalde. bi-m. ISSN 0002-497X

**University of Texas at Austin. Humanities Research Center**
Box 7219, Austin, TX 78712.
- Library Chronicle. s-a. ISSN 0024-2241
- University of Texas. Humanities Research Center. Bibliographical Monograph Series. irreg. ISSN 0564-6855
- University of Texas. Humanities Research Center. Tower Bibliographical Series. irreg. ISSN 0563-2595

**University of Texas at Austin. Law School Foundation**
2500 Red River, Austin, TX 78705.
- American Journal of Criminal Law. 3 per yr. ISSN 0092-2315

**University of Texas at Austin. Lyndon B. Johnson School of Public Affairs**
Austin, TX 78712.
- Guide to Texas State Agencies. irreg; 5th ed., 1977.
- Public Affairs Comment. q. ISSN 0033-3395
- Texas Legislative Issues: Report of the Texas Legislature Pre-Session Conference; judicial reorganization, revenue sharing, property taxation and school finance. biennial
- University of Texas, Austin. County Auditors' Institute. Proceedings. a. ISSN 0082-3406 (Co-sponsor: County Auditors Association of Texas)
- University of Texas, Austin. Institute for Tax Assessors. Proceedings. a. ISSN 0082-3430 (Co-sponsors: Texas Association of Assessing Officers; Texas Municipal League)
- University of Texas, Austin. Lyndon B. Johnson School of Public Affairs. Occasional Papers. irreg.
- University of Texas, Austin. Lyndon B. Johnson School of Public Affairs. Seminar Research Report. irreg.

**University of Texas at Austin. Natural Fibers Economic Research**
Box 8180, University Station, Austin, TX 78712.
- Texas Cotton Review. a. ISSN 0082-3392 (Co-sponsor: Natural Fibers & Food Protein Commission of Texas)
- University of Texas, Austin. Natural Fibers Economic Research. Research Report. irreg. ISSN 0082-3384 (Co-sponsor: Natural Fibers & Food Protein Commission of Texas)

**University of Texas at Austin. School of Law**
2500 Red River, Austin, TX 78705.
- Checklist of Human Rights Documents. m. (prep. by its Tarlton Law Library)

**University of Texas at Austin. Tarlton Law Library**
2500 Red River, Austin, TX 78705.
- Tarlton Law Library. Notes. bi-m. ISSN 0029-4020
- University of Texas, Austin. Tarlton Law Library. Legal Bibliography Series. irreg. ISSN 0085-7092

**University of Texas at Dallas**
P.O. Box 688, Richardson, TX 75080.
- Engineering Economist. q. ISSN 0013-791X (American Society for Engineering Education. Engineering Economy Division)
- Flora of Texas. irreg. ISSN 0071-5808
- Texas Research Foundation, Renner. Contributions. irreg., 1970, vol. 6. ISSN 0082-3139
- Wrightia; a botanical journal. irreg., vol. 5, no. 3, 1974. ISSN 0084-2648

**University of Texas at El Paso**
El Paso, TX 79968.
- Nova. q. ISSN 0029-4985
- Southwestern Studies. Monographs. (pub. by Texas Western Press)

**University of Texas at El Paso. Bureau of Business and Economic Research**
Box 180, El Paso, TX 79968.
- El Paso Economic Review. m. ISSN 0013-4031

**University of Texas at Galveston. Medical Branch**
Galveston, TX 77550.
- Texas Reports on Biology and Medicine. q. ISSN 0040-4675
- University Medical. bi-m. ISSN 0042-014X

**University of Texas at Port Aransas. Marine Science Institute**
Port Aransas Marine Laboratory, Port Aransas, TX 78373.
- Contributions in Marine Science. a.

**University of Texas at San Antonio. Center for Archeological Research**
Box 6005, San Antonio, TX 78285.
- Lithic Technology. 3 per yr.

**University of Texas. M.D. Anderson Hospital and Tumor Institute**
Texas Medical Center, Houston, TX 77025.
- Anderson Hospital and Tumor Institute, Houston, Texas. General Report. biennial ISSN 0066-1627
- Anderson Hospital and Tumor Institute, Houston, Texas. Research Report. biennial. ISSN 0066-1635
- Cancer Bulletin. (pub. by Medical Arts Publishing Foundation)
- Clinical Conference on Cancer. Papers. (pub. by Year Book Medical Publishers, Inc.)
- Current Articles on Neoplasia. w. (prep. by its Research Medical Library)
- Mammalian Chromosomes Newsletter. q. (prep. by its Section of Cell Biology)

**University of Texas Press**
Austin, TX 78712.
- Journal of Library History, Philosophy and Comparative Librarianship. q. ISSN 0022-2259
- Research in African Literatures. 3 per yr. ISSN 0034-5210 (University of Texas at Austin. African and Afro-American Studies and Research Center)
- Social Science Quarterly. q. ISSN 0038-4941 (Southwestern Social Science Association) (Co-Sponsor: University of Texas)
- Texas Quarterly. q. ISSN 0040-4659 (University of Texas at Austin)
- Texas Studies in Literature and Language; a journal of the humanities. 4 per yr. ISSN 0040-4691 (University of Texas at Austin)
- Walter Prescott Webb Memorial Lectures. a. ISSN 0083-713X (University of Texas at Arlington)

**University of the Pacific**
Stockton, CA 95204.
- Pacific Historian. q. ISSN 0030-8676

**University of the Pacific. Association of Students**
Stockton, CA 95204.
- Pacifican. w. ISSN 0030-8994

**University of the Pacific. McGeorge School of Law**
3201 Donner Way, Sacto, CA 95817.
- Pacific Law Journal. s-a. ISSN 0030-8757

**University of the Pacific. Pacific Marine Station**
Dillon Beach, CA 94929.
- Pacific Marine Station, Dillon Beach, California. Research Report. irreg. ISSN 0078-7604

**University of the Pacific. School of Dentistry**
2155 Webster St., San Francisco, CA 94115.
- Contact Point. q. ISSN 0010-7301

**University of the Pacific. School of Pharmacy**
Attn.: Dr. M. H. Malone, Stockton, CA 95211
- American Journal of Pharmaceutical Education. 5 per yr. ISSN 0002-9459 (American Association of Colleges of Pharmacy) (Subscr. to: Amer. Assn of Colleges of Pharmacy, 4630 Montgomery Ave., Suite 201, Bethesda, MD 20014)
- Pacific Information Service on Street-Drugs. 6 per yr.

**University of the South**
Sewanee, TN 37375.
- Sewanee News. q. ISSN 0037-3044
- Sewanee Review. q. ISSN 0037-3052

**University of the South. School of Theology**
Sewanee, TN 37375.
- St. Luke's Journal of Theology. q.

**University of Toledo. College of Business Administration**
Business Research Center, 2801 W. Bancroft St., Toledo, OH 43606.
- University of Toledo. Business Research Center. Business Administration and Economics Reference Service. irreg.
- University of Toledo. Business Research Center. Miscellaneous Papers. irreg; latest issue, 1977.
- University of Toledo. Business Research Center. Occasional Papers. irreg; latest issue, 1977.
- University of Toledo. Business Research Center. Regional Research Reports. irreg; latest issue, 1977.
- University of Toledo. Business Research Center. Studies in Financial Institutions. irreg; latest edition, 1976.
- University of Toledo. Business Research Center. Working Papers in Operations Analysis. irreg; latest edition, 1974.

**University of Toledo. College of Education**
- Journal of Abstracts in International Education. (pub. by University of Toledo Press)

**University of Toledo. College of Law**
Student Bar Assn., Toledo, OH 43606.
- Discovery (Toledo) ISSN 0012-3633
- University of Toledo Law Review. 3 per yr. ISSN 0042-0190

**University of Toledo Press**
Toledo, OH 43606
(Subscr. Address: c/o Malcolm Campbell, Bowling Green State Univ., Bowling Green, OH 43403)
- Journal of Abstracts in International Education. s-a. ISSN 0094-2383 (University of Toledo. College of Education) (Co-sponsors: Bowling Green State University, University of Akron)

**University of Tulsa**
Tulsa, OK 74104.
- James Joyce Quarterly. q. ISSN 0021-4183
- Nimrod; an individual review. s-a. ISSN 0029-053X

**University of Tulsa College of Law**
3120 E. Fourth Place, Tulsa, OK 74104.
- Tulsa Law Journal. q. ISSN 0041-4050

**University of Tulsa. Department of English**
600 S. College Ave., Tulsa, OK 74104.
- University of Tulsa. Department of English. Monograph Series. irreg., 1972, no. 14. ISSN 0082-6812

**University of Tulsa. Information Services Department**
1133 N. Lewis, Tulsa, OK 74110.
- Alphabetic Subject Index to Petroleum Abstracts. s-m. ISSN 0002-6441
- Dual Dictionary Coordinate Index to Petroleum Abstracts. s-a. ISSN 0012-6853
- Petroleum Abstracts. w. ISSN 0031-6423

**University of Utah**
258 O S H, Salt Lake City, UT 84112.
- Western Political Quarterly. q. ISSN 0043-4078 (Western Political Science Association) (Co-sponsors: Pacific Northwest Political Science Association; Southern California Political Science Association)

**University of Utah. Bureau of Economic and Business Research**
Salt Lake City, UT 84112.
- Utah Construction Report. q. ISSN 0042-1383
- Utah Economic and Business Review. m. ISSN 0042-1405
- Utah Export Directory. irreg., latest issue, 1975. ISSN 0092-2374 (Co-Sponsor: University of Utah Center for Economic and Community Development)

**University of Utah. College of Law**
Salt Lake City, UT 84112.
- Journal of Contemporary Law. s-a.
- Utah Law Review. q. ISSN 0042-1448 (Utah Law Review Society)

**University of Utah. Department of Economics**
Salt Lake City, UT 84112.
- Intermountain Economic Review. s-a. ISSN 0020-5664

**University of Utah. Department of English**
Salt Lake City, UT 84112.
- Possible Sack. m.
- Western Humanities Review. q. ISSN 0043-3845

**University of Utah. Eccles Medical Sciences Library**
Extension Services, Salt Lake City, UT 84112.
- Hospital Library Handbook. irreg.

**University of Utah. Electrical Engineering Department**
3054 Merrill Engineering Bldg., Salt Lake City, UT 84112.
- University of Utah. Microwave Device and Physical Electronics Laboratory Quarterly Report. q. ISSN 0026-2870 (prep. by its Microwave Device and Physcial Electronics Lab)

**University of Utah. Institute of Industrial Relations**
227 College of Business, Salt Lake City, UT 84112.
- University of Utah. Institute of Industrial Relations. Bulletin. irreg. ISSN 0083-4912

**University of Utah. Office of Institutional Studies**
Salt Lake City, UT 84112.
- University of Utah. Office of Institutional Studies. Statistical Summaries. a. ISSN 0083-4920

**University of Utah Press**
Salt Lake City, UT 84112.
- Publications in the American West. irreg., latest issue, 1978. ISSN 0085-5227 (American West Center)
- University of Utah Anthropological Papers. irreg., 1973, no. 95. ISSN 0083-4947

**University of Vermont. Cooperative Extension Service**
Morrill Hall, Burlington, VT 05401.
- Vermont Resources Research Center Series. irreg., latest, no. 20.

**University of Vermont. Department of English**
Burlington, VT 05401.
- Exercise Exchange; a journal for teachers of English in high schools and colleges. s-a.

**University of Virginia**
Newcomb Hall, Charlottesville, VA 22903.
- Cavalier Daily. 5 per w. ISSN 0008-8609
- Virginia Law Weekly. w. ISSN 0042-661X
- Virginia Quarterly Review; a national journal of literature and discussion. q. ISSN 0042-675X

**University of Virginia. Corcoran Department of History**
History Club, Randall Hall, Charlottesville, VA 22903.
- Essays in History. a. ISSN 0071-1411

**University of Virginia. Institute of Government**
207 Minor Hall, Charlottesville, VA 22903.
- University of Virginia News Letter. 12 per yr. ISSN 0042-0271

**University of Virginia Library**
Charlottesville, VA 22901.
- University of Virginia. Library. Microfilm Publications. irreg., 1969, no. 8. ISSN 0083-6559 (prep. by its Department of Photographic Services)

**University of Virginia. School of Law**
Charlottesville, VA 22900.
- Legwork. bi-m (Sep-May) (prep. by its Legal Environment Group)
- Virginia Journal of International Law. q. ISSN 0042-6571 (Virginia Journal of International Law Association)
- Virginia Law Review. 8 per yr. ISSN 0042-6601 (Virginia Law Review Association)

**University of Virginia. School of Medicine**
Medical Library, Charlottesville, VA 22901.
- Virginia Union List of Biomedical Serials. irreg., 1975, 5th ed. ISSN 0083-6540

**University of Washington**
4045 Brooklyn Ave. N.E., Seattle, WA 98105.
- Modern Language Quarterly. q. ISSN 0026-7929
- Pacific Northwest Quarterly. q. ISSN 0030-8803
- Poetry Northwest. q. ISSN 0032-2113

**University of Washington. Black Student Union**
Hub, Seattle, WA 98105.
- Black Voice. ISSN 0006-4300

**University of Washington. College of Architecture & Urban Planning**
Seattle, WA 98195.
- University of Washington. College of Architecture and Urban Planning. Development Series. irreg.

**University of Washington. College of Business Administration**
105 Mackenzie Hall, Seattle, WA 98195.
- University of Washington. College of Business Administration. Occasional Paper. irreg., no. 25, 1971. ISSN 0511-2834

**University of Washington. College of Education**
Seattle, WA 98105.
- University of Washington. College of Education Record. bi-m(Nov.-May) ISSN 0042-0301

**University of Washington. College of Engineering**
Office of the Dean of Engineering, Seattle, WA 98195.
- Trend in Engineering. q. ISSN 0041-2317

**University of Washington. College of Fisheries**
- University of Washington Publications in Fisheries. (pub. by University of Washington Press)

**University of Washington. College of Fisheries and Fisheries Institute**
Seattle, WA 98105.
- Research in Fisheries. a. ISSN 0083-7555

**University of Washington. Department of English**
Seattle, WA 98105.
- Assay. ISSN 0004-5004
- Autumn. irreg; 1973, vol. 29.

**University of Washington. Department of Environmental Health**
461 Health Sciences Building, Dept. of Environmental Health Sc-34, Seattle, WA 98195.
- Environmental Health and Safety News. m. (prep. by its School of Public Health and Community Medicine)

**University of Washington. Department of Oceanography**
Seattle, WA 98105.
- University of Washington. Department of Oceanography. Contribution. irreg. ISSN 0083-7520
- University of Washington. Department of Oceanography. Fishery Report. irreg. ISSN 0083-7539
- University of Washington. Department of Oceanography. Special Report. irreg. ISSN 0083-7547

**University of Washington. Division of Marine Resources**
4059 Roosevelt Way N.E., Seattle, WA 98105.
- AIDJEX Bulletin. approx. 5 per yr. ISSN 0091-3480

**University of Washington. Graduate School of Business Administration**
Seattle, WA 98195.
- Journal of Contemporary Business. q.
- Journal of Financial and Quantitative Analysis. 5 per yr. ISSN 0022-1090 (Western Finance Association)

**University of Washington. Graduate School of Public Affairs**
- Public Policy Issues in Resource Management. (pub. by University of Washington Press)

**University of Washington. Henry Art Gallery**
Seattle, WA 98195.
- Index of Art in the Pacific Northwest. irreg., no. 7, 1975. ISSN 0085-1760

**University of Washington. Institute for Comparative & Foreign Area Studies**
- Publications on Asia. (pub. by University of Washington Press)
- Publications on Russia and Eastern Europe. (pub. by University of Washington Press)

**University of Washington. Institute for Environmental Studies**
211 Engineering Annex 7M-12, Seattle, WA 98195.
- Environmental Outlook. m.

**University of Washington Libraries**
Seattle, WA 98195.
- Washington Library Letter. s-m. ISSN 0511-3202

**University of Washington Press**
Seattle, Wa 98105.
- Asian Law Series. irreg., no. 5, 1976.
- B B C Music Guides. irreg., no. 33, 1975. ISSN 0084-8018

- Biology Series (Seattle) irreg.
- International Conference on Causes of Sudden Death in Infants. Proceedings. irreg., 2nd, 1970.
- Public Policy Issues in Resource Management. irreg., vol. 5, 1973. ISSN 0079-7634 (University of Washington. Graduate School of Public Affairs)
- Publications on Asia. irreg., no. 31, 1977. ISSN 0079-7782 (University of Washington. Institute for Comparative & Foreign Area Studies)
- Publications on Russia and Eastern Europe. irreg., no. 8, 1977. ISSN 0079-7790 (University of Washington. Institute for Comparative & Foreign Area Studies)
- University of Washington Publications in Fisheries. irreg., vol. 6, 1975. ISSN 0085-7939 (University of Washington. College of Fisheries)
- Walker-Ames Lectures. irreg.

**University of Washington. School of Law**
Condon Hall, Seattle, WA 98105.
- Washington Law Review. 4 per yr. ISSN 0043-0617

**University of Washington School of Medicine. Health Sciences Information Services**
E-305, Health Sciences Center SC-60, Seattle, WA 98195.
- University of Washington Medicine. q. ISSN 0094-2006

**University of West Florida**
John C. Pace Library, Pensacola, FL 32504.
- Gulf Coast Conference Proceedings. biennial. (Gulf Coast History and Humanities Conference)

**University of West Los Angeles**
Law Review, 11000 Washington Blvd., Culver City, CA 90230.
- University of West Los Angeles Law Review. a. ISSN 0083-4068

**University of Wisconsin. Department of English**
- Modine Gunch. (pub. by Modine Gunch Press)

**University of Wisconsin. Department of German**
- Monatshefte fuer Deutschen Unterricht. (pub. by University of Wisconsin Press)

**University of Wisconsin-La Crosse**
La Crosse, WI 54601.
- Racquet. w.(during school yr) ISSN 0033-930X

**University of Wisconsin-La Crosse. Center for Contemporary Poetry**
Murphy Library, La Crosse, WI 54601.
- Voyages to the Inland Sea. a.

**University of Wisconsin-La Crosse. Institute for Minority Studies**
101 Main Hall, Lacrosse, WI 54601.
- National Association of Interdisciplinary Ethnic Studies. Newsletter. 3 per yr.

**University of Wisconsin-Madison**
Social Science Bldg., Madison, WI 53706.
- Land Economics; a quarterly journal devoted to the study of economic and social institutions. q. ISSN 0023-7639

**University of Wisconsin-Madison. African Studies Program**
Madison, WI 53706.
- University of Wisconsin. African Studies Program. Occasional Papers. irreg.

**University of Wisconsin-Madison. Applied Population Laboratory**
Madison, WI 53706.
- University of Wisconsin, Madison. Applied Population Laboratory. Population Note. irreg., no. 12, 1969. ISSN 0084-0734
- University of Wisconsin, Madison. Applied Population Laboratory. Population Series. irreg., no. 24, 1970. ISSN 0084-0742

**University of Wisconsin, Madison. Cartographic Laboratory**
Science Hall, Madison, WI 53706.
- University of Wisconsin, Madison. Cartographic Laboratory. Paper. irreg.

**University of Wisconsin, Madison. Center for Women's and Family Living Education**
North Lake St., Madison, WI 53706.
- Wisconsin Women Newsletter. irreg. ISSN 0085-8242

University of Wisconsin-Madison. Center System
Libraries
2218 University Ave., Madison, WI 53706.
● Off Center. m. ISSN 0048-1491

University of Wisconsin-Madison. Department of
African Languages and Literature
1450 Van Hise Hall, Madison, WI 53706.
● Ba Shiru. s-a. ISSN 0045-1282

University of Wisconsin, Madison. Department of Art
1913 Shepherd St. N.W., Madison, WI 53706.
● Wisconsin Monographs of Visual Arts Education.
s-a.

University of Wisconsin-Madison. Department of East
Asian Languages and Literature
Madison, WI 53706.
● Wisconsin China Series. irreg. ISSN 0084-053X

University of Wisconsin-Madison. Department of
English
● Contemporary Literature. (pub. by University of
Wisconsin Press)

University of Wisconsin-Madison. Department of
French & Italian
618 van Hise, Madison, WI 53706.
● Sub-Stance. 3 per yr. ISSN 0049-2426

University of Wisconsin-Madison. Department of
German
Box 413, Milwaukee, WI 53201.
● New German Critique; an interdisciplinary journal
of German studies. 3 per yr. ISSN 0094-033X

University of Wisconsin-Madison. Engineering
Experiment Station
Madison, WI 53706.
● Univeristy of Wisconsin, Madison. Engineering
Experiment Station. Annual Report. a. ISSN
0084-0882

University of Wisconsin-Madison. Extension
Departments of Mathematics
Business Office, 432 North Lake Street, Madison,
WI 53706.
● Delta. s-a. ISSN 0011-801X

University of Wisconsin-Madison. Extension Services
in Pharmacy
Rm 155 Pharmacy Bldg., Madison, WI 53706.
● Wisconsin Pharmacy Extension Bulletin. m. ISSN
0043-6593

University of Wisconsin-Madison. Graduate School of
Business
1155 Observatory Dr., Madison, WI 53706.
● University of Wisconsin. Bureau of Business
Research and Service. Monographs. irreg. ISSN
0512-0918

University of Wisconsin-Madison. Institute for
Research in the Humanities
Madison, WI 53706.
● Nestor. m. ISSN 0028-2812

University of Wisconsin-Madison. Institute for
Research on Poverty
Social Science Building, 1180 Observatory Drive,
Madison, WI 53706.
● University of Wisconsin. Institute for Research on
Poverty. Monograph Series. (pub. by Academic
Press, Inc.)
● University of Wisconsin, Madison. Institute for
Research on Poverty. Research Report. s-a. ISSN
0092-847X
● University of Wisconsin, Madison. Institute for
Research on Poverty. Reprint Series. irreg., 1971,
no. 61. ISSN 0084-0769

University of Wisconsin-Madison. Land Tenure
Center
1525 Observatory Dr., 310 King Hall, Madison, WI
53706.
● L T C Newsletter. irreg; no. 53, 1976. ISSN 0084-
0785
● L T C Paper. irreg; no. 112, 1976. ISSN 0084-
0793
● Land Economics Monographs. (pub. by University
of Wisconsin Press)
● University of Wisconsin, Madison. Land Tenure
Center. Reprint. irreg; no. 129, 1974. ISSN 0084-
0807
● University of Wisconsin, Madison. Land Tenure
Center. Research Paper. irreg; no. 70, 1976. ISSN
0084-0815

● University of Wisconsin, Madison. Land Tenure
Center. Training and Methods Series. irreg; no.
26, 1975. ISSN 0084-0823

University of Wisconsin-Madison. Law School
975 Bascom Mall, Madison, WI 53706.
● Wisconsin Law Review. 4 per yr. ISSN 0043-
650X

University of Wisconsin-Madison. Office of Research
Publications
110 Commerce Building, 1155 Observatory Dr.,
Madison, WI 53706.
● Wisconsin Business Monographs. irreg; no. 10,
1976. ISSN 0084-0513
● Wisconsin Economy Studies. irreg., 1973, no. 14.
ISSN 0084-0599

University of Wisconsin-Madison. Program in African
Economic History
Madison, WI 53706.
● African Economic History Review. irreg. ISSN
0360-6333

University of Wisconsin-Madison. Regional
Rehabilitation Research Institute
Madison, WI 53706.
● Wisconsin Studies in Vocational Rehabilitation.
Monographs. irreg. ISSN 0512-5456

University of Wisconsin-Madison. Seminar on the
Acquisition of Latin American Library Materials
Memorial Library, Madison, WI 53706.
● University of Wisconsin, Madison. Seminars on
the Acquisition of Latin American Library
Materials. Microfilm Projects Newsletter. a.

University of Wisconsin-Madison. University Center
for Cooperatives
Madison, WI 53706.
● International Journal of Cooperative
Development/Revista Internacional de Desarrollo
Cooperativo. q. ISSN 0090-9580

University of Wisconsin-Madison. University-Industry
Research Program
1215 WARF Bldg., 610 Walnut St., Madison, WI
53706.
● U I R Research Newsletter. (University Industry
Research) q. ISSN 0041-512X

University of Wisconsin. Mathematical Research
Center
● University of Wisconsin. Mathematical Research
Center Series. (pub. by John Wiley & Sons, Inc)

University of Wisconsin-Milwaukee. Center for Latin
America
Milwaukee, WI 53201.
● Conference on Latin American History
Newsletter. s-a. ISSN 0010-5570 (Conference on
Latin American History)
● University of Wisconsin. Center for Latin
America. Center Essays. irreg. ISSN 0084-084X
● University of Wisconsin, Milwaukee. Center for
Latin America. Discussion Papers. irreg., no. 60,
1976.
● University of Wisconsin, Milwaukee. Center for
Latin America. Essay Series. irreg; no. 7, 1976.
● University of Wisconsin, Milwaukee. Center for
Latin America. Special Studies Series. irreg., no.
2, 1974.

University of Wisconsin-Milwaukee. Institute of
World Affairs
Milwaukee, WI 53201.
● Global Focus Series. irreg., no. 16, 1974. ISSN
0072-4742

University of Wisconsin-Milwaukee Library
2311 E. Hartford Ave., Milwaukee, WI 53201.
● U W M Library Newsletter. 3 per yr.

University of Wisconsin-Oshkosh
c/o Dr. David Lippert, 800 Algoma Blvd., Oshkosh,
WI 54901.
● Oshkosh Advance-Titan. w. ISSN 0300-676X
● Wisconsin Review. q. ISSN 0043-6631

University of Wisconsin-Platteville. Institute of
Public Affairs
Platteville, WI 53818.
● Forum on Public Affairs. s-a. ISSN 0015-8550

University of Wisconsin Press
Journals Dept., Box 1379, Madison, WI 53701.
● Arctic Anthropology. biennial. ISSN 0066-6939

● Contemporary Literature. 4 per yr. ISSN 0010-
7484 (University of Wisconsin-Madison.
Department of English)
● Financial Management. q. ISSN 0046-3892
(Financial Management Association)
● International Organization. q. ISSN 0020-8183
(World Peace Foundation)
● Journal of Human Resources; education,
manpower and welfare policies. q. ISSN 0022-
166X (Industrial Relations Research Institute)
(Co-Sponsor: Institute for Research on Poverty)
● Land Economics Monographs. irreg. ISSN 0075-
7837 (University of Wisconsin-Madison. Land
Tenure Center)
● Literary Monographs. irreg. ISSN 0075-9902
● Luso-Brazilian Review; devoted to the culture of
the Portuguese speaking world. s-a. ISSN 0024-
7413
● Monatshefte fuer Deutschen Unterricht. q. ISSN
0026-9271 (University of Wisconsin. Department
of German)
● Publications in Medieval Science. irreg. ISSN
0079-7685
● Studies in Eighteenth Century Culture; American
Society for Eighteenth Century Studies.
Proceedings of the Annual Meeting. irreg., vol. 4,
1975.

University of Wyoming. Agricultural Experiment
Station
Box 3354, Laramie, WY 82071.
● Wyoming. Agricultural Experiment Station,
Laramie. Bulletin. irreg. ISSN 0084-313X
● Wyoming. Agricultural Experiment Station,
Laramie. Research Journal. irreg., 1968, no. 20.
ISSN 0084-3148
● Wyoming. Agricultural Experiment Station,
Laramie. Science Monograph. irreg., 1971, no. 23.
ISSN 0084-3156

University of Wyoming. College of Law
Box 3035, University Sta., Laramie, WY 82070.
● Land and Water Law Review. s-a. ISSN 0023-
7612 (Co-Sponsors: Wyoming State Bar; Water
Resources Research Institute)

University of Wyoming. Department of Geology
Box 3006, Laramie, WY 82071.
● Unversity of Wyoming. s-a. ISSN 0010-7980

University of Wyoming. Division of Adult Education
and Community Service
Box 3274, University Station, Laramie, WY 82070.
● University of Wyoming. Division of Adult
Education and Community Service. Report. a.
ISSN 0084-3172

University of Wyoming Library
Box 3334, Univ. Sta., Laramie, WY 82071.
● University of Wyoming Publications. irreg. ISSN
0084-3199

University of Wyoming. Natural Resources Research
Institute
P.O.B. 3038, Laramie, WY 82071.
● University of Wyoming. Natural Resources
Research Institute. Information Circular. irreg.,
1970, no. 74. ISSN 0084-3180

University of Wyoming. Water Resources Research
Institute
Box 3067, University Station, Laramie, WY 82071.
● University of Wyoming. Water Resources
Research Institute. Annual Report. a. ISSN 0084-
3202
● University of Wyoming. Water Resources
Research Institute. Water Resources Series. irreg.
ISSN 0084-3210

University of Wyoming. Wyoming Educational Center
Laramie, WY 82070.
● Brainstorm. bi-m.

University Park Press
(Subsidiary of: American Medical Publishers)
Chamber of Commerce Bldg., Baltimore, MD
21202.
● Advances in Sex Hormone Research. irreg (approx
1 vol. per yr.)
● Biological Council. Coordinating Committee for
Symposia on Drug Action. Symposium
Proceedings. irreg. ISSN 0520-1802
● Biology and Environment. irreg.
● Gann Monographs. irreg.(approx. 2 issues per
year); 1970, no. 9. ISSN 0072-0151 (Japanese
Cancer Association)
● International Congress of Psychosurgery.
Proceeding. irreg.

- International Series on Sports Sciences. irreg.
- M T P International Review of Science. Inorganic Chemistry, Series 1. irreg. ISSN 0076-1753
- M T P International Review of Science. Organic Chemistry. irreg. ISSN 0076-1761
- M T P International Review of Science. Physical Chemistry. irreg. ISSN 0076-177X
- Recent Advances in Studies on Cardiac Structure and Metabolism. irreg., vol. 4, 1974 (approx. 2 vols. per yr.) (International Study Group for Research in Cardiac Metabolism)
- Reviews in Perinatal Medicine. a. ISSN 0362-5699
- West Coast Cancer Symposium. Proceedings. a.

**University Photographers Association of America**
Box 500, North Amherst, MA 01059.
- U. P. A. Journal. q. ISSN 0041-5383

**University Press Book Service Inc.**
302 Fifth Ave., New York, NY 10001.
- New Scholarly Books in America. q.
- New Scientific & Technical Books in America. s-a.

**University Press of Hawaii**
2840 Kolowalu St., Honolulu, HI 96822.
- Asian Perspectives; a journal of archaeology and prehistory of Asia and the Pacific. s-a. ISSN 0066-8435 (University of Hawaii)
- Asian Studies at Hawaii Monograph Series. irreg., no. 19, 1977. ISSN 0066-8486 (University of Hawaii. Asian Studies Program)
- Association for Social Anthropology in Oceania. Monograph Series. irreg. ISSN 0066-9172
- East-West Bibliographical Series. irreg., 1972, no. 2.
- Hawaii Topical Conference in Particle Physics. Proceedings. biennial. ISSN 0073-1153
- Oceanic Linguistics. s-a. ISSN 0029-8115 (University of Hawaii)
- Oceanic Linguistics. Special Publications. irreg., no. 14, 1976. ISSN 0078-3188 (University of Hawaii. Social Sciences and Linguistics Institute)
- Pacific History Series. irreg. ISSN 0078-7507 (Australian Subscr. Address: Australian National University Press, P.O. Box 4, Canberra, A.C.T., 2600, Australia)
- Pacific Science; devoted to the biological and physical sciences of the Pacific Region. q. ISSN 0030-8870 (University of Hawaii)
- Philosophy East and West; a quarterly journal of Asian and comparative thought. q. ISSN 0031-8221 (University of Hawaii)

**University Press of Kentucky**
Lexington, KY 40506.
- Kentucky Nature Studies. irreg., latest issue, 1974. ISSN 0075-5524
- Studies in Anthropology. irreg, no. 13, 1970. ISSN 0085-6843
- Studies in Romance Languages. irreg. ISSN 0085-6894

**University Press of Virginia**
Box 3608 University Station, Charlottesville, VA 22903.
- Studies in Bibliography. a. ISSN 0081-7600 (Bibliographical Society of the University of Virginia)
- Virginia Historical Society. Documents. irreg; vol. 11, 1975. ISSN 0083-6389
- Virginia Independence Bicentennial Publications. irreg; vol. 3, 1977.
- Virginia Legal Studies. irreg.
- Williamburg in American Series. irreg; vol. 10, 1975. ISSN 0084-0297
- Winterthur Conference Report. a. ISSN 0084-0408 (Henry Francis DuPont Winterthur Museum)
- Winterthur Portfolio. a. ISSN 0084-0416 (Henry Francis DuPont Winterthur Museum)

**University Presses of Florida**
15 N. W. 15th St., Gainesville, FL 32601.
- Caribbean Conference Series. a. ISSN 0069-0457
- Consortium on Revolutionary Europe. Proceedings. a. ISSN 0093-2574
- Handbook of Latin American Studies. Humanities. irreg.
- Handbook of Latin American Studies. Social Sciences. irreg.
- International Organization of Citrus Virologists. Proceedings of the Conference. triennial, 1969, 6th, Japan. ISSN 0074-7203
- Latin American Monographs. irreg; no. 20, 1976. ISSN 0075-8108 (University of Florida. Center for Latin American Studies)

- Southern Conference on Gerontology Report. a. ISSN 0071-6111
- University of Florida. Center for Gerontology. Studies and Programs. a. ISSN 0071-6103
- University of Florida. Department of Accounting. Accounting Series. irreg., latest issue no. 8, (1971, no 7) ISSN 0071-6065
- University of Florida Monographs. Humanities. irreg., 3 nos. a year. ISSN 0071-6189
- University of Florida Monographs. Social Sciences. irreg., (approx. 4 per yr) ISSN 0071-6197

**University Printing**
4133 University Way N.E., Seattle, WA 98105.
- Pacific Northwest Merchandiser and Apparel Journal. irreg., latest issue, 1975.

**University Professors for Academic Order**
635 S.W. 4th St., Corvallis, OR 97330.
- Universitas. 9 per yr. ISSN 0146-9061

**University Publications**
Box 47, Blacksburg, VA 24060.
- Frontiers of Economics. irreg. ISSN 0362-6911
- Industrial Organization Review. 3 per yr. (Physical Biological Sciences Ltd.)
- Journal of Biological Physics. q. ISSN 0092-0606 (Physical Biological Sciences Ltd.)

**Universum Sokol Publications Inc**
283 Oak St., Perth Amboy, NJ 08861.
- New York Denik; Slovak American political, cultural and economic weekly. w. ISSN 0048-0002

**Unmuzzled Ox**
Box 840, Canal St. Sta., New York, NY 10013.
- Unmuzzled Ox. q. ISSN 0049-5557

**Unnatural Acts**
c/o Bernadette Mayer, Ed., General Delivery, Worthington, MA 01098.
- Unnatural Acts. 2-3 per yr.

**Unspeakable Visions of the Individual**
Box 439, California, PA 15419.
- Unspeakable Visions of the Individual. 1-3 per yr. ISSN 0049-559X

**Up Against the Wall Street Journal Collective**
1511 S.A.B., Univ. of Michigan, Ann Arbor, MI 48104.
- Up against the Wall Street Journal. 17 per yr. ISSN 0042-0662

**Up from Under Inc.**
339 Lafayette St., New York, NY 10012.
- Up from Under; by, for, and about women. q. ISSN 0042-0670

**Upholsterers' International Union**
25 North Fourth St., Philadelphia, PA 19106.
- U. I. U. Journal. m. ISSN 0041-5162

**Upjohn Co.**
Kalamazoo, MI 49001
(Orders to: 666 Fifth Ave., New York, NY 10019)
- Guidelines to Metabolic Therapy. q.
- Guidelines to Professional Pharmacy. q.

**Upper Midwest Council**
250 Marquette Ave., Minneapolis, MN 55480.
- Upper Midwest Economic Study. Progress Report. irreg. ISSN 0083-4610
- Upper Midwest Economic Study. Technical Paper. irreg., 1964, no. 11. ISSN 0083-4637
- Upper Midwest Economic Study. Urban Report. irreg., 1964, no. 8. ISSN 0083-4645

**Upper Moreland Education Association**
Box 81, Willow Grove, PA 19090.
- U M E A Replay. m, sept-june.

**Upper Room**
1908 Grand Ave., Nashville, TN 37203.
- Alive Now. bi-m. (Co-sponsor: United Methodist Church)

**Upper Snake River Valley Historical Society**
P. O. Box 244, Rexburg, ID 83440.
- Snake River Echoes. q.

**Upshaw Family Journal**
c/o Ted O. Brooke, Ed., 79 Wagonwheel Ct., N.E., Marietta, GA 30062.
- Upshaw Family Journal. q. ISSN 0098-8960

**Upton Country Genealogical Society**
P.O. Box 6, Rankin, TX 79778.
- Trails and Tales. irreg. ISSN 0091-6455

**Urban Affairs Institute**
955 S. Western Ave., Suite 210, Los Angeles, CA 90006.
- Black Politician. q. ISSN 0006-422X

**Urban Alternatives Group**
Box 303, Worthington, OH 43085.
- Doing It; practical alternatives for humanizing city life. bi-m.

**Urban Institute**
2100 M St. N.W., Washington, DC 20037.
- Search (Washington, D.C.); a report from the urban institute. bi-m. ISSN 0048-9921
- Urban Institute. Annual Report. a. ISSN 0092-7481

**Urban Institute. Cable Television Information Center**
2100 M Street, N.W., Washington, DC 20037.
- Cable Television Information Center. Urban Institute. Notes from the Center. irreg.

**Urban Land Institute**
1200 18 St. N.W., Washington, DC 20036.
- Dollars and Cents of Shopping Centers. triennial. ISSN 0070-704X
- Environmental Comment. m.
- Land Use Digest. m. ISSN 0023-768X
- Urban Land; news and trends in land development. m.(except July-Aug) ISSN 0042-0891
- Urban Land Institute. Research Report. irreg., 1972, no. 19. ISSN 0083-470X
- Urban Land Institute. Technical Bulletin. irreg., 1972, no. 67. ISSN 0083-4718
- Urban Land Institute Project Reference File. 20 per yr.

**Urban Libraries Council**
c/o Cleveland Public Library, 325 Superior Avenue, Cleveland, OH 44114.
- Lamp.

**Urban Observatory of San Diego**
202 C St., San Diego, CA 92101.
- Urban Observatory of San Diego. Special Report. irreg.

**Urban Periodicals, Inc.**
25 West 45th St., New York, NY 10036.
- New York Affairs. q. ISSN 0090-9920

**Urban Planning Aid**
2 Park Sq., Rm. 305, Boston, MA 02116.
- Community Press Features. m.

**Urban Planning Aid. Occupational Health & Safety Project**
639 Massachusetts Ave., Cambridge, MA 02139.
- Survial Kit; a health & safety newsletter. bi-m.

**Urban Publishing Co.**
3079 Campbellton Rd. S.W., Atlanta, GA 30311.
- Urban Health; the journal of health care in the cities. 8 per yr.

**Urban Research Corp.**
5464 South Shore Drive, Chicago, IL 60615.
- Urban Read-Out. s-m. ISSN 0049-5670

**Urban Telecommunications Workshop**
c/o Ed. & Pub. Glenn Ralston, 276 Riverside Dr., New York, NY 10025.
- Urban Telecommunications Forum. m. ISSN 0092-9441 (Co-Sponsor: Rutgers Univ. Urban Communications Teaching and Research Center)

**Laurence Urdang, Ed. & Pub.**
Essex, CT 06426.
- Verbatim. q.

**Urner-Barry Publications, Inc.**
Box 389, Toms River, NJ 08753.
- Producers' Price-Current. d.(Mon-Fri) ISSN 0032-9711

**Urology Times, Inc.**
79 Madison Ave., New York, NY 10016.
- Urology Times. m.

**Monida Urquhart, Ed. & Pub.**
4603 Palm Drive, Box 722, La Canada, CA 91011.
- Western Cleaner and Launderer. m. ISSN 0049-738X

**Uruguay Collectors Club**
Box 1214, Des Plaines, IL 60016.
- Uruguay Philatelist. q.

**US 1 Worksheets**
73 Fairfield Ave., Lawrenceville, NJ 08648.
- US 1 Worksheets. 2-3 per yr.

**Artist USA, Inc.**
1315 Walnut St., Philadelphia, PA 19107.
- Award Winning Architecture - USA. a. ISSN 0093-8254 (Co-Sponsor: American Institute of Architects)

**Utah. Department of Agriculture**
147 North 200 West, Salt Lake City, UT 84103.
- Utah. State Department of Agriculture. Biennial Report. biennial.
- Utah Agricultural Statistics. a. (Co-Sponsor: U.S. Department of Agriculture, Statistical Reporting Service)

**Utah. Department of Employment Security. Committee on Industrial and Employment-Planning**
174 Social Hall Ave., Salt Lake City, UT 84111.
- Directory of Utah Manufacturers. biennial. ISSN 0070-6566

**Utah. Department of Public Instruction. Annual Report of the State Superintendent of Public Instruction**
1400 University Club Bldg., 136 East South Temple, Salt Lake City, UT 84111.
- Utah. Department of Public Instruction. Annual Report of the State Superintendent of Public Instruction. a. ISSN 0094-8314

**Utah. Department of Social Security. Division of Aging**
345 S. Sixth E., Salt Lake City, UT 84102.
- Better Tomorrows. q. ISSN 0006-0232

**Utah. Department of Social Services. Division of Family Services**
333 South 2nd E., Salt Lake City, UT 84111.
- Family Services in Utah: Annual Report. a. ISSN 0361-4158

**Utah. Department of Social Services. Division of Health**
44 Medical Dr., Salt Lake City, UT 84113.
- Utah Vital Statistics Annual Report. a.

**Utah. Department of Transportation**
Salt Lake City, UT 84100.
- Utah. Department of Transportation. Highway Safety Program, Annual Report. a. ISSN 0361-5332

**Utah. Division of Wildlife Resources**
1596 W. North Temple, Salt Lake City, UT 84116.
- Utah. Division of Wildlife Resources. Biennial Report. biennial. ISSN 0360-800X

**Utah. Forestry and Fire Control**
1596 West North Temple, Salt Lake City, UT 84103.
- Utah. Forestry and Fire Control. R C and D Release. irreg. ISSN 0092-9638

**Utah. Geological and Mineral Survey**
606 Black Hawk Way, Salt Lake City, UT 84108.
- Utah Geological and Mineral Survey. Bulletin. irreg. ISSN 0098-4825
- Utah Geological and Mineral Survey. Survey Notes. q.
- Utah Geology. s-a.

**Utah. State Archives and Records Service**
Salt Lake City, UT 84111.
- Utah Administrative Rule Making Bulletin. m. ISSN 0093-8955

**Utah. State Board of Education**
1400 University Club Building, 136 East South Temple, UT 84111.
- Utah. State Board of Education. Opinions of the Utah State Superintendent of Public Instruction. irreg., latest issue 1972. ISSN 0093-0040
- Utah Public School Directory. a.

**Utah. State Board of Education. Division of Research and Development**
1670 University Club Bldg., Salt Lake City, UT 84111.
- Utah. State Board of Education. Division of Research and Development. Career Development, Dropout Prevention Program, Experimental Prgorams, Teacher Leadership Program, Regional Service Units; Annual Report. a. ISSN 0094-5374

**Utah. State Board of Regents**
136 E. South Temple, Suite 1201, Salt Lake City, UT 84111.
- Utah State Board of Regents. Annual Report of the Governor and the Legislature. a. ISSN 0083-4866
- Utah System Summary; news of Utah higher education. irreg (2-3 per yr.)

**Utah. State Library Commission**
2150 S. 300 W., Suite 16, Salt Lake City, UT 84115.
- Horsefeathers. m. ISSN 0018-5205

**Utah Academy of Science, Arts and Letters**
c/o Ed. Ernest L. Olsen, Brigham Young University, Provo, UT 84602.
- Utah Academy of Science, Arts and Letters. Proceedings. a. ISSN 0083-4823

**Utah Cattlemen's Association**
150 S. Sixth E., Suite 10B, Salt Lake City, UT 84102.
- Utah Cattleman. m. ISSN 0042-1375

**Utah Congress of Parents & Teachers**
1037 East South Temple, Salt Lake City, UT 84102.
- Sound-off. 10 per yr.

**Utah Education Association**
875 E. 5180 South, Murray, UT 84107.
- U E A Action. m. ISSN 0042-1413

**Utah Foundation**
32 East First South, Salt Lake City, UT 84111.
- Statistical Review of Government in Utah. a.
- Utah Foundation. Research Report. m.

**Utah Genealogical Association**
Box 1144, Salt Lake City, UT 84110.
- Genealogical Journal. q.
- Utah Genealogical Association. Genealogical Journal. q.

**Utah Geological Association**
P.O. Box 11334, Salt Lake City, UT 84111.
- Utah Geological Association. Annual Guidebook. a. ISSN 0083-484X

**Utah Holiday Publishing Co.**
246 West First South, Salt Lake City, UT 84101.
- Utah Holiday; life in Utah. m.

**Utah Juvenile Court**
339 South 6th East, Salt Lake City, UT 84102.
- Utah. Juvenile Court. Annual Report. a. ISSN 0566-4152

**Utah Law Review Society**
- Utah Law Review. (pub. by University of Utah College of Law)

**Utah Library Association**
Utah State Library Commission, 2150 South 2nd West, Salt Lake City, UT 84602.
- Mormon Americana. (pub. by Brigham Young University. Library)
- Utah Libraries. s-a. ISSN 0042-1456

**Utah Magazine Inc.**
65 Fayette, Salt Lake City, UT 84101.
- Utah. m.

**Utah Nurses Association**
1058 E. 9th South, Salt Lake City, UT 84105.
- U N A Communique. m.

**Utah Peace Officers Association**
Box 11657, Salt Lake City, UT 84111.
- Code 10-5. q.

**Utah Plumbing, Heating, Cooling Contractors**
669 So. 2nd East, Salt Lake City, UT 84111.
- Plumbers Friend. a. ISSN 0085-4905

**Utah Press Association, Inc.**
Box 1327, Salt Lake City, UT 84110.
- Utah Publisher and Printer. m. ISSN 0042-1499

**Utah Retail Grocers' Association**
606 Beneficial Life Bldg., Salt Lake City, UT 84101.
- Intermountain Food Retailer. m. ISSN 0020-5680

**Utah Rose Society**
2100 Pheasant Way, Salt Lake City, UT 84121.
- Rosette. q. ISSN 0048-8623

**Utah Schools for the Deaf and the Blind**
846 20th St., Ogden, UT 84401.
- Utah Eagle. 8 per yr. ISSN 0042-1391

**Utah State Historical Society**
603 E. South Temple, Salt Lake City, UT 84102.
- Utah Historical Quarterly. q. ISSN 0042-143X
- Utah History Research Bulletin. a.
- Utah State Historical Society Newsletter. bi-m. ISSN 0042-1529

**Utah State Medical Association**
42 S. 5th E., Salt Lake City, UT 84102.
- Utah Medical Bulletin. m. ISSN 0042-1464

**Utah State University of Agriculture and Applied Science**
Logan, UT 84321.
- U S U Staff News. w. ISSN 0041-5561
- Utah Science. q. ISSN 0042-1502
- Utah State University of Agriculture and Applied Science. Monograph Series. irreg., 1968, vol. 15, no. 2. ISSN 0083-4858
- Western Historical Quarterly. q. ISSN 0043-3810 (Western History Association)

**Ute Indian Tribe**
Box 129, Fort Duchesne, UT 84026.
- Ute Bulletin. m. ISSN 0300-6808

**Utica College**
Box 304, Burrstone Rd., Utica, NY 13502.
- Tangerine. w. ISSN 0039-940X

**Utility Workers Union of America A F L - C I O Local 1-2**
386 Park Ave. South, New York, NY 10016.
- Record. 4 per yr. ISSN 0034-1541

**V. Baker Enterprises**
2300 Fairview Rd., Costa Mesa, CA 92626.
- Tuning Board. m. ISSN 0362-6091

**V. U. Publishing Co.**
1744 N. Farwell Ave. Suite 208, Milwaukee, WI 53202.
- Journal of Instructional Psychology. 4 per yr. ISSN 0094-1956

**Vagabond Press**
c/o John Bennett, Box 879, Ellensburg, WA 98926.
- Vagabond. q. ISSN 0042-2193
- Vagabond Chapbook. irreg.

**Vajradhatu**
1111 Pearl St., Boulder, CO 80302.
- Garuda. a. ISSN 0046-5445

**Valkyrie Press, Inc.**
2135 First Ave. S., St. Petersburg, FL 33712.
- Poetry Venture. irreg., latest issue 1977. ISSN 0032-2199

**Valley Automobile Club**
303 Market St., Kingston, PA 18704.
- Valley Motorist. bi-m.

**Valley Forge Historical Society**
Valley Forge, PA 19481.
- Picket Post. q. ISSN 0031-9619

**Valley National Bank of Arizona**
Box 71, Phoenix, AZ 85001.
- Arizona Progress. m.
- Eagle (Phoenix). m.

**Valley Studio**
c/o T. Leabhart, Ed., Rt. 3, Spring Green, WI 53588.
- Mime Journal. s-a.

**Valor & Arms Press**
P.O. Box 2243, Ft. Collins, CO 80522.
- By Valor & Arms; journal of American military history. q.

**Valparaiso University**
- Cresset. (pub. by Valparaiso University Press)

**Valparaiso University Press**
Valparaiso, IN 46383.
- Cresset; a review of literature, the arts and public affairs. m.(Sept-June) ISSN 0011-1198 (Valparaiso University)

**Valparaiso University. School of Law**
Valparaiso, IN 46383.
- Valparaiso University Law Review. 3 per yr. ISSN 0042-2363

**Value Trend Analysis**
7440 Girard Ave., Suite 4, La Jolla, CA 92037.
- Investment Quality Trends; for the enlightened investor. s-m. ISSN 0021-0110

**Van Allen Publishing Co.**
Box 354, Hicksville, NY 11802.
- New York Auto Repairs. m. ISSN 0028-713X

**Van Dahl Publications Inc.**
Box 10, 520 E. First Ave., Albany, OR 97321.
- Stamp Collector. w.

**Marinus W. Van der Steen, Jr., Ed. & Pub.**
Box 42085, Los Angeles, CA 90042.
- Holland Report. w. ISSN 0300-8800

**Phyllis Van Kriedt, Ed. & Pub.**
Box 70, Mill Valley, CA 94941.
- California Wineletter. s-m. ISSN 0008-1655

**R.C. Van Ness**
717 Webster St., P. O. Box 260, Algonquin, IL 60102.
- Midwest Eighty-Eight Manufacturing. bi-m. ISSN 0026-3354

**D. Van Nostrand Books**
(Subsidiary of: Litton Educational Publishers)
450 W. 33 St., New York, NY 10001.
- A C S Monographs. irreg., 1974, no. 169. ISSN 0065-7719 (American Chemical Society)
- New Perspectives in Political Science. irreg., 1970, no. 24. ISSN 0077-8613
- Van Nostrand Mathematical Studies. irreg., 1969, no. 24. ISSN 0083-5145

**Van Nostrand Reinhold Co.**
300 Pike St., Cincinnati, OH 45202.
- Vacuum Metallurgy Conference. Proceedings. irreg. (American Vacuum Society)

**Van Steenwyk News Letter**
c/o E. Bos, 2522 Walnut St., Cedar Falls, IA 50613.
- Van Steenwyk News Letter. q. ISSN 0042-2460

**Richard S. Van Winkle**
244 Highland Ave., Ridgewood, NJ 07450.
- Surfing East. bi-m. ISSN 0039-6052

**Vance Publishing Corporation (Chicago)**
300 W. Adams St., Chicago, IL 60606.
- Home Center Magazine. m.
- Modern Beauty Shop Magazine. m. ISSN 0026-7511
- Modern Styles and How-To's. a.
- Modern's Market Guide. a. ISSN 0544-7178
- Wood & Wood Products; the national authority on wood & allied products management and operations. m. ISSN 0043-7662
- Wood & Wood Products Reference Data/Buying Guide. a. ISSN 0084-1080

**Vance Publishing Corporation (Kansas City)**
One Gateway Center, Kansas City, KS 66101.
- Drovers Journal. w. ISSN 0012-6454
- Grower. m.
- Packer; devoted to the interest of commercial growers, packers, shippers, receivers and retailers of fruits, vegetables and other products. w. ISSN 0030-9168 (And, 300w. Adams St. Chicago, IL 60606 or 133 E. 58 St., New York, NY 10022)

**Vance Publishing Corporation (New York)**
746 Lexington Ave., New York, NY 10022.
- Lockwood'S Directory of the Paper and Allied Trades. a. ISSN 0076-0277
- Paper Trade Journal. w. ISSN 0031-1197

**Vanderbilt Bar Association**
- Dicta. (pub. by Vanderbilt University. School of Law)

**R.T. Vanderbilt Co., Inc.**
30 Winfield St., Norwalk, CT 06855.
- Vanderbilt Rubber Handbook. irreg. ISSN 0083-5218

**Vanderbilt Student Communications, Inc.**
Box 1504-B, Nashville, TN 37235.
- Vanderbilt Hustler. s-w. ISSN 0042-2517

**Vanderbilt Television News Archive**
Joint University Libraries, Nashville, TN 37203.
- Television News Index and Abstracts. irreg. ISSN 0085-7157

**Vanderbilt University**
Box 6309, Sta. B, Nashville, TN 37235.
- Soundings; an interdisciplinary journal. q. ISSN 0038-1861 (Co-Publisher: Society for Religion in Higher Education)

**Vanderbilt University. Center for Latin American Studies**
Box 1806, Nashville, TN 37235.
- Vanderbilt University. Center for Latin American Studies. Occasional Paper. irreg. ISSN 0083-5234

**Vanderbilt University. Department of English**
c/o Frank Judge, Box 4756, Station B, Nashville, TN 37203.
- Vanderbilt Poetry Review. q.

**Vanderbilt University. Department of Environmental and Water Resources Engineering**
Box 6304, Station B, Nashville, TN 37235.
- Vanderbilt University. Department of Environmental and Water Resources Engineering. Technical Reports. irreg.

**Vanderbilt University. Department of Sociology and Anthropology**
Box 1532, Nashville, TN 37235.
- Vanderbilt University. Department of Sociology and Anthropology. Publications in Anthropology. irreg.

**Vanderbilt University Press**
Box 1813 Station B, Nashville, TN 37235.
- Abraham Flexner Lectures in Medicine. irreg.
- Vanderbilt Sociology Conference. Proceedings. irreg. ISSN 0083-5226

**Vanderbilt University. Publications Office**
117 Alumni Hall, Nashville, TN 37240.
- Vanderbilt University. Abstracts of Theses. irreg.

**Vanderbilt University. School of Law**
Nashville, TN 37203.
- Dicta. every 3 weeks during school year. ISSN 0417-4542 (Vanderbilt Bar Association)
- Vanderbilt Journal of Transnational Law. q. ISSN 0090-2594
- Vanderbilt Law Review. 6 per yr. ISSN 0042-2533

**Vanderbilt University. W. T. Bandy Center for Baudelaire Studies**
Box 1830, Sta. B, Nashville, TN 37235.
- Bulletin Baudelairien. s-a. ISSN 0007-4128

**Vanguard Productions**
203 Clayton St., San Francisco, CA 94117.
- Vanguard (San Francisco) m. (approx.) ISSN 0042-255X

**Vanity Fair**
5512 Wayne Ave., Philadelphia, PA 19144.
- Movies. 10 per yr. ISSN 0027-2795

**Al Vann**
400 E. 56th St., New York, NY 10022.
- Music & Arts. bi-m. ISSN 0047-8423

**Dan Vap Press**
R.R. 1, Norfolk, NE 68701.
- Amateur Archaeologist. q. ISSN 0363-969X

**Variety, Inc.**
154 W. 46th St., New York, NY 10036.
- Variety. w. ISSN 0042-2738

**Vassar College**
Poughkeepsie, NY 12601.
- Hudson River Anthology. a.
- Vassar Quarterly. q. ISSN 0042-2851

**Vegetable Growers Association of New Jersey Inc.**
Cook College, Blake Hall, Box 231, New Brunswick, NJ 08903.
- Garden Stater. 3 per yr. ISSN 0016-4615

**Vegetarian Society of New York**
277 Broadway, Rm. 1301, New York, NY 10007.
- Vegetarian Courier. m. ISSN 0049-5905

**Vegetarian Times**
Box A 3104, Chicago, IL 60690.
- Vegetarian Times. bi-m.

**Vegetarian World**
Suite 216, 8235 Santa Monica Blvd., Los Angeles, CA 90046.
- Vegetarian World. q.

**Vellez Music News**
24208 Alliene Ave., Lomita, CA 90717.
- Vellez Music News. q. ISSN 0042-3246

**Venceremos Brigade. National Office**
GPO Box 3169, New York, NY 10001.
- Venceremos. m.

**Vending Times, Inc.**
211 E. 43 St., New York, NY 10036.
- International Vending Buyer's Guide and Directory. a.
- Vending Times. m. ISSN 0042-3327

**Vends Annual Market Data and Directory**
2160 Patterson St., Cincinnati, OH 45214.
- Vends Annual Market Data and Directory. a.

**Ventura County Historical Society**
100 East Main St., Ventura, CA 93001.
- Heritage and History. m.
- Ventura County Historical Society Quarterly. q. ISSN 0042-3491

**Vergilian Society**
c/o C. P. Twichell, The Choate School, Wallingford, CT 06492.
- Vergilius. a. ISSN 0506-7294

**Vergilian Society (Willoughby)**
c/o Adele Knight, 37946 Barber Ave., Willoughby, OH 44094.
- Vergilian Society Newsletter. a.

**Geneva Alice Verkennes, Ed. & Pub.**
1395 James St., Burton, MI 48529.
- Aeolian-Harp. biennial.
- Aloha to Hawaii. irreg.

**Vermilion County Museum Society**
116 N.Gilbert St., Danville, IL 61832.
- Heritage of Vermilion County. q. ISSN 0018-0718

**Vermont. Agency of Development & Community Affairs**
Ed. Brian Vachon, 61 Elm St., Montpelier, VT 05602.
- Vermont Life. q. ISSN 0042-417X

**Vermont. Agency of Environmental Conservation**
Montpelier, VT 05602.
- Vermont. Agency of Environmental Conservation. Biennial Report. biennial. ISSN 0360-3059

**Vermont. Department of Banking and Insurance. Division of Banking**
120 State St., Montpelier, VT 05602.
- Vermont. Commissioner of Banking and Insurance. Annual Report of the Bank Commissioner. a. ISSN 0083-5730

**Vermont. Department of Corrections**
Director of Volunteer Services, 79 River St., Heritage II Office Bldg., Montpelier, VT 05602.
- Vermont Corrections Volunteer. q.

**Vermont. Department of Education**
State Office Building, Montpelier, VT 05602.
- Vermont Educational Directory. a.

**Vermont. Department of Employment Security**
Montpelier, VT 05602.
- Vermont. Department of Employment Security. Statistical Tables. irreg. ISSN 0095-1382
- Vermont Labor Force. m. ISSN 0506-7472

**Vermont. Department of Libraries. Law and Document Library**
Montpelier, VT 05602.
- Checklist of Available Vermont State Publications. a.

**Vermont. Geological Survey**
Montpelier, VT 05602
(Order from: Vermont Dept. of Libraries, 111 State St., Montpelier VT 05602)
- Environmental Geology. irreg. ISSN 0071-0857
- Studies in Vermont Geology. irreg. ISSN 0081-8747

- Vermont. Geological Survey. Bulletin. irreg. ISSN 0083-5757
- Vermont. Geological Survey. Special Publication. irreg. ISSN 0083-5765

**Vermont. Office of Statistical Coordination**
State Capitol, Montpelier, VT 05602.
- Vermont Facts and Figures. irreg. ISSN 0092-5144

**Vermont Agricultural Experiment Station**
University of Vermont, Burlington, VT 05401.
- Vermont. Agricultural Experiment Station, Burlington. Research Report. irreg., no. 80, 1974. ISSN 0083-5706
- Vermont. Agricultural Experiment Station, Burlington. Station Bulletin Series. irreg., no. 679, 1974. ISSN 0083-5714
- Vermont. Agricultural Experiment Station, Burlington. Station Pamphlet Series. irreg., no. 40, 1975. ISSN 0083-5722

**Vermont Catholic Press Association**
209 College St., Burlington, VT 05401.
- Vermont Catholic Tribune. w. ISSN 0042-4145

**Vermont Education Association**
138 Main St., Montpelier, VT 05602.
- V E A Today. m.(Sept.-June)

**Vermont Historical Society**
Pavilion Bldg., 109 State St., Montpelier, VT 05602.
- Vermont History. q. ISSN 0042-4161

**Vermont Industrial Development Authority**
Pavilion Office Building, Montpelier, VT 05602.
- Vermont Industrial Development Authority. Annual Report. a. ISSN 0363-2067

**Vermont Library Association**
Vermont Dept. of Libraries, Montpelier, VT 05602.
- Vermont Libraries. 6 per yr. ISSN 0049-5956

**Vermont Music Educators Association**
126 Hinesburg Rd., South Burlington, VT 05401.
- Vermont Music News. 4 per yr. ISSN 0042-4188

**Vermont Philatelic Society**
c/o Peter G. Huntsman, 18 Fuller St., Montpelier, VT 05602.
- Vermont Philatelist. q.

**Vermont School Boards Association**
Box 339, 62 State St., Montpelier, VT 05602.
- V S B A Newsletter. m.

**Verona Fathers-Sons of the Sacred Heart**
2104 St. Michael St., Cincinnati, OH 45204.
- Verona Fathers Missions. 6 per yr. ISSN 0042-4234

**Lawrence Verry, Inc. (U.S. Distrib.)**
Mystic, CT 06355.
- Natal Regional Survey. Additional Report. irreg., no. 7, 1973. ISSN 0077-2895 (University of Natal SA)

**Verse Writers' Guild of Ohio**
c/o J. A. Margeson, 6501 Dobson Square E., Columbus, OH 43229.
- Dream Shop. q.

**Vertical Marketing Inc.**
500 N. Michigan Ave., Chicago, IL 60611.
- Sphere; the magazine for the discerning woman. m.

**Vestal Central Schools**
Vestal, NY 13850.
- Status of Your Vestal Schools. 10 per yr. ISSN 0039-0755

**Veteran Motor Club of America**
15 Newton St., Brookline, MA 02146.
- Bulb Horn. bi-m. ISSN 0045-3471

**Veterans Information Service**
P.O. Box 111, East Moline, IL 61244.
- What Every Veteran Should Know. a. ISSN 0083-9108

**Veterans of Foreign Wars of the United States**
c/o John L. Smith, Broadway at 34th St., Kansas City, MO 64111.
- V. F. W. Magazine. m. ISSN 0042-1820
- Washington Action Reporter. m.

**Veterans of Foreign Wars of the United States. Department of Minnesota**
Veterans Service Bldg., St. Paul, MN 55155.
- Gopher Oversea'r. 11 per yr.

**Veterans of Foreign Wars of the United States. Ladies Auxiliary**
406 W. 34th St., Kansas City, MO 64111.
- V F W Auxiliary. 10 per yr.

**Veterinary Medicine Publishing Co.**
144 N. Nettleton, Bonner Springs, KS 66012.
- Veterinary Medicine/Small Animal Clinician. m. ISSN 0042-4889

**Veterinary Practice Publishing Co.**
Box 4457, Santa Barbara, CA 93103.
- Canine Practice; the journal of canine medicine & surgery for the practitioner. bi-m. ISSN 0094-4904
- Feline Practice; the journal of feline medicine & surgery for the practitioner. bi-m. ISSN 0046-3639

**Vibration**
Box 08152, Cleveland, OH 44108.
- Vibration. q. ISSN 0049-6073

**Vickers Petroleum Corporation**
Box 2240, Wichita, KS 67201.
- Vickers Voice. q. ISSN 0042-5087

**Able David Victor, Inc.**
29 E. 61st St., New York, NY 10021.
- New York Insider; an unconventional guide to a good time in New York. bi-m.

**Victorian Society in America**
219 South Sixth St., Philadelphia, PA 19106.
- Nineteenth Century. 4 per yr. ISSN 0097-5184
- Victorian Society in America. Bulletin. bi-m.

**Victorians Institute Journal**
Old Dominion University, Norfolk, VA 23508.
- Victorians Institute.Journal. a.

**Nikolajs Vieglais, Ed. & Pub.**
1900 Essex Street, Berkeley, CA 94703.
- Po Stopam Christa/Following the Steps of Christ. q.

**Vienybe**
192 Highland Blvd., Brooklyn, NY 11207.
- Vienybe. fortn.

**Vietnam Bulletin**
Embassy of Vietnam, 2251 R St., N.W., Washington, DC 20008.
- Vietnam Bulletin. w. ISSN 0042-5729

**Viewpoints Institute, Inc.**
117 West 9th, Los Angeles, CA 90015.
- Viewpoint Publications. irreg. ISSN 0083-6222

**Vigo County Public Library**
222 N. Seventh St., Terre Haute, IN 47801.
- Vigo County Public Library Staff Bulletin. m. ISSN 0042-6059

**Richard A. Viguerie Co., Inc.**
7777 Leesburg Pike, Falls Church, VA 22043.
- Right Report. s-m.

**Viking Press, Inc**
625 Madison Ave, New York, NY 10022.
- Documents of 20th Century Art. irreg.
- Viking Critical Library. irreg.

**Village Press**
6 Odd Fellows Ave., Concord, NH 03301.
- Among the Deep Sea Fishers. ISSN 0003-1976 (International Grenfell Association)

**Village Voice**
80 University St., New York, NY 10003.
- Village Voice. w. ISSN 0042-6180

**Villanova University Law School**
Villanova, PA 19085.
- Villanova Law Review. bi-m. ISSN 0042-6229

**Viltis**
c/o V. F. Beliajus, Box 1226, Denver, CO 80201.
- Viltis; a folklore magazine. bi-m. ISSN 0042-6253

**Vintage Magazine Inc.**
Box 2739, Boulder, CO 80302.
- Vintage; for people who like wine & food. 12 per yr. ISSN 0049-6456

**Vintage Records**
Box 2144, Anaheim, CA 91804.
- Record Exchanger. bi-m. ISSN 0557-9147

**Viola da Gamba Society of America, Inc.**
Fiddlers' Hill, Edgewater, MD 21037
(Subscr. to: Rev. Gordon Fischer, All Hallows Rectory, Davidsonville, MD 21035)
- Viola da Gamba Society of America Journal. a. ISSN 0507-0252

**Virginia. Air Pollution Control Board**
Rm 1106, Ninth St. Office Building, Richmond, VA 23219.
- Virginiair. q.

**Virginia. Commission for Children and Youth**
1200 State Office Bldg., Richmond, VA 23219.
- Virginia's Children and Youth; a report to the governor and general assembly. biennial. ISSN 0083-6567

**Virginia. Commission of Game and Inland Fisheries**
Box 11104, Richmond, VA 23230.
- Virginia Wildlife. m. ISSN 0042-6792

**Virginia. Council on the Environment**
Box 790, Richmond, VA 23206.
- Impact (Richmond) bi-m.

**Virginia. Department of Agriculture and Commerce**
Box 1165, Richmond, VA 23209.
- Virginia. Agricultural Opportunities Development Program. Annual Report. a. ISSN 0362-6490
- Virginia. Department of Agriculture. Bulletin. m.(except Jan) ISSN 0042-6482

**Virginia. Department of Agriculture and Commerce. Division of Product and Industry Regulation**
203 N. Governor St., Room 304, Richmond, VA 23219.
- Virginia. Division of Product and Industry Regulation. Inspection Service Section. Annual Report. a. ISSN 0362-3661

**Virginia. Department of Conservation and Economic Development. Division of Mineral Resources**
Box 3667, Charlottesville, VA 22903.
- Virginia. Division of Mineral Resources. Publications. irreg.
- Virginia Minerals. q. ISSN 0042-6652

**Virginia. Department of Corrections. Bureau of Management Information**
22 E. Cary, Richmond, VA 23219.
- Report of Probation Supervision Workload. a. ISSN 0362-7489

**Virginia. Department of Education**
9Th St. Office Bldg., Richmond, VA 23216.
- National Seminar on Year-Round Education. Proceedings. a. ISSN 0095-2451
- Pilot Studies Approved for State Aid in Public School Systems in Virginia. a. ISSN 0079-2071 (prep. by its Division of Educational Research)
- Public Education in Virginia. q.
- Virginia Educational Directory. a. ISSN 0083-6354
- Virginia's Supply of Public School Instructional Personnel. a. ISSN 0083-6575 (prep. by its Division of Teacher Education)

**Virginia. Department of Health. Bureau of Health Education**
Richmond, VA 23219.
- Virginia Health Bulletin. q. ISSN 0042-6520

**Virginia. Department of Health. Medical Examiner Division**
9 North 14th St., Richmond, VA 23219.
- Medico-Legal Bulletin. m. ISSN 0025-8164

**Virginia. Department of Highways and Transportation**
1221 E. Broad St., Richmond, VA 23219.
- Virginia Department of Highways and Transportation Bulletin. b1-m.
- Virginia Highway and Transportation Conference. Proceedings. a. (Co-sponsor: Virginia Military Institute)

**Virginia. Department of Labor and Industry. Division of Research and Statistics**
Richmond, VA 23232.
- Virginia. Department of Labor and Industry. Division of Research and Statistics. Occupational Injuries and Illnesses by Industry. ISSN 0095-8174

**Virginia. Department of Vocational Rehabilitation**
Box 11045, 4615 W. Broad St, Richmond, VA 23230.
- Challenge (Richmond) q. ISSN 0009-1073

**Virginia. Division of Aeronautics**
P.O. 7716, Richmond, VA 23231.
- Virginia Aviation. q.

**Virginia. Division of Justice and Crime Prevention**
8501 Mayland Dr., Richmond, VA 23229.
- Criminal Justice Plan (Richmond) irreg. ISSN 0362-8353

**Virginia. Drug Abuse Advisory Council**
Richmond, VA 23219.
- Imprint. a. ISSN 0095-1714

**Virginia. Employment Commission**
Richmond, VA 23219.
- Virginia. Employment Commission. Manpower Research Division. Economic Assumptions. irreg. ISSN 0095-3075
- Virginia Economic Indicators. m. ISSN 0042-6490

**Virginia. Law Enforcement Officers Training Standards Commission**
Richmond, VA 23219.
- Virginia. Law Enforcement Officers Training Standards Commission. Biennial Report. biennial. ISSN 0095-1846

**Virginia. Office of the Attorney General**
Supreme Court Bldg., 1101 E. Broad St., Richmond, VA 23219.
- Virginia. Attorney General's Office. Civil Digest. irreg. ISSN 0097-790X

**Virginia. Port Authority**
1600 Maritime Tower, Norfolk, VA 23510.
- Virginia Port Authority. Board of Commissioners. Annual Report. a. ISSN 0083-6532
- Virginia Port Authority. Foreign Trade Annual Report: The Ports of Virginia. a. ISSN 0083-6516

**Virginia. State Council of Higher Education**
911 E. Broad St., 10th Floor, Richmond, VA 23219.
- Higher Education in Virginia; selected characteristics, degree programs, student fees in public and private institutions. q.
- Resident and off-Campus Enrollment/Virginia State-Supported Institutions of Higher Education. a.

**Virginia. State Library**
12th & Capital Streets, Richmond, VA 23219.
- Virginia. State Library. Publications. irreg. ISSN 0083-6524
- Virginia Cavalcade. q. ISSN 0042-6474
- Virginia State Library News. irreg.

**Virginia. State Library. Historical Publications Division**
Richmond, VA 23219.
- Virginia State Publications in Print. a. ISSN 0507-102X

**Virginia. State Library. Library Development Branch**
Richmond, VA 23219.
- Statistics of Virginia Public Libraries. irreg. ISSN 0095-3490

**Virginia. State Water Control Board**
2111 N. Hamilton St., P.O. Box 11143, Richmond, VA 23230.
- Virginia. State Water Control Board. Annual Report. a. ISSN 0095-1978

**Virginia Academy of Science**
- Virginia Journal of Science. (pub. by Medical College of Virginia)

**Virginia Association of Plumbing-Heating-Cooling Contractors**
2117 Lake Ave., Richmond, VA 23230.
- Virginia P H C C Image. m.

**Virginia Association of Teachers of English**
- Virginia English Bulletin. (pub. by F.N. Wimer, Ed. & Pub.)

**Virginia Baptist Historical Society**
Box 34, University of Richmond, VA 23173.
- Virginia Baptist Register. a. ISSN 0083-6311

**Virginia Bar Association**
T.C. Williams School of Law, University of Richmond, Richmond, VA 23173.
- Virginia Bar Association Journal. biennial. ISSN 0360-3857

**Virginia-Carolina Peanut Association**
- Peanut Journal and Nut World. (pub. by Peanut Journal Publishing Co.)

**Virginia Commonwealth University. Adult Education Program**
- Community/Junior College Research Quarterly. (pub. by Hemisphere Publishing Corporation)

**Virginia Commonwealth University. University Computer Center**
1015 Floyd Ave, Box 174, Richmond, VA 23220.
- Computereport. m.

**Virginia Congress of Parents and Teachers**
3810 Augusta Ave., Richmond, VA 23230.
- Virginia P T A Bulletin. m.(except Jul. & Aug.) ISSN 0042-6709

**Virginia Education Association**
116 South Third St., Richmond, VA 23219.
- V E A News. m (Sept.-May) ISSN 0042-1790
- Virginia Journal of Education. m.(Sept-May) ISSN 0042-6563

**Virginia Education Association. School Librarians Department**
116 S. Third St., Richmond, VA 23219.
- Librachat. s-a. ISSN 0024-211X

**Virginia Food Dealers Association**
1001 E. Main St., Richmond, VA 23219.
- Foodsman. m. ISSN 0015-6728

**Virginia Forests, Inc.**
One North 5th St., Richmond, VA 23219.
- Virginia Forests. q.

**Virginia Gazette Inc.**
Williamsburg, VA 23185.
- Virginia Gazette. w. ISSN 0049-6480

**Virginia Geographical Society**
- Virginia Geographer. (pub. by Mary Washington College. Department of Geography)

**Virginia High School League**
c/o School of Continuing Education, Univ. of Virginia, Box 3697, University Sta., Charlottesville, VA 22903.
- Leaguer. q. ISSN 0023-9666

**Virginia Highway Users Association**
P.O. Box 1397, Richmond, VA 23211.
- Virginia Trucker. bi-m.

**Virginia Historical Society**
Box 7311, Richmond, VA 23221.
- Virginia Historical Society. Documents. (pub. by University Press of Virginia)
- Virginia Historical Society. Occasional Bulletin. s-a. ISSN 0042-6555
- Virginia Magazine of History and Biography. q. ISSN 0042-6636

**Virginia Institute of Marine Science**
Gloucester Point, VA 23062.
- Estuarine Research Federation. Publication E R F. irreg.
- Virginia Institute of Marine Science, Gloucester Point. Data Reports. irreg; no. 13, 1975. ISSN 0083-6419
- Virginia Institute of Marine Science, Gloucester Point. Educational Series. irreg; no. 18, 1975. ISSN 0083-6427
- Virginia Institute of Marine Science, Gloucester Point. Marine Resources Advisory Series. irreg; no. 11, 1976. ISSN 0083-6435
- Virginia Institute of Marine Science, Gloucester Point. Marine Resource Information Bulletin. 1-2 per mo. (prep. by its I & E Office)
- Virginia Institute of Marine Science, Gloucester Point. Special Report in Applied Marine Science and Ocean Engineering. irreg; no. 118, 1976.

- Virginia Institute of Marine Science, Gloucester Point. Special Scientific Report. irreg; no. 76, 1975. ISSN 0083-6443
- Virginia Institute of Marine Science, Gloucester Point. Translation Series. irreg; no. 27, 1976. ISSN 0083-6397

**Virginia Institute of Pastoral Care, Inc.**
c/o John L. Florell, 507 N. Lombardy St., Richmond, VA 23220.
- Pastoral Care and Counseling Abstracts. a. (National Clearing House. Joint Council on Research)

**Virginia Journal of International Law Association**
- Virginia Journal of International Law. (pub. by University of Virginia. School of Law)

**Virginia Law Review Association**
- Virginia Law Review. (pub. by University of Virginia. School of Law)

**Virginia Library Association**
Box 12445, Richmond, VA 23241.
- Virginia Librarian. q. ISSN 0042-6628

**Virginia Military Institute**
Preston Library, Lexington, VA 24450.
- Virginia Military Institute, Lexington. Publications, Theses, and Dissertations of the Staff and Faculty. a. ISSN 0083-6451

**Virginia Municipal League**
700 Travelers Bldg., Richmond, VA 23219.
- Virginia Town & City. m. ISSN 0042-6784

**Virginia Museum of Fine Arts**
Blvd. and Grove Ave., Richmond, VA 23221.
- Arts in Virginia. 3 per yr. ISSN 0004-4032
- Virginia Museum Bulletin. m.(Sept-May) ISSN 0042-6687

**Virginia Nurses Association**
312 W. Grace St., Richmond, VA 23220.
- Virginia Nurse. q.

**Virginia Pharmaceutical Association**
3119 West Clay St., Richmond, VA 23230.
- Virginia Pharmacist. m. ISSN 0042-6717

**Virginia Place Name Society**
c/o Mannuscripts Department, University of Virginia Library, Charlottesville, VA 22901.
- Virginia Place Name Society. Occasional Papers. irreg. ISSN 0083-646X

**Virginia Polytechnic Institute and State University. Center for Study of Public Choice**
Blacksburg, VA 24061.
- Public Choice. q. ISSN 0048-5829 (Public Choice Society)

**Virginia Polytechnic Institute and State University. Department of Sociology**
Blacksburg, VA 24061.
- Sociological Symposium. 4 per yr. ISSN 0038-027X

**Virginia Polytechnic Institute and State University. Department of Geological Sciences**
Blacksburg, VA 24061.
- Virginia Polytechnic Institute and State University. Department of Geological Sciences. Geological Guidebooks. irreg., latest issue 1971. ISSN 0507-1259

**Virginia Polytechnic Institute and State University. Extension Division**
Dept. of Agricultural Economics, Blacksburg, VA 24061.
- Virginia Agricultural Economics. m. ISSN 0042-6466
- Virginia Polytechnic Institute and State University. Extension News. m. ISSN 0042-6725

**Virginia Polytechnic Institute and State University. News Services**
200 Media Bldg., 301 Burruss Hall, Blacksburg, VA 24061.
- Head, Heart, Hands & Health. m. ISSN 0017-8713

**Virginia Polytechnic Institute and State University. Research Division**
Blacksburg, VA 24061.
- Insects of Virginia. irreg. ISSN 0098-1222
- Virginia Polytechnic Institute and State University. Research Division. Report. irreg.

**Virginia Polytechnic Institute and State University. School of Forestry and Wildlife Resources**
Blacksburg, VA 24061.
- Social Sciences in Forestry; forestry economics, including related materials-a current selected bibliography. 3 per yr.

**Virginia Polytechnic Institute and State University. Water Resources Research Center**
225 Norris Hall, Blacksburg, VA 24061.
- Environmental Legislation Reporter. w. ISSN 0362-5400
- Water Resources Research in Virginia, Annual Report. a. ISSN 0095-1250

**Virginia Polytechnic Institute and State University. Wood Research and Wood Construction Laboratory**
Blacksburg, VA 24061.
- Virginia Polytechnic Institute and State University. Wood Research and Wood Construction Laboratory. Special Report. irreg. ISSN 0083-6508

**Virginia Poultry Federation**
Box 1036, Harrisonburg, VA 22801.
- Virginia Poultryman. m. ISSN 0042-6733

**Virginia Press Association**
Virginia Bldg., Richmond, VA 23219.
- Virginia's Press. m.

**Virginia Publishers Wing, Inc.**
301 E. Franklin St., Drawer 2Y, Richmond, VA 23205.
- Virginia Record. m. ISSN 0042-6768

**Virginia School Boards Association**
Peabody Hall, Univ. of Va., Charlottesville, VA 22903.
- Virginia School Boards Association Newsletter. m.(except Oct. July, Aug.) ISSN 0042-6776

**Virginia Society of Certified Public Accountants**
700 E. Main St., Suite 1010, Richmond, VA 23219.
- Virginia Accountant. q. ISSN 0042-644X

**Virginia Society of Ornithology**
Ed. F. R. Scott, 115 Kennondale Lane, Richmond, VA 23226.
- Raven. 4 per yr. ISSN 0034-0146

**Virginia Sports Publications, Inc.**
P.O. Box 305, Alexandria, VA 22313.
- Fishing in Virginia. a. ISSN 0085-056X

**Virginia State Bar. Criminal Law Section**
Fredericksburg, VA 22401.
- Virginia. State Bar. Criminal Law Section. Criminal Law Seminar. a. ISSN 0099-0795 (Co-sponsor: Virginia Bar Association)

**Virginia State Bar. Young Lawyers Conference**
700 Bldg., 700 E. Main St., Richmond, VA 23219.
- Virginia State Bar. Young Lawyers Conference. Newsletter. q.

**Virginia State Chamber of Commerce**
611 E. Franklin, Richmond, VA 23219.
- Commonwealth. m. ISSN 0010-3365
- Directory of Virginia Manufacturing and Mining. biennial. ISSN 0070-6574

**Virginia State Dental Association**
2015 Staples Mill Rd., Suite 331, Richmond, VA 23230.
- Virginia Dental Journal. bi-m. ISSN 0049-6472

**Virginia State Reading Association**
Longwood College, Farmville, VA 23901.
- Reading in Virginia. s-a.

**Virginia Wesleyan College. Department of English**
Norfol, VA 23502.
- Inlet. a. ISSN 0085-1884

**Virgo Enterprises**
58 N. Main St., Union City, PA 16438.
- Pro Archer. m.

**Viridian Starfire**
1623 Brown St., Napa, CA 94558.
- Viridian Starfire. irreg. ISSN 0085-7831

**Visage Press, Inc.**
3409 Wisconsin Ave. N.W., Washington, DC 20016.
- Victimology; an international journal. q. ISSN 0361-5170

**Visible Language**
Box 1972 CMA, Cleveland, OH 44106.
- Visible Language. q. ISSN 0022-2224

**Vision, Inc.**
641 Lexington Ave., New York, NY 10022.
- Progreso. 9 per yr. ISSN 0033-0485
- Vision Letter; a political and economic report on Latin America. fortn. ISSN 0042-6962

**Visiting Nurse Association of Brooklyn. Department of Resources Development**
138 South Oxford St., Brooklyn, NY 11217.
- V N A Newsletter. 3 per yr.

**Visitors East**
663 Fifth Ave., New York, NY 10022.
- Visitors East. m. ISSN 0042-6997

**Vista Hill Foundation**
7798 Starling Drive, San Diego, CA 92123.
- Drug Abuse and Alcoholism Newsletter. 10 per yr.

**Visual Arts Research and Resource Center Relating to the Caribbean. Phelps Stoke Fund**
10 E. 87 St., New York, NY 10028.
- Pre-Columbian Research Resources Review; visual arts in the Caribbean. q.

**Visual Dialog**
P.O. Box 1438, Los Altos, CA 94022.
- Visual Dialog. q. ISSN 0360-4225

**Visual Resources Inc.**
One Lincoln Plaza, New York, NY 10023.
- Art & Cinema. 3 per yr.

**Visual Science Information Center**
School of Optometry, University of California, Berkeley, CA 94720.
- Current Abstracts on Contact Lenses. m.

**Visual Studies Workshop**
4 Elton St., Rochester, NY 14607.
- Afterimage. m(10 per yr) ISSN 0300-7472

**Visual Ventures Publishing**
Box 4725, Diamond Bar, CA 91765.
- Therapist; the magazine devoted to the selected health fields. bi-m.

**Viva International Ltd.**
909 Third Ave., New York, NY 10022.
- Viva. m.

**Vocational Guidance Manuals**
620 S. Fifth St., Louisville, KY 40202.
- Vocational Guidance Manuals. Career Series. irreg.

**Vocational Industrial Clubs of America, Inc.**
105 N. Virginia Ave., Falls Church, VA 22046.
- V I C A. 4 per yr. ISSN 0042-1839

**Vocations for Social Change, Inc.**
353 Broadway, Cambridge, MA 02139.
- People's Yellow Pages. biennial. (American Friends Service Committee, Inc.)

**Vocations for Social Change, Inc. (Oakland)**
5951 Canning St., Oakland, CA 94609.
- Workforce. bi-m.

**Voice of Brotherhood**
423 Seward St., Juneau, AK 99801.
- Voice of Brotherhood. m. ISSN 0300-6913

**Voice of India**
223 E. 32nd St., New York, NY 10016.
- Voice of India. m.

**Voice of Liberty Association**
Box 164, 692 Sunnybrook Dr., Decatur, GA 30031.
- Voice of Liberty. q. ISSN 0042-8159

**Voice of Prison**
Subscription Dept., Box 520, Walla Walla, WA 99362.
- Voice of Prison. bi-m.

**Voice of the Basques**
Boise, ID 83706.
- Voice of the Basques. m.

**Voice of the Black Community**
857 N. Jasper, Decatur, IL 62521.
- Voice of the Black Community. ISSN 0042-8183

**Voice of the Nazarene, Inc.**
Finleyville, PA 15332.
- Voice of the Nazarene-a Universal Challenger. m. ISSN 0042-8213

**Voicespondence Club**
Box 207, Shillington, PA 19607.
- Voicespondent. q. ISSN 0042-8299

**Volkswagen of America, Inc.**
Box 400, Nevada, IA 50201.
- Small World. 5 per yr. ISSN 0037-7279

**Volunteer Lawyers for the Arts**
36 W. 44th St., New York, NY 10036.
- Arts and the Law. 10 per yr.

**Volunteer Services for the Blind**
919 Walnut St., Philadelphia.
- Jack and Jill Magazine (Braille Edition) m.
- Ladies Home Journal (Braille Edition) m.

**Volunteers in Technical Assistance**
3706 Rhode Island Ave., Mt. Rainier, MD 20822.
- V I T A News. q.

**Von Kleinsmid Institute of International Affairs**
Univ. of Southern California, School of International Relations, VKC 330, Univ. Park, Los Angeles, CA 90007.
- Studies in Comparative Communism; an international interdisciplinary journal. q. ISSN 0039-3592

**Edward Vondrak**
6225 S. Kedzie Ave., Chicago, IL 60629.
- Southwest News-Herald. w. ISSN 0038-4704

**Vort Works Ink**
1708 Tilton Dr., Silver Spring, MD 20902.
- Vort. 4 per yr.

**Vortex Institute, Inc.**
P.O. Box 73152, Fairbanks, AK 99707.
- Universe. irreg. (approx. a.), vol. 7, 1974.

**Voter Education Project Inc.**
52 Fairlie St. N.W., Atlanta, GA 30303.
- Roster of Black Elected Officials in the South. irreg. ISSN 0093-9951

**Voyages, Inc.**
Box 4862, Washington, DC 20008.
- Voyages; a national literary magazine. irreg. ISSN 0042-9031

**Voyageur**
Box 7246, Powderhorn Sta., Minneapolis, MN 55487.
- Voyageur. q. ISSN 0042-904X

**W B**
c/o Patricia Jones, Ed., 188 E. 3rd St., New York, NY 10009.
- W B. 2-3 per yr.

**W F M T, Inc.**
500 N. Michigan, Chicago, IL 60611.
- Chicago. m.

**W I S E**
see **World Information Systems Exchange (W I S E)**

**W M D Publications**
P.O. Box 198, Islip, NY 11751.
- Commercial Directories of the United States. biennial.

**W M S E Publications**
Box 1003, Leesburg, VA 22075.
- World Military and Social Expenditures. irreg. ISSN 0363-4795

**W N Y C**
2500 Municipal Bldg., New York, NY 10007.
- Masterwork Bulletin. bi-m.

**W T S Pharmcraft**
Div. of Wallace and Tiernan Inc., 642 Broad St., Clifton, NJ 08109.
- Podiatry Management Letter. bi-m. ISSN 0024-0990

**W. W. Publications**
110 E. 59 St., New York, NY 10022.
● Working Woman. m.

**W W R**
324 C St., S. E., Washington, DC 20003.
● W W R. (Women's Washington Representative)
m.

**W - W Twentyfirst Corporation**
● Weight Watchers. (pub. by Family Media, Inc.)

**W W W W W Information Services, Inc.**
1595 Elmwood Ave., Rochester, NY 14620
(Subscr. to: Box 36601, Rochester, N.Y. 14609)
● Business Travel Hotline. m.
● Buyerism Newsletter. m.
● Careerism Newsletter. s-m.

**Wabash Valley Genealogical Society, Inc.**
Box 85, Terre Haute, IN 47805.
● Sycamore Leaves. q.

**Wachovia Bank and Trust Company, N.A.**
Box 3099, 301 N. Main St., Winston-Salem, NC
27102.
● North Carolina Agribusiness. m. ISSN 0300-6727

**Wade Publishing Co.**
230 California St., Box 3019, San Francisco, CA
94119.
● Daily Construction Service. d. ISSN 0011-5401

**Wadley Institutes of Molecular Medicine**
9000 Harry Hines Blvd., Dallas, TX 75235.
● Journal of Clinical Hematology and Oncology. q.

**Wadsworth Publishing Co.**
10 Davis Dr., Belmont, CA 94002.
● American History Research Series. irreg.
● Basic Concepts in Health Science Series. irreg.
● Fundamentals of Botany Series. irreg.
● Man-Environment System in the Late Twentieth
Century. irreg.
● Problems in a Business Society. irreg.
● Wadsworth Accounting Series. irreg.
● Wadsworth Botany Series. irreg.
● Wadsworth Continuing Education Series. irreg.
● Wadsworth Developmental Mathematics Series.
irreg.
● Wadsworth Guides to Literary Study. irreg.
● Wadsworth Guides to Science Teaching. irreg.
● Wadsworth Music Series. irreg.
● Wadsworth Series: Explorations in the Black
Experience. irreg.
● Wadsworth Series in American Politics. irreg.
● Wadsworth Series in Analytic Ethnography. irreg.
● Wadsworth Series in Chemistry. irreg.
● Wadsworth Series in Curriculum and Instruction.
irreg.
● Wadsworth Series in Finance. irreg.
● Wadsworth Series in Labor Economics and
Industrial Relations. irreg.
● Wadsworth Series in Sociology. irreg.
● Wadsworth Series in Special Education. irreg.
● Wadsworth Series in World Politics. irreg.
● Wadsworth Studies in Philosophical Criticism.
irreg.

**Arnold L. Wagner, Ed. & Pub.**
1130 N. Cottage, Salem, OR 97301.
● Pro; the voice of the cartooning world. m. ISSN
0032-9061

**J. H. Wagner, Ed. & Pub.**
Box 4875, Washington, DC 20008.
● Alpine Information; monthly report for
mountaineers. 8 per yr. ISSN 0145-2371
● Defense Business. w. ISSN 0364-9008
(Government Business Worldwide Reports)
● Defense Survey & Directory. m. ISSN 0099-166X
● Government Businesss Worldwide Reports. irreg.

**J. Richard Wagner, Ed. & Pub.**
P.O. Box 3413, Tucson, AZ 85722.
● Tipsico Bulletin. bi-m.

**Wagner College. Horrmann Library**
Staten Island, NY 10301.
● Markham Review. 4 per yr. ISSN 0025-3820

**Wagon & Star Publishers**
4032 W. Century Blvd., Inglewood, CA 90304.
● Dion. 4 per yr.(approx.) ISSN 0012-3064

**Waikiki Aquarium**
2777 Kalakaua Ave., Honolulu, HI 96815.
● Directory of Aquarium Specialists. irreg.

● Directory of the Public Aquaria of the World.
irreg; latest issue 1976. ISSN 0085-0039

**Waikiki Publishing Co. Inc.**
1441 Kapiolani Blvd., Suite 909, Honolulu, HI
96814.
● Here's Hawaii. s-m.

**Wake Forest University**
Winston-Salem, NC 27109.
● North Carolina English Teacher. q. (North
Carolina English Teachers Association)

**Wake Forest University. Overseas Research Center**
Raynolda Sta., Winston Salem, NC 27106.
● Developing Nations Monograph Series. irreg.

**Wake Forest University. School of Law**
Winston-Salem, NC 27109.
● Wake Forest Law Review. q. ISSN 0043-003X

**Wakeman-Walworth, Inc.**
P.O. Box 1144, Darien, CT 06820.
● Resource Recovery & Energyreview. bi-m. ISSN
0361-2562

**Wakra Publishing Group**
Box 404, Prudential Center Sta., Boston, MA
02199.
● Wakra. q. ISSN 0049-6855

**Walden - Mott Corporation**
466 Kinderkamack Rd., Oradell, NJ 07649.
● Walden's A B C Guide and Paper Production
Yearbook. a. ISSN 0083-7024
● Walden's Paper Report. s-m.

**Walker and Co.**
720 Fifth Ave., New York, NY 10019.
● Problems of History Series. irreg.
● World Trade Annual. a. ISSN 0512-3739 (United
Nations Statistical Office UN)
● World Trade Annual Supplement. a. ISSN 0512-
3747 (United Nations Statistical Office UN)

**Walker Art Center**
Vineland Place, Minneapolis, MN 55403.
● Design Quarterly. 4 per yr. ISSN 0011-9415

**Walker-Davis Publications, Inc.**
2500 Office Center, Willow Grove, PA 19090.
● Plant & Industrial Engineer's Digest. m.

**Walker Publishing Co., Inc.**
2016 W. Main, Sedalia, MO 65301.
● Full Cry. m. ISSN 0016-2620

**Walker's Manual Incorporated**
5855 Naples Plaza, Suite 101, Long Beach, CA
90803.
● Walker's Manual of Western Corporations. a.
ISSN 0092-749X
● Walker's Manual Supplement. 12 per yr. ISSN
0300-6549

**Wall Street Publishing Institute Inc.**
16 School St., Yonkers, NY 10701.
● Stock Market Magazine. m.(Sept-June) ISSN
0039-1638

**Wall Street Reports Publishing Corp.**
120 Wall St., New York, NY 10005.
● Antiques Investment Report. fortn.
● Art Investment Report. fortn. ISSN 0090-9211
● Wall Street Reports. m. ISSN 0043-0099

**Wall Street Transcript Corp.**
120 Wall St., New York, NY 10005.
● Wall Street Transcript; a professional publication
for the business and financial community. w.
ISSN 0043-0102

**Wallace-Homestead Co.**
Box 1317, Des Moines, IA 50305.
● Farm Tax Saver; tips for income tax and estate
planning. m. ISSN 0363-7840
● Wallaces Farmer. s-m. ISSN 0043-0129

**Wallace Publishing Co., Inc.**
P.O. Box 4021, Mountain View, CA 94040.
● Textile Services Management. m. ISSN 0040-5183

**Walnut Grove Publishing, Inc.**
611 Delsea Dr., Westville, NJ 08093.
● D V B Magazine. (Delaware Valley Business) m.

**Walt Disney Production**
Disneyland, P.O. Box 3232, Anaheim, CA 92803.
● Vacationland. 3 per yr.

**David Walter Associates**
107 Northern Blvd., Great Neck, NY 11021.
● Walter Report. w.

**Roy W. Walter & Associates**
60 Glen Ave., Glen Rock, NJ 07452.
● Behavioral Sciences Newsletter. fortn.

**Walters Art Gallery**
600 N. Charles St., Baltimore, MD 21201.
● Walters Art Gallery. Bulletin. m.(Oct-May) ISSN
0043-0188
● Walters Art Gallery. Journal. a. (occasionally
biennial) ISSN 0083-7156

**Wanderer Printing Co.**
128 E. 10th St., St. Paul, MN 55101.
● Wanderer. w.

**Karl Wang, Ed. & Pub**
102-40 62nd Ave., Apt. 6C, Forest Hills, NY
11375.
● Soft Stone; an international journal of the arts.
irreg., 1-2 per yr.

**Wang Laboratories**
836 North St., Tewksbury, MA 01876.
● Programmer; a Swap Users Society publication. q.
ISSN 0033-0418

**War Resisters League**
339 Lafayette St., New York, NY 10012.
● W R L News. bi-m. ISSN 0042-9791

**War Resisters League, Southeast**
Box 7477, Atlanta, GA 30357.
● W.R.L. S.E. Newsletter. q.

**Jim Ward, Ed. & Pub.**
Rt. 8, Thorngrove Pike, Knoxville, TN 37914.
● Wild West Stars; cowboy film corral. bi-m.

**Ward's Communications, Inc.**
28 W. Adams St., Detroit, MI 48226.
● Ward's Auto World. 12 per yr. ISSN 0043-0315
● Ward's Automotive Reports. w.
● Ward's Automotive Yearbook. a. ISSN 0083-7229
● Ward's Engine Update. fortn.
● Ward's Who's Who Among U.S. Motor Vehicle
Manufacturers. irreg.

**Ward's Natural Science Establishment**
Box 1712, Rochester, NY 14603.
● Ward's Bulletin. 3 per yr. ISSN 0043-0323

**Warner Press, Inc.**
Box 2499, Anderson, IN 46011.
● Climb. w. ISSN 0009-8965 (Church of God)
● Learn; we learn about God. q. ISSN 0023-9682
(Church of God)
● Reach. m. ISSN 0034-0308
● Vital Christianity. fortn. ISSN 0042-7381 (Church
of God)

**Warp Four**
c/o John R. Racano, Ed., 113 Cleveland Ave.,
Colonia, NJ 07067.
● Warp Four; the magazine of science fiction,
fantasy and horror. q.

**Warren Burkett**
854 National Press Bldg., Washington, DC 20045.
● Urban Growth Letter. 22 per yr.

**Warren County Historical Society**
Box 223, Lebanon, Ohio.
● Historicalog. m.

**Warren Education Association**
● Harbinger (Detroit) (pub. by Harpress
Publications)

**Warren, Gorham and Lamont, Inc.**
210 South St., Boston, MA 02111.
● Bank Auditing and Accounting Report. m. ISSN
0522-2478
● Bank Automation Newsletter. m. ISSN 0572-5933
● Bank Director's Report. m. ISSN 0522-2494
● Bank Executive's Report. s-m.
● Bank Executive's Seminar Series. m.
● Bank Holding Company Reporter (Supplement)
supplements issued periodically to update base
volume.
● Bank Loan Officers Report. m.

- Bank Marketing Report. m.
- Bank Officers Handbook of Commercial Banking Law (Supplement) supplements issued periodically to update base volume.
- Bank Operations Report. m. ISSN 0045-1487
- Bank Personnel Report. m.
- Bank Security Report. m.
- Bank Tax Report. s-m.
- Bank Teller's Report. m.
- Banker & Tradesman. w. ISSN 0005-5409
- Bankers Diary and Guide. a.
- Bankers Handbook of Federal Aids to Financing (Supplement) supplements issued periodically to update base volume.
- Banker's Letter of the Law. m. ISSN 0005-5433
- Bankers Magazine. q. ISSN 0005-545X
- Banking Law Journal. 10 per yr. ISSN 0005-5506
- Banking Law Journal Digest (Supplement) supplements issued periodically to update set of 2 base volumes.
- Bittker and Eustice's Federal Income Taxation of Corporations and Shareholders (Supplement) supplements issued periodically to update base volume.
- Bittker Forms Book (Supplement) supplements issued periodically to update base volume.
- Brady on Bank Checks (Supplement) supplements issued periodically to update base volume.
- Branch Banker's Report. m.
- Business and Society Review; a quarterly forum on the role of business in a free society. q. ISSN 0045-3609
- Computer Law & Tax Report. m. ISSN 0361-7203
- Condominium Development Guide (Supplement) supplements issued periodically to update base volume.
- Consolidated Tax Return (Supplement) supplements issued periodically to update base volume.
- Consumer Credit and Truth-In-Lending Compliance Report. m. ISSN 0300-6034
- Corporation Law and Tax Report. s-m.
- Criminal Law Bulletin. bi-m. ISSN 0011-1317
- Criminal Law Digest (Supplement); digests of leading federal and state cases. supplements issued periodically to update base volume.
- Equal Credit Opportunity Manual (Supplement) supplements issued periodically to update base volume.
- Executive Compensation Report. m.
- Fair Credit Reporting Manual. irreg., 2nd edt. 1977; supplements issued periodically to update base vol.
- Federal Banking Laws (Supplement) supplements issued periodically to update base volume.
- Federal Income Taxation of Banks and Financial Institutions (Supplement) supplements issued periodically to update base volume.
- Freeman and Freeman's Tax Practice Deskbook (Supplement) supplements issued periodically to update base volume.
- Index to Federal Tax Articles (Supplement) supplements issued periodically to update base volumes.
- Investment Companies; mutual funds and other types. a.(with quarterly updating) ISSN 0075-0271 (Wiesenberger Services, Inc.)
- Journal of Corporate Taxation. q. ISSN 0094-0593
- Journal of Pedodontics. q.
- Journal of Real Estate Taxation. q. ISSN 0093-5107
- Kess Tax Practice Report. s-m.
- Law of Bank Deposits, Collections and Credit Cards (Supplement) supplements issued periodically to update base volume.
- Management Results. q. (Wiesenberger Services, Inc.)
- Modern Accounting and Auditing Checklists (Supplement) supplements issued periodically to update base volume.
- Modern Bank Accounting and Auditing Forms (Supplement) supplements issued periodically to update base volume.
- Modern Banking Checklists (Supplement) supplements issued periodically to update base volume.
- Modern Banking Forms. supplements issued periodically to update set of two base volumes.
- Modern Condominium Forms (Supplement) supplements issued periodically to update base volume.
- Modern Construction Forms (Supplement) supplements issued periodically to update base volume.
- Modern Corporation Checklists (Supplement) loose-leaf supplements issued periodically to update base volume.

- Modern Health Care Forms (Supplement) supplements issued periodically to update base volume.
- Modern Personnel Forms (Supplement) supplements issued periodically to update base volume.
- Modern Real Estate and Mortgage Forms (Supplement) supplements issued periodically to update base volume.
- Modern Real Estate Ownership and Investment Forms (Supplement) supplement issued periodically to update base volume.
- Modern Securities Transfers (Supplement) supplement issued periodically to update base volume.
- Modern Trust Checklists (Supplement) loose-leaf supplements issued periodically to update base volume.
- Modern Trust Forms (Supplement) supplements issued periodically to update base volume.
- Mortgage and Real Estate Executives Report. s-m. ISSN 0047-813X
- Mutual Fund Performance Monthly. m. ISSN 0047-8490 (Wiesenberger Services, Inc.)
- Mutual Funds Current Performance & Dividend Record. m. (Wiesenberger Services, Inc.)
- Pension Regulation Manual (Supplement) supplements issued periodically to update base volumes.
- Real Estate Law Digest (Supplement) supplements issued periodically to update base volume.
- Real Estate Law Journal. q. ISSN 0048-6868
- Real Estate Law Report. m.
- Real Estate Review. q. ISSN 0034-0790
- Real Estate Review Portfolio Series. m.
- Real Estate Tax Ideas. m.
- Review of Taxation of Individuals. q.
- Robinson Federal Income Taxation of Real Estate. supplements issued periodically to update base volume.
- S E C Accounting Report. m.
- Securities Regulation Law Journal. q. ISSN 0097-9554
- Stanley and Kilcullen's Federal Income Tax Law (Supplement) supplements issued periodically to update base volume.
- Stephens, Maxfield and Lind's Federal Estate and Gift Taxation (Supplement) supplements issued periodically to update base volume.
- Tax Court Practice (Supplement) supplements issued periodically to update base volume.
- Tax Fraud and Evasion (Supplement) supplements issued periodically to update base volume.
- Tax Law Review. q. ISSN 0040-0041 (New York University. Law Publications)
- Taxation of Closely Held Corporations (Supplement) supplements issued periodically to update base volume.
- Taxation of Patents, Trademarks, Copyrights and Know-How (Supplement) supplements issued periodically to update base volume.
- Thorndike Encyclopedia of Banking and Financial Tables (Supplement) annual supplements update base volume.
- Truth-in-Lending Manual (Supplement) supplements issued periodically to update set of two base volumes.
- Uniform Commercial Code Law Journal. q. ISSN 0041-672X
- Uniform Commercial Code Law Letter. m. ISSN 0503-1966
- Wiesenberger Report. q. (Wiesenberger Services, Inc.)

**Warren Publishing Co.**
145 E. 32nd St., New York, NY 10016.
- Famous Monsters of Filmland. 9 per yr. ISSN 0014-7443

**Washburn University. School of Law**
Topeka, KS 66621.
- Washburn Law Journal. 3 per yr. ISSN 0043-0420

**Robert E. Washer, Ed. & Pub.**
82 E. 8th St., Oneida Castle, NY 13421.
- T. Q. C. B/Queen Canon Bibliophile. q. ISSN 0039-8489

**Washington (State) Attorney General's Office**
Dexter Horton Bldg., Seattle, WA 98104.
- Consumer Protection Newsletter. q.
- Washington (State). Attorney General's Office. Directory of Charitable Organizations and Trusts Registered with the Office of Attorney General. irreg. ISSN 0093-6693

**Washington (State) Department of Commerce and Economic Development**
Olympia, WA 98504.
- Announced New Plants and Expansions in the State of Washington. q.
- Directory of Washington Manufacturers. a. ISSN 0419-3857 (prep. by its Trade Development Division)

**Washington (State) Department of Commerce and Economic Development. Department of Foreign Trade**
General Administration Bldg., Olympia, WA 98504.
- Washington Foreign Trade Trends. bi-m.

**Washington (State) Department of Ecology**
Olympia, WA 98504.
- Air Watch. q.
- Washington (State). Department of Ecology. Water Quality Assessment Report. a. ISSN 0362-6369

**Washington (State) Department of Fisheries**
General Administration Building, Olympia, WA 98501.
- Washington (State). Department of Fisheries. Fisheries Research Papers. irreg., 1970, vol. 3, no. 2. ISSN 0083-744X (prep. by its Research Division)
- Washington (State). Department of Fisheries. Research Bulletin. irreg., 1970, no. 9. ISSN 0083-7466 (prep. by its Research Division)
- Washington (State) Department of Fisheries. Technical Report. irreg., no. 24, 1977. ISSN 0083-7474

**Washington (State) Department of Highways**
Highway Administration Bldg., Olympia, WA 98504.
- Highway & Ferry System Motorists Information Report. m. (prep. by its Public Affairs Office)
- Washington Highway News. m. ISSN 0511-3180

**Washington (State) Department of Motor Vehicles**
Research & Technology, Olympia, WA 98504.
- Washington (State). Department of Motor Vehicles. Research and Technology. Research Report. irreg. ISSN 0092-3583

**Washington (State) Department of Motor Vehicles. Information Office**
Highways - Licenses Bldg, Olympia, WA 98504.
- D M Views. m.

**Washington (State) Department of Natural Resources**
Olympia, WA 98504.
- Totem. m. ISSN 0040-9723
- Washington (State). Natural Areas Advisory Committee. Biennial Report. biennial. ISSN 0362-8906

**Washington (State) Department of Natural Resources. Division of Geology and Earth Resources**
Olympia, WA 98501.
- Washington (State) Division of Geology and Earth Resources. Information Circular. irreg.
- Washington Geologic Newsletter. q. ISSN 0094-2820

**Washington (State) Department of Revenue**
Olympia, WA 98504.
- Washington (State). Department of Revenue. Forest Tax Report. irreg. ISSN 0362-7462
- Washington (State). Department of Revenue. Research and Information Division. Comparative State/Local Taxes. a.
- Washington (State). Department of Revenue. Research and Information Division. Property Tax Levy and Collection Statistics. a.
- Washington (State) Department of Revenue. Revenue Newsletter. s-m.

**Washington (State) Department of Social and Health Services**
Box 1788 Olympia Airport, Olympia, WA 98504.
- Environmental Radiation Surveillance in Washington State; Annual Report. a. ISSN 0509-769X (prep. by its Health Services Division)
- Overview. m.
- Washington (State) Department of Social and Health Services. Income Maintenance, Community Social Services and Medical Assistance. m. (prep. by its Office of Program Analysis and Technical Standards)

- Washington (State). Department of Social and Health Services. Jail Inspection Report. irreg. ISSN 0091-7265

**Washington (State) Department of Social and Health Services. Office on Aging**
OB-433G, Olympia, WA 98504.
- Washington (State) Department of Social and Health Services. Office on Aging. Senior Newsletter. q.

**Washington (State) Department of Social and Health Services. Office of Community Health Service**
MS 5-2, Olympia, WA 98504.
- Alerts. q.

**Washington (State) Employment Security Department**
5000 Capitol Blvd., Olympia, WA 98501.
- Washington (State) Employment Security Department. Local Labor Market Developments. m.
- Washington Economic Indicators. bi-m. ISSN 0511-2400 (prep. by its Research and Statistics Branch)

**Washington (State) Fruit Commission**
Box 2696, 622 W. Yakima Ave., Yakima, WA 98902.
- Goodfruit Grower. s-m. ISSN 0046-6174
- Goodgrape Grower. q.

**Washington (State) Game Department**
600 N. Capitol Way, Olympia, WA 98501.
- Washington (State) Game Department. Applied Research Section. Bulletin. irreg. ISSN 0095-3253
- Washington Wildlife. q. ISSN 0049-6952

**Washington (State) Indian Assistance Division. Office of Community Development**
1677 2nd Ave., Tumwater, WA 98504.
- Washington (State). Indian Assistance Diviision. Indian Economic Employment Assistance Program. Annual Report. a. ISSN 0360-4837

**Washington (State) Law and Justice Planning Office**
Olympia, WA 98504.
- State of Washington Comprehensive Plan for Crime Control and the Administration of Justice. irreg. ISSN 0363-5643

**Washington (State) Legislature**
Olympia, WA 98504.
- Washington (State) Legislature. Pictorial Directory. irreg., latest issue 1975. ISSN 0091-8253

**Washington (State) Legislature. Transportation Committee**
Olympia, WA 98501.
- Washington (State) Legislature. Transportation Committee. Report. irreg. ISSN 0095-6082

**Washington (State) Real Estate Division**
Box 247, Highways Licenses Bldg., Olympia, WA 98405.
- Washington Real Estate News. bi-m.

**Washington (State) State Library**
Olympia, WA 98504.
- Public Administration; recent additions to the Washington State Library collection. m.

**Washington (State) State Office of Program Planning and Fiscal Management**
Information Service Division, House Office Bldg., Olympia, WA 98504
(Dist. by: State Library, Olympia WA 98504)
- Washington (State). Human Resources Agencies. Annual Report. a. ISSN 0091-4312
- Washington (State) Natural Resources and Recreation Agencies. Annual Report. a.
- Washington (State) Office of Program Planning and Fiscal Management. Population and Enrollment Section. Population Trends. a. ISSN 0083-7482
- Washington (State). Transportation Agencies. Annual Report. a. ISSN 0091-4967

**Washington (State) State Patrol**
Olympia, WA 98501.
- Washington State Traffic Accident Facts. a. ISSN 0509-7967

**Washington (State) Superintendent of Public Instruction**
Old Capitol Bldg., Olympia, WA 98504.
- Washington Education Directory. (pub. by Barbara Krohn and Associates)
- Your Public Schools. fortn. ISSN 0044-1104

**Washington (State) Utilities and Transportation Commission**
Highways-License Bldg., Olympia, WA 98504.
- Washington (State) Utilities and Transportation Commission. Transportation Report. a. ISSN 0083-758X

**Washington (State) Vocational Rehabilitation Services Division**
P.O. Box 1788, Olympia, WA 98504.
- Washington (State). Vocational Rehabilitation Services Division. State Facilities Plan. irreg. ISSN 0092-5543

**Washington (State) Water Research Center**
Washington State University, Pullman, WA 99163.
- Washington (State) Water Research Center, Pullman. Report. irreg., latest issue no. 16. ISSN 0083-7598

**Washington Academy of Sciences**
9650 Rockville Pike, Bethesda, MD 20014.
- Washington Academy of Sciences. Journal. q. ISSN 0043-0439

**Washington Alaska Regional Medical Program**
500 Univ. District Bldg., Seattle, WA 98105.
- R M P Results. (Regional Medical Program) bi-m. ISSN 0033-7013

**Washington & Jefferson College**
Washington, PA 15301.
- Red and Black. w. ISSN 0034-1940
- Topic; a journal of the liberal arts. a. ISSN 0049-4127
- Washington and Jefferson Literary Journal. a. ISSN 0043-0455

**Washington and Lee University**
Box 722, Lexington, VA 24450.
- Shenandoah; Washington and Lee University Review. q. ISSN 0037-3583

**Washington and Lee University. Office of Publications**
Lexington, VA 24450.
- W & L. q. ISSN 0042-952X

**Washington and Lee University. School of Law**
Lexington, VA 24450.
- Washington & Lee Law Review. 4 per yr. ISSN 0043-0463

**Washington Archaeologist**
Box 84, University Station, Seattle, WA 98105.
- Washington Archaeologist. irreg. ISSN 0511-3091

**Washington Area Council on Alcoholism & Drug Abuse, Inc.**
1330 New Hampshire Ave. N.W., Washington, DC 20036.
- Coping Catalog; a guide to resources in the greater Washington area for alcohol and drug addiction problems. a.

**Washington Association of Sheriffs and Police Chiefs**
1222 Second Ave., Seattle, WA 98101.
- Washington Law Enforcement Journal. q. (Co-sponsor: Washington State Law Enforcement Association)

**Washington Association of Wheat Growers**
301 W. Main, Ritzville, WA 99169.
- Wheat Life. m. ISSN 0043-4701

**Washington Banktrends**
Suite 503, 734 15th St. N.W., Washington, DC 20005.
- Washington Banktrends. w.

**Washington Board of Realtors, Inc.**
1511 K St. N.W., Washington, DC 20005.
- Realtor. m.

**Washington Business Information, Inc.**
1080 National Press Bldg., Washington, DC 20045.
- Devices & Diagnostics Letter. w. ISSN 0098-7573
- Food and Drug Letter. bi-w. ISSN 0362-6466
- Product Safety Letter. w. ISSN 0098-7530

**Washington Center of Foreign Policy Research**
- Studies in International Affairs. (pub. by Johns Hopkins University Press)

**Washington Community Video Center, Inc.**
Box 21068, Washington, DC 20009.
- TeleVISIONS. bi-m.

**Washington Consortium of Universities**
- Potomac Review. (pub. by Potomac Review, Inc.)

**Washington County (Arkansas) Historical Society**
118 E. Dickson St., Fayetteville, AR 72701.
- Flashback. q.

**Washington County (Maryland)) Board of Education**
Box 730, Commonwealth Ave., Hagerstown, MD 21740.
- Washington County Education News. 5 per yr. ISSN 0043-051X

**Washington County (Ohio) Historical Society**
401 Aurora St., Marietta, OH 45750.
- Tallow Light. q. ISSN 0049-2914

**Washington County World**
92 River St., Montpelier, VT 05602.
- Washington County World. w.

**Washington Crime News Services**
7620 Little River Tpke., Annandale, VA 22003.
- Corrections Digest; a complete information exchange for the rehabilitation and correction professional. bi-w. ISSN 0010-9045
- Court Systems Digest; significant trends in judicial management and administration. m.
- Crime Control Digest. w. ISSN 0011-1295
- Juvenile Justice Digest. fortn. ISSN 0094-2413
- Narcotics Control Digest. fortn. ISSN 0027-786X
- Security Systems Digest. fortn. ISSN 0037-069X
- Training Aids Digest. m.

**Washington Criminal Justice Education and Training Center**
Providence Heights, Issaquah, WA 98027.
- Washington Criminal Justice Education and Training Center. Journal. q.

**Washington Crop and Livestock Reporting Service**
3136 Federal Office Bldg., Seattle, WA 98174.
- Washington Agricultural Statistics. irreg. ISSN 0095-4330

**Washington Data Processing Service Center**
Room 110, Gen. Admin. Bldg., Olympia, WA 98504.
- W D P S C Happenings. bi-m.

**Washington Dental Service**
2208 N. W. Market St., Seattle, WA 98107.
- Washington Dental Service Newsletter. q. ISSN 0043-0536

**Washington-District of Columbia Pharmaceutical Association, Inc.**
Suite 26, 5506 Connecticut Ave., N.W., Washington, DC 20015.
- National Capital Pharmacist. m. ISSN 0027-8890

**Washington Folk Strums**
9937 Cottrell Terrace, Silver Spring, MD 20903.
- Washington Folk Strums. irreg. ISSN 0091-9020

**Washington Insurance Newsletter, Inc.**
1365 National Press Bldg., Washington, DC 20045.
- Washington Insurance Newsletter. w. ISSN 0043-0595

**Washington International Arts Letter**
Townhouse Four, Harbour Square, 1321 4th St., S.W., Washington, DC 20024.
- Arts Patronage Series. irreg. ISSN 0066-8168

**Washington Journalism Center**
- Critical Issues Series. (pub. by Publishing Sciences Group, Inc.)

**Washington Law Reporter Co.**
1625 Eye St. N.W., Room 814, Washington, DC 20006.
- Daily Washington Law Reporter. d.

**Washington Library Association. O.P.E.N. Interest Group**
Washington State Library, Olympia, WA 98504.
- O.P.E.N. Newsletter. (Outreach Programs for Essential Needs) q.

**Washington Literary Society**
Randolph-Macon College, Ashland, VA 23005.
- Stylus (Ashland) s-a. ISSN 0039-4300

**Washington Magazine Inc.**
1828 L St. N.W., Suite 200, Washington, DC
20036.
- Washingtonian. m. ISSN 0043-0897

**Washington Metropolitan Area Transit Authority**
600 Fifth St. N.W., Washington, DC 20001.
- Metro Memo. bi-m. ISSN 0026-1378

**Washington Monitor, Inc.**
201 Massachusetts Ave. N.E., Washington, DC
20002.
- Congressional Monitor; daily listing of all
scheduled Congressional committee hearings, with
witnesses. d, with weekly supplements. ISSN
0010-5902
- Congressional Record Scanner; outline of contents
of the Congressional Record. 180 per yr.
- Congressional Yellow Book; loose-leaf directory of
members of congress, their committees, and their
key aides. 4 per yr.
- Monday Monitor; weekly listing of all scheduled
Congressional committee hearings, with witnesses.
w.

**Washington Monthly Co.**
1028 Connecticut Ave. N.W., Washington, DC
20036.
- Washington Monthly. m. ISSN 0043-0633

**Washington Music Educator's Association**
c/o C. G. Burnett, 913 E. 8th Ave., Ellensburg, WA
98926.
- Voice of Washington Music Educators. 5 per yr.

**Washington Newspaper Publishers' Association, Inc.**
3838 Stone Way North, Seattle, WA 98103.
- Washington Newspaper. m. ISSN 0043-0684

**Washington Performing Arts Society**
425 13th St. N. W., Suite 712, Washington, DC
20004.
- W.P.A.S.Museletter. several times a year. ISSN
0092-4113

**Washington Poets Association**
3837 134th N.E., Bellevue, WA 98005.
- Yawp. 4 per yr.

**Washington Recreation and Park Society, Inc.**
Box 512, Olympia, WA 98507.
- W R P S News. q. ISSN 0042-9805

**Washington Reports to Africa**
Box 687, Glen Echo, MD 20768.
- Washington Reports to Africa. w.

**Washington Researchers Information Report**
910 17th St. N.W., No. 325, Washington, DC
20006.
- Washington Researchers Information Report. q.

**Washington Review: a Quarterly Review of the Arts**
404 10th Street, S.E., Washington, DC 20003.
- Washington Review: a Quarterly Review of the
Arts. q.

**Washington School of Psychiatry. Forum on
Psychiatry and the Humanities**
- Psychiatry and the Humanities. (pub. by Yale
University Press)

**Washington Science Fiction Association**
- S F & F Journal. (pub. by M Press)

**Washington Spectator, Inc.**
Box 32280, Washington, DC 20007
- Washington Spectator/Between the Lines. s-m.
(Subsc. to:, Box 1750, Annapolis, MD 21404)

**Washington State Association of Counties**
6730 Martin Way N.E., Olympia, WA 98506.
- Washington County News. m.

**Washington State Association of School Librarians**
18605 104th St., N.E, Bothell, WA 98011.
- Library Leads/Library Leads. q. ISSN 0043-0765

**Washington State Coaches Association**
Auditorium Building, 24th and Colby, Everett, WA
98201
(Subscr. Address: Don Burnett, 9322 21st Ave.,
NW, Seattle, Wash. 98104)
- Washington Coach. q. ISSN 0043-0501

**Washington State Dental Association**
Box 9824, Seattle, WA 98109.
- W S D A News. m. ISSN 0042-983X
- Washington State Dental Journal. a. ISSN 0083-
7431

**Washington State Entomological Society**
Department of Entomology, Washington State
University, Pullman, WA 99163.
- Melanderia. irreg., no. 26, 1976. ISSN 0076-6224
- Washington State Entomological Society
Proceedings. irreg., 1-2 per yr. ISSN 0043-0773

**Washington State Food Dealers Association**
120 6th Ave. North, Seattle, WA 98109.
- Washington Food Dealer Magazine. m. ISSN
0043-0560

**Washington State Grange**
3104 Western Ave., Seattle, WA 98121.
- Washington Grange News. s-m. ISSN 0043-0587

**Washington State Horticultural Association**
Box 136, Wenatchee, WA 98801.
- Washington State Horticultural Association.
Proceedings. a.

**Washington State Nurses Association**
1117 Second Avenue, Room 200, Seattle, WA
98118.
- W S N A Mini Journal. irreg. (approx. 4 per yr)
- Washington State Journal of Nursing. q. ISSN
0043-0781

**Washington State Pharmaceutical Association**
1305 3rd Ave., Suite 204, Seattle, WA 98101.
- Washington Pharmacist. bi-m.

**Washington State Research Council**
1071 Capitol Way, Olympia, WA 98501.
- Washington State Research Council Monthly
Report. m. ISSN 0043-0803

**Washington State School Directors' Association**
200 E. Union, Olympia, WA 98501.
- Compass (Olympia) bi-m.
- Signal (Olympia) 22 per yr.

**Washington State University**
Pullman, WA 99163.
- Poe Studies. 2-3 per yr. ISSN 0090-5224

**Washington State University. College of Engineering**
Pullman, WA 99163.
- Engineering and Society Series. irreg., no. 3, 1974.
ISSN 0094-7288

**Washington State University. Department of English**
Pullman, WA 99163.
- E S Q. (Emerson Society Quarterly); journal of
the American Renaissance. q. ISSN 0013-6670
- Kamadhenu. 2 per yr.

**Washington State University. Department of Pure
and Applied Mathematics**
Pullman, WA 99163.
- Washington State University. Mathematics Notes.
q. ISSN 0043-082X

**Washington State University. Engineering Extension
Service**
College of Engineering, Pullman, WA 99164.
- Northwest Wood Products Clinic. Proceedings. a.
ISSN 0078-1797 (Co-sponsors: Spokane Chamber
of Commerce, Timber Products Bureau;
University of Idaho; Montana State University)
- Quest (Pullman); seeking for knowledge. q. ISSN
0033-6327
- Road Builder's Clinic. Proceedings. a. ISSN 0080-
3278 (Co-sponsor: University of Idaho, College of
Engineering)
- Symposium on Particleboard. Proceedings. a.
ISSN 0082-089X
- Symposium on the Nondestructive Testing of
Wood. Proceedings. irreg., 1970, no. 3. ISSN
0082-0970
- Washington State University. College of
Engineering. Annual Report. a. ISSN 0083-7512
- Wood Industry Abstracts. 6 per yr. ISSN 0360-
3083 (Co-Sponsor; Forest Product Research
Society)

**Washington State University Library. Library Staff
Association**
Pullman, WA 99163.
- Washington. State University, Pullman. Library
Staff Association. L S A Open Stacks. 12 per yr.
ISSN 0083-7563

**Washington State University Press**
Pullman, WA 99163.
- Northwest Science. q. ISSN 0029-344X
(Northwest Scientific Association)
- Washington State University. Bureau of Economic
and Business Research. Study. irreg., no. 49,
1972. ISSN 0083-7504
- Washington State University. Research Studies. q.
ISSN 0043-0838

**Washington University**
- Student Life. (pub. by Campus Publications, Inc.)

**Washington University. Institute for Urban &
Regional Studies**
St. Louis, MO 63130.
- Washington University, St. Louis. Institute for
Urban and Regional Studies. Working Paper.
irreg., 1970, no. 8. ISSN 0085-798X

**Washington University. Library**
St. Louis, MO 63130.
- Washington University Librarian. q. ISSN 0049-
6944

**Washington University. School of Law**
St. Louis, MO 63130.
- Washington University Law Quarterly. 5 per yr.
ISSN 0043-0862

**Washington University. School of Medicine Library**
4580 Scott Ave., St. Louis, MO 63110.
- Washington University. School of Medicine
Library. Library Notes; an occasional publication.
8 per yr. ISSN 0024-242X

**Washington University. Student Union**
Box 1068, Washington University, Clayton, MO
63130.
- A C I I D. (Critical Insight into Israel's
Dilemmas) 2 per yr. ISSN 0044-5630

**Washington Watch, Inc.**
- Washington Watch. (pub. by Shrikumar Poddar)

**Washington Women's Art Center**
1821 Q St.,N.W., Washington, DC 20009.
- Womensphere. bi-m.

**Washington Workshops**
1329 E St. N.W., Suite 1111, Washington, DC
20004.
- Youth Info Digest. a.

**Washout Publishing Co.**
Box 2752, Schenectady, NY 12309.
- Washout Review. q.

**Washtenaw Community College**
- Ann Arbor Review. (pub. by Ann Arbor Review
Press)

**Watauga Association of Genealogists**
East Tennessee State University, Sherrod Library,
Room 301, Johnson City, TN 37601.
- Watauga Association of Genealogists. Bulletin. s-a.
ISSN 0091-8857

**Watch on the Atomic Energy Commission Citizen's
Energy Council**
Box 285, Allendale, NJ 07401.
- Watch on the AEC. m.

**Watchtower Bible & Tract Society, Inc.**
117 Adams St., Brooklyn, NY 11201.
- Awake. s-m. ISSN 0005-237X
- Jehovah's Witnesses Yearbook. a. ISSN 0075-3602
(Jehovah's Witnesses)
- Watchtower; announcing Jehovah's kingdom. s-m.
ISSN 0043-1087 (Jehovah's Witnesses)

**Water Information Center, Inc.**
7 High St., Huntington, NY 11743.
- Ground Water Newsletter. s-m.
- Water Newsletter; water supply, waste disposal,
conservation, pollution. s-m. ISSN 0043-1273

**Water Pollution Control Federation**
2626 Pennsylvania Ave. N.W., Washington, DC
20037.
- Deeds and Data. m. ISSN 0091-3634
- Water Pollution Control Federation. Journal. m.
ISSN 0043-1303
- Water Pollution Control Federation Conference.
Abstracts of Technical Papers. a.
- Water Pollution Control Federation Highlights. m.
ISSN 0049-6987

**Water Polo Scoreboard**
1913 Nipomo Ave., Long Beach, CA 90815.
- Water Polo Scoreboard. m. except Mar., Dec. ISSN 0043-1311

**Water Resources Association of the Delaware River Basin**
901 Stephen Girard Building, 21 South 12th St., Philadelphia, PA 19107.
- Delaware Basin Bulletin. irreg. ISSN 0045-9844

**Water Resources Information System**
Dept. of Ecology, Olympia, WA 98504.
- Basin Bibliography. irreg. ISSN 0092-0355

**Water Resources Publications**
1912 Sequoia St., Fort Collins, CO 80521.
- Bilateral U S-Japan Seminar in Hydrology. triennial.

**Water Spectrum**
Washington, DC 20310
- Water Spectrum. q. ISSN 0043-1435

**Watershed Foundation**
- Black Box. (pub. by Black Box)

**Waterways Journal, Inc.**
319 N. Fourth St., 666 Security Bldg., St. Louis, MO 63102.
- Inland River Guide. a.
- Inland River Record. a. (Subscr. to: 121 River Ave., Sewickley, PA 15143)
- Waterways Journal; devoted to the marine profession and commercial interest of all inland waterways. w. ISSN 0043-1524

**Sylvestre C. Watkins, Ed. & Pub.**
11372 Links Dr., Reston, VA 22090.
- Black Heritage. bi-m.

**Watman Educational Services**
Box 457, Henniker, NH 03242.
- W. E. S. Authors' and Publishers' Service Newsletter. 6 per yr.

**Ann Watson**
P.O. Box 22296, San Diego, CA 92122.
- Ann Watson Report. m.

**Neale Watson Academic Publications, Inc.**
156 Fifth Ave., New York, NY 10010.
- Comparative Medicine East & West. q.
- Milbank Memorial Fund Quarterly/Health and Society. q. ISSN 0026-3745
- Yale Journal of Biology and Medicine. bi-m. ISSN 0044-0086 (Yale University)

**Watson-Guptill Publications, Inc.**
One Astor Plaza, New York, NY 10036.
- Annual of Advertising, Editorial & Television Art & Design with the Annual Copy Awards. a. (Art Directors Club of New York) (Co-Sponsor: Copy Club of New York)

**Watson Publications**
5 S. Wabash Ave., Chicago, IL 60603.
- Modern Railroads/Rail Transit. m.

**Watt Publishing Co.**
Mount Morris, IL 61054.
- American Dairy Review. m. ISSN 0002-8169
- Broiler Business. m.
- Farm Supplier; serving farm supply, feed, and fertilizer, dealers. m. ISSN 0014-813X
- Industria Avicola. m. ISSN 0019-7467
- Pig International. m. ISSN 0031-9767
- Poultry International. m. ISSN 0032-5767
- Poultry Tribune; covering egg production, processing & marketing. m. ISSN 0032-5805
- Turkey World. m. ISSN 0041-4271
- Who's Who in the Egg and Poultry Industries. a. ISSN 0510-4130

**Franklin Watts Inc.**
750 Fifth Ave., New York, NY 10019.
- Jane's Ocean Technology (New York) a. ISSN 0360-4950

**Waukesha County Historical Society**
20245 W. National Ave., New Berlin, WI 53151.
- Landmark. q.

**Wax Publications, Inc.**
1239 Vine St., Philadelphia, PA 19107.
- Film Bulletin. m. ISSN 0015-1165

**Way Out West Tent**
1111 Larra Bee St. No. 3, Los Angeles, CA 90069.
- Pratfall; the way out west periodical tribute to Stan and Ollie. 3-4 per yr. ISSN 0032-6887 (Sons of the Desert)

**Wayfarer Corporation**
Suite 225 First National Bank Bldg., 165 Cannon St., Charleston, SC 29403.
- Charleston-City of Charm. a.

**Wayne State University**
Detroit, MI 48202.
- Michigan College Personnel Association Journal. s-a. ISSN 0026-2080
- South End. q. ISSN 0038-3430

**Wayne State University. Archives of Labor History and Urban Affairs**
Detroit, MI 48202.
- Archives of Labor History and Urban Affairs Newsletter. q. ISSN 0044-8729

**Wayne State University. Center for the Study of Cognitive Processes**
768 Mackenzie Hall, Detroit, MI 48202.
- Wayne State University. Center for the Study of Cognitive Processes. Dissertations in Cognitive Processes. a. ISSN 0083-7741

**Wayne State University. College of Engineering**
Detroit, MI 48202.
- Wayne Engineer. bi-m. ISSN 0049-7037

**Wayne State University. College of Pharmacy**
Detroit, MI 48202.
- Stephen Wilson Annual Pharmacy Seminar. Report. a. ISSN 0585-2471

**Wayne State University. Division of University Relations**
Detroit, MI 48202.
- Wayne State University Alumni News. q. ISSN 0043-163X

**Wayne State University Law School**
468 W. Ferry, Detroit, MI 48202.
- Wayne Law Review. 5 per yr. ISSN 0043-1621

**Wayne State University. Medical Library**
4325 Brush St., Detroit, MI 48201.
- Selected List of Biomedical Serials in Metropolitan Detroit. irreg., 6th edt. 1974. ISSN 0511-392X
- Union List of Serials in the Wayne State University Libraries. q. ISSN 0082-7681
- Wayne State University, Detroit. Medical Library. Report. irreg., no. 62, 1974. ISSN 0083-775X

**Wayne State University Press**
5959 Woodward Ave., Detroit, MI 48202.
- American Imago; a psychoanalytic journal for culture, science and the arts. q. ISSN 0065-860X (Association for Applied Psychoanalysis)
- American Journal of Political Science. q. ISSN 0092-5853 (Midwest Conference of Political Scientists)
- American Orthopsychiatric Association. Papers Presented at the Annual Convention. a.
- Criticism; a quarterly for literature and the arts. q. ISSN 0011-1589
- Human Biology. q. ISSN 0018-7143
- Lafayette Clinic Handbooks in Psychiatry. irreg. ISSN 0075-7608
- Lafayette Clinic Monographs in Psychiatry. irreg. ISSN 0075-7616
- Walt Whitman Review. q. ISSN 0043-017X

**Wayside Gardens**
Box 1, Hodges, SC 29695.
- Wayside Gardener. q.

**Wayside Press**
Charlottsville, VA 22903.
- Speech and Hearing Association of Virginia. Journal. s-a. ISSN 0038-7150

**Wayside Press (Cottonwood)**
P.O. Box 475, Cottonwood, AR 86326.
- Wayside Quarterly. q.

**We Are One**
1000 River Road, Teaneck, NJ 07666.
- We Are One. q.

**Webb Co.**
1999 Shepard Rd., St. Paul, MN 55116.
- Beef. m. ISSN 0005-7738

- Canoe. bi-m. ISSN 0360-7496 (American Canoe Association)
- Consumer Life. q.
- Farm Industry News. 8 per yr. ISSN 0014-7990
- Irrigation Age. m. ISSN 0021-1656
- National Hog Farmer. m. ISSN 0027-9447
- Snow Goer Trade. 7 per yr.
- T W A Ambassador. m. ISSN 0039-8632 (Trans World Airlines)

**Arthur Weber**
Il 60646, Chicago, IL 60659.
- Consumers Digest. bi-m. ISSN 0010-7182

**J. F. Weber, Ed. & Pub.**
1 Jewett Place, Utica, NY 13501.
- Discography Series. a (includes 5 separate nos. issued together)

**Weber Publications Inc.**
3975 E. Bayshore Rd., Palo Alto, CA 94303.
- Microwave Systems News. m. ISSN 0047-7214

**Webster College**
Webster Groves, MO 63119.
- Webster Review. q.

**Wedgwood International Seminar**
55 van Dam St., New York, NY 10013.
- American Wedgwoodian. q. ISSN 0569-9053

**Weed Science Society of America**
113 N. Neil St., Champaign, IL 61820.
- Weed Science. bi-m. ISSN 0043-1745
- Weed Science Society of America. Abstracts.
- Weeds Today. (pub. by Bill Dorn Associates, Inc.)

**Weekly Bulletin of Leather and Shoe News Co.**
215 Canal St., Manchester, NH 03101.
- Weekly Bulletin of Leather and Shoe News. w.

**Weekly California Citator**
c/o Marshall F. Johnson, 528 Fifth Ave., Sacremento, CA 95818.
- Weekly California Citator. w. ISSN 0092-2560

**Weekly Gayzette**
Box 15786, Philadelphia, PA 19103.
- Weekly Gayzette. w.

**Weekly Guardian Associates Inc.**
33 W. 17th St., New York, NY 10011.
- Guardian; independent radical newsweekly. w. ISSN 0017-5021

**Weight Watchers of Philadelphia**
113 S. Easton Rd., Glenside, PA 19038.
- Small Talk. bi-m.

**Weimaraner Club of America**
Box 6086 Heatherdowns Station, Toledo, OH 43614.
- Weimaraner. m. ISSN 0049-710X

**Weis Laboratories**
4563 2nd Ave. North, St. Petersburg, FL 33713.
- Biology Career Bulletin. bi-m.

**Robert F. Welch, Ed. & Pub.**
14006 Ventura Blvd., Sherman Oaks, CA 91423.
- Walls & Ceilings. m. ISSN 0043-0161

**Robert Welch, Inc.**
395 Concord Ave., Belmont, MA 02178.
- American Opinion; a conservative review. 11 per yr. ISSN 0003-0236

**Welding Research Council**
345 E. 47th St., New York, NY 10017.
- Welding Research Abroad. m. ISSN 0043-2318
- Welding Research Council Bulletin. 11 per yr. ISSN 0043-2326

**Wellesley College. Department of Music**
Wellesley, MA 02181.
- Wellesley Edition. irreg. ISSN 0083-7881
- Wellesley Edition Cantata Index Series. irreg. ISSN 0083-7873

**Wellman Press, Inc.**
200 N. Cedar St., Lansing, MI 48901.
- Michigan Master Plumber & Mechanical Contractor. m. (Michigan Plumbing & Mechanical Contractors Association)

**Mark Wells, Jr., Ed. & Pub.**
3200 Wilshire Blvd., Los Angeles, CA 90010.
- Insurance Journal. fortn. ISSN 0020-4714

**Wells Fargo Bank. Economics Department**
Box 44000, San Francisco, CA 94144.
- Wells Fargo Bank Business Review. m. ISSN 0043-2415

**Welt Publishing Co.**
1511 K St., N.W. (316), Washington, DC 20005.
- Soviet Business & Trade. fortn. ISSN 0092-4695

**Wenco Enterprises**
P.O. Box 4263, Portland, OR 97208.
- Wenco International Trade Directory. irreg. ISSN 0091-9705

**Wenner-Gren Foundation for Anthropological Research**
14 E. 71 St., New York, NY 10021.
- Wenner-Gren Foundation for Anthropological Research. Report. a. ISSN 0083-7997

**Werbel Publishing Co., Inc.**
595 Old Willets Path, Smithtown, NY 11787.
- General Insurance Guide. q. ISSN 0016-6545

**Werner & Werner Corporation**
606 Wilshire Blvd., Santa Monica, CA 90401.
- Aviation Annual. a.
- Golf Score. 8 per yr.
- Plane & Pilot. m. ISSN 0032-0617

**Werner Management Consultants, Inc.**
1450 Broadway, New York, NY 10018.
- Focus: a Textile Executive Report. 5 per yr.
- Texscope. European Textile Distribution. irreg.
- Texscope: European Overview. irreg.
- Texscope: Open End Spinning. irreg., latest issue 1974.
- Texscope: Textile Technological Investment Climate. irreg.
- Texscope; U S A Textile Industry Overview. irreg., latest issue 1975. ISSN 0092-3540

**Frank D. Wesley**
Box 510, 1510 Commercial Park Dr., Lakeland, FL 33802.
- Florida Contractor; plumbing-heating-cooling. m. ISSN 0046-4112 (Associated Plumbing & Mechanical Contractors of Florida)

**Wesleyan Christian Advocate**
159 Forrest Ave., N.E., Atlanta, GA 30303.
- Wesleyan Christian Advocate. w.

**Wesleyan Church**
- Encounter. (pub. by Wesleyan Publishing House)
- In-Touch. (pub. by Wesleyan Publishing House)
- Primary Friend. (pub. by Wesleyan Publishing House)
- Wesleyan Advocate. (pub. by Wesleyan Publishing House)

**Wesleyan Church Youth Department**
- Wind. (pub. by Wesleyan Publishing House)

**Wesleyan College**
Forsyth Rd, Macon, GA 31201.
- Times and Challenge. m. ISSN 0040-7879

**Wesleyan College Alumnae Association**
4760 Forsyth Rd., Macon, GA 31201.
- Wesleyan College Now. 5 per yr.

**Wesleyan Publishing House**
Box 2000, Marion, IN 46952.
- Encounter. w. (Wesleyan Church)
- In-Touch. w. (Wesleyan Church)
- Primary Friend. w. ISSN 0032-8286 (Wesleyan Church)
- Wesleyan Advocate. fortn. ISSN 0043-289X (Wesleyan Church)
- Wind. m. (Wesleyan Church Youth Department)

**Wesleyan Theological Society**
22101 Osborne Road, Lakeville, IN 46536.
- Wesleyan Theological Journal. a. ISSN 0092-4245

**Wesleyan University Press**
55 High St., Middletown, CT 06457.
- American Maritime Library. irreg. ISSN 0065-9207 (Mystic Seaport, Inc.)
- History and Theory; studies in the philosophy of history. 4 per yr. ISSN 0018-2656
- Wesleyan Poetry Program. s-a. ISSN 0511-4934

**West Aurora Public Schools**
District 129, Box 552, Aurora, IL 60507.
- Chalkboard. q. ISSN 0043-1540

**West Bend News**
102 So. 6th Ave, West Bend, WI 53095.
- West Bend Shoppers Guide. w.

**West Central Kentucky Family Research Association**
P.O. 1465, Owensboro, KY 42301.
- West Central Kentucky Family Research Association. Bulletin. q.

**West Central Missouri Genealogical Society**
705 Broad, Warrensburg, MO 64093.
- Prairie Gleaner. q. ISSN 0032-6623

**West Chester State College**
West Chester, PA 19380.
- College Literature. 3 per yr. ISSN 0093-3139

**West Coast Dry Kiln Association**
Oregon State University, School of Forestry, Corvallis, OR 97331.
- Western Dry Kiln Clubs. Proceedings. a.

**West Coast Poetry Review**
Ed. W. L. Fox, 1127 Codel Way, Reno, NV 89503.
- West Coast Poetry Review. q. ISSN 0049-7215

**West End**
Box 354, Jerome Ave. Station, Bronx, NY 10468.
- West End; a magazine of poetry and politics. q. ISSN 0049-7223

**West Georgia College**
Carrollton, GA 30117.
- West Georgia College Review. q. ISSN 0043-3136

**West Georgia College. Division of Social Sciences**
Carrollton, GA 30117.
- West Georgia College Studies in the Social Sciences. a. ISSN 0081-8682

**West Publishing Co.**
50 W. Kellogg Blvd., St. Paul, MN 55102
- American Ethnological Society. Monographs. irreg., vol. 55, 1973. ISSN 0065-8197 (American Ethnological Society) (Vols. before 1972 dist. by: University of Washington Press, Seattle, WA 98105)
- American Ethnological Society. Proceedings of Spring Meeting. a. ISSN 0065-8200
- Applied Psychological Measurement. q.
- Arizona Legislative Service. irreg. ISSN 0094-4246
- Delaware Reporter. irreg. ISSN 0091-5564
- Directory of Law Teachers. a. ISSN 0070-573X (Association of American Law Schools)
- Report of Cases Argued and Determined in the Supreme Court of the State of Arizona. irreg. (Arizona. Supreme Court)
- Report of Cases Determined in the Supreme Court and Court of Appeals of the State of New Mexico. irreg. ISSN 0094-7148 (New Mexico. Supreme Court)

**West Side Association of Commerce, Inc.**
230 W. 41st St., New York, NY 10036.
- Magazine of New York Business; magazine of New York business. 3 per yr. ISSN 0091-6137

**West Tennessee Historical Society**
c/o James H. Edmonson, Ed., Memphis State University, Box 82260, Memphis, TN 38152.
- West Tennessee Historical Society. Papers. a.

**West Texas Chamber of Commerce**
Box 1561, Abilene, TX 79601.
- This Is West Texas. bi-m. ISSN 0040-6201

**West Texas Geological Society**
Box 1595, V and J Tower, Midland, TX 79701.
- West Texas Geological Society. Publications. irreg.

**West Texas Livestock Weekly**
Box 3306, San Angelo, TX 76901.
- West Texas Livestock Weekly. w. ISSN 0049-724X

**West Texas State University. College of Education**
Box 208, WT Station, Canyon, TX 79016.
- Studies in Education. a.

**West Virginia. Board of Regents**
950 Kanawha Blvd. E., Charleston, WV 25301.
- Fact Book and Report of the West Virginia State System of Higher Education. irreg. ISSN 0093-8831
- Physical Facilities at Institutions of Higher Education in West Virginia. irreg. ISSN 0093-884X

- Student Enrollment Report; West Virginia Institutions of Higher Education. a. ISSN 0091-8938
- West Virginia's State System of Higher Education; Annual Report, Current Operating Revenues and Expenditur:s. a. ISSN 0091-6196

**West Virginia. Commission on Aging**
State Capitol, Charleston, WV 25305.
- West Virginia. Commission on Aging. Annual Progress Report. a. ISSN 0083-8438

**West Virginia. Commission on Mental Retardation**
Room 308, Embleton Building, Charleston, WV 25301.
- Journal on the Handicapped Child. q. ISSN 0047-2905
- Promise M/R. bi-m. ISSN 0048-5543
- West Virginia. Commission on Mental Retardation. Annual Report. a. ISSN 0083-8446

**West Virginia. Department of Agriculture**
Charleston, WV 25305.
- West Virginia. Department of Agriculture. Market Bulletin. s-m. ISSN 0025-3545

**West Virginia. Department of Archives and History**
State Capitol Bldg., Charleston, WV 25305.
- West Virginia History. q. ISSN 0043-325X

**West Virginia. Department of Commerce**
State Capitol, Charleston, WV 25305.
- Goldenseal. q. ISSN 0099-0159 (Co-Sponsor: West Virginia Arts and Humanities Council)
- West Virginia. Department of Commerce. Annual Report. a. ISSN 0083-8454
- West Virginia Economic Profile. irreg. ISSN 0097-7675 (prep. by its Industrial Development Division)

**West Virginia. Department of Education**
Capitol Complex, Bldg B-016, Charleston, WV 25305.
- West Virginia Education Directory. a. ISSN 0085-8099

**West Virginia. Department of Employment Security. Research and Statistics Division**
112 California Ave., Charleston, WV 25305.
- West Virginia. Department of Employment Security. Area Manpower Summary. s-a.
- West Virginia Economic Indicators. m. ISSN 0049-7258
- West Virginia Employment and Earnings Trends: Annual Summary. a.

**West Virginia. Department of Health**
State Office Bldg. No. 1, Charleston, WV 25305.
- West Virginia. Department of Health. Bi-Weekly Morbidity Report. fortn.

**West Virginia. Department of Mines**
State Capitol Bldg., Rm. 151-E, Charleston, WV 25305.
- West Virginia. Department of Mines. Directory of Mines. a. ISSN 0083-8462

**West Virginia. Department of Natural Resources**
Charleston, WV 25305.
- West Virginia. Department of Natural Resources. Annual Report on the Comprehensive Water Resources Plan. a. ISSN 0095-4659
- Wonderful West Virginia. m. ISSN 0030-7157

**West Virginia. Division of Vocational Rehabilitation**
1427 Lee St. East, Charleston, WV 25301.
- Comeback. q.

**West Virginia. Geological and Economic Survey**
Morgantown, WV 26505.
- Current Geological Research in West Virginia. a. ISSN 0093-240X
- West Virginia Geological Survey. Archaeological Series. irreg. ISSN 0083-8489
- West Virginia Geological Survey. Bulletin. irreg. ISSN 0083-8500
- West Virginia Geological Survey. Circulars. irreg. ISSN 0083-8519
- West Virginia Geological Survey. Coal-Geology Bulletin. irreg.
- West Virginia Geological Survey. Environmental Geology Bulletin. irreg.
- West Virginia Geological Survey. Geological Publications. Volumes. irreg. ISSN 0083-8527
- West Virginia Geological Survey. Mineral Resources Series. irreg.
- West Virginia Geological Survey. Newsletter. irreg. ISSN 0083-8470

- West Virginia Geological Survey. Reports of Archaeological Investigations. irreg. ISSN 0083-8535
- West Virginia Geological Survey. Reports of Investigations. irreg. ISSN 0083-8543
- West Virginia Geological Survey. River Basin Basic Data Reports. irreg.
- West Virginia Geological Survey. River Basin Bulletins. irreg. ISSN 0083-856X
- West Virginia Geological Survey. State Park Bulletins. irreg. ISSN 0083-8578

**West Virginia. Governor's Committee on Crime, Delinquency, and Corrections**
1212 Lewis St., Ste. 321, Charleston, WV 25305.
- West Virginia. Governor's Committee on Crime, Delinquency, and Corrections. Comprehensive Criminal Justice Plan. irreg. ISSN 0094-0275
- West Virginia Criminal Justice Review. m.

**West Virginia. Human Rights Commission**
P. & G. Bldg., 2019 E. Washington St., Charleston, WV 25305.
- West Virginia. Human Rights Commission. Report. a. ISSN 0083-8594

**West Virginia. Office of Emergency Services**
806 Greenbrier St., Charleston, WV 25311.
- W.V.O.E.S. Annual Report. a. ISSN 0099-0671

**West Virginia Chamber of Commerce**
Box 2789, Charleston, WV 25330.
- West Virginia Business Index. Annual Review Number. a. ISSN 0083-839X

**West Virginia Coal Association**
P.O. Box 1111, Charleston, WV 25324.
- West Virginia Coal Facts. a. ISSN 0091-5513

**West Virginia Coal Mining Institute**
213 White Hall, Morgantown, WV 26506.
- West Virginia Coal Mining Institute. Proceedings. a. ISSN 0083-842X

**West Virginia Dental Association**
408 Davidson Bldg., Box 1946, Charlestown, WV 25327.
- West Virginia Dental Journal. q. ISSN 0043-3225

**West Virginia Echoer**
398 National Rd., Wheeling, WV 26003.
- West Virginia Echoer. bi-m.

**West Virginia Education Association**
1558 Quarrier St., Charleston, WV 25311.
- West Virginia School Journal (1976) bi-m. (Jan.-May); m (Jun.-Dec.)

**West Virginia Free Press**
Box 381, Institute, WV 25112.
- West Virginia Free Press. irreg. ISSN 0043-3233

**West Virginia Highlands Conservancy**
206 Union St., Webster Springs, WV 26288.
- Highlands Voice. m.

**West Virginia Hillbilly**
Ed. Jim Comstock, Richwood, WV 26261.
- West Virginia Hillbilly. w. ISSN 0043-3241

**West Virginia Hills and Streams, Inc.**
P. O. Box 38, Durbin, WV 26264.
- West Virginia Hills & Streams. m.

**West Virginia Library Association**
c/o Ed. Donald E. Riggs, Rt. 1, Box 289-L, Princeton, WV 24740.
- West Virginia Libraries. q. ISSN 0043-3276

**West Virginia Motor Truck Association**
Box 4416, Charleston, WV 25304.
- West Virginia Transporter. m.

**West Virginia Music Educators Association, Inc.**
West Liberty State College, West Liberty, WV 26074.
- Notes a Tempo. m (Sept.-Jun.) ISSN 0029-3946

**West Virginia Nurses Association**
47 Capital City Bldg., Charleston, WV 25301.
- Weather Vane. bi-m. ISSN 0043-1664

**West Virginia Record and West Virginia Merchant**
Box 3112, Charleston, WV 25331.
- West Virginia Record and West Virginia Merchant. bi-m. ISSN 0300-6530

**West Virginia Research League Inc.**
1214 Charleston National Plaza, Charleston, WV 25301.
- West Virginia Research League. Statistical Handbook; a digest of selected data on state and local government in West Virginia. a. ISSN 0091-6102

**West Virginia School Boards Association**
Box 1008, Charleston, WV 25324.
- Communicator (Charleston) q.

**West Virginia Society of Certified Public Accountants**
Box 1142, Charleston, WV 25324.
- West Virginia C.P.A. q. ISSN 0043-3217

**West Virginia State Medical Association**
Box 1031, Charleston, WV 25324.
- West Virginia Medical Journal. m. ISSN 0043-3284

**West Virginia University**
Morgantown, WV 26506.
- Castanea. q. ISSN 0008-7475
- Daily Athenaeum. d.(Sept.-June); w.(July-Aug.) ISSN 0011-5371
- Victorian Poetry. q. ISSN 0042-5206 (Orders to:, 129 Armstrong Hall)
- West Virginia University Magazine. q. ISSN 0043-3349

**West Virginia University. Agricultural Experiment Station**
Morgantown, WV 26506.
- West Virginia. Agricultural Experiment Station, Morgantown. Current Report. irreg., 1971, no. 58. ISSN 0083-8381

**West Virginia University. Bureau of Business Research**
Morgantown, WV 26506.
- Bibliography of Publications of University Bureaus of Business and Economic Research. a. ISSN 0066-8761 (Association for University Business and Economic Research)
- Business Law Review. s-a. (Co-publisher: National Association of Business Law Teachers, Inc.)
- Journal of Small Business Management. q. ISSN 0047-2778 (National Council of Small Business Management Development)
- West Virginia Statistical Handbook. irreg. ISSN 0511-6775
- West Virginia University. Business and Economic Studies. irreg., vol. 13, 1975. ISSN 0068-4392

**West Virginia University. Center for Extension and Continuing Education**
Office of Research and Development, 17 Grant Ave., Morgantown, WV 26506.
- West Virginia University. Center for Extension and Continuing Education. Research Series. irreg., no. 19, 1976.

**West Virginia University. College of Agriculture and Forestry**
Morgantown, WV 26506.
- West Virginia Agriculture & Forestry. q. ISSN 0043-3195

**West Virginia University. Department of Biology**
University Office of Publications, Morgantown, WV 26506.
- West Virginia University. Department of Biology. Core Arboretum Bulletin. s-a.

**West Virginia University. Engineering Experiment Station**
College of Engineering, Morgantown, WV 26506.
- Appalachian Gas Measurement Short Course, West Virginia University. Proceedings. a. ISSN 0066-5371
- Appalachian Underground Corrosion Short Course, West Virginia University. Proceedings. a. ISSN 0066-538X
- Forest Engineering Symposium. Proceedings. a. ISSN 0071-7444
- Industrial Engineering Conference. Proceedings. a. ISSN 0073-7445
- West Virginia University. Engineering Experiment Station. Bulletin. irreg. ISSN 0083-8640
- West Virginia University. Engineering Experiment Station. Report. irreg., 1970, no.11. ISSN 0083-8659

**West Virginia University Law Center**
Morgantown, WV 26506.
- West Virginia Law Review. q. ISSN 0043-3268

**West Virginia University Library**
Main Office, Morgantown, WV 26506.
- Appalachian Outlook; new sources of regional information. q. ISSN 0003-6625
- Archives of British History and Culture. a.
- West Virginia Union List of Serials. a. ISSN 0512-4743

**West Virginia Wildwater Association**
2737 Daniels Ave., South Charleston, WV 25303.
- Wild Water Splashes. m.

**Westana Publications**
World Trade Center, Suite 314, San Francisco, CA 94111.
- Printing Journal. m.

**Westart**
Box 1396, Auburn, CA 95603.
- Westart; West Coast's art news scene. s-m. ISSN 0043-3357

**Westburg Associates, Publishers**
1745 Madison Ave., Fennimore, WI 53809.
- North American Mentor. q. ISSN 0549-7078

**Westchester Academy of Medicine**
Purchase, NY 10577.
- Westchester Bulletin. 10 per yr.

**Westchester County Board of Realtors, Inc.**
188 E. Post Rd., White Plains, NY 10601.
- Westchester Realtor. m. ISSN 0043-339X

**Westchester County Historical Society**
43 Read Ave., Tuckahoe, NY 10707.
- Westchester Historian. q. ISSN 0049-7266

**Westchester Law Journal Inc.**
Ed. Frances M. Stachnik, 175 Main St., White Plains, NY 10601.
- Westchester Law Journal. w. ISSN 0049-7274

**Western Agricultural Economics Association**
315 Extension Hall, Oregon University, Corvallis, OR 97331.
- Western Agricultural Economics Association. Proceedings. a.

**Western Airlines**
- Western's World. (pub. by Frank M. Hiteshew & Associates)

**Western Association of Africanists**
- Western Association of Africanists. Newsletter. (pub. by University of Nebraska-Lincoln)

**Western Association of Graduate Schools**
c/o Pacific Lutheran University, Tacoma, WA 98447.
- Western Association of Graduate Schools. Proceedings of the Annual Meeting. a. ISSN 0511-6848

**Western Association of Insurance Brokers**
962 Russ Bldg., 235 Montgomery St., San Francisco, CA 94104.
- Broker. m.

**Western Association of Map Libraries**
Univ. Library, Univ. of California, Santa Cruz, CA 95064.
- Western Association of Map Libraries. Information Bulletin. 3 per yr. ISSN 0049-7282
- Western Association of Map Libraries. Occasional Papers. irreg.

**Western Association of Schools and Colleges**
1499 Bayshore Highway, Burlingame, CA 94010.
- Western Association of Schools and Colleges Directory. a.

**Western Association of State Game and Fish Commissioners**
c/o Robert L. Salter, Box 25, Boise, ID 83707.
- Western Association of State Game and Fish Commissioners. Proceedings. a. ISSN 0085-8102

**Western Builder Publishing Co.**
6526 River Parkway, Milwaukee, WI 53213.
- Western Builder. w. ISSN 0043-3535

**Western Business Publications**
274 Brannan St., San Francisco, CA 94107.
- Meetings: Pacific. a.
- Pacific Travel News. m. ISSN 0030-8951 (Pacific Area Travel Association)

**Western Carolina University. Division of Economic Development**
Cullowhee, NC 28723.
- Western Carolina Business Review. q. (prep. by its Center for Improving Mountain Living)

**Western Christian Leadership Conference**
4802 McKinley, Los Angeles, CA 90011.
- W C L C Newsletter. m. ISSN 0042-9570

**Western Communications. Ltd.**
1741 Ivar Ave., Suite 116, Los Angeles, CA 90028.
- Pharmacy West. m.

**Western Confectioners and Tobacconist Co.**
Box 1107, Santa Monica, CA 90406.
- American Buyer's Review. bi-m.

**Western Conservation Journal**
314 Lloyd Bldg., Seattle, WA 98101.
- Western Conservation Journal. 5 per yr. ISSN 0043-3608

**Western Construction Magazine, Inc.**
Box 2328, Eugene, OR 97402.
- Western Construction. m. ISSN 0043-3616

**Western Dental Society**
8939 S. Sepulveda Blvd., No. 420, Los Angeles, CA 90045.
- Western Dental Society. Newsletter. 8 per yr.

**Western Economic Association**
California State University, Dept. of Economics, Long Beach, CA 90840.
- Economic Inquiry. 4 per yr.

**Western Educational Society for Telecommunications**
c/o Robert P. Slingland, Box 5346, Tacoma, WA 98403.
- W E S T Telememo. irreg.

**Western Electric Co., Inc.**
195 Broadway, New York, NY 10007
- Western Electric Engineer. 4 per yr. ISSN 0043-3659 (Subscr. to:, 222 Broadway, New York, NY 10038)

**Western Electric Co. Inc. Organization 400**
555 Union Boulevard, Allentown, PA 18103.
- Technical Digest. m.

**Western Electronic Manufacturers Association**
2600 El Camino Real, Palo Alto, CA 94306.
- W E M A Directory. a. ISSN 0509-5190

**Western Electronic Show and Convention**
- W E S C O N Technical Papers. (pub. by Western Periodicals Co.)

**Western Farm Equipment**
c/o M. A. Johnson, Ed., Box 1452, Lake Oswego, OR 97034.
- Western Farm Equipment. 8 per yr. ISSN 0043-3691

**Western Finance Association**
- Journal of Financial and Quantitative Analysis. (pub. by University of Washington. Graduate School of Business Administration)

**Western Flyer**
c/o Dave Sclair, Ed., Box 44400, Tacoma, WA 98444.
- Western Flyer. s-m.

**Western Forestry and Conservation Association**
1326 American Bank Bldg., Portland, OR 97205.
- Western Forestry & Conservation Association. Permanent Association Committees. Proceedings. a.
- Western Forestry Conference. Proceedings. a.

**Western Forestry Center**
4033 S. W. Canyon Rd., Portland, OR 97221.
- Western Forestry Center. Annual Report. a.

**Western Fraternal Life Association**
1900 1st Ave. , N.E., Cedar Rapids, IA 52402.
- Bratrsky Vestnik/Fraternal Herald. m. ISSN 0006-9256

**Western Growers Association**
Box 2130, Newport Beach, CA 92663.
- Western Grower & Shipper; the business magazine of the Western row crop industry. m. ISSN 0043-3799

**Western Heart Publishing Co.**
Box 2940, Mesa, AZ 85204.
- Western Heart. bi-m. ISSN 0043-3802

**Western Highway Institute**
333 Pine St., San Francisco, CA 94104.
- Western Highway Institute. Research Committee. Report. irreg. ISSN 0083-8918
- Western Highway Institute. State Motor Carriers Handbook. biennial. ISSN 0083-890X

**Western History Association**
- Western Historical Quarterly. (pub. by Utah State University of Agriculture and Applied Science)

**Western Horseman, Inc.**
Box 7980, Colorado Springs, CO 80933.
- Western Horseman; devoted mainly to Western or stock horse. m. ISSN 0043-3837

**Western Illinois University**
Macomb, IL 61455.
- Journal of Developing Areas. q. ISSN 0022-037X

**Western Illinois University. Center for Business and Economic Research**
Macomb, IL 61455.
- Journal of Behavioral Economics. s-a. ISSN 0090-5720

**Western Illinois University. College of Education**
Danville, IL 61455.
- Timely Issues in Education; a journal of research, writing and observation. a. (Phi Delta Kappa at Western Illinois University) (Co-Sponsor: Western Illinois University, College of Education)

**Western Illinois University. Department of English**
Macomb, IL 61455.
- Essays in Literature. s-a.
- Mississippi Valley Review. 2 per yr.

**Western Industrial Advertisers**
P.O. Box 22250, Los Angeles, CA 90022.
- Earth. bi-m.

**Western Institute of Multivariate Experimental Psychology**
c/o Dr. Charles Burdsal, Ed., Department of Psychology, Wichita State University, Wichita, KS 67208.
- Multivariate Experimental Clinical Research. q.

**Western Interstate Commission for Higher Education**
P.O. Drawer P, Boulder, CO 80302.
- Reports on Higher Education. q. ISSN 0034-4869

**Western Interstate Library Coordinating Organization**
Drawer P, Boulder, CO 80302.
- W I L C O Newsletter. bi-m. ISSN 0361-9478

**Western Interstate Nuclear Board**
Lakewood, CO 80215.
- Western Interstate Nuclear Board. Annual Report. a. ISSN 0090-1598

**Western Literature Association**
Utah State Univ., UMC 32, Logan, UT 84322.
- Western American Literature. q. ISSN 0043-3462

**Western Livestock Reporter, Inc.**
Box 30758, Billings, MT 59107.
- Western Livestock Reporter. w.

**Western Management Sciences Institute**
- Interdisciplinary Colloquium on Mathematics in the Behavioral Sciences. (pub. by University of California, Los Angeles. Graduate School of Management)

**Western Massachusetts Genealogical Society**
Box 206, Forest Park Station, Springfield, MA 01108.
- American Elm. q.

**Western Merchandise Mart**
1355 Market St., San Francisco, CA 94103.
- Western Merchandiser. s-a.

**Western Michigan University**
Kalamazoo, MI 49001.
- Charles C. Adams Center for Ecological Studies. Occasional Papers. irreg. ISSN 0009-1766
- Reading Horizons. q. ISSN 0034-0502

**Western Michigan University. Department of English**
Kalamazoo, MI 49008.
- Comparative Drama. q. ISSN 0010-4078

**Western Michigan University. Medieval Institute**
Kalamazoo, MI 49001.
- Studies in Medieval Culture. irreg., 1973, no. 3. ISSN 0085-6878

**Western Michigan University. Office of Research Services**
Kalamazoo, MI 49008.
- Directory of National Science Foundation Programs. bi-m. (U.S. National Science Foundation Directory Service)

**Western Michigan University. School of Librarianship**
Kalamazoo, MI 49008.
- Western Michigan University. School of Librarianship. Bulletin. a.

**Western Mining News**
Suite 227 Peyton Bldg., Spokane, WA 99201
- Western Mining News. w. ISSN 0300-662X

**Western New York Genealogical Society, Inc.**
c/o Mrs. H. J. Miller, 209 Nassau Ave., Kenmore, NY 14217.
- Western New York Genealogical Society Journal. q.

**Western News Printing and Publishing**
1210 California St., Denver, CO 80204.
- Western News; journal devoted to Scandinavian interests. s-m.

**Western Newspaper Publishing Co.**
537 E. Ohio St., Indianapolis, IN 46204.
- Indiana Architect. bi-m. (Indiana Society of Architects)

**Western Outdoors Publications**
3939 Birch St., Box 2027, Newport Beach, CA 92663.
- Western Outdoor News. w. ISSN 0049-7479
- Western Outdoors. m. ISSN 0043-4000

**Western Pennsylvania Bluegrass Committee**
Box 10223, Pittsburgh, PA 15232.
- Western Pennsylvania Bluegrass Committee. Newsletter. m.

**Western Pennsylvania Genealogical Society**
4338 Bigelow Blvd., Pittsburgh, PA 15219.
- Jots from the Point. m.
- Western Pennsylvania Genealogical Quarterly. q. ISSN 0095-0866

**Western Pennsylvania School for Blind Children**
201 Bellefield Ave., Pittsburgh, PA 15213.
- Illuminator. 3 per yr. ISSN 0019-2376

**Western Periodicals Co.**
13000 Raymer St., North Hollywood, CA 91605.
- American Institute of Aeronautics and Astronautics. A I A A Los Angeles Section. Monographs. irreg., latest vol. 20. ISSN 0065-8685
- Ancient Interface. a. ISSN 0097-8442
- Asilomar Conference on Circuits and Systems. Conference Record. a. ISSN 0571-3218 (University of Santa Clara) (Co-sponsor: Naval Post-Graduate School)
- Hawaii International Conference on System Sciences. Proceedings. a. ISSN 0073-1129 (University of Hawaii. Department of Electrical Engineering) (Co-sponsor: Information Sciences Program)
- Journal of Cybernetics and Information Science. 4 per yr. (American Society for Cybernetics)
- Symposium on Nondestructive Evaluation of Components and Materials in Aerospace, Weapons Systems and Nuclear Applications. biennial. ISSN 0082-0857 (American Society for Nondestructive Testing. South Texas Section) (Co-sponsor: Southwest Research Center)
- Symposium on Nonlinear Estimation Theory and Its Applications. Proceedings. irreg.
- W E S C O N Technical Papers. a. ISSN 0083-8837 (Western Electronic Show and Convention)
- West Coast Reliability Symposium. irreg., 12th, 1971. ISSN 0083-8217 (American Society for Quality Control. Los Angeles Section)

**Western Pharmacology Society**
c/o Peter Lomax, Ed., Dept. of Pharmacology,
U.C.L.A. School of Medicine, Los Angeles, CA
90024.
- Western Pharmacology Society. Proceedings. a.
ISSN 0083-8969

**Western Plains Library System**
Box 627, Clinton, OK 73601.
- Western Plains Library System Newsletter. m.
ISSN 0043-4051

**Western Plastics News Inc.**
1704 Colorado Ave., Santa Monica, CA 90404.
- Plastics. m.

**Western Poetry Press**
3253-Q San Amadeo, Laguna Hills, CA 92653.
- Western Poetry Quarterly. q.

**Western Political Science Association**
- Western Political Quarterly. (pub. by University of
Utah)

**Western Printing & Publishing Co.**
Box 601, Sparks, NV 89431.
- Nevada Livestock and Agriculture Journal. m.
ISSN 0047-9470 (Nevada Farm Bureau
Federation)

**Western Psychological Services**
12031 Wilshire Blvd, Los Angeles, CA 90025.
- Human Basics Library. irreg., 1966, no. 3. ISSN
0073-3822
- W P S Professional Handbook Series. irreg. ISSN
0083-8977

**Western Publications, Inc. (Austin)**
Box 3338, Austin, TX 78764.
- Badman; rustlers, gunfighters, owl hoot, lawmen,
renegades, the works. irreg., 1971, vol. 1, no. 2.
ISSN 0067-2874
- Frontier Times; the true west. bi-m. ISSN 0016-
2124
- Gold; lost mines, gold rush, buried treasure, the
works. irreg., 1972, no. 6. ISSN 0072-4920
- Old West. q. ISSN 0030-2058
- Relics; a link with our pioneer heritage. bi-m.
ISSN 0034-3900
- True West. bi-m. ISSN 0041-3615
- Wanderlust; true adventure in far places. q. ISSN
0083-7172

**Western Publishing Co., Inc.**
1220 Mound Ave., Racine, WI 53404.
- Buying and Selling United States Coins. a. ISSN
0068-4562
- Catalog of Modern World Coins. irreg. (every 18
mos.-2 years) ISSN 0069-102X
- Current Coins of the World. irreg. ISSN 0070-
1882
- Dark Shadows. q. ISSN 0011-6688
- Guidebook of English Coins, Nineteenth and
Twentieth Centuries. irreg; 8th ed., 1975. ISSN
0072-8802
- Guidebook of Modern United States Currency.
irreg; 7th ed., 1975. ISSN 0072-8810
- Guidebook of United States Coins. a. ISSN 0072-
8829
- Handbook of United States Coins. a. ISSN 0072-
9949
- Ripley's Believe It or Not; true ghost stories. 7
per yr. ISSN 0035-5518

**Western Railway Club**
332 S. Michigan, Chicago, IL 60604.
- Western Railway Club. Official Proceedings. 5 per
yr. ISSN 0043-4116

**Western Regional Science Association**
c/o Western Washington State College, Dept. of
Economics, Bellingham, WA 98225.
- Annals of Regional Science. 3 per yr.

**Western Reserve Historical Society**
Quail Bldg., Cleveland, OH 44106.
- Western Reserve Historical Society, Cleveland.
Publications. irreg., 1968, no. 120. ISSN 0083-
8985

**Western Reserve Magazine**
Box 243, Garrettsville, OH 44231.
- Western Reserve Magazine. bi-m. ISSN 0361-
333X

**Western Retail Implement & Hardware Association**
Kansas City, MO 64111.
- Hardware & Farm Equipment. m. ISSN 0017-
7679

**Western Ski Promotions, Inc.**
Box 5029, University Station, Seattle, WA 98105.
- Northwest Skier. 20 per yr. ISSN 0029-3458
(Pacific Northwest Ski Association)

**Western Snow Conference**
Room 360, Court House, Spokane, WA 99201.
- Western Snow Conference. Proceedings. a.

**Western Social Science Association**
Colorado State Univ., Social Science Bldg., Fort
Collins, CO 80523.
- Social Science Journal. 3 per yr.
- Western Social Science Association Monograph
Series. irreg.

**Western Social Science Association (Boulder)**
Univ. of Colorado, Boulder, CO 80302
- Western Social Science Association Newsletter. s-
a. (Subscr. to:, c/oProf. William W. Ray, Dept. of
Urban Studies, Texas Christian University, Ft.
Worth, TX 76129)

**Western Society of Engineers**
176 W. Adams St. , Suite 1835, Chicago, IL 60603.
- Midwest Engineer; serving the engineering
profession. m. (Sep.-May) ISSN 0026-3370

**Western Society of Malacologists**
Pomona, CA 91766
- Western Society of Malacologists. Annual Report.
a. ISSN 0361-1175 (Order from: Bertram C.
Draper, Treas., 8511 Bleriot Ave., Los Angeles,
CA 90045)

**Western Society of Weed Science**
c/o J. Lamar Anderson, Department of Plant
Science, UMC 48, Utah State University, Logan,
UT 84322.
- Western Society of Weed Science. Proceedings. a.
ISSN 0091-4487
- Western Society of Weed Science. Research
Progress Report. a. ISSN 0511-8107

**Western Speech Communication Association**
c/o Exec. Secty. Robert W. Vogelsang, Portland
State Univ., Portland, OR 97207.
- Western Speech Communication. q.

**Western States Publications**
17835 Ventura Blvd., Suite 312, Encino, CA 91316.
- Western Floors. m. ISSN 0049-7398

**Western Theological Seminary**
Holland, MI 49423.
- Reformed Review. 3 per yr. ISSN 0034-3064 (Co-
Sponsor: Reformed Church in America)

**Western Trade Magazine Publishers**
3870 Cody St, Wheat Ridge, CO 80033.
- Recorder. m. (except Dec.) ISSN 0034-1649

**Western Washington State College**
Bellingham, WA 98225.
- Jeopardy; a magazine of creative arts. s-a. ISSN
0021-5880
- Journal of English Linguistics. a. ISSN 0075-4242

**Western Washington State College. Aquatic Studies
Program**
Bellingham, WA 98225.
- Western Washington State College. Aquatic
Studies Program. Technical Report Series. irreg.

**Western Washington State College. College of Ethnic
Studies**
Bellingham, WA 98225.
- Journal of Ethnic Studies. q. ISSN 0091-3219

**Western Washington State College. Department of
English**
Bellingham, WA 98225.
- Concerning Poetry. s-a. ISSN 0010-5201

**Western Washington State College. Dept. of History**
Bellingham, WA 98225.
- Studies in History and Society. s-a. ISSN 0039-
369X

**Western Washington State College. Program in East
Asian Studies**
Bellingham, WA 98225.
- Western Washington State College. Program in
East Asian Studies. Occasional Papers. irreg.,
approx. 2 per yr.

**Western Wood Products Association**
1500 Yeon Bldg., Portland, OR 97204.
- Barometer. w.
- Western Lumber Facts. m. ISSN 0511-7704
- Western Wood Products Association. Statistical
Yearbook. a. ISSN 0511-8301

**Western World Press**
Box 2714, Culver City, CA 90230.
- Western World Review. q. ISSN 0043-4299

**Western World Publishers**
511 Harrison St., San Francisco, CA 94105.
- Western Collector; pioneer for today's collector.
m. ISSN 0043-3578

**Western Writers of America, Inc.**
105-49th Ave. W., Bradenton, FL 33507.
- Roundup. m. ISSN 0035-855X

**Westerners International**
Box 2304, La Placita Station, Tucson, AZ 85702.
- Buckskin Bulletin. q. ISSN 0045-3307
- Droppings. (pub. by Omaha Westerners)

**Westerners. Kansas City Posse**
- Trail Guide. (pub. by Lowell Press)

**Westerners. Kansas Corral**
P.O. Box 531, Abilene, KS 67410.
- Prairie Scout. a.

**Westerners. Los Angeles Corral**
c/o Ed. Donald Duke, Box 8136, San Marino, CA
91108.
- Branding Iron. q. ISSN 0006-9078

**Westerners, San Diego Corral**
P.O. Box 7174, San Diego, CA 92107.
- Wrangler. 4 per yr. ISSN 0512-4077

**Westernlore Press**
5117 Eagle Rock Blvd., Los Angeles, CA 90041.
- Great West and Indian Series. irreg. ISSN 0072-
7342
- Westernlore Ghost Town Series. irreg. ISSN 0083-
9019

**Westigan Review of Poetry**
Univ. of Utah, c/o Don Stap, English Dept., Salt
Lake City, UT 84112.
- Westigan Review of Poetry. irreg.

**Westigan Review Press**
c/o John Knapp, 2nd, Swetman Hall, State
University College, Oswego, NY 13126.
- Westigan Review Chapbooks. irreg.

**Westminster Press**
Witherspoon Bldg, Philadelphia, PA 19107.
- New Testament Library. irreg. ISSN 0077-8834
- Old Testament Library. irreg. ISSN 0078-4567

**Westminster Theological Seminary**
Chestnut Hill, Philadelphia, PA 19118.
- Westminster Theological Journal. 3 per yr. ISSN
0043-4388

**Westmoreland County Motor Club**
Box 458, Greensburg, PA 15601.
- Westmoreland Traveler. m. ISSN 0043-4396

**Weston School of Theology**
3 Phillips Place, Cambridge, MA 02138
- New Testament Abstracts; a reccord of current
literature. 3 per yr. ISSN 0028-6877 (Subscr. to:
Council on the Study of Religion, Wilfrid Laurier
University, Waterloo, Ont. N2L 3C5, Canada)

**Westview Press**
1898 Flatiron Ct., Boulder, CO 80301.
- Ancient Peoples and Places. irreg. ISSN 0570-
023X
- Current Bibliographic Survey of National Defense.
q.
- Current Bibliographic Survey of National Defense.
q.
- International Organisations in World Politics
Yearbook. a. ISSN 0363-7123
- R. U. S. I. and Brassey's Defence Yearbook. a.
ISSN 0305-6155 (Royal United Services Institute)

● Research Institute on International Change. Studies. irreg.

**Wetlands**
c/o Thomas S. Zawyrucha, 14 Sutton Court, Box 252, NY 11795.
● Wetlands; new writers forum. q.

**Weyerhaeuser Company**
Tacoma, WA 98401.
● Weyerhaeuser News. m.

**Whaley-Eaton Corporation**
National Press Bldg., Washington, DC 20045.
● American Letter; the standard Washington authority. w.
● Transportation Business Report. fortn. ISSN 0300-6506
● Whaley-Eaton Foreign Letter. w. ISSN 0043-4477

**Wharton School of Finance and Commerce**
*see under* University of Pennsylvania

**Wheaton College. Alumni Association**
Wheaton, IL 60187.
● Wheaton Alumni. 10 per yr.

**Wheelwright, Bond, Company**
Porter's Landing, Freeport, ME 04032.
● Maine That Was Series. irreg., 1967, no. 2. ISSN 0076-2709

**Whiskey, Women, And...**
c/o Daniel Kochakian, Ed., 39 Pine Ave., Haverhill, MA 01830.
● Whiskey, Women, And... irreg (approx. every 3-4 mos.) ISSN 0091-7664

**Whisman Educators Association**
c/o Lorraine Scott, Educators Professional Center, 2483 Old Middlefield Rd., Mountain View, CA 94043.
● W. E. A. Spark. bi-m.

**Whispers**
c/o Stuart David Schiff, Ed., Box 1492-W, Azalea St., Browns Mills, NJ 08015.
● Whispers. q.

**White Bones Press**
R.D. 1, Box 265, Otego, NY 13825.
● Bones. irreg., 1973, no. 4. ISSN 0006-7105

**White County Historical Society**
Box 327, Searcy, AR 72143.
● White County Heritage. q. ISSN 0043-4906

**White Farm Equipment**
2625 Butterfield Rd., Oak Brook, IL 60521.
● Better Farming for Better Living. q.

**White Mountain Apache Tribe**
Box 708, Whiteriver, AZ 85941.
● Fort Apache Scout. bi-m.

**White Pine**
c/o Dennis Maloney, Ed., 15 Mount Vernon Ave., Buffalo, NY 14210.
● White Pine. 4 per yr.

**White Rose AAA Motor Club**
118 E. Market St., York, PA 17405.
● White Rose Motorist. bi-m. ISSN 0043-4981

**White Urp Press**
5011-2 Green Mtn. Circle, Columbia, MD 21044.
● Abbey; the journal of literary brouhaha. q.

**White, Weld and Co.**
300 Park Ave., New York, NY 10022.
● International Bonds. a. ISSN 0093-6766

**White Wing Publishing House**
Box 1039, Cleveland, TN 37311.
● White Wing Messenger. w. ISSN 0043-5007 (Church of God of Prophecy)

**Whitestone Publications**
Fawcett Bldg, Greenwich, CT 06832.
● Baseball Annual. a. ISSN 0067-4257

**Whiting Press, Inc.**
Rochester, MN 55901
● American Ophthalmological Society. Transactions. a, 1973, no. 71. ISSN 0065-9533 (Subscr. to: Dr. Robert W. Hollenhorst, Sec.-Treas., American Ophthalmological Society, 200 First St. S. W., Rochester, MN 55901)

**Whitmark Associates**
4120 Main St., Suite 100, Dallas, TX 75226.
● Whitmark Directory; source book of talent, fashion and audio visual services for the Southwest. a. ISSN 0511-8794
● Whitmark News & Views. m.

**C. M. Whitmore, Jr., Ed. & Pub**
Box 2386, Evansville, IN 47714.
● Plate Block Comments. irreg (approx. 5 per yr.)

**Whitney Communications Corporation**
205 E. 42nd St., New York, NY 10017
● Art Letter. 10 per yr.
● Boating Industry. m. ISSN 0006-5404
● Boating Industry Marine Buyers Guide. a
(Subscr. to: Boating Industry, 270 St. Paul St., Denver, CO 80206)
● Boating Industry Showtime Showcase. s-a.

**Whitney Communications Corporation. Magazine Division**
150 E. 58th St., New York, NY 10022
(Subscr. to: Department 698, Hightstown, NJ 08520)
● Interior Design. m. ISSN 0020-5508
● Interior Design Buyers Guide. a.

**Whitney Enterprises**
30 E. 40th St., New York, NY 10016.
● Graphic Science; the magazine of engineering services. m. ISSN 0017-3398

**Whitney Museum of American Art**
945 Madison Ave. at 75 St., New York, NY 10021.
● Whitney Review. a. ISSN 0511-8824

**Whitston Publishing Co. Inc.**
P.O. Box 322, Troy, NY 12181.
● Abortion Bibliography. a. ISSN 0092-9522
● American Dissertations on Foreign Education; a bibliography with abstracts. irreg.
● American Humanities Index. q.
● Bibliography of Noise. a. ISSN 0092-5756
● Drug Abuse Bibliography. a. ISSN 0093-2515
● Population and the Population Explosion: a Bibliography. a. ISSN 0091-2263
● Sickle Cell Hemoglobinopathies: a Comprehensive Bibliography. irreg.
● Venereal Disease Bibliography. a. ISSN 0090-8479

**Whittier Clubs of Haverhill and Amesbury**
c/o Ed. John B. Pickard, Department of English, University of Florida, Gainesville, FL 32611.
● Whittier Newsletter. a. ISSN 0511-8832

**Whittier College. Associated Students**
Quaker Campus, Whittier, CA 90608.
● Quaker Campus. w. ISSN 0033-5045

**Who Put the Bomp**
Box 7112, Burbank, CA 91510.
● Who Put the Bomp. 4 per yr. ISSN 0039-7873

**Whole Earth Catalog**
558 Santa Cruz Ave., Menlo Park, CA 95205.
● Whole Earth Catalog. ISSN 0043-5031

**Who's Who Among Black Americans, Inc., Publishing Co.**
Northbrook, IL 60062.
● Who's Who Among Black Americans. irreg. ISSN 0362-5753

**Who's Who Among Students**
Box 2029, Tuscaloosa, AL 35401.
● Who's Who Among Students in American Junior Colleges. a. ISSN 0511-8891

**Who's Who Historical Society**
1331 Cordell Pl., Los Angeles, CA 90069.
● Who's Who in California. biennial. ISSN 0511-8948

**Who's Who in Advertising**
Box 556, Rye, NY 10580.
● Who's Who in Advertising. biennial. ISSN 0511-8905

**Who's Who in Pro Basketball**
P.O. 221, Pleasantville, NY 10036.
● Who's Who in Pro Basketball. a.

**Who's Who Publications, Inc.**
108 N.W. Ninth Ave., Portland, OR 07209.
● Traffic Manager. bi-m. ISSN 0041-0705

**Wichita Area Chamber of Commerce**
350 W. Douglas, Wichita, KS 67202.
● Wichita. bi-m. ISSN 0043-5228

**Wichita-Sedgwick County Metropolitan Area Planning Dept.**
104 South Main, Wichita, KS 67202.
● Wichita-Sedgwick County Metropolitan Area Planning Department Newsletter. bi-m.

**Wichita State University. College of Business Administration**
Wichita, KS 67208.
● Kansas Economic Indicators. m. (prep. by its Center for Business and Economic Research)

**Wichita State University. Department of Logopedics**
Wichita, KS 67208.
● Kansas Speech and Hearing Association Journal. s-a. ISSN 0022-8788

**Wichita State University. School of Music**
Wichita, KS 67208.
● Kansas Music Review. 5 per yr. ISSN 0022-8702

**Wichita State University Student Government Association**
c/o Marsha Mills, Ed., Wichita State University Post Office, Wichita, KS 67208.
● Gazebo; a poetry journal. s-a.

**Wickstrom Publishers, Inc.**
2701 S. Bayshore Dr., Suite 501, Miami, FL 33133.
● Aloft. bi-m. ISSN 0002-631X
● Florida Sportsman. m. ISSN 0015-3885

**Wider Horizons Project Newsletter**
70 Hereford St., Boston, MA 02115.
● Wider Horizons Project Newsletter. q.

**Wiesenberger Services, Inc.**
● Investment Companies. (pub. by Warren, Gorham and Lamont, Inc.)
● Management Results. (pub. by Warren, Gorham and Lamont, Inc.)
● Mutual Fund Performance Monthly. (pub. by Warren, Gorham and Lamont, Inc.)
● Mutual Funds Current Performance & Dividend Record. (pub. by Warren, Gorham & Lamont, Inc.)
● Wiesenberger Report. (pub. by Warren, Gorham & Lamont, Inc.)

**Wilbur Register**
Wilbur, WA 99185.
● Tribal Tribune. bi-m.

**Wilcox Publishing Co.**
Box 4227, 2632 N. Forgeus Ave., Tucson, AZ 85717.
● International Nautical Index; a comprehensive reference guide for the modern yachting public. q. ISSN 0363-261X

**Wild Country**
Box 296, Goleta, CA 93017.
● Wild Country. m.

**Wild Raspberry**
Box 1541, Hartford, CT 06101.
● Wild Raspberry. fortn. ISSN 0017-7997

**Wildcrafters Press**
Box 7, Looneyville, WV 25259.
● Herb Collector's Manual & Marketing Guide; gingseng growers and collectors' handbook. irreg., latest 1977.

**Wilderness Press**
2440 Bancroft Way, Berkeley, CA 94704.
● Wilderness Press Trail Guide Series. irreg.

**Wilderness Research Foundation**
3100 Prudential Plaza, Chicago, IL 60601.
● Quetico-Superior Wilderness Research Center, Ely, Minnesota. Annual Report. a. ISSN 0079-9211
● Quetico-Superior Wilderness Research Center, Ely, Minnesota. Technical Notes. irreg., 1968, no. 5. ISSN 0079-922X

**Wilderness Society**
1901 Pennsylvania Ave., N.W., Washington, DC 20006.
- Living Wilderness. q. ISSN 0024-5305
- Wilderness Report. 10 per yr. ISSN 0084-0114

**Wildlife Disease Association**
Box 886, Ames, IA 50010.
- Journal of Wildlife Diseases. q. ISSN 0090-3558

**Wildlife Management Institute**
709 Wire Bldg., Washington, DC 20005.
- North American Wildlife and Natural Resources Conference. Transactions. a. ISSN 0078-1355
- Outdoor News Bulletin. fortn. ISSN 0030-7092

**Wildlife Society**
7101 Wisconsin Ave. N.W., Washington, DC 20014.
- Journal of Wildlife Management. q. ISSN 0022-541X
- Wildlife Monographs. irreg., no. 51, 1976. ISSN 0084-0173

**Wildlife Society (Lawrence)**
1041 N. H. St., Lawrence, KS 66044.
- Wildlife Society Bulletin. q. ISSN 0091-7648

**John Wiley & Sons, Inc.**
605 Third Ave., New York, NY 10016.
- Adsorption and Adsorbents. irreg. ISSN 0092-8089
- Advances in Satellite Meteorology. irreg., vol. 2, 1974. ISSN 0094-5307
- Chemical Analysis; a series of monographs on analytical chemistry and its applications. irreg., 1976, vol. 47. ISSN 0069-2883
- Clinical Monographs in Obstetrics and Gynecology. irreg.
- Curriculum Inquiry. q. ISSN 0362-6784
- Hayes & Becker Information Sciences Series. irreg., 1974, latest vol. unnumbered.
- International Journal of Chemical Kinetics. bi-m. ISSN 0538-8066
- Journal of Clinical Ultrasound. q. ISSN 0091-2751
- Lower Palaeozic Rocks of the New World. irreg., vol. 2, 1974. ISSN 0076-1389
- New Techniques in Biophysics and Cell Biology. irreg.
- Origins of Behavior Series.
- Public Policy. q. ISSN 0033-3646 (Harvard University. John F. Kennedy School of Government)
- Research Advances in Alcohol & Drug Problems. a. ISSN 0093-9714
- Science Education. q. (incl. ERIC Bibliography) ISSN 0036-8326
- Selective Organic Transformations. irreg., 1972, vol. 2. ISSN 0080-8660
- Series in Decision and Control. irreg., unnumbered, latest vol. 1972. ISSN 0080-8962
- Society of Rheology. Transactions. q. ISSN 0038-0032
- Soil Engineering Series. irreg., unnumbered, latest vol. 1976.
- Space Science Text Series. irreg., 1971, latest vol., unnumbered.
- Techniques of Chemistry. irreg., 1976, vol. 11. ISSN 0082-2531
- University of California Engineering and Physical Sciences Extension Series. irreg. latest vol. 1972. ISSN 0068-631X
- University of Wisconsin. Mathematical Research Center Series. irreg. latest vol. 27. ISSN 0084-0890
- Wiley American Republic Series. irreg., 1975 latest vol. ISSN 0084-0181
- Wiley Monographs in Crystallography. irreg., latest 1976.
- Wiley Series in Computing. irreg., unnumbered, 1976 latest vol.
- Wiley Series on Systems Engineering and Analysis. irreg., unnumbered, 1977 latest vol. ISSN 0084-019X
- Wiley Series on the Science and Technology of Materials. irreg., 1974 latest vol. ISSN 0084-0203

**Wiley Hamilton Publishing Group**
(Subsidiary of: John Wiley & Sons, Inc.)
John Wiley & Sons, Inc., 1129 State St., Santa Barbara, CA 93101.
- Wiley Hamilton. irreg., 1974 latest vol. unnumbered.

**Wiley Interscience**
605 Third Ave., New York, NY 10016.
- Advances in Analytical Chemistry and Instrumentation. irreg., 1973, vol. 11. ISSN 0065-2148
- Advances in Biomedical Engineering and Medical Physics. irreg., 1971, vol. 4. ISSN 0065-2261
- Advances in Chemical Physics. irreg., vol. 35, 1976. ISSN 0065-2385
- Advances in Electrochemistry and Electrochemical Engineering. irreg., 1973, vol. 9. ISSN 0567-9907
- Advances in Environmental Sciences and Technology. irreg., vol. 8, 1977. ISSN 0065-2563
- Advances in Enzymology and Related Areas of Molecular Biology. irreg., vol. 44, 1976. ISSN 0065-258X
- Advances in Organic Chemistry; methods and results. irreg., vol. 9, 1976. ISSN 0065-3047
- Advances in Photochemistry. irreg., vol. 9 latest issue. ISSN 0065-3152
- Advances in Plasma Physics. irreg., vol. 6, 1976. ISSN 0065-3187
- Advances in Psychobiology. irreg., vol. 3, 1976. ISSN 0065-3241
- Advances in Radiation Chemistry. irreg., vol. 5, 1976. ISSN 0065-3306
- American Academy of Psychoanalysis. Journal. q. ISSN 0090-3604
- Applied Polymer Symposium. Papers. irreg., 1977, no. 55. ISSN 0066-5517 (Brooklyn Polytechnic Institute)
- Biochemical Preparations. irreg., 1971, vol. 13. ISSN 0067-8686
- Biomedical Engineering and Health Systems: A Wiley-Interscience Series. irreg., unnumbered, 1975 latest vol.
- Biomedical Materials Research Symposia. irreg., latest vol. 7.
- Biopolymers; an international journal of research on biological macromolecules. m. ISSN 0006-3525
- Biotechnology and Bioengineering. m. plus symposium. ISSN 0006-3592
- Biotechnology & Bioengineering Symposia. irreg., 1976, no. 6. ISSN 0572-6565
- Business Data Processing: a Wiley Series. irreg., unnumbered, 1975 latest vol.
- Chemistry of Functional Groups. irreg., unnumbered, 1975 latest vol. ISSN 0069-3146
- Chemistry of Heterocyclic Compounds; a series of monographs. irreg., 1974, vol. 29. ISSN 0069-3154
- Chemistry of Organometallic Compounds. irreg., 1973, latest vol. unnumbered.
- Color Research and Application. q. ISSN 0361-2317 (Co-sponsors: Inter-Society Color Council: Color Group; Canadian Society for Color)
- Communications on Pure and Applied Mathematics. bi-m. ISSN 0010-3640 (New York University. Courant Institute of Mathematical Sciences)
- Comparative Studies in Behavioral Science: A Wiley Series. irreg., latest vol. 1975.
- Contemporary Religious Movements: A Wiley-Interscience Series. irreg., unnumbered, 5 vols. to date.
- Corrosion Monograph Series. irreg., unnumbered, 1975 latest vol.
- Crystal Structures. irreg., 1971, vol. 6 pt. 2. ISSN 0070-167X
- Current Concepts in Nutrition. irreg., 1976 vol. 4.
- Desitter Regional Geology Series. irreg., latest vol. 1974, unnumbered.
- Developmental Psychobiology; an international journal. q. ISSN 0012-1630
- Earth Surface Processes. q.
- Electrochemical Society Series. irreg., unnumbered, latest vol., 1976. (Electrochemical Society, Inc.)
- Environmental Science and Technology: a Wiley-Interscience Series of Texts and Monographs. irreg., unnumbered, latest vol., 1976.
- Guides to Information Sources in Science and Technology. irreg. ISSN 0072-8934
- High Polymers; a series of monographs on the chemistry, physics and technology of high polymeric substances. irreg., 1973, vol. 28. ISSN 0073-2109
- International Association for Child Psychiatry and Allied Professions. Yearbook. irreg., 1974, vol. 3. ISSN 0074-963X
- International Journal of Quantum Chemistry. bi-m., includes symposia. ISSN 0020-7608
- Interscience Monographs and Texts in Physics and Astronomy. irreg., vol. 29, 1976. ISSN 0074-9931
- Interscience Tracts on Physics and Astronomy. irreg., 1972, vol. 29. ISSN 0074-9958

- Journal of Applied Polymer Science. m.(plus symposia) ISSN 0021-8995
- Journal of Biomedical Materials Research. bi-m(including symposia) ISSN 0021-9304
- Journal of Graph Theory. q.
- Journal of Neurobiology; an international journal. q. ISSN 0022-3034
- Journal of Polymer Science. Polymer Chemistry Edition. m. (incl. symposia Macromolecular Reviews) ISSN 0360-6376
- Journal of Polymer Science. Polymer Letters Edition. m. (incl. symposia and Macromolecular Reviews) ISSN 0361-1027
- Journal of Polymer Science. Polymer Physics Edition. m. (incl. symposia & Macromolecular Reviews) ISSN 0098-1273
- Journal of Polymer Science. Polymer Symposia Edition. m?
- Journal of Research in Science Teaching. 4 per yr. ISSN 0022-4308 (National Association for Research in Science Teaching) (Co-Sponsor: Association for the Education of Teachers in Science)
- Lowdin Symposia; Proceedings of the International Symposium on Atomic, Molecular, and Solid-State Theory and Quantum Biology. irreg., 1975, vol. 9. ISSN 0076-1370 (Dist. by: Ars Polona-Ruch, Krakowskie Przedmiescie 7, Warsaw, Poland)
- Macromolecular Reviews. irreg., vol. 11 latest issue. ISSN 0076-2083
- Macromolecular Syntheses. irreg., 1977, vol. 6. ISSN 0076-2091
- Marine Ecology; a comprehensive, integrated treatise on life in oceans and coastal waters. irreg., vol. 4, 1976.
- Mechanisms of Molecular Migrations. irreg., 1971, vol.4. ISSN 0076-5791
- Methods and Techniques in Geophysics. irreg., 1966, vol. 2. ISSN 0076-6836
- Methods of Biochemical Analysis. irreg., vol. 23, 1976. ISSN 0076-6941
- Networks; an interdisciplinary journal. 4 per yr. ISSN 0028-3045
- Ocean Engineering: a Wiley Series. irreg., 1976 latest vol.
- Organic Electronic Spectral Data. irreg., vol. 11, 1975. ISSN 0078-6136
- Organic Photochemical Syntheses. irreg., vol. 2, 1977. ISSN 0078-6144
- Organic Reaction Mechanisms. Annual Survey. irreg., vol. 10, 1976. ISSN 0078-6160
- Organic Reactions. irreg., vol. 24, 1976. ISSN 0078-6179
- Organic Syntheses. a. ISSN 0078-6209
- Organic Syntheses Collective Volumes. irreg., 1973, vol. 5. ISSN 0078-6217
- Organometallic Reactions Series. irreg., vol. 5, 1975. ISSN 0078-6497
- Perspectives in Nephrology and Hypertension. irreg., unnumbered, 1977 latest vol. ISSN 0092-2900
- Physics and Chemistry of the Organic Solid State. irreg., 1967, vol. 3. ISSN 0079-1954
- Polymer Engineering and Technology Series. irreg., 1969, vol. 10. ISSN 0079-3728
- Polymer Reviews. irreg., 1971, vol.18. ISSN 0079-3736
- Problems of Human Reproduction: A Wiley Biomedical Series. irreg., vol. 2, 1974.
- Progress in Bio-Organic Chemistry. irreg., vol. 4, 1976. ISSN 0079-6077
- Progress in Inorganic Chemistry. irreg., vol. 22, 1977. ISSN 0079-6379
- Progress in Physical Organic Chemistry. irreg., vol. 11, 1974. ISSN 0079-6662
- Progress in Phytochemistry. irreg., 1973, vol. 3. ISSN 0079-6689
- Pure and Applied Mathematics: A Wiley Interscience Series of Texts, Monographs and Tracts. irreg., latest vols. 1976.
- Quantitative Methods for Biologists and Medical Scientists. irreg., latest vol. 1967, unnumbered.
- Quarterly Journal of Economics. q. ISSN 0033-5533 (Harvard University. Department of Economics)
- Reactive Intermediates in Organic Chemistry. irreg., latest vol. 1975. ISSN 0486-0748
- Real Estate for Professional Practitioners: a Wiley Series. irreg., 1977, latest vol.
- Society of Plastics Engineers Monographs. irreg., unnumbered, 1977 latest vol.
- Solvay Conference Proceedings - Chemistry. irreg.,1971, 14th. ISSN 0081-1998 (Solvay Institute of Chemistry)
- Solvay Conference Proceedings - Physics. irreg., 1971, 14th. ISSN 0081-2005 (Solvay Institute of Physics)

- Stanford Series on Methods and Techniques in the Clinical Laboratory. irreg., 1975 latest vol.
- Surface and Colloid Science. irreg., vol. 9, 1976. ISSN 0081-9573
- Synthetic Procedures in Nucleic Acid Chemistry. irreg., vol. 2, 1973. ISSN 0082-1152
- Techniques in Pure and Applied Microbiology. irreg., unnumbered, 1975 latest vol. ISSN 0082-2515
- Techniques of Biochemical and Biophysical Morphology. irreg., vol. 2, 1975. ISSN 0082-2523
- Techniques of Electrochemistry. irreg., 1973, vol. 2. ISSN 0082-254X
- Techniques of Metals Research. irreg., 1976, vol. 7, pt. 2. ISSN 0082-2558
- Topics in Phosphorous Chemistry. irreg., 1977, vol. 9. ISSN 0082-4992
- Topics in Stereochemistry. irreg., 1976, vol. 9. ISSN 0082-500X
- Treatise of Skin. irreg.
- Treatise on Analytical Chemistry. Part 1: Theory and Practice of Analytical Chemistry. irreg., 1976, vol. 12. ISSN 0082-6243
- Treatise on Analytical Chemistry. Part 2: Analytical Chemistry of the Elements; Analytical Chemistry of Organic and Inorganic Compounds. irreg., 1976, vol. 15. ISSN 0082-6251
- Treatise on Analytical Chemistry. Part 3: Analytical Chemistry in Industry. irreg., 1976, vol. 3. ISSN 0082-626X
- Wiley Monographs in Chemical Physics. irreg., latest vol. 1974, unnumbered.
- Wiley Series in Behavior. irreg., latest 1976.
- Wiley Series in Human Factors. irreg., unnumbered, latest vol. 1976.
- Wiley Series in Urban Research. irreg., unnumbered, latest vol. 1975.
- Wiley Series on Systems and Controls for Financial Management. irreg., unnumbered, latest vol. 1976.

**Wiley-Medical**
(Subsidiary of: John Wiley & Sons, Inc.)
605 Third Ave., New York, NY 10016.
- Medical Ultrasound. q.

**Paul H. Wilkinson, Ed. & Pub.**
5900 Kingswood Rd., N.W., Washington, DC 20014.
- Aircraft Engines of the World. irreg. ISSN 0065-4892

**Will County Federation of Labor**
- Labor Record. (pub. by Labor Record Publishing Co., Inc.)

**Willa Cather Pioneer Memorial & Educational Foundation**
Red Cloud, NE 68970.
- Willa Cather Pioneer Memorial & Educational Foundation Newsletter. q.

**Willamette Management Associates, Inc.**
220 S.W. Alder, Portland, OR 97204.
- Northwest Investment Review; monitoring the Publicly Traded Securities of the Great Northwest. s-m. ISSN 0300-6824
- Northwest Stock Guide; investment information on all Major Northwest Corporations. m.

**Willamette University. College of Law**
Salem, OR 97301.
- Willamette Law Journal. 3 per yr. ISSN 0043-5562

**Willem Mengelberg Society**
2132 N. 70th St., Wauwatosa, WI 53213.
- Willem Mengelberg Society. Newsletter. 3 per yr.

**Willett & Gray, Inc.**
P.O. Box N, Brightwaters, NY 11718.
- Weekly Statistical Sugar Trade Journal. w. ISSN 0043-1923

**William Alanson White Psychiatric Foundation Inc**
1610 New Hampshire Ave., N. W., Washington, DC 20009.
- Psychiatry; journal for the study of interpersonal processes. q. ISSN 0033-2747

**William Alanson White Psychoanalytic Institute**
20 W. 74th St., New York, NY 10023.
- W A W Newsletter. q. ISSN 0042-9511

**William-Frederick Press**
55 E. 86 St., New York, NY 10028.
- Index to Early American Periodical Literature, 1728-1870; a survey of American literature. irreg. ISSN 0073-5914
- Pamphleteer Monthly; a buying-guide to worthwhile reading. m.(Sept-June) ISSN 0031-0557
- Prospects for America. irreg. ISSN 0079-7014
- William-Frederick Poets Series. irreg., no. 166, 1974. ISSN 0084-0238

**William Jewell College**
Liberty, MO 64068.
- Bulletin on Current Research in Soviet and East European Law. 3 per yr.
- Forensic. q. ISSN 0015-735X (Pi Kappa Delta) (Subscr. to: Theodore O. H. Karl, Communication Arts, Pacific Lutheran Univ., Tacoma, WA 98447)

**William-Lawrence Corp.**
Box 2830, Newport Beach, CA 92713
- Motorcycle Dealernews. m.

**Williams & Wilkins Co.**
428 E. Preston St., Baltimore, MD 21202.
- Acta Cytologica; the journal of clinical cytology. 6 per yr. ISSN 0001-5547 (International Academy of Cytology)
- Acute Myocardial Infarction Symposium. Proceedings. a.
- American Association of Pathologists and Bacteriologists. Symposium. Monographs. ISSN 0065-7298
- American Journal of Optometry and Physiological Optics. m. ISSN 0093-7002 (American Academy of Optometry)
- American Journal of Physical Medicine. bi-m. ISSN 0002-9491
- American Pediatric Society and Society for Pediatric Research. Program and Abstracts; abstracts of the annual meeting. a.
- Bergey's Manual of Determinative Bacteriology. a.
- Cancer Research. m. ISSN 0008-5472 (American Association for Cancer Research) (Editorial Office: Fels Research Institute, Temple University School of Medicine, Philadelphia, PA 19140)
- Clinical Neurosurgery; Proceedings. a. ISSN 0069-4827 (Congress of Neurological Surgeons)
- Critical Care Medicine. bi-m. ISSN 0090-3493 (Society of Critical Care Medicine)
- Drug Metabolism and Disposition; the biological fate of chemicals. bi-m. ISSN 0090-9556 (American Society for Pharmacology and Experimental Therapeutics)
- Gastroenterology. m. ISSN 0016-5085 (American Gastroenterological Association)
- Handbook of Physiology. irreg. ISSN 0072-9876 (American Physiological Society)
- Investigative Urology. bi-m. ISSN 0021-0005
- Journal of Criminal Law & Criminology. q. ISSN 0091-4169 (Northwestern University. School of Law)
- Journal of Histochemistry and Cytochemistry. m. ISSN 0022-1554 (Histochemical Society)
- Journal of Immunology. m. ISSN 0022-1767 (American Association of Immunologists)
- Journal of Investigative Dermatology. m. ISSN 0022-202X (Society for Investigative Dermatology)
- Journal of Nervous and Mental Disease; an educational journal of neuropsychiatry. m. ISSN 0022-3018
- Journal of Pharmacology and Experimental Therapeutics. m.(4 vols per yr) ISSN 0022-3565 (American Society of Pharmacology and Experimental Therapeutics, Inc)
- Journal of Trauma. m. ISSN 0022-5282 (American Association for the Surgery of Trauma)
- Journal of Urology. m. ISSN 0022-5347 (American Urological Association)
- Laboratory Investigation; a journal of experimental methods and pathology. m. ISSN 0023-6837 (International Academy of Pathology)
- Medicine; analytical reviews of general medicine, neurology, psychiatry, dermatology and pediatrics. bi-m. ISSN 0025-7974
- Monographs in Pathology. irreg. ISSN 0077-0922 (International Academy of Pathology)
- Obstetrical and Gynecological Survey. m. ISSN 0029-7828

- P. A. Journal; a journal for the new health practitioners. q. ISSN 0091-4614 (American Academy of Physicians' Assistants) (Editorial address:, 2341 Jefferson Davis Hwy., Suite 700, Arlington, VA 22202)
- Pediatric Research; international journal of human developmental biology. m. ISSN 0031-3998 (International Pediatric Research Foundation Inc)
- Pharmacological Reviews. q. ISSN 0031-6997 (American Society for Pharmacology and Experimental Therapeutics) (Co-sponsors: British Pharmacological Society, Scandinavian Pharmacological Society)
- Plastic and Reconstructive Surgery. m. ISSN 0032-1052 (American Society of Plastic & Reconstructive Surgeons)
- Radiologic Technology. bi-m. ISSN 0033-8397 (American Society of Radiologic Technologists)
- Seminars in Medicine. bi-m.
- Soil Science. m. ISSN 0038-075X (Rutgers University)
- Stain Technology; a journal for microtechnic and histochemistry. bi-m. ISSN 0038-9153 (Biological Stain Commission)
- Survey of Anesthesiology. bi-m. ISSN 0039-6206
- Symposia on Fundamental Cancer Research. Papers. a. ISSN 0082-0733 (Co-Sponsors: University of Texas M.D. Anderson Hospital; Tumor Institute, Houston; University of Texas Graduate School of Biomedical Sciences)
- Transplantation. m. ISSN 0041-1337 (Transplantation Society)
- Urological Survey. bi-m. ISSN 0042-1146

**Williams College**
P.O. Box 633, Williamstown, MA 01267.
- Berkshire Review. s-a. ISSN 0005-920X
- Pamoja Tutashinda. s-a.

**Richard T. & Mildred C. Williams, Eds. & Pubs.**
Box 307, Danboro, PA 18916.
- Pennsylvania Traveler-Post. q.
- Williams' Family Bulletin; records published for the numerous Williams descendants. q. ISSN 0043-5627

**Williams Market Analysis**
P.O. Box 170, Elmwood, NE 68349.
- U S Statistical Atlas. biennial.

**Grant Williams Publishing Co.**
943 Plymouth Bldg., 12 South 6th St., Minneapolis, MN 55402.
- Digest for Home Furnishers. q.

**Wilmington Public Schools**
Box 869, Wilmington, DE 19899.
- Wilmington Public Schools. Profile. bi-m. ISSN 0043-5635

**Wilsir Publications**
1271 Avenue of the Americas, Suite 3560, New York, NY 10020.
- Sew Business. m. ISSN 0029-4292

**Wilson Associates**
Box 1950, Hollywood, CA 90028.
- Audience; informal commentary on film & television. m. ISSN 0004-7503

**Evan Wilson Associates, Inc.**
1206 Temple Gardens, Baltimore, MD 21217.
- Alfantics. m. ISSN 0094-0259 (Alfa Romeo Owners Club. Capital Chapter)

**H.W. Wilson Co.**
950 University Ave., Bronx, NY 10452.
- Abridged Readers' Guide to Periodical Literature. m.(Sept-May)(annual cumulations) ISSN 0001-334X
- Applied Science and Technology Index; a cumulative subject index to English language periodicals in the fields of aeronautics and space science, automation, chemistry, construction, earth sciences, electricity and electronics, etc. m. (except July) ISSN 0003-6986
- Art Index; an author and subject index to domestic and foreign art periodicals and museum bulletins covering archaeology, architecture, art history, arts and crafts, city planning, fine arts, graphic arts, industrial design etc. q.(annual cumulations) ISSN 0004-3222
- Bibliographic Index; a subject list of bibliographies in English and foreign languages. 3 per yr. (3rd issue cumulates all three issues) ISSN 0006-1255
- Biography Index; a quarterly index to biographical material in books and magazines. q. (annual and 3 year cumulations) ISSN 0006-3053

- Biological and Agricultural Index; a subject index to periodicals in the fields of biology and agriculture and related sciences. m.(except Aug) (annual cumulation) ISSN 0006-3177
- Book Review Digest; an index to reviews of current books. m (except Feb. and July) (annual cumulations) ISSN 0006-7326
- Business Periodicals Index; a cumulative subject index to English language periodicals in the fields of accounting, advertising and public relations, automation, banking, communications, economics, finance and investments, insurance, labor, management, etc. m.(except Aug) ISSN 0007-6961
- Children's Catalog. quinquennial, with a. supplements.
- Cumulative Book Index; a world list of books in the English Language. 11 per yr (quarterly and annual cumulations) ISSN 0011-300X
- Current Biography. m. (exc. Dec.) ISSN 0011-3344
- Current Biography Yearbook. a. ISSN 0084-9499
- Current Book Review Citations. m. except Aug. ISSN 0360-1250
- Education Index; an author-subject index to educational publications in the English language. m.(Sept-June) (annual cumulation) ISSN 0013-1385
- Essay and General Literature Index; an index to collections of essays and works of a composite nature that have reference value. s-a(annual and 5 year cumulations) ISSN 0014-083X
- Fiction Catalog. quinquennial w. annual supplements.
- Humanities Index; an author and subject index to periodicals in the fields of archaeology and classical studies, area studies, folklore, history, language and literature, literary and political criticism, performing arts, philosophy, religion and theology, and related subjects. q (annual cumulations)
- Index to Legal Periodicals. m.(Oct-Aug)(annual and 3 year cumulations) ISSN 0019-4077
- Library Literature; an index to library and information science. bi-m.(annual and 2 year cumulations) ISSN 0024-2373
- Public Library Catalog. quinquennial, with a. supplements.
- Readers' Guide to Periodical Literature; an author subject index to selected general interest periodicals of reference value in libraries. s-m.(Sept-June); m.(July-Aug) (quarterly and annual cumulations) ISSN 0034-0464
- Senior High School Library Catalog. quinquennial, with a. supplements.
- Social Sciences Index; an author and subject index to periodicals in the fields of anthropology, area studies, economics, environmental science, geography, law and criminology, medical sciences, political science, psychology, public administration, sociology and related subjects. q.(annual cumulations) ISSN 0094-4920
- Vertical File Index; a subject and title index to selected pamphlet material. m.(Sep.-July) ISSN 0042-4439
- Wilson Library Bulletin. m.(Sept-June) ISSN 0043-5651

**Wilson College**
Chambersburg, PA 17201.
- Billboard (Chambersburg) w. (Wilson College Government Association)

**Wilson College Government Association**
- Billboard (Chambersburg) (pub. by Wilson College)

**Howard Wilson, Ed. & Pub.**
185 Marlboro, Boston, MA 02116.
- Kitchen Times. m.

**Thomas B. Wilson, Ed. & Pub.**
38 Swan St., Lambertville, NJ 08530.
- Ontario Register. q. ISSN 0030-3070

**Wilson Ornithological Society**
c/o Dr. Jerome A. Jackson, Ed., Dept. of Zoology, Mississippi State Univ., MS 39762.
- Wilson Bulletin; a quarterly magazine of ornithology. q. ISSN 0043-5643

**Phil Wilson Publishing Company**
1939 W. Gray, Houston, TX 77019.
- Geologic Field Trip Guidebooks of North America; a Union List Incorporating Monographic Titles. irreg. 2nd, 1971. ISSN 0533-7356
- Texas List of Scientific and Technical Serial Publications. a.

**Wilton Enterprises**
833 W. 115th St., Chicago, IL 60643.
- Celebrate 2; the annual for cake decorators. a. ISSN 0361-0896

**F.N. Wimer, Ed. & Pub.**
309 North Ninth Street, Richmond, VA 23219.
- Virginia English Bulletin. s-a. ISSN 0504-426X (Virginia Association of Teachers of English)

**U Kyaw Win, Ed. & Pub.**
Box 1891, Costa Mesa, CA 92626.
- Burma Bulletin. q.

**Winchell Publishing Co.**
1315 Cherry St, Philadelphia, PA 10107.
- Crier. q. ISSN 0016-8939

**Wind**
c/o Quentin R. Howard, R.F.D. Route No. 1, Box 810, Pikeville, KY 41501.
- Wind. 3-4 per yr.

**Wind Drifters Balloon Club**
2814 Empire Ave., Burbank, CA 91504.
- Hot-Air. m.

**Wind Power Digest**
Rt. 2, Box 489, Bristol, IN 46507.
- Wind Power Digest. q.

**Windflower Press**
1720 1/2 C. St., Lincoln, NE 68502.
- New Salt Creek Reader. irreg. (approx. 3-4 per yr.)

**Wine Guild**
Box 851, New York, NY 10010.
- Wine News. q.

**Wine Journal, Inc.**
575 West End Ave., New York, NY 10024.
- Wine Now. bi-m. ISSN 0094-5153

**Wine Rings**
c/o Joyce Odam, Ed., Rt. 1, Box 821, Wilton, CA 95693.
- Wine Rings. q. ISSN 0146-6356

**Wing Publications**
Box 2012, Arlington, VA 22202.
- Virginia Legionnaire. m. (American Legion. Department of Virginia)

**Wing Publications, Inc.**
Box 9248, Charlotte, NC 28299.
- Carolina Golfer. bi-m. ISSN 0008-6770
- Carolina Sportsman. bi-m. ISSN 0008-6800
- Southern Gardens. bi-m. ISSN 0038-4143

**Winpoint Corp.**
505 8th Ave., New York, NY 10018.
- Winning Points. 19 per yr.

**Winrod Letter**
P.O. 1193, Homer, AK 99603.
- Winrod Letter. m.

**Stephen W. Winship and Co.**
Box 1108, Concord, NH 03301.
- New England Guide; guide to travel and history. a. ISSN 0077-8222
- New Hampshire Camping Guide. a. ISSN 0077-8354 (New Hampshire Campground Owners Association)
- New Hampshire Vacation Guide. a. ISSN 0077-8419

**V. H. Winston and Sons, Inc.**
1511 K St. N.W., Washington, DC 20005.
- American Journal of Community Psychology; feminist review of the news. q. ISSN 0091-0562
- Journal of Applied Social Psychology. q. ISSN 0021-9029
- Series in General Psychiatry. irreg.

**Winston Paramount Books**
- Best Poets of the Twentieth Century on Man and Environment. (pub. by J. Mark Press)

**Winston Press**
General Book Division of Mine Publications, 25 Groveland Terrace, Minneapolis, MN 55403.
- Viewpoints (Minneapolis) irreg.

**William Winter, Ed. & Pub.**
9350 Wilshire Boulevard, Beverly Hills, CA 90212.
- William Winter Comments-on Current World Affairs. s-m.

**Henry Francis DuPont Winterthur Museum**
- Winterthur Conference Report. (pub. by University Press of Virginia)
- Winterthur Portfolio. (pub. by University Press of Virginia)

**Wion Publications**
Pier 38-40, San Francisco, CA 94107.
- May Day Pictorial News. m. ISSN 0025-6129

**Wire Association International**
- Wire Journal. (pub. by Wire Journal, Inc.)
- Wire Journal Directory/Catalog. (pub. by Wire Journal, Inc.)

**Wire Journal, Inc.**
1570 Boston Post Rd., Guilford, CT 06437.
- Wire Journal. m. ISSN 0043-602X (Wire Association International)
- Wire Journal Directory/Catalog. a. ISSN 0512-5405 (Wire Association International)

**Wire Service Guild. Local 222**
133 W. 44th St., New York, NY 10036.
- Wireport. m. ISSN 0043-6070

**Wire Technology Inc.**
P.O. Box 480, Stamford, CT 06904.
- Wire Technology. bi-m. ISSN 0361-4565
- Wire Technology Buyer's Guide. a.

**Wisconsin. Bureau of Planning and Budget. Management Information Systems Unit**
Madison, WI 53702.
- Wisconsin Population Projections. a. ISSN 0091-5254

**Wisconsin. Commissioner of Securities**
P.O. Box 1768, Madison, WI 53701.
- Wisconsin. Commissioner of Securities. Biennial Report. biennial since 1967.

**Wisconsin. Department of Administration**
202 South Thornton Ave., Madison, WI 53702.
- Wisconsin Blue Book.
- Wisconsin Statistical Abstract. irreg., 2nd 1972.

**Wisconsin. Department of Administration. Bureau of Financial Operations**
Madison, WI 53702.
- Wisconsin. Department of Administration. Annual Fiscal Report. a. ISSN 0085-8226

**Wisconsin. Department of Health and Social Services. Division of Mental Hygiene**
1 W. Wilson St., Madison, WI 53702.
- Wisconsin Mental Hygiene Review. q. ISSN 0043-6550

**Wisconsin. Department of Industry, Labor and Human Relations. Bureau of Research and Statistics**
Box 608, Madison, WI 53701.
- Occupational Opportunities Information for Wisconsin. irreg. ISSN 0512-6355

**Wisconsin. Department of Natural Resources**
Madison, WI 53701.
- Wisconsin. Department of Natural Resources. Annual Water Quality Report to Congress. a. ISSN 0362-5354
- Wisconsin. Department of Natural Resources. Technical Bulletin. irreg. ISSN 0084-0564
- Wisconsin Natural Resources. bi-m.

**Wisconsin. Department of Public Instruction**
126 Langdon St., Madison, WI 53702.
- Wisconsin. Department of Public Instruction. Newsletter. m. (Aug.-May)
- Wisconsin Public School Directory. a.

**Wisconsin. Department of Public Instruction. Division for Library Services**
126 Langdon St., Madison, WI 53702.
- Channel D L S. m (Sept.-July-Aug.)
- Tips from C.L.I.P. (pub. by Coordinated Library Information Program, Inc.)
- Wisconsin Library Bulletin. bi-m. ISSN 0043-6526
- Wisconsin Library Service Record. a. ISSN 0361-2848

**Wisconsin. Department of Transportation**
Madison, WI 53702.
● Wisconsin Accident Facts. a.

**Wisconsin. Department of Transportation. Bureau of Budget, Finance. & Audit**
4802 Sheboygan Ave., Madison, WI 53702.
● Wisconsin. Department of Transportation. State Summary: Type and Amount of Aids Paid to All Local Governmental Units and Counties. a. ISSN 0090-1067

**Wisconsin. Department of Transportation. Division of Planning**
Hill Farms State Office Bldg., 5802 Sheboygan Ave., Madison, WI 53702.
● Wisconsin. Department of Transportation. Division of Planning. Highway Mileage Data. a. ISSN 0084-0572

**Wisconsin. Department of Transportation. Travel Statistics and Data Coordination Section**
Madison, WI 53702.
● Wisconsin. Department of Transportation. Automatic Traffic Recorder Data; monthly average daily traffic. irreg.
● Wisconsin. Department of Transportation. Division of Planning. Highway Traffic. a. ISSN 0084-0580

**Wisconsin. Division of Corrections. Bureau of Planning, Development, and Research**
Madison, WI 53701.
● Huber Law Survey. irreg. ISSN 0094-0763
● Wisconsin. Division of Corrections. Bureau of Planning, Development, and Research. Adult and Juvenile Probation Admissions. a.
● Wisconsin. Division of Corrections. Bureau of Planning, Development, and Research. Adult Probation Admissions. ISSN 0095-4004
● Wisconsin. Division of Corrections. Bureau of Planning, Development, and Research. Admissions to Juvenile Institutions. a.
● Wisconsin. Division of Corrections. Bureau of Planning, Development, and Research. Juvenile Probation Admissions. ISSN 0095-4306
● Wisconsin. Division of Corrections. Bureau of Planning, Development, and Research. Probation and Parole Terminations. a.
● Wisconsin. Division of Corrections. Bureau of Planning, Development, and Research. Releases from Juvenile Institutions. a.
● Wisconsin. Division of Corrections. Bureau of Planning, Development, and Research. Work Release-Study Release Program. irreg. ISSN 0095-0564

**Wisconsin. Division of Health**
Box 309, Madison, WI 53702.
● Wisconsin's Health. q. ISSN 0043-6747

**Wisconsin. Division of Highway Safety Coordination**
Office of the Governor, Room 1121 - State Office Building, 1 W. Wilson St., Madison, WI 53702.
● Wisconsin. Division of Highway Safety Coordination. Highway Safety Report to the Legislature. a. ISSN 0098-5082

**Wisconsin. Education Communications Board**
732 North Midvale Boulevard, Madison, WI 53705.
● Wisconsin. Educational Communications Board. Biennial Report. biennial. ISSN 0361-2120

**Wisconsin. Geological and Natural History Survey**
1815 University Ave., Madison, WI 53706.
● Wisconsin. Geological and Natural History Survey. Information Circulars. irreg. ISSN 0512-0640

**Wisconsin. Governor's Advocacy Committee on Children and Youth**
106 E. Doty St., Suite 208, Madison, WI 53703.
● Wisconsin. Governor's Advocacy Committee on Children and Youth Annual Report. a. ISSN 0084-0602

**Wisconsin. Office of the Commissioner of Securities**
Box 1768, Madison, WI 53701.
● Wisconsin Franchise Bulletin. q.
● Wisconsin Security Bulletin. m.

**Wisconsin. State Laboratory of Hygiene**
Univ. of Wisconsin, 465 Henry Mall, Madison, WI 53706.
● Wisconsin State Laboratory of Hygiene. Laboratory Newsletter. m. ISSN 0043-6682

**Wisconsin Academy of Sciences, Arts and Letters**
1922 University Ave., Madison, WI 53705.
● Academy Triforium. m.
● Wisconsin Academy of Sciences, Arts and Letters, Transactions. a. ISSN 0084-0505

**Wisconsin Alliance Press, Inc.**
2140 Atwood Ave., Madison, WI 53704.
● Wisconsin Patriot. m.

**Wisconsin Alumni Association**
650 N. Lake St., Madison, WI 53706.
● Wisconsin Alumnus. bi-m.

**Wisconsin American Legion**
812 E. State St., Milwaukee, WI 53202.
● Badger Legionnaire. m. ISSN 0005-3767

**Wisconsin Archeological Society**
Box 1292, Milwaukee, WI 53201.
● Wisconsin Archeologist. q. ISSN 0043-6364

**Wisconsin Association of School Boards**
Box 160, Winneconne, WI 54986.
● Wisconsin School News. m.

**Wisconsin Audiovisual Association**
Educational Media Dept., University of Wisconsin-La Crosse, La Crosse, WI 54601.
● W A V A Dispatch. 4 per yr. ISSN 0049-772X (Co-sponsor: Milwaukee Public Schools)

**Wisconsin Coalition for Education Reform**
3019 N. Farwell Ave., Milwaukee, WI 53211.
● Wisconsin Coalition for Educational Reform. Newsletter. irreg.

**Wisconsin Congress of Parents and Teachers Inc.**
223 N Baldwin St., Madison, WI 53703.
● Wisconsin Parent Teacher Bulletin. 9 per yr(Sept-May) ISSN 0043-6577

**Wisconsin Council of Teachers of English**
c/o Nicholas J. Karolides, Ed., University of Wisconson-River Falls, River Falls, WI 54022.
● Wisconsin Council of Teachers of English. Service Bulletin Series. irreg.
● Wisconsin English Journal. 3 per yr. ISSN 0512-1213

**Wisconsin County Boards Association**
22 West Washington Ave., Room 200, Madison, WI 53703.
● Wisconsin Counties. m.

**Wisconsin County Lands**
Box 119, Wisconsin Dells, WI 53965.
● Wisconsin County Lands. 12 per yr.

**Wisconsin Crime Information Bureau**
P.O. Box 2718, Madison, WI 53701.
● Wisconsin Criminal Justice Information, Crime and Arrests. a.

**Wisconsin Dental Association**
Suite 523-30, Clark Bldg., 633 W. Wisconsin Ave., Milwaukke, WI 53203.
● Wisconsin Dental Association. Journal. m. ISSN 0091-4185

**Wisconsin Electric Cooperative Association**
1810 South Park Street, Madison, WI 53701.
● Wisconsin R E C News. m.

**Wisconsin Engineering Journal Association**
276 Mechanical Engineering Bldg., Univ. of Wisconsin, Madison, WI 53705.
● Wisconsin Engineer. m.(Oct-May) ISSN 0043-6453

**Wisconsin Evangelical Lutheran Synod**
● Northwestern Lutheran. (pub. by Northwestern Publishing House)

**Wisconsin Farm Bureau Federation**
Box 5550, Madison, WI 53705.
● Badger Farm Bureau News. m. ISSN 0005-3740

**Wisconsin Farmer Co., Inc.**
Box 4420, Madison, WI 53711.
● Wisconsin Agriculturist; a farm progress publication. s-m. ISSN 0043-6356

**Wisconsin Geological Society**
c/o William C. Bode, 1601 So. Sherwood Dr., New Berlin, WI 53151.
● Trilobite. 10 per yr. ISSN 0041-2988

**Wisconsin Institute of Certified Public Accountants**
600 E. Mason, Milwaukee, WI 53202.
● Wisconsin C P A. q. ISSN 0043-6402

**Wisconsin Jewish Publications Foundation**
1360 N. Prospect Ave., Milwaukee, WI 53202.
● Wisconsin Jewish Chronicle. w. ISSN 0043-6488

**Wisconsin Library Association**
Public Library, Madison, WI 53703.
● Wisconsin Library Association. President's Newsletter. bi-m. ISSN 0032-7778

**Wisconsin Manufacturers' Association**
324 E. Wisconsin Ave., Milwaukee, WI 53202.
● Classified Directory of Wisconsin Manufacturers. a. ISSN 0069-4525

**Wisconsin Nurses Association**
161 W. Wisconsin Ave., Room 6012, Milwaukee, WI 53203.
● Stat. bi-m. ISSN 0038-9986

**Wisconsin Optometric Association**
5721 Odana Rd., Madison, WI 53719.
● Wisconsin Optometric Association. Journal. bi-m.

**Wisconsin Petroleum Association**
202 N. Midvale Blvd., Madison, WI 53705.
● W I S P A Informer. m.

**Wisconsin Poetry Magazine Illustrated**
Box 187, Milwaukee, WI 53201.
● Wisconsin Poetry Magazine Illustrated. s-a. ISSN 0043-6607

**Wisconsin Research and Development Center for Cognitive Learning**
1025 West Johnson St., Madison, WI 53706.
● Wisconsin Research and Development Center for Cognitive Learning. Practical Papers. irreg., 1972, no. 13. ISSN 0084-0629
● Wisconsin Research and Development Center for Cognitive Learning. Theoretical Papers. irreg., 1972, no. 41. ISSN 0084-0637
● Wisconsin Research and Development Center for Cognitive Learning. Technical Reports. irreg., 1972, no. 245. ISSN 0084-0645

**Wisconsin Restaurant Association**
122 W. Washington Ave., Madison, WI 53703.
● Wisconsin Restaurateur. m.

**Wisconsin Retailers Review**
c/o Bob Shinners, Box 37, Hartland, WI 53029.
● Wisconsin Retailers Review. m.

**Wisconsin School Music Association**
115 W. Main St., Madison, WI 53703.
● Wisconsin School Musician. 4 per yr. ISSN 0043-6658

**Wisconsin Secondary School Administrators Association**
New Berlin High School, 18695 W. Cleveland Ave., New Berlin, WI 53151.
● Wisconson Secondary School Administrators Association. Bulletin. 3 per yr. ISSN 0361-5391

**Wisconsin Sheriffs and Deputy Sheriffs Association**
Box 145, Chippewa Falls, WI 54724.
● Wisconsin Sheriff and Deputy. q.

**Wisconsin Society for Ornithology, Inc**
38552 Genesee Lake Rd., Oconomowoc, WI 53066.
● Passenger Pigeon; a magazine of Wisconsin bird study. q. ISSN 0031-2703

**Wisconsin Sociological Association**
Univ. of Wisconsin-Eau Claire, Eau Claire, WI 54701.
● Wisconsin Sociologist. q. ISSN 0043-6666

**Wisconsin Sportsman, Inc.**
Box 1307, Oshkosh, WI 54901.
● Wisconsin Sportsman. bi-m. ISSN 0361-9451

**Wisconsin State Historical Society**
816 State St., Madison, WI 53706.
● Badger History. q.(during school year) ISSN 0005-3759
● Wisconsin State Historical Society. Urban History Group. Newsletter. irreg. ISSN 0084-067X

**Wisconsin State University**
River Falls, WI 54022.
● Student Voice. w. ISSN 0039-2804

**Wisconsin Tales and Trails, Inc.**
P.O. Box 5650, Madison, WI 53705.
- Wisconsin Trails; magazine of life in the Badger State. q.

**Wisconsin Union Labor News Publishing Co.**
1406 Emil St., Box 1725, Madison, WI 53701.
- Union Labor News. m. ISSN 0041-6924 (Co-Sponsors: Madison Federation of Labor A F L-C I O and Others)

**Wm. H. Wise & Co., Inc.**
336 Mountain Rd, Union City, NJ 07087.
- World Shopping Encyclopedia. 4 per yr. (Caravan, Inc)

**Wistar Institute Press**
36th St. at Spruce, Philadelphia, PA 19104.
- American Journal of Anatomy. m. ISSN 0002-9106
- American Journal of Physical Anthropology. bi-m. ISSN 0002-9483 (American Association of Physical Anthropologists)
- Anatomical Record. m. ISSN 0003-276X (American Association of Anatomists)
- Journal of Cellular Physiology. m. ISSN 0021-9541
- Journal of Comparative Neurology. fortn. ISSN 0021-9967
- Journal of Experimental Zoology. m. ISSN 0022-104X
- Journal of Morphology. m. ISSN 0022-2887
- Teratology; the journal of abnormal development. bi-m. ISSN 0040-3709 (Teratology Society)

**Witches International Craft Associaties; Witches Liberation Movement**
- Witchcraft Digest. (pub. by Hero Press)

**Witches Trine**
Box 23243, Oakland, CA 94623.
- Witches Trine. 8 per yr.

**Wittenborn and Co.**
1018 Madison Ave., New York, NY 10021.
- Documents of Modern Art. irreg.

**Dean Witter and Co.**
45 Montgomery St., San Francisco, CA 94106.
- Thursday Letter. fortn.

**Wofford College. Sandor Teszler Library**
Spartanburg, SC 29301.
- Wofford Bibliopolist. 2-3 per yr. ISSN 0043-714X

**Woldon Communications, Inc.**
(Subsidiary of: Billboard Publications, Inc.)
1 Astor Plaza, New York, NY 10036.
- Group Travel. m. ISSN 0017-4750

**Wolf House Books**
Box 209-K, Cedar Springs, MI 49319.
- London Collector. s-a. ISSN 0047-5033

**Wolfe Publishing Co., Inc.**
Box 3030, Prescott, AZ 86301.
- Handloader. bi-m. ISSN 0017-7393
- Rifle Magazine. bi-m. ISSN 0035-5216

**Wolfe Publishing, Inc.**
Box 1094, Snyder, TX 79549.
- General Aviation Business: the Blue Sheet. m.
- General Aviation News: the Green Sheet. fortn.

**Wolfer Printing Co., Inc.**
422 Wall St., Los Angeles, CA 90013.
- Patterson's California Beverage Gazetteer. m. ISSN 0031-3238

**Henry Wolfrath, Ed. & Pub.**
Box 44, Northport, NY 11768.
- Long Island Investor. 5 per yr.

**Woman Activist, Inc.**
2310 Barbour Rd., Falls Church, VA 22043.
- Woman Activist; an action bulletin for women's rights from the courthouse to the White House. m. ISSN 0049-7770

**Woman Becoming**
6664 Woodwell St., Pittsburgh, PA 15217.
- Woman Becoming. s-a.

**Woman Talk**
Box 356, Blackwood, NJ 08012.
- Woman Talk. m.

**Womanchild**
One Hawthorne St., No. 2, Worcester, MA 01610.
- Womanchild. q.

**Woman's National Farm & Garden Association, Inc.**
2375 Walton Blvd., Rochester, MI 48063.
- Woman's National Magazine. q. ISSN 0043-7352

**Woman's Soul Publishing, Inc**
P.O. Box 11646, Milwaukee, WI 53211.
- Paid My Dues; journal of women & music. 3-4 per yr. ISSN 0097-8035

**Woman's World Joint Venture**
575 Madison Ave., New York, NY 10022.
- Woman's World Family Crafts. bi-m.

**WomanSpirit**
Box 263, Wolf Creek, OR 97497.
- WomanSpirit. 4 per yr.

**Women**
3028 Greenmount Ave., Baltimore, MD 21218.
- Women. q. ISSN 0043-7433

**Women for Constitutional Government**
310 W. Robb St., Box 220, Summit, MS 39666.
- Woman Constitutionalist. m. ISSN 0043-728X

**Women for Sobriety, Inc.**
344 Franklin St., Quakertown, PA 18951.
- Sobering Thoughts. m.

**Women in Communications, Inc.**
National Headquarters, Box 9561, Austin, TX 78766.
- Matrix; a magazine for women in journalism & communications. q. ISSN 0025-598X

**Women in Struggle**
Box 324, Winneconne, WI 54986.
- Women in Struggle. bi-m. ISSN 0049-7819

**Women Library Workers**
555 29th St., San Francisco, CA 94131.
- Women Library Workers Newsletter. bi-m.

**Women - Poems**
23 Meriam St., Lexington, MA 02173.
- Women - Poems. irreg.

**Women Strike for Peace**
799 Broadway, New York, NY 10003.
- Women Strike for Peace. q. ISSN 0042-9864

**Women Writing Newsletter**
Rd. 3, Newfield, NY 14867.
- Women Writing Newsletter. bi-m.

**Women's American ORT**
1250 Broadway, New York, NY 10001.
- Women's American O R T Reporter. bi-m. ISSN 0043-7514

**Women's Center (Venice)**
P.O. Box 597, Venice, CA 90231.
- Sister Feminist Paper. m.

**Women's Circle Home Cooking**
Box 428, Seabrook, NH 03874.
- Women's Circle Home Cooking.

**Women's Equity Action League. National Capital Chapter**
621 National Press Bldg., Washington, DC 20024.
- W E A L Washington Report. 6 per yr. ISSN 0300-6867

**Women's History Research Center**
2325 Oak St., Berkeley, CA 94708.
- Directory of Films by and/Or About Women. biennial.
- Female Artists Past and Present. biennial.

**Women's International Bowling Congress, Inc.**
5301 S. 76th St., Greendale, WI 53129.
- Woman Bowler. m. ISSN 0043-7255
- Women's International Bowling Congress. Playing Rules. a. ISSN 0361-3976

**Women's International League for Peace and Freedom (Philadelphia)**
1213 Race St., Philadelphia, PA 19107.
- Peace and Freedom. 9 per yr. ISSN 0015-9093

**Women's International Network**
187 Grant St., Lexington, MA 02173.
- W I N News. q.

**Women's Law Journal**
Box 130, 308 Westwood Plaza, Los Angeles, CA 90024.
- Women's Law Journal. s-a.

**Women's League for Conservative Judaism**
48 E. 74 St., New York, NY 10021.
- Women's League Outlook. q. ISSN 0043-7557

**Women's Lobby, Inc.**
1345 G St. S.E., Washington, DC 20003.
- Women's Lobby Quarterly; analysis of legislation affecting women. q.

**Women's National Abortion Action Coalition**
156 Fifth Ave., New York, NY 10011.
- W O N A A C Newsletter. m.

**Women's Poetry Collective**
- Gravida. (pub. by Gravida, Ltd.)

**Women's Press Collective**
Box 562, Eugene, OR 97401.
- Womens Press; a womens news journal. m. ISSN 0049-786X

**Women's Rights Law Reporter, Inc.**
180 University Ave., Newark, NJ 07102.
- Women's Rights Law Reporter. q. ISSN 0085-8269

**Women's Track and Field World Publications, Inc.**
Box 371, Claremont, CA 91711.
- Women's Track and Field World. m. ISSN 0043-7573

**Women's Work, Inc.**
1302 18th St. N.W., Suite 203, Washington, DC 20036.
- Women's Work. bi-m.

**Wonderworld**
Box 16168, Long Beach, CA 90806.
- Wonderworld. q.

**Gilbert Woo, Ed. & Pub.**
4114 California St., San Francisco, CA 94118
(Subscr. to: 809 Stockton St., Suite 101, San Francisco, CA 94108)
- Chinese Pacific Weekly. w.

**Wood County Board of Education**
1210 13th St., Parkersburg, WV 26101.
- Wood County Board of Education. News & Views. m.

**Wood, Wire and Metal Lathers' International Union**
AFL-CIO Bldg., 815 16th St., N.W., Washington, DC 20006.
- Lather. q. ISSN 0023-8716

**Wood - Woods Family Magazine**
c/o Mrs. Charles C. Alexander, Ed. & Pub., 903 Myers Ave., Columbia, TN 38401.
- Wood - Woods Family Magazine. a. ISSN 0091-6706

**W. C. Woodall, Ed. & Pub.**
106 16th St., Columbus, Ga.
- Industrial Index. m. ISSN 0019-8404

**Woodall Publishing Co.**
500 Hyacinth Pl., Highland Park, IL 60035.
- Better Camping; four seasons of outdoor living. m. ISSN 0006-0070
- Campground Management. 12 per yr.
- Hiking (Highland Park) ISSN 0094-0291
- Trailer Travel Magazine. m. ISSN 0041-0802
- Woodall's Campground Directory. a.
- Woodall's Campground Directory. Eastern Edition. a.
- Woodall's Campground Directory. Florida Campgrounds Edition. a. ISSN 0090-5151
- Woodall's Campground Directory. North American Edition. a.
- Woodall's Campground Directory. Western Edition. a.
- Woodall's Directory of Mobile Home Communities. a. ISSN 0094-1891
- Woodall's Mobile-Modular Living. a. ISSN 0093-7274
- Woodall's Retirement Communities Directory. a.

**Woodbine Publishers Inc.**
90 Bagby Rd., Suite 222, Birmingham, AL 35209.
- Annals of Ophthalmology. m. ISSN 0003-4886 (American Society of Contemporary Ophthalmology)

- Contact Lens Journal. q. (Contact Lens Society of America)

**Woodenboat**
Box 4933, Manchester, NH 03108.
- Woodenboat; the magazine for wooden boat owners, builders and designers. bi-m. ISSN 0095-067X

**Woodmen of the World Life Insurance Society**
1700 Farnam St., Omaha, NE 68102.
- Woodmen of the World Magazine. m. ISSN 0043-7751

**Woodrow Wilson Foundation**
- Papers of Woodrow Wilson. (pub. by Princeton University Press)

**Woodrow Wilson International Center for Scholars**
Smithsonian Institution Bldg., Washington, DC 20560
- Wilson Quarterly. q. ISSN 0363-3276 (Subscr. to:, Box 2450, Greenwich, CT 06830)
- Woodrow Wilson International Center for Scholars. Annual Report. a. ISSN 0092-4261

**Woodrow Wilson National Fellowship Foundation**
32 Nassau Street, Princeton, NJ 08540.
- Woodrow Wilson National Fellowship Foundation. Newsletter. irreg.(approx. 3 times a year) ISSN 0084-1137
- Woodrow Wilson National Fellowship Foundation. Report. a. ISSN 0084-1145

**Woods Hole Oceanographic Institution**
Woods Hole, MA 02543.
- Oceanus. q. ISSN 0029-8182

**Woodson County Historical Society**
Yates Center, KS 66783.
- In the Beginning. q. ISSN 0019-3275

**Woolknit Associates, Inc.**
501 Madison Ave., New York, NY 10022.
- Woolknit Annual. a. ISSN 0084-1234

**J. Howard Woolmer - Books**
Gladstone Hollow, Andes, NY 13731.
- Focus Series. irreg., approx. biennial. ISSN 0071-6316

**Worcester Art Museum**
55 Salisbury St., Worcester, MA 01608.
- Worcester Art Museum Bulletin. 3 per yr.

**Worcester District Medical Society**
57 Cedar St., Worcester, MA 01609.
- Worcester Medical News. bi-m. ISSN 0043-7905

**Worcester Polytechnic Institute. Alumni Association**
Worcester, MA 01609.
- W P I Journal. 5 per yr. ISSN 0043-7913

**Word, Inc.**
4800 Waco Dr., Waco, TX 76710.
- Catalyst (Waco); a resource for Christian leaders. m.
- Faith/At/Work Magazine. 8 per yr.

**Word of Truth Productions**
Box 288, Ballston Spa, NY 12020.
- Bible and Spade; a quarterly digest of biblical archaeology. q.

**Word Smith**
1817 S. Vodges St., Philadelphia, PA 19143.
- Word Smith. s-a.

**Word to the Wise**
Box 139, Lancaster, MA 01561.
- Word to the Wise. q.

**Wordens Weekly Report**
1915 Floranda Rd., Fort Lauderdale, FL 33308.
- Wordens Weekly Report. w.

**Words News & Interview, Inc.**
Box 16099, Louisville, KY 40216.
- Christian Contemporary. bi-m.

**Wordsworth Circle**
c/o Marilyn Gaull, Ed., Dept. of English, Temple Univ., Philadelphia, PA 19122.
- Wordsworth Circle. q. ISSN 0043-8006

**Work in America Institute, Inc.**
700 White Plains Rd., Scarsdale, NY 10583.
- World of Work Report. m.

**Workers Defense League**
150 Fifth Ave., New York, NY 10011.
- W D L News. q.

**Workers World Party**
- Workers World. (pub. by World View Publishers, Inc.)

**Working Craftsman, Inc.**
Box 42, 150 Shermen Road, Northbrook, IL 60062.
- Working Craftsman; the magazine for working craftsmen. q.

**Workmen's Benefit Fund of the United States of America**
714 Seneca Ave., Brooklyn, NY 11227.
- Solidarity. m(excepting combined issues in Jan.-Feb., Jun-Jul.; Aug.-Sep.) ISSN 0038-1152

**Workmen's Circle**
45 E. 33 St., New York, NY 10016.
- Call (New York) bi-m. ISSN 0008-1698
- Inner Circle. 5 per yr.
- Kinderzeitung. bi-m. ISSN 0023-1533
- Kultur Un Lebn. 5 per yr. ISSN 0023-513X (prep. by its Yiddish Division)
- Workmen's Circle Call. bi-m. ISSN 0043-8111

**World Affairs Council of Northern California**
406 Sutter St., San Francisco, CA 94108.
- Booknotes. m.

**World Airline Record**
327 S. Lasalle St., Chicago, IL 60604.
- Airline Newsletter: World Airline Record Newsletter. s-m. ISSN 0002-2748

**World Archaeological Society**
c/o Ron Miller, Dir., Lake Rd. 65-48, Star Rt. 140-D, Hollister, MO 65672.
- W. A. S. Newsletter. 4 per yr.
- World Archaeological Society. Special Publication. irreg.

**World Association for the Advancement of Veterinary Parasitology**
c/o Sec. Treas. Dr. S. M. Gafar, Department of Veterinary Microbiology, Purdue University, Lafayette, IN 47901.
- World Association for the Advancement of Veterinary Parasitology. Proceedings of Conference. biennial, 1969, 4th, Univ. of Glasgow. ISSN 0084-1404

**World Association of Estonians, Inc.**
243 E. 34th St., Box 123, New York, NY 10016.
- Meie Tee. s-m. ISSN 0025-8768

**World Bank**
For publications of this agency see section for UNITED NATIONS

**World Book and Travel Report**
2000-B Governor's Circle, Houston, TX 77092.
- World Book and Travel Report. 4 per yr.

**World Co.**
Sixth and New Hampshire, Lawrence, KS 66044.
- Kansas English. 3 per yr. (Kansas Association of Teachers of English)

**World Community Association**
- International Financing and Investment. (pub. by Oceana Publications, Inc.)

**World Council of Credit Unions**
1617 Sherman Ave., P.O. Box 431, Madison, WI 53701.
- World Council of Credit Unions. Newsletter. m.
- World Council of Credit Unions. Yearbook. a.
- World Reporter. q. ISSN 0043-8952

**World Crafts Council**
29 West 53 St., New York, NY 10019.
- World Crafts Council. General Assembly. Proceedings of the Biennial Meeting. biennial; 6th, Toronto, 1974. ISSN 0084-1706

**World Cutter and Chariot Racing Association**
- Cutter and Chariot Racing World. (pub. by Harris Publishing, Inc. (Idaho Falls))

**World Data Center A for Glaciology**
*see under* U. S. Environmental Data Service

**World Education**
1414 Sixth Ave., New York, NY 10019.
- World Education Reports; a journal of program developments in the field of functional education for family life planning. 9 per yr. ISSN 0300-7006

**World Education Markets Inc.**
Box 30037, Washington, DC 20014.
- W E M Newsletter; the international news report for the education industry. s-m. ISSN 0042-9635

**World Federalist Educational Fund**
1424 16th St. N.W., Washington, DC 20036.
- New Federalist Papers. a.

**World Federalists, USA**
1424 Sixteenth St., NW, Washington, DC 20036.
- World Citizen/Federalist Letter. m. (10 per yr.)

**World Federation of Hungarian Jews**
136 E. 39th St., New York, NY 10016.
- Hungarian Jewish Studies. irreg., 1973, vol. 3.

**World Future Society**
4916 St. Elmo Ave., Washington, DC 20014.
- Futurist; a journal of forecasts, trends, and ideas about the future. bi-m. ISSN 0016-3317
- World Future Society Bulletin. bi-m. ISSN 0049-8092

**World Future Society. Special Studies Division**
4916 St. Elmo Ave., Washington, DC 20014.
- Careers Tomorrow. bi-m.
- Communications Tomorrow. bi-m.
- Education Tomorrow. bi-m.
- Habitats Tomorrow. bi-m.
- Human Values Tomorrow. bi-m.
- Life-Styles Tomorrow. bi-m.

**World Gift Review**
616 9th St., Union City, NJ 07087.
- World Gift Review Monthly Newsletter. m. ISSN 0049-8106

**World Goodwill**
866 United Nations Plaza, Suite 566-7, New York, NY 10017
(or 1 rue de Varembe (3e), C. P. 31, 1211 Geneva 20, Switzerland; or 235 Finchley Rd., Hampstead, London NW3 6LS, England)
- World Goodwill Commentary; a bulletin on current trends in world affairs. q.

**World Health Organization. Pan American Health Organization**
For publications of this agency see section for UNITED NATIONS

**World Information Systems Exchange (W I S E)**
Box 2-J, Tempe, AZ 85282.
- Graphics Expo - World Communications in Graphics Technology. q.
- LeCOURT - Global Communications in Legal Information Systems. q.
- Monitor - Perceptions of Change in Medical Information Science. q.

**World Information Systems Exchange (W I S E) Library and Information Science Division**
Publications Dept., Box 349, Phoenix, AZ 85001.
- Automated Activities in Health Sciences Libraries. q.
- Network: International Communications in Library Automation. q.

**World Institute Council**
777 United Nations Plaza, New York, NY 10017.
- Fields Within Fields...Within Fields; the methodology of the creative process. q. ISSN 0015-0770

**World Leisure and Recreation Association**
345 E. 46th St., New York, NY 10017.
- W L R A Bulletin. s-m (except Jul. & Aug.)

**World Medical Association, Inc.**
10 Columbus Circle, New York, NY 10019.
- International Medical Directory. irreg. (prep. by its U.S. Committee)
- International News Items. q. ISSN 0020-8086
- World Medical Association. General Assembly. Proceedings. a, 1947, 29th, Sweden. ISSN 0084-1897
- World Medical Journal. bi-m. ISSN 0049-8122

**World Meetings Information Center, Inc.**
824 Boylston St., Chestnut Hill, MA 02167.
- Current Programs. (pub. by Data Courier, Inc.)

- Current Programs. Annual Index. (pub. by Data Courier Inc.)
- World Meetings: Outside U.S.A. and Canada. q. ISSN 0043-8677
- World Meetings: Social & Behavioral Sciences, Education & Management. q. ISSN 0043-8685
- World Meetings: United States and Canada. q. ISSN 0043-8693

**World Methodist Council**
Lake Junaluska, NC 28745.
- World Parish. m(Sept.-June) ISSN 0043-8839

**World Methodist Historical Society**
World Methodist Bldg., Lake Junaluska, NC 28745.
- World Methodist Historical Society. News Bulletin. q.

**World Neighbors**
5116 North Portland, Oklahoma City, OK 73112.
- Soundings from Around the World. q.

**World News Corporation**
730 Third Ave., New York, NY 10017.
- Star. w.

**World of Comic Art Publications**
P.O. Box 507, Hawthorne, CA 90250.
- World of Comic Art; the historical journal of comic art and caricature. q.(plus special annual no.) ISSN 0043-8766

**World Peace Foundation**
- International Organization. (pub. by University of Wisconsin Press)

**World Peace News**
777 United Nations Plaza, Eleventh Floor, New York, NY 10017.
- World Peace News. 9 per yr. ISSN 0049-8130 (American Movement for World Government, Inc.)

**World Peace Through Law Center**
839-17th St., N.W., Washington, DC 20006.
- Law and Computer Technology. q. ISSN 0023-9178 (prep. by its Section on Law & Computer Technology)
- World Law Review. biennial, 1971, no. 5, Belgrade.
- World Legal Directory. irreg. ISSN 0075-8213

**World Pen Pals**
1690 Como Ave., St. Paul, MN 55108.
- Silver Lining. a.

**World Poetry, Inc.**
1616 Walnut, Rm. 405, Philadelphia, PA 19103.
- American Poetry Review. bi-m.

**World Presbyterian Missions, Inc.**
901 N. Broom St., Wilmington, DE 19806.
- W P M Newletter. m. ISSN 0042-9783

**World Products**
99 Church St., Box 3224, Church St. Sta., New York, NY 10008.
- World Products. m.

**World Prophetic Ministry, Inc.**
P.O. Drawer 907, Colton, CA 92324.
- Prophetic Newsletter; the news in the light of the Bible. m. ISSN 0033-1341

**World Publications**
Box 366, Mountain View, CA 94040.
- Bike Book Quarterly. q.
- Bike World. m.
- Down River. m.
- Marathon Handbook. a. ISSN 0360-9928
- Nordic World. issued seasonally.
- Runner's Book Series. m.
- Runner's World. m. ISSN 0035-9939
- Soccer World. m.

**World Publishing, Inc.**
9 N. Fourth St., Minneapolis, MN 55401.
- American Jewish World. w. ISSN 0002-9084

**World Redemption**
Box 1925, Independence, MO 64055.
- Zion's Warning. bi-m.

**World Research, Inc.**
11722 Sorrento Valley Road, San Diego, CA 92121.
- Occasional Review; a journal of contemporary thought in the arts, humanities, and social sciences. s-a.

- World Research INK. m.

**World Science Education**
Box 683, Princeton, NJ 08540.
- Adventures in Experimental Physics; a selection of papers & personal discovery stories dealing with innovative, unconventional & adventurous experimentation. s-a. ISSN 0044-6386

**World Science Fiction Association**
- Aussiecon Flyer. (pub. by Unicorn Press)

**World Ship Society. Port of New York Branch**
Box 2411, New York, NY 10001.
- P. O. N. Y. Express. (Port of New York) q.

**World Socialist Party of the United States**
295 Huntington Ave., Boston, MA 02115.
- Western Socialist; journal of scientific socialism in the Western Hemisphere. bi-m. ISSN 0043-4191 (Co-sponsor: Socialist Party of Canada)

**World Sports Publishers**
1511 K. St., N.W., Suite 1036, Washington, DC 20005.
- World-Wide Golf Directory. a. ISSN 0093-2477

**World Team Tennis (Organization)**
Newport Beach, CA 92660.
- World Team Tennis Official Magazine. irreg. ISSN 0361-3429

**World Trade Academy Press, Inc.**
50 E. 42nd St., New York, NY 10017.
- American Register of Inter-Corporate Ownership. irreg. ISSN 0065-9975
- Directory of American Firms Operating in Foreign Countries. irreg., 1974, 8th ed. ISSN 0070-5071
- Directory of Foreign Firms Operating with the United States. irreg. ISSN 0070-5543
- Directory of Professional and Occupational Licensing in the United States. irreg. ISSN 0070-6132 (Dist. by Simon & Schuster, Inc., Technical and Reference Book Division, 1 W. 39 St., New York, NY 10018)
- International Reference Handbook of Marketing, Management and Advertising Organizations. irreg.
- Looking for Employment in Foreign Countries Reference Handbook. biennial.
- Modern Vocational Trends. m. ISSN 0026-8550
- Multinational Marketing & Employment Directory. irreg. ISSN 0363-4426
- National Register of Scholarships and Fellowships. irreg., 1973, 5th ed. ISSN 0077-538X

**World Trade Academy Press, Inc. Technical and Reference Book Division**
50 E. 42 St., New York, NY 10017
- Modern Vocational Trends Reference Handbook. irreg., 1969, 7th ed. ISSN 0077-0167 (Dist. by Simon & Schuster, Inc., Technical and Reference Book Division, 1 W. 39 St., New York NY 10018)

**World Tribune Press**
1351 Ocean Front, Santa Monica, CA 90401.
- N.S.A. Photo Album. irreg. (Nichiren Shoshu Academy)
- N.S.A. Quarterly. q. (Nichiren Shoshu Academy)
- World Tribune. 5 per wk. ISSN 0049-8165 (Nichiren Shoshu Academy) (Subscr. to:, Box 1427, Santa Monica CA 90406)

**World Union of National Socialists**
2507 N. Franklin Rd., Arlington, VA 22201.
- W U N S Bulletin. q.

**World United Formosans for Independence**
Box D, Kearny, NJ 07032.
- Independent Taiwan. 11 issues a yr. in Chinese; 1 issue in English.

**World University Service**
20 West 40th St., New York, NY 10018.
- E U M E N Action. (Entr'aide Universitaire Mondiale) irreg. ISSN 0424-0227
- World University Service. Annual Report. a. ISSN 0084-2419
- World University Service. Programme of Action. biennial. ISSN 0084-2427

**World View Publishers, Inc.**
46 W. 21st St., New York, NY 10010.
- Workers World. w. ISSN 0043-809X (Workers World Party)

**World Vision International**
919 West Huntington Drive, Monrovia, CA 91016.
- Christian Leadership Letter. m.
- World Vision. m. ISSN 0043-9215

**World Ways**
Route 18, Morristown, NJ 07960.
- World Ways; journal of recreational linguistics. q.

**World Wide Gun Report, Inc.**
Box 111, Aledo, IL 61231.
- Gun Report; dedicated to the interests of gun enthusiasts everywhere. m. ISSN 0017-5617

**World Wide Trade Service**
P.O. Box 283, Medina, WA 98039.
- American Drop-Shippers Directory. a. ISSN 0065-8103
- Importers and Exporters Trade Promotion Guide. biennial. ISSN 0073-5604

**World Wide Wrestling Federation**
80 Riverside Drive, New York, NY 10024.
- Wrestling Where It's at. bi-m.

**World Zionist Organization-American Section Inc. Department of Education and Culture in the Diaspora**
515 Park Ave., New York, NY 10022.
- La-Mathil (American Edition); a voweled Hebrew newspaper. w.

**World's Poultry Science Association**
c/o W. R. Jenkins, Sec.- Treas., USA Branch - W P S A, ES-USDA, 5509 South Agriculture, Washington, DC 20250.
- World's Poultry Science Association. Report of the Proceedings of International Congress. quadrennial. ISSN 0084-2532

**Worldwide Culture Society**
Box 9453, North Hollywood, CA 91609.
- World Club Directory. a.

**Wormsloe Foundation**
- Wormsloe Foundation. Publications. (pub. by University of Georgia Press)

**Wormwood Review Press**
Box 8840, Stockton, CA 95204.
- Wormwood Review. q. ISSN 0043-9401

**Worn-out Press**
101 East Sycamore St., Normal, IL 61761.
- McClean County Poetry Review. q.

**Worth International Communications Corp.**
Box 2226, Hollywood, FL 33022.
- Communique (Hollywood) m. ISSN 0015-4180
- Recommend: Florida. m. ISSN 0034-1452

**Wotanin Press**
Box 493, Poplar, MT 59255.
- Wotanin-Wowapi. s-m. (Fort Peck Tribes)

**Ron Wray, Ed. & Pub.**
502 E. 38th St., Apt 14-B, Indianapolis, IN 46205.
- Primer. q.

**Wrecking & Salvage Journal**
P.O. Box 130, Hingham, MA 02043.
- Demo Memo. w.

**Wright Investors' Service**
Wright Bldg., 500 State St., Bridgeport, CT 06604.
- Wright Bankers' Service; investment advice & recommendations. w.

**Wright Publishing Co.**
2949 Century Place, Costa Mesa, CA 92626.
- Dune Buggies & Hot VWs; the fun car journal. m. ISSN 0012-7132

**Wright State University**
Eugene W. Kettering Center, 140 East Monument Ave., Dayton, OH 45402.
- National Conference on Energy and the Environment. Proceedings. irreg. (American Institute of Chemical Engineers. Dayton & Ohio Valley Sections)
- Nexus. 3 per yr.

**Wright State University. College of Education**
Dayton, OH 45431.
- Ohio English Bulletin. q.

**Wright State University. English Department**
Dayton, OH 45431.
- Images. 3 per yr.

**Write on Publishing House, Inc.**
2025 York St., Denver, CO 80206.
- Mountain Gazette. m.

**Writer, Inc.**
8 Arlington St., Boston, MA 02116.
- Writer. m. ISSN 0043-9517
- Writer's Handbook. a. ISSN 0084-2710

**Writers Digest**
9933 Alliance Rd., Cincinnati, OH 45242.
- Artists' Market. a. ISSN 0361-607X
- Writer's Market. (pub. by F & W Publishing Corp.)
- Writer's Yearbook. (pub. by F & W Publishing Corp.)

**Writers Guild of America, East**
22 W. 48th St., New York, NY 10036.
- Writers Guild of America, East. Newsletter. m.

**Writers Guild of America, West**
8955 Beverly Blvd., Los Angeles, CA 90048.
- Writers Guild of America/West. Newsletter. m. ISSN 0043-9533

**Writers' Resources**
12 Cooney St., Somerville, MA 02143.
- Writers' Resources. bi-m.

**Wyandotte General Hospital**
2333 Biddle Ave., Wyandotte, MI 48192.
- Capsule. bi-m.

**Wycliffe Bible Translators, Inc.**
19891 Beach Blvd., Huntington Beach, CA 92648.
- In Other Words. m.
- Notes on Translation. (pub. by Academic Publications)

**Wyoming. Archives and Historical Department**
Barrett Bldg., Cheyenne, WY 82002.
- Annals of Wyoming. s-a. ISSN 0003-4991
- Wyoming History News. bi-m. ISSN 0043-972X

**Wyoming. Department of Administration and Fiscal Control. Research and Statistics Division**
302 Emerson Building, Cheyenne, WY 82002.
- Wyoming. State of Wyoming Annual Report. a.
- Wyoming Data Handbook. biennial.

**Wyoming. Department of Economic Planning and Development**
Barrett Bldg., Cheyenne, WY 82002.
- Wyoming Progress Reports. m. ISSN 0043-9762

**Wyoming. Department of Education**
Cheyenne, WY 82001.
- Guidance in Wyoming Schools. irreg. ISSN 0097-9201 (prep. by its Office of School Pupil Services)
- Wyoming Adult Education. Adult Education Plan. a. ISSN 0361-2171
- Wyoming Educator. m.(Sept.-May) ISSN 0043-969X

**Wyoming. Department of Environmental Quality**
Cheyenne, WY 82001.
- Wyoming. Department of Environmental Quality. Annual Report. a. ISSN 0099-1279
- Wyoming. Water Quality Division. Wyoming State Plan. irreg. ISSN 0098-0846 (prep. by its Water Quality Division)

**Wyoming. Department of Health and Social Services**
Cheyenne, WY 82001.
- Wyoming. Department of Health and Social Services. Annual Report. a. ISSN 0098-6984

**Wyoming. Department of Labor and Statistics**
304 Capitol Building, Cheyenne, WY 82001.
- Wyoming. Department of Labor and Statistics. Survey of Occupational Injuries and Illnesses. a.

**Wyoming. Department of Revenue and Taxation**
220 Carey Ave., Cheyenne, WY 82002.
- Wyoming. Department of Revenue and Taxation. Annual Report. a. ISSN 0094-9019

**Wyoming. Division of Educational Data Systems and Statistical Service**
Cheyenne, WY 82002.
- Wyoming. Division of Education Data Systems and Statistical Services. Wyoming Public Schools: General Fund Accounting. a.

**Wyoming. Division of Planning, Evaluation and Information Services**
Cheyenne, WY 82001.
- Wyoming. Division of Planning, Evaluation and Information Services. Statistical Report Series. irreg. ISSN 0093-5530

**Wyoming. Division of Public Assistance and Social Services**
State Office Building, Central Ave., Cheyenne, WY 82001.
- Wyoming. Division of Public Assistance and Social Services. Quarterly Statistical Report. q.

**Wyoming. Employment Security Commission**
Box 2760, Casper, WY 82601.
- Wyoming Employment Outlook. m. ISSN 0043-9703

**Wyoming. Employment Security Commission. Research and Analysis Section**
Casper, Box 2760, WY 82601.
- Wyoming. Employment Security Commission. Research and Analysis Section. Farm Labor Report. a. ISSN 0095-389X
- Wyoming Area Manpower Review. s-a. ISSN 0097-739X

**Wyoming. Game and Fish Department**
Cheyenne, WY 82002.
- Wyoming. Game and Fish Commission. Bulletin. irreg.
- Wyoming Wildlife. m. ISSN 0043-9819

**Wyoming. Geological Survey**
University of Wyoming, Box 3008, University Sta., Laramie, WY 82070.
- Wyoming. Geological Survey. Bulletin. irreg.

**Wyoming. Governor's Office of Highway Safety**
Cheyenne, WY 82001.
- Wyoming. Governor's Office of Highway Safety. Annual Report. a. ISSN 0098-5058

**Wyoming. Recreation Commission**
604 E. 25th, Cheyenne, WY 82002.
- Wyoming. Recreation Commission. Annual Report. a. ISSN 0085-8323

**Wyoming. State Library**
Supreme Court Bldg., Cheyenne, WY 82002.
- Outrider. m. ISSN 0030-7319
- Wyoming Library Roundup. q. ISSN 0043-9738

**Wyoming Congress of Parents and Teachers**
183 El Rancho Dr., Rawlins, WY 82301.
- Wyoming P T A News. 4 per yr. ISSN 0043-9754

**Wyoming Education Association**
115 E. 22nd St., Cheyenne, WY 82001.
- Wyoming Education News. m.(Sept-May) ISSN 0043-9681

**Wyoming Farm Bureau Federation**
406 South 21st St., Box 1348, Laramie, WY 82070.
- Wyoming Agriculture. m (Jul.-Aug. combined)

**Wyoming Geological Association**
Box 545, Casper, WY 82601.
- Earth Science Bulletin. q. ISSN 0012-8236
- Wyoming Geological Association. Guidebook, Annual Field Conference. a. (Dist. by: Petroleum Info Corp)
- Wyoming Geological Association. Publications. irreg.

**Wyoming Nurses Association**
Seminoedam, WY 82333.
- Wyoming Nurse. irreg.

**Wyoming School Board Association**
Box 3274, University Station, Laramie, WY 82071.
- Wyoming School Boards Bulletin. bi-m. ISSN 0043-9789

**Wyoming State Medical Society**
Box 4009, Cheyenne, WY 82001.
- Medical Wire. q.

**Wyoming State Rural Electric Association**
301 Pacific Western Bldg., Casper, WY 82601.
- Wyoming Rural Electric News. m. ISSN 0043-9770

**Wyoming Stock Growers Association**
Box 206, Cheyenne, WY 82001.
- Cow Country. m.

**Wyoming Stockman-Farmer Publishing Co.**
110 E. 17th St., Cheyenne, WY 82001.
- Wyoming Stockman Farmer. m. ISSN 0043-9800

**Wyoming Wool Growers Association**
Box 115, 300 North Center, Casper, WY 82601.
- Wyoming Wool Grower. m. ISSN 0043-9827

**Wyrd Publications**
324 Candy Lane, Santa Rosa, CA 95401.
- Wyrd.

**Wythe County Historical Review**
245 S. 10th St., Wytheville, VA 24382.
- Wythe County Historical Review. q.

**Xaverian Brothers**
St. Joseph Province, Danvers, MA 01923.
- Working for Boys. q. ISSN 0043-8103

**Xaverian Missionary Fathers**
101 Summer St., Holliston, MA 01746.
- Xaverian Missions Newsletter. 9 per yr.

**Xavier Society for the Blind**
154 E. 23rd St., New York, NY 10010.
- Catholic Review (New York) 11 per yr. ISSN 0008-8323

**Xavier University**
c/o Ed. Dr. Vytautas Bieliauskas, Psychology Dept., Cincinnati, OH 45207.
- P I R I Newsletter. (Psychologists Interested in Religious Issues) q.

**Xavier University of Louisiana**
New Orleans, LA 70125.
- Xavier University Studies; journal of critical and creative scholarship. 2 per yr. ISSN 0043-9894

**Xerox Corporation**
Xerox Square 021, Rochester, CT 06904.
- Xerox Disclosure Journal. bi-m. ISSN 0361-4190
- Xerox World. m.

**Xerox Education Publications**
1250 Fairwood Ave., Columbus, OH 43216.
- Bubblegum Gazette. w.(during summer vacation)
- Current Events (Braille Edition) w.
- Current Events (Inkprint Edition) fortn. ISSN 0011-3492
- Current Science (Braille Edition); for students in junior high classes, grades 7-9. fortn.
- Current Science (Inkprint Edition); for students in junior high classes, grades 7-9. fortn. ISSN 0011-3905
- Jellybean Jamboree. w.(during summer vacation)
- Know Your World. 28 per yr. ISSN 0023-2483
- My Weekly Reader (Grades 5-6 edition) 28 per yr.
- My Weekly Reader (Kindergarten-4th grade edition) 28 per yr.
- O P T: the Magazine on People and Things Teacher's Edition. s-m. (Subscr. to: Xerox Education Center, 1250 Fairwood Ave., Columbus, OH 43216)
- Peppermint Press. w.(during summer vacation)
- Read Magazine. fortn. ISSN 0034-0359
- You and Your World. 28 per yr. ISSN 0044-068X

**Xi Psi Phi Fraternity**
1005 E. Main St., Suite 7, Medford, OR 97501.
- Xi Psi Phi Quarterly. q. ISSN 0049-8262

**Yacht Racing**
c/o Knowles L. Pittman, 143 Rowayton Ave., Rowayton, CT 06853.
- Yacht Racing. m.

**Yachting Publishing Corporation**
50 W. 44 St., New York, NY 10036.
- Boat Owner's Buyers Guide. a. ISSN 0067-9321
- Yachting; power and sail. m. ISSN 0043-9940

**Yakima Tribe**
Box 386, Toppenish, WA 98948.
- Yakima Nation Review. bi-m.

**Richard B. Yale**
2626 San Diego Ave., San Diego, CA 92110.
- Butterfield Express. m. ISSN 0007-7283

**Yale Alumni Publications**
149 York St., New Haven, CT 06509.
- Yale Alumni Magazine. m. ISSN 0044-0051

**Yale Banner Publications**
243-A Yale Sta., New Haven, CT 06520.
- Yale Lit. 5 per yr.

**Yale Forestry Alumni Association**
- Yale Forest School News. (pub. by Yale University. School of Forestry)

**Yale Law Journal Co., Inc.**
401-A Yale Sta., New Haven, CT 06520.
- Yale Law Journal. 8 per yr. ISSN 0044-0094

**Yale Law Library**
Yale Law School, New Haven, CT 06520.
- Yale Law Library. Selected Acquisitions. 9 per yr.

**Yale Scientific Publications, Inc.**
244-A Yale Sta., New Haven, CT 06520.
- Yale Scientific Magazine. m.(Oct-May) ISSN 0044-0140 (Yale University)

**Yale Speleological Society**
2027 Yale Station, New Haven, CT 06520.
- Yale Speleological Society. Journal. 2 per yr. ISSN 0044-0159

**Yale Studies in World Public Order,Inc.**
Box 2102,Yale Station, New Haven, CT 06520.
- Yale Studies in World Public Order. s-a.

**Yale University**
323 W.L. Harkness Hall, New Haven, CT 06520.
- Excavations at Dura-Europos. (pub. by J. J. Augustin, Inc.)
- Yale French Studies. s-a. ISSN 0044-0078
- Yale Journal of Biology and Medicine. (pub. by Neale Watson Academic Publications, Inc.)
- Yale Review. q. ISSN 0044-0124 (Ed. Office: 28 Hillhouse Ave., New Haven, CT 06520)
- Yale Scientific Magazine. (pub. by Yale Scientific Publications, Inc.)

**Yale University. Afro- American Cultural Center**
211 Park St., New Haven, CT 06520.
- Renaissance Two; Journal of Afro-American Studies. q.

**Yale University Art Gallery**
New Haven, CT 06520.
- Yale University Art Gallery. Bulletin. irreg. ISSN 0084-3539

**Yale University. Department of Anthropology**
New Haven, CT 06502.
- Yale University. Department of Anthropology. Publications in Anthropology. irreg.

**Yale University. Department of Music**
- Collegium Musicum: Yale University. (pub. by A-R Editions, Inc.)

**Yale University. Economic Growth Center**
Box 1987, Yale Station, New Haven, CT 06520.
- Yale University. Economic Growth Center. Report. triennial. ISSN 0084-3547

**Yale University Library**
New Haven, CT 06520.
- Bibliographical Series from the Yale University Library Collections. irreg.
- Western Historical Series. irreg. ISSN 0513-1545
- Yale University Library Gazette. q. ISSN 0044-0175

**Yale University Press**
92 A Yale Station, New Haven, CT 06520.
- American Academy of Child Psychiatry. Journal. q. ISSN 0002-7138 (American Academy of Child Psychiatry)
- Caribbean Series. irreg., no. 15, 1975. ISSN 0069-0538
- Cowles Foundation for Research in Economics at Yale University. Monographs. irreg.,no. 25, 1975. ISSN 0084-9413
- Elizabethan Club Series. irreg., 1972, no. 5. ISSN 0085-0225
- James K. Whittemore Lectures in Mathematics Given at Yale University. irreg., latest 1974.
- Psychiatry and the Humanities. a. ISSN 0363-8952 (Washington School of Psychiatry. Forum on Psychiatry and the Humanities)
- Studies in British Art. irreg; latest, 1976.
- Thomas More Lectures. irreg., 1969, no. 3. ISSN 0082-4208
- Yale College Series. irreg; no. 14, 1976. ISSN 0084-3318
- Yale Fastbacks. irreg., no, 18, 1977. ISSN 0084-3326

- Yale Germanic Studies. irreg., no. 6, 1976. ISSN 0084-3334
- Yale Historical Publications (Miscellany) irreg; no. 110, 1976. ISSN 0084-3350
- Yale Judaica Series. irreg., latest issue, 1972. ISSN 0084-3369
- Yale Linguistic Series. irreg; latest, 1976. ISSN 0513-4412
- Yale Linguistic Series: Chinese. irreg; latest, 1975.
- Yale Mathematical Monographs. irreg., no. 6, 1975. ISSN 0084-3377
- Yale Near Eastern Researches. irreg; no. 7, 1977. ISSN 0084-3385
- Yale Oriental Series. Babylonian Texts. irreg., vol. 13, 1972.
- Yale Publications in American Studies. irreg., 1970, no. 20. ISSN 0084-3393
- Yale Publications in Religion. irreg., no. 18, 1974. ISSN 0084-3407
- Yale Publications in the History of Art. irreg., no. 26, 1974. ISSN 0084-3415
- Yale Romanic Studies. Second Series. irreg; no. 26, 1976. ISSN 0084-3423
- Yale Russian and East European Studies. irreg., no. 13, 1977. ISSN 0084-3431
- Yale Scene; University Series. irreg., no. 3, 1974. ISSN 0084-344X
- Yale Series in Economic History. irreg., latest, 1976.
- Yale Series in the Sciences. irreg., latest 1972.
- Yale Series of Younger Poets. irreg; no. 71, 1976. ISSN 0084-3458
- Yale Southeast Asia Studies. irreg., 1970, no. 7. ISSN 0084-3466
- Yale Studies in English. irreg., no. 186, 1975. ISSN 0084-3482
- Yale Studies in Political Science. irreg., no. 26, 1974. ISSN 0084-3490
- Yale Studies in the History of Music. irreg., 1969, no. 5. ISSN 0084-3504
- Yale Studies in the History of Science and Medicine. irreg; no. 11, 1976. ISSN 0084-3512
- Yale Studies of the City. irreg. ISSN 0084-3520
- Yale University. University Series. irreg.
- Yale Western Americana Paperbounds. irreg., 1966, no. 17. ISSN 0084-3555
- Yale Western Americana Series. irreg., no. 28, 1976. ISSN 0084-3563

**Yale University. School of Art**
Department of Graphic Design, 180 York St., New Haven, CT 06520
(Dist. by George Wittenborn, Inc., 1018 Madison Ave., New York, N.Y. 10021)
- Still: Yale Photography Annual. a. ISSN 0081-5586

**Yale University. School of Drama**
Box 2046, Yale Sta., New Haven, CT 06520.
- Yale/Theatre. 3 per yr. ISSN 0044-0167

**Yale University. School of Forestry**
205 Prospect St., New Haven, CT 06511.
- Yale Forest School News. s-a. (Yale Forestry Alumni Association)
- Yale University. School of Forestry. Bulletin. irreg.

**Yale University. School of Law**
New Haven, CT 06520.
- Yale Law School Studies. irreg. ISSN 0513-1405

**Yale University. School of Medicine**
333 Cedar St., New Haven, CT 06510.
- Yale Medicine; alumni bulletin. 3 per yr. ISSN 0044-0116

**Yale University School of Medicine. Department of Microbiology**
310 Cedar St., New Haven, CT 06510.
- Neurospora Newsletter. a. ISSN 0028-3975

**Yale University. School of Music**
New Haven, CT 06520.
- Journal of Music Theory. s-a. ISSN 0022-2909

**Yale University. Sears Foundation for Marine Research**
Box 2025 Yale Sta., New Haven, CT 06520.
- Sears Foundation for Marine Research. Memoirs. irreg.

**Yale University. Southeast Asia Studies**
77 Prospect St., New Haven, CT 06520
- Yale Southeast Asia Studies. Monograph Series. irreg. ISSN 0513-4501 (Dist. by: Cellar Book Shop, 18090 Wyoming, Detroit, MI 48221)

**Yamaha International Corp.**
6600 Orangethorpe Ave., Buena Park, CA 90620.
- Music Notes. irreg.

**Yankee Gardener**
10 Rumford Park Ave., Woburn, MA 01801.
- Yankee Gardener. m.

**Yankee, Inc.**
Dublin, NH 03444.
- New Englander. m. ISSN 0028-4947
- Old Farmer's Almanac. a. ISSN 0078-4516
- Yankee. m. ISSN 0044-0191
- Yankee Guide to the New England Countryside. s-a.

**Yankee Milk Inc.**
100 Milk Lane, Newington, CT 06111.
- Yankeemilk News. m.

**Yanks Abroad**
c/o Myron Kandel, 200 W. 57 St., New York, NY 10019.
- Yanks Abroad. m.

**Yardage Publications**
Box 528, Georgetown, CT 06829.
- Yardage; the monthly report on textile selling. m. ISSN 0044-0221

**Yardbird Pub. Cooperative**
Box 2370, Station A, Berkeley, CA 94701.
- Yardbird Reader. ISSN 0093-6103

**Yavneh**
156 5th Ave., 11th Floor, New York, NY 10010.
- Kol Yavneh. q.
- Yavneh Studies. 5-10 per yr. ISSN 0044-0256

**Ye Olde Genealogie Shoppe**
c/o Walter Gooldy, 9430 Vandergriff Rd., Indianapolis, IN 46239.
- Gooldy Grapevine. s-a.

**Year, Inc.**
Box 380, Petaluma, CA 94952.
- News Front; the management trends magazine. bi-m. ISSN 0028-9191
- Year: the World In... a. ISSN 0084-3571

**Year Book Medical Publishers, Inc.**
35 E. Wacker Dr., Chicago, IL 60601.
- Advances in Internal Medicine. a. ISSN 0065-2822
- Advances in Nephrology from the Necker Hospital. a. ISSN 0084-5957
- Advances in Pediatrics. a. ISSN 0065-3101
- Advances in Surgery. a. ISSN 0065-3411
- Clinical Conference on Cancer. Papers. a. ISSN 0069-4800 (University of Texas. M.D. Anderson Hospital and Tumor Institute) (Co-Sponsors: Tumor Institute, Houston; University of Texas Graduate School of Biomedical Sciences)
- Current Problems in Diagnostic Radiology. bi-m.
- Current Problems in Pediatrics/C P P. m. ISSN 0045-9380
- Current Problems in Surgery. m. ISSN 0011-3840
- D M/Disease-A-Month. m. ISSN 0011-5029
- Year Book Color Atlas Series. irreg.
- Year Book of Anesthesia. a. ISSN 0084-3652
- Year Book of Cancer. a. ISSN 0084-3679
- Yearbook of Cardiology. a.
- Year Book of Dentistry. a. ISSN 0084-3717
- Year Book of Dermatology. a. ISSN 0084-3725
- Year Book of Diagnostic Radiology. a. ISSN 0098-1672
- Year Book of Drug Therapy. a. ISSN 0084-3733
- Year Book of Endocrinology. a. ISSN 0084-3741
- Year Book of Medicine. a. ISSN 0084-3873
- Year Book of Nuclear Medicine. a. ISSN 0084-3903
- Year Book of Obstetrics and Gynecology. a. ISSN 0084-3911
- Year Book of Ophthalmology. a. ISSN 0084-392X
- Year Book of Orthopedics and Traumatic Surgery. a. ISSN 0084-3938
- Year Book of Pathology and Clinical Pathology. a. ISSN 0084-3946
- Year Book of Pediatrics. a. ISSN 0084-3954
- Year Book of Plastic and Reconstructive Surgery. a. ISSN 0084-3962
- Year Book of Psychiatry and Applied Mental Health. a. ISSN 0084-3970
- Year Book of Surgery. a. ISSN 0090-3671

- Year Book of the Ear, Nose and Throat. a. ISSN 0084-4055
- Year Book of Urology. a. ISSN 0084-4071

**Years Press**
ATL EBH, Michigan State University, East Lansing, MI 48824.
- Centering. irreg.

**Yellow Press, Inc.**
2394 Blue Island, Chicago, IL 60608.
- Milk Quarterly. irreg.

**Yellow Seed Center**
1006 Winter St., Philadelphia, PA 19107.
- Yellow Seeds. m.

**Yerkes Regional Primate Research Center**
Emory Univ., Atlanta, GA 30322.
- Yerkes Regional Primate Research Center. Newsletter. irreg. ISSN 0084-4179

**Yeshiva University**
500 W. 185 St, New York, NY 10033.
- Hamevaser. m. ISSN 0017-7040
- Studies in Judaica. irreg., vol. 6, 1975. ISSN 0585-6833

**Yeshiva University. Albert Einstein College of Medicine**
Dept of Anatomy, Eastchester Rd. & Morris Park Ave., Bronx, NY 10461.
- Bibliographia Neuroendocrinologica. q. ISSN 0006-1247

**Yeshiva University. Belfer Graduate School of Science**
- Yeshiva University, New York. Belfer Graduate School of Science. Annual Science Conference Proceedings. (pub. by Academic Press, Inc)

**Yeshiva University. Sephardic Studies Program**
500 W. 185 St., New York, NY 10033.
- American Sephardi. s-a. ISSN 0003-102X
- Sephardic Scholar. a. (American Society of Sephardic Studies)
- Yeshiva University Sephardic Bulletin. q.

**Yeshiva University. Wurzweiler School of Social Work**
55 Fifth Ave., New York, NY 10003.
- Jewish Social Work Forum. a. ISSN 0021-6712 (prep. by its Alumni Association)

**Yeshiva University. Yeshiva College Student Council**
500 W. 185th St., New York, NY 10033.
- Commentator. bi-w.(Sept.-June) ISSN 0010-2652
- Tempo. s-a. ISSN 0040-3008

**Michael Yessis, Ed. & Pub.**
Dept. of Physical Education, California State University, Fullerton, 800 North State College Blvd., Fullerton, CA 92634.
- Yessis Review of Soviet Physical Education and Sports. q. ISSN 0513-5389

**Yid Pub Association**
260 Broadway, Brooklyn, NY 11211.
- Yid; voice of the American Orthodox jewry. bi-w. ISSN 0044-040X

**Yiddisher Kultur Farband Inc.**
80 Fifth Ave., New York, NY 10011.
- Yiddishe Kultur. 10 per yr. ISSN 0044-0426

**YIVO Institute for Jewish Research**
1048 Fifth Ave., New York, NY 10028.
- Guides to Jewish Subjects in Social and Humanistic Research; doctoral dissertations and master's theses accepted by American institutions of higher learning. a. ISSN 0533-5620
- News of the Yivo. q. ISSN 0028-9302
- Recent Additions to the YIVO Collections. 3 per yr. (prep. by its Library and Archives)
- Yidishe Shprakh/Yiddish Language. a. ISSN 0044-0442
- Yivo Annual of Jewish Social Science. irreg; vol. 16, 1976. ISSN 0084-4209
- Yivo Bleter/Yivo Pages. irreg; vol. 45, 1975. ISSN 0084-4217

**YIVO Institute for Jewish Research. Max Weinreich Center for Advanced Jewish Studies**
1048 Fifth Ave., New York, NY 10028.
- Working Papers in Yiddish and East European Jewish Studies/In Gang Fun Arbet: Yidish Un Mizrakh Eyropeishe Yidishe Shtudies. m.

**John W. Yopp Publications, Inc.**
770 Spring St., N.W., Atlanta, GA 30308.
- Refrigeration. m. ISSN 0034-3137
- Southern Cemetery. bi-m. ISSN 0038-397X
- Southern Funeral Director; a business and professional journal devoted to the interests of funeral directors in the South and Southwest. m. ISSN 0038-4135

**York Barbell Co**
- Strength & Health Magazine. (pub. by Strength & Health Publishing Co.)

**York College. Department of Foreign Languages**
Jamaica, NY 11451.
- Bilingual Review/Revista Bilingue; a journal dedicated to the study of the linguistics and literature of the English-Spanish bilingualism in the United States. 3 per yr. ISSN 0094-5366

**York Research Publishing Co.**
Box 4671, Springdale, CT 06907.
- Science News Reporter. bi-m. ISSN 0036-8431

**York Rite Publishing Co.**
Box 529, 305 W. 12th St., Trenton, MO 64683.
- Royal Arch Mason. q. ISSN 0035-8649 (Royal Arch Masons, General Grand Chapter)

**Yorke Medical Group**
- Cutis. (pub. by Dun-Donnelley Publishing Corp.)

**Yorktown Printing & Pennysaver Corp.**
c/o John W. Chase, 1761 Front St., Yorktown Heights, NY 10598.
- Pennysaver. w.

**Thomas Yoseloff, Inc.**
c/o A. S. Barnes & Co., Inc., Box 421, Cranbury, NJ 08512.
- Bucknell Review; a scholarly journal of letters, arts and science. 2 per yr. ISSN 0007-2869
- International Photography Yearbook. a. ISSN 0074-736X (A.S. Barnes and Co., Inc.)

**You: the Quest**
Dept Y, P.O. Box 281, Kansas City, MO 64141.
- You: the Quest. s-m.

**J.R. Young**
Box 4189, Station B, Anderson, SC 29621.
- Safety Journal. bi-m. ISSN 0036-2506

**Young Adult Alternative Newsletter**
c/o Carol Starr, Ed., 37167 Mission Blvd., Fremont, CA 94536.
- Young Adult Alternative Newsletter. irreg.; latest issue, 1975.

**Arthur Young & Co.**
277 Park Ave., New York, NY 10017.
- Arthur Young Journal. 3 per yr. ISSN 0004-3613

**Young Athlete Enterprises**
Box 513, Edmonds, WA 98020.
- Young Athlete. bi-m. (Subscr. to: Box 246, Mount Morris, IL 61054)

**Young Calvinist Federation**
Box 7244, 1333 Alger S.E., Grand Rapids, MI 49510.
- Insight (Grand Rapids) 10 per yr. ISSN 0020-1928

**Young Communication**
51 Mountain Ave., Larchmont, NY 10538.
- Tube Talk; a children's guide to the best in television. m.

**Young-Conway Publications, Inc.**
347 Madison Ave., New York, NY 10017.
- Food & Equipment Product News. 9 per yr. ISSN 0015-6280

**Young-Conway Publishing Co**
5455 Wilshire Blvd. Ste. 711, Los Angeles, CA 90036.
- Western Foodservice. 12 per yr.

**James Dean Young, Ed. & Pub.**
c/o Georgia Institute of Technology, Department of English, Atlanta, GA 30332.
- Critique: Studies in Modern Fiction. 3 per yr. ISSN 0011-1619

**Young Lords Party**
352 Willis Ave, Bronx, NY 10454.
- Palante; Latin revolutionary news service. s-m. ISSN 0031-0271

**Young Men's and Young Women's Hebrew Association of New York**
1393 Lexington Ave., New York, NY 10028.
- Y Bulletin. bi-m.

**Young Men's Institute**
50 Oak St., San Francisco, CA 94102.
- Young Men's Institute. Institute Journal. bi-m. ISSN 0020-2673

**Young People's Socialist League**
112 East 19th St., New York, NY 10003.
- Social Democrat. q.

**Young Scientists of America Foundation, Inc.**
Box 9066, Phoenix, AZ 85068.
- Young Engineer & Scientist; the science youth magazine. q.(during school year) ISSN 0044-0752

**Young Socialist Alliance**
Box 471 Cooper Station, New York, NY 10003.
- Young Socialist. m.

**Young Way Publishing**
Box 27183, Honolulu, HI 96817.
- Sandwich Isles Gazette. w. during summer.

**Young Women's Christian Association**
600 Lexington Ave., New York, NY 10022.
- Y W C A Interchange. 7 per yr.
- Young Women's Christian Association. National Board. Report. a. (prep. by its National Board)
- Young Women's Christian Association of the United States of America. The Printout. a. ISSN 0084-4306 (prep. by its National Board)

**Your Story Magazine**
c/o Ed. James G. O'Brien, 131 Hammell Place, Maywood, NJ 07607.
- Your Story Magazine. bi-m.

**Your Tomorrow**
8742 Buffalo Ave., Niagara Falls, NY 14304.
- Your Tomorrow. m.

**Youth Correctional Institution**
Bordentown, NJ 08505.
- Youth Correctional Institution, Bordentown, N.J. Annual Report. a. ISSN 0092-4539

**Youth for Christ International**
Box 419, Wheaton, IL 60187.
- Campus Life. m. ISSN 0008-2538

**Youth Institute for Peace in the Middle East**
275 7th Ave., 25th Fl., New York, NY 10001.
- Crossroads. m. ISSN 0011-2054

**Youth International Party**
9 Bleeker St., New York, NY 10012.
- Yipster Times. irreg.(3-4 per yr)

**Youth Liberation Press, Inc.**
2007 Washtenaw Ave., Ann Arbor, MI 48104.
- F P S: a Magazine of Young People's Liberation. q.

**Youth Organization for Black Unity**
Box 2413, Washington, DC 20013.
- African World. m. ISSN 0044-6637

**Youth Specialties**
861 Sixth Ave., Suite 411, San Diego, CA 92101.
- Wittenburg Door. bi-m.

**Youthways Corporation**
34 W. Putnam Ave., Greenwich, CT 06830.
- Flip. m. ISSN 0015-3745

**Yugntruf**
3328 Bainbridge Ave., New York, NY 10467.
- Yugntruf; yiddish student quarterly. q.

**Yugoslav Information Center**
488 Madison Ave., New York, NY 10022.
- Yugoslav Facts and Views. m. ISSN 0427-8968

**Z Press, Inc.**
c/o Ken Ward Elmslie, Ed., Calais, VT 05648.
- Z. s-a.

**David Zackin**
95 N. Main St., Waterbury, CT 06702.
- Drycleaners News. m. ISSN 0012-6802
- Northeast Outdoors. m.

**Zeirei Agudath Israel of America**
5 Beekman St., New York, NY 10038.
- Zeirei Forum. irreg.

**Zeitgeist, Inc.**
Box 595, Saugatuck, MI 49453.
- Zeitgeist. q. ISSN 0044-2119

**Zen Center (Rochester)**
7 Arnold Park, Rochester, NY 14607.
- Zen Bow. q. ISSN 0044-3956

**Zen Center (San Francisco)**
300 Page St., San Francisco, CA 94102.
- Wind Bell. 3 per yr. ISSN 0043-5708

**Zen Center of Los Angeles**
927 S. Normandie Ave., Los Angeles, CA 90006.
- Z.C.L.A. Journal. 3 per yr. ISSN 0360-991X

**Zephyros**
1201 Stanyan St., San Francisco, CA 94117.
- Zephyros. s-a.

**Zero Population Growth, Inc.**
1346 Connecticut Ave. N.W., Washington, DC 20036.
- Z P G National Reporter. 10 per yr. ISSN 0049-8718

**Zetetic Press**
P.O. Box 6, Folsom, CA 95630.
- Unfold. irreg.

**Zetlan Picture Libraries**
Summit Ave., Central Valley, NY 10917.
- Colonial Life Picture Library. m.

**Zeugma**
22 Jeanette Ave., Belmont, MA 02178.
- Zeugma. q.

**Zien Enterprises, Inc.**
606 W. Wisconsin Ave., Milwaukee, WI 53203.
- Wisconsin Beverage Journal. m. ISSN 0043-6399

**Ziff-Davis Publishing Co.**
1 Park Ave., New York, NY 10016
- Aerospace Daily. 5 per wk.
- Boating. m. ISSN 0006-5374
- Business and Commercial Aviation. m. ISSN 0007-6570
- Business Aviation; the weekly of business aviation. w. ISSN 0045-3617
- Car and Driver. m. ISSN 0008-6002
- Car and Driver Buyers Guide. a.
- Color Photography. a. ISSN 0069-5998
- Communications Handbook. a. ISSN 0069-777X
- Cycle. m.
- Cycle Buyers Guide. a. ISSN 0070-2277
- Electronic Experimenter's Handbook. a.
- Flying. m. ISSN 0015-4806
- Flying Annual and Pilot' Buying Guide. a.
(Dist. by Sportshelf, P.O. Box 634, New Rochelle, N.Y. 10802)
- Hotel and Travel Index; the world wide hotel directory. q. ISSN 0018-6112
- Invitation to Photography. s-a. ISSN 0075-0301
- Meetings and Conventions. m. ISSN 0025-8652
- Modern Bride; a complete guide for the bride to be. bi-m. ISSN 0026-7546
- Official Hotel & Resort Guide. 10 per yr.
- Photography Annual. a. ISSN 0079-1849
- Photography Directory and Buying Guide. a. ISSN 0079-1857
- Photomethods. m.
- Popular Electronics. m. ISSN 0032-4485
- Popular Photography. m. ISSN 0032-4582
- Psychology Today. m. ISSN 0033-3107
- Skiing. 7 per yr.(Sept-Mar) ISSN 0037-6264
- Skiing Trade News. s-a. ISSN 0037-6299
- Stereo Directory & Buying Guide. a. ISSN 0090-6786
- Stereo Review. m. ISSN 0039-1220
- Tape Recording & Buying Guide. a. ISSN 0082-1691
- Thirty Five M.M. Photography. 3 per yr.
- Travel Weekly. s-w. ISSN 0041-2082
- World Aviation Directory. s-a. ISSN 0043-826X

**Ziff-Davis Publishing Co. Public Transportation and Travel Division**
1 Park Ave., New York, NY 10016.
- Aviation Daily. 5 per w.
- Aviation Daily's Airline Statistical Annual. a. ISSN 0092-2862
- Official Meeting Facilities Guide. ISSN 0094-5242

**Zim-Mer Trade Publications, Inc.**
6 Harrison St., New York, NY 10013.
- Produce News. w. ISSN 0032-969X

**Harold O. Zimman, Inc.**
156 Broad St., Lynn, MA 01901.
- United States Lawn Tennis Association. Yearbook. a. ISSN 0083-1557

**Donald R. & Robert H. Zimmer, Eds. & Pubs.**
Box 118, Pierce, NE 68767.
- Iowa Smoke-Eater. m.

**Toni Ortner Zimmerman, Ed. & Pub.**
Bell Hollow Rd., Putnam Valley, NY 10579.
- Connections. s-a.

**Zionist Organization of America**
4 E. 34th St., New York, NY 10016.
- American Zionist. m.(except July and Aug) ISSN 0003-1550

**Zionist Organization of America. Masada Youth Movement**
Z. O. A. House, 4 E. 34th St., New York, NY 10016.
- Ayin l'Tzion. 5 per yr.

**Zondervan Publishing House**
1415 Lake Drive S.E., Grand Rapids, MI 49506.
- Rozell'S Complete Lessons. a. ISSN 0080-4746
- Zondervan Pastor's Annual. a. ISSN 0084-5558

**Zoological Society of San Diego**
Box 551, San Diego, CA 92112.
- Zoonooz. m. ISSN 0044-5282

**Mike Zotti**
P.O. Box 89, Barton, FL 33830.
- Citrus World. m. ISSN 0009-7608 (Lake Region Publishing Corp.)

**Gerald A. Zucker**
Box 11597, Philadelphia, PA 19116.
- Advisor Suburban. w.
- Advisor: West. w.

**Zulch and Zulch, Inc.**
P.O. Box 4427, Sylmar, CA 91342.
- Big Book of Metalworking Machinery. irreg. ISSN 0045-1983

**3M National Ad. Co.**
1700 Walnut St., Philadelphia, PA 19103.
- Where; a Travelaide publication. w.

**8 X 10 Art Portfolios**
Box 363, New York, NY 10013.
- 8 X 10 Art Portfolios. irreg.

**13th Moon, Inc.**
Box 3, Inwood Sta., New York, NY 10034.
- 13th Moon. s-a. ISSN 0094-3320

**20th Century Christian, Inc.**
2809 Granny White Pike, Nashville, TN 37204.
- Power for Today. bi-m. ISSN 0032-6011
- 20th Century Christian. m.

**21st Century Communications, Inc.**
635 Madison Ave., New York, NY 10022.
- Best of National Lampoon. irreg. ISSN 0092-5306

**73 Inc.**
Peterborough, NH 03458.
- Seventy-Three; Amateur Radio. m. ISSN 0037-3036

**100 Flowers Bookstore**
186 Hampshire St., Cambridge, MA 02139.
- 100 Flowers Re-View. bi-m.

**613 Magazine**
Box 168, 530 Ave. R., Brooklyn, NY 11223.
- 613 Magazine. 10 per yr.

# UPPER VOLTA

**Centre Voltaique de la Recherche Scientifique**
B.P. 6, Ouagadougou, Upper Volta.
- Etudes Voltaiques. irreg (approx. 1 per yr.)
- Notes et Documents Voltaiques; bulletin trimestriel d'information scientifique. q. ISSN 0550-0923
- Recherches Voltaiques; collection de travaux de sciences humaines sur la Haute-Volta. irreg. ISSN 0486-1426

**Chambre de Commerce, d'Agriculture et d'Industrie de Haute-Volta**
Box 502, Ouagadougou, Upper Volta.
- Courrier Consulaire de la Haute Volta. m. ISSN 0574-3370

**Comite Interafricain d'Etudes Hydrauliques**
*see* Interafricain Committee for Hydraulic Studies

**Communaute Economique du Betail et de la Viande**
Secretariat, Ouagadougou, Upper Volta.
- C E B V. irreg.

**Instituteurs et Animateurs de Haute-Volta**
B.D.604, Ouagadougou, Upper Volta.
- Action Culture Reflexion. m.

**Interafrican Committee for Hydraulic Studies**
B.P. 369, Ouagadougou, Upper Volta.
- Interafrican Committee for Hydraulic Studies. Liaison Bulletin. q.

**Mouvement de Liberation Nationale**
B.P. 606, Ouagadougou, Upper Volta.
- Ecclaire. bi-m. ISSN 0046-1032

**Soleil de Haute-Volta.**
B.P. 1095, Ave. de la Liberte, Ouagadougou, Upper Volta.
- Soleil de Haute-Volta. w.

**Upper Volta. Comite de Coordination du Developpement Rural**
Secretariat Permanent, B.P. 7007, Ouagadougou, Upper Volta.
- Essor Rural; bulletin de liaison et d'information technique et professionnelle. m.

**Upper Volta. Direction de l'Hydraulique et de l'Equipement Rural. Service I.R.H.**
Ministere du Plan, du Developpement Rural, de l'Environnement et du Tourisme, Ouagadougou, Upper Volta.
- Upper Volta. Direction de l'Hydraulique et de l'Equipement Rural. Service I.R.H. Rapport d'Activites. irreg.

**Upper Volta. Direction des Eaux et Forets et de la Conservation des Sols**
Ouagadougou, Upper Volta.
- Upper Volta. Direction des Eaux et Forets et de la Conservation des Sols. Rapport Annuel. a.

**Upper Volta. Institut National de la Statistique et de la Demographie**
Ouagadougou, Upper Volta.
- Upper Volta. Institut National de la Statistique et de la Demographie. Bulletin Annuaire d'Information Statistique et Economique. a.

**Upper Volta. Service des Statistiques Agricoles**
Ministere du Plan, du Developpement Rural, de l'Environnement et du Tourisme, Ouagadougou, Upper Volta.
- Upper Volta. Service des Statistiques Agricoles. Annuaire. a.

# URUGUAY

**Arca**
Colonia 1263, Montevideo, Uruguay.
- Aqui. irreg. ISSN 0066-5606
- Aves del Arca. irreg. ISSN 0067-2637
- Bolsilibros. irreg. ISSN 0067-9909
- Ensayo y Testimonio. irreg. ISSN 0071-0679
- Grandes Todos. irreg. ISSN 0072-5439
- Narradores de Arca. irreg. ISSN 0077-2801
- Narrativa Latinoamericana. irreg. ISSN 0077-2844
- Poesia. irreg. ISSN 0079-2462
- Politica. irreg. ISSN 0079-3027

- Pupila: Libros de Nuestro Tiempo. irreg. ISSN 0079-8061
- Sociedad Uruguaya. irreg. ISSN 0081-0649

**Asistencia Reciproca Petrolera Estatal Latinoamericana**
Box 1006, Montevideo, Uruguay.
- A R P E L. Boletin Informativo. q.
- A R P E L. Boletin Tecnico. q.

**Asocacion Odontologica Uruguaya**
Av. Agraciada 1464, Piso 13, Montevideo, Uruguay.
- Odontologia Uruguaya. s-a. ISSN 0029-8425

**Asociacion de Bancos del Uruguay**
Rincon 468, Montevideo, Uruguay.
- A E B U. m. ISSN 0001-1010

**Asociacion de Escribanos del Uruguay**
Av. 18 de Julio 1730, Montevideo, Uruguay.
- Asociacion de Escribanos del Uruguay. Revista. bi-m.

**Asociacion Latinoamericana de Armadores**
Rio Negro 1394-Of. 502, Casilla de Correo 767, Montevideo, Uruguay.
- A L A M A R Informativo. w.

**Asociacion Latinoamericana de Libre Comercio**
Oficina de Ventas, Cebollati 1461, Montevideo, Uruguay.
- A L A L C Carta Informativa. bi-m.
- Asociacion Latinoamericana de Libre Comercio. Boletin Bibliografico. irreg. ISSN 0571-3854
- Asociacion Latinoamericana de Libre Comercio. Comercio Exterior Argentina. Exportacion. irreg. ISSN 0571-3870
- Asociacion Latinoamericana de Libre Comercio. Comercio Exterior Argentina. Importacion. irreg. ISSN 0571-3889
- Asociacion Latinoamericana de Libre Comercio. Comercio Exterior Brasil. Exportacion. irreg. ISSN 0571-3897
- Asociacion Latinoamericana de Libre Comercio. Comercio Exterior Brazil. Importacion. irreg. ISSN 0571-3900
- Asociacion Latinoamericana de Libre Comercio. Documentacion A L A L C. irreg. ISSN 0571-3919
- Asociacion Latinoamericana de Libre Comercio. Indice Alfabetico de Mercaderias. irreg. ISSN 0571-3927
- Asociacion Latinoamericana de Libre Comercio. Informe de las Actividades. irreg. ISSN 0518-9519
- Asociacion Latinoamericana de Libre Comercio. Lista Consolidada de Concesiones. irreg. ISSN 0571-3935
- Asociacion Latinoamericana de Libre Comercio. Lista Nacional de Brasil. irreg. ISSN 0571-396X
- Asociacion Latinoamericana de Libre Comercio. Lista Nacional de Chile. irreg. ISSN 0571-3978
- Asociacion Latinoamericana de Libre Comercio. Lista Nacional de Colombia. irreg. ISSN 0571-3986
- Asociacion Latinoamericana de Libre Comercio. Lista Nacional de Ecuador. irreg. ISSN 0571-3994
- Asociacion Latinoamericana de Libre Comercio. Lista Nacional de la Republica Argentina. irreg. ISSN 0571-4001
- Asociacion Latinoamericana de Libre Comercio. Lista Nacional de Mexico. irreg. ISSN 0571-401X
- Asociacion Latinoamericana de Libre Comercio. Lista Nacional de Paraguay. irreg. ISSN 0571-4028
- Asociacion Latinoamericana de Libre Comercio. Lista Nacional de Peru. irreg. ISSN 0571-4036
- Asociacion Latinoamericana de Libre Comercio. Listas de Concesiones Arancelarias para Ecuador y Paraguay. irreg. ISSN 0571-4052
- Asociacion Latinoamericana de Libre Comercio. Serie Estadistica. irreg. ISSN 0571-4079
- Asociacion Latinoamericana de Libre Comercio. Serie Instrumentos. irreg. ISSN 0571-4087
- Boletin de Informacion Comercial. m.
- L A F T A. Newsletter. bi-m. ISSN 0460-1947
- Sintesis. bi-m (with supplements) ISSN 0037-5802

**Asociacion Rural del Uruguay**
Avda. Uruguay 864, Montevideo, Uruguay.
- Asociacion Rural del Uruguay. Revista. s-m. ISSN 0044-9326

**Asociacion Uruguaya de Derecho Internacional**
Montevideo, Uruguay.
- Revista Uruguaya de Derecho Internacional. irreg.

**Banco Central del Uruguay**
Montevideo, Uruguay.
- Banco Central del Uraguay. Departamento de Investigaciones Economicas. Importaciones Cumplidas, Estado Por Pais, Rubro y Subrubro. m.
- Banco Central del Uruguay. Boletin Estadistico Mensual. m. ISSN 0005-4747
- Banco Central del Uruguay. Indicadores de la Actividad Economica-Financiera. irreg.
- Banco Central del Uruguay. Seleccion de Temas Economicos. m. ISSN 0005-4755

**Biblioteca Americana de Autores. Boletin**
Casilla Correo 5033, Montevideo, Uruguay.
- Biblioteca Americana de Autores. Boletin. m. ISSN 0006-162X

**Biblioteca "Jose Artigas"**
25 de Mayo 609, Montevideo, Uruguay.
- Biblioteca "Jose Artigas". Boletin. q. ISSN 0006-1697

**Olaf Blixen, Ed. & Pub.**
P.O. Box 495, Montevideo, Uruguay.
- Moana; Estudios de Antropologia Oceanica. a. ISSN 0076-9770

**Boletin Uruguayo de Sociologia**
Juncal 1395, Casilla de Correo 1122, Montevideo, Uruguay.
- Boletin Uruguayo de Sociologia. 3 per yr. ISSN 0006-6508

**Mario Bon Espasandin, Ed. & Pub.**
Calle Juncal 1395, Piso 2, Escritorio 5, Montevideo, Uruguay.
- Boletin Uruguayo de Sociologia. q. ISSN 0006-6508

**C I N T E R F O R**
*see* **Centro Interamericano de Investigacion y Documentacion Sobre Formacion Profesional**

**Camara de Comercio Uruguayo Britanica**
Av. Agraciada 1641, Montevideo, Uruguay.
- Camara de Comercio Uruguayo-Britanica. Revista. m. ISSN 0008-1914

**Camara de Industrias del Uruguay**
Avda Agraciada 1670, Piso 1, Montevideo, Uruguay.
- Camara de Industrias del Uruguay. Guia de Socios y de Productos. m.

**Centro de Estudios Arqueologicos y Antropologicos Americanos**
Zubillaga 1117, Montevideo, Uruguay.
- Amerindia; revista de prehistoria y etnologia de America. biennial.

**Centro de Estudios y Publicaciones de la Industria y la Produccion**
Vazquez 1429, Montevideo, Uruguay.
- Diccionario de la Produccion y de la Industria. a.

**Centro de Investigacion, Informacion y Difusion de la Joven Poesia Uruguaya**
Avda. Centenario 3923 Ap. 008 Blok.H., Montevideo, Uruguay.
- Torre de los Panoramas. q.

**Centro de Investigaciones Sociales de Montevideo**
- Revista Uruguaya de Ciencias Sociales. (pub. by Libreria Anticuaria Americana)

**Centro Interamericano de Investigacion y Documentacion Sobre Formacion Profesional**
Casilla de Correo 1761, Montevideo, Uruguay (Dist. in U.S. by International Labour Office, Washington Branch Office, 666 11th St., N.W., Washington, D.C. 20001)
- C I N T E R F O R. Estudios y Monografias. irreg. ISSN 0577-2931
- C I N T E R F O R - Documentacion. 3 per yr. ISSN 0577-2915
- Catalogo de Publicaciones Latinoamericanas Sobre Formacion Profesional. a. ISSN 0069-1046
- Centro Interamericano de Investigacion y Documentacion Sobre Formacion Profesional. Boletin. 6 per yr. ISSN 0577-2907
- Centro Interamericano de Investigacion y Documentacion Sobre Formacion Profesional. Cuadro Comparativo y Fichas Descriptivas. a.
- Centro Interamericano de Investigacion y Documentacion Sobre Formacion Profesional. Catalogo de Manuales Latinoamericanos Sobre Formacion Profesional. irreg.

- Centro Interamericano de Investigacion y Documentacion Sobre Formacion Profesional. Informes. irreg.
- Centro Interamericano de Investigacion y Documentacion Sobre Formacion Profesional. Indice de los Documentoa Referentes a los Proyectos. a.
- Centro Interamericano de Investigacion y Documentacion Sobre Formacion Profesional. Resumenes de Formacion Profesional. 3 per yr.
- Centro Interamericano de Investigacion y Documentacion Sobre Formacion Profesional. Serie Bibliografica. irreg.
- Colecciones Basicas C I N T E R F O R. irreg.

**Centro Latinoamericano de Economia Humana**
Casilla de Correo 998, Montevideo, Uruguay.
- Cuadernos Latinoamericanos de Economia Humana. 3 per yr. ISSN 0011-2526

**Cine Club del Uruguay**
Rincon 567, Montevideo, Uruguay.
- Cine Club del Uruguay. Cuadernos. irreg.(approx. 1 issue per year) ISSN 0069-4118

**Colegio de Doctores en Ciencias Economicas y Contadores del Uruguay.**
Av. Agraciada 1464, Montevideo, Uruguay.
- Revista de Economia, Finanzas y Administracion. 3 per yr.

**Comentarios Bibliograficos Americanos**
- C B A Boletin Informativo. (pub. by Eduardo Darino, Ed. & Pub.)

**Comision de Integracion Electrica Regional**
Bulevar Artigas 996, Montevideo, Uruguay.
- Comision de Integracion Electrica Regional. Catastro de los Servicios de Consultoria en los Paises de la C I E R. a. (prep. by its Secretaria General)
- Comision de Integracion Electrica Regional. Directorio del Sector Electrico. irreg.; latest issue, 1971.
- Comision de Integracion Electrica Regional. Recursos Energeticos de los Paises de la C I E R. biennial.

**Confederacion Latinoamericana de Asociaciones Cristianas de Jovenes**
Colonia 1884, P.3, Montevideo, Uruguay.
- Asociacion. q.
- Confederacion Latinoamericana de Asociaciones Cristianas de Jovenes. Carta. irreg.
- Educacion para el Desarrollo. q.

**Consejo Interamericano de Comercio y Produccion**
*see* **Inter-American Council of Commerce and Production**

**Norberto Costabel, Ed. & Pub.**
San Jose 215, Juan Lacaze, Uruguay.
- Claridad. 3 per wk. ISSN 0009-823X

**Eduardo Darino, Ed. & Pub.**
Casilla de Correo 1677, Montevideo, Uruguay (U.S. Subscr. to: E. Dartno, P.O. Box 5173, Grand Central Sta., New York, NY)
- C B A Boletin Informativo. m. ISSN 0007-7917 (Comentarios Bibliograficos Americanos) (Subscr. to Eduardo Darino, P.O. Box 5173, Grand Central Station, New York, N.Y. 10017)
- Comentarios Bibliograficos Americanos. 5 per yr. ISSN 0010-2237
- Comentarios Bibliograficos Americanos. Anuario. a. ISSN 0084-893X
- Guia de Latinoamerica. biennial.
- Hispanicamerican Arts; reference magazine to the hispanicamerican arts. bi-m.
- Revistero; el mas completo informe sobre las publicaciones periodicas de America Latina. a. ISSN 0085-5642

**Destellos Evangelicos**
Casilla de Correo 2110, Montevideo, Uruguay.
- Destellos Evangelicos. m. ISSN 0011-9547

**Eco d'Italia**
Ituzaingo 1482, Montevideo, Uruguay.
- Eco d'Italia; unico settimanale Italiano dell'Uruguay. w. ISSN 0012-9534

**Escuela Hermetica Occidental**
Casilla de Correo 51, Montevideo, Uruguay.
- Luz del Cosmos; orden cosmica. q. ISSN 0024-7723

**Estacion Experimental Dr. Mario Cassinoni**
Paysandu, Uruguay.
- Boletin Produccion Animal. 1-2 per yr. ISSN 0006-6486
- Estacion Experimental. Dr. Mario Cassinoni. Facultad de Agronomia. Boletin Tecnico. s-a. ISSN 0014-1127

**Libreria Amalio Fernandez**
Montevideo, Uruguay.
- Revista de Derecho, Jurisprudencia y Administracion. m. ISSN 0034-7906

**Fundacion de Cultura Universitaria**
25 de Mayo 537, Galeria 18, Gaboto-Local 4, Montevideo, Uruguay.
- Cuadernos de Literatura. 6 per yr. ISSN 0011-2445

**Hospital de Clinicas "Dr. Manuel Quintela"**
Universidad de la Republica, Avda. Italia S/N, Montevideo, Uruguay.
- Universidad de la Republica. Hospital de Clinicas. Informe Estatistico. a. ISSN 0041-8455

**Iglesia y Sociedad en America Latina**
Casilla de Correo 179, Montevideo, Uruguay.
- Iglesia y Sociedad en America Latina. Carta. irreg. ISSN 0579-3114
- Iglesia y Sociedad en America Latina. Fichas. m.

**Instituto de Filosofia**
Cerrito 73, Montevideo, Uruguay.
- Galileo; publicacion dedicada a problemas metacientificos. irreg. ISSN 0016-4062

**Instituto de Higiene**
Depto. de Parasitologia, Av. Alfredo Navarro 3051, Montevideo, Uruguay.
- Revista Uruguaya de Patologia Clinica y Microbiologia. s-a. (Sociedad Uruguaya de Patologia Clinica) (Co-sponsor: Sociedad Uruguaya de Microbiologia)

**Instituto de Neurologia**
Hospital de Clinicas, 2 Piso, Montevideo, Uruguay.
- Acta Neurologica Latinamericana. q. ISSN 0001-6306

**Instituto Interamericano de Ciencias Agricolas de la O E A**
Casilla 1217, Montevideo, Uruguay.
- Actividades de la Zona sur. bi-m.

**Instituto Interamericano del Nino**
Avda. 8 de Octubre 2904, Montevideo, Uruguay.
- Instituto Interamericano del Nino. Boletin. q. ISSN 0020-4056
- Instituto Interamericano del Nino. Publicaciones Sobre Servicio Social. irreg.
- Interamerican Children's Institute. Report of the General Director. a.

**Instituto Nacional de Carnes. Departamento de Exportaciones**
Montevideo, Uruguay.
- Instituto Nacional de Carnes. Departmento du Exportaciones. Exportacion de Carnes, Estadisticas. a.

**Inter-American Children's Institute**
*see* Instituto Interamericano del Nino

**Inter-American Council of Commerce and Production**
Misiones 1400, Montevideo, Uruguay.
- Inter-American Council of Commerce and Production. Uruguayan Section. Publicaciones. irreg. ISSN 0538-3048

**International Journal of Neurology**
Calle Buenos Aires 363, Montevideo, Uruguay.
- International Journal of Neurology. q. ISSN 0020-7446

**Latin American Free Trade Association**
*see* Asociacion Latinoamericana de Libre Comercio

**Latinamerican Arts**
Casilla de Correo 1677, Montevideo, Uruguay
- Latinamerican Arts; all you want or must know, about everything, in all the fields of Hispanic American arts. q.

**Libreria Anticuaria Americana**
Juan Carlos Gomez, 1418, Montevideo, Uruguay.
- Revista Uruguaya de Ciencias Sociales. a. (Centro de Investigaciones Sociales de Montevideo)

**Museo Historico Nacional**
Casa de Rivera, Rincon 437, Montevideo, Uruguay, MN 55084.
- Revista Historica. a.

**Museo Nacional de Historia Natural**
Casilla de Correos 399, Montevideo, Uruguay.
- Montevideo. Museo de Historia Natural. Communicaciones Zoologicas. 6-8 per yr. ISSN 0027-0113
- Montevideo. Museo de Historia Natural. Comunicaciones Botanicas. 4-6 per yr. ISSN 0027-0121
- Museo Nacional de Historia Natural. Anales. irreg; latest issue, 1974.
- Museo Nacional de Historia Natural. Communicaciones Antropologicas. irreg. ISSN 0077-1244
- Museo Nacional de Historia Natural. Communicaciones Paleontologicas. irreg.

**Ovum**
Casilla 2454, La Cruz de Carrasco, Montevideo, Uruguay.
- Ovum. 10 per yr. ISSN 0018-7054

**Pan American Federation of Engineering Societies**
Rincon 454 Esc 414, Montevideo, Uruguay.
- Pan American Federation of Engineering Societies. Bulletin. a. ISSN 0078-8791

**Public Instituto de Tisiologia**
Larranha 1392, Montevideo, Uruguay.
- Hoja Tisiologica. s-a. ISSN 0018-3326

**Carlos Quijano, Ed. & Pub.**
Bartolome Mitre 1414, Montevideo, Uruguay.
- Marcha. w. ISSN 0025-2824

**Radio Manual**
Javier Barrios Amarin 1586, Montevideo, Uruguay.
- Radio Manual. m.

**Carlos M. Rama**
Coronel Alegre 1340, Montevideo, Uruguay.
- Gacetilla Austral. bi-m. ISSN 0016-3899

**Revista de Biologia del Uruguay**
c/o Dr. Fernando Mane-Garzon, Ed., Casilla de Correo 157, Montevideo, Uruguay.
- Revista de Biologia del Uruguay. a.

**Revista de Derecho Comercial**
25 de Mayo 555, Montevideo, Uruguay.
- Revista de Derecho Comercial. 3 per mo. ISSN 0034-7876

**Revista de Economia**
Rincon 593, Montevideo, Uruguay.
- Revista de Economia. q.

**Sociedad de Cirugia del Uruguay**
Hospital de Clinicas "Dr. Manuel Quintela", Piso 4, Montevideo, Uruguay.
- Cirugia del Uruguay. bi-m (with supplements) ISSN 0009-7381

**Sociedad de Cirugia Plastica del Uruguay**
Av. Agraciada 1464, Montevideo, Uruguay.
- Cirugia Plastica Uruguaya. q. ISSN 0009-7403

**Sociedad de Medicina del Trabajo del Uruguay**
Av. Agraciada 1464, Montevideo, Uruguay.
- Revista de Medicina Social y del Trabajo. q. ISSN 0034-8562

**Sociedad de Tisiologia y Enfermedades del Torax**
Casilla de Correo 835, Montevideo, Uruguay.
- Torax. q. ISSN 0049-4143 (Co-sponsor: Sociedad de Cardiologia)

**Sociedad Malacologica del Uruguay**
Casilla 1401, Montevideo, Uruguay.
- Gazeta de Baixada. s-a. ISSN 0037-8607

**Sociedad Uruguaya de Patologia Clinica**
- Revista Uruguaya de Patologia Clinica y Microbiologia. (pub. by Instituto de Higiene)

**Sociedad Uruguaya de Pediatria**
Av. Agraciada 1464, Montevideo, Uruguay.
- Archivos de Pediatria del Uruguay. m. ISSN 0004-0584

**Unesco. Regional Office of Science and Technology for Latin America**
For publications of this agency see section for UNITED NATIONS

**Universidad de la Republica**
18 de Julio 1824, Montevideo, Uruguay.
- Gaceta de la Universidad. q. ISSN 0016-3759

**Universidad de la Republica. Facultad de Arquitectura**
Av. 18 de Julio 1824, Montevideo, Uruguay.
- Universidad de la Republica. Facultad de Arquitectura. Revista. m. ISSN 0014-6714

**Universidad de la Republica. Facultad de Ciencias Economicas y de Administracion**
Casilla de Correo 5052, Montevideo, Uruguay.
- Universidad de la Republica. Facultad de Ciencias Economicas y Administracion. Instituto de Estadistica. Indice de Precios al Consumidor. m. ISSN 0041-8439
- Universidad de la Republica. Facultad de Ciencias Economicas y de Administracion. Revista. irreg.

**Universidad de la Republica. Facultad de Humanidades y Ciencias**
Casilla de Correo, 157, Montevideo 157, Uruguay.
- Revista de Biologia del Uruguay. irreg.
- Universidad de la Republica. Facultad de Humanidades y Ciencias. Publicaciones. ISSN 0041-8447 (prep. by its Departamento de Documentacion y Biblioteca)

**Universidad de la Republica. Facultad de Ingeniera**
Herrera y Reissig 565, Montevideo, Uruguay.
- Montevideo Universidad. Facultad de Ingenieria y Agrimensura. Boletin. bi-m. ISSN 0027-013X

**Universidad de la Republica. Facultad de Odontologia**
Gral. las Heras 1925, Montivideo, Uruguay.
- Universidad de la Republica. Facultad de Odontologia. Anales. irreg. ISSN 0083-4785

**Universidad de la Republica. Instituto de Administration**
18 de Julio 1953 4p, Montevideo, Uruguay.
- Universidad de la Republica. Instituto de Administration. Cuaderno. irreg.; no. 65, 1975. ISSN 0077-1287

**Universidad de Uruguay. Departamento de Literatura Iberoamericana**
Montevideo, Uruguay.
- Universidad de Uruguay. Departamento de Literatura Iberoamericana Publicaciones. irreg. ISSN 0077-1252

**Universidad de Uruguay. Facultad de Agronomia**
Avda. Garzon 780, Montevideo, Uraguay.
- Universidad de la Republica. Facultad de Agronomia. Publicacion Miscelanea. irreg. ISSN 0077-1279
- Universidad de Uruguay. Facultad de Agronomia. Boletin. irreg. ISSN 0077-1260

**Universidad de Uruguay. Instituto de Matematica y Estadistica**
J. Herrera y Reissig 565, Montevideo, Uruguay.
- Universidad de Uruguay. Instituto de Matematica y Estadistica. Publicaciones Didacticas. irreg., 1969, no. 2. ISSN 0077-1295

**Uruguay. Biblioteca Nacional**
Guayabo 1795, Montevideo, Uruguay.
- Anuario Bibliografico Uruguayo. a.

**Uruguay. Centro de Estadisticas Nacionales y Comercio Internacional**
Misiones 1361, Montevideo, Uruguay.
- Ec-Co; economia y comercio de los paises Iberoamericanos. bi-m.

**Uruguay. Ministerio de Defensa Nacional**
Montevideo, Uruguay.
- Gaceta Militar y Naval. ISSN 0016-383X
- Revista Militar y Naval. q. ISSN 0035-015X

**Uruguay. Ministerio de Salud Publica. Departamento de Estadistica**
Montevideo, Uruguay.
- Morbilidad. irreg.

**Uruguay. Servicio de Oceanografia e Hidrografia**
Capurro 980, Casilla de Correo No. 1381, Montevideo, Uruguay.
- Uruguay. Servicio de Oceanografia e Hidrografia. Avisos a los Navegantes. m.

**Uruguay Filatelico**
Box 518, Montevideo, Uruguay.
- Uruguay Filatelico. 4 per yr. ISSN 0042-1189

**World Association for Animal Production**
c/o Dr. Hernan Caballero, Secretary General,
Casilla de Correos 1217, Montevideo, Uruguay.
- World Conference on Animal Production.
Proceedings. irreg., 1973, 3rd, Melbourne. ISSN
0084-1552

# USSR

**Akademiya Budivnystva i Arkhitektury Ukrainskoi S.S.R.**
Kiev, U.S.S.R.
- Budivel'ni Materialy i Konstruktsii. (pub. by Vydavnytstvo Budivelnyk)
- Promyshlennoe Stroitel'stvo i Inzhenernye Sooruzheniya. bi-m. ISSN 0033-1198

**Akademiya Meditsinskikh Nauk S. S. S. R.**
Ul. Solyanka, 14, 109801 Moscow, U. S. S. R.
- Akademiya Meditsinskikh Nauk S. S. S. R. Vestnik. m. ISSN 0002-3027
- Arkhiv Anatomii, Gistologii i Embriologii. (pub. by Izdatel'stvo Meditsina)
- Bulletin of Experimental Biology and Medicine. (pub. by Consultants Bureau US)
- Meditsinskaya Radiologiya. m. ISSN 0025-8334
- Patologicheskaya Fiziologiya i Eksperimental'naya Terapiya. bi-m. ISSN 0031-2991
- Voprosy Meditsinskoi Khimii. (pub. by Izdatel'stvo Meditsina)

**Akademiya Meditsinskikh Nauk S.S.S.R. Nauchno-Issledovatel'skaya Laboratoriya Eksperimental'no-Biologicheskikh Modelei**
Moskovskaya Oblast', G. Khimki, Pos. Svetlie Gory, U.S.S.R.
- Biologiya Laboratornykh Zhivotnykh. irreg.

**Akademiya Nauk Armyanskoi S.S.R.**
Ul. Barekamutian, 24, Erevan, U. S. S. R.
- Aiastani Kensabanakan Andes. m. ISSN 0017-8683
- Aikakan Himiakan Amsagir/Armenian Chemical Journal. m. ISSN 0002-2101
- Akademiya Nauk Armyanskoi S.S.R. Doklady. 10 per yr.
- Akademiya Nauk Armyanskoi S. S. R. Izvestiya. Seriya Fizika. bi-m. ISSN 0002-3035
- Akademiya Nauk Armyanskoi S. S. R. Izvestiya. Seriya Matematika. bi-m. ISSN 0002-3043
- Akademiya Nauk Armyanskoi S. S. R. Izvestiya. Seriya Mekhanika. bi-m. ISSN 0002-3051
- Akademiya Nauk Armyanskoi S. S. R. Izvestiya. Seriya Tekhnicheskikh Nauk. bi-m. ISSN 0002-306X
- Astrophysics. (pub. by Consultants Bureau US)
- Biologicheskii Zhurnal Armenii. 10 per yr. ISSN 0002-2969
- Geologicheskii Zhurnal Armenii. bi-m. ISSN 0016-769X
- Lraber Asarakakan Gitutyunneri. m. ISSN 0024-7111
- Zhurnal Eksperimental'noi i Klinicheskoi Meditsiny. bi-m. ISSN 0013-3310

**Akademiya Nauk Azerbaidzhanskoi S. S. R.**
Poselok Musabekova, 571, Baku, U. S. S. R.
(Subscr. Tl: Mezhdunarodnaya Kniga, Moscow, G-200, U. S. S. R.)
- Akademiya Nauk Azerbaidzhanskoi S. S. R. Doklady. (pub. by Izdatel'stvo Elm)
- Akademiya Nauk Azerbaidzhanskoi S. S. R. Izvestiya. Seriya Biologicheskikh Nauk. (pub. by Izdatel'stvo Elm)
- Akademiya Nauk Azerbaidzhanskoi S. S. R. Izvestiya. Seriya Ekonomicheskikh Nauk. (pub. by Izdatel'stvo Elm)
- Akademiya Nauk Azerbaidzhanskoi S. S. R. Izvestiya. Seriya Fiziko - Tekhnicheskikh i Matematicheskikh Nauk. (pub. by Izdatel'stvo Elm)
- Akademiya Nauk Azerbaidzhanskoi S. S. R. Izvestiya. Seriya Istoriya, Filosofiya i Pravo. q. ISSN 0002-3116
- Akademiya Nauk Azerbaidzhanskoi S. S. R. Izvestiya. Seriya Nauki o Zemle. bi-m. ISSN 0002-3124
- Akademiya Nauk Azerbaidzhanskoi S. S. R. Izvestiya. Seriya Yazykoznanie, Literatura i Iskusstvo. q. ISSN 0002-3132

- Azerbaidzhan Tibb Zhurnaly/Azerbaidzhanskii Meditsinskii Zhurnal. m. ISSN 0005-2523
- Azerbaidzhanskii Khimicheskii Zhurnal. bi-m. ISSN 0005-2531

**Akademiya Nauk Estonskoi S.S.R.**
Ul. Kokhtu, 6, 200103 Tallinn, U. S. S. R.
- Akademiya Nauk Estonskoi S. S. R. Izvestiya. Biologiya/Eesti N. S. V. Teaduste Akadeemia Toimetised. Bioloogia. (pub. by Kirjastus Perioodika)
- Akademiya Nauk Estonskoi S.S.R. Izvestiya. Fizika. Matematika/Eesti Nsv Teaduste Akadeemia. Toimetised. Fuusika. Matemaatika. (pub. by Kirjastus Perioodika)
- Akademiya Nauk Estonskoi S. S. R. Izvestiya. Obshchestvennye Nauki. q. ISSN 0002-3159
- Keel Ja Kirjandus. m. ISSN 0022-9601
- Sovetskoe Finnougrovedenie. (pub. by Kirjastus Perioodika)

**Akademiya Nauk Gruzinskoi S.S.R.**
Ul. Dzerzhinskogo 8, Tbilisi, U.S.S.R.
- Akademiya Nauk Gruzinskoi S.S.R. Izvestiya. Seriya Biologicheskaya. bi-m.
- Akademiya Nauk Gruzinskoi S.S.R. Izvestiya. Seriya Khimicheskaya. q.
- Akademiya Nauk Gruzinskoi S. S. R. Soobshcheniya. m. ISSN 0002-3167

**Akademiya Nauk Kazakhskoi S. S. R.**
Ul. Shevchenko, 28, 480591 Alma - Ata, U. S. S. R.
- Akademiya Nauk Kazakhskoi S. S. R. Izvestiya. Seriya Biologicheskaya. bi-m. ISSN 0002-3183
- Akademiya Nauk Kazakhskoi S. S. R. Izvestiya. Seriya Fiziko - Matematicheskaya. bi-m. ISSN 0002-3191
- Akademiya Nauk Kazakhskoi S. S. R. Izvestiya. Seriya Geologicheskaya. bi-m. ISSN 0002-3175
- Akademiya Nauk Kazakhskoi S. S. R. Izvestiya. Seriya Khimicheskaya. bi-m. ISSN 0002-3205
- Akademiya Nauk Kazakhskoi S. S. R. Vestnik. (pub. by Izdatel'stvo Nauka. Otdelenie v Kazakhstane)

**Akademiya Nauk Kirgizskoi S. S. R.**
Ul. 23. Parts'ezda, 265-a, Frunze, U. S. S. R.
- Akademiya Nauk Kirgizskoi S. S. R. Izvestiya. bi-m. ISSN 0002-3221

**Akademiya Nauk Latviiskoi S. S. R.**
- Akademiya Nauk Latviiskoi S. S. R. Izvestiya/Latvijas P. S. R. Zinatnu Akademijas. Vestis. (pub. by Izdevnieciba Zinatne)
- Akademiya Nauk Latviiskoi S. S. R. Izvestiya. Seriya Fizicheskikh i Tekhnicheskikh Nauk. (pub. by Izdevnieciba Zinatne)
- Akademiya Nauk Latviiskoi S. S. R. Izvestiya. Seriya Khimicheskaya. (pub. by Izdevnieciba Zinatne)
- Chemistry of Heterocyclic Compounds. (pub. by Consultants Bureau US)
- Contributions to the History of Science and Technology in Baltics/Iz Istorii Estestvoznaniya i Tekhniki Pribaltiki. (pub. by Izdevnieciba Zinatne)
- Khimiya Drevesiny. (pub. by Izdevnieciba Zinatne)
- Magnetohydrodynamics. (pub. by Consultants Bureau US)
- Magnitnaya Gidrodinamika. (pub. by Izdevnieciba Zinatne)
- Polymer Mechanics. (pub. by Consultants Bureau US)

**Akademiya Nauk Latviiskoi S.S.R. Institut Elektroniki i Vychislitel'noi Tekhniki**
Ul. Turgeneva, 19, Riga, U.S.S.R.
- Akademiya Nauk Latviiskoi S. S. R. Elektronikas un Skaitlosanas Tehnikas Instituts. Raspoznavanie Obrazov. irreg.
- Analogo-Diskretnye Preobrazovaniya Signalov. (pub. by Izdevnieciba Zinatne)

**Akademiya Nauk Latviiskoi S.S.R. Institut Mekhaniki Polimerov**
- Mekhanika Polimerov. (pub. by Izdevnieciba Zinatne)

**Akademiya Nauk Litovskoi S.S.R**
Lenino Prospektas 3, Vilnius, U. S. S. R.
- Akademiya Nauk Litovskoi S. S. R. Trudy. Seriya A. Obshchestvennye Nauki. 4 per yr. ISSN 0024-2985

- Akademiya Nauk Litovskoi S. S. R. Trudy. Seriya B. Khimiya, Tekhnika, Fizicheskaya Geografiya. 6 per yr. ISSN 0024-2993
- Akademiya Nauk Litovskoi S. S. R. Trudy. Seriya C. Biologicheskie Nauki. q. ISSN 0024-3000
- Baltica. biennial. ISSN 0067-3064
- Geografinis Metrastis/Geographical Annual. irreg. ISSN 0072-0917
- Lietuvos Fizikos Rinkinys/Litovskii Fizicheskii Sbornik. bi-m. ISSN 0024-2969
- Litovskii Matematicheskii Sbornik. q. ISSN 0024-2977

**Akademiya Nauk Litovskoi S.S.R. Institut Fiziko-Tekhnicheskikh Problem Energetiki**
Metalo 4, 233684 Kaunas, U. S. S. R.
- Silumine Fizika/Teplofizika. irreg., no. 7, 1975. ISSN 0082-4089
- Technine Kibernetika/Tekhnicheskaya Kibernetika. (pub. by Izdatel'stvo Mintis)

**Akademiya Nauk Litovskoi S. S. R. Lietuviu Kalbos Ir Literaturos Institutas**
Vilnius, U. S. S. R.
- Kalbos Kultura. s-a. ISSN 0022-7900

**Akademiya Nauk Moldavskoi S.S.R.**
Prospekt Lenina 1, Kishinev, U.S.S.R.
- Akademiya Nauk Moldavskoi S.S.R. Izvestiya. Seriya Biologicheskikh i Khimicheskikh Nauk. bi-m.
- Akademiya Nauk Moldavskoi S. S. R. Izvestiya. Seriya Fiziko - Tekhnicheskikh i Matematicheskikh Nauk. 3 per yr.
- Akademiya Nauk Moldavskoi S.S.R. Izvestiya. Seriya Obshchestvennykh Nauk. (pub. by Izdatel'stvo Shtiintsa)
- Elektronnaya Obrabotka Materialov. bi-m. ISSN 0013-5739

**Akademiya Nauk S. S. S R**
Leninskii prospekt, 14, Moscow V-71, U.S.S.R.
- Academy of Sciences of the U S S R. Biology Bulletin. (pub. by Consultants Bureau US)
- Academy of Sciences of the U S S R. Chemistry Bulletin. (pub. by Consultants Bureau US)
- Academy of Sciences of the U S S R. Mathematical Notes. (pub. by Consultants Bureau US)
- Agrokhimiya. (pub. by Izdatel'stvo Nauka)
- Akademiya Nauk S. S. S. R. Doklady. (pub. by Izdatel'stvo Nauka)
- Akademiya Nauk S. S. S. R. Izvestiya. Energetika i Transport. (pub. by Izdatel'stvo Nauka)
- Akademiya Nauk S. S. S. R. Izvestiya. Seriya Biologicheskaya. (pub. by Izdatel'stvo Nauka)
- Akademiya Nauk S. S. R. Izvestiya. Seriya Fizika Atmosfery i Okeana. (pub. by Izdatel'stvo Nauka)
- Akademiya Nauk S. S. S. R. Izvestiya. Seriya Fizika Zemli. (pub. by Izdatel'stvo Nauka)
- Akademiya Nauk S. S. S. R. Izvestiya. Seriya Geologicheskaya. (pub. by Izdatel'stvo Nauka)
- Akademiya Nauk S. S. S. R. Izvestiya. Seriya Khimicheskaya. (pub. by Izdatel'stvo Nauka)
- Akademiya Nauk S. S. S. R. Izvestiya. Seriya Matematicheskaya. (pub. by Izdatel'stvo Nauka)
- Akademiya Nauk S. S. S. R. Izvestiya. Seriya Neorganicheskie Materialy. (pub. by Izdatel'stvo Nauka)
- Akademiya Nauk S. S. S. R. Vestnik. m. ISSN 0002-3442
- Akusticheskii Zhurnal. (pub. by Izdatel'stvo Nauka)
- Algebra and Logic. (pub. by Consultants Bureau US)
- Applied Biochemistry and Microbiology. (pub. by Consultants Bureau US)
- Biochemistry. (pub. by Consultants Bureau US)
- Biokhimiya. m. ISSN 0006-307X
- Bioorganicheskaya Khimiya. (pub. by Izdatel'stvo Nauka)
- Chemistry and Technology of Fuels and Oils. (pub. by Consultants Bureau US)
- Colloid Journal of the U S S R. (pub. by Consultants Bureau US)
- Cosmic Research. (pub. by Consultants Bureau US)
- Doklady Biochemistry. (pub. by Consultants Bureau US)
- Doklady Biological Sciences. (pub. by Consultants Bureau US)
- Doklady Biophysics. (pub. by Consultants Bureau US)
- Doklady Botanical Sciences. (pub. by Consultants Bureau US)

- Doklady Chemistry. (pub. by Consultants Bureau US)
- Doklady Physical Chemistry. (pub. by Consultants Bureau US)
- Elektrichestvo. m. ISSN 0013-5380
- Engineering Cybernetics. (pub. by Scripta Publishing Co. US)
- Entomological Review. (pub. by Scripta Publishing Co. US)
- Exakt. (pub. by Deutsche Verlagsanstalt GmbH GW)
- Fibre Chemistry. (pub. by Consultants Bureau US)
- Fizika i Khimiya Obrabotki Materialov. bi-m. ISSN 0015-3214
- Fizika i Tekhnika Poluprovodnikov. m. ISSN 0015-3222
- Fizika Metallov i Metallovedenie. m. ISSN 0015-3230
- Fizika Plazmy. (pub. by Izdatel'stvo Nauka)
- Fizika Tverdogo Tela. m. ISSN 0015-3249
- Fiziologicheskii Zhurnal. (pub. by Izdatel'stvo Nauka. Leningradskoe Otdelenie)
- Fiziologiya Cheloveka. (pub. by Izdatel'stvo Nauka)
- Fluid Dynamics. (pub. by Consultants Bureau US)
- Functional Analysis and Its Applications. (pub. by Consultants Bureau US)
- Funktsional'nyi Analiz i Ego Prilozheniya. q. ISSN 0016-285X
- Genetika. m. ISSN 0016-6758
- Geomagnetizm i Aeronomiya. bi-m. ISSN 0016-7940
- Glass and Ceramics. (pub. by Consultants Bureau US)
- High Energy Chemistry. (pub. by Consultants Bureau US)
- High Temperature Physics. (pub. by Consultants Bureau US)
- Human Physiology. (pub. by Consultants Bureau US)
- Inorganic Materials. (pub. by Consultants Bureau US)
- Instruments and Experimental Techniques. (pub. by Consultants Bureau US)
- Journal of Analytical Chemistry of the US S R. (pub. by Consultants Bureau US)
- Journal of Applied Chemistry of the U S S R. (pub. by Consultants Bureau US)
- Journal of Evolutionary Biochemistry and Physiology. (pub. by Consultants Bureau US)
- Journal of General Chemistry of the U S S R. (pub. by Consultants Bureau US)
- Journal of Ichthyology/Problemy Ikhtiologii. (pub. by Scripta Publishing Co. US)
- Journal of Organic Chemistry of the U S S R. (pub. by Consultants Bureau US)
- Journal of Structural Chemistry. (pub. by Consultants Bureau US)
- Khimiya i Zhizn' m. ISSN 0023-1142
- Khimiya Tverdogo Topliva. bi-m. ISSN 0023-1177
- Kinetics and Catalysis. (pub. by Consultants Bureau US)
- Kolloidnyi Zhurnal; journal of physico-chemistry of surface phenomenon and dispersed systems. bi-m. ISSN 0023-2912
- Kosmicheskie Issledovaniya. bi-m. ISSN 0023-4206
- Kristallografiya. bi-m. ISSN 0023-4761
- Lithology and Mineral Resources. (pub. by Consultants Bureau US)
- Mashinovedenie. bi-m. ISSN 0025-4576
- Matematicheskie Zametki. m. ISSN 0025-567X
- Microbiology. (pub. by Consultants Bureau US)
- Mikologiya i Fitopatologiya. bi-m. ISSN 0026-3648
- Molecular Biology. (pub. by Consultants Bureau US)
- Molekulyarnaya Biologiya. bi-m. ISSN 0026-8984
- Movoznavstvo. (pub. by Izdatel'stvo Naukova Dumka)
- Neftekhimiya. bi-m. ISSN 0028-2421
- Neirofiziologiya/Neurophysiology. (pub. by Izdatel'stvo Naukova Dumka)
- Optika i Spektroskopiya. (pub. by Izdatel'stvo Nauka. Leningradskoe Otdelenie)
- Paleontological Journal. (pub. by Scripta Technica, Inc. US)
- Parazitologiya. bi-m. ISSN 0031-1847
- Pharmaceutical Chemistry Journal. (pub. by Consultants Bureau US)
- Power Engineering. (pub. by Allerton Press, Inc. US)
- Pribory i Tekhnika Eksperimenta. bi-m. ISSN 0032-8162
- Prikladnaya Matematika i Mekhanika. bi-m. ISSN 0032-8235
- Priroda; populyarnyi estestvenno nauchnyi zhurnal. m. ISSN 0032-874X

- Problems of Information Transmission. (pub. by Consultants Bureau US)
- Problems of the Contemporary World/Problemes du Monde Contemporain/Problemas del Mundo Contemporaneo. irreg. ISSN 0079-5763
- Programming and Computer Software. (pub. by Consultants Bureau US)
- Radio Engineering and Electronic Physics. (pub. by Scripta Publishing Co. US)
- Radiobiologiya. bi-m. ISSN 0033-8192
- Radiokhimiya. bi-m. ISSN 0033-8311
- Radiotekhnika i Elektronika. m. ISSN 0033-8494
- Rastitel'nye Resursy. q. ISSN 0033-9946
- Social Sciences. q. ISSN 0049-0911
- Solar System Research. (pub. by Consultants Bureau US)
- Soviet Atomic Energy. (pub. by Consultants Bureau US)
- Soviet Atomic Energy. Supplement. (pub. by Consultants Bureau US)
- Soviet Electrochemistry. (pub. by Consultants Bureau US)
- Soviet Genetics. (pub. by Consultants Bureau US)
- Soviet Journal of Bioorganic Chemistry. (pub. by Consultants Bureau US)
- Soviet Journal of Coordination Chemistry. (pub. by Consultants Bureau US)
- Soviet Journal of Developmental Biology. (pub. by Consultants Bureau US)
- Soviet Journal of Glass Physics and Chemistry. (pub. by Consultants Bureau US)
- Soviet Journal of Marine Biology. (pub. by Consultants Bureau US)
- Soviet Microelectronics. (pub. by Consultants Bureau US)
- Soviet Plant Physiology. (pub. by Consultants Bureau US)
- Soviet Radiochemistry. (pub. by Consultants Bureau US)
- Soviet Soil Science. (pub. by Scripta Publishing Co. US)
- Teoreticheskie Osnovy Khimicheskoi Tekhnologii. bi-m. ISSN 0040-3571
- Theoretical and Mathematical Physics. (pub. by Consultants Bureau US)
- Theoretical Foundations of Chemical Engineering. (pub. by Consultants Bureau US)
- Thermal Engineering. (pub. by Pergamon Press, Inc. US)
- Tsitologiya i Genetika. bi-m. ISSN 0041-4883
- Uspekhi Fizicheskikh Nauk. m. ISSN 0042-1294
- Uspekhi Khimii. m. ISSN 0042-1308
- Uspekhi Matematicheskikh Nauk. (pub. by Izdatel'stvo Nauka)
- Uspekhi Sovremennoi Biologii. bi-m. ISSN 0042-1324
- Water Resources. (pub. by Consultants Bureau US)
- Yadernaya Fizika. m. ISSN 0044-0027
- Zashchita Metallov. bi-m. ISSN 0044-1856
- Zemlya i Vselennaya. (pub. by Izdatel'stvo Nauka)
- Zhurnal Analiticheskoi Khimii. m. ISSN 0044-4502
- Zhurnal Eksperimental'noi i Teoreticheskoi Fiziki. m. ISSN 0044-4510
- Zhurnal Evolyutsionnoi Biokhimii i Fiziologii. bi-m. ISSN 0044-4529
- Zhurnal Fizicheskoi Khimii. m. ISSN 0044-4537
- Zhurnal Nauchnoi i Prikladnoi Fotografii i Kinematografii. bi-m. ISSN 0044-4561
- Zhurnal Obshchei Khimii. m. ISSN 0044-460X
- Zhurnal Prikladnoi Khimii. (pub. by Izdatel'stvo Nauka. Leningradskoe Otdelenie)
- Zhurnal Strukturnoi Khimii. bi-m. ISSN 0044-4634
- Zhurnal Tekhnicheskoi Fiziki. m. ISSN 0044-4642
- Zhurnal Vychislitel'noi Matematiki i Matematicheskoi Fiziki. bi-m. ISSN 0044-4669

**Akademiya Nauk S.S.S.R. Astrosovet**
- Astronomicheskii Zhurnal. (pub. by Izdatel'stvo Nauka)
- Pis'ma v Astronomicheskii Zhurnal. (pub. by Izdatel'stvo Nauka)

**Akademiya Nauk S.S.S.R. Chemical Technology Section**
- Doklady Chemical Technology. (pub. by Consultants Bureau US)

**Akademiya Nauk S.S.S.R. Dagestanskii Filial**
Ul. Gadzhieva, 45, Makhachkala, Daghestan, U.S.S.R.
- Dagestanskii Etnograficheskii Sbornik. irreg. (prep. by its Institut Istorii, Yazyka i Literatury)

**Akademiya Nauk S. S. S. R. Dal'nevostochnyi Nauchnyi Tsentr**
Ul. Leninskaya 50, Vladivostok, U.S.S.R.
- Ekonomiko-Matematicheskie Metody Planirovaniya i Upravleniya. irreg.
- Voprosy Ekonomiki Sel'skogo Khozyaistva Dal'nego Vostoka. irreg.

**Akademiya Nauk S. S. S. R. Institut Arkheologii**
Ul. D. Ulyanova, 19, Moscow B-36, U. S. S. R.
- Sovetskaya Arkheologiya. q. ISSN 0038-5034

**Akademiya Nauk S. S. S. R. Institut Automatiki i Telemekhaniki**
- Avtomatika i Telemekhanika. (pub. by Izdatel'stvo Nauka)

**Akademiya Nauk S.S.S.R. Institut Biologicheskoi Fiziki**
Akademgorodok, 142292 Pushchino, U. S. S. R.
- Biofizika Zhivoi Kletki. irreg. ISSN 0301-2425

**Akademiya Nauk S.S.S.R. Institut Ekonomiki**
- Voprosy Ekonomiki. (pub. by Izdatel'stvo Pravda)

**Akademiya Nauk S.S.S.R. Institut Elementoorganicheskikh Soedinenii**
Ul. Vavilova, 14, Moscow, U. S. S. R.
- Progress Polimernoi Khimii. irreg. ISSN 0079-6883

**Akademiya Nauk S.S.S.R. Institut Etnografii**
- Akademiya Nauk S.S.S.R. Institut Etnografii. Polevye Issledovaniya. (pub. by Izdatel'stvo Nauka)
- Sovetskaya Etnografiya. (pub. by Izdatel'stvo Nauka)

**Akademiya Nauk S. S. S. R. Institut Filosofii**
- Voprosy Filosofii. (pub. by Izdatel'stvo Pravda)

**Akademiya Nauk S.S.S.R. Institut Fiziki im. P. N. Lebedeva**
- Soviet Physics-Lebedev Institute Reports. (pub. by Allerton Press, Inc. US)

**Akademiya Nauk S. S. S. R. Institut Fiziki Zemli**
B. Gruzinskaya ul. 10, Moscow, U.S.S.R.
- Voprosy Teorii Razrabotki Mestorozhdenii Poleznykh Iskopaemykh. a.

**Akademiya Nauk S.S.S.R. Institut Geokhimii i Analitichnoi Khimii im. V. I. Vernadskogo**
Vorobevskoe Shosse, 47a, Moscow, U. S. S. R.
(Subscr. to: Mezhdunarodnaya Kniga, Moscow, G-200, U.S.S.R.)
- Geokhimiya. m. ISSN 0016-7525

**Akademiya Nauk S. S. S. R. Institut Geologii Rudnykh Mestorozhdenii, Petrografii, Mineralogii i Geokhimii**
Starometnyi Per., 35, Moscow, U. S. S. R.
- Akademiya Nauk S. S. S. R. Institut Geologii Rudnykh Mestorozhdenii, Petrografii, Mineralogii i Geokhimii. Trudy. 6 per yr. ISSN 0002-3299

**Akademiya Nauk S.S.S.R. Institut Gosudarstva i Prava**
- Sovetskoe Gosudarstvo i Pravo. (pub. by Izdatel'stvo Nauka)

**Akademiya Nauk S. S. S. R. Institut Istorii S. S. S. R.**
- Istoriya S. S. S. R. (pub. by Izdatel'stvo Nauka)

**Akademiya Nauk S.S.S.R. Institut Latinskoi Ameriki**
- Latinskaya Amerika. (pub. by Izdatel'stvo Nauka)

**Akademiya Nauk S. S. S. R. Institut Matematiki**
Ul. Vavilova, 42, Moscow V-333, U. S. S. R.
- Matematicheskii Sbornik. m. ISSN 0025-5157 (Co-sponsor: Moskovskoe Matematicheskoe Obshchestvo)
- Teoriya Veroyatnostei i Ee Primenenie. q. ISSN 0040-361X

**Akademiya Nauk S.S.S.R. Institut Mirovoi Ekonomiki i Mezhdunarodnykh Otnoshenii**
- Mirovaya Ekonomika i Mezhdunarodnye Otnosheniya. (pub. by Izdatel'stvo Pravda)

**Akademiya Nauk S. S. S. R. Institut Narodov Azii**
- Aziya i Afrika Segodnya. (pub. by Izdatel'sto Nauka)

**Akademiya Nauk S. S. S. R. Institut Nauchnoi Informatsii i Fundamentalnaya Biblioteka po Obshchestvennym Naukam**
Ul. Frunze, 11, 121019 Moscow, U.S.S.R.
- Mezhdunarodnoe Rabochee Dvizhenie; bibliograficheskii byulleten. m.
- Novaya Literatura po Gosudarstvu i Pravu za Rubezhom; bibliograficheskii byulleten. m.
- Novaya Sovetskaya Literatura po Gosudarstvu i Pravu. Novaya Yuridicheskaya Literatura v S. S. S. R; bibliograficheskii byulleten. m.

**Akademiya Nauk S. S. S. R. Institut Obshchei i Neorganicheskoi Khimii im. N.S. Kurnakova**
- Zhurnal Neorganicheskoi Khimii. (pub. by Izdatel'stvo Nauka)

**Akademiya Nauk S.S.S.R. Institut Okeanologii**
Letnaya ul. 1, Lyublino, U.S.S.R.
- Akademiya Nauk S. S. S. R. Institut Okeanologii. Trudy. 2 per yr. ISSN 0002-3450

**Akademiya Nauk S. S. S. R. Institut Paleontologii**
- Paleontologicheskii Zhurnal. (pub. by Izdatel'stvo Nauka)

**Akademiya Nauk S.S.S.R. Institut Russkogo Yazyka**
- Russkaya Rech' (pub. by Izdatel'stvo Nauka)
- Russkii Yazyk za Rubezhom/Russian Abroad. (pub. by Izdatel'stvo Moskovskii Universitet)

**Akademiya Nauk S.S.S.R. Institut Vodnykh Problem**
- Vodnye Resursy. (pub. by Izdatel'stvo Nauka)

**Akademiya Nauk S.S.S.R. Institut Vostokovedeniya**
- Narody Azii i Afriki. (pub. by Izdatel'stvo Nauka)

**Akademiya Nauk S. S. S. R. Institut Vseobshchei Istorii**
Ul. D. Ulyanova, 19, Moscow B-36, U. S. S. R.
- Novaya i Noveishaya Istoriya. bi-m. ISSN 0029-5124
- Vestnik Drevnei Istorii/Journal of Ancient History. (pub. by Izdatel'stvo Nauka)

**Akademiya Nauk S. S. S. R. Institut Yazykoznaniya**
Ul. Marksa i Engel'sa 1/14, Moscow, U.S.S.R.
- Lingvisticheskie Issledovaniya. irreg.
- Voprosy Yazykoznaniya. (pub. by Izdatel'stvo Nauka)

**Akademiya Nauk S.S.S.R. Kol'skii Filial**
Apatity, Akademgorodok, U. S. S. R.
- Voprosy Ekonomiki Narodnogo Khozyaistva Murmanskoi Oblasti. irreg. (prep. by its Otdel Ekonomicheskikh Issledovanii)

**Akademiya Nauk S.S.S.R. Krymskaya Astrofizicheskaya Observatoriya**
- Krymskaya Astrofizicheskaya Observatoriya. Izvestiya. (pub. by Izdatel'stvo Nauka)

**Akademiya Nauk S.S.S.R. Laboratoriya Teorii Protsessov Perenosa**
Leninskii prospekt, 14, Moscow V-71, U.S.S.R.
- Chislennye Metody v Dinamike Razrezhennykh Gazov. irreg.

**Akademiya Nauk S.S.S.R. Mezhduvedomstvennyi Geofizicheskii Komitet**
Molodezhnaya ul., 3, Moscow, U. S. S. R.
- Geofizicheskii Byulleten/Geophysical Bulletin. (pub. by Izdatel'stvo Nauka)
- Glyatsiologiya/Glaciology. irreg. ISSN 0568-6245

**Akademiya Nauk S.S.S.R. Nauchnyi Sovet po Istorii Mirovoi Kul'tury**
- Pamyatniki Kul'tury. Novye Otkrytiya/ Monuments of Culture. New Discoveries. (pub. by Izdatel'stvo Nauka)

**Akademiya Nauk S.S.S.R. Okeanografichnaya Komissiya**
Leninskii prospekt, 14, Moscow V-71, U.S.S.R.
- Okeanologiya. bi-m. ISSN 0030-1574

**Akademiya Nauk S. S. S. R. Otdelenie Biokhimii, Biofiziki i Khimii Fiziologicheski Aktivnykh Soedinenii**
- Biofizika. (pub. by Izdatel'stvo Nauka)

**Akademiya Nauk S.S.S.R. Otdelenie Fiziko-tekhnicheskikh Problem Energetiki**
Leninskii prospekt, 14, Moscow V-71, U.S.S.R.
- Teplofizika Vysokikh Temperatur. bi-m. ISSN 0040-3644

**Akademiya Nauk S.S.S.R. Otdelenie Fiziologii im. I.P. Pavlova**
Leninskii prospekt, 14, Moscow V-71, U.S.S.R.
- Zhurnal Vysshei Nervnoi Deyatel'nosti. bi-m. ISSN 0044-4677

**Akademiya Nauk S.S.S.R. Otdelenie Geologii, Geofiziki, Geokhimii**
Staromonetnyi Per. 35, Moscow G-17, U. S. S. R.
(Subscr. to: Mezhdunarodnaya Kniga, Moscow, G-200, U. S. S. R.)
- Geologiya Rudnykh Mestorozhdenii. bi-m. ISSN 0016-7908

**Akademiya Nauk S. S. S. R. Otdelenie Mekhaniki i Protsessov Upravleniya**
Leninskii Pr., 14, Moscow, U.S.S.R.
- Akademiya Nauk S. S. S. R. Izvestiya. Tekhnicheskaya Kibernetika. (pub. by Izdatel'stvo Nauka)
- Inzhenerno- Fizicheskii Zhurnal. m.

**Akademiya Nauk S. S. S. R. Otdelenie Nauk o Zemle**
Leninskii prospekt, 14, Moscow V-71, U. S. S. R.
- Geotektonika. bi-m. ISSN 0016-853X
- Litologiya i Poleznye Iskopaemye. bi-m. ISSN 0024-497X

**Akademiya Nauk S.S.S.R. Otdelenie Obshchei Biologii**
Leninskii prospekt, 14, Moscow V-71, U.S.S.R.
- Biologiya Morya/Marine Biology. (pub. by Izdatel'stvo Nauka. Dal'nevostochnoe Otdelenie)
- Voprosy Ikhtiologii. bi-m. ISSN 0042-8752
- Zhurnal Obshchei Biologii. bi-m. ISSN 0044-4596
- Zoologicheskii Zhurnal. m. ISSN 0044-5134

**Akademiya Nauk S.S.S.R. Otdelenie Obshchei i Tekhnicheskoi Khimii**
Leninskii prospekt, 14, Moscow V-71, U.S.S.R.
- Vysokomolekulyarnye Soedineniya. m. ISSN 0042-9368
- Vysokomolekulyarnye Soedineniya. Kratkie Soobshcheniya. m.

**Akademiya Nauk S.S.S.R. Sektor Istochnikovedeniya i Vspomogatel'nykh Istoricheskikh Distsiplin**
- Istochnikovedenie Otechestvennoi Istorii. (pub. by Izdatel'stvo Nauka)

**Akademiya Nauk S. S. S. R. Sibirskoe Otdelenie**
Prospekt Nauki, 21, Novosibirsk, U. S. S. R.
- Akademiya Nauk S. S. S. R. Sibirskoe Otdelenie Izvestiya. Seriya Biologicheskikh i Meditsinskikh Nauk. 3 per yr. ISSN 0002-3418
- Akademiya Nauk S. S. S. R. Sibirskoe Otdelenie. Izvestiya. Seriya Khimicheskikh Nauk. 6 per yr. ISSN 0002-3426
- Akademiya Nauk S. S. S. R. Sibirskoe Otdelenie. Izvestiya. Seriya Tekhnicheskikh Nauk. 3 per yr. ISSN 0002-3434
- Combustion, Explosion and Shock Waves. (pub. by Consultants Bureau US)
- Geologiya i Geofizika. m. ISSN 0016-7886 (prep. by its Institut Geologii i Geofiziki)
- Journal of Applied Mechanics and Technical Physics. (pub. by Consultants Bureau US)
- Koltsa; Bibliografiya. irreg. (prep. by its Institut Matematiki)
- Optimizatsiya. irreg (approx 5-6 per yr) (prep. by its Institut Matematiki)
- Problemy Severa; tekushchii ukazatel' literatury. q. (prep. by its Gosudarstvennaya Publichnaya Nauchno- Tekhnicheskaya Biblioteka)
- Rastitel'nyi Mir Sibiri i Dal'nego Vostoka; tekushchii ukazatel' literatury. irreg.
- Regional'naya Nauka o Razmeshchenii Proizvoditel'nykh Sil; sbornik referativnykh rabot. irreg. (prep. by its Institut Ekonomiki i Organizatsii Promyshlennogo Proizvodstva)
- Siberian Mathematical Journal of the Academy of Sciences of the U. S. S. R., Novosibirsk. (pub. by Consultants Bureau US)
- Sibirskii Matematicheskii Zhurnal. bi-m. ISSN 0037-4474
- Soviet Mining Science. (pub. by Consultants Bureau US)
- Zhurnal Prikladnoi Mekhaniki i Tekhnicheskoi Fiziki. bi-m. ISSN 0044-4626

**Akademiya Nauk S.S.S.R. Uralskii Nauchnyi Tsentr**
Ul. Pervomaiskaya, 91, Sverdlovsk, U.S.S.R.
- Akademiya Nauk S. S. S. R. Sibirskoe Otdelenie Uralskii Nauchnyi Tsentr. Institut Elektrkhimii. Trudy. irreg. ISSN 0568-6776

**Akademiya Nauk S.S.S.R. Vostochno- Sibirskii Filial**
Ul. Favorskogo, 1, 664033 Irkutsk, U.S.S.R.
- Akademiya Nauk S. S. S. R. Sibirskoe Otdelenie. Vostochno- Sibirskii Filial. Institut Geokhimii. Ezhegodnik. irreg. (prep. by its Institut Geokhimii)

**Akademiya Nauk S. S. S. R. Vsesoyuznoe Botanicheskoe Obshchestvo**
Leninskii prospekt, 14, Moscow, U. S. S. R.
- Botanicheskii Zhurnal. m. ISSN 0006-8136

**Akademiya Nauk S. S. S. R. Vsesoyuznoe Obshchestvo Pochvovedeniya**
- Pochvovedenie. (pub. by Izdatel'stvo Nauka)

**Akademiya Nauk S. S. S. R. Vychislitel'nyi Tsentr**
Ul. Vavilova, 40, Moscow V-333, U.S.S.R.
- Dinamika Izluchayushchego Gaza. irreg.
- Issledovania po Teorii Algorifmov i Matematicheskoi Logike. irreg.
- Matematicheskie Problemy Geofiziki. irreg.
- Obrabotka Simvol'noi Informatsii. irreg.

**Akademiya Nauk Tadzhikskoi S. S. R.**
Ul. Aym, 121, Dushanbe, U. S. S. R.
- Akademiya Nauk Tadzhikskoi S. S. R. Doklady. m. ISSN 0002-3469
- Akademiya Nauk Tadzhikskoi S. S. R. Izvestiya. Otdelenie Biologicheskikh Nauk. q. ISSN 0002-3477
- Akademiya Nauk Tadzhikskoi S. S. R. Izvestiya. Otdelenie Fiziko- Matematicheskikh i Geologo- Khimicheskikh Nauk. q. ISSN 0002-3485

**Akademiya Nauk Tadzhikskoi S.S.R. Institut Ekonomiki**
Prospekt Lenina 37, Dushanbe, U.S.S.R.
- Ekonomiko-Matematicheskie Metody v Planirovanii Narodnogo Khozyaistva. irreg.

**Akademiya Nauk Tadzhikskoi S. S. R. Tsentralnaya Nauchnaya Biblioteka**
Ul. Aym, 121, Dushanbe, U.S.S.R.
- Obshchestvennye Nauki v Tadzhikistane; Ukazatel' Literatury. q.

**Akademiya Nauk Turkmenskoi S.S.R.**
Ul. Gogolya, 15, Ashkhabad, U.S.S.R.
- Akademiya Nauk Turkmenskoi S. S. R. Izvestiya. Seriya Biologicheskikh Nauk. bi-m. ISSN 0002-3493
- Akademiya Nauk Turkmenskoi S. S. R. Izvestiya. Seriya Fiziko- Tekhnicheskikh, Khimicheskikh i Geologicheskikh Nauk. bi-m. ISSN 0002-3507
- Akademiya Nauk Turkmenskoi S.S.R. Izvestiya. Seriya Obshchestvennykh Nauk. bi-m.

**Akademiya Nauk Turkmenskoi S. S. R. Institut Pustyni**
Sad Keshi, Ashkhabad, U. S. S. R.
- Problemy Osvoeniya Pustyn/Problems of Desert Development. bi-m. ISSN 0032-9428

**Akademiya Nauk Ukrainskoi S. S. R.**
- Akademiya Nauk Ukrains'koi Rsr. Dopovidi. Seria a Fiziko- Matematichni ta Tekhnichni Nauki. (pub. by Izdatel'stvo Naukova Dumka)
- Akademiya Nauk Ukrainskoi S. S. R. Dopovidi. Seriya Geologiya, Geofizyka, Khimiya ta Biologiya. (pub. by Izdatel'stvo Naukova Dumka)
- Cybernetics. (pub. by Consultants Bureau US)
- Fizika Nizkikh Temperatur/Low Temperature Physics. (pub. by Izdatel'stvo Naukova Dumka)
- Fiziologichnyi Zhurnal. (pub. by Izdatel'stvo Naukova Dumka)
- Geologichnii Zhurnal. (pub. by Izdatel'stvo Naukova Dumka)
- Kibernetika. (pub. by Izdatel'stvo Naukova Dumka)
- Klinicheskaya Khirurgiya. (pub. by Izdatel'stvo Naukova Dumka)
- Konstitutsiya i Svoista Mineralov. (pub. by Izdatel'stvo Naukova Dumka)
- Prikladnaya Mekhanika. (pub. by Izdatel'stvo Naukova Dumka)
- Soviet Applied Mechanics. (pub. by Consultants Bureau US)
- Soviet Materials Science. (pub. by Consultants Bureau US)
- Strength of Materials. (pub. by Consultants Bureau US)
- Ukrainski Khimicheskii Zhurnal/Ukrains'kyi Kimichnyi Zhurnal. (pub. by Izdatel'stvo Naukova Dumka)

**Akademiya Nauk Ukrainskoi S.S.R. Fiziko-Tekhnicheskii Institut Nizkikh Temperatur**
Pr. Lenina 47, Kharkov, U.S.S.R.
- Matematicheskaya Fizika i Funktsionalnyi Analiz. irreg.
- Voprosy Gidrodinamiki i Teploobmena v Kriogennykh Sistemakh. irreg.

**Akademiya Nauk Ukrainskoi S.S.R. Glavnaya Astronomicheskaya Observatoriya**
- Astrometriya i Astrofizika/Astrometry and Astrophysics. (pub. by Izdatel'stvo Naukova Dumka)

**Akademiya Nauk Ukrainskoi S.S.R. Institut Biokhimii**
Ul. Leontovicha, 9, 252030 Kiev 30, U. S. S. R.
- Ukrains'kyi Biokhimichnyi Zhurnal. 6 per yr. ISSN 0041-610X

**Akademiya Nauk Ukrainskoi S.S.R. Institut Botaniki**
- Ukrains'kyi Botanichnyi Zhurnal. (pub. by Izdatel'stvo Naukova Dumka)

**Akademiya Nauk Ukrainskoi S. S. R. Institut Ekonomiki**
- Ekonomika Radyanskoi Ukrainy. (pub. by Izdatel'stvo Radyanska Ukraina)

**Akademiya Nauk Ukrainskoi S.S.R. Institut Elektrosvarki im. E. O. Patona**
Ul. Gor'kogo, 69, Kiev, U.S.S.R.
- Avtomaticheskaya Svarka. m. ISSN 0005-2302

**Akademiya Nauk Ukrainskoi S.S.R. Institut Gaza**
- Kataliticheskaya Konversiya Uglevodorodov. (pub. by Izdatel'stvo Naukova Dumka)

**Akademiya Nauk Ukrainskoi S.S.R. Institut Istorii**
- Mynule i Suchasne Pivnichnoi Bukovyny/Proshloe i Nastoyaschchee Severnoi Bukoviny. (pub. by Izdatel'stvo Naukova Dumka)
- Ukrains'kyi Istorychnyi Zhurnal. (pub. by Izdatel'stvo Naukova Dumka)

**Akademiya Nauk Ukrainskoi S.S.R. Institut Kibernetiki**
- Soviet Automatic Control. (pub. by Scripta Publishing Co. US)

**Akademiya Nauk Ukrainskoi S.S.R. Institut Literatury im. T.G. Shevchenko**
Ul. Kirova, 4, Kiev, U. S. S. R.
- Radyans'ke Literaturoznavstvo. m. ISSN 0033-8613

**Akademiya Nauk Ukrainskoi S.S.R. Institut Matematiki**
- Ukrainian Mathematical Journal. (pub. by Consultants Bureau US)
- Ukrainskii Matematicheskii Zhurnal/Ukrains'kyi Matematychnyi Zhurnal. (pub. by Izdatel'stvo Naukova Dumka)

**Akademiya Nauk Ukrainskoi S. S. R. Institut Mikrobiologii**
- Mikrobiologichnyi Zhurnal. (pub. by Izdatel'stvo Naukova Dumka)

**Akademiya Nauk Ukrainskoi S.S.R. Institut Prikladnoi Matematiki i Mekhaniki**
- Teoriya Sluchainykh Protsessov. (pub. by Izdatel'stvo Naukova Dumka)

**Akademiya Nauk Ukrainskoi S.S.R. Institut Problem Mashinostroeniya**
- Problemy Mashinostroeniya. (pub. by Izdatel'stvo Naukova Dumka)

**Akademiya Nauk Ukrainskoi S.S.R. Institut Problem Materialovedeniya**
Ul. Krzhizanovskogo, 3, Akademgorodok, Kiev, U. S. S. R.
- Poroshkovaya Metallurgiya. m. ISSN 0032-4795

**Akademiya Nauk Ukrainskoi S.S.R. Institut Problem Prochnosti**
- Problemy Prochnosti. (pub. by Izdatel'stvo Naukova Dumka)

**Akademiya Nauk Ukrainskoi S.S.R. Institut Zoologii**
Ul. Lenina, 15, Kiev, U. S. S. R.
- Parazyty, Parazytozy ta Shliakhyikh Likvidatsii. irreg.

**Akademiya Nauk Ukrainskoi S.S.R. Instytut Mystetsvo-znavstva, Folkloru ta Etnografii**
- Narodna Tvorchist' ta Etnografiya. (pub. by Izdatel'stvo Naukova Dumka)

**Akademiya Nauk Ukrainskoi S.S.R. Kiberneticheskii Tsentr**
- Upravlyayuchie Sistemy i Mashiny. (pub. by Izdatel'stvo Naukova Dumka)

**Akademiya Nauk Ukrainskoi S.S.R. Material Sciences Institute**
- Soviet Powder Metallurgy and Metal Ceramics. (pub. by Consultants Bureau US)

**Akademiya Nauk Uzbekskoi S.S.R.**
Ul. Kuibysheva 15, Tashkent, U.S.S.R.
- Akademiya Nauk Uzbekskoi S.S.R. Izvestiya. Seriya Fiziko-Matematicheskikh Nauk. bi-m.
- Akademiya Nauk Uzbekskoi S. S. R. Izvestiya. Seriya Tekhnicheskikh Nauk. bi-m.
- Chemistry of Natural Compounds. (pub. by Consultants Bureau US)
- Geliotekhnika. bi-m. ISSN 0016-6022
- Khimiya Prirodnykh Soedinenii. bi-m. ISSN 0023-1150
- Obshchestvennye Nauki v Uzbekistane. m. ISSN 0029-7763
- Uzbekskii Biologicheskii Zhurnal. bi-m. ISSN 0042-1685
- Uzbekskii Geologicheskii Zhurnal. bi-m. ISSN 0042-1693
- Uzbekskii Khimicheskii Zhurnal. bi-m. ISSN 0042-1707

**Akademiya Nauk Uzbekskoi S.S.R. Institut Matematiki im V. I. Romanovskogo**
Astronomicheskii tup., 11, Tashkent, U. S. S. R.
- Kraevye Zadachi dlya Differentsial'nykh Uravnenii. irreg.

**Akademiya Navuk Belarusskai S. S. R.**
Leninskii prospekt, 68, Minsk, U. S. S. R.
- Akademiya Navuk Belarusskai S. S. R. Doklady. m. ISSN 0002-354X
- Akademiya Navuk Belarusskai S.S.R. Vesti. Seryya Biyalagichnykh Navuk. bi-m. ISSN 0002-3558
- Akademiya Navuk Belarusskai S. S. R. Vestsi. Seryya Fizika- Matematychnykh Navuk. bi-m. ISSN 0002-3574
- Akademiya Navuk Belarusskai S. S. R. Vestsi. Seryya Fizika- Tekhnichnykh Navuk. q. ISSN 0002-3566
- Akademiya Navuk Belarusskai S. S. R. Vestsi. Seryya Gramadskikh Navuk. bi-m. ISSN 0002-3582
- Akademiya Navuk Belarusskai S. S. R. Vestsi. Seryya Khimichnykh Navuk. bi-m. ISSN 0002-3590
- Akademiya Navuk Belarusskai S. S. R. Vestsi. Seryya Sel'skagaspadarchykh Navuk. q. ISSN 0002-3604
- Differential Equations. (pub. by Consultants Bureau US)
- Energeticheskoe Khozyaistvo Belorusskoi S.S.R. s-a.
- Journal of Engineering Physics. (pub. by Consultants Bureau US)
- Problemy Poles'ya. irreg.

**Akademiya Navuk Belorusskoi S. S. R. Institut Yazikoznaniya im. Yakuba Kolasa**
Leninskii Prospekt, 68, 220072 Minsk, U.S.S.R.
- Belarusskaya Linhvistika. s-a.

**Akademiya Pedagogicheskikh Nauk S.S.S.R.**
Bolshaya Polyanka, 58, 113095 Moscow, U.S.S.R.
- Sem'ya i Shkola. m. ISSN 0037-2048
- Voprosy Psikhologii. (pub. by Izdatel'stvo Prosveshchenie)

**Akademiya Pedagogicheskikh Nauk S.S.S.R. Nauchno - Issledovatel'skii Institut Pedagogicheskoi Metodologii Standartov**
Ul. Makarenko 5-16, Moscow K-64, U.S.S.R.
- Sovetskaya Pedagogika. m. ISSN 0038-5093

**Armenian Society for Friendship and Cultural Relations with Foreign Countries**
Ul. Abovian, 3, Erevan, U. S. S. R.
- Armenia Today. q. ISSN 0004-2293

**Armyanskaya S. S. R. Ministerstvo Kul'tury**
Ul. Isahakian, 28, Erevan, U. S. S. R.
- Sovetakan Arvest. m. ISSN 0038-500X
- Sovetakan Mankavarzh. m. ISSN 0038-5026

**Belorusskaya S.S.R. Ministerstvo Kul'tury**
Minsk, U.S.S.R.
- Literatura i Mastatstva. 2 per wk. ISSN 0024-4686

**Belorusskaya S.S.R. Ministerstvo Zdravookhraneniya**
Minsk, U.S.S.R.
- Zdravookhranenie Belorussii. m. ISSN 0044-1961

**Belorusskii Gosudarstvennyi Institut Narodnogo Khozyaistva**
- Ekonomika i Organizatsiya Promyshlennogo Proizvodstva. (pub. by Izdatel'stvo Vysshaya Shkola B. S. S. R.)

**Belorusskii Politekhnicheskii Institut**
Leninskii prosp. 65, 220027 Minsk, U.S.S.R.
- Izvestiya Vysshikh Uchebnykh Zavedenii. Seriya Energetika. m. ISSN 0579-2983 (U. S. S. R. Ministerstvo Vysshego i Srednego Spetsial'nogo Obrazovaniya)

**Vydavnytstvo Budivelnyk**
Volodymyzska, 24, Kiev, U. S. S. R.
- Budivel'ni Materialy i Konstruktsii. bi-m. ISSN 0007-2974 (Akademiya Budivnystva i Arkhitektury Ukrainskoi S. S. R.)

**Chelyabinskii Gosudarstvennyi Pedagogicheskii Institut**
Chelyabinsk, U.S.S.R.
- Voprosy Fiziki Tverdogo Tela. irreg.

**Chuvashskii Gosudarstvennyi Universitet**
Moskovskii prospekt, 15, Cheboksary, U.S.S.R.
- Teoriya Funktsii Kompleksnogo Peremennogo i Kraevye Zadachi. irreg.

**Committee for Cultural Relations with Armenians Abroad**
Alverdian Str. 37, Erevan, U. S. S. R.
- Areiniki Dzain. w. ISSN 0017-8705

**Dalnevostochnoe Knizhnoe Izdatel'stvo. Sakhalinskoe Otdelenie**
Ul. Dzerzhinskogo, 34, Yuzhno-Sakhalinsk, U.S.S.R.
- Literatura o Sakhalinskoi Oblasti. a. (Sakhalinskaya Oblastnaya Biblioteka)

**Izdatel'stvo DOSAAF**
Novo - Ryazanskaya ul. 26, Moscow B-66, U.S.S.R.
- Kryl'ya Rodiny. m. ISSN 0023-4974
- Voennye Znaniya. m. ISSN 0042-9074

**Izdatel'stvo Ekonomika**
Berezhkovskaya Nab., 6, 2121864 Moscow, U. S. S. R.
(Subscr. to: Mezhdunarodnaya Kniga, Moscow, G-200, U.S.S.R.)
- Ekonomika i Zhizn'. m. ISSN 0013-3051
- Organizatsiya Upravleniya. irreg.

**Izdatel'stvo Elm**
Ul. Narimanova, 31, Baku 370073, U. S. S. R.
(Subscr. to: Mezhdunarodnaya Kniga, Moscow, G-200, U. S. S. R.)
- Akademiya Nauk Azerbaidzhanskoi S. S. R. Doklady. m. ISSN 0002-3078
- Akademiya Nauk Azerbaidzhanskoi S. S. R. Izvestiya. Seriya Biologicheskikh Nauk. bi-m. ISSN 0002-3086
- Akademiya Nauk Azerbaidzhanskoi S. S. R. Izvestiya. Seriya Ekonomicheskikh Nauk. q. ISSN 0002-3094
- Akademiya Nauk Azerbaidzhanskoi S. S. R. Izvestiya. Seriya Fiziko - Tekhnicheskikh i Matematicheskikh Nauk. bi-m. ISSN 0002-3108

**Izdatel'stvo Energiya**
Slyuzovaya Nab., 10, Moscow z-114, U.S.S.R.
(Subscr. to: Mezhdunarodnaya Kniga, Moscow G-200, U.S.S.R.)
- Elektricheskie Stantsii. m. ISSN 0013-5372 (U. S. S. R. Ministerstvo Energetiki i Elektrifikatsii)
- Energetik. m. ISSN 0013-7278
- Teploenergetika. m. ISSN 0040-3636

**Izdatel'stvo Finansy**
Ul. Chernyshevskogo 7, Moscow K-142, U. S. S. R.
(Subscr. to: Mezhdunarodnaya Kniga, Moscow, G-200, U.S.S.R.)
- Den'gi i Kredit. m. ISSN 0011-8362 (Gosbank S. S. R.)
- Finansy S.S.S.R. m. ISSN 0015-2161 (U.S.S.R. Ministerstvo Finansov)

**Izdatel'stvo Fizkul'tura i Sport**
Kalayaevskaya Ul., 27, Moscow, U. S. S. R.
(Subscr. to: Mezhdunarodnaya Kniga, Moscow, G-200, U.S.S.R.)
- Fizkul'tura i Sport. m. ISSN 0015-332X (U. S. S. R. Komitet po Fizicheskoi Kul'ture i Sportu pri Sovete Ministrov)
- Katera i Yakhty. bi-m. ISSN 0022-930X
- Konevodstvo i Konnyi Sport. m. ISSN 0023-3285
- Legkaya Atletika. m. ISSN 0024-4155 (Soyuz Sportivnykh Obshchestv i Organizatsii S. S. S. R.)
- Okhota i Okhotnich'e Khozyaistvo. m. ISSN 0030-1582
- Shakhmatnyi Byulleten' m. ISSN 0037-3230 (U. S. S. R. Komitet po Fizicheskoi Kul'ture i Sportu pri Sovete Ministrov)
- Shakhmaty v S. S. S. R. m. ISSN 0037-3249 (U. S. S. R. Komitet po Fizicheskoi Kul'ture i Sportu pri Sovete Ministrov)
- Sport in the USSR. m. ISSN 0038-7908
- Sportivnaya Zhizn' Rossii. m. ISSN 0038-8092 (Soyuz Sportivnykh Obshchestv i Organizatsii Rossiiskoi S.F.S.R.)
- Sportivnye Igry. m. ISSN 0038-8106 (Soyuz Sportivnykh Obshchestv i Organizatsii S.S.S.R.)
- Teoriya i Praktika Fizicheskoi Kul'tury. m. ISSN 0040-3601 (U. S. S. R. Komitet po Fizicheskoi Kul'ture i Sportu pri Sovete Ministrov)

**Geograficheskoe Obshchestvo S.S.S.R. Zabaikal'skii Filial**
Chita, U. S. S. R.
- Klimat i Gidrografiya Zabaikal'ya. irreg.

**Gidrometeoizdat**
Vasilevskii Ostrov, Leningrad V-53, U.S.S.R.
(Subscr. To: Mezhdunarodnaya Kniga, Moscow G-200, U.S.S.R.)
- Fizika Nizhnei Atmosfery. irreg. (Institut Eksperimentalnoi Meteorologii)
- Meteorologiya i Gidrologiya. m. ISSN 0026-119X

**Glavnaya Geofizicheskaya Observatoriya im. A. I. Voeikova**
Karbysheva, 7, Leningrad K-18, U.S.S.R.
- A. I. Voeikov Main Geophysical Observatory, Leningrad. Data of Measurements of Electric Field Strength of the Atmosphere at Various Altitudes by the Results of Soundings. irreg. ISSN 0065-0080
- A. I. Voeikov Main Geophysical Observatory, Leningrad. Results of Ground Observations of Atmospheric Electricity. Additional Issue. a. ISSN 0065-0099
- Solnechnaya Radiatsiya i Radiatsionnyi Balans (Mirovaya Set)/Solar Radiation and Radiation Balance Data (the World Network) m. (Co-Sponsor: World Meteorological Organization)

**Gosbank S. S. S. R.**
- Den'gi i Kredit. (pub. by Izdatel'stvo Finansy)

**Gosteleradio S. S. S. R.**
Ul. Pyatnitskaya, 25, Moscow, U. S. S. R.
- Krugozor. m. ISSN 0454-5508

**Gosudarstvennaya Biblioteka Belorusskoi S. S. R. im V. I. Lenina**
Krasnoznamennaya ul., 9, Minsk, U.S.S.R.
- Letopis' Pechati B. S. S. R. m.
- Raionnye Biblioteki Belorussii; analiz sostoyaniya raboty i metodicheskie rekomendatsii. a.

**Gosudarstvennaya Biblioteka S.S.S.R. im. V.I. Lenina**
Pr. Kalinina 3, 121019 Moscow Tsentr, U. S. S. R.
(Subscr. to: Mezhdunarodnaya Kniga, Moscow G-200, U.S.S.R.)
- Bibliotekar' m. ISSN 0006-1808
- Bibliotekovedenie i Bibliografiya za Rubezhom. 5 per yr. ISSN 0519-9514
- Gosudarstvennaya Biblioteka S. S. S. R. im. V. I. Lenina. Informatsionnyi Byulleten' Novykh Inostrannykh Knig, Postupivshikh v Biblioteku. Seriya 1: Fiziko - Matematicheskie i Khimicheskie Nauki; Nauki o Zemle; Tekhnika i Tekhnicheskie Nauki. 3 per mo. ISSN 0041-8072
- Gosudarstvennaya Biblioteka S. S. S. R. im. V. I. Lenina. Informatsionnyi Byulleten' Novykh Inostrannykh Knig, Postupivshikh v Biblioteku. Seriya 3: Obshchestvennye Nauki; Khudozhestvennaya Literatura; Iskusstvo. 3 per m. ISSN 0041-8080
- Letopis' Zhurnal'nykh Statei. w and q. ISSN 0024-1202

**Gosudarstvennyi Astronomicheskii Institut im. P. K. Shternberga**
- Gosudarstvennyi Astronomicheskii Institut im. P. K. Shternberga. Soobshcheniya. (pub. by Izdatel'stvo Moskovskii Universitet)
- Gosudarstvennyi Astronomicheskii Institut im. P. K. Shternberga. Trudy. (pub. by Izdatel'stvo Moskovskii Universitet)

**Gosudarstvennyi Muzei Izobrazitel'nykh Iskusstv im. Pushkina**
Volkhonka 12, 121019 Moscow, U.S.S.R.
- Gosudarstvennyi Muzei Izobrazitel'nykh Iskusstv im. Pushkina. Soobshcheniya. irreg. ISSN 0077-1562

**Institut Eksperimentalnoi Meteorologii**
- Fizika Nizhnei Atmosfery. (pub. by Gidrometeoizdat)

**Institut Mekhanobr**
21 Liniya, 8a, Leningrad B-26, U.S.S.R.
- Obogashchenie Rud. bi-m. ISSN 0029-7623

**Institut Vodnogo Transporta, Leningrad**
- Institut Vodnogo Transporta, Leningrad. Gidrotekhnicheskaya Laboratoriya. Materialy. (pub. by Izdatel'stvo Transport. Leningradskoe Otdelenie)

**International Anatomical Congress**
C/O Prof. Dr. Shdanow, Karl Marx Prospekt 18, Moscow K-9, U.S.S.R.
- International Anatomical Congress. Proceedings. quinquennial, 1970, 9th, Leningrad. ISSN 0074-1353

**International Federation for Documentation. Committee on Research on the Theoretical Basis of Information**
Hofweg 7, 2511 AA The Hague, Netherlands
- F I D/R I Meetings Reports. irreg., no. 2, 1974. (And Vsesoyuznyi Institut Nauchno-Tekhnicheskoi Informatsii, Ul. Baltiiskaya 14, Moscow, U.S.S.R.)

**International Geographical Union**
Inquire: Dr. Yuri/Medvedkov.,Sec. Gen., Soviet Organizing Committee, Staromonetnyi Per. 29, Moscow 109017, U.S.S.R.
- International Geographical Union. Report of Congress. quadrennial; 23rd, Moscow 1976. ISSN 0074-6134

**International Grassland Congress**
Inquire: Dr. V. Igloviv, All-Union Research Forage Institute, Moscow Region, Lugovaya, USSR.
- International Grassland Congress. Proceedings. irreg., 1974, 12th, Moscow. ISSN 0074-6185

**Irkutskii Gosudarstvennyi Universitet im. A. A. Zhdanova**
Ul. Karla Marksa, 1, Irkutsk, U.S.S.R.
- Asimptoticheskie Metody v Teorii Sistem. irreg.

**Izdatel'stvo Iskusstvo**
Tsvetnoi bulvar, 25, Moscow K-51, U. S. S. R.
- Iskusstvo. m. ISSN 0021-177X (U. S. S. R. Ministerstvo Kul'tury) (Co-sponsor: Soyuz Khudozhnikov S. S. S. R.)
- Repertuar Khudozhestvennoi Samodeyatel'nosti. s-m. ISSN 0034-4648
- Stikhi. irreg.
- Teatr; zhurnal dramaturgii i teatra. m. ISSN 0040-0777 (U.S.S.R. Ministerstvo Kul'tury) (Co-sponsor: Soyuz Pisatelei S.S.S.R.)

**Ivanovskii Tekstil'nyi Institut**
Ivanovo, U.S.S.R.
- Izvestiya Vysshikh Uchebnykh Zavedenii. Seriya Tekhnologiya Tekstil'noi Promyshlennosti. bi-m. ISSN 0021-3497

**Izdatel'stvo Izvestiya**
Pl. Pushkina, 5, 103798 Moscow, U.S.S.R.
(Subscr. to: Eastern News Distributors, 155 West 15 Street, New York, N. Y. 10011 U. S. A.)
- Druzhba Narodov. m. ISSN 0012-6756 (Soyuz Pisatelei S.S.S.R.)
- Foreign Trade/Vneshnyaya Torgovlya. m. ISSN 0042-7721 (U.S.S.R. Ministerstvo Vneshnei Torgovli)
- Novyi Mir; literaturno-khudozhestvennyi i obshchestvenno-politicheski zhurnal. m. ISSN 0029-5329 (Soyuz Pisatelei S.S.S.R.)
- Sovety Deputatov Trudyashchikhsya. m. ISSN 0038-5247

- Soviet Literature/Sovetskaya Literatura. m. ISSN 0038-5557 (Soyuz Pisatelei S.S.S.R.)
- Voprosy Literatury. m. ISSN 0042-8795 (Soyuz Pisatelei S.S.S.R.) (Co-sponsor: Akademiya Nauk S.S.S.R. Institut Mirovoi Literatury im. A. M. Gor'kogo)

**Izdatel'stvo Kainar**
Kashgarskaya ul., 64, Alma-Ata, U.S.S.R.
- Vestnik Sel'skokhozyaistvennoi Nauki Kazakhstana. m. ISSN 0042-4684 (Kazakhskaya S.S.R. Ministerstvo Sel'skogo Khozyaistva)

**Kalininskii Nauchno-Issledovatel'skii Institut Tekstilnoi Promyshlennosti**
Kalinin, U.S.S.R.
- Kalininskii Nauchno-issledovatel'skii Institut Tekstil'noi Promyshlennosti. Nauchno-issledovatel'skie Trudy. irreg.

**Izdatel'stvo Kamenyar**
Vul. Vatutina 6, Lvov, U.S.S.R.
- Zhovten; literaturno-mystetz'kyi ta hromads'kopolitychnyi zhurnal. m. ISSN 0044-4499 (Soyuz Pisatelei Ukrainskoi S.S.R.)

**Kazakhskaya S.S.R. Ministerstvo Sel'skogo Khozyaistva**
- Vestnik Sel'skokhozyaistvennoi Nauki Kazakhstana. (pub. by Izdatel'stvo Kainar)

**Kazakhskii Gosudarstvennyi Universitet**
Ul. Lenina 18, Alma-Ata, U.S.S.R.
- Biologicheskie Nauki. irreg.
- Filosofskie Nauki. irreg.

**Kazakhskii Nauchno-Issledovatel'skii Institut Onkologii i Radiologii**
Alma-Ata, U.S.S.R.
- Kazakhskii Nauchno-issledovatel'skii Institut Onkologii i Radiologii. Trudy. a. ISSN 0075-529X

**Kazanskii Gosudarstvennyi Pedagogicheskii Institut**
Ul. Mezjlauk, 1, 420021 Kazan, U.S.S.R.
- Kazanskii Gosudarstvennyi Pedagogicheskii Institut. Voprosy Istorii, Teorii Muzyki i Muzykal'nogo Vospytaniya. Sbornik. biennial.

**Kazanskii Universitet**
Ul. Lenina, 4/5, Kazan, U.S.S.R.
- Izvestiya Vysshikh Uchebnykh Zavedenii. Seriya Matematika. m. ISSN 0021-3446
- Kazanskii Universitet. Sbornik Aspirantskikh Rabot: Teoriya Plastin i Obolochek. irreg.
- Paramagnitnyi Rezonans. irreg.
- Romantizm v Russkoi i Sovetskoi Literature. irreg.

**Khabarovskoe Knizhnoe Izdatel'stvo**
Ul. Lenina, 181, Blagoveshchensk, U.S.S.R.
- Priamur'e Moe; literaturno-khudozhestvennyi sbornik. irreg.

**Kharkivskyi Politekhnichnyi Instytut**
Ul. Frunze, 21, Kharkov, U.S.S.R.
- Ekonomika Promyslovosti. irreg.
- Elektroenergetika i Avtomatizatsiya Energoustanovok. irreg.
- Elektrovymiriuvalna Tekhnika. irreg.
- Magnitnoimpulsnaya Obrabotka Metallov. irreg.

**Kharkovskii Gosudarstvennyi Universitet**
Kharkov, U.S.S.R.
- Kharkovskii Gosudarstvennyi Universitet. Filolohiya. irreg.
- Kharkovskii Gosudarstvennyi Universitet. Radiofizyka i Elektronika. irreg.

**Izdatel'stvo Khimiya**
Novaya pl., 10, Moscow K-12, U.S.S.R.
- Khimicheskaya Promyshlennost' m. ISSN 0023-110X (U.S.S.R. Ministerstvo Khimicheskoi Promyshlennosti)
- Khimicheskie Volokna. bi-m. ISSN 0023-1118
- Khimiya i Tekhnologiya Topliv i Masel. m. ISSN 0023-1169

**Izdatel'stvo Khudozhestvennaya Literatura**
Novo - Basmannay ul., 19, Moscow B-66, U.S.S.R.
- Detskaya Literatura. m. ISSN 0011-9717

**Izdatel'stvo Khudozhestvennaya Literatura. Leningradskoe Otdelenie**
Ul. Mokhovaya, 20, Leningrad D-28, U. S. S. R.
(Subscr. to: Mezhdunarodnaya Kniga, Moscow, G-200, U. S. S. R.)
- Neva. m. ISSN 0028-4009 (Soyuz Pisatelei Rossiiskoi S.F.S.R.)

- Zvezda; literaturno-khudozhestvennyi i obshchestvenno-politicheski zhurnal. m. ISSN 0039-7105 (Soyuz Pisatelei S.S.S.R.)

**Izdatel'stvo Kievskii Universitet**
Bul'var Tarasa Shevchenko, 14, Kiev, U.S.S.R.
- Fizika Aerodispersnykh Sistem. irreg. (Subscr. to: Mezhdunarodnaya Kniga, Moscow, G-200, U. S. R.)
- Theory of Probability and Mathematical Statistics. (pub. by American Mathematical Society US)

**Izdatel'stvo Kniga**
Ul. Nezhdanovoi, 8-10, Moscow K-9, U. S. R.
- Letopis' Gazetnykh Statei. s-m. ISSN 0024-1172 (U. S. S. R. Komitet po Pechati Soveta Ministrov)
- Letopis' Pechatnykh Proizvedenii Izobrazitel'nogo Iskusstva. q. ISSN 0024-1199 (U. S. S. R. Komitet po Pechati Soveta Ministrov)
- Notnaya Letopis' q. ISSN 0029-4462 (U. S. S. R. Komitet po Pechati Soveta Ministrov)
- Poligrafiya. m. ISSN 0032-2717 (U. S. S. R. Komitet po Pechati Soveta Ministrov)
- Sovetskaya Bibliografiya. bi-m. ISSN 0038-5042 (U. S. S. R. Komitet po Pechati Soveta Ministrov)
- V Mire Knig. m. ISSN 0042-188X (U. S. S. R. Komitet po Pechati Soveta Ministrov)

**Izdatel'stvo Kolos**
Sadovaya-Spasskaya, 18, 107807 Moscow, U. S. S. R.
(Subscr. to: Mezhdunarodnaya Kniga, Moscow, G-200, U. S. S. R.)
- Ekonomika Sel'skogo Khozyaistva. m. ISSN 0013-3094 (U. S. S. R. Ministerstvo Sel'skogo Khozyaistva)
- Gidrotekhnika i Melioratsiya. m. ISSN 0016-9722 (U. S. S. R. Ministerstvo Sel'skogo Khozyaistva)
- Khlopkovodstvo. m. ISSN 0023-1231 (U. S. S. R. Ministerstvo Sel'skogo Khozyaistva)
- Mekhanizatsiya i Elektrifikatsiya Sotsialisticheskogo Sel'skogo Khozyaistva. m. ISSN 0025-8881 (U. S. S. R. Ministerstvo Sel'skogo Khozyaistva)
- Sel'skoe Khozyaistvo za Rubezhom. Seriya: Rasteneivodstvo i Zhivotnovodstvo. m. ISSN 0037-1653 (Vsesoyuznaya Akademiya Sel'skokhozyaistvennykh Nauk im. V. I. Lenina)
- Tekhnika v Sel'skom Khozyaistve. m. ISSN 0040-2265 (U. S. S. R. Ministerstvo Sel'skogo Khozyaistva)
- Vsesoyuznyi Nauchno-Issledovatel'skii Institut Zernovogo Khozyaistva. Trudy. irreg. (Vsesoyuznaya Akademiya Sel'skokhozyaistvennykh Nauk im. V. I. Lenina)
- Zemledelie. m. ISSN 0044-3913 (U.S.S.R. Ministerstvo Sel'skogo Khozyaistva)
- Zernovoe Khozyaistvo. m. (U.S.S.R. Ministerstvo Sel'skogo Khozyaistva)

**Komitet Sovetskikh Zhenshchin**
- Soviet Woman/Sovetskaya Zhenshchina. (pub. by Izdatel'stvo Pravda)

**Kommanduyushchii Artilleriei Vooruzhennykh Sil' S. S. R.**
Moscow, U.S.S.R.
- Artilleriiskii Zhurnal. m. ISSN 0004-3818

**Kommunisticheskaya Partiya Armyanskoi S.S.R. Tsentral'nyi Komitet**
Erevan, U.S.S.R.
- Leninyan Ugiov. m. ISSN 0024-0869

**Kommunisticheskaya Partiya Belorussii. Tsentral'nyi Komitet**
Leninskii Prospekt, 77, 220041, Minsk, U.S.S.R.
- Kommunist Belorussii/Komunist Belarusii. (pub. by Izdatel'stvo Zvyazda)
- Politinformator i Agitator. s-m.

**Kommunisticheskaya Partiya Sovetskogo Soyuza. Tsentral'nyi Komitet**
- Kommunist. (pub. by Izdatel'stvo Pravda)
- Partiinaya Zhizn' (pub. by Izdatel'stvo Pravda)
- Politicheskoe Samoobrazovanie. (pub. by Izdatel'stvo Pravda)

**Kommunisticheskaya Partiya Tadzhikskoi S. S. R. Tsentral'nyi Komitet**
Pr. Lenina, 46, Dushanbe, U. S. S. R.
(Subscr. to: Mezhdunaroodnaya Kniga, Moscow, G-200, U. S. S. R.)
- Kommunisti Tochikiston. m. ISSN 0023-3129

**Kommunisticheskaya Partiya Ukrainy. Tsentral'nyi Komitet**
- Kommunist Ukrainy/Komunist Ukraini. (pub. by Izdatel'stvo Radyanska Ukraina)

**Konstruktorsko-Tekhnologicheskii Institut Avtomatizatsii Avtomobilstroeniya**
Chelyabinsk, U.S.S.R.
- Konstruktorsko-Tekhnologicheskii Institut Avtomatizatsii Avtomobilstroeniya. Sbornik Trudov. irreg.

**Krasnoyarskii Institut Tsvetnykh Metallov**
- Liteinoe Proizvodstvo, Metallovedenie i Obrabotka Metallov Davleniem. (pub. by Krasnoyarskoe Knizhnoe Izdatel'stvo)

**Krasnoyarskoe Knizhnoe Izdatel'stvo**
Prospekt Mira, 89, Krasnoyarsk, U.S.S.R.
- Liteinoe Proizvodstvo, Metallovedenie i Obrabotka Metallov Davleniem. irreg. (Krasnoyarskii Institut Tsvetnykh Metallov)

**Latviiskaya S.S.R. Gosudarstvennyi Nauchno-tekhnicheskii Komitet Soveta Ministrov**
Riga, U.S.S.R.
- Nauka i Tekhnika/Zinatne Un Tekhnika. m. ISSN 0028-1255

**Latviiskaya S.S.R. Ministerstvo Kultury**
Riga, U.S.S.R.
- Shakhs/Shakhmaty. s-m. ISSN 0558-1613

**Latviiskaya S. S. R. Valsts Gramatu Palata**
Bibliotekas 5, Riga, U. S. S. R.
- Latvijas P S R Preses Hronika. m. ISSN 0023-8910

**Latviiskii Gosudarstvennyi Universitet. Kafedra Statistiki i Planirovaniya Narodnogo Khozyaistva S.S.S.R.**
Bulvar Raynisa 19, Riga, U. S. S. R.
- Voprosy Statistiki. irreg.

**Latviiskii Nauchno-issledovatel'skii Institut Gidrotekhniki i Melioratsii**
Ul. Revoliutsiias, 43, Elgava, Latvia, U.S.S.R.
- Polimery v Melioratsii i Vodnom Khozyaistve. irreg.

**Leningrad. Gorodskoi Sovet Deputatov Trudyashchikhsya. Ispolnitel'nyi Komitet**
- Stroitel'stvo i Arkhitektura Leningrada. (pub. by Lenizdat)

**Leningradskii Gornyi Institut**
Leningrad, U.S.S.R.
- Novye Issledovaniya v Gornoi Elektromekhanike. irreg.
- Novye Issledovaniya v Khimii, Metallurgii i Obogashchenii. irreg.

**Leningradskii Institut Tochnoi Mekhaniki i Optiki**
Leningrad, U.S.S.R.
- Izvestiya Vysshikh Uchebnykh Zavedenii. Seriya Priborostroenie. m. ISSN 0021-3454

**Leningradskii Universitet**
Universitetskaya nab. 7/9, Leningrad B-164, U.S.S.R.
- Avtomatizirovannye Sistemy Upravleniya. irreg. (Rossiiskaya S. F. S. R. Ministerstvo Vysshego i Srednego Spetsial'nogo Obrazovaniya)
- Leningradskii Universitet. Uchenye Zapiski. Seriya Geologicheskikh Nauk. irreg. ISSN 0459-0805
- Leningradskii Universitet. Vestnik. Seriya Biologiya. (pub. by Izdatel'stvo Nauka. Leningradskoe Otdelenie)
- Leningradskii Universitet. Vestnik. Seriya Ekonomika, Filosofiya i Pravo. (pub. by Izdatel'stvo Nauka. Leningradskoe Otdelenie)
- Leningradskii Universitet. Vestnik. Seriya Fizika i Khimiya. (pub. by Izdatel'stvo Nauka. Leningradskoe Otdelenie)

- Leningradskii Universitet. Vestnik. Seriya Geologiya i Geografiya. (pub. by Izdatel'stvo Nauka. Leningradskoe Otdelenie)
- Leningradskii Universitet. Vestnik. Seriya Istoriya, Yazyk i Literatura. (pub. by Izdatel'stvo Nauka. Leningradskoe Otdelenie)
- Leningradskii Universitet. Vestnik. Seriya Matematika, Mekhanika i Astronomiya. (pub. by Izdatel'stvo Nauka. Leningradskoe Otdelenie)
- Litologiya i Paleogeografiya. triennial.
- Molekulyarnaya Fizika i Biofizika Vodnykh Sistem. (pub. by Lenizdat)
- Nekotorye Filosofskie Voprosy Sovremennogo Estestvoznaniya. (pub. by Lenizdat)
- Prikladnaya Mekhanika i Priborostroenie. (pub. by Lenizdat)
- Slavyanskaya Filologiya. irreg.
- Slavyanskaya Filologiya.
- Voprosy Teorii Sistem Avtomaticheskogo Upravleniya. irreg.

**Leningradskii Universitet. Geologicheskii Fakultet**
- Leningradskii Universitet. Uchenye Zapiski. Seriya Geologicheskikh Nauk.

**Leningradskii Universitet. Kafedra Litologii i Morskoi Geologii**
- Litologiya i Paleogeografiya.

**Leninskii Kommunisticheskii Soyuz Molodezhi Belorusskoi S.S.R.**
- Byarozka. (pub. by Izdatel'stvo Zvyazda)
- Maladosts' (pub. by Izdatel'stvo Zvyazda)

**Leninskii Kommunisticheskii Soyuz Molodezhi Ukrainskoi S.S.R.**
- Dnipro. (pub. by Izdatel'stvo Molod)
- Malyatko. (pub. by Izdatel'stvo Molod)
- Pioneriya. (pub. by Izdatel'stvo Molod)

**Lenizdat**
Fontanka, 59, Leningrad, U.S.S.R.
- Molekulyarnaya Fizika i Biofizika Vodnykh Sistem. irreg. (Leningradskii Universitet)
- Nekotorye Filosofskie Voprosy Sovremennogo Estestvoznaniya. irreg. (Leningradskii Universitet)
- Prikladnaya Mekhanika i Priborostroenie. irreg. (Leningradskii Universitet)
- Stroitel'stvo i Arkhitektura Leningrada. m. ISSN 0039-2413 (Leningrad. Gorodskoi Sovet Deputatov Trudyashchikhsya. Ispolnitel'nyi Komitet) (Co-sponsors: Soyuz Arkhitektorov S. S. S. R., Leningradskoe Otdelenie)

**Izdatel'stvo Lesnaya Promyshlennost'**
Ul. 25 Oktyabrya, 8, Moscow K-12, U. S. S. R.
(Subscr. to: Mezhdunarodnaya Kniga, Moscow, G-200, U. S. S. R.)
- Derevoobrabatyvayushchaya Promyshlennost' m. ISSN 0011-9008 (U. S. S. R. Ministerstvo Derevoobrabatyvayushchei Promyshlennosti)
- Lesnoe Khozyaistvo. m. ISSN 0024-1113

**Izdatel'stvo Literaturnaya Gazeta**
Pisemskogo 7, Moscow, U.S.S.R
(Subscr. to: Mezhdunarodnaya Kniga, Moscow, G-200, U. S. S. R.)
- Nash Sovremennik; literaturno-khudozhestvennyi i obshchestvenno-politicheskii zhurnal. m. ISSN 0027-8238 (Soyuz Pisatelei Rossiiskoi S. F. S. R.)

**Litovskaya S. S. R. Aukstuju Mokyklu Mokslo Darbai**
Vilnius, U. S. S. R.
- Elektrotechnika ir Mechanika. irreg.
- Mekhanicheskaya Tekhnologiya/Mechanine Technologija. irreg.

**Litovskaya S. S. R. Ministerstvo Vysshego Obrazovaniya**
- Baltistica. (pub. by Izdatel'stvo Mintis)

**Izdatel'stvo Mashinostroenie**
Pervyi Basmanny Per., 3, Moscow, U.S.S.R.
(Subscr. to: Mezhdunarodnaya Kniga, Moscow, G-200, U.S.S.R.)
- Kuznechno-shtampovochnoe Proizvodstvo. m. ISSN 0023-5806
- Mashinostroitel' m. ISSN 0025-4568
- Mekhanizatsiya Stroitel'stva. m. ISSN 0025-8903 (U.S.S.R. Gosstroi)

- Optiko-mekhanicheskaya Promyshlennost' m. ISSN 0030-4042
- Pribory i Sistemy Upravleniya. m. ISSN 0032-8154 (U. S. S. R. Ministerstvo Priborostroeniya)
- Sel'skii Mekhanizator. m. ISSN 0037-1645
- Shveinaya Promyshlennost' bi-m. ISSN 0037-4431
- Stanki i Instrumenty. m. ISSN 0038-9811
- Stroitel'nye i Dorozhnye Mashiny. m. ISSN 0039-2391 (U. S. S. R. Ministerstvo Stroitel'nogo, Dorozhnogo i Kommunal'nogo Mashinostroeniya)
- Stroitel'stvo Truboprovodov. m. ISSN 0039-2448
- Svarochnoe Proizvodstvo. m. ISSN 0491-6441
- Transportnoe Stroitel'stvo. m. ISSN 0041-1701

**Izdatel'stvo Meditsina**
Petroverigskii per., 6-8, Moscow K-142, U. S. S. R. (Subscr. to: Mezhdunarodnaya Kniga, Moscow, G-200, U. S. S. R.)
- Akusherstvo i Ginekologiya. m. ISSN 0002-3906
- Antibiotiki. m. ISSN 0003-5637
- Arkhiv Anatomii, Gistologii i Embriologii. m. ISSN 0004-1947 (Akademiya Meditsinskikh Nauk S. S. S. R.)
- Arkhiv Patologii. m. ISSN 0004-1955 (U. S. S. R. Ministerstvo Zdravookhraneniya) (Co-sponsor: Akademiya Meditsinskikh Nauk S. S. S. R.)
- Byulleten' Eksperimental'noi Biologii i Meditsiny. m. ISSN 0006-4041
- Eksperimental'naya Khirurgiya i Anesteziologiya. bi-m. ISSN 0013-3329
- Grudnaya Khirurgiya. bi-m. ISSN 0017-4866
- Kardiologiya. m. ISSN 0022-9040
- Khimiko-farmatsevticheskii Zhurnal. m. ISSN 0023-1134 (U.S.S.R. Ministerstvo Meditsinskoi Promyshlennosti)
- Klinicheskaya Meditsina. m. ISSN 0023-2149
- Laboratornoe Delo (po Voprosam Meditsiny) m. ISSN 0023-6748
- Meditsinskaya Parazitologiya i Parazitarnye Bolezni. bi-m. ISSN 0025-8326
- Meditsinskaya Sestra. m. ISSN 0025-8342
- Meditsinskaya Tekhnika. bi-m. ISSN 0047-6617 (U. S. S. R. Ministerstvo Meditsinskoi Promyshlennosti)
- Ortopediya, Travmatologiya i Protezirovaniye. m. ISSN 0030-5987
- Pediatriya. m. ISSN 0031-403X
- Problemy Endokrinologii. bi-m.
- Problemy Tuberkuleza. m. ISSN 0032-9533
- Stomatologiya. bi-m. ISSN 0039-1735
- Sudebno-meditsinskaya Ekspertiza. q. ISSN 0039-4521 (Vsesoyuznoe Nauchnoe Obshchestvo Sudebnykh Medikov)
- Terapevticheskii Arkhiv. m. ISSN 0040-3660
- Vestnik Dermatologii i Venerologii. m. ISSN 0042-4609
- Vestnik Khirurgii. m. ISSN 0042-4625
- Vestnik Oftal'mologii. bi-m. ISSN 0042-465X
- Vestnik Otorinolaringologii. bi-m. ISSN 0042-4668
- Vestnik Rentgenologii i Radiologii. bi-m. ISSN 0042-4676
- Voprosy Kurortologii, Fizioterapii i Lechebnoi Fizicheskoi Kul'tury. bi-m. ISSN 0042-8787
- Voprosy Meditsinskoi Khimii. bi-m. ISSN 0042-8809 (Akademiya Meditsinskikh Nauk S. S. S. R.)
- Voprosy Neirokhirurgii. bi-m. ISSN 0042-8817
- Voprosy Okhrany Materinstva i Detstva. m. ISSN 0042-8825
- Voprosy Revmatizma. q. ISSN 0042-885X
- Zhurnal Mikrobiologii, Epidemiologii i Immunobiologii. m. ISSN 0049-8726
- Zhurnal Nevropatologii i Psikhiatrii im S.S. Korsakova. m. ISSN 0044-4588
- Zhurnal Ushnykh, Nosovykh i Gorlovykh Boleznei. bi-m. ISSN 0044-4650

**Izdatel'stvo Meditsina. Leningradskoe Otdelenie**
Ul. Nekrasova, 10, 192104 Leningrad, U. S. S. R. (Subscr. to: Mezhdunarodnaya Kniga, Moscow, G-200, U. S. S. R.)
- Voprosy Onkologii. m. (U. S. S. R. Ministerstvo Zdravookhraneniya) (Co-sponsor: Vsesoyuznoe Nauchnoe Obshchestvo Onkologov)

**Izdatel'stvo Meditsina. Otdelenie v Uzbekistane**
Ul. Navoi, 30, Tashkent, U.S.S.R.
- Meditsinskii Zhurnal Uzbekistana. m. ISSN 0025-830X

**Izdatel'stvo Metallurgiya**
2-i Obydenski Per. 14, Moscow G-34, U.S.S.R. (Subscr. To: Mezhdunarodnaya Kniga, Moscow G-200, U.S.S.R.)
- Koks i Khimiya. m. ISSN 0023-2815 (U. S. S. R. Ministerstvo Chernoi Metallurgii) (Co-sponsor: Nauchno-tekhnicheskoe Obshchestvo Chernoi Metallurgii)

- Metallovedenie i Termicheskaya Obrabotka Metallov. m. ISSN 0026-0819
- Metallurg. m. ISSN 0026-0827 (U.S.S.R. Ministerstvo Chernoi Metallurgii) (Co-sponsor: Profsoyuz Rabochikh Metallurgicheskoi Promyshlennosti)
- Moskovskii Institut Stali i Splavov. Nauchnye Trudy. irreg.
- Ochistka Vodnogo i Vozdushnogo Basseinov na Predpriyatiyakh Chernoi Metallurgii. irreg. (U. S. S. R. Ministerstvo Chernoi Metallurgii)
- Stal' m. ISSN 0038-920X (U. S. S. R. Ministerstvo Chernoi Metallurgii) (Co-sponsor: Nauchno - Tekhnicheskoe Obshchestvo Chernoi Metallurgii)
- Tsvetnye Metally. m. ISSN 0041-4891 (U. S. S. R. Ministerstvo Tsvetnoi Metallurgii)
- Zavodskaya Laboratoriya; zhurnal po analiticheskoi khimii, fizicheskim, matematicheskim i mekhanicheskim metodam issledovaniya materialov. m. ISSN 0044-1910 (U.S.S.R. Ministerstvo Chernoi Metallurgii) (Co-sponsor: Nauchno-tekhnicheskoe Obshchestvo Chernoi Metallurgii)

**Mezhdunarodnaya Demokraticheskaya Federatsiya Zhenshchin**
Moscow, U.S.S.R.
- Zhenshchiny Mira. q. ISSN 0044-4456

**Mezhdunarodnaya Kniga (Distributor)**
Moscow G-200, U.S.S.R.
- Kozhevenno-Obuvnaya Promyshlennost' m. ISSN 0023-4354
- Standarty i Kachestvo. m. ISSN 0038-9692

**Minskii Radiotekhnicheskii Institut**
- Automatika i Vychislitel'naya Tekhnika. (pub. by Izdatel'stvo Vysshaya Shkola B.S.S.R.)

**Izdatel'stvo Mintis**
Lenino Prosp. 3, Vilnius, U. S. S. R. (Subscr. to: Mezhdunarodnaya Kniga, Moscow, G-200, U. S. S. R.)
- Baltistica; studies in Baltic linguistics. 2 per yr. ISSN 0045-1371 (Litovskaya S. S. R. Ministerstvo Vysshego Obrazovaniya)
- Technine Kibernetika/Tekhnicheskaya Kibernetika. irreg. (Akademiya Nauk Litovskoi S.S.R.. Institut Fiziko--Tekhnicheskikh Problem Energetiki)

**Izdatel'stvo Molod**
Khreshchatyk 10, 5-i Poverkh, Kiev, U.S.S.R.
- Dnipro; literaturno-khudozhnii ta hromads'kopolitychnyi zhurnal. m. ISSN 0012-4354 (Leninskii Kommunisticheskii Soyuz Molodezhi Ukrainskoi S.S.R.)
- Malyatko. m. ISSN 0025-1453 (Leninskii Kommunisticheskii Soyuz Molodezhi Ukrainskoi S.S.R.)
- Pioneriya. m. ISSN 0032-0102 (Leninskii Kommunisticheskii Soyuz Molodezhi Ukrainskoi S.S.R.)
- Start. m. ISSN 0038-9935 (Soyuz Sportivnykh Obshchestv i Organizatsii Ukrainskoi S.S.R.)

**Izdatel'stvo Molodaya Gvardiya**
Ul. Sushevskaya, 21, Moscow a-55, U.S.S.R. (Subscr. to: Mezhdunarodnaya Kniga, Moscow G-200, U.S.S.R.)
- Masterskaya; uroki literaturnogo masterstva. irreg.
- Molodaya Gvardiya. m. ISSN 0026-9050 (Vsesoyuznyi Leninskii Kommunisticheskii Soyuz Molodezhi. Tsentral'nyi Komitet)
- Molodoi Kommunist. m. ISSN 0026-9077 (Vsesoyuznyi Leninskii Kommunisticheskii Soyuz Molodezhi. Tsentral'nyi Komitet)
- Murzilka. m.
- Sputnik Sel'skoi Molodezhi. a.
- Tekhnika - Molodezhi. m. ISSN 0040-2257 (Vsesoyuznyi Leninskii Kommunisticheskii Soyuz Molodezhi. Tsentral'nyi Komitet)
- Veselye Kartinki. m. ISSN 0504-0523 (Vsesoyuznyi Leninskii Kommunisticheskii Soyuz Molodezhi. Tsentral'nyi Komitet)
- Vokrug Sveta. m. ISSN 0042-8485 (Vsesoyuznyi Leninskii Kommunisticheskii Soyuz Molodezhi. Tsentral'nyi Komitet)
- Vozhatyi. m. ISSN 0042-9104 (Vsesoyuznyi Leninskii Kommunisticheskii Soyuz Molodezhi. Tsentral'nyi Komitet)
- Yunyi Naturalist. m. ISSN 0044-1392 (Vsesoyuznyi Leninskii Kommunisticheskii Soyuz Molodezhi. Tsentral'nyi Komitet)
- Yunyi Tekhnik. m. ISSN 0044-1406 (Vsesoyuznyi Leninskii Kommunisticheskii Soyuz Molodezhi. Tsentral'nyi Komitet)

**Moskovskaya Patriarkhiya**
Novodevichii pr., 1, Moscow G-435, U.S.S.R.
- Zhurnal Moskovskoi Patriarkhii/Journal of the Moscow Patriarchate. m. ISSN 0044-4553

**Moskovskaya Publichnaya Biblioteka**
Moscow, U.S.S.R.
- Prognozirovanie Razvitiya Bibliotechnogo Dela v S.S.S.R. irreg.

**Moskovskii Gorodskii Sovet Deputatov Trudyashchikhsya**
Ul. Gor'kogo, 9, Moscow, U.S.S.R
(Subscr. to: Mezhdunarodnaya Kniga, Moscow G-200,U.S.S.R.)
- Stroitel'stvo i Arkhitektura Moskvy. m. ISSN 0039-2421

**Moskovskii Gosudarstvennyi Institut Kul'tury**
Moscow, U.S.S.R.
- Bibliotekovedenie, Bibliografiya i Informatika. irreg.

**Moskovskii Gosudarstvennyi Pedagogicheskii Institut Inostrannykh Yazykov**
Rostokinskii pr., 13, Moscow B-14, U.S.S.R.
- Sbornik Statei po Frantsuzskoi Lingvistike i Metodike Prepodavaniya Inostrannogo Yazika v VUZE. irreg.

**Moskovskii Institut Geologii i Razvedki**
Prospekt Marksa 18, Mgri, Moscow, U. S. S. R. (Subscr. to: Mezhdunarodnaya Kniga, Moscow, G-200, U. S. S. R.)
- Izvestiya Vysshikh Uchebnykh Zavedenii. Seriya Geologiya i Razvedka. m. ISSN 0016-7762 (U.S.S.R. Ministerstvo Vysshego i Srednego Spetsial'nogo Obrazovaniya)

**Moskovskii Institut Stali i Splavov**
- Moskovskii Institut Stali i Splavov. Nauchnye Trudy. (pub. by Izdatel'stvo Metallurgiya)

**Moskovskii Universitet**
Leninskie Gory, Moscow V-234, U.S.S.R. (Subscr. to: Mezhdunarodnaya Kniga, Moscow, G-200, U. S. S. R.)
- Gosudarstvennyi Astronomicheskii Institut im. P. K. Shternberga. Soobshcheniya. q. ISSN 0038-1489
- Gosudarstvennyi Astronomicheskii Institut im. P. K. Shternberga. Trudy. s-a. ISSN 0041-3453
- Moscow University Mechanics Bulletin. (pub. by Allerton Press, Inc. US)
- Moscow University Soil Science. (pub. by Allerton Press, Inc. US)
- Moskovskii Universitet. Biblioteka. Rukopisnaya i Pechatnaya Kniga v Fondakh. irreg.
- Moskovskii Universitet. Vestnik. Seriya 1: Matematika i Mekhanika. bi-m.
- Moskovskii Universitet. Vestnik. Seriya 2: Khimiya. bi-m.
- Moskovskii Universitet. Vestnik. Seriya 3: Fizika, Astronomiya. bi-m.
- Moskovskii Universitet. Vestnik. Seriya 4: Geologiya. bi-m.
- Moskovskii Universitet. Vestnik. Seriya 5: Geografiya.
- Moskovskii Universitet. Vestnik. Seriya 5: Geografiya. bi-m. ISSN 0027-1381
- Moskovskii Universitet. Vestnik. Seriya 6: Biologiya, Pochvovedenie. bi-m.
- Moskovskii Universitet. Vestnik. Seriya 7: Ekonomika. bi-m.
- Moskovskii Universitet. Vestnik. Seriya 7: Ekonomika.
- Moskovskii Universitet. Vestnik. Seriya 8: Filosofiya. bi-m.
- Moskovskii Universitet. Vestnik. Seriya 9: Istoriya. bi-m.
- Moskovskii Universitet. Vestnik. Seriya 10: Filologiya. bi-m.
- Moskovskii Universitet. Vestnik. Seriya 11: Zhurnalistika. bi-m.
- Moskovskii Universitet. Vestnik. Seriya 12: Pravo. bi-m. ISSN 0027-1357
- Moskovskii Universitet. Vestnik. Seriya 12: Pravo.
- Moskovskii Universitet. Vestnik. Seriya 13: Teoriya Nauchnogo Kommunizma. bi-m.
- Moskovskii Universitet. Vestnik. Seriya 14: Vostokovedenie. s-a.

- Moskovskoe Obshchestvo Ispytatelei Prirody. Biologicheskii Otdel. Byulleten/Moscow Society of Naturalists. Biological Series. Bulletin. bi-m. ISSN 0027-1403
- Moskovskoe Obshchestvo Ispytatelei Prirody. Geologicheskii Otdel. Byulleten/Moscow Society of Naturalists. Geological Series. Bulletin. 1917. ISSN 0007-7682
- Problemy Istorii Matematiki i Mekhaniki. irreg.
- Russkii Yazyk za Rubezhom/Russian Abroad. bi-m. ISSN 0036-0384 (Akademiya Nauk S.S.S.R.. Institut Russkogo Yazyka)

**Moskovskii Universitet. Kafedra Gruntovedeniya i Inzhenernoi Geologii**
Leninskie Gory, Moscow V-234, U.S.S.R.
- Voprosy Inzhenernoi Geologii i Gruntovedeniya; proceedings of the seminar of the chair of the theory elasticity under the guidance A.A. Ilushin. biennial.

**Moskovskoe Obshchestvo Ispytatelei Prirody**
- Moskovskoe Obshchestvo Ispytatelei Prirody. Biologicheskii Otdel. Byulleten/Moscow Society of Naturalists. Biological Series. Bulletin. (pub. by Izdatel'stvo Moskovskii Universitet)
- Moskovskoe Obshchestvo Ispytatelei Prirody. Geologicheskii Otdel. Byulleten/Moscow Society of Naturalists. Geological Series. Bulletin. (pub. by Izdatel'stvo Moskovskii Universitet)

**Izdatel'stvo Muzyka**
Neglinnaya ul., 14, Moscow K-45, U.S.S.R.
- Muzykal'noe Vospitanie v Shkole. irreg.

**Izdatel'stvo Mysl**
Leninskii Prospekt 15, 117071 Moscow B-71, U.S.S.R.
- Kommunisticheskaya Partiya Sovetskogo Soyuza. Vysshaya Partiinaya Shkola. Uchenye Zapiski. irreg.

**Nauchno- Issledovatelski Institut po Bezopasnosti Rabot V Gornoi Promyshlennosti, Makeevka**
- Bor'ba s Gazom v Ugol'nykh Shakhtakh. (pub. by Izdatel'stvo Nedra)

**Nauchno-Issledovatel'skii Institut Kholodil'noi Promyshlennosti S.S.S.R.**
Ul. Kostyakova 12, Moscow A-422, U.S.S.R.
- Kholodil'naya Tekhnika. m. ISSN 0023-124X

**Nauchno-issledovatel'skii Institut Kul'tury. Otdel' Narodnogo Tvorchestva**
- Voprosy Uchebno-vospitatel'noi Raboty v Samodeyatel'nykh Kollektivakh. (pub. by Izdatel'stvo Sovetskaya Rossiya)

**Nauchno-Issledovatel'skii Institut Kul'tury. Otdel' Sotsiologicheskikh Issledovanii**
- Sotsiologiya Kul'tury. (pub. by Izdatel'stvo Sovetskaya Rossiya)

**Nauchno-Issledovatel'skii Institut po Tsenoobrazovaniyu**
Vtoraya Yaroslavskaya ul., 3, Moscow, U.S.S.R.
- Novaya Literatura po Tsenoobrazovaniyu, Opublikovannaya v S.S.S.R; annotirovannyi ukazatel' irreg.

**Nauchno-issledovatel'skii Konyunkturnyi Institut**
Ul. Pudovkina 4, Moscow, U.S.S.R.
- Byulleten' Inostrannoi Kommercheskoi Informatsii. 3 per w. ISSN 0007-7674

**Nauchno-tekhnicheskoe Obshchestvo Pishchevoi Promyshlennosti**
Kuznetskii most, 19, Moscow, U.S.S.R.
- Khlebopekarnaya i Konditerskaya Promyshlennost' m. ISSN 0023-1215
- Tabak. q. ISSN 0039-873X

**Nauchno-tekhnicheskoe Obshchestvo Radiotekhniki i Elektrosvyazi im. A. S. Popova**
Kuznetskii most 20, 103031 Moscow, U.S.S.R.
- Elektrosvyaz' (pub. by Izdatel'stvo Svyaz')
- Radiotekhnika. m. ISSN 0033-8486

**Izdatel'stvo Nauka**
Podsosenskii Per., 21, Moscow K-62, U.S.S.R (Subscr. to: Mezhdunarodnaya Kniga, Moscow, G-200, U.S.S.R.)
- Agrokhimiya. m. ISSN 0002-1881 (Akademiya Nauk S. S. S. R.) (Co-sponsor: U. S. S. R. Ministerstvo Sel'skogo Khozyaistva)
- Akademiya Nauk S. S. S. R. Doklady; svodnyi vypusk. 36 per yr. ISSN 0002-3264

- Akademiya Nauk S.S.S.R. Institut Etnografii. Polevye Issledovaniya. irreg.
- Akademiya Nauk S. S. S. R. Izvestiya. Energetika i Transport. bi-m. ISSN 0002-3310
- Akademiya Nauk S. S. S. R. Izvestiya. Seriya Biologicheskaya. bi-m. ISSN 0002-3329
- Akademiya Nauk S. S. S. R. Izvestiya. Seriya Fizika Atmosfery i Okeana. m. ISSN 0002-3515
- Akademiya Nauk S. S. S. R. Izvestiya. Seriya Fizika Zemli. m. ISSN 0002-3337
- Akademiya Nauk S. S. S. R. Izvestiya. Seriya Geologicheskaya. m. ISSN 0002-3345
- Akademiya Nauk S. S. S. R. Izvestiya. Seriya Khimicheskaya. m. ISSN 0002-3353
- Akademiya Nauk S. S. S. R. Izvestiya. Seriya Matematicheskaya. bi-m. ISSN 0002-3361
- Akademiya Nauk S. S. S. R. Izvestiya. Seriya Neorganicheskie Materialy. m. ISSN 0002-337X
- Akademiya Nauk S. S. S. R. Izvestiya. Tekhnicheskaya Kibernetika. bi-m. ISSN 0002-3388
- Akusticheskii Zhurnal. bi-m. ISSN 0002-3914 (Akademiya Nauk S.S.S.R.)
- Astronomicheskii Zhurnal. bi-m. ISSN 0004-6299 (Akademiya Nauk S.S.S.R. Astrosovet)
- Aviatsiya i Kosmonavtika. m. ISSN 0005-2183
- Avtomatika i Telemekhanika. m. ISSN 0005-2310 (Akademiya Nauk S. S. S. R.. Institut Avtomatiki i Telemekhaniki)
- Avtomobil'nye Dorogi. m. ISSN 0005-2353
- Aziya i Afrika Segodnya. m. ISSN 0005-2574 (Akademiya Nauk S. S. S. R.. Institut Narodov Azii) (Co-sponsor: Institut Afriki)
- Biofizika. bi-m. ISSN 0006-3029 (Akademiya Nauk S. S. S. R.. Otdelenie Biokhimii, Biofiziki i Khimii Fiziologicheski Aktivnykh Soedinenii)
- Bioorganicheskaya Khimiya. m. (Akademiya Nauk S.S.S.R.)
- Fizika Plazmy. bi-m. (Akademiya Nauk S.S.S.R)
- Fiziko-tekhnicheskie Problemy Razrabotki Poleznykh Iskopremykh. bi-m. ISSN 0015-3273
- Fiziologiya Cheloveka. bi-m. (Akademiya Nauk S.S.S.R.)
- Fiziologiya Rastenii. bi-m. ISSN 0015-3303
- Geofizicheskii Byulleten/Geophysical Bulletin. irreg., approx. 2 per yr. ISSN 0072-1182 (Akademiya Nauk S.S.S.R.. Mezhduvedomstvennyi Geofizicheskii Komitet)
- Istochnikovedenie Otechestvennoi Istorii. irreg. (Akademiya Nauk S.S.S.R.. Sektor Istochnikovedeniya i Vspomogatel'nykh Istoricheskikh Distsiplin)
- Istoriya S. S. S. R. bi-m. ISSN 0021-2660 (Akademiya Nauk S. S. S. R.. Institut Istorii S. S. S. R.)
- Kauchuk i Rezina. m. ISSN 0022-9466
- Khimiya Vysokikh Energii/High Energy Chemistry. bi-m. ISSN 0023-1193
- Kosmicheskaya Biologiya i Aviakosmicheskaya Meditsina. bi-m.
- Krymskaya Astrofizicheskaya Observatoriya. Izvestiya. s-a. (Akademiya Nauk S.S.S.R.. Krymskaya Astrofizicheskaya Observatoriya)
- Latinskaya Amerika. bi-m (Spanish edt. q) ISSN 0044-748X (Akademiya Nauk S.S.S.R.. Institut Latinskoi Ameriki)
- Narody Azii i Afriki; istoriya, ekonomika, kultura. bi-m. ISSN 0027-8041 (Akademiya Nauk S.S.S.R.. Institut Vostokovedeniya) (Co-sponsor: Akademiya Nauk S.S.S.R. Institut Afriki)
- Paleontologicheskii Zhurnal. q. ISSN 0031-031X (Akademiya Nauk S. S. S. R.. Institut Paleontologii)
- Pamyatniki Kul'tury. Novye Otkrytiya/ Monuments of Culture. New Discoveries. a. (Akademiya Nauk S.S.S.R.. Nauchnyi Sovet po Istorii Mirovoi Kul'tury)
- Pis'ma v Astronomicheskii Zhurnal. m. (Akademiya Nauk S.S.S.R.. Astrosovet)
- Pochvovedenie. m. ISSN 0032-180X (Akademiya Nauk S. S. S. R.. Vsesoyuznoe Obshchestvo Pochvovedeniya)
- Russkaya Rech' bi-m. ISSN 0036-0368 (Akademiya Nauk S.S.S.R.. Institut Russkogo Yazyka)
- Smena. s-m. (Vsesoyuznyi Leninskii Kommunisticheskii Soyuz Molodezhi. Tsentral'nyi Komitet)
- Sovetskaya Etnografiya. bi-m. ISSN 0038-5050 (Akademiya Nauk S. S. R.. Institut Etnografii)
- Sovetskoe Gosudarstvo i Pravo. m. ISSN 0038-5204 (Akademiya Nauk S.S.S.R.. Institut Gosudarstva i Prava)
- Uspekhi Matematicheskikh Nauk. bi-m. ISSN 0042-1316 (Akademiya Nauk S. S. S. R.) (Co-sponsor: Moskovskoe Matematicheskoe Obshchestvo)

- Vestnik Drevnei Istorii/Journal of Ancient History. q. ISSN 0042-4617 (Akademiya Nauk S.S.S.R.. Institut Vseobshchei Istorii)
- Vodnye Resursy. bi-m. (Akademiya Nauk S.S.S.R.. Institut Vodnykh Problem)
- Voprosy Yazykoznaniya. bi-m. ISSN 0042-8868 (Akademiya Nauk S. S. S. R.. Institut Yazykoznaniya)
- Zemlya i Vselennaya. bi-m. ISSN 0044-3948 (Akademiya Nauk S.S.S.R.)
- Zhurnal Neorganicheskoi Khimii. m. ISSN 0044-457X (Akademiya Nauk S. S. S. R.. Institut Obshchei i Neorganicheskoi Khimii im. N.S. Kurnakova)

**Izdatel'stvo Nauka. Dal'nevostochnoe Otdelenie**
690022 Vladivostok, U.S.S.R.
- Biologiya Morya/Marine Biology. bi-m. (Akademiya Nauk S.S.S.R.. Otdelenie Obshchei Biologii) (Co-sponsor: Akademiya Nauk S.S.S.R. Dal'nevostochnyi Nauchnyi Tsentr)

**Izdatel'stvo Nauka. Leningradskoe Otdelenie**
Mendeleevskaya lin., 3/5, Leningrad V-164, U.S.S.R.
(Subscr. to: Mezhdunarodnaya Kniga, Moscow, G-200, U. S. S. R.)
- Fiziologicheskii Zhurnal. m. ISSN 0015-329X (Akademiya Nauk S.S.S.R.)
- Leningradskii Universitet. Vestnik. Seriya Biologiya. q. ISSN 0024-080X
- Leningradskii Universitet. Vestnik. Seriya Ekonomika, Filosofiya i Pravo. q. ISSN 0024-0818
- Leningradskii Universitet. Vestnik. Seriya Fizika i Khimiya. q. ISSN 0024-0826
- Leningradskii Universitet. Vestnik. Seriya Geologiya i Geografiya. q. ISSN 0024-0834
- Leningradskii Universitet. Vestnik. Seriya Istoriya, Yazyk i Literatura. q. ISSN 0024-0842
- Leningradskii Universitet. Vestnik. Seriya Matematika, Mekhanika i Astronomiya. q. ISSN 0024-0850
- Optika i Spektroskopiya. m. ISSN 0030-4034 (Akademiya Nauk S. S. S. R.)
- Tsitologiya/Cytology. m. ISSN 0041-3771
- Vsesoyuznoe Geograficheskoe Obshchestvo. Izvestiya. bi-m. ISSN 0042-9252
- Zhurnal Prikladnoi Khimii. m. ISSN 0044-4618 (Akademiya Nauk S. S. S. R.)

**Izdatel'stvo Nauka. Otdelenie v Kazakhstane**
28 Shevchenko, Alma-Ata, U.S.S.R.
- Akademiya Nauk Kazakhskoi S. S. R. Vestnik. m. ISSN 0002-3213

**Izdatel'stvo Naukova Dumka**
Ul. Repina 3, Kiev, U. S. S. R.
(Subscr. to: Mezhdunarodnaya Kniga, Moscow, G-200, U.S.S.R.)
- Akademiya Nauk Ukrains'koi Rsr. Dopovidi. Seria a Fiziko- Matematichni ta Tekhnichni Nauki. m. ISSN 0002-3531
- Akademiya Nauk Ukrainskoi S. S. R. Dopovidi. Seriya Geologiya, Geofizyka, Khimiya ta Biologiya. m. ISSN 0002-3523
- Astrometriya i Astrofizika/Astrometry and Astrophysics. q. ISSN 0582-8201 (Akademiya Nauk Ukrainskoi S.S.R.. Glavnaya Astronomicheskaya Observatoriya)
- Doshkil'ne Vykhovannya. m. ISSN 0012-5601
- Farmatsevtychnyi Zhurnal. bi-m. ISSN 0014-8342 (Akademiya Nauk Ukrainskoi S.S.R.)
- Fizika Nizkikh Temperatur/Low Temperature Physics. m. (Akademiya Nauk Ukrainskoi S.S.R.)
- Fiziologichnyi Zhurnal. bi-m. ISSN 0015-3311 (Akademiya Nauk Ukrainskoi S.S.R.)
- Geologichnii Zhurnal. bi-m. ISSN 0016-7703 (Akademiya Nauk Ukrainskoi S.S.R.)
- Kataliticheskaya Konversiya Uglevodorodov. irreg. (Akademiya Nauk Ukrainskoi S.S.R.. Institut Gaza)
- Kibernetika. bi-m. ISSN 0023-1274 (Akademiya Nauk Ukrainskoi S.S.R.)
- Klinicheskaya Khirurgiya. m. ISSN 0023-2130 (Akademiya Nauk Ukrainskoi S. S. R.)
- Konstitutsiya i Svoista Mineralov. a. ISSN 0454-3343 (Akademiya Nauk Ukrainskoi S.S.R.)
- Mekhanizatsiya Sil'skogo Gospodarstva. m. ISSN 0025-889X
- Mikrobiologichnyi Zhurnal. bi-m. ISSN 0026-3664 (Akademiya Nauk Ukrainskoi S. S. R.. Institut Mikrobiologii)
- Movoznavstvo. bi-m. ISSN 0027-2833 (Akademiya Nauk Ukrainskoi S.S.R.)
- Mynule i Suchasne Pivnichnoi Bukovyny/Proshloe i Nastoyashchee Severnoi Bukoviny. irreg. (Akademiya Nauk Ukrainskoi S.S.R.. Institut Istorii)

- Narodna Tvorchist' ta Etnografiya. bi-m. ISSN 0027-7924 (Akademiya Nauk Ukrainskoi S.S.R.. Instytut Mystetsvo-znavstva, Folkloru ta Etnografii)
- Neirofiziologiya/Neurophysiology. bi-m. ISSN 0028-2561 (Akademiya Nauk S.S.S.R.) (Co-sponsor: Akademiya Nauk Ukrainskoi S.S.R.)
- Prikladnaya Mekhanika. m. ISSN 0032-8243 (Akademiya Nauk Ukrainskoi S.S.R.)
- Problemy Mashinostroeniya. irreg. (Akademiya Nauk Ukrainskoi S.S.R.. Institut Problem Mashinostroeniya)
- Problemy Prochnosti. m. ISSN 0556-171X (Akademiya Nauk Ukrainskoi S.S.R.. Institut Problem Prochnosti)
- Teoriya Sluchainykh Protsessov. irreg., no. 3, 1975. (Akademiya Nauk Ukrainskoi S.S.R.. Institut Prikladnoi Matematiki i Mekhaniki)
- Ukrainski Khimicheskii Zhurnal/Ukrains'kyi Kimichnyi Zhurnal. m. ISSN 0041-6045 (Akademiya Nauk Ukrainskoi S.S.R.)
- Ukrainskii Fizicheskii Zhurnal/Ukrains'kyi Fizychnyi Zhurnal. m. ISSN 0041-6126
- Ukrainskii Matematicheskii Zhurnal/Ukrains'kyi Matematychnyi Zhurnal. bi-m. ISSN 0041-6053 (Akademiya Nauk Ukrainskoi S.S.R.. Institut Matematiki)
- Ukrains'kyi Botanichnyi Zhurnal. bi-m. ISSN 0041-6118 (Akademiya Nauk Ukrainskoi S.S.R.. Institut Botaniki)
- Ukrains'kyi Istorychnyi Zhurnal. m. ISSN 0041-6134 (Akademiya Nauk Ukrainskoi S.S.R.. Institut Istorii)
- Upravlyayuchie Sistemy i Mashiny. bi-m. (Akademiya Nauk Ukrainskoi S.S.R.. Kiberneticheskii Tsentr)

**Izdatel'stvo Nedra**
Tretyakovskii proezd, 1, Moscow K-12, U.S.S.R.
- Bor'ba s Gazom v Ugol'nykh Shakhtakh. irreg. (Nauchno- Issledovatelski Institut po Bezopasnosti Rabot V Gornoi Promyshlennosti, Makeevka)
- Gazovaya Promyshlennost' m. ISSN 0016-5581 (U. S. S. R. Ministerstvo Gazovoi Promyshlennosti) (Co-sponsor: Nauchno - Tekhnicheskoe Obshchestvo Neftyanoi i Gazovoi Promyshlennosti)
- Geologiya Nefti i Gaza. m. ISSN 0016-7894 (U. S. S. R. Ministerstvo Geologii) (Co-sponsor: U. S. S. R. Ministerstvo Gazovoi Promyshlennosti; U. S. S. R. Ministerstvo Neftedobyvayushchei Promyshlennosti)
- Inzhener - Neftyanik. m.
- Neftegazonosnye i Perspektivnye Kompleksy Tsentralnykh i Vostochnykh Oblastei Russkoi Platformy. irreg. (Vsesoyuznyi Nauchno - Issledovatel'skii Geologorazvedochnyi Neftyanoi Institut)
- Razvedka i Okhrana Nedr. m. ISSN 0034-026X (U. S. S. R. Ministerstvo Geologii) (Co-sponsor: Profsoyuz Rabochikh Geologorazvedochnykh Rabot)

**Novosibirskii Gosudarstvennyi Universitet**
Novosibirsk, 99 Akademgorodok, U.S.S.R.
- Aktual'nye Problemy Leksikologii i Slovoobrazovaniya. irreg.

**Novosti Press Agency**
Pl. Pushkina, 2, Moscow, U.S.S.R
(Subscr. to: Eastern News Distributors, 155 West 15 Street, New York, Nn. Y. 10011 U. S. A.)
- Socialism: Theory and Practice. m.
- Sputnik; monthly digest of Soviet press and literature. m. ISSN 0038-8718

**Obshchestvo Krasnyi Krest**
Moscow, U.S.S.R
(Subscr. to: Mezhdunarodnaya Kniga, Moscow, G-200, U. S. S. R.)
- Sovetskii Krasnyi Krest. m. ISSN 0038-5131

**Izdatel'stvo Pedagogika**
3d Proezd Maryinoi Roshchi, 41, Moscow, U.S.S.R.
- Shkola i Proizvodstvo. m. ISSN 0037-4024 (Rossiiskaya S.F.S.R. Ministerstvo Prosveshcheniya)
- Vospitanie Shkol'nikov. bi-m. ISSN 0042-8957

**Kirjastus Perioodika**
Pikk Tan. 37, Tallinn, U. S. S. R.
(Subscr. to: Mezhdunarodnaya Kniga, Moscow, G-200, U. S. S. R.)
- Akademiya Nauk Estonskoi S. S. R. Izvestiya. Biologiya/Eesti N. S. V. Teaduste Akadeemia Toimetised. Bioloogia. q. ISSN 0013-2144

- Akademiya Nauk Estonskoi S.S.R. Izvestiya. Fizika. Matematika/Eesti Nsv Teaduste Akadeemia. Toimetised. Fuusika. Matemaatika. q. ISSN 0002-3140
- Eesti Loodus/Estonian Nature. m. ISSN 0013-2136
- Looming; kirjanduslik ja uhiskondlik-poliitiline ajakiri. m. ISSN 0024-6441
- Sovetskoe Finnougrovedenie. q. ISSN 0038-5182 (Akademiya Nauk Estonskoi S. S. R.)

**Permskii Gosudarstvennyi Pedagogicheskii Institut**
Perm, U.S.S.R.
- Eksperimental'noe Issledovanie Lichnosti i Temperamenta. irreg.

**Politehniskais Instituts, Riga**
Ul. Lenina, 1, Riga, U.S.S.R.
- Teploprovodnost' i Diffuziya. irreg.

**Politekhnichnyi Instytut, Kiev**
Brets-Litovskii pr., 39, Kiev, U.S.S.R.
- Izvestiya Vysshikh Uchebnykh Zavedenii. Seriya Radioelektronika. m. ISSN 0021-3470
- Politekhnichnyi Instytut Kiev. Vestnik. Seriya Mashinostroeniya. irreg.

**Polutehniline Instituut**
Ehitajate tee 5, Tallinn, U.S.S.R.
- Polutehniline Instituut Tallinn. Matematika i Teoreticheskaya Mekhanika. irreg.
- Tallinskii Politekhnicheskii Institut. Trudy. irreg., no. 375, 1975.

**Izdatel'stvo Polymya**
Minsk, U. S. S. R.
- Belarus' m. ISSN 0005-8319 (Sayuz Pismennikaw Belarusskai S. S. R.)
- Neman. m. ISSN 0028-2588 (Soyuz Pisatelei Belorusskoi S.S.R.)
- Polymya. m. ISSN 0032-3985 (Soyuz Pisatelei Belorusskoi S.S.R.)

**Izdatel'stvo Pravda**
Ul. Pravdy, 24, Moscow 125047, U. S. S. R.
(Subscr. to: Mezhdunarodnaya Kniga, Moscow, G-200, U. S. S. R.)
- Ekonomicheskaya Gazeta. w. ISSN 0013-3132
- Kommunist; teoreticheskii i politicheskii zhurnal. 18 per yr. ISSN 0023-3099 (Kommunisticheskaya Partiya Sovetskogo Soyuza. Tsentral'nyi Komitet)
- Krokodil. 3 per mo. ISSN 0023-4877
- Mirovaya Ekonomika i Mezhdunarodnye Otnosheniya. m. ISSN 0026-5829 (Akademiya Nauk S.S.S.R.. Institut Mirovoi Ekonomiki i Mezhdunarodnykh Otnoshenii)
- Moscow News. w. ISSN 0027-1306
- Nauka i Zhizn; nauchno-populyarnyi zhurnal. m. ISSN 0028-1263 (Vsesoyuznoe Obshchestvo "Znanie")
- Ogonek. w. ISSN 0030-0721
- Oktyabr' m. ISSN 0030-1957 (Soyuz Pisatelei Rossiiskoi S. F. S. R.)
- Partiinaya Zhizn' 24 per yr. ISSN 0031-2509 (Kommunisticheskaya Partiya Sovetskogo Soyuza. Tsentral'nyi Komitet)
- Pioner. m. ISSN 0032-003X (Vsesoyuznyi Leninskii Kommunisticheskii Soyuz Molodezhi. Tsentral'nyi Komitet)
- Politicheskoe Samoobrazovanie. m. ISSN 0032-3225 (Kommunisticheskaya Partiya Sovetskogo Soyuza. Tsentral'nyi Komitet)
- Sovetskii Ekran. s-m. ISSN 0038-5123 (U.S.S.R. Gosudarstvennyi Komitet po Kinematografii Soveta Ministrov)
- Soviet Film/Sovetskii Fil'm. m. ISSN 0038-5395
- Soviet Union/Sovetskii Soyuz. m. ISSN 0038-514X
- Soviet Woman/Sovetskaya Zhenshchina; devoted to social and political problems, literature and art. m. ISSN 0038-5913 (Komitet Sovetskikh Zhenshchin)
- Voprosy Ekonomiki. m. ISSN 0042-8736 (Akademiya Nauk S.S.S.R.. Institut Ekonomiki)
- Voprosy Filosofii. m. ISSN 0042-8744 (Akademiya Nauk S. S. R.. Institut Filosofii)
- Voprosy Istorii. m. ISSN 0042-8779
- Yunost' m. ISSN 0021-3233 (Soyuz Pisatelei S. S. R.)
- Za Rubezhom; weekly review of foreign press. w. ISSN 0044-1554
- Zdorov'e. m. ISSN 0044-1945 (U.S.S.R. Ministerstvo Zdravookhraneniya)
- Zhurnalist. m. ISSN 0022-5568 (Soyuz Zhurnalistov S. S. S. R.)

**Privolzhskoe Knizhnoe Izdatel'stvo**
Ul. Goncharova, 52, Ulyanovsk, U.S.S.R.
- Issledovanie, Konstruirovanie i Raschet Rezbovykh Soedinenii. irreg. (Ulyanovskii Politekhnicheskii Institut)

**Profizdat**
Ul. Kirova, 13, Moscow, U. S. S. R.
(Subscr. to: Mezhdunarodnaya Kniga, Moscow, G-200, U. S. S. R.)
- Klub i Khudozhestvennaya Samodeyatel'nost' a-m. (Vsesoyuznyi Tsentral'nyi Sovet Professional'nykh Soyuzov)
- Okhrana Truda i Sotsial'noe Strakhovanie. m. ISSN 0030-1590 (Vsesoyuznyi Tsentral'nyi Sovet Professional'nykh Soyuzov)
- Sovetskie Profsoyuzy. s-m. ISSN 0038-5174 (Vsesoyuznyi Tsentral'nyi Sovet Professional'nykh Soyuzov)
- Sovetskii Shakhter. m. ISSN 0038-5158 (Profsoyuz Rabochikh Ugol'noi Promyshlennosti S.S.S.R.. Tsentral'nyi Komitet)
- Turist. m. ISSN 0041-4182
- Vsemirnoe Profsoyuznoe Dvizhenie. m. ISSN 0042-9236 (World Federation of Trade Unions)

**Profsoyuz Rabochikh Ugol'noi Promyshlennosti S.S.S.R. Tsentral'nyi Komitet**
- Sovetskii Shakhter. (pub. by Profizdat)

**Izdatel'stvo Progress**
Zubovskii bulvar, 21, Moscow G-21, U.S.S.R.
- Sovremennaya Khudozhestvennaya Literatura za Rubezhom; informatsionnyi sbornik. bi-m. (Vsesoyuznaya Gosudarstvennaya Biblioteka Inostrannoi Literatury)

**Izdatel'stvo Prosveshchenie**
3-i Proezd Mar'inoi Roshchi, 41, Moscow, U.S.S.R.
(Subscr. to: Mezhdunarodnaya Kniga, Moscow, G-200, U. S. S. R.)
- Doshkol'noe Vospitanie. m. ISSN 0012-561X (Rossiiskaya S.F.S.R. Ministerstvo Prosveshcheniya)
- Geografiya v Shkole. bi-m. ISSN 0016-7207 (U.S.S.R. Ministerstvo Prosveshcheniya)
- Matematika v Shkole. bi-m. ISSN 0025-5181 (U.S.S.R. Ministerstvo Prosveshcheniya)
- Narodnoe Obrazovanie. m. ISSN 0027-8033 (U.S.S.R. Ministerstvo Prosveshcheniya)
- Russkii Yazyk v Shkole. bi-m. ISSN 0036-0376 (Rossiiskaya S.F.S.R. Ministerstvo Prosveshcheniya)
- Voprosy Psikhologii. bi-m. ISSN 0042-8841 (Akademiya Pedagogicheskikh Nauk S.S.S.R.)

**Izdatel'stvo Radyanska Ukraina**
Brest-Litovskii Prospekt, 94, Kiev, U. S. S. R.
(Subscr. to: Mezhdunarodnaya Kniga, Moscow, G-200, U. S. S. R.)
- Ekonomika Radyanskoi Ukrainy. m. ISSN 0013-3086 (Akademiya Nauk Ukrainskoi S. S. R.. Institut Ekonomiki)
- Kommunist Ukrainy/Komunist Ukraini. m. ISSN 0023-3110 (Kommunisticheskaya Partiya Ukrainy. Tsentral'nyi Komitet)
- Lyudyna i Svit. m. ISSN 0024-7871
- News from the Ukraine. w. ISSN 0549-110X
- Perets. fortn. ISSN 0031-5176
- Ukraina; hromads'ko-politychnyi, literaturno-khudozhnii ilyustrovanyi tyzhnevyk. w. ISSN 0041-6088
- Ukraine. q.

**Izdatel'stvo Radyanskii Pismennik**
Bul'var Lesi Ukrainki, 20, U. S. S. R., U.S.S.R.
- Literaturna Ukrayina. 2 per wk. ISSN 0024-4821 (Soyuz Pisatelei Ukrainskoi S.S.R.)
- Prapor; literaturno-khudozhnii ta hromads'ko-politychnyi zhurnal. m. ISSN 0032-6860 (Soyuz Pisatelei Ukrainskoi S.S.R.)
- Raduga. m. ISSN 0033-8591 (Soyuz Pisatelei Ukrainskoi S.S.R.)
- Vitchyzna; literaturno-khudozhnii ta hromads'kopolitychnyi misyachnyk. m. ISSN 0042-7470 (Soyuz Pisatelei Ukrainskoi S.S.R.)
- Vsesvit; literaturno-khudozhnii ta hromads 'kopolitychnyi zhurnal. m. ISSN 0042-9279 (Soyuz Pisatelei Ukrainskoi S.S.R.)

**Rossiiskaya S. F. S. R. Ministerstvo Avtomobil'nogo Transporta i Shosseinykh Dorog**
Moscow, U.S.S.R.
- Avtomobil'nyi Transport. m. ISSN 0005-2345

**Rossiiskaya S.F.S.R. Ministerstvo Kommunal'nogo Khozyaistva**
Ul. Razina 7, Moscow, U.S.S.R.
- Zhilishchnoe i Kommunal'noe Khozyaistvo. m. ISSN 0044-4464 (Co-sponsor: Profsoyuz Rabochikh Mestnoi Promyshlennosti i Kommunal'nogo Khozyaistva)

**Rossiiskaya S.F.S.R. Ministerstvo Kul'tury**
Moscow, U.S.S.R.
- Teatral'naya Zhizn' s-m. ISSN 0040-0785 (Co-sponsors: Vserossiiskoe Teatral'noe Obshchestvo; Soyuz Pisatelei Rossiiskoi S.F.S.R.)

**Rossiiskaya S.F.S.R. Ministerstvo Prosveshcheniya**
Ul. Pogodinskaya 8, Moscow G-117, U.S.S.R.
- Doshkol'noe Vospitanie. (pub. by Izdatel'stvo Prosveshchenie)
- Nachal'naya Shkola. m. ISSN 0027-7371
- Prepodavanie Istorii v Shkole. bi-m. ISSN 0032-7506
- Russkii Yazyk v Shkole. (pub. by Izdatel'stvo Prosveshchenie)
- Shkola i Proizvodstvo. (pub. by Izdatel'stvo Pedagogika)

**Rossiiskaya S.F.S.R. Ministerstvo Rechnogo Flota**
- Rechnoi Transport. (pub. by Izdatel'stvo Transport)

**Rossiiskaya S. F. S. R. Ministerstvo Sotsial'nogo Obespecheniya**
- Sotsial'noe Obespechenie. (pub. by Izdatel'stvo Sovetskaya Rossiya)

**Rossiiskaya S. F. S. R. Ministerstvo Vysshego i Srednego Spetsial'nogo Obrazovaniya**
- Avtomatizirovannye Sistemy Upravleniya. (pub. by Izdatel'stvo Leningradskii Universitet)

**Rossiiskaya S.F.S.R. Ministerstvo Zdravodkhraneniya**
Moscow, U.S.S.R.
- Zdravookhranenie Rossiiskoi Federatsii. m. ISSN 0044-197X

**Ryazanskii Radiotekhnicheskii Institut**
Ul. Gagarina 59/1, 390024 Ryazan, U.S.S.R.
- Magnito-Poluprovodnikovye i Elektromashinnye Elementy Avtomatiki. irreg.

**Sakhalinskaya Oblastnaya Biblioteka**
- Literatura o Sakhalinskoi Oblasti. (pub. by Dalnevostochnoe Knizhnoe Izdatel'stvo. Sakhalinskoe Otdelenie)

**Saratovskii Universitet**
Saratov, U.S.S.R.
- Issledovaniya v Oblasti Khimii Redkozemel'nykh Elementov. irreg.

**Sayuz Pismennikaw Belarusskai S. S. R.**
- Belarus' (pub. by Izdatel'stvo Polymya)

**Severno- Kavkazskii Gornometallurgicheskii Institut**
Ordzhonikidze, U.S.S.R.
- Izvestiya Vysshikh Uchebnykh Zavedenii. Seriya Chernaya Metallurgiya. m. ISSN 0021-3438

**Izdatel'stvo Shtiintsa**
Ul. Akademicheskaya, 3, Kishinev 277028, U.S.S.R. (Subscr. to: Mezhdunarodnaya Kniga, Moscow, G-200, U. S. S. R.)
- Akademiya Nauk Moldavskoi S.S.R. Izvestiya. Seriya Obshchestvennykh Nauk. 3 per yr.

**Izdatel'stvo Sovetskaya Rossiya**
Proezd Sapunova 13-15, Moscow K-12, U.S.S.R.
- Kul'tura i Zhizn/Culture and Life. m. ISSN 0023-5199 (Soyuz Sovetskikh Obshchestv Druzhby i Kul'turnoi Svyazi s Zarubezhnymi Stranami)
- Sotsial'noe Obespechenie. m. ISSN 0038-1713 (Rossiiskaya S. F. S. R. Ministerstvo Sotsial'nogo Obespecheniya)
- Sotsiologiya Kul'tury. a. (Nauchno-Issledovatel'skii Institut Kul'tury. Otdel' Sotsiologicheskikh Issledovanii)
- Voprosy Uchebno-vospitatel'noi Raboty v Samodeyatel'nykh Kollektivakh. irreg. (Nauchno-issledovatel'skii Institut Kul'tury. Otdel' Narodnogo Tvorchestva)

**Izdatel'stvo Sovetskii Khudozhnik**
Ul. Chernyakhovskogo, 4a, Moscow A-319, U.S.S.R.
- Tvorchestvo. m. ISSN 0041-4565 (Soyuz Khudozhnikov S.S.S.R.)

**Sovetskii Komitet Zashchity Mira**
Kropotkinskaya, 10, Moscow, U.S.S.R.
- Twentieth Century and Peace/Bek XX i Mir; bulletin of the Soviet Peace Committee. m.

**Izdatel'stvo Sovetskii Kompozitor**
Naberezhnaya Morisa Toreza, 30, Moscow W-35, U.S.S.R.
- Muzykal'naya Folkloristika. irreg. (Soyuz Kompozitorov Rossiiskoi S.F.S.R.. Folklornaya Komissiya)
- Muzykal'naya Zhizn' s-m. ISSN 0027-5352 (Soyuz Kompozitorov S.S.S.R.)
- Sovetskaya Muzyka. m. ISSN 0038-5085 (Soyuz Kompozitorov S.S.S.R.) (Co-sponsor: U.S.S.R. Ministerstvo Kul'tury)
- V Mire Muzyki; Kalendar' a.

**Soyuz Arkhitektorov S.S.S.R.**
- Zodchestvo. (pub. by Stroiizdat)

**Soyuz Khudozhnikov S. S. S. R.**
Gogolevskii bul., 10, Moscow, U. S. S. R.
- Khudozhnik. m. ISSN 0023-1258
- Tvorchestvo. (pub. by Izdatel'stvo Sovetskii Khudozhnik)

**Soyuz Kompozitorov Rossiiskoi S.F.S.R. Folklornaya Komissiya**
- Muzykal'naya Folkloristika. (pub. by Izdatel'stvo Sovetskii Kompozitor)

**Soyuz Kompozitorov S.S.S.R.**
- Muzykal'naya Zhizn' (pub. by Izdatel'stvo Sovetskii Kompozitor)
- Sovetskaya Muzyka. (pub. by Izdatel'stvo Sovetskii Kompozitor)

**Soyuz Pisatelei Armyanskoi S. S. R.**
Erevan, U. S. S. R.
- Literaturnaya Armeniya. m. ISSN 0024-483X
- Sovetakan Grakanutiun. m. ISSN 0038-5018

**Soyuz Pisatelei Azerbaidzhanskoi S.S.R.**
Ul. Khagani 25, Baku, U.S.S.R.
- Literaturnyi Azerbaidzhan. m. ISSN 0024-4864

**Soyuz Pisatelei Belorusskoi S.S.R.**
- Neman. (pub. by Izdatel'stvo Polymya)
- Polymya. (pub. by Izdatel'stvo Polymya)

**Soyuz Pisatelei Kazakhskoi S.S.R.**
Kommunisticheskii Prospekt 103/105, Alma-Ata, U.S.S.R.
- Prostor; literaturno-khudozhestvennyi i obshchestvennopoliticheskii illyustrirovannyi zhurnal. m. ISSN 0033-1597

**Soyuz Pisatelei Rossiiskoi S.F.S.R.**
Moscow, U.S.S.R.
- Literaturnaya Rossiya. w. ISSN 0024-4856 (Co-sponsor: Moskovskaya Pisatel'skaya Organizatsiya)
- Moskva; literary magazine. m. ISSN 0027-1411
- Nash Sovremennik. (pub. by Izdatel'stvo Literaturnaya Gazeta)
- Neva. (pub. by Izdatel'stvo Khudozhestvennaya Literatura. Leningradskoe Otdelenie)
- Oktyabr' (pub. by Izdatel'stvo Pravda)

**Soyuz Pisatelei Rossiiskoi S.F.S.R. Rostovskoe Oblastnoe Otdelenie**
Krasnoarmeiskaya 23, Rostov-na-Donu, GSP-6, U.S.S.R.
- Don; literaturno-khudozhestvennyi i obshchestvenno-politicheskii zhurnal. m. ISSN 0012-5393

**Soyuz Pisatelei S.S.S.R.**
Moscow, U.S.S.R.
(Subscr. to: Mezhdunarodnaya Kniga, Moscow, G-200, U. S. S. R.)
- Druzhba Narodov. (pub. by Izdatel'stvo Izvestiya)
- Literaturnaya Gazeta. w. ISSN 0024-4848
- Novyi Mir. (pub. by Izdatel'stvo Izvestiya)
- Soviet Literature/Sovetskaya Literatura. (pub. by Izdatel'stvo Izvestiya)
- Voprosy Literatury. (pub. by Izdatel'stvo Izvestiya)
- Yunost' (pub. by Izdatel'stvo Pravda)
- Znamya; literaturno-khudozhestvennyi i obshchestvenno-politicheski zhurnal. m. ISSN 0044-4898
- Zvezda. (pub. by Izdatel'stvo Khudozhestvennaya Literatura. Leningradskoe Otdelenie)

**Soyuz Pisatelei Ukrainskoi S.S.R.**
- Literaturna Ukrayina. (pub. by Izdatel'stvo Radyanskii Pismennik)
- Prapor. (pub. by Izdatel'stvo Radyanskii Pismennik)
- Raduga. (pub. by Izdatel'stvo Radyanskii Pismennik)
- Vitchyzna. (pub. by Izdatel'stvo Radyanskii Pismennik)
- Vsesvit. (pub. by Izdatel'stvo Radyanskii Pismennik)
- Zhovten' (pub. by Izdatel'stvo Kamenyar)

**Soyuz Rabotnikov Kinematografii S.S.S.R.**
Ul. Usievicha, 9, Moscow A-319, U.S.S.R.
- Iskusstvo Kino. m. ISSN 0021-1788

**Soyuz Sovetskikh Obshchestv Druzhby i Kul'turnoi Svyazi s Zarubezhnymi Stranami**
- Kul'tura i Zhizn/Culture and Life. (pub. by Izdatel'stvo Sovetskaya Rossiya)

**Soyuz Sportivnykh Obshchestv i Organizatsii Rossiiskoi S.F.S.R.**
- Sportivnaya Zhizn' Rossii. (pub. by Izdatel'stvo Fizkul'tura i Sport)

**Soyuz Sportivnykh Obshchestv i Organizatsii S. S. S. R.**
- Legkaya Atletika. (pub. by Izdatel'stvo Fizkul'tura i Sport)
- Sportivnye Igry. (pub. by Izdatel'stvo Fizkul'tura i Sport)

**Soyuz Sportivnykh Obshchestv i Organizatsii Ukrainskoi S.S.R.**
- Start. (pub. by Izdatel'stvo Molod)

**Soyuz Zhurnalistov S.S.S.R.**
Moscow, U.S.S.R.
- Sovetskoe Foto. m. ISSN 0038-5190
- Zhurnalist. (pub. by Izdatel'stvo Pravda)

**Spilka arkhitektiv Ukrayiny**
Kiev, U.S.S.R.
- Stroitel'stvo i Arkhitektura. m. ISSN 0039-2405

**Izdatel'stvo Statistika**
Ul. Kirova, 39, Moscow K-450, U.S.S.R.
- Vestnik Statistiki. m. ISSN 0042-4692 (U.S.S.R. Tsentral'noe Statisticheskoe Upravlenie pri Sovete Ministrov)

**Stroiizdat**
Kuznetskii most, 9, Moscow, U.S.S.R.
(Subscr. Address: Mezhdunarodnaya Kniga, Moscow G-200, U.S.S.R.
- Na Stroikakh Rossii. m. ISSN 0027-7312
- Nauka i Suspil'stvo. m. ISSN 0028-1247
- Osnovaniya, Fundamenty i Mekhanika Gruntov. bi-m. ISSN 0030-6223 (U.S.S.R. Gosstroi)
- Stroitel'. m. ISSN 0039-2375
- Stroitel'naya Mekhanika i Raschot Sooruzhenii. bi-m. ISSN 0039-2383 (U.S.S.R. Gosstroi)
- Tsement. m. ISSN 0041-4867 (U. S. S. R. Ministerstvo Promyshlennosti Stroitel'nykh Materialov)
- Zodchestvo. irreg. (Soyuz Arkhitektorov S.S.S.R.)

**Izdatel'stvo Sudostroenie**
Ul. Gogolya, 8, Leningrad D-65, U.S.S.R.
- Sudostroenie. m. ISSN 0039-4580 (U.S.S.R. Ministerstvo Sudostroeniya) (Co-sponsor: Nauchno-tekhnicheskoe Obshchestvo Sudostroitel'noi Promyshlennosti im. A. N. Krylov)

**Izdatel'stvo Svyaz'**
Chistoprudnyi bul'var, 2, Moscow, U.S.S.R.
- Elektrosvyaz' m. ISSN 0013-5771 (Nauchno-tekhnicheskoe Obshchestvo Radiotekhniki i Elektrosvyazi im. A. S. Popova)
- Vestnik Svyazi. m. ISSN 0042-4706

**Tbilisi Universitet**
Chavchavadze Ave., Tbilisi, U.S.S.R.
- Tbilisi Universitet. Institut Prikladnoi Matematiki. Seminar. Annotatsii Dokladov. irreg., 1971, no. 4. ISSN 0082-2191

**Izdatel'stvo Tekhnika**
Pushkinskaya 28, Kiev, U.S.S.R.
- Ugol' Ukrainy. m. ISSN 0041-5804

**Tekhnolohichnyi Instytut Lehkoy Promyslovosti**
Kiev, U.S.S.R.
- Izvestiya Vysshikh Uchebnykh Zavedenii. Seriya Tekhnologiya Legkoi Promyshlennosti. bi-m. ISSN 0021-3489

**Timiryazevskaya Sel'skokhozyaistvennaya Akademiya**
Ul. Timiryazevskaya, 49, Moscow a-8, U.S.S.R.
- Timiryazevskaya Sel'skokhozyaistvennaya Akademiya. Izvestiya. bi-m. ISSN 0021-342X

**Tomskii Meditsinskii Institut. Tsentralnaya Nauchno-Issledovatelskaya Laboratoriya**
- Voprosy Radiobiologii i Biologicheskogo Deistviya Tsitostaticheskikh Preparatov. (pub. by Izdatel'svo Tomskii Universitet)

**Tomskii Universitet**
Prospekt Lenina, 36, Tomsk-10, U.S.S.R.
- Izvestiya Vysshikh Uchebnykh Zavedenii. Seriya Fizika. m. ISSN 0021-3411
- Voprosy Radiobiologii i Biologicheskogo Deistviya Tsitostaticheskikh Preparatov. irreg. (Tomskii Meditsinskii Institut. Tsentralnaya Nauchno-Issledovatelskaya Laboratoriya)

**Izdatel'stvo Transport**
Basmannyi Tupik, 6a, Moscow B-175, U.S.S.R.
(Subscr. to: Mezhdunarodnaya Kniga, Moscow, G-200, U. S. S. R.)
- Avtomatika, Telemekhanika i Svyaz. m. ISSN 0005-2329 (U. S. S. R. Ministerstvo Putei Soobshcheniya)
- Morskoi Flot; journal of USSR merchant marine. m. ISSN 0027-1217 (U.S.S.R. Ministerstvo Kommercheskogo Flota)
- Rechnoi Transport. m. ISSN 0034-1290 (Rossiiskaya S.F.S.R. Ministerstvo Rechnogo Flota)
- Zheleznodorozhnyi Transport. m. ISSN 0044-4448 (U.S.S.R. Ministerstvo Putei Soobshcheniya)

**Izdatel'stvo Transport. Leningradskoe Otdelenie**
Ul. Dekabristov, 33, 190121 Leningrad, U. S. S. R.
- Institut Vodnogo Transporta, Leningrad. Gidrotekhnicheskaya Laboratoriya. Materialy. irreg.

**Izdatel'stvo Trud**
Pl. Pushkina, Moscow 103782 GSP, U.S.S.R.
- Novoe Vremya/New Times. w. ISSN 0029-5280

**Tsentral'nyi Nauchno-Issledovatel'skii Institut Patentnoi Informatsii i Tekhniko-Ekonom'cheskikh Issledovanii**
Raushskaya Nab. 4, 113035 Moscow, U.S.S.R.
- Otkrytiya, Izobreteniya, Promyshlennye Obraztsy, Tovarnye Znaki/Bulletin for Inventions, Designs, and Trademarks. 4 per mo. ISSN 0007-4020

**U. S. S. R. Glavnoe Arkhivnoe Upravlenie**
Pirogovskaya 17, Moscow G-435, U. S. S. R.
- Sovetskie Arkhivy. bi-m. ISSN 0038-5166

**U. S. S. R. Glavnoe Upravlenie Geodezii i Kartografii pri Sovete Ministrov**
Moscow, U. S. S. R.
- Geodeziya i Kartografiya. m. ISSN 0016-7126

**U. S. S. R. Gosplan**
Ul. Gor'kovo 5/6, Moscow, Tsentr, U. S. S. R.
- Planovoe Khozyaistvo. m. ISSN 0032-0757

**U. S. S. R. Gosstroi**
Moscow, U.S.S.R.
- Beton i Zhelezobeton. m. ISSN 0005-9889
- Byulleten' Stroitel'noi Tekhniki. m. ISSN 0007-7690
- Mekhanizatsiya Stroitel'stva. (pub. by Izdatel'stvo Mashinostroenie)
- Osnovaniya, Fundamenty i Mekhanika Gruntov. (pub. by Stroiizdat)
- Promyshlennoe Stroitel'stvo. m. ISSN 0033-118X
- Stroitel'naya Mekhanika i Raschot Sooruzhenii. (pub. by Stroiizdat)
- Vodosnabzhenie i Sanitarnaya Tekhnika. m. ISSN 0042-7918
- Zhilishchnoe Stroitel'stvo. m. ISSN 0044-4472

**U. S. S. R. Gosudarstvennyi Komitet Autotraktornogo i Sel'skokhozyaistvennogo Mashinostroeniya pri Gosplane**
Neglinnaya 23, Moscow I-51, U.S.S.R.
- Avtomobil'naya Promyshlennost' m. ISSN 0005-2337

**U. S. S. R. Gosudarstvennyi Komitet Khimicheskogo i Neftyanogo Mashinostroeniya pri Gosplane**
Moscow, U.S.S.R.
- Khimicheskoe i Neftyanoe Mashinostroenie. m. ISSN 0023-1126

**U. S. S. R. Gosudarstvennyi Komitet Khimicheskoi Promyshlennosti pri Gosplane**
Moscow, U.S.S.R.
- Khimiya v Sel'skom Khozyaistve. m. ISSN 0023-1185

**U. S. S. R. Gosudarstvennyi Komitet po Chernoi i Tsvetnoi Metallurgii**
Proezd Vladimirova, 6, Moscow K-12, U. S. S. R.
- Gornyi Zhurnal. m. ISSN 0017-2278

**U. S. S. R. Gosudarstvennyi Komitet po Grazhdanskomu Stroitel'stvu i Arkhitekture**
Ul. Shchuseva 3, Komn. 16, Moscow K-1, U.S.S.R.
- Arkhitektura S S S R. m. ISSN 0004-1939 (Co-sponsor: Soyuz Arkhtektorov S. S. S. R.)

**U. S. S. R. Gosudarstvennyi Komitet po Ispol'zovaniyu Atomnoi Energii S. S. S. R.**
Ul. Kirova 18, Moscow, U. S. S. R.
- Atomnaya Energiya. m. ISSN 0004-7163

**U. S. S. R. Gosudarstvennyi Komitet po Khimii pri Sovete Ministrov**
Moscow, U. S. S. R.
- Lakokrasochnye Materialy i Ikh Primenenie. bi-m. ISSN 0023-737X

**U. S. S. R. Gosudarstvennyi Komitet po Kinematografii Soveta Ministrov**
Leningradskii Prosp. 47, 125167, GSP, Moscow, U. S. S. R.
- Sovetskii Ekran. (pub. by Izdatel'stvo Pravda)
- Tekhnika Kino i Televideniya. m. ISSN 0040-2249

**U. S. S. R. Gosudarstvennyi Komitet po Torgovle**
Ul. Razina 28, Moscow, U. S. S. R.
- Sovetskaya Torgovlya. m. ISSN 0038-5107

**U. S. S. R. Gosudarstvennyi Komitet Soveta Ministrov po Nauke i Tekhnike**
Prospekt Mira 106, Moscow i-164, U. S. S. R.
- Konservnaya i Ovoshchesushil'naya Promyshlennost' m. ISSN 0023-3587
- Vinodelie i Vnogradarstvo S.S.S.R. 8 per yr. ISSN 0042-6318
- Torfyanaya Promyshlennost' m. ISSN 0040-9472
- Vestnik Mashinostroeniya. m. ISSN 0042-4633

**U. S. S. R. Gosudarstvennyi Komitet Soveta Ministrov po Pechati**
Moscow, U. S. S. R., U.S.S.R.
(Subscr. to: Mezhdunarodnaya Kniga, Moscow, G-200, U.S.S.R.)
- Ekspress-Informatsiya. Knizhnaya Torgoulya. m. ISSN 0023-236X
- Knizhnoe Obozrenie. w. ISSN 0023-2378

**U. S. S. R. Gosudarstvennyi Komitet Soveta Ministrov po Voprosam Truda i Zarabotnoi Platy**
Pl. Kuibysheva 1, Moscow K-12, U. S. S. R.
- Sotsialisticheskii Trud. m. ISSN 0037-8216
- U. S. S. R. Gosudarstvennyi Komitet Soveta Ministrov po Voprosam Truda i Zarabotnoi Platy. Byulleten. m. ISSN 0007-7666

**U. S. S. R. Gosudarstvennyi Komitet Standartov Mer i Izmeritel'nykh Priborov**
Shchuseva 4, Moscow K-1, U.S.S.R.
- Izmeritel'naya Tekhnika. m. ISSN 0021-3349

**U. S. S. R. Gosudarstvennyi Komitet Tyazhelego, Energeticheskogo i Transportnogo Mashinostroenie pri Gosplane**
Moscow, U. S. S. R.
- Energomashinostroenie/Power Machinery Construction. m. ISSN 0013-7456

**U.S.S.R. Komitet po Delam Izobretenii i Otkrytii Soveta Ministrov S.S.S.R.**
Moscow, U.S.S.R.
- Izobretatel' i Ratsionalizator. m. ISSN 0021-3365

**U.S.S.R. Komitet po Delam Stroitel'stva Soveta Ministrov S.S.S.R.**
Moscow, U.S.S.R., U. S. S R
(Subscr. to: Mezhdunarodnaya Kniga, Moscow, G-200, U.S.S.R.)
- Ekonomika Stroitel'stva. m. ISSN 0013-3116

**U. S. S. R. Komitet po Fizicheskoi Kul'ture i Sportu pri Sovete Ministrov**
- Fizkul'tura i Sport. (pub. by Izdatel'stvo Fizkul'tura i Sport)
- Shakhmatnyi Byulleten' (pub. by Izdatel'stvo Fizkul'tura i Sport)
- Shakhmaty v S. S. S. R. (pub. by Izdatel'stvo Fizkul'tura i Sport)
- Teoriya i Praktika Fizicheskoi Kul'tury. (pub. by Izdatel'stvo Fizkul'tura i Sport)

**U. S. S. R. Komitet po Pechati Soveta Ministrov**
- Letopis' Gazetnykh Statei. (pub. by Izdatel'stvo Kniga)
- Letopis' Pechatnykh Proizvedenii Izobrazitel'nogo Iskusstva. (pub. by Izdatel'stvo Kniga)
- Notnaya Letopis' (pub. by Izdatel'stvo Kniga)
- Poligrafiya. (pub. by Izdatel'stvo Kniga)
- Sovetskaya Bibliografiya. (pub. by Izdatel'stvo Kniga)
- V Mire Knig. (pub. by Izdatel'stvo Kniga)

**U. S. S. R. Ministerstvo Chernoi Metallurgii**
- Koks i Khimiya. (pub. by Izdatel'stvo Metallurgiya)
- Metallurg. (pub. by Izdatel'stvo Metallurgiya)
- Ochistka Vodnogo i Vozdushnogo Basseinov na Predpriyatiyakh Chernoi Metallurgii. (pub. by Izdatel'stvo Metallurgiya)
- Stal' (pub. by Izdatel'stvo Metallurgiya)
- Zavodskaya Laboratoriya. (pub. by Izdatel'stvo Metallurgiya)

**U. S. S. R. Ministerstvo Derevoobrabatyvayushchei Promyshlennosti**
- Derevoobrabatyvayushchaya Promyshlennost' (pub. by Izdatel'stvo Lesnaya Promyshlennost')

**U.S.S.R. Ministerstvo Elektricheskoi Promyshlennosti**
Moscow, U.S.S.R.
- Elektrotekhnika. m. ISSN 0013-5860

**U.S.S.R. Ministerstvo Energetiki i Elektrifikatsii**
Bol'shoi Cherkasskii Per., 2, Moscow K-12, U.S.S.R.
- Elektricheskie Stantsii. (pub. by Izdatel'stvo Energiya)
- Gidrotekhnicheskoe Stroitel'stvo. m. ISSN 0016-9714
- Promyshlennaya Energetika. m. ISSN 0033-1155 (Co-sponsor: Nauchno-tekhnicheskoe Obshchestvo Energetiki i Energeticheskoi Promyshlennosti)

**U. S. S. R. Ministerstvo Finansov**
Moscow, U. S. S. R.
- Bukhgalterskii Uchet. m. ISSN 0007-3776
- Finansy S.S.S.R. (pub. by Izdatel'stvo Finansy)

**U. S. S. R. Ministerstvo Gazovoi Promyshlennosti**
- Gazovaya Promyshlennost' (pub. by Izdatel'stvo Nedra)

**U.S.S.R. Ministerstvo Geologii**
Moscow, U.S.S.R.
- Geologiya Nefti i Gaza. (pub. by Izdatel'stvo Nedra)
- Razvedka i Okhrana Nedr. (pub. by Izdatel'stvo Nedra)
- Sovetskaya Geologiya. m. ISSN 0038-5069

**U. S. S. R. Ministerstvo Grazhdanskoi Aviatsii**
Moscow, U.S.S.R.
- Grazhdanskaya Aviatsiya. m. ISSN 0017-3606

**U.S.S.R. Ministerstvo Khimicheskoi Promyshlennosti**
- Khimicheskaya Promyshlennost' (pub. by Izdatel'stvo Khimiya)

**U.S.S.R. Ministerstvo Kommercheskogo Flota**
- Morskoi Flot. (pub. by Izdatel'stvo Transport)

**U. S. S. R. Ministerstvo Kul'tury**
Moscow, U. S. S. R.
- Iskusstvo. (pub. by Izdatel'stvo Iskusstvo)
- Kinomekhanik. m. ISSN 0023-1681
- Teatr. (pub. by Izdatel'stvo Iskusstvo)

**U.S.S.R. Ministerstvo Legkoi Promyshlennosti**
Moscow, U.S.S.R.
(Subscr. To: Mezhdunarodnaya Kniga, Moscow G-200, U.S.S.R.)
- Tekstil'naya Promyshlennost' m. ISSN 0040-2397

**U.S.S.R. Ministerstvo Meditsinskoi Promyshlennosti**
- Khimiko-farmatsevticheskii Zhurnal. (pub. by Izdatel'stvo Meditsina)
- Meditsinskaya Tekhnika. (pub. by Izdatel'stvo Meditsina)

**U.S.S.R. Ministerstvo Myasnoi i Molochnoi Promyshlennosti**
Moscow, U.S.S.R.
- Molochnaya Promyshlennost' m. ISSN 0026-9026
- Myasnaya Industriya S.S.S.R. m. ISSN 0027-5492

**U.S.S.R. Ministerstvo Neftyanoi Promyshlennosti**
Moscow, U.S.S.R
(Subscr. to: Mezhdunarodnaya Kniga, Moscow, G-200, U.S.S.R.)
- Neftyanik. m. ISSN 0028-243X
- Neftyanoe Khozyaistvo. m. ISSN 0028-2448

**U.S.S.R. Ministerstvo Oborony**
- Voenno-Istoricheskii Zhurnal. (pub. by Voenizdat)
- Voennyi Vestnik. (pub. by Voenizdat)

**U.S.S.R. Ministerstvo Pishchevoi Promyshlennosti**
Chistye Prudy, 12, Moscow, U.S.S.R.
- Maslozhirovaya Promyshlennost' m. ISSN 0025-4649
- Mukomol'no-elevatornaya i Kombikormovaya Promyshlennost' m. ISSN 0027-3090

**U. S. S. R. Ministerstvo Priborostroeniya**
- Pribory i Sistemy Upravleniya. (pub. by Izdatel'stvo Mashinostroenie)

**U.S.S.R. Ministerstvo Promyshlennosti Stroitel'nykh Materialov**
Moscow, U.S.S.R.
- Steklo i Keramika. m. ISSN 0039-1115
- Tsement. (pub. by Stroiizdat)

**U.S.S.R. Ministerstvo Prosveshcheniya**
Pogodinskaya Ul. 8, Moscow G-117, U.S.S.R.
- Geografiya v Shkole. (pub. by Izdatel'stvo Prosveshchenie)
- Literatura v Shkole. bi-m. ISSN 0024-4724
- Matematika v Shkole. (pub. by Izdatel'stvo Prosveshchenie)
- Narodnoe Obrazovanie. (pub. by Izdatels'stvo Prosveshchenie)

**U.S.S.R. Ministerstvo Putei Sooshcheniya**
Novoryazanskaya ul., 12, Moscow 228, U.S.S.R
(Subscr. to: Mezhdunarodnaya Kniga, Moscow, G-200, U. S. S. R.)
- Avtomatika, Telemekhanika i Svyaz. (pub. by Izdatel'stvo Transport)
- Put' i Putevoe Khozyaistvo. m. ISSN 0033-4715
- Zheleznodorozhnyi Transport. (pub. by Izdatel'stvo Transport)

**U.S.S.R. Ministerstvo Rybnogo Khozyaistva**
Moscow, U.S.S.R
(Subscr. to: Mezhdunarodnaya Kniga, Moscow, G-200, U.S.S.R.)
- Rybnoe Khozyaistvo. m. ISSN 0036-049X

**U. S. S. R. Ministerstvo Sel'skogo Khozyaistva**
Moscow, U.S.S.R.
- Ekonomika Sel'skogo Khozyaistva. (pub. by Izdatel'stvo Kolos)
- Gidrotekhnika i Melioratsiya. (pub. by Izdatel'stvo Kolos)
- Kartofel' i Ovoshchi. m. ISSN 0022-9148
- Khlopkovodstvo. (pub. by Izdatel'stvo Kolos)
- Krolikovodstvo i Zverovodstvo. bi-m. ISSN 0023-4885
- Kukuruza. m. ISSN 0023-5040
- Len i Konoplya. m. ISSN 0024-418X
- Mekhanizatsiya i Elektrifikatsiya Sotsialisticheskogo Sel'skogo Khozyaistva. (pub. by Izdatel'stvo Kolos)
- Mezhdunarodnyi Sel'skokhozyaistvennyi Zhurnal; nauchno-proizvodstvennyi zhurnal po obmenu dostizheniyami nauki i peredovoga opyta v sel'skom khozyaistve stran-uchastnits Soveta Ekonomicheskoi Vzaimopomoschi. bi-m. ISSN 0026-1882
- Molochnoe i Myasnoe Skotovodstvo. m. ISSN 0026-9034
- Ovtsevodstvo. m. ISSN 0030-7572
- Ptitsevodstvo. m. ISSN 0033-3239

- Rybovodstvo i Rybolovstvo. bi-m. ISSN 0036-0503
- Sadovodstvo. m. ISSN 0036-2298
- Sakharnaya Promyshlennost' m. ISSN 0036-3340
- Sakharnaya Svekla. m. ISSN 0036-3359
- Selektsiya i Semenovodstvo. bi-m. ISSN 0037-1459
- Svinovodstvo. m. ISSN 0039-713X
- Tekhnika v Sel'skom Khozyaistve. (pub. by Izdatel'stvo Kolos)
- Tsvetovodstvo. m. ISSN 0041-4905
- Veterinariya. m. ISSN 0042-4846
- Zashchita Rastenii. m. ISSN 0044-1864
- Zemledelie. (pub. by Izdatel'stvo Kolos)
- Zernovoe Khozyaistvo. (pub. by Izdatel'stvo Kolos)
- Zhivotnovodstvo. m. ISSN 0044-4480

**U.S.S.R. Ministerstvo Stankostroitel'noi i Instrumental'noi Promyshlennosti**
Moscow, U.S.S.R.
- Liteinoe Proizvodstvo. m. ISSN 0024-449X
- Mekhanizatsiya i Avtomatizatsiya Proizvodstva. m. ISSN 0025-8873

**U.S.S.R. Ministerstvo Stroitel'nogo, Dorozhnogo i Kommunal'nogo Mashinostroeniya**
Moscow G-200, U.S.S.R.
- Montazhnye i Spetsial'nye Raboty v Stroitel'stve. m. ISSN 0027-0040
- Stroitel'nye i Dorozhnye Mashiny. (pub. by Izdatel'stvo Mashinostroenie)

**U.S.S.R. Ministerstvo Sudostroeniya**
- Sudostroenie. (pub. by Izdatel'stvo Sudostroenie)

**U.S.S.R. Ministerstvo Svyazi**
Moscow, U.S.S.R.
- Radio. m. ISSN 0033-765X (Co-sponsor:: Vsesoyuznoe Dobrovol'noe Obshchestvo Sodeistviya Armii, Aviatsii i Flotu)

**U.S.S.R. Ministerstvo Tselyulozno-bumazhnoi Promyshlennosti**
Ul. 25 Oktyabrya, Moscow K-12, U.S.S.R.
- Bumazhnaya Promyshlennost' m. ISSN 0007-5817
- Gidroliznaya i Lesokhimicheskaya Promyshlennost' 8 per yr. ISSN 0016-9706

**U. S. S. R. Ministerstvo Tsvetnoi Metallurgii**
- Tsvetnye Metally. (pub. by Izdatel'stvo Metallurgiya)

**U.S.S.R. Ministerstvo Ugol'noi Promyshlennosti**
Moscow, U.S.S.R.
- Ekonomika Ugol'noi Promyshlennosti. irreg.
- Ugol' m. ISSN 0041-5790

**U.S.S.R. Ministerstvo Visshego i Srednego Spetsialnogo Obrazovaniya**
- Soviet Mathematics. (pub. by Allerton Press, Inc. US)

**U.S.S.R. Ministerstvo Vneshnei Torgovli**
- Foreign Trade/Vneshnyaya Torgovlya. (pub. by Izdatel'stvo Izvestiya)

**U. S. S. R. Ministerstvo Vysshego i Srednego Spetsial'nogo Obrazovaniya**
Moscow, U. S. S. R.
- Ekonomicheskie Nauki. (pub. by Izdatel'stvo Vysshaya Shkola)
- Filologicheskie Nauki. (pub. by Izdatel'stvo Vysshaya Shkola)
- Filosofskie Nauki. (pub. by Izdatel'stvo Vysshaya Shkola)
- Izvestiya Vysshikh Uchebnykh Zavedenii. Seriya Energetika. (pub. by Belorusskii Politekhnicheskii Institut)
- Izvestiya Vysshikh Uchebnykh Zavedenii. Seriya Geologiya i Razvedka. (pub. by Moskovskii Institut Geologii i Razvedki)
- Izvestiya Vysshikh Uchebnykh Zavedenii. Seriya Radiofizika. m. ISSN 0021-3462
- Srednee Spetsial'noe Obrazovanie. m. ISSN 0038-8785
- Vestnik Vysshei Shkoly. m. ISSN 0042-4757

**U. S. S. R. Ministerstvo Zdravookhraneniya**
Moscow, U.S.S.R.
- Arkhiv Patologii. (pub. by Izdatel'stvo Meditsina)
- Biomedical Engineering. (pub. by Consultants Bureau US)
- Farmakologiya i Toksikologiya. bi-m. ISSN 0014-8318
- Fel'dsher i Akusherka. m. ISSN 0014-9772
- Gigiena i Saritariya. m. ISSN 0016-9900

- Gigiena Truda i Professional'nye Zabolevaniya. m. ISSN 0016-9919
- Khirurgiya. m. ISSN 0023-1207
- Meditsinskaya Gazeta. s-w. ISSN 0025-8318
- Sovetskoe Zdravookhranenie. m. ISSN 0038-5239
- Urologiya i Nefrologiya. bi-m. ISSN 0042-1154
- Voprosy Onkologii. (pub. by Izdatel'stvo Meditsina. Leningradskoe Otdelenie)
- Voprosy Pitaniya. bi-m. ISSN 0042-8833
- Zdorov'e. (pub. by Izdatel'stvo Pravda)

**U.S.S.R. Prokuratura**
Moscow, U.S.S.R.
- Sotsialisticheskaya Zakonnost' m. ISSN 0038-1691 (Co-sponsor: U.S.S.R. Verkhovnyi Sud)

**U.S.S.R. Tsentral'noe Statisticheskoe Upravlenie pri Sovete Ministrov**
- Vestnik Statistiki. (pub. by Izdatel'stvo Statistika)

**U. S. S. R. Verkhovnyi Sovet**
Prospekt Kalinina 4/22, Moscow, U. S. S. R.
- Verkhovnyi Sovet S.S.S.R. Vedomosti. w. ISSN 0042-3017

**Ukrainskaya S.S.R. Ministerstvo Kul'tury**
Kiev, U.S.S.R.
- Kul'tura i Zhyttya. s-w. ISSN 0023-5180
- Sotsialistychna Kul'tura. m. ISSN 0038-1705

**Ukrainskaya S.S.R. Ministerstvo Osvity**
Kiev, U.S.S.R.
- Radyans'ka Osvita. s-w. ISSN 0033-8605
- Ukrains'ka Mova i Literatura v Shkoli; metodychnyi zhurnal. m. ISSN 0041-6096

**Ukrainskaya S.S.R. Ministerstvo Zdorovya**
Kiev, U.S.S.R.
- Oftal'mologicheskii Zhurnal. 8 per yr. ISSN 0030-0675
- Pediatriya, Akusherstvo ta Ginekologiya. bi-m. ISSN 0031-4048

**Ulyanovskii Politekhnicheskii Institut**
- Issledovanie, Konstruirovanie i Raschet Rezbovykh Soedinenii. (pub. by Privolzhskoe Knizhnoe Izdatel'stvo)

**Izdatel'stvo Urozhai**
Bol'shaya Podvalnaya ul., 10, Kiev 34, U. S. S. R.
- Khliborob Ukrainy. m. ISSN 0023-1223

**Vilnius Universitet**
Ciurlionio g-ve 21/27, Vilnius 31, U.S.S.R.
- Geografija ir Geologija. irreg. ISSN 0072-0976

**Vneshtorgreklama**
Ul. Kahovka 31, Korp. 2, Moscow 113461, U.S.S.R.
- Soviet Export. bi-m. ISSN 0490-1274

**Voenizdat**
Bol'shoi Kisel'nyi Per., 14, Moscow, U.S.S.R.
(Subscr. to: Mezhdunarodnaya Kniga, Moscow, G-200, U.S.S.R.)
- Soviet Military Review/Sovetskoe Voennoe Obozrenie. m. ISSN 0038-5220
- Voenno-Istoricheskii Zhurnal. m. ISSN 0042-9058 (U.S.S.R. Ministerstvo Oborony)
- Voenno - Meditsinskii Zhurnal. m. ISSN 0047-7397
- Voennyi Vestnik. m. ISSN 0042-9066 (U.S.S.R. Ministerstvo Oborony)

**Voronezhskii Gosudarstvennyi Universitet**
Universitetskaya ploshchad, 1, Voronezh, U. S. S. R.
- Filosofiya i Fizika.

**Vserossiiskoe Teatral'noe Obshchestvo**
Ul. Gorkogo, 16, Moscow, U. S. S. R.
- Voprosy Teatra; sbornik statei i materialov. a. ISSN 0507-3952 (Co-sponsor: Institut Istorii Iskusstv)

**Vsesoyuznaya Akademiya Sel'skokhozyaistvennykh Nauk im. V. I. Lenina**
Bolshoi Kharitonevskii per., 21, Moscow, U.S.S.R.
- Sel'skoe Khozyaistvo za Rubezhom. Seriya: Rasteneivodstvo i Zhivotnovodstvo. (pub. by Izdatel'stvo Kolos)
- Sel'skokhozyaistvennaya Biologiya. bi-m. ISSN 0037-167X
- Sel'skokhozyaistvennaya Literatura S. S. S. R. m. ISSN 0037-1688
- Vsesoyuznaya Akademiya Sel'skokhozyaistvennykh Nauk im. V. I. Lenina. Doklady. m. ISSN 0042-9244

- Vsesoyuznyi Nauchno-Issledovatel'skii Institut Zernovogo Khozyaistva. Trudy. (pub. by Izdatel'stvo Kolos)

**Vsesoyuznaya Gosudarstvennaya Biblioteka Inostrannoi Literatury**
Ulyanovskaya 1, Moscow, U.S.S.R.
- Informatsiya o Bibliotechnom Dele i Bibliografii za Rubezhom. bi-m. ISSN 0019-9826
- Sovremennaya Khudozhestvennaya Literatura za Rubezhom. (pub. by Izdatel'stvo Progress)

**Vsesoyuznoe Geograficheskoe Obshchestvo**
- Vsesoyuznoe Geograficheskoe Obshchestvo. Izvestiya. (pub. by Izdatel'stvo Nauka. Leningradskoe Otdelenie)

**Vsesoyuznoe Mineralogicheskoe Obshchestvo**
Leninskii prospekt, 14, Moscow V-71, U.S.S.R.
- Vsesoyuznoe Mineralogicheskoe Obshchestvo. Zapiski. bi-m. ISSN 0042-9260

**Vsesoyuznoe Nauchnoe Obshchestvo Sudebnykh Medikov**
- Sudebno-meditsinskaya Ekspertiza. (pub. by Izdatel'stvo Meditsina)

**Vsesoyuznoe Obshchestvo Filatelistov**
Moscow, U. S. S. R.
- Filateli'ya S. S. S. R. m. ISSN 0015-0983

**Vsesoyuznoe Obshchestvo "Znanie"**
Proezd Serova, 4, Moscow, U.S.S.R.
- International Affairs/Mezhdunarodnaya Zhizn' m. ISSN 0020-5869
- Nauka i Religiya. m. ISSN 0028-1239
- Nauka i Zhizn' (pub. by Izdatel'stvo Pravda)

**Vsesoyuznyi Institut Assortimenta Izdelii Legkoi Promyshlennosti i Kul'tury Odezhdy**
Kuznetskii most, 14, Moscow, U.S.S.R.
- Zhurnal Mod. q. ISSN 0044-4545

**Vsesoyuznyi Institut Nauchno-Tekhnicheskoi Informatsii (VINITI)**
Baltiiskaya ul., 14, Moscow, A-219, U.S.S.R. (Subscr. to: Mezhdunarodnaya Kniga, Moscow G-200, U.S.S.R.)
- Ekspress-Informatsita. Aviastroenie. 48 per yr. ISSN 0013-3345
- Ekspress-Informatsiya. Astronavtika i Raketodinamika. 48 per yr.
- Ekspress-Informatsiya. Automobilestroenie. 48 per yr. ISSN 0013-3353
- Ekspress-Informatsiya. Avtomaticheskie Linii i Metallorezhushchie Stanki. 48 per yr.
- Ekspress-Informatsiya. Avtomatizirovannyi Elektroprivod. Elektrotekhnologiya. Elektrosnabzhenie. Silovaya Preobrazovatel'naya Tekhnika. 48 per yr.
- Ekspress-Informatsiya. Burenie. 24 per yr.
- Ekspress-Informatsiya. Detali Mashin. 48 per yr. ISSN 0013-3388
- Ekspress-Informatsiya. Ekonomicheskie i Mezhdunarodno-Pravovye Voprosy Mirovogo Rybolovstva. m.
- Ekspress-Informatsiya. Eksperimenty i Metody v Mineralogii i Geokhimii. 48 per yr.
- Ekspress-Informatsiya. Elektricheskie Mashiny i Apparaty. 48 per yr. ISSN 0013-3396
- Ekspress-Informatsiya. Elektricheskie Stantsii, Seti i Sistemy. 48 per yr. ISSN 0013-340X
- Ekspress-Informatsiya. Elektronika. 48 per yr. ISSN 0013-3418
- Ekspress-Informatsiya. Fotokinoapparatura. Nauchnaya i Prikladnaya Fotografiya. 48 per yr. ISSN 0013-3426
- Ekspress-Informatsiya. Garazhi i Garazhnoe Oborudovanie. 48 per yr. ISSN 0013-3434
- Ekspress-Informatsiya. Gidroenergetika. 48 per yr. ISSN 0013-3442
- Ekspress-Informatsiya. Gornorudnaya Promyshlennost' 48 per yr. ISSN 0013-3450
- Ekspress-Informatsiya. Gorodskoi Transport. 48 per yr. ISSN 0013-3469
- Ekspress-Informatsiya. Iskusstvennye Sooruzheniya na Avtomobil'nykh Dorogakh. 48 per yr. ISSN 0013-3477
- Ekspress-Informatsiya. Ispytatel'nye Pribory i Stendy. 48 per yr. ISSN 0013-3485
- Ekspress-Informatsiya. Izdatel'skoe Delo. m.
- Ekspress-Informatsiya. Khimia i Tekhnologiya Neorganicheskikh Veshchestv. 48 per yr. ISSN 0013-3515
- Ekspress-Informatsiya. Khimicheskaya Tekhnologiya Pererabotki Vysokopolimernykh Materialov. 48 per yr. ISSN 0013-3493

- Ekspress-Informatsiya. Khimiya i Pererabotka Nefti i Gaza. 48 per yr. ISSN 0013-3507
- Ekspress-Informatsiya. Kibernetika v Khimii i Khimicheskoi Tekhnologii. 48 per yr.
- Ekspress-Informatsiya. Kontrol'no-Izmeritel'naya Tekhnika. 48 per yr. ISSN 0013-3523
- Ekspress-Informatsiya. Korrozia i Zashchita Metallov. 48 per yr. ISSN 0013-3531
- Ekspress-Informatsiya. Kozhevennaya Promyshlennost' 24 per yr.
- Ekspress-Informatsiya. Kozhlagalantereinaya Promyshlennost' m.
- Ekspress-Informatsiya. Kvantovaya Radiotekhnika. 48 per yr.
- Ekspress-Informatsiya. Lokomotivostroenie Vagonostroenie. 48 per yr. ISSN 0013-3558
- Ekspress-Informatsiya. Mekhovaya Promyshlennost' m.
- Ekspress-Informatsiya. Myasnaya i Molochnaya Promyshlennost' 48 per yr. ISSN 0013-3574
- Ekspress-Informatsiya. Nadezhnost' i Kontrol' Kachestva. 48 per yr.
- Ekspress-Informatsiya. Nefte- i Gazodobyvayushchaya Promyshlennost' 48 per yr. ISSN 0013-3582
- Ekspress-Informatsiya. Neftegazovaya Geologiya i Geofizika. 24 per yr.
- Ekspress-Informatsiya. Neftepromyslovoe Delo. 24 per yr.
- Ekspress-Informatsiya. Neftepromyslovoe Stroitel'stvo. 24 per yr.
- Ekspress-Informatsiya. Novye Lekarstvennye Preparaty. m.
- Ekspress-Informatsiya. Obogashchenie Poleznykh Iskopaemykh. 48 per yr. ISSN 0013-3590
- Ekspress-Informatsiya. Obrabotka Ryby i Moreproduktov. m.
- Ekspress-Informatsiya. Obuvnaya Promyshlennost' m.
- Ekspress-Informatsiya. Onkologiya. m.
- Ekspress-Informatsiya. Organizatsiya i Bezopasnost' Dorozhnogo Dvizheniya. 48 per yr.
- Ekspress-Informatsiya. Organizatsiya Perevozok, Avtomatica, Telemekhanica i Svyaz' na Zheleznykh Dorogakh. 48 per yr. ISSN 0013-3604
- Ekspress-Informatsiya. Peredacha Informatsii. 48 per yr.
- Ekspress-Informatsiya. Pererabotka Nefti i Neftekhimiya. 36 per yr.
- Ekspress-Informatsiya. Pishchevaya Promyshlennost' 48 per yr. ISSN 0013-3612
- Ekspress-Informatsiya. Pobochnye Deistviya Lekarstvennykh Veshchestv. m.
- Ekspress-Informatsiya. Pod'emno-Tekhnicheskoe, Vodolaznye i Sudopod'emnye Raboty. 48 per yr.
- Ekspress-Informatsiya. Pod'emno-Transportnoe Mashinostroenie. 48 per yr. ISSN 0013-3620
- Ekspress-Informatsiya. Poligraficheskaya Promyshlennost' m.
- Ekspress-Informatsiya. Porshnevye i Gazoturbinnye Dvigateli. 48 per yr. ISSN 0013-3639
- Ekspress-Informatsiya. Pozharnaya Okhrana. 48 per yr.
- Ekspress-Informatsiya. Pribory i Elementy Avtomatiki i Vychislitel'noi Tekhniki. 48 per yr.
- Ekspress-Informatsiya. Promyshlennoe Rybolovstvo. m.
- Ekspress-Informatsiya. Promyshlennost' Iskusstvennoi Kozhi. m.
- Ekspress-Informatsiya. Promyshlennyi Organicheskii Sintez. 48 per yr. ISSN 0013-3663
- Ekspress-Informatsiya. Promyshlennyi Transport. 48 per yr. ISSN 0013-3671
- Ekspress-Informatsiya. Promyslovaya Okeanologiya. m.
- Ekspress-Informatsiya. Protsessy i Apparaty Khimicheskikh Proizvodstv. 48 per yr. ISSN 0013-368X
- Ekspress-Informatsiya. Put' i Stroitel'stvo Zheleznykh Dorog. 48 per yr. ISSN 0013-3698
- Ekspress-Informatsiya. Radiolokatsiya, Televidenie, Radiosvyaz' 48 per yr. ISSN 0013-3701
- Ekspress-Informatsiya. Radiotekhnika Sverkhvysokikh Chastot. 48 per yr.
- Ekspress-Informatsiya. Rezhushchie Instrumenty. 48 per yr. ISSN 0013-3728
- Ekspress-Informatsiya. Rybnaya Promyshlennost' 48 per yr. ISSN 0013-3736
- Ekspress-Informatsiya. Rybokhozyaistvennoe Ispol'zovanie Resursov Mirovogo Okeana. m.
- Ekspress-Informatsiya. Rybokhozyaistvennoe Ispol'zovanie Vnutrennikh Vodoemov. m.

- Ekspress-Informatsiya. Sel'skokhozyaistvennye Mashiny i Orudiya. Mekhanizatsiya Sel'skokhozyaistvennykh Rabot. 48 per yr. ISSN 0013-3744
- Ekspress-Informatsiya. Shveinaya Promyshlennost' m.
- Ekspress-Informatsiya. Silikatnye Stroitel'nye Materialy. 48 per yr. ISSN 0013-3752
- Ekspress-Informatsiya. Sinteticheskie Vysokopolimernye Materialy. 48 per yr. ISSN 0013-3760
- Ekspress-Informatsiya. Sistemy Avtomaticheskogo Upravleniya. 48 per yr. ISSN 0013-3779
- Ekspress-Informatsiya. Steklo, Keramika i Ogneupory. 48 per yr. ISSN 0013-3787
- Ekspress-Informatsiya. Stroitel'stvo i Ekspluatatsiya Avtomobilnykh Dorog. 48 per yr. ISSN 0013-3795
- Ekspress-Informatsiya. Sudostroenie. 48 per yr. ISSN 0013-3809
- Ekspress-Informatsiya. Tara i Upakovka. Konteinery. 48 per yr.
- Ekspress-Informatsiya. Tedriya i Praktika Nauchnoi Informatsii. s-m. ISSN 0013-3892
- Ekspress-Informatsiya. Tekhnicheskaya Ekspluatatsiya Podvizhnogo Sostava i Tyaga Poezdov. 48 per yr. ISSN 0013-3833
- Ekspress-Informatsiya. Tekhnicheskaya Kibernetika. 48 per yr. ISSN 0013-3841
- Ekspress-Informatsiya. Tekhnika i Tekhnologiya Burovykh i Gornykh Razvedochnykh Rabot. 48 per yr.
- Ekspress-Informatsiya. Tekhnologicheskoe Oborudovanie Dlya Obrabotki Ryby. m.
- Ekspress-Informatsiya. Tekhnologiya i Oborudovanie Kuznechno-Shtampovochnogo Proizvodstva. 48 per yr. ISSN 0013-385X
- Ekspress-Informatsiya. Tekhnologiya i Oborudovanie Liteinogo Proizvodstva. 48 per yr. ISSN 0013-3868
- Ekspress-Informatsiya. Tekhnologiya i Oborudovanie Mekhanosborochnogo Proizvodstva. 48 per yr. ISSN 0013-3876
- Ekspress-Informatsiya. Tekstil'naya Promyschlennost' 48 per yr. ISSN 0013-3884
- Ekspress-Informatsiya. Teploenergetika. 48 per yr. ISSN 0013-3906
- Ekspress-Informatsiya. Termostoikie Plastiki. 48 per yr.
- Ekspress-Informatsiya. Traktorostroenie. 48 per yr. ISSN 0013-3914
- Ekspress-Informatsiya. Transport i Khranenie Nefti i Gaza. 48 per yr. ISSN 0013-3922
- Ekspress-Informatsiya. Transport i Khranenie Nefti i Nefteproduktov. 24 per yr.
- Ekspress-Informatsiya. Trikotazhnaya Promyshlennost' m.
- Ekspress-Informatsiya. Tsellyulozno-Bumazhnaya Promyshlennost' 48 per yr. ISSN 0013-3930
- Ekspress-Informatsiya. Ugol'naya Promyshlennost' 48 per yr. ISSN 0013-3957
- Ekspress-Informatsiya. Vakuumnaya Tekhnika. 48 per yr.
- Ekspress-Informatsiya. Vodnyi Transport. 48 per yr. ISSN 0013-3965
- Ekspress-Informatsiya. Vozdushnyi Transport. 48 per yr. ISSN 0013-3973
- Ekspress-Informatsiya. Vychislitel'naya Tekhnika. 48 per yr. ISSN 0013-3981
- Ekspress-Informatsiya. Zabolevaniya Serdechno-Sosudistoi Sistemy. m.
- Ekspress-Informatziya. Avtomobil'nyi Transport. 48 per yr. ISSN 0013-3361
- Itogi Nauki i Tekhniki: Genetika Cheloveka. a.
- Itogi Nauki i Tekhniki: Geomagnetizm i Vysokie Sloi Atmosfery. a.
- Itogi Nauki i Tekhniki: Stratigrafiya, Paleontologiya. a.
- Itogi Nauki i Tekhniki: Tekhnologiia Organicheskikh Veshchestv. a.
- Nauchno-tekhnicheskaya Informatsiya. m. ISSN 0028-1131
- Referativnyi Zhurnal. Astronomiya. m. ISSN 0486-2236
- Referativnyi Zhurnal. Aviatsionnye i Raketnye Dvigateli. m.
- Referativnyi Zhurnal. Avtomatika, Telemekhanika i Vychislitel'naya Tekhnika. m. ISSN 0034-2289
- Referativnyi Zhurnal. Avtomobil'nye Dorogi. m. ISSN 0486-2252
- Referativnyi Zhurnal. Avtomobil'nyi i Gorodskoi Transport. m. ISSN 0034-2297
- Referativnyi Zhurnal. Biofizika. m.
- Referativnyi Zhurnal. Biologicheskaya Khimiya. s-m. ISSN 0486-2260
- Referativnyi Zhurnal. Biologiya. m. ISSN 0034-2300

- Referativnyi Zhurnal. Dvigateli Vnutrennego Sgoraniya. m. ISSN 0486-2279
- Referativnyi Zhurnal. Ekonomika Promyshlennosti. m. ISSN 0034-2319
- Referativnyi Zhurnal. Elektronika i ee Primenenie. m. ISSN 0486-2287
- Referativnyi Zhurnal. Elektrosvyaz' m. ISSN 0486-2295
- Referativnyi Zhurnal. Elektrotekhnika i Energetika. m. ISSN 0034-2327
- Referativnyi Zhurnal. Farmakologiya. Khimioterapevticheskie Sredstva. Toksikologiya. m. ISSN 0034-2335
- Referativnyi Zhurnal. Fizika. m. ISSN 0034-2343
- Referativnyi Zhurnal. Fotokinotekhnika. m. ISSN 0484-2235
- Referativnyi Zhurnal. Geodeziya Aeros' Emka. m.
- Referativnyi Zhurnal. Geofizika. m. ISSN 0034-236X
- Referativnyi Zhurnal. Geografiya. m. ISSN 0034-2378
- Referativnyi Zhurnal. Geologiya. ISSN 0486-2309
- Referativnyi Zhurnal. Gornoe Delo. m. ISSN 0034-2386
- Referativnyi Zhurnal. Gornoe i Neftepromyslovye Mashinostroenie. m.
- Referativnyi Zhurnal. Informatika. m. ISSN 0486-235X
- Referativnyi Zhurnal. Issledovanie Kosmicheskogo Prostranstva. m. ISSN 0034-2408
- Referativnyi Zhurnal. Khimia. s-m. ISSN 0486-2325
- Referativnyi Zhurnal. Khimicheskoe, Neftepererabatyvayschchee i Polimernoe Mashinostroenie. m.
- Referativnyi Zhurnal. Kibernetika. m. ISSN 0486-2333
- Referativnyi Zhurnal. Kommunal'noe, Bytovoe i Torgovoe Oborudovanie. m. ISSN 0484-2286
- Referativnyi Zhurnal. Korroziya i Zashchita ot Korrozii. m.
- Referativnyi Zhurnal. Kotlostroenie. m. ISSN 0034-2424
- Referativnyi Zhurnal. Legkaya Promyshlennost' m. ISSN 0034-2432
- Referativnyi Zhurnal. Lesovedenie i Lesovodstvo. m. ISSN 0034-2440
- Referativnyi Zhurnal. Mashinostroitel'nye Materialy, Konstruktsii i Raschet Detale; Mashin. Gidroprivod. m. ISSN 0034-2459
- Referativnyi Zhurnal. Matematika. m. ISSN 0034-2467
- Referativnyi Zhurnal. Meditsinskaya Geografiya. m. ISSN 0034-2475
- Referativnyi Zhurnal. Mekhanika. m. ISSN 0034-2483 (Subscr. to: Mezhdunarodnaya Kniga, Moscow, G-200, U.S.S.R.)
- Referativnyi Zhurnal. Metallurgiya. m. ISSN 0034-2491
- Referativnyi Zhurnal. Metrologiya i Izmeritel'naya Tekhnika. m. ISSN 0034-2505 (Subscr. to: Mezhdunarodnaya Kniga, Moscow, G-200, U.S.S.R.)
- Referativnyi Zhurnal. Nasosostroenie i Kompressorostroenie. Kholodil'noe Mashinostroenie. m.
- Referativnyi Zhurnal. Oborudovanie Pishchevoi Promyshlennosti. m. ISSN 0034-2521
- Referativnyi Zhurnal. Obshchie Voprosy Patologii. m.
- Referativnyi Zhurnal. Okhrana Prirody i Vosproizvodstvo Prirodnykh Resursov. m.
- Referativnyi Zhurnal. Onkologiya. m.
- Referativnyi Zhurnal. Organizatsiya i Bezopasnost' Dorozhnogo Dvizheniya. m.
- Referativnyi Zhurnal. Organizatsiya Upravleniya. m.
- Referativnyi Zhurnal. Pochvovedenie i Agrokhimiya. m. ISSN 0034-2548
- Referativnyi Zhurnal. Pozharnaya Okhrana. m.
- Referativnyi Zhurnal. Promyshlennyi Transport. 12 per yr. ISSN 0034-2556
- Referativnyi Zhurnal. Radiatsionnaya Biologiya. m.
- Referativnyi Zhurnal. Radiotekhnika. m. ISSN 0034-267X
- Referativnyi Zhurnal. Raketostroenie. m. ISSN 0034-2564
- Referativnyi Zhurnal. Rastenievodstvo (Biologicheskie Osnovy) m. ISSN 0486-2384
- Referativnyi Zhurnal. Stroitel'nye i Dorozhnye Mashiny. m. ISSN 0484-2472
- Referativnyi Zhurnal. Svarka. m. ISSN 0034-2572
- Referativnyi Zhurnal. Tekhnologiya i Oborudovanie Tsellyulozno-vumazhnogo i Poligraficheskogo Proizvodstva. m. ISSN 0034-2580

- Referativnyi Zhurnal. Tekhnologiya Mashinostroeniya. m. ISSN 0034-2599
- Referativnyi Zhurnal. Teploenergetika. m. ISSN 0484-2502
- Referativnyi Zhurnal. Traktory i Sel'skokhozyaistvennye Mashiny i Orudiya. m. ISSN 0034-2602
- Referativnyi Zhurnal. Truboprovodnyi Transport. m. ISSN 0034-2610
- Referativnyi Zhurnal. Turbostroyeniye. m. ISSN 0034-2629
- Referativnyi Zhurnal. Vodnyi Transport. m. ISSN 0484-2537
- Referativnyi Zhurnal. Voprosy Tekhnicheskogo Progressa i Organizatsii Proizvodstva v Mashinostroenii. m. ISSN 0034-2637
- Referativnyi Zhurnal. Vozdushnyi Transport. m. ISSN 0484-2561
- Referativnyi Zhurnal. Vzaimodeistvie Raznykh Vidov Transporta i Konteinernye Perevozki. m. ISSN 0034-2645
- Referativnyi Zhurnal. Yadernye Reaktory. m. ISSN 0034-2653
- Referativnyi Zhurnal. Zheleznodorozhnyi Transport. m. ISSN 0484-2596
- Referativnyi Zhurnal. Zhivotnovodstvo i Veterinariya. m. ISSN 0034-2661
- Voprosy Informatsionnoi Teorii i Praktiki. irreg.

**Vsesoyuznyi Issledovatel'skii Institut Morskoi Geologii i Geofiziki**
Ul. Lacpliesa, 13, Riga, U. S. S. R.
- Morskaya Geologiya i Geofizika/Marine Geology and Geophysics. biennial. ISSN 0076-4477

**Vsesoyuznyi Leninskii Kommunisticheskii Soyuz Molodezhi. Tsentral'nyi Komitet**
Moscow, U.S.S.R.
- Molodaya Gvardiya. (pub. by Izdatel'stvo Molodaya Gvardiya)
- Molodoi Kommunist. (pub. by Izdatel'stvo Molodaya Gvardiya)
- Pioner. (pub. by Izdatel'stvo Pravda)
- Pionerskaya Pravda. s-w. ISSN 0032-0048
- Smena. (pub. by Izdatel'stvo Nauka)
- Tekhnika - Moladezhi. (pub. by Izdatel'stvo Molodaya Gvardiya)
- Veselye Kartinki. (pub. by Izdatel'stvo Molodaya Gvardiya)
- Vokrug Sveta. (pub. by Izdatel'stvo Molodaya Gvardiya)
- Vozhatyi. (pub. by Izdatel'stvo Molodaya Gvardiya)
- Yunyi Naturalist. (pub. by Izdatel'stvo Molodaya Gvardiya)
- Yunyi Tekhnik. (pub. by Izdatel'stvo Molodaya Gvardiya)

**Vsesoyuznyi Nauchno - Issledovatel'skii Geologorazvedochnyi Neftyanoi Institut**
- Neftegazonosnye i Perspektivnye Kompleksy Tsentralnykh i Vostochnykh Oblastei Russkoi Platformy. (pub. by Izdatel'stvo Nedra)

**Vsesoyuznyi Nauchno-Issledovatelskii Institut Prirodnykh Gazov. Tyumenskii Filial**
Tyumen, U.S.S.R.
- Prirodnyi Gaz Sibiri. irreg.

**Vsesoyuznyi Nauchno-issledovatel'skii Institut Vagonostroeniya**
Moscow, U. S. S. R.
- Vsesoyuznyi Nauchno-issledovatel'skii Institut Vagonostroeniya. Trudy. irreg.

**Vsesoyuznyi Nauchno-Issledovatelskii Institut Zheleznodorozhnogo Transporta**
Moscow, U.S.S.R.
- Vsesoyuznyi Nauchno-Issledovatel'skii Institut Zheleznodorozhnogo Transporta. Vestnik. 8 per yr. ISSN 0042-4749

**Vsesoyuznyi Tsentral'nyi Sovet Professional'nykh Soyuzov**
- Klub i Khudozhestvennaya Samodeyatel'nost' (pub. by Profizdat)
- Okhrana Truda i Sotsial'noe Strakhovanie. (pub. by Profizdat)
- Sovetskie Profsoyuzy. (pub. by Profizdat)

**Izdatel'stvo Vysshaya Shkola**
Neglinnaya, 29, Moscow K-51, U. S. S. R
- Ekonomicheskie Nauki. m. ISSN 0013-3019 (U. S. S. R. Ministerstvo Vysshego i Srednego Spetsial'nogo Obrazovaniya)
- Filologicheskie Nauki. bi-m. ISSN 0028-1212 (U. S. S. R. Ministerstvo Vysshego i Srednego Spetsial'nogo Obrazovaniya)

- Filosofskie Nauki. bi-m. ISSN 0015-1858 (U. S. S. R. Ministerstvo Vysshego i Srednego Spetsial'nogo Obrazovaniya)

**Izdatel'stvo Vysshaya Shkola B.S.S.R.**
Minsk, U.S.S.R.
- Automatika i Vychislitel'naya Tekhnika. bi-m. (Minskii Radiotekhnicheskii Institut)
- Ekonomika i Organizatsiya Promyshlennogo Proizvodstva. irreg. (Belorusskii Gosudarstvennyi Institut Narodnogo Khozyaistva)

**World Federation of Trade Unions**
- Vsemirnoe Profsoyuznoe Dvizhenie. (pub. by Izdatel'stvo Profizdat)

**Izdatel'stvo Zdorovya**
Ul. Yavarskaya, 1, Kiev 52, U.S.S.R.
- Vrachebnoe Delo. m. ISSN 0049-6804

**Izdevnieciba Zinatne**
Turgeneva iela, 19, Riga, U. S. S. R.
- Akademiya Nauk Latviiskoi S. S. R. Izvestiya/Latvijas P. S. R. Zinatnu Akademijas. Vestis. m. ISSN 0023-8929
- Akademiya Nauk Latviiskoi S. S. R. Izvestiya. Seriya Fizicheskikh i Tekhnicheskikh Nauk. bi-m. ISSN 0002-323X
- Akademiya Nauk Latviiskoi S. S. R. Izvestiya. Seriya Khimicheskaya. bi-m. ISSN 0002-3248
- Analogo-Diskretnye Preobrazovaniya Signalov. irreg. (Akademiya Nauk Latviiskoi S.S.R.. Institut Elektroniki i Vychislitel'noi Tekhniki)
- Contributions to the History of Science and Technology in Baltics/Iz Istorii Estestvoznaniya i Tekhniki Pribaltiki. a or biennial. ISSN 0069-9713 (Akademiya Nauk Latviiskoi S. S. R.)
- Khimiya Drevesiny. bi-m. (Akademiya Nauk Latviiskoi S.S.R.)
- Magnitnaya Gidrodinamika. q. ISSN 0025-0015 (Akademiya Nauk Latviiskoi S. S. R.)
- Mekhanika Polimerov. bi-m. ISSN 0025-8865

**Izdatel'stvo Znanie**
Novaya pl., 3-4, 101835 Moscow, U.S.S.R.
- Nauka Segodnya. a.

**Izdatel'stvo Zvyazda**
Leninskii prospekt, 77, Minsk, U. S. S. R.
(Subscr. to: Mezhdunarodnaya Kniga, Moscow, G-200, U. S. S. R.)
- Byarozka. m. ISSN 0007-7429 (Leninskii Kommunisticheskii Soyuz Molodezhi Belorusskoi S.S.R.)
- Golos Radzimy. s-w. ISSN 0017-1948
- Kommunist Belorussii/Komunist Belarusii. m. ISSN 0023-3102 (Kommunisticheskaya Partiya Belorussii. Tsentral'nyi Komitet)
- Maladosts; literaturno-khudozhestvennyi i obshchestvenno-politicheski zhurnal TzK lKSM Belorussiyi. m. ISSN 0025-1208 (Leninskii Kommunisticheskii Soyuz Molodezhi Belorusskoi S.S.R.)

# VATICAN CITY

**Academia Alfonsiana**
C.P. 2458, 00100 Rome, Italy.
- Studia Moralia. a. ISSN 0081-6736

**Fondazione Latinitas**
Vatican City, Italy.
- Latinitas; commentarii linguae latinae excolendae. q. ISSN 0023-883X

**Monumenti Musei e Gallerie Pontificie**
Citta del Vaticano, Rome, Italy.
- Pontifico Museo Missionario Etnologico. Annali. a.

**Pontifical Commission Justice and Peace**
Palazzo San Calisto, Vatican City, Italy.
- Justitia et Pax. q.

**Pontifical Society for Priestly Vocations**
- Seminarium. (pub. by Vatican Press)

**Pontificia Accademia Teologica Romana**
Palazzo Canonici, 00120 Vatican City, Italy.
- Divinitas. 3 per yr. ISSN 0012-4222

**Pontificia Universita Lateranese**
Palazzo Canonici, Postale 1/2349, 00120 Vatican City.
- Lateranum. s-a.

**Specola Vaticana**
Vatican City.
- Specola Astronomica Vaticana, Castel Gandolfo, Italy. Annual Report. a. ISSN 0081-3575
- Specola Astronomica Vaticana, Castel Gandolfo, Italy. Miscellanea Astronomica. irreg. ISSN 0081-3583
- Specola Astronomica Vaticana, Castel Gandolfo, Italy. Ricerche Astronomiche. irreg. ISSN 0081-3591
- Specola Astronomica Vaticana, Castel Gandolfo, Italy. Ricerche Spettroscopiche. irreg. ISSN 0081-3605
- Vatican Observatory Publications. irreg. ISSN 0083-5293

**Vatican. Segretaria di Stato. Ufficio Centrale di Statistica della Chiesa**
- Annuarium Statisticum Ecclesiae/Statistique de l'Eglise/Statistical Yearbook of the Church. (pub. by Libreria Editrice Vaticana)

**Vatican Press**
Sacred Congregation for Catholic Education, 00120 Vatican City, Italy.
- Seminarium; a review for seminaries, ecclesiastical vocations, universities. q. (Pontifical Society for Priestly Vocations)

**Libreria Editrice Vaticana**
Citta del Vaticano, Rome, Italy.
- Acta Apostolicae Sedis. Commentarium Officiale. fortn. ISSN 0001-5199
- Annuarium Statisticum Ecclesiae/Statistique de l'Eglise/Statistical Yearbook of the Church. a. (Vatican. Segretaria di Stato. Ufficio Centrale di Statistica della Chiesa)
- Communicationes. s-a.
- Notitiae. m. ISSN 0029-4306
- Nuntia. s-a.
- Seminarium. q. ISSN 0582-6314

# VENEZUELA

**Academia de Ciencias Fisicas Matematicas y Naturales**
Aptdo 1421, Palacio de las Academias, Caracas 101, Venezuela.
- Academia de Ciencias Fisicas Matematicas y Naturales. Boletin. q.

**Academia Nacional de la Historia**
Palacio de las Academias, Antigua Universidad Central, Caracas, Venezuela.
- Academia Nacional de la Historia. Boletin. q. ISSN 0001-382X

**Academia Nacional de Medicina**
Palacio de las Academias, Antigua Universidad Central, Caracas, Venezuela.
- Gaceta Medica de Caracas. bi-m. (Co-sponsor: Congreso Venezolano de Ciencias Medicas)

**Academia Venezolana de la Lengua**
Palacio de las Academias, Antigua Universidad Central, Caracas, Venezuela.
- Academia Venezolana de la Lengua, Correspondiente de la Espanola. Boletin. s-a.

**Arbol de Fuego: Poesia**
Apdo. de Correos 59.055, Los Chaguaramos, Caracas, Venezuela.
- Arbol de Fuego: Poesia. m. ISSN 0003-7915

**Archivo Historico de Miraflores**
Palacio Blanco, Av. Urbaneta, Caracas, Venezuela.
- Archivo Historico de Miraflores. Boletin. bi-m. ISSN 0042-3386

**Arte**
Aptdo. 19211, Quinta Crespo, Caracas 101, Venezuela.
- Arte. s-m.

**Arte e Investigacion**
Apdo. de Correos 16116, El Coliseo, Caracas, Venezuela.
- Arte e Investigacion. m.

**Asociacion Cultural Humboldt**
Apartado 60.501, Caracas, Venezuela.
- Asociacion Cultural Humboldt. Boletin. 1-2 per yr. ISSN 0004-4792

**Asociacion de Tecnicos Azucareros de Venezuela**
Estacion Experimental de Occidente, Yaritaguce, Yaracuy, Venezuela.
- A T A V E Boletin Informativo. irreg. ISSN 0084-683X

**Asociacion Interamericana de Presupuesto Publico**
Apartado Postal 8139, Caracas 101, Venezuela.
- Asociacion Interamericana de Presupuesto Publico Revista. q.

**Asociacion Venezolana Benefico Social "Hogar" Virgen de las Dolores**
Monzon a Barcenas No. 135, Caracas, Venezuela.
- Ecos. bi-m. ISSN 0013-0680

**Asociacion Venezolana de Archiveros**
Archivo General de la Nacion, Av. Urdaneta 15, Caracas, Venezuela.
- Asociacion Venezolana de Archiveros. Coleccion Doctrina. irreg. ISSN 0066-8591

**Asociacion Venezolana de Enfermeras Profesionales**
Edificio Sur, 4 Piso, Oficina 412, el Silencio, Caracas, Venezuela.
- Asociacion Venezolana de Enfermeras Profesionales. Boletin. irreg. ISSN 0066-8613

**Asociacion Venezolana de Hospitales**
Apartado No. 4841, Caracas, Venezuela.
- Tecnica Hospitalaria. q. ISSN 0040-182X

**Asociacion Venezolana de Ingenieria Electrica**
Apartado 6255, Caracas, Venezuela.
- Energia e Industria. bi-m.

**Asociacion Venezolana de Ingenieria Electrica y Mecanica**
Apdo. 6255, Caracas, Venezuela.
- Ingenieria Electrica y Mecanica. bi-m. ISSN 0020-1049

**Asociacion Venezolana de Orientacion Familiar y Sexual**
Aptdo. 80442, Caracas, Venezuela.
- A V O F Y S Boletin. q.

**Asociacion Venezolana de Periodistas**
Casa Nacional del Periodista, Avenida Andres Bello, Caracas, Venezuela.
- Periodista. m. ISSN 0048-3370

**Asociacion Venezolana de Planificacion Familiar**
La. Av. los Palos Grandes No. 23, Caracas 106, Venezuela.
- Germinal. q.

**Asociacion Venezolana de Sociologia**
Caracas, Venezuela.
- Sociologia. a. ISSN 0583-9750

**Asociacion Venezolana para el Avance de la Ciencia**
Apdo. del Este 61843, Caracas 107, Venezuela.
- Acta Cientifica Venezolana. 6 per yr. ISSN 0001-5504

**Associacion Interciencia**
Apdo. 51842, Caracas 105, Venezuela.
- Interciencia.

**Editorial Axial**
Apartado Postal 62, Merida, Venezuela.
- Axial; revista de poesia. q. ISSN 0005-2426 (Grupo Literario Axial)

**Banco Central de Venezuela**
Esquina de las Carmelitas, Caracas, Venezuela.
- Banco Central de Venezuela. Informe Economico. a. ISSN 0067-3250
- Banco Central de Venezuela. Memoria. a. ISSN 0067-3269
- Banco Central de Venezuela. Revista. q. ISSN 0005-4720
- Revista de Economia Latinoamericana. q. ISSN 0034-804X

**Banco de Venezuela**
Avenida Universidad 7, Caracas, Venezuela.
- Banco de Venezuela. Informe Semestral. s-a.
- Economia y Finanzas. m. ISSN 0005-4844
- Fomento Agropecuario. m.

**Camara de Comercio de la Guaira**
Frente a la Plaza el Consul, Edificio "camara de Comercio", Maiquetia, Apartado 150 la Guaira Departamento Vargas, Venezuela.
- Camara de Comercio de la Guaira. Boletin Estadistico. a. ISSN 0008-1876

- Guaira. m. ISSN 0017-4971

**Camara de Industriales de Caracas**
Edificio Camara de Industriales Esquina Puente Anauco, Caracas, Venezuela.
- Produccion. m. ISSN 0032-9681 (Co-sponsor: Consejo Venezolano de la Industria)

**Camara Industriales Joyeria y Relojes**
Apartado de Correos 51839, Caracas 105, Venezuela.
- Precision. bi-m. ISSN 0032-7131

**Camara Venezolano Britanica de Comercio e Industria**
Apto. 5713, Caracas 106, Venezuela.
- Camara Venezolano Britanica de Comercio e Industria. Anuario. a.

**Miguel Angel Capriles, Ed. & Pub.**
Torre de la Prensa, Plaza del Panteon, Caracas, Venezuela.
- Elite. w.
- Paginas. w.
- Venezuela Grafica. w.

**Lubio Cardozo y Juan Pinto, Eds & Pubs.**
Apartado 410, Herida, Venezuela.
- K; revista de poesia. 6 per yr. ISSN 0047-3030

**Centro de Estudios Latinoamericanos Romulo Gallegos**
Apdo. Postal 29076, Caracas, Venezuela.
- Araisa. a.

**Centro de Historia del Estado Falcon**
Coro, Venezuela.
- Centro de Historia del Estado Falcon. Boletin. ISSN 0008-9990

**Centro Nacional de Investigaciones Agropecuarias**
Apdo. 653, Maracay, Edo. Aragua, Venezuela.
- Agronomia Tropical. bi-m. ISSN 0002-192X

**Centro Simon Bolivar**
Torre sur, Piso 6 Officina 652, Caracas, Venezuela.
- COVENIN Boletin. q. (Comision Venezolana de Normas Industriales)

**Ciencia Aeronautica**
Av. Urdaneta, Edificio Cipriano Morales, Caracas, Venezuela.
- Ciencia Aeronautica. m. ISSN 0009-6717

**Cisoria Arte**
Apartado 5053, Caracas 105, Venezuela.
- Cisoria Arte. q.

**Club Filatelico de Caracas**
Apartado 61197, Caracas 106, Venezuela.
- Club Filatelico de Caracas. Revista. q. ISSN 0529-9853

**Colegio de Ingenieros de Venezuela**
Apdo 20006, Bosque los Caobos, Caracas, Venezuela.
- Colegio de Ingenieros de Venezuela. Boletin Informativo. m. ISSN 0010-0625

**Colegio de Medicos del Distrito Federal**
Plaza de Bellas Artes, Avda de Bellas Artes, Los Chaguaramos, Caracas, Venezuela.
- Sociedad Venezolana de Cirugia Boletin.

**Colegio de Profesores de Venezuela**
Apartado de Correo 6642, Caracas 101, Venezuela.
- Colegio de Profesores de Venezuela. Seccional No. 1. Boletin. Informativo. 8 per yr. ISSN 0010-0633

**Comision Venezolana de Normas Industriales**
- COVENIN Boletin. (pub. by Centro Simon Bolivar)

**Compania Anonima de Administracion y Fomento Electrico**
Caracas, Venezuela.
- Compania Anonima de Administracion y Fomento Electrico. Informe Anual. a.

**Consejo Nacional de Investigaciones Cientificas y Tecnologicas. Departamento de Educacion**
Apartado 70617 Los Ruices, Caracas, Venezuela.
- Consejo Nacional de Investigaciones Cientificas y Tecnologicas. Departamento de Educacion. Directorio Nacional de Cursos de Postgrado. irreg.

**Corporacion de los Andes**
Edificio Sede, La Isla, Merida, Venezuela.
● Corporacion de los Andes. Revista. q.

**Corporacion Venezolana de Fomento. Unidad de Estudios**
Edificio Norte, Centro Simon Bolivar, Caracas, Venezuela.
● Cuadernos de Informacion Economica. s-a.

**Corriere de Caracas, C. A.**
Apartado 2560, Caracas, Venezuela.
● Corriere di Caracas; settimanale italiano indipendente. w. ISSN 0010-9231

**Distribuidora Venezolana de Azucares. Departamento de Promocion Industrial**
Edificio Torre Europa, Av. de Miranda, Caracas 106, Venezuela.
● Directorio Industrial Azucarero. irreg.

**Edicion Edime**
Comision Editora, Caracas, Venezuela.
● Archivos Venezolanos de Folklore. a. ISSN 0570-7196 (Universidad Central de Venezuela. Instituto de Antropologia e Historia) (Co-sponsor: Instituto de Filologia Andres Bello)

**En Haa**
Apartado 19211, Quinta Crespo, Caracas, Venezuela.
● En Haa. 1-2 per yr. ISSN 0013-6956

**Escuela Naval de Venezuela**
Meseta de Mamo, Dpto Vargas, DF, Venezuela.
● Galeon. 4 per yr. ISSN 0016-402X (Venezuela. Ministerio de la Defensa. Oficina Tecnica)

**Frente Nacional Pro Defensa del Petroleo Venezolano**
Apto. 50514, Caracas 105, Venezuela.
● Frente Nacional pro-Defensa del Petroleo Venezolano. Actuaciones. irreg.

**Fundacion John Boulton**
Apdo. 929, Caracas, Venezuela.
● Fundacion John Boulton. Boletin Historico. 3 per yr. ISSN 0016-2701

**Fundacion la Salle de Ciencias Naturales. Instituto Caribe de Antropologia y Sociologia**
Apartado 8150, Caracas 101, Venezuela.
● Antropologica. 3 per yr. ISSN 0003-6110

**Fundacion Servicio para el Agricultor**
Estacion Experimental de Cagua, Cagua (Estado Aragua), Venezuela.
● Fundacion Servicio para el Agricultor. Noticias Agricolas. m. ISSN 0029-4160

**Ganagrinco**
Ed. Rafael Salom, Apartado de Correo 4216, Caracas 101, Venezuela.
● Ganagrinco; ganaderia-agricultura-industria-comercio. q. ISSN 0046-5399

**Dr. Rafael M. Gonzalez, Ed. & Pub.**
Colegio de Odontologos de Venezuela, Apdo. 1341, Caracas, Venezuela.
● Venezuela Odontologia. bi-m. ISSN 0042-3424

**Editora Grafos**
Edificio Paris, Plaza Candelaria, Sotano, Venezuela (Distr. by: Difusora Venezolano del Libro, Edificio Partenio, Local D, Avda. Universidad, Esq. Coliseo, Caracas, Venezuela)
● Politica; ideas para una America Nueva. m.

**Grupo Escritores de Venezuela**
Apartado 4023, Carmelitas 101, Caracas, Venezuela.
● Galaxia 71. bi-m.

**Grupo Literario Axial**
● Axial. (pub. by Editorial Axial)

**Guibanca**
Av. las Acacias, Esquina Sabana Grande, Edificio Arismendi, Caracas, Venezuela.
● Guibanca; guia nacional de bancos, companias de seguros, entidades de ahorro y prestamo, sociedades financieras. a.

**Hospital Vargas**
Caracas, Venezuela.
● Hospital Vargas. Archivos. q. ISSN 0018-5884

**Ideas Concretas.**
Avenida Liberatador -Esquina las Acacias, Edificio las Vegas, Caracas, Venezuela.
● Ideas Concretas. bi-m.

**Instituto Celis Perez**
Apartado Postal 163, Valencia, Venezuela (Subscr. Address: Medicina Libros, Edif. Pax Cruce, Av. Avila y Caracas, Caracas, Venezuela)
● Revista Otorrinolaringologica. q.

**Instituto de Credito Agricola y Pecuario**
Barquisimeto, Venezuela.
● Instituto de Credito Agricola y Pecuario. Boletin Mensual. m.

**Instituto de Geografia y Conservacion de Recursos Naturales**
Universidad de los Andes, Facultad de Ciencias Forestales, Merida, Venezuela.
● Revista Geografica. s-a.

**Instituto de Investigaciones Veterinarias**
Division de Investigaciones Veterinarias, Apdo. Postal 70, Maracay 300, Venezuela.
● Instituto de Investigaciones Veterinarias. Boletin. irreg. ISSN 0074-0128

**Instituto de Materiales y Modelos Estructurales**
Unversidad Central de Venezuela, Facultad de Ingenieria, Apartado 50361 Sabana Grande, Caracas, Venezuela.
● I. M. M. E. Boletin. q. ISSN 0020-3971

**Instituto Forestal Latinoamericano de Investigacion y Capacitacion**
Apartado 36, Merida, Venezuela.
● Instituto Forestal Latinoamericano de Investigacion y Capacitacion. Bibliographical Bulletin. q.
● Instituto Forestal Latinoamericano de Investigacion y Capacitacion. Boletin Bibliografico. q. ISSN 0046-9971
● Instituto Forestal Latinoamericano de Investigacion y Capacitacion. Boletin. 3 per yr (aprox.) ISSN 0538-1126

**Instituto Nacional de Cultura y Bellas Artes**
Oficina Central de Informacion, Box 6238, Caracas, Venezuela.
● Carta Cultural de Venezuela. m. ISSN 0008-6983
● Cuadernos para Estudiantes: Los Poetas. irreg. ISSN 0070-1785
● Revista Venezolana de Folklore. s-a(approx.) ISSN 0035-0575

**Instituto Nacional de Nutricion**
Apdo. 2049, Caracas, Venezuela.
● Archivos Latinoamericanos de Nutricion. q. ISSN 0004-0622

**Instituto Nacional de Obras Sanitarias**
Caracas, Venezuela.
● Instituto Nacional de Obras Sanitarias, Caracas. Division de Hidrologia. Anuario Climatologico. a.

**Instituto Oceanografico. Biblioteca**
Universidad de Oriente, Cumana, Venezuela.
● Lagena. s-a. ISSN 0023-7256

**Instituto para la Conservacion del Lago de Valencia**
Apartado 761, Valencia, Venezuela.
● Lago. bi-m. ISSN 0047-3898

**International Rural Housing Association**
Apto. 16224, Caracas, Venezuela.
● Revista Internacional de Vivienda Rural/ International Rural Housing Journal. irreg. (1-2 per yr.)

**Jakemate**
Apdo. de Correos 59051, Chaguaramos, 104, Caracas, Venezuela.
● Jakemate. q. ISSN 0047-1712

**Editorial Momento C.A.**
Ferrenquin a la Cruz 153, Caracas, Venezuela.
● Momento; la mejor revista de Venezuela. w. ISSN 0026-9131

**Museo Boggio**
Esquina las Monjas, Caracas, Venezuela.
● Museo Boggio. Cuadernos de Arte. irreg.

**Museo de Ciencias Naturales**
Apdo. 8011, Caracas, Venezuela.
● Museo de Ciencias Naturales. Boletin. q. ISSN 0027-3899

**Nueva Sociedad Ltda.**
Apartado 61712, Chacao, Caracas 106, Venzuela.
● Nueva Sociedad. bi-m.

**Ortiz & Asociados s.r.l.**
Apdo. 50.045, Caracas, Venezuela.
● Automovil de Venezuela. m. ISSN 0005-1616

**Editorial Petro-Nave**
Edificio Zingg No. 221-222-223, 2 piso, Caracas, Venezuela.
● Aeronaves. bi-m.
● Banca y Seguros. m. ISSN 0408-3075
● Petroleo y Mineria de Venezuela. m. ISSN 0031-6415

**Petrolero**
Box 12554, Caracas, Venezuela.
● Petrolero. fortn. ISSN 0021-7492

**Poesia de Venezuela**
Apdo. Postal 1114, Caracas 101, Venezuela.
● Poesia de Venezuela. bi-m. ISSN 0032-1893

**Press Agencias, S.A.**
Puento Nuevo a Pto. Escondido, Edif. el Nacional, Caracas, Venezuela.
● Resumen. w.

**Proceso Politico**
Apartado 70850, Caracas 107, Venezuela.
● Proceso Politico. irreg.

**Publiprint s.r.l.**
Primera Avenida las Delicias de Sabana Grande No 18, Apartado 60773, Caracas 105, Venezuela.
● Foton; fotografia, cine y sonida (photography, amateur movie and sound) m. ISSN 0015-8895

**Editora de Revistas, C.A.**
Apartado 2935, Caracas, Venezuela.
● Gaceta Hipica. w. ISSN 0016-3775

**Sociedad Bolivariana de Venezuela**
Apdo. 874, Caracas, Venezuela.
● Sociedad Bolivariana de Venezuela. Revista. q. ISSN 0037-8402

**Sociedad Civil Cine al Dia**
Apdo. 50446, Sabana Grande, Caracas, Venezuela.
● Cine al Dia. 8 per yr. ISSN 0009-692X

**Sociedad de Ciencias Naturales la Salle**
Edif. Fundacion la Salle-Ph., Av. Cota Mil, Apartado 8150, Caracas, 101, Venezuela.
● Natura; revista trimestral de divulgacion cientifica, tecnica y cultural. q. ISSN 0028-064X
● Novedades Cientificas. Serie Botanica. irreg.; latest issue, 1971. ISSN 0078-2548
● Novedades Cientificas. Serie Zoologica. irreg.; latest issue, 1971. ISSN 0078-2556
● Sociedad de Ciencias Naturales la Salle. Memoria. q. ISSN 0037-8518

**Sociedad de Obstetricia y Ginecologia de Venezuela**
Biblioteca, Apartado 20081, Avenida San Martin, Caracas, Venezuela.
● Revista de Obstetricia y Ginecologia de Venezuela. q. ISSN 0048-7732

**Sociedad Latinoamericana de Microscopia Electronica**
P.O. Box 63, Merida, Edo. Merida, Venezuela.
● Revista de Microscopia Electronica. q. ISSN 0300-3426

**Sociedad Latinoamericana de Tuberosas**
Box 97, Maracay, Venezuela.
● Noticiero Tuberosas. irreg. ISSN 0085-4387

**Sociedad Odontologica Latino-Americano de Implantes Aloplasticos y Trasplantes**
Clinica los Andes, Avenida Lincoln, Sabana Grande, Caracas, Venezuela.
● S. O. L. A. I. A. T. q. ISSN 0036-1771

**Sociedad Venezolana de Filosofia**
Caracas, Venezuela.
● Estudios Filosoficos. irreg.

**Sociedad Venezolana de Gastroenterologia**
Av. Los Palos Grandes, Caracas, Venezuela.
● G. E. N. bi-m. ISSN 0016-3503

**Sociedad Venezolana de Puericultura y Pediatria**
Colegio de Medicos del Distrito Federal, Caracas, Venezuela.
● Archivos Venezolanos de Puericultura y Pediatria. q. ISSN 0004-0649

**Sociedad Venezolana de Radiologia**
Policlinica Mendez Gimon, Avda. Andres Bello, Caracas, Venezuela.
- Radiologia y Medicina Nuclear. s-a. ISSN 0033-8370

**Sociedad Venezolana de Urologia**
Colegio de Medicos del D.F., Caracas, Venezuela.
- Revista Venezolana de Urologia. q. ISSN 0035-0591

**Temas Economicos**
Conde a Pinango 22, Apdo. 2570, Caracas, Venezuela.
- Temas Economicos. m. ISSN 0495-0615

**Teoria y Praxis**
Avenida Andres Bello, Edificio A.V.P., Piso 1, Oficina No. 5, Apdo de Correos, No. 40274 (Nueva Granada), Caracas, Venezuela.
- Teoria y Praxis; revista Venezolana de ciencias sociales. q. ISSN 0301-701X

**Territorio Federal, Venezuela. Direccion de Educacion y Cultura. Departamento de Extension Cultural**
Delta Amacuro, Tucupita, Venezuela.
- Correo del Delta. q. ISSN 0010-9096

**Universidad Catolica Andres Bello. Centro de Estudios del Futuro de Venezuela**
La Vega, Montalban, Apdo. 13228, Caracas, Venezuela.
- Prospeccion Siglo XXI. Venezuela Ano 2000. q.

**Universidad Catolica Andres Bello. Facultad de Letras**
Departamento de Humanidades, Apartado 29068, Caracas, Venezuela.
- Montalban. a.

**Universidad Catolica Andres Bello. Instituto de Investigaciones Economicas**
Facultad de Economia, Esquina de Jesuitas 37, Caracas, Venezuela.
- Saman. irreg., 1968, no. 14. ISSN 0080-5750

**Universidad Central de Venezuela**
Facultad de Derecho, Caracas, Venezuela.
- Instituto de Derecho Privado. Boletin. s-a. ISSN 0020-3823 (prep. by its Instituto de Derecho Privado)

**Universidad Central de Venezuela. Academia de Ciencias Politicas y Sociales**
Caracas, Venezuela.
- Universidad Central de Venezuela. Academia de Ciencias Politicas y Sociales. Boletin. irreg.

**Universidad Central de Venezuela. Biblioteca Central**
Apartado de Correo 71-175, Caracas 107, Venezuela.
- Coleccion "Foros y Seminarios." Serie Foros. irreg., 1968, no. 5. ISSN 0069-5084

**Universidad Central de Venezuela. Consejo de Desarrollo Cientifico y Humanistico**
Caracas, Venezuela.
- Universidad Central de Venezuela. Consejo de Desarrollo Cientifico y Humanistico. Catalogo de la U. C. V. triennial. ISSN 0083-5439

**Universidad Central de Venezuela. Direccion de Cultura**
Ciudad Universitaria, Caracas, Venezuela.
- Coleccion "Aniversarios Culturales". irreg., 1968, no. 4. ISSN 0069-5033
- Coleccion "Foros y Seminarios." Serie Seminarios. irreg. ISSN 0069-5092
- Coleccion "Humanism y Ciencia". irreg., 1969, no. 8. ISSN 0069-5114
- Cultura Universitaria. 3 per yr.

**Universidad Central de Venezuela. Escuela de Biologia**
Apdo 10098, Caracas, Venezuela.
- Acta Biologica Venezuelica. 4 per yr. ISSN 0001-5326

**Universidad Central de Venezuela. Facultad de Agronomia**
Comision de Informacion y Documentacion, Apartado 4579, Maracay, Venezuela.
- Universidad Central de Venezuela. Revista de la Facultad de Agronomia. irreg.; vol. 8, no.1, 1974. ISSN 0041-8285

**Universidad Central de Venezuela. Facultad de Ciencias Economicas y Sociales**
Caracas, Venezuela.
- Economia y Ciencias Sociales. q. ISSN 0012-9895

**Universidad Central de Venezuela. Facultad de Ciencias Veterinarias**
Apdo. de Correos 4563, Maracay-Edo. Aragua., Venezuela.
- Revista de Medicina Veterinaria y Parasitologia. 4 per yr. ISSN 0048-7724

**Universidad Central de Venezuela. Facultad de Derecho**
Caracas, Venezuela
(Subscr. to: Servicio de Distribucion y Venta, Biblioteca Central, Universidad Central, Caracas, Venezuela)
- Antologias del Pensamiento Politico. irreg. ISSN 0066-4936 (prep. by its Instituto de Estudios Politicos)
- Documentos; revista de informacion politica. q. ISSN 0012-4753 (prep. by its Instituto de Estudios Politicos)
- Politeia. a. (prep. by its Instituto de Estudios Politicos)
- Universidad Central de Venezuela. Facultad de Derecho. Revista. q. ISSN 0041-8293
- Universidad Central de Venezuela. Instituto de Ciencias Penales y Criminologicas. Anuario. a; latest edt., no. 3. ISSN 0507-570X (prep. by its Instituto de Ciencias Penales y Criminologicas)
- Universidad Central de Venezuela. Instituto de Estudios Politicos. Cuadernos. irreg.; latest issue. 1974. ISSN 0083-5420

**Universidad Central de Venezuela. Facultad de Farmacia**
Apto. 40109, Nueva Granada, Caracas, Venezuela.
- Universidad Central de Venezuela. Facultad de Farmacia. Revista. q. ISSN 0041-8307

**Universidad Central de Venezuela. Facultad de Humanidades y Educacion**
Director de la Escuela de Biblioteconomia y Archivos, Caracas, Venezuela.
- Codex; boletin de la escuela de biblioteconomia y archivos. q. ISSN 0010-0196

**Universidad Central de Venezuela. Facultad de Odontologia**
Caracas, Venezuela.
- Acta Odontologica Venezolana. q. ISSN 0001-6365

**Universidad Central de Venezuela. Instituto de Antropologia e Historia**
Caracas, Venezuela.
- Archivos Venezolanos de Folklore. (pub. by Edicion Edime)
- Instituto de Antropologia e Historia. Anuario. a.

**Universidad Central de Venezuela. Instituto de Estudios Hispanoamericanos**
Avenida la Colina Qta. "Mitaqueri" Cruce Con Avenida Minerva, Urbanizacion las Acacias, Venezuela.
- Universidad Central de Venezuela. Instituto de Estudios Hispanoamericanos. Anuario. a.

**Universidad de Carabobo. Centro de Investigaciones Penales y Criminologicas**
Valencia, Venezuela.
- Relacion Criminologica. s-a. ISSN 0486-350X

**Universidad de los Andes**
Apdo. 277, Merida, Venezuela.
- Actual. 3 per yr. ISSN 0001-7639

**Universidad de los Andes. Centro de Investigaciones Literarias**
Merida, Venezuela.
- Universidad de los Andes. Centro de Investigaciones Literarias. Serie Bibliografica. irreg.

**Universidad de los Andes. Escuela de Letras**
Merida, Venezuela.
- Universidad de los Andes. Escuela de Letras. Anuario. a.

**Universidad de Los Andes. Facultad de Derecho**
Centro de Jurisprudencia, Merida, Venezuela.
- Universidad de los Andes. Facultad de Derecho. Anuario. a. ISSN 0076-6550

**Universidad de Los Andes. Facultad de Odontologia, Biblioteca**
Merida, Venezuela.
- Revista Odontologica de Merida. q. ISSN 0035-0273

**Universidad de los Andes. Instituto de Derecho Agrario y Estudios Rurales**
Merida, Venezuela.
- Derecho y Reforma Agraria. a.

**Universidad de Los Andes. Instituto de Geografia y Conservacion de Recursos Naturales**
Merida, Venezuela.
- Universidad de Los Andes. Instituto de Geografia y Conservacion de Recursos Naturales. Cuadernos Geograficos. irreg., no. 7, 1974. ISSN 0076-6569 (prep. by its Facultad de Ciencias Forestales)

**Universidad de Los Andes. Instituto de Investigaciones Economicas**
Facultad de Economia, Merida, Venezuela.
- Anuario Estadistico de Los Andes; Venezuela. a. ISSN 0066-5185
- Economia. a. ISSN 0070-8399

**Universidad de Oriente. Escuela de Ciencias Sociales**
Apdo. Postal 245, Cumana, Venezuela.
- Ciencias Sociales. s-a.

**Universidad de Oriente. Escuela de Geologia y Minas**
La Sabanita, Ciudad Bolivar, Venezuela.
- Geominas. q. ISSN 0016-7975

**Universidad de Oriente. Instituto Oceanografico**
Cumana, Venezuela.
- Instituto Oceanografico. Boletin. s-a. ISSN 0020-417X (prep. by its Bilbioteca)
- Universidad de Oriente. Instituto Oceanografico Biblioteca. Boletin Bibliografico. a; no. 11, 1974. ISSN 0590-3343
- Universidad de Oriente. Instituto Oceanografico. Registro de Datos Oceanograficos y Meteorologicos. irreg.

**Universidad del Zulia. Escuela de Comunicacion Social**
Maracaibo, Venezuela.
- Asunto. irreg.

**Universidad del Zulia. Facultad de Agronomia**
Apartado 526, Maracaibo, Venezuela.
- Luz. irreg; 1975, vol. 3, no. 2.

**Universidad del Zulia. Facultad de Derecho**
Maracaibo, Venezuela.
- Universidad del Zulia. Facultad de Derecho. Revista. 3 per yr.

**Universidad del Zulia. Facultad de Humanidades y Educacion**
Apdo. 526, Maracaibo, Venezuela.
- Anuario de Filologia. a; biennial. ISSN 0066-507X
- Cain. a. ISSN 0068-5259
- Cuadernos de Orientacion. irreg. ISSN 0070-170X
- Cuadernos de Pedagogia. irreg. ISSN 0070-1718
- Revista de Filosofia. s-a.
- Universidad Nacional del Zulia. Facultad de Humanidades y Educacion. Artes y Letras. irreg. ISSN 0076-4337
- Universidad Nacional del Zulia. Facultad de Humanidades y Educacion. Conferencias y Coloquios. irreg. ISSN 0076-4345
- Universidad Nacional del Zulia. Facultad de Humanidades y Educacion. Fuera de Serie. irreg. ISSN 0076-4353
- Universidad Nacional del Zulia. Facultad de Humanidades y Educacion. Manuales de la Escuela de Educacion. irreg. ISSN 0076-4361
- Universidad Nacional del Zulia. Facultad de Humanidades y Educacion. Monografias y Ensayos. irreg. ISSN 0076-437X

**Universidad del Zulia. Facultad de Medicina**
Dept. de Medicina Tropical, Maracaibo, Venezuela.
- Kasmera. irreg. ISSN 0075-5222

**Universidad del Zulia, Instituto de Investigacion Clinica. Facultad de Medicina**
Aptdo. Postal 1151, Maracaibo, Venezuela.
- Investigacion Clinica. q. (prep. by its Instituto de Investigacion Clinica)

**Universidad Simon Bolivar**
Caracas, Venezuela.
- Colecciondina Mica y Siembra. irreg.

**Universidad Simon Bolivar. Departamento de Filosofia**
Apartado Postal No. 5354, Caracas, Venezuela.
- Revista Venezolana de Filosofia. s-a. (Co-sponsor: Sociedad Venezolana de Filosofia)

**Editorial Universitaria**
Apdo. 1151, Maracaibo, Venezuela.
- Universidad del Zulia. Revistas. q. ISSN 0041-8811

**Ve Venezuela**
Apdo. del Este 60182, Caracas, Venezuela.
- Ve Venezuela. q. ISSN 0042-2932

**Venezuela. Administracion General del Impuesto Sobre la Renta. Division de Coordinacion y Supervision Legal y Tecnica**
Caracas, Venezuela.
- Doctrine y Jurisprudencia. q.

**Venezuela. Archivo General de la Nacion**
Santa Capilla a Carmelitas, 15, Avenida Urdaneta, Caracas, Venezuela.
- Venezuela. Archivo General de la Nacion. Boletin. s-a. ISSN 0042-3378

**Venezuela. Biblioteca Nacional**
Caracas 101, Venezuela.
- Bibliografia Venezolana. q. ISSN 0006-1085

**Venezuela. Departamento de Hacienda**
- Venezuela. Cuenta General de Ingresos y Gastos Publicos, Bienes Nacionales, Inclusive Materias, y Cuenta del Departamento de Hacienda: Ingresos y Gastos. (pub. by Venezuela. Imprimeria Nacional)

**Venezuela. Direccion de Hidrografia y Navegacion. Seccion de Climatologia**
Departamento de Meteorologia, Caracas, Venezuela.
- Venezuela. Direccion de Hidrografia y Navegacion. Seccion de Climatologia. Boletin Climatologico Anual. a.
- Venezuela. Direccion de Hidrografia y Navegacion. Seccion de Climatologia. Promedios Climatologicos de las Estaciones. irreg.

**Venezuela. Direccion de Normalizacion y Certificacion de Calidad**
Avda. Boyaca, Caracas, Venezuela.
- Boletin Normalizacion. q.

**Venezuela. Division de Economica Petrolera**
Caracas, Venezuela.
- Venezuelan Petroleum Industry; statistical data. a. ISSN 0506-5283

**Venezuela. Imprimeria Nacional**
Caracas, Venezuela.
- Venezuela. Cuenta General de Ingresos y Gastos Publicos, Bienes Nacionales, Inclusive Materias, y Cuenta del Departamento de Hacienda: Ingresos y Gastos. a. (Venezuela. Departamento de Hacienda)

**Venezuela. Ministerio de Agricultura y Cria**
Caracas, Venezuela.
- Agricultor Venezolano. bi-m. ISSN 0002-1326

**Venezuela. Ministerio de Agricultura y Cria. Direccion de Planificacion y Estadistica**
Division de Estadistica, Caracas, Venezuela.
- Encuesta Agropecuaria. a.
- Produccion Agricola - Periodo de Invierno. a; latest issue 1975.
- Produccion Agricolo-Periodo de Verano. a; latest issue 1975.
- Venezuela. Ministerio de Agricultura y Cria. Boletin de Precios de Productos Agropecuarios. m.
- Venezuela. Ministerio de Agricultura y Cria. Direccion de Economica y Estadistica Agropecuaria. Anuario Estadistica Agropecuario. a. ISSN 0083-5366
- Venezuela. Ministerio de Agricultura y Cria. Direccion de Planificacion y Estadistica. Estadisticas Agropecuarias de las Entidades Federales. biennial.
- Venezuela. Ministerio de Agricultura y Cria. Division de Estadistica. Encuesta Avicola Nacional. a.
- Venezuela. Ministerio de Agricultura y Cria. Division de Estadistica. Encuesta da Ganado Procino. a.

**Venezuela. Ministerio de Agricultura y Cria. Insituto Botanico**
Apartado 2156, Caracas, Venezuela.
- Acta Botanica Venezuelica. irreg. ISSN 0084-5906

**Venezuela. Ministerio de Educacion**
Departamento de Publicaciones, Salvador de Leon a Coliseo No. 29, Caracas 101, Venezuela.
- Educacion; revista para el magisterio. q. ISSN 0013-1075
- Tricolor; revista Venezolana para los ninos. 9 per yr. ISSN 0041-2902
- Venezuela. Departamento de Investigaciones Educacionales. Seccion de Estadistica. Estadisticas Educacionales. a. (prep. by its Departamento de Investigaciones Educacionales)

**Venezuela. Ministerio de Educacion. Direccion de Cultura y Bellas Artes**
Apdo. de Correos 6238, Caracas, Venezuela.
- Instituto de Folklore. Boletin. irreg (2-3yr)

**Venezuela. Ministerio de Educacion Nacional. Museo de Ciencias Naturales**
Apartado de Correos 8011, Caracas, Venezuela.
- Folia Antropologica. irreg. ISSN 0428-8254

**Venezuela. Ministerio de Energia y Minas**
Caracas, Venezuela.
- Venezuela. Ministry of Mines and Hydrocarbons. Monthly Bulletin. m. ISSN 0042-3416

**Venezuela. Ministerio de Fomento**
Centro Simon Bolivar, Edificio sur, Caracas, Venezuela.
- Boletin de la Propiedad Industrial. m. ISSN 0006-6338 (prep. by its Officina de Registro de la Propiedad Industrial)
- Estadistica Venezolana. irreg. (prep. by its Direccion General de Estadistica y Censos Nacionales)
- Estadisticas del Comercio Exterior de Venezuela. Boletin. irreg. (prep. by its Direccion General de Estadistica y Censos Nacionales)
- Venezuela. Departamento de Estadistica Vital. Informe Especial. q. (prep. by its Departamento de Estadistica Vital)

**Venezuela. Ministerio de Fomento. Direccion General de Estadistica y Censos Nacionales**
Centro Simon Bolivar, Edificio sur, Caracas, Venezuela.
- Encuesta Industrial: Resultados Nacionales. irreg. (prep. by its Direccion General de Estadistica y Censos Nacionales)
- Indicadores Socioeconomicos y de Coyuntura. irreg. (prep. by its Direccion General de Estadistica y Censos Nacionales)

**Venezuela. Ministerio de Hacienda. Direccion General de Finanzas Publicas**
Centro Simon Bolivar, Edificio Norte, Caracas, Venezuela.
- Revista de Hacienda. q. (prep. by its Direccion de Investigaciones Economicas)
- Venezuela. Ministerio de Hacienda. Direccion General de Finanzas Publicas. Boletin Estadistico. m. (prep. by its Direccion de Investigaciones Economicas)
- Venezuela. Ministerio de Hacienda. Direccion General de Finanzas Publicas. Suplemento Estadistico. biennial. (prep. by its Direccion de Investigaciones Economicas)

**Venezuela. Ministerio de Justicia**
Apdo. Postal 2084, Caracas, Venzuela.
- Venezuela. Ministerio de Justicia. Revista. q.

**Venezuela. Ministerio de Justicia. Comision Indigenista Nacional**
Edificio Lincoln, Calle Real de Sabana Grande, Caracas, Venezuela.
- Gaceta Indigenista. bi-m. ISSN 0433-0854

**Venezuela. Ministerio de la Defensa. Las Fuerzas Armadas**
Caracas, Venezuela.
- Revista de las Fuerzas Armadas. m. ISSN 0034-8473

**Venezuela. Ministerio de la Defensa. Oficina Tecnica**
- Galeon. (pub. by Escuela Naval de Venezuela)

**Venezuela. Ministerio de la Defensa. Servicio de Sanidad Militar**
Hospital Central de las Fuerzas Armadas, San Martin, Caracas, Venezuela.
- Salus Militiae. s-a. ISSN 0036-3642
- Venezuela. Hospital Central de la Fuerzas Armadas. Boletin Medico. q.

**Venezuela. Ministerio de Minas e Hidrocarburos**
Torre Norte, Centro Simon Bolivar, Caracas, Venezuela.
- Actividades Petroleras. q. ISSN 0001-7582
- Boletin de Geologia. 2-3 per yr. ISSN 0006-6281
- Venezuela. Ministerio de Minas e Hidrocarburos. Carta Semanal. w. ISSN 0042-3394
- Venezuela. Ministerio de Minas e Hidrocarburos. Memoria y Cuenta. a. ISSN 0083-5374
- Venezuela. Ministerio de Minas e Hidrocarburos. Oficina de Economia Minera. Hierro y Otros Datos Estadisticos. a. ISSN 0083-5382
- Venezuela. Ministerio de Minas e Hidrocarburos. Oficina de Economia Petrolera. Petroleo y Otros Datos Estadisticos. a. ISSN 0083-5390
- Venezuela. Ministry of Mines and Hydrocarbons. Informations. bi-m. ISSN 0042-3408

**Venezuela. Ministerio de Sanidad y Asistencia Social**
Oficina de Publicaciones, Biblioteca y Archivo, Centro Simon Bolivar, Edificio Sur, Caracas, Venezuela.
- Revista Venezolana de Sanidad y Asistencia Social. q. ISSN 0035-0583
- Venezuela. Ministerio de Sanidad y Asistencia Social. Memoria y Cuenta. a.

**Venezuela. Ministerio de Sanidad y Assistencia Social. Direccion de Salud Publica**
Caracas, Venezuela.
- Boletin de Salud Publica. q. (prep. by its Direccion de Salud Publica)

**Venezuela. Ministerio del Trabajo**
Servicio de Publicaciones, Caracas, Venezuela.
- Revista de Trabajo. q. ISSN 0034-8988

**Venezuela. Oficina Central de Informacion**
Apdo. de Correos 192, Caracas, Venezuela.
- Indice Cultural de Venezuela. m. ISSN 0019-6991
- Venezuela Ahora. w.

**Venezuela. Secretaria de la Presidencia**
Caracas, Venezuela.
- Archivo Historico de Miraflores Boletin. bi-m. ISSN 0004-0444

**Venezuela. Sociedad Venezolana de Ingeniera Hidraulica**
Colegio de Ingenieros de Venezuela, Apdo. 2006, Los Caobos, Venezuela.
- Agua. q. ISSN 0044-6890 (Co-sponsors: Venezuela. Direccion General de Recursos Hidraulicos; Laboratorio de Hidraulica; Instituto Nacional de Obras Sanitarias; Comision de Plan Nacional de Aprovechamiento de los Recursos Hidraulicos)

**Venezuelan-American Chamber of Commerce and Industry**
Apartado 5181, Caracas, Venezuela.
- Business Venezuela. bi-m. ISSN 0045-3641
- Venezuelan-American Chamber of Commerce and Industry. Yearbook and Membership Directory. a.

# VIETNAM

**Courrier du Vietnam**
46 Tran Hung Dao, Hanoi, Vietnam.
- Courrier du Vietnam. w. ISSN 0045-8902

**Federation des Syndicats du Vietnam**
82 Tran Hung Dao, Hanoi, Vietnam.
- Syndicats Vietnamiens. q. ISSN 0049-2744

**South Vietnam National Front for Liberation**
Dazimina Hanoi 19, Hai Ba Trung, Hanoi, Vietnam.
- South Vietnam in Struggle. w. ISSN 0049-1535

**Vietnam**
79 Ly Thuong Kiet, Hanoi, Vietnam.
- Vietnam. m. ISSN 0042-5710

**Vietnam. Directorate of Archives and Libraries**
P.O. Box 2094, Saigon, Vietnam.
- Vietnam. Directorate of Archives and Libraries. Catalogue of Books. a.

**Vietnam Women's Hanoi**
39- Hang Chuoi, Hanoi, Vietnam.
- Women of Vietnam. m. ISSN 0512-1825

**Vietnam Youth Federation**
64 Ba Trieu St., Hanoi, Vietnam.
- Vietnam Youth. q. ISSN 0049-6375

**Vietnamese Studies**
Xunhasaba 32, Hai Ba Trung, Hanoi, Vietnam.
- Vietnamese Studies. irreg. ISSN 0085-7823

**Xunhasaba**
32 Hai Ba Trung, Hanoi, Vietnam.
- Etudes Vietnamiennes. q. ISSN 0531-206X
- Vietnam Courier. m.

## VIRGIN ISLANDS (BRITISH)

**British Virgin Islands. Finance Department**
Tortola, British Virgin Islands.
- Tourism in the British Virgin Islands. a.

## VIRGIN ISLANDS (U. S.)

**College of the Virgin Islands. Caribbean Islands Research Institute**
St. Thomas, Virgin Islands.
- Caribbean Research Institute. Report. irreg; latest, tenth anniv. issue, 1975.

**St. Croix Library Association**
Box 6760, Sunny Isles, St. Croix, VI 00820.
- Studies in Virgin Islands Librarianship. irreg.

**Sunrise Publications Inc.**
Box 4085, Christiansted, St. Croix, Virgin Islands.
- Caribbean Sunrise. q.

**Virgin Islands (U.S.) Department of Commerce. Division of Trade and Industry**
Charlotte Amalie 00801, St. Thomas, Virgin Islands.
- Virgin Islands (U.S.). Division of Trade and Industry. External Trade Statistics with Foreign Countries. a. ISSN 0083-6303

**Virgin Islands Archaeological Society**
Havensight Road, St. Thomas, VI 00801.
- Virgin Islands Archaeological Society Journal. q.

**Virgin Islands Nurses Association**
Box 2866, Charlotte Amalie, St. Thomas, Virgin Islands.
- V I N A Quarterly. q. ISSN 0049-6464

## WESTERN SAMOA

**Department of Economic Development**
Apia, Western Samoa.
- Western Samoa. Department of Economic Development. Development of Western Samoa. a.

**Samoa Times Ltd.**
Box 1160, Apia Western Samoa, Oceania.
- Samoa Times. w. ISSN 0036-3839

## YEMEN

**Central Bank of Yemen**
Box 59, San'a, Yemen.
- Central Bank of Yemen. Annual Report. a.
- Foreign Trade Statistics of Yemen Arab Republic. a. (prep. by its Research Department)

**Yemen. Central Statistical Office**
Sana'a, Yemen.
- Yemen. Central Statistical Office. Statistical Yearbook.

## YEMEN, SOUTHERN

**British Petroleum Refinery (Aden) Ltd.**
P.O.Box 3003, Aden, Southern Yemen.
- Aden Magazine/Magallat Aden. a. ISSN 0065-1923

## YUGOSLAVIA

**Advokatska Komora Bosne i Hercegovine**
Saloma Albaharija 2, Sarajevo, Yugoslavia.
- Advokatura Bosne i Hercegovine. q.

**Advokatska Komora Srbije**
Mose Pijade 13, Belgrade, Yugoslavia.
- Advokatura. q.

**Advokatska Komora Vojvodine**
Zmaj Jovina 20, 21000 Novi Sad, Yugoslavia.
- Gasnik Advokatske Komore Vojvodine. m. ISSN 0017-0933

**Agentstvo Pechati "Novosti"**
Strahinjica Bana 50, Belgrade, Yugoslavia.
- Zemlja Sovjeta; ilustrovani casopis Novinske agencije "Novosti" (APN) fortn. ISSN 0044-3921

**Agrotehnicar**
Trg Republike 3/I, Zagreb, Yugoslavia.
- Agrotehnicar; Jugoslavenski list za mehanizaciju u poljoprivredi. fortn. ISSN 0002-1989

**Akademija Nauka i Umjetnosti Bosne i Hercegovine. Centar za Balkanoloska Ispitivanja**
Sarajevo, Yugoslavia.
- Akademija Nauka i Umjetnosti Bosne i Hercegovine. Centar za Balkanoloska Ispitivanja. Godisnjak. a.

**Akademija Nauka i Umjetnosti Bosne i Hercegovine. Hemijski Institut**
Vojvode Putnika 43, Sarajevo, Yugoslavia.
- Glasnik Hemicara i Tehnologa Bosne i Hercegovine. irreg. ISSN 0367-4444

**Akademija Nauka i Umjetnosti Bosne i Hercegovine. Odeljenje Drustvenih Nauka**
Obala Vojvode Stepe 42, Sarajevo, Yugoslavia.
- Akademija Nauka i Umjetnosti Bosne i Hercegovine. Odeljenje Drustvenih Nauka. Radovi. ISSN 0350-0039

**Akademija Nauka i Umjetnosti Bosne i Hercegovine. Odeljenje Medicinskih Nauka**
Obala Vojvode Stepe 42, Sarajevo, Yugoslavia.
- Akademija Nauka i Umjetnosti Bosne i Hercegovine. Odeljenje Medicinskih Nauka. Radovi. irreg. ISSN 0350-0071

**Akademija Nauka i Umjetnosti Bosne i Hercegovine. Odjeljenje Istorijsko Filoloskih Nauk**
Obala Vojvode Stepe 42, Sarajevo, Yugoslavia.
- Akademija Nauka i Umjetnosti Bosne i Hercegovine. Odjeljenje Istorijsko Filoloskih Nauk. Djela. irreg.

**Albus (Fabrika Sapuna i Hemijskih Proizvoda)**
Novi Sad, Yugoslavia.
- Albus. m. ISSN 0002-4961

**Andragoski Centar**
Vojnoviceva 42, Zagreb, Yugoslvaia.
- Andragogija. bi-m. ISSN 0029-764X

**Arenaturist**
Pula, Yugoslavia.
- Arenaturist. a.

**Arheoloski Muzej Istre u Puli**
M. Balote 3, Pula, Yugoslavia.
- Historia Archaeologica. s-a.

**Association of Croat Writers**
*see* Drustvo Knjizevnika Hrvatske

**Association of Yugoslav Insurance Organizations**
*see* Udruzeni Zavod za Osiguranje i Reosiguranje

**Association of Yugoslav Surgeons**
*see* Udruzenje Hirurga Jugoslavije

**Auto-Moto Savez Jugoslavije**
Ruzveltova 18, Belgrade, Yugoslavia.
- Moto Revija. m. ISSN 0027-1683

**Bagdala**
Zakiceva 11, Krusevac, Yugoslavia.
- Bagdala; mesecni list za knjizevnost, umetnost i kulturu. m. ISSN 0005-3880

**Belgrade. Skupstina Grada**
Cika Ljubina 16, Belgrade, Yugoslavia.
- Privredno Pravni Prirucnik; za pravnu opstu i kadrovsku sluzbu privrednih i ostalih radnih organizacija. m. ISSN 0032-9002

**Beogradski Izdavacko-Graficki Zavod**
Bulevar Vojvode Misica 17, Box 340, Belgrade, Yugoslavia.
- Savremenik; mesecni knjizevni casopis. m. ISSN 0036-519X

**Borba**
Trg Marksa i Engelsa 7, Belgrade, Yugoslavia.
- Autosport; specijalizovano nedeljno izdanje jugoslavenskog sportskog lista "Sport". w. ISSN 0005-173X
- Borbin Informator; list radnih ljudi NIGP Borba. m.
- Celik; casopis Udruzenja jugoslovenskih zelezara. bi-m. ISSN 0008-8722
- Nedeljne Novosti. w. ISSN 0028-1999
- Pionir-Kekec; jugoslovenski pionirski list. w. ISSN 0032-0099
- Poletarac. m. ISSN 0032-2547

**Borec**
Miklosiceva 28, Ljubljana, Yugoslavia.
- Borec. m. ISSN 0006-7725

**Boris Kidric Institute of Nuclear Sciences**
*see* Institut za Nuklearne Nauke "Boris Kidric"

**Bosko Buha Informativni Centar**
Matija Gupca 2, Virovitica, Yugoslavia.
- Viroviticki List. w. ISSN 0042-6849 (Socijalisticki Savez Radnog Naroda Opcine Virovitica)

**Bosnia and Hercegovina. Arhiv**
Save Kovacevica 6, 71000 Sarajevo, Yugoslavia.
- Glasnik Arhiva i Drustava Arhivskih Radnika Bosne i Hercegovine. a.

**Bosnia and Hercegovina. Zavod za Statistiku**
Jugoslavenske Narodne Armije 54, Sarajevo, Yugoslavia.
- Statisticki Pregled Socijalisticke Republike Bosne i Hercegovine. m. ISSN 0039-0542

**Bratstvo**
Kej 29 Dekemvri 8, Nis, Yugoslavia.
- Bratstvo; vestnik na bulgarskata narodnost v sFR Jugoslavija. w. ISSN 0006-9272

**Brodogradnja**
Box 68, Miramarska 22-V, 41000 Zagreb, Yugoslavia.
- Brodogradnja; casopis za pitanje brodogradnje i brodogradevne industrije. bi-m. ISSN 0007-215X

**Cehoslovacki Savez v SR Hrvatskoj**
Trg marsala Tita 7, Daruvar, Yugoslavia.
- Jednota. w. ISSN 0021-5791

**Centar za Idejni i Teorijski Rad CK SKH**
Setaliste Karla Marxa 2, 4100 Zagreb, Yugoslavia.
- Nase Teme. m. ISSN 0547-3101

**Centar za Informacije i Publicitet**
Miramarska 15a, Zagreb 41000, Yugoslavia.
- Udruzeni Rad; jugoslavenski strucni casopis za pitanja iz medjusobnih odnosa u udruzenom radu. bi-m.

**Centar za Istrazivanje Biblije Dokumentaciju i Informacije**
Krajiska 14, Zagreb, Yugoslavia.
- Znaci Vremena; porodicni casopis za hriscansku renesansu. q.

**Centar za Kulturno-Propagandni i Informativni Rad Vukovar**
Nazorova 12/1, Vukovar, Yugoslavia.
- Vukovarske Novine. w. ISSN 0042-9309 (Socijalisticki Savez Radnog Naroda Vukovar)

**Centar za Proucavanje i Suzbijanje Alkoholizma i Drugih Ovisnosti**
Vinogradska 29, 41000 Zagreb, Yugoslavia.
- Alcoholism; journal on alcoholism and related addictions. s-a. ISSN 0002-502X (Co-sponsor: International Council on Alcoholism and Addictions)
- Centar za Proucananje i Suzbijanje Alkoholizma i Drugih Ovisnosti. Radovi. irreg. ISSN 0033-8567

**Centar za Proucavanje Prirodnih Zdravstvenih Nacela**
Maksimirska 9, Zagreb, Yugoslavia.
- Zivot i Zdravije. q.

**Centar za Unapredjivanje Saha**
7 Jula 30, Box 739, Belgrade, Yugoslavia.
- Sahovski Informator/Chess Informant/Sahmatnyj Informator. s-a. ISSN 0045-6586 (World Chess Federation - FIDE)

**Centar za Vojnonaucnu Dokumentaciju i Informacije**
Balkanska 53, Belgrade, Yugoslavia.
- Bibliografija Domacih i Stranih Knjiga. 6 per yr. ISSN 0350-1450

**Croatia. Arhiv Hrvatske**
Marulicev trg 21, 41000 Zagreb, Yugoslavia.
- Arhivski Vjesnik. a.

**Croatia. Odvjetnicka Komora**
Zrinjski trg 15, Zagreb, Yugoslavia
- Odvjetnik; glasilo odvjetnika Hrvatske. bi-m. ISSN 0029-8530 (Subscr. to: "Mladost" Export Import, Ilica 30, 41000 Zagreb, Yugoslavia)

**Croatia. Vrhovni Sud**
- Pregled Sudske Prakse. (pub. by Narodne Novine, Zagreb)

**Croatia Zajednica Osiguranja**
Miramarska 22, Box 868, 41001 Zagreb, Yugoslavia.
- Osiguranje i Privreda; casopis za teoriju i praksu osiguranja. m. ISSN 0030-6193 (Udruzeni Zavod za Osiguranje i Reosiguranje)

**Cuvar Jadrana**
Saveznicka Obala 18, Split, Yugoslavia.
- Cuvar Jadrana. s-m. ISSN 0011-4200

**Delo**
Tomsiceva 1-3, 61001 Ljubljana, Yugoslavia.
- Avto; jugoslovanska avtomobilisticna revija. fortn.
- I T D; ilustrirani tednik dnevnika Delo. w.

**Dnevnik**
Bulevar 23. Oktobra 31, Novi Sad, Yugoslavia.
- Osmeh; humoristicki magazin. m.
- Savremena Poljoprivreda/Contemporary Agriculture. m. ISSN 0581-8850
- Veseli Svet; humoristicki magazin. m. ISSN 0042-4536

**Drustvo Arhivskih Radnika SR Srbije**
c/o Radomir Jemnovic, Karnegijeva 2, Belgrade, Yugoslavia.
- Arhivski Pregled. s-a. ISSN 0004-1297

**Drustvo Bibliotekara Bosne i Hercegovine**
Vojvode Stepe Obala 42, Sarajevo, Yugoslavia.
- Bibliotekarstvo. q. ISSN 0006-1832

**Drustvo Bibliotekara Srbije**
Skerliceva 1, 11000 Belgrade, Yugoslavia.
- Bibliotekar. bi-m. ISSN 0006-1816

**Drustvo Bibliotekarjev Slovenije**
Turjaska 1, Ljubljana, Yugoslavia.
- Knjiznica. q. ISSN 0023-2424

**Drustvo Dijabeticara Hrvatske**
Sirkoviceva 8, Zagreb, Yugoslavia.
- Dijabeticar; casopis za socijalno medicinska pitanja dijabeticara. q.

**Drustvo Dubrovcana i Prijatelja Dubrovacke Starine**
Kunscak 61, Zagreb, Yugoslavia.
- Dubrovacki Horizonti. 3 per yr.

**Drustvo Istoricara SR Srbije**
Cika Ljubina 18-20, Belgrade, Yugoslavia.
- Istorijski Glasnik. s-a. ISSN 0021-2644

**Drustvo Knjizevnika Hrvatske**
Trg Republike 7, 41000 Zagreb, Yugoslavia.
- Bridge/Most/Bruecke/Ponte; literary review. 6 per yr. ISSN 0006-9833

**Drustvo Lekara Vojvodine**
Vase Stajica 9, Novi Sad, Yugoslavia.
- Medicinski Pregled. bi-m. ISSN 0025-8105

**Drustvo Livarjev Slovenije**
Lepi Pot 6, Ljubljana, Yugoslavia.
- Livarski Vestnik. bi-m. ISSN 0024-5135

**Drustvo Ljevaca SR Hrvatske**
Dure Salaja 1, Box 194, Zagreb, Yugoslavia.
- Ljevarstvo; glasilo Drustava Ljevaca SRH. 3 per yr. ISSN 0024-5402

**Drustvo Matematicara i Fizicara SR Hrvatske**
Marulicev Trg. 19, Zagreb, Yugoslavia.
- Glasnik Matematicki. s-a. ISSN 0017-095X

**Drustvo Medicinskih Radnika Srbije**
Zmaja Od Nocaja 9/4, Belgrade, Yugoslavia.
- Medicinski Radnik; casopis za strucna i drustvena pitanja. bi-m. ISSN 0025-8113

**Drustvo Medicinskih Sestara i Medicinskih Tehnicara Hrvatske**
Mlinarska 38, Zagreb, Yugoslavia.
- Vjesnik Medicinskih Sestara i Medicinskih Tehnicara Hrvatske. q.

**Drustvo Parazitologa Jugoslavije**
Rockfelerova 7, Zagreb, Yugoslavia.
- Acta Parasitologica Iugoslavica. irreg.

**Drustvo Socijalnih Radnika Hrvatske**
Nazorava 51, Zagreb, Yugoslavia.
- Socijalni Rad. q. ISSN 0038-0105

**Drustvo za Srpskohrvatski Jezik i Knjizevnost Srbije**
Knez Mihailova 35, Belgrade, Yugoslavia.
- Knjizevnost i Jezik. q. (Co-sponsor: Drustvo za Srpskohrvatski Jezik i Knjizevnost Crne Gore)

**Drustvo za Tehniku Zavarivanja Hrvatske**
Djure Salaja 1, Zagreb, Yugoslavia.
- Zavarivanje. m. ISSN 0044-1902 (Savez Drustava za Tehniku Zavarivanja Jugoslavije)

**Drustvo Zobozdrastvenih Delavcev Slovenije**
Hrvatski trg 6, Ljubljana, Yugoslavia.
- Zobozdravstveni Vestnik. bi-m. ISSN 0044-4928

**Drustvoto na Arhivskite Rabotnici i Arhivite vo Makedonija**
Kej Dimitar Vlahov 66, Skopje, Yugoslavia.
- Makedonski Arhivist. s-a. ISSN 0350-1728

**Drustvoto za Makedonski Jazik i Literatura**
Grigor Prlicev 5, 91000 Skopje, Yugoslavia.
- Literaturen Zbor. s-a. ISSN 0024-4791 (Co-Sponsor: Institut za Makedonski Jazik, Skopje)

**Drzavna Zalozba Slovenije**
Stritarjeva 3/2, Box 50-1, Ljubljana, Yugoslavia.
- Sodobnost. m. ISSN 0038-0482

**Duga**
Bulevar vojvode Misica 17, Belgrade, Yugoslavia.
- Galaksija; casopis za popularizaciju nauke. m.
- Prakticna Zena. fortn. ISSN 0032-6747

**Ekonomski Biro**
Marsala Tita 4, Belgrade, Yugoslavia.
- Ekonomska Analiza/Economic Analysis. q. ISSN 0013-3213

**Ekonomski Fakultet u Beogradu**
- Ekonomski Anali. (pub. by Savremena Praksa)

**Elektrotehnicki Institut Poduzeca "Rade Koncar"**
Fallerovo Set. 22, Zagreb, Yugoslavia.
- Informacije Rade Koncar. irreg. ISSN 0033-7536

**Elektrotehniska Zveza Slovenije**
Trzaska 25, Box 92-II, 61001 Ljubljana, Yugoslavia.
- Elektrotehniski Vestnik. bi-m. ISSN 0013-5852

**Enigmatski Klub**
Bulevar Vojvode Misica 67, Box 219, Belgrade, Yugoslavia.
- Enigma; zabavni casopis: ukrstene reci, rebusi. w. ISSN 0013-8436
- Mala Ukrstenica. m. ISSN 0025-1178
- Razonoda Miliona; ukrstene reci, rebusi, zagonetke. irreg. ISSN 0034-0243

**Etnografski Muzej na Cetinju**
Trg Revolucije, Cetinje, Yugoslavia.
- Etnografski Muzej na Cetinju. Glasnik. irreg.

**Etnografski Muzej u Beogradu**
Studentski trg 13, Belgrade, Yugoslavia.
- Etnografski Muzej u Beogradu. Glasnik. a.
- Etnoloski Pregled/Revue d'Ethnologie. a. (Etnolosko Drustvo Jugoslavije)

**Etnolosko Drustvo Jugoslavije**
- Etnoloski Pregled/Revue d'Ethnologie. (pub. by Etnografski Muzej u Beogradu)

**Export Press**
Francuska 27, Belgrade, Yugoslavia.
- Journal Export; export-import, international, forwarding agencies, industry, mining, agriculture, finance, films, tourism, hunting, information. fortn. ISSN 0021-8227
- Journal of Yugoslav Foreign Trade. q. ISSN 0022-5452
- Trgovinski Glasnik; informativni list za trgovinu. m. ISSN 0041-2457

**Farmaceutsko Drustvo Hrvatske**
Masarykova 2, Zagreb 1, Yugoslavia.
- Farmaceutski Glasnik. m. ISSN 0014-8202

**Farmaceutsko Drustvo Srbije**
Terazije 12, Box 664, Belgrade, Yugoslavia.
- Arhiv za farmaciju. 6 per yr. ISSN 0004-1963

**Farmaceutsko Drustvo Vojvodine**
Bulevar Revolucije 32, Novi Sad, Yugoslavia.
- Farmaceut. bi-m.

**Filmska Kultura**
Aleja Borisa Kidrica 46, 41020 Zagreb, Yugoslavia.
- Filmska Kultura; Jugoslavenski casopis za filmska pitanja. bi-m. ISSN 0015-170X

**Filozofsko Drustvo Srbije**
Studentski trg 1, 11000 Belgrade, Yugoslavia.
- Filozofija; jugoslovenski casopis za filozofiju. q. ISSN 0015-1866

**Filozofsko-Teoloski Insitut Druzbe Isusove**
Jordanovac 110, Zagreb, Yugoslavia.
- Obnovljeni Zivot/Life Renewed; dvomjesecnik za religioznu kulturu. bi-m.

**Forum, Novi Sad**
Vojvode Misica 1, Novi Sad, Yugoslavia.
- Kepes Ifjusag. w.
- Magyar Szo Naptara. a. ISSN 0541-9344

**Forum, Subotica**
Trg Slobode 2, Subotica, Yugoslavia.
- Letunk; tarsadalom, tudomany, kultura. bi-m.

**Franjevacka Visoka Bogoslovija, Makarska**
Zrtava Fasizma 1, 58300 Makarska, Yugoslavia.
- Sluzba Bozja; liturgijsko-pastoralna revija. q. ISSN 0037-7074

**Galenika**
Ul. Masarikova 5, 11000 Belgrade, Yugoslavia.
- Medicinska Revija; casopis za medicinu i farmaciju. q. ISSN 0025-8067

**Galerije Grada Zagreba**
Katarinin trg 2, 41000 Zagreb, Yugoslavia.
- Bit International; television today. irreg.
- Spot; casopis za fotografiju. q.

**Geografsko Drustvo Bosne i Hercegovine**
Vojvode Putnika 66, Sarajevo, Yugoslavia.
- Geografski List. bi-m.

**Geografsko Drustvo Hrvatske**
Marulicev Trg 19/2, Zagreb, Yugoslavia.
- Geografski Horizont. q. ISSN 0016-7266

**Geografsko Drustvo Slovenije**
Askerceva 12, Ljubljana, Yugoslavia.
- Geografski Obzornik; casopis za geografsko vzgojo in izobrazbo. q. ISSN 0016-7274

**Geoloski Zavod Ljubljana. Institut za Geologiju**
- Geologija. (pub. by Slovensko Geolosko Drustvo)

**Geotehnika**
Kupska 2, Zagreb, Yugoslavia.
- Geotehnika; informativno glasilo radne zajednice Geotehnika. irreg.

**Glas Istre**
Obala Marsala Tita 10, Pula, Yugoslavia.
- Glas Istre. w. ISSN 0017-0771 (Socijalisticki Savez Radnog Naroda Istre, Hrvatskog primorja i Gorskog kotara)
- Istarski Mozaik; casopis za drustvena, knjizevna i umjetnicka pitanja Istre. q. ISSN 0021-2415
- Istra; kultura, knjizevnost drustvena pitana. m.

**Glas Podrinja**
Karadjordjeva 17, Sabac, Yugoslavia.
- Glas Podrinja; list za drustvena i politicka pitanja.
w. ISSN 0017-081X

**Glavni Zadruzni Savez**
Kneza Milosa 26/I, Belgrade, Yugoslavia.
- Socijalisticka Poljoprivreda; mesecnik za
poljoprivredu i zemiljoradnicko zadrugarstvo. m.

**Gospodarski Vestnik**
Miklosiceva 38, 61000 Ljubljana, Yugoslavia.
- Economic Echo from Yugoslavia; review for the
international exchange of goods and services. 8
per yr. ISSN 0012-916X

**Gradina, Izdavacka Ustanova**
Pobede 38, 18000 Nis, Yugoslavia.
- Gradina; casopis za umetnost, nauku i drustveni
pitanja. m.

**Hidrografski Institut Jugoslavenske Ratne Mornarice**
58000 Split, Yugoslavia.
- Oglas za Pomorce/Notices to Mariners. m. ISSN
0030-0713

**Horizont-Yugoslavia**
Draskoviceva 44, Zagreb, Yugoslavia.
- Yugoslavia; review for international and Yugoslav
economic, technological, social and cultural issues.
q. ISSN 0049-8483

**Hortikulturna Drustva Hrvatske**
Setaliste 1. Maja 8, Split, Yugoslavia.
- Hortikultura. q. ISSN 0018-5337

**Hrvatski Filatelisticki Savez**
Draskoviceva 27, Zagreb, Yugoslavia.
- Filatelija. bi-m. ISSN 0015-0967

**Hrvatsko Bibliotekarsko Drustvo**
- Vjesnik Bibliotekara Hrvatske. (pub. by
Nacionalna i Sveucilisna Biblioteka)

**Hrvatsko Filolosko Drustvo**
Djure Salaja 3, 41000 Zagreb, Yugoslavia.
- Jezik; casopis za kulturu hrvatskoga knjizevnog
jezika. bi-m. ISSN 0021-6925
- Knjizevna Smotra; casopis za svjetsku knjizevnost.
q. ISSN 0455-0463

**Hrvatsko Filolosko Drustvo. Sekcija za Strane Jezike**
Djure Salaja 3, Zagreb, Yugoslavia.
- Strani Jezici. 4 per yr. (prep. by its Institut za
Lingvistiku)

**Hrvatsko Geolosko Drustvo**
- Geoloski Vjesnik. (pub. by Institut za Geoloska
Istrazivanja u Zagrebu)

**Hrvatsko Kemijsko Drustvo**
Marulicev trg 19, Zagreb, Yugoslavia.
- Croatica Chemica Acta. q. ISSN 0011-1643 (Co-
sponsor: Sveuciliste u Zagrebu)

**Hrvatsko Narodno Kazaliste u Osijeku**
Prolaz Radoslava Bacica 1, Osijek, Yugoslavia.
- Kazaliste; revija za scensku glazbu i kulturu. q.

**Ibarske Novosti, Novinsko Izdavacka i Radio
Ustanova**
Mire Cukulica 9, Kraljevo, Yugoslavia.
- Ibarske Novosti; list za politicka i drustvena
pitanja. w. ISSN 0019-0977

**Imunoloski Zavod**
Rockefellerova 2, 41000 Zagreb, Yugoslavia.
- Imunoloski Zavod. Radovi. 1-2 per yr. ISSN
0033-8559

**Informativni Centar Daruvar**
Matije Gupca 7, Daruvar, Yugoslavia.
- Vjesnik Komune; glasilo OKSSRN Daruvar. m.
ISSN 0042-7624

**Informativni Centar, Sombor**
Gradska Kuca 226-35, Sombor, Yugoslavia.
- Pokret. m. ISSN 0032-2407
- Somborske Novine. w. ISSN 0038-1276

**Informativno Dokumentarni Centar, Koprivnica**
Trg Marsala Tita 1, Koprivnica, Yugoslavia.
- Glas Podravine. w. ISSN 0017-0801

**Informator**
Masarykova 1, Zagreb, Yugoslavia.
- Ekonomist. q. ISSN 0013-3191 (Savez
Ekonomista Jugoslavije)

- Marketing; casopis Jugoslavenskog udruzenja za
marketing JUMA. q. ISSN 0581-1023
(Jugoslovensko Udruzenje za Marketing (JUMA))

**Institut Drustvenih Nauka u Beogradu. Centar za
Demografska Istrazivanja**
Narodnog Fronta 45, Belgrade, Yugoslavia.
- Stanovnistvo. q. ISSN 0038-982X

**Institut za Arhitekturu i Urbanizam Srbije**
Bulevar Revolucije 73/II, Belgrade, Yugoslavia.
- Institut za Arhitekturu i Urbanizam Srbije.
Zbornik Radova. a.

**Institut za Crkvenu Glazbu u Zagrebu**
Trg. Kralja Tomislava 21, 41000 Zagreb, Yugoslavia.
- Sveta Cecilija; casopis za duhovnu glazbu. m.

**Institut za Dokumentaciju Zastite na Radu, Nis**
Stanka Paunovica 17, Nis, Yugoslavia.
- Jugoslovenska i Inostrana Dokumentacija Zastite
na Radu. m. ISSN 0022-6068

**Institut za Drvo, Zagreb**
Ul. 8 Maja 82, 41001 Zagreb, Yugoslavia.
- Drvna Industrija. m. ISSN 0012-6772

**Institut za Film, Belgrade**
Cika Ljubina 15, Belgrade, Yugoslavia.
- Kinematografija u Srbiji. a. ISSN 0350-2651

**Institut za Folklor, Skopje**
Ruzveltova 3, Box 319, 91000 Skopje, Yugoslavia.
- Makedonski Folklor. s-a.

**Institut za Geoloska Istrazivanja u Zagrebu**
Sachsova 2, Zagreb, Yugoslavia.
- Geoloski Vjesnik. irreg. ISSN 0016-7924
(Hrvatsko Geolosko Drustvo)

**Institut za Historiju Radnickog Pokreta Hrvatske**
Opaticka 10, Zagreb, Yugoslavia.
- Casopis za Suvremenu Povjest/Magazine of
Contemporary History. 3 per yr.

**Institut za Istrazivanje i Razvoj Obrazovanja**
Draze Pavlovica 15, Belgrade, Yugoslavia.
- Institut za Istrazivanje i Razvoj Obrazovanja.
Bibliografija; lista bibliografskih podataka
novonabavljenih knjiga i clanaka iz domace i
inostrane pedagoske literature. m.

**Institut za Kriminoloska i Socioloska Istrazivanja**
Gracanicka 18, 11000 Belgrade, Yugoslavia.
- Institut za Kriminoloska i Socioloska Istrazivanja.
Zbornik. a.

**Institut za Makedonski Jazik, Skopje**
Grigor Prlicev 5, 91000 Skopje, Yugoslavia.
- Makedonski Jazik. s-a. ISSN 0025-1089

**Institut za Medicinska Istrazivanja i Medicinu Rada**
Mose Pijade 158, Box 291, 41001 Zagreb,
Yugoslavia.
- Arhiv za Higijenu Rada i Toksikologiju/Archives
of Industrial Hygiene and Toxicology. q. ISSN
0004-1254 (Co-sponsors: Udruzenja za Medicinu
Rada SFRJ; Udruzenje Toksikologa Jugoslavije)

**Institut za Medjunarodni Radnicki Pokret**
Trg Marksa i Engelsa Br. 11, 11000 Belgrade,
Yugoslavia.
- Medjunarodni Radnicki Pokret. q. (Institut za
Medjunarodnu Politiku i Privredu u Beogradu)

**Institut za Medjunarodnu Politiku i Privredu u
Beogradu**
Makedonska 25, Box 750, Belgrade, Yugoslavia.
- Institut za Medjunarodnu Politiku i Privredu u
Beogradu. Godisnjak. a.
- Institute of International Politics and Economics.
Documentation Bulletin. irreg.
- Medjunarodni Problemi. q. ISSN 0025-8555
- Medjunarodni Radnicki Pokret. (pub. by Institut
za Medjunarodni Radnicki Pokret)
- Spoljnopoliticka Dokumentacija. bi-m. ISSN 0038-
7754

**Institut za Nacionalna Istorija, Skopje**
Boris Kidric 66, 91000 Skopje, Yugoslavia.
- Institut za Nacionalna Istorija, Skopje. Glasnik/
Institut d'Histoire Nationale, Skopje. Revue. 3 per
yr. ISSN 0583-4961

**Institut za Naucno-Tehnicku Dokumentaciju i
Informacije**
Kataniceva 15, Box 667, Belgrade, Yugoslavia.
- Bibliografija Prispelih Knjiga Clanaka Iz Strucnih
Casopisa i Drugih Dokumenata. m. ISSN 0006-
1166

**Institut za Nuklearne Nauke "Boris Kidric"**
Box 522, Vinca, 11000 Belgrade, Yugoslavia.
- Boris Kidric Institute of Nuclear Sciences.
Bulletin. irreg. ISSN 0006-7784

**Institut za Oceanografiju i Ribarstvo**
Mose Pijade 63, Box 114, 58001 Split, Yugoslavia.
- Acta Adriatica. irreg. ISSN 0001-5113

**Institut za Organizaciju i Razvoj, Belgrade**
Milana Rakica 35, Belgrade, Yugoslavia.
- Organizacija i Kadrovi/Organization and
Personnel. m. ISSN 0048-217X

**Institut za Psihomedicinu Saobracaja**
Park Lenjina 2, Osijek, Yugoslavia.
- Psihomedicina Saobracaja/Psychomedicine of
Traffic. s-a.

**Institut za Rehabilitaciju, Belgrade**
Sokobanjska, Belgrade, Yugoslavia.
- Povratak u Zivot. bi-m. ISSN 0032-5880

**Institut za Sigurnost, Zagreb**
Cakovecka 17, 41000 Zagreb, Yugoslavia.
- Sigurnost; strucno naucni casopis. q. ISSN 0037-
508X

**Institut za Spoljnu Trgovinu**
Mose Pijade 8, Belgrade, Yugoslavia.
- Jugoslovensko Vinogradarstvo i Vinarstvo. m.
ISSN 0022-6130
- Problemi Spoljne Trgovine i Konjunkture/Foreign
Trade & Business Cycles Problems. q. ISSN 0032-
938X

**Institut za Srpskohrvatski Jezik**
Knez Mihajlova 35, Belgrade, Yuoslavia.
- Nas Jezik. 5 per yr. ISSN 0027-8084

**Institut za Strucno Usavrsavanje i Specijalizaciju
Zdrastvenih Radnika Srbije**
Nusiceva 25/I, Belgrade, Yugoslavia.
- Medicina Danas; casopis za strucno usavrsavanje
lekara. 6 per yr. ISSN 0025-7796

**Institut za Uporedno Pravo, Belgrade**
Terazije 41, 11000 Belgrade, Yugoslavia.
- Pregled Zakonodavstva u Stranim Drzavama. q.
ISSN 0032-731X
- Strani Pravni Zivot. Serija D: Teorija,
Zakonodavstvo, Praksa. q. ISSN 0039-2138
- Yugoslav Law/Droit Yougoslav. 3 per yr. ISSN
0350-2252 (Union of Jurists Associations of
Yugoslavia)

**Institut za Vodoprivredu "Jaroslav Cerni"**
Bulevar vojvode Misica 43, Belgrade, Yugoslavia.
- Hidrotehnicka Bibliografija. bi-m. ISSN 0018-1358

**Institut za Zastitu Majki i Djece**
Klaiceva 16, Zagreb, Yugoslavia.
- Arhiv za Zastitu Majke i Djeteta. bi-m. ISSN
0004-1289

**Institute of Linguistics, Zagreb**
Djure Salaja 3, 41000 Zagreb, Yugoslavia.
- Yugoslav Serbo-Croatian-English Contrastive
Project. Series B: studies. irreg.

**Interesna Zaednica na Kulturata, Prilep**
Joska Jordanoski 2, Prilep, Yugoslavia.
- Stremez; spisanie za literatura, umetnost i kultura.
10 per yr. ISSN 0039-2294

**International Centre of Onomastics**
Blijde- Inkomsstr. 5, 3000 Louvain, Belgium
(Order 11th Congress Proceedings from Bulgarische
Akademie der Wissenschaften, 1 rue 7 Noemvri,
Sofia)
- International Committee of Onomastic Sciences.
Congress Proceedings. triennial; 11th, Sofia,
Bulgaria, 1972. ISSN 0074-2791

**International Hop Growers Convention**
Titova 19, Ljubljana, Yugoslavia.
- International Hop Growers Convention. Report of
Congress. a, 25th, 1975, Warsaw. ISSN 0074-
6223

**International Institute for the Science of Sintering**
- Science of Sintering. (pub. by Jugoslovenski Komitet za Elektroniku i Telekomunikacije, Automatizaciju i Nuklearnu Tehniku (ETAN))

**International Union of Prehistoric and Protohistoric Sciences**
Institute of Archaeology, Knez Mihajlova 35/2, Belgrade, Yugoslavia.
- International Union of Prehistoric and Protohistoric Sciences. Proceedings of Congress. irreg; 1-3rd, belgrade, 1971-1973. ISSN 0074-9478

**Istorijski Institut SR Crne Gore, Titograd**
Naselje Krusevac, Box 101, 81000 Titograd, Yugoslavia.
- Istorijski Zapisi. q. ISSN 0021-2652 (Co-Sponsor: Drustvo Istoricara Crne Gore)

**Izdavacko Preduzece Rad**
Moshe Pijade 12, Belgrade, Yugoslavia.
- Knjizevna Kritika; casopis za umetnicku, istorijsku i filosofsku kritiku. bi-m.

**Jedinstvo**
Marsala Tita 49, Pristina, Yugoslavia.
- Jedinstvo. s-w. ISSN 0021-5775 (Socijalisticki Savez Radnog Naroda Kosova)

**Jez**
Terazije 27, Belgrade, Yugoslavia.
- Jez. w. ISSN 0021-6917

**JUCEMA**
Prilaz JNA 30, Zagreb, Yugoslavia.
- Cement; casopis industrije cementa jugoslavije. q. ISSN 0008-882X

**Jugobanka**
Titova 32, Ljubljana, Yugoslavia.
- Novice; glasilo delovne skupnosti Jugobanke. m.

**Jugopetrol**
23. Oktobar 27, Novi Sad, Yugoslavia.
- Jugopetrol, Trgovinsko Preduzece za Promet Nafte i Naftinih Derivata. Bilten. irreg.

**Jugoslavenska Akademija Znanosti i Umjetnosti. Historijski Institut**
Dubrovnik., Yugoslavia.
- Jugoslavenska Akademija Znanosti i Umjetnosti. Historijski Institut, Dubrovnik. Anali. a. ISSN 0449-3648

**Jugoslavenska Akademija Znanosti i Umjetnosti. Institut za Filozofiju Znanosti i Mir**
Marulicev trg 19/I, 41000 Zagreb, Yugoslavia.
- Encyclopaedia Moderna. 4 per yr. ISSN 0013-7138

**Jugoslavenska Akademija Znanosti i Umjetnosti. Razred za Prirodne Znanosti**
Zrinski trg 11, Zagreb, Yugoslavia.
- Annales Forestales/Anali za Sumarstvo. a.

**Jugoslavenska Akademija Znanosti i Umjetnosti. Razred za Suvremenu Knjizevnost**
Brace Kavurica 1, 41000 Zagreb, Yugoslavia.
- Forum. 8 per yr. ISSN 0015-8445

**Jugoslavenski Komitet Svjetskog Kongresa za Naftu**
Savska Cesta 64, Zagreb, Yugoslavia.
- Nafta. m. ISSN 0027-755X

**Jugoslavensko Drustvo za Primjenu Goriva i Maziva**
Berislaviceva 6, 41000 Zagreb, Yugoslavia.
- Goriva i Maziva/Fuels and Lubricants. bi-m.

**Jugoslavensko Sportsko Drustvo "Partizan"**
Terazije 29, Belgrade, Yugoslavia.
- Partizanov Vesnik. fortn. ISSN 0031-255X

**Jugoslavija Film, Import-Export of Motion Pictures**
Knez Mihailova 19, 11000 Belgrade, Yugoslavia.
- News-Jugoslavija Film. irreg. ISSN 0448-021X

**Jugoslovenska Investiciona Banka**
Terazije 9, Box 152, 11001 Belgrade, Yugoslavia.
- Investbanka; list radne zajednice jugoslovenske investicione banke. m.
- Jugoslovenska Investiciona Banka. Annual Report. a. ISSN 0075-4536

**Jugoslovenska Revija**
Terazije 31, Belgrade, Yugoslavia.
- Jugoslavija; ezemesjacnyj illustrirovanyi zurnal. m. ISSN 0022-6033

- Review; yugoslav monthly magazine. m. ISSN 0034-6357

**Jugoslovenski Bibliografski Institut**
Terazije 26, Belgrade, Yugoslavia.
- Bibliografija Jugoslavije/Bibliography of Yugoslavia; clanci i prilozi u casopisima i listovima. s-m. ISSN 0006-114X
- Bibliografija Jugoslavije. Knjige, Brosure i Muzikalije. fortn. ISSN 0523-2201
- Bibliografija Jugoslavije. Serija A. Drustvene Nauke; clanci i prilozi u casopisima, listovima i zbornicima. bi-m. ISSN 0373-6369
- Bibliografija Jugoslavije. Serija B. Prirodne i Primenjene Nauke; clanci i prilozi u casopisima, listovima i zbornicima. m. ISSN 0523-218X
- Bibliografija Jugoslavije. Serija C. Umetnost, Sport, Filologija, Knjizevnost i Muzikalije; clanci i prilozi u casopisima, listovima i zbornicima. m. ISSN 0373-6377
- Bibliografija Jugoslovenske Periodike/Bibliography of Yugoslav Periodicals. q. ISSN 0006-1158

**Jugoslovenski Centar za Tehnicku i Naucnu Dokumentaciju**
Sl. Penezica-Krcuna 29-31, Box 724, 11000 Belgrade, Yugoslavia.
- Bilten Dokumentacije. Analiticka Hemija/Bulletin of Documentation. Analytical Chemistry. m. ISSN 0350-0101
- Bilten Dokumentacije. Biljna Proizvodnja/Bulletin of Documentation. Plant Production. m. ISSN 0006-257X
- Bilten Dokumentacije. Drzavni Organi. Drustvene Politicke Zajednice. Privreda. Drustvene Sluzbe. Pravo/Bulletin of Documentation. State Authorities. Social and Political Communities. Economy. Social Services. Law. m. ISSN 0350-0454
- Bilten Dokumentacije. Elektrotehnika/Bulletin of Documentation. Electrical Engineering. m. ISSN 0006-2588
- Bilten Dokumentacije. Goriva i Maziva/Bulletin of Documentation. Fuel Technology and Lubricants. m. ISSN 0006-2596
- Bilten Dokumentacije. Gradevinarstvo i Arhitektura/Bulletin of Documentation. Civil Engineering and Architecture. m. ISSN 0006-260X
- Bilten Dokumentacije. Hemija i Hemijska Industrija/Bulletin of Documentation. Chemistry and Chemical Industry. m. ISSN 0006-2618
- Bilten Dokumentacije. Industrija Tekstila i Papira/Bulletin of Documentation. Textile and Paper Industry. m. ISSN 0006-2626
- Bilten Dokumentacije. Informatika/Bulletin of Documentation. Informatics. m. ISSN 0350-0357
- Bilten Dokumentacije. Iskoriscenje Otpadaka/Bulletin of Documentation. Waste Utilization. m. ISSN 0350-0209
- Bilten Dokumentacije. Masinska Tehnologija i Radne Masine/Bulletin of Documentation. Mechanical Technology. m. ISSN 0006-2634
- Bilten Dokumentacije. Metalurgija/Bulletin of Documentation. Metallurgy. m. ISSN 0006-2642
- Bilten Dokumentacije. Otpadne Vode i Zagadjenje Vazduha/Bulletin of Documentation. Water and Air Pollution. m. ISSN 0350-0152
- Bilten Dokumentacije. Pogonske Masine i Masinski Delovi/Bulletin of Documentation. Power Engines and Machine Parts. m. ISSN 0006-2650
- Bilten Dokumentacije. Prehrambena Industrija/Bulletin of Documentation. Food Industry. m. ISSN 0006-2669
- Bilten Dokumentacije. Rudarstvo i Geologija/Bulletin of Documentation. Mining and Geology. m. ISSN 0006-2677
- Bilten Dokumentacije. Saobracaj/Bulletin of Documentation. Traffic. m. ISSN 0006-2685
- Bilten Dokumentacije. Savremena Organizacija i Ekonomika Radnih Organizacija/Bulletin of Documentation. Modern Organization and Business Management. m. ISSN 0303-223X
- Bilten Dokumentacije. Silikatna Industrija/Bulletin of Documentation. Glass, Ceramic and Refractory Industries. m. ISSN 0006-2693
- Bilten Dokumentacije. Stocna Proizvodnja i Veterinarstvo/Bulletin of Documentation. Stockbreeding. m. ISSN 0006-2707
- Bilten Dokumentacije. Sumarstvo i Drvna Industrija/Bulletin of Documentation. Forestry and Wood Industry. m. ISSN 0006-2715
- Bilten Dokumentacije. Zastita na Radu/Bulletin of Documentation. Safety Precautions. m. ISSN 0350-0306
- Bilten Dokumentacije. Zavarivanje/Bulletin of Documentation. Welding. m. ISSN 0350-0055

- Bilten Tehnickih Informacija Iz Oblasti Industrije Gume. m. ISSN 0350-025X
- Informatika. q. ISSN 0019-9923
- Naucni i Strucni Skupovi u Jugoslavii i u Inostranstvu/Scientific and Professional Meetings in Yugoslavia and Foreign Countries. s-a. ISSN 0350-011X
- O A P. Automatska Obrada Podataka. Bibliografija/Automatic Data Processing. Bibliography. m. ISSN 0350-0403

**Jugoslovenski Gradjevinski Centar**
Bulevar Revolucije 84, 11000 Belgrade, Yugoslavia.
- Dokumentacija za Gradevinarstvo i Arhitekturu. m. ISSN 0012-5024

**Jugoslovenski Komitet za Elektroniku i Telekomunikacije, Automatizaciju i Nuklearnu Tehniku (ETAN)**
Kneza Milosa 9, Belgrade, Yugoslavia.
- Science of Sintering. 3 per yr. (International Institute for the Science of Sintering) (Co-sponsor: Srpska Akademija Nauka i Umetnosti)

**Jugoslovenski Komitet za Elektroniku i Telekomunikacije, Automatizaciju i Nuklearnu Tehniku (ETAN) Savezni Strucni Odbor za Automatizaciju**
Unska 17, Zagreb, Yugoslavia.
- Automatika; journal of technical board for automation of the Yugoslav Committee ETAN. bi-m. ISSN 0572-2241

**Jugoslovenski Pregled**
Mose Pijade 8, Belgrade, Yugoslavia.
- Jugoslovenski Pregled; informativno-dokumentarne sveske. m. ISSN 0022-6114
- Yugoslav Survey; a record of facts and information. q. ISSN 0044-1341

**Jugoslovenski Zavod za Produktivnost Rada**
Uzum Mirkova 1, Belgrade, Yugoslavia.
- Produktivnost. m. ISSN 0032-9975

**Jugoslovensko Drustvo za Mehaniku**
Kneza Milosa 8, Belgrade, Yugoslavia.
- Teorijska i Primenjena Mehanika/Theoretical and Applied Mechanics. q.

**Jugoslovensko Entomolosko Drustvo**
Zagreb, Yugoslavia.
- Acta Entomologica Jugoslavica. s-a.

**Jugoslovensko Naucno Vocarsko Drustvo**
Vojvode Stepe 9, Cacak, Yugoslavia.
- Jugoslovensko Vocarstvo/Journal of Yugoslav Pomology. q. ISSN 0350-2155

**Jugoslovensko Udruzenje Matematickih i Fizickih Drustava. Komisija za Fiziku**
Gric 3, 41003 Zagreb, Yugoslavia.
- Fizika; a journal of experimental and theoretical physics. q. ISSN 0015-3206

**Jugoslovensko Udruzenje za Krivicno Pravo i Kriminologiju**
Gracanicka 18, 11000 Belgrade, Yugoslavia.
- Jugoslovenska Revija za Kriminologiju i Krivicno Pravo. q. ISSN 0022-6076

**Jugoslovensko Udruzenje za Marketing (JUMA)**
- Marketing. (pub. by Informator)

**Jugoslovensko Udruzenje za Medjunarodno Pravo**
Bulevar Revolucije 67, Belgrade, Yugoslavia.
- Jugoslovenska Revija za Medjunarodno Pravo. 3 per yr. ISSN 0022-6084

**Jugoslovensko Udruzenje za Sociologiju**
Studentski trg 1, 11000 Belgrade, Yugoslavia.
- Sociologija; casopis za sociologiju, socijalnu, psihologiju i socijalnu antropologiju. q. ISSN 0038-0318

**Jugosovenski Institut za Novinarstvo, Beograd**
Trg Republike 5, Box 541, Belgrade, Yugoslavia.
- Novinarstvo. q. ISSN 0029-5175

**Jugovinil**
Kastel Sucurac, Split, Yugoslavia.
- Jugovinil; list Poduzeca za proizvodnju plasticnih masa i kemijskih proizvoda. q. ISSN 0022-6149

**Karlovacki Tjednik**
Mihoviliceva 2, Karlovac, Yugoslavia.
- Karlovacki Tjednik. w. ISSN 0022-9059

**Katedra**
Ob Parku 5, Maribor, Yugoslavia.
- Katedra; studentski list. s-m. ISSN 0022-9296

**Kinoloski Savez SR Hrvatske**
Ilica 61, Zagreb, Yugoslavia.
- Moj Pas. m. ISSN 0026-8895

**Klinicka Bolnica "Dr. M. Stojanovic" u Zagrebu**
Vinogradska 29, 41000 Zagreb, Yugoslavia.
- Anali Klinicke Bolnice "Dr. M. Stojanovic". q.
ISSN 0301-2255

**Klinicka Bolnica "Dr. M. Stojanovic" u Zagrebu.
Klinika za Otorinolaringologiju i Cervikofacijalnu
Kirurgiju**
- Symposia Otorhinolaryngologica Iugoslavica. (pub.
by Zavod za Proucavanje i Zastitu Uha i Disnih
Organa)

**Kmecki Glas**
Miklosiceva 4-I, 61001 Ljubljana, Yugoslavia.
- Kmecki Glas. w. ISSN 0023-2238

**Knjizevne Novine**
Francuska 7, Belgrade, Yugoslavia.
- Knjizevne Novine; list za knjizevnost i kulturu.
fortn. ISSN 0023-2416

**Komisija za Ekonomsku Historiju Jugoslavije**
Strossmayerov trg 2, Zagreb, Yugoslavia.
- Acta Historico-Oeconomica Iugoslaviae; casopis
za ekonomsku istoriju jugoslavije. a.

**Komuna**
Brace Tatica 6, Kikinda, Yugoslavia.
- Komuna; list za drustvena i politicka pitanja. w.
ISSN 0023-1398

**Komunist**
Trg Marksa i Engelsa 11, 11000 Belgrade,
Yugoslavia.
- Komunist. w. ISSN 0023-320X (Savez Komunista
Jugoslavije)
- Questions Actuelles du Socialisme. q. ISSN 0033-
6351
- Socialist Thought and Practice. m.
- Socijalizam; casopis Saveza komunista Jugoslavije.
m. ISSN 0489-5967 (Savez Komunista
Jugoslavije)
- Yugoslav Information Bulletin. m.

**Konferencija za Drustvenu Aktivnost Zena
Jugoslavije**
Bulevar Lenjina No.6, Belgrade, Yugoslavia.
- Faits et Tendances; revue traitant des questions
sociales. 3 per yr. ISSN 0014-7052

**Krajina**
Marsala Tita 6, Bihac, Yugoslavia.
- Krajina. w. ISSN 0023-446X

**Krmiva**
Gunduliceva 45, Zagreb, Yugoslavia.
- Krmiva; mjesecnik za pitanje ishrane stoke i
proizvodnje stocne hrane. m. ISSN 0023-4850
(Poslovno Udruzenje Industrije Stocne Hrane)

**Kulturen Zivot**
Rabotnicki Dom 5, Box 85, 91001 Skopje,
Yugoslavia.
- Kulturen Zivot/Cultural Life; kultura, umetnost,
opstestveni prasanja. m. ISSN 0047-3731 (Co-
Sponsor: Kulturno-Prosvetna Zaednica na
Makedonija)
- Macedonian Review; history, culture, literature,
arts. 3 per yr. ISSN 0350-3089

**Kulturni Zivot**
Box 286, Belgrade, Yugoslavia.
- Kulturni Zivot. m. ISSN 0023-5261 (Zajednica
Kulturno-Prosvetnih Organizacija Jugoslavije)

**Kulturno-Prosvetna Zaednica na Makedonija**
Radnjanska 17, Skopje, Yugoslavia.
- Prosveta; vesnik za obrazovanie i kultura. bi-w.
ISSN 0033-1619

**Kulturno Prosvetna Zajednica Opstine Kraljevo**
Cara Dusana 36, Kraljevo, Yugoslavia.
- Oktobar; list za knjizevnost, umetnost i kulturu.
m. ISSN 0030-1949

**Kulturno Prosvetna Zajednica Opstine Pozarevac**
Pozarevac, Yugoslavia.
- Branicevo; casopis za knjizevna kulturna i
drustvena pitanja. s-m. ISSN 0006-9140

**Kulturno-Prosvjetna Zajednica Bosne i Hercegovine**
Hasana Kikica 12, Sarajevo, Yugoslavia.
- Odjek; revija za umjetnost nauku i drustvena
pitanja. fortn. ISSN 0029-8387

**Lek, Tovarna Farmacevtskih in Kemicnih Izdelkov**
Celovska Cesta 135, 61001 Ljubljana, Yugoslavia.
- Pro Medico. s-a. ISSN 0032-9088

**Libertatea**
Zarka Zrenjanina 7, Pancevo, Yugoslavia.
- Lumina.

**Lidhjes Se Rinise Se Kosoves**
- Zeri i Rinise. (pub. by Rilindja)

**Lovacka Knjiga**
V. Nazora 61, Zagreb, Yugoslavia.
- Lovacki Vjesnik. m. ISSN 0024-6999 (Lovacki
Savez Hrvatske)

**Lovacki Savez Hrvatske**
- Lovacki Vjesnik. (pub. by Lovacka Knjiga)

**Lovska Zveza Slovenije**
Zupanciceva 9, Ljubljana, Yugoslavia.
- Lovec. bi-m. ISSN 0024-7014

**Makedonska Akademija na Naukite i Umetnostite**
Lermontova 1, Box 428, Skopje, Yugoslavia.
- Makedonska Akademija na Naukite i Umetnostite.
Oddelenie za Opstestveni Nauki. Prilozi. irreg.
ISSN 0350-1698
- Makedonska Akademija na Naukite i Umetnostite.
Oddelenie za Prirodno-Matematicki Nauki.
Prilozi. irreg.

**Makedonsko Izdanie na Komunist**
Box 313, Skopje, Yugoslavia.
- Pogledi; spisanie za opstestveni prasanja. bi-m.
ISSN 0032-2245

**Marksisticki Centar, Titograd**
- Praksa. (pub. by Pobjeda)

**Matematicki Institut, Beograd**
Knez Mihailova 35/1, Belgrade, Yugoslavia.
- Matematicki Vesnik. 4 per yr. ISSN 0025-5165

**Matica Hrvatska**
Zagrebacka 1, Zadar, Yugoslavia.
- Zadarska Revija. bi-m. ISSN 0044-1589

**Matica Iseljenika Bosne i Hercegovine**
Omladinska 5, Sarajevo, Yugoslavia.
- Nas Svijet. m. ISSN 0027-8106

**Matica Iseljenika Hrvatske**
Trnjanska bb, Zagreb, Yugoslavia.
- Matica; list iseljenika Hrvatske. m. ISSN 0025-
5920

**Matica Srpska**
Matice Srpske 1, Novi Sad, Yugoslavia.
- Letopis Matice Srpske. m. ISSN 0025-5939
- Zbornik za Drustvene Nauke. a. ISSN 0044-1937
- Zbornik za Slavistiku/Review of Slavic Studies. s-
a. ISSN 0350-0470

**Matica Srpska. Odeljenje za Drustvene Nauke**
Matice Srpske 1, Novi Sad, Yugoslavia.
- Zbornik za Istoriju. 2 per yr.

**Medicinska Knjiga**
Mate Vidakovica 24, 11001 Belgrade, Yugoslavia.
- Acta Ophthalmologica Iugoslavica. 4 per yr. ISSN
0001-6403 (Udruzenje Oftalmologa Jugoslavije)
(Co-sponsor: Savez Lekarskih Drustava SFR
Jugoslavije)

**Medicinski Fakultet u Rijeci**
see Sveuciliste u Rijeci. Medicinski Fakultet

**Medjimurje**
Sajmiste 66, Cakovec, Yugoslavia.
- Medjimurje. w. ISSN 0025-8229

**Medjunarodna Politika**
Nemanjina 34, 11000 Belgrade, Yugoslavia.
- Diplomatic Corps of Belgrade. a. ISSN 0070-4946
- Medjunarodna Politika. fortn.
- Review of International Affairs. fortn. ISSN 0486-
6096

- Revue de Politique Internationale. fortn. ISSN
0035-1695

**Medjunarodni Slavisticki Centar SR Hrvatske**
Djure Salaja 3, Zagreb, Yugoslavia.
- Zbornik Zagrebacke Slavisticke Skole. irreg.

**Medjunarodni Slavisticki Centar SR Srbije**
Studetski trg 3/1, Belgrade, Yugoslavia.
- Naucni Sastanak Slavista u Vukove Dane. Referati
i Saopstenja. a.

**Medjurepublicka Zajednica Kulture Sava**
Borisa Kidrica 44, Sabac, Yugoslavia.
- Provincija. q.

**Mestni Muzej v Idrii**
Idrija, Yugoslavia.
- Idrijski Razgledi. q. ISSN 0019-1523

**Meteoroloski Zavod SR Slovenije. SAS za
Agrometeorologijo**
Ljubljana, Yugoslavia.
- Agrometeorolosko Porocilo. m.(Dec.-Feb.) 3 per
mo.(Mar.-Nov.) ISSN 0002-189X

**Mlado Pokolenje**
Proletarskih Brigada 8, Belgrade, Yugoslavia.
- Bilten Zavoda za Osnovno Obrazovanje i
Obrazovanje Nastavnika Sr Srbije. q. ISSN 0006-
2758

**Mladost**
Marsala Tita 2, Belgrade, Yugoslavia.
- Ideje; jugoslovenski studentski casopis. bi-m.
(Savez Socijalisticke Omladine Jugoslavije)
- Mladost. w. ISSN 0026-7031 (Savez Socijalisticke
Omladine Jugoslavije)

**Moderna Organizacija**
Tomsiceva 7, 64001 Kranj, Yugoslavia.
- Organizacija in Kadri. m. ISSN 0350-1531

**Muzejsko Drustvo Hrvatske**
Savska Cesta 18, 41000 Zabreb, Yugoslavia.
- Vijesti Muzealaca i Konzervatora Hrvatske. bi-m.
ISSN 0042-6083 (Co-sponsor: Drustvo
Konzervatora Jugoslavije)

**Muzicka Akademija u Zagrebu. Muzikoloski Zavod**
Gunduliceva 6, 41001 Zagreb, Yugoslavia.
- Arti Musices/Musicological Yearbook. a. ISSN
0587-5455

**Muzicka Omladina Osijek**
Bulevar JNA, Osijek, Yugoslavia.
- Muzicka Omladina; list Osnovne zajednice
Muzicke omladine Osijek. m. ISSN 0027-5271

**Nacionalna i Sveucilisna Biblioteka**
Marulicev trg 21, Zagreb, Yugoslavia.
- Vjesnik Bibliotekara Hrvatske. q. (Hrvatsko
Bibliotekarsko Drustvo)

**Nadbiskupija Splitsko-Makarska**
Zrinsko-Frankopanska 14, 58001 Split, Yugoslavia.
- Crkva u Svijetu. q.
- Vjesnik Nadbiskupije Splitsko-Makarske. bi-m.
ISSN 0042-7659

**Nadbiskupski Ordinarijat u Beogradu**
Svetozara Markovica 20, 11000 Belgrade,
Yugoslavia.
- Blagovest; verski mesecnik. m. ISSN 0006-4505

**Napred**
Vojvode Misica 21, Valjevo, Yugoslavia.
- Napred; list za politicka i drustvena pitanja. w.
ISSN 0027-7843 (Socijalisticki Savez Radnog
Naroda Opstine Valjevskog Sreza)

- Pingrin; nedeljni ilustrovani zabavnik. w. ISSN
0031-9880

**Narodna Armija**
Mose Pijade 29, Belgrade, Yugoslavia.
- Front. w. ISSN 0016-2027
- Narodna Armija; list jugoslavenske narodne
armije. w. ISSN 0027-7908

**Narodna Banka Jugoslavije**
Bulevar Revolucije 15, Box 1010, 11001 Belgrade,
Yugoslavia.
- National Bank of Yugoslavia. Annual Report. a.
ISSN 0077-2798

- National Bank of Yugoslavia. Quarterly Bulletin. q.

**Narodna Biblioteka Srbije**
Skerliceva 1, 11000 Belgrade, Yugoslavia.
- Bibliografija Prinovljenih Domacih Publikacija. bi-m.

**Narodna in Univerzitetna Knjiznica**
Turjaska 1, 61001 Ljubljana, Yugoslavia.
- Narodna in Univerzitetna Knjiznica, Ljubljana. Zbornik. irreg.
- Obvestila Republiske Maticne Knjiznice. irreg.
- Slovenska Bibliografija. a.

**Narodne Novine, Nis**
Balkanska 2, Nis, Yugoslavia.
- Glas Omladine; list mladih. bi-w. ISSN 0017-0798
- Narodne Novine; list za drustvena i politicka pitanja. w. ISSN 0027-7932 (Subscr. to: "Mladost" Export Import, Ilica 30, 41000 Zagreb, Yugoslavia)

**Narodne Novine, Zagreb**
Ratkajev Prolaz 4, Zagreb, Yugoslavia.
- Pregled Sudske Prakse. irreg. (Croatia. Vrhovni Sud) (Co-sponsors: Croatia. Ustavni Sud; Visi Privredni Sud u Zagrebu)
- Vjesnik Rada; casopis za pitanja rada, radnih odnosa, zaposljavanja i socijalnog osiguranja. m. ISSN 0042-7632

**Narodni List**
Lenjinovo Setaliste 4, Zadar, Yugoslavia.
- Narodni List. w. ISSN 0027-7975

**Narodno Pozoriste**
Tuzla, Yugoslavia.
- Pozoriste; casopis za pozorisnu umjetnost. bi-m. ISSN 0032-616X

**Narodno Sveuciliste "Bozidar Maslaric". Centar za Kulturu i Umjetnost**
Vukovarska 31, Osijek 54000, Yugoslavia.
- Revija; casopis za knjizevnost, kulturu i drustvena pitanja. bi-m. ISSN 0034-6888

**Narodno Sveuciliste Juraj Kokot**
Zagrebacka 37, Velika Gorica, Yugoslavia.
- Velikogoricki List. fortn. ISSN 0042-322X

**Nasa Knjiga, Skopje**
Partizanski Odredi 17, 91000 Skopje, Yugoslavia.
- Tribina; vesnik za selo vo SR Makedonija. w. ISSN 0041-266X

**Nasa Rec, Leskovac**
Masarikov trg 7, Leskovac, Yugoslavia.
- Nasa Rec. w. ISSN 0027-8122 (Socijalisticki Savez Leskovacke Opstine)

**Nasa Rijec**
Fadila Jahica Spanca 8, Zenica, Yugoslavia.
- Nasa Rijec; list za drustvena i politicka pitanja. w. ISSN 0027-8130

**Naucno Delo**
Vuka Karadzica 5, Belgrade, Yugoslavia.
- Academie Serbe des Sciences et des Arts. Bulletin. Classe des Sciences Mathematiques et Naturelles. Nouvelle Serie. ISSN 0001-4184 (Srpska Akademija Nauka i Umetnosti. Odeljenje Prirodno-Matematickih Nauka)

**Naucno Drustvo za Istoriju Zdravstvene Kulture Jugoslavije**
Fruskogorska 47, Novi Sad, Yugoslavia.
- Acta Historica Medicinae, Pharmaciae, Veterinae. q' ISSN 0001-5865

**Nedeljne Novine**
Trg Bratstva i Jedinstva 32, Backa Palanka, Yugoslavia.
- Nedeljne Novine. w. ISSN 0028-1980 (Socijalisticki Savez Radnog Naroda Backa Palanka)

**Neuroloski-Psihijatrijska Klinika Rebro, Zagreb**
Rebro, Zagreb, Yugoslavia.
- Neuropsihijatrija; casopis za neurologiju, psihijatriju i granicna podrucja. q. ISSN 0047-9438 (Udruzenje Neurologa i Psihijatara Jugoslavije)

**Nolit**
Terazije 31, Belgrade, Yugoslavia.
- Delo; mesecni knjizevni casopis. m. ISSN 0011-7935

**Nova Makedonija**
Bulevar Jugoslovenske Narodne Armije 68, Skopje, Yugoslavia, Skopje, Yugoslavia.
- Drugarce. s-m. ISSN 0012-6632
- Osten; satiricno-humoristicen vesnik. fortn. ISSN 0030-6363

**Novinsko Informativna Ustanova u Osnivanju**
Seste Licke Divizije 3, Gospic, Yugoslavia.
- Licke Novine. fortn. ISSN 0024-2888 (Socijalisticki Savez Radnog Naroda Zajednice Opcina Gospic)

**Obzor**
Novi Sad, Yugoslavia.
- Hlas l'Udu. w. ISSN 0018-2869 (Socijalisticki Svaz Pracujucich Vojvodiny Pre Slovakov)

**Ogranomatik**
Insitut za Organizacija Rada i Automatizaciju Poslovanja, Milana Rakica 35, Box 999, Belgrade, Yugoslavia.
- Industrijska Istrazivanja; casopis za pitanja primene metoda operacionih i drugih istrazivanja. 6 per yr. ISSN 0019-9419

**Onkoloski Institut**
Register Raka za Slovenijo, Zaloska 2, 61000 Ljubljana, Yugoslavia.
- Rak v Sloveniji. Tabele/Cancer in Slovenia. Tables. a. ISSN 0079-9580

**Opca Bolnica "Dr. Josip Kajfes"**
Miskine 64, Zagreb, Yugoslavia.
- Bibliografija Medicinske Periodike Jugoslavije/ Index Medicus Iugoslavicus. a. ISSN 0067-6799

**Opstestveno Politickite Organizacii na SR Makedonija**
Ilinldenska 66, Skopje, Yugoslavia.
- Opstestveno Politickite Organizacii na SR Makedonija. Bilten. m.

**Opstinska Konferencija Muzicke Omladine**
AVNOJ-a 5, Bihac, Yugoslavia.
- Lira. m. ISSN 0024-4244

**Opstinska Zajednica Kulture Subotica**
Gradska kuca 2, Subotica, Yugoslavia.
- Rukovet; casopis za knjizevnost, umetnost i drustvena pitanja. bi-m. ISSN 0035-9793

**Oslobodjenje**
Marsala Tita 13, Sarajevo, Yugoslavia.
- Privredne Novine. w.

**Pancevac**
Zarka Zrenjanina 7, Pancevo, Yugoslavia.
- Pancevac. w. ISSN 0031-0662

**Pavliha**
Gradisce 4, Ljubljana, Yugoslavia.
- Antena. w. ISSN 0003-536X
- Karavana. q. ISSN 0047-3219
- Pavliha. w. ISSN 0031-3289

**Pcelarski Savez SR Hrvatske**
Heinzelova 55, Zagreb, Yugoslavia.
- Pcela. m. ISSN 0031-3416 (Co-sponsor: Savez Pcelara SR Bosne i Hercegovine)

**Pedagoska Akademija, Split**
Zrtava Fasizma 6, Box 118, Split, Yugoslavia.
- Skolski Vjesnik; casopis za pedagoska i prosvjetna pitanja. q. ISSN 0037-654X

**Pedagoska Akademija u Gospicu**
Marka Oreskovica 24/2, Gospic, Yugoslavia.
- Dostignuca; casopis za skolstvo, prosvjetu i kultura. irreg. ISSN 0012-5636

**Pedagosko Drustvo SR Hrvatske**
Trg Marsala Tita 4, Zagreb, Yugoslavia.
- Pedagoski Rad. bi-m. ISSN 0031-384X

**Pedagosko Drustvo SR Srbije**
Terazije 26, Belgrade, Yugoslavia.
- Nastava i Vaspitanje. 6 per yr.

**Planinarski Savez Hrvatske**
Kozarceva 22, 41000 Zagreb, Yugoslavia.
- Nase Planine. bi-m. ISSN 0027-819X

**Pobeda**
Trg Marsala Tita 66, Krusevac, Yugoslavia.
- Pobeda. w. ISSN 0032-1796

**Pobjeda**
Bulevar Revolucije, 81000 Titograd, Yugoslavia.
- Praksa; casopis za drustvena pitanja. bi-m. ISSN 0032-6704 (Marksisticki Centar, Titograd)

**Polimlje**
Vladimira Perica Valtera 50, Prijepolje, Yugoslavia.
- Polimlje; list za politicka i drustvena pitanja. w. ISSN 0032-2733

**Politika**
Makedonska 29, Belgrade, Yugoslavia.
- Ilustrovana Politika. w. ISSN 0019-2570
- N I N/Nedeljne Informativne Novine. w. ISSN 0027-6685
- Politika-Ekspres; nedeljna revija. w. ISSN 0032-3381
- Politikin Zabavnik. w. ISSN 0032-339X
- Tempo; ilustrovani nedelnji sportski list. w. ISSN 0040-3024

**Poslovna Politika**
c/o Hotel Jugoslavija, 11181 Belgrade, Yugoslavia.
- Poslovna Politika; Jugoslovenski casopis za upravljanje sistemom poslovanja. m.

**Poslovno Udruzenje Industrije Stocne Hrane**
- Krmiva. (pub. by Krmiva)

**Poslovno Udruzenje Proizvodaca Mineralnih Dubriva**
Nemanjina 7, Belgrade-Zemun, Yugoslavia.
- Agrohemija; casopis za hemizaciju poljoprivrede i sumarstva. bi-m. ISSN 0002-1865 (Co-Sponsor: Jugoslovensko Drustvo za Proucavanje Zemljista)

**Poslovno Udruzenje Ribarske Privrede**
Nehajska 15.3, Zagreb, Yugoslavia.
- Morsko Ribarstvo/Maxime Fisheries; jugoslavenski strucno-popularni casopis za pitanja ribarske privrede na moru. q. ISSN 0027-1209

**Pravoslavni Bogoslovski Fakultet u Beogradu**
7 Jula 2, Belgrade, Yugoslavia, Yugoslavia.
- Bogoslovlje. s-a. ISSN 0006-5714

**Preduzece za Proizvodnju i Montazu Aluminijumskih i Celicnih Konstrukcija**
Francuska 52, Belgrade, Yugoslavia.
- Beograd. m.

**Presernova Druzba**
Borsetova 27, Ljubljana, Yugoslavia.
- Obzornik; mesecna lujdska revija Presernove druzbe. m. ISSN 0029-7860

**Prirodnjacki Muzej u Beogradu**
Njegoseva 51, Belgrade, Yugoslavia.
- Prirodnjacki Muzej u Beogradu. Glasnik. Serija A: Mineralogija, Geologija, Paleontologija. irreg. ISSN 0367-4983
- Prirodnjacki Muzej u Beogradu. Glasnik. Serija B: Bioloske Nauke. irreg. ISSN 0373-2134
- Prirodnjacki Muzej u Beogradu. Glasnik. Serija C: Sumarstvo i Lov. irreg.

**Prirodonaucen Muzej na Makedonija**
Bulevar Ilinden bb, 91000 Skopje, Yugoslavia.
- Fragmenta Balcanica Musei Macedonici Scientiarum Naturalium. 5-9 per yr. ISSN 0015-9298

**Prirodoslovno Drustvo Slovenije**
Novi trg 4, Ljubljana, Yugoslavia, Yugoslavia.
- Proteus; ilustriran casopis za poljudno prirodoznanstvo. m. ISSN 0033-1805

**Privredni Pregled**
Marsala Birjuzova 3, 11000 Belgrade, Yugoslavia.
- Direktor; casopis za teoriju i praksu rukovodjenja i upravljanja. m.
- Economic Review. m. ISSN 0013-0303
- Finansije. m. ISSN 0015-2145
- Glasnik Poljoprivredne Proizvodnje, Prerade i Plasmana. m. ISSN 0017-0976
- Nova Trgovina. m. ISSN 0469-0281
- Prosvetni Pregled; list prosvetnih, naucnih i kulturnih radnika SR Srbije. w. ISSN 0033-1651
- Yugoslavia; Hotel and Tourist Directory. irreg.

**Privredni Vjesnik**
Rooseveltov Trg 2, Box 631, Zagreb, Yugoslavia.
- A B C Privrede Jugoslavije. irreg.
- Privredni Vjesnik; drustveno-ekonomski tjednik. w. ISSN 0032-8995
- U T; jugoslavenska revija za ugostiteljstvo i turizam. m. ISSN 0041-557X

**Progres**
Stevana Sremca 13, Novi Sad, Yugoslavia.
• Panorama. w. ISSN 0031-0883

**Prosveta**
Dobracina 30, Belgrade, Yugoslavia
(Subscr. to: Strahinjica Bana 9/111, Box 555,
Belgrade, Yugoslavia)
• Knjizevnost. m. ISSN 0023-2408

**Prosveten Rabotnik**
Rabotnicki Dom II/VIII, Soba 185, Skopje,
Yugoslavia.
• Prosveten Rabotnik. fortn. ISSN 0033-1635

**Prosveteno Delo**
Mito Hadzi Vasiljev, Baraka Jasmin, Skopje,
Yugoslvaia.
• Prosveten Glasnik. bi-m. ISSN 0033-1627 (Savetot
za Prosveta na SR Makedonija) (Co-sponsor:
Savetot za Kultura na SR Makedonija)

**Prosvetno-Pedagoski Zavod Zrenjanin**
Ul. Dr. M. Tirsa 2, Zrenjanin, Yugoslavia.
• Pedagoski Zivot; bilten Prosvetno pedagoskog
zavoda zrenjanin. 3 per yr. ISSN 0031-3858

**Prosvjetni Sabor Hrvatske**
Socijalisticke Revolucije 17, Box 437, Zagreb,
Yugoslavia.
• Kulturni Radnik. bi-m. ISSN 0023-5253

**Prosvjetno Pedagoski Zavod Mostar**
Ante Zuanica 14, Mostar, Yugoslavia.
• Skola Danas. q. ISSN 0037-6450

**Ptujski Tednik**
Vosnjakova 5, Ptuj, Yugoslavia.
• Uradni Vestnik Obcin Ormoz in Ptuj. m. ISSN
0042-0778

**Radiotelevizija Zagreb**
Cvjetna cesta 66, Zagreb, Yugoslavia.
• Skolska Televizija. 4 per yr. ISSN 0037-6523

**Radnicko Sveuciliste "Mosa Pijade"**
Proletarskih Brigada 68, Zagreb, Yugoslavia.
• Informativni Bilten Radnickog Sveucilista "Mosa
Pijade". m. ISSN 0020-0638
• Petnaest Dana/Fifteen Days; casopis za kulturu i
umjetnost. m. ISSN 0031-6296

**Rafinerija Nafte, Sisak**
Sisak, Yugoslavia.
• Rafinerijski List. fortn.

**Razgledi**
Ul. Ivo Ribar-Lola 66, Box 345, 91000 Skopje,
Yugoslavia.
• Razgledi; spisanie za literatura, umetnost i kultura.
m. ISSN 0034-0227

**Rec Naroda**
Lenjinova 4, Pozarevac, Yugoslavia.
• Rec Naroda; list za drustvena i politicka pitanja.
w. ISSN 0034-1142 (Socijalisticki Savez Radnog
Naroda Opstine Pozarevac)

**Republicki Zavod za Zastitu Spomenika Kulture**
Bozidara Adzije 11, Belgrade, Yugoslavia.
• Zbornik Zastite Spomenika Kulture/Recueil des
Travaux sur la Protection des Monuments
Historiques. irreg.

**Rilindja**
Rruga Beogradi 29a, Prishtine, Yugoslavia.
• Zeri i Rinise. w. ISSN 0514-7352 (Lidhjes Se
Rinise Se Kosoves)

**Rudarski Institut, Belgrade**
Batajnicki Put 2, Belgrade, Yugoslavia.
• Rudarski Glasnik/Bulletin of Mines. q. ISSN
0035-9637

**Rudarski Institut, Ljubljana**
Askerceva 20, Box 594, 61001 Ljubljana,
Yugoslavia.
• Rudarsko-Metalurski Zbornik/Mining and
Metallurgy Quarterly. q. ISSN 0035-9645 (Co-
sponsor: Univerza V Ljubljani. Fakulteta za
Naravoslovje in Tehnologijo)

**Sarajevska Armijska Oblast**
Box 01-25, Sarajevo, Yugoslavia.
• Narodni Borac; list Sarajevske armijske oblasti.
fortn. ISSN 0027-7959

**Savetot za Prosveta na SR Makedonija**
• Prosveten Glasnik. (pub. by Prosveteno Delo)

**Savez Arheoloskih Drustava Jugoslavije**
Cara Urosa 20, Belgrade, Yugoslavia.
• Balcanoslavica. s-a. ISSN 0350-0179

**Savez Arhitekata Hrvatske**
Trg Republike 3/I, 41000 Zagreb, Yugoslavia.
• Arhitektura; arhitektura, urbanizam, dizajn. q.
• Covjek i Prostor; arhitektura, kiparstvo, slikarstvo
i primijenjena umjetnost. m. ISSN 0011-0728

**Savez Drustava Arhivskih Radnika Jugoslavije**
Karnedzijeva 2, Belgrade, Yugoslavia.
• Arhivist. s-a. ISSN 0350-2856 (Co-sponsor: Savez
Drustava Arhivskih Radnika Jugoslavije i Arhiva
u Jugoslavii)

**Savez Drustava Defektologa Jugoslavije**
Kosovska 8, Belgrade, Yugoslavia.
• Specijalna Skola. bi-m. ISSN 0038-6936

**Savez Drustava Istoricara Jugoslavije**
Karnedzijeva 2, Box 545, Belgrade, Yugoslavia.
• Jugoslovenski Istorijski Casopis. q.

**Savez Drustava Pravnika Hrvatske**
Savska 41, Zagreb, Yugoslavia
• Nasa Zakonitost. m. ISSN 0027-8165 (Co-
Sponsors: Udruzenje za Upravne Znanosti i
Praksu Hrvatske; Republicki Zavod za Javnu
Upravu SR Hrvatske) (Subscr. to: "Mladost"
Export Import, Ilica 30, 41000 Zagreb,
Yugoslavia)

**Savez Drustava Psihologa SFR Jugoslavije**
Salajeva 8, Zagreb, Yugoslavia.
• Revija za Psihologiju; casopis Saveza drustava
psihologa SFR Jugoslavije. s-a. (Co-sponsor:
Filozofski Fakultet u Zagrebu, Odsjek za
Psihologiju)

**Savez Drustava za Strane Jezike i Knjizevnosti SFRJ**
Knez Mihajlova 35, Belgrade, Yugoslavia.
• Filoloski Pregled. q. ISSN 0015-1807

**Savez Drustava za Tehniku Zavarivanja Jugoslavije**
• Zavarivanje. (pub. by Drustvo za Tehniku
Zavarivanja Hrvatske)

**Savez Ekonomista Bosne i Herzegovine**
Trg Oslobodenja 1, Sarajevo, Yugoslavia.
• Ekonomski Glasnik. q. ISSN 0013-3272

**Savez Ekonomista Hrvatske**
Berislaviceva 6, Zagreb, Yugoslavia.
• Ekonomski Pregled. m.

**Savez Ekonomista Jugoslavije**
• Ekonomist. (pub. by Informator)

**Savez Ekonomista Srbije**
Marsala Tita 16, Belgrade, Yugoslavia.
• Ekonomika Udruzenog Rada. m.
• Ekonomska Misao. q. ISSN 0013-323X

**Savez Ekonomista Vojvodine**
Bulevar Marsala Tita 9-4, 21000 Novi Sad,
Yugoslavia.
• Privredna Izgradnja. q. ISSN 0032-8979

**Savez Elektrotehnickih Inzenjera i Tehnicara
Hrvatske**
Berislaviceva 6/I, Zagreb, Yugoslavia.
• Elektrotehnika. 6 per yr. ISSN 0013-5844

**Savez Energeticara SR Hrvatske**
Ilica 34-1, Zagreb, Yugoslavia.
• Energeticar. q.

**Savez Farmaceutskih Drustava Jugoslavije**
Trg Marsala Tita 3, 41000 Zagreb, Yugoslavia.
• Acta Pharmaceutica Jugoslavica. q. ISSN 0001-
6667

**Savez Geodetskih Inzenjera i Geometara S F R J**
• Geodetski List. (pub. by Savez Geodetskih
Inzenjera i Geometara SR Hrvatske)

**Savez Geodetskih Inzenjera i Geometara SR
Hrvatske**
Berislaviceva 6, Zagreb, Yugoslavia.
• Geodetski List. m. ISSN 0016-710X (Savez
Geodetskih Inzenjera i Geometara S F R J)
• Savez Geodetskih Inzenjera i Geometara
Hrvatske. Obavijesti. 2-3 per yr. ISSN 0029-7461

**Savez Gluvih i Nagluvih Jugoslavije**
Svetog Save 16-18, Belgrade, Yugoslavia.
• Nas Glas. m. ISSN 0027-8076

**Savez Gradjevinskih Inzenjera i Tehnicara SR Srbije**
Kneza Milosa 7-11, Belgrade, Yugoslavia.
• Izgradnja. m. (Co-sponsors: Savez Drustava
Arhitekata SR Srbije; Savet za Gradjevinarstvo
Privredne Komore SR Srbije)

**Savez Hemicara i Tehnologa Jugoslavije**
Kneza Milosa 9, Box 648, 11000 Belgrade,
Yugoslavia.
• Hemijska Industrija/Chemical Industry. m. ISSN
0367-598X
• Industrija Secera. m.

**Savez Inzenjera i Tehnicara Jugoslavije**
Kneza Milosa 9, Box 187, 11000 Belgrade,
Yugoslavia.
• I T Novine. w. ISSN 0019-0837
• Masinstvo. m. ISSN 0461-2531
• Nase Gradevinarstvo. m.
• Rudarstvo - Geologija - Metalurgija. m.
• Tehnika. m. ISSN 0040-2176

**Savez Inzenjera i Tehnicara Sumarstva i Industrije za
Preradu Drveta SR BiH**
M. Tita 5, Sarajevo, Yugoslavia, Yugoslavia.
• Narodni Sumar; strucni casopis za sumarstvo i
industriju za preradu drveta. bi-m. ISSN 0027-
7983

**Savez Inzenjera i Tehnicara Tekstilaca SR Srbije**
Kneza Milosa 7/II, 11000 Belgrade, Yugoslavia.
• Tekstilna Industrija. m. ISSN 0040-2389

**Savez Jevrejskih Opstina Jugoslavije**
7. Jula 71a, Belgrade, Yugoslavia, Yugoslavia.
• Jevrejski Pregled. m. ISSN 0021-6240
• Kadima. m. ISSN 0022-748X (Federation of
Jewish Communities in Yugoslavia)

**Savez Kemicara i Tehnologa Hrvatske**
Berislaviceva 6/1, Box 697, 41001 Zagreb,
Yugoslavia.
• Kemija u Industriji; casopis kemicara i tehnologa
Jugoslavije. m. ISSN 0022-9830

**Savez Kompozitora Jugoslavije**
Radiceva 15/3, Sarajevo, Yugoslavia.
• Zvuk; Jugoslovenska muzicka revija. q. ISSN
0044-555X

**Savez Komunista Jugoslavije**
• Komunist. (pub. by Komunist)
• Socijalizam. (pub. by Komunist)

**Savez Lekarskih Drustava SFR Jugoslavije**
Zeleni Venac 1/I, Belgrade, Yugoslavia.
• Medicinski Glasnik. m. ISSN 0025-8091

**Savez Novinara Jugoslavije**
Trg Republike 5, Belgrade, Yugoslavia.
• Nasa Stampa. m. ISSN 0027-8149

**Savez Omladine Gimnazije, Vladimir Vitasovic"**
Kuslanova 52, Zagreb, Yugoslavia.
• Mi Mladi. q. ISSN 0026-1939

**Savez Omladine Hrvatske**
Dezmanova C, Zagreb, Yugoslavia.
• Polet; mjesecnik mladih za kulturu, umjetnost i
drustvena pitanja. m. ISSN 0032-2520

**Savez Omladine Vojvodine**
Pokrajinski Komitet, Novi Bulevar B.B., Novi Sad,
Yugoslavia.
• Savez Omladine. m. ISSN 0036-5092

**Savez Organizacija za Socijalisticko Vaspitanje i
Brigu o Djeci Bosne i Hercegovine**
JNA 28/I, Sarajevo, Yugoslavia.
• Porodica i Dijete. m. ISSN 0032-4787

**Savez Organizacija za Tehnicku Kulturu Jugoslavije**
• Tehnicke Novine. (pub. by Tehnicka Knjiga,
Belgrade)

**Savez Pedagoskih Drustava Jugoslavije**
Mose Pijade 12, Box 331, 11001 Belgrade,
Yugoslavia.
• Pedagogija; casopis Saveza pedagoskih drustava. q.
ISSN 0031-3807

**Savez Poljoprivrednih Inzenjera i Tehnicara Hrvatske**
Berislaviceva 6, Zagreb, Yugoslavia.
• Agronomski Glasnik. m. ISSN 0002-1954

**Savez Poljoprivrednih Inzenjera i Tehnicara Jugoslavije**
Kneza Milosa 9-13/I, Belgrade, Yugoslavia.
- Arhiv za Poljoprivredne Nauke. bi-m. ISSN 0004-1262
- Ekonomika Proizvodnje Hrane. m.

**Savez Radio-Amatera Jugoslavije**
- Radio-Amater. (pub. by Tehnicka Knjiga, Belgrade)

**Savez Rezervnih Vojnih Staresina Beograda**
Trg Bratstva i Jedinstva 9, Belgrade, Yugoslavia.
- Odbrana. bi-m. ISSN 0029-8336

**Savez Sindikata Jugoslavije**
Trg Marksa i Engelsa 5, 11000 Belgrade, Yugoslavia.
- Rad. w. ISSN 0033-7463
- Yugoslav Trade Unions. bi-m. ISSN 0044-135X
- Yugoslavskie Profsoyuzy; gazeta Soyuza profsoyuzov Yugoslavii. bi-m. ISSN 0022-6041

**Savez Sindikata Jugoslavije. Sluzba za Informacije i Dokumentaciju**
Trg Marksa i Engelsa 5, Belgrade, Yugoslavia.
- Savez Sindikata Jugoslavije. Centralni Vec. Bilten. m. ISSN 0006-2561

**Savez Socijalisticke Omladine Bosne i Hercegovine**
Marsala Tita 44, Sarajevo, Yugoslavia.
- Nasi Dani. w. ISSN 0027-8262

**Savez Socijalisticke Omladine Crne Gore**
Novaka Miloseva 12, Titograd, Yugoslavia.
- Omladinski Pokret. m.

**Savez Socijalisticke Omladine Hrvatske, Zagreb. Centar Drustvenih Djelatnosti**
Opaticka 10, 41001 Zagreb, Yugoslavia.
- Pitanja; mjesecnik: drustvo, znanost, kultura. m.

**Savez Socijalisticke Omladine Hrvatske, Zagreb. Sveucilisna Konferencija**
Trg zrtava fasizma 13, 41001 Zagreb, Yugoslavia.
- SL. (Studentski List) w. ISSN 0039-288X

**Savez Socijalisticke Omladine Jugoslavije**
- Ideje. (pub. by Mladost)
- Mladost. (pub. by Mladost)

**Savez Socijalisticke Omladine Vojvodine. Pokrajinska Konferencija**
- Polja. (pub. by Tribuna Mladih)

**Savez Sportskih Ribolovnih Drustava SR Hrvatske**
Palmoticeva 7/1, Zagreb, Yugoslavia.
- Ribolov; casopis za unapredenje ribolovnog sporta i turizma. bi-m.

**Savez Sportskih Ribovolovaca Bosne i Hercegovine**
Pere Kosarica 10, Sarajevo, Yugoslavia.
- Ribarski List. q. ISSN 0035-4953

**Savez Strojarskih i Brodogradjevnih Inzenjera i Tehnicara Hrvatske**
- Strojarstvo. (pub. by Izdavacki Savjet Casopisa Strojarstvo)

**Savez Studenata Beograda**
Balkanska 4, Belgrade, Yugoslavia.
- Student; list beogradskih studenata. w. ISSN 0039-2693

**Savez Studenata Jugoslavije**
c/o Beogradski Univerzitet, Univerzitetski Odbor Saveza Studenata Jugoslavije, Knez Mihajlova 40/4, Belgrade, Yugoslavia.
- Vidici; knjizevnost, film, likovne umetnosti, filozofija, pozoriste, muzika, arhitektura. m. ISSN 0042-529X

**Savez Studenata Medicinskih Fakulteta u Zagrebu i Rijeci**
Salata 3, Zagreb, Yugoslavia.
- Medicinar; strucni casopis Saveza studenata. bi-m. ISSN 0025-7966 (Co-Sponsor: Stomatoloski Fakultet u Zagrebu)

**Savez Udruzenja Borca Narodno Oslobodilacgot Rata. Opcinski Odbor Dalmacije**
Livanjska 5, Split, Yugoslavia.
- Poruka Borca. 7 per yr. ISSN 0032-5171

**Savez Udruzenja Folklorista Jugoslavije**
Kneza Mihaila 35, Belgrade, Yugoslavia.
- Narodno Stvaralastvo - Folklor. q. ISSN 0027-8017

**Savez Udruzenja Pravnikov Jugoslavije**
Proleterskih Brigada 74, Box 179, Belgrade, Yugoslavia.
- Arhiv za Pravne i Drustvene Nauke. q. ISSN 0004-1270

**Savez Udruzenog Pravoslavnog Svestenstva SFRJ**
Francuska 31-1, Belgrade, Yugoslavia.
- Pravoslavna Misae. s-a. ISSN 0032-700X

**Savez Veterinara i Veterinarskih Tehnicara SFRJ. Odbor za Izdavacku Delatnost**
Bulevar JNA 18, Belgrade, Yugoslavia.
- Peradarstvo; casopis za problematiku peradarske proizvodnje. m. ISSN 0031-6792

**Savez Zeleznicara Esperantista Jugoslavije**
Mihanoviceva 12, Zagreb, Yugoslavia.
- Jugoslavia Pervojisto. bi-m. ISSN 0022-6025

**Savezni Zavod za Zdravstvenu Zastitu, Belgrade**
Slobodana Penezica-Krcuna 35, Belgrade, Yugoslavia.
- Narodno Zdravlje/Yugoslav Journal of Public Health. m. ISSN 0027-8025

**Savjet Organizacija za Pomoc Mentalno Retardiranim Osobama u SFRJ**
Prilaz JNA 43/Iii, Zagreb, Yugoslavia.
- Pregled Problema Mentalno Retardiranih Osoba. bi-m. ISSN 0032-7298

**Savremena Praksa**
Knez Mihajlova 6, Belgrade, Yugoslavia.
- Ekonomski Anali. q. ISSN 0013-3264 (Ekonomski Fakultet u Beogradu)
- Savremena Praksa; list za privredna i pravna pitanja radnih organizacija. w. ISSN 0036-5173

**Serbia. Republicki Zavod za Unapredjivanje Vaspitanja i Obrazovanja SR Srbije**
Nemanjina 24/V, Box 45-29, 11124 Belgrade, Yugoslavia.
- Aktuelnosti u Vaspitanju i Obrazovanju. 10 per yr.
- Revija Skolstva i Prosvetna Dokumentacija. q. ISSN 0034-6896

**Serbia. Zavod za Statistiku**
Milana Rakica 5, Belgrade, Yugoslavia.
- Mesecni Statisticki Pregled. m.

**Sindikat Delavcev Vzgoje in Izobrazevanja SRS**
Poljanska 6, Ljubljana, Yugoslavia.
- Prosvetni Delavec; list delavcev v vzgojnoizobrazevalnih zavodih. bi-w. ISSN 0033-1643

**Sindikat Radnika Drustvenih Djelatnosti Crne Gore**
Novaka Miloseva 9a, Box 253, Titograd, Yugoslavia.
- Prosvjetni Rad; list prosvjetnih i naucnih radnika socijalisticke republike Crne Gore. bi-w. ISSN 0033-1686

**Sindikat Radnika Drustvenih Djelatnosti SR Bosne i Hercegovine**
Dure Dakovica 4, Sarajevo, Yugoslavia.
- Prosvjetni List. fortn. ISSN 0033-1678

**Skola za Obrazovanje Kvalifikovanih Radnika SR Srbije**
Kralja Milutina 66, Box 558, Belgrade, Yugoslavia.
- Nasa Strucna Skola. m. ISSN 0027-8157 (Co-sponsor: Savez Pedagoskih Drustava Jugoslavije)

**Skolska Knjiga**
Masarykova 28, Zagreb, Yugoslavia.
- Savremena Metodika Nastave Hrvatskog ili Srpskog Jezika. q.

**Skolske Novine**
Trg Marsala Tita 4, Box 785, 41000 Zagreb, Yugoslavia, Yugoslavia.
- Skolske Novine. w. ISSN 0037-6531

**Skupnost Slovenskih Obcan**
Cankarjeva 5, Ljubljana, Yugoslavia.
- Obcan. w' ISSN 0029-747X

**Skupstina Opcine Karlovac**
Banjavciceva 9, Karlovac, Yugoslavia.
- Sluzbene Novine Opcine Karlovac. bi-w. ISSN 0037-7104

**Skupstina Opcine Krizevci**
Mose Pijade 12, Krizevci, Yugoslavia.
- Sluzbeni Vjesnik Opcine Krizevci. ISSN 0037-7163

**Skupstina Opcine Podravska Slatina**
Trg marsala Tita 5, Podravska Slatina, Yugoslavia.
- Opcina Podravska Slatina. Sluzbeni Glasnik. m. ISSN 0037-7112

**Skupstina Opcine Rovinj**
Ul. Matteotti 1/1, Rovinj, Yugoslavia.
- Sluzbeni Glasnik Opcine Rovinj. 8-12 per yr. ISSN 0037-7120

**Slavisticno Drustvo Slovenije**
Askerceva 12, Ljubljana, Yugoslavia.
- Jezik in Slovstvo. 8 per yr. ISSN 0021-6933
- Slavisticna Revija. (pub. by Zalozba Obzorja Maribor)

**Slobodna Dalmacija**
Splitskog odreda 4, Split, Yugoslavia.
- Nedeljna Dalmacija. w.

**Slovenia. Privredna Komora**
Bulevar JNA 13, Osijek, Yugoslavia.
- Privreda; casopis za privredna pitanja Slavonije i Baranje. m. ISSN 0032-8960 (Co-sponsor: Baranja. Privredna Komora)

**Slovenia. Republiski Sekretarijat za Notranje Zadeve SR Slovenije**
Kidriceva 2, 61000 Ljubljana, Yugoslavia.
- Revija za Kriminalistiko in Kriminologijo. q. ISSN 0034-690X

**Slovenska Akademija Znanosti in Umetnosti. Institut za Arheologijo**
Novi trg 3, 61000 Ljubljana, Yugoslavia.
- Arheoloski Vestnik/Acta Archaeologica. bi-m.

**Slovenska Akademija Znanosti in Umetnosti. Razred za Filoloske in Literarne Vede**
Novi Trg 5/1, Ljubljana, Yugoslavia.
- Traditiones. irreg.

**Slovenska Akademija Znanosti in Umetnosti. Razred za Prirodoslovne Vede**
Novi trg 3, Ljubljana, Yugoslavia.
- Acta Carsologica/Krasoslovni Zbornik. a.

**Slovenska Evanjelicka A.V. Cirkva v SFR Juhoslavii**
Karadziceva 2, Novi Sad, Yugoslavia.
- Evanjelicky Hlasnik. m. ISSN 0014-3642

**Slovenska Izseljenska Matica**
Cankarjeva 1, Box 169, 61001 Ljubljana, Yugoslavia.
- Rodna Gruda; revija za Slovence po svetu. m. ISSN 0557-2282

**Slovenske Rimskokatoliske Skofije**
Cankarjevo Nabrezje 3, 6100 Ljubljana, Yugoslavia.
- Cerkev v Sedanjem Svetu. bi-m. ISSN 0009-0387

**Slovenski Etnografski Muzej**
Presernova cesta 20, Ljubljana, Yugoslavia.
- Slovenski Etnograf. a.

**Slovensko Farmacevtsko Drustvo**
Box 01-247, Dalmatinova 10/II, 61001 Ljubljana, Yugoslavia.
- Farmacevtski Vestnik. q. ISSN 0014-8229

**Slovensko Geolosko Drustvo**
Parmova Ul. 33, 1000 Ljubljana, Yugoslavia.
- Geologija; razprave in porocila. a. ISSN 0016-7789 (Geoloski Zavod Ljubljana. Institut za Geologijo)

**Slovensko Zdravnisko Drustvo**
Komenskega 4, Box 26, 61001 Ljubljana, Yugoslavia.
- Zdravstveni Vestnik/Medical Journal of Slovenia. m. ISSN 0350-0063

**Sluzben Vesnik na Socialisticka Republika Makedonija**
29 Noemvri 10a, Skopje, Yugoslavia.
- Sluzben Vesnik na Socialisticka Republika Makedonija. irreg. ISSN 0037-7147

**Sluzbeni Vjesnik Opcine Buje, Novigrad i Umag**
Partizanska 2, Buje, Yugoslavia.
- Sluzbeni Vjesnik Opcine Buje, Novigrad i Umag. s-m. ISSN 0037-7155

**Socijalisticki Savez Leskovacke Opstine**
- Nasa Rec. (pub. by Nasa Rec, Leskovac)

**Socijalisticki Savez Radnog Naroda Backa Palanka**
- Nedeljne Novine. (pub. by Nedeljne Novine)

**Socijalisticki Savez Radnog Naroda Istre, Hrvatskog primorja i Gorskog kotara**
- Glas Istre. (pub. by Glas Istre)

**Socijalisticki Savez Radnog Naroda Kosova**
- Jedinstvo. (pub. by Jedinstvo)

**Socijalisticki Savez Radnog Naroda Opcine Bjelovar**
Trg Jedinstva 11, Bjelovar, Yugoslavia.
- Bjelovarski List. w. ISSN 0006-4068

**Socijalisticki Savez Radnog Naroda Opcine Dubrovnik**
Miha Pracaıa 1, Dubrovnik, Yugoslavia.
- Dubrovacki Vjesnik; list Socijalistickog saveza radnog naroda opoine Dubrovnik. w. ISSN 0012-690X

**Socijalisticki Savez Radnog Naroda Opcine Virovitica**
- Viroviticki List. (pub. by Bosko Buha Informativni Centar)

**Socijalisticki Savez Radnog Naroda Opstine Ivangrad**
Polimska 9, Ivangrad, Yugoslavia.
- Sloboda. bi-w. ISSN 0037-6876

**Socijalisticki Savez Radnog Naroda Opstine Pozarevac**
- Rec Naroda. (pub. by Rec Naroda)

**Socijalisticki Savez Radnog Naroda Opstine Titograd**
Lenjinov bulevar 66, Titograd, Yugoslavia.
- Titogradska Tribina. w. ISSN 0040-8204

**Socijalisticki Savez Radnog Narodna Opstine Trebinje**
Mija Zupcevica 9, Trebinje, Yugoslavia.
- Glas Trebinja; list Socijalistickog saveza radnog naroda opstine Trebinje. m. ISSN 0017-0828

**Socijalisticki Savez Radnog Naroda Opstine Valjevskog Sreza**
- Napred. (pub. by Napred)

**Socijalisticki Savez Radnog Naroda Opstine Vranje**
29 Novembra 10, Vranje, Yugoslavia.
- Slobodna Rec; list za drustvena i politicka pitanja. w. ISSN 0037-6884

**Socijalisticki Savez Radnog Naroda Suboticke Opstine**
Maksima Gorkog 8, Subotica, Yugoslavia.
- Suboticke Novine. w. ISSN 0039-436X

**Socijalisticki Savez Radnog Naroda Varazdin**
- Varazdinske Vijesti. (pub. by Varazdinske Vijesti)

**Socijalisticki Savez Radnog Naroda Vinkovacke Komune**
Djure Djakovica 29, Vinkovci, Yugoslavia.
- Novosti. w. ISSN 0029-5272

**Socijalisticki Savez Radnog Naroda Vukovar**
- Vukovarske Novine. (pub. by Centar za Kulturno-Propagandni i Informativni Rad Vukovar)

**Socijalisticki Savez Radnog Naroda Zajednice Opcina Gospic**
- Licke Novine. (pub. by Novinsko Informativna Ustanova u Osnivanju)

**Socijalisticki Svaz Pracujucich Vojvodiny Pre Slovakov**
- Hlas l'Udu. (pub. by Obzor)

**Socijalna Politika**
Mose Pijade 12, Belgrade, Yugoslavia.
- Socijalna Politika. m. ISSN 0038-0091

**Sociolosko Drustvo Hrvatske**
Tomislavov trg 21, 41000 Zagreb, Yugoslavia.
- Revija za Socijologiju/Sociological Review. q. ISSN 0350-154X

**Sojuz na Istoriskite Drustva na SR Makedonija**
Boris Kidric 66, 91000 Skopje, Yugoslavia.
- Istorija. s-a.

**Sojuz na Zdruzenijata na Pravnicite na Makedonija**
Box 452, Skopje, Yugoslavia.
- Pravna Misla; spisanie za pravni i opstestveni prasanja. bi-m. ISSN 0032-695X

**Sojuz Rusinoh i Ukraincoh Gorvatskej**
Pionirske Naselene 10, Vukovar, Yugoslavia.
- Nova Dumka. irreg.

**Sojuzot na Drustvata na Ekonomistite na SR Makedonija**
Box 489, Skopje, Yugoslavia.
- Stopanski Pregled/Economic Review; spisanie na Sojuzot na drustvata na ekonomistite od SR Makedonija. bi-m. ISSN 0039-1816

**Sojuzot na Fizicka Kultura na Makedonija**
Cetinska 24, Skopje, Yugoslavia.
- Sluzben Glasnik na Sojuzot za Fizicka Kultura na Makedonija. m. ISSN 0037-7090

**Sojuzot na Geodetskite Inzeneri i Geometri na Makedonija**
Skopje, Yugoslavia.
- Geodetski Pregled. irreg.

**Sojuzot na Socijalistickata Mladina na Makedonija**
Cvetan Dimov 66, Skopje, Yugoslavia.
- Mlad Borec. w. ISSN 0026-7023

**Sojuzot na Trudovite Invalidi na Makedonija**
Marsala Tita, Box 437, Skopje, Yugoslavia.
- Trudov Invalid. m. ISSN 0041-3445
- Zastita. m. ISSN 0044-1872

**Sovremenost**
Ivo Ribar Lola 66, Skopje, Yugoslavia.
- Sovremenost; literatura, umetnost, opstestveni prasanja. bi-m. ISSN 0038-5972

**Sportsko Drustvo Crvena Zvezda**
Uzun Mirkova 10, Belgrade, Yugoslavia.
- Zvezdina Revija. m. ISSN 0044-5533

**Srecanja**
Presernov trg 4, Ljubljana, Yugoslavia.
- Srecanja. m. ISSN 0038-8777

**Sredisnji Institut za Tumore i Slicne Bolesti**
Ilica 197, 41000 Zagreb, Yugoslavia.
- Libri Oncologici; casopis kancerologa Jugoslavije. q.

**Srpska Akademija Nauka i Umetnosti**
Knez Mihailova 35, 11001 Belgrade, Yugoslavia
- Academie Serbe des Sciences et des Arts. Bulletin. Classe des Sciences Mathematiques et Naturelles. Nouvelle Serie. (pub. by Naucno Delo)
- Izvori Srpskog Prava/Sources de Droit Serbe/ Serbische Rechtsquellen. irreg.
- Srpska Akademija Nauka i Umetnosti. Odeljenje Drustvenih Nauka. Glas. irreg. ISSN 0081-394X (Dist. by: Prosveta, Terazije 16, Belgrade, Yugoslavia)
- Srpska Akademija Nauka i Umetnosti. Odeljenje Drustvenih Nauka. Posebna Izdanja. irreg. ISSN 0081-3982 (Dist. by: Prosveta, Terazije 16, Belgrade, Yugoslavia)
- Srpska Akademija Nauka i Umetnosti. Odeljenje Drustvenih Nauka. Spomenik. irreg. ISSN 0081-4059 (Dist. by: Prosveta, Terazije 16, Belgrade, Yugoslavia)
- Srpska Akademija Nauka i Umetnosti. Odeljenje Jezika i Knjizevnosti. Posebna Izdanja. irreg. ISSN 0081-3990 (Dist. by: Prosveta, Terazije 16, Belgrade, Yugoslavia)
- Srpska Akademija Nauka i Umetnosti. Odeljenje Jezika i Knjizevnosti. Glas. irreg. ISSN 0081-3958 (Dist. by: Prosveta, Terazije 16, Belgrade, Yugoslavia)
- Srpska Akademija Nauka i Umetnosti. Odeljenje Likovne i Muzicke Umetnosti. Muzicka Izdanja. irreg. ISSN 0490-6659
- Srpska Akademija Nauka i Umetnosti. Odelenje Likovne i Muzicke Umetnosti. Posebna Izdanja. irreg. ISSN 0081-4008 (Dist. by: Prosveta, Terazije 16, Belgrade, Yugoslavia)
- Srpska Akademija Nauka i Umetnosti. Odeljenje Medicinskih Nauka. Glas. irreg. ISSN 0081-3966 (Dist. by: Prosveta, Terazije 16, Belgrade, Yugoslavia)
- Srpska Akademija Nauka i Umetnosti. Odeljenje Medicinskih Nauka. Posebna Izdanja. irreg. ISSN 0081-4016 (Dist. by: Prosveta, Terazije 16, Belgrade, Yugoslavia)
- Srpska Akademija Nauka i Umetnosti. Odeljenje Prirodno-Matematickih Nauka. Posebna Izdanja. irreg., 1972, no. 39. ISSN 0081-4024 (Dist. by: Prosveta, Terazije 16, Belgrade, Yugoslavia)
- Srpska Akademija Nauka i Umetnosti. Odeljenje Tehnickih Nauka. Glas. irreg. ISSN 0081-3974 (Dist. by: Prosveta, Terazije 16, Belgrade, Yugoslavia)

- Srpska Akademija Nauka i Umetnosti. Odeljenje Tehnickih Nauka. Posebna Izdanja. irreg. ISSN 0081-4040 (Dist. by: Prosveta, Terazije 16, Belgrade, Yugoslavia)
- Srpska Akademija Nauka i Umetnosti. Povremena Izdanja. irreg.
- Srpska Akademija Nauka i Umetnosti. Predavanja. irreg. ISSN 0561-7383
- Srpska Akademija Nauka i Umetnosti Spomenica. irreg. ISSN 0081-4032 (Dist. by: Prosveta., Terazije 16, Belgrade, Yugoslavia)
- Srpski Etnografski Zbornik. Naselja i Poreklo Stanovnistva. irreg. ISSN 0081-4067 (Dist. by: Prosveta, Terazije 16, Belgrade, Yugoslavia)
- Srpski Etnografski Zbornik. Rasprave i Gradja. irreg. ISSN 0081-4075 (Dist. by: Prosveta, Terazije 16, Belgrade, Yugoslavia)
- Srpski Etnografski Zbornik. Srpske Narodne Umotvorine. irreg. ISSN 0081-4083 (Dist. by: Prosveta, Terazije 16, Belgrade, Yugoslavia)
- Srpski Etnografski Zbornik. Zivot i Obicaji Narodni. irreg. ISSN 0081-4091 (Dist. by: Prosveta, Terazije 16, Belgrade, Yugoslavia)
- Zbornik Istorije Knjizevnosti/Recueil des Travaux de l'Histoire de la Litterature. irreg. ISSN 0084-5183 (Dist. by: Prosveta, Terazije 16, Belgrade, Yugoslavia)
- Zbornik za Istoriju, Jezik i Knjizevnost Srpskog Naroda. Fontes Rerum Slavorum Meridionalium. irreg. ISSN 0084-5191 (Dist. by: Prosveta, Terazije 16, Belgrade, Yugoslavia)
- Zbornik za Istoriju, Jezik i Knjizevnost Srpskog Naroda. Spomenici na Srpskom Jeziku. irreg. ISSN 0084-5205 (Dist. by Prosveta, Terazije 16, Belgrade, Yugoslavia)
- Zbornik za Istoriju, Jezik i Knjizevnost Srpskog Naroda. Spomenici na Tudjim Jezicima. irreg. ISSN 0084-5213 (Dist. by: Prosveta, Terazije 16, Belgrade, Yugoslavia)

**Srpska Akademija Nauka i Umetnosti. Etnografski Institut**
Vuka Karadzica 5, Belgrade, Yugoslavia.
- Srpska Akademija Nauka i Umetnosti. Etnografski Institut. Glasnik. irreg.
- Srpska Akademija Nauka i Umetnosti. Etnografski Institut. Zbornik Radova. irreg.

**Srpska Akademija Nauka i Umetnosti. Koordinacioni Medjuakademski Odbor za Balkanologiju**
Belgrade, Yugoslavia.
- Balcanica. a. (Co-sponsor: Srpska Akademija Nauka i Umetnosti. Balkanoloski Institut)

**Srpska Patrijarsija**
7 Jula 5, Belgrade, Yugoslavia.
- Teoloski Pogledi. q.

**Srpsko Hemijsko Drustvo**
Karnegijeva 4, 11001 Belgrade, Yugoslavia.
- Glasnik Hemijskog Drustva/Societe Chimique, Belgrade. Bulletin. 10 per yr. ISSN 0017-0941
- Hemijski Pregled. bi-m. ISSN 0440-6826

**Srpsko Kulturno Drustvo "Prosvjeta"**
Berislaviceva 10-I, Zagreb, Yugoslavia.
- Prosvjeta. m. ISSN 0033-166X

**Srpsko Lekarsko Drustvo**
Narodnog Fronta 1, Belgrade, Yugoslavia.
- Srpski Arhiv za Celokupno Lekarstvo/Serbian Archives of Entire Medicine. m. ISSN 0049-0210

**Srpsko Lekarsko Drustvo. Podruznica u Nisu**
Nis, Yugoslavia.
- Acta Medica Medianae. bi-m. ISSN 0365-4478

**Srpsko Lekarsko Drustvo. Redakcija za Stomatoloski Glasnik Srbije**
Rankeova 4, Belgrade, Yugoslavia.
- Stomatoloski Glasnik Srbije. bi-m. ISSN 0039-1743

**Srpsko Sociolosko Drustvo**
Marsala Tita 16, Belgrade, Yugoslavia.
- Socioloski Pregled/Sociological Review. 3 per yr.
ISSN 0085-6320

**Stalna Konferencija Gradova Jugoslavije**
Makedonska 22/X, Box 414, Belgrade, Yugoslavia.
- Komuna; casopis za pitanja teorije i prakse
komunalnih zajednica. m. ISSN 0023-3161

**Stanbiro, Poduzece za Organizaciju Informacije
Ekonomske i Ostale Usluge**
Tkalciceva 48-50, Zagreb, Yugoslavia.
- Poduzece Banka. m.

**Sterijino Pozorje**
Zmaj Jovina 22, 21000 Novi Sad, Yugoslavia.
- Scena; casopis za pozorisnu umetnost. bi-m. ISSN
0036-5734

**Izdavacki Savjet Casopisa Strojarstvo**
Berislaviceva 6, 41000 Zagreb, Yugoslavia.
- Strojarstvo; casopis za teoriju i praksu u
strojarstvo/journal for the theory and application
in mechanical engineering. 6 per yr. (Savez
Strojarskih i Brodogradjevnih Inzenjera i
Tehnicara Hrvatske)

**Stvaranje**
Bulevar revolucije 11, Box 37, 81000 Titograd,
Yugoslavia.
- Stvaranje; casopis za knjizevnost i kulturu. m.
ISSN 0039-422X

**Sveti Arhijerejski Sinod Srpske Pravoslavne Crkve**
7 Jula 5, Belgrade, Yugoslavia.
- Glasnik. m. ISSN 0017-0925

**Svetlost**
21 Oktobra 66, Kragujevac, Yugoslavia.
- Svetlost. w. ISSN 0039-7059

**Sveuciliste u Rijeci. Medicinski Fakultet**
Olge Ban 20, Rijeka, Yugoslavia.
- Acta Facultatis Medicae Fluminensis. irreg. ISSN
0065-1206 (Co-sponsor: Sveuciliste u Zagrebu)

**Sveuciliste u Zagrebu. Fakultet Politickih Nauka**
Dolac 1, 41000 Zagreb, Yugoslavia.
- Politicka Misao/Political Thought; casopis za
politicke nauke. q. ISSN 0032-3241 (Co-sponsor:
Centar za Kulturnul Djelatnost SSD Zagreba)

**Sveuciliste u Zagrebu. Fakultet Strojarstva i
Brodogradaje**
Dure Salaja 7, Zagreb, Yugoslavia.
- Sveuciliste u Zagrebu Fakultet Strojarstva i
Brodogradaje. Zbornik. a.

**Sveuciliste u Zagrebu. Fakultet za Defectologiju**
Kuslanova 59a, Zagreb, Yugoslavia.
- Defektologija/Defectology. s-a.

**Sveuciliste u Zagrebu. Filozofski Fakultet**
Dure Salaja 3, 41000 Zagreb, Yugoslavia,
Yugoslavia.
- Govor; revija za teoretsku i primenjenu fonetiku. 3
per yr. ISSN 0533-8859
- Studia Romanica et Anglica - Zagrebiensia. s-a.
ISSN 0039-3339

**Sveuciliste u Zagrebu. Institut za Drustvena
Istrazivanja**
Amruseva 8/III, 41000 Zagreb, Yugoslavia.
- Sociologija Sela. q. ISSN 0038-0326 (prep. by its
Centar za Sociologiju Sela Grada i Prostora)

**Sveuciliste u Zagrebu. Medicinski Fakultet**
Salata 3, Zagreb, Yugoslavia.
- Radovi Medicinskog Fakulteta u Zagrebu/Acta
Facultatis Medicae Zagrabiensis. 3 per yr. ISSN
0033-8575

**Sveuciliste u Zagrebu. Referalni Centar**
Trg Marsala Tita 3, Box 327, 41001 Zagreb,
Yugoslavia.
- Informatologia Yugoslavica. q. ISSN 0046-9483

**Sveuciliste u Zagrebu. Stomatoloski Fakultet**
Gunduliceva 5, Zagreb, Yugoslavia.
- Acta Stomatologica Croatica. q. ISSN 0001-7019

**Svijet**
Vladimira Parica Valtera 3, Sarajevo, Yugoslavia.
- Svijet; nedelniji ilustrovani list. w. ISSN 0039-
7121

**Izdavacko Preduzece Svjetlost**
Leze Perere 36, Sarajevo, Yugoslavia.
- Izraz; casopis za knjizevnu i umjetnicku kritiku.
m. ISSN 0021-3381

**Tanjug Economic Service**
Oblicev venac 2, Belgrade, Yugoslavia.
- Privreda i Rukovodjenje. m.

**Tanjug News Agency**
Box 609, Nemanjina 34, 11001 Belgrade,
Yugoslavia.
- Yugoslav Life. m. ISSN 0044-1333

**Tednik**
Vosnjakov 5, Ptuj, Yugoslavia.
- Tednik; glasilo Socijalisticne zveze delovnega
ljudstva. w. ISSN 0040-1978

**Tehnicka Knjiga, Belgrade**
7. Jula 26, Belgrade, Yugoslavia.
- Foto-Kino Revija; jugoslovenski casopis za
fotografijui amaterski film. m. ISSN 0015-8704
- Radio-Amater; casopis Saveza radio-amatera
Jugoslavije. m. ISSN 0033-8168 (Savez Radio-
Amatera Jugoslavije)
- Tehnicke Novine. 10 per yr. (Savez Organizacija
za Tehnicku Kulturu Jugoslavije)

**Tehnicka Knjiga, Zagreb**
Jurisiceva 10, Zagreb, Yugoslavia.
- Elektrotehnicar; casopis za elektro, radio, TV i
kinotehniku. m. ISSN 0013-5828

**Tehnicka Zalozba Slovenije**
Lepi Pot 6, Ljubljana, Yugoslavia.
- TIM; revija za tehnicno in znanstveno dejavnost
mladine. m. ISSN 0040-7712

**Teoloska Fakulteta v Ljubljani**
Poljanska 4, 61000 Ljubljana, Yugoslavia.
- Bogoslovni Vestnik. q. ISSN 0006-5722

**Timok**
Ljube Nesica 33, Zajecar, Yugoslavia.
- Razvitak. bi-m. ISSN 0034-0278

**Tortenelmi Leveltar**
24400 Senta, Yugoslavia.
- Zentai Fuzetek. irreg.

**Tribuna Mladih**
Katolicka Porta 5, Box 190, 21000 Novi Sad,
Yugoslavia.
- Polja; casopis za kulturu, umetnost i drustvena
pitanja. m. ISSN 0032-3578 (Savez Socijalisticke
Omladine Vojvodine. Pokrajinska Konferencija)

**Trudbenik**
12 Udarne brigade 3 a, Skopje, Yugoslavia.
- Trudbenik; vesnik na sindikalnite organizacii vo
Makedonija. w. ISSN 0041-3437

**Turisticka Stampa**
Knez Mihailova 21, Belgrade, Yugoslavia.
- Jugoslawische Touristenzeitung/Yugoslav Tourist
News. m. ISSN 0022-605X
- Turisticke Novine. w. ISSN 0041-4204
- Umetnost; casopis za likovne umetnosti i kritiku.
bi-m. ISSN 0041-6320

**Turisticna Zveza Slovenije**
Miklosiceva 38, Ljubljana, Yugoslavia.
- Turisticni Vestnik; strokovno in organizaciono
glasilo turizma in gostinstva Slovenie. bi-m. ISSN
0041-4212

**Udruzena Elektroprivreda SR Hrvatske**
Proletarskih Brigada 37, Zagreb, Yugoslavia.
- Energija; casopis elektroprivrede Hrvatske. m.
ISSN 0013-7448

**Udruzeni Zavod za Osiguranje i Reosiguranje**
- Osiguranje i Privreda. (pub. by Croatia Zajednica
Osiguranja)

**Udruzenje Banka Jugoslavije**
Masarikova 5, Belgrade, Yugoslavia.
- Jugoslovensko Bankarstvo. m.

**Udruzenje Dermatovenerologa Jugoslavije**
Komenskega 4, Ljubljana, Yugoslavia.
- Acta Dermatovenerologica Iugoslavica. q. ISSN
0302-4466

**Udruzenje Emajliraca Jugoslavije**
Srebrnjak 169, 41000 Zagreb, Yugoslavia.
- Emajl-Keramika-Staklo. q. ISSN 0013-6506

**Udruzenje Ginekologa-Opstetricara Jugoslavije**
Petrova 13, Zagreb, Yugoslavia.
- Jugoslavenska Ginekologija i Opstetricija. 6 per yr.
ISSN 0017-002X

**Udruzenje Hirurga Jugoslavije**
c/o Hirurska Klinika, Vodnjanska 17, Skopje,
Yugoslavia.
- Acta Chirurgica Iugoslavica. q. ISSN 0001-5474

**Udruzenje Knijigovoda Hrvatske**
8. Maja 1945, 42, Zagreb, Yugoslavia.
- Knjigovoda; glasilo za financijsko-racunovodstvene
kadrove. m. ISSN 0023-2386

**Udruzenje Knjigovoda Srbije**
Njegoseva 19, Box 403, Belgrade, Yugoslavia.
- Knjigovodstvo; casopis za pitanja knjigovodstva.
m. ISSN 0023-2394

**Udruzenje Knjizevnih Prevodilaca Srbije**
Francuska 7, Belgrade, Yugoslavia.
- Mostovi. q.

**Udruzenje Komercijalista Jugoslavije**
Zmaja od Nocaja 9, Belgrade, Yugoslavia.
- Komercijalist; jugoslovenski strucno informativni
casopis za unapredjenje komercijalnog poslovanja.
bi-m. ISSN 0350-1019

**Udruzenje Mlekarskih Radnika SR Hrvatske**
Ilica 31, Zagreb, Yugoslavia.
- Mljekarstvo; list za unapredenje mljekarstva. m.
ISSN 0026-704X

**Udruzenje Muzickih Pedagoga Hrvatske**
Socijalisticke Revolucije, 17, Zagreb, Yugoslavia.
- Muzika. q. ISSN 0027-531X

**Udruzenje Neurologa i Psihijatara Jugoslavije**
- Neuropsihijatrija. (pub. by Neuroloski-
Psihijatrijska Klinika Rebro, Zagreb)

**Udruzenje Oftalmologa Jugoslavije**
- Acta Ophthalmologica Iugoslavica. (pub. by
Medicinska Knjiga)

**Udruzenje Pravoslavnog Svestenstva SFR Jugoslavije.
Glavni Savez**
Francuska 31-1, Belgrade, Yugoslavia.
- Vesnik Glavnog Saveza Undruzenog Pravoslavnog
Svestenstva SFR Jugoslavije. fortn. ISSN 0042-
4552

**Udruzenje za Tehnologiju Vode**
Mije Kovacevica 7, Belgrade, Yugoslavia.
- Voda i Sanitarna Tehnika. bi-m.

**Unija Bioloskih Naucnih Drustava Jugoslavije**
Nemanjina 6, Belgrade-Zemun, Yugoslavia.
- Biosistematika/Biosystematics. a.
- Genetika/Genetics. irreg. (Co-sponsor: Drustvo
Geneticara Jugollavije)
- Jugoslavica Physiologica et Pharmacologica. q.
ISSN 0021-3225

**Union of Jurists Associations of Yugoslavia**
- Yugoslav Law/Droit Yougoslave. (pub. by Institut
za Uporedno Pravo, Belgrade)

**Union of Yugoslav Youth**
Bulevar Lenjina 6, 11070 Belgrade, Yugoslavia.
- Union of Yugoslav Youth. Newsletter. m.

**Univerza v Ljubljani**
Trg Osvobodite 11, Ljubljana, Yugoslavia.
- Univerza v Ljubljani. Vestnik. a.

**Univerza v Ljubljani. Fakulteta za Sociologijo,
Politicne Vede in Novinarstvo**
Titova Cesta 102, Ljubljana, Yugoslavia.
- Teorija in Praksa; revija za druzbena vprasanja. m.
ISSN 0040-3598

**Univerza v Ljubljani. Fakulteta za Strojnistvo**
Murnikova 2, Box 197/IV, 61000 Ljubljana,
Yugoslavia.
- Strojniski Vestnik/Mechanical Journal. bi-m. ISSN
0039-2480

**Univerza v Ljubljani. Filozofska Fakulteta**
Askerceva 12, Ljubljana, Yugoslavia.
- Acta Neophilologica. a. ISSN 0567-784X
- Linguistica. irreg., vol. 15, 1975. ISSN 0024-3922
- Muzikoloski Zbornik/Musicological Annual. a.
ISSN 0580-373X (prep. by its Oddelek za
Muzikologijo)

**Univerza v Ljubljani. Medicinska Fakulteta**
Vrazov Trg 2, 61000 Ljubljana, Yugoslavia.
- Medicinski Razgledi. q. ISSN 0025-8121

**Univerza v Ljubljani. Pravni Fakultet**
Trg Osvoboditve 11, Box 209, 61001 Ljubljana, Yugoslavia.
- Vestnik Instituta za Javno Upravo. q. ISSN 0350-0365 (prep. by its Institut za Javno Upravo)

**Univerzitet u Beogradu**
Studentski trg 16, Belgrade, Yugoslavia.
- Dijalektika/Dialectics; casopis za metodolosko filozofske probleme matematickih, prirodnih i tehnickih nauka. q. ISSN 0350-1272
- Gledista. m. ISSN 0017-1166 (Co-sponsor: Republicka Konferencija Saveza Omladine Srbije)

**Univerzitet u Beogradu. Elektrotehnicki Fakultet**
Studentski trg 1, Belgrade, Yugoslavia.
- Beogradski Univerzitet. Elektrotehnicki Fakultet. Publikacije. Serija: Elektronika, Telekomunikacije, Automatika. irreg.

**Univerzitet u Beogradu. Filoloski Fakultet**
c/o Fond za Publikacije, Studentski trg 3/I, 11000 Belgrade, Yugoslavia.
- Prilozi za Knjizevnost, Jezik, Istoriju i Folklor. s-a.

**Univerzitet u Beogradu. Institut za Botaniku i Botanicke Baste**
Takovska 43, Belgrade, Yugoslavia.
- Univerzitet u Beogradu. Institut za Botaniku i Botanicke Baste. Glasnik. a.

**Univerzitet u Beogradu. Pravni Fakultet**
Bulevar Revolucije 67, Belgrade, Yugoslavia.
- Beogradski Univerzitet. Pravni Fakultet. Anali. q. ISSN 0003-2565

**Univerzitet u Beogradu. Prirodno-Matematicki Fakultet**
Studentski trg 16, 11000 Belgrade, Yugoslavia.
- University of Beograd. Faculty of Sciences. Department of Astronomy. Publications. a. (prep. by its Katedra za Astronomiju)

**Univerzitet u Beogradu. Tehnicki Fakultet**
Ruzveltova 1a, 11000 Belgrade, Yugoslavia.
- Tehnicka Fizika/Journal of Engineering Physics. s-a. ISSN 0350-0594 (prep. by its Zavod za Fiziku)

**Univerzitet u Nisu**
Mike Paligorica 2/47, Nis, Yugoslavia.
- Naucni Podmladak. Drustvene Nauke; strucni casopis studenata univerziteta u nisu. q.

**Univerzitet u Novom Sadu. Prirodno-Matematicki Fakultet**
21001 Novi Sad, Yugoslavia.
- Univerzitet u Novom Sadu. Prirodno - Matematicki Fakultet. Zbornik Radova. a.

**Univerzitet u Sarajevu**
Vojvode Stepe obala 7/111, 71000 Sarajevo, Yugoslavia.
- Pregled; casopis za drustvena pitanja. m. ISSN 0032-7271
- Univerzitet u Sarajevu. Doktorske Disertacije. Rezimei. a.

**Univerzitet u Sarajevu. Gradjevinski Fakultet**
Stjepana Tomica 5, Sarajevo, Yugoslavia.
- Gradjevinski Fakultet. Institut za Materijale i Konstrukcije. Zbornik Istrazivackih Radova. a. ISSN 0350-1701 (prep. by its Institut za Materijale i Konstrukcije)

**Univerzitet u Sarajevu. Poljoprivredni Fakultet**
Zagrebacka 18, Sarajevo, Yugoslavia.
- Radovi Poljoprivrednog Fakuteta Univerziteta u Sarajevu. 19 per yr. ISSN 0033-8583

**Univerzitet u Zagrebu**
*see* Sveuciliste u Zagrebu

**Univerzitet vo Skoplje. Ekonomskiot Fakultet**
Skoplje, Yugoslavia.
- Univerzitet vo Skoplje. Ekonomskiot Fakultet. Godisnik. a.

**Univerzitet vo Skoplje. Medicinski Fakultet**
Karpos 11, Box 105, 91000 Skopje, Yugoslavia.
- Godisen Zbornik na Medicinskiot Fakultet vo Skopje/Acta Facultatis Medicinae Skopiensis. a. ISSN 0065-1214

**Urbanisticni Institut SR Slovenije**
Dimiceva 12/II, Box 346-VII, Ljubljana, Yugoslavia.
- Urbanizem. s-m.

**Urednistvo Socijalne Politike**
Marsala Tita 21, Belgrade, Yugoslavia.
- Ergonomija. bi-m. (Co-sponsor: Institut za Dokumentaciju Zastite na Radu u Nisu)
- Revija Rada. bi-m.

**Varazdinske Vijesti**
Trg Bozidara Adzije 7, Varazdin, Yugoslavia.
- Varazdinske Vijesti. w. ISSN 0042-2711 (Socijalisticki Savez Radnog Naroda Varazdin)

**Visoka Ekonomsko Komercialna Sola**
Razlagova 14, Maribor, Yugoslavia.
- Nase Gospodarstvo/Our Economy: Review of Current Problems in Economics. m. (Co-Sponsor: Drustvo Ekonomistov)

**Vjesnik**
Ljubice Gerovac 1, 41000 Zagreb, Yugoslavia.
- Arena; informativni drustveno politicki ilustrirani tjednik. w.
- Studio; tjedni informativni list za televiziju, radio, film, teatar i muziku. w. ISSN 0039-4106
- Svijet; jugoslavenska zenska revija. s-m. ISSN 0039-7113
- Vjesnik U Srijedu; jugoslavenski informativni tjednik. w. ISSN 0042-7640

**Vojna Akademija Rodova Kopnene Vojske i Intendantske Sluzbe**
Veljka Lukica-Kurjaka 33, Belgrade, Yugoslavia.
- Akademac. m.

**Vojni Muzej, Belgrade**
- Vesnik Vojnog Muzeja Jugoslovenske Narodne Armije. (pub. by Vojnoizdavacki Zavod)

**Vojnoistorijski Institut**
Bircaninova Br.5, Belgrade, Yugoslavia.
- Vojnoistorijski Glasnik. 4 per yr. ISSN 0042-8442

**Vojnoizdavacki Zavod**
Balkanska 53, 11002 Belgrade, Yugoslavia.
- Mornaricki Glasnik. bi-m. ISSN 0027-1136 (Yugoslavia. Ratna Mornarica)
- Vesnik Vojnog Muzeja Jugoslovenske Narodne Armije. a. ISSN 0067-5660 (Vojni Muzej, Belgrade)
- Vojni Glasnik; strucni casopis rodova vojske i sluzbi jNA. m. ISSN 0042-840X (Dist. by Jugoslovenska Knjiga, Box 36, 11001 Belgrade, Yugoslavia)
- Vojno Delo; opstevojni teorijski casopis. bi-m. ISSN 0042-8426 (Dist. by Jugoslovenska Knjiga, Box 36, 11001 Belgrade, Yugoslavia)
- Vojnotehnicki Glasnik. bi-m. ISSN 0042-8469 (Yugoslavia. Savezni Sekretarijat za Narodnu Odbranu)

**Vojvodjansko Drustvo za Poljoprivrednu Tehniku**
Vlahoviceva 2, Novi Sad, Yugoslavia.
- Savremena Poljoprivredna Tehnika/Contemporary Agricultural Technic. q. ISSN 0350-2953
- Savremena Poljoprivredna Tehnika/Contemporary Agricultural Technic. q. ISSN 0350-2953

**World Chess Federation - FIDE**
- Sahovski Informator/Chess Informant/Sahmatnyj Informator. (pub. by Centar za Unapredjivanje Saha)

**Yugoslavia. Beogradska Armijska Oblast**
Nemanjina 9, Belgrade, Yugoslavia.
- Vojnik; ilustravani list. fortn. ISSN 0042-8418

**Yugoslavia. Privredna Komora**
- Yugoslav Export-Import Directory. (pub. by Yugoslaviapublic)
- Yugoslavia Export. (pub. by Yugoslaviapublic)

**Yugoslavia. Ratna Mornarica**
- Mornaricki Glasnik. (pub. by Vojnoizdavacki Zavod)

**Yugoslavia. Ratno Vozduhoplovstvo i Protivvazdusne Odbrane**
Marsala Tita 1, Zemun, Belgrade, Yugoslavia.
- Krila Armije. fortn. ISSN 0023-4672

**Yugoslavia. Savezna Komisija za Nuklearnu Energiju**
Kosancicev Venac 29, Belgrade, Yugoslavia.
- Nuklearna Energija. bi-m. ISSN 0029-5914

**Yugoslavia. Savezni Sekretarijat za Inostrane Poslove**
Belgrade, Yugoslavia.
- Liste des Membres du Corps Diplomatique a Beograd. s-a.

**Yugoslavia. Savezni Sekretarijat za Narodnu Odbranu**
Kneza Milosa 37, Belgrade, Yugoslavia.
- Bilten Pravne Sluzbe J N A. q. ISSN 0006-2731
- Odbrana i Zastita. bi-m. ISSN 0029-8344
- Vojnotehnicki Glasnik. (pub. by Vojnoizdavacki Zavod)

**Yugoslavia. Savezni Sekretarijat za Narodnu Odbranu. Sanitetska Uprava**
Pasterova 3, 11000 Belgrade, Yugoslavia.
- Vojnosanitetski Pregled/Military Medical and Pharmaceutical Review; casopis lekara i farmaceuta jugoslovenske narodne armije. bi-m. ISSN 0042-8450

**Yugoslavia. Savezni Sekretarijat za Unutresnje Poslove**
Kneza Milosa 92, Box 870, Belgrade, Yugoslavia.
- Trinaesti Maj; casopis saveznog sekretarijata za unutresnje poslove. bi-m. ISSN 0041-302X

**Yugoslavia. Savezni Zavod za Patente**
Marsala Tita 2, Belgrade, Yugoslavia.
- Patentni Glasnik; Sluzbeni list Saveznog Zavoda za Patente. bi-m. ISSN 0031-2908

**Yugoslavia. Savezni Zavod za Statistiku**
Kneza Milosa 20, Belgrade, Yugoslavia.
- Demografska Statistika. a. ISSN 0084-4357
- Drustveni Proizvod i Narodni Dohodak. a. ISSN 0300-2527
- Indeks; mesecni pregled Privredne Statistike SFR Jugoslavije. m. ISSN 0019-3585
- Industrijski Proizvodi. a.
- Investicije. a.
- Licni Dohoci. a. ISSN 0300-2535
- Neki Pokazatelji Tehnickog Razvoja Privrede Jugoslavije. a. ISSN 0300-2497
- Statistika Spoljne Trgovine SFR Jugoslavije. a. ISSN 0084-4373
- Yugoslavia. Savenzi Zavod za Statistiku. Statisticki Bilten. irreg. ISSN 0084-4365
- Yugoslavia. Savezni Zavod za Statistiku. Anketa O Ostvarivanju Prava Radnika Iz Radnog Odnosa. irreg.
- Yugoslavia. Savezni Zavod za Statistiku. Anketa O Porodicnim Budzetima Radnickih Domacinstava. irreg.
- Yugoslavia. Savezni Zavod za Statistiku. Industrijske Organizacije. irreg.
- Yugoslavia. Savezni Zavod za Statistiku. Komunalni Fondovi u Gradskim Naseljima. irreg.
- Yugoslavia. Savezni Zavod za Statistiku. Osnovna i Srednje.
- Yugoslavia. Savezni Zavod za Statistiku. Radne Organizacije Prema Visini Najnizeg i Najviseg Neto Licnog Dohotka. s-a.
- Yugoslavia. Savezni Zavod za Statistiku. Samoupravljanje u Privredi. irreg.
- Yugoslavia. Savezni Zavod za Statistiku. Samoupravljanje u Ustanovama Drustvenih Sluzbi. irreg.
- Yugoslavia. Savezni Zavod za Statistiku. Saobracaj i Veze. ISSN 0513-0794
- Yugoslavia. Savezni Zavod za Statistiku. Statisticka Revija. q. ISSN 0039-0534 (Co-sponsor: Jugoslovensko Statisticko Drustvo)
- Yugoslavia. Savezni Zavod za Statistiku. Turizam. a.
- Yugoslavia. Savezni Zavod za Statistiku. Ucenici u Privredi. ISSN 0513-0832
- Yugoslavia. Savezni Zavod za Statistiku. Zaposleno Osoblje. ISSN 0513-0883
- Yugoslavia. Savezni Zavod za Statistiku. Zaposleno Osoblje i Neto Licni Dohoci po Grupama Delatnosti. s-a.
- Yugoslavia. Savezni Zavod za Statistiku. Zaposlenost. s-a. ISSN 0513-0891

**Yugoslaviapublic**
Knez Mihailova 10, Box 447, 11001 Belgrade, Yugoslavia.
- Yugoslav Export-Import Directory. a. ISSN 0084-4349 (Yugoslavia. Privredna Komora)
- Yugoslavia Export. m. ISSN 0044-1368 (Yugoslavia. Privredna Komora)

**Za Domovinu**
Socijalisticke Revolucije 14, Zagreb, Yugoslavia.
- Za Domovinu; list zagrebacke armijske oblasti. fortn. ISSN 0044-152X

**Zagreb Academy of Music. Institute of Musicology**
Gunduliceva 6, 41001 Zagreb, Yugoslavia.
- International Review of the Aesthetics and Sociology of Music. s-a. (Co-sponsor: International Committee for Aesthetic Studies)

**Zagreb Univerzitet**
see Sveuciliste u Zagrebu

**Zajednica**
Vojvode Putnika 62, Sarajevo, Yugoslavia.
- Zajednica. fortn. ISSN 0044-1716

**Zajednica Jugoslovenske Elektroprivrede**
Balkanska 13-15, Belgrade, Yugoslavia.
- Elektroprivreda. bi-m. ISSN 0013-5755

**Zajednica Jugoslovenskih Posta, Telegrafe i Telefona**
Palmoticeva 2/2, Box 1110, Belgrade, Yugoslavia.
- Telekomunikacije. q. ISSN 0040-2605

**Zajednica Jugoslovenskih Univerziteta**
Palmoticeva 22, Belgrade, Yugoslavia.
- Univerzitet Danas. m. ISSN 0042-0425

**Zajednica Kulturno-Prosvetnih Organizacija Jugoslavije**
- Kulturni Zivot. (pub. by Kulturni Zivot)

**Zalozba Obzorja Maribor**
Partizanska 5, 62000 Maribor, Yugoslavia.
- Slavisticna Revija; journal for linguistics and literary sciences. q. (Slavisticno Drustvo Slovenije)

**Zastita Rada**
Jelene Cetkovic 3, Box 723, Belgrade, Yugoslavia.
- Zastita Rada. m. ISSN 0044-1880

**Zavod SR Slovenija za Spomenisko Varstvo**
Plecnikov trg 2, Ljubljana, Yugoslavia.
- Varstvo Narave/Nature Conservation. s-a. ISSN 0506-4252

**Zavod SR Slovenije za Statistiko**
Vozarski Pot 12, Ljubljana, Yugoslavia.
- Prikazi in Studije. m. ISSN 0032-8227
- Zaposleni po Obcinah. irreg.

**Zavod SR Slovenije za Varstvo Pri Delu**
Bohoriceva 22/a, 61000 Ljubljana, Yugoslavia.
- Delo in Varnost; revija za varstvo pri delu. bi-m. ISSN 0011-7943

**Zavod za Casopisno in Radijsko Dejavnost Murska Sobota**
Titova 29/I, Murska Sobota, Yugoslavia.
- Vestnik; glasilo obcinskih konferenc sZDL Murska Sobota, Gornja Radgona, Lendava in Ljutomer. w. ISSN 0042-4587

**Zavod za Ekonomske Ekspertize**
Palmira Toljatija 3, Belgrade, Yugoslavia.
- Automatizacija Poslovanja; unapredenje poslovne politike preduzeca. m. ISSN 0005-1268
- Organizacija Samoupravljanja OUR; casopis za pitanja stimulativne raspodele i obracuna po ekonomskim jedinicama. m.
- Planiranje i Analiza Poslovanja. m. ISSN 0554-2537

**Zavod za Javnu Upravu, Belgrade**
Nemanjina 22, Belgrade, Yugoslavia.
- Opstina; casopis za pitanja drustvenog samoupravljanja. m. ISSN 0030-3895

**Zavod za Mentalno Zdravlje**
Palmoticeva 37, 11000 Belgrade, Yugoslavia.
- Psihijatrija Danas. q. ISSN 0350-2538

**Zavod za Novinsko Izdavacku i Propagandnu Delatnost JZ**
Nemanjina 6, Belgrade, Yugoslavia.
- Carinski Pregled. fortn. ISSN 0008-6592

**Zavod za Organizaciju i Ekonomiku Zdravstva. Centar za Lijekove**
Savska 41/VII, 41000 Zagreb, Yugoslavia.
- Pharmaca; casopis za probleme farmakodinamije i farmakoterapije. q. ISSN 0031-6857 (Co-sponsor: Savez Zajednica Zdravstvenih Radnih Organizacija SR Hrvatske)

**Zavod za Organizaciju i Upravljanje Poslovnim Sistemom u Organizacijama Udruzenog Rada**
Ul. 29 Novembra Br. 48/III, Belgrade, Yugoslavia.
- Organizacija Poslovanja. m.

**Zavod za Pedagoska i Kulturno Prosvjetna Pitanja**
Strossmayerova 6, Osijek, Yugoslavia.
- Zivot i Skola; casopis za pedagoska i kulturnoprosvjetna pitanja. bi-m. ISSN 0044-4855

**Zavod za Proucavanje i Zastitu Uha i Disnih Organa**
Vinogradska 29, 41000 Zagreb, Yugoslavia.
- Symposia Otorhinolaryngologica Iugoslavica. q. ISSN 0586-9145 (Klinicka Bolnica "Dr. M. Stojanovic" u Zagrebu. Klinika za Otorinolaringologiju i Cervikofacijalnu Kirurgiju)

**Zavod za Proucavanje Kulturnog Razvitka**
Nemanjina 24/II, 11000 Belgrade, Yugoslavia.
- Kultura; casopis za teoriju i sociologiju kulture i kulturnu politiku. q. ISSN 0023-5164

**Zavod za Tehnologiju Zita i Brasna**
Rumenacka 103, Novi Sad, Yugoslavia.
- Zito Hleb; casopis za tehnologiju zita i brasna. bi-m.

**Zavod za Transfuziju Krvi, Belgrade**
Svetosavska 39, Belgrade, Yugoslavia.
- Bilten za Hematologiju i Transfuziju. a. (Co-sponsor: Udruzenje Hematologa i Transfuziologa Jugoslavije)

**Zavod za Trzisna Istrazivanja**
Mose Pijade 8/I, 11001 Belgrade, Yugoslavia.
- Konjunkturni Barometar. m. ISSN 0023-3471
- Trziste Stoke i Stochih Proizoda; konjunkturne informacije. s-m. ISSN 0041-3755

**Zavod za Trzisna Istrazivanja. Centar za Istrazivanje Konjukture**
Mose Pijade 8/I, 11001 Belgrade, Yugoslavia.
- Konjunkturni Pregled. m. ISSN 0023-348X

**Zavod za Unapredivanje Osnovnog Obrazovanja SR Hrvatske**
Joze Vlahovica 6, Zagreb, Yugoslavia.
- Pogledi i Iskustva u Odgoju i Obrazovanju. 8 per yr. ISSN 0032-2253

**Zavod za Unapredjenje Domacinstva Bosne i Hercegovine**
Skenderija 70, Sarajevo, Yugoslavia.
- Savremeno Domacinstvo. q. ISSN 0036-5203

**Zavod za Zdravstvenu Zastitu SR Srbije**
Dr. Subotica 5, 11000 Belgrade, Yugoslavia.
- Zavod za Zdravstvenu Zastitu SR Srbije. Glasnik; casopis za preventivnu i socijalnu medicinu sa organizacijom zdravstvene. q. ISSN 0409-0314

**Zbor Lijecnika Hrvatske. Sekcija za Maksilofacijalnu i Plasticnu Kirurgiju**
Subiceva 9, Zagreb, Yugoslavia.
- Chirurgia Maxillofacialis and Plastica. 3 per yr. ISSN 0009-4781

**Zbor Lijecnika u Rijeci**
Borisa Kidrica 40, 51000 Rijeka, Yugoslavia.
- Medicina; strucni casopis Zbora lijecnika Rijeka. q. ISSN 0025-7729

**Zdruzene PTT Organizacije Slovenije**
Cigaletova 15, Ljubljana, Yugoslavia, Yugoslavia.
- P T T Novice; glasilo P T T delavcev Slovenije. fortn.

**Zdruzenie na Smetkovodstveno-Finansiskite Rabotnici na Makedonija**
Box 267, Skopje, Yugoslavia.
- Sovremeno Pretprijatie; spisanie za smetkovodstveno-finansiska i organizaciona problematika na rabotnite organizacii. bi-m. ISSN 0038-5964

**Zdruzenje Anatomov Jugoslavije**
Zaloska 4, Ljubljana, Yugoslavia.
- Folia Anatomica Iugoslavica. a. ISSN 0350-0233

**Zdruzenje Bank SR Slovenije**
Subiceva 2, 61001 Ljubljana, Yugoslavia.
- Bancni Vestnik; revija za denarnistvo in bancnistvo. m. ISSN 0005-4631

**Zemaljski Muzej Bosne i Hercegovine**
Vojvode Putnika 7, Sarajevo, Yugoslavia.
- Wissenschaftliche Mitteilungen des Bosnisch-Herzegowinischen Landesmuseums. Archaeologie. irreg.
- Wissenschaftliche Mitteilungen des Bosnisch-Herzegowinischen Landesmuseums. Naturwissenschaft. irreg. ISSN 0350-0012

**Zemaljski Muzej Bosne i Hercegovine. Glasnik. Arheologija. a.** ISSN 0581-7501
**Zemaljski Muzej Bosne i Hercegovine. Glasnik. Etnologija. a.** ISSN 0581-751X
**Zemaljski Muzej Bosne i Hercegovine. Glasnik. Prirodne Nauke. a.**

**Zena**
Vlaska 70a/III, Zagreb, Yugoslavia.
- Zena. bi-m.

**Zgodovinsko Drustvo za Slovenijo**
Mestni trg 27, Ljubljana, Yugoslavia.
- Kronika; casopis za Slovensko krajevno zgodovino. 3 per yr. ISSN 0023-4923

**Zveza Arhitektov Slovenije**
Erjavceva Cesta 15-1, 61000 Ljubljana, Yugoslavia.
- Sinteza; revija za likovno kulturo. ɔ. ISSN 0049-0601 (Co-sponsor: Drustvo Likovnih Umetnikov Slovenije)

**Zveza Drustev Glasbenih Pedagogov Slovenije**
Vegova 7, Ljubljana, Yugoslavia.
- Grlica; revija za glasbeno vzgojo. 5 per yr. ISSN 0017-4343

**Zveza Drustev Pravnikov SR Slovenije**
Subiceva 2, 61000 Ljubljana, Yugoslavia
- Pravnik; revija za pravno teorijo in prakso. q. ISSN 0032-6976 (Subscr. to: CZ Uradni List, Veselova 11, 61000 Ljubljana, Yugoslavia)

**Zveza Ekonomistov Slovenije**
Titova 19/1, Ljubljana, Yugoslavia.
- Ekonomska Revija. q. ISSN 0013-3256

**Zveza Gradbenih Inzenirjev in Tehnikov Slovenije**
Erjavceva 15, Ljubljana, Yugoslavia.
- Gradbeni Vestnik. m. ISSN 0017-2774

**Zveza Inzenirjev in Tehnikov Gozdarstva in Lesarstva SR Slovenije**
Erjavceva Cesta 15, Ljubljana, Yugoslavia.
- Gozdarski Vestnik. 10 per yr. ISSN 0017-2723
- Les; revija za lesno gospodarstvo. m. ISSN 0024-1067

**Zveza Inzenirjev in Tehnikov Slovenije**
Erjavceva 15, Ljubljana, Yugoslavia.
- Nova Proizvodnja; obzornik napredka v tehniki in gospodarstvu. bi-m. ISSN 0029-5051

**Zveza Kulturnih Delavcev v Mariboru**
Rotovski trg 1, Maribor, Yugoslavia.
- Dialogi. m. ISSN 0012-2068

**Zveza Kulturno Prosvetnih Organizacij Slovenije**
Dalmatinova 4, Ljubljana, Yugoslavia.
- Ekran; revija za film in televizijo. 10 per yr. ISSN 0013-3302
- Nasi Zbori. bi-m. ISSN 0027-8270

**Zveza Pedagoskih Drustev Slovenije**
Gosposka 3/1, Ljubljana, Yugoslavia.
- Sodobna Pedagogika. ISSN 0038-0474

**Zveza Prijateljev Mladine Slovenije**
Miklosiceva Cesta 16, Ljubljana, Yugoslavia.
- Otrok in Druzina; revija za druzinsko in druzbeno vzgojo. m. ISSN 0030-6681

**Zveza Sindikatov Slovenije**
Dalmatinova 4, Box 313-VI, Ljubljana, Yugoslavia.
- Delavska Enotnost. w. ISSN 0011-7722

**Zveza Socialisticne Mladine Slovenije. Univerzitetna Konferenca**
Box 86, Trg Osvoboditve 1/II, 61000 Ljubljana, Yugoslavia.
- Tribuna; studentski list. fortn. ISSN 0041-2724

**Zvezda, Trgovinska i Radna Organizacija**
Zona Pristanista i Skladista 66, Novi Sad, Yugoslavia.
- Zvezda; list za internu upotrebu i samoupravno dogovaranje. m.

# ZAIRE

**Association Nationale des Entreprises Zairoises**
B. P. 7247, Kinshasa, Zaire.
- Association Nationale des Entreprises Zairoises. Circulaire d'Information. irreg.

**Banque Commerciale Zairoise**
B.P. 2798, Kinshasa, Zaire.
- Banque Commerciale Zairoise. Reports and Balance Sheets. a.

**Banque du Zaire**
B.P. 2697, Kinshasa, Zaire.
- Banque du Zaire. Bulletin Mensuel de la Statistique. m.
- Banque du Zaire. Rapport Annuel. a. ISSN 0300-1172

**Bibi**
33 Av. Victoire, Kinshasa, Zaire.
- Bibi. m.

**Centre d'Etudes des Religions Africaines**
*see under* **Universite Nationale du Zaire, Kinshasa**

**Centre d'Etudes Ethnologiques**
Bandundu, Zaire.
- Centre d'Etudes Ethnologiques. Publications. Serie 3: Travaux Linguistiques. irreg.

**Centre d'Etudes pour l'Action Sociale**
9, rue Pere Boka, B.P. 3375, Kinshasa, Zaire.
- Zaire-Afrique; economie-culture-vie sociale. m. ISSN 0049-8513

**Centre d'Execution de Programmes Sociaux et Economiques**
208, Av. Kasa-Vubu, Box 1873, Lubumbashi, Zaire.
- Problemes Sociaux Zairois. q.

**Centre de Recherches Industrielles en Afrique Centrale**
B. P. 54, Lubumbashi, Zaire.
- Sciences, Techniques, Informations C R I A C. irreg.

**Centre Interdisciplinaire pour le Developpement et l'Education Permanente**
Kinshasa, Zaire.
- Etudes Zairoises. s-a.

**Congo Disque**
B.P. 6112, Kinshasa 6, Zaire.
- Congo Disque; revue de la musique congolaise moderne. ISSN 0010-5775

**Dionga**
2 rue Dima, Immeuble Amassio, B.P. 8031, Kinshasa, Zaire.
- Dionga. m.

**Documentation et Information Africaines**
B.P. 2598, Kinshasa, Zaire.
- Documentation et Information Africaines. d.

**Dombi**
Guest House O.N.R.D., 10 E rue Limete, B. P. 3498, Kalima, Kinshasa, Zaire.
- Dombi; revue Congolaise des lettres et des arts. bi-m. ISSN 0046-0532

**Edition du Secretariat-General**
Kinshasa-Combe, Zaire.
- Annuaire de l'Eglise Catholique au Zaire. a.

**GECAMINES**
*see* **Generale des Carrieres et Mines du Zaire**

**Generale des Carrieres et Mines du Zaire**
B.P. 450, Lubumbashi, Zaire.
- GECAMINES. Annual Report. a. (prep. by its Division des Relations Publiques)
- Maadini; bulletin d'information de la Gecamines. q. (prep. by its Division des Relations Publiques)

**Institut de Gestion de Portefeuille. Department du Portefeuille**
B.P. 3473, Kinhasa/Gombe, Zaire.
- Portefeuille; revue d'informatton economique et financiere. irreg.

**Institut de Recherches Economiques et Sociale**
*see under* **Universite Nationale du Zaire, Kinshasa**

**Institut Geographique du Zaire**
B.P. 3086, Kinshasa, Zaire.
- Institut Geographique du Zaire. Rapport Annuel. a. ISSN 0443-3173

**Institut National de Preparation Professionnelle**
B. P. 7248, Kinshasa 1, Zaire.
- Institut National de Preparation Professionnelle. Cahier. irreg.

**Institut National pour l'Etude et la Recherche Agronomique**
B.P. 1513, Kisangani, Zaire.
- Institut National pour l'Etude et la Recherche Agronomique. Rapport Annuel. a.

**Institut pour la Recherche Scientifique en Afrique Centrale**
Lwiro- Bukavu, Zaire.
- Chronique de l' I R S A C. 3 per yr. ISSN 0009-6040

**Maison d'Editions "Jeunes pour Jeunes"**
B.P. 9624, Kinshasa 1, Zaire.
- Likembe. bi-m.

**Mission Catholique**
B.P. 276, Coquilhatville, Zaire.
- Aequatoria. q.

**Ngabu**
Building Sonas, Ex-Avenue Ministere Rubbens No. 18, Kinshasa, Zaire.
- Ngabu; revue Zairoise des assurances. q.

**Office National de la Recherche et du Developpement**
B.P. 3474, Kinshasa, Zaire.
- Cahiers Zairois de la Recherche et du Developpement. irreg.
- Cultures au Zaire et en Afrique. q. (prep. by its Section des Sciences de l'Homme)
- Revue Zairoise de Droit. s-a.

**Panafrican Trade Union Information Center. African-American Consultative Committee**
P.O. 1788, Kinshasa, Zaire.
- Labor in Perspective. m.

**Presses Universitaires du Zaire**
Documentation et Diffusion, B.P. 8815, Kinshasa 1, Zaire.
- Revue de Pedagogie Appliquee. q.
- Universite Nationale du Zaire, Kinshasa. Faculte de Droit. Annales. irreg.

**Societe d'Etudes Juridiques du Katanga**
B. P. 510, Lubumbashi, Zaire.
- Revue Juridique du Zaire. 3 per yr.

**Societe Generale des Editions Africaines**
B.P. 391, Limete, Kinshasa, Zaire.
- Tribune Diplomatique.

**Societe Nationale d'Electricite**
Building I.N.S.S., Boulevard du 30-Juin, Boite Postale 500, Kinshasa 1, Zaire.
- Energie et Progres. q.

**Societe Zairoise d'Edition et d'Information**
Kinshasa, Zaire.
- Horizons 80; hebdomadaire zairois d'information economique. w.

**Union des Ecrivains Zairois**
Kinshasa, Zaire.
- Culture et Authenticite; revue zairoise d'orientation culturelle. m.

**Union des Jeunesses Revolutionnaires Congolaises**
Maison Patrice Lumumba, Mulongwe (Kivu), Kinshasa, Zaire.
- Eclair. m. ISSN 0012-9380

**Union Internationale Chretienne des Dirigeants d'Enterprise. Centre Chretien d'Action pour les Dirigeants et Cadres des Enterprise**
32B Avenue Tombalbaye, Kinshasa, Zaire.
- Cadicec. q.

**Universite Nationale du Zaire. Junction des Etudiants**
Bloc VIII No 1109, B.P. 945, Lubumbashi, Zaire.
- Forum Universitaire. q.

**Universite Nationale du Zaire, Kinshasa. Centre d'Etudes des Religions Africaines**
B.P. 756, Kinshasa 11, Zaire.
- Cahiers des Religions Africaines. s-a. ISSN 0008-0047

**Universite Nationale du Zaire, Kinshasa. Faculte du Droit**
- Universite Nationale du Zaire, Kinshasa. Faculte de Droit. Annales. (pub. by Presses Universitaires du Zaire)

**Universite Nationale du Zaire, Kinshasa. Institut de Recherches Economiques et Sociales**
Box 257, Kinshasa 11, Zaire.
- Cahiers Economiques et Sociaux. q. ISSN 0008-0209
- Universite Nationale du Zaire, Kinshasa. Institut de Recherches Economiques et Sociales. Lettre Mensuelle. m.
- University Nationale du Zaire, Kinshasa. Institut de Recherches Economiques et Sociale. Document du Mois. q.

**Universite Nationale du Zaire, Kisangani. Centre de Recherches Interdisciplinaires pour le Developpement de l'Education**
B.P. 2012, Kisangani, Zaire.
- Revue Zairoise de Psychologie et de Pedagogie. 2 per yr.

**Universite Nationale du Zaire, Lubumbashi**
B.P. 945, Lubumbashi, Zaire.
- Elimu; revue des sciences humaines. q.

**Universite Nationale du Zaire, Lubumbashi. Centre de Linguistique Theorique et Appliquee**
B.P. 1607, Lumbumbashi, Zaire.
- Universite Nationale du Zaire, Lubumbashi. Centre de Linguistique Theorique et Appliquee. Bulletin d'Information. bi-m.

**Universite Nationale du Zaire, Lubumbashi. Department d'Histoire**
B.P. 1825, Lubumbashi, Zaire.
- Etudes d'Histoire Africaine/Studies in African History. a. ISSN 0071-1993 (Co-sponsor: Musee Royale de l'Afrique Centrale, Belgium)

**Universite Nationale du Zaire, Lubumbashi. Department de Philosophie**
B. P. 1825, Lubumbashi, Zaire.
- Cahiers Philosophiques Africains/African Philosophical Journal. irreg.

**Universite Nationale du Zaire, Lubumbashi. Faculte de Philosophie et Lettres**
B. P. 2896, Lubumbashi, Zaire.
- Cahiers de Litterature et de Linguistique Applique. s-a. ISSN 0045-3749

**Universite Nationale du Zaire, Lubumbashi. Faculte des Sciences Socials, Politiques et Administratives**
B.P. 2896, Lubumbashi, Zaire.
- Cahiers Zairois d'Etudes Politiques et Sociales. q.

**Zaire. Conseil Legislatif National**
Kinshasa, Zaire.
- Zaire. Conseil Legislatif National. Compte Rendu Analytique. irreg.

**Zaire. Conseil Permanent de la Comptabilite**
Secretariat General de la Comptabilite, 17, Ave. du Port, Building S.N.C.Z., B.P. 308, Kinshasa, Zaire.
- Conseiller Comptable. q.

**Zaire. Direction des Archives et Bibliotheques**
B.P. 3090, Kinshasa Kalina, Zaire.
- Zaire. Direction des Archives et Bibliotheques. Bibliographie Nationale.

**Zaire. Direction Generale des Finances**
B.P. 12997, Kinshasa, Zaire.
- Zaire. Direction Generale des Finances. Bulletin des Finances. bi-m. (prep. by its Division des Etudes et de la Documentation)

**Zaire. Direction Generale et Administration**
1 rue Luozi Kasa-Vubu, B. P. 8246, Kinshasa, Zaire.
- Zaire Ya Sika. bi-m.

**Zaire. Institut National de la Statistique**
Kinshasa, Zaire.
- Zaire. Institut National de la Statistique. Annuaire des Statistiques du Commerce Exterieur. a. ISSN 0304-5692

**Zaire. Ministere de la Culture et des Arts. Direction des Archives et Bibliotheques**
*see* **Zaire. Direction des Archives et Bibliotheques**

**Zaire Business**
3986, rue Ex-Belgika, Building Amasco, B.P. 9839, Kinshasa, Zaire.
- Zaire Business. w.

# ZAMBIA

**African National Congress of South Africa**
Box 1791, Lusaka, Zambia.
- Mayibuye. fortn. ISSN 0025-6188

**Associated Reviews Ltd.**
Lufunsa Avenue, Box 717, Ndola, Zambia.
- Zambian Industrial Directory. irreg. ISSN 0084-5116

**Bank of Zambia**
Director of Research, Box 80, Lusaka, Zambia.
- Bank of Zambia. Quarterly Statistical Review. q.

**Central Fisheries Research Institute**
*see* Zambia. Central Fisheries Research Institute

**Copper Industry Service Bureau**
Kitwe, Zambia
(Dist. by American Metal Climax, Inc., 1270 Ave. of the Americas, New York, N.Y. 10026)
- Zambia Mining Yearbook. a; latest issue 1975. ISSN 0076-9010

**Copperbelt Education**
P.O. Box 1552, Ndola, Zambia.
- Copperbelt Education. 1-2 per yr.

**Historical Association of Zambia**
c/o University of Zambia, Box 2379, Lusaka, Zambia.
- History in Zambia. irreg., 1974, no. 5.

**Literature Clearing House**
Africa Literature Centre, P.O. 1319, Kitwe, Zambia.
- Christian Communications Journal in Africa. bi-m. ISSN 0045-6799

**Livingstone Museum**
Box 498, Livingstone, Zambia.
- Zambia Journal. s-a.

**Lusaka Theatre Club**
Box 615, Lusaka, Zambia.
- Stage. bi-m.

**Mindolo Ecumenical Foundation**
P.O. Box 1493, Kitwe, Zambia.
- Mindolo News Letter. irreg., 1970, no. 33. ISSN 0076-8901

**Mission Press**
Box 1581, Ndola, Zambia.
- Icengelo; christian monthly magazine. m.

**Mphala Creative Society**
c/o International House 5-13, University of Zambia, P.O. Box 2379, Lusaka, Zambia.
- Jewel of Africa; a literary and cultural magazine from Zambia. m. ISSN 0021-6259

**National Council for Scientific Research**
*see* Zambia. National Council for Scientific Research

**New Writers Group**
Box 1889, Lusaka, Zambia.
- New Writing from Zambia. q. ISSN 0028-7083

**Roan Consolidated Mines Ltd.**
Kalewa Rd., North Rise, P.O. Box 1605, Ndola, Zambia.
- Mining Mirror; Zambia's mining industry newspaper. fortn. (Co-sponsor: Nchanga Consolidated Copper Mines Limited)

**T B M Publicity Enterprises Ltd.**
P. O. 40, Kitwe, Zambia.
- Outlook. m. ISSN 0030-7262

**United National Independence Party. Youth Wing**
Box 302, Lusaka, Zambia.
- Youth. fortn.

**University of Zambia**
Box 2379, Lusaka, Zambia.
- Zango/Forum; Zambian journal of contemporary issues. 3 per yr.

**University of Zambia. Institute for African Studies**
Box 900, Lusaka, Zambia
- African Social Research. (pub. by Manchester University Press UK)

- University of Zambia. Institute for African Studies. Communication. a. ISSN 0084-5108
(Dist. by: Humanities Press, Inc., 171 First Ave., Atlantic Highlands, NJ 07016)

**University of Zambia. School of Law**
Box 2379, Lusaka, Zambia.
- Zambia Law Journal. s-a.

**Wildlife Conservation Society of Zambia**
P.O. Box 255, Lusaka, Zambia.
- Black Lechwe. q. ISSN 0045-219X

**Zambia. Central Fisheries Research Institute**
Box 100, Chilanga, Zambia.
- Fisheries Research Bulletin of Zambia. irreg. ISSN 0084-4713

**Zambia. Central Statistical Office**
P.O. Box 1908, Lusaka, Zambia.
- Census of Industrial Production in Zambia. a, latest 1973. ISSN 0069-1429
- Zambia. Central Statistical Office. Agricultural and Pastoral Production. a, latest 1975 (preliminary report) ISSN 0080-1305
- Zambia. Central Statistical Office. Annual Statement of External Trade. a, latest 1975. ISSN 0084-4489
- Zambia. Central Statistical Office. Balance of Payments Statistics. a, latest 1974.
- Zambia. Central Statistical Office. Employment and Earnings. irreg. (report covers 3 years); latest 1972-74. ISSN 0084-4500
- Zambia. Central Statistical Office. Financial Statistics of Government Sector (Economic and Functional Analysis) a, latest 1972.
- Zambia. Central Statistical Office. Financial Statistics of Public Corporations. a, latest 1969. ISSN 0084-4519
- Zambia. Central Statistical Office. Fisheries Statistics (Natural Waters) a, latest 1971. ISSN 0514-8731
- Zambia. Central Statistical Office. Insurance Statistics. a, latest 1969. ISSN 0084-4535
- Zambia. Central Statistical Office. Migration Statistics. a, latest 1975. ISSN 0084-4543
- Zambia. Central Statistical Office. Monthly Digest of Statistics. m. ISSN 0027-0377
- Zambia. Central Statistical Office. Statistical Year Book. a, ISSN 0084- 4551
- Zambia. Central Statistical Office. Transport Statistics. q. ISSN 0514-5392
- Zambia. Central Statistical Office. Vital Statistics. a, latest 1975. ISSN 0084-456X

**Zambia. Commission for Investigation**
Lusaka, Zambia
(Orders to: Government Printer, Box 136, Lusaka, Zambia)
- Zambia. Commission for Investigation. Annual Report. a.

**Zambia. Commission for the Preservation of Natural and Historical Monuments and Relics**
P.O. Box 124, Livingstone, Zambia.
- Archaeologia Zambiana. 1-2 per yr. ISSN 0570-6068
- Zambia. Commission for the Preservation of Natural and Historical Monuments and Relics. Annual Report. a. ISSN 0084-4586

**Zambia. Geological Survey**
P.O. Box R.W. 135, Lusaka, Zambia.
- Annotated Bibliography and Index of the Geology of Zambia. irreg, latest issue 1970-1971. ISSN 0066-2410
- Zambia. Geological Survey. Annual Reports. a, latest issue 1974. ISSN 0084-473X
- Zambia. Geological Survey. Economic Reports. irreg. ISSN 0084-4748
- Zambia. Geological Survey. Occasional Papers. irreg. ISSN 0084-4756
- Zambia. Geological Survey. Reports. irreg, latest issue 1976. ISSN 0084-4764
- Zambia. Geological Survey. Technical Reports. irreg.

**Zambia. Government Printer**
P.O. Box 136, Lusaka, Zambia.
- Zambia. Department of Community Development. Report. a (approx.), latest 1975. ISSN 0084-4608
- Zambia. Department of Cooperatives. Annual Report. a. ISSN 0514-5430
- Zambia. Department of Labour. Report. a. ISSN 0084-4632
- Zambia. Department of Social Welfare. Report. a. ISSN 0084-4667

- Zambia. Department of Social Welfare. Social Welfare Research Monographs. irreg. ISSN 0081-0533
- Zambia. Department of Taxes. Annual Report of the Commissioner of Taxes. a. ISSN 0084-4675
- Zambia. Department of the Administrator-General and Official Receiver. Report. a. ISSN 0084-4683
- Zambia. Department of Water Affairs. Hydrological Branch. Hydrological Year Book. a. ISSN 0084-4691
- Zambia. Department of Water Affairs. Report. a. ISSN 0084-4705
- Zambia. Educational and Occupational Assessment Service. Annual Report. a. ISSN 0514-5457
- Zambia. General Post Office. Annual Report of the Postmaster-General. a. ISSN 0084-5019
- Zambia. Immigration Department. Report. a. ISSN 0084-4802
- Zambia. Mines Development Department. Annual Report. a. ISSN 0084-4845
- Zambia. Ministry of Agriculture. Annual Report. a. ISSN 0084-4853
- Zambia. Ministry of Health. Report. a. ISSN 0084-4918
- Zambia. Office of the Auditor-General. Report of the Auditor-General. a. ISSN 0084-4497
- Zambia. Office of the Conservator of Natural Resources. Report. a.
- Zambia. Pneumoconiosis Medical and Research Bureau and Pneumoconiosis Compensation Board. Annual Reports. a. ISSN 0084-5000
- Zambia. Prisons Department. Report. a. ISSN 0084-4659
- Zambia. Public Service Commission. Report. a. ISSN 0084-5035
- Zambia. Sports Directorate. Report. a. ISSN 0084-506X
- Zambia. Survey Department. Report. a. ISSN 0084-5078
- Zambia. Teaching Service Commission. Annual Report. a. ISSN 0084-5086
- Zambia. Victoria Falls Electricity Board. Report. a. ISSN 0083-6001

**Zambia. Health and Welfare Department**
P.O. Box 789, Lusaka, Zambia.
- Zambia. Health and Welfare Department. Annual Report of the Medical Officer of Health. a.

**Zambia. Information Services**
Box RW 20, Lusaka, Zambia
(Orders to: Government Printer, Box 136, Lusaka, Zambia)
- About Zambia. irreg. ISSN 0065-0374
- Intanda. fortn. ISSN 0020-4854
- Tsopano. fortn. ISSN 0041-378X
- Z; monthly magazine in English. m. ISSN 0044-1422
- Zambia. Information Services. Annual Report. a. ISSN 0084-4810

**Zambia. Meteorological Department**
Box 200, Lusaka, Zambia
(Orders to: Government Printer, Box 136, Lusaka, Zambia)
- Zambia. Meteorological Department. Totals of Monthly and Annual Rainfall; for selected stations in Zambia.
- Zambian Climatological Summary; Surface and Upper Air Data. irreg.

**Zambia. Ministry of Education**
Box RW 93, Lusaka, Zambia
- Zambia. Ministry of Education. Report. a. ISSN 0084-487X (Orders to: Government Printer, Box 136, Lusaka, Zambia)
- Zambia Educational Journal. a.

**Zambia. Ministry of Education. Curriculum Development Centre**
Private Bag RW 18, Lusaka, Zambia.
- Orbit; magazine for young Zambians. 9 per yr.

**Zambia. Ministry of Planning and Finance**
Box RW 62, Lusaka, Zambia
(Orders to: Government Printer, Box 136, Lusaka, Zambia)
- Zambia. Ministry of Planning and Finance. Annual Report. a.

**Zambia. Ministry of Rural Development**
Box RW 197, Lusaka, Zambia.
- Farming in Zambia. q. ISSN 0014-8504
- Zambia . Ministry of Rural Development. Quarterly Agricultural Statistical Bulletin. q. (prep. by its Statistics Section)

**Zambia. Ministry of Rural Development. Land Use Branch**
Mount Makulu Research Station, Box 7, Chilanga, Zambia.
- Zambia. Ministry of Rural Development. Land Use Branch. Soil Survey Report. irreg.

**Zambia. National Archives**
Box RW 10, Ridgeway, Lusaka, Zambia.
- National Archives of Zambia. Annual Report. a; latest 1974. ISSN 0084-4942
- National Archives of Zambia. National Archives Occasional Paper. irreg.
- National Bibliography of Zambia. a.

**Zambia. National Council for Scientific Research**
Box CH 158, Chelston, Lusaka, Zambia
- Zambia. National Council for Scientific Research. Annual Report. a. ISSN 0084-4950 (Orders to: Government Printer, Box 136, Lusaka, Zambia)
- Zambia Journal of Science and Technology. q.

**Zambia. National Food and Nutrition Commission**
Box 2669, Lusaka, Zambia.
- Nutrition News in Zambia. irreg.(approx. 2-4 issues per year) ISSN 0078-284X
- Zambia. National Food and Nutrition Commission. Annual Report. a. ISSN 0084-4969

**Zambia. National Museums Board**
c/o Livingstone Museum, Box 498, Livingstone, Zambia.
- Zambia. National Museums Board. Report. a. ISSN 0084-4977
- Zambia Museums Journal. a.

**Zambia. National Parks and Wildlife Service**
Private Bag 1, Chilanga, Zambia
(Orders to: Government Printer, Box 136, Lusaka, Zambia)
- Puku. irreg., 1973, no. 7. ISSN 0079-7901

**Zambia Association for Scientific Education**
Box R.W. 335, Lusaka, Zambia.
- Science Education in Zambia. q.

**Zambia Congress of Trade Unions**
Box 652, Kitwe, Zambia.
- Workers Voice. m.

**Zambia Electricity Supply Corporation**
Box 3304, Lusaka, Zambia.
- Zambia Electricity Supply Corporation. Annual Report. a, latest 1973-74.

**Zambia Geographical Association**
P.O. Box R.W. 287, Lusaka, Zambia.
- Z G A Bibliographic Series. irreg; no. 2, 1975.
- Z G A Occasional Studies. irreg.
- Zambia Geographical Association. Conference Handbook. irreg.
- Zambian Geographical Journal. q.

**Zambia Industrial and Mining Corp. Ltd.**
Box 90, Lusaka, Zambia.
- Enterprise. q.
- Survey of Zambian Industry. q.

**Zambia Library Association**
Box 2839, Lusaka, Zambia.
- Zambia Library Association Journal. q. ISSN 0049-853X

**Zambia Medical Association**
Box 717, Ndola, Zambia.
- Medical Journal of Zambia. bi-m. ISSN 0047-651X

**Zambia Nurses Association**
Box 2104, Kitwe, Zambia.
- Zambia Nurse. 3 per yr.

**Zambia Publishing Company**
Box 1421, Lusaka, Zambia.
- Zambia Daily Mail. d.

**Zambian Ornithological Society**
P.O. Box 3944, Lusaka, Zambia.
- Zambian Ornithological Society. Bulletin. s-a.
- Zambian Ornithological Society. Newsletter. m.

**Zimbabwe African Peoples Union**
Box 1657, Lusaka, Zambia
- Revolution. bi-m. (Orders outside Africa: 7 Countess Rd., London N.W. 5, England)

# Sources of Serials
# International Index

Editrice A   (IT)
A A A Motor Club of N.E. Pennsylvania   (US)
A A Grapevine, Inc.   (US)
A A R P   (UK)

A & A Enterprises Inc.   (LB)
A & P Publications   (II)
A & U Publishing Co., Ltd.   (JA)
Editorial A B C   (CK)
A B C - Arab Trade Reference: Arab & Middle East
   Countries   (UA)

A B C-CLIO
   see American Bibliographic Center-Clio Press   (US)
A B C der Deutschen Wirtschaft   (GW)
A B C Directory   (US)
A B C Historic Publications   (UK)
A B C Leisure Magazines, Inc.   (US)
A B C Schwann Publications, Inc.   (US)
A B C Travel Guides Ltd.   (UK)

A B C voor Handel en Industrie C. V.   (NE)
A. B. E. Publications   (UK)
A B M R Publications Ltd.   (UK)
A B W A Co., Inc.   (US)
A B Z Druck und Verlagsanstalt Hamann und Sinek
   (AU)

A.C. and E. Publishing Co.   (US)
A C P Publishers Ltd.   (UK)
A.C.T.-Action Press   (US)
A.D.A. Edita Tokyo Co., Ltd   (JA)

A D A-Vakpers   (NE)
A D C Publications   (AT)
A D E G-Oesterreich Handelsaktiengesellschaft
   (AU)

A D F Publishing, Inc.   (US)
A. D. P.   (FR)
A.D.P.S.   (FR)
A. D. Publications, Inc.   (US)

A E C I Ltd.   (SA)
A. E. C. R.   (FR)
A E G-Telefunken   (GW)
A F - Architekturforum   (AU)

A. F. E. R. L. A.   (FR)
A.F.E.S. Graduate Fellowship of Australia   (AT)
A.F.I.   (US)
A F L-C I O   (US)
A F L-C I O. Committee on Political Education   (US)

A F L-C I O. Industrial Union Department   (US)
A.F.L.-C.I.O. Labor Organizations   (US)
A-F Producciones Ltda   (PE)
A F T A C Enterprises   (US)
A F Z -Fischwaid Verlagsgesellschaft mbH   (GW)
A G A Corporation   (US)
A.G.E.   (IT)
A. G. Publications Ltd.   (IS)

A.-G.-T.-Verlag Georg Thum   (GW)
A I D
   see U.S. Agency for International Development
   (US)
A I E A
   see International Atomic Energy Agency   (UN)
A.I.F. Services   (FR)
A I G A
   see International Association of Geomagnetism and
   Aeronomy   (JA)
A I M   (MX)
A I M Report   (US)
A I R
   see India. All India Radio   (II)
A L A   (AG)
Ediciones A. L. P. E.   (MX)
A la Votre   (US)
A-Lehdet Oy   (FI)
A M C K   (BE)
A.M. Dogliotti College of Medicine
   see under University of Liberia   (LB)
A. M. G. International   (GR)
A M K-Verlag   (AU)
A.M.O.   (UK)
A M R International, Inc.   (US)
A M S Press, Inc.   (US)
A.N.A.R.E. Club   (AT)
A.N.F.A.N.O.M.A.   (FR)
A.N.I.C.A.   (IT)
A N N Y Publications Inc.   (US)
A. N. S. I. Societa A. R. L.   (IT)
A.N. Sinha Institute of Social Studies
   see Sinha Institute of Social Studies   (II)
A O E   (AU)
A P B A Journal   (US)
A.P. Publications Ltd.   (UK)
A P S   (US)
A P S Publications   (US)
A-Press   (CS)
A Press Ltd.   (US)
A Q Verlag   (GW)
Editrice A R C O   (IT)
A. R. E. P.- Aime Reboul Editions Publicite   (FR)
A-R Editions, Inc.   (US)
A R G Publishing Co.   (US)
A.R.T.E.   (IT)
A.S. Barnes and Co., Inc.   (US)
A S C U   (US)
A. S. E. A. Electric Australia Pty. Ltd.   (AT)
A S G Industries, Inc.   (US)
A S I Publications Ltd.   (UK)
A S M P-Society of Photographers in Communications
   (US)
A S T M S   (UK)
A S T M S. Pearl Section Gazette Committee   (UK)
A S U C L A Communications Board   (US)
Editions A. T. D. Science et Service   (FR)
A T-Fachverlag GmbH   (GW)
A. T. S. I. L   (IT)

Ediciones A U C A   (CL)
A und O Handelsgesellschaft mbH und Co. KG
   (GW)
A V A Magazine   (UK)
A.V.A. Promotions Ltd.   (HK)
A V A R D
   see Association of Voluntary Agencies for Rural
   Development   (II)
A V D Verlag GmbH   (GW)
Editrice A.V.E   (IT)
A Wake Newslitter Press   (UK)
Editoriale A. Z   (IT)
A-4 Publications Ltd.   (UK)
Aabo Akademi   (FI)
Aabo Akademi. Statsvetenskapliga   (FI)
Aabo Swedish University School of Economics.
   Institute of Commercial Geography
   see Handelshoegskolan vid Aabo Akademi.
   Ekonomisk-Geografiska Institutionen   (FI)
Aachener Geschichtsverein   (GW)
AAFAQ Monthly   (UK)
Aahlens och Aakerlunds Foerlag AB   (SW)
Uitgeverij Aarde en Kosmos   (NE)
Aargauer Tagblatt AG   (SZ)
Aarhus Frimaerkehandel   (DK)
Aarhus Universitet. Botanical Institute   (DK)
Aarhus Universitet. Institut for Jysk Sprog- og
   Kulturforskning   (DK)
Aarhus Universitet. Matematisk Institut   (DK)
Aaron Burr Association   (US)
Aarox Publishing Ltd.   (UK)
Paul Aastroems Foerlag   (SW)
Aavesh   (II)
Publicaciones de l' Abadia de Montserrat   (SP)
Abadia de Santo Domingo de Silos   (SP)
Antonio Abarca Benito, Ed. & Pub.   (SP)
Emilio L. Abarico, Ed. & Pub.   (PH)
Abayuma Seismological Observatory
   see under Kyoto University   (JA)
Abba   (US)
Abbaco   (IT)
Abbaye Benedictine de Mont-Laurier   (CN)
Abbaye de Lerins   (FR)
Abbaye de Maredsous   (BE)
Editions de l' Abbaye de Solesmes   (FR)
Abbaye du Mont-Cesar   (BE)
Abbey Garden Press   (US)
Abbey National Building Society   (UK)
Abbey Press   (UK)
Abbey Press   (US)
Abbotsbury Publications   (UK)
Abbott, Langer & Associates   (US)
Abdij van Berne   (NE)
Abdullahi Bayero College   (NR)
Z. Abedin, Ed. & Pub.   (II)
Abeille de France, S.A.R.L.   (FR)
Abeilles et Fleurs   (FR)
Abel News Agencies   (US)
Abelard-Schuman   (US)

Accountants' Pubiishing Co. Ltd. (UK)
Accounting Association of Australia and New Zealand (AT)
Accounting Corporation of America (US)
Ace Books (US)
Acero (MX)
Eduardo Acevedo, Ed. & Pub. (CK)
Achaab Publishing (MR)
Achalm-Verlag (GW)
Achdut Ha-Avoda-Poale Zion of Canada (CN)
Achievement Disabled Action Group, Inc. (US)
Achiever Publishing House (IS)
Achkhar (FR)
Ackermann Advertising and News Service Ltd. (CN)
Ackroyd Publications S. A. (BE)
Acme Boot Co., Inc. (US)
Acme Newspapers Inc. (US)
Acopsis (FR)
Acorn Press (US)
Acorn Publishing Co. Pty. Ltd. (AT)
Acorn Sporting Publications (UK)
Acoustic Corporation of America (US)
Acoustical and Board Products Association (US)
Acoustical Publications, Inc. (US)
Acoustical Society of America (US)
Acquarius Publications (PH)
Acquire Publishing Co., Inc. (US)
Acres, Inc. (US)
Acropolis Books (US)
Acta Anaesthesiologica (IT)
Acta Embryologiae Experimentalis (IT)
Acta Gastroenterologica Latinoamericana (AG)
Acta Iberica Radiologica-Cancerologica (SP)
Publications Acta Medica Belgica (BE)
Acta Obstetrica y Ginecologica Hispano-Lusitania (SP)
Acta Pediatrica Espanola (SP)
Acta Press (CN)
Acta Radiologica (SW)
Acta Universitatis Gothoburgensis (SW)
Actio Catholica (HU)
Actio Catholica Hungarorum in Exteris (IT)
ACTION
 see U. S. ACTION (US)
Action Catholique Generale Feminine (FR)
Action Chretienne en Orient (FR)
Action Cinematographique (BE)
Action Committee Against Narcotics (HK)
Action for Children's Television (US)
Action Municipale (FR)
Editions Action Poetique (FR)
Action Populaire (DM)
Action Publishers, Inc. (US)
Activa Publishing Ltd. (US)
Activites Musicales (FR)
Actors Equity Association (US)
Acts 29 (US)
Actual Size Press (US)
Actualidad Filatelica (SP)
Actualidad Pastoral (AG)
Actualidades Economicas (PO)
Actualite Agricole (CN)
Actualite en Copie Conforme S.P.R.L. (BE)
Actualite Fiduciaire (FR)
Actualite Juridique: Edition Droit Administratif (FR)
Actualite Magazine Quebec Ltd. (CN)
SARL Actualites Agricoles (FR)
Actuarieel Genootschap (NE)
Acupuncture Letter (US)
Ad Arts Associates (US)
Ad East Enterprises (US)
Ad Search: the National Want Ad Newspaper (US)
ADAC Verlag GmbH (GW)
Adalbert Stifter-Institut des Landes Oberoesterreich (AU)
Adam International Review (UK)
Adam Publishing Ltd. (UK)
Alger L. Adams, Ed. & Pub. (US)
Stuart M. Adams Holdings Pty. Ltd. (AT)
Adarsh Seva Sangha (II)
Adcraft Club of Detroit (US)
Addiction Research Foundation of Ontario (CN)
Addis Ababa University (ET)
Addis Ababa University. College of Technology (ET)
Addis Ababa University. Educational Research Centre (ET)
Addis Ababa University. Faculty of Law (ET)
Addis Ababa University. Geophysical Observatory (ET)
Addis Ababa University. Institute of Development Research (ET)
Addis Ababa University. Institute of Ethiopian Studies (ET)
Addis Ababa University. University Testing Center (ET)
Lloyd Addison, Ed. & Pub. (US)
Addison-Wesley Publishing Co. Advanced Book Program (US)

Addressograph-Multigraph (Pty.) Ltd. (SA)
Adela Investment Company S.A. (PE)
Adelaide City Council (AT)
Adelaide Women's Liberation Movement (AT)
Adelphi University (US)
Adelphi University School of Social Research (US)
Adept Publications (US)
Adex, C. V. (NE)
Adhesion Society of Japan (JA)
Albert Adib, Ed. & Pub. (LE)
P. Adimoolam, Ed. & Pub. (II)
Adirondack Life (US)
Adirondack Mountain Club, Inc. (US)
Adis Press (Australasia) Pty. Ltd. (NZ)
Adis Press Australasia Pty. Ltd. (AT)
Adlai Stevenson Institute (US)
Adlodorum (SA)
Admap Publications Ltd. (UK)
Administracao-Geral do Porto de Lisboa (PO)
Administracion General de Puertos (AG)
Administration in Mental Health (US)
Administrative and Clerical Officers Association (AT)
Administrative Change (II)
Administrative Management Society (US)
Administrative Staff College of India (II)
Adobe News, Inc. (US)
Adoptees' Liberty Movement Association (US)
Adrenal Metabolic Research Society (US)
Adressbuch-Gesellschaft Berlin mgH (GW)
Deutscher Adressbuch-Verlag (GW)
Adriatico (IT)
Adriatrca Editrice (IT)
Adult Education Association in Massachusetts, Inc. (US)
Adult Education Association of Israel (IS)
Adult Education Association of the United States of America (US)
Advaita Ashrama (II)
Advance Yoeman Press (US)
Advanced Institute for Analytic Psychotherapy (US)
Advanced Management Research (US)
Advanced Mile-Posts Publications Ltd. (UK)
Advanced Research Projects Agency (US)
Advanced Technology Publications, Inc. (US)
Advancement and Placement Institute (US)
Advancing Frontiers of Plant Sciences (II)
Adventure Guides, Inc. (US)
Adventurers (US)
Adventures in Poetry (US)
Adventuresses of Sherlock Holmes (US)
Editions Adversaires (SZ)
Adverse Drug Reaction Research Unit (UK)
Advertising and Media Consultants Ltd. (TH)
Advertising Association (UK)
Advertising Checking Bureau, Inc. (US)
Advertising Data Ltd. (UK)
Advertising Research & Marketing Services Ltd. (LE)
Advertising Research Foundation (US)
Advertising Specialty Institute (US)
Advertising Standards Authority Ltd. (UK)
Advertising Trade Publications, Inc. (US)
Advisory Centre for Education (UK)
Advisory Enterprises, Inc. (US)
Advisory Information Services Ltd. (UK)
Advisory Information Services Ltd (US)
Advocate (New York) (US)
Advocate (Providence) (US)
Advocate (San Mateo) (US)
Advocate House (US)
Advocate Newspaper Pty. Ltd. (AT)
Advokatska Komora Bosne i Hercegovine (YU)
Advokatska Komora Srbije (YU)
Advokatska Komora Vojvodine (YU)
Adyar Library and Research Centre (II)
Adyar-Verlagsvereinigung (AU)
Aegir Corp. (US)
Aegis-Verlag (GW)
Aemmepi Editrice (IT)
Aeolian Press (US)
Aer Lingus (IE)
Aerial Phenomena Research Organization (US)
Aero Club de Portugal (PO)
Aero-Club der Schweiz (SZ)
Aero Publishers, Inc. (US)
Aero West Magazine Inc. (US)
Aeroguia S.A. (SP)
Aeroklub CSSR (CS)
Aeromexico (MX)
Aeronautica & Air Label Collectors Club (US)
Aeronautica Macchi S.p.A. (IT)
Aeronautical Press Ltd. (NZ)
Aeronautical Publications of India Private Limited (II)
Aeronautical Research Institute of Sweden
 see Flygtekniska Foersoeksanstalten (SW)
Aeronautical Society of India (II)

Aeronews (IT)
Aerophile (US)
Aeroport de Paris (FR)
Aeropress (NE)
Aeropuertos y Servicios Auxiliares (MX)
Aeroquip Corp. (US)
Aerosol Industry Association of Japan (JA)
Aerosol Techniques, Inc. (US)
Aerospace Industries Association of America, Inc. (US)
Aerospace Medical Association (US)
Deutscher Aerzte-Verlag GmbH (GW)
Aerztekammer Berlin (GW)
Aerztekammer Bremen (GW)
Aerztekammer Niedersachsen (GW)
Aerztekammer Nordrhein (GW)
Aesthetik und Kommunikation Verlags-GmbH (GW)
Aetherius Society (US)
Aetna Life and Casualty (US)
Afars and Issas. Ministry of the Interior (FT)
Foerlags AB Affaersekonomi (SW)
Affairs Publishing Ltd. (CN)
Affiches d'Alsace et de Lorraine-Moniteur des Soumissions et des Ventes de Bois de l'Est (FR)
Affiliate Artists, Inc. (US)
Afghanistan. Department of Statistics (AF)
Afghanistan. Ministry of Education (AF)
Afghanistan. Ministry of Information and Culture (AF)
Afram Associates (US)
Africa Bibliographic Center (KE)
Africa Bureau (UK)
Africa Contemporary Record Ltd. (UK)
Africa Evangelical Fellowship (UK)
Africa Evangelistic Band (SA)
Africa Inland Mission (US)
Africa Inland Mission (KE)
Africa Institute of South Africa (SA)
Africa Investors & Placement Services, Inc. (US)
Africa Journal Ltd. (UK)
Africa News Service Inc. (US)
Africa Podium (FR)
Africa Publications (India) (II)
Africa Publications Trust (UK)
Africa Research Ltd. (UK)
Africa Today Associates (US)
Africaine (FR)
African-American Chamber of Commerce (US)
African American Institute (US)
African-American Labor Center (US)
African American Teachers Association (US)
African Association of St. Augustine (IT)
African Bibliographic Center (US)
African Clarion (SW)
African Cultures Publications Ltd. (NR)
African Development Bank (IV)
African Development Magazine Ltd. (UK)
African Education Press (NR)
African Institute for Economic and Social Development
 see Institut Africain pour le Developpement Economique et Social (IV)
African Institute for Economic Development and Planning (SG)
African Insurance Record (SA)
African International Publishing Co. (Pty) Ltd. (SA)
African Law Association in America, Inc. (US)
African Library Association of South Africa (SA)
African Literary and Scientific Publications Ltd. (NR)
African Literature Association (US)
African Methodist Episcopal Church (US)
African Methodist Episcopal Church (New York) (US)
African Methodist Episcopal Church. Division of Christian Education (US)
African Methodist Episcopal Zion Church (US)
African Methodist Episcopal Zion Church. Church Board of Publications (US)
African Music Society (SA)
African National Congress of South Africa (UK)
African National Congress of South Africa (ZA)
African National Council (RH)
African Newspapers of Nigeria Ltd. (NR)
African Oxygen Ltd (SA)
African Peoples Party (US)
African People's Socialist Party (US)
African Picture & Information Service (US)
African Publishing House, Ltd. (LB)
African Society (UA)
African Studies Association (US)
African Studies Association. Archives-Libraries Committee (US)
African Studies Association of the United Kingdom (UK)
African Studies Association of the West Indies (JM)
African Succulent Plant Society (UK)
African Violet Society of America, Inc. (US)

Ajia Keizai Kenkyusho
  *see* Institute of Developing Economies   (JA)
Ajia Seikei Gakkai
  *see* Society for Asian Political and Economic
  Studies   (JA)
Ajoy Bhavan   (II)
Akademia Ekonomiczna, Krakow   (PL)
Akademia Ekonomiczna, Poznan   (PL)
Akademia Ekonomiczna, Wroclaw   (PL)
Akademia Gorniczo-Hutnicza im. Stanislawa Staszica
  (PL)
Akademia Medyczna, Bialystok   (PL)
Akademia Medyczna, Krakow   (PL)
Akademia Medyczna, Warsaw   (PL)
Akademia Medyczna, Wroclaw   (PL)
Akademia Rolnicza, Krakow   (PL)
Akademia Rolnicza, Poznan   (PL)
Akademia Rolnicza, Szczecin   (PL)
Akademia Rolnicza, Warsaw   (PL)
Akademia Rolnicza, Wroclaw   (PL)
Akademia Rolniczo-Techniczna   (PL)
Akademiai Kiado, Publishing House of the Hungarian
  Academy of Sciences   (HU)
Akademie der Landwirtschaftswissenschaften der DDR
  (GE)
Akademie der Landwirtschaftswissenschaften der
  DDR. Institut fuer Landwirtschaftliche Information
  und Dokumentation   (GE)
Akademie der Paedagogischen Wissenschaften der
  DDR   (GE)
Akademie der Paedagogischen Wissenschaften der
  DDR. Zentralstelle fuer Paedagogische Information
  und Dokumentation   (GE)
Akademie der Wissenschaften. Vienna   (AU)
Akademie der Wissenschaften der DDR   (GE)
Akademie der Wissenschaften der DDR.
  Geodaetisches Institut   (GE)
Akademie der Wissenschaften der DDR.
  Geographisches Institut   (GE)
Akademie der Wissenschaften der DDR. Institut fuer
  Griechisch-Roemische Altertumskunde   (GE)
Akademie der Wissenschaften der DDR. Institut fuer
  Meereskunde, Warnemuende   (GE)
Akademie der Wissenschaften der DDR. Institut fuer
  Wirtschaftsgeschichte   (GE)
Akademie der Wissenschaften der DDR.
  Nationalkomitee fuer Geodaesie und Geophysik
  (GE)
Akademie der Wissenschaften der DDR. Rat fuer
  Sprachwissenschaft   (GE)
Akademie der Wissenschaften der DDR.
  Zentralinstitut fuer Alte Geschichte und
  Archaeologie   (GE)
Akademie der Wissenschaften der DDR.
  Zentralinstitut fuer Ernaehrung   (GE)
Akademie der Wissenschaften der DDR.
  Zentralinstitut fuer Genetik und
  Kulturpflanzenforschung Gatersleben   (GE)
Akademie der Wissenschaften der DDR.
  Zentralinstitut fuer Geschichte   (GE)
Akademie der Wissenschaften der DDR.
  Zentralinstitut fuer Isotopen- und Strahlenforschung
  (GE)
Akademie der Wissenschaften der DDR.
  Zentralinstitut fuer Literaturgeschichte   (GE)
Akademie der Wissenschaften der DDR.
  Zentralinstitut fuer Mathematik und Mechanik
  (GE)
Akademie der Wissenschaften der DDR.
  Zentralinstitut fuer Physik der Erde   (GE)
Akademie der Wissenschaften der DDR.
  Zentralinstitut fuer Sprachwissenschaft   (GE)
Akademie der Wissenschaften der DDR.
  Zentralinstitut fuer Wirtschaftswissenschaften   (GE)
Akademie der Wissenschaften, Goettingen   (GW)
Akademie der Wissenschaften und der Literatur,
  Mainz   (GW)
Akademie der Wissenschaften und der Literatur,
  Mainz. Kommission fuer Geschichte des Altertums
  (GW)
Akademie der Wissenschaften und der Literatur,
  Mainz. Kommission fuer Geschichte der Medizin
  und der Naturwissenschaften   (GW)
Akademie der Wissenschaften und der Literatur,
  Mainz. Mathematisch-Naturwissenschaftliche Klasse
  (GW)
Akademie fuer Aerztliche Fortbildung der DDR
  (GE)
Akademie fuer Fuehrungskraefte der Wirtschaft
  (GW)
Akademie fuer Oeffentliches Gesundheitswesen
  (GW)
Akademie fuer Staats und Rechtswissenschaft der
  DDR   (GE)
Akademie fuer Staats und Rechtswissenschaft der
  DDR. Informationszentrum Staat und Recht   (GE)

Akademie Verlag GmbH.   (GE)
Akademiet for de Tekniske Videnskaber   (DK)
Akademifoerlaget   (SW)

Akademiia na Selskostopanskite Nauki   (BU)
Akademija Nauka i Umjetnosti Bosne i Hercegovine.
  Centar za Balkanoloska Ispitivanja   (YU)
Akademija Nauka i Umjetnosti Bosne i Hercegovine.
  Hemijski Institut   (YU)
Akademija Nauka i Umjetnosti Bosne i Hercegovine.
  Odeljenje Drustvenih Nauka   (YU)
Akademija Nauka i Umjetnosti Bosne i Hercegovine.
  Odjeljenje Istorijsko Filoloskih Nauk   (YU)
Akademija Nauka i Umjetnosti Bosne i Hercegovine.
  Odeljenje Medicinskih Nauka   (YU)
Akademin Foer Tekniska Vetenskaper
  *see* Teknillisten Tieteiden Akatemia   (FI)
Akademische Druck- und Verlagsanstalt   (AU)
Akademische Verlagsgesellschaft   (GW)
Akademisches Gymnasium. Elternvereinigung   (AU)
Akademisk Forlag   (DK)
Akademiya Budivnystva i Arkhitektury Ukrainskoi
  S.S.R.   (UR)
Akademiya Meditsinskikh Nauk S. S. S. R.   (UR)
Akademiya Meditsinskikh Nauk S.S.S.R. Nauchno-
  Issledovatel'skaya Laboratoriya Eksperimental'no-
  Biologicheskikh Modelei   (UR)
Akademiya Nauk Armyanskoi S.S.R.   (UR)
Akademiya Nauk Azerbaidzhanskoi S. S. R.   (UR)
Akademiya Nauk Estonskoi S.S.R.   (UR)
Akademiya Nauk Gruzinskoi S.S.R.   (UR)
Akademiya Nauk Kazakhskoi S. S. R.   (UR)
Akademiya Nauk Kirgizskoi S. S. R.   (UR)
Akademiya Nauk Latviiskoi S. S. R.   (UR)
Akademiya Nauk Latviiskoi S.S.R. Institut Mekhaniki
  Polimerov   (UR)
Akademiya Nauk Litovskoi S.S.R   (UR)
Akademiya Nauk Litovskoi S.S.R. Institut Fiziko-
  Tekhnicheskikh Problem Energetiki   (UR)
Akademiya Nauk Litovskoi S. S. R. Lietuviu Kalbos Ir
  Literaturos Institutas   (UR)
Akademiya Nauk Moldavskoi S.S.R.   (UR)
Akademiya Nauk S. S. S R   (UR)
Akademiya Nauk S.S.S.R. Astrosovet   (UR)
Akademiya Nauk S.S.S.R. Chemical Technology
  Section   (UR)
Akademiya Nauk S.S.S.R. Dagestanskii Filial   (UR)
Akademiya Nauk S. S. S. R. Dal'nevostochnyi
  Nauchnyi Tsentr   (UR)
Akademiya Nauk S. S. S. R. Institut Arkheologii
  (UR)
Akademiya Nauk S. S. S. R. Institut Automatiki i
  Telemekhaniki   (UR)
Akademiya Nauk S.S.S.R. Institut Biologicheskoi
  Fiziki   (UR)
Akademiya Nauk S.S.S.R. Institut Ekonomiki   (UR)
Akademiya Nauk S.S.S.R. Institut
  Elementoorganicheskikh Soedinenii   (UR)
Akademiya Nauk S.S.S.R. Institut Etnografii   (UR)
Akademiya Nauk S. S. S. R. Institut Filosofii   (UR)
Akademiya Nauk S.S.S.R. Institut Fiziki im. P. N.
  Lebedeva   (UR)
Akademiya Nauk S. S. S. R. Institut Fiziki Zemli
  (UR)
Akademiya Nauk S.S.S.R. Institut Geokhimii i
  Analitichnoi Khimii im. V. I. Vernadskogo   (UR)
Akademiya Nauk S. S. S. R. Institut Geologii
  Rudnykh Mestorozhdenii, Petrografii, Mineralogii i
  Geokhimii   (UR)
Akademiya Nauk S.S.S.R. Institut Gosudarstva i Prava
  (UR)
Akademiya Nauk S. S. S. R. Institut Istorii S. S. S. R.
  (UR)
Akademiya Nauk S.S.S.R. Institut Latinskoi Ameriki
  (UR)
Akademiya Nauk S. S. S. R. Institut Matematiki
  (UR)
Akademiya Nauk S.S.S.R. Institut Mirovoi Ekonomiki
  i Mezhdunarodnykh Otnoshenii   (UR)
Akademiya Nauk S. S. S. R. Institut Narodov Azii
  (UR)
Akademiya Nauk S. S. S. R. Institut Nauchnoi
  Informatsii i Fundamentalnaya Biblioteka po
  Obshchestvennym Naukam   (UR)
Akademiya Nauk S. S. S. R. Institut Obshchei i
  Neorganicheskoi Khimii im. N.S. Kurnakova   (UR)
Akademiya Nauk S.S.S.R. Institut Okeanologii   (UR)
Akademiya Nauk S. S. S. R. Institut Paleontologii
  (UR)

Akademiya Nauk S.S.S.R. Institut Russkogo Yazyka
  (UR)
Akademiya Nauk S.S.S.R. Institut Vodnykh Problem
  (UR)
Akademiya Nauk S.S.S.R. Institut Vostokovedeniya
  (UR)
Akademiya Nauk S. S. S. R. Institut Vseobshchei
  Istorii   (UR)
Akademiya Nauk S. S. S. R. Institut Yazykoznaniya
  (UR)
Akademiya Nauk S.S.S.R. Kol'skii Filial   (UR)
Akademiya Nauk S.S.S.R. Krymskaya
  Astrofizicheskaya Observatoriya   (UR)
Akademiya Nauk S.S.S.R. Laboratoriya Teorii
  Protsessov Perenosa   (UR)
Akademiya Nauk S.S.S.R. Mezhduvedomstvennyi
  Geofizicheskii Komitet   (UR)
Akademiya Nauk S.S.S.R. Nauchnyi Sovet po Istorii
  Mirovoi Kul'tury   (UR)
Akademiya Nauk S.S.S.R. Okeanografichnaya
  Komissiya   (UR)
Akademiya Nauk S. S. S. R. Otdelenie Biokhimii,
  Biofiziki i Khimii Fiziologicheski Aktivnykh
  Soedinenii   (UR)
Akademiya Nauk S.S.S.R. Otdelenie Fiziko-
  tekhnicheskikh Problem Energetiki   (UR)
Akademiya Nauk S.S.S.R. Otdelenie Fiziologii im. I.P.
  Pavlova   (UR)
Akademiya Nauk S.S.S.R. Otdelenie Geologii,
  Geofiziki, Geokhimii   (UR)
Akademiya Nauk S. S. S. R. Otdelenie Mekhaniki i
  Protsessov Upravleniya   (UR)
Akademiya Nauk S. S. S. R. Otdelenie Nauk o Zemle
  (UR)
Akademiya Nauk S.S.S.R. Otdelenie Obshchei Biologii
  (UR)
Akademiya Nauk S.S.S.R. Otdelenie Obshchei i
  Tekhnicheskoi Khimii   (UR)
Akademiya Nauk S.S.S.R. Sektor Istochnikovedeniya i
  Vspomogatel'nykh Istoricheskikh Distsiplin   (UR)
Akademiya Nauk S. S. S. R. Sibirskoe Otdelenie
  (UR)
Akademiya Nauk S.S.S.R. Uralskii Nauchnyi Tsentr
  (UR)
Akademiya Nauk S.S.S.R. Vostochno- Sibirskii Filial
  (UR)
Akademiya Nauk S. S. S. R. Vsesoyuznoe
  Botanicheskoe Obshchestvo   (UR)
Akademiya Nauk S. S. S. R. Vsesoyuznoe
  Obshchestvo Pochvovedeniya   (UR)
Akademiya Nauk S. S. S. R. Vychislitel'nyi Tsentr
  (UR)
Akademiya Nauk Tadzhikskoi S. S. R.   (UR)
Akademiya Nauk Tadzhikskoi S.S.R. Institut
  Ekonomiki   (UR)
Akademiya Nauk Tadzhikskoi S. S. R. Tsentralnaya
  Nauchnaya Biblioteka   (UR)
Akademiya Nauk Turkmenskoi S.S.R.   (UR)
Akademiya Nauk Turkmenskoi S. S. R. Institut
  Pustyni   (UR)
Akademiya Nauk Ukrainskoi S. S. R.   (UR)
Akademiya Nauk Ukrainskoi S.S.R. Fiziko-
  Tekhnicheskii Institut Nizkikh Temperatur   (UR)
Akademiya Nauk Ukrainskoi S.S.R. Glavnaya
  Astronomicheskaya Observatoriya   (UR)
Akademiya Nauk Ukrainskoi S.S.R. Institut Biokhimii
  (UR)
Akademiya Nauk Ukrainskoi S.S.R. Institut Botaniki
  (UR)
Akademiya Nauk Ukrainskoi S. S. R. Institut
  Ekonomiki   (UR)
Akademiya Nauk Ukrainskoi S.S.R. Institut
  Elektrosvarki im. E. O. Patona   (UR)
Akademiya Nauk Ukrainskoi S.S.R. Institut Gaza
  (UR)
Akademiya Nauk Ukrainskoi S.S.R. Institut Istorii
  (UR)
Akademiya Nauk Ukrainskoi S.S.R. Institut
  Kibernetiki   (UR)
Akademiya Nauk Ukrainskoi S.S.R. Institut Literatury
  im. T.G. Shevchenko   (UR)
Akademiya Nauk Ukrainskoi S.S.R. Institut
  Matematiki   (UR)
Akademiya Nauk Ukrainskoi S. S. R. Institut
  Mikrobiologii   (UR)
Akademiya Nauk Ukrainskoi S.S.R. Institut Prikladnoi
  Matematiki i Mekhaniki   (UR)
Akademiya Nauk Ukrainskoi S.S.R. Institut Problem
  Mashinostroeniya   (UR)
Akademiya Nauk Ukrainskoi S.S.R. Institut Problem
  Materialovedeniya   (UR)
Akademiya Nauk Ukrainskoi S.S.R. Institut Problem
  Prochnosti   (UR)
Akademiya Nauk Ukrainskoi S.S.R. Institut Zoologii
  (UR)

Akademiya Nauk Ukrainskoi S.S.R. Instytut
    Mystetsvo-znavstva, Folkloru ta Etnografii  (UR)
Akademiya Nauk Ukrainskoi S.S.R. Kiberneticheskii
    Tsentr  (UR)
Akademiya Nauk Ukrainskoi S.S.R. Material Sciences
    Institute  (UR)
Akademiya Nauk Uzbekskoi S.S.R.  (UR)
Akademiya Nauk Uzbekskoi S.S.R. Institut Matematiki
    im V. I. Romanovskogo  (UR)
Akademiya Navuk Belarusskai S. S. R.  (UR)
Akademiya Navuk Belorusskoi S. S. R. Institut
    Yazikoznaniya im. Yakuba Kolasa  (UR)
Akademiya Pedagogicheskikh Nauk S.S.S.R.  (UR)
Akademiya Pedagogicheskikh Nauk S.S.S.R. Nauchno
    - Issledovatel'skii Institut Pedagogicheskoi
    Metodologii Standartov  (UR)
Akaroa Mail Co. Ltd.  (NZ)
Akashvani Group of Journals  (II)
Akedemi Gizi  (IO)
H. Akerets Erben AG  (SZ)
Akhbar el Yom Publishing House  (UA)
Al-Akhbar Printing Establishment  (UA)
Akhil Mithila Maithili Pracharak Sangh  (II)
Akhila Bharatiya Sanskrit Parishad  (II)
Akim-Israel Association for Rehabilitation of the
    Mentally Handicapped  (IS)
Akita Association of Rural Medicine  (JA)
Akita-ken Noson Igakkai
    see Akita Association of Rural Medicine  (JA)
Akiyoshi-dai Science Museum  (JA)
Akron Consolidated Ltd.  (NZ)
Akron Dental Society  (US)
Akron-Summit County Public Library  (US)
Akros Publications  (UK)
Forlaget Aktuel Viden A-S  (DK)
Aktuell Verlagsgesellschaft mbH  (GW)
Akvariet Publications  (SW)
Al Helal Printing and Publishing Co. Ltd.  (BG)
ALA Schweizerische Gesellschaft fuer Vogelkunde und
    Vogelschutz
    see Schweizerische Gesellschaft fuer Vogelkunde
    und Vogelschutz  (SZ)
Alabama. Commission on Higher Education  (US)
Alabama. Department of Archives and History  (US)
Alabama. Department of Conservation and Natural
    Resources  (US)
Alabama. Department of Conservation and Natural
    Resources. Marine Resources Div.  (US)
Alabama. Department of Education  (US)
Alabama. Department of Industrial Relations  (US)
Alabama. Department of Pensions and Security  (US)
Alabama. Department of Public Heaalth  (US)
Alabama. Development Office  (US)
Alabama. Division of Vital Statistics  (US)
Alabama. Division of Vocation Education and
    Community Colleges  (US)
Alabama. Law Enforcement Planning Agency  (US)
Alabama. Public Library Service  (US)
Alabama Academy of Science  (US)
Alabama Archaeological Society  (US)
Alabama Association of Secondary School Principals
    (US)
Alabama Baptist Historical Society  (US)
Alabama Chamber of Commerce  (US)
Alabama Dental Association  (US)
Alabama Education Association  (US)
Alabama Farm Bureau Federation  (US)
Alabama Food Council  (US)
Alabama Forestry Association  (US)
Alabama Geological Society  (US)
Alabama Historical Association  (US)
Alabama Junior College Library Association  (US)
Alabama League of Municipalities  (US)
Alabama Library Association, Inc.  (US)
Alabama Personnel and Guidance Association  (US)
Alabama Solar Energy Association  (US)
Alabama State Bar Association  (US)
Alabama State Council on the Arts and Humanities
    (US)
Alabama State Nurses Association  (US)
Alabama Trucking Association  (US)
Alabaster Passamore, Ltd.  (UK)
Alakendu Bodh Niketan  (II)
Alamal Magazine  (UA)
Alameda- Contra Costa Medical Association  (US)
Alameda-Contra Costa Transit District  (US)
Alamo Area Council of Governments  (US)
Alanno  (IT)
Editorial Alas  (SP)
Alaska. Board of Registration for Architects, Engineers
    and Land Surveyors  (US)
Alaska. Criminal Investigation Bureau  (US)
Alaska. Department of Agriculture. Statistical
    Reporting Service  (US)
Alaska. Department of Economic Development.
    Division of Economic Enterprise  (US)
Alaska. Department of Fish and Game  (US)

Alaska. Department of Fish and Game. Auke Bay
    (US)
Alaska. Department of Fish and Game. Game Division
    (US)
Alaska. Department of Health and Social Services
    (US)
Alaska. Department of Health and Social Services.
    Division of Medical Assistance  (US)
Alaska. Department of Health and Social Services.
    Office of Alcoholism  (US)
Alaska. Department of Labor. Employment Security
    Division  (US)
Alaska. Department of Natural Resources. Division of
    Geological and Geophysical Surveys  (US)
Alaska. Department of Natural Resources. Division of
    Lands  (US)
Alaska. Department of Natural Resources. Division of
    Oil and Gas  (US)
Alaska. Department of Public Safety. Planning and
    Research  (US)
Alaska. Department of Revenue  (US)
Alaska. Division of Family and Children Services
    (US)
Alaska. Division of Public Health  (US)
Alaska. Division of State Libraries  (US)
Alaska. Legislative Budget and Audit Committee
    (US)
Alaska. Office of Ombudsman  (US)
Alaska. Office of the Governor  (US)
Alaska. State Council on the Arts  (US)
Alaska. Violent Crimes Compensation Board  (US)
Alaska Bar Association  (US)
Alaska Conservation Society  (US)
Alaska Construction News, Inc.  (US)
Alaska Directory Corp.  (US)
Alaska Education Association  (US)
Alaska Geographic Society  (US)
Alaska Information & Research Service  (US)
Alaska Library Association  (US)
Alaska Methodist University Press  (US)
Alaska Native Medical Center  (US)
Alaska Northwest Publishing Co.  (US)
Alaska Travel Guide  (US)
Alaska Women's Resource Center  (US)
Alba Stamp Group  (UK)
Albania. Ministere de l'Agriculture  (AA)
Albania. Ministere de l'Enseignement et de la Culture
    (AA)
Albania. Ministere de la Sante Publique  (AA)
Albanian American Islamic Center New York- New
    Jersey  (US)
Albanian Orthodox Diocese of America  (US)
Albanians of Yugoslavia, Union of the Kossovars
    (US)
Albany Law School  (US)
Albany Medical College  (US)
Albany Medical College. Department of
    Ophthalmology  (US)
P. Francisco Albarracin Pascual, S.J.  (SP)
Editions Albatros  (FR)
Albatros, Nakladatelstvi pro Deti a Mladez  (CS)
Albee-Campbell, Inc.  (US)
Albemarle County Historical Society  (US)
Karl Alber GmbH  (GW)
Albert Press  (PK)
Albert Steffen Stiftung  (SZ)
Alberta. Alberta Council on Aging  (CN)
Alberta. Alcoholism & Drug Abuse Commission
    (CN)
Alberta. Bureau of Statistics  (CN)
Alberta. Business Development and Tourism. Business
    Services Branch  (CN)
Alberta. Department of Agriculture  (CN)
Alberta. Department of Agriculture. Horticultural
    Research Center  (CN)
Alberta. Department of Agriculture. Market Analysis
    Branch  (CN)
Alberta. Department of Education  (CN)
Alberta. Department of Health and Social
    Development  (CN)
Alberta. Department of Industry and Commerce
    (CN)
Alberta. Department of Recreation, Parks and Wildlife.
    4-H and Junior Forest Ranger Branch  (CN)
Alberta. Department of the Environment  (CN)
Alberta. Department of the Environment.
    Communications Branch  (CN)
Alberta. Energy Resources Conservation Board  (CN)
Alberta. Environment Conservation Authority  (CN)
Alberta Association for the Mentally Retarded  (CN)
Alberta Association of Registered Nurses  (CN)
Alberta Association of Registered Nursing Orderlies
    (CN)
Alberta Bowhunters and Archers Association  (CN)
Alberta Certified Nursing Aide Association  (CN)
Alberta Chamber of Commerce  (CN)
Alberta Disaster Services Agency  (CN)
Alberta Federation of Labour  (CN)

Alberta Genealogical Society  (CN)
Alberta Government Telephones  (CN)
Alberta Hail and Crop Insurance Corporation  (CN)
Alberta Hog Producers Marketing Board  (CN)
Alberta Home Economics Association  (CN)
Alberta Hospital Association  (CN)
Alberta Information Retrieval Association. Western
    Canada Chapter of A.S.I.S.  (CN)
Alberta Landrace Swine Association  (CN)
Alberta Motor Association  (CN)
Alberta Native Communications Society  (CN)
Alberta Opportunity Co.  (CN)
Alberta Pharmaceutical Association  (CN)
Alberta Research Council  (CN)
Alberta School Trustees Association  (CN)
Alberta Teachers' Association  (CN)
Alberta Teachers' Association. Professional
    Development Department  (CN)
Alberta Trucking Association  (CN)
Alberta-Westmorland-Kent Regional Library.
    Extension Department  (CN)
Albion Village Press  (UK)
Albrecht-Altdorfer-Gymnasium, Regensburg  (GW)
E. Albrecht-Verlags-KG  (GW)
Album  (UK)
Albuquerque Archaeological Society  (US)
Albuquerque Bar Association  (US)
Albus (Fabrika Sapuna i Hemijskih Proizvoda)  (YU)
Ediciones Alcala S.A.  (SP)
Alcan Aluminiumwerke GmbH  (GW)
Alcan Canada Products  (CN)
Alcan Smelters and Chemicals Ltd.  (CN)
Alchemist  (CN)
Editorial Alcion  (SP)
Alcohol and Drug Concerns Inc.  (CN)
Alcoholics Anonymous in South Africa & South-West
    Africa  (SA)
Alcoholics Anonymous World Services, Inc.  (US)
Alcoholism and Drug Addiction Research Foundation
    of Ontario
    see Addiction Research Foundation of Ontario
    (CN)
Alcuin Society  (CN)
Alvaro Aldana y Cia Ltd.  (CK)
Aldebaran  (US)
Alden Press (Oxford) Ltd.  (UK)
Aldine Publishing Co.  (US)
Rex W. Alding, Ed. & Pub.  (NZ)
Aldria Securities Ltd.  (UK)
Aldrich Chemical Company, Inc.  (US)
Aldrich Entomology Club  (US)
Aldrig Mere Krig  (DK)
Alektor-Verlag  (GW)
Alemas  (SP)
Aleph Ltd.  (US)
Publications Alerte  (CN)
Alessandria. Amministrazione Provinciale di
    Alessandria  (IT)
Alexander Graham Bell Association for the Deaf, Inc.
    (US)
Alexander Hamilton Institute  (US)
Alexander Research and Communications, Inc.
    Downtown Research & Development Center  (US)
Alexander von Humboldt-Stiftung  (GW)
Alexandria Medical Association  (UA)
Alexandrian Society  (US)
Alexanor  (FR)
Alfa  (CS)
ALFA Edizioni  (IT)
Alfa Romeo Owners Club  (US)
Alfa Romeo Owners Club. Capital Chapter  (US)
Ediciones Alfaguara S.A.  (SP)
Alfateh University. Faculty of Science  (LY)
Alfred P. Sloan Foundation  (US)
Algemeen Belgisch Vlasverbond  (BE)
Algemeen Christelijk Werkersverbond  (BE)
Algemeen Nederlands Verbond  (NE)
Algemeen Publiciteitskantoor B.V.  (NE)
Algemeen Verbond Bouw Bedrijf  (NE)
Algemeen Verbond van Ondernemers in het
    Schildersbedrijf  (NE)
Algemeen Verbond van Volkstuinders Vereenigingen in
    Nederland  (NE)
Algemeene Vereeniging "Radio Omroep"  (NE)
Algemene Bank Nederland  (NE)
Algemene Bond van Onderwijzend Personeel  (NE)
Algemene Conferentie der Nederlandse Letteren
    (NE)
Algemene Nederlandse Bond van
    Schoonheidsinstituten  (NE)
Algemene Nederlandse Grafische Bond  (NE)
Algemene Nederlandse Unie van Muziekverenigingen
    (NE)
Algemene Nederlandse Vereniging voor Sociale
    Geneeskunde  (NE)
Algemene Nederlandse Vredesactie  (NE)
Algemene Pharmaceutische Bond  (BE)
Algemene Speeltuinvereniging Prinsejagt  (NE)

Algemene Vereniging van Naaimachinehandelaren (NE)
Algemene Vereniging van Ondernemers in het Loodgieters-, Sanitair- en Gasverwarmingsinstallatiebedrijf (NE)
Algemene Vereniging van Zeevarenden (NE)
Algemene Vereniging voor de Centrale Verwarmings- en Luchtbehandelingsindustrie (NE)
Algeria. Bibliotheque Nationale (AE)
Algeria. Commissariat National a l'Informatique (AE)
Algeria. Direction des Douanes (AE)
Algeria. Direction des Statistiques (AE)
Algeria. Institut National Algerien du Commerce Exterieur (AE)
Algeria. Ministere de l'Industrie et de l'Energie. Direction des Mines et de la Geologie. Service Geologique
    see Algeria. Service Geologique (AE)
Algeria. Ministere de l'Information et de la Culture (AE)
Algeria. Office Algerien d'Action Economique et Touristique (AE)
Algeria. Office National Algerien du Tourisme (AE)
Algeria. Service Geologique (AE)
Algerie Economique (AE)
Alian Publications Inc. (US)
Alianza de Pueblos Libres (US)
Alice James Poetry Cooperative (US)
Alice Lloyd College (US)
Alieia (GR)
Aligarh Muslim University (II)
Aligarh Muslim University. Center for Advanced Study (II)
Aligarh Muslim University. Department of History (II)
Aligarh Muslim University. Department of Political Science (II)
Aligarh Muslim University. Geographical Society (II)
S. M. Alimuddin, Ed. & Pub. (II)
Alive & Kicking (US)
Alkebu-Lan Books (US)
All-American Conference to Combat Communism (US)
All Americas Publishers Service, Inc. Canterbury Export Group (US)
All Bengal Teachers' Association (II)
All-British Pigeon Racing Publishing Co. Ltd. (UK)
All-Church Press Newspapers (US)
All England Netball Association (UK)
All England Women's Lacrosse Association (UK)
All in (UK)
All India Administrative Offices Employees Union (II)
All India Air Conditioning and Refrigeration Association (II)
All India Anglo-Indian Association (II)
All India Association for Christian Higher Education (II)
All India Association of Mental Retardation (II)
All-India Automobile and Ancillary Industries Association (II)
All India Bank Employees Federation (II)
All India Basic Education Council (II)
All-India Bee Keepers Association (II)
All India Catholic University Federation (II)
All India Central Land Development Banks Cooperative Union Ltd. (II)
All India Coffee Workers Cooperative Societies Federation Ltd. (II)
All India Commercial Association (II)
All India Congress Committee (II)
All India Congress Committee. Women's Department (II)
All India Council of Mayors (II)
All India Crime Prevention Society (II)
All India Federation of Education Associations (II)
All India Federation of Master Printers (II)
All India Federation of University and College Teachers Organisations (II)
All-India Fine Arts and Crafts Society (II)
All India Food Preservers' Association (II)
All India Handloom Exporters Guide (II)
All India Homeopathic Association (II)
All India Indo-Korean Friendship Association (II)
All India Institute of Homeopathy (II)
All India Institute of Local Self Government (II)
All India Institute of Medical Sciences (II)
All India Institute of Medical Sciences. Department of Orthopaedic Surgery (II)
All India Instrument Manufacturers and Dealers Association (II)
All India Iron and Steel Stockholders Federation (II)
All India Kasiraja Trust (II)
All India Magic Circle (II)
All India Management Association (II)
All-India Manufacturers' Organization (II)
All India Non-Edible Oil Association (II)

All India Occupational Therapists' Association (II)
All India Ophthalmological Society (II)
All India Organisation of Employers (II)
All India Panchayat Parishad (II)
All India Radio
    see India. All India Radio (II)
All India Reporter Ltd. (II)
All India Sai Samaj (II)
All India State Cooperative Banks Federation (II)
All India Trade Union Congress (II)
All India Youth Federation (II)
All Kerala Homeopathic Physicians Association (II)
All-Pakistan Islamic Education Conference (PK)
All Pakistan Women's Association (PK)
All Saints' Church, Plumstead (SA)
All Seasons Publishing Co. (CN)
All This & Less Publishers (US)
Alla Bottega (IT)
Allahabad Geographical Society (II)
Allahabad Law Journal Co., Ltd. (II)
Allahabad Mathematical Society (II)
Allahabad University
    see University of Allahabad (II)
Allan Hancock Foundation (US)
Ian Allan Ltd. (UK)
Allegany Mountain Press (US)
Allegheny Continental and Ozark Airlines (US)
Allegheny County Bar Association (US)
Allegheny County Medical Society (US)
Allegheny County Pharmaceutical Association (US)
Allegheny Ludlum Steel Corp. (US)
George A. Allen, Jr., Ed. & Pub. (US)
Paul C. Allen, Ed. & Pub. (US)
W. H. Allen & Co. Ltd. (UK)
George Allen & Unwin (Publishers) Ltd. (UK)
Allen County Historical Society (US)
G. R. Allen, Ed. & Pub. (NZ)
Howard Allen Enterprises (US)
J. A. Allen Ltd. (UK)
Allen-Pacific Co. (US)
Allen Press Inc. (US)
Allens (Clerkenwell) Ltd. (UK)
Aller Press A-S (DK)
Allergy Information Association (CN)
A-S Allers Familie-Journal (NO)
Allers Foerlag AB (SW)
Allerton Press, Inc. (US)
Allgemeine Aerztliche Gesellschaft fuer Psychotherapie (GW)
Allgemeine Anthroposophische Gesellschaft (SZ)
Allgemeine Geschichtsforschende Gesellschaft der Schweiz (SZ)
Allgemeine Gesellschaft fuer Philosophie in Deutschland e.V. (GW)
Allgemeine Ortskrankenkasse (GW)
Allgemeine Sparkasse in Linz (AU)
Allgemeine Unfallversicherungsanstalt. Unfallverhuetungsdienst (AU)
Allgemeine Waermetechnik (GW)
Allgemeiner Caecilien-Verband (GW)
Allgemeiner Deutscher Automobil-Club e.V. (GW)
Allgemeiner Deutscher Tanzlehrer Verband (GW)
Alliance Chorale Canadienne (CN)
Alliance College. Department of English (US)
Alliance des Jeunes pour le Socialisme (FR)
Alliance des Professeurs de Montreal (CN)
Alliance Internationale de Tourisme
    see International Touring Alliance (SZ)
Alliance Israelite Universelle en France (FR)
Alliance Marxiste Revolutionnaire (FR)
Alliance Nationale des Mutualites Chretiennes (BE)
Alliance of American Insurers (US)
Alliance Party of Northern Ireland (UK)
Alliance Syndicaliste, Paris (FR)
Alliance-Zendings-Centrum Parousia (NE)
Allianz Versicherungs-AG (GW)
Allied Artists of America (US)
Allied Business Consultants, Inc. (US)
Allied Gasoline Retailers Association of Florida, Inc. (US)
Allied Graphic Arts (US)
Allied Industrial Workers of America (US)
Allied Newspapers (TH)
Allied Publishers Private Ltd. (II)
Allied Publishing Ltd. (SA)
Allied Trades Association (II)
Allis-Chalmers Corp. (US)
Allmaenna Foerlaget
    see Liber Foerlag (SW)
Allmaenna Foersvarsfoereningen (SW)
Allotrope (UK)
Allsport Publishing Corp. (US)
Allstate Enterprises, Inc. (US)
Kommanditbolaget Allt om Hobby AB och Co. (SW)
Alltech Publishing Co. (US)
Editrice Alluminio (IT)
Allured Publishing Corp. (US)
Allyn and Bacon, Inc. (US)

Alma Verlag (SZ)
Almanac Co. (US)
Almanach-Verlags-Gesellschaft (GW)
Badan Penerbit Almanak Jakarta (IO)
Editora Almanaque da Paraiba Ltda (BL)
Almindelige Danske Laegeforening (DK)
Almqvist and Wiksell International (SW)
Almwirtschaftlicher Verein Oberbayern (GW)
Aloka Bharati (II)
Aloy Steel Producers Association of India (II)
G. Alparone, Ed. & Pub. (IT)
Edizioni Alpe (IT)
Alpeninstitut fuer Umweltforschung und Entwicklungsplanung in der GFL (GW)
Alpha Beta Alpha, National Library Science Fraternity (US)
Alpha Beta Company (US)
Alpha Delta Kappa, Honorary Sorority for Women Educators (US)
Alpha Delta Sigma (US)
Alpha Epsilon Delta (US)
Alpha Epsilon Rho. Alpha Omega Chapter (US)
Alpha Kappa Alpha Sorority (US)
Alpha Kappa Delta - National Sociology Honor Society (US)
Alpha Omega Alpha Honor Medical Society (US)
Alpha Pi Mu, Industrial Engineering Honor Society (US)
Alpha Psi Omega National Theatre Honorary (US)
Alpha Publications (NR)
Alphaville Books (US)
Alpine Club (UK)
Alpine Club of Canada (CN)
Alpine Club of Canada. Edmonton Section (CN)
Alpine Garden Society (UK)
Editions Alsatia (FR)
Alt-Katholische Kirche Oesterreichs (AU)
Harry Alter, Ed. & Pub. (US)
Alter S.A. (SP)
Alternative England and Wales (UK)
Alternative Press Centre, Inc. (US)
Alternative Press Syndicate (US)
Alternative Sources of Energy (US)
Alternative to Alienation (CN)
Alternative Verlag GmbH (GW)
Alternatives (US)
Altherrenverband der Saengerschaft Franco-Palatia Bayreuth (GW)
Altra Italia (IT)
Altrafrica (IT)
Altri Termini (IT)
Aluminium Development Council of Australia (AT)
Aluminium-Verlag GmbH (GW)
Aluminium-Zentrale e.V. (GW)
Aluminiumraadet (DK)
Aluminum Association (US)
Aluminum Association. Statistical & Commercial Research Policy Committee (US)
Aluminum Workers International Union (US)
Ediciones Jose Luis Alvarez (SP)
Robert S. Alvarez, Ed. & Pub. (US)
Fachverlag Ernst Aly (GW)
Alyeska Reports (US)
Am Oved Ltd. Publishers (IS)
Ama (SP)
Amaco (NE)
AMACOM
    see American Management Associations (US)
Amagasinet (NO)
Amakusa Marine Biological Laboratory
    see under Kyushu University (JA)
Amakusa Rinkai Jikkensho
    see Kyushu University. Amakusa Marine Biological Laboratory (JA)
Amalgamated Clothing Textile Workers Union (US)
Amalgamated Clothing Workers of America (US)
Amalgamated Engineering Union (SA)
Amalgamated Jewelry, Diamond and Watchcase Worker's Union. Local No. 1 (US)
Amalgamated Metal Workers' Union (AT)
Amalgamated Milk Vendors Association of New South Wales (AT)
Amalgamated Press (II)
Amalgamated Press (Pty) Ltd. (SA)
Amalgamated Society of Woodworkers of South Africa (SA)
Amalgamated Transit Union (US)
Amalgamated Union of Engineering Workers. Engineering Section (UK)
Amalgamated Union of Engineering Workers. Foundry Section (UK)
Amalgamated Union of Engineering Workers. Technical, Administrative & Supervisory Section (UK)
Amalgamated Wireless (Australasia) Ltd. (AT)
Albert Amann Verlag (GW)
Amanzimtoti Printing & Publishing Co. (Pty) Ltd. (SA)

American Association of University Women. New York Division (US)

American Association of Variable Star Observers (US)

American Association of Veterinary Laboratory Diagnosticians (US)

American Association of Workers for the Blind, Inc. (US)

American Association of Zoo Veterinarians (US)

American Association of Zoological Parks and Aquariums (US)

American Association on Mental Deficiency (US)

American Astronautical Society, Inc. (US)

American Astronomical Society (US)

American Atheists (US)

American Austin-Bantam Club (US)

American Automobile Association (US)

American Automobile Association. East Florida Division (US)

American Automobile Association. Texas Division (US)

American Automobile Association. Wisconsin Division (US)

American Baby Inc. (US)

American Bandmasters Association (US)

American Banker, Inc. (US)

American Bankers Association (US)

American Bantam Association (US)

American Baptist Churches in the U.S.A. (US)

American Baptist Historical Society (US)

American Bar Association (US)

American Bar Association. Commission on Correctional Facilities & Services (US)

American Bar Association. Consortium on Legal Services & the Public (US)

American Bar Association. Department of Professional Standards (US)

American Bar Association. Law Student Division (US)

American Bar Association. Ombudsman Committee (US)

American Bar Association. Section of Administrative Law (US)

American Bar Association. Section of Antitrust Law (US)

American Bar Association. Section of Bar Activities (US)

American Bar Association. Section of Corporation, Banking and Business Law (US)

American Bar Association. Section of Criminal Justice (US)

American Bar Association. Section of Economics of Law Practice (US)

American Bar Association. Section of Family Law (US)

American Bar Association. Section of General Practice (US)

American Bar Association. Section of Individual Rights and Responsibilities (US)

American Bar Association. Section of Insurance, Negligence and Compensation Law (US)

American Bar Association. Section of International and Comparative Law (US)

American Bar Association. Section of Labor Relations Law (US)

American Bar Association. Section of Legal Education and Admissions to the Bar (US)

American Bar Association. Section of Litigation (US)

American Bar Association. Section of Local Government Law (US)

American Bar Association. Section of Natural Resources Law (US)

American Bar Association. Section of Public Contract Law (US)

American Bar Association. Section of Real Property, Probate and Trust Law (US)

American Bar Association. Section of Science and Technology (US)

American Bar Association. Section of Taxation (US)

American Bar Association. Special Committee on Environmental Law (US)

American Bar Association. Standing Committee on Lawyers' Title Guaranty Funds (US)

American Bar Association. Standing Committee on Legal Assistance for Military Personnel (US)

American Bar Association. Young Lawyers Section (US)

American Bar Foundation (US)

American Bard (US)

American Beekeeping Federation (US)

American Begonia Society, Inc. (US)

American Bell Association (US)

American Benedictine Review, Inc. (US)

American Berkshire Association (US)

American Better Health Publications (US)

American Bible Society (US)

American Bibliographic Service (US)

American Bibliographical Center-Clio Press (US)

American Bicentennial Communications Inc. (US)

American Biographical Institute (US)

American Birding Association (US)

American Blake Foundation, Inc. (US)

American Board for Certification in Orthotics and Prosthetics (US)

American Board of Missions to the Jews (US)

American Board of Professional Psychology (US)

American Boccaccio Association (US)

American Booksellers Association (US)

American Bowling Congress, Inc. (US)

American Boxwood Society (US)

American Brewer Publishing Corp. (US)

American Broncho-Esophagological Association (US)

American Bryological & Lichenological Society (US)

American Bureau for Medical Aid to China (US)

American Bureau of Metal Statistics Inc. (US)

American Bureau of Shipping (US)

American Business Communication Association (US)

American Business Law Association (US)

American Business Men's Research Foundation (US)

American Business Press, Inc. (US)

American Business Women's Association (US)

American Camellia Society (US)

American Camping Association (US)

American-Canadian Publishers, Inc. (US)

American Cancer Society, Inc. (US)

American Cancer Society, Inc. Connecticut Division (US)

American Cancer Society, Inc. Louisiana Division (US)

American Cancer Society, Inc. Minnesota Division (US)

American Canoe Association (US)

American Carbon Committee (US)

American Carpatho-Russian Orthodox Greek Catholic Diocese (US)

American Cat Fanciers Association (US)

American Catholic Historical Association (US)

American Catholic Historical Society of Philadelphia (US)

American Catholic Philosophical Association (US)

American Cemetery Association (US)

American Ceramic Society, Inc. (US)

American Chain & Cable Co. Inc. (US)

American Challenge (US)

American Chamber of Commerce (United Kingdom) (UK)

American Chamber of Commerce for Brazil (BL)

American Chamber of Commerce in Argentina (AG)

American Chamber of Commerce in Australia (AT)

American Chamber of Commerce in France (FR)

American Chamber of Commerce in Italy (IT)

American Chamber of Commerce in Japan (JA)

American Chamber of Commerce in Morocco (MR)

American Chamber of Commerce in Thailand (TH)

American Chamber of Commerce in the Netherlands (NE)

American Chamber of Commerce of Mexico (MX)

American Chamber of Commerce of the Philippines (PH)

American Chamber of Commerce Researchers Association (US)

American Checker Federation (US)

American Chemical Society (US)

American Chemical Society. Chicago Section (US)

American Chemical Society. Cleveland Section (US)

American Chemical Society. Delaware Section (US)

American Chemical Society. Division of Chemical Education (US)

American Chemical Society. Division of Environmental Chemistry (US)

American Chemical Society, Florida Section (US)

American Chemical Society. Indiana Section (US)

American Chemical Society. Lehigh Valley Section (US)

American Chemical Society. Minnesota Section (US)

American Chemical Society. New Jersey Section & New York Section (US)

American Chemical Society. Philadelphia Section (US)

American Chemical Society. Pittsburgh Section (US)

American Chemical Society. Rochester Section (US)

American Chemical Society. Rubber Division (US)

American Chemical Society. St. Louis Section (US)

American Chemical Society. Southern California Section (US)

American Chemical Society. Syracuse Section (US)

American Chemical Society. Virginia Section (US)

American Chiropractic Association, Inc. (US)

American Choral Directors Association (US)

American Choral Foundation, Inc. (US)

American Church Union Inc. (US)

American Cinema Editors, Inc. (US)

American Citizen (US)

American Citizen's Band Radio Association (US)

American Civil Defense Association (US)

American Civil Liberties Union (US)

American Civil Liberties Union of New Jersey (US)

American Civil Liberties Union of Southern California (US)

American Civil Liberties Union of Washington (US)

American Civil War Round Table of Australia (AT)

American Classical College. Institute for Economic and Financial Research (US)

American Classical College. Institute for Economic & Political World Strategic Studies (US)

American Classical College. Research Center for Economic Psychology (US)

American Classical League (US)

American Cleft Palate Association (US)

American Clinical and Climatological Association (US)

American Coin Club (US)

American Collectors Association, Inc. (US)

American College Health Association (US)

American College in Paris (FR)

American College of Allergists (US)

American College of Apothecaries (US)

American College of Cardiology (US)

American College of Chest Physicians (US)

American College of Clinical Pharmacology (US)

American College of Dentists (US)

American College of Emergency Medical Technicians (US)

American College of Emergency Physicians (US)

American College of Foot Orthopedists (US)

American College of Gastroenterology (US)

American College of General Practioners in Osteopathic Medicine and Surgery (US)

American College of Hospital Administrators (US)

American College of Legal Medicine (US)

American College of Life Underwriters (US)

American College of Neuropsychiatrists (US)

American College of Nurse-Midwives (US)

American College of Nursing Home Administrators (US)

American College of Obstetricians and Gynecologists (US)

American College of Orgonomy (US)

American College of Osteopathic Surgeons (US)

American College of Physicians (US)

American College of Preventive Medicine (US)

American College of Probate Counsel (US)

American College of Psychiatrists (US)

American College of Radiology (US)

American College of Sports Medicine (US)

American College of Surgeons (US)

American College of Veterinary Pathologists (US)

American College of Veterinary Toxicologists (US)

American College Testing Program (US)

American Collegiate Employment Institute. Summer Employment Division (US)

American Committee on Italian Migration (US)

American Communications Network (US)

American Comparative Literature Association (US)

American Concrete Institute (US)

American Conference of Academic Deans (US)

American Conference of Governmental Industrial Hygienists (US)

American Conference of Governmental Industrial Hygienists. Committee on Industrial Ventilation (US)

American Conference of Therapeutic Self Help, Self Health, Social Clubs A.C.T. (US)

American Congregational Association (US)

American Congress of Rehabilitation Medicine (US)

American Congress on Surveying & Mapping (US)

American Congress on Surveying and Mapping. Arizona Section (US)

American Consulting Engineers Council (US)

American Contract Bridge League, Inc. (US)

American Coptic Association (US)

American Correctional Association (US)

American Corrective Therapy Association (US)

American Council for Curricular Evaluation (US)

American Council for Judaism (US)

American Council for Nationalities Service (US)

American Council of Independent Laboratories Inc. (US)

American Council of Industrial Arts Teacher Educators (US)

American Council of Learned Societies (US)

American Council of Life Insurance (US)

American Council of Polish Cultural Clubs (US)

American Council of Teachers of Uncommonly Taught Asian Languages (US)

American Council of the Blind (US)

American Council of Voluntary Agencies for Foreign Service, Inc (US)

American Council on Consumer Interests (US)

American Council on Education (US)

American Council on Education for Journalism (US)

American Council on Industrial Arts Teacher Education (US)

American Council on Pharmaceutical Education (US)

American Institute of Plant Engineers  (US)
American Institute of Public Opinion  (US)
American Institute of Real Estate Appraisers  (US)
American Institute of Steel Construction, Inc.  (US)
American Institute of the History of Pharmacy  (US)
American Institute of Ultrasound in Medicine  (US)
American Institutes for Research  (US)
American Institutes for Research (Pittsburgh)  (US)
American Instructors of the Deaf  (US)
American Instrument Co. Inc.  (US)
American Insurance Association  (US)
American-International Charolais Association  (US)
American International Investment Corporation  (US)
American Investment Co.  (US)
American Iron and Steel Institute  (US)
American-Israel Chamber of Commerce and Industry,
   Inc.  (US)
American Israel Ventures Corp.  (US)
American Italian Historical Association  (US)
American Jersey Cattle Club  (US)
American Jewish Alternatives to Zionism, Inc.  (US)
American Jewish Committee  (US)
American Jewish Committee. Institute of Human
   Relations  (US)
American Jewish Committee. National Labor Service
   (US)
American Jewish Congress  (US)
American Jewish Congress. Commission on Law and
   Social Actions  (US)
American Jewish Historical Society  (US)
American Jewish Life  (US)
American Jewish Times-Outlook  (US)
American Journal of Acupuncture  (US)
American Journal of Ancient History  (US)
American Journal of Economics & Sociology, Inc.
   (US)
American Journal of Nursing Co.  (US)
American Journal of Science  (US)
American Judges Association  (US)
American Judicature Society  (US)
American Junior Bowling Congress  (US)
American Kennel Club, Inc.  (US)
American Kidney Fund  (US)
American Labor Conference on International Affairs,
   Inc.  (US)
American Lancia Club  (US)
American Land Development Association  (US)
American Land Title Association  (US)
American Landrace Association  (US)
American Laryngological Association  (US)
American Laryngological Rhinological and Otological
   Society  (US)
American Latvian Association in the U. S., Inc.  (US)
American Law Enforcement Officers Association
   (US)
American Law Institute  (US)
American Law Institute-American Bar Association
   Committee on Continuing Professional Education
   (US)
American Lawn Bowls Association  (US)
American Leather Chemists Association  (US)
American Lebanese Serian Associated Charities  (US)
American Legion  (US)
American Legion. Department of Colorado  (US)
American Legion. Department of Indiana  (US)
American Legion. Department of Iowa  (US)
American Legion. Department of Mississippi  (US)
American Legion. Department of Missouri  (US)
American Legion. Department of Montana  (US)
American Legion. Department of Nebraska  (US)
American Legion. Department of South Dakota  (US)
American Legion. Department of Texas  (US)
American Legion. Department of Virginia  (US)
American Legion. Department of West Virginia  (US)
American Legion Auxiliary  (US)
American Legion Magazine  (US)
American Legion Press Association  (US)
American Library Association  (US)
American Library Association. Advisory Committee
   for Liaison with Japanese Libraries  (US)
American Library Association. Conference
   Arrangements Office  (US)
American Library Association. Education Division
   (US)
American Library Association. Government
   Documents Round Table  (US)
American Library Association. Health and
   Rehabilitative Library Services Division  (US)
American Library Association. Information Science
   and Automation Division  (US)
American Library Association. Intellectual Freedom
   Committee  (US)
American Library Association. International Relations
   Round Table  (US)
American Library Association. Junior Members Round
   Table  (US)
American Library Association. Library Administration
   Division  (US)

American Library Association. Library Education
   Division  (US)
American Library Association. Library Technology
   Program  (US)
American Library Association. Reference & Adult
   Services Division  (US)
American Library Association. Reference and
   Subscription Books Review Committee  (US)
American Library Association. Resources and
   Technical Services Division  (US)
American Library Association. Social Responsibilities
   Round Table  (US)
American Library Association. Staff Organization
   Round Table  (US)
American Library Association. Washington Office
   (US)
American Library Trustee Association  (US)
American Life Foundation  (US)
American Life Insurance Association  (US)
American-Lithuanian Medical Association  (US)
American-Lithuanian Press Radio Association  (US)
American-Lithuanian R.C. Women's Alliance  (US)
American Littoral Society  (US)
American Logistics Association  (US)
American Lung Association  (US)
American Lung Association of New York State  (US)
American Lutheran Church  (US)
American Lutheran Church and Lutheran Church in
   America  (US)
American Lutheran Church. Commission on
   Evangelism  (US)
American Lutheran Church Women  (US)
American Lutheran Publicity Bureau  (US)
American Malacological Union, Inc.  (US)
American Management Associations  (US)
American Management Associations. Executive
   Compensation Service  (US)
American Marine Register  (US)
American Maritime Cases, Inc.  (US)
American Marketing Association  (US)
American Marketing Association. Committee on
   Attitude Research  (US)
American Marketing Association. New York Chapter
   (US)
American Mathematical Society  (US)
American Matthay Association  (US)
American Medical Association  (US)
American Medical Association Auxiliary, Inc.  (US)
American Medical Association. Center for Health
   Services Research and Development  (US)
American Medical Association. Council on Foods and
   Nutrition  (US)
American Medical Association. Council on Medical
   Education  (US)
American Medical Electroencephalographic
   Association  (US)
American Medical Record Association  (US)
American Medical Student Association  (US)
American Medical Technologists  (US)
American Medical Women's Association, Inc  (US)
American Medical Writers Association  (US)
American Mensa Ltd.  (US)
American Merchant Marine Library Association
   (US)
American Metal Climax, Inc.  (US)
American Metal Stamping Association  (US)
American Meteorological Society  (US)
American Metric Journal Publishing Co.  (US)
American-Mexican Medical Association  (MX)
American Microscopical Society  (US)
American Military Institute  (US)
American Milking Shorthorn Society  (US)
American Mining Congress  (US)
American Montessori Society  (US)
American Morgan Horse Association, Inc.  (US)
American Mosaic Literary Publications  (US)
American Mosquito Control Association  (US)
American Motor Carrier  (US)
American Motorcyclist Association  (US)
American Mountaineering and Rockclimbing Magazine
   (US)
American Movement for World Government, Inc.
   (US)
American Museum of Natural History  (US)
American Music Center  (US)
American Musicological Society  (US)
American Musicological Society. Greater New York
   Chapter  (US)
American Mutual Life Association  (US)
American Name Society  (US)
American National Heritage Association  (US)
American National Metric Council  (US)
American National Red Cross  (US)
American National Standards Institute  (US)
American National Standards Institute. Committee Z-
   39  (US)
American Nature Study Society  (US)
American Navion Society  (US)

American Near East Refugee Aid, Inc.  (US)
American Newspaper Boy Press  (US)
American Newspaper Markets, Inc.  (US)
American Newspaper Publishers Association. Research
   Institute  (US)
American Nuclear Society  (US)
American Numismatic Association  (US)
American Numismatic Association, Junior Members
   (US)
American Numismatic Society  (US)
American Nurses Association  (US)
American Nurses Association. Council for State
   Boards of Nursing  (US)
American Nurses' Association. National League for
   Nursing  (US)
American Nurses Association. Statistics Department
   (US)
American Nurses' Foundation, Inc.  (US)
American Occupational Medical Association  (US)
American Occupational Therapy Association, Inc.
   (US)
American Oil Chemists' Society  (US)
American Old Time Fiddlers Association  (US)
American Ophthalmological Society  (US)
American Optical Corp.  (US)
American Optometric Association  (US)
American Orchid Society Inc.  (US)
American Orff Schulwerk Association  (US)
American Oriental Society  (US)
American Ornithologists Union  (US)
American Ornithologists' Union (Chicago)  (US)
American Orthopaedic Society for Sports Medicine
   (US)
American Orthopsychiatric Association  (US)
American Orthotic and Prosthetic Association  (US)
American Osteopathic Academy of Orthopedics  (US)
American Osteopathic Association  (US)
American Osteopathic College of Radiology  (US)
American Osteopathic Hospital Association  (US)
American Otological Society  (US)
American Paint Journal Co.  (US)
American Paper Institute, Inc.  (US)
American Patent Law Association  (US)
American Peace Society  (US)
American Peanut Research and Education Association
   (US)
American Pedestrian Association  (US)
American Pediatric Directory  (US)
American Personnel and Guidance Association  (US)
American Petroleum Institute  (US)
American Petroleum Institute. Central Abstracting and
   Indexing Service  (US)
American Petroleum Institute. Committee for Air and
   Water Conservation  (US)
American Petroleum Institute. Committee on Medicine
   and Environmental Health  (US)
American Petroleum Institute. Division of Refining
   (US)
American Petroleum Institute. Division of Statistics
   and Economics  (US)
American Petroleum Institute. Editorial Department
   (US)
American Petroleum Institute. Statistical Publications
   Section  (US)
American Pharmaceutical Association  (US)
American Philatelic Congress  (US)
American Philatelic Research Library  (US)
American Philatelic Society, Inc.  (US)
American Philatelic Society. Writers Unit No. 30
   (US)
American Philological Association  (US)
American Philosophical Association  (US)
American Philosophical Society  (US)
American Philosophical Society. Library  (US)
American Philosophical Society. Survey of Sources for
   the History of Biochemistry and Molecular Biology
   (US)
American Physical Society  (US)
American Physical Therapy Association  (US)
American Physiological Society  (US)
American Phytopathological Society  (US)
American Pigeon Journal Co.  (US)
American Plant Life Society  (US)
American Podiatry Association  (US)
American Poetry and Poetics  (US)
American Poets Fellowship Society  (US)
American Polar Society  (US)
American Political Research Corp.  (US)
American Political Science Association  (US)
American Polled Hereford Association  (US)
American Polled Hereford Publications, Inc.  (US)
American Polygraph Association  (US)
American Pomological Society  (US)
American-Portuguese Overseas Information
   Organization  (US)
American Portuguese Society  (US)
American Postal Workers Union - AFL-CIO  (US)
American Postcard Journal  (US)

American Powder Metallurgy Institute (US)
American Power Boat Association (US)
American Power Conference (US)
American Press (US)
American Primrose Society (US)
American Printing History Association (US)
American Printing House for the Blind (US)
American Printing House for the Blind. Department of Educational Research (US)
American Proctologic Society (US)
American Production and Inventory Control Society, Inc. (US)
American Professors for Peace in the Middle East (US)
American Protestant Defense League (US)
American Protestant Hospital Association (US)
American Psychiatric Association (US)
American Psychiatric Association Gay Caucus (US)
American Psychoanalytic Association (US)
American Psychological Association (US)
American Psychological Association. Division of Clinical Psychology (US)
American Psychological Association. Division of Educational Psychology (US)
American Psychological Association. Division Two (US)
American Psychological Association. Educational Affairs Office (US)
American Psychological Association. Section on Clinical Child Psychology (US)
American Psychopathological Association (US)
American Psychosomatic Society (US)
American Public Gas Association (US)
American Public Health Association (US)
American Public Power Association (US)
American Public Transit Association (US)
American Public Welfare Association (US)
American Public Works Association (US)
American Quarter Horse Association (US)
American Rabbit Journal (US)
American Radio Association (US)
American Radio Relay League, Inc. (US)
American Railway Bridge and Building Association (US)
American Railway Engineering Association (US)
American Real Estate and Urban Economics Association (US)
American Record (US)
American Recorder Society Inc. (US)
American Recorder Society. Metropolitan New York Chapter (US)
American Register (US)
American Research Center in Egypt (US)
American Revenue Association (US)
American Rheumatism Association (US)
American Rhododendron Society (US)
American Risk and Insurance Association (US)
American Road and Transportation Builders Association (US)
American Road Builders Association (US)
American Rock Garden Society (US)
American Roentgen Ray Society (US)
American Rose Society, Inc. (US)
American Sabbath Tract Society (US)
American Safe Deposit Association (US)
American Samoa Bar Association (AS)
American-Scandinavian Foundation (US)
American School Counselor Association (US)
American School Food Service Association (US)
American School Health Association (US)
American School of Classical Studies at Athens (US)
American Schools of Oriental Research (US)
American Scientific Affiliation (US)
American Scientific Glassblowers Society (US)
American Security Council (US)
American Security Council Press (US)
American Servicemen's Union (US)
American Shih Tzu Club (US)
American Shore and Beach Preservation Association (US)
American Simmental Association (US)
American Social Health Association (US)
American Society for Adolescent Psychiatry (US)
American Society for Aesthetics (US)
American Society for Artificial Internal Organs (US)
American Society for Cell Biology (US)
American Society for Church Architecture (US)
American Society for Clinical Investigation (US)
American Society for Conservation Archaeology (US)
American Society for Cybernetics (US)
American Society for Eastern Arts (US)
American Society for Eighteenth-Century Studies (US)
American Society for Engineering Education (US)
American Society for Engineering Education. Chemical Engineering Division (US)

American Society for Engineering Education. Computers in Education Division (US)
American Society for Engineering Education. Continuing Engineering Studies Division (US)
American Society for Engineering Education. Engineering Design Graphics Division (US)
American Society for Engineering Education. Engineering Economy Division (US)
American Society for Environmental History (US)
American Society for Ethnohistory (US)
American Society for Gastrointestinal Endoscopy (US)
American Society for Horticultural Science (MX)
American Society for Horticultural Science (US)
American Society for Indian Arts and Culture (US)
American Society for Industrial Security (US)
American Society for Information Science (US)
American Society for Information Science, Pacific Northwest Chapter (US)
American Society for Information Science. Special Interest Group on Education for Information Science (US)
American Society for Information Science. Special Interest Group on Information Analysis Centers (US)
American Society for International Law (US)
American Society for Legal History (US)
American Society for Medical Technology (US)
American Society for Metals (US)
American Society for Metals. Metals Information (US)
American Society for Microbiology (US)
American Society for Neurochemistry (US)
American Society for Nondestructive Testing. South Texas Section (US)
American Society for Personnel Administration (US)
American Society for Pharmacology and Experimental Therapeutics (US)
American Society for Photobiology (US)
American Society for Political and Legal Philosophy (US)
American Society for Psychical Research, Inc. (US)
American Society for Psychoprophylaxis in Obstetrics (Berkeley) (US)
American Society for Psychoprophylaxis in Obstetrics Inc. (US)
American Society for Public Administration (US)
American Society for Public Administration. Section on International and Comparative Administration (US)
American Society for Public Instruction. National Capital Area Chapter (US)
American Society for Quality Control (US)
American Society for Quality Control. Food, Drug and Cosmetic Division (US)
American Society for Quality Control. Los Angeles Section (US)
American Society for Reformation Research (US)
American Society for Surgery of the Hand (US)
American Society for Testing & Materials (US)
American Society for the Prevention of Cruelty to Animals (US)
American Society for Theatre Research (US)
American Society for Training and Development (US)
American Society of Abdominal Surgeons (US)
American Society of Agricultural Engineers (US)
American Society of Agronomy, Inc. (US)
American Society of Allied Health Professions (US)
American Society of Anesthesiologists (US)
American Society of Animal Science (US)
American Society of Animal Science. Western Section (US)
American Society of Appraisers (US)
American Society of Arms Collectors (US)
American Society of Association Executives (US)
American Society of Bakery Engineers (US)
American Society of Bariatric Physicians (US)
American Society of Biological Chemists (US)
American Society of Bookplate Collectors and Designers (US)
American Society of Brewing Chemists (US)
American Society of Cartographers (US)
American Society of Certified Engineering Technicians (US)
American Society of Chartered Life Underwriters (US)
American Society of Church History (US)
American Society of Cinematographers Corporation (US)
American Society of Civil Engineers (US)
American Society of Civil Engineers. Boston Society of Civil Engineers Section (US)
American Society of Civil Engineers. Texas Section (US)
American Society of Clinical Hypnosis (US)
American Society of Clinical Nutrition, Inc. (US)
American Society of Clinical Pathologists (US)

American Society of Clinical Pathologists. Commission on Continuing Education (US)
American Society of Composers, Authors and Publishers (US)
American Society of Consultant Pharmacists (US)
American Society of Contemporary Medicine and Surgery (US)
American Society of Contemporary Ophthalmology (US)
American Society of Criminology (US)
American Society of Dentistry for Children (US)
American Society of Dowsers (US)
American Society of Electroencephalographic Technologists (US)
American Society of Enologists (US)
American Society of Farm Managers and Rural Appraisers (US)
American Society of Group Psychotherapy and Psychodrama (US)
American Society of Heating, Refrigerating and Air-Conditioning Engineers, Inc. (US)
American Society of Hospital Pharmacists (US)
American Society of Human Genetics (US)
American Society of Ichthyologists and Herpetologists (US)
American Society of Internal Medicine (US)
American Society of International Law (US)
American Society of Landscape Architects (US)
American Society of Law & Medicine, Inc. (US)
American Society of Limnology and Oceanography (US)
American Society of Lubrication Engineers (US)
American Society of Mammalogists (US)
American Society of Mechanical Engineers (US)
American Society of Mechanical Engineers. Heat Transfer Division (US)
American Society of Mechanical Engineers. Incinerator Division (US)
American Society of Mechanical Engineers. Machine Design Division (US)
American Society of Mechanical Engineers. Pressure Vessel Division (US)
American Society of Mechanical Engineers. Rail Transportation Division (US)
American Society of Mechanical Engineers. Research Committee on Fluid Meters (US)
American Society of Medical Technologists (US)
American Society of Mexico, A.C. (MX)
American Society of Military Comptrollers (US)
American Society of Military Insignia Collectors (US)
American Society of Missiology (US)
American Society of Naturalists (US)
American Society of Naval Engineers, Inc. (US)
American Society of Newspaper Editors (US)
American Society of Notaries (US)
American Society of Ocularists (US)
American Society of Ophthalmologic and Otolaryngologic Allergy (US)
American Society of Parasitologists (US)
American Society of Pension Actuaries (US)
American Society of Pharmacognosy (US)
American Society of Pharmacology and Experimental Therapeutics, Inc (US)
American Society of Photogrammetry (US)
American Society of Photogrammetry. Cartography Division (US)
American Society of Planning Officials (US)
American Society of Plant Physiologists (US)
American Society of Plant Taxonomists (US)
American Society of Plastic & Reconstructive Surgeons (US)
American Society of Plastic and Reconstructive Surgery. Educational Foundation (US)
American Society of Plumbing Engineers (US)
American Society of Polar Philatelists (US)
American Society of Psychosomatic Dentistry and Medicine (US)
American Society of Radiologic Technologists (US)
American Society of Safety Engineers (US)
American Society of Sanitary Engineering (US)
American Society of Sephardic Studies (US)
American Society of Sugar Beet Technologists (US)
American Society of the French Legion of Honor, Inc. (US)
American Society of Traffic and Transportation, Inc. (US)
American Society of Travel Agents (US)
American Society of Tropical Medicine and Hygiene (US)
American Society of University Composers (US)
American Society of Veterinary Clinical Pathologists (US)
American Society of Zoologists (US)
American Sociological Association (US)
American Sokol Organization (US)
American Soybean Association (US)
American Speech and Hearing Association (US)

American Spelean History Association (US)
American Square Dance Society (US)
American Stamp Dealers' Association, Inc. (US)
American Statistical Association (US)
American Stock Exchange, Inc (US)
American String Teachers Association (US)
American Student Dental Association (US)
American Studies Association (US)
American Studies Association. Kentucky-Tennessee
Chapter (US)
American Studies Association of Korea (KO)
American Studies Research Centre (II)
American Suffolk Sheep Society (US)
American Sugar Cane League of the U. S. A. (US)
American Surgical Association (US)
American Surgical Trade Association (US)
American Swedish Institute (US)
American-Swiss Association Inc. (US)
American Symphony Orchestra League (US)
American Technical Education Association, Inc. (US)
American Technical Society (US)
American Telephone & Telegraph Company (US)
American Telephone and Telegraph Company. Long
Lines Department (US)
American Theatre Association (US)
American Theatre Association. Childrens Theatre
Association of America (US)
American Theatre Organ Society (US)
American Theological Library Association (US)
American Thoracic Society (US)
American Tool, Die & Stamping News Co. (US)
American Topical Association, Inc. (US)
American Topical Association, Inc. Biology Unit
(US)
American Topical Association, Inc. Casey Jones
Railroad Unit (US)
American Topical Association, Inc. Geology Study
Unit (US)
American Topical Association, Inc. Ships on Stamps
Unit (US)
American Trade Magazines, Inc. (US)
American Train Dispatchers Association (US)
American Transcendental Quarterly (US)
American Translators Association (US)
American Traveler, Inc. (US)
American Trial Lawyers Association (US)
American Trucking Associations (US)
American Type Culture Association (US)
American Underwriter (US)
American Universal Artforms Corp. (US)
American Universities Field Staff, Inc. (US)
American University (US)
American University. Center for the Study of Private
Enterprise (US)
American University. Jewish Studies Program (US)
American University. Office of University
Development (US)
American University. School of Business
Administration (US)
American University. School of Education (US)
American University. Washington College of Law
(US)
American University in Cairo (UA)
American University in Cairo. Division of Public
Service (UA)
American University of Beirut (LE)
American University of Beirut. Economic Research
Institute (LE)
American Urological Association (US)
American Vacuum Society (US)
American Vecturist Association (US)
American Vegetarian Union (US)
American Venereal Disease Association (US)
American Veterans Committee, Inc. (US)
American Veterans of World War II, Korea and Viet
Nam (AMVETS) (US)
American Veterinary Medical Association (US)
American Veterinary Medical Association. Student
Chapter (US)
American Veterinary Publications, Inc. (US)
American Veterinary Radiology Society (US)
American Vocational Association (US)
American Vocational Association. Trade and Industrial
Division (US)
American Vocational Education Research Association
(US)
American Water Resources Association (US)
American Water Works Association (US)
American Water Works Association. Southwest and
Texas Sections (US)
American Watercolor Society (US)
American Way Publications (US)
American Welding Society (US)
American West Center (US)
American Whitewater Affiliation (US)
American Woman's Society of Certified Public
Accountants (US)
American Women's Club of Korea (KO)

American Wood Preservers Association (US)
American Wood Preservers Institute (US)
American Yorkshire Club, Inc. (US)
American Youth Hostels, Inc. (US)
American Youth Hostels, Inc. Metropolitan New York
Council (US)
American Zionist Federation (US)
American Zionist Youth Foundation (US)
Companhia Editora Americana (BL)
Americana Annual (US)
Americans Exiled in Canada (CN)
Americans for Constitutional Action (US)
Americans for Democratic Action (US)
Americans for Effective Law Enforcement (US)
Americans for Middle East Understanding, Inc. (US)
Americans United for Separation of Church and State
(US)
Americas Future Inc (US)
Americke Velvyslanectvi (CS)
Amerika Instituut (NE)
Amerikai Magyar Szo (US)
Amerikas Latviesu Apvieniba (US)
Amerikas Latvietis (US)
Ameron, Inc. (US)
Amerpub Co. (US)
Ames Company (US)
Ames Publishing Co. (US)
Amfetex Inc. (US)
Amherst College. Alumni Council (US)
Ami du Charcutier, du Boucher et du Salaisonnier
(FR)
Ami du Peuple (FR)
Amicale Anciens Fonctionnaires de Police Francais
Maroc (FR)
Amici del Museo del Risorgimento (IT)
Amici Thomae Mori (FR)
Amicizia (IT)
Amicizia Ebraico-Cristiana di Firenze (IT)
Amis de l'Histoire de la Perade (CN)
Amis de la Tradition Celticum (FR)
Amis de Pezenas (FR)
Amis de Rimbaud (FR)
Amis de Svedectvi (FR)
Amis des Cahiers Haut-Marnais (FR)
Amis des Cahiers Libres de Leon Emery (FR)
Amis du Lexique Francais (FR)
Amis du Vieux Calais (FR)
Amish Church (CN)
Amish Mennonite Publishing Association (US)
Amitie Judeo-Arabe (FR)
Amities Internationales Napoleoniennes (FR)
Amities Philosophiques Internationales (FR)
Amities Spirituelles (FR)
Amman in the Evening (JO)
Ammark Publishing Co., Inc. (US)
Amministrazione per le Attivita Assistenziale Italiane e
Internazionali (IT)
Amministrazione Provinciale di Cremona (IT)
Amministrazione Socialista (IT)
Ammon Hennacy House of Hospitality (US)
Ammonitore (IT)
Amnesty International (UK)
Amnesty International (Toronto Group) (CN)
Amnesty International of the U. S. A. (US)
Amoco Enterprises, Inc. (US)
Amon-Ra Fine Art Ltd. (UK)
Amordian Press, Inc. (US)
Amos Press, Inc. (US)
Amoxtli (MX)
Editions Ampere (FR)
Ampersand Publishing Services (CN)
Amphoto (US)
Ampleforth Abbey (UK)
Amsterdam. Bureau van Statistiek (NE)
Amsterdam. Gemeentelijke Sociale Dienst (NE)
Amsterdam. Stadsdrukkerij (NE)
Amsterdam-Rotterdam Bank N.V. (NE)
Amt fuer Fremdenverkehr und Kongresswesen (GW)
Amterre Development Inc. (US)
Amtsraadsforningen i Danmark (DK)
Amtsvejinspektoerforeningen i Danmark (DK)
Amundsen Publications, Inc. (US)
An Claidheamh Soluis, Inc. (US)
An Cosantoir Army Headquarters (IE)
An Foras Taluntais (IE)
An Lef Kernewek (UK)
Editions de l' An 2000 (FR)
Ana-Maskin Aktiebolag (SW)
Anaesthesiology and Resuscitation Research Forum
(II)
Anahata Nada (US)
Anales de Cirugia (AG)
Analisis Confirmado (AG)
Analisis S.A.I.C. (AG)
Analog Sounds (US)
Analytical Psychology Club of New York, Inc. (US)

Anametrics, Inc. (US)
Ananda Marga Society (US)
Anarcho Surrealist Insurrectionary Feminists
Collective (AT)
George Anastasopoulos, Ed. & Pub. (GR)
Anatomical Society of Great Britain and Ireland
(UK)
Anatomical Society of India (II)
Anatomische Gesellschaft (GE)
Anbar Publications Ltd. (UK)
Anchor Books Pty. Ltd. (AT)
Anchor Press (CN)
Anchor Society (US)
Ancienne Maison l'Homme et Argy (FR)
Ancient Iranian Cultural Society (IR)
Ancient Monuments Society (UK)
Ancient Order of Foresters Friendly Society (UK)
Editrice Ancora (IT)
Ancram Restoration., Inc. (US)
Andaktsbokselskapet (NO)
Andalan (SP)
Andar per Ceramiche (IT)
Andean Report (PE)
Andelsbogtrykkeriet (DK)
Andelsselskap av Lastbileiere (NO)
Andelsudvalget (DK)
Walter G. Anderson, Ed. & Pub. (US)
W. H. Anderson Co. (US)
Anderson Advertisers (GW)
Ronald Anderson & Associates (AT)
Anderson College (US)
Anderson Group, Inc. (US)
Anderson, M.D., Hospital and Tumor Institute
see under University of Texas (US)
The Anderson Ranch Arts Foundation (US)
Andes (BO)
Andhra Agricultural Union (II)
Andhra Pradesh. Department of Archaeology and
Museums (II)
Andhra Pradesh. Department of Information and
Public Relations (II)
Andhra Pradesh. Director of State Archives (II)
Andhra Pradesh. Directorate of Marketing (II)
Andhra Pradesh. Office of the Comptroller and
Auditor-General (II)
Andhra Pradesh. State Council of Educational
Research and Training (II)
Andhra Pradesh Productivity Council (II)
Andhra Pradesh State Financial Corporation (II)
Andhra University (II)
Andhra University Press and Publications (II)
Andover Newton Theological School (US)
Andragoski Centar (YU)
Andrew W. Mellon Foundation (US)
Andrews Paper & Chemical Co. Inc. (US)
Andrews University Press (US)
Andrews University. Student Association (US)
Editions Andrillon (FR)
Anees Publishing Co. (AF)
Aneks Press (UK)
ANFAVEA (BL)
Ang Bayani (PH)
Ange Gardien (FR)
Angeletti Editore (IT)
Franco Angeli Editore (IT)
Angelicum (IT)
Angelicum-Convento di S.Angelo (IT)
Angestelltenverband Deutscher Milchkontroll- und
Tierzuchtangestellten (GW)
Verlag fuer Angewandte Psychologie (GW)
Angiology Research Foundation (US)
Angle Orthodontists Research & Education
Foundation, Inc. (US)
Anglers Cooperative Association (UK)
Anglesey Antiquarian Society and Field Club (UK)
Anglica Society (JA)
Anglican & Eastern Churches Association (UK)
Anglican Church in Western Australia (AT)
Anglican Church of Canada (CN)
Anglican Church of Canada. Diocese of Caledonia
(CN)
Anglican Church of Canada. General Synod (CN)
Anglican Diocese of Kimberley and Kuruman (SA)
Anglican Pacifist Fellowship (UK)
Anglican Theological Review, Inc. (US)
Angling Times Ltd. (UK)
Anglo-American Associates (US)
Anglo American Corporation (SA)
Anglo American Directory of Mexico (MX)
Anglo Arab Association (UK)
Anglo-Byelorussian Society (UK)
Anglo Chilean Society (UK)
Anglo-Continental Dental Society (UK)
Anglo-German Association (UK)
Anglo-Israel Chamber of Commerce (UK)
Anglo-Japanese Economic Institute (UK)
Anglo-Jewish Publishers (CN)
Anglo-Lat (US)

Anglo-Spanish Society (UK)
Angola. Biblioteca Nacional (AO)
Angola. Direccao dos Servicos de Estatistica (AO)
Angola. Direccao Provincial dos Servicos de Geologia e Minas (AO)
Angola. Imprensa Nacional (AO)
Angola. Secretaria Provincial de Saude, Trabalho, Previdencia e Assistencia (AO)
Angola Comite (NE)
Angora Goat Stud Breeders Society (SA)
Angora Mohair Association of Australia (AT)
Angus Publishers (US)
R.N.S. Anil, Ed. & Pub. (II)
Animal Anti-Cruelty League (SA)
Animal Defence League of Canada (CN)
Animal Health Foundation (US)
Animal Health Trust (UK)
Animal Protection Institute of America (US)
Animal Rescue League of Boston (US)
Animal Welfare Institute (US)
Anjuman Taraggi Urdu (Hind) (II)
Ankara Universitesi. Tip Fakultesi
    see University of Ankara. Medical Faculty (TU)
Ankara Universitesi. Veteriner Fakultesi
    see University of Ankara. Faculty of Veterinary Medicine (TU)
Uitgeverij Ankh-Hermes B.V. (NE)
Ankho International Inc. (US)
Ann Arbor Publishers (US)
Ann Arbor Review Press (US)
Ann Arbor Science Publishers, Inc. (US)
Casa Editrice Giacomo d' Anna (IT)
Annales de Normandie (FR)
Annales Homeopathiques Francaises (FR)
Annali di Medicina Navale (IT)
Annals Publishing Co. (US)
Annamalai University. Department of Economics (II)
Annenberg School Press (US)
Annonsoerfoereningens Service AB (SW)
Annotated Bibliography of Bibliographies on Selected Government Publications & Supplementary Guides to the Superintendent of Documents Classification System. Supplement (US)
Annuaire Catholique de France (FR)
Annuaire de l'Education Nationale (FR)
Annuaire de la Presse et de la Publicite (FR)
Annuaire des Architectes (FR)
Annuaire des Communautes d'Enfants (FR)
Annuaire du Spectacle (FR)
Annuaire General de la Pharmacie Francaise (FR)
Annuaire Paris: Bijoux (FR)
Annual Reviews Inc. (US)
Peter Annunziata (US)
Editorial Ano dos Mil, S. A. (MX)
Another Mother for Peace (US)
Anritsu Electric Co., Ltd. (JA)
ANRO Inc. (US)
Ansett Airlines of Australia (AT)
Ansgarsfoerbundet Inom Svenska Kyrkan (SW)
Anson & Co Ltd. (UI)
Pressverband Anstoss und Argumente (AU)
Antena de Telecommunicacion (SP)
Antenna Edicoes Tecnicas Ltda (BL)
Editrice Antenore (IT)
Anthelion Press, Ltd. (US)
Anthol Publications (CN)
Anthropological Association of Canada (CN)
Anthropological Publications (NE)
Anthropological Society of Bombay (II)
Anthropological Society of Japan (JA)
Anthropological Society of New South Wales (AT)
Anthropological Survey of India (II)
Anthropologike Hetaireia Tes Hellados (GR)
Anthropologische Gesellschaft in Wien (AU)
Editions Anthropos (FR)
Anthropos Institut (SZ)
Anthroposophical Society in America (US)
Anthroposophical Society in Great Britain (UK)
Anthroposophische Gesellschaft in Deutschland (GW)
Anti-Apartheid Movement (UK)
Anti-Defamation League of B'nai B'rith (US)
Anti-Friction Bearing Manufacturers Association, Inc. (US)
Anti-Revolutionaire Partij (NE)
Anti-Stalinism Study Group (US)
Antiauto Sport (IT)
Antibioticos, S.A. (SP)
Antibolschewistisches Block der Nationen (GW)
Antigua Libreria Robredo (MX)
Antilles Publications, Inc. (US)
Antioch College (US)
Antioch Review, Inc. (US)
Antioquia, Colombia. Departamento Administrativo de Planeacion Biblioteca (CK)
Antioquia, Colombia. Secretaria de Educacion y Cultura (CK)
Antipode: A Radical Journal of Geography (US)

Antiquarian and Landmarks Society of Connecticut, Inc. (US)
Antiquarian Bookman (US)
Antiquarian Horological Society (UK)
Antique Airplane Association (US)
Antique & General Advertising Ltd. (UK)
Antique & Historical Arms Collectors Guild of Victoria (AT)
Antique Automobile Club of America (US)
Antique Collector (UK)
Antique Collectors Club (UK)
Antique Finder Ltd. (UK)
Antique Wireless Association Inc (US)
Antiquer (US)
Antiquities Service of the Sudan (UK)
Antiquity Publications Ltd. (UK)
Antiseptic (II)
Antitrust Law and Economics Review, Inc. (US)
John A. Antonsen A-S (NO)
Antonson Publishing Co., Ltd. (CN)
Antropos (AG)
Antwerp Bee-Argus (US)
Antwerp Bibliophile Society
    see Vereeniging der Antwerpsche Bibliophielen (BE)
Antwerp Chamber of Commerce and Industry
    see Chambre de Commerce et d'Industrie d'Anvers (BE)
Anuario F.H.I. Argentina: Frutas y Hortalizas Industriarizadas y Frescas (AG)
Anvil Press (US)
Anvil Press (Liverpool) (UK)
Any-All Printers (US)
Aoki Shoten (JA)
Aomori Local Meteorological Observatory (JA)
Aomori Prefecture Agricultural Improvement Association (JA)
Aonde Vamos (BL)
Aoyama-Gakuin University (JA)
APA-Holland University Press (NE)
Apalachee Correctional Institution (US)
Apartment Association of Orange County (US)
Apartment News Publications, Inc. (US)
Apartment Owners and Managers Association of America (US)
Apartment Owners Publishing Co. (US)
Apartments for Rent, Inc. (US)
APEC Editora S.A. (BL)
Aperture (US)

Apex Publishers & Publicity Ltd. (CN)
Aphra (US)
Apollo Magazine (UK)
Apostles of Infinite Love (CN)
Apostleship of Prayer (CN)
Apostleship of the Sea (UK)
Apostolaat van het Gebed (NE)
Apostolate, Inc. (US)
Apostolic Lutheran Church of America (US)
Apostolischer Visitator fuer Klerus und Glaeubige des Ermlandes (GW)
Apotekarsocieteten (SW)
Deutscher Apotheker-Verlag (GW)
Appalachian Associates, Inc. (US)
Appalachian Mountain Club (US)
Appalachian Regional Commission
    see U. S. Appalachian Regional Commission (US)
Appalachian State University (US)
Appalachian State University. Department of History (US)
Appalachian Trail Conference (US)
Appaloosa Horse Club Inc. (US)
Appalshop Inc. (US)
Apparel Publishing Ltd. (NZ)
Apple & Pear Board (AT)
Apple Publishers, Designers and Photographers (Pty) Ltd. (SA)
Apple River Journal (US)
Apple Tree Press (US)
Applegarth Follies (CN)
Appleton-Century-Crofts (US)
Applied Chemicals Pty. Ltd. (AT)
Applied Computer Research (US)
Applied Forestry Research Institute (US)
Applied Library Resources (US)
Applied Mathematics Group, MIT (US)
Applied Parking Techniques, Inc. (US)
Applied Probability Trust (UK)
Applied Science Center for Archaeology (US)
Applied Science Publishers Ltd. (UK)
Applied Scientific Research Corporation of Thailand (TH)
Applied Technology Publications Ltd. (UK)
Appointments Market Weekly (II)
Appraisal Institute of Canada Inc. (CN)
Approach 13-30 Corp. (US)
Kustannusosakeyhtio Apulehti (FI)

Apuntes de la Linea (AG)
Aqua-Field Publications (US)
Aqua Pura (AT)
Aquarian Advertising Associates (US)
Aquarian Publishing Co. (US)
Aquarimantims (CK)
Aquario (AG)
Aquarium Society of New South Wales (AT)
Aquarius (PR)
Aquarius (SA)
Aquarius (UK)
Aquatic Research Institute (US)
Aquila Publishing Co. Ltd. (UK)
R. Aquiles (PO)
Aquinas College of Higher Studies (CE)
Arab Academy of Damascus (SY)
Arab Book Information Centre (UA)
Arab Federation of Petroleum Mining & Chemical Workers (UA)
Arab Film & Television Centre
    see under Lebanon. Ministry of Information (LE)
Arab Fund for Economic and Social Development (KU)
Arab Horse Society (UK)
Arab Information Center (US)
Arab Lawyers Union (UA)
Arab League Educational Scientific and Cultural Organization (UA)
Arab League Information Centre (CN)
Arab Markets (BA)
Arab Oil Review (LY)
Arab Palestinian Resistance (SY)
Arab Petroleum Research Center (LE)
Arab Report and Record (UK)
Arab Republic of Egypt Embassy
    see Embassy of the Arab Republic of Egypt (II)
Arab Veterinary Medical Association (UA)
Arabian American Oil Co.(ARAMCO) (SU)
Arabic Literature Mission (UK)
Arabic Publishing House (IS)
Arabidopsis Information Service (GW)
Arachnological Society of East Asia (JA)
Periodici Aracne Nuova Editrice (IT)
Arak College of Science (IR)
Aral AG (GW)
Aralabs Inc. (US)
Casa Editrice Araldo della Verite (IT)
ARAMCO
    see Arabian American Oil Co. (ARAMCO) (SU)
Aramco (NE)
Aramtek Corporation (US)
Editorial Aranzadi (SP)
Arawak Press Ltd. (JM)
Arbeiderspers (BE)
B. V. de Arbeiderspers (NE)
Verlag Arbeit und Beruf (GW)
Arbeiterwohlfahrt Bundesverband E.V (GW)
Arbeitsausschuss des Evangelischen Kirchenbautages und Dioezesan-Kunstvereins, Linz (GW)
Arbeitsgemeinschaft Allensbach e.V. (GW)
Arbeitsgemeinschaft Berliner Haus-, Grund-, und Ruinenbesitzervereine e. V. (GW)
Arbeitsgemeinschaft Cinema (SZ)
Arbeitsgemeinschaft der Berufsvertretungen Deutscher Apotheker (GW)
Arbeitsgemeinschaft der Bitumen-Industrie E.V. (GW)
Arbeitsgemeinschaft der Dioezesansekretariate der Cursillo-Bewegung (AU)
Arbeitsgemeinschaft der Familienkundlichen Gesellschaften in Hessen (GW)
Arbeitsgemeinschaft der Karpatendeutschen aus der Slowakei (GW)
Arbeitsgemeinschaft der Oeffentlich-rechtlichen Rundfunkanstalten der Bundesrepublik Deutschland (GW)
Arbeitsgemeinschaft der Oesterreichischen Gemeinwirtschaft (AU)
Arbeitsgemeinschaft der Parlaments- und Behoerdenbibliotheken (GW)
Arbeitsgemeinschaft der Verbaende der Technischen Haendler (GW)
Arbeitsgemeinschaft der Verbraucher E.V. (AGV) (GW)
Arbeitsgemeinschaft Deutscher Krankenhausapotheker (GW)
Arbeitsgemeinschaft Deutscher Schweineerzeuger e.V. (GW)
Arbeitsgemeinschaft Deutscher Tierzuechter (GW)
Arbeitsgemeinschaft Deutscher Verkehrsflughaefen (GW)
Arbeitsgemeinschaft die Moderne Kueche (GW)
Arbeitsgemeinschaft Ethnomedizin, Hamburg (GW)
Arbeitsgemeinschaft Europaeischer Kalibreure (GW)
Arbeitsgemeinschaft Fernwaerme e.V. (GW)
Arbeitsgemeinschaft Frau und Mutter (GW)
Arbeitsgemeinschaft fuer Berlin-Brandenburgische Kirchengeschichte (GW)

Arbeitsgemeinschaft fuer Betriebliche Altersversorgung
e.V. (GW)
Arbeitsgemeinschaft fuer Buch- und Schrifttum der
Katholischen Aktion Oesterreichs (AU)
Arbeitsgemeinschaft fuer Datenverarbeitung (AU)
Arbeitsgemeinschaft fuer Elektrische
Nachrichtentechnik (SZ)
Arbeitsgemeinschaft fuer Evangelische Kinderpflege
(GW)
Arbeitsgemeinschaft fuer Finanzwissenschaftliche
Forschung und Information (AU)
Arbeitsgemeinschaft fuer Historische Sozialkunde
(AU)
Arbeitsgemeinschaft fuer Jugendhilfe (GW)
Arbeitsgemeinschaft fuer Juristisches Bibliotheks- und
Dokumentationswesen (GW)
Arbeitsgemeinschaft fuer Kameradenwerke und
Traditionsverbaende (GW)
Arbeitsgemeinschaft fuer Lebensniveauvergleiche
(AU)
Arbeitsgemeinschaft fuer Medizinisches
Bibliothekswesen (GW)
Arbeitsgemeinschaft fuer Pharmazeutische
Verfahrenstechnik e. V. (GW)
Arbeitsgemeinschaft fuer Psychotechnik in Oesterreich
(AU)
Arbeitsgemeinschaft fuer Rheinische Musikgeschichte
e. V. (GW)
Arbeitsgemeinschaft fuer Salesianische Studien (GW)
Arbeitsgemeinschaft fuer Getreideforschung (GW)
Arbeitsgemeinschaft Industriebau e.V. (GW)
Arbeitsgemeinschaft Korrosion (GW)
Arbeitsgemeinschaft Landwirtschaftlicher
Gefluegelzuechter Oesterreichs (AU)
Arbeitsgemeinschaft Moebeltransport Bundesverband
e.V. (GW)
Arbeitsgemeinschaft Oesterreichischer Entomologen
(AU)
Arbeitsgemeinschaft ostdeutscher Familienforscher,
Herne (GW)
Arbeitsgemeinschaft Sozialwissenschaftlicher Institute
e.V. (GW)
Arbeitsgemeinschaft Spekulative Thematik (GW)
Arbeitsgemeinschaft Verstaerkte Kunststoffe e. V.
(GW)
Arbeitsgemeinschaft Waermebehandlung und
Werkstoff-Technik e.V. (GW)
Arbeitsgemeinschaft zur Foerderung der Partnerschaft
in der Wirtschaft e.V. (GW)
Arbeitsgruppe fuer Empirische Bildungsforschung
(GW)
Arbeitskammer des Saarlandes (GW)
Arbeitskreis der Kampftruppen (GW)
Arbeitskreis Deutscher Bildungsstaetten e.V. (GW)
Arbeitskreis fuer Jugendliteratur (GW)
Arbeitskreis fuer Kunst und Sprache (AU)
Arbeitskreis fuer Wehrforschung (GW)
Arbeitskreis Progressive Kunst (GW)
Arbeitskreis Sozialwissenschaftliche Informationen
(GW)
Arbeitsring fuer Paedagogische Elternhilfe E. V.,
Aachen (GW)
Arbeitsstelle Jugend- und Bildungsdienst (SZ)
Arbejdsgiversammenslutningen Dansk Snedker- og
Toemrerhaandverk, Moebel og Bygningsindustri
(DK)
Arbetaren (SW)
Arbetarnas Bildningsfoerbund (SW)
Arbiter (IT)
Arbo S. A. C. E. I. (AG)
Arbol de Fuego: Poesia (VE)
Arboricultural Association (UK)
Arbutus Publications Ltd. (CN)
L'Arc (FR)
Arca (UY)
Arcade Stamp Shop (SA)
Arcadie (FR)
Arch-Way Publishers Ltd. (CN)
Archaeological Centre (UK)
Archaeological Institute of America (US)
Archaeological News Letter (UK)
Archaeological Research Associates (US)
Archaeological Society of B. C. (CN)
Archaeological Society of Central New York (US)
Archaeological Society of Connecticut (US)
Archaeological Society of Delaware (US)
Archaeological Society of Japan (JA)
Archaeological Society of New Jersey (US)
Archaeological Society of New Mexico (US)
Archaeological Society of North Carolina (US)
Archaeological Society of Ohio (US)
Archaeological Society of Victoria (AT)
Archaeology Abroad Service (UK)
Archai (CN)
Archbishop of Karachi (PK)
Archconfraternity of Christian Mothers (US)
Archdiocesan Major Seminary (PH)
Archdiocese of Cape Coast (GH)

Archdiocese of Chicago (US)
Archdiocese of Montreal (CN)
Archdiocese of New York (US)
Archdiocese of San Francisco (US)
Archery Association of Australia (AT)
Archeveche de Bourges (FR)
Archeveche de Lyon (FR)
Archeveche de Toulouse (FR)
Archeveque Catholique Romain de Quebec (CN)
Archigram Group (UK)
Archimedia, Inc. (US)
Editions de l' Archipel (FR)
Archistra: Archives-Histoire-Traditions (FR)
Architect & Contractor (US)
Architects Publishing Corp. of India (II)
Architectural and Archaeological Society of Durham
and Northumberland (UK)
Architectural Association (UK)
Architectural Association of Kenya (KE)
Architectural Index (US)
Architectural Institute of Japan (JA)
Architectural Metals (US)
Architectural Metalwork Association (UK)
Architectural Press Ltd. (UK)
Architectural Register of America (US)
Architecture and Building Industry (II)
Architecture-France (FR)
Architectuur en Beeldende Kunsten (NE)
Verlag Architektur und Baudetail GmbH (GW)
Archiv fuer Energiewirtschaft (GW)
Archiv fuer Psychiatrie und Nervenkrankheiten
(GW)
Archive of Social Innovation (US)
Archives and Records Association (NZ)
Archives Authority of New South Wales (AT)
Archives de Meurthe et Moselle (FR)
Archives for the Performing Arts (US)
Archives Internationales Claude Bernard (FR)
Archives Internationales de Pharmacodynamie et de
Therapie (BE)
Archives Medicales de l'Ouest (FR)
Archives of American Art
    see under Smithsonian Institution (US)
Archives of Child Health (II)
Archives of Vancouver Society (CN)
Archives Suisses d'Anthropologie Generale (SZ)
Archivio-Biblioteca-Museo Civico (IT)
Archivio Botanico e Biogeografico Italiano (IT)
Archivio di Studi Urbani e Regionali (IT)
Archivio Storico per la Calabria e la Lucania (IT)
Archivio Trimestrale (IT)
Archivo Historico de Miraflores (VE)
Archivo Historico del Guayas (EC)
Archivos Argentinos de Dermatologia (AG)
Archon Books (US)
Arcispedale S. Anna di Ferrara (IT)
Arco Corp. (US)
Arco Publishing Co. Inc. (US)
Arctic Institute of North America (CN)
Arctic Publications & Productions (US)
Arctinurus Co. (US)
Ardis Publishers (US)
Area Auto Racing News, Inc. (US)
Areito (US)
Arellano University (PH)
Arena Forfatternes Forlag (DK)
Arena Magazine Co. (US)
Arena Publications Association (AT)
Arena Publications Ltd. (UK)
Arenaturist (YU)
Arens Corp. (US)
Aret Runt (SW)
Arete (San Francisco) (US)
Arete Activities, Inc. (US)
Aretusa Editrice srl. (IT)
Armando Argalia Editore (IT)
Editions d' Argenson (FR)
Argentina (AG)
Argentina. Biblioteca del Congreso (AG)
Argentina. Caja Federal de Ahorro y Prestamo para la
Vivienda (AG)
Argentina. Centro de Investigacion Documentaria
(AG)
Argentina. Centro Nacional de Documentacion e
Informacion Educativa (AG)
Argentina. Comision Nacional de Valores (AG)
Argentina. Consejo Federal de Inversiones (AG)
Argentina. Consejo Nacional de Desarrollo (AG)
Argentina. Consejo Nacional de Investigaciones
Cientificas y Tecnicas (AG)
Argentina. Departamento de Estudios Historicos
Navales (AG)
Argentina. Departamento de Lecheria (AG)
Argentina. Direccion General de Sanidad (AG)

Argentina. Direccion Nacional de Asistencia Nacional
(AG)
Argentina. Direccion Nacional de Energia y
Combustibles. Departamento de Estadistica (AG)
Argentina. Direccion Nacional de Migraciones.
Instituto Etnico Nacional (AG)
Argentina. Direccion Nacional de Programacion e
Investigacion (AG)
Argentina. Division de Estadisticas Sociales (AG)
Argentina. Empresa Nacional de Correos y Telegrafos
(AG)
Argentina. Instituto Antartico Argentino (AG)
Argentina. Instituto de Asuntos Tecnicos. Direccion de
Estadistica (AG)
Argentina. Instituto Forestal Nacional (AG)
Argentina. Instituto Nacional de Derecho Aeronautico
y Espacial (AG)
Argentina. Instituto Nacional de Estadistica y Censos
(AG)
Argentina. Instituto Nacional de Planificacion
Economica (AG)
Argentina. Instituto Nacional de Tecnologia
Agropecuaria (AG)
Argentina. Instituto Nacional de Tecnologia
Agropecuaria. Estacion Experimental Regional
Agropecuaria del Alto Valle (AG)
Argentina. Instituto Nacional de Tecnologia
Agropecuaria. Estacion Experimental Regional
Agropecuaria Pergamino (AG)
Argentina. Instituto Nacional de Tecnologia
Agropecuria. Estacion Experiemntal Agropecuaria
Manfredi (AG)
Argentina. Instituto Nacional de Tecnologia Industrial
(AG)
Argentina. Mercado Nacional de Hacienda (AG)
Argentina. Ministerio de Comercio (AG)
Argentina. Ministerio de Cultura y Educacion (AG)
Argentina. Ministerio de Defensa. Escuela de Defensa
Nacional (AG)
Argentina. Ministerio de Economia (AG)
Argentina. Ministerio de Economia. Junta Nacional de
Carnes (AG)
Argentina. Ministerio de Economia. Secretaria de
Estado de Hacienda (AG)
Argentina. Ministerio de Economia. Secretaria de
Estado de Programacion y Coordinacion Economica
(AG)
Argentina. Ministerio de Economia. Secretaria de
Recursos Naturales y Ambiente Humano (AG)
Argentina. Ministerio de Relaciones Exteriores (AG)
Argentina. Ministerio del Ejercito (AG)
Argentina. Oficina de Estudios para la Colaboracion
Economica Internacional (AG)
Argentina. Oficina Sectorial de Desarrollo de Energia.
Departamento de Informacion e Investigacion
Aplicada (AG)
Argentina. Policia Federal Argentina (AG)
Argentina. Santa Fe Centro de Documentacion e
Informacion Educativa (AG)
Argentina. Secretaria de Estado de Agricultura y
Ganaderia (AG)
Argentina. Secretaria de Estado de Ciencia y
Tecnologia (AG)
Argentina. Secretaria de Estado de Salud Publica
(AG)
Argentina. Secretaria de Estado de Trabajo (AG)
Argentina. Secretaria de Guerra (AG)
Argentina. Servicio de Hidrografia Naval (AG)
Argentina. Servicio de Inteligencia Naval (AG)
Argentina. Servicio de Intelligencia Naval. Bibliotecas
de la Armada (AG)
Argentina. Servicio Nacional de Parques Nacionales
(AG)
Argentina. Servicio Nacional de Pesca (AG)
Argentina. Servicio Nacional Minero Geologico
(AG)
Argentine Science Fiction Review Publications (AG)
Argentine Society of Angiology (AG)
Argentino (AG)
Argentinos Lietuviu Balsas (AG)
Argileto Editore (IT)
Argout Editions (FR)
Argument for Frihet och Raett (SW)
Argument-Verlag GmbH (GW)
Argus and Australasian Ltd. (AT)
Argus Books Ltd. (UK)
Argus des Pharmaciens (FR)
Argus du Livre (FR)
Argus Press Ltd. (UK)
Argus Publishers Corp. (US)
Argus-Verlag (GW)
P. C. Argyle-Stuart, Ed. & Pub. (US)
Arheoloski Muzej Istre u Puli (YU)
Arhiva Nationala de Filme (RM)
Ediciones Ariadna (AG)

Uitgeverij Ariadne B.V. (NE)
Arid Zone Research Association of India (II)
Ariel (HO)
Ediciones Ariel, S.A. (SP)
Aries Corp. (US)
John Arigho & Sons (1974) Ltd. (IE)
Edizioni Ariminum (IT)
Arion's Dolphin (US)
Aristo-Werke Dennert und Pape KG (GW)
Aristotelian Society (UK)
Arizona. Advisory Commission on Arizona
 Environment (US)
Arizona. Advisory Council for Vocational Education
 (US)
Arizona. Commission on the Arts and Humanities
 (US)
Arizona. Department of Administration. Finance
 Division (US)
Arizona. Department of Administration. Personnel
 Division (US)
Arizona. Department of Economic Security (US)
Arizona. Department of Economic Security. Office of
 Planning (US)
Arizona. Department of Education (US)
Arizona. Department of Health Services (US)
Arizona. Department of Health Services. Bureau of Air
 Quality Control (US)
Arizona. Department of Public Safety (US)
Arizona. Department of Transportation (US)
Arizona. Office of Economic Planning and
 Development (US)
Arizona. Office of the Post Auditor (US)
Arizona. Oil & Gas Conservation Commission (US)
Arizona. State Dental Board (US)
Arizona. State Land Department. Division of Forestry
 (US)
Arizona. Supreme Court (US)
Arizona. Water Commission (US)
Arizona Academy of Science (US)
Arizona Archaeological and Historical Society (US)
Arizona Association for Supervision and Curriculum
 Development (US)
Arizona Automobile Association (US)
Arizona Bank (US)
Arizona Blue Book: a Guide to the State of Arizona
 (US)
Arizona Cactus & Native Flora Society (US)
Arizona Education Association (US)
Arizona English Teachers Association (US)
Arizona Federation of Stamp Clubs, Inc. (US)
Arizona Geological Society (US)
Arizona Grocers Publishing Co. Inc (US)
Arizona Highways (US)
Arizona Historical Society (US)
Arizona Jim Co-Op (US)
Arizona Library Extension Service. Division of Library
 Archives and Public Records (US)
Arizona Medical Association (US)
Arizona Motor Transport Association (US)
Arizona Nurses Association (US)
Arizona Pharmaceutical Association (US)
Arizona Small Mine Operators Association (US)
Arizona Society of Mental Health Technology (US)
Arizona Society of Professional Engineers (US)
Arizona-Sonora Desert Museum, Inc. (US)
Arizona Speech & Hearing Association (US)
Arizona State Dental Association (US)
Arizona State University (US)
Arizona State University. Bureau of Publishing (US)
Arizona State University. Center for Asian Studies
 (US)
Arizona State University. Center for Latin American
 Studies (US)
Arizona State University. Center for Public Affairs
 (US)
Arizona State University. College of Business
 Administration (US)
Arizona State University. College of Education (US)
Arizona State University. College of Law (US)
Arizona State University. Department of Anthropology
 (US)
Arizona State University. Faculty of Industrial
 Engineering (US)
Arizona State University. Music Department (US)
Arizona Trailer Publications (US)
Ark (AT)
Ark Ozark Publishing Co. Inc. (US)
Wydawnictwo Arkady (PL)
Arkansas. Bureau of Vital Statistics (US)
Arkansas. Commission on Crime and Law
 Enforcement (US)
Arkansas. Department of Education (US)
Arkansas. Department of Mental Retardation (US)
Arkansas. Department of Parks and Tourism. Travel
 Division (US)
Arkansas. Department of Planning. Environmental
 Preservation Commission (US)
Arkansas. Division of Health Statistics (US)

Arkansas. Division of Human Services (US)
Arkansas. Division of Rehabilitation Services (US)
Arkansas. Employment Security Division. Research
 and Statistics (US)
Arkansas. Game and Fish Commission (US)
Arkansas. Geological Commission (US)
Arkansas. Industrial Development Commission (US)
Arkansas. Judicial Department (US)
Arkansas. Manpower Council (US)
Arkansas. Securties Department (US)
Arkansas. State Board of Nursing (US)
Arkansas. State Highway Department (US)
Arkansas Almanac (US)
Arkansas Archeological Society (US)
Arkansas Archeological Survey (US)
Arkansas Bankers Association (US)
Arkansas-Best Freight System, Inc. (US)
Arkansas Cattlemen's Association (US)
Arkansas Community Organizations for Reform Now
 (ACORN) (US)
Arkansas Education Association (US)
Arkansas Electric Cooperatives (US)
Arkansas Free Enterprise Association (US)
Arkansas Grocer Publishing Co. (US)
Arkansas Historical Association (US)
Arkansas Industrial Development Foundation (US)
Arkansas Library Association (US)
Arkansas LP Gas Association, Inc. (US)
Arkansas Medical Society (US)
Arkansas Municipal League (US)
Arkansas Oil & Gas Commission (US)
Arkansas Poultry Federation (US)
Arkansas Rehabilitation Research and Training Center
 (US)
Arkansas State Dental Association (US)
Arkansas State University. Division of English,
 Philosophy and Languages (US)
Arkansas Survey (US)
Arkansas Tech University (US)
Arkansas Valley Journal, Inc (US)
Arkeologisk Museum i Stavanger (NO)
Arkitekt (TU)
Arkitektens Forlag (DK)
Arktisk Institut (DK)
Arlington Books (Publishers) Ltd. (UK)
Arlington Historical Society, Inc. (US)
Arlington Publishing Co (US)
Arlis (Art Libraries Society) (UK)
Armada de Chile (CL)
Armadillo Press (US)
L. Armand, Ed. & Pub. (FR)
Casa Editrice Armando Armando (IT)
Armchair Press (US)
Armco Steel Corporation (US)
Armco Steel Corporation. Metal Products Division
 (US)
Armed Forces Communications and Electronics (US)
Armed Forces Journal International (US)
Armed Forces Medical College (PK)
Armee du Salut (FR)
Armenian Catholic Patriarchate (LE)
Armenian Democratic Liberal Organization (US)
Armenian Evangelical Brotherhood Church (LE)
Armenian Evangelical Church (CN)
Armenian General Benevolent Union of America, Inc.
 (US)
Armenian Literary Society-New York, Inc. (US)
Armenian Missionary Association of America (US)
Armenian Patriarchate (IS)
Armenian Relief Society, Inc. (US)
Armenian Reporter, Inc. (US)
Armenian Society for Friendship and Cultural
 Relations with Foreign Countries (UR)
Armenian Welfare Association of New York, Inc.
 (US)
Armenian Youth Federation. Simon Zavarian Chapter
 (CN)
Armestaben (SW)
Armidale and District Historical Society (AT)
Armitage Press, Inc. (US)
Armorial Francais (BE)
Arms and Armour Society (UK)
Armstrong Cork Co. (US)
Army Aviation Association of America, Inc. (US)
Army Cadet Force Association (UK)
Army, Navy and Air Force Veterans Association in
 Canada (CN)
Army Pension Share Hospital (GR)
Army Quarterly and Defence Journal (UK)
Army Times Publishing Co. (US)
Armyanskaya S. S. R. Ministerstvo Kul'tury (UR)
Arnall & Jackson Pty. Ltd. (AT)
Arnamagnaean Institute (DK)
Arne-Verlag (GW)
Arnell Publications, Inc. (US)
Arner Publications, Inc. (US)
Librairie Arnette (FR)
Arnhem. Gemeentearchief (NE)

Arnhem Advertising. International Patent Developers,
 Inc. (US)
Arno Press (US)
Arnold Air Society (US)
Arnold Arboretum (US)
Arnold Bennett Newsletter (US)
Verlag Ernst Arnold GmbH (GW)
Arnold Select Publishing Co. (US)
Jason Aronson, Inc. (US)
Arquitectura Mexico (MX)
Arquivo de Bibliografia Portuguesa (PO)
Arquivos Brasileiros de Oftalmologia (BL)
Arquivos de Tisiologia. Estancia Sanatorial (PO)
Arrivi e Partenze (IT)
Ars Medici et Nouveautes Medicales (BE)
Ars Moriendi (US)
Ars Sutoria S.A.S. (IT)
Ars Una (FR)
Ars-Uomo (IT)
Art Adress Verlag Mueller KG (GW)
Art & Architecture (IR)
Art and Artists of the Monterey Peninsula (US)
Art & Language Press (UK)
Art and Literary Society (CN)
Art and Nature (US)
Art Chretien (FR)
Art Craft Teachers Association (AT)
Editions de l' Art de Vivre (FR)
Art Dialogue Press (AT)
Art Digest, Inc. (US)
Art Direction Magazine (US)
Art Directions Book Co. (US)
Art Directors Club Milano (IT)
Art Directors Club of New York (US)
Art Directors Club of Tokyo (JA)
Art et Maitrise Publicite (FR)
Art et Technique (BE)
Art Gallery of Greater Victoria (CN)
Art Gallery of Hamilton (CN)
Art Gallery of Ontario (CN)
Art Gallery of South Australia (AT)
Art History Museums, Antwerp
 see Kunsthistorische Musea, Antwerp (BE)
Art in America, Inc. (US)
Art Institute of Chicago (US)
Art Instruction Schools (US)
Art Libraries Society of North America (US)
Art Magazine Inc. (CN)
Art Net Ltd. (UK)
Art Official Inc. (CN)
Art Press (FR)
Art Sales Index Ltd. (UK)
Art Students League of New York (US)
Art Study Centre (II)
Art Teachers Association of Victoria (AT)
Art Vivant (FR)
Art Voices, Inc. (US)
Art Workers Guild (UK)
Arte (IT)
Arte (VE)
Edizioni d' Arte Alfieri (IT)
Arte e Investigacion (VE)
Arte Fotografico S.L. (SP)
Arte Grafico Editorial Argentino S.A. (AG)
Arte Informa (AG)
Arte-Literatura (PY)
Edizioni Arte Lombarda (IT)
Arte Nuova (IT)
Editorial Arte y Letras de America (AG)
Arteditorial Co. (CN)
Arteguia (SP)
Artes (BL)
Artes de Mexico y del Mundo S.A. (MX)
Artes Visuales (PR)
Editions H. Artese (FR)
Artforum, Inc. (US)
Editions B. Arthaud (FR)
Arthika Cetana (II)
Arthritis and Rheumatism Council (UK)
Arthritis Foundation (US)
Arthritis Foundation. American Rheumatism
 Association Section (US)
Arthritis Foundation. Michigan Chapter (US)
Arthur Machen Society (US)
Arthur Wilson Memorial Foundation (AT)
Arthurs Publications Ltd. (CN)
Arti Grafiche Friulane (IT)
Artia (CS)
Artibus Asiae Publishers (SZ)
Artificial Breeding Board of Tasmania (AT)
Artilleriklubben (SW)
Artilleriofficersforeningen (DK)
Artillery Association (II)
Artisan Staff Association (SA)
Artist Publishing Co. Ltd. (UK)
Artistes et Varietes (FR)
Artists Associates (HK)
Artists' Association of Finland

*see* Suomen Taiteilijaseura (FI)
Artists' Guild of Australia (AT)
Artists - U S A: Guide to Contemporary American Art (US)
Artman's Press (US)
Artnews (US)
Editions ARTO (BE)
Editions d' Artrey (FR)
Arts Alliance Corp. (US)
Arts Asiatiques (FR)
Arts Council of Great Britain (UK)
Arts Council of Great Britain. Eastern Arts Association (UK)
Arts et Objets du Maroc (FR)
Arts, Lettres et Progres (FR)
Arts of Asia Publications (HK)
Arts Reporting Service (US)
Artsake Studios (US)
Artweek, Inc. (US)
Wydawnictwa Artystyczne i Filmowe (PL)
Wydawnictwa Artystyczno-Graficzne RSW "Prasa-Ksiazka-Ruch" (PL)
Arum Holdings Ltd. (CN)
Arun Group of Publications (II)
Arusha-Konakri Institute (UFOMI) Inc. (US)
Arussi Rural Development Unit (ET)
Arut Perum Jothi (II)
Arya Mehr University of Technology (IR)
Arzneimittel-Informationsdienst GmbH (A.T.I.) (GW)
Arzobispado de Madrid-Alcala (SP)
Arzobispado de Sevilla. Oficina Diocesana de Informacion (SP)
Verlag fuer Arztrecht (GW)
Asahi Evening News (JA)
Asahi Glass Co., Ltd. (JA)
Asahi Shimbun (JA)
Asakumo Shimbunsha (JA)
Asbarez Publishing Co. (US)
Asbestos Cement Service Co. Ltd. (IT)
Asbestos Textile Institute (US)
Asbury Theological Seminary (US)
H. Aschehoug & Co. (W. Nygaard) A-S (NO)
Aschendorffsche Verlagsbuchhandlung (GW)
Ascot Publishing Enterprises, Inc (US)
Asea AB (SW)
Asfaltindustriens Oplysningskontor for Vejbygning (DK)
Asgard Publishing Ltd. (UK)
Asgard-Verlag Dr. Werner Hippe KG (GW)
Asheville Area Chamber of Commerce (US)
Ashford Press (US)
Ashire Publishing Ltd. (UK)
Ashland Oil, Inc. (US)
Ashlee Publishing Co., Inc. (US)
Ashleys of America, Inc. (US)
Ashok Prakashan Mandir (II)
Ashoka Publications Ltd. (UK)
Ashuach (IS)
Asia Christian Colleges Association (UK)
Asia Documentation and Research Center
  *see under* Universite de Geneve (SZ)
Asia Electronics United (JA)
Asia Foundation (US)
Asia Letter Ltd (HK)
Asia Publishing House (II)
Asia Publishing House, Inc. (US)
Asia Research (Private) Ltd (SI)
Asia Society (US)
Asia Society. Performing Arts Program (US)
Asia Society. South East Asia Development Advisory Group (US)
Asia Trade Journals Ltd. (HK)
Asian and Pacific Council (CH)
Asian and Pacific Council. Cultural and Social Centre (KO)
Asian Beacon Fellowship (MY)
Asian Cultural Center (CH)
Asian Cultural Centre for Unesco (JA)
Asian Development Bank (PH)
Asian Development Institute
  *see under* United Nations Economic and Social Commission for Asia and the Pacific (UN)
Asian Family Affair, Inc. (US)
Asian Federation of Obstetrics and Gynaecology (SI)
Asian Finance Publications Ltd. (HK)
Asian Information Center for Geotechnical Engineering (TH)
Asian Institute
  *see under* Pahlavi University (IR)
Asian Institute of Technology (TH)
Asian Labor Education Center (PH)
Asian Mass Communication Research and Information Centre (SI)
Asian Music Publications (US)
Asian Outlook (CH)
Asian-Pacific Dental Federation (PH)
Asian Pacific Dental Student Association (JA)

Asian-Pacific Society of Cardiology (US)
Asian Parliamentarians' Union (JA)
Asian Peoples' Anti-Communist League - Republic of China (CH)
Asian Productivity Organization (JA)
Asian Regional Institute for School Building Research (CE)
Asian Research Service (HK)
Asian Studies Press (II)
Asian Trade Publications (BG)
Asiatic Research Center (KO)
Asiatic Society, Bombay (II)
Asiatic Society, Calcutta (II)
Asiatic Society of Bangladesh (BG)
Asien Buecherei (GW)
Asistencia Reciproca Petrolera Estatal Latinoamericana (UY)
Foerlags AB ASK (SW)
ASLIB (UK)
ASLIB. Library Association, Audiovisual Groups (UK)
ASLIB. Transport and Planning Group (UK)
ASLIB. Youth Libraries Group (UK)
Aslin Advertising Co. (CN)
Asmeccanica (IT)
Asocacion Odontologica Uruguaya (UY)
Asociacion Archivistica Argentina (AG)
Asociacion Argentina Amigos de la Astronomia (AG)
Asociacion Argentina Criadores de Cebu (AG)
Asociacion Argentina Criadores de Cerdos (AG)
Asociacion Argentina de Actores (AG)
Asociacion Argentina de Ciencia Politica (AG)
Asociacion Argentina de Mineralogia, Petrologia y Sedimentologia (AG)
Asociacion Argentina de Psiquiatria Social (AG)
Asociacion Argentina de Quimicos y Coloristas Textiles (AG)
Asociacion Argentina de Semiotica (AG)
Asociacion Argentina para el Progreso de las Ciencias (AG)
Asociacion Asturiana de Amigos de la Naturaleza (SP)
Asociacion Bioquimica Argentina (AG)
Asociacion Colombiana de Archivistas. Archivo Nacional (CK)
Asociacion Colombiana de Facultades de Medicina (CK)
Asociacion Colombiana para al Estudio Cientifico de la Poblacion (CK)
Asociacion Comercial Hispano-Sueca (SP)
Asociacion Costarricense de Bibliotecarios (CR)
Asociacion Cubano de las Naciones Unidas (CU)
Asociacion Cultural Humboldt (VE)
Asociacion de Academias de la Lengua Espanola Comision Permanente. Boletn (SP)
Asociacion de Agencias de Viajes y Turismo (PY)
Asociacion de Bancos del Uruguay (UY)
Asociacion de Bibliotecarios del Paraguay (PY)
Asociacion de Bibliotecarios Profesionales de Rosario (AG)
Asociacion de Bibliotecas Universitarias y Especializadas de Nicaragua (NQ)
Asociacion de Centros Farmaceuticos de Espana S.A. (SP)
Asociacion de Escribanos del Uruguay (UY)
Asociacion de Estudios Cooperativos (SP)
Asociacion de Ex-Alumnos de la Escuela Nacional de Bibliotecarios (AG)
Asociacion de Exportadores (PE)
Asociacion de Guias de Mexico (MX)
Asociacion de Hidalgos a Fuero de Espana (SP)
Asociacion de Industriales Metalurgicos (AG)
Asociacion de Ingenieros Aeronauticos (SP)
Asociacion de Ingenieros de Minas, Metalurgistas y Geologos de Mexico (MX)
Asociacion de Ingenieros de Montes (SP)
Asociacion de Ingenieros del I. C. A. I. (SP)
Asociacion de Ingenieros Navales (SP)
Asociacion de Ingenieros Petroleros de Mexico, A.D. (MX)
Asociacion de Ingenieros y Arquitectos de Mexico (MX)
Asociacion de Investigacion Industrial Electrica (SP)
Asociacion de Investigacion Tecnica de la Industria Papelera Espanola (SP)
Asociacion de Investigacion Tecnica de las Industrias de la Madera (SP)
Asociacion de Investigacion Textil Algodonera (SP)
Asociacion de la Prensa de Lugo (SP)
Asociacion de la Prensa Medica Espanola (SP)
Asociacion de la Prensa Tecnica Argentina (AG)
Asociacion de Maestros de Puerto Rico (PR)
Asociacion de Maestros Pintores de Barcelona (SP)
Asociacion de Medicina Interna de Mexico (MX)

Asociacion de Medicos Especialistas de la Salud Publica de Costa Rica (CR)
Asociacion de Obstetricia y Ginecologia (SP)
Asociacion de Prensa Hondurena (HO)
Asociacion de Quimicos y Coloristas Textiles (SP)
Asociacion de San Jorge de Alcoy (SP)
Asociacion de Tecnicos Azucareros de Cuba (CU)
Asociacion de Tecnicos Azucareros de Venezuela (VE)
Asociacion de Tecnicos en Alimentos de Mexico, A.C. (MX)
Asociacion del Congreso Panamericano de Ferrocarriles (AG)
Asociacion Demografica Costarricense (CR)
Asociacion Dental Mexicana (MX)
Asociacion Dominicana pro Bienestar de la Familia (DR)
Asociacion Electrotecnia Argentina (AG)
Asociacion Espanola Contra el Cancer (SP)
Asociacion Espanola de Amigos de los Castillos (SP)
Asociacion Espanola de Cirujanos (SP)
Asociacion Espanola de la Carretera (SP)
Asociacion Espanola de la Prensa Tecnica (SP)
Asociacion Espanola de Lucha Contra el Fuego (SP)
Asociacion Espanola de Lucha Contra la Contaminacion Ambiental (SP)
Asociacion Espanola de Orientalistas (SP)
Asociacion Espanola de Technicos de Cerveza y Malta (SP)
Asociacion Espanola de Tecnicos de Maquinaria para la Construccion y Obras Publicas (SP)
Asociacion Espanola de Urologia (SP)
Asociacion Espanola Hematologia y Hemoterapia (SP)
Asociacion Espanola para el Control de la Calidad (SP)
Asociacion Espanola para el Progreso de las Ciencias (SP)
Asociacion Filatelica de Guatemala (GT)
Asociacion Filatelica de la Republica Argentina (AG)
Asociacion Franco-Mexicana de Ingenieros y Tecnicos (MX)
Asociacion General de Agricultores (GT)
Asociacion General de Archivistas de el Salvador (ES)
Asociacion Interamericana de Bibliotecarios y Documentalistas Agricolas (CR)
Asociacion Interamericana de Presupuesto Publico (VE)
Asociacion International de Galdosianos (US)
Asociacion Latino Americana de Facultades de Odontologia (GT)
Asociacion Latino-Americana de Filosofos Catolicos (BL)
Asociacion Latinoamericana de Armadores (UY)
Asociacion Latinoamericana de Ciencias Fisiologicas (AG)
Asociacion Latinoamericana de Escuelas de Bibliotecologia y Ciencias de la Informacion (MX)
Asociacion Latinoamericana de Libre Comercio (UY)
Asociacion Latinoamericana de Patologos (MX)
Asociacion Medica Argentina (AG)
Asociacion Medica de Corrientes y Sociedad de Cirugia (AG)
Asociacion Medica de los Ferrocarriles Nacionales de Mexico (MX)
Asociacion Medica de Puerto Rico (PR)
Asociacion Mexicana de Bibliotecarios, A.C. (MX)
Asociacion Mexicana de Caminos (MX)
Asociacion Mexicana de Facultades y Escuelas de Medicina (MX)
Asociacion Mexicana de Hoteles y Moteles (MX)
Asociacion Mexicana de Orquideologia AC (MX)
Asociacion Mexicana de Restaurantes (MX)
Asociacion Mexicana de Sociologia (MX)
Asociacion Nacional Automovilistica, A.C. (MX)
Asociacion Nacional de Agricultores Pequenos. Secretaria Ideologica (CU)
Asociacion Nacional de Bibliotecarios, Archiveros y Arqueologos (AG)
Asociacion Nacional de Contratistas de Instalaciones Sanitarias e Hidraulicas (MX)
Asociacion Nacional de Enfermeras de Colombia (CK)
Asociacion Nacional de Industriales (CK)
Asociacion Nacional de Ingenieros Industriales. Agrupacion de Tataluna (SP)
Asociacion Nacional de Ingenieros Industriales de Espana (SP)
Asociacion Nacional de Instituciones Financieras (CK)
Asociacion Nacional de la Industria Quimica (MX)
Asociacion Nacional de Medicos Forenses (SP)
Asociacion Nacional de Peritos e Ingenieros Tecnico Industriales (SP)
Asociacion Nacional de Quimicos de Espana (SP)
Asociacion Nacional de Universidades e Institutos de Ensenanza Superior (MX)

Association d'Humanisme et Renaissance   (SZ)
Association d'Interpretes et de Traducteurs   (SZ)
Association d'Organisation Scientifique du Travail
   (SZ)
Association Dahomeene de Geographie   (DM)
Association de Botanique Tropicale. Laboratoire de
   Phanerogamie   (FR)
Association de Developpement et d'Industrialisation de
   la Region Alsace   (FR)
Association de Etablissements Canton aux
   d'Assurances Contre l'Incendie
   see Vereinigung Kantonaler
   Feuerversicherungsanstalten   (SZ)
Association de Geographes Francais   (FR)
Association de l'Ecole Nationale Superieure des
   Bibliothecaires   (FR)
Association de la Construction de Montreal et du
   Quebec   (CN)
Association de la Revue d'Orthopedie Dento-Faciale
   (FR)
Association de la Revue Militaire Suisse   (SZ)
Association de Pedagogie Cybernetique   (FR)
Association de Solidarite France-Arabe   (FR)
Association des Amis d'Alain   (FR)
Association des Amis d'Alfred de Vigny   (FR)
Association des Amis d'Andre Gide   (FR)
Association des Amis de Jean Cocteau   (FR)
Association des Amis de l'Assistance Publique   (FR)
Association des Amis de l'E.N.S.B.A.N.A.   (FR)
Association des Amis de la Comedie de l'Ouest   (FR)
Association des Amis de la Polynesie Francaise   (FR)
Association des Amis de la Radiesthesie   (FR)
Association des Amis de la Revue de Geographie de
   Lyon   (FR)
Association des Amis de Milosz   (FR)
Association des Amis de Pierre Teilhard de Chardin
   (FR)
Association des Amis de Vergy   (FR)
Association des Amis du Musee des Beaux-Arts   (FR)
Association des Amis du Musee International des
   Hussards   (FR)
Association des Amis et Ancien Eleves du Laboratoire
   de Geologie, I   (FR)
Association des Anatomistes   (FR)
Association des Anciens Eleves de l'Ecole Centrale
   des Arts et Manufactures   (FR)
Association des Anciens Eleves de l'Ecole Francaise
   des Attaches de Presse   (FR)
Association des Anciens Eleves de l'Ecole Nationale
   d'Administration   (FR)
Association des Anciens Eleves de l'Ecole Superieur
   de Commerce de Paris   (FR)
Association des Anciens Eleves de l'Ecole Superieure
   de Fonderie   (FR)
Association des Anciens Eleves de l'Ecole Technique
   d'Aeronautique et de Construction Automobile
   (FR)
Association des Anciens Eleves de l'Institut
   d'Oenologie de Bordeaux   (FR)
Association des Anciens Eleves des Ecoles Techniques
   Superieures de Geneve   (SZ)
Association des Anciens Eleves des Facultes des
   Lettres de Paris   (FR)
Association des Anesthesiologistes Francais   (FR)
Association des Archives Spartacus   (FR)
Association des Archivistes du Quebec   (CN)
Association des Archivistes et Bibliothecaires de
   Belgique   (BE)
Association des Archivistes Francais   (FR)
Association des Assureurs-Vie du Canada   (CN)
Association des Bibliothecaires Francais   (FR)
Association des Bibliotheques Ecclesiastiques de
   France   (FR)
Association des Chefs d'Entreprises Libres (A.C.E.L.)
   (FR)
Association des Cineastes de Marseille-Provence
   (FR)
Association des Demographes du Quebec   (CN)
Association des Diplomes de Microbiologie de la
   Faculte de Pharmacie de Nancy   (FR)
Association des Diplomes de Polytechniques   (CN)
Association des Ecrivains Belges de Langue Francaise
   (BE)
Association des Editeurs Canadiens   (CN)
Association des Educateurs Specialises pour Inadaptes
   du Quebec   (CN)
Association des Eglises Baptistes Evangeliques   (CN)
Association des Eleves de l'Ecole Centrale de Lyon
   (FR)
Association des Eleves de l'Ecole Speciale des Travaux
   Publics   (FR)
Association des Enseignants Franco-Ontariens   (CN)
Association des Etudes Tsiganes   (FR)
Association des Fabricants Belges et Explosifs   (BE)
Association des Francais Libres   (FR)
Association des Guides Catholiques du Canada   (CN)
Association des Hautes Etudes Hospitalieres   (FR)
Association des Historiens Africains   (CM)

Association des Horticulteurs de la Suisse Romande
   (SZ)
Association des Infirmieres Catholiques du Canada
   (CN)
Association des Ingenieurs Anciens Eleves de l'Institut
   National Polytechnique de Grenoble   (FR)
Association des Ingenieurs de Chauffage et de
   Ventilation de France   (FR)
Association des Ingenieurs de la Faculte Polytechnique
   de Mons   (BE)
Association des Ingenieurs des Postes et
   Telecommunications   (FR)
Association des Ingenieurs des Villes de France   (FR)
Association des Ingenieurs et Anciens Eleves de
   l'Ecole Superieure d'Ingenieurs et Techniciens pour
   l'Agriculture (E.S.IT.P.A.)   (FR)
Association des Ingenieurs et Techniciens Africains de
   Cote d'Ivoire   (IV)
Association des Ingenieurs Techniciens Chimistes de
   St. Ghislain-Hornu   (BE)
Association des Instituteurs Reunis du Grand-Duche
   de Luxembourg   (LU)
Association des Jeunes Romanistes   (FR)
Association des Joueurs d'Echecs Par Correspondance
   (FR)
Association des Juifs Originaires d'Algerie Installes en
   France   (FR)
Association des Licencies et Ingenieurs Commerciaux
   (BE)
Association des Maires de France   (FR)
Association des Maitres-Cuisiniers de France   (FR)
Association des Maitres Imprimeurs de Montreal
   (CN)
Association des Medecins de Langue Francaise du
   Canada   (CN)
Association des Medecins Israelites de France   (FR)
Association des Officiers de la Ville de Paris   (FR)
Association des Paralyses de France   (FR)
Association des Peintres Officiels de la Marine   (FR)
Association des Pharmaciens Directeurs de
   Laboratoires d'Analyses Biologiques   (FR)
Association des Pharmacologistes   (FR)
Association des Photographes Professionnelle de la
   Province de Quebec   (CN)
Association des Professeurs d'Arts Plastiques du
   Quebec   (CN)
Association des Professeurs de Langues Vivantes
   (BE)
Association des Professeurs de Mathematiques de
   l'Enseignement Public. Regionale Parisienne   (FR)
Association des Professeurs de Philosophie de
   l'Enseignement Public   (FR)
Association des Professionnels de l'Activite Physique
   du Quebec   (CN)
Association des Reeducateurs de la Parole et du
   Langage Oral et Ecrite (A.R.P.L.O.E.)   (FR)
Association des Sages-Femmes de l'Ecole
   d'Accouchement de la Maternite de Nancy   (FR)
Association des Scouts de France   (FR)
Association des Secretaires Generaux des Parlements
   see Association of Secretaries General of
   Parliaments   (FR)
Association des Services Geologiques Africains   (FR)
Association des Societes et Fonds Francais
   d'Investissement   (FR)
Association des Societes Scientifiques Medicales
   Belges   (BE)
Association des Techniciens d'Animaux de Laboratoire
   (FR)
Association des Technologistes Agricoles Inc.   (CN)
Association des Traducteurs et Interpretes de l'Ontario
   (CN)
Association des Universitaires de Geneve   (SZ)
Association des Universites Partiellement Ou
   Entierement de Langue Francaise   (CN)
Association des Universites Partiellement Ou
   Entierement de Langue Francaise. Bureau Africain
   (SG)
Association des Viticulteurs d'Alsace   (FR)
Association du Diabete du Quebec Inc.   (CN)
Association du Magnificat   (FR)
Association du Theatre pour l'Enfance et la Jeunesse
   (FR)
Association Economie et Humanisme   (FR)
Association en Biologie Appliquee   (FR)
Association Evangile et Liberte   (FR)
Association Feminine d'Education et d'Action Sociale
   (CN)
Association for Applied Psychoanalysis   (US)
Association for Asian Studies   (CH)
Association for Asian Studies, Inc.   (US)
Association for Asian Studies, Inc. Committee on East
   Asian Libraries   (US)
Association for Asian Studies, Inc. Committee on
   Research Materials   (US)
Association for Canadian Studies in the United States
   (US)

Association for Childhood Education International
   (US)
Association for Children with Aphasic and Perceptual
   Difficulties   (AT)
Association for Children with Learning Disabilities
   (US)
Association for Christian Social Studies   (AT)
Association for Clinical Pastoral Education   (US)
Association for Commonwealth Literature and
   Language Studies   (II)
Association for Communication Administration   (US)
Association for Comparative Economic Studies   (US)
Association for Computational Linguistics   (US)
Association for Computing Machinery   (US)
Association for Computing Machinery. Programming
   Language Committee   (US)
Association for Computing Machinery. San Francisco
   Bay Area Chapters   (US)
Association for Computing Machinery. Special Interest
   Group on Applications of Computer Technology
   (US)
Association for Computing Machinery. Special Interest
   Group on Automata and Compatability Theory
   (US)
Association for Computing Machinery. Special Interest
   Group on Business Data Processing   (US)
Association for Computing Machinery. Special Interest
   Group on Computer Uses in Education   (US)
Association for Computing Machinery. Special Interest
   Group on Graphics   (US)
Association for Computing Machinery. Special Interest
   Group on Language Analysis and Studies in the
   Humanities   (US)
Association for Computing Machinery. Special Interest
   Group on Microprogramming   (US)
Association for Computing Machinery. Special Interest
   Group on Numerical Analysis   (US)
Association for Computing Machinery. Special Interest
   Group on Operating Systems   (US)
Association for Computing Machinery. Special Interest
   Group on Programming Languages   (US)
Association for Consumer Education   (AT)
Association for Continuing Higher Education   (US)
Association for Documentation in Economics   (JA)
Association for Economic Development   (JA)
Association for Education in Journalism   (US)
Association for Education in Journalism. International
   Division   (US)
Association for Education in Journalism. Mass
   Communications and Society Division   (US)
Association for Education of the Visually
   Handicapped, Inc.   (US)
Association for Educational Communications and
   Technology   (US)
Association for Educational Data Systems   (US)
Association for Evolutionary Economics   (US)
Association for Field Archaeology   (US)
Association for Field Services in Teacher Education
   (US)
Association for French Studies in Southern Africa
   (SA)
Association for Group Psychoanalysis and Process
   (UK)
Association for Hospital Medical Education   (US)
Association for Humanistic Education and
   Development   (US)
Association for Humanistic Psychology   (US)
Association for Institutional Research   (US)
Association for Intercollegiate Athletics for Women
   (US)
Association for International Medical Study, Inc.
   (US)
Association for Jewish Studies   (US)
Association for Literary and Linguistic Computing
   (UK)
Association for Media and Technology in Education in
   Canada   (CN)
Association for Non-White Concerns in Personnel and
   Guidance   (US)
Association for Peace   (IS)
Association for Preservation Technology   (CN)
Association for Professional Education for Ministry
   (US)
Association for Programmed Learning and Educational
   Technology   (UK)
Association for Protection of Fur-Bearing Animals
   (CN)
Association for Psychiatric Treatment of Offenders
   (UK)
Association for Radical East Asian Studies   (UK)
Association for Recorded Sound Collections   (US)
Association for Research and Enlightenment   (US)
Association for Research in Growth Relationships
   (US)
Association for Research in Nervous and Mental
   Disease   (US)
Association for Research in Vision and Ophthalmology
   (UK)

Association for Research in Vision and Ophthalmology (US)
Association for School, College and University Staffing (US)
Association for Science Education (UK)
Association for Scottish Literary Studies (UK)
Association for Self Management (US)
Association for Social Anthropology in Oceania (US)
Association for Social Economics (US)
Association for Studies in Economic Behavior (JA)
Association for Supervision and Curriculum Development (US)
Association for Symbolic Logic (NE)
Association for Symbolic Logic, Inc (US)
Association for Systems Management (US)
Association for Teacher Education in Africa. Western Council (NR)
Association for the Advancement of Agricultural Sciences in Africa (ET)
Association for the Advancement of Baltic Studies (US)
Association for the Advancement of Behavior Therapy (US)
Association for the Advancement of Medical Instrumentation (US)
Association for the Advancement of Psychoanalysis (US)
Association for the Advancement of Psychotherapy (US)
Association for the Advancement of Science of Malawi (MW)
Association for the Care of the Child (JA)
Association for the Coordination of University Religious Affairs (US)
Association for the Development of Computer-Based Instructional Systems (US)
Association for the Development of Religious Information Systems (US)
Association for the Education of Pupils from Overseas (UK)
Association for the Help of Retarded Children. New York City Chapter (US)
Association for the Journal of Religious History (AT)
Association for the Preservation of Virginia Antiquities (US)
Association for the Promotion of Science Education (II)
Association for the Reform of Latin Teaching (UK)
Association for the Sociological Study of Jewry (US)
Association for the Sociology of Religion (US)
Association for the Study of Afro-American Life and History, Inc (US)
Association for the Study of Animal Behaviour (UK)
Association for the Study of Dada & Surrealism (US)
Association for the Study of Law and Politics
  see under Keio University (JA)
Association for the Study of Man-Environment Relations (US)
Association for the Study of Medical Education (UK)
Association for the Study of Nationalities (U.S.S.R. and East Europe), Inc. (US)
Association for the Study of Oriental Insects (II)
Association for the Study of Perception (US)
Association for the Study of Religion (US)
Association for the Study of the World Refugee Problems (AU)
Association for the Understanding of Man (US)
Association for Therapeutic Education (UK)
Association for Union Democracy (US)
Association for University Business and Economic Research (US)
Association for Voluntary Sterilization, Inc. (US)
Association for Women in Science (US)
Association for World Education (US)
Association Forestiere Quebecoise (CN)
Association Francaise d'Etudes Americaines (FR)
Association Francaise d'Experts de la Cooperation Technique Internationale (FR)
Association Francaise d'Hygiene et de Medecine Scolaires et Universitaires (FR)
Association Francaise de Chirurgie (FR)
Association Francaise de Criminologie (FR)
Association Francaise de l'Eclairage (FR)
Association Francaise de Normalisation (AFNOR) (FR)
Association Francaise des Amis d'Albert Schweitzer (FR)
Association Francaise des Amis des Chemins de Fer (FR)
Association Francaise des Banques (FR)
Association Francaise des Collectionneurs et Amis d'Ex Libris (A.F.C.E.L) (FR)
Association Francaise des Documentalistes et des Bibliothecaires Specialises (FR)
Association Francaise des Enseignants de Francais (FR)
Association Francaise des Femmes Diplomees des Universites (FR)

Association Francaise des Ingenieurs du Caoutchouc et des Plastiques (FR)
Association Francaise des Ingenieurs et Chefs d'Entretien (FR)
Association Francaise des Ophtalmologistes Praticiens (FR)
Association Francaise des Relations Publiques (FR)
Association Francaise des Techniciens des Peintures, Vernis, Encres d'Imprimerie, Colles et Adhesifs (FR)
Association Francaise des Techniciens du Petrole (FR)
Association Francaise des Techniciens et Ingenieurs de Securite et des Medecins du Travail (FR)
Association Francaise du Froid (FR)
Association Francaise pour l'Avancement des Sciences (FR)
Association Francaise pour l'Etude des Eaux (FR)
Association Francaise pour l'Etude du Cancer (FR)
Association Francaise pour l'Etude du Quaternaire (FR)
Association Francaise pour l'Etude du Sol (FR)
Association Francaise pour la Cybernetique Economique et Technique (FR)
Association Francaise pour la Sauvegarde de l'Enfance et de l'Adolescence (FR)
Association Francaise pour le Controle Industriel de Qualite (FR)
Association Francaise pour le Developpement de l'Enseignement Technique (FR)
Association Francaise pour les Recherches et Etudes Camerounaises (FR)
Association France Etats Unis (FR)
Association France-Malte (FR)
Association Franco Ukrainienne (FR)
Association Generale des Conservateurs, des Collections Publiques de France (FR)
Association Generale des Etudiants de l'Universite de Sherbrooke (CN)
Association Generale des Etudiants Guadeloupeens (FR)
Association Generale des Hygienistes et Techniciens Municipaux (FR)
Association Generale des Medecins de France (FR)
Association Generale des Meuniers Belges (BE)
Association Generale des Psychologues Francophones d'Afrique et de Madagascar (SG)
Association Geographes de l'Est (FR)
Association Graphique et Artistique (BE)
Association Guillaume Bude (FR)
Association H.E.C. (FR)
Association Homoeopathique Belge (BE)
Association in Canada Serving Organizations for Human Settlements (CN)
Association Inter-Africaine d'Editions (SG)
Association Internationale d'Etudes du Sud-Est Europeen (RM)
Association Internationale d'Experts Scientifiques du Tourisme
  see International Association of Scientific Experts in Tourism (SZ)
Association Internationale d'Information Scolaire Universitaire et Professionnelle
  see International Association for Educational and Vocational Information (FR)
Association Internationale de Bibliophilie (FR)

Association Internationale de Broncho-Pneumologie
  see International Broncho-Pneumologic Association (FR)

Association Internationale de Cybernetique
  see International Association for Cybernetics (BE)

Association Internationale de Geodesie
  see International Association of Geodesy (BE)

Association Internationale de la Securite Sociale
  see International Social Security Association (SZ)

Association Internationale de Linguistique Appliquee (GW)

Association Internationale de Presse pour l'Etude des Problems d'Outre-Mer (FR)
Association Internationale des Docteurs (Lettres) de l'Universite de Paris (FR)
Association Internationale des Etudes Byzantines
  see International Association for Byzantine Studies (GR)
Association Internationale des Etudes Francaises (FR)
Association Internationale des Etudiants en Sciences Economiques et Commerciales
  see International Association of Students in Business and Economics (BE)
Association Internationale des Numismates Professionnels
  see International Association of Professional Numismatists (FR)

Association Internationale des Parlementaires de Langue Francaise (FR)
Association Internationale des Ponts et Charpentes
  see International Association for Bridge and Structural Engineering (SZ)
Association Internationale des Societes d'Assurance Mutuelle
  see International Association of Mutual Insurance Companies (FR)
Association Internationale des Travailleurs (FR)
Association Internationale du Film d'Animation
  see International Animated Film Association (FR)
Association Internationale Futuribles
  see International Association Futuribles (FR)
Association Internationale Permanente des Congres de la Route
  see Permanent International Association of Road Congresses (FR)
Association Internationale pour l'Histoire du Verre
  see International Association for the History of Glass (BE)
Association Internationale pour la Defence de la Liberte Religieuse
  see International Association for the Defence of Religious Liberties (SZ)
Association Internationale pour la Recherche Medicale (FR)
Association Interprofessionnelle des Centres Medicaux et Sociaux de la Region Parisienne (FR)
Association Interprofessionnelle pour l'Etude du Travail (FR)
Association Jean-Favard pour le Developpement de la Linguistique Quantitative (FR)
Association "l'Education" (FR)
Association l'Eglise Reformee Vous Parle (FR)
Association Laitiere Francaise (FR)
Association le Christianisme au 20th Siecle (FR)
Association les Amis de l'Homme (FR)
Association les Amis de Napoleon 3rd (FR)
Association Litteraire et Artistique Internationale
  see International Literary and Artistic Association (FR)
Association Luxembourgeoise des Ingenieurs et Industriels (LU)
Association Mars et Mercure (BE)
Association Mondiale des Corses (FR)
Association Mutualiste de l'Industrie Hoteliere (FR)
Association Nationale d'Aide aux Handicapes Mentaux (BE)
Association Nationale d'Economie (FR)
Association Nationale de la Meunerie Francaise (FR)
Association Nationale de la Presse Mutualiste (FR)
Association Nationale de la Recherche Technique (FR)
Association Nationale de Lutte Contre les Fleaux Atmospheriques (FR)
Association Nationale des Anciennes Deportees et Internees de la Resistance (FR)
Association Nationale des Assistants de Service Social (FR)
Association Nationale des Chasseurs de Gibier d'Eau (FR)
Association Nationale des Docteurs en Droit (FR)
Association Nationale des Docteurs es-Sciences Economiques (FR)
Association Nationale des Entreprises Zairoises (ZR)
Association Nationale des Maitres Agricoles (FR)
Association Nationale des Parents d'Enfants Aveugles (FR)
Association Nationale des Poetes et Ecrivains Camerounais (CM)
Association Nationale des Polios de France (FR)
Association Nationale des Veuves Civiles Chefs de Famille (FR)
Association Nationale "Notre-Dame des Gitans" (FR)
Association Nationale pour l'Etude de la Communaute de la Loire et de ses Affluents (FR)
Association Nationale pour la Defense de la Qualite Francaise (FR)
Association Nationale pour la Formation Professionnelle des Adultes (A.F.P.A.) (FR)
Association Nationale pour la Protection Contre l'Incendie (BE)
Association Nationale pour le Developpement des Techniques de Marketing (ADETEM) (FR)
Association Normandie Protestante (FR)
Association of Acrobats (AT)
Association of African Universities (GH)
Association of Afrikaans Rhodesians (RH)
Association of American Chambers of Commerce in Latin America (US)
Association of American Colleges (US)
Association of American Editorial Cartoonists (US)
Association of American Feed Control Officials (US)
Association of American Geographers (US)
Association of American Geographers. Southeastern Division (US)

Association of American Law Schools  (US)
Association of American Law Schools. Committee on
 Libraries  (US)
Association of American Law Schools. Law School
 Admission Council  (US)
Association of American Law Schools. Section on
 Foreign Exchanges of Law Teachers and Students
 (US)
Association of American Library Schools  (US)
Association of American Medical Colleges  (US)
Association of American Medical Colleges. Division of
 Educational Measurement and Research  (US)
Association of American Pesticide Control Officials,
 Inc.  (US)
Association of American Physicians  (US)
Association of American Physicians & Surgeons, Inc.
 (US)
Association of American Plant Food Control Officials
 (US)
Association of American Publishers  (US)
Association of American Railroads  (US)
Association of American Rhodes Scholars  (US)
Association of American State Geologists  (US)
Association of American Veterinary Medical Colleges
 (US)
Association of American Women Dentists  (US)
Association of Americans and Canadians for Aliyah
 (US)
Association of Americans and Canadians in Israel
 (Jerusalem Region)  (IS)
Association of Apex Clubs  (AT)
Association of Applied Biologists  (UK)
Association of Archivists and Librarians of Belgium
 see Association des Archivistes et Bibliothecaires de
 Belgique  (BE)
Association of Aroostook Indians, Inc.  (US)
Association of Art Historians. Department of Art
 History  (UK)
Association of Artists' Run Galleries  (US)
Association of Asian-American Chambers of
 Commerce  (US)
Association of Asphalt Paving Technologists  (US)
Association of Assistant Librarians  (UK)
Association of Attenders and Alumni of the Hague
 Academy of International Law  (NE)
Association of Australian Slovaks  (AT)
Association of Balloon and Airship Constructors
 (US)
Association of Banks in Lebanon  (LE)
Association of Baptist Professors of Religion  (US)
Association of Bay Area Governments  (US)
Association of Belgian Writers in the French Language
 see Association des Ecrivains Belges de Langue
 Francaise  (BE)
Association of British Adoption and Fostering
 Agencies  (UK)
Association of British Dental Surgery Assistants
 (UK)
Association of British Launderers & Cleaners  (UK)
Association of British Riding Schools  (UK)
Association of British Spectroscopists  (UK)
Association of British Travel Agents  (UK)
Association of British Tree Surgeons & Arborists
 (UK)
Association of Broadcasting & Allied Staffs  (UK)
Association of Burglary Insurance Surveyors  (UK)
Association of Business Archives
 see Likearkistoyhdistys  (FI)
Association of California School Administrators  (US)
Association of California Water Agencies  (US)
Association of Canadian Archivists  (CN)
Association of Canadian Community Colleges  (CN)
Association of Canadian Faculties of Dentistry  (CN)
Association of Canadian Law Teachers  (CN)
Association of Canadian Map Libraries  (CN)
Association of Canadian Medical Colleges  (CN)
Association of Canadian Television and Radio Artists
 (ACTRA)  (CN)
Association of Canadian University Teachers of
 English  (CN)
Association of Caribbean Universities and Research
 Institutes  (PR)
Association of Caribbean University and Research
 Libraries  (PR)
Association of Cashiers Ltd.  (UK)
Association of Chambers of Commerce of South Africa
 (SA)
Association of Child Psychology and Psychiatry  (US)
Association of Child Psychotherapists  (UK)
Association of Choral Conductors  (US)
Association of Christian Teachers  (UK)
Association of Cinematograph, Television and Allied
 Technicians  (UK)
Association of Clinical Biochemists  (UK)
Association of Clinical Pathologists  (UK)
Association of Clinical Scientists  (US)
Association of Co-Operative Building Societies of N.
 S. W. Ltd.  (AT)

Association of College and Research Libraries  (US)
Association of College and University Auditors  (US)
Association of College and University Housing
 Officers  (US)
Association of College Honor Societies  (US)
Association of College Unions-International  (US)
Association of College, University and Community
 Arts Administrators, Inc.  (US)
Association of Colleges for Further and Higher
 Education  (UK)
Association of Collegiate Schools of Architecture, Inc.
 (US)
Association of Collegiate Schools of Planning  (US)
Association of Commonwealth Universities  (UK)
Association of Commonwealth Universities. U.K.
 Committee of Vice-Chancellors & Principals  (UK)
Association of Community Schools  (UK)
Association of Computer Programmers and Analysts
 (US)
Association of Conference Executives  (UK)
Association of Consulting Engineers of Canada  (CN)
Association of Consulting Foresters  (US)
Association of Contemporary Historians  (UK)
Association of Cost Engineers  (UK)
Association of County Councils  (UK)
Association of Croat Writers
 see Drustvo Knjizevnika Hrvatske  (YU)
Association of Czechoslovak Plastic Surgeons  (CS)
Association of Danish Landscape Architects  (DK)
Association of Data Processing Service Organizations
 (US)
Association of Departments of English  (US)
Association of Departments of Foreign Languages
 (US)
Association of Dispensing Opticians  (UK)
Association of District Councils  (UK)
Association of Economic Geographers  (JA)
Association of Education Committees  (UK)
Association of Engineering Geologists  (US)
Association of Engineers and Architects in Israel  (IS)
Association of Engineers, India  (II)
Association of Engineers, Kerala State  (II)
Association of Environmental Hygiene  (SW)
Association of Estonians in Great Britain  (UK)
Association of European Operational Research
 Societies  (NE)
Association of Evangelicals for Italian Missions  (US)
Association of Existential Psychology and Psychiatry
 (US)
Association of Exploration Geochemists  (NE)
Association of Exploration Geologists  (US)
Association of Faculties of Pharmacy of Canada
 (CN)
Association of Feminist Consultants  (US)
Association of Finnish Chemical Societies  (FI)
Association of Finnish Civil Engineers  (FI)
Association of Food and Drug Officials of the United
 States  (US)
Association of Food Scientists and Technologists
 (India)  (II)
Association of Foremen and Supervisors  (AT)
Association of Geography Teachers of India  (II)
Association of Governing Boards of Universities and
 Colleges  (US)
Association of Government Accountants  (US)
Association of Government Supervisors and Radio
 Officers  (UK)
Association of Hebrew Writers of Southern Africa
 (SA)
Association of Highway Officials of the North Atlantic
 States  (US)
Association of History Teachers  (NR)
Association of Icelandic Wholesalers and Importers
 see Felag Islenzkra Storkaupmanna  (IC)
Association of Idaho Cities  (US)
Association of Illinois Electric Cooperatives  (US)
Association of Immigration and Nationality Lawyers
 (US)
Association of Independent Colleges and Schools
 (US)
Association of Independent Colleges and Schools.
 Accrediting Commission  (US)
Association of Independent Copy Machine Dealers
 and Manufacturers  (US)
Association of Indian Engineering Industry  (II)
Association of Indian Pharmaceutical Manufacturers
 (II)
Association of Industrial Accident Boards and
 Commissions  (US)
Association of Institutes for European Studies  (SZ)
Association of Institutional Distributors  (US)
Association of Insurance Brokers  (UK)
Association of International Accountants  (UK)
Association of International Law  (JA)
Association of International Libraries  (EI)
Association of Interstate Commerce Commission
 Practitioners  (US)
Association of Iron and Steel Engineers  (US)

Association of Island Marine Laboratories of the
 Caribbean  (PR)
Association of Japanese Geographers  (JA)
Association of Jewish Ex-Servicemen and Women,
 (Cardiff)  (UK)
Association of Jewish Libraries  (US)
Association of Jewish Refugees in Great Britain  (UK)
Association of Junior Leagues, Inc.  (US)
Association of Kinsmen Clubs  (CN)
Association of Law and Political Science
 see under Tohoku University  (JA)
Association of Law Societies of the Republic of South
 Africa  (SA)
Association of Law Teachers  (UK)
Association of Libertarian Feminists  (US)
Association of Life Insurance Medical Directors  (US)
Association of Lithuanian Foresters in Exile  (US)
Association of Lithuanian Workers  (US)
Association of Little Presses of Great Britain  (UK)
Association of London Clearing Banks  (UK)
Association of Lunar and Planetary Observers  (US)
Association of Man-Made Fibre Industry  (II)
Association of Marian Helpers  (US)
Association of Marshall Scholars and Alumni  (US)
Association of Mary Immaculate  (CN)
Association of Medical Group Psychoanalysts  (US)
Association of Medical Rehabilitation Directors &
 Coordinators, Inc.  (US)
Association of Medical Technologists  (II)
Association of Medical Women in India  (II)
Association of Mental Health Administrators  (US)
Association of Metal Sprayers  (SA)
Association of Metropolitan Authorities  (UK)
Association of Microbiologists of India  (II)
Association of Midwest Fish and Wildlife
 Commissioners  (US)
Association of Military Surgeons of the U. S.  (US)
Association of Mining, Electrical & Mechanical
 Engineers  (UK)
Association of Mining Labor Accident Prevention
 (JA)
Association of Missouri Electric Cooperatives, Inc.
 (US)
Association of Musical Instrument Industries, London
 (UK)
Association of Muslim Scientists and Engineers of
 North America  (US)
Association of National Advertisers, Inc.  (US)
Association of New Brunswick Land Surveyors  (CN)
Association of New Jersey Environmental
 Commissions  (US)
Association of Norwegian Road Engineers  (NO)
Association of Notaries  (IR)
Association of Obstetrics and Gynecology of the
 Republic of China  (CH)
Association of Occupational Therapists  (UK)
Association of Official Analytical Chemists  (US)
Association of Official Seed Analysts  (US)
Association of Oilwell Servicing Contractors  (US)
Association of Old Crows  (US)
Association of Ontario Land Surveyors  (CN)
Association of Operating Room Nurses, Inc.  (US)
Association of Operating Room Technicians, Inc.
 (US)
Association of Ophthalmic Opticians  (IE)
Association of Ophthalmic Opticians in Finland
 see Suomen Silmaoptikkojen Liitto  (FI)
Association of Orthodox Jewish Scientists  (US)
Association of Otolaryngologists of India  (II)
Association of Pacific Coast Geographers  (US)
Association of Pediatricians of Pakistan  (PK)
Association of Pharmaceutical Teachers of India  (II)
Association of Photographic Laboratories  (UK)
Association of Physicians of Great Britain and Ireland
 (UK)
Association of Physicians of India  (II)
Association of Physiologists and Pharmacologists of
 India  (II)
Association of Polish Students and Graduates in Exile
 (UK)
Association of Political and Social Science  (JA)
Association of Private Camps  (US)
Association of Private Telephone Companies in
 Finland
 see Puhelinlaitosten Liitto  (FI)
Association of Professional Directors of YMCA's
 (US)
Association of Professional Engineers, Australia  (AT)
Association of Professional Engineers, Geologists &
 Geophysicists of Alberta  (CN)
Association of Professional Engineers of British
 Columbia  (CN)
Association of Professional Engineers of Manitoba
 (CN)
Association of Professional Engineers of
 Newfoundland  (CN)
Association of Professional Engineers of Nova Scotia
 (CN)

Association of Professional Engineers of Saskatchewan (CN)
Association of Professional, Executive, Clerical and Computer Staff (UK)
Association of Professional Foresters (UK)
Association of Professors of Missions (US)
Association of Public Address Engineers (UK)
Association of Public Lighting Engineers (UK)
Association of Railway Preservation Societies (UK)
Association of Recognised English Language Schools (UK)
Association of Registered Bank Holding Companies (US)
Association of Registered Professional Foresters of New Brunswick (CN)
Association of Rehabilitation Nurses (US)
Association of Research Libraries (US)
Association of Research Libraries. Center for Chinese Research Materials (US)
Association of Research Libraries. Systems and Procedures Exchange Center (US)
Association of Russian-American Scholars in U.S.A. (US)
Association of Scandinavian Slavicists and Baltologists (DK)
Association of School Business Officials of the United States and Canada (US)
Association of Scientific Workers (UK)
Association of Scientific Workers of India (II)
Association of Secondary School Teachers of English in Israel (IS)
Association of Secretaries General of Parliaments (FR)
Association of Social Anthropologists of the Commonwealth (UK)
Association of Southeast Asian Institutions of Higher Learning (TH)
Association of Southeast Asian Librarians (SI)
Association of Southeastern Biologists, Inc. (US)
Association of Special Libraries of the Philippines (PH)
Association of State Library Agencies (US)
Association of State Road Transport Undertakings (II)
Association of Supervisory and Executive Engineers (UK)
Association of Surgeons of Gt. Britain and Ireland (UK)
Association of Surgeons of India (II)
Association of Surgeons of South Africa (SA)
Association of Swedish Automobile Manufacturers and Wholesalers (SW)
Association of Swiss Ironmongers (SZ)
Association of Swiss Macaroni Manufacturers (SZ)
Association of Systematics Collections (US)
Association of Teacher Educators (US)
Association of Teachers in Colleges and Departments of Education (UK)
Association of Teachers of Domestic Science (UK)
Association of Teachers of English as a Foreign Language (AT)
Association of Teachers of Japanese (US)
Association of Teachers of Management (UK)
Association of Teachers of Mathematics (UK)
Association of Teachers of Mathematics of New York City (US)
Association of Teachers of Preventive Medicine and Community Health (US)
Association of Teachers of Printing and Allied Subjects (UK)
Association of Teachers of Russian (UK)
Association of Teachers of Social Studies in the City of New York (US)
Association of Texas Electric Cooperatives (US)
Association of the Bar of the City of New York (US)
Association of the British Pharmaceutical Industry (UK)
Association of the Deaf and Mute in Israel. Helen Keller Home (IS)
Association of the Graduates of the Institutes and Faculties of Education (UA)
Association of the Guilds of Weavers, Spinners and Dyers (UK)
Association of the Research Institutes
  see under Tohoku University (JA)
Association of the Research Institutes for Tuberculosis of National Universities in Japan (JA)
Association of the Teachers of Mathematics in New England (US)
Association of the United States Army (US)
Association of the University Library School Graduates (TU)
Association of Theological Schools (US)
Association of Theological Schools in South East Asia (PH)
Association of Track and Field Statisticians (US)
Association of Trial Lawyers of America (US)

Association of Ukranian Former Combatants in Great Britain (UK)
Association of Unit Trust Managers (UK)
Association of Universities and Colleges of Canada (CN)
Association of Universities for Research in Astronomy (US)
Association of University Architects (US)
Association of University Radiologists (US)
Association of University Summer Sessions (US)
Association of University Teachers (UK)
Association of Urban and Community Symphony Orchestras (US)
Association of Urban Authorities (MF)
Association of Urban Universities (US)
Association of Var Naring (SW)
Association of Veterinary Students of Great Britain and Ireland (IE)
Association of Veterinary Surgeons Malaysia (MY)
Association of Voluntary Action Scholars (US)
Association of Voluntary Agencies for Rural Development (AVARD) (II)
Association of Working Press, Inc. (US)
Association of Yeshivah-Day School Principals of General Studies (US)
Association of Yugoslav Insurance Organizations
  see Udruzeni Zavod za Osiguranje i Reosiguranje (YU)
Association of Yugoslav Surgeons
  see Udruzenje Hirurga Jugoslavije (YU)
Association of Zoo Directors of Australia and New Zealand (AT)
Association on American Indian Affairs (US)
Association Pax Christi (FR)
Association Peinture (FR)
Association Permanente des Congres Belges de la Route (BE)
Association Pharmaceutique Belge (BE)
Association Poesie Vivante France (FR)
Association pour Defendre la Memoire du Marechal Petain (FR)
Association pour l'Avancement des Sciences et des Techniques de la Documentation (FR)
Association pour l'Encouragement a l'Union des Revues Techniques Belges (BE)
Association pour l'Etude des Problemes d'Outre Mer (FR)
Association pour l'Etude des Problemes de l'Europe (IT)
Association pour l'Etude Taxonomique de la Flore d'Afrique Tropicale (BE)
Association pour l'Histoire de Belle Ile-En-Mer (FR)
Association pour l'Histoire des Sciences de la Nature (FR)
Association pour l'Information Culturelle (BE)
Association pour la Connaissance de l'Allemagne d'Aujourd'hui (FR)
Association pour la Democratie et l'Education Locale et Sociale (A D E L S) (FR)
Association pour la Diffusion de la Documentation Hydraulique (FR)
Association pour la Diffusion de la Pensee Francaise (FR)
Association pour la Diffusion et l'Animation Musicales en Aquitaine (FR)
Association pour la Diffusion et l'Usage de la Langue Latine (FR)
Association pour la Promotion de l'Etude des Langues Modernes (BE)
Association pour la Promotion de l'Orgue dans la Region Grenobloise (FR)
Association pour la Promotion de la Couture Personnelle (FR)
Association pour la Promotion Industrie-Agriculture (FR)
Association pour la Promotion Sociale et la Formation Professionelle dans les Transports Routiers (FR)
Association pour la Protection Automobile (CN)
Association pour la Recherche et Intervention Psychosociologiques (FR)
Association pour la Traduction Automatique et la Linguistique Appliquee (FR)
Association pour le Bon Usage du Francais dans l'Administration (FR)
Association pour le Developpement des Bibliotheques de Religieuses-A D B R (FR)
Association pour le Developpement des Oeuvres Sociales des Sapeurs-Pompiers de Paris (FR)
Association pour le Developpement des Techniques de Transport, d'Environnement et de Circulation (A.T.E.C.) (FR)
Association pour le Developpement et la Diffusion de l'Information Militaire (FR)
Association pour le Development Industriel de l'Ouest Atlantique (FR)
Association pour le Perfectionnement et l'Expansion de la Chocolaterie et de la Confiserie de France (FR)

Association pour le Rayonnement des Lettres, des Arts et des Sciences (FR)
Association pour les Aveugles (FR)
Association pour les Espaces Naturels (FR)
Association pour les Etudes et Recherches de Zoologie Appliquee et de Phytopathologie (BE)
Association pour Une Libre Vie de l'Esprit (FR)
Association pour Une Meilleure Connaissance de l'Asie (FR)
Association Professionnelle des Dessinateurs et Techniciens du Batiment et des Travaux Publics (FR)
Association Professionnelle des Meuniers du Quebec (CN)
Association Psychanalytique de France (FR)
Association Quebecoise des Pharmaciens Proprietaries (CN)
Association Quebecoise des Techniques de l'Eau (CN)
Association Quebecoise du Transport et des Routes Inc. (CN)
Association Quebecoise pour l'Etude Comparative du Droit (CN)
Association Reconnue d'Utilite Publique (FR)
Association Regionale pour l'Etude et la Recherche Scientifiques (FR)
Association Reparatrice (FR)
Association Royale des Anciens Eleves des Ecoles de Brasserie Gand, Bruxelles et Louvain (BE)
Association Saint-Ambroise (FR)
Association Saint-Yves (FR)
Association Scientifique de la Precontrainte (FR)
Association Scientifique et Technique pour la Recherche en Informatique Documentaire (BE)
Association Senegalaise d'Etudes et de Recherches Juridiques (SG)
Association Senegalaise pour l'Etude du Quaternaire Africain (SG)
Association Spiritus (FR)
Association Stenographique Unitaire (FR)
Association-Sterling Films (US)
Association Strasbourgeoise des Periodiques de Sciences Humaines (FR)
Association Suisse Chateaux et Ruines (SZ)
Association Suisse de Science Politique (SZ)
Association Suisse des Electriciens (SZ)
Association Suisse des Geologues et Ingenieurs
  see Vereinigung Schweizerischer Petroleum-Geologen und -Ingenieure (SZ)
Association Suisse des Magasins d'Horlogerie Specialises
  see Verband Schweizerischer Uhrenfachgeschaefte (SZ)
Association Syndicale des Cadres de l'Edition et de la Librairie Francaise (FR)
Association Technique de Fonderie (FR)
Association Technique de Fonderie de Belgique (BE)
Association Technique de l'Industrie du Gaz en France (FR)
Association Technique de l'Industrie Papetiere (FR)
Association Technique Maritime et Aeronautique (FR)
Association U F O-Quebec (CN)
Association Valentin Hauy pour le Bien des Aveugles (FR)
Association Viticole Champenoise (FR)
Associations des Anciens Eleves des Ecoles des Mines (FR)
Associations Publications, Inc. (US)
Associazione Alpinistica "Giovane Montagna" (IT)
Associazione Amici di Castel San Angelo (IT)
Associazione Antiquari d'Italia (IT)
Associazione ARES (IT)
Associazione Artiglieri d'Italia (IT)
Associazione Bancaria Italiana (IT)
Associazione Biblica Italiana (IT)
Associazione Cenacolo (IT)
Associazione Commercianti di Reggio Emilia (IT)
Associazione Cotoniera Italiana (IT)
Associazione Cultural della Provincia di Rieti (IT)
Associazione Culturale Progresso Grafico (IT)
Associazione degli Africanisti Italiani (IT)
Associazione degli Industriali di Arezzo (IT)
Associazione degli Industriali di Siena (IT)
Associazione dei Librai della Svizzera Italiana
  see Schweizerischer Buchhaendler- und Verleger-Verband (SZ)
Associazione dei Medici Provinciali Italiani (IT)
Associazione dei Medici Scrittori Italiani (IT)
Associazione del Mercato Alimentari Coloniali Oli Grassi e Prodotti Chimici Industriali (IT)
Associazione di Storia Ecclesiastica Novarese (IT)
Associazione Elettrotecnica ed Elettronica Italiana (IT)
Associazione Emilia Romagna Contro la Tubercolosi e la Malatie Polmonari (IT)
Associazione Enotecnici Italiani (IT)

Associazione Ex Allievi Istituto Sperimentale di Caseificio  (IT)

Associazione fra i Costruttori in Acciaio Italiani  (IT)

Associazione fra Industrie Chimico-Farmaceutiche  (IT)

Associazione fra le Cassa di Risparmio Italiana  (IT)

Associazione fra le Societa Italiana per Azioni  (IT)

Associazione Frigorifera Italiana  (IT)

Associazione Friulana Donatori di Sangue  (IT)

Associazione Generale delle Cooperative Italiane  (IT)

Associazione Generale Italiana dello Spettacolo  (IT)

Associazione Genetica Italiana  (IT)

Associazione Genitori  (IT)

Associazione Geofisica Italiana.  (IT)

Associazione Geotecnica Italiana  (IT)

Associazione Grossisti Ortofrutticoli  (IT)

Associazione Gruppi Archeologici d'Italia  (IT)

Associazione Industriale Lombarda  (IT)

Associazione Industriali  (IT)

Associazione Industrie Siderurgiche Italiane  (IT)

Associazione Ingegneri della Provincia di Bologna  (IT)

Associazione Insegnanti Ebrei d'Italia  (IT)

Associazione Internazionale della Stampa Medica  (IT)

Associazione Internazionale di Poesia  (IT)

Associazione Irrigazione Est Sesia  (IT)

Associazione Italiana Allevatori  (IT)

Associazione Italiana Assistenza Spastici  (IT)

Associazione Italiana Barmen e Sostenitori  (IT)

Associazione Italiana Biblioteche  (IT)

Associazione Italiana Condizionamento dell 'Aria, Riscaldamento Refrigerazione  (IT)

Associazione Italiana Culturale Aeronautica  (IT)

Associazione Italiana de Ricerca Operativa  (IT)

Associazione Italiana dei Centri Trasfusionali  (IT)

Associazione Italiana dei Pubblici Istitute di Credito Su Pegno  (IT)

Associazione Italiana del Vuoto  (IT)

Associazione Italiana di Aeronautica e Astronautica  (IT)

Associazione Italiana di Cartografia  (IT)

Associazione Italiana di Cultura Classica  (IT)

Associazione Italiana di Genio Rurale  (IT)

Associazione Italiana di Idroclimatologia, Talassologia e Terapia Fisica  (IT)

Associazione Italiana di Illuminazione  (IT)

Associazione Italiana di Metallurgia  (IT)

Associazione Italiana Editori  (IT)

Associazione Italiana Filatelia Religiosa "San Gabriele"  (IT)

Associazione Italiana Giuristi Democratici  (IT)

Associazione Italiana Industriali Tintori, Stampatori e Finitori Tessili  (IT)

Associazione Italiana Laringectomizzati  (IT)

Associazione Italiana Maestri Cattolici  (IT)

Associazione Italiana Manufatturieri Pelli-Cuoio e Succedanei  (IT)

Associazione Italiana Ottici  (IT)

Associazione Italiana per gli Studi di Marketing  (IT)

Associazione Italiana per gli Studi di Politica Estera  (IT)

Associazione Italiana per i Rapporti Culturali Con l'Unione Sovietica  (IT)

Associazione Italiana per il Calcolo Automatico  (IT)

Associazione Italiana per Il Consiglio dei Comuni d'Europa  (IT)

Associazione Italiana per Il Controllo della Qualita  (IT)

Associazione Italiana per Il Progresso dell'Industria del Latte  (IT)

Associazione Italiana per l'Arbitrato  (IT)

Associazione Italiana Prefabbricazione per l'Edilizia Industrializzata  (IT)

Associazione Italiana Santa Cecilia  (IT)

Associazione Italiana Scientifica di Metapsichica  (IT)

Associazione Italiana Societa Concessionarie Autostrade e Trafori  (IT)

Associazione Italiana Strumentisti  (IT)

Associazione Italiana Studi Americanistici  (IT)

Associazione Italiana Studi del Paranormale  (IT)

Associazione Italiana Tecnici del Latte  (IT)

Associazione Italiana Tecnico Economica del Cemento  (IT)

Associazione Libraio Italiani  (IT)

Associazione Linguistica Salentina  (IT)

Associazione Lombarda Dirigenti Aziende Industriali  (IT)

Associazione Mazziniana Italiana  (IT)

Associazione Medica Chirurgica di Tivoli e della Val d'Aniene  (IT)

Associazione Medici Dentisti Italiani  (IT)

Associazione Mineraria Italiana  (IT)

Associazione Nationale fra le Industrie Automobilistche  (IT)

Associazione Nazionale Allevatori Bovini di Razza Piemontese  (IT)

Associazione Nazionale Alpini  (IT)

Associazione Nazionale Armieri Affini  (IT)

Associazione Nazionale Autoriparatori e Autoricambisti  (IT)

Associazione Nazionale Bieticoltori  (IT)

Associazione Nazionale Ciclo, Motociclo e Accessori  (IT)

Associazione Nazionale Combattenti e Reduci Federazione Provinciale di Milano  (IT)

Associazione Nazionale Costruttori Edili  (IT)

Associazione Nazionale degli Industriali dei Laterizi  (IT)

Associazione Nazionale dei Musei Italiani  (IT)

Associazione Nazionale dei Procuratori e Patrocinatori Legali  (IT)

Associazione Nazionale del Libero Pensiero "Giordano Bruno"  (IT)

Associazione Nazionale dell'Industria Chimica  (IT)

Associazione Nazionale dell'Industria della Saponeria della Detergenza e dei Prodotti d'Igiene  (IT)

Associazione Nazionale delle Bonifiche, delle Irrigazioni e dei Miglioramenti Fondiari  (IT)

Associazione Nazionale di Ingegneria Sanitaria  (IT)

Associazione Nazionale di Vernicatura Decorazione e Stuccatura  (IT)

Associazione Nazionale Esercenti Spettacoli Vaggianti  (IT)

Associazione Nazionale Ex Internati  (IT)

Associazione Nazionale Fabbricanti Giocattoli  (IT)

Associazione Nazionale fra le Imprese Assicuratrici  (IT)

Associazione Nazionale Fra le Industrie Automobilistche  (IT)

Associazione Nazionale fra le Industrie della Gomma  (IT)

·ssociazione Nazionale fra le Industrie della Gomma Cavi Elettrici ed Affini  (IT)

Associazione Nazionale Giovani Agricoltori  (IT)

Associazione Nazionale Industriali Laterizi  (IT)

Associazione Nazionale Industrie Elettrotecniche ed Elettroniche  (IT)

Associazione Nazionale Industrie Metalli Non Ferrosi  (IT)

Associazione Nazionale Ingegneri e Architetti Italiani  (IT)

Associazione Nazionale Instituti Autonomi e Case Consorzi Popolari  (IT)

Associazione Nazionale Invalidi Esiti Poliomielite  (IT)

Associazione Nazionale Italia Albania  (IT)

Associazione Nazionale Italiana Grossisti Orologiai  (IT)

Associazione Nazionale Italiana Industrie Grafiche Cartotecniche e Trasformatrici  (IT)

Associazione Nazionale Italiana per l'Automazione  (IT)

Associazione Nazionale "L.Luzzatti"  (IT)

Associazione Nazionale Laureati in Scienze Biologiche  (IT)

Associazione Nazionale Lavoratori Anziani di Azienda  (IT)

Associazione Nazionale Medici Direttori di Ospedali  (IT)

Associazione Nazionale Mutilati e Invalidi di Guerra  (IT)

Associazione Nazionale Partigiani d'Italia  (IT)

Associazione Nazionale per Aquileia  (IT)

Associazione Nazionale per Il Controllo della Combustione  (IT)

Associazione Nazionale per Il Progresso della Scuola Italiana  (IT)

Associazione Nazionale per la Tutela del Patrimonio Storico Artistico e Naturale della Nazione  (IT)

Associazione Nazionale Reduci Dalla Prigionia  (IT)

Associazione Nazionale Sottufficiali Marina Fuori Servizio  (IT)

Associazione Nazionale Tecnici Zucchero ed Alcole  (IT)

Associazione Nazionale Termotecnici e Aerotecnici  (IT)

Associazione Nazionale Uccelatori ed Uccellinai  (IT)

Associazione Nazionale Ufficiali Aeronautica  (IT)

Associazione Nazionale Ufficiali Sanitari Medici Igienisti  (IT)

Associazione Orafo Valenzano  (IT)

Associazione Ottica Italiana  (IT)

Associazione Piccole e Medie Industrie  (IT)

Associazione Piemontese Orafi Orologiai  (IT)

Associazione Piscicultori Italiani  (IT)

Associazione pro Padova  (IT)

Associazione Problemistica Italiana  (IT)

Associazione Professionale Autonoma Cineoperatori  (IT)

Associazione Profumieri Milano  (IT)

Associazione Provinciale Agricoltori  (IT)

Associazione Radiotecnica Italiana  (IT)

Associazione Relazioni Culturali Spagna, Portogallo e America Latina  (IT)

Associazione Relazioni Sociali  (IT)

Associazione Romana di Entomologia  (IT)

Associazione Scientifica di Produzione Animale  (IT)

Associazione Scout Cattolici Italiani  (IT)

Associazione Siciliana contro la Tubercolosi  (IT)

Associazione Tecnica dell' Automobile  (IT)

Associazione Termotecnica Italiana  (IT)

Associazione Turistica pro Empoli  (IT)

Associazioni Dottori in Scienze Agrarie di Bari  (IT)

Associazioni Italiana Societa Concessionarie Autostrade e Trafori  (IT)

Associes de Neuve-France  (CN)

Assofermet  (IT)

Assogiocattoli  (IT)

Assurances Generales de France  (FR)

Assyrian-American Federation  (US)

Assyrian Star Inc.  (US)

Editorial Aster  (PO)

Editions Asteria  (FR)

Asthma Foundation of New South Wales  (AT)

Asthma Publications Society  (US)

Astrado Prouvencalo  (FR)

Astral S.C.L.  (IT)

Astro-Gator Astronomy Club  (US)

Astro Media Corp  (US)

Astrolabio  (IT)

Astrologisk Akademi  (DK)

Astrology and Athrishta  (II)

Astrology Services International, Inc.  (US)

Astronomical Endeavours Publishing Co.  (US)

Astronomical Society of Australia  (AT)

Astronomical Society of India  (II)

Astronomical Society of Japan  (JA)

Astronomical Society of New South Wales  (AT)

Astronomical Society of New York  (US)

Astronomical Society of South Australia  (AT)

Astronomical Society of Southern Africa  (SA)

Astronomical Society of the Pacific  (US)

Astronomical Society of Victoria  (AT)

Astronomical Society of Western Australia  (AT)

Astronomisches Rechen-Institut  (GW)

Astronomisk Selskab  (DK)

At Rise  (US)

Atalanta Press  (US)

Editions de l' Atalante  (FR)

Atar SA  (SZ)

Atchison, Topeka and Santa Fe Railway Co.  (US)

ATCOM, Inc.  (US)

Atcost Ltd.  (UK)

Atelier du Coeur- Meurtry  (FR)

Atelier du Monastere Sainte Catherine  (FR)

Atelier Parisien d'Urbanisme  (FR)

Ateliers de Constructions Electriques de Charleroi  (BE)

Ateliers Proteges  (FR)

Atena S. p. A.  (IT)

Ateneo  (ES)

Edizioni dell' Ateneo  (IT)

Ateneo Bruzio  (IT)

Ateneo de Manila University  (PH)

Ateneo de Manila University. Institute of Philippine Culture  (PH)

Ateneo de Manila University. Loyola School of Theology  (PH)

Ateneo de Manila University Press  (PH)

Ateneo Veneto  (IT)

Ateneu Angrense de Letras e Artes  (BL)

Athanor Press  (US)

Athena Mediterranea  (IT)

Athenaeum-Verlag GmbH  (GW)

Athene A-S  (DK)

Athenes-Presse Libre  (FR)

Atheneum Publishers  (US)

Athens Center of Ekistics  (GR)

Athens Chamber of Commerce and Industry  (GR)

Athens College  (GR)

Athens Cultural Center  (GR)

Athens International Film Festival  (US)

Athens Technological Organization. Athens Center of Ekistics
    see Athens Center of Ekistics  (GR)

Verlagsanstalt Athesia  (IT)

Athletic Journal Publishing Co.  (US)

Athletic Publishing Co.  (US)

Athletica Press  (CN)

Athletik-Verlag  (GW)

Athlone Press  (UK)

Atkinson College Students' Association  (CN)

Atlanta Chamber of Commerce  (US)

Atlanta Gazette, Inc.  (US)

Atlanta Regional Commission  (US)

Atlanta University  (US)

Atlanta Voice  (US)

Atlanta Workshop in Nonviolence  (US)

Atlanteans Association Ltd.  (UK)

Atlantic Advertising  (US)

Australia. National Capital Development Commission
(AT)
Australia. National Library of Australia   (AT)
Australia. National Library of Australia. Australian
Advisory Council on Bibliographical Services   (AT)
Australia. National Library of Australia. Film Division
(AT)
Australia. National Library of Australia. Resources
Organizations and Development Branch   (AT)
Australia. National Library of Australia. Selection,
Acquisition and Processing Section   (AT)
Australia. Patent Office   (AT)
Australia. Post-Master General's Department. Stamps
and Philatelic Section   (AT)
Australia. Postmaster General's Department. Research
Laboratories   (AT)
Australia. Public Service Board. Personnel
Development Branch   (AT)
Australia. Repatriation Department   (AT)
Australia. Social Welfare Commission   (AT)
Australia and New Zealand Banking Group Ltd.
(AT)
Australia & New Zealand Teachers of the Visually
Handicapped   (NZ)
Australia and South Pacific Temperance Council
(AT)
Australia Indonesia Association of New South Wales
(AT)
Australia International Press   (AT)
Australia-Japan Economic Institute   (AT)
Australia-Japan Society-Ichido of New South Wales
(AT)
Australia Mineral Development Laboratories   (AT)
Australia New Zealand Association   (CN)
Australia Party. Victorian Branch   (AT)
Australian Academy of Forensic Sciences   (AT)
Australian Academy of Science   (AT)
Australian Academy of Science. National Committee
for Antarctic Research   (AT)
Australian Academy of the Humanities   (AT)
Australian Accounting Research Foundation   (AT)
Australian Agricultural Council   (AT)
Australian Agricultural Economic Society   (AT)
Australian Amateur Weight Lifting Federation   (AT)
Australian-American Association   (AT)
Australian and New Zealand American Studies
Association   (AT)
Australian and New Zealand Association for Medieval
and Renaissance Studies   (AT)
Australian and New Zealand Association for the
Advancement of Science   (AT)
Australian and New Zealand Association of Bellringers
(AT)
Australian and New Zealand College of Psychiatrists
(AT)
Australian and New Zealand History of Education
Society   (AT)
Australian Anglers Association   (AT)
Australian Asphalt Pavement Association   (AT)
Australian Associated Stock Exchanges   (AT)
Australian Association for Cultural Freedom   (AT)
Australian Association for Research in Education
(AT)
Australian Association for the Mentally Retarded
(AT)
Australian Association for the Teaching of English
(AT)
Australian Association of Adult Education   (AT)
Australian Association of Adult Education. Division of
Postgraduate Extension Studies   (AT)
Australian Association of Mathematics Teachers
(AT)
Australian Association of Neurologists   (AT)
Australian Association of Permanent Building Societies
(AT)
Australian Association of Social Workers   (AT)
Australian Association of Speech and Hearing   (AT)
Australian Association of Teachers of the Deaf   (AT)
Australian Bank Officials Association   (AT)
Australian Bank Officials Association. State Savings
Bank of Victoria Division   (AT)
Australian Bankers' Association. Research Directorate
(AT)
Australian Baptist Publishing Co.   (AT)
Australian Biochemical Society   (AT)
Australian Book Publishers Association   (AT)
Australian Book Review   (AT)
Australian Boot Trade Employees Federation   (AT)
Australian Brahman Breeders' Association   (AT)
Australian Breeders Service   (AT)
Australian Broadcasting Commission   (AT)
Australian Builder Publishing Co., Pty. Ltd.   (AT)
Australian Bulletin of Labour
Australian Bureau of Statistics
see Australia. Australian Bureau of Statistics   (AT)
Australian Catholic Historical Society   (AT)
Australian Ceramic Society   (AT)

Australian Chamber of Commerce   (AT)
Australian Chemical Engineering   (AT)
Australian Chess Federation   (AT)
Australian Chicken Meat Council   (AT)
Australian Chiropractors Association   (AT)
Australian Christian Endeavour Union Inc.   (AT)
Australian Citrus Growers' Federation   (AT)
Australian Clay Target Association   (AT)
Australian Coal Industry Research Laboratories Ltd
(AT)
Australian College of Education   (AT)
Australian College of Ophthalmologists   (AT)
Australian College of Paediatrics   (AT)
Australian Comparative Education Society   (AT)
Australian Computer Society   (AT)
Australian Computer Society, Inc. Canberra Branch
(AT)
Australian Computer Society Inc. New South Wales
Branch   (AT)
Australian Computer Society, Inc. Queensland Branch
(AT)
Australian Computer Society Inc. Victorian Branch
(AT)
Australian Conservation Foundation   (AT)
Australian Consolidated Press   (AT)
Australian Consumers' Association   (AT)
Australian Copyright Council   (AT)
Australian Council for Educational Research   (AT)
Australian Council for Educational Standards   (AT)
Australian Council for Health, Physcial Education and
Recreation   (AT)
Australian Council for Overseas Aid   (AT)
Australian Council of Social Service   (AT)
Australian Council of Trade Unions   (AT)
Australian Council on Ageing   (AT)
Australian Council on Awards in Advanced Education
(AT)
Australian Cricket Society   (AT)
Australian Cricket Society. A. C. T. Branch   (AT)
Australian Crime Prevention Council   (AT)
Australian Croquet Council   (AT)
Australian Dental Association   (AT)
Australian Dental Association. Western Australian
Branch   (AT)
Australian Dried Fruits Association   (AT)
Australian Drug Information Services Pty. Ltd.   (AT)
Australian Electric Traction Association   (AT)
Australian Entomological Society   (AT)
Australian Esperanto Association   (AT)
Australian Farm Management Society   (AT)
Australian Federation of Air Pilots   (AT)
Australian Federation of Modern Languages Teachers
Associations   (AT)
Australian Federation of University Women   (AT)
Australian Federation of Wizo   (AT)
Australian Fish Trades Review   (AT)
Australian Flying Corps and Royal Australian Air
Force Association   (AT)
Australian Forest Industries Journal Pty. Ltd.   (AT)
Australian Forestry Council   (AT)
Australian Foundry Institute   (AT)
Australian Frontier   (AT)
Australian Gas Association   (AT)
Australian Geography Teachers' Association   (AT)
Australian Group for the Scientific Study of Mental
Deficiency   (AT)
Australian Guild of Professional Cooks   (AT)
Australian Hereford Society Ltd.   (AT)
Australian Hi-Fi Publications Pty. Ltd.   (AT)
Australian Hockey Association   (AT)
Australian Honey Board   (AT)
Australian Hospital Association   (AT)
Australian Hotels Association   (AT)
Australian Hotels Association. South Australian
Branch   (AT)
Australian Hotels Association. Tasmanian Branch
(AT)
Australian Hotels Association. Victoria Branch   (AT)
Australian Hotels Association. Western Australia
Branch   (AT)
Australian Industries Development Association   (AT)
Australian Information Service   (US)
Australian Inland Mission Frontier Service   (AT)
Australian Institute of Aboriginal Studies   (AT)
Australian Institute of Agricultural Science   (AT)
Australian Institute of Archaeology   (AT)
Australian Institute of Building   (AT)
Australian Institute of Cartographers   (AT)
Australian Institute of Construction Supervisors   (AT)
Australian Institute of Credit Management   (AT)
Australian Institute of Credit Management. Victorian
Division   (AT)
Australian Institute of Criminology   (AT)
Australian Institute of Dairy Factory Managers and
Secretaries   (AT)
Australian Institute of Drycleaning   (AT)
Australian Institute of Engineering Associates   (AT)

Australian Institute of Hospital Administrators   (AT)
Australian Institute of International Affairs   (AT)
Australian Institute of Management   (AT)
Australian Institute of Management. New South Wales
Division   (AT)
Australian Institute of Marine and Power Engineers
(AT)
Australian Institute of Metals   (AT)
Australian Institute of Navigation   (AT)
Australian Institute of Parks & Recreation   (AT)
Australian Institute of Petroleum Ltd.   (AT)
Australian Institute of Physics   (AT)
Australian Institute of Political Science   (AT)
Australian Institute of Refrigeration, Air Conditioning
and Heating, Inc   (AT)
Australian Institute of Steel Construction   (AT)
Australian Institute of Urban Studies   (AT)
Australian Institute of Urban Studies. Queensland
Division   (AT)
Australian Institute of Valuers   (AT)
Australian Institute of Weights and Measures   (AT)
Australian Institution of Refrigeration, Air
Conditioning and Heating   (AT)
Australian Insurance Institute   (AT)
Australian Jaycees   (AT)
Australian Jersey Herd Society   (AT)
Australian Jewish Historical Society   (AT)
Australian Jewish Times   (AT)
Australian Jewish Welfare and Relief Society   (AT)
Australian Jockey Club   (AT)
Australian Journalists' Association   (AT)
Australian Journalists' Association. Western Australia
District   (AT)
Australian Labor Party. Australian Capital Territory
Branch   (AT)
Australian Labor Party. New South Wales Branch
(AT)
Australian Labor Party. Western Australia Branch
(AT)
Australian Ladies Golf Union   (AT)
Australian Language Research Centre   (AT)
Australian Law Librarians' Group   (AT)
Australian Lead Development Association   (AT)
Australian League of Rights   (AT)
Australian Left Review   (AT)
Australian Legal Aid Review Committee   (AT)
Australian Library Promotions Council   (AT)
Australian Liquified Petroleum Gas Association   (AT)
Australian Litho Club   (AT)
Australian Littoral Society   (AT)
Australian Mammal Society   (AT)
Australian Map Curators Circle   (AT)
Australian Mathematical Society   (AT)
Australian Meat Board   (AT)
Australian Meat Research Committee   (AT)
Australian Medical Association   (AT)
Australian Mensa Inc.   (AT)
Australian Metal Trades Export Group   (AT)
Australian Meteorological Association   (AT)
Australian Mineral Foundation   (AT)
Australian Mineral Industries Research Association
(AT)
Australian Mining Industry Council   (AT)
Australian Model Railway Association   (AT)
Australian Museum   (AT)
Australian National Association for Mental Health
(AT)
Australian National Cat Federation   (AT)
Australian National Committee on Large Dams   (AT)
Australian National University   (AT)
Australian National University   (PP)
Australian National University. Centre for Continuing
Education   (AT)
Australian National University. Computer Centre
(AT)
Australian National University. Department of Far
Eastern History   (AT)
Australian National University. Department of
International Relations   (AT)
Australian National University. Department of Pacific
and Southeast Asian History   (AT)
Australian National University. Department of
Political Science   (AT)
Australian National University. Department of Pure
Mathematics   (AT)
Australian National University. Faculty of Asian
Studies   (AT)
Australian National University. Forestry Department
(AT)
Australian National University. Geology Department
(AT)
Australian National University Gliding Club   (AT)
Australian National University. Historical Society
(AT)
Australian National University Press   (AT)
Australian National University. Research School of
Biological Sciences   (AT)

B A S F Landwirtschaftliche Versuchsstation   (GW)
B.B. Bks   (UK)
B B C Brown, Boveri & Co., Ltd.   (SZ)
B B D O, Inc.   (US)
B C P R Communications   (US)
B.C.S.I.R.
   see Bangladesh Council of Scientific and Industrial
   Research   (BG)
B. C. Teachers' Federation   (CN)
B D U   (NE)
B.E.D. Business Journals Ltd.   (UK)
B E N E L U X Documentatie Centrum   (BE)
B E N E L U X Economic Union   (BE)
B E N E L U X Economic Union. Central Economic
   Council   (BE)
B E N E L U X Merkenbureau   (NE)
B.F. B   (IT)
B F L Communications Inc.   (US)
B. I. E. P.   (FR)
B.I.R.E. Entreprise de Presse   (FR)
B I T
   see International Labour Office   (UN)
B-J Paperback Books Suggestion Guide   (US)
B. K. T. Publishing Co.   (UK)
B L V Verlagsgesellschaft mbH   (GW)
B. M. G. Publications Ltd.   (UK)
B M I Canada Limited   (CN)
B M T Publications, Inc.   (US)
B O A P W Ltd.   (US)
B P A Byggproduction AB   (SW)
B P I Publishing Co.   (US)
B P S Exhibitions   (UK)
B.R.E.S.   (FR)
B.S.C.   (IT)
B U C International Corp.   (US)
B W S Publishing Ltd.   (UK)
B. Y. B. Ltd.   (UK)
Baarns Lyceum   (NE)
Baas Becking Geobiological Laboratory   (AT)
Baatliv   (NO)
Babani Press   (UK)
Babbling Bookworm   (US)
Babcox Publications, Inc.   (US)
Babka Publishing Co.   (US)
Babson College   (US)
Babson's Reports Inc.   (US)
Baby John   (US)
Verlag Bachem und Sohn   (GW)
J. P. Bachem Verlag GmbH   (GW)
Back Door   (US)
Backpacker   (US)
Backstage Publications, Inc.   (US)
Editions de la Baconniere S. A.   (SZ)
Baden-Wuerttemberg. Innenministerium   (GW)
Baden- Wuerttemberg. Kommission fuer
   Geschichtliche Landeskunde   (GW)
Baden-Wuerttemberg. Landesdenkmalamt   (GW)
Baden-Wuerttemberg. Landesgewerbeamt   (GW)
Baden-Wuerttemberg. Landeswohlfahrtswerk   (GW)
Baden-Wuerttemberg. Ministerium fuer Arbeit,
   Gesundheit und Sozialordnung   (GW)
Baden-Wuerttemberg. Ministerium fuer Ernaehrung,
   Landwirtschaft und Umwelt   (GW)
Baden-Wuerttembergischer Luftfahrtverband e.V.
   (GW)
Mrs. M.D. Badenhorst, Ed. & Pub.   (SX)
Badia Greca di Grottaferrata   (IT)
Badische Anilin- und Soda-Fabrik A.G.   (GW)
Badischer Landesverein fuer Naturkunde und
   Naturschutz e.V   (GW)
Badlands Natural History Association   (US)
Badminton Association of England   (UK)
Rheinisch-Westfaelischer Baecker-Verlag GmbH
   (GW)
Baeder und Kurverwaltung   (GW)
Baeren-Druck   (GW)
Baerenreiter Verlag   (GW)
Baeuerlicher Presseverein   (AU)
Bagdala   (YU)
August Bagel Verlag   (GW)
Baghdad Chamber of Commerce   (IQ)
Bagin   (LE)
Baha Matbaas   (TU)
Baha'i World Centre   (IS)
Bahama out Islands Promotion Board   (BF)
Bahamas. Department of Statistics   (BF)
Bahamas. Ministry of Works   (BF)
Bahamas Magazine Ltd.   (BF)
Bahamian Review   (BF)
Ediciones Bahia   (SP)
Bahia, Brazil. Centro de Planejamento   (BL)
Bahia, Brazil. Divisao de Informacao Industrial e
   Promocao de Investimentos   (BL)
Bahia, Brazil. Fundacao de Pesquisa. Secretaria do
   Planejamento Ciencia e Tecnologia   (BL)
Bahia, Brazil. Secretaria das Minas e Energia   (BL)
Bahia, Brazil. Secretaria de Saude   (BL)

Bahnsport Aktuell Verlag   (GW)
Bahrain. Ministry of Information   (BA)
Bahrain Chamber of Commerce and Industry   (BA)
Bahrain Petroleum Co. Ltd.   (BA)
Bahrain Trade Directory   (BA)
Bahri Publications Ltd.   (II)
Alexander Baier-Presse   (GW)
Baikar Association, Inc.   (US)
F. Bailey & Son Ltd.   (UK)
Sheila Baille & Associates   (SA)
J. B. Bailliere et Fils   (FR)
Bailliere Tindall   (UK)
J. H. Baird Publishing Co.   (US)
Bairnsdale Field Naturalists' Club   (AT)
Maya Bajapeyi, Ed. & Pub.   (II)
Baker & Bowden   (US)
Baker and Taylor Companies   (US)
Baker-og Konditormestrenes Landsforening   (NO)
Bakers Union   (US)
Bakery and Confectionery Workers' International
   Union of America, AFL-CIO-CLC   (US)
Simon Bakht, Ed. & Pub.   (LE)
Baking Trade Federation of Australia. South Australian
   Branch   (AT)
Balai Penelitian Ferkebunan Bogor
   see Research Institute for Estate Crops   (IO)
Balai Penyelidikan Purusahaan Perkebunan Gula
   see Experimental Station of the Sugar Industry
   (IO)
Balance, Inc.   (US)
Balatroswerke H. Rost und Co.   (GW)
Balboa Park Information Center. Master Calendar
   (US)
John Balding (Publishing & Publicity) Ltd.   (IE)
O. Baldinger, Ed. & Pub.   (SZ)
Bale Catalogue of Palestine and Israel Postage Stamps
   (UK)
Bale Publications   (US)
Baleen Press   (US)
Joost Baljeu, Ed. & Pub.   (NE)
A. A. Balkema Ltd.   (SA)
John Ball Publications Ltd.   (UK)
Ball State University   (US)
Ball State University. College of Business   (US)
Ball State University. Department of Geography and
   Geology   (US)
Ball State University. Department of History   (US)
Ball State University. Teachers College   (US)
Ballantine Books   (US)
Ballard Printing & Publishing Co.   (US)
Ballena Press   (US)
Ballet Dancer   (US)
Ballet Nacional de Cuba   (CU)
Ballinger Publishing Co.   (US)
Ballistocardiography Research Society   (SZ)
Balloon Federation of America   (US)
Balnearios   (MX)
Balneological Society of Japan   (JA)
Balshon Printing Co.   (US)
Edizioni Alessandro Baltadori   (IT)
Balthazar Publishing House   (PH)
Baltic Philatelist Club   (CN)
Baltimore. Health Department. Bureau of Health
   Information   (US)
Baltimore City Public Schools. Division of Publications
   and Public Information   (US)
Baltimore College of Dental Surgery
   see under University of Maryland   (US)
Baltimore County Public Library   (US)
Baltimore Jewish Times   (US)
Baltimore Women's Liberation Center   (US)
Verlag Baltische Briefe Wolf J. von Kleist   (GW)
Baltische Gesellschaft in Deutschland e.V.   (GW)
Bamah Association   (IS)
Bamrung Nukoulkit Press   (TH)
Banana Growers Federation   (AT)
Banana Productions   (US)
Bananas Publishing   (UK)
Banaras Hindu University   (II)
Banaras Hindu University. Institute of Medical
   Sciences   (II)
Editora Banas, S.A.   (BL)
Banasthali-Vidyapith   (II)
Banbury Historical Society   (UK)
Banca d'Italia   (IT)
Banca Nazionale del Lavoro   (IT)
Banca Nazionale dell'Agricoltura   (IT)
Banca Nazionale Somala
   see Somali National Bank   (SO)
Banca y Comercio   (MX)
Paolo F. Bancale Ed. & Pub.   (IT)
Bancaria Editrice S.p.A.   (IT)
Bancas y Bancarios de Colombia   (CK)
Banco Bamerindus do Brazil   (BL)
Banco Central   (SP)
Banco Central de Bolivia   (BO)

Banco Central de Chile   (CL)
Banco Central de Costa Rica   (CR)
Banco Central de Costa Rica. Departamento
   Monetario   (CR)
Banco Central de Costa Rica. Division de Asuntos
   Economicas   (CR)
Banco Central de Honduras. Departamento de
   Estudios Economicos   (HO)
Banco Central de la Republica Argentina   (AG)
Banco Central de la Republica Dominicana   (DR)
Banco Central de Nicaragua   (NQ)
Banco Central de Nicaragua. Biblioteca y Servicios de
   Informacion   (NQ)
Banco Central de Nicaragua. Departamento de
   Estudios Economicos   (NQ)
Banco Central de Reserva de el Salvador   (ES)
Banco Central de Reserva del Peru. Seccion
   Publicaciones   (PE)
Banco Central de Venezuela   (VE)
Banco Central del Ecuador   (EC)
Banco Central del Ecuador. Biblioteca   (EC)
Banco Central del Paraguay   (PY)
Banco Central del Uruguay   (UY)
Banco Central do Brasil S. A.   (BL)
Banco Centroamericano de Integracion Economica
   (HO)
Banco da Amazonia. Centro de Documentacao e
   Biblioteca   (BL)
Banco de Alicante   (SP)
Banco de Bilbao   (SP)
Banco de Chile. Gerencia de Estudios   (CL)
Banco de Credito de Peru   (PE)
Banco de Desenvolvimento do Parana, S.A.   (BL)
Banco de Espana. Servicio de Estudios   (SP)
Banco de Financiacion Industrial   (SP)
Banco de Guatemala   (GT)
Banco de la Provincia de Buenos Aires   (AG)
Banco de la Republica. Departamento de
   Investigaciones Economicas   (CK)
Banco de la Vivienda de Nicaragua. Caja Central de
   Ahorro y Prestamo   (NQ)
Banco de Mexico   (MX)
Banco de Mexico. Departamento de Investigaciones
   Industriales   (MX)
Banco de Nordeste do Brasil   (BL)
Banco de Santander. Publicidad y Estudios   (SP)
Banco de Venezuela   (VE)
Banco de Vizcaya   (SP)
Banco di Napoli   (IT)
Banco di Napoli. Direzione Generale   (IT)
Banco di Roma   (FR)
Banco di Roma   (IT)
Banco di Sardegna   (IT)
Banco di Sicilia   (IT)
Banco do Brasil S.A.   (BL)
Banco do Brasil S.A. Departamento Geral de Selecao e
   Desenvolvimento do Pessoal   (BL)
Banco do Estado de Pernambucco   (BL)
Banco do Nordeste do Brasil   (BL)
Banco do Nordeste do Brasil. Departamento de
   Estudos Economicos do Nordeste   (BL)
Banco Exterior de Espana   (SP)
Banco Ganadero Argentino   (AG)
Banco Guipuzcoano   (SP)
Banco Hispano Americano   (SP)
Banco Interamericano de Desarrollo. Instituto para la
   Integracion de America Latina   (AG)
Banco Lar Brasileiro S.A.   (BL)
Banco Minero del Peru. Division de Planeamiento
   (PE)
Banco Nacional de Comercio Exterior, S.A.
   Departamento de Publicaciones   (MX)
Banco Nacional de Fomento   (EC)
Banco Nacional de Mexico, S.A.   (MX)
Banco Nacional de Panama   (PN)
Banco Nacional de Panama. Asesoria Economica y
   Planificacion   (PN)
Banco Nacional do Desenvolvimento Economico
   (BL)
Banco Nacional Hipotecaria Urbano y de Obras
   Publicas   (MX)
Banco National de Fomento   (HO)
Bancroft-Parkman, Inc.   (US)
Bancroft-Whitney Company   (US)
Drukkerij Banda B.V.   (NE)
Siba Prosad Banerjee, Ed. & Pub.   (II)
Nilratan Banerji, Ed. & Pub.   (II)
Banff Centre Press   (CN)
Bangalore Printing & Publishing Co. Ltd.   (II)
Verlag der Schillerbuchhandlung Hans Banger   (GW)
Bangkok Bank Ltd. Economic Research Division
   (TH)
Bangkok Bank Ltd. Planning & Analysis Department
   (TH)
Bangkok English Language Center   (TH)
Bangla Academy   (BG)
Bangladesh. Bureau of Statistics   (BG)

Heinrich Bauer Verlag Muenchen (GW)
Bauernverband Wuerttemberg-Baden (GW)
Bauer's Witwe und Co. (AU)
Baufachverlag Wien Ges. m. b. H. (AU)
Franklin P. Baugh, Ed. & Pub. (US)
Verlag E. C. Baumann KG (GW)
Baumgartner-Verlag (GW)
Bausch & Lomb Inc. (US)
Bausparkasse Wuestenrot (AU)
Bausparkasse Wuestenrot (GW)
Bauverlag GmbH (GW)
Bauverlag GmbH. Zweigniederlassung Berlin (GW)
VEB Verlag fuer Bauwesen (GE)
Bax Society (UK)
Baxter Brothers (US)
Baxter County Historical Society (US)
Baxter Publishing Co. (CN)
Bay Area Air Pollution Control District (US)
Bay Area International Monthly (US)
Bay Area Review Course, Inc. (US)
Bay County Genealogical Society (US)
Bay Guardian Co. (US)
Bay State Business World (US)
Bayard Presse (FR)
Bayard Publications, Inc. (US)
Publicaciones Bayarri (SP)
Bayer (Schweiz) AG (SZ)
Bayer (Sverige) AB, Agro-Kemi (SW)
Bayer AG (GW)
Bayer AG (US)
Bayer Australia Ltd. (AT)
Bayer do Brasil Industrias Quimicas S.A. (BL)
N.V. Bayer Gorsac S.A. (BE)
Bayer Italia S. p. A. (IT)
Bayer Nederland B.V. (NE)
Bayer Phytochim (FR)
Bayer Portugal S A R L (PO)
Bayer UK Ltd. Agrochem Division (UK)
Bayerische Akademie der Schoenen Kuenste (GW)
Bayerische Akademie der Wissenschaften (GW)
Bayerische Akademie der Wissenschaften. Institut fuer
  Volkskunde (GW)
Bayerische Akademie der Wissenschaften. Kommission
  fuer Bayerische Landesgeschichte (GW)
Bayerische Botanische Gesellschaft (GW)
Bayerische Jungbauernschaft e.V. (GW)
Bayerische Landesaerztekammer (GW)
Bayerische Landeszahnaerztekammer (GW)
Bayerische Numismatische Gesellschaft (GW)
Bayerische Staatliche Bibliotheken (GW)
Bayerische Staatsbibliothek (GW)
Bayerische Staatssammlung fuer Palaeontologie und
  Historische Geologie (GW)
Bayerischer Bauernverband (GW)
Bayerischer Beamtenbund (GW)
Bayerischer Landessportverband e.V. (GW)
Bayerischer Landesverein fuer Familienkunde e.V.
  (GW)
Bayerischer Lehrer- und Lehrerinnenverband (GW)
Bayerischer Lehrer- und Lehrerinnenverband.
  Bezirksverbaende Niederbayern und Oberpfalz
  (GW)
Bayerischer Reallehrerverband e.V. (GW)
Bayerischer Rundfunk (GW)
Bayerischer Schachbund e.V. (GW)
Bayerischer Turnverband e.V. (GW)
Bayerisches Geologisches Landesamt (GW)
Druckerei und Verlagsanstalt Bayerland (Anton
  Steigenberger) (GW)
Bayern. Generaldirektion der Bayerischen Staatlichen
  Bibliotheken (GW)
Bayern. Hauptstaatsarchiv (GW)
Bayern. Landesamt fuer Brand- und
  Katastrophenschutz (GW)
Bayern. Landesamt fuer Denkmalpflege (GW)
Bayern. Landesamt fuer Wasserwirtschaft (GW)
Bayern. Staatsministerium der Justiz (GW)
Bayern. Staatsministerium des Innern (GW)
Bayern. Staatsministerium fuer Arbeit und
  Sozialordnung (GW)
Bayern. Staatsministerium fuer Unterricht und Kultus
  (GW)
Bayern. Statistisches Landesamt (GW)
Bayernbund e.V. (GW)
Bayernpartei (GW)
Bayland Publishing, Inc. (US)
Baylor College of Dentistry. Alumni and Public
  Information Office (US)
Baylor College of Medicine. Cardiovascular Research
  Center (US)
Baylor University. Armstrong Browning Library (US)
Baylor University. Department of Geology (US)
Baylor University. Hankamer School of Business
  (US)
Baylor University. J.M. Dawson Studies in Church and
  State (US)
Baylor University. Law School (US)
Baylor University Medical Center (US)

Baylor University Press (US)
Ernest Bayly, Ed. & Pub (UK)
Baymer Publications, Inc. (US)
Baywood Publishing Co., Inc. (US)
Mahlon F. Beach, Ed. & Pub. (CN)
Beacon House Inc. (US)
Beacon Press (US)
Beacon Publications Ltd. (JM)
Beacon-Verlag Koerber oHG (GW)
Beaconsfield Press Pty., Ltd. (AT)
Bead Journal (US)
Colin Beale, Ed. & Pub. (CN)
Bean Improvement Cooperative (US)
Bear Flag Productions, Inc. (US)
Bear Tribe Medicine Society (US)
Beardsley Publishing Corp. (US)
Pierre Bearn, Editor and Publisher (FR)
Beau Geste Press (UK)
Editons Beauchesne (FR)
Laboratoires Beaufour (FR)
Editions Beaulieu (FR)
Beauterama (FR)
Beauty Fashion, Inc. (US)
Beauty World, Inc. (US)
Beaux-Arts (CN)
Beaux-Arts et Culture (SZ)
Beaver Dan Michigan Enterprises Ltd. (US)
Fitzgerald Beaver, Ed. & Pub. (US)
Beaverbrook Art Gallery (CN)
Beaverbrook Newspapers Ltd. (UK)
Felice del Beccaro, Ed. & Pub. (IT)
Joergen Beck, Ed. & Pub. (DK)
AB Wilh. Becker (SW)
Beckman Instruments GmbH (GW)
Beckman Instruments, Inc. Spinco Div. (US)
Verlag Eduard F. Beckmann KG (GW)
C. H. Beck'sche Verlagsbuchhandlung (GW)
Bedford Institute of Oceanography (CN)
Bedford Stuyvesant Youth in Action, Inc. (US)
Bedfordshire Area Health Authority (UK)
Bedfordshire Historical Record Society (UK)
Bedriftsoekonomens Forlag (NO)
Bedrijfschap voor de Lederwarenindustrie (NE)
Bedrijfslaboratorium voor Grond- en Gewasonderzoek
  (NE)
Bedste fra Reader's Digest ApS (DK)
Beecham Foods (UK)
Beecham Society
  see Sir Thomas Beecham Society (US)
Beefmaster Breeders Universal (US)
Uitgeversmaatschappij L.A. van Beek B.V. (NE)
Beer Wholesaler Publishing Co. (US)
De Beers Industrial Diamond Division Pty. Ltd.
  (UK)
Imprimerie J. Beffort (LU)
Verlag Begegnung (GE)
Behavioral Neuropsychiatry Medical Publishers, Inc.
  (US)
Behavioral Publications, Inc. (US)
Behavioral Research Laboratories (US)
Behavioral Research Survey Center (US)
Behaviormetric Society of Japan (JA)
Behavioural Sciences Centre (II)
Behn-Miller Publishers, Inc. (US)
Behring-Werke, Marburg (GW)
B. Behr's Verlag GmbH (GW)
A. Beig Verlag (GW)
Forlaget Beilin og Johansen ApS (DK)
Beirat fuer Wirtschafts und Sozialfragen (AU)
Verlag das Beispiel (GW)
Beklaednadsarbetarnes Foerbund (SW)
Bela Abela Publications (II)
Jerome D. Belager, Ed. & Pub. (US)
Belaruskaja Vydaveckaja Siabrynia (US)
Belenes Publications Ltd. (IE)
Belfast Natural History and Philosophical Society
  (UK)
Editions P. Belfond (FR)
Belgian American Chamber of Commerce in the U.S.
  (US)
Belgian Centre for Geochronology (BE)
Belgian Chamber of Commerce in Great Britain
  (UK)
Belgian Consulate General. Industrial Section (US)
Belgian Federation of Food Trade
  see Federation Belge du Commerce Alimentaire
  (BE)
Belgian Federation of Ironmongers (BE)
Belgian Geological Society
  see Societe Geologique de Belgique (BE)
Belgian Information and Documentation Institute
  see Institut Belge d'Information et de
  Documentation (BE)
Belgian Institute of Political Science
  see Institut Belge de Science Politique (BE)
Belgian National Library
  see Bibliotheque Royal Albert 1er (BE)
Belgian Society for Geographical Studies

  see Societe Belge d'Etudes Geographiques (BE)
Belgian Society of Musicology
  see Societe Belge de Musicologie (BE)
Belgian Society of Photogrammetry
  see Societe Belge de Photogrammetrie (BE)
Belgian Society of Tropical Medicine
  see Societe Belge de Medicine Tropicale (BE)
Belgicatom (BE)
Belgisch Instituut Tot Verbetering van de Biet
  see Institut Belge pour l'Amelioration de la
  Betterave (BE)
Belgisch Instituut voor Voorlichting en Documentatie
  see Institut Belge d'Information et de
  Documentation (BE)
Belgisch Instituut voor Wetenschap de Politiek
  see Institut Belge de Science Politique (BE)
Belgisch Israelitisch Weekblad (BE)
Belgisch Petroleum Instituut
  see Institut Belge du Petrole (BE)
Belgische Boerenbond. Economaat (BE)
Belgische Duivensport (BE)
Belgische Fruittelersorganisaties (BE)
Belgische Nationale Federatie voor Bont en Kleinvel
  see Federation Nationale Belge de la Fourrure et de
  la Peau en Poil (BE)
Belgische Vereniging voor Documentatie
  see Association Belge de Documentation (BE)
Belgische Vereniging voor Geologie
  see Societe Belge de Geologie (BE)
Belgische Vereniging voor Psychologie
  see Societe Belge de Psychologie (BE)
Belgische Vereniging voor Verlamden
  see Association Belge des Paralyses (BE)
Belgium. Administration de l'Education Physique, des
  Sports et de la Vie en Plein Air (BE)
Belgium. Administration de l'Energie (BE)
Belgium. Administration de la Marine et de la
  Navigation Interieure (BE)
Belgium. Administration des Eaux et Forets (BE)
Belgium. Administration des Mines (BE)
Belgium. Administration du Commerce. Service de la
  Propriete Industrielle et Commerciale
  see Belgium. Service de la Propriete Industrielle et
  Commerciale (BE)
Belgium. Administration Penitentiare (BE)
Belgium. Belgische Dienst voor de Buitenlandse
  Handel
  see Belgium. Office Belge du Commerce Exterieur
  (BE)
Belgium. Bestuur Strafinrichtingen
  see Belgium. Administration Penitentiaire (BE)
Belgium. Bestuur van het Zeewezen en van de
  Binnenvaart
  see Belgium. Administration de la Marine et de la
  Navigation Interieure (BE)
Belgium. Bureau National de Documentation sur le
  Bois (BE)
Belgium. Centre d'Etude de l'Energie Nucleaire
  see Centre d'Etude de l'Energie Nucleaire (BE)
Belgium. Commissariat General au Tourisme (BE)
Belgium. Conseil National de la Politique Scientifique
  (BE)
Belgium. Conseil National du Travail (BE)
Belgium. Counseil Superieur des Classes Moyennes
  (BE)
Belgium. Cour de Cassation (BE)
Belgium. Fonds National de la Recherche Scientifique
  (BE)
Belgium. Force Navale (BE)
Belgium. Hoge Raad voor de Middenstand
  see Belgium. Conseil Superieur des Classes
  Moyennes (BE)
Belgium. Institut National d'Assurance Maladie
  Invalidite (BE)
Belgium. Institut National d'Assurances Sociales pour
  Travailleurs Independants (BE)
Belgium. Institut National de Statistique (BE)
Belgium. Institut National du Logement (BE)
Belgium. Institut Royal Meteorologique (BE)
Belgium. Ministere de l'Agriculture (BE)
Belgium. Ministere de l'Agriculture. Administration
  des Eaux et Forets
  see Belgium. Administration des Eaux et Forets
  (BE)
Belgium. Ministere de l'Agriculture. Bestuur der
  Economische Diensten (BE)
Belgium. Ministere de l'Education Nationale et de la
  Culture Francaise (BE)
Belgium. Ministere de l'Education Nationale et de la
  Culture Francaise. Administration de l'Education
  Physique, des Sports et de la Vie en Plein Air
  see Belgium. Administration de l'Education
  Physique, des Sports et de la Vie en Plein Air
  (BE)
Belgium. Ministere de l'Education Nationale et de la
  Culture Francaise. Direction Generale de
  l'Organisation des Etudes (BE)
Belgium. Ministere de l'Emploi et du Travail (BE)

Belgium. Ministere de la Defense Nationale  (BE)
Belgium. Ministere de la Justice. Administration
  Penitentiaire
    see Belgium. Administration Penitentiaire  (BE)
Belgium. Ministere de la Prevoyance Sociale  (BE)
Belgium. Ministere de la Sante Publique et de la
  Famille  (BE)
Belgium. Ministere des Affaires Economiques  (BE)
Belgium. Ministere des Affaires Economiques.
  Administration de l'Energie
    see Belgium. Administration de l'Energie  (BE)
Belgium. Ministere des Affaires Economiques.
  Administration des Mines
    see Belgium. Administration des Mines  (BE)
Belgium. Ministere des Affaires Economiques. Institut
  National de Statistique
    see Belgium. Institut National de Statistique  (BE)
Belgium. Ministere des Affaires Economiques. Service
  de la Metrologie
    see Belgium. Service de la Metrologie  (BE)
Belgium. Ministere des Affaires Economiques. Service
  de la Propriete Industrielle et Commerciale
    see Belgium. Service de la Propriete Industrielle et
    Commerciale  (BE)
Belgium. Ministere des Affaires Etrangeres  (BE)
Belgium. Ministere des Affaires Etrangeres.
  Administration des Relations Culturelles
    see Belgium. Administration des Relations
    Culturelles  (BE)
Belgium. Ministere des Communications  (BE)
Belgium. Ministere des Communications.
  Administration de la Marine et de la Navigation
  Interieure
    see Belgium. Administration de la Marine et de la
    Navigation Interieure  (BE)
Belgium. Ministere des Finances. Administration
  Centrale des Contributions  (BE)
Belgium. Ministere des Trauvaux Public  (BE)
Belgium. Ministerie van Economische Zaken
    see Belgium. Ministere des Affaires Economiques
    (BE)
Belgium. Ministerie van Landbouw
    see Belgium. Ministere de l'Agriculture  (BE)
Belgium. Ministerie van Nationale Opvoeding en
  Nederlandse Cultuur  (BE)
Belgium. Ministerie van Verkeerswezen
    see Belgium. Ministere des Communications  (BE)
Belgium. Ministerie van Volksgezondheid en van Het
  Gezin
    see Belgium. Ministere de la Sante Publique et de la
    Famille  (BE)
Belgium. Nationaal Arbeidsraad
    see Belgium. Conseil National du Travail  (BE)
Belgium. Nationaal Instituut voor de Huisvesting
    see Belgium. Institut National du Logement  (BE)
Belgium. Nationaal Instituut voor de Statistiek
    see Belgium. Institut National de Statistique  (BE)
Belgium. National Dairy Office  (BE)
Belgium. Nationale Centrale Landbouw-Service  (BE)
Belgium. Nationale Dienst voor Opgravingen
    see Belgium. Service National des Fouilles  (BE)
Belgium. Office Belge du Commerce Exterieur  (BE)
Belgium. Office National de l'Emploi  (BE)
Belgium. Parlement  (BE)
Belgium. Regie des Postes Belges  (BE)
Belgium. Rijksinstituut voor Ziekte- en
  Invaliditeitsverzekering
    see Belgium. Institut National d'Assurance Maladie
    Invalidite  (BE)
Belgium. Rijksstation voor Landbowtechniek  (BE)
Belgium. Rijksstation voor Sierplantenteelt  (BE)
Belgium. Rijksstation voor Zeevisserij  (BE)
Belgium. Service de la Metrologie  (BE)
Belgium. Service de la Propriete Industrielle et
  Commerciale  (BE)
Belgium. Service Geologique de Belgique.
  Administration des Mines
    see Belgium. Administration des Mines  (BE)
Belgium. Service National des Fouilles  (BE)
Belgium. Service Social des Postes  (BE)
Belgium. Services de Programmation de la Politique
  Scientifique  (BE)
Belgrade. Skupstina Grada  (YU)
Belize. Government Information Service  (BH)
Belize Institute of Social Research and Action  (BH)
Bell & Howell Co. Newspaper Indexing Center,
  Microphoto Division  (US)
G. Bell & Sons Ltd.  (UK)
Bell-Arm Corp.  (US)
Bell Bryant Pty. Ltd.  (AT)
Bell Directory Publishers Inc.  (US)
Bell-Northern Research Ltd.  (CN)
Bell Publications  (US)
Bell Publishers  (CN)
Bell Publishing Ltd.  (UK)
Bell Telephone Company of Canada  (CN)
Bell Telephone Laboratories, Inc.  (US)

Bell Telephone Laboratories, Inc. Libraries and
  Information Systems Center  (US)
Bella  (FR)
Editions Bellarmin  (CN)
Editions Bellefaye  (FR)
A. Bellinvia, Ed. & Pub.  (IT)
Bellman Publishing Co.  (US)
Bellrock Press Association  (CN)
Bell's Fashion Bureau (1940) Ltd.  (UK)
Belmont Education Association  (US)
Belmont-Maitland Ltd.  (UK)
A.H. Belo Corp.  (US)
Beloit Poetry Journal  (US)
Belorusskaya S.S.R. Ministerstvo Kul'tury  (UR)
Belorusskaya S.S.R. Ministerstvo Zdravookhraneniya
  (UR)
Belorusskii Gosudarstvennyi Institut Narodnogo
  Khozyaistva  (UR)
Belorusskii Politekhnicheskii Institut  (UR)
Editions Henri Belouze  (FR)
Chr. Belser Verlag  (GW)
Beltone Corp.  (US)
Beltone Institute for Hearing Research  (US)
Verlag Julius Beltz  (GW)
Verlag Beltz Basel  (SZ)
Ben-Gurion University of the Negev  (IS)
Benalla Art Gallery Society  (AT)
Bench Advisors  (US)
Bendel State. Ministry of Home Affairs and
  Information  (NR)
Matthew Bender & Co., Inc.  (US)
Bender Publications  (US)
Bendigo Field Naturalist Club  (AT)
Benedict Lust Publications  (US)
Benedictine Sisters of Perpetual Adoration  (US)
Benediktinerabtei Braunau  (GW)
Benediktinerabtei Muensterschwarzach  (GW)
Benediktinerabtei Niederaltaich  (GW)
Benevolent and Protective Order of Elks of the United
  States of America  (US)
Bengal Engineering College  (II)
Bengal Library Association  (II)
Bengali International  (II)
Bengali Literature  (II)
Benin. Institut National de la Statistique et de
  l'Analyse Economique  (DM)
Benjamin Company  (US)
Benjamin Franklin Stamp Club  (US)
W. A. Benjamin Inc.  (US)
John Benjamins B. V.  (NE)
Benn Brothers Ltd.  (UK)
B. M. Bennani, Ed. & Pub.  (US)
Frank P. Bennett & Co, Inc.  (US)
Bennett, Coleman & Co., Ltd. Times of India  (II)
Bennett, Coleman & Co., Ltd. Times of India, Bombay
  (II)
Bennett-Scott Publishing Corp.  (US)
Bennington College  (US)
Bent  (CN)
Benteli-Verlag  (SZ)
Bentham-Moxon Trust  (UK)
Hans W. Bentz  (GW)
Benwill Publishing Corp.  (US)
Verlagsgenossenschaft Beobachter AG  (SZ)
Beogradski Izdavacko-Graficki Zavod  (YU)
Beratungsstelle fuer Autogentechnik GmbH  (GW)
Beratungsstelle fuer Stahlverwendung  (GW)
Berben Verlag  (GW)
Berea Board of Education  (US)
Berea College Alumni Association  (US)
Berea College Appalachian Center  (US)
Berean Bible Society  (US)
Editions Jacques Bereny  (FR)
Sigurd Troels Berg  (DK)
Berg-Verlag GmbH  (GW)
Bergakademie Freiberg  (GE)
Bergakademie Freiberg. Wissenschaftliches
  Informationszentrum  (GE)
Bergbau-Berufsgenossenschaft  (CW)
Bergen Bank  (NO)
Bergen County (New Jersey) Historical Society  (US)
Bergen Turlag  (NO)
Bergens Kjoepmannsforening  (NO)
Bergens Sjoefart Museum  (NO)
Imprimerie et Librairie Berger-Levrault  (FR)
Verlag Ferdinand Berger und Soehne OHG  (AU)
Bergischer Geschichtsverein e. V.  (GW)
Bergman Publishers, Inc.  (US)
Verlag Siegfried Bergmann  (GW)
Bergmann-Kameradschaft 137. Inf. Div.  (AU)
Bergmann und Co.  (GW)
Drukkerij Bergmans-MCH  (NE)
Bergverks-Nytt  (NO)
Verlag Berichthaus  (SZ)
Berita Publishing Sdn. Bhd:  (MY)
Berkeley Enterprises, Inc.  (US)
Berkeley Poets' Workshop and Press  (US)

Berkley Publishing Corp.  (US)
Berkshire Archaeological Society  (UK)
Bill Berkson, Ed. & Pub.  (US)
Berl Publications Ltd.  (NZ)
Berlage Lyceum School Alliance  (NE)
Gustav Berle  (US)
Berlin (West) Senator fuer Inneres  (GW)
Berlin (West) Senator fuer Wirtschaft  (GW)
Berlin (West) Statistisches Landesamt  (GW)
Berlin (West) Verkehrsamt  (GW)
Berlin-Information  (GE)
Berlin Verlag  (GW)
Berlin Wertpapierboerse  (GW)
Berliner Bank Aktiengesellschaft  (GW)
Berliner Flughafen-GmbH  (GW)
Berliner Hausbesitz Verlag, Manfred Schoeneck
  (GW)
Berliner Historische Kommission  (GW)
Berliner Kraft- und Licht-(Bewag) Aktiengesellschaft
  (GW)
Berliner Missionswerk  (GW)
Berliner Turnerbund E.V.  (GW)
Berliner-Verlag  (GE)
Berliner Wort Verlagsgesellschaft mbH.  (GW)
Clayton G. Berling  (US)
Francesco Berlingieri, Ed. & Pub.  (IT)
Berlingske Forlag  (DK)
Bermont Books  (US)
Bermuda. Finance Department. Statistical Office
  (BM)
Bermuda Book Stores  (BM)
Bermuda Historical Society  (BM)
Bermudian Publishing Co. Ltd.  (BM)
Bernan Associates, Inc.  (US)
Bernard Amtmann Inc.  (CN)
Bernard Price Institute for Palaeontological Research
  see under University of the Witwatersrand,
  Johannesburg  (SA)
Bernard und Graefe Verlag fuer Wehrwesen  (GW)
Berndorf. Stadtgemeinde Berndorf  (AU)
Berne (Canton) Kantonale Steuerverwaltung  (SZ)
Editions de Berne et Cie  (FR)
Verlag A. Bernecker  (GW)
Berner Boersenverein  (SZ)
Judy Berner Publishing Co.  (US)
Arnold Bernhard & Co., Inc.  (US)
Bernice Pauahi Bishop Museum  (US)
Bernice Pauahi Bishop Museum. Department of
  Anthropology  (US)
Bernice Pauahi Bishop Museum. Department of
  Entomology  (US)
Bernporter Books  (US)
Navin Berry, Ed. & Pub.  (II)
Berryhill  (US)
William Berssen, Ed. & Pub.  (US)
Bertelsen Publishing Co.  (US)
Bertelsmann-Fachverlag  (GW)
Bertelsmann Fachzeitschriften GmbH  (GW)
Verlagsgruppe Bertelsmann GmbH  (GW)
W. Bertelsmann Verlag KG  (GW)
Raoul Bertolo, Pub.  (FR)
Livraria Bertrand S A R L  (PO)
Berufsfoerderungsinstitut  (AU)
Berufsgenossenschaft der Chemischen Industrie
  (GW)
Berufsgenossenschaft der Feinmechanik und
  Elektrotechnik  (GW)
Berufsverband der Augenaerzte Deutschlands e.V.
  (GW)
Berufsverband der Deutschen Chirurgen, e-V.  (GW)
Berufsverband der Deutschen Urologen  (GW)
Berufsverband der Frauenaerzte e. V.  (GW)
Berufsverband der Heilpraktiker Nordrhein-Westfalen
  e.V.  (GW)
Berufsverband der Kinderaerzte Deutschlands e.V.
  (GW)
Berufsverband Deutscher Internisten  (GW)
Berufsverband Deutscher Psychologen  (GW)
Berufsverband Oesterreichischer Diplomfuersorger
  (AU)
Rene de Berval, Ed. & Pub.  (JA)
Besant Cultural Centre. Kalakshetra (International Arts
  Centre)  (II)
Fachverlag N. Besselich  (GW)
Bessire & Company, Inc.  (US)
Best Books Private Ltd.  (II)
A. M. Best Co.  (US)
Best Friends  (US)
Det Beste A-S  (NO)
Beste aus Reader's Digest AG  (SZ)
Verlag das Beste GmbH  (GW)
Verlag Adalbert Bestgen  (GW)
Bet Midrash le-Torah ve-Hora Ah  (US)
Bet Midrash Lerabanim  (IS)
Beta Beta Beta National Biological Society  (US)
Beta Phi Mu, International Honor Society  (US)

Beth Sar Shalom  (US)
Bethal Printing Works  (SA)
Bethel College  (US)
Verlagsbuchhandlung Bethel - Dirk Dolman und Co.
  KG Nachfolger  (GW)
Bethlehem Express Printing & Publishing Co. (Pty)
  Ltd.  (SA)
Bethune Jones  (US)
Beton Arme  (FR)
Beton-Verlag GmbH  (GW)
Betriebswirtschaftliche Beratungsstelle fuer den
  Einzelhandel  (GW)
Better America  (US)
Better Business Bureau of Eastern Massachusetts, Inc.
  (US)
Better Business Bureau of Metropolitan New York Inc.
  (US)
Better Education  (US)
Better Farming Association  (JA)
Better Healthkeeping, Inc.  (US)
Better Homes and Gardens Idea Publications  (US)
Better Life Movement  (II)
Beuroner Kunstverlag GmbH  (GW)
Beuth Verlag GmbH  (GW)
Beverage Journal Inc.  (US)
Beverage Media Ltd.  (US)
Beverage News Inc.  (US)
Beverage Publications, Inc.  (US)
Beverage Publishing Co. of Rhode Island, Inc.  (US)
Beverage Retailer Weekly  (US)
Beverly Hills Bar Association  (US)
Beverly Review  (US)
Bexley Christadelphians Ecclesia  (UK)
Studioverlag Beyer  (AU)
Beyond Baroque Foundation  (US)
Beyond Our Control  (US)
Beyond Reality Magazine, Inc.  (US)
Paul E. Bezanker, Ed. & Pub.  (US)
De Bezige Bij  (NE)
Bhabha Atomic Research Centre  (II)
Bhagalpur University  (II)
Bhagyavati Library  (II)
Bhaktivedanta Book Trust  (US)
S. K. Bhanot, Ed. & Pub.  (II)
Bharari  (II)
Bharat Krishak Samaj  (II)
Bharat Sevak  (II)
Bharat Sevashram Sangha  (II)
Bharat Sevashram Sangha  (UK)
Bharata Ganita Parisad  (II)
Bharata Manisha  (II)
Bharathan Publications Private Ltd.  (II)
Bharatiya Adimjati Sevak Sangh  (II)
Bharatiya Janasangh Kerala Pradesh  (II)
Bharatiya Natya Sangh  (II)
Bharatiya Vidya Bhavan  (II)
T. E. Bhaskaran, Ed. & Pub.  (II)
Sant Ram Bhatia, Ed. & Pub.  (II)
T.A. Bhatt, Ed. & Pub.  (KE)
Brojendra K. Bhattacharya, Ed. & Pub.  (II)
Bhavan's College of Mass Communication  (II)
Bhopal University Research Council  (II)
Bhubaneswar Review  (II)
Biafra Time Ltd.  (NR)
John Bialas, Ed. & Pub.  (US)
Bialostockie Towarzystwo Naukowe  (PL)
Vito Bianco, Ed. & Pub.  (IT)
Bibbia e Oriente  (IT)
Bibelbund  (GW)
Bibi  (ZR)
Bible Advocate Press  (US)
Bible College of New Zealand, Inc.  (NZ)
Bible Holiness Movement  (CN)
Bible Land Mission  (LE)
Bible Sabbath Association International  (US)
Bible Science Association  (US)
Bible Society of South Africa  (SA)
Biblical Archaeology Society  (US)
Biblical Evangelism Press  (US)
Biblical Institute Press  (IT)
Biblical Theology Bulletin  (US)
Editions Biblio-Mer  (BE)
Bibliografia Medica Internacional  (SP)
Editrice Bibliografica s.r.l.  (IT)
Bibliograma  (AG)
Bibliographic Information Center for the Study of
  Political Science  (US)
Bibliographic Press Ltd.  (UK)
Bibliographic Services  (AT)
Bibliographical Society  (UK)
Bibliographical Society of America  (US)
Bibliographical Society of Australia & New Zealand
  (AT)
Bibliographical Society of Canada  (CN)
Bibliographical Society of the University of Virginia
  (US)
VEB Bibliographisches Institut  (GE)
Bibliographisches Institut AG  (GW)

Bibliography Newsletter  (US)
Bibliography of Literature Relating to the
  Assassination of President John F. Kennedy  (US)
Biblioteca  (AG)
Biblioteca Americana de Autores. Boletin  (UY)
Biblioteca Argentina para Ciegos  (AG)
Biblioteca Cantonale Lugano  (SZ)
Biblioteca Centrala de Stat a Republicii Socialiste
  Romania  (RM)
Biblioteca Centrala Pedagogica  (RM)
Biblioteca de Menendez Pelayo  (SP)
Biblioteca do Sejur  (BL)
Biblioteca Forteguerriana  (IT)
Biblioteca Francescana  (IT)
Biblioteca "Jose Artigas"  (UY)
Biblioteca Judeteana Constanta  (RM)
Biblioteca Labronica Notiziario  (IT)
Biblioteca Malatestiana  (IT)
Biblioteca Marsilio  (IT)
Biblioteca Nacional Jose Marti  (CU)
Biblioteca Nacional Jose Marti. Departamento de
  Coleccion Cubana  (CU)
Biblioteca Nacional Jose Marti. Departmento de
  Hemeroteca e Informacion de Humanidades  (CU)
Biblioteca Nazionale Centrale di Firenze  (IT)
Biblioteca Statale e Libreria Civica, Cremona  (IT)
Biblioteca Statale Isontina di Gorizia  (IT)
Biblioteca Universitaria y Provincial de Barcelona
  (SP)
Biblioteca y Hemeroteca de Servicios Electricos del
  Gran Buenos Aires  (AG)
Biblioteka Kornicka  (PL)
Biblioteka Narodowa  (PL)
Biblioteka Narodowa. Instytut Bibliograficzny  (PL)
Biblioteka Slaska  (PL)
Bibliotekarforbundet  (DK)
Bibliotekscentralen  (DK)
Bibliotekstjaenst AB  (SW)
Bibliotheca Bogoriensis  (IO)
Bibliotheca Islamica Booksellers  (US)
Bibliotheca Polyglotta  (CN)
Bibliotheca Rosenthaliana  (NE)
Bibliothek fuer Zeitgeschichte, Stuttgart  (GW)
Bibliothekar-Lehrinstitut des Landes Nordrhein-
  Westfalen  (GW)
Bibliotheque Africaine  (BE)
Bibliotheque des Ecoles Francaises d'Athenes et de
  Rome  (FR)
Bibliotheque Historique de la Ville de Paris  (FR)
Bibliotheque Interuniversitaire de Bordeaux  (FR)
Bibliotheque Interuniversitaire de Medecine et de
  Pharmacie. Bibliotheque de Medecine et de
  Pharmacie  (FR)
Bibliotheque Nationale  (FR)
Bibliotheque Nationale. Cabinet des Estampes  (FR)
Bibliotheque Nationale. Departement de la
  Phonotheque Nationale et de l'Audiovisuel  (FR)
Bibliotheque Nationale du Quebec  (CN)
Bibliotheque Nationale Suisse
  see Switzerland. Bibliotheque Nationale Suisse
  (SZ)
Bibliotheque Royale Albert 1er  (BE)
Bibliotheque Universitaire, Grenoble  (FR)
Biblos: Ukrainian Bibliography  (US)
Bicentennial Publishing Corp.  (US)
Bicycle Bibliography  (US)
Bielefelder Verlagsanstalt KG  (GW)
Bien  (US)
Verlag die Biene  (GW)
Bienvenidos - Welcome  (MX)
Editions Biere  (FR)
Biermann KG  (GW)
Big Deal  (US)
Big Deal Press  (US)
Big Farmer, Inc.  (US)
Big Mama Rag  (US)
Bigfoot Information Center  (US)
Bihar. Directorate of Industries  (II)
Bihar Research Institute of Prakit, Jainology, and
  Ahimsa  (II)
Bihar Research Society  (II)
Bihar State Digamber Jain Youth Association  (II)
Bijenhuis-Wageningen  (NE)
Bijutsu-shi Gakkai
  see Japan Art History Society  (JA)
Bijutsu Shuppan-sha  (JA)
Bilder-Zeitung G.m.b.H.  (AU)
Verlag Bildpost  (GW)
Bildungspolitische Verlagsanstalt  (GW)
Bilgummiverkstedenes Landsforbund  (NO)
Bill Communications, Inc.
  see also Hartman Communications, Inc. Rubber
  World  (US)
Bill Communications Inc.  (US)
Bill Communications Inc. Automotive Division  (US)
Billboard Directories  (US)

Billboard Ltd.  (UK)
Billboard Publications Inc.  (US)
Billboard Publications, Inc. Amusement Business
  Division  (US)
Billboard Publications, Inc. (New York)  (US)
Billiard Congress of America  (US)
Billy Graham Evangelistic Association  (US)
Billy Graham Evangelistic Association Deutschland
  e.V.  (GW)
A B Bilstatistik  (SW)
Zeitschriftenverlag Dr. Bilz und Dr. Fraund KG
  (GW)
Bim  (BB)
Binay Bhushan Bhattacharya  (II)
Clive Bingley (Journals) Ltd.  (UK)
Verlag Max Binkert AG  (SZ)
Binnenschiffahrts-Verlag GmbH  (GW)
Binsted Publications  (UK)
Bio-Dynamic Farming and Gardening Association, Inc.
  (US)
Bio-Feedback Technology Inc.  (US)
Biochemical Society (Book Depot)  (UK)
Biochemischer Bund Deutschlands e.V.  (GW)
Biodeterioration Information Centre  (UK)
Biodynamica  (US)
Biofeedback Research Society  (US)
Biogeographical Society of Japan  (JA)
Biographical Research Institute  (PK)
Biographies Canadienness-Francaises, Ltee.  (CN)
Biologia Gabonica  (FR)
Biologia Maritima  (NE)
Biological Engineering Society  (UK)
Biological Photographic Association  (II)
Biological Photographic Association, Inc.  (US)
Biological Sciences Curriculum Study  (US)
Biological Society  (NZ)
Biological Society of Nevada  (US)
Biological Society of Pakistan  (PK)
Biological Society of Washington  (US)
Biological Stain Commission  (US)
Biologie Medicale  (FR)
Biologie Verlag  (GW)
Biologische Anstalt Helgoland  (GW)
Biologische Bundesanstalt fuer Land- und
  Forstwirtschaft  (GW)
Biologische Bundesanstalt fuer Land- und
  Forstwirtschaft in Berlin- Dahlem  (GW)
Biology Teachers Association of the Philippines  (PH)
Biomass Energy Institute  (CN)
Biomedical Information Corp.  (US)
Biomedical Information Service  (UK)
Biometeorological Research Centre  (NE)
Biometric Society  (US)
Biometrika Trust  (UK)
Bionomica-Gemeinschaft e.V.  (GW)
Bionomica-Verlag  (GW)
Biophysical Society  (US)
Biophysical Society of Japan  (JA)
Bioradii Publications  (IC)
BioSciences Information Service of Biological
  Abstracts  (US)
Biosophia  (IT)
Birbal Sahni Institute of Palaeobotany  (II)
Bircher-Benner Verlag Dr. Ralph Bircher und Co.
  (SZ)
Bird Banders' Association of Australia  (AT)
Bird Effort Press  (US)
Bird Observers Club  (AT)
Birds and Country  (UK)
Kaare Messel Birkelund, Ed. & Pub.  (NO)
Birkhaeuser Verlag  (SZ)
Birla Institute of Art and Music  (II)
Birmingham and Midland Society for Genealogy and
  Heraldry  (UK)
Birmingham & Warwickshire Archaeological Society
  (UK)
Birmingham Area Chamber of Commerce  (US)
Birmingham Art Association  (US)
Birmingham Bar Association  (US)
Birmingham Chamber of Industry and Commerce
  (UK)
Birmingham Education Association  (US)
Birmingham Medical and Dental Schools  (UK)
Birmingham Medical Society  (UK)
Birmingham Post & Mail Ltd.  (UK)
Birmingham Publishing Co.  (US)
Birmingham World  (US)
Birth and the Family Journal  (US)
Bischoeflicher Stuhl, Passau  (GW)
Bischoeflicher Stuhl Regensburg  (GW)
Bischoefliches Generalvikariat, Essen  (GW)
Bischoefliches Ordinariat Sanct Poelten  (AU)
Bischoefliches Seelsogeamt Klagenfurt  (AU)
Biseibutsubyo Kenkyusho
  see Osaka University. Research Institute for
  Microbial Diseases  (JA)
Bishop Museum
  see Bernice Pauahi Bishop Museum  (US)

Bishop Museum Press  (US)
Bishops University. Students' Executive Council
  (CN)
Bispedoemmeraadenes Fellesraad--Kirkeraadet  (NO)
Bit  (DK)
Bit Information Service  (UK)
Bit-Verlag  (GW)
Verlag Bitaon Ltd.  (IS)
Bits and Pieces  (US)
Bitter Oleander Press  (US)
Bittersweet, Inc.  (US)
Bituminous Coal Research, Inc.  (US)
Bitzaron, Inc.  (US)
Bix Beiderbecke Memorial Society  (US)
Bizarre Acres Publications  (UK)
Edizione Bizzari  (IT)
Bokaforlag Odds Bjoernssonar  (IC)
Blabandsrorelsens Barnversamhet  (SW)
J. J. Black  (UK)
Black Affairs  (US)
Black American Law Student Association  (US)
Black Art  (US)
Black Ascensions  (US)
Black Book  (US)
Black Box  (US)
Black Business Digest  (US)
Black Child Development Institute  (US)
Black Collegiate Services, Inc.  (US)
Black Community Programmes  (SA)
Black Country Society  (UK)
Black Cultural Center of Trenton, Inc.  (US)
Black Diamond Co., Inc.  (US)
Black Dwarf  (UK)
Black Economic Research Center  (US)
Black Ecumenical Commission of Massachusetts
  (US)
Black Employees of the Library of Congress  (US)
Black Forum Magazine  (US)
Black Graphics International  (US)
Black Hills Genealogy Club  (US)
Black Hills State College. Journalism Graphics
  Department  (US)
Black History Museum  (US)
Black Jack  (US)
Black-Jewish Information Center. Media Project  (US)
Black List  (US)
Black Literature and Arts Congress  (SA)
A. & C. Black Ltd.  (UK)
Black Maria Collective, Inc.  (US)
Black News  (US)
Black Panther Party  (US)
Black Photographers Annual Inc.  (US)
Black Powder Times  (US)
Black Sash  (SA)
Black Secretariat Archdiocese of Detroit  (US)
Black Silent Majority Committee  (US)
Black Sparrow Press  (US)
Black Stone Press  (US)
Black Times Publishing Corp.  (US)
Black Warrior Review  (US)
Black Watch  (UK)
Black Wax Magazine  (UK)
Black Women's Community Development Foundation
  (US)
Black World Foundation  (US)
Blackberry  (US)
Blackberry (Albuquerque)  (US)
Blackbird Press  (US)
Blackface Sheep Breeders' Association  (UK)
Blackfish  (CN)
Blackfriars  (UK)
Blackfriars Press Periodicals Ltd.  (UK)
Blackpool Gazette & Herald Ltd.  (UK)
Blackpool Hotel and Guest House Association Ltd.
  (UK)
Black's Guide to the Office Space Market  (US)
Blackstaff Press Ltd.  (UK)
Basil Blackwell & Mott Ltd.  (UK)
Blackwell Scientific Publications Ltd.  (UK)
Blackwent Publishing Co.  (US)
William Blackwood & Sons Ltd.  (UK)
Bladkompaniet A-S  (NO)
Blaisdell Family National Association  (US)
Blaisdell Institute for Advanced Study of World
  Cultures and Religions  (US)
Blake Enterprises, Inc.  (US)
Blakeham Publications Ltd.  (UK)
Blakes (Norfolk Broads Holidays) Ltd.  (UK)
Aldo Blanc, Ed. & Pub  (IT)
Aguet Blanc Redaz, Ed. & Pub.  (IT)
William F. Bland Co.  (US)
Blandford Business Press  (UK)
Blandford Press Ltd.  (UK)
Blankenbergs Literair Archief Trefpunt  (BE)
Blantyre Printing & Publishing Co. Ltd.  (MW)
Blantyre Water Board  (MW)
Blasmusikverlag  (GW)
Blaues Kreuz in Deutschland e.V.  (GW)

Blaukreuz-Verlag  (GW)
Blaukreuz-Verlag  (SZ)
Bleb Press  (US)
Blessed Sacrament Fathers  (US)
Blesston Printers & Publishers  (SA)
Blest Co.  (US)
Blewett Co., Inc.  (US)
Blick und Bild Verlag S. Kappe KG  (GW)
Blinded Veterans Association  (US)
Blinden- und Sehschwachen-Verband der DDR.
  Deutsche Zentralbuecherei fuer Blinde zu Leipzig
  (GE)
Blindenbibliotheek "Le Sage ten Broek"  (NE)
Blink Publications Ltd.  (UK)
Bliss & Laughlin Industries  (US)
Bliss Classification Association  (UK)
Blitz  (US)
Blitz Publications Private Ltd.  (II)
Olaf Blixen, Ed. & Pub.  (UY)
Bloc de la Liberte Linguistique  (BE)
Bloch Editores S.A.  (BL)
Bloemfontein. Development Officer  (SA)
H. W. Blok Uitgeverij B.V.  (NE)
Blonder-Tongue Labs, Inc.  (US)
Blood Information Service  (US)
Bloodhorse Breeder's Association of Australia. South
  Australian Division  (AT)
Bloom & Co., Inc.  (US)
Bloomfield Public Library  (US)
Bloomington Independent Publishing Co.  (US)
Librairie Bloud et Gay  (FR)
Blue Anchor, Inc.  (US)
Blue Army of Our Lady of Fatima in U.S. and Canada
  (US)
Blue Book of Europe AB  (SW)
Blue Cross Association  (US)
Blue Cross of Switzerland  (SZ)
Blue Cross of Wisconsin  (US)
Blue-J, Inc.  (US)
Blue Pig  (US)
Blue Rose Ministry  (US)
Blue Sky  (US)
Bluebell Railway Ltd.  (UK)
Bluebell Railway Preservation Society  (UK)
Blueberry Hill Publishing Co.  (US)
Bluebonnets and Silver Shoes of Texas  (US)
Editora Edgard Bluecher Ltda.  (BL)
Bluegrass Unlimited Inc.  (US)
Bluenose Rambler  (CN)
Blues  (BE)
Blues  (CN)
Blues and Swing  (FR)
Blues Unlimited  (UK)
Editorial Blume  (SP)
Blundell Bros. Ltd.  (NZ)
Blyth Standard  (CN)
B'minhal Hachinuch  (IS)
B'nai B'rith  (US)
B'nai B'rith. Career and Counseling Services  (US)
B'nai B'rith Hillel Foundation  (US)
B'nai B'rith Hillel Foundation at Brooklyn College
  (US)
Bnai B'rith Messenger, Inc.  (US)
B'nai B'rith. Metropolitan Conference  (US)
B'nai B'rith Women  (US)
B'nai B'rith Youth Commission  (US)
Board for Social Responsibility of the General Synod
  (UK)
Board of Celtic Studies  (UK)
Board of Education of the General Synod  (UK)
Board of Fire Commissioners of New South Wales
  (AT)
Board of Foreign Trade  (CH)
Board of Jewish Education, Inc.  (US)
Board of Jewish Education of Greater New York
  (US)
Board of Jewish Education of Greater New York.
  Department of Art  (US)
Board of Management  (II)
Boardroom Reports, Inc.  (US)
Boardwalk Publications  (US)
Boast  (US)
Boat Enquiries Ltd.  (UK)
Boat Owners Association of the United States  (US)
Boat World Publications  (UK)
Boating Industry Association  (US)
Boating Publications, Inc.  (US)
Boats & Harbors  (US)
Bob Jones University  (US)
Bobbin Publications, Inc.  (US)
Bobbs-Merrill Co., Inc.  (US)
Bobeck Laboratories B E N E L U X  (BE)
Bobit Publishing Co.  (US)
Boc-Murex  (UK)
Boca Raton Historical Society  (US)

Diffusion de Boccard  (FR)
Boccherini's Minuet  (FR)
Verlag Bockau und Freese  (GW)
Verlag Bodet und Link  (GW)
Bodine Electric Co.  (US)
Bodleian Library  (UK)
Andre-Pierre Body, Ed. & Pub.  (FR)
Henning C. Boe, Ed. & Pub.  (US)
Boehlau-Verlag  (GW)
Hermann Boehlaus Nachf.  (AU)
Hermann Boehlaus Nachfolger  (GE)
Boei-cho Koku Igaku Jikkentai
  see Japan Air Self Defense Force. Aeromedical
    Laboratory  (JA)
Boei Daigakko
  see National Defense Academy  (JA)
Boei Gakkai  (JA)
Boekencentrum B.V.  (NE)
Drukkerij G.W. den Boer  (NE)
C. de Boer Jr. N. V.  (NE)
Alfred G. Boerger, Ed. & Pub.  (US)
Boerne- og Ungdomspaedagogernes Landsorganisation
  (DK)
Forlaget Boersen A-S  (DK)
Boersenverein der Deutschen Buchhaendler.
  Historische Kommission  (GE)
Boersenverein des Deutschen Buchhandels  (GW)
Dr. Julius Boese, Ed. & Pub.  (AU)
Bogazici Universitesi  (TU)
Bogazici University
  see Bogazici Universitesi  (TU)
Bogden and Quigley, Inc.  (US)
Bogor Zoological Museum
  see Museum Zoologicum Bogoriense  (IO)
Bogota, Colombia. Camara de Comercio  (CK)
Bohemian Freethinking School Society  (US)
Bohmann Verlag K.G.  (AU)
Bohman Industrial Traffic Consultants, Inc.  (US)
Bohn, Scheltema en Holkema  (NE)
Boian News Service  (US)
Editions Boileau  (FR)
Boink  (US)
Bois  (FR)
Editions du Boisbaudry  (FR)
Boise State University. Department of English  (US)
Boixareu Editores, S.A.  (SP)
Bokautgafa Menningarsjod  (IC)
Bokcafet  (SW)
Bolaffi e Mondadori  (IT)
Boldt Verlag KG  (GW)
Francis Bolen, Ed. & Pub.  (BE)
Editora Boletin de Custos Ltda.  (BL)
Boletin Diplomatico  (MX)
Boletin Uruguayo de Sociologia  (UY)
Drukkerij Bolhuis B.V.  (NE)
Boligselskabernes Landsforening  (DK)
Bolivia. Caja Nacional de Seguridad Social  (BO)
Bolivia. Instituto Nacional de Estadistica  (BO)
Bolivia. Ministerio de Cultura, Informacion y Turismo
  (BO)
Bolivia. Ministerio de Defensa Nacional  (BO)
Bolivia. Secretaria General de Deportes  (BO)
Bolivia. Servicio Geologico de Bolivia  (BO)
Bolivia. Servicio Nacional de Caminos  (BO)
Bolivia. Subsecretaria de Justicia  (BO)
Bolivia's Bibliographical Society  (BO)
Casa Editrice Bolletino Metallografico  (IT)
Bollettino Bibliografico Sardo e Archivio Tradizioni
  Popolari  (IT)
Bollettino dei Prezzi All'ingrosso  (IT)
Bollettino di Collegamento  (IT)
Bollettino Tributario d'Informazioni  (IT)
Verlag Jacques Bollmann AG  (SZ)
Bolsa de Cereales  (AG)
Bolsa de Comercio de Buenos Aires  (AG)
Bolsa de Comercio de Mendoza  (AG)
Bolsa de Comercio de Rosario  (AG)
Bolsa de Valores de Mexico  (MX)
Bolsa de Valores de Sao Paulo  (BL)
Bolsa de Valores do Rio de Janeiro  (BL)
Bolton College of Education  (UK)
Bolton Fine Art Litho Works  (II)
Bolton Publications (Pty) Ltd.  (SA)
Bolyai Janos Matematikai Tarsulat  (HU)
Bombay Art Society  (II)
Bombay Biological Association  (II)
Bombay Chartered Accountants' Society  (II)
Bombay Duck  (US)
Bombay Hospital Trust  (II)
Bombay Labour Institute  (II)
Bombay Law Reporter Pvt. Ltd.  (II)
Bombay Market  (II)
Bombay Natural History Society  (II)
Bombay Oilseeds & Oils Exchange Ltd.  (II)
Bombay University
  see University of Bombay  (II)

Bombay Zionist Association  (II)
Bombshelter Press  (US)
Bon Appetit  (US)
Bon Appetit (Kansas City)  (US)
Mario Bon Espasandin, Ed. & Pub.  (UY)
Bonanza Press Ltd.  (CN)
B.V. Uitgeversmaatschappij Bonaventura  (NE)
Bond Buyer  (US)
Bond Heemschut  (NE)
Bond Nederlands Israel  (NE)
Bond Street Publishers Ltd.  (UK)
Bond van Nederlandse Fotodetailhandelaren  (NE)
Bond van Politieambtenaren in Nederland tot
    Bescherming van Dieren  (NE)
Bond voor Materialenkennis  (NE)
Bond voor Staatspensionering  (NE)
Bond Wheelwright Co.  (US)
Bondholder's Register (Publishers) Ltd.  (UK)
Johann L. Bondi und Sohn  (AU)
Francesco Boneschi, Ed. & Pub.  (IT)
Verlag Aurel Bongers  (GW)
Michel Bongrand S.A.  (FR)
Bonifacius-Druckerei  (GW)
Bonifatiuswerk der Deutschen Katholiken e.V.  (GW)
Bonn. Verein fuer Niederdeutsche Sprachforschung
    (GW)
Bonn. Werbe und Verkehrsamt  (GW)
Bonne Table et Tourisme  (FR)
Bonnell Publications, Inc.  (US)
Bonner Heimat- und Geschichtsverein  (GW)
Bonneterie-Mercerie-Habillement  (FR)
Howard T. Bonnett, Ed. and Pub.  (US)
Albert Bonniers Foerlag AB  (SW)
Bonsai in Australia  (AT)
Bonsai Press--Jama Press  (US)
Bonsai Society of Greater New York, Inc.  (US)
Forlaget Bonytt AS  (NO)
Book Associates, Inc.  (US)
Book Club of California  (US)
Book Collectors of America  (US)
Book Collectors' Society of Australia  (AT)
Book Digest Company, Inc.  (US)
Book News, Inc.  (US)
Book-Of-The-Month Club  (US)
Book Review  (II)
Book Society of Persia  (IR)
Booklegger Press  (US)
Booklet Pane Society  (US)
Books About Birds  (US)
Books & Friends  (US)
Books & Journals Private Ltd.  (II)
Books for Libraries, Inc.  (US)
Books for Your Children  (UK)
Books International of DH-TE International, Inc.
    (US)
Books Ireland  (IE)
Booksellers Association of Great Britain & Ireland
    (UK)
Bookswest Magazine  (US)
Bookworm  (US)
Boom-Pers  (NE)
Boone, Inc  (US)
Joseph Boonin, Inc.  (US)
Richard Boorberg Verlag (Muenchen)  (GW)
Richard Boorberg Verlag (Stuttgart)  (GW)
Boosey and Hawkes, Inc.  (US)
Boosey & Hawkes Music Publishers Ltd.  (UK)
Boost  (UK)
Boot and Shoe Workers' Union (AFL-CIO)  (US)
Verlag fuer Bootswirtschaft  (GW)
Bor- es Cipoipari Tarsasag  (HU)
Edizioni Bora S.N.C. di P. Prandin & C.  (IT)
Borax Consolidated Ltd  (UK)
Borba  (YU)
Bord Failte  (IE)
Bord na Mona  (IE)
Bordeaux Chirurgical  (FR)
Bordeaux Medical  (FR)
Border-Mountain Press  (US)
Border Press Agency Ltd.  (UK)
Boreal  (CN)
Boreal Institute for Northern Studies  (CN)
Borec  (YU)
Borgens Forlag  (DK)
Borghese  (IT)
Verkehrsblattverlag Dr. Borgmann  (GW)
Editoriale Il Borgo  (IT)
Boris Kidric Institute of Nuclear Sciences
    see Institut za Nuklearne Nauke "Boris Kidric"
    (YU)
Verlag Born  (GW)
Uitgeversmaatschappij Born B. V.  (NE)
Borneo Research Council  (US)
Eli Bornstein, Ed. & Pub.  (CN)
Gebrueder Borntraeger Verlagsbuchhandlung  (GW)
Borodin Communications Ltd.  (UK)

Yehuda Borovik  (IS)
Borromaeusverein  (GW)
Borsa Valori di Torino  (IT)
Borsod Megyei Lapkiado Vallalat  (HU)
Bosai Kenkyusho
    see Kyoto University. Disaster Prevention Research
    Institute  (JA)
Bosch en Keuning N. V.  (NE)
Robert Bosch GmbH. Abteilung FSD  (GW)
Robert Bosch GmbH. Geschaeftsbereich Elektronik
    (GW)
Bose Institute  (II)
Ed Bosin, Jr., Ed. & Pub.  (US)
Bosko Buha Informativni Centar  (YU)
Bosnia and Hercegovina. Arhiv  (YU)
Bosnia and Hercegovina. Zavod za Statistiku  (YU)
Bosporus University
    see Bogazici Universitesi  (TU)
Gustav Bosse Verlag  (GW)
Boston. School Department  (US)
Boston & Maine Railroad  (US)
Boston Architectural Center  (US)
Boston Board of Fire Underwriters, Inc.  (US)
Boston Children's Medical Center  (US)
Boston City Record  (US)
Boston College  (US)
Boston College. Graduate School of Social Work
    (US)
Boston College. Law School  (US)
Boston College. Peripatology Program  (US)
Boston Critic Inc.  (US)
Boston Daughters of Bilitis  (US)
Boston Eagle  (US)
Boston Marine Guide Publishing, Inc.  (US)
Boston Museum of Fine Arts  (US)
Boston Phoenix  (US)
Boston Society for Gerontologic Psychiatry, Inc.
    (US)
Boston Street Railway Association  (US)
Boston Symphony Orchestra  (US)
Boston Technical Publishers, Inc.  (US)
Boston University  (US)
Boston University. African Studies Center  (US)
Boston University. African Studies Library  (US)
Boston University. College of Basic Studies  (US)
Boston University Medical Center  (US)
Boston University Scholarly Publications  (US)
Boston University School of Law  (US)
Boston University. School of Public Communication
    (US)
Boston Wesleyan Association  (US)
Boston Women's Collective, Inc.  (US)
Bostonian Society  (US)
Bostwick Press  (US)
Botanic Gardens  (SI)
Botanical Institute of Barcelona  (SP)
Botanical Research Institute  (SA)
Botanical Society of America, Inc.  (US)
Botanical Society of Bengal  (II)
Botanical Society of Edinburgh  (UK)
Botanical Society of Egypt  (UA)
Botanical Society of Japan  (JA)
Botanical Society of South Africa  (SA)
Botanical Society of the British Isles  (UK)
Botanisch-Zoologische Gesellschaft Liechtenstein-
    Sargans-Werdenberg  (LH)
Botanische Staatssammlung Muenchen  (GW)
Botaniske Institutionerna, Uppsala  (SW)
Libreria y Ediciones Botas S. A.  (MX)
Botswana. Central Statistics Office  (BS)
Botswana. Commissioner of the Police  (BS)
Botswana. Department of Health  (BS)
Botswana. Department of Income Tax  (BS)
Botswana. Department of Wildlife and National Parks
    (BS)
Botswana. Forest Department  (BS)
Botswana. Geological Survey and Mines Department
    (BS)
Botswana. Government Printer  (BS)
Botswana. Information Department  (BS)
Botswana. Ministry of Agriculture  (BS)
Botswana. Ministry of Agriculture. Division of Co-
    Operative Development  (BS)
Botswana. National Library Service  (BS)
Botswana Development Corporation  (BS)
Botswana National Library Service
    see Botswana. National Library Service  (BS)
Botswana Society  (BS)
Bottler & Packer Ltd.  (UK)
Robert M. Bottorff, Ed. & Pub.  (US)
Editions Edouard Boucherit  (FR)
Verlag Bouer und Wohner  (SZ)
Bougainville Copper Pty. Ltd.  (AT)
Georges Bouillon, Ed. & Pub.  (BE)
Pierre Boujut, Pub.  (FR)
Boukoumanis Publications  (GR)
Boulder Valley Education Association  (US)
Boulevard Publications  (US)

G.F. Boullier, Ed. & Pub.  (FR)
Claude Boumendil  (FR)
Boumi Temple A.A.O.N.M.S. Oasis of Baltimore
    (US)
Boundary Historical Society  (CN)
Bourg-Bourger  (LU)
C. Bourgeois, Editeur  (FR)
Bourke & District Historical Society  (AT)
Bourne Society  (UK)
J. Bout en Zoon  (NE)
Bouteille a la Mer  (FR)
Boutiques de France  (FR)
Bouverie Publishing Co. Ltd.  (UK)
Bouvier Verlag Herbert Grundmann  (GW)
Uitgave van de N.V. Drukkerij de Bouwkroniek  (BE)
Bow Publications Ltd.  (UK)
Bowdoin College. Hawthorne-Longfellow Library
    (US)
Bowdoin College. Museum of Art  (US)
Bowers and Ruddy Galleries, Inc.  (US)
Bowes Publishers Ltd.  (CN)
R. R. Bowker Company  (US)
R. R. Bowker Company. Jaques Cattell Press  (US)
Bowker Publishing Co. Ltd.  (UK)
Bowley Publications  (UK)
Bowling Green Popular Press  (US)
Bowling Green State University. Center for
    Communications Research  (US)
Bowling Green State University. Creative Writing
    Program  (US)
Bowling Green State University. Department of
    English  (US)
Bowling Green State University. Department of
    Geography  (US)
Bowling Green State University. Department of
    Sociology  (US)
Bowling Green State University. Environmental
    Studies Center  (US)
Bowling Green State University. Library  (US)
Bowling Green State University. Office of
    Experimental Studies  (US)
Bowling Green State University. Philosophy
    Documentation Center  (US)
Bowling Proprietors' Association of America, Inc.
    (US)
Boxe Ring s.r.l.  (IT)
Boy Scouts of America  (US)
Boyce Thompson Institute for Plant Research  (US)
Westholsteinische Verlagsanstalt Boyens und Co.
    (GW)
William H. Boyer, Ed. & Pub.  (US)
Boynton & Associates  (US)
Boys' Brigade, Inc.  (UK)
Boys' Clubs of America  (US)
Boys' Outfitter Co., Inc.  (US)
Gianni Baget Bozzo, Ed. & Pub.  (IT)
Brabant. Dienst voor Geschiedkundige en
    Folkloristische Opzoekingen
    see Brabant. Service de Recherches Historiques et
    Folkloriques  (BE)
Brabant. Service de Recherches Historiques et
    Folkloriques  (BE)
Verlag Friedrich Brabec  (AU)
W. B. Bradbury Co., Inc.  (US)
Braddock Publications  (US)
Bradfield College  (UK)
Bradford & Halifax Chambers of Commerce  (UK)
Bradford County Historical Society  (US)
Bradford's Directory  (US)
Bradley Publications Ltd.  (CN)
Bradley Pulverizer Co.  (UK)
Bradley University. Evening College  (US)
Herbert W. Bradnick  (UK)
Brador Publications  (US)
Bradwell Abbey Field Centre  (UK)
Bragg Briefs  (US)
Brahmana-Gaurava  (II)
Brahms-Gesellschaft Hamburg  (GW)
Zeitschriftenverlag Dr. Hildegard Braig  (AU)
Braille Institute of America, Inc.  (US)
Brain Information Service-Brain Research Institute
    (US)
Brainchild  (US)
Brakeley, John Price Jones Inc.  (US)
Bramson Publishing Co.  (US)
Branch Line Society  (UK)
Brandeis University. English Department  (US)
Brandeis University. Office of Public Affairs  (US)
Brandeis University Press  (US)
Brandeis University. Research Liaison Committee
    (US)
Brandenburgh en Co.  (NE)
Herbert A. Brandon  (US)
Brandon House, Inc.  (US)
Brandshare Ltd.  (UK)
Druckerei H. Brandt  (GW)
Louis E. Brandt  (US)
Braniff International  (US)

P.H. Brans Ltd. (BE)
Branschtidningsfoerlaget (SW)
Branstead Press (CN)
Brant Wright Associates Ltd. (UK)
Brantwood Publications, Inc. (US)
John C. Brasfield Publishing Corp. (US)
Brasil Ilustrado (BL)
Impressora Brasileira (BL)
Editora Brasileira de Agricultura S.A. (BL)
Empresa Brasileira de Telecomunicacoes (BL)
Empresa Brasileira de Turismo (BL)
Brasilia, Brazil. Departamento de Estradas de
  Rodagem. Diretoria Geral (BL)
Editora Brasiliense (BL)
Brass Bulletin (SZ)
Brass Press (US)
Bratstvo (CN)
Bratstvo (YU)
Wilhelm Braumueller, Universitaets -
  Verlagsbuchhandlung GmbH (AU)
Verlag G. Braun GmbH (GW)
Braunschweigischer Geschichts Verein e.V. (GW)
Bravado Feature Service (US)
Brave Beaver Pressworks Ltd. (CN)
Brazil. Arquivo Nacional (BL)
Brazil. Banco Nacional da Habitacao. Assessoria
  Tecnica de Documentacao (BL)
Brazil. Banco Nacional da Habitacao. Secretaria de
  Divulgacao (BL)
Brazil. Biblioteca Nacional (BL)
Brazil. Camara dos Deputados. Centro de
  Documentacao e Informacao (BL)
Brazil. Comissao Central de Levantamento e
  Fiscalizacao das Safras Triticolas (BL)
Brazil. Comissao de Financiamento da Producao
  (BL)
Brazil. Comissao Executiva do Plano da Lavoura
  Cacaneira (BL)
Brazil. Conselho de Desenvolvimento Economico
  (BL)
Brazil. Conselho Federal de Farmacia (BL)
Brazil. Conselho Nacional de Petroleo. Secao de
  Relacoes Publicas (BL)
Brazil. Departamento Administrativo do Pessoal Civil
  (BL)
Brazil. Departamento Estadual de Estatistica (BL)
Brazil. Departamento Nacional de Mao-de Obra.
  Secao de Documentacao (BL)
Brazil. Departamento Nacional de Obras Contra as
  Secas (BL)
Brazil. Departamento Nacional de Obras Contra as
  Secas. Centro de Pesquisas Ictiologicas (BL)
Brazil. Departamento Nacional de Obras Contras as
  Secas. Servico de Piscicultura (BL)
Brazil. Departamento Nacional de Obras de
  Saneamento (BL)
Brazil. Departamento Nacional de Pesquisa
  Agropecuaria. (BL)
Brazil. Diretoria de Intendencia da Marinha (BL)
Brazil. Fundacao Nacional do Indio (BL)
Brazil. Fundacao Nacional do Indio. Museu do Indio
  (BL)
Brazil. Instituto de Pesquisas Agropecuarias do Norte
  (BL)
Brazil. Instituto do Acucar e do Alcool (BL)
Brazil. Instituto do Acucar e do Alcool. Divisao de
  Estudo e Planejamento (BL)
Brazil. Instituto Nacional de Previdencia Social (BL)
Brazil. Instituto Nacional de Tecnologia (BL)
Brazil. Instituto Nacional do Livro (BL)
Brazil. Ministerio da Aeronautica (BL)
Brazil. Ministerio da Agricultura (BL)
Brazil. Ministerio da Agricultura. Conselho Nacional
  de Desenvolvimento de Pecuaria (BL)
Brazil. Ministerio da Agricultura. Departamento de
  Assistencia ao Cooperativismo (BL)
Brazil. Ministerio da Agricultura. Departamento
  Nacional de Producao Animal (BL)
Brazil. Ministerio da Agricultura. Escritorio de
  Estatistica (BL)
Brazil. Ministerio da Agricultura. Instituto Nacional de
  Colonizacao e Reforma Agraria (BL)
Brazil. Ministerio da Agricultura. Subsecretaria de
  Planejamento e Orcamento (BL)
Brazil. Ministerio da Educacao e Cultura (BL)
Brazil. Ministerio da Educacao e Cultura. Campanha
  de Defesa do Folclore Brasileiro (BL)
Brazil. Ministerio da Educacao e Cultura.
  Departamento de Assuntos Universitaries (BL)

Brazil. Ministerio da Educacao e Cultura.
  Departamento de Educacao Fisica e Desportos
  (BL)
Brazil. Ministerio da Educacao e Cultura. Directoria
  do Patromonio Historico e Artistico Nacional (BL)
Brazil. Ministerio da Educacao e Cultura. Servico de
  Estatistica da Educacao e Cultura (BL)
Brazil. Ministerio da Fazenda (BL)
Brazil. Ministerio da Fazenda. Assesoria de Estudos,
  Planejamento e Avalicao (BL)
Brazil. Ministerio da Fazenda. Delegacio no Estado do
  Rio de Janeiro (BL)
Brazil. Ministerio da Fazenda. Subsecretaria de
  Economia e Financas (BL)
Brazil. Ministerio da Guerra (BL)
Brazil. Ministerio da Industria e do Comercio.
  Superintendencia da Borracha (BL)
Brazil. Ministerio da Justicia (BL)
Brazil. Ministerio da Marinha. Diretoria de
  Comunicacoes e Eletronica da Marinha (BL)
Brazil. Ministerio da Marinha. Servico de
  Documentacao Geral da Marinha (BL)
Brazil. Ministerio da Saude (BL)
Brazil. Ministerio da Saude. Coordenacao de
  Assistencia Medica e Hospitalar (BL)
Brazil. Ministerio da Saude. Servico Nacional da
  Enfermidade Mental (BL)
Brazil. Ministerio das Minas e Energia. Departamento
  Nacional da Producao Mineral (BL)
Brazil. Ministerio das Relacoes Exteriores (BL)
Brazil. Ministerio das Relacoes Exteriores, Biblioteca.
  (BL)
Brazil. Ministerio das Relacoes Exteriores. Divisao de
  Documentacao Diplomatica. Biblioteca (BL)
Brazil. Ministerio de Educacao e Cultura. Instituto
  Nacional de Estudos e Pesquisas Educacionais
  (BL)
Brazil. Ministerio do Interior (BL)
Brazil. Ministerio do Interior, Secretaria Geral (BL)
Brazil. Ministerio do Trabalho e Previdencia Social.
  Centro de Documentacao e Informatica (BL)
Brazil. Ministerio do Trabalho, Industria e Comercio
  (BL)
Brazil. Ministerio dos Transportes. Departamento
  Nacional de Estradas de Rodagem (BL)
Brazil. Ministerio dos Transportes. Operacao Maua
  (BL)
Brazil. Observatorio Nacional (BL)
Brazil. Rede Ferroviaria Federal. Departamento
  Geral de Estadistica (BL)
Brazil. Rede Ferroviaria Federal. Regional do
  Nordeste (BL)
Brazil. Rede Ferroviaria Federal. Superintendencia
  Geral de Coordenacao e de Planejamento (BL)
Brazil. Secretaria da Agricultura. Coordenadoria da
  Pesquisa de Recursos Naturais (BL)
Brazil. Secretaria da Agricultura. Instituto de
  Zootecnia (BL)
Brazil. Secretaria da Agricultura. Instituto Florestal
  (BL)
Brazil. Secretaria da Receita Federal. Centro de
  Informacoes Economico- Fiscais (BL)
Brazil. Secretaria de Coordenacao e Planejamento.
  Fundacao de Economia e Estatistica (BL)
Brazil. Secretaria de Estado de Educacao de Cultura
  (BL)
Brazil. Secretaria de Obras Publicas (BL)
Brazil. Secretaria de Planejamento da Presidencia da
  Republica (BL)
Brazil. Secretaria de Planejamento. Instituto de
  Planejamento Economico e Social (BL)
Brazil. Secretaria do Saneamento, Habitacao e Obras
  (BL)
Brazil. Secretaria-Geral do Exercito (BL)
Brazil. Senado Federal (BL)
Brazil. Servico de Estatistica da Educacao e Cultura
  (BL)
Brazil. Servico Federal de Processamento de Dados
  (BL)
Brazil. Servico Social do Comercio (BL)
Brazil. Servico Social do Comercio. Administracao
  Regional do Estado de Sao Paulo (BL)
Brazil. Servico Social do Comercio. Divisao de
  Documentacao e Intercambio (BL)
Brazil. Superintendencia do Desenvolvimento da
  Amazonia (BL)
Brazil. Superintendencia do Desenvolvimento da
  Amazonia. Departamento Administrativo (BL)
Brazil. Superintendencia do Desenvolvimento da
  Regiao Sul (BL)

Brazil. Superintendencia do Desenvolvimento do
  Nordeste (BL)
Brazil. Superintendencia do Desenvolvimento do
  Nordeste. Coordenacao de Informatica (BL)
Brazil. Superintendencia do Desenvolvimento do
  Nordeste. Departamento de Agricultura e
  Abastecimento (BL)
Brazil. Superintendencia do Desenvolvimento do
  Nordeste. Departamento de Recursos Naturais
  (BL)
Brazil. Superintendencia do Desenvolvimento do
  Nordeste. Departamento de Servicos Basicos da
  Sudene (BL)
Brazil. Superintendencia Nacional da Marinha
  Mercante. Assessoria de Relacoes Publicas (BL)
Brazil. Supremo Tribunal Federal (BL)
Brazil. Tribunal Regional do Trabalho (BL)
Brazilian-American Chamber of Commerce, Inc. (US)
Brazilian Center
  see under Sophia University (JA)
Brazilian College of Angiology (BL)
Brazilian Embassy (BL)
Brazilian Government Trade Bureau (US)
Brazilian Institute of Economic Studies (BL)
George Braziller, Inc. (US)
Breakthru Publications (UK)
Breandan Breathnach, Ed. & Pub. (IE)
Breda Publications (AT)
Brede-Verlag (GW)
Verlag Friedl Brehm (GW)
Breifne Historical Society (IE)
Breitkopf und Haertel (GW)
Bremen. Senator fuer Bildung, Wissenschaft und Kunst
  (GW)
Bremer Gesellschaft fuer Vorgeschichte (GW)
Bremische Evangelische Kirche (GW)
Bremische Hafenvertretung e. V. (GW)
Verlag Joh. Brendow und Sohn (GW)
Brentwood Publishing Corp. (US)
Bres' (NE)
Robert D. Breth Organization (US)
Brethren Journal Association (US)
Brethren Missionary Herald Co. (US)
Breuberg-Bund (GW)
Keith Breusch Pty. Ltd. (AT)
Breve, Il Gruppo, la Cultura, l'Idee (IT)
Brevillier-Urban Aktiengesellschaft (AU)
C. Brewer & Co. Ltd. (US)
Brewers Guild Publications Ltd. (UK)
Brewing and Malting Barley Research Institute (CN)
Brewing Research Foundation (UK)
Brewing Science Research Institute (JA)
Brewster Printing Co. (UK)
George W. Bricker, Ed. & Pub. (US)
Arthur Brickman Associates (US)
Bridge Magazine (US)
Bridge West Publications (UK)
Bridge World Magazine Inc. (US)
Bridgeport Hospital (US)
Bridgeport News Inc. (US)
Rose Mary Bridger (US)
Bridgestone Tire Co. (JA)
Brigade in Action (US)
Brigham Young University (US)
Brigham Young University. Asian Studies Program
  (US)
Brigham Young University. Center for
  Thermochemical Studies (US)
Brigham Young University. College of Engineering
  Sciences and Technology (US)
Brigham Young University. College of Family Living
  (US)
Brigham Young University. Department of
  Anthropology and Archaeology (US)
Brigham Young University. Department of Geology
  (US)
Brigham Young University. J. Reuben Clark Law
  School (US)
Brigham Young University. Law Library (US)
Brigham Young University. Library (US)
Brigham Young University. New World Archaeological
  Foundation (US)
Brigham Young University Press (US)
Bright Lights (US)
Brighton College (UK)
Brighton Head and Freak Magazine (UK)
Brighton Historical Society (AT)
Brighton Park Life (US)
Alice Briley (US)
E. J. Brill (NE)
E. J. Brill GmbH (GW)
Brilliant Corners (US)
Brimicombe Magazines (UK)
Bernadita Bringcula (PH)
J. B. van den Brink en Co. B.V. (NE)
Russ Brinkley, Ed. & Pub. (US)
Brisbane Development Association (AT)

Bristol and Gloucestershire Archaeological Society (UK)
Bristol & West of England Engineering Manufacturers Association Ltd. (UK)
Bristol Arts Centre (UK)
Bristol City Museum. Bristol Archaeological Research Group (UK)
Bristol Evening Post (UK)
Bristol Industrial Archaeological Society (UK)
Bristol Medico Chirurgical Society (UK)
Bristol Naturalists' Society (UK)
Bristol University Medical Students Club (UK)
Britain First Press (UK)
Britain's Sun Club (UK)
Brith Hasmoll (IS)
British Academy (UK)
British Academy of Forensic Sciences (UK)
British Agents Register (UK)
British Agricultural and Garden Machinery Association Ltd. (UK)
British Agricultural History Society (UK)
British Air Line Pilots Association (UK)
British Aircraft Corp. (UK)
British Airways (UK)
British Airways. Travel Div. (UK)
British Amateur Athletic Board (UK)
British Amateur Press Association (UK)
British Amateur Scientific Research Association (UK)
British America Publishing Co. Ltd. (CN)
British & Commonwealth Shipping Co., Ltd. (UK)
British and Foreign Bible Society (UK)
British and Irish Communist Organisation (UK)
British Antarctic Survey (UK)
British Antique Dealers Association (UK)
British Arachnological Society (UK)
British Archaeological Association (UK)
British Association for American Studies (UK)
British Association for Commercial and Industrial Education (UK)
British Association of Accountants and Auditors, Ltd. (UK)
British Association of Americn Square Dance Clubs (UK)
British Association of Chemists (UK)
British Association of Colliery Management (UK)
British Association of Green Crop Driers Ltd. (UK)
British Association of Industrial Editors (UK)
British Association of Organisers and Lecturers in Physical Education (UK)
British Association of Orientalists (UK)
British Association of Plastic Surgeons (UK)
British Association of Removers (UK)
British Association of Rheumatology and Rehabilitation (UK)
British Association of Singapore (SI)
British Association of Social Workers (UK)
British Association of Teachers of the Deaf (UK)
British Association of Urological Surgeons (UK)
British Astronomical Association (UK)
British Automobile Racing Club (UK)
British Bee-Keepers' Association (UK)
British Bee Publications Ltd. (UK)
British Beer-mat Collectors Society (UK)
British Blind & Shutter Association (UK)
British Book Centre (US)
British Boot and Shoe Institution (UK)
British Broadcasting Corp. (UK)
British Broadcasting Corp. Arabic Service (UK)
British Bromeliad Society (UK)
British Bureau of Television Advertising (UK)
British Caledonian Airways Ltd (UK)
British Campaign for the Release of Indonesian Political Prisoners (UK)
British Canadian Trade Association (CN)
British Canoe Union (UK)
British Carbonization Research Association (UK)
British Cardiac Society (UK)
British Caribbean Philatelic Study Group (US)
British Carpet Manufacturers Association (UK)
British Cartographic Society (UK)
British Cast Iron Research Association (BCIRA) (UK)
British Cave Research Association (UK)
British Ceramic Plant & Machinery Manufacturers' Association (UK)
British Ceramic Research Association (UK)
British Ceramic Society (UK)
British Chamber of Commerce (FR)
British Chamber of Commerce in Brazil (BL)
British Chamber of Commerce in Mexico (MX)
British Chamber of Commerce in Spain (SP)
British Chamber of Commerce of Turkey (TU)
British Chess Federation (UK)
British Chess Magazine Ltd. (UK)
British Chess Problem Society (UK)
British Club Year Book & Directory Ltd. (UK)
British Coke Research Association (UK)

British Columbia. Alcohol and Drug Commission (CN)
British Columbia. Bureau of Economics and Statistics (CN)
British Columbia. Cancer Foundation (CN)
British Columbia. Department of Human Resources (CN)
British Columbia. Department of Labour. Research Branch (CN)
British Columbia. Department of Lands, Forests and Water Resources. Water Resources Service (CN)
British Columbia. Department of Recreation and Conservation (CN)
British Columbia. Department of Travel Industry (CN)
British Columbia. Energy Commission (CN)
British Columbia. Environment and Land Use Committee (CN)
British Columbia. Forest Service (CN)
British Columbia. Library Development Commission (CN)
British Columbia. Ministry of Economic Development (CN)
British Columbia. Ministry of Labour. Research and Planning Branch (CN)
British Columbia. Ministry of Mines and Petroleum Resources (CN)
British Columbia. Ministry of Recreation and Conservation (CN)
British Columbia. Ministry of the Environment. Water Investigation Branch (CN)
British Columbia. Provincial Archives. Aural History (CN)
British Columbia. Royal Commission on Family and Children's Law (CN)
British Columbia Art Teachers Association (CN)
British Columbia Association for the Mentally Retarded (CN)
British Columbia Association of Mathematics Teachers (CN)
British Columbia Association of Teachers of Classics (CN)
British Columbia Bond Dealers Association (CN)
British Columbia Civil Liberties Association (CN)
British Columbia English Teachers' Association (CN)
British Columbia Federation of Labour (CN)
British Columbia Fruit Growers Association (CN)
British Columbia Genealogical Society (CN)
British Columbia Health Association (CN)
British Columbia Historical Association (CN)
British Columbia Institute for Economic Policy (CN)
British Columbia Library Association (CN)
British Columbia Medical Association (CN)
British Columbia Mountaineering Club (CN)
British Columbia Museums Association (CN)
British Columbia Music Educators' Association (CN)
British Columbia Native Indian Teachers' Association (CN)
British Columbia Physical Education Teachers Association (CN)
British Columbia Primary Teachers' Association (CN)
British Columbia Provincial Judges' Association (CN)
British Columbia Research Council (CN)
British Columbia School Counsellors' Association (CN)
British Columbia School Trustees Association (CN)
British Columbia Science Teachers Association (CN)
British Columbia Social Studies Teachers Association (CN)
British Columbia Society for Crippled Children (CN)
British Columbia Thoroughbred Breeders Society (CN)
British Columbia Tuberculosis Christmas Seal Society (CN)
British Columbia Voice of Women (CN)
British Combustion Equipment Manufacturers Association (UK)
British Computer Society (UK)
British Correspondence Chess Association (UK)
British Council (UK)
British Council (US)
British Council. English-Teaching Information Centre (UK)
British Council. Medical Department (UK)
British Council for Rehabilitation of the Disabled (UK)
British Council of Churches (UK)
British Country Music Association (UK)
British Cycling Federation (UK)
British Deaf Association (UK)
British Decorators Association (UK)
British Dental Association (UK)
British Diabetic Association (UK)
British Direct Mail Marketing Association (UK)
British Ecological Society (UK)
British Educational Administration Society (UK)
British Educational Research Association (UK)

British Epilepsy Association (UK)
British Equine Veterinary Association (UK)
British Esperanto Association (UK)
British European Associated Publishers Ltd. (UK)
British Farmer and Stockbreeder Ltd. (UK)
British Federation of Film Societies (UK)
British Federation of Folk Clubs (UK)
British Federation of Master Printers (UK)
British Federation of Music Festivals (UK)
British Film Fund Agency (UK)
British Film Institute (UK)
British Fire Services Association (UK)
British Flower Industry Association (UK)
British Food Manufacturing Industries Research Association (UK)
British Footwear Manufacturers Federation (UK)
British Friesian Cattle Society of Great-Britain & Ireland (UK)
British Frozen Food Federation (UK)
British Fuchsia Society (UK)
British Gas Corporation (UK)
British Geriatric Society (UK)
British Glass Industry Research Association (UK)
British Gliding Association (UK)
British Goat Society (UK)
British Golf Greenkeepers Association (UK)
British Grassland Society (UK)
British Hardware Federation (UK)
British Herpetological Society (UK)
British Homoeopathic Association (UK)
British Horological Institute (UK)
British Hospitals Contributory Schemes Association (UK)
British Hotels, Restaurants and Caterers Association (UK)
British Humanist Association (UK)
British Hydromechanics Research Association (UK)
British Ichthyological Society (UK)
British Independent Steel Producers Association (UK)
British Industrial and Scientific International Translation Service (UK)
British Industrial Biological Research Association (UK)
British Industrial Publicity Overseas Ltd. (UK)
British Information Services. Policy and Reference Division (US)
British Institute in Eastern Africa (UK)
British Institute of Archaeology at Ankara (UK)
British Institute of Cleaning Science (UK)
British Institute of History & Archaeology in East Africa (KE)
British Institute of International and Comparative Law (UK)
British Institute of Management (UK)
British Institute of Management Foundation (UK)
British Institute of Non-Destructive Testing (UK)
British Institute of Radiology (UK)
British Institute of Recorded Sound (UK)
British Interlingua Society (UK)
British Internal Combustion Engine Research Institute (UK)
British Interplanetary Society (UK)
British Iris Society (UK)
British Israel World Federation (UK)
British Israel World Federation (Canada) Inc. (CN)
British-Italian Society (UK)
British Jazz Society (UK)
British Jewellery & Giftware Federation Ltd. (UK)
British Kinematograph Sound and Television Society (UK)
British Leprosy Relief Association (UK)
British Liberals (UK)
British Library (UK)
British Library. Bibliographic Services Division (UK)
British Library. Board (UK)
British Library Lending Division (UK)
British Library. Reference Division (UK)
British Library. Research and Development Department (UK)
British Library of Political and Economic Science (UK)
British Lichen Society (UK)
British Mahabodhi Society (UK)
British Medical Association (UK)
British Midland Airways Limited (UK)
British Model Soldier Society (UK)
British Monomarks Ltd. (UK)
British Mountaineering Council (UK)
British Museum (Natural History) (UK)
British Music Information Centre (UK)
British Mycological Society (UK)
British National Association for Soviet and East European Studies (UK)
British-National Association of Toy Retailers (UK)
British National Committee for Geodesy and Geophysics. Geodesy Subcommittee. (UK)
British National Export Council (UK)

British Natural Hygiene Society  (UK)
British Naturalists Association  (UK)
British Naturopathic and Osteopathic Association  (UK)
British North America Philatelic Society  (CN)
British-North American Research Association  (UK)
British Nuclear Energy Society  (UK)
British Nuclear Forum  (UK)
British Numismatic Society  (UK)
British Occupational Hygiene Society  (UK)
British Optical Association  (UK)
British Ornithologists' Club  (UK)
British Ornithologists' Union  (UK)
British Orthoptic Society  (UK)
British Paedodontic Society  (UK)
British Paper and Board Industry Federation  (UK)
British Paper and Board Industry Federation. Technical Division  (UK)
British Parachute Association  (UK)
British Peace Committee  (UK)
British Pelagorium and Germanium Society  (UK)
British Petroleum Co. Ltd.  (UK)
British Petroleum Refinery (Aden) Ltd.  (YS)
British Pharmacological Society  (UK)
British Philatelic Federation Ltd.  (UK)
British Photobiology Society  (UK)
British Phycological Journal  (UK)
British Plastics Federation  (UK)
British Polio Fellowship  (UK)
British-Portuguese Chamber of Commerce  (PO)
British Post Office  (UK)
British Printing Industries Federation  (UK)
British Property Federation  (UK)
British Psychological Society  (UK)
British Pteridological Society  (UK)
British Publications, Inc.  (US)
British Puppet and Model Theatre Guild  (UK)
British Quarrying & Slag Federation  (UK)
British Rabbit Council  (UK)
British Racing & Sports Car Club  (UK)
British Railways Board  (UK)
British Records Association  (UK)
British Rheumatism and Arthritis Association  (UK)
British Rubber Manufacturers' Association Ltd.  (UK)
British Safety Council  (UK)
British Sailors' Society  (UK)
British School at Athens  (UK)
British School at Rome  (UK)
British School of Archaeology in Iraq  (UK)
British School of Archaeology in Jerusalem  (UK)
British Schools Exploring Society  (UK)
British Science Fiction Association Ltd.  (UK)
British Ship Research Association  (UK)
British Sign Association  (UK)
British Small Animal Veterinary Association  (UK)
British Social Biology Council  (UK)
British Society for Immunology  (UK)
British Society for Middle East Studies  (UK)
British Society for Middle Eastern Studies  (UK)
British Society for Music Therapy  (UK)
British Society for Phenomenology  (UK)
British Society for Research in Agricultural Engineering  (UK)
British Society for Social Responsibility in Science  (UK)
British Society for Strain Measurement  (UK)
British Society for Surgery of the Hand  (UK)
British Society for the History of Pharmacy  (UK)
British Society for the History of Science  (UK)
British Society for the Philosophy of Science  (UK)
British Society for the Study of Mental Subnormality  (UK)
British Society of Aesthetics  (UK)
British Society of Animal Production  (UK)
British Society of Commerce  (UK)
British Society of Dowsers  (UK)
British Society of Gastroenterology  (UK)
British Society of Rheology  (UK)
British Society of Russian Philately  (UK)
British Society of Soil Science  (UK)
British Society of the Study of Orthodontics  (UK)
British Sociological Association  (UK)
British Solomon Islands. Department of Posts and Telecommunications  (BP)
British South Africa Police  (RH)
British Soviet Friendship Society  (UK)
British Standards Institution  (UK)
British Stationery & Office Products Federation  (UK)
British Steel Corp.  (UK)
British Steel Corp. Corporate Development Laboratory  (UK)
British Steel Corp. Market Promotion Dept.  (UK)
British Steelmaker Ltd.  (UK)
British Stock Car Association  (UK)
British Sugar Corp., Ltd.  (UK)
British Sulphur Corp. Ltd.  (UK)
British Surrealist Group  (UK)

British-Swedish Chamber of Commerce in Sweden  (SW)
British-Swiss Chamber of Commerce in Switzerland  (SZ)
British Tar Industry Association  (UK)
British Textile Confederation  (UK)
British Theatre Association  (UK)
British Theatre Institute  (UK)
British Tourist Authority  (UK)
British Toy Manufacturers Association  (UK)
British Trades Alphabet Ltd.  (UK)
British Transport Docks Board  (UK)
British Trust for Ornithology  (UK)
British Unidentified Flying Object Research Association  (UK)
British Union Conference of Seventh-Day Adventists  (UK)
British Union for the Abolition of Vivisection  (UK)
British Universities Film Council Ltd.  (UK)
British Veterinary Association  (UK)
British Virgin Islands. Finance Department  (VB)
British Watch and Clock Makers Guild  (UK)
British Water Ski Federation  (UK)
British Waterfowl Association  (UK)
British Waterways Board  (UK)
British Women Pilots Association  (UK)
British Women's Temperance Association  (UK)
Brivais Vards  (AT)
Bro- Dart Publishing Co.  (US)
Broadband Information Services, Inc.  (US)
Broadcast Education Association  (US)
Broadcast Information Bureau Inc.  (US)
Broadcast Magazine  (UK)
Broadcast Music Inc.  (US)
Broadcasting Council of New Zealand  (NZ)
Broadcasting Publications, Inc.  (US)
Broadfields (Technical Publishers) Ltd.  (UK)
Broadman Press  (US)
Broadsheet  (US)
Broadsheet Collective  (NZ)
Broadside Press  (US)
Broadsider  (US)
Broadwater Press Ltd.  (UK)
Brock University. Department of Geological Sciences  (CN)
Verlag F.A. Brockhaus  (GW)
R. Brockhaus Verlag  (GW)
Brockhouse Limited  (UK)
Studienverlag Dr. N. Brockmeyer  (GW)
Brodogradnja  (YU)
Bob Broedel Ed. & Pub.  (US)
Broenner-Verlag  (GW)
Broken Hill Proprietary Co., Ltd  (AT)
Brome County Historical Society  (CN)
Bromeliad Society  (US)
Bromeliad Society of Australia  (AT)
Bromley Weekly Review Ltd.  (UK)
Bronfman & Cohen, Publishers Ltd.  (IS)
Bronte Parsonage Museum  (UK)
Bronx Board of Realtors  (US)
Bronx Chamber of Commerce, Inc.  (US)
Bronx Community College. Evening Student Association  (US)
Bronx Council on the Arts Inc.  (US)
Bronx County Dental Society  (US)
Bronx County Historical Society  (US)
Bronx County Medical Society  (US)
Bronx Real Estate and Building News, Inc.  (US)
Bronxville Women's Club, Inc.  (US)
Brookdale Hospital Medical Center  (US)
Simon Brooke and Associates  (SA)
Brookhaven National Laboratory  (US)
Brookings Institution  (US)
Brooklyn Arts and Cultural Association  (US)
Brooklyn Bar Association  (US)
Brooklyn Botanic Garden  (US)
Brooklyn College of the City University of New York  see under City University of New York  (US)
Brooklyn Engineers Club  (US)
Brooklyn Heights Periodicals Inc.  (US)
Brooklyn Insurance Brokers Association  (US)
Brooklyn Law School  (US)
Brooklyn Museum  (US)
Brooklyn Polytechnic Institute  (US)
Brooklyn Polytechnic Institute. Microwave Institute Symposium Committee  (US)
Brooklyn Public Library  (US)
Brooklyn Tuberculosis and Respiratory Disease Association Inc.  (US)
Brooks Bird Club  (US)
Brooks-Cole Publishing Co.  (US)
Brooks Memorial Art Gallery  (US)
Broom and Broom Corn News  (US)
Brophy Preparatory School  (US)
Broteria: Ciencias Naturais  (PO)
Brother  (UK)
Brotherhood of Locomotive Engineers  (US)
Brotherhood of Maintenance of Way Employes  (US)

Brotherhood of Railroad Signalmen  (US)
Brotherhood of Railway, Airline, Steamship Clerks, Freight Handlers, Express and Station Employes  (US)
Brotherhood of Railway Carmen of America  (US)
Brotherhood of Railway Running Trades  (CN)
Brotherhood of St. Herman of Alaska  (US)
Brotherhood of St Laurence  (AT)
Brothers of the Holy Eucharist  (US)
Brown, Boveri & Cie. Aktiengesellschaft  (GW)
Brown, Boveri & Co., Ltd.
  see B B C Brown, Boveri & Co., Ltd.  (SZ)
Wm. C. Brown Company Publishers  (US)
S.E.D. Brown, Ed. & Pub.  (SA)
Brown Gold Publications  (US)
Brown, Son and Ferguson Ltd.  (UK)
Brown Swiss Cattle Breeders Association  (US)
Brown University  (US)
Brown University. Afro-American Studies  (US)
Brown University. Alumni Association  (US)
Brown University Library. Friends of the Library  (US)
Brown University Press  (US)
Brown University. Psychology Department  (US)
Browning Institute, Inc.  (US)
Browning Society of London  (UK)
Michael Bruce Associates  (US)
Bruce County Historical Society  (CN)
Verlag F. Bruckmann KG  (GW)
Bruckner Society of America Inc.  (US)
Brud Nevez  (FR)
Bruderverlag  (GW)
Bruecke  (SA)
Verlag die Bruecke GmbH  (GW)
Bruecke-Museum  (GW)
Bruel og Kjaer Industri A-S  (DK)
J.D. Ter Brugge, Ed. & Pub.  (NE)
Brulot  (FR)
Brunei. State Secretariat. Information Service  (BX)
Brunei Museum  (BX)
Brunel University Students Union  (UK)
Editions Brunier  (FR)
Brunnen-Verlag GmbH  (GW)
Brunner-Mazel, Inc.  (US)
Brunner Verlag  (AU)
Brunner Verlag AG  (SZ)
Brunnquell-Verlag  (GE)
Brunswick Publishing Co.  (US)
Brussels Society for Latin Studies
  see Societe d'Etudes Latines de Bruxelles  (BE)
Etablissements Emile Bruylant  (BE)
Bryan Publications, Inc.  (US)
Bryant Press  (CN)
S.M. Bryde Forlag  (NO)
Bryn Mawr College and Haverford College. Haverford Student Council  (US)
Bryn Mawr College. Career Planning Office  (US)
Bryologisch-Lichenologische Arbeitsgemeinschaft fuer Mittel-Europa  (GW)
Edizioni Bucalo  (IT)
Bucaramanga, Colombia. Camara de Comercio  (CK)
Zeit-Verlag Gerd Bucerius  (GW)
VEB Verlag fuer Buch- und Bibliothekswesen  (GE)
Buchalter-Zeitung  (AU)
Verlag C.J. Bucher AG  (SZ)
Buchexport  (GE)
Buchhaendler-Vereinigung GmbH  (GW)
Libreria Buchholz  (CK)
Hugo Buchser S.A.  (SZ)
B.J. Buck  (US)
Buck Investment Service  (US)
Buckeye Association of School Administrators  (US)
Buckeye Review Publishing Company, Inc  (US)
Buckingham Publishing Co.  (CN)
Buckley Press Ltd.  (UK)
Bucknell University College of Engineering  (US)
Bucks County Bar Association  (US)
Bucks County Planning Commission  (US)
Paul C. Bucy & Associates  (US)
Budapesti Izraelita Hitkozseg  (HU)
Budapesti Muszaki Egyetem  (HU)
Budapesti Muszaki Egyetem. Kozponti Konyvtar  (HU)
BUDAVOX Telecommunication Foreign Trading Company Ltd.  (HU)
Buddhist Bookstore  (US)
Buddhist Missionary Society  (MY)
Buddhist Publication Society  (CE)
Buddhist Publications  (CE)
Buddhist Society  (UK)
Buddhist Vihara Society  (US)
Buddhistisches Kultur- und Meditationszentrum Scheibbs  (AU)
Budgerigar Society  (UK)
Vydavnytstvo Budivelnyk  (UR)
Budo Bond Nederland  (NE)
Budo-Centrum AB  (SW)
Budtail Publishing  (UK)

Buecher-Herzog  (AU)
Buechergilde Gutenberg Verlagsgesellschaft mbH
  (GW)
Verlag Buecherschiff Walter Reutin  (GW)
Buechler und Co. AG  (SZ)
Buehnenschriften-Vertriebs-Gesellschaft  (GW)
Buenos Aires (Province) Direccion de Vialidad  (AG)
Buenos Aires (Province) Direccion Provincial de
  Cultura  (AG)
Buenos Aires Musical  (AG)
Buerger Deutscher Herkunft in Ausland  (GE)
Buero- und Organisationstechnik Verlagsgesellschaft
  Dr. H. Benad  (GW)
Buffalo and Erie County Historical Society  (US)
Buffalo and Erie County Public Library  (US)
Buffalo Area Chamber of Commerce  (US)
Buffalo Fan  (US)
Buffalo Museum of Science  (US)
Buffalo Society of Natural Sciences  (US)
Buhre's Forlag  (NO)
Buijten en Schipperheijn, B. V.  (NE)
Builders Association of Fort Worth & Tarrant County
  (US)
Builders Association of India  (II)
Builders Publications of India (P) Ltd.  (II)
Building & Contract Journals Ltd.  (UK)
Building and Engineering Review  (UK)
Building and Estate Management Society  (SI)
Building & Realty Record  (US)
Building Centre, Bristol  (UK)
Building Centre of Israel  (IS)
Building for Profit  (US)
Building Industries Federation (South Africa)  (SA)
Building Industry Congress of Western Australia
  (AT)
Building News, Inc.  (US)
Building Officials and Code Administrators
  International  (US)
Building Owners & Managers Association International
  (US)
Building Owners Managers Association  (CN)
Building Publishers Ltd.  (UK)
Building Publishing Co. Pty. Ltd.  (AT)
Building Research Advisory Board  (US)
Building Research Institute
  see Japan. Building Research Institute  (JA)
Building Science Forum of Australia  (AT)
Building Services Research and Information
  Association  (UK)
Building Societies Institute  (UK)
Building Stone Institute  (US)
Building Trades Employers Association of the City of
  New York  (US)
Building Workers' Industrial Union of Australia.
  Victorian Branch  (AT)
Buitenlandse Boek  (NE)
Bulgaria. Ministerstvo na Finansite  (BU)
Bulgaria. Ministerstvo na Informatsiiata i
  Suobshteniiata  (BU)
Bulgaria. Ministerstvo na Khimicheska Promishlenost
  (BU)
Bulgaria. Ministerstvo na Lekata Promishlenost  (BU)
Bulgaria. Ministerstvo na Mashinostroeneto i
  Metalurgiiata  (BU)
Bulgaria. Ministerstvo na Narodnata Otbrana  (BU)
Bulgaria. Ministerstvo na Narodnoto Zdrave  (BU)
Bulgaria. Ministerstvo na Stroezhite i Arkhitekturata
  (BU)
Bulgaria. Ministerstvo na Transporta  (BU)
Bulgaria. Ministerstvo na Transporta. Glavno
  Upravlene na Putushtata  (BU)
Bulgaria. Ministerstvo na Vutreshnita Turgoviia i
  Uslugite  (BU)
Bulgaria. Ministerstvo na Zemedelieto i Khranitelna
  Promishlenost  (BU)
Bulgarian Social Democratic Party in Exile  (AU)
Bulgarreklama Agency  (BU)
Bulgarska Akademiia na Naukite  (BU)
Bulgarska Akademiia na Naukite. Mikrobiologicheski
  Institut  (BU)
Bulgarska Akademiia na Naukite. Arkheologicheski
  Institut i Muzei  (BU)
Bulgarska Akademiia na Naukite. Botanicheski Institut
  (BU)
Bulgarska Akademiia na Naukite. Fizicheski i
  Matematicheski Institut  (BU)
Bulgarska Akademiia na Naukite. Geofizichni Institut
  (BU)
Bulgarska Akademiia na Naukite. Geografski Institut
  (BU)
Bulgarska Akademiia na Naukite. Geologicheski
  Institut  (BU)
Bulgarska Akademiia na Naukite. Ikonomicheski
  Institut  (BU)
Bulgarska Akademiia na Naukite. Institut po Filosofiia
  (BU)

Bulgarska Akademiia na Naukite. Institut po Istoriia
  (BU)
Bulgarska Akademiia na Naukite. Institut po
  Khidrologiia i Meteorologiia  (BU)
Bulgarska Akademiia na Naukite. Institut po
  Mikrobiologiia  (BU)
Bulgarska Akademiia na Naukite. Institut po
  Morfologiia  (BU)
Bulgarska Akademiia na Naukite. Institut po Obshta i
  Sravnitelna Patalogiia  (BU)
Bulgarska Akademiia na Naukite. Institut po
  Sotsiologiia  (BU)
Bulgarska Akademiia na Naukite. Institut po
  Tekhnicheska Kibernetika  (BU)
Bulgarska Akademiia na Naukite. Institut po Vodni
  Problemi  (BU)
Bulgarska Akademiia na Naukite. Institut za
  Balkanistika  (BU)
Bulgarska Akademiia na Naukite. Institut za Bulgarski
  Ezik  (BU)
Bulgarska Akademiia na Naukite. Institut za Istoriia
  (BU)
Bulgarska Akademiia na Naukite. Institut za
  Izkustvoznanie  (BU)
Bulgarska Akademiia na Naukite. Institut za Literatura
  (BU)
Bulgarska Akademiia na Naukite. Institut za
  Muzikoznanie  (BU)
Bulgarska Akademiia na Naukite. Institut za Pravni
  Nauki  (BU)
Bulgarska Akademiia na Naukite.
  Nauchnoizsledovatelski Tsentur za Africa i Aziia
  (BU)
Bulgarska Akademiia na Naukite. Sektsiia po
  Astronomiia  (BU)
Bulgarska Akademiia na Naukite. Tsentralna Biblioteka
  (BU)
Bulgarska Akademiia na Naukite. Tsentralna
  Khelmintologichna Laboratoriia  (BU)
Bulgarska Akademiia na Naukite. Tsentralna
  Laboratoriia po Biomekhanika  (BU)
Bulgarska Akademiia na Naukite. Tsentralna
  Laboratoriia po Geodeziia  (BU)
Bulgarska Akademiia na Naukite. Zoologicheski
  Institut  (BU)
Bulgarska Turgovska Promishlena Palata  (BU)
Bulgarski Profesionalni Suiuzi  (BU)
Bulgarsko Istorichesko Druzhestvo  (BU)
Bulkowsky Verlag  (GW)
Hans Bulla und Sohn  (AU)
Bulletin Biologique de la France et de la Belgique
  (FR)
Bulletin de l'Antiquaire et du Brocanteur  (FR)
Bulletin de l'Oeuvre d'Orient  (FR)
Bulletin de Paris  (FR)
Bulletin Europeen de Physiopathologie Respiratoire
  (FR)
Bulletin of Concerned Asian Scholars  (US)
Bulletin Publishing Co.  (US)
Editions des Bulletins Reunis  (FR)
Bullinger's Guides, Inc.  (US)
T.V. Bulpin  (SA)
Bulwer Lytton Circle  (UK)
Bulzoni Editore  (IT)
Bunadarfelag Islands  (IC)
Bund Demokratischer Sozialisten  (AU)
Bund der Berliner und Freunde Berlins e.V.
  Kreisverband Muenchen  (GW)
Bund der Blindenfreunde e.V.  (GW)
Bund der Deutschen Zollbeamten  (GW)
Bund der Fliegergeschaedigten, Evakuierten,
  Waehrungsgeschaedigten  (GW)
Bund der Freien Waldorfschulen e.V.  (GW)
Bund der Ingenieure des Gartenbaues  (GW)
Bund der Kriegsblinden Deutschlands e. V.  (GW)
Bund der Mitteldeutschen  (GW)
Bund der Oeffentlich Bestellten Vermessungsingenieure
  e.V.  (GW)
Bund der Sozialversicherungs-Beamten und -
  Angestellten  (GW)
Bund der Theatergemeinden e.V.  (GW)
Bund der Verfolgten des Naziregimes Berlin e.V.
  (GW)
Bund der Versorgungsbeamten  (GW)
Bund der Vertriebenen. Landesverband Niedersachsen
  e.V.  (GW)
Bund Deutscher Architekten  (GW)
Bund Deutscher Baumeister, Architekten und
  Ingenieure e.V.  (GW)
Bund Deutscher Blasmusikverbaende e.V.  (GW)
Bund Deutscher Champignonzuechter e.V.  (GW)
Bund Deutscher Fallschirmjaeger e.V.  (GW)
Bund Deutscher Forstmaenner  (GW)
Bund Deutscher Forstmaenner. Landesverband Bayern
  e.V.  (GW)
Bund Deutscher Hebammen  (GW)
Bund Deutscher Kriminalbeamter  (GW)
Bund Deutscher Philatelisten e.V.  (GW)

Bund Deutscher Rassegefluegelzuechter e.V.  (GW)
Bund Deutscher Rechtspfleger  (GW)
Bund Deutscher Steuerbeamten  (GW)
Bund Deutscher Taubstummenlehrer  (GW)
Bund Deutscher Zimmermeister  (GW)
Bund Evangelisch-Freikirchlicher Gemeinden  (GW)
Bund Freireligioeser Gemeinden Deutschlands  (GW)
Bund fuer Deutsche Schrift  (GW)
Bund gegen Alkohol im Strassenverkehr e.V.  (GW)
Bund Katholischer Religions Lehrervereinigungen
  (GW)
Bund Sozialistischer Akademiker, Intellektueller und
  Kuenstler  (AU)
Bund Sozialistischer Freiheitskaempfer und Opfer des
  Faschismus  (AU)
Bund und Land  (GW)
Bund und Landesverbaende der Wasser - und
  Kulturbauingenieure  (GW)
Bund-Verlag GmbH  (GW)
Bunda College of Agriculture  (MW)
Bundaberg Newspaper Co  (AT)
Bundes Arbeitsgemeinschaft der Mittel- und
  Grossbetriebe des Einzelhandels e.V.  (GW)
Bundes-Blindenerziehungsinstitut  (AU)
Bundes- und Landesinnungen der Dachdecker  (AU)
Bundes- und Landesinnungen der Glaserer  (AU)
Bundes- und Landesinnungen des Taxigewerbes  (AU)
Bundesaerztekammer  (GW)
Bundesanstalt fuer Alpenlaendische Landwirtschaft
  Gumpenstein  (AU)
Bundesanstalt fuer Pflanzenbau und Samenpruefung
  (AU)
Bundesarbeitsgemeinschaft Hilfe fuer Behinderte
  (GW)
Bundesarchitektenkammer  (GW)
Bundesberufsgruppen des Landmaschinenhandels und
  Landmaschinenhandwerks Oesterreichs  (AU)
Bundesfachgruppe fuer Zahn-,Mund-und
  Kieferheilkunde  (AU)
Bundesfachverband Fleischereibedarf- Grosshandel
  e.V., Wuppertal  (GW)
Bundesfachverband fuer Grosskuechen  (GW)
Bundesforschungsanstalt fuer Fischerei  (GW)
Bundesgewerbeverband Imbissbetriebe E. V.  (GW)
Bundesgremium fuer Schulphotographie  (GW)
Bundesgrosshandelsverband fuer Uhren- und
  Uhrentechnischen Bedarf e.V.  (GW)
Bundesholzwirtschaftsrat  (GW)
Bundesinnung der Cafetiers  (AU)
Bundesinnung der Chemischreiniger, Waescher und
  Faerber  (AU)
Bundesinnung der Elektrotechniker und
  Radiomechaniker  (AU)
Bundesinnung der Kraftfahrzeugmechaniker  (AU)
Bundesinnung der Mechaniker  (AU)
Bundesinnung der Schuhmacher  (AU)
Bundesinnung der Zahntechniker  (AU)
Bundesinnung des Wirtschaftlichen Werbewesens
  (AU)
Bundesinnung und Landesinnung der Tischler
  Oesterreichs  (AU)
Bundesinnung und Landesinnungen der Installateure
  Oesterreichs  (AU)
Bundesinnungsverband des Gebaeudereiniger-
  Handwerks  (GW)
Bundesinnungsverband des
  Orthopaedieschuhmacherhandwerks  (GW)
Bundesinstitut fuer Berufsbildungsforschung  (GW)
Bundesinstitut fuer Ostwissenschaftliche und
  Internationale Studien  (GW)
Bundesinstitut fuer Sportwissenschaft  (GW)
Bundeskammer der Gewerblichen Wirtschaft  (AU)
Bundeskammer der Tieraerzte Oesterreichs  (AU)
Bundeskonvikt Wien  (AU)
Bundesnotarkammer  (GW)
Bundesobstbauverband Oesterreichs  (AU)
Bundesstelle fuer Aussenhandelsinformation
  see under Germany, Federal Republic  (GW)
Bundessteuerberaterkammer  (GW)
Bundesverband der Agraringenieure (BAI) e.V.  (GW)
Bundesverband der Betriebskrankenkassen  (GW)
Bundesverband der Deutschen Binnenschiffahrt E.V.
  (GW)
Bundesverband der Deutschen Brot- und
  Backwarenindustrie e.V  (GW)
Bundesverband der Deutschen Ernaehrungsindustrie
  (GW)
Bundesverband der Deutschen Feinkostindustrie e. V.
  (GW)
Bundesverband der Deutschen Fleischwarenindustrie
  e.V.  (GW)
Bundesverband der Deutschen Gas- und
  Wasserwirtschaft  (GW)
Bundesverband der Deutschen Industrie  (GW)
Bundesverband der Deutschen Schrottwirtschaft
  (GW)
Bundesverband der Deutschen Standesbeamten e.V
  (GW)

Bundesverband der Deutschen Zahnaerzte e.V. (GW)
Bundesverband der Deutschen Ziegelindustrie e.V.
  (GW)
Bundesverband der Dolmetscher und Uebersetzer e. V.
  (GW)
Bundesverband der Erwerbsgaertner Oesterreichs
  (AU)
Bundesverband der Innungskrankenkassen (GW)
Bundesverband der Lehrer an Beruflichen Schulen
  (GW)
Bundesverband der Naturstein-Industrie (GW)
Bundesverband der Ortskrankenkassen (GW)
Bundesverband der Soldaten der ehemaligen Waffen-
  SS e.V. (GW)
Bundesverband der Weinbautreibenden Oesterreichs
  (AU)
Bundesverband des Deutschen Farbengrosshandels
  (GW)
Bundesverband des Deutschen Gueternah- und
  Gueterfernverkehrs (GW)
Bundesverband des Deutschen Gueterverkehrs e.V
  (GW)
Bundesverband des Deutschen
  Personenverkehrsgewerbes (GW)
Bundesverband des Deutschen Schuheinzelhandels
  (GW)
Bundesverband des Deutschen Seiler-, Segel-und
  Netzmacherhandwerks e.V. (GW)
Bundesverband des Deutschen Textileinzelhandels e.V.
  (GW)
Bundesverband des Elektro-Grosshandels (VEG) e.V.
  (GW)
Bundesverband des Schmuckwarengrosshandels
  (GW)
Bundesverband des Werbenden Buch- und
  Zeitschriftenhandels E.V. (GW)
Bundesverband Deutschen Beton- und Fertigteil-
  Industrie (GW)
Bundesverband Deutscher Banken e.V. (GW)
Bundesverband Deutscher Baustoffhaendler e.V.
  (GW)
Bundesverband Deutscher Kleingaertner e.V. (GW)
Bundesverband Deutscher Mittelstandsbrauereien e.V.
  (GW)
Bundesverband Deutscher Stahlhandel (GW)
Bundesverband Deutscher Versicherungskaufleute
  (BVK) (GW)
Bundesverband Deutscher Volks- und Betriebswirte
  e.V. (GW)
Bundesverband Deutscher Zeitungsverleger (GW)
Bundesverband Druck e.V. (GW)
Bundesverband Freischaffender Architekten und
  Bauingenieure e.V. (GW)
Bundesverband fuer den Selbstschutz (GW)
Bundesverband fuer Spastisch Gelaehmte und andere
  Koerperbehinderte e.V. (GW)
Bundesverband Materialwirtschaft und Einkauf e.V.
  (GW)
Bundesverband Metall (GW)
Bundesverband Oelfeuerungen und Gasfeuerungen E.
  V. (GW)
Bundesverband Oesterreichischer Widerstandskaempfer
  und Opfer des Faschismus (AU)
Bundesverband Ring Deutscher Makler (RDM) E.V
  (GW)
Bundesvereinigung der Deutschen
  Arbeitgeberverbaende e.V. (GW)
Bundesvereinigung Evangelischer Eltern und Erzieher
  E.V (GW)
Bundesvereinigung Lebenshilfe fuer Geistig Behinderte
  e.V (GW)
Bundesversicherungsanstalt fuer Angestellte. Dezernat
  fuer Presse- und Oeffentlichkeitsarbeit (GW)
Bundesvorstand des FDGB (GE)
Bundesvorstand des Sozialistischen Hochschulbundes
  (GW)
Deutscher Bundeswehr-Verlag GmbH (GW)
Bundeszentrale fuer Politische Bildung (GW)
Bunhill Publications Ltd. (UK)
Bunrin-do Co. Ltd. (JA)
Bunsengesellschaft fuer Physikalische Chemie (GW)
Bunting and Lyon (US)
Verlag Aenne Burda (GW)
Burda Verlag GmbH (GW)
Burdick Enterprises (US)
Bureau a Tours (FR)
Bureau d'Etudes Cooperatives et Communautaires
  (FR)
Bureau d'Etudes et de Recherches Theoriques
  (BERTHE) (FR)
Bureau d'Informations et de Previsions Economiques
  (B. I. P. E.) (FR)
Bureau des Relations Exterieures et Sociales (FR)
Bureau des Relations Publiques de l'Industrie Sucriere
  see Public Relations Office of the Sugar Industry
  (MF)
Bureau Dienstverlening Overlegorganen (NE)
Bureau Dit (NE)

Bureau Ellens (NE)
Bureau et Informatique (FR)
Bureau Euristop (EI)
Bureau for International Language Coordination
  (UK)
Bureau International d'Education
  see Unesco. International Bureau of Education
  (UN)
Bureau International de l'Heure (FR)
Bureau International de Liaison et de Documentation
  (FR)
Bureau International de Relations Publiques (FR)
Bureau International des Containers (FR)
Bureau International des Poids et Mesures (FR)
Bureau International des Societes Gerant les Droits
  d'Enregistrement et de Reproduction Mecanique
  (FR)
Bureau International du Travail
  see International Labour Office (UN)
Bureau Issue Association (US)
Bureau of Business Practice (US)
Bureau of Educational and Psychological Research
  (II)
Bureau of Foreign Languages (US)
Bureau of Hygiene and Tropical Diseases (UK)
Bureau of Lebanese and Arab Documentation (LE)
Bureau of Medical Practitioner Affairs Ltd. (UK)
Bureau of National Affairs, Inc. (US)
Bureau of Social Science Research Inc. (US)
Bureau of Sugar Experiment Stations (AT)
Bureau Universitaire de Recherche Operationnelle
  (FR)
Bureau van Vliet B.V. (NE)
Bureau Veritas (FR)
Burgen- und Schloessererhaltungsverein (AU)
Burgenlaendische Gemeinschaft (AU)
Burgenland. Amt der Burgenlaendischen
  Landesregierung (AU)
Burgenland. Burgenlaendische Landwirtschaftskammer
  (AU)
Burgenland Verlag, G.m.b.H. (AU)
Burgess Publishing Co. (US)
Hans Burghagen Verlag (GW)
Buri Druck und Verlag (SZ)
Louis Burke (CN)
Alan Burke Inc. (US)
Edgar P. Burke (US)
Burke House Periodicals Ltd. (UK)
Burke's Peerage Ltd. (UK)
Burleigh Press Ltd. (UK)
Burlington Magazine Publications Ltd. (UK)
Burlington Publishing Company(1942) Ltd. (UK)
Burma Medical Association (BR)
Burmah Oil Trading Ltd (UK)
Eric Burmann, Ed. & Pub. (FR)
Burnard Printing Co. (CN)
Burnham Corporation. Lord & Burnham Division
  (US)
John S. Burns and Sons (UK)
Burns Federation (UK)
Burrelle's Press Clipping Service (US)
Burroughs Bibliophiles (US)
Burroughs Corp. (US)
Burroughs Wellcome Co. (US)
J. Burrow & Co. Ltd. (UK)
Roy Douglass Burrow, Ed. & Pub. (US)
Burundi. Departement de la Presse (BD)
Burundi. Secretariat General a la Presidence Charge du
  Bureau Technique d'Etudes. Department des Etudes
  et Statistiques (BD)
Bush League (US)
Bush Music Club (AT)
Aubrey Bush Publications (UK)
Bushell Publishing Co. Pty. Ltd. (AT)
Business & Economics Book Guide (US)
Business and Industry (US)
Business and Industry: Taiwan (CH)
Business and Professional People for the Public
  Interest (US)
Business Books Ltd. (UK)
Business Borrower (US)
Business Committee for the Arts, Inc. (US)
Business Communications (US)
Business Communications Co., Inc. (Stamford) (US)
Business Communications, Inc. (US)
Business Communications Review (US)
Business Extension Bureau (US)
Business Graduates Association (UK)
Business Guides, Inc. (US)
Business-Industry Political Action Committee. Political
  Education Division (US)
Business Intercommunication, Inc. (JA)
Business International Asia-Pacific (HK)
Business International Corp. (US)
Business International S.A. (SZ)
Business Journals, Inc. (US)
Business Journals of America, Inc. (US)

Business Masters International (PH)
Business News Publishing Co. (US)
Business Press, Inc. (US)
Business Press Ltd. (HK)
Business Press Private Ltd. (II)
Business Publications, Inc. (US)
Business Publications International (II)
Business Publications Ltd. (HK)
Business Publications Service (US)
Business Publicity Ltd. (TH)
Business Publishers, Inc. (US)
Business Review (TH)
Business Science Corporation (US)
Business Surveys Ltd. (UK)
Business Systems & Equipment (UK)
Business Trends (PH)
Business Week Holdings Ltd (SA)
Business West Publishing Co (US)
Business World Inc. (US)
Businessman (II)
Verlag Helmut Buske (GW)
Bussei Kenkyusho
  see University of Tokyo. Institute for Solid State
  Physics (JA)
J. H. de Bussy (NE)
De Bussy, Eilerman Harms N. V. (NE)
Bust Press (CN)
Bustamante Press, Inc. (PH)
Butane-Propane News, Inc. (US)
Butcher Workman Educational and Benevolent
  Association, Inc. (US)
Michael Butler & Kemble Williams, Eds. & Pubs.
  (UK)
Butt Press (US)
Butte County Historical Society (US)
Buttenheim Publishing Corp. (US)
Butterfly (FR)
Butterick Fashion Marketing Co. (US)
Butterick Fashion Marketing Co. Butterick Pattern
  Service (US)
Butterworth & Co.(Canada) Ltd. (CN)
Butterworth & Co. (Publishers) Ltd. (UK)
Butterworth & Co. (South Africa) (Pty.) Ltd. (SA)
Butterworths of New Zealand Ltd. (NZ)
Butterworths Pty. Ltd. (AT)
Buttonwood Farms, Inc. (US)
Verlag Butzon und Bercker (GW)
Buxom Belles International, Inc. (US)
Buyer's Guide to Indian Art (US)
Buyers Laboratory, Inc. (US)
Buyers Market of Canada (CN)
Buyers Purchasing Digest (US)
Buzz Christian Ministries (UK)
Foerlaget By och Bygd (SW)
Byblos Productions Ltd. (UK)
Bydgoskie Towarzystwo Naukowe (PL)
Byelorussian American Association, Inc. (US)
Byelorussian-American Union (US)
Byelorussian-American Youth Organization (US)
Byelorussian Institute of Arts and Sciences, Inc. (US)
Byelorussian Literary Association (CN)
Byelorussian Times (US)
Byers Associates (CN)
Bygge Fagene (DK)
Byggenytt (NO)
Byggfoerlaget (SW)
AB Byggmaestarens Foerlag (SW)
Byggnadsingenjoren- Team (SW)
Foerlags AB Tidning Foer Byggnadskonst (SW)
Byggnadsvaerlden AB (SW)
Byomkes Chakrabarti (II)
Byron Society Journal Ltd. (UK)
Byte Publications, Inc. (US)
Byways (UK)
C A E Industries Ltd. (CN)
Editions C A M (FR)
Edizioni C A M (IT)
Editions C A M S (FR)
C A P News, Inc. (US)
Editions C A S C (CN)
C & P Research, Inc. (US)
C B A International (JA)
C.B.D. Research Ltd. (UK)
C B I
  see Cement- och Betonginstitutet (SW)
C B I A Service Corp. (US)
C B Media Limited (CN)
C B S Consumer Publishing-West (US)
C B S Publications. Popular Magazine Group (US)
C B-Verlag Carl Boldt
C C F Publishing and Printing Co. Ltd. (CN)
C C H Australia Ltd. (AT)
C C H Canadian Ltd. (CN)
Edizioni C D (IT)
C D P Information and Intelligence Unit (UK)
Ediciones C E A C (SP)
C E C A

*see* European Coal and Steel Community.
Consultative Committee (EI)
Edizioni C.E.D.A.M.
*see* Casa Editrice Dott. Antonio /Milani (IT)
C. E. D. I. (FR)
C E D I P S (SZ)
C E D-Samsom, N.V. (BE)
C E E A
*see* European Atomic Energy Community (EI)
C E Enterprises Inc. (US)
C.E.L. (FR)
C E L A D E
*see* United Nations. Centro Latinoamericano de
Demografia (UN)
C. E. P.
*see* Compagnie Europeenne d'Editions (FR)
C E P A L
*see* United Nations Economic Commission for Latin
America (UN)
C. E. R. B. O. M.
*see* Centre d'Etudes et de Recherches de Biologie et
d'Oceanographie Medicale (C. E. R. B. O. M.)
(FR)
C.E.R.E.S.
*see* Universite de Tunis. Centre d'Etudes et de
Recherches Economiques et Sociales (TI)
C E R N
*see* European Organization for Nuclear Research
(SZ)
C E S E S (IT)
Edizioni C E S I (IT)
C E S P E T R O L (IT)
C.E.S. Publishing Corp. (US)
C.E.T.I.A.T. (FR)
C E T I S A
*see* Compania Espanola de Editoriales
Technologicas Internacionales, S.A. (SP)
C F D T (FR)
C. F. E.
*see* Compagnie Francaise d'Editions (FR)
C F F S Index Committee (CN)
C F P Publications, Ltd. (CN)
C. G. Jung Foundation for Analytical Psychology, Inc.
(US)
C. G. Jung Institute of Los Angeles, Inc. (US)
C. H. E. A. R., Inc (US)
Editions C.I.B. (BE)
C. I. B. (FR)
C I B-N A C M Corp. (US)
C I D E L T (FR)
C I D E S A
*see* International Centre for African Social and
Economic Documentation (BE)
Empresa C I L U de Jornalismo (BL)
C I N T E R F O R
*see* Centro Interamericano de Investigacion y
Documentacion Sobre Formacion Profesional (UY)
C.I.R. (IT)
C I R E S (IV)
C I R I E C
*see* International Centre of Research and
Information on Public and Cooperative Economy
(BE)
C I R P
*see* International Institution for Production
Engineering Research (SZ)
C I S
*see* International Labour Office. International
Occupational Safety and Health Information Centre
(UN)
C.I.S.E. S.p.A. (IT)
C I S I A
*see* Centro Italiano Sviluppo Impeighi Acciaio (IT)
C.I.S.L. (IT)
Editrice C.I.S.P.E.L. (IT)
C M G Publications (US)
C M N Publications (US)
C M P Publications, Inc. (US)
C M R (II)
C.N.A. (HK)
C.N.A. Publications (UK)
Editions C.N.C. (FR)
C. N. D. P. - Documentation Migrants (FR)
C. N. R. A. (FR)
C O F I E C (EC)
C O M A (Year Book) Ltd. (UK)
C O P A (CN)
C O R E Publications (US)
C O R E S T A (FR)
C O S M E P, Inc. (US)
C O S M I C (US)
C P C Communications, Inc. (US)
C Q (US)
Editora C Q, Ltda. (BL)
C Q Publishing Co. (JA)
C R C Press, Inc. (US)
C R E

*see* Standing Conference of Rectors and Vice-
Chancellors of the European Universities (SZ)
C R E D R Corp. (US)
C. R. E. E. (FR)
C. R. E. S. (FR)
C R I & P Railroad Co. (US)
C R I C
*see* Centre National de Recherches Scientifiques et
Techniques pour l'Industrie Cimentiere (BE)
C S A Press (US)
C S I Press, Inc. (US)
C. S. I. R.
*see* India. Council of Scientific and Industrial
Research (II)
C. S. I. R. O. (AT)
C. S. I. R. O. Division of Animal Health (AT)
C. S. I. R. O. Division of Animal Production (AT)
C. S. I. R. O. Division of Applied Geomechanics
(AT)
C. S. I. R. O. Division of Applied Mineralogy (AT)
C. S. I. R. O. Division of Atmospheric Physics (AT)
C. S. I. R. O. Division of Building Research (AT)
C. S. I. R. O. Division of Chemical Technology (AT)
C. S. I. R. O. Division of Computing Research (AT)
C. S. I. R. O. Division of Entomology (AT)
C. S. I. R. O. Division of Fisheries and Oceanography
(AT)
C.S.I.R.O. Division of Food Research (AT)
C. S. I. R. O. Division of Forest Research (AT)
C. S. I. R. O. Division of Horticultural Research
(AT)
C.S.I.R.O. Division of Irrigation Research (AT)
C. S. I. R. O. Division of Land Use Research (AT)
C. S. I. R. O. Division of Mathematical Statistics
(AT)
C. S. I. R. O. Division of Mechanical Engineering
(AT)
C. S. I. R. O. Division of Plant Industry (AT)
C. S. I. R. O. Division of Radiophysics (AT)
C. S. I. R. O. Division of Soils (AT)
C. S. I. R. O. Division of Textile Physics (AT)
C. S. I. R. O. Division of Tropical Pastures (AT)
C.S.I.R.O. Division of Wildlife Research (AT)
C. S. I. R. O. Forest Products Laboratory (AT)
C. S. I. R. O. Marine Biochemistry Unit (AT)
C.S.I.R.O. Minerals Research Laboratories (AT)
C. S. I. R. O. National Measurement Laboratory
(AT)
C. S. I. R. O. National Standards Laboratory (AT)
C. S. I. R. O. Wheat Research Unit (AT)
C. S. I. R. O. Wool Research Laboratories (AT)
C S M Marketing, Inc. (US)
C. S. Publications Ltd. (UK)
C.S.R. Building Materials (AT)
C S S R (IT)
C T B-McGraw Hill (US)
C T Corporation System (US)
C. T. I. C. M.
*see* Centre Technique Industrial de la Construction
Metallique (FR)
C T R Publications (CN)
C V J M Gesamtverband in Deutschland e.V. C V J
M- Westbund (GW)
C V 2 (CN)
Cab Stand (US)
Cabaret Co. (US)
Cabildo Insular de Gran Canaria, las Palmas (SP)
Cable Communications Corp. (US)
Cable Television Association of Great Britain (UK)
Cable TV World, Inc. (US)
Cablecommunications Resource Center (US)
Cabon Publishing Co. Pty Ltd. (AT)
Cacciatore Siciliano (IT)
Cactus and Succulent Society of Great Britain (UK)
Cactus Inc. (CN)
Cactus Place (UK)
Cactus Press (US)
Cactus Publications (II)
Cadbury Ltd. (UK)
Cadernos de Biblioteconomia, Arquivistica e
Documentacao (PO)
Gruppo Editoriale Cadmos (IT)
Caducee (FR)
Editions le Caducee, Inc. (CN)
Caedmon Literature (US)
Cafeteria (US)
Caffe (IT)
Forlaget Cahier (DK)
Cahier de l'Humanisme Libertaire (FR)
Cahiers Bretons (FR)
Cahiers Bruxellois (BE)
Cahiers de l'Homme Espirit (FR)
Editions des Cahiers de la Ceramique (FR)
Cahiers de la Cinematheque (FR)
Cahiers de la Renaissance Vaudoise (SZ)
Editons Cahiers de la Republique (FR)
Cahiers de Litterature et de Poesie: Poetes et Leurs
Amis (FR)

Cahiers des Ingenieurs Agronomes (FR)
Cahiers du Medecin Specialiste (FR)
Cahiers du Yachting (FR)
Cahiers Fiscaux Europeens (FR)
Cahiers Franco-Ecossais de Normandie (FR)
Cahiers Medicaux de France (FR)
Cahiers Pierre Loti (FR)
Cahners Publishing Co., Inc. (US)
Cahners Publishing Co., Inc. (Boston) (US)
Caim (US)
Cairngorm Club (UK)
Cairnmillar Institute (AT)
Cairns Folk Club (AT)
Cairo Chamber of Commerce (UA)
Caisse Nationale des Monuments Historiques (FR)
Caja Central de Ahorros y Prestamos. Seccion
Estadistica (CL)
Caja de Ahorros de Ronda (SP)
Caja de Ahorros y Monte de Piedad de las Baleares
(SP)
Caja de Ahorros y Monte de Piedad de Zaragoza
(SP)
Caja de Credito Agrario, Industrial y Minero (CK)
Cajal Club (US)
Cal-Neva Wildlife (US)
Michele Calabrese, Ed. & Pub. (IT)
Calabria - Domani (IT)
Calabria Letteraria (IT)
Calatomic (US)
Calavo Growers of California (US)
Alberto Calcagno, Ed. & Pub. (IT)
Calcutta. Superintendent of Printing (II)
Calcutta Historical Society (II)
Calcutta Management Association (II)
Calcutta Mathematical Society (II)
Calcutta Medical Club (II)
Calcutta Motor Dealers' Association (II)
Calcutta Press (P) Ltd. (II)
Calcutta Retail Dealer's Samity (II)
Calcutta Statistical Association (II)
Calcutta University
*see* University of Calcutta (II)
Calcutta University Press
*see also* University of Calcutta (II)
Calcutta University Press (II)
John Calder (Publishers) Ltd. (UK)
Caldwell Communications, Inc. (US)
Caledon Venster Printing Works (Pty.) Ltd. (SA)
Calendar Magazines Ltd. (UK)
Calf News, Inc. (US)
Calgary Aquarium Society (CN)
Calgary Fish and Game Association (CN)
Calgary Indian Friendship Centre (CN)
Calgary Livestock Market Journal (CN)
Calgary Sports Car Club (CN)
Calgary Zoological Society (CN)
Calgon Corporation (US)
Calico Museum of Textiles (II)
Calicut University
*see* University of Calicut (II)
California. Administrative Office of the California
Courts (US)
California. Air Resources Board (US)
California. Attorney General's Office (US)
California. Commission on the Status of Women
(US)
California. Department of Aging (US)
California. Department of Commerce (US)
California. Department of Commerce. Division of
International Trade (US)
California. Department of Consumer Affairs.
Contractor's State License Board (US)
California. Department of Corporations (US)
California. Department of Education (US)
California. Department of Education. Bureau of
Publications (US)
California. Department of Education. Bureau of School
Apportionments and Reports (US)
California. Department of Education. Gifted and
Talented Education Management Team (US)
California. Department of Education. Office of
Program Evaluation and Research (US)
California. Department of Fish and Game (US)
California. Department of Food and Agriculture.
Division of Plant Industry (US)
California. Department of Forestry (US)
California. Department of Health. Bureau of Maternal
and Child Health (US)
California. Department of Health. Comprehensive
Health Planning Program (US)
California. Department of Health. Facilities Licensing
Section (US)
California. Department of Health. Vector and Waste
Management (US)
California. Department of Housing and Community
Development (US)
California. Department of Industrial Relations (US)

Camberwell Council on Alcoholism   (UK)
Cambridge Entomological Club   (US)
Cambridge Group for History of Population and Social
   Structure   (UK)
Cambridge Historical Society   (UK)
Cambridge Institute of Education   (UK)
Cambridge Medical Publication Ltd.   (UK)
Cambridge Philological Society   (UK)
Cambridge Philosophical Society   (UK)
Cambridge Quarterly   (UK)
Cambridge Scientific Abstracts, Inc.   (US)
Cambridge University   (UK)
Cambridge University. Cambridge School of
   Architecture   (UK)
Cambridge University. Department of Architecture
   (UK)
Cambridge University Engineering Society   (UK)
Cambridge University. Institute of Criminology   (UK)
Cambridge University. Law Faculty   (UK)
Cambridge University Library   (UK)
Cambridge University. Library Management Research
   Unit   (UK)
Cambridge University Mathematical Society   (UK)
Cambridge University Medical Society   (UK)
Cambridge University. Middle East Centre   (UK)
Cambridge University Press   (UK)
Cambridgeshire & Isle of Ely Naturalists Trust   (UK)
Cambridgeshire Life Ltd.   (UK)
Camden County Record   (US)
Camden History Society   (UK)
Paul Camelio, Pub.   (FR)
Camels Coming Newsletter   (US)
Camera Club   (UK)
Camera di Comercio Industria, Artigianato e
   Agricoltura di Reggio Emilia   (IT)
Camera di Commercio di Asti   (IT)
Camera di Commercio Industria, Artigianato e
   Agricoltura Ancona   (IT)
Camera di Commercio, Industria, Artigianato e
   Agricoltura della Spezia   (IT)
Camera di Commercio Industria Artigianato e
   Agricoltura di Arezzo   (IT)
Camera di Commercio Industria Artigianato e
   Agricoltura di Belluno   (IT)
Camera di Commercio, Industria, Artigianato e
   Agricoltura di Brindisi   (IT)
Camera di Commercio Industria Artigianato e
   Agricoltura di Cuneo   (IT)
Camera di Commercio, Industria, Artigianato e
   Agricoltura di Ferrara   (IT)
Camera di Commercio Industria Artigianato e
   Agricoltura di Forli   (IT)
Camera di Commercio Industria Artigianato e
   Agricoltura di Livorno   (IT)
Camera di Commercio Industria Artigianato e
   Agricoltura di Milano   (IT)
Camera di Commercio, Industria, Artigianato e
   Agricoltura di Padova   (IT)
Camera di Commercio Industria Artigianato e
   Agricoltura di Palermo   (IT)
Camera di Commercio Industria Artigianato e
   Agricoltura di Pavia   (IT)
Camera di Commercio Industria, Artigianato e
   Agricoltura di Perugia   (IT)
Camera di Commercio Industria Artigianato e
   Agricoltura di Roma   (IT)
Camera di Commercio Industria Artigianato e
   Agricoltura di Teramo   (IT)
Camera di Commercio Industria Artigianato e
   Agricoltura di Torino   (IT)
Camera di Commercio Industria Artigianato e
   Agricoltura di Trento   (IT)
Camera di Commercio Industria Artigianato e
   Agricoltura di Treviso   (IT)
Camera di Commercio Industria Artigianato e
   Agricoltura di Venezia   (IT)
Camera di Commercio Industria Artigianato e
   Agricoltura, Modena   (IT)
Camera di Commercio Industria, Artiginato e
   Agricoltura di Pesaro   (IT)
Camera di Commercio Industria e Agricoltura di
   Cagliari   (IT)
Camera di Commercio Industria e Agricoltura di
   Firenze   (IT)
Camera di Commercio Industria e Agricoltura di
   Mantova   (IT)
Camera di Commercio Industria e Agricoltura di
   Reggio Emilia   (IT)
Camera Francese di Commercio ed Industria in Italia
   (IT)
Camera Thirty-Five   (US)
CamerArt, Inc.   (JA)
Kenneth W. Cameron   (US)
Quentin Cameron, Ed. & Pub.   (AT)
Cameroon. Bureau Information Presse de Forces
   Armees   (CM)

Cameroon. Department of Statistics and National
   Accounts   (CM)
Cameroon. Direction des Affaires Culturelle   (CM)
Cameroon. Direction des Mines et de la Geologie
   (CM)
Cameroon. Regie Nationale des Chemins de Fer
   (CM)
Cameroon. Service d'Hydrometeorologie   (CM)
Cameroon Development Corporation   (CM)
Rosso Pio Camillo, Ed. & Pub.   (IT)
Cammino   (IT)
Cammino Economico   (IT)
Camp de l'Arpa   (SP)
Camp Fire Girls, Inc.   (US)
Campagnie Internationale d'Editions Populaires   (BE)
Campaign Associates   (US)
Campaign for Comprehensive Education   (UK)
Campaign for Nuclear Disarmament   (UK)
Campaign Publications   (SA)
Campaigner Publications, Inc.   (US)
Campana Contra el Hambre en el Mundo   (SP)
Alex N. Campbell, Jr.   (US)
Camper's Guide to Area Campgrounds   (US)
Campground Marketing Associates   (US)
Campgrounds Unlimited   (US)
Campi & C. S.p.A.   (IT)
Campillos Ltd.   (UK)
Campina Grande, Brazil. Comissao Cultural do
   Municipio Prefeitura   (BL)
Campinas, Brazil. Instituto Agronomico. Servico de
   Divulgacao Tecnico-Cientifica   (BL)
Camping & Sports Equipment Ltd.   (UK)
Camping Club of Great Britain and Ireland Ltd.
   (UK)
Campo   (BL)
Campo   (MX)
Editrice Il Campo   (IT)
Campus Communications, Inc.   (US)
Campus Crusade for Christ   (US)
Campus Publications, Inc.   (US)
Can-Am Media, Inc.   (US)
Can Manufacturers Institute   (US)
Canada. Agriculture Canada. Animal Research
   Institute   (CN)
Canada. Agriculture Canada. Economics Branch
   (CN)
Canada. Agriculture Canada. Experimental Farm
   (CN)
Canada. Agriculture Canada. Information Division
   (CN)
Canada. Agriculture Canada. International Liaison
   Service   (CN)
Canada. Agriculture Canada. Library   (CN)
Canada. Agriculture Canada. Market Information
   Service   (CN)
Canada. Agriculture Canada. Pesticide Technical
   Information Office   (CN)
Canada. Agriculture Canada. Research Branch   (CN)
Canada. Agriculture Canada. Research Institute   (CN)
Canada. Agriculture Canada. Research Program
   Services   (CN)
Canada. Agriculture Canada. Research Station   (CN)
Canada. Air Pollution Control Directorate   (CN)
Canada. Anti-Dumping Tribunal   (CN)
Canada. Atmospheric Environment Service   (CN)
Canada. Bureau of Intellectual Property   (CN)
Canada. Canadian Penitentiary Service. National
   Parole Service   (CN)
Canada. Centre for Inland Waters   (CN)
Canada. Centre for Mineral and Energy Technology
   (CN)
Canada. Commissioner of Official Languages   (CN)
Canada. Correctional Investigator   (CN)
Canada. Department of Agriculture   (CN)
Canada. Department of Agriculture. Economics
   Branch   (CN)
Canada. Department of Agriculture. Food Research
   Institute   (CN)
Canada. Department of Agriculture. Health of Animals
   Branch   (CN)
Canada. Department of Agriculture. Information
   Division   (CN)
Canada. Department of Agriculture. Microbiology
   Research Institute   (CN)
Canada. Department of Agriculture. Poultry Division
   & Markets Information Section   (CN)
Canada. Department of Communications. Engineering
   Support Division   (CN)
Canada. Department of Communications. Information
   Services   (CN)
Canada. Department of Consumer & Corporate Affairs
   (CN)
Canada. Department of Consumer and Corporate
   Affairs. Patent Office   (CN)

Canada. Department of Energy, Mines and Resources
   (CN)
Canada. Department of Energy, Mines and Resources.
   Energy Policy Sector   (CN)
Canada. Department of Energy, Mines and Resources.
   Mineral Development Sector   (CN)
Canada. Department of External Affairs   (CN)
Canada. Department of Finance   (CN)
Canada. Department of Indian and Northern Affairs
   (CN)
Canada. Department of Industry, Trade and
   Commerce   (CN)
Canada. Department of Industry, Trade and
   Commerce. Office of Design   (CN)
Canada. Department of Labour   (CN)
Canada. Department of Labour. Collective Bargaining
   Division   (CN)
Canada. Department of Labour. Women's Bureau
   (CN)
Canada. Department of Manpower and Immigration
   (CN)
Canada. Department of Manpower and Immigration.
   Economic Analysis and Forecasts Branch   (CN)
Canada. Department of Manpower and Immigration.
   Pacific Region Office   (CN)
Canada. Department of Manpower and Immigration.
   Regional Economic Services Branch   (CN)
Canada. Department of Manpower and Immigration.
   Strategic Planning and Research   (CN)
Canada. Department of National Defence   (CN)
Canada. Department of National Health and Welfare
   (CN)
Canada. Department of National Health and Welfare.
   Fitness and Amateur Sport Branch   (CN)
Canada. Department of National Health and Welfare.
   Health Programs Branch   (CN)
Canada. Department of National Health and Welfare.
   Library   (CN)
Canada. Department of National Revenue. Customs
   and Excise Branch   (CN)
Canada. Department of Regional Economic Expansion
   (CN)
Canada. Department of Transport. Marine
   Telecommunications & Electronics Branch   (CN)
Canada. Department of Transport. Public Affairs
   Branch   (CN)
Canada. Department of Veterans Affairs   (CN)
Canada. Earth Physics Branch. Division of Seismology
   (CN)
Canada. Eastern Forest Products Laboratory   (CN)
Canada. Fisheries and Environment Canada (CN)
Canada. Fisheries and Environment Canada. Canadian
   Environmental Advisory Council   (CN)
Canada. Fisheries and Environment Canada. Canadian
   Forestry Service   (CN)
Canada. Fisheries and Environment Canada. Canadian
   Wildlife Service   (CN)
Canada. Fisheries and Environment Canada. Fisheries
   and Marine Service   (CN)
Canada. Fisheries and Environment Canada. Fisheries
   Management   (CN)
Canada. Fisheries and Environment Canada. Forest
   Fire Research Institute   (CN)
Canada. Fisheries and Environment Canada. Forest
   Management Institute   (CN)
Canada. Fisheries and Environment Canada. Inland
   Waters Directorate   (CN)
Canada. Fisheries and Environment Canada. Insect
   Pathology Research Institute   (CN)
Canada. Fisheries and Environment Canada. Lands
   Directorate   (CN)
Canada. Fisheries and Environment Canada. Maritimes
   Regional Library   (CN)
Canada. Fisheries and Environment Canada. Northern
   Forest Research Centre   (CN)
Canada. Fisheries and Environment Canada. Western
   Forest Products Laboratory   (CN)
Canada. Food Prices Review Board   (CN)
Canada. Geological Survey of Canada   (CN)
Canada. Grain Commission. Economics and Statistics
   Division   (CN)
Canada. Grains Council   (CN)
Canada. Health and Welfare Canada   (CN)
Canada. Labour Canada   (CN)
Canada. Labour Canada. Public Relations Branch
   (CN)
Canada. Law Reform Commission   (CN)
Canada. Marine Environmental Data Service   (CN)
Canada. Marine Sciences Directorate. Pacific Region
   (CN)
Canada. Maritimes Forest Research Centre   (CN)

Canada. Marketing and Trade Division (CN)

Canada. Ministry of Treasury, Economics and Intergovernmental Affairs (CN)

Canada. Ministere de l'Industrie et du Commerce (CN)

Canada. Ministry of State for Science and Technology (CN)

Canada. Ministry of State for Urban Affairs (CN)

Canada. Ministry of Transport. Canadian Air Transportation Administration (CN)

Canada. National Energy Board (CN)

Canada. Northern Administration Branch. Resources Division (CN)

Canada. Parks Canada (CN)

Canada. Permanent Committee on Geographical Names. Surveys and Mapping Branch (CN)

Canada. Radio-Television and Telecommunications Commission (CN)

Canada. Research Station (CN)

Canada. Road and Motor Vehicle Traffic Safety Branch (CN)

Canada. Statistics Canada (CN)

Canada. Supply and Services Canada (CN)

Canada. Supreme Court (CN)

Canada. Tax Review Board (CN)

Canada. Transport Commission (CN)

Canada. Treasury Board Secretariat (CN)

Canada. Unemployment Insurance Commission (CN)

Canada Council (CN)

Canada Institute for Scientific and Technical Information (CN)

Canada Japan Trade Council (CN)

Canada Jaycees-Jaycees du Canada (CN)

Canada Law Book Ltd. (CN)

Canada-Mongolia Society (CN)

Canada Rides Publications Ltd. (CN)

Canada Safety Council (CN)

Canada Ski Magazine (CN)

Canada-United Kingdom Chamber of Commerce (UK)

Canada West Publications (CN)

Canada's Foundry Journal (CN)

Canada's Wings (CN)

Canadian Aberdeen Angus Association (CN)

Canadian Aeronautics and Space Institute (CN)

Canadian Air Mail Collectors Club (US)

Canadian Air Traffic Control Association, Inc. (CN)

Canadian Amateur Boxing Association (CN)

Canadian Amateur Radio Federation Inc. (CN)

Canadian Amateur Softball Association (CN)

Canadian Anaesthetists' Society (CN)

Canadian Analyst Ltd. (CN)

Canadian Appaloosa Horse Association (CN)

Canadian Arabian Horse Registry (CN)

Canadian Arctic Resources Committee (CN)

Canadian Arthritis and Rheumatism Society (CN)

Canadian Association for Adult Education (CN)

Canadian Association for American Studies (CN)

Canadian Association for Children with Learning Disabilities (CN)

Canadian Association for Health, Physical Education & Recreation (CN)

Canadian Association for Laboratory Animal Science (CN)

Canadian Association for Publishing in Philosophy (CN)

Canadian Association for South Asian Studies (CN)

Canadian Association for the Mentally Retarded (CN)

Canadian Association in Support of the Native People (CN)

Canadian Association of Administrative Sciences (CN)

Canadian Association of African Studies (CN)

Canadian Association of College and University Libraries (CN)

Canadian Association of College and University Student Services (CN)

Canadian Association of Departments of Extension and Summer School (CN)

Canadian Association of Exhibitions (CN)

Canadian Association of Geographers (CN)

Canadian Association of Geographers. Education Committee (CN)

Canadian Association of Geographers. Western Division (CN)

Canadian Association of Information Science (CN)

Canadian Association of Law Libraries (CN)

Canadian Association of Management Consultants (CN)

Canadian Association of Marine Equipment Industries (CN)

Canadian Association of Music Libraries (CN)

Canadian Association of Occupational Therapists (CN)

Canadian Association of Optometrists (CN)

Canadian Association of Physicists (CN)

Canadian Association of Radiologists (CN)

Canadian Association of Rehabilitation Personnel (CN)

Canadian Association of Schools of Social Work (CN)

Canadian Association of Slavists (CN)

Canadian Association of Slavists. Ottawa Branch (CN)

Canadian Association of Social Workers (CN)

Canadian Association of Special Libraries & Information Services (CN)

Canadian Association of Sport Sciences (CN)

Canadian Association of University Teachers (CN)

Canadian Association of University Teachers of German (CN)

Canadian Authors Association (CN)

Canadian Authors Association. Edmonton Branch (CN)

Canadian Automobile Association (CN)

Canadian Aviation Historical Society (CN)

Canadian Band Directors Association (CN)

Canadian Bankers Association (CN)

Canadian Bar Association (CN)

Canadian Bar Association. British Columbia Branch (CN)

Canadian Bar Association. Toronto Branch (CN)

Canadian Book Publishers' Council (CN)

Canadian Botanical Association (CN)

Canadian Broadcasting Corporation (CN)

Canadian Brotherhood of Railway, Transport and General Workers (CN)

Canadian Bureau for International Education (CN)

Canadian Cable Television Association (CN)

Canadian Cancer Society (CN)

Canadian Canoe Association (CN)

Canadian Catholic Historical Association (CN)

Canadian Caver Magazine (CN)

Canadian Century Publishers (CN)

Canadian Century Publishing Co. (CN)

Canadian Ceramic Society (CN)

Canadian Certified General Accountants' Association (CN)

Canadian Chamber Concerts Press (CN)

Canadian Children's Literature Association (CN)

Canadian Children's Magazine (CN)

Canadian Children's Press (CN)

Canadian Chiropractic Association (CN)

Canadian Church Historical Society (CN)

Canadian Circulations Audit Board, Inc. (CN)

Canadian Coin News (CN)

Canadian College of Teachers (CN)

Canadian Commission for Unesco (CN)

Canadian Communist League (Marxist-Leninist) (CN)

Canadian Comparative Literature Association (CN)

Canadian Conference of Catholic Bishops. Publications Service (CN)

Canadian Conference of the Arts (CN)

Canadian Construction Association (CN)

Canadian Cooperative Wool Growers Ltd. (CN)

Canadian Copper and Brass Development Association (CN)

Canadian Corporation for Studies in Religion (CN)

Canadian Council of Christians and Jews (CN)

Canadian Council of Churches (CN)

Canadian Council of Professional Engineers (CN)

Canadian Council of Teachers of English (CN)

Canadian Council of the Blind (CN)

Canadian Council on Social Development (CN)

Canadian Council on Urban and Regional Research (CN)

Canadian Criminology and Corrections Association (CN)

Canadian Cultural Society of the Deaf in Canada (CN)

Canadian Curling News (CN)

Canadian Daily Quotation Service Ltd. (CN)

Canadian Dental Association (CN)

Canadian Dental Hygienists Association (CN)

Canadian Diabetic Association (CN)

Canadian Dietetic Association (CN)

Canadian Economics Association (CN)

Canadian Education Association (CN)

Canadian Educational Programmes (CN)

Canadian Egg Producers' Council (CN)

Canadian Electrical Distributors Association (CN)

Canadian Embassy. Public Affairs Division (US)

Canadian Engineering Publications Ltd. (CN)

Canadian Enterprise Corporation (US)

Canadian Environmental Law Research Foundation (CN)

Canadian Export Association (CN)

Canadian Family Camping Federation (CN)

Canadian Federation of Biological Societies (CN)

Canadian Federation of Business and Professional Women's Clubs (CN)

Canadian Federation of Humane Societies (CN)

Canadian Federation of Mayors and Municipalities (CN)

Canadian Federation of Music Teachers' Association (CN)

Canadian Fiction (CN)

Canadian Field Hockey Council (CN)

Canadian Figure Skating Association (CN)

Canadian Figure Skating Association. Central Ontario Section (CN)

Canadian Film Archives (CN)

Canadian Film Development Corporation (CN)

Canadian Film Institute (CN)

Canadian Flight Publishing Co. (CN)

Canadian Folk Music Society (CN)

Canadian Forces Base (CN)

Canadian Forces Base Edmonton (CN)

Canadian Forces Base Montreal (CN)

Canadian Forces Base Winnipeg (CN)

Canadian Forces Headquarters (CN)

Canadian Forces Headquarters - Directorate of Flight Safety (CN)

Canadian Foresters Life Insurance Society (CN)

Canadian Forestry Association (CN)

Canadian Forestry Association of B.C. (CN)

Canadian Forwarder (CN)

Canadian Fruit Wholesalers Association (CN)

Canadian Gas Association (CN)

Canadian Gay Activists Alliance (CN)

Canadian Gladiolus Society (CN)

Canadian Government Office of Tourism (CN)

Canadian Gregg Association (CN)

Canadian Guernsey Breeders Association (CN)

Canadian Guild of Organists (CN)

Canadian Gypsum Co. Ltd. (CN)

Canadian H & G Publishing Ltd. (CN)

Canadian Hackney Horse Society (CN)

Canadian Health Record Association (CN)

Canadian Hearing Society (CN)

Canadian Heart Foundation (CN)

Canadian Hemophilia Society (CN)

Canadian Hemophilia Society. Ontario Chapter (CN)

Canadian High Commission. Counsellor (Public Affairs) (UK)

Canadian Historical Association (CN)

Canadian Home Economics Association (CN)

Canadian Horticultural Council (CN)

Canadian Hospital Association (CN)

Canadian Imperial Bank of Commerce (CN)

Canadian Importers Association, Inc. (CN)

Canadian Indemnity Co. (CN)

Canadian Independent Adjusters' Conference (CN)

Canadian Industrial Traffic League (CN)

Canadian Industries Ltd. (CN)

Canadian Information Processing Society (CN)

Canadian Institute of Chartered Accountants (CN)

Canadian Institute of Food Science and Technology (CN)

Canadian Institute of Forestry (CN)

Canadian Institute of International Affairs (CN)

Canadian Institute of Mining & Metallurgy (CN)

Canadian Institute of Onomastic Sciences (CN)

Canadian Institute of Planners (CN)

Canadian Institute of Quantity Surveyors (CN)

Canadian Institute of Surveying (CN)

Canadian Institute of Timber Construction (CN)

Canadian Intelligence Publications (CN)

Canadian International Development Agency (CN)

Canadian International DX Radio Club (CN)

Canadian Jersey Cattle Club (CN)

Canadian Jewish Magazine (CN)

Canadian Jewish News (CN)

Canadian Jewish Outlook (CN)

Canadian Journal of Neurological Sciences, Inc. (CN)

Canadian Journalism Foundation, Inc. (CN)

Canadian Labour Congress (CN)

Canadian Ladies' Golf Association (CN)

Canadian Lawn Tennis Association (CN)

Canadian Library Association (CN)

Canadian Library Association. Microfilm Project (CN)

Canadian Library Trustees' Association (CN)

Canadian Life Insurance Association (CN)

Canadian Limousin Association (CN)

Canadian Linguistic Association (CN)

Canadian Livestock Feed Board (CN)

Canadian Manufacturers Association (CN)

Canadian Mass Publications (CN)

Canadian Mathematical Congress (CN)

Canadian Mathematical Congress. Research Committee (CN)

Canadian Medical Association (CN)

Canadian Mental Health Association (CN)

Canadian Meteorological Society (CN)
Canadian Mime Theatre (CN)
Canadian Miner Publishing Co. (CN)
Canadian Mobile Home Association (CN)
Canadian Motorist (CN)
Canadian Murray Grey Association (CN)
Canadian Museums Association (CN)
Canadian Music Centre (CN)
Canadian Music Council (CN)
Canadian Music Educators Association (CN)
Canadian Musical News Co. (CN)
Canadian National Institute for the Blind (CN)
Canadian National Railways (CN)
Canadian Nationalist Party (CN)
Canadian Native Friendship Centre (CN)
Canadian Nature Federation (CN)
Canadian Negro Publishing Association (CN)
Canadian News Synthesis Project (CN)
Canadian Newspaper Services International Ltd.
  (CN)
Canadian Notes & Queries (CN)
Canadian Nuclear Association (CN)
Canadian Numismatic Research Society (CN)
Canadian Nursery Trades Association (CN)
Canadian Nurses' Association (CN)
Canadian Office Machine Dealers Association (CN)
Canadian Opera Company (CN)
Canadian Ophthalmological Society (CN)
Canadian Oral History Association (CN)
Canadian Orienteering Federation (CN)
Canadian Osteopathic Association (CN)
Canadian Otolaryngological Society (CN)
Canadian Paper Money Society (CN)
Canadian Paraplegic Association (CN)
Canadian Paraplegic Association. British Columbia
  Division (CN)
Canadian Paraplegic Association. Central Western
  Division (CN)
Canadian Paraplegic Association. New Brunswick
  Division (CN)
Canadian Parks Recreation Association (CN)
Canadian Peace Research Institute (CN)
Canadian Petroleum Association (CN)
Canadian Pharmaceutical Association (CN)
Canadian Philatelic Society of Great Britain (UK)
Canadian Philosophical Association (CN)
Canadian Photopress Publishing Ltd. (CN)
Canadian Physiological Society (CN)
Canadian Physiotherapy Association (CN)
Canadian Phytopathological Society (CN)
Canadian Plains Research Center (CN)
Canadian Podiatry Association (CN)
Canadian Political Science Association (CN)
Canadian Postmasters Association (CN)
Canadian Psychiatric Association (CN)
Canadian Psychological Association (CN)
Canadian Public Health Association (CN)
Canadian Pulp and Paper Association (CN)
Canadian Quarter Horse Association (CN)
Canadian Railroad Historical Association (CN)
Canadian Railway Club, Inc. (CN)
Canadian Real Estate Association (CN)
Canadian Red Book (CN)
Canadian Red Cross Society (CN)
Canadian Red Cross Society. Alberta - Northwest
  Territories Division (CN)
Canadian Rehabilitation Council for the Disabled
  (CN)
Canadian Religious Conference (CN)
Canadian Research Centre for Anthropology (CN)
Canadian Retail Hardware Association (CN)
Canadian Review of Studies in Nationalism, Inc.
  (CN)
Canadian Rodeo Cowboys' Association (CN)
Canadian Rodeo News Ltd. (CN)
Canadian Rose Society (CN)
Canadian Scene (CN)
Canadian Schizophrenia Foundation (CN)
Canadian School Library Association (CN)
Canadian Seed Growers Association (CN)
Canadian Semiotics Research Association (CN)
Canadian Shorthorn Association (CN)
Canadian Ski Association (CN)
Canadian Slovak Benefit Society (CN)
Canadian Slovak League (CN)
Canadian Society for Asian Studies (CN)
Canadian Society for Chemical Engineering (CN)
Canadian Society for Education Through Art (CN)
Canadian Society for Immunology (CN)
Canadian Society for Legal History (CN)
Canadian Society for Mechanical Engineering (CN)
Canadian Society for the Study of Education (CN)
Canadian Society for the Study of Higher Education
  (CN)
Canadian Society of Agricultural Engineering (CN)
Canadian Society of Agronomy (CN)
Canadian Society of Animal Production (CN)
Canadian Society of Biblical Studies (CN)

Canadian Society of Clinical Chemists (CN)
Canadian Society of Creative Leathercraft (CN)
Canadian Society of Environmental Biologists (CN)
Canadian Society of Exploration Geophysicists (CN)
Canadian Society of Forensic Science (CN)
Canadian Society of Hospital Pharmacists (CN)
Canadian Society of Immunology (CN)
Canadian Society of Laboratory Technologists (CN)
Canadian Society of Petroleum Geologists (CN)
Canadian Society of Radiological Technicians (CN)
Canadian Society of Respiratory Technologists (CN)
Canadian Society of Rural Extension (CN)
Canadian Sociology and Anthropology Association
  (CN)
Canadian Speech and Hearing Association (CN)
Canadian Sport Parachuting Association (CN)
Canadian Stage and Arts Publications, Ltd. (CN)
Canadian Standards Association (CN)
Canadian Tax Foundation (CN)
Canadian Teachers' Federation (CN)
Canadian Technical Asphalt Association (CN)
Canadian Technical Publications Ltd. (CN)
Canadian Textile Journal Publishing Co. Ltd. (CN)
Canadian Theatre Review Publications (CN)
Canadian Theological College (CN)
Canadian Toy Manufacturers Association (CN)
Canadian Tribune (CN)
Canadian Trotting Association (CN)
Canadian Tuberculosis and Respiratory Disease
  Association (CN)
Canadian Union of General Employees (CN)
Canadian Union of Public Employees (CN)
Canadian University Service Overseas (CN)
Canadian Urban Transit Association (CN)
Canadian Veterinary Medical Association (CN)
Canadian Vocational Association (CN)
Canadian Volleyball Association (CN)
Canadian Volleyball Publications (CN)
Canadian War Records Office (CN)
Canadian Wheelmen's Association (CN)
Canadian Wild Horse Society (CN)
Canadian Wildlife Federation (CN)
Canadian Woodmen of the World (CN)
Canadian Youth Hostels Association, North West
  Region (CN)
Canadian Youth Hostels Association Region. Pacific
  Region (CN)
Canary Breeders' Association of Australia (AT)
Canberra Alpine Club (AT)
Canberra & District Historical Society Inc. (AT)
Canberra Bushwalking Club (AT)
Canberra College of Advanced Education. Students'
  Association (AT)
Canberra Consumers, Inc. (AT)
Canberra Gliding Club (AT)
Canberra Kennel Association (AT)
Canberra Mathematical Association (AT)
Canberra Post (AT)
Cancer Care, Inc. (US)
Cancer Control Society (US)
Cancer Institute (JA)
Cancer Letter (US)
Cancer Research Campaign (UK)
Cancer Research Institute
  see under Sapporo Medical College (JA)
Cancer Society of Finland
  see Suomen Syopayhdistys (FI)
Candar Publishing Co. (US)
Candidate Press (US)
Candido (IT)
Candour League of Rhodesia (RH)
Aurelio Canevari Editore (IT)
Canine Information Center (US)
Canning Publications, Inc (US)
Canning Trade, Inc. (US)
Cano Isaza & Cia (CK)
Canoe Camping Club (UK)
Canoe Kayak Club de France (FR)
Canon Law Society of Great Britain (UK)
Libreria Editrice Canova (IT)
Canterbury and York Society (US)
Canterbury Archaeological Scoiety (UK)
Canterbury Botanical Society (NZ)
Canterbury Chamber of Commerce (NZ)
Canterbury Diocesan House (UK)
Canterbury Horticultural Society, Inc. (NZ)
Luigi Cantone, Ed. & Pub. (IT)
Editio Cantor KG (GW)
Cantorial Council of America (US)
Cantrills Filmnotes (AT)
Cantwell-Conteville Family Association (US)
Dr. J.A. Canut, Ed. & Pub. (SP)
Canvas Products Association International (US)
Canvet Publications Ltd. (CN)
Canyon Cinema Cooperative (US)
Canyouth Publications (CN)
Editions du Cap (MC)
Cape Horners - Australia (AT)

Cape of Good Hope. Cape School Board (SA)
Cape of Good Hope. Department of Nature
  Conservation (SA)
Cape Piscatorial Society (SA)
Cape Provincial Library Service (SA)
Cape Town Photographic Society (SA)
Cape Verde. Direccao Nacional de Informacao (CV)
Capilano College (CN)
Capilla Alfonsina. Boletin (MX)
Capital de la Poesia (AG)
Capital Energy Letter (US)
Capital Ledger (US)
Capital Management Publications (US)
Capital Publishers, Inc. (US)
Capital Publishing Corporation (US)
Capital Region Planning Commission (US)
Capital University Law School (US)
Capitalist Reporter Inc. (US)
Capitol District Communications (US)
Capitol Publications, Inc. (US)
Capitol Publications, Inc. Education News Services
  Division (US)
Capitol Publications, Inc. Health News Services
  Division (US)
Capitulo Colombiano de la Academia Americana de
  Pediatria (CK)
Capla Publications, Inc. (US)
Ronald Caplan, Ed. & Pub. (CN)
J. W. Cappelens Forlag (NO)
Casa Editrice Licinio Cappelli (IT)
Capra Press (US)
Capricornio (AO)
Miguel Angel Capriles, Ed. & Pub. (VE)
Capuchin Fathers of the Pokrof-Monastery (NE)
Capuchin-Franciscan Order (IT)
Capuchin Missions (US)
Capuchin Publications (IE)
Car and Locomotive Cyclopedia (US)
Car Classics Publishing Co. (US)
Car Ferry Enquiries Ltd. (UK)
Cara (US)
Carabela (SP)
Giuseppe Caraciolo, Ed. & Pub. (IT)
Caracola (SP)
Editions Caracteres (FR)
Caravan Club (UK)
Caravan Club of Sweden (SW)
Caravan, Inc (US)
Caravan Publications (Pty) Ltd. (SA)
Empresa Grafica Carazinhense Ltda. (BL)
Carcanet Press Ltd. (UK)
Card Memorabilia Association (US)
Cardamom Board
  see India. Cardamom Board (II)
Cardiff Area Students Association (UK)
Cardiff Medical Society (UK)
Cardinal Mindszenty Foundation, Inc. (US)
Cardinal Publishing Co. (US)
Mario Cardinali, Ed. & Pub. (IT)
Cardinallar Ltd (UK)
Cardio-Vascular Bulletin (IR)
Cardiological Society of India (II)
Lubio Cardozo y Juan Pinto, Eds & Pubs. (VE)
Care (NZ)
CARE, Inc. (US)
Career Consultants Ltd. (UK)
Career Education Center (US)
Careers Research and Advisory Centre (UK)
Caret (UK)
Carfax Publishing Co. (UK)
Carga Util (SP)
Cargill, Inc. (US)
Carib Publicity Co. Ltd. (BB)
Caribbean Archives Association (GP)
Caribbean Congress of Labour (TR)
Caribbean Conservation Association (BB)
Caribbean Consumers Documentation Centre (BB)
Caribbean Contact (TR)
Caribbean Development Bank. Board of Governors
  (BB)
Caribbean Food and Nutrition Institute
  see under World Health Organization. Pan
  American Health Organization (UN)
Caribbean Free Trade Association (TR)
Caribbean Journal of Science and Mathematics (US)
Caribbean Review Inc. (US)
Caribbean Tourism Association (UK)
Caribbean Universities Press (BB)
Editoria del Caribe (DR)
Caribook Ltd. (CN)
Caritas India (II)
Caritas Internationalis (IT)
Buchhandlung Adalbert Carl (GW)
CARL Communications Ltd. (UK)
Verlag Hans Carl KG (GW)
Carleton Board of Education (CN)
Carleton College (US)
Carleton Press (CN)

Ediciones CEDEL  (SP)
Editions du Cedre  (FR)
Cehoslovacki Savez v SR Hrvatskoj  (YU)
Ceilings and Interior Systems Contractors Association
  (US)
Camilo Jose Cela Trulock  (SP)
Celal Tevfik Karasapan  (TU)
Celanese Fibers Marketing Co. Customer Information
  Services  (US)
Celebration  (US)
Celebrity Publications, Ltd.  (US)
Celebrity Service, Inc.  (US)
Celebrity Service Ltd.  (UK)
Celebrity Sports  (US)
Cellulose Research Institute  (IO)
Celmer & Twente Associates  (US)
Eliecer Celnik, Ed. & Pub.  (CK)
Celo Press  (US)
Celtic League  (IE)
Celtut Matbaasi  (TU)
Celuloide  (PO)
Cement and Concrete Association  (UK)
Cement Association of Japan  (JA)
Cement Manufacturers' Association  (II)
Cement- och Betonginstitutet  (SW)
Cement Research Institute of India  (II)
Cemento-Hormigon  (SP)
Cemetery Research, Inc.  (US)
Cenaclul Literar "Menora"  (IS)
Cenacolo di Cultura "Publius Ovidius Naso"  (IT)
Cencus Publications  (II)
Cendex Corp.  (US)
Cenobio  (SZ)
Centar za Idejni i Teorijski Rad CK SKH  (YU)
Centar za Informacije i Publicitet  (YU)
Centar za Istrazivanje Biblije Dokumentaciju i
  Informacije  (YU)
Centar za Kulturno-Propagandni i Informativni Rad
  Vukovar  (YU)
Centar za Proucavanje i Suzbijanje Alkoholizma i
  Drugih Ovisnosti  (YU)
Centar za Proucavanje Prirodnih Zdravstvenih Nacela
  (YU)
Centar za Unapredjivanje Saha  (YU)
Centar za Vojnonaucnu Dokumentaciju i Informacije
  (YU)
Centaur & Company  (US)
Centauros  (AG)
Centenary College  (US)
Centennial Commission  (CN)
Center for Adult Diseases, Osaka  (JA)
Center for Agricultural Economic Research  (IS)
Center for Applied Linguistics  (US)
Center for Arabic and Afro-Asian Studies  (IS)
Center for Autonomous Social Action. General
  Brotherhood of Workers  (US)
Center for Bibliographical Studies, Uppsala  (SW)
Center for Book Arts, Inc.  (US)
Center for Business and Economic Research  (US)
Center for California Public Affairs  (US)
Center for Computer-Oriented Research in Biblical
  and Related Ancient Literatures  (US)
Center for Conflict Resolution  (US)
Center for Consumer Education Services  (US)
Center for Continuing Education in Podiatric Medicine
  (CCEPM)  (US)
Center for Cuban Studies  (US)
Center for Cybernetic Systems Synergism  (US)
Center for Defense Information  (US)
Center for Disease Control
  see U.S. Center for Disease Control  (US)
Center for Economic, Financial and Social Research
  and Documentation  (LE)
Center for Educational Reform, Inc.  (US)
Center for Environmental Education  (US)
Center for Equal Education  (US)
Center for Foreign Study  (US)
Center for Global Perspectives  (US)
Center for Growth Alternatives  (US)
Center for Hermeneutical Studies  (US)
Center for Immunology  (SZ)
Center for Information and Numerical Data Analysis
  and Synthesis  (US)
Center for Information on America  (US)
Center for Inter-American Relations  (US)
Center for International Education and Research in
  Accounting
  see under University of Illinois at Urbana-
  Champaign  (US)
Center for International Environment Information
  (US)
Center for Japanese Social & Political Studies  (JA)
Center for Law and Education, Inc.  (US)
Center for Louisiana Studies  (US)
Center for Marketing Communications  (US)
Center for Migration Studies of New York, Inc.  (US)
Center for New Images  (US)
Center for Personalized Instruction  (US)

Center for Policy Analysis  (US)
Center for Policy Process  (US)
Center for Population Research
  see under U.S. Center for Population Research
  (US)
Center for Process Studies  (US)
Center for Productive Public Management  (US)
Center for Psychosocial Studies  (US)
Center for Public Libraries  (IS)
Center for Reformation Research  (US)
Center for Reformation Research. Sixteenth Century
  Studies Conference  (US)
Center for Research Libraries  (US)
Center for Science in the Public Interest  (US)
Center for Teaching About Peace and War  (US)
Center for the Development of Human Resources
  (US)
Center for the Rights of Campus Journalists  (US)
Center for the Study of Armament and Disarmament
  see under California State University, Los Angeles
  (US)
Center for the Study of Democratic Institutions  (US)
Center for the Study of Federalism  (US)
Center for the Study of Instruction  (US)
Center for the Study of Popular Culture  (US)
Center for the Study of Public Policy, Inc.  (US)
Center for the Study of the Future  (US)
Center for the Study of the Presidency  (US)
Center for the Teaching of the Americas  (US)
Center for U F O Studies  (US)
Center for Women's Studies & Services  (US)
Center on Evaluation, Development and Research
  (US)
Center on International Race Relations  (US)
Center Press  (US)
Centexbel  (BE)
Centraal Bureau van de Tuinbouwveilingen in
  Nederland  (NE)
Centraal Bureau van Sobrietas  (NE)
Centraal Bureau voor de Schapenfokkerij  (NE)
Centraal Bureau voor de Varkensfokkerij  (NE)
Centraal Bureau voor het Katholiek Onderwijs  (NE)
Centraalbureau voor Schimmelcultures  (NE)
Centrais Eletricas Brazileiras S.A. Assessoria de
  Relacoes Publicas de Eletrobras  (BL)
Central Africa Historical Association  (RH)
Central African Journal of Medicine  (RH)
Central African Power Corporation  (RH)
Central African Republic. Direction de la Statistique
  Generale et des Etudes Economiques  (CX)
Central African Zionist Organisation  (RH)
Central America Report  (GT)
Central American Institute of Public Administration
  see Instituto Centroamericano de Administracion
  Publica  (CR)
Central Archives for the History of the Jewish People
  (IS)
Central Asian Mission  (UK)
Central Asian Research Centre  (UK)
Central Association of Finnish Forest Industries
  see Suomen Metsateollisuuden Keskusliitto  (FI)
Central Association of Finnish Photographic
  Organizations
  see Suomen Valokuvajarjestojen Keskusliitto
  Finnfoto  (FI)
Central Association of the Miraculous Medal  (US)
Central Bank of Barbados  (BB)
Central Bank of Ceylon  (CE)
Central Bank of China  (CH)
Central Bank of China. Economic Research
  Department  (CH)
Central Bank of Cyprus  (CY)
Central Bank of Egypt  (UA)
Central Bank of Gambia  (GM)
Central Bank of Iceland
  see Sedlabanki Islands  (IC)
Central Bank of Iran
  see Bank Markazi Iran  (IR)
Central Bank of Iraq  (IQ)
Central Bank of Ireland  (IE)
Central Bank of Jordan  (JO)
Central Bank of Kenya  (KE)
Central Bank of Kuwait  (KU)
Central Bank of Malta  (MM)
Central Bank of Nigeria  (NR)
Central Bank of Syria  (SY)
Central Bank of the Bahamas  (BF)
Central Bank of the Philippines  (PH)
Central Bank of the Republic of Turkey  (TU)
Central Bank of Trinidad and Tobago  (TR)
Central Bank of Yemen  (YE)
Central Baptist Church  (US)
Central Baptist Theological Seminary of Minneapolis
  (US)
Central Board for Workers Education  (II)
Central Building Research Institute

  see India. Central Building Research Institute  (II)
Central Bureau for Educational Visits and Exchanges
  (UK)
Central Bureau for Jewish Aged  (US)
Central Bureau for Satellite Geodesy
  see under International Association of Geodesy
  (GR)
Central Coffee Research Institute  (II)
Central Committee for Conscientious Objectors  (US)
Central Committee for Conscientious Objectors. San
  Francisco  (US)
Central Committee of the Communist Party of Cuba
  (CU)
Central Committee of the Union of Agricultural
  Working People of Korea  (KN)
Central Conference of American Rabbis  (US)
Central Conference of Teamsters  (US)
Central Constructor Corp.  (US)
Central Cotton Committee
  see Pakistan. Pakistan Central Cotton Committee
  (PK)
Central Council for Agricultural and Horticultural Co-
  Operation  (UK)
Central Council for British Naturism  (UK)
Central Council for Research in Indian Medicine and
  Homoeopathy  (II)
Central Council of Church Bell Ringers  (UK)
Central Council of Land Surveyors of South Africa
  (SA)
Central de Numismatica y Medallistica  (MX)
Central Electric Railfans' Association  (US)
Central Electrochemical Research Institute
  see India. Central Electrochemical Research
  Institute  (II)
Central European Federalists  (UK)
Central Fisheries Research Institute
  see Zambia. Central Fisheries Research Institute
  (ZA)
Central Flower News, Inc.  (US)
Central Food Technological Research Institute
  see India. Central Food Technological Research
  Institute  (II)
Central Fraser Valley Star Publications  (CN)
Central Glass and Ceramic Research Institute
  see India. Central Glass and Ceramic Research
  Institute  (II)
Central Hall Artists Inc.  (US)
Central Health Education Bureau
  see India. Central Health Education Bureau  (II)
Central Homoeopathic and Biochemic Association
  (II)
Central Industrial Secretariat  (AT)
Central Inland Fisheries Research Institute  (II)
Central Institute of Education  (II)
Central Institute of Education. Alumni Association
  (II)
Central Institute of Research and Training in Public
  Cooperation  (II)
Central Leather Research Institute
  see India. Central Leather Research Institute  (II)
Central Library for Biological Sciences and Agriculture
  see Bibliotheca Bogoriensis  (IO)
Central Library of Trinidad and Tobago  (TR)
Central Literary Magazine  (UK)
Central London Adult Education Institute  (UK)
Central Marine Fisheries Research Institute  (II)
Central Mechanical Engineering Research Institute
  see India. Central Mechanical Engineering Research
  Institute  (II)
Central Michigan University  (US)
Central Michigan University. Department of English
  (US)
Central Mining Research Station
  see India. Central Mining Research Station  (II)
Central Missouri State University  (US)
Central Mortgage and Housing Corporation  (CN)
Central National Organization for Applied Scientific
  Research in the Netherlands  (NE)
Central Naugatuck Valley Regional Planning Agency
  (US)
Central New York Academy of Medicine  (US)
Central New York Genealogical Society  (US)
Central News Agency Ltd.  (SA)
Central Party  (US)
Central Philippine University  (PH)
Central Publicity  (AT)
Central Road Research Institute
  see India. Central Road Research Institute  (II)
Central Salt and Marine Chemicals Research Institute
  see India. Central Salt and Marine Chemicals
  Research Institute  (II)
Central Scientific Instruments Organization
  see India. Central Scientific Instruments
  Organization  (II)
Central Scotland Chamber of Commerce  (UK)
Central Silk Board
  see India. Central Silk Board  (II)
Central Social Welfare Board  (II)

Chattanooga Audubon Society  (US)
Chattanooga Coin and Stamp Co.  (US)
Chattanooga Science Fiction Convention  (US)
R. N. Chatterjee, Pub.  (II)
K. Chatterji  (II)
Amala Chaudhuri, Ed. & Pub.  (II)
Manjari Chaudhuri  (II)
S. B. Chaudhuri, Ed. & Pub.  (II)
Chauffoerernes Forbund i Danmark  (DK)
Chaukhambha Orientalia  (II)
Chaussons et Petits Rats  (FR)
Chavhata Weekly  (II)
Check Collectors Round Table  (US)
Checkpoint Council  (AT)
Chedwato Service  (US)
Cheering Words  (UK)
Cheese Reporter Publishing Co., Inc.  (US)
Cheever Publishing, Inc.  (US)
Chekhov Publishing Corporation  (US)
Chelsea Associates, Inc.  (US)
Chelsea College. Students Union  (UK)
Chelsea Speleological Society  (UK)
Chelyabinskii Gosudarstvennyi Pedagogicheskii Institut
  (UR)
Chemical Abstracts Service  (US)
Chemical Bank  (BE)
Chemical Daily Co., Ltd.  (JA)
Chemical Economic Services  (US)
Chemical Economy Research Institute  (JA)
Chemical India Annual  (II)
Chemical Industries Association Ltd.  (UK)
Chemical Institute of Canada  (CN)
Chemical Process Industries of India  (II)
Chemical Publishing Co.  (US)
Chemical Society  (UK)
Chemical Society of Japan  (JA)
Chemical Society of the Philippines  (PH)
Chemical Society of Turkey  (TU)
Chemical Spotlight Inc.  (US)
Chemical Take-Off  (II)
Chemicals & Allied Products Export Promotion
  Council  (II)
Chemie Gruenenthal GmbH  (GW)
Verlag Chemie International, Inc.  (US)
Chemiefaser Lenzing AG  (AU)
Chemin  (FR)
Chemische Gesellschaft der DDR  (GE)
Verlag fuer Chemische Industrie  (GW)
Chemisches Forschungsinstitut der Wirtschaft
  Oesterreichs  (AU)
Prof. Chien-Fu Chen, Ed. & Pub.  (CH)
Cherokee Boys Club, Inc.  (US)
Cherokee Nation of Oklahoma  (US)
Cherokee Times  (US)
Cherravuru Nagabhushanacharyulu  (II)
Cherry Valley Editions  (US)
Chesapeake and Ohio Historical Society, Inc.  (US)
Chesapeake Bay Communications, Inc.  (US)
Chesapeake Bay Foundation  (US)
Cheshire Foundation Homes  (UK)
Chesopiean Archaeological Association  (US)
Chess (Sutton Coldfield) Ltd  (UK)
Chess Digest  (US)
Chess Endgame Study Circle  (UK)
Chesswood House Publishing Ltd.  (CN)
Chest and Heart Association. Scottish Branch  (UK)
Chest Disease Research Institute
  see under Kyoto University  (JA)
Chest Heart and Stroke Association  (UK)
Chester County Press  (US)
Chester White Swine Record Association  (US)
Chestnut Hill Community Association  (US)
Chetham Society  (UK)
Chevalier Press  (AT)
Chevaliers du Colomb du Quebec  (CN)
Chevrolet Motor Division  (US)
Chevron Petroleum Maatschappij (Nederland) N.V
  (NE)
Chhandita  (II)
Chi Epsilon  (US)
Chi Luen Press  (HK)
Chiang Mai University. Faculty of Medicine  (TH)
Chiba Daigaku
  see Chiba University  (JA)
Chiba Igakkai
  see Chiba Medical Society  (JA)
Chiba Medical Society  (JA)
Chiba University. Faculty of Engineering  (JA)
Chiba University. Faculty of Horticulture  (JA)
Chiba University. Faculty of Humanities and Social
  Sciences  (JA)
Chicago. Chicago Transit Authority  (US)
Chicago. Crime Commission  (US)
Chicago. Department of Development and Planning
  (US)
Chicago. Department of Environmental Control  (US)
Chicago. Department of Urban Renewal  (US)
Chicago Academy of Sciences  (US)

Chicago and Illinois Restaurant Association  (US)
Chicago Area Transportation Study  (US)
Chicago Association of Commerce and Industry  (US)
Chicago Athletic Association  (US)
Chicago B.S.I.  (US)
Chicago Bowler Publishing Co.  (US)
Chicago Bridge and Iron Company  (US)
Chicago Clergy and Laity Concerned  (US)
Chicago Commission on Human Relations  (US)
Chicago Dental Society  (US)
Chicago Federation of Labor and Industrial Union
  Council  (US)
Chicago Fireman's Association-Local 2  (US)
Chicago Gay Crusader  (US)
Chicago Genealogical Society  (US)
Chicago Herpetological Society  (US)
Chicago Historical Society  (US)
Chicago Independent  (US)
Chicago Jewish Student Press  (US)
Chicago Library System  (US)
Chicago Linguistic Society  (US)
Chicago Medical Society  (US)
Chicago Mercantile Exchange  (US)
Chicago, Milwaukee, St. Paul and Pacific Railroad Co.
  (the Milwaukee Road)  (US)
Chicago New Art Association  (US)
Chicago Public Library  (US)
Chicago Retail Druggists' Association  (US)
Chicago Shimpo, Inc.  (US)
Chicago Society of Biblical Research  (US)
Chicago State University  (US)
Chicago Sun-Times  (US)
Chicago Unlimited, Inc.  (US)
Chicago Zoological Society  (US)
Chicano Community Newspaper  (US)
Chicano Law Student Association  (US)
Chicano Times  (US)
Chicano Training Center, Inc.  (US)
Chichester Diocese  (UK)
Chicorel Library Publishing Corp.  (US)
Chief Engineers & Chief Mechanical Engineers of the
  Major Ports of India  (II)
Chief Engineers Association of Chicago  (US)
Chien d'Or  (CN)
Chiesa Santa Rosalia  (IT)
Chiesa Universale Giuris-Davidica  (IT)
Chigaku Kyoshitsu
  see Kyoto University. Institute of Earth Science
  (JA)
Chigwell Local History Society  (UK)
Chikusan Shikenjo
  see Japan. National Institute of Animal Industry
  (JA)
Chikyu Butsurigaku Kyoshitsu
  see Kyoto University. Geophysical Institute  (JA)
George Chilaris, Ed. & Pub.  (GR)
Child and Youth Research Center  (PH)
Child Evangelism Fellowship Inc.  (US)
Child Guidance Clinic of Greater Winnipeg  (CN)
Child Guidance School Society  (II)
Child Poverty Action Group  (UK)
Child Study Press  (US)
Child Welfare League of America, Inc.  (US)
Childbirth Without Pain Education Association  (US)
Children and Youth Aliyah Committee for Great
  Britain  (UK)
Childrens Activities Time Society Inc.  (AT)
Children's Aid Society  (US)
Children's Aid Society of Metropolitan Toronto
  (CN)
Children's Aid Society of Ottawa  (CN)
Children's Apparel Manufacturers Association  (CN)
Childrens Art Foundation  (US)
Childrens Book Centre Ltd.  (UK)
Children's Book Council, Inc.  (US)
Children's Book Council of Australia  (AT)
Children's Book Review Service Inc.  (US)
Children's Book Trust  (II)
Children's Foundation  (US)
Children's Hospital Medical Center, Boston  (US)
Children's Hospital National Medical Center  (US)
Children's Hospital of Los Angeles. University
  Affiliated Program  (US)
Children's Hospital of Philadelphia  (US)
Children's House, Inc.  (US)
Children's Science Book Review Committee  (US)
Children's Television Workshop  (US)
Children's Theatre Conference  (US)
Chile. Ferrocarriles del Estado  (CL)
Chile. Fuerza Aerea  (CL)
Chile. Instituto de Investigaciones Agropecuarias
  (CL)
Chile. Instituto Nacional de Estadisticas  (CL)
Chile. Ministerio de Agricultura. Servicio Agricola y
  Ganadero  (CL)
Chile. Ministerio de Educacion Publica. Centro de
  Documentacion Pedagogica  (CL)

Chile. Ministerio de Hacienda. Direccion de
  Presupuestos  (CL)
Chile. Ministerio del Trabajo y Prevision Social.
  Superintendencia de Seguridad Social  (CL)
Chile. Oficina de Planificacion Nacional.
  Departamento de Estudios y Planificacion Urbano
  (CL)
Chile. Servicio Nacional de Salud  (CL)
Chile. Superintendencia de Bancos  (CL)
Chilton Book Co.  (US)
Chilton Co., Inc.  (US)
Chilton Co., Inc. Automotive Editorial Dept.  (US)
S. S. Chimanlal, Ed. & Pub.  (II)
Chimo Media Ltd.  (CN)
Chin-Tan Society  (KO)
China Academy  (CH)
China-Burma-India Veterans Association  (US)
China Consultants International, Ltd.  (US)
China Development Corporation  (CH)
China Economic News Service  (CH)
China External Trade Development Council  (CH)
China Forum Incorporation  (CH)
China Medical Board of New York  (US)
China Philatelic Society  (CH)
China Policy Study Group  (UK)
China Productivity Center  (CH)
China Publishing Company  (CH)
China Rebuilding Federation  (JA)
China, Republic. Department of Social Affairs  (CH)
China, Republic. Directorate-General of Budget,
  Accounting and Statistics  (CH)
China, Republic. Economic Planning Council  (CH)
China, Republic. Ministry of Communications.
  Tourism Bureau  (CH)
China, Republic. Ministry of Economic Affairs.
  Industrial Development & Investment Center  (CH)
China, Republic. Ministry of Finance. Department of
  Statistics  (CH)
China, Republic. Ministry of the Interior  (CH)
China, Republic. Telecommunications Laboratories
  (CH)
China Society  (CH)
China Stamp Collector's Club of Australasia  (AT)
China Study Centre  (II)
China Welfare Institute  (CC)
Chinese-American Cultural Association, Inc.  (US)
Chinese Buddhist Society of Australia  (AT)
Chinese-Canadian Press  (CN)
Chinese Chemical Society  (CH)
Chinese-English Translation Assistance Group  (US)
Chinese for Affirmative Action  (US)
Chinese Historical Society of America  (US)
Chinese Information Service  (US)
Chinese Institute of Chemical Engineers  (CH)
Chinese Institute of Civil and Hydraulic Engineering
  (CH)
Chinese Institute of Mining & Metallurgical Engineers.
  Industrial Technology Research Institute  (CH)
Chinese Language Teachers Association  (US)
Chinese Medical Association  (CC)
Chinese Petroleum Corporation. Exploration Division
  (CH)
Chinese Physiological Society  (CH)
Chinese Pictorial Review Ltd.  (SI)
Chinese Psychological Association  (CH)
Chinese Publicity Bureau Ltd.  (CN)
Chinese Society of Microbiology  (CH)
Chinese University of Hong Kong  (HK)
Chinese University of Hong Kong. Chung Chi College
  (HK)
Chinese University of Hong Kong. Economic Research
  Centre  (HK)
Chinese University of Hong Kong. Institute of Chinese
  Studies  (HK)
Chinese University of Hong Kong. Translation Centre
  (HK)
Chinese Voice Publishing & Printing Co. Ltd  (CN)
Rev. Peter P. S. Ching., Ed. & Pub.  (US)
Ching Hsin Chih Tso Kung Ssu Chu Pan Pu
  see Fresh Productions  (HK)
Ching Sui Printing Works Co., Ltd.  (CH)
Chinook Chemicals Corp.  (CN)
Chirimo  (RH)
Chiriotti Editori  (IT)
Chirurgia Triveneta  (IT)
Chitralekha Karyalaya  (II)
Chittagong Port Trust  (BG)
Chittaranjan Publishers  (II)
Chizu Kyokai
  see Map Society  (JA)
Verlag Chmielorz GmbH und Co  (GW)
CHOBISCO
  see Chambre Syndicale des Grossistes en
  Confiserie-Chocolaterie-Biscuits et Autres Derives
  du Sucre  (BE)
Choice  (US)
Choisir  (SZ)
Choix Artistique et Litteraire  (FR)

Chomo Uri  (US)
Choomia  (US)
Chopmen Enterprises  (SI)
Ramesh Chopra, Ed. & Pub.  (II)
Choshi Local Meteorological Observatory  (JA)
P.S. Chowdary, Ed. & Pub.  (II)
Chowder Press  (US)
Chretiens dans le Monde Rural  (FR)
Christ Church College  (II)
Verlagsverein der Christ im Zwanzigsten Jahrhundert
  (GW)
A. Christ Zeitschriftenverlag GmbH und Co. KG
  (GW)
Christadelphian Magazine and Publishing Association
  Ltd.  (UK)
Christavashram Press  (II)
Christelijk-Historische Jongeren Organisatie  (NE)
Christelijk Jongeren Verbond  (NE)
Christelijk Nationaal Vakverbond in Nederland  (NE)
Christelijk-Sociale Jeugd Organisatie-Werkende Jeugd
  (NE)
Christelijk Syndicaat van Personeel van Spoorwegen,
  Posterijen  (BE)
Christelijk Vlaams Kunstenaarsverbond  (BE)
Christelijke Arbeidersbeweging
  see Catholic Workers Movement  (BE)
Christelijke Blindenbibliotheek  (NE)
Christelijke Bond van Schoenmakers-Patroons in
  Nederland  (NE)
Christelijke Gereformeerde Kerken in Nederland.
  Zendingsdeputaten  (NE)
Christelijke Middenstands- en Burgersvrouwen  (BE)
Christendom Educational Corporation  (US)
Christian and Missionary Alliance  (US)
Christian Anti-Communism Crusade  (US)
Christian Association for Psychological Studies  (US)
Christian Beacon Press  (US)
Christian Board of Publication  (US)
Christian Booksellers Association  (US)
Christian Booksellers of Southern Africa  (SA)
Christian Brothers  (IE)
Christian Brothers of the Australian and N.Z.
  Provinces  (AT)
Christian Camping International  (US)
Christian Century Foundation  (US)
Christian Children's Fund  (US)
Christian Chronicle Inc.  (US)
Christian Church-Disciples of Christ  (US)
Christian Citizens Crusade Inc.  (US)
Christian Conference of Asia  (JA)
Christian Council of Nigeria  (NR)
Christian Democratic World Union  (IT)
Christian Echoes National Ministry  (US)
Christian Education Movement  (UK)
Christian Educators Journal Association  (US)
Christian Endeavour Union of Great Britain and
  Ireland  (UK)
Christian Evidence League  (US)
Christian Family Movement  (US)
Christian Government Movement  (US)
Christian Herald Association Inc.  (US)
Christian Herald Co. Ltd.  (UK)
Christian Herald Inc.  (US)
Christian Institute for Ethnic Studies in Asia  (PH)
Christian Institute for the Study of Religion and
  Society  (II)
Christian Institute of Southern Africa  (SA)
Christian Institutes of Islamic Studies  (II)
Christian Interfaith Media Evaluation Center, Ltd.
  (US)
Christian Labor Association  (US)
Christian Librarian's Fellowship, Inc.  (US)
Christian Life Publications, Inc.  (US)
Christian Literature Crusade Inc.  (JM)
Christian Medical Association of India  (II)
Christian Medical Association of India. Christian
  Nurses League  (II)
Christian Medical College Hospital  (II)
Christian Medical Society  (US)
Christian Missions in Many Lands, Inc.  (US)
Christian Nationalist Crusade  (US)
Christian Nationalist Party  (CN)
Christian News Ltd.  (UK)
Christian Order  (UK)
Christian Peace Conference  (CS)
Christian Press Ltd.  (CN)
Christian Record Braille Foundation, Inc  (US)
Christian Reformed Church  (US)
Christian Reformed Immigration Societies in Canada
  (CN)
Christian Reformed Publishing House  (US)
Christian Research Institute  (US)
Christian Restoration Association  (US)
Christian Rural Fellowship  (US)
Christian Scholar's Review  (US)
Christian Science Publishing Society  (US)
Christian Service Brigade  (US)
Christian Socialist Movement  (UK)
Christian Spiritual Alliance Inc.  (US)

Christian Study Centre on Chinese Religion and
  Culture  (HK)
Christian Theological Seminary  (US)
Christian Transportation Inc. Bus Division  (CN)
Christian Unity Press  (US)
Christian Weekly Newspapers Ltd.  (UK)
Christian Witness to Israel  (UK)
Christian Women Concerned  (AT)
Christian Women's Conventions International  (AT)
Christian Writers Institute  (US)
Verlag Dr. Ing. Paul Christiani  (GW)
Christianity and Crisis, Inc.  (US)
Christianity on Campus  (US)
Christianity Today, Inc.  (US)
Hans Christians Verlag  (GW)
Christlich-Demokratische Union (CDU)
  Frauenvereinigung  (GW)
Christlich-Soziale Kollegenschaft  (GW)
Christliche Allianz  (GW)
Werk Christliche Innerlichkeit  (AU)
Christliche Postvereinigung in Deutschland  (GW)
Christliche Verlagsgesellschaft mbH  (GW)
Christlicher Zeitschriftenverlag  (GW)
Christliches Verlagshaus GmbH  (GW)
Christoffel Blindenmission e. V.  (GW)
Christophers, Inc.  (US)
Christ's Mission  (US)
Christus Rex Society  (IE)
Chronicle Guidance Publications, Inc.  (US)
Chronicle House  (UK)
Chronicle of the Horse, Inc.  (US)
Chronicle Publications  (PK)
Chronique des Lettres Francaises  (FR)
Chronique Sociale de France  (FR)
Chrzescijanskie Stowarzyszenie Spoleczne  (PL)
Chubu Institute of Technology  (JA)
Chugoku Electric Power Co., Inc.  (JA)
Nicholas N. Chuhnov, Ed. & Pub  (US)
Chulalongkorn University. Institute of Population
  Studies  (TH)
Chulalongkorn University. School of Dentistry  (TH)
Chung-Ang Herald  (KO)
Chung Hwa Information Service  (CH)
Chung Kuang Yu Hsien Kung Ssu  (HK)
Chung-Kuo Tai Chi Chuan Hsueh Shu Yen Chiu Hui
  (CH)
Chung Tai Publishing Co.  (CH)
Chuo Daigaku Keizai Shogakkai
  see Chuo University. Economic and Commercial
  Society  (JA)
Chuo University. Economic and Commercial Society
  (JA)
Chuo University. Faculty of Law  (JA)
Chuo University. Faculty of Science and Engineering
  (JA)
Chuo University. Institute of Comparative Law in
  Japan  (JA)
Church and Synagogue Library Association  (US)
Church Army  (UK)
Church Army in Canada  (CN)
Church Center Press  (US)
Church Council of Greater Seattle  (US)
Church Extension Service, Inc.  (US)
Church Herald Inc.  (US)
Church History Association of India  (II)
Church in Wales Publications  (UK)
Church Information Office  (UK)
Church Lads Brigade  (UK)
Church Management, Inc.  (US)
Church Missionary Society of Australia  (AT)
Church Music Association of America  (US)
Church of All Worlds  (US)
Church of Christ Literature Services  (SA)
Church of England  (UK)
Church of England. Board for Social Responsibility
  (UK)
Church of England. Central Readers' Conference
  (UK)
Church of England Children's Society  (UK)
Church of England. Diocese of Adelaide  (AT)
Church of England, Dioceses of Melbourne & Bendigo
  (AT)
Church of England Historical Society  (AT)
Church of God  (US)
Church of God of Prophecy  (US)
Church of Jesus Christ of Latter-Day Saints  (NE)
Church of Jesus Christ of Latter-day Saints  (US)
Church of Jesus Christ of Latter-day Saints.
  Corporation of the First Presidency  (US)
Church of Jesus Christ of Latter-day Saints. Manti
  Region  (US)
Church of Light  (US)
Church of North India  (II)
Church of Scientology  (UK)
Church of Scientology. Celebrity Center  (US)
Church of Scientology in South Africa (Pty) Ltd.
  (SA)
Church of Scientology of California  (US)

Church of Scientology of California. New American
  Saint Hall Organization  (US)
Church of Scotland  (UK)
Church of South India  (II)
Church of the Brethren. General Board  (US)
Church of the Eternal Source  (US)
Church of the Hermetic Sciences  (US)
Church of the Lutheran Brethren  (US)
Church of the Lutheran Confession  (US)
Church of the Nazarene  (US)
Church of the Province of South Africa  (SA)
Church of the United Brethren in Christ  (US)
Church Pastoral Aid Society  (UK)
Church Press Ltd.  (AT)
Church Publications  (US)
Church Service Society  (UK)
Church Society  (UK)
Church Union  (UK)
Church Women United  (US)
Church World  (US)
Churches of Christ  (NE)
Churches of God. General Conference  (US)
J. & A. Churchill  (UK)
Churchman Co.  (US)
Church's Ministry Among the Jews  (UK)
Chusho Kigyo Joho Senta
  see Small Business Information Centre  (JA)
Chuto Chosakai
  see Middle East Institute of Japan  (JA)
Chutzpah Collective  (US)
Chuvashskii Gosudarstvennyi Universitet  (UR)
CIBA-Geigy Ltd.  (SZ)
Ciba-Geigy Plastics and Additives Co.  (UK)
CIBA Pharmaceutical Co.  (US)
Cibis Publishers  (KE)
Ciceroniana  (IT)
Ciclismo d'Italia  (IT)
Editorial Ciclo  (AG)
Cider Press  (US)
Cidue Edizioni s.r.l.  (IT)
Cie de Publication Rurale  (CN)
Cie Electro-Mecanique  (FR)
Ciencia Aeronautica  (VE)
Editorial Ciencias y Tecnologia, S.A.  (MX)
Libreria Cientifica Medinaceli  (SP)
Publicaciones de el Ciervo, S.A.  (SP)
Cigar Association of America  (US)
Editorial Ciguena  (SP)
Cimaise  (FR)
Cimarron Zen Center  (US)
Cimas  (SP)
CIMBRA  (SP)
Ciments Canada Lafarge Ltd.  (CN)
Cimone  (IT)
Cina Esperanto Ligo  (CC)
Cincinnati. Division of Police  (US)
Cincinnati Art Museum  (US)
Cincinnati Bar Association  (US)
Cincinnati Dental Society  (US)
Cincinnati Historical Society  (US)
Cincinnati Milacron B.V.  (NE)
Cinderella Stamp Club  (UK)
Cine Advance  (II)
Cine-Asesor  (SP)
Cine Central  (II)
Cine Club del Uruguay  (UY)
Cine Cubano  (CU)
Cine-Revue S. A.  (BE)
Cine Technicians' Association of South India  (II)
Cineaste  (US)
Cineclub Nucleo  (AG)
Cineclube do Porto  (PO)
Cinecorriere  (IT)
Cinema-Canada (Montreal)  (CN)
Cinema Magazine  (UK)
Cinema Organ Society  (UK)
Cinema-Quebec  (CN)
Cinema Sourcebook  (US)
Cinemabook  (US)
Cinemagic  (US)
Cinemasud  (IT)
Cinematography Committee  (BU)
Edizione Cinemeccanica  (IT)
Cinestudio  (SP)
Cinethique  (FR)
Cinmay Smrti Pathagara  (II)
Cinque Foil  (US)
Editrice Ciranna Latina  (IT)
Circle Books  (UK)
Circle Forum  (US)
Circle K International  (US)
Circle of State Librarians  (UK)
Circle Publications, Ltd.  (US)
Circolo Artistico di Bologna  (IT)
Circolo Cooperazione Concordia  (IT)
Circolo Culturale A.F. Formiggini  (IT)
Circolo Culturale G. Faldella  (IT)
Circolo del Cinema di Rovigo  (IT)

Circolo Speleologico Romano   (IT)
Circulo Catolico Polaco en la Republica Argentina   (AG)
Circulo Culturale Costa Rossa   (IT)
Circulo de Aeronautica   (AG)
Circulo de Bellas Artes   (SP)
Circulo de Cultura Panamericano   (US)
Circulo de Estudos Linguisticos   (BL)
Circulo Fraternal de Cooperacao Escotista   (PO)
Circulo Odontologico de Cordoba   (AG)
Circulo Odontologico de Rosario   (AG)
Circus Fans Association of America   (US)
Circus Historical Society   (US)
CIRIEC Canada   (CN)
Cisalpino-Goliardica   (IT)
Cisoria Arte   (VE)
CIStems, Inc.   (US)
Cistercienser in Mehrerau   (AU)
Edizioni Cisterciensi   (IT)
Citadel Press   (AT)
Citadel Press, Inc.   (US)
The Citadel-the Military College of South Carolina   (US)
Citeaux V.Z.W.   (BE)
Citibank   (US)
Citibank. Foreign Information Service   (US)
Citicorp   (US)
Citizen Publications   (II)
Citizen Publishing Co., Inc.   (US)
Citizen World Press, Inc.   (US)
Citizens Advisory Council to the Pennsylvania Department of Environmental Resources   (US)
Citizens and Scientists Concerned About Dangers in Environment   (US)
Citizens Band Publishing Industries, Inc.   (US)
Citizens Committee for Protection of the Environment   (US)
Citizens Committee for the Right to Keep and Bear Arms   (US)
Citizen's Constitutional Committee   (US)
Citizens Council, Inc.   (US)
Citizens Councils of America   (US)
Citizens for Clean Air, Inc.   (US)
Citizens for Decency Through Law, Inc.   (US)
Citizens for Farm Labor   (US)
Citizens for Local Democracy   (US)
Citizens Gazette   (II)
Citizens' Governmental Research Bureau   (US)
Citizens League of Minneapolis   (US)
Citizen's Movement for Safe and Efficient Energy   (US)
Citizens Public Expenditure Survey, Inc.   (US)
Citizens' Research Foundation   (US)
Citizens Union of the City of New York   (US)
Citoyens du Cosmos   (CN)
Citroen-Daal   (NA)
Citrum   (SA)
Citrus Engineering Conference   (US)
Citrus Industry   (US)
Citta di Vita   (IT)
Citta e Societa   (IT)
Edizioni Citta Eterna   (IT)
Citta Futura   (IT)
Citta Nuova   (IT)
City and Guilds College Union   (UK)
City Business Library   (UK)
City Club of New York   (US)
City College of New York   (US)
City College of New York. Alumni Association   (US)
City College of New York. Engineering School   (US)
City College of New York. Library   (US)
City College of New York. School of Education   (US)
City College of New York. Workshop Center for Open Education   (US)
City Geese   (US)
City Lights Books   (US)
City Magazines Ltd.   (UK)
City Moon   (US)
City News Publishing Co.   (US)
City of Aberdeen. Public Relations Department   (UK)
City of Birmingham Symphony Orchestra   (UK)
City of Burlington Common Council   (US)
City of London Phonograph & Gramophone Society   (UK)
City of London Polytechnic. Mansfield Law Club   (UK)
City of London Weekly Ltd.   (UK)
City of Ottawa Coin Club   (CN)
City of Perth   (AT)
City of Westminster Chamber of Commerce   (UK)
City of York Art Gallery   (UK)
City Planning Association of Japan   (JA)
City Printers and Stationers (Pty) Ltd.   (RH)
City University of New York   (US)
City University of New York. Bernard M. Baruch College   (US)
City University of New York, Brooklyn College   (US)

City University of New York, Brooklyn College. Africana Institute   (US)
City University of New York, Brooklyn College. Center for Responsive Psychology   (US)
City University of New York, Brooklyn College. Graduate Student Association   (US)
City University of New York. Comparative Urban Studies Center   (US)
City University of New York, Graduate Center. Environmental Psychology Program   (US)
City University of New York. Graduate School and University Center   (US)
City University of New York, Graduate School and University Center. Center for Social Research   (US)
City University of New York. Hunter College   (US)
City University of New York. Queens College   (US)
City University of New York, Queens College. Center for Instructional Development   (US)
City University of New York, Queens College. Department of English   (US)
City University of New York, Queens College. Graduate Political Science Association   (US)
City University of New York. Research Center for Musical Iconography   (US)
City University Union Society   (UK)
Ciudadano   (SP)
Civic-Data Corp.   (US)
Civic Garden Centre   (CN)
Civic Trust   (UK)
Civica Biblioteca A. Maj   (IT)
Civica Stazione Idrobiologica di Milano   (IT)
Civil Affairs Association   (US)
Civil and Public Services Association   (UK)
Civil Rights Court Digest   (US)
Civil Service National Whitley Council   (UK)
Civil Service Sports Council   (UK)
Civil Service Union   (UK)
Civil War Round Table Associates   (US)
Civil War Token Society   (US)
Civilfoersvarsfoerbundets Foerlags AB   (SW)
Civilingenjoersfoerbundets Tidskrift   (SW)
Civilisation Libertaire   (FR)
Civilta Cattolica   (IT)
Civilta Italica   (IT)
Civitan International   (US)
Edizioni Civitas   (IT)
Civitas dei Foundation   (US)
Civitec   (FR)
Librairie Clairafrique   (SG)
Claitor's Publishing Division   (US)
Clan Casselberry-Casselbury-Castleberry-Castlebury of America   (US)
Clan Donald Association of Nova Scotia   (CN)
Clan MacNeil Association of America   (US)
Clan McLaren Society, U S A   (US)
Clanalder Press   (AT)
Clancy Publications, Inc   (US)
Clapper Publishing Company, Inc.   (US)
Claremont College   (US)
Claremont Institute for Administrative Studies. Claremont Graduate School   (US)
Claremont Men's College. Department of Political Science   (US)
Clarence Publishing Co.   (AT)
Clarendon Press   (UK)
Claretian Fathers   (SP)
Claretian Juridical Institute in Rome   (IT)
Claretian Publications   (US)
Clarion Call Memorial Publications   (US)
Clarion Press   (US)
Clarity Publishing, Inc.   (US)
Arthur H. Clark Co.   (US)
Donald D. Clark & Associates, Inc.   (US)
Dean M. Clark   (US)
Raymond B. Clark, Jr., Ed. & Pub.   (US)
Clark Boardman Co., Ltd.   (US)
Clark County Board of Education   (US)
Clark Publishing (Highland Park)   (US)
Clark Publishing Co.   (US)
Clark University   (US)
Clark University. Graduate Board   (US)
Clark University Press   (US)
James Clarke & Co. Ltd.   (UK)
Clarke & Hunter (London) Ltd.   (UK)
Frederick S. Clarke, Ed & Pub.   (US)
Clarke Institute of Psychiatry   (CN)
Clarke, Irwin & Co., Ltd.   (CN)
Richard Clarke Associates   (US)
Editions Claspy Zurich   (SZ)
E. W. Classey Ltd.   (UK)
Classic Car Club of America   (US)
Classic M G Yearbook   (US)
Classic Partners   (US)
Classic Publications Ltd.   (UK)
Classic Publishing (Pty.) Ltd.   (SA)
Classical Association   (US)
Classical Association of Canada   (CN)

Classical Association of New England   (US)
Classical Association of South Africa   (SA)
Classical Association of the Atlantic States   (US)
Classical Association of the Middle West and South, Inc.   (US)
Classical Association of the Pacific Northwest   (US)
Classical Association of the Southwestern United States   (US)
Classical Folia Associates   (US)
Classified Media Ltd.   (UK)
Claude Bernard Guide Europeen de l'Immobilier   (FR)
Alice Moser Claudel, Ed. & Pub.   (US)
Hans Clavin, Ed. & Pub.   (NE)
Rufus Clay   (US)
Clay Minerals Society   (US)
Clay Publishing Co. Ltd.   (CN)
Clay Science Society of Japan   (JA)
Editions Clayton   (FR)
Chris Clayton, Ed. & Pub   (US)
Sharon Clayton   (US)
Clayton Junior College   (US)
Editions CLE   (CM)
La Cle des Champs   (FR)
Clean Air Society of Australia & New Zealand   (AT)
Clearinghouse for Options in Children's Education   (US)
Clearinghouse for U F O News and Information   (US)
Clearinghouse on Development Communication   (US)
Clemens-Sels-Museum   (GW)
Clemson University. Clemson Architectural Foundation   (US)
Clemson University. College of Industrial Management and Textile Science   (US)
Clemson University. Cooperative Extension Service   (US)
Clemson University. Department of English   (US)
Clemson University. Department of Forestry   (US)
Clemson University. Department of Political Science   (US)
Clemson University. Poultry Science Department   (US)
Clemson University. Water Resources Research Institute   (US)
Editions de Clermont   (FR)
Cleveland Advertising Club   (US)
Cleveland Automobile Club-AAA   (US)
Cleveland Citizen Publishing Co.   (US)
Cleveland Clinic Foundation   (US)
Forrest F. Cleveland, Ed. & Pub.   (US)
Cleveland Engineering Society   (US)
Cleveland Food Dealers Association   (US)
Cleveland Foundation   (US)
Cleveland Institute of Music   (US)
Cleveland Jewish Publication Co.   (US)
Cleveland Ltda.   (BL)
Cleveland Magazine Co.   (US)
Cleveland Medical Library Association   (US)
Cleveland Museum of Art   (US)
Cleveland Museum of Natural History   (US)
Cleveland Public Library Staff Association   (US)
Cleveland State University. College of Law   (US)
Cleveland State University. Department of Philosophy   (US)
Cleveland State University. Department of Religion   (US)
Cleveland Trust Company   (US)
Cleworth Publishing Co., Inc.   (US)
Client's Monthly Alert, Inc.   (US)
Ralph L. Clifford, Ed. & Pub.   (US)
Cliggott Publishing Co.   (US)
Clima y Ambiente   (SP)
Climax Molybdenum Co.   (US)
Climax Molybdenum Co. Technical Information Department. AMAX Specialty Metals Corp.   (US)
Climbing, Ltd.   (US)
Clinch River Breeder Reactor Project   (US)
Clinica Chirurgica dell'Universita   (IT)
Clinica della Malattie Nervose e Mentali   (IT)
Edizioni Clinica Europea   (IT)
Clinica Mexicana de Cirugia y Radioterapie   (MX)
Clinica Oculistica   (IT)
Clinica Ostetrica e Ginecologica   (IT)
Clinica Ostetrica e Ginecologia "L. Mangiagalli"   (IT)
Clinica Pediatrica   (IT)
Clinica Pediatrica Universitaria de Lisboa   (PO)
Clinical Chiropractic Publishing Co., Inc   (US)
Clinical Electron Microscopy Society of Japan   (JA)
Clinical Lab Products, Inc.   (US)
Clinical Psychiatry News   (US)
Clinical Psychology Publishing Co., Inc.   (US)
Clinton Essex-Franklin Library System   (US)
CLIO   (IT)
CLIO Awards Enterprises, Inc.   (US)
Clio Press Ltd.   (UK)
Clique Ltd.   (UK)
Cloquet Publications, Inc.   (US)

Close, Martin, Schreiber & Co. (US)
Clothing Institute (UK)
Cloud Chamber (US)
Cloudburst Press (CN)
Clover Patch, Inc. (US)
Clovernook Printing House for Blind (US)
Clown War (US)
Clowns of America, Inc (US)
Club Alpin Francais (FR)
Club Alpin Francais. Section Rhone-Alpes (FR)
Club Alpin Suisse (SZ)
Club Alpino Italiano (IT)
Club Alpino Italiano Sezioni Trivenete (IT)
Club Atletico de Madrid (SP)
Club de Commone (IT)
Club de la Grammaire (SZ)
Club de Radiorama (SP)
Club del Ejecutivo de Seguros (SP)
Club des Ornithologues du Quebec, Inc. (CN)
Club du Cirque (FR)
Club du Griffon, d'Arret a Poil Dur Korthals (FR)
Club Familiar, Inc. (US)
Club Filatelico de Caracas (VE)
Club Francais de la Medaille (FR)
Club International Alhambra (SP)
Club Juventud Panadera (SP)
Club of Arts Amateurs (JO)
Club Pleins Feux (FR)
Club Politikon e.V. (GW)
Clube de Campismo de Lisboa (PO)
Clube de Engenharia (BL)
Clube Filatelico de Portugal (PO)
Clube Militar Naval (PO)
Clube Naval. Departamento Cultural (BL)
Clubes Rotarios de la Republica (HO)
CNK International (UK)
Co-Existence (UK)
Coach & Athlete, Inc. (US)
Coach House Press (CN)
Coachella Valley Sun (US)
Coaching News (UK)
Coal Consumers Association of India (II)
Coal Industry Advisory Committee to the Ohio River
  Valley Water Sanitation Commission (US)
COAS Publishing and Research (US)
Coast (US)
Coast and Mountain Walkers of New South Wales
  (AT)
Coastal Anti-Pollution League (UK)
Coastal Bend Council of Governments (US)
Coastal Plains Center for Marine Development
  Services (US)
Cobra Foerlags (SW)
Coburger Landesstiftung (GW)
Coca-Cola Export Corporation (Holland Branch)
  (NE)
Libreria Cocco (IT)
Cochin Port Trust (II)
Cochin University
  see University of Cochin (II)
Cockatrice Press Ltd. (UK)
Cockerel Print (NZ)
Cockpit-Uitgeverij (NE)
Cockrel Corporation (US)
Cocoa Research Institute (GH)
Coconut Research Institute (CE)
Coda Publications (CN)
Codecri Ltda. (BL)
Cody Publications, Inc. (US)
Coe College (US)
Coe College Student Senate (US)
Coe Laboratories (US)
Dietrich Coelde Verlag GmbH (GW)
Coffee Gallery (US)
Coffee House; Contemporary Greek Arts and Letters
  (US)
Anita Coffelt, Ed. & Pub. (US)
Cogitations (US)
Cognizant Corp. (US)
Gabriel M. Cohen, Ed. & Pub. (US)
Stanley Cohen, Ed. & Pub. (US)
Verlag B. Cohn (US)
Coimbra Editora (PO)
Coin Arts, Inc. (US)
Coin Investment Communique (US)
Coinamatic Trade Publishing Co., Inc. (US)
Cointra, S.A. (SP)
Coker College (US)
Colby College Library (US)
Cold Spring Harbor Laboratory (US)
Colegio Anchieta. Centro de Estudos Sociais (BL)
Colegio Antioqueno de Abogados (CK)
Colegio de Abogados (CR)
Colegio de Abogados de Honduras (HO)
Colegio de Abogados de la Ciudad de Buenos Aires
  (AG)
Colegio de Abogados de Medellin (CK)
Colegio de Abogados de Puerto Rico (PR)

Colegio de Abogados de Zaragoza. (SP)
Colegio de Agentes de Cambio y Bolsa de Barcelona.
  Servicio de Estudios e Informacion (SP)
Colegio de Bibliotecarios de la Provincia de Buenos
  Aires (AG)
Colegio de Cirujanos Dentistas de Puerto Rico (PR)
Colegio de Dentistas de Chile (CL)
Colegio de Doctores en Ciencias Economicas y
  Contadores del Uruguay (UY)
Colegio de Farmaceuticos de Costa Rica (CR)
Colegio de Graduados en Ciencias Economicas (AG)
Colegio de Ingenieros Agronomos de Mexico, A.C.
  (MX)
Colegio de Ingenieros Arquitectos y Agrimensores de
  Puerto Rico (PR)
Colegio de Ingenieros de Caminos, Canales y Puertos
  (SP)
Colegio de Ingenieros de Venezuela (VE)
Colegio de Medicos del Distrito Federal (VE)
Colegio de Medicos y Cirujanos (CR)
Colegio de Medicos y Cirujanos de Nicaragua (NQ)
Colegio de Mexico (MX)
Colegio de Mexico. Biblioteca (MX)
Colegio de Postgraduados (MX)
Colegio de Profesores de Venezuela (VE)
Colegio de San Ignacio. Asociacion Antiguos Alumnos
  (SP)
Colegio Dominicano de Ingenieros, Arquitectos y
  Agrimensores (DR)
Colegio Hondureno Economistas (HO)
Colegio Ibero-Latino-Americano de Dermatologia
  (PO)
Colegio Medico de El Salvador (ES)
Colegio Medico del Peru (PE)
Colegio Militar do Rio de Janeiro (BL)
Colegio Nacional de Economistas (MX)
Colegio Nacional de Enfermeras (MX)
Colegio Nacional General Primo de Rivera (SP)
Colegio Oficial de Arquitectos de Cataluna y Baleares
  (SP)
Colegio Oficial de Arquitectos de Madrid (SP)
Colegio Ofieial de Farmaceuticos de la Provincia de
  Barcelona (SP)
Colegio Oficial de Ingenieros Tecnicos en Topografia
  (SP)
Colegio Salesiano (PE)
Colegio Sindical Nacional de Agentes de Seguros
  (SP)
Colegio Teologado "Felipe Scio" (SP)
Charles Coleman, Buch- und Zeitschriften-Verlag KG
  (GW)
Erwin Coleman, Inc. (US)
Coleopterists Society (US)
Coleopterists Society (Washington) (US)
Colgate Alumni Corporation (US)
Colgate University (US)
Colgate University Press (US)
Librairie Armand Colin (FR)
Collectable Old Advertising (US)
Collectif Jeune Cinema (FR)
Collections Baur (SZ)
Collections et Monnaies (FR)
Collective Bargaining Forum (US)
Collective Black Arts, Inc. (US)
Collectivites-Express (FR)
Collector Books (US)
Collector Ltd. (UK)
Collectors Club (US)
Collector's Media, Inc. (US)
Collectors Quarterly (US)
College Ahuntsic (CN)
College and University Personnel Association (US)
College Art Association of America (US)
College Athletics Publishing Service (US)
College Band Directors National Association (US)
College Bound Journal (US)
College d'Europe (BE)
College de France. Institut des Hautes Etudes
  Chinoises (FR)
College de Pataphysique (FR)
College English Association (US)
College Entrance Examination Board (US)
College Entrance Examination Board. Admissions
  Testing Program (US)
College Entrance Examination Board. College
  Scholarship Service (US)
College Francais de Medecine Interne (FR)
College Francais de Pathologie Vasculaire (FR)
College International pour l'Etude Scientifique des
  Techniques de Production Mecanique
  see International Institution for Production
  Engineering Research (SZ)
College Language Association (US)
College Music Society (US)
College of Agriculture and Animal Husbandry (IR)
College of American Pathologists (US)
College of Dairy Agriculture (JA)
College of Emporia Alumni Society (US)

College of Engineering (II)
College of Engineering Technology (II)
College of Family Physicians of Canada (CN)
College of Insurance (US)
College of Librarianship Wales (UK)
College of Medicine, Mosul (IQ)
College of Medicine of South Africa (SA)
College of New Caledonia (CN)
College of Physicians and Surgeons (US)
College of Physicians and Surgeons of British
  Columbia (CN)
College of Physicians and Surgeons of Ontario (CN)
College of Physicians of Philadelphia (US)
College of Preceptors (UK)
College of Psychic Studies (UK)
College of Radiographers (UK)
College of St. Thomas (US)
College of Social Welfare and Research Centre (BG)
College of Speech Therapists (UK)
College of Teachers of the Blind (UK)
College of Textile Technology, Serampore (II)
College of the Virgin Islands. Caribbean Islands
  Research Institute (VI)
College of William and Mary (US)
College of William and Mary. Department of Modern
  Languages (US)
College of William and Mary. School of Business
  Administration (US)
College of Wooster (US)
College Philosophique et Theologique S.J. St.-Albert
  (BE)
College Placement Council, Inc. (US)
College Placement Services, Inc. (US)
College Press Service (US)
College-Rater, Inc. (US)
College Reading Association (US)
College Saint Pierre (HT)
College Sports Information Directors of America
  (US)
College Store Catalog (US)
College Swimming Coaches Association of America
  (US)
College Theology Society (US)
College Universitaire de Hearst
  see University College of Hearst (CN)
Collegiate Scene (US)
Collegio Alberoni (IT)
Collegio Alla Querce (IT)
Collegio Araldico (IT)
Collegio Assistenti (IT)
Collegio dei Geometri di Torino e Provincia e
  dell'Union Regionale Collegi Geometri del Piemonte
  e della Valle d'Aosta (IT)
Collegio Ingegneri Ferroviari Italiani (IT)
Collegio Internazionale S. Lorenzo da Brindisi (IT)
Collegio San Bonaventura. Commissione Storica (IT)
Collegium Ad Studium Historiae Medicae (JA)
Collegium Carolinum (GW)
Collegium Internationale Allergologicum (SZ)
Collegium Internationale Chirugiae Digestivae (IT)
Collegium Romanicium Helvetiorum a Curatoribus
  Vocis Romanicae (SZ)
Collier Books (US)
Rex Collings Ltd. (UK)
Editrice Collins (IT)
James H. Collyer (CN)
Cologne. Museen der Stadt Koeln (GW)
Cologne. Oberstadtdirektor (GW)
Cologne. Statistisches Amt (GW)
Cologne. Verkehrsamt (GW)
Colombia. Corporacion Nacional de Turismo (CK)
Colombia. Departamento Administrativo Nacional de
  Estadistica. Banco Nacional de Datos (CK)
Colombia. Departamento Nacional de Planeacion
  (CK)
Colombia. Direccion General del Presupuesto (CK)
Colombia. Escuela Superior de Guerra. Fuerzas
  Militares de Colombia (CK)
Colombia. Fuerza Aerea (CK)
Colombia. Instituto Colombiana de Seguros Sociales
  (CK)
Colombia. Ministerio de Agricultura (CK)
Colombia. Ministerio de Defensa (CK)
Colombia. Ministerio de Educacion Nacional. Division
  de Educacion de Adultos (CK)
Colombia. Ministerio de Educacion Nacional. Instituto
  Colombiano de Antropologia (CK)
Colombia. Ministerio de Educacion Nacional. Instituto
  Colombiano para el Fomento de la Educacion
  Superior (CK)
Colombia. Ministerio de Educacion Nacional.
  Extension Cultural (CK)
Colombia. Ministerio de Gobierno. Instituto
  Linguistico de Verano (CK)
Colombia. Ministerio de Minas y Energia (CK)

*see* International Committee on the History of Art (FR)
Comite Intersyndical des Biologistes Francais (FR)
Comite Judio Americano (AG)
Comite Maritime International
  *see* International Maritime Committee (BE)
Comite Nacional Brasileiro da Conferencia Mundial da Energia (BL)
Comite Nacional Lechero (SP)
Comite National Contre le Tabagisme (FR)
Comite National de Defense Contre l'Alcoolisme (FR)
Comite National de l'Enfance (FR)
Comite National de l'Organisation Francaise (FR)
Comite National de la Gravure Francaise (FR)
Comite National de Propagande pour la Consommation des Produits de la Mer (FR)
Comite National du Secours Routiers Francais (FR)
Comite National Francais de Geodesie et Geophysique (FR)
Comite Professionnel du Petrole (FR)
Comite Regional de Recursos Hidraulicos (HO)
Comites de Lutte des Handicapes (FR)
Comitetul Central al Uniunii Tineretului Comunist (RM)
Comitetul de Cultura si Educatie Socialista al Judetului Brasov (RM)
Comitetul de Cultura si Educatie Socialista al Judetului Iasi (RM)
Comitetul de Cultura si Educatie Socialista al Judetului Mures (RM)
Comitetul de Cultura si Educatie Socialista al Judetului Sibiu (RM)
Comitetul National Pentru Apararea Pacii din Republica Socialista Romania (RM)
Comitetul Pentru Cultura si Educatie Socialista a Municipiului Bucuresti (RM)
Commanders' Conference Information Exchange Program (US)
Comment Publishing Co. (NZ)
Editrice Commentarium pro Religiosis (IT)
Commerce (1935) Limited (II)
Commerce & Industry Monthly Journal (BG)
Commerce Clearing House, Inc. (US)
Commerce Editions (FR)
Commerce Law Services, Inc. (US)
Commerce Publishing Co. (US)
Commerce Publishing Corp. (US)
Commercial & Technical Publications (II)
Commercial Bank of Australia Ltd. (AT)
Commercial Bank of Ethiopia (ET)
Commercial Bank of Greece (GR)
Commercial Fisheries Laboratory (PR)
Commercial Fishing Enterprises Ltd. (UK)
Commercial Herald (US)
Commercial Law League of America (US)
Commercial Magazine Co. (CN)
Commercial Products Ltd. (II)
Commercial Publications of S. A. Pty. Ltd. (AT)
Commercial Publishing Co. (US)
Commercial Syndicate Ltd. (KE)
Commercial Transport Magazine Ltd. (UK)
Commercial Travellers' Guild (AT)
Commercial West (US)
Publications Commerciales Francaises (CN)
Commercianti Italiani Filatelici (IT)
Commercio del Colore (IT)
Commercio del Popolo (IT)
Commercio Italiana per la Gran Bretagna e il Commonwealth (IT)
Commerical Publications Bureau (II)
Commerzbank AG (GW)
Commerzia-Verlag (GW)
Commissariat of St. Stephen's Franciscan Province (US)
Commissariato Nazionale per Il Terz' Ordine Francescano (IT)
Commissie voor de Ontwikkeling van Beleidsanalyse (NE)
Commission Belge de Bibliographie (BE)
Commission de la Bourse (BE)
Commission de la Carte Geologique du Monde (CN)
Commission des Communautes Europeennes
  *see* Commission of the European Communities (EI)
Commission Economique pour l'Afrique
  *see* United Nations Economic Commission for Africa (UN)
Commission Francaise des Archives Juives (FR)
Commission Generale de la Securite et de la Salubrite dans la Siderurgie
  *see* General Commission on Safety and Health in the Iron and Steel Industry (EI)
Commission Internationale des Industries Agricoles et Alimentaires
  *see* International Commission for Agricultural Industries (FR)

Commission Internationale des Irrigations et du Drainage
  *see* International Commission on Irrigation and Drainage (II)
Commission Internationale Technique de Sucrerie
  *see* International Commission of Sugar Technology (BE)
Commission Interuniversitaire Suisse de Linguistique Appliquee (SZ)
Commission of the European Communities (EI)
Commission of the European Communities. Centre d'Information et de Documentation (EI)
Commission of the European Communities. Commission Generale de la Securite et de la Salubrite dans la Siderurgie
  *see* General Commission on Safety and Health in the Iron and Steel Industry (EI)
Commission of the European Communities. Directorate General for Press and Information. Division for Industrial and Scientific Information
  *see* Commission of the European Communities. Division for Industrial and Scientific Information (EI)
Commission of the European Communities. Directorate General for Social Affairs. Vocational Guidance and Training Division
  *see* Commission of the European Communities. Vocational Guidance and Training Division (EI)
Commission of the European Communities. Directorate of Taxation (EI)
Commission of the European Communities. Division for Industrial and Scientific Information (EI)
Commission of the European Communities. Dublin Office (EI)
Commission of the European Communities. General Commission on Safety and Health in the Iron and Steel Industry
  *see* General Commission on Safety and Health in the Iron and Steel Industry (EI)
Commission of the European Communities Library (EI)
Commission of the European Communities. Terminology Office (EI)
Commission of the European Communities. Vocational Guidance and Training Division (EI)
Commission on Professional and Hospital Activities (US)
Commission on Rehabilitation Medicine (US)
Commission on Voluntary Service & Action (US)
Commissione delle Comunita Europee (IT)
Commissioner of Patents (AT)
Committee Against Racism (US)
Committee for a Free China (US)
Committee for an Independent Canada (CN)
Committee for Babylonian Jewry (UK)
Committee for Better Transit, Inc. (US)
Committee for Cultural Relations with Armenians Abroad (UR)
Committee for Economic Development (US)
Committee for Economic Development of Australia (AT)
Committee for Freedom in Mozambique, Angola and Guinea (UK)
Committee for Freedom of Choice in Cancer Therapy, Inc. (US)
Committee for International Cooperation in Information Retrieval Among Examining Patent Offices (SZ)
Committee for International Coordination of National Research in Demography
  *see* Comite International de Coordination des Recherches Nationales en Demographie (FR)
Committee for Jewish Culture (IS)
Committee for Monetary Research and Education, Inc. (US)
Committee for Prisoner Humanity & Justice (US)
Committee for the Advancement of Kurdistan (US)
Committee for the Furtherance of Torah Observance (US)
Committee for the Future, Inc. (US)
Committee for the Support of Human Rights in South Korea (US)
Committee of Black Performing Arts (US)
Committee of Civil Rights League (SA)
Committee of Communist Revolutionaries (II)
Committee of Concerned Indian Philosophers for Social Action (II)
Committee of Direction of Fruit and Vegetable Marketing (AT)
Committee of Directors of Polytechnics (UK)
Committee of Greek Agronomists (GR)
Committee of Interns and Residents (US)
Committee of London Clearing Bankers (UK)
Committee of Southern Churchmen Inc. (US)
Committee of the Kyoto University Africa Primatological Expedition
  *see under* Kyoto University (JA)

Committee of University Industrial Relations Librarians (US)
Committee on Canadian Labour History (CN)
Committee on Institutional Cooperation (US)
Committee on Invisible Exports (UK)
Committee on Research in Dance (US)
Committee on Space Research (FR)
Committee to Combat Huntington's Disease, Inc. (US)
Committee to End Violence Against the Next Generation (US)
Commodities Magazine, Inc. (US)
Commodity Advisory Service (US)
Commodity Exchange, Inc. (US)
Commodity Futures Trading Commission (US)
Commodity Research Bureau Inc. (US)
Common Cause (US)
Common Law Reports Ltd. (UK)
Common Market Law Reports (UK)
Common Wealth (UK)
Commons, Open Spaces and Foot Paths Preservation Society (UK)
Commonweal Publishing Co., Inc. (US)
Commonwealth Agricultural Bureaux (UK)
Commonwealth Air Transport Council (UK)
Commonwealth & Continental Church Society (UK)
Commonwealth Banking Corp. (AT)
Commonwealth Broadcasting Association (UK)
Commonwealth Bureau of Animal Health (UK)
Commonwealth Bureau of Dairy Science and Technology (UK)
Commonwealth Bureau of Horticulture and Plantation Crops (UK)
Commonwealth Bureau of Nutrition (UK)
Commonwealth Bureau of Pastures and Yield Crops (UK)
Commonwealth Bureau of Plant Breeding and Genetics (UK)
Commonwealth Bureau of Soils (UK)
Commonwealth Club of California (US)
Commonwealth Committee on Mineral Resources and Geology. Geological Liaison Office (UK)
Commonwealth Council for Educational Adminstration (AT)
Commonwealth Forestry Bureau (UK)
Commonwealth Forestry Institute. Forest Economics Section (UK)
Commonwealth Foundation (UK)
Commonwealth Human Ecology Council (UK)
Commonwealth Industrial Gases Ltd. (AT)
Commonwealth Institute (UK)
Commonwealth Institute of Biological Control (TR)
Commonwealth Institute of Entomology (UK)
Commonwealth Institute of Helminthology (TR)
Commonwealth Institute of Helminthology (UK)
Commonwealth Library Association (JM)
Commonwealth Magistrates' Association (UK)
Commonwealth Mycological Institute (UK)
Commonwealth Parliamentary Association (AT)
Commonwealth Parliamentary Association (CN)
Commonwealth Parliamentary Association (UK)
Commonwealth Police Officers Association (AT)
Commonwealth Press Union (UK)
Commonwealth Producers' Organization (UK)
Commonwealth Scientific and Industrial Research Organization
  *see* C. S. I. R. O. (AT)
Commonwealth Secretariat. Commonwealth Youth Programme (UK)
Commonwealth Secretariat. Education Division (UK)
Commonwealth Secretariat. General Trade and Commodities Division (UK)
Commonwealth Secretariat. Information Division (UK)
Commonwealth Taxation Board of Review (AT)
Commonwealth Teaching Service (AT)
Communaute de Taize (FR)
Communaute Economique du Betail et de la Viande (UV)
Communaute Europeene de l'Energie
  *see* European Atomic Energy Community (EI)
Communaute Europeene du Charbon et de l'Acier
  *see* European Coal and Steel Community (EI)
Communaute Non Violente (FR)
Communication and Cognition (BE)
Communication Arts Books (US)
Communication Channels Inc. (US)
Communication Consultants, Inc. (US)
Communication Industries Association of Japan (JA)
Communication Research and Services (US)
Communications Board (UK)
Communications Counselors. Inc (US)
Communications for Health (US)
Communications House (US)

Confederation Nationale des Syndicats Dentaires (FR)
Confederation Nationale du Commerce Charbonnier (FR)
Confederation Nationale du Travail (FR)
Confederation of British Industry (UK)
Confederation of Free German Trade Unions (GE)
Confederation of Health Service Employees (UK)
Confederation of Indian Industrial Editors (II)
Confederation of Irish Industry (IE)
Confederation Royale Horeca (BE)
Confederazione Cooperativa Italiana (IT)
Confederazione delle Libere Associazioni Artigane Italiane (IT)
Confederazione Generale Agricoltura Italiana (IT)
Confederazione Generale dell' Industria Italiana (IT)
Confederazione Italiana d'Azienda (IT)
Confederazione Italiana dei Servizi Pubblici degli Enti Locali (IT)
Confederazione Italiana Servizi Pubblici degli Enti Locali (IT)
Confederazione Italiana Sindacati Lavoratori (IT)
Confederazione Nazionale Coltivatori Diretti (IT)
Conference Board in Canada (CN)
Conference Board, Inc. (US)
Conference Board of the Mathematical Sciences (US)
Conference Catholique Canadienne. Office National de Liturgie (CN)
Conference des Ordinaires du Rwanda et Burundi (BD)
Conference for Secondary School English Department Chairmen (US)
Conference Group for Social and Administrative History (US)
Conference of Mennonite Brethren Churches of Canada (CN)
Conference of Muslim Lecturers and Senior Staff of All Nigerian Universities (NR)
Conference of Presidents of Major American Jewish Organizations (US)
Conference of Public Health Laboratory Directors (US)
Conference of Socialist Economists (UK)
Conference on Alternative State and Local Public Policies (US)
Conference on Biological Sonar and Diving Mammals. Proceedings (US)
Conference on British Studies (US)
Conference on Chinese Oral and Performing Literature (US)
Conference on Christianity and Literature (US)
Conference on College Composition and Communication (US)
Conference on Faith and History (US)
Conference on Jewish Social Studies (US)
Conference on Latin American History (US)
Conference on Scottish Studies (CN)
Conference Permanente des Recteurs et Vice Chanceliers des Universites Europeennes
  see Standing Conference of Rectors and Vice-Chancellors of the European Universities (SZ)
Conference Universitaire Suisse (SZ)
Conferences & Exhibitions Publications Ltd. (UK)
Conferences du Cenacle (LE)
  Editorial Confidencias, S. A. (MX)
  Editions de la Confiserie (FR)
Confluence Press, Inc. (US)
Confluencia (US)
Confluent Education and Research Center (US)
Confrontation Press (UK)
Confucius-Mencius Society of the Republic of China (CH)
Congenital Anomalies Research Association of Japan (JA)
Ivan A. Conger, Ed. & Pub. (US)
Congo. Service de la Statistique (CF)
Congo Disque (ZR)
Congregacao do Santissimo Redentor (BL)
Congregation of Marian Fathers (US)
Congregation of Marians (US)
Congregational Library (US)
Congregational Memorial Hall Trust Ltd. (UK)
Congregazione dei Missionari di S. Carlo (IT)
Congregazione di S. Giuseppe (Giuseppini del Murialdo) (IT)
Congregazione Universale della Santa Casa (IT)
Congres de Psychiatrie et de Neurologie de Langue Francaise (FR)
Congreso Judio Latinoamericano (AG)
Congress for Jewish Culture, Inc. (US)
Congress of Afrikan People (US)
Congress of Astrological Organizations (US)
Congress of County Medical Societies (CCMS) Publishing Co. (US)
Congress of Illinois Historical Societies & Museums (US)

Congress of Jewish Culture (US)
Congress of Neurological Surgeons (US)
Congress of Organizations of the Physically Handicapped, Inc. (US)
Congress of Racial Equality (US)
Congressional Black Caucus (US)
Congressional Digest Corp. (US)
Congressional Information Bureau Inc. (US)
Congressional Information Service (US)
Congressional Quarterly Inc. (US)
Congressional Staff Directory (US)
Connaissance des Hommes (FR)
Connecticut. Advisory Council on Vocational and Career Education. (US)
Connecticut. Auditors of Public Accounts (US)
Connecticut. Commission on Human Rights and Opportunities (US)
Connecticut. Commission to Study and Investigate the Problems of Deaf and Hearing-Impaired Persons (US)
Connecticut. Connecticut Agricultural Experiment Station (US)
Connecticut. Council on Environmental Quality (US)
Connecticut. Department of Community Affairs (US)
Connecticut. Department of Corrections. Research Section (US)
Connecticut. Department of Environmental Protection (US)
Connecticut. Department of Health (US)
Connecticut. Department of Transportation. Bureau of Staff Services (US)
Connecticut. Department on Aging (US)
Connecticut. Energy Advisory Board (US)
Connecticut. Judicial Department (US)
Connecticut. Labor Department (US)
Connecticut. Office of the Bank Commissioner (US)
Connecticut. Permanent Commission on the Status of Women (US)
Connecticut. State Library (US)
Connecticut. Treasury Department (US)
Connecticut Academy of Arts and Sciences (US)
Connecticut Association of Boards of Education, Inc. (US)
Connecticut Audiovisual Education Association (US)
Connecticut Bar Association, Inc. (US)
Connecticut Business & Industry Association (US)
Connecticut College (US)
Connecticut Conservation Association (US)
Connecticut Correctional Institution (US)
Connecticut Directory Co., Inc. (US)
Connecticut Education Association (US)
Connecticut Hospital Research and Education Foundation, Inc. (US)
Connecticut Junior Republic (US)
Connecticut Library Association (US)
Connecticut Nurses Association (US)
Connecticut Public Expenditure Council, Inc. (US)
Connecticut River Valley Covered Bridge Society (US)
Connecticut School Library Association (US)
Connecticut Society of Certified Public Accountants. Educational and Research Foundation (US)
Connecticut State Dental Association (US)
Connecticut State Medical Society (US)
Connecticut Writers League (US)
Conner Prairie Pioneer Settlement (US)
Connerly & Associates, Inc. (US)
Connolly Books Ltd. (UK)
Conocimiento de la Nueva Era (AG)
Conococheague Associates, Inc. (US)
Conquest (US)
Gerhard Conrad (GW)
Conradh na Gaeilge (IE)
Conseil d'Expansion Economique Inc. (CN)
Conseil de l'Europe
  see Council of Europe (FR)
Conseil de l'Hotellerie et de la Restauration (CN)
Conseil des Affaires Sociales et de la Famille (CN)
Conseil des Arts du Canada. Office des Tournees (CN)
Conseil des Musees Nationaux (FR)
Conseil des Recherches Agricoles du Quebec (CN)
Conseil des Sciences du Canada (CN)
Conseil du Quebec de l'Enfance Exceptionnelle (CN)
Conseil Economique Regional de Wallonie (BE)
Conseil Europeen pour la Recherche Nucleaire
  see European Organization for Nuclear Research (SZ)
Conseil International de l'Action Sociale
  see International Council on Social Welfare (FR)
Conseil International de la Langue Francaise (FR)
Conseil International des Agences Benevoles
  see International Council of Voluntary Agencies (SZ)
Conseil International des Machines a Combustion
  see International Council on Combustion Engines (FR)
Conseil International pour l'Exploration de la Mer

  see International Council for the Exploration of the Sea (DK)
Conseil International sur les Problemes de l'Alcoolisme et des Toxicomanies
  see International Council on Alcohol and Addictions (SZ)
Conseil Luxembourgeois du Mouvement Europeen (LU)
Conseil National des Economies Regionales et de la Productivite (C.N.E.R.P.) (FR)
Conseil National du Mouvement de la Paix (FR)
Conseil National du Patronat Francais (FR)
Conseil Oecumenique des Eglises
  see World Council of Churches (SZ)
Conseil Regional de Paris de l'Ordre des Architectes (FR)
Conseil Superieur de la Peche (FR)
Conseil Superieur du Livre (CN)
Conseiller des Assurances et de la Finance (FR)
Consejo de Direccion (CU)
Consejo Economica y Social de las Naciones Unidas
  see United Nations Economic and Social Council (UN)
Consejo Economico Sindical Nacional (SP)
Consejo General de Colegios de Odontologos y Estomatologos (SP)
Consejo Interamericano de Comercio y Produccion
  see Inter-American Council of Commerce and Production (UY)
Consejo Latinoamericano de Ciencias Sociales (AG)
Consejo Nacional de Ayudantes Tecnicos Sanitarios (SP)
Consejo Nacional de Ciencia y Tecnologia (MX)
Consejo Nacional de Enfermeras (SP)
Consejo Nacional de Investigaciones Cientificas y Tecnologicas. Departamento de Educacion (VE)
Consejo Nacional para la Ensenanza de la Biologia (MX)
Consejo Nacional para la Ensenanza e Investigacion en Psicologia (MX)
Consejo Nacional Tecnico de la Educacion (MX)
Consejo Superior de Colegios de Ingenieros de Minas (SP)
Consejo Superior de Colegios Oficiales de Aparejadores y Arquitectos Tecnicos (SP)
Consejo Superior Universitario Centroamericano (ES)
Consejo Superior Universitario Centroamericano (NQ)
Consejo Superior Universitario Centroamericano (CR)
Consejo Tecnico de Telecomunicacion (SP)
Conselho Estadual de Educacao de Sao Paulo (BL)
Conselho Federal de Cultura (BL)
Conselho Nacional de Desenvolvimento Cientifico e Tecnologico (BL)
Conselho Nacional de Economia (BL)
Conselho Nacional de Pesquisas (BL)
Conselho Nacional de Pesquisas, Sociedade Brasileira de Geologia (BL)
Consensus, Inc. (US)
Conservation Committee of California Oil Producers (US)
Conservation Contractor's Association of Texas (US)
Conservation Council of Ontario (CN)
Conservation Education Association (US)
Conservation Foundation (US)
Conservation Society of New South Wales (AT)
Conservative & Unionist Central Office (UK)
Conservative Baptist Foreign Mission Society (US)
Conservative Society of America (US)
Conservatoire Botanique de la Ville de Geneve (SZ)
Conservatoire de Musique de Geneve (SZ)
Conservatoire National des Arts et Metiers (FR)
Conservatorio Nacional de Musica (MX)
Conservatorul "George Dima" (RM)
Consiglio della Gioventu Evangelica Italiana (IT)
Consiglio Nazionale degli Ingegneri (IT)
Consiglio Nazionale delle Ricerche (IT)
Consiglio Nazionale delle Ricerche. Istituto di Elaborazione della Informazione (IT)
Consiglio Nazionale per la Professione; Federazione Nazionale dei Periti Industriali (IT)
Consiglio Regionale della Miniere (!T)
Consiliul Culturii si Educatiei Socialiste (RM)
Consiliul General A.R.L.U.S. (RM)
Consiliul National al Apelor (RM)
Consiliul National al Femeilor din Republica Socialista Romania (RM)
Consiliul Suprem al Dezvoltarii Economice si Sociale. Institutul Central de Cercetari Economice (RM)
Consistoire Israelite de Paris (FR)
Consociato Internationalis Musicae Sacrae (LU)
Consolidated Artists Inc. (US)
Consolidated Drake Press (US)
Consolidated Edison Company of New York, Inc. (US)
Consolidated Marketing Services, Inc. (US)
Consolidated Press Printing Co., Inc. (US)

Cornell University Libraries. Department of
  Manuscripts and University Archives   (US)
Cornell University Libraries. John M. Olin Library
  (US)
Cornell University Medical College. Alumni
  Association, Inc.   (US)
Cornell University. Office of International Agriculture
  (US)
Cornell University Press   (US)
Cornell University. Sage School of Philosophy   (US)
Cornell University. School of Hotel Administration
  (US)
Cornell University. Southeast Asia Program   (US)
Cornell Veterinarian, Inc.   (US)
Cornelsen-Velhagen und Klasing GmbH und Co.
  (GW)
Cornerstone Genealogical Society   (US)
Cornhusker Press   (US)
Corning Museum of Glass   (US)
Cornmarket Press Ltd.   (UK)
Cornwall Archaeological Society   (UK)
Corona Publishing Co., Ltd.   (JA)
Coronelli-Weltbund der Globusfreunde   (AU)
Corpcom Services, Inc.   (US)
Corpo Nazionale Giovani Esploratori Italiani. Clan
  Nazionale Seniores   (IT)
Corporacion Boliviana de Fomento   (BO)
Corporacion de Estudios y Publicaciones   (EC)
Corporacion de los Andes   (VE)
Corporacion del Cobre. Departamento Estudios y
  Analisis de Mercados   (CL)
Corporacion Editorial, S.A.   (MX)
Corporacion Financiera Colombiana S.A.
  Departamento Tecnico-Economico   (CK)
Corporacion Hotelera de Colombia   (CK)
Corporacion Minera de Bolivia. Dept. de Relaciones
  Publicas   (BO)
Corporacion Venezolana de Fomento. Unidad de
  Estudios   (VE)
Corporate Information Center   (US)
Corporate Reorganization Reporter, Inc.   (US)
Corporate Report, Inc.   (US)
Corporate Responsibility   (US)
Corporate Shareholder, Inc.   (US)
Corporation des Bibliothecaires Professionnels du
  Quebec   (CN)
Corporation des Createurs Artisans de l'Est du Quebec
  (CN)
Corporation des Electroniciens du Quebec   (CN)
Corporation for Public Broadcasting   (US)
Corporation of Lloyds   (UK)
Corporation of London   (UK)
Corporation of Master Electricians of Quebec   (CN)
Corporation of Professional Social Workers   (CN)
Corporation of the National Museums of Canada
  (CN)
Corporation Professionnelle des Conseillers
  d'Orientation du Quebec   (CN)
Corporation Professionnelle des Medecins du Quebec
  (CN)
Corporation Service Co.   (US)
Corps of Engineers. Waterborne Commerce Statistics
  Center   (US)
Corpus Publishers Services Ltd.   (CN)
Corpus Scriptorum Christianorum Orientalium de
  Louvain-Washington   (BE)
Correctional Association of New York   (US)
Correctional Information Service, Inc.   (US)
Ediciones Corregidor   (AG)
Correio Portugues   (CN)
Correios e Telecomunicacoes de Portugal. Servicos
  Culturais   (PO)
Correo Hispano-Americano   (CN)
Correspondence Chess League of Australia   (AT)
Corriedale Sheep Society (Inc.)   (NZ)
Corriere de Caracas, C. A.   (VE)
Corriere del Teatro   (IT)
Editoriale del Corriere della Sera   (IT)
Corriere Internazionale del Teatro   (IT)
Corriere Internazionale della Musica   (IT)
Corriere Nuova Europa   (IT)
Corrispondenza Socialista   (IT)
Corrodentia Society   (US)
Corrosion and Protection Association   (US)
Corrosion Prevention and Control   (UK)
Corso Andrea Podesta   (IT)
Cortex   (IT)
Corvallis Environmental Research Laboratory   (US)
Corvus Publishing Group Ltd.   (CN)
Cosmatom   (UK)
Cosme Matias Menezes Pvt. Ltd.   (II)
Cosmetic, Toiletry & Fragrance Association   (US)
Cosmetic World News   (UK)
Cosmetology Accrediting Commission   (US)
Cosmic Circus   (US)
Cosmic Information Agency   (US)
Cosmic Media   (SI)

Cosmic-Ray Research Laboratory
  see under Nagoya University   (JA)
Cosmopolitan Institute of Public Affairs   (II)
Cosmorama Cultural Enterprise Co. Ltd.   (HK)
Editorial Cosmos   (MX)
Cosmos   (UK)
Cosmos Press Ltd.   (CY)
Cosretic Laboratories   (US)
Livraria Sa da Costa   (PO)
Editorial Costa Rica   (CR)
Costa Rica. Archivo Nacional   (CR)
Costa Rica. Direccion General de Estadistica y Censos
  (CR)
Costa Rica. Ministerio de Cultura, Juventud y
  Deportes   (CR)
Costa Rica. Ministerio de Educacion Publica.
  Direccion General de Artes y Letras   (CR)
Costa Rica. Ministerio de Hacienda. Oficina del
  Presupuesto   (CR)
Costa Rica. Ministerio de Obras Publicas y
  Transportes. Instituto Geografico Nacional   (CR)
Norberto Costabel, Ed. & Pub.   (UY)
Gregg Costikyan, Ed. & Pub.   (US)
Costituente di Destra   (IT)
Costume Society   (UK)
Costume Society of America   (US)
Costume Society of Ontario   (CN)
Richard Cotten, Ed. & Pub.   (US)
Cotton Corporation of India   (II)
Cotton Digest Co., Inc.   (US)
Cotton Exporters Association   (UA)
Cotton Gin and Oil Mill Press   (US)
Cotton Public Corporation   (SJ)
Cotton Research Corp   (UK)
Cotton Research Institute, Gatooma   (RH)
Cotton Textiles Export Promotion Council.   (II)
Cottonwood Review   (US)
Couleurs   (FR)
Richard L. Coulton, Ed. & Pub.   (CN)
Council Bluffs Central Labor Union   (US)
Council for a Department of Peace   (US)
Council for Advancement and Support of Education
  (US)
Council for Agricultural and Chemurgic Research
  (US)
Council for Basic Education   (US)
Council for British Archaeology   (UK)
Council for Civil Liberties   (AT)
Council for Educational Technology for the United
  Kingdom   (UK)
Council for European Studies   (US)
Council for Exceptional Children   (US)
Council for Exceptional Children. Canadian
  Committee   (CN)
Council for Financial Aid to Education   (US)
Council for Interdisciplinary Communication in
  Medicine   (US)
Council for International Exchange of Scholars.
  Conference Board of Associated Research Council
  (US)
Council for International Organizations of Medical
  Sciences   (SZ)
Council for Islamic Studies and Research   (BG)
Council for Kentish Archaeology   (UK)
Council for Law Reporting   (GH)
Council for Nature   (UK)
Council for Nautical Archaeology   (UK)
Council for Old World Archaeology   (US)
Council for Planning & Conservation   (US)
Council for Political Studies   (II)
Council for Scientific and Industrial Research   (GH)
Council for Scientific and Industrial Research, Ghana.
  Forest Products Research Institute   (GH)
Council for Scientific and Industrial Research   (SA)
Council for Scientific and Industrial Research.
  Department of Nature Conservation   (SA)
Council for Scientific and Industrial Research.
  National Building Research Institute
  see National Building Research Institute   (SA)
Council for Scientific and Industrial Research.
  National Institute for Personnel Research
  see National Institute for Personnel Research   (SA)
Council for Scientific and Industrial Research.
  National Institute for Transport and Road Research
  see National Institute for Transport and Road
  Research   (SA)
Council for Scientific and Industrial Research.
  National Institute for Telecommunication Research
  see National Institute for Telecommunication
  Research   (SA)
Council for Scientific and Industrial Research.
  National Mechanical Engineering Research Institute
  see National Mechanical Engineering Research
  Institute   (SA)
Council for Scientific and Industrial Research.
  National Research Institute for Mathematical
  Sciences

see National Research Institute for Mathematical
  Sciences   (SA)
Council for Scientific and Industrial Research.
  Scientific Committee for Antarctic Research   (SA)
Council for Scientific and Industrial Research. South
  African Wool and Textile Research Institute
  see South African Wool and Textile Research
  Institute   (SA)
Council for Social Development   (II)
Council for the Defence of Government Schools. NSW
  Branch   (AT)
Council for the Development of Economic and Social
  Research in Africa   (SG)
Council for the Protection of Rural England   (UK)
Council for the Protection of Rural Wales   (UK)
Council for the Single Mother and Her Child   (AT)
Council for the Social Sciences in East Africa. Social
  Science Conference   (TZ)
Council for Tobacco Research--U.S.A. Inc.   (US)
Council for World Mission (Congregational and
  Reformed)   (UK)
Council of Australian Food Technology Association
  (AT)
Council of Behavioral Research   (II)
Council of Better Business Bureaus   (US)
Council of Biological and Medical Abstracts   (US)
Council of Biology Editors   (US)
Council of British Manufacturers of Petroleum
  Equipment   (UK)
Council of Christians and Jews   (UK)
Council of Churches in Indonesia   (IO)
Council of Communication Societies   (US)
Council of Earth Religions   (US)
Council of Educational Facility Planners   (US)
Council of Europe   (FR)
Council of Europe. Documentation Centre for
  Education in Europe
  see Documentation Centre for Education in Europe
  (FR)
Council of Europe. European Commission of Human
  Rights
  see European Commission of Human Rights   (FR)
Council of Europe. European Committee on Crime
  Problems
  see European Committee on Crime Problems   (FR)
Council of Europe. European Conference of Local
  Authorities
  see European Conference of Local Authorities
  (FR)
Council of Europe. European Information Centre for
  Nature Conservation
  see European Information Centre for Nature
  Conservation   (FR)
Council of European National Youth Committees
  (BE)
Council of Graduate Schools in the U.S.   (US)
Council of Higher Educational Institutions in New
  York City   (US)
Council of Jewish Federations and Welfare Funds, Inc.
  (US)
Council of Law Reporting for New South Wales
  (AT)
Council of Legal Education   (UK)
Council of Michigan Foundations   (US)
Council of Ministers of the European Communities
  see Council of the European Communities   (EI)
Council of Northern California Philatelic Societies
  (US)
Council of Ontario Universities   (CN)
Council of Planning Librarians   (US)
Council of Planning Librarians. Exchange
  Bibliographies   (US)
Council of Profit Sharing Industries   (US)
Council of Scientific and Industrial Research
  see India. Council of Scientific and Industrial
  Research   (II)
Council of Social Service of the A.C.T.   (AT)
Council of State Governments   (US)
Council of State Governments. Conference of Chief
  Justices   (US)
Council of State Governments. Southern Legislative
  Conference   (US)
Council of State Planning Agencies   (US)
Council of Supervisors and Administrators of the City
  of New York   (US)
Council of T A V R Associations   (UK)
Council of the European Communities   (EI)
Council of the Forest Industries of B.C.   (CN)
Council of the Scottish Law Agents Society   (UK)
Council of the Sephardi Community   (IS)
Council of the Southern Mountains, Inc.   (US)
Council of the Stock Exchange   (UK)
Council on Abandoned Military Posts   (US)
Council on American Affairs   (US)
Council on Anthropology and Education   (US)
Council on Economic Priorities   (US)

Cuba. Ministerio de Salud Publica  (CU)
Cuba. Ministerio de Salud Publica. Centro Nacional de
  Informacion de Ciencias Medicas  (CU)
Cuba. Ministerio del Commercio Exterior  (CU)
Cuba. Oficina Nacional de Invenciones, Informacion
  Tecnica y Marcas  (CU)
Cuba Internacional  (CU)
Cuba Resource Center  (US)
Cucina Italiana  (IT)
Cuckfield Baptist Church  (UK)
Cudahy Publishing Co.  (US)
Cue Publishing Co.  (US)
Cuento  (MX)
Cuerpo Medico Beneficencia Provincia de Madrid
  (SP)
Cuestionario  (AG)
Editions Cujas  (FR)
Editorial Cul - Tec s.r.l.  (AG)
Culinary Alliance, Local 681 and Bartenders, Local
  686  (US)
Culinary Institute of America  (US)
Culinary Reviews Inc.  (US)
Cullen Egan Dell Australia  (AT)
William Culross & Son Ltd.  (UK)
Edizioni di Cultura Contemporanea  (IT)
Cultura nel Mondo  (IT)
Cultura y Ciencia Politica  (MX)
Cultural Activist  (US)
Cultural and Social Centre for the Asian and Pacific
  Region  (KO)
Cultural Comercial  (HO)
Cultural Correspondence  (US)
Cultural Distribuidora de Livros  (BL)
Cultural Motivation Publications Inc.  (US)
Cultural Research Institute  (II)
Ediciones Culturales Mexicanas, S.A.  (MX)
Culture, Arts et Loisirs  (FR)
Editions "Culture et Civilisation"  (BE)
Culture Francaise  (FR)
Culture Vulture Publishing Ltd.  (CN)
Cultureel Jongeren Paspoort Noord-Holland  (NE)
Cultures et Developpement  (BE)
Cultuurtechnische Vereniging  (NE)
Culver Press  (US)
Culver-Stockton College  (US)
Cumann Leabharlannaithe Scoile  (IE)
Cumberland and Coles Genealogical Society  (US)
Cumberland Industrial Association  (UK)
Cumberland Presbyterian Church  (US)
Editorial Cumbre, S. A.  (MX)
Cummins Publishing Co.  (US)
Cumulative Stock Profits Advisor  (US)
Cumulus Corp.  (US)
Edizioni Curci s.r.l.  (IT)
Curia Arcivescovile di Ferrara  (IT)
Curia Arcivescovile di Monreale  (IT)
Curia Episcopalis Bauzanensis-Brixinensis  (IT)
Curia Metropolitana di Reggio Calabria  (IT)
Curia Patriarcale di Venezia  (IT)
Curia Vescovile di Verona  (IT)
Curiospress International  (FR)
Current  (PK)
Current Events  (II)
Current History, Inc.  (US)
Current Indian Statutes  (II)
Current Law Publishers  (II)
Current Podiatry Publications  (US)
Current Publications Private Ltd.  (II)
Current Science Association  (II)
Current Tax Reporter (Supreme Court)  (II)
Current Technical Literature Co. Pvt. Ltd.  (II)
Current World Leaders  (US)
Currents Information Systems, Inc  (US)
Curriculum Advisory Service  (US)
Curriculum Innovations, Inc.  (US)
Phillip J. Currie, Ed. & Pub.  (CN)
Currituck County Historical Society  (US)

Curtis Guild & Co. Publishers, Inc.  (US)
Curtis International Ltd.  (US)
Curtis Publishing Co.  (US)
Curwood Collector Society  (US)
Cusanus-Gesellschaft  (GW)
Empresa Editorial Cusco S.A.  (PE)
Elliott L. Cushman  (US)
Stephen P. Cushman  (US)

Cushman Foundation for Foraminiferal Research
  (US)

Custom Tailors and Designers Association of America,
  Inc.  (US)

Customart Press, Inc.  (US)
Customs Officer's Association of Australia. Fourth
  Division  (AT)
Cutlands Press Ltd.  (UK)
Cutler-Hammer, Inc.  (US)
Cutler Publications, Inc.  (US)
Ediciones Cutor S. A.  (SP)

Cuvar Jadrana  (YU)
Cuyahoga County Regional Planning Commission
  (US)
Cwmni Urdd Gobaith Cymru  (UK)
Cycle News, Inc.  (US)
Cycle World Magazine  (US)
Cycling Press, Inc.  (US)
Cycling Publications  (SA)
Cyclists' Touring Club  (UK)
Cyclotouriste  (FR)
Cyclotron Trading Services  (US)
Cygnet Enterprises  (UK)
Cykel-och Mopedfraemjandet  (SW)
Cykel- och Sporthandlarnes Riksfoerbund
  Serviceaktiebolag  (SW)
Cykelfoerbundet  (SW)
Cymbidium Society of America, Inc.  (US)
Cyngor Llyfrau Cymraeg  (UK)
Cyngor Ysgolion Ac Addysg Grefyddol Cymru  (UK)
Cypher  (UK)
Cyprus. Agricultural Research Institute  (CY)
Cyprus. Department of Agriculture. Soils and Plant
  Nutrition Section  (CY)
Cyprus. Department of Antiquities  (CY)
Cyprus. Department of Social Welfare Services  (CY)
Cyprus. Department of Statistics and Research  (CY)
Cyprus. Geological Survey Department  (CY)
Cyprus. Government Printing Office  (CY)
Cyprus. Ministry of Education  (CY)
Cyprus. Ministry of Education. Nicosia School
  Committee  (CY)
Cyprus. Ministry of Finance. Department of Statistics
  and Research
  see Cyprus. Department of Statistics and Research
  (CY)
Cyprus. Ministry of Labour and Social Insurance
  (CY)
Cyprus. Public Information Office  (CY)
Cyprus Educational Research Association  (CY)
Cyprus Geographical Association  (CY)
Cyprus Research Centre  (CY)
Cyrano de Paris  (FR)
Cystic Fibrosis Foundation  (US)
Wydawnictwa Czasopism Technicznych, N.O.T.  (PL)
Czech Ecumenical Council  (CS)
Czech Music Fund. Music Information Centre  (CS)
Czech Union of Fire Brigades  (CS)
Czechoslovak Cybernetic Association  (CS)
Czechoslovak Filmexport  (CS)
Czechoslovak Publishing Co.  (US)
Czechoslovak Society of Arts and Sciences in
  America, Inc.  (US)
Czechoslovakia. Archivni Sprava  (CS)
Czechoslovakia. Ceskoslovenska Atomova Komise
  (CS)
Czechoslovakia. Ceskoslovenska Lidova Armada.
  Hlavni Politicka Sprava  (CS)
Czechoslovakia. Federalni Ministerstvo Dopravy
  (CS)
Czechoslovakia. Federalni Ministerstvo Financi  (CS)
Czechoslovakia. Federalni Ministerstvo Hutnictvi a
  Tezkeho Strojirenstvi  (CS)
Czechoslovakia. Federalni Ministerstvo Kultury  (CS)
Czechoslovakia. Federalni Ministerstvo Narodni
  Obrany. Hlavni Politicka Sprava  (CS)
Czechoslovakia. Federalni Ministerstvo Paliv a
  Energetiky  (CS)
Czechoslovakia. Federalni Ministerstvo Prace a
  Socialnich Veci  (CS)
Czechoslovakia. Federalni Ministerstvo pro Technicky
  a Investicni Rozvoj  (CS)
Czechoslovakia. Federalni Ministerstvo Spoju  (CS)
Czechoslovakia. Federalni Ministerstvo Vnitra  (CS)
Czechoslovakia. Federalni Ministerstvo Zemedelstvi a
  Vyzivy  (CS)
Czechoslovakia. Federalni Statisticky Urad  (CS)
Czechoslovakia. Ministerstvo Kultury Ceske
  Socialisticke Republiky  (CS)
Czechoslovakia. Ministerstvo Lesniho a Vodniho
  Hospodarstvi Ceske Socialistike Republiky  (CS)
Czechoslovakia. Ministerstvo Obchodu Ceske
  Socialisticke Republiky  (CS)
Czechoslovakia. Ministerstvo Priemyslu Slovenskej
  Socialistickej Republiky  (CS)
Czechoslovakia. Ministerstvo Prumyslu Ceske
  Socialisticke Republiky  (CS)
Czechoslovakia. Ministerstvo Skolstva Slovenskej
  Socialistickej Republiky  (CS)
Czechoslovakia. Ministerstvo Skolstvi Ceske
  Socialisticke Republiky  (CS)
Czechoslovakia. Ministerstvo Spravedlnosti Ceske
  Socialisticke Republiky  (CS)
Czechoslovakia. Ministerstvo Stavebnictva Slovenskej
  Socialistickej Republiky  (CS)
Czechoslovakia. Ministerstvo Stavebnictvi Ceske
  Socialisticke Republiky  (CS)
Czechoslovakia. Ministerstvo Zemedelstvi a Vyzivy
  Ceske Socialisticke Republiky  (CS)

Czechoslovakia. Nejvyssi Soud  (CS)
Czechoslovakia. Statni Banka Ceskoslovenska  (CS)
Czechoslovakia. Statni Knihovna  (CS)
Czechoslovakia. Statni Pedagogicka Knihovna
  Komenskeho - Ustredni Pedagogicka Knihovna C S
  S R  (CS)
Czechoslovakia. Statni Planovaci Komise  (CS)
Czechoslovakia. Statni Ustav pro Zdravotnickou a
  Dokumentacni Sluzbu  (CS)
Verlag Ingrid Czwalina  (GW)
D.A.T.A., Inc.  (US)
D.A.V. College. Post-Graduate Department of Political
  Science  (II)
D.A.Y. Association  (US)
D C C -Wirtschaftsdienst und -Verlag GmbH  (GW)
D. C. Gazette  (US)
D D K-Verlag Ingeborg Weber  (GW)
D. de Giorgio, Ed. & Pub.  (IT)
D E E A Studio for Shortfilms  (GE)
D G Bank (Deutsche Genossenschaftsbank)  (GW)
D. H. Lawrence Review  (US)
D I S A Elektronik A-S  (DK)
D. J. H., Publishers  (US)
D K S Publications  (US)
D. L. Blair Corp.  (US)
D L G Verlag
  see Deutsche Landwirtschafts-Gesellschaft-Verlags
  GmbH  (GW)
D L W Aktiengesellschaft  (GW)
D M S Inc.  (US)
D N A-People's Legal Services, Inc.  (US)
D O X A  (IT)
D'Pastrana Editores, S.A.  (MX)
D R Publications Ltd.  (UK)
D R W-Verlag Weinbrenner-KG  (GW)
D S N Publications, Inc.  (US)
D S z Druckschriften- und Zeitungs-Verlag GmbH
  (GW)
D.U.L.J.V.A.  (FR)
D'Urso  (IT)
D V G-Deutsche Verlagsgesellschaft mbH  (GW)
Da Capo Press, Inc.  (US)
Da Gama Publishers (Pty) Ltd.  (SA)
Dacca University
  see University of Dacca  (BG)
Dacca University Geography Association  (BG)
Daco-Verlag Guenter Blaese  (GW)
Dacotah Territory - Territorial Press  (US)
Dadant & Sons, Inc.  (US)
Dadazine  (US)
DAF Nederland Bedrijfswagen B.V.
  see Doorne's Bedrijfswagenfabriek DAF B.V.  (NE)
Daffodil Society  (UK)
DAFSA Documentation  (FR)
Dag Hammarskjoeld Foundation  (SW)
DAGROFA  (DK)
Joseph F. Dahdah, Ed. & Pub.  (LE)
Dahlia Books  (SW)
Daido Gakkan Shuppan-bu  (JA)
Daiichi Kangyo Bank Ltd.  (JA)
Daiichi Kogyo Seiyaku Co. Ltd.  (JA)
Daiichi Seiyaku Co., Ltd.  (JA)
Daiichi Shuppan K. K.  (JA)
Daiichi Shuppan Senta  (JA)
R. Daillie, Pub.  (FR)
Daily Automotive News Co., Ltd.  (JA)
Daily Express Books Department  (UK)
Daily Telegraph Ltd.  (NZ)
Daily Telegraph Ltd.  (UK)
Daily Times of Nigeria Ltd.  (NR)
Daily Variety Ltd.  (US)
Casa Editrice G. Dainese  (IT)
Dainichi-Nippon Cables Ltd.  (JA)
Dainihon Suisankai
  see Japan Fisheries Association  (JA)
Dairy Editorial Services, Inc.  (US)
Dairy Farmers Inc.  (US)
Dairy Goat Journal Publishing Corp.  (US)
Dairy Industry Authority of New South Wales  (AT)
Dairy Research Inc.  (US)
Dairy Society International  (US)
Dairylea Cooperative, Inc.  (US)
Daisons Press Ltd.  (CN)
Daisy Publishing Co. , Inc  (US)
Dakota-North Plains Corp.  (US)
Dale Corporation  (US)
Dalesman Publishing Co. Ltd.  (UK)
Imprimerie Dalex a Montrouge  (FR)
Dalhousie Gazette Publishing Society  (CN)
Dalhousie University  (CN)
Dalhousie University. Computer Centre  (CN)
Dalhousie University. Faculty of Law  (CN)
Dalhousie University. Institute of Public Affairs  (CN)
Dalhousie University Press Ltd.  (CN)
Dalhousie University. School of Library Service  (CN)
Dalhousie University. Sir James Dunn Law Library
  (CN)
Dalka  (SO)

Deccan College Research Institute. Postgraduate &
  Research Institute  (II)
Deccan Geographical Society  (II)
December  (US)
Decennie  (FR)
Deciduous  (US)
R.v. Decker's Verlag, G. Schenk GmbH  (GW)
Pierre Decoulx, Ed. & Pub.  (FR)
Joel Decupper, Ed. & Pub.  (SG)
Edizioni Dedalo  (IT)
Dee Publishing Co.  (US)
Deepsadhana Publications  (II)
Deer Sportsman of America, Inc.  (US)
Deere & Company  (GW)
Deere & Company  (US)
John Deere S.A.  (SP)
Dees Communications  (US)
Defence Employees Welfare Council, New Delhi  (II)
Defence Journal  (PK)
Defender Publishing Co., Inc.  (US)
Defenders of the American Constitution, Inc.  (US)
Defense de l'Occident SARL  (FR)
Defense des Distillateurs Ambulants et des Bouilleurs
  de Cru  (FR)
Defense des Libertes Scolaires et Familiales  (FR)
Defense Information School  (US)
Defense Research Institute, Inc.  (US)
Defensor-Chieftain  (US)
Defiance College  (US)
Verlag Degener und Co.  (GW)
Joseph Deghaye  (BE)
J. Dehantschutter  (BE)
Edizioni Dehoniane  (IT)
Centro Editoriale Dehoniano  (IT)
Dehqan-e Ruz  (IR)
Deike-Verlag  (GW)
Deirdre  (IE)
Editions Jean Deit  (FR)
Deitenbeck Publishing Co., Inc.  (US)
Dekalb Community College  (US)
Dekalb Community College-South. Department of
  Business Administration  (US)
Dekalb Musicians Supply Co.  (US)
Dekker en Van de Vegt  (NE)
Marcel Dekker, Inc.  (US)
Marcel Dekker Journals  (US)
Delacorte Press  (US)
Delane Press  (UK)
Delano Historical Society  (US)
Delap's Fantasy and Science Fiction Review  (US)
Editions Jean Pierre Delarge  (FR)
Delaware. Department of Health and Social Services
  (US)
Delaware. Department of Health and Social Services.
  Division of Social Services  (US)
Delaware. Department of Highways and
  Transportation  (US)
Delaware. Department of Justice  (US)
Delaware. Department of Natural Resources and
  Environmental Control  (US)
Delaware. Department of Public Instruction  (US)
Delaware. Geological Survey  (US)
Delaware. Office of Management, Budget & Planning
  (US)
Delaware. Office of Minority Business Enterprises
  (US)
Delaware. State Board of Education  (US)
Delaware. State Treasurer  (US)
Delaware Army National Guard Headquarters  (US)
Delaware Art Museum  (US)
Delaware County Pharmaceutical Association  (US)
Delaware Learning Resources Association  (US)
Delaware Library Association, Inc.  (US)
Delaware Museum of Natural History  (US)
Delaware Nurses Association  (US)
Delaware State Chamber of Commerce  (US)
Delaware Today, Inc.  (US)
Delaware Valley Outdoor News  (US)
Delaware Valley Regional Planning Commission  (US)
Delawarr Laboratories Ltd.  (UK)
Delbridge Publishing Co.  (US)
Delegacion Vallvidrera del C. E. A.  (SP)
Delegates World Bulletin  (US)
Delegation a l'Amenagement du Territoire et a
  l'Action Regionale  (FR)
Delek, Israel Fuel Corporation  (IS)
Editoriale Delfino  (IT)
Delft University Press  (NE)
Delfts Bouwkundig Studenten Gezelschap Stylos
  (NE)
Delhi. Labour Commissioner  (II)
Delhi Law Times  (II)
Delhi Library Association  (II)
Delhi Medical Association  (II)
Delhi Press Samachar Patra  (II)
Delhi Sangita Samaj  (II)
Delhi Surgical Society  (II)
Delhi University

*see* University of Delhi  (II)
Delhi University Botanical Society  (II)
Delhi Writers Club  (II)
Delirante  (FR)
Verlag Delius, Klasing und Co.  (GW)
J. Dell'Acquo-Bascourt  (FR)
Dell Publishing Co. Inc.  (US)
Dellcrest Children's Centre  (CN)
Delmarva Advisory Council  (US)
Delmarva Advisory Council. Technology Acquisition
  Unit  (US)
Editions J. Delmas et Cie  (FR)
Delo  (YU)
Delphinium Society  (UK)
Editora Delta  (BL)
Delta  (UK)
Delta Air Lines  (US)
Delta Communications, Inc.  (US)
Delta Distributing Co.  (US)
Delta Farm Press, Inc.  (US)
Delta Kappa Epsilon Fraternity  (US)
Delta Kappa Gamma Society International  (US)
Delta Mu Delta National Honor Society in Business
  Administration  (US)
Delta Nu Alpha Transportation Fraternity  (US)
Delta Omicron International Music Fraternity  (US)
Delta Pi Epsilon Graduate Business Education
  Fraternity  (US)
Delta Psi Kappa  (US)
Delta Scene Corporation  (US)
Delta Sigma Delta  (US)
Delta Sigma Delta Fraternity. Arkansas Graduate
  Chapter  (US)
Delta Theta Phi Law Fraternity  (US)
Delta-Verlag Martin Buske  (GW)
Deltiologists of America  (US)
G. Delwel, B. V.  (NE)
Demag AG  (GW)
Carlos Esteban Demalde  (AG)
Karl Demeter Verlag  (GW)
Democrat Publishing Co., Ltd.  (CN)
Democratic Action Party of Malaysia  (MY)
Democratic Forum  (II)
Democratic National Party  (SA)
Democratic Republican Party (S. Korea)  (KO)
Democratic Research Service  (II)
Democratic Socialist Club  (SI)
Democratic Socialist Organizing Committee  (US)
Democrazia Cristiana  (IT)
Demografiska Forskargruppen  (SW)
Demographic Publications, Inc.  (US)
Demographic Research Centre, Baroda  (II)
Demokrit-Verlag  (GW)
Verlag fuer Demoskopie  (GW)
Dempa Publications, Inc  (US)
Dempa Publications Inc.  (JA)
Casa Editrice Denaro  (IT)
Dende Press, Inc.  (US)
Lou Deneumoustier, Ed. & Pub.  (US)
Deneway Guides and Travel Ltd.  (UK)
Denison Scientific Association  (US)
Denison University  (US)
Denki Kagaku Kyokai
  *see* Electrochemical Society of Japan  (JA)
Denki Seiko Kenkyukai
  *see* Electric Furnace Steel Research Association
  (JA)
Denki Tsushin Daigaku
  *see* University of Electro-Communications  (JA)
Denki Tsushin Kyokai
  *see* Telecommunications Association  (JA)
Denkisha Kenkyukai
  *see* Institute of Electric Rolling Stock  (JA)
Denmark. Atomenergikommissionen Forsoegsanslaeg
  Risoe  (DK)
Denmark. Boligministeriet  (DK)
Denmark. Danida  (DK)
Denmark. Danmarks Fiskeri- og Havundersoegelser
  (DK)
Denmark. Danmarks Geologiske Undersoegelse  (DK)
Denmark. Danmarks Statistik  (DK)
Denmark. Danske Statsbaner  (DK)
Denmark. Direktoratet for Kriminalforsorgen  (DK)
Denmark. Direktoratet for Toldvaesenet  (DK)
Denmark. Farvandsdirektoratet. Nautisk Afdeling
  (DK)
Denmark. Fiskeriministeriet Forsoegslaboratorium
  (DK)
Denmark. Folketing  (DK)
Denmark. Forskningssekretariatet  (DK)
Denmark. Groenlands Geologiske Undersogelse  (DK)
Denmark. I.D.E., Danmarks Institut for International
  Udveksling  (DK)
Denmark. Jordfordelingssekretariatet  (DK)
Denmark. Justitsministeriet. Direktoratet for
  Kriminalforsorgen
  *see* Denmark. Direktoratet for Kriminalforsorgen
  (DK)

Denmark. Kommissionen for Videnskabelige
  Undersogelser i Groenland  (DK)
Denmark. Kongelige Bibliotek  (DK)
Denmark. Landoekomiske Driftsbureau  (DK)
Denmark. Landsnaevnet for Boerne- og
  Ungdomsforsorg  (DK)
Denmark. Ministeriet for Groenland. Statistisk Kontor
  (DK)
Denmark. Ministry of Foreign Affairs
  *see* Denmark. Udenrigsministeriet  (DK)
Denmark. Nationalmuseet  (DK)
Denmark. Nationalmuseet. Nationaldiskoteket  (DK)
Denmark. Nordisk Statistisk Sekretariat  (DK)
Denmark. Planlaegningsraadet  (DK)
Denmark. Post- og Telegrafvaesenet  (DK)
Denmark. Rigsarkivet  (DK)
Denmark. Rigsbibliotekarembedet  (DK)
Denmark. Socialforskningsinstituttet  (DK)
Denmark. Socialstyrelsen  (DK)
Denmark. Statens Bygningsfredningsfond  (DK)
Denmark. Statens Filmcentral  (DK)
Denmark. Statens Forstlige Forsoegsvaesen  (DK)
Denmark. Statens Husdyrbrugsudvalg  (DK)
Denmark. Statens Husholdningsraad  (DK)
Denmark. Statens Kunstmuseumsnaevn  (DK)
Denmark. Statens Planteavlsudvalg  (DK)
Denmark. Udenrigsministeriet  (DK)
Denmark. Udenrigsministeriet. Handelsafdelingen
  (DK)
Denmark. Undervisningsministeriet. Oekonomisk-
  Statistiske Konsulent  (DK)
Denmark. Vildtbiologisk Station  (DK)
Editions Denoel  (FR)
Denpa Koho Kenkyukai
  *see* Japanese Committee for Radio Aids to
  Navigation  (JA)
Denshi Shashin Gakkai
  *see* Society of Electro Photography of Japan  (JA)
Denshi Tsushin Gakkai
  *see* Institute of Electronics and Communication
  Engineers of Japan  (JA)
J. M. Dent & Sons Ltd.  (UK)
Benjamin Dent Publications Ltd.  (UK)
Dental Association of South Africa  (SA)
Dental Laboratory Association  (US)
Dental Publications Ltd  (UK)
Dental Society of the State of New York  (US)
Dental Students' Association  (CE)
Dental Survey Publications  (US)
Dental Technician Ltd.  (UK)
Dentists Association of Iran  (IR)
Dentoscope  (FR)
Dentsu Advertising Ltd.  (JA)
Denver Art Museum  (US)
Denver Chamber of Commerce  (US)
Denver Field Ornithologists  (US)
Denver Freethinkers' Society  (US)
Denver Public Library  (US)
Denver Public Library. Fish and Wildlife Reference
  Service  (US)
Denver Public Library. Young Adult Services  (US)
Denver Research Institute
  *see under* University of Denver  (US)
Denver Weekly News  (US)
Denyse and Co. Inc.  (US)
Departamento del Valle del Cauca  (CK)
Department for National Savings  (UK)
Department Store Employees Union. Local 21  (US)
Department Store Workers' Union, Local 1- S  (US)
Depeche Commerciale et Agricole  (FR)
Depeche Mode  (FR)
Dependable Lists, Inc.  (US)
Depository Trust Company  (US)
Depot Press  (US)
W. H. Depperman, Ed. & Pub.  (US)
Deprem Arastirma Enstitusu
  *see* Earthquake Research Institute  (TU)
Deputazione di Storia Patria Florence  (IT)
Deputazione di Storia Patria per l'Umbria  (IT)
Derby and Derbyshire Chamber of Commerce  (UK)
Derby Societa Editrice  (IT)
Derbyshire Archaeological Society  (UK)
Derbyshire Countryside Ltd.  (UK)
Derbyshire Publishing Co. Inc.  (US)
Rufus Dercksen, Ed. & Pub.  (SA)
Editoriales de Derecho Reunidas, S.A.  (SP)
Editions Dereume  (BE)
Derivation and Tabulation Associates
  *see* D.A.T.A.  (US)
Dermatologische Gesellschaft der DDR  (GE)
DeRoche Publications  (US)
Editions Derouaux  (BE)
Editions Jean Derrier S A R L  (FR)
Derus Media Service  (US)
Derwent Publications Ltd.  (UK)

Desarrollo Agropecuario del Pais. Grupo Hidraulico (CU)
Desarrollo Economico (MX)
Desarrollo Indoamericano (CK)
Descant (CN)
Desclee de Brouwer (FR)
Deseret News (US)
Desert (US)
Desert Botanical Garden (US)
Desert First Works Press (US)
Desert Horse Corp. (US)
Desert Locust Control Organization for Eastern Africa (ET)
Desert Silhouette Publishing (US)
Design (IT)
Design and Industries Association (UK)
Design Council (UK)
Design International (GW)
Design Methods Group (US)
Designer Bookbinders Review (UK)
Designers West (US)
Desoer S.A. (BE)
Desperado (US)
Desperate Living (US)
Etablissement Dessart (BE)
Dessin et Technique (FR)
Destellos Evangelicos (UY)
Destin (SZ)
Detail-Papirhandlerforeningen i Danmark (DK)
Detective Publications, Inc. (US)
Gustav Detjen, Jr., Ed. & Pub. (US)
Detroit Athletic Club (US)
Detroit Bar Association (US)
Detroit Board of Education (US)
Detroit College of Law (US)
Detroit Diesel Allison (US)
Detroit District Dental Society (US)
Detroit Federation of Teachers. Local 231, AFL-CIO (US)
Detroit Historical Society (US)
Detroit Institute of Arts (US)
Detroit Publication Consultants (US)
Detroit Society for Genealogical Research (US)
Detroit Sun, Inc. (US)
Detroit Yacht Club (US)
Franz Deuticke (AU)
Deutsch-Arabische Handelskammer (UA)
Samuel Deutsch, Ed. & Pub. (US)
Deutsch-Indische Gesellschaft (GW)
Deutsch-Russlaendische Gesellschaft E.V. (GW)
Deutsche Akademie der Landwirtschaftswissenschaften (GE)
Deutsche Akademie der Naturforscher Leopoldina (GE)
Deutsche Akademie der Naturforscher Leopoldina. Archiv fuer Geschichte der Naturforschung und Medizin (GE)
Deutsche Akademie der Wissenschaften zu Berlin (GW)
Deutsche Akademie fuer Psychoanalyse (GW)
Deutsche Akademie fuer Sprache und Dichtung, Darmstadt (GW)
Deutsche Akademie fuer Staedtebau und Landesplanung (GW)
Deutsche Angestellten-Gewerkschaft (GW)
Verlag der Deutsche Apotheker (GW)
Deutsche Arbeitsgemeinschaft Vakuum (GW)
Deutsche B P Aktiengesellschaft (GW)
Deutsche Bausparkasse (GW)
Deutsche Bibliothek (GW)
Deutsche Bibliothek. Abteilung Deutsches Musikarchiv (GW)
Deutsche Blindenstudienanstalt (GW)
Deutsche Bodenkundliche Gesellschaft (GW)
Deutsche Botanische Gesellschaft (GW)
Deutsche Buch-Gemeinschaft (GW)
Deutsche Buecherei (GE)
Deutsche Bundesbahn (GW)
Deutsche Bundesbahn. Werbe- und Auskunftsamt fuer den Personen- und Gueterverkehr (GW)
Deutsche Bundesbank (GW)
Deutsche Bundespost (GW)
Deutsche Burgenvereinigung e.V. (GW)
Deutsche Dendrologische Gesellschaft (GW)
Deutsche Dermatologische Gesellschaft (GW)
Deutsche Entomologische Gesellschaft (GW)
Deutsche Evangelische Missionshilfe Verlag (GW)
Deutsche Exlibris-Gesellschaft e.V. (GW)
Deutsche Forschungs- und Versuchsanstalt fuer Luft- und Raumfahrt e.V. (GW)
Deutsche Forschungsgemeinschaft (GW)
Deutsche Forschungsgemeinschaft. Hegel Kommission (GW)
Deutsche Forschungsgesellschaft fuer Druck- und Reproduktionstechnik e.V. (FOGRA) (GW)
Deutsche Friedensgesellschaft-Vereinigte Kriegsdienstgegner (DFG-VK) (GW)
Deutsche Gemmologische Gesellschaft e.V. (GW)

Deutsche Geodaetische Kommission (GW)
Deutsche Gesellschaft fuer Agrarrecht (GW)
Deutsche Gesellschaft fuer Amerikastudien (GW)
Deutsche Gesellschaft fuer Anaesthesie und Wiederbelebung (GW)
Deutsche Gesellschaft fuer Anaesthesie und Wiederbelebung. Berufsverband Deutscher Anaesthesisten (GW)
Deutsche Gesellschaft fuer Anthropologie (GW)
Deutsche Gesellschaft fuer Arbeitsschutz e.V. (GW)
Deutsche Gesellschaft fuer Auswaertige Politik e.V. (GW)
Deutsche Gesellschaft fuer Bewaesserungswirtschaft E.V (GW)
Deutsche Gesellschaft fuer Biomedizinische Technik (GW)
Deutsche Gesellschaft fuer Chemisches Apparatewesen e.V. - DECHEMA (GW)
Deutsche Gesellschaft fuer Chirurgie (GW)
Deutsche Gesellschaft fuer Chronometrie e. V. (GW)
Deutsche Gesellschaft fuer die Vereinten Nationen (GW)
Deutsche Gesellschaft fuer Dokumentation e.V. (GW)
Deutsche Gesellschaft fuer Dokumentation e.V. Komitee fuer Terminologie und Sprachfragen (GW)
Deutsche Gesellschaft fuer Elektronenmikroskopie e.V. (GW)
Deutsche Gesellschaft fuer Erd-und Grundbau (GW)
Deutsche Gesellschaft fuer Ernaehrung (GW)
Deutsche Gesellschaft fuer Fettwissenschaft e. V. (GW)
Deutsche Gesellschaft fuer Gartenkunst und Landschaftspflege (GW)
Deutsche Gesellschaft fuer Gerontologie (GW)
Deutsche Gesellschaft fuer Geschichte der Medizin, Naturwissenschaft und Technik e.V. (GW)
Deutsche Gesellschaft fuer Gynaekologie (GW)
Deutsche Gesellschaft fuer Hals- , Nasen- , Ohrheilkunde, Kopf- und Halschirurgie (GW)
Deutsche Gesellschaft fuer Hauswirtschaft e.V. (GW)
Deutsche Gesellschaft fuer Heereskunde e.V. (GW)
Deutsche Gesellschaft fuer Herpetologie und Terrarienkunde e.V. (GW)
Deutsche Gesellschaft fuer Holzforschung (GW)
Deutsche Gesellschaft fuer Hygiene und Mikrobiologie (GW)
Deutsche Gesellschaft fuer Innere Medizin (GW)
Deutsche Gesellschaft fuer Kartographie e.V (GW)
Deutsche Gesellschaft fuer Kieferorthopaedie (GW)
Deutsche Gesellschaft fuer Kinderheilkunde (GW)
Deutsche Gesellschaft fuer Klinische Chemie (GW)
Deutsche Gesellschaft fuer Kommunikationsforschung (GW)
Deutsche Gesellschaft fuer Kreislaufforschung (GW)
Deutsche Gesellschaft fuer Luft- und Raumfahrt e.V. (GW)
Deutsche Gesellschaft fuer Lungen- und Atmungsforschung (GW)
Deutsche Gesellschaft fuer Manuelle Medizin (GW)
Deutsche Gesellschaft fuer Metallkunde e. V. (GW)
Deutsche Gesellschaft fuer Mineraloelwissenschaft und Kohlechemie (GW)
Deutsche Gesellschaft fuer Musik des Orients (GW)
Deutsche Gesellschaft fuer Neurologie (GW)
Deutsche Gesellschaft fuer Operations Research (GW)
Deutsche Gesellschaft fuer Orthopaedie und Traumatologie (GW)
Deutsche Gesellschaft fuer Ostasienkunde (GW)
Deutsche Gesellschaft fuer Osteuropakunde (GW)
Deutsche Gesellschaft fuer Parasitologie (GW)
Deutsche Gesellschaft fuer Pathologie (GW)
Deutsche Gesellschaft fuer Phaenomenologische Forschung (GW)
Deutsche Gesellschaft fuer Photogrammetrie (GW)
Deutsche Gesellschaft fuer Polarforschung (GW)
Deutsche Gesellschaft fuer Psychiatrie und Nervenheilkunde (GW)
Deutsche Gesellschaft fuer Psychologie (GW)
Deutsche Gesellschaft fuer Qualitaet (GW)
Deutsche Gesellschaft fuer Rechtsmedizin (GW)
Deutsche Gesellschaft fuer Rheumatologie (GW)
Deutsche Gesellschaft fuer Saeugetierkunde (GW)
Deutsche Gesellschaft fuer Schiffahrts-und Marinegeschichte e. V. (GW)
Deutsche Gesellschaft fuer Sexualforschung (GW)
Deutsche Gesellschaft fuer Thorax-, Herz- und Gefaesschirurgie (GW)
Deutsche Gesellschaft fuer Unfallheilkunde, Versicherungs-, Versorgungs- und Verkehrsmedizin (GW)
Deutsche Gesellschaft fuer Ur- und Fruehgeschichte (GW)

Deutsche Gesellschaft fuer Verdauungs- und Stoffwechselkrankheiten (GW)
Deutsche Gesellschaft fuer Versicherungsmathematik (GW)
Deutsche Gesellschaft fuer Voelkerkunde (GW)
Deutsche Gesellschaft fuer Volkskunde e.V. (GW)
Deutsche Gesellschaft fuer Volkskunde e.V. Kommission fuer Ostdeutsche Volkskunde (GW)
Deutsche Gesellschaft fuer Wehrmedizin und Wehrpharmazie (GW)
Deutsche Gesellschaft fuer Zahn-, Mund- und Kieferheilkunde (GE)
Deutsche Gesellschaft fuer Zahn-, Mund- und Kieferheilkunde (GW)
Deutsche Gesellschaft fuer Zuechtungskunde e.V. (GW)
Deutsche Gesellschaft zur Foerderung der Hoer- Sprach-Geschaedigten e.V. (GW)
Deutsche Glastechnische Gesellschaft (GW)
Deutsche Gustav Freytag Gesellschaft (GW)
Deutsche Haematologische Gesellschaft (US)
Deutsche Handelskammer in Oesterreich (AU)
Deutsche Heilpraktikerschaft e.V. (GW)
Deutsche Hochschule fuer Koerperkultur Leipzig (GE)
Deutsche Hochschule fuer Musik "Hanns Eisler". Leitstelle fuer Information und Dokumentation "Musik" (GE)
Deutsche Industriemeistervereinigung e.V (GW)
Deutsche Kakteen Gesellschaft (GW)
Deutsche Katholik in Kanada (CN)
Deutsche Keramische Gesellschaft e.V. (GW)
Deutsche Kolpingsfamilie e.V. (GW)
Deutsche Krankenhausgesellschaft (GW)
Deutsche Krebsgesellschaft (GW)
Deutsche Kriminologische Gesellschaft (GW)
Deutsche Landwirtschafts-Gesellschaft e. V. (GW)
Deutsche Landwirtschafts-Gesellschaft-Verlags-GmbH (GW)
Deutsche Meteorologische Gesellschaft (GW)
Deutsche Mineralogische Gesellschaft (GW)
Deutsche Morgenlaendische Gesellschaft (GW)
Deutsche Morgenlaendische Gesellschaft Beirut. Orient-Institut (LE)
Deutsche Mozart-Gesellschaft e.V. (GW)
Deutsche Orchestervereinigung (GW)
Deutsche Orient-Gesellschaft (GW)
Deutsche Ornithologen-Gesellschaft e.V. (GW)
Deutsche Pestalozzi-Gesellschaft (GW)
Deutsche Pharmakologische Gesellschaft (GW)
Deutsche Pharmazeutische Gesellschaft (GW)
Deutsche Philatelisten-Jugend E.V. (GW)
Deutsche Photo-und Kinohaendler-Bund (GW)
Deutsche Physikalische Gesellschaft (GW)
Verlagsanstalt Deutsche Polizei GmbH (GW)
Deutsche Postgewerkschaft (GW)
Deutsche Roentgengesellschaft (GW)
Verlag Deutsche Saengerzeitung GmbH (GW)
Deutsche Schiller-Gesellschaft (GW)
Der Deutsche Schreiner, Verlags-GmbH (GW)
Deutsche Schuhfachschule Pirmasens (GW)
Deutsche Schutzvereinigung fuer Wertpapierbesitz e.V. (GW)
Deutsche Shakespeare Gesellschaft (GE)
Deutsche Shakespeare-Gesellschaft West (GW)
Deutsche Staatsbibliothek (GE)
Deutsche Staatsbibliothek. Theodor Fontane Archiv (GE)
Deutsche Statistische Gesellschaft (GW)
Deutsche Stiftung fuer Internationale Entwicklung (GW)
Deutsche Stiftung fuer Internationale Entwicklung. Zentralstelle fuer Ernaehrung und Landwirtschaft (GW)
Deutsche Theatertechniker Gesellschaft (GW)
Deutsche Tieraerzteschaft e.V. (GW)
Deutsche Tropenmedizinische Gesellschaft (GW)
Deutsche Ueberseeische Bank (GW)
Deutsche UFO-Studiengesellschaft (DUIST e. V.) (GW)
Deutsche UNESCO-Kommission (GW)
Deutsche Vereinigung fuer die Rehabilitation Behinderter (GW)
Deutsche Vereinigung fuer Gewerblichen Rechtsschutz und Urheberrecht (GW)
Deutsche Vereinigung fuer Internationales Steuerrecht (GW)
Deutsche Vereinigung fuer Parlamentsfragen (GW)
Deutsche Verkehrswissenschaftliche Gesellschaft (GW)
Deutsche Verlagsanstalt GmbH (GW)
Deutsche Viehhandelsgesellschaft MbH Fachverlag (GW)
Deutsche Volksgesundheits-Bewegung E.V. (GW)
Deutsche Volkswirtschaftliche Gesellschaft (GW)

Deutsche Wissenschaftliche Kommission fuer Meeresforschung (GW)
Verlag Deutsche Wohnungswirtschaft GmbH (GW)
Deutsche Zeitung Christ und Welt Verlag GmbH (GW)
Deutsche Zoologische Gesellschaft (GW)
Deutscher Adressbuch-Verlag (GW)
Deutscher Aero Club (GW)
Deutscher Agrarverlag GmbH (GW)
Deutscher Akademischer Austauschdienst (DAAD) (GW)
Deutscher Alpenverein (GW)
Deutscher Altphilologen-Verband (GW)
Deutscher Amateur-Radio-Club (GW)
Deutscher Anglerverband der DDR (GE)
Deutscher Anwaltverein e.V. (GW)
Deutscher Apotheker-Verein (GW)
Deutscher Arbeitsring fuer Laermbekaempfung e.V. (GW)
Deutscher Badminton Verband (GW)
Deutscher Bauernverband e V. (GW)
Deutscher Beamtenbund (GW)
Deutscher Beamtenbund, Landesbund Bremen e.V. (GW)
Deutscher Beamtenbund. Landesbund Rheinland-Pfalz (GW)
Deutscher Beamtenbund. Verband der Beamten der Obersten Bundesbehoerden (GW)
Deutscher Berufsverband fuer Krankenpflege (GW)
Deutscher Bibliotheksverband e.V. (GW)
Deutscher Bibliotheksverband e.V. Arbeitsstelle fuer das Bibliothekswesen (GW)
Deutscher Blindenverband e.V. (GW)
Deutscher Boots- und Schiffbauer-Verband (GW)
Deutscher Buehnenverein e.V. (GW)
Deutscher Bund fuer Naturgemasse Lebens- und Heilweise e.V. (GW)
Deutscher Bundeswehr-Verband e.V (GW)
Deutscher Camping-Club e.V. (GW)
Deutscher Caritasverband (GW)
Deutscher Demokratischer Rundfunk. Staatliches Rundfunkkomitee (GE)
Deutscher Diabetikerbund e.V. (GW)
Deutscher Drucker Verlagsgesellschaft mbH und Co. KG (GW)
Deutscher Edelkatzenzuechter-Verband e.V. (GW)
Deutscher Erfinderring e.V. (GW)
Deutscher Evangelischer Missionsrat (GW)
Deutscher Fachverlag GmbH (GW)
Deutscher Feuerwehrverband (GW)
Deutscher Fleischerverband (GW)
Deutscher Forschungsdienst (GW)
Deutscher Forstverein (GW)
Deutscher Frauenrat (GW)
Deutscher Fussball-Bund (GW)
Deutscher Genossenschafts-Verlag GmbH (GW)
Deutscher Germanisten-Verband (GW)
Deutscher Gewerkschaftsbund (GW)
Deutscher Gewerkschaftsbund. Wirtschafts- und Sozialwissenschaftliches Institut (GW)
Deutscher Handelsvereinigung Spar (GW)
Deutscher Harmonikaverband e.V. (GW)
Deutscher Hochseesportverband Hansa e.V. (GW)
Deutscher Hotel- und Gaststaettenverband E.V. (DEHOGA) (GW)
Deutscher Hugenotten-Verein e.V. (GW)
Deutscher Imkerbund e.V. (GW)
Deutscher Instituts-Verlag GmbH (GW)
Deutscher Journalisten-Verband e.V (GW)
Deutscher Kanu-Verband e.V. (GW)
Deutscher Kommunal-Verlag GmbH (GW)
Deutscher Konditorenbund (GW)
Deutscher Koordinierungsrat der Gesellschaften fuer Christlichjuedische Zusammenarbeit (GW)
Deutscher Landkreistag (GW)
Deutscher Lehrerverband (GW)
Deutscher Lehrerverein Sued- und Suedwestafrikas (SA)
Deutscher Medizinischer Informationsdienst e. V. (GW)
Deutscher Mieterbund e.V. (GW)
Deutscher Modelleisenbahn-Verband der DDR (GE)
Deutscher Motoryachtverband e.V. (GW)
Deutscher Musikrat (GW)
Deutscher Oekumenischer Ausschuss (GW)
Deutscher Paritaetischer Wohlfahrtsverband E.V. (GW)
Deutscher Radio- und Fernseh- Fachverband e.V. (GW)
Deutscher Radsport-Verband der DDR (GE)
Deutscher Raiffeisenverband e.V. (GW)
Deutscher Rat der Europaeischen Bewegung e.V. (GW)
Deutscher Richterbund (GW)
Deutscher Ringer-Bund (GW)
Deutscher Saengerbund e.V. (GW)
Deutscher Sauna-Bund e.V. (GW)
Deutscher Schach-Verband (GE)

Deutscher Schaedlingsbekaempfer-Verband (GW)
Deutscher Schuetzenbund (GW)
Deutscher Sparkassen- und Giroverband e.V. (GW)
Deutscher Sparkassenverlag GmbH (GW)
Deutscher Sportlehrerverband e.V. (GW)
Deutscher Staedte- und Gemeindebund (GW)
Deutscher Stenografenbund e. V. (GW)
Deutscher Studenten-Anzeiger (GW)
Deutscher Supplement Verlag KG (GW)
Deutscher Teckelklub (GW)
Deutscher Textilreinigungs-Verband e.V. (GW)
Deutscher Turn- und Sportbund (GE)
Deutscher Turnerbund (GW)
Deutscher Verband der Jugenbuende fuer Entschiedenes Christentum e.V. (GW)
Deutscher Verband Frau und Kultur e.V. (GW)
Deutscher Verband fuer Material Pruefung (GW)
Deutscher Verband fuer Schweisstechnik e.V. (GW)
Deutscher Verband fuer Wasserwirtschaft e.V. (GW)
Deutscher Verband fuer Wohnungswesen, Staedtebau und Raumplanung e.V. (GW)
Deutscher Verein fuer Gesundheitspflege e. V. (GW)
Deutscher Verein fuer Kunstwissenschaft (GW)
Deutscher Verein fuer Oeffentliche und Private Fuersorge (GW)
Deutscher Verein fuer Vermessungswesen (GW)
Deutscher Verein fuer Versicherungswissenschaft e.V. (GW)
Deutscher Vieh und Fleischhandelsbund (GW)
Deutscher Volkshochschulverband. Paedagogische Arbeitsstelle (GW)
Deutscher Weinbauverband (GW)
Deutscher Werkbund E.V. (GW)
Deutscher Wetterdienst (GW)
Deutscher Wetterdienst. Seewetteramt (GW)
Deutscher Wissenschaftler Verband (GW)
Deutscher Zentralverein Homoeopatischer Aerzte e.V. (GW)
Deutsches Afrika-Korps e.V. (GW)
Deutsches Archaeologisches Institut (GW)
Deutsches Archaeologisches Institut, Athens (GR)
Deutsches Archaeologisches Institut. Kommission fuer Alte Geschichte und Epigraphik (GW)
Deutsches Archaeologisches Institut. Roemisch-Germanische Kommission (GW)
Deutsches Amforum e.V. (GW)
Deutsches Bucharchiv, Muenchen (GW)
Deutsches Computer Forum (GW)
Deutsches Evangelisches Institut fuer Altertumwissenschaft des Heiligen Landes (GW)
Deutsches High-Fidelity Institut (GW)
Deutsches Historisches Institut in Rom (IT)
Deutsches Hydrographisches Institut (GW)
Deutsches Institut fuer Aerztliche Mission (GW)
Deutsches Institut fuer Afrika-Forschung (GW)
Deutsches Institut fuer Betriebswirtschaft (GW)
Deutsches Institut fuer Erforschung des Mittelalters (GW)
Deutsches Institut fuer Filmkunde (GW)
Deutsches Institut fuer Internationale Paedagogische Forschung (GW)
Deutsches Institut fuer Normung e.V. (GW)
Deutsches Institut fuer Normung e.V. Ausschuss fuer Klassifikation (GW)
Deutsches Institut fuer Normung e.V. Fachnormenausschuss Photo Technik (GW)
Deutsches Institut fuer Normung e.V. Normenausschuss Schiffbau (GW)
Deutsches Institut fuer Puppenspiel (GW)
Deutsches Institut fuer Urbanistik (GW)
Deutsches Institut fuer Vormundschaftswesen (GW)
Deutsches Institut fuer Wirtschaftsforschung (GW)
Deutsches Jugendherbergswerk (GW)
Deutsches Jugendinstitut e.V. (GW)
Deutsches Komitee fuer Elektrowaerme (GW)
Deutsches Krebsforschungszentrum (GW)
Deutsches Kunststoff-Institut (GW)
Deutsches Leichtathletik-Verband (GW)
Deutsches Mode Institut (GE)
Deutsches Museum (GW)
Deutsches Orient-Institut (GW)
Deutsches Paedagogisches Zentralinstitut, Berlin (GE)
Deutsches Patentamt (GW)
Deutsches Rotes Kreuz (GW)
Deutsches Volksheimstaettenwerk e.V. (GW)
Deutsches Volksliederarchiv (GW)
Deutsches Wirtschaftswissenschaftliches Institut fuer Fremdenverkehr (GW)
Deutsches Wissenschaftliches Steuerinstitut der Steuerberater und Steuerbevollmaechtigten e.V. (GW)
Deutsches Wollforschungsinstitut (GW)
Deutsches Zentralinstitut fuer soziale Fragen (GW)
Deutsches Zentralkommittee zur Bekaempfung der Tuberkulose (GW)
Deutschland-Berichte (GW)
Verlag Deutschland Magazin (GW)

Deutschland Stiftung e.V. (GW)
Deutschlandfunk (GW)
Deutschschweizerischer Sprachverein (SZ)
Deutschsprachige Arbeitsgemeinschaft fuer Handchirurgie (GW)
Devastan Enterprises (US)
Dev Dutt, Ed. & Pub. (II)
Development Academy of the Philippines (PH)
Development and Progress (IE)
Development Bank of Indonesia
    see Bank Pembangunan Indonesia (IO)
Development Corp. for Wales (UK)
Development Dialogue (SW)
Development Finance Company of Kenya (KE)
Development Publications Ltd. (CN)
Development West, Inc. (US)
Devenir Historico (AG)
Deventer Landbouwers Vereniging Nji Sri (NE)
V. Lakshmi Devi (II)
Devon and Cornwall Notes and Queries Publishing Co. (UK)
Devon Archaeological Society (UK)
Devon Beekeepers Association (UK)
Devon Cattle Breeders' Society (UK)
Dewan Bahasa dan Pustaka Malaysia. Cawangan Sarawak (MY)
DeWitt & Co. (US)
Dewitt County Genealogical Society (US)
Dey Biswas Enterprises (II)
Dhanvantari Karyalaya (II)
Dharma Publishing (US)
Dharmaram College (II)
Dharmaram College. Centre for the Study of World Religions (II)
Ramasarana Dhaundiyala (II)
Pankaj Dhawan, Pub. (II)
Dhondt Foundation
    see Fondation Jan Dhondt (BE)
Di Baio Editore (IT)
Di Cyan & Brown (US)
Di Modica (IT)
Diabetes Federation of Australia (AT)
Diabetes Outlook, Inc. (US)
Diabetic Association of India (II)
Diagnosis News Inc. (US)
Diagrama Comunicacoes (BL)
Diakoniewerk Kaiserswerth (GW)
Diakonisches Werk der Evangelischen Kirche im Rheinland (GW)
Diakonisches Werk in Hessen und Nassau (GW)
Dialectica (SZ)
Dialetti d'Italia (IT)
Dialog, Inc. (US)
Dialoghi (IT)
Dialogos (IT)
Dialogue (SA)
Dialogue Foundation (US)
Dialogue Publications (II)
Dialogue Publications, Inc. (US)
Dialysis & Transplantation Inc. (US)
Gary L. Diamond, Ed. & Pub. (US)
Diamond Lead Co. (JA)
Diamond News (Pty) Ltd. (SA)
Diamond Publications Inc (US)
Diamond Publishing Co. (US)
Diamond Reo Trucks, Inc. (US)
Diamond Walnut Growers Inc. (US)
Diamondhead Corp. (US)
Diana (AG)
Diana (FR)
Diana (IT)
Diana's Bimonthly Press (US)
Diapason, Inc. (US)
Diapason S. A. (FR)
Diarios Associados (BL)
Dr. Jose Dias, Ed. & Pub. (PO)
Editions de la Diaspora Francaise (FR)
Diaz de Santos (SP)
Dibco Press, Inc. (US)
Dibrugarh University. Centre for Sociological Study of Frontier Region (II)
Diccionario de Especialidades Farmaceuticas (MX)
Dickens Fellowship (UK)
Dickens Press Ltd. (US)
Dickinson Robinson Group Africa (Pty) Ltd. (SA)
Dickinson School of Law (US)
Dickinson State College (US)
Judson Dicks, Ed. & Pub. (US)
Dickson and Johnson Pty. Ltd. (AT)
Didactic, Inc. (US)
Didaktischer Dienst (GW)
Ediciones Didascalia (SP)
Librairie Marcel Didier (BE)
Librairie Marcel Didier (FR)
Societe Didot Bottin (FR)
Eugen Diederichs Verlag (GW)
Dierenpark Wassenaar Zoo (NE)
Diesel and Gas Turbine (US)

Diesel Fuel Services Inc. (US)
Diesel Publications, Inc. (US)
Verlag Moritz Diesterweg (GW)
Dietetique d'Aujourd'hui (FR)
Dietmeier-van Zevern Publications, Inc. (US)
Felix Dietrich Verlag (GW)
Dietz Verlag (GE)
Diffusion Artistique et Graphique (FR)
Diffusion de la Pensee Francaise (FR)
Diffusions et Relations Officielles (FR)
Digest Books, Inc. (US)
Digest of Advices, Inc (US)
Digest Reporting Service Ltd. (CN)
Digital Equipment Computer Users Society (US)
Digital Equipment Corp. (US)
Dignity, Inc. (US)
Drukkerij Dijkstra Niemeyer B.V. (NE)
Dikegorikos Syllogos Athenon (GR)
Uitgeversmaatschappij Diligentia B. V. (NE)
George O. Dillon, Ed. & Pub. (US)
Diloutremer (FR)
Dimensioni (IT)
J. Clency Dinan, Ed. & Pub. (MF)
Dinas Intelijen Medan dan Geografi Jawatan Topografi
  T.N.I.-A.D. (IO)
Diners Club de France (FR)
Diners Club Inc. (US)
James Dines & Co. (US)
Dio e Popolo (IT)
Diocese de Paris (FR)
Diocese de Petropolis (BL)
Diocese of Arua (UG)
Diocese of Bristol (UK)
Diocese of Churchill Hudson's Bay (CN)
Diocese of Fargo (US)
Diocese of Harrisburg (US)
Diocese of Jamaica (JM)
Diocese of Lilongwe (MW)
Diocese of Reno (US)
Diocese of Richmond (US)
Diocese of San Angelo (US)
Diocese of San Diego (US)
Diocese of Singapore (SI)
Diocese of Songea (TZ)
Diocese of the Armenian Church of America (US)
Diocesi Cattolica, Comacchio (IT)
Diocesi di Cremona (IT)
Dioecesis St. Poelten (AU)
Dioezese Linz, Pastoralamt. Sozialreferat (AU)
Dionga (ZR)
Diplomat (PK)
Diplomatic and Consular Officers, Retired.
  Membership Directory (US)
Diplomatic Press and Publishing Co. (UK)
Editions Diplomatiques Africaines (SZ)
Diplomatist Associates Ltd. (UK)
Diprepu Co. Ltd. (UK)
Diputacion Foral de Navarra. Institucion Principe de
  Viana (SP)
Diputacion Provincial de Barcelona. Instituto de
  Ciencias Sociales (SP)
Diputacion Provincial de Barcelona. Servicios de
  Bibliotecas (SP)
Diputacion Provincial de Caceres (SP)
Direccion Central de la Accion Catolica Espanola
  (SP)
Direccion General de Archivos y Bibliotecas (SP)
Direccion General de Seguridad (SP)
Direct Mail-Marketing Association (US)
Direct Mail-Marketing Association (Washington)
  (US)
Direct Publications Pty. Ltd. (AT)
Direct Publications, West Australian Newspapers, Ltd.
  (AT)
Direct Selling Association (US)
Direction des Journaux Officiels (FR)
Direction du Pelerinage de Lisieux (FR)
Directional Advertising, Inc. (US)
Director General of the Ordnance Survey (UK)
Director Publications Inc (US)
Directories International (US)
Directories of Industry, Inc. (US)
Directories Publishing Co. (US)
Directors Art Institute (US)
Directors Guild of America, Inc. (US)
Directory of Alternative Periodicals (UK)
Directory of Educational Specialists (US)
Directory of Graduate Law Study (US)
Directory of Somalia (UK)
Directory of Specific Learning Disability Services
  (US)
Direzione Belle Arti del Comune di Venezia (IT)
Direzione Civici Musei (IT)
Diritti della Scuola (IT)
Disabled American Veterans and Auxiliary (US)
Disabled Driver's Association (UK)
Disabled Drivers' Motor Club (UK)

Disabled War Veterans Association of Finland (FI)
Disaster Prevention Research Institute
  see under Kyoto University (JA)
Disc Collectors Newsletter (US)
Discalced Carmelite Fathers (US)
Discalced Carmelite Fathers (IE)
Discalced Carmelite Fathers. Washington Province
  (US)
Disco Times International (US)
Discobolo (SP)
Discographer (US)
Discographical Forum (UK)
Discos Colombia. Promotion Department (SP)
Casa Editrice Discoteca s.r.l. (IT)
Discotheque National de Belgique (BE)
Discovery Productions (US)
Diseno (MX)
Diskus-Verlag (GW)
Dispensario Antituberculoso "Max Arias Schreiber"
  (PE)
Dissemination and Assessment Center for Bilingual
  Education (US)
Dissent Publishing Co., Inc. (US)
Distilled Spirits Council of the United States, Inc.
  (US)
Distillers Feed Research Council (US)
Distinctive Publications Ltd. (UK)
Distribuidora Venezolana de Azucares. Departamento
  de Promocion Industrial (VE)
Distribution Codes Inc. (US)
Distribution-Verlag GmbH (GW)
Distributive Education Clubs of America (US)
Distributive Workers of America (US)
District of Columbia. City Council (US)
District of Columbia. Department of Environmental
  Services. Air and Water Monitoring Division (US)
District of Columbia. Department of Manpower (US)
District of Columbia Dental Society (US)
District of Columbia Library Association (US)
District of Columbia Sociological Society (US)
Editions "Distrigraph" s.p.r.l. (BE)
Distrito de Riego No. 38, Rio Mayo (MX)
Ditchley Foundation (UK)
Divadelni Ustav (CS)
Diversion Magazine (US)
Divine Life Society (II)
Divine Light Mission (US)
Divine Science Federation International (US)
Divine Word University (PH)
Divine World Missionaries (IT)
N. Divinsky, Ed. & Pub. (CN)
Divulgacao da Pesca Maritima Ltda. (BL)
Divulgotecnica. Agencia Publicitaria de Investimentos
  e Representacoes (PO)
Divultec S. A. (SP)
Editrice Divus Thomas (IT)
Diwanchand Institute of National Affairs (II)
Dixie Contractor, Inc. (US)
Dixie Dung Beetle Press (US)
Dixie Publications and Arts Co. (US)
Dixie Publishers (US)
Dixon Springs Agricultural Center (US)
Djassin'foue (IV)
Djeich (AE)
Dnevnik (YU)
Do It Now Foundation (US)
Doane Agricultural Service, Inc (US)
Gildeverlag Hans Gerhard Dobler GmbH (GW)
Musikverlag Ludwig Doblinger (AU)
Doboku Gakkai
  see Japan Society of Civil Engineers (JA)
Dobson Books Ltd. (UK)
Editions Docis (FR)
Documentacion Espanola Contemporanea, S.L. (SP)
Documentation Abstracts, Inc. (US)
Documentation Agricole (FR)
Documentation Associates Information Services, Inc.
  (US)
Documentation Center of Architecture and Urban and
  Regional Planning (IT)
Documentation Centre for Education in Europe (FR)
Documentation Centre for Modern Indonesia (NE)
Documentation et Information Africaines (ZR)
Documentation Francaise (FR)
Documentation Professionnelle (FR)
Documentations Industrielles et Techniques (FR)
Documenti di Attualita Politica (IT)
Documenti Sul Comunismo (IT)
Dodd, Mead & Co., Inc (US)
Dodson Publishing Co. (US)
William Dogan Publications (US)
Dogar Bros. (PK)
Dogliotti College of Medicine
  see under University of Liberia (LB)
Doin Editeurs (FR)
Editora Dois Irmaos Ltda (BL)
Dojindo Laboratories (JA)

Dojo Hiryo Gakkai
  see Japanese Society of Soil and Manure (JA)
Verlag Dokumentation (GW)
Dokumentationsarchiv des Oesterreichischen
  Widerstandes (AU)
Dokumentationsring Paedagogik (GW)
Dokumentationsstelle fuer Schul- und Bildungsfragen
  see Centre Suisse de Documentation en Matiere
  d'Enseignement et d'Education (SZ)
Dokumente-Verlag (FR)
Alfred F. Dolbey (US)
Dolfinarium Harderwijk (NE)
Doll Castle News (US)
Dolmen Press (IE)
Dolmetsch Foundation (UK)
Dolnoslaskie Towarzystwo Oswiatowe (PL)
Dolphin Press (SA)
Domani (IT)
Societa Editrice Domani S.p.A. (IT)
Dombi (ZR)
Domenico Del Bianco (IT)
Domestic Equipment Publications Ltd (UK)
Domestic Heating Society (UK)
Domestic Petroleum Publishers, Inc. (US)
Dominica. House of Assembly (DQ)
Dominica. Ministry of Agriculture, Trade and Natural
  Resources (DQ)
Dominica. Treasury Department (DQ)
Dominica Agricultural and Industrial Development
  Bank (DQ)
Dominican Convent Friars-Fatima. Secretariado
  Nacional do Rosario (PO)
Dominican Fathers (US)
Dominican Fathers, Province of St. Albert the Great
  (US)
Dominican Fathers, Province of St. Joseph (US)
Dominican Fathers Publishers (US)
Dominican Republic. Centro Dominicano de
  Promocion de Exportaciones (DR)
Dominican Republic. Centro Nacional de
  Investigaciones Agropecuarias. Laboratorio de
  Sanidad Vegetal (DR)
Dominican Republic. Direccion General de Bellas
  Artes (DR)
Dominican Republic. Ejercito Nacional (DR)
Dominican Republic. Oficina Nacional de Presupuesto
  (DR)
Dominican Republic. Secretaria de Estado de
  Agricultura y Colonisacion (DR)
Dominican Republic. Secretaria de Estado de Industria
  y Comercio (DR)
Dominican Republic. Secretaria de Estado de Justicia
  y Trabajo (DR)
Dominican Republic. Secretaria de Estado de las
  Fuerzas Armadas (DR)
Dominican Republic. Secretaria de Estado de Obras
  Publicas y Comunicaciones (DR)
Dominican Sisters of Sinsinawa (US)
Dominicos de Andalucia. Studium Generale (SP)
Dominion Astrophysical Observatory (CN)
Dominion Engineering Works Ltd. (CN)
Dominion Life Assurance Co. (CN)
Dominion Press (US)
Dominion Press Ltd. (UK)
VEB Domowina Verlag (GE)
Editoriale Domus (IT)
Domus-Verlag GmbH (GW)
Ediciones Don Bosco (SP)
Don-Verlag Henry Ferling (GW)
V. V. Donald (NZ)
Donaldson, Lufkin and Jenrette, Inc (US)
Donato Editore (IT)
Donau-Verlag (GW)
Donaueuropaeisches Institut (AU)
Donauschwaebischer Heimatverlag (GW)
Donegal Democrat (IE)
Donemus Foundation (NE)
Donizetti Society (UK)
Donna di Casa (IT)
Eric Donne, Ed. & Pub. (US)
Reuben H. Donnelley Corp. (US)
Reuben H. Donnelley Corp. (Chicago) (US)
Reuben H. Donnelley Corp. (San Francisco) (US)
Reuben H. Donnelley Corp. Transportation Guides
  and Services (US)
Reuben H. Donnelley Corp. Travel Magazines
  Division (US)
Donovan Ltd. (CN)
Duane Doolittle, Ed. & Pub. (US)
Door (US)
Door and Hardware Institute (US)
Van Doorne's Bedrijfswagenfabriek DAF B.V. (NE)
Dopolavoro Ferroviario (IT)
Dopress (SP)
Sandy Dorbin, Ed. & Pub. (US)
Dordius AB (SW)
Editions J. M. Dore, Inc. (CN)

Dorec Verlags AG (SZ)
Doric Publishing Co., Inc. (US)
Doris Publications (UK)
John Frederick Dorman, Ed. & Pub. (US)
Bill Dorn Associates, Inc. (US)
William J. Dornan, Inc. (US)
Dornier AG (GW)
Dorotheum (AU)
Dorset County Museum (UK)
Dorset Down Sheep Breeders' Association (UK)
Dorset Natural History and Archaeological Society
  (UK)
Dorset Publishing Co. (UK)
Izdatel'stvo DOSAAF (UR)
Doshisha Daigaku
  see Doshisha University (JA)
Doshisha University. Economic Society (JA)
Doshisha University. English Literary Society (JA)
Doshisha University. Gaikoku Bungakukai (JA)
Doshisha University. School of Theology (JA)
Doshisha University. Science and Engineering
  Research Institute (JA)
Dositey Obradovich Circle (UK)
Editora Dosmil (CK)
Douai Abbey (UK)
Doubleday & Company, Inc. (US)
Doubleday Canada Ltd. (CN)
Douglas College. English and Communications
  Division (CN)
Douglas County Historical Society (US)
Orestis B. Doumanis, Ed. & Pub. (GR)
Dove Communications (AT)
Don Dover, Ed. & Pub. (US)
Dover Publications, Inc. (US)
Dow Chemical Co. (US)
Dow Jones & Co., Inc. (US)
Dow, Jones, & Co., Inc. Dow Jones Books (US)
Dow Theory Forecasts, Inc. (US)
Dow Theory Letters, Inc (US)
Dowden, Hutchinson & Ross, Inc. (US)
Downe Communications, Inc. (US)
Downey Communications, Inc. (US)
Downhill Only Club (UK)
Downstate Medical Center (US)
Downtown Athletic Club (US)
Downtown-Lower Manhattan Association (US)
Doxiadis Associates International Co., Ltd. (GR)
Ediciones Doyma, S.A. (SP)
Dr. Abrahram Kuyperstichting ter Bevordering van de
  Studie der Antirevolutionaire Beginselen (NE)
Draegerwerk AG (GW)
Dragoco, Inc. (US)
Dragon Runners' Chronicle (US)
Dragonfly (US)
Draka Kabel B.V. (NE)
Marjorie Look Drake, Ed. & Pub. (US)
Drake Publishers, Inc. (US)
Drake University. Law School (US)
Drama Book Shop (US)
Drama Book Specialists (US)
Dramatic Artistic & Literary Rights Organisation (Pty)
  Ltd. (SA)
Dramatika Produce (US)
Dramatists Guild, Inc. (US)
Dramrite Printers Ltd. (UK)
Drapalik Verlag (SZ)
Draper World Population Fund (US)
Dravo Corp. (US)
Dream Journal (US)
Dreams and Inner Spaces (US)
Drehpunkt (SZ)
Dreibrunnen-Verlag (GW)
Dreistern Verlag (GW)
Drejtoria Qendrore e Librit (AA)
Drentse Genootschap (NE)
Dresdner Bank A.G. (GW)
Julius Dressler Buch- und Zeitschriftenverlag (AU)
Kenneth Drew (US)
Walter R. Drew, Ed. & Pub. (US)
Drew University Theological School (US)
Drexel University (US)
Drexel University. Graduate School of Library Science
  (US)
Drift Publications (II)
N. Drikakes, Ed. & Pub. (GR)
Drive Publications Ltd. (UK)
Drivers License Guide Company (US)
Walter Drobich, Pub. (CN)
B. V. Drogistenpers (NE)
Droit de Vivre (FR)
Dropsie University (US)
Drorbaugh Publications Inc (US)
Droste-Verlag GmbH (GW)
Droughtmaster Stud Breeders' Society (AT)
Librarie Droz (SZ)
M. D. Drucker (US)
Druckspiegel-Fachzeitschriftenverlags- Gesellschaft
  mbH und Co. KG (GW)

Druffel-Verlag (GW)
Drug Abuse Council, Inc. (US)
Drug, Chemical and Allied Trades Association (US)
Drug Intelligence & Clinical Pharmacy, Inc (US)
Drug Merchandising (CN)
Drug Research & Control Centre (UA)
Drum (Amherst) (US)
Drum Corps News, Inc. (US)
Drum Publications (Nigeria) Ltd. (NR)
Drum Publications (UK) Ltd. (UK)
Drum Publishers Ltd. (CN)
Drusberg Verlag (SZ)
Drustvo Arhivskih Radnika SR Srbije (YU)
Drustvo Bibliotekara Bosne i Hercegovine (YU)
Drustvo Bibliotekara Srbije (YU)
Drustvo Bibliotekarjev Slovenije (YU)
Drustvo Dijabeticara Hrvatske (YU)
Drustvo Dubrovcana i Prijatelja Dubrovacke Starine
  (YU)
Drustvo Istoricara SR Srbije (YU)
Drustvo Knjizevnika Hrvatske (YU)
Drustvo Lekara Vojvodine (YU)
Drustvo Livarjev Slovenije (YU)
Drustvo Ljevaca SR Hrvatske (YU)
Drustvo Matematicara i Fizicara SR Hrvatske (YU)
Drustvo Medicinskih Radnika Srbije (YU)
Drustvo Medicinskih Sestara i Medicinskih Tehnicara
  Hrvatske (YU)
Drustvo Parazitologa Jugoslavije (YU)
Drustvo Socijalnih Radnika Hrvatske (YU)
Drustvo za Srpskohrvatski Jezik i Knjizevnost Srbije
  (YU)
Drustvo za Tehniku Zavarivanja Hrvatske (YU)
Drustvo Zobozdrastvenih Delavcev Slovenije (YU)
Drustvoto na Arhivskite Rabotnici i Arhivite vo
  Makedonija (YU)
Drustvoto za Makedonski Jazik i Literatura (YU)
Druzba Sv. Mohorja (AU)
Druzhestvo na Psikholozite (BU)
Dry Mount Press (US)
Dryad Press Inc. (US)
Drzavna Zalozba Slovenije (YU)
Du Pont de Nemours & Co.
  see E.I. Du Pont de Nemours & Co. (US)
Duaal Publishing Corp. (US)
Herbert T. Duane, Jr. (US)
Jose Venancio Duarte Sosa, Ed. & Pub. (PY)
Howard S. Dubin, Ed. & Pub. (US)
Dublin Chamber of Commerce (IE)
Dublin Institute for Advanced Studies (IE)
Dublin University (IE)
Dublin University Press Ltd. (IE)
Dubuque Leader (US)
Editions Duc (FR)
Duck (US)
Leonard G. Duck, Ed. & Pub. (US)
Ducks Unlimited (Canada) (CN)
Ducks Unlimited, Inc. (US)
Editions J. Duculot a Gembloux, S.A. (BE)
Robin Dudding, Ed. & Pub. (NZ)
Dude Ranchers Association (US)
Dudgeon Publications (US)
Dudley Observatory (US)
Dudley Public Libraries (UK)
Duemmlers Verlag (GW)
Verlag Duerrsche Buchhandlung (GW)
Duesseldorf. Amt fuer Fremdenverkehr und
  Wirtschaftsfoerderung (GW)
Duesseldorf. Amt fuer Statistik und Wahlen (GW)
Duesseldorf. Hauptstaatsarchiv (GW)
Duesseldorf. Presseamt (GW)
Duff's Turf Guide (Pty.) Ltd. (SA)
James Duffy & Co. Ltd. (IE)
Duga (YU)
Dugith Publishers (IS)
Duiker Apparatenfabriek N.V. (NE)
Duiwebenodigdhede (Edms) Bpk (SA)
Editions Dujarric (FR)
Duke Bar Association (US)
Duke Endowment (US)
Duke University. Commonwealth Studies Center
  (US)
Duke University. Council on Aging and Human
  Development (US)
Duke University. Department of Classical Studies
  (US)
Duke University. Divinity School (US)
Duke University. Geology Department (US)
Duke University. Library (US)
Duke University Marine Laboratory. Cooperative
  Oceanographic Program (US)
Duke University Medical Center Library. Library
  Systems and Communications Division (US)
Duke University Press (US)
Duke University. Program in Comparative Studies on
  Southern Asia (US)
Duke University. School of Engineering (US)
Duke University. School of Law (US)

Dulac et Cie (FR)
Editions du Dulbea (BE)
Duluth Area Chamber of Commerce (US)
Dumbarton Oaks Center for Byzantine Studies (US)
Dumbarton Oaks Garden Library (US)
Dumbarton Oaks Research Library and Collections.
  Center for Pre-Columbian Studies (US)
Dumfriesshire and Galloway Natural History and
  Antiquarian Society (UK)
Richard H. Dummer (US)
Dun and Bradstreet (Australia) Pty. Ltd. (AT)
Dun & Bradstreet, Inc. (US)
Dun & Bradstreet, Inc. Business Economics
  Department (US)
Dun and Bradstreet, Inc. Credit Services (US)
Dun & Bradstreet, Inc. Marketing Services Division
  (US)
Dun & Bradstreet International (US)
Dun and Bradstreet Ltd. (UK)
Dun & Bradstreet of Canada (CN)
Dun & Bradstreet - Stubbs Ltd. (IE)
Dun-Donnelley Publishing Corp. (US)
Dun-Donnelley Publishing Corp. Graphic Arts
  Division (US)
Duncan Enterprises, Inc. (US)
Duncker und Humblot (GW)
Dundalgan Press (W. Tempest) Ltd. (IE)
Dundee and Tayside Chamber of Commerce and
  Industry (UK)
Dungadhiwasa (II)
Dunia Usaha (IO)
Dunlop Estates Berhad (MY)
Dunlop Industrial Products (Pty.) Ltd (SA)
Dunn & Hargitt (US)
Duodecimal Society of America, Inc. (US)
Duodecimal Society of Great Britain (UK)
Publications Paul Dupont (FR)
Etienne Dupuch, Jr. Publications (BF)
Editions Jean Dupuis (BE)
T. N. Dupuy Associates (US)
Duquesne University. Department of Modern
  Languages (US)
Duquesne University. Institute of Man (US)
Duquesne University Press (US)
Duquesne University. School of Law (US)
Duquesne University. School of Music (US)
Miguel Duran-Loriga, Ed. & Pub. (SP)
Durban High School Old Boys' Club (SA)
Durban Museum (SA)
Durban Progressive Jewish Congregation (SA)
Durham County Local History Society (UK)
Durlacher Press (UK)
Durzhavno Voenno Izdatelstvo (BU)
Dushkin Publishing Group (US)
Dustbooks (UK)
Dustbooks (US)
Dustri-Verlag Dr. Karl Feistle (GW)
Dutch-Australian Publishing Co. Pty. Ltd. (AT)
Dutch Canadian Association (CN)
Dutch Canadian Toronto Credit Union (CN)
Dutch College of Surgeons (NE)
Dutch Handball Federation (NE)
Dutch Historical Association (NE)
Dutch Liberal Reformed Association
  see Vereniging van Vrijzinnig Hervormden in
  Nederland (NE)
Dutch Reformed Mission Church
  see Nederduitse Gereformeerde Sendingkerk (SA)
Dutch Volkswagen Organization (NE)
Dutchess County Genealogical Society (US)
E. P. Dutton & Co., Inc. (US)
Delamer Duverus Coordinates (US)
Dwarf Iris Society (US)
E. J. Dwyer Pty. Ltd. (AT)
Dybfrost Instituttet (DK)
Dynamit Nobel AG. Sprengtechnischer Dienst (GW)
Dynastat, Inc. (US)
Dyrefondet (DK)
E A E C
  see European Atomic Energy Community (EI)
E C A
  see United Nations Economic Commission for
  Africa (UN)
E.C. Boone Advertising Ltd. (CN)
E C E
  see United Nations Economic Commission for
  Europe (UN)
E C L A
  see United Nations Economic Commission for Latin
  America (UN)
Edizioni E C O (IT)
E C O C Ltda. (CK)
E C O S O C
  see United Nations Economic and Social Council
  (UN)
E.C. Publications, Inc. (US)

Edizioni E.C.R.A. (IT)
E C S C
    see European Coal and Steel Community (EI)
E C W A
    see United Nations Economic Commission for
        Western Asia (UN)
E C W A Productions Ltd. (NR)
E D A (IT)
E D A Corp. (US)
Casa Editrice E D A M (IT)
E D I M A (FR)
E D P News Services Inc. (US)
E. D. Publications Ltd. (UK)
E E C
    see European Economic Community (EI)
E F B - Verlag (GW)
E F S (SW)
E G & G Inc. (US)
E. G. C. M. (FR)
Editions E.G.E. (FR)
E G G (US)
Editions "E.G.P." (BE)
E. G. P. (FR)
E-Go Enterprises (US)
E I B
    see European Investment Bank (EI)
E. I. du Pont de Nemours & Co. (US)
E I P, Inc. (US)
E.K.B. Boktrykkeri (NO)
E K H E Advertising (US)
E K S F-Zentralstelle (GW)
E L-Information ELRA (DK)
Editions E.L.T.A. (FR)
E. Leitz, Inc. (US)
E. M. A. P National Publications Ltd. (UK)
E. M. G. Handmade Gramophones Ltd. (UK)
E M N I D-Institut GmbH (GW)
E M Publications (CN)
E. O. Kroon Levensmiddelenorganisatie N.V. (NE)
E. P. C. I. (FR)
E P I E Institute (US)
E.P.I.S.A. (AG)
E. P. I. S.A. Editeurs (FR)
E.P.T. (IT)
E R C Publishing Co. (CN)
E R I C (US)
E R I C. Clearinghouse on Early Childhood Education
    (US)
E R I C Clearinghouse on Educational Management
    (US)
E R I C. Clearinghouse on Higher Education (US)
E R I C Clearinghouse on Urban Education (US)
E R I Edizioni (IT)
E R i S S.p.A. (IT)
E.S.A.V. (IT)
E S C A F E
    see United Nations Economic and Social
        Commission for Asia and the Pacific (UN)
E S C A P
    see United Nations Economic and Social
        Commission for Asia and the Pacific (UN)
E S E California (US)
E S - Espana Cultural (SP)
E S P Research Associates Foundation (US)
E. S. T. E. C. (FR)
E.S.T. Editrice (IT)
E.T.A. (IT)
E.T.A.C.A. (FR)
E.T.A. Hoffmann-Gesellschaft (GW)
E. T. A. I. (FR)
E U N S A
    see Ediciones Universidad de Navarra S.A. (SP)
E U R A T O M
    see European Atomic Energy Community (EI)
E U R O S T A T
    see Statistical Office of the European Communities
        (EI)
E V A N-G
    see Committee to End Violence Against the Next
        Generation (US)
E W Communications, Inc. (US)
E Z Maid Inc. (US)
Eagle (NR)
Ealing Publications Ltd. (UK)
Ealing Technical College. School of Librarianship
    (UK)
Ear Magazine-New York (US)
Ear Press (US)
Ear Research Institute (US)
Earby Mine Research Group (UK)
Earl Heywood Fan Club (AT)
Earlsport Ltd. (UK)
Early American Industries Association (US)
Early American Society (US)
Early Childhood Education Council, Manitoba (CN)
Early English Text Society (US)
Early Ford V-8 Club of America (US)
Early Music Laboratory (US)

Earnshaw Publications Inc. (US)
Earth Garden (AT)
Earth Guild Inc (US)
Earth Religious Supplies, Inc. (US)
Earth Research (CN)
Earth Science Publishing Co. (US)
Earthmovers and Road Contractors Association of
    Australia Ltd. (AT)
Earthquake Research Institute
    see under University of Tokyo (JA)
Earthquake Research Institute (TU)
Earth's Daughters (US)
Earwig Graphics (NZ)
Eason & Son, Ltd. (IE)
East Africa Natural History Society (KE)
East Africa Womens League (KE)
East African Academy (KE)
East African Agricultural and Forestry Research
    Organization (KE)
East African Community. Statistical Department
    (KE)
East African Directory Company (KE)
East African Freshwater Fisheries Research
    Organization (UG)
East African Harbours Corporation (KE)
East African High Commission. Customs and Excise
    Department (KE)
East African Institute of Social and Cultural Affairs
    (KE)
East African Literature Bureau (KE)
East African Medical Research Council (KE)
East African Publishing House (KE)
East African Research Information Centre (KE)
East African Staff College (KE)
East African Standard (Newspapers) Ltd. (KE)
East African Venture Co. (KE)
East African Wildlife Society (UK)
East Anglian Magazine Ltd. (UK)
East Asia Publishing Co. Ltd. (JA)
East Asia Travel Association (JA)
East Asian Pastoral Institute (PH)
East Carolina University. Department of English
    (US)
East Carolina University. Department of History
    (US)
East Carolina University. Department of Political
    Science (US)
East Carolina University Poetry Forum Press (US)
East Central Illinois Criminal Justice Commission, Inc.
    (US)
East End Publishers, Inc. (US)
East Flanders. Provinciebestuur (BE)
East India Hotels Ltd. (II)
East London Arts Magazine Society (UK)
East London History Society (UK)
East London Photographic Society (SA)
East Midland Allied Press Ltd. (UK)
East Midlands Arts (UK)
East Midlands Geological Society (UK)
East of England Agricultural Society (UK)
East Pakistan Co-operative Society (BG)
East Publications, Inc. (JA)
East Riding Archaeological Society (UK)
East Side Chamber of Commerce (US)
East Side Express (US)
East Tennessee Development District (US)
East Tennessee Historical Society (US)
East Tennessee State University. Research Advisory
    Council (US)
East Texas Chamber of Commerce (US)
East Texas School Study Council (US)
East Texas State University (US)
East-West Center (US)
East-West Center. Communications Institute (US)
East-West Center. Culture Learning Institute (US)
East-West Center. East-West Technology and
    Development Institute (US)
East-West Center. Population Institute (US)
East-West Foundation (NE)
East-West Network, Inc. (US)
East-West Publishing Co. (US)
East-West S.P.R.L. (BE)
East-West Trade Council (US)
East Yorkshire Local History Society (UK)
Eastbourne College (UK)
Easter Publishing (US)
Eastern Airlines (US)
Eastern Apicultural Society (US)
Eastern Association of Student Financial Aid
    Administrators (US)
Eastern Automotive Journal (US)
Eastern Band of Cherokee Indians. Tribal Council
    (US)
Eastern Buddhist Society (JA)
Eastern Canada Association of the Deaf, Inc. (CN)
Eastern Canada Centre of Slavists and East European
    Specialists (CN)
Eastern Centre of International Studies (II)

Eastern Communication Association (US)
Eastern Counties Newspapers Ltd. (UK)
Eastern Dental Society (US)
Eastern Economic Association (US)
Eastern Economist Ltd. (II)
Eastern Electricity Board (UK)
Eastern Esplanade (UK)
Eastern Finance Association (US)
Eastern Horizon Press (HK)
Eastern Illinois University. Student Publications (US)
R. F. Eastern Ltd. (UK)
Eastern Massachusetts Regional Library System (US)
Eastern Michigan University. Department of English
    (US)
Eastern Milk Producers (US)
Eastern Montana Catholic Diocese (US)
Eastern Nebraska Genealogical Society (US)
Eastern New Mexico University. Department of
    Anthropology (US)
Eastern New Mexico University. Natural Sciences
    Research Institute (US)
Eastern New Mexico University. Paleo-Indian Institute
    (US)
Eastern North Carolina Genealogical Society (US)
Eastern Ontario Regional Library System (CN)
Eastern Pennsylvania Psychiatric Institute (US)
Eastern Pharmacist (II)
Eastern Press Services (India) (II)
Eastern Psychiatric Association (US)
Eastern Publishing Co. (US)
Eastern Railway Magazine (II)
Eastern Regional Organisation for Planning and
    Housing (II)
Eastern Regional Research Center (US)
Eastern Review, Inc. (US)
Eastern School Law Review (US)
Eastern States Archeological Federation (US)
Eastern Trade Press Co. (II)
Eastern Washington State College. Department of
    History (US)
Eastern - Western Quarter Horse Journal (US)
Eastland Publications Private Ltd. (II)
Robert Eastman, Ed. & Pub. (US)
Eastman Kodak Co. (US)
Eastman Kodak Co. Eastman Organic Chemicals
    (US)
S.C. Easton (UK)
Easy Money Refund Bulletin (US)
Eaton House Publishers Ltd. (UK)
Eaton-Williams Publications (UK)
Ebasco Services Incorporated (US)
Ebel-Doctorow Publications, Inc. (US)
Ebenezer Society (US)
Ebertin-Verlag (GW)
Josef Ebner, Ed. & Pub. (AU)
Ebner Verlag GmbH und Co. KG (GW)
Ebsco Industries (US)
Ecco Press Ltd. (US)
Echidna Epics Co. Ltd. (UK)
Echo Africain (FR)
Echo de la Finance (FR)
Echo de la Timbrologie (FR)
S.A. Echo des Bois (BE)
Echo Magazine Co. (CH)
Echo of Iran (IR)
Echos de Brehat (FR)
Echter-Verlag (GW)
Kommissions-Verlag Eckardt und Messtorff (GW)
Eckart-Verlag (GW)
A. Ross Eckler, Ed. & Pub. (US)
Publications Eclair Ltee (CN)
Eclaireuses et Eclaireurs Unionistes de France (FR)
Eclecta (FR)
Eclectic Magazine Co. (US)
Eclipse Publications Ltd. (UK)
Eco Contemporaneo (AG)
Eco d'Italia (UY)
Eco de Nayarit (MX)
Eco del Chisone (IT)
Eco del Seguro (SP)
Eco Dominicana, S. A. (DR)
Eco-Logos (US)
Eco Motori (IT)
Editorial ECO, S.A. (SP)
Editions de l' Ecole (FR)
Ecole Biblique et Archeologique de Jerusalem (FR)
Ecole d'Alfort (FR)
Ecole de Danse Simone Suter (SZ)
Ecole de Specialisation de l'Artillerie Anti-Aerienne
    (FR)
Ecole des Haute Etudes Commerciales (CN)
Ecole des Hautes Etudes Commerciales et Consulaires
    de Liege. Association des Licencies et Ingenieurs
    Commerciaux (BE)

Ecole des Hautes Etudes en Sciences Sociales (FR)

Ecole des Hautes Etudes en Sciences Sociales. Centre d'Etudes Chinoise (FR)

Ecole des Hautes Etudes en Sciences Sociales. Section des Sciences Economiques et Sociales (FR)

Ecole des Hautes Etudes Hispaniques (FR)

Ecole des Parents (FR)

Ecole du Genie (BE)
Ecole Francaise d'Athenes (GR)
Ecole Francaise d'Extreme-Orient (FR)
Ecole Moderne Francaise - Pedagogie Freinet (FR)
Ecole Nationale d'Administration. Centre de Recherches et d'Etudes Administratives (TI)
Ecole Nationale du Genie Rural, des Eaux et des Forets (FR)
Ecole Nationale Superieure de Techniques Avancees (FR)
Ecole Nationale Superieure des Bibliotheques (FR)
Ecole Normale Israelite Orientale (FR)
Ecole Normale Veterinaire d'Alfort (FR)
Ecole Polytechnique Federale de Lausanne (SZ)
Ecole Polytechnique Federale de Lausanne. Chaire de Systemes Logiques (SZ)
Ecole Polytechnique Federale de Lausanne. Institut d'Entomologie (SZ)
Ecole Pratique des Hautes Etudes (FR)
Ecole Pratique des Hautes Etudes. Centre d'Etudes Arctiques et Finno-Scandinaves (FR)
Ecole Pratique des Hautes Etudes. Centre d'Etudes de Planification Socialiste (FR)
Ecole Pratique des Hautes Etudes. Centre d'Etudes des Communications de Masse (FR)
Ecole Pratique des Hautes Etudes. Centre d'Etudes des Techniques Economiques Modernes (FR)
Ecole Pratique des Hautes Etudes. Centre d'Etudes Pre- et Protohistoriques (FR)
Ecole Pratique des Hautes Etudes. Centre de Documentation sur l'Extreme-Orient (Section Chine) (FR)
Ecole Pratique des Hautes Etudes. Centre de Documentation sur l'U.R.S.S. et les Pays Slaves (FR)
Ecole Pratique des Hautes Etudes, Centre de Mathematique Sociale (FR)
Ecole Pratique des Hautes Etudes. Centre de Psychiatrie Sociale (FR)
Ecole Pratique des Hautes Etudes, Centre de Recherches (FR)
Ecole Pratique des Hautes Etudes. Centre de Recherches d'Histoire et de Philologie (FR)
Ecole Pratique des Hautes Etudes. Centre de Recherches Historiques (FR)
Ecole Pratique des Hautes Etudes. Centre de Sociologie Europeenne (FR)
Ecole Pratique des Hautes Etudes. Centre International de Recherches d'Histoire des Sciences et des Techniques (FR)
Ecole Pratique des Hautes Etudes. Division des Aires Culturelles (FR)
Ecole Pratique des Hautes Etudes. Laboratoire d' Anthropologie (FR)
Ecole Pratique des Hautes Etudes. Laboratoire d'Anthropologie Sociale (FR)
Ecole Pratique des Hautes Etudes. Laboratoire de Micropaleontologie (FR)
Ecole Speciale Militaire de Saint-Cyr (FR)
Ecole Superieure d'Agriculture I.T.P.A. (FR)
Ecole Superieure des Sciences Economiques et Commerciales (FR)
Ecoles Nationales Veterinaires de Lyon et de Toulouse (FR)
Ecological Society of America (US)
Ecological Society of Australia (AT)
Ecological Society of Japan (JA)
Ecologist (UK)
Ecology Action (AT)
Ecology Action East (US)
Ecology Center (US)
Ecology Center of Ann Arbor (US)
Econ-Verlag GmbH (GW)
Econocast Services (US)
Econometric Society (US)
Economia Internacional (SP)
Economia Mundial (SP)
Economia Nacional Internacional de la Empresa (SP)
Economia Sociale Contrattuale (IT)
Economic Affairs Bureau, Inc. (US)
Economic and Business Research Information and Advisory Service (TR)
Economic and Industrial Publications (PK)
Economic and Scientific Research Foundation (II)
Economic and Social Commission for Asia and the Far East

    *see* United Nations Economic and Social Commission for Asia and the Pacific (UN)
Economic and Social Commission for Asia and the Pacific
    *see* United Nations Economic and Social Commission for Asia and the Pacific (UN)
Economic and Social Committee of the European Communities (EI)
Economic and Social Council
    *see* United Nations Economic and Social Council (UN)
Economic and Social Council. International Narcotics Control Board
    *see* International Narcotics Control Board (UN)
Economic and Social History Society of Ireland (UK)
Economic and Social Research Institute (IE)
Economic and Social Review (IE)
Economic and Social Science Research Association (UK)
Economic Association of Malaysia (MY)
Economic Commission for Africa
    *see* United Nations Economic Commission for Africa (UN)
Economic Commission for Europe
    *see* United Nations Economic Commission for Europe (UN)
Economic Commission for Latin America
    *see* United Nations Economic Commission for Latin America (UN)
Economic Commission for Western Asia
    *see* United Nations Economic Commission for Western Asia (UN)
Economic Cooperation Study Group (II)
Economic Council of Canada (CN)
Economic Council of Limburg
    *see* Limburgse Economische Raad (BE)
Economic Development Administration (PR)
Economic Development Foundation (PH)
Economic Geology Publishing Co. (US)
Economic History Association (US)
Economic History Society (UK)
Economic Information & Agency (HK)
Economic League Ltd. (UK)
Economic News Agency Inc. (US)
Economic Research Center, Inc. (US)
Economic Society of Australia and New Zealand (AT)
Economic Society of Australia and New Zealand. New South Wales and Victorian Branches (AT)
Economic Society of Australia and New Zealand. Queensland Branch (AT)
Economic Society of Australia and New Zealand. Western Australian Branch (AT)
Economic Society of Finland
    *see* Ekonomiska Samfundet i Finland (FI)
Economic Society of Ghana (GH)
Economic Society of South Africa (SA)
Economic Statistics Bureau of Washington, D.C. (US)
Economic Studies & Journals Publishing Co. (II)
Economica (EC)
Economical Driver (US)
Economics and Commercial Teachers' Association of New South Wales (AT)
Economics and Technology Inc. (US)
Economics Association (UK)
Economics Press Inc. (US)
Economie (FR)
Economie et Politique (FR)
Economisch Instituut voor het Midden- en Kleinbedrijf (NE)
Economisch Technologisch Instituut voor Noord-Brabant (NE)
Economisch Technologisch Instituut voor Zuid-Holland (NE)
Economisch-Technologische Dienst voor Noord-Holland (NE)
Economist Intelligence Unit, Ltd (UK)
Economist Newspaper Ltd. (UK)
Economist Publishing Co. (US)
Economista (SP)
Ecosources (US)
Editorial Ecro (AG)
Compania Editora del Ecuador (EC)
Ecuador. Centro de Desarrollo Industrial del Ecuador (EC)
Ecuador. Comision de Valores. Corporacion Financiera Nacional (EC)
Ecuador. Direccion de Aviacion Civil (EC)
Ecuador. Instituto Nacional de Estadistica (EC)
Ecuador. Instituto Nacional de Higiene "Leopoldo Izquieta Perez" (EC)
Ecuador. Instituto Nacional de Meteorologia e Hidrologia (EC)
Ecuador. Instituto Nacional de Pesca del Ecuador (EC)
Ecuador. Instituto Nacional de Prevision (EC)

Ecuador. Ministerio de Defensa Nacional. Comandancia General de Marina (EC)
Ecuador. Ministerio de Finanzas. Direccion General de Recaudaciones (EC)
Ecuador. Ministerio de Industrias, Comercio e Integracion (EC)
Ecuador. Ministerio de Recursos Naturales y Energeticos (EC)
Ecuador. Ministerio de Recursos Naturales y Energeticos. Direccion General de Geologia y Minas (EC)
Ecuador. Ministerio de Relaciones Exteriores (EC)
Ecuador. Ministerio de Salud Publica. Departamento Nacional de Poblacion (EC)
Ecuador. Superintendencia de Bancos (EC)
Ecuadorian-American Association Inc. (US)
Ecumenical Institute (US)
Ecumenical Theological Research Fraternity in Israel (IS)
Ed-U Press (US)
Gruppo Giornalistico Edagricole (IT)
Eddy Dance Foundation (US)
Edece-Edicoes Culturais Ltda. (BL)
Edeka Verlag GmbH (GW)
Morris Edelson, Ed. & Pub. (US)
Eden Press (UK)
Eden Valley Press (US)
M. Edenlund, Ed. & Pub. (SW)
Edgar Wallace Society (UK)
Edgeworks (US)
Edi-Clef (FR)
Edi-Monde (FR)
Edi-Publi-France (FR)
Edi-Quebec Inc. (CN)
Ediafric - la Documentation Africaine (FR)
Edibat Publicite (FR)
Edicao S.A. (BL)
EDICEF (FR)
Ediciones Catalanes de Paris (FR)
Editions Edifor (FR)
Edilerner (SP)
Edilstampa (IT)
Edima (FR)
Casa Editrice Edimark (IT)
Edicion Edime (VE)
Edimedica S.A. (SP)
Edimoda (IT)
Edinat S.A.R.L. (FR)
Edinburgh Academy (UK)
Edinburgh Architectural Association (UK)
Edinburgh College of Commerce (UK)
Edinburgh Mathematical Society (UK)
Edinburgh Medical Missionary Soceity (UK)
Edinburgh Pictorial Ltd. (UK)
Edinburgh University Press (UK)
Edinburgh University Student Publications Board (UK)
Edipress (SP)
Ediregie (FR)
EDIREP (FR)
EDISAFRIC
    *see* Editions Diplomatiques Africaines (SZ)
Edisette s.r.l. (IT)
Julian I. Edison, Ed. & Pub. (US)
Edison Electric Institute (US)
Edisport (FR)
Edisport, S.I. (SP)
Edisport S.P.A. (IT)
Edistampa s.r.l. (IT)
Edita S.A. (SZ)
Editalia (IT)
Editecnia, S.A. (SP)
Editecnica Italiana s.r.l. (IT)
Editem (FR)
Editepsa (SP)
EDITESA S. A. (AG)
Editest (BE)
Editeur Officiel du Quebec (CN)
Editeurs de Presse Associes (FR)
Editgraf (IT)
Casa Editrice Edithema (IT)
Editing Service Group S.A. (BE)
Edition Collection Scientifique-Progres de l'Homme (FR)
Edition du Secretariat-General (ZR)
Edition Text und Kritik GmbH (GW)
Editions Caracteres (FR)
Editions Commerciales Europeennes (FR)
Editions Commerciales Francaises (FR)
Editions d'Informatique (FR)
Editions d'Organisation (FR)
Editions d'Utovie (FR)
Editions de l'Universite d'Ottawa (CN)
Editions de l'Universite de Bruxelles (BE)
S.A.R.L. Editions de la Francite (FR)
Editions de la Publicite (FR)
Editions de la Tete de Feuille (FR)
Editions de la Vie Medicale (FR)

El Salvador. Ministerio de Educacion  (ES)
El Salvador. Ministerio de Planificacion y
  Coordinacion del Desarrollo Economico y Social.
  Seccion de Investigaciones Estadisticas  (ES)
El Salvador. Servicio e Investigaciones Hidrologicas.
  (ES)
El Salvador. Superintendencia de Bancos y Otras
  Instituciones Financieras  (ES)
Elan S.A.  (AG)
Eland Press (Pty) Ltd  (SA)
Eland Publishing Co. Pty. Ltd.  (AT)
Elanders Boktryckeri AB  (SW)
Elbe-Wochenblatt Verlagsgesellschaft MbH  (GW)
Elbiom Forlagsaktieselskab  (DK)
Elder Churchman.  (US)
Elder Citizens in British Columbia  (CN)
Aethelred Eldridge, Ed. & Pub.  (US)
Gruppo Editoriale Electa S.p.A.  (IT)
Electoral Reform Society  (UK)
Electric Component Industries Association  (II)
Electric Furnace Steel Research Association  (JA)
Electric Machinery Mfg. Co.  (US)
Electric Power Associations of Mississippi  (US)
Electric Power Research Institute  (US)
Electric Railroaders' Association  (US)
Electric Railway Society  (UK)
Electric Supply Authority Engineers' Institute  (NZ)
Electric Vehicle Council  (US)
Electrical & Electronic Engineering Society  (SI)
Electrical and Electronic Manufacturers Association
  (CN)
Electrical Consultant  (US)
Electrical Contractors' Association  (UK)
Electrical Contractors Association of New South
  Wales  (AT)
Electrical Contractors' Association of Queensland
  (AT)
Electrical Contractors Association of S.A. Inc.  (AT)
Electrical Contractors Federation (Victoria)  (AT)
Electrical Development Association of Victoria  (AT)
Electrical Electronic and Telecommunication-
  Plumbing Union  (UK)
Electrical-Electronic Press Ltd.  (UK)
Electrical Equipment Representatives Association
  (US)
Electrical Information Publications, Inc.  (US)
Electrical Power Engineers' Association  (UK)
Electrical Supply Authorities Association of New
  Zealand  (NZ)
Electrical Trade Unions of Australia  (AT)
Electricite Automobile  (FR)
Electricite de France  (FR)
N. V. Electriciteitsmaatschappij Aeg  (NE)
Electricity Council  (UK)
The Electrification Council  (US)
Electro Medical Trade Association Ltd.  (UK)
Electrochemical Society Inc.  (US)
Electrochemical Society of India  (II)
Electrochemical Society of Japan  (JA)
Electrographic Corp.  (US)
Electron Microscopy Society of America  (US)
Electronic Connector Study Group, Inc.  (US)
Electronic Defense Association  (US)
Electronic Engineering Association  (UK)
Electronic Industries Association  (US)
Electronic Periodicals, Inc  (US)
Electronic Representatives Association  (US)
Electronics Association of Japan  (JA)
Electronics Commission  (II)
Electronics of America  (US)
Electronique Professionnelle Belge  (BE)
Electrophysiological Technologists' Association  (UK)
Empresa Editorial Electrotecnica, Ltda.  (PO)
Electrowatt Engineering Services Ltd.  (SZ)
Eleftherotypia  (GR)
G.C. Eleftheroudakis S.A.  (GR)
Elek Books Ltd.  (UK)
Elektor Publishers Ltd.  (UK)
Elektrik Muhendisleri Odasi
  see Institute of Electrical Engineers  (TU)
Elektriska Installatoersorganisationen  (SW)
Elektrizitaets- und Metallwaren-Industrie Gesellschaft
  (EUMIG)  (AU)
Verlags- und Wirtschafts- Gesellschaft der
  Elektrizitaetswerke mbH  (GW)
Elektro-Welt Verlag Dr. Huethig
  see Huethig Verlag GmbH  (GW)
Elektroingenjoersfoerbundet  (FI)
Elektroinstallatoerenes Landsforbund  (NO)
Verlag der Elektromonteur AG  (SZ)
Elektron-Verlag  (AU)
Elektrotehnicki Institut Poduzeca "Rade Koncar"
  (YU)
Elektrotehniska Zveza Slovenije  (YU)
Elektrowirtschaft  (SZ)
Uitgeversmaatschappij Elektuur B.V.  (NE)
Element-Verlag GmbH  (GW)
Elevator World  (US)

Eleventh District Dental Society  (US)
H. Wayne Eley Associates Inc.  (US)
Aba Elhanani, Ed. and Publ.  (IS)
Eli Lilly & Co.  (US)
Editrice Elia  (IT)
Robert J. Elias, Ed. & Pub.  (CN)
Elim Pentecostal Church  (UK)
Elisha Mitchell Scientific Society  (US)
Elite Publishing Corp.  (US)
Elitera-Verlag GmbH  (GW)
Elizabeth Cady Stanton Publishing Co.
  see Stanton  (US)
Editorial Elizondo, S. A.  (MX)
Elle  (FR)
Ellen Glasgow Newsletter  (US)
Ellenberg Publishers Ltd.  (GW)
Ellen's Old Alchemical Press  (US)
Ellinikos Organismos Tourismou
  see National Tourist Organization of Greece  (GR)
Elliot Brothers (London) Ltd.  (UK)
Elliott Publications Ltd.  (UK)
R. C. Ellis  (CN)
Elizabeth Prather Ellsberry  (US)
Izdatel'stvo Elm  (UR)
Elmfield Press  (UK)
Elmside Echoes  (US)
Eloquenza  (IT)
Elsevier North-Holland, Inc., New York  (US)
Elsevier-North Holland Scientific Publishers Co., Ltd.
  (IE)
Elsevier Scientific Publishing Co.  (NE)
Elsevier Sequoia S.A.  (SZ)
Elsim Co.  (UK)
Otto Elsner Verlagsgesellschaft  (GW)
Elvy & Gibbs  (UK)
Werbegemeinschaft Elwert und Meurer  (GW)
N.G. Elwert Verlag  (GW)
Elwi-Verlag  (GW)
Email Metal  (FR)
Embajada Argentina  (SP)
Embajada de U R S S  (MX)
Embajada del Peru en Bolivia  (BO)
Embalajes  (SP)
A-S Emballering  (NO)
Embankment Press Ltd.  (UK)
Embassy  (UK)
Embassy of Bolivia, London  (UK)
Embassy of Chile. Press Office  (US)
Embassy of Ghana  (US)
Embassy of Greece  (US)
Embassy of Greece in Argentina  (AG)
Embassy of Japan in Argentina  (AG)
Embassy of Mexico, London  (UK)
Embassy of Pakistan. Information Division  (US)
Embassy of Paraguay, London  (UK)
Embassy of South Africa in Argentina  (AG)
Embassy of Switzerland  (US)
Embassy of the Arab Republic of Egypt  (II)
Embassy of the Arab Republic of Egypt  (KE)
Embassy of the Federal Republic of Germany  (II)
Embassy of the Federal Republic of Germany  (US)
Embassy of the Khmer Republic  (US)
Embassy of the Philippines  (FR)
Embassy of the Republic of Iraq  (II)
Embassy of the Republic of South Africa  (IT)
Embassy of the Republic of Uganda  (US)
Embassy of the Republic of Vietnam  (UK)
Embassy of the State of Qatar  (US)
Embassy of the U. S. S. R. in India
  see U. S. S. R. Embassy in India  (II)
Embassy of the U S S R in the U S A  (US)
Embassy of the United Republic of Tanzania  (US)
Embassy of the United States in Japan  (JA)
Embassy of Venezuela  (US)
Ember Press  (UK)
Embroiderers' Guild  (UK)
Embroiderers Guild of America  (US)
Editora Ementario Forense Ltda.  (BL)
Editions Emer  (FR)
Emerald City Press  (US)
Emergency Care Research Institute  (US)
Emergency Department Nurses Association  (US)
Emergency Librarian  (CN)
Emergency Medical Services, Inc.  (US)
Emerson Review  (US)
Emha-Verlag  (GW)
EMI Cinemas Ltd.  (UK)
Emigrante  (UK)
Emma (Printers & Publishers)  (UK)
Editoriale Emme Elle s.r.l.  (IT)
Emmentaler Druck  (SZ)
Emmess Press  (US)
Emory University  (US)
Emory University. Candler School of Theology  (US)
Emory University. Center for Research in Social
  Change  (US)
Emory University Family Planning Program  (US)
Emory University. Information Services  (US)

Emory University. Office of Alumni Publications
  (US)
Emory University. School of Law  (US)
Emphysema Anonymous, Inc  (US)
Empire City Pharmaceutical Society Inc.  (US)
Empire Life Insurance Co.  (CN)
Empire of India Philatelic Society  (II)
Empire Stamp Corporation Ltd.  (CN)
Empire State College. Learning Resources Center
  (US)
Empire State Iris Society  (US)
Empire State Numismatic Association  (US)
Empire State Railway Museum  (US)
Empire State Report, Inc.  (US)
Employee Relocation Council  (US)
Employers' Federation of New South Wales  (AT)
Employers Insurance of Texas  (US)
Employment Conditions Abroad Ltd.  (UK)
Emporia Kansas State College  (US)
Emporia Kansas State College. Alumni Association
  (US)
Emporia Kansas State College. Division of Biology
  (US)
Emporia Kansas State College. School of Library
  Science  (US)
Emporike Trapeza Tes Hellados
  see Commercial Bank of Greece  (GR)
Empreiteiro Ltda  (BL)
Empresa Brasileira de Pesquisa Agropecuaria  (BL)
Empresa de Pesquisa Agropecuaria de Minas Gerais
  (BL)
Empresa de Pesquisa Agropecuaria de Minas Gerais.
  Biblioteca  (BL)
Empresa Editorial s.r.l.  (AG)
Empress Chinchilla Breeders Cooperative, Inc.  (US)
Empty Boat Press  (US)
Empty Closet  (US)
Empty Elevator Shaft  (US)
En Haa  (VE)
En Passant Poetry Quarterly  (US)
En Punta  (SP)
Enablement Inc.  (US)
Enabling Co.  (US)
Encee Technical Publications Corporation  (II)
Edizioni Encia  (IT)
Encounter Ltd.  (UK)
Encres Vives  (FR)
Encuentro  (AG)
Encyclopaedia Africana Project  (GH)
Encyclopaedia Britannica, Inc.  (US)
Encyclopedie Medico Chirurgicale  (FR)
The End (and Variations Thereof)  (US)
James G. Endicott, Ed. & Pub.  (CN)
Endocrine Society  (US)
Endymion  (US)
Eneguess Publishing Co.  (US)
Energiagazdalkodasi Tudomanyos Egyesulet  (HU)
Energieonderzoek Centrum Nederland  (NE)
Energiewirtschaft und Technik Verlagsgesellschaft
  mbH  (GW)
Izdatel'stvo Energiya  (UR)
Editions de l' Energumene  (FR)
Energy Blacksouth Press  (US)
Energy Communications, Inc.  (US)
Energy Daily  (US)
Energy Economics Research Ltd.  (UK)
Energy Research Corporation  (US)
Energy Resources Conservation Board  (CN)
Engei Gakkai
  see Japanese Society for Horticultural Science
  (JA)
Verlag N. P. Engel  (GW)
Verlag der Engel des Herrn  (GW)
Andi Engel, Ed. & Pub.  (UK)
Engeldrum Publishing Corp.  (US)
Verlag Alfred Engelmann  (GW)
Engetec Ltda.  (BL)
Engineer of Southern California  (US)
Engineering Alloys Digest, Inc.  (US)
Engineering Contractors Associations  (US)
Engineering Export Promotion Council  (II)
Engineering Foundation  (US)
Engineering Foundation. Column Research Council
  (US)
Engineering Index, Inc.  (US)
Engineering Industries Association  (UK)
Engineering Industries Association. Northern Region
  (UK)
Engineering Institute of Canada  (CN)
Engineering Materials and Design  (UK)
Engineering News-Record  (US)
Engineering Research Institute
  see under Kyoto University  (JA)
Engineering Research Institute  (II)
Engineering Sciences Data Unit Ltd.  (UK)
Engineering Societies of New England  (US)
Engineering Society of Baltimore, Inc.  (US)
Engineering Society of Detroit  (US)

Escuela Superior de Tecnica Empresarial  (SP)
Casa Editrice ESEDRA  (IT)
Eska Tijdschriften B. V.  (NE)
Eskimo-Iglo Ges. m.b.H.  (AU)
Eskimo, Indian, Aleut Publishing Co.  (US)
Esoteric Philosophy Center, Inc.  (US)
Espaces  (FR)
Espaces et Societes  (FR)
Prensa Espanola  (SP)
Esparavel  (CK)
Espasa-Calpe, S.A.  (SP)
Esperanto Association of North America, Inc.  (US)
Esperanto Book Service  (US)
Esperanto-Editions  (FR)
Esperanto League for North America  (US)
Esperanto Teachers Association  (UK)
Editoriale Esperienza  (IT)
Espirito Santo. Empresa de Assistencia Tecnica e
    Extensao Rural  (BL)
ESPress, Inc.  (US)
Esprit Createur  (US)
Esprit et Vie  (FR)
Esprit Libre  (FR)
Editions Esprit S.A.R.L.  (FR)
Esquire, Inc.  (US)
Editorial Esquiu S. A.  (AG)
Essandess Special Editions  (US)
Essay Proof Society  (US)
Edizioni ESSE  (IT)
Esselte Kartfoerlagen  (SW)
Esselte Studium AB  (SW)
Essen. Stadtbibliothek  (GW)
Essence Communications Inc.  (US)
Essener Verlag fuer Sozialversicherung GmbH  (GW)
Esseno Publications, Inc.  (US)
Essential Oil Association of India  (II)
Essential Press  (US)
Esser Scientific Press  (NE)
Essex County Council  (UK)
Essex County Library  (UK)
Essex County Medical Society  (US)
Essex Editors, Inc.  (US)
Essex Education Committee  (UK)
Essex Field Club  (UK)
Essex Hall Bookshop  (UK)
Essex Institute  (US)
Essex Naturalists' Trust Ltd.  (UK)
Essex Society for Family History  (UK)
J. Esslinger Druckerei und Verlag  (GW)
Esso Italiana  (IT)
Esso Malaysia Berhad  (MY)
Esso Nederland B. V.  (NE)
Esso Petroleum Co., Ltd.  (UK)
Esso Standard Oil Co.  (JA)
Estacion Experimental Delta del Parana  (AG)
Estacion Experimental Dr. Mario Cassinoni  (UY)
Estado Mayor del Ejercito  (CL)
Estates Gazette Ltd.  (UK)
Estes Industries  (US)
Estetica Ambrosiana  (IT)
Estlandssvenskarna i Sverige  (SW)
Estonian Information Centre  (SW)
Estonian Publishing Co. Toronto Ltd.  (CN)
Fidel Estrada Navarro, Ed. & Pub.  (MX)
Estrel Editions  (FR)
Estuaire  (CN)
Estudiantes y Egresados de Cursos en Israel  (IS)
Estudio Teologico Agustiniano  (SP)
Estudio Teologico de San Esteban  (SP)
Estudios Comerciales s.r.l.  (PE)
Empresa Editora de Estudos Medicos, Ltda.  (PO)
Et ve Balik Kurumu  (TU)
Etablissements des Editions du Togo  (TG)

Editions ETAPE  (FR)

Etas Kompass Periodici Tecnici S.p.A.  (IT)
Etas Periodici del Tempo Libri S.p.A.  (IT)

Etat-Major General de la Force Terrestre. Direction
    du Genie  (BE)
Nira Etchenique  (AG)
Etegil-Edit.Tecn.Graf.Ind.Ltda.  (BL)
Eternal Network  (CN)
Eternity Science Fiction  (US)
Ethical Publishing Co. (Pty.) Ltd.  (SA)
Ethiope Publishing Corporation  (NR)
Ethiopia. Central Statistical Office  (ET)
Ethiopia. Civil Aviation Administration. Climatological
    Branch  (ET)
Ethiopia. Customs Head Office  (ET)
Ethiopia. Department of Labour and Employment
    (ET)
Ethiopia. Public Employment Administration  (ET)
Ethiopia. Smallpox Eradication Programme  (ET)
Ethiopian Chamber of Commerce  (ET)
Ethiopian Library Association  (ET)
Ethiopian Manuscript Microfilm Library  (ET)
Ethiopian Medical Association  (ET)
Ethiopian Students Union in North America  (US)

Ethiopian Tourist Office  (ET)
Ethiopian Wildlife and Natural History Society  (ET)
Ethiopian Women's Welfare Association  (ET)
Ethnic American Coalition  (US)
Ethnic Millions Political Action Committee  (US)
Ethnike Trapeza Tes Hellados
    see National Bank of Greece  (GR)
Ethnikon Idrimatos "Vassilefs Pavlos"
    see National Foundation "King Paul"  (GR)
Ethnographic & Folk Culture Society  (II)
Ethnos Publishers  (US)
Blaine Ethridge-Books  (US)
Ethyl Corporation. Research Laboratories  (US)
Etnografiska Museet  (SW)
Etnografski Muzej na Cetinju  (YU)
Etnografski Muzej u Beogradu  (YU)
Etnologia-Antropologia Culturale  (IT)
Etnolosko Drustvo Jugoslavije  (YU)
Etoile de la Foire  (BE)
Etoile Promotion  (FR)
N.A. Etrogy Publishing Company  (IS)
S. A. les Etudes  (FR)
Etudes Classiques  (BE)
Etudes Sociales et Syndicales  (FR)
Etudes Sovietiques  (FR)
Etudiants Catholiques de la Region Parisienne  (FR)
Etudiants de la Restauration Nationale  (FR)
Etzb'omi Publishing House  (IS)
Eugenia Dorothy Blount Lamar Lectures at Mercer
    University, Macon, Georgia  (US)
Eugenics Society  (UK)
Eura Press, Edizioni Italiane  (IT)
Euramerica, S.A.  (SP)
Eurap Publishing Co. Ltd.  (UK)
Euratom
    see European Atomic Energy Community  (EI)
Eureka  (FR)
Eureka  (SW)
Eureka Press  (US)
Euro Fair B. V.  (NE)
Euro Publications Ltd.  (UK)
EUROFIMA
    see European Company for the Financing of
    Railway Rolling Stock  (SZ)
EUROFINAS
    see European Federation of Finance House
    Associations  (BE)
Eurograph-Bernardoni  (IT)
Eurographik  (IT)
Euromed Publications  (UK)
Euromoney Publications Ltd.  (UK)
Euromonitor Publications Ltd.  (UK)
Europ-Elite N.V.  (BE)
Europ Export Edition GmbH  (GW)
Libreria Europa  (SP)
Europa-Fachpresse-Verlag GmbH  (GW)
Europa Illustrata e l'Italia Illustrata  (IT)
Europa Instituut
    see under Universiteit van Amsterdam  (NE)
Europa Kurier Pty. Ltd.  (AT)
Europa Libera  (IT)
Europa Publications Ltd.  (UK)
Edizioni Europa s.r.l.  (IT)
Europa Study Unit  (US)
Europa-Union Deutschland e.V.  (GW)
Europa Union Verlag GmbH  (GW)
Europa-Verlag  (GW)
Europa-Verlag AG  (AU)
Europa Verlag AG  (SZ)
Europaeisch-Festlaendische Brueder-Unitaet  (GW)
Europaeische Foederalistische Bewegung  (GW)
Europaeische Gemeinschaft fuer Kohle und Stahl
    see European Coal and Steel Community  (EI)
Europaeische Union der Pianomacher-Fachverbaende
    (GW)
Europaeische Vereinigung fuer Veterinaerchirurgie
    (GW)
Europaeische Verlagsanstalt GmbH  (GW)
Verlag Europaeische Wehrkunde GmbH  (GW)
Europaeisches Bau-Forum  (LU)
Europaeisches Erzieherbund (European Assn. of
    Teachers)  (AU)
Europaeisches Institut fuer Politische, Wirtschaftliche
    und Soziale Fragen e.V.  (GW)
Europaeisches Parlament
    see European Parliament  (EI)
Europahaus Wallersee-Salzburg  (AU)
Europautomation  (FR)
Europe  (FR)
Europe and Asia Association  (JA)
Europe House Publishing Ltd.  (UK)
Europe Orientale  (FR)
Editions Europe Sud-Est  (GR)
European Abstracts Service  (SW)
European American Bank and Trust Co.  (US)
European and Mediterranean Plant Protection
    Organization  (FR)
European Association for American Studies  (NE)

European Association for Animal Production  (NE)
European Association for Animal Production  (IT)
European Association for Engineering Education
    (NE)
European Association for Industrial Marketing
    Research  (NE)
European Association for Maxilofacial Surgery
    (GW)
European Association for Micro-Processing and Micro-
    Programming  (FR)
European Association for Personnel Management
    (FR)
European Association for Potato Research  (NE)
European Association for Research on Plant Breeding.
    (NE)
European Association for the Study of Diabetes  (US)
European Association of Advertising Agencies  (BE)
European Association of Endocrinology  (SZ)
European Association of Experimental Social
    Psychology  (US)
European Association of Exploration Geophysicists
    (NE)
European Association of Neurological Societies  (BE)
European Association of Perinatal Medicine  (SZ)
European Association of Scientific Information
    Dissemination Centers  (IT)
European Association of Teachers. Irish Section  (IE)
European Association of Urology  (SZ)
European Atomic Energy Community  (EI)
European Atomic Energy Community. Bureau
    Euristop
    see Bureau Euristop  (EI)
European Banks International  (BE)
European Biological Research Association  (SZ)
European Brewery Convention  (NE)
European Broadcasting Union  (SZ)
European Bureau of Adult Education  (NE)
European Cell Biology Organization  (GW)
European Cement Association  (FR)
European Centre for Population Studies  (NE)
European Ceramic Association  (FR)
European Chemoreception Organization  (UK)
European Christian Democratic Union  (IT)
European Coal and Steel Community. Consultative
    Committee  (EI)
European Coil Coating Association  (UK)
European Commission of Human Rights  (FR)
European Committee for Concrete  (FR)
European Committee on Crime Problems  (FR)
European Communities. Economic and Social
    Committee
    see Economic and Social Committee of the
    European Communities  (EI)
European Community Information Service  (NE)
European Community Institute for University Studies
    (BE)
European Community Institute for University Studies
    (EI)
European Company for the Financing of Railway
    Rolling Stock  (SZ)
European Confederation for Physical Therapy  (FR)
European Conference of Local Authorities  (FR)
European Conference of Ministers of Transport  (FR)
European Conference on Electron Microscopy  (IS)
European Congress of Anaesthesiology  (SP)
European Consortium for Political Research  (NE)
European Consortium for Political Research. Data
    Information Service  (NO)
European Coordination Centre for Research and
    Documentation in Social Sciences  (NE)
European Council for Education by Correspondence
    (BE)
European Council of Jewish Community Services
    (FR)
European Court of Human Rights  (GW)
European Cultural Foundation. Council for Cultural
    Co-Operation  (FR)
European Data Publishing Co.  (UK)
European Economic Community Savings Bank Group
    (EI)
European Economic Data Publishing Co., Ltd.  (UK)
European Federation for Intercultural Learning  (BE)
European Federation for the Protection of Waters
    (SZ)
European Federation of Chemical Engineering  (GW)
European Federation of Corrosion.  (UK)
European Federation of Finance House Associations
    (BE)
European Federation of Physical and Rehabilitation
    Medicine  (IT)
European Federation of Purchasing  (BE)
European Foundation for Management Development
    (EFMD)  (GW)
European Free Trade Association  (SZ)
European Grassland Federation  (SW)
European Home Study Council  (UK)
European Information Centre for Nature Conservation
    (FR)

European Institute of Business Administration (FR)
European Investment Bank (EI)
European Jewish Publications, Ltd. (UK)
European Lead Development Committee (UK)
European League for Economic Cooperation (BE)
European Malacological Union (AU)
European Movement (UK)
European Organization for Caries Research (SZ)
European Organization for Civil Aviation Electronics (FR)
European Organization for Nuclear Research (SZ)
European Organization for Quality Control (SZ)
European Organization for the Safety of Air Navigation (BE)
European Orthodontic Society (UK)
European Parliament (EI)
European Peptide Symposium (NE)
European Physical Society (SZ)
European Pressure Die Casting Committee (UK)
European Primary Aluminum Association (GW)
European Report (BE)
European Scientific Association of Applied Economics (NE)
European Social Fund (EI)
European Society for Experimental Surgery (SZ)
European Society for Opinion and Marketing Research (NE)
European Society for Opinion Surveys and Market Research (UK)
European Society for Rural Sociology (NE)
European Society for the Study of Drug Toxicity (NE)
European Society of Cardiology (BE)
European Society of Linguistics (GW)
European Society of Neuroradiology (US)
European Society of Ophthalmology (SZ)
European Society on Microcirculation (SZ)
European Southern Observatory (GW)
European Space Agency (FR)
European Studies Committee (UK)
European Technical Coverage Inc. (US)
European Transport Law (BE)
European Travel Commission (UK)
European University News (FR)
European Weed Research Council (UK)
Europese Bibliotheek (NE)
Europinion (FR)
Europlast (IT)
Europublica Verlagsgesellschaft G.m.b.H. (AU)
Eurosell B. V. (NE)
Verlag Eurosport (AU)
Eurostat
   see Statistical Office of the European Communities (EI)
Euroviande (FR)
Euthanasia Educational Council (US)
Wirtschafts- und Forstverlag Euting KG (GW)
Evangelical Churches of West Africa (NR)
Evangelical Congregational Church (US)
Evangelical Covenant Church of America (US)
Evangelical Covenant Church of America. Pacific Southwest Conference (US)
Evangelical Fellowship of India (II)
Evangelical Foundation (US)
Evangelical Free Church of America (US)
Evangelical Friends Alliance (US)
Evangelical Lutheran Church in South Africa. Western Diocese (SA)
Evangelical Lutheran Church of Canada (CN)
Evangelical Lutheran Church of Tanzania. North Western Diocese (TZ)
Evangelical Lutheran Synod (US)
Evangelical Magazine (UK)
Evangelical Missions Information Service (US)
Evangelical Teacher Training Association (US)
Evangelical Theological Society (US)
Evangelical Voice (CN)
Evangelicka Cirkev Ceskobratrska (CS)
Evangeliipress (SW)
Evangelisatie-Boekhandel en Uitgeverij Horizont (NE)
Evangelisch-Kirchliche Vereinigung in der Schweiz (SZ)
Evangelisch-Lutherische Dreikoenigsgemeinde (GW)
Evangelisch-Lutherischer Landeskirchenrat (GW)
Evangelisch-Lutherisches Landeskirchenamt Sachsens (GE)
Evangelisch-methodistische Kirche (GW)
Evangelisch-Methodistische Kirche in der DDR (GE)
Evangelische Akademie Berlin (GW)
Evangelische Akademie Rheinland-Westfalen (GW)
Evangelische Akademie Tutzing (GW)
Evangelische Akademie von Kurhessen-Waldeck (GW)
Evangelische Akademikerschaft in Deutschland (GW)
Evangelische Buchhilfe e.V. (GW)

Evangelische Gemeinde A.B. Wien-Waehring (AU)
Evangelische Gemeinde Koeln-Kalk-Humboldt (GW)
Evangelische Gemeindepresse GmbH (GW)
Evangelische Gesellschaft fuer Deutschland e.V. (GW)
Evangelische Kirche in Deutschland (GW)
Evangelische Kirche in Hessen und Nassau in Frankfurt. Amt fuer Kirchenmusik (GW)
Evangelische Landjugend Bayern (GW)
Evangelische-Lutheranische Kirchengemeinde Bayreuth (GW)
Evangelische Maatschappij (NE)
Evangelische Pfarrgemeinde Purkersdorf (AU)
Evangelische Studentengemeinde in der Bundesrepublik Deutschland und Berlin (West)
Evangelische Verlagsanstalt GmbH (GE)
Evangelische Weibliche Jugend in Bayern e.V. (GW)
Evangelische Zentralstelle fuer Weltanschauungsfragen (GW)
Evangelischer Bund in Oesterreich (AU)
Verlag Evangelischer Gemeindeblatt Berlin (GW)
Evangelischer Missionsverlag GmbH (GW)
Evangelischer Oberkirchenrat (GW)
Evangelischer Oberkirchenrat Karlsruhe (GW)
Evangelischer Oberkirchenrat Stuttgart (GW)
Evangelischer Presseverband fuer Baden e.V. (GW)
Evangelischer Presseverband fuer Bayern e.V. (GW)
Gemeinschaftswerk der Evangelischer Publizistik (GW)
Evangelisches Bibliothekar-Lehrinstitut, Goettingen (GW)
Evangelisches Jugendwerk in Oesterreich (AU)
Evangelisches Pfarramt Melk (AU)
Evangelisches Verlagswerk GmbH (GW)
Evangelistic Enterprises Society (CN)
M. Evans and Co., Inc. (US)
Hugh Evans & Sons Ltd. (UK)
R. W. Evans Associates Ltd. (CN)
Evans Brothers Ltd. (UK)
Evans-Methuen Educational (UK)
Evans-Novak Political Report Company (US)
Evansville Public Library (US)
Evelyn Waugh Society (US)
Evensongs Association (CH)
Events Publications Inc. Ltd. (CN)
Everbody's Money (US)
Editorial Everest (SP)
Everett Grant Pty. Ltd. (AT)
Everglades Publishing Co. (US)
Harry T. Everingham, Ed. & Pub (US)
Everson Museum of Art of Syracuse and Onondaga County (US)
Evert Communications Ltd. (CN)
Everton Publishers, Inc. (US)
Every Woman (US)
Everybodys Press Inc. (US)
Everything for Everybody (US)
Everyweek Educational Press Ltd. (UK)
Eve's Weekly Ltd. (II)
Ewell Neil Dental Society (US)
Ewha Women's University. College of Law and Politcal Science (KO)
Ex-Editora (BL)
Ex Libris (US)
Ex Libris et Guilde du Disque (SZ)
Ex Libris-Verlag (GW)
Ex-Service (1943) Association (UK)
Exakt-Verlag (SZ)
Exarchat du Patriarche de Moscou (FR)
Excelsior Publications (FR)
Compania Editorial Excelsior S. C. L. (MX)
Excerpta Medica (NE)
Exchangiste Universel (FR)
Executive Business Media, Inc. (US)
Executive Communications, Inc. (US)
Executive Compensation Service
   see under American Management Associations (US)
Executive Council of the Episcopal Church (US)
Executive Enterprises Publications Co., Inc. (US)
Executive Publications (US)
Executive Publications, Inc. (Washington) (US)
Executive Review Publishers (US)
Executive Sciences Institute, Inc. (US)
Executive Strategy Services Co. (US)
Executive Woman (US)
Executor and Trustee Institute (AT)
Exhibitor Services, Inc (US)
Exile & Exile Editions (CN)
EXIM-INDEX Dr. E. Goldberger (SZ)
Eximbank
   see Export- Import Bank of the United States (US)
Exp-Press (NE)
Expanded Shale, Clay and Slate Institute (US)
Editora Expansao Ltda. (BL)
Expansion (MX)
Expansion Scientifique (FR)

Expatriate Review (US)
Experiment in International Living (US)
Experiment Press (US)
Experimental Aircraft Association, Inc. (US)
Experimental Psychology Society (UK)
Experimental Station of the Sugar Industry (IO)
Expertise Institute Inc. (US)
Explorations Institute (US)
Explorers Club (US)
Explorers Enterprises Inc, (US)
Explosion Hunger-1975 (II)
Exponent Two (US)
Export Council of Norway (NO)
Export-Import Bank of Japan (JA)
Export-Import Bank of the United States (US)
Export Press (YU)
Export Times Publishing Ltd. (UK)
Exportad Pty. Ltd. (AT)
Exporters-Importers Club (II)
Express (FR)
Express Documents (FR)
Express Newspapers Ltd. (AT)
Express Transport Company Ltd. (SE)
Express-Trykkeriet (DK)
Express Wieczorny (PL)
Expression One (UK)
Editoriale l' Expresso S.p. A. (IT)
Editorial Extemporaneos (MX)
Extended Sweet's Mill (US)
Extension Journal, Inc. (US)
Exxon Aviation Marketing Affiliates (US)
Exxon Chemical Co. (US)
Exxon Company, U.S.A. (US)
Exxon Corporation (US)
Exxon International Co. (US)
F A O
   see Food and Agriculture Organization of the United Nations (UN)
F. A. Publications, Inc. (US)
F A S E B
   see Federation of American Societies for Experimental Biology (US)
F A T M Press (US)
F & F Publications (US)
F & W Publishing Corp. (US)
F B G Enterprises, Inc. (US)
F.B.P. Publishing, Inc. (US)
F C I News Agency (UK)
F.C.N.G.R. (AG)
F C X, Inc. (US)
F D M-Huset (DK)
F E P International Ltd. (SI)
F E P Productions Ltd. (NZ)
F F A
   see Flygtekniska Foersoeksanstalten (SW)
F I E L
   see Fundacion de Investigaciones Economicas Latinoamericanas (AG)
F K K Vereinigung Gymnasion (AU)
F L M (IT)
F M Music Program Guide, Inc. (US)
F N C E T A (FR)
F. P. B. Enterprises (US)
F. S. Publications (US)
F T A (DK)
Editora F T D (BL)
Edicoes F U C M T (BL)
F. U. Research Institute, Inc. (US)
F. van Landschot Bankiers (NE)
F. W. Publications (AT)
Fratelli Fabbri Editori (IT)
Redazione Fabbrica e Stato (IT)
Fabian Chemical Co. (CN)
Ethel H. Fabian, Ed. & Pub. (US)
Fabian Society (UK)
Fabrangen (US)
FABRIMETAL
   see Federation des Entreprises de l'Industrie des Fabrications Metalliques (BE)
Fabritius og Soenner Forlag (NO)
Fabulous Las Vegas (US)
Facets Multimedia, Inc. (US)
VEB Fachbuchverlag (GE)
Fachgruppe Ladenbau (SZ)
Fachgruppenvereinigung des Krankenpflegepersonals und verwandter Berufe (AU)
Fachinstitut der Steuerberater (GW)
Fachschriften-Verlag GmbH (GW)
Fachverband der Bayerischen Standesbeamten E.V. (GW)
Fachverband der Chemischen Industrie Oesterreichs. Gruppe Kunststoffverarbeitende Industrie (AU)
Fachverband der Futtermittelindustrie e.V. (GW)
Fachverband der Maschinen und Stahlbauindustrie Oesterreichs (AU)
Fachverband der Oesterreichischen Standesbeamten (AU)
Fachverband der Reprografie e.V. (GW)

Fachverband des Deutschen Fliesengewerbes (GW)
Fachverband des Deutschen Teppich- und Gardinenhandels e.V. (GW)
Fachverband Deutscher Eisenwaren-und Hausrathaendler e.V (GW)
Fachverband Deutscher Floristen e.V (GW)
Fachverband Lichtwerbung (GW)
Fachverband Machinenbau (GE)
Fachverband Stickstoffindustrie (GW)
Fachvereinigung der Trafikanten im Freien Wirtschaftsverband (AU)
Fachvereinigung der Verwaltungsleiter Deutscher Krankenanstalten e.V. (GW)
Fachverlag fuer das Oesterreichische Bekleidungsgewerbe (AU)
Fackliga Vaerldsrorelsen (SW)
Facolta Biblica (IT)
Facolta di Medicina Veterinaria (IT)
Fact Technical Society (II)
Editorial Facta (SP)
Factory Mutual Engineering Corp. (US)
Factory Outlet Shopping Guide Publications (US)
Facts & Comparisons, Inc. (US)
Facts and Figures (II)
Facts on File Inc. (US)
Faculadade de Odontologia de Pernambuco. Biblioteca (BL)
Faculdade de Ciencias de Lisbon. Laboratorio de Fisica (PO)
Faculdade de Ciencias Medicas da Santa Casa de Sao Paulo (BL)
Faculdade de Farmacia e Odontologia de Ribeirao Preto (BL)
Faculdade de Filosofia, Braga (PO)
Faculdade de Filosofia, Ciencias e Letras de Araraquara. Cadeira de Politica (BL)
Faculdade de Filosofia, Ciencias e Letras de Araraquara. Cadeira de Sociologia e Fundamentos Sociologicos da Educao (BL)
Faculdade de Filosofia, Ciencias e Letras de Assis (BL)
Faculdade de Filosofia, Ciencias e Letras de Assis. Departamento de Filosofia (BL)
Faculdade de Filosofia, Ciencias e Letras de Assis. Departamento de Historia (BL)
Faculdade de Filosofia, Ciencias e Letras de Cataguases (BL)
Faculdade de Filosofia, Ciencias e Letras de Marilia (BL)
Faculdade de Filosofia de Mariana (BL)
Faculdade Municipal de Ciencias Economicas e Administrativa de Osasco (BL)
Faculdades Integradas Estacio de Sa (BL)
Faculdades Unidas Catolicas de Mato Grosso. Faculdade Dom Aquino de Filosofia, Ciencias e Letras (BL)
Facultad de la Escuela de Trabajo Social (PR)
Facultad de Teologia, Granada (SP)
Facultad de Teologia San Federico de Borja (SP)
Facultad Teologica del Norte de Espana. Facultad de Teologia (SP)
Facultades de Filosofia de la Compania de Jesus en Espana (SP)
Facultas Buch- und Zeitschriftenverlag fuer Medizin und Pharmazie GmbH (AU)
Faculte de Medecine de Besancon (FR)
Faculte de Medecine de Marseille (FR)
Faculte de Pharmacie de Strasbourg (FR)
Faculte de Philosophie et de Theologie (FR)
Faculte des Lettres et Sciences Humaines de Tunis (TI)
Faculte des Lettres et Sciences Humaines, Meched (IR)
Faculte des Sciences (FR)
Faculte des Sciences Agronomiques de l'Etat a Gembloux (BL)
Faculte des Sciences de Paris. Laboratoire de Geographie Physique (FR)
Faculte Medicine de Caen (FR)
Facultes Catholiques de Lille (FR)
Faculty Association of California Community Colleges (US)
Faculty of Actuaries in Scotland (UK)
Faculty of Building (UK)
Faculty of Homoeopathy (UK)
Faculty of Radiologists (UK)
Faculty of Teachers in Commerce Limited (UK)
Faculty Press (UK)
Faculty Press (US)
Faculty Press (New York) (US)
Faellesforeningen for Danmarks Brugsforeninger (DK)
Faellesraadet for Markedsfoering (DK)
Faellesrepraesentationen for Danmarks Biografteatre (DK)
Faellesrepraesentationen for Funktionaerer ved Koebenhavns Havnevaesen (DK)

Faellesudralget Mellem Erhvervsvejledningsraadet og Folkeskolens Laeseplansudvalg (DK)
Faenza Editrice S.p.A. (IT)
Editions Henry Fagne (BE)
A-S Fagpresseforlaget (NO)
Fahlbeckska Stiftelsen (SW)
Verlagsgesellschaft C. J. Fahle (GW)
Foerlags AB Thorsten Fahlskog (SW)
Roy Faiers Ltd. (UK)
Faims et Soifs des Hommes (FR)
Faipari Tudomanyos Egyesulet (HU)
Fair (US)
Fair Lawn Education Association (US)
Fairbanks Native Association (US)
Fairchild Books (US)
Fairchild Publications, Inc. (US)
Fairchild Tropical Garden (US)
John Fairfax & Sons Ltd. (AT)
Fairleigh Dickinson University (US)
Fairleigh Dickinson University. Department of English (US)
Fairleigh Dickinson University. Florham-Madison Campus (US)
Fairmont State College (US)
Fairplay Publications, Ltd. (UK)
Faith and Life Press (US)
Faith for Daily Living Foundation (SA)
Faith for Today (US)
Fakultetsforeningen Veneficus (NO)
Falcon Publications (US)
Falkland Islands Journal (FK)
Editions Georges Fall (FR)
Falling Wall Press Ltd. (UK)
Editorial Fama (MX)
Societa Editrice la Famiglia (IT)
Forlaget Familien A-S (NO)
Familienkundliche Kommission fuer Niedersachsen und Bremen (GW)
Familienverband Avenarius e.V. (GW)
Family Circle, Inc. (US)
Family Circle Publications Ltd. (AT)
Family Health (US)
Family Lines System (US)
Family Media, Inc. (US)
Family Motor Coach Association (US)
Family Pet (US)
Family Planning Association (UK)
Family Planning Association of China (CH)
Family Planning Association of India (II)
Family Planning Association of Kenya (KE)
Family Planning Association of Nepal (NP)
Family Planning Association of Pakistan (PK)
Family Planning International Assistance (US)
Family Process, Inc. (US)
Family Service Association of America (US)
Family Therapy Institute of Marin (US)
Family Welfare Association (UK)
Fan Press (US)
Fan Publications, Inc. (US)
Fandom Unlimited Enterprises (US)
Juan Fanning, Ed. & Pub. (PE)
Fantasy Association (US)
Fantasy Publishing Co., Inc. (US)
Fante di Quadri (IT)
Far East Oceania Information Services, Ltd. (NZ)
Far East Reporter (US)
Far East Reporters, Inc. (JA)
Far East Trade Press Ltd. (HK)
Far East Trade Service, Inc. (CH)
Far Eastern Economic Review Ltd. (HK)
Far Eastern University (PH)
Far Eastern University. Institute of Law (PH)
FAR-MAR-Co., Inc. (US)
Far West Publishing Co. (US)
Far West Ski Association (US)
Far Western Philosophy of Education Society (US)
Farall Instruments (US)
Editorial Farbat s.r.l. (AG)
Fares Stephen (US)
Joseph I. Farley Publishing Co., Inc. (US)
Farleys (Fareham) Ltd (UK)
Farm & Home Publications (US)
Farm and Ranch Vacations, Inc. (US)
Farm Buildings Information Centre (UK)
Farm Business Ltd. (UK)
Farm Credit Banks of New Orleans (US)
Farm Credit Banks of Omaha (US)
Farm Credit Corporation (CN)
Farm Holiday Guides Ltd. (UK)
Farm Implement Publishing Co. (US)
Farm Journal, Inc. (US)
Farm Machinery Industrial Research Corp. (JA)
Farm Management Association (UK)
Farm Papers Ltd. (CN)

Farm Tempo U. S. A (US)
Farm Wife, Inc. (US)
Societa Editoriale Farmaceutica (IT)
Farmaceutico Publishing Co., Inc. (US)
Farmaceutiska Fakultetsfoereningen (SW)
Farmaceutsko Drustvo Hrvatske (YU)
Farmaceutsko Drustvo Srbije (YU)
Farmaceutsko Drustvo Vojvodine (YU)
Farmacia Nueva (IT)
Farmacisti d'Italia (IT)
Editoriale Il Farmaco (IT)
Farmand (NO)
Farmer Genealogy Co. (US)
Farmer-Labor Press Publishing Co. Inc. (US)
Farmer-Stockman Publishing Co. (US)
Farmers and Manufacturers Beet Sugar Association (US)
Farmers Club (UK)
Farmers Digest, Inc. (US)
Farmers Educational & Cooperative Union of America. South Dakota Division (US)
Farmers' Forum, India
  see Bharat Krishak Samaj (II)
Farmers' Friend (CH)
Farmers Friend and Rural Reporter (US)
Farmers' Parliamentary Forum (II)
Farmers' Union of Wales (UK)
Farmers Union of Western Australia (Inc.) (AT)
Farmers Union Publishing Co. (US)
Farmers Weekly Newspaper Co. Ltd. (AT)

Farming Press Ltd. (UK)

Farmland Industries, Inc. (US)

Farmunione-Associazione Nazionale dell'Industria Farmaceutica Italiana (IT)

Ibrahim Farrah, Inc. (US)
Farrar, Straus & Giroux, Inc. (US)
Farrell Lines Inc. (US)
Farrell Publishing Co. (US)
Farriers Journal Publishing Co. Ltd. (UK)
Fash, New York (US)
Fashion Buyer Ltd. (UK)
Fashion Newsletter Inc. (US)
Fashion Textiles Mode Publishing Ltd. (CN)
Fasquelle Editeurs (FR)
Fatebenefratelli (IT)
Fathar (US)
Fatty Acid Producers Council (US)
Faulkner County Historical Society (US)
Fault (US)
Fauna Preservation Society (UK)
Fauno Editore (IT)
J. Faura - Soler, Ed. & Pub. (SP)
J. Faust & Co. (US)
Faust-Gesellschaft (GW)
Faversham House (UK)
Faversham Society (UK)
Fawcett Publications, Inc. (US)
Fax Forecast (US)
Fax Publishing Inc. (CN)
F. W. Faxon Co., Inc. (US)
Librairie Fayard (FR)
Fazal Printing Bureau (II)
Fearnly & Egers Chartering Co. Ltd. (NO)
Feature Publications, Inc. (US)
FEBECA
  see Federation Belge du Commerce Alimentaire (BE)
FEBECOOP
  see Federation Belge des Cooperatives (BE)
Uitgeverij FED B. V. (NE)
Fedemetal (CK)
Federacao Brasileira das Sociedades de Otorinolaringologia e Broncoesofagologia (BL)
Federacao Brasileira de Associacao de Bibliotecarios (BL)
Federacao Brasileira de Medicina Desportiva. Centro de Documentacao e Informacao Em Ciencias do Esporte (BL)
Federacao das Industrias (BL)
Federacao das Industrias do Estado da Bahia (BL)
Federacao das Industrias do Estado de Minas Gerais (BL)
Federacao das Industrias do Estado do Espirito Santo (BL)
Federacao das Industrias do Estado do Rio de Janeiro (BL)
Federacao das Industrias do Estado do Rio Grande do Norte (BL)
Federacao das Industrias do Estado do Rio Grande do Sul (BL)
Federacao dos Trabalhadores na Agricultura do Estado do Parana (BL)
Federacao e Centro das Industrias do Estado de Sao Paulo (BL)

Federation Internationale de Philatelie
  *see* International Philatelic Federation (LU)
Federation Internationale de Rugby Amateur
  *see* International Amateur Rugby Federation (FR)
Federation Internationale des Editeurs de Journaux et
  Publications
  *see* International Federation of Newspaper
  Publishers (FR)
Federation Internationale des Ingenieurs Conseils
  *see* International Federation of Consulting Engineers
  (NE)
Federation Internationale des Instituts de Recherches
  Socio-Religieuses
  *see* International Federation of Institutes for Social
  and Socio-Religious Research (BE)
Federation Internationale des Organisations de
  Donneurs de Sang (FR)
Federation Internationale des Producteurs Agricoles
  *see* International Federation of Agricultural
  Producers (FR)
Federation Internationale des Producteurs de Jus de
  Fruits
  *see* International Federation of Fruit Juice
  Producers (FR)
Federation Internationale des Professeurs de Francais
  (FR)
Federation Internationale des Societes et Instituts pour
  l'Etude de la Renaissance
  *see* International Federation of Societies and
  Institutes for the Study of the Renaissance (SZ)
Federation Internationale des Syndicats Chretiens
  d'Ouvriers Agricoles (BE)
Federation Internationale Motocycliste (SZ)
Federation Interprofessionnelle de la Congelation
  Ultra-Rapide (FR)
Federation Interprofessionnelle de la Region Parisienne
  (FR)
Federation Intersyndicale des Maisons de Sante
  Privees de France et d'Outremer (FR)
Federation Mondiale des Villes-Cites Unies
  *see* United Towns Organization (FR)
Federation Mondiale pour la Protection des Animaux
  *see* World Federation for the Protection of Animals
  (SZ)
Federation Nationale Belge de la Fourrure et de la
  Peau en Poil (BE)
Federation Nationale Belge des Tapissiers-Garnisseurs
  et Decorateurs d'Interieur (BE)
Federation Nationale d'Habitat Rural (FR)
Federation Nationale de Commercants de France
  (FR)
Federation Nationale de l'Industrie de la Chaussure de
  France (FR)
Federation Nationale de l'Industrie Laitiere (FR)
Federation Nationale de la Coiffure (FR)
Federation Nationale de la Maroquinerie (FR)
Federation Nationale de la Presse Francaise (FR)
Federation Nationale de la Propriete Agricole (FR)
Federation Nationale de la Sante (AE)
Federation Nationale des Agents Commerciaux (FR)
Federation Nationale des Anciens Combattants et
  Caolets des Transmissions (FR)
Federation Nationale des Anciens Combattants,
  Prisonniers, Deportes, Resistants et Victimes de
  Guerre des Chemins de Fer Francais (ENCAC)
  (FR)
Federation Nationale des Anciens des Forces
  Francaises en Allemagne et en Autriche, Rhenanie,
  Ruhr & Tyrol (FR)
Federation Nationale des Artisans Electriciens (FR)
Federation Nationale des Boissons (FR)
Federation Nationale des Chambres Syndicales (BE)
Federation Nationale des Clubs (FR)
Federation Nationale des Clubs Automobiles de
  France (FR)
Federation Nationale des Combattants Prisonniers de
  Guerre et Combattants d'Algerie, Tunisie, Maroc.
  (FR)
Federation Nationale des Comites de Vigilance (FR)
Federation Nationale des Commissaires de Police et
  Commissaires de Police Adjoints de Belgique (BE)
Federation Nationale des Compagnies de Theatre et
  d'Animation (FR)
Federation Nationale des Conseils Juridiques et
  Fiscaux (FR)
Federation Nationale des Cooperatives de
  Consommation (FR)
Federation Nationale des Cooperatives Ouvrieres de
  Production du Batiment, des Travaux Publics et des
  Activites Annexes (FR)
Federation Nationale des Enseignants Quebecois
  (CN)
Federation Nationale des Foyers Ruraux de France
  (FR)
Federation Nationale des Groupements de Protection
  des Cultures (FR)
**Federation Nationale des Groupements des Entreprises**
  **Francaises dans la Lutte Contre le Cancer** (FR)

Federation Nationale des Industries Electroniques
  (FR)
Federation Nationale des Infirmieres Belges (BE)
Federation Nationale des Jeunes Alliances Paysannes
  (BE)
Federation Nationale des Medecins Omnipraticiens
  Francais (FR)
Federation Nationale des Mineurs CFDT (FR)
Federation Nationale des Negociants en Materiaux de
  Construction (FR)
Federation Nationale des Organisations Sanitaires
  Apicoles Departementales (FR)
Federation Nationale des Plus Grands Invalides de
  Guerre (FR)
Federation Nationale des Poissonniers Detaillants
  Belges (BE)
Federation Nationale des Producteurs de l'Horticulture
  et des Pepinieres. (FR)
Federation Nationale des Promoteurs-Constructeurs
  (F. N. P. C.) (FR)
Federation Nationale des Republicains Independants.
  (FR)
Federation Nationale des Sapeurs-Pompiers Francais
  (FR)
Federation Nationale des Societes Cooperatives
  d'H.L.M. (FR)
Federation Nationale des Societes d'Economie Mixte
  de Construction, d'Amenagement et de Renovation
  (FR)
Federation Nationale des Syndicats. Departement des
  Medicins Electro- Radiologistes Qualifies (FR)
Federation Nationale des Syndicats d'Exploitants
  Agricoles (FR)
Federation Nationale des Syndicats d'Ingenieurs et de
  Cadres (FR)
Federation Nationale des Syndicats de Droguistes
  (FR)
Federation Nationale des Syndicats de Proprietaires
  Forestiers (FR)
Federation Nationale des Syndicats de Societes de
  Commerce Exterieur (FR)
Federation Nationale des Travaux Publics (FR)
Federation Nationale des Travaux Publics et des
  Syndicats Affilies (FR)
Federation Nationale du Batiment (FR)
Federation Nationale du Commerce des Engrais et
  Produits Connexes (FR)
Federation Nationale du Commerce et de l'Artisanat
  Automobile (FR)
Federation Nationale du Commerce et de la
  Reparation du Cycle & Motocycle (FR)
Federation Nationale du Credit Agricole (FR)
Federation Nationale "les Fils des Tues" (FR)
Federation Nationale Teinture et Apprets (FR)
Federation of African Women's Clubs (RH)
Federation of American Hospitals (US)
Federation of American Scientists (US)
Federation of American Societies for Experimental
  Biology (US)
Federation of Arab Canadian Societies (CN)
Federation of Asian Pharmaceutical Associations
  (PH)
Federation of Australian Astrologers Co-Operative
  (Vic.) Ltd. (AT)
Federation of Australian Commercial Broadcasters.
  Research and Promotion Division (AT)
Federation of Australian Universities Staff Associations
  (AT)
Federation of Biocommunication Societies (US)
Federation of British Artists (UK)
Federation of British Columbia Naturalists (CN)
Federation of Canadian Archers (CN)
Federation of Children's Book Groups (UK)
Federation of Civil Engineering Contractors (SA)
Federation of Commonwealth and British Chambers of
  Commerce (UK)
Federation of Danish Architects (DK)
Federation of Dutch Naturist-Organisations (NE)
Federation of Egyptian Industries (UA)
Federation of Engineering Industries (NO)
Federation of European Biochemical Societies (NE)
Federation of European Microbiological Societies
  (NE)
Federation of Evangelical Lutheran Churches in India
  (II)
Federation of Family History Societies (UK)
Federation of Finnish Film Societies (FI)
Federation of Free Byelorussian Journalists (CN)
Federation of Genealogical Societies (US)
Federation of Genealogical Societies. Chicago Regional
  Office (US)
Federation of Greek Industries (GR)
Federation of Hotel and Restaurant Associations of
  India (II)
Federation of Icelandic Master-Craftsmen
  *see* Landssamband Idnadarmanna (IC)
Federation of Indian Chambers of Commerce and
  Industry (II)

Federation of Insurance Counsel (US)
Federation of Insurance Institutes (II)
Federation of Irish Beekeeping Associations (IE)
Federation of Japan Confectionary Associations (JA)
Federation of Jewish Agencies of Greater Philadelphia
  (US)
Federation of Junior Chambers of Commerce in
  Scotland (UK)
Federation of Karnataka Chambers of Commerce &
  Industry (II)
Federation of Kibbutz Movements (IS)
Federation of Master Builders (UK)
Federation of Migros Cooperatives (SZ)
Federation of Motion Picture Councils (US)
Federation of New York State Bird Clubs,Inc (US)
Federation of Obstetric & Gynaecological Societies of
  India (II)
Federation of Old Cornwall Societies (UK)
Federation of Ontario Naturalists (CN)
Federation of Orthodontic Associations (US)
Federation of Pakistan Chambers of Commerce and
  Industry (PK)
Federation of Personnel Services (UK)
Federation of Playgoers Society (UK)
Federation of Publishers & Booksellers Associations in
  India (II)
Federation of Saskatchewan Indians (CN)
Federation of Scandinavian Paint and Varnish
  Technicians (DK)
Federation of Societies for Coatings Technology (US)
Federation of Societies of Professional Engineers
  (SA)
Federation of South African Gem & Mineral Societies
  (SA)
Federation of Southern Cooperatives (US)
Federation of Staff Associations of Australian Colleges
  of Advanced Education (AT)
Federation of State Medical Boards of the United
  States (US)
Federation of Swiss Physicians
  *see* Schweizerische Aerzteorganisation (SZ)
Federation of Swiss Watch Manufacturers (SZ)
Federation of Synagogues of South Africa (SA)
Federation of Tax Administrators (US)
Federation of the Covenant People (SA)
Federation of the Friends of History
  *see* Historian Ystavain Liitto (FI)
Federation of Tobacco Manufacturers in Belgium
  *see* Federation Belgo-Luxembourgeoise des
  Industries du Tabac (BE)
Federation of Victorian Film Societies (AT)
Federation of Women Teachers Associations of
  Ontario (CN)
Federation of Women Zionists of Great Britain and
  Ireland (UK)
Federation of Women's Institutes (SA)
Federation of Worker's Singing Societies of the U.S.A
  (US)
Federation pour le Respect de l'Homme et de
  l'Humanite (F.R.H.) (FR)
Federation Protestante de France (FR)
Federation Quebecoise de la Faune (CN)
Federation Romande de Metiers du Batiment (SZ)
Federation Romande Immobiliere (SZ)
Federation Romandes des Maitres Menuisiers,
  Ebenistes, Charpentiers, Fabricants de Meubles et
  Parqueteurs (SZ)
Federation Royale Belge du Yachting (BE)
Federation Royale des Associations Belges
  d'Ingenieurs Civils et d'Ingenieurs Agronomes
  (BE)
Federation Sportive et Culturelle de France (FR)
Federation Sportive et Gymnique du Travail (FR)
Federation Suisse des Avocats
  *see* Schweizerischer Anwaltsverband (SZ)
Federation Suisse des Cheminots
  *see* Schweizerischer Eisenbahnerverband (SZ)
Federation Suisse des Marchands de Tabacs
  *see* Verband Schweizerischer Tabakhaendler (SZ)
Federation Suisse des Typographes (SZ)
Federation Suisse-Liechtentein des Sports Populaires
  (SZ)
Federation Touristique du Brabant (BE)
Federation Unie des Auberges de Jeunesse (FR)
Federazione Automobilistica Italiana (IT)
Federazione Bowling Italiana (IT)
Federazione Cattolica Italiana (AT)
Federazione Ciclistica Italiana (IT)
Federazione Circoli Giovanili (IT)
Federazione delle Associazioni Italiane Alberghi e
  Tourismo (IT)
Federazione Fra le Associazioni Piccole e Medie
  Industrie, Regione Piemontese (IT)
Federazione Ginnastica d'Italia (IT)
Federazione Impiegati Operai Metallurgici (IT)
Federazione Istituti di Attivita Educative (IT)
Federazione Italian Tabaccai (IT)
Federazione Italiana Amministratori Enti Locali (IT)

Finland. National Board of Agriculture. Statistics Office
see Finland. Maatilahallitus. Statistics Office (FI)
Finland. National Board of Building
see Finland. Rakennushallituksen Tutkimus-ja Kehitystoiminnan (FI)
Finland. National Board of Social Welfare
see Finland. Sosiaalihallitus (FI)
Finland. National Board of Trade and Consumers Interests
see Finland. Elinkeinohallitus (FI)
Finland. Patentti- ja Rekisterihallitus (FI)
Finland. Posti-Ja Lennatinlaitos (FI)
Finland. Rakennushallitus. Tutkimus-ja Kehitystoiminnan (FI)
Finland. Social Security Institution
see Finland. Kansanelakelaitos (FI)
Finland. Sosiaali- Ja Terveysministerio (FI)
Finland. Sosiaalihallitus (FI)
Finland. Statistikcentrale
see Finland. Tilastokeskus (FI)
Finland. Tilastokeskus (FI)
Finland. Tullihallitus (FI)
Finland. Tyovoimaministerio (FI)
Finland. Ulkoasiainministerio (FI)
Finland. Valtion Painatuskeskus (FI)
Finland. Valtionrautatiet (FI)
Finlands Arkitektfoerbund (FI)
Finlands Bank
see Suomen Pankki (FI)
Finlands Forstmaestarefoerbund
see Suomen Metsanhoitajaliitto (FI)
Finlands Fysioterapeutfoerbund
see Suomen Laakintavoimistelijaliitto (FI)
Finlands Husdjursavelsfoerening
see Suomen Kotielainjalostusyhdistys (FI)
Finlands Journalistfoerbund
see Suomen Sanomalehtimiesten Liitto (FI)
Finlands Juristfoerbund
see Suomen Lakimiesliitto (FI)
Finlands Svenska Koepmannafoerbund (FI)
Finlands Utrikeshandelsfoerbund
see Finnish Foreign Trade Association (FI)
Finlands Vetenskapliga Bibliotekssamfund
see Suomen Tieteellinen Kirjastoseura (FI)
Editrice Finlavoro (IT)
Ruth Finley, Ed. & Pub. (US)
Finnfacts Instituutii (FI)
Finnish Academy of Science and Letters
see Suomalainen Tiedeakatemia (FI)
Finnish Academy of Technical Sciences
see Teknillisten Tieteiden Akatemia (FI)
Finnish Aeronautical Association
see Suomen Ilmailuliitto (FI)
Finnish American Chamber of Commerce (US)
Finnish-American Historical Society of the West (US)
Finnish American League for Democracy (US)
Finnish American Publishing Co. (US)
Finnish Animal Breeding Association
see Suomen Kotielainjalostusyhdistys (FI)
Finnish Boat and Motor Association (FI)
Finnish Broadcasting Company. Section for Long-Range Planning (FI)
Finnish Co-Operative Wholesale Society
see Suomen Osuuskauppojen Keskeskunta (FI)
Finnish Cultural Foundation (FI)
Finnish Dental Society
see Suomen Hammaslaakariseura (FI)
Finnish Economic Association
see Kansantaloudellinen Yhdistys (FI)
Finnish Electric Workers' Union
see Suomen Sahkoalantyontekijian Liitto (FI)
Finnish Employers' Confederation
see Suomen Tyonantajain Keskuslitto (FI)
Finnish Federation of Nurses
see Suomen Sairaanhoitajaliitto (FI)
Finnish Federation of Physical Therapists
see Suomen Laakintayoimistelaliitto (FI)
Finnish Fisheries Association
see Suomen Kalastusyhdistys (FI)
Finnish Foreign Trade Association (FI)
Finnish Forest Research Institute
see Finland. Metsantutkimuslaitos (FI)
Finnish Game and Fisheries Research Institute (FI)
Finnish Game and Fisheries Research Institute. Fisheries Division (FI)
Finnish Geodetic Institute
see Suomen Geodeettinen Laitos (FI)
Finnish Hard of Hearing Union
see Kuulonhuoltoliitto (FI)
Finnish Hardware and Builders' Merchants Association
see Suomen Rauta- ja Koneliikkeiden Yhdistys (FI)
Finnish Historical Society
see Suomen Historiallinen Seura (FI)

Finnish Hotel and Restaurant Association (FI)
Finnish Institute of International Affairs
see Ulkopoliittinen Instituutti (FI)
Finnish Insurance Society (FI)
Finnish Literature Society
see Suomalaisen Kirjallisuuden Seura (FI)
Finnish Materials Management Association (FI)
Finnish Medical Association
see Suomen Laakariliitto (FI)
Finnish Medical Society Duodecim (FI)
Finnish Music Teachers Association (FI)
Finnish Musicians Union
see Suomen Muusikkojen Liitto (FI)
Finnish Newspaper Co. Inc. (US)
Finnish Newspaper Publishers Association
see Sanomalehtien Liitto (FI)
Finnish Oriental Society
see Suomen Itamainen Seura (FI)
Finnish Ornithological Society
see Suomen Lintutieteellinen Yhdistys (FI)
Finnish Packaging Association
see Suomen Pakkausyhdistys (FI)
Finnish Paper and Timber Journal Publishing Co. (FI)
Finnish Pentacostal Churches of the U.S. and Canada (CN)
Finnish Political Science Association (FI)
Finnish Population and Family Welfare Federation
see Vaestontutkimuslaitos (FI)
Finnish Research Library Association
see Suomen Tieteellinen Kirjastoseura (FI)
Finnish Road Association
see Suomen Tieyhdistys (FI)
Finnish Tourist Board (FI)
Finnish Union of Chemists
see Suomen Kemistiliitto (FI)
Finnish Union of Survey Engineers (FI)
Finnlands Aussenhandelsverband
see Finnish Foreign Trade Association (FI)
Finska Jaern- och Maskinaffaererenas Foerening
see Suomen Rauta- ja Koneliikkeiden Yhdistys (FI)
Finska Laekaresaellskapet (FI)
Fiona Press, Inc. (US)
Libreria Editrice Fiorentina (IT)
F. Fiorentini & C. (IT)
Fire Exit (US)
Fire Fly Reporter (US)
Fire Independent, Inc. (US)
Fire Marshals Association of North America (US)
Fire Protection Association (UK)
Firenze Agricola (IT)
Fireweed (US)
Firma Dr. Karl Eisenhardt und Soehne (AU)
Firma Eisner Baumaschinen Ges. m.b.H. (AU)
First Atomic Power Industry Group (JA)
First Boston Corp. (US)
First Catholic Slovak Union (US)
First Century Fellowship (US)
First Church of Christ, Scientist (US)
First Coinvestors Inc. (US)
First District Dental Society (US)
First Hawaiian Bank (US)
First Issue (US)
First Jersey National Bank (US)
First National Bank of Boston (US)
First National Bank of Boston, Buenos Aires Branch (AG)
First National Bank of Chicago. Business & Economic Research Division (US)
First National City Bank (LB)
First National City Bank (New York)
see Citibank (US)
First Pan African Cultural Festival (AE)
First Things First, Inc. (US)
First Unitarian Church of Berkeley (US)
First Unitarian Church of Harvard (US)
First World Foundation (US)
Fiscal Press Ltd. (UK)
J. A. Fisch Associates Pty. Ltd. (SA)
Librairie Fischbacher (FR)
Verlag Michael Fischer (AU)
AG Buchdruckerei B. Fischer (SZ)
Fischer-Bergst-Verlag (GW)
Carl Fischer, Inc. (US)
Fischer Medical Publications, Inc. (US)
Fischer Taschenbuch Verlag (GW)
VEB Gustav Fischer Verlag (GE)
Gustav Fischer Verlag (GW)
S. Fischer Verlag GmbH (Frankfurt) (GW)
F. L. Fischer-Werbung (GW)
Fischwirtschaftliches Marketing-Institut (GW)
Fish Friers Review Ltd. (UK)
Fish Trades Review (AT)
Jack I. Fishbein, Ed. & Pub. (US)
Fisheries Association of British Columbia (CN)
Fisheries Association of Iceland
see Fiskifelag Islands (IC)
Fisheries Council of Canada (CN)
Fisheries Laboratory (UK)

Fisheries Organization Society Ltd. (UK)
Fisherman Publishing Society (CN)
Fishermen's News, Inc. (US)
Fishing Club of America (US)
Fishing Gazette Publishing Corp (US)
Fishing in Maryland, Inc. (US)
Fishing Tackle Trade News, Inc. (US)
Fishpaste (UK)
A-S Fiskaren (NO)
Fiskehandlerforeningen for Koebenhavn og Omegn (DK)
Fiskeri- og Soefartsmuseet. Saltvandsakvariet (DK)
Fiskeribladet (NO)
Fiskerifoereningen i Finland
see Suomen Kalastusyhdistys (FI)
Fiskerinytt A-S (NO)
Fiskifelag Islands (IC)
William C. Fitt, Ed. & Pub. (US)
Fitzgerald Communications, Inc. (US)
Fitzgerald Publishing Co., Inc. (US)
Fitzken Publishers (UK)
Fitzroy Ecumenical Centre (AT)
James Fitzsimmons, Ed. & Pub. (SZ)
Fitzsimons Army Medical Center
see under U.S. Army (US)
Five Arches Press (UK)
Five Associated University Libraries (US)
Five Windsors Publishing Co. Ltd. (CN)
Fixdruck (GW)
Izdatel'stvo Fizkul'tura i Sport (UR)
S. F. Flaccovio Editore (IT)
Flag Research Center (US)
Flambeau (BE)
Flambeaux Publishing Co. (US)
Flamencos Internacional Association (US)
Flammability News Bulletin, Inc. (US)
Flammarion (FR)
Flammarion Medecine Sciences (FR)
Flammes Vives (FR)
Fleet Publications Canada Ltd. (CN)
Fleet Reserve Association (US)
Fleet Street Letter Ltd. (UK)
Fleet Street Patent Law Reports Ltd (UK)
Verlag Hermann Fleischhauer und Co. (GW)
Max C. Fleischmann College of Agriculture
see under University of Nevada (US)
Al Fleming Communications, Inc. (US)
Flemish Association of Gastro-Enterology (BE)
Flemmings Verlag (GW)
Flensburger Zeitungsverlag GmbH (GW)
Flesch Financial Publications (Pty) Ltd (SA)
Fleurop GmbH (GW)
Fleurus-Presse International (FR)
Flexographic Technical Association (US)
Flight Safety Foundation, Inc. (US)
Flinders University of South Australia. History and Politics Society (AT)
Flinders University of South Australia. School of Social Sciences (AT)
Flintshire Historical Society (UK)
Floating Island Publications (US)
Florafax International, Inc. (US)
Florence. Ufficio della Provincia (IT)
Florida. Bureau of Local Government Finance (US)
Florida. Comptroller of Florida (US)
Florida. Crop and Livestock Reporting Service (US)
Florida. Department of Administration (US)
Florida. Department of Administration. Division of Retirement (US)
Florida. Department of Administration. Division of State Planning (US)
Florida. Department of Agriculture and Consumer Services (US)
Florida. Department of Agriculture and Consumer Services. Division of Forestry (US)
Florida. Department of Agriculture and Consumer Services. Division of Plant Industry (US)
Florida. Department of Commerce (US)
Florida. Department of Commerce. Division of Economic Development (US)
Florida. Department of Community Affairs. Division of Technical Assistance (US)
Florida. Department of Education (US)
Florida. Department of Education. Division of Elementary and Secondary Education (US)
Florida. Department of Education. Division of Vocational Education (US)
Florida. Department of Education. Professional Practices Council (US)
Florida. Department of Health and Rehabilitative Services (US)
Florida. Department of Health and Rehabilitative Services. Public Health Statistics Section (US)
Florida. Department of Highway Safety and Motor Vehicles. Division of Motor Vehicles (US)
Florida. Department of Natural Resources (US)
Florida. Department of Natural Resources. Division of Resource Management (US)

Florida. Department of Natural Resources. Marine Research Laboratory (US)
Florida. Department of State. Bureau of Historic Sites and Properties (US)
Florida. Department of State. Division of Archives, History and Records Management (US)
Florida. Department of State. Division of Elections (US)
Florida. Department of Transportation (US)
Florida. Division of Corrections (US)
Florida. Division of Family Services (US)
Florida. Division of Mental Health (US)
Florida. Farm Labor and Rural Manpower Service (US)
Florida. Game and Fresh Water Fish Commission (US)
Florida. Governor's Commission on the Status of Women (US)
Florida. Legislature. Joint Legislative Management Committee (US)
Florida. Legislature. Senate (US)
Florida. Mental Health Program Office (US)
Florida. State Library (US)
Florida. State Manpower Planning Council (US)
Florida A & M University (US)
Florida Academy of Family Physicians (US)
Florida Academy of Sciences, Inc. (US)
Florida Anthropological Society, Inc. (US)
Florida Association for Media in Education (US)
Florida Association of Realtors (US)
Florida Atlantic University (US)
Florida Atlantic University-Florida International University. Joint Center for Environment and Urban Problems (US)
Florida Audubon Society (US)
Florida Bankers Association (US)
Florida Bar (US)
Florida Chamber of Commerce (US)
Florida Citrus Mutual (US)
Florida Co-Operative Apartment Owners Association Inc (US)
Florida Confederation of Historical Societies (US)
Florida Congress of Parents and Teachers (US)
Florida Conservation Foundation (US)
Florida Consumer Information Bureau, Inc. (US)
Florida Council of Teachers of English (US)
Florida Dental Association (US)
Florida Education Association (US)
Florida Educational Research and Development Council (US)
Florida Engineering Society (US)
Florida English Journal (US)
Florida Entomological Society (US)
Florida F L Reporter (US)
Florida Farm Bureau Federation (US)
Florida Funeral Directors Association (US)
Florida Group Childcare Association (US)
Florida Historical Society (US)
Florida Industrial Arts Association (US)
Florida Law Revision Council (US)
Florida League of Cities (US)
Florida Library Association (US)
Florida Medical Association, Inc. (US)
Florida Music Educators Association (US)
Florida Nurses Association (US)
Florida Ocean Sciences Institute (US)
Florida Pharmaceutical Association (US)
Florida Psychological Association (US)
Florida Restaurant Association (US)
Florida Roofing, Sheet Metal & Air Conditioning Contractors Association, Inc. (US)
Florida Rural Electric Cooperatives Association (US)
Florida School for the Deaf and the Blind (US)
Florida Society of Geographers (US)
Florida Speech Communication Association (US)
Florida Speleological Society (US)
Florida State Board of Independent Colleges and Universities (US)
Florida State Firemen's Association (US)
Florida State Museum (US)
Florida State Reading Council (US)
Florida State University (US)
Florida State University. Center for Yugoslav-American Studies, Research, and Exchanges (US)
Florida State University. College of Law (US)
Florida State University. Department of Anthropology (US)
Florida State University. Department of Biological Sciences (US)
Florida State University. Department of Classics (US)
Florida State University. Department of Education (US)
Florida State University. Department of Philosophy (US)
Florida State University. Developmental Research School (US)

Florida State University. Institute for Social Research (US)
Florida State University. Instructional Media Center (US)
Florida State University. Office of the Provost, Graduate Studies & Research (US)
Florida State University. School of Library Science (US)
Florida State University System (US)
Florida Supermarket Association (US)
Florida Technological University (US)
Florida Trucking Association, Inc. (US)
Floristisch-Soziologische Arbeitsgemeinschaft (GW)
Florists Telegraph Delivery Association (UK)
Raymond Flory, Ed. & Pub. (US)
Von Flotow (GW)
Flour Milling and Baking Research Association (UK)
Flournoy & Associates (US)
Floyd Junior College. Humanities Division (US)
Verlag Fluessiges Obst GmbH (GW)
Flughafen Hamburg GmbH (GW)
Fluor Corporation (US)
Fly Fisherman Magazine, Inc. (US)
Flyfishers Club (UK)
Flygfoerlaget AB (SW)
Flygtekniska Foersoeksanstalten (SW)
Flying Physician Association, Inc. (US)
Flying Saucer News Co. (US)
Flyvevaabnets Soldaterforening (DK)
Focolare Movement for Men (PH)
Focus Foerlag (SW)
Focus Guide Magazine Group (PN)
Focus-Midwest Publishing Co., Inc. (US)
Focus News (US)
Focus Philippines (PH)
Focus Publications (UK)
Focus Publications Council (UK)
Focus-Verlag (SZ)
Fodens Ltd. (UK)
Foerbundet Svenska Finlandsfrivilliga (SW)
Foerderer Verein "Nemzetor" (GW)
Foerderungsgemeinschaft der Kartoffelwirtschaft E.V (GW)
Foereningen Flottans Maen (SW)
Foereningen Foer Arbetarskydd (SW)
Foereningen Foer Inre Vattenvaegar (SW)
Foereningen Foer Samhaellsplanering (SW)
Foereningen Foer Svensk Kulturhistoria (SW)
Foereningen Foer Vaestgoetalitteratur (SW)
Foereningen Foer Vattenhygien (SW)
Foereningen Granskaren (FI)
Foereningen Heimdal (SW)
Foereningen Kurskamraterna (SW)
Foereningen NEFA-Norden (SW)
Foereningen Norden (SW)
Foereningen Opuscula Medica (SW)
Foereningen Svensk Fjaederfaeskoetsel (SW)
Foereningen Svensk Form (SW)
Foereningen Svenska Tonsattares Internationella Musikbyra (SW)
Foereningen Svenska Verktygsmaskintillverkare (SW)
Foereningen Sveriges Flotta (SW)
Foereningen Sveriges Saendareamafoerer (SW)
Foereningen Unga Filosoter (SW)
Tidskriftaktiebolaget Foeretagsekonomi (SW)
Foeroya Frodskaparfelag (FA)
Foersikringsbranschens Serviceaktiebolag (SW)
Foersvarets Civila Tjaenstemannafoerbund (SW)
Foersvarets Forskningsanstalt (SW)
Casa Editrice Foglio (IT)
Foi et le Temps (BE)
Foi et Vie (FR)
Jorge Foix, Ed. & Pub. (SP)
Fokker-VFW B.V. Bedrijf Drechtsteden (NE)
Folclore do Maranhao (BL)
Folger Shakespeare Library (US)
Folha Carioca Editora S.A. (BL)
Folio Magazine Publishing Corp. (US)
Folio Society Ltd. (UK)
Folk Dance Association (US)
Folk Dance Federation of California, South (US)
Folk Dance Magazine (US)
Folk Lore Society of Victoria (AT)
Folk Music Society of Ireland (IE)
Folk Review Ltd. (UK)
Folkbildningsfoerbundet (SW)
Folkeligt Oplysnings Forbund (DK)
Folkeuniversitetet (NO)
Folkevirke (DK)
Folklore Centre (IQ)
Folklore Feminists Communication (US)
Folklore Forum, Inc. (US)
Folklore Society (UK)
Folklore Society of Greater Washington (US)
Folkparkernas Centralorganisation (SW)
Folkpartiet Riksorganisation (SW)
Folkpartiets Ungdomsfoerbund (SW)
Folkscene Publication (US)

Follia di New York (US)
Follow up (UK)
Fomento de las Artes Decorativas. Agrupacion de Diseno Industrial (SP)
Fomento del Trabajo Nacional (SP)
Fomento Martinense. Grupo Espeleologico (SP)
Fondation Calouste Gulbenkian (FR)
Fondation Charles Plisnier (BE)
Fondation de l'Afrique du Sud
    see South Africa Foundation (SA)
Fondation Egyptologique Reine Elisabeth (BE)
Fondation Eugene Ysaye (BE)
Fondation Francaise d'Etudes Nordiques (FR)
Fondation Hardt pour l'Etude de l'Antiquite Classique (SZ)
Fondation Jan Dhondt (BE)
Fondation Nationale des Politiques et Direction de la Documentation (FR)
Fondation Nationale des Sciences Politiques (FR)
Fondation Nationale pour l'Enseignement de la Creativite (FR)
Fondation Nationale pour l'Enseignement de la Gestion des Entreprises (FR)
Fondation pour la Recherche et le Developpement dans l'Ocean Indien (RE)
Fondation pour la Recherche Sociale (FR)
Fondation Singer-Polignac (FR)
Fondazione Cini (IT)
Fondazione "Claudio Monteverdi" (IT)
Fondazione Diritto del Lavoro (IT)
Fondazione Giangiacomo Feltrinelli (IT)
Fondazione Giorgio Cini (IT)
Fondazione Latinitas (VC)
Fondazione Lerici Prospezioni Archeologiche (IT)
Fondazione Ugo Bordoni (IT)
Fondo Colombiano de Investigaciones Cientificas (CK)
Fondo Cultural de la Cuna de America (DR)
Fondo de Cultura Economica (MX)
Fonds des Nations Unies pour l'Enfance
    see Unicef (UN)
Editora Fontana Ltda (BL)
Edicoes Maria da Fonte (PO)
Fontessa Publications Ltd. (UK)
Food and Agriculture Organization of the United Nations (UN)
Food and Agriculture Organization of the United Nations. Regional Office for Asia and the Far East (UN)
Food and Agriculture Organization of the United Nations. Regional Office for Latin America (UN)
Food and Nutrition Institute of Iran (IR)
Food and Nutrition Research Institute
    see Philippines. Food and Nutrition Research Institute (PH)
Food Chemical News, Inc. (US)
Food Corporation of India (II)
Food Distribution Research Society (US)
Food Education Society (UK)
Food Farming and Agriculture (II)
Food Hygienic Society of Japan (JA)
Food Industries Credit Bureau (US)
Food Marketing Institute (US)
Food Processing Machinery and Supplies Association (US)
Food Research and Action Center (US)
Food Science Co., Ltd. (JA)
Food Selling Publications, Inc. (US)
Food Service Executives Association, Inc. (US)
Food Trade Press Ltd. (UK)
Foodgrain Technologists' Research Association of India (II)
Foodland International Corp. (US)
Football Association (UK)
Football Forecaster (US)
Football News Co. (US)
G. W. Foote & Co. (UK)
Foote Mineral Company (US)
Foothills Trader (US)
Footnote (UK)
Footwear News (US)
For Now (US)
Forbes Inc. (US)
Forbes Publications Ltd. (UK)
Forbrukerraadet (NO)
Force Four Motoring Publications Ltd. (UK)
Ford Associates Inc. (US)
Ford Foundation (US)
Ford Motor Co. (US)
Ford Motor Co. Ford Truck Division (US)
Ford Motor Co., Ltd. Tractor Operations (UK)
Ford-Werke AG (GW)
Fordham University (US)
Fordham University Press (US)
Fordham University. School of Law (US)
Ford's Travel Guides (US)
Forecast (AT)
Forecast Publications (UK)

Forecaster Publishing Co. (US)
Foreign Affairs Association of Japan (JA)
Foreign Affairs Publishing Co. (UK)
Foreign Area Materials Center (US)
Foreign Correspondents Ltd. (UK)
Foreign Credit Insurance Association (US)
Foreign Credit Interchange Bureau. National
　Association of Credit Management (US)
Foreign Language Association of the Red River (US)
Foreign Languages Press (RM)
Foreign Medical School Information Center (US)
Foreign Policy Association (US)
Foreign Policy Research Institute (US)
Foreign Resources Associates (US)
Foreign Student Service Council (US)
Foreign Tax Law Association (US)
Foreign Trade Publishing House (KN)
Evan H. Foreman, Ed. & Pub. (US)
Foremost Foods Company, S.F (US)
Foremost Press Ltd. (UK)
Forenede Danske Motorejere (DK)
Forenedetidsskrifters Forlag (DK)
Forening for Boghaandvaerk (DK)
Foreningen af Arbejdsledere i Danmark (DK)
Foreningen af Danske Civiloekonomer (DK)
Foreningen af Danske Medicinfabrikker (DK)
Foreningen af Kioskejere i Danmark (DK)
Foreningen af Registrerede Revisorer (DK)
Foreningen af Statsautoriserede Revisorer (DK)
Foreningen af Sygehusadministratorer i Danmark
　(DK)
Foreningen Dansk Erhvervsfjerkrae (DK)
Foreningen Nordens Forbund (NO)
Foreningen til Norske Fortidsminnesmerkers Bevaring
　(NO)
Foreningen til Ski-Idrettens Fremme (NO)
Foreningen til Soefartens Fremme (DK)
Foreningen til Svampekundskabens Fremme (DK)
Forensic Publishing Co. (UK)
Forensic Science Society (UK)
Foresight Publishing Co. (UK)
Forest Farmers Association (US)
Forest History Society (US)
Forest Industries Committee on Timber Valuation and
　Taxation (US)
Forest Industries Council (US)
Forest Products Research and Industries Development
　Commission
　see Philippines. Forest Products Research and
　Industries Development Commission (PH)
Forest Products Research Institute
　see under Council for Scientific and Industrial
　Research (GH)
Forest Products Research Society (US)
Forest Research Institute (BG)
Forest Research Institute (NZ)
Forest Research Institute (IO)
Forest Research Institute & Colleges (II)
Forestry Association of Nigeria (NR)
Foret Privee (FR)
Foreword Press, Inc. (US)
Forges (CN)
Forging Industry Association (US)
Forkel Verlag GmbH (GW)
Verlag Form GmbH (GW)
Formaluce (IT)
Formez (IT)
Formosan Association for Advancement of Science
　(CH)
Formosan Medical Association (CH)
Formula Enterprises (US)
Fornminnesfoereningen i Goeteborg (SW)
Foro Padano (IT)
FORPRIDECOM
　see Philippines. Forest Products Research and
　Industries Development Commission (PH)
Forrest Publications Inc. (US)
Forretningsbankenes Konjunkturinstitutt (NO)
Forschunginstitut fuer Deutsche Sprache, Marburg
　(GW)
Forschunginstitut fuer Wirtschaftsverfassung und
　Wettbewerb e.V. (GW)
Forschungsgesellschaft fuer das Strassenwesen e.V.
　(GW)
Forschungsgesellschaft fuer Genossenschaftswesen,
　Muenster (GW)
Forschungsgesellschaft fuer Wohnen, Bauen und
　Planen (AU)
Forschungsinstitut der Eidgenoessischen Turn- und
　Sportschule Magglingen (SZ)
Forschungsring fuer Biologisch-Dynamische
　Wirtschaftsweise (GW)
Forschungsstelle fuer den Handel, Berlin (GW)
Forschungsstelle fuer Jagdkunde und
　Wildschadenverhuetung (GW)
Forschungsstelle fuer Juristische Dokumentation,
　Frankfurt (GW)

Forschungsstelle fuer Politische Wissenschaft (SZ)
Forschungsvereinigung Antriebstechnik e. V. (GW)
A-S Forsikringsletteratur (NO)
Forskningsbiblioteksraadet (SW)
Forskningsraadens Naemnd Foer
　Forskningsinformation (SW)
Forster-Verlag AG (SZ)
Forstliche Fachvereine und Standesorganisationen
　Oesterreichs (AU)
Forstliche Forschungsanstalt Muenchen (GW)
Fort Beaufort Advocate (AT)
Fort Belknap Genealogical Association (US)
Fort Belknap Society (US)
Fort Burgwin Research Center, Inc. (US)
Fort Collins Audubon Society (US)
Fort Concho Museum (US)
Fort Dodge Laboratories (US)
Fort Hare University Press (SA)
Fort Hays Kansas State College (US)
Fort Lauderdale Historical Society, Inc. (US)
Fort Peck Tribes (US)
Fort Smith Public Schools in Action (US)
Fort Ticonderoga Association (US)
Fort Vancouver Historical Society (US)
Fort Victoria-Zimbabwe Publicity Association (RH)
Fort Wayne Public Library (US)
Fort Worth Area Chamber of Commerce (US)
Fort Worth Commercial Recorder (US)
Fort Worth Como Monitor (US)
Fort Worth Genealogical Society (US)
Fort Worth Star Telegram (US)
Fortean Times (UK)
Fortlett Publishing Corp. (US)
Fortnightly (US)
Fortress Press (US)
Verlag Fortschritte der Medizin M B Schwappach und
　Co. - GmbH und Co. (GW)
Fortuna Italiana (IT)
Fortune Society (US)
Foerlagsfoereningen Forum (FI)
Editions du Forum (FR)
Editrice Forum (IT)
Forum A.S.B.L. (BE)
Forum for Behavioural Technology (US)
Forum for Interdisciplinary Mathematics (II)
Forum for Sociologists (II)
Forum for the Advancement of Students in Science
　and Technology, Inc. (US)
Forum for the Advancement of Toxicology in Colleges
　of Pharmacy (US)
Forum House Publishing Co. (CN)
Forum International (UK)
Forum International (US)
Forum Italiano dell'Energia Nucleare (IT)
Forum Literario (US)
Forum, Novi Sad (YU)
Forum of Industrial Technologists (II)
Forum Press Ltd. (UK)
Forum Publications, Inc. (US)
Forum Stadtpark (AU)
Forum, Subotica (YU)
Forum-Verlag GmbH (GW)
Forumverlag (AU)
Forward Times (US)
Foseco Inc. (US)
G. Fossataro, Ed. & Pub. (IT)
Foster Associates (US)
G. W. Foster Associates Ltd. (UK)
Foster Wheeler Corp. (US)
Editorial Fotografia Universal (AG)
Fotografisk Forlag (NO)
VEB Fotokinoverlag Leipzig (GE)
Foton Publishing B.V. (NE)
Fotoptica S-A (BL)
Fotorotar AG (SZ)
W. Foulsham & Co. Ltd. (UK)
Foundation Byzantine (BE)
Foundation Center (US)
Foundation Church of the Millennium (US)
Foundatlon "de Paladijn" (NE)
Foundation Documenta de Medicina Geographica et
　Tropica (NE)
Foundation Euphytica (NE)
Foundation Flora Malesiana (NE)
Foundation for Business Responsibilities (UK)
Foundation for Change (US)
Foundation for Christian Living (US)
Foundation for Coast to Coast Opera Publication
　(CN)
Foundation for Cooperative Housing (US)
Foundation for Economic Education, Inc. (US)
Foundation for Education, Science and Technology
　(SA)
Foundation for Environmental Conservation (SZ)
Foundation for European Judaism (UK)
Foundation for International Philosophical Exchange
　(US)
Foundation for Management Education

see University of Cochin. Foundation for
　Management Education (II)
Foundation for National Progress (US)
Foundation for Promoting International Economic
　Information (SZ)
Foundation for Psychiatric Research in Finland (FI)
Foundation for Religious Action in the Social and
　Civil Order (US)
Foundation for Research in the Afro-American
　Creative Arts, Inc. (US)
Foundation for Research on the Nature of Man (US)
Foundation for Student Communication, Inc. (US)
Foundation for the Advancement of International
　Business Administration, Inc. (US)
Foundation for the Community of Artists (US)
Foundation for the Future (US)
Foundation for the Promotion of the Translation of
　Dutch Literary Works (NE)
Foundation for the Study of Cycles (US)
Foundation Janus (NE)
Foundation Management Inc. (US)
Foundation of Clinical Oncology (JA)
Foundation Press, Inc. (US)
Foundation Prometheus (NE)
Foundation Publications Ltd. (UK)
Foundation University (PH)
Foundation University. School of Law (PH)
Foundry News (II)
Four Decades (CN)
Four Points Intertribal Council (US)
Four Seasons Foundation (US)
Four Seasons Publications (US)
Four Swords, Inc. (US)
Four Wheeler Publishing Co. (US)
Four Zoas Press (US)
Fourah Bay College
　see under University of Sierra Leone (SL)
Fourman Holdings Ltd. (NZ)
Fourth Class Cancellation Club (US)
Fourth Estate (US)
Fourth Estate (US)
Fourth Estate Publishing Co. (NZ)
Fourth International - Posadist. International
　Secretariat (IT)
Fourth Seacoast Publishing Co. Inc. (US)
Fovarosi Szabo Ervin Konyvtar (HU)
Foxfire Fund, Inc. (US)
Foxlow Publications Ltd. (UK)
Foyer Bulgare (BL)
Fraenkische Geographische Gesellschaft (GW)
Fragment (UK)
Fragments (NZ)
Fragua (SP)
Fraktefartoyenes Rederiforening (NO)
Frameworks Press (UK)
Editions du Franc-Canada (CN)
Francaise d'Edition et de Publication (FR)
Editions de France (FR)
France. Archives Nationales (FR)
France. Bibliotheque Nationale
　see Bibliotheque Nationale (FR)
France. Bureau de Documentation Miniere. Division
　de Documentation (FR)
France. Bureau de Recherches Geologiques et
　Minieres (FR)
France. Bureau National d'Information Scientifique et
　Technique (FR)
France. Caisse Nationale de Credit Agricole (FR)
France. Caisse Nationale de l'Assurance Maladie des
　Travailleurs Salaries (FR)
France. Caisse Nationale des Allocations Familiales
　(FR)
France. Centre de Diffusion et d'Informations
　Administratives (FR)
France. Centre de Documentation et Informations
　(FR)
France. Centre de Recherches sur les Zones Arides
　(FR)
France. Centre National d'Etudes des
　Telecommunications (FR)
France. Centre National d'Etudes des
　Telecommunications. Departement Mesures
　Ionespheriques et Radioelectriques (FR)
France. Centre National de Coordination des Etudes
　et Recherches sur la Nutrition et l'Alimentation
　(FR)
France. Centre National de la Recherche Scientifique
　see Centre National de la Recherche Scientifique
　(FR)
France. Centre National pour l'Exploitation des
　Oceans (FR)
France. Comite des Travaux Historiques et
　Scientifiques (FR)
France. Comite Monetaire de la Zone Franc (FR)
France. Commision Centrale pour la Navigation du
　Rhin (FR)
France. Commissariat a l'Energie Atomique (FR)

France. Commission d'Histoire Economique et Sociale de la Revolution Francaise   (FR)
France. Commission des Operations de Bourse   (FR)
France. Commission Nationale de l'Amenagement du Territoire   (FR)
France. Commission Technique des Ententes   (FR)
France. Conseil National de la Comptabilite   (FR)
France. Delegation a l'Informatique   (FR)
France. Delegation Generale a la Recherche Scientifique et Technique   (FR)
France. Departement des Statistiques de Transport. Service des Affaires Economiques et Internationales   (FR)
France. Direction de l'Amenagement Foncier et de l'Urbanisme   (FR)
France. Direction de l'Equipement et des Transports. Bureau A2   (FR)
France. Direction de la Documentation   (FR)
France. Direction de la Prevision   (FR)
France. Direction des Journaux Officiels
   see Direction des Journaux Officiels   (FR)
France. Direction du Batiment, des Travaux Publics et de la Conjoncture   (FR)
France. Direction du Gaz, de l'Electricite et du Charbon   (FR)
France. Direction General de la Concurrence et des Prix   (FR)
France. Direction Generale a l'Aviation Civile   (FR)
France. Direction Generale de la Protection de la Nature   (FR)
France. Direction Generale des Douanes et Droits Indirects   (FR)
France. Direction Generale des Impots   (FR)
France. Documentation Francaise
   see Documentation Francaise   (FR)
France. Imprimerie Nationale
   see Imprimerie Nationale   (FR)
France. Inspection Generale des Finances   (FR)
France. Institut National d'Etudes Demographiques   (FR)
France. Institut National de Gestion Previsionnelle et de Controle de Gestion   (FR)
France. Institut National de la Propriete Industrielle   (FR)
France. Institut National de la Recherche Agronomique   (FR)
France. Institut National de la Recherche Agronomique. Departement d'Economie et de Sociologie Rurales   (FR)
France. Institut National de la Sante et de la Recherche Medicale   (FR)
France. Institut National de la Statistique et des Etudes Economiques   (FR)
France. Institut National de Recherche et de Documentation Pedagogiques   (FR)
France. Institut National de Recherche et de Securite pour la Prevention des Accidents du Travail et des Maladies Professionelles   (FR)
France. Laboratoire Central des Ponts et des Chaussees   (FR)
France. Ministere de l'Agriculture et du Developpement Rural   (FR)
France. Ministere de l'Agriculture et du Developpement Rural. Service Central des Enquetes et Etudes Statistiques   (FR)
France. Ministere de l'Agriculture et du Developpement Rural. Service des Forets   (FR)
France. Ministere de l'Agriculture et du Developpement Rural. Service Regional de Statistique Agricole
   see France. Service Regional de Statistique Agricole   (FR)
France. Ministere de l'Amenagement du Territoire, de l'Equipement du Logement et des Transports   (FR)
France. Ministere de l'Amenagement du Territoire, de l'Equipement du Logement et des Transports. Direction du Batiment et des Travaux Public et de la Conjoncture
   see France. Direction du Batiment et des Travaux Public et de la Conjoncture   (FR)
France. Ministere de l'Economie et des Finances   (FR)
France. Ministere de l'Economie et des Finances. Commission Centrale des Marches   (FR)
France. Ministere de l'Economie et des Finances. Direction de la Prevision
   see France. Direction de la Prevision   (FR)
France. Ministere de l'Economie et des Finances. Direction du Tresor
   see France. Direction du Tresor   (FR)

France. Ministere de l'Economie et des Finances. Direction Generale des Impots
   see France. Direction Generale des Impots   (FR)
France. Ministere de l'Economie et des Finances. Direction General de la Concurrence et des Prix
   see France. Direction Generale de la Concurrence et des Prix   (FR)
France. Ministere de l'Education Nationale. Office Francais des Techniques Modernes d'Education
   see France. Office Francais des Techniques Modernes d'Education   (FR)
France. Ministere de l'Industrie et de la Recherche   (FR)
France. Ministere de l'Industrie et de la Recherche. Service de Relations Publiques et d'Information   (FR)
France. Ministere de l'Interieur. Service d'Information et de Relations Publiques (S.I.R.P.)   (FR)
France. Ministere de la Cooperation   (FR)
France. Ministere de la Defense Nationale   (FR)
France. Ministere de la Defense Nationale. Antenne Air   (FR)
France. Ministere de la Protection de la Nature et de l'Environment   (FR)
France. Ministere de la Sante   (FR)
France. Ministere des Affaires Culturelles   (FR)
France. Ministere des Affaires Etrangeres   (FR)
France. Ministere des Affaires Etrangeres. Department of Cultural, Scientific and Technical Relations   (FR)
France. Ministere des Affaires Etrangeres. Direction du Personnel et de l'Administration Generale   (FR)
France. Ministere des Armees   (FR)
France. Ministere des Postes et Telecommunications   (FR)
France. Ministere du Travail   (FR)
France. Ministre d'Etat Charge des Departements et Territories d'Outre-Mer   (FR)
France. Office des Cooperatives et des Collectivites   (FR)
France. Office Francais des Techniques Modernes d'Education   (FR)
France. Office National d'Etudes et de Recherches Aerospatiales   (FR)
France. Office National d'Immigration. Section Documentation-Statistiques   (FR)
France. Office National d'Information sur les Enseignements et les Professions   (FR)
France. Office National de Publications Culturelles   (FR)
France. Parlement. Assemblee Nationale   (FR)
France. Secretariat d'Etat a la Marine   (FR)
France. Secretariat d'Etat au Tourisme   (FR)
France. Secretariat d'Etat aux Affaires Etrangeres Charge de la Cooperation. Direction de l'Aide au Developpement   (FR)
France. Secretariat d'Etat aux Postes et Telecommunications. Service de l'Information et de Relations Publiques   (FR)
France. Secretariat d'Etat aux Universites. Service des Bibliotheques   (FR)
France. Secretariat des Missions d'Urbanisme et d'Habitat   (FR)
France. Service de Documentation et de Cartographie Geographiques   (FR)
France. Service des Forets   (FR)
   see France. Ministere de l'Agriculture et du Developpement Rural. Service des Forets
France. Service Hydrographique et Oceanographique de la Marine   (FR)
France. Service Regional de Statistique Agricole   (FR)
France a Table   (FR)
France Catholique-Ecclesia   (FR)
France Diffusion Presse   (FR)
France Dimanche   (FR)
Editions France-Empire   (FR)
Editions et Publicite France-Etranger   (FR)
France Europe Publicitec   (FR)
France Expansion   (FR)
France Forum   (FR)
France-Iberie Recherche. Theses et Documents. Institut d'Etudes Hispaniques, Hispanoamericaines   (FR)
France Lafayette   (FR)
Editions de la France Libre   (FR)
France Pharmacie   (FR)
France Protestante   (FR)
France-Selection   (FR)
France U. R. S. S. Magazine   (FR)
France Viticole   (FR)
Editions de Francia   (FR)
Ennio Francia Ed. & Pub.   (IT)
Francis A. Countway Library of Medicine   (US)
Francis Bacon Society Inc.   (UK)
Francis I. Dupont & Co.   (US)
Francis Thompson Society   (UK)
Franciscan Fathers   (US)
Franciscan Fathers of California, Inc.   (US)

Franciscan Fathers of Maine   (US)
Franciscan Fathers of the Commissariat of the Most Holy Savior   (US)
Franciscan Fathers. Slovenian Chaplaincy   (AT)
Franciscan Friars of St. John the Baptist Province   (US)
Franciscan Herald Press   (US)
Franciscan House of Formation of Australian - New Zealand Province   (AT)
Franciscan Printing Press   (IS)
Franciscan Publishers   (US)
Franciscan Sisters of Allegany   (US)
Editorial Franciscana   (PO)
Franciscanos Espanoles   (SP)
Franciscanos, Custody of the Most Holy Savior   (US)
Emiliano A. Francisco, Ed. & Pub.   (US)
Francite   (US)
Editons R. Franck   (FR)
Francke Verlag   (SZ)
Franckh'sche Verlagshandlung W. Keller und Co.   (GW)
Librairie le Francois   (FR)
Franey and Co. Ltd.   (UK)
Franjevacka Visoka Bogoslovija, Makarska   (YU)
Frank Browne's Things I Hear   (AT)
Verlag H. G. Franke   (SZ)
Frankenbund - Vereinigung fuer Fraenkische Landeskunde und Kulturpflaege e.V.   (GW)
Frankfurt am Main. Statistisches Amt und Wahlamt   (GW)
Druck- und Verlagshaus Frankfurt am Main GmbH   (GW)
Frankfurt Book Fair   (GW)
Frankfurter Allgemeine Zeitung   (GW)
Frankfurter Bund fuer Volksbildung GmbH   (GW)
Frankfurter Fachverlag   (GW)
Frankfurter Geographische Gesellschaft   (GW)
Frankfurter Societaetsdruckerei GmbH   (GW)
Burt Franklin & Co., Inc.   (US)
Franklin and Marshall College   (US)
Franklin Broadcasting Co.   (US)
Franklin Carrack Co.   (AT)
Franklin County (Tennessee) Historical Society   (US)
Franklin County (Washington) Historical Society   (US)
Franklin D. Roosevelt Philatelic Society   (US)
Franklin Institute   (US)
Franklin Institute Press   (US)
Franklin Institute Research Laboratories   (US)
Franklin Mint   (US)
Franklin Mint Collectors Society   (US)
Franklin Press (Baton Rouge)   (US)
Franklin Press (Denver)   (US)
Franklin Printing Company   (US)
R Franks Publishing Ranch   (US)
Franz-Sales-Verlag   (GW)
Franzis-Verlag   (GW)
Fraser & Co.(Pte)   (SI)
Fraser Group   (CN)
Fraser Island Defender's Organization, Ltd.   (AT)
Fraser Management Associates   (US)
Fraser Pearce Ltd.   (UK)
Fraser Valley Milk Producers' Association   (CN)
Fratelli Jovane   (IT)
Fratelli Lega Editori   (IT)
Fraternal Actuarial Association   (US)
Fraternal Order of Eagles   (US)
Fraternal Order of Police   (US)
Fraternites du Saint-Esprit   (FR)
Frati Minori Cappuccini della Provincia Consentina   (IT)
Fratini Missionari di Recco. Collegio Serafico   (IT)
Fraunhofer-Gesellschaft   (GW)
Fraunhofer Gesellschaft. Dokumentationsstelle fuer Bautechnik   (GW)
Fraunhofer-Gesellschaft. Dokumentationszentrale Wasser   (GW)
Frayed Page Collective   (US)
J. Myrick Frazier, Ed. & Pub.   (US)
Freark Brownelbeck Press   (US)
Freas-Rooke Computer Center   (US)
Fred and Eleanor Schonell Educational Research Centre   (AT)
Dr. H. T. Fredeen, Ed. & Pub.   (CN)
Frederiksberg Frimaerke Forening   (DK)
Fredette's   (US)
Fredrika-Bremer Foerbundet   (SW)
Free Albania Committee   (US)
Free Asia Association   (JA)
Free Church Federal Council   (UK)
Free Church of Scotland Publications Committee   (UK)
Free Commonwealth Group, Ltd.   (UK)
Free-Economy Association, Inc.   (US)
Free Evangelical Churches of Greece   (GR)
Free Lance Poets and Prose Workshop, Inc.   (US)
Free Library of Philadelphia. Reader Development Program   (US)

Free Methodist Church of North America (US)
Free Methodist Church of North America.
　Department of Christian Education (US)
Free News & Feature Service Publishers (II)
Free People Inc. (US)
Free Press (UK)
Free Press (US)
Free Press Publications (Western) Ltd. (CN)
Free Thinkers of America (US)
Free Thought Opinion (US)
Free University of Brussels
　see Universitie Libre de Bruxelles; Vrije Universiteit
　Brussel (The two universities have been separate
　institutions since 1970) (BE)
Free Venice Beachhead (US)
Free Voice of Labor Association (US)
Freebizak, Inc. (US)
Freed Publishing Co. (US)
Freedom (PK)
Freedom Fellowship Church (US)
Freedom House (US)
Freedom Leadership Foundation Inc. (US)
Freedom News, Inc. (US)
Freedom of Information Center (US)
Freedom of Vision (UK)
Freedom Press (UK)
Freedom Press, Inc. (US)
Freedom to Read Foundation (US)
Freedomways Associates (US)
Freeland Family Association (US)
Freeland League for Jewish Territorial Colonization
　(US)
Freeland Press Ltd. (UK)
Robert Freeman Publishing Corp. (US)
W.H. Freeman and Co. (US)
Freeman, Cooper & Co. (US)
Miller Freeman Publications, Inc. (US)
Miller Freeman Publications Ltd. (UK)
Miller Freeman Publications S.A. (BE)
Freeman Publishing Co. Inc. (US)
Freemen Institute (US)
Freer Gallery of Art (US)
Freezer Family Ltd. (UK)
Attilio Fregoli, Ed. & Pub. (IT)
Freiburger Studentenschaft (GE)
Freidenker-Vereinigung der Schweiz (SZ)
Freie Demokratische Partei. Landesverband Berlin
　(GW)
Freie Demokratische Partei Saar (GW)
Freie Universitaet Berlin. Institut fuer Meteorologie
　(GW)
Freie Universitaet Berlin. Institut fuer Publizistik
　(GW)
Freie Universitaet Berlin. John F. Kennedy-Institut
　fuer Nordamerika-Studien (GW)
Freie Universitaet Berlin. Leitstelle Politische
　Dokumentation (GW)
Freie Universitaet Berlin. Osteuropa-Institut (GW)
Freie Universitaet Berlin. Zentralinstitut fuer
　Sozialwissenschaftliche Forschung (GW)
Verlag der Freien Volksbuehne Berlin e.V. (GW)
Freier Verband Deutscher Zahnaerzte e.V. (GW)
Freies Deutsches Hochstift (GW)
Verlag Freies Geistesleben GmbH (GW)
Freight Transport Association (UK)
Freighter Travel Club of America (US)
Freiheitliche Partei Oesterreichs (AU)
Freiheitliche Partei Oesterreichs. Freiheitliche
　Betriebsorganisation in der Voeest (AU)
Freiheitliche Partei Oesterreichs. Landesgruppe
　Oberoesterreich (AU)
Freiheitlicher Oberoesterreichischer Landeslehrerverein
　(AU)
Freireligioese Landesgemeinde Baden (GW)
Freireligioese Verlagsbuchhandlung (GW)
Freisinnig-Demokratische Partei der Schweiz (SZ)
Freisoziale Union (GW)
Fremad A-S (DK)
Fremantle Port Authority (AT)
Fremdenverkehrsverband fuer Wien (AU)
Fremdenverkehrszentrale Hamburg (GW)
Jean Fremon (FR)
Fremont Unified School District (US)
French-American Review (US)
French Chamber of Commerce in Great Britain (UK)
French Chamber of Commerce of the United States
　Inc. (US)
French Embassy. Cultural Services (US)
French Forum Inc. (US)
French Institute-Alliance Francaise (US)
French Institute of Oriental Archaeology
　see Institut Francais d'Archeologie Orientale (UA)
French Notes & Queries (US)
Laurence French Publications Ltd. (UK)
Frenkel Mailing Service (UK)
Otto Frensel Material para Lacticinios Ltda. (BL)
Frente de Afirmacion Hispanista A.C. (MX)

Frente Nacional Pro Defensa del Petroleo Venezolano
　(VE)
Frente Obrero (US)
Fresh Productions (HK)
Freshman English News (US)
Freshwater Biological Research Foundation (US)
Freshwater Fisheries Research Laboratory
　see Japan. Freshwater Fisheries Research
　Laboratory (JA)
Freshwater Press, Inc (US)
Fresno County Medical Society (US)
Fresno Genealogical Society (US)
Fresno-Madera Dental Society (US)
Fresno Teachers Association (US)
Fretted Instrument Guild of America (US)
Dr. Filippo Fretto, Ed. & Pub. (IT)
Verlag Gebrueder Fretz (SZ)
Freund Publishing House Ltd. (IS)
Freunde des Wallraf-Richartz-Museums (GW)
Freunde Mainfraenkischer Kunst und Geschichte
　(GW)
Verlag Jean Frey AG (SZ)
Hans Frey, Ed. & Pub. (SZ)
Friction Materials Standards Institute, Inc. (US)
Dr. Heinz F. Friederichs (GW)
Ira J. Friedman (US)
Friedrich-Alexander-Universitaet, Nuernberg (GW)
Friedrich-Ebert-Stiftung (GW)
Friedrich-Ebert-Stiftung. Forschung Institut (GW)
Friedrich-Schiller-Universitaet Selbstverlag (GE)
Erhard Friedrich Verlag (GW)
Friend Publications Ltd. (UK)
Friendly Publications (US)
Friends Church, Northwest Yearly Meeting (US)
Friends Committee on Legislation of California (US)
Friends Committee on National Legislation (US)
Friends Conference on Religion and Psychology (US)
Friends Historical Association (US)
Friends Historical Society (UK)
Friends of Asia House Gallery (US)
Friends of Columbia Libraries. Butler Library (US)

Friends of Covent Garden Ltd. (UK)
Friends of Duke University Library (US)
Friends of Free Palestine (US)
Friends of Haiti (US)
Friends of Morris Library (US)
Friends of N U S G W U E (CN)
Friends of Osler Library (CN)
Friends of Photography (US)
Friends of the Bancroft Library (US)
Friends of the Detroit Public Library, Inc. (US)
Friends of the Earth (US)
Friends of the Grosse Pointe Public Library (US)
Friends of the la Trobe Library (AT)
Friends of the Lithuanian Front (US)
Friends of the Midrashia, Israel (IS)
Friends of the Milwaukee Public Museum (US)
Friends of the Nassau County Museum (US)
Friends of the National Zoo (US)
Friends of the New York Academy of Medicine.
　Friends of the Rare Book Room, Inc. (US)
Friends of the Oak Park Public Library (US)
Friends of the Princeton University Library (US)
Friends of the Rosenberg Library (US)
Friends of the Trees (II)
Friends of the Turnbull Library (NZ)
Friends of the University of Iowa Libraries (US)
Friends of the University of Miami Library (US)
Friends of the University of Pennsylvania Library
　(US)
Friends of the USC Libraries (US)
Friends of the Washington Review of the Arts (US)
Friends of the Western Buddhist Order (UK)
Friends of the World Council of Churches, Inc. (US)
Friends of the Written Word (US)
Friends of Vietnam (Australia) (AT)
Friends of Youth, Inc. (US)
Friends Publishing Corp. (US)
Friends Service Council (UK)
Friends Suburban Project (US)
Friends United Meeting (Quakers) (US)
Friends United Press Board (US)
Friends World Committee (UK)
Friendship Press (US)
Friendship Publications, Inc. (US)
Friendship Society Finland - USSR (FI)
Fries Instituut
　see under Rijksuniversiteit Te Groningen (NE)
Friesch Rundvee-Stamboek en Bond van K. I. (NE)
Friese Maatschappij van Landbouw (NE)
Friesland Cattle Breeder's Association of South Africa
　(SA)
Frihetlig Socialistisk Tidskrift (SW)
Robert F. Frink, Ed. & Pub. (US)
Frisporg (NO)
Frit Nordens Forlag (DK)
David Frith Publications (AT)

Fritidsfiskarna (SW)
Werner Fritsch Verlag (GW)
Fritz Reiner Society (US)
Fritzsche-D & O (US)
Frobenius-Institut (GW)
From beyond the Dark Gate (US)
From the Kennels (US)
Friedrich Fromman Verlag Guenther Holzboog KG
　(GW)
Verlag Georg Fromme und Co. (AU)
Front Page Record, Inc. (US)
Front Portugais de Liberation (FR)
Front Rouge (FR)
Fronte del Lavoro (IT)
Fronte Italiano di Liberazione Femminile (IT)
Frontier Airlines (US)
Frontier Nursing Service (US)
Frontier Press, Inc. (US)
Frontiers International (US)
Frontul Unitatii Socialiste (RM)
Walter B. Frost & Co. (US)
Arne Frost-Hansens Forlag (DK)
Frozen Food Age Publishing Corp. (US)
Editions Fructidor (FR)
Fructidor International (FR)
Verlag A. Fruehmorgen (GW)
Fruit World Pty. Ltd. (AT)
Editions Fruits et Primeurs (FR)
Frukt og Tobakkhandlernes Landsforbund (NO)
Frye-Williamson Press, Inc. (US)
Frysk Orkest (NE)
Fryske Akademy (NE)
Fu-Min Geographical Institute of Economic
　Development (CH)
Fudge & Co. Ltd. (UK)
H. H. Fuehring (GW)
Fuel and Metallurgical Journals Ltd. (UK)
Don J. Fuelsch, Ed. & Pub. (US)
Verlag Fuer die Frau (GE)
Fueri-Lamy (FR)
Fuerza Nueva (SP)
Fuerzas Armadas Revolucionarias (CU)
Laureano Fueyo (SP)
Fuji Bank Ltd. (JA)
Fuji Electric Manufacturing Co., Ltd. (JA)
Fuji Marketing Research Co., Ltd. (JA)
Fujikura Cable Works Co., Ltd. (JA)
Fujisawa Pharmaceutical Co. Ltd. (JA)
Fujitsu Limited (JA)
Fukien Humanities Society (CH)
Fukui Daigaku
　see Fukui University (JA)
Fukui University. Faculty of Education (JA)
Fukuoka Daigaku
　see Fukuoka University (JA)
Fukuoka District Meteorological Observatory (JA)
Fukuoka Entomological Society (JA)
Fukuoka Kanku Kishodai
　see Fukuoka District Meteorological Observatory
　(JA)
Fukuoka Medical Society (JA)
Fukuoka University. Faculty of Literature (JA)
Fukushima Medical Society (JA)
Fuldaer Geschichtsverein (GW)
Fulfillment Management Association (US)
Full Circle Marketing Corp. (US)
Fuller & Dees (US)
Fuller Theological Seminary (US)
Fuller Theological Seminary. Overseas Crusades (US)
Fullerton & Lloyd (Publishers) Ltd. (UK)
Fullerton College (US)
Fullerton Publishing Co. (CN)
Fulton County Historical & Genealogical Society
　(US)
Fumin Kyokai Shuppan-bu
　see Better Farming Association (JA)
Funch Press (US)
"Fund"
　see International Monetary Fund (UN)
Fund for Animals Inc. (US)
Fund for Assistance to Private Education (PH)
Fund for the Replacement of Animals in Medical
　Experiments (UK)
Fund Raising Institute (US)
Fundacao Armando Alvares Penteado. Faculdade de
　Administracao (BL)
Fundacao Calouste Gulbenkian (PO)
Fundacao Carlos Chagas. Departamento de Pesquisas
　Educacionais (BL)
Fundacao Casa Dr. Blumenau (BL)
Fundacao Centro de Pesquisas Economicas e Sociais
　do Piaui (BL)
Fundacao Cultural de Curitiba (BL)
Fundacao de Assistencia dos Municipios do Estado do
　Parana (BL)
Fundacao de Economia e Estatistica (BL)
Fundacao Faculdade Catolica de Medicina. Centro
　Academico XXII de Marco (BL)

Fundacao Getulio Vargas (BL)
Fundacao Getulio Vargas. Servico de Publicacoes
  (BL)
Fundacao Instituto Brasileiro de Geografia e Estatistica
  (BL)
Fundacao Instituto Brasileiro de Geografia e
  Estatistica. Departmento de Estatisticas Industriais,
  Comerciais e de Servicos (BL)
Fundacao Joao Pinheiro (BL)
Fundacao Metropolitana Paulista (BL)
Fundacao Nacional do Bem-Estar do Menor (BL)
Fundacao para o Livro do Cego no Brasil (BL)
Fundacao para o Progresso da Cirugia (BL)
Fundacao Servicos de Saude Publica. Centro de
  Investigacoes Epidemiologicas (BL)
Fundacao Zoobotanica do Rio Grande do Sul. Museu
  de Ciencias Naturais (BL)
Fundacion Acta Fondo para la Salud Mental. (AG)
Fundacion Bariloche (AG)
Fundacion de Cultura Universitaria (UY)
Fundacion de Investigaciones Economicas
  Latinoamericanas (AG)
Fundacion Dominicana de Desarrollo (DR)
Fundacion Dr. Jose Maria Mainetti para el Progreso
  de la Medicina (AG)
Fundacion Educacional Roberto Bellarmino (CL)
Fundacion Foessa (SP)
Fundacion Jimenez Diaz (SP)
Fundacion John Boulton (VE)
Fundacion Juan March (SP)
Fundacion la Salle de Ciencias Naturales. Instituto
  Caribe de Antropologia y Sociologia (VE)
Fundacion Lazaro Galdiano (SP)
Fundacion Miguel Lillo (AG)
Fundacion Nuestra Historia (AG)
Fundacion Puigvert (SP)
Fundacion Romulo Raggio (AG)
Fundacion Roux-Ocefa (AG)
Fundacion Servicio para el Agricultor (VE)
Fundex Ltd. (UK)
Fundicator Inc. (US)
Fundo de Comercializacao (AO)
Fundy Group Publications Ltd. (CN)
Funk & Wagnalls (US)
William F. Funkhouser, Ed. & Pub. (US)
Funny Funny World (US)
Edizioni Il Fuoco (IT)
Fur Age Weekly (US)
Fur Parade (US)
Fur Review Publishing Co. (UK)
Fur Takers of America Inc. (US)
Fur Vogue Publishing Co. (US)
Fur Weekly News Ltd. (UK)
Furche-Verlag H. Rennebach KG (GW)
Die Furche Zeitschriften-Betriebsgesellschaft mbH und
  Co. KG (AU)
Furman University (US)
Furnishing Media Pty. Ltd. (AT)
Furniture History Society (UK)
Furniture Industry Research Association (UK)
Furniture Methods & Materials (US)
Furniture Today Publishing Inc. (US)
Furniture World- Furniture South (US)
Al-Furqan (II)
Furrow Trust (IE)
Buchdruckerei K. Furter (SZ)
Fusion Energy Foundation (US)
Fussball Club Pforzheim (GW)
Futura Communications, Inc. (US)
Futura Publishing Co. (US)
Future Communications (US)
Future Farmers of America (US)
Future Farmers of America. California Association
  (US)
Future Farmers of America. Florida Association (US)
Future Farmers of America. Georgia Association
  (US)
Future Farmers of America. Texas Association (US)
Future Farmers of America. Wyoming Association
  (US)
Future Homemakers of America (US)
Future Requirements Agency (US)
Futuremics, Inc. (US)
Futuro (AG)
Futurum Forlag A-S (NO)
G A T T
  see General Agreement on Tariffs and Trade (UN)
G. B. Pant University of Agriculture and Technology
  (II)
G.B.W. Publications, Inc. (US)
G. C. Conn, Ltd. (US)
G C N Inc. (US)
G. C. Publishing Corporation (US)
G D R Peace Council (GE)

G. E. C.-Marconi Electronics Ltd. (UK)
G E D I M (FR)
Edizioni G E P (IT)
G F W Verlag GmbH (GW)
G.I. Counselling Center (GW)
G.I.E. Gedimat (FR)
G.I.E. Informatique et Gestion (FR)
G.I. Movement-Yokosuka (JA)
G I T-Verlag Ernst Giebeler (GW)
G.K. Chesterton Society (CN)
G. K. W. Publications Ltd. (UK)
G M L Corporation (US)
G M T (DK)
G M T Medical Information Systems, Inc. (US)
G.P.A. (MW)
G.P.I. Corporation (US)
G. P. I. Corporation. Keyboard Players International
  (US)
G. R. E. C. E.
  see Groupement de Recherche et d'Etudes pour la
  Civilisation Europeenne (FR)
G T E-Automatic Electric (US)
G T E Laboratories, Inc. (US)
G.U.Z. (NE)
Gaba Publications (KE)
J. Gabalda et Cie (FR)
Gabinete de Estudos das Pescas (PO)
Betriebswirtschaftlicher Verlag Dr. Th. Gabler KG
  (GW)
Gabon. Direction de l'Enseignement du Premier Degre
  (GO)
Gabon. Direction de la Statistique et des Etudes
  Economiques (GO)
Gabon. Direction Generale des Finances et du Budget
  (GO)
Gabon. Institut Pedagogique National (GO)
Gabon. Ministere de l'Education Nationale. Direction
  de l'Administration Generale et de la Planification
  (GO)
Gabonese Press and Publishing Co. (GO)
Gabriel Italiana (IT)
Gaceta Agricola (MX)
Gaceta Economica (BO)
Gaceta Ilustrada, S.A. (SP)
Gaceta Publishing Co. (US)
Gaceta Textil (AG)
Gaertnerische Verlagsgesellschaft (GW)
W. J. Gage, Ltd. (CN)
Gaimusho Joho Bunkakyoku (JA)
Gaines Dog Research Center (US)
Gairm Publications (UK)
Ediciones Gaisa (SP)
Gakki Shohosha (JA)
Gakushuin Daigaku
  see Gakushuin University (JA)
Gakushuin University. Department of Economics
  (JA)
Gala International (IT)
Galactic Approximation Press (US)
Editorial Galaxia (SP)
Galaxy Music Corp (US)
Galaxy Press (US)
Galaxy Publication Ltd. (UK)
Gale & Polden Ltd. (UK)
Gale Research Co. (US)
Galenika (YU)
Galerie. Jardin des Arts (FR)
Verlag die Galerie GmbH (AU)
Galerie Nierendorf (GW)
Galerie Raymond Creuze (FR)
Galerie Sanct Lucas (AU)
Galerije Grada Zagreba (YU)
Editorial Galerna (SP)
Galesburg Trades & Labor Assembly (US)
Editoriale Galfa (IT)
Galicia y Rio de la Plata (AG)
Galilee (BE)
Gallagher Report Inc. (US)
Editions Bertil Galland (SZ)
A. R. Gallant (UK)
Gallant Publishing Co., Inc. (US)
Gallard, Johanet & Cie. (FR)
Gallaudet College. Alumni Association (US)
Gallaudet College. Department of English (US)
Gallaudet College. Office of Alumni & Public
  Relations (US)
Luis Gallego, Ed. & Pub. (SP)
Galleon World Travel Association Ltd. (UK)
Galleria del Cavallino (IT)
Galleria la Medusa (IT)
Gallery (UK)
Gallery First Nighters' Club (AT)
Gallery One Publishing Company (LE)
Gallery Publications Ltd. (CN)
Editions Gallimard (FR)
Gallimaufry (US)
Gallo (IT)
Gallo Publishing Corporation (US)

Galloway Cattle Society (UK)
Galloway Publications (US)
Galpin Society (UK)
Galton Foundation (UK)
S.A.R.L. Galvano (FR)
Galvanotecnica (IT)
Gam on Yachting (CN)
Editorial Gama Moda (SP)
Gambi Publications, Inc. (US)
Gambia. Central Statistics Division (GM)
Gambia. Education Department (GM)
Gambia. Information Services (GM)
Gambia. Produce Marketing Board (GM)
Gambia Family Planning Association (GM)
Gambler's Book Club (US)
Gamit Enterprises, Inc. (US)
Editions Gamma (BE)
Gamma Alpha Chi National Office (US)
Gamma Publishing Co. (US)
Poul Gammelbo, Ed. & Pub. (DK)
Editrice Gan (IT)
Gán Kenkyusho
  see Sapporo Medical College. Cancer Research
  Institute (JA)
Ganado (SP)
Ganagrinco (VE)
Gandhi Peace Foundation (II)
Gandhian Institute of Studies (II)
Gandhian Thought (II)
Giacomo Gandolfi S.p.A. (IT)
Ganganatha Jha Kendriya Sanskrit Vidyapeetha (II)
Ganglia Press (CN)
Gita Ganguli (II)
Ganterie-Vetements de Peau (FR)
Gar Publishing Co. (US)
Garage & Service Station News Publishing Co. (CN)
Garavi Gujarat Publications (UK)
Joaquin Garcia Morato (SP)
Julio Garcia Peri Editor (SP)
Garda Review Ltd. (IE)
Koninklijke Drukkerij van de Garde N. V. (NE)
Garden Center of Greater Cleveland (US)
Garden Club of America (US)
Garden History Society (UK)
Garden State Numismatic Association (US)
Garden State Publishing Co. (US)
Garden Writers Association of America (US)
Gardeners' Sunday Organisation (UK)
Gardner Printing and Publishing Pty. Ltd. (AT)
Gardner Publications, Inc. (US)
Garg Publishing Co. (II)
Editions Garnier Freres (FR)
Editions Robert Garouel et Adaut (FR)
Garratt Printing Co. Ltd. (NZ)
Garretson Graphics (US)
Garrett County Historical Society (US)
Garrett-Evangelical Theological Seminary (US)
Garrett Park Press (US)
Editorial Garsi (SP)
Gartenbau-Verlag (SZ)
Garuda Indonesian Airways (IO)
Gary Public Library (US)
Gary's Enterprises (US)
Aldo Garzanti Editore (IT)
Gas (US)
Gas and Fuel Corporation of Victoria (AT)
Gas Chromatography Discussion Group (UK)
Gas Digest (US)
Gas Industries Equipment and Appliance News, Inc.
  (US)
Gas Magazines, Inc. (US)
Gas Processors Association (US)
Gas Turbine Publications, Inc. (US)
Gas Workers Public Relations Council (US)
Gasoline News Publishing Company (US)
E.F. Gasser (SZ)
Buchdruckerei Gassmann AG (SZ)
Gast- und Schankbetriebe (AU)
L. D. Gasteiger (US)
Gastgewerbe Verlag (GW)
Gastronomie Magazine: l'Art Culinaire (FR)
Gaswaerme- Institut Essen (GW)
Gateway Publications (UK)
Gateway to the West-Ohio (US)
Gaudeamus Foundation (NE)
Gauge "O" Guild Gazette (UK)
Gauhati University. Department of Anthropology (II)
Gauldal Historielag (NO)
Editions Gautier-Languereau (FR)
Jessyca Russell Gaver, Ed. & Pub. (US)
Gaveshana (II)
Gavin-Jobson Associates (US)
Reginald Gay, Ed. & Pub. (US)
Gay Liberation Press (AT)
Gay News Ltd. (UK)
Gay Peoples Union at Stanford (US)
Gay Publishing Collective (NZ)
Gay Sunshine Press, Inc. (US)

Gay Women's Advocate Office  (US)
Gaya Ciencia  (SP)
Gaylord Bros. Inc.  (US)
Gaylords  (US)
Gayre & Nigg  (UK)
Gaz de France  (FR)
Gaz de France. Departement Profor  (FR)
Gaz de France. Direction Commerciale  (FR)
Gaz de France. Direction Regionale de la Distribution
  Paris  (FR)
Gazeta da Farmacia Ltda.  (BL)
Gazeta de Pinheiros Ltda.  (BL)
La Gazette  (FR)
Gazette Apicole  (FR)
Gazette du Palais et du Notariat  (FR)
Gazette Medicale de France  (FR)
Gazette Publications  (US)
Gazette Publishing Co.  (US)
Gazette Publishing Co., Inc.  (US)
Gazzetta delle Arti  (IT)
Gazzetta Farmaceutica  (IT)
Gazzetta Zeitschriften Ges. mbH  (AU)
Gazzettino del Jonio  (IT)
Gazzettino della Scuola  (IT)
Gazzettino Numismatico  (IT)
Gazzettino Pty. Ltd.  (AT)
Gdanskie Towarzystwo Naukowe  (PL)
Gdanskie Towarzystwo Przyjaciol Sztuki  (PL)

Editions GEAD  (FR)

Gebbie Press  (US)

Gebetsapostolat  (GW)

Gebetsliga  (AU)

GECAMINES
  see Generale des Carrieres et Mines du Zaire  (ZR)
Geci Verlag  (GW)
Henry L. Geddie, Ed. & Pub.  (US)
Gee & Co. (Publishers) Ltd.  (UK)
Geelong Historical Society  (AT)
Geer Publishing Co. Inc.  (US)
Akademische Verlagsgesellschaft Geest und Portig
  K.G.  (GE)
Geetha Book House  (II)
Gegenschein  (AT)
Gegenschein Press  (US)
Verlag Dr. Max Gehlen  (GW)
Industrie-Verlag Carlheinz Gehlsen  (GW)
Gehoerlosen- und Schwerhoerigenverband der DDR
  (GE)
Edizioni Geiger  (IT)
Geillustreerde Pers B.V.  (NE)
Geirui Kenkyusho
  see Whales Research Institute  (JA)
Richard E. Geis, Ed. & Pub.  (US)
Verlag Gebr. Geiselberger  (GW)
Geisinger Medical Center  (US)
Verlag W. Geissler-Werry  (GW)

Gekkan Gasorin Sutandosha  (JA)

Gelatiere Italiano  (IT)

Uitgeversmaatschappij de Gelderlander Vakpers BV
  (NE)
Geloso S.p.A.  (IT)
Gem and Jewellery Information Centre of India  (II)
Gem Publishers Inc.  (US)
Gemac Corp.  (US)
Gemeindejugendwerk  (GW)
Gemeinnuetzige Verwaltungsgesellschaft fuer
  Wissenschaftspflege MbH  (GW)
Gemeinschaft der Jagdflieger  (GW)
Gemeinschaft der Wohnungseigentuemer  (AU)
Gemeinschaft Evangelischer Erzieher in Baden  (GW)
Gemeinschaftsverlag GmbH  (GW)
Gemini Foundation  (US)
Gemini Press  (US)
Gemmological Association of Australia  (AT)
Gemmological Association of Great Britain  (UK)
Gemological Institute of America  (US)
Genbaku Hoshano Kenkyusho
  see Hiroshima University. Research Institute for
  Nuclear Medicine and Biology  (JA)
Genbaku Shogai Chosa Iinkai
  see Radiation Effects Research Foundation  (JA)
Gendaisha Publishing Co. Ltd.  (JA)
Genealogical Forum of Portland Oregon  (US)
Genealogical Institute of Oklahoma  (US)
Genealogical Periodical Annual Index  (US)
Genealogical Reference Builders  (US)
Genealogical Research  (US)
Genealogical Society of East Alabama  (US)
Genealogical Society of Finland
  see Suomen Sukututkimusseura  (FI)
Genealogical Society of Greater Miami  (US)
Genealogical Society of New Jersey  (US)
Genealogical Society of Old Tryon County  (US)
Genealogical Society of Pennsylvania  (US)
Genealogical Society of Riverside  (US)

Genealogical Society of South Africa  (SA)
Genealogical Society of Southwestern Pennsylvania
  (US)
Genealogical Society of Tidewater Virginia  (US)
Genealogical Society of Victoria  (AT)
Genealogische Gesellschaft, Sitz Hamburg e.V.  (GW)
Genealogiska Samfundet i Finland
  see Suomen Sukututkimusseura  (FI)
Genealogist  (US)
Genealogists, Inc.  (US)
Genealogy Club of America  (US)
Geneeskundige Kring van Antwerpen  (BE)
Genera  (UK)
General Advertising & Publishing, Inc.  (US)
General Agreement on Tariffs and Trade  (UN)
General and Municipal Workers' Union  (UK)
General Assembly of Unitarian Free Christian
  Churches  (UK)
General Association of Regular Baptist Churches
  (US)
General Aviation Safety Committee  (UK)
General Church of the New Jerusalem  (SW)
General Commission on Chaplains and Armed Forces
  Personnel  (US)
General Commission on Safety and Health in the Iron
  and Steel Industry  (EI)
General Conference of Seventh Day Adventists  (US)
General Conference of the Church of God  (US)
General Conference of the New Church  (UK)
General Council of British Shipping  (UK)
General Council of the Assemblies of God  (US)
General Dealer (Pty) Ltd.  (SA)
General Dental Council  (UK)
General Electric Co. Ltd. Hirst Research Centre
  (UK)
General Electric Co. Ltd. of England  (UK)
General Electric Co. Research and Development
  Center  (US)
General Enterprises  (SA)
General Espanola de Seguros, S.A.  (SP)
General Executive Services, Inc.  (US)
General Federation of the Labourers Union  (JO)
General Federation of Trade Unions  (UK)
General Federation of Trade Unions of Korea. Central
  Committee  (KN)
General Federation of Women's Clubs  (US)
General Gramophone Publications Ltd.  (UK)
General Medical Council  (UK)
General Motors, Philippines  (PH)
General Publications  (MW)
General Society of Mayflower Descendants  (US)
General Technical Services  (US)
General Treaty on Central American Economic
  Integration. Permanent Secretariat  (GT)
General Workers Union  (MM)
Generale des Carrieres et Mines du Zaire  (ZR)
Generalist  (US)
Generalstabens Lithografiske Anstalt  (SW)
Genesis  (AG)
Genesis Publishing Inc.  (US)
Genesis Way Inc.  (US)
Genetical Society of Great Britain  (UK)
Genetics Clearinghouse  (US)
Genetics Society of America  (US)
Genetics Society of Canada  (CN)
Genetics Society of Japan  (JA)
Genkenku Shisetsu
  see Osaka University. Institute for Cancer Research
  (JA)
Uitgeverij van Gennep  (NE)
Genootschap Amstelodamum  (NE)
Genootskap vir Afrikaanse Volkskunde  (SA)
Genossenschaft Deutscher Buehnenangehoeriger
  (GW)
Genossenschaftliche Zentralbank AG  (SZ)
Genova. Ripartizione Censimenti e Statistica  (IT)
Steven H. Gens, Ed. & Pub.  (US)
Genshi Enerugi Kenkyusho
  see Kyoto University. Institute of Atomic Energy
  (JA)
Genshikaku Kenkyusho
  see University of Tokyo. Institute for Nuclear Study
  (JA)
Genshiryoku Anzen Kenkyu Kyokai
  see Nuclear Safety Research Association  (JA)
Genshiryoku Iinkai
  see Japan. Japan Atomic Energy Commission  (JA)
Gentle Folk and Other Creatures  (AT)
Gentlemen's Quarterly  (US)
A. W. Gentner Verlag  (GW)
Genyosha Publications, Inc.  (JA)
Geo Abstracts Ltd  (UK)
Geo-Buch Verlag  (GW)
Geo Center, International Map Center  (GW)
Geochemical Society of India  (II)
Geochemical Society of Japan  (JA)
Geochron Laboratories, Inc.  (US)
Geodetic Society of Japan  (JA)

Geodex International, Inc.  (US)
Geoffrita Productions, Ltd.  (US)
Geografia Universal  (MX)
Geograficheskoe Obshchestvo S.S.S.R. Zabaikal'skii
  Filial  (UR)
Geografilararnas Riksfoerening  (SW)
Geografiska Saellskapet i Finland
  see Suomen Maantieteelinen Seura  (FI)
Geografsko Drustvo Bosne i Hercegovine  (YU)
Geografsko Drustvo Hrvatske  (YU)
Geografsko Drustvo Slovenije  (YU)
Geographia Ltd.  (UK)
Geographic and Area Study Publications  (US)
Geographical Association  (UK)
Geographical Association of Tanzania  (TZ)
Geographical Field Group  (UK)
Geographical Publications Ltd.  (UK)
Geographical Research Centre  (II)
Geographical Research Institute  (US)
Geographical Society of Finland
  see Suomen Maantieteelinen Seura  (FI)
Geographical Society of India  (II)
Geographical Society of Ireland  (IE)
Geographical Society of Kenya  (KE)
Geographical Society of New South Wales  (AT)
Geographical Survey Institute
  see Japan. Geographical Survey Institute  (JA)
Geographikos Homilos Kyprou
  see Cyprus Geographical Association  (CY)
Geographisch-Ethnographische Gesellschaft Zurich
  (SZ)
Geographische Gesellschaft der DDR  (GE)
Geographische Gesellschaft e.V., Muenchen  (GW)
Geographisches Institut der Hochschule fuer
  Welthandel  (AU)
Geography Club, Montreal  (CN)

Geography Teachers Association of Queensland  (AT)

Geography Teachers Association of South Australia
  (AT)

Geography Teachers Association of Victoria  (AT)

Geological Association of Canada  (CN)

Geological, Mining and Metallurgical Society of India
  (II)

Geological Society of America  (US)
Geological Society of Australia  (AT)
Geological Society of Denmark
  see Dansk Geologisk Forening  (DK)
Geological Society of Egypt  (UA)
Geological Society of Finland
  see Suomen Geologinen Seura  (FI)
Geological Society of India  (II)
Geological Society of Iraq  (IQ)
Geological Society of Jamaica  (JM)
Geological Society of Japan  (JA)
Geological Society of London  (UK)
Geological Society of Malaysia  (MY)
Geological Society of South Africa  (SA)
Geological Society of the Oregon Country  (US)
Geological Society of the Philippines  (PH)
Geological Survey of Canada
  see Canada. Geological Survey of Canada  (CN)
Geological Survey of Greenland
  see Denmark. Groenlands Geologiske Undersogelse
  (DK)
Geological Survey of Ireland  (IE)
Geological Survey of Japan
  see Japan. Geological Survey of Japan  (JA)
Geological Survey of Queensland  (AT)
Geological Survey of Sweden
  see Sweden. Sveriges Geologiska Undersoekning
  (SW)
Geological Survey of Victoria  (AT)
Wydawnictwa Geologiczne  (PL)
Geologische Bundesanstalt  (AU)
Geologische Gesellschaft in Wien  (AU)
Geologiska Foereningen i Stockholm  (SW)
Geologists' Association  (UK)
Geoloski Zavod Ljubljana. Institut za Geologijo  (YU)
Geophysical Directory, Inc.  (US)
Geophysical Institute
  see under Kyoto University  (JA)
Barbara George  (US)
Herbert George, Ed. & Pub.  (US)
George Mason University  (US)
George Peabody College for Teachers  (US)
George Peabody College for Teachers. Alumni
  Association  (US)
George Peabody College for Teachers. Division of
  Surveys & Field Services  (US)
George Peabody College for Teachers. School of
  Library Science  (US)
George S. May International Company  (US)
George Street Press  (UK)
George Washington University  (US)
George Washington University. American Studies
  Program  (US)

George Washington University. Government Contracts Program (US)
George Washington University Hatchet (US)
George Washington University Medical Center. Population Information Program (US)

George Washington University. National Law Center (US)

Georgeson & Co. (US)

Georgetown Chamber of Commerce (GY)
Georgetown Law Journal Association (US)

Georgetown Medical Bulletin (US)
Georgetown University (US)
Georgetown University. Center for Strategic and International Studies (US)
Georgetown University. Joseph and Rose Kennedy Institute for the Study of Human Reproduction and Bioethics (US)
Georgetown University Law Center (US)
Georgetown University. Medical Center (US)
Georgetown University. School of Languages & Linguistics (US)
Georgetowner, Inc. (US)
Verlag Dr. Rudolf Georgi OHG (GW)
Georgi Publishing Co. (SZ)
Georgia. Bureau of Industry & Trade. Tourist Division (US)
Georgia. Department of Agriculture (US)
Georgia. Department of Community Development (US)
Georgia. Department of Education (US)
Georgia. Department of Human Resources. Division of Physical Health (US)
Georgia. Department of Natural Resources (US)
Georgia. Department of Natural Resources. Earth and Water Division (US)
Georgia. Department of Natural Resources. Environmental Protection Division (US)
Georgia. Employment Security Agency (US)
Georgia. Forestry Commission (US)
Georgia. State Data Center (US)
Georgia. State Economic Opportunity Office (US)
Georgia Academy of Science. (US)
Georgia Association of Plumbing-Heating-Cooling Contractors (US)
Georgia College (US)
Georgia Congress of Parents and Teachers (US)
Georgia Conservancy (US)
Georgia Council for the Social Sciences (US)
Georgia Educational Improvement Council (US)
Georgia Entomological Society (US)
Georgia Farm Bureau Federation (US)
Georgia Historical Society (US)
Georgia Institute of Technology (US)
Georgia Institute of Technology. Engineering Experiment Station (US)
Georgia Institute of Technology. Industrial Development Division (US)
Georgia Journal of International and Comparative Law, Inc. (US)
Georgia Law Review Association Inc (US)
Georgia Library Association (US)
Georgia Life (US)
Georgia Motor Trucking Association (US)
Georgia Municipal Association (US)
Georgia Museum of Art
  see under University of Georgia (US)
Georgia Music Educators Association (US)
Georgia Nurses Association (US)
Georgia Ornithological Society (US)
Georgia Peanut Commission (US)
Georgia Political Science Association (US)
Georgia Ports Authority (US)
Georgia Press Association (US)
Georgia School Boards Association (US)
Georgia Society of Certified Public Accountants, Inc. (US)
Georgia Society of Professional Engineers (US)
Georgia Southern College. English Department (US)
Georgia State Lodge Fraternal Order of Police (US)
Georgia State University (US)
Georgia State University. College of Business Administration (US)
Georgia State University. College of Urban Life (US)
Georgia State University. Department of English (US)
Georgia State University. Department of Psychology (US)
Georgia State University. Foreign Language Department (US)
Georgia State University. Hospital Administration Program (US)
Georgia State University. Library (US)
Georgia Straight Publishing Ltd. (CN)
Georgia Tech National Alumni Association (US)

Georgia Water & Pollution Control Association (US)
Georgian Bay Regional Library System (CN)
Georgian National Alliance (US)
Geoscience Information Society (US)
Geosystems (UK)
Geotehnika (YU)
Geoteknisk Institut (DK)
Geothermal Energy Association (US)
Geothermal Resources Council (US)
Gepipari Tudomanyos Egyesulet (HU)
Fachverlag Gerardi KG (GW)
H. E. & H. S. Gerber, Eds. & Pubs. (US)
Ernst Gerdes Verlag (GW)
Ash Gerecht, Ed. & Pub. (US)
Gereformeerd Historisch Instituut (NE)
Gereformeerd Maatschappelijk Verbond (NE)
Gereformeerd Politiek Verbond (NE)
Gereformeerde Kerk in Suid-Afrika
  see Reformed Church in South Africa (SA)
Gereformeerde Kerken in Classis Harderwijk en Nijkerk (NE)
Gereformeerde Persvereniging, Rotterdam (NE)
Gereja Methodist Malaysia (MY)
Geriatrics Publishing Co. (AT)
Gerlach en Co. B. V. (NE)
Germain Publishing Co. Inc. (US)
German American Chamber of Commerce, Inc. (US)
German-American National Congress, Inc. (US)
German Church of God in U. S. A. (US)
German Congress of Scholars of English (GW)
German Philatelic Society (CN)
German Philatelic Society (US)
German Publications Ltd. (CN)
German Shepherd Dog Club of America, Inc. (US)
German Society of Winnipeg (CN)
Germanisches Nationalmuseum Nuernberg (GW)
Germany, Democratic Republic. Amt fuer Erfindungs- und Patentwesen (GE)
Germany, Democratic Republic. Amt fuer Erfindungs- und Patentwesen der DDR. Abteilung Dokumentembereitstellung (GE)
Germany, Democratic Republic. Amt fuer Standardisierung, Messwesen und Warenpruefung (GE)
Germany, Democratic Republic. Meteorologischer Dienst (GE)
Germany, Democratic Republic. Ministerium fuer Auswaertige Angelegenheiten (GE)
Germany, Democratic Republic. Ministerium fuer Auswaertige Angelegenheiten. Presseabteilung (GE)
Germany, Democratic Republic. Ministerium fuer Gesundheitswesen (GE)
Germany, Democratic Republic. Ministerium fuer Hoch- und Fachschulwesen. Beirat fuer das Wissenschaftliche Bibliothekswesen und die Wissenschaftliche Information (GE)
Germany, Democratic Republic. Ministerium fuer Hoch- und Fachschulwesen (GE)
Germany, Democratic Republic. Ministerium fuer Justiz (GE)
Germany, Democratic Republic. Ministerium fuer Kultur. Rat fuer Museumswesen (GE)
Germany, Democratic Republic. Ministerium fuer Land-, Forst- und Nahrungsgueterwirtschaft (GE)
Germany, Democratic Republic. Ministerium fuer Verkehrswesen (GE)
Germany, Democratic Republic. Ministerium fuer Verkehrswesen. Hauptverwaltung der Zivilen Luttfahrt (GE)
Germany, Democratic Republic. Ministerium fuer Volksbildung (GE)
Germany, Democratic Republic. Presseamt beim Vorsitzenden des Ministerrates der DDR (GE)
Germany, Democratic Republic. Seehydrographischer Dienst (GE)
Germany, Democratic Republic. Staatliche Archivverwaltung (GE)
Germany, Democratic Republic. Staatliche Zentralverwaltung fuer Statistik (GE)
Germany, Democratic Republic. Staatssekretariat fuer Arbeit und Loehne. Zentrales Forschunginstitut fuer Arbeit (GE)
Germany, Democratic Republic. Zentralinstitut fuer Berufsbildung (GE)
Germany, Democratic Republic. Zentralinstitut fuer Bibliothekswesen (GE)
Germany, Federal Republic. Bundesanstalt fuer Arbeit (GW)
Germany, Federal Republic. Bundesanstalt fuer Arbeit. Institut fuer Arbeitsmarkt- und Berufsforschung (GW)
Germany, Federal Republic. Bundesanstalt fuer Bodenforschung (GW)
Germany, Federal Republic. Bundesanstalt fuer Gewaesserkunde (GW)
Germany, Federal Republic. Bundesanstalt fuer Landeskunde (GW)

Germany, Federal Republic. Bundesanstalt fuer Materialpruefung (GW)
Germany, Federal Republic. Bundesanstalt fuer Milchforschung (GW)
Germany, Federal Republic. Bundesanstalt fuer Strassenwesen (GW)
Germany, Federal Republic. Bundesanstalt fuer Vegetationskunde, Naturschutz und Landschaftspflege (GW)
Germany, Federal Republic. Bundesaufsichtsamt fuer das Versicherungswesen (GW)
Germany, Federal Republic. Bundesforschungsanstalt fuer Fischerei (GW)
Germany, Federal Republic. Bundesforschungsanstalt fuer Fischerei. Institut fuer Fangtechnik (GW)
Germany, Federal Republic. Bundesforschungsanstalt fuer Forst- und Holzwirtschaft in Reinbeck (GW)
Germany, Federal Republic. Bundesforschungsanstalt fuer Landeskunde und Raumordnung (GW)
Germany, Federal Republic. Bundesforschungsanstalt fuer Rebenzuechtung Geilweilerhof (GW)
Germany, Federal Republic. Bundesgesundheitsamt (GW)
Germany, Federal Republic. Bundesgesundheitsamt. Kunststoff-Kommission (GW)
Germany, Federal Republic. Bundesminister fuer Innerdeutsche Beziehungen (GW)
Germany, Federal Republic. Bundesministerium der Finanzen (GW)
Germany, Federal Republic. Bundesministerium der Justiz (GW)
Germany, Federal Republic. Bundesministerium der Verteidigung (GW)
Germany, Federal Republic. Bundesministerium des Innern (GW)
Germany, Federal Republic. Bundesministerium des Innern. Schutzkommission (GW)
Germany, Federal Republic. Bundesministerium fuer Arbeit und Sozialordnung (GW)
Germany, Federal Republic. Bundesministerium fuer Bildung und Wissenschaft (GW)
Germany, Federal Republic. Bundesministerium fuer das Post - und Fernmeldewesen (GW)
Germany, Federal Republic. Bundesministerium fuer Ernaehrung, Landwirtschaft und Forsten (GW)
Germany, Federal Republic. Bundesministerium fuer Forschung und Technologie (GW)
Germany, Federal Republic. Bundesministerium fuer Raumordnung, Bauwesen und Staedtebau (GW)
Germany, Federal Republic. Bundesministerium fuer Unterricht (GW)
Germany, Federal Republic. Bundesministerium fuer Verkehr (GW)
Germany, Federal Republic. Bundesministerium fuer Wirtschaft (GW)
Germany, Federal Republic. Bundesministerium fuer Wirtschaftliche Zusammenarbeit (GW)
Germany, Federal Republic. Bundessortenamt (GW)
Germany, Federal Republic. Bundesstelle fuer Aussenhandelsinformation (GW)
Germany, Federal Republic. Bundesversicherungsamt (GW)
Germany, Federal Republic. Deutscher Bundestag. Abteilung Wissenschaftliche Dokumentation (GW)
Germany, Federal Republic. Presse und Informationsamt (GW)
Germany, Federal Republic. Sachverstaendigenrat zur Begutachtung der Gesamtwirtschaftlichen Entwicklung (GW)
Germany, Federal Republic. Statistisches Bundesamt (GW)
Germinal Publications (P) Ltd. (II)
Gernsback Publications, Inc. (US)
Gerold und Appel Verlagsgesellschaft (GW)
Gerold und Co. (AU)
Geron-X, Inc. Publishers (US)
Gerontological Society (US)

Gerontologie (FR)

Gerpresse (FR)

Gershire Ltd. (UK)

Verlag Dr. H. A. Gerstenberg (GW)

Gesamtdeutsches Institut (GW)
Gesamtverband Bueromaschinen-Technik B.V. (GW)
Gesamtverband der Christlichen Gewerkschaften Deutschlands (GW)
Gesamtverband der Deutschen Geschichts- und Altertumsvereine (GW)
Gesamtverband der Evangelischen Kirchengemeinden in Marburg (GW)
Gesamtverband der Kraftfahrzeug- Vermieter Deutschlands e.V. (GW)
Gesamtverband der Nichtsesshaftenhilfe (GW)
Gesamtverband Deutscher Musikfachgeschaefte e.V. (GW)
Gesamtverband Deutscher Nervenaerzte (GW)
Gesamtverband Deutscher Realschullehrer (GW)

Gesamtverband Kunststoffverarbeitende Industrie e.V.
  (GW)
Gesamtverband Neuzeitliche Textilpflege- Betriebe
  Deutschlands e.V.  (GW)
Geschichtsverein fuer Goettingen und Umgebung
  (GW)
Geschichtsverein fuer Kaernten  (AU)
Gesellschaft Boden und Gesundheit  (GW)
Gesellschaft der Augenaertzte der DDR  (GE)
Gesellschaft der Bibliophilen  (GW)
Gesellschaft der Circusfreunde in Deutschland e.V.
  (GW)
Gesellschaft der Freunde Alter Musikinstrumente
  (SZ)
Gesellschaft der Freunde Carnuntums  (AU)
Gesellschaft der Freunde der Oesterreichischen
  Nationalbibliothek  (AU)
Gesellschaft der Freunde der Stadt Linz  (AU)
Gesellschaft der Orgelfreunde e.V.  (GW)
Gesellschaft der Redakteure der Neuen Freien Presse
  (AU)
Gesellschaft der Staudenfreunde e.V.  (GW)
Gesellschaft des Schweizerische Hals- Nasen- und
  Ohrenaerzte  (SZ)
Gesellschaft Deutscher Chemiker  (GW)
Gesellschaft Deutscher Chemiker. Fachgruppe
  Analytische Chemie  (GW)
Gesellschaft Deutscher Chemiker. Fachgruppe
  Wasserchemie  (GW)
Gesellschaft Deutscher Metallhuetten und Bergleute
  e.V.  (GW)
Gesellschaft Deutscher Naturforscher und Aerzte
  (GW)
Gesellschaft fuer Agrargeschichte und Agrarsoziologie
  (GW)
Gesellschaft fuer Anaesthesiologie und Reanimation
  der DDR  (GE)
Gesellschaft fuer angewandte Mathematik und
  Mechanik  (GW)
Gesellschaft fuer Angewandtes Marketing mbH
  (GW)
Gesellschaft fuer Arbeitswissenschaft e. V.  (GW)
Gesellschaft fuer Bedrohte Voelker  (GW)
Gesellschaft fuer Bibliothekswesen und Dokumentation
  des Landbaues  (GW)
Gesellschaft fuer Bronchopneumonologie und
  Tuberkulose der DDR  (GE)
Gesellschaft fuer Chirurgie der DDR  (GE)
Gesellschaft fuer Chirurgie der DDR. Sektion
  Experimentelle Chirurgie  (GE)
Gesellschaft fuer das Oeffentliche Haushaltswesen
  (AU)
Gesellschaft fuer das Schweizerischen Volkstheater
  (SZ)
Gesellschaft fuer Deutsch-Sowjetische Freundschaft
  Westberlin  (GW)
Gesellschaft fuer Deutsch-Sowjetische Freundschaft.
  Zentralvorstand  (GE)
Gesellschaft fuer deutsche Postgeschichte  (GW)
Gesellschaft fuer Deutsche Sprache  (GW)
Gesellschaft fuer die gesamte Hygiene  (GE)
Gesellschaft fuer die Gesamte Kriminologie  (GW)
Gesellschaft fuer die Geschichte und Bibliographie des
  Brauwesens  (GW)
Gesellschaft fuer Dokumentation Bodenmechanik und
  Grundbau e.V.  (GW)
Gesellschaft fuer Endokrinologie und
  Stoffwechselkrankheiten  (GE)
Gesellschaft fuer Erdkunde zu Berlin  (GW)
Gesellschaft fuer Familienkunde in Franken e.V.
  (GW)
Gesellschaft fuer Ganzheitsforschung  (AU)
Gesellschaft fuer Gastroenterologie der DDR  (GE)
Gesellschaft fuer Gerontologie der DDR  (GE)
Gesellschaft fuer Geschwulstbekaempfung der DDR
  (GE)
Gesellschaft fuer Griechische und Hellenistische
  Rechtsgeschichte  (AU)
Gesellschaft fuer Gynaekologie und Geburtshilf der
  DDR  (GE)
Gesellschaft fuer Historische Waffen- und
  Kostuemkunde  (GW)
Gesellschaft fuer Innere Medizin der DDR  (GE)
Gesellschaft fuer Internationale Geldgeschichte  (GW)
Gesellschaft fuer Internationale Sprache e.V.  (GW)
Gesellschaft fuer Kernforschung mbH  (GW)
Gesellschaft fuer Klassische Philologie in Innsbruck
  (AU)
Gesellschaft fuer Klinische Medizin der DDR  (GE)
Gesellschaft fuer Klinische und Experimentelle
  Immunologie der DDR  (GE)
Gesellschaft fuer Konservative Publizistik e.V.  (GW)
Gesellschaft fuer Konsum-, Markt- und
  Absatzforschung  (GW)
Gesellschaft fuer Laender- und Voelkerkunde  (GW)
Gesellschaft fuer Militaerische Bautechnik  (SZ)

Gesellschaft fuer Mittelrheinische Kirchengeschichte
  (GW)
Gesellschaft fuer Musikforschung  (GW)
Gesellschaft fuer Natur, Technik und Wirtschaft
  (AU)
Gesellschaft fuer Naturkunde in Wuerttemberg  (GW)
Gesellschaft fuer Nuclear-Medizin  (GW)
Gesellschaft fuer Oeffentliche Wirtschaft und
  Gemeinwirtschaft e.V.  (GW)
Gesellschaft fuer Organisation e.V.  (GW)
Gesellschaft fuer Orthopaedie der DDR  (GE)
Gesellschaft fuer Ost- und Suedostkunde  (AU)
Gesellschaft fuer Pediatrie der DDR  (GE)
Gesellschaft fuer Physikalische und Mathematische
  Biologie der DDR  (GE)
Gesellschaft fuer Physiotherapie der DDR  (GE)
Gesellschaft fuer Pommersche Geschichte,
  Altertumskunde und Kunst  (GW)
Gesellschaft fuer Praktische Psychologie e.V  (GW)
Gesellschaft fuer Psychiatrie und Neurologie  (GE)
Gesellschaft fuer Psychologie der DDR  (GE)
Gesellschaft fuer Rechtsvergleichung  (GW)
Gesellschaft fuer Regionalforschung  (GW)
Gesellschaft fuer Schleswig-Holsteinische Geschichte
  (GW)
Gesellschaft fuer Sozialen Fortschritt E.V., Bonn
  (GW)
Gesellschaft fuer Sport und Technik  (GE)
Gesellschaft fuer Sportmedizin der DDR  (GE)
Gesellschaft fuer Stenografie und Maschinenschreiben
  der DDR  (GE)
Gesellschaft fuer Stomatologie der DDR  (GE)
Gesellschaft fuer Tribologie und Schmierungstechnik
  (GW)
Gesellschaft fuer Uebernationale Zusammenarbeit e.V.
  (GW)
Gesellschaft fuer Unternehmungsgeschichte  (GW)
Gesellschaft fuer Urologie der DDR  (GE)
Gesellschaft fuer Voelkerkunde  (GW)
Gesellschaft fuer Volkskunde, Basel. Abteilung Film
  (SZ)
Gesellschaft fuer Wehrkunde e.V.  (GW)
Gesellschaft fuer Wirtschafts- und Sozialwissenschaften
  (GW)
Gesellschaft fuer Wissenschaftliche Symbolforschung
  (GW)
Gesellschaft fuer Zukunftsfragen e.V.  (GW)
Gesellschaft Mariae in Oesterreich und Deutschland
  (AU)
Gesellschaft Naturforschender Freunde zu Berlin
  (GW)
Gesellschaft pro Vindonissa  (SZ)
Gesellschaft Schweizer Monatshefte  (SZ)
Gesellschaft Schweizerische Musikzeitung  (SZ)
Gesellschaft Schweizerischer Landwirte  (SZ)
Gesellschaft Schweizerischer Maler, Bildhauer und
  Architekten  (SZ)
Gesellschaft Schweizerischer Tieraerzte  (SZ)
Gesellschaft Schweizerischer Zeichenlehrer  (SZ)
Gesellschaft zur Dompropstei  (GW)
Gesellschaft zur Foerderung der Inneren Kolonisation
  (GFK)  (GW)
Gesellschaft zur Foerderung der Kunststofftechnik
  (AU)
Gesellschaft zur Foerderung der Unabhaengigen Presse
  (AU)
Gesellschaft zur Foerderung des New Orleans Jazz
  (GW)
Gesellschaft zur Foerderung Tiefenpsychologischer und
  Psychotherapeutischer Forschung und Weiterbildung
  (GW)
Gesellschaft zur Pflege der Maerchengutes der
  Europaeischen Voelker  (GW)
Gestions Hospitalieres  (FR)
Gesture  (US)
Gesualdi Editore Roma  (IT)
Gesuiti di Sicilia  (IT)
Getting Together  (US)
Librairie Orientaliste Paul Geuthner  (FR)
Gewerbliches Guetertransportwesen Oesterreichs
  (AU)
Gewerkschaft der Arbeiter in der Land und Forst-
  Wirtschaft  (AU)
Gewerkschaft der Eisenbahner Deutschlands  (GW)
Gewerkschaft der Oeffentlich Bediensteten.
  Bundessektion Hoehere Schule  (AU)
Gewerkschaft der Polizei  (GW)
Gewerkschaft Druck und Papier  (AU)
Gewerkschaft Erziehung und Wissenschaft  (GW)
Gewerkschaft Erziehung und Wissenschaft.
  Landesverband Bayern  (GW)
Gewerkschaft Erziehung und Wissenschaft.
  Landesverband Nordrhein-Westfalen  (GW)
Gewerkschaft Gartenbau, Land- und Forstwirtschaft
  (GW)
Gewerkschaft Handel, Banken und Versicherungen
  (GW)
Gewerkschaft Holz und Kunststoff  (GW)

Gewerkschaft Leder  (GW)
Gewerkschaft Oeffentliche Dienste, Transport und
  Verkehr. Hauptabteilung Polizei  (GW)
Neuer Deutscher Gewerkschafts-Verlag GmbH  (GW)
Gewestelijke Economische Raad voor Vlaanderen
  (BE)
Geyer-Edition  (AU)
Geyer-McAllister Publications  (US)
Ghana. Central Bureau of Statistics  (GH)
Ghana. Cocoa Marketing Board  (GH)
Ghana. Information Services Department  (GH)
Ghana. Meteorological Services Department  (GH)
Ghana. Ministry of Education  (GH)
Ghana. Ministry of Social Welfare and Community
  Development  (GH)
Ghana. National Council for Higher Education  (GH)
Ghana. National Redemption Council  (GH)
Ghana. Railway and Ports Administration  (GH)
Ghana Broadcasting Corporation  (GH)
Ghana Catholic Hierarchy  (GH)
Ghana Commercial Bank  (GH)
Ghana Geographical Association  (GH)
Ghana Home Scientist Association  (GH)
Ghana Institute of Management and Public
  Administration  (GH)
Ghana Institution of Engineers  (GH)
Ghana Library Association  (GH)
Ghana Medical Association  (GH)
Ghana Publishing Corporation  (GH)
Ghana Sociological Association  (GH)
Ghana Water & Sewerage Corporation  (GH)
P. Ghosh  (II)
Amal Ghosh-hajra, Ed. & Pub.  (II)
Ghost Dance Press  (US)
Ghurfat al-Tijarah Wa-al-Sinaah Bi-al-Jazair  (IQ)
Giannini Foundation of Agricultural Economics  (US)
H. Gianotten B.V.  (NE)
G. Giappichelli Editore  (IT)
Giardini Editori e Stampatori in Pisa  (IT)
D. Parke Gibson International, Inc.  (US)
Gideons International in Canada  (CN)
Gidra Inc.  (US)
Gidrometeoizdat  (UR)
Gidwaney's Publishing Co.  (II)
Gebr. Giehrl  (GW)
Wolfgang Gielow Verlag  (GW)
Gieseking-Verlag  (GW)
Fachverlag Giesserei-Erfahrungsaustausch  (GW)
Giesserei-Verlag GmbH  (GW)
Gifu Daigaku
  see Gifu University  (JA)
Gifu University. Faculty of Agriculture  (JA)
Gifu University. School of Medicine  (JA)
Gig Enterprises, Inc.  (US)
Editoriale Giganti del Basket s. r. l.  (IT)
Gilan Business College  (IR)
Gilbert and Sullivan Journal  (UK)
Gerry Gilbert, Ed. & Pub.  (CN)
Gilbertson & Page Ltd.  (UK)
Thomas Giles  (US)
Gilgamesh Publishing Co.  (US)
Editorial Gustavo Gili, S.A.  (SP)
Margo V. Gill, Ed. & Pub.  (SI)
R. V. Gill Publishing Co.  (US)
Gillelije Sten och Grus  (SW)
Ray Gillem, Ed. & Pub.  (CN)
Gilmore Publications  (CN)
Gingerbread, Association for One Parent Families
  (UK)
H. Marvin Ginn Corporation  (US)
GINSI  (IO)
Ralph Ginzburg  (US)
Armando Giordano, Ed. & Pub.  (IT)
Alfonso Giordano, Ed. & Pub. (Milan)  (IT)
Irmao di Giorgio  (BL)
Gruppo Editoriale Il Giornale d'Italie S.p.A.  (IT)
Giornale di Clinica Medica  (IT)
Giornale di Geologia  (IT)
Giornale di Medicina e Pneumologia  (IT)
Giornale Italiano delle Malattie del Torace  (IT)
Giornale Italiano di Chirurgia  (IT)
Giornalista Mario Borretti  (IT)
Giorno Poetry Systems Institute, Inc.  (US)
Giovane Critica  (IT)
Girard Associates Inc.  (US)
Frank Girard, Ed. & Pub.  (US)
Girard Home News, Inc.  (US)
Verlag W. Girardet  (GW)
Girl Crusaders' Union  (UK)
Girl Guides Association  (UK)
Girl Guides Association (N.S.W.)  (AT)
Girl Guides Association of Papua New Guinea  (PP)
Girl Guides of Canada  (CN)
Girl Scouts of the U.S.A.  (US)
Girl Talk  (US)
Girls Brigade  (AT)
Girls' Brigade  (UK)
Girls Brigade International  (UK)

Girls Clubs of America  (US)
Girls' Rodeo Association News  (US)
GIROD  (FR)
Editions Spes: Jean-Paul Gisserot  (FR)
Gita Press  (II)
Gita Publishing House  (II)
Verlag Dieter Gitzel  (GW)
Casa Editrice Dott. A. Giuffre  (IT)
Giunta Centrale per gli Studi Storici  (IT)
Giunta Diocesana di A.C.  (IT)
Giunti-Barbera  (IT)
Giustizia e Costituzione  (IT)
Edizioni Giustizia Nuova  (IT)

Giustizia Penale  (IT)
Jul. Gjellerups Boghandel A-S  (DK)
J. Gjellerups Forlag A-S  (DK)
Gladney Publishing Group Ltd.  (CN)
Glamorgan History Society  (UK)
Glanville Publishers, Inc .  (US)
Editorial Glarma, S.A.  (SP)
Glarmesterlauget i Danmark  (DK)
Glas Istre  (YU)
Glas Podrinja  (YU)
Glasblaeser-Vereinigung  (SZ)
Alfred B. Glaser  (US)
Glasforskningsinstitutet  (SW)
Glasgow Archaeological Society  (UK)
Glasgow Art Gallery  (UK)
Glasgow Art Gallery and Museums Association  (UK)
Glasgow Chamber of Commerce  (UK)
Glasgow Mathematical Society  (UK)
Mary Glasgow Publications Ltd.  (UK)
Glass Art Magazine, Inc.  (US)
Glass Containers Manufacturers Institute  (US)
Glass Manufacturers Federation  (UK)
Glass's Dealers Guide Pty. Ltd.  (AT)
Glass's Guide Service Ltd.  (UK)
Glassworks Press  (US)
Glavnaya Geofizicheskaya Observatoriya im. A. I.
    Voeikova  (UR)
Glavni Zadruzni Savez  (YU)
Glavno Politichesko Upravlenie na Narodnata Armiia
    (BU)
Gleaner Company Ltd.  (JM)
Gleason Publishing Co. Inc.  (US)
Glenbow Alberta Institute  (CN)
Glendale Adventist Medical Center Publications
    Service  (US)
Glenmary Home Missioners  (US)
Glenmary Sisters  (US)
Peter Glenn Publications, Inc.  (US)
Glenvale Publications Pty. Ltd.  (AT)
Glenwood State Hospital-School  (US)
Glide Publications  (US)
Gliding Club of Victoria  (AT)
Gliding Federation of Australia  (AT)
Global Dialogue Publications Inc.  (US)
Global Engineering Documentation Services, Inc.
    (US)
Global Village  (US)
Globe and Mail Ltd.  (CN)
Globe Communications Corp.  (CN)
Globe Publishing Co. Pty. Ltd.  (AT)
Editoriale Globo  (IT)
Globus-Verlag  (AU)
Globus-Verlagsanstalt  (GW)
Glock und Lutz Verlag  (GW)
Glos Ludowy  (US)
Glossa Society  (CN)
Glowna Biblioteka Lekarska  (PL)
Glowny Instytut Gornictwa  (PL)
Verlag Glueckauf GmbH  (GW)
Glueckstelle Mihalovits  (AU)
Glun na Buaidhe  (IE)
Glyndebourne Festival Opera  (UK)
Glyndebourne Productions Ltd.  (UK)
Gnananada Ashram  (II)
Go Publishing Ltd.  (CN)
Goa, Daman, and Diu. Bureau of Economics,
    Statistics, and Evaluation  (II)
Goa, Daman, and Diu. Department of Information and
    Tourism  (II)
Goa Publications  (II)
Goat Breeders' Society of Australia  (AT)
Goathair Press  (CN)
Goddard Space Flight Center  (US)
Godfrey Memorial Library  (US)
David Godine Publisher  (US)
George Godwin Ltd.  (UK)
K. Godzinski, Ed. & Pub.  (CN)
Publications Paul Goebel  (FR)
Dr. Klaus Goebel  (GW)
Verlag Goecke und Evers  (GW)
Goeller-Verlag  (GW)
G. V. W. F. Goelst  (NE)
Imprimerie J. Goemaere  (BE)
Verlag Carl Th. Goerg KG  (GW)

Goerres-Gesellschaft  (GW)
Dieter Goeschl Buch- und Zeitschriftenverlag  (AU)
Alois Goeschl und Co.  (AU)
Goetabanken  (SW)
Goeteborg. Stadskontor  (SW)
Goeteborgs Kungliga Segelsaellskap  (SW)
Goeteborgs Kungliga Vetenskaps- och Vitterhets-
    Samhaelle  (SW)
Goeteborgs Museer. Etnografiska Museet  (SW)
Goeteborgs Tandlaekare Saellskap  (SW)
Goeteborgs Universitet  (SW)
Goeteborgs Universitet. Bibliotek  (SW)
Goeteborgs Universitet. Demographic Research
    Institute  (SW)
Goeteborgs Universitet. Department of Psychology
    (SW)
Goeteborgs Universitet. Ekonomisk-Historiska
    Institutionen  (SW)
Goeteborgs Universitet. Sociologiska Institutionen
    (SW)
Goeteborgs Universitet. Statistiska Institutionen  (SW)
Goethe-Gesellschaft, Weimar  (GE)
Goethe-Institut, Munich  (GW)
Goethe-Institut zur Pflege Deutscher Sprache und
    Kultur im Ausland  (GW)
Goetheana Periodico Literario  (AG)
Goettinger Arbeitskreis e.V.  (GW)
Goettinger Druckerei- und Verlagsgesellschaft mbH
    (GW)
Buch und Offsetdruck W. Goetz  (AU)
M. N. Gogate, Ed. & Pub.  (II)
Goias, Brazil. Secretaria da Educacao e Cultura.
    Instituto Goiano de Folclore  (BL)
Goias, Brazil. Secretaria da Industria e Comercio
    (BL)
Goias, Brazil. Secretaria do Planejamento e
    Coordenacao  (BL)
Gokhale Institute of Politics and Economics  (II)
Gokhale Institute of Public Affairs  (II)
Ed. & Pub. Fay Gold  (US)
Gold Coast Pictorial, Inc.  (US)
Gold Coin Newsletter  (US)
Gold Flower Collective  (US)
Golden Arc Publishing and Typesetting Ltd.  (CN)
Golden Film Productions (Edms) Bpk  (SA)
Golden Gate Foundation for Group Treatment  (US)
Golden Gate North Publishing Co.  (US)
Golden Gate University. School of Law  (US)
Golden Temple Enterprises  (CN)
Golden Years  (UK)
Goldenrod Publications  (US)
Goldermood Rainbow Press  (US)
Goldhawk Press Ltd.  (UK)
Wilhelm Goldmann Verlag GmbH  (GW)
Gwenyth D. Goldsberry, Ed. & Pub.  (US)
Buchdruckerei Rudolf Goldschagg  (GE)
Goldsmith-Nagan, Inc.  (US)
Goldstein Associates  (US)
Goldwater Publications  (II)
Dan Golenpaul Associates  (US)
Golf Course Superintendents Association of America
    (US)
Golf Digest, Inc.  (US)
Golf Digest, Inc. Tennis Features, Inc.  (US)
Golf Singapore Review  (SI)
Golf World Associates Ltd.  (UK)
Golf World, Inc.  (US)
Milton Golin, Ed. & Pub.  (US)
Editorial Golova s.r.l.  (AG)
Verlag Erich Goltze KG  (GW)
Gomer Press  (UK)
Livio Gomez, Ed. & Pub.  (PE)
Diego Gomez Florez, Ed. & Pub.  (SP)
Carlos Goncalves Fidalgo, Ed. & Pub  (BL)
J. B. Goncharsky, Ed. & Pub.  (US)
Gondolier Enterprises Inc.  (US)
Editions du Gonfalon  (FR)
Gong Verlag  (GW)
Miguel J. Goni Fernandez, Ed. & Pub.  (SP)
C. W. Gonick  (CN)
Gontran Trottier  (CN)
Gonzaga University  (US)
Gonzaga University School of Law  (US)
Dr. Rafael M. Gonzalez, Ed. & Pub.  (VE)
Eladio Gonzalez Nunez, Ed. & Pub.  (PY)
Good Earth Press  (CH)
Good Gay Poets Collective  (US)
Good Gay Poets Press  (US)
Good Neighbours Retired Citizens Association  (CN)
Good News Broadcasting Association, Inc.  (US)
Good News Missionary Society  (SA)
Good Outdoor Manners Association  (US)
Good Publishing Co.  (US)
Good Road Ltd.  (UK)
Goodfellow  (US)
Goodheart-Willcox Co., Inc.  (US)
C. Goodliffe Neale Ltd.  (UK)
Goodyear Industrial Products Division  (US)

Goodyear Tire & Rubber Co.  (US)
Goodyear Tyre and Rubber Co. Australia, Ltd.  (AT)
Gooi en Sticht B.V.  (NE)
Gopali Printers  (II)
Van Gorcum  (NE)
Editions Gaston Gorde  (FR)
Verlag Gordian-Max Rieck GmbH  (GW)
Fernando Gordillo Escudero, Ed. & Pub.  (SP)
Maynard M. Gordon, Ed. & Pub  (US)
Gordon and Breach Science Publishers  (US)
Gordon and Breach Science Publishers Ltd.  (UK)
Gordon Blackwell  (US)
Gordon Publications, Inc.  (US)
Gordon Technical College  (AT)
June Gorentz  (US)
Rev. Daniel Gorham, Ed. & Pub.  (US)
Gorkhapatra Corporation  (NP)
Gorlich Editore S.p.A.  (IT)
Gorman Publishing Co.  (US)
Gosbank S. S. S. R.  (UR)
Goshen College  (US)
Gospel Association for the Blind, Inc.  (US)
Gospel Herald Foundation  (CN)
Gospel Mission Publishers  (CN)
Gospel Music Association  (US)
Gospel Publishing House  (US)
Gospel Standard Publications  (UK)
Gospel Tract Distributors  (US)
Gospodarski Vestnik  (YU)
Zalozba (Casa Editrice) Gospodarstvo  (IT)
Gosteleradio S. S. S. R.  (UR)
Gosudarstvennaya Biblioteka Belorusskoi S. S. R. im
    V. I. Lenina  (UR)
Gosudarstvennaya Biblioteka S.S.S.R. im. V.I. Lenina
    (UR)
Gosudarstvennyi Astronomicheskii Institut im. P. K.
    Shternberga  (UR)
Gosudarstvennyi Muzei Izobrazitel'nykh Iskusstv im.
    Pushkina  (UR)
Ediciones Gota de Agua  (AG)
Gothenburg Chamber of Commerce  (SW)
Gothenburg Retail Association  (SW)
Gothic Castle Publishing Co. Inc.  (US)
Gothique Publications  (UK)
Gotlands Historical Museum  (SW)
Gottfried-Wilhelm-Leibniz Gesellschaft e.V.  (GW)
Gotthelf Verlag  (SZ)
Gottlieb Duttweiler Institute for Economic & Social
    Studies  (GW)
Gottlieb Duttweiler Institute for Economic & Social
    Studies  (SZ)
Annie Gottlieb, Ed. & Pub.  (US)
Verlag Max Gottschalk  (GW)
Martin Gottschalk  (US)
Gouda Quint B.V.  (NE)
Goulandris Natural History Museum  (GR)
Gould's Position, Inc.  (US)
G. Gourdon, Ed. and Pub.  (FR)
Gourmet Inc.  (US)
Gourmet's Notebook  (US)
Dorina de Gouvea Nowill  (BL)
Government and Opposition Ltd.  (UK)
Government and Public Administration Society  (SI)
Government Business Worldwide Reports  (US)
Government College. Department of Economics  (PK)
Government College. Department of English Language
    and Literature  (PK)
Government College. Department of History and
    Political Science  (PK)
Government College. Department of Psychology
    (PK)
Government College. Research Council  (PK)
Government Data Publications  (US)
Government Dental College and Hospital  (II)
Government Development Bank for Puerto Rico
    see Puerto Rico. Banco Gubernamenta de Fomento
    (PR)
Government Development Bank for Puerto Rico
    (US)
Government Forest Experiment Station
    see Japan. Government Forest Experiment Station
    (JA)
Government Industrial Development Laboratory,
    Hokkaido
    see Japan. Government Industrial Development
    Laboratory, Hokkaido  (JA)
Government Industrial Research Institute, Kyushu
    see Japan. Government Industrial Research
    Institute, Kyushu  (JA)
Government Information Services  (US)
Government Printer  (TR)
Government Publications Service Center  (JA)
Government R and D Report  (US)
Government Research Co.  (US)
Governmental Research Association, Inc.  (US)

Governors State University (US)
Govi-Verlag GmbH (GW)
Gown Trust. Students' Union (UK)
Editions Gozlan (FR)
Van der Graaf en Co's Uitgeversmaatschappij B. V. (NE)
N. V. Uitgeversmaatschappij de Graafschap (NE)
Grabert-Verlag (GW)
Gracas do Servo de Deus: Padre Cruz (PO)
Grace Hospital (US)
Grace Magazine Trust (UK)
Gradina Botanica a Universitatii Bucuresti (RM)
Gradina, Izdavacka Ustanova (YU)
Gradiva (US)
Graduate Business Admissions Council (US)
Graduate Institute of International Studies
    see Universite de Geneve. Institut Universitaire de Hautes Etudes Internationales (SZ)
Graenges AB (SW)
Graf und Neuhaus (SZ)
Grafenwerther Musen Werk- und Foerderkreis fuer Literatur, Kunst und Wissenschaft e.V. (GW)
Grafica Toscana (IT)
Grafische Industrie van Eerd B.V. (NE)
Grafiska Arbetsgivare-och Industriorganisationerna (SW)
Grafiska Fackfoerbundet (SW)
Grafiska Faktors- och Tjaenstemannafoerbundet (SW)
Grafiske Bedrifters Landsforening (NO)
Editora Grafos (VE)
Grafton Publications, Inc. (US)
Graham Publishing Co. (Pvt.) Ltd. (RH)
Grail (UK)
Grain and Farm Service Centers (US)
Grain Dealers Mutual Insurance Co. (US)
Grain Elevators Board of New South Wales (AT)
Gralla Publications (US)
Gramophone Company of India (II)
Grand Cru (US)

Grand East of the Netherlands (NE)

Grand Island Biological Co. (US)

Grand Lodge Free and Accepted Masons of Indiana (US)

Grand Lodge Free and Accepted Masons of the State of New York (US)
Grand Lodge of Montana, Ancient Free & Accepted Masons (US)
Grand Lodge of Oklahoma, Ancient Free and Accepted Masons (US)
Grand Manan Historical Society (CN)
Grand Orange Lodge of Canada (CN)
Grand Orient de France (FR)
Grand River Dam Authority (US)
Grand United Order of Oddfellows (AT)
Grande Ronde Review (US)
Verlag G. Grandpierre (GW)
Grandremy (FR)
Publications des Grands Lacs Inc. (CN)
Grange Bateliere S.A. (FR)
Granite Cutters International Association of America (US)
Granite Publications (UK)
Granite Publications (US)
Chapman Grant, Ed. & Pub. (US)
Granta (UK)
Grantechs (US)
Grantsmanship Center (US)
Grapevine (US)
Grapevine (Saratoga) (US)
Graphic Arts International Union (US)
Graphic Arts International Union. Contract & Research Department (US)
Graphic Arts Technical Foundation (US)
Graphic Arts Trade Journal International Inc. (US)
Graphic Corporation (GH)
Graphic Export Centre (NE)
Graphic Publications (SI)
Graphic Publications, Inc. (US)
Graphic Publishing Corporation (US)
Graphikum (GW)

Graphmitre Ltd. (UK)

Grass Roots General Store (AT)

Grass Roots Publishing Co. (US)
Editions Bernard Grasset (FR)
Giuseppe Grassi, Ed. & Pub. (IT)
Grassland Research Institute (UK)
Grassland Society of Southern Africa (SA)
Grassland Society of Victoria (AT)
Grasso's Koninklijke Machinefabrieken N.V. (NE)
Grassroots Collective (US)
Gratz College (US)
Kenneth V. Graves (US)
Earl G. Graves Publishing Co. (US)
Gravida, Ltd. (US)

Gravure Research Institute (US)
Gravure Research Institute. Environmental and O S H A Committee (US)
Gravure Technical Association Inc. (US)
Gray Book (II)
Gray Panther News (US)
Graybar Electric Co. (US)
Graycroft Press (US)
Gray's Inn Press Ltd. (UK)
Gray's Sporting Journal Co. (US)
Graziers' Association of New South Wales (AT)
Great Blafigria-IS (II)
Gt. Brit. Agricultural Development and Advisory Service (UK)
Gt. Brit. Agricultural Research Council. Institute of Animal Physiology (UK)
Gt. Brit. Atomic Energy Research Establishment (UK)
Gt. Brit. Board of Inland Revenue (UK)
Gt. Brit. British Airports Authority (UK)
Gt. Brit. British Antarctic Survey (UK)
Gt.Brit. Cabinet Office (UK)
Gt. Brit. Central Health Services Council (UK)
Gt. Brit. Central Office of Information (UK)
Gt. Brit. Central Statistical Office (UK)
Gt. Brit. Civil Aviation Authority (UK)
Gr.Brit. Civil Service Department (UK)
Gt. Brit. Civil Service Department. Central Computer Agency (UK)
Gt. Brit. Commission on Industrial Relations (UK)
Gt. Brit. Customs and Excise Department (UK)
Gt. Brit. Department of Agriculture and Fisheries for Scotland (UK)
Gt. Brit. Department of Education and Science (UK)
Gt. Brit. Department of Employment (UK)
Gt. Brit. Department of Energy (UK)
Gt. Brit. Department of Health and Social Security (UK)
Gt. Brit. Department of Health and Social Security. Committee on Safety of Medicines (UK)
Gt. Brit. Department of Health and Social Security. National Health Service (UK)
Gt. Brit. Department of Industry (UK)
Gt. Brit. Department of Industry. Business Statistics Office (UK)
Gt. Brit. Department of the Environment (UK)
Gt. Brit. Department of the Environment. Ancient Monuments Board (UK)
Gt.Brit. Department of the Environment. Building Research Establishment (UK)
Gt. Brit. Department of the Environment. Committee on Synthetic Detergents (UK)
Gt. Brit. Department of the Environment. Fire Research Station (UK)
Gt.Brit. Department of the Environment. Headquarters Library, Research Section (UK)
Gt. Brit. Department of the Environment. Housing and Construction (UK)
Gt. Brit. Department of the Environment. Property Services Agency (UK)
Gt. Brit. Department of the Environment. Transport and Road Research Laboratory (UK)
Gt. Brit. Department of Trade (UK)
Gt.Brit. Department of Trade. H. M. Coastguard (UK)
Gt. Brit. Department of Transport (UK)
Gt. Brit. Departments of the Environment and Transport (UK)
Gt.Brit. Departments of the Environment & Transport. Library (UK)
Gt. Brit. Electricity Council (UK)
Gt. Brit. Foreign and Commonwealth Office (UK)
Gt. Brit. Foreign and Commonwealth Office. Overseas Development Administration (UK)
Gt. Brit. Forestry Commission (UK)
Gt. Brit. General Register Office, Scotland (UK)
Gt. Brit. H.M. Nautical Almanac Office (UK)
Gt. Brit. H.M.S.O. (UK)
Gt. Brit. H.M.S.O. (N. Ireland) (UK)
Gt. Brit. H.M. Treasury (UK)
Gt. Brit. Herring Industry Board (UK)
Gt. Brit. Home Office (UK)
Gt. Brit. Home Office. Police Research Services Unit (UK)
Gt. Brit. Home Office. Prison Department (UK)
Gt. Brit. Hydraulics Research Station (UK)
Gt. Brit. Institute of Geological Sciences (UK)
Gt. Brit. Institute of Terrestrial Ecology (UK)
Gt. Brit. Medical Research Council (UK)
Gt. Brit. Medical Research Council. Laboratory Animals Centre (UK)
Gt. Brit. Meteorological Office (UK)

Gt. Brit. Ministry of Agriculture, Fisheries and Food (UK)
Gt. Brit. Ministry of Agriculture, Fisheries and Food. Pest Infestation Control Laboratory (UK)
Gt. Brit. Ministry of Agriculture, Fisheries and Food. White Fish Authority (UK)
Gt. Brit. Ministry of Defence (UK)
Gt. Brit. Ministry of Defense (Army) Royal Army Chaplains' Department Centre (UK)
Gt.Brit. Ministry of Defense. Royal Air Force (UK)
Gt.Brit. Ministry of Defense. Royal Navy (UK)
Gt. Brit. Ministry of Overseas Development (UK)
Gt. Brit. Ministry of Overseas Development. Centre for Overseas Pest Research (UK)
Gt. Brit. Ministry of Overseas Development. Directorate of Overseas Surveys (UK)
Gt.Brit. National Coal Board (UK)
Gt. Brit. National Economic Development Office (UK)
Gt. Brit. National Savings Committee for England and Wales (UK)
Gt. Brit. Natural Environment Research Council (UK)
Gt. Brit. Office of Fair Trading (UK)
Gt.Brit. Office of Population Censuses and Surveys (UK)
Gt. Brit. Public Works Loan Board (UK)
Gt. Brit. Royal Botanic Gardens (UK)
Gt. Brit. Royal Botanic Gardens (Edinburgh) (UK)
Gt. Brit. Royal Commission on Historical Manuscripts (UK)
Gt. Brit. Royal Commission on Historical Monuments (UK)
Gt. Brit. Royal Electrical & Mechanical Engineers (UK)
Gt. Brit. Royal Greenwich Observatory (UK)
Gt. Brit. Royal Mint (UK)
Gt.Brit. Royal Navy Communications Branch (UK)
Gt. Brit. Science Research Council (UK)
Gt. Brit. Scottish Health Service Planning Council (UK)
Gt. Brit. Scottish Law Commission (UK)
Gt. Brit. Scottish Office (UK)
Gt. Brit. Social Science Research Council (UK)
Gt.Brit. Soil Survey (UK)
Gt. Brit. University Grants Committee (UK)
Gt. Brit. Victoria and Albert Museum (UK)
Gt. Brit. Water Pollution Research Laboratory (UK)
Gt. Brit. Water Resources Board (UK)

Great Britain Philatelic Society (UK)
Great Dane Club of Victoria (AT)
Great Falls Genealogical Society (US)
Great Lakes Basin Commission (US)
Great Lakes Commission (US)
Great Lakes Fishery Commission (US)
Great Lakes Historical Society (US)
Great Lakes Maritime Institute (US)
Great Lakes Press (US)
Great Neck Newsmagazine Group Ltd. (US)
Great North of Scotland Railway Association (UK)
Great Northwest Publications (US)
Great Plains National Instructional Television Library (US)
Great Society Press (US)
Great Turtle Enterprises, Inc. (US)
Great Western Press Ltd. (CN)
Great Western Society Ltd. (UK)
Great Works (US)
Greater Bombay and Thana District Cooperative Housing Federation Ltd. (II)
Greater Boston Diabetes Society Inc. (US)
Greater Cincinnati Chamber of Commerce (US)
Greater Cleveland Genealogy Society (US)
Greater Cleveland Growth Association (US)
Greater Detroit Building Trade Council (US)
Greater Detroit Chamber of Commerce (US)
Greater Europe Mission (US)
Greater Freehold Chamber of Commerce (US)
Greater Harrisburg Region Central Labor Council (US)
Greater Hartford Council on Alcoholism. Capitol Region Drug Information Center (US)
Greater Hartford Publishing Co. Inc. (US)
Greater Kansas City Dental Society (US)
Greater London Arts Association (UK)
Greater London Council (UK)
Greater London Council. Department of Public Health Engineering (UK)
Greater London Council. Intelligence Unit (UK)
Greater Milwaukee Dental Association (US)
Greater Milwaukee Federation of Lutheran Churches-Missouri Synod (US)
Greater Minneapolis Chamber of Commerce (US)
Greater New York Bridge Association (US)
Greater New York Taxpayers Association (US)
Greater Newark Chamber of Commerce (US)
Greater North Dakota Association (US)

Greater Omaha Chamber of Commerce (US)
Greater Publications Pty. Ltd. (AT)
Greater St. Louis Dental Society (US)
Greater San Antonio Chamber of Commerce (US)
Greater San Francisco Chamber of Commerce (US)
Greater World Association (UK)
Greater Yakima Chamber of Commerce (US)
Editorial Gredos (SP)
Gredzens (AT)
Greece. Department of Antiquities and Archaeological
  Restoration
    see Greece. General Direction of Antiquities and
    Restoration (GR)
Greece. General Direction of Antiquities and
  Restoration (GR)
Greece. Hypourgeion Koinonikon Hyperesion
    see Greece. Ministry of Social Services (GR)
Greece. Ministry of Social Services (GR)
Greece. National Statistical Service (GR)
Greece. Office National de Statistique
    see Greece. National Statistical Service (GR)
Greece. Secretariat General of Press and Information
  (GR)
Greek-American Review (US)
Greek Archdiocese Press (US)
Greek Institute (UK)
Greek Institute for Foreign and International Law
    see Hellenic Institute of International and Foreign
    Law (GR)
Greek Mathematical Society (GR)
Greek National Committee for Astronomy (GR)
Greek National Tourist Organization
    see National Tourist Organization of Greece (GR)
Greek Observer (UK)
Greek Orthodox Archdiocese of America (US)
Greek Pharmaceutical Society (GR)
Greek Report (UK)
Greek Speleological Society (GR)
Greek Sunday News (US)
Greek World Press (US)
F. F. Greeley, Ed. & Pub. (US)
Warren H. Green (US)
Green & Co. (UK)
W. Green & Son Ltd. (UK)
Dr. Jerry Green, Ed. & Pub. (CN)
Green Island (UK)
Green Mountain Club, Inc. (US)
Green Mountain Editions (US)
Green Mountain Post (US)
Victor Green Publications Ltd. (UK)
Green River Community College. Associated Student
  Body (US)
Green River Press, Inc. (US)
Green World (US)
Greencrest Industrial Publications (CN)
Greenfield Publishing Co. (US)
Percy Greene, Ed. & Pub. (US)

Greenfield Review Press (US)
Green's Magazine (US)
Greensboro Printing Co. (US)
Greentree Publishing Corporation (US)
Greenwich Meridian (CN)
Henry Greenwood & Co. Ltd. (UK)
Greenwood Press (US)
William Greer, Ed. & Pub. (US)
Greey de Pencier Publications (CN)
Gregg Publishing Co. (CN)
Gregor Mendel Institute for Medical Genetics and
  Twin Studies. Permanent Committee (IT)
Gregorian University Press (IT)
Libreria Gregoriana Editrice (IT)
Gremio de Ferreteria de Barcelona (SP)
Gremio dos Industriais do Transportes Em
  Automoveis (PO)
Gremio Nacional dos Bancos e Casas Bancarias (PO)
Gremio Sindical de la Electricidad (SP)
Gremio Sindical de Libreros de Barcelona (SP)
Gremio Sindical Nacional de Detallistas de
  Alimentacion (SP)
Grenada. Government Printing Office (GD)
Grennan Publication (AT)
Grenzverlag (AU)
Willi Gressner Verlag (GW)
Greven Verlag Koeln (GW)
Grey Advertising Pty. Ltd. (AT)
Greyhound & Sporting Press Ltd. (IE)
Greyhound Corporation (US)
Greyhound Magazine Co. Ltd. (UK)
Greyhound News Pty. Ltd. (AT)
Greyhound Owner Ltd. (UK)
Greyhound Racing Control Board (Victoria) (AT)
Greyhound Recorder (AT)
Greystone Park Psychiatric Hospital (US)
Greystone Publishers, Inc. (US)
Greyton H. Taylor Wine Museum (US)
Griekenland Werkgroepen in Nederland en Belgie
  (NE)

W. B. Griffin (US)
Griffin Press (AT)
Griffin Publishing Co., Inc. (US)
E. V. Griffith, Ed. & Pub. (US)
Griffith Observatory (US)
Samuel Griffiths and Co. (Pty) Ltd. (SA)
Grille (IE)
Grilled Flowers (US)
Grimes School of Law
    see under University of Liberia (LB)
Grimsby Independent (CN)
Le Griot (CM)
Grist Press (US)
Denny Griswold, Ed. & Pub. (US)
Grit Publishing Co. (US)
Grive (FR)
Grocer's Advisor (US)
Grocer's Gazette Ltd. (UK)
Grocers Publishing Co. Inc. (US)
Grocery Distribution Magazine (US)
Grocery Industry Services, Inc. (US)
Grocery Trade Publishing Co. (US)
B.V. Drukkerij J. J. Groen en Zoon (NE)
Groen van Prinsterer Kweekschool (NE)
Groendahl og Soens Boktrykkeri (NO)
Groene Amsterdammer N.V. (NE)
Groenlands Geologiske Undersogelse
    see Denmark. Groenlands Geologiske Undersogelse
    (DK)
Groenlands Landsraad (DK)
Groenlandske Selskab (DK)
Grolier Yearbook, Inc. (US)
Groninger Maatschappij van Landbouw (NE)
Julius Groos Verlag (GW)
Verlag Grossbild - Technik GmbH (GW)
Grosse Point Public Library (US)
Grosse Point Yacht Club (US)
Grosse Verlag GmbH (GW)
Grosset & Dunlap (US)
Grosseteste Review Books (UK)
Richard Grossinger, Ed. & Pub. (US)
Grossman Publishers, Inc. (US)
Grossmont Education Association (US)
Sergio Grossu, Ed. & Pub. (FR)
G. Grote'sche Verlagsbuchhandlung KG (GW)
G. Grote'sche Verlagsbuchhandlung KG (Stuttgart)
  (GW)
Grotta della Vipera (IT)
Ground Zero (US)
Group for the Advancement of Psychiatry (US)
Group for the Study of Atoms and Molecules from
  Radio-Electric Research (NE)
Group Health Association of America, Inc. (US)
Group of Japanese Pedologists (JA)
Group Research Inc. (US)
Groupe Creations (FR)
Groupe d'Acoustique Musicale (FR)
Groupe d'Etude du Film (SZ)
Groupe d'Etudes Balzaciennes (FR)
Groupe d'Etudes de Psychiatrie Psychologie et
  Sciences Sociales (FR)
Groupe d'Etudes Prospectives Internationales du
  C.F.C.E. (FR)
Groupe de Recherche et d'Information Feministes
  (BE)
Groupe de Sociologie des Religions (FR)
Groupe Expansion (FR)
Groupe Intersyndical de l'Industrie Nucleaire (FR)
Groupe J.A. (FR)
Groupe L.C.C.E (FR)
Groupe, Union, Defense (FR)
Groupe Voie Lactee (SZ)
Groupement d'Edition et d'Information Technique,
  Economique et Culturelle (FR)
Groupement de Recherche et d'Etudes pour la
  Civilisation Europeenne (FR)
Groupement des Associations de Proprietaires
  d'Appareils a Vapeur et Electriques (FR)
Groupement des Directeurs Publicitaires de France
  (FR)
Groupement des Industries Francaises Aeronautiques
  et Spatiales (G.I.F.A.S) (FR)
Groupement des Societes Immobilieres
  d'Investissement (FR)
Groupement Europeen la Recherche Scientifique en
  Stomatologie et Odontologie (BE)
Groupement Genealogique de la Region du Nord
  (FR)
Groupement International pour la Recherche
  Scientifique en Stomatologie
    see International Group for Scientific Research in
    Stomatology (BE)
Groupement Medical d'Etudes sur l'Alcoolisme (FR)
Groupement National pour l'Organisation de la
  Medecine Auxiliaire (FR)
Groupement pour l'Etude des Transports Urbains
  Modernes (FR)

Groupes Bibliques Universitaires de Suisse Romande
  (SZ)
Grove Press (US)
Grow Publishers (AT)
Grower Publications Ltd. (UK)
Growing Point (UK)
Growing Room Collective (CN)
Growth Fund Guide (US)
Growth Industry News (US)
Growth Publishing Co. Inc. (US)
Growth Stock Outlook Inc. (US)
Verlag Dr. Carl Grueb (GW)
Fred Gruenberger (US)
B. R. Gruener B.V. (NE)
Matthias Gruenewald Verlag (GW)
Editora Gruenwald Ltda. (BL)
Grumman Aerospace Corporation (US)
Grundig AG (GW)
VEB Deutscher Verlag fuer Grundstoffindustrie (GE)

Grune & Stratton, Inc. (US)

Gruner und Jahr GmbH und Co. (GW)

Grupo de Trabalho Permanente para a Documentacao
  e Informacao Economico Social (PO)
Grupo Escritores de Venezuela (VE)
Grupo Espeleologico Vizcaino (SP)
Grupo Juventud S.A. (MX)
Grupo Literario Axial (VE)
Grupo Local de Panaderia de Barcelona (SP)
Grupo Poesia (PE)
Gruppe Internationaler Marxisten. Deutsche Sektion
  der IV. Internationale (GW)
Gruppe Revolutionaere Marxisten (AU)
Gruppi Grotte Italiani (IT)
Gruppo Agrochimica (IT)
Gruppo di Studio Sul Societa e Istituzioni (IT)
Gruppo Finanziario Tessile (IT)
Gruppo Otologi Ospedalieri Italiani (IT)
Gruppo Savoia (IT)
Walter de Gruyter und Co. (GW)
Gryphon House (US)
Gryphon Press (UK)
Gryphon Press (US)
Editora Guadalupe Ltda. (CK)
Guajana (PR)
Guam. Department of Commerce (GU)
Guam. Department of Public Health and Social
  Services (GU)
Guam. Department of Revenue and Taxation (GU)
Guanabara, Brazil. Secretaria de Ciencia e Tecnologia.
  Instituto de Conservacao da Natureza (BL)
Antonio Guarasci, Ed. & Pub. (IT)
Guardia di Finanza (IT)
Guardian and Manchester Evening News Ltd. (UK)
Guardian Publishing (CN)
Guatemala. Direccion General de Estadistica (GT)
Guatemala. Ministerio de Educacion. Instituto
  Indigenista Nacional (GT)
Guatemala. Observatorio Nacional de Guatemala (GT)
Guatemala. Oficina de Planeamiento Integral de la
  Educacion (GT)
Guayacan (GT)
Guentter-Staib Verlag (GW)
Guepes (FR)
Guerre de Classes (FR)
Guest and Bell (AT)
Guest Relations Association (US)
Guetersloher Verlagshaus Gerd Mohn (GW)
Guggenheim Laboratories (UK)
Editora Guia Aeronautico Ltda (BL)
Guia Industrial y Comercial de Puerto Rico, Inc.
  (PR)
Editora de Guias Ltda (BL)
Guibanca (VE)
H. Guichou, Ed. & Pub. (FR)
Libreria Internazionale Guida (IT)
Guida Monaci (IT)
Guidance Exchange (US)
Guidance Publications (US)
Guide des Ports: France, Maghreb, Algerie, Tunisie,
  Maroc, Afrique Noire (FR)
Guide des Relais Routiers (FR)
Guide International de l'Energie Atomique et des
  Etudes Spatiales (FR)
Guide Publications (II)
Guide Publishing (CN)
Guide Services, Inc. (US)
Guide to Reprints, Inc. (US)
Guidelines Publications (US)
Guideposts Associates, Inc. (US)
Guides Equestres (FR)
Guides to Multinational Business, Inc. (US)
Francis A. Guido, Ed. and Pub. (US)
Guild Book Service (US)
Guild for Religious Architecture (US)
Guild for the Promotion of Welsh Music (UK)

Guild of British Newspaper Editors   (UK)
Guild of Carillonneurs in North America   (US)
Guild of Catholic Doctors   (UK)
Guild of Freemen of the City of London   (UK)
Guild of Health   (UK)
Guild of Our Lady of Ransom   (UK)
Guild of Prescription Opticians of America   (US)
Guild of Professional Translators   (US)
Guild of Shaker Crafts   (US)
Guild of Undergraduates   (UK)
Guilde du Livre   (SZ)
Guildford Poets Press   (UK)
Guildhall Library   (UK)
Guildhall Poets   (UK)
Guilds of Weavers, Spinners and Dyers   (UK)
Guilford College. Department of Mathematics   (US)
Guimaraes, Portugal. Arquivo Municipal "Alfredo
   Pimenta"   (PO)
Guinness Superlatives Ltd.   (UK)
Guitar   (UK)
Guitar Players International   (US)
Guitare et Musique Chansons Poesie   (FR)
Demetrio Guitierrez Alarcon   (SP)
Gujarat. Bureau of Economics and Statistics   (II)
Gujarat. Directorate of Geology and Mining   (II)
Gujarat. Directorate of Manpower, Employment and
   Training   (II)
Gujarat. Office of the Commissioner of Labour   (II)
Gujarat Ayurveda University   (II)
Gujarat Industrial Development Corporation   (II)
Gujarat Pustakalaya Sahayak Sahakari Mandal Ltd.
   (II)
Gujarat Research Society   (II)
Gujarat State Financial Corporation   (II)
Gujarat University   (II)
Gulcher   (US)
Guldsmedefagets Faellesraad   (DK)
Gulf and Caribbean Fisheries Institute   (US)
Gulf Coast History and Humanities Conference   (US)
Gulf Coast Lumberman   (US)
Gulf Coast News Digest   (US)
Gulf Coast Publishing Corp.   (US)
Gulf Coast Research Laboratory   (US)
Gulf General Atomic Inc.   (US)
Gulf Oil Corporation   (US)
Gulf Publishing Co.   (US)
Gulf Weekly Mirror   (BA)
Gulfshore Publishing Company, Inc.   (US)
Bill Gulley, Ed. & Pub.   (US)
Gumma Daigaku
   see Gumma University   (JA)
Gumma University. Faculty of Education   (JA)
Gumma University. Institute of Endocrinology   (JA)
Gumma University. School of Medicine   (JA)
Gummessons Bokfoerlag   (SW)
S. R. Gunjal, Ed. & Pub.   (II)
Gunma University
   see Gumma University   (JA)
Guns Annual Book of Handguns   (US)
Guns Magazine   (US)
P.T. Gunung Agung   (IO)
Guozi Shudian (China Publications Centre)   (CC)
Bibash Gupta, Ed. & Pub.   (II)
G. S. Balarma Gupta, Ed. & Pub.   (II)
J. C. Gupta, Ed. & Pub.   (II)
Gura Sandesha   (II)
Gurafikkusha   (JA)
Guru Nanak Dev University. Department of Guru
   Nanak Studies   (II)
Gurukul Kangri University   (II)
N. Gurulingam, Ed. & Pub.   (II)
Gustav-Adolph-Werk   (GW)
Gustav Werner Stiftung   (GW)
Gustavus Adolphus College   (US)
Gut   (CN)
Gutenberg-Gesellschaft   (GW)
Gutenberghus Bladene   (DK)
Guthrie Foundation for Medical Research   (US)
C. B. Guthrie Tariff Bureau   (US)
Guthrie Theater Co   (US)
Guy & Co.   (IE)
Hubert P. Guy, Ed. & Pub.   (US)
Guyana. Central Agricultural Station. Research
   Division   (GY)
Guyana. Geological Survey Department   (GY)
Guyana. Hydrometeorological Serivce   (GY)
Guyana. Ministry of Agriculture   (GY)
Guyana. Ministry of External Affairs   (GY)
Guyana. Ministry of Information and Culture   (GY)
Guyana. National Library   (GY)
Guyana. Office of the Ombudsman   (GY)
Guyana Association of Professional Engineers   (GY)
Guyana Institute for Social Research and Action
   (GY)
Guyana Library Association   (GY)
Guyana Rice Producers Association   (GY)
Guy's Hospital   (UK)
Augusto Guzzo, Ed. & Pub.   (IT)

Gwalwa Daraniki Association   (AT)
Gwasg Y Sir   (UK)
Gwinnet Historical Society   (US)
Gyldendal Norsk Forlag   (NO)
Gyldendalske Boghandel-Nordisk Forlag A-S   (DK)
Gymnasieskolernes Laererforening   (DK)
Gyogynoveny Kutato Intezet   (HU)
Gypsy Table Series   (US)
Gyst Publications   (US)
H. A. Lanzer Co.   (US)
H. B. Publishers   (CN)
H C C C Inc.   (US)
H.C.M. State Institute of Public Administration   (II)
H D C Publications   (US)
H. G. Wells Society   (UK)
H I A S Inc.   (US)
H.I.C. Corporation   (US)
H.M.S. Mercury   (UK)
H P A   (UK)
H P Publishing Co. Inc.   (US)
H. Q. Royal Artillery   (UK)
H. R. Industries, Inc.   (US)
H S B Riksfoerbund   (SW)
H T H Publishers   (US)
H.T.S. Corps   (NE)
H.V. Chapman and Associates Ltd.   (CN)
H. W. Moore Equipment Co.   (US)
H W W A - Institut fuer Wirtschaftsforschung,
   Hamburg   (GW)
Ediciones H Y M S A
   see Hogar y la Moda, S.A.   (SP)
VEB Hermann Haack   (GE)
Haagse Jazz Club   (NE)
Haaken Ohlssons Foerlag   (SW)
Verlag Otto Haase   (GW)
Helmut Haase-Verlag   (GW)
Haasenstein'scher Verlag KG   (GW)
Habari Barua   (US)
Verlag Josef Habbel   (GW)
Habegger Verlag   (SZ)
Rudolf Habelt Verlag   (GW)
Habibi Publications   (US)
Foerlags AB Habit   (SW)
Habitante   (AG)
Hablemos de Cine   (PE)
Habonim Labor Zionist Youth   (US)
Hacettepe Universitesi. Cucak Sagligi Enstitusu
   see University of Hacettepe. Institute of Child
   Health   (TU)
Hacettepe Universitesi. Nufus Etutleri Enstitusu
   see University of Hacettepe. Institute of Population
   Studies   (TU)
Hacettepe University Press   (TU)
Librairie Hachette   (FR)
Hacienda, Inc.   (US)
Hackney Horse Society   (UK)
Hackney Junior Libraries   (UK)
Hackney Library Services   (UK)
Hackney People's Press   (UK)
Hackney Publications Inc.   (US)
Hadassah Medical Organization   (IS)
Hadassah, the Women's Zionist Organization of
   America   (US)
Hadassah Vocational Guidance Institute   (IS)
Hadassah Zionist Youth Commission   (US)
Dr. Wilhelm Hadmovsky, Ed. & Pub.   (AU)
Hadoar Association, Inc.   (US)
Hadtortenelmi Intezet   (HU)
Dr. Curt Haefner Verlag   (GW)
Haenssler-Verlag   (GW)
Haentjens Dekker en Gumbert   (NE)
F. Haer & Co.   (US)
Hafenbautechnische Gesellschaft   (GW)
Hafenkurier   (NE)

Hafner Publishing Co., Inc.   (US)

Hagedorn Publishing Co.   (US)
Ten Hagen B. V.   (NE)
The Hague. Afdeling Voorlichting   (NE)
Hague Conference on Private International Law.
   Permanent Bureau   (NE)
M. W. Hague, Ed. & Pub.   (II)
Hahn-Meitner-Institut fuer Kernforschung Berlin
   (GW)
Hahnemann Homoeopathic Pharmacy   (II)
Verlag Hahnsche Buchhandlung   (GW)
Joseph Haiek, Ed. & Pub.   (US)
Haifa Music Museum and Amli Library   (IS)
Haifa University   (IS)
Haigh and Hochland Ltd.   (UK)
Haiku Press   (CN)
Verlag Anton Hain KG   (GW)
Hair and Beauty Publications Ltd.   (UK)
Hairenik Association, Inc.   (US)
Haiti. Administration Generale des Douanes   (HT)
Haiti. Bureau d'Ethnologie   (HT)

Haiti. Departement du Travail et du Bien-Etre Social
   (HT)
Haiti. Institut Haitien de Statistique. Departement des
   Finances et des Affaires Economique   (HT)
Haiti. Office d'Assurance Accidents du Travail,
   Maladie et Maternite   (HT)
Haiti-Culture   (HT)
Haitian Unity Council   (US)
Hakibbutz Hameuchad Publishing House Ltd.   (IS)
A. M. Hakkert Ltd.   (CN)
Hakko Kenkyusho
   see Institute for Fermentation   (JA)
Hakluyt Society   (UK)
Hakodate Technical College   (JA)
Halcyon Business Publications, Inc.   (US)
Haldane Publishing Co. Pty. Ltd.   (AT)
Robert G. Halford, Ed. & Pub.   (CN)
Halgo Publishing Co.   (US)
Halifax Board of Trade   (CN)
Halifax Visitors and Convention Bureau   (CN)
Halifax Wildlife Association   (CN)
Alan W. Hall (Publications) Ltd.   (UK)
G. K. Hall and Co.   (US)
George D. Hall Company   (US)
Sir John Hall, Ed. & Pub.   (UK)
Josef Hall KG   (GW)
Wilton E. Hall Publisher   (US)
Hall Associates   (US)
Hall Publications   (US)
Hall Radio Report   (US)
Halle Concerts Society   (UK)
Hallwag AG   (SZ)
Eds. & Pubs. John Halmaghi & Vasile Posteuca   (US)
Verlag Alfred Halscheidt   (GW)
Halsted Press   (US)
Hambro Life Assurance   (UK)

Hamburg. Statistisches Landesamt   (GW)
Hamburger Arzte-Verlag GmbH   (GW)
Hamburger Gesellschaft fuer Voelkerrecht und
   Auswaertige Politik   (GW)
Hamburger Hochbahn Aktiengesellschaft   (GW)
Hamburger Kunsthalle   (GW)
Hamburger Museumsverein   (GW)
Hamburger Sport-Verein e.V.   (GW)
Hamburger Sportbund e.V.   (GW)
Hamburgisches Museum fuer Voelkerkunde   (GW)
Hamburgisches Zoologisches Museum und Institut
   (GW)

Hamdard Foundation
   see under Institute of Health and Tibbi Research
   (PK)

Hamel Publishing Co., Inc.   (US)
Hamibantu Publications   (UK)
Hamid & Co.   (PK)
Hamilton College   (US)
Hamilton College. Trustees of Hamilton College   (US)
Hamilton County Pharmaceutical Association   (US)
Hamish Hamilton Ltd.   (UK)
Hamilton Naturalists' Club   (CN)
Hamline University. Midwestern School of Law   (US)
Hamlyn Group   (US)
Paul Hamlyn Pty. Ltd.   (AT)
Hammer and Coffin Society   (US)
Hammer and Steel Newsletter   (US)
F. M. Hammerle Textilwerke AG   (AU)
Anne M. Hammerman, Ed. & Pub.   (US)
Hammond Almanac, Inc.   (US)
Hampden-Sydney Poetry Review   (US)
Hampshire College   (US)
Hampshire Field Club   (UK)
Hampshire Genealogical Society   (UK)
Hampshire Swine Registry   (US)
Hampton Books   (US)
Hampton Institute   (US)
Hampton Roads Educational Television Association,
   Inc.   (US)
Hampton Roads Science Fiction Association   (US)
Juanita Hancock, Ed. & Pub.   (US)
Hand Book   (US)
Albert Hand Publications Ltd.   (UK)
Hand Vol Pluis   (NE)
Hand Weavers' and Spinners' Guild of Australia
   (AT)
Handbook of Florida Securities   (US)
Handcrafters News   (US)
Handelens Samarbeidsorgan for Jordbruksvarer   (NO)
Handels- og Soefartsmuseet paa Kronborg   (DK)
Verlag Handels- und Werbepraxis GmbH   (GW)
Neuer Handels-Verlag GmbH und Co. KG   (GW)
Handelsanstaelldas Foerbund   (SW)
Handelsbestyrer Forbundet   (NO)
Handelsblatt GmbH   (GW)
B.V. de Handelsdrukkerij van 1874   (NE)
Handelshoegskolan i Stockholm. Bibliotek   (SW)
Handelshoegskolan i Stockholm. Ekonomiska
   Forskningsinstitutet   (SW)

Handelshoegskolan Vid Aabo Akademi. Ekonomisk-
   Geografiska Institutionen (FI)
Handelshoejskolen i Koebenhavn. Instituttet for
   Udenrigshandel (DK)
Handelskammer Bremen (GW)
Handelskammer Hamburg (GW)
Handelskammer Niederoesterreich (AU)
Handelskammer Oberoesterreich (AU)
Handicapped Persons Association of Japan National
   Railways (JA)
Handikappinstitutet (SW)
Handjuawg (IO)
Handweavers Guild of America, Inc. (US)
Verlag fuer Handwerk und Gewerbe GmbH (GW)
Handwerkskammer Stuttgart (GW)
Handy and Harman (US)
Carlton Haney Publications (US)
Hanging Loose Press (US)
Han'guk Chungdung Kyoyukhoe (KO)
Hani Publications (US)
Franz Hanke, Editor and Publisher (AU)
Hanns-Seidel-Stiftung e.V. (GW)
Hanover Books Ltd. (UK)
Hanover Insurance Co. (US)
Hans-Bredow-Institut (GW)
Hans Christian Andersens Hus (DK)
Hans-Pfitzner-Gesellschaft e.V. (GW)
Hansa Publishers Ltd. (CE)
Hansen Publishing Inc. (US)
Carl Hanser Verlag (GW)
Hansischer Geschichtsverein (GW)
Hansischer Gildenverlag (GW)
Hansom Books (UK)
Lennart Hansson (SW)
Peter Hanstein Verlag GmbH (GW)
Industrie- und Handelswerbung A. Hanuschik (GW)
Haolam Hazeh Ltd. (IS)
Hapdong News Agency (KO)
Harangue (FR)
Haraton Ltd. (UK)
Harbor Dental Society (US)
Harbor Lights (US)
Harbour Newspaper & Publishing Co. Ltd. (AT)
Harcourt Brace Jovanovich Health Care Publications
   (US)
Harcourt Brace Jovanovich, Inc. (US)
Hard Cheese (UK)
Hard Core News Printing Co-Op (US)
Hard Rain, Inc. (US)
Hardin-Simmons University (US)
A. R. Harding Publishing Co. (US)
Hardware Retailer Publishing Co. (AT)
Hardware Retailers Association of New South Wales
   (AT)
Hardwood Plywood Manufacturers Association (US)
Hardy & Ally (II)
William G. Hare, Ed. & Pub. (US)
Hare Publications (US)
Harian Publications (US)
P. Haridas, Ed. & Pub. (II)
Shukla Hariprasad, Ed. & Pub. (II)
Harishchandra Mathur State Institute of Public
   Administration (II)
Harlang og Toksvig Bladforlag A-S (DK)
Harlequin Enterprises Ltd. (CN)
Harley-Davidson Motor Co., Inc. (US)
Harlo Press (US)
Harmonikaverband Oesterreichs (AU)
Harmsworth Press Ltd. (UK)
Harness Horse, Inc. (US)
Harness Horsemen International, Inc. (US)
Miguel de Haro Serrano, Ed. & Pub (SP)
Harper and Row Publishers, Inc. (US)
Harper & Row Publishers, Inc. Medical Department
   (US)
Harper Hospital (Detroit) Department of Gynecology
   and Obstetrics (US)
Harper Square Press (US)
Harper Trade Journals Ltd. (UK)
Harper's Magazine Co. (US)
Harpress Publications (US)
George G. Harrap & Co. Ltd. (UK)
Verlag Otto Harrassowitz (GW)
G. W. Harris (UK)
Phillip Harris, Ed. & Pub. (US)
Harris Auction Galleries, Inc. (US)
Harris Communications (US)
Paul T. Harris, Ed. & Pub. (CN)
Harris Press (US)
Harris Publications Ltd. (UK)
Harris Publishing Co. (Cleveland) (US)
Harris Publishing, Inc. (Idaho Falls) (US)
Rick Harris, Ed. & Pub. (CN)
Harrisburg Catholic Publishing Associates (US)
Harrison Mayer Ltd. (UK)
Harrison Street Review (US)
Harry Frank Guggenheim Foundation (US)
Harry S. Truman Library Institute (US)

Harsh Publishing Co. (US)
Karl Hart (GW)
Hart-Davis Educational (UK)
Hart Publications, Inc. (Denver) (US)
Hart Publishing Co. (New York) (US)
Hartford Hospital (US)
Hartford Insurance Group (US)
Hartford Seminary Foundation (US)
Hartford Steam Boiler Inspection and Insurance Co.
   (US)
A. Hartleben (AU)
W. P. P. Hartman (NE)
Hartman Communications, Inc. (US)
Richard F. Hartmann (GW)
Hartmannbund - Verband der Aertzte Deutschlands
   e.V. (GW)
K. Hartofylakadis, Ed. & Pub. (GR)
Marion T. Hartung (US)
Hartung und Karl (GW)
Hartwell Co. (US)
Harvard Divinity School (US)
Harvard Lampoon, Inc. (US)
Harvard Law Review Association (US)
Harvard Magazine, Inc. (US)
Harvard Public Health Alumni Association (US)
Harvard School of Dental Medicine (US)
Harvard School of Public Health. Department of
   Nutrition (US)
Harvard Ukrainian Research Institute (US)
Harvard University (US)
Harvard University. Aiken Computation Laboratory
   (US)
Harvard University. Botanical Museum (US)
Harvard University. Center for International Affairs
   (US)
Harvard University. Center for Middle Eastern Studies
   (US)
Harvard University. Center for Studies in Education
   and Development (US)
Harvard University. Charles Warren Center for Studies
   in American History (US)
Harvard University Comics Society (US)
Harvard University. Department of Economics (US)
Harvard University. Department of Germanic
   Languages and Literatures (US)
Harvard University. Department of History (US)
Harvard University. Department of Linguistics (US)
Harvard University. Department of Romance
   Languages and Literature (US)
Harvard University. East Asian Research Center
   (US)
Harvard University. Graduate School of Business
   Administration (US)
Harvard University. Graduate School of Business
   Administration. Baker Library (US)
Harvard University Graduate School of Design (US)
Harvard University. Graduate School of Education
   (US)
Harvard University. Gray Herbarium (US)
Harvard University. Institute of Politics (US)
Harvard University. John F. Kennedy School of
   Government (US)
Harvard University. Laboratory for Computer
   Graphics and Spatial Analysis (US)
Harvard University Law School (US)
Harvard University Law School. Legislative Research
   Bureau (US)
Harvard University. Law School Library (US)
Harvard University. Law School Record Corp. (US)
Harvard University Library (US)
Harvard University Medical School. Department of
   Biophysics (US)
Harvard University. Museum of Comparative Zoology
   (US)
Harvard University Peabody Museum of Archaeology
   and Ethnology
   see Peabody Museum of Archaeolgy and Ethnology
   (US)
Harvard University Press (US)
Harvard University. Program for Science and
   International Affairs (US)
Harvard University. Program on Information
   Technologies and Public Policy (US)
Harvard University. Program on Regional and Urban
   Economics (US)
Harvard University. Widener Library (US)
Harvard-Yenching Institute (US)
Harvard-Yenching Library (US)
Harvest Farm Magazine (CH)
Harvest House, Ltd. (CN)
Harvest Publications (Evanston) (US)
Harvest Publishers (Santa Barbara) (US)
Harvest Publishing Co. (Cleveland) (US)
Harvester Press Ltd. (UK)
Harvey & Blythe Ltd. (UK)
Harwood & Charles Publishing Co. (US)
Haryana
   see also Punjab (II)

Haryana. Department of Education (II)
Haryana. Department of Labour (II)
Haryana. Director of Public Relations (II)
Haryana. State Health Education Bureau (II)
Haryana Agricultural University (II)
Haryana Agricultural University. College of Veterinary
   Medicine (II)
Haryana Agricultural University. Directorate of
   Research (II)
Haryana Cooperative Union Ltd. (II)
Haryana State Electricity Board (II)
Harzverein fuer Geschichte und Altertumskunde
   .
V. Hase und Koehler Verlag (GW)
Hashomer Hatzair Zionist Youth Movement (US)
Haskins & Sells (US)
Hasler Ltd. (SZ)
Hastings College of Law (US)
Hastings House Publishers, Inc. (US)
Hastings Press, Inc. (US)
W. C. Hatch Publishing Co. (US)
Librarie A. Hatier (FR)
Hatra Research Centre for Knitting, Dyeing and
   Making-up (UK)
Hatton, Brown & Co. Inc. (US)
Hattori Botanical Laboratory (JA)
Haude und Spenersche Verlagsbuchhandlung GmbH
   (GW)
Haueisen Verlag KG (GW)
Hauenstein-Verlag (SZ)
Karl F. Haug Verlag GmbH (GW)
Verlag B. Haugg KG (GW)
Haughton Publishing Co. of Texas (US)
Paul Haupt AG (SZ)
Hauptberatungsstelle fuer Elektrizitaetsanwendung e.V
   (GW)
Hauptverband der Bundesbahn-Landwirtschaft e.V.
   (GW)
Hauptverband der Deutschen Bauindustrie (GW)
Hauptverband der Deutschen Filmtheater e.V. (GW)
Hauptverband der Gewerblichen
   Berufsgenossenschaften e.V. (GW)
Hauptverband der Graphischen Unternehmungen
   Oesterreichs (AU)
Hauptverband der Oesterreichischen
   Sozialversicherungstraeger (AU)
Hauptverband der Oesterreichischen Sparkassen
   (AU)
Hauptverband des Deutschen Maler- und
   Lackiererhandwerks (GW)
Hauptverband des Oesterreichischen Buchhandels
   (AU)
Haus der Technik e.V., Essen (GW)
Verlag Haus und Grund GmbH (GW)
Die Hausfrau, Inc. (US)
Dr. Ernst Hauswedell und Co., Verlag (GW)
Haute Coiffure Francaise (FR)
Havenloods (NE)
Haverford College (US)
Havering Central Library. London Borough (UK)
Al-Hawadess Press & Publishing Co. S.A.L. (LE)
Hawaii. Agricultural Reporting Service (US)
Hawaii. Commission on Aging (US)
Hawaii. Criminal Injuries Compensation Commission
   (US)
Hawaii. Department of Agriculture (US)
Hawaii. Department of Defense. Civil Defense
   Division (US)
Hawaii. Department of Education (US)
Hawaii. Department of Education. Office of Business
   Services (US)
Hawaii. Department of Education. Office of
   Instructional Services (US)
Hawaii. Department of Education. Office of Library
   Services (US)
Hawaii. Department of Health (US)
Hawaii. Department of Health. Comprehensive Health
   Planning Office (US)
Hawaii. Department of Health. Health Education
   Office (US)
Hawaii. Department of Health. Mental Health Division
   (US)
Hawaii. Department of Health. Research and Statistics
   Office (US)
Hawaii. Department of Labor and Industrial Relations.
   Research and Statistics Office (US)
Hawaii. Department of Land and Natural Resources
   (US)
Hawaii. Department of Planning and Economic
   Development (US)
Hawaii. Insurance Division (US)
Hawaii. Judiciary Department (US)
Hawaii. Legislative Reference Bureau (US)
Hawaii. Office of Information and Youth Affairs
   (US)
Hawaii. Office of the Auditor (US)
Hawaii. Office of the Lieutenant Governor (US)
Hawaii. Office of the Ombudsman (US)

Hawaii. State Commission on the Status of Women (US)
Hawaii. State Law Enforcement and Juvenile Delinquency Planning Agency (US)
Hawaii. State Library. Office of Library Services (US)
Hawaii Agricultural Experiment Station (US)
Hawaii Audubon Society (US)
Hawaii Beverage Guide (US)
Hawaii Business Publishing Corporation (US)
Hawaii Council (US)
Hawaii Dental Association (US)
Hawaii Foundation for American Freedoms, Inc. (US)
Hawaii Institute of Geophysics (US)
Hawaii Institute of Marine Biology (US)
Hawaii Library Association (US)
Hawaii Medical Association (US)
Hawaii National Guard Association (US)
Hawaii Observer Corporation (US)
Hawaii State Federation of Labor (US)
Hawaii Tourist News, Inc. (US)
Hawaii Visitors Bureau (US)
Hawaiian Entomological Society (US)
Hawaiian Historical Society (US)
Hawaiian Malacological Society (US)
Hawaiiana Almanac Publishing Co. (US)
D. A. Hawkins Ltd. (KE)
Hawkins Publishing Co., Inc. (US)
Haworth Press (US)
Hawthorn Press Pty. Ltd. (AT)
Hay Associates (US)
Hayden Publishing Co. Inc. (US)
Edward N. Hayes, Ed. & Pub. (US)
Hayes Historical Society (US)
Julius Hayman Ltd. (CN)
Haymarket Press (US)
Haymarket Publishing Ltd. (UK)
Haymarket Publishing Ltd. (IE)
Verlag A. W. Hayn's Erben (GW)
Hays County Historical and Genealogical Society (US)
Haywood House (US)
Hazelwood Publishing Pty. Ltd. (AT)
Headland Publications (UK)
Headley Bros. Ltd. (UK)
Headmasters Association (UK)
Headmasters' Conference (UK)
Headquarters Air Cadets R.A.F. (UK)
Healdsburg Tribune-Enterprise and Scimitar (US)
Healer Publishing Co. Ltd. (UK)
Health (II)
Health Affairs Press (US)
Health and Strength Publishing Co. (UK)
Health and Welfare Council of Central Maryland, Inc. (US)
Health Culture Inc. (CN)
Health Economics Service (AT)
Health Education Council (UK)
Health Education Council of Western Australia (AT)
Health Insurance Association of America. Consumer and Professional Relations Division (US)
Health Insurance Institute (US)
Health League of Canada (CN)
Health Manpower Council of California. Annual Health Manpower Conference (US)
Health of the People (NZ)
Health Physics Society (US)
Health Policy Advisory Center (US)
Health Science Research Association (JA)
Health Sciences Communications Association (US)
Health Sciences Publishing Corp. (US)
Health Services Manpower Review (UK)
Health Visitors Association (UK)
HealthRight, Inc., Women's Health Forum (US)
Heanor Record Centre (UK)
Heard Heritage (US)
Hearing Aid Journal (US)
Hearst Books. Motor Book Department (US)
Hearst Magazines (US)
Hearst Magazines. Book Division (US)
Heart (AT)
Hearthstone Press (US)
Heartland Publications, Ltd. (US)
Hearts of Oak Benefit Society (UK)
D.C. Heath & Company (US)
Heather Enterprises, Inc. (US)
Heather Society (UK)
Heating and Ventilating Contractors' Association (UK)
Heating and Ventilating Publications Ltd. (UK)
Heavy & Chemical Industries News Agency (JA)
Heavy Engineering Corporation (II)
Hebauf Travel Press (GW)
Hebbel-Gesellschaft (GW)
Hebrew Literary Foundation (US)
Hebrew Publications for Children Inc. (US)

Hebrew Union College. Jewish Institute of Religion (US)
Hebrew Union College. Jewish Institute of Religion. Library (US)
Hebrew Union College. Jewish Institute of Religion (New York) (US)
Hebrew University of Jerusalem (IS)
Hebrew University of Jerusalem. Alumni Association (IS)
Hebrew University of Jerusalem. Graduate Library School (IS)
Hebrew University of Jerusalem. H.S. Truman Research Institute (IS)
Hebrew University of Jerusalem. Hadassah Medical School (IS)
Hebrew University of Jerusalem. Institute of Archaeology (IS)
Hebrew University of Jerusalem. Institute of Criminology (IS)
Hebrew University of Jerusalem. Institute of Languages and Literatures (IS)
Hebrew University of Jerusalem. Institute of Urban & Regional Studies (IS)
Hebrew University of Jerusalem. Leonard Davis Institute of International Relations (IS)
Hebrew University of Jerusalem. Students' Union (IS)
Hebrew Writers Association in Israel (IS)
Hecate (AT)
Hechal Shlomo (IS)
Hechos y Dichos (SP)
Connie Hechter (US)
Heckners Verlag (GW)
Hedgpeth Newsletter (US)
Hedmark Slektshistorielag (NO)
Heenayana (II)
H. Heenemann GmbH (GW)
Heering Verlag GmbH (GW)
W. Heffer & Sons Ltd. (UK)
Heffers Printers Ltd. (UK)
Hegel-Gesellschaft (GW)
Hegel Society of America (US)
Verlag Dr. Heger (GW)
Heibonsha Ltd. (JA)
Verlag fuer Wissenschaft und Leben Georg Heidecker (GW)
Heideland-Orbis (BE)
Heidelberg Graphics (US)
Heider-Verlag (GW)
The Heights Inc. (US)
Arthur J. Heighway Publications, Ltd. (UK)
G. en W. Heijboer, Ed. & Pub. (NE)
Firma J. Heijnis Tsz (NE)
Verlag Dr. H. Heilmaier (GW)
Heilsarmee GmbH (GW)
Heim Gallery (London) Ltd. (UK)
Zeitungs- und Zeitschriften-Verlag Heim und Welt (GW)
Verlag fuer Heimat und Werk (GW)
Heimatbund Allgaeu (GW)
Heimatkreis Roemerstadt-Altxater e.V. (GW)
Heimatland-Verlag (AU)
Heimatliche Verlags- und Vertriebsgesellschaft MbH (GW)
Heimatverband fuer den Kreis Pinneberg (GW)
Heimatverein des Kreises Segeberg (GW)
Heimatverein Porz e.V. (GW)
Heimatvertriebene aus Suedosteuropa (GW)
Heimdal (FR)
Heimevernsbladet (NO)
Verlag die Heimstatt (GW)
Heineman Foundation Laboratories (US)
James H. Heineman, Inc (US)
Heinemann Educational Books Ltd. (UK)
Heinemann Medical Books Ltd. (UK)
Heinmann Pan Books (UK)
Verlag Dr. Adolf Heinrich (AU)
Heinrich-Heine-Institut, Duesseldorf (GW)
Fachzeitschriftenverlag Heinrichs (GW)
Heinrichs Verlag KG (GW)
Heinrichshofen's Verlag (GW)
Heinze Verlag GmbH und Co. (GW)
Heirs, Inc. (US)
Hekisuto Japan K. K.
    see Hoechst Japan, Ltd. (JA)
Helbing und Lichtenhahn Verlag AG (SZ)
Andre Helbo (BE)
Heldref Publications (US)
Helen Diner Memorial Womens Center (US)
Helen Dwight Reid Educational Foundation (HELDREF) (US)
Helfer-Verlag E. Schwabe (GW)
Helgelsefoerbundet (SW)
Helicon (II)
Helictite (US)
Helioda-Verlag (SZ)
Heliopolis Press (US)

Hellcoal Press (US)
A. Hellendoorn Verlag (GW)
Hellenews Ltd. (GR)
Hellenic-American Chamber of Commerce (US)
Hellenic American Society (US)
Hellenic Dental Association (GR)
Hellenic Herald Pty. Ltd. (AT)
Hellenic Industrial Development Bank (GR)
Hellenic Institute of International and Foreign Law (GR)
Hellenic Junior Red Cross (GR)
Hellenic Numismatic Society (GR)
Hellenic Olympic Committee (GR)
Hellenic Philotelic Federation (GR)
Hellenic Review (UK)
Hellenic Shipping International (UK)
Hellenic Society for Aesthetics (GR)
Hellenic Society for Philosophical Studies (GR)
Hellenic Society of Marine Molecular Biology (GR)
Hellenic Youth Association of Western Australia (AT)
Hellenike Mathematike Hetaireia
    see Greek Mathematical Society (GR)
Hellenike Nomismatike Hetaireia
    see Hellenic Numismatic Society (GR)
Hellenike Spelaiologike Hetaria
    see Greek Speleological Society (GR)
Hellenike Trapeza Biomechanikes Anaptyxeos
    see Hellenic Industrial Development Bank (GR)
Hellenism (US)
Hellequin (FR)
Hellinicos Erythros Stavros
    see Hellenic Junior Red Cross (GR)
Hellric Publications (US)
Helmars Rudzitis (US)
Helminthological Society of India (II)
Helminthological Society of Washington (US)
Helpt Elkander (NE)
Helsingen Kauppakorkeakoulu. Kirjasto (FI)
Helsingin Yliopisto. Kasvatustieteen Laitos (FI)
Helsingin Yliopisto. Kirjasto (FI)
Helsingin Yliopisto. Seismologian Laitos (FI)
Helsingin Yliopisto. Tahtitieteellinen Observatorio (FI)
Helsinki. City Statistical Center (FI)
Helsinki School of Economics
    see Helsingin Kauppakorkeakoulu (FI)
Verlag Helvetica Chimica Acta (SZ)
Hem Publishers Private Ltd. (II)
Hemelspleet (NE)
Hemisphere Publishing Corporation (US)
Verlag Marie Hemmerle (GW)
Hemmets Journal AB (SW)
Hemmings Motor News (US)
Hemvaernets Stiftelse (SW)
Henderson & Henderson (US)
Hendrickson Publishing Co., Inc. (US)
Henkel GmbH (GW)
G. Henle Verlag (GW)
Aloys Henn Verlag KG (GW)
Henna (PK)
Hennepin County Board of Commissioners (US)
Hennepin County Library. Technical Services Division (US)
Hennepin County Medical Society (US)
Editions Hennessen (FR)
Edizioni Hennessen Italia (IT)
Gisbert Hennessen Verlag (GW)
Hennessen Verlag KG (AU)
Hennessey & Ingalls, Inc. (US)
Henry F. Henrichs Publications, Inc. (US)
Henrietta Szold Institute (IS)
Henriettenstiftung Hannover (GW)
Henry County Historicalog (US)
Henry Dunant Institute (NE)
Coulston R. Henry, Ed. & Pub. (US)
Henry Ford Community College (US)
Henry Ford Hospital (US)
Henry George Institute (US)
Henry George League (AT)
Henry George School of Social Science (US)
Henschelverlag Kunst und Gesellschaft (GE)
Herald Advisory Services (UK)
Herald & Weekly Times, Ltd. (AT)
Herald Books (US)
Herald of Freedom (US)
Herald Publishing Co. (Houston) (US)
Herald Publishing Company (US)
Herald Publishing House (US)
Herald Travel Bureau (AT)
Heraldisch-Genealogische Gesellschaft Adler (AU)
Heraldo Club (AG)
Heraldo del Cine (AG)
Heraldo Dental (CK)
Heraldry Society (UK)
Heraldry Society of Australia (AT)
Heraldry Society of Canada (CN)
Heraldry Society of Southern Africa (SA)

Heras Institute of Indian History and Culture  (II)
Herausgeberkommission und Historischer Verein des
    Kantons Bern  (SZ)
Herb Grower Magazine  (US)
Herb Society of America  (US)
Herbarium. Bradeanum  (BL)
Herbarium Bogariense  (IO)
Herbarium of the Royal Botanic Gardens, Kew  (UK)
Alfred Herbert Ltd.  (UK)
Herbicide Recommendations  (AT)
Hercules Inc.  (US)
Herd Book Charolais  (FR)
Herd Book F.F.P.N.  (FR)
Georg Herde  (GW)
Walter Herdeg Graphis Press  (SZ)
Verlag Herder  (AU)
Herder Editrice s.r.l.  (IT)
Verlag Herder KG  (GW)
Here Now  (UK)
Hereford Herd Book Society  (UK)
Hereford Press  (UK)
Hereford Publications, Inc.  (US)
Herforder Verein fuer Heimatkunde  (GW)
Verlag Klaus Edgar Herfurth  (GW)
Verlag W. Herget  (AU)
Heriot-Watt University  (UK)
Heritage Music Press  (US)
Heritage Papers  (US)
Heritage Publishers  (II)
Heritage Publishing Co.  (US)
Heritage Publishing Co. (North Little Rock)  (US)
John Herlings Labor Letter, Inc.  (US)
Editions Hermann  (FR)
Hermann-Oberth-Gesellschaft  (GW)
Hermes Verlags- und Werbe-Gesellschaft mbH  (GW)
Hermods Foundation  (SW)
Amado F. Hernandez, Ed. & Pub.  (US)
Jeng Herney-Shorng, Ed. & Pub.  (CH)
Industrieverlag von Hernhaussen KG  (GW)
Hero Press  (US)
Verlag des Herold Herbert Sexauer KG  (GW)
John S. Herold, Inc.  (US)
Herold Vereinigte Anzeigen-Gesellschaft M.B.H.
    (AU)
Herold-Verlag Dr. Franz Wetzel und Co. KG  (GW)
Heroldo de Esperanto  (BE)
E. T. Heron & Co. Ltd.  (UK)
Heron Publishing Co. (Pty) Ltd.  (SA)
Herpetological Information Search Systems  (US)
Herpetologists League  (US)
Lorenzo Herranz, Ed. & Pub  (SP)
Mario Herrera Gray, Ed. & Pub.  (PE)
Publicaciones Herrerias, S.A.  (MX)
Herrick Public Library  (US)
Hertfordshire Chamber of Commerce  (UK)
Hertfordshire Local History Council  (UK)
Hervey Bay Writers' Workshop  (AT)
Hervormd Opleidingscentrum  (NE)
Hervormde Bond voor Inwendige Zending  (NE)
Hervormde Gemeente Arnhem  (NE)
Hervormde Gemeente, Hoenderloo  (NE)
Hervormde Gemeente Kerkelijk Bureau  (NE)
Hervormde Jeugdraad  (NE)
Hervormde Vereniging  (NE)
Herz und Co.  (AU)
Rudolf Herzfeldt Verlag  (GW)
Herzog-August-Bibliothek, Wolfenbuettel  (GW)
Verlag Guenther Heske  (GW)
Hessen. Hessisches Landesamt fuer Geschichtliche
    Landeskunde  (GW)
Hessen. Kultusministerium  (GW)
Hessen. Landeszentrale fuer Politische Bildung  (GW)
Hessen. Minister der Justiz  (GW)
Hessen. Ministerium fuer Landwirtschaft und Umwelt
    (GW)
Hessen. Staatskanzlei  (GW)
Hessen. Statistisches Landesamt  (GW)
Hessischer Jugendring  (GW)
Hessischer Volkshochschulverband  (GW)
Hestesport  (DK)
Hestra-Verlag  (GW)
Hetaireia Makedonikon Spoudon
    see Society for Macedonian Studies  (GR)
HeteroCorporation  (US)
Heterofonia  (MX)
Heugel  (FR)
Hanseatisches Werbekontor Heuser und Co.  (GW)
Hewitt Bros.  (US)
Peter Hewitt Publications Ltd.  (UK)
Hewlett Packard Co. (Palo Alto)  (US)
Hewlett Packard Co. (Santa Clara)  (US)
Hewlett Packard Co. (Waltham)  (US)
Hewlett-Woodmere Public Library  (US)
Heyden & Son Ltd.  (UK)
Carl Heymanns Verlag KG  (GW)
Heythrop College (University of London)  (UK)
Hi-Fi Trade Journal Limited  (UK)

Hi-Rise Weekly  (US)
Hi-Torque Publications, Inc.  (US)
Hiaring Co.  (US)
Hibernia National Review Ltd.  (IE)
Hibiscus Press  (US)
Hibueras  (HO)
T. & C. Hicks  (UK)
Hidrografski Institut Jugoslavenske Ratne Mornarice
    (YU)
Anton Hiersemann Verlag  (GW)
Higdon Family Newsletter  (US)
William J. Higginson, Ed. & Pub.  (US)
Higginson Press  (US)
High Authority
    see Commission of the European Communities
    (EI)
High Commissioner for New Zealand in Britain  (UK)
High Orchard Press  (UK)
High Plains Publishers, Inc.  (US)
High Polymer Publishing Association  (JA)
High Society Magazine, Inc.  (US)
High Times Pty. Ltd.  (AT)
High Voltage Engineering Corporation  (US)
Robin Higham, Ed. & Pub.  (US)
Dean Coughenour & Robin Higham, Eds. & Pubs.
    (US)
Highland Farmers & Settlers Association  (PP)
Highland Herald Ltd.  (UK)
Highland Press, Inc.  (US)
Highlander, Inc.  (US)
Highlands and Islands Development Board  (UK)
Highlands Press (Hampden)  (US)
Highlands Press (Radford)  (US)
Highlights  (II)
Highlights for Children, Inc.  (US)
Highway Book Shop  (CN)
Highway Loss Data Institute  (US)
Highway Mail (Pty) Ltd.  (SA)
Highway Safety Institute  (US)
Highway Users Federation  (US)
Hikosan Biological Laboratory  (JA)
Hilfsgemeinschaft Aller Menschen Guten Willens
    (AU)
Hilfsgemeinschaft der Blinden und Sehschwachen
    Oesterreichs  (AU)
Hilfskomitee der Galiziendeutschen  (GE)
Adam Hilger Ltd.  (UK)
Craig Hill, Ed. & Pub.  (US)
Jesse Hill, Jr.  (US)
Hill and Wang  (US)
Leonard Hill Books  (UK)
Hill Group Publications  (AT)
Hill International Publications  (US)
Hillsdale College. Center for Constructive Alternative
    (US)
Hilmir H.F.  (IC)
Hilton Head Island Chamber of Commerce  (US)
Hilversum. Bureau voor Sociaal-Wetenschappelijk
    Onderzoek  (NE)
Himachal Pradesh. Department of Agriculture  (II)
Himachal Pradesh. Department of Education  (II)
Himachal Pradesh. Directorate of Economics and
    Statistics  (II)
Himachal Pradesh. State Museum, Simla  (II)
Himalangue  (NP)
Himalayan Club  (II)
Himalayan Economist  (NP)
Himalayan Federation  (NP)
Himalayan Observer Press  (II)
Himmat Publications Trust  (II)
Hind Kusht Nivaran Sangh
    see Indian Leprosy Association  (II)
Hind Mazdoor Sabha  (II)
Hindustan Antibiotics Ltd.  (II)
Hindustan Chamber of Commerce  (II)
Hindustan Machine Tools Ltd.  (II)
Hindustan Publishing Corp.  (II)
Hindustan Shipyard Ltd.  (II)
Hindustan Steel Limited  (II)
Hindustan Steel Limited. Bhilai Steel Plant  (II)
Hindustan Thompson Associates  (II)
Hindustan Times  (II)
Hine's Legal Directory, Inc.  (US)
Hinstorff Verlag  (GE)
Hinterbruehl. Marktgemeinde Hinterbruehl.
    Gemeindeamt  (AU)
Hip Society  (US)
Hippokrates-Verlag GmbH  (GW)
Hiradastechnikai Tudomanyos Egyesulet  (HU)
Hiram College  (US)
Hiram College. English Department  (US)
Hire Purchase Trade Association  (UK)
Hirlapkiado Vallalat  (HU)
Hirosaki Daigaku
    see Hirosaki University  (JA)
Hirosaki University. Faculty of Agriculture  (JA)
Hirosaki University. Faculty of Science  (JA)
Hiroshima Botanical Club  (JA)

Hiroshima Daigaku
    see Hiroshima University  (JA)
Hiroshima Daigaku Genbaku Hoshano Kenkyusho
    see Hiroshima University. Research Institute for
    Nuclear Medicine and Biology  (JA)
Hiroshima Medical Association  (JA)
Hiroshima Shinagakkai
    see Sinological Society of Hiroshima  (JA)
Hiroshima University. Botanical Institute  (JA)
Hiroshima University. Department of Geology and
    Mineralogy  (JA)
Hiroshima University. Department of Mathematics
    (JA)
Hiroshima University. Faculty of Engineering  (JA)
Hiroshima University. Faculty of General Education
    (JA)
Hiroshima University. Faculty of Science  (JA)
Hiroshima University. Laboratory for Amphibian
    Biology  (JA)
Hiroshima University. Research Institute for Nuclear
    Medicine and Biology  (JA)
Hiroshima University. Research Institute for
    Theoretical Physics  (JA)
Hiroshima University. School of Medicine  (JA)
Hiroshima University Dental Society  (JA)
Hirsch Organization, Inc.  (US)
Harro V. Hirschheydt  (GW)
Verlag Ferdinand Hirt GmbH  (AU)
S. Hirzel Verlag  (GE)
S. Hirzel Verlag  (GW)
Hispamerica  (US)
Hispania  (FR)
Hispanic and Luso-Brazilian Council  (UK)
Hispanic Foundation  (US)
Hispanic Institute of the United States
    see under Columbia University  (US)
Hispano  (US)
Hispano Americana, S.A.  (AG)
G. W. Hissink and Co.  (NE)
Hissu Aminosan Kenkyu Iinkai
    see Research Committee on Essential Amino Acids
    (JA)
Histadrut  (IS)
Histadrut. Union of Clerical, Administrative and Public
    Service Employees  (IS)
Histadruth Ha-Morim  (IT)
Histadruth Ivrith of America  (US)
Histochemical Society  (US)
Histonium  (AG)
Historama  (FR)
Historia Natural y pro Natura  (GT)
Historian Ystavain Liitto  (FI)
Historians Film Committee  (US)
Historic Commercial Vehicle Club  (UK)
Historic Madison, Inc.  (US)
Historic Schaefferstown Inc.  (US)
Historic Society of Lancashire and Cheshire  (UK)
Historical Aircraft Decal Inc.  (US)
Historical & Genealogical Society of Somerset County,
    Inc.  (US)
Historical and Scientific Society of Manitoba  (CN)
Historical Association  (US)
Historical Association of Kenya  (KE)
Historical Association of Southern Florida  (US)
Historical Association of Sweden  (SW)
Historical Association of Tanzania  (TZ)
Historical Association of Zambia  (ZA)
Historical Breechloading Smallarms Association  (UK)
Historical Communications Inc.  (US)
Historical Conservation Society  (PH)
Historical Evaluation and Research Organization
    (US)
Historical Firearms Society of South Africa  (SA)
Historical Metallurgy Society  (UK)
Historical Society of Afghanistan  (AF)
Historical Society of Alberta  (CN)
Historical Society of Alberta. Whoop up Country
    Chapter  (CN)
Historical Society of Berks County  (US)
Historical Society of Cape Town  (SA)
Historical Society of Delaware  (US)
Historical Society of Ghana  (GH)
Historical Society of Haddonfield  (US)
Historical Society of Israel  (IS)
Historical Society of Japan  (JA)
Historical Society of Mecklenburg Upper Canada
    (CN)
Historical Society of Nanyang University  (SI)
Historical Society of Nigeria  (NR)
Historical Society of Pennsylvania  (US)
Historical Society of Port Elizabeth  (SA)
Historical Society of South Africa  (SA)
Historical Society of Southern California  (US)
Historical Society of the Church in Wales  (UK)
Historical Society of the Presbyterian Church of Wales
    (UK)
Historical Society of Western Pennsylvania  (US)
Historical Times Ltd.  (UK)

Historiker-Gesellschaft der DDR. Hansische Arbeitsgemeinschaft (GE)
Historiographisches Institut GmbH (Solothurn) (GW)
Historisch-Antiquarischer Verein Obwalden (SZ)
Historische Kommission fuer Niedersachsen und Bremen (GW)
Historische Kommission fuer Ost- und Westpreussische Landesforschung (GW)
Historische Kommission Zu Berlin (GW)
Historische und Antiquarische Gesellschaft zu Basel (SZ)
Historischer Verein der Pfalz (GW)
Historischer Verein des Kantons St. Gallen (SZ)
Historischer Verein Dillingen an der Donau (GW)
Historischer Verein fuer Hessen (GW)
Historischer Verein fuer Oberfranken (GW)
Historischer Verein fuer Steiermark (AU)
Historischer Verein fuer Wuerttembergisch Franken (GW)
Historisk Samfund for Als og Sundeved (DK)
Historisk Samfund for Fyns Stift (DK)
Historisk Samfund for Holback (DK)
Historisk Samfund for Ribe Amt (DK)
Historisk Samfund for Ringkoebing Amt (DK)
Historisk Samfund for Skive og Omegn (DK)
Historisk Samfund for Soenderjylland (DK)
Historisk Samfund for Vendsyssel (DK)
Historisk Samfund for Viborg Amt (DK)
Historisk-Topografisk Selskab for Soelleroed Kommune (DK)
Historiska Foereningen (FI)
History and Social Science Teacher Inc. (CN)
History Book Club, Inc. (US)
History in Africa (US)
History of Anthropology Newsletter (US)
History of Education Society (UK)
History of Education Society (US)
History of Science Society (US)
History of Science Society of Japan (JA)
History Teachers' Association of New South Wales (AT)
History Workshop Journal (UK)
Histrionic Publishing Corp. (US)
Hitachi, Ltd. (JA)
Hitachi Zosen Technical Research Institute (JA)
Hitahdut Oley Britannia (IS)
Hitahdut Oley Bukovina (IS)
Hitchcock Publishing Co. (US)
Roy Hitchcock, Jr., Ed. & Pub. (US)
Frank M. Hiteshew & Associates (US)
Hitotsubashi Academy (JA)
Hitotsubashi Daigaku
    see Hitotsubashi University (JA)
Hitotsubashi University (JA)
Hitotsubashi University. Institute of Economic Research (JA)
Hjemkundskabslaererforeningen (DK)
A-S Hjemmet (NO)
Hjemmevaernsbladet (DK)
Hjukrunarfelags Islands (IC)
Hoad's Technical Publications Pty. Ltd. (AT)
W. D. Hoard and Sons Co. (US)
Hob-Nob (US)
Hobart and William Smith Colleges (US)
Hobart Brothers Co. (US)
Hobart Walking Club (AT)
Hobbies and Things (US)
Editorial Hobby Comercial e Industrial (AG)
Hobby House Press (US)
Hobby International (BG)
Hobby Publications, Inc. (US)
Hobsons Press (UK)
Verlag Hoch und Tiefbau (SZ)
Hochschul-Informations-System GmbH (GW)
Hochschule fuer Bodenkultur (AU)
Hochschule fuer Bodenkultur. Forstliche Abteilung (AU)
Hochschule fuer Film und Fernsehen der DDR (GE)
Hochschule fuer Oekonomie (GE)
Hochschule fuer Politik (GW)
Hochschule fuer Sozial- und Wirtschaftswissenschaften, Linz (AU)
Hochschule fuer Sozial- und Wirtschaftswissenschaften, Linz. Oesterreichisches Institut fuer Arbeitsmarkt Politik (AU)
Hochschule fuer Verkehrswesen "Friedrich List" (GE)
Hochschule fuer Wirtschaft und Politik, Hamburg (GW)
Hochschule St. Gallen fuer Wirtschafts- und Sozialwissenschaften. Forschungsinstitut fuer Absatz und Handel (SZ)
Hochschule St. Gallen fuer Wirtschafts- und Sozialwissenschaften. Institut fuer Betriebswirtschaft (SZ)
Hochschule St. Gallen fuer Wirtschafts- und Sozialwissenschaften. Institut fuer Fremdenverkehr und Verkehrswirtschaft (SZ)

Hochschule St. Gallen fuer Wirtschafts- und Sozialwissenschaften. Schweizerisches Institut fuer Aussenwirtschafts-, Struktur- und Marktforschung (SZ)
Hochschullehrerbund (GW)
Philip Hochstein, Ed. & Pub. (US)
Hochuli AG (SZ)
Hockey & Arena Biz (US)
Hockey Association (UK)
Hockey Illustrated Ltd. (CN)
Hod Mother Earth Tribe (US)
William Hodge & Co. Ltd. (UK)
C. E. Hodge, Ed. & Pub. (UK)
Hodges Figgis & Co. Ltd. (IE)
Peter Hodgkiss, Ed. & Pub. (UK)
Francis Hodgson (F.H. Books Ltd.) (UI)
C. F. Hodgson & Son Ltd. (UK)
Hoechst AG (GW)
Hoechst Japan, Ltd. (JA)
Hoefling Verlag Dr. V. Mayer (GW)
Hoehere Graphische Bundes Lehr und Versuchsanstalt (AU)
Editore Ulrico Hoepli (IT)
Hoerbiger Institut (AU)
Verlag Hoergeschaedigte Kinder (GW)
Verlag K. Hoerning GmbH (GW)
Van der Hoeven Foundation for Theoretical Biology
    see Prof. Dr. Jan van der Hoeven Foundation for Theoretical Biology (NE)
E. M. Hoffman, Ed. & Pub. (CN)
Hoffman Printing Co. (US)
Hoffman Publications, Inc. (US)
Verlag H. Hoffmann (GW)
Verlag Dieter Hoffmann (Mainz) (GW)
Verlag Dr. Hoffmann KG (GW)
F. Hoffmann-La Roche & Co., Ltd. (SZ)
Hoffmann und Campe Verlag (GW)
Otto Hoffmanns Verlag (GW)
Fritz S. Hofheimer, Inc. (US)
Verlag Karl Hofmann (GW)
Rudolf Hofmann Verlag (GW)
VEB Friedrich Hofmeister Musikverlag (GE)
Hofstad Vakpers B.V. (NE)
Hofstra University (US)
Hofstra University Press (US)
Hofstra University. School of Business (US)
Hofstra University. School of Law (US)
Hogakkai
    see Tohoku University. Association of Law and Political Science (JA)
Hogaku Kenkyukai
    see Keio University. Association for the Study of Law and Politics (JA)
Hogaku Kyokai
    see Jurisprudence Association (JA)
Edward J. Hogan, Ed. & Pub. (US)
Betsy Hogan Associates (US)
Hogar del Libro, S. A. (SP)
Hogar y Arquitectura (SP)
Hogar y la Moda, S.A. (SP)
Hogarth Press Ltd. (UK)
Hoger Instituut voor Bestuur- en Handelswetenschappen (BE)
Hoger Instituut voor Grafisch Onderwijs (BE)
Hoger Katechetisch Instituut, Nijmegen (NE)
Hogeschool te Tilburg. Instituut voor Arbeidsvraagstukken (NE)
Hogeschool te Tilburg. John F. Kennedy Institute (NE)
Noel Farr Hoggard, Ed. & Pub. (NZ)
Hohasen Igaku Sogo Kenkyusho
    see National Institute of Radiological Sciences (JA)
Hohenzollerischer Geschichtsverein (GW)
Hoke Communications, Inc. (US)
Hokekyo Bunka Kenkyujo
    see Rissho University. Institute for the Comprehensive Study of Lotus Sutra (JA)
Hoken Kagaku Kenkyukai
    see Kyorin-Shoin (Health Science Research Association) (JA)
Hokkaido Artificial Insemination Technician Association (JA)
Hokkaido Central Fisheries Experimental Station (JA)
Hokkaido Daigaku
    see Hokkaido University (JA)
Hokkaido Daigaku Oyo Denki Kenkyusho
    see Hokkaido University. Research Institute of Applied Electricity (JA)
Hokkaido Daigaku Shokubai Kenkyusho Kiyo
    see Hokkaido University. Research Institute for Catalysis (JA)
Hokkaido Dental Association (JA)
Hokkaido Juishikai
    see Hokkaido Veterinary Medical Association (JA)
Hokkaido Kachiku Jinko Juseishi Kyokai

    see Hokkaido Artificial Insemination Technician Association (JA)
Hokkaido Kogai Boshi Kenkyujo
    see Hokkaido Research Institute for Environmental Pollution (JA)
Hokkaido Kogyo Kaihatsu Shikenjo
    see Japan. Government Industrial Development Laboratory, Hokkaido (JA)
Hokkaido Kyoiku Daigaku
    see Hokkaido University of Education (JA)
Hokkaido Librarians Study Circle (JA)
Hokkaido National Agricultural Experiment Station
    see Japan. Hokkaido National Agricultural Experiment Station (JA)
Hokkaido Orthopedic and Traumatic Surgery Society (JA)
Hokkaido Research Institute for Environmental Pollution (JA)
Hokkaido Seikei Saigai Geka Gakkai
    see Hokkaido Orthopedic and Traumatic Surgery Society (JA)
Hokkaido Shika Ishikai
    see Hokkaido Dental Association (JA)
Hokkaido Toshokan Kenkyukai
    see Hokkaido Librarians Study Circle (JA)
Hokkaido University (JA)
Hokkaido University. Faculty of Agriculture (JA)
Hokkaido University. Faculty of Economics and Business Administration (JA)
Hokkaido University. Faculty of Engineering (JA)
Hokkaido University. Faculty of Fisheries (JA)
Hokkaido University. Faculty of Science (JA)
Hokkaido University. Faculty of Veterinary Medicine (JA)
Hokkaido University. Institute of Algological Research (JA)
Hokkaido University. Institute of Immunological Science (JA)
Hokkaido University. Institute of Low Temperature Science (JA)
Hokkaido University. Research Institute for Catalysis (JA)
Hokkaido University. Research Institute of Applied Electricity (JA)
Hokkaido University. Urakawa Seismological Observatory (JA)
Hokkaido University of Education (JA)
Hokkaido Veterinary Medical Association (JA)
Hokkaidoritsu Chuo Suisan Shijenko
    see Hokkaido Central Fisheries Experimental Station (JA)
Hokuno-Kai (JA)
Holden Arboretum (US)
Holden-Day, Inc. (US)
Holdsworth Natural Resource Center (US)
Holec NV (NE)
Holiday Fellowship Ltd (UK)
Holiness Union Mission (SA)
Holland Genealogical Society (US)
Holland Society of New York (US)
Holland University Press
    see APA-Holland University Press (NE)
Hollands Diep (NE)
Hollandsche Molen (NE)
Hollar, Skupina Ceskoslovenskych Umelcu-Grafiku (CS)
Lee A. Holley, Ed. & Pub. (US)
Brueder Hollinek (AU)
Hollinger Mines Ltd. (CN)
Harry Hollingsworth, Ed. & Pub. (US)
Hollins College (US)
Hollis Directories (UK)
Hollow Spring Review of Poetry (US)
Holly Society of America, Inc. (US)
Hollycroft Press, Inc. (US)
Hollywood Congregational Center for Study and Service (US)
Holm Seminar on Electrical Contacts (US)
A. J. Holman Co. (US)
W. & R. Holmes (Books) (UK)
Holmes & Meier Publishers, Inc. (US)
Michael I. Holmes, Ed. & Pub. (US)
Holmes Forlag (NO)
Holmes McDougall Ltd. (UK)
John F. Holmes Publishing Co., Inc. (US)
Arthur Holmes Society (UK)
Joergen Holst, AD Promotion-Forlag (DK)
Holstein-Friesian Association of Canada (CN)
Holstein-Friesian World, Inc. (US)
T. J. Holt & Co., Inc. (US)
Holt, Rinehart and Winston, Inc. (US)
Holt Rinehart and Winston of Canada, Ltd. (CN)
Steven Holtzman, Ed. & Pub. (US)
Holy Childhood Society (UK)
Holy Cross Greek Orthodox School of Theology. Hellenic College (US)
Holy Cross Monastery (US)
Holy Cross Orthodox Press (US)

Holy Name Society  (AT)
Holy Synod of the Church of Greece  (GR)
Holy Trinity Monastery  (US)
Holyoke Community College  (US)
Holyrood Publications Ltd.  (IE)
Holz-Verlag GmbH  (GW)
Adolf Holzhausens Nachfolger  (AU)
Ferdinand Holzmann Verlag  (GW)
Hans Holzmann Verlag KG  (GW)
Holzner-Verlag  (GW)
Holzwarth und Berger  (AU)
Home Builders Association of Alabama, Inc.  (US)
Home Builders Association of Maryland  (US)
Home Economics Association of Australia  (AT)
Home Economics Education Association  (US)
Home Planet Publications  (US)
Home Science Association of India  (II)
Home Words Printing & Publishing Co. Ltd.  (UK)
Homebuyers Journal (Westchester County Edition)
    (US)
Homefinders (1915) Ltd.  (UK)
Homeo Doctor  (PK)
Homeopathic Herald  (II)
Homeopathic Medical Society of the State of
    Pennsylvania  (US)
Homersham Advertising Agency  (CN)
Homesewing Trade News  (US)
Homin Ukrainy Publishing Co.  (CN)
Homme Libre  (FR)
Homme Nouveau  (FR)
Publications Michel Hommell  (FR)
Hommes et Migrations  (FR)
Editions Hommes et Techniques  (FR)
Hommes Libres  (FR)
Hommes Volants  (FR)
Homoeopathic Education Society  (II)
Homosexual Information Center  (US)
Honduras. Corte Suprema de Justicia  (HO)
Honduras. Empresa Nacional de Energia Electrica.
    Departamento de Planificacion Economica  (HO)
Honduras. Instituto Hondureno de Seguridad Social.
    Departamento de Estadistica y Actuarial  (HO)
Honduras Industrial, S. A.  (HO)
Honegger S.A.  (AG)
Honeywell B.V.  (NE)
Hong Kong. Census and Statistics Department  (HK)
Hong Kong. Education Department  (HK)
Hong Kong. Fisheries Research Station  (HK)
Hong Kong. Government Information Services  (HK)
Hong Kong. Government Publications Centre  (HK)
Hong Kong. Royal Observatory  (HK)
Hong Kong Economic Association  (HK)
Hong Kong General Chamber of Commerce  (HK)
Hong Kong Geographical Association  (HK)
Hong Kong Junior Chamber  (HK)
Hong Kong Library Association  (HK)
Hong Kong Management Association  (HK)
Hong Kong Medical Association  (HK)
Hong Kong Nurses Association  (HK)
Hong Kong Tourist Association  (HK)
Hong Kong Trade Development Council  (HK)
Hong Kong Trade Development Council  (US)
Hong Kong University Press  (HK)
Honolulu. Department of Civil Service  (US)
Honolulu. Mayor's Committee on the Status of
    Women  (US)
Honolulu. Police Department  (US)
Honolulu Publishing Co. Ltd.  (US)
Honourable Artillery Company  (UK)
Honourable Company of Master Mariners  (UK)
Hood's Texas Brigade Association  (US)
Hoofdbedrijfschap Ambachten  (NE)
Hoofdbestur der Belastingen  (BE)
Hoofdproduktschap voor Akkerbouwprodukten  (NE)
Hoofs and Horns Publishing Co.  (US)
Hooker Chemicals & Plastics Corp. Durez Division
    (US)
Hoosier Challenger  (US)
Hoosier Folklore Society  (US)
Hoosier Motor Club  (US)
Hoosier Publications Inc.  (US)
Hoosier State Press Association, Inc.  (US)
Hoover Institution  (US)
Hoover Institution Press  (US)
Hopfenverlag  (GW)
Hopi Action Program  (US)
Hopital Boucicaut-Paris. Laboratoire d'Eutonologie
    (FR)
Hopital Chicoutimi, Inc.  (CN)
Hopital des Enfants Malades. Centre d'Estudes sur les
    Maladies du Metabolisme Chez l'Enfant  (FR)
Hopital, Information Therapeutique  (FR)
Hopital Necker. Clinique Nephrologique  (FR)
Hopital Universitaire Brugmann. Clinique de
    Gynecologie et d'Obstetrique  (BE)
Ralph Hopkins, Jr., Ed. & Pub.  (US)

Roland G. Hopkins, Ed. & Pub.  (US)
Hopkins Publications  (US)
Hopkins Quarterly  (CN)
Verlag Hoppenstedt und Co.  (GW)
Horace Mann-Lincoln Institute  (US)
Horace Mann School  (US)
Horan & Wall  (AT)
Horatio Alger Society  (US)
Horitsu Bunka Sha  (JA)
Horizon House  (US)
Horizon Publications Ltd.  (UK)
Editions Horizons de France  (FR)
Horizons du Fantastique  (FR)
Horizont-Yugoslavia  (YU)
Editorial Horizonte  (PE)
Livros Horizonte  (PO)
Horn Book, Inc.  (US)
Horn Speaker  (US)
Horological Guild of Australasia. Victorian Branch
    (AT)
Horological Institute of Japan  (JA)
Horry County Historical Society  (US)
Horse Lover's National  (US)
Horsebreeder  (US)
Horseless Carriage Club of America, Inc.  (US)
Horselframjandets Riksforbund  (SW)
Horseman Publishing Co.  (US)
Horsemen's Benevolent and Protective Association
    (US)
Horses  (US)
Horsetrader, Inc.  (US)
De Horstink  (NE)
Horticultural and Agricultural Research Station  (UK)
Horticultural Data Processors  (US)
Horticultural Education Association  (UK)
Horticultural Press Pty. Ltd.  (AT)
Horticultural Research Station  (AT)
Horticultural Society of India  (II)
Horticulture Publications Ltd.  (CN)
Hortikulturna Drustva Hrvatske  (YU)
Horton Publishing Co.  (US)
Hortus-Verlag GmbH  (GW)
John F. Horty, Ed. & Pub.  (US)
Hosakai
    see Lawyer's Association  (JA)
Hoseasons  (UK)
Hosei Daigaku
    see Hosei University  (JA)
Hosei Gakkai
    see Kyushu University. Institute of Law and Politics
    (JA)
Hosei University. Economics Society  (JA)
Hoshasen Eikyo Kenkyusho
    see Radiation Effects Research Foundation  (JA)
Hosiery and Textile Journal  (II)
Margaret Hosni, Ed. & Pub.  (UA)
Hospital Association of New York State  (US)
Hospital Boards' Association of New Zealand, Inc.
    (NZ)
Hospital de Clinicas "Dr. Manuel Quintela"  (UY)
Hospital de Juqueri  (BL)
Hospital dos Servidores do Estado  (BL)
Hospital Employees Association  (SA)
Hospital Financial Management Association  (US)
Hospital for Joint Diseases & Medical Center  (US)
Hospital for Sick Children  (CN)
Hospital for Sick Children  (UK)
Hospital for Special Surgery  (US)
Hospital Infantil de Mexico  (MX)
Hospital Medicine Publications Ltd.  (UK)
Hospital Municipal Dr. Enrique Tornu. Sociedad de
    Tisiologia y Neumologia  (AT)
Hospital Oftalmologico de Nuestra Senora de la Luz
    (MX)
Hospital Psiquiatrico de la Habana  (CU)
Hospital Publications, Inc.  (US)
Hospital Research and Educational Trust  (US)
Hospital Research and Testing Institute  (US)
Hospital Topics, Inc.  (US)
Hospital Vargas  (VE)
Hospitalis Verlag AG  (SZ)
Hospitalized Veterans Writing Project  (US)
Uitgeverij J. Hoste N.V.  (BE)
Hot Club de France. Bulletin  (FR)
Hotel and Restaurant Employee and Bartenders
    International Union  (US)
Hotel Association of New Zealand  (NZ)
Hotel Association of Rhodesia  (RH)
Hotel Catering & Institutional Management
    Association  (UK)
Hotel-Dieu. Clinique Medico-Sociale du Diabete et des
    Maladies Metaboliques  (FR)
Hotel Herald Co.  (US)
Hotel, Motel & Club Employees Union Local 6  (US)
Hotel-Motel Greeters International, Lone Star Charter
    (US)
Hotel Sales Management Association  (US)
Hotel Service Inc.  (US)

Hotel Tipton Enterprises  (US)
Hotel- und Gaststaetten-Vereinigung Frankfurt am
    Main e.V.  (GW)
Hotel Verlag  (AU)
Hotels de la France  (FR)
Hotline Quarterly  (US)
Hottinger Baldwin Messtechnik GmbH  (GW)
C. W. Hotze  (US)
P.K. Houdek, Ed. & Pub.  (US)
Houghton Mifflin Co.  (US)
Houille Blanche  (FR)
Houilleres du Bassin du Nord et du Pas-De-Calais
    (FR)
Houilleres du Centre-Midi  (FR)
House-Builders' Federation  (UK)
House Information Services Ltd.  (UK)
House of Greystoke  (US)
House of Love and Prayer Publications  (US)
House of White Birches  (US)
House of Words  (US)
Houseman & Co.  (TH)
Housewife's Trust  (UK)
Housing Australia Publishing Co.  (AT)
Housing Centre Trust  (UK)
Housing Industry Association  (AT)
Housman Society  (UK)
Houston Chamber of Commerce  (US)
Houston Engineer Publishing Company  (US)
Houston Engineering & Scientific Society  (US)
Houston Geological Society  (US)
Houston Law Review Inc.  (US)
Houston Standard Publications Ltd.  (CN)
Houston Teachers Association  (US)
Hovedorganisationen af Officerer af a-Linien  (DK)
Hovedsorganisationen af Mesterforeninger i
    Byggefagne i Danmark  (DK)
Hover Club of Great Britain Ltd.  (UK)
Cloyde P. Howard Consultants  (US)
Howard League for Penal Reform  (UK)
Howard Needles Tammen and Bergendoff  (US)
Howard Publications  (UK)
Howard Publications, Inc.  (US)
Howard Publishing Co.  (US)
Howard University  (US)
Howard University. African Studies Department  (US)
Howard University. Bureau of Educational Research
    (US)
Howard University. Department of History  (US)
Howard University. Department of University
    Relations and Publications  (US)
Howard University. Morland Spingarn Research
    Center  (US)
Howard University Press  (US)
Howard University. School of Business & Public
    Administration  (US)
Howard University. School of Law  (US)
Howard University. School of Religion  (US)
George L. Howe Press Service Ltd.  (UK)
C. D. Howe Research Institute  (CN)
Howell Publishing Co.  (US)
Howes Waldon Associates Ltd.  (CN)
Howey Foundation  (UK)
Howmark Publishing Corporation, Inc.  (US)
Hoyts Theatres Ltd.  (AT)
Hrvatski Dom  (AT)
Hrvatski Filatelisticki Savez  (YU)
Hrvatsko Bibliotekarsko Drustvo  (YU)
Hrvatsko Filolosko Drustvo  (YU)
Hrvatsko Filolosko Drustvo. Sekcija za Strane Jezike
    (YU)
Hrvatsko Geolosko Drustvo  (YU)
Hrvatsko Kemijsko Drustvo  (YU)
Hrvatsko Narodno Kazaliste u Osijeku  (YU)
Hsiang-kang Chi-tu Chiao Kung Yeh Wei Yuan Hui
    (HK)
Hsiang-Kang Kung i Chih Pin Chang Fa Chan Hsieh
    Hui.  (HK)
Hsing-Tao Pao Yeh Yu Hsien Kung Ssu  (HK)
Hsinhua News Agency  (HK)
Empresa Editora Huaral Magazine S.A.  (PE)
Hub Publications Ltd.  (UK)
Hub Rail, Inc.  (US)
Hubbard High School  (US)
Hubbord Industries  (US)
Verlag Hans Huber  (SZ)
Huber und Co. AG  (SZ)
Hubertusverlag  (AU)
Stan Hubsher  (US)
Huddleston Family Newsletter  (US)
Hudson County Dental Society  (US)
Howard Penn Hudson & Mary E. Hudson, Eds. &
    Pubs.  (US)
Hudson-Fachpresse  (SZ)
Hudson Family Association (South)  (US)
Hudson Heritage House  (US)
Hudson Home Guides  (US)
Hudson Institute  (US)
Hudson Publications Ltd.  (UK)

Hudson Publishing Co. (US)
Hudson Research Europe Ltd. (FR)
Hudson Review, Inc. (US)
Hudson River Press (US)
Hudson's Bay Co. (CN)
Hermann Huebener Verlag KG (GW)
Max Hueber Verlag (GW)
Lee W. Huebner, Ed. & Pub. (US)
Huebner Publications, Inc. (US)
Hadayatullah Huebsch (GW)
Hueck Family Association (US)
Chemische Werke Huels AG (GW)
Editorial Huemul S.A. (AG)
Huerta (US)
Huethig und Pflaum Verlag (GW)
Huethig und Wepf Verlag (SZ)
Dr. Alfred Huethig Verlag GmbH (GW)
Musikverlag Hug und Co. (SZ)
Hug-Verlag AG (SZ)
John R. Hughes, Ed. & Pub. (US)
Hughes, Sanders & Howard Ltd. (UK)
Hugo-Obermaier-Gesellschaft (GW)
Hugo von Hofmannstahl-Gesellschaft (GW)
Huguenot Society of Canada (CN)
Huguenot Society of London (UK)
Huguenot Society of Utrecht (NE)
N. V. Uitgeverij "Het Huis van Linnaeus" (NE)
Huisvrou Press (Pty) Ltd. (SA)
Huletts Aluminum Ltd. (SA)
Roger Hull, Ed. & Pub. (US)
Hulton House (UK)
Hulton Technical Press Ltd. (UK)
Human Dimensions Institute Inc. (US)
Human Ergology Research Association (JA)
Human Events, Inc. (US)
Human Factor: A Journal of Radical Sociology (US)
Human Factors Society (US)
Human Geography Society of Japan (JA)
Human Life Foundation, Inc. (US)
Human Life Foundation, Inc. (Washington) (US)
Human Relations Area Files, Inc. (US)
Human Resources Research Organization (US)
Human Rights for Women, Inc. (US)
Human Sciences Press (US)
Human Sciences Research Council (SA)
Human Sciences Research Council. Institute for
Historical Research (SA)
Human Sciences Research Council. Institute of
Manpower Research (SA)
Human Service Press (US)
Humana Press, Inc. (US)
Humane Education Society (UK)
Humane Society of the United States (US)
Humanistisch Verbond (NE)
Humanistische Stichting Socrates (NE)
Humanistische Union e.V. (GW)
Verlag Humanitas (GW)
Humanite Rouge (FR)
Humanities Association of Canada (CN)
Humanities Press, Inc. (US)
Humanities Research Council of Canada (CN)
Humanity Foundation (CN)
Humberside (UK)
Humboldt State University. Department of Sociology
(US)
Humboldt-Universitaet zu Berlin (GE)
Humboldt-Universitaet zu Berlin. Institut fuer
Mathematische Logik (GE)
Humboldt-Universitaet zu Berlin. Museum fuer
Naturkunde (GE)
Humes Ltd. (AT)
Humor Exchange Network (US)
John Humphries (UK)
Hungara Esperanto Asocio (HU)
Hungarian Baptist Union of America (US)
Hungarian Central Technical Library and
Documentation Centre-Technoinform (HU)
Hungarian Lutheran Conference (AT)
Hungarian National Committee (US)
Hungarian P.E.N. Club (HU)
Hungarian Readers' Service Inc. (CN)
Hungarian Turul Society Inc. (CN)
Hungarian Word (US)
Hungarofilm (HU)
Hungary. Belkereskedelmi Miniszterium (HU)
Hungary. Egeszsegugyi Miniszterium (HU)
Hungary. Epitesugyi es Varosfejlesztesi Miniszterium
(HU)
Hungary. Koho- es Gepipari Miniszterium.
Ipargazdasagi, Szervezesi es Szamitastechnikai
Intezet (HU)
Hungary. Koho- es Gepipari Miniszterium.
Tudomanyos-Muszaki Tajekoztato Intezet (HU)
Hungary. Kozponti Statisztikai Hivatal (HU)
Hungary. Kulugymininszterium (HU)
Hungary. Mezogazdasagi es Elelmezesugyi
Miniszterium (HU)

Hungary. Mezogazdasagi es Elelmezesugyi
Miniszterium. Informacios Kozpont (HU)
Hungary. Minisztertanacs (HU)
Hungary. Orszagos Idegenforgalmi Hivatal (HU)
Hungary. Orszagos Meresugyi Hivatal (HU)
Hungary. Orszagos Muemlekvedelmi Bizottsag (HU)
Hungary. Orszagos Szabadalmi Hivatal (HU)
Hungary. Orszagos Termeszetvedelmi Hivatal (HU)
Hungary. Orszagos Vizugyi Foigazgatosag (HU)
Hungary. Penzugyminiszterium (HU)
Hungary. Vizgazdalkodasi Tudomanyos Kutato Intezet
(HU)
Hal W. Hunt, Ed. & Pub. (US)
J. L. Hunt Publications Ltd. (CN)
Kendall Hunt Publishing Co. (US)
Edward Hunter, Ed. & Pub. (US)
Hunter & Barney Ltd. (UK)
Hunter College
see under City University of New York (US)
Hunter Mountain Ski Bowl (US)
Hunter Museum of Art (US)
Hunter Publishing Co. (US)
Hunter Valley Research Foundation (AT)
Hunterdon County Democrat Inc. (US)
Hunterdon County Historical Society (US)
Hunter's Horn, Inc. (US)
Hunting Dog Publishing Co., Inc. (US)
Hunting Group (UK)
Huntingdon College (US)
Huntingdonshire Local History Society (UK)
Huntington Library, Art Gallery and Botanical
Gardens (US)
Huntsville Association of Folk Musicians (US)
Huntsville Literary Association (US)
Huntsville-Madison County Historical Society (US)
Huon Newspaper Co. Pty. Ltd. (AT)
Hurad Ltd. (UK)
Huron Review (US)
Huron Road Hospital (US)
C. Hurst and Co. (UK)
Hurst House Inc. (US)
Hus og Hjem (DK)
Hushaallslaerarnas Riksfoerening (SW)
Husholdningslaereren (Vaeloese) (DK)
Husholdningslaererforeningen (DK)
Husmodersfoerbundet Hem och Samhaelle (SW)
Syed Hussain Publications (Sdn) Bhd. (MY)
Hustler (US)
Phillips Huston, Ed. & Pub. (US)
Hutchinson Educational Ltd. (UK)
Annelies Huter Verlag (GW)
Hutsul Association, Inc. (US)
Hvidvarebranchens Faellesraad (DK)
Hwa-Kang Publishing Co. (CH)
Hyacinths and Biscuits (US)
Hyborean Legion (US)
Hyde Chemical Publishing Co. Ltd. (UK)
Harry Hyde, Jr., Ed. & Pub. (US)
Hydro Products (US)
Hydro-Quebec (CN)
Hydrometeorologicky Ustav (CS)
Hydrometeorologicky Ustav, Bratislava (CS)
Neuer Hygiene Verlag in der Medizinisch-Literarische
Verlagsgesellschaft mbH (GW)
Hymn Society of America (US)
Hype (US)
Hyperion Poetry Journal (US)
Hyresgaesternas Foerlags AB (SW)
Hyresgaesternas Riksfoerbund (SW)
I A C I C O (IT)
I. A. C. P.
see Indian Association of Clinical Psychologists
(II)
I A E A
see International Atomic Energy Agency (UN)
I A G A
see International Association of Geomagnetism and
Aeronomy (JA)
I A R C
see International Agency for Research on Cancer
(UN)
I A S L I C
see Indian Association of Special Libraries and
Information Centres (II)
I- Am Publishing Corp. (US)
I B E
see Unesco. International Bureau of Education
(UN)
I B F Publications (UK)
I B M Deutschland GmbH (GW)
I B M Nederland N.V. (NE)
I B P A Electronic Publications (BE)
I B R D
see International Bank for Reconstruction and
Development (UN)
I C A-Foerlaget AB (SW)

I C A O
see International Civil Aviation Organization (UN)
I C E M
see Intergovernmental Committee for European
Migration (SZ)
I C F T U
see International Condeferation of Free Trade
Unions (II)
Edizioni I.C.I. (IT)
I C I C (Directory Publishers) Ltd. (NR)
I C I D
see International Commission on Irrigation and
Drainage (II)
I C I United States Inc. (US)
I C J
see International Court of Justice (UN)
I C Update Master (US)
I D A
see International Development Association (UN)
I. D. E.
see Institute of Developing Economies (JA)
I. D. E., Danmarks Institut for International
Udveksling
see Denmark. I. D. E., Danmarks Institut for
International Udveksling (DK)
I D O C-North America Inc. (US)
I D W Verlag GmbH (GW)
I E N-Europe S.A. (BE)
I E P Ediciones (PE)
I E R S
see Unesco. International Bureau of Education.
International Educational Reporting Service (UN)
I F C
see International Finance Corporation (UN)
I. F. C. E. (FR)
I F O Institut fuer Wirtschaftsforschung (GW)
I.F.P. (FR)
I H C Holland (NE)
I I E P
see International Institute for Educational Planning
(UN)
I I E S. Latin American Institute for Economic and
Social Planning
see International Institute for Labour Studies (UN)
I I F T
see Indian Institute of Foreign Trade (II)
I I L S
see International Institute for Labour Studies (UN)
I I S E E
see Japan. International Institute of Seismology and
Earthquake Engineering (JA)
I I T C
see Indian International Trade Center (II)
I I T Research Institute (US)
I K O'S Laeremidler A-S (NO)
I.L.A.R.I. (FR)
I L O
see International Labour Office (UN)
I.L.T.A.M. Corporation for Planning and Research
(IS)
I M C O
see Intergovernmental Maritime Consultative
Organization (UN)
I M F
see International Monetary Fund (UN)
I M S America, Ltd. (US)
I M S International Inc. (New York) (US)
I. M. Systems (US)
I N (AG)
Ediciones I N A P (MX)
Ediciones I N A P P (SP)
I N A S (IT)
I N C A-F I E J Research Association (IFRA) (GW)
I N C B
see International Narcotics Control Board (UN)
I N F A Publications (II)
I N F O R Journal (CN)
I M I S
see International Atomic Energy Agency.
International Nuclear Information System (UN)
I. N. L. Print Ltd. (NZ)
I N R O, Inc, (International Naval Research
Organization) (US)
I.N.R.S (FR)
I N S D O C
see Indian National Scientific Documentation
Centre (II)
I O L
see Institute of Librarians (II)
I O S H
see International Labour Office. International
Occupational Safety and Health Information Centre
(UN)
I P A G
see Electronics Commission (Information, Planning
and Analysis Group) (II)
I.P.A.G. (IT)
I P C Building and Contract Journals Ltd. (UK)

I P C Business Press (Australia) Pty. Ltd.  (AT)
I P C Business Press Information Services Ltd.  (UK)
I P C Business Press Ltd.  (UK)
I P C Consumer Industries Press Ltd.  (UK)
I P C Electrical-Electronic Press Ltd.  (UK)
I P C Industrial Press Ltd.  (UK)
I P C Magazines Ltd.  (UK)
I P C Newspapers Ltd.  (UK)
I P C Science and Technology Press Ltd.  (UK)
I P C Specialist & Professional Press Ltd.  (UK)
I P C Transport Press Ltd.  (UK)
I.P.E.C.  (FR)
I P P J
    see Nagoya University. Institute of Plasma Physics
    (JA)
I P S S
    see Institute of Political and Social Studies  (II)
I. R. C.
    see Indian Roads Congress  (II)
I R C A
    see International Railway Congress Association
    (BE)
I R F E D  (FR)
I. S. E. Publications Ltd.  (UK)
Ediciones I S L A  (BO)
I. S. P. of Canada  (CN)
I S P T Journal of Research  (II)
I T A - Uffici Informazioni Specializzati  (IT)
I T E C Editrice  (IT)
I. T. F. Regional Office  (PE)
I T U
    see International Telecommunication Union  (UN)
Iade Argentina S.A.  (AG)
Ian Buchan Fell Research Project on Housing  (AT)
Ibadan Renaissance Society  (NR)
Ibadan University Geographical Society  (NR)
Ibadan University Library
    see University of Ibadan. Library  (NR)
Ibadan University Press  (NR)
Ibaraki Daigaku
    see Ibaraki University  (JA)
Ibaraki University. Faculty of Science  (JA)
Ibarske Novosti, Novinsko Izdavacka i Radio
    Ustanova  (YU)
Iberflora  (SP)
Iberica Europea de Ediciones, S.A.  (SP)
Ibero-American Bureau of Education  (SP)
Ibero-Amerikanisches Institut  (GW)
Ibero-Amerikanisches Institut Preussischer Kulturbesitz
    Berlin  (GW)
Ibid, Inc.  (US)
Ice Cream Alliance  (UK)
Iceland. Hagstofa Islands  (IC)
Iceland. Statistical Bureau
    see Iceland. Hagstofa Islands  (IC)
Icelandic Canadian Club  (CN)
Icelandic Natural History Society
    see Islenzka Natturufraedifelag  (IC)
Icelandic Nurses' Association
    see Hjukrunarfelags Islands  (IC)
Icelandic Scientific Society
    see Visindafelag Islendinga  (IC)
Ichthyological Society of Japan  (JA)
Ichthyophile  (IS)
Ichthys-Verlag  (GW)
Ichud Habonim  (IS)
Ichud Habonim S.A.  (SA)
Ichud Ha'kvutzot Ve'hakibbutzim. Youth Division
    (IS)
Ici-Paris  (FR)
ICOMOS
    see International Council of Monuments and Sites
    (BE)
Iconoclast  (US)
Iconolatre Publications  (UK)
Iconomatrix  (CN)
Idaho. Bureau of Mines and Geology  (US)
Idaho. Department of Agriculture  (US)
Idaho. Department of Education  (US)
Idaho. Department of Employment  (US)
Idaho. Department of Fish and Game  (US)
Idaho. Department of Health and Welfare. Bureau of
    Research and Statistics  (US)
Idaho. Department of Labor and Industrial Services
    (US)
Idaho. Department of Parks and Recreation  (US)
Idaho. Department of Social and Rehabilitation
    Services  (US)
Idaho. Department of Water Resources  (US)
Idaho. Division of Budget, Policy Planning &
    Coordination  (US)
Idaho. Division of Tourism and Industrial
    Development  (US)
Idaho. Division of Veterans' Services  (US)
Idaho. Law Enforcement Planning Commission  (US)
Idaho. State Board for Vocational Education  (US)
Idaho. State Board of Education  (US)

Idaho. State Board of Nursing  (US)
Idaho. State Superintendent of Public Instruction
    (US)
Idaho. State Tax Commission  (US)
Idaho. Statistical Reporting Service. Crop and
    Livestock Reporting Service  (US)
Idaho. Traffic Safety Commission  (US)
Idaho. Transportation Department  (US)
Idaho Cattlemen's Association  (US)
Idaho Education Association  (US)
Idaho Heritage  (US)
Idaho Library Association. Publications Committee
    (US)
Idaho Pea & Lentil Commission  (US)
Idaho Personnel & Guidance Association  (US)
Idaho Potato Commission  (US)
Idaho Retailers & Food Dealers Association  (US)
Idaho School Trustees Association  (US)
Idaho State Historical Society  (US)
Idaho State Nurses Association  (US)
Idaho State Pharmaceutical Association  (US)
Idaho State University. College of Liberal Arts  (US)
Idaho State University Museum  (US)
Idaho State University Press  (US)
Idaho Water Resources Research Institute  (US)
Idara-I-Farogh-I-Urdu  (II)
Idea Centro Studi Roma  (IT)
Idea Source Guide  (US)
Idea Treasury, Inc.  (US)
Ideal  (US)
Ideal Companion  (NR)
Ideal Publishing Corp.  (US)
Ideals Publishing Corp.  (US)
Ideas  (HO)
Ideas  (US)
Ideas Concretas.  (VE)
Idees pour Tous  (FR)
Idees-Service  (FR)
Casa Editrice Idelson  (IT)
Ideologia y Sociedad  (CK)
Ideos, Inc.  (US)
Wydawnictwo Idisz Buch  (PL)
Idlewilde International Publishing Ltd.  (CN)
IDOCET
    see International Documentary Centre for
    Electronic Technology  (BE)
Ifjusagi Lapkiado Vallalat  (HU)
IG-TNO Research Institute for Environmental
    Hygiene  (NE)
IGA Iberica  (SP)
Igaku Kenkyusho
    see University of Tokyo. Institute of Medical
    Science  (JA)
Igaku no Sekaisha  (JA)
Igaku Shoin Ltd.  (JA)
Igbo Philosophical Association  (NR)
Igitur Revista Literaria  (AG)
Iglesia Adventista del Septima Dia  (AG)
Iglesia Evangelica del Rio de la Plata  (AG)
Iglesia Evangelica Dominicana  (DR)
Iglesia Metodista de Mexico. Secretaria de Educacion
    Cristiana  (MX)
Iglesia Metodista el Mesias  (MX)
Iglesia y Sociedad en America Latina  (UY)
Igman Pty. Ltd.  (AT)
Karl Ihl und Co. KG  (GW)
Ikatan Akuntan Indonesia  (IO)
Ikatan Hakim Indonesia. Tjabang Semarang  (IO)
Ikhwanul Muslimoon Inc.  (US)
Ikon Publications  (SA)
Ileostomy Association of Great Britain & Ireland
    (UK)
Ilford Ltd.  (UK)
Iliff School of Theology  (US)
Illiana Genealogical & Historical Society  (US)
Illinois. Administrative Office of Illinois Courts  (US)
Illinois. Board of Higher Education  (US)
Illinois. Bureau of Employment Security. Research and
    Statistics Section  (US)
Illinois. Cities and Villages Municipal Problems
    Commission  (US)
Illinois. Community College Board  (US)
Illinois. Department of Business and Economic
    Development  (US)
Illinois. Department of Children and Family Services.
    Office of Community Relations  (US)
Illinois. Department of Conservation  (US)
Illinois. Department of Corrections. Division of
    Research and Long Range Planning  (US)
Illinois. Department of Insurance  (US)
Illinois. Department of Mental Health and
    Developmental Disabilities  (US)
Illinois. Department of Mental Health and
    Developmental Disabilities. Drug Abuse Program
    (US)
Illinois. Department of Public Aid  (US)
Illinois. Department of Public Health  (US)
Illinois. Department of Public Instruction  (US)

Illinois. Department of Public Instruction. Publications
    and Library Resources Section  (US)
Illinois. Department of Transportation  (US)
Illinois. Department of Transportation. Division of
    Water Resource Management  (US)
Illinois. Division of Fire Prevention  (US)
Illinois. Division of Vocational and Technical
    Education  (US)
Illinois. Energy Resources Commission  (US)
Illinois. Environmental Protection Agency  (US)
Illinois. Environmental Protection Agency. Division of
    Air Pollution Control  (US)
Illinois. Environmental Protection Agency. Operator
    Certification Section  (US)
Illinois. Fire Protection Personnel Standards and
    Education Commission  (US)
Illinois. Housing Development Authority  (US)
Illinois. Judicial Inquiry Board  (US)
Illinois. Law Enforcement Commission  (US)
Illinois. Legislative Investigating Commission  (US)
Illinois. Office of Education  (US)
Illinois. Office of Education. Migrant Education
    Section  (US)
Illinois. Secretary of State  (US)
Illinois. State Archives  (US)
Illinois. State Board of Investment  (US)
Illinois. State Geological Survey  (US)
Illinois. State Library  (US)
Illinois Academy of Family Physicians  (US)
Illinois Association for Advancement of Archaeology
    (US)
Illinois Association for Health, Physical Education and
    Recreation  (US)
Illinois Association for Supervision and Correction
    (US)
Illinois Association of Plumbing-Heating-Cooling
    Contractors  (US)
Illinois Association of School Boards  (US)
Illinois Association of School Librarians  (US)
Illinois Association of Teachers of English  (US)
Illinois Audubon Society  (US)
Illinois Bankers Association  (US)
Illinois Baptist State Assocation  (US)
Illinois Bell Telephone Co.  (US)
Illinois Beverage Media, Inc.  (US)
Illinois Central Gulf Railroad  (US)
Illinois Contractors Trade Directory, Inc.  (US)
Illinois Country Opry Inc.  (US)
Illinois Dental Hygienists Association  (US)
Illinois Education Association  (US)
Illinois Federation of the Blind  (US)
Illinois Geographical Society  (US)
Illinois Handcrafts Directory  (US)
Illinois Horticultural Experiment Station  (US)
Illinois Institute for Environmental Quality  (US)
Illinois Institute of Technology  (US)
Illinois Institute of Technology. Chicago-Kent College
    of Law  (US)
Illinois Institute of Technology. Department of
    Electrical Engineering  (US)
Illinois Institute of Technology. National Conference
    on Power Transmission  (US)
Illinois Issues  (US)
Illinois Junior College Music Association  (US)
Illinois Labor History Society  (US)
Illinois Landscape Contractors Association  (US)
Illinois Library Association  (US)
Illinois Lumber and Material Dealers Association
    (US)
Illinois Lung Association  (US)
Illinois Magazine  (US)
Illinois Metro East Industrial Development
    Corporation  (US)
Illinois Mining Institute  (US)
Illinois Municipal League  (US)
Illinois Music Educators Association  (US)
Illinois Natural History Survey  (US)
Illinois Nurses Association  (US)
Illinois Nurses Association. Chicago District  (US)
Illinois Optometric Association  (US)
Illinois Park & Recreation Society  (US)
Illinois Petroleum Marketers Association  (US)
Illinois Police Association  (US)
Illinois Press Association  (US)
Illinois Regional Library Council  (US)
Illinois Society for Medical Research  (US)
Illinois Society of Professional Engineers  (US)
Illinois State Academy of Sciences  (US)
Illinois State Bar Association  (US)
Illinois State Chamber of Commerce  (US)
Illinois State Dental Society  (US)
Illinois State Federation of Labor and Congress of
    Industrial Organizations  (US)
Illinois State Genealogical Society  (US)
Illinois State Historical Library  (US)
Illinois State Historical Society  (US)
Illinois State Medical Society  (US)
Illinois State Museum  (US)

Illinois State Poetry Society  (US)
Illinois State University  (US)
Illinois State University. Alumni Office  (US)
Illinois State University. Dept. of Educational
  Administration  (US)
Illinois State University. News and Publications
  Service  (US)
Illinois Trucking Associations  (US)
Illinois Wesleyan University  (US)
Illinois Wildlife Federation  (US)
Illovo Sugar Estates Ltd.  (SA)
Illuminating Engineering Institute of Japan  (JA)
Illuminating Engineering Society  (UK)
Illuminating Engineering Society  (US)
Illuminating Engineering Society of Australia  (AT)
Illumination of the Morning Star  (US)
Illustrated County Magazine Group Ltd.  (UK)
Illustrated Liverpool News  (UK)
Illustrated Speedway News  (US)
Illustrazione Pubblicitaria  (IT)
Illustrierte Rundschau der Gendarmerie  (AU)
Ilustre Colegio Provincial de Abogados de San
  Sebastian  (SP)
IMADOS (Institut Mantpulacnich, Dopravnich,
  Obalovych a Skladovacich Systemu)  (CS)
Editora Imagem Nova  (BL)
Images du Transport  (FR)
Imago Mundi Ltd.  (UK)
Imera Publishing Co.  (GR)
Immaculate Heart Missions  (US)
Immedia Ltd.  (UK)
Immedia Pte. Ltd.  (SI)
Immeuble Azarie  (LE)
Immeuble Chidiac  (LE)
Immigration Control Association  (AT)
Immigration History Society  (US)
Immunbiologische Informationen e.V.  (GW)
Imono Kenkyushitsu
  see Waseda University. Casting Research
  Laboratory  (JA)
Impact  (AT)
Impact  (UK)
Impact (Belgium)  (BE)
Impact Films Inc.  (US)
Impact Publications (Chicago)  (US)
Impact Publications (Estes Park)  (US)
Impact Publications Pvt. Ltd.  (II)
Impact Publishers, Inc.  (US)
Arthur J. Imparato Associates  (US)
Impart Publishers  (US)
Impegno Settanta  (IT)
Imperial Cancer Research Fund  (UK)
Imperial Chemical Industries Ltd. Plant Protection
  Division  (UK)
Imperial Embassy of Iran. Economic Section  (US)
Imperial Iran Academy of Philosophy  (IR)
Imperial Oil Ltd.  (CN)
Imperial Order Daughters of the Empire  (CN)
Imperial Society of Teachers of Dancing  (UK)
Imperial Tobacco Ltd.  (UK)
Imperial War Museum  (UK)
Impex India  (II)
Publicaciones Importantes S.A.  (MX)
Importers & Exporters Association of Taipei  (CH)
Editions de l' Impossible  (FR)
Imprendinvest Italiana s.r.l.  (IT)
Imprensa Nacional  (MH)
Imprensa Universitaria do Ceara  (BL)
L' Impresa Edizioni s.r.l.  (IT)
Impresa Generale Pubblicita  (IT)
Impresa Mossen Alcover  (SP)
Impresiones, S.A.  (MX)
Impresos y Ediciones, S.A.  (SP)
Imprimerie Catholique  (LE)
Imprimerie du Messager S.A.  (FR)
Imprimerie du Sud-Est  (FR)
Imprimerie Nationale  (FR)
Societe des Editions de l' Imprimerie Nouvelle  (FR)
Imprimerie Siciliano  (FR)
Impulse  (CN)
IMSWORLD Publications Ltd.  (UK)
Imunoloski Zavod  (YU)
In-Flight Publishing Co.  (US)
In Particular  (UK)
In Search  (NE)
Inbavan Tanah Air  (IO)
Incept  (UK)
Incidenza  (IT)
Income Tax Payers' Association of Ceylon  (CE)
Incomes Data Services Ltd.  (UK)
Incontri  (IT)
Incontro  (IT)
Incorporated Association of Architects & Surveyors
  (UK)
Incorporated Association of Architects and Surveyors.
  Fire Surveyors Section  (UK)
Incorporated Association of Organists  (UK)

Incorporated Association of Preparatory Schools
  (UK)
Incorporated British Institute of Certified Carpenters
  (UK)
Incorporated Council of Law Reporting for England
  and Wales  (UK)
Incorporated Council of Law Reporting for the State
  of Queensland  (AT)
Incorporated Law Society  (UK)
Incorporated Law Society of Sri Lanka  (CE)
Incorporated Practitioners in Radio & Electronics
  (UK)
Incorporated Society of Musicians  (UK)
Incorporated Society of Organ Builders  (UK)
Incorporated Society of Planters  (MY)
Incorporated Society of Valuers & Auctioneers  (UK)
Ind Coope Hotels (Allied Breweries Ltd.)  (UK)
Indcom Publications Ltd.  (UK)
Editions Indelec  (FR)
Independent Bankers Association of America  (US)
Independent Battery Manufacturers Association, Inc.
  (US)
Independent Board for Presbyterian Foreign Missions
  (US)
Independent Broadcasting Authority  (UK)
Independent Buyers Association Inc.  (US)
Independent College Funds of America  (US)
Independent Cultural Association  (SA)
Independent Educational Services  (US)
Independent Fundamental Churches of America  (US)
Independent Grocers Alliance  (US)
Independent Insurance Agents Association of
  California  (US)
Independent Insurance Agents Association of New
  York, Inc.  (US)
Independent Insurance Agents of America, Inc.  (US)
Independent Insurance Agents of Wisconsin  (US)
Independent-Journal Newspapers  (US)
Independent Lithuanian Printing Co. Ltd.  (CN)
Independent Magazines Ltd.  (UK)
Independent Newspapers  (RH)
Independent Newspapers Ltd.  (IE)
Independent Order of Foresters  (CN)
Independent Order of Odd Fellows  (UK)
Independent Order of Odd Fellows of Oklahoma
  (US)
Independent Order of Rechabites  (UK)
Independent Order of Svithiod  (US)
Independent Peruvian Association  (PE)
Independent Petroleum Association of America  (US)
Independent Petroleum Association of Canada  (CN)
Independent Press  (US)
Independent Schools Association Inc  (UK)
Independent Schools Association of the Central States
  (US)
Independent Schools Association of the Southwest
  (US)
Independent Schools Careers Organization  (UK)
Independent Survey Co. Ltd.  (CN)
Independent Television Publications Ltd.  (UK)
Index Inc.  (US)
Index to Australian Innovative Schools  (AT)
India. All India Radio  (II)
India. Archaeological Survey of India  (II)
India. Armed Forces Medical Services  (II)
India. Botanical Survey of India  (II)
India. Bureau of Public Enterprises
  see also India. Ministry of Finance  (II)
India. Bureau of Public Enterprises  (II)
India. Cardamom Board  (II)
India. Central Board of Irrigation and Power  (II)
India. Central Board of Revenue  (II)
India. Central Building Research Institute  (II)
India. Central Bureau of Investigation  (II)
India. Central Electrochemical Research Institute  (II)
India. Central Food Technological Research Institute
  (II)
India. Central Glass and Ceramic Research Institute
  (II)
India. Central Health Education Bureau  (II)
India. Central Leather Research Institute  (II)
India. Central Mechanical Engineering Research
  Institute  (II)
India. Central Mining Research Station  (II)
India. Central Road Research Institute  (II)
India. Central Salt and Marine Chemicals Research
  Institute  (II)
India. Central Scientific Instruments Organization
  (II)
India. Central Silk Board  (II)
India. Central Statistical Organization  (II)
India. Central Vigilance Commission  (II)
India. Coffee Board  (II)
India. Coir Board  (II)
India. Committee on Science and Technology  (II)
India. Council of Scientific and Industrial Research
  (II)

India. Department of Atomic Energy  (II)
India. Department of Commercial Intelligence and
  Statistics  (II)
India. Department of Company Affairs
  see also India. Ministry of Industrial Development
  (II)
India. Department of Company Affairs  (II)
India. Department of Culture  (II)
India. Department of Economic Affairs  (II)
India. Department of Family Planning  (II)
India. Department of Labour and Employment
  see India. Ministry of Labour  (II)
India. Department of Personnel and Administrative
  Reforms  (II)
India. Department of Power  (II)
India. Department of Publication  (II)
India. Department of Science and Technology  (II)
India. Department of Science and Technology.
  Botanical Survey of India
  see India. Botanical Survey of India  (II)
India. Department of Science and Technology. Khadi
  and Village Industries Commission
  see India. Khadi and Village Industries Commission
  (II)
India. Department of Space  (II)
India. Director of Military Training  (II)
India. Directorate General of Factory Advice and
  Labour Institutes  (II)
India. Directorate General of Health Services. Central
  Health Education Bureau
  see India. Central Health Education Bureau  (II)
India. Directorate General of Mines Safety  (II)
India. Directorate of Arecanut and Spices
  Development  (II)
India. Directorate of Cashew Nut Development  (II)
India. Directorate of Coconut Development  (II)
India. Directorate of Cotton Development  (II)
India. Directorate of Extension  (II)
India. Directorate of Inspection  (II)
India. Directorate of Jute Development  (II)
India. Directorate of Marketing and Inspection  (II)
India. Directorate of Oilseeds Development  (II)
India. Directorate of Sugarcane Development  (II)
India. Directorate of Tobacco Development  (II)
India. Finance Department  (II)
India. Forest Research Institute & Colleges  (II)
India. Forward Markets Commission  (II)
India. Geological Survey of India  (II)
India. Government of India Press  (II)
India. Indian Bureau of Mines  (II)
India. Khadi and Village Industries Commission  (II)
India. Labour Bureau
  see also India. Ministry of Labour  (II)
India. Labour Bureau  (II)
India. Meteorological Department  (II)
India. Ministry of Agriculture  (II)
India. Ministry of Agriculture and Irrigation.
  Department of Agriculture. Directorate of Arecanut
  and Spices Development
  see India. Directorate of Arecanut and Spices
  Development  (II)
India. Ministry of Agriculture and Irrigation.
  Department of Agriculture. Directorate of Oilseeds
  Development
  see India. Directorate of Oilseeds Development
  (II)
India. Ministry of Agriculture and Irrigation.
  Department of Agriculture. Directorate of Tobacco
  Development
  see India. Directorate of Tobacco Development
  (II)
India. Ministry of Agriculture and Irrigation.
  Department of Agriculture  (II)
India. Ministry of Agriculture and Irrigation. National
  Sugar Institute
  see India. National Sugar Institute  (II)
India. Ministry of Agriculture. Directorate of Coconut
  Development
  see India. Directorate of Coconut Development
  (II)
India. Ministry of Agriculture. Directorate of
  Extension
  see India. Directorate of Extension  (II)
India. Ministry of Agriculture. Directorate of
  Marketing and Inspection
  see India. Directorate of Marketing and Inspection
  (II)
India. Ministry of Agriculture. Directorate of Tobacco
  Development
  see India. Directorate of Tobacco Development
  (II)
India. Ministry of Commerce  (II)
India. Ministry of Commerce and Industry.
  Department of Commercial Intelligence and
  Statistics
  see India. Department of Commercial Intelligence
  and Statistics  (II)
India. Ministry of Commerce. Cardamom Board

Institut d'Etudes Semitiques  (FR)
Institut d'Etudes Slaves, Paris  (FR)
Institut d'Etudes Sociales de l'Etat a Bruxelles  (BE)
Institut d'Etudes Socialistes, Paris  (FR)
Institut d'Histoire de l'Amerique Francaise  (CN)
Institut d'Histoire du Christianisme
    see under Universite Libre de Bruxelles  (BE)
Institut d'Hygiene des Mines  (BE)
Institut d'Odontostomatologie  (FR)
Institut d'Optique. Centre de Documentation  (FR)
Institut de Botanique, Strasbourg  (FR)
Institut de Cancerologie et d'Immunogenetique  (FR)
Institut de Ceramique Francaise  (FR)
Institut de Documentation Scientifique  (SZ)
Institut de Droit International  (FR)
Institut de Formation et d'Etudes Psycho-
    Sociologiques et Pedagogiques  (FR)
Institut de France  (FR)
Institut de France. Academie des Inscriptions et
    Belles-Lettres
    see Academie des Inscriptions et Belles-Lettres
    (FR)
Institut de France. Academie des Sciences
    see Academie des Sciences  (FR)
Institut de France. Academie Francaise
    see Academie Francaise  (FR)
Institut de Geographie Alpine  (FR)
Institut de Geographie, Paris. Bibliotheque  (FR)
Institut de Gestion de Portefeuille. Department du
    Portefeuille  (ZR)
Institut de la Communaute Europeenne pour les
    Etudes Universitaires
    see European Community Institute for University
    Studies  (BE)
Institut de Linguistique de Louvain  (BE)
Institut de Litterature et de Techniques Artistiques de
    Masse  (FR)
Institut de Mathematiques  (SZ)
Institut de Medecine Legale et de Medecine Sociale
    (FR)
Institut de Medecine Tropicale  (FR)
Institut de Pastorale  (CN)
Institut de Pharmacie A. Gilkinet
    see Universite de Liege. Institut de Pharmacie
    (BE)
Institut de Philosophie de Louvain  (BE)
Institut de Promotion Internationale  (FR)
Institut de Recherche en Informatique et Automatique
    (FR)
Institut de Recherche et d'Histoire des Textes, Paris
    (FR)
Institut de Recherches Agronomiques. Laboratoire
    Regional Veterinaire  (LE)
Institut de Recherches Agronomiques Tropicales et des
    Cultures Vivrieres  (FR)
Institut de Recherches Appliquees du Dahomey
    (DM)
Institut de Recherches de l'Europe Centrale  (BE)
Institut de Recherches du Coton et des Textiles
    Exotiques  (FR)
Institut de Recherches Economiques et Sociale
    see under Universite Nationale du Zaire, Kinshasa
    (ZR)
Institut de Recherches en Economie de la Production
    (FR)
Institut de Recherches pour les Huiles et Oleagineux
    (FR)
Institut de Recherches Psychologiques, Inc.  (CN)
Institut de Recherches sur les Fruits et Agrumes
    (IRFA)  (FR)
Institut de Science Financiere  (FR)
Institut de Sciences Mathematiques et Economiques
    Appliquees, Paris  (FR)
Institut de Soudure  (FR)
Institut der Deutschen Wirtschaft  (GW)
Institut der Wirtschaftspruefer in Deutschland e.V.
    (GW)
Institut des Actuaires Francais  (FR)
Institut des Assureurs-Vie Agrees du Canada  (CN)
Institut des Belles Lettres Arabes  (TI)
Institut des Corps Gras (ITERG)  (FR)
Institut des Etudes Augustiniennes  (FR)
Institut des Etudes Francaises  (US)
Institut des Etudes Pedagogiques  (AA)
Institut des Hautes Etudes de l'Amerique Latine
    (FR)
Institut des Hautes Etudes Scientifiques, Paris  (FR)
Institut des Industries de Fermentation  (BE)
Institut des Peches Maritimes  (MR)
Institut des Sciences Humaines  (ML)
Institut des Sciences Humaines Appliquees, Paris
    (FR)
Institut des Sciences Juridiques, Politiques et
    Administratives. Faculte de Droit et des Sciences
    Economiques d'Alger  (AE)
Institut Drustvenih Nauka u Beogradu. Centar za
    Demografska Istrazivanja  (YU)
Institut du Transport Aerien, Paris  (FR)

Institut du Verre  (FR)
Institut Economique Agricole  (BE)
Institut Economique et Social des Classes Moyennes
    (BE)
Institut Eksperimentalnoi Meteorologii  (UR)
Institut Emile Vandervelde  (BE)
Institut Europeen d'Enseignement Culturel et
    Professionnel  (FR)
Institut "Finanzen und Steuern." e.V.  (GW)
Institut Fondamental d'Afrique Noire  (SG)
Institut Fondamental d'Afrique Noire. Centre de Cote-
    d'Ivoire  (IV)
Institut Fondamental d'Afrique Noire. Centre de
    Mauritanie  (SG)
Institut Fondamental d'Afrique Noire. Centre de Saint-
    Louis de Senegal  (SG)
Institut Fondamental d'Afrique Noire. Centre du Niger
    (NG)
Institut for Dansk Dialektforskning  (DK)
Institut Francais d'Archeologie d'Istanbul  (FR)
Institut Francais d'Archeologie de Beyrouth  (FR)
Institut Francais d'Archeologie Orientale  (UA)
Institut Francais d'Etude et d'Information Culturelles
    et Techniques  (FR)
Institut Francais d'Etudes Andines  (PE)
Institut Francais d'Etudes Strategiques  (FR)
Institut Francais d'Histoire Sociale  (FR)
Institut Francais d'Indologie  (II)
Institut Francais de la Cooperation  (FR)
Institut Francais de Navigation  (FR)
Institut Francais de Pondichery  (II)
Institut Francais des Combustibles et de l'Energie
    (FR)
Institut Francais des Experts Comptables  (FR)
Institut Francais du Cafe, du Cacao et Autres Plantes
    Stimulantes  (FR)
Institut Francais du Petrole  (FR)
Institut Franco-Iranien. Departement d'Iranologie
    (FR)
Institut fuer Afrika-Kunde  (GW)
Institut fuer Allgemeine Botanik und Botanischer
    Garten  (GW)
Institut fuer Angewandte Geodaesie  (GW)
Institut fuer Angewandte Sozial und
    Wirtschaftsforschung  (AU)
Institut fuer Asienkunde  (GW)
Institut fuer Auslandsbeziehungen, Stuttgart  (GW)
Institut fuer Bildungs- und Entwicklungsforschung
    (AU)
Institut fuer Binnenfischerei  (GE)
Institut fuer Bueroorganisation  (SZ)
Institut fuer Demoskopie, Allensbach  (GW)
Institut fuer den Wissenschaftlichen Film  (GW)
Institut fuer Deutsche Militaergeschichte  (GE)
Institut fuer Deutsche Nachkriegsgeschichte  (GW)
Institut fuer Deutsche Sprache  (GW)
Institut fuer Dokumentation und Information ueber
    Sozialmedizin und Oeffentliches Gesundheitswesen
    (GW)
Institut fuer Dokumentationswesen  (GW)
Institut fuer Ehe- und Familienwissenschaft  (SZ)
Institut fuer Energetik. Zentralstelle fuer Rationale
    Energieanwendung  (GE)
Institut fuer Europaeische Politik, Bonn  (GW)
Institut fuer Europaeisches und Internationales
    Wirtschaftsrecht  (GW)
Institut fuer Festkoerperforschung.
    Kernforschungsanlage Juelich  (GW)
Institut fuer Film- und Fernsehrecht  (GW)
Institut fuer Finanzwissenschaft und Steuerrecht
    (AU)
Institut fuer Forstwissenschaften  (GE)
Institut fuer Gesellschaftspolitik  (AU)
Institut fuer Gewerbeforschung  (AU)
Institut fuer Heilpaedagogik  (SZ)
Institut fuer Iberoamerika-Kunde  (GW)
Institut fuer Industrieforschung  (AU)
Institut fuer Internationale Beziehungen der DDR
    (GE)
Institut fuer Internationale Politik und Wirtschaft
    (GE)
Institut fuer Internationale Schulbuchforschung  (GW)
Institut fuer Internationales Recht und Internationale
    Beziehungen  (SZ)
Institut fuer Interne Revision  (GW)
Institut fuer Kirchenrecht  (AU)
Institut fuer Kommunalwirtschaft  (GE)
Institut fuer Konstruktiven Ingenieurbau  (GW)
Institut fuer Kunst und Aesthetik  (GW)
Institut fuer Landwirtschaftliche Marktforschung
    Braunschweig  (GW)
Institut fuer Leichtbau und Oekonomische
    Verwendung von Werkstoffen  (GE)
Institut fuer Meeres Forschung, Bremerhaven  (GW)
Institut fuer Menschen- und Menschheitskunde
    (GW)
Institut fuer Museumswesen der Deutschen
    Demokratischen Republik  (GE)

Institut fuer Musikalische Volkskunde  (GW)
Institut fuer Oesterreichische Kunstforschung  (AU)
Institut fuer Oesterreichkunde  (AU)
Institut fuer Ostdeutsche Kirchen- und
    Kulturgeschichte  (GW)
Institut fuer Ostrecht, Munich  (GW)
Institut fuer Paedogogik
    see Unesco Institute for Education  (UN)
Institut fuer Pflanzenschutzforschung. Abteilung
    Taxonomie der Insekten  (GE)
Institut fuer Politologische Zeitfragen  (SZ)
Institut fuer Raumordnung  (GW)
Institut fuer Reaktorsicherheit der Technischen
    Ueberwachungs-Vereine  (GW)
Institut fuer Rundfunktechnik GmbH  (GW)
Institut fuer Schiffbau  (GE)
Institut fuer Seeverkehrswirtschaft Bremen  (GW)
Institut fuer Sozialpolitik und Sozialreform (Dr. Karl
    Kummer-Institut)  (AU)
Institut fuer Staedtebau, Raumplanung und
    Raumordnung  (GW)
Institut fuer Technologie Kultureller Einrichtungen
    (GE)
Institut fuer Voelkerkunde  (AU)
Institut fuer Weiterbildung Mittlerer Medizinischer
    Fachkraefte  (GE)
Institut fuer Weltanschauliche Fragen  (SZ)
Institut fuer Weltwirtschaft, Kiel  (GW)
Institut fuer Wissenschaft und Kunst  (AU)
Institut fuer Wissenschaftliche Information aus der
    Sowjetunion  (GW)
Institut fuer Wissenschaftliche Zusammenarbeit
    (GW)
Institut fuer Zeitgeschichte  (GW)
Institut Geographique du Zaire  (ZR)
Institut Geographique National. Service de la
    Documentation Geographique  (FR)
Institut Grand-Ducal de Luxembourg. Section de
    Linguistique, de Folklore et de Toponymie  (LU)
Institut Gustave Roussy  (FR)
Institut "Haus der Barmherzigkeit"  (AU)
Institut Hellenique de Droit International et Etranger
    see Hellenic Institute of International and Foreign
    Law  (GR)
Institut Henri Poincare
    see under Universite de Paris VI  (FR)
Institut Historique Augustinien  (BE)
Institut Historique Belge de Rome  (BE)
Institut Historique et Archeologique Neerlandais de
    Stamboull  (TU)
Institut Hygieny a Epidemiologie  (CS)
Institut International d'Administration Publique  (FR)
Institut International d'Etudes Sociales.
    see International Institute for Labour Studies  (UN)
Institut International d'Etudes sur l'Education
    see International Institute for Studies on Education
    (BE)
Institut International de Psychagogie et de
    Psychotherapie  (SZ)
Institut International de Recherches Graphologiques
    (FR)
Institut International pour les Methodes
    d'Alphabetisation des Adultes
    see International Institute for Adult Literacy
    Methods  (IR)
Institut J. Solomides  (FR)
Institut Jugend Film Fernsehen e.V.  (GW)
Institut Jules Destree pour la Defense et l'Illustration
    de la Wallonie  (BE)
Institut Jupiter
Institut Keguruan dan Ilmu Pendidikan  (IO)
Institut Konsumenten- und Sozialanalysen  (SZ)
Institut Litteraire  (FR)
Institut Maurice Thorez  (FR)
Institut Mekhanobr  (UR)
Institut Metaphysique International  (FR)
Institut Michael Pacha. Laboratoire Maritime de
    Physiologie  (FR)
Institut National Algerien du Commerce Exterieur
    see Algeria. Institut National Algerien du
    Commerce Exterieur  (AE)
Institut National d'Etude du Travail et d'Orientation
    Professionnelle  (FR)
Institut National de Bois  (FR)
Institut National de la Recherche Agronomique de
    Tunisie  (TI)
Institut National de Preparation Professionnelle  (ZR)
Institut National des Appellations d'Origine des Vins
    et Eaux-de-Vie.  (FR)
Institut National des Industries Extractives  (BE)
Institut National des Langues et Civilisations
    Orientales  (FR)
Institut National des Sciences Humaines  (CD)
Institut National Genevois  (SZ)
Institut National pour l'Etude et la Recherche
    Agronomique  (ZR)

Institut Oceanographique (FR)
Institut Panafricain pour le Developpement
  see Pan-African Institute for Development (CM)
Institut Pasteur (FR)
Institut Pasteur d'Algerie (AE)
Institut Pasteur de la Guyane Francaise (FG)
Institut Pasteur de Lille (FR)
Institut Pasteur de Lyon (FR)
Institut Pasteur de Madagascar (MG)
Institut Pasteur de Tunis (TI)
Institut Pasteur Hellenique (GR)
Institut po Voena Istoriia (BU)
Institut pour l'Encouragement de la Recherche
  Scientifique dans l'Industrie et l'Agriculture. Centre
  d'Ecologie Forestiere et Rurale
  see Centre d'Ecologie Forestiere et Rurale (BE)
Institut pour la Recherche Scientifique en Afrique
  Centrale (ZR)
Institut pre Dalsie Vzdelavanie Lekarov a Farmaceutov
  (CS)
Institut Protestant de Theologie (FR)
Institut Prumysloveho Designu (CS)
Institut Royal des Relations Internationales (BE)
Institut Royal du Patrimoine Artistique (BE)
Institut Royal Meteorologique de Belgique
  see Belgium. Institut Royal Meteorologique. (BE)
Institut Scientifique et Technique des Peches
  Maritimes (FR)
Institut Suisse de Recherche sur les Pays de l'Est
  see Schweizerisches Ost-Institut (SZ)
Institut Suisse de Rome (IT)
Institut Superieur de l'Etat de Traducteurs et
  d'Interpretes (BE)
Institut Superieur des Carrieres Artistiques (FR)
Institut Technique de l'Aviculture (ITAVI) (FR)
Institut Technique de l'Elevage Ovin et Caprin (FR)
Institut Technique de la Vigne et du Vin (FR)
Institut Technique des Administrations Publiques
  (FR)
Institut Technique du Batiment et des Travaux Publics.
  Annales (FR)
Institut Teknologi Bandung. Ikatan Mahasiswa
  Arsitektur "Gunadharma" (IO)
Institut Textile de France (FR)
Institut Togolais des Sciences Humaines (TG)
Institut und Museum fuer Geschichte der Stadt
  Dresden (GE)
Institut Universitaire de Hautes Etudes Internationales
  see under Universite de Geneve (SZ)
Institut Universitaire de Hautes Etudes Internationales.
  Asia Documentation and Research Center
  see Universite de Geneve. Asia Documentation and
  Research Center (SZ)
Institut Vodnogo Transporta, Leningrad (UR)
Institut y Solomides (FR)
Institut za Arhitekturu i Urbanizam Srbije (YU)
Institut za Crkvenu Glazbu u Zagrebu (YU)
Institut za Dokumentaciju Zastite na Radu, Nis (YU)
Institut za Drvo, Zagreb (YU)
Institut za Film, Belgrade (YU)
Institut za Folklor, Skopje (YU)
Institut za Geoloska Istrazivanja u Zagrebu (YU)
Institut za Historiju Radnickog Pokreta Hrvatske
  (YU)
Institut za Istrazivanje i Razvoj Obrazovanja (YU)
Institut za Kriminoloska i Socioloska Istrazivanja
  (YU)
Institut za Makedonski Jazik, Skopje (YU)
Institut za Medicinska Istrazivanja i Medicinu Rada
  (YU)
Institut za Medjunarodni Radnicki Pokret (YU)
Institut za Medjunarodnu Politiku i Privredu u
  Beogradu (YU)
Institut za Nacionalna Istorija, Skopje (YU)
Institut za Naucno-Tehnicku Dokumentaciju i
  Informacije (YU)
Institut za Nuklearne Nauke "Boris Kidric" (YU)
Institut za Oceanografiju i Ribarstvo (YU)
Institut za Organizaciju i Razvoj, Belgrade (YU)
Institut za Psihomedicinu Saobracaja (YU)
Institut za Rehabilitaciju, Belgrade (YU)
Institut za Sigurnost, Zagreb (YU)
Institut za Spoljnu Trgovinu (YU)
Institut za Srpskohrvatski Jezik (YU)
Institut za Strucno Usavrsavanje i Specijalizaciju
  Zdrastvenih Radnika Srbije (YU)
Institut za Uporedno Pravo, Belgrade (YU)
Institut za Vodoprivredu "Jaroslav Cerni" (YU)
Institut za Zastitu Majki i Djece (YU)
Institute Chartered Life Underwriters (CN)
Institute Danois des Echanges
  see Denmark. I.D.E., Danmarks Institut for
  International Udveksling (DK)
Institute for Advanced Philosophical Research (US)
Institute for Advanced Studies, Vienna (AU)
Institute for African Studies (UK)
Institute for Agricultural Research
  see under Tohoku University (JA)

Institute for American Democracy (US)
Institute for Application of Computing Technique in
  Control (CS)
Institute for Atomic Energy
  see under Rikkyo University (JA)
Institute for Atomic Sciences in Agriculture (NE)
Institute for Balkan Studies (GR)
Institute for Business Planning, Inc. (US)
Institute for Byzantine and Modern Greek Studies
  (US)
Institute for Cancer Research
  see under Osaka University (JA)
Institute for Chemical Research
  see under Kyoto University (JA)
Institute for Clay Technology (UK)
Institute for Clinical Science (US)
Institute for Communication Research (KO)
Institute for Comparative Studies of Culture (JA)
Institute for Consumer and Social Research
  see Institut Konsumenten- und Sozialanalysen (SZ)
Institute for Continuing Professional Development,
  Inc. (US)
Institute for Cross-Cultural Research (US)
Institute for Defence Studies and Analyses (II)
Institute for Defense Analyses (US)
Institute for Development of Educational Activities,
  Inc. (US)
Institute for Early Iberian Christian Studies (US)
Institute for Economic and Financial Research.
  see under American Classical College (US)
Institute for Economic and Social Research, Education
  and Information (IO)
Institute for Economic Research
  see under Shiga University (JA)
Institute for Education
  see Unesco Institute for Education (UN)
Institute for Educational Finance (US)
Institute for Electoral Studies (II)
Institute for Fermentation (JA)
Institute for Financial Management and Research,
  Madras (II)
Institute for Fiscal Studies (UK)
Institute for Futures Research and Education (IT)
Institute for German-American Studies (US)
Institute for Graduate Dentists. Alumni Association
  (US)
Institute for Historical Research
  see under Human Sciences Research Council (SA)
Institute for Humane Studies (US)
Institute for Industrial Education (SA)
Institute for Industrial Research and Standards (IE)
Institute for Inter-American Legal Studies (US)
Institute for International Research (UK)
Institute for International Research Ltd. (US)
Institute for International Sociological Research
  (GW)
Institute for International Sociological Research (IS)
Institute for Invention and Innovation, Inc. (US)
Institute for Land and Water Management Research
  see Instituut voor Cultuurtechniek en
  Waterhuishouding (NE)
Institute for Laser Documentation (US)
Institute for Local Self Reliance (US)
Institute for Manpower Research
  see under Human Sciences Research Council (SA)
Institute for Marine Environmental Research (UK)
Institute for Medical and Dental Engineering
  see under Tokyo Medical and Dental University
  (JA)
Institute for Migration (FI)
Institute for Monetary Research (US)
Institute for New Communications, Inc. (US)
Institute for Nuclear Study
  see under University of Tokyo (JA)
Institute for Optical Research
  see under Tokyo Kyoiku University (JA)
Institute for Palestine Studies (LE)
Institute for Petroleum Research and Geophysics (IS)
Institute for Phytopathological Research
  see Instituut voor Plantenziektenkundig Onderzoek
  (NE)
Institute for Profit Planning Inc. (US)
Institute for Protection of Mothers and New Born
  (IR)
Institute for Protein Research
  see under Osaka University (JA)
Institute for Psychoanalysis (US)
Institute for Rational Living (US)
Institute for Research and Planning in Science and
  Education. Iranian Documentation Centre (IR)
Institute for Research and Planning in Science and
  Education. Tehran Book Processing Centre (IR)
Institute for Research on Land and Water Resources
  (US)
Institute for Research on Poverty
  see under University of Wisconsin-Madison (US)
Institute for Responsive Education (US)
Institute for Science of Labour (JA)

Institute for Scientific Co-Operation (GW)
Institute for Scientific Information (US)
Institute for Social Sciences and Humanity
  see under Tokyo Metropolitan University (JA)
Institute for Socioeconomic Studies (US)
Institute for Solid State Physics
  see under University of Tokyo (JA)
Institute for Southern Studies (US)
Institute for Studies in American Music (US)
Institute for the Certification of Computer
  Professionals (US)
Institute for the Certification of Engineering
  Technicians (US)
Institute for the Comparative Study of Political
  Systems (US)
Institute for the Comprehensive Study of Lotus Sutra
  see under Rissho University (JA)
Institute for the Development of Indian Law (US)
Institute for the History of Christianity
  see Universite Libre de Bruxelles. Institut d'Histoire
  du Christianisme (BE)
Institute for the Intellectual Development of Children
  and Young Adults (IR)
Institute for the Study and Treatment of Delinquency
  (UK)
Institute for the Study of Chinese Communist
  Problems (CH)
Institute for the Study of Christianity and Culture
  see under International Christian University (JA)
Institute for the Study of Conflict (UK)
Institute for the Study of Drug Addiction (US)
Institute for the Study of Drug Dependence (UK)
Institute for the Study of English in Africa
  see under Rhodes University (SA)
Institute for the Study of Human Issues (US)
Institute for the Study of Human Reproduction
  see under University of Santo Tomas (PH)
Institute for the Study of Man in Africa (SA)
Institute for the Study of Man Inc. (US)
Institute for the Study of Nineteenth Century Europe
  (US)
Institute for the Study of Nonviolence (US)
Institute for the Study of the USSR (GW)
Institute for the Translation of Hebrew Literature
  (IS)
Institute for Tropical Medicine
  see under Nagasaki University (JA)
Institute for Virus Research
  see under Kyoto University (JA)
Institute for Water and Air Pollution Research
  see Sweden. Institutet Foer Vatten- och
  Luftvaardsforskning (SW)
Institute for Workers Control (UK)
Institute of Accident Surgery (UK)
Institute of Acoustics (UK)
Institute of Actuaries (UK)
Institute of Actuaries of Australia and New Zealand
  (AT)
Institute of Administration & Commerce of South
  Africa (SA)
Institute of Administrative Accounting (UK)
Institute of Adult Education (TZ)
Institute of Advanced Legal Studies (UK)
Institute of Advanced Motorists (UK)
Institute of Advanced Studies of World Religions
  (US)
Institute of Advanced Thinking (US)
Institute of Afro-Asian and World Affairs (II)
Institute of Agricultural Economics (UK)
Institute of Agricultural Engineering (IS)
Institute of Agricultural Research (ET)
Institute of Amateur Cinematographers (US)
Institute of Andean Studies (US)
Institute of Animal Technicians (UK)
Institute of Applied Linguistics
  see Instituut voor Toegepaste Linguistiek (BE)
Institute of Applied Manpower Research (II)
Institute of Applied Metaphysics (CN)
Institute of Applied Microbiology
  see under University of Tokyo (JA)
Institute of Arbitrators (UK)
Institute of Army Education. Foreign Language
  Section (UK)
Institute of Association Executives (CN)
Institute of Atomic Energy
  see under Kyoto University (JA)
Institute of Australian Geographers (AT)
Institute of Australian Photography (AT)
Institute of Automotive Mechanical Engineers (Inc.)
  (AT)
Institute of Ayurvedic Studies and Research (II)
Institute of Bankers (PK)
Institute of Bankers (UK)
Institute of Bankers in Ireland (IE)
Institute of Bankers in Scotland (UK)
Institute of Bankers in South Africa (SA)
Institute of Baths Management (UK)
Institute of Biology (UK)

Institute of Biology. Committee on Biological Information   (UK)
Institute of Brewing   (UK)
Institute of British Carriage and Automobile Manufacturers   (UK)
Institute of British Foundrymen   (UK)
Institute of British Geographers   (UK)
Institute of Building   (UK)
Institute of Burial & Cremation Administration Inc   (UK)
Institute of Certified Ambulance Personnel   (UK)
Institute of Certified Public Accountants in Israel   (IS)
Institute of Certified Travel Agents   (US)
Institute of Chartered Accountants in Australia   (AT)
Institute of Chartered Accountants in England and Wales   (UK)
Institute of Chartered Accountants in Ireland   (IE)
Institute of Chartered Accountants of India   (II)
Institute of Chartered Accountants of Nigeria   (NR)
Institute of Chartered Accountants of Pakistan   (PK)
Institute of Chartered Accountants of Scotland   (UK)
Institute of Chartered Accountants of Sri Lanka   (CE)
Institute of Chartered Financial Analysts   (US)
Institute of Chartered Secretaries and Administrators. Australian Division   (AT)
Institute of Chartered Secretaries and Administrators. Canadian Division   (CN)
Institute of Chiropodists   (UK)
Institute of Civil Defence   (UK)
Institute of Club Managers and Secretaries Ltd.   (AT)
Institute of Commerce   (UK)
Institute of Commerical and Industrial Security Executives   (AT)
Institute of Commonwealth Studies   (UK)
Institute of Community Psychiatry and Mental Health   (II)
Institute of Company Secretaries of India.   (II)
Institute of Comparative Law in Japan
   see under Chuo University   (JA)
Institute of Constitutional and Parliamentary Studies   (II)
Institute of Constitutional Medicine
   see under Kumamoto University   (JA)
Institute of Consulting Engineers   (II)
Institute of Contemporary Arts   (UK)
Institute of Cost and Management Accountants   (UK)
Institute of Cost and Management Accountants of Pakistan   (PK)
Institute of Cost and Works Accountants of India   (II)
Institute of Craft Education   (UK)
Institute of Credit Management   (UK)
Institute of Criminology of Sri Lanka   (CE)
Institute of Data Processing   (UK)
Institute of Defence Management   (II)
Institute of Developing Economies   (JA)
Institute of Development Management   (TZ)
Institute of Directors   (UK)
Institute of Directors in Australia   (AT)
Institute of Directors, India   (II)
Institute of Directors. Manchester Branch   (UK)
Institute of Domestic Heating Engineers   (UK)
Institute of Early American History & Culture   (US)
Institute of Earth Science
   see under Kyoto University   (JA)
Institute of East Asian Studies   (KO)
Institute of Eastern Culture   (JA)
Institute of Economic Affairs   (UK)
Institute of Economic Democracy   (AT)
Institute of Economic Geography   (II)
Institute of Economic Growth, Delhi   (II)
Institute of Economic Research   (II)
Institute of Electric Rolling Stock   (JA)
Institute of Electrical and Electronics Engineers Inc.   (US)
Institute of Electrical and Electronics Engineers, Inc. Aerospace and Electronic Systems Society   (US)
Institute of Electrical and Electronics Engineers, Inc. Computer Society   (US)
Institute of Electrical and Electronics Engineers, Inc. Engineering Management Society   (US)
Institute of Electrical & Electronics Engineers, Inc. Philadelphia Section   (US)
Institute of Electrical and Electronics Engineers, Inc. San Francisco Section   (US)
Institute of Electrical and Electronics Engineers, Inc. United States Activities Committee   (US)
Institute of Electrical and Electronics Engineers. Seccion Mexico   (MX)
Institute of Electrical Engineers   (TU)
Institute of Electrical Engineers of Japan   (JA)
Institute of Electrical Inspectors   (AT)
Institute of Electrolysis   (UK)
Institute of Electronics and Communication Engineers of Japan   (JA)
Institute of Endemic Diseases   (IQ)
Institute of Energy Economics   (JA)

Institute of Engineers   (BG)
Institute of Engineers and Technicians   (UK)
Institute of Environmental Sciences   (US)
Institute of Estonian Language and Literature
   see Eesti Keele ja Kirjanduse Instituut   (SW)
Institute of European Studies   (US)
Institute of Export   (UK)
Institute of Export Development   (PH)
Institute of Factory Management   (UK)
Institute of Farm Income Research   (IS)
Institute of Field and Garden Crops   (IS)
Institute of Fisheries Management   (UK)
Institute of Food Science and Technology of the United Kingdom   (UK)
Institute of Food Technologists   (US)
Institute of Forest Genetics   (KO)
Institute of Foresters of Australia   (AT)
Institute of Foresters of Great Britain   (UK)
Institute of Freight Forwarders Ltd.   (UK)
Institute of Freshwater Research   (SW)
Institute of Fuel   (UK)
Institute of Fuel. British Flame Research Committee   (UK)
Institute of Fuel. Northern Ireland Section   (UK)
Institute of Gas Technology   (US)
Institute of General Semantics   (US)
Institute of Geology and Paleontology
   see under Tohoku University   (JA)
Institute of Groundsmanship   (UK)
Institute of Group Analysis   (UK)
Institute of Health and Tibbi Research. Hamdard National Foundation   (PK)
Institute of Health Education   (UK)
Institute of Health Service Administrators   (UK)
Institute of Heating & Air Conditioning Industries   (US)
Institute of Hematology   (II)
Institute of Heraldic and Genealogical Studies   (UK)
Institute of Historical Research   (UK)
Institute of Historical Studies   (II)
Institute of History of Medicine   (II)
Institute of Hospital Engineering   (UK)
Institute of Housing   (UK)
Institute of Human Study   (II)
Institute of Hygiene and Preventive Medicine   (PK)
Institute of In-Depth Evangelism   (CR)
Institute of Incorporated Photographers   (UK)
Institute of Indian Foundrymen   (II)
Institute of Industrial and Commercial Research
   see under Tokyo College of Economics   (JA)
Institute of Industrial and Labor Relations. College of Business and Public Administration   (US)
Institute of Industrial Engineers   (AT)
Institute of Industrial Health   (JA)
Institute of Industrial Launderers   (US)
Institute of Industrial Science
   see under University of Tokyo   (JA)
Institute of Information Scientists   (UK)
Institute of Instrumentation and Control, Australia. (I.I.C.A.)   (AT)
Institute of Insurance Research Co. Ltd.   (JA)
Institute of Internal Auditors, Inc.   (US)
Institute of International Education   (US)
Institute of International Relations   (CH)
Institute of International Studies   (US)
Institute of Islamic Culture   (PK)
Institute of Jamaica   (JM)
Institute of Jazz Studies   (US)
Institute of Jewish Affairs   (UK)
Institute of Jewish Studies   (UK)
Institute of Judicial Administration   (US)
Institute of Judicial Administration. Juvenile Justice Standards Project   (US)
Institute of Labor and Industrial Relations   (US)
Institute of Laboratory Animal Resources. Division of Prological Sciences-Assembly of Life Sciences   (US)
Institute of Law and Politics
   see under Kyushu University   (JA)
Institute of Legal Executives   (UK)
Institute of Librarians (I.O.L.)   (II)
Institute of Life Insurance   (US)
Institute of Linguistics, Zagreb   (YU)
Institute of Linguists   (UK)
Institute of Living   (US)
Institute of Local Government Administrators   (UK)
Institute of Local Government Studies   (UK)
Institute of Management   (IS)
Institute of Management Sciences   (US)
Institute of Manpower Studies   (UK)
Institute of Marine Engineers   (UK)
Institute of Marine Molecular Biology   (GR)
Institute of Marine Research
   see Finland. Merentutkimuslaitos   (FI)
Institute of Market Officers   (UK)
Institute of Marketing   (UK)
Institute of Marketing and Management   (II)
Institute of Materials Handling   (UK)

Institute of Maternal and Child Health   (PH)
Institute of Mathematical Sciences   (II)
Institute of Mathematical Statistics   (US)
Institute of Mathematics
   see under Rikkyo University   (JA)
Institute of Mathematics and its Applications   (UK)
Institute of Measurement and Control   (UK)
Institute of Mechanical Engineers   (UK)
Institute of Medical & Biological Illustration   (UK)
Institute of Medical and Veterinary Science   (AT)
Institute of Medical Laboratory Sciences   (UK)
Institute of Medical Laboratory Technology   (UK)
Institute of Medical Laboratory Technology of Nigeria   (NR)
Institute of Medical Science
   see under University of Tokyo   (JA)
Institute of Medical Sciences
   see under Banaras Hindu University   (II)
Institute of Medicine of Chicago   (US)
Institute of Medieval Canon Law   (US)
Institute of Mental Measurements   (US)
Institute of Metal Finishing   (UK)
Institute of Microbiology   (IT)
Institute of Mine Surveyors of South Africa   (SA)
Institute of Municipal Administration   (AT)
Institute of Municipal Administration. Queensland Division   (AT)
Institute of Municipal Assessors of Ontario   (CN)
Institute of Municipal Treasurers and Accountants South Africa   (SA)
Institute of Naval Medicine   (UK)
Institute of Navigation   (US)
Institute of New Communications   (US)
Institute of New Zealand Health Inspectors Inc.   (NZ)
Institute of Newspaper Controllers and Finance Officers, Inc.   (US)
Institute of Noise Control Engineering   (US)
Institute of Oceanographic Sciences   (UK)
Institute of Office Management (India)   (II)
Institute of Open Education   (US)
Institute of Operation Theatre Technicians   (UK)
Institute of Ophthalmology   (UK)
Institute of Outdoor Drama   (US)
Institute of Paper Chemistry   (US)
Institute of Papua and New Guinea Studies   (PP)
Institute of Park and Recreation Administration   (UK)
Institute of Park & Recreation Administration (Southern Africa)   (SA)
Institute of Pastoral Psychology   (US)
Institute of Patentees and Inventors   (UK)
Institute of Personnel Management   (UK)
Institute of Personnel Management (Australia)   (AT)
Institute of Petroleum   (UK)
Institute of Pharmacy Management International   (UK)
Institute of Philippine Culture
   see under Ateneo de Manila University   (PH)
Institute of Physical and Chemical Research   (JA)
Institute of Physics.   (UK)
Institute of Plasma Physics
   see under Nagoya University   (JA)
Institute of Plumbing   (UK)
Institute of Political and Social Studies   (II)
Institute of Polymer Industry, Inc.   (JA)
Institute of Population Problems
   see Japan. Institute of Population Problems   (JA)
Institute of Positive Education   (US)
Institute of Power Engineers   (CN)
Institute of Power Engineers, Toronto   (CN)
Institute of Practitioners in Work Study, Organization and Methods   (UK)
Institute of Printing   (UK)
Institute of Psycho-Analysis   (UK)
Institute of Psychology and Graphology   (II)
Institute of Psychophysical Research   (II)
Institute of Public Administration   (SJ)
Institute of Public Administration   (IE)
Institute of Public Administration, New York   (US)
Institute of Public Administration of Canada   (CN)
Institute of Public Affairs   (AT)
Institute of Public Enterprises   (II)
Institute of Public Health
   see Japan. Institute of Public Health   (JA)
Institute of Public Health   (SA)
Institute of Public Relations   (UK)
Institute of Purchasing   (SA)
Institute of Purchasing and Supply   (UK)
Institute of Purchasing and Supply Management   (AT)
Institute of Quality Assurance   (UK)
Institute of Quantity Surveyors   (UK)
Institute of Quarrying   (UK)
Institute of Race Relations   (UK)
Institute of Radiation Breeding
   see Japan. Institute of Radiation Breeding   (JA)
Institute of Rail Transport   (II)

Instituto de Estudios Sindicales, Sociales y
Cooperativos  (SP)
Instituto de Estudios Sobre Armas Antiguas  (SP)
Instituto de Estudios Tarraconenses Ramon Berenguer
IV  (SP)
Instituto de Estudos Avancados en Educacao  (BL)
Instituto de Farmacologia Espanola  (SP)
Instituto de Filologia Hispanica "Miguel de
Cervantes". Departamento de Dialectologia y
Tradiciones Populares  (SP)
Instituto de Filologia y Literaturas Hispanicas "Dr.
Amado Alonso"  (AG)
Instituto de Filosofia  (UY)
Instituto de Filosofia "Luis Vives"  (SP)
Instituto de Filosofia Practica  (AG)
Instituto de Fomento Pesquero  (CL)
Instituto de Genetica y Antropologia  (SP)
Instituto de Geografia Aplicada  (SP)
Instituto de Geografia e Historia Militar do Brazil.
Ministerio do Exercito  (BL)
Instituto de Geografia y Conservacion de Recursos
Naturales  (VE)
Instituto de Ginecologia  (BL)
Instituto de Higiene  (UY)
Instituto de Higiene e Medicina Tropical  (PO)
Instituto de Historia del Arte  (AG)
Instituto de Historia "Jeronimo Zurita"  (SP)
Instituto de Implantodontologia  (AG)
Instituto de Informacion y Documentacion en
Biomedicina  (SP)
Instituto de Informacion y Documentacion en Ciencia
y Tecnologia  (SP)
Instituto de Ingenieros de Minas de Chile  (CL)
Instituto de Ingenieros de Minas del Peru  (PE)
Instituto de Investigacao Agronomica de Angola
(AO)
Instituto de Investigacao Agronomica de Mocambique.
Centro de Documentacao Agraria  (MZ)
Instituto de Investigacao Cientifica de Angola.
Departamento de Documentacao e Informacao
(AO)
Instituto de Investigacao Cientifica de Mocambique.
Centro de Documentacao Cientifica  (MZ)
Instituto de Investigacao Veterinaria de Mocambique
(MZ)
Instituto de Investigacion Cultural para la Educacion
Popular  (BO)
Instituto de Investigacion de Recursos Naturales
(CL)
Instituto de Investigacion Operativa y Estadistica
(SP)
Instituto de Investigacion Textil y de Cooperacion
Industrial  (SP)
Instituto de Investigaciones de Historia del Derecho
(AG)
Instituto de Investigaciones Geologicas  (CL)
Instituto de Investigaciones Medicas  (ES)
Instituto de Investigaciones Sociales y Economicas
A.C.  (MX)
Instituto de Investigaciones Tecnologicas  (CK)
Instituto de Investigaciones Veterinarias  (VE)
Instituto de la Caza Fotografica y Ciencias de la
Naturaleza.  (SP)
Instituto de la Grasa y sus Derivados  (SP)
Instituto de la Opinion Publica  (SP)
Instituto de la Patagonia  (CL)
Instituto de Matematica  (AG)
Instituto de Matematica Beppo Levi  (AG)
Instituto de Matematica Pura e Aplicada  (BL)
Instituto de Materiales y Modelos Estructurales  (VE)
Instituto de Maternidad "Alberto Peralata Ramos".
Asociacion Medica  (AG)
Instituto de Medicina Tropical de Sao Paulo  (BL)
Instituto de Neurocirugia e Investigaciones Cerebrales
(CL)
Instituto de Neurologia  (UY)
Instituto de Nutricao  (BL)
Instituto de Nutricion de Centro America y Panama
see United Nations. Institute of Nutrition of Central
America and Panama  (UN)
Instituto de Optica "Daza de Valdes"  (SP)
Instituto de Organizacao Racional do Trabalho  (BL)
Instituto de Parasitologia, "Lopez-Neyra"  (SP)
Instituto de Pastoral Andina  (PE)
Instituto de Pedagogia  (SP)
Instituto de Pesquisa Agropecuaria do l'Este  (BL)
Instituto de Pesquisa Veterinarias Desiderio Finamor
(BL)
Instituto de Pesquisas e Experimentacao Agropecuarias
do Norte  (BL)
Instituto de Pesquisas e Experimentacao Agropecuarias
do Sul  (BL)
Instituto de Pesquisas Rodoviarias  (BL)
Instituto de Plastico y Caucho  (SP)
Instituto de Prehistoria y Arqueologia de la Diputacion
Provincial de Barcelona  (SP)

Instituto de Previdencia do Estado da Guanabara.
Servico de Relacoes Publicas  (BL)
Instituto de Previdencia e Assistencia dos Servidores
do Estado. Divisao de Relacoes Publicas  (BL)
Instituto de Prevision Social  (PY)
Instituto de Publicaciones y Estadisticas S.A.  (AG)
Instituto de Resseguros do Brasil. Assessoria de
Relacoes Publicas  (BL)
Instituto de Sociologia Aplicada  (SP)
Instituto de Sociologia. Facultad de Ciencias Sociales
(CK)
Instituto de Sociologia y Desarrollo del Area Iberica
(SP)
Instituto de Soldadura  (PO)
Instituto de Tecnicas Sociales de la Fundacion Fondo
Social Universitario  (SP)
Instituto de Tecnologia de Alimentos  (BL)
Instituto de Teologia "Francisco Suarez"  (SP)
Instituto de Terapeutica Purissimus S.A.  (AG)
Instituto de Tonantzintla  (MX)
Instituto de Vivienda y Urbanismo  (PN)
Instituto de Zootecnia. Facultad de Veterinaria  (SP)
Instituto del Cemento Portland Argentino  (AG)
Instituto del Mar del Peru  (PE)
Instituto Dexeus  (SP)
Instituto Diego Velazquez  (SP)
Instituto do Azeite e Produtos Oleaginosos  (PO)
Instituto do Desenvolvimento Economico Social do
para  (BL)
Instituto do Trabalho, Previdencia e Accao Social de
Angola  (AO)
Instituto dos Produtos Florestais  (PO)
Instituto Ecuatoriano de Ciencias Naturales  (EC)
Instituto Ecuatoriano de Folklore  (EC)
Instituto Eduardo Torroja de la Construccion y del
Cemento  (SP)
Instituto Espanol de Arqueologia  (SP)
Instituto Espanol de Emigracion  (SP)
Instituto Espanol de Entomologia  (SP)
Instituto Espanol de Estudios Mediterraneos  (SP)
Instituto Espanol de Medicina Tropical  (SP)
Instituto Espanol de Oceanografia  (SP)
Instituto Espanol del Envase y Embalaje  (SP)
Instituto Estadual de Hematologia Arthur de Siqueira
Cavalcanti  (BL)
Instituto Femenino de Investigaciones Historicas
(PY)
Instituto Figlie di Maria Ausiliatrice Salesiane di Don
Bosco  (IT)
Instituto Filologia Hispanica "Miguel de Cervantes"
(SP)
Instituto Filosofico de Balmesiana  (SP)
Instituto Forestal. Division Estudios Economicos
(CL)
Instituto Forestal Latinoamericano de Investigacion y
Capacitacion  (VE)
Instituto Francisco de Vitoria. Escuela de Estudios
Juridicos del Ejercito  (SP)
Instituto Gemologico Espanol  (SP)
Instituto Genealogico Brasileiro  (BL)
Instituto Geofisico do Infante D. Luis  (PO)
Instituto Geografico "Agustin Codazzi"  (CK)
Instituto Geografico e Geologico  (BL)
Instituto Geografico y Catastral. Seccion de
Geomagnetismo y Aeronomia  (SP)
Instituto Gregoriano de Lisboa  (PO)
Instituto Historico e Geografico Brasileiro  (BL)
Instituto Historico e Geografico de Juiz de Fora  (BL)
Instituto Hondureno de Antropologia e Historia
(HO)
Instituto Hondureno de Cultura Interamericana  (HO)
Instituto IBYS  (SP)
Instituto Indigenista Interamericano  (MX)
Instituto Indigenista Nacional  (NQ)
Instituto Ingenieros Civiles de Espana  (SP)
Instituto Interamericano  (US)
Instituto Interamericano de Ciencias Agricolas de la O
E A  (GT)
Instituto Interamericano de Ciencias Agricolas de la O
E A  (UY)
Instituto Interamericano de Ciencias Agricolas de la O
E A. Centro Interamericano de Documentacion e
Informacion Agricola  (CR)
Instituto Interamericano de Ciencias Agricolas de la O
E A. Secretariado  (CR)
Instituto Interamericano de Ciencias Agricolas de la O
E A. Technical Advisory Council  (CR)
Instituto Interamericano del Nino  (UY)
Instituto Internacional de Filosofia, A.C.  (MX)
Instituto Internacional de Gencalogia y Heraldica y
Federacion de Corporacion es Afines  (SP)

Instituto Internacional de Literatura Iberoamericana
(US)
Instituto Italiano di Cultura in Portogallo  (PO)
Instituto Jaime Ferran de Microbiologia  (SP)
Instituto Jalisciense de Antropologia e Historia  (MX)
Instituto Joaquim Nabuco de Pesquisas Sociais  (BL)
Instituto Jorge Juan de Matematicas  (SP)
Instituto Jose Celestino Mutis  (SP)
Instituto Juan Sebastian Elcano  (SP)
Instituto "la Casa"  (IT)
Instituto Latinoamericano de Planificacion Economica y
Social  (UN)
Instituto Latinoamericano de Relacianas
Internacionales  (AG)
Instituto Latinoamericano de Relaciones
Internacionales (I.L.A.R.I)  (FR)
Instituto Latinoamericano del Fierro y el Acero  (CL)
Instituto Linguistico de Verano
see also under Colombia. Ministerio de Gobierno.
Instituto Linguistico de Verano
see also under United States Summer Institute of
Linguistics
Instituto Linguistico de Verano  (PE)
Instituto Lucchelli Bonadeo  (AG)
Instituto Mexicano de Contadores Publicos  (MX)
Instituto Mexicano de Control de Calidad. Division de
Divalgacion  (MX)
Instituto Mexicano de Estudios Sociales  (MX)
Instituto Mexicano de Ingenieros Quimicos  (MX)
Instituto Mexicano del Cafe  (MX)
Instituto Mexicano del Cemento y del Concreto, A. C.
(MX)
Instituto Mexicano del Petroleo  (MX)
Instituto Mexicano del Seguro Social  (MX)
Instituto Mexicano del Seguro Social. Departamento
de Investigacion Cientifica  (MX)
Instituto Mexicano del Seguro Social. Subdireccion
General Medica  (MX)
Instituto Montecristeno de Arqueologia  (DR)
Instituto Nacional de Administracion Publica  (MX)
Instituto Nacional de Antropologia e Historia  (MX)
Instituto Nacional de Antropologia e Historia.
Departamento de Monumentos Coloniales  (MX)
Instituto Nacional de Antropologia e Historia.
Departamento de Monumentos Prehispanicos
(MX)
Instituto Nacional de Bellas Artes. Museo de Arte
Moderno  (MX)
Instituto Nacional de Cancerologia  (MX)
Instituto Nacional de Cardiologia  (MX)
Instituto Nacional de Carnes. Departamento de
Exportaciones  (UY)
Instituto Nacional de Cultura. Museo Nacional de
Historia  (PE)
Instituto Nacional de Cultura y Bellas Artes  (VE)
Instituto Nacional de Deportes, Educacion Fisica y
Recreacion  (CU)
Instituto Nacional de Edafologia y Agrobiologia  (SP)
Instituto Nacional de Educacion Fisica  (SP)
Instituto Nacional de Energia Nuclear. Department of
Libraries and Documentation Services  (MX)
Instituto Nacional de Enfermedades Neoplasicas
(PE)
Instituto Nacional de Ensenanza Media "Alfonso X el
Sabio"  (SP)
Instituto Nacional de Estudios de Teatro  (AG)
Instituto Nacional de Estudios Juridicos  (SP)
Instituto Nacional de Geofisica  (SP)
Instituto Nacional de Geologia  (SP)
Instituto Nacional de Industria  (SP)
Instituto Nacional de Investigaciones Agrarias  (SP)
Instituto Nacional de Investigaciones Agricolas.
Departamento de Divulgacion Tecnica  (MX)
Instituto Nacional de Investigaciones Folkloricas
(AG)
Instituto Nacional de Investigaciones Geologico
Mineras  (CK)
Instituto Nacional de Investigaciones Pecuarias.
Rancho Experimental la Campana  (MX)
Instituto Nacional de la Pesca de Cuba  (CU)
Instituto Nacional de la Pesca de Cuba. Centro de
Investigaciones Pesqueras  (CU)
Instituto Nacional de la Vivienda  (SP)
Instituto Nacional de Nutricion  (VE)
Instituto Nacional de Obras Sanitarias,  (VE)
Instituto Nacional de Pesquisas da Amazonia  (BL)
Instituto Nacional de Pesquisas da Amazonia. Museu
Paraense Emilio Goeldi  (BL)
Instituto Nacional de Planificacion  (MX)
Instituto Nacional de Seguros  (CR)
Instituto Nacional de Seguros. Division de Mercadeo
(CR)
Instituto Nacional del Libro Espanol  (SP)
Instituto Nacional Indigenista  (MX)
Instituto Nazionale della Previdenza Sociale  (IT)
Instituto Neo Pitagorico  (BL)

Instituto Oceanografico. Biblioteca (VE)
Instituto Oswaldo Cruz (BL)
Instituto Otavaleno de Antropologia. Centro de Documentacion (EC)
Instituto Panamericano de Geografia e Historia (BO)
Instituto Panamericano de Geografia e Historia (MX)
Instituto Panamericano de Geografia e Historia (PE)
Instituto Panamericano de Geografia e Historia (EC)
Instituto Panamericano de Geografia e Historia. Comite del Folklore (MX)
Instituto para la Conservacion del Lago de Valencia (VE)
Instituto Paranaense de Botanica (BL)
Instituto Peruano de Administracion de Empresas (PE)
Instituto Politecnico Nacional. Comision de Operacion y Fomento de Actividades Academicas (MX)
Instituto Politecnico Nacional. Escuela National de Ciencias Biologicas (MX)
Instituto Politecnico Nacional. Escuela Superior de Economia (MX)
Instituto Politecnico Nacional. Escuela Superior de Medicina (MX)
Instituto Politecnico Nacional. Unidad Professional de Zacatenco (MX)
Instituto Portugues de Heraldica (PO)
Instituto Portugues de Oncologia de Francisco Gentil (PO)
Instituto Quimico de Sarria (SP)
Instituto Quimico de Sarria. Asociacion de Quimicos (SP)
Instituto Rio Grandese do Arroz (BL)
Instituto Salazar y Castro (SP)
Instituto Salvadoreno de Cultura Hispanica (ES)
Instituto Salvadoreno de Turismo (ES)
Instituto Sancho de Moncado (SP)
Instituto Sindical de Formacion Cooperativa (SP)
Instituto Superior de Bibliotecologia (AG)
Instituto Superior de Ciencias Morales (SP)
Instituto Superior de Filosofia (SP)
Instituto Superior Economico e Social (PO)
Instituto Superior Tecnico (PO)
Instituto Tecnologico de Aeronautica (BL)
Instituto Tecnologico do Rio Grande do Sul (BL)
Instituto Tecnologico y de Estudios Superiores de Monterrey (MX)
Instituto Tecnologico y de Estudios Superiores de Monterrey. Departamento de Seguridad Industrial (MX)
Instituto Tecnologico y de Estudios Superiores de Monterrey. Division de Ciencias Agropecuarias y Maritimas (MX)
Instituto Torcuato di Tella (AG)
Institutt for Kristen Oppeding (NO)
Instituttet for Markedsfoering (NO)
Instituttet for Merkantil Informasjon A-S (NO)
Institulul Agronomic "Dr. Petru Groza" (RM)
Institulul Agronomic "Ion Ionescu de la Brad" (RM)
Institulul Central de Cercetari Chimice (RM)
Institulul de Cercetari Pedagogice si Psihologice (RM)
Institulul de Cercetari Pentru Cultura Cartofului si Sfeclei de Zahar (RM)
Institulul de Cercetari si Proiectari Alimentare (RM)
Institulul de Fizica Atomica (RM)
Institulul de Fizica, Bucharest (RM)
Institulul de Geologie si Geofizica (RM)
Institulul de Medicina si Farmacie din Tirgu-Mures (RM)
Institulul de Meteorologie si Hidrologie (RM)
Institulul de Microbiologie, Parazitologie si Epidemiologie "Dr. I. Cantacuzino" (RM)
Institulul de Mine Petrosani (RM)
Institulul de Studii, Cercetari si Proiectari Pentru Gospodarirea Apelor (RM)
Institulul de Studii Istorice si Social Politice (RM)
Institulul de Studii si Proiectari Energetice (RM)
Institulul de Studii Sud-Est Europene (RM)
Institulul National de Informare si Documentare Stiintifica si Tehnica (RM)
Institulul Pedagogic Oradea (RM)
Institulul Politehnic "Gheorghe Asachi" din Iasi (RM)
Institulul Politehnic "Gheorghe Gheorghiu-Dej" (RM)
Institulul Politehnic "Traian Vuia" (RM)
Institutum Balticum (GW)
Institutum Canarium (AU)
Institutum Carmelitanum (IT)

Institutum Historicum Polonicum Romae (IT)
Institutum Historicum Societatis Iesu (IT)
Institutum Iudaicum, Tuebingen (GW)
Institutum Judaicum Delitzschianum (NE)
Institutum Liturgicum Ratisbonense (GW)
Institutum Patristicum Augustinianum (IT)
Instituttutet Foer Metallforskning (SW)
Instituut Schoevers B.V. (NE)
Instituut voor Byzantijnse en Oecumenische Studies te Nijmegen (NE)
Instituut voor Cultuurtechniek en Waterhuishouding (NE)
Instituut voor de Veredeling van Tuinbouwgewassen (NE)
Instituut voor Doven (NE)
Instituut voor Franciscaanse Geschiedenis (BE)
Instituut voor Grafische Techniek TNO (NE)
Instituut voor Hygiene en Epidemiologie (BE)
Instituut voor Kernphysisch Onderzoek (NE)
Instituut voor Landbouwcooperatie in Friesland (NE)
Instituut voor Nederlandse Lexicologie (NE)
Instituut voor Plantenziektenkundig Onderzoek (NE)
Instituut voor Pluimveeonderzoek "Het Spelderholt" (NE)
Instituut voor Staatkundige Vorming (BE)
Instituut voor Toegepaste Linguistick (BE)
Instituut voor Veevoedingsonderzoek "Hoorn" (NE)
Instructor Publications, Inc. (US)
Instrument Society of America (US)
Instrumental Fair Inc. (US)
Instrumentalist Co. (US)
Instytut Automatyki Systemow Energetycznych (PL)
Instytut Badan Jadrowych. Zaklad Radiobiologii i Ochrony Zdrowia (PL)
Instytut Badania Prawa Sadowego (PL)
Instytut Badawczy Drog i Mostow (PL)
Instytut Balneoklimatyczny (PL)
Instytut Ciezkiej Syntezy Organicznej (PL)
Instytut Doskonalenia Kadr Kierowniczych Administracji Panstwowej (PL)
Instytut Ekonomiki Uslug i Drobnej Wytworczosci (PL)
Instytut Elektrotechniki (PL)
Instytut Geologiczny (PL)
Instytut Informacji Naukowej, Technicznej i Ekonomicznej (PL)
Instytut Koniunktur i Cen Handlu Zagranicznego (PL)
Instytut Lacznosci (PL)
Instytut Lotnictwa (PL)
Instytut Maszyn Matematycznych (PL)
Instytut Materialow Ogniotrwalych (PL)
Instytut Mechaniki Precyzyjnej (PL)
Instytut Medycyny Morskiej i Tropikalnej w Gdyni (PL)
Instytut Medycyny Pracy i Higieny Wsi (PL)
Instytut Metali Niezelaznych (PL)
Instytut Meteorologii i Gospodarki Wodnej (PL)
Instytut Naftowy (PL)
Instytut Naukowo-Badawczy (PL)
Instytut Naukowy Kultury Fizycznej (PL)
Instytut Obrobki Plastycznej (PL)
Instytut Obrobki Skrawaniem (PL)
Instytut Ochrony Roslin (PL)
Instytut Onkologii (PL)
Instytut Organizacji, Zarzadzania i Ekonomiki Przemyslu Budowlanego (PL)
Instytut Przemyslu Zielarskiego (PL)
Instytut Technologii Drewna (PL)
Instytut Technologii Elektronowej (PL)
Instytut Tele-i Radiotechniczny (PL)
Instytut Transportu Samochodowego (PL)
Instytut Warzywnictwa (PL)
Instytut Weterynarii (PL)
Instytut Wydawniczy "Nasza Ksiegarnia" (PL)
Instytut Wydawniczy Znak (PL)
Instytut Zachodni (PL)
Instytut Zachodnio - Pomorski (PL)
Instytut Ziemniaka, Bonin (PL)
Instytut Zywnosci i Zywienia (PL)
Ediciones y Publicaciones de Insula (SP)
Insular Publishers Corp (PR)
Insurance Accounting & Statistical Association (US)
Insurance Adjuster (US)
Insurance and Actuarial Society of Glasgow (UK)
Insurance Brokers Association of the Province of Quebec (CN)
Insurance Economics Society of America (US)
Insurance Field Co., Inc. (US)
Insurance Flash (US)
Insurance Forum, Inc. (US)
Insurance Information Institute (US)
Insurance Institute for Highway Safety (US)
Insurance Institute of Canada (CN)
Insurance Institute, Rhodesia (RH)
Insurance News (US)
Insurance Producers Services Corp. (US)
Insurance Publishing & Printing Co. (UK)

Insurance Stock Market Service (US)
Insurance Week, Inc. (US)
Insurance Workers International Union (US)
Intec Press Ltd. (UK)
Integrated Bar of the Philippines (PH)
Integrated Education Associates (US)
Integrated Management (II)
Integration (IS)
Integrity (US)
Intelligence International Ltd. (UK)
Inter Afrique Presse (IV)
Inter American Regional Organisation of Workers
  see Organizacion Regional Interamericana de Trabajadores (MX)
Inter American University of Puerto Rico (PR)
Inter American University of Puerto Rico. Alumni Association (PR)
Inter American University Press (PR)
Inter Auto-Route-Inter Auto-Ecoles de France (FR)
Inter City Publishing Co. (CN)
Inter Counties Publications Ltd. (UK)
Inter Nationes (GW)
Interactive Data Services, Inc. (US)
Interafrican Committee for Hydraulic Studies (UV)
Inter-African Council for Philosophy (DM)
Inter-African Phyto-Sanitary Commission (CM)
Inter-American Affairs Press (US)
Interamerican Association for Democracy and Freedom. U S Committee (US)
Interamerican Association of Sanitary Engineers (MX)
Inter-American Bar Association (US)
Inter-American Bibliographical and Library Association (US)
Inter-American Bilingual Teacher Newsletter (US)
Inter-American Center of Tax Administrators (PN)
Inter-American Children's Institute
  see Instituto Interamericano del Nino (UY)
Interamerican College of Radiology (US)
Inter-American Commission of Women (C I M) (US)
Inter-American Commission on Human Rights (US)
Inter-American Committee on Bibliography (US)
Inter-American Council of Commerce and Production (UY)
Interamerican Defense College (US)
Inter-American Development Bank (US)
Inter-American Development Bank. Institute for Latin American Integration
  see Banco Interamericano de Desarrollo. Instituto para la Integracion de America Latina (AG)
Inter-American Institute of Agricultural Sciences
  see Instituto Interamericano de Ciencias Agricolas de la OEA (CR)
Interamerican Press Association (US)
Interamerican Society of Psychology (US)
Inter-American Statistical Institute (US)
Inter-American Tropical Tuna Commission (US)
Interasia Publications (HK)
Interavia S.A. (SZ)
Interchange Foundation (US)
Inter-Church Holiness Convention (US)
Intercity Publications (N. W.) Ltd. (UK)
Intercollegiate Association of Women Students (US)
Intercollegiate Broadcasting System, Inc. (US)
Intercollegiate Case Clearing House (US)
Intercollegiate Studies Institute, Inc. (US)
Inter-Com, Inc. (US)
Intercom; the Newsletter for California Community College Librarians (US)
Intercommunications, Inc. (US)
Interconair (SZ)
Intercontinental Marketing Corp. (JA)
Intercontinental Medical Book Corporation (US)
Inter-Continental Press Guide (CU)
Intercontinental Press Publishing Association (US)
Intercontinental Publications, Inc. (US)
S.A.R.L. Inter-Continents Promotion (IV)
Inter-County Publishers, Inc. (US)
InterCulture Associates (US)
Interdenomination Foreign Mission Association of North America, Inc. (US)
Interdenominational Theological Center (US)
Interdisciplinary Communications Media Inc. (US)
Inter-Documentation Company (SZ)
Interdok Corp. (US)
Interedi, SARL (FR)
Interesna Zaednica na Kulturata, Prilep (YU)
Interessengemeinschaft der Schweizerischen Aluminium,-Huetten, -Walz- und -Presswerke (SZ)
Interessengemeinschaft deutschsprachiger Autoren (GW)
Inter-Europeenne de Presse (FR)
Interface Learning Collective Inc. (US)
Interface Periodicals Ltd. (UK)
Interface Press (US)
Interfaith Center on Corporate Responsibility (US)
Interfaith Observer (US)
Interflora British Unit Ltd. (UK)

Interflora Norge AS (NO)
Interflora Sweden (SW)
Interfraternity Research and Advisory Council (US)
Intergovernmental Bureau for Informatics (IT)
Intergovernmental Committee for European Migration (SZ)
Intergovernmental Council for Automatic Data Processing (IS)
Intergovernmental Council of Copper Exporting Countries (FR)
Inter-Governmental Maritime Consultative Organization (UN)
Inter-Grafik (MY)
Inter-Groupe Folklore. Region Parisienne (FR)
Interia Shuppan (JA)
Interia Shuppan K. K. (JA)
Interim Books (US)
Interkantonale Kontrollstelle fuer Heilmittel (SZ)
Interlibrary Users Association (US)
Interline and Air Travel News (UK)
Interline, Inc. (US)
Editiones Interlingua (SZ)
Interlingue Institute (SZ)
Interlochen Arts Academy. National Music Camp (US)
Intermed Communications Inc. (US)
Intermedia (US)
Intermedia News and Feature Service (US)
Uitgeverij Intermediair B.V. (NE)
Intermediaire des Chercheurs et Curieux (FR)
Intermediate Technology Publications Ltd. (UK)
Intermission (US)
Intermodal World, Inc. (US)
Intermode Verlag (SZ)
Intermountain Contractor, Inc. (US)
Intermountain Farmers Association (US)
Intermountain Jewish News (US)
Intermountain Logging News (US)
Internacia Asocio de Bibliistoj Kaj Orientalistoj (IT)

International Abolitionist Federation (FR)

International Academy at Santa Barbara. Environmental Studies Institute (US)

International Academy of Cytology (US)
International Academy of Indian Culture (II)
International Academy of Legal Medicine and Social Medicine (BE)
International Academy of Legal Medicine and Social Medicine (IT)
International Academy of Oral Pathology (US)
International Academy of Orthodontics (US)
International Academy of Pathology (UK)
International Academy of Pathology (US)
International Academy of Proctology (US)
International Academy of the History of Medicine (NE)
International Academy of Wood Science (US)
International Actuarial Association (BE)
International Actuarial Association. Astin Section (NE)
International Advancement (US)
International Advertising Association (US)
International Advertising Association (KO)
International Advertising Association. United Kingdom Chapter (UK)
International Aeronautic Federation (FR)
International African Institute (UK)
International African Law Association (UK)
International Agencies (SL)
International Agency for Research in Library History (II)
International Agency for Research on Cancer (UN)
International Agricultural Aviation Congress (NE)
International Agricultural Centre (NE)
International Air Transport Association (CN)
International Air Transport Association (SZ)
International Al Jolson Society (CN)
International Alliance of Hospital Volunteers (CN)
International Alliance of Theatrical Stage Employees and Moving Picture Machine Operators of the United States and Canada (US)
International Alliance of Theatrical Stage Employees and Moving Picture Machine Operators of the United States and Canada. Local 659 (US)
International Alliance of Women (UK)
International Amateur Basketball Federation (GW)
International Amateur Boat Building Society (US)
International Amateur Radio Union (US)
International Amateur Rugby Federation (FR)
International Anatomical Congress (UR)
International and Tri-States Oil Mill Superintendent's Association (US)
International Anesthesia Research Society (US)
International Animated Film Association (FR)
International Antonio Vivaldi Society (DK)
International Archery Federation (UK)
International Armaments Press (US)

International Arthur Schnitzler Research Association (US)
International Arthurian Society (UK)
International Arthurian Society (US)
International Aryan League (II)
International Association for Accident and Traffic Medicine (SW)
International Association for Advancement of Earth & Environmental Sciences (US)
International Association for Analytical Psychology (SZ)
International Association for Bridge and Structural Engineering (SZ)
International Association for Byzantine Studies (GR)
International Association for Cereal Chemistry (AU)
International Association for Child Psychiatry and Allied Professions (NE)
International Association for Classical Archaeology (IT)
International Association for Cross-Cultural Psychology (CN)
International Association for Cross-Cultural Psychology (US)
International Association for Cultural Freedom (NR)
International Association for Cultural Freedom (UK)
International Association for Cybernetics (BE)
International Association for Dental Research (US)
International Association for Dutch Studies (NE)
International Association for Earthquake Engineering (UK)
International Association for Ecology (NE)
International Association for Educational and Vocational Guidance (GW)
International Association for Educational and Vocational Information (FR)
International Association for Great Lakes Research (US)
International Association for Hydraulic Research (NE)
International Association for Hydrogen Energy (US)
International Association for Identification (US)
International Association for Life Saving and First Aid to the Injured (NE)
International Association for Mass Communication Research (UK)
International Association for Mathematical Geology (US)
International Association for Mathematics and Computers in Simulation (US)
International Association for Patristic Studies (NE)
International Association for Plant Taxonomy (NE)
International Association for Plant Taxonomy. International Bureau for Plant Taxonomy and Nomenclature (NE)
International Association for Plant Tissue Culture (UK)
International Association for Pollution Control (US)
International Association for Reformed Faith and Action (UK)
International Association for Religious Freedom. North American Chapter (US)
International Association for Research in Income and Wealth (US)
International Association for Scientific Study of Mental Deficiency (US)
International Association for Semiotic Studies (NE)
International Association for Shell and Spatial Structures. (SP)
International Association for the Advancement of Educational Research (BE)
International Association for the Advancement of Ethnology and Eugenics (US)
International Association for the Defence of Religious Liberties (SZ)
International Association for the Exchange of Students for Technical Experience (AU)
International Association for the History of Agriculture (II)
International Association for the History of Glass (BE)
International Association for the History of Religions (NE)
International Association for the Study of Pain (NE)
International Association for Water Law (IT)
International Association Futuribles (FR)
International Association of Agricultural Economists (UK)
International Association of Agricultural Librarians and Documentalists (NE)
International Association of Allergology (NE)
International Association of Allergology (US)
International Association of Applied Linguistics (UK)
International Association of Applied Psychology (BE)

International Association of Applied Psychology (UK)
International Association of Art Critics (SW)
International Association of Asbestos Workers (US)
International Association of Assessing Officers (US)
International Association of Bibliophiles
   see Association Internationale de Bibliophie (FR)
International Association of Bridge, Structural and Ornamental Iron Workers (US)
International Association of Business Communicators (US)
International Association of Cancer Victims and Friends (US)
International Association of Chain Stores (FR)
International Association of Chiefs of Police, Inc. (US)
International Association of Coroners and Medical Examiners (US)
International Association of Counseling Services, Inc. (US)
International Association of Country Music (US)
International Association of Cytology (JA)
International Association of Democratic Lawyers (BE)
International Association of Dredging Companies (NE)
International Association of Drilling Contractors (US)
International Association of Electrical Inspectors (US)
International Association of Engineering Geology (GW)
International Association of Fire Chiefs, Inc. (US)
International Association of French Studies
   see Association Internationale des Etudes Francaises (FR)
International Association of Geodesy (FR)
International Association of Geodesy. Central Bureau for Satellite Geodesy (GR)
International Association of Geodesy. Commission Permanente des Marees Terrestres (BE)
International Association of Geomagnetism and Aeronomy (JA)
International Association of Group Psychotherapy (US)
International Association of Hail Insurers (SZ)
International Association of Health Underwriters (US)
International Association of Hydrogeologists (FR)
International Association of Hydrological Sciences (UK)
International Association of Independent Producers (US)
International Association of Individual Psychology (UK)
International Association of Insurance Counsel (US)
International Association of Jazz Record Collectors (US)
International Association of Labor History Institutions (SZ)
International Association of Laryngectomees (US)
International Association of Law Libraries (GW)
International Association of Lawyers (BE)
International Association of Lighthouse Authorities (FR)
International Association of Logopedics and Phoniatrics (SW)
International Association of Machinists and Aerospace Workers (US)
International Association of Master Penmen and Teachers of Handwriting (CN)
International Association of Meteorology and Atmospheric Physics (CN)
International Association of Meteorology and Atmospheric Physics (US)
International Association of Microbiological Societies (CN)
International Association of Microbiological Societies. International Committee on Systematic Bacteriology (US)
International Association of Microbiological Societies. Virology Section (SZ)
International Association of Milk Control Agencies (US)
International Association of Milk, Food and Environmental Sanitarians, Inc. (US)
International Association of Museums of Arms and Military History (UK)
International Association of Music Libraries (GW)
International Association of Music Libraries (US)
International Association of Music Libraries (U. K. Branch) (UK)
International Association of Mutual Insurance Companies (FR)
International Association of Oral Surgeons (DK)
International Association of Orientalist Librarians (UK)

International Association of Papyrologists   (UK)
International Association of Personnel in Employment
    Security   (US)
International Association of Philatelic Journalists
    (FR)
International Association of Physical Education and
    Sports for Girls and Women   (JA)
International Association of Plumbing and Mechanical
    Officials   (US)
International Association of Ports and Harbors   (JA)
International Association of Printing House Craftsmen
    (US)
International Association of Professional Numismatists
    (FR)
International Association of Pupil Personnel Workers
    (US)
Inter-National Association of Refrigerated Warehouses
    (US)
International Association of School Librarianship
    (US)
International Association of Schools of Social Work
    (US)
International Association of Science and Technology
    for Development   (CN)
International Association of Scientific Experts in
    Tourism   (SZ)
International Association of Sedimentologists  (UK)
International Association of Seed Crushers   (UK)
International Association of Sound Archives   (NE)
International Association of Space Philatelists   (US)
International Association of State Lotteries   (SZ)
International Association of Students in Business and
    Economics   (BE)
International Association of Technological Universities
    Libraries   (UK)
International Association of Thalasso-Theraphy   (FR)
International Association of Theoretical and Applied
    Limnology   (US)
International Association of Torch Clubs   (US)
International Association of Universities   (FR)
International Association of University Professors &
    Lecturers   (UK)
International Association of Volcanology and
    Chemistry of the Earth's Interior   (IT)
International Association of Wall and Ceiling
    Contractors, Inc.   (US)
International Association of Wiping Cloth
    Manufacturers   (US)
International Association of Women Ministers   (US)
International Association of Workers for Maladjusted
    Children   (FR)
International Association on the Artificial Prolongation
    of the Human Specific Lifespan   (BE)
International Association on Water Pollution Research
    (US)
International Astronomical Union   (NE)
International Astronomical Union   (SZ)
International Atlantic Salmon Foundation   (CN)
International Atomic Energy Agency   (UN)
International Atomic Energy Agency. International
    Centre for Theoretical Physics   (UN)
International Atomic Energy Agency. International
    Nuclear Information System   (UN)
International Authority on Visual Merchandising
    (US)
International Automobile Parade   (SZ)
International Baccalaureate Office   (SZ)
International Badminton Federation   (UK)
International Bank for Reconstruction and
    Development   (UN)
International Bank Note Society   (UK)
International Banker Association, Inc.   (US)
International Bar Assocation   (US)
International Bar Association   (UK)
International Bee Research Association   (UK)
International Bio-Medical Information Service, Inc.
    (US)
International Biological Programme   (US)
International Black Writers Conference Inc.   (US)
International Board on Books for Young People
    (AU)
International Board on Books for Young People. U.S.
    National Section   (US)
International Bonhoeffer Archive and Research
    Committee. English Language Section   (US)
International Book House, Ltd.   (II)
International Botanical Congress   (US)
International Brain Research Organization   (US)
International Brangus Breeders Association   (US)
International Broadcasters Society   (NE)
International Broncho-Pneumologic Association   (FR)
International Brotherhood of Electrical Workers (AFL-
    CIO)   (US)
International Brotherhood of Electrical Workers (AFL-
    CIO) Local Union No. 3   (US)
International Brotherhood of Electrical Workers (AFL-
    CIO) Local 1470   (US)
International Brotherhood of Magicians   (US)

International Brotherhood of Painters & Allied Trades
    (US)
International Brotherhood of Pottery and Allied
    Workers   (US)
International Brotherhood of Teamsters, Chauffeurs,
    Warehousemen and Helpers of America   (US)
International Bureau for the Study of the Problems in
    the Teaching of Greek and Latin   (BE)
International Bureau of Education
    see under Unesco   (UN)
International Bureau of Fiscal Documentation   (NE)
International Bureau of Weights and Measures
    see Bureau International des Poids et Mesures
    (FR)
International Business Contacts   (NE)
International Business-Government Counsellors Inc.
    (US)
International Business Machines Corp.   (US)
International Business Machines Corp. Data Processing
    Division   (US)
International Cardiovascular Society   (IT)
International Cargo Handling Coordination Association
    (UK)
International Cartographic Association   (GW)
International Catholic Migration Commission   (SZ)
International Catholic Movement for Intellectual and
    Cultural Affairs   (SZ)
International Catholic Rural Association   (IT)
International Center for Advanced Studies   (US)
International Center for Arid and Semi-Arid Land
    Studies   (US)
International Center of Information on Antibiotics
    (BE)
International Center of Medieval Art   (US)
International Centre for African Social and Economic
    Documentation   (BE)
International Centre for Kathakali   (II)
International Centre for Local Credit   (NE)
International Centre for Mechanical Sciences   (US)
International Centre for Religious Education   (BE)
International Centre for the Settlement of Investment
    Disputes   (US)
International Centre for Theoretical Physics
    see under International Atomic Energy Agency
    (UN)
International Centre for Training and Research in
    Development Studies. Institute of Social Studies
    (UK)
International Centre of Fertilizers   (SZ)
International Centre of Films for Children and Young
    People   (FR)
International Centre of Free Trade Unionists in Exile
    (UK)
International Centre of Heat and Mass Transfer   (US)
International Centre of Insect Physiology and Ecology
    (KE)
International Centre of Onomastics   (BE)
International Centre of Onomastics   (YU)
International Centre of Research and Information on
    Public and Cooperative Economy   (BE)
International Centre of Research and Information on
    Public and Cooperative Economy. Israeli Section.
    (IS)
International Chamber of Commerce   (FR)
International Chamber of Commerce. Iranian
    Committee   (IR)
International Chamber of Commerce. United States
    Council   (US)
International Chemical and Nuclear Corp   (US)
International Chemical Workers Union   (US)
International Chess Federation   (CS)
International Childbirth Education Association   (US)
International Children's Centre   (FR)
International Chiropractors Association   (US)
International Christian Broadcasters   (US)
International Christian Communications, Inc.   (US)
International Christian Gypsy Movement   (FR)
International Christian University   (JA)
International Christian University. Institute for the
    Study of Christianity and Culture   (JA)
International Church of the Foursquare Gospel   (US)
International City Management Association   (US)
International Civil Airport Association   (UK)
International Civil Aviation Organization   (UN)
International Civil Defence Organization   (SZ)
International Claim Association   (US)
International Clarinet Society   (US)
International Cliff Richard Movement   (NE)
International Co-Operative Alliance   (UK)
International Co-Operative Alliance. Regional Office
    and Education Centre for South-East Asia   (II)
International College of Applied Nutrition   (US)
International College of Dentists   (US)
International College of Dentists (San Mateo)   (US)
International College of Dentists. European Section
    (GW)
International College of Pediatrics   (SZ)

International College of Psychosomatic Medicine
    (SZ)
International College of Surgeons   (US)
International Commercial Bank of China   (CH)
International Commercial Bank of China. Head Office-
    Economic Research Dept.   (CH)
International Commercial Network Ltd.   (UK)
International Commission for Agricultural Industries
    (FR)
International Commission for the Conservation of
    Atlantic Tunas.   (SP)
International Commission for the Northwest Atlantic
    Fisheries   (CN)
International Commission for the Prevention of
    Alcoholism   (US)
International Commission for the Protection of the
    Rhine Against Pollution   (GW)
International Commission for the Scientific
    Exploration of the Mediterranean Sea   (FR)
International Commission for Uniform Methods of
    Sugar Analysis   (UK)
International Commission of Agricultural Engineering
    (FR)
International Commission of Jurists   (SZ)
International Commission of Sugar Technology   (BE)
International Commission on Cloud Physics   (CN)
International Commission on Illumination   (FR)
International Commission on Irrigation and Drainage
    (II)
International Commission on Irrigation and Drainage.
    Greek National Committee   (GR)
International Commission on Large Dams   (US)
International Commission on Radiological Protection
    (UK)
International Commission on Radiological Protection
    (US)
International Commission on the History of
    Mathematics   (CN)
International Committee for Histochemistry and
    Cytochemistry   (US)
International Committee for Historical Science   (FR)
International Committee for Social Sciences
    Documentation   (NE)
International Committee for the Standardization of
    Angiological Methods   (SZ)
International Committee of Catholic Nurses   (BE)
International Committee of Food Science and
    Technology   (US)
International Committee of Historical Sciences.
    Commission for the History of State Assemblies
    (BE)
International Committee of Military Medicine and
    Pharmacy   (FR)
International Committee of Photobiology. King's
    College   (UK)
International Committee of the Red Cross   (SZ)
International Committee of Weights and Measures
    (US)
International Committee on General Relativity and
    Gravitation   (US)
International Committee on Laboratory Animals
    (NO)
International Committee on the History of Art   (FR)
International Committee on Urgent Anthropological
    and Ethnological Research   (AU)
International Communication Association   (US)
International Communist Party   (FR)
International Comparative Literature Association
    (HU)
International Computer Education Center   (US)
International Computer Programs, Inc.   (US)
International Confederation for Agricultural Credit
    (SZ)
International Confederation for Disarmament & Peace
    (UK)
International Confederation of Arab Trade Unions
    (UA)
International Confederation of Art Dealers   (BE)
International Confederation of Free Trade Unions
    (BE)
International Confederation of Free Trade Unions
    (ICFTU) Asian Regional Organization   (II)
International Confederation of Free Trade Unions.
    African Regional Organisation   (NR)
International Confederation of Midwives   (UK)
International Confederation of Societies of Authors
    and Composers   (FR)
International Confederation of Thermal Analysis
    (UK)
International Conference of Building Officials   (US)
International Conference of Human Genetics   (NE)
International Conference of Police Associations   (US)
International Conference of Weekly Newspaper
    Editors   (US)
International Conference on Cybernetics and Society
    (US)
International Conference on Ion Implantation in
    Semiconductors   (US)

International Conference on Large High Voltage Electric Systems (FR)
International Conference on Social Welfare (US)
International Conference on Sociology of Religion (FR)
International Conference on Soil Mechanics and Foundation Engineering. Proceedings (MX)
International Congress of Pharmacology (US)
International Congress of Prehistoric and Protohistoric Sciences (GW)
International Congress of Psychopathology of Expression (SZ)
International Congress on Automotive Safety (US)
International Congresses of Entomology (UK)
International Congresses on Tropical Medicine and Malaria (GR)
International Construction Machinery Fair, Munich (B A U M A) (GW)
International Construction Reporter (US)
International Consultants (ICCONSULT) Ltd. (IS)
International Consumer Credit Association (US)
International Contacts Office (GR)
International Convention Facilities Directory (US)
International Cooperation Council, Inc. (US)
International Coordinating Committee for the Presentation of Science and the Development of out-of-School Scientific Activities (BE)
International Copyright Society (GW)
International Correspondence Schools (ICS) (US)
International Cosmetic Manufacturing Conference (US)
International Cotton Advisory Committee (US)
International Council for Adult Education (CN)
International Council for Bird Preservation (UK)
International Council for Bird Preservation. British Section (UK)
International Council for Building Research, Studies and Documentation (NE)
International Council for Educational Development (US)
International Council for Educational Media (FR)
International Council for Educational Media (UK)
International Council for Environmental Law (SZ)
International Council for Philosophy and Humanistic Studies (FR)
International Council for Philosophy and Humanistic Studies (IT)
International Council for the Exploration of the Sea (DK)
International Council of Christian Churches (US)
International Council of Graphic Design Associations (UK)
International Council of Home Help Services (NE)
International Council of Jews from Czechoslovakia (UK)
International Council of Monuments and Sites (BE)
International Council of Museums (ICOM) (FR)
International Council of Nurses (SZ)
International Council of Psychologists, Inc. (US)
International Council of Scientific Unions (FR)
International Council of Scientific Unions. Abstracting Board (FR)
International Council of Scientific Unions. Committee on Data for Science and Technology (FR)
International Council of Scientific Unions. Inter-Union Commission of Solar Terrestrial Physics (US)
International Council of Shopping Centers (US)
International Council of Societies of Industrial Design (UK)
International Council of Sport and Physical Education. Research Committee (FR)
International Council of the Aeronautical Sciences (US)
International Council of the Aeronautical Sciences (IS)
International Council of Voluntary Agencies (SZ)
International Council of Women (FR)
International Council on Alcohol and Addictions (SZ)
International Council on Archives (FR)
International Council on Archives. East and Central African Regional Branch (KE)
International Council on Archives. Southeast Asian Regional Branch (MY)
International Council on Combustion Engines (FR)
International Council on Environmental Law (GW)
International Council on Health, Physical Education and Recreation (GW)
International Council on Health, Physical Education and Recreation (GW)
International Council on Social Welfare (FR)
International Council on Social Welfare (II)
International Council on Social Welfare (US)
International Council on Social Welfare. Japanese National Committee (JA)
International Court of Justice (UN)
International Courtly Literature Society, Temple University (US)

International Creative Center (SZ)
International Criminal Police Organization-Interpol (FR)
International Crosby Circle (UK)
International Currency Review Ltd. (UK)
International Customs Tariffs Bureau (BE)
International Dachau Committee (BE)
International Dairy Federation (BE)
International Dance Teachers Association Ltd (UK)
International Data Corp. (US)
International Defense and Aid Fund for Southern Africa (US)
International Dental Federation (UK)
International Development Association (UN)
International Development Research Center see under Indiana University (US)
International Development Research Centre (SG)
International Development Research Centre (SI)
International Development Research Centre. Devsis Study Team (CN)
International Diabetes Federation (NE)
International Diabetes Federation (UK)
International District Heating Association (US)
International Documentation and Communication Center (IT)
International Documentation Bureau (BE)
International Double Reed Society (US)
International Edsel Club (US)
International Egg Commission (AU)
International Electrochemical Institute (US)
International Electrotechnical Commission (SZ)
International English Shepherd Registry, Inc (US)
International Epidemiological Association (UK)
International Executive Newsletters Co. (US)
International Exhibition for the Food and Allied Industries (UK)
International Experimental and Art Film Theatres Confederation (FR)
International Export Association (UK)
International Eye Foundation (US)
International Fabricare Institute (US)
International Fabricare Institute. I F I Research Center (US)
International Falcon Movement (AU)
International Falcon Movement - Socialist Educational International (AU)
International Federation for Automatic Control (US)
International Federation for Documentation (NE)
International Federation for Documentation. Classification Research Committee (GW)
International Federation for Documentation. Comision Latinoamericana (CK)
International Federation for Documentation. Commission for Asia and Oceania (AT)
International Federation for Documentation. Committee on Classification Research (NE)
International Federation for Documentation. Committee on Developing Countries (NE)
International Federation for Documentation. Committee on Education and Training (NE)
International Federation for Documentation. Committee on Linguistics in Documentation (NE)
International Federation for Documentation. Committee on Research on the Theoretical Basis of Information (NE)
International Federation for Documentation. Committee on Research on the Theoretical Basis of Information (UR)
International Federation for Home Economics (FR)
International Federation for Housing and Planning (NE)
International Federation for Hygiene, Preventive Medicine and Social Medicine (IT)
International Federation for Information Processing (SZ)
International Federation for Information Processing (UK)
International Federation for Information Processing. Applied Information Processing Group (NE)
International Federation for Medical Electronics and Biological Engineering (UK)
International Federation for Medical Psychotherapy (SZ)
International Federation for Modern Languages and Literature (AT)
International Federation for Theatre Research (UK)
International Federation of Agricultural Producers (FR)
International Federation of Air Traffic Controllers' Associations (GW)
International Federation of Air Traffic Controllers Associations (SZ)
International Federation of Asian and Western Pacific Contractors Associations (PH)
International Federation of Association Football (SZ)
International Federation of Associations of Textile Chemists and Colorists (SZ)

International Federation of Audit Bureaus of Circulations (UK)
International Federation of Automatic Control (NE)
International Federation of Automatic Control (GW)
International Federation of Automatic Control. Comite Espanol (SP)
International Federation of Automobile Engineers' and Technicians' Associations (JA)
International Federation of Beekeepers' Associations "Apimondia" (RM)
International Federation of Blood Donors Organizations see Federation Internationale des Organisations de Donneurs de Sang (FR)
International Federation of Building and Woodworkers (SZ)
International Federation of Business and Professional Women (UK)
International Federation of Catholic Universities (FR)
International Federation of Cell Biology (NE)
International Federation of Clinical Chemistry (SZ)
International Federation of Clinical Chemistry (UK)
International Federation of Commercial Clerical and Technical Employees (SZ)
International Federation of Consulting Engineers (NE)
International Federation of Cotton and Allied Textile Industries (SZ)
International Federation of Employees in Public Service (BE)
International Federation of Fruit Juice Producers (FR)
International Federation of Gynaecology and Obstetrics (SW)
International Federation of Gynaecology and Obstetrics (SZ)
International Federation of Institutes for Social and Socio-Religious Research (BE)
International Federation of Journalists and Travel Writers (FR)
International Federation of Landscape Architects (SZ)
International Federation of Library Associations (GW)
International Federation of Library Associations and Institutions (NE)
International Federation of Library Associations. Children's Section (UK)
International Federation of Library Associations. Office for UBC (UK)
International Federation of Library Associations. Special Libraries Section (GW)
International Federation of Medical Students' Associations (FI)
International Federation of Municipal Engineers (IS)
International Federation of Newspaper Publishers (FR)
International Federation of Operational Research Societies (NE)
International Federation of Operational Research Societies. Airline Group (US)
International Federation of Ophthalmological Societies (FR)
International Federation of Park and Recreation Administration (UK)
International Federation of Pedestrians (NE)
International Federation of Petroleum and Chemical Workers (US)
International Federation of Physical Medicine and Rehabilitation (NE)
International Federation of Plantation, Agricultural and Allied Workers (SZ)
International Federation of Prestressing (UK)
International Federation of Professional and Technical Engineers (US)
International Federation of Secondary Education Teachers (FR)
International Federation of Societies and Institutes for the Study of the Renaissance (SZ)
International Federation of Societies for Electroencephalography and Clinical Neurophysiology (US)
International Federation of Societies for Electroencephalography and Clinical Neurophysiology (IE)
International Federation of Sportive Medicine (IT)
International Federation of Surveyors (US)
International Federation of Teachers of French see Federation Internationale des Professeurs de Francais (FR)
International Federation of the Cinematographic Press (FR)
International Federation of Trade Unions of Transport (BE)
International Federation of Translators (BE)
International Federation on Ageing (US)
International Fellowship of Reconciliation (BE)

International Fertility Association  (AG)
International Fiction Association  (CN)
International Film and Television Council  (IT)
International Film Collector  (UK)
International Film Importers and Distributors of America  (US)
International Film Theatre  (AT)
International Finance Corporation  (UN)
International Fiscal Association  (NE)
International Fluidics Services Ltd.  (UK)
International Flying Farmers, Inc.  (US)
International Folk Music Council  (CN)
International Food Information Service  (UK)
International Foodservice Manufacturers Association (US)
International Fortean Organization  (US)
International Foundation for Studies in Reproduction, Inc.  (US)
International Foundation for Telemetering  (US)
International Foundation for Theoretical Research (US)
International Foundation of Employee Benefit Plans (US)
International Foundations of Education Quarterly (US)
International Free-Lancers' Organization  (IS)
International Friendship League  (NE)
International Friendship League  (UK)
International Friendship Society  (KO)
International Frozen Food Association  (US)
International Game Fish Association  (US)
International Gas Union  (UK)
International General  (US)
International Geneva Association, Inc.  (US)
International Geographical Union  (FR)
International Geographical Union  (GW)
International Geographical Union  (UR)
International Geographical Union. World Land Use Survey Commission  (UK)
International Geranium Society  (US)
International Glaciological Society  (UK)
International Grafik  (DK)
International Grain Legume Information Centre (NR)
International Graphical Federation  (SZ)
International Graphics Corp.  (US)
International Graphoanalysis Society  (US)
International Grassland Congress  (UR)
International Gravimetric Bureau  (FR)
International Grenfell Association  (US)
International Group for Research on Women  (CN)
International Group for Scientific Research in Stomatology  (BE)
International Gymnastic Federation  (SZ)
International Harpsichord Society  (US)
International Harvester Co.  (US)
International Harvester Company of Canada Ltd (CN)
International Hebrew Christian Alliance  (UK)
International Hockey Federation  (BE)
International Homoeopathic League  (GW)
International Honorary Society for High School Journalists  (US)
International Hop Growers Convention  (YU)
International Hospital Federation  (UK)
International Hotel Association  (FR)
International Hotel Association  (UK)
International Hotel Association. Deutsche Sektion (GW)
International Hotel Directories Ltd.  (US)
International Humanist and Ethical Union  (NE)
International Hydrographic Organization  (MC)
International I U P A C Congress of Pesticide Chemistry  (US)
International Inflammation Research Society  (US)
International Information Center  (AT)
International Information Centre for Terminology, Vienna  (AU)
International Institute for Adult Literacy Methods (IR)
International Institute for Aerial Survey and Earth Sciences  (NE)
International Institute for Applied Systems Analysis (AU)
International Institute for Children's Literature and Reading Research  (AU)
International Institute for Conservation of Historic and Artistic Works  (UK)
International Institute for Educational Planning  (UN)
International Institute for Geothermal Research, Pisa, Italy  (IT)
International Institute for Human Rights  (NE)
International Institute for Labour Studies  (UN)
International Institute for Land Reclamation and Improvement  (NE)
International Institute for Peace  (AU)
International Institute for Population Studies  (II)
International Institute for Rural Reconstruction  (US)

International Institute for Social History  (NE)
International Institute for Strategic Studies  (UK)
International Institute for Studies on Education  (BE)
International Institute for the Science of Sintering (YU)
International Institute for the Study of Religions, Inc. (JA)
International Institute for the Unification of Private Law  (IT)
International Institute of Administrative Sciences (BE)
International Institute of Administrative Sciences (BL)
International Institute of Communications  (UK)
International Institute of Conservation  (US)
International Institute of Differing Civilizations  (BE)
International Institute of Ibero-American Literature (US)
International Institute of Philosophy  (FR)
International Institute of Public Finance  (GW)
International Institute of Refrigeration  (FR)
International Institute of Seismology and Earthquake Engineering
    see Japan. International Institute of Seismology and Earthquake Engineering  (JA)
International Institute of Social Economics  (UK)
International Institute of Space Law  (FR)
International Institute of Space Law  (US)
International Institute of Synthetic Rubber Producers (US)
International Institute of Tamil Studies  (II)
International Institute of Tropical Agriculture  (NR)
International Institute of Welding  (UK)
International Institution for Production Engineering Research  (SZ)
International Intertrade Index  (US)
International Invention Register  (US)
International Iron and Steel Institute  (BE)
International Jazz Federation  (AU)
International Jewish Labor Bund  (US)
International Joint Commission. Great Lakes Regional Office  (CN)
International Joint Commission. Great Lakes Research Advisory Board  (CN)
International Journal of Forensic Dentistry  (UK)
International Journal of Neurology  (UY)
International Journal of Sexology  (II)
International Journal of Transport Economics  (IT)
International Kart Federation  (US)
International Labor Press Association  (US)
International Labour Office  (UN)
International Labour Office. International Institute for Labour Studies
    see International Institute for Labour Studies  (UN)
International Labour Office. International Occupational Safety and Health Information Centre  (UN)
International Labour Organisation
    see International Labour Office  (UN)
International Ladies Garment Workers' Union  (US)
International Ladies Garment Workers Union. Local 66  (US)
International Language Centre  (UK)
International Law Association  (UK)
International Law Association. American Branch (US)
International Law Book Co.  (II)
International Law Fund  (US)
International Law Perspective  (US)
International Lead and Zinc Study Group  (US)
International Lead Zinc Research Organization, Inc. (US)
International League against Epilepsy  (US)
International League for the Rights of Man  (US)
International League of Antiquarian Booksellers (NE)
International League of Dermatological Societies (US)
International League of Liberal Christian Women (US)
International League of Societies for the Mentally Handicapped  (BE)
International Legal Sciences Association  (JA)
International Leprosy Association  (US)
International Library-Book Publishers  (US)
International Library of African Music  (SA)
International Licensing Ltd.  (UK)
International Linguistic Association  (US)
International Literary and Artistic Association  (FR)
International Longshoremen's & Warehousemen's Union  (US)
International Longshoremen's Association, A F L-C I O. Local 1814  (US)
International Lutheran Laymen's League  (US)
International Machine Tool Design and Research Conference  (UK)
International Maize and Wheat Improvement Center
    see Centro Internacional de Mejoramiento de Maiz y Trigo  (MX)

International Management Association of Japan  (JA)
International Management Services  (CJ)
International Management Services  (US)
International Maritime Committee  (BE)
International Marketing Federation  (NE)
International Markets Advertising Agency  (UK)
International Markets Advertising Agency  (US)
International Marxist Group(British Section, 4th International)  (UK)
International Mass Media Research Center  (US)
International Material Management Society  (US)
International Mathematical Union  (AT)
International Mathematical Union  (SW)
International Measurement Confederation. IMEKO Secretariat  (HU)
International Medical Association for the Study of Living Conditions and Health  (FR)
International Medical Society of Japan  (JA)
International Medical Society of Paraplegia  (UK)
International Medieval Bibliography  (UK)
International Metallographic Society Inc  (US)
International Metalworkers Federation  (SZ)
International Metaphysical Festivals, Inc.  (US)
International Meteorological Institute in Stockholm (SW)
International Micrographic Congress  (US)
International Microwave Power Institute  (CN)
International Military Sports Council  (BE)
International Mimes & Pantomimists  (US)
International Mineralogical Association  (US)
International Mobile Air Conditioning  (US)
International Molders' and Allied Workers' Union (US)
International Monetary Fund  (UN)
International Movement of Radical Anthropologists. Etnografisk Afdeling  (DK)
International Multidisciplinary Research Association (US)
International Municipal Signal Association  (US)
International Music Centre  (AU)
International Music Council. International Institute for Comparative Music Studies and Documentation (IT)
International Musicological Society  (GW)
International Musicological Society  (SZ)
International Narcotic Enforcement Officers Association  (US)
International Narcotics Control Board  (UN)
International Naturist Federation  (GW)
International Netsuke Collectors Society Journal (US)
International New Thought Alliance  (US)
International News Keyus, Inc.  (US)
International News, Photo, Correspondence & Hobby Club  (NE)
International Newspaper Collectors' Club  (US)
International Newspaper Promotion Association  (US)
International Nickel Co. Inc.  (US)
International Nickel Co. Inc. Huntington Alloys  (US)
International Nickel Company of Canada Ltd.  (CN)
International Nonwovens & Disposables Association (US)
International North Pacific Fisheries Commission (CN)
International Numismatic Directory  (UK)
International Occupational Safety and Health Information Centre
    see under International Labour Office  (UN)
International Oceanographic Foundation  (US)
International Office of Bibliography  (BE)
International Office of Cocoa and Chocolate  (BE)
International Oil Scouts Association  (US)
International Olive Growers Federation  (SP)
International Olive Oil Council  (SP)
International Olympic Academy  (GR)
International Olympic Committee  (SZ)
International Order of Odd Fellows  (US)
International Order of Odd Fellows. Grand Lodge of Oregon  (US)
International Organization for Ancient Languages Analysis by Computer  (BE)
International Organization for Biological Control of Noxious Animals and Plants  (FR)
International Organization for Standardization  (SZ)
International Organization for Succulent Plant Study (US)
International Organization for the Study of Group Tensions  (US)
International Organization for the Study of the Old Testament  (NE)
International Organization of Biological Control  (SZ)
International Organization of Citrus Virologists  (US)
International Organization of Consumers Unions (NE)
International Organization of Journalists  (CS)
International Organization of Journalists. Graphic Club (HU)

International Organization of Old Testament Scholars (NE)
International Organization of Supreme Audit Institutions (CN)
International Organizing Committee of World Mining Congresses (PL)
International Ornithological Congress (NE)
International P. E. N. (UK)
International P. E. N. Taipei Chinese Center (CH)
International Pacific Halibut Commission (US)
International Pacific Salmon Fisheries Commission (CN)
International Palaeontological Association (NO)
International Peace Research Association (FI)
International Peace Research Institute (FI)
International Peat Society (FI)
International Pediatric Research Foundation Inc (US)
International Penpals Pool (II)
International Pentecostal Holiness Church (US)
International Percussion Reference Library (US)
International Permanent Committee on Canned Foods. French Delegation (FR)
International Personnel Management Association (US)
International Pharmaceutical Federation (NE)
International Pharmaceutical Students Federation (NE)
International Philatelic Federation (LU)
International Phonetic Association (UK)
International Phycological Society (UK)
International Physical Index, Inc. (US)
International Planned Parenthood Federation (UK)
International Planned Parenthood Federation (US)
International Planned Parenthood Federation. Africa Regional Office (KE)
International Planned Parenthood Federation. East & South East Asia and Oceania Region (MY)
International Planned Parenthood Federation. Europe Region (UK)
International Plant Breeders Association for the Protection of New Varieties (FR)
International Plant Protection Center (US)
International Plastic Modelers' Society (US)
International Plastic Modelers Society-U.S.A. (US)
International Plastic Modelers Society. U.S.A. Branch-Northern Delaware Chapter (US)
International Plastic Modellers Society (UK)
International Plastic Modellers Society-Canada (CN)
International Playground Association (UK)
International Poetry Forum (US)
International Poetry Review (Greensboro) (US)
International Poetry Society (UK)
International Polar Motion Service. Central Bureau (JA)
International Police Association (UK)
International Police Association. Australian Section (AT)
International Police Association. British Section (UK)
International Political Science Association (CN)
International Political Science Association (FR)
International Potash Institute (SZ)
International Press Cutting Service (II)
International Press Institute (UK)
International Press Journal (CN)
International Press Ltd. (CN)
International Press Telecommunications Council (UK)
International Primatological Society (US)
International Printing and Graphic Communications Union (US)
International Prisoners' Aid Association (US)
International Project in the Field of Food Irradiation (GW)
International Prospect (UK)
International Psycho-Analytical Association (UK)
International Public Policy Institute (US)
International Public Relations Pty. Ltd. (AT)
International Publications Ltd. (TR)
International Publications Service (US)
International Publishers Association (SZ)
International Publishing and Marketing Co. (TH)
International Publishing Co. of America (US)
International Publishing Corp. (UK)
International Publishing Enterprises (IT)
International Puppeteers Union. French Section (FR)
International Radio and Television Organization (CS)
International Radio and Television Society, Inc. (US)
International Railway Congress Association (BE)
International Railway Publishing Co. Ltd. (CN)
International Railway Union (IT)
International Rayon and Synthetic Fibres Committee (FR)
International Reading Association, Inc. (US)
International Reading Association, Inc. Indiana State Council (US)

International Reading Association, Inc. Ohio Council (US)
International Real Estate Federation (FR)
International Reference Organization in Forensic Medicine & Sciences (US)
Editions International Registry of Who's Who S.A. (Geneva) (SZ)
International Religious Liberty Association (US)
International Remote Sensing Institute (US)
International Reports, Inc. (US)
International Reprographic Blueprint Association (US)
International Rescue Committee (US)
International Research Center for Energy and Economic Development (US)
International Research Center on Rural Cooperative Communities (IS)
International Research Centre (KO)
International Research Communications System (IRCS) (UK)
International Review (CN)
International Review Service, Inc. (US)
International Rice Research Institute (PH)
International Road Federation (US)
International Road Transport Union (SZ)
International Rodeo Association (US)
International Rubber Study Group (UK)
International Rural Housing Association (VE)
International Savings Banks Institute (SZ)
International Scholarly Book Services Inc. (US)
International Scientific Communications, Inc. (US)
International Scientific Film Association (FR)
International Scientific Publications (II)
International Seaweed Symposium (NO)
International Secretariat for the University Study of Education (BE)
International Secretariat for Volunteer Service (SZ)
International Secretariat of Entertainment Trade Unions (BE)
International Seed Testing Association (NO)
International Seismological Centre (UK)
International Serials Data System. International Centre (FR)
International Shade Tree Conference, Inc. (US)
International Shooting Union (GW)
International Silk Association (FR)
International Skating Union (SZ)
International Skeletal Society (US)
International Social Science Council (NE)
International Social Security Association (SZ)
International Socialist Publishing Co (US)
International Society for Animal Blood Group Research (NE)
International Society for Astrological Research, Inc. (US)
International Society for Burn Injuries (NE)
International Society for Burn Injuries (UK)
International Society for Business Education (SZ)
International Society for Cell Biology (US)
International Society for Chronobiology (IT)
International Society for Community Development (US)
International Society for Educational Information, Inc. (JA)
International Society for Electrosleep and Electroanaesthesia (AU)
International Society for Experimental Hematology (DK)
International Society for Fluoride Research (US)
International Society for General Semantics (US)
International Society for Horticultural Science (NE)
International Society for Human and Animal Mycology (UK)
International Society for Hybrid Microelectronics (UK)
International Society for Japanese Philately (US)
International Society for Jazz Research (Graz, Austria) (AU)
International Society for Krishna Consciousness (US)
International Society for Labor Law and Social Security. United States National Committee (US)
International Society for Labour Law and Social Legislation (SZ)
International Society for Music Education (GW)
International Society for Paediatric Neurosurgery (SZ)
International Society for Performing Arts, Libraries and Museums (FR)
International Society for Photogrammetry (NE)
International Society for Portuguese Philately (US)
International Society for Prospective Medicine (LH)
International Society for Research on the Moors (AU)
International Society for Rock Mechanics (PO)

International Society for Soil Mechanics and Foundation Engineering (GW)
International Society for Soil Mechanics and Foundation Engineering (US)
International Society for Stereology (US)
International Society for Technology Assessment (US)
International Society for Terrain-Vehicle Systems (US)
International Society for the Comparative Study of Civilization, American Branch (US)
International Society for the Study of Medieval Philosophy (BE)
International Society for the Study of Significs (NE)
International Society for the Study of Symbols (US)
International Society for Tropical Ecology (II)
International Society of Aesthetic Plastic Surgery (US)
International Society of Art and Psychopathology (FR)
International Society of Art and Psychopathology (SZ)
International Society of Audiology (SZ)
International Society of Bassists (US)
International Society of Bible Collectors (US)
International Society of Biometeorology (NE)
International Society of Blood Transfusion (FR)
International Society of Blood Transfusion (SZ)
International Society of Cardiology (SZ)
International Society of Christian Endeavor (US)
International Society of Criminology (FR)
International Society of Cybernetic Medicine (IT)
International Society of Digestive Endoscopy (US)
International Society of Educational Planners (CN)
International Society of Endocrinology (NE)
International Society of Food Service Consultants (US)
International Society of Geographical Pathology (SZ)
International Society of Hematology (SZ)
International Society of Hematology (US)
International Society of Hematology. European Division (SZ)
International Society of Heraldry & Family Trees (US)
International Society of Heterocyclic Chemistry (US)
International Society of History of Medicine (FR)
International Society of Ichthyology and Hydrobiology (II)
International Society of Internal Medicine (SZ)
International Society of Lymphology (GW)
International Society of Medical Hydrology and Climatology (IT)
International Society of Military Collectors (UK)
International Society of Nephrology (SZ)
International Society of Nephrology (US)
International Society of Neuroendocrinology (SZ)
International Society of Organbuilders (GW)
International Society of Orthopedic Surgery and Traumatology (BE)
International Society of Performing Arts Administrators (US)
International Society of Phonetic Sciences (SZ)
International Society of Planetarium Educators (US)
International Society of Plant Morphologists (II)
International Society of Radiology (SZ)
International Society of Reply Coupon Collectors (US)
International Society of Soil Science (FR)
International Society of Soil Science (IT)
International Society of Sports Psychology (IT)
International Society of Sugarcane Technologists (US)
International Society of Surgery (BE)
International Society of Tropical Dermatology (US)
International Society of United Modern Enterprise (NR)
International Society of Urology (FR)
International Society of Weekly Newspaper Editors (US)
International Society on Biotelemetry (SZ)
International Society on Metabolic Eye Disease (US)
International Society on Thrombosis and Haemostasis (GW)
International Society on Toxicology (US)
International Sociological Association (UK)
International Sociological Association. Research Committee on Sociolinguistics (US)
International Solar Energy Society (US)
International Solar Energy Society. American Section (US)
International Solar Energy Society. Australian and New Zealand Section (AT)
International Solid Waste and Public Cleansing Association (SZ)
International Speleological Union (AU)
International Sporting Press Association (FR)

International Standing Committee on Physiology and Pathology of Animal Reproduction  (UK)

International Star Class Yacht Racing Association  (US)

International Statistical Institute   (NE)

International Statistical Institute   (UK)

International Studies Association  (US)

International Studies Association. Comparative Interdisciplinary Studies Section  (US)

International Study Group for Mathematics Learning  (UK)

International Study Group for Research in Cardiac Metabolism  (US)

International Sugar Journal Ltd.  (UK)

International Sugar Organization  (US)

International Sugar Research Foundation, Inc.  (US)

International Superphosphate and Compound Manufacturers Association Ltd.  (UK)

International Superphosphate Manufacturers' Association Ltd.  (FR)

International Symposium on Animal and Plant Toxins  (US)

International Symposium on Stochastic Hydraulics  (US)

International Tape Association  (US)

International Taxicab Association  (US)

International Telecommunication Union   (UN)

International Telephone and Telegraph Corp.  (UK)

International Telephone and Telegraph Corporation  (GW)

International Telex Corp.  (US)

International Telugu Institute  (II)

International Textile, Garment and Leather Workers' Federation  (BE)

International Textiles BV   (NE)

International Theatre Institute  (FR)

International Theatre Institute of the United States  (US)

International Theatre Institute. Polish Center   (PL)

International Thespian Society  (US)

International Tin Council  (UK)

International Tin Research Council  (UK)

International Tin Research Institute  (BE)

International Tin Research Institute  (UK)

International Touring Alliance  (SZ)

International Trade and Finance Review  (US)

International Trade Fair Association  (II)

International Trade News Letter  (US)

International Trade Publications Ltd.  (UK)

International Trade Union of Miners  (CS)

International Translations Centre  (NE)

International Transport Workers' Federation  (UK)

International Trust for Zoological Nomenclature  (UK)

International Turquoise Association  (US)

International Typeface Corp.  (US)

International Typographical Union  (US)

International U F O Observer Corps.  (JA)

International Understanding  (II)

International Union Against Cancer  (SZ)

International Union Against Cancer  (US)

International Union Against the Venereal Diseases  (UK)

International Union Against Tuberculosis  (FR)

International Union Against Tuberculosis  (UK)

International Union for Applied Ornithology. Institut fuer Biologie, Umwelt und Lebensschutz  (GW)

International Union for Child Welfare  (SZ)

International Union for Conservation of Nature and Natural Resources  (SZ)

International Union for Health Education  (SZ)

International Union for Inland Navigation  (BE)

International Union for Moral and Social Action  (BE)

International Union for Pure & Applied Biophysics (UK)

International Union for the Scientific Study of Population  (BE)

International Union for Vacuum Science Technique and Applications  (UK)

International Union of Academies  (BE)

International Union of Air Pollution Prevention Associations  (US)

International Union of Alpine Associations  (SZ)

International Union of Angiology  (FR)

International Union of Anthropological and Ethnological Sciences  (GW)

International Union of Architects
    see  Union Internationale des Architectes

International Union of Biochemistry  (NE)

International Union of Biochemistry  (UK)

International Union of Biochemistry  (US)

International Union of Biological Sciences  (NE)

International Union of Bricklayers and Allied Craftsmen  (US)

International Union of Building Societies and Savings Associations  (UK)

International Union of Crystallography   (NE)

International Union of Crystallography   (DK)

International Union of Electrical, Radio and Machine Workers, AFL-CIO, CLC  (US)

International Union of Elevator Constructors  (US)

International Union of Food and Allied Workers' Associations  (SZ)

International Union of Forest Research Organizations  (NO)

International Union of Geodesy and Geophysics  (CN)

International Union of Geodesy and Geophysics  (FR)

International Union of Geological Sciences   (NE)

International Union of Local Authorities   (NE)

International Union of Operating Engineers  (US)

International Union of Petroleum & Industrial Workers  (US)

International Union of Pharmacology  (US)

International Union of Physiological Sciences   (FR)

International Union of Physiological Sciences   (HU)

International Union of Prehistoric and Protohistoric Sciences  (YU)

International Union of Producers and Distributors of Electrical Energy  (FR)

International Union of Psychological Science   (FR)

International Union of Psychological Science   (US)

International Union of Public Transport   (BE)

International Union of Pure and Applied Chemistry  (UK)

International Union of Pure and Applied Chemistry  (US)

International Union of Pure and Applied Physics  (CN)

International Union of Pure and Applied Physics  (FR)

International Union of Pure and Applied Physics  (UK)

International Union of Pure and Applied Physics. Commission on Atomic and Molecular Physics and Spectroscopy  (CN)

International Union of Railways  (FR)

International Union of School and University Health and Medicine  (FR)

International Union of Socialist Youth   (AU)

International Union of Speleology  (SZ)

International Union of Students  (CS)

International Union of Testing and Research Laboratories for Materials and Structures  (FR)

International Union of Theoretical and Applied Mechanics  (DK)

International Union of Theoretical and Applied Mechanics  (US)

International Universities Press, Inc.  (US)

International Veterinary Association for Animal Production  (SP)

International Vine and Wine Office
    see Office International de la Vigne et du Vin  (FR)

International Violin and Guitar Makers Association  (US)

International Wages for Housework. London Wages for Housework Committee  (UK)

International Water Resources Association  (US)

International Water Supply Association  (UK)

International Waterfowl Research Bureau  (UK)

International Wealth Success  (US)

International Weightlifting Federation  (UK)

International Whaling Commission  (UK)

International Wheat Council  (UK)

International Wizard of Oz Club, Inc.  (US)

International Wood Trade Publications, Inc.  (US)

International Woodworkers of America, AFL-CIO, CLC  (US)

International Woodworkers of America. Regional Council No. 1   (CN)

International Word Processing Association  (US)

International Work Group for Indigenous Affairs  (DK)

International Year & Hand-Books S.r.l.  (IT)

International Year Book and Statesmen's Who's Who  (UK)

International 505 Association  (AT)

Internationale Arbeitsgemeinschaft fuer Hymnologie  (GW)

Internationale Brecht-Gesellschaft  (GW)

Internationale Buergermeister-Union  (GW)

Internationale Congress Union  (GW)

Internationale Gemeenschap van Christenen  (NE)

Internationale Gesellschaft fuer Geschichte der Pharmazie  (GW)

Internationale Gesellschaft fuer Kiefer-Gesichts-Chirurgie  (GE)

Internationale Gesellschaft fuer Orientforschung  (NE)

Internationale Gesellschaft fuer Religionspsychologie  (GW)

Internationale Heinrich Schuetz-Gesellschaft e.V.  (GW)

Internationale Lenau-Gesellschaft   (AU)

Verlag fuer Internationale Politik GmbH  (GW)

Internationale School voor Wijsbegeerte   (NE)

Internationale Sozialistische Publikationen GmbH  (GW)

Internationale Stefan Zweig-Gesellschaft   (AU)

Internationale Stiftung Mozarteum   (AU)

Internationale Uitlotingsdienst   (NE)

Internationale Vereinigung Beratender Ingenieure
    see International Federation of Consulting Engineers  (NE)

Internationale Vereinigung Christlicher Geschaeftsleute. Gruppe Zurich   (SZ)

Internationale Vereinigung fuer Brueckenbau und Hochbau
    see International Association for Bridge and Structural Engineering  (SZ)

Internationale Vereinigung fuer Rechts- und Sozialphilosophie  (GW)

Internationale Vereinigung fuer Soziale Sicherheit
    see International Social Security Association  (SZ)

Internationale Vereinigung fuer theoretische und angewandte Limnologie  (GW)

Internationale Vereniging Bellamy   (NE)

Internationale Vereniging voor Nederlandistiek   (NE)

Internationale Werbegesellschaft m.b.H.   (AU)

Internationale Zentralinstitut fuer das Jugend-und Bildungsfernsehen  (GW)

Internationaler Bodensee Verkehrsverein  (GW)

Internationaler Genfer Verban - Landesteil Oesterreich  (AU)

Internationaler Rat zur Bekaempfung des Alkoholismus und der Suchtgefahren
    see International Council on Alcohol and Addictions  (SZ)

Internationales Entomologisches Verein  (GW)

Internationales Esperanto-Museum in Wien  (AU)

Internationales Forschungszentrum fuer Grundfragen der Wissenschaften, Salzburg  (AU)

Internationales Institut fuer den Frieden  (AU)

Internationales Institut fuer Missionswissenschaftliche Forschungen  (GW)

Internationales Katholisches Missionswerk e.V.  (GW)

Internationales Musikzentrum   (AU)

Internationales Wollsekretariat Geschaeftsstelle fuer Oesterreich  (AU)

Internationella Kvinnofoerbundet foer Fred och Frihet. Svenska Sektionen
    see Women's International League for Peace and Freedom. Swedish Section  (SW)

Societa Editrice Internazionale   (IT)

Compagnia Edizione Internazionali  (IT)

Internews  (US)

Inter-Parliamentary Union   (SZ)

Interplanetary Space Travel Research Association (United Kingdom)  (UK)

Interpol
    see International Criminal Police Organization-Interpol  (FR)

Polska Agencja Interpress   (PL)

Interpress Publications Ltd.  (CN)

Interpress Publishing Co.  (HU)

Interprovincial School for the Deaf   (CN)

Interpub Co. Ltd.  (IR)

Interreligious Foundation for Community Organization  (US)

Edizioni Interrogations  (IT)

Inter-School & Inter-Varsity Christian Fellowship Ltd.  (JM)

Intersection, Inc.  (US)

Intersistemas, S.A. de C.V.  (MX)

Inter-Society Color Council  (US)

Intersociety Committee on Pathology Information  (US)

Interstate  (US)

Interstate Commission on the Potomac River Basin  (US)

Interstate Oil Compact Commission  (US)

Interstate Printers & Publishers, Inc.  (US)

Intertec Publishing Corp.  (US)

Inter-Tribal Council of California  (US)

Inter-Tribal Council of Nevada, Inc.  (US)

Inter-Union Commission on Geodynamics  (CN)

Interuniversitair Centrum voor Hedendaagse Geschiedenis
    see Centre Interuniversitaire d'Histoire Contemporaine  (BE)

Interuniversitair Centrum voor Studie en Documentatie van Latijns Amerika  (NE)

Inter-University Case Program  (US)

Interuniversity Centre for European Studies  (CN)

Interuniversity Communications Council  (US)

Inter-University Consortium for Political and Social Research  (US)

Inter-University Seminar on Armed Forces & Society  (US)

Inter-Varsity Christian Fellowship  (US)
Inter-Varsity Press  (UK)
Intervention Collective  (AT)
Interview Enterprises, Inc.  (US)
Interwing Group Ltd.  (PK)
Intlaw Publishers Corporation  (II)
Intra-Science Research Foundation  (UK)
Intra-Science Research Foundation  (US)
Intramurale Gezondheidszorg  (NE)
Intrepid Press  (US)
Intrigue Publications, Inc.  (US)
P. Introzzi, Ed. & Pub.  (IT)
Editora Inubia S.A.  (BL)
Inummart  (CN)
Invalidiliitto r.y.  (FI)
Inventors Society of Australia  (AT)
Inventors Workshop International  (US)
Inverell and District Historical Society  (AT)
Investarama Club  (US)
Investment & Marketing  (PK)
Investment Company Institute  (US)
Investment Dealers Digest (IDD) Inc.  (US)
Investor Responsibility Research Center  (US)
Investors Chronicle Publication  (UK)
Investors' Institute, Inc.  (US)
Investors League Inc.  (US)
Invicta Publications  (AT)
Invictus Publishing Co.  (US)
IOGT-NTO  (SW)
Iona College  (US)
Iona Print Ltd.  (IE)
Iowa. Bureau of Labor. Research and Statistics
  Division  (US)
Iowa. Civil Rights Commission  (US)
Iowa. Department of Health. Division of Records and
  Statistics  (US)
Iowa. Department of Public Instruction  (US)
Iowa. Drug Abuse Authority  (US)
Iowa. Employment Security Commission  (US)
Iowa. Geological Survey  (US)
Iowa. Higher Education Facilities Commission  (US)
Iowa. Office for Planning and Programming  (US)
Iowa. State Conservation Commission  (US)
Iowa. State Library Commission  (US)
Iowa Academy of Science  (US)
Iowa Archaelogical Society  (US)
Iowa Association for Lifelong Learning  (US)
Iowa Association of Electric Cooperatives  (US)
Iowa Association of Plumbing, Heating, Cooling
  Contractors, Inc.  (US)
Iowa Association of School Administrators  (US)
Iowa Association of School Boards  (US)
Iowa Congress of Parents and Teachers  (US)
Iowa Council of Teachers of English  (US)
Iowa Crop and Livestock Reporting Service  (US)
Iowa Dental Association  (US)
Iowa Dental Hygienists' Association  (US)
Iowa Development Commission  (US)
Iowa Educational Media Association  (US)
Iowa Farm Bureau Federation  (US)
Iowa Genealogical Society  (US)
Iowa Grain and Feed Association  (US)
Iowa Library Association  (US)
Iowa Lumbermens Association  (US)
Iowa Medical Society  (US)
Iowa Motor Truck Association  (US)
Iowa Music Educators Association  (US)
Iowa Nurses' Association  (US)
Iowa Ornithologists' Union  (US)
Iowa Poetry Association  (US)
Iowa Regional Medical Program  (US)
Iowa Restaurant Association  (US)
Iowa Retail Food Dealers Association  (US)
Iowa Society of Certified Public Accountants  (US)
Iowa State Education Association  (US)
Iowa State Historical Society. Division of Historical
  Museum and Archives  (US)
Iowa State Penitentiary at Fort Madison  (US)
Iowa State Policeman's Association  (US)
Iowa State University  (US)
Iowa State University. Department of English  (US)
Iowa State University. Engineering Research Institute
  (US)
Iowa State University Library  (US)
Iowa State University Press  (US)
Iowa State University. Publications Distribution Center
  (US)
Iowa State University. Student Counseling Service
  (US)
Iowa United Methodist Church  (US)
Iowa United Methodist Communications  (US)
Iparmuveszeti Muzeum  (HU)
Ipirotiki Estia  (GR)
Iqbal Academy Pakistan  (PK)
Iran. Geological Survey  (IR)
Iran. Ministry of Culture and Arts. Centre for Iranian
  Anthropology  (IR)

Iran. Ministry of Culture and Arts. General
  Department of Cultural and Artistic Cooperations
  (IR)
Iran. Ministry of Finance and Economic Affairs  (IR)
Iran. Ministry of Health. Family Planning Division
  (IR)
Iran. Ministry of Industries and Mines  (IR)
Iran. Ministry of Information and Tourism  (IR)
Iran. National Library  (IR)
Iran. State Civil Defence Organization  (IR)
Iran. Statistical Centre  (IR)
Iran. Supreme Commander's Staff  (IR)
Iran American Chamber of Commerce, Inc.  (US)
Iran Marketing Co.  (IR)
Iran Philatelic Study Circle  (UK)
Iran Press Organization  (IR)
Iran Society  (II)
Iranian Association for the United Nations  (IR)
Iranian Association of Obstetricians and Gynecologists
  (IR)
Iranian Bankers' Association  (IR)
Iranian Chamber of Commerce and Industry and
  Mines  (IR)
Iranian Documentation Centre
  see under Institute for Research and Planning in
  Science  (IR)
Iranian Library Association  (IR)
Iranian Mathematical Society  (IR)
Iranian Orthopaedic Association  (IR)
Iranian Petroleum Institute  (IR)
Iranian Public Health Association  (IR)
Iraq. Al-Jihaz al-Markazi Lil-Ihsa
  see Iraq. Central Statistical Organization  (IQ)
Iraq. Central Statistical Organization  (IQ)
Iraq. Central Statistical Organization. Department of
  Foreign Trade Statistics  (IQ)
Iraq. Central Statistical Organization. Industrial
  Statistics Department  (IQ)
Iraq. Department of Tourism Services  (IQ)
Iraq. Directorate General of Antiquities  (IQ)
Iraq. Ministry of Culture and Information  (IQ)
Iraq. Ministry of Education  (IQ)
Iraq. Ministry of Health. Institute of Endemic Diseases
  see Institute of Endemic Diseases  (IQ)
Iraq. Ministry of Justice. Legal Drafting Department
  (IQ)
Iraq National History Museum  (IQ)
Iraq Natural History Research Centre  (IQ)
Iraqi Federation of Industries  (IQ)
Iraqi Medical Professions' Association  (IQ)
Ireland. Central Statistics Office  (IE)
Ireland. Department of Agriculture and Fisheries
  (IE)
Ireland. Department of Education  (IE)
Ireland. Department of External Affairs. Information
  Section  (IE)
Ireland. Department of Finance  (IE)
Ireland. Department of Industry and Commerce  (IE)
Ireland. Government Publications Sales Office  (IE)
Irgun Haganaim B'israel  (IS)
Irgun Hayatsivim  (IS)
Ha-Irgun le-Milhamah ve-Tipul Be-Hatsalat Rekhush
  Yehudi  (IS)
Irgun Oley Merkaz Europa  (IS)
Irish Agricultural Organization Society Ltd.  (IE)
Irish American Cultural Institute  (US)
Irish Ancestor  (IE)
Irish Association for the Blind  (IE)
Irish Association of Master Bakers  (UK)
Irish Astronomical Journal  (UK)
Irish Communist Organization  (UK)
Irish Congress of Trade Unions Research Service
  (IE)
Irish Contracts Weekly  (IE)
Irish Countrywomens Association  (IE)
Irish Creamery Managers Association  (IE)
Irish Creamery Milk Suppliers Association  (IE)
Irish Dairy Board  (IE)
Irish Dental Association  (IE)
Irish Dominican Fathers  (IE)
Irish Engineering Publications Ltd.  (IE)
Irish Federation of Women's Clubs  (IE)
Irish Georgian Society  (IE)
Irish Guild of Catholic Nurses  (IE)
Irish Hardware and Allied Trader Ltd.  (IE)
Irish Historical Society  (IE)
Irish Hotel and Catering Institute  (IE)
Irish Linen Guild  (UK)
Irish Management Institute  (IE)
Irish Medical Association  (IE)
Irish Messenger Publications  (IE)
Irish National Teachers Organization  (UK)
Irish Naturalists' Journal Committee  (UK)
Irish Nurses' Organization  (IE)
Irish People, Inc.  (US)
Irish Pigs & Bacon Commission  (IE)
Irish Province of the Society of Jesus  (IE)
Irish Publication Surveys Ltd.  (IE)

Irish Publishing Co. Ltd.  (IE)
Irish Republican Movement  (IE)
Irish Road Transport Association  (IE)
Irish Sea Fisheries Board  (IE)
Irish Sisters of Charity  (IE)
Irish Society for Archives  (IE)
Irish Sugar Co.  (IE)
Irish Tatler & Sketch Ltd.  (IE)
Irish Times Ltd.  (IE)
Irish Trade and Technical Publications Ltd.  (IE)
Irish Transport & General Workers' Union  (IE)
Irish University Review  (IE)
Irish Wildbird Conservancy  (IE)
Irish World  (US)
Irkutskii Gosudarstvennyi Universitet im. A. A.
  Zhdanova  (UR)
Irmanaultson Realizacoes  (BL)
Iron and Steel Institute of Japan  (JA)
Iron and Steel Statistics Bureau  (UK)
Iron and Steel Trades Confederation  (UK)
Iron Castings Society  (US)
Iron Man Publishing Co.  (US)
Iron Press  (UR)
Ironwood Press  (US)
Irrigation Research & Extension Committee  (AT)
Irus-Verlag  (GW)
Irvine World Publishers  (US)
Irving-Cloud Publishing Co.  (US)
Iryo Dokokai
  see Medical Treatment Association  (JA)
Peter Isaacson Publications  (AT)
Isar-Post, Druck- und Verlagsgesellschaft mbH  (GW)
Ishikawajima-Harima Heavy Industries Co., Ltd.  (JA)
Ishiyaku Publishers, Inc.  (JA)
Izdatel'stvo Iskusstvo  (UR)
Islam and the Modern Age Society  (II)
Islamic Cultural Centre  (UK)
Islamic Culture Board  (II)
Islamic Missionary Society  (SA)
Islamic Political Party of Malaysia  (MY)
Islamic Research Academy  (PK)
Islamic Research Institute
  see Pakistan. Ministry of Religious Affairs. Islamic
  Research Institute  (PK)
Islamic Students' Union of the University of Malaya
  (MY)
Island Press Ltd.  (BM)
Isle of Man Examiner Ltd.  (UK)
Isle of Man Natural History and Antiquarian Society
  (UI)
Isle of Wight County Press Ltd.  (UK)
Islenzka Natturufraedifelag  (IC)
Ispettorato Provinciale dell'Agricoltura  (IT)
Ispettorato Provinciale dell' Agricoltura Pesaro  (IT)
N. Israel  (NE)
Israel. Air Force  (IS)
Israel. Atomic Energy Commission  (IS)
Israel. Central Bureau of Statistics  (IS)
Israel. Commissioner for Complaints from the Public
  (IS)
Israel. Department of Customs and Excise  (IS)
Israel. Department of Surveys  (IS)
Israel. Environmental Protection Agency  (IS)
Israel. Geological Survey  (IS)
Israel. Government Press Office  (IS)
Israel. Hydrological Service  (IS)
Israel. Knesset  (IS)
Israel. Meteorological Service  (IS)
Israel. Ministry for Foreign Affairs  (IS)
Israel. Ministry of Agriculture. Agriculture and
  Settlement Planning and Development Center  (IS)
Israel. Ministry of Agriculture. Dept. of Fisheries
  (IS)
Israel. Ministry of Commerce and Industry  (IS)
Israel. Ministry of Commerce and Industry. Foreign
  Trade Division  (IS)
Israel. Ministry of Communications  (IS)
Israel. Ministry of Education and Culture  (IS)
Israel. Ministry of Health  (IS)
Israel. Ministry of Justice. Patent Office  (IS)
Israel. Ministry of Labour  (IS)
Israel. Ministry of Religious Affairs  (IS)
Israel. Ministry of Social Welfare  (IS)
Israel. Ministry of the Interior  (IS)
Israel. Ministry of Tourism  (IS)
Israel. National Council for Research and
  Development  (IS)
Israel. National Council for Research and
  Development. Center of Scientific and
  Technological Information  (IS)
Israel. State Revenue Administration  (IS)
Israel Academy of Sciences and Humanities  (IS)
Israel Association for International Cooperation  (IS)
N.V. Boekhandel en Antiquariaat B.M. Israel B.V.
  (NE)
Israel Bar Association  (IS)
Israel Business Books Ltd.  (IS)
Israel Chess Federation  (IS)

Italian Books and Periodicals (IT)
Italian Center for Applied Linguistics (IT)
Italian Chamber of Commerce for the U K and the Commonwealth
  *see* Commercio Italiana per la Gran Bretagna e il Commonwealth (IT)
Italian Chamber of Commerce in Australia (AT)
Italian Chamber of Commerce in Chicago (US)
Italian Chamber of Commerce of Toronto (CN)
Italian Committee (IT)
Italian Cultural Institute (CN)
Italian Embassy in the United States. Commercial Office (US)
Italian Heritage Newsletter (US)
Italian Historical Society of America (US)
Italian Institute for Foreign Trade
  *see* Istituto Nazionale per Il Commercio Estero (IT)
Italian Medical Association (IT)
Italian National Institute of Higher Mathematics Conventions (IT)
Italian National Olympic Committee (IT)
Italian Quarterly (US)
Italian Socialist Democratic Party (IT)
Italian Society for the Prevention and Diagnosis of Tumors (IT)
Italian Society for the Study of Sterility and Fertility (IT)
Italian Society of Anesthesiology (IT)
Italian Society of Biochemistry (IT)
Italian Society of Gastroenterology (IT)
Italian Society of Immunology and Immunopathology (IT)
Italian Society of Neurosurgery (IT)
Italian Society of Urology (IT)
Italian Sulfur Corporation
  *see* Ente Zolfi Italian (IT)
Italian Tribune Publishing Co. (US)
Editoriale Italiana (IT)
Compagnia Editoriale Italiana (IT)
Italiani nel Mondo (IT)
Italiano Ltd. (UK)
Italimuse Inc (US)
Italo-American Times Publishing Co. (US)
Italo Di Castri (IT)
Italy. Aeronautica Militare Italiana. Ispettorato Telecomunicazione e Assistenza al Volo (IT)
Italy. Consiglio dell'Ordine dei Medici di Torino. Bollettino Ordine dei Medici (IT)
Italy. Ente Nazionale Idrocarburi (IT)
Italy. Istituto Centrale di Statistica (IT)
Italy. Istituto Nazionale per Lo Studio della Congiuntura (IT)
Italy. Istituto Poligrafico dello Stato (IT)
Italy. Laboratorio di Studi Sulla Ricerca e Sulla Documentazione (IT)
Italy. Ministera della Pubblica Istruzione (IT)
Italy. Ministero dei Lavori Pubblici-Consiglio Superiore (IT)
Italy. Ministero dei Trasporti e dell'Aviazione Civile (IT)
Italy. Ministero dei Trasporti e dell' Aviazione Civile. Azienda Autona Dellle Ferrovie dello Stato (IT)
Italy. Ministero del Bilancio (IT)
Italy. Ministero del Commercio Con l'Estero (IT)
Italy. Ministero del Lavoro e della Previdenza Sociale (IT)
Italy. Ministero dell'Industria del Commercio e dell'Artigianato (IT)
Italy. Ministero dell'Interno (IT)
Italy. Ministero della Difesa-Aeronautico (IT)
Italy. Ministero della Difesa-Esercito (IT)
Italy. Ministero della Difesa. Servizio dei Informazione Pubblica (IT)
Italy. Ministero della Pubblica Istruzione (IT)
Italy. Ministero della Sanita (IT)
Italy. Ministero delle Finanze (IT)
Italy. Ministero delle Poste e delle Telecomunicazioni (IT)
Italy. Ministero di Grazia e Guistizia. Centro Studi Penitenziaria (IT)
Italy. Ministero per i Beni Culturali e Ambientali (IT)
Italy. Officio della Proprieta Letteraria (IT)
Italy. Presidenza del Consiglio dei Ministri (IT)
Italy. Presidenza del Consiglio dei Ministri. Servizio Informazioni (IT)
Italy. Stato Maggiore Aeronautica (IT)
Italy-America Chamber of Commerce, Inc. (US)
Ithaca College. Dept. of Sociology (US)
Itineraires (FR)
Itinerario-Guia del Viajero (SP)
Itsuu Laboratory (JA)
Ittihad al-Kuttab al-Arab (SY)
Ittihad al-Sinaat al-Misriyah
  *see* Federation of Egyptian Industries (UA)

Ivanovskii Tekstil'nyi Institut (UR)
Ivimey and Associates Pty. Ltd. (AT)
Ivory Coast. Bibliotheque Nationale (IV)
Ivory Coast. Bureau de Developpement Industriel (IV)
Ivory Coast. Bureau National d'Etudes Techniques de Developpement (IV)
Ivory Coast. Direction des Affaires Economiques et des Relations Economiques Exterieures (IV)
Ivory Coast. Direction des Mines et de la Geologie (IV)
Ivory Coast. Direction du Budget Special d'Investissement et d'Equipment (IV)
Ivory Coast. Ministere de l'Agriculture (IV)
Ivory Coast. Ministere de l'Economie et des Finances (IV)
Ivory Coast. Ministere du Plan (IV)
Ivory Coast. Ministry of Information (IV)
Ivory Coast. Service de la Statistique (IV)
Iwanami Shoten Publishers (JA)
Iwate Daigaku
  *see* Iwate University (JA)
Iwate Igakkai
  *see* Iwate Medical Association (JA)
Iwate Medical Association (JA)
Iwate University. Faculty of Engineering (JA)
Iwate University. Mountains Land Use Research Station (JA)
Iyo Kizai Kenkyusho
  *see* Tokyo Medical and Dental University. Institute for Medical and Dental Engineering (JA)
Izaak Walton League of America (US)
Izdavacko Preduzece Rad (YU)
Izumi and Co., Ltd. (JA)
Izdatel'stvo Izvestiya (UR)
J A A D Publishing Co. (US)
J A E C
  *see* Japan. Japan Atomic Energy Commission (JA)
J A E R I
  *see* Japan Atomic Energy Research Institute (JA)
J A I Press (US)
J A P I C
  *see* Japan Pharmaceutical Information Centre (JA)
J A P O S Study Group (US)
J A S D F
  *see* Japan Air Self Defense Force (JA)
J. & M. Associates (US)
J. B. Printing (US)
J-B Publishing Co. (US)
J.C.E. (IT)
J E O L Ltd. (JA)
J.E.P. and Associates (UK)
J E R C
  *see* Japan Economic Research Center (JA)
J E T R O
  *see* Japan External Trade Organization (JA)
J F J Educational Services, Inc. (US)
J.-G.-Herder-Institut (GW)
J H M Publications (US)
J I C A
  *see* Japan International Cooperation Agency (JA)
J I C S T
  *see* Japan Information Center of Science and Technology (JA)
J.J. Group of Hospitals (II)
J.K. Lasser Tax Institute (US)
J.K. Publications (II)
J.L.B. Smith Institute of Ichthyology
  *see under* Rhodes University (SA)
J. M. P. Services (West Africa) Ltd. (NR)
J. N. R.
  *see* Japanese National Railways (JA)
J P O Inc. (US)
J. Paul Getty Museum (US)
J. S. C.
  *see* Science Council of Japan (JA)
Jean Jachymiak, Pub. (FR)
John Jackson and Associates Pty. Ltd. (AT)
Jackson County Historical Society (US)
Jackson County Medical Society (US)
Jackson Laboratory (US)
Jacksonville Area Chamber of Commerce (US)
Jacksonville Children's Museum (US)
Jacksonville Genealogical Society (US)
Jacksonville State University. Board of Publications (US)
John I. Jacobs & Co. Ltd. (UK)
Jacobsen Publishing Co. (US)
Editions Jacquemart (FR)
Jadavpur University. Department of Comparative Literature (II)
Jaeger-Verlag GmbH (GW)
W. Jaeggi AG (SZ)
Jag Inc. (US)
Jagdgebrauchshundverband (GW)
Jagdspaniel-Klub (GW)
Jaguar Books (UK)
Jaguar Clubs of Australia (AT)

B. O. Jahnsson, Ed. & Pub. (SW)
John Jahr Verlag KG (GW)
Verlag Jahrbuch der Lehrer der Hoeheren Schulen (GW)
Jahrbuch-Verlag (GW)
Jahreszeiten-Verlag GmbH (GW)
Jai Hind (II)
Jaideva Bros. (II)
Jain Bhawan (II)
S. C. Jain, Ed. & Pub. (II)
N. Jaiswal, Ed. & Pub. (II)
Jakemate (VE)
Jal-Verlag (GW)
JALA Internationaal B.V. (NE)
Jalart House Inc. (US)
Jalisco. Comision Forestal del Estado de Jalisco (MX)
Jam To-Day (US)
Al-Jamaheer Press House (IQ)
Jamaica (B.W.I.) Study Group (US)
Jamaica. Department of Statistics (JM)
Jamaica. Ministry of Health and Environmental Control. Bureau of Health Education (JM)
Jamaica. Ministry of Pensions and Social Secuirty (JM)
Jamaica Agricultural Society (JM)
Jamaica Chamber of Commerce (JM)
Jamaica Geographical Society (JM)
Jamaica Industrial Development Corp. (JM)
Jamaica Tourist Board (JM)
Jamaican Historical Society (JM)
Jamawu Publications (SL)
James Conran Pty. Ltd. (AT)
James Cook University of North Queensland (AT)
James Cook University of North Queensland. Dept. of English (AT)
James Cook University of North Queensland. Department of Geography (AT)
James Cowan Associates (S.E. Asia) Pte Ltd. (SI)
Derek James, Ed. & Pub. (UK)
James Ford Bell Library (US)
James Ford Bell Technical Center (US)
James Sprunt Foundation, Inc. (US)
James Willard Schultz Society (US)
Al-Jamhour - al-Jadid (LE)
Jamiyat-ul-Falah Karachi (PK)
Jammu and Kashmir. Directorate of Economics and Statistics (II)
Jammu and Kashmir. High Court (II)
Jammu and Kashmir. Legislative Council. Comittee on Privileges (II)
Jammu and Kashmir Academy of Art Culture and Languages (II)
Jammu and Kashmir Cooperative Union (II)
Jammu University
  *see* University of Jammu (II)
Janlen Enterprises (US)
Janmabhoomi Group of Newspapers (II)
Jannersten Foerlag AB (SW)
Anthony J. Jannetti, Inc. (US)
Acke Janson, Ed. & Pub. (SW)
Januz Marketing Communications (US)
Japadre Editore (IT)
Japan
  *see also* Japanese (JA)
Japan. Atomic Energy Research Institute
  *see* Japan Atomic Energy Research Institute (JA)
Japan. Building Research Institute (JA)
Japan. Bureau of Statistics (JA)
Japan. Director of Statistical Standards (JA)
Japan. Economic Planning Agency (JA)
Japan. Economic Planning Agency. Economic Research Institute
  *see* Japan. Economic Research Institute (JA)
Japan. Economic Research Institute (JA)
Japan. Fermentation Research Institute (JA)
Japan. Fisheries Agency. Freshwater Fisheries Research Laboratory
  *see* Japan. Freshwater Fisheries Research Laboratory (JA)
Japan. Fisheries Agency. Japan Sea Regional Fisheries Research Laboratory
  *see* Japan. Japan Sea Regional Fisheries Research Laboratory (JA)
Japan. Fisheries Agency. Tohoku Regional Fisheries Research Laboratory
  *see* Japan. Tohoku Regional Fisheries Research Laboratory (JA)
Japan. Fisheries Agency. Tokai Regional Fisheries Research Laboratory
  *see* Japan. Tokai Regional Fisheries Research Laboratory (JA)
Japan. Forestry Agency (JA)
Japan. Forestry Agency. Government Forest Experiment Station

Japan Association of Physical Education for Women
 and Girls   (JA)
Japan Association of Rehabilitation Medicine   (JA)
Japan Atomic Energy Commission
 see Japan. Japan Atomic Energy Commission   (JA)
Japan Atomic Energy Research Institute. Tokai
 Research Establishment   (JA)
Japan Atomic Energy Society
 see Atomic Energy Society of Japan   (JA)
Japan Atomic Industrial Forum, Inc.   (JA)
Japan Audio-Visual Education Association   (JA)
Japan Audiological Society   (JA)
Japan Automobile Federation   (JA)
Japan Automobile Manufacturers Association   (JA)
Japan Bicycle Industry Association   (JA)
Japan Broadcast Publishing Co., Ltd.(Nippon Hoso
 Shuppan Kyokai)   (JA)
Japan Broadcasting Corp.   (JA)
Japan Broadcasting Corp. Radio & TV Culture
 Research Institute   (JA)
Japan Broadcasting Corp. Technical Research
 Laboratories   (JA)
Japan Broncho- Esophagological Society   (JA)
Japan Cartographers Association   (JA)
Japan Center for Area Development Research   (JA)
Japan Chamber of Commerce and Industry   (JA)
Japan Chemical Fibres Association   (JA)
Japan Chemical Industry Association   (JA)
Japan Christian Medical Association   (JA)
Japan Concrete Institute   (JA)
Japan Cotton Traders' Association   (JA)
Japan Dental Association   (JA)
Japan Development Bank   (JA)
Japan Diabetic Society   (JA)
Japan Documentation Society   (JA)
Japan Echo Inc.   (JA)
Japan Economic Journal   (JA)
Japan Economic Research Center   (JA)
Japan Economic Review   (JA)
Japan Electric Power Survey Committee   (JA)
Japan Emergency Christian Conference on Korean
 Problems   (JA)
Japan Endocrine Society   (JA)
Japan Endocrine Society. Eastern Branch   (JA)
Japan Engineering News, Inc.   (JA)
Japan Environmental Sanitation Center   (JA)
Japan Evangelical Missionary Association   (JA)
Japan Experimental Animal Research Association
 (JA)
Japan External Trade Organisation   (AT)
Japan External Trade Organization   (CN)
Japan External Trade Organization   (JA)
Japan F A O Association   (JA)
Japan Federation of Composers   (JA)
Japan Federation of Economic Organizations   (JA)
Japan Feed Trade Association   (JA)
Japan Fisheries Association   (JA)
Japan Foundation
 see Kokusai Koryu Kikin   (IT)
Japan Foundation   (JA)
Japan Foundation for Shipbuilding Advancement
 (JA)
Japan Foundrymen's Society   (JA)
Japan Gas Association   (JA)
Japan General Foundry Center Foundation   (JA)
Japan Group   (US)
Japan Heat Management Association   (JA)
Japan Hematological Society   (JA)
Japan Hospital Equipment Association   (JA)
Japan Industrial & Vocational Training Association
 (JA)
Japan Industrial Location Center   (JA)
Japan Industrial Safety Association   (JA)
Japan Industrial Vehicles Association   (JA)
Japan Industry and Trade Research Association   (JA)
Japan Information Center of Science and Technology
 (JA)
Japan Institute for Biological Science
 see Nippon Institute for Biological Science   (JA)
Japan Institute for International Study   (JA)
Japan Institute of Industrial Engineering   (JA)
Japan Institute of Labour   (JA)
Japan Institute of Metals   (JA)
Japan Institution for Library Science   (JA)
Japan International Cooperation Agency   (JA)
Japan Investors Ltd.   (JA)
Japan Iron and Steel Exporter's Association   (JA)
Japan Iron & Steel Federation   (JA)
Japan Journal, Inc.   (JA)
Japan Knitwear Designer's Association   (JA)
Japan Lead Zinc Development Association   (JA)
Japan Library Association   (JA)
Japan Light Metal Association   (JA)
Japan Lumber Journal, Inc.   (JA)
Japan Machinery Federation   (JA)
Japan Management Science Institute   (JA)
Japan Map Center   (JA)
Japan Medical Association (Nihon Ishikai)   (JA)

Japan Medical Association (Nippon Igaku Kyokai)
 (JA)
Japan Medical Library Association   (JA)
Japan Medical Publishers, Inc. (Nihon Gakujutsu
 Shuppansha)   (JA)
Japan Mental Health Society   (JA)
Japan Meteorological Agency
 for publications of this agency, see Japan Weather
 Association   (JA)
Japan Microphotography Association   (JA)
Japan Monkey Centre   (JA)
Japan National Tourist Organization   (JA)
Japan Neurosurgical Society   (JA)
Japan Orthodontic Society   (JA)
Japan Patent Center, Inc.   (JA)
Japan Pediatric Society   (JA)
Japan Petroleum Consultants, Ltd.   (JA)
Japan Petroleum Institute   (JA)
Japan Pharmaceutical Information Centre   (JA)
Japan Pharmaceutical Library Association   (JA)
Japan Pharmaceutical, Medical & Dental Supply
 Exporter's Association   (JA)
Japan Pharmaceutical Traders' Association   (JA)
Japan Phonograph Record Association   (JA)
Japan Plant Protection Association   (JA)
Japan Plastics Industry Federation   (JA)
Japan Plastics Journal Ltd.   (JA)
Japan Polar Research Association   (JA)
Japan Press & Service International Co., Ltd.   (JA)
Japan Press, Ltd.   (JA)
Japan Printers' Association   (JA)
Japan Printing News Publishing Co.   (JA)
Japan Public Law Association   (JA)
Japan Publications Trading Co. Ltd.   (US)
Japan Publications Trading Co. Ltd.   (JA)
Japan Publishing House   (JA)
Japan Radiation Research Society   (JA)
Iapan Radioisotope Association   (JA)
Japan Radiological Society
 see Nippon Societas Radiologica   (JA)
Japan Railway Civil Engineering Association   (JA)
Japan Railway Cybernetics Association   (JA)
Japan Railway Engineer's Association   (JA)
Japan Real Estate Institute   (JA)
Japan Refrigeration and Air Conditioning Press   (JA)
Japan Research Association for Textile End-Uses
 (JA)
Japan Road Association   (JA)
Japan Science Foundation   (JA)
Japan Science Society   (JA)
Japan Scientists' Association   (JA)
Japan Sea Regional Fisheries Research Laboratory
 see Japan. Japan Sea Regional Fisheries Research
 Laboratory   (JA)
Japan Securities Research Institute   (JA)
Japan Sewage Works Association   (JA)
Japan Shipping Exchange, Inc.   (JA)
Japan Snake Institute   (JA)
Japan Society for Aeronautical and Space Sciences
 (JA)
Japan Society for Cancer Therapy   (JA)
Japan Society for Cell Biology   (JA)
Japan Society for Technology of Plasticity   (JA)
Japan Society for the Promotion of Science   (JA)
Japan Society of Air Pollution   (JA)
Japan Society of Bakery Technology   (JA)
Japan Society of Chemotherapy   (JA)
Japan Society of Civil Engineers   (JA)
Japan Society of Clinical Pathology   (JA)
Japan Society of Colour Materials   (JA)
Japan Society of Earth Science Education   (JA)
Japan Society of Histochemistry and Cytochemistry
 (JA)
Japan Society of Histological Documentation
 (Societatis Histochemicae Japonicae)   (JA)
Japan Society of Human Genetics   (JA)
Japan Society of International Economics   (JA)
Japan Society of Library Science   (JA)
Japan Society of Logopedics and Phoniatrics   (JA)
Japan Society of London   (UK)
Japan Society of Lubrication Engineers   (JA)
Japan Society of Materials Science   (JA)
Japan Society of Mathematical Education   (JA)
Japan Society of Mechanical Engineers   (JA)
Japan Society of Medical Electronics and Biological
 Engineering   (JA)
Japan Society of Neonatology   (JA)
Japan Society of Precision Engineering   (JA)
Japan Society of Smooth Muscle Research   (JA)
Japan Society of Tropical Medicine   (JA)
Japan Steel & Tube Corporation   (JA)
Japan Steel Works, Ltd.   (JA)
Japan Storage Battery Association   (JA)
Japan Sugar Refiners' Association   (JA)
Japan Surgical Society   (JA)

Japan Tariff Association   (JA)
Japan Teachers' Union   (JA)
Japan Telegraph and Telephone Public Corporation
 (JA)
Japan Textiles and Fibers Research Institute   (JA)
Japan Times, Ltd.   (JA)
Japan Tourist Association   (JA)
Japan Trade Centre   (CN)
Japan Trade Publications Ltd.   (JA)
Japan Travel Bureau, Inc.   (JA)
Japan Typography Association   (JA)
Japan Ukiyo-e Society   (JA)
Japan Union of Associations of Economic Sciences
 (JA)
Japan Water Works Association   (JA)
Japan Weather Association   (JA)
Japan Weather Association. Hokkaido Branch   (JA)
Japan Weather Association. Kagoshima Local
 Meteorological Observatory   (JA)
Japan Welding Society   (JA)
Japan Wood Research Society   (JA)
Japana Esperanto Instituto   (JA)
Japanese
 see also Japan   (JA)
Japanese Aerospace Directory   (JA)
Japanese American Citizens League   (US)
Japanese American News   (US)
Japanese American Philatelic Society   (US)
Japanese Anatomical Association   (JA)
Japanese Archaeologists Association   (JA)
Japanese Association for Dental Science   (JA)
Japanese Association for Infectious Diseases   (JA)
Japanese Association for the Prevention of Venereal
 Diseases and Treponematoses   (JA)
Japanese Association of American Studies   (JA)
Japanese Association of Criminal Psychology   (JA)
Japanese Association of Educational Psychology   (JA)
Japanese Association of Groundwater Hydrology
 (JA)
Japanese Association of Indian and Buddhist Studies
 (JA)
Japanese Association of Leather Technology   (JA)
Japanese Association of Marine Standardization   (JA)
Japanese Association of Mineralogists, Petrologists and
 Economic Geologists   (JA)
Japanese Association of Museums   (JA)
Japanese Association of Physical Medicine, Balneology
 and Climatology   (JA)
Japanese Association of Refrigeration   (JA)
Japanese Association of Theoretical Economics   (JA)
Japanese Association of Transportation Medicine
 (JA)
Japanese Biochemical Society   (JA)
Japanese Cancer Association   (US)
Japanese Cancer Association   (JA)
Japanese Circulation Society   (JA)
Japanese Climatological Seminar   (JA)
Japanese College of Angiology   (JA)
Japanese Committee for Radio Aids to Navigation
 (JA)
Japanese Commune Movement   (JA)
Japanese Dermatological Association   (JA)
Japanese Forestry Society   (JA)
Japanese Foundation for Cancer Research
 see Cancer Institute   (JA)
Japanese Institute of Culture   (IT)
Japanese Journal of Applied Physics   (JA)
Japanese Labour Law Association   (JA)
Japanese Leprosy Association   (JA)
Japanese Literature Association   (JA)
Japanese Medical Society of Alcohol Studies   (JA)
Japanese Musicological Society   (JA)
Japanese National Committee on Large Dams   (JA)
Japanese National Railways   (JA)
Japanese National Railways. Railway Technical
 Research Institute   (JA)
Japanese Neurochemical Society   (JA)
Japanese Nursing Association   (JA)
Japanese Ophthalmological Society   (JA)
Japanese Orthopaedic Assocation   (JA)
Japanese Pathological Society   (JA)
Japanese Pharmacological Society   (JA)
Japanese Physical Fitness Society   (JA)
Japanese Political Science Association   (JA)
Japanese Poultry Science Association   (JA)
Japanese Psychological Association   (JA)
Japanese Red Cross Society   (JA)
Japanese Rocket Society   (JA)
Japanese Shipowners' Association   (JA)
Japanese Social Labour College   (JA)
Japanese Society for Bacteriology   (JA)
Japanese Society for Crippled Children   (JA)
Japanese Society for Dental Health   (JA)
Japanese Society for Horticultural Science   (JA)
Japanese Society for Hygiene   (JA)
Japanese Society for Psychiatry and Neurology   (JA)
Japanese Society for Public Administration   (JA)
Japanese Society for Tuberculosis   (JA)

Japanese Society of Allergology  (JA)
Japanese Society of Applied Entomology and Zoology  (JA)
Japanese Society of Biological Scientists  (JA)
Japanese Society of Child Health  (JA)
Japanese Society of Comparative Law  (JA)
Japanese Society of Criminology  (JA)
Japanese Society of Developmental Biologists  (JA)
Japanese Society of Electron Microscopy  (JA)
Japanese Society of Ethnology  (JA)
Japanese Society of Fertility and Sterility  (JA)
Japanese Society of Fisheries Oceanography  (JA)
Japanese Society of Food and Nutrition  (JA)
Japanese Society of Food Science and Technology  (JA)
Japanese Society of Gastroenterology  (JA)
Japanese Society of Internal Medicine  (JA)
Japanese Society of Limnology  (JA)
Japanese Society of Neurology  (JA)
Japanese Society of Neurology and Psychiatry  (JA)
Japanese Society of Nuclear Medicine  (JA)
Japanese Society of Oral Surgeons  (JA)
Japanese Society of Parasitology  (JA)
Japanese Society of Pediatric Neurology  (JA)
Japanese Society of Pharmacognosy  (JA)
Japanese Society of Phycology  (JA)
Japanese Society of Physical Education  (JA)
Japanese Society of Plant Physiologists  (JA)
Japanese Society of Public Economy  (JA)
Japanese Society of Scientific Fisheries  (JA)
Japanese Society of Sericultural Science  (JA)
Japanese Society of Soil Mechanics and Foundation Engineering  (JA)
Japanese Society of Starch Science  (JA)
Japanese Society of Veterinary Science  (JA)
Japanese Society of Zootechnical Science  (JA)
Japanese Sociological Society  (JA)
Japanese Stomatological Society  (JA)
Japanese Technical Association of the Pulp and Paper Industry  (JA)
Japanese Tissue Culture Association  (JA)
Japanese Urological Association  (JA)
Japanese Urological Association. Nishi Nihon Section  (JA)
Japanese Weekly on Pharmacy and Chemistry  (JA)
Jardin Botanique de Montreal  (CN)
Jardin Botanique National de Belgique  (BE)
Javaharicam  (II)
Jawaharlal Nehru Agricultural University
　see Jawaharlal Nehru Krishi Vishwa Vidyalala  (II)
Jawaharlal Nehru Krishi Vishwa Vidyalaya  (II)
Jawaharlal Nehru Technological University. Regional Engineering College  (II)
Jawaharlal Nehru University Literary Society  (II)
Jawaharlal Nehru University. School of International Studies  (II)
Jawaharlal Nehru University. School of Languages  (II)
Jay Kay Publications  (AT)
Jay Publishing  (US)
Melville Jayathissa, Ed. & Pub.  (MY)
Jaycees International  (US)
Jayell Publishing Co.  (US)
Jazz Hot  (FR)
Jazz Journal  (UK)
Jazz Monographs  (US)
Jazz Report  (US)
Jazzband  (AG)
Jean-Paul Gesellschaft  (GW)
Jedinstvo  (YU)
Jednota Ceskoslovenskych Matematiku a Fyziku  (CS)
Jeevak Anshathlya  (II)
Jefferson Communications, Inc.  (US)
Jefferson Law Book Co.  (US)
Jefferson Medical College. Alumni Association  (US)
Jegu S.A.  (FR)
Kommunalschriften-Verlag J. Jehle  (GW)
Jehovah's Witnesses  (UK)
Jehovah's Witnesses  (US)
Jemma Publications Ltd.  (IE)
Jenaische Burschenschaft Arminia auf dem Burgkeller  (GW)
Jeng-Yih Lin  (CH)
Jenoptik Jena GmbH  (GE)
Olafs Jenssonar Loeknir  (IC)
Jeon la Bug-do Gyo Yug Yeon Gu Won  (KN)
Jeppe High Schools' Quondam Club  (SA)
Jernkontoret  (SW)
Jerome Press  (US)
Jersey Cattle Breeders' Society of S.A.  (SA)
Jersey Cattle Society of the U.K.  (UK)
Jersey Society of Parapsychology  (US)
Jerusalem Academic Press  (IS)
Jerusalem and the Middle East Church Association  (UK)
Jerusalem International Book Fair  (IS)
Jerusalem Philosophical Society  (IS)

Jerusalem Post Publications, Ltd.  (IS)
Jerusalem Publishing House, Ltd.  (IS)
Jerusalem Quarterly  (IS)
Jerusalemsverein  (GW)
T. C. Jervay, Ed. & Pub.  (US)
Jesuit East Asian Assistancy  (PH)
Jesuit Fathers  (GR)
Jesuit Fathers  (IE)
Jesuit Seminary Guild  (US)
Jesuitenkolleg  (AU)
Jesus Activity Media  (AT)
Jesus to the Communist World, Inc.  (US)
Jetline Schedules Ltd.  (UK)
Maison d'Editions "Jeunes pour Jeunes"  (ZR)
Jeunesse et Orgue  (FR)
Jeunesse Ouvriere Chretienne  (FR)
Jeunesses Litteraires de France  (FR)
Jeunnesses Musicales de Suisse Romande et Italienne  (SZ)
Jewish Agency for Israel  (IS)
Jewish Art Quarterly  (US)
Jewish Board of Guardians  (US)
Jewish Book Council
　see under National Jewish Welfare Board  (US)
Jewish Boston, Inc.  (US)
Jewish Braille Institute of America, Inc.  (US)
Jewish Chronicle Enterprises, Inc.  (CN)
Jewish Chronicle Publications  (UK)
Jewish Community Council of Ottawa  (CN)
Jewish Community of British Columbia  (CN)
Jewish Currents, Inc.  (US)
Jewish Defense League  (US)
Jewish Defense League. Youth Movement  (US)
Jewish Demographic Society  (US)
Jewish Digest Association  (US)
Jewish Echo Ltd.  (UK)
Jewish Educational Ventures, Inc.  (US)
Jewish Federation & Council of Greater Seattle  (US)
Jewish Federation of Delaware  (US)
Jewish Federation of St. Louis  (US)
Jewish Floridian  (US)
Jewish Gazette Ltd.  (UK)
Jewish Herald (Pty) Ltd.  (SA)
Jewish Historical Society of England  (UK)
Jewish Labor Committee  (US)
Jewish Ledger  (US)
Jewish Literary Trust Ltd.  (UK)
Jewish Look  (US)
Jewish Media Service  (US)
Jewish Monitor  (US)
Jewish Museum  (US)
Jewish Music Research Centre  (IS)
Jewish National and University Library  (IS)
Jewish National Fund  (IS)
Jewish News Publishing Co.  (US)
Jewish Peace Fellowship  (US)
Jewish People  (US)
Jewish Public Library  (CN)
Jewish Publication Society of America  (US)
Jewish Reconstructionist Foundation  (US)
Jewish Record  (US)
Jewish Society of America, Inc.  (US)
Jewish Spectator  (US)
Jewish Standard Co.  (US)
Jewish Star  (US)
Jewish Student Projects of Greater Boston, Inc.  (US)
Jewish Telegraph Ltd.  (UK)
Jewish Telegraphic Agency  (US)
Jewish Times  (US)
Jewish Vegetarian & Natural Health Society  (UK)
Jewish War Veterans of the U.S.A.  (US)
Jewish Weekly Dispatch  (US)
Jewish Welfare Federation  (US)
Jez  (YU)
Jhr. Mr. A. F. de Savornin Lohman Stichting  (NE)
Jicarilla Apache Tribe  (US)
Jiells Bokfoerlag  (SW)
Jiji Press, Ltd.  (JA)
Jikei University School of Medicine  (JA)
Jim Clarke Foundation  (UK)
Jimbun Kagaku Kenkyujo
　see Kyoto University. Research Institute for Humanistic Studies  (JA)
Jinbun Chiri Gakkai
　see Human Geography Society of Japan  (JA)
Jinbun Gakkai
　see Tokyo Metropolitan University. Institute for Social Sciences and Humanity  (JA)
Jinko Mondai Kenkyusho
　see Japan. Institute of Population Problems  (JA)
Jinrui Dotaigaku Kenkyukai
　see Human Ergology Research Association  (JA)
Jinsen Igaku Committee  (JA)
Jishin Gakkai
　see Seismological Society of Japan  (JA)
Jishin Kenkyusho
　see University of Tokyo. Earthquake Research Institute  (JA)

Jiwaji University  (II)
Jnana Sadhak Publishing Company  (II)
Jo-Ro Press  (US)
Joachimsthal Publishers  (NE)
Joanneum. Abteilung fuer Botanik  (AU)
Joanneum. Abteilung fuer Geologie, Palaeontologie und Bergbau  (AU)
Joanneum. Abteilung fuer Zoologie  (AU)
Jobson Publishing Corporation  (US)
Jobson's Publications  (AT)
Jochi University
　see Sophia University  (JA)
Jockey Club of Buenos Aires  (AG)
Jodhpur University
　see University of Jodhpur  (II)
Editions Louis Johanet  (FR)
Pierre Johanet et ses Fils  (FR)
Johann Adam Moehler-Institut Paderborn  (GW)
Johanna Stichting Revalidatie Centrum  (NE)
Johannes Wagner Schriftgiesserei und Messinglinienfabrik  (GW)
Johannesburg. Produce Market Department  (SA)
Johannesburg College of Education  (SA)
Johannesburg Drukkery  (SA)
Johannesburg Film Society  (SA)
Johannesburg Jaycees  (SA)
Johannesburg Laundry & Dry Cleaners Association  (SA)
Johannesburg Stock Exchange  (SA)
John Brown Book Club  (US)
John Carroll University. School of Business  (US)
John Coutts Library Service Ltd.  (CN)
John Crerar Library  (US)
John Dewey Society  (US)
John Dewey Society for the Study of Education and Culture  (US)
John E. Owens Memorial Foundation, Inc.  (US)
John Edwards Memorial Foundation, Inc.  (US)
John G. Neihardt Foundation, Inc.  (US)
John Jay College of Criminal Justice. Newspaper Society  (US)
John Marshall Bar Association  (US)
John Marshall Law School  (US)
John Milton Society for the Blind  (US)
John Player & Sons Ltd.  (UK)
John Rylands University Library  (UK)
John Steinbeck Society  (US)
Johnny Appleseed Patriotic Publications  (US)
Johns Hopkins Hospital School of Nursing  (US)
Johns Hopkins University  (US)
Johns Hopkins University. Applied Physics Laboratory  (US)
Johns Hopkins University. Department of Earth and Planetary Sciences  (US)
Johns Hopkins University. Milton E. Eisenhower Library  (US)
Johns Hopkins University. Office of Student Affairs  (US)
Johns Hopkins University Press  (US)
Johns Hopkins University. School of Hygiene and Public Health  (US)
Johns Hopkins University School of Medicine  (US)
Johns-Manville Corporation  (US)
Johnson C. Smith University  (US)
Johnson Hill Press, Inc.  (US)
Johnson Management Institute  (US)
Johnson, Matthey & Co. Ltd.  (UK)
Johnson Publications  (BF)
Johnson Publishing Co., Inc  (US)
Johnson Publishing Co. (Loveland)  (US)
Johnson Society of London  (UK)
Johnson's Charts, Inc.  (US)
Johnson's of Hendon Ltd.  (UK)
Bruce Johnston  (CN)
Johnston & Neville (Pty) Ltd.  (SA)
Johnston International Publishing Corp  (HK)
Johnston International Publishing Corporation  (LE)
Johnston International Publishing Corporation  (US)
Johnstown Motor Club  (US)
Joho Shori Gakkai
　see Information Processing Society of Japan  (JA)
Joint Association of Classical Teachers  (UK)
Joint British Committee for Stress Analysis  (UK)
Joint Center for Political Studies  (US)
Joint Center for Urban Studies  (US)
Joint Committee on Powder Diffraction Standards.  (US)
Joint Council of Teamsters No. 37  (US)
Joint Council of Teamsters No. 42  (US)
Joint Council on Economic Education  (US)
Joint Council on Educational Broadcasting Television  (US)
Joint Federal-State Land Use Planning Commission for Alaska  (US)
Joint Fire Prevention Publicity Committee Inc.  (CN)
Joint Institute for Laboratory Astrophysics  (US)
Joint Nuclear Research Center, Ispra, Italy  (EI)

Joint Planning Commission, Lehigh-Northampton
  Counties (US)
Joint Reference Library. Public Administration Service
  (US)
Joint Strategy and Action Committee (US)
Ediciones Joker (SP)
Don Jolly & Associates (US)
Jonah Publishing Ltd. (CN)
Edward L. Jones, Ed. & Pub. (US)
H. Jones, Ed. & Pub. (US)
Milton W. Jones (US)
Jones Lang Wootton (US)
David F. Jones Ltd. (NZ)
Jones Medical Publications (US)
Jonge Muziek (BE)
Jordan (JO)
Jordan. Armed Forces (JO)
Jordan. Department of Agricultural Marketing (JO)
Jordan. Department of Culture and Arts (JO)
Jordan. Department of Statistics (JO)
Jordan. Ministry of Agriculture (JO)
Jordan. Ministry of Culture and Information (JO)
Jordan. Ministry of Education (JO)
Jordan. Ministry of Health (JO)
Jordan. Ministry of National Economy (JO)
Jordan. Ministry of National Economy. Department of
  Agricultural Marketing
  see Jordan. Department of Agricultural Marketing
  (JO)
Jordan. Ministry of Tourism & Antiquities (JO)
Jordan Bar Association (JO)
Jordan Cooperative Organization (JO)
Jordan Dataquest Ltd. (UK)
Clyde C. Jordan, Ed. & Pub. (US)
Jordan Information Bureau (US)
Jordan Library Association (JO)
Jordan Medical Association (JO)
Jordan University. Accounting Society (JO)
Jordan University. Department of Information &
  Public Relations (JO)
Jordan University. Economic Studies Society (JO)
Jordan University. Public Administration and Political
  Sciences Society (JO)
Jordanian Youth and Sports Organization (JO)
Jornal Brasileiro de Doencas Toracicas (BL)
Jornal de Letras (BL)
Jornal de Letras e Artes (PO)
Jornal de Poesia (BL)
Jornal do Brasil (BL)
Empresa do Jornal do Comercio (PO)
Jornal Portugues de Economic e Financas (PO)
Empresa Jornalistica (BL)
Companhia Editora Jorues (BL)

Wilfried Josch, Editor and Publisher (AU)

Josep Communications (US)

Michael Joseph (UK)
V. J. Joseph, Ed. & Pub. (II)
Joseph Haas-Gesellschaft (GW)
Joseph-Haydn-Institut e.V. (GW)
Joseph Jacobs Organization (US)
Josephite Society (US)
Joshi Foundation (II)
Joshi Hospital (II)
Joslin Diabetes Foundation, Inc. (US)
Joslyn Art Museum (US)
Jossey-Bass, Inc., Publishers (US)
Jour-Azur S.A. (FR)
Journal and Bulletin Agency (US)
Journal Constructo (CN)
Journal de Conchyliologie (AT)
Journal de la Construction de la Suisse Romande
  (SZ)
Journal de la Marine Marchande, S.A. (FR)
Journal de Medecine de Lyon (FR)
Journal de Medecine et de Chirurgie Pratiques (FR)
Journal de Tanger (MR)
Journal des Combattants (FR)
Journal des Communes (FR)
Journal des Finances (FR)
Journal des Mots Croises S.A. (FR)
Journal des Notaires et des Avocats (FR)
Journal des Oiseaux du Monde (FR)
Journal des Sciences Medicales de Lille (FR)
Journal du Batiment et des Travaux Publics (FR)
Journal Europeen du Collectionneur d'Ordres et
  Decorations (SZ)
Journal of Advertising (US)
Journal of Applied Communications Research (US)
Journal of Belizean Affairs (BH)
Journal of Black Poetry (US)
Journal of Clinical Computing, Inc. (US)
Journal of Collective Chemistry and Physics (UK)
Journal of Commerce (US)
Journal of Commerce and Shipping Telegraph Ltd.
  (UK)
Journal of Commerce Ltd. (CN)
Journal of Contemporary Asia (SW)

Journal of Contemporary Poets (US)
Journal of Correctional Education (US)
Journal of Dermatologic Surgery, Inc. (US)
Journal of Drug Issues (US)
Journal of Genetics (II)
Journal of Hispanic Philology Inc. (US)
Journal of Neuropathology and Experimental
  Neurology (US)
Journal of Nursing Administration, Inc. (US)
Journal of Park Administration Ltd. (UK)
Journal of Philosophy, Inc. (US)
Journal of Refrigeration Ltd. (UK)
Journal of Reproductive Medicine, Inc. (US)
Journal of Rheumatology (CN)
Journal of Southern African Affairs (US)
Journal of Taxation, Ltd. (US)
Journal of the History of Medicine and Allied
  Sciences, Inc. (US)
Journal of the History of Philosophy, Inc. (US)
Journal of Undergraduate Psychological Research
  (US)
Journal on Political Repression, Inc. (US)
Journal Press (US)
Journal Publications (II)
Journal Publications (Camden) (US)
Journal Publishers, Inc. (Ft. Collins) (US)
Journal Publishing Affiliates (US)
Journal Publishing Co. (Irvington) (US)
Journal-Record Publishing Co. (US)
Journal Thirty One (US)
Journal Verlagsgesellschaft mbH (GW)
Journalism Education Association, Inc. (US)
Journee Vinicole (FR)
Journee Vinicole Export (FR)
Casa Editrice Dott. Eugenio Jovene (IT)
Jovenes de la Accion Catolica (AG)
Jovenes Educadores del Peru (PE)
Joy Dev Ray (II)
Joy Manufacturing Co. Denver Equipment Division
  (US)
Joynson-Bruwers Ltd. (UK)
Jozo Kagaku Kenkyusho
  see Brewing Science Research Institute (JA)
Jozsef Attila Tudomanyegyetem (HU)
JR Rider (CN)
JUCEMA (YU)
Helen & Felix Juda Collection (US)
Judaica Bibliography and News (US)
Judaica Post (CN)
Judaica Verlag (SZ)
Judo Illustrated Inc. (US)
Judo, Ltd. (UK)
Judo Regionale (IT)
Juedische Presse GmbH (GW)
Verlag Juergens KG (GW)
Jugend und Volk Verlagsgesellschaft (AU)
Jugendhaus Duesseldorf E.V. (GW)
Jugobanka (YU)
Jugopetrol (YU)
Jugoslavenska Akademija Znanosti i Umjetnosti.
  Historijski Institut (YU)
Jugoslavenska Akademija Znanosti i Umjetnosti.
  Institut za Filozofiju Znanosti i Mir (YU)
Jugoslavenska Akademija Znanosti i Umjetnosti.
  Razred za Prirodne Znanosti (YU)
Jugoslavenska Akademija Znanosti i Umjetnosti.
  Razred za Suvremenu Knjizevnost (YU)
Jugoslavenski Komitet Svjetskog Kongresa za Naftu
  (YU)
Jugoslavensko Drustvo za Primjenu Goriva i Maziva
  (YU)
Jugoslavensko Sportsko Drustvo "Partizan" (YU)
Jugoslavija Film, Import-Export of Motion Pictures
  (YU)
Jugoslovenska Investiciona Banka (YU)
Jugoslovenska Revija (YU)
Jugoslovenski Bibliografski Institut (YU)
Jugoslovenski Centar za Tehnicku i Naucnu
  Dokumentaciju (YU)
Jugoslovenski Gradjevinski Centar (YU)
Jugoslovenski Komitet za Elektroniku i
  Telekomunikacije, Automatizaciju i Nuklearnu
  Tehniku (ETAN) (YU)
Jugoslovenski Komitet za Elektroniku i
  Telekomunikacije, Automatizaciju i Nuklearnu
  Tehniku (ETAN) Savezni Strucni Odbor za
  Automatizaciju (YU)
Jugoslovenski Pregled (YU)
Jugoslovenski Zavod za Produktivnost Rada (YU)
Jugoslovensko Drustvo za Mehaniku (YU)
Jugoslovensko Entomolosko Drustvo (YU)
Jugoslovensko Naucno Vocarsko Drustvo (YU)
Jugoslovensko Udruzenje Matematickih i Fizickih
  Drustava. Komisija za Fiziku (YU)
Jugoslovensko Udruzenje za Krivicno Pravo i
  Kriminologiju (YU)
Jugoslovensko Udruzenje za Marketing (JUMA)
  (YU)

Jugoslovensko Udruzenje za Medjunarodno Pravo
  (YU)
Jugoslovensko Udruzenje za Sociologiju (YU)
Jugosovenski Institut za Novinarstvo, Beograd (YU)
Jugovinil (YU)
Juigaku Kenkyusho
  see Nihon University. Research Institute for
  Veterinary Science (JA)
Juilliard School (US)
Editions Julliard (FR)
Jump Cut (US)
Junction Enterprises (US)
Jundi Shapur University. College of Education (IR)
Jundi Shapur University. Faculty of Medicine (IR)
Junge Christliche Arbeitnehmer (GW)
Junge Generation in der Volkspartei (AU)
Verlag Junge Kirche (GW)
Verlag Junge Welt (GE)
Junior Academy of the Ohio Academy of Science
  (US)
Junior Astronomical Society (UK)
Junior Astronomy Club (US)
Junior Bookshelf (UK)
Junior Club Publications Ltd. (UK)
Junior High School Association of Illinois (US)
Junior Hospital Doctors" Association (UK)
Junior League of Halifax (CN)
Junior Philatelic Society of America (US)
Junior Statesman (II)
Junior Statesmen Foundation (US)
Juniper Editions (US)
Juniper Journals Ltd. (UK)
Juniper Press (US)
Dr. W. Junk B. V. Publishers (NE)
Junta Central de Fiestas (SP)
Junta da Accao Social. Centro de Estudos Sociais e
  Corporativos (PO)
Junta de Colonizacao Interna (PO)
Junta de Energia Nuclear (SP)
Junta de Estudios Historicos de Mendoza (AG)
Junta de Investigacaoes do Ultramar (PO)
Junta de Investigacaoes do Ultramar. Centro de
  Estudos Historicos Ultramarinos (PO)
Junta de Investigacoes do Ultramar. Centro de
  Documentacao Cientifica Ultramarina (PO)
Junta del Acuerdo de Cartagena (PE)
Junta del Acuerdo de Cartagena. Unidad
  Administrativa (PE)
Juntendo Medical Society (JA)
Juntendo University. School of Medicine (JA)
Junularo Esperantista de Nord-Ameriko (US)
Jupiter Verlag GmbH (AU)
Jurid Werke GmbH (GW)
Editorial Juridica de Chile (CL)
Editora Juridica Ltda. (BL)
Juridical Digests Institute (US)
Ediciones Juridicas (PE)
Juridiska Foereningen i Finland (FI)
Jurisprudence Association (JA)
Jurisprudence Generale Dalloz (FR)
Jurist- och Samhaellsvetare Foerbundet (SW)
Jurist Publishing Co. (IE)
Juristischer Verlag W. Ellinghaus und Co. GmbH
  (GW)
Jury Verdict Research, Inc. (US)
Jus (MX)
Editorial Jus (PE)
Jus Gentium (IT)
Editorial Jus, S. A. (MX)
Just Compensation, Inc. (US)
Justice of the Peace (Holdings) Ltd. (UK)
Justices' Clerks' Society (UK)
Juta & Co. Ltd. (SA)
Drukkerij Juten (NE)
Juventa Verlag (GW)
Juventus F.C. S.p.A. (IT)
Juzen Medical Society of Kanazawa University (JA)
Jysk Selskab for Historie (DK)
Jyvaskylan Yliopisto. Department of Physics (FI)
Jyvaskylan Yliopisto. Kasvatustieteiden Tutkimuslaitos
  (FI)
Jyvaskylan Yliopisto. Kirjasto (FI)
Jyvaskylan Yliopisto. Matematiikan Laitos (FI)
K & K Publishing Inc. (US)
K & M Publications Inc (US)
K-Dee Publishing Co. (US)
K E I D A N R E N
  see Japan Federation of Economic Organizations
  (JA)
K E M A (NE)
K. K. K. Istanbul Askeri Basimevi (TU)
K-Konsult (SW)
K L M Royal Dutch Airlines (NE)
K. M. Manju Joshi Memorial Society (II)
K N A Forlaget A-S (NO)
K. of C. Auto & Travel Club (US)
K. Publications (London) Ltd. (UK)
K R C Associates (US)

Karachi University Library Science Alumni Association  (PK)
Karamu Association  (US)
Karate Association of Malaysia  (MY)
Karate Budokan International Inc.  (MY)
Karawane Verlag  (GW)
S. Karger AG  (SZ)
Karger Libri AG  (SZ)
Karikazo  (US)
Norman Kark Publications Ltd.  (UK)
Karl Marx Universitaet  (GE)
Karl-Marx-Universitaet. Herder-Institut  (GE)
Karl-Marx-Universitaet. Universitaetsbibliothek  (GE)
Karl-May-Gesellschaft  (GW)
Karlovacki Tjednik  (YU)
Karmel  (NE)
Edward J. Karnarkowski, Ed. & Pub.  (US)
Karnatak Law Journal  (II)
Karnatak University  (II)
Karnatak University. College of Education  (II)
Karnatak University. Department of Social Anthropology  (II)
Karnatak University Library Association  (II)
Karnataka
    see also Mysore  (II)
Karnataka. Commissioner of Labour  (II)
Karnataka. Department of Agriculture. Farm Advisory and Extension Services
    see Karnataka. Farm Advisory and Extension Services  (II)
Karnataka. Department of Information and Tourism  (II)
Karnataka. Farm Advisory and Extension Services  (II)
Karnataka. Finance Department  (II)
Karnataka. Mysore Minerals Ltd.  (II)
Karnataka. Mysore Sales International Limited  (II)
Karnataka Patrika Private Limited  (II)
Karnataka Small Industries Development Corporation Ltd.  (II)
Karnataka State Education Federation  (II)
Karolinska Institutet  (SW)
Deutscher Kartei-Verlag  (GW)
Kartellverband Katholischer Deutscher Studentenvereine  (GW)
Karting Magazine Ltd.  (UK)
Panstwowe Przedsiebiorstwo Wydawnictw Kartograficznych  (PL)
Karyalaya Natya Kala Kendram Institute  (II)
Kasetsart University  (TH)
Kasetsart University. Museum of Fisheries  (TH)
Kashmir Affairs  (II)
Kashmir University
    see University of Kashmir  (II)
Kasr el-Aini Clinical Society. Faculty of Medicine  (UA)
Kasr-El-Aini Journal of Surgery  (UA)
Kastner und Oehler  (AU)
Yuzuru Katagiri, Ed. & Pub.  (JA)
Kate Greenaway Society  (US)
Kate Smith U.S.A. Friends Club  (US)
Katechetisches Institut  (AU)
Katedra  (YU)
Kates-Boylston Publications, Inc.  (US)
Kathell  (US)
Katholiek Centrum voor Lectuurinformatie en Bibliotheekvoorziening  (BE)
Katholiek Documentatie Centrum  (NE)
Katholiek Onderwijs Verbond  (NE)
Katholiek Vormingswerk voor Landelijke Vrouwen  (BE)
Katholieke Artsenvereniging  (NE)
Katholieke Nederlandse Boeren- en Tuindersbond  (NE)
Katholieke Universiteit te Leuven
    see also Universite Catholique de Louvain (the two universities have been separate institutions since 1970)  (BE)
Katholieke Universiteit te Leuven  (BE)
Katholieke Universiteit te Leuven. Centrum voor Ziekenhuiswetenschap  (BE)
Katholieke Universiteit te Leuven. Department Orientalistiek  (BE)
Katholieke Universiteit te Leuven. Faculteit der Economische en Toegepaste Economische Wetenschappen  (BE)
Katholieke Universiteit te Leuven. Faculty of Social Science  (BE)
Katholieke Universiteit te Leuven. Faculty of Theology  (BE)
Katholieke Universiteit te Leuven. Fakulteit der Landbouwwetenschappen  (BE)
Katholieke Universiteit Te Leuven. Instituut voor Middeleeuwse Studies  (BE)
Katholieke Universiteit te Leuven. Instituut voor Naamkunde  (BE)

Katholieke Universiteit te Leuven. Seminarium Philologiae Humanisticae  (BE)
Katholieke Vereniging van Directies, Docenten en Consulten bij het Beroepsonderwijs en het Leerlingwezen  (NE)
Katholieke Vereniging van Leerkrachten in de Lichamelijke Oefening "St. Thomas van Aquino"  (NE)
Katholische Bundesarbeitsgemeinschaft Land  (GW)
Katholische Filmkommission fuer Oesterreich  (AU)
Katholische Hochschuljugend Oesterreichs  (AU)
Katholische Jungschar Oesterreichs  (AU)
Katholische Landesarbeitsgemeinschaft fuer Jugendsozialarbeit  (GW)
Katholische Lehrerschaft Oesterreichs  (AU)
Katholische Oesterreichische Studentenverbindung "Borussia" im MKV  (AU)
Katholischer Akademikerverband Deutschland  (GW)
Katholischer Deutscher Frauenbund  (GW)
Katholischer Familienverband Oesterreichs  (AU)
Katholischer Krankenhausverband Deutschlands e.V.  (GW)
Katholischer Siedlungsdienst e.V.  (GW)
Katholisches Bibelwerk e.V.  (GW)
Katholisches Bistum der Alt-Katholiken in Deutschland  (GW)
Katholisches Frauenwerk in Oesterreich  (AU)
Katholisches Jugendwerk Oesterreichs  (AU)
Katholisches Militaerbischofsamt  (GW)
Katolicki Uniwersytet Lubelski  (PL)
Katolieke Filmliga  (BE)
Menke Katz, Ed. & Pub.  (US)
Kauka-Verlag  (GW)
Kauppa Koti Oy  (FI)
Kauppateknikko  (FI)
Kauppiaitten Kustannus Oy  (FI)
Kawai Pharmaceutical Co., Ltd.  (JA)
Kawata Publicity Inc.  (JA)
Kay Publishing Co.  (US)
Kayak Books, Inc.  (US)
Kaye Publishing Corporation  (US)
Kayhan Group of Newspapers  (IR)
Kayttokirjat Oy  (FI)
Kayward Publications  (US)
Kazakhskaya S.S.R. Ministerstvo Sel'skogo Khozyaistva  (UR)
Kazakhskii Gosudarstvennyi Universitet  (UR)
Kazakhskii Nauchno-Issledovatel'skii Institut Onkologii i Radiologii  (UR)
Dr. Artin Kazandjian, Pub.  (LE)
Kazanskii Gosudarstvennyi Pedagogicheskii Institut  (UR)
Kazanskii Universitet  (UR)
Kearney State College  (US)
Keats Publishing, Inc.  (US)
Keats-Shelley Association of America, Inc.  (US)
Keats-Shelley Memorial Association  (UK)
George S. Keenan  (US)
Keep America Beautiful, Inc.  (US)
Keeping Abreast Journal  (US)
Keeping up with Music Education  (US)
Keepsake Press  (UK)
Internationale Drukkerij en Uitgeverij Keesing N.V.  (BE)
KEIDANREN
    see Japan Federation of Economic Organizations  (JA)
L. Keidel  (GW)
Keie Kindaika Kenkyusho
    see Management Science Research Institute  (JA)
Keikinzoku Kyokai
    see Japan Light Metal Association  (JA)
Keio Daigaku
    see Keio University  (JA)
Keio Economic Society
    see under Keio University  (JA)
Keio Gijuku Daigaku Igaku Joho Senta
    see Keio University. Medical Library and Information Center  (JA)
Keio Gijuku Hogaku Kenkyukai
    see Keio University. Asssociation for the Study of Law and Politics  (JA)
Keio University. Association for the Study of Law and Politics  (JA)
Keio University. Faculty of Engineering  (JA)
Keio University. Institute of Management and Labor Studies  (JA)
Keio University. Keio Economic Society  (JA)
Keio University. Medical Library and Information Center  (JA)
Keio University. School of Medicine  (JA)
Keio University Society of Business and Commerce  (JA)
Keiron  (AG)
Keisatsu-cho Kagaku Keisatsu Kenkyusho
    see Japan. National Research Institute of Police Science  (JA)
Henry A. Keitel, Ed. & Pub.  (US)

Keizai Chiri Gakkai
    see Association of Economic Geographers  (JA)
Keizai Dantai Rengokai
    see Japan Federation of Economic Organizations  (JA)
Keizai Hatten Kyokai
    see Association for Economic Development  (JA)
Keizai Kikakucho
    see Japan. Economic Planning Agency  (JA)
Keizai Riron Gakkai
    see Society of Political Economy  (JA)
Kekkaku Kyobu Shikkan Kenkyusho
    see Kyoto University. Chest Disease Research Institute  (JA)
Kekkaku Yobokai
    see Japan Anti-Tuberculosis Association  (JA)
Thomas R. Kellaway, Ed. & Pub.  (US)
J. J. Keller & Associates, Inc.  (US)
Keller Publishing Corporation  (US)
Keller und Co., Druckerei und Verlag  (SZ)
Josef Keller Verlag  (GW)
Kelley Blue Book  (US)
Augustus M. Kelley Publishers  (US)
Kellogg Co. (Battle Creek)  (US)
M. W. Kellogg Co. (Houston)  (US)
Kellogg Continental B. V.  (NE)
Robert Kelly, Ed. & Pub.  (US)
Kelly's Directories Ltd.  (UK)
Keltner Statistical Service, Inc.  (US)
Kelvin Publications (Pty) Ltd.  (SA)
Kemian Kustannus Oy  (FI)
Kemp's Group (Printers & Publishers) Ltd.  (UK)
Kempter Verlag  (GW)
Ken-yusha, Inc.  (JA)
Kenchiku Gijutsusha  (JA)
Kendalch Keltiek  (FR)
Kendervic Ltd.  (UK)
P. J. Kenedy & Sons  (US)
Kenko na Kurashi No Kai  (JA)
Kenkyusho Rengokai
    see Tohoku University. Association of the Research Institutes  (JA)
Kenlis Publications Ltd.  (IE)
Kennecott Copper Corporation  (US)
Kennedy and Co. Ltd.  (UK)
Kennedy & Kennedy, Inc.  (US)
Kennedy Brothers (Publishing) Ltd.  (UK)
Kennedy Galleries, Inc.  (US)
Kennel Club  (UK)
Kenroy Publishers Ltd.  (CN)
Kensetsu-cho Kenchiku Kenkyusho Kokusai Jishin Kogakuino
    see Japan. International Institute of Seismology and Earthquake Engineering  (JA)
Kensetsu-sho Doboku Kenkyusho
    see Japan. Public Works Research Institute  (JA)
Kensetsu-sho Kokudo Chiri-in
    see Japan. Geographical Survey Institute  (JA)
Kent Archaeological Society  (UK)
Kent County Council  (UK)
Kent Family History Society  (UK)
Kent Feeds, Inc.  (US)
Kent Historical Society  (CN)
George Kent Ltd.  (UK)
Kent Messenger  (UK)
Kent State University. Center for Business and Economic Research  (US)
Kent State University. Department of English  (US)
Kent State University. Department of History  (US)
Kent State University Libraries  (US)
Kent State University Press  (US)
Kent State University. Student Publications Policy Committee  (US)
Kenton Bible Hall, Inc.  (US)
Kentron Erevnis tes Hellenikes Philosophias  (GR)
Kentucky. Adjutant-General's Office  (US)
Kentucky. Crop and Livestock Reporting Service  (US)
Kentucky. Department of Child Welfare  (US)
Kentucky. Department of Commerce  (US)
Kentucky. Department of Commerce. Division of Research and Planning  (US)
Kentucky. Department of Education  (US)
Kentucky. Department of Education. Bureau of Administration and Finance  (US)
Kentucky. Department of Fish and Wildlife  (US)
Kentucky. Department of Health  (US)
Kentucky. Department of Health. Department for Human Resources  (US)
Kentucky. Department of Natural Resources  (US)
Kentucky. Office for Local Government  (US)
Kentucky Academy of Family Physicians  (US)
Kentucky Academy of Science  (US)
Kentucky Agricultural Experiment Station  (US)
Kentucky Association for Health, Physical Education & Recreation  (US)
Kentucky Association of Communication Arts  (US)
Kentucky Association of Electric Cooperatives  (US)

Kentucky Association of Highway Contractors (US)
Kentucky Association of Plumbing-Heating-Cooling Contractors (US)
Kentucky Association of School Librarians (US)
Kentucky Association on Alcohol Abuse and Alcoholism, Inc. (US)
Kentucky Bankers Association (US)
Kentucky Baptist Convention (US)
Kentucky Bar Association (US)
Kentucky Civil War Round Table (US)
Kentucky Council of Economic Advisors (US)
Kentucky Council of Teachers of English (US)
Kentucky Council on Public Higher Education (US)
Kentucky Dental Association (US)
Kentucky Education Association (US)
Kentucky Elementary School Principal (US)
Kentucky Farm Bureau Federation (US)
Kentucky Federation of the Blind (US)
Kentucky Folklore Society (US)
Kentucky Geological Survey (US)
Kentucky Historical Society (US)
Kentucky Law Enforcement Council (US)
Kentucky Library Association (US)
Kentucky Manpower Development, Inc. (US)
Kentucky Medical Association (US)
Kentucky Municipal League (US)
Kentucky Music Teachers Association (US)
Kentucky Nurses Association (US)
Kentucky Poetry Review (US)
Kentucky Press Association (US)
Kentucky Society of Certified Public Accountants (US)
Kentucky State AFL-CIO (US)
Kenya. Board of Adult Education (KE)
Kenya. Central Bureau of Statistics (KE)
Kenya. Coffee Board (KE)
Kenya. Dairy Board (KE)
Kenya. Director of Aerodromes (KE)
Kenya. Government Printing and Stationery Department (KE)
Kenya. Mines and Geological Department (KE)
Kenya. Ministry of Commerce and Industry (KE)
Kenya. Ministry of Finance and Planning (KE)
Kenya. Ministry of Finance and Planning. Central Bureau of Statistics
   see Kenya. Central Bureau of Statistics (KE)
Kenya. Ministry of Information and Broadcasting (KE)
Kenya. Ministry of Tourism and Wildlife (KE)
Kenya. National Housing Corporation (KE)
Kenya. National Irrigation Board (KE)
Kenya. National Library Service Board (KE)
Kenya. National Museum (KE)
Kenya Education Journal (KE)
Kenya Institute of Administration (KE)
Kenya Library Association (KE)
Kenya Medical Association (KE)
Kenya Museum Society (KE)
Kenya National Chamber of Commerce and Industry (KE)
Kenya National Union of Teachers (KE)
Kenya Press Centre (KE)
Kenya Railways (KE)
Kenyon College (US)
Kephart Communications Inc. (US)
Kepler-Kommission (GW)
P. Keppler Verlag KG (GW)
Kerala. Department of Industries and Commerce (II)
Kerala. Directorate of Archives (II)
Kerala. Kerala Legislature (II)
Kerala. Kerala State Planning Board (II)
Kerala. Labour and Industrial Bureau (II)
Kerala. State Co-Operative Union (II)
Kerala Academy of Biology (II)
Kerala Agricultural University. College of Agriculture (II)
Kerala Aided Primary Teachers' Union (II)
Kerala Arya Prathinidhi Sabha (II)
Kerala Industry (II)
Kerala Institute of Marxist Studies (II)
Kerala Law Times (II)
Kerala Sree (MY)
Kerala State Productivity Council (II)
Kerala University
   see University of Kerala (II)
Keramik-Freunde der Schweiz (SZ)
Kombinat VEB Keramische Werke Hermsdorf (GE)
Robert Kerdasha, Ed. & Pub. (US)
Keren Hayesod (IS)
Kereskedelmi Munka- es Uzemszervezesi Intezet (KERORG) (HU)
Editons Kerfan (FR)
Kerk en Vrede (NE)
Kerkeraad Hervormde Gemeente (NE)
Kerkjeugvereniging (SA)
Kern County Dental Society (US)
Kern County Historical Society (US)
Kern Institute (NE)

Druck und Verlag Kern und Birner (GW)
Alfred Kernen Verlag (GW)
Kerrwil Publications Ltd. (CN)
Kerry Archaeological and Historical Society (IE)
Kerslake, Billens & Humphrey, Ltd. (NZ)
A. S. Kerswill Ltd. (UK)
Kesari-Mahratta Trust Publication (II)
Kesatuan Akademis Universiti Singapura (SI)
Osheen Keshishian, Ed. & Pub. (US)
Kesho Publications (KE)
Keter Publishing House Ltd. (IS)
Kettering Laboratory (US)
Eugen Ketterl (AU)
Kexue Chuban She (CC)
Key Club International (US)
Key Dayton Scene (US)
Key Markets Publishing Co. (US)
Key Organization (US)
Key Publishers Ltd. (CN)
Key-This Week in Chicago (US)
Keyboard World, Inc. (US)
Keystone Automobile Club AAA (US)
Keystone Publishing Co. (US)
KFUK-KFUM's Riksfoerbund (SW)
Khabarovskoe Knizhnoe Izdatel'stvo (UR)
Khalsa Publications (II)
Kharkivskyi Politekhnichnyi Instytut (UR)
Kharkovskii Gosudarstvennyi Universitet (UR)
Khartoum University Press (SJ)
Khasmik Poetry Quarterly (AT)
Khatoon-e-Mashriq (II)
M. S. R. Khemchand, Ed. & Pub. (II)
Izdatel'stvo Khimiya (UR)
Khosla Publishing Co. (II)
Izdatel'stvo Khudozhestvennaya Literatura (UR)
Izdatel'stvo Khudozhestvennaya Literatura. Leningradskoe Otdelenie (UR)
Kianja (MG)
Kibbutz Artzi Hashomer Hatzair (IS)
Lu Kibler, Ed. & Pub. (US)
Kick to Corruption (II)
Friedrich Kiehl Verlag GmbH (GW)
Kiel. Wasser-und Schiffahrtsdirektion Nord (GW)
Izdatel'stvo Kievskii Universitet (UR)
Kigyo Horonsha (JA)
Kihara Institute for Biological Research (JA)
Kijk op het Noorden (NE)
Kikogaku Danwakai
   see Tokyo University of Education. Laboratory of Climatology (JA)
Kilbrittain Newspapers Ltd. (IE)
Kildonan Promotions Ltd. (CN)
Kilgore's Tree (US)
Killaly Press (CN)
Kimberly Communications Corporation (US)
Kime's International Law Directory, Ltd (UK)
Kimport Dolls (US)
Henry Kimpton Ltd. (UK)
Kindai-Eiga Corp. (JA)
Kindai Kagaku Ltd. (JA)
Kindaikenchiku-sha Ltd. Co. (JA)
Kinder- und Jugenddorf Klinge e.V. (GW)
Kindness Club (CN)
King & Hutchings (UK)
Ralph W. King & Yuill (AT)
King County Library System (US)
King County Medical Society (US)
King Enterprises (US)
King Publications (US)
King Publications Ltd. (UK)
Kingdom Digest (US)
The Kingdom Press (US)
King's College (US)
Kings College Hospital Medical School (UK)
Kings Cross Publishing Co. (UK)
Kings Regiment (UK)
Kingsclere Publications (UK)
Kingston Arts Council (CN)
Kingston Field Naturalists (CN)
Kingston Press Services Ltd. (UK)
Kinki Agricultural Administration Bureau
   see Japan. Kinki Agricultural Administration Bureau (JA)
Kinki Chugoku Agricultural Research Association (JA)
Kinki University. Faculty of Pharmaceutical Sciences (JA)
Kinoloski Savez SR Hrvatske (YU)
Kinzoku Hyomen Gijutsu Kyokai
   see Metal Finishing Society of Japan (JA)
Kinzoku Kogyo Jigyodan
   see Japan. Metal Mining Agency (JA)
Editions du Kiosque (FR)
Kipen Publishing Corporation (US)
Kipling Society (UK)
Kiplinger Washington Editors, Inc. (US)
Verlag Kirchheim und Co. GmbH (GW)
Jack & Viola Kirecofe, Eds. & Pubs. (US)

Kirin Brewery Co. Ltd. (JA)
Kirklanda Esperanto-Centro (US)
Kirklees Chamber of Commerce Inc. (West Yorkshire) (UK)
Kirkley Press Inc. (US)
Kirkus Service, Inc. (US)
Kirloskar Press (II)
Kirolak (SP)
Verlag A. Kirsch (AU)
Kirschbaum Verlag (GW)
Verlag Therese Kirschner GmbH (AU)
Sandra D. Kirshenbaum, Ed. & Pub. (US)
Kiruna Geophysical Institute (SW)
Kisho-cho (Japan Meteorological Agency)
   for publications of this agency, see Japan Weather Association (JA)
Kisho-cho Kisho Kenkyusho
   see Meteorological Research Institute (JA)
Nawal Kishore, Ed. & Pub. (II)
Kisipari Szovetkezetek Orszagos Szovetsege (OKISZ) (HU)
Kiso Butsurigaku Kenkyusho Riron Butsurigaku Kankokai
   see Kyoto University. Research Institute for Fundamental Physics (JA)
Kissan Products Ltd. (II)
Kissei Pharmaceutical Co., Ltd. (JA)
Kita Nihon Byogaichu Kenkyukai
   see Society of Plant Protection of North Japan (JA)
Kitakanto Medical Society (JA)
Kitano Hospital
   see Tazuke Kofukai Medical Research Institute (JA)
Kitazato Institute for Infectious Diseases (JA)
Kite Books (US)
Kitt Peak National Observatory (US)
R. Kitzinger (GW)
Kiver-Patterson Publishing (UK)
M. S. Kiver Publications, Inc (US)
Kivukoni College (TZ)
Kiwanis International (US)
Kjellberg-ESAB GmbH (GW)
Kjoebenhavns Handelsbank
   see Copenhagen Handelsbank (DK)
Kjoettbransjens Landsforbund (NO)
Klagenfurt. Magistrat der Landeshauptstadt Klagenfurt (AU)
Verlag W.W. Ed. Klambt KG (GW)
Klas Publishing Co. (US)
Sholom Klass, Ed. & Pub. (US)
Klass Publications, Inc (US)
Klassillis - Filologinen Yhdistys (FI)
Klaus-Groth-Gesellschaft (GW)
Anthony C. Kleber (US)
Bernard A. Klein (US)
B. Klein Publication, Inc. (US)
Kleinhans Co. (US)
Ernst Klett Verlag (GW)
Klevens Publications, Inc. (US)
Kliatt Paperback Book Guide (US)
Editions Klincksieck (FR)
Charles H. Kline & Co., Inc. (US)
Kline Geology Laboratory (US)
Ralph A. Kling (US)
Curtis C. Klinger (US)
Klinicka Bolnica "Dr. M. Stojanovic" u Zagrebu (YU)
Klinicka Bolnica "Dr. M. Stojanovic" u Zagrebu. Klinika za Otorinolaringologiju i Cervikofacijalnu Kirurgiju (YU)
Verlag Julius Klinkhardt (GW)
Oskar Klokow, Verlag und Versandbuchhandlung (GW)
Vittorio Klostermann (GW)
Klub der Kinoamateure Oesterreichs (AU)
Klub Slovenischer Studenten in Wien (AU)
Verlag Wilhelm Kluge (GW)
Kluwer B.V. (NE)
Kluwer Schoolboeken B.V. (NE)
Kmecki Glas (YU)
Manfred Kmoch (AU)
KMW Commodity Consultants Ltd. (CN)
Moises Knaphais, Ed. & Pub. (AG)
Ed. & Pub. Horst Knapp (AU)
Fritz Knapp Verlag GmbH (GW)
Knave Publications, Inc. (US)
Kneipp-Verlag GmbH (GW)
Knickerbocker Club, New York (US)
Izdatel'stvo Kniga (UR)
Knighton Publications (UK)
Knights of Columbus (US)
Knights of Columbus in the Philippines (PH)
Knights of Columbus. Service Dept. (US)
Knights of Lithuania (US)
Knights of the Southern Cross (AT)
Knjizevne Novine (YU)
Alfred A. Knopf (US)

Know (US)

Know, Inc. (US)

Knowledge Industry Publications, Inc. (US)

Donald D. Knowles, Ed. & Pub. (US)

Knox College (US)

Knox County Illinois Genealogical Society (US)

Knudsens Reklamebyraa (NO)

Uitgeverij Frits Knuf B. V. (NE)

Knuth Beth (US)

Ko Hsueh Chu Pan She. Chung-Kuo Kuo Chi Shu
Tien (CC)

Ko-Operatieve Wijnbouwers Vereniging van Z.A.
(SA)

Kobe Daigaku
see Kobe University (JA)

Kobe-shi Shokubutsu Boekisho
see Japan. Kobe Plant Protection Station (JA)

Kobe University. Faculty of Economics (JA)

Kobe University Law Review Association (JA)

Kobe University Medical Society (JA)

Kobe University. Research Institute for Economics and
Business Administration (JA)

Kobe University. School of Business Administration
(JA)

Kobe University. School of Medicine (JA)

Verlag Harald Kobold (GW)

Kobundo (JA)

Kobunshi Gakkai
see Society of Polymer Science (JA)

Kobunshi Kankokai
see High Polymer Publishing Association (JA)

Kobzar Publishing Co. Ltd. (CN)

Irvin Koch, Ed. & Pub. (US)

Verlagsanstalt Alexander Koch GmbH (GW)

Henerik Kocher, Ed. & Pub. (BL)

Kochi Daigaku
see Kochi University (JA)

Kochi University. Earthquake Observatory (JA)

Kockums AB (SW)

Kodak Ag (GW)

Kodak-Pathe. Division Marches et Graphiques (FR)

Kodansha International Ltd (JA)

Kodansha Ltd. (JA)

Kodex-Verlag GmbH (GW)

Koebenhavns Bogtrykkerforening (DK)

Koebenhavns Cykelhandler Forening (DK)

Koebenhavns Philatelist Klub (DK)

Koebenhavns Universitet (DK)

Koebenhavns Universitet. Arnamagnaeanske Institut
see Arnamagnaean Institute (DK)

Koebenhavns Universitet. Centralinstitut for Nordisk
Asienforskning
see Scandinavian Institute of Asia Studies (DK)

Koebenhavns Universitet. Geologisk Centralinstitut
(DK)

Koebenhavns Universitet. Historisk Institut (DK)

Koebenhavns Universitet. Institut d'Etudes Romanes
(DK)

Koebenhavns Universitet. Institut for Anvendt og
Matematisk Lingvistik (DK)

Koebenhavns Universitet. Institut for Filmvidenskab
(DK)

Koebenhavns Universitet. Institut for Matematisk
Statistik (DK)

Koebenhavns Universitet. Institute of Art History
(DK)

Koebenhavns Universitet. Marinbiologisk Institut
(DK)

Koebenhavns Universitet. Medicinisk-Historiske
Institut og Museum (DK)

Koebenhavns Universitet. Sociologisk Institut (DK)

Hein Koehler (GW)

Koehler und Foltmer (GW)

Koehlers Verlagsgesellschaft mbH (GW)

Koeletekniske Foreninger i Skandinavien (DK)

Koelner Vortraege zur Sozial- und
Wirtschaftsgeschichte (GW)

Otto Koeltz Antiquariat (GW)

Allen Koenigsberg (US)

Koepmannens Foerlags AB (SW)

Verlag Valentin Koerner (GW)

Koerner GmbH (GW)

Koettbranschens Riksfoerbund (SW)

Kogaku Kenkyujo
see Kyoto University. Engineering Research
Institute (JA)

Kogaku Kenkyusho
see Tokyo Kyoiku University. Institute for Optical
Research (JA)

Kogan Page Ltd. (UK)

Drukkerij t Koggeschip B.V. (NE)

Kogos International Corp. (US)

Kogyo Gijutsuin Biseibutsu Kogyo Gijutsu Kenkyusho
see Japan. Fermentation Research Institute (JA)

Kogyo Keizai Kenkyosho
see Industrial Chemical Consultants, Inc. (JA)

Kogyo Rodo Saigai Boshi Kyokai

see Association of Mining Labor Accident
Prevention (JA)

Koh-i-Noor Hardtmuth S.p.A. (IT)

Verlag Carl Kohler (GW)

C. C. Kohler (UK)

W. Kohlhammer GmbH (Koeln) (GW)

W. Kohlhammer GmbH (Stuttgart) (GW)

W. Kohlhammer-Verlag GmbH. Abt.
Veroeffentlichungen des Statistischen Bundesamtes
(GW)

Kojunsha (JA)

J. H. Kok B. V. (NE)

Kokugakuin University. Faculty of Economics (JA)

Kokugakuin University. Faculty of Law and Politics
(JA)

Kokuritsu Bosai Kagaku Gijutsu Senta
see National Research Center for Disaster
Prevention (JA)

Kokuritsu Eisei Shikenjo
see National Institute of Hygienic Sciences (JA)

Kokuritsu Gan Senta
see Japan. National Cancer Center (JA)

Kokuritsu Idengaku Kenkyusho
see Japan. National Institute of Genetics (JA)

Kokuritsu Kagaku Hakubutsukan
see National Science Museum (JA)

Kokuritsu Kokkai Toshokan
see National Diet Library (JA)

Kokuritsu Kokugo Kenkyusho
see National Language Research Institute (JA)

Kokuritsu Koshu Eisei-in
see Japan. Institute of Public Health (JA)

Kokuritsu Kyokuchi Kenkyujyo
see National Institute of Polar Research (JA)

Kokuritsu Tama Kenkyusho
see Japan. National Institute for Leprosy Research
(JA)

Kokuritsu Tokushu Kyoiku Sogo Kenkyujo
see National Institute for Special Education (JA)

Kokusai Christian University (JA)

Kokusai Keizai Gakkai
see Japan Society of International Economics (JA)

Kokusai Koryu Kikin (IT)

Kokusai Kowan Kyokai
see International Association of Ports and Harbors
(JA)

Kokusai Kyoku-Undo Kansoku Jigyo Chuo-Kyoku
see International Polar Motion Service (JA)

Kokusai Nogyo-Sha K.K. (JA)

Kokusai Saibo Gakkai
see International Association of Cytology (JA)

Kokusai Shokuryo Nogyo Kyokai
see Japan F A O Association (JA)

Kokusaiho Gakkai
see Association of International Law (JA)

Kokusaiho Kyokai Nihon- Shibu
see International Legal Sciences Association (JA)

Kokuseido Publishing Co., Ltd. (JA)

Kokushikan Daigaku Kyoyo Gakkai
see Kokushikan University. Society of Liberal Arts
(JA)

Kokushikan University. Society of Liberal Arts (JA)

Kokuzeicho
see Japan. National Tax Agency (JA)

Mykola Kolankiwsky, Ed.. & Pub. (CN)

Peter Kolbe Verlag (GW)

Verlag H. Kolbenstetter (GW)

Kollek and Sons (IS)

James Koller, Ed. & Pub. (US)

Kolloid- Gesellschaft (GW)

Kolonihaveforbundet for Danmark (DK)

Izdatel'stvo Kolos (UR)

Komal Patra (II)

Kombinat Technische Gebaeudeausruestung Institut
(GE)

Komisija za Ekonomsku Historiju Jugoslavije (YU)

Komitet far Yidisher Kultur in Yisroel (IS)

Komitet Sovetskikh Zhenshchin (UR)

Komitet za Izkustvo i Kultura (BU)

Komitet za Nauka, Tekhnicheski Progres i Visshe
Obrazovanie (BU)

Komitet za Otdikh i Turizum (BU)

Komitet za Televiziia i Radio (BU)

Kommanditgesellschaft Verlag Horst Axtmann GmbH
und Co. (GW)

Kommanduyushchii Artilleriei Vooruzhennykh Sil' S.
S. S. R. (UR)

Verlag die Kommenden GmbH (GW)

Kommission fuer Geschichtliche Landeskunde in
Baden-Wuerttemberg (GW)

Kommission fuer Literaturwissenschaft. (AU)

Kommissionsverlag der Oesterreichischen
Staatsdruckerei (AU)

Kommunalarbetarefoerbundet (SW)

Kommunale Kinematografers Landsforbund (NO)

Kommunalwissenschaftliches Dokumentationszentrum
(AU)

Kommunernes Landsforening (DK)

Kommunisticheskaya Partiya Armyanskoi S.S.R.
Tsentral'nyi Komitet (UR)

Kommunisticheskaya Partiya Belorussii. Tsentral'nyi
Komitet (UR)

Kommunisticheskaya Partiya Sovetskogo Soyuza.
Tsentral'nyi Komitet (UR)

Kommunisticheskaya Partiya Tadzhikskoi S. S. R.
Tsentral'nyi Komitet (UR)

Kommunisticheskaya Partiya Ukrainy. Tsentral'nyi
Komitet (UR)

Kommunistischer Arbeiterbund Deutschlands (KABD)
(GW)

Kommunistischer Bund fuer den Proletarischen
Internationalismus (GW)

Kommunistischer Bund Westdeutschland (GW)

Kommunistischer Bund Wien (AU)

Kommunistiska Foerbundet (SW)

Forlaget Kompas-Denmark (DK)

Kompass Belgium S.A. (BE)

Kompass Espana SA (SP)

Kompass Hong Kong (HK)

Kompass International AG (SZ)

Kompass Maroc-Veto (MR)

Kompass Nederland N.V. (NE)

Kompass Norge A-S (NO)

Kompass Publishers Ltd. (UK)

Kompass Sweden (SW)

Komuna (YU)

Wydawnictwa Komunikacji i Lacznosci (PL)

Komunist (YU)

Komunisticka Strana Ceskoslovenska (CS)

Kona Communications, Inc. (US)

Konditorei, Verlagsgesellschaft mbH (GW)

Koneviestin Ammattilehdet Oy (FI)

Lisbet Konfeld (SZ)

Konferencija za Drustvenu Aktivnost Zena Jugoslavije
(YU)

Kongelig Dansk Aeroklub (DK)

Kongelig Norsk Automobilklub (NO)

Kongelig Norsk Motorbaat Forbund (NO)

Kongelige Danske Geografiske Selskab (DK)

Kongelige Danske Landhusholdningsselskab (DK)

Kongelige Danske Selskab for Faedrelandets Historie
(DK)

Kongelige Danske Videnskabernes Selskab (DK)

Kongelige Norske Videnskabers Selskab (NO)

Kongelige Veterinaer- og Landbohoejskole (DK)

Kongeriget Danmarks Handels-Kalender (DK)

Konglomerati Press (US)

Kongressgesellschaft fuer Aerztliche Fortbildung e.V.
(GW)

Koninklijk Belgisch Instituut voor
Natuurwetenschappen (BE)

Koninklijk Genootschap voor Landbouwwetenschap
(NE)

Koninklijk Instituut voor de Tropen (NE)

Koninklijk Instituut voor Het Kunstpatrimonium
see Institut Royal du Patrimoine Artistique (BE)

Koninklijk Instituut voor Taal-, Land- en Volkenkunde
(NE)

Koninklijk Museum voor Midden-Afrika
see Musee Royal de l'Afrique Centrale (BE)

Koninklijk Natuurwetenschappelijk Genootschap
Dodonaea (BE)

Koninklijk Nederlands Aardrijkskundig Genootschap
(NE)

Koninklijk Nederlands Geologisch Mijnbouwkundig
Genootschap (NE)

Koninklijk Nederlands Korfbal Verbond (NE)

Koninklijk Nederlandsch Genootschap voor Geslacht-
en Wapenkunde (NE)

Koninklijk Technicum PBNA (NE)

Koninklijk Verbond van Ondernemers (NE)

Koninklijke Academie voor Nederlandse Taal- en
Letterkunde (BE)

Koninklijke Academie voor Overzeese Wetenschappen
see Academie Royale des Sciences d'Outre-Mer
(BE)

Koninklijke Algemeene Vereeniging voor
Bloembollencultuur (NE)

Koninklijke Automobiel Club van Belgie (BE)

Koninklijke Bibliotheek Albert I
see Bibliotheque Royal Albert 1er (BE)

Koninklijke Confederatie Horeca
see Confederation Royale Horeca (BE)

Koninklijke Maatschappij voor Dierkunde van
Antwerpen
see Societe Royale de Zoologie d'Anvers (BE)

Koninklijke Marine (NE)

Koninklijke Musea voor Schone Kunsten van Belgie
see Musees Royaux des Beaux-Arts de Belgique
(BE)

Koninklijke Nationale Bond voor Reddingwezen en
Eerste Hulp Bij Ongelukken "Het Oranje Kruis"
(NE)

Koninklijke Nederlandsche Athletiek-Unie   (NE)
Koninklijke Nederlandsche Cricket Bond   (NE)
Koninklijke Nederlandsche Maatschappij Tot
   Bevordering der Geneeskunst   (NE)
Koninklijke Nederlandsche Roeibond   (NE)
Koninklijke Nederlandsche Voetbalbond   (NE)
Koninklijke Nederlandse Akademie van
   Wetenschappen   (NE)
Koninklijke Nederlandse Akademie van
   Wetenschappen. Sociaal-Wetenschapplijk Informatie
   en Documentatiecentrum   (NE)
Koninklijke Nederlandse Akademie van
   Wetenschappen. Sociaal-Wetenschappelijke Raad
   (NE)
Koninklijke Nederlandse Baseball en Softball Bond
   (NE)
Koninklijke Nederlandse Bosbouw Vereniging   (NE)
Koninklijke Nederlandse Botanische Vereniging   (NE)
Koninklijke Nederlandse Centrale Vereniging tot
   Bestrijding der Tuberculose   (NE)
Koninklijke Nederlandse Chemische Vereniging   (NE)
Koninklijke Nederlandse Dambond   (NE)
Koninklijke Nederlandse Maatschappij Ter
   Bevordering der Pharmacie   (NE)
Koninklijke Nederlandse Maatschappij voor
   Diergeneeskunde   (NE)
Koninklijke Nederlandse Maatschappij voor Tuinbouw
   en Plantkunde   (NE)
Koninklijke Nederlandse Militaire Bond pro Rege
   (NE)
Koninklijke Nederlandse Natuurhistorische Vereniging
   (NE)
Koninklijke Nederlandse Natuurhistorische Vereniging.
   Bryology Group   (NE)
Koninklijke Nederlandse Oudheidkundige Bond   (NE)
Koninklijke Nederlandse Redersvereniging   (NE)
Koninklijke Nederlandse Schaakbond   (NE)
Koninklijke Nederlandse Schutters Associatie   (NE)
Koninklijke Nederlandse Toeristenbond ANWB   (NE)
Koninklijke Nederlandse Vereniging "Ons Leger"
   (NE)
Koninklijke Nederlandse Vereniging Onze Vloot
   (NE)
Koninklijke Nederlandse Vereniging van Leraren en
   Onderwijzers in de Lichamelijke Opvoeding   (NE)
Koninklijke Nederlandse Vereniging van
   Transportondernemingen   (NE)
Koninklijke Nederlandse Vereniging voor Luchtvaart
   (NE)
Koninklijke Nederlandse Vereniging voor Luchtvaart.
   Afdeling Parachutespringen   (NE)
Koninklijke Nederlandse Vereniging voor Luchtvaart.
   Afdeling Zweefvliegen   (NE)
Koninklijke Nationale Broederschap   (NE)
Koninklijke Vereniging "Het Nederlandsche Rundvee-
   Stamboek"   (NE)
Koninklijke Vereniging "Onze Luchtmacht"   (NE)
Koninklijke Vereniging ter Beoefening van de
   Krijgswetenschap   (NE)
Koninklijke Vereniging van Gasfabrikanten in
   Nederland   (NE)
Koninklijke Vereniging voor Facultatieve Crematie
   (NE)
Koninklijke Vlaamse Ingenieursvereniging   (BE)
Konkordanter-Verlag   (GW)
Sipapu Konocti Books   (US)
Konpyuta Eijisha
   *see* Computer Age Co., Ltd.   (JA)
Konrad-Adenauer-Stiftung fuer Politische Bildung und
   Studienfoerderung e.V. Politische Akademie
   Eichholz   (GW)
Konradin-Verlag Robert Kohlhammer GmbH   (GW)
Verlag fuer Konservative Publizistik   (GW)
Konservatorium-Vereniging   (SA)
Universitaetsverlag Konstanz GmbH   (GW)
Konsthistoriska Saellskapet   (SW)
Konstnaersgillet i Finland
   *see* Suomen Taiteilijaseura   (FI)
Konstruktorsko-Tekhnologicheskii Institut
   Avtomatizatsii Avtomobilstroeniya   (UR)
Konsumtionsandelslagens Centralfoerbund
   *see* Kulutusosuuskuntien Keskusliitto (KK) r.y.
   (FI)
Kontakt   (CN)
Kontakt   (II)
Kontexts Publications   (UK)
Kontorteknisk Landsforening   (NO)
Kontrollraadet foer Betongvaror   (SW)
Kooperatieve Utjowery   (NE)
Kooperation Evangelischer Kirchen und Missionen
   (SZ)
Kooperativa Foerbundet   (SW)
Kooperativa Ledares Foerbund   (SW)
Kooperative Faellesforbund i Danmark   (DK)
Kopfklinik   (GW)
Koranyi Sandor Tarsasag   (HU)
Korea Amateur Sports Association   (KO)
Korea Development Bank   (KO)

Korea Directory Co.   (KO)
Korea Exchange Bank   (KO)
Korea Information Service Inc.   (KO)
Korea Institute of Science and Technology   (KO)
Korea Photo News, Inc.   (KO)
Korea, Republic. Bureau of Planning   (KO)
Korea, Republic. Bureau of Statistics   (KO)
Korea, Republic. Central Meteorological Office   (KO)
Korea, Republic. Economic Planning Board   (KO)
Korea, Republic. Ministry of Agriculture & Fishery.
   Office of Rural Development   (KO)
Korea, Republic. Ministry of Education   (KO)
Korea, Republic. Ministry of Science and Technology
   (KO)
Korea Research and Publication, Inc.   (US)
Korea Scientific and Technological Information Center
   (KO)
Korea Stamp Society, Inc.   (US)
Korea Trade Promotion Corp.   (KO)
Korea University. College of Science and Engineering
   (KO)
Korea Week Publishing Co.   (US)
Korean Association for Conservation of Nature   (KN)
Korean Association of International Law   (KO)
Korean Association of International Relations   (KO)
Korean Democratic Women's Union. Central
   Committee   (KN)
Korean Institute for Family Planning   (KO)
Korean Institute of International Studies   (KO)
Korean Library Association   (KO)
Korean Library Science Society   (KO)
Korean Medical Association   (KO)
Korean Micro-Library Association   (KO)
Korean National Commission for UNESCO   (KO)
Korean Nurses' Association   (KO)
Korean Otolaryngological Society   (KO)
Korean Overseas Information Service   (KO)
Korean Physiological Society   (KO)
Korean Publishers Association   (KO)
Korean Reconstruction Bank   (KO)
Korean Research Center   (KO)
Korean Research Council   (KO)
Korean Social Science Research Institute   (KO)
Korean Society for Future Studies   (KO)
Korean Standards Association   (KO)
Korean Studies Institute   (KO)
Korean Traders Association, Inc   (US)
Herbert Kornblitt, Ed. & Pub.   (US)
Koronasha
   *see* Corona Publishing Co., Ltd.   (JA)
Korrosionscentralen, ATV   (DK)
Drukkerij Korthuis   (NE)
Kosciuszko Foundation   (US)
Kosei-cho Kokuritsu Eiyo Kenkyusho
   *see* Japan. National Institute of Health   (JA)
Kosei-sho Jinko Mondai Kenkyusho
   *see* Japan. Institute of Population Problems   (JA)
Kosei-sho Kokuritsu Tama Kenkyusho
   *see* Japan. National Institute for Leprosy Research
   (JA)
Verlag Adolf Kosel   (AU)
P. J. Koshy, Ed. & Pub.   (II)
Kosmon Church   (UK)
Kosmon Press   (UK)
Livraria Kosmos Editora   (BL)
Kosmos Gesellschaft der Naturfreunde   (GW)
Koss Corp.   (US)
Kossuth Konyvkiado   (HU)
Kossuth Lajos Tudomanyegyetem   (HU)
Kostnicka Jednota   (CS)
Kotaigun Seitaigakkai
   *see* Society of Population Ecology   (JA)
M. V. Kotak, Ed. & Pub.   (II)
Kothari & Sons   (II)
Kothari Publications   (II)
Kotikielen Seura   (FI)
Kotitalousopettajien Liitto   (FI)
Kotiteollisuuden Keskusliitto r.y.   (FI)
Helen Panopalis Kotsonis, Ed. & Pub.   (GR)
G. P. Koushal, Ed. & Pub.   (II)
Van Kouteren's Publishing Co.   (NE)
N. A. Kovach, Ed. & Pub.   (US)
Kovner Publications Inc.   (US)
Kowan Gijutsu Kenkyusho
   *see* Japan. Port and Harbour Technical Research
   Institute   (JA)
K. S. Kowshik   (II)
Kozlekedestudomanyi Egyesulet   (HU)
Kozponti Kolorisztikai Kutato Laboratorium   (HU)
Kracht van Omhoog   (NE)
Verlag Karl Kraemer und Co.   (SZ)
Karl Kraemer Verlag   (GW)
David Kraft Publishing Company   (IS)
Kraftfahrt-Bundesamt   (GW)
Kraftfornytt   (NO)
Matthias Kraintschan, Ed. & Pub.   (AU)
Krajina   (YU)
Krajowa Agencja Wydawnicza   (PL)

Krajowe Wydawnictwo Czasopism   (PL)
Michael J. Krajsa   (US)
Krak   (DK)
Krakowskie Wydawnictwo Prasowe RSW "Prasa -
   Ksiazka - Ruch"   (PL)
Kralco Printing Co. Pty. Ltd.   (AT)
Verlag Dr. Waldemar Kramer   (GW)
Verlag A. Krammer und Co.   (GW)
Kranti Parishad   (II)
Krasnoyarskii Institut Tsvetnykh Metallov   (UR)
Krasnoyarskoe Knizhnoe Izdatel'stvo   (UR)
Kratville Publications   (US)
Kraus- Thomson Organization Ltd.
   *see* K T O Press   (US)
Krause Publications, Inc.   (US)
Kraushar Andrews and Eassie Ltd   (UK)
Krausskopf-Verlag fuer Wirtschaft GmbH   (GW)
Krauth Memorial Library   (US)
Krax   (UK)
G. Krebs Verlagsbuchhandlung AG   (SZ)
Kredietbank   (BE)
Kreisgemeinschaft Osterode Ostpreussen   (GW)
Kresge Art Center Gallery   (US)
Kresge Foundation   (US)
Kreuz-Verlag   (GW)
Phyllis van Kriedt, Ed. & Pub.   (US)
Krieger Publishing Co., Inc.   (US)
Kriegsopferverband Steiermark   (AU)
Krigskoleutdannede Offiserers Landsforening   (NO)
Krigsvidenskabelige Selskab   (DK)
Krikos Ltd.   (UK)
Verlag fuer Kriminalistische Fachliteratur   (GW)
Dr. F. Krins   (GW)
Krishnamurti Foundation   (II)
Kristall Editrice   (IT)
Kristelig Folkeparti   (NO)
Kristelig Legeforening i Norge   (NO)
Kristen Demokratisk Samling   (SW)
Kristliga Esperantofoerbund   (SW)
Kristlik Fryske Folsbibleteek   (NE)
Kristna Samfundens Nykterhetsroerelse   (SW)
Kritika   (II)
Krmiva   (YU)
Kroc Foundation   (US)
Kroeber Anthropological Society   (US)
Kroegers Buch- und Verlagsdruckerei   (GW)
Alfred Kroener Verlag   (GW)
Kroghs Skolehandbog   (DK)
Barbara Krohn and Associates   (US)
Kronos Press   (US)
Kroon Levensmiddelenorganisatie N.V.
   *see* E. O. Kroon Levensmiddelenorganisatie N.V.
   (NE)
Diane Kruchkow, Ed. & Pub.   (US)
Verlag Dr. Krueger KG   (GW)
Krueger-Verlag   (GW)
N.V. de Kruidenier-l'Epicier   (BE)
Krul's Maandblad voor Stoom- en Chemische
   Wasserijen Ververijen en Wassalons   (NE)
Krupp GmbH   (GW)
Uitgeversmaatschappij Kruyt   (NE)
Wydawnictwo Ksiazka i Wiedza   (PL)
Ktaadn   (US)
Kuala Lumpur Stock Exchange   (MY)
H. Kuchling   (AU)
Kuden Kenkyusho
   *see* Nagoya University. Research Institute of
   Atmospherics   (JA)
Kudzu   (US)
Kuehl KG   (GW)
Verlag Werner Kuehn   (GW)
Kuehn-Verlag   (GW)
Michael Kuehnle, Ed. & Pub.   (SZ)
Kuemmerly und Frey AG   (SZ)
Kuestenausschuss Nord- und Ostsee, Kiel   (GW)
F. William Kuethe, Jr., Ed. & Pub.   (US)
Kugelfischer Georg Schaefer & Co.   (GW)
Kuhlman Electric Company   (US)
G. Kuhlmann   (GW)
Kuki Chowa Eisei Kogakkai
   *see* Society of Heating, Air Conditioning, and
   Sanitary Engineers of Japan   (JA)
Kuksu Press   (US)
Hubert Fabian Kulterer, Editor and Publisher   (AU)
Kulttuurikeskus Kriittisen Korkeakoulun
   Kannatusyhdistys r.y.   (FI)
Kultur   (AU)
Buch- und Zeitschriften-Verlag Kultur und Wissen
   GmbH und Co. KG   (GW)
Kultura (Distributor)   (HU)
Kulturbuch-Verlag GmbH   (GW)
Kulturbund der DDR   (GE)
Kulturbund der DDR. Pirckheimer-Gesellschaft   (GE)
Kulturbund der DDR. Zentraler Arbeitskreis Esperanto
   (GE)
Kulturen Zivot   (YU)
Kulturhistoriska Foereningen Foer Soedra Sverige
   (SW)

Kulturni Zivot  (YU)
Kulturno-Prosvetna Zaednica na Makedonija  (YU)
Kulturno Prosvetna Zajednica Opstine Kraljevo  (YU)
Kulturno Prosvetna Zajednica Opstine Pozarevac
  (YU)
Kulturno-Prosvjetna Zajednica Bosne i Hercegovine
  (YU)
Kulturplatz Dammweg e.V.  (GW)
Kulturwerk Schlesien e.V.  (GW)
Kultuurraad voor Vlaanderen  (BE)
Kulutusosuuskuntien Keskusliitto (KK) r.y.  (FI)
Kumamoto Daigaku
  see Kumamoto University  (JA)
Kumamoto Igakkai
  see Kumamoto Medical Society  (JA)
Kumamoto Medical Society  (JA)
Kumamoto University. Faculty of Engineering  (JA)
Kumamoto University. Faculty of Science  (JA)
Kumamoto University. Institute of Constitutional
  Medicine  (JA)
Kumamoto University Medical School  (JA)
K. Kumar, Ed. & Pub.  (II)
Shiva Kumar, Ed. & Pub.  (II)
Kumar Karyalaya Ltd.  (II)
Kungliga Armemuseum  (SW)
Kungliga Automobil Klubben  (SW)
Kungliga Gustav Adolfs Akademien  (SW)
Kungliga Krigsvetenskapsakademien  (SW)
Kungliga Oerlogsmannasaellskapet  (SW)
Kungliga Skogs- och Lantbruksakademien  (SW)
Kungliga Skogshoegskolan. Institutionen Foer
  Virkeslaera  (SW)
Kungliga Svenska Aeroklubben  (SW)
Kungliga Svenska Vetenskapsakademien  (SW)
Kungliga Tekniska Hoegskolan  (SW)
Kungliga Tekniska Hoegskolan. Division of
  Photogrammetry  (SW)
Kungliga Tekniska Hoegskolan. Flygtekniska
  Institutionen  (SW)
Kungliga Vetenskaps-Societeten  (SW)
Kungliga Vetenskapsakademien  (SW)
Kungliga Vitterhets-, Historie- och Antikvitets
  Akademien  (SW)
Verlag Kunst und Stein  (SZ)
Kunst und Technik Verlagsgesellschaft mbH  (GW)
Verlag fuer Kunst und Wissenschaft  (GE)
Kunstakademiets Bibliotek  (DK)
Kunsthistorische Musea, Antwerp  (BE)
Kunsthistorisches Institut in Florenz  (IT)
Kunsthistorisches Museum in Wien  (AU)
Kunstindustrimuseet i Oslo  (NO)
Verlag Kunstkreis AG  (SZ)
Kunstmuseum Bern  (SZ)
Kunststoff-Verlag  (GW)
Deutscher Kunstverlag GmbH  (GW)
Deutscher Verlag fuer Kunstwissenschaft  (GW)
Henry Kuntz, Jr., Ed. & Pub  (US)
Kupat Holim Health Insurance Institution  (IS)
Kupijai und Prochnow, Verlag und Druckerei  (GW)
Kuppuswami Sastri Research Institute  (II)
Kuratorium fuer Technik und Bauwesen in der
  Landwirtschaft e.V.  (GW)
Kuratorium fuer Verkehrssicherheit  (AU)
Kuratorium fuer Verkehrssicherheit.
  Verkehrspychologisches Institut  (AU)
Mohammad Yusef Kureshy, Ed. & Pub.  (PK)
George Kurian Reference Books  (US)
Kurinji Quarterly  (II)
Kurpil  (SP)
Kursbuch Verlag  (GW)
Kurume Daigaku
  see Kurume University  (JA)
Kurume Medical Association  (JA)
Kurume University School of Medicine  (JA)
Kurverwaltung Bad Homburg  (GW)
Kustartilleriklubben  (SW)
Kutztown State College. English Department  (US)
Kuulonhuoltoliitto  (FI)
Kuwait. Central Statistical Office  (KU)
Kuwait. Ministry of Guidance & Information  (KU)
Kuwait Medical Association  (KU)
Kuwait Oil Co. Ltd.  (KU)
Kuyperstichting ter Bevordering van de Studie der
  Antirevolutionaire Beginselen
  see Dr. Abraham Kuyperstichting ter Bevordering
  van de Studie der Antirevolutionaire Beginselen
  (NE)
Kvaekarna
  see Vaenner Samfund i Sverige  (SW)
Kvakera Esperantista Societo  (UK)
Kvenfelagasamband Islands  (IC)
Kvidinge Sockens Hembygdsfoerening  (SW)
Kwame Nkrumah Institute of Writers and Journalists
  (UK)
Kwang Wen Book Co.  (CH)
Kwara State. Ministry of Home Affairs and
  Information  (NR)
Kyiw Publishing House  (US)

Kyklos-Verlag  (SZ)
Kyle Publishing Co.  (US)
Kyorin Shoin  (JA)
Kyoritsu Shuppan Co., Ltd.  (JA)
Kyoto Association for International Culture and
  Tourism  (JA)
Kyoto Daigaku
  see Kyoto University  (JA)
Kyoto Daigaku Afurika Ruijin'en Gakujutsu Chosatai
  see Kyoto University. Committee of the Kyoto
  University Africa Primatological Expedition  (JA)
Kyoto Daigaku Bosai Kenkyusho
  see Kyoto University. Disaster Prevention Research
  Institute  (JA)
Kyoto Daigaku Genshi Enerugi Kenkyusho
  see Kyoto University. Institute of Atomic Energy
  (JA)
Kyoto Daigaku Jimbun Kagaku Kenkyujo
  see Kyoto University. Research Institute for
  Humanistic Studies  (JA)
Kyoto Daigaku Kagaku Kenkyusho
  see Kyoto University. Institute for Chemical
  Research  (JA)
Kyoto Daigaku Kekkaku Kyobu Shikkan Kenkyusho
  see Kyoto University. Chest Disease Research
  Institute  (JA)
Kyoto Daigaku Kogaku Kenkyujo
  see Kyoto University. Engineering Research
  Institute  (JA)
Kyoto Daigaku Rigakubu Chikyu Butsurigaku
  Kyoshitsu
  see Kyoto University. Geophysical Institute  (JA)
Kyoto Daigaku Rigakubu Fuzoku Otsu Rinko
  Jikkensho
  see Kyoto University. Otsu Hydrobiological Station
  (JA)
Kyoto Daigaku Rigakubu Fuzoku Seto Rinkai
  Jikkensho
  see Kyoto University. Seto Marine Biological
  Laboratory  (JA)
Kyoto Daigaku Shokuryo Kogaku Kenkyusho
  see Kyoto University. Research Institute for Food
  Science  (JA)
Kyoto Daigaku Suri Kaiseki Kenkyusho
  see Kyoto University. Research Institute for
  Mathematical Sciences  (JA)
Kyoto Daigaku Uirusu Kenkyusho
  see Kyoto University. Institute for Virus Research
  (JA)
Kyoto Daigaku Zinbun Kagata Kenkynsyo
  see Kyoto University. Institute for Humanistic
  Studies  (JA)
Kyoto Fire Prevention Association  (JA)
Kyoto-furitsu Daigaku
  see Kyoto Prefectural University  (JA)
Kyoto-furitsu Ika Diagaku
  see Kyoto Prefectural University of Medicine  (JA)
Kyoto Kogei Sen'i Daigaku
  see Kyoto Technical University  (JA)
Kyoto Kyoiku Daigaku
  see Kyoto University of Education  (JA)
Kyoto Prefectural University  (JA)
Kyoto Prefectural University of Medicine  (JA)
Kyoto Shobo Henshu Iinkai
  see Kyoto Fire Prevention Association  (JA)
Kyoto Technical University. Faculty of Industrial Arts
  (JA)
Kyoto University. Abuyama Seismological Observatory
  (JA)
Kyoto University. Chest Disease Research Institute
  (JA)
Kyoto University. College of Agriculture  (JA)
Kyoto University. Committee of the Kyoto University
  Africa Primatological Expedition  (JA)
Kyoto University. Data Processing Center  (JA)
Kyoto University. Department of Architecture  (JA)
Kyoto University. Department of Civil Engineering
  (JA)
Kyoto University. Disaster Prevention Research
  Insitute  (JA)
Kyoto University. Economic Society  (JA)
Kyoto University. Engineering Research Institute
  (JA)
Kyoto University. Faculty of Engineering  (JA)
Kyoto University. Faculty of Medicine  (JA)
Kyoto University. Faculty of Science  (JA)
Kyoto University. Geophysical Institute  (JA)
Kyoto University. Institute for Chemical Research
  (JA)
Kyoto University. Institute for Virus Research  (JA)
Kyoto University. Institute of Atomic Energy  (JA)
Kyoto University. Institute of Earth Science  (JA)
Kyoto University. Misaki Marine Biological Institute
  (JA)
Kyoto University. Otsu Hydrobiological Station  (JA)
Kyoto University. Research Institute for Food Science
  (JA)

Kyoto University. Research Institute for Fundamental
  Physics  (JA)
Kyoto University. Research Institute for Humanistic
  Studies  (JA)
Kyoto University. Research Institute for Mathematical
  Sciences  (JA)
Kyoto University. Seto Marine Biological Laboratory
  (JA)
Kyoto University of Education  (JA)
Kyoyo Gakkai
  see Kokushikan University. Society of Liberal Arts
  (JA)
Kyrkomusikernas Riksfoerbund  (SW)
Kyushu American Literature Society  (JA)
Kyushu Association of Neuro-Psychiatry  (JA)
Kyushu Daigaku
  see Kyushu University  (JA)
Kyushu Daigaku Hosei Gakkai
  see Kyushu University. Institute of Law and Politics
  (JA)
Kyushu Daigaku Oyo Rikigaku Kenkyusho
  see Kyushu University. Research Institute for
  Applied Mechanics  (JA)
Kyushu Daigaku Rigakubu Fuzoku Amakusa Rinkai
  Jikkensho
  see Kyushu University. Amakusa Marine Biological
  Laboratory  (JA)
Kyushu Daigaku Tokei Kagaku Kenkyukai
  see Kyushu University. Research Association of
  Statistical Sciences  (JA)
Kyushu Institute of Technology  (JA)
Kyushu Kogyo Daigaku
  see Kyushu Institute of Technology  (JA)
Kyushu Kogyo Gijutsu Shikenjo
  see Japan. Government Industrial Research
  Institute, Kyushu  (JA)
Kyushu Sangyo University  (JA)
Kyushu Shinkei Seishin Gakkai
  see Kyushu Association of Neuro-Psychiatry  (JA)
Kyushu University. Amakusa Marine Biological
  Laboratory  (JA)
Kyushu University. College of General Education
  (JA)
Kyushu University. Department of Fisheries  (JA)
Kyushu University. Faculty of Agriculture  (JA)
Kyushu University. Faculty of Engineering  (JA)
Kyushu University. Faculty of Medicine  (JA)
Kyushu University. Faculty of Science  (JA)
Kyushu University. Institute of Law and Politics  (JA)
Kyushu University. Research Association of Statistical
  Sciences  (JA)
Kyushu University. Research Institute for Applied
  Mechanics  (JA)

L B I News  (US)
L.D.C. Publications  (UG)
L. D. Pankey Alumni Association  (US)
L.E.N., Inc.  (US)
Editions L E P S  (FR)
Edizioni L.E.T.I  (IT)
L G Z Landis und Gyr Zug AG  (SZ)
L. H. Bailey Hortorium  (US)
L. H. Publishing Co.  (US)
L K B-Produkter AB  (SW)
L. Loffredo Editore  (IT)
L N S News Service, Inc.  (US)
L'Officiel-U S A, Inc.  (US)
L.Q.C. Lamar Society of International Law  (US)
L. S. B. Leakey Foundation  (US)
L S M Information Center  (CN)
L. S. W. Associates  (US)
L T R Editora Ltda.  (BL)
L.V.A. "Ramove" Inc.  (US)
L.W. & T.S. Nominees  (AT)
L-5 Society  (US)
La Leche League International, Inc  (US)
Ignacio H. de La Mota, Ed. & Pub.  (SP)
La Motte Enterprises  (US)
Editions La Presse  (CN)
La Salette Fathers  (US)
La Salle College  (US)
La Trobe University. Historical Association  (AT)
La Trobe University. Students Representative Council
  (AT)
Laban Art of Movement Guild  (UK)
Labo-France  (FR)
Editions Labo Pharma  (FR)
Labor  (IT)
Labor Challenge Publications  (CN)
Labor Cooperative Educational & Publishing Society,
  Inc  (US)
Labor Council of New South Wales  (AT)
Labor et Fides S.A.  (SZ)
Labor Herald Publishing Co.  (US)
Labor News Company  (US)
Labor Record Publishing Co., Inc.  (US)
Labor Research Association  (US)
Labor Today Associates  (US)

Langham House (Pty) Ltd. (SA)
Language Americas Association (US)
Language and Literature Bureau (BX)
Language Association of Eastern Africa (KE)
Language by Radio Interest Group (US)
Language Learning Systems Inc (US)
Editoriale Laniera S.p.A. (IT)
Lantbrukarnas Ekonomi AB (SW)
Lantbrukarnas Riksfoerbund (SW)
Lantbrukshoegskolan (SW)
Lantbrukshoegskolan. Institutionen Foer
   Markvetenskap (SW)
Lantbruksnytt (SW)
Lantmannens Tryckeri-Forening (SW)
Laographike Kypros (CY)
Lapidary Journal, Inc. (US)
Lapidary Publications (UK)
Lapidary Rock & Mineral Society of British Columbia
   (CN)
Lapin Tutkimusseura (FI)
Lapkiado Vallalat (HU)
Verlag Heinrich Lapp (GW)
Maison Ferdinand Larcier S.A. (BE)
Librairie Lardanchet (FR)
Large Families of America, Inc. (US)
Editoriale Lariana S.p. A. (IT)
Larimi Communications Ltd. (US)
Editions Lariviere (FR)
Larkin Publications, Inc. (US)
Larousse (FR)
Publicite Larrey (FR)
William Larsen, Jr., Ed. & Pub. (US)
Larue D. Carter Memorial Hospital (US)
Laryngoscope Co. (US)
Las Vegas Israelite (US)
Las Vegas Voice Inc. (US)
Las Villas, Cuba. Consejo Nacional de Cultura (CU)
Laser (UK)
Lasersphere (US)
J. K. Lasser Institute (US)
Ed. & Pub. J. Lassieur (FR)
Verlag Michael Lassleben (GW)
Lastensuojelun Keskusliitto (FI)
Latham Publications Inc. (US)
Tony Lathrop (US)
Norman Lathrop Enterprises (US)
Latimer Publications (US)
Latin America Recorder (II)
Latin America Review of Books, Ltd. (UK)
Latin American Documentation (US)
Latin American Free Trade Association
   see Asociacion Latinoamericana de Libre Comercio
   (UY)
Latin American Free Trade Association (AG)
Latin American Index, Ltd. (US)
Latin American Institute for Economic and Social
   Planning
   see Instituto Latinoamericano de Planificacion
   Economica y Social (UN)
Latin American Newsletters Ltd. (UK)
Latin American Notaphilic Society (UK)
Latin American Perspectives, Inc. (US)
Latin American Policy Alternatives Group (US)
Latin American Studies Association (US)
Latin American Working Group (CN)
Latin Language Mathematicians' Group (RM)
Latin New York (US)
Latinamerican Arts (UY)
Latinamerika-Institutet (SW)
Latinoamericana Editores (PE)
Andrea Latorre Editore (IT)
Lattante (IT)
Lattbetong AB (SW)
Latvian Literary Society Celinieks (US)
Latvian Relief Society of Canada (Daugavas Vanagi)
   (CN)
Latviiskaya S.S.R. Gosudarstvennyi Nauchno-
   tekhnicheskii Komitet Soveta Ministrov (UR)
Latviiskaya S.S.R. Ministerstvo Kultury (UR)
Latviiskaya S. S. R. Valsts Gramatu Palata (UR)
Latviiskii Gosudarstvennyi Universitet. Kafedra
   Statistiki i Planirovaniya Narodnogo Khozyaistva
   S.S.S.R. (UR)
Latviiskii Nauchno-issledovatel'skii Institut
   Gidrotekhniki i Melioratsii (UR)
Verlag Latvija (GW)
Latvija Amerika Publishing Ltd. (CN)
Laubach Literacy Inc. (US)
Laufer Publishing Co. (US)
Laughing Bear (US)
C.J. Laumanns (GW)
Laurance Press Co (US)
Laurel Press (US)
Laurence, Scott & Electromotors Ltd. (UK)
Laurentian University (CN)
Lava Publications (II)
Editions Charles Lavauzelle et Cie (FR)
Laventhol & Horwath (US)

Librairie Lavoisier (FR)
Edizioni del Lavoro (IT)
Law Academy (II)
Law and Local Government Publications Ltd. (UK)
Law and Society Association (US)
Law-Arts Publishers Inc. (US)
Law Book Co. (II)
Law Book Co. Ltd. (AT)
Law Book Co. Ltd. Queensland Branch (AT)
Law Book Co. Ltd. Victoria Branch (AT)
Law Bulletin Publishing Co. (US)
Law Council of Australia (AT)
Law Development Centre (UG)
Moody T. Law, Ed. & Pub. (US)
Law Guardian Publishing Co. Ltd. (UK)
Law in American Society Foundation (US)
Law Institute of Victoria (AT)
Law Journal Publication (II)
Law Notes Lending Library Ltd. (UK)
Law Publications, Inc. (US)
Law Referencer (II)
Law Reporters (II)
Law Reprints, Inc. (US)
Law Review Ltd. (II)
Law Society (UK)
Law Society of New South Wales (AT)
Law Society of Scotland (UK)
Law Society of Upper Canada (CN)
Bryon Lawes, Ed. & Pub. (CN)
Gary Lawless, Ed. & Pub. (US)
William Lawrence Corp. (US)
Lawrence Publishing Co, Pty. Ltd. (AT)
Laws of India Private Ltd. (II)
Lawsearch, Inc. (US)
Lawyer-Pilots Bar Association (US)
Lawyer to Lawyer Consultation Panel (US)
Lawyer's Association (JA)
Lawyers Association of the G.D.R. (GE)
Lawyers Co-Operative Publishing Co. (US)
Lawyers Title Insurance Corporation (US)
Verlag August Lax (GW)
Lay Theology in Ireland (IE)
Laymen's Home Missionary Movement (US)
Laymen's Movement for a Christian World, Inc.
   (US)
Lazio (IT)
Lazio Ieri e Oggi (IT)
Lea & Febiger (US)
Frederic Leach, Ed. & Pub. (CN)
Stephen Leacock Associates (CN)
Lead Development Association (London) (UK)
Lead Industries Association, Inc. (US)
Leader (IT)
Leader-Observer, Inc. (US)
Leader Publications Inc. (US)
Leader Publishing Co. (AT)
Leadership Publications (UG)
Leadership Resources (Washington) (US)
Leadership Resources Inc. (US)
League for Economic Democracy (US)
League for Industrial Democracy (US)
League for International Food Education (US)
League for Socialist Reconstruction (US)
League of Arab States (US)
League of Arab States Mission (II)
League of California Cities (US)
League of Canadian Poets. Executive Committee
   (CN)
League of Iowa Municipalities (US)
League of Islamic Sciences (JO)
League of Kansas Municipalities (US)
League of Minnesota Cities (US)
League of Minnesota Poets (US)
League of Nebraska Municipalities (US)
League of Red Cross Societies (SZ)
League of the German Democratic Republic for
   Friendship Among the Peoples (GE)
League of United Latin American Citizens (LULAC)
   (US)
League of Welldoers (UK)
League of Wisconsin Municipalities (US)
League of Women Voters of Massachusetts (US)
League of Women Voters of the City of New York
   (US)
League of Women Voters of the U.S. (US)
League of Women Voters of Washington (US)
R. D. Leakey, Ed. & Pub. (UK)
Lealtad (AG)
Learning Exchange (AT)
Learning Exchange (US)
Learning Resources Corporation (US)
Leasco Corporation (US)
Leather Export Promotion Council (II)
Leather Industries Research Institute
   see under Rhodes University (SA)
Leather Wear (UK)
Leathercraftsman, Inc. (US)

Lebanese Association of Armenian University
   Graduates (LE)
Lebanese Dental Council (LE)
Lebanese Journal of Political Science (LE)
Lebanon. Direction Centrale de la Statistique (LE)
Lebanon. Direction General des Transports (LE)
Lebanon. Ministry of Information. Arab Film &
   Television Centre (LE)
Lebanon Valley College Student Council (US)
Leben Verlag AG (LH)
Lebhar-Friedman, Inc. (US)
Edward T. LeBlanc, Ed. & Pub. (US)
G. Leblanc Corporation (US)
LeBlanc Research Corporation (US)
Editions Lecerf (FR)
LECTO Libreria (SP)
Editorial Lectura y Estudio S.A. (SP)
Lectures Francaises (FR)
Lecturis B.V. Eindhoven (NE)
Lederle Laboratories (US)
Libreria Ledi (IT)
Editions Christian Ledoux (FR)
Lee County Historical Society (US)
Hubert F. Lee, Ed. & Pub. (US)
Lee Foundation (SI)
Lee Kong Chian Museum of Asian Culture (SI)
Lee Publishing Co. (US)
Leech Printing Ltd. (CN)
Leeds Arts Collections Fund (UK)
Leeds Chamber of Commerce and Industry (UK)
Leeds Grammar School (UK)
Leeds Labour Publishing Society Ltd. (UK)
Leeds Philosophical and Literary Society (UK)
Leeds University Union (UK)
Buchdruckerei und Verlag Leemann AG (SZ)
Curtis E. Lees and Associates (US)
Lee's Mardi Gras Enterprises, Inc. (US)
Lee's Philatelist (US)
Leeward Publications Inc. (US)
Rene Lefeuvre (FR)
Left Curve (US)
Lega degli Stati Arabi a Roma (IT)
Lega dei Comuni (IT)
Lega Italiana Contro Fumi e Rumori (IT)
Lega Italiana di Igiene e Profilassi Mentale (IT)
Lega Missionaria Studenti (IT)
Lega Navale Italiania (IT)
Lega Nazionale delle Cooperative e Mutue (IT)
Lega per le Autonomie e i Poteri Locali (IT)
Legal Action Group (UK)
Legal-Medical Studies, Inc. (US)
Legal Medicine Press (US)
Legal Research Institute, Inc. (US)
Legation of Latvia (US)
Jean Pascal Legen (FR)
Leger des Heils (NE)
Legiao Brasileira de Assistencia (BL)
Legion Cabs Trading Co-Operative Society Ltd (AT)
Legion for Survival of Freedom Inc. (US)
Legion of the Frontiersmen of the Commonwealth.
   New Zealand Division (NZ)
Legislacion Economica Ltda. (CK)
Legislative Research International (US)
Legislator (II)
Legitimerade Sjukgymnasters Riksfoerbund (SW)
Legnickie Towarzystwo Przyjaciol Nauk (PL)
F. Legrand, Ed. & Pub. (IT)
Lehigh University (US)
Lehigh Valley Labor Council and AFL-CIO Union
   Council of Northampton and Warren County (US)
Lehigh Valley Motor Club (US)
J. F. Lehmanns Verlag (GW)
Lehrerbund der O V P Steiermark (AU)
Lehrervereinigung Duesseldorf (GW)
Lehtimiehet Oy (FI)
Herbert Leibowitz, Ed. & Pub. (US)
Leicester & County Chamber of Commerce (UK)
Leicester University Press (UK)
Leicestershire Local History Council (UK)
Leiden University Press (NE)
Leidsche Drukkerij B.V. (NE)
Leinster Leader (IE)
Leisurability Publications Inc. (CN)
Leisure (CE)
Leisure Boating and Speedway Magazines Pty. Ltd.
   (AT)
Leisure Publications, Inc. (US)
Leisure Time Institute (US)
Leisureguides, Inc. (US)
Russell G. Leiter, Ed. & Pub. (US)
Verlag B. M. Leitner (AU)
Lejernes Landsorganisation (DK)
Editions de Lejeunia (BE)
Lek, Tovarna Farmacevtskih in Kemicnih Izdelkov
   (YU)
Lem Editrice (IT)
Leman Publications, Inc. (US)
Lembaga Administrasi Negara (IO)

Lembaga Biologi Nasional. Herbarium Bogoriense
    see Herbarium Bogoriense (IO)
Lembaga Biologi Nasional. Museum Zoologicum
    Bogoriense
    see Museum Zoologicum Bogoriense (IO)
Lembaga Biologi Nasional. Pusat Pewelitian Botani
    see Treub Laboratory (IO)
Lembaga Biologi Nasional. Treub Laboratory
    see Treub Laboratory (IO)
Lembaga Ilmu Pengetahuan Indonesia
    see Indonesian Institute of Sciences (IO)
Lembaga Ilmu Pengetahuan Indonesia. Pusat
    Dokumentasi Ilmiah Nasional
    see National Scientific Documentation Centre (IO)
Lembaga Meteorological dan Geofisika
    see Meteorological and Geophysical Institute (IO)
Lembaga Oseanologi Nasional
    see Indonesia. National Institute of Oceanography
    (IO)
Lembaga Penelitian, Pendidikan dan Penerangan
    Ekonomi dan Sosial
    see Institute for Economic and Social Research,
    Education and Information (IO)
Lembaga Penelitian Selulose
    see Cellulose Research Institute (IO)
Lembeck-Verlag (GW)
Alberto S. Lemos, Ed. & Pub. (US)
Lemoyne College (US)
Len Jury Ltd. (NZ)
Lending Law Forum, Inc. (US)
Leningrad. Gorodskoi Sovet Deputatov
    Trudyashchikhsya. Ispolnitel'nyi Komitet (UR)
Leningradskii Gornyi Institut (UR)
Leningradskii Institut Tochnoi Mekhaniki i Optiki
    (UR)
Leningradskii Universitet (UR)
Leningradskii Universitet. Geologicheskii Fakultet
    (UR)
Leningradskii Universitet. Kafedra Litologii i Morskoi
    Geologii (UR)
Leninskii Kommunisticheskii Soyuz Molodezhi
    Belorusskoi S.S.R. (UR)
Leninskii Kommunisticheskii Soyuz Molodezhi
    Ukrainskoi S.S.R. (UR)
Lenizdat (UR)
Lennards-Instituut (NE)
Lenoir Rhyne College. English Dept. (US)
Lenore Schwartz Leukemia Research Foundation.
    Research Information Service (US)
Lenox Hill Publishing and Distributing Corporation
    (US)
Gebr. Lensing, Verlagsanstalt KG (GW)
Leo Baeck Institut (IS)
Leo Baeck Institute (UK)
Leo Publications (Pty) Ltd. (SA)
Leon. Ayuntamiento de Leon (SP)
J. H. Leonard (CN)
Leonard Theological College (II)
Leonardo Edizioni Scientifiche (IT)
Lepetit Colloquia on Biology and Medicine (NE)
Gruppo Lepetit S.p.A. (IT)
Lepidoptera Research Foundation, Inc. (US)
Lepidopterists Society (US)
Lepidopterological Society of Japan (JA)
Lepidopterologisk Forening (DK)
Leprosy Mission (UK)
Leprosy Research Laboratory and Training Center
    see Philippines. Leprosy Research Laboratory and
    Training Center (PH)
Lepus Books (UK)
Verlag Robert Lerche (GW)
Verlag Robert Lerche. Abt. Praeger Nachrichten
    (GW)
Lernhurst Publications Ltd. (UK)
Editorial Victor Leru (AG)
Lerums Boktryckeri AB (SW)
Publications Les Affaires Inc. (CN)
Le'sbeinformed (US)
Lesbian Alliance Newsletter (US)
Lesbian Feminist (US)
Lesbian Front (US)
Lesbian Resource Center (US)
Lesbian Switchboard (US)
Lesen Verlag GmbH (GW)
Bernard Leser Publications Pty. Ltd. (AT)
Leserinitiative Publik e.V. (GW)
Leske Verlag und Budrich GmbH (GW)
Izdatel'stvo Lesnaya Promyshlennost' (UR)
Lesotho. Auditor General (LO)
Lesotho. Ministry of Education and Culture (LO)
Lesotho. Treasury (LO)
Editions Olivier Lesourd (FR)
Lessing Society (GW)
Lesstrang Publishing Corporation (US)
Lesterstar Ltd. (UK)
Imprimerie Leteyf (LE)
Letra Viva (AG)
Letras Nacionales (CK)

Letras Potosinas (MX)
Letters from Asia (HK)
Letters of Interest Associates (CN)
Letterstedtska Foereningen (SW)
Lettres Eoliennes (GR)
Lettres Francaises (FR)
Letture (IT)
Letz Co. Inc. (US)
Leuven University Press (BE)
Leuvense Bijdragen (BE)
Carlo de Leva, Ed. & Pub. (IT)
Editions du Levain (FR)
Forlaget Levende Billeder A-S (DK)
Leviathan (US)
Leviathan House (UK)
Editions Philippe Levie (BE)
Levin Publishing Co., Inc. (US)
S. Jay Levy, Ed. & Pub. (US)
Lewis & Clark Law School (US)
Lewis & Clark Trail Heritage Foundation, Inc. (US)
H. K. Lewis & Co. Ltd. (UK)
A.F. Lewis and Co. of New York, Inc. (US)
Lewis Carroll Society (UK)
Lewis Carroll Society of North America (US)
George Q. Lewis, Ed. & Pub. (US)
Lewis Publications Ltd. (UK)
Lewis Publishing Co. (US)
Lewis University. Correctional Programs (US)
Lex Editoria S. A. (BL)
Lexington Books (US)
Lexington Library (US)
Lexington Philharmonic Society (US)
Lexington School for the Deaf. Parents Association
    (US)
Lexington Theological Seminary (US)
Ley Hunter (UK)
Ediciones la Ley S.A. (AG)
Leybold-Heraeus GmbH und Co. KG (GW)
Peter Li, Inc (US)
Liaisons Sociales (FR)
Liber Foerlag (SW)
Libera Universita Internazionale degli Studi Sociali pro
    Deo. Istituto di Sociologia (IT)
Liberal Catholic Church (UK)
Liberal Catholic Church in Australia (AT)
Liberal News (UK)
Liberal Party in Alberta (CN)
Liberal Party in Ontario (CN)
Liberal Party of Australia. Federal Secretariat (AT)
Liberal Party of South Africa (SA)
Liberal Party Organisation (UK)
Liberal Religious Youth, Inc. (US)
Liberation (II)
Liberation (UK)
Liberation News Services (UK)
Liberation Publications (Milwaukee) (US)
Liberation Support Movement (US)
Liberation War (II)
Liberator Press (US)
Liberia. Bureau of the Budget (LB)
Liberia. Department of State (LB)
Liberia. General Services Agency (LB)
Liberia. Ministry of Agriculture (LB)
Liberia. Ministry of Commerce, Industry and
    Transportation (LB)
Liberia. Ministry of Finance (LB)
Liberia. Ministry of Foreign Affairs (LB)
Liberia. Ministry of Information, Cultural Affairs and
    Tourism (LB)
Liberia. Ministry of Justice (LB)
Liberia. Ministry of Labour, Youth & Sports (LB)
Liberia. Ministry of Local Government, Rural
    Development & Urban Reconstruction (LB)
Liberia. Ministry of National Defense (LB)
Liberia. Ministry of Planning and Economic Affairs
    (LB)
Liberia. Ministry of Public Works (LB)
Liberia Baptist Missionary and Educational
    Convention (LB)
LiberLaeromedel (SW)
LiberLaeromedel, Malmoe (SW)
Libero Artigianato e Piccole Aziende Modenesi (IT)
Libertarian Alternative Newsletter (US)
Libertarian Enterprises of Canada (CN)
Libertarian Forum (US)
Libertarian Press Service (US)
Libertarian Republican Alliance (US)
Libertarian Review, Inc. (US)
Libertarian Scholar (US)
Libertatea (YU)
Liberty Bell Publications (US)
Liberty Library Corp. (US)
Liberty Lowdown (US)
Armando Libotte, Ed. & Pub. (SZ)
Libra House Ltd. (IE)
Libra Publishers, Inc. (US)
Librairie Ancienne et Moderne. Bulletin (FR)
Librairie Beauchemin Limitee (CN)

Librairie de la Faculte de Sciences (FR)
Librairie de Rome (BE)
Librairie des Cinq Continents (FR)
Librairie des Facultes de Medecine et de Pharmacie
    (FR)
Librairie Generale de Droit et de Jurisprudence (FR)
Librairie Generale de l'Enseignement (FR)
Librairie Mariale et Franciscaine (FR)
Librairie Orientale (LE)
Librairie Sociale et Economique (FR)
Editrice Libraria Tuscolana (IT)
Libraries Board of South Australia (AT)
Libraries Unlimited, Inc. (US)
Librart s.r.l. (AG)
Library (II)
Library Action Group (UK)
Library Associates, Inc. (US)
Library Associates of Brooklyn College, Inc. (US)
Library Association (UK)
Library Association. Branch and Mobile Libraries
    Group (UK)
Library Association. Cataloguing and Indexing Group
    (UK)
Library Association. Colleges, Institutes and Schools of
    Education Group (UK)
Library Association. East Midlands Branch (UK)
Library Association. Eastern Branch (UK)
Library Association. Hospital Libraries and
    Handicapped Readers Group (UK)
Library Association. Industrial Group (UK)
Library Association. International and Comparative
    Librarianship Group (UK)
Library Association. Library Education Group (UK)
Library Association. Library History Group (UK)
Library Association. North Western Group (UK)
Library Association of Alberta (CN)
Library Association of Australia. A.C.T. Branch (AT)
Library Association of Australia. Queensland Branch
    (AT)
Library Association of Australia. School and Children's
    Libraries Sections (AT)
Library Association of Australia. Universities &
    College Libraries Section (AT)
Library Association of Barbados (BB)
Library Association of Finland
    see Suomen Kirjastoseura (FI)
Library Association of Ireland (UK)
Library Association of Singapore (SI)
Library Association of the City University of New
    York (US)
Library Association of Trinidad and Tobago (TR)
Library Association. Scottish Group (UK)
Library Association. West Midland Branch (UK)
Library Automated Systems Information Exchange
    (AT)
Library Binding Institute (US)
Library Board of Queensland (AT)
Library-College Associates, Inc. (US)
Library Literature House (II)
Library of Congress
    see U. S. Library of Congress (US)
Library of Congress Professional Association (US)
Library of New South Wales (AT)
Library of Tibetan Works and Archives (II)
Library Publicity Clippings (US)
Library Trustees Foundation of New York State (US)
Library World (UA)
Libreria Anticuaria Americana (UY)
Libreria Cientifica Medinaceli (SP)
Libreria de Porrua Hermanos y Cia S.A. (MX)
Edtrice Libreria Dottrina Cristiana (IT)
Libreria Internacional (MX)
Libreria Internazionale Guida (IT)
Libya. Census and Statistical Department (LY)
Libya. Ministere de l'Information et de la Culture
    (LY)
Licensed Beverage Journal Inc. (US)
Licensed Practical Nurses of New York, Inc. (US)
Licensed Vintners' Associations (IE)
Licensing Executives Society, Inc. (US)
F. O. Licht KG (GW)
Lichthoeve (NE)
Lichttechnische Gesellschaft e.V. (GW)
Lichtwark-Stiftung (GW)
Lick Observatory. Library (US)
Licosa S.p.A. (IT)
Licosa-Sansoni S.p.A. (IT)
Editions Lidec (FR)
Lidhjes Se Rinise Se Kosoves (YU)
Lieber-Atherton, Inc. (US)
Liechtensteinische Akademische Gesellschaft (LH)
Liechtenstein. Press and Information Office (LH)
VEB Lied der Zeit Musikverlag (GE)
Life & Vision Publications (AT)
Life Foundation, Inc. (US)
Life Insurance Marketing and Research Association
    (LIMRA) (US)
Life Insurers Conference (US)

Life Office Management Association  (US)
Life Science Co., Ltd.  (JA)
Life Underwriters Association of Canada  (CN)
Life Underwriters Association of South Africa  (SA)
Life Underwriters Association of the City of New
  York  (US)
Lifestyle Publishing Co., Inc.  (US)
Liga Alvaro Bahia Contra a Mortalidade Infantil
  (BL)
Liga Brasileira de Esperanto  (BL)
Liga de Almaceneros Minoristas y Afines  (AG)
Liga Maritima de Chile  (CL)
Liga pro Comportamiento Humano  (AG)
Liga Socialista Puertorriquena  (PR)
Editions Ligel  (FR)
J. Liger, Ed. & Pub.  (FR)
John Liggins Ltd.  (UK)
Light  (US)
Light and Life Press  (US)
Light of Life Society of India  (II)
Light Railway Transport League  (UK)
Light Steam Power  (UK)
The Lighter Than Air Society  (US)
Lightner Publishing Corporation  (US)
Ligne Creatrice  (FR)
Kathleen Lignell, Ed. & Pub.  (US)
Ligo Internacia de Blindaj Esperantistoj  (FR)
Ligue Antituberculeuse de Quebec  (CN)
Ligue d'Action Nationale  (CN)
Ligue des Bibliotheques Europeennes de Recherche
  (UK)
Ligue des Droits de l'Homme  (FR)
Ligue des Jeune Socialistes  (CN)
Ligue Francaise de l'Enseignement et de l'Education
  Permanente  (FR)
Ligue Francaise du Coin de Terre et du Foyer  (FR)
Ligue Francaise pour les Auberges de la Jeunesse
  (FR)
Ligue Marxiste Revolutionaire  (SZ)
Ligue Nationale Francaise Contre le Cancer  (FR)
Ligue Nationale pour la Liberte des Vaccinations
  (FR)
Ligue Suisse pour la Litterature de la Jeunesse
  see Schweizerischer Bund fuer Jugendliteratur  (SZ)
Ligue Urbaine et Rurale  (FR)
Ligues Pomologiques Wallonnes  (BE)
Guiseppe Liguori, Ed. & Pub.  (IT)
Liguria-Sabatelli Editori  (IT)
Liikearkistoyhdistys r.y.  (FI)
Kustannusliike Liikejulkaisut Oy  (FI)
Liiketaloudellinen  (FI)
Likuni Press and Publishing House  (MW)
Lilith Publications, Inc.  (US)
Lillooet District Historical Society  (CN)
Eli Lilly & Co.  (US)
Albert Limbach Verlag  (GW)
Limburg (Province) Culturele Dienst  (BE)
Limburgs Geschied- en Oudheidkundig Genootschap
  (NE)
Limburgse Economische Raad  (BE)
Limestone Publications  (UK)
Limnological Society of Southern Africa  (SA)
Lincoln College  (NZ)
Lincoln College. Department of Farm Management
  and Rural Valuation  (NZ)
Lincoln College. Department of Horticulture  (NZ)
Lincoln College. New Zealand Agricultural
  Engineering Institute  (NZ)
Lincoln Electric Co. (Australia)  (AT)
Lincoln Library  (US)
Lincoln Memorial University Press  (US)
Lincoln National Life Insurance Co.  (US)
Lincoln Park Zoological Society  (US)
Lincoln University  (US)
Lincoln University College of Law  (US)
Lincolnshire and South Humberside Arts  (UK)
Lincolnshire Life Ltd  (UK)
Industrieverlag Peter Linde GmbH  (AU)
L. A. van der Linden  (NE)
Linden-Museum fuer Voelkerkunde  (GW)
Lindencroft Publications Inc.  (US)
Herbert Linder, Ed. & Pub.  (US)
Linders-Adremo B.V.  (NE)
H. L. Lindquist Publications, Inc.  (US)
Lindsey Press  (UK)
Linea Dura  (AG)
Linear & Circular Permutations  (US)
Lineastruttura  (IT)
Linen Supply Association of America  (US)
Carl Ling Presse GmbH  (GW)
Linge Gowda Detective & Security Chambers  (II)
Linguistic Circle of Canberra  (AT)
Linguistic Circle of Copenhagen  (DK)
Linguistic Research Inc.  (CN)
Linguistic Society of America  (US)
Linguistic Society of India  (II)
Linguistic Society of Japan  (JA)
Linguistic Society of the Philippines  (PH)

Verlag Linguistica Biblica  (GW)
Linguistics Association of Great Britain  (UK)
Lingvologia Revuo  (AT)
Link House Publications Ltd  (UK)
Linkage for Ancestral Research  (US)
Linley Publishing Co., Inc.  (US)
Linn County Publishing Co.  (US)
Linnaean Society of New York  (US)
Linnean Society of London  (UK)
Linnean Society of N.S.W.  (AT)
V.D. Linnepe Verlagsgesellschaft KG  (GW)
Linnett Books  (US)
Linz. Archiv der Stadt Linz  (AU)
Linz. Magistrat  (AU)
Lionhead Publishing  (US)
Lions International  (SW)
Lions International  (US)
Lions International  (IT)
Lions International. Australian Branch  (AT)
Lions International District "A"  (CN)
Lipid Research, Inc.  (US)
Lipika Foundation  (II)
Verlag Karl M. Lipp  (GW)
Louis Lippens, Ed. & Pub.  (FR)
J. B. Lippincott Co.  (US)
Lippischer Heimatbund  (GW)
Lipscombe & Associates  (AT)
Lipsius & Tischer  (GW)
Lirica nel Mondo  (IT)
Tijdschriftenfonds J.J. Lispet  (NE)
Alan R. Liss, Inc  (US)
Lissot  (FR)
List and Index Society  (UK)
List and Index Society. Public Record Office  (UK)
Listening  (US)
Listening Library, Inc.  (US)
Lister Hill Center for Biomedical Communications
  (US)
John Lister Ltd.  (UK)
Liszt Society Ltd.  (UK)
Literamed Publications Nigeria, Ltd.  (NR)
Literarische Union e.V.  (GW)
Literary Guild  (US)
Literary Press  (II)
Literary Publications Foundations Inc.  (US)
Literary Studies  (II)
Verlag der Literat  (GW)
Literature & History  (UK)
Literature Clearing House  (ZA)
Literature Searchers  (US)
Izdatel'stvo Literaturnaya Gazeta  (UR)
Litho Services (Pvt.) Ltd.  (RH)
Lithuanian Alliance of America  (US)
Lithuanian American Community  (US)
Lithuanian Cooperative Publishing Society, Inc.  (US)
Lithuanian Historical Society, Inc.  (US)
Lithuanian House Ltd.  (UK)
Lithuanian National Foundation, Inc.  (US)
Lithuanian National League of America  (US)
Lithuanian Social Democratic Party in Exile  (UK)
Lithuanian Workers Literary Association  (US)
Litis  (BL)
Litmus  (US)
Litomerice (Okres) Okresni Muzeum  (CS)
Litovskaya S. S. R. Aukstuju Mokyklu Mokslo Darbai
  (UR)
Litovskaya S. S. R. Ministerstvo Vysshego
  Obrazovaniya  (UR)
Littell Families of America  (US)
Little Big Horn Associates  (US)
Little Brothers of the Good Shepherd  (US)
Little, Brown & Co.  (US)
Little Face, Inc  (US)
Little-Flower Press  (II)
Little Free Press  (US)
Arthur D. Little, Inc.  (US)
Little Magazine  (US)
Little People of America, Inc  (US)
Little Publications, Inc.  (US)
Little Review Press  (US)
Little Rock Chamber of Commerce  (US)
Little Ship Club  (UK)
Little Word Machine Publications  (UK)
Litton Charolais Ranch, Inc.  (US)
Litton Publication, Inc.  (US)
Lituanus Foundation, Inc.  (US)
Liturgical Conference  (US)
Liturgical Ecumenical Center Trust  (NE)
Liturgical Press  (US)
Edizioni Liturgiche e Vincenzian  (IT)
Liturgisches Institut Trier  (GW)
Live Free, Inc.  (US)
Live Leads Corp.  (US)
Livermore Research Center of California, Inc.  (US)
Liverpool Corp.  (UK)
Liverpool Cotton Services Ltd.  (UK)
Liverpool Council for Voluntary Service  (UK)
Liverpool Council of Social Service  (UK)

Liverpool School of Tropical Medicine  (UK)
Liverpool University Press  (UK)
Livestock Breeder Journal, Inc.  (US)
Livestock Market Digest, Inc  (US)
Livestock Service, Inc.  (US)
Livestock Services  (US)
Liviana Editrice  (IT)
Living Blues Publications  (US)
Living Church Foundation, Inc.  (US)
Living Hand  (US)
Living History Centre  (US)
Living in the Ozarks Newsletter  (US)
Living Today News  (AT)
Leo Livingston, Ed. & Pub.  (US)
R. W. Livingston, Ed. & Pub.  (US)
E. & S. Livingstone  (UK)
Livingstone Museum  (ZA)
Livrangol Editores  (AO)
Livre Canadien  (CN)
Livre Contemporain et les Bibliophiles Francosuisses
  (FR)
Editions Lizon  (CN)
Ljudtekniska Saellskapet  (SW)
Ljuskultur  (SW)
Llano Estacado Heritage, Inc.  (US)
Publicaciones Llergo  (MX)
Llewellyn Publications  (US)
Magda Llohis Serra, Ed. & Pub.  (SP)
Luis Llongueras Batlle, Ed. & Pub.  (SP)
Lloyd Anversois S.A.  (BE)
Lloyd Library and Museum  (US)
Lloyd Publications of Canada  (CN)
Lloyds Australian Register of Trades & Commerce
  Pty. Ltd.  (AT)
Lloyds Bank International Ltd.  (UK)
Lloyds Bank Ltd.  (UK)
Lloyd's Hearing Aid Corp.  (US)
Lloyd's of London Press Ltd.  (UK)
Lloyd's Register of Shipping  (UK)
Lloyd's Register of Shipping  (US)
Lluvia de Rosas  (SP)
Llyfrfa's Methodistiaid Calfinaid  (UK)
Loblolly Inc.  (US)
Lobrecht Verlag Max Rauscher KG  (GW)
Local and Short Haul Carriers National Conference
  (US)
Local Autonomy College  (JA)
Local Government Association of South Australia
  (AT)
Local Government Institute  (BG)
Local Government Operational Research Unit  (UK)
Local Pennsylvanian, Inc.  (US)
Local Population Studies  (UK)
Local Self-Government  (II)
Locale Publishing Co.  (US)
Lock Haven State College  (US)
Locke Newsletter  (UK)
Lockheed-California Co.  (US)
Edward B. Lockwood, Inc.  (US)
Lockwood Press Ltd.  (US)
Lockwood Trade Journal Co. Inc.  (US)
Loco-Revue  (FR)
Locomotive Maintenance Officers Association  (US)
Marcel Locquin, Ed. & Pub.  (FR)
Locus Publications  (US)
Locus Science Publishers  (UK)
Lodestar Press Inc.  (US)
Lodzkie Towarzystwo Naukowe  (PL)
Baxter Loe, Ed. & Pub.  (US)
Loefgrenia  (BL)
E. Loepfe-Benz AG Graphische Anstalt  (SZ)
Editore Loescher  (IT)
Empresa Jornalistica Ulrich Loew S.A.  (BL)
Loewenthal Publications Inc.  (US)
Luigi Loffredo, Ed. & Pub.  (IT)
Logan Brown Communications  (CN)
Logberg-Heimskringla Publishing Co. Ltd.  (CN)
Loggers World, Inc.  (US)
Van Loghum Slaterus  (NE)
Editions Logitec  (FR)
Logos International Fellowship Inc.  (US)
Loisirs & Nature  (FR)
Loisirs Nautiques  (FR)
Lok-Milap Trust  (II)
Lolfa  (UK)
Loma Linda University. Department of Archives and
  Special Collections  (US)
Loma Linda University. Geoscience Research Institute
  (US)
Loma Linda University. School of Dentistry Alumni
  Association  (US)
Editions du Lombard  (BE)
Editoriale Lombarda S.p.A.  (IT)
Lomond Publications  (US)
London and Continental Publishing Ltd.  (UK)
London and Home Counties Regional Advisory
  Council for Technological Education  (UK)
London and Middlesex Archaeological Society  (UK)

London and Sheffield Publishing Co. Ltd.  (UK)
London Archaeologist Association  (UK)
London Borough of Barking  (UK)
London Boroughs Association  (UK)
London Bureau  (UK)
London Chamber of Commerce & Industry  (UK)
London Cigarette Card Co. Ltd.  (UK)
London City Mission  (UK)
London Corn Circular Ltd.  (UK)
London Diary Publications Ltd.  (UK)
London Hospital League of Nurses  (UK)
London Information (Rowse Muir) Ltd.  (UK)
London Institute of World Affairs  (UK)
London Letter  (UK)
London Magazine  (UK)
London Mathematical Society  (UK)
London Medieval Society  (UK)
London Natural History Society  (UK)
London Northwest  (US)
G. C. London Publishing Corp.  (US)
London Record Society  (UK)
London Review  (UK)
London School of Economics  (UK)
London School of Economics and Political Science
  (UK)
London School of Economics and Political Science.
  Students' Union  (UK)
London School of Hygiene & Tropical Medicine
  (UK)
London Society  (UK)
London Stage Project  (US)
London Welsh Association  (UK)
London Writer Circle  (UK)
Long Distance Road Transport Association of
  Australia  (AT)
Long Island Builders Institute  (US)
Long Island Commercial Review Inc.  (US)
Long Island Fisherman Publishing Co.  (US)
Long Island Historical Society  (US)
Long Island Institute for Mental Health  (US)
Long Island Kegler Enterprises  (US)
Long Island Lighting Co.  (US)
Long Island Poetry Collective, Inc.  (US)
Long Island Police News  (US)
Long Island Sportsmen's Society  (US)
Long Island University. Brooklyn Center  (US)
Long Island University. English Department  (US)
Long Island University Press  (US)
Long Island University. SALENA Library Learing
  Center  (US)
Long Island University. School of Business
  Administration  (US)
Long Publishing, Inc.  (US)
Long Term Credit Bank of Japan Ltd.  (JA)
Long Time Coming  (CN)
Long View Publishing Co., Inc.  (US)
Longmac Ltd.  (UK)
Longman Group Ltd.  (UK)
Longman Group Ltd. Keesing's Publications  (UK)
Longman Ltd.  (UK)
Longmans Canada, Ltd.  (CN)
Angelo Longo Editore  (IT)
Longonesi e Co.  (IT)
Henri Longpre  (CN)
Longwood Program  (US)
Lonja Compania Editora Argentina S.A.C.  (AG)
Lonsdale Publications Ltd.  (UK)
Looking Glass Publications  (US)
Lookout Publications  (SP)
Loon  (US)
Francisco Lopez Canis  (SP)
Jose Lopez del Arco y Soler, Ed. & Pub.  (SP)
Lopez Publications, Inc.  (US)
Lorain County Community College. Student Activities
  Office  (US)
Loras College  (US)
Loras College. Delta Epsilon Sigma  (US)
Lord International  (II)
Lord's Day Observance Society  (UK)
Verlag Lorenz  (AU)
Lorenz Industries  (US)
Carlesi Loris, Ed. & Pub.  (IT)
Lorne, Caldough Ltd.  (UK)
Lorton Publications  (SA)
Los Alamos Scientific Laboratory  (US)
Los Amigos del Libro  (BO)
Los Angeles (County) Air Pollution Control District
  (US)
Los Angeles (County) Department of Regional
  Planning  (US)
Los Angeles (County) Public Library  (US)
Los Angeles Area Chamber of Commerce  (US)
Los Angeles Athletic Club  (US)
Los Angeles Catholic Worker  (US)
Los Angeles Cinematheque, Inc.  (US)
Los Angeles College of Chiropractic  (US)
Los Angeles Commercial News  (US)
Los Angeles County Bar Association  (US)

Los Angeles County Federation of Labor  (US)
Los Angeles County Medical Association  (US)
Los Angeles County Museum of Art  (US)
Los Angeles Geographical Society  (US)
Los Angeles Hillel Council. Jewish Federation-Council,
  los Angeles  (US)
Los Angeles Institute of Contemporary Art  (US)
Los Angeles Junior Chamber of Commerce  (US)
Los Angeles Valley College Library. Periodicals
  Department  (US)
Los Yebenes, Spain. Ayuntamiento  (SP)
Loto-Quebec  (CN)
Lott Publishing Co.  (US)
Jack Lotto, Ed. & Pub.  (US)
Lou Pais  (FR)
Publications Louchel  (FR)
Loughborough University of Technology  (UK)
Loughborough University of Technology. Department
  of Economics  (UK)
Loughborough University of Technology. Students
  Union  (UK)
Imprimerie R. Louis  (BE)
Louis Arthur Grimes School of Law
  see under University of Liberia  (LB)
Louis Harris and Associates, Inc.  (US)
Louisburg College  (US)
Louise Bao  (HK)
Louisiana  (DK)
Louisiana. Advisory Commission on Coastal and
  Marine Resources  (US)
Louisiana. Commissioner of Securities  (US)
Louisiana. Department of Agriculture  (US)
Louisiana. Department of Agriculture. Milk Division
  (US)
Louisiana. Department of Art, Historical and Cultural
  Preservation  (US)
Louisiana. Department of Commerce and Industry
  (US)
Louisiana. Department of Employment Security  (US)
Louisiana. Department of Public Safety  (US)
Louisiana. Department of Public Works  (US)
Louisiana. Division of Mental Health  (US)
Louisiana. Geological Survey  (US)
Louisiana. Health and Human Resources
  Administration  (US)
Louisiana. Health and Social and Rehabilitation
  Services Administration  (US)
Louisiana. State Board of Nurse Examiners  (US)
Louisiana. State Planning Office  (US)
Louisiana. Wild Life and Fisheries Commission  (US)
Louisiana Academy of Sciences  (US)
Louisiana Archaeological Society  (US)
Louisiana Association of Insurance Agents, Inc.  (US)
Louisiana Bankers Association  (US)
Louisiana Contractor  (US)
Louisiana Council of Teachers of English  (US)
Louisiana Dental Association  (US)
Louisiana Engineering Society  (US)
Louisiana Folklore Society  (US)
Louisiana Forestry Association  (US)
Louisiana Gridweek  (US)
Louisiana Historical Association  (US)
Louisiana Indian Hobbyist Association, Inc.  (US)
Louisiana Library Association  (US)
Louisiana LP-Gas Association  (US)
Louisiana Motor Transportation Association  (US)
Louisiana Municipal Association  (US)
Louisiana Oil Marketers Association  (US)
Louisiana Polytechnic Institute. Agricultural
  Engineering Department  (US)
Louisiana School Boards Association  (US)
Louisiana State Medical Society  (US)
Louisiana State Nurses Association  (US)
Louisiana State Pharmaceutical Association  (US)
Louisiana State University  (US)
Louisiana State University. Agricultural Experiment
  Station  (US)
Louisiana State University. Alumni Federation  (US)
Louisiana State University. Animal Science
  Department  (US)
Louisiana State University. College of Business
  Administration  (US)
Louisiana State University. College of Engineering
  (US)
Louisiana State University. Cooperative Wildlife
  Research Unit  (US)
Louisiana State University. Division of Business and
  Economic Research  (US)
Louisiana State University. Division of Continuing
  Education  (US)
Louisiana State University. Law School  (US)
Louisiana State University Library  (US)
Louisiana State University. Museum of Geoscience
  (US)
Louisiana State University. Office of Information
  Services  (US)
Louisiana State University. Office of Sea Grant
  Development  (US)

Louisiana State University Press  (US)
Louisiana State University. School of Forestry and
  Wildlife Management  (US)
Louisiana State University. School of Geoscience
  (US)
Louisiana Studies Institute  (US)
Louisiana Teacher's Association  (US)
Louisiana Tech University  (US)
Louisiana Tech University. Division of Administration
  and Business Research  (US)
Louisiana Tech University. Division of Life Sciences
  Research  (US)
Louisiana Tech University. Prescott Library  (US)
Louisiana Tourist Commission  (US)
Louisiana Water Resources Research Institute  (US)
Louisville Area Chamber of Commerce  (US)
Louisville Board of Education  (US)
Louvain Medical  (BE)
Lovacka Knjiga  (YU)
Lovacki Savez Hrvatske  (YU)
H. D. Love & Associates Pty. Ltd.  (AT)
Love Conspiracy  (US)
Love Project  (US)
Love Publishing Co.  (US)
Lovejoy's College Guide Inc.  (US)
Loverseed Press  (UK)
Lovska Zveza Slovenije  (YU)
Low Gear Fellowship  (AT)
Low Income Family Emancipation Society  (II)
Benjamin Lowe, Ed. & Pub.  (US)
James L. Lowe, Ed. & Pub.  (US)
Robson Lowe Ltd.  (UK)
Lowell Observatory  (US)
Lowell Press  (US)
Lowell University  (US)
Lower Albany Historical Society  (SA)
Lower Cape Fear Historical Society  (US)
Lowlands Review  (US)
Ken Lowman Ed. & Pub.  (US)
Lowry Enterprises  (US)
Loxton Publishers Ltd  (UK)
Loyal Order of Ancient Shepherds (Ashton Unity)
  Friendly Society  (UK)
Loyal Order of Moose  (US)
Loyola Law School  (US)
Loyola Marymount University  (US)
Loyola School of Theology
  see under Ateneo de Manila University  (PH)
Loyola Students Association  (CN)
Loyola University  (US)
Loyola University of Chicago  (US)
Loyola University of Chicago. Center for Research in
  Urban Government  (US)
Loyola University of Chicago. Department of English
  (US)
Loyola University of Chicago. School of Dentistry
  (US)
Wydawnictwo Lubelskie  (PL)
Lubranopublicitas  (IT)
Lucas Industries Ltd.  (UK)
Rev. Silas Emmitt Lucas, Jr. Ed. & Pub.  (US)
Luchterhand Verlag  (GW)
Lucille Press  (US)
Dr. W.O. Lucin, Ed. & Pub.  (US)
Lucis Publishing Co.  (US)
Luckiamute  (US)
Lucknow Publishing House  (II)
Lucknow University
  see University of Lucknow  (II)
Ludd's Mill Poetry Publishing Co- Operative  (UK)
Ludwig Boltzmann-Institut fuer Umweltwissenschaften
  und Naturschutz  (AU)
Luebecker Nachrichten GmbH  (GW)
Dr. Ernst Lueddemann und Sohn  (GW)
Luedin AG  (SZ)
Lufkin Industries, Inc.  (US)
Luftfahrt-Verlag Walter Zuerl  (GW)
Luftwaffen-Ring e.V.  (GW)
Luggage and Leather Goods Manufacturers of America
  (US)
Drukkerij Joh. Luijk N.V.  (NE)
Philip Luker  (AT)
N. V. Drukkerij-Uitgeverij Lumax  (NE)
Lumber Co-Operator, Inc.  (US)
Lumbermens Credit Association, Inc.  (US)
Imprenta Editorial Lumen S.A.  (PE)
Lumen Vitae Press  (BE)
Lumiere et Vie  (FR)
Horst Lummert  (GW)
Luna Publications  (US)
Lunatic Fringe  (US)
A. A. Lund Associates  (US)
Lund Humphries  (UK)
Lunde Forlag og Bokhandel A-S  (NO)
Lundequistka Bokhandeln  (SW)
Lunds Universitet. Department of Geography  (SW)
Lunds Universitet. Faculty of Odontology  (SW)
Lunds Universitet. Historiska Museum  (SW)

Lunds Universitet. Institute of Art History (SW)
Lunds Universitet. Institute of Economic History (SW)
Lunds Universitet. Institutionen Foer Nordiska Spraak (SW)
Lunds Universitet. Psychological Laboratory (SW)
Lunds Universitet. Slaviska Institutionen (SW)
Lunds Universitet. Tandlaekarhoegskolan. Odontologiska Fakulteten
   see Lunds Universitet. Faculty of Odontology (SW)
Luce Luongo, Ed. & Pub. (IT)
Luptonian (US)
Lure of Litchfield Hills (US)
Lusaka Theatre Club (ZA)
Sally Luscomb, Ed. & Pub. (US)
Luso-Americano Co., Inc. (US)
Lute Society (UK)
Lute Society of America (US)
H. Lutgens, Ed. & Pub. (US)
Luther-Gesellschaft (GW)
Luther-Verlag (GW)
Lutheran Academy for Scholarship (US)
Lutheran Book Depot (SA)
Lutheran Braille Evangelism Association (US)
Lutheran Center Association (US)
Lutheran Church in America (US)
Lutheran Church in America. Board of Publication (US)
Lutheran Church in America. Division for World Mission and Ecumenism (US)
Lutheran Church in America. Eastern Canada Synod (CN)
Lutheran Church in America. Minnesota Synod (US)
Lutheran Church in America. New Jersey Synod (US)
Lutheran Church in America. Western Canada Synod (CN)
Lutheran Church in Liberia (LB)
Lutheran Church Library Association (US)
Lutheran Church, Missouri Synod (US)
Lutheran Church-Missouri Synod. Board of Missions for the Blind (US)
Lutheran Church, Missouri Synod. Board of Youth Ministry (US)
Lutheran Church-Missouri Synod, Hong Kong Mission (HK)
Lutheran Church-Missouri Synod. Michigan District (US)
Lutheran Church of Australia (AT)
Lutheran Church Women (US)
Lutheran Community Services (US)
Lutheran Council in Canada (CN)
Lutheran Council in the U.S.A. (US)
Lutheran Education Association (US)
Lutheran General Hospital (US)
Lutheran Human Relations Association (US)
Lutheran News, Inc. (US)
Lutheran Publications in New Jersey (US)
Lutheran Publishing House (AT)
Lutheran Society for Worship, Music and the Arts (US)
Lutheran Theological Seminary (US)
Lutheran Women of Australia (AT)
Lutheran World Federation (SZ)
Lutherisches Verlagshaus GmbH (GW)
Luton & Dunstable Hospital (UK)
Luton, Dunstable & District Chamber of Commerce (UK)
Lutte Ouvriere (FR)
Editions Lux (FR)
Erika Lux Verlag (AU)
Luxembourg. Administration de l'Emploi (LU)
Luxembourg. Bibliotheque Nationale (LU)
Luxembourg. Caisse d'Epargne de l'Etat (LU)
Luxembourg. Inspection Generale de la Securite Sociale (LU)
Luxembourg. Ministere des Finances (LU)
Luxembourg. Ministere du Travail et da la Securite Sociale. Inspection Generale de la Securite Sociale
   see Luxembourg. Inspection Generale de la Securite Sociale (LU)
Luxembourg. Service Central de la Statistique et des Etudes Economiques (LU)
Luz (AG)
Luz (Denver) (US)
Luz Magazine, Inc. (US)
Empresa Editorial Luz, S. A. (GT)
Luzac & Co., Ltd. (UK)
Luzern (Canton) Staatskanzlei (SZ)
Harald Lyche og Co. A-S (NO)
Lykes Bros. Steamship Co. Inc. (US)
Lyle Printing & Publishing Co. (US)
Lyle Publishing (UK)
R. W. Lyman (Canada Co.) (CN)
Lynatrace, Inc. (US)
Lynch-Bowes, Inc. (US)
Lynchburg Foundry (US)

Lynge og Soen (DK)
Lynx House Press (US)
Lyone Publications Ltd. (CN)
Lyons Band (US)
Lyric Opera of Chicago (US)
Lyric Theatre (UK)
Lysteknisk Selskab (DK)
M A M (CY)
M and W Publications (UK)
M B A Communications, Inc. (US)
M C B (European Marketing & Customer Studies) (UK)
M C B (Management Decision) Ltd. (UK)
M C B (Managerial Finance) Ltd. (UK)
M C B (Managerial Law) Ltd. (UK)
M C B (Physical Distribution Management) Ltd. (UK)
M C B (Social Economics) Ltd. (UK)
M.C.B. (European Training) Ltd. (UK)
M C-B Manufacturing Chemists (US)
M C P Publications (US)
M. D. Anderson Hospital and Tumor Institute
   see under University of Texas (US)
M D Publications (Canada) Ltd. (CN)
M D Publications, Inc. (US)
Editrice M E M A s.r.l. (IT)
Impremerie M.E.N. (ML)
M F C Services (US)
M. F. Enterprises Inc. (US)
M Farmaceutico Publishing Co., Inc. (US)
M.G.A. Publications Pty. Ltd. (AT)
M-G Publications (US)
M. G. Textile School (II)
M. H. Information Center (JA)
M.I.M.S. (Pty) Ltd (SA)
M I N Publishing (US)
M I T Press (US)
M L F (SZ)
M M C School of Management (II)
M M L Centre for Rheumatic Diseases (II)
M.M. Publications Ltd. (PK)
M. O. D. E. F. (FR)
M.O. Publishing Company (US)
M O T A M A R
   see World Muslim Congress (PK)
M. P. I. Publishers (Motive Power International) (CN)
M P L A Solidarity Committee (US)
M P R C (Asia) Sdn. Berhad (MY)
M P R Publishing Services Ltd. (UK)
M Press (US)
M.R.A.
   see Societe Nouvelles des Publications M. R. A. (FR)
M S Foerbundet (SW)
M. S. Publishing (UK)
M.S.S. Information Corporation (US)
M. S. University of Baroda
   see Maharaja Sayajirao University of Baroda (II)
M. W. Prince Hall Grand Lodge (US)
M W Publishers (UK)
Maanedsskrift for Praktisk Laegegerning (DK)
Maanmittaustieteiden Seura r.y. (FI)
Maanpudustuslehden Kustannus Oy (FI)
Maarakentajain Kustannus Oy (FI)
Maatalouden Tutkimuskeskus (FI)
Maatschappij der Nederlandse Letterkunde (NE)
B.V. Maatschappij voor Bedrijfswetenschappelijke Uitgaven (NE)
MAC Publications Inc. (US)
Macabre (US)
McAnally & Associates, Inc. (US)
Maccabi World Union (IS)
McCall Pattern Co. (US)
McCall Publishing Co. (US)
Maccan Publishing Co. (CN)
Casa Editrice Maccari (IT)
McCarron Bird Pty. Ltd. (AT)
Pat McCarty (US)
A. Mario Macchi (IT)
Gaetano Macchiaroli Editore (IT)
Lowell McClellan (US)
J. C. McColl & Associates Pty. Ltd., Farm Management Consultants (AT)
George E. McCracken, Ed. & Pub (US)
Robert M. McCune (US)
McCutchan Publishing Corp. (US)
Ames McDaniel, Ed. & Pub. (US)
Macdaniel Publications Ltd. (US)
M. MacDonald (UK)
Macdonald and Co. (UK)
Macdonald and Evans Ltd. (UK)
Macdonald & Jane's Publishers Ltd. (UK)
McDonald Publications of London Ltd. (UK)
MacDonald Publishing Co. (US)
McDonnell Douglas (US)
Macedonian Patriotic Organization (US)
Ralph McElroy Co., Inc. (US)

McElroy Family Newsletter (US)
McFadden Business Publications (US)
Macfadden Women's Media, Inc. (US)
Macfarland Co. (US)
McGill Medical Undergraduate Society (CN)
McGill-Queen's University Press (CN)
McGill University (CN)
McGill University. Brace Research Institute (CN)
McGill University. Centre for Developing-Area Studies (CN)
McGill University. Dental Students' Society (CN)
McGill University. Department of Classics (CN)
McGill University. Department of Geography (CN)
McGill University. Department of Meteorology (CN)
McGill University. Department of Physics (CN)
McGill University. Engineering Undergraduate Society (CN)
McGill University. Faculty of Education (CN)
McGill University. Faculty of Law (CN)
McGill University. Graduate Business Students' Society (CN)
McGill University. Graduates' Society (CN)
McGill University. Industrial Relations Centre (CN)
McGill University. Institute of Air and Space Law (CN)
McGill University. Macdonald Physics Laboratory (CN)
McGill University. Marine Sciences Centre (CN)
McGill University. Mechanical Engineering Department (CN)
McGill University. Osler Library (CN)
McGill University. Redpath Museum (CN)
McGill University. School of Nursing (CN)
Richard M. McGrath (US)
McGrath Publishing Co. (US)
McGraw Hill Book Co. (US)
McGraw-Hill Book Co. Gregg Division (US)
McGraw-Hill Book Co. (U.K.) Ltd. (UK)
McGraw-Hill, Inc. (US)
McGraw-Hill Information Systems Co. Sweet's Division (US)
McGraw-Hill Information Systems Company of Canada Ltd. (CN)
McGraw-Hill Publications Co (US)
McHenry Publishing Co. (US)
Machinery and Allied Products Institute (US)
Machinery Dealers National Association (US)
Machinery Dealers National Information System Inc. (US)
Machinery Market Ltd. (UK)
Machinery Publishing Co. Ltd. (UK)
Machlett Laboratories, Inc (US)
McIntish Publishing Co. Ltd. (CN)
George McIntosh (UK)
Don L. Macintyre, Ed. & Pub. (US)
Mack Associates (US)
Mack Brooks Exhibitions, Ltd. (UK)
David McKay Co. (US)
Mackay Publishing Corporation (US)
McKeand Publications, Inc (US)
McKellar Publications (US)
Mackenzie & Arthur Ltd. (UK)
W. & J. Mackey Ltd. (UK)
Mackinac Island State Park Commission (US)
McKinsey & Co. Inc. (US)
Mackintosh Publications (UK)
McKnight Medical Communications, Inc. (US)
McKnight Publishing Company (US)
Maclaren Publishers Ltd. (UK)
McLean Guide to Kennels of America (US)
McLean Hospital (US)
Maclean-Hunter Ltd. (CN)
Maclean-Hunter Ltd. (UK)
Maclean-Hunter Ltd. (Calgary) (CN)
Maclean-Hunter Ltd. (Montreal) (CN)
Maclean-Hunter Publishing Corporation (US)
McLelland & Stewart (CN)
Dan Macleod, Ed. & Pub. (CN)
Fred McMahon, Ed. & Pub. (US)
McMahon Publishing Co. (US)
McMaster Association for 18th Century Studies (CN)
McMaster University (CN)
McMaster University. Department of Anthropology (CN)
McMaster University. Institute for Materials Research (CN)
McMaster University Library Press (CN)
MacMillan Bloedel Ltd. (CN)
Macmillan, Inc. (US)
Macmillan Information (US)
Macmillan Journals Ltd. (UK)
Macmillan London Ltd. (UK)
Macmillan Press Ltd. (UK)
Macmillan Professional Magazines, Inc. (US)
Macmillan Publishers Ltd. (UK)
Macmillan Publishing Co. (US)
Macmillan Publishing Co., Inc. (US)
Macmillan Science Co., Inc. (US)

McMullin Publishers Ltd. (CN)
MacNair- Dorland Co., Inc. (US)
McNamara Publishing Co. Inc. (US)
Macnaughtan and Sinclair Ltd. (UK)
Macniven and Wallace (UK)
Maco Publishing Co., Inc. (US)
Macomb County Circuit Court (US)
Macquarie University. Centre for Advancement of
    Teaching (AT)
Macquarie University. School of English & Linguistics
    (AT)
Macquarie University. School of History, Philosphy
    and Politics (AT)
Macquarie University. School of Modern Languages
    (AT)
MacRae's Blue Book Co. (US)
William H. McRee, Ed. & Pub. (US)
Macro-Comm Corp. (US)
Editorial Macrometrica (SP)
Macula (FR)
McVay-McVeigh-McVey Family Archives Quarterly
    (US)
Madan Printers (II)
Madawaska Limitee (CN)
Made In...Publicity (CS)
Made in Europe Marketing Organization GmbH & Co.
    KG (GW)
Maden Te†kik ve Arama Enstitusu
    see Mineral Research and Exploration Institute
    (TU)
Madhya Pradesh. Directorate of Tribal Welfare (II)
Madhya Pradesh. Planning and Development
    Department (II)
Madhya Pradesh Varshiki (II)
Madisen Publishing Division (US)
Madison Area Committee on Southern Africa (US)
Madison Avenue Magazine, Inc. (US)
Madison Metropolitan School District (US)
Madison Teachers Inc. (US)
Madness Network News (US)
Madoc-Tweed Art & Writing Centre (CN)
Madonna di Castelmonte (IT)
Madonna House Apostolate (CN)
Madras
    see also Tamil Nadu (II)
Madras Institute of Development Studies (II)
Madras Institute of Technology (II)
Madras Law Journal Office (II)
Madras Psychology Society (II)
Madras Reporters Guild (II)
Madras University
    see University of Madras (II)
Madrigaal V.Z.W. (BE)
Madure-Madagascar (FR)
Maeght Editeur (FR)
Maerkischer Kreis (GW)
Mafeking Mail (Pty) Ltd. (SA)
Magadh University (II)
Magazine Art Pty. Ltd. (AT)
Magazine Associates (AT)
Magazine-Expansion (FR)
Magazine Management Co. Inc. (US)
Magazine of Bibliographies (US)
Magazine Press Ltd. (NZ)
Magazine Printers (AT)
Magazine Publishers Association, Inc. (US)
Magazines-Creative, Inc. (US)
Magazines for Industry, Inc. (US)
VEB Magdeburger Armaturenwerke "Karl Marx"
    (GE)
Magelan S.A.R.L. (FR)
Magic Industries (US)
Magisterio Espanol, S.A. (SP)
Magistrates' Association (UK)
Magistrates' Association of South Africa and South-
    West Africa (SA)
Magistratura Democratica (IT)
Editoriale Magna Graecia (IT)
Magna Publishing Co. (US)
Editions Magnard (FR)
Magnes Press (IS)
Magnet (CS)
Magnum Publications Ltd. (UK)
Magnum-Royal Publications Inc. (US)
Al Magnuson, Ed. & Pub. (US)
Sven Magnusson, Ed. and Pub. (SW)
John Magor, Ed. & Pub. (CN)
Magveto Kiado (HU)
Magyar Allami Eotvos Lorand Geofizikai Intezet
    (HU)
Magyar Elektrotechnikai Egyesulet (HU)
Magyar Elelmezesipari Tudomanyos Egyesulet (HU)
Magyar Elettani Tarsasag (HU)
Magyar Epitomuveszek Szovetsege (HU)
Magyar Eszperanto Szovetseg
    see Hungara Esperanto Asocio (HU)
Magyar Filmtudomanyi Intezet (HU)
Magyar Fogorvosok Egyesulete (HU)

Magyar Foldrajzi Tarsasag (HU)
Magyar Fotomuveszek Szovetsege (HU)
Magyar Geofizikusok Egyesulete (HU)
Magyar Gyogyszereszeti Tarsasag (HU)
Magyar Hidrologiai Tarsasag (HU)
Magyar Irodalomtorteneti Tarsasag (HU)
Magyar Irok Szovetsege (HU)
Magyar Jogasz Szovetseg (HU)
Magyar Kemikusok Egyesulete (HU)
Magyar Kereskedelmi Kamara (HU)
Magyar Kommunista Ifjusagi Szovetseg (HU)
Magyar Konyvkiadok es Konyvterjesztok Egyesulese
    (HU)
Magyar Korhazszovetseg (HU)
Magyar Kozgazdasagi Tarsasag (HU)
Magyar Kulugyi Intezet (HU)
Magyar Muhely (FR)
Magyar Munkasmozgalmi Muzeum (HU)
Magyar Nemzeti Muzeum (HU)
Magyar Neprajzi Tarsasag (HU)
Magyar Neurologiai es Pszichiatriai Tarsasag (HU)
Magyar Orszagos Leveltar (HU)
Magyar Pedagogiai Tarsasag (HU)
Magyar Radiologiai Tarsasag (HU)
Magyar Rakkutatok Tarsasaga (HU)
Magyar Szocialista Munkaspart (MSZMP) Kozponti
    Bizottsag (HU)
Magyar Szocialista Munkaspart (MSZMP)
    Tarsadalomtudomanyi Intezet (HU)
Magyar Tavirati Iroda (HU)
Magyar Termeszettudomanyi Muzeum (HU)
Magyar Testnevelesi Foiskola (HU)
Magyar Tortenelmi Tarsulat (HU)
Magyar Tudomanyos Akademia (HU)
Magyar Tudomanyos Akademia. Agrargazdasagi
    Kutato Intezet (HU)
Magyar Tudomanyos Akademia. Agrokemiai Kutato
    Intezet (HU)
Magyar Tudomanyos Akademia. Allam-es
    Jogtudomanyi Intezet (HU)
Magyar Tudomanyos Akademia. Atommag Kutato
    Intezet (HU)
Magyar Tudomanyos Akademia. Foldrajztudomanyi
    Kutato Intezet (HU)
Magyar Tudomanyos Akademia. Ipargazdasagtani
    Kutatocsoport (HU)
Magyar Tudomanyos Akademia. Irodalomtudomanyi
    Intezet (HU)
Magyar Tudomanyos Akademia. Izotop Intezet (HU)
Magyar Tudomanyos Akademia.
    Kozgazdasagtudomanyi Intezet (HU)
Magyar Tudomanyos Akademia. Kozponti Fizikai
    Kutato Intezet (HU)
Magyar Tudomanyos Akademia. Mikrobiologiai Kutato
    Intezet (HU)
Magyar Tudomanyos Akademia. Neprajzi Kutato
    Csoport (HU)
Magyar Tudomanyos Akademia. Nepzenekutato
    Csoport (HU)
Magyar Tudomanyos Akademia. Nyelvtudomanyi
    Intezet (HU)
Magyar Tudomanyos Akademia. Regeszeti Intezet
    (HU)
Magyar Tudomanyos Akademia. Szociologiai Intezet
    (HU)
Magyar Tudomanyos Akademia. Tortenettudomanyi
    Intezet (HU)
Magyar Uttorok Szovetsege (HU)
Magyar Zenemuveszek Szovetsege (HU)
Magyarhoni Foldtani Tarsulat (HU)
Maha Bodhi Society of India (II)
Mahajan Brothers (II)
Maharaja Sayajirao University of Baroda (II)
Maharaja Sayajirao University of Baroda. Centre for
    Advanced Study in Education (II)
Maharaja Sayajirao University of Baroda. Department
    of Archaeology and Ancient History (II)
Maharaja Sayajirao University of Baroda. Department
    of History (II)
Maharaja Sayajirao University of Baroda. Department
    of Museology (II)
Maharaja Sayajirao University of Baroda. Faculty of
    Education and Psychology (II)
Maharashtra. Bureau of Economics and Statistics (II)
Maharashtra. Commissioner of Labour and Director of
    Employment (II)
Maharashtra. Department of Agriculture (II)
Maharashtra. Department of Archives (II)
Maharashtra. Directorate of Geology, Mining, and
    Groundwater Development (II)
Maharashtra. Directorate of Information and Public
    Relations (II)
Maharashtra. Maharashtra Information Centre (II)
Maharashtra. Maharashtra State Institute of Education
    (II)
Maharashtra Economic Development Council (II)
Maharashtra Rajya Sahakari Sangh
    see Maharashtra State Co-Operative Union (II)

Maharashtra Small Scale Industries Association (II)
Maharashtra State Co-Operative Union (II)
Maharashtra State Financial Corporation (II)
Mahatma Gandhi Memorial Research Centre (II)
Mahenjodaro (II)
Maher Publications, Inc. (US)
William F. Mahler, Ed. & Pub. (US)
Mahoning Mimeograph and Pamphlet Service (US)
Kailash Mahto (II)
Casa Editrice Maia (IT)
Otto Maier Verlag (GW)
Mail
Mailbox Club, Inc. (US)
Maille, SARL (FR)
Steven L. Maimes, Ed. & Pub. (US)
Main Lafrentz & Co. (Certified Public Accountants)
    (US)
Maine. Bureau of Labor and Industry. Department of
    Commerce and Industry (US)
Maine. Bureau of Labor and Industry. Department of
    Manpower Affairs (US)
Maine. Bureau of Property Taxation (US)
Maine. Commission on the Arts and the Humanities
    (US)
Maine. Criminal Justice Planning & Assistance Agency
    (US)
Maine. Department of Conservation (US)
Maine. Department of Environmental Protection
    (US)
Maine. Department of Health and Welfare (US)
Maine. Department of Inland Fisheries and Wildlife
    (US)
Maine. Department of Manpower Affairs. Employment
    Security Commission (US)
Maine. Department of Marine Resources (US)
Maine. Department of the Attorney General. Criminal
    Division (US)
Maine. Department of the Attorney General. Law
    Enforcement Education Section (US)
Maine. Department of Transportation (US)
Maine. Geological Survey (US)
Maine. Higher Education Facilities Commission (US)
Maine. Labor Market Evaluation and Planning Section
    (US)
Maine. Manpower Research Division (US)
Maine. School Administrative District 70 (US)
Maine. Soil and Water Conservation Commission
    (US)
Maine. State Development Office (US)
Maine. State Library (US)
Maine. State Planning Office (US)
Maine A F L-C I O (US)
Maine Agricultural Experiment Station (US)
Maine Antique Digest, Inc. (US)
Maine Digest Inc (US)
Maine Edition (US)
Maine Genealogical Inquirer (US)
Maine Good Roads Association (US)
Maine Guarantee Authority (US)
Maine Historical Society (US)
Maine Medical Association (US)
Maine Municipal Association (US)
Maine National Bank (US)
Maine Nature (US)
Maine Organic Farmer and Gardener (US)
Maine Potato Council (US)
Maine State Grocers Association (US)
Maine State Museum (US)
Maine Teachers' Association (US)
Maine Times (US)
Maine Water Utilities Association (US)
Maine Writers' Conference (US)
Mainichi Daily News (JA)
Mainichi Newspapers (JA)
Mainichi Newspapers, Osaka. Braille Mainichi Section
    (JA)
Mainmise (CN)
Mainoshoitajain Yhdistys (FI)
Mainzer Altertumsverein (GW)
Mainzer Verlagsanstalt und Druckerei Will und Rothe
    KG (GW)
Libreria Maiolo (IT)
Maioricensis Schola Lullistica (SP)
Maison de la Chasse et de la Nature (FR)
Maison de Marie Claire (FR)
Maison des Sciences de l'Homme (FR)
Maison Internationale de la Poesie (BE)
Adrien Maisonneuve (FR)
Editions Maisonneuve et Larose (FR)
Maisons d'Enfants et d'Adolescents de France (FR)

Leon Maister (Pty) Ltd. (SA)

Majalle-Ye Tarikh-e Eslam (IR)

Maji-Maji (US)

Majlis Pengeluar-Pengeluar Getah Tanah Melayu
    see Rubber Producers Council of Malaysia (MY)

Major Magazines, Inc. (US)
Majority Report Co. (US)
Makabayan Publishing Corp. (PH)
Makar Press (AT)
Makara Publishing & Design Co-Operative (CN)
Makedonska Akademija na Naukite i Umetnostite (YU)
Makedonsko Izdanie na Komunist (YU)
Makerere Institute of Social Research (UG)
Makerere Law Society (UG)
Makerere Political Society (UG)
Makerere University. Department of Geography (UG)
Makerere University. Department of History (UG)
Makerere University. Department of Literature (UG)
Makerere University. Department of Religious Studies and Philosophy (UG)
Makerere University. Department of Rural Economy and Extension (UG)
Makerere University. East African Institute of Social Research (UG)
Makerere University. Faculty of Agriculture (UG)
Makerere University. Faculty of Arts & Social Sciences (UG)
Makerere University. Faculty of Education (UG)
Makerere University. Faculty of Law (UG)
Makerere University. Library (UG)
Makerere University Medical Students Association (UG)
Makerere University. Science Faculty (UG)
Makerere University. Sociological Society (UG)
Makhteshim Agan (IS)
Makina Muhendisleri Odasi (TU)
Makki Publications (SA)
Malacological Society of Australia (AT)
Malacological Society of Japan (JA)
Malaga. Camara Oficial de la Propiedad Urbana de la Provincia (SP)
Malaga. Diputacion Provincial (SP)
Malagasy Republic. Bibliotheque Nationale (MG)
Malagasy Republic. Direction de la Recherche Scientifique et Technique. Section de Demographie (MG)
Malagasy Republic. Institut National de la Statistique et de la Recherche Economique (MG)
Malagasy Republic. Ministere des Finances et du Plan. Institut National de la Statistique et de la Recherche Economique
  see Malagasy Republic. Institut National de la Statistique et de la Recherche Economique (MG)
Malago Archives Committee (UK)
Malawi. Department of Agricultural Research (MW)
Malawi. Department of Information (MW)
Malawi. Fisheries Department (MW)
Malawi. Geological Survey (MW)
Malawi. Government Printer (MW)
Malawi. Meteorological Services (MW)
Malawi. National Library (MW)
Malawi. National Statistical Office (MW)
Malawi. Post Office Savings Bank (MW)
Malawi Railways, Ltd. (MW)
Malawi Young Pioneers (MW)
Malaya Railway Administration (MY)
Malayan Law Journal (Pte) Ltd. (SI)
Malayan Medical Association (SI)
Malayan Nature Society (MY)
Malayan Pineapple Industry Board (MY)
Malayan Tin Bureau (US)
Malaysia. Bahagian Perikanan
  see Malaysia. Fisheries Division (MY)
Malaysia. Department of Statistics (MY)
Malaysia. Department of Tourism (MY)
Malaysia. Federal Agricultural Marketing Authority (MY)
Malaysia. Fisheries Division (MY)
Malaysia. Geological Survey (MY)
Malaysia. Government Printer (MY)
Malaysia. Jabatan Galian
  see Malaysia. Mines Department (MY)
Malaysia. Kementerian Buroh dan Tenaga Raayat
  see Malaysia. Ministry of Labour and Manpower (MY)
Malaysia. Kementerian Luar Negeri
  see Malaysia. Ministry of Foreign Affairs (MY)
Malaysia. Kementerian Pertanian dan Tanah
  see Malaysia. Ministry of Agriculture and Lands (MY)
Malaysia. Kementerian Pertanian dan Tanah. Bahagian Perikanan
  see Malaysia. Fisheries Division (MY)
Malaysia. Lembaga Pemasara Pertanian Persekutuan
  see Malaysia. Federal Agricultural Marketing Authority (MY)
Malaysia. Meteorological Service (MY)
Malaysia. Mines Department (MY)
Malaysia. Ministry of Agricultural and Lands. Fisheries Division
  see Malaysia. Fisheries Division (MY)

Malaysia. Ministry of Agriculture and Lands (MY)
Malaysia. Ministry of Foreign Affairs (MY)
Malaysia. Ministry of Labour and Manpower (MY)
Malaysia. National Archives (MY)
Malaysia. National Family Planning Board (MY)
Malaysia. National Library (MY)
Malaysia. Perbendaharaan
  see Malaysia. Treasury (MY)
Malaysia. Perkhidmatan Kajicuaca Malaysia
  see Malaysia. Meteorological Service (MY)
Malaysia. Survey Department (MY)
Malaysia. Treasury (MY)
Malaysia Inter-Religious Organisation (MY)
Malaysia. Jabatan Perangkaan
  see Malaysia. Department of Statistics (MY)
Malaysian Agricultural Research and Development Institute (MY)
Malaysian Branch of the Royal Asiatic Society (MY)
Malaysian Centre for Development Studies (MY)
Malaysian Chinese Association (MY)
Malaysian Forester (MY)
Malaysian Historical Society (MY)
Malaysian Industrial Development Finance Berhad (MY)
Malaysian Institute of Chemistry (MY)
Malaysian Institute of Management (MY)
Malaysian Mathematical Society (MY)
Malaysian Medical Association (MY)
Malaysian Multi-Purpose Cooperative Society (MY)
Malaysian Press Institute (MY)
Malaysian Rubber Bureau (GW)
Malaysian Rubber Bureau (MY)
Malaysian Rubber Producers' Research Association. Malaysian Rubber Research & Development Board (UK)
Malaysian Rubber Research and Development Board (MY)
Malaysian Society of Applied Biology (MY)
Malaysian Sociological Research Institute (MY)
Malaysian Timber Industry Board (MY)
Malaysian Trades Union Congress (MY)
Malaysian Veterinary Association (MY)
Robert Malcomson, Ed. & Pub. (US)
Maledicta Press (US)
Malermestrenes Landsforbund (NO)
Malfasi Editore (IT)
Mali. Ministere de l'Enseignement Superieur Secondaire et de la Recherche Scientifique. Institut Pedagogique National (ML)
Mali. Service de la Statistique Generale, de la Comptabilite Nationale et de la Mecanographie (ML)
Malim Dulta (II)
Malki Museum, Inc. (US)
Mallasjuomalehti Oy (FI)
Mallett & Co. (UK)
Walter Mallin Verlag (GW)
L.C.G. Malmberg B.V. (NE)
Malmborg och Hedstrom Foerlags AB (SW)
Malmborg og Hedstroem Forlag A-S (DK)
Librairie Maloine (FR)
Malpractice Lifeline, Inc. (US)
Malraux Society (US)
Malta. Central Office of Statistics (MM)
Malta. Department of Health (MM)
Malta Chamber of Commerce (MM)
Malta Library Association (MM)
Malta Service Bureau (CN)
Malta Union of Teachers (MM)
Maltzeff (SZ)
Mamane International Academy (II)
Mambo Press (RH)
Mamelle (US)
Mammal Society (UK)
Mammalia (FR)
Mamme e Bimbi (IT)
Giovanni Mammucari, Ed. & Pub. (IT)
Man and His Music (US)
Man & Manager Inc. (US)
Man-Flight Systems, Inc. (US)
Man in India (II)
Man in the Northeast (US)
Man-to-Man (UK)
Management Centre Europe (BE)
Management Consultants (NP)
Management Consultants Ltd. (UK)
Management Decision Monographs (UK)
Management Development Centre (II)
Management Information Corporation (US)
Management Information Service (US)
Management Publications Ltd. (UK)
Management Reports Inc. (US)
Management Resources, Inc. (US)
Management Science Publishing Inc. (US)
Management Science Research Institute (JA)
Management-Scope (US)
Management Services Associates (US)
Management Training and Advisory Center (UG)

Manager Magazin Verlagsgesellschaft mbH (GW)
Manana (MX)
Manas Publishing Co. (US)
Manasayan (II)
Giuseppe Manassero, Ed. & Pub. (IT)
Manchester Association of Engineers (UK)
Manchester Business School (UK)
Manchester Chamber of Commerce and Industry (UK)
Manchester College. Old Students' Association (UK)
Manchester District Association of Unitarian and Free Christian Churches (UK)
Manchester Guardian Society for the Protection of Trade (UK)
Manchester Literary and Philosophical Society (UK)
Manchester Mensa. (UK)
Manchester University Folk Song Society (UK)
Manchester University Press (UK)
Mario Mancini Editore (IT)
Andrew R. Mandala, Ed. & Pub. (US)
Mandragora (BE)
W.S. Maney & Sons Ltd. (UK)
Mangineer Publications (US)
Fr. Mangold'sche Buchhandlung (GW)
Mangum Family Bulletin (US)
Manhattan Arts Review, Inc. (US)
Manhattan Center for Advanced Psychoanalytic Studies, Inc. (US)
Manhattan College. Department of English and World Literature (US)
Manhattan College. School of Engineering (US)
Manicomio Judiciario Heitor Carrilho (BL)
Manifold (UK)
Editorial Manila (MX)
Manila. Department of Public Works & Communications (PH)
Manila Bay Co. (CN)
Manila Central University (PH)
Manila Secondary Teachers (PH)
Manion Forum (US)
Manitoba. Bureau of Statistics (CN)
Manitoba. Department of Agriculture (CN)
Manitoba. Department of Co-Operative Development (CN)
Manitoba. Department of Education (CN)
Manitoba. Department of Health and Social Development (CN)
Manitoba. Department of Industry and Commerce (CN)
Manitoba. Department of Labour (CN)
Manitoba. Department of Mines, Resources and Environment. Exploration & Geological Survey Branch (CN)
Manitoba. Department of Tourism, Recreation and Cultural Affairs (CN)
Manitoba. Department of Tourism, Recreation and Cultural Affairs. Research and Planning Branch (CN)
Manitoba. Environmental Council (CN)
Manitoba. Health Services Commission (CN)
Manitoba. Horse Racing Commission (CN)
Manitoba. Land Value Appraisal Commission (CN)
Manitoba. Lotteries Commission (CN)
Manitoba. Police Commission (CN)
Manitoba. Public Library Services (CN)
Manitoba. Welfare Advisory Committee (CN)
Manitoba Archaeological Society (CN)
Manitoba Association of Registered Nurses (CN)
Manitoba Association of Teachers of English (CN)
Manitoba Cancer Treatment and Research Foundation (CN)
Manitoba Classic and Antique Auto Club (CN)
Manitoba Dental Association (CN)
Manitoba Educational Research Council (CN)
Manitoba Historical Society (CN)
Manitoba Library Association (CN)
Manitoba Museum of Man and Nature (CN)
Manitoba Naturalists' Society (CN)
Manitoba Pool Elevators (CN)
Manitoba Record Society (CN)
Manitoba School Library Audio Visual Association (CN)
Manitoba Society of Radiological Technologists Inc. (CN)
Manitoba Teachers' Society (CN)
Manitoba Telephone System (CN)
Manitoba Theatre Centre (CN)
Manitoba Tourist Association (CN)
Manitoba Water Services Board (CN)
Manitowoc County Historical Society (US)
Mankato State University (US)
Mankind Publishing Co. (US)
Mankind Quarterly (UK)
Verlag Th. Mann (GW)
Verlag Mann und Bartels GmbH (GW)
Gebr. Mann Verlag (GW)
Manning Rapley Publishing Ltd. (UK)
Manningham Press (UK)

George Mannion, Ed. & Pub.  (CN)
Mannus-Verlag Peter Wegener  (GW)
Mano Enterprises, Inc.  (US)
Manohar Book Service  (II)
Manoir Notre-Dame de Grace  (CN)
Manomet Bird Observatory  (US)
A. Manoury  (FR)
Editrice la Manovella s.r.l.  (IT)
ManRoot  (US)
Man's Magazine  (US)
Mansell Information-Publishing Ltd.  (UK)
Mansfield State College. Department of English  (US)
Manson Western Corp.  (US)
Mantatoforos  (UK)
Manteia  (FR)
Manual de Impuestos - Regimen Legal Tributario
  (CK)
Manufactured Housing Reporter  (US)
Manufacturer Publishing Co.  (US)
Manufacturer Publishing Co. Pty. Ltd.  (AT)
Manufacturers' Agent Publishing Co., Inc.  (US)
Manufacturers Agents Association  (UK)
Manufacturers' Agents National Association  (US)
Manufacturers Association of Nigeria  (NR)
Manufacturers Hanover Trust Co. International
  Division  (US)
Manufacturer's News, Inc.  (US)
Manufacturing Chemists Association  (US)
Manufacturing Confectioner Publishing Co.  (US)
Manufacturing Jewelers and Silversmiths of America,
  Inc  (US)
Manx Museum and National Trust  (UK)
Manz Verlag  (GW)
Manzi Pietro  (IT)
Manzsche Verlags- und Universitaetsbuchhandlung
  (AU)
Maori Education Foundation  (NZ)
Map Collectors Circle  (UK)
Map Society  (JA)
Mapa Fiscal Editora S.A.  (BL)
Mapat Publications Inc.  (US)
Mapix  (US)
Maple Creek News Ltd.  (CN)
Maple Leaf Club  (US)
Mappin & Curran (Philatelists) Pty. Ltd.  (AT)
Maps  (US)
Maquettes-Plastiques  (FR)
Mara Institute of Technology  (MY)
Imprimerie et Publicite du Marais S.A.  (BE)
Maranatha Revival Crusade  (II)
Marathon Oil Co.  (US)
Marathon Publications  (IE)
Marathwada University  (II)
D. L. Marayana, Ed. & Pub.  (II)
Marburger Bund  (GW)
Marburger Publishing Co., Inc.  (US)
Marcel Quellet  (US)
Marcham Manor Press  (UK)
Editions du Marchand Quebecois  (CN)
Marche  (BE)
Marcolli Editore  (IT)
Marcom-West, Inc.  (US)
Marconi Co. Ltd.  (UK)
Marconi Instruments Ltd.  (UK)
Editora Marcos Ltda.  (BL)
Marden-Kane, Inc.  (US)
Marebesi Salvatore  (IT)
Editions Marechal  (FR)
Marg Publications  (II)
Marga Institute (Sri Lanka Centre for Development
  Studies)  (CE)
Margins  (US)
Margutta  (IT)
Carl Marhold Verlagsbuchhandlung  (GW)
Mariah Publications  (US)
Mariahilf, Pfarre  (AU)
Mariale Werken  (BE)
Marian Association for Young Girls  (FR)
Marian Library  (US)
Mariannhill Mission Society  (SA)
Maricopa Urban Teachers Association  (US)
Marie-Claire  (FR)
Marie Selby Botanical Gardens  (US)
Mariemou  (MU)
Marietta College  (US)
Editions Marigny  (FR)
Marilyn  (US)
Marina de Guerra  (CU)
Marina News, Inc.  (US)
Marine Advisory Service  (US)
Marine and General Publicity Ltd.  (IE)
Marine Annuals, Inc.  (US)
Marine Aquarist Publications, Inc.  (US)
Marine Biological Association of the United Kingdom
  (UK)
Marine Biological Laboratory  (US)
Marine Board of Hobart  (AT)
Marine Business  (US)

Marine Corps Association  (US)
Marine Digest Inc.  (US)
Marine Engineers Beneficial Association  (US)
Marine Historical Associations, Inc.  (US)
Marine Hobbyist News  (US)
Marine Laboratory, Aberdeen. Scotland  (UK)
Marine Media Management Ltd.  (UK)
Marine Park Research Station
  see Sabiura Marine Park Research Station  (JA)
Marine Pollution Information Centre. Marine
  Biological Association of the United Kingdom
  (UK)
Marine Products Export Development Authority  (II)
Marine Publications  (US)
Marine Retailer  (US)
Marine Safety Council  (US)
Marine Technology Society  (US)
A. J. Marineau  (US)
Marinnytt  (SW)
Mario Negri Institute for Pharmacological Research
  (US)
Mario Press  (IO)
Giovanna Mariotti, Ed. & Pub.  (IT)
Maritime Activity Reports, Inc.  (US)
Maritime Association of the Port of N.Y.  (US)
Maritime Bank of Israel, Ltd  (IS)
Maritime Co-Operative Printers, Ltd.  (CN)
Maritime Command  (CN)
Maritime Folk Music Society  (CN)
Maritime Law Book Co.  (CN)
Maritime Lumber Bureau  (CN)
Maritime Postmark Society  (US)
Maritime Press Foundation  (IO)
Maritime Professional Photographers Association
  (CN)
Maritime Professional Publishing Co.  (CN)
Maritime Research, Inc.  (US)
Maritime Safety Agency
  see Japan. Maritime Safety Agency  (JA)
Maritime Union of India  (II)
Maritime World Ltd.  (UK)
Marjorie Pollard Publications Ltd.  (UK)
Mark-Age, Inc.  (US)
Mark Distributors  (US)
Mark II  (CN)
J. Mark Press  (US)
Mark-Tier's Economy Report  (AT)
Mark Twain Journal  (US)
Mark Twain Research Foundation, Inc.  (US)
Mark 40 Enterprises,Inc.  (US)
Markaz al-Istilamat al-Islami al- Filibbini  (PH)
Markell Publishing Co.  (US)
Market Bulletin  (PK)
Market Chronicle  (US)
Market Communications Inc.  (US)
Market Indicators Digest  (SA)
Market Industries News  (AT)
Market Intelligence Ltd.  (UK)
Market News Publishing Corporation  (US)
Market Place Publications  (US)
Market Research Africa (Pty) Ltd.  (SA)
Market Research Society  (UK)
Market-Show Publications, Inc.  (US)
Marketeer  (II)
Marketing & Economic Research Bureau  (II)
Marketing & Publishing Ltd.  (KE)
Marketing Development  (US)
Marketing Economics Institute, Ltd.  (US)
Marketing Forum Magazine  (US)
Marketing Handbooks Inc.  (US)
Marketing House Publishers Ltd  (UK)
Marketing News, Inc.  (US)
Marketing Programs and Services Group, Inc.  (US)
Marketing Publications Inc.  (US)
Marketing Science Institute  (US)
Marketing Services Group International  (US)
Marketplace Publications Inc.  (US)
Markham House Press Ltd.  (UK)
Markham Publishing Co.  (US)
Marking Devices Publishing Co., Inc.  (US)
Markkinointijarjestojen Yheistyoelin  (FI)
Markos Publicity N. V.  (NE)
D. L. Marks  (AT)
Marksisticki Centar, Titograd  (YU)
Markson Science Inc.  (US)
Marktgemeinde  (AU)
Markus Verlagsgesellschaft mbH  (GW)
Harold Markusoff  (CN)
Editrice Maro  (IT)
Marpep Publishing Ltd.  (CN)
Marple's Business Roundup, Inc.  (US)
Marquetry Society  (UK)
Marquette Engineer  (US)
Marquette University  (US)
Marquette University. Aristotelean Society  (US)
Marquette University. College of Business
  Administration  (US)
Marquette University. Law School  (US)

Marquette University Press  (US)
Marquette University. School of Dentistry  (US)
Marquette University. Slavic Institute  (US)
Dr. Alfredo Marquez Campos, Ed. & Pub.  (MX)
Marquis Academic Media  (US)
Editions Marquis Ltee  (CN)
Marquis Who's Who Inc.  (US)
Marriott Corporation  (US)
Hans Marseille Verlag  (GW)
Marshall, Morgan & Scott Ltd.  (UK)
Marshall-Wythe School of Law  (US)
Marsilio Editori S.p.A.  (IT)
Marstellar Inc.  (US)
Martec Publishing Group Ltd.  (UK)
C. F. Martin and Co.  (US)
Martin & Harris Private Ltd.  (II)
Martin Center  (US)
Martin Co., Inc.  (US)
Colin Martin, Ed. & Pub.  (SZ)
Gloria A. Martin, Ed. & Pub.  (US)
Robert L. Martin, Ed. & Pub.  (US)
Martin Luther King, Jr. Center for Social Change
  (US)
Martin-Luther-Universitaet Halle-Wittenberg  (GE)
Martin-Luther-Universitaet Halle-Wittenberg.
  Mathematisch-Naturwissenschaftliche Fakultaet
  (GE)
Franklin H. Martin Memorial Foundation  (US)
Martin Psychiatric Research Foundation  (US)
Martin Publications (Sacramento)  (US)
Martin Publishing Co.  (US)
Martindale-Hubbell, Inc.  (US)
Martinella di Milano  (IT)
Laboratoires Martinet  (FR)
Carlos Martinez  (CK)
Maria Martini Editore  (IT)
Martonair Ltd.  (UK)
Marttaliitto r.y.  (FI)
Maruee  (II)
Marunouchi Research Center Co., Ltd.  (JA)
Gianni Marussi Ed. & Pub.  (IT)
Marvel Comics Group  (US)
Robert B. Marvin, Ed. & Pub.  (US)
Marx Karoly Kozgazdasagtudomanyi Egyetem  (HU)
Marx Memorial Library  (UK)
Verlag Manfred Marx und Co.  (SZ)
Marxist-Leninistiska Kampforbundet  (SW)
Marxistische Blaetter GmbH  (GW)
Mary Washington College. Department of Geography
  (US)
Maryborough Adult Education Centre  (AT)
Maryland. Bureau of Air Quality Control  (US)
Maryland. Bureau of Traffic Engineering  (US)
Maryland. Commission on Intergovernmental
  Cooperation  (US)
Maryland. Correctional Training Commission  (US)
Maryland. Council for Higher Education  (US)
Maryland. Crime Investigating Commission  (US)
Maryland. Department of Economic and Community
  Development  (US)
Maryland. Department of Economic and Community
  Development. Maryland Office of Tourism  (US)
Maryland. Department of Education  (US)
Maryland. Department of Education. Division of
  Library Development and Services  (US)
Maryland. Department of Education. Division of
  Library Development and Services, School Media
  Services Section  (US)
Maryland. Department of Employment and Social
  Services  (US)
Maryland. Department of Fiscal Services. Division of
  Fiscal Research  (US)
Maryland. Department of Health and Mental Hygiene
  (US)
Maryland. Department of Human Resources  (US)
Maryland. Department of Juvenile Services  (US)
Maryland. Department of Legislative Reference  (US)
Maryland. Department of Natural Resources  (US)
Maryland. Department of State Planning  (US)
Maryland. Division of Correction  (US)
Maryland. Division of Marketing  (US)
Maryland. Division of Social Security  (US)
Maryland. Division of State Documents  (US)
Maryland. Geological Survey  (US)
Maryland. Governor's Commission on Law
  Enforcement and the Administration of Justice
  (US)
Maryland. Hall of Records Commission  (US)
Maryland. Social Services Administration  (US)
Maryland. State Board for Community Colleges  (US)
Maryland Bankers Association  (US)
Maryland Center of Public Broadcasting  (US)
Maryland Congress of Parents and Teachers Inc.
  (US)
Maryland-Delaware-D.C. Press Association  (US)
Maryland English Journal  (US)
Maryland Genealogical Society  (US)
Maryland Herpetological Society  (US)

Maryland Historical Society  (US)
Maryland Historical Trust  (US)
Maryland Horse Breeders Association  (US)
Maryland Library Association  (US)
Maryland Media, Inc.  (US)
Maryland Motor Truck Association, Inc.  (US)
Maryland Municipal League Inc.  (US)
Maryland Nurses Association  (US)
Maryland Ornithological Society, Inc.  (US)
Maryland Pharmaceutical Association  (US)
Maryland Police Training Commission  (US)
Maryland Port Administration  (US)
Maryland School for Blind  (US)
Maryland State Bar Association  (US)
Maryland State Dental Association  (US)
Maryland State Horticultural Society  (US)
Maryland State Teachers Association  (US)
Maryland Writers Council  (US)
Marylebone Press Ltd.  (UK)
Publicaciones Marynka, S. A.  (MX)
Casa Editrice Bemporad Marzocco  (IT)
Marzorati Editore  (IT)
Maschinenfabrik Augsburg-Nuernberg AG  (GW)
Maschinenfabrik Fahr AG  (GW)
Mash Family Bulletin  (US)
Izdatel'stvo Mashinostroenie  (UR)
Mashoor Press  (PK)
Al-Mashriq  (US)
Masihi Avaza  (II)
Maskinentreprenoerenes Forbund  (NO)
Maskinkontakt AB  (SW)
Maskinmestrenes Forening  (DK)
George Mason  (US)
Phillip Mason, Ed. & Pub.  (US)
Mason and Associates, Financial Consultants  (US)
Mason-Charter Publishers. Petrocelli Division  (US)
Mason Clinic  (US)
Mason Contractors Association of America, Inc.
 (US)
Kenneth Mason Publications Ltd.  (UK)
Masonic Record Ltd.  (UK)
Librairie Francois Maspero  (FR)
Librairie Francois Maspero  (UK)
Masque Enterprises  (UK)
Masque Publications  (AT)
Mass Communications Pty. Ltd.  (AT)
Mass Media Ministries, Inc.  (US)
Mass Retailing Institute  (US)
Mass Spectrometry Data Centre  (UK)
Mass Transit  (US)
Massachusetts. Aeronautics Commission  (US)
Massachusetts. Board of Higher Education  (US)
Massachusetts. Bureau of Curriculum Services  (US)
Massachusetts. Bureau of Library Extension  (US)
Massachusetts. Committee on Criminal Justice  (US)
Massachusetts. Criminal History Systems Board  (US)
Massachusetts. Department of Civil Service and
 Registration. Board of Public Accountancy  (US)
Massachusetts. Department of Community Affairs.
 Bureau of Regional Planning  (US)
Massachusetts. Department of Correction  (US)
Massachusetts. Department of Education  (US)
Massachusetts. Department of Mental Health  (US)
Massachusetts. Department of Public Health  (US)
Massachusetts. Department of Public Welfare. State
 Advisory Board  (US)
Massachusetts. Division of Employment Security
 (US)
Massachusetts. Division of Fisheries and Game  (US)
Massachusetts. Division of Mineral Resources  (US)
Massachusetts. Governor's Highway Safety Bureau
 (US)
Massachusetts. Rehabilitation Commission  (US)
Massachusetts. Security and Privacy Council  (US)
Massachusetts Advocacy Center  (US)
Massachusetts Archaeological Society, Inc.  (US)
Massachusetts Audubon Society  (US)
Massachusetts Bar Association  (US)
Massachusetts College of Pharmacy  (US)
Massachusetts Council for the Social Studies  (US)
Massachusetts Council on the Arts and Humanities
 (US)
Massachusetts Dental Society  (US)
Massachusetts Foreign Languages Association  (US)
Massachusetts Herpetological Society  (US)
Massachusetts Historical Society  (US)
Massachusetts Horticultural Society  (US)
Massachusetts Housing Finance Agency  (US)
Massachusetts Institute of Technology  (US)
Massachusetts Institute of Technology. Alumni
 Association  (US)
Massachusetts Institute of Technology. Center for
 International Studies  (US)
Massachusetts Institute of Technology. Flight
 Transportation Laboratory  (US)
Massachusetts Institute of Technology. Neurosciences
 Research Program  (US)

Massachusetts Institute of Technology. Political
 Science Department  (US)
Massachusetts Institute of Technology Press
 see M I T Press  (US)
Massachusetts Institute of Technology. Research
 Laboratory of Electronics  (US)
Massachusetts Law Reform Institute  (US)
Massachusetts League of Cities and Towns  (US)
Massachusetts Library Association  (US)
Massachusetts Medical Society  (US)
Massachusetts Motor Truck Association, Inc.  (US)
Massachusetts Music Educators Association, Inc.
 (US)
Massachusetts Nurses Association  (US)
Massachusetts Physician, Inc.  (US)
Massachusetts Port Authority  (US)
Massachusetts Psychological Center, Inc.  (US)
Massachusetts Review, Inc.  (US)
Massachusetts Secondary School Principals
 Association  (US)
Massachusetts Society for the Prevention of Cruelty to
 Animals  (US)
Massachusetts Society of Certified Public Accountants,
 Inc.  (US)
Massachusetts Society of Professional Engineers  (US)
Massachusetts State Labor Council, AFL-CIO  (US)
Massachusetts Taxpayers Foundation  (US)
Massachusetts Teachers Association  (US)
Editions Richard Masse  (FR)
Massenet Society  (UK)
Massey-Ferguson (United Kingdom) Ltd.  (UK)
Massey University. Geography Department  (NZ)
Massey University. School of Business  (NZ)
Editions Charles Massin et Cie  (FR)
A. H. Massina & Co. Pty. Ltd.  (AT)
Masson  (FR)
Masson Italia Editori S.p.A.  (IT)
Masson Services  (FR)
Luigi Massoni, Ed. & Pub.  (IT)
Verlag der Massstaebe  (GW)
Master Bakers Association  (AT)
Master Brewers Association of America  (US)
Master Builders Association  (AT)
Master Builders Association of New South Wales
 (AT)
Master Builders' Association of Tasmania  (AT)
Master Builders Association of Victoria & Builders
 Exchange  (AT)
Master Carriers' Association of New South Wales
 (AT)
Master Drawings Association, Inc.  (US)
Master Grocers' Association of Victoria Ltd.  (AT)
Master Indicator of the Stock Market  (US)
Master Ladies Hairdressers Association  (AT)
Master Ladies Hairdressers' Association of New South
 Wales  (AT)
Master Pastrycooks Association of New South Wales
 (AT)
Master Photographers Association  (UK)
Master Plan Service, Inc.  (US)
Master Plumbers & Mechanical Services Association
 (AT)
Master Plumbers Association of New South Wales
 (AT)
Master Plumbers Association of Queensland  (AT)
Master Publications (Minneapolis)  (US)
Master Publications, Inc.  (US)
Master Teacher, Inc.  (US)
Master Wineletter  (FR)
J.J. Masterson, Ed. & Pub.  (AT)
Matagiri  (US)
Match  (US)
Editoriale Match-Ball S.p.A.  (IT)
Mate  (NZ)

Matemaattisten Aineiden Opettajien Liitto  (FI)

Matematicki Institut, Beograd  (YU)
Matematisk Institutt  (NO)
Materdei Community Centre  (IT)
Materials Management Journal of India  (II)
Materialy Zrodlowe do Dziejow Kosciola w Polsce
 (PL)
Materiel d'Entreprise  (FR)
Maternity Center Association  (US)
Mathematical Association  (UK)
Mathematical Association of America  (US)
Mathematical Association of India  (II)
Mathematical Association of Nigeria  (NR)
Mathematical Association of South Australia  (AT)
Mathematical Association of Tanzania  (TZ)
Mathematical Association of Victoria  (AT)
Mathematical Association of Western Australia  (AT)
Mathematical Pie  (UK)
Mathematical Programming Society  (NE)
Mathematical Society  (II)
Mathematical Society of Japan  (JA)
Mathematics Associations of Two-Year Colleges
 Journal, Inc.  (US)

Mathematics Education  (II)
Mathematika Sciences Society  (II)
Mathematische Gesellschaft der DDR  (GE)
Mather and Platt Ltd.  (UK)
Mathilda and Terence Kennedy Institute of
 Rheumatology  (UK)
Mathilde-Zimmer-Stiftung e.V.  (GW)
Mathrubhumi Press  (II)
Matica Hrvatska  (YU)
Matica Iseljenika Bosne i Hercegovine  (YU)
Matica Iseljenika Hrvatske  (YU)
Matica Slovenska  (CS)
Matica Srpska  (YU)
Matica Srpska. Odeljenje za Drustvene Nauke  (YU)
Matilda Ziegler Publishing Co. for the Blind, Inc.
 (US)
Mato Grosso, Brazil. Servico do Acordo de
 Classificacao  (BL)
Matrix  (US)
Matsushita Electric Industrial Co., Ltd.  (JA)
Paul R. Matt  (US)
Mattachine Society of the Niagara Frontier  (US)
Matterhorn Sports Club  (US)
Matthaes Verlag GmbH  (GW)
Matthew's Printing  (US)
Mattingley Publishing Co., Inc.  (US)
Matus-Cernak-Institut  (GW)
Verlag Wilhelm Maudrich  (AU)
Maulai Enterprise  (PK)
Maumee Valley Historical Society  (US)
Neil L. Maurer, Ed. & Pub.  (US)
Carl Maurersche Buchdruckerei  (GW)
Achille Mauri Editore  (IT)
Maurice Falk Institute for Economic Research in Israel
 (IS)
Mauritania. Direction de la Statistique et des Etudes
 Economiques  (MU)
Mauritius. Archives  (MF)
Mauritius. Central Electricity Board  (MF)
Mauritius. Central Statistical Office  (MF)
Mauritius. Customs and Excise Department  (MF)
Mauritius. Government Printing Office  (MF)
Mauritius. Ministry of External Affairs, Tourism and
 Immigration  (MF)
Mauritius. Ministry of Social Security  (MF)
Mauritius. Registrar of Insurance  (MF)
Mauritius People's Progressive Party  (MF)
Mauritius Times Publication  (MF)
Maury County Historical Society  (US)
Maverick Media, Inc.  (US)
Maverick Publications  (US)
Max  (US)
Max-Planck-Gesellschaft zur Foerderung der
 Wissenschaften  (GW)
Max-Planck-Institut fuer Auslaendisches Oeffentliches
 Recht und Voelkerrecht  (GW)
Max-Planck-Institut fuer Auslaendisches und
 Internationales Privatrecht  (GW)
Max-Planck-Institut fuer Bildungsforschung  (GW)
Max-Planck-Institut fuer Kohlenforschung. Institut fuer
 Strahlenchemie  (GW)
Max-Planck-Institut fuer Landarbeit und Landtechnik
 (GW)
Max-Planck-Institut fuer Stroemungsforschung  (GW)
Max-Planck-Institute for Foreign and International
 Patent, Copyright and Competitition Law, Munich
 (GW)
Max-Reger-Institut  (GW)

Nigen A. Maxey, Ed. & Pub.  (US)
Maximilian-Gesellschaft e.V.  (GW)
Maximilian-Verlag  (GW)
Maxwell Publicity  (IE)
May & Baker Ltd.  (UK)
May & Brett Ltd.  (UK)
Maya Deb  (II)
Mayday  (CN)
Karl Mayer GmbH  (GW)
F. C. Mayer Verlag  (GW)
Mayhew-McCrimmon Ltd.  (UK)
Mayhill Publications, Inc.  (US)
Editora Mayo  (BL)
Mayo Clinic  (US)
Mayo Foundation. Alumni Association  (US)
Mazamas  (US)
Editions d'Art Lucien Mazenod  (FR)
Mazenod Institute  (LO)
MD Promotions Ltd.  (UK)
Me Jane  (AT)
Mead & McGrouther (Pty) Ltd.  (SA)
Meadowlark Publishing Ltd.  (CN)
Katherine F. Meadows, Ed. & Pub.  (US)
Meadville-Lombard Theological School  (US)
Meal Expenditure Analysis Ltd.  (UK)
Means Co., Inc.  (US)
Measurements and Data Corp.  (US)
Meat and Allied Trades Federation of Australia  (AT)

Mercedes Publishing Co. (AT)
Mercer County Community College (US)
Mercer University. Walter F. George School of Law (US)
Merchandise Mart Directory (US)
Merchandiser Publishing Co. (New York) (US)
Merchandising Magazines Pty. Ltd. (AT)
Merchandising Publications Co. (US)
Merchant Magazine, Inc. (US)
Merchant Navy and Airline Officers Association (UK)
Merchants and Manufacturers Association (US)
Mercia Publicity (UK)
Merck and Co. Inc (US)
Merck Sharp & Dohme (Pty) Ltd. (SA)
Mercure (BE)
Editions Mercure (FR)
N V V-Bond Mercurius (NE)
Mercury House Publications Ltd. (UK)
Mercury Press, Inc (US)
Mercury Productions, Inc. (US)
Mercury Publications Ltd. (CN)
Mercury-Walch Pty. Ltd. (AT)
Mercyhurst College (US)
Meredith Corporation (US)
Merestechnikai es Automatizalasi Tudomanyos Egyesulet (HU)
Mergers & Acquisitions, Inc. (US)
Editions Mericourt (FR)
Meridiano Dodici (IT)
Editorial Meridiano, S. A. (MX)
Editori Meridionali Riuniti (IT)
Merino Stud Breeders' Association of South Africa (SA)
Meriupseeriyhdistys (FI)
Ha-Merkaz Ha-Artsi Shel Irgune Ha-Kablanim Veha-Bonim Be-Yisrael (IS)
Universitaetsbuchhandlung Rudolf Merkel (GW)
Merkonomiliitto r.y. (FI)
Merkos l'Inyonei Chinuch, Inc. (US)
Merksa-Servicio de Estudios de Mercado, S.A. (SP)
Merkur (CS)
Merkur Wechselseitige Versicherungsanstalt (AU)
Merlin Press (UK)
Merlin Publishing Co. (CN)
Merrill Analysis Inc. (US)
Merrill-Palmer Institute (US)
Charles E. Merrill Publishing Co. (US)
Merriman Publishing Co. (US)
Verlag Merseburger Berlin GmbH (GW)
Merseyside Arts Association (UK)
Merseyside Social Credit Association (UK)
Mershon Center for Education in National Security (US)
Merton Publications Ltd. (CN)
Mesquita and Silver, Inc. (US)
Messageries M.B.P. (FR)
Edizioni Messagero (IT)
Messagers Catholiques de la Bible (CN)
Messaggerie Italiane S.p.A. (IT)
Messaggerie Musicali (IT)
Edizioni Messaggero (IT)
Messenger Press (US)
Messenger Publications Pty. Ltd. (AT)
Messenger Publishing Co. (Kansas City) (US)
Messenger Publishing House (UK)
Messerschmitt-Boelkow-Blohm GmbH (GW)
Messianic Jewish Alliance of America (US)
Mestni Muzej v Idrii (YU)
Metaalcompagnie "Brabant" B.V. (NE)
Metaalunie (NE)
Metal Building Review (US)
Metal Bulletin Ltd. (UK)
Metal Center News (US)
Metal Fabricating Institute Inc. (US)
Metal Finishing Society of Japan (JA)
Metal Mining Agency
    see Japan. Metal Mining Agency (JA)
Metal Polishers, Buffers, Platers and Helpers International Union (US)
Metal Powder Industries Federation (US)
Metal Trades Industry Association of Australia (AT)
Metal Tube Packaging Council of North America (US)
Metall-Verlag GmbH (GW)
Metallgesellschaft AG (GW)
Editions la Metallurgie Francaise (FR)
Izdatel'stvo Metallurgiya (UR)
Metals and Ceramics Information Center (US)
Metals and Plastics Publications, Inc. (US)
Metals Society (UK)
Metanoia (US)
Metaphysische Rundschau (AU)
Kyriakos H. Metaxas, Ed. & Pub. (UK)
Editorial Meteci, S.A. (MX)
Editions Meteore (FR)
Meteoritical Society (US)
Meteorological and Geophysical Institute (IO)

Meteorological Research Institute (JA)
Meteorological Society of Japan (JA)
Meteorologische Gesellschaft der DDR (GE)
Meteoroloski Zavod SR Slovenije. SAS za Agrometeorologijo (YU)
Methodist Board of Publication (UK)
Methodist Church. Division of Education and Youth (UK)
Methodist Church in New South Wales (AT)
Methodist Church in South Australia (AT)
Methodist Church in Southern Asia (II)
Methodist Church Music Society (UK)
Methodist Church of South Africa (SA)
Methodist Church of Victoria & Tasmania (AT)
Methodist Church Overseas Division (UK)
Methodist Department of Communication (AT)
Methodist Federation for Social Action (US)
Methodist Hospital of Dallas (US)
Methodist Local Preachers Aid Association (UK)
Methodist Newspaper Co., Ltd. (UK)
Methodist Overseas Missions (AT)
Methodist Publishing House (UK)
Methods-Time Measurement Association for Standards and Research (US)
Methuen and Co. Ltd. (UK)
Metiers d'Art du Quebec Inc. (CN)
Ha-Metivta (IS)
Metmenys Corp. (US)
Metodistkyrkans i Sverige (SW)
Editora Metodos Ltda (BL)
METRA (FR)
Metraton Publications (UK)
Metric Commission (CN)
Metric Information Service Bulletin (UK)
Metric Supply International (US)
METRO
    see New York Metropolitan Reference & Research Library Agency (US)
Metro Magazine, Inc. (US)
Metro Printers (CE)
Metro-Sud (CN)
Metrologic Instruments Inc. (US)
Metropolitan Air Post Society (US)
Metropolitan Almanac (US)
Metropolitan Area Planning Council (US)
Metropolitan Atlanta Rapid Transit Authority (M A R T A) (US)
Metropolitan Baltimore Chamber of Commerce (US)
Metropolitan Church Association (US)
Metropolitan Community Church (US)
Metropolitan Council of the Twin Cities Area (US)
Metropolitan Council on Housing (US)
Metropolitan Detroit AFL-CIO (US)
Metropolitan Electricity Authority (TH)
Metropolitan Fund, Inc. (US)
Metropolitan Library Service Agency (US)
Metropolitan Life Insurance Company (US)
Metropolitan Milwaukee Association of Commerce (US)
Metropolitan Museum of Art (US)
Metropolitan Nashville Board of Education (US)
Metropolitan New York Council (US)
Metropolitan Opera Guild, Inc. (US)
Metropolitan Opera National Council. Central Opera Service (US)
Metropolitan Pensioners Welfare Association (CN)
Metropolitan Petroleum Company (US)
Metropolitan Pittsburgh Public Broadcasting (US)
Metropolitan Police. Traffic Division (UK)
Metropolitan Restaurant News, Inc. (US)
Metropolitan School Study Council (US)
Metropolitan Technical College (JA)
Metropolitan Toronto Library Board (CN)
Metropolitan Toronto Library Board. Theatre Section (CN)
Metropolitan Tulsa Chamber of Commerce (US)
Metropolitan Washington Board of Trade (US)
Metropolitan Washington Builders Association (US)
Metropolitan Washington Council of Governments (US)
Metropolitan Water District of Southern California (US)
Metru (IO)
Metsastajain Keskusjarjesto (FI)
Metsataloudellinen Aikakauskirja Oy (FI)
Metzgereipersonal-Verband der Schweiz (SZ)
J. B. Metzlersche Verlagsbuchhandlung (GW)
Alfred Metzner Verlag GmbH (GW)
Meubles et Decors S.A. (BE)
Meulenhoff-Bruna B.V. (NE)
Editorial Mex-Ameris, S.A. (MX)
Mexican Academic Clearing House (US)
Mexican Air Line Pilots Association (MX)
Mexican-American Legal Defense and Educational Fund (US)
Mexican Investor (MX)
Mexican Society for Soil Mechanics (MX)
Mexican Society of Behavior Analysis (MX)

Editora Mexico (MX)
Mexico. Archivo General de la Nacion (MX)
Mexico. Comision Federal de Electricidad (MX)
Mexico. Comision Nacional Bancaria y de Seguros (MX)
Mexico. Comision Nacional de Valores (MX)
Mexico. Comison Nacional de los Salarios Minimos (MX)
Mexico. Consejo Nacional de Ciencia y Tecnologia (MX)
Mexico. Direccion de Estadistica y Estudios Economicos (MX)
Mexico. Direccion General de Estadistica (MX)
Mexico. Direccion General de Estadistica. Departamento de Estadisticas Economicas Basicas (MX)
Mexico. Direccion General de Investigacion en Salud Publica (MX)
Mexico. Direccion General de la Prensa, Memorias, Bibliotecas y Publicaciones. Departamento de Asuntos Internacionales (MX)
Mexico. Ministerio de Hacienda y Credito Publico (MX)
Mexico. Secretaria de Agricultura y Ganaderia. Departamento de Divulgacion Forestal y de la Fauna (MX)
Mexico. Secretaria de Agricultura y Ganaderia. Direccion General de Sanidad Vegetal (MX)
Mexico. Secretaria de Educacion Publica (MX)
Mexico. Secretaria de Industria y Comercio (MX)
Mexico. Secretaria de Industria y Comercio. Direccion General de Estadistica (MX)
Mexico. Secretaria de la Defensa Nacional (MX)
Mexico. Secretaria de la Defensa Nacional. Departamento de la Industria Militar (MX)
Mexico. Secretaria de la Presidencia (MX)
Mexico. Secretaria de Obras Publicas (MX)
Mexico. Secretaria de Recursos Hidraulicos (MX)
Mexico. Secretaria de Recursos Hidraulicos. Instituto Nacional de Investigaciones Pecuarias (MX)
Mexico. Secretaria de Salubridad y Asistencia (MX)
Mexico. Secretaria del Trabajo y Prevision Social (MX)
Mexico. Servicio Nacional A R M O
    see Mexico. Servicio Nacional de Adiestramiento Rapido de la Mano de Obra en la Industria (MX)
Mexico. Servicio Nacional de Adiestramiento Rapido de la Mano de Obra de la Industria. Centro de Informacion Tecnica y Documentacion (MX)
Mexico. Servicio Nacional de Adiestramiento Rapido de la Mano de Obra en la Industria (MX)
Mexico. Servico Nacional de Adiestramiento Rapido de la Mano de Obra en la Industria. Centro de Informacion Tecnica y Documentacion (MX)
Mexico Agricola (MX)
Mexico Industrial (MX)
Mexletter Investment Counsel (MX)
Jean de Mey, Ed. & Pub. (BE)
Editions Meyer et Cie (SZ)
Verlag G. Meyers Erben (SZ)
Mezhdunarodnaya Demokraticheskaya Federatsiya Zhenshchin (UR)
Mezhdunarodnaya Kniga (Distributor) (UR)
Thomas Mezick (US)
Mezinarodni Politika (CS)
Miami Magazine, Inc. (US)
Miami Malacological Society (US)
Miami University (US)
Miami University-Middletown (US)
Miami Valley Milk Producers Association (US)
Guido Miano Editore (IT)
Miba-Verlag (GW)
Michael Reese Hospital & Medical Center (US)
Michael's Thing (US)
Editions Albin Michel (FR)
Michelin (FR)
Michelin Tyre Co.Ltd. (UK)
Geographische Buchhandlung R. Michels (GW)
Michie Co. (US)
Michigan. Advisory Commission on Physician Assistants (US)
Michigan. Advisory Council for Vocational Education (US)
Michigan. Aeronautics Commission (US)
Michigan. Bureau of Medical Assistance (US)
Michigan. Center for Health Statistics (US)
Michigan. Department of Agriculture. Division of Plant Industry (US)
Michigan. Department of Civil Rights (US)
Michigan. Department of Commerce (US)
Michigan. Department of Commerce. Corporation & Securities Bureau (US)
Michigan. Department of Education (US)

Michigan. Department of Education. Division of Vocational Education  (US)
Michigan. Department of Education. State Library Services  (US)
Michigan. Department of Management and Budget  (US)
Michigan. Department of Mental Health  (US)
Michigan. Department of Natural Resources  (US)
Michigan. Department of Natural Resources. Geology Division  (US)
Michigan. Department of Natural Resources. Institute for Fisheries Research  (US)
Michigan. Department of Natural Resources. Natural Resources Council  (US)
Michigan. Department of Natural Resources. Office of Surveys and Statistics  (US)
Michigan. Department of Public Health  (US)
Michigan. Department of Public Health. Bureau of Industrial Health  (US)
Michigan. Department of Social Services  (US)
Michigan. Department of Social Services. Bureau of Quality Control and Statistical Analysis  (US)
Michigan. Department of State. Michigan History Division  (US)
Michigan. Department of State Police  (US)
Michigan. Employment Security Commission  (US)
Michigan. Environmental Protection Branch  (US)
Michigan. Geological Survey  (US)
Michigan. Manpower Commission  (US)
Michigan. Office of Criminal Justice Programs  (US)
Michigan. Office of Highway Safety Planning  (US)
Michigan. Office of the Court Administrator  (US)
Michigan. State Housing Development Authority  (US)
Michigan A F L-C I O News, Inc.  (US)
Michigan Academy of Science, Arts and Letters  (US)
Michigan Association for Media in Education  (US)
Michigan Association for Supervision and Curriculum Development  (US)
Michigan Association of Chiefs of Police  (US)
Michigan Association of Health and Physical Education  (US)
Michigan Association of Home Builders  (US)
Michigan Association of Osteopathic Physicians and Surgeons, Inc.  (US)
Michigan Association of School Administrators  (US)
Michigan Association of School Boards, Inc.  (US)
Michigan Association of Secondary School Principals  (US)
Michigan Audubon Society  (US)
Michigan Beverage News Inc.  (US)
Michigan Botanical Club  (US)
Michigan Business Education Association  (US)
Michigan Christian Advocate Publishing Co.  (US)
Michigan Corrections Association  (US)
Michigan Dental Association  (US)
Michigan Dental Hygienists Association  (US)
Michigan Education Association  (US)
Michigan Education Association. Region Six  (US)
Michigan Engineering Society  (US)
Michigan Entomological Society  (US)
Michigan Farm Bureau  (US)
Michigan Food Dealers Association  (US)
Michigan Fraternal Order of Police  (US)
Michigan Hospital Association  (US)
Michigan Independent Press, Inc.  (US)
Michigan Institute of Psychosynthesis  (US)
Michigan Law Review Association  (US)
Michigan Library Association  (US)
Michigan Linguistic Society  (US)
Michigan Milk Producers Association  (US)
Michigan Municipal League  (US)
Michigan Museum Association  (US)
Michigan Music Educators Association  (US)
Michigan Music Theory Society  (US)
Michigan Nurses Association  (US)
Michigan Optometric Association  (US)
Michigan Personnel & Guidance Association  (US)
Michigan Pharmacists Association  (US)
Michigan Plumbing & Mechanical Contractors Association  (US)
Michigan Restaurateur  (US)
Michigan Society for Respiratory Therapy  (US)
Michigan Society of Architects  (US)
Michigan Speech and Hearing Association  (US)
Michigan State Chamber of Commerce  (US)
Michigan State Florist Association  (US)
Michigan State Medical Society  (US)
Michigan State University  (US)
Michigan State University. African Studies Center  (US)
Michigan State University. Agricultural Experiment Station  (US)
Michigan State University. Agriculture and Natural Resources Education Institute  (US)
Michigan State University. Alumni Association  (US)
Michigan State University. Asian Studies Center  (US)

Michigan State University. Bureau of Business and Economic Research  (US)
Michigan State University. Center for International Programs  (US)
Michigan State University. Center for Rural Manpower & Public Affairs  (US)
Michigan State University. Computer Laboratory  (US)
Michigan State University. Continuing Education Service  (US)
Michigan State University. Cooperative Extension Service  (US)
Michigan State University. Department of Agricultural Economics  (US)
Michigan State University. Department of Animal Husbandry  (US)
Michigan State University. Department of English  (US)
Michigan State University. Department of Entomology  (US)
Michigan State University. Department of Physics  (US)
Michigan State University. Department of Secondary Education and Curriculum  (US)
Michigan State University. Department of Sociology  (US)
Michigan State University. Graduate School of Business Administration  (US)
Michigan State University. Institute for Community Development and Services  (US)
Michigan State University. Institute for International Studies in Education  (US)
Michigan State University. Institute of Water Research  (US)
Michigan State University. Latin American Studies Center  (US)
Michigan State University. Learning Systems Institute  (US)
Michigan State University Libraries. International Library  (US)
Michigan State University. Museum  (US)
Michigan State University. Outdoor Education Project  (US)
Michigan State University. Public Administration Program  (US)
Michigan State University. Sahel Documentation Center  (US)
Michigan State University. School of Labor and Industrial Relations  (US)
Michigan State University. Special Programs  (US)
Michigan Technic  (US)
Michigan Technological University. Library  (US)
Michigan Trucking Association  (US)
Michigan United Conservation Clubs Inc  (US)
Michigan Water Pollution Control Association  (US)
Microbiology Research Foundation  (JA)
Microcard Edition Books  (US)
Microcard Editions  (US)
Microcomputer Associates, Inc.  (US)
Microcritica  (AG)
Microfiche Foundation  (NE)
Microfilm Association of Great Britain  (UK)
Microfilm Publishing, Inc.  (US)
Microfilming Corporation of America  (US)
Microform Review, Inc.  (US)
Microforms International Marketing Corporation  (US)
Micrography  (NE)
Microinfo Ltd.  (UK)
Micromedia Ltd.  (CN)
Micronesian Area Research Center
  see under University of Guam  (GU)
Micronitor News and Printing Co.  (TT)
Micropaleontology Press  (US)
Microscope Publications Ltd.  (UK)
Mid-America Dairymen, Inc.  (US)
Mid-America Lumbermens Service Corporation  (US)
Mid-America Publishing Corporation  (US)
Mid-America Publishing Corporation (Shenandoah)  (US)
Mid-Atlantic Regional Archives Conference  (US)
Mid-Continent Banker  (US)
Mid-Continent Regional Science Association  (US)
Mid-Continent Scientific  (US)
Mid-East Commerce  (LE)
Mid-Eastern Cooperatives  (US)
Mid-Hudson Genealogical Journal  (US)
Mid-Hudson Library System  (US)
Mid-Hudson School Study Council  (US)
Mid-Ohio Regional Planning Commmission  (US)
Midatlantic Review  (US)
Midcontinent American Studies Association  (US)
Midcontinent Farmers Association  (US)
Middaugh Printers at Sugarcreek  (US)
Midden Noord-Holland Combinatie  (NE)
Midden Oosten Instituut  (NE)
Middle East Commercial Information Center  (LE)
Middle East Economic Consultants  (UK)

Middle East Economic Digest Ltd.  (UK)
Middle East Enterprise  (US)
Middle East Information Media Ltd.  (IS)
Middle East Institute  (US)
Middle East Institute of Japan  (JA)
Middle East International Publishers  (UK)
Middle East Librarians Association  (US)
Middle East Magazine Ltd.  (UK)
Middle East News Agency  (UA)
Middle East Observer  (UA)
Middle East Perspective, Inc.  (US)
Middle East Petroleum and Economic Publications  (LE)
Middle East Research and Action Group  (UK)
Middle East Research & Information Project  (US)
Middle East Research and Publishing Center  (LE)
Middle East Review  (UK)
Middle East Studies Association of North America, Inc.  (US)
Middle East Technical University  (TU)
Middle East Trade Publications Ltd.  (UK)
Middle Eastern Regional Radioisotope Centre for the Arab Countries  (UA)
Middle States Association of Colleges and Secondary Schools  (US)
Middlebury College  (US)
Middlesex & Surrey League for the Hard of Hearing  (UK)
Middlesex County Library  (CN)
Middlesex Hospital Medical School  (UK)
Middlesex Publishing Co., Ltd.  (UK)
MidEast Report, Inc.  (US)
Midiscope Pyrenees  (FR)
Midland Bank Ltd.  (UK)
Midland Cooperatives, Inc.  (US)
Midland Genealogical Society  (US)
Midland Lutheran College  (US)
Midland Medical Institute  (UK)
Midland Mutual Life Insurance Co.  (US)
Midland News Association Ltd.  (UK)
Midland Publications  (II)
Midlands Club Cricket Conference  (UK)
Midlands New Towns Society  (UK)
Midmarch Associates  (US)
Midnight Publishing Corp. Ltd.  (CN)
Midori-Shobo Co., Ltd.  (JA)
Midrex Corporation  (US)
Midwest Agricultural Relations, Inc.  (US)
Midwest Art  (US)
Midwest Association for Latin American Studies  (US)
Midwest Beverage Publications  (US)
Midwest Chaparral Poets  (US)
Midwest Conference of Political Scientists  (US)
Midwest Genealogical Society  (US)
Midwest History of Education Society  (US)
Midwest Modern Langage Association  (US)
Midwest Newsclip  (US)
Midwest Oil Register, Inc.  (US)
Midwest Outdoors  (US)
Midwest Petroleum Marketers Association  (US)
Midwest Publishers (Ann Arbor)  (US)
Midwest Publishing Co., Inc. (Skokie)  (US)
Mid-West Publishing Company, Inc. (Topeka)  (US)
Midwest Racing News, Inc.  (US)
Mid-West Records Inc  (US)
Midwest Research Institute  (US)
Midwest Review of Public Administration, Inc.  (US)
Midwest Sociological Society  (US)
Mid-West Tennessee Genealogical Society  (US)
Midwest Traders Ltd.  (US)
Midwest Wool Marketing Cooperative  (US)
Midwest World  (US)
Midwestern Association of Graduate Schools  (US)
Mid-Western Banker  (US)
Mie Daigaku
  see Mie University  (JA)
Mie-kenritsu Daigaku
  see Mie Prefectural University  (JA)
Mie Prefectural University. Faculty of Fisheries  (JA)
Mie Prefecture. Environmental Science Institute  (JA)
Mie University. School of Medicine  (JA)
Verlag Ista Mielke und Co.  (GW)
S. Migliarino  (IT)
Mignon  (MX)
Migraine Trust  (UK)
Migrant Legal Action Program  (US)
Mike Causey's Federal Employe Newsletter  (US)
Mil-Mac Publications Ltd.  (CN)
Milady Publishing Corporation  (US)
Milan. Federazione Provinciale Cooperative e Mutue  (IT)
Milan Law Publishers  (II)
Casa Editrice Dott. Antonio Milani  (IT)
Milano Sole Editore  (IT)
Milapweekly  (UK)
Milbank Memorial Fund  (US)
Miles Laboratories Inc.  (US)

Milestone Car Society Inc.  (US)
Militaergeschichtliches Forschungsamt  (GW)
Militaertekniska Foereningen  (SW)
Militaerverlag der Deutschen Demokratischen
  Republik  (GE)
Militancia  (AG)
Militancia: Temas del Socialismo  (MX)
Militant  (FR)
Militant  (UK)
Militant Publishing Association  (US)
Military Chaplains Association of the United States of
  America  (US)
Military Collectors News  (US)
Military Communications  (US)
Military Historical Society  (UK)
Military Historical Society of Australia  (AT)
Military History Associates, Inc.  (US)
Military History Society of Ireland  (IE)
Military Law Project  (US)
Military Order of the World Wars  (US)
Milk, Inc.  (US)
Milk Industry Foundation  (US)
Milk Marketing Board  (UK)
Milk Marketing Board for Northern Ireland  (UK)
Milky Way Press (San Francisco)  (US)
Milky Way Productions Inc.  (US)
Mill Hollow Corp.  (US)
Mill Trade Journal  (US)
Millennium Publishing Group  (UK)
Miller & Fink Corp.  (US)
William J. Miller Associates, Inc.  (US)
Ole Miller, Ed. & Pub.  (DK)
Miss Lee Miller, Ed. & Pub.  (US)
Miller Electric Manufacturing Co.  (US)
Miller Index  (US)
Miller Publishing Co.  (US)
Milli Kutuphane
  see Turkey. National Library  (TU)
Millimeter Magazine Inc.  (US)
Millinery and Boutique  (UK)
Millinery Research Corporation  (US)
Million Dollar Round Table  (US)
Millionaires of Today or Tomorrow  (US)
Societe d'Editions Millot et Cie  (FR)
Mills and Boon Ltd.  (UK)
Mills College. Associated Students  (US)
Milton College Student Senate  (US)
Milton Helpern Library of Legal Medicine  (US)
Milton Publishing Co. Ltd.  (UK)
Milton Society of America  (US)
Milwaukee. Bureau of Budget and Management
  Analysis  (US)
Milwaukee County News  (US)
Milwaukee District Nurses' Association  (US)
Milwaukee Fire Department Athletic Association
  (US)
Milwaukee Public Library  (US)
Milwaukee Public Museum  (US)
Milwaukee Public Schools  (US)
Mimar  (IT)

Mimram Books  (UK)

Lettres Modernes (Minard)  (FR)

Minaret  (II)

Minas Gerais, Brazil. Departamento de Estradas de
  Rodagem. Servico de Transito  (BL)
Mind Association  (US)
Mindanao State University. Research Center  (PH)
Mindolo Ecumenical Foundation  (ZA)
Mine Medical Officers' Association of South Africa
  (SA)
Mine Surface Officials' Association of South Africa
  (SA)
Mine Ventilation Society of South Africa  (SA)
Mineracao Metalurgia  (BL)
Mineral Digest, Ltd.  (US)
Mineral Research and Exploration Institute of Turkey
  (TU)
Mineraloelwirtschafts Verband e.V.  (GW)
Mineralogical Association of Canada  (CN)
Mineralogical Record, Inc.  (US)
Mineralogical Society  (UK)
Mineralogical Society of America  (US)
Mineralogical Society of India  (II)
Mineralogical Society of Japan  (JA)
Minerals and Metals Trading Corp. of India Ltd.  (II)
Miners Federation of Australia  (AT)
Miners' International Federation  (UK)
Edizioni Minerva Medica  (IT)
Minerva-Verlag  (GW)
Minerva-Verlag Thinnes und Nolte  (GW)
Mini-Micro Systems  (US)
Miniature Armoured Fighting Vehicle Association
  (UK)
Minimax  (II)
Mining and Allied Machinery Corporation  (II)
Mining and Metallurgical Society of Finland

  see Vuorimiesyhdistys  (FI)
Mining Association of Canada  (CN)
Mining Engineering Society of Turkey  (TU)
Mining Engineers Association  (II)
Mining Equipment News  (US)
Mining, Geological & Metallurgical Institute of India
  (II)
Mining Journal Ltd.  (UK)
Mining Research & Service Organization  (CH)
Ministerial Sisterhood Unitarian Universalist  (US)

Ministers Life Resources, Inc.  (US)

Wydawnictwo Ministerstwa Obrony Narodowej  (PL)

Ministikok  (CN)

Ministry of Christ Church  (US)

Minkus Publications Inc.  (US)

Minneapolis Athletic Club  (US)

Minneapolis District Dental Journal  (US)
Minneapolis Medical Research Foundation, Inc.  (US)
Minneapolis Society of Fine Arts  (US)
Minnesota. Criminal Justice Information Section
  (US)
Minnesota. Department of Administration  (US)
Minnesota. Department of Agriculture  (US)
Minnesota. Department of Corrections  (US)
Minnesota. Department of Economic Development
  (US)
Minnesota. Department of Education  (US)
Minnesota. Department of Education. Office of Public
  Libraries and Interlibrary Cooperation  (US)
Minnesota. Department of Employment Services
  (US)
Minnesota. Department of Health  (US)
Minnesota. Department of Human Rights  (US)
Minnesota. Department of Natural Resources  (US)
Minnesota. Department of Natural Resources. Division
  of Fish and Wildlife  (US)
Minnesota. Department of Public Safety  (US)
Minnesota. Department of Public Welfare  (US)
Minnesota. Department of Public Welfare. Public
  Information, Education Section  (US)
Minnesota. Department of Revenue  (US)
Minnesota. Geological Survey  (US)
Minnesota. Governor's Commission on Crime
  Prevention and Control  (US)
Minnesota. Health Statistics Section  (US)
Minnesota. Office of Ombudsman for Corrections
  (US)
Minnesota. Office of Revisor of Statutes  (US)
Minnesota. Pollution Control Agency  (US)
Minnesota. State Board of Health  (US)
Minnesota. State Manpower Council  (US)
Minnesota. State Planning Agency. Development
  Planning Division  (US)
Minnesota. State Planning Agency. Environmental
  Planning Section  (US)
Minnesota Academy of Science  (US)
Minnesota Association of Plumbing-Heating-Cooling
  Contractors Inc.  (US)
Minnesota Center for Philosophy of Science  (US)
Minnesota Congress of Parents, Teachers and Students
  (US)
Minnesota Dental Association  (US)
Minnesota Education Association  (US)
Minnesota Education Association. Northern Division
  (US)
Minnesota Federated Women's Clubs  (US)
Minnesota Food Retailers Association  (US)
Minnesota Geographic Society  (US)
Minnesota Great Lakes Commission  (US)
Minnesota Historical Society  (US)
Minnesota Law Review Foundation  (US)
Minnesota Leader  (US)
Minnesota League for Nursing  (US)
Minnesota Motor Transport Association  (US)
Minnesota Music Educators Association  (US)
Minnesota Newspaper Association  (US)
Minnesota Nurses Association  (US)
Minnesota Optometric Association  (US)
Minnesota Ornithologist's Union  (US)
Minnesota Police & Peace Officers Association  (US)
Minnesota Private College Fund  (US)
Minnesota Review  (US)
Minnesota Sentinel Publishing Co.  (US)
Minnesota Society of Architects  (US)
Minnesota Speech and Hearing Association  (US)
Minnesota State Automobile Association  (US)
Minnesota State Horticultural Society  (US)
Minnesota State Medical Association  (US)
Minnesota State Pharmaceutical Association  (US)
Minnesota State Sheriffs Association  (US)
Minnesota Turkey Growers Association  (US)
Minnesota Vocational Association  (US)
Minnesota Women's Center  (US)
R. B. Minogue  (US)

Minority Business Information Institute  (US)

Minority Forum  (II)
Minority Report  (II)
Minority Research Center  (US)
Minority Rights Group  (UK)
Minot State College. Publications Board  (US)
Minotaur Press  (US)
Minskii Radiotekhnicheskii Institut  (UR)
Izdatel'stvo Mintis  (UR)
Editions de Minuit  (FR)
Minutemen  (US)
Raul M. Mir Rague, Ed. & Pub.  (SP)
Mira  (II)
Editorial Mirador  (AG)
Mirage  (US)
Mirage Press (Baltimore)  (US)
Miramar Publishing Co.  (US)
Miramoor Publications Ltd.  (UK)
Mirchandi & Co. Pvt. Ltd.  (II)
Alberto Mirkin  (AG)
Mirror  (CN)
Mirror Class Association of Australia  (AT)
Mirror Newspapers Ltd.  (AT)
Mirror Northwest  (US)
Karlo Mirth, Ed. & Pub.  (US)
G. Rabbani Mirza, Ed. & Pub.  (PK)
Misaki Marine Biological Station
  see under University of Tokyo  (JA)
Casa Editrice Miscellanea Francescana  (IT)
Mise en Page  (FR)
Mise-en-Scene  (US)
Misioneros Combonianos. Congregacion Misionera
  (SP)
Misioneros del Sagrado Corazon  (SP)
Misioneros Hijos del Corazon de Maria (Claretianos)
  (SP)
Misioneros Javerianos  (SP)
Basudeo Misra, Ed. & Pub.  (II)
Miss Black America  (US)
Missao de Estudos Agronomicos do Ultramar  (PO)
Misset-Amersfoort  (NE)
Uitgeversmaatschappij C. Misset B. V.  (NE)
Missi  (FR)
Missiezusters van Sint Petrus Claver  (NE)
Mission Archeologique et Ethnologique Francaise au
  Mexique  (MX)
Mission Aviation Fellowship  (US)
Mission Catholique  (ZR)
Mission Journal, Inc.  (US)
Mission of the State of Kuwait to the United Nations
  (US)
Mission Press  (SA)
Mission Press  (ZA)
Missionaires de la Consolata  (CN)
Missionaires Volontaires Adventistes  (FR)
Missionare von Mariannhill  (AU)
Missionari Comboniani  (IT)
Missionari del Preziosissimo Sangue  (IT)
Missionaries of the Sacred Heart  (AT)
Missionarissen van Scheut  (NE)
Missionary Oblates of Mary Immaculate  (LO)
Missionary Society of St. Paul the Apostle in the State
  of New York  (US)
Missionary Society of the Oblate Fathers of Texas
  (US)
Missionhurst, Inc.  (US)
Missioni della Compagnia di Gesu  (IT)
Missionnaires du Sacre-Coeur  (CN)
Missionnaires Oblats de Marie Immaculee  (FR)
Missions Advanced Research & Communication
  Center  (US)
Missions des Peres des Sainte-Croix  (CN)
Missions Education  (US)
Missions to Seamen  (UK)
Missionsanstalt der Pallottiner  (GW)
Missionsbund zur Ausbreitung des Evangeliums
  (GW)
Missionshaus Bibelschule Wiedenest  (GW)
Missionssaellskapet Bibeltrogna Vaenner  (SW)
Missionwerk Neues Leben e.V.  (GW)
Mississauga Public Library  (US)
Mississippi. Agricultural & Industrial Board  (US)
Mississippi. Board of Architecture  (US)
Mississippi. Department of Education  (US)
Mississippi. Game and Fish Commission  (US)
Mississippi. Governor's Office of Human Resources
  (US)
Mississippi Library Commission  (US)
Mississippi Agricultural and Forestry Experiment
  Station  (US)
Mississippi Arts Commission  (US)
Mississippi Association of Educators  (US)
Mississippi Band of Choctaw Indians  (US)
Mississippi Bankers Association  (US)
Mississippi Baptist Convention Board  (US)
Mississippi Board of Trustees of State Institutions of
  Higher Learning  (US)
Mississippi Cattlemen's Association  (US)
Mississippi Congress of Parents and Teachers  (US)

Mississippi Council for Geographic Education   (US)
Mississippi Dental Association   (US)
Mississippi Farm Bureau Federation   (US)
Mississippi Folklore Society   (US)
Mississippi Hereford Association   (US)
Mississippi Historical Society   (US)
Mississippi Library Association   (US)
Mississippi Marine Resources Council   (US)
Mississippi Modern Language Association   (US)
Mississippi Mud   (US)
Mississippi Municipal Association   (US)
Mississippi Music Educators Association   (US)
Mississippi Nurses' Association   (US)
Mississippi Rag, Inc.   (US)
Mississippi Research and Development Center   (US)
Mississippi Retail Grocers Association   (US)
Mississippi State Medical Association   (US)
Mississippi State University. Christian Student Center
   (US)
Mississippi State University. College of Arts and
   Sciences   (US)
Mississippi State University. College of Business &
   Industry   (US)
Mississippi State University. Forest Products
   Utilization Laboratory   (US)
Mississippi State University. Graduate School   (US)
Mississippi State University. Mitchell Memorial
   Library   (US)
Mississippi State University. Water Resources
   Research Institute   (US)
Mississippi Valley Publishing Co.   (US)
Missouri. Air Conservation Commission   (US)
Missouri. Center for Health Statistics   (US)
Missouri. Department of Community Affairs   (US)
Missouri. Department of Conservation   (US)
Missouri. Department of Elementary and Secondary
   Education   (US)
Missouri. Department of Higher Education   (US)
Missouri. Department of Mental Health. Division of
   Alcoholism and Drug Abuse   (US)
Missouri. Department of Natural Resources   (US)
Missouri. Department of Natural Resources. Division
   of Geology and Land Survey   (US)
Missouri. Department of Public Health and Welfare.
   Division of Mental Health   (US)
Missouri. Department of Revenue   (US)
Missouri. Department of Social Services. Division of
   Health   (US)
Missouri. Disaster Planning and Operations Office
   (US)
Missouri. Division of Commerce and Industrial
   Development   (US)
Missouri. Division of Fisheries   (US)
Missouri. Division of Highway Safety   (US)
Missouri. Division of Insurance   (US)
Missouri. Division of Youth Services   (US)
Missouri. Public Service Commission   (US)
Missouri. State Library   (US)
Missouri Academy of General Practice   (US)
Missouri Archaeological Society   (US)
Missouri Area Bluegrass Committee   (US)
Missouri Association of Osteopathic Physicians and
   Surgeons   (US)
Missouri Association of Teachers of English   (US)
Missouri Association of Trial Attorneys   (US)
Missouri Baptist Convention   (US)
Missouri Bar   (US)
Missouri Beef Cattleman, Inc.   (US)
Missouri Botanical Garden   (US)
Missouri Congress of Parents and Teachers
   Associations   (US)
Missouri Council of Architects, Inc.   (US)
Missouri Dental Association   (US)
Missouri Farm Bureau Federation   (US)
Missouri Historical Society   (US)
Missouri L P Gas Association   (US)
Missouri Library Association   (US)
Missouri Life, Inc.   (US)
Missouri Municipal League   (US)
Missouri Music Educators Association   (US)
Missouri Nurses Association   (US)
Missouri Oil Jobbers Association   (US)
Missouri Pacific Railroad Co.   (US)
Missouri Pharmaceutical Association   (US)
Missouri Police Chiefs Association   (US)
Missouri Political Science Association   (US)
Missouri Power & Light Co.   (US)
Missouri Press Association   (US)
Missouri Province Educational Institute   (US)
Missouri Regional Medical Program   (US)
Missouri River Basin Commission   (US)
Missouri School Boards Association   (US)
Missouri Society of Professional Engineers   (US)
Missouri Speleological Society   (US)
Missouri Speleological Survey, Inc.   (US)
Missouri State Medical Association   (US)
Missouri State Teachers Association   (US)
Missouri Training Center for Men   (US)

Missouri Valley Adult Education Association   (US)
Missouri Valley Economic Association   (US)
Missouri Veterinary Medical Association   (US)
Mita Society for Library and Information Science
   (JA)
Mitchell College of Advanced Education. Business and
   Administration Society   (AT)
George Mitchell, Ed. & Pub.   (CN)
Dwight Emerson Mitchell, Ed. & Pub.   (US)
Gary D. Mitchell, Ed. & Pub.   (US)
Mitchell Manuals, Inc.   (US)
Mithila Research Institute   (II)
Dhiren Mitra, Ed. & Pub.   (II)
Mitra & Ghosh Publishers Pvt. Ltd.   (II)
Mitsubishi Bank   (JA)
Mitsubishi Economic Research Institute   (JA)
Mitsubishi Electric Corporation   (JA)
Mitsubishi Electric Corporation. Central Research
   Laboratory   (JA)
Mitsubishi Heavy Industries Ltd.   (JA)
Mitsui and Co. Australia, Ltd.   (AT)
Mitsui & Co., Ltd.   (JA)
Mitsui Engineering & Shipbuilding Co., Ltd.   (JA)
Mittag- Lefflers Matematiska Stiftelse   (SW)
Mitteldeutscher Saengerbund e.V.   (GW)
Seymour Mittlemark Organization Inc.   (US)
Verlag E. S. Mittler und Sohn GmbH   (GW)
Mitzion Tetzeh Torah, Ltd.   (IS)
Miyazaki University. Faculty of Engineering   (JA)
Mizrachi Federation   (CN)
Mizrachi Women's Organization of America   (US)
Mlada Fronta   (CS)
Mlado Pokolenje   (YU)
Mladost   (YU)
Mo-Kan Bi-State Planning Commission   (US)
Mobay Chemical Corporation. Chemagro Agricultural
   Division   (US)
Mobil Oil Portuguesa   (PO)
Mobile Area Chamber of Commerce   (US)
Mobile Genealogical Society   (US)
Mobile Post Office Society   (US)
Mobile Publications Ltd.   (CN)
Mobilia Press A-S   (DK)
Mockingbird Press   (US)
Mode International   (FR)
Model Aeroplane Gazette   (UK)
Model & Allied Publications Ltd.   (UK)
Model T Ford Club of America   (US)
Modelisme   (FR)
Modellbahnen-Welt Verlags-GmbH   (GW)
Societa Tipografia Editrice Modenese   (IT)
Moderata Samlingspartiets Riksorganisation   (SW)
Moderata Ungdomsforbundet   (SW)
Modern Book Depot   (PK)
Modern Brewery Age Publishing Co.   (US)
Modern Byggteknik Team   (SW)
Modern Churchmen's Union   (UK)
Modern Country Music Association   (AT)
Modern Cycle Publishing Co. Inc.   (US)
Modern Data Services, Inc.   (US)
Modern Day Periodicals, Inc.   (US)
Modern Greek Society: a Newsletter.   (US)
Modern Greek Studies Association   (US)
Modern Handcraft, Inc.   (US)
Modern Housing Inc.   (US)
Modern Humanities Research Association   (UK)
Modern Keyboard Review   (US)
Modern Language Association   (UK)
Modern Language Association. English X Group
   (US)
Modern Language Association of America   (US)
Modern Language Association of America. Center for
   Editions of American Authors   (US)
Modern Language Association of America.
   Comparative Romance Linguistics Section   (US)
Modern Language Association of America Conference
   (US)
Modern Language Association of America. Conference
   on Research Opportunities in Renaissance Drama
   (US)
Modern Language Association of America. Early
   American Literature Group   (US)
Modern Language Association of America, Old
   English Group   (US)
Modern Language Association of America. Oriental-
   Western Literary Relations Group   (US)
Modern Language Association of America, Popular
   Literature Section   (US)
Modern Language Association of America. Southern
   Conference on Language Teaching   (US)
Modern Language Association of America. Spanish I
   Section   (US)
Modern Language Association. Seminar on Science-
   Fiction   (US)
Modern Language Society
   see Uusfilologinens Yhdistys   (FI)
Modern Language Teachers' Association of New South
   Wales   (AT)

Modern Language Teachers Association of Sweden
   see Riksfoereningen Foer Laerarna i Moderna
   Spraak   (SW)
Modern Language Teachers Association of Victoria
   (AT)
Modern Magaz.nes (Holdings) Ltd.   (AT)
Modern Medicine of Australia Pty. Ltd.   (AT)
Modern Medicine of New Zealand Ltd.   (NZ)
Modern Metals Publications Ltd.   (UK)
Modern Microfilm Co.   (US)
Modern Newspapers (Pty) Ltd.   (SA)
Modern People Productions   (US)
Modern Photography   (US)
Modern Poetry Association   (US)
Modern Poetry in Translation Ltd.   (UK)
Modern Poetry Studies   (US)
Modern Productions Ltd   (NZ)
Modern Psychoanalytic Publications   (US)
Modern Publications   (RH)
Modern Publications Co. Ltd.   (NR)
Modern Publications Ltd.   (NZ)
Modern Teaching Methods Association   (AT)
Moderna Organizacija   (YU)
Modernage   (US)
Moderne Databehandling   (NO)
Moderne Industrie Publikationsgesellschaft   (GW)
Edizioni Moderne Internazionali   (IT)
Moderner Verlag   (GW)
Modernist Studies: Literature and Culture, 1920-1940
   (CN)
Modine Gunch Press   (US)
Modino Press Ltd.   (UK)
Moditalia   (IT)
Modus Publications (Pvt.) Ltd.   (RH)
Moebelhandlernes Landsforbund   (NO)
Moebelindustrins Service AB   (SW)
Verlag der Moebelspediteur   (GW)
Heinrich Moeller Soehne GmbH   (GW)
Heinz Moeller-Verlag   (GW)
R. Moellerfors, Ed. & Pub.   (SW)
Moench Verlagsgesellschaft mbH   (GW)
Moffat Publishing Co. Ltd.   (UK)
Mofussil   (UK)
Abdul Hafez Mohammad, Ed. & Pub.   (JO)
S. S. Mohan   (II)
Mohawk Nation. Program in American Studies   (US)
Mohegan Fine Arts Committee   (US)
Verlag J.C.B. Mohr (Paul Siebeck)   (GW)
Mojo Navigator(e)   (US)
Mokuzai Kenkyusho
   see Wood Research Institute   (JA)
H. N. & A. L. Moldenke, Eds. & Pubs.   (US)
Peter Moll Africa Ltd.   (KE)
Izdatel'stvo Molod   (UR)
Izdatel'stvo Molodaya Gvardiya   (UR)
Edgardo Moltoni, Ed. & Pub.   (IT)
Moment Magazine Associates   (US)
Momento   (IT)
Editorial Momento C.A.   (VE)
Momentum Press   (US)
Momo's Press   (US)
Publications Mon Bebe   (CN)
Mon Jardin et Ma Maison   (FR)
Mona   (CS)
Monarch International - Gold and Silver Exchange
   (CN)
Monarchist League   (UK)
Monarchist League of Canada   (CN)
Monarchist Press Association   (UK)
Monaro Conservation Society   (AT)
Monash University   (AT)
Monash University. Anthropology and Sociology
   Society   (AT)
Monash University. Centre of Southeast Asian Studies
   (AT)
Monash University. Department of Civil Engineering
   (AT)
Monash University. Department of Classical Studies
   (AT)
Monash University. Department of French   (AT)
Monash University. Department of Geography   (AT)
Monash University. English Department   (AT)
Monash University. Faculty of Law   (AT)
Monash University. Higher Education Advisory and
   Research Unit   (AT)
Monash University. Monash Engineering Students
   Society   (AT)
Monash University. Science Fiction Association   (AT)
Monastere Benedictin, Chevetogne   (BE)
Monastere de Saint Andre   (BE)
Monastero esarchico di Grottaferrata   (IT)
Monastero S. Benedetto   (IT)
Monbu-sho Kokuritsu Idengaku Kenkyusho
   see Japan. National Institute of Genetics   (JA)
Arnoldo Mondadori Editore   (IT)
Monday Morning Press   (US)
Monde   (FR)
Mondes Asiatiques   (FR)

Mondo Afro-Asiatico (IT)
Mondo Bancario (IT)
Mondo Cinese (IT)
Societa Editoriale Mondo Economico (IT)
Mondo Occulto (IT)
Editorial Moneda y Credito (SP)
Monetary Research Ltd (BM)
Monete e Medaglie (IT)
Monex International Ltd. (US)
Editorial Monex S. de R.L. y C.V. (MX)
Money Digest Press, Inc. (US)
Money Making Reporter (US)
Money Market Directories, Inc. (US)
Money Market Investor, Inc. (US)
Mongolia Society (US)
Moniposti (FI)
Moniteur Africain (SG)
Moniteur des Travaux Publics et du Batiment (FR)
Monitor Book Co. Inc. (US)
Monitor Consultants (UK)
Monitor Publications (Miami) (US)
Monitor Publishing (Washington) (US)
Monitor Trade Publications Inc. (US)
Monitor-Verlag (GW)
Monks of St. John's Abbey (US)
Monks Wood Experimental Station (UK)
Monmouth College (US)
Monmouth County Education Association (US)
Monmouth-Ocean Development Council (US)
Monnaie de Paris (FR)
Casa Editrice Felice le Monnier (IT)
Monogram Publications (UK)
Monograph Association of India (II)
Monographies de l'Industrie et du Commerce en France (FR)
Monotype Corp. Ltd. (UK)
Juan A. Monroy (SP)
Monsalvat (SP)
Monster Times Publishing Co., Inc. (US)
Montag Publications (US)
Montagu Ventures Ltd. (UK)
Empresa Editorial Federico Montagud de Miguel (SP)
Montan- und Wirtschaftsverlag GmbH (GW)
Montana. Advisory Council for Vocational Education (US)
Montana. Bureau of Mines and Geology (US)
Montana. Criminal Justice Data Center (US)
Montana. Department of Business Regulation (US)
Montana. Department of Health and Environmental Services (US)
Montana. Department of Livestock. Animal Health Division (US)
Montana. Department of Military Affairs (US)
Montana. Department of Natural Resources and Conservation (US)
Montana. Department of Public Instruction (US)
Montana. Department of Social and Rehabilitation Services (US)
Montana. Division of Planning and Economic Development (US)
Montana. Environmental Quality Council (US)
Montana. Office of Budget & Program Planning (US)
Montana. Office of Public Instruction (US)
Montana. Office of the Legislative Auditor (US)
Montana. State Library (US)
Montana. Water Resources Division (US)
Montana Archaeological Society (US)
Montana Associated Utilities (US)
Montana Education Association (US)
Montana Farm Bureau Federation (US)
Montana Food Distributors Association (US)
Montana Forest and Conservation Experiment Station (US)
Montana Grain Growers Association (US)
Montana Historical Society (US)
Montana Law Enforcement Academy (US)
Montana League of Cities & Towns (US)
Montana Motor Transport Association, Inc. (US)
Montana Music Educators Association (US)
Montana Oil Journal, Inc. (US)
Montana Press Association (US)
Montana Reconnaissance Project (US)
Montana State University (US)
Montana State University. Associated Students (US)
Montana State University. Cooperative Extension Service (US)
Montana State University. Mathematics Department (US)
Montana Stockgrowers Association (US)
Montana University Joint Water Resources Research Center (US)
Montana Wool Growers Association (US)
Montaneros de Aragon (SP)
Montcalm Publishing Corp. (US)
Editions Montchrestien (FR)
Montclair Art Museum (US)
Montclair Board of Education (US)

Montclair State College. Center for Economic Education (US)
Montclair State College. Department of Adult Continuing Education (US)
Monte dei Paschi di Siena (IT)
Montebello Teachers Association (US)
Publications Paul Montel (FR)
Montemora Foundation Inc. (US)
Montepio de Perfumistas y Drogueros (SP)
Monterey Savings and Loan Association (US)
Fernando Montes Matte S. J. (CL)
Montfort Fathers (CN)
Montfort Missionaries (US)
Montgomery-Bucks County Dental Society (US)
Monthly Film Making (UK)
Monthly Guardian (PK)
Monthly Review, Inc. (US)
Monthly Review of Management Research (US)
Montreal Baseball Club Ltd. (CN)
Montreal Catholic School Commission (CN)
Montreal Children's Hospital (CN)
Montreal General Hospital (CN)
Montreal International Airport (CN)
Montreal Museum of Fine Arts (CN)
Montreal Standard Publishing Co. (CN)
Montreal Stock Exchange (CN)
Montreal Teachers Association (CN)
Montreal Urban Community Policemen's Brotherhood Inc. (CN)
Montreaux TV Symposium (SZ)
Monument Builders of North America (US)
Monument Press (US)
Monumenta Serica Institute (GW)
Monumenti Musei e Gallerie Pontifice (VC)
Moodies Services, Ltd. (UK)
Moody Bible Institute of Chicago (US)
Moody's Investors Service, Inc. (US)
S. C. Mookerjee (II)
Moonbeam Publications (US)
Moonraker Press (UK)
Moonshine (UK)
Moorbad Neydharting (AU)
K. E. Moore, Ed. & Pub. (US)
Moorhead State College (US)
Moorpack College (US)
Moot: Thirkill - Threlkeld Family Newsletter (UK)
Mora Ferenc Konyvkiado (HU)
J. Victor Morais, Ed. & Pub. (MY)
Moral Education Forum (US)
D. Antonio Morales Rodriguez, Ed. & Pub. (SP)
Morality in Media, Inc. (US)
Donald Norman Moran, Ed. & Pub. (US)
Moravian Church in America-North and South (US)
Moravian Church in Great Britain (UK)
Moravian Music Foundation (US)
Moravske Muzeum (CS)
Moravske Muzeum. Numismaticke Oddeleni (CS)
Moray Publications (UK)
Charles C. Morchand Co., Inc. (US)
Editrice Morcelliana (IT)
Moreana Publications (FR)
Morehead State University (US)
Morehouse-Barlow Co. (US)
Morehouse College (US)
Morehouse College. Public Relations and Alumni Affairs Office (US)
Moreland School District (US)
Rene Moreux et Cie (FR)
Robert Morey Associates (US)
Morgan & Morgan, Inc. (US)
G. Russell Morgan, Ed. & Pub. (US)
Morgan-Grampian (Construction Press) Ltd. (UK)
Morgan-Grampian (Professional Press) Ltd. (UK)
Morgan-Grampian (Publishers) Ltd. (UK)
Morgan- Grampian, Inc. (US)
Morgan Guaranty Trust Co. of New York (US)
Morgan Guaranty Trust Co. of New York. Trust and Investment Division (US)
Morgan Press (US)
A. E. Morgan Publications Ltd. (UK)
Roy Morgan Research Centre Pty. Ltd. (AT)
Nigel Morland, Ed. & Pub. (UK)
Kay Titus Mormino, Ed. & Pub. (US)
Mormon History Association (US)
Morning (JO)
Morning Star Press (US)
Morocco. Direction de la Statistique (MR)
Morocco. Direction des Mines et de la Geologie (MR)
Morocco. Division des Antiquites (MR)
Morpeth-Northumbrian Gathering Committee (UK)
Sydney Morrell & Co. Inc. (US)
Morris Arboretum (US)
Robert Morris Associates (US)
Morris Harvey College Publications (US)
William Morris Society (UK)

A. B. Morse Co. (US)
Morsingboernes Forening (DK)
Morski Instytut Rybacki (PL)
Wydawnictwo Morskie (PL)
Ernst G. Mortensens Forlag (NO)
Mortgage Bankers Association of America (US)
Morton Arboretum (US)
Morton Associates Ltd. (UK)
Morton Newspapers Ltd. (UK)
Morton Publications Ltd. (UK)
Editora Morumbi (BL)
Mosaic Press (CN)
Mosaisk Troessamfund (DK)
Mosaiska Forsamlingens Committee for Judar i Sovjet (SW)
C. V. Mosby Co. (US)
Mosca Profana (CU)
Moscow Narodny Bank Quarterly Review (UK)
Moskovskaya Patriarkhiya (UR)
Moskovskaya Publichnaya Biblioteka (UR)
Moskovskii Gorodskii Sovet Deputatov Trudyashchikhsya (UR)
Moskovskii Gosudarstvennyi Institut Kul'tury (UR)
Moskovskii Gosudarstvennyi Pedagogicheskii Institut Inostrannykh Yazykov (UR)
Moskovskii Institut Geologii i Razvedki (UR)
Moskovskii Institut Stali i Splavov (UR)
Moskovskii Universitet (UR)
Moskovskii Universitet. Kafedra Gruntovedeniya i Inzhenernoi Geologii (UR)
Moskovskoe Obshchestvo Ispytatelei Prirody (UR)
Moss Side Press (UK)
Ignacio H. de la Mota, Ed. & Pub. (SP)
Motamar
   see World Muslim Congress (PK)
Motamar al-Alam al-Islam
   see World Muslim Congress (PK)
Mother Cabrini League (US)
Mother Earth News, Inc. (US)
Mothers' Manual Inc. (US)
Mothers' Union (UK)
Mothers' Union in Australia (AT)
Motion Canada Media Productions Ltd. (CN)
Motion Picture Editor's Federal Credit Union (US)
Motor Agents Association Ltd. (UK)
Motor Cargo, Inc. (US)
Motor Carrier Service Inc. (US)
Motor Club of America (US)
Motor Industries Federation (SA)
Motor Industry Research Association (UK)
Motor Italia (IT)
Motor Mundial, S.A. (SP)
Motor News Market Place (UK)
Motor Publications (US)
Motor Sport Magazine Ltd. (UK)
Motor Traders Association of N.S.W. (AT)
Motor Transport Association of Connecticut (US)
Motor Transport Fact Book (US)
Motor Transport Owners' Association in South Africa (SA)
Motor Transportation Association of South Carolina, Inc. (US)
Motor Vehicle Manufacturers Association of the U.S. Inc. (US)
Vereinigte Motor-Verlage GmbH und Co. KG (GW)
Motorboat, Inc (US)
Motorbranschens Foerlag (SW)
Motorbranschens Riksfoerbund (SW)
Motorfoerernes Avholdsforbund (NO)
Mototidningen Kart (SW)
Mount Allison University (CN)
Mount Allison University. Federated Alumni (CN)
Mount Alverno Press (US)
Mount Desert Island Biological Laboratory (US)
Mount Holyoke College. Alumnae Association (US)
Mount Saint Mary's College (US)
Mount St. Scholastica Convent (US)
Mount Salus Press (IE)
Mount Saviour Monastery (US)
Mount Sinai Hospital (US)
Mount Washington Observatory Inc. (US)
Mountain Business Publishing (US)
Mountain Call, Inc. (US)
Mountain Club of Maryland (US)
Mountain Empire Publishing, Inc. (US)
Mountain Life Ltd. (UK)
Mountain Magazine Ltd. (UK)
Mountain Plains Adult Education Association (US)
Mountain-Plains Library Association (US)
Mountain Press (US)
Mountain Publishing Co Inc (US)
Mountain Safety Research (US)
Mountain States Publishing Co. (US)
Mountaineers (US)
Mountains Land Use Research Laboratory
   see under Iwate University (JA)
Mountainside Publishing, Inc (US)

Mouth (US)
Mouth of the Dragon (US)
Mouthpiece Publications (UK)
Editions Mouton et Cie (FR)
Mouton Publishers (NE)
Mouvement contre le Racisme l'Antisemitisme et pour la Paix (FR)
Mouvement de la Condition Masculine (FR)
Mouvement de Liberation Nationale (UV)
Mouvement des Cadres, Ingenieurs et Dirigeants Chretiens (M.C.C.) (FR)
Mouvement des Sionistes Originaires. d'A.F.N. (Afrique Francaise du Nord) (FR)
Mouvement Eucharistique du Canada (CN)
Mouvement Federaliste European (FR)
Mouvement Federaliste Francaise (FR)
Mouvement International de la Reconciliation (FR)
Mouvement Missionnaire Interieur Laique (FR)
Mouvement pour le Desarmement, la Paix et la Liberte (FR)
Mouvement Rural de Jeunesse Chretienne (FR)
Movement (UK)
Movement for Economic Justice (US)
Movement Shorthand Society (US)
Movie Magazine Ltd. (UK)
Movie-TV Marketing (JA)
Ediciones del Movimento (SP)
Movimento Adulti Scouts e Guide Cattolici Italiani (IT)
Movimento Circoli della Didattica (IT)
Movimento Familiar Cristao (BL)
Movimento Gaetano Salvemini (IT)
Movimento Laureati di Azione Cattolica (IT)
Movimento Politico dei Lavoratori (IT)
Movimento Universale de Ordine Integrale (IT)
Prensa del Movimiento (SP)
Movimiento de Reconciliacion en la Argentina (AG)
Movimiento Internacional de Estudiantes Catolicos (PE)
Moving On (US)
Moving Out (US)
Moxxom Magazines (Pty) Ltd. (SA)
Mozambique. Direccao dos Services das Alfandegas (MZ)
Mozambique. Direccao dos Servicos dos Portos, Caminhos de Ferro e Transportes (MZ)
Mozambique. Harbours, Railways and Transports Administration
  see Mozambique. Direccao dos Servicos dos Portos, Caminhos de Ferro e Transportes (MZ)
Mozambique. Inspeccao Provincial de Educacao (MZ)
Mozambique. Servico Meteorologico (MZ)
Mozartgemeinde Wien (AU)
Mphala Creative Society (ZA)
Mr. Cogito (US)
Ms. Atlas Press (US)
Ms Magazine Corporation (US)
Mt. Isa Writers Workshop (AT)
Mu Alpha Theta (US)
Mu Beta Psi National Honorary Musical Fraternity (US)
Mu Phi Epsilon International Music Sorority (US)
Verlag Hermann Mucke. Astronomisches Buero (AU)
Verlag Walter G. Muehlau (GW)
Verlagsgesellschaft Rudolf Mueller (GW)
Buchdruckerei Robert Mueller AG (SZ)
Mueller Electric Co (US)
Verlag Lambert Mueller GmbH (GW)
C.F. Mueller GmbH (Karlsrune) (GW)
Otto Mueller Verlag (AU)
Muenchen. Amt fuer Statistik und Datenanalyse (GW)
Muenchner Entomologische Gesellschaft (GW)
Muenchner Handelsverein (GW)
Muenchner Kammerspiele (GW)
Kommissions-Verlag Muenstermann (GW)
Muenzen und Medaillen AG (SZ)
Mugwumps' Instrument (US)
Muhammads Mosque No. 2 (US)
Muiderkring B.V. (NE)
Mujer de America (CK)
Mukherjee Library (II)
Societa Editrice Il Mulino (IT)
Mullard Ltd. (UK)
Mullen Publications, Inc. (US)
Arthur W. Muller, Ed. & Pub. (US)
Multi-Communication Ministries, Inc. (US)
Multi-Science Publishing Co. Ltd. (UK)
Multidex Computing Co. (US)
Multimedia Education Inc. (US)
Multiple Sclerosis Society (UK)
Multiscience Publications Ltd. (CN)
Multnomah County Medical Society (US)
Mundartfreunde Oesterreichs (AU)
Publicaciones Mundial (SP)

Mundo Cultural (BL)
Mundo Financiero (SP)
Mundo Gastronomico (MX)
Ediciones Mundo Hispanico (SP)
Mundo Israelita (AG)
Mundo Madereru (AG)
Ediciones Mundo Marina S.A. (MX)
Mundo Medico (MX)
Ediciones Mundo, S. A. (SP)
Mundus (IT)
Munford Publications, Inc. (US)
Munich Roundup (GW)
Municipal Association of Tasmania (AT)
Municipal Association of Victoria (AT)
Municipal Bond News Inc. (US)
Municipal Clerks Association of N.J. Inc. (US)
Municipal Corporation of Greater Bombay (II)
Municipal Engineering Publications Ltd. (UK)
Municipal Engineers of the City of New York (US)
Municipal Finance Officers Association (US)
Municipal Forms Ltd. (CN)
Municipal Journal Ltd. (UK)
Municipal Law Reports, Inc. (US)
Municipal League of Seattle & King County (US)
Municipal Publications (UK)
Municipal Publications, Inc. (Boston) (US)
Municipal Publications, Inc. (Philadelphia) (US)
Municipal Reference Library (US)
Municipal Research and Services Center of Washington (US)
Municipal Tramways Trust (AT)
Municipal World Ltd. (CN)
Municipalia (SP)
Municipality of Metropolitan Toronto (CN)
Municipio de San Juan (PR)
Munin-Verlag Gmbh (GW)
Munksgaard (DK)
Munno Publications (UG)
Munro Barr Publications Ltd. (UK)
Munroe Publications, Inc (US)
Munson-Williams-Proctor Institute (US)
Munzinger-Archiv (GW)
Ahmad Eed Murad, Ed. & Pub. (CN)
Egidio Muraglia, Ed. & Pub. (IT)
Murerfagets Oplysningsraad (DK)
Roberto Murillo Rocha, Ed. & Pub. (MX)
D. J. Murphy (Publishers) Ltd. (UK)
Murphy-Richter Publishing Company (US)
John Murray (Publishers) Ltd. (UK)
Murray Goulburn Co-Op Ltd. (AT)
Murray Grey Beef Cattle Society (AT)
Murray Hill News Corp. (US)
Murray Park College of Advanced Education. Department of History and Australian Studies (AT)
Murray Publishing Co. (US)
K.G. Murray Publishing Co. Pty. Ltd. (AT)
Murray State University. College of Business and Public Affairs (US)
Murray Valley Development League (AT)
Mursia Editore (IT)
Musashino Art University (JA)
Muscle Man Inc. (US)
Muscular Dystrophy Association, Inc. (US)
Muscular Dystrophy Association of Canada (CN)
Muscular Dystrophy Group of Great Britain (UK)
Muse Publishing Co., Inc. (US)
Muse Publishing Co., Inc. (US)
Musee d'Art Contemporain (CN)
Musee d'Art et Archeologie de l'Universite de Madagascar (MG)
Musee d'Art et d'Histoire, Geneva (SZ)
Musee d'Ethnographie de la Ville de Geneve (SZ)
Musee de Beaux Arts (FR)
Musee de l'Homme (FR)
Musee de l'Hotel Gouin (FR)
Musee de Mariemont (BE)
Musee Guimet. Paris (FR)
Musee National des Arts et Traditions Populaires (FR)
Musee National des Sciences Naturelles (CN)
Musee National Suisse
  see Schweizerisches Landesmuseum (SZ)
Musee Neuchatelois (SZ)
Musee Pyreneen du Chateau-Fort de Lourdes. Societe des Amis de Musee (FR)
Musee Royal de l'Afrique Centrale (BE)
Museen der Stadt Erfurt (GE)
Musees Royaux des Beaux-Arts de Belgique (BE)
Musen Jujisha Kyoiku Kyokai (JA)
Museo Americanista de Antropologia, Historia, Numismatica y Ciencias Naturales (AG)
Museo Antropologico "Antonio Santiana" (EC)
Museo Argentino de Ciencias Naturales Bernardino Rivadavia (AG)
Museo Arqueologico de Cachi (AG)
Museo Arqueologico Nacional (SP)
Museo Bodoniano (IT)
Museo Boggio (VE)

Museo Civici Veneziani (IT)
Museo Civico di Storia Naturale "G. Doria" (IT)
Museo Civico di Storia Naturale, Verona (IT)
Museo de Ciencias Naturales (VE)
Museo de Historia Natural de la Ciudad de Mexico (MX)
Museo de Historia Natural de San Rafael (AG)
Museo de Zoologia (SP)
Museo del Barrio (US)
Museo del Hombre Dominicano (DR)
Museo dell'Impero Romano (IT)
Museo Egizio, Turin (IT)
Museo Etnografico (PY)
Museo Etnografico Municipal Damaso Aree. Instituto de Investigaciones Antropologicas (AG)
Museo Historico Nacional (UY)
Museo Internazionale delle Ceramiche (IT)
Museo Nacional de Antropologia y Arqueologia (PE)
Museo Nacional de Costa Rica (CR)
Museo Nacional de Historia Natural (CL)
Museo Nacional de Historia Natural (UY)
Museo Nazionale d'Arte Orientale (IT)
Museo Nazionale del Cinema (IT)
Museo Nazionale della Scienza e della Tecnica Leonarda da Vinci (IT)
Museo Social Argentino (AG)
Museo Trentino del Risorgimento e della Lotta per la Liberta (IT)
Museu de Arqueologia e Etnologia (BL)
Museu de Dundo (AO)
Museu de Etnografia e Historia (PO)
Museu do Indio (BL)
Museu e Laboratorio Zoologico e Antropologico, (Museu Bocage) (PO)
Museu Nacional (BL)
Museu Nacional de Antropologia (MX)
Museum Boymans-van Beuningen (NE)
Museum d'Histoire Naturelle (RE)
Museum d'Histoire Naturelle (SZ)
Museum fuer Geschichte der Stadt Dresden (GE)
Museum fuer Ur- und Fruehgeschichte, Potsdam (GE)
Museum fuer Ur- und Fruehgeschichte, Schwerin (GE)
Museum fuer Ur- und Fruehgeschichte Thueringens (GE)
Museum fuer Voelkerkunde (AU)
Museum fuer Voelkerkunde, Berlin (GW)
Museum fuer Voelkerkunde, Leipzig (GE)
Museum fuer Voelkerkunde und Vorgeschichte (GW)
Museum G. Frey. Entomologisches Institut (GW)
Museum Haaretz (IS)
Museum National d'Histoire Naturelle (FR)
Museum National d'Histoire Naturelle. Association de Botanique Tropicale (FR)
Museum National d'Histoire Naturelle. Bibliotheque Centrale (FR)
Museum National d'Histoire Naturelle. Laboratoire d'Ethnobotanique (FR)
Museum National d'Histoire Naturelle. Laboratoire de Palynologie (FR)
Museum of American Folk Art (US)
Museum of Antiquites of Tel-Aviv-Yafo (IS)
Museum of Fine Arts, Houston (US)
Museum of Fine Arts, St. Petersburg (US)
Museum of New Mexico Press (US)
Museum of Northern Arizona (US)
Museum of the City of New York (US)
Museum of the Confederacy (US)
Museum of the Fur Trade (US)
Museum of the Great Plains (US)
Museum of Varberg (SW)
Museum Restoration Service (CN)
Museum Zoologicum Bogoriense (IO)
Museums Association (UK)
Museums Association of Pakistan (PK)
Museumsverein Alsergrund (AU)
Mushroom Growers' Association (UK)
Mushroom Media Inc. (PH)
Music Academy (II)
Music and Letters Ltd. (UK)
Music Article Guide (US)
Music Association of Ireland (IE)
Music Business Reference, Inc. (US)
Music City News Publishing Co., Inc. (US)
Music Educators National Conference (US)
Music Group of the Communist Party (UK)
Music Industry Publications (UK)
Music Journal Inc. (US)
Music Library Association (US)
Music Notes (Chicago) (US)
Music Teachers Association (US)
Music Trades Corporation (US)
Musica (US)
Musica Iberoamericana Co. (JA)
Musical Box Society International (US)

Musical Box Society of Great Britain   (UK)
Musical Newsletter, Inc.   (US)
Musical Opinion Ltd.   (UK)
Musicalbrande   (IT)
Casa Editrice Musicale Carrara   (IT)
Musicana Collector   (US)
Musicdata, Inc.   (US)
Musician's Guide Publications   (US)
Musicological Society of Australia   (AT)
VEB Deutscher Verlag fuer Musik   (GE)
Musikalische Jugend Deutschlands   (GW)
Musikhandel Verlagsgesellschaft mbH   (GW)
Musikhistoriska Museet   (SW)
Verlag das Musikinstrument   (GW)
Muslim Intellectuals' International   (PK)
Muslim News International   (PK)
Muslim Review   (II)
Muslim World League   (SU)
T. Musolini Editore   (IT)
Musterschmidt-Verlag   (GW)
Muszaki es Termeszettudomanyi Egyesuletek
  Szovetsege   (HU)
Muszaki es Termeszettudomanyi Egyesuletek
  Szovetsege. Baranya Megyei Szervezet   (HU)
Muszaki Konyvkiado   (HU)
Mut-Verlag   (GW)
Muth-Verlag   (GW)
Mutua Sabadellense de Seguros   (SP)
Mutual Beneficial Association of Rail Transportation
  Employees, Inc.   (US)
Mutual Benefit Life Insurance Co.   (US)
Mutual Funds Scoreboard   (US)
Mutual Of New York Life Insurance Co. Public
  Relations Department   (US)
Mutual U F O Network, Inc.   (US)
Mutualite Sociale Agricole de la Corse   (FR)
Mutuelle Generale de la Police Francaise   (FR)
Mutuelle Nationale des Etudiants de France   (FR)
J. Muusses B.V.   (NE)
Muzejsko Drustvo Hrvatske   (YU)
Muzeul Banatului   (RM)
Muzeul de Istorie Naturala "Gr. Antipa"   (RM)
Muzeul de Istorie si Arheologie Alba Julia   (RM)
Muzeul Literaturii Romane   (RM)
Muzeum Archeologiczne, Gdansk   (PL)
Muzeum Archeologiczne i Etnograficzne, Lodz   (PL)
Muzeum Archeologiczne, Krakow   (PL)
Muzeum Archeologiczne, Poznan   (PL)
Muzeum Archeologiczne, Wroclaw   (PL)
Muzeum Etnograficzne, Wroclaw   (PL)
Muzeum Gornoslaskie   (PL)
Muzeum Historii Polskiego Ruchu Rewolucyjnego
  (PL)
Muzeum Mazurskie   (PL)
Muzeum Narodowe, Szczecin   (PL)
Muzeum Narodowe, Warsaw   (PL)
Muzeum Narodowe, Wroclaw   (PL)
Muzeum w Bialymstoku   (PL)
Muzicka Akademija u Zagrebu. Muzikoloski Zavod
  (YU)
Muzicka Omladina Osijek   (YU)
Muziek Expres B. V.   (NE)
Polskie Wydawnictwo Muzyczne   (PL)
Izdatel'stvo Muzyka   (UR)
Muzzle Loaders Association of Great Britain   (UK)
My Little Salesman, Inc,   (US)
Philip Myaboo   (II)
Myastenia Gravis Foundation   (CN)
Myasthenia Gravis Foundation Inc.   (US)
Mycological Society of America   (US)
Mycological Society of Japan   (JA)
Mycotaxon, Ltd.   (US)
John Bernard Myers, Ed. & Pub.   (US)
Myers Publishing Co., Inc.   (US)
O. Mygind   (DK)
M. Myogo, Pub.   (FR)
Myriad Publishing   (CN)
Myrianyn - the Layman   (US)
Myrin Institute for Adult Education   (US)
Myrjon Press   (US)
Izdatel'stvo Mysl   (UR)
Mysl Polska   (UK)
Mysore
  see also Karnataka   (II)
Mysore Economic Review   (II)
Mysore Horticultural Society   (II)
Mysore University
  see University of Mysore   (II)
Mystery & Detection Annual.   (US)
Mystery Trader   (UK)
Mystery Writers of America, Inc.   (US)
Mystic Seaport, Inc.   (US)
Mystic Seaport, Inc. G.W. Blunt White Library   (US)
Mythic Society   (II)
Mythical Press   (CN)
Mythopoeic Society   (US)
N A A C P

  see National Association for the Advancement of
  Colored People   (US)
N.A.D.A.
  see National Automobile Dealers Association   (US)
N.A.G. Press Ltd.   (UK)
N A S A
  see U. S. National Aeronautics and Space
  Administration   (US)
N B Enterprises, Inc.   (US)
N C A A Publishing Service   (US)
N. C. R. A.   (FR)
N C R Corporation   (US)
N D L
  see National Diet Library   (JA)
N.E.B. Editions Scientifiques   (FR)
N E G M Publishing Co.   (US)
N. E. I. D. Informations   (FR)
N. E. M. F.
  see Nouvelles Editions Medicales Francaise
  (NEMF)   (FR)
N E T A   (FR)
N F E R Publishing Co., Ltd.   (UK)
N H K
  see Japan Broadcasting Corp.   (JA)
N I D O C
  see National Information and Documentation
  Centre   (UA)
N I G Editrice   (IT)
N I K K I R E N
  see Japan Machinery Federation   (JA)
N I K K Y O S O
  see Japan Teachers' Union   (JA)
N I M M Educational Media Service, Inc.   (US)
N J M Associates   (US)
N L S P, Inc.
  see National Live Stock Publishing   (US)
N O I International   (AU)
N O K Publishers, Ltd.   (US)
N P M   (UK)
N R C Publishing Co.   (CN)
N R F
  see Sweden. Statens Naturvetenskapliga
  Forskningsraad   (SW)
N T L Institute for Applied Behavioral Science   (US)
N T V
  see Nippon Television Network Corp.   (JA)
N. V. Tot Keuring van Elektrotechnische Materialen
  see K E M A   (NE)
N Y A Argus   (FI)
N.Y.M. Company of California   (US)
N Y M Corporation   (US)
N Y R E V, Inc.   (US)
N.Z. Forest Products Ltd.   (NZ)
Naa   (NO)
Editions Naaman   (CN)
Nabya Bangla Natya Parishad   (II)
Franco Nacci   (IT)
Nachrichten fuer Unzufrieden   (SZ)
Nachrichten-Verlags-Gesellschaft mbH   (GW)
Nachrichtentechnische Gesellschaft im VDE (NTG)
  (GW)
Nacion   (MX)
Editora Nacional   (BO)
Editora Nacional   (SP)
Empresa Nacional de Publicidade   (PO)
Nacional Financiera, S.A.   (MX)
Nacional Quimantu Ltda.   (CL)
Editores Nacionales   (EC)
Nacionalna i Sveucilisna Biblioteka   (YU)
Naciones Unidas
  see United Nations   (UN)
Naczelna Dyrekcja Archiwow Panstwowych   (PL)
Naczelna Organizacja Techniczna   (PL)
Naczelna Organizacja Techniczna. Oddzial w
  Rzeszowie   (PL)
Naczelna Rada Spoldzielcza   (PL)
Nadbiskupija Splitsko-Makarska   (YU)
Nadbiskupski Ordinarijat u Beogradu   (YU)
Nadi al-Tijarah   (UA)
Naeringslivets Arkivraad   (SW)
Naeringslivets Tidningsstiftelse   (SW)
Naftika Chronika Ltd.   (GR)
Nagaland. Cultural Research and State Museum   (II)
Nagaland. Director of Information, Publicity &
  Tourism   (II)
Nagaland. Directorate of Education   (II)
Nagaland Nationalist Cooperative Society Ltd.   (II)
Nagano Medical Society   (JA)
Nagaoka Technical College   (JA)
Nagasaki Daigaku
  see Nagasaki University   (JA)
Nagasaki Daigaku Netti Igaku Kenkyusho
  see Nagasaki University. Institute for Tropical
  Medicine   (JA)
Nagasaki University. Institute for Tropical Medicine
  (JA)
Nagasaki University. School of Medicine   (JA)
Editions Nagel S.A.   (SZ)

Nagoya. Environmental Pollution Research Institute
  (JA)
Nagoya City University. Medical Association   (JA)
Nagoya City University. Medical School   (JA)
Nagoya Daigaku
  see Nagoya University   (JA)
Nagoya Daigaku Kankyo Igaku Kenkyusho
  see Nagoya University. Research Institute of
  Environmental Medicine   (JA)
Nagoya Daigaku Kuden Kenkyusho
  see Nagoya University. Research Institute of
  Atmospherics   (JA)
Nagoya Daigaku Purazuma Kenkyusho
  see Nagoya University. Institute of Plasma Physics
  (JA)
Nagoya Daigaku Rigakubu Uchusen Boenkyo
  see Nagoya University. Cosmic Ray Research
  Laboratory   (JA)
Nagoya Daigaku Suishitsu Kagaku Kenky Shisetsu
  see Nagoya University. Water Research Institute
  (JA)
Nagoya Port Authority   (JA)
Nagoya-shiritsu Daigaku
  see Nagoya City University   (JA)
Nagoya University. Cosmic-Ray Research Laboratory
  (JA)
Nagoya University. Department of Earth Sciences
  (JA)
Nagoya University. Department of Economics   (JA)
Nagoya University. Department of Mathematics   (JA)
Nagoya University. Faculty of Engineering   (JA)
Nagoya University. Institute of Plasma Physics   (JA)
Nagoya University. Research Institute of Atmospherics
  (JA)
Nagoya University. Research Institute of
  Environmental Medicine   (JA)
Nagoya University. School of Medicine   (JA)
Nagoya University. Water Research Institute   (JA)
Nagoyako Kanri Kumai
  see Nagoya Port Authority   (JA)
M. L. Nahar, Ed. & Pub.   (II)
Nahrungs- und Genussmittel-Fachverlag A.Gordian
  GmbH & Co. KG   (GW)
Natabar Naik, Ed. & Pub.   (II)
Naikahoken Kankokai   (JA)
S. K. Nair, Ed. & Pub.   (II)
Nakladatelstvi Dopravy a Spoju   (CS)
Nakladatelstvi Svazu Ceskych Vytvarnych Umelcu
  (CS)
A. K. Krishna Nambiar, Ed. & Pub.   (II)
Names of Distinction, Inc.   (US)
Names Society   (UK)
Namgyal Institute of Tibetology   (SK)
G. R. Namias, Ed. & Pub.   (IT)
Namib Desert Research Station   (SX)
Namib Times   (SA)
Namos Verlagsgesellschaft   (GW)
Nan-Sea Publications   (CN)
Nanaimo Old Time Bottle Association   (CN)
Nananom Publishers   (GH)
Editorial Nande   (PY)
R. N. Nandy   (II)
Nankodo Co., Ltd.   (JA)
Nanogens International   (US)
Nantucket Maria Mitchell Association   (US)
Nantucket Review   (US)
Nanyang Orchid Association   (SI)
Nanyang Univ. Nan-Yang ta Hsueh Chung-Kuo Yu
  Wen Hsueh Hui   (SI)
Nanyang University   (SI)
Nanyang University. Biology Society   (SI)
Nanyang University. Lee Kong Chian Institute of
  Mathematics   (SI)
Nanzando Co., Ltd.   (JA)
Napa-Solano Dental Society   (US)
Naples, Italy. Consorzio Autonomo del Porto   (IT)
Napoleone Editore   (IT)
Napoleonic Society   (UK)
Societa Editrice Napoletana s.r.l.   (IT)
Compagnia Editrice Napoletano   (IT)
Napred   (YU)
Naprstkovo Muzeum Asijskych, Africkych a
  Americkych Kultur   (CS)
Nara Advertising Ltd.   (NR)
Nara Medical Association   (JA)
C. P. Narang, Ed. & Pub.   (II)
Narayananda Universal Yoga Ashrama   (DK)
Chitra Narayann, Ed. & Pub.   (II)
Narciso   (IT)
Narcotics Education, Inc.   (US)
Narcotics Education Service   (AT)
Narod Press   (UK)
Narodna Armija   (YU)
Narodna Banka Jugoslavije   (YU)
Narodna Biblioteka "Kiril i Metodii"   (BU)
Narodna Biblioteka Srbije   (YU)
Narodna in Univerzitetna Knjiznica   (YU)

Narodne Novine, Nis (YU)
Narodne Novine, Zagreb (YU)
Narodni Fronta (CS)
Narodni List (YU)
Narodni Muzeum (CS)
Narodni Muzeum. Ustredni Muzeologicky Kabinet (CS)
Narodni Technicke Muzeum (CS)
Narodni Vybory (CS)
Narodno Pozoriste (YU)
Narodno Sveuciliste "Bozidar Maslaric". Centar za Kulturu i Umjetnost (YU)
Narodno Sveuciliste Juraj Kokot (YU)
Naropa Institute (US)
Narrow Gauge Railway Society (UK)
Narula Dwakhana (II)
NASA
    see U.S. National Aeronautics and Space Administration (US)
Nasa Knjiga, Skopje (YU)
Nasa Rec, Leskovac (YU)
Nasa Rijec (YU)
Nase Vojsko, Publishing House of the Czechoslovak Army (CS)
Jay R. Nash, Ed. & Pub. (US)
Nashotah House (US)
Nasim Book Depot (II)
Nasionale Tydskrifte (SA)
Nasjonalforeningen for Folkehelsen (NO)
Nassau & Paradise Island Promotion Board (BF)
Nassau Community College (US)
Nassau County. Department of Recreation and Parks (US)
Nassau County Bar Association (US)
Nassau County Medical Center (US)
Nassau Herald (US)
Nassau Library System (US)
Nassau-Suffolk Regional Planning Board (US)
Natal. Education Department (SA)
Natal. Parks, Game & Fish Preservation Board (SA)
Natal. Provincial Library Services (SA)
Natal Agricultural Union (SA)
Natal Hunters & Game Conservation Association (SA)
Natal Society (SA)
Natale Onderwysersunie (SA)
Manian Natesan (II)
Librairie Fernand Nathan (FR)
Stella Nathan (US)
Nathanael Literature Distributors (CN)
Nathaniel Hawthorne Society (US)
Nation (IQ)
Nation Co. Inc. (US)
Nation Europa Verlag GmbH (GW)
Nation Newspapers Ltd. (KE)
Nation Trust (II)
Nationaal Centrum voor Geestelijke Volksgezondheid (NE)
Nationaal Centrum voor Oudheidkundige Navorsingen in Belgie
    see Centre National de Recherches Archeologiques en Belgique (BE)
Nationaal Centrum voor Wetenschappelijk en Technisch Onderzoek der Cementnijverheid
    see Centre National de Recherches Scientifiques et Techniques pour l'Industrie Cimentierre (BE)
Nationaal Rheumafonds (NE)
Nationaal Sekretariaat van Het Katholiek Onderwijs (BE)
Nationaal Verbond Haarkappers (BE)
Nationaal Verbond voor Volkstuinen (BE)
Zeitungsverlag National (GE)
National Academy of Art (II)
National Academy of Code Administration (US)
National Academy of Letters (II)
National Academy of Music, Dance and Drama (II)
National Academy of Sciences (II)
National Academy of Sciences (US)
National Academy of Sciences. Committee on Fire Research (US)
National Academy of Sciences. Committee on Scholarly Communication with the Peoples Republic of China (US)
National Academy of Sciences. Conference on Electrical Insulation and Dielectric Phenomena (US)
National Academy of Sciences. Institute of Laboratory Animal Resources (US)
National Academy of Sciences. National Committee on Tunneling Technology (US)
National Academy of Sciences. Ocean Affairs Board (US)
National Academy of Sciences Transportation Research Board (US)
National Accreditation Council for Agencies Serving the Blind and Visually Handicapped (US)
National Acoustic Laboratories (AT)

National Action Committee on the Status of Women (CN)
National Acupuncture Association (US)
National Advanced Drivers' Association (UK)
National Advertising Co-Op (US)
National Advisory Council on Supplementary Centers and Services (US)
National Aeronautic Association of the U.S.A. (US)
National Aeronautical Laboratory
    see India. National Aeronautical Laboratory (II)
National Aeronautics and Space Administration
    see U.S. National Aeronautics and Space Administration (US)
National Aerospace Association (US)
National Aerospace Laboratory
    see Japan. National Aerospace Laboratory (JA)
National Affairs (US)
National Affairs Inc. (US)
National Affiliation for Literacy Advance (US)
National African Chamber of Commerce (SA)
National Agricultural Institute (US)
National Agricultural Library
    see U.S. National Agricultural Library (US)
National Agricultural Marketing Federation of India Limited (II)
National Agricultural Society of Ceylon (CE)
National Alliance for Family Life (US)
National Alliance of Postal and Federal Employees (US)
National Alliance of Young Entrepreneurs (II)
National Alliance Television and Electronic Service Associations (US)
National Amateur Press Association (US)
National American Studies Connections Collective (US)
National-American Wholesale Grocer's Association, Inc. (US)
National Americanism Commission (US)
National & Commercial Banking Group Ltd. (UK)
National and Local Government Officers Association (UK)
National Anti-Vivisection Society Ltd. (UK)
National Appliance and Radio-Electronic Dealers Association (US)
National Archaeological Institute of Indonesia. Department of Prehistory (IO)
National Architectural Accrediting Board, Inc. (US)
National Archives
    see India. National Archives of India (II)
National Archives and Records Service
    see U.S. National Archives and Records Service (US)
National Art Education Association (US)
National Art Material Trade Association (US)
National Arts Centre (CN)
National Asphalt Pavement Association (US)
National Assembly Library (KO)
National Assembly of Religious Brothers (US)
National Assembly of Women Religious (N.A.W.R.) (US)
National Assessment of Educational Progress. Education Commission of the States (US)
National Association for Better Broadcasting (US)
National Association for Business Teacher Education (US)
National Association for Community Development (US)
National Association for Core Curriculum, Inc. (US)
National Association for Creative Children and Adults (US)
National Association for Deaf-Blind and Rubella Children (UK)
National Association for Environmental Education (UK)
National Association for Environmental Education (US)
National Association for Foreign Student Affairs (US)
National Association for Girls and Women in Sport (US)
National Association for Hearing and Speech Action (US)
National Association for Humanities Education (US)
National Association for Mental Health (US)
National Association for Music Therapy, Inc. (US)
National Association for Non-Parents (US)
National Association for Photographic Art (CN)
National Association for Physical Education of College Women (US)
National Association for Practical Nurse Education and Service, Inc. (US)
National Association for Public Continuing and Adult Education (US)
National Association for Regional Ballet (US)

National Association for Research in Science Teaching (US)
National Association for Retarded Citizens (US)
National Association for Stock Car Auto Racing, Inc. (US)
National Association for the Advancement of Colored People (US)
National Association for the Blind (II)
National Association for the Care and Resettlement of Offenders. (UK)
National Association for the Education of Young Children (US)
National Association for the Teaching of English (UK)
National Association for Uniformed Services (US)
National Association for Women Deans, Administrators and Counselors (US)
National Association of Accountants (US)
National Association of Almshouses (UK)
National Association of Amateur Oarsmen (US)
National Association of American Balloon Corps Veterans (US)
National Association of Animal Breeders (US)
National Association of Attorneys General (US)
National Association of Australian State Road Authorities (AT)
National Association of Auto Trim Shops (US)
National Association of Bank Women (US)
National Association of Bedding Manufacturers (US)
National Association of Biology Teachers (US)
National Association of Black Psychologists (US)
National Association of Blackfeet Indians (US)
National Association of Blue Shield Plans (US)
National Association of Boys' Clubs (UK)
National Association of Broadcast Employees and Technicians (US)
National Association of Broadcasters (US)
National Association of Business and Educational Radio (US)
National Association of Business Law Teachers, Inc. (US)
National Association of Chain Drug Stores (US)
National Association of Christian Schools (US)
National Association of College Admissions Counselors (US)
National Association of College and University Attorneys (US)
National Association of College and University Business Officers (US)
National Association of College Deans and Registrars (US)
National Association of College Stores, Inc. (US)
National Association of College-University Food Services (US)
National Association of College Wind & Percussion Instructors (US)
National Association of Colleges and Teachers of Agriculture (US)
National Association of Collegiate Directors of Athletics (US)
National Association of Congregational Christian Churches (US)
National Association of Conservation Districts (US)
National Association of Cooperative Officials (UK)
National Association of Corrosion Engineers (US)
National Association of Counties (US)
National Association of Counties. Research Foundation (US)
National Association of Credit Management (US)
National Association of Cycle Traders (UK)
National Association of Demolition Contractors (US)
National Association of Dental Laboratories (US)
National Association of Dramatic and Speech Arts (US)
National Association of Educational Broadcasters (US)
National Association of Educational Buyers (US)
National Association of Educational Negotiators (US)
National Association of Educational Secretaries (US)
National Association of Electric Companies (US)
National Association of Electrical Distributors (US)
National Association of Elementary School Principals (US)
National Association of Evangelicals (US)
National Association of Federally Licensed Firearms Dealers (US)
National Association of Fire Investigators (US)
National Association of Fleet Administrators, Inc. (US)
National Association of Flight Instructors (US)
National Association of Flower Arrangement Societies (UK)
National Association of Friendship Centres (CN)
National Association of Geology Teachers (US)
National Association of Glove Manufacturers (US)
National Association of Goldsmiths (UK)

National Association of Health Services Executives (US)
National Association of Home Builders of the United States (US)
National Association of Hosiery Manufacturers (US)
National Association of Housing and Redevelopment Officials (US)
National Association of Housing Cooperatives (US)
National Association of Human Rights Workers (US)
National Association of Independent Insurance Adjusters (US)
National Association of Independent Insurers (US)
National Association of Independent Schools (US)
National Association of Industrial and Technical Teacher Educators (US)
National Association of Insectocutor Manufacturers (US)
National Association of Installment Companies (US)
National Association of Institutional Laundry Managers (US)
National Association of Insurance Brokers, Inc. (US)
National Association of Insurance Commissioners (US)
National Association of Intercollegiate Athletics (US)
National Association of Interdisciplinary Ethnic Studies (US)
National Association of Investment Clubs (US)
National Association of Jazz Educators (US)
National Association of Jewish Center Workers (US)
National Association of Jewish Homes for the Aged (US)
National Association of Laboratory Schools (US)
National Association of Language Laboratory Directors (US)
National Association of Letter Carriers (A.F.L.-C.I.O.) (US)
National Association of Letter Carriers. N Y L C Branch 36 (US)
National Association of Life Underwriters (US)
National Association of Local Councils (UK)
National Association of Manufacturers (US)
National Association of Manufacturers. Fiscal & Economic Policy Department (US)
National Association of Master Bakers, Confectioners & Caterers (UK)
National Association of Materials Management (II)
National Association of Metal Finishers (US)
National Association of Minority C.P.A. Firms (US)
National Association of Music Merchants Inc. (US)
National Association of Mutual Insurance Companies (US)
National Association of Mutual Savings Banks (US)
National Association of Naturopathic Physicians (US)
National Association of Nurses in Israel (IS)
National Association of Organ Teachers (US)
National Association of Pattern Manufacturers (US)
National Association of Pediatric Nurse Associates and Practitioners (US)
National Association of Pension Funds (UK)
National Association of Persons Handicapped by Tuberculosis and Other Pulmonary Diseases
see Tuberkuloosi ja Keuhkovammaisten Liitto (FI)
National Association of Postal Supervisors (US)
National Association of Postmasters of the United States (US)
National Association of Power Engineers, Inc. (US)
National Association of Printing Ink Makers (US)
National Association of Prison Visitors (UK)
National Association of Private Psychiatric Hospitals (US)
National Association of Probation Officers (UK)
National Association of Professors of Hebrew (US)
National Association of Public Insurance Adjusters (US)
National Association of Purchasing Agents (US)
National Association of Rabbit Breeders (IT)
National Association of Radiotelephone Systems (US)
National Association of Real Estate Investment Trusts (US)
National Association of Realtors (US)
National Association of Regional Councils (US)
National Association of Regulatory Utility Commissioners (US)
National Association of Relay Manufacturers (US)
National Association of Retail Druggists (US)
National Association of Retail Grocers of Australia (NARGA) (AT)
National Association of Retired Federal Employees (US)
National Association of School Psychologists (US)
National Association of Schools of Art (US)
National Association of Schools of Music (US)
National Association of Schools of Public Affairs and Administration (US)
National Association of Science Writers Inc. (US)

National Association of Secondary School Principals (US)
National Association of Securities Dealers Inc. (US)
National Association of Small Business Investment Companies (US)
National Association of Social Workers (US)
National Association of Soft Drinks Manufacturers Ltd. (UK)
National Association of State Budget Officers (US)
National Association of State Universities and Land-Grant Colleges (US)
National Association of Student Personnel Administrators (US)
National Association of Suggestion Systems (US)
National Association of Teachers' Agencies (US)
National Association of Teachers in Colleges and Departments of Education (UK)
National Association of Teachers in Further and Higher Education (UK)
National Association of Teachers of Singing, Inc. (US)
National Association of Teachers of the Mentally Handicapped (UK)
National Association of Temple Educators (US)
National Association of Testing Authorities (AT)
National Association of the Deaf (US)
National Association of the Partners of the Alliance
see Partners of the Americas (US)
National Association of Theatre Nurses (UK)
National Association of Tobacco Distributors, Inc. (US)
National Association of Trade and Technical Schools (US)
National Association of Trailer Owners, Inc. (US)
National Association of Training Schools and Juvenile Agencies (US)
National Association of Underwater Instructors (US)
National Association of Watch and Clock Collectors (US)
National Association of Wholesaler-Distributors (US)
National Association of Women Artists (US)
National Association of Women Lawyers (US)
National Association of Womens & Childrens Apparel Salesmen (US)
National Association to Keep and Bear Arms Inc. (US)
National Asthma Center (US)
National Astrological Society (US)
National Athletic Trainers Association (US)
National Auctioneers Association (US)
National Audio-Visual Association, Inc. (US)
National Audiovisual Center
see U.S. National Audiovisual Center (US)
National Audubon Society (US)
National Audubon Society. Nature Center Planning Division (US)
National Auricula & Primula Society (UK)
National Auto Auction Association (US)
National Auto Research Canada (CN)
National Automobile Association (US)
National Automobile Club (US)
National Automobile Dealers Association (US)
National Automobile Dealers Association. Appraisal Guides (US)
National Automotive Radiator Service Association (US)
National Awami Party of Bangla Desh (UK)
National Bank of Australasia Ltd. (AT)
National Bank of Commerce. International Banking Department (TZ)
National Bank of Egypt (UA)
National Bank of Ethiopia (ET)
National Bank of Greece (GR)
National Bank of Liberia (LB)
National Bank of Pakistan (PK)
National Baseball Congress (US)
National Begonia Society (UK)
National Beta Club (US)
National Bible Knowledge Association (US)
National Bible Society of Scotland (UK)
National Bilingual Education Association (US)
National Biological Institute. Bogor Zoological Museum
see Museum Zoologicum Bogoriense (IO)
National Biological Institute. Herbarium Bogoriense
see Herbarium Bogoriense (IO)
National Biological Institute. Treub Laboratory
see Treub Laboratory (IO)
National Black Gazette (US)
National Blue Books, Inc. (US)
National Bluegrass Association (US)
National Board of Medical Examiners (US)
National Board of Review of Motion Pictures, Inc. (US)
National Book Centre of Bangladesh (BG)
National Book Council of Pakistan (PK)
National Book Critics Circle Inc. (US)

National Book Development Council of Singapore (SI)
National Book League (UK)
National Book League. Scottish Office (UK)
National Botanic Gardens
see India. National Botanic Gardens (II)
National Botanic Gardens of South Africa (SA)
National Braille Association (US)
National Braille Press Inc. (US)
National British Women's Total Abstinence Union (UK)
National Building Research Institute (SA)
National Buildings Organisation
see India. National Buildings Organisation (II)
National Bureau of Economic Research (US)
National Bureau of Standards
see U.S. National Bureau of Standards (US)
National Burglar & Fire Alarm Association (US)
National Business Education Association (US)
National Business Forms Association (US)
National Business Publications Ltd. (CN)
National Button Society (US)
National Cable Television Institute (US)
National Cancer Association of South Africa (SA)
National Cancer Center
see Japan. National Cancer Center (JA)
National Cancer Conference (US)
National Cancer Institute
see U.S. National Cancer Institute (US)
National Cancer Institute of Canada (CN)
National Candy Wholesalers Association, Inc. (US)
National Canners Association (US)
National Capital Planning Commission
see U. S. National Capital Planning Commission (US)
National Cartographic Information Center
see U. S. National Cartographic Information Center (US)
National Catholic Cemetery Conference (US)
National Catholic Educational Association (US)
National Catholic Educational Association. Special Education Department (US)
National Catholic News Service (US)
National Catholic Reporter Publishing Co., Inc. (US)
National Catholic Rural Life Conference (US)
National Catholic Women's Union (US)
National Caucus of Labor Committees (US)
National Center for Atmospheric Research (US)
National Center for Audio Tapes (US)
National Center for Community Action (US)
National Center for Education Communications
see U. S. National Center for Education Communications (US)
National Center for Education Statistics
see U.S. National Center for Education Statistics (US)
National Center for Educational Brokering (US)
National Center for Health Statistics
see U.S. National Center for Health Statistics (US)
National Center for Law-Focused Education (US)
National Center for Resource Recovery, Inc. (US)
National Center for Social and Criminological Research (UA)
National Center for Social Statistics
see U. S. National Center for Social Statistics (US)
National Center for State Courts (US)
National Center for the Study of Collective Bargaining in Higher Education (US)
National Center for Voluntary Action (US)
National Center on Educational Media and Materials for the Handicapped (US)
National Central Library (CH)
National Central Library. Bureau of International Exchange of Publications (CH)
National Centre for the Performing Arts (II)
National Centre of Social Research (GR)
National Cheerleaders Association (US)
National Chemical Laboratory for Industry
see Japan. National Chemical Laboratory for Industry (JA)
National Chengchi University (CH)
National Chengchi University. Program of African Studies (CH)
National Child Labor Committee (US)
National Children's Bureau (UK)
National Children's Wear Association (UK)
National China and Glass Federation of France (FR)
National Chinchilla Breeders of Canada (CN)
National Christian Association (US)
National Christian Council of Japan (JA)
National Christian Council of Japan. N C C Center for the Study of Japanese Religions (JA)
National Christian News (US)
National Christian Temperance Movement (NE)
National Christmas Tree Association (US)
National Chrysanthemum Society (UK)
National Civic Council (AT)

National Civic League, Inc.  (US)
National Civil Service League  (US)
National Classification Management Society  (US)
National Clearinghouse for Alcohol Information
    see U. S. National Clearinghouse for Alcohol
    Information  (US)
National Clearinghouse for Drug Abuse Information
    see U. S. National Clearinghouse for Drug Abuse
    Information  (US)
National Clearinghouse for Legal Services, Inc.  (US)
National Clearinghouse for Poison Control Centers
    see U. S. National Clearinghouse for Poison Control
    Centers  (US)
National Clearinghouse for Smoking and Health
    see U. S. National Clearinghouse for Smoking and
    Health  (US)
National Clearinghouse on Offender Employment
    Restrictions  (US)
National Climatic Center
    see U.S. National Climatic Center  (US)
National Coal Association  (US)
National Coffee Association of U.S.A. Inc.  (US)
National College of Astrology  (II)
National College of Criminal Defense Lawyers and
    Public Defenders  (US)
National College of the State Judiciary  (US)
National College Physical Education Association for
    Men  (US)
National Collegiate Athletic Association  (US)
National Collegiate Players  (US)
National Commercial Finance Conference Inc.  (US)
National Commission for Unesco  (PH)
National Commission on Human Life, Reproduction
    and Rhythm  (US)
National Commission on Resources for Youth  (US)
National Committee Against Discrimination, Inc.
    (US)
National Committee Against Repressive Legislation
    (US)
National Committee for Audio-Visual Aids in
    Education  (UK)
National Committee for Labor Israel Inc.  (US)
National Committee for Monetary Reform  (US)
National Committee for Prevention of Child Abuse
    (US)
National Committee on Indian Work  (US)
National Committee on the Emeriti  (US)
National Committee on U.S.-China Relations  (US)
National Committee on Uniform Traffic Laws and
    Ordinances  (US)
National Computer Program Abstract Service  (US)
National Computer Systems  (US)
National Computing Centre Ltd.  (UK)
National Concrete Masonry Association  (US)
National Condominium Owners Association (N C O
    A)  (US)
National Confederation of Parent Teacher Associations
    (UK)
National Conference of Bankruptcy Judges  (US)
National Conference of Bar Examiners  (US)
National Conference of Black Political Scientists
    (US)
National Conference of Canadian Universities and
    Colleges Committee  (CN)
National Conference of Catholic Charities  (US)
National Conference of Commissioners on Uniform
    State Laws  (US)
National Conference of Editorial Writers  (US)
National Conference of Jewish Communal Service
    (US)
National Conference of South African Surveyors
    (SA)
National Conference of Standards Laboratories  (US)
National Conference of State Legislatures  (US)
National Conference of State Social Security
    Administrators  (US)
National Conference of Synagogue Youth  (US)
National Conference on Fluid Power  (US)
National Conference on Social Welfare  (US)
National Conference on Soviet Jewry  (US)
National Conference on Weights and Measures  (US)
National Congress of American Indians  (US)
National Congress of Parents and Teachers  (US)
National Consumer Finance Association  (US)
National Consumers League  (US)
National Contest  (US)
National Contract Management Association  (US)
National Cooperative Consumers' Federation  (II)
National Cooperative Development Corporation  (II)
National Cooperative Union of India  (II)
National Cooperative Union of India. Committee for
    Cooperative Training  (II)
National Coordinating Council on Drug Education
    (US)
National Cottonseed Products Association  (US)
National Council for Chartered Accountants  (SA)

National Council for Civil Liberties  (UK)
National Council for Community Services to
    International Visitors  (US)
National Council for Consumer Goods and Consumer
    Information
    see Sweden. Statens Konsumentraad  (SW)
National Council for Critical Analysis  (US)
National Council for Geographic Education  (US)
National Council for Homemaker Home Health Aide
    Services, Inc.  (US)
National Council for Jewish Education  (US)
National Council for Research
    see Sudan. National Council for Research  (SJ)
National Council for Science Education  (II)
National Council for Scientific Research
    see Zambia. National Council for Scientific
    Research  (ZA)
National Council for Scientific Research  (LE)
National Council for Social Research. Department of
    Education, Arts and Science  (SA)
National Council for Special Education  (UK)
National Council for the Care of Cripples in South
    Africa  (SA)
National Council for the Social Studies  (US)
National Council for the Traditional Arts, Inc.  (US)
National Council for U.S.-China Trade  (US)
National Council for Universal & Unconditional
    Amnesty  (US)
National Council of Administrative Women in
    Education  (US)
National Council of Applied Economic Research  (II)
National Council of Architectural Registration Boards
    (US)
National Council of Associations for Policy Sciences
    (US)
National Council of Building Material Producers
    (UK)
National Council of Churches. Division of Education
    and Ministry  (US)
National Council of College Publications Advisers
    (US)
National Council of Educational Research and
    Training  (II)
National Council of Educational Research and
    Training. Regional College of Education  (II)
National Council of Engineering Examiners  (US)
National Council of Farmer Cooperatives  (US)
National Council of Jewish Women. Tulsa Section
    (US)
National Council of Juvenile Court Judges  (US)
National Council of La Raza  (US)
National Council of Negro Women, Inc.  (US)
National Council of Physical Distribution Management
    (US)
National Council of Secondary School Athletic
    Directors  (US)
National Council of Small Business Management
    Development  (US)
National Council of Social Service Inc.  (UK)
National Council of Social Welfare  (JA)
National Council of State Garden Clubs, Inc.  (US)
National Council of Teachers of English  (US)
National Council of Teachers of Mathematics  (US)
National Council of the Churches of Christ in the
    U.S.A.  (US)
National Council of the Churches of Christ in the
    U.S.A. Division of Overseas Ministries  (US)
National Council of the Knights of Peter Claver  (US)
National Council of the Paper Industry for Air and
    Stream Improvement, Inc.  (US)
National Council of the Realist Writers Groups  (AT)
National Council of the Third Order of Saint Francis
    (SP)
National Council of United States Magistrates  (US)
National Council of Women in India  (II)
National Council of Women of Australia  (AT)
National Council of Women of South Africa  (SA)
National Council of Wool Selling Brokers of Australia
    (AT)
National Council of Y M C As  (US)
National Council of YMCA's of India  (II)
National Council of Young Israel  (US)
National Council on Alcoholism  (US)
National Council on Black Aging, Inc.  (US)
National Council on Crime and Delinquency  (US)
National Council on Crime and Delinquency. Research
    Center  (US)
National Council on Drug Abuse  (US)
National Council on Educational Materials  (US)
National Council on Family Relations  (US)
National Council on Measurement in Education  (US)
National Council on Radiation Protection and
    Measurements  (US)
National Council on the Aging  (US)
National Cowboy Hall of Fame and Western Heritage
    Center  (US)
National Credit Office  (US)
National Credit Union Administration

    see U.S. National Credit Union Administration
    (US)
National Criminal Justice Information and Statistics
    Service
    see U. S. National Criminal Justice Information and
    Statistics Service  (US)
National Crushed Stone Association  (US)
National Cutting Horse Association  (US)
National CYO Federation  (US)
National Dahlia Society (Great Britain)  (UK)
National Dairy Council  (US)
National Dairy Council of Canada  (CN)
National Dairymen's Association, Inc.  (UK)
National Deaf Childrens Society  (UK)
National Decorating Products Association  (US)
National Defence College  (UK)
National Defence Headquarters  (CN)
National Defense Academy  (JA)
National Defense College of the Philippines  (PH)
National Defense Medical Society  (JA)
National Defense Research Institute
    see Sweden. Foersvarets Forskningsanstalt  (SW)
National Defense Transportation Association  (US)
National Democratic Forum  (US)
National-Demokratische Partei Deutschlands  (GE)
National Dental Association  (US)
National Development Bank  (SL)
National Development Corporation  (TZ)
National Diet Library  (JA)
National Directory Service, Inc.  (US)
National District Attorneys Association  (US)
National Documentation Centre for Sport, Physical
    Education and Recreation  (UK)
National Dog Owners' Association  (UK)
National Drug & Chemical Co. of Canada Ltd.  (CN)
National Earthquake Information Center
    see under U. S. Geological Survey  (US)
National Easter Seal Society for Crippled Children &
    Adults  (US)
National Economic Development Office  (UK)
National Education Association  (US)
National Education Program  (US)
National Education Society of Sri Lanka  (CE)
National Educational Film Center  (US)
National Educator  (US)
National Electrical Contractors Association  (US)
National Electrical Manufacturers Association  (US)
National Electronic Distributors Association, Inc.
    (US)
National Electronic Injury Surveillance System
    see U.Snational Electronic Injury Surveillance
    System  (US)
National Electronic Service Dealers Association  (US)
National Electronics Conference  (US)
National Electronics Council  (UK)
National Emergency Civil Liberties Committee  (US)
National Emergency Planning Establishment  (CN)
National Employers Directory Service  (US)
National Employment Association  (US)
National Endowment for the Arts
    see U. S. National Endowment for the Arts  (US)
National Endowment for the Humanities
    see U. S. National Endowment for the Humanities
    (US)
National Energy Information Center
    see entry for U.S. Federal Energy Administration
    (US)
National Enquirer, Inc.  (US)
National Entertainment and Campus Activities
    Association  (US)
National Entertainment Conference  (US)
National Environmental Engineering Research
    Institute
    see India. National Environmental Engineering
    Research Institute  (II)
National Environmental Health Association  (US)
National Environmental Research Center  (US)
National Environmental Research Center (Research
    Triangle Park)  (US)
National Environmental Research Council  (UK)
National Epilepsy League, Inc.  (US)
National Equine Defence League  (UK)
National Exchange Club  (US)
National Extension College  (UK)
National Eye Institute
    see U.S. National Eye Institute  (US)
National Eye Research Foundation  (US)
National Fantasy Fan Federation. Games Bureau
    (US)
National Farm and Power Services, Inc.  (US)
National Farm-City Council, Inc.  (US)
National Farmers Union  (CN)
National Farmers' Union  (UK)
National Farmers Union  (US)
National Farmers' Union County Publications Ltd.
    (UK)
National Features Syndicate, Inc  (US)

National Interreligious Service Board for Conscientious Objectors (US)
National Intervenors (US)
National Investigations Committee on Aerial Phenomena (US)
National Investment Bank (GH)
National Investment Publishing Co. (US)
National Investor Relations Institute (US)
National Iranian Oil Company (IR)
National Jewish Welfare Board (US)
National Jewish Welfare Board. Jewish Book Council (US)
National Jogging Association (US)
National Josep Publishing Co. (US)
National Junior Classical League (US)
National Junior College Athletic Association (US)
National Junior Horticultural Association (US)
National Kappa Kappa Iota (US)
National Keyboard Arts Associates (US)
National Kidney Foundation (US)
National Knitted Outerwear Association (US)
National L P-Gas Association (US)
National Labor Relations Board
    see U.S. National Labor Relations Board (US)
National Language Research Institute (JA)
National Lawyers Guild (US)
National Lawyers Guild (New York) (US)
National Lawyers Guild (Seattle) (US)
National Laymen's Council, Church League of America (US)
National League for Nursing (US)
National League of American Pen Women, Inc. (US)
National League of Cities (US)
National League of Families of American Prisoners and Missing in Action in Southeast Asia (US)
National League of Postmasters (US)
National League of the Blind and Disabled (UK)
National Learning Corp. (US)
National Legal Aid and Defender Association (US)
National Librarians Association (US)
National Library
    see India. National Library (II)
    see National Diet Library (JA)
National Library (SI)
National Library Literary Review (US)
National Library of Australia
    see Australia. National Library of Australia (AT)
National Library of Canada (CN)
National Library of Medicine
    see U.S. National Library of Medicine (US)
National Library of New Zealand (NZ)
National Library of New Zealand. General Services Division (NZ)
National Library of Wales (UK)
National Life Insurance Company of Vermont (US)
National Live Stock and Meat Board (US)
National Live Stock Publishing (US)
National Livestock Feeders Association, Inc. (US)
National Lubricating Grease Institute (US)
National Macaroni Manufacturers Association (US)
National Machine Tool Builders' Association (US)
National Magazine Co., Ltd. (UK)
National Magazines Ltd. (SA)
National Management Association (US)
National Maple Syrup Digest (US)
National Marine Electronics Association (US)
National Marine Engineers Beneficial Association (US)
National Marine Fisheries Service
    see U.S. National Marine Fisheries Service (US)
National Maritime Board (UK)
National Maritime Museum (UK)
National Maritime Museum (IS)
National Maritime Union of America. A F L - C I O (US)
National Marriage Guidance Council (UK)
National Master Farriers Blacksmiths (UK)
National Mechanical Engineering Research Institute (SA)
National Mediation Board
    see U.S. National Mediation Board (US)
National Medical Association (US)
National Medical Audiovisual Center
    see U.S. National Medical Audiovisual Center (US)
National Medical Fellowships Inc. (US)
National Medical Library
    see India. National Medical Library (II)
National Merit Scholarship Corporation (US)
National Meteorological Center
    see U.S. National Meteorological Center (US)
National Microfilm Association (US)
National Microfilm Association. Metropolitan New York Chapter (US)
National Micrographics Association (US)
National Middle School Association (US)
National Milk Producers Federation (US)
National Minority Business Campaign (US)

National Mirror Inc. (US)
National Model Railroad Association (US)
National Moroccan Tourist Office (MR)
National Motor Museum Trust (UK)
National Multiple Sclerosis Society (US)
National Municipal League (US)
National Museum, Bloemfontein (SA)
National Museum of Man (CN)
National Museum of Man. History Division (CN)
National Museum of Modern Art, Tokyo (JA)
National Museum of Natural Sciences (CN)
National Museum of Tanzania (TZ)
National Museum of the Philippines (PH)
National Museum of Victoria (AT)
National Museum of Wales (UK)
National Museum. Trustees Board (NZ)
National Museums and Monuments of Rhodesia (RH)
National Museums of Canada (CN)
National Music Council (US)
National Mutual House (UK)
National Muzzle Loading Rifle Association (US)
National Neighbors (US)
National News Service, Inc. (US)
National Newspaper Association (US)
National Newspaper Publishers Association (US)
National Notary Association (US)
National Nudist Council (US)
National Nurses Association of Kenya (KE)
National Nutrition Society (JA)
National Nutritional Foods Association (US)
National Occupational Safety Association (SA)
National Ocean Survey
    see U.S. National Ocean Survey (US)
National Oceanographic Data Center
    see U.S. National Oceanographic Data Center (US)
National Oceanographic Instrumentation Center
    see U.S. National Oceanographic Instrumentation Center (US)
National Office for Black Catholics (US)
National Office Machine Dealers Association (US)
National Office Products Association (US)
National Opera Association, Inc. (US)
National Operatic and Dramatic Association (UK)
National Opinion Research Center (US)
National Organization for Women. Atlanta Chapter (US)
National Organization for Women. Central New Jersey Chapter (US)
National Organization for Women. Eastern Massachusetts Chapter (US)
National Organization for Women. Houston, Texas Chapter (US)
National Organization for Women. Madison Chapter (US)
National Organization for Women. Metropolitan Detroit Chapter (US)
National Organization for Women. Pennsylvania Chapter (US)
National Organization for Women. San Diego County Chapter (US)
National Organization for Women. San Francisco Chapter (US)
National Organization for Women. San Joaquin Chapter (US)
National Organization for Women. Washington, D.C. Chapter (US)
National Organization on Legal Problems of Education (US)
National Ornamental and Miscellaneous Metals Association (US)
National Packaging Association of Australia (AT)
National Packaging Association of Australia. Queensland Division (AT)
National Paint and Coatings Association (US)
National Palace Museum (CH)
National Park Service
    see U.S. National Park Service (US)
National Parking Association (US)
National Parks and Conservation Association (US)
National Parks Association of N.S.W. (AT)
National Particleboard Association (US)
National Pawnbrokers Association (Inc.) (UK)
National Peach Council (US)
National Periodical Library (US)
National Petroleum News (US)
National Pharmaceutical Association (UK)
National Pharmaceutical Association, Inc. (US)
National Philatelic Society (UK)
National Philatelic Society (US)
National Physical Laboratory
    see India. National Physical Laboratory (II)
National Pig Breeders' Association (UK)
National Pilots Association (US)
National Planning Association (US)
National Poetry Foundation, Inc. (US)
National Poetry Press (US)

National Police Chiefs & Sheriffs Information Bureau (US)
National Police Gazette (CN)
National Police Officers Association of America, Inc. (US)
National Pontius Association (US)
National Prep Sports Network, Inc. (US)
National Press Club (US)
National Press Council of the Republic of China (CH)
National Press Ltd. (MY)
National Press Photographers Association (US)
National Prisoners' Reform Association (US)
National Productivity Council (II)
National Property Law Digests, Inc. (US)
National Provisioner, Inc. (US)
National Psychological Association for Psychoanalysis, Inc. (US)
National Publications Service (PK)
National Publishers Ltd. (CN)
National Publishers Press
National Publishing Co. (Pty) Ltd. (SA)
National Publishing Corporation (US)
National Publishing Group Ltd. (IE)
National Racquetball Club, Inc. (US)
National Radio Institute (US)
National Radiological Protection Board (UK)
National Railway Historical Society. Pacific Northwest Chapter (US)
National Railway Historical Society. Tacoma Chapter (US)
National Railway Publication Co. (US)
National Reading Conference, Inc. (US)
National Ready Mixed Concrete Association (US)
National Recreation and Park Association (US)
National Reform Association (US)
National Register of Prominent Americans (US)
National Register Publishing Co., Inc. (US)
National Rehabilitation Association (US)
National Religious Broadcasters, Inc (US)
National Remodelers Association (US)
National Renaissance Party (US)
National Renderers Association (US)
National Reprographic Centre for documentation (UK)
National Research Bureau Inc. (US)
National Research Center for Disaster Prevention (JA)
National Research Council. Commission on Human Resources (US)
National Research Council. Committee on Polar Research (US)
National Research Council. Division of Biological Science (US)
National Research Council. Highway Research Board (US)
National Research Council of Canada (CN)
National Research Council of Canada. Associate Committee on Air Cushion Technology (CN)
National Research Council of Canada. Associate Committee on Geotechnical Research (CN)
National Research Council of Canada. Associate Committee on Scientific Criteria for Environmental Quality (CN)
National Research Council of Canada. Canada Institute for Scientific and Technical Information (CISTI) (CN)
National Research Council of Canada. Canadian National Committee for the I.U.G.G. (CN)
National Research Council of Canada. Division of Building Research (CN)
National Research Council of Canada. Division of Mechanical Engineering (CN)
National Research Council of Canada. Office of Grants & Scholarships (CN)
National Research Council of Canada. Public Information Branch (CN)
National Research Council of the Philippines (PH)
National Research Council. Transportation Research Board (US)
National Research Development Corporation of India
    see India. National Research Development Corporation of India (II)
National Research Institute for Mathematical Sciences (SA)
National Research Institute for Metals (JA)
National Research Institute for Pollution and Resources
    see Japan. National Research Institute for Pollution and Resources (JA)
National Research Institute of Police Science
    see Japan. National Research Institute of Police Science (JA)
National Research Laboratory of Metrology
    see Japan. National Research Laboratory of Metrology (JA)
National Restaurant Association (US)
National Retail Hardware Association (US)

National Retail Merchants Association  (US)
National Retail Merchants Association. Financial
  Executives Division  (US)
National Retired Teachers Association  (US)
National Review, Inc.  (US)
National Rifle Association of America  (US)
National Right to Work Committee  (US)
National Road Safety Council  (SA)
National Roads and Motorists Association  (AT)
National Rose Society of Australia  (AT)
National Rural Electric Cooperative Association  (US)
National Rural Letter Carriers Association  (US)
National Safety Council  (II)
National Safety Council  (US)
National Safety Council. Lehigh Valley Chapter  (US)
National Safety Council of Australia  (AT)
National Safety Council of Western Australia. Road
  Safety Division  (AT)
National Sales Development Institute  (US)
National Salesmen's Organizations, Inc.  (US)
National Sand and Gravel Association  (US)
National Sash & Door Jobbers Association  (US)
National Savings and Loan League  (US)
National Savings Committee for England and Wales
  (UK)
National Scholarship First Fund  (US)
National Scholarship Service and Fund for Negro
  Students  (US)
National Scholastic Press Association  (US)
National School Boards Association  (US)
National School Development Council  (US)
National School Public Relations Association  (US)
National School Volunteer Program, Inc.  (US)
National School Yearbook-Newspaper Association
  (US)
National Science Council of Sri Lanka  (CE)
National Science Council of the Republic of China
  (CH)
National Science Development Board
  see Philippines. National Science Development
  Board  (PH)
National Science Foundation
  see U.S. National Science Foundation  (US)
National Science Museum  (JA)
National Science Teachers Association  (US)
National Scientific Documentation Centre  (IO)
National Sculpture Society  (US)
National Sea Grant Depository  (US)

National Secretaries Association (International)  (US)
National Securities & Research Corp.  (US)
National Security Traders Association  (US)
National Seed Advisory Council  (IT)
National Service Secretariat, Inc.  (US)
National Sharecroppers Fund & Rural Advancement
  Fund  (US)
National Shellfisheries Association  (US)
National Sheriffs' Association  (US)
National Shoe Retailers Association  (US)
National Shorthand Reporters Association  (US)
National Skeet Shooting Association  (US)
National Ski Areas Association  (US)
National Slovak Society of U.S.A.  (US)
National Small-Bore Rifle Association  (UK)
National Small Business Association  (US)
National Socialist White People's Party  (US)
National Society for Autistic Children  (UK)
National Society for Autistic Children  (US)
National Society for Clean Air  (UK)
National Society for Hebrew Day Schools  (US)
National Society for Medical Research  (US)
National Society for Mentally Handicapped Children
  (UK)
National Society for Performance and Instruction
  (US)
National Society for Preservation of Covered Bridges
  Inc.  (US)
National Society for the Prevention of Blindness, Inc.
  (US)
National Society for the Prevention of Cruelty to
  Children  (UK)
National Society for the Study of Education  (US)
National Society of Accountants for Cooperatives
  (US)
National Society of Master Patternmakers  (UK)
National Society of Professional Engineers  (US)
National Society of Public Accountants  (US)
National Society of Scabbard and Blade  (US)
National Society of the Daughters of the American
  Revolution  (US)
National Society of the Sons of the American
  Revolution  (US)
National Solid Wastes Management Association  (US)
National Soybean Processors Association  (US)
National Speleological Society. Cascade Grotto  (US)
National Speleological Society. Huntsville Grotto
  (US)
National Speleological Society, Inc.  (US)

National Spiritual Assembly of the Baha'is of the
  United States  (US)
National Spiritualist Association of Churches  (US)
National Sporting Goods Association  (US)
National Spotlight  (US)
National Spotted Swine Record, Inc.  (US)
National Standards Association, Inc.  (US)
National States Rights Party  (US)
National Story League  (US)
National Strategy Information Center  (US)
National Student Nurses' Association  (US)
National Student Volunteer Program
  see U. S. National Student Volunteer Program
  (US)
National Sugar Institute
  see India. National Sugar Institute  (II)
National Supply Distributors Association Inc.  (US)
National Survey  (US)
National Swahili Council  (TZ)
National Taiwan Normal University. Department of
  Social Education  (CH)
National Taiwan Normal University. Graduate
  Institute of Education  (CH)
National Taiwan University. College of Agriculture
  (CH)
National Taiwan University. College of Engineering
  (CH)
National Taiwan University. College of Law  (CH)
National Taiwan University. College of Medicine
  (CH)
National Taiwan University. College of Science  (CH)
National Taiwan University. Department of
  Agricultural Chemistry  (CH)
National Taiwan University. Department of
  Archaeology and Anthropology  (CH)
National Taiwan University. Department of Geography
  (CH)
National Taiwan University. Department of Geology
  (CH)
National Taiwan University. Department of Sociology
  (CH)
National Taiwan University. Graduate Institute of
  Electrical Engineering  (CH)
National Taiwan University. Institute of Fishery
  Biology  (CH)
National Taiwan University. Institute of Oceanography
  (CH)
National Tank Truck Carriers, Inc.  (US)
National Tatler  (US)
National Tax Agency
  see Japan. National Tax Agency  (JA)
National Tax Association-Tax Institute of America
  (US)
National Teachers College, Kyambago  (UG)
National Technical Information Service
  see U.S. National Technical Information Service
  (US)
National Technical Information Service  (US)
National Telephone Cooperative Association  (US)
National Terrazo and Mosaic Association, Inc.  (US)
National Textbook Co.  (US)
National Therapeutic Recreation Society  (US)
National Tire Dealers and Retreaders Association
  (US)
National Tonnage Club of Farmers  (II)
National Tool Die and Precision Machining
  Association  (US)
National Tourist Organisation of Greece  (GR)
National Traction Engine Club  (UK)
National Trades Union Congress  (SI)
National Traffic Law News  (US)
National Training Center of Lie Detection, Inc.  (US)
National Training Council  (AT)
National Transit Newsletter  (US)
National Translations Center  (US)
National Treasury Employees Union  (US)
National Trust for Historic Preservation  (US)
National Trust for Scotland  (UK)
National Trust of Australia (New South Wales)  (AT)
National Trust of South Australia, Barmera Branch
  (AT)
National Tyre Distributors Association  (UK)
National Underwriter Co.  (US)
National Union of Agricultural Workers  (UK)
National Union of Bank Employees  (MY)
National Union of Bank Employees  (UK)
National Union of Christian Schools  (US)
National Union of Hospital and Health Care
  Employees  (US)
National Union of Insurance Workers. Prudential
  Section  (UK)
National Union of Journalists  (UK)
National Union of Journalists (India)  (II)
National Union of Licensed Victuallers  (UK)
National Union of Plantation Workers  (MY)
National Union of Railwaymen of Australia  (AT)
National Union of Seamen  (UK)

National Union of Sheet Metal Workers,
  Coppersmiths, Heating and Domestic Engineers
  (UK)
National Union of Southern African Students  (SA)
National Union of Students  (UK)
National Union of Students United Kingdom. Health
  Student Section  (UK)
National Union of Teachers  (UK)
National Union of Teachers of Malaysia  (MY)
National Union of the Footwear Leather and Allied
  Trades  (UK)
National Union of Townswomen's Guilds  (UK)
National Unity Party of Canada  (CN)
National University  (UK)
National University Extension Association  (US)
National University of Iran. Dental School  (IR)
National University of Ireland  (IE)
National University of Lesotho. School of Education
  (LO)
National University of Malaysia  (MY)
National University of Malaysia, Department of
  Geography  (MY)
National University of Malaysia. Historical Society
  (MY)
National University of Malaysia. Persatuan
  Kajimanusia Dan Kajimasharakat  (MY)
National Urban Coalition  (US)
National Urban League  (US)
National Urban League. Council of Executive
  Directors  (US)
National Vegetable Society  (UK)
National Verbond der Textieldetaillanten  (BE)
National Vocational Guidance Association  (US)
National Vulcan Engineering Insurance Group Ltd.
  (UK)
National Water Council  (UK)
National Water Supply Improvement Association
  (US)
National Water Well Association of Australia  (AT)
National Waterways Conference, Inc.  (US)
National Weather Service
  see U.S. National Weather Service  (US)
National Westminster Bank Ltd  (UK)
National Wildlife Federation, Inc.  (US)
National Woman's Christian Temperance Union  (US)
National Wool Growers Association  (US)
National Writers Club  (US)
National Young Judea  (US)
National Youth Alternatives Project  (US)
National Youth Bureau  (UK)
National Youth Leadership Training Institute  (SI)
National Zoological Gardens of South Africa  (SA)
National 4-H Council  (US)
Nationale Centrale voor Kleine en Middelgrote
  Levensmiddellenbedrijven  (BE)
Nationale Commissie tegen het Alkoholisme  (NE)
Nationale Confederatie V.D.  (BE)
Nationale Confederatie van Het Kaderpersoneel
  see Confederation Nationale des Cadres  (BE)
Nationale Cooperatieve Raad voor Land- en
  Tuinbouw.  (NE)
Nationale Kruisvereniging  (NE)
Nationale Nederlanden Insurance  (NE)
Nationale Organisatie voor Buurtwerk  (NE)
Nationale Vereniging Tot Voorkoming van
  Arbeidsongevallen  (BE)
Nationalekonomiska Foereningen  (SW)
Nationales Komitee fuer Gesundheitserziehung der
  DDR  (GE)
Nationalist Newspaper Co. Ltd.  (IE)
Nationaloekonomisk Forening  (DK)
Nationless Worldwide Assn.  (FR)
Nations Unies
  see United Nations  (UN)
Nationwide Building Society  (UK)
Nationwide Papers  (US)
Native American Rights Fund  (US)
Native American Student Alliance  (US)
Native American Training Associates Institute  (US)
Native Brotherhood of British Columbia and Raven
  Society  (CN)
Native Communications Society of Nova Scotia
  (CN)
Native Communications Society of the Western
  N.W.T.  (CN)
Native Council of Canada  (CN)
Native Voice Publishing Society  (CN)
Izdatelstvo Natsionalen Suvet na Otechestveniia Front
  (BU)
Natun Thikana  (II)
Natura Mosana  (BE)
Natural Environmental Research Council  (UK)
Natural Food Publications Ltd.  (UK)
Natural Hazards Research and Applications
  Information Center  (US)
Natural Health World  (US)
Natural High  (US)

Nederlandse Klokkenspel-Vereniging   (NE)
Nederlandse Kring voor Wetenschap der Politiek
   (NE)
Nederlandse Malacologische Vereniging   (NE)
Nederlandse Melkhandelaren Organisatie   (NE)
Nederlandse Natuurkundige Vereniging. Fysisch
   Laboratorium   (NE)
Nederlandse Onderwatersport Bond   (NE)
Nederlandse Operastichting   (NE)
Nederlandse Orchideeen Vereniging   (NE)
Nederlandse Orde van Accountants-
   Administratieconsulenten   (NE)
Nederlandse Organisatie van Pluimveehouders   (NE)
Nederlandse Organisatie van Tijdschriftuitgevers
   (NE)
Nederlandse Organisatie voor Internationale
   Ontwikkelingssamenwerking   (NE)
Nederlandse Organisatie voor Zuiver-Wetenschappelijk
   Onderzoek   (NE)
Nederlandse Ornithologische Unie   (NE)
Nederlandse Planteziektenkundige Vereniging   (NE)
Nederlandse Rode Kruis   (NE)
Nederlandse Spaarbankbond   (NE)
N. V. Nederlandse Spoorwegen   (NE)
Nederlandse Sport Federatie   (NE)
Nederlandse Stikstofmestoffen Industrie.
   Landouwkundig Bureau   (NE)
Nederlandse Toeristen Kampeerclub   (NE)
Nederlandse Unie van Opticiens   (NE)
Nederlandse Vacuumvereiniging   (NE)
Nederlandse Vereniging Bescherming Voetgangers
   (NE)
Nederlandse Vereniging "de Rijwiel- en Automobiel
   Industrie"   (NE)
Nederlandse Vereniging ter Bevordering van het
   Levensverzekeringwezen   (NE)
Nederlandse Vereniging tot Beoefening van de Sociale
   Geschiedenis   (NE)
Nederlandse Vereniging tot Steun aan het Koningin
   Wilhelmina Fonds voor de Kankerbestrijding   (NE)
Nederlandse Vereniging van Assurantieadviseurs
   (NE)
Nederlandse Vereniging van Belangstellenden in het
   Spoor- en Tramwegwezen   (NE)
Nederlandse Vereniging van Bouwondernemers   (NE)
Nederlandse Vereniging van Elektroencefalografie
   Laboranten   (NE)
Nederlandse Vereniging van Handelaren in
   Verwarmings- en Huishoudelijke Artikelen   (NE)
Nederlandse Vereniging van Huisvrouwen   (NE)
Nederlandse Vereniging van Journalisten   (NE)
Nederlandse Vereniging van Maatschappelijk Werkers
   (NE)
Nederlandse Vereniging van Modelbouwers   (NE)
Nederlandse Vereniging van Ondernemers in het
   Carosseriebedrijf   (NE)
Nederlandse Vereniging van Radiologisch Laboranten
   (NE)
Nederlandse Vereniging van Rubberfabrikanten   (NE)
Nederlandse Vereniging van Veiligheidstechnici   (NE)
Nederlandse Vereniging van Vrijzinnige
   Zondagsscholen en Leidraad voor de Leiding   (NE)
Nederlandse Vereniging van Vrouwen met
   Academische Opleiding   (NE)
Nederlandse Vereniging van Wasserijen   (NE)
Nederlandse Vereniging voor de Landelijke Eigendom
   (NE)
Nederlandse Vereniging voor de Verenigde Naties
   (NE)
Nederlandse Vereniging voor Geodesie   (NE)
Nederlandse Vereniging voor Herpetologie en
   Terrariumkunde   (NE)
Nederlandse Vereniging voor Internationaal Recht
   (NE)
Nederlandse Vereniging voor Koeltechniek   (NE)
Nederlandse Vereniging voor Management (Nive)
   (NE)
Nederlandse Vereniging voor Personeelbeleid   (NE)
Nederlandse Vereniging voor Psychiaters in
   Dienstverband   (NE)
Nederlandse Vereniging voor Revalidatie   (NE)
Nederlandse Vereniging voor Sexuele Hervorming
   (NE)
Nederlandse Vereniging voor Slechthorenden   (NE)
Nederlandse Vereniging voor Zeegeschiedenis   (NE)
Nederlandse Volksdansvereniging   (NE)
Nederlandse Volleybal Bond   (NE)
Nederlandse Waterski Bond   (NE)
Nederlandse Zending   (NE)
Nederlandse Zendingsraad   (NE)
Izdatel'stvo Nedra   (UR)
Needle and Bobbin Club   (US)
Needlepoint, Inc.   (US)
Needlework Guild of America   (US)
Neerlands Postduiven Orgaan   (NE)
NEF Publishing Co.   (US)
Negocios   (MX)
Negocios y Bancos   (MX)

M. J. Negre, Pub.   (FR)
Negro Airmen International, Inc.   (US)
Negro Educational Review, Inc.   (US)
Negro Lawmaker Journal   (US)
Negro Universities Press   (US)
Neighbourhood Publications Cooperative Society Ltd.
   (II)
Dr. Neinhaus Verlag GmbH   (GW)
Nelson Africa Ltd.   (KE)
Thomas Nelson and Sons   (US)
A. Verner Nelson Associates   (US)
Nelson Gallery-Atkins Museum   (US)
Nelson-Hall Publishing Co.   (US)
Nematological Society of India   (II)
Nemzetkozi Zenei Versenyek es Fesztivalok Irodaja
   (HU)
Neo Aftokinito   (GR)
Neo-American Church   (US)
Neos Kosmos   (AT)
Nepal. Central Bureau of Statistics   (NP)
Nepal. Department of Agricultural Education and
   Research   (NP)
Nepal. Department of Archaeology   (NP)
Nepal. Department of Commemoration   (NP)
Nepal. Department of Electricity   (NP)
Nepal. National Planning Commission   (NP)
Nepal Bank Limited   (NP)
Nepal Digest Publication   (NP)
Nepal Economic and Commerce Research Centre
   (NP)
Nepal Geographical Society   (NP)
Nepal Industrial Development Corporation   (NP)
Nepal Medical Association   (NP)
Nepal Nature Conservation Society   (NP)
Nepal Press Digest (Pvt) Ltd.   (NP)
Nepal Rastra Bank   (NP)
Nepal Red Cross Society   (NP)
Nepalese Association for World Understanding   (NP)
Nepalese Journal of Science   (NP)
Nepali Janavadi Krantikari Samskritika Sangha   (NP)
Nepmuvelesi Propaganda Iroda   (HU)
Neprajzi Muzeum   (HU)
Nepszava Lapkiado Vallalat   (HU)
Neptune Productions   (US)
Neptune's Kingdom   (IE)
Hans Nesser   (SZ)
Neste Oy   (FI)
Netaji Subhas National Institute of Sports   (II)
Nether Press   (UK)
Netherlands. Bureau voor de Industriele Eigendom.
   Octrooiraad   (NE)
Netherlands. Centraal Bureau voor de Statistiek   (NE)
Netherlands. Commissie Zeehavenoverleg   (NE)
Netherlands. Gevangeniswezen. Centraal Wervings- en
   Opleidingsinstituut   (NE)
Netherlands. Hydrografisch Bureau   (NE)
Netherlands. Inspectie voor het Brandweerwezen
   (NE)
Netherlands. Kabinet Nederlandse Antillen   (NE)
Netherlands. Koninklijke Landmacht   (NE)
Netherlands. Koninklijke Luchtmacht   (NE)
Netherlands. Koninklijke Luchtmacht. Afdeling
   Bedrijfsveiligheid Koninklijke Luchtmachtstaf
   (NE)
Netherlands. Ministerie van Binnenlandse Zaken
   (NE)
Netherlands. Ministerie van Binnenlandse Zaken.
   Inspectie voor het Brandweerwezen
   see Netherlands. Inspectie voor het
   Brandweerwezen   (NE)
Netherlands. Ministerie van Buitenlandse Zaken.
   Voorlichtingsdienst Ontwikkelingssamenwerking
   (NE)
Netherlands. Ministerie van Cultuur Recreatie en
   Maatschappelijk Werk   (NE)
Netherlands. Ministerie van Defensie   (NE)
Netherlands. Ministerie van Economische Zaken.
   Economische Voorlichtingsdienst   (NE)
Netherlands. Ministerie van Justitie.   (NE)
Netherlands. Ministerie van Justitie. Gevangeniswezen
   see Netherlands. Gevangeniswezen   (NE)
Netherlands. Ministerie van Justitie. Wetenschappelijk
   Onderzoek- en Documentatiecentrum   (NE)
Netherlands. Ministerie van Landbouw en Visserij
   (NE)
Netherlands. Ministerie van Landbouw en Visserij.
   Statistics and Documentation Section   (NE)
Netherlands. Ministerie van Sociale Zaken. Library
   and Documentation Service   (NE)
Netherlands. Ministerie van Volksgezondheid en
   Milieuhygiene   (NE)
Netherlands. Ministerie van Volkshuisvesting en
   Ruimtelijke Ordening. Afdeling Voorlichting   (NE)
Netherlands. Persraad   (NE)
Netherlands. Raad voor de Beroepskeuzevoorlichting
   (NE)
Netherlands. Rijks Geologische Dienst   (NE)
Netherlands. Rijkscommissie voor Geodesie   (NE)

Netherlands. Rijksmuseum   (NE)
Netherlands. Rijksmuseum voor Volkenkunde   (NE)
Netherlands. Rijksvoorlichtingsdienst   (NE)
Netherlands. Sociaal en Culturkeel Planbureau   (NE)
Netherlands. Sociale Verzekeringsraad   (NE)
Netherlands. Staatsbedrijf der Posterijen Telegrafie en
   Telefonie   (NE)
Netherlands. Staatsuitgeverij   (NE)
Netherlands. Tariefcommissie   (NE)
Netherlands A D P Research Centre   (NE)
Netherlands Antilles. Bureau voor de Statistiek   (NA)
Netherlands Antilles. Departement Sociale and
   Economische Zaken   (NA)
Netherlands Association of Journalists
   see Nederlandse Vereniging van Journalisten   (NE)
Netherlands-British Chamber of Commerce   (UK)
Netherlands Cement Industry B.V.   (NE)
Netherlands Central Organization for Applied
   Scientific Research TNO   (NE)
Netherlands Centre of the International Theatre
   Institute   (NE)
Netherlands Chamber of Commerce in U.S.   (US)
Netherlands Consulate General. Economic Information
   Service   (US)
Netherlands Council for Trade Promotion. Economic
   Information Service   (US)
Netherlands Electronics and Radio Society.   (NE)
Netherlands Emigration Service   (NE)
Netherlands Federation of Trade Unions   (NE)
Netherlands Grain Centre   (NE)
Netherlands Hydrobiological Society   (NE)
Netherlands Institute for Sea Research   (NE)
Netherlands Institute for the Middle East   (NE)
Netherlands Institute of Transport   (NE)
Netherlands Investment Bank for Developing
   Countries   (NE)
Netherlands-Ireland Institute   (NE)
Netherlands Maritime Institute. Maritime Economic
   Research Centre   (NE)
Netherlands Organisation for Applied Scientific
   Research   (NE)
Netherlands Royal Army
   see Netherlands. Koninklijke Landmacht   (NE)
Netherlands Society of Royal Navy Officers
   see Vereniging van Marine-Officieren   (NE)
Netherlands Sociological Society   (NE)
Netherlands Universities Foundation for International
   Cooperation   (NE)
Netherlands Youth Council
   see Nederlandse Federatie Jeugd en Jongerenwerk
   (NE)
Nettai Nogyo Gakkai
   see Tropical Agriculture Research Association of
   Japan   (JA)
Nettennis, Inc.   (US)
Neturei Karta of U.S.A.-Guardians of the Holy City
   (US)
Network   (UK)
Neue Bachgesellschaft, Internationale Vereinigung
   (GE)
Verlag Neue Deutsche Hefte   (GW)
Neue Deutsche Schule Verlagsgesellschaft MbH
   (GW)
Verlag Neue Gesellschaft GmbH   (GW)
Verlag Neue Musik   (GE)
Verlag Neue Physik   (AU)
Neue Religioes-Soziale Vereinigung   (SZ)
Verlag Neue Technik   (AU)
Verlag Neue Technik AG   (SZ)
Verlag fuer Neue Werbung GmbH   (GW)
Verlag Neue Wirtschafts-Briefe GmbH   (GW)
Neue Zeitung   (US)
Neue Zuercher Zeitung   (SZ)
Neuer Konkret Verlag   (GW)
Verlag Neuer Merkur GmbH   (GW)
Neuer Vorwaerts Verlag   (GW)
Neuer Vorwaerts-Verlag Nau und Co.   (GW)
Verlag Neuer Weg GmbH   (GW)
Neues Leben   (AU)
Neues Optikerjournal Verlag   (GW)
Verlag Dr. Neufang KG   (GW)
Wolfgang Neugebauer   (AU)
Neuland-Verlagsgesellschaft mbH   (GW)
Sociedade Editora da Revista Neurobiologia   (BL)
Neuroelectric Society, Inc.   (US)
Neurological Society of India   (II)
Neuroloski-Psihijatrijska Klinika Rebro, Zagreb   (YU)
Neurotics Anonymous International Liaison, Inc.
   (US)
Neuwerk-Gemeinschaft e.V.   (GW)
Nevada. Advisory Council for Manpower Training and
   Career Education   (US)
Nevada. Bureau of Mines and Geology   (US)
Nevada. Commission on Crime, Delinquency, and
   Corrections   (US)

Nevada. Department of Economic Development (US)
Nevada. Department of Education (US)
Nevada. Department of Highways (US)
Nevada. Division of Personnel (US)
Nevada. Employment Security Department (US)
Nevada. Gaming Control Board. Economic Research Unit (US)
Nevada. Office of Legislative Auditor (US)
Nevada. Public Works Board (US)
Nevada. Research and Education Planning Center (US)
Nevada. State Board for Vocational Education (US)
Nevada. State Library (US)
Nevada. State Planning Coordinators Office (US)
Nevada. Tax Commission (US)
Nevada Cattlemen's Association (US)
Nevada Farm Bureau Federation (US)
Nevada Historical Society (US)
Nevada League of Cities (US)
Nevada Library Association (US)
Nevada Music Educators Association (US)
Nevada Publishing Co. (US)
Nevada Society of Professional Engineers (US)
Nevada State Education Association (US)
Nevada State Medical Association (US)
Nevada State Museum (US)
Francisco Ferretra Neves, Ed. & Pub. (PO)
Nevesole (IT)
Nevil Interagency Referral Service (US)
New Age Communications Inc. (US)
New Age Press (II)
New Age Teachings (US)
New Alaskan Publishing Co. (US)
New Alchemy Institute - West (US)
New American Library (US)
New American Library (New York) (US)
New American Movement (US)
New Asia College. Institute of Advanced Chinese Studies and Research (HK)
New Atlantean Research Society (US)
New Awareness Publishing Co., Inc. (US)
New Banner Institute, Inc. (US)
New Books (US)
New Breed Organization Ltd. (NR)
New Broom (US)
New Brunswick. Correctional Program (CN)
New Brunswick. Department of Agriculture and Rural Development (CN)
New Brunswick. Department of Agriculture & Rural Development. Horticulture Division (CN)
New Brunswick. Department of Agriculture and Rural Development. Plant Industry Branch (CN)
New Brunswick. Department of Fisheries (CN)
New Brunswick. Department of Health (CN)
New Brunswick. Department of Labour (CN)
New Brunswick. Department of Municipal Affairs (CN)
New Brunswick. Department of Natural Resources (CN)
New Brunswick. Department of Youth (CN)
New Brunswick. Economic Advisor's Office (CN)
New Brunswick. Field Services Branch (CN)
New Brunswick. Health Services Advisory Council (CN)
New Brunswick. Liquor Control Commission (CN)
New Brunswick. Research and Productivity Council (CN)
New Brunswick Development Corporation (CN)
New Brunswick Electric Power Commission (CN)
New Brunswick Federation of Naturalists (CN)
New Brunswick Home Economics Association (CN)
New Brunswick Industrial Safety Council (CN)
New Brunswick Information Service (CN)
New Brunswick Museum (CN)
New Brunswick Public Employees Association (CN)
New Brunswick Teachers' Association (CN)
New Caledonia. Service de la Statistique (NL)
New Caledonia. Service des Mines (NL)
New Canadian Publisher (CN)
New Century Publishing Co.Ltd. (UK)
New Chamber Orchestra of Canada (CN)
New Chemical Publications (Pty) Ltd. (SA)
New China Publication Service (CH)
New Christian (UK)
New Chronicle Printery Ltd. (DQ)
New Church Press (UK)
New City Songster (UK)
New Collage Press (UK)
New Community Press Ltd. (UK)
New Daily Cardinal Corporation (US)
New Day Publishing Co. (US)
New Democratic Party of British Columbia (CN)
New Departures (UK)
New Detroit, Inc. (US)
New Diffusionist Press (UK)
New Dimensions (US)
New Dimensions in Education, Inc. (US)

New Directions (UK)
New Directions for Women, Inc. (US)
New Earth Books (US)
New East, Inc. (US)
New England Association of Teachers of English (US)
New England Beverage Publications, Inc. (US)
New England Board of Higher Education (US)
New England Botanical Club, Inc. (US)
New England Bride (US)
New England Caller, Inc. (US)
New England Council of Optometrists (US)
New England Crop and Livestock Reporting Service (US)
New England Fuel Institute (US)
New England Furniture News (US)
New England Gardening (US)
New England Genealogical Society. Committee on Heraldry (US)
New England Hardware Publications (US)
New England Historic Genealogical Society (US)
New England History Teachers Association (US)
New England Interstate Water Pollution Control Commission (US)
New England Library Board (US)
New England Library Information Network (US)
New England Prisoner's Association (US)
New England Program in Teacher Education (US)
New England Railroad Club (US)
New England Reading Association (US)
New England River Basins Commission (US)
New England Road Builders Association (US)
New England School Development Council (US)
New England School of Law (US)
New England Science Fiction Association Inc. (US)
New England Telephone Co. (US)
New England Water Works Association (US)
New Environment Association (US)
New Era Books (UK)
New Era Educational Society, Inc. (US)
New Era Magazine (UK)
New Farm Press (Grimsby) Ltd. (UK)
New Fiction Society (UK)
New Gay Life (US)
New Gospel Treasure Publishing Co (US)
New Guinea News Service (Pty.) Ltd. (PP)
New Guyana Co. Ltd. (GY)
New Hampshire. Bureau of Vital Statistics (US)
New Hampshire. Commission on Crime and Delinquency (US)
New Hampshire. Council on Aging (US)
New Hampshire. Department of Agriculture. Bureau of Markets (US)
New Hampshire. Department of Education (US)
New Hampshire. Department of Education. Food and Nutrition Service (US)
New Hampshire. Department of Employment Security (US)
New Hampshire. Division of Public Health. Program on Alcohol & Drug Abuse (US)
New Hampshire. Employment Service Bureau (US)
New Hampshire. Fish and Game Department (US)
New Hampshire. Fish and Game Department. Game Management and Research Division (US)
New Hampshire. State Library (US)
New Hampshire Archeological Society Inc. (US)
New Hampshire Archeological Society, Inc. (Manchester) (US)
New Hampshire Association of Conservation Commissions (US)
New Hampshire Campground Owners Association (US)
New Hampshire Dental Society (US)
New Hampshire Education Association (US)
New Hampshire Historical Society (US)
New Hampshire Library Association (US)
New Hampshire Music Educators Association (US)
New Hampshire Nurses Association (US)
New Hampshire School Administrators Association (US)
New Hampshire School Boards Association (US)
New Hampshire Social Welfare Council (US)
New Hampshire Truck Owners Association (US)
New Hebrides. Condominium Bureau of Statistics (NN)
New Hebrides. Condominium Geological Survey (NN)
New Hellas (CN)
New Horizons Communications Group Press (US)
New Horse Play (US)
New Internationalist Publications Ltd. (UK)
New Internationalist Publications Ltd. (US)
New Japan Casting and Forging Society (JA)
New Japanese Doctors' Association (JA)
New Jersey. Advisory Commission on the Status of Women (US)

New Jersey. Bureau of Community Mental Health Services (US)
New Jersey. Bureau of Geology and Topography (US)
New Jersey. Bureau of Statistical Analysis and Social Research (US)
New Jersey. Department of Agriculture (US)
New Jersey. Department of Community Affairs. Division of Local Government Services (US)
New Jersey. Department of Corrections (US)
New Jersey. Department of Education (US)
New Jersey. Department of Education. Division of Curriculum and Instruction (US)
New Jersey. Department of Education. Division of Vocational Education (US)
New Jersey. Department of Environmental Protection (US)
New Jersey. Department of Environmental Protection. Division of Water Resources (US)
New Jersey. Department of Environmental Protection. New Jersey Clean Air Council (US)
New Jersey. Department of Human Services. Division of Youth and Family Services (US)
New Jersey. Department of Labor and Industry (US)
New Jersey. Department of Labor and Industry. Division of Planning and Research. (US)
New Jersey. Department of Labor and Industry. Office of Business Economics (US)
New Jersey. Department of Law and Public Safety. Division of Civil Defense-Disaster Control (US)
New Jersey. Department of the Treasury. Division of Taxation (US)
New Jersey. Department of Transportation (US)
New Jersey. Developmental Disabilities Council (US)
New Jersey. Division of Administrative Procedure (US)
New Jersey. Division of Banking (US)
New Jersey. Division of Criminal Justice. Appellate Section (US)
New Jersey. Highway Authority. Garden State Parkway (US)
New Jersey. Office of Economic Policy (US)
New Jersey. Office of International Trade (US)
New Jersey. State Health Benefits Commission (US)
New Jersey. State Law Enforcement Planning Agency (US)
New Jersey. State Legislature. Office of Fiscal Affairs (US)
New Jersey. State Library (US)
New Jersey. State Office on Aging (US)
New Jersey. Violent Crimes Compensation Board (US)
New Jersey Academy of Science (US)
New Jersey Association for Health, Physical Education and Recreation (US)
New Jersey Association of Certified Dental Laboratories, Inc. (US)
New Jersey Association of Certified Dental Laboratories, Inc. (Springfield) (US)
New Jersey Association of Osteopathic Physicians & Surgeons (US)
New Jersey Association of Realtors (US)
New Jersey Audubon Society (US)
New Jersey Bankers Association (US)
New Jersey Bell Telephone Co (US)
New Jersey Civil Service Association (US)
New Jersey Classical Association (US)
New Jersey Committee for the Humanities (US)
New Jersey Comprehensive Health Planning Agency (US)
New Jersey Congress of Parents and Teachers (US)
New Jersey Cooperative Extension Service (US)
New Jersey Council of School Administrators (US)
New Jersey Council on Alcohol Problems (US)
New Jersey Crop Reporting Service (US)
New Jersey Dental Association (US)
New Jersey Division of Savings and Loan Associations (US)
New Jersey Federation of Business & Professional Woman's Clubs, Inc. (US)
New Jersey Federation of Planning Officials (US)
New Jersey Federation of Shade Tree Commissions (US)
New Jersey Genesis Quarterly (US)
New Jersey Historical Commission (US)
New Jersey Historical Society (US)
New Jersey Institute of Technology (US)
New Jersey Jazz Society (US)
New Jersey Law Journal Publishing Co. (US)
New Jersey Library Association (US)
New Jersey Manufacturers Association (US)
New Jersey Mortgage Finance Agency (US)
New Jersey Mosquito Control Association, Inc (US)
New Jersey Motor Truck Association (US)
New Jersey Music and Arts (US)
New Jersey Optometric Association (US)
New Jersey Pharmaceutical Association (US)
New Jersey Poetry Society (US)

New Jersey Postal History Society  (US)
New Jersey Press Association  (US)
New Jersey Real Estate Commission  (US)
New Jersey Savings League  (US)
New Jersey School Boards Association  (US)
New Jersey School Development Council  (US)
New Jersey Shield Publishing Co., Inc.  (US)
New Jersey Shore Builders Association  (US)
New Jersey Society of Architects  (US)
New Jersey Society of Professional Engineers, Inc.
(US)
New Jersey Speech and Hearing Association  (US)
New Jersey Speech and Hearing Association (Rocky
Hill)  (US)
New Jersey State Agency for Social Security  (US)
New Jersey State Bar Association  (US)
New Jersey State Federation of Women's Clubs  (US)
New Jersey State League of Municipalities  (US)
New Jersey State Museum  (US)
New Jersey State Nurses' Association  (US)
New Jersey State Patrolmen's Benevolent Association
(US)
New Jersey State Safety Council  (US)
New Journal at Yale, Inc.  (US)
New Journal of Statistics and Operational Research
(UK)
New Journalist  (AT)
New Korea  (US)
New Leaf Publications  (CN)
New Left Review Ltd.  (UK)
New Life Publications  (UK)
New Magazine, Inc.  (US)
New Medical Journals Ltd.  (UK)
New Mexico. Bureau of Mines and Mineral Resources
(US)
New Mexico. Department of Agriculture  (US)
New Mexico. Department of Development  (US)
New Mexico. Department of Education. Veterans
Approval Division  (US)
New Mexico. Department of Game and Fish  (US)
New Mexico. Department of State Forestry  (US)
New Mexico. Employment Security Commission
(US)
New Mexico. Governor's Council on Criminal Justice
Planning  (US)
New Mexico. Secretary of State  (US)
New Mexico. State Planning Office  (US)
New Mexico. State Records Center and Archives.
Publications Management Division  (US)
New Mexico. Supreme Court  (US)
New Mexico. Veterans' Service Commission  (US)
New Mexico Association of Elementary School
Principals  (US)
New Mexico Book League  (US)
New Mexico Cattle Growers Association  (US)
New Mexico Committee on Children and Youth
(US)
New Mexico Educational Association  (US)
New Mexico Farm & Ranch, Inc.  (US)
New Mexico Geological Society  (US)
New Mexico Motor Carriers' Association, Inc.  (US)
New Mexico Municipal League  (US)
New Mexico Music Educators Association  (US)
New Mexico Pharmaceutical Association  (US)
New Mexico Review and Legislative Journal  (US)
New Mexico Rural Electrification Cooperative
Association  (US)
New Mexico Society of Professional Engineers  (US)
New Mexico Solar Energy Association  (US)
New Mexico State University Press  (US)
New Mexico State University. Rio Grande Historical
Collections Library  (US)
New Mexico State University. Writing Center  (US)
New Moon Communications  (US)
New Morality  (IT)
New Nation Publications  (SA)
New Nigeria Development Company Ltd.  (NR)
New Nippon Electric Company Ltd.  (JA)
New Orleans Academy of Ophthalmology  (US)
New Orleans Jazz Club  (US)
New Orleans Jazz Club of California  (US)
New Orleans Jazz Club of Southern California  (US)
New Orleans Public Library  (US)
New Orleans Retail Grocers Association  (US)
New Orleans Socialist Union  (US)
New Pathway Publishing Co. Ltd  (CN)
New Politics Publishing Co.  (US)
New Prima Press  (II)
New Property Press  (UK)
New Readers' Press  (US)
New Renaissance  (US)
New Republic  (US)
New Review Books  (CN)
New Review Inc.  (US)
New Review Ltd.  (UK)
New Scholar  (US)
New School for Social Research  (US)

New School for Social Research. Center for New York
City Affairs  (US)
New Schools Exchange  (US)
New Scientist  (UK)
New Sense  (US)
New Skete Monastery  (US)
New Social Perspectives, Inc.  (US)
New South Press  (US)
New South Wales. Attorney-General. Bureau of Crime
Statistics and Research  (AT)
New South Wales. Attorney General Justice
Department  (AT)
New South Wales. Department of Agriculture  (AT)
New South Wales. Department of Agriculture.
Division of Marketing and Economics  (AT)
New South Wales. Department of Decentralisation and
Development  (AT)
New South Wales. Department of Education  (AT)
New South Wales. Department of Labour and Industry
(AT)
New South Wales. Department of Lands  (AT)
New South Wales. Department of Main Roads  (AT)
New South Wales. Department of Mines  (AT)
New South Wales. Department of Technical Education
(AT)
New South Wales. Department of Tourism  (AT)
New South Wales. Directorate of Aboriginal Welfare
(AT)
New South Wales. Fire Service  (AT)
New South Wales. Forestry Commission  (AT)
New South Wales. Forestry Commission. Department
of Conservation  (AT)
New South Wales Government Printer  (AT)
New South Wales. Health Commission  (AT)
New South Wales. Health Commission. Division of
Health Education  (AT)
New South Wales. Higher Education Authority  (AT)
New South Wales. Industrial Commission  (AT)
New South Wales. Law Reform Commission  (AT)
New South Wales. Maritime Services Board. Public
Relations Section  (AT)
New South Wales. Metric Conversion Board  (AT)
New South Wales. National Parks and Wildlife Service
(AT)
New South Wales. State Fisheries  (AT)
New South Wales. Supreme Court  (AT)
New South Wales. Teachers Federation  (AT)
New South Wales Association of Special Education
Teachers  (AT)
New South Wales Conservatorium of Music  (AT)
New South Wales Dairy Farmers Association  (AT)
New South Wales Humanist Society  (AT)
New South Wales Independent Teachers Association
(AT)
New South Wales Institute of Freshwater Fishermen
(AT)
New South Wales League of Women Voters  (AT)
New South Wales Maritime Services Board  (AT)
New South Wales Military Historical Society  (AT)
New South Wales Nurses Association  (AT)
New South Wales Retail Tobacco Traders Association
(AT)
New South Wales Rugby League  (AT)
New South Wales Soil Conservation Service  (AT)
New Square Publications Ltd.  (IE)
New Statements  (CN)
New Straits Times Press (Malaysia) Berhad  (MY)
New Times Communications Corp.  (US)
New Times, Inc.  (US)
New Times, Inc. (Tempe)  (US)
New Towns Association  (UK)
New Tribes Mission  (US)
New Unity  (US)
New Venture Publishing  (US)
New Viewpoints  (US)
New Vision  (TR)
New Voices  (TR)
New Voices  (US)
New Wave Society  (II)
New Way Enterprises, Ltd.  (US)
New Woman, Inc.  (US)
New Women's Magazine Society  (CN)
New World Arts Workshop  (US)
New World Associates  (GY)
New World Club, Inc.  (US)
New World Forum, Inc.  (US)
New World Haiku  (US)
New World Press  (US)
New World Publishers Ltd.  (UK)
New World Publishing Co., Inc.  (US)
New World Review Publications, Inc.  (US)
New Worlds Publishing  (UK)
New Writers Group  (ZA)
New York (City) Addiction Services Agency  (US)
New York (City) Board of Education  (US)
New York (City) Bureau of the Budget  (US)
New York (City) Comptrollers Office  (US)
New York (City) Department for the Aging  (US)

New York (City) Department of Health  (US)
New York (City) Department of Public Works. Bureau
of Gas & Electricity  (US)
New York (City) Department of Social Services.
Human Resources Administration  (US)
New York (City) Fire Department  (US)
New York (City) Health Systems Agency of New
York City  (US)
New York (City) Housing Authority  (US)
New York (City) Metropolitan Transportation
Authority  (US)
New York (City) Office of Labor Relations  (US)
New York (City) Office of the Mayor  (US)
New York (City) Police Department  (US)
New York (City) Post Office  (US)
New York (City) Transit Authority  (US)
New York (State) Consumer Protection Board  (US)
New York (State) Crime Victims Compensation Board
(US)
New York (State) Department of Audit and Control
(US)
New York (State) Department of Commerce  (US)
New York (State) Department of Environmental
Conservation  (US)
New York (State) Department of Labor. Division of
Research and Statistics  (US)
New York (State) Department of Labor. Labor Staff
Academy Library  (US)
New York (State) Department of Law  (US)
New York (State) Department of Law. Environmental
Protection Bureau  (US)
New York (State) Department of Mental Hygiene
(US)
New York (State) Department of Social Services
(US)
New York (State) Department of State  (US)
New York (State) Department of Taxation and
Finance  (US)
New York (State) Division of Criminal Justice Services
(US)
New York (State) Division of the Budget. Office of
Statistical Coordination  (US)
New York (State) Drug Abuse Control Commission
(US)
New York (State) Education Department  (US)
New York (State) Education Department. Bureau of
Educational Finance Research  (US)
New York (State) Education Department. Division of
Education Management Services  (US)
New York (State) Education Department. Information
Center on Education  (US)
New York (State) Education Department. Office of
Health, Pupil and Non-Pupil Public School Service
(US)
New York (State) Education Department. Office of
Occupational Education  (US)
New York (State) Education Department. Office of
State History  (US)
New York (State) Energy Research and Development
Authority  (US)
New York (State) Foreign Area Materials Center
(US)
New York (State) Geological Survey  (US)
New York (State) Health and Mental Hygiene
Facilities Improvement Corporation  (US)
New York (State) Insurance Department  (US)
New York (State) Interdepartmental Committee on
Indian Affairs  (US)
New York (State) Medical Care Facilities Finance
Agency  (US)
New York (State) Office for the Aging  (US)
New York (State) Office of Parks and Recreation
(US)
New York (State) Office of Planning Services  (US)
New York (State) Office of Welfare Inspector General
(US)
New York (State) Public Employment Relations Board
(US)
New York (State) State Library  (US)
New York (State) State Library. Division of Library
Development  (US)
New York (State) State Police  (US)
New York (State) Urban Development Corporation
(US)
New York (State) Workmen's Compensation Board
(US)
New York Academy of Dentistry  (US)
New York Academy of Medicine  (US)
New York Academy of Medicine. Library  (US)
New York Academy of Sciences  (US)
New York Association of Teachers of English  (US)
New York Athletic Club  (US)
New York Botanical Garden  (US)
New York C.S. Lewis Society  (US)
New York Cactus & Succulent Society, Inc.  (US)
New York Chamber of Commerce and Industry  (US)
New York City Central Labor Council. AFL-CIO
(US)

New Zealand Institute of Chemistry (NZ)
New Zealand Institute of Economic Research (NZ)
New Zealand Institute of Electricians Inc (NZ)
New Zealand Institute of Food Science & Technology
(NZ)
New Zealand Institute of Local Authority
Administration (NZ)
New Zealand Institute of Management (NZ)
New Zealand Institute of Medical Laboratory
Technology (NZ)
New Zealand Institute of Public Administration (NZ)
New Zealand Institute of Surveyors (NZ)
New Zealand Institute of Valuers (NZ)
New Zealand Institution of Engineers (NZ)
New Zealand Library Association (NZ)
New Zealand Library Association. Archives
Committee. (NZ)
New Zealand Licensee Co. Ltd. (NZ)
New Zealand Marine Sciences Society. Fisheries
Research Division (NZ)
New Zealand Medical Records Officers' Association
(NZ)
New Zealand Merchant Engineers (NZ)
New Zealand Military Historical Society (NZ)
New Zealand Model Railway Guild Inc. (NZ)
New Zealand Monthly Review Society Inc. (NZ)
New Zealand National Society for Earthquake
Engineering (NZ)
New Zealand National Travel Association (NZ)
New Zealand Newspapers Ltd. (NZ)
New Zealand Nurses Association (NZ)
New Zealand Oceanographic Institute (NZ)
New Zealand Operational Research Society (NZ)
New Zealand Planning Institute (NZ)
New Zealand Pony Clubs Association (NZ)
New Zealand Portland Cement Association (NZ)
New Zealand Potter (NZ)
New Zealand Pottery and Ceramics Research
Association (NZ)
New Zealand Poultry Board (NZ)
New Zealand Printing & Related Trades Industrial
Union of Workers (NZ)
New Zealand Pschological Society (NZ)
New Zealand Railway and Locomotive Society, Inc
(NZ)
New Zealand Rationalist Association Inc. (NZ)
New Zealand Red Cross Society Inc. (NZ)
New Zealand Socialist Unity Party (NZ)
New Zealand Society of Accountants (NZ)
New Zealand Society of Periodontology (NZ)
New Zealand Society of Physiotherapists (NZ)
New Zealand Speech Therapists Association (NZ)
New Zealand Student Christian Movement (NZ)
New Zealand Tablet Co. Ltd. (NZ)
New Zealand Teachers' Colleges' Association (NZ)
New Zealand Theater Federation (NZ)
New Zealand Theatre Trust (NZ)
New Zealand Urban Public Passenger Transport
Council (NZ)
New Zealand Veterinary Association (NZ)
New Zealand Wholesale Hardware Guilds' Federation
(NZ)
New Zealand Wool Marketing Corporation (NZ)
Newark Museum Association (US)
Newark Public Library (US)
Newberry College (US)
Newberry Library (US)
Newberry Library. Hermon Dunlap Smith Center for
the History of Cartography (US)
Newbury House, Publishers, Inc. (US)
Donald Newby Publications, Ltd. (UK)
Newcastle Chronicle and Journal (UK)
Newcastle Flora & Fauna Protection Society (AT)
Newcastle Public Library (AT)
Newcastle University. Department of Physiology
(UK)
Newcastle University Philosophy Club (AT)
Newcastle University Students" Representative
Council (UK)
Newcastle Upon Tyne Polytechnic (UK)
Newcomen Society for the Study of the History of
Engineering and Technology (UK)
Newedi Press (US)
Newest Press (CN)
Newfoundland. Department of Fisheries (CN)
Newfoundland. Department of Mines and Energy
(CN)
Newfoundland. Department of Social Services (CN)
Newfoundland Association of Public Employees
(CN)
Newfoundland Medical Association (CN)
Newfoundland Medical Board (CN)
Newfoundland Outdoors (CN)
Newfoundland Public Libraries Board. Public Library
Services (CN)
Newfoundland Teachers Association (CN)
Newhall Co. (US)
Newkirk Associates (US)

Newkirk Products, Inc. (US)
Newlaw Media Inc. (US)
W. Newman and Co. (II)
Newman Association (UK)
Newman Bookshop (UK)
Newman Foundation of Toronto (CN)
Newman Publishing Ltd. (UK)
Newnes-Butterworths (UK)
Newport Historical Society (US)
Newport News Shipbuilding (US)
News (PO)
News & Book Trade Review & Stationers Gazette Ltd.
(UK)
News & Letters Committees (US)
News Bank, Inc. (US)
News Circle (US)
News from Neasden (UK)
News Group Newspapers Ltd. (UK)
News Leader, Inc. (US)
News Media Ownership Ltd. (NZ)
News Publications Ltd. (UK)
News Publishers Ltd. (KE)
Newscribes Group (US)
Newsletter for Birdwatchers (II)
Newsletters, Inc. (US)
Newsletters International (US)
Newspaper Advertising Bureau, Inc. (US)
Newspaper and Mail Deliverers' Union (US)
Newspaper Archive Developments Ltd. (UK)
Newspaper Enterprise Association, Inc. (US)
Newspaper Fund, Inc. (US)
Newspaper Guild (US)
Newspaper Guild of New York (US)
Newspaper Representations (S.A.) (Pty.) (SA)
Newspaper Society (UK)
Newspread International (KE)
Newsprint Information Committee (US)
Newsweb (US)
Newsweek Books (US)
Newsweek, Inc. (US)
Newton Mann Ltd. (UK)
Next (US)
Next Year Country Magazine Inc. (CN)
Neydharting Verlag (AU)
Ngabu (ZR)
Auguste Nguyen (FR)
Niagara Frontier Transportation Authority. (US)
Niagara Magazine (US)
Niagara Parks Commission (CN)
Aktiebolaget NIBO (SW)
Nicaragua. Direccion General de Aduanas (NQ)
Nicaragua. Guardia Nacional de Nicaragua. Oficina
del Encargado General de Abastos (NQ)
Nicaragua. Oficina Ejecutiva de Encuestos y Censos
(NQ)
Nicaragua. Secretaria de Informacion y Prensa (NQ)
Giuseppe Niccolai, Ed. and Pub. (IT)
Nichifutsu Ikakai
see Societe Franco-Japonaise de Medecine (JA)
Nichifutsu Kogyo Gijutsukai
see Societe Franco-Japonaise des Techniques
Industrielles (JA)
Nichiren Shoshu Academy (US)
Nichiren Shoshu Francaise (FR)
Nichols College (US)
Nicholson and Bass Ltd (IE)
Nicholson's Pty. Ltd. (AT)
Nickelodeon Graphics Arts Service (US)
Nickerson & Collins Co. (US)
Nickle Publications Co. Ltd. (CN)
Lewis Nicolas Co.,Inc. (US)
Niederlaendische Handelskammer fuer Oesterreich
(AU)
Niederoesterreich. Amt der Niederoesterreichische
Landesregierung. Presseabteilung (AU)
Niederoesterreich. Niederoesterreichische Landes-
Landwirtschaftskammer (AU)
Niederoesterreichischer Landesfeuerwehrverband.
Landesfeuerwehrkommando (AU)
Niederoesterreichischer Landesjagdverband (AU)
Niederrheinische Industrie- und Handelskammer
Duisburg-Wesel-Kleve zu Duisburg (GW)
Niedersachsen. Kultusministerium (GW)
Niedersachsen. Ministerium der Justiz (GW)
Niedersachsen. Niedersaechsischer Gemeindetag
(GW)
Niedersaechsische Staats- und Universitaetsbibliothek
(GW)
Niedersaechsisches Landesmuseum, Hannover (GW)
Niekas Publications (US)
A.C. Nielsen Co. (US)
Nieman Foundation (US)
Max Niemeyer Verlag (GW)
N. V. Uitgeversmij. Nieuwe Limburger (NE)
Nieuwe Rotterdamse Courant N.V. (NE)
Nieuwe Vereniging van Aannemers Grootbedrijf
(NE)
Nieuws Uit Zuid-Afrika (SA)

Nieuwsdienst Morele Herbewapening (NE)
NIFRA Publishers (LH)
Niger. Direction de la Statistique et des Comptes
Nationaux (NG)
Niger. Ministere de l'Information (NG)
Niger. Office des Postes et Telecommunications
(NG)
Nigeria (NR)
Nigeria. Anti-Inflation Task Force (NR)
Nigeria. Federal Department of Fisheries (NR)
Nigeria. Federal Department of Forest Research
(NR)
Nigeria. Federal Institute of Industrial Research,
Oshodi (NR)
Nigeria. Federal Ministry of Industries. Federal
Institute of Industrial Research, Oshodi
see Nigeria. Federal Institute of Industrial Research,
Oshodi (NR)
Nigeria. Federal Ministry of Labour (NR)
Nigeria. Federal Office of Statistics (NR)
Nigeria. Meteorological Service (NR)
Nigeria. National Electric Power Authority (NR)
Nigeria. National Library (NR)
Nigeria. National Manpower Board (NR)
Nigeria. Nigerian National Advisory Council for the
Blind (NR)
Nigeria. Nigerian Ports Authority (NR)
Nigeria Business Directory (NR)
Nigeria Civil Service Union. Western State Branch
(NR)
Nigeria Confidential Co. (NR)
Nigeria English Studies Association (NR)
Nigeria Lawyers' Quarterly (NR)
Nigeria Union of Teachers (NR)
Nigerian Association of French Teachers (NR)
Nigerian Broadcasting Corporation (NR)
Nigerian Chamber of Mines (NR)
Nigerian Consulate General (US)
Nigerian Current Affairs Society (NR)
Nigerian Economic Society (NR)
Nigerian Geographical Association (NR)
Nigerian Industrial Development Bank (NR)
Nigerian Institute for Oil Palm Research (NR)
Nigerian Institute of International Affairs (NR)
Nigerian Institute of Management (NR)
Nigerian Institute of Social and Economic Research
(NR)
Nigerian Library Association (NR)
Nigerian Library Association. Lagos Division (NR)
Nigerian Medical Association (NR)
Nigerian Mining, Geological and Metallurgical Society
(NR)
Nigerian National Advisory Council for the Blind
see Nigeria. Nigerian National Advisory Council for
the Blind (NR)
Nigerian Pharmaceutical & Medical Company (NR)
Nigerian Ports Authority
see Nigeria. Nigerian Ports Authority (NR)
Nigerian Society of International Affairs (NR)
Nigerian Tobacco Company (NR)
Nigerian Tourist Association (NR)
Nightwings Press (US)
Nihon
see also Nippon (JA)
Nihon Allergy Gakkai
see Japanese Society of Allergology (JA)
Nihon Arukoru Igakkai
see Japanese Medical Society of Alcohol Studies
(JA)
Nihon Boeki Shuppansha
see Japan Trade Publications Ltd. (JA)
Nihon Bungaku Kyokai
see Japanese Literature Association (JA)
Nihon Bunko Gakkai
see Spectroscopical Society of Japan (JA)
Nihon Butsuri Gakkai
see Physical Society of Japan (JA)
Nihon Butsuri Kagaku Kenkyukai
see Physico-Chemical Society of Japan (JA)
Nihon Byoin Setsubi Kyokai
see Japan Hospital Equipment Association (JA)
Nihon Byori Gakkai
see Japanese Pathological Society (JA)
Nihon Cast Iron Foundry Association (JA)
Nihon Chigaku Kyoiku Gakkai
see Japan Society of Earth Science Education (JA)
Nihon Chiiki Kaihatsu Senta
see Japan Center for Area Development Research
(JA)
Nihon Chikudenchi Kogyokai
see Japan Storage Battery Association (JA)
Nihon Chikusan Gakkai
see Japanese Society of Zootechnical Science (JA)
Nihon Chikyu Denki Jiki Gakkai
see Society of Terrestrial Magnetism and Electricity
of Japan (JA)
Nihon Chikyu Kagakkai
see Geochemical Society of Japan (JA)

Nihon Chishitsu Gakkai
see Geological Society of Japan (JA)
Nihon Chizu Senta
see Japan Map Center (JA)
Nihon Cho Gakkai
see Ornithological Society of Japan (JA)
Nihon Dai Damu Kaigi
see Japanese National Committee on Large Dams (JA)
Nihon Daigaku
see Nihon University (JA)
Nihon Daigaku Igakkai
see Nihon University Medical Association (JA)
Nihon Daigaku Juigaku Kenkyusho
see Nihon University. Research Institute for Veterinary Science (JA)
Nihon Daigaku Keizaigaku Shogaku Kenkyu-kai
see Nihon University. Economic and Commercial Research Society (JA)
Nihon Daigaku Rikogaku Kenkyusho
see Nihon University. Research Institute of Science and Technology (JA)
Nihon Denki Gakkai
see Institute of Electrical Engineers of Japan (JA)
Nihon Denki Seiki K. K.
see Nippon Electric Industry Co., Ltd. (JA)
Nihon Denpun Gakkai
see Japanese Society of Starch Science (JA)
Nihon Denryoku Chosa Iinkai
see Japan Electric Power Survey Committee (JA)
Nihon Densenbyo Gakkai
see Japanese Association for Infectious Diseases (JA)
Nihon Denshi K. K.
see J E O L Ltd. (JA)
Nihon Denshi Kenbikyo Gakkai
see Japanese Society of Electron Microscopy (JA)
Nihon Dobutsu Gakkai
see Zoological Society of Japan (JA)
Nihon Dokumenteshon Kyokai
see Japan Documentation Society (JA)
Nihon Doro Kyokai
see Japan Road Association (JA)
Nihon Eibungakkai
see English Literary Society of Japan (JA)
Nihon Eisei Gakkai
see Japanese Society for Hygiene (JA)
Nihon Eiyo to Shokuryo Gakkai
see Japanese Society of Food and Nutrition (JA)
Nihon Funin Gakkai Zasshi
see Japanese Society of Fertility and Sterility (JA)
Nihon Gakujutsu Kaigi
see Science Council of Japan (JA)
Nihon Gan Chiryo Gakkai
see Japan Society for Cancer Therapy (JA)
Nihon Gan Gakkai
see Cancer Institute (JA)
Nihon Ganka Gakkai
see Japanese Ophthalmological Society (JA)
Nihon Ganseki Kobutsu Kosho Gakkai
see Japanese Association of Minerologists, Petrologists and Economic Geologists (JA)
Nihon Gas Kyokai
see Japan Gas Association (JA)
Nihon Geka Gakkai
see Japan Surgical Society (JA)
Nihon Gengogakkai
see Linguistic Society of Japan (JA)
Nihon Genshiroku Gakkai
see Atomic Energy Society of Japan (JA)
Nihon Genshiryoku Kenkyusho
see Japan Atomic Energy Research Institute (JA)
Nihon Genshiryoku Sangyo Kaigi
see Japan Atomic Industrial Forum, Inc. (JA)
Nihon Gesuido Kyokai
see Japan Sewage Works Association (JA)
Nihon Gijutsu Koho Kyokai
see Japan Association for Technical Information (JA)
Nihon Ginko
see Bank of Japan (JA)
Nihon Gomu Kyokai
see Society of Rubber Industry (JA)
Nihon Gyorui Gakkai
see Ichthyological Society of Japan (JA)
Nihon Hakubutsuken Kyokai
see Japanese Association of Museums (JA)
Nihon Hanzai Gakkai
see Japanese Society of Criminology (JA)
Nihon Hassei Seibutsu Gakkai
see Japanese Society of Developmental Biologists (JA)
Nihon Hebizoku Gakujutsu Kenkyusho
see Japan Snake Institute (JA)
Nihon Heikatsukin Gakkai
see Japan Society of Smooth Muscle Research (JA)
Nihon Hifuka Gakkai

see Japanese Dermatological Association (JA)
Nihon Hifukagakkai Osaka Chihokai
see Osaka Dermatological Association (JA)
Nihon Hikaku Gijutsu Kyokai
see Japanese Association of Leather Technology (JA)
Nihon Hikakuho Kenkyusho
see Chuo University. Institute of Comparative Law in Japan (JA)
Nihon Hinyokika Gakkai
see Japanese Urological Association (JA)
Nihon Hinyokika Gakkai Nishi Nihon Rengo
see Japanese Urological Association. Nishi Nihon Section (JA)
Nihon Hoi Gakkai
see Medico-Legal Society of Japan (JA)
Nihon Hoshasei Doigenso Kyokai
see Japan Radioisotope Association (JA)
Nihon Hoso Times Co. Ltd. (JA)
Nihon Igaku Toshokan Kyokai
see Japan Medical Library Association (JA)
Nihon Ikakikai Gakkai
see Medical Instrument Society of Japan (JA)
Nihon Imono Kogyokai
see Nihon Cast Iron Foundry Association (JA)
Nihon Indasutoriaru Enjiniaringu Kyokai
see Japan Institute of Industrial Engineering (JA)
Nihon Indogaku- Bukkyogakukai
see Japanese Association of Indian and Buddhist Studies (JA)
Nihon Insatsu Gakkai
see Technical Association of Graphic Arts of Japan (JA)
Nihon Insatsu Shinbunsha
see Japan Printing News Publishing Co. (JA)
Nihon Ishikai
see Japan Medical Association (JA)
Nihon Iyaku Joho Senta
see Japan Pharmaceutical Information Centre (JA)
Nihon Iyakuhin Yushutsu Kumiai
see Japan Pharmaceutical, Medical and Dental Supply Exporter's Association (JA)
Nihon Jibi Inkoka Gakkai
see Oto-Rhino-Laryngological Society of Japan (JA)
Nihon Jido Seigyo Kyokai
see Japan Association of Automatic Control Engineers (JA)
Nihon Jidosha Kogyokai
see Japan Automobile Manufacturers Association (JA)
Nihon Jikken Dobutsu Kenkyukai
see Japan Experimental Animal Research Association (JA)
Nihon Jinrui Iden Gakkai
see Tokyo Medical and Dental University. Department of Human Genetics (JA)
Nihon Jinruigaku Gakkai
see Anthropological Society of Japan (JA)
Nihon Juigakkai
see Japanese Society of Veterinary Science (JA)
Nihon Junkanki Gakkai
see Japanese Circulation Society (JA)
Nihon Junkatsu Gakkai
see Japan Society of Lubrication Engineers (JA)
Nihon Kagaku Gijutsu Joho Senta
see Japan Information Center of Science and Technology (JA)
Nihon Kagaku Gijutsu Renmei
see Union of Japanese Scientists and Engineers (JA)
Nihon Kagaku Gijutsu Shinko Zaidan
see Japan Science Foundation (JA)
Nihon Kagaku Kogyo Kyokai
see Japan Chemical Industry Association (JA)
Nihon Kagaku Ryoho Gakkai
see Japan Society of Chemotherapy (JA)
Nihon Kagakusha Kaigi
see Japan Scientists' Association (JA)
Nihon Kaibo Gakkai
see Japanese Anatomical Association (JA)
Nihon Kaihatsu Ginko
see Japan Development Bank (JA)
Nihon Kairui Gakkai
see Malacological Society of Japan (JA)
Nihon Kaiun Shukaijo
see Japan Shipping Exchange, Inc. (JA)
Nihon Kaiyo Gakkai
see Oceanographical Society of Japan (JA)
Nihon Kakin Gakkai
see Japanese Poultry Science Association (JA)
Nihon Kaku Igakkai
see Japanese Society of Nuclear Medicine (JA)
Nihon Kango Kyokai
see Japanese Nursing Association (JA)
Nihon Kankyo Eisei Senta
see Japan Environmental Sanitation Center (JA)
Nihon Katei Seikatsu Mondai Kenkyu Kyokai (JA)

Nihon Kazan Gakkai
see Volcanological Society of Japan (JA)
Nihon Keiei Kagaku Kenkyusho
see Japan Management Science Institute (JA)
Nihon Keieisha Dantai Remmei Kohobu (JA)
Nihon Keiho Gakkai
see Criminal Law Society of Japan (JA)
Nihon Keizai Kenkyu Senta
see Japan Economic Research Center (JA)
Nihon Keizai Shinbunsha
see Japan Economic Journal (JA)
Nihon Kekkaku Yobokai
see Japan Anti-Tuberculosis Association (JA)
Nihon Kekkakubyo Gakkai
see Japan Society for Tuberculosis (JA)
Nihon Kenchiku Gakkai
see Architectural Institute of Japan (JA)
Nihon Ketsueki Gakkai
see Japan Hematological Society (JA)
Nihon Kikai Gakkai
see Japan Society of Mechanical Engineers (JA)
Nihon Kikon Shokudoka Gakkai
see Japan Broncho-Esophagological Society (JA)
Nihon Kinzoku Gakkai
see Japan Institute of Metals (JA)
Nihon Kirisutosha Ika Renmai
see Japan Christian Medical Association (JA)
Nihon Kiseichu Gakkai
see Japanese Society of Parasitology (JA)
Nihon Kisho Gakkai
see Meteorological Society of Japan (JA)
Nihon Kisho Kyokai
see Japan Weather Association (JA)
Nihon Kobutsu Gakkai
see Mineralogical Society of Japan (JA)
Nihon Kogyo Keiei Gakkai
see Japan Industrial Management Association (JA)
Nihon Kogyo Ritchi Senta
see Japan Industrial Location Center (JA)
Nihon Kogyo Shimbun (JA)
Nihon Koko Gakkai
see Archaeological Society of Japan (JA)
Nihon Koku Gakkai
see Japan Society for Aeronautical and Space Sciences (JA)
Nihon Koku Seibi Kyokai
see Japan Aeronautical Engineers' Association (JA)
Nihon Koku Uchu Gakkai
see Japan Society for Aeronautical and Space Sciences (JA)
Nihon Kokuka Gakkai
see Japanese Stomatological Society (JA)
Nihon Kokusai Chizu Gakkai
see Japan Cartographers Association (JA)
Nihon Kokusai Igaku Kyokai
see International Medical Society of Japan (JA)
Nihon Kokuyu Tetsudo
see Japanese National Railways (JA)
Nihon Konkuriito Kogaku Kyokai
see Japan Concrete Institute (JA)
Nihon Kosei Busshitsu Gakujutsu Kyogikai
see Japan Antibiotics Research Association (JA)
Nihon Koseibutsu Gakkai
see Palaeontological Society of Japan (JA)
Nihon Kotsu Igakkai Kyushu Chihokai
see Japanese Association of Transportation Medicine (JA)
Nihon Kozan Chishitsu Gakkai
see Society of Mining Geologists of Japan (JA)
Nihon Kuki Seijo Kyokai
see Japan Air Cleaning Association (JA)
Nihon Kyoiku-shinri Gakkai
see Japanese Association of Educational Psychology (JA)
Nihon Kyoikuho Gakkai (JA)
Nihon Kyosei Shika Gakkai
see Japan Orthodontic Society (JA)
Nihon M-E Gakkai
see Japan Society of Medical Electronics and Biological Engineering (JA)
Nihon Maikuro Shashin Kyokai
see Japan Microphotography Association (JA)
Nihon Menka Kyokai
see Japan Cotton Traders' Association (JA)
Nihon Minkan Kyoiku Kenkyu Dantai Renrakukai (JA)
Nihon Minzoku Gakkai
see Japanese Society of Ethnology (JA)
Nihon Mokuzai Gakkai
see Japan Wood Research Society (JA)
Nihon Mokuzai Kako Gijutsu Kyokai
see Wood Technological Association of Japan (JA)
Nihon Monki Senta
see Japan Monkey Centre (JA)
Nihon Myakkan Gakkai
see Japanese College of Angiology (JA)
Nihon Naibunpi Gakkai Tobu-Bukai

*see* Japan Endocrine Society. Eastern Branch (JA)

Nihon Naika Gakkai
*see* Japanese Society of Internal Medicine (JA)

Nihon Namari Aen Juyo Kenkyukai
*see* Japan Lead Zinc Development Association (JA)

Nihon Netsu Enerugi Gijutsu Kyokai
*see* Japan Heat Management Association (JA)

Nihon Nettai Igakkai
*see* Nissan Diesel Motor Co., Ltd. (JA)

Nihon Nissan Jizeru Kogyo K. K.
*see* Japan Nissan Diesel Motor Co., Ltd. (JA)

Nihon Nitto Uea Dezain Kyokai
*see* Japan Knitwear Designers Association (JA)

Nihon Nogaku Toshokan Kyogikai
*see* Japan Association of Agricultural Librarians and Documentalists (JA)

Nihon Nogyo Keizai Gakkai
*see* Agricultural Economic Society of Japan (JA)

Nihon Norin Kikaku Kyokai
*see* Japan Agricultural Standards Association (JA)

Nihon Noshinkei Geka Gakkai
*see* Japan Neurosurgical Society (JA)

Nihon Ojioroji Gakkai
*see* Japan Audiological Society (JA)

Nihon Onsei Gengo Igakkai
*see* Japan Society of Logopedics and Phoniatrics (JA)

Nihon Onsen Kiko Butsuri Igakkai
*see* Japanese Association of Physical Medicine, Balneology and Climatology (JA)

Nihon Opereshonzu Risachi Gakkai
*see* Operations Research Society of Japan (JA)

Nihon Oyo Dobutsu Konchu Gakkai
*see* Japanese Society of Applied Entomology and Zoology (JA)

Nihon Oyo Igakkai
*see* Society of Applied Medicine (JA)

Nihon Pan Gijutsusha Kyokai
*see* Japan Society of Bakery Technology (JA)

Nihon Porarogurafu Gakkai
*see* Polarographic Society of Japan (JA)

Nihon Purasuchikkusu Shinposa
*see* Japan Plastics Journal Ltd. (JA)

Nihon Rai Gakkai
*see* Japanese Leprosy Association (JA)

Nihon Reito Kyokai
*see* Japanese Association of Refrigeration (JA)

Nihon Reito Reibo Shinbunsha
*see* Japan Refrigeration and Air Conditioning Press (JA)

Nihon Rikusui Gakkai
*see* Japanese Society of Limnology (JA)

Nihon Ringyo Kyokai
*see* Japanese Forestry Society (JA)

Nihon Rodo Kyokai
*see* Japan Institute of Labour (JA)

Nihon Rodosho
*see* Japan. Ministry of Labour (JA)

Nihon Roketto Kyokai
*see* Japanese Rocket Society (JA)

Nihon Sakumotsu Gakkai Kiji
*see* Crop Science Society of Japan (JA)

Nihon Sangyo Eisei Gakkai
*see* Japan Association of Industrial Health (JA)

Nihon Sangyo Kunren Kyokai
*see* Japan Industrial and Vocational Training Association (JA)

Nihon Sangyo Sharyo Kyokai
*see* Japan Industrial Vehicles Association (JA)

Nihon Sanshi Gakkai
*see* Japanese Society of Sericultural Science (JA)

Nihon Seibutsu Kagakusha
*see* Japanese Society of Biological Scientists (JA)

Nihon Seibyo Yobo Kyokai
*see* Japanese Association for Prevention of Venereal Diseases and Treponematoses (JA)

Nihon Seiji Gakkai
*see* Japanese Political Science Association (JA)

Nihon Seikagakkai
*see* Japanese Biochemical Society (JA)

Nihon Seikosho
*see* Japan Steel Works, Ltd. (JA)

Nihon Seiri Gakkai
*see* Physiological Society of Japan (JA)

Nihon Seishin Eiseikai
*see* Japan Mental Health Society (JA)

Nihon Seito Kogyokai
*see* Japan Sugar Refiners Association (JA)

Nihon Sekiyu Konsarutanto K. K.
*see* Japan Petroleum Consultants, Ltd. (JA)

Nihon Sen'i Kikai Gakkai
*see* Textile Machinery Society of Japan (JA)

Nihon Sen'i Seihin Shohi Kagakkai
*see* Japan Research Association for Textile End-Uses (JA)

Nihon Sen'i Shinbun Co., Ltd. (JA)

Nihon Senpaku Hyojun Kyokai
*see* Japanese Association of Marine Standardization (JA)

Nihon Senshu Kyokai
*see* Japanese Shipowners' Association (JA)

Nihon Senten Ijo Gakkai
*see* Congenital Anomalies Research Association of Japan (JA)

Nihon Setchaku Kyokai
*see* Adhesion Society of Japan (JA)

Nihon Shakai-jigyo Daigaku
*see* Japanese Social Labour College (JA)

Nihon Shakaito
*see* Socialist Party of Japan (JA)

Nihon Shashin Gakkai
*see* Society of Photographic Science and Technology of Japan (JA)

Nihon Shashin Kyokai
*see* Photographic Society of Japan (JA)

Nihon Shika Daigaku
*see* Nippon Dental College (JA)

Nihon Shika Daigaku Shigakkai
*see* Society of Nippon Dental College (JA)

Nihon Shika Ishikai
*see* Japan Dental Association (JA)

Nihon Shinkei Gakkai
*see* Japanese Society of Neurology (JA)

Nihon Shinri Gakkai
*see* Japanese Psychological Association (JA)

Nihon Shiseniji Gakkai
*see* Japan Society of Neonatology (JA)

Nihon Shitai Fujiyuji Kyokai
*see* Japanese Society for Crippled Children (JA)

Nihon Shizai Kanrishi Kyokai
*see* Japan Materials Management Association (JA)

Nihon Shokakibyo Gakkai
*see* Japanese Society of Gastroenterology (JA)

Nihon Shokubutsu Boeki Kyokai
*see* Japan Plant Protection Association (JA)

Nihon Shokubutsu Byori Gakkai
*see* Phytopathological Society of Japan (JA)

Nihon Shokubutsu Gakkai
*see* Botanical Society of Japan (JA)

Nihon Shokubutsu Seiri Gakkai
*see* Japanese Society of Plant Physiologists (JA)

Nihon Shoni Hoken Kyokai
*see* Japanese Society of Child Health (JA)

Nihon Shoni Shinkeigaku Kenkyukai
*see* Japanese Society of Pediatric Neurology (JA)

Nihon Shonika Gakkai
*see* Japan Pediatric Society (JA)

Nihon Shoyaku Gakkai
*see* Japanese Society of Pharmacognosy (JA)

Nihon Sosei Kako Gakkai
*see* Japan Society for Technology of Plasticity (JA)

Nihon Soshiki Baiyo Gakkai
*see* Japanese Tissue Culture Association (JA)

Nihon Soshiki Kagakkai
*see* Japan Society of Histological Documentation (JA)

Nihon Soshiki Saibo Kagakkai
*see* Japan Society of Histochemistry and Cytochemistry (JA)

Nihon Sugakkai
*see* Mathematical Society of Japan (JA)

Nihon Suisan Gakkai
*see* Japanese Society of Scientific Fisheries (JA)

Nihon Taiiku Gakkai
*see* Japanese Society of Physical Education (JA)

Nihon Tairyoku Igakkai
*see* Japanese Physical Fitness Society (JA)

Nihon Tekko Kyokai
*see* Iron and Steel Institute of Japan (JA)

Nihon Tekko Renmei
*see* Japan Iron and Steel Federation (JA)

Nihon Tekko Yushutsu Kumiai
*see* Japan Iron and Steel Exporters Association (JA)

Nihon Tenmon Gakkai
*see* Astronomical Society of Japan (JA)

Nihon Tetsudo Gijutsu Kyokai
*see* Japan Railway Engineer's Association (JA)

Nihon Tetsudo Saibanetikkusu Kyogikai
*see* Japan Railway Cybernetics Association (JA)

Nihon Tonyobyo Gakkai
*see* Japan Diabetic Society (JA)

Nihon Toshokan Kyokai
*see* Japan Library Association (JA)

Nihon Uirusu Gakkai
*see* Society of Japanese Virologists (JA)

Nihon University. Atomic Energy Research Institute (JA)

Nihon University. Economic and Commercial Research Society (JA)

Nihon University Medical Association (JA)

Nihon University. Research Institute for Veterinary Science (JA)

Nihon University. Research Institute of Science and Technology (JA)

Nihon University. School of Dentistry (JA)

Nihon Wakkusuman Zaidan
*see* Waksman Foundation of Japan (JA)

Nihon Yakugakkai
*see* Pharmaceutical Society of Japan (JA)

Nihon Yakugaku Toshokan Kyogikai
*see* Japan Pharmaceutical Library Association (JA)

Nihon Yakuri Gakkai
*see* Japanese Pharmacological Society (JA)

Nihon Yogashi Kyogai Rengokai
*see* Federation of Japan Confectionary Associations (JA)

Nihon Zairyo Gakkai
*see* Japan Society of Materials Science (JA)

Nihon Zosen Shinko Zaidan
*see* Japan Foundation for Shipbuilding Advancement (JA)

Niigata Airglow Observatory (JA)

Niigata Daigaku Rigakubu Fuzoku Sado Rinko Jikkenjo Kenkyu
*see* Niigata University. Sado Marine Biological Station (JA)

Niigata Igakkai
*see* Niigata Medical Society (JA)

Niigata Medical Society (JA)

Niigata University. Faculty of Agriculture (JA)

Niigata University. Faculty of Science (JA)

Niigata University. Sado Marine Biological Station (JA)

Niigata University. School of Medicine (JA)

Martinus Nijhoff (NE)

Nikkan Jidosha Shimbun-sha
*see* Daily Automotive News Co., Ltd. (JA)

Nikkan Kogyo Shimbunsha
*see* Industrial Daily News Ltd. (JA)

Nikkei Mc-Graw Hill Inc. (JA)

Nikkyoso
*see* Japan Teachers' Union (JA)

Vinko Nikolic (SP)

Nilkant Industries Pvt. Ltd. (II)

Nimbkar Rehabilitation Trust (II)

Nimrod Publications (AT)

Nimrod Publications Ltd (CN)

Ningen Igakusha (JA)

Nippon
*see also* Nihon (JA)

Nippon Bitamin Gakkai
*see* Japan Vitamin Society (JA)

Nippon Chikasui Gakkai
*see* Japanese Association of Groundwater Hydrology (JA)

Nippon Chiri Gakkai
*see* Association of Japanese Geographers (JA)

Nippon Denki Garasu
*see* Nippon Electric Glass Co. Ltd. (JA)

Nippon Denki K. K.
*see* Nippon Electric Co. Ltd. (JA)

Nippon Dental College (JA)

Nippon Dojo Hiryo Gakkai
*see* Japanese Society of Soil and Manure (JA)

Nippon Electric Co. Ltd. (JA)

Nippon Electric Glass Co. Ltd. (JA)

Nippon Electric Industry Co., Ltd. (JA)

Nippon Export Times (JA)

Nippon Gakushiin
*see* Japan Academy (JA)

Nippon Ginko
*see* Bank of Japan (JA)

Nippon Gyosei Gakkai
*see* Japanese Society for Public Administration (JA)

Nippon Hoso Kyokai
*see* Japan Broadcasting Corp. (JA)

Nippon Hoso Shuppan Kyokai
*see* Japan Broadcast Publishing Co., Ltd. (JA)

Nippon Hyoronsha (JA)

Nippon Igaku Hoshasen Gakkai
*see* Nippon Societas Radiologica (JA)

Nippon Igaku Kyokai
*see* Japan Medical Association (JA)

Nippon Ika Daigaku
*see* Nippon Medical School (JA)

Nippon Institute for Biological Science (JA)

Nippon Jui Chikusan Daigaku Kiyo
*see* Nippon Veterinary and Zootechnical College (JA)

Nippon Kagakkai
*see* Chemical Society of Japan (JA)

Nippon Kagaku Gijutsu Renmei
*see* Union of Japanese Scientists and Engineers (JA)

Nippon Kagaku Kyokai
*see* Japan Science Society (JA)

Nippon Kagakushi Gakkai
*see* History of Science Society of Japan (JA)

Nippon Kikai-Kogyo Rengokai (NIKKIREN)

Norin-sho Kachiku Eisei Shikenjo
  see Japan. National Institute of Animal Health
  (JA)
Norin-sho Kinki Nosei-kyoku
  see Japan. Kinki Agricultural Administration Bureau
  (JA)
Norin-sho Nogyo Gijutsu Kenkyusho
  see Japan. National Institute of Agricultural
  Sciences (JA)
Norin-sho Nogyo Gijutsu Kenkyusho Hoshasen
  see Japan. Institute of Radiation Breeding (JA)
Norin-sho Nogyo Sogo Kenkyusho
  see Japan. National Research Institute of
  Agriculture (JA)
Norin-sho Ringyo Shikenjo Kyusha Shijo
  see Japan. Government Forest Experiment Station.
  Kyushu Branch (JA)
Norin-sho Sanshi Shikenjo
  see Japan. Sericultural Experiment Station (JA)
Norin-sho Shikoku Nogyo Shikenjo
  see Japan. Shikoku Agricultural Experiment Station
  (JA)
Norin-sho Sochi Shikenjo
  see Japan. National Grassland Research Institute
  (JA)
Norin-sho Yokohama Shokubutsu Boekisho
  see Japan. Yokohama Plant Protection Station
  (JA)
Norm (II)
Norma Editora e Publicidade Ltda. (BL)
Wydawnictwa Normalizacyjne (PL)
Norman Bethune Institute of Ideological Studies
  (CN)
Norman Glenn Publications, Inc. (US)
Norman Mackenzie Art Gallery (CN)
Norman Publishing Corp. (US)
P. G. Normandin (CN)
James Normington, Ed. & Pub. (US)
Editorial del Noroeste, S. A. C. I. (AG)
Noroil Publishing House Ltd. (NO)
Norois (FR)
Luther Norris (US)
Norrlandsfoerbundet (SW)
Norrona Publishing Co. (CN)
Harold Norse, Ed. & Pub. (US)
Norsk Aero Klubb (NO)
Norsk Apoteknikerforbund (NO)
Norsk Arbeidsgiverforening (NO)
Norsk Arkeologisk Selskap (NO)
Norsk Baatinformasjon (NO)
Norsk Botanisk Forening (NO)
Norsk Brannvern Forening (NO)
Norsk Bygningsindustriarbeiderforbund (NO)
Norsk Dampkjelforening (NO)
Norsk Elektriker- og Kraftstasjonforbund (NO)
Norsk Entomologisk Forening (NO)
Norsk Esperanto- Forbund
  see Norvega Esperantista Ligo (NO)
Norsk Faktorforbund (NO)
Norsk Farmaceutisk Selskap (NO)
Norsk Filatelistforbund (NO)
Norsk Fjoerfeavlslag (NO)
Norsk Folkemuseum (NO)
Norsk Forening for Luftrett (NO)
Norsk Forening for Sosialt Arbeide (NO)
Norsk Forening for Varme- , Ventilasjon- og
  Sanitaerteknikk (NO)
Norsk Forstmannsforening (NO)
Norsk Galvano Teknisk Landsforening (NO)
Norsk Gartnerforbund (NO)
Norsk Geologisk Forening (NO)
Norsk Hotell og Restaurantforbund (NO)
Norsk Innkjoepslederforbund (NO)
Norsk Institutt for By- og Regionforskning (NO)
Norsk Institutt for Vannforskning (NO)
Norsk Instituut for Kosmisk Fysikk (NO)
Norsk Journalistag (NO)
Norsk Kafeforbund (NO)
Norsk Kennel Klub (NO)
Norsk Kjemisk Selskap (NO)
Norsk Laererlag (NO)
Norsk Landbruksakademikerforbund (NO)
Norsk Lektorlag (NO)
Norsk Musikerforbund (NO)
Norsk Musikksamling (NO)
Norsk Ornitologisk Forening (NO)
Norsk Pedagogikklag (NO)
Norsk Plastforening (NO)
Norsk Polarinstitutt (NO)
Norsk Psykologforening (NO)
Norsk Renseriforbund (DK)
Norsk Revmatike Forbund (NO)
Norsk Rikskringkasting (NO)
Norsk Sau- og Geitalslag (NO)
Norsk Senter for Informatikk (NO)
Norsk Sjoefartsmuseum (NO)
Norsk Sjoemannsforbund (NO)
Norsk Skattebetaleforening (NO)

Norsk Skog- og Landarbeiderforbund (NO)
Norsk Skogindustri (NO)
Norsk Slektshistorisk Forening (NO)
Norsk Speiderguttforbund (NO)
Norsk Spraakraad (NO)
Norsk Styrmandsforening (NO)
Norsk Sveiseteknisk Forening (NO)
Norsk Sykepleierforbund (NO)
Norsk Tannvern (NO)
Norsk Teknisk Museum. (NO)
Norsk Tekstil Teknisk Forbund (NO)
Norsk Tidsskrift for Sjakk (NO)
Norsk Utenrikspolitisk Institutt (NO)
Norsk Yrkes- og Husstellaererlag (NO)
Norsk Zoologisk Forening (NO)
Norske Advokatforening (NO)
Norske Arbeiderparti (NO)
Norske Arkitekters Landsforbund (NO)
Norske Avisers Landsforbund (NO)
Norske Baatbyggeriers Landsforening (NO)
Norske Bankforening (NO)
Norske Baptistsamfunn (NO)
Norske Bokhandlerforening (NO)
Norske Boligbyggelags Landsforbund (NO)
Norske Doeves Landsforbund (NO)
Norske Elverksjefers Forening (NO)
Norske Flyktningeraad (NO)
Norske Fysioterapeuters Forbund (NO)
Norske Geografiske Selskab (NO)
Norske Gutters Forlag (NO)
Norske Hageselskap (NO)
Norske Handelsreisende (NO)
Norske Handverks og Industribedrifters Forbund
  (NO)
Norske Historiske Forening (NO)
A-S Norske Husdyrtidsskrifter (NO)
Norske Jord- og Myrselskap (NO)
Norske Jordmorforening (NO)
Norske Kokkemesteres Landsforening (NO)
Norske Kommuners Sentralforbund (NO)
Norske Kunst- og Kulturhistoriske Museer (NO)
Norske Laegeforening (NO)
Norske Maskinistforbund (NO)
Norske Mejerifolks Landsforening (NO)
Norske Meteorologiske Institutt
  see Norway. Norske Meteorologiske Institutt
  (NO)
Norske Murmesteres Landsforening (NO)
Norske Musikklaereres Landsforbund (NO)
Norske Papirhandleres Landsforbund (NO)
Norske Radio - TV Handlereslandsforbund (NO)
Norske Roerleggerbedrifters Landsforening (NO)
Norske Samlaget (NO)
Norske Sivilingenioeers Forening (NO)
Norske Sjoeretts-Forening (NO)
Norske Skogselskap (NO)
Norske Socialoekonomers Forening (NO)
Norske Sykehusadministrasjons Landsforbund (NO)
Norske Sykehusforening (NO)
Norske Tannlaegeforening (NO)
Norske Trevarefabrikkers Landsforbund (NO)
Norske Veritas (NO)
Norske Veterinaerforening (NO)
Norske Videnskaps-Akademi (NO)
Norstedts Tryckeri AB (SW)
Editorial Norte (AG)
North American Association of Summer Sessions
  (US)
North American Baptist Conference (US)
North American Benefit Association (US)
North American Bird Bander (US)
North American Congress on Latin America, Inc.
  (US)
North American Council on Adoptable Children
  (NACAC) (US)
North American Dostoevsky Society (US)
North American Fireman's Association (US)
North American Game Breeders and Shooting
  Preserve Operators Association (US)
North American Gladiolus Council (US)
North American Gladiolus Council. Commercial
  Growers Division (US)
North American Jewish Students Network (US)
North American Limousin Foundation (US)
North American Mycological Association (US)
North American Patristics Society (US)
North American Pizza Association, Inc. (US)
North American Publishing Co. (US)
North American Review (US)
North American Saxophone Alliance (US)
North American Securities Administrators Association,
  Inc. (US)
North American Simulation and Gaming Association
  (US)
North American Society for Corporate Planning (N A
  S C P) (US)
North American Society for Sport History (US)

North American Student Cooperative Organization
  (N.A.S.C.O.) (US)
North American Trackless Trolley Association (CN)
North American Vegetarian Society (US)
North Atlantic Treaty Organization (BE)
North Atlantic Treaty Organization (NE)
North Atlantic Treaty Organization. Committee on the
  Challenges of Modern Society (BE)
North Atlantic Treaty Organization. Scientific Affairs
  Division (BE)
North Atlantic Treaty Organization. Scientific Affairs
  Division (NE)
North Cal-Neva Resource Conservation and
  Development Project (US)
North California State Dental Hygienists Association
  (US)
North Carolina. Commission on Higher Education
  Facilities (US)
North Carolina. Council on State Goals and Policy
  (US)
North Carolina. Criminal Justice Training and
  Standards Council (US)
North Carolina. Department of Agriculture (US)
North Carolina. Department of Community Colleges
  (US)
North Carolina. Department of Cultural Resources
  (US)
North Carolina. Department of Human Resources
  (US)
North Carolina. Department of Human Resources.
  Division of Health Services (US)
North Carolina. Department of Human Resources.
  Division of Social Services (US)
North Carolina. Department of Natural and Economic
  Resources. Division of Economic Development
  (US)
North Carolina. Department of Natural and Economic
  Resources. Geology and Mineral Resources Section
  (US)
North Carolina. Department of Natural and Economic
  Resources. Groundwater Section (US)
North Carolina. Department of Revenue (US)
North Carolina. Division of Archives and History
  (US)
North Carolina. Division of Commerce and Industry.
  Research and Statistics Section (US)
North Carolina. Governor's Highway Safety Program
  (US)
North Carolina. Human Relations Council (US)
North Carolina. Office of Intergovernmental Relations
  (US)
North Carolina. Secretary of State (US)
North Carolina. State Bar (US)
North Carolina. Wildlife Resources Commission (US)
North Carolina Association of Educators (US)
North Carolina Association of Plumbing-Heating-
  Cooling Contractors, Inc. (US)
North Carolina Bankers Association (US)
North Carolina Central University (US)
North Carolina Citizens Association, Inc. (US)
North Carolina Education Association. Division of
  Principals (US)
North Carolina Electric Membership Corp. (US)
North Carolina English Teachers Association (US)
North Carolina Folklore Society (US)
North Carolina Genealogical Society (US)
North Carolina Independent Publishing Co. Inc. (US)
North Carolina Law Enforcement Officers Association
  (US)
North Carolina League for Nursing (US)
North Carolina League of Municipalities (US)
North Carolina Library Association (US)
North Carolina Medical Society (US)
North Carolina Motor Carriers Association, Inc.
  (US)
North Carolina Museum of Art (US)
North Carolina Music Teachers Association (US)
North Carolina Nurses Association (US)
North Carolina School Boards Association (US)
North Carolina Speech and Drama Association (US)
North Carolina State University (US)
North Carolina State University. Agricultural
  Experiment Station (US)
North Carolina State University. D.H. Hill Library
  (US)
North Carolina State University. Department of Adult
  and Community College Education (US)
North Carolina State University. Department of
  Computer Science (US)
North Carolina State University. Department of Crop
  Science (US)
North Carolina State University. Department of
  Economics and Business (US)
North Carolina State University. Department of
  English (US)
North Carolina State University. Department of
  Foreign Languages and Literatures (US)

Norway. Statens Arbeidstilsyn Direktoratet  (NO)
Norway. Statens Bibliotektilsyn  (NO)
Norway. Statens Institutt for Alkoholforskning  (NO)
Norway. Statistisk Sentralbyraa  (NO)
Norway. Teledirektoratet  (NO)
Norway. Velferdstjenesten for Handelsflaaten  (NO)
Norway. Veterinaerdirektoratet  (NO)
Norway-America Association  (NO)
Norwegian Agency for International Development
   see Norway. Direktoratet for Utviklingshjelp  (NO)
Norwegian American Chamber of Commerce, Inc.
   (US)
Norwegian-American Historical Association  (US)
Norwegian Association for Students of Technology
   (NO)
Norwegian Chamber of Commerce (London) Inc.
   (UK)
Norwegian Electro-technical Society  (NO)
Norwegian Federation of Business Economists  (NO)
Norwegian Geotechnical Institute
   see Norges Geotekniske Institutt  (NO)
Norwegian Information Service  (US)
Norwegian Institute of Technology
   see Universitetet i Trondheim. Norges Tekniske
   Hoegskole  (NO)
Norwegian Police Athletic and Sports Association
   (NO)
Norwegian Research Council for Science and the
   Humanities
   see Norges Almenvitenskapelige Forskningsraad
   (NO)
Norwegian Singers Association of America, Inc.  (US)
Norwegian Society of Professional Engineers  (NO)
Norwegian Technical Press
   see Teknisk Presse A-S  (NO)
Norwegian Textile Retailers Association  (NO)
Nor'westing Inc.  (US)
Nosferatu Press  (US)
Nosotros  (MX)
Nostalgia News  (US)
Editrice le Nostre Scuole  (IT)
Nostro Tempo  (IT)
Notebook Press  (US)
Notes and Queries for Somerset and Dorset  (UK)
Notes and Sketches  (US)
Notes on Contemporary Literature  (US)
Notes on Modern American Literature  (US)
Nothing Doing (Formally of London)  (UK)
Noticiario da Moda  (BL)
Noticias Caninas  (BL)
Noticiero del Plastico  (AG)
Noticioso Perea  (AG)
Notitas Musicales  (MX)
Notiziario Famiglie Numerose  (IT)
Notre Dame de Sion  (FR)
Notre Dame English Association  (US)
Notre Dame of Jolo College  (PH)
Notre Dame University. Graduate School  (PH)
Notre Voix  (FR)
Nottingham & Nottinghamshire Field Club  (UK)
Nottingham and Nottinghamshire Technical
   Information Service  (UK)
Nottingham UFO Investigation Society  (UK)
Nottingham Union Students Union  (UK)
Nottinghamshire Chamber of Commerce and Industry
   (UK)
Nouveau Quartier Latin  (FR)
Nouveaux Rythmes du Monde  (BE)
Nouvel Observateur  (FR)
Nouvelle Barre du Jour  (CN)
Editions de la Nouvelle Critique  (FR)
Nouvelle Frontiere  (FR)
Nouvelle Hygiene  (FR)
Nouvelle Imprimerie Commerciale et Industrielle S.C.
   (BE)
Nouvelle Revue Franc-Comtoise  (FR)
Nouvelle Revue Socialiste  (FR)
Nouvelle Societe Anonyme la Vie Ouvriere  (FR)
Nouvelle Societe Presence Africaine  (FR)
Nouvelles du Monde  (FR)
Nouvelles Editions Africaines  (SG)
Nouvelles Editions de la Publicite  (FR)
Nouvelles Editions de Publications Agricoles  (FR)
Nouvelles Editions Latines  (FR)
Nouvelles Editions Medicales Francaises  (FR)
Nouvelles Editions Musicales Modernes et Cie  (FR)
Nouvelles Etudes Marxistes  (FR)
Nouvelles Litteraires, Arts, Sciences, Spectacles  (FR)
Nova  (CK)
Editions Nova  (FR)
Nova Agep  (IT)

Bokfoerlaget Nova Ecclesia  (SW)
Nova Hrvatska Ltd.  (UK)
Nova Makedonija  (YU)
Nova Press  (GW)
Nova Scotia. Department of Agriculture and
   Marketing  (CN)
Nova Scotia. Department of Agriculture and
   Marketing. Horticulture and Biology Services
   Branch  (CN)
Nova Scotia. Department of Development  (CN)
Nova Scotia. Department of Education  (CN)
Nova Scotia. Department of Education. Health and
   Physical Education Office  (CN)
Nova Scotia. Department of Labour  (CN)
Nova Scotia. Department of Labour. Economics and
   Research Division  (CN)
Nova Scotia. Department of Public Health  (CN)
Nova Scotia. Department of Recreation  (CN)
Nova Scotia. Department of Social Services  (CN)
Nova Scotia. Emergency Measures Organization
   (CN)
Nova Scotia. Environmental Control Council  (CN)
Nova Scotia. Office of the Ombudsman  (CN)
Nova Scotia Bird Society  (CN)
Nova Scotia College of Art & Design  (CN)
Nova Scotia Communications and Information Centre
   (CN)
Nova Scotia Drama League  (CN)
Nova Scotia Fruit Growers Association  (CN)
Nova Scotia Historical Society  (CN)
Nova Scotia Land Surveyors Association  (CN)
Nova Scotia Museum  (CN)
Nova Scotia Power Corporation  (CN)
Nova Scotia Research Foundation  (CN)
Nova Scotia Springhill Penitentiary  (CN)
Nova Scotia Teachers Union  (CN)
Nova Scotia Technical College. School of Architecture
   (CN)
Nova Scotian Institute of Science  (CN)
Nova Sociedade Angolana  (AO)
Robert Novak, Ed. & Pub.  (US)
Novaro Internacional, S.A.  (MX)
Novello and Co. Ltd.  (UK)
Novinar  (CS)
Novinsko Informativna Ustanova u Osnivanju  (YU)
Noviny Vnitrniho Obchodu  (CS)
Novographos, S.A.  (SP)
Novosibirskii Gosudarstvennyi Universitet  (UR)
Novosti Press Agency  (UR)
Novosti Press Agency in Ethiopia  (ET)
Novy Domov  (CN)
Now Voyager  (US)
Nowhere Press  (II)
Nowi Dni Publications Ltd.  (CN)
John L. Noyce, Ed. & Pub.  (UK)
Noyes Data Corporation  (US)
Nu?  (US)
Nuclear Assurance Corporation  (US)
Nuclear Energy Society  (CH)
Nuclear Safety Research Association  (JA)
Nuernberg. Stadtbibliothek  (GW)
Nuernberg. Stadtverwaltung  (GW)
Verlag Nuernberger Presse  (GW)
Nuestro Anhelo  (AG)
Ediciones Nuestro Tiempo  (AG)
Nueva  (EC)
Nueva Editorial Interamericana, S. A. de C. V.  (MX)
Nueva Forma  (SP)
Nueva Sociedad Ltda.  (VE)
Libreria Nueva Vision  (AG)
Nuevas Ediciones, S.A.  (SP)
Nuevos Aires  (AG)
Editions Nuit et Jour  (FR)
Nukada Institute for Medical and Biological Research
   (JA)
Numeridex, Inc  (US)
Numismatic Association of Southern California  (US)
Numismatic Directories  (UK)
Numismatic Fine Arts, Inc.  (US)
Numismatic Publishing Co.  (UK)
Numismatic Society of India  (II)
Uitgeverij Numismatica Nederland N. V.  (NE)
Numismaticke Listy  (CS)
Numismatique & Change  (FR)
Numismatische Gesellschaft e.V.  (GW)
Numismatische Gesellschaft zu Berlin  (GW)
Nuorten Keskus R.Y.  (FI)
Editrice Nuova Alba  (IT)
Nuova Antologia  (IT)
Nuova Corrente  (IT)
Nuova Editrice s.r.l.  (IT)
Nuova Era  (IT)
Nuova Fotografia  (IT)
Nuova Italia Editrice  (IT)
Nuova Mercurio S.p.A.  (IT)
Nuova Rivista Pedagogica  (IT)
Nuova Rivista Tributaria  (IT)
Editrice Nuova Societa S.p.A.  (IT)

Nuova Vallecchi Editore S.p.A.  (IT)
Societa Editoriale Nuove Cronache Italiane  (IT)
Nuove Edizioni Operaie s.r.l.  (IT)
Nuove Iniziative Editoriali S.p.A.  (IT)
Editrice Nuovi Orientamenti  (IT)
Nuovo Agora Omaggio  (IT)
Nuovo Bollettino Bibliografico Sardo  (IT)
Nuovo Chirone  (IT)
Nuovo Diritto  (IT)
Nuovo Impegno  (IT)
Edizioni Nuovo Mezzogiorno  (IT)
Nuovo Osservatore  (IT)
Nuovo Pensiero Militare  (IT)
Nazir Ahmad Nuri  (II)
Nursery World  (UK)
Nurses Association of Jamaica  (JM)
Nurses Association of the American College of
   Obstetricians and Gynecologists  (US)
Nurses Association of the Counties of Long Island
   (US)
Nurses Association of the Republic of China  (CH)
Nurses Reform Association of New Zealand  (NZ)
Nursing Digest, Inc.  (US)
Nursing Home Report  (US)
Nursing Notes Ltd.  (UK)
Nursing Publications, Inc.  (US)
Nutrition Foundation, Inc.  (US)
Nutrition Society  (UK)
Nutrition Today, Inc.  (US)
Nuttall Ornithological Club  (US)
Nuwe Protestantse Kerk in Afrika  (SA)
Ny Carlsberg Glyptotek  (DK)
Forlaget Ny Teknik A-S  (DK)
Nya Bokfoerlags AB  (SW)
Anders Nyborg A-S  (DK)
Nye Family of America Association  (US)
Nyegaard & Co. A-S  (NO)
Forlaget P.E. Nygaard  (DK)
Gerald Nygaard, Ed. & Pub.  (US)
Nykterhetsroerelsens Scoutfoerbund  (SW)
Nykylehdet Oy  (FI)
Nykytekstiili Oy  (FI)
Nymphenburger Verlagshandlung  (GW)
Nystrom Publishing Co., Inc.  (US)
Nyt Nordisk Forlag  (DK)
Nyt Presse Bureau  (DK)
O A B Press Service Ltd.  (NR)
O A C I
   see International Civil Aviation Organization  (UN)
O A Kyokai
   see Europe and Asia Association  (JA)
O.D.E.G.E. Presse S.A.  (FR)
O.G.E.T.  (IT)
O. G. P. P.  (FR)
O. Henry House  (US)
O I C S
   see International Narcotics Control Board  (UN)
O M I Farm News  (US)
O M P I
   see World Intellectual Property Organization  (UN)
O M S
   see World Health Organization  (UN)
O. N. I. S. E. P
   see under France. Office National d'Information sur
   les Enseignements et les Professions  (FR)
O. P. B. International S.p.A.  (IT)
O.P. Books Pty. Ltd.  (AT)
O. P. E. R. A.  (FR)
O. P. Publications Corp.  (US)
Edizioni O.R.G.A  (IT)
O R L Publications Ltd.  (CN)
O.R.S.T.O.M.  (NL)
O.S. & S. Ltd.  (UK)
O S I Publications  (US)
O S P (Oficina Sanitaria Panamericana)
   see World Health Organization. Pan American
   Health Organization  (UN)
Oahu Development Conference  (US)
Oak Publications  (US)
Oak Ridge Associated Universities, Inc.  (US)
Oak Ridge National Laboratory  (US)
Oakham School  (UK)
Oakland Public Library  (US)
Oakwood Press  (UK)
Oan Vap Press  (US)
OARCA - Freie Akademie zur Koordinierung von
   Esoterik und Wissenschaft e.V.  (GW)
Oasis Books  (UK)
O'Bannon Genealogist  (US)
Obedinenie Pervopokhodnikov  (US)
Oberflaechenbearbeitung Metallischer und
   Nichtmetallischer Werkstoffe  (GW)
Oberhessische Gesellschaft fuer Natur- und Heilkunde,
   Giessen  (GW)
Librairie Oberlin  (FR)
Oberlin College  (US)
Oberlin College. Allen Memorial Art Museum  (US)
Oberlin College. Alumni Association  (US)

Oesterreichisches Forschungsinstitut fuer Wirtschaft und Politik  (AU)
Oesterreichisches Institut fuer Bauforschung  (AU)
Oesterreichisches Institut fuer Raumplanung  (AU)
Oesterreichisches Institut fuer Schul-und Sportstaettenbau  (AU)
Oesterreichisches Institut fuer Verpackung  (AU)
Oesterreichisches Institut fuer Wirtschaftsforschung  (AU)
Oesterreichisches Jugendrotkreuz  (AU)
Oesterreichisches Kolpingwerk  (AU)
Oesterreichisches Kulturinstitut, Rom  (IT)
Oesterreichisches Kuratorium fuer Sicherheit im Bergland  (AU)
Oesterreichisches Lateinamerika-Institut  (AU)
Oesterreichisches Luftfahrt Archiv  (AU)
Oesterreichisches Museum fuer Volkskunde  (AU)
Oesterreichisches Nationalinstitut  (AU)
Oesterreichisches Ost- und Suedosteuropa Institut  (AU)
Oesterreichisches Rotes Kreuz  (AU)
Oesterreichisches Staatsarchiv  (AU)
Oesterreichisches Volksliedwerk  (AU)
Oesterreichisches Wirtschaftsinstitut fuer Strukturforschung und Strukturpolitik  (AU)
Oesterreichisches Zentrum fuer Wirtschaftlichkeit und Produktivitaet (OPWZ)  (AU)
Oeuvre Apostolique pour les Missions de Fondation Francaise a l'Etranger  (FR)
Oeuvre de Saint Pierre Apotre  (FR)
Oeuvre Nationale de l'Enfance  (BE)
Of Sea & Shore Publications  (US)
Off-Beat Digest  (US)
Off Duty  (GW)
Off-Licence Journal  (UK)
Off Off Broadway Alliance  (US)
Off Our Backs Inc.  (US)
Verlag Offene Worte  (GW)
Offensiv  (SZ)
Office and Professional Employees International Union  (US)
Office Arabe de Presse et de Documentation  (SY)
Office Belge du Commerce Exterieur
   see Belgium. Office Belge du Commerce Exterieur  (BE)
Office Belge pour l'Accroissement de la Productivite  (BE)
Office Central de la Cooperation a l'Ecole  (FR)
Office Central des Chemins de Fer d'Outremer  (FR)
Office de Justification de la Diffusion  (FR)
Office de la Recherche Scientifique et Technique Outre-Mer de M'Bour. Centre de Geophysique  (SG)
Office de la Recherche Scientifique et Technique Outre-Mer. Service des Publications  (FR)
Office de Publicite et d'Edition Lutetia  (FR)
Office de Tourisme de Paris  (FR)
Office de Vulgarisation Pharmaceutique  (FR)
Office des Assureurs de Belgique  (BE)
Office des Communications Sociales  (CN)
Office des Nouvelles Internationales  (FR)
Office des Publications Officielles des Communautes Europeennes
   see Office for Official Publications of the European Communities  (EI)
Office Diocesain d'Information  (FR)
Office du Baccalaureat International
   see International Baccalaureate Office  (SZ)
Office Education Association  (US)
Office for Official Publications of the European Communities  (EI)
Office Forestier Central Suisse  (SZ)
Office Francais de Presse Specialisee  (FR)
Office Genealogique et Heraldique de Belgique  (BE)
Office General de la Musique  (FR)
Office General de Presse et de Publicite  (FR)
Office Intercantonal de Controle de Medicaments
   see Interkantonale Kontrollstelle fuer Heilmittel  (SZ)
Office International de l'Enseignment Catholique
   see Catholic International Education Office  (BE)
Office International de la Vigne et du Vin  (FR)
Office International de Librairie  (BE)
Office International du Cacao et de Chocalat
   see International Office of Cocoa and Chocolate  (BE)
Office International Oeuvres Formation Civique  (FR)
Office National de la Recherche et du Developpement  (ZR)
Office of Health Economics  (UK)
Office of the Australian Official Representative  (AT)
Office of the Chancellor of the Swedish Universities
   see Sweden. Universitetskanslersaembetet  (SW)
Office Publications, Inc.  (US)
Office Publicitaire du Centre  (FR)
Office Research Institute  (US)
Office Rwandais d'Information
   see Rwanda. Office Rwandais d'Information  (RW)

Office Statistique des Communautes Europeenes
   see Statistical Office of the European Communities  (EI)
Office Suisse d'Expansion Commerciale
   see Schweizerische Zentrale fuer Handelsfoerderung  (SZ)
Office Technique pour l'Utilisation de l'Acier  (FR)
Office Universitaire de Recherche Socialiste  (FR)
Officers Association of the Royal Norwegian Air Forces  (NO)
Officers' Christian Union  (UK)
Officers' Pensions Society Ltd.  (UK)
Official Meeting Facilities Guide  (US)
Official Motor Carrier Directory, Inc.  (US)
Official Motor Freight Guide, Inc.  (US)
Official Organ Blue Book  (US)
Officiel de la Couture et de la Mode de Paris S.A.  (FR)
Officiel de la Photographie et du Cinema  (FR)
Officiel des Galeries  (FR)
Officiel des Spectacles  (FR)
Officiel Francais des Guides d'Achets Professionnels  (FR)
Officiel S.A.  (FR)
Officium Libri Catholic  (IT)
John Offord (Publications) Ltd.  (UK)
Offset-Haus AG  (SZ)
Offshore Information Literature  (UK)
Editorial Ofice  (SP)
Oficina de Educacion Iberoamericana  (SP)
Oficina de Informacion Holandesa  (AG)
Oficina Informativa de Comercio Exterior  (SP)
Oficina Internacional de Informacion y Observacion del Espanol  (SP)
Oficina Sanitaria Panamericana
   see World Health Organization. Pan American Health Organization  (UN)
Ogata Institute for Medical and Chemical Research  (JA)
Ogranomatik  (YU)
Ohara Institute for Agricultural Biology
   see Okayama University. Ohara Institute fuer Landwirtschaftliche Biologie  (JA)
Ohara Institute fuer Landwirtschaftliche Biologie
   see under Okayama University  (JA)
Ohio. Administration of Justice Division  (US)
Ohio. Advisory Council for Vocational Education  (US)
Ohio. Attorney General's Office  (US)
Ohio. Board of Regents  (US)
Ohio. Bureau of Employment Services  (US)
Ohio. Commission on Aging  (US)
Ohio. Department of Economic and Community Development  (US)
Ohio. Department of Economic and Community Development. Bureau of Business Research  (US)
Ohio. Department of Education. Division of Special Education  (US)
Ohio. Department of Health  (US)
Ohio. Department of Industrial Relations. Division of Mines  (US)
Ohio. Department of Mental Health and Mental Retardation  (US)
Ohio. Department of Mental Health and Mental Retardation. Office of Developmental Disabilities  (US)
Ohio. Department of Natural Resources. Division of Geological Survey  (US)
Ohio. Department of Natural Resources. Division of Wildlife  (US)
Ohio. Department of State Personnel  (US)
Ohio. Division of Safety and Hygiene  (US)
Ohio. State Library  (US)
Ohio Academy of Family Physicians  (US)
Ohio Academy of Science  (US)
Ohio AFL-CIO  (US)
Ohio Agricultural Research and Development Center  (US)
Ohio Arts Council  (US)
Ohio Association of Garden Clubs  (US)
Ohio Association of Secondary School Administrators  (US)
Ohio Bankers Association  (US)
Ohio Biological Survey  (US)
Ohio Brass Co  (US)
Ohio College Library Center  (US)
Ohio Congress of Parents & Teachers, Inc.  (US)
Ohio Contractors Association  (US)
Ohio Cooperative Wildlife Research Unit  (US)
Ohio Council on Economic Education  (US)
Ohio Education Association  (US)
Ohio Educational Library Media Association  (US)
Ohio Farm Bureau Federation and Affiliated Co-Operatives  (US)
Ohio Florists Association  (US)
Ohio Forestry Association, Inc.  (US)
Ohio Genealogical Society  (US)
Ohio Historical Society  (US)

Ohio Jersey Breeders Association Inc.  (US)
Ohio Journal  (US)
Ohio Library Association  (US)
Ohio Library Trustees Association  (US)
Ohio Municipal League  (US)
Ohio Music Education Association  (US)
Ohio Music Education Association (Akron)  (US)
Ohio Northern University  (US)
Ohio Nurses Association  (US)
Ohio Osteopathic Association of Physicians and Surgeons  (US)
Ohio School Boards Association  (US)
Ohio Society of Certified Public Accountants  (US)
Ohio Society of Professional Engineers  (US)
Ohio State Bar Association  (US)
Ohio State Grange  (US)
Ohio State Medical Association  (US)
Ohio State Pharmaceutical Association  (US)
Ohio State University  (US)
Ohio State University  (US)
Ohio State University. Alumni Association  (US)
Ohio State University. Center for Business and Economic Research  (US)
Ohio State University. Center for Vocational Education  (US)
Ohio State University. College of Administrative Science  (US)
Ohio State University. College of Biological Sciences  (US)
Ohio State University. College of Education  (US)
Ohio State University. College of Engineering  (US)
Ohio State University. College of Law  (US)
Ohio State University. Disaster Research Center  (US)
Ohio State University. Engineering Experiment Station  (US)
Ohio State University. Extension Entomologists  (US)
Ohio State University. Graduate Institute for World Affairs  (US)
Ohio State University Hospitals. Department of Communications and Public Affairs  (US)
Ohio State University. Institute of Polar Studies  (US)
Ohio State University Libraries  (US)
Ohio State University Marion Campus  (US)
Ohio State University. Medical Administration Center  (US)
Ohio State University Press  (US)
Ohio State University. Project on Linguistic Analysis  (US)
Ohio State University. School of Allied Medical Professions  (US)
Ohio State University. School of Journalism  (US)
Ohio State University. School of Music  (US)
Ohio State University. Service Center for Teachers of Asian Studies  (US)
Ohio State University. Slavic Languages Department  (US)
Ohio State University. Theatre Research  (US)
Ohio State University. Water Resources Center  (US)
Ohio Testing Services  (US)
Ohio Trucking Association  (US)
Ohio University  (US)
Ohio University. Center for Educational Research & Service  (US)
Ohio University. Center for International Studies  (US)
Ohio University. Department of English  (US)
Ohio University Press  (US)
Ohio University Press Administrative Annex  (US)
Ohio University. Student Publications Board  (US)
Ohio Valley Area Libraries  (US)
Ohio Valley Philosophy of Education Society  (US)
Ohio Valley Retailer  (US)
Ohio Veterinary Medical Association  (US)
Ohio Wesleyan University  (US)
Ohioana Library Association  (US)
Lillies Ohlsson, Ed. & Pub.  (SW)
Verlag Arthur Ohm  (GW)
Oiga  (PE)
Oikoumenikon  (IT)
Oil & Colour Chemists Association  (UK)
Oil & Natural Gas Commission, Dehradun  (II)
Oil Buyers Guide  (US)
Oil, Chemical and Atomic Workers International Union  (US)
Oil Information, Inc.  (US)
Oil Men's Association of America  (US)
Oil Review Publishing Co.  (US)
Oil Technologists Association of India  (II)
KG Oil-Telegram GmbH und Co.  (GW)
Oildom Publishing Co.  (US)
Oilgas S.A.  (SP)
Oise Peasants Organizations  (FR)
Oita Daigaku
   see Oita University  (JA)
Oita University. Economic Research Society  (JA)
Oita University. Research Institute of Economics  (JA)

Okajima's Folia Anatomica Japonica  (JA)
Okayama Daigaku
  see Okayama University  (JA)
Okayama Daigaku Nogyo Seibutsu Kenkyusho
  see Okayama University. Ohara Institute fuer
  Landwirtschaftliche Biologie  (JA)
Okayama Daigaku Rigakubu Kaimen-kagaku Kenkyu
  Shisetsu
  see Okayama University. Research Laboratory for
  Surface Science  (JA)
Okayama University. Ohara Institute for Agricultural
  Biology
  see Okayama University. Ohara Institute fuer
  Landwirtschaftliche Biologie  (JA)
Okayama University. Department of Biology  (JA)
Okayama University. Department of Mathematics
  (JA)
Okayama University. Ohara Institute fuer
  Landwirtschaftliche Biologie  (JA)
Okayama University. Research Laboratory for Surface
  Science  (JA)
Okayama University. School of Engineering  (JA)
Okayama University. School of Medicine  (JA)
Okeechobee Waterway Association  (US)
Okike  (NR)
Okinawa. Statistics Department  (JA)
Okinawa-ken Tokeika
  see Okinawa. Statistics Department  (JA)
Okinawa Library Association  (JA)
Okinawa Toshokan Kyokai
  see Okinawa Library Association  (JA)
Oklahoma. Aeronautics Commission  (US)
Oklahoma. Attorney General's Office  (US)
Oklahoma. Board of Medicolegal Investigations. Office
  of the Chief Medical Examiner  (US)
Oklahoma. Conservation Commission  (US)
Oklahoma. Department of Education. Curriculum
  Improvement Commission  (US)
Oklahoma. Department of Health  (US)
Oklahoma. Department of Highways. Planning
  Division  (US)
Oklahoma. Department of Industrial Development
  (US)
Oklahoma. Department of Institutions Social and
  Rehabilitative Services  (US)
Oklahoma. Department of Libraries  (US)
Oklahoma. Department of Mental Health  (US)
Oklahoma. Department of Public Welfare  (US)
Oklahoma. Department of Wildlife Conservation
  (US)
Oklahoma. Division of Maternal and Child Health
  (US)
Oklahoma. Drug Abuse Division  (US)
Oklahoma. Employment Security Commission.
  Actuarial Division  (US)
Oklahoma. Employment Security Commission.
  Research & Planning Division  (US)
Oklahoma. Geological Survey  (US)
Oklahoma. Indian Affairs Commission  (US)
Oklahoma. Industrial Development Department  (US)
Oklahoma. Office of Community Affairs and Planning
  (US)
Oklahoma. State Board of Public Accountancy  (US)
Oklahoma. Tax Commission. Ad Valorem Division
  (US)
Oklahoma. Turnpike Authority  (US)
Oklahoma. Water Resources Board  (US)
Oklahoma Academy of Science  (US)
Oklahoma Agricultural Experiment Station  (US)
Oklahoma Anthropological Society  (US)
Oklahoma Art Center  (US)
Oklahoma Association of Electric Cooperatives  (US)
Oklahoma Bankers Association  (US)
Oklahoma Bar Association  (US)
Oklahoma Bluegrass Club Inc.  (US)
Oklahoma Cattlemen's Association  (US)
Oklahoma City Chamber of Commerce  (US)
Oklahoma City Geological Society  (US)
Oklahoma Congress of Parents and Teachers  (US)
Oklahoma Council on Economic Education  (US)
Oklahoma County Libraries  (US)
Oklahoma Dental Association  (US)
Oklahoma Education Association  (US)
Oklahoma Farm Bureau  (US)
Oklahoma Farmers Union  (US)
Oklahoma Fishery Research Laboratory  (US)
Oklahoma Historical Society  (US)
Oklahoma Library Association  (US)
Oklahoma LP-Gas Association  (US)
Oklahoma Oil Marketers Association  (US)
Oklahoma Ornithological Society  (US)
Oklahoma Reading Council  (US)
Oklahoma Restaurant Association  (US)
Oklahoma Retail Grocers Association  (US)
Oklahoma Retailer Publishing Co.  (US)
Oklahoma River Basin Survey  (US)
Oklahoma Society of Professional Engineers Inc.
  (US)

Oklahoma State Medical Association  (US)
Oklahoma State Nurses Association  (US)
Oklahoma State University. College of Arts and
  Sciences  (US)
Oklahoma State University. College of Business
  Administration  (US)
Oklahoma State University. College of Engineering
  (US)
Oklahoma Today  (US)
Oklahoma University College of Law  (US)
Oklahoma Water Resources Research Institute  (US)
Oklahomans for Indian Opportunity  (US)
Okra Press  (US)
Old Athlone Society  (IE)
Old Calabar and Ogoja Youth Organization  (NR)
Old Car Value Guide  (US)
Old Colfeians Association  (UK)
Old Contemptible  (UK)
Old Dartmouth Historical Society  (US)
Old Dominion University. Conference on Scottish
  Studies  (US)
Old Dublin Society  (IE)
Old Fort Genealogical Society of Southeastern Kansas
  (US)
Old Friends  (US)
Old-House Journal Corporation  (US)
Old Lyme Investment Co.  (US)
Old Marble Press  (US)
Old Motor Magazine Ltd.  (UK)
Old Nun Publications  (CN)
Old Rhodian Union  (SA)
Old Salem, Inc.  (US)
Old Soldiers of Baker Street of the Two Saults  (US)
Old Sturbridge Village  (US)
Old Time Music  (UK)
R. Oldenbourg Verlag GmbH  (GW)
Oldenburgische Gesellschaft fuer Familienkunde
  (GW)
Oleander Press  (UK)
Oleander Press  (US)
Oleo  (SP)
Editoriale Olimpia  (IT)
Olivant Press  (US)
Jose Soares de Oliveira, Ed. & Pub.  (PO)
Michael Oliver  (US)
Oliver & Boyd  (UK)
C. Dalley Oliver, Ed. & Pub.  (US)
Oliver Press  (US)
Oliver's Guides  (UK)
C. Olivetti & Co., S.p.A.  (IT)
Olle und Wolter GmbH und Co.  (GW)
Georg Olms Verlag GmbH  (GW)
Olmstead's Genealogy Recorded  (US)
Paul C. Olrik, Ed. & Pub.  (DK)
Casa Editrice Leo S. Olschki  (IT)
Humphrey A. Olsen, Ed. & Pub.  (US)
David E. Olson, Ed. & Pub.  (US)
Olympia  (CS)
Olympia-Verlag GmbH  (GW)
Olympic Club  (US)
Olympic Genealogical Society  (US)
Olympic Media Information  (US)
Olyslager Organisation  (NE)
Guenter Olzog Verlag  (GW)
Om  (US)
Om Rama - Yoga Sangam  (II)
Oma Press  (NR)
Omaha-Council Bluffs Metropolitan Area Planning
  Agency  (US)
Omaha District Dental Society  (US)
Omaha Jewish Federation  (US)
Omaha Westerners  (US)
Oman Publishing Co.  (US)
Omega Epsilon Phi Fraternity  (US)
Omega Group Ltd.  (US)
Omen Press Inc.  (US)
Omens  (UK)
Omicron Delta Epsilon Fraternity  (US)
Omicron Nu Home Economics Honor Society  (US)
Ommation Press  (US)
Omni Industries, Inc.  (US)
Omni Publications Bulletin  (US)
Edizioni Omnia Medica  (IT)
Omnibus Society  (UK)
Verlag J.G. Oncken Nachf. GmbH  (GW)
One Parent Community  (US)
One People's Australia League  (AT)
One-Size-Fits-All Press  (US)
One World Spotlight  (GH)
Jerome H. O'Neil  (US)
William O'Neil & Co., Inc.  (US)
Ongaku Gakkai
  see Japanese Musicological Society  (JA)
Ongaku No Tomo Sha Corp.  (JA)
Onibonoje Press  (NR)
Onkoloski Institut  (YU)
Online, Inc.  (US)
Onlooker Publications Pvt. Ltd.  (II)

Drukkerij Onnes B.V.  (NE)
Onrea  (BE)
Uitgeverij "Ons Huis"  (NE)
Ons Vee  (NE)
Onslow Historical Society  (NZ)
Ontario. Division of Mines. Geological Branch  (CN)
Ontario. Government Services  (CN)
Ontario. Labour Relations Board  (CN)
Ontario. Ministry of Agriculture and Food  (CN)
Ontario. Ministry of Colleges and Universities  (CN)
Ontario. Ministry of Community and Social Services
  (CN)
Ontario. Ministry of Consumer and Commercial
  Relations  (CN)
Ontario. Ministry of Culture and Recreation.
  Provincial Library Service  (CN)
Ontario. Ministry of Education  (CN)
Ontario. Ministry of Energy  (CN)
Ontario. Ministry of Government Services. Printing
  Services Branch  (CN)
Ontario. Ministry of Housing  (CN)
Ontario. Ministry of Industry and Tourism  (CN)
Ontario. Ministry of Labour. Research Library  (CN)
Ontario. Ministry of Natural Resources.  (CN)
Ontario. Ministry of Natural Resources. Division of
  Forests  (CN)
Ontario. Ministry of the Environment  (CN)
Ontario. Ministry of the Environment. Information
  Services Branch  (CN)
Ontario. Ministry of the Environment. Water
  Resources Branch  (CN)
Ontario. Ministry of Transportation and
  Communications  (CN)
Ontario. Ministry of Treasury, Economics and
  Intergovernmental Affairs. Ontario Statistical Centre
  (CN)
Ontario Archaeological Society  (CN)
Ontario Archaeological Society. Ottawa Chapter
  (CN)
Ontario Association for Curriculum Development
  (CN)
Ontario Association for Emotionally Disturbed
  Children  (CN)
Ontario Association for Geographic and
  Environmental Education  (CN)
Ontario Association for Mathematics Education
  (CN)
Ontario Association of Children's Aid Societies  (CN)
Ontario Bird Banding Association  (CN)
Ontario Cancer Treatment and Research Foundation
  (CN)
Ontario College of Pharmacists  (CN)
Ontario Crafts Council  (CN)
Ontario Criminal Injuries Compensation Board  (CN)
Ontario Dental Association  (CN)
Ontario Dental Hygienists' Association  (CN)
Ontario Educational Association  (CN)
Ontario Educational Research Council  (CN)
Ontario Energy Board  (CN)
Ontario English Catholic Teachers Association  (CN)
Ontario Federation of Agriculture  (CN)
Ontario Federation of Labour  (CN)
Ontario Film Association Inc.  (CN)
Ontario Folk Dance Association  (CN)
Ontario Forest Information Service  (CN)
Ontario Forestry Association  (CN)
Ontario Fruit and Vegetable Growers Association
  (CN)
Ontario Genealogical Society  (CN)
Ontario Handgun Association  (CN)
Ontario Historical Society  (CN)
Ontario Hog Producers Association  (CN)
Ontario Hospital Association  (CN)
Ontario Human Rights Commission  (CN)
Ontario Hydro  (CN)
Ontario Institute for Studies in Education  (CN)
Ontario Insurance Adjusters Association  (CN)
Ontario Insurance Agents and Brokers Association.
  Consumer Liaison Committee  (CN)
Ontario Library Association  (CN)
Ontario Lung Association  (CN)
Ontario Medical Association  (CN)
Ontario Medical Wives Association  (CN)
Ontario Metis & Non-Status Indian Association
  (CN)
Ontario Milk Marketing Board  (CN)
Ontario Modern Language Teachers' Association
  (CN)
Ontario Motor League. Ottawa Club  (CN)
Ontario Numismatist  (CN)
Ontario Petroleum Institute Inc.  (CN)
Ontario Plumbing Inspectors Association  (CN)
Ontario Progressive Conservative Association  (CN)
Ontario Psychological Association  (CN)

Ontario Public School Trustees Association (CN)
Ontario Puppetry Association (CN)
Ontario Report (CN)
Ontario Research Foundation (CN)
Ontario Retail Gasoline and Automotive Service Association (CN)
Ontario Review (CN)
Ontario Secondary School Teachers' Federation (CN)
Ontario Securities Commission (CN)
Ontario Shade Tree Council (CN)
Ontario Showcase Publishing Co. Ltd. (CN)
Ontario Society of Medical Technologists (CN)
Ontario Speech and Hearing Association (CN)
Ontario Status of Women Council (CN)
Ontario Teachers' Federation (CN)
Ontario Trucking Association (CN)
Uitgeverij S.M. Ontwikkeling (BE)
Oomoto and Universal Love and Brotherhood Association (JA)
Oost en West (NE)
Oostelike Transvaalse Kooperasie Beperk (SA)
Oostenrijkse Handelsdelegatie in Nederland (NE)
Op Cit (IT)
Op Safari (Pty) Ltd. (SA)
Opca Bolnica "Dr. Josip Kajfes" (YU)
Open-Air Mission (UK)
Open Book (AT)
Open Court Publishing Co. (US)
Open Door International (BE)
Open Press (IE)
Open Road Publishing Co. (US)
Open University (UK)
Open University Press (UK)
Open Window Society, Inc. (US)
Opera Aperta (IT)
Opera Buona Stampa (IT)
Opera della Regalita' di N.S.G.C. (IT)
Opera di Santa Rita di Roccaporena di Cascia (IT)
Opera Madonna delle Grazie (IT)
Opera Nazionale: Maternita e Infanzia (IT)
Opera North (UK)
Opera, Subtitle (FR)
Operational Research Society (UK)
Operational Research Society of India (II)
Operational Research Society of India, Calcutta Branch (II)
Operations Research Society of America (US)
Operations Research Society of Japan (JA)
Operative Plasterers' and Cement Masons' International Association of the United States and Canada (US)
Opettajien Ammattijarjesto (FI)
Diffusion Ophrys (FR)
Ophthalmic Publishing Co. (US)
Ophthalmological Society of Egypt (UA)
Opinion Europeenne (IT)
Opinion Publications (US)
Opinion Publications, Inc. (US)
Opinione Repubblicana (IT)
Opolskie Towarzystwo Przyjaciol Nauk (PL)
Oporto, Portugal. Camara Municipal, Oporto (PO)
Theodor Oppermann Verlag (GW)
Opportunities Press, Inc. (US)
Opportunities Unlimited Publications (US)
Opportunity Publishing Co. (US)
Opstestveno Politickite Organizacii na SR Makedonija (YU)
Opstinska Konferencija Muzicke Omladine (YU)
Opstinska Zajednica Kulture Subotica (YU)
Editions Opta (FR)
Opthalmological Society of the Republic of China (CH)
Optical Publishing Co., Inc (US)
Optical Society of America, Inc. (US)
Optical Society of India (II)
Optical World Ltd. (UK)
Opticians and Optometrists Association of N.S.W. (AT)
Opticians Association of America (US)
Opticien Belge (BE)
Optikai, Akusztikai es Filmtechnikai Egyesulet (HU)
Option Weekly (US)
Options Publishing Co. (US)
Optosonic Press (US)
Opus (CS)
O'Quinn Studios, Inc. (US)
Verlag Orac (AU)
Oracle of Maat Publishing Company (US)
Oral History Association (US)
Oral Roberts Evangelistic Association Inc. (US)
Orange County Bar Association (US)
Orange County Califoia Genealogical Society (US)
Orange County Cooperative Extension (US)
Orange County Illustrated, Inc. (US)
Orange Free State. Director of Hospital Services (SA)
Orange Free State. Education Department (SA)

Orange Free State. Library Service (SA)
Orange Free State. Nature Conservation Division (SA)
Orange Press (US)
Orangeburg Historical and Genealogical Society (US)
Uitgeverij A. J. Oranje (NE)
Orario Nuovo Grippaudo (IT)
Oratoire de France (FR)
Oratoire Saint-Joseph du Mont-Royal (CN)
Orbe Publications Inc. (US)
Orbis (CS)
Orbis Publishing Ltd. (UK)
Orbis-Verlag (GW)
Orbit Books (UK)
Orbit Weekly (II)
Orcadian (UK)
Orchid Review Ltd. (UK)
Orchid Society of New South Wales (AT)
Orchid Society of South East Asia (SI)
Ordem dos Advogados do Brasil (BL)
Ordem dos Economistas de Sao Paulo (BL)
Orden de las Escuelas Pias (SP)
Orden de los Frailes Menores Capuchinos (AG)
Order of Agrologists of Quebec (CN)
Order of Ahepa (US)
Order of Demolay. International Supreme Council (US)
Order of Engineers of Quebec (CN)
Order of Friars Minor (US)
Order of Nurses of Quebec (CN)
Order of Physicians in Lebanon (LE)
Order of Runeberg (US)
Order of Saint Augustine. Curia Generalizia (IT)
Order of Saint Basil-The-Great (CN)
Order of St. Francis. Curia Generalis (IT)
Order of St. John (UK)
Order of St. John. Priory for South Africa (SA)
Order of the Road (UK)
Order of the Sons of Italy in America. Grand Lodge of California (US)
Order of the Sons of Italy in America. Grand Lodge of Massachusetts (US)
Order of United Commercial Travelers of America (US)
Orders and Medals Society of America (US)
Ordina Editions (BE)
Ordine degli Ingegneri della Provincia di Catania (IT)
Ordine dei Medici della Provincia di Parma (IT)
Ordine dei Medici di Torino e Provincia (IT)
Ordine del Combattentismo Attivo (IT)
Ordine del Dottori Commercialisti di Milano (IT)
Ordine Ospedaliero di S. Giovanni di Dio (IT)
Ordre des Architectes (FR)
Ordre des Architectes du Quebec (CN)
Ordre des Arpenteurs-Geometres du Quebec (CN)
Ordre des Dentistes du Quebec (CN)
Ordre des Experts Comptables et des Comptables Agrees. Conseil Superieur (FR)
Ordre des Geometres Experts (FR)
Ordre National des Chirurgiens- Dentistes. Conseil National (FR)
Ordre National des Medecins (FR)
Ordre National des Medicins. Conseil Departemental des Hauts-de-Seine (FR)
Ordre Professionnelle des Ingenieurs Forestiers du Quebec (CN)
Ordre Souveraia Militaire Hospitalier de St. Jean de Jerusalem de Rhodes et de Malte (IT)
Ordre Souverain de Malte (SZ)
Ore (UK)
Oregon. Department of Agriculture (US)
Oregon. Department of Economic Development (US)
Oregon. Department of Education (US)
Oregon. Department of Fish and Wildlife (US)
Oregon. Department of Forestry (US)
Oregon. Department of Geology and Mineral Industries (US)
Oregon. Department of Revenue (US)
Oregon. Department of Transportation. Mass Transit Division (US)
Oregon. Department of Transportation. Motor Vehicles Division (US)
Oregon. Department of Transportation. State Parks and Recreation Branch (US)
Oregon. Educational Coordinating Commission (US)
Oregon. Fish Commission (US)
Oregon. Governor's Commission on Youth (US)
Oregon. Governor's Steering Committee for Management Selection and Development (US)
Oregon. Office of Community Health Services (US)
Oregon. Public Utility Commissioner (US)
Oregon. Public Welfare Division (US)
Oregon. Secretary of State (US)
Oregon. State Advisory Council for Career and Vocational Education (US)
Oregon. State Board of Accountancy (US)

Oregon. State Employment Division. Research & Statistics (US)
Oregon. State Health Division (US)
Oregon. State Health Division. Office of Health Planning Services (US)
Oregon. State Library (US)
Oregon. Workmen's Compensation Board. Accident Prevention Division (US)
Oregon Archaeological Society (US)
Oregon Association for Supervision and Curriculum Development (US)
Oregon Association of Nurserymen (US)
Oregon Cattlemen's Association, Inc. (US)
Oregon College of Education. Humanities Department (US)
Oregon Daily Emerald Publishing Co., Inc. (US)
Oregon Dental Association (US)
Oregon Education Association (US)
Oregon Educational Media Association (US)
Oregon Environmental Council (US)
Oregon Farm Bureau Federation (US)
Oregon Feed, Seed & Supplies Association (US)
Oregon Historical Society (US)
Oregon Library Association (US)
Oregon Licensee, Inc. (US)
Oregon Music Educator (US)
Oregon Nurses Association (US)
Oregon Optometric Association (US)
Oregon Outdoors Publishing Co. (US)
Oregon Psychological Association (US)
Oregon Regional Medical Program (US)
Oregon Regional Primate Research Center (US)
Oregon Research Institute (US)
Oregon Rural Electrical Cooperative Association (US)
Oregon School Study Council (US)
Oregon Science Teachers Association (US)
Oregon State Association of Plumbing-Heating-Cooling Contractors, Inc. (US)
Oregon State Bar (US)
Oregon State Grange (US)
Oregon State System of Higher Education (US)
Oregon State University. Air Resources Center (US)
Oregon State University. Department of Horticulture (US)
Oregon State University. Environmental Health Sciences Center (US)
Oregon State University. Forest Research Laboratory (US)
Oregon State University. Genetics Insitute (US)
Oregon State University. Marine Advisory Program (US)
Oregon State University Press (US)
Oregon State University. School of Engineering (US)
Oregon State University. School of Forestry (US)
Oregon State University. Sea Grant College Program (US)
Oregon State University. Water Resources Research Institute (US)
Oregon Voter Digest (US)
Orelfa Editora (AG)
Orell Fuessli Graphische Betriebe AG (SZ)
Orfanotrofio Antoniano dei PP. Rogazionisti (IT)
Orfeo (CL)
Orff-Schulwerk Association of Queensland (AT)
Organ Club (UK)
Organ Historical Society, Inc. (US)
Organe Internationale de Controle des Stupefiants see International Narcotics Control Board (UN)
Organic Farming & Gardening Society (AT)
Organic Preparations and Procedures, Inc. (US)
Organisakous Agricole (FR)
Organisasjonen Vern og Velferd (NO)
Organisation Commune Africaine et Mauricienne (CX)
Organisation de l'Aviation Civile Internationale see International Civil Aviation Organization (UN)
Organisation des Communistes de Suisse (M.L.) (SZ)
Organisation des Nations pour l'Education, la Science et la Culture see Unesco (UN)
Organisation for the Prevention of Accidents (GR)
Organisation Francaise du Mouvement Europeen (FR)
Organisation Intergouvernementale Consultative de la Navigation Maritime see Intergovernmental Maritime Consultative Organization (UN)
Organisation Internationale pour l'Etude des Langues Anciennes Par Ordinateur see International Organization for Ancient Languages Analysis by Computer (BE)
Organisation Mondiale de la Propriete Intellectuelle see World Intellectual Property Organization (UN)
Organisation Mondiale de la Sante see World Health Organization (UN)
Organisation Mondiale pour l'Education Prescolaire (IE)

Organisation of Angolan Women   (TZ)
Organisation of European Aluminium Smelters   (GW)
Organisation Revolutionnaire Anarchiste   (FR)
Organisation Sioniste de France   (FR)
Organisations Chretiennes-Sociales   (SZ)
Organisme Professionnel de Prevention du Batiment et
   des Travaux Publiques   (FR)
Organizacao Provincial de Voluntarios e Defesa Civil
   de Angola   (AO)
Organizacion Continental Latino Americana de
   Estudiantes   (CU)
Organizacion Mundial de la Propriedad Intelectual
   see World Intellectual Property Organization   (UN)
Organizacion Sindical Espanola   (SP)
Organizacion Sindical Leridana   (SP)
Organizacion Universitaria de Intercambio
   Panamericano   (AG)
Organization for Defense of Four Freedoms for
   Ukraine Inc.   (US)
Organization for Economic Cooperation and
   Development   (FR)
Organization for Economic Cooperation and
   Development. Nuclear Energy Agency   (FR)
Organization for Flora Neotropica   (US)
Organization for the Rebirth of Ukraine   (US)
Organization of African Unity. Health, Sanitation and
   Nutrition Commission   (ET)
Organization of African Unity. Inter- African Bureau
   for Soils   (CX)
Organization of African Unity. Scientific Technical
   and Research Commission   (NG)
Organization of American Historians   (US)
Organization of American Kodaly Educators   (US)
Organization of American States   (US)
Organization of American States. Department of Social
   Affairs   (US)
Organization of Arab Petroleum Exporting Countries
   (KU)
Organization of Black American Culture, Writers'
   Workshop   (US)
Organization of Historical Studies   (US)
Organization of North American Indian Students
   (US)
Organization of Petroleum Exporting Countries   (AU)
Organization of Solidarity of the Peoples of Asia,
   Africa and Latin America   (CU)
Organization of the Cooperatives of America   (PE)
Organizing Committee for a Fifth Estate   (US)
Organizzazione Editoriale Medico Farmaceutica   (IT)
Organizzazione Internationale dei Trasporti a Fune
   (AU)
Organizzazione "X"   (IT)
Organizzazione Zeppieri   (IT)
Organizzazioni Speciali   (IT)
Organon Nederland B.V.   (NE)
Orgonomic Publications Inc.   (US)
Orhanizatsiia Ukra Inok Kanady   (CN)
Oriens Institute for Religious Research   (JA)
Orient   (PK)
Orient Longman Ltd.   (II)
Editora Orientador Ltda.   (BL)
Oriental Art Magazine Ltd.   (UK)
Oriental Economist   (JA)
Oriental Institute   (II)
Oriental Library   (JA)
Oriental Medical Publications   (II)
Oriental Publicity Service   (HK)
Oriental Research Institute   (II)
Oriental Rug Importers Association of America   (US)
Oriental Tide Society   (JA)
Oriental Watchman Publishing House   (II)
Oriflama Edicions, S.A.   (SP)
Origins Publications   (CN)
Orijin Denki K. K.   (JA)
Orion   (US)
Orion Press   (US)
Orissa. Director of Public Instruction   (II)
Orissa. Finance Department   (II)
Orissa. State Family Planning Bureau   (II)
Orissa Government Press   (II)
Orissa State Auroville Committee   (II)
Orkester Journalen AB   (SW)
Orleans Parish Medical Society   (US)
Ormanci Gazetesi   (TU)
Ornithological Society of Japan   (JA)
Ornithological Society of New Zealand Inc.   (NZ)
Ornithologische Gesellschaft in Bayern   (GW)
Ornitologia Rondo Esperantlingva   (NE)
Ornitologische Vereniging de Wielewaal   (BE)
Editrice Orobica   (IT)
D. Emilio Oromi, Ed. & Pub.   (SP)
Orphelinat Mutualiste de la Police Nationale   (FR)
Orr-Flanagan Co.   (US)
Dr. Hector Orrego Puelma, Ed. & Pub.   (CL)
Orsa Maggiore Editrice   (IT)
Tipografico Editrice dell' Orso   (IT)
Orszagos Erdeszeti Egyesulet   (HU)

Orszagos Filharmonia   (HU)
Orszagos Konyvtarugyi es Dokumentacios Tanacs
   (HU)
Orszagos Magyar Banyaszati es Kohaszati Egyesulet
   (HU)
Orszagos Muszaki Konyvtar es Dokumentacios
   Kozpont
   see Hungarian Central Technical Library and
   Documentation Centre - Technoinform   (HU)
Orszagos Orvostudomanyi Konyvtar es Dokumentacios
   Kozpont   (HU)
Orszagos Szechenyi Konyvtar   (HU)
Orszagos Szechenyi Konyvtar. Konyvtartudomanyi es
   Modszertani Kozpont   (HU)
Orszagos Szovetkezeti Tanacs   (HU)
Orta Dogu Teknik Universitesi
   see Middle East Technical University   (TU)
Orthodox Church in America   (US)
Orthodox Lore Of the Gospel of Our Savior Mission
   (US)
Orthodox Reformed Publishing Society   (US)
Orthopedic Nurses Association   (US)
Ortiz & Asociados s.r.l.   (VE)
Ortodox Kyrkotidnings Foerlag   (SW)
Orton Society, Inc.   (US)
Verlag der Ortskrankenkassen   (GW)
Orvos- es Egeszsegugyi Dolgozok Szakszervezete
   (HU)
Oryx Press   (US)
Osaka (City) Port and Harbour Bureau   (JA)
Osaka (Prefecture) Osaka District Meteorological
   Observatory   (JA)
Osaka (Prefecture) Radiaton Center   (JA)
Osaka City Medical Center   (JA)
Osaka City University. Department of Geosciences
   (JA)
Osaka City University. Faculty of Economics   (JA)
Osaka City University. Faculty of Engineering   (JA)
Osaka College of Music   (JA)
Osaka Daigaku
   see Osaka University   (JA)
Osaka Daigaku Biseibutsubyo Kenkyusho
   see Osaka University. Research Institute for
   Microbial Diseases   (JA)
Osaka Daigaku Igakubu
   see Osaka University Medical School   (JA)
Osaka Daigaku Igakubu Fuzoku Genkenku Shisetsu
   see Osaka University. Institute for Cancer Research
   (JA)
Osaka Daigaku Sangyo Kagaku Kenkyusho
   see Osaka University. Institute of Scientific and
   Industrial Research   (JA)
Osaka Daigaku Shigakkai
   see Osaka University Dental Society   (JA)
Osaka Daigaku Tanpakushitsu Kenkyusho
   see Osaka University. Institute for Protein Research
   (JA)
Osaka Dental University   (JA)
Osaka Dermatological Association   (JA)
Osaka-furitsu Daigaku
   see University of Osaka Prefecture   (JA)
Osaka-furitsu Hohasen Chuo Kenkyusho
   see Osaka (Prefecture). Radiation Center   (JA)
Osaka Ika Daigaku
   see Osaka Medical College   (JA)
Osaka Institute of Technology   (JA)
Osaka Kanku Kishodai
   see Osaka (Prefecture). Osaka District
   Meteorological Observatory   (JA)
Osaka Kogyo Daigaku
   see Osaka Institute of Technology   (JA)
Osaka Medical College   (JA)
Osaka Museum of Natural History   (JA)
Osaka Odontological Society   (JA)
Osaka Ongaku Daigaku
   see Osaka College of Music   (JA)
Osaka Prefectural University
   see University of Osaka Prefecture   (JA)
Osaka Science and Technology Center   (JA)
Osaka Senken Ltd.   (JA)
Osaka-shi Igakkai
   see Osaka City Medical Center   (JA)
Osaka Shika Daigaku
   see Osaka Dental University   (JA)
Osaka Shika Gakkai
   see Osaka Odontological Society   (JA)
Osaka-shiritsu Daigaku
   see Osaka City University   (JA)
Osaka-shiritsu Shizenkagaku Hakubutsukan
   see Osaka Museum of Natural History   (JA)
Osaka University. College of General Education   (JA)
Osaka University. Department of Economics   (JA)
Osaka University. Department of Mathematics   (JA)
Osaka University. Faculty of Engineering   (JA)
Osaka University. Faculty of Pharmaceutical Sciences
   (JA)
Osaka University. Institute for Cancer Research   (JA)
Osaka University. Institute for Protein Research   (JA)

Osaka University. Institute of Scientific and Industrial
   Research   (JA)
Osaka University. Laboratory of Nuclear Study   (JA)
Osaka University Dental Society   (JA)
Osaka University Medical School   (JA)
Osaka University Medical School. Department of
   Hygiene   (JA)
Osaka University Medical School. Department of
   Ophthalmology   (JA)
Osaka University. Research Institute for Microbial
   Diseases   (JA)
Osang Verlag   (GW)
Alan Osborne & Associates   (UK)
Osbornes Advertising Service   (UK)
Osiris   (US)
Oslo Boers   (NO)
Oslo Brannkorpsforening   (NO)
Oslo Bymuseum   (NO)
Oslo City Hospital Ward   (NO)
Oslo Faktorforening   (NO)
Oslo Import- og Export- Agenter Forening   (NO)
Oslo Kamera Klubb   (NO)
Oslo Kjoepmannsforening   (NO)
Oslo Militaere Samfund   (NO)
Oslo og Omegns Vaktmesterforening   (NO)
Oslobodjenje   (YU)
Osmania University. Centre of Exploration Geophysics
   (II)
Osmania University. Department of Commerce   (II)
Osmania University. Department of Linguistics   (II)
Osmania University. Department of Psychology   (II)
Ospedale al Mare   (IT)
Ospedale Maria Vittoria   (IT)
Ospedale Neuropsichiatrico Provinciale   (IT)
Ospedale Psichiatrico Provinciale   (IT)
Ospirio S. Famiglia   (IT)
Osram-Gesellschaft   (GW)
Osservatore Politico Letterario   (IT)
Osservatore Tributario e Rassegna Tributaria   (IT)
Osservatorio Astronomico di Roma   (IT)
Osservatorio Astronomico di Torino   (IT)
Osservatorio di Economia Agraria per l'Europa   (IT)
Osservatorio Geofisico Sperimentale   (IT)
Osservatorio Regionale per le Malattie della Vite   (IT)
Ossolineum, Publishing House of the Polish Academy
   of Sciences   (PL)
Ost-West-Kontakte Verlags- und Werbegesellschaft
   mbH   (GW)
Ostehandlerforeningen for Danmark   (DK)
Osterhus Publishing House, Inc.   (US)
Osteuropa-Institut, Munich   (GW)
Ostfriesische Landschaft   (GW)
Ostkirchenwerk Catholica Unio   (SZ)
Ostkirchliches Institut der Deutschen Augustiner
   (GW)
Ostomercato S. p.A.   (IT)
Verlag Ostschweiz   (SZ)
Ostschweizerische Gesellschaft fuer Hoehlenforschung
   (SZ)
Ostseegesellschaft e.V.   (GW)
Osuuskunta Kirjapainotaito   (FI)
Osveta   (CS)
Osvetovy Ustav   (CS)
Oswego County Historical Society   (US)
Oswego Press   (US)
Otago Daily Times Ltd.   (NZ)
Otago Law Review Trust Board   (NZ)
Otago Museum Trust Board   (NZ)
Otago University. Science Students' Association
   (NZ)
Kustannusosakeyhtio Otava   (FI)
Othello Outlook   (US)
Other Scenes Inc.   (UK)
Other Side   (US)
Other Woman Collective   (CN)
Oto-Laryngological Society of Australia   (AT)
Oto-Rhino-Laryngological Society of Japan   (JA)
Otsu Hydrobiological Station
   see under Kyoto University   (JA)
Otsu Rinko Jikkensho
   see Kyoto University. Otsu Hydrobiological Station
   (JA)
Otsuka Pharmaceutical Factory   (JA)
Editrice Ottavi s.r.l.   (IT)
Ottawa. Board of Trade   (CN)
Ottawa Civil Service Recreational Association   (CN)
Ottawa Field-Naturalists' Club   (CN)
Ottawa Public Library   (CN)
Ottawa Valley Western Horse Association   (CN)
Otterbein College   (US)
Otto Rank Association   (US)
Oude Paden   (NE)
Oudtshoorn Courant (Pty) Ltd.   (SA)
Ouest Industriel, Maritime, Agricole et Commercial
   (FR)

Our American Heritage Committee News Bulletin (US)
Our Dogs Publishing Co. Ltd. (UK)
Our Generation Press (CN)
Our People's Underworld (US)
Our Sunday Visitor, Inc. (US)
Our Town (US)
Editions Ouranos (FR)
Out There (US)
Outdoor Canada Magazine Limited (CN)
Outdoor Eduquip (US)
Outdoor Empire Publishing, Inc. (US)
Outdoor Times (US)
Outdoor Writers Association of America, Inc. (US)
Outdoors Unlittered (CN)
Outdoorsman Publishing Co. (US)
Outfitters Professional Society, Inc. (US)
Outlook (CE)
Outlook (TU)
Outlook Publications (US)
Outlook Publications, Inc. (US)
Outlook Publications Pty. Ltd. (SA)
Outlook Publishers, Inc. (US)
Outposts Publications (UK)
George Outram & Co. Ltd. (UK)
Outrigger Publications Ltd. (NZ)
Outside the Net (US)
Outworlds (US)
Over-The-Counter Securities Review (US)
Over the Garden Fence, Inc. (US)
Overbrook School for the Blind (US)
Overland (AT)
The Overseas American, Inc. (UK)
Overseas Crusades, Inc. (US)
Overseas Development Council (US)
Overseas Development Institute (UK)
Overseas Economic Cooperation Fund (JA)
Overseas Electrical Industry Survey Institute (JA)
Overseas Missionary Fellowship (US)
Overseas Newspapers (Agencies) Ltd. (UK)
Overseas Press and Media Association (UK)
Overseas Press Club of America, Inc. (US)
Overseas Telecommunications Commission (Australia) (AT)
Overseas Trade Research Fund (UK)
Overspill (UK)
Ovidius (IT)
Ovum (UY)
Mohammad Owais, Ed. & Pub. (PK)
Peter Owen Ltd. (UK)
Owen's Commerce and Travel Ltd. (UK)
Owens Valley Indian Education Center (US)
Owl's Head Press (CN)
Owner Drivers Society (UK)
Owner Publication (UK)
Ox Head Press (US)
Oxbridge Communications, Inc. (US)
Oxfam (UK)
Oxford and Cambridge Philological Societies (UK)
Oxford & IBH Publishing Co. (II)
Oxford Bibliographical Society (UK)
Oxford Centre for Postgraduate Hebrew Studies (UK)
Oxford Consumers Group (UK)
Oxford Industries, Inc. (US)
Oxford Mission (UK)
Oxford Society (UK)
Oxford Student Publications Ltd. (UK)
Oxford University Press (CN)
Oxford University Press (II)
Oxford University Press (UK)
Oxford University Press (US)
Oxford University Press (East African Branch) (KE)
Oxford University Press (Nigerian Branch) (NR)
Oxford University Scientific Society (UK)
Oxfordshire Architectural and Historical Society (UK)
Oyez S.A. (BE)
Oyo Biseibutsu Kenkyusho
  see University of Tokyo. Institute of Applied
  Microbiology (JA)
Oyo Biseibutsugaku Kenkyu Shoreikai
  see Microbiology Research Foundation (JA)
Oyo Denki Kenkyusho
  see Hokkaido University. Research Institute of
  Applied Electricity (JA)
Oyo Rikigaku Kenkyusho
  see Kyushu University. Research Institute for
  Applied Mechanics (JA)
Oz Publications (US)
Ozarks Mountaineer (US)
Jerome S. Ozer Publisher Inc. (US)
P A H O
  see World Health Organization. Pan American
  Health Organization (UN)
P A I A Electronics, Inc. (US)
P.A.N. Editrice (IT)

P A R C
  see Pacific-Asia Resources Center (JA)
P A S T I C
  see Pakistan Scientific and Technological
  Information Centre (PK)
P & J Press (UK)
Editions P.B.M. (FR)
P C A Inc. (US)
P C A Publications Ltd. (UK)
P. C. M. (FR)
P C Moderner Verlag (GW)
P C S I R
  see Pakistan Council of Scientific and Industrial
  Research (PK)
P C V A Publications Ltd. (UK)
P. D. Consultants (AT)
P.D.O. de Kesel (BE)
P E A L (US)
P.E.C.H. Society (PK)
P E M F (FR)
P.E.N. All-India Centre (II)
P. E. N. American Center (US)
P-EN Publications Inc. (US)
P.F. Publications (UK)
P.G. Sports Service Inc. (US)
P-H-C Information Services (US)
P H P Institute, Inc. (JA)
P.H. Press Ltd. (UK)
P.I.M.E. Missionaries (US)
P J D Publications (US)
P J S Publications, Inc. (US)
P. K. Endowment for Library and Information Science (II)
P. L. D. Publishers (PK)
P.M. Inc. (US)
P M S Publishing Co. Inc. (US)
P. N. C. (PH)
P. N. M. Publishing Co. Ltd. (TR)
P N Review (UK)
P N Y X Publishing Co. (US)
P P A Publications, Inc. (US)
P P D Publications (UG)
P P G Industries, Inc. (US)
P. P. Layouts (UK)
P.R.E.E.S. (FR)
P R, Inc. (Partisan Review) (US)
P R M Science & Technology Agency (UK)
P R Productions (CN)
P. R. Publications (II)
P R Publishing Co., Inc. (US)
P S C Publications Committee (US)
P S Communications, Inc. (US)
P. S. G. & Sons Charities (II)
P S L Publications Ltd. (UK)
P.S.R.L. (AG)
P S W (Educational) Publications (UK)
P.T.J. Publishing, Inc. (US)
P T N Publishing Corp. (US)
P T P Publishing Services (Pty) Ltd (SA)
P U D O C (NE)
P V Publications (UK)
P W Communications (US)
P. W. P. (CN)
P. W. Publishing Co. Inc. (US)
P Y C Edition (FR)
P y S (MX)
Paarl Printing Co. (Pty.) Ltd (SA)
Tipografia della Pace (IT)
Pace Publications (US)
Pacemaker Publications (IE)
Pacific Area Travel Association (UK)
Pacific Area Travel Association (US)
Pacific Area Travel Association. Indonesia Chapter (IO)
Pacific-Asia Resources Center (JA)
Pacific Basin Reports (US)
Pacific Books, Publishers (US)
Pacific Coast Archaeological Society, Inc. (US)
Pacific Coast Aviation Directory (US)
Pacific Coast Council on Latin American Studies (US)
Pacific Coast Electrical Association, Inc. (US)
Pacific Coast Entomological Society (US)
Pacific Coast Obstetrical and Gynecological Society (US)
Pacific Coast Renderers Association (US)
Pacific Coast Slavic Baptist Association, Inc. (US)
Pacific Coast Society of Orthodontists (US)
Pacific County Historical Society Inc. (US)
Pacific Daily Ltd. (FJ)
Pacific Horticultural Foundation (US)
Pacific Hotel-Motel News (US)
Pacific Inter-Club Yacht Association of Northern California (US)
Pacific Islands Studies and Notes (US)
Pacific Journal of Mathematics (US)
Pacific Lutheran Theological Seminary (US)
Pacific Magazines Ltd. (HK)

Pacific Marine Fisheries Commission (US)
Pacific Mutual Life Insurance Co. (US)
Pacific Northwest Aviation Historical Foundation (US)
Pacific Northwest Bird and Mammal Society (US)
Pacific Northwest Conference on Foreign Languages (US)
Pacific Northwest Humanist Publications (CN)
Pacific Northwest Library Association (US)
Pacific Northwest River Basins Commission (US)
Pacific Northwest Ski Association (US)
Pacific Orchid Society of Hawaii (US)
Pacific Peoples' Action Front in Suva (FJ)
Pacific Perceptions, Inc. (US)
Pacific Periodicals Ltd. (FJ)
Pacific Press, Inc. (US)
Pacific Press Publishing Association (US)
Pacific Publications (US)
Pacific Publications (Australia) Pty. Ltd. (AT)
Pacific Publishing Foundation Inc. (US)
Pacific Railroad Society Inc. (US)
Pacific Science Association (AT)
Pacific Science Association (US)
Pacific Scientific Information Center (US)
Pacific Search (US)
Pacific Shippers, Inc. (US)
Pacific Sociological Association (US)
Pacific Southwest Airlines (US)
Pacific Stamp Journal (NZ)
Pacific Studies Center (US)
Pacific Sun Publishing Co. Inc. (US)
Pacific Travel Directory (AT)
Pacific Trollers' Association (CN)
Pacific Tropical Botanical Garden (US)
Pacific West Publications Ltd. (CN)
Pacific Western Agricultural Publications (US)
Pacific Wilderness Journal (US)
Pacific Yearbooks (AT)
Pacifica Foundation WBAI (US)
Editorial Pacifico (CK)
Pacini Editore (IT)
Packaging Machinery Manufacturers Institute (US)
Packard Automobile Classics (US)
Padan Aram (US)
Paddle Steamer Preservation Society (UK)
Padres Carmelitas Descalzas (SP)
Padres Jesuitas de la Iglesia de San Jose (EC)
Edizioni dei Padri Carmelitani Scalzi (IT)
Paedagogische Hochschule, Potsdam (GE)
Paedagogisches Institut der Stadt Wien (AU)
Paedagogisches Institut des Bundes in Oberoesterreich (AU)
Paedagogisches und Berufspaedagogisches Institut des Bundes in Salzburg (AU)
Paencor, Inc. (PH)
Paeroa and District Historical Society (NZ)
Pagan Movement in Britain and Ireland (UK)
Ralph Page, Ed. & Pub. (US)
Tony Page, Ed. & Pub. (US)
G. P. Page Publications (CN)
Page Publications Pty. Ltd. (AT)
C. A. Page Publishing Co (US)
Pageant (CN)
Pages (UK)
Editorial Paginas y Tapas s.r.l. (AG)
Pahala (II)
Pahl-Rugenstein Verlag (GW)
Pahlavi University. Asian Institute (IR)
Pahlavi University. Faculty of Agriculture (IR)
Pahlavi University. Faculty of Engineering (IR)
Pahlavi University Publications (IR)
Pahlavi University. School of Medicine (IR)
Pai Wan Chuang (CC)
Paideia Editrice (IT)
Paideia Press (US)
Paikallislehtien Liitto (FI)
Imprimerie F. Paillart (FR)
Paint Research Association (UK)
Painted Bride Quarterly, Inc. (US)
Painter AVO (LE)
Painters District Council Nine of New York City (US)
Painting and Decorating Contractors of America (US)
Paisano Publications Inc. (US)
Pajarito Publications (US)
Pak Publishers (PK)
Pakistan. Agricultural Research Council (PK)
Pakistan. Air Force (PK)
Pakistan. Bureau of Labour Publications (PK)
Pakistan. Central Bureau of Education (PK)
Pakistan. Central Statistical Office
  see Pakistan. Statistical Division (PK)
Pakistan. Department of Archaeology and Museums (PK)
Pakistan. Department of Civil Aviation (PK)
Pakistan. Department of Insurance (PK)

Pakistan. Directorate of Livestock Farms  (PK)
Pakistan. Directorate of Rural Works Programme
 (PK)
Pakistan. Export Promotion Bureau  (PK)
Pakistan. Finance Division  (PK)
Pakistan. Geological Survey of Pakistan  (PK)
Pakistan. Krishi Gabe Shona Parishad
 see Pakistan. Agricultural Research Council  (PK)
Pakistan. Meteorological Department  (PK)
Pakistan. Military Training Directorate  (PK)
Pakistan. Ministry of Commerce  (PK)
Pakistan. Ministry of Commerce. Trade Marks
 Registry
 see Pakistan. Trade Marks Registry  (PK)
Pakistan. Ministry of Education. Central Bureau of
 Education
 see Pakistan. Central Bureau of Education  (PK)
Pakistan. Ministry of Education. Directorate of
 Archives and Libraries  (PK)
Pakistan. Ministry of Education. Documentation
 Section  (PK)
Pakistan. Ministry of Finance
 see also Pakistan. Office of the Economic Adviser
 (PK)
 see also Pakistan. Statistical Division  (PK)
 see also Pakistan. Finance Division  (PK)
Pakistan. Ministry of Finance  (PK)
Pakistan. Ministry of Finance, Planning and Economic
 Affairs. Statistical Division
 see Pakistan. Statistical Division  (PK)
Pakistan. Ministry of Food, Agriculture and Rural
 Development. Food and Agriculture Division  (PK)
Pakistan. Ministry of Food, Agriculture and Rural
 Development. Rural Development Division  (PK)
Pakistan. Ministry of Food and Agriculture. Pakistan
 Central Cotton Committee
 see Pakistan. Pakistan Central Cotton Committee
 (PK)
Pakistan. Ministry of Foreign Affairs  (PK)
Pakistan. Ministry of Religious Affairs. Islamic
 Research Institute  (PK)
Pakistan. National Assembly  (PK)
Pakistan. Office of the Economic Adviser  (PK)
Pakistan. Official Language Committee  (PK)
Pakistan. Pakistan Central Cotton Committee  (PK)
Pakistan. Planning Commission  (PK)
Pakistan. Post Office Department  (PK)
Pakistan. State Bank of Pakistan  (PK)
Pakistan. Statistical Division  (PK)
Pakistan. Supreme Court  (PK)
Pakistan. Survey of Pakistan  (PK)
Pakistan. Trade Marks Registry  (PK)
Pakistan Academy of Sciences  (PK)
Pakistan Administrative Staff College  (PK)
Pakistan Association for the Advancement of Science
 (PK)
Pakistan Atomic Energy Commission  (PK)
Pakistan Botanical Society  (PK)
Pakistan Boy Scouts Association  (PK)
Pakistan Cardiac Society  (PK)
Pakistan Central Cotton Committee
 see Pakistan. Pakistan Central Cotton Committee
 (PK)
Pakistan Co-operative Fruit Development Board  (PK)
Pakistan Council of Scientific and Industrial Research
 (PK)
Pakistan Dental Review  (PK)
Pakistan Economic Association  (PK)
Pakistan Forest Institute  (PK)
Pakistan Group for the Study of Local Government
 (PK)
Pakistan Herald Publications  (PK)
Pakistan Historical Society  (PK)
Pakistan Industrial Credit and Investment Corporation
 (PK)
Pakistan Industrial Development Corporation  (PK)
Pakistan Institute of Development Economics  (PK)
Pakistan Institute of Management  (PK)
Pakistan Insurance Corporation  (PK)
Pakistan Journal of Surgery, Gynaecology, and
 Obstetrics  (PK)
Pakistan Law House  (PK)
Pakistan Library Association  (PK)
Pakistan Medical Association  (PK)
Pakistan Medical Research Council  (PK)
Pakistan National Tuberculosis Association  (PK)
Pakistan Nurses Federation  (PK)
Pakistan Paint Manufacturers' Association  (PK)
Pakistan Perspective  (US)
Pakistan Petroleum Ltd.  (PK)
Pakistan Philatelic Association  (PK)
Pakistan Philosophical Congress  (PK)
Pakistan Press International  (PK)
Pakistan Publications  (PK)
Pakistan Publishers & Booksellers Association  (PK)
Pakistan Railways  (PK)
Pakistan Scientific and Technological Information
 Centre  (PK)

Pakistan Society  (UK)
Pakistan Society of Biochemists  (PK)
Pakistan Society of Leather Technologists  (PK)
Pakistan Standards Institution  (PK)
Pakistan Statistical Association  (PK)
Pakistan University of Engineering and Technology
 (PK)
Pakistan Water and Power Development Authority
 (PK)
Palabra  (US)
Palacio Foz  (PO)
Palaeobotanical Society  (II)
Palaeological Association of Japan, Inc.  (JA)
Palaeontological Society of Japan  (JA)
Palaeovertebrata  (FR)
Palaestra  (IT)
Palais de la Decouverte  (FR)
Palais des Beaux-Arts  (BE)
Palatinate Office  (UK)
Palatines to America  (US)
Edizioni Palatino in Roma  (IT)
Aldo Palazzi Editore  (IT)
Palazzi Editrice S.p.A.  (IT)
Palazzo Marino  (IT)
Casa Editrice Palazzo Vecchio  (IT)
Paldor Publications  (US)
Paleari Edizioni Milano  (IT)
Paleari Industria Grafica s.r.l.  (IT)
Paleis voor Schone Kunsten
 see Palais des Beaux Arts  (BE)
Paleontological Research Institution  (US)
Paleontological Society  (US)
Paleontologische Gesellschaft e.V.  (GW)
Librairie Palestine  (FR)
Palestine Exploration Fund  (UK)
Palestine National Liberation Movement  (CN)
Palestine Solidarity Committee  (US)
Palgrave Publishing Co. Ltd.  (UK)
Pali Buddhist Union  (UK)
Palle Fogtdals A-S  (DK)
Pallottiner Druck und Lahn-Verlag  (GW)
Palm Beach County Genealogy Society  (US)
Palm Beach Newspapers, Inc.  (US)
Palm Publications Co.  (LB)
Palm Society, Inc.  (US)
Palm Springs Life  (US)
G. J. Palmer & Sons Ltd.  (UK)
Palmer Publications  (US)
Palmer Publications Inc.  (US)
Palmerton Publishing Co., Inc.  (US)
Ugo Palmisano, Ed. & Pub.  (IT)
Paloalan Jarjestot  (FI)
Fratelli Palombi Editori  (IT)
Palomino Horse Breeders of America  (US)
Nino Palumbo, Ed. & Pub.  (IT)
Edizioni Palutan Grafica  (IT)
Palynological Society of India  (II)
Pamatnik Narodniho Pisemnictvi  (CS)
Pamatnik Terezin  (CS)
Pammatone  (IT)
Pamposh Publications  (II)
Pan  (MX)
Pan-African Institute  (US)
Pan-African Institute for Development  (CM)
Pan Africanist Congress  (UK)
Pan Africanist Congress of Azania (South Africa)
 (SA)
Pan-Afriscope (Nigeria) Ltd.  (NR)
Pan American Cancer Cytology Society  (US)
Pan-American Coffee Bureau  (US)
Pan American Development Foundation  (US)
Pan American Federation of Engineering Societies
 (UY)
Pan American Health Organization
 see under World Health Organization  (UN)
Pan American Institute of Comparative Law  (US)
Pan American Medical Women's Alliance  (US)
Pan American Railway Congress Associaton  (AG)
Pan American Sanitary Bureau
 see World Health Organization. Pan American
 Health Organization  (UN)
Pan American University  (US)
Pan American World Airways  (US)
Pan Pacific Centers  (US)
PAN Publishing House  (CY)
Panache  (US)
Panafrican Trade Union Information Center. African-
 American Consultative Committee  (ZR)
Panama. Contraloria General. Direccion de
 Contabilidad  (PN)
Panama. Departamento de Beneficencia Cultural.
 Loteria Nacional de Beneficencia  (PN)
Panama. Direccion de Estadistica y Censos  (PN)
Panama. Direccion General de Recursos Naturales
 Renovables  (PN)
Panama. Ministerio de Agricultura y Ganaderia  (PN)
Panama Canal Co.  (PN)

Panama Canal Co. Engineering Division  (PN)
Panama Tribune  (PN)
Panamerican Federation of Associations of Medical
 Schools  (CK)
Panamerican Federation of Endocrine Societies  (AG)
Panamin Foundation  (PH)
Panax Newspapers, Inc.  (US)
Pancevac  (YU)
Pandas Publishing and Advertising Service  (AT)
Pandecte Neon Noman Kediataghmaton  (GR)
L. K. Pandey, Ed. & Pub.  (II)
O. N. Pandeya, Ed. & Pub.  (II)
R. V. Pandit, Ed. & Pub.  (HK)
C. M. Pandit, Ed. & Pub.  (II)
Pandon Publications, Ltd.  (UK)
Pandora Press  (US)
Pandulipi Club  (II)
Panel Publishers  (US)
Panel Publishers. Cantor Fitzgerald Group Ltd.  (US)
Panhandle Eastern Pipe Line Co.  (US)
Panhellenic Confederation of Agricultural Cooperatives
 (GR)
Panhellenic Pharmaceutical Association  (GR)
Panjab University
 see University of the Punjab  (PK)
Panjab University  (II)
Panjab University. Extension Library  (II)
Panjabi University
 see Punjabi University  (II)
Panjandrum Press  (US)
Panorama  (AG)
Panorama  (AT)
Panorama Africain  (SG)
Panorama Bonaerense  (AG)
Panorama D.D.R. - Auslandspresseagentur  (GE)
Panorama de la Mode  (FR)
Panorama de la Musique  (FR)
Panorama International Inc.  (US)
Panorama of Las Vegas, Inc.  (US)
Panorama Publicita Marketing  (IT)
Panorama Verlagsgesellschaft m.b.H.  (AU)
Panstwowa Wyzsza Szkola Muzyczna  (PL)
Panstwowe Przedsiebiorstwo "Skladnica Ksiegarska"
 (PL)
Panstwowe Wydawnictwo Ekonomiczne  (PL)
Panstwowe Wydawnictwo Naukowe  (PL)
Panstwowe Wydawnictwo Naukowe. Oddzial we
 Wroclawiu  (PL)
Panstwowy Zaklad Higieny  (PL)
Panstwowy Zaklad Wydawnictw Lekarskich  (PL)
Mario Pantaleo, Ed. & Pub  (IT)
Pantheon Books, Inc.  (US)
Pantheon Press- General Enterprises  (US)
Edizioni Paoline  (IT)
Paon Press  (US)
Papa Bach Paperbacks  (US)
C. Papagheorghiou  (GR)
John Papamichalakis, Ed. & Pub.  (GR)
Papelaria Fernandes  (PO)
Paper and Twine Journal  (US)
Paper Bag Institute  (US)
Paper House, Inc.  (US)
Paper Industry Management Association  (US)
Paper Jacks  (CN)
Paper Makers Advertising Association  (US)
Paper, Printing & Packaging Industries Research
 Association  (UK)
Paper Publications Society  (NE)
Papier- und Buchgewerblicher Verlag  (AU)
Papiermacher Berufsgenossenschaft  (GW)
Papir- es Nyomdaipari Muszaki Egyesulet  (HU)
Papua & New Guinea Scientific Society  (PP)
Papua New Guinea. Bureau of Statistics  (PP)
Papua New Guinea. Department of Agriculture, Stock
 and Fisheries  (PP)
Papua New Guinea. Department of Business
 Development  (PP)
Papua New Guinea. Department of Education  (PP)
Papua New Guinea. Department of Education.
 Curriculum Branch  (PP)
Papua New Guinea. Department of Information and
 Extension Services  (PP)
Papua New Guinea. Department of Labour  (PP)
Papua New Guinea. Department of Social
 Development and Home Affairs  (PP)
Papua New Guinea. Government Printer  (PP)
Papua-New Guinea. Literature Bureau  (PP)
Papua, New Guinea. Manpower Planning Unit.
 Manpower Studies  (PP)
Papua New Guinea. Office of Local Government
 (PP)
Papua-New Guinea Cave Exploration Group  (PP)
Papua New Guinea Institute of Medical Research
 (PP)
Papua New Guinea University of Technology  (PP)
Par les Loisirs et le Tourisme  (FR)
Parabas  (II)

Parabola  (US)
Parachute Publications  (CN)
Parachute Regiment and Airborne Forces  (UK)
Parade Publications (Pty) Ltd.  (RH)
Paragon Publications  (AT)
Paragon Publications, Inc.  (US)
Paraguay. Armada Nacional  (PY)
Paraguay. Centro Military y Naval  (PY)
Paraguay. Direccion General de Estadistica y Censos
   (PY)
Paraguay. Ministerio de Industria y Comercio  (PY)
Paraguay. Ministerio de Industria y Comercio.
   Division de Registro y Estadistica Industrial  (PY)
Ediciones Paralelo Cero  (EC)
Parallelo Trentotto  (IT)
Paralyzed Veterans of America, Inc.  (US)
Parana, Brazil. Secretaria de Estado para os Negocios
   da Fazenda  (BL)
Parana em Paginas  (BL)
Paraplegic-Quadraplegic Association of Western
   Australia  (AT)
Parapsychological Association  (US)
Parapsychology Foundation  (US)
Parapsychology Press  (US)
L. Pardi, Ed. & Pub.  (IT)
Libreria Pardo  (AG)
Pardon Verlagsgesellschaft mbH  (GW)
F. M. Pareja, Ed. & Pub.  (SP)
Parent Cooperative Preschools International  (CN)
Parent Cooperative Preschools International  (US)
P. E. Parent, Ed. & Pub.  (CN)
Parent-Teacher Association of Connecticut, Inc.  (US)
Alfredo Parente, Ed. & Pub.  (IT)
J. N. Parenteau, Ed. & Pub.  (CN)
Parenteral Drug Association, Inc.  (US)
Parents Magazine Enterprises, Inc.  (US)
Parents National Educational Union  (UK)
Parents' Theosophical Research Group  (US)
Parents Without Partners Inc.  (US)
Verlag Paul Parey (Berlin)  (GW)
Verlag Paul Parey (Hamburg)  (GW)
Parfymehandlernes Landsforbund  (NO)
Marjorie Parham  (US)
Parichiti Cultural Association  (II)
PariPassu  (US)
Paris-Bijoux Exportation  (FR)
Paris-Cote-d'Azur  (FR)
Paris Match  (FR)
Paris Publications, Inc.  (US)
Paris Regie  (FR)
Paris Review, Inc.  (US)
Pariser Kurier  (FR)
Parish Visitors of Mary Immaculate  (US)
Gerard Parizeau & Cie, Inc.  (CN)
Park College  (US)
Park East News Inc.  (US)
Park Region Publishing Co.  (US)
Park Street Publishing (London) Ltd.  (UK)
Parkdale Young Liberal Association  (CN)
Parker and Son Publications, Inc.  (US)
S. E. Parker, Ed. & Pub.  (UK)
Parker Publishing Co. Inc.  (US)
Parker School of Foreign and Comparative Law
   see under Columbia University  (US)
Parkins Publishing Co. Ltd.  (CN)
Parkway Printing and Publishing Ltd.  (CN)
Parlameto  (IT)
Parlement Europeen
   see European Parliament  (EI)
Parliamentary Digest Ltd.  (UK)
Parliamentary Research Services  (UK)
Edizioni Luigi Parma  (IT)
Parnassos, Greek Cultural Society of New York  (US)
Parochial Clergy Association  (UK)
Parola del Popolo Publishing Association  (US)
Parole e le Idee  (IT)
Parousia Press  (US)
W. Parr & Co.  (UK)
Parrett & Neves Ltd.  (UK)
Parrocchia  (IT)
Parrocchia S. Gerardo  (IT)
Parroquia Immaculada Concepcion  (SP)
Parroquia "San Roque"  (AG)
Parroquia Santisima Trinidad Rufino  (AG)
Donald Parsons & Co. Ltd.  (UK)
Russell O. Parta  (US)
Parti Communiste Francais. Comite Central  (FR)
Parti Democratique Senegalais  (SG)
Parti du Travail d'Albanie  (AA)
Parti Liberal du Quebec  (CN)
Parti Nationaliste Occitan  (FR)
Parti Radical-Democratique Suisse
   see Freisinnig-Demokratische Partei der Schweiz
   (SZ)
Parti Socialiste et Cercle d'Etudes Socialistes Jean
   Jaures  (FR)
Parti Socialiste Unifie  (FR)
Participation Projects Foundation  (US)

Particle Science and Technology Information Service
   (UK)
Particulier  (FR)
Partido Comunista  (AG)
Partido Liberal. Consejo Central Ejecutivo  (HO)
Partido Revolucionario Institucional  (MX)
Partido Socialista Puertorriqueno  (PR)
Partido Unido de la Revolucion Socialista Cubana
   (CU)
Partidul Comunist Roman. Comitetul Central  (RM)
Partij van de Arbeid. Federatie van Jongerengroepen
   (NE)
Partir  (FR)
Partito Comunista d'Italia. Comitato Centrale  (IT)
Partito Comunista Italiano  (IT)
Partito Comunista Rivoluzionario  (IT)
Partito Liberale Italiano  (IT)
Partito Popolare Italiano  (IT)
Partito Socialista Italiano  (IT)
Partners of the Americas  (US)
Verlag Parzeller und Co.  (GW)
Pasadena City College  (US)
Pasaules Brivo Latviesu Apvieniba  (US)
Pascack Historical Society  (US)
Paschim Maharashtra Pradeshik Sahakari Mandal, Ltd.
   (II)
Paseo del Rio Association of San Antonio  (US)
Pashto Academy  (PK)
Pasold Research Fund Ltd.  (UK)
Pass Editrice  (IT)
Passaic County Dental Society  (US)
Passaic County Historical Society  (US)
Passaic County Medical Society  (US)
Passaic County Technical and Vocational High School
   (US)
Verlag Passavia  (GW)
Passionist Fathers  (IE)
Passionist Fathers  (IT)
Passionist Missions, Inc.  (US)
Passionisti  (IT)
Past and Present Society  (UK)
Pastoral Misionera  (SP)
Edizioni Pastorali  (IT)
Pastoralist and Graziers Association of W.A. (Inc.)
   (AT)
Marvin Patchen, Inc.  (US)
J. R. Patel, Ed. & Pub.  (II)
L. M. Patel, Ed. & Pub.  (II)
Patent and Trademark Institute of Canada  (CN)
Patent Office  (UK)
Patent Publications, Inc.  (US)
Patent Searching Service  (US)
Patentanwaltskammer  (GW)
Paternoster Press Ltd.  (UK)
Paters Camillianen Sint Camillushuis  (NE)
Paters Montfortanen  (NE)
Paterson Redevelopment Division  (US)
Pathe Baby Portugal  (PO)
S. R. Pather, Ed. & Pub  (SA)
Pathfinder Travel Parks  (CN)
Pathikrit Association  (II)
Pathological Society of Great Britain and Ireland
   (UK)
Pathway Publishing Corporation  (CN)
G. V. Patil  (II)
Patmos Verlag  (GW)
Patna University  (II)
George Gordon Paton & Co.  (US)
Patria Publishing Co. Ltd.  (CN)
Patriarchal Parishes of the Russian Orthodox Church
   in the U.S.A.  (US)
Patrice Lumumba Printing Office  (GV)
Patrolmen's Benevolent Association of New York City
   (US)
Casa Editrice Patron  (IT)
Patronato ACLI  (IT)
Patronato de Obras Docentes del Movimiento  (SP)
Patronato Genovese pro Natura "A. Anfossi"  (IT)
Patrys  (SA)
Patten Co., Inc.  (US)
Pattern Makers' League of North America  (US)
Pattern Recognition Society  (US)
Patterns  (AT)
Patterson Publishing Co.  (US)
Patterson Publishing Pty. Ltd.  (AT)
Patterson Smith Publishing Corporation  (US)
Patzer-Verlag GmbH und Co. KG  (GW)
Hauke (Hank) Paul  (GW)
Stanley Paul & Co. Ltd.  (UK)
Paul-Ehrlich-Gesellschaft  (GW)
Paul-Ehrlich-Institut  (GW)
Paul-Ernst-Gesellschaft  (GW)
Paul-Hindemith-Institut  (GW)
John Paul Productions Ltd.  (NZ)
Kegan Paul, Trench, Trubner Ltd.  (UK)
Ediciones Paulinas  (AG)
Ediciones Paulinas  (CK)
Editions Paulines  (CN)

Paulinus-Verlag  (GW)
Paulist Press  (US)
Empresa Grafica Editorial Paulista  (BL)
Paull & Goode Publishing Ltd.  (UK)
Paul's Press  (II)
Paulus-Verlag GmbH  (SZ)
Paulus-Verlag Karl Geyer  (GW)
N. Pauwels, Ed. & Pub.  (BE)
Pauwels Fils  (BE)
Pavliha  (YU)
Panagiotis Pavlouros, Ed. & Pub.  (GR)
Pavlov Institute  (II)
Pavlovian Society of America  (US)
Publizistisches Archiv Karl R. Pawlas  (GW)
Editorial Pax  (CK)
Instytut Wydawniczy "Pax"  (PL)
Pax  (SW)
Pax Christi Centre  (UK)
Pax Christi International. French Section  (FR)
Pax Forlag  (NO)
John Paxton & Associates  (UK)
Payment Systems, Incorporated  (US)
Josephine Payne, Ed. & Pub.  (US)
Imprenta Fray Payo  (GT)
Editions Payot  (FR)
Paysan du Midi  (FR)
Payton Pty. Ltd.  (AT)
Editora Paz e Terra  (BL)
Paz y Justicia  (AG)
Alexander Pazandak  (US)
Pcelarski Savez SR Hrvatske  (YU)
Pea River Historical and Genealogical Society  (US)
Pea Vine Music Co.  (US)
Peabody Institute. Conservatory of Music  (US)
Peabody Museum of Archaeology and Ethnology
   (US)
Peabody Museum of Natural History  (US)
Peabody Museum of Salem  (US)
Peace Council of the German Democratic Republic
   (GE)
Peace News Ltd.  (UK)
Peace Plans  (AT)
Peace Pledge Union  (UK)
H. L. Peace Publications  (US)
Peace Publishers & Co.  (US)
Peace Research Laboratory  (US)
Peace Science Society (International)  (US)
Peacemaker  (UK)
Peacemaker Movement  (US)
Peacock Business Press, Inc.  (US)
F. E. Peacock Publishers  (US)
Peak District Mines Historical Society  (UK)
Peak Publications Society  (CN)
Peanut Journal Publishing Co.  (US)
Pearl  (II)
Peat, Marwick, Mitchell & Co.  (US)
Melvin A. Peavey, Ed. & Pub.  (US)
Pebble  (US)
Pecheurs d'Hommes  (FR)
Peco Publications & Publicity Ltd.  (UK)
Pecsi Tudomanyegyetem  (HU)
Pedagogicka Fakulta, Presov. Kabinet pre Vyskum
   Krajiny  (CS)
Pedagogicka Fakulta v Ostrave  (CS)
Pedagogicka Fakulta v Usti nad Labem  (CS)
Izdatel'stvo Pedagogika  (UR)
Pedagoska Akademija, Split  (YU)
Pedagoska Akademija u Gospicu  (YU)
Pedagosko Drustvo SR Hrvatske  (YU)
Pedagosko Drustvo SR Srbije  (YU)
Editorial Pedeca  (SP)
Creighton Peden  (US)
Bo Torp Pedersen, Ed. and Pub.  (DK)
C. F. Pederson  (DK)
Pedestrian Press  (US)
Pedestrians Association for Road Safety  (UK)
Pediatre Parisien SARL  (FR)
Pediatric Association of the Republic of China  (CH)
Pediatric Clinics of India  (II)
Pediatric Portfolio  (US)
Pedolojisto Kondankai
   see Group of Japanese Pedologists  (JA)
Editions A. Pedone  (FR)
Pedra e Cal  (BL)
Ennio Pedrini  (IT)
Willem Pee, Ed. & Pub.  (BE)
Editions Peeters s.p.r.l.  (BE)
Uitgeverij Pegasus  (NE)
Pegasus  (II)
Pegasus Press  (NZ)
Pegasus Public Relations  (AT)
Johanny Peillon  (MR)
Matthew W. Pelczynski, Ed. & Pub.  (US)
Pelham Books Ltd.  (UK)
Pelican Publishing Co., Inc.  (US)
Editrice Pellegrini  (IT)
B. Pellerano & S. del Gaudia  (IT)
Pellervo-Seura  (FI)

F. P. Pellicano, Ed. & Pub.   (IT)
Tipografia A. Pelligrini (Udine)   (IT)
Pelosi Alexandre   (IT)
Dr. Pelzer Verlag   (GW)
Pembroke State University   (US)
Pembrokeshire Local History Society   (UK)
Pen & Pencil Set   (US)
Pendejo Press   (US)
Pender Bros. Pty. Ltd.   (AT)
Pendle Hill, a Quaker Center for Study and
  Contemplation   (US)
Pendle Hill Publications   (US)
Pendleton Publications   (US)
Pendragon House Ltd.   (CN)
Editions Penelope   (CN)
Penfer   (US)
Penguin Books, Inc.   (US)
Barry Penhale   (CN)
Peninsula Bulletin Publishing Co.   (US)
Peninsula Electronics News   (US)
Peninsula Hospital Center   (US)
Peninsula Motor Club   (US)
Peninsula Newspapers, Inc.   (US)
Peninsula Publishing Co.   (US)
Peninsular State Philatelic Society   (US)
Penjerdel Corporation   (US)
Penman Publishing Co.   (US)
Penn Central Transportation Co.   (US)
A-S Penn-Inform   (NO)
Penn Valley Community College   (US)
Pennant Publishing Co. Inc   (US)
Pennine Platform   (UK)
Betty L. Pennington, Ed. & Pub.   (US)
Pennmarva Dairymen's Cooperative Federation   (US)
Pennsylvania. Board of Probation and Parole. Research
  and Statistical Division   (US)
Pennsylvania. Bureau of Aviation   (US)
Pennsylvania. Civil Service Commission. Bureau of
  Examinations   (US)
Pennsylvania. Commonwealth Child Development
  Committee   (US)
Pennsylvania. Crime Commission   (US)
Pennsylvania. Crop Reporting Service   (US)
Pennsylvania. Department of Commerce   (US)
Pennsylvania. Department of Commerce. Bureau of
  International Commerce   (US)
Pennsylvania. Department of Commerce. Bureau of
  Statistics, Research & Planning   (US)
Pennsylvania. Department of Commerce. Bureau of
  Travel Development   (US)
Pennsylvania. Department of Community Affairs
  (US)
Pennsylvania. Department of Education   (US)
Pennsylvania. Department of Education. Bureau of
  Educational Statistics   (US)
Pennsylvania. Department of Education. Bureau of
  Information and Publications   (US)
Pennsylvania. Department of Education. Bureau of
  Vocational, Technical and Continuing Education
  (US)
Pennsylvania. Department of Environmental Resources
  (US)
Pennsylvania. Department of Environmental
  Resources. Bureau of Topographic and Geologic
  Survey   (US)
Pennsylvania. Department of Justice. Bureau of
  Criminal Justice Statistics   (US)
Pennsylvania. Department of Public Health. Air
  Management Services   (US)
Pennsylvania. Department of Public Welfare   (US)
Pennsylvania. Fish Commission   (US)
Pennsylvania. Game Commission   (US)
Pennsylvania. Historical and Museum Commission
  (US)
Pennsylvania. Human Relations Commission   (US)
Pennsylvania. Labor Relations Board   (US)
Pennsylvania. Office of the Budget   (US)
Pennsylvania. State Advisory Council for Vocational
  Education   (US)
Pennsylvania. State Board of Vocational Rehabilitation
  (US)
Pennsylvania Academy of Ophthalmology and
  Otolaryngology   (US)
Pennsylvania Association for Retarded Citizens, Inc.
  (US)
Pennsylvania Association for the Blind   (US)
Pennsylvania Association of Plumbing Contractors,
  Inc.   (US)
Pennsylvania Association of Secondary School
  Principals   (US)
Pennsylvania Automotive Association   (US)
Pennsylvania Chamber of Commerce   (US)
Pennsylvania Chiefs of Police Association   (US)
Pennsylvania Classical Association   (US)
Pennsylvania Commission for Women   (US)
Pennsylvania Council of Teachers of English   (US)
Pennsylvania Dental Association   (US)
Pennsylvania Economy League   (US)

Pennsylvania Economy League. Eastern Division
  (US)
Pennsylvania Federation of Sportsmen's Clubs   (US)
Pennsylvania Fish Culturists Association   (US)
Pennsylvania Flower Growers   (US)
Pennsylvania Folklife Society   (US)
Pennsylvania Folklore Society   (US)
Pennsylvania Forestry Association   (US)
Pennsylvania German Society   (US)
Pennsylvania Grocers Association   (US)
Pennsylvania Historical Association   (US)
Pennsylvania Holstein Association   (US)
Pennsylvania Home Rule Association   (US)
Pennsylvania Hotel-Motor Inn Association   (US)
Pennsylvania Illustrated   (US)
Pennsylvania Institute of Certified Public Accountants
  (US)
Pennsylvania Labor News Publishing Co.   (US)
Pennsylvania Library Association   (US)
Pennsylvania Manufactured Housing Association
  (US)
Pennsylvania Medical Society   (US)
Pennsylvania Music Educators Association, Inc.   (US)
Pennsylvania Newspaper Publishers Association   (US)
Pennsylvania Nurses Association   (US)
Pennsylvania P T A   (US)
Pennsylvania Pharmaceutical Association   (US)
Pennsylvania Prison Society   (US)
Pennsylvania Restaurant Association   (US)
Pennsylvania S.P.C.A.   (US)
Pennsylvania School Boards Association   (US)
Pennsylvania School Study Council   (US)
Pennsylvania Society of Professional Engineers   (US)
Pennsylvania State Association for Health, Physical
  Education and Recreation   (US)
Pennsylvania State Association of Township
  Supervisors   (US)
Pennsylvania State Education Association   (US)
Pennsylvania State Grange   (US)
Pennsylvania State Modern Language Association
  (US)
Pennsylvania State University. Audio-Visual Services
  (US)
Pennsylvania State University. Center for Air
  Environment Studies   (US)
Pennsylvania State University. Coal Research Section
  (US)
Pennsylvania State University. College of Agriculture
  (US)
Pennsylvania State University. College of Business
  Administration   (US)
Pennsylvania State University. College of Earth and
  Mineral Sciences   (US)
Pennsylvania State University. College of Earth &
  Mineral Sciences, Earth & Mineral Sciences
  Continuing Education   (US)
Pennsylvania State University. Cooperative Extension
  Service   (US)
Pennsylvania State University. Dept. of Anthropology
  (US)
Pennsylvania State University. Department of Classics
  (US)
Pennsylvania State University. Department of English
  (US)
Pennsylvania State University. Department of French
  (US)
Pennsylvania State University. Engineering
  Publications   (US)
Pennsylvania State University. Institute for Research
  on Land and Water Resources   (US)
Pennsylvania State University Press   (US)
Pennsylvania State University. University Libraries
  (US)
Pennsylvania State University. Vice President for
  Research and Graduate Studies   (US)
Penny Pincher   (US)
Penny Press   (US)
Pennzoil Co.   (US)
Penombra   (IT)
Pense et Lutte   (FR)
Pensee Nationale   (FR)
Pensiero Nazionale   (IT)
Pensiero Scientifico   (IT)
Pension Publications   (UK)
Pension Trends   (US)
Pensionistenverband Oesterreichs   (AU)
Penstock Publications   (CN)
Pentagramma   (IT)
Pentamas Ltd.   (CN)
Pentecostal Assemblies of Canada   (CN)
Pentecostal Fellowship of North America   (US)
Pentecostal Protestant Church   (SA)
Penthouse Photo World Ltd.   (US)
Penthouse Poster Press   (US)
Penthouse Publications Ltd.   (UK)
Penton-IPC   (US)
People Against Racism in Education   (US)

People Newspapers Ltd.   (IE)
People of the Living God   (US)
People to People   (HK)
People-to-People Health Foundation   (US)
People-To-People International   (US)
People United to Save Humanity. P.U.S.H.-Operation
  Push   (US)
People's Alternative Press   (CN)
Peoples Business Commission   (US)
Peoples Christian Coalition   (US)
Peoples Church of Chicago   (US)
People's Computer Co.   (US)
Peoples Democracy   (UK)
Peoples Dispensary for Sick Animals   (UK)
People's Movement for the Liberation of Angola
  (TZ)
People's National Movement Publishing Co.   (TR)
People's News Service   (UK)
People's Party   (US)
People's Party of India   (II)
People's Progressive Party   (GY)
People's Publishing Co., Inc.   (US)
People's Publishing Co. Ltd.   (NR)
People's Publishing House Private Ltd.   (II)
People's Voice   (NZ)
Peoplesmedia Inc.   (US)
Peoria Academy of Science   (US)
Peoria Labor News   (US)
Pepinieristes Horticulteurs Maraichers   (FR)
Pepperdine University. School of Law   (US)
Pequot Press   (US)
Pequot Publishing, Inc.   (US)
Per Jacobsson Foundation   (US)
Peramiho Publications   (TZ)
Perceptual and Motor Skills   (US)
Percival Publishing Co.   (NZ)
Percival Publishing Co. Pty. Ltd.   (AT)
Percussive Arts Society, Inc.   (US)
Peter Peregrinus Ltd.   (UK)
Perennial Books Ltd.   (UK)
Perennial Education, Inc.   (US)
Peres Blancs de Sainte-Anne de Jerusalem   (IS)
Peres de la Compagnie de Jesus   (CN)
Peres Jesuits   (UA)
Peres Montfortains   (CN)
Henry Perez   (US)
Perfekt Verlag   (AU)
Perfins Club   (US)
Performance Guide Publications, Inc   (US)
Performance Publications   (US)
Performing Arts Council, Orange Free State   (SA)
Performing Arts Council Transvaal   (SA)
Performing Arts Journal   (US)
Performing Arts Social Society, Inc.   (US)
Performing Right Society Ltd.   (UK)
Perfumeria Moderna   (MX)
Edizioni Pergamena   (IT)
Pergamon Press, Inc.   (US)
Pergamon Press Ltd.   (UK)
Peri-Med Verlag Dr. D. Straube   (GW)
Periodica   (DK)
Prensa Periodica, S.A.   (SP)
Periodico Delta SCA.   (AG)
Periodiques Parisiens   (FR)
Periodiques Reader's Digest Ltee.   (CN)
Periodismo Especializado, S.A.   (MX)
Periodistas y Publicistas Asociados de Mexico, S.A.
  (MX)
Kirjastus Perioodika   (UR)
Periscoop   (BE)
Perkhidmatan Kajicuaca Malaysia
  see Malaysia. Meteorological Service   (MY)
Perkin-Elmer Corp.   (US)
Perkin-Elmer Corp. Instrument Division   (US)
Perkins School for the Blind   (US)
Permail Pty. Ltd.   (AT)
Editora Permanencia   (BL)
Permanent and International Committee of
  Underground Town Planning and Construction
  (FR)
Permanent Building Societies Association Ltd.   (AT)
Permanent Bureau of Afro-Asian Writers   (UA)
Permanent Commission and International Association
  on Occupational Health   (JA)
Permanent International Altaistic Conference   (US)
Permanent International Association of Navigation
  Congresses   (BE)
Permanent International Association of Road
  Congresses   (FR)
Permanent International Committee for the Study of
  Life Assurance Medicine   (SZ)
Permanent International Committee of Linguists
  (NE)
Permanent International Committee on Canned Foods
  (FR)
Permanent Mission of Oman to the U.N.   (US)
Permanent Press   (US)
Permanent Way Institution   (UK)

Permian Basin District Dental Society (US)
Permskii Gosudarstvennyi Pedagogicheskii Institut (UR)
Perna Editore (IT)
Pernambuco, Brazil. Conselho de Desenvolvimento. Instituto de Desenvolvimento de Pernambuco (BL)
Pernambuco, Brazil. Governo do Estado (BL)
Peronismo y Liberacion (AG)
Peronismo y Socialismo (AG)
Perpetual Help Center (US)
Editorial Perpetuo Socorro (SP)
A. Perrault (CN)
Editions G. M. Perrin (FR)
Perry Publications (US)
Peter Perry Publishing Ltd. (CN)
Perry Rhodan Science Fiction Magazine (US)
Persatuan Economi Malaysia
    see Economic Association of Malaysia (MY)
Persatuan Mahasiswa Islam Universiti Malaya
    see Islamic Students' Union of the University of Malaya (MY)
Persatuan Perpustakaan Malaysia (MY)
Perskorporasie van S.A. (Edms) Bpk. (SA)
Personal Rights Association (UK)
Personhistoriska Samfundet (SW)
Personnel Journal, Inc. (US)
Personnel Psychology, Inc. (US)
Perspecta (US)
Perspective Publications Pvt. Ltd. (II)
Perspectives Euro Africaines (MR)
Perspectives, Inc. (US)
Perspectives of New Music, Inc. (US)
Pertadbiran Keretapi Tanah Malaya
    see Malaya Railway Administration (MY)
Pertamina (IO)
Perth City Council (AT)
Perth Observatory (AT)
Peru. Archivo General de la Nacion (PE)
Peru. Biblioteca Nacional (PE)
Peru. Caja Nacional de Seguro Social (PE)
Peru. Centro Nacional de Productividad (PE)
Peru. Consejo Nacional de Justicia (PE)
Peru. Empresa Nacional de Telecomunicaciones (PE)
Peru. Escuela Naval del Peru (PE)
Peru. Fuerza Aerea (PE)
Peru. Instituto Nacional de Cultura (PE)
Peru. Ministerio de Educacion Publica. Oficina Sectorial de Planificacion (PE)
Peru. Ministerio de Guerra y Marina (PE)
Peru. Ministerio de Relaciones Exteriores (PE)
Peru. Ministerio de Salud (PE)
Peru. Ministerio del Interior. Direccion de Sanidad (PE)
Peru. Oficina Regional de Desarrollo del Norte (PE)
Peru Indigena (PE)
Ediciones Peruanas (PE)
Peruvian Society of Cancerology (PE)
Alberto Peruzzo (IT)
Editorial Pesca y Marina S.A. (US)
Pescara Enterprises (US)
Peshawar (City) Pakistan Academy for Rural Development (PK)
Peshawar University
    see University of Peshawar (PK)
Editora Pesquisa Brasileiro do Disco (BL)
Pest Megyei Muzeumok Igazgatosaga (HU)
Pestalozzi-Froebel-Verband (GW)
Pestalozzi Kinder- und Jugenddorf Wahlwies (GW)
Peter Martin Associates (CN)
Peter Publications (US)
Peter Warlock Society (UK)
Verlag C. F. Peters (GW)
F.E. Peters Co. (US)
C. F. Peters Corporation (US)
Eric C. Peters, Ed. & Pub. (US)
A. Peters, Pub. (II)
Peters Publishing Co. of Texas (US)
Petersen og Bratvolds Bladforlag (DK)
Petersen Public Relations (DK)
Petersen Publishing Co. (US)
Fred. L. Peterson, Ed. & Pub. (US)
George Peterson, Inc. (US)
Peterson Publishing Co. Ltd. (UK)
Peterson's Guides Inc. (US)
Petheric Press Ltd. (CN)
A. J. Petrando (US)
Petranis Press (AT)
Petrine Publications (UK)
Editorial Petro-Nave (VE)
Petrocelli Books (US)
Petroleo Brasileiro S.A. (BL)
Petroleo Brasileiro S.A. Centro de Pesquisas e Desenvolvimento (BL)
Petroleo Brasileiro, S. A. Servicio de Pessoal (BL)
Petrolero (VE)
Petroleum Digests (UK)
Petroleum Geology: a Digest of Russian Literature on Petroleum Geology (US)

Petroleum Information Corp. (US)
Petroleum Information Service (II)
Petroleum Intelligence Weekly (US)
Petroleum Legislation (US)
Petroleum Mirror (FR)
Petroleum Press Bureau Ltd. (UK)
Petroleum Publishers Inc. (US)
Petroleum Publishing Co. (US)
Petroleum Publishing Co. Dental Economics Division (US)
Petroleum Publishing Co. (Houston) (US)
Publicazioni Petrolifere S.p.A. (IT)
Petronio (IT)
Petty Papers (US)
Petulengro Publications (UK)
Editions Peuples Amis (FR)
Peuser S.A. (AG)
Pewter Collectors' Club of America (US)
Peylim-Yad l'Achim (IS)
Pez y la Serpiente (NQ)
Pfadfinderinnenschaft St. Georg (GW)
Pfaelzer Bauernverlag GmbH (GW)
Pfaelzer Saenger (GW)
Pfaelzische Bauern- und Winzerschaft e.V. (GW)
Pfaelzische Gesellschaft zur Foerderung der Wissenschaften in Speyer (GW)
Pfaelzischer Saengerbund (GW)
Pfarre Perchtolsdorf (AU)
Ph. Pfeiffer's Buchdruckereien und Verlage (GW)
Pfizer Europe Management Center (BE)
Pflanzenschuetzer (AU)
Richard Pflaum Verlag KG (GW)
Udo Pfriemer Verlag GmbH (GW)
Phaedrus, Inc. (US)
Phaeton Press, Inc. (US)
Phaidon Press Ltd. (UK)
Phantasmicom Press (US)
Phare (BE)
Pharmaceutical Association of Israel (IS)
Pharmaceutical Business Analysis Service (UK)
Pharmaceutical Manufacturers Association (US)
Pharmaceutical Promotion Ltd. (UK)
Pharmaceutical Research Association (JA)
Pharmaceutical Research Institute (JA)
Pharmaceutical Society of Egypt (UA)
Pharmaceutical Society of Great Britain (UK)
Pharmaceutical Society of Ireland (IE)
Pharmaceutical Society of Japan (JA)
Pharmaceutical Society of South Africa (SA)
Pharmaceutical Society of the State of New York (US)
Pharmaceutical Society of Victoria (AT)
Pharmachim (BU)
Pharmacien de Reserve (FR)
Pharmacien Rural (FR)
Pharmaco-Medical Documentation, Inc. (US)
Pharmacy Board of New Zealand (NZ)
Pharmacy Reports, Inc. (US)
Pharmapress-Verlagsgesellschaft (GW)
Pharmazeutische Gesellschaft der DDR (GE)
Pharmazeutischer Verlag (GW)
PharmChem Research Foundation (US)
Pharos (II)
Pharos Press (UK)
Phi Alpha Theta. Beta Alpha Chapter (US)
Phi Alpha Theta International Honor Society in History (US)
Phi Beta Kappa
    see United Chapters of Phi Beta Kappa (US)
Phi Chi Theta (US)
Phi Delta Epsilon (US)
Phi Delta Kappa (US)
Phi Delta Kappa at Western Illinois University (US)
Phi Delta Kappa Educational Foundation (US)
Phi Delta Theta Fraternity (US)
Phi Epsilon Kappa Fraternity (US)
Phi Kappa Phi (US)
Phi Kappa Tau Fraternity (US)
Phi Lambda Upsilon, Honorary Chemical Society (US)
Phi Mu Alpha Sinfonia Fraternity of America, Inc. (US)
Phi Rho Sigma Medical Society (US)
Phi Sigma Iota Honor Society (US)
Phi Sigma Society (US)
Phi Sigma Tau (US)
Phi Upsilon Omicron (US)
Philadelphia Art Alliance (US)
Philadelphia Association for Psychoanalysis (US)
Philadelphia Association of Retail Druggists (US)
Philadelphia Bar Association (US)
Philadelphia College of Pharmacy and Science (US)
Philadelphia College of Textiles and Science. Alumni Association (US)
Philadelphia County Dental Society (US)
Philadelphia County Medical Society (US)
Philadelphia Dental Laboratory Association (US)
Philadelphia Gas Works (US)

Philadelphia Jewish Times (US)
Philadelphia Museum of Art (US)
Philadelphia Port Corporation (US)
Philadelphia Society of Clinical Psychologists (US)
Philadelphia Task Force on Women in Religion (US)
Philadelphia Tribune (US)
Philadelphia Yearly Meeting of Friends (US)
Philaprint (FR)
Philatelic Exporter Ltd. (UK)
Philatelic Federation of Southern Africa (SA)
Philatelic Guild (US)
Philatelic Traders Society Ltd. (UK)
Philatelists Union of the Democratic People's Republic of Korea (KN)
George Philip & Son Ltd. (UK)
Philippine Airlines, Inc. (PH)
Philippine Association, Inc. (PH)
Philippine Association of Entomologists (PH)
Philippine Association of Social Workers (PH)
Philippine Atmospheric, Geophysical and Astronomical Services Administration
    see Philippines. Philippine Atmospheric, Geophysical and Astronomical Services Administration (PH)
Philippine Atomic Energy Commission
    see Philippines. Philippine Atomic Energy Commission (PH)
Philippine Cancer Society (PH)
Philippine Center for Advanced Studies
    see under University of the Philippines (PH)
Philippine Chamber of Industries (PH)
Philippine Chinese Historical Association (PH)
Philippine Christian College (PH)
Philippine Coconut Authority. Agricultural Research Department
    see Philippines. Philippine Coconut Authority. Agricultural Research Department (PH)
Philippine Commercial and Industrial Bank. (PH)
Philippine Council of Management (PH)
Philippine Dental Association (PH)
Philippine Economic Society (PH)
Philippine Federation of Private Medical Practitioners (PH)
Philippine Geographical Society (PH)
Philippine Index Service, Inc. (PH)
Philippine Institute of Certified Public Accountants (PH)
Philippine Inventors Commission
    see Philippines. Philippine Inventors Commission (PH)
Philippine Journal of Education Co., Inc. (PH)
Philippine Journalists Inc. (PH)
Philippine Library Association (PH)
Philippine Lumberman, Inc. (PH)
Philippine Marketing Association (PH)
Philippine Medical Association (PH)
Philippine Medical-Dental Publications (PH)
Philippine Mental Health Association (PH)
Philippine National Red Cross (PH)
Philippine Normal College. Community-School Health Education Center (PH)
Philippine Normal College. Language Study Center (PH)
Philippine Nurses Association (PH)
Philippine Pediatric Society (PH)
Philippine Public School Teachers Association (PH)
Philippine Society of International Law (PH)
Philippine Society of Ophthalmology (PH)
Philippine Sociological Society (PH)
Philippine Statistical Association (PH)
Philippine Sugar Association (PH)
Philippine Sugar Institute (PH)
Philippine Tax Journal (PH)
Philippine Women's University (PH)
Philippines. Agricultural Meteorology Division (PH)
Philippines. Board of Investments (PH)
Philippines. Bureau of Agricultural Economics (PH)
Philippines. Bureau of Animal Industry (PH)
Philippines. Bureau of Disease Control. Leprosy Research Laboratory and Training Center
    see Philippines. Leprosy Research Laboratory and Training Center (PH)
Philippines. Bureau of Mines (PH)
Philippines. Bureau of National and Foreign Information (PH)
Philippines. Bureau of Plant Industry (PH)
Philippines. Bureau of Vocational Education (PH)
Philippines. Civil Service Commission (PH)
Philippines. Department of Agrarian Reform. Planning Service (PH)
Philippines. Department of Agriculture and Natural Resources. Agricultural Information Division (PH)
Philippines. Department of Agriculture and Natural Resources. Bureau of Animal Industry
    see Philippines. Bureau of Animal Industry (PH)
Philippines. Department of Agriculture and Natural Resources. Fisheries Commission
    see Philippines. Fisheries Commission (PH)

Philippines. Department of Commerce and Industry (PH)
Philippines. Department of Foreign Affairs. Office of Press and Public Affairs (PH)
Philippines. Department of Natural Resources (PH)
Philippines. Department of Trade. Research and Information Division (PH)
Philippines. Fisheries Commission (PH)
Philippines. Food and Nutrition Research Institute (PH)
Philippines. Forest Products Research and Industries Development Commission (PH)
Philippines. Forest Research Institute (PH)
Philippines. Government Printing Office (PH)
Philippines. Labor Statistics Service (PH)
Philippines. Leprosy Research Laboratory and Training Center (PH)
Philippines. National Archives. Bureau of Records Management (PH)
Philippines. National Census and Statistics Office (PH)
Philippines. National Economic and Development Authority (PH)
Philippines. National Grains Authority (PH)
Philippines. National Institute of Science and Technology (PH)
Philippines. National Library (PH)
Philippines. National Media Production Center (PH)
Philippines. National Science Development Board (PH)
Philippines. National Science Development Board. Food and Nutrition Research Institute
  see Philippines. Food and Nutrition Research Institute (PH)
Philippines. National Science Development Board. Forest Products Research and Industries Development Commission
  see Philippines. Forest Products Research and Industries Development Commission (PH)
Philippines. National Science Development Board. National Institute of Science and Technology
  see Philippines. National Institute of Science and Technology (PH)
Philippines. National Science Development Board. Philippine Inventors Commission
  see Philippines. Philippine Inventors Commission (PH)
Philippines. National Science Development Board. Scientific Library and Documentation Division (PH)
Philippines. National Tax Research Center (PH)
Philippines. Office of Press and Public Affairs
  see under Philippines. Department of Foreign Affairs (PH)
Philippines. Philippine Atmospheric, Geophysical and Astronomical Services Administration (PH)
Philippines. Philippine Atomic Energy Commission (PH)
Philippines. Philippine Coconut Authority. Agricultural Research Department (PH)
Philippines. Philippine Inventors Commission (PH)
Philippines. Population Commission (PH)
Philippines Daily Express Publishing Corp. (PH)
Philippines Labor Relations Journal (PH)
Philips Electrical Pty. Ltd. (AT)
Philips Electron Devices (CN)
Philips Electronic Instruments, Inc. (US)
N.V. Philips Gloeilampenfabrieken (NE)
Philips GmbH (GW)
Philips India Ltd.-ELCOMA (Electronic Components and Materials) (II)
Philips Roxane Laboratories, Inc. (US)
Philips S.p.A. (IT)
Philips' Telecommunicatie Industrie B.V. (NE)
Phillie Newsletter (US)
Phillimore & Co. Ltd. (UK)
Phillips Academy (US)
Geoff Phillips & Associates Pty. Ltd. (AT)
Phillips Exeter Academy (US)
Phillips Petroleum Company (US)
Phillips Publishing, Inc. (US)
Phillips University (US)
Phillumenists Worldring (GW)
Philo Institute (US)
Philologenverband Baden-Wuerttemberg (GW)
Philological Association of the Pacific Coast (US)
Philological Soceity (UK)
Philologikos Syllogos Parnassos (GR)
Philomathean Society (US)
Philosophic Society for the Study of Sport (US)
Philosophical Association of Kenya (KE)
Philosophical Forum, Inc. (US)
Philosophical Research Society Inc. (US)
Philosophical Society of the Sudan (SJ)
Philosophisch-Theologische Hochschule der Dioezese Linz (AU)
Philosophisch-Theologische Hochschule, Passau. Institut fuer Ostbairische Heimatforschung (GW)

Philosophische Gesellschaft Oesterreichs (AU)
Philosophy Documentation Center (US)
Philosophy Education Society, Inc. (US)
Philosophy of Education Society (US)
Philosophy of Education Society of Australasia (AT)
Philosophy of Science Association (US)
Phoenix-Capital (US)
Phoenix Jewish News, Inc. (US)
Phonemic Spelling Council (US)
Phono-Log Publishing (US)
Phonogram International B.V. (NE)
Ovo/Photo. English Edition (CN)
Photo Gallery (US)
Photo Marketing Association (US)
Photo-Memo (CN)
Photo News Publishers, Inc (US)
Photo Pictorialists of Milwaukee, Inc. (US)
Photo Publishing Co. (AT)
Photogrammetric Society (UK)
Photogrammetric Society of South Africa (SA)
Photographic Historical Society of New York (US)
Photographic Industry Council of Australia (AT)
Photographic Society of America, Inc. (US)
Photographic Society of Ireland (IE)
Photographic Society of Japan (JA)
Photographic Society of New Zealand (NZ)
Photographic Workers Union (DK)
Photojournalist Ltd. (UK)

Photon (US)

Shashi Phukan, Ed. & Pub. (II)

Phycological Society of America (US)
Physica-Verlag Rudolf Liebing GmbH und Co. (GW)
Physica-Verlag Rudolf Liebing KG (AU)
Physical Biological Sciences, Ltd. (US)
Physical Education Association (UK)
Physical Education Association. M. Hankinson Trust) (UK)
Physical Education Association of Great Britain & Northern Ireland (UK)
Physical Education Publications (US)
Physical Education Society of the YMCA'S of North America (US)
Physical Research Laboratory (II)
Physical Society of Japan (JA)
Physicians' Association of Madras (II)
Physicians Drug Manual, Inc. (US)
Physicians International Press, Inc. (US)
Physicians Postgraduate Press (US)
Physician's Record Co. (US)
Physicians World, Inc. (US)
Physico-Chemical Society of Japan (JA)
Physics Trust Publications (UK)
Physikalisch-Medizinische Sozietaet Erlangen (GW)
Physikalisch-Technische Bundesanstalt (GW)
Physikalische Gesellschaft der DDR (GE)
Physiognomy (DK)
Physiological Society, London (UK)
Physiological Society of Japan (JA)
Phytogeographical Society (JA)
Phytopathological Society of Japan (JA)
Uitgeverij Pi B.V. (NE)
Edizioni Pi-Erre (IT)
Pi Gamma Mu, National Social Science Honor Society (US)
Pi Kappa Delta (US)
Pi Lambda Theta (US)
Pi Mu Epsilon (US)
Pia Sociedade Filhas de Sao Paulo (BL)
Pia Societa San Paolo (IT)
Compagnia Editoriale Pianeta s.r.l. (IT)
Piano Quarterly, Inc. (US)
Piano Technicians Guild, Inc. (US)
Piano Trade Publishing Co. (US)
Editions A. et J. Picard (FR)
Piccin Editore (IT)
A. Pichlers Witwe und Sohn (AU)
Pick Publications (UK)
Pick Publishing Corp. (US)
Pick-Verlag (US)
Pickaway County Historical Society (US)
Pickering & Inglis Ltd. (UK)
Pick'n' and Sing'n' Gather'n', Inc. (US)
Pictorial News Review Publications (PK)
Pictorial Publications (GH)
Pictures Publishing Co. (US)
A. Pidhainy (CN)
Piedmont CB Directory (US)
Pienteollisuuden Keskusliitto (FI)
Ed. Piepersche Buchdruckerei und Verlagsanstalt (GW)
Pierce-Arrow Society, Inc. (US)
Pierian Press (US)
Rachetto Piero, Ed. & Pub. (IT)
Pierre Fauchard Academy (US)
Pierson Printing Co. (US)
Romaine Pierson Publishers, Inc. (US)
Guido Pietroni, Ed. & Pub. (IT)

Pig Breeders Weekly (UK)
Pigeon Fancier (AT)
Pigiron Press (US)
Wilson Pignagnoli (IT)
Pig's Arse Press (AT)
Pikes Peak Ar a Council of Governments (US)
Pikeville College. Appalachian Studies Center (US)
Verlag Piletzky (AU)
Ellen Pilger (GW)
Pilgrim Publishers (US)
Pilgrim Society (US)
A. Sivasubramonia Pillai, Ed. & Pub. (II)
Jean-Guy Pilon, Ed. & Pub. (CN)
Pilot Books (US)
Pilote (CN)
G. Pilz (AU)
Pimienta Publishing Corp. (US)
Pinatel (FR)
Pinecrest State School (US)
Pinel-Publikationen (GW)
Joaquin Pineros Corpus (CK)
Fratelli Pini Editori S.p.A. (IT)
Editora Pini Ltda. (BL)
Pink Triangle Press (CN)
Pinkus-Genossenschaft (SZ)
Philippe Pinquier (FR)
Pinto Horse Association of America Inc. (US)
Pion Ltd. (UK)
Pioneer America (Louisiana State University) (US)
Pioneer America Society (US)
Pioneer Girls, Inc. (US)
Pioneer Press (US)
Pioneer Publications Ltd. (UK)
Pioneer Total Abstinence Association (IE)
Pioneer Women- The Women's Labor Zionist Organization of America (US)
Pioneerikilta r.y. (FI)
Pipe Club of Australia (AT)
Pipe Club of Great Britain Ltd. (UK)
Pipe World Est. (IT)
Piraiki-Patraiki Cotton Manufacturing Co. Inc. (GR)
Industrie Pirelli S. p. A. (IT)
Pirquet Society of Clinical Medicine, Inc. (US)
Pisces Publishing Corp. (US)
Pit and Quarry Publications, Inc. (US)
Pithead Press (Pty) Ltd. (SA)
Pitman Medical Publishing Co. Ltd. (UK)
Pitman Periodicals Ltd. (UK)
Pitra Editoriale (IT)
Pittsburg State University (US)
Pittsburgh Athletic Association (US)
Pittsburgh Catholic Publishing Associates (US)
Pittsburgh History and Landmarks Foundation (US)
Pittsburgh Musical Society (US)
Pittsburgh Regional Library Center (US)
Pittsburgh Symphony Society (US)
Pittsburgh Teachers Education Association (US)
Pitysmont Post (US)
Pius-Parsch-Institut (AU)
Pivovary a Sladovny (CS)
Pizza and Pasta Publishing Co. (US)
Place of Herons Press (US)
Verlag Plaedoyer (SZ)
Plaid Cymru (Welsh Nationalist Party) (UK)
Plain Dirt (US)
Plain Rapper (US)
Plain Truth (US)
Plains Conference (US)
Plainsong (US)
Plaisir de France (FR)
Plaistow Press (UK)
Editions Plan et But (FR)
Plan Magazines Ltd. (UK)
Planarian Research Group (US)
Planet (UK)
Planet-Drum Foundation (US)
Editorial Planeta S. a (SP)
Planetary Legion for Peace - PLP (US)
Planinarski Savez Hrvatske (YU)
Planned Parenthood Association of Ghana (GH)
Planned Parenthood Federation of America, Inc. The Alan Guttmacher Institute (US)
Planned Parenthood League of Connecticut, Inc. (US)
Planned Parenthood-World Population (US)
Planning and Transport Research and Computation (International) Co. (UK)
Planning Executives Institute (US)
Planning Institute of British Columbia (CN)
Planning Transport Associates, Inc. (US)
Metallwerk Plansee AG (AU)
Plant and Equipment Publications Ltd. (UK)
Plant Assessment (London) Ltd. (UK)
Plant Biochemical Society (II)
Plant Breeding Institute (UK)
Plant News Ltd. (UK)
Plant Pests and Diseases Research Institute (IR)
Plant Protection Center (CH)

Planteo (AG)
Plantie Talleres Graficos S.A. (AG)
Plants Inc. (US)
Die Planung Verlagsgesellschaft mbH (GW)
Plast-Ukrainian Youth Organization (CN)
Plastic Aircraft Modellers (UK)
Plasticos (PO)
Plasticos em Revista Editora Ltda. (BL)
Plastics Age Co. Ltd. (JA)
Plastics and Rubber Institute (UK)
Plastics Focus Publishing Co., Inc. (US)
Plastics Institute of South Africa (SA)
Plastics Investigations (UK)
R. S. Platou A-S (NO)
Platt Saco Lowell (US)
Platt Saco Lowell Bulletin (UK)
Platt Saco Lowell. Replacement Parts Center (US)
Plattdeutsche Post (US)
Platte Publishing Co. (US)
Platt's Oilgram News Service (US)
Play (AT)
Play Meter (US)
Play Schools Association (US)
Playbill Inc (US)
Playboy Enterprises Inc. (US)
Playboy Publications Inc. (US)
Players International Publications (US)
Playfair Publishing Group (AT)
Plays, Inc. (US)
J. Plaza, Ed. & Pub. (CK)
Plaza y Janes S.A. (SP)
Bengt Pleijel, Ed. & Pub. (SW)
Publications Plein Air (CN)
Plein Chant (FR)
Plenhurst Ltd. (UK)
Plenum Press (US)
Plenum Publishing Co. Ltd. (UK)
Plenum Publishing Corp.
  see also Consultants Bureau (US)
Plenum Publishing Corp. (US)
Plenum Publishing Corp. I.F.I.--Plenum Data Co.
  (US)
Plessey Telecommunications Ltd. Electronic Systems
  Ltd. (UK)
Plexus (US)
Plexus Publishing, Inc. (US)
Plough Publicity (Hull) Ltd. (UK)
Ploughshares, Inc. (US)
Plug Press (US)
Pluma (CK)
Plumbing & Mechanical Contractors Council of Harris
  County, Inc. (US)
Plus Media, Inc. (US)
Plus Publications (US)
Plus Publications, Inc. (US)
Editorial Plus Ultra (AG)
Pluto Press (UK)
Plymouth College (UK)
Plymouth Four and Six Cylinder Owners Club (US)
Pneumatique (FR)
Poale Zion (UK)
L. Wilson Poarch, Jr., Ed. & Pub. (US)
Pobeda (YU)
Pobjeda (YU)
Editorial Pocho che (US)
Pocket Pal (US)
S. K. Poddar, Ed. & Pub. (II)
Empresa Jornalistico o Poder (BL)
Podiatry Record Publishing Co., Inc. (US)
Podiatry Society of the State of New York (US)
Poema Convidado (US)
Poemes Inedits (CN)
H. Poeppinghaus (GW)
Carl Ernst Poeschel Verlag (GW)
Poesia de Venezuela (VE)
Poesia-Poesia (AG)
Poesie (FR)
Poesie (SZ)
Poeticart Club (AT)
Poetry Book Society (UK)
Poetry Eastwest Publications (US)
Poetry Miscellany (US)
Poetry Nippon Press (JA)
Poetry Project (US)
Poetry Society Inc. (UK)
Poetry Society of America (US)
Poetry Society of Australia (AT)
Poetry Society of Japan (JA)
Poetry Society of Michigan (US)
Poetry - Windsor - Poesie (CN)
Poets' and Painters Press (UK)
Poets & Writers, Inc. (US)
Poets' Guild (US)
Poet's League of Greater Cleveland (US)
Poets Press of Osgoldcross (UK)
Pohl Druckerei und Verlagsanstalt (GW)
Henry A. Pohs, Ed. & Pub. (US)
Guiseppe Poidomani, Pub. (IT)

Poiken Keskus r.y. (FI)
Point Blanc Press (US)
Point du Jazz (BE)
Point Foundation (US)
Point Loma Publications, Inc. (US)
Point of View (US)
Point Veterinaire (FR)
Pointblank Times (US)
Points et Contrepoints (FR)
Poison Pen Press (US)
Rev. Jerome Pokorny, Ed. & Pub (US)
Pola Editrice s.r.l. (IT)
Polak en Van Gennep Uitgeversmaatschappij B.V.
  (NE)
Polana AG (SZ)
Poland. Glowne Biuro Studiow i Projektow
  Gorniczych (PL)
Poland. Glowny Urzad Statystyczny (PL)
Poland. Ministerstwo Gornictwa i Energetyki (PL)
Poland. Ministerstwo Handlu Zagranicznego i
  Gospodarki Morskiej (PL)
Poland. Ministerstwo Komunikacji (PL)
Poland. Ministerstwo Kultury i Sztuki. Generalny
  Konserwator Zabytkow (PL)
Poland. Ministerstwo Nauki, Szkolnictwa Wyzszego i
  Techniki (PL)
Poland. Ministerstwo Oswiaty i Wychowania (PL)
Poland. Ministerstwo Przemyslu Chemicznego (PL)
Poland. Ministerstwo Zdrowia i Opieki Spolecznej
  (PL)
Poland. Urzad Patentowy (PL)
Poland China Record Association (US)
Poland Music Association (NE)
Polarographic Society of Japan (JA)
K. R. Polavarapu, Ed. & Pub. (II)
Wydawnictwa Handlu Zagranicznego Polexportpress
  (PL)
Franco Poli, Ed. & Pub. (IT)
Police (FR)
Police Association of N.S.W. (AT)
Police College, Bramshill (UK)
Police Federation (UK)
Police Forces of Australia (AT)
Police Officers Journal Inc. (US)
Police Press Inc. (US)
Police Review Publishing Co. Ltd. (UK)
Police Training College (KE)
Policia Portuguesa (PO)
Editorial Policial (AG)
Policlinica Geral do Rio de Janeiro (BL)
Policy Studies Organization (US)
Poliedrica Editrice (IT)
Edizioni Il Polifilo (IT)
Poliisimies (FI)
Polimlje (YU)
Polish American Historical Association (US)
Polish Army Veterans Association of America, Inc.
  (US)
Polish Association of South Australia (AT)
Polish Communities in Australia and New Zealand
  (AT)
Polish Cultural Foundation Ltd. Editorial Committee
  (UK)
Polish Embassy in London (UK)
Polish Falcons of America (US)
Polish Historical Society in Great Britain (UK)
Polish Institute and Sikorski Museum (UK)
Polish Institute of Arts and Sciences in America
  (US)
Polish Library (UK)
Polish Museum of America (US)
Polish National Alliance (US)
Polish National Alliance of Brooklyn (US)
Polish National Alliance. Sports Youth Commission
  (US)
Polish National Union of America (US)
Polish Populist Party (UK)
Polish Press Ltd. (CN)
Polish Roman Catholic Union of America (US)
Polish Socialist Party in Exile (UK)
Polish Society of Anaesthesiologists (PL)
Polish Society of Arts and Sciences Abroad (UK)
Polish Star Publishing Co. Inc. (US)
Polish Tatra Mountaineers Alliance (US)
Polish Voice Publishing Co. (CN)
Polish Western Association of America (US)
Polish Women's Alliance of America (US)
Polisidrott (SW)
Editorial Politea (AG)
Politechnika Czestochowska (PL)
Politechnika Gdanska (PL)
Politechnika Krakowska (PL)
Politechnika Lodzka (PL)
Politechnika Poznanska (PL)
Politechnika Slaska (PL)
Politechnika Warszawska (PL)
Politechnika Wroclawska (PL)

Politehniskais Instituts, Riga (UR)
Politekhnichnyi Instytut, Kiev (UR)
Giancarlo Politi Editore (IT)
Politica Estera (IT)
Politica y Economia (AG)
Political Affairs Publishers, Inc. (US)
Political and Economic Planning (UK)
Political Quarterly Publishing Co. Ltd. (UK)
Political Research, Inc. (US)
Political Science Association of South Africa (SA)
Political Student's Association (NR)
Political Studies Association of the United Kingdom
  (UK)
Politics and Money Publishing Co. (UK)
Politiembetsmennenes Landsforening (NO)
Politika (YU)
Politiken Weekly (DK)
Politique Hebdo (FR)
Polizei Technik Verkehr, Verlagsgesellschaft mbH und
  Co. KG (GW)
Polizeigewerkschaft im Deutschen Beamtenbund
  (GW)
R.L. Polk & Co. (US)
R. L. Polk & Co. Ltd. (CN)
Polk County Medical Society (US)
Pollustop (FR)
Pollution Equipment News (US)
Pollyhaugh Press Ltd. (UK)
Polo Petroquimico da Bahia (BL)
Wydawnictwo Polonia (PL)
Polska Agencja Prasowa (PL)
Polska Akademia Nauk (PL)
Polska Akademia Nauk. Biblioteka (PL)
Polska Akademia Nauk. Biblioteka Gdanska (PL)
Polska Akademia Nauk. Biblioteka, Krakow (PL)
Polska Akademia Nauk. Centrum Obliczeniowe (PL)
Polska Akademia Nauk. Committee on Research and
  Peaceful Uses of Outer Space (PL)
Polska Akademia Nauk. Committee on the Science of
  Science (PL)
Polska Akademia Nauk. Instytut Badan Literackich
  (PL)
Polska Akademia Nauk. Instytut Biologii
  Doswiadczalnej im. M. Nenckiego (PL)
Polska Akademia Nauk. Instytut Botaniki (PL)
Polska Akademia Nauk. Instytut Budownictwa
  Wodnego (PL)
Polska Akademia Nauk. Instytut Chemii Fizycznej
  (PL)
Polska Akademia Nauk. Instytut Ekologii (PL)
Polska Akademia Nauk. Instytut Farmakologii (PL)
Polska Akademia Nauk. Instytut Filozofii i Socjologii
  (PL)
Polska Akademia Nauk. Instytut Fizyki (PL)
Polska Akademia Nauk. Instytut Genetyki Roslin
  (PL)
Polska Akademia Nauk. Instytut Geofizyki (PL)
Polska Akademia Nauk. Instytut Geografii (PL)
Polska Akademia Nauk. Instytut Historii (PL)
Polska Akademia Nauk. Instytut Historii Kultury
  Materialnej (PL)
Polska Akademia Nauk. Instytut Immunologii i Terapii
  Doswiadczalnej (PL)
Polska Akademia Nauk. Instytut Jezyka Polskiego
  (PL)
Polska Akademia Nauk. Instytut Krajow
  Socjalistycznych (PL)
Polska Akademia Nauk. Instytut Maszyn
  Przeplywowych (PL)
Polska Akademia Nauk. Instytut Matematyczny (PL)
Polska Akademia Nauk. Instytut Nauk Prawnych
  (PL)
Polska Akademia Nauk. Instytut Organizacji i
  Kierowania (PL)
Polska Akademia Nauk. Instytut Panstwa i Prawa
  (PL)
Polska Akademia Nauk. Instytut Podstaw Inzynierii
  Srodowiska (PL)
Polska Akademia Nauk. Instytut Podstawowych
  Problemow Techniki (PL)
Polska Akademia Nauk. Instytut Reumatologiczny
  (PL)
Polska Akademia Nauk. Instytut Sztuki (PL)
Polska Akademia Nauk. Instytut Teatru (PL)
Polska Akademia Nauk. Instytut Zoologii (PL)
Polska Akademia Nauk. Komitet Akustyki (PL)
Polska Akademia Nauk. Komitet Architektury i
  Urbanistyki (PL)
Polska Akademia Nauk. Komitet Astronomii (PL)
Polska Akademia Nauk. Komitet Automatyki i
  Cybernetyki Technicznej (PL)
Polska Akademia Nauk. Komitet Badan i Prognoz
  "Polska 2000" (PL)
Polska Akademia Nauk. Komitet Badan Morza (PL)

Al Preiss Ltd. (US)
Prejepscot Press (US)
Julien Prelat (FR)
Premier Publicity Service Ltd. (UK)
Premiere (US)
Premiere Imprimerie Ukrainienne en France (FR)
Premio (IT)
Prenatal Moeder en Kind N.V. (NE)
Prensa Confidencial (AG)
Prensa Latina, Agencia Informativa Latinoamericana (FR)
Prensa Latinoamericana S.A. (CL)
Prensa Literaria Centroamericana (NQ)
Prensa Medica Argentina, S.R.L. (AG)
Prensa Mexicana, S.A. (MX)
Prensachil Ltda (CL)
William B. Prentice & Associates (CN)
Prentice-Hall, Inc. (US)
Prentice-Hall, Inc. General Book Mktg. Div. (US)
Prentice-Hall of Canada, Ltd. (CN)
Presbyterian Book Depot (GH)
Presbyterian Church in Canada (CN)
Presbyterian Church in Ireland (UK)
Presbyterian Church in the United States (US)
Presbyterian Church of Australia (AT)
Presbyterian Church of New Zealand (NZ)
Presbyterian Church of Southern Africa (SA)
Presbyterian Church of Wales (UK)
Presbyterian Church U.S. Synod of Red River (US)
Presbyterian Comment (CN)
Presbyterian Guardian Publishing Corp. (US)
Presbyterian Historical Society (US)
Presbyterian Lay Committee (US)
Presbyterium der Evangelischen Gemeinde Wien-Favoriten-Christuskirche (AU)
Presence du Cinema (FR)
Presence, S.A.R.L. (FR)
Presence Socialiste (FR)
Editorial Presencia Ltda (CK)
Presencia, S.A. (SP)
Presernova Druzba (YU)
Preservation Society of Charleston (US)
Presgraves Reunion (US)
President, Inc. (US)
President Publications (US)
President's Committee on Employment of the Handicapped (US)
Press Agencias, S.A. (VE)
Press and Information Service of the European Communities (EI)
Press and Public Relations Association (II)
Press and Publications Agency (II)
Press Council of India (II)
Press Export, S.A. (SP)
Press Foundation of Asia (PH)
Press Institute of India (II)
Press of the Times (US)
Press-Tech, Inc. (US)
Pressdram Ltd. (UK)
Presse Corporative Francaise (FR)
Presse et Information (FR)
Presse et Loisirs S.A. (BE)
Editions de la Presse Europeenne (BE)
Presse Immobiliere (FR)
La Presse Libre (FR)
Presse Ltee. (CN)
Presse Periodique Professionnelle (FR)
Editions Presse Professionnelle (FR)
Edition Presse Specialisee (FR)
Presse und Bildung GmbH (GW)
Presse und Sport (GW)
Pressed Curtains (UK)
Editions Presselec (FR)
Presselec S.P.R.L. (BE)
Presses Academiques (BE)
Presses Centrales Lausanne S.A. (SZ)
Presses Continentales (FR)
Presses d'Europe (FR)
Presses de l'Ecole Normale Superieure (FR)
Presses de l'Universite de Montreal (CN)
Presses de l'Universite du Quebec (CN)
Presses de l'Universite Laval (CN)
Presses de la Fondation Nationale des Sciences Politiques (FR)
Presses de la Tour Saint-Jacques (FR)
Presses du Palais Royal (FR)
Presses du Temps Present (FR)
Presses Universitaires de Brussels (BE)
Presses Universitaires de France (FR)
Presses Universitaires de Grenoble (FR)
Presses Universitaires du Zaire (ZR)
Presseverlag (GW)
Presshouse Publications Ltd. (UK)
Pressmedia Ltd. (UK)
Presso Galleria S. Giorgio (IT)
Pressure Technology Corporation of America (US)
Prestel-Verlag (GW)

Prestige Books of Canada (CN)
Prestige Journals of India (II)
Prestige Publication Co. (NR)
Prestige Publications (II)
Prestige Publications, Ltd. (UK)
Prestige Publishing Pty. Ltd. (AT)
Preston and District Chamber of Commerce and Industry (UK)
Preston Polytechnic (UK)
Preston Publications, Inc. (US)
Prestressed Concrete Institute (US)
Preti della Missione della Provincia di Roma (IT)
Pretoria College for Advanced Technical Education (SA)
Pretoria Horticultural Society (SA)
Pretoria Photographic Society (SA)
Pretres Diocesains (FR)
Prevention Routiere dans l'Entreprise (FR)
Previdenza Sociale nell'Agricoltura (IT)
Preview of Bermuda, Ltd. (BM)
Edizioni Previsionali (IT)
Renan Prevost, Ed. & Pub. (US)
Priapus (UK)
Robert C. Price, Ed. & Pub. (US)
Price Guide Publishers (US)
Price Institute for Palaeontological Research
   see under University of the Witwatersrand, Johannesburg (SA)
Price Waterhouse & Co. (US)
Pride Publications (US)
Pride Publications, Inc. (US)
Priests' Eucharistic League (US)
Priests of Holy Cross. Indiana Province (US)
Priests of the Sacred Heart (US)
Primal Institute (US)
Primalinea (IT)
Primary Education Pty. Ltd. (AT)
Primary English Teachers Association of New South Wales (AT)
Primary Sources (US)
Primeira Escola de Tecelagem (BL)
Primer Acto, S.A. (SP)
Editorial Primera Plana s.r.l. (AG)
Primicia (BO)
Prince Edward Island. Civil Service Commission (CN)
Prince Edward Island. Department of Agriculture (CN)
Prince Edward Island. Department of Community Services (CN)
Prince Edward Island. Department of Development (CN)
Prince Edward Island. Department of Environment (CN)
Prince Edward Island. Department of Fisheries (CN)
Prince Edward Island. Department of Health (CN)
Prince Edward Island. Department of Industry and Commerce (CN)
Prince Edward Island. Department of Labour (CN)
Prince Edward Island. Department of the Environment and Tourism (CN)
Prince Edward Island. Public Utilities Commission (CN)
Prince Edward Island Land Development Corporation (CN)
Prince George's County Genealogical Society (US)
Prince George's County Memorial Library System (US)
Prince Publishing Group (AT)
Princeton Arts Journal (US)
Princeton Theological Seminary (US)
Princeton University (US)
Princeton University. Art Museum (US)
Princeton University. Center of International Studies (US)
Princeton University. Department of Electrical Engineering (US)
Princeton University. Department of Psychology (US)
Princeton University. Econometric Research Program (US)
Princeton University. Graduate School (US)
Princeton University. Industrial Relations Section (US)
Princeton University. International Finance Section (US)
Princeton University. Library (US)
Princeton University. Library Staff Association (US)
Princeton University Press (US)
Princeton University. School of Engineering and Applied Science (US)
Princo B.V. (NE)
Prindle Weber and Schmidt Inc. (US)
Print Collector's Newsletter Inc. (US)
Print Craft Publishers (II)
Print Media Services, Ltd. (US)
Printable Arts Society, Inc. (US)
Printer (US)

Printerhall Ltd. (UK)
Printers News Pty. Ltd. (AT)
Printing and Allied Trades Employers' Federation (AT)
Printing and Publishing Industry Training Board (UK)
Printing Craftsmen, Inc. (US)
Printing Historical Society (UK)
Printing Industries Federation of New Zealand (Inc.) (NZ)
Printing News, Inc. (US)
Printing Platemakers Association, Inc. (US)
Printoff Printers & Publishers (PK)
Printway, Inc. (US)
Printworkshop (UK)
Printwrite (AT)
Priory Press (US)
Priroda (CS)
Prirodnjacki Muzej u Beogradu (YU)
Prirodonaucen Muzej na Makedonija (YU)
Prirodoslovno Drustvo Slovenije (YU)
Prism Publications Ltd. (UK)
Prison Action Group (US)
Prison Arts Foundation (CN)
Prison Officers Association (UK)
Prisoners Aid Association of South Australia (Inc.) (AT)
Prisoners Union (US)
Pritchard Publications (US)
Pritchard Publishing Co. (US)
Privacy Journal (US)
Editions Edouard Privat (FR)
Private Carrier Conference, Inc. (US)
Private Development Corporation of the Philippines (PH)
Private Libraries Association (UK)
Private Motorist Protection Association (IE)
Private Police Publishers (US)
Private Printer & Private Press (UK)
Editore Privitera (IT)
Privolzhskoe Knizhnoe Izdatel'stvo (UR)
Privredni Pregled (YU)
Privredni Vjesnik (YU)
E. L. Prizer, Ed. & Pub. (US)
PRM Science & Technology Agency Ltd. (UK)
Pro Arte-Sociedade de Artes, Letras e Ciencias (BL)
Pro Civitate Christiana (IT)
Pro Ecclesia Foundation (US)
Pro Football Weekly, Inc. (US)
Pro Mundi Vita. Centrum Informationis. Special Notes (BE)
Pro Padova (IT)
Pro Rege Pers (SA)
Pro Se Collective (US)
Pro Veritate (Pty) Ltd. (SA)
Probation Officers' Association of Victoria (AT)
Probe (UK)
Probe (Santa Barbara) (US)
Probe, Inc. (US)
Problemi (IT)
Problemi della Pedagogia (IT)
Procedes et Equipements Electroniques (FR)
Proceedings in Print, Inc. (US)
Proceso Politico (VE)
Processed Foods Exports Promotion Council (II)
Processlabs Private Ltd. (II)
Procrastinators' Club of America (US)
Walter T. Proctor, Ed. & Pub. (US)
Procuradoria das Estudantes Ultramarinos (PO)
Procure des Missions du Levant (FR)
Prodace, S. A. (SP)
Prodei (SP)
Prodotto Alimentare Italiano (IT)
Produce Marketing Association (US)
Producers' Council, Inc. (US)
Producers Guild of America (US)
Producers Publications (Pty) Ltd. (PP)
Production Engineering Research Association (UK)
Production et Gestion (FR)
Production Press (US)
Production Publishing Co. (US)
Productions, Ltd. (US)
Productivity Promotion Council of Australia (AT)
Produktschap voor Siergewassen (NE)
Prodyut Kumar Som (II)
Proefstation de voor Groenten- en Fruitteelt onder Glas (NE)
Prof. Dr. Jan van der Hoeven Foundation for Theoretical Biology (NE)
Professeurs de l'Ancienne Faculte de Medecine d'Alger (FR)
Professional & Scientific Publications (UK)
Professional Association of Trained Nurses of Nigeria (NR)
Professional Books Ltd. (UK)
Professional Breeding Services Inc. (US)
Professional Communications Associates (US)

Professional Corporation of Nursing Assistants of Quebec (CN)
Professional Development Associates (US)
Professional Exchange (US)
Professional Fishermen's Association of Tasmania (AT)
Professional Golfers' Association of America (US)
Professional Grounds Management Society (US)
Professional Information Sources, Inc. (US)
Professional Installer (US)
Professional Institute of the Public Service of Canada (CN)
Professional Insurance Agents (US)
Professional Liability Reporter (US)
Professional Medical Services Co. (US)
Professional Officers' Association (AT)
Professional Photographers of America (US)
Professional Photographers of California, Inc. (US)
Professional Photographers of Canada (CN)
Professional Players Union of Holland (NE)
Professional Press, Inc. (US)
Professional Productivity Associates (US)
Professional Publication Producers (US)
Professional Publications (II)
Professional Publications, Inc. (US)
Professional Publications, Inc. (Atlanta) (US)
Professional Publications, Inc. (Columbus) (US)
Professional Publishing Corp. (US)
Professional Rehabilitation Workers with the Adult Deaf, Inc. (US)
Professional Rodeo Cowboys Association (US)
Professional Staff Congress - City University of New York (US)
Professional Training & Review Academy (PH)
Profile Books Ltd. (UK)
Profiles Publishing Corp. (US)
Profils Poetiques des Pays Latins (FR)
Profit Press, Inc. (US)
Izdatelstvo Profizdat (BU)
Profizdat (UR)
Profsoyuz Rabochikh Ugol'noi Promyshlennosti S.S.S.R. Tsentral'nyi Komitet (UR)
Progetto 80 (IT)
Programa de Desarrollo de la Comunidad (GT)
Editions Programme (FR)
Progres (YU)
Progres Agricole et Viticole (FR)
Progres Medical (FR)
Progresos de Obstetricia y Ginecologia (SP)
Izdatel'stvo Progress (UR)
Progress Books (CN)
Progress Printing & Publishing Co. Ltd. (CN)
Progress Publishing Company, Ltd. (CN)
Progress-Register (US)
Progressive Conservative Association of Alberta (CN)
Progressive Conservative Party of Ontario (CN)
Progressive Farmer Co. (US)
Progressive Grocer Publishing Co. (US)
Progressive, Inc. (US)
Progressive Labor Party (US)
Progressive League (UK)
Progressive Papers Limited (PK)
Progressive Publishing Co. (US)
Progressive Students for Israel (CN)
Progressive Workers Movement (CN)
Progressiven Organisationen (SZ)
Prointer-Ediciones (SP)
Project Concern, Inc. (US)
Project - Guidelines to Equal Opportunity (US)
Project House Foundation, Inc. (US)
Project Innovation (US)
Project Magazine Inc. (US)
Project Management Corp. (US)
Project on Linguistic Analysis (US)
Prol Publishing Co. (US)
Proletarian Path (II)
Promapress (FR)
Promark S.p.A. (IT)
Promenade Magazines, Inc. (US)
Promethee (FR)
Promocao-Da-Familia Editora (BL)
Ediciones de Promocion Cultural, S.A. (SP)
Promocion Popular Cristiana (SP)
Promocion y Ventes S. A. I. C. (AG)
Promociones Turisticas de Panama y el Caribe, S.A. (PN)
Editora Promocoes e Publicidade, Assessoria de Relacoes Publicas Ltda. (BL)
Promodis (FR)
Promotia-Zeitschriftenverlagsges. m.b.H. (AU)
Promotion-Presse-Internationale (P.P.I.) (FR)
Promotor Verlags- und Forderungsgesellschaft mbH (GW)
Promotora de Publicaciones, S.A. (SP)
Promovere (BE)
Proof (US)
Proofreaders Club of New York (US)

Propaganda Editoriale Grafica S.p. A. (IT)
Editora Propaganda S.A. (BL)
Propagation de la Foi (FR)
Propeller Club of the United States (US)
Properties (US)
Property Services Agency (UK)
Prophet Press, Taipei (CH)
Prophetic Witness Movement International (UK)
Proprieta Fondiaria Agricola (IT)
Proprietary Association (US)
Proscenium Press (US)
Proscenium Publications (US)
Proscope (CN)
Prospect (UK)
Prospecta (FR)
Prospective Medicale (FR)
Prospector Research Services, Inc. (US)
Prospectors' Club International (US)
Prospetti (IT)
Prospettive Regionali (IT)
Prost und Meiner-Verlag (GW)
Prostaglandin Information Center (US)
Izdatel'stvo Prosveshchenie (UR)
Prosveta (YU)
Prosveten Rabotnik (YU)
Prosveteno Delo (YU)
Prosvetno-Pedagoski Zavod Zrenjanin (YU)
Prosvjetni Sabor Hrvatske (YU)
Prosvjetno Pedagoski Zavod Mostar (YU)
Protection et Securite du Public (FR)
Protein-Calorie Advisory Group of the United Nations System (UN)
Protestant Episcopal Cathedral Foundation (US)
Protestant Episcopal Church in the U.S.A. (US)
Protestant Truth Society Inc. (UK)
Protestants-Christelijke Artsen-Organisatie in Nederland (NE)
Protestants Christelijke Onderwijsvakorganisatie (NE)
Protestantse Stichting tot Bevordering van het Bibliotheekwezen en de Lektuurvoorlichting in Nederland (NE)
Proteus Press (US)
Protexin Americana S.A. (AG)
Edizioni di Protezione Civile s.r.l. (IT)
Proud-Bailey Co. Ltd. (UK)
Dr. J. R. Prous, Ed. & Pub (SP)
Proust Research Association (US)
Providence Hospital (US)
Province of St. Joseph of the Capuchin Order (US)
Provinces Belge l'Expression Francaise (BE)
Provincia di Genova dei Frati Minori Cappuccini (IT)
Provincia Iblea (IT)
Provincia Occidental Claretianos de Colombia (CK)
Provincia Religiosa dei Frati Minori Conventuali di Puglia (IT)
Provincia Romana dei Frati Predicatori (IT)
Provinciaal Genootschap van Kunsten en Wetenschappen in Noord-Brabant. (NE)
Provincial Association of Catholic Teachers of Quebec (CN)
Provincial Bank of Canada. Economic Research Department (CN)
Provincial Insurance Co. Ltd. (UK)
Provincial Intermediate Teachers (CN)
Provincial Newspapers Association (IE)
Provincial Trade Press Ltd. (UK)
Provinciale Bibliotheek van Limburg (BE)
Provinciale Vereniging Het Limburgse Groene Kruis (NE)
Editions Provinciales (BE)
Provinzialat der Brueder der Christlichen Schulen (AU)
Provinzialinstitut fuer Westfaelische Landes- und Volksforschung (GW)
Provo Radicale (IT)
Provoker (US)
Provveditorato al Porto di Venezia (IT)
Proyecto Hidrometeorologico Centroamericano (HO)
Prudential Financial Corp. of Los Angeles (US)
Prudential Insurance Co. of America (US)
Pruefer-Werbung (GW)
Pruitt- Scott Publications (US)
Pryde Publications (CN)
Przemyslowy Instytut Elektroniki (PL)
Przemyslowy Instytut Maszyn Rolniczych. Branzowy Osrodek Informacji Naukowej, Technicznej i Ekonomicznej (PL)
Przemyslowy Instytut Telekomunikacji (PL)
Psi Chi National Office (US)
Psi Omega Fraternity (US)
Psicologia Contemporanea (IT)
Psionic Medical Society (UK)
Psy-Ed Corp. (US)
Psychiatria Fennica (FI)
Psychiatric Institute Foundation. Center for Group Studies (US)

Psychiatric Nurses Association of Canada (CN)
Psychiatry Association (JO)
Psychiatry Digest (US)
Psychic Magazine, Inc. (US)
Psychic Press Ltd. (UK)
Psychic Society of Athens (GR)
Psychical Research Foundation, Inc. (US)
Psychoanalytic Quarterly, Inc (US)
Psychodiagnostic Test Co. (US)
Psycholinguistic Association of India (II)
Psychologia Society (JA)
Psychological Association of the Philippines (PH)
Psychological Association of Trinidad and Tobago (TR)
Psychological Institute of the Republic of South Africa (SA)
Psychological Record (US)
Psychological Reports (US)
Psychological Society of Ireland (IE)
Verlag fuer Psychologie (GW)
Psychologische Lehr- und Beratungsstelle (SZ)
Psychologist Magazine Ltd. (UK)
Psychologists for Social Action (US)
Psychology (US)
Psychology Society (SA)
Psychometric Society (US)
Psychonomic Society, Inc. (US)
Psychophysikalische Gesellschaft e.V. (P.P.G.) (GW)
Psychosynthesis Institute (US)
Psychotechnisches Institut (AU)
Psywar Society (UK)
Ptujski Tednik (YU)
Edizioni Pubbli Re (IT)
Pubblicista (IT)
Pubblicita e Vendita (IT)
Pubblicita Editoriale Italiana (IT)
Societa Editrice Pubblicitaria (IT)
Pubbliemme (IT)
Pubbliturist (IT)
Publi- Contact (BE)
Publi-Export (FR)
Editions Publi-Guid (FR)
Publi-Inter (FR)
Publi-Lux (LU)
Publi - Representaciones S.A. (MX)
Publi-Ric (FR)
Publi-Service Fandrosoana (MG)
Edition Publi-Team-Elysees (FR)
Publiart S.A. (SP)
Publibanif S.A. (SP)
Public Affairs Council (US)
Public Affairs Information Service, Inc. (US)
Public Affairs Research Council of Louisiana (US)
Public Choice Society (US)
Public Citizen (US)
Public Citizen Platform (US)
Public Citizen's Tax Reform Research Group (US)
Public Education Association Information Service (US)
Public Finance Verlag (GW)
Public Health Inspectors' Association (UG)
Public Instituto de Tisiologia (UY)
Public Interest Briefs (US)
Public Interest Economics Foundation (US)
Public Issues Research Bureau, Inc. (US)
Public Law Education Institute (US)
Public Libraries Board (UG)
Public Library Association (US)
Public Library of Cincinnati and Hamilton County (US)
Public Library of Des Moines (US)
Public Library of Newark (US)
Public Library of Youngstown and Mahoning County (US)
Public Press Ltd. (CN)
Public Relations Aids, Inc. (US)
Public Relations Association of Korea (KO)
Public Relations Board Inc. (US)
Public Relations Institute of South Africa (SA)
Public Relations Office of the Sugar Industry (MF)
Public Relations Plus, Inc. (US)
Public Relations Society of America, Inc. (US)
Public Safety Personnel Research Institute, Inc. (US)
Public Servants Association of South Africa (SA)
Public Service Alliance of Canada (CN)
Public Service Association of South Australia Inc. (AT)
Public Service Commission (CN)
Public Service Magazine, Inc. (US)
Public Service Materials Center (US)
Public Services Laboratory (US)
Public Utilities Reports, Inc (US)
Public Works Journal Corporation (US)
Public Works Research Institute
    see Japan. Public Works Research Institute (JA)
Publica S.A. (SP)
Publicaciones Controladas, S.A. (SP)
Publicaciones Espanolas (SP)

Publicaciones Especializadas Internacionales, S.A. (SP)
Publicaciones Importantes, S. A. (MX)
Publicaciones Internacionales S.A. (SP)
Publicaciones y Promociones Impresas (MX)
Publicaciones y Revistas, S.A. (SP)
Publicacoes Associadas Paulista Ltda (BL)
Editora de Publicacoes Cientificas Ltda (BL)
Publicacoes Executivas Brasileiras Ltda (BL)
Publicacoes Informativas Ltda. (BL)
Editora Publicacoes Technicas Ltda. (BL)
Publican (US)
Publicat (FR)
Publication House, Inc. (US)
Publications d'Art et d'Archeologie (FR)
Publications de la Soudure Autogene (FR)
Publications de la Vie Catholique (FR)
Publications des Cahiers Mode
    see P.C.M. (FR)
Publications du Nord-Ouest (CN)
Publications Enfantines (FR)
Publications Fiduciaires (FR)
Publications for Industry (US)
Publications Image (US)
Publications International Ltd. (US)
Publications Office of the European Communities
    see Office for Official Publications of the European
    Communities (EI)
Publications Periodiques Parisiennes (FR)
Publications Periodiques Specialisees (FR)
Publications Planning (US)
Publications South, Inc. (US)
Publicidad Delta (SP)
Publicidad Nacional (GT)
Publicidad Profesional y Revistas S.A. (MX)
Publicisa (SP)
Publicite B. M. Inc. (CN)
Uitgeversbedrijf "Publiciteit" Schiedam (NE)
Publicity Club of Boston (US)
Publicity Press Ltd. (AT)
Publicity Society of India (II)
Publiclair (FR)
Publicness (FR)
N. V. Publico (NE)
Publiepi (IT)
Publigraf (IT)
Publijudo (FR)
Publimedia Editrice (IT)
Publimondex (BE)
Publindex s.r.l. (IT)
Publinform Publicacoes Informativas Ltda. (BL)
Editions Publiplast (FR)
Publipress S.A. (SZ)
Publiprint s.r.l. (VE)
Publishers Advertising Co. (US)
Publishers Association for Cultural Exchange (JA)
Publishers Development Corp. (US)
Publishers Group (PR)
Publisher's Inc. (US)
Publishers' Information Bureau Inc. (US)
Publishers Printing House, Inc. (US)
Publishers Professional Services (US)
Publishers Service Inc. (US)
Publishing & Distributing Co. Ltd. (UK)
Publishing Associates (US)
Publishing Center for Cultural Resources (US)
Publishing Center, Inc. (US)
Publishing Committee of Industry of Free China
    (CH)
Publishing Dynamics, Inc. (US)
Publishing House of the Bulgarian Academy of
    Sciences (BU)
Publishing Research Associates (JA)
Publishing Sciences Group, Inc. (US)
Publisicula S.N.C. (IT)
Publistyl (FR)
Publitec Publications (LE)
Publitra P.V.B.A. (BE)
Publiturist (IT)
Publitype (IT)
Publivog S.P.R.L. (BE)
Verlag fuer Publizitaet (GW)
Pubsun Corp. (US)
Pueblo Education Association, Inc. (US)
Pueblo of Zuni (US)
Puerta del Sol (DR)
Puerto Rican Solidarity Community (US)
Puerto Rico. Banco Gubernamental de Fomento (PR)
Puerto Rico. Bureau of Labor Statistics. Wage Analysis
    and Occupational Studies Division (PR)
Puerto Rico. Bureau of the Budget (PR)
Puerto Rico. Comision de Derechos Civiles (PR)
Puerto Rico. Departamento de la Vivienda. Urban
    Renewal and Housing Corporation (PR)
Puerto Rico. Department of Agriculture (PR)
Puerto Rico. Department of Education (PR)
Puerto Rico. Department of Health. Cancer Control
    Program (PR)

Puerto Rico. Department of Health. Division of Health
    Facilites (PR)
Puerto Rico. Department of Labor (PR)
Puerto Rico. Department of Labor. Bureau of Labor
    Statistics (PR)
Puerto Rico. Department of State (PR)
Puerto Rico. Department of State. Caribbean Regional
    Library (PR)
Puerto Rico. Department of the Treasury (PR)
Puerto Rico. Division of Demographic Registry and
    Vital Statistics (PR)
Puerto Rico. Planning Board. Economic Indices
    Section (PR)
Puerto Rico. Planning Board. Statistics Coordination
    Section (PR)
Puerto Rico. Ports Authority. Office of Economic
    Research (PR)
Puerto Rico Living (PR)
Fred C. Pugarelli, Ed. & Pub. (US)
Puget Sound Maritime Historical Society (US)
Puhelinlaitosten Liitto R.Y. (FI)
Pulgyo Munhwa (KO)
Pullen Walker Publishing Co. (US)
Pullman Standard (US)
Pulp (US)
Pulp and Paper Research Institute of Canada (CN)
Pulp Era Press (US)
Pulp Press (CN)
Pulsar, S.A. (SP)
Pulse of Youth (II)
Punch (Nigeria) Ltd. (NR)
Punch Publications Ltd. (UK)
Pungolo del Sud (IT)
Pungolo Verde (IT)
Punjab
    see also Haryana (II)
Punjab. Bureau of Education (PK)
Punjab. Department of Agriculture (PK)
Punjab. Economic and Statistical Organisation (II)
Punjab Agricultural University (II)
Punjab Law Reporter (II)
Punjab Medical Journal (II)
Punjab National Bank, Ltd. (II)
Punjab Pharmacists' Federation; All India Medical
    Practitioners' Association; All India Homoepathic
    League (II)
Punjab Punch (PK)
Punjab State Cooperative Fruit Development
    Federation Ltd (II)
Punjab State Industrial Development Corporation (II)
Punjab University
    see University of the Punjab (PK)
    see Panjab University (II)
Punjabi Sahitya (UK)
Punjabi University (II)
Punjabi University. Department of Linguistics (II)
Punjabi University. Department of Religious Studies
    (II)
Punk Publications, Inc. (US)
Punto de Contacto-Point of Contact, Inc. (US)
Punto Omega (AG)
Puppeteers of America (US)
Purabi Publishers (II)
Purazuma Kenkyusho
    see Nagoya University. Institute of Plasma Physics
    (JA)
Purchasing Agents Association of Rochester (US)
Purchasing and Management Personnel (US)
Purchasing Management Association (US)
Purchasing Management Association of Alabama
    (US)
Purchasing Management Association of Arizona (US)
Purchasing Management Association of Boston, Inc.
    (US)
Purchasing Management Association of Buffalo, Inc.
    (US)
Purchasing Management Association of Canada.
    British Columbia District (CN)
Purchasing Management Association of Carolinas-
    Virginia, Inc. (US)
Purchasing Management Association of Chicago (US)
Purchasing Management Association of Cincinnati,
    Inc. (US)
Purchasing Management Association of Cleveland, Inc.
    (US)
Purchasing Management Association of Florida, Inc.
    (US)
Purchasing Management Association of Indianapolis,
    Inc. (US)
Purchasing Management Association of Kansas City
    (US)
Purchasing Management Association of Louisville
    (US)
Purchasing Management Association of Northern
    California, Inc. (US)
Purchasing Management Association of Oregon (US)
Purchasing Management Association of Philadelphia,
    Inc. (US)

Purchasing Management Association of Syracuse and
    Central New York (US)
Purchasing Management Association of Tulsa (US)
Purchasing Management Association of Washington,
    Inc. (US)
Purchasing Management Associations of New York
    and New Jersey (US)
Purchasing Management Associations of Texas,
    Louisiana and New Mexico (US)
Purdue Alumni Association (US)
Purdue Musical Organizations (US)
Purdue Opinion Panel (US)
Purdue University. Agricultural Experiment Station
    (US)
Purdue University. Department of Agricultural
    Economics (US)
Purdue University. Dept. of English (US)
Purdue University Libraries and Audio Visual Center
    (US)
Purdue University. Materials Research Business Office
    (US)
Purdue University. Office of Manpower Studies (US)
Purdue University. School of Civil Engineering (US)
Purdue University. School of Electrical Engineering
    (US)
Purdue University. School of Pharmacy (US)
Purdue University. Undergraduates of the University
    (US)
Pure Life Society (MY)
Purnell & Sons Ltd. (UK)
Purnell Books (UK)
Pusat Dokumentasi Ilmiah Nasional
    see National Scientific Documentation Centre (IO)
Pusat Penelitian Botani
    see Treub Laboratory (IO)
Pusat Pengajian Pembangunan Malaysia
    see Malaysian Centre for Development Studies
    (MY)
Pushikorogia-kai
    see Psychologia Society (JA)
Universitaetsverlag Anton Pustet (AU)
Verlag Friedrich Pustet (GW)
Put Money in the Bank Refunders Bulletin (US)
Putman Publishing Co. (US)
Putman Publishing Company (US)
G. P. Putnam's Sons (US)
Puumiesten Liitto (FI)
Puzz (IT)
Pym Editeur (FR)
Pyramid Books (US)
Pyramid Publications, Inc. (US)
Pyrethrum Bureau (KE)
Pyro Press Publications (US)
Q. C. Correspondence Circle Ltd. (UK)
Q I M P Quarterly (PK)
Qantas Airways Ltd. (AT)
Qaumi Ekta Trust (II)
Quad Publications (US)
Quaderni di Critica (IT)
Quaderni di Dibattito Politico (IT)
Quaderni Piacentini (IT)
Quadriga-Drukwerken (NE)
Quaid-i-Azam University (PK)
Quaid-i-Azam University. Department of Pakistan
    Studies (PK)
Quaid-i-Azam University. International Forum (PK)
Quaid-i-Azam University Press (PK)
Quaintance & Co. (Publishers) Ltd. (UK)
Quaker Fellowship of the Arts (UK)
Quaker Oats. Corporate Affairs Department (US)
Quaker Theological Discussion Group (US)
Quaker Yeomen (US)
Qualified Remodeler, Inc. (US)
Quantum Science Corp. (US)
Quapaw Quarter Association (US)
Quarry (CN)
Quarry (SA)
Quarry Managers' Journal Ltd. (UK)
Quartel-General de Intendencia do Exercito (BL)
Quarter Century Wireless Association, Inc. (US)
Quarter Racing Publishers, Inc. (US)
Quarter Racing World, Inc. (US)
Quarterbacks, Delta Canada (CN)
Quarterly Review of Literature (US)
Quartet (US)
Quarto Potere (IT)
Quasi (IT)
Quatre Verites (FR)
J. Quatreboeufs (FR)
Quebec (Province) Bureau of Statistics (CN)
Quebec (Province) Bureau of Statistics. Division des
    Peches (CN)
Quebec (Province) Bureau of Statistics. Service du
    Travail et de la Main d'Oeuvre (CN)
Quebec (Province) Centrale des Bibliotheques (CN)
Quebec (Province). Commission des Services
    Juridiques (CN)
Quebec (Province) Department of Agriculture (CN)

Quebec (Province) Department of Intergovernmental Affairs  (CN)
Quebec (Province) Department of Natural Resources  (CN)
Quebec (Province) Department of Natural Resources. Service de l'Hydrometrie  (CN)
Quebec (Province) Department of Tourism, Fish and Game  (CN)
Quebec (Province) Health Insurance Board  (CN)
Quebec (Province) Ministere de l'Industrie et du Commerce  (CN)
Quebec (Province) Ministere des Affaires Culturelles  (CN)
Quebec (Province) Ministere des Communications  (CN)
Quebec (Province) Ministere des Consommateurs, Cooperatives et Institutions Financieres  (CN)
Quebec (Province) Ministere des Richesses Naturelles  (CN)
Quebec (Province) Ministere des Terres et Forets  (CN)
Quebec (Province) Ministere des Terres et Forets. Conseil Consultatif des Reserves Ecologiques  (CN)
Quebec (Province) Ministere du Travail et de la Main d'Oeuvre  (CN)
Quebec (Province) National Assembly  (CN)
Quebec (Province) National Assembly. Parliamentary Documents Service  (CN)
Quebec (Province) Office de la Langue Francaise  (CN)
Quebec (Province) Office de la Protection du Consommateur  (CN)
Quebec (Province) Pension Board  (CN)
Quebec (Province) Service de Consultation et Assistance en Toxicomanies  (CN)
Quebec (Province) Service de l'Hydrometrie  (CN)
Quebec Automobile Club  (CN)
Quebec Camping Association  (CN)
Quebec Federation of Home and School Associations  (CN)
Quebec Forest Industries Association  (CN)
Quebec Industrial Development Corporation  (CN)
Quebec Society for the Protection of Plants  (CN)
Queen Alexandra Solarium for Crippled Children Society  (CN)
Queen Anne Press Ltd.  (UK)
Queen Charlotte Islands Musuem Society  (CN)
Queen of All Hearts  (US)
Queen Victoria Museum  (AT)
Queens Borough Public Library  (US)
Queens Botanical Garden Society Inc  (US)
Queens Chamber of Commerce  (US)
Queens College
    see under City University of New York  (US)
Queens College Press  (US)
Queens Council on the Arts. Literary Arts Division  (US)
Queens County Bar Association  (US)
Queen's Nursing Institute  (UK)
Queens Own Highlanders  (UK)
Queen's Printer, Alberta  (CN)
Queen's Printer, Canada  (CN)
Queen's Printer, Newfoundland  (CN)
Queen's Printer, Prince Edward Island  (CN)
Queen's Printer, Saskatchewan  (CN)
Queen's University  (CN)
Queen's University. Department of Electrical Engineering  (CN)
Queen's University. Department of Mathematics  (CN)
Queen's University. Engineering Society  (CN)
Queen's University. Industrial Relations Centre  (CN)
Queen's University. Institute for Economic Research  (CN)
Queen's University. Institute of Local Government  (CN)
Queen's University Law School  (CN)
Queen's University. Law Students Society  (CN)
Queens University Medical Library  (UK)
Queen's University of Belfast  (UK)
Queensland. Air Pollution Council  (AT)
Queensland. Bureau of Sugar Experiment Stations  (AT)
Queensland. Department of Commercial and Industrial Development  (AT)
Queensland. Department of Education  (AT)
Queensland. Department of Education. Information and Publications Branch  (AT)
Queensland. Department of Education. Primary Curriculum Committee  (AT)
Queensland. Department of Education. Research and Curriculum Branch  (AT)
Queensland. Department of Forestry  (AT)
Queensland. Department of Health  (AT)
Queensland. Department of Mines  (AT)
Queensland. Department of Primary Industries  (AT)
Queensland. Department of Primary Industries. Fisheries Branch  (AT)

Queensland. Department of Primary Industries. Marketing Services Branch  (AT)
Queensland. Government Printer  (AT)
Queensland. Land Administration Commission  (AT)
Queensland. Main Roads Department  (AT)
Queensland. State Government Insurance Office  (AT)
Queensland Automobile Chamber of Commerce Inc.  (AT)
Queensland Chamber of Manufactures  (AT)
Queensland Conservation Council  (AT)
Queensland Council of State School Organisations  (AT)
Queensland Country Life Pty. Ltd.  (AT)
Queensland Country Women's Association  (AT)
Queensland Dairymen's Organization  (AT)
Queensland Historical Review  (AT)
Queensland History Teachers Association  (AT)
Queensland Hotels Association  (AT)
Queensland Institute for Educational Research  (AT)
Queensland Master Builders Association  (AT)
Queensland Museum  (AT)
Queensland Naturalists' Club  (AT)
Queensland Newspapers Pty. Ltd.  (AT)
Queensland Police Union of Employees  (AT)
Queensland Primary Producers' Co-Operative Association  (AT)
Queensland Professional Officers Association  (AT)
Queensland Retail Tobacco Traders' Association  (AT)
Queensland Retail Traders' Association  (AT)
Queensland Shopkeepers' Association  (AT)
Queensland Society of Sugar Cane Technologists  (AT)
Queensland Teachers Union  (AT)
Queensland Writers' Workshop  (AT)
Quekett Microscopical Club  (UK)
Quell Verlag  (GW)
Quelle und Meyer  (GW)
Quercy Recherche  (FR)
Editrice Queriniana  (IT)
Quest  (CN)
Quest (Washington, D.C.)  (US)
Quest Productions  (US)
Quest Publication  (US)
Quest Publishing  (US)
Quest Publishing Co.  (US)
Quest Research Publications Ltd.  (UK)
Questitalia  (IT)
Quick Books  (US)
Don Quick Publications  (CN)
Quickenings in Trillum Land  (US)
Quiet Birdmen  (US)
Quigley Publishing Co.  (US)
Carlos Quijano, Ed. & Pub.  (UY)
Quill & Scroll Society  (US)
Quill Publications  (SA)
Quiltmakers Time  (US)
Quincy College  (US)
Quinlan Publishing Co. Inc.  (US)
Quinn Publications, Inc. (Compton)  (US)
Quinn Publications, Inc. (Ft. Worth)  (US)
Quintaparete  (IT)
Editorial Dante Quintero S. A.  (AG)
Buch- und Zeitschriften-Verlag die Quintessenz W. Haase  (GW)
Quirindi & District Historical Society  (AT)
Editorial Quiris S.A.  (SP)
Quirk's Reviews  (US)
Quiz-Set Publishing Co.  (US)
Editions Quo Vadis  (FR)
M. Sharif Qurshi, Ed. & Pub.  (PK)
R.A.F. Provost Branch  (UK)
R.A.I.P.  (FR)
R A Productions, Inc.  (US)
R. & B Enterprises  (US)
R & D Press  (US)
R. & W. Management Co. Inc.  (US)
R C A
    see Radio Corporation of America  (US)
R.C.A. North Ryde Pty. Ltd.  (AT)
R C C Press  (UK)
R C G Publications Ltd.  (UK)
R-C Modeler Corp.  (US)
R.C.P. Edition  (FR)
R C P Publications, Inc.  (US)
R C Publications, Inc.  (US)
R. C. Publications, Inc. (New York)  (US)
R D Communications  (US)
R E C O E X  (SP)
R F D  (US)
R. F. W. W. Publications Ltd.  (UK)
R G H Publishing Corp.  (US)
R.G. Lewis & Co. Ltd.  (CN)
R. H. M Associates Inc.  (US)
R I A S - Funkuniversitaet  (GW)
R I B A Publications Ltd.  (UK)
Editora R J Ltda  (BL)

R L D Group, Inc.  (US)
R. M. Bucke Memorial Society  (CN)
R N Publications  (US)
R O C  (FR)
R P C Publications  (US)
R P M Music Publications Ltd.  (CN)
R S A World  (SA)
R.S.H. Publications  (US)
R S H Publications Worldwide  (US)
R. S. P. C. A.  (UK)
R S T Corp.  (US)
R S V P  (UK)
R T S Music Gazette  (US)
R T T Y Journal  (US)
R.V.K. Publishing Co  (US)
R. W. Beck and Associates  (US)
R X Golf and Travel, Inc.  (US)
Verlag Dr. Josef Raabe  (GW)
Raabe-Gesellschaft  (GW)
Raad vir Geesteswetenskaplike Navorsing
    see Human Sciences Research Council  (SA)
Rabbi Isaac Elchanan Theological Seminary  (US)
Rabbinical Alliance of America  (US)
Rabbinical Assembly  (US)
Rabbinical Council of America  (US)
Rabindra Bharati University  (II)
Race Relations Board  (UK)
Raceform Ltd.  (UK)
Racehorse Ltd.  (UK)
Racing Car News Pty. Ltd.  (AT)
Racing Pictorial Magazine  (US)
Racing Pigeon Publishing Co. Ltd  (UK)
Racquet and Paddle Publications, Inc.  (US)
Rada Prasy Technicznej  (PL)
Radakrishna Indraprastha Estate  (II)
Radcap Inc.  (US)
Radcliffe College. Alumnae Association  (US)
Radha Soami Satsang Beas  (SA)
Radiation Effects Research Foundation  (JA)
Radiation Shielding Information Center  (US)
Radical America  (US)
Radical de Gauche  (FR)
Radical-Democratic Party
    see Freisinnig-Demokratische Partei der Schweiz  (SZ)
Radical Education  (UK)
Radical Education Project  (US)
Radical Jewish Union  (US)
Radical Science Journal  (UK)
Radical Therapist, Inc.  (US)
Radicals Against Poverty  (US)
Peter Radielovic, Ed. & Pub.  (US)
Radiesthesie Magazine  (FR)
Radikale Venstre  (DK)
Radio Amateur Callbook, Inc.  (US)
Radio and Electronic Officers Union  (UK)
Radio and Television Weekly  (US)
Radio Chassis Television  (AG)
Radio Club of America, Inc.  (US)
Radio Clube de Mozambique  (MZ)
Radio Corporation of America Broadcast Systems  (US)
Radio Corporation of America. Corporate Engineering Services  (US)
Radio Corporation of America Laboratories  (US)
Radio Corporation of America, Sydney  (AT)
Radio Corporation of America. Technical Services Training  (US)
Radio, Electricity & Furniture Association  (SA)
Radio-Holland B. V.  (NE)
Radio Manual  (UY)
Radio Nederland Wereldomroep  (NE)
Radio Research Laboratories
    see Japan. Ministry of Posts and Telecommunications. Radio Research Laboratories  (JA)
Radio Society of Great Britain  (UK)
Radio Society of Ontario, Inc.  (CN)
Radio Society of Rhodesia  (RH)
Radio Technical Commission for Aeronautics  (US)
Radio Telefis Eireann  (IE)
Radio Television News Directors Association  (US)
Radio-Transistronic Constructor  (II)
Radiobranchens Informationstjeneste  (DK)
Radioliikkeiden Liitto  (FI)
Radiological Society of North America, Inc.  (US)
Radionic Association  (UK)
Radiotelegrafistforenigen  (DK)
Radiotelevizija Zagreb  (YU)
Radiotronics Publishers  (HK)
Radiovy Konstrukter  (CS)
Uitgeverij C. E. Radius en P. Gruppelaar  (NE)
Radius Group Inc.  (US)
Radius-Verlag GmbH  (GW)
Radix (Berkeley)  (US)
Radnicko Sveuciliste "Mosa Pijade"  (YU)
Radnorshire Society  (UK)
Izdatel'stvo Radyanska Ukraina  (UR)

Izdatel'stvo Radyanskii Pismennik   (UR)
Raeber AG   (SZ)
Rafinerija Nafte, Sisak   (YU)
Rag Collective   (US)
Lawrence Ragan Communications, Inc.   (US)
Raggi Verlag   (SZ)
P. Raghavan, Ed. & Pub.   (II)
Ragioni Critiche   (IT)
Maria Ragno   (IT)
Rags   (US)
Ragtime Society   (CN)
A. Ragunathan   (MY)
Rahla   (FR)
Emil Rahm, Ed. & Pub.   (SZ)
RAI-Radiotelevisione Italiana   (IT)
Norman W. Raies   (US)
Raifu Saiensu
    see Life Science Co., Ltd.   (JA)
Rail-Europe   (US)
Rail Travel News   (US)
Railroad Enthusiasts, New York Division, Inc.   (US)
Railroad Research Information Service   (US)
Railroad Station Historical Society   (US)
Railroad Yardmasters of America   (US)
Railton Publications Ltd.   (CN)
Railway and Canal Historical Society   (UK)
Railway and Locomotive Historical Society   (US)
Railway Development Association   (UK)
Railway Digest International   (UK)
Railway Enthusiasts Society, Inc.   (NZ)
Railway Equipment and Publication Co.   (US)
Railway Fuel and Operating Officers Association
    (US)
Railway Industry Association of Great Britain   (UK)
Railway Invigoration Society   (UK)
Railway Preservation Society of Ireland   (UK)
Railway Research Index Division   (NE)
Railway Technical Research Institute
    see under Japanese National Railways   (JA)
Railway Tie Association   (US)
Railways Institute Council   (AT)
Rain Umbrella, Inc.   (US)
Rainbow Book Co. Educational Publishers   (II)
Rainbow Press   (US)
Raincoast Historical Society   (CN)
Rainer Foundation   (UK)
Rainforth Foundation   (US)
Raith Verlag   (GW)
Raivaaja Publishing Co.   (US)
Baldev Raj, Ed. & Pub.   (II)
Raja Rammohan Sarani   (II)
S. Raja   (II)
Rajasthan. Board of Secondary Education   (II)
Rajasthan. Directorate of Economics and Statistics
    (II)
Rajasthan. Directorate of Medical, Health, and Family
    Planning Services   (II)
Rajasthan. Forest Department   (II)
Rajasthan. State Institute of Education   (II)
Rajasthan Agricultural Research Workers Association
    (II)
Rajasthan Ayurvedic Research Laboratories   (II)
Rajasthan Library Association   (II)
Rajasthan State Warehousing Corporation   (II)
Rajasthan University Library   (II)
Rajesh Publications   (II)
Rajneesh Publications   (II)
Rajo Publications, Inc.   (US)
Rajshahi University
    see University of Rajshahi   (BG)
Rakennusmestarien Keskusliitto   (FI)
Kustannus Oy Rakennustekniikka   (FI)
Rakentajain Tiedotus r.y.   (FI)
Rakuno Gakuen Daigaku
    see College of Dairy Agriculture   (JA)
Carlos M. Rama   (UY)
K. N. Ramachandran, Ed. & Pub.   (II)
C. Ramakrishna, Ed. & Pub.   (II)
Ramakrishna Mission Institute of Culture   (II)
Ramakrishna Order   (II)
Editorial Ramallo   (PR)
Raman Publications   (II)
Ramanath Publications Private Ltd.   (II)
Ramblers' Association   (UK)
Ramco Publishing Co   (US)
Ramcon, Inc.   (US)
Rami Press   (II)
Ruben A. Ramirez Mitchell, Ed. & Pub.   (AG)
Ramo Editoriale degli Agricoltori   (IT)
Editions de la Rampe   (SZ)
Rampe (Linz)   (AU)
Ramsay Society of Chemical Engineers   (UK)
Ramsay, Son & Parker (Pty) Ltd.   (SA)
Ramsay, Ware Publishing Pty. Ltd.   (AT)
Ran Tan Plan   (BE)
Ranchi University   (II)
Ranchi University. Department of Anthropology   (II)
Ranchi University. Department of History   (II)

Ranchi University. Department of Mathematics   (II)
Ranchi University. Department of Political Science
    (II)
Rancho Santa Ana Botanic Garden   (US)
Rand Afrikaans University   (SA)
Rand Corporation   (US)
Rand McNally & Co.   (US)
Randall Publishing Co.   (US)
Randi Printers   (II)
Randolph-Macon College   (US)
Random House   (US)
Random Lengths Publications, Inc.   (US)
Randse Afrikaanse Universiteit
    see Rand Afrikaans University   (SA)
Rangefinder Publishing Co.   (US)
David Rangel Medina, Ed. & Pub.   (MX)
Rani Suhasini Roy   (II)
Rank and File Teachers Group   (UK)
Rank Strand Electric   (UK)
Rank Xerox-U.K.   (UK)
Rankin County News   (US)
Dr. Herta Ranner   (AU)
C. M. Rao, Ed. & Pub.   (II)
Nageswara Rao Estates Private Ltd.   (II)
T. S. K. Rao, Ed. & Pub.   (II)
T.S.N. Rao, Ed. & Pub.   (II)
Rapeseed Association of Canada   (CN)
William E. Rapfogel, Ed. & Pub.   (US)
Rapid, Foreign Trade Publicity Corporation   (CS)
Rapistan, Inc.   (US)
Rapport Publishing Co., Inc.   (US)
Raptakos, Brett & Co., Ltd   (II)
Rare-Earth Information Center   (US)
Rare Journeys, Inc.   (US)
Rasi Palam   (II)
Rassegna Alpina   (IT)
Rassegna dei Lavori Pubblici   (IT)
Rassegna di Cultura e Vita Scolastica   (IT)
Rassegna di Diritto Cinematografico, Teatrale e della
    Radiotelevisione   (IT)
Rassegna di Diritto e Technica dell' Alimentazione
    (IT)
Rassegna di Diritto e Tecnica Doganale e delle
    Imposte di Fabbricazione   (IT)
Rassegna di Politica e di Storia   (IT)
Rassegna di Studi Psichiatrici   (IT)
Rassegna Europea   (IT)
Rassegna Giuridica Ed Economica sui Danni di
    Guerra   (IT)
Rassegna Grafica Editrice   (IT)
Rassegna Internazionale di Logica   (IT)
Rassegna Melodrammatica   (IT)
Rassegna Mensile della Imposte Dirette   (IT)
Rassegna Modi di Abitare Oggi   (IT)
Rassemblement pour le Civisme, le Dialogue et le
    Renouveau   (FR)
Oy Rastor AB   (FI)
Rat fuer Formgebung   (GW)
Ratcliffe College   (UK)
Rath en Doodeheefver N. V.   (NE)
Rating and Valuation Association   (UK)
Rating Publishers Ltd.   (UK)
Rational Transportation   (US)
Rationalisierungskuratorium der Deutschen Wirtschaft
    (GW)
Rationalisointiliitto   (FI)
Rationalist Association, Inc.   (US)
Rationalist Association of Australia Ltd.   (AT)
Rationalist Association of N.S.W.   (AT)
Rationalist Press Association   (UK)
Rationalist Society of Australia Ltd.   (AT)
Ratna Dhar Jha   (II)
Ratna Pustak Bhandar   (NP)
Raunchy Rock Publishing   (US)
Rautatievirkamiesliitto   (FI)
Verlag Gerhard Rautenberg   (GW)
Ravan Press (Pty.) Ltd.   (SA)
Raven Press   (US)
Ravenhill Publishing Co. Ltd.   (UK)
Ravenswood Post   (US)
Ravenswood Publications. Ltd.   (UK)
Ravenswood Publishing Co   (US)
Ravikrupa Trust   (II)
Oy Ravintolalehti   (FI)
Allen Raymond, Inc.   (US)
Raymond International Inc.   (US)
Raymond Lee Organization, Inc.   (US)
Rayon Publishing Corp.   (US)
Raytheon Co.   (US)
La Raza Associates   (US)
Razgledi   (YU)
Editorial Razon y Fe S.A.   (SP)
RDP (Data Services) Ltd.   (UK)
Libreria L. de Re   (IT)
Read Hudson Organization Ltd.   (UK)
Reader   (US)
Reader's Club of Canada Ltd.   (CN)
Reader's Digest AB

    see Valitut Palat   (FI)
Reader's Digest AB   (SW)
Reader's Digest Association Far East Ltd.   (HK)
Readers Digest Association, Inc.   (US)
Reader's Digest Association Ltd.   (SA)
Reader's Digest Association Ltd.   (UK)
Reader's Digest Association Private Ltd.   (II)
Reader's Digest Association Pty. Ltd.   (AT)
Reader's Digest Chile Limitada   (CL)
Reader's Digest Magazines Ltd.   (CN)
Uitgeversmaatschappij The Reader's Digest N.V.
    (NE)
Reader's Digest of Japan, Ltd.   (JA)
Reader's Digest S.A.   (BE)
Readex Microprint Corp.   (US)
Reading Reform Foundation   (US)
Reading University. Graduate School of Contemporary
    European Studies   (UK)
Real Academia de Ciencias Exactas, Fisicas y
    Naturales   (SP)
Real Academia de Cordoba de Ciencias, Bellas Letras
    y Nobles Artes   (SP)
Real Academia de Farmacia   (SP)
Real Academia de la Historia   (SP)
Real Academia Espanola   (SP)
Real Academia Nacional de Medicina   (SP)
Real Aero Club de Espana   (SP)
Real Conservatorio Superior de Musica   (SP)
Real Escuela Oficial y Superior de Avicultura   (SP)
Real Estate Agents & Valuers Society   (AT)
Real Estate and Stock Institute of Victoria   (AT)
Real Estate Board of Greater Vancouver   (CN)
Real Estate Forum, Inc.   (US)
Real Estate Institute of New South Wales   (AT)
Real Estate Institute of Queensland   (AT)
Real Estate News Inc.   (US)
Real Estate Success Secrets   (US)
Real Monasterio del Escorial   (SP)
Real Property Inventory of Metropolitan Cleveland
    (US)
Real Resources Group   (US)
Real Sociedad Arquelogica Tarraconense   (SP)
Real Sociedad Espanola de Fisica y Quimica   (SP)
Real Sociedad Espanola de Historia Natural   (SP)
Real Sociedad Vascongada de los Amigos del Pais
    (SP)
Real World   (US)
Realist   (US)
Realites 5-6   (FR)
Realities Library   (US)
Realities Series   (US)
Reality   (SA)
Reality Evangelism   (US)
Reason Enterprises   (US)
Rebirth, Inc.   (US)
Reblooming Iris Reporter   (US)
Rec Naroda   (YU)
Recherche et Architecture   (FR)
Recherche et Diffusion Economique   (BE)
Verlagsgesellschaft Recht und Wirtschaft mbH   (GW)
Deutsche Rechtsprechung, Verlags-Gesellschaft mbH
    und Co. KG   (GW)
Rechtsverlag GmbH   (GW)
Recien Nacido   (SP)
Recife, Brazil. Secretaria de Assuntos Juridicos   (BL)
Reclame Technische Uitgevers Maatschappij NZ
    (NE)
Record Collector   (UK)
Record Handbook   (US)
Record Mart   (UK)
Record Publishing Co.   (US)
Record Publishing Co. (Dallas)   (US)
Record Publishing, Inc.   (US)
Record Research   (US)
Record Stockman Inc.   (US)
Record World Publishing Co. Inc.   (US)
Recorded Sound Research   (US)
Recorder Group Publications, Inc.   (US)
Recorder Press Ltd.   (UK)
Recorder Review   (US)
Recording and Broadcasting Publications   (US)
Recording Engineer-Producer   (US)
Recording for the Blind   (US)
Recordkeeper Tax Publications, Inc.   (US)
Recovers and Growers of Australia   (AT)
Recreation Consultants   (US)
Recreational Vehicle Dealers of America   (US)
Recuperation   (FR)
Red Angus Association of America   (US)
Red Candle Press   (UK)
Red Cloud Indian School, Inc.   (US)
Red Comb Co-Operative   (AT)
Red Deer College. Learning Resources Centre   (CN)
Red Dust Inc.   (US)
Red Hill Press   (US)
Red House   (UK)
Red Maple Publishing Co.   (CN)
Red Pen Publications   (AT)

Red Poll Cattle Club of America (US)
Red River Valley Historical Association (US)
Red Weather (US)
Redactor-Verlag GmbH (GW)
Redbook Publishing Co. (US)
Redbridge & Waltham Forest Area Health Authority.
  East Roding Health District (UK)
Editorial Reddis S.A. (SP)
Redeemer's Voice (CN)
Redemptorist Fathers (NE)
Redemptorist Fathers (US)
Redemptorist Fathers of New York (US)
Redemptorist Fathers. Ste-Anne de Beaupre Province
  (CN)
Redemptorist Publications (UK)
Redemptorist Publications (IE)
Rederiforeningen for Mindre Skibe (DK)
Redgrave Information Resources (US)
Redgrave Publishing Co. (US)
Reds Alert (US)
Redstockings (DK)
Redwood Empire Dental News (US)
A. H. & A. W. Reed (AT)
A.H. & A.W. Reed (NZ)
Stanley Foster Reed, Ed. & Pub. (US)
Thomas Reed, Ed. & Pub. (US)
William Reed Ltd. (UK)
Reed Printing and Publishing Co. (US)
Thomas Reed Publications Ltd. (UK)
Reeducation (FR)
Bjarne H. Reenskaug A-S (NO)
Arbeiterkampf-Verlag J. Reents (GW)
Reese Publishers (US)
Reese Publishing Co. Inc. (US)
Referees' Association (UK)
Reference & Index Services (US)
Refik Saydam Merkez Hifzissihha Enstituso (TU)
B. V. Uitgeversmaatschappij Reflex (NE)
Reform Synagogues of Great Britain (UK)
Reforme (FR)
Reformed Baptist Movement (UK)
Reformed Church in America (US)
Reformed Church in South Africa (SA)
Reformed Ecumenical Synod (US)
Reformed Presbyterian Fellowship in the Great
  Congregation (Ps.40,10) (NE)
Reformed Theological Review (AT)
Reformverband Oesterreichischer Hausbesitzer (AU)
Refractories Association of Great Britain (UK)
Refractory (AT)
Refrigeration Press, Ltd. (UK)
Regency International Publications Ltd. (UK)
Regency Press (UK)
Verlag Regensberg (GW)
Verlag Regensburger Bistumsblatt (GW)
Regie de l' Assurance-Maladie du Quebec (CN)
Regie Publicite Industrielle (FR)
Regiment Publications (US)
Region (SP)
Region Cynegetique du Sud-Ouest (FR)
Regional & Technical Publications (IE)
Regional Center for Demographic Training and
  Research in Latin America
    see United Nations. Centro Latinoamericano de
    Demografia (UN)
Regional Centre for Education in Science and
  Mathematics (MY)
Regional Clearinghouse Service for Population
  Education (TH)
Regional Council for Education (KE)
Regional Cultural Institute (IR)
Regional Educational Building Institute of Africa (SJ)
Regional Engineering College
    see Jawaharlal Nehru Technological University.
    Regional Engineering College (II)
Regional Institute of Social Welfare Research (US)
Regional Plan Association, Inc. (US)
Regional Postgraduate Institute for Medicine and
  Dentistry, Newcastle-Upon-Tyne (UK)
Regional Science Association (US)
Regional Science Association, India (II)
Regional Science Research Institute (US)
Regional Studies Association (US)
Regional Training Directors Association (US)
Regione Calabrese (IT)
Regione e Potere Locale (IT)
Regione Toscana (IT)
Registered Clubs Association of Australia (AT)
Registered Nurses Association of British Columbia
  (CN)
Registered Nurses Association of Nova Scotia (CN)
Registered Nurses Association of Ontario (CN)
Regmi Research (Pvt) Ltd. (NP)
Regular Baptist Press (US)
Regular Common Carrier Conference (US)
Rehabilitation Industries Corporation Ltd. (II)
Rehabilitation Institute of Oregon (US)
Rehabilitation International (US)

Rehabilitation International USA (US)
Rehabilitation Psychology (US)
Rehabilitations-Verlag Gmbh (GW)
Reich Verlag AG (SZ)
Dr. Ludwig Reichert Verlag (GW)
Reichsverband Oesterreichischer Kleintierzuechter
  (AU)
D. Reidel Publishing Co. (NE)
Reilly-Lake Shore Graphics (US)
Reilly Publishing Co. (US)
A. Reiman (NE)
Dietrich Reimer Buchhandlung (GW)
Reinecke-Verlag GmbH (GW)
Reinhardt-Keymer Publishing Co., Inc. (US)
Ernst Reinhardt Verlag (GW)
Friedrich Reinhardt Verlag (SZ)
Reinhold Publishing Co., Inc. (US)
Reisbureau de Magneet N.V. (NE)
Reise Verlag (GW)
Verlag Franz Reisinger (AU)
J. Reisinger, Ed. & Pub. (US)
Otto F. Reiss Co. (US)
C. A. Reitzels Forlag (DK)
Relaciones Publicas (SP)
Relations Exterieures et Diffusion (FR)
Relations Latines (IT)
Relazioni (IT)
Relazioni Pubbliche Informazioni s.r.l. (IT)
Reldt Pty. Ltd. (AT)
Release News (UK)
Release the World for Christ Foundation (US)
Releim Publishing Corp. (US)
Relgocrest Ltd. (UK)
Relief for Africans in Need in the Sahel (US)
Religioese Bildungsarbeit Stuttgart GmbH (GW)
Religion and Society Inc. (US)
Religion Newswriters Association (US)
Religionsgemeinschaft Deutsche Unitarier e.V. (GW)
Religious & Theological Abstracts Inc. (US)
Religious Book Review Press, Inc. (US)
Religious Education Association (US)
Religious Liberty Publishing Association (US)
Religious Publishing Co. (US)
Religious Research Association (US)
Relim Publishing Company, Inc. (US)
Relis Namurwes A.S.B.L. (BE)
Remember When (US)
Remington Review, Inc. (US)
Remonstrantse Gemeente Groningen (NE)
Renacimiento, Inc. (US)
Renaissance du Livre S.A. (BE)
Renaissance House (US)
Renaissance Society of America (US)
Editions Rencontre Orient Occident (SZ)
Editions Rencontre S.A. (SZ)
Rencontres Sous le Signe de la Langue Francaise
  (FR)
Rendez-Vous (CN)
Rendiconti (IT)
Renfro Valley Press (US)
Klaus Renner Verlag (GW)
Editions le Renouveau Inc. (CN)
Renown Publications Inc. (US)
C. V. Rensburg Publications (SA)
Rensselaer Polytechnic Institute (US)
Rensselaer Polytechnic Institute. Center for Urban and
  Environmental Studies (US)
Rensselaerville Historical Society (US)
Reorganized Church of Jesus Christ of Latter Day
  Saints (US)
Reparation Society of the Immaculate Heart of Mary,
  Inc. (US)
Repartee (US)
Reparticao de Assistencia Tecnica e Vulgarizacao
  (PO)
Repertoire Analytique de Litterature Francaise (FR)
Repertoire des Voyages (FR)
Repertoire du Marketing et du Management (FR)
Repertoire Internationale d'Iconographie Musicale.
  Research Center for Musical Iconography (US)
Repertorio Latinoamericano S.A. (AG)
Replay Publishing (US)
Editorial Replica (AG)
Editions Replique (FR)
Reportage (IT)
Reportajes: Documentos para la Historia (BO)
Reporter (US)
Empresa Jornalistica o Reporter de Santo Andre Ltda.
  (BL)
Reporter Newspapers Co. (AT)
Reporter Publishing Co. (San Francisco) (US)
Reporters Committee for Freedom of the Press (US)
Reporting on Governments, Inc. (US)
Reports Corp. (US)
Reports, Inc. (US)
Repository Press (CN)
Repress, S.A. (SP)

Reproduction Research Information Service Ltd.
  (UK)
Repsol Publications (IE)
Republic Forge Company (II)
Republic National Life Insurance Co. (US)
Republic of Iraq Embassy
    see Embassy of the Republic of Iraq (II)
Republican Delta (US)
Republican Educational Department (IE)
Republican Journal (US)
Republican National Committee (US)
Republican News Agency (Pty) Ltd. (SA)
Republicki Zavod za Zastitu Spomenika Kulture
  (YU)
Res (AG)
N.V. Res (NE)
Res Publica (Pty) Ltd. (SA)
Technischer Verlag Resch KG (GW)
Research and Development Associates for Military
  Food & Packaging Systems Inc. (US)
Research and Documentation Centre (UK)
Research & Documentation Corp. (US)
Research and Review Service of America, Inc. (US)
Research Association of Powder Technology, Japan
  (JA)
Research Association of Statistical Sciences
    see under Kyushu University (JA)
Research Center for Religion & Human Rights in
  Closed Societies (US)
Research Committee on Essential Amino Acids (JA)
Research Company of America (US)
Research Corporation (US)
Research Group for European Migration Problems
  (NE)
Research Group, Inc. (US)
Research in Electrocardiology, Inc. (US)
Research in Librarianship (UK)
Research in Psychotherapy (US)
Research Institute for Applied Mechanics
    see under Kyushu University (JA)
Research Institute for Estate Crops (IO)
Research Institute for Humanistic Studies
    see under Kyoto University (JA)
Research Institute for Mathematical Sciences
    see under Kyoto University (JA)
Research Institute for Microbial Diseases
    see under Osaka University (JA)
Research Institute for Nuclear Medicine and Biology
    see under Hiroshima University (JA)
Research Institute for Ocean Economics (JA)
Research Institute for Scientific Measurements
    see under Tohoku University (JA)
Research Institute for Strength and Fracture of
  Materials
    see under Tohoku University (JA)
Research Institute for Tuberculosis, Leprosy and
  Cancer
    see under Tohoku University (JA)
Research Institute for Veterinary Science
    see under Nihon University (JA)
Research Institute of America (US)
Research Institute of America, Inc. (US)
Research Institute of Applied Electricity
    see under Hokkaido University (JA)
Research Institute of Asian Economies (KO)
Research Institute of Atmospherics
    see under Nagoya University (JA)
Research Institute of Crude Oil and Hydrocarbon
  Gases (CS)
Research Institute of Economics
    see under Oita University (JA)
Research Institute of Electrical Communication
    see under Tohoku University (JA)
Research Institute of Environmental Medicine
    see under Nagoya University (JA)
Research Institute of International Trade and Industry
  (Tsusho Sangiyo Chosakai) (JA)
Research Institute of Logopedics and Phoniatrics
    see under University of Tokyo (JA)
Research Institute of Mineral Dressing and Metallurgy
    see under Tohoku University (JA)
Research Institute of Northern Canada (CN)
Research Institute of Science and Technology
    see under Nihon University (JA)
Research Laboratory for Surface Science
    see under Okayama University (JA)
Research Library on African Affairs (GH)
Research Press Co. (US)
Research Publications (US)
Research Publications Pty. Ltd. (AT)
Research Publications Services Ltd. (UK)
Research Society for Victorian Periodicals (CN)
Research Society of Pakistan (PK)
Researched News and Commentary (US)
Reseau des Emetteurs Francais (FR)
Reserve Bank of Australia (AT)
Reserve Bank of India
    see India. Reserve Bank of India (II)

Reserve Bank of Malawi (MW)
Reserve Bank of New Zealand (NZ)
Reserve Forces Benefit Association (US)
Reserve Officers Association of U.S. (US)
Reserve Research, Ltd. (US)
Residential Care Association (UK)
Residenz Verlag (AU)
Resist (US)
Resistenza (IT)
Resisters Inside the Army (RITA) (FR)
Herbert Resnick (US)
Resophonic Echoes (US)
Resort & Motel Administration (CN)
Resort Management, Inc. (US)
Resource Publications (US)
Resources Exploitation Institute (JA)
Resources for the Future, Inc. (US)
Responsible Parenthood Council (PH)
Ressorgiment (AG)
Restaurant Association of Metro Washington (US)
Restaurant Association of the State of Washington
  (US)
Restaurant Business Inc. (US)
Restaurator Press (DK)
Reston Publishing Company, Inc. (US)
Resumen (MX)
Resumen (US)
Resurgence Trust (UK)
Resuscitation Press (UK)
Retail Clerks International Association (US)
Retail Council of Canada (CN)
Retail Credit Federation (UK)
Retail Directions, Inc. (US)
Retail Fruit Trade Federation Ltd. (UK)
Retail Gasoline Dealers Association of Monroe,
  Wayne, Ontario & Livingston Counties (US)
Retail Grocers and Storekeepers' Association of
  Western Australia (Inc.) (AT)
Retail Grocers Association (US)
Retail Grocers Association of Arizona (US)
Retail Grocery Dairy and Allied Trade Association
  (IE)
Retail Journals Ltd (UK)
Retail Merchants Association of Canada
  (Saskatchewan) Inc. (CN)
Retail Reporting Bureau (US)
Retail Storekeeper's Association of S.A. Inc. (AT)
Retail Tobacco Sellers Association of Victoria (AT)
Retail Traders Association of Tasmania (AT)
Retail Wholesale and Department Store Union (US)
Retail Wholesale, Chain Store Food Employees Union.
  Local 338 (US)
Retail World Pty. Ltd. (AT)
Retailer (II)
Retailer and Marketing News (US)
Reticuloendothelial Society (US)
Retired Officers' Association (US)
Retirement Choice Magazine Co. Ltd. (UK)
Retirement Living Publishing Co. (US)
A. Retlaw & Associates (US)
Retreading Consultant Services, Inc. (US)
Retrieval (AT)
Retsforbundets Presse (DK)
Retsvideustabelige Institut (DK)
Returned Services League of Australia. New South
  Wales Branch (AT)
Returned Services League of Australia. Victorian
  Branch (AT)
Editions Retz (FR)
Reumatologiai Tarsasag (HU)
Reunert & Lenz Ltd. (SA)
Imprimeries Reunies (SZ)
Reunion des Endocrinologistes de Langue France
  (FR)
Reunion Lyonnaise de Pediatrie (FR)
Reveil de l'Arrondissement de Fougeres (FR)
Reveille Newspapers Ltd. (UK)
Revelation (LB)
Revelation (UK)
Fleming H. Revell Co. (US)
Revenue Sharing Advisory Service (US)
Revere Publishing, Inc. (US)
Reverend Oblate Fathers (US)
Review (UK)
Review and Herald Publishing Association (US)
Review for Religious (US)
Review la Bouche (US)
Review of Religions (PK)
Review of the News Inc. (US)
Review of the River Plate (AG)
Review Publications (II)
Review Publications Pty. Ltd. (AT)
Review Publishing Co., Inc (US)
Reville Publishing Co. (AT)
Revista Agropecuaria (CR)
Revista Canadiense de Estudios Hispanicos (CN)
Revista Clinica Espanola (SP)
Revista Colombiana del Trabajo (CK)

Revista Comercial de Nicaragua (NQ)
Revista Continente: Chile Hacia el Mundo (CL)
Revista de Biologia del Uruguay (UY)
Revista de Ciencias de la Educacion (AG)
Revista de Cultura Brasilena (SP)
Revista de Cultura Vozes (BL)
Revista de Derecho Comercial (UY)
Revista de Derecho Laboral (AG)
Revista de Economia (PO)
Revista de Economia (UY)
Revista de Ferreteria y Ramos Generales (AG)
Revista de Ginecologia e d'Obstetricia (BL)
Revista de Jurisprudencia Argentina (AG)
Revista de Menorca (SP)
Revista de Nutricion y Aterosclerosis (AG)
Revista de Obras Sanitarias de la Nacion (AG)
Revista de Occidente, S.A. (SP)
Revista Diplomatica e Internacional (BO)
Revista do Esporte (BL)
Revista do Trabalho (BL)
Editora Revista dos Tribunais (BL)
Revista Espanola de Seguros (SP)
Revista Financiera (SP)
Editora Revista Fiscal Ltda. (BL)
Revista Fotoarte Ltda. (BL)
Revista Ilustrade de las Carnes Argentinas (AG)
Revista Latinoamericana de Microbiologia (MX)
Revista Literaria Azor (SP)
Revista Luterana (AG)
Revista Manizales (CK)
Revista Mensal de Exportacao Ltda. (BL)
Revista Mexicana de Fianzas (MX)
Revista Mexicana del Petroleo (MX)
Revista Odonto-Estomatologica (BL)
Revista para Jubilados y Pensionados (AG)
Revista Peruana de Ciencias Juridicas y Sociales (PE)
Revista Sur (AG)
Editora Revista Tamaulipas (MX)
Revista Tecnica e Informativa Ltda. (BL)
Revista Tecnica Iem (MX)
Editora de Revistas, C.A. (VE)
Revolution Africaine (AE)
Revolutionaere Socialisters Forbund (DK)
Revolutionary Communist Group (UK)
Revolutionary Marxist Group (AT)
Revolutionary Socialist Party (II)
Revue Action Canada France Inc. (CN)
Revue Administrative (FR)
Revue Algologique (FR)
Revue Archeologique de l'Est et du Centre-Est (FR)
Revue Archeologique du Centre de la France (FR)
Revue Belge de Psychologie et de Pedagogie (BE)
Revue Bryologique et Lichenologique (FR)
Revue Commerce (CN)
Revue d'Acoustique (FR)
Revue d'Economie et de Droit Immobilier (FR)
Revue d'Etudes Militaires, Aeriennes et Navales
  (FR)
Revue d'Histoire de la Spiritualite (FR)
Revue de Droit International de Sciences
  Diplomatiques et Politiques (SZ)
Revue de Droit Penal et de Criminologie (BE)
Revue de Gerontologie d'Expression Francaise (FR)
Revue de Jurisprudence Commerciale (FR)
Revue de l'Enseignement Superieur (FR)
Revue de Laryngologie (FR)
Revue de Metallurgie (FR)
Revue de Mycologie (FR)
Revue de Theologie et de Philosophie (SZ)
Revue des Finances Communales (FR)
Revue des Hotesses (FR)
Revue du Materiel d'Entreprise (FR)
Revue du Rouergue (FR)
Revue du Vieux Geneve (SZ)
Revue du Vivarais (FR)
Revue Generale de l'Electricite (FR)
Revue Generale des Caoutchoucs et Plastiques (FR)
Revue Generale des Routes et des Aerodromes (FR)
Revue Hippique (CN)
Revue Historique de Bordeaux et du Departement de
  la Gironde (FR)
Revue Historique et Archeologique du Maine (FR)
Revue Internationale des Cadres (FR)
Revue Internationale des Tabacs (FR)
Revue Internationale du Droit d'Auteur (FR)
Revue Mabillon (FR)
Revue Medicale de Liege (BE)
Revue Moderne (FR)
Revue Montalembert (FR)
Revue Municipale Inc. (CN)
Revue Neuchateloise (SZ)
Revue Nouvelle (BE)
Revue Politique et Parlementaire (FR)
Revue Pratique de Droit Social (FR)
Revue Spiritus (FR)
Revue Stomato-Odontologique du Nord de la France
  (FR)
Revue 9 et 2 (FR)

SARL Revues Internationales (FR)
Rexair Inc, (US)
Rexall Drug Co. (US)
Rexwood Publications Ltd. (CN)
Editorial "Alfonso Reyes" (MX)
Raimundo de los Reyes, Ed. & Pub. (SP)
Reynolds Publishing Co., Inc. (US)
Rhea, Greiner & Co., Inc. (US)
Rheinisch-Bergische Druckerei- und Verlagsgesellschaft
  mbH (GW)
Rheinisch-Westfaelische Akademie der Wissenschaften
  (GW)
Rheinisch-Westfaelische Boerse zu Duesseldorf.
  (GW)
Rheinisch-Westfaelisches Institut fuer
  Wirtschaftsforschung, Essen (GW)
Rheinische Friedrich-Wilhelms-Universitaet. Institut
  fuer Soziologie (GW)
Rheinische Vereinigung fuer Volkskunde (GW)
Rheinischer Landwirtschaftsverlag GmbH (GW)
Rheinischer Verband fuer Schwarzbundt-Rinderzucht
  (GW)
Rheinisches Landesmuseum, Bonn (GW)
Rheinisches Landesmuseum, Trier (GW)
Rheinland-Pfalz. Landesarchivverwaltung (GW)
Rheinland Verlag (GW)
Rhenania Fachverlag GmbH (GW)
Rho Pi Phi International Pharmaceutical Fraternity
  (US)
Rhode Island. Department of Economic Development
  (US)
Rhode Island. Department of Education (US)
Rhode Island. Department of Employment Security
  (US)
Rhode Island. Department of Health (US)
Rhode Island. Department of Mental Health,
  Retardation and Hospitals (US)
Rhode Island. Department of State Library Services
  (US)
Rhode Island. Manpower Planning Council (US)
Rhode Island. State Library (US)
Rhode Island Agricultural Experiment Station (US)
Rhode Island Bar Association (US)
Rhode Island College (US)
Rhode Island College Alumni Association (US)
Rhode Island Education Association (US)
Rhode Island Historical Society (US)
Rhode Island Jewish Historical Association (US)
Rhode Island Library Association (US)
Rhode Island Medical Society (US)
Rhode Island School of Design (US)
Rhode Island School of Design. Student Board (US)
Rhode Island State Council on the Arts (US)
Rhode Island State Dental Society (US)
Rhode Island Statewide Planning Program (US)
Rhode Island Yearbook Foundation, Inc. (US)
Rhodes Publishing Co., Inc. (US)
Rhodes University (SA)
Rhodes University. Department of Philosophy (SA)
Rhodes University. Institute for the Study of English
  in Africa (SA)
Rhodes University. J. L. B. Smith Institute of
  Ichthyology (SA)
Rhodes University. Leather Industries Research
  Institute (SA)
Rhodes University. Speech and Drama Department
  (SA)
Rhodes University. Students' Representative Council
  (SA)
Rhodesia. Army (RH)
Rhodesia. Central Statistical Office (RH)
Rhodesia. Department of Meteorological Services
  (RH)
Rhodesia. Government Printer (RH)
Rhodesia. Ministry of Agriculture (RH)
Rhodesia. Ministry of Education. Branch of
  Community Development Training (RH)
Rhodesia. Ministry of Finance (RH)
Rhodesia. Ministry of Information, Immigration and
  Tourism (RH)
Rhodesia. Ministry of Internal Affairs (RH)
Rhodesia. Ministry of Water Development (RH)
Rhodesia. National Archives (RH)
Rhodesia. Registrar of Insurance (RH)
Rhodesia. Tobacco Research Board (RH)
Rhodesia, a Field for Investment (RH)
Rhodesia Broadcasting Corporation (RH)
Rhodesia Calls (Pvt.) Ltd. (RH)
Rhodesia Library Association (RH)
Rhodesia National Farmers' Union (RH)
Rhodesia National Tourist Board (RH)
Rhodesia Nurses Association (RH)
Rhodesia Railway Worker's Union (RH)
Rhodesia Railways (RH)
Rhodesia Teachers' Association (RH)
Rhodesian Caravan Association (RH)
Rhodesian Economic Society (RH)
Rhodesian Farmer Publications (RH)

Rhodesian Financial Gazette (RH)
Rhodesian Information Office (US)
Rhodesian Journals Ltd. (RH)
Rhodesian Motor Trade Association (RH)
Rhodesian Ornithological Society (RH)
Rhodesian Philatelic Agencies (Pvt) Ltd. (RH)
Rhodesiana Society (RH)
Rhodos, International Science and Art Publishers (DK)
Rhone-Poulenc-Specia (FR)
Rhythm (II)
Rhythm (US)
Milton Riback, Inc. (US)
Francisco Jose Ribeiro de Vasconcellos (BL)
Rican Journal Inc. (US)
Dr. Franco Ricciardi, Ed. & Pub. (IT)
Rice Journal Enterprises (US)
Rice University (US)
Rice University. History Department (US)
Rice University. Program of Development Studies (US)
Ricegrowers' Co-Operative Mills Ltd. (AT)
Rich Publishing, Inc. (US)
Richard and Co. (US)
Richard de Boo Ltd. (CN)
Richard Foncke Gallery (BE)
Richard 3rd Society (UK)
Richards Industries, Inc. (US)
Richards, Lawrence & Co. (US)
Richards Rosen Press (US)
Eileen Richardson, Ed. & Pub. (CN)
Richardson Heritage Society (US)
Verlag Hans Richarz (GW)
Editions Richelieu (FR)
Paul Richenbacher Verlag (SZ)
Edizioni Richerche (IT)
Paul Richmond and Co. (US)
Richmond Chamber of Commerce (US)
Richmond County Historical Society (US)
Richmond Heights General Hospital (US)
Richmond Historian (US)
Richmond Publishing Co. Ltd. (UK)
Marc Richter (BE)
Rickard Publishing Co. (US)
Rickenbacker Report Corp. (US)
Rickey de Montrond (US)
Pierre Ricouard Syndic (FR)
R.G. Riddell Pty.Ltd. (AT)
Peter de Ridder Press (NE)
Ridge Association of Retarded Citizens (US)
Ridge Runners (US)
Ridgewood Pentecostal Church (US)
Ridings Publishing Co. (UK)
Oskar Riedel, Ed. & Pub. (AU)
Dr. Riederer Verlag GmbH (GW)
Editions Riegel (FR)
Riegel Publications (CN)
Riemenschneider Bach Institute (US)
H. K. Rigg, Ed. & Pub. (US)
Ted Riggs, Ed. & Pub. (US)
Rijk der Vrouw (BE)
Rijksherbarium (NE)
Rijksinstituut Sociale Verzekeringen der Zelfstandigen (BE)
Rijksinstituut voor het Rassenonderzoek van Cultuurgewassen (NE)
Rijksinstituut voor Oorlogsdocumentatie (NE)
Rijkslandbouwconsulentschap voor Plantenziekten (NE)
Rijksmuseum Kroeller-Mueller (NE)
Rijksmuseum van Geologie en Mineralogie (NE)
Rijksmuseum van Natuurlijke Historie (NE)
Rijksmuseum van Natuurlijke Historie. Delta Onderzoek Hydrobiologisch Institut (NE)
Rijkstuinbouwconsulentschap (NE)
Rijksuniversiteit Te Gent (BE)
Rijksuniversiteit Te Gent. Centrale Bibliotheek (BE)
Rijksuniversiteit Te Gent. Centrum voor Onkruidonderzoek (BE)
Rijksuniversiteit te Gent. Dienst voor Franse Linguistiek (BE)
Rijksuniversiteit te Gent. Faculteit Landbouwetenschapen. Centrum voor Onkruidonderzoek
    see Rijksuniversiteit Te Gent. Centrum voor Onkruidonderzoek (BE)
Rijksuniversiteit Te Gent. Faculteit Landbouwetenschappen (BE)
Rijksuniversiteit te Gent. Faculteit van de Economische Wetenschappen (BE)
Rijksuniversiteit Te Gent. Geologisch Instituut (BE)
Rijksuniversiteit Te Gent. Laboratorium voor Experimentele, Differentiele en Genetische Psychologie (BE)
Rijksuniversiteit Te Gent. Section de Philologie Romane (BE)
Rijksuniversiteit Te Gent. Sektie Germaanse Philologie (BE)

Rijksuniversiteit Te Gent. Seminarie voor Musicologie (BE)
Rijksuniversiteit Te Gent. Seminarie voor Sociologie (BE)
Rijksuniversiteit te Gent. Seminaries voor Historische en voor Vergelijkende Pedagogiek (BE)
RIjksuniversiteit te Gent. Sterrenkungid Observatorium (BE)
Rijksuniversiteit te Groningen. Fries Instituut (NE)
Rijksuniversiteit te Groningen. Nedersaksisch Instituut (NE)
Rijksuniversiteit te Groningen. Polemologisch Instituut (NE)
Rijksuniversiteit te Groningen. Stichting Gronings Universiteitsblad (NE)
Rijksuniversiteit te Leiden (NE)
Rijksuniversiteit te Leiden. Documentation Office for East European Law (NE)
Rijksuniversiteit te Leiden. Geologisch en Mineralogisch Instituut (NE)
Rijksuniversiteit te Leiden. Institute for Prehistory (NE)
Rijksuniversiteit te Utrecht (NE)
Rijksuniversiteit te Utrecht. Archaeological Institute (NE)
Rijksuniversiteit te Utrecht. Bibliotheek (NE)
Rijksuniversiteit te Utrecht. Department of Stratigraphy and Paleontology (NE)
Rijksuniversiteit te Utrecht. Geografisch Instituut (NE)
Rijksuniversiteit te Utrecht. Geologisch Instituut (NE)
Rijksuniversiteit te Utrecht. Instituut de Vooys voor Nederlandse Taal- en Letterkunde (NE)
Rijksuniversiteit te Utrecht. Instituut voor Oosterse Talen (NE)
Rijksuniversiteit te Utrecht. Kunsthistorisch Instituut (NE)
Rijnlands Lyceum (NE)
Rikagaku Kenkyusho Saikurotoron Kenkyushitsu
    see Institute of Physical and Chemical Research (JA)
Rikka Publishing House (CN)
Rikkyo Daigaku Rigakubu Sugaku Kyoshitsu
    see Rikkyo University. Institute of Mathematics (JA)
Rikkyo University (JA)
Rikkyo University. Institute for Atomic Energy (JA)
Rikogaku Kenkyusho
    see Nihon University. Research Institute of Science and Technology (JA)
Rikogaku Kenkyusho
    see Waseda University. Science and Engineering Research Laboratory (JA)
Riksfoerbundet DX-Alliansen (SW)
Riksfoerbundet Foer Hembygdsvaard (SW)
Riksfoerbundet foer Hjaert- och Lungsjuka (SW)
Riksfoerbundet Hem och Skola (SW)
Riksfoerbundet Mot Alkoholmissbruk (SW)
Riksfoerbundet mot Allergi (SW)
Riksfoerbundet Mot Reumatism (SW)
Riksfoerbundet Svensk Traedgaard (SW)
Riksfoereningen Foer Laerarna i Moderna Spraak (SW)
Riksfoereningen Foer Svenskhetens Bevarande i Utlandet (SW)
Rikshospitalet (NO)
Riksidrottsfoerbundets Foerlags AB (SW)
Rikuyosha (JA)
Rilindja (YU)
Ben Rinaldo Co. (US)
Rinderzuchtzentrale Angeln (GW)
Ring Freiheitlicher Jugend (AU)
Ring, Inc. (US)
Foulek Ringelheim, Ed. & Pub. (BE)
Ringier und Co. (SZ)
Ringling Museum of Art (US)
Ringsport Publications (UK)
Ringyo Shikenjo
    see Japan. Government Forest Experiment Station (JA)
Rinkai Jikkensho
    see University of Tokyo. Misaki Marine Biological Station (JA)
Societa Editrice Il Rinnovamento (IT)
Rinsho-Shikasha (JA)
Rin'ya-cho
    see Japan. Forestry Agency (JA)
Rinzai-Ji, Inc. (US)
Editora Rio (BL)
Rio de Janeiro. Servico Social do Comercio (BL)
Rio de Janeiro, Brazil (City) Empresa de Turismo do Municipio (BL)
Rio de Janeiro, Brazil. Imprensa Oficial (BL)
Rio de Janeiro, Brazil. Secretaria de Saude. Departamento de Recursos Humanos (BL)

Rio Grande do Sul, Brazil. Departamento Autonomo del Estradas de Rodagem. Divisao de Servicos Especiais (BL)
Rio Grande do Sul, Brazil. Departamento da Saude (BL)
Rio Grande do Sul, Brazil. Rio Grande do Sul Consultoria-Geral (BL)
Rio Grande Educational Association (US)
Rio Grande Writers Association (US)
Ripon College (US)
Ripon Society, Inc. (Charlestown) (US)
Risalat (II)
Rising Sign: the Astrology Newspaper (US)
Rising Sun (II)
Risk and Insurance Management Society, Inc. (US)
Rissho Daigaku Hokekyo Bunka Kenkyujo
    see Rissho University. Institute for the Comprehensive Study of Lotus Sutra (JA)
Rissho University. Institute for the Comprehensive Study of Lotus Sutra (JA)
Risveglio (IT)
Ritchie County Historical Society (US)
Ritena (SP)
Ritenour Consolidated School District (US)
Ritsumeikan University. Economic Society (JA)
Verlag Matthias Ritthammer KG (GW)
Rittmann Ltd. (SZ)
Riunioni Medico-Chirurgiche Internazionali (IT)
Editori Riuniti (IT)
River Bend Library System (US)
River Bottom (US)
River City Enterprises, Inc. (US)
River City Press (US)
Rivers State. Ministry of Agriculture and Natural Resources (NR)
Rivers State. Ministry of Information (NR)
Rivers State Council for Arts & Culture (NR)
Riverside County Farm Bureau Inc. (US)
Riverside County Publishing Co. (US)
Riverside Public Library (US)
Riverside Quarterly (US)
Riviera Eco (IT)
Riviera Printers & Publishers Inc. (CN)
Rivista Abruzzese (IT)
Rivista Amministrativa della Repubblica Italiana (IT)
Rivista dei Lavori Pubblici (IT)
Rivista del Colore (IT)
Rivista di Estetica (IT)
Rivista di Etnografia (IT)
Rivista di Patologia Vegetale (IT)
Rivista di Polizia (IT)
Rivista di Scienze Preistoriche (IT)
Rivista di Suinicoltura (IT)
Rivista Internazionale di Economia dei Trasporti (IT)
Rivista Italiana di Paleontologia e Stratigrafia (IT)
Edizioni Rivista Mediche (IT)
Rivista Militare della Svizzera Italiana (SZ)
Rivista Tributaria (IT)
Rizzoli Editore (IT)
Elena Rizzotti, Ed. & Pub. (IT)
Rjettur (IC)
Ro Zai Ho (JA)
Road Ahead Publishing Co. Pty Ltd. (AT)
Road Apple Press (US)
Road Haulage Association (UK)
Road King Magazine (US)
Road Runner Press (US)
Road Transport Association of Western Australia (AT)
Roadcap and Associates (US)
Roadmasters and Maintenance of Way Association of America (US)
Roads and Transportation Association of Canada (CN)
Roan Consolidated Mines Ltd. (ZA)
Roanoke College (US)
Roanoke Tribune (US)
Roanoke Valley Chamber of Commerce (US)
Roanoke Valley Historical Society (US)
Roband Publications (US)
Robar Industries, Inc. (US)
Editions E. Robert (FR)
Robert Dumm Piano Review (US)
Robert Kahn and Associates (US)
Robert Schalkenbach Foundation (US)
Robert Wood Johnson Foundation (US)
Martin Roberts & Associates, Inc. (US)
F. M. Roberts Enterprises (US)
Roberts Publishing Corp. (US)
Ruby A. Roberts (US)
Sanford and Patricia Roberts (US)
Martin Robertson & Co. Ltd. (UK)
Robertson Publishing Co. (US)
Robertson Review (US)

R. D. Robinson Publishing Co. (CN)

R. L. Robinson (US)

Shepard D. Robinson, Ed. & Pub. (US)

Royal Australian Planning Institute. Queensland Division  (AT)
Royal Automobile Association of South Australia Inc.  (AT)
Royal Automobile Club of Queensland, Brisbane  (AT)
Royal Automobile Club of Tasmania  (AT)
Royal Automobile Club of Victoria  (AT)
Royal Automobile Club of Western Australia  (AT)
Royal Bank of Canada  (CN)
Royal Belgian Society of Political Economy
  see Societe Royale d'Economie Politique de Belgique  (BE)
Royal Botanic Gardens  (UK)
Royal Botanic Gardens and National Herbarium  (AT)
Royal Botanical Gardens  (CN)
Royal British Legion  (UK)
Royal British Legion Scotland  (UK)
Royal Caledonian Curling Club  (UK)
Royal Canadian Academy of Arts  (CN)
Royal Canadian Air Force Association  (CN)
Royal Canadian Geographical Society  (CN)
Royal Canadian Institute  (CN)
Royal Canadian Mounted Police  (CN)
Royal Children's Hospital  (AT)
Royal College of Art  (UK)
Royal College of Midwives  (UK)
Royal College of Music  (UK)
Royal College of Nursing  (UK)
Royal College of Nursing. Library  (UK)
Royal College of Obstetricians and Gynaecologists  (UK)
Royal College of Organists  (UK)
Royal College of Pathologists of Australia  (AT)
Royal College of Physicians & Surgeons of Canada  (CN)
Royal College of Physicians of Edinburgh  (UK)
Royal College of Psychiatrists  (UK)
Royal College of Surgeons  (IE)
Royal College of Surgeons of Edinburgh  (UK)
Royal College of Surgeons of England  (UK)
Royal Commonwealth Society  (UK)
Royal Commonwealth Society. New South Wales Branch  (AT)
Royal Corps of Transport  (UK)
Royal Courts of Justice (Ulster)  (UK)
Royal Danish Academy of Sciences and Letters
  see Kongelige Danske Videnskabernes Selskab  (DK)
Royal Danish Agricultural Society
  see Kongelige Danske Landhusholdningsselskab  (DK)
Royal Danish Automobile Club  (DK)
Royal Danish Geographical Society
  see Kongelige Danske Geografiske Selskab  (DK)
Royal Dublin Society  (IE)
Royal Dutch Geographical Society
  see Koninklijk Nederlands Aardrijkskundig Genootschap  (NE)
Royal Dutch Motorcycle Union (KNMV)  (NE)
Royal Economic Society  (UK)
Royal Entomological Society  (UK)
Royal Far West Children's Health Scheme  (AT)
Royal Flemish Association of Engineers
  see Koninklijke Vlaamse Ingenieursvereniging  (BE)
Royal Forest and Bird Protection Society of New Zealand Inc.  (NZ)
Royal Forestry Society of England, Wales and Northern Ireland  (UK)
Royal Geographical Society  (UK)
Royal Geographical Society of Australasia. South Australian Branch  (AT)
Royal Geographical Society of Australia. Queensland Branch  (AT)
Royal Geological and Mining Society of the Netherlands
  see Koninklijk Nederlands Geologisch Mijnbouwkundig Genootschap  (NE)
Royal Globe Insurance Co.  (US)
Royal Greenwich Observatory  (UK)
Royal Highland and Agricultural Society of Scotland  (UK)
Royal Historical Society  (UK)
Royal Historical Society of Queensland  (AT)
Royal Horticultural Society  (UK)
Royal Horticultural Society of Victoria  (AT)
Royal Humane Society  (UK)
Royal Institute for Linguistics and Anthropology
  see Koninklijk Instituut voor Taal-, Land- en Volkenkunde  (NE)
Royal Institute of British Architects  (UK)
Royal Institute of British Architects. East Midlands Region  (UK)
Royal Institute of British Architects. Northern Region  (UK)
Royal Institute of British Architects. West Midlands Region  (UK)

Royal Institute of British Architects. Yorkshire Region  (UK)
Royal Institute of International Affairs  (UK)
Royal Institute of Navigation  (UK)
Royal Institute of Philosophy  (UK)
Royal Institute of Public Administration  (UK)
Royal Institute of Public Administration. Australian Regional Groups  (AT)
Royal Institute of Public Health and Hygiene  (UK)
Royal Institute of the Architects of Ireland  (IE)
Royal Institution of Chartered Surveyors  (UK)
Royal Institution of Engineers in the Netherlands  (NE)
Royal Institution of Great Britain  (UK)
Royal Institution of Naval Architects  (UK)
Royal Irish Academy  (IE)
Royal Irish Academy of Music  (IE)
Royal Jersey Agricultural & Horticultural Society  (UI)
Royal Life Saving Society  (UK)
Royal Marines  (UK)
Royal Melbourne Institute of Technology  (AT)
Royal Meteorological Society  (UK)
Royal Microscopical Society  (UK)
Royal Military College of Australia  (AT)
Royal Military College of Canada  (CN)
Royal Military Police  (UK)
Royal Musical Association  (UK)
Royal N.S.W. Bowling Association  (AT)
Royal National Institute for the Blind  (UK)
Royal National Institute for the Blind. Moon Branch  (UK)
Royal National Institute for the Deaf  (UK)
Royal National Life-Boat Institution  (UK)
Royal National Mission to Deep Sea Fishermen  (UK)
Royal National Rose Society  (UK)
Royal Naval Engineering College  (UK)
Royal Naval Sailing Association  (UK)
Royal Neighbors of America  (US)
Royal Netherlands Association of Architects  (NE)
Royal Netherlands Hockey Association  (NE)
Royal Netherlands Lawn Tennis Association  (NE)
Royal Netherlands Meterological Institute  (NE)
Royal Netherlands Shipowners Association
  see Koninklijke Nederlandse Redersvereniging  (NE)
Royal Netherlands Society for Agricultural Science
  see Koninklijk Genootschap voor Landbouwwetenschap  (NE)
Royal New Zealand Institute of Horticulture  (NZ)
Royal Norwegian Council for Scientific and Industrial Research
  see Norges Teknisk-Naturvitenskapelige Forskningsraad  (NO)
Royal Norwegian Society of Science
  see Kongelige Norske Videnskabers Selskab  (NO)
Royal Numismatic Society  (UK)
Royal Numismatic Society of New Zealand, Inc.  (NZ)
Royal Ontario Museum  (CN)
Royal Over-Seas League  (UK)
Royal Philatelic Society  (UK)
Royal Philatelic Society of Canada  (CN)
Royal Philatelic Society of New Zealand  (NZ)
Royal Philatelic Society of Victoria  (AT)
Royal Philosophical Society of Glasgow  (UK)
Royal Photographic Society of Great Britain  (UK)
Royal Pigeon Racing Association  (UK)
Royal Pioneer Corps and Association  (UK)
Royal Queensland Bowls Association  (AT)
Royal Regiment of Canadian Artillery  (CN)
Royal Regiment of Fusiliers  (UK)
Royal School of Church Music  (UK)
Royal School of Mines Association  (UK)
Royal Scottish Forestry Society  (UK)
Royal Scottish Geographical Society  (UK)
Royal Society  (UK)
Royal Society for Asian Affairs  (UK)
Royal Society for the Prevention of Accidents  (UK)
Royal Society for the Prevention of Cruelty to Animals  (UK)
Royal Society for the Protection of Birds  (UK)
Royal Society of Antiquaries of Ireland  (IE)
Royal Society of Arts  (UK)
Royal Society of Canada  (CN)
Royal Society of Edinburgh  (UK)
Royal Society of Health  (UK)
Royal Society of Literature of the United Kingdom  (UK)
Royal Society of London  (UK)
Royal Society of London. British National Committee for Geodesy and Geophysics  (UK)
Royal Society of Medicine  (UK)
Royal Society of New South Wales  (AT)
Royal Society of New Zealand  (NZ)
Royal Society of Queensland  (AT)
Royal Society of S.A.  (AT)

Royal Society of South Africa  (SA)
Royal Society of Tasmania  (AT)
Royal Society of Tropical Medicine and Hygiene  (UK)
Royal Society of Ulster Architects  (IE)
Royal Society of Victoria  (AT)
Royal Society of Western Australia  (AT)
Royal South Australian Bowling Association  (AT)
Royal South Australian Society of Arts  (AT)
Royal Statistical Society  (UK)
Royal Swedish Academy of Agriculture and Forestry
  see Kungliga Skogs- och Lantbruksakademien  (SW)
Royal Swedish Academy of Engineering Sciences
  see Ingenioersvetenskapsakademien  (SW)
Royal Swedish Academy of Sciences
  see Kungliga Vetenskapsakademien  (SW)
Royal Tank Regiment Publications Ltd.  (UK)
Royal Tehran Hilton  (IR)
Royal Television Society  (UK)
Royal Town Planning Institute  (UK)
Royal Tropical Institute
  see Koninklijk Instituut voor de Tropen  (NE)
Royal United Service Institute for Defence Studies  (UK)
Royal United Services Institute  (US)
Royal University Students' Theological Association  (MM)
Royal Volunteer Coastal Patrol  (AT)
Royal Western Australian Historical Society  (AT)
Royal Winnipeg Ballet  (CN)
Royal Yachting Association  (UK)
Royal Zoological Society of New South Wales  (AT)
Royal Zoological Society of Scotland  (UK)
Royale Federation Colombophile Belge  (BE)
Royalton College Press  (US)
H.G. Rozas, S.A.  (PE)
Rozvoj Mistniho Hospodarstvi  (CS)
Rubber and Plastics Digest  (II)
Rubber and Plastics Research Association of Great Britain  (UK)
Rubber Manufacturers Association  (US)
Rubber Producers' Council of Malaysia  (MY)
Rubber Research Institute of Malaysia  (MY)
Rubber Research Institute of Sri Lanka  (CE)
S. M. Rubel & Co.  (US)
Samuel K. Rubin, Ed. & Pub.  (US)
Rudarski Institut, Belgrade  (YU)
Rudarski Institut, Ljubljana  (YU)
Rude Pravo  (CS)
Ruder and Finn Inc.  (US)
Rudinger Foundation  (US)
Rudolf Steiner Nachlassverwaltung  (FR)
Rudolf Virchow Medical Society  (US)
Friedrich Rudy  (AU)
Editions Ruedo Iberico  (FR)
Ruehle-Diebener Verlag GmbH und Co. KG  (GW)
Verlag Ruetten und Loenig  (GE)
Verlag Ruetten und Loening  (GE)
Ruffin Publications, Inc.  (US)
Rugby Football League  (UK)
Ruggieri S. Ed C. Editori  (IT)
Ruhr-Universitaet, Bochum. Institut fuer Entwicklungsforschung und Entwicklungspolitik  (GW)
Ruhrlaendische Verlags-Gesellschaft mbH  (GW)
Juan Ruiz Pena, Ed. & Pub.  (SP)
Rumanian Free Democratic Committee  (UK)
Rumford Publishing Co.  (US)
Rumpf Publishing Division  (US)
Rundfunk-und Fernsehtechnisches Zentralamt  (GE)
Rundschau-Verlag, Otto G. Koeniger GmbH und Co  (GW)
Runestone  (US)
Runnymede Trust  (UK)
Rupambara  (II)
Rural Advancement Fund of the National Sharecroppers Fund  (US)
Rural Bank of New South Wales  (AT)
Rural Education Association  (US)
Rural Electrification Corporation  (II)
Rural Gravure Service Inc.  (US)
Rural Housing Alliance  (US)
Rural Music Schools Association  (UK)
Rural Reconstruction Authority of Western Australia  (AT)
Editora Rural, S.A.  (SP)
Rural Sociological Society (Auburn)  (US)
Rural Sociological Society (College Point)  (US)
Editora e Grafica o Ruralista Ltda.  (BL)
Ruralite Services, Inc.  (US)
Ruritan National, Inc.  (US)
Rusconi Editore S.p.A.  (IT)
Rush-Presbyterian-St. Luke's Medical Center and Its Alumni Foundation  (US)
Rush Publishing Co., Inc.  (US)
Russell Fenton Co.  (AT)
Bertrand Russell Peace Foundation  (UK)

Russell's Guides, Inc. (US)
Russian Brotherhood Organization of the U. S. (US)
Russian Life, Inc. (US)
Russian Orthodox Catholic Mutual Aid Society (US)
Russian Petroleum Press Review (SZ)
Russian Review, Inc. (US)
Russky Golos Publishing Corp. (US)
Russland und Wir - Verlag und Handlung (GW)
Ruta Dominicana (DR)
Rutas de Cataluna (SP)
Rutgers Center of Alcohol Studies. Publications
  Division (US)
Rutgers University (US)
Rutgers University. Bureau of Biological Research
  (US)
Rutgers University. Center for Urban Policy Research
  (US)
Rutgers University. College of Engineering (US)
Rutgers University. Cook College (US)
Rutgers University. Department of Alumni Relations
  (US)
Rutgers University. Department of Botany (US)
Rutgers University. Graduate School of Business
  Administration (US)
Rutgers University. Graduate School of Library
  Science (US)
Rutgers University. Institute of Management and
  Labor Relations (US)
Rutgers University Library. Associated Friends of the
  Library (US)
Rutgers University Press (US)
Rutgers University. School of Law (US)
Rutgers University. School of Law (Camden) (US)
Rutherford B. Hayes Library (US)
Rutherford Laboratory. Scientific Administration
  Department (UK)
Rutland Historical Society (US)
Rutward Mail Order Publications (US)
Rwanda. Bureau de l'Enseignement Familial (RW)
Rwanda. Direction de la Documentation et des
  Statistiques (RW)
Rwanda. Office Rwandais d'Information (RW)
Ryan Publications (AT)
Ryazanskii Radiotekhnicheskii Institut (UR)
Ryde District Historical Society (AT)
Thomas O. Ryder (US)
Rydge Publications Pty. Ltd. (AT)
Ryela, S.A. (AG)
Ryerson Polytechnical Institute. Student's Union
  (CN)
Ryska Bibelsaellskapet (SW)
Ryukei Shosha (JA)
Ryukyu Philatelic Specialist Society (US)
S A B A M
  see Societe Belge des Auteurs, Compositeurs et
  Editeurs (BE)
S.A. Blind Workers Organisation (SA)
S. A. D. E. P. (FR)
S.A. des Editions de la Mode Chic de Paris (FR)
S.A. Engine Driver's, Firemen's and Operators'
  Association (SA)
S A F International, Inc. (US)
S A F O
  see Swedish Atomic Forum (SW)
S A F P (FR)
S A G S A S.p.A. (IT)
S.A. Germanistenverband (SA)
S. A. M., Inc. (US)
S.A.P.E.F. (SG)
S.A.R.P.E (SP)
S. A. Road Transport Association Inc (AT)
Edizioni S A S I P (IT)
S A S M I R A
  see Silk and Art Silk Mills' Research Association
  (II)
S. A. Scientific Committee for Antarctic Research
  see Council for Scientific and Industrial Research.
  Scientific Committee for Antarctic Research (SA)
S A T R (FR)
S. & H. Publications (UK)
S B R, Inc. (US)
S B 67 Verlagsgesellschaft mbH (GW)
S C J (AT)
S C M Press Ltd. (UK)
S. D. M. S. (FR)
S.E.B.A.M. (FR)
S E C T I (IT)
S. E. D. A. (FR)
S.E.D.A.C. Editions (FR)
S E D I P A (FR)
S. E. D. I. T (FR)
S. E. F. A. G. (FR)
S E G E D O (FR)
S.E.G. Public Relations (Pty) Ltd. (SA)
S.E.I.D. (FR)
S E I T S.N.C. (IT)
S E L I S la Quinzaine Litteraire (FR)
S. E. M. A. D

see Societe d'Editions Medicales et Alimentaires
  Relatives au Diabete (FR)
S. E. M. I. S. (FR)
S E N D O C (Small Enterprises National
  Documentation Center)
  see Small Industry Extension Training Institute
  (II)
S E N T O K Y O
  see Special Libraries Association, Japan (JA)
S.E.P.A. (FR)
S.E.P.A. (IT)
S. E. P. A. I. C
  see Societe d'Edition et de Publicite Agricoles,
  Industrielles et Commerciales (FR)
S.E.P.E.
  see Societe Europeenne de Presse et d'Edition
  (FR)
S E P Edition (FR)
Editrice S.E.P.I. (IT)
S.E.R.A. (FR)
S E R-Jobs for Progress, Inc. (US)
S E R-Schaktkonsult AB (SW)
S.E.T.A. s.r.l.
  see Societa Edizioni Techniche Arredamento (IT)
S. E. T. I. C. (FR)
S E V
  see Schweizerischer Eisenbahnerverband (SZ)
S F Booklog (US)
S. F. Camera Publishing Co. Inc. (US)
S F Commentary (AT)
S Gaugian (US)
S H A W C O
  see University of Cape Town. Students Health and
  Welfare Centres Organisation (SHAWCO) (SA)
S.H.Y. (GR)
Editions S I C (BE)
S.I.C. Publishing Corp. (US)
S.I.E. (FR)
S I E M (FR)
S.I.P.E. (FR)
Editore S.I.P.I.
  see Servicio Italiana Pubblicazioni Internazionali
  s.r.l. (IT)
S.I.R.P.E. (FR)
S.L.E.E.S (FR)
S. K. F. Ball Bearing (Australia) Pty. Ltd. (AT)
S M A Fathers (IE)
Editions S.M.E. (FR)
S. N. E. M. (FR)
S-N Publications, Inc. (US)
S.O.C.I.D.O.C. (FR)
S O C O T E L (FR)
S. O. D. Publishing, Inc. (US)
S.O.E. (Societe Occidentale d'Edition) (FR)
S.O.F.I.A.C. (FR)
S. O. G. E. T. A. P. (FR)
Editorial S O P E C S.A. (SP)
S O P I C (FR)
S O P P E P (FR)
S O P R A L (FR)
Editions S.O.S. (FR)
S.O.S. Amitie France (FR)
S O S Kinderdorf (AU)
Editions S.O.S.P. (FR)
S. O. S. U. S. A., Ship of State (US)
S P Books (US)
S P E A K, Inc. (US)
S.P.E.B. (FR)
S. P. E. K. (La Maison des Kinesitherapeutes) (FR)
S.P.E.L.D. (FR)
S. P. E. O. C.
  see Societe de Presse et d'Edition Ovine et Caprine
  (S.P.E.O.C.) (FR)
S. P. E. R. (FR)
S P I C (SP)
S.P.O.T. Publicite (FR)
S P R Charter (US)
S. P. Technical Publications Ltd. (UK)
S.R.C. Press (SA)
S R M Foundation of Great Britain (UK)
Edizioni e S S E (IT)
Edizioni S T E M- MUCCHI
  see Societa Tipografica Editrice Modenese (IT)
S T E P E
  see Societe Technique d'Editions pour l'Entreprise
  (S T E P E) (FR)
S.W.A. Scientific Society (SX)
S X O Corp. (US)
S Z (AU)
SAAB-SCANIA (SW)
SAAB-SCANIA. SCANIA Division (SW)
Saalburg-Museum (GW)
Saarbruecken. Kulturamt (GW)
Saatkorn-Verlag GmbH (GW)
Sabah. Department of Agriculture. Agricultural
  Economics Division (MY)

Sabah. Department of Statistics (MY)
Sabah. Forest Department (MY)
Sabah. Marine Department (MY)
Sabah Society (MY)
Sabatelli Editori (IT)
Sabena Belgian World Airlines (BE)
Sabin's Discount Records (US)
Sabiura Marine Park Research Station (JA)
Forlaget Sabroe A-S (DK)
Verlag W. Sachon (GW)
Sacramento Area Central Labor Council. Building
  Trades Council, Printing Trades Council (US)
Sacramento City Teachers Association (US)
Sacramento Metropolitan Chamber of Commerce
  (US)
Sacramento State College (US)
Sacred Heart University
  see University of the Sacred Heart (JA)
Sacred Heart University (US)
Kase Sadako, Ed. & Pub. (JA)
Saddle and Bridle (US)
Saddlers and Upholsterer's Guild (DK)
Sadesi (SZ)
Ralph Sadgrove (UK)
Sadhana Publications (II)
Sadhna Prakashan (II)
Sadie's Chatter (US)
Sado Marine Biological Station
  see under Niigata University (JA)
Sado Rinko Jikkenjo Kenkyu
  see Niigata University. Sado Marine Biological
  Station (JA)
Saechsische Akademie der Wissenschaften, Leipzig
  (GE)
Saechsische Akademie der Wissenschaften, Leipzig.
  Historische Kommission (GE)
Saechsische Akademie der Wissenschaften, Leipzig.
  Mathematisch-Naturwissenschaftliche Klasse (GE)
Saechsische Akademie der Wissenschaften, Leipzig.
  Philologisch-Historische Klasse (GE)
Saechsische Landesbibliothek (GE)
Saellskapet Bokvaennera (SW)
Saellskapet Foer Studier i Arbetarroerelsens Historia
  (SW)
Saemann Verlagsgesellschaft mbH (GW)
Safeco Insurance Companies (US)
Safety Electronics, Inc. (US)
Safety First Association (SA)
Safety in Mines Research Establishment (UK)
Sagamore Publishing Company, Inc. (US)
Sage Brush Ventures (CN)
Sage Publications, Inc. (US)
Sage Publications Ltd. (UK)
Sage School of Philosophy
  see under Cornell University (US)
Sageret (FR)
Saggiatore S.p.A. (IT)
Sahitya Akademi
  see National Academy of Letters (II)
Saifia College. Department of Zoology (II)
Johann Michael Sailer Verlag GmbH (GW)
Sailing the Road Clear (US)
Jacques Saillot, Ed. & Pub. (FR)
St. Albertus Magnus Apothekergilde e.V. (GW)
St. Andrews Presbyterian College (US)
St. Anthony Messenger Press (US)
St. Anthonys' Press (UK)
St. Augustine Historical Society (US)
St. Augustine's Center for American Indians (US)
Saint Augustine's College (US)
St. Bartholomew's Hospital. Students Union (UK)
St. Bernard Charities (CN)
St. Bonaventure University (US)
St. Bonaventure University. Franciscan Institute (US)
St. Charles Seminary (US)
St. Clair County Historical Society (US)
St. Cloud State College (US)
St. Columban's Foreign Mission Society (US)
St. Croix Library Association (VI)
St. David's University College (UK)
St. Dunstan's for Men and Women Blinded on War
  Service (UK)
St. Edwards University (US)
St. Elizabeth Mission Society (US)
St. Francis Xavier University (CN)
St. Gallen Graduate School of Economics, Business
  and Public Administration
  see Hochschule St. Gallen fuer Wirtschafts- und
  Sozialwissenschaften (SZ)
St. George Association of the U.S.A. (US)
St. George's College (JM)
St. George's Hospital Medical School (UK)
Saint Hubert Club de France (FR)
St. James Armenian Apostolic Church (US)
St. James Press (UK)
St. James Press Publications Ltd. (UK)
St. Joan's Alliance (FR)
St. John Medical Center (US)

Saint John's Abbey (US)
St. John's College. Office of College Relations (US)
St. John's University. Business Research Institute (US)
St. John's University. Hill Monastic Manuscript Library (US)
St. John's University Press (US)
St. John's University. School of Law (US)
St. Joseph County's Official Museum (US)
St. Joseph Light & Power Co. (US)
St. Joseph Museum (US)
Saint Joseph's College (Collegeville) (US)
Saint Joseph's College (Philadelphia) (US)
St. Joseph's Hospital (US)
St. Labre Indian School (US)
Saint Lawrence Seaway Development Corporation
    see U.S. Saint Lawrence Seaway Development Corporation (US)
St. Lawrence University (US)
St. Lawrence University. Department of English (US)
St. Lazarus Trust (US)
St. Louis. Board of Police Commissioners (US)
St. Louis (County) Health Department. Conference of Local Environmental Health Administrators (US)
St. Louis Art Museum (US)
St. Louis College of Pharmacy (US)
St. Louis Genealogical Society (US)
St. Louis Jewish Light, Inc. (US)
St. Louis Park Medical Center (US)
St. Louis Pharmacists' Association (US)
St. Louis Public Library (US)
St. Louis Regional Commerce and Growth Association (US)
Saint Louis University (PH)
St. Louis University (US)
St. Louis University. College of Philosophy and Letters (US)
Saint Louis University. Graduate School of Arts and Sciences (PH)
St. Louis University. Pius XII Memorial Library (US)
St. Louis University. School of Divinity (US)
St. Louis University School of Law (US)
St. Louis Westerners (US)
St. Luke's College (UK)
St. Luke's Hospital (MM)
St. Luke's Hospital Medical Staff (US)
St. Mark's Institute of Theology (AT)
St. Martin-In-The-Fields Church (UK)
St. Martin's Press (UK)
St. Martin's Press (US)
Saint Mary's College (PH)
Saint Mary's College (US)
St. Mary's Hospital Medical School Students' Union (UK)
St. Mary's University. Division of Continuing Education (CN)
St. Mary's University. English Department (CN)
St. Mary's University School of Law (US)
St. Mary's University Student Council (CN)
St. Mawr Jazz Poetry Project (US)
St. Meinrad Archabbey (US)
St. Olaf College (US)
St.-Otto-Verlag (GW)
St. Patrick's College (AT)
St. Patrick's College. Editorial Committee (IE)
St. Patrick's College. Educational Research Centre (IE)
St. Patrick's Parish House (US)
Editions Saint Paul (FR)
Editions Saint-Paul (SZ)
St. Paul. Metropolitan Transit Commission (US)
Saint Paul. St. Paul (US)
St. Paul Area Chamber of Commerce (US)
St. Paul Athletic Club (US)
St. Paul Companies Inc. (US)
St. Paul Public Library (US)
Saint Paul Society (CN)
Saint Paul University (CN)
Saint Paul University. Institute of Mission Studies (CN)
St. Paul's Abbey (US)
St. Paul's Economic Society (JA)
St. Paul's Indian Mission (US)
St. Paul's University
    see Rikkyo University (JA)
Imprimerie Saint Paulus, S. A. (LU)
Verlag St. Peter (AU)
St. Peter's Abbey (CN)
St. Peter's Press (CN)
Uitgegeven voor de St. Pietersabdij van Steenbrugge (BE)
St. Regis Paper Co. (US)
St. Regis Publications, Inc. (US)
St. Rita School for the Deaf (US)
St. Stephens Mission (US)
St. Thomas More College (CN)
St. Thomas More Society (AT)
St. Thomas's Hospital Medical School (UK)

St. Vincent. Government Information Service (XM)
St. Vincent de Paul Superior Council for Southern Africa (SA)
St. Vladimir's Orthodox Theological Seminary (US)
St. Wilfrid's Church (SA)
St. Xavier College (US)
Sairaalatalousyhdistys r.y (FI)
Saitama University (JA)
Armando Saitta, Ed. & Pub. (IT)
Saiva Siddhanta Mahasamajam (II)
Saiva Sithantha Sungum of South Africa (Universal Mission) (SA)
Saiwai Shoho (JA)
Sajit Print (II)
Saket Economic Survey (II)
Sakhalinskaya Oblastnaya Biblioteka (UR)
Sakthi Sugars Ltd. (II)
Editorial Sal Terrae (SP)
Sala Foundation (PR)
Salamon e Agustoni Editori (IT)
Frank Salantrie, Ed. & Pub. (US)
Salar Jung Museum (II)
Salart House Inc. (US)
Editorial Salcedo, S. A. (MX)
SALCO (NE)
Salem County Historical Society (US)
Salem State College. Student Government Association (US)
Editrice Salentina - Galatina (IT)
Sales and Marketing Executives International, Inc. (US)
Sales Association of the Chemical Industry, Inc. (US)
Sales Executives Club of New York (US)
Sales Tax Practitioners' Association (II)
Salesian Missions (US)
Salesman's Guide, Inc. (US)
Salisbury State College (US)
Salisbury Times, Inc. (US)
Salk Institute for Biological Studies (US)
Salome (US)
Salon International de la Confiserie Chocolaterie Biscuiterie (FR)
Salon International de la Machine Agricole (FR)
Salon Ltd. (US)
Salone Nautico Internazionale di Genoa (IT)
Salotto Culturale (IT)
Salt Lake Area Chamber of Commerce (US)
Salt Lick Press (US)
Salt Water Sportsman, Inc. (US)
Salted Feathers (US)
Saltzman Companies (US)
Salvage Bids (US)
Salvat Editores, S.A. (SP)
Salvation Army (AT)
Salvation Army (NZ)
Salvation Army (NR)
Salvation Army (SA)
Salvation Army (UK)
Salvation Army (US)
Salvation Army (KE)
Salvation Army. Canada Territorial Headquarters (CN)
Salvation Army in Malaysia and Singapore (SI)
Salvationist Publishing and Supplies, Ltd. (UK)
Gaetano Salveti, Ed. & Pub. (IT)
Salvo Imprevisti (IT)
Arti Grafiche A. Salvoni e Co., S.A. (SZ)
Salzburg. Bundesland Salzburg (AU)
Salzburg. Stadtverkehrsbuero Salzburg (AU)
Salzburger Aktiengesellschaft fuer Elektrizitaetswirtschaft (AU)
Sam Houston State University. English Department (US)
Sam Houston State University. Institute of Contemporary Corrections and the Behavioral Sciences (US)
Sam Lusky (US)
Samatat Prakashan (II)
Sambandan International Press (MY)
Samford University (US)
Samfundet de Nio (SW)
Samfundet for Dansk Genealogi og Personalhistorie (DK)
Samisdat (US)
Samizdat (UK)
Sammenslutningen af Lokalhistoriske Arkiver (DK)
Samoa Times Ltd. (WS)
Samriddhi Publications (II)
Howard W. Sams & Co., Inc. (US)
Samsom Publications Ltd. (UK)
Samsom Uitgeverij B. V. (NE)
T. J. Samuel, Ed. & Pub. (CN)
Samvirkende Danske Haveselskaber (DK)
Samvirkende Koebmandsforeninger i Danmark (DK)
San Antonio Development Agency (US)
San Antonio District Dental Society (US)
San Beda College (PH)
San Bernardino County Library (US)

San Bernardino County Museum Association (US)
San Diego (City) City Planning Department (US)
San Diego (County) County Planning Department (US)
San Diego (County) Department of Education (US)
San Diego (County) Integrated Planning Office (US)
San Diego Applause Magazine, Inc. (US)
San Diego Biomedical Symposium. Proceedings (US)
San Diego Chamber of Commerce (US)
San Diego County Dental Society (US)
San Diego County Labor Council (US)
San Diego County Medical Society (US)
San Diego Floral Association (US)
San Diego Genealogical Society (US)
San Diego Historical Society (US)
San Diego Law Review Association (US)
San Diego Magazine Publishing Co. (US)
San Diego Museum of Man (US)
San Diego Numismatic Society Inc. (US)
San Diego Society of Natural History (US)
San Diego State University. Bureau of Business and Economic Research (US)
San Diego State University Press (US)
San Francisco Aquarium Society Inc. (US)
San Francisco Bay Area Dance Coalition (US)
San Francisco Bay Area Rapid Transit District (US)
San Francisco Bay Conservation and Development Commission (US)
San Francisco Labor Council, AFL-CIO (US)
San Francisco Labor Council Newspaper Association (US)
San Francisco Maritime Museum (US)
San Francisco Medical Society (US)
San Francisco Phoenix (US)
San Francisco Planning and Urban Renewal Association (US)
San Francisco Publishing Co. (US)
San Francisco Review of Books (US)
San Francisco Society for the Prevention of Cruelty to Animals (US)
San Francisco State University. Adan E. Treganza Anthropology Museum (US)
San Francisco State University. Alumni Association (US)
San Francisco State University. Audio Visual Center (US)
San Francisco State University. Journalism Department (US)
San Francisco Sunday Examiner & Chronicle (US)
San Francisco Theological Seminary (US)
San Francisco Unified School District (US)
San Gabriel Valley Dental Society (US)
Imprenta San Jose (CL)
San Jose State University (US)
San Jose State University. School of Business (US)
San Jose Teachers Association (US)
San Juan. Gobierno Municipal (PR)
San Luis Obispo County Historical Society (US)
San Luis Valley Historical Society, Inc. (US)
Editrice San Marco (IT)
San Marino. Segreteria di Stato per gli Affari Esteri (SM)
San Mateo County Dental Society (US)
Javier San Roman, Ed. & Pub. (SP)
Sanatorio di Collinaia (IT)
Sanaullah Publications (PK)
Sanborn Map Company, Inc. (US)
Ramon Sanchez Contreras, Ed. (MX)
Luis C. Sanchez Fogarty, Ed. & Pub. (MX)
Sanctuary Press Ltd. (UK)
Sand and Gravel Association Limited (UK)
Sandbach Parochial Church Council (UK)
Karl Sandels, Ed. & Pub. (SW)
Sanders Worldwide, Inc. (US)
T. K. Sanderson Organization (US)
Sanderson Publications Ltd. (CN)
Sandes Soldiers' & Airmen's Homes (UK)
Sandoz AG (SZ)
Sandoz Pharmaceuticals. Drug Information Association (US)
SANE: A Citizens' Organization for a Sane World (US)
Sanford Evans Publishing Ltd. (CN)
Sangamon State University (US)
Sangamon State University. Illinois Legislative Studies Center (US)
Sangeet Natak Akademi
    see National Academy of Music, Dance and Drama (II)
Sangre de Cristo Press (US)
Sangyo Boeki Kenkyusho
    see Tokyo College of Economics. Institute of Industrial and Commercial Research (JA)
Sangyo Kagaku Kenkyusho
    see Osaka University. Institute of Scientific and Industrial Research (JA)
Sangyo Press Ltd. (JA)
Sanitary Maintenance (US)

Sanity Now  (US)
S. Sankaran, Ed. & Pub.  (II)
Sankore  (ML)
Sankt Gallische Naturwissenschaftliche Gesellschaft
  (SZ)
Sankyo Co. Ltd.  (JA)
Sankyo Co., Ltd. Central Research Laboratories  (JA)
Sankyo K. K. Chuo Kenkyusho
  see Sankyo Co., Ltd., Research Laboratories  (JA)
Sanoma Osakeyhtio  (FI)
Sanomalehtien Liitto  (FI)
Sanpo Inc.  (JA)
Sanshi Shikenjo
  see Japan. Sericultural Experiment Station  (JA)
Sanskrit College. Department of Postgraduate Training
  and Research  (II)
Casa Editrice G. C. Sansoni S.p.A.  (IT)
Sant Sipahi  (II)
Santa Barbara Museum of Natural History  (US)
Santa Clara (County) County Planning Department
  (US)
Santa Clara County Historical and Genealogical
  Society  (US)
Santa Fe, Argentina. Centro Provincial de
  Documentacion e Informacion. Educativa,  (AG)
Santa Gertrudis Breeders' (Australia) Association
  (AT)
Santamaria e Correa Ltda.  (BL)
Sante et Sport  (FR)
Santiago del Estero, Argentina. Direccion General de
  Investigaciones Estadistica y Censos  (AG)
Santuari Francescani Valle di Rieti  (IT)
Editora Santuario  (BL)
Santuario de la Virgen del Rosario  (AG)
Santuario della Madonna del Perpetuo Soccorso  (IT)
Santuario di Nettuno  (IT)
Santuario Madonna di Barbana  (IT)
Santuario S. Giuseppe da Copertino  (IT)
Sanve Publishing, Inc.  (PH)
Sanyo Chemical Industries Ltd.  (JA)
Livraria Sao Jose  (BL)
Sao Paulo, Brazil (City) Biblioteca Municipal Mario de
  Andrade  (BL)
Sao Paulo, Brazil. Centrais Eletricas. Setor de Estudos
  de Mercado  (BL)
Sao Paulo, Brazil. Departamento de Aguas e Energia
  Eletrica. Secretaria dos Servicos e Obras Publica
  (BL)
Sao Paulo, Brazil. Departamento de Edificios e Obras
  Publicas  (BL)
Sao Paulo, Brazil. Instituto de Saude. Divisao de
  Hansenologia e Dermatologia Sanitaria  (BL)
Sao Paulo, Brazil. Secretaria da Agricultura do Estado.
  Instituto de Economia Agricola  (BL)
Sao Paulo, Brazil. Secretaria da Agricultura. Instituto
  de Economia Agricola  (BL)
Sao Paulo, Brazil. Secretaria da Educacao  (BL)
Sao Paulo, Brazil. Secretaria de Economia e
  Planejamento. Coordenadoria de Planejamento
  (BL)
Sao Paulo. Servico Social do Comercio. Conselho
  Tecnico de Economia, Sociologia e Politica  (BL)
Sao Paulo, Brazil. Superintendencia de Saneamento
  Ambiental  (BL)
Sao Tome e Principe. Reparticao Provincial dos
  Servicos de Estatistica  (SF)
Sappho Publications Ltd.  (UK)
Sapporo Ika Daigaku
  see Sapporo Medical College  (JA)
Sapporo Ika Daigaku Fuzoka Gan Kenkyusho
  see Sapporo Medical College. Cancer Research
  Institute  (JA)
Sapporo Medical College  (JA)
Sapporo Medical College. Cancer Research Institute
  (JA)
Sarada Ranganathan Endowment for Library Science,
  Bangalore  (II)
Sarah Lawrence College  (US)
Sarajevska Armijska Oblast  (YU)
Sarasota Publishing Corp.  (US)
Sarasvat  (II)
Sarathi Karyalaya  (II)
Saratovskii Universitet  (UR)
Sarawak. Department of Agriculture. Research Branch
  (MY)
Sarawak. Department of Statistics  (MY)
Sarawak. Government Printing Office  (MY)
Sarawak Economic Development Corporation  (MY)
Sarawak Electricity Supply Corporation  (MY)
Editrice Sarda Fossataro Cagliari  (IT)
Sardar Patel Institute of Economics and Social
  Research  (II)
Sardar Patel University  (II)
Sardar Patel University. Department of Economics
  (II)
Sarganserlaendische Buchdruckerei AG  (SZ)
Porter Sargent Publishers, Inc.  (US)
SARP Uitgewers  (SA)

Sartotecnica S.p.A.  (IT)
Sarvadeshik Arya Pratinidhi Sabha  (II)
Sarvodaya Prachuralayam  (II)
Sarvotkrushta Marathi Katha  (II)
Saskatchewan. Alcoholism Commission  (CN)
Saskatchewan. Bureau of Statistics  (CN)
Saskatchewan. Department of Agriculture. Family
  Farm Improvement Branch  (CN)
Saskatchewan. Department of Culture and Youth
  (CN)
Saskatchewan. Department of Finance  (CN)
Saskatchewan. Department of Highways  (CN)
Saskatchewan. Department of Highways and
  Transportation. Planning Branch  (CN)
Saskatchewan. Department of Industry and Commerce
  (CN)
Saskatchewan. Department of Labour. Research and
  Planning Division  (CN)
Saskatchewan. Department of Mineral Resources
  (CN)
Saskatchewan. Department of Mineral Resources.
  Mineral Records Branch  (CN)
Saskatchewan. Department of the Environment  (CN)
Saskatchewan. Department of Tourism and Renewable
  Resources  (CN)
Saskatchewan. Highway Traffic Board  (CN)
Saskatchewan. Medical Care Insurance Commission
  (CN)
Saskatchewan Archaeological Society  (CN)
Saskatchewan Archives Board  (CN)
Saskatchewan Association for the Mentally Retarded.
  Regina Branch  (CN)
Saskatchewan Association of Educational Media
  Specialists  (CN)
Saskatchewan Association of Housing and Nursing
  Homes  (CN)
Saskatchewan Association of Rural Municipalities
  (CN)
Saskatchewan Centre of the Arts  (CN)
Saskatchewan Council of Social Studies Teachers
  (CN)
Saskatchewan Council on Educational Administration
  (CN)
Saskatchewan Educational Research Association
  (CN)
Saskatchewan English Teachers Association  (CN)
Saskatchewan Farmstart Corporation  (CN)
Saskatchewan Genealogical Society  (CN)
Saskatchewan Government Employees' Association
  (CN)
Saskatchewan Government Insurance Office  (CN)
Saskatchewan Guidance and Counseling Association
  (CN)
Saskatchewan Gun Collectors Association  (CN)
Saskatchewan Home Economics Teachers' Association
  (CN)
Saskatchewan Housing Corporation  (CN)
Saskatchewan Industrial Education Association  (CN)
Saskatchewan Library Association  (CN)
Saskatchewan Motor Club  (CN)
Saskatchewan Natural History Society  (CN)
Saskatchewan Oil and Gas Corporation  (CN)
Saskatchewan Poetry Society  (CN)
Saskatchewan Provincial Library  (CN)
Saskatchewan Registered Nurses' Association  (CN)
Saskatchewan Research Council  (CN)
Saskatchewan Research Council Library  (CN)
Saskatchewan School Trustees Association  (CN)
Saskatchewan Science Teachers' Society  (CN)
Saskatchewan Society for Education Through Art
  (CN)
Saskatchewan Teachers' Federation  (CN)
Saskatchewan Teachers' Federation. Early Childhood
  Education Council  (CN)
Saskatchewan Telecommunications  (CN)
Saskatchewan Tourist Association  (CN)
Saskatchewan Trucking Association  (CN)
Saskatchewan Water Supply Board  (CN)
Saskatchewan Wildlife Federation  (CN)
Saskatchewan Writers Guild  (CN)
Sasquatch Publishing, Inc.  (US)
Sastu Sahitya Mudranalaya Trust  (II)
Satellite Video Exchange Society  (CN)
Joel Sater, Ed. & Pub.  (US)
Satire-Verlag  (GW)
Sepp Sattelberger, Editor  (AU)
Saturday Centre  (AT)
Saturday Evening Post Company  (US)
Saturday Review Book Club  (US)
Saturday Review Inc.  (US)
Saudi Arabia. Central Department of Statistics  (SU)
Saudi Arabia. Ministry of Finance and National
  Economy. Central Department of Statistics
  see Saudi Arabia. Central Department of Statistics
  (SU)
Saudi Arabia. Ministry of Hajj and Aukaf  (SU)
Saudi Arabian Monetary Agency  (SU)
Verlag Sauerlaender  (SZ)

J.D. Sauerlaender's Verlag  (GW)
Saugar University
  see University of Saugar  (II)
Sauna-Verlag Werner Thomas  (GW)
W. B. Saunders Co.  (US)
W. B. Saunders Co. Ltd.  (UK)
Sauvage  (FR)
Savacou  (JM)
Savage  (US)
Savanna Forestry Research Station  (NR)
Savannah Magazine, Inc.  (US)
Savannah State College  (US)
Editions J. Savaron  (FR)
Save on Shopping Directory  (US)
Save the Children Fund  (UK)
Save the Kangaroo Committee  (AT)
Save the Nation  (KO)
Savetot za Prosveta na SR Makedonija  (YU)
Savez Arheoloskih Drustava Jugoslavije  (YU)
Savez Arhitekata Hrvatske  (YU)
Savez Drustava Arhivskih Radnika Jugoslavije  (YU)
Savez Drustava Defektologa Jugoslavije  (YU)
Savez Drustava Istoricara Jugoslavije  (YU)
Savez Drustava Pravnika Hrvatske  (YU)
Savez Drustava Psihologa SFR Jugoslavije  (YU)
Savez Drustava za Strane Jezike i Knjizevnosti SFRJ
  (YU)
Savez Drustava za Tehniku Zavarivanja Jugoslavije
  (YU)
Savez Ekonomista Bosne i Herzegovine  (YU)
Savez Ekonomista Hrvatske  (YU)
Savez Ekonomista Jugoslavije  (YU)
Savez Ekonomista Srbije  (YU)
Savez Ekonomista Vojvodine  (YU)
Savez Elektrotehnickih Inzenjera i Tehnicara Hrvatske
  (YU)
Savez Energeticara SR Hrvatske  (YU)
Savez Farmaceutskih Drustava Jugoslavije  (YU)
Savez Geodetskih Inzenjera i Geometara S F R J
  (YU)
Savez Geodetskih Inzenjera i Geometara SR Hrvatske
  (YU)
Savez Gluvih i Nagluvih Jugoslavije  (YU)
Savez Gradjevinskih Inzenjera i Tehnicara SR Srbije
  (YU)
Savez Hemicara i Tehnologa Jugoslavije  (YU)
Savez Inzenjera i Tehnicara Jugoslavije  (YU)
Savez Inzenjera i Tehnicara Sumarstva i Industrije za
  Preradu Drveta SR BiH  (YU)
Savez Inzenjera i Tehnicara Tekstilaca SR Srbije
  (YU)
Savez Jevrejskih Opstina Jugoslavije  (YU)
Savez Kemicara i Tehnologa Hrvatske  (YU)
Savez Kompozitora Jugoslavije  (YU)
Savez Komunista Jugoslavije  (YU)
Savez Lekarskih Drustava SFR Jugoslavije  (YU)
Savez Novinara Jugoslavije  (YU)
Savez Omladine Gimnazije, Vladimir Vitasovic"
  (YU)
Savez Omladine Hrvatske  (YU)
Savez Omladine Vojvodine  (YU)
Savez Organizacija za Socijalisticko Vaspitanje i Brigu
  o Djeci Bosne i Hercegovine  (YU)
Savez Organizacija za Tehnicku Kulturu Jugoslavije
  (YU)
Savez Pedagoskih Drustava Jugoslavije  (YU)
Savez Poljoprivrednih Inzenjera i Tehnicara Hrvatske
  (YU)
Savez Poljoprivrednih Inzenjera i Tehnicara Jugoslavije
  (YU)
Savez Radio-Amatera Jugoslavije  (YU)
Savez Rezervnih Vojnih Staresina Beograda  (YU)
Savez Sindikata Jugoslavije  (YU)
Savez Sindikata Jugoslavije. Sluzba za Informacije i
  Dokumentaciju  (YU)
Savez Socijalisticke Omladine Bosne i Hercegovine
  (YU)
Savez Socijalisticke Omladine Crne Gore  (YU)
Savez Socijalisticke Omladine Hrvatske, Zagreb.
  Centar Drustvenih Djelatnosti  (YU)
Savez Socijalisticke Omladine Hrvatske, Zagreb.
  Sveucilisna Konferencija  (YU)
Savez Socijalisticke Omladine Jugoslavije  (YU)
Savez Socijalisticke Omladine Vojvodine. Pokrajinska
  Konferencija  (YU)
Savez Sportskih Ribolovnih Drustava SR Hrvatske
  (YU)
Savez Sportskih Ribovolovaca Bosne i Hercegovine
  (YU)
Savez Strojarskih i Brodogradjevnih Inzenjera i
  Tehnicara Hrvatske  (YU)
Savez Studenata Beograda  (YU)
Savez Studenata Jugoslavije  (YU)
Savez Studenata Medicinskih Fakulteta u Zagrebu i
  Rijeci  (YU)
Savez Udruzenja Borca Narodno Oslobodilacgot Rata.
  Opcinski Odbor Dalmacije  (YU)
Savez Udruzenja Folklorista Jugoslavije  (YU)

Savez Udruzenja Pravnikov Jugoslavije (YU)
Savez Udruzenog Pravoslavnog Svestenstva SFRJ (YU)
Savez Veterinara i Veterinarskih Tehnicara SFRJ. Odbor za Izdavacku Delatnost (YU)
Savez Zeleznicara Esperantista Jugoslavije (YU)
Savezni Zavod za Zdravstvenu Zastitu, Belgrade (YU)
Savigny-Stiftung (GE)
Saving Grace (AT)
Savings Association League of New York State (US)
Savings Bank Association of New York State (US)
Savings Banks Association of Massachusetts (US)
Savings Banks Insitute (UK)
Savjet Organizacija za Pomoc Mentalno Retardiranim Osobama u SFRJ (YU)
De Savornin Lohman Stichting
  see Jhr. Mr. A. F. de Savornin Lohman Stichting (NE)
Savremena Praksa (YU)
Sawell Publications Ltd. (UK)
Sawmill Clinic (US)
Editions de Saxe (FR)
Saxon och Lindstroems Foerlags AB (SW)
Sayuz Pismennikaw Belarusskai S. S. R. (UR)
Scalabrini Fathers (UK)
Oy Scan-Auto AB (FI)
Scandalous Bohemians of New Jersey (US)
Scandia (SW)
Scandinavia Philatelic Society (UK)
Scandinavian Airlines (SW)
Scandinavian American Bulletin (US)
Scandinavian Association for Research on Latin America (SW)
Scandinavian Association for Thoracic and Cardiovascular Surgery (SW)
Scandinavian Association of Geneticists (SW)
Scandinavian Association of Obstetricians and Gynaecologists (SW)
Scandinavian Association of Plastic Surgeons (SW)
Scandinavian Association of Urology (SW)
Scandinavian Blues Association (SW)
Scandinavian Building Research Congress (DK)
Scandinavian Institute of African Studies
  see Nordiska Afrikainstitutet (SW)
Scandinavian Institute of Asian Studies (DK)
Scandinavian Media Ltd. (DK)
Scandinavian Media Service (NO)
Scandinavian News Co. (CN)
Scandinavian Oil Gas Magazine (NO)
Scandinavian Orthopaedic Association (DK)
Scandinavian Philatelic Services Corp. (US)
Scandinavian Physiological Society (SW)
Scandinavian Science Press Ltd. (DK)
Scandinavian Society for Clinical Chemistry and Clinical Physiology (NO)
Scandinavian Society for Economic and Social History and Historical Geography (NO)
Scandinavian Society for Plant Physiology (DK)
Scandinavian Society of Rheumatologists (SW)
Scandinavian Sociological Association (NO)
Scanpet (Scandinavian Petroleum) A-S (NO)
Scarboro Foreign Mission Society (CN)
Scarborough College. Students Council (CN)
Scarborough Publishing Co. (US)
Scarecrow Books (US)
Scarecrow Press, Inc. (US)
Scena Illustrata (IT)
Scenograficky Ustav (CS)
Schaafsma en Brouwer (NE)
Verlag Deutsche Schachblaetter (GW)
Schachklub Hietzing (AU)
Schacht Verlag GmbH (GW)
Schachverlag Gerhard Katzer (GW)
Verlag Moritz Schaefer (GW)
Hans Schaefer, Ed. & Pub. (GW)
Sidney Schafer (US)
L. Schaffrath (GW)
Verlag M. und H. Schaper (GW)
R. & M. Scharfenberg Literature Searchers (US)
Scharnhorst-Buchkameradschaft GmbH (GW)
F. K. Schattauer Verlag (GW)
Meyer Schattner (US)
Schechter Report-Labs (US)
Hansisches Verlagskontor H. Scheffler (GW)
Verlag A. Schendl (AU)
Schenkman Publishing Company, Inc. (US)
Leo Schepman (NE)
Scherma (IT)
Fachverlag Schiele und Schoen GmbH (GW)
Verlag Schiffahrt und Weltverkehr AG (SZ)
Schiffahrtmedizinisches Institut der Marine (GW)
Schiffahrts-Verlag Hansa C. Schroedter und Co. (GW)
Schiffahrts-Verlag Rheinschiffahrt (GW)
Schiffbautechnische Gesellschaft e.V. (GW)

Schiffli Lace and Embroidery Manufacturers Association (US)
Schild-Verlag GmbH (GW)
Schillerschule (GW)
Max Schimmel Verlag OHG (GW)
Schimmelpfeng GmbH (GW)
G. Schindele Verlag GmbH (GW)
Victor O. Schinnerer & Co. (US)
Buchdruckerei Schippert und Co. (SZ)
G. Schirmer, Inc. (US)
Schlach Peremohy (GW)
Charles Schlacks, Jr., Ed. & Pub. (US)
Phyllis Schlafly (US)
Schleswig-Holstein. Innenministerium (GW)
Schleswig-Holstein. Kultusministerium (GW)
Schleswig-Holstein. Landesamt fuer Wasserhaushalt und Kuesten (GW)
Schleswig- Holsteinischer Heimatbund (GW)
Willy Schleunung GmbH und Co. KG (GW)
Schluetersche Verlagsanstalt und Druckerei (GW)
Schlumberger Well Services (US)
Schmalenbach-Gesellschaft (GW)
Verlag Schmid GmbH (Freiburg) (GW)
Verlag Dr. Otto Schmidt KG (GW)
Max Schmidt-Roemhild Verlag (GW)
Reinhold Schmidt Verlag (AU)
Kurt Schmidt Verlag (GE)
Erich Schmidt Verlag (Berlin) (GW)
Erich Schmidt Verlag (Bielefeld) (GW)
Verlag Franz Schmitt OHG (GW)
Drukkerij Schmitz B.V. (NE)
Wilhelm Schmitz Verlag (GW)
P.-A. Schmueking (GW)
Verlag Lambert Schneider (GW)
Schnell Publishing Co. (US)
Verlag Schnell und Steiner (GW)
Uitgeverij L.C.E. Schnitger-Noyon (NE)
Schoch und Co. (SZ)
Schocken Books, Inc. (US)
Arnold Schoenberg Institute (US)
Ferdinand Schoeningh (GW)
Schoharie County Historical Society (US)
Scholar House Publishing (CN)
Scholarly Resources, Inc. (US)
Scholars Press (US)
Scholastic Magazines, Inc. (US)
School Administration Publications (US)
School Arts Magazine (US)
School for Parents (CY)
School Government Publishing Co. Ltd. (UK)
School Law Digest Corporation (US)
School Law Review (US)
School Library Association (UK)
School Library Association of New South Wales (AT)
School Library Association of Queensland (AT)
School Library Association of the Northern Territory (AT)
School Library Association of Victoria (AT)
School Management Study Group (US)
School Management Study Group (Fremont) (US)
School Natural Science Society (UK)
School of Living (US)
School of Modern Photography (US)
School of Natural Science Life in Action (US)
School of Oriental and African Studies, University of London (UK)
School of Ozarks Troglophiles (US)
School of Planning and Architecture (II)
School of Tropical Medicine, Calcutta (II)
School of Truth Ltd. (SA)
School of Universal Philosophy & Healing (UK)
School Science and Mathematics Association, Inc. (US)
School Sisters of Notre Dame. Mequon Province (US)
School Vocational Center (Marion County) (US)
School Yarn Publications, Ltd. (UK)
Schoolmaster Publishing Co. Ltd. (UK)
Schools Council (UK)
Schoonmaker Associates (US)
Schopenhauer Gesellschaft e.V. (GW)
Schott & Co. Ltd. (UK)
B. Schott's Soehne (GW)
B. Schott's Soehne (IT)
Schrader und Partner (GW)
Verlag Willy Schrickel (Duesseldorf) (GW)
Schriften zur Zeit GmbH (AU)
Schriftenmissions-Verlag (GW)
Schriftstellerverband der Deutschen Demokratischen Republik (GE)
Schriks' Drukkerij B. V. (NE)
Hermann Schroeder Verlag (Hannover) (GW)
Hermann Schroedel Verlag KG (Darmstadt) (GW)
Horst Schroeder Verlag (GW)
Verlag Anton Schroll und Co. (AU)
Anton Schroll und Co. (GW)

Simon Schuchat, Ed. and Pub. (US)
Schueck Soehne AG (SZ)
Carl Schuenemann Verlag (GW)
Bayerischer Schulbuch-Verlag (GW)
Verlagsgesellschaft Schulfernsehen (GW)
Schulthess Polygraphischer Verlag AG (SZ)
J. H. Schultz Forlag (DK)
Krafthand Verlag Walter Schulz (GW)
Hans Ferdinand Schulz Verlag (GW)
Schutzbund fuer Hausbesitz (GW)
Schutzverband gegen unlauteren Wettbewerb (AU)
Schuyler County Historical Museum (US)
Schuyler County Historical Society (US)
Heinrich Schwab Verlag (GW)
Schwabe und Co. (SZ)
Schwalbe, Deutsche Vereinigung fuer Problemschach (GW)
Schwaneberger Verlag GmbH (GW)
Paedagogischer Verlag Schwann Gmbh (GW)
Verlag Otto Schwartz und Co. (GW)
Verlag Adalbert Schweiger (GW)
Deutscher Verlag fuer Schweisstechnik GmbH (GW)
J. Schweitzer Verlag (GW)
Schweizer Brauerei-Rundschau (SZ)
Schweizer Heimatschutz (SZ)
Schweizer Heimatwerk (SZ)
Verlag Schweizer Kavallerist (SZ)
Schweizer Kneippverband (SZ)
Verlagsgenossenschaft Schweizer Soldat (SZ)
Schweizer Spiegel Verlag AG (SZ)
Schweizer Wirteverband (SZ)
E. Schweizerbart'sche Verlagsbuchhandlung (GW)
Schweizerische Aerzteorganisation (SZ)
Schweizerische Akademie der Medizinischen Wissenschaften (SZ)
Schweizerische Aktion fuer Menschenrechte (SZ)
Schweizerische Amerikanisten-Gesellschaft
  see Societe Suisse des Americanistes (SZ)
Schweizerische Apotheker-Verein
  see Societe Suisse de Pharmacie (SZ)
Schweizerische Bibliophilen-Gesellschaft (SZ)
Schweizerische Botanische Gesellschaft (SZ)
Schweizerische Chemische Gesellschaft (SZ)
Schweizerische Entomologische Gesellschaft (SZ)
Schweizerische Fahrrad und Motorrad Gewerbe Verband (SZ)
Schweizerische Galvanotechnische Gesellschaft (SZ)
Schweizerische Gefluegelzeitung (SZ)
Schweizerische Geisteswissenschaftliche Gesellschaft (SZ)
Schweizerische Gemeinnuetzige Gesellschaft (SZ)
Schweizerische Geologische Gesellschaft (SZ)
Schweizerische Gesellschaft der Offiziere der Sanitatstruppen (SZ)
Schweizerische Gesellschaft der Offiziere des Munitionsdienstes (SZ)
Schweizerische Gesellschaft fuer Asienkunde (SZ)
Schweizerische Gesellschaft fuer Chirurgie (SZ)
Schweizerische Gesellschaft fuer Geschichte der Medizin und der Naturwissenschaften (SZ)
Schweizerische Gesellschaft fuer Gynaekologie (SZ)
Schweizerische Gesellschaft fuer Klinische Chemie (SZ)
Schweizerische Gesellschaft fuer Lebensmittelwissenschaft und- Technologie (SZ)
Schweizerische Gesellschaft fuer Marktforschung (SZ)
Schweizerische Gesellschaft fuer Psychiatrie (SZ)
Schweizerische Gesellschaft fuer Sportmedizin (SZ)
Schweizerische Gesellschaft fuer Statistik und Volkswirtschaft (SZ)
Schweizerische Gesellschaft fuer Theaterkultur (SZ)
Schweizerische Gesellschaft fuer Ur- und Fruehgeschichte (SZ)
Schweizerische Gesellschaft fuer Ur- und Fruehgeschichte. Institut fuer Ur- und Fruehgeschichte der Schweiz (SZ)
Schweizerische Gesellschaft fuer Vogelkunde und Vogelschutz (SZ)
Schweizerische Gesellschaft fuer Volkskunde. (SZ)
Schweizerische Gesellschaft pro Technorama (SZ)
Schweizerische Kartellkommission (SZ)
Schweizerische Katholische Bibelbewegung (SZ)
Schweizerische Konferenz fuer Oeffentliche Fuersorge (SZ)
Schweizerische Kreditanstalt
  see Credit Suisse (SZ)
Schweizerische Kriminalistische Gesellschaft (SZ)
Schweizerische Landesbibliothek
  see Switzerland. Bibliotheque Nationale Suisse (SZ)
Schweizerische Lithographenbund (SZ)
Schweizerische Meteorologische Zentralanstalt
  see Switzerland. Schweizerische Meteorologische Zentralanstalt (SZ)
Schweizerische Musikforschende Gesellschaft (SZ)
Schweizerische Nationalbank (SZ)
Schweizerische Naturforschende Gesellschaft (SZ)

Schweizerische Neurologische Gesellschaft (SZ)
Schweizerische Offiziersgesellschaft (SZ)
Schweizerische Organisation der Homophilen (SZ)
Schweizerische Public Relations Gesellschaft (SZ)
Schweizerische Rueckversicherungs-Gesellschaft (SZ)
Schweizerische Schiffahrtsvereinigung (SZ)
Schweizerische Spenglermeister- und Installateur-
Verband (SZ)
Schweizerische Staatsbuergerliche Gesellschaft (SZ)
Schweizerische Stiftung fuer das Alter (SZ)
Schweizerische Treuhand- und Revisionskammer
(SZ)
Schweizerische Verein fuer Straf- Gefaengniswesen
und Schutzaufsicht (SZ)
Schweizerische Vereinigung der
Versicherungsmathematiker (SZ)
Schweizerische Vereinigung fuer Atomenergie (SZ)
Schweizerische Vereinigung von Textilfachleuten
(SZ)
Schweizerische Verkehrszentrale (SZ)
Schweizerische Volksbank
see Banque Populaire Suisse (SZ)
Schweizerische Zahntechniker-Vereinigung (SZ)
Schweizerische Zentrale fuer Handelsfoerderung (SZ)
Schweizerischen Baumeisterverbandes (SZ)
Schweizerischen Corrosserie Industrie (SZ)
Schweizerischen Kynologischen Gesellschaft (SZ)
Schweizerischen Mathematischen Gesellschaft (SZ)
Schweizerischen Physikalischen Gesellschaft (SZ)
Schweizerischer Aero-Club (SZ)
Schweizerischer Alpwirtschaftlicher Verein (SZ)
Schweizerischer Anwaltsverband (SZ)
Schweizerischer Arbeitslehrerinnen-Verein (SZ)
Schweizerischer Aufklaerungsdienst (SZ)
Schweizerischer Bankverein (SZ)
Schweizerischer Baukaderverband (SZ)
Schweizerischer Berufsverband fuer Tanz und
Gymnastik (SZ)
Schweizerischer Buchdruckerverein (SZ)
Schweizerischer Buchhaendler- und Verleger-Verband
(SZ)
Schweizerischer Bund fuer Jugendherbergen (SZ)
Schweizerischer Bund fuer Jugendliteratur (SZ)
Schweizerischer Bund fuer Naturschutz (SZ)
Schweizerischer Chemiker-Verband (SZ)
Schweizerischer Drogistenverband (SZ)
Schweizerischer Eisenbahnamateur- und
Modellbauclubs (SZ)
Schweizerischer Eisenbahnerverband (SZ)
Schweizerischer Elektrotechnischer Verein (SZ)
Schweizerischer Feldpostverein (SZ)
Schweizerischer Feldweibelverband (SZ)
Schweizerischer Feuerwehrverband (SZ)
Schweizerischer Floristenverband (SZ)
Schweizerischer Forstverein (SZ)
Schweizerischer Fourierverband (SZ)
Schweizerischer Gewerbeverband (SZ)
Schweizerischer Gewerkschaftsbund (SZ)
Schweizerischer Jaegerverband zur Hebung der
Patentjagd und des Wildschutzes (SZ)
Schweizerischer Katholischer Anstalter-Verband (SZ)
Schweizerischer Kaufmaennischer Verein (SZ)
Schweizerischer Kunstverein (SZ)
Schweizerischer Lehrerverein (SZ)
Schweizerischer Lichtspieltheater-Verband (SZ)
Schweizerischer Lithographenbund (SZ)
Schweizerischer Maler und Gipsermeister Verband
(SZ)
Schweizerischer Mechanikermeister-Verband (SZ)
Schweizerischer Metall- und Uhrenarbeitnehmer-
Verband (SZ)
Schweizerischer Musikerverband (SZ)
Schweizerischer Obstverband Zug (SZ)
Schweizerischer Pfadfinderbund (SZ)
Schweizerischer Photographenverband (SZ)
Schweizerischer Reklameverband (SZ)
Schweizerischer Schachverband (SZ)
Schweizerischer Studentenverein (SZ)
Schweizerischer Technischer Verband (SZ)
Schweizerischer Tierschutzverband (SZ)
Schweizerischer Turnverein (SZ)
Schweizerischer Typographenbund (SZ)
Schweizerischer Verband Angestellter Drogisten (SZ)
Schweizerischer Verband des Schmiede,
Landmaschinen, Metall und Holzgewerbe (SZ)
Schweizerischer Verband Evangelischer Arbeitnehmer
(SZ)
Schweizerischer Verband fuer Behindertensport (SZ)
Schweizerischer Verband fuer Beruflichen Unterricht
(SZ)
Schweizerischer Verband fuer Berufsberatung (SZ)
Schweizerischer Verband Staatlich Anerkannter
Physiotherapeuten (SZ)
Schweizerischer Verband Technischer Betriebskader
(SZ)
Schweizerischer Verband von Fachleuten fuer
Alkoholgefaehrdeten- und Suchtkrankenhilfe (SZ)
Schweizerischer Verein fuer Kaeltetechnik (SZ)

Schweizerischer Verein fuer Schweisstechnik (SZ)
Schweizerischer Verein von Gas- und
Wasserfachmaennern (SZ)
Schweizerischer Wasserwirtschaftsverband (SZ)
Schweizerischer Wissenschaftsrat (SZ)
Schweizerischer Zeitungsverleger-Verband (SZ)
Schweizerischer Zentralverband des Musikhandels und
der Angeschlossen Verbaende (SZ)
Schweizerisches Bundesarchiv
see Switzerland. Schweizerisches Bundesarchiv
(SZ)
Schweizerisches Gutenbergmuseum (SZ)
Schweizerisches Institut fuer Gewerbliche Wirtschaft
(SZ)
Schweizerisches Institut fuer Hauswirtschaft (SZ)
Verlag Schweizerisches Katholisches Bibelwerk (SZ)
Schweizerisches Landesmuseum (SZ)
Schweizerisches Ost-Institut (SZ)
Schweizerisches Sozialarchiv (SZ)
Schweizerisches Tropeninstitut (SZ)
Journal-Verlag Schwend GmbH (GW)
Schwenkfelder Church. General Conference (US)
Die Schwesternrevue GmbH (GW)
Luigi Scialpi Editore (IT)
Salvatore Sciascia (IT)
Science Activities Publishing Co. (US)
Science & Behavior Books, Inc. (US)
Science and Engineering Research Laboratory
see under Waseda University (JA)
Science and Government Report Inc. (US)
Science & Medicine Publications (US)
Science and Medicine Publishing Co., Inc. (US)
Science and Society, Inc. (US)
Science and Technology (US)
Science and Technology Agency (UK)
Science Associates International Inc. (US)
Science Association of Nigeria (NR)
Science Council of Canada (CN)
Science Council of Japan (JA)
Science Editors, Inc. (US)
Science et Industrie (FR)
Science Fiction Book Review Index (US)
Science Fiction Foundation (UK)
Science Fiction Research Association (US)
Science Fiction Review Monthly (US)
Science Fiction Writers of America (US)
Science for the People (US)
Science Foundation for Physics (AT)
Science Foundation of the Philippines (PH)
Science History Publications Ltd. (UK)
Science House Publishers (US)
Science Museum Library (UK)
Science Museum of Minnesota (US)
Science Museum of Victoria (AT)
Science of Man (US)
Science of Mind Publications (US)
Science Policy Foundation (UK)
Science Research Associates (US)
Science Research Council (UK)
Science-Service (FR)
Science Service, Inc. (Marion) (US)
Science Service, Inc. (Washington) (US)
Science Teachers Association of New South Wales
(AT)
Science Teachers Association of New York State
(US)
Science Teachers Association of Queensland (AT)
Science Teachers Association of Tasmania (AT)
Science Teachers Association of Victoria (AT)
Science Teachers Association of Western Australia
(AT)
Sciences de l'Information (FR)
Sciences et Avenir (FR)
Scientia (IT)
Scientia Paedagogica Experimentalis (BE)
Scientia Verlag (GW)
Scientiarum Historia (BE)
Scientific Agricultural Society of Finland
see Suomen Maataloustieteellinen Seura (FI)
Scientific American Inc. (US)
Scientific Ballooning and Radiations Monitoring
Organization (FR)
Scientific Committee for Antarctic Research
see under Council for Scientific and Industrial
Research (SA)
Scientific Documentation Centre Ltd. (UK)
Scientific Exploration Society (UK)
Scientific Indexing & Retrieval Service (UK)
Scientific Information Consultants Ltd. (UK)
Scientific Instrument Co. Ltd. (II)
Scientific Manpower Commission (US)
Scientific Meetings Publications (US)
Scientific Newsletters, Inc. (US)
Scientific Press Ltd. (UK)
Scientific Research Committee, Uttar Pradesh (II)
Scientific Research Council (JM)
Scientific Society of Pakistan (PK)

Scientific Society of the Medical Care Organization
(UA)
Scientific Surveys Ltd. (UK)
Editrice Scientifica (Milan) (IT)
Editoriale Scientifica (Naples) (IT)
Libreria Scientifica Editrice (IT)
Edizioni Scientifiche Inglesi Americane (IT)
Edizioni Scientifiche Italiane S.p.A. (IT)
Edizioni Scientifiche Techniche Europee (IT)
Scientists Institute for Public Information (New York)
(US)
Scientists Institute for Public Information (St. Louis)
(US)
Scienza dell'Alimentazione (IT)
Scienza e Tecnica (IT)
Scienze S.p.A. (IT)
Editura Scinteia (RM)
Sciweizerischer Buchhaendler- und Verleger-Verband
(SZ)
Scope Enterprises, Inc. (US)
Scope Publications Inc. (US)
Scope Publishing Co (TR)
Scotia (UK)
Scotia Publications (US)
Scotian Pen Guild (CN)
Scots Independent (Newspapers) Ltd. (UK)
Scots Philosophical Club (UK)
Scots Secretariat Pamphlets Organisation (UK)
E. P. Scott (US)
Scott Advertising & Publishing Co. (US)
Scott Air Force Base (US)
W. D. Scott & Co. (AT)
T. G. Scott and Son Ltd. (UK)
O. M. Scott & Sons (US)
Colin Scott, Ed. & Pub. (UK)
Scott Periodicals Corp. (US)
Scott Polar Research Institute (UK)
Scott Publications (Pty) Ltd. (SA)
Scott Publishing Company (US)
Scottish Academic Press Ltd. (UK)
Scottish & Universal Newspapers Ltd. (UK)
Scottish Area National Union of Mineworkers (UK)
Scottish Association of Master Bakers (UK)
Scottish Association of Opticians (UK)
Scottish Braille Press (UK)
Scottish Catholic Historical Association (UK)
Scottish Centre for Ornithology & Bird Protection
(UK)
Scottish Children's League of Pity (UK)
Scottish Clubman Ltd. (UK)
Scottish Council for Research in Education (UK)
Scottish Economic Society (UK)
Scottish Episcopal Church (UK)
Scottish Farmer Publications Ltd. (UK)
Scottish Folk Directory (UK)
Scottish Genealogy Society (UK)
Scottish Georgian Society (UK)
Scottish Graphical Association (UK)
Scottish Grocer (UK)
Scottish Group of the University. College and
Research Section of the Library Association (UK)
Scottish Hardware and Drysalters Association (UK)
Scottish Home and Health Department (UK)
Scottish Institute of Adult Education (UK)
Scottish Institute of Missionary Studies (UK)
Scottish Landowners' Federation (UK)
Scottish Library Association (UK)
Scottish Local Authorities Special Housing Group
(UK)
Scottish Marine Biological Association (UK)
Scottish Milk Marketing Board (UK)
Scottish Mountaineering Club (UK)
Scottish Opera Club (UK)
Scottish Ornithologists Club (UK)
Scottish Pharmacist (UK)
Scottish Pipe Band Association (UK)
Scottish Planning Exchange (UK)
Scottish Postmark Group (UK)
Scottish Reformation Society (UK)
Scottish Rock Garden Club (UK)
Scottish Society for Industrial Archaeology (UK)
Scottish Society for Prevention of Vivisection (UK)
Scottish Stock Exchange Association (UK)
Scottish Sub Aqua Club (UK)
Scottish Tartans Society (UK)
Scottish Temperance Alliance (UK)
Scottish Tourist Board (UK)
Scottish Tramway Museum Society (UK)
Scottish Typographical Association (UK)
Scottish Union of Students (UK)
Scottish Wildlife Trust (UK)
Scout Association (UK)
Scout Association of Australia (AT)
Scout Association of Australia. Victoria Branch (AT)
Scout Memorabilia (US)
Scout Union of Finland (FI)
Scouts de France (FR)
Scowrers & Molly Maguires of San Francisco (US)

Scrambling Press (US)
Scranton Publishing Co. (US)
Scree (US)
Screen Actors Guild (US)
Screen Actors Guild. New York Branch (US)
Screw Machine Publishing Co., Inc. (US)
Scribe (US)
Charles Scribner's Sons (US)
Scrip Services (UK)
Scripps Clinic and Research Foundation (US)
Scripps Institution of Oceanography (US)
Script Publications (UK)
Scripta Mathematica (US)
Scripta Mercaturae Verlag (GW)
Scripta Publishing Co. (US)
Scripta Technica, Inc. (US)
Editions Scriptar S.A. (SZ)
Forlaget Scriptor (DK)
Scripture Gift Mission (UK)
Scripture Press Publications, Inc. (US)
Scripture Union (US)
Scruncheons (CN)
Sculpture in the Environment (US)
Scuola Archeologica di Atene (IT)
Scuola Artigiana del Libro- Pubblico Passeggio (IT)
Scuola Beato Angelico (IT)
Scuola di Guerra, Biblioteca (IT)
Scuola Normale Superiore di Pisa (IT)
Editrice la Scuola S.p.A. (IT)
Sdruzeni Ceskoslovenskych Filatelistu (CS)
Sdruzeni pro Odbyt Dehtovych Barviv (CS)
Sdruzenia Slovenskych Katolikyo (US)
Sea Cadet Corps of the United Kingdom (UK)
Sea Spray (AT)
Sea Turtle Inc. (US)
Seabird Group (UK)
Seaboard Subscription Agency (US)
Seabury Press (US)
B. A. Seaby Ltd. (UK)
Seacoast Newspaper Ltd. (UK)
Seafarers Education Service (UK)
Seafarers International Union of Canada (CN)
Seafarers' International Union of North America
  (US)
Seafood Exporters Association of India (II)
Seaforth Advertising (UK)
Seal Club Chatter (US)
Seal Publishing Co. (Pty) Ltd. (SA)
Seamen's Church Institute of New York (US)
Seamen's Union of Australia (AT)
SEAMEO Central Coordinating Board for Tropical
  Medicine & Public Health (TH)
Sean Dorman Manuscript Society (UK)
Seaport Publishing Co. (US)
Seara Medica Neurocirurgica (BL)
Empresa de Publicidade Seara Nova, S.A.R.L. (PO)
Search Group Inc. (US)
G. D. Searle and Co. (US)
G.D. Searle & Co. Management Information Services
  (US)
Sears Foundation for Marine Research (US)
Seaside Topics (US)
Seatrade Publications Ltd. (UK)
Seattle Audubon Society (US)
Seattle Chamber of Commerce (US)
Seattle Film Society (US)
Seattle-First National Bank (US)
Seattle Folklore Society (US)
Seattle Genealogical Society (US)
Seattle-King County Dental Society (US)
Seattle Opportunities Industrialization Center (US)
Seattle Professional Engineering Employees
  Association (US)
Seattle Public Library (US)
Seattle Repertory Theatre (US)
Seattle Teachers Association (US)
Seattle University (US)
Seattle University. Department of English (US)
Sebald Druck und Verlag (GW)
Secker & Warburg (UK)
Second Back Row Press (AT)
Second Coming Press (US)
Second Foundation (US)
Second Page, Inc. (US)
Second Wave (US)
Secondary School Theatre Conference (US)
Secondary Student Union of Western Australia (AT)
Ediciones Secretariado Trinitario (SP)
Secretariat International de l'Enseignement
  Universitaire des Sciences Pedagogiques
    see International Secretariat for the University
    Study of Education (BE)
Secretariat of the National Assembly (KO)
Secretaries and Managers Association (AT)
Secular Subjects (US)
Securitas (FR)
Securities Industry Association, Inc. (US)

Securities Industry Association, Inc. (Washington)
  (US)
Securities Investor Protection Corp. (US)
Security Education (Australasia) Pub. Co. (AT)
Security Gazette Ltd. (UK)
Security Letter, Inc. (US)
Security Pacific National Bank (US)
Security World Publishing Co., Inc. (US)
Sedlabanki Islands (IC)
Sedmay Ediciones (SP)
Sedo S.A (SZ)
Editions Sedom (FR)
Sedona Life (US)
SARL Sedotourmovico (FR)
See Magazines (US)
Karl Seebacher, Ed. & Pub. (US)
Seed Publications Ltd. (UK)
Seed World (US)
Seehafen-Verlag Erik Blumenfeld (GW)
Seeing Eye Inc. (US)
Seel House Press Ltd. (UK)
Seely Genealogical Society (US)
Seems (US)
Seer Ox (US)
Seer's Catalogue Inc. (US)
Gerd Segers, Ed. & Pub. (BE)
Editrice Segesta S.p.A. (IT)
Editions Seghers (FR)
Editrice Segisa (IT)
Segretariato Diocesano Malati (IT)
Jean Seguin & Associates (CN)
Narender K. Sehgal, Ed. & Pub. (II)
Seibundo Shinkosha Publishing Co., Ltd. (JA)
Seido Language Institute (JA)
Seiki Gakkai
  see Japan Society of Precision Engineering (JA)
Verlag Seiler und Co. (GW)
Seilsport Maritimt Forlag (NO)
Seisan Gijutsu Kenkyusho
  see University of Tokyo. Institute of Industrial
  Science (JA)
Seishin Igaku Institute of Psychiatry (JA)
Seismological Society of America (US)
Seismological Society of America. Eastern Section
  (US)
Seismological Society of Japan (JA)
Sekai Sekiyu Kaigi Nihon Kokunai Iinkai
  see World Petroleum Congress. Japanese National
  Committee (JA)
Sekiyu Gakkai
  see Japan Petroleum Institute (JA)
Sekiyu Kogyo Jihyo-sha (JA)
Sekretariat Pemerintah Daerah (IO)
Selby Botanical Gardens
  see Marie Selby Botanical Gardens (US)
Selby's Laboratory News (AT)
Selcuklu Tarih ve Medeniyeti Enstitusu (TU)
Selden Society (UK)
Selecciones del Reader's Digest (Iberia) S.A. (SP)
Selecciones Tauro S.A. (PE)
Selecoes do Readers Digest (BL)
Selecoes Odontologicas Editora e Publicidade Ltda
  (BL)
Select (PH)
Select Information Exchange (US)
Select Publishing Co. (US)
Selecta-Verlag (GW)
Selected Bibliography of Gerbil Research Publications
  (US)
Selection du Reader's Digest S.A.
  see Beste aus Reader's Digest AG (SZ)
Selection du Reader's Digest, S.A. (FR)
Selection Sketsmasa (IO)
Selections Medicales et Scientifiques (FR)
Selektiv Reklam AB (SW)
Selektiv Reklame A-S (DK)
Selenium & Tellurium Development Association, Inc.
  (US)
Selepress S.p. A. (IT)
Selezione Dal Reader's Digest S.p.A. (IT)
Self-Realization Fellowship, Inc. (US)
Self Reliance Association of American Ukrainians
  (US)
Emmerich Selinger, Ed. & Pub. (AU)
A. R. L. Selkirk (UK)
Sell's Publications Ltd. (UK)
Selmer Company (US)
Selskabet for Dansk Skolehistorie (DK)
Selskabet for de Norske Fiskeriers Fremme (NO)
Selskabet for Historie og Samfundsoekonomi (DK)
Selskabet for Naturlaerens Udbredelse (DK)
Selskabet for Oslo Byes Vel (NO)
Selskabet for Stuekulturer i Danmark (DK)
Selvejende Institution Politisk Revy (DK)
Selvigs Forlag A-S (NO)
Semaine des Hopitaux (FR)
Semana, S.A. (SP)
Semana Vitivinicola (SP)

Ediciones Semanales Gallegas, S.A. (SP)
Editorial Semanario Israelita S. A. (AG)
Semanario Sabado (EC)
Seminar for Arabian Studies (UK)
Seminar fuer Freiheitliche Ordnung (GW)
Seminar on the Acquisition of Latin American Library
  Materials (US)
Seminarhilfswerk Innsbruck (AU)
Seminarie Vlaamse Dialektologie te Gent (BE)
Seminaries voor Historische en voor Vergelijkende
  Pedagogiek
    see under Rijksuniversiteit Te Gent (BE)
Seminario Arcivescovile di Milano (IT)
Seminario de Argueologia y Numismatica Aragonesas
  (SP)
Seminario de Filologia Vasca Julio de Urquijo (SP)
Seminario de Historia Social y Economica (SP)
Seminario Francescano di Giaccherino (IT)
Seminario Matematico Garcia de Galdeano. Facultad
  de Ciencias (SP)
Seminario Nacional de Controle de Qualidade (BL)
Seminario Xavier Zubiri (SP)
Seminex (US)
Seminole Junior College. Student Government
  Association (US)
Semiotext (e), Inc. (US)
Semmelweis Orvostorteneti Muzeum (HU)
Semmon Toshokan Kyogikai
  see Special Libraries Association, Japan (JA)
Uitgeverij Semper Agendo (NE)
Semplex of U.S.A. (US)
David Senahi, Ed. & Pub. (US)
Senales (AG)
Senate of Canada (CN)
Senckenbergische Naturforschende Gesellschaft
  (GW)
Sendai Fukusokan Kagaku Kenkyusho
  see Sendai Institute of Heterocyclic Chemistry
  (JA)
Sendai Institute of Heterocyclic Chemistry (JA)
SENDOC (Small Enterprises National Documentation
  Centre)
  see Small Industry Extension Training Institute
  (II)
Seneca College (CN)
Senegal. Archives (SG)
Senegal. Centre d'Etude des Civilisations (SG)
Senegal. Direction de l'Exploitation Meteorologique
  (SG)
Senegal. Direction de la Statistique (SG)
Senegal. Imprimerie Nationale (SG)
Senegal. Ministere de l'Information et de
  Telecommunications. Direction de l'Information
  (SG)
Senegal. Ministere des Finances et des Affaires
  Economiques. Direction de la Statistique
    see Senegal. Direction de la Statistique (SG)
Senegal. Office de Radiodiffusion-Television (SG)
Senger Annoncen (SZ)
Sen'i Gakkai
  see Society of Fiber Science and Technology (JA)
Sen'i Kenkyusha Co. (JA)
Senior Citizen News (US)
Senior Citizens Association of Los Angeles County
  (US)
Senior Citizens Today (US)
Senior Golf Publications Co. (US)
Senior World Publications (US)
Senmon Toshokan Kyogikai
  see Special Libraries Association, Japan (JA)
Sennacieca Asocio Tutmonda (FR)
Sensen-Verlag Ernst Schwarcz (AU)
Senterpartiets Hovedorganisasjon (NO)
Sentinel Publishing Co. (US)
Sentinel Publishing Association (SA)
Sentinel Publishing Co. (CN)
Sentry Books Inc. (US)
Seoul Journal of Medicine (KO)
Seoul National University (KO)
Seoul National University. College of Commerce
  (KO)
Seoul National University. Institute of Economic
  Research (KO)
Seoul National University. Institute of Management
  Research (KO)
Seoul National University. Population and
  Development Studies Center (KO)
Seoul National University. School of Public Health
  (KO)
SEPEG (SZ)
SEPeM s.r.l. (IT)
Sepher-Hermon Press, Inc. (US)
Sepreco S.A.R.L (FR)
Sept-Jours Inc. (CN)
P. T. Septenarius (IO)
Septieme Aurore (FR)
SEPTIMA (FR)
Sequences (CN)

Sequoia Institute at Claremont (US)
Umberto Serafini (IT)
Serbia. Republicki Zavod za Unapredjivanje Vaspitanja
    i Obrazovanja SR Srbije (YU)
Serbia. Zavod za Statistiku (YU)
Serbian Cultural Club "St. Sava" in New South Wales
    (AT)
Serbian League of Canada (CN)
Serbian Literary Association (US)
Serbian National Defence (AT)
Serbian National Shield Society (CN)
Serengeti Research Institute (TZ)
Bruno Sereni, Ed. & Pub. (IT)
I. N. Serges (GR)
Sericultural Experiment Station
    see Japan. Sericultural Experiment Station (JA)
Serina Press (US)
Patrick Sermadiras (FR)
Servants of the People Society (II)
Service Biblique Evangile et Vie (FR)
Service Central d'Organisation et Methodes (FR)
Service Commercial. Division Relations Publiques
    Commerciales (IV)
Service d'Exploitation Industrielle des Tabacs et
    Allumettes (FR)
Service d'Information des Communautes Europeennes
    (EI)
Service de Centralisation des Etudes Genealogiques et
    Demographiques de Belgique (BE)
Service de Presse Economique des Industries
    Alimentaires (FR)
Service de Presse, Edition, Information (FR)
Service de Recherches Juridiques Comparatives (FR)
Service de Renseignements du Repertoire Industriel
    (FR)
Service des Instruments de Mesure (FR)
Service des Relations Publiques de Houilleres du Nord
    et du Pas-de-Calais (FR)
Service Employees International Union (US)
Service Monde-Ami. Secretariat National (CN)
Service Publications, Inc. (US)
Service Publishing Co. (US)
Service Social d'Aide aux Emigrants (FR)
Service Station Association of N.S.W. Ltd. (AT)
Service Station Publications Ltd. (UK)
Service Technique pour l'Education (FR)
Service to Youth Council Inc. (AT)
Services and Centres of Mental Hygiene (IT)
Editions Services Interentreprises (BE)
Services Techniques et Commerciaux de la Reunion
    des Musees Nationaux (FR)
Servicio Comercial de la Industria Textil Algodonera
    (SP)
Servicio de Extension Agraria (SP)
Servicio de Publicaciones Agrarias (SP)
Servicio de Transmisiones del Ejercito (MX)
Servicio Informativo Espanol (SP)
Servicio Latino-Americano y Asiatico de Vivienda
    Popular (CK)
Servicio Municipal de Parques y Jardines de Barcelona
    (SP)
Servicios Industriales Pesqueros S.A. (SP)
Servico de Publicacoes da M.P. (PO)
Servico Nacional de Appendizagem Comerical -
    SENAC (BL)
Servico Nacional de Cancer (BL)
Servico Social da Industria. Divisao de Orientacao
    Social (BL)
Servicos de Publicacoes Especializadas Ltda (BL)
Servir Mieux (FR)
Servisads Ltd. (UK)
Servizio di Sanita Aeronautica (IT)
Servizio Italiana Pubblicazioni Internazionali s.r.l.
    (IT)
William Sessions Ltd. (UK)
Seth G.S. Medical College and K.E.M. Hospital. Staff
    Society (II)
Mrs. Padma Seth, Ed. & Pub. (II)
Sarabjeet Seth, Ed. & Pub. (II)
Seto Marine Biological Laboratory
    see under Kyoto University (JA)
Seto Rinkai Jikkensho
    see Kyoto University. Seto Marine Biological
    Laboratory (JA)
Seton Hall University (US)
Seton Hall University. School of Business
    Administration (US)
Seton Hall University. Student Center (US)
Settanta Anni di Calcio (IT)
Settlement Study Center, Rehovot (IS)
Editions du Seuil (FR)
Sevak Publications (II)
Swami Bholananda Sevamandal (II)
Seven (US)
Seven Arts Press, Inc. (US)
Seven Square Press (US)
Seventh-Day Adventist Church (SA)
Seventh-Day Adventist Church (US)

Seventh-Day Adventist Church in Britain (UK)
Seventh-Day Adventist Church. Trans-Africa Division
    (SA)
Seventh-Day Adventist Reform Movement (US)
Seventh-Day Adventists (II)
Seventh-Day Adventists (US)
Seventh-Day Adventists. Australasian Division (AT)
Seventies Press (US)
Severn-Wylie Jewett Co. (US)
Severno- Kavkazskii Gornometallurgicheskii Institut
    (UR)
Severoceske Nakladatelstvi (CS)
Sewing Machine Times Ltd. (UK)
Sex Information and Education Council of the U.S.
    (US)
Sexpol Association (FR)
Sexual Law Reporter (US)
Seybold Publications, Inc. (US)
Seychelles. National Archives and Museum (SE)
Seychelles Farmers Association (SE)
Seychelles People's United Party (SE)
Seychellois Press Ltd. (SE)
Seymour Press Ltd. (UK)
Seyse s.r.l. (AG)
Editrice Sfera (IT)
Sha-Sim Enterprises, Inc. (US)
Shaare Zedek Hospital. Falk Schlesinger Institute for
    Medical Halachic Research (IS)
Shaded Room Press (US)
Shaftesbury Society (UK)
Navalchad T. Shah & Co. (II)
P. M. Shah, Ed. & Pub. (II)
Shahpar (II)
Shakai Hosho Kenkyusho
    see Social Development Research Institute (JA)
Shakai-jinruigakkai
    see under Tokyo Metropolitan University (JA)
Shakai Kagaku Kenkyusho
    see University of Tokyo. Institute of Social Science
    (JA)
Shakespeare Newsletter (US)
Shakespeare Society of Japan (JA)
Shakespearean Authorship Society (UK)
Shalom Ltda. (BL)
Shama Magazine (II)
Shaman, Inc. (US)
Shambhala Publications Inc. (US)
Shameless Hussy Press (US)
Shamie Publishing Co. (US)
Shamrock Agencies (TZ)
Shankpainter (US)
Shannon County Historical Society (US)
Shantarani Sons & Co. (II)
Shanti Sadan (UK)
Shantih (US)
Shanty Hollow Corporation (US)
M. E. Shapre, Inc. (US)
Sharada Ranganathan Endowment for Library Science
    (US)
Sharing (US)
Sharing: a Journal of Community (US)
L. K. Sharma (II)
S. K. Sharma, Pub. (II)
Sudhir Sharma, Ed. & Pub. (II)
M. E. Sharpe, Inc. (US)
J. Sharpe Publications (Pty) Ltd. (SA)
Shasta Historical Society (US)
Dennis Shattuck (US)
Shaver Poultry Breeding Farms, Ltd (CN)
Shaw & Sons Ltd. (UK)
Shaw Society of California (US)
SHAWCO
    see University of Cape Town. Students Health and
    Welfare Centres Organisation (SHAWCO) (SA)
Shawnee Nation (US)
William K. Shearer, Ed. & Pub. (US)
Carl B.E. Shedd (US)
Sheet Metal Industries (UK)
Sheet Metal Workers' International Association (US)
Sheffer Co. (US)
Sheffield Chamber of Commerce (UK)
Sheffield University Metallurgical Society (UK)
Shejzat (IT)
Shelby Publishing Co. Inc. (US)
Shelby Publishing Corporation (US)
Sheldon Memorial Art Gallery (US)
Shell (US)
Shell Austria AG (AU)
Shell Canada Ltd. (CN)
Shell Eastern Petroleum Ltd. (SI)
Shell International Petroleum Co. Ltd. (UK)
Shell-Mex. and B.P. Ltd (UK)
Shell Nederland B.V. (NE)
Shell Nederland Raffinaderij B.V. (NE)
Shell Oil Co. (US)
Shell Southern Africa (Pty) Ltd. (SA)
Shellac Export Promotion Council (II)
Shelter Publications, Inc. (US)

Herbert M. Shelton, Ed. & Pub. (US)
Shennen Publishing & Publicity Co. (AT)
Shepard's Citations, Inc. (US)
Sheperd College (US)
Sheppard Press, Ltd. (UK)
Sheriff & Police Reporter (US)
Sheriffs' Association of Texas (US)
Sherlock Holmes Society of London (UK)
Dean Sherman, Inc. (US)
John Sherratt & Son Ltd. (UK)
Sherwood Anderson Society (US)
Sherwood Publishing Co. (AT)
Shetland Council of Social Service (UI)
Shevchenko Scholastic Society (US)
Shevchenko Scientific Society (US)
Shia Imami Ismailia Association for Kenya (KE)
Shield Publishing Co. (US)
Shiga University. Institute for Economic Research
    (JA)
Shigaku-kai
    see Historical Society of Japan (JA)
Shigen Sogo Kaihatsu Kenkyusho
    see Resources Exploitation Institute (JA)
Shih Chieh Wen Wu Kung Ying She Tsung Ching
    Hsiao (CH)
Shikizai Kyokai
    see Japan Society of Colour Materials (JA)
Shikoku Agricultural Experiment Station
    see Japan. Shikoku Agricultural Experiment Station
    (JA)
Shikoku Entomological Society (JA)
Shikoku Konchu Gakkai
    see Shikoku Entomological Society (JA)
Shikshak Publishing House (II)
C. W. Shilling Auditory Research Center, Inc. (US)
Shimer College (US)
Shimizu Construction Co. Ltd (JA)
Shin Buddhist Association (UK)
Shin Gijutsu-sha
    see M. H. Information Center (JA)
Shin Nihon Chutanzo Kyokai
    see New Japan Casting and Forging Society (JA)
Shin Nihon Ishi Kyokai
    see New Japanese Doctors' Association (JA)
Shin-Norinsha Co., Ltd. (JA)
Shindan to Chiryosha Co. (JA)
Shining Waters Press (US)
Shinohara Publishers, Inc. (JA)
Shinrigaku Hyoron Kankokai (JA)
Shinseikatsu Undo Kyokai (JA)
Shinshu Konchu Gakkai
    see Entomological Society of Shinshu (JA)
Shinshu University. Faculty of Engineering (JA)
Shinshu University. Faculty of Medicine (JA)
Shinshu University. Faculty of Science (JA)
Shinshu University. Faculty of Textile Science and
    Technology (JA)
Ship Research Institute
    see Japan. Ship Research Institute (JA)
Ship Research Institute of Norway
    see Norges Skipsforskningsinstitutt (NO)
Shipbuilders Council of America (US)
Shiplovers Society of Victoria (AT)
Shipping and Port Review (II)
Shipping Digest Inc. (US)
Shipping Newspapers (W.A.) Ltd. (AT)
Shipyard General Workers' Federation of British
    Columbia (CN)
Shire Horse Society (UK)
Shire Publications (UK)
Shirl Olympius (US)
Shirley Institute (UK)
Shiryo Yushutsunyu Kyogikai
    see Japan Feed Trade Association (JA)
Shiryoku Inc. (US)
Shivaji University (PK)
Shizuoka University. Faculty of Science (JA)
Sh'ma Inc. (US)
Shoe and Allied Trades Research Association
    (SATRA) (UK)
Shoe Service Institute of America (US)
Shoe String Press Inc. (US)
Shoe-the-Coast Shoe Reporter (US)
Shoe Trades Publishing Co. (US)
Shokokusha Publishing Co., Inc. (JA)
Shokubai Kenkyusho Kiyo
    see Hokkaido University. Research Institute for
    Catalysis (JA)
Shokubutsu Bunri Chiri Gakkai
    see Phytogeographical Society (JA)
Shokuryo Keizai Shimbun Sha (JA)
Shokuryo Kogaku Kenkyusho
    see Kyoto University. Research Institute for Food
    Science (JA)
Shomei Gakkai
    see Illuminating Engineering Institute of Japan
    (JA)
Shoni Aiiku Kyokai

*see* Association for the Care of the Child  (JA)
Shooting Federation of Canada  (CN)
Shopping Center Digest  (US)
Shore Publishing Co.  (US)
Short Brothers & Harland Ltd.  (UK)
Short Wave Magazine Ltd.  (UK)
Shorthorn Society of the United Kingdom of Great
 Britain and Ireland  (UK)
Shortland Publications  (NZ)
Shot Publications  (II)
Shout  (UK)
Show-Business  (FR)
Show Reporter Publishing Co., Inc.  (US)
Showa Medical Association  (JA)
Showa University. School of Medicine  (JA)
Showbill Publications Ltd.  (CN)
Showcase Publishing Co., Inc.  (US)
Showcast  (AT)
Showunie  (NE)
Shree Gurudev Ashram  (II)
Shree Jiwaji Observatory  (II)
Shreveport Chamber of Commerce  (US)
Shreveport Sun, Inc.  (US)
Shri Chhatrapati Shivaji University  (II)
Shri Ram Centre for Industrial Relations & Human
 Resources  (II)
Shri Ram College of Commerce  (II)
Shrikumar Poddar  (US)
Izdatel'stvo Shtiintsa  (UR)
Shugoofa  (II)
U. Shukla, Ed. & Pub.  (II)
Leo Shull Publications  (US)
Shuppan News Co. Ltd.  (JA)
Shuttle Craft Guild  (US)
Paul Shuttleworth, Ed. & Pub.  (US)
Satyendra Shyam, Ed. & Pub.  (II)
SIACH (Israeli New Left)  (IS)
Siam Publications Ltd.  (TH)
Siam Society  (TH)
Siberian Husky Club of America, Inc.  (US)
Sibyl-Child Press, Inc.  (US)
Sicilia del Lunedi  (IT)
SIDA
 *see* Sweden. Styrelsen Foer Internationell
 Utveckling  (SW)
Sidarth Publications  (II)
Siddha Yoga Dham  (II)
Sideler  (FR)
Siderurgia Brasileira  (BL)
Siebel Publishing Co.  (US)
Horst Siebert Verlag  (GW)
Siecle a Mains  (UK)
Siegel-Verlag Otto Mueller  (GW)
Siegler und Co. Verlag fuer Zeitarchive GmbH  (GW)
Sielkundige Instituut van die Republiek van Suid-
 Afrika
 *see* Psychological Institute of the Republic of South
 Africa  (SA)
Siemens Aktiengesellschaft  (GW)
Siemens-Albis  (SZ)
Siemens, S.A.  (SP)
Siempre Inc.  (US)
Siena College  (US)
Sierra Club  (US)
Sierra Club. Atlantic Chapter  (US)
Sierra Club International Program  (US)
Sierra Club. New York City Group  (US)
Sierra Club. Oklahoma Chapter  (US)
Sierra Commercial Enterprise  (SL)
Sierra Economic Services  (US)
Sierra Leone. Central Statistics Office  (SL)
Sierra Leone. Ministry of Education  (SL)
Sierra Leone. Ministry of Finance  (SL)
Sierra Leone. Ministry of Information and
 Broadcasting  (SL)
Sierra Leone Geographical Association  (SL)
Sierra Leone Library Association  (SL)
Sierra Leone Society  (SL)
Sigalert Enterprises Ltd.  (CN)
Sigert-Verlag GmbH  (GW)
Sigma Alpha Iota, International Music Fraternity for
 Women  (US)
Sigma Delta Kappa  (US)
Sigma Gamma Epsilon  (US)
Sigma Nu Phi Fraternity (Legal)  (US)
Sigma Theta Tau National Honor Society of Nursing
 (US)
Sigma Xi, Scientific Research Society of North
 America  (US)
Sigma Zeta  (US)
Signal  (CS)
Signalert Corporation  (US)
Editions Revue Signature  (FR)
Editions les Signes des Temps  (FR)
Significant Advances in Science  (US)
Editora Signo Ltda  (BL)
Oscar Signorini, Ed. & Pub.  (IT)
Signpost Press  (US)

Signpost Publications  (US)
Signs of the Times Publishing Co.  (US)
Siipikarjanhoitajain Liito  (FI)
A. W. Sijthoff International Publishing Co.  (NE)
Sikh Cultural Centre  (II)
Sikh Cultural Society of Great Britain  (UK)
Uitgeverij de Sikkel N.V.  (BE)
Uitgeverij de Sikkel N.V.  (NE)
Sikorsky Aircraft  (US)
Silayan Filipino Community Center  (CN)
Silent Majority V.O.I.C.E.  (US)
Silent Press Inc.  (US)
Silex  (FR)
A.S.B.L. Silicates Industriels  (BE)
Silk and Art Silk Mills' Research Association  (II)
Silk and Rayon Textiles Export Promotion Council
 (II)
Silky Terrier Club of America, Inc.  (US)
Egon Siller Verlag  (GW)
Silliman University  (PH)
Sillon Catholique  (FR)
M. L. Silva Haydu & Cia. Ltda.  (BL)
Editions Andre Silvaire  (FR)
Silver and Gold Report  (US)
Silver Institute  (US)
Silver Publishing Co. Inc.  (US)
Silver Scarab Press  (US)
Sima Publishers  (US)
M. I. Simansky, Pub.  (FR)
Editions la Simarre  (FR)
SIMEP Editions  (FR)
Simes S.p.A.  (IT)
Simian Society of America, Inc.  (US)
Simmental Journal, Inc.  (US)
Simmenthal S.p.A.  (IT)
Simmons-Boardman Publishing Corporation  (US)
Simmons College. Alumnae Association  (US)
Simmons College. School of Library Science  (US)
Simmons Kinfolk  (US)
R. Richard Simmons Ltd.  (UK)
Q. K. Simms  (US)
Geo. Alex. Simon  (CN)
Simon and Schuster, Inc.  (US)
Simon & Schuster of Canada, Ltd.  (CN)
H.K. Simon Co., Inc.  (US)
Simon Fraser University  (CN)
Simon Public Relations, Inc.  (US)
Simon van der Stel Foundation  (SA)
Simon's Town Historical Society  (SA)
Simplicity Pattern Co., Inc.  (US)
Simpson Publishing Co.  (US)
Sims Printing Co., Inc.  (US)
Simulation Councils, Inc.  (US)
Simulation-Gaming-News, Inc.  (US)
Simulations Publications, Inc.  (US)
Sin Nombre, Inc.  (PR)
SIN-Staedtebauinstitut  (GW)
Sinai Hospital of Detroit  (US)
David Sinclair Publications  (US)
Sind University
 *see* University of Sind  (PK)
Sind University Press  (PK)
Sindacato di Mogliano  (IT)
Sindacato Direttivi delle Ferrovie Dello Stato  (IT)
Sindacato Italiano Lavoratori Bonifica Irrigazione
 (IT)
Sindacato Italiano Postelgrafonico  (IT)
Sindacato Nazionale Autonomo della Scuola
 Elementare  (IT)
Sindacato Nazionale Estetisi Diplomati  (IT)
Sindacato Nazionale Ingegneri Liberi Professionisti
 Italiani  (IT)
Sindacato Nazionale Odontotecnici  (IT)
Sindacato Nazionale Presidi e Professori di Ruolo
 (IT)
Sindacato Nazionale Scuola Media  (IT)
Sindacato Unitario Medici d'Italia  (IT)
Editrice Sindicale Italia s.r.l.  (IT)
Sindicato da Industria da Construcao Civil do Estado
 da Guanabara  (BL)
Sindicato de Trabajadores Ferrocarrileros de la
 Republica Mexicana  (MX)
Sindicato dos Bancarios de Sao Paulo
 *see* Sindicato dos Empregados Em Estabelecimentos
 Bancarios de Sao Paulo  (BL)
Sindicato dos Bancos do Estado da Guanabara.
 Assessoria Economica  (BL)
Sindicato dos Empregados em Estabelecimentos
 Bancarios de Sao Paulo  (BL)
Sindicato dos Lojistas do Comercio de Sao Paulo
 (BL)
Sindicato Nacional da Industria de Tratores,
 Caminhoes, Automoveis e Veiculos Similares  (BL)
Sindicato Nacional de Industria Quimicas  (SP)
Sindicato Nacional de la Pesca  (SP)
Sindicato Nacional de la Piel  (SP)
Sindicato Nacional de Trabajadores de la Aviacion
 (CU)

Sindicato Nacional del Metal  (SP)
Sindicato Nacional dos Editores de Livros. Centro de
 Bibliotecnia  (BL)
Sindicato Nacional dos Oficiais Maquinistas da
 Marinha Mercante  (PO)
Sindicato Nacional Textil  (SP)
Sindikat Delavcev Vzgoje in Izobrazevanja SRS  (YU)
Sindikat Radnika Drustvenih Djelatnosti Crne Gore
 (YU)
Sindikat Radnika Drustvenih Djelatnosti SR Bosne i
 Hercegovine  (YU)
Sing out, Inc.  (US)
Singapore. Department of Statistics  (SI)
Singapore. Economic Development Board  (SI)
Singapore. Family Planning and Population Board
 (SI)
Singapore. Government Printing Office  (SI)
Singapore. Housing and Development Board  (SI)
Singapore. Metrication Board  (SI)
Singapore. Ministry of Culture  (SI)
Singapore. Ministry of Finance  (SI)
Singapore. Ministry of Health  (SI)
Singapore. Ministry of Labour  (SI)
Singapore. Ministry of Science and Technology  (SI)
Singapore. Ministry of the Environment  (SI)
Singapore. Monetary Authority  (SI)
Singapore. National Maritime Board  (SI)
Singapore. National Statistical Commission  (SI)
Singapore. National Statistical Commission. Library-
 Cum-Archive  (SI)
Singapore. Primary Production Department  (SI)
Singapore. Science Council  (SI)
Singapore Armed Forces Education Department-
 Personnel Research & Education Department (SI)
Singapore Buddhist Youth Organisations Joint
 Celebrations Committee  (SI)
Singapore Chinese Chamber of Commerce  (SI)
Singapore Cine Club  (SI)
Singapore Computer Society  (SI)
Singapore Guppy Club  (SI)
Singapore Indian Chamber of Commerce  (SI)
Singapore Institute of Architects  (SI)
Singapore Institute of Planners  (SI)
Singapore International Chamber of Commerce  (SI)
Singapore Investor  (SI)
Singapore Linguistic Society  (SI)
Singapore Manufacturers' Association  (SI)
Singapore National Institute of Chemistry  (SI)
Singapore National Printers Ltd.  (SI)
Singapore Police Academy  (SI)
Singapore Polytechnic Building Society  (SI)
Singapore Polytechnic Draughting Society,  (SI)
Singapore Polytechnic Engineering Society  (SI)
Singapore Polytechnic Polymer Society  (SI)
Singapore Securities Research Institute  (SI)
Singapore Society of Accountants  (SI)
Singapore Sports Council  (SI)
Singapore Tourist Promotion Board  (SI)
Singapore Trained Nurses' Association  (SI)
Singer Company. Kearfott Division  (US)
Raman K. Singh, Ed. & Pub.  (US)
G. Singh, Ed. & Pub.  (II)
M. Gulab Singh & Sons (P). Ltd.  (II)
Pritam Singh  (II)
Sardar Amar Singh & Sons  (II)
Singhal House  (II)
Singing News  (US)
Single Parent Resource Center  (US)
Single Service Institute  (US)
Singles-Mingles, Inc.  (US)
Singles World Corporation  (US)
A. N. Sinha Institute of Social Studies  (II)
Sinha Publishing House  (II)
Sinister Wisdom  (US)
V. M. Sinkar, Ed. & Pub.  (II)
Sinn Fein the Workers' Party  (IE)
Sino-American Buddhist Association  (US)
Sino-American Cultural and Economic Association
 (CH)
Sino-British Trade Council  (UK)
Sinological Society of Hiroshima  (JA)
Sinsinawa Publications  (US)
Sint-Adelbertabdij  (NE)
Sint-Bernardinuscollege  (NE)
Sint Ignatiuscollege  (NE)
Sint Janscollege  (NE)
Sinter Press  (SZ)
Sioux City Magazine  (US)
Sioux City Newspapers, Inc.  (US)
Sioux Falls College Student Association  (US)
Giani Balwant Singh Sant Sipahi , Ed. & Pub.  (II)
Sipario Editrice S.R.L.  (IT)
Sir George Williams University Day Students
 Association  (CN)
Sir Isaac Pitman & Sons Ltd.  (UK)
Sir James Whitney School  (CN)

Sir Thomas Beecham Society  (UK)
Sir Thomas Beecham Society (Cleveland)  (US)
Sir Thomas Beecham Society (Redondo Beach)  (US)
Sira Institute Ltd.  (UK)
Sirene  (NO)
Editions Sirey  (FR)
Sirjana  (NP)
Siskiyou County Historical Society  (US)
Sisson and Parker Ltd.  (UK)
Sistema Bancos de Comercio  (MX)
Sister Cities International  (US)
Sister Courage  (US)
Sisterhood  (US)
Sisters Disciples of the Divine Master  (IT)
Sisters of Homophile Equality  (NZ)
Sisters of Mercy  (US)
Sisters of St. Joseph of Peace  (US)
Sisters of Service  (CN)
Site, Inc.  (US)
Sivananda School of Yoga  (SA)
Six Thirteen  (US)
Sixpack, Inc.  (US)
Sixteen & Vine Church of Christ  (US)
Sixteen Magazines, Inc.  (US)
Sjakkstikka  (NO)
Sjaloom  (NE)
Sjoemannsforeningen  (NO)
Sjomilitaere Samfund  (NO)
A-S Skagerak  (NO)
Skandinavisk Byggfackpress AB  (SW)
Skandinavisk Emballage- och Transport- Tidskrift
  (SW)
Skandinavisk Motor Presse  (DK)
Skandinavisk U F O Information  (DK)
Skandinaviska Enskilda Banken  (SW)
Skarien & Associates  (US)
Skarland Press A-S  (NO)
Skate Magazine  (UK)
Skattebetalarnas Foerening  (SW)
Skema s.r.l.  (IT)
Skeptic Magazine, Inc.  (US)
Aktiebolaget SKF  (SW)
Ski America Enterprises  (US)
Ski Club News, Inc.  (US)
Ski Club of Great Britain  (UK)
Ski-Flash-Neige et Glace  (FR)
Ski Racing, Inc.  (US)
Ski Specialists  (UK)
Skidmore College  (US)
Skiklub Duesseldorf  (GW)
Skil Corporation  (US)
Skillings' Mining Review  (US)
Thomas Skinner Directories  (UK)
Anthony F. Skirius  (US)
Skisport  (US)
T. Skjel Annonsebyraa  (NO)
Panstwowe Przedsiebiorstwo "Skladnica Ksiegarska"
  (PL)
Georg P. Skogberg  (SW)
Skogbrukets og Skogindustrienes Forskningsraad
  (NO)
Skol Vreizh  (FR)
Skola za Obrazovanje Kvalifikovanih Radnika SR
  Srbije  (YU)
Skolaerien Ha Kelennerien Ar Falz  (FR)
Skolepsykologernes Landsforening  (DK)
Skolledarfoerbundet  (SW)
Skolska Knjiga  (YU)
Skolske Novine  (YU)
Skolta Esperanto Ligo  (NE)
Skota Federacio Esperantista  (UK)
Forlaget Skribella A-S  (DK)
Spraakfoerlaget Skriptor  (SW)
Skupnost Slovenskih Obcan  (YU)
Skupstina Opcine Karlovac  (YU)
Skupstina Opcine Krizevci  (YU)
Skupstina Opcine Podravska Slatina  (YU)
Skupstina Opcine Rovinj  (YU)
Sky Diver  (US)
Sky Publishing Corporation  (US)
Skylark  (II)
Skyline Publishers, Inc.  (US)
Skywriter Press  (US)
Skywriting  (US)
Charles B. Slack, Inc.  (US)
George O. Slankard, Ed. & Pub.  (US)
Wydawnictwo "Slask"  (PL)
Slaski Instytut Naukowy  (PL)
Slate Services  (US)
Slavic Gospel Association  (US)
Slavisticno Drustvo Slovenije  (YU)
Sleep Learning Association  (UK)
Slesse News  (CN)
Carl Slienger  (UK)
Slimming Magazine Ltd.  (UK)
R. A. Slinn Ltd.  (UK)
Slit Wrist Magazine  (US)
Sloan-Kettering Institute for Cancer Research  (US)

Slobodna Dalmacija  (YU)
Editions Slog  (FR)
Jacob Slonim Publishing Ltd.  (IS)
Slovak-American Cultural Center  (US)
Slovak Engineering Society  (CS)
Slovak Institute  (US)
Slovak Jesuit Fathers in Canada  (CN)
Slovak League of America  (US)
Slovak V Amerike Weekly Newspaper  (US)
Sloveni in Italia  (IT)
Slovenia. Privredna Komora  (YU)
Slovenia. Republiski Sekretarijat za Notranje Zadeve
  SR Slovenije  (YU)
Slovenian National Federation of Canada  (CN)
Slovenian Women's Union of America  (US)
Slovenska Akademia Vied  (CS)
Slovenska Akademia Vied. Archeologicky Ustav  (CS)
Slovenska Akademia Vied. Ekonomicky Ustav  (CS)
Slovenska Akademia Vied. Filozoficky Ustav  (CS)
Slovenska Akademia Vied. Fyzikalny Ustav  (CS)
Slovenska Akademia Vied. Geofyzikalny Ustav  (CS)
Slovenska Akademia Vied. Geologicky Ustav D. Stura
  (CS)
Slovenska Akademia Vied. Historicky Ustav  (CS)
Slovenska Akademia Vied. Jazykovedny Ustav L.
  Stura  (CS)
Slovenska Akademia Vied. Kabinet Orientalistiky
  (CS)
Slovenska Akademia Vied. Literarnovedny Ustav
  (CS)
Slovenska Akademia Vied. Narodopisny Ustav  (CS)
Slovenska Akademia Vied. Sociologicky Ustav  (CS)
Slovenska Akademia Vied. Umenovedny Ustav  (CS)
Slovenska Akademia Vied. Ustav Dendrobiologie
  (CS)
Slovenska Akademia Vied. Ustav Experimentalnej
  Farmakologie  (CS)
Slovenska Akademia Vied. Ustav Mechaniky Strojov
  (CS)
Slovenska Akademia Vied. Ustav Slovenskej Literatury
  (CS)
Slovenska Akademia Vied. Ustav Statu a Prava  (CS)
Slovenska Akademia Vied. Ustav Stavebnictva a
  Architektury  (CS)
Slovenska Akademia Vied. Ustav Svetovej Literatury a
  Jazykov  (CS)
Slovenska Akademia Vied. Ustav Teorie a Dejin
  Umenia  (CS)
Slovenska Akademia Vied. Ustav Vlastnosti Hornin
  (CS)
Slovenska Akademia Vied. Virologicky Ustav  (CS)
Slovenska Akademija Znanosti in Umetnosti. Institut
  za Arheologijo  (YU)
Slovenska Akademija Znanosti in Umetnosti. Razred
  za Filoloske in Literarne Vede  (YU)
Slovenska Akademija Znanosti in Umetnosti. Razred
  za Prirodoslovne Vede  (YU)
Slovenska Chemicka Spolocnost  (CS)
Slovenska Entomologicka Spolocnost  (CS)
Slovenska Evanjelicka A.V. Cirkva v SFR Juhoslavii
  (YU)
Slovenska Izseljenska Matica  (YU)
Slovenska Narodna Galeria  (CS)
Slovenska Odborova Rada  (CS)
Slovenska Spolocnost pre Racionalnu Vyzivu  (CS)
Slovenske Narodne Muzeum  (CS)
Slovenske Narodne Muzeum. Archeologicky Ustav
  (CS)
Slovenske Pedagogicke Nakladatelstvo  (CS)
Slovenske Rimskokatolicke Skofije  (YU)
Slovenskeho Katolickeho Sokola  (US)
Slovenski Etnografski Muzej  (YU)
Slovensko Farmacevtsko Drustvo  (YU)
Slovensko Geolosko Drustvo  (YU)
Slovensko Zdravnisko Drustvo  (YU)
Slovensky Muzicky Fond  (CS)
Slovensky Spisovatel  (CS)
Slovenskych Otcov Benediktinov  (US)
Slow Learning Childrens Group of W.A.  (AT)
Sluzben Vesnik na Socijalisticka Republika Makedonija
  (YU)
Sluzbeni Vjesnik Opcine Buje, Novigrad i Umag
  (YU)
Small Business Information Centre  (JA)
Small Businessman's Clinic  (US)
Small Farm Press  (US)
Small Industry Extension Training Institute  (II)
Small Pond  (US)
Small Towns Institute  (US)
Smaller Manufacturers Council  (US)
Smar International  (PK)
Smeets International Publications  (NE)
J. B. Smith  (UK)
Albert E. Smith (Printers) Ltd.  (UK)
Al Smith, Ed. & Pub.  (US)
Raymond D. Smith  (US)
Richard Arlen Smith, Ed. & Pub.  (US)
Gladys Smith & Associates  (US)

Wilbur Smith and Associates  (US)
Bruce Main Smith & Co. Ltd.  (UK)
Smith Bucklin and Associates  (US)
H. Royer Smith Co.  (US)
Allen Smith Co., Inc.  (US)
Smith College  (US)
Smith College. School for Social Work  (US)
Smith Institute of Ichthyology
  see under Rhodes University  (SA)
Smith Publications, Inc.  (US)
W.R.C. Smith Publishing Co.  (US)
Smith Publishing Company  (CN)
Smiths Industries Ltd. Aviation Division  (UK)
Smithsonian Institution  (US)
Smithsonian Institution. Archives of American Art
  (US)
Smithsonian Institution Astrophysical Observatory
  (US)
Smithsonian Institution. Center for Short Lived
  Phenomena  (US)
Smithsonian Institution. History of Science Society
  (US)
Smithsonian Institution. Information Systems Division
  (US)
Smithsonian Institution. Museum of History and
  Technology  (US)
Smithsonian Institution Press  (US)
Smithsonian Science Information Exchange  (US)
Smits-N. V.  (NE)
Smitweld N.V.  (NE)
Smoke-Eater Publications  (US)
Smoke Signals Publishing Committee  (AT)
Smudge on the Window  (US)
Ray Smutek, Ed. & Pub.  (US)
Snail Enterprises  (UK)
P. Snelders-Beckmann  (NE)
Foster D. Snell, Inc.  (US)
Snell Publishing Co. Inc.  (US)
Snia Viscosa  (IT)
Snibbe Publications, Inc.  (US)
Snips Magazine, Inc.  (US)
Snoeck-Ducaju en Zoon N.V.  (BE)
Snow Brand Milk Products Co. Ltd.  (JA)
Snow Goer  (US)
Snowmobiler's Race & Rally Magazine  (US)
Snowsports Publications, Inc.  (US)
Snowy Mountains Engineering Corporation  (AT)
Arlis M. Snyder, Ed. & Pub.  (US)
Thelma H. Snyder, Ed. & Pub.  (US)
F. K. Soans, Ed. & Pub.  (II)
Soap and Detergent Association  (US)
Jose Soares de Oliveira, Ed. & Pub.  (PO)
Soaring Society of America, Inc.  (US)
Sobeli  (BE)
Soccer Associates, Inc.  (US)
Soccer File Ltd.  (UK)
Soccer Life Publishing Co.  (US)
Soccer World Publishing Co. Pty. Ltd.  (AT)
Sociaal Economische Raad  (NE)
Sociadade Brasileira de Instrucao  (BL)
Social Administration Association  (UK)
Social Concern, Inc.  (US)
Social Credit Co-Ordinating Centre  (UK)
Social Democratic Party  (DK)
Social Democrats, U.S.A.  (US)
Social Development Research Institute  (JA)
Social Education Society of China  (CH)
Social Impact Foundation  (PH)
Social Innovation Information Service  (US)
Social Legislation Information Service  (US)
Social Life  (II)
Social Psychiatry Research Institute  (US)
Social Science Education Consortium  (US)
Social Science History Association  (US)
Social Science Research Council  (UK)
Social Science Research Council  (US)
Social Science Research Council of Canada  (CN)
Social Science Research Council. Postgraduate Awards
  Division  (UK)
Social Service Board of North Dakota  (US)
Social Service Employees Union. Local 371  (US)
Social Service Publications  (US)
Social Tidsskrift  (DK)
Social Work  (SA)
Publicaciones Sociales Mexicanas  (MX)
Socialist Action Publishing Association  (NZ)
Socialist Commentary Publications Ltd.  (UK)
Socialist Digest  (II)
Socialist Forum  (US)
Socialist International  (UK)
Socialist Labor Party  (US)
Socialist Labor Party of Canada  (CN)
Socialist Left Party  (NO)
Socialist Party of Australia  (AT)
Socialist Party of Great Britain  (UK)
Socialist Party of Japan  (JA)
Socialist World  (II)
Socialist Youth Alliance  (AT)

Socialista (BE)
Socialistes Chretiens de Langue Francaise (SZ)
Socialisticka Akademia Slovenskej Socialistickej Republiky (CS)
Socialisticke Zemedelstvi (CS)
Socialisticky Svaz Mladeze (CS)
Socialisticky Svaz Mladeze. Pionyrska Organizace (CS)
Socialistische Uitgeverij Nijmegen (NE)
Socialmedicinsk Tidskrift (SW)
Sociedad Agronomica de Chile (CL)
Sociedad Americana de Oftalmologia y Optometria (CK)
Sociedad Antioquena de Ingenieros (CK)
Sociedad Argentina de Biologia (AG)
Sociedad Argentina de Cardiologia (AG)
Sociedad Argentina de Escritores (AG)
Sociedad Argentina de Estudios Geograficos (AG)
Sociedad Argentina de Gastroenterologia (AG)
Sociedad Argentina de Investigacion Clinica (AG)
Sociedad Argentina de Investigadores en Ciencia de la Ingenieria Quimica y Quimica Aplicada (AG)
Sociedad Argentina de Leprologia (AG)
Sociedad Argentina de Metales (AG)
Sociedad Argentina de Mineria y Geologia (AG)
Sociedad Argentina de Neuropatologia (AG)
Sociedad Argentina de Oftalmologia (AG)
Sociedad Argentina de Ortodoncia (AG)
Sociedad Argentina de Pediatria (AG)
Sociedad Argentina de Profesores de Santa Escritura (AG)
Sociedad Argentina de Radiologia (AG)
Sociedad Argentina de Urologia (AG)
Sociedad Astronomica de Mexico (MX)
Sociedad Bolivariana de Venezuela (VE)
Sociedad Boliviana de Historia Natural (BO)
Sociedad Canaria de Pediatria (SP)
Sociedad Castellano-Astur-Leonosa de Pediatria (SP)
Sociedad Castellonense de Cultura (SP)
Sociedad Catalana de Seguridad y Medicina del Trabajo (SP)
Sociedad Chihuahuense de Estudios Historicos (MX)
Sociedad Chilena de Historia y Geografia (CL)
Sociedad Chilena de Obstetricia y Ginecologia (CL)
Sociedad Chilena de Otorrinolaringologia (CL)
Sociedad Chilena de Pediatria (CL)
Sociedad Chilena de Quimica (CL)
Sociedad Chilena Entomologia (CL)
Sociedad Cientifica Argentina (AG)
Sociedad Civil Cine al Dia (VE)
Sociedad Colombiana de Arquitectos (CK)
Sociedad Colombiana de Arquitectos. Seccional de Antioquia (CK)
Sociedad Colombiana de Economistas (CK)
Sociedad Colombiana de Matematicas (CK)
Sociedad Colombiana de Obstetricia y Ginecologia y Federacion Colombiana de Sociedades de Obstetricia y Ginecologia (CK)
Sociedad Colombiana de Ortodoncia (CK)
Sociedad Colombiana de Planificacion (CK)
Sociedad Colombiana de Psiquiatria (CK)
Sociedad Colombiana de Quimicos Farmaceuticos (CK)
Sociedad Cubana de Historia de la Medicina (CU)
Sociedad Cubana de Ingenieros (CU)
Sociedad Cultural Amigos del Arte de Baena (SP)
Sociedad de Abogados (HO)
Sociedad de Agricultores de Colombia (CK)
Sociedad de Autores Puertorriquenoes (PR)
Sociedad de Autores y Compositores de Musica (MX)
Sociedad de Bibliotecarios de Puerto Rico (PR)
Sociedad de Biologia de Concepcion (CL)
Sociedad de Ciencias Naturales Aranzadi (SP)
Sociedad de Ciencias Naturales la Salle (VE)
Sociedad de Cirugia de Rosario (AG)
Sociedad de Cirugia del Uruguay (UY)
Sociedad de Cirugia Plastica del Uruguay (UY)
Sociedad de Escritores Hispano-Filipinos (PH)
Sociedad de Fomento de la Cria Caballar de Espana (SP)
Sociedad de Fomento Fabril (CL)
Sociedad de Historia de Rosario (AG)
Sociedad de Historia Natural de Baleares (SP)
Sociedad de Industriales de las Artes Graficas (MX)
Sociedad de la Raza (US)
Sociedad de Legislacion Comparada. Comite Peruano (PE)
Sociedad de Medicina del Trabajo del Uruguay (UY)
Sociedad de Medicina Veterinaria de Chile (CL)
Sociedad de Neurologia. Psiquiatria y Neurocirugia (CL)
Sociedad de Obstetricia y Ginecologia de Buenos Aires (AG)
Sociedad de Obstetricia y Ginecologia de Venezuela (VE)
Sociedad de Patologia Respiratoria (SP)

Sociedad de Pediatria y Puericultura del Paraguay (PY)
Sociedad de Tisiologia y Enfermedades del Torax (UY)
Sociedad Dental de el Salvador (ES)
Sociedad Dominicana de Geografia (DR)
Sociedad Dominicana de Pediatria (DR)
Sociedad Entomologica del Peru (PE)
Sociedad Espanola de Acustica (SP)
Sociedad Espanola de Alergia (SP)
Sociedad Espanola de Anatomia Patologica (SP)
Sociedad Espanola de Anestesiologia y Reanimacion (SP)
Sociedad Espanola de Bromatologia (SP)
Sociedad Espanola de Ceramica y Vidrio (SP)
Sociedad Espanola de Gerontologia (SP)
Sociedad Espanola de Historia de la Medicina (SP)
Sociedad Espanola de Linguistica (SP)
Sociedad Espanola de Oftalmologia (SP)
Sociedad Espanola de Oncologia (SP)
Sociedad Espanola de Optica (SP)
Sociedad Espanola de Otorrinolaringologia (SP)
Sociedad Espanola de Patologia Digestiva (SP)
Sociedad Espanola de Problemistas de Ajedrez (SP)
Sociedad Espanola de Quimicos Cosmeticos (SP)
Sociedad Espanola de Radiodifusion (SP)
Sociedad Espanola de Radiologia y Electrologia Medicas y de Medicina Nuclear (SP)
Sociedad Espanola de Rehabilitacion (SP)
Sociedad Espanola de Socorros Mutuos y Beneficencia (AG)
Sociedad Folklorica de Mexico (MX)
Sociedad Forestal Mexicana A.C. (MX)
Sociedad Geografica de Lima (PE)
Sociedad Geologica del Peru (PE)
Sociedad Ginecologica Espanola (SP)
Sociedad Hebraica Argentina (AG)
Sociedad Honoraria Hispanica for Secondary Schools (US)
Sociedad Ibero-American de Estudios Numismaticos (SP)
Sociedad Latinoamericana de Microscopia Electronica (VE)
Sociedad Latinoamericana de Tuberosas (VE)
Sociedad Luso-Espanola de Neurocirugia (SP)
Sociedad Malacologica del Uruguay (UY)
Sociedad Matematica Mexicana (MX)
Sociedad Medica de Santiago (CL)
Sociedad Medica de Valparaiso (CL)
Sociedad Medica del Centro Materno-Infantil Gral. Maximino Avila Camacho (MX)
Sociedad Medica del Hospital de Mexico, S.S.A. (MX)
Sociedad Mexicana de Alergia e Inmunologia, A.C. (MX)
Sociedad Mexicana de Fisica (MX)
Sociedad Mexicana de Fotogrametria, Fotointerpretacion y Geodesia (MX)
Sociedad Mexicana de Geografia y Estadistica (MX)
Sociedad Mexicana de Historia de la Ciencia y de la Tecnologia (MX)
Sociedad Mexicana de Ingenieria de Costos, A.C. (MX)
Sociedad Mexicana de Micologia (MX)
Sociedad Mexicana de Neumologia y Cirugia de Torax (MX)
Sociedad Mexicana de Neurologia y Psiquiatria (MX)
Sociedad Mexicana de Ortopedia (MX)
Sociedad Mexicana de Pediatria (MX)
Sociedad Mexicana de Planificacion (MX)
Sociedad Nacional de Agricultura (CL)
Sociedad Neurologica Argentina (AG)
Sociedad Nuevoleonesa de Historia, Geografia y Estadistica (MX)
Sociedad Odontologica Antioquena (CK)
Sociedad Odontologica de Chile (CL)
Sociedad Odontologica Latino-Americano de Implantes Aloplasticos y Trasplantes (VE)
Sociedad Peruana de Derecho Internacional (PE)
Sociedad Petrolifera Espanola, Shell, S.A. (SP)
Sociedad Quimica del Peru (PE)
Sociedad Rural Argentina (AG)
Sociedad Salvadorena de Odontologia Infantil (ES)
Sociedad Uruguaya de Patologia Clinica (UY)
Sociedad Uruguaya de Pediatria (UY)
Sociedad Vasco Navarra de Pediatria (SP)
Sociedad Venezolana de Filosofia (VE)
Sociedad Venezolana de Gastroenterologia (VE)
Sociedad Venezolana de Puericultura y Pediatria (VE)
Sociedad Venezolana de Radiologia (VE)
Sociedad Venezolana de Urologia (VE)
Sociedad y Derecho (PE)
Sociedade Brasileira de Anestesiologia (BL)
Sociedade Brasileira de Angiologia (BL)
Sociedade Brasileira de Cardiologia (BL)
Sociedade Brasileira de Cultura (BL)

Sociedade Brasileira de Dermatologia (BL)
Sociedade Brasileira de Direito Internacional (BL)
Sociedade Brasileira de Economistas Rurais (BL)
Sociedade Brasileira de Educacao (BL)
Sociedade Brasileira de Entomologia (BL)
Sociedade Brasileira de Estudos Sobre Discos Voadores (BL)
Sociedade Brasileira de Filosofos Catolicos (BL)
Sociedade Brasileira de Fisica (BL)
Sociedade Brasileira de Geografia (BL)
Sociedade Brasileira de Matematica (BL)
Sociedade Brasileira de Medicina Tropical (BL)
Sociedade Brasileira de Microbiologia (BL)
Sociedade Brasileira de Oftalmologia (BL)
Sociedade Brasileira de Patologia Clinica (BL)
Sociedade Brasileira de Pediatria (BL)
Sociedade Brasileira para o Progresso da Ciencia (JL)
Sociedade Brasileira para Professores de Linguistica (BL)
Sociedade Civil de Bem-Estar Familiar No Brasil (BL)
Sociedade das Ciencias Medicas de Lisboa (PO)
Sociedade de Estudos de Mocambique (MZ)
Sociedade de Farmacia e Quimica de Sao Paulo (BL)
Sociedade de Lingua Portuguesa (PO)
Sociedade de Medicina e Cirurgia de Sao Jose do Rio Preto (BL)
Sociedade de Medicina e Cirurgia do Rio de Janeiro (BL)
Sociedade de Neurologia, Psiquiatria e Higiene Mental do Brasil. Hospital das Clinicas Pedro II (BL)
Sociedade de Pediatria de Sao Paulo (BL)
Sociedade de Psicologia de Sao Paulo (BL)
Sociedade Entomologica do Brasil (BL)
Sociedade Farmaceutica Lusitana (PO)
Sociedade Industrial Farmaceutica (PO)
Sociedade Martins Sarmento (PO)
Sociedade Nacional de Agricultura (BL)
Sociedade Paranaense de Matematica (BL)
Sociedade Paulista de Medicina Veterinaria (BL)
Sociedade Paulista de Ortodontia (BL)
Sociedade Portuguesa de Antropologia e Etnologia (PO)
Sociedade Portuguesa de Ciencias Veterinarias (PO)
Sociedade Portuguesa de Estomatologia (PO)
Sociedade Portuguesa de Numismatica (PO)
Sociedade Portuguesa de Quimica (PO)
Sociedade Portuguesa de Reumatologia (PO)
Sociedade Visconde de Sao Leopoldo (BL)
Sociedades Hispanas Confederados de los Estados Unidos de America (US)
Societa Accademica Romana (IT)
Societa Archeologica Comense (IT)
Societa Astronomica Italiana (IT)
Societa Botanica Italiana (IT)
Societa Chimica Italiana (IT)
Societa Culturale Opere Tipografiche (IT)
Societa degli Ingegneri e degli Architetti in Torino (IT)
Societa di Banca Svizzera
    see Schweizerischer Bankverein (SZ)
Societa di Cultura per Il Friuli Occidentale (IT)
Societa di Cultura per la Lucania (IT)
Societa di Etnografia Italiana (IT)
Societa di Medicina e Scienze Naturali di Parma (IT)
Societa di Ricerche in Chirurgia (IT)
Societa di San Vincenzo de Paoli. Consiglio Superiore Italiano (IT)
Societa di Storia Patria per la Sicilia Orientale (IT)
Societa di Studi Geografici di Firenze (IT)
Societa di Studi Romagnoli (IT)
Societa di Studi Valdesi (IT)
Societa Elettronica Lombarda (IT)
Societa Entomologica Italiana (IT)
Societa Farmaceutici Italia (IT)
Societa Filologica Friulana (IT)
Societa Filosofica Calabrese (IT)
Societa Generale di Telefonia ed Elettronica (IT)
Societa Geografica Italiana (IT)
Societa Industrie Riunite Editorial: Siciliane (IT)
Societa Internazionale di Psicologia della Scrittura and Centro Internazionale di Ipnosi Medica e Psicologica (IT)
Societa Italiana Amici dei Fiori (IT)
Societa Italiana Autori Drammatici (IT)
Societa Italiana di Biochimica Clinica (IT)
Societa Italiana degli Autori Ed Editori (IT)
Societa Italiana di Agopuntura (IT)
Societa Italiana di Agronomia (IT)
Societa Italiana di Biologia Sperimentale (IT)
Societa Italiana di Cardiologia (IT)
Societa Italiana di Chemioterapia (IT)
Societa Italiana di Economia Demografia e Statistica (IT)
Societa Italiana di Filosofia Giuridica e Politica (IT)
Societa Italiana di Fisica (IT)
Societa Italiana di Fisiologia (IT)

Societe Technique d'Editions pour l'Entreprise (S T E P E)  (FR)
Societe Theosophique de France  (FR)
Societe Tunisienne des Sciences Medicales  (TI)
Societe Universitaire d'Editions et de Librairie  (FR)
Societe Vaudoise d'Histoire et d'Archeologie  (SZ)
Societe Vaudoise des Sciences Naturelles  (SZ)
Societe Vega, Engraver  (CN)
Societe Versaillaise des Sciences Naturelles  (FR)
Societe Zairoise d'Edition et d'Information  (ZR)
Societe Zoologigue de Quebec, Inc.  (CN)
Societe Zoologique de France  (FR)
Societes de Medecine du Travail de France  (FR)
Societes des Eleveurs des Bovins et des Chevaux Canadiens  (CN)
Society & Commerce Publications (Pvt) Ltd.  (II)
Society and Screen  (PK)
Society for a Classical America  (US)
Society for Academic Achievement  (US)
Society for Advancement of Continuing Education for Ministry  (US)
Society for Advancement of Electrochemical Science and Technology  (II)
Society for Advancement of Management  (US)
Society for African Church History  (UK)
Society for American Archaeology  (US)
Society for American Indian Studies  (US)
Society for Analytical Chemistry  (UK)
Society for Analytical Chemistry. Chemical Society Division  (UK)
Society for Ancient Numismatics  (US)
Society for Anesthesiology and Resuscitation of the GDR  (GE)
Society for Anglo-Chinese Understanding  (UK)
Society for Animal Rights, Inc.  (US)
Society for Applied Bacteriology  (UK)
Society for Applied Learning Technology  (US)
Society for Applied Spectroscopy  (US)
Society for Army Historical Research  (UK)
Society for Art Publications  (CN)
Society for Asian Folklore  (JA)
Society for Asian Music  (US)
Society for Asian Music (New York)  (US)
Society for Cinema Studies  (US)
Society for Clinical and Experimental Hypnosis  (US)
Society for Clinical Oncology  (UK)
Society for College and University Planning  (US)
Society for Computer Simulation  (US)
Society for Coptic Archaeology  (UA)
Society for Cultural Relations with the U.S.S.R.  (UK)
Society for Czechoslovak Philately, Inc.  (US)
Society for Democracy in Greece  (US)
Society for Economic Botany  (US)
Society for Education in Film and Television  (UK)
Society for Education in Laissez-Faire  (US)
Society for Education Through Art  (UK)
Society for Endocrinology  (UK)
Society for Environmental Education  (UK)
Society for Epidemiologic Research  (US)
Society for Ethnomusicology  (US)
Society for Experimental and Descriptive Malacology  (US)
Society for Experimental Biology  (UK)
Society for Experimental Biology and Medicine  (US)
Society for Experimental Stress Analysis  (US)
Society for Finnish Philology
    see Kotikielen Seura  (FI)
Society for Folk Life Studies  (UK)
Society for French - American Affairs  (US)
Society for French Historical Studies  (US)
Society for General Microbiology  (UK)
Society for General Systems Research  (US)
Society for Geographical Studies, Kanpur  (II)
Society for Geography  (SA)
Society for Geology Applied to Mineral Deposits  (US)
Society for German-American Studies  (US)
Society for Growing Australian Plants  (AT)
Society for Health and Human Values  (US)
Society for Historians of American Foreign Relations (S.H.A.F.R.)  (US)
Society for Historical Archaeology  (US)
Society for History Education  (US)
Society for Human Ecology  (SZ)
Society for Indian and Northern Education  (CN)
Society for Individual Liberty  (US)
Society for Individual Liberty (Warminster)  (US)
Society for Industrial and Applied Mathematics  (US)
Society for Industrial Archeology  (US)
Society for Information Display  (US)
Society for International Development  (FR)
Society for International Development  (US)
Society for International Development. Israel Chapter (IS)
Society for International Education, Training and Research  (US)
Society for International Numismatics  (US)
Society for Investigative Dermatology  (US)

Society for Iranian Studies  (US)
Society for Italian Historical Studies  (US)
Society for Italic Handwriting  (UK)
Society for Japanese Studies  (US)
Society for Lincolnshire History & Archaeology (UK)
Society for Long Range Planning  (US)
Society for Louisiana Irises  (US)
Society for Macedonian Studies  (GR)
Society for Mass Media and Resource Technology (AT)
Society for Medical Anthropology  (US)
Society for Medical Studies  (GR)
Society for Medieval Archaeology  (UK)
Society for Nautical Research  (UK)
Society for Near Eastern Studies in Japan  (JA)
Society for Neuroscience  (US)
Society for Nutrition Education  (US)
Society for Old Testament Study  (UK)
Society for Pennsylvania Archaeology  (US)
Society for Personality and Social Psychology  (US)
Society for Personality Assessment, Inc.  (US)
Society for Personality Research Inc.  (NZ)
Society for Photographic Education  (US)
Society for Post-Medieval Archaeology  (UK)
Society for Promoting Christian Knowledge  (UK)
Society for Psychical Research  (UK)
Society for Psychophysiological Research  (US)
Society for Range Management  (US)
Society for Rapid Publication of Medical and Biological Papers  (JA)
Society for Renaissance Studies  (UK)
Society for Research in Child Development, Inc. (US)
Society for Research in Psychology of Music and Music Education  (UK)
Society for Science & Technical Documents Utilization Promotion  (JA)
Society for Slovene Studies  (US)
Society for South India Studies  (US)
Society for Spanish and Portuguese Historical Studies (US)
Society for Spreading the Knowledge of True Prayer (UK)
Society for Technical Communication  (US)
Society for the Advancement of Agricultural Sciences (PK)
Society for the Advancement of Anaesthesia in Dentistry  (UK)
Society for the Advancement of Botany  (II)
Society for the Advancement of Education  (US)
Society for the Advancement of Food Service Research  (US)
Society for the Advancement of Material and Process Engineering  (US)
Society for the Advancement of Scandinavian Study (US)
Society for the Bibliography of Natural History  (UK)
Society for the Experimental Analysis of Behavior, Inc.  (US)
Society for the Experimental Analysis of Behavior, Inc. (Lawrence)  (US)
Society for the History of Discoveries  (NE)
Society for the History of Discoveries  (US)
Society for the History of Technology  (US)
Society for the Investigation of the Unexplained  (US)
Society for the Preservation and Encouragement of Barber Shop Quartet Singing in America, Inc. (US)
Society for the Preservation of Birds of Prey  (US)
Society for the Preservation of Long Island Antiquities (US)
Society for the Preservation of New England Antiquities  (US)
Society for the Prevention of Heart Disease and Rehabilitation  (II)
Society for the Progress of Science  (II)
Society for the Promoting of Emigration Research (SW)
Society for the Promotion of Art History Publications in Canada  (CN)
Society for the Promotion of Hellenic Studies  (UK)
Society for the Promotion of International Otorhinolaryngology  (JA)
Society for the Promotion of Nature Reserves  (UK)
Society for the Promotion of Roman Studies  (UK)
Society for the Propagation of the Faith  (US)
Society for the Protection of Nature in Israel  (IS)
Society for the Protection of New Hampshire Forests (US)
Society for the Protection of the Environment  (SA)
Society for the Protection of Unborn Children  (UK)
Society for the Psychological Study of Social Issues (US)
Society for the Rehabilitation of the Facially Disfigured, Inc.  (US)
Society for the Scientific Study of Sex  (US)

Society for the Study of Addiction to Alcohol and other Drugs  (UK)
Society for the Study of Alchemy and Early Chemistry (UK)
Society for the Study of Amphibians and Reptiles (US)
Society for the Study of Early China  (US)
Society for the Study of Evolution  (US)
Society for the Study of Human Biology  (UK)
Society for the Study of Industrial Medicine  (II)
Society for the Study of Industrial Medicine, Bombay Branch  (II)
Society for the Study of Labour History  (UK)
Society for the Study of Medical Ethics  (UK)
Society for the Study of Midwestern Literature  (US)
Society for the Study of Reproduction  (US)
Society for the Study of Social Biology  (US)
Society for the Study of Social Problems  (US)
Society for the Study of Social Sciences  (II)
Society for the Study of State Governments  (II)
Society for the Study of Welsh Labour History  (UK)
Society for Theatre Research  (UK)
Society for Underwater Technology  (UK)
Society for Walloon Language and Literature
    see Societe de Langue et de Litterature Wallonnes (BE)
Society of Actuaries  (US)
Society of Agricultural Meteorology of Japan  (JA)
Society of Airway Pioneers  (US)
Society of Alabama Geographers  (US)
Society of Allied Weight Engineers  (US)
Society of American Archivists  (US)
Society of American Florists. Ornamental Horticulturists  (US)
Society of American Foresters  (US)
Society of American Magicians  (US)
Society of American Travel Writers  (US)
Society of Analytical Psychology  (UK)
Society of Animal Artists  (US)
Society of Animal Morphologists & Physiologists  (II)
Society of Antiquaries of London  (UK)
Society of Antiquaries of Scotland  (UK)
Society of Applied Medicine  (JA)
Society of Applied Microbiology  (UA)
Society of Archer-Antiquaries  (UK)
Society of Architectural Historians  (US)
Society of Architectural Historians of Great Britain (UK)
Society of Archivists  (UK)
Society of Assistants Teaching in Preparatory Schools (UK)
Society of Audio Consultants  (US)
Society of Australian Genealogists  (AT)
Society of Authors  (UK)
Society of Automotive Engineers  (US)
Society of Automotive Engineers-Australasia  (AT)
Society of Automotive Engineers of Japan  (JA)
Society of Biblical Literature  (US)
Society of Biological Chemists  (II)
Society of Biological Psychiatry  (US)
Society of Border Leicester Sheep Breeders  (UK)
Society of British Aerospace Companies Ltd.  (UK)
Society of Cable Television Engineers  (UK)
Society of Cable Television Engineers  (US)
Society of Carbide and Tool Engineers  (US)
Society of Catholic Medical Missionaries, Inc.  (US)
Society of Certified Consumer Credit Executives (US)
Society of Chartered Property & Casualty Underwriters  (US)
Society of Chemical Engineers  (JA)
Society of Chemical Engineers of Japan  (US)
Society of Chemical Industry  (UK)
Society of Chiropodists  (UK)
Society of Christ for Polish Emigrants  (US)
Society of Civil and Public Servants  (UK)
Society of Colonial Wars  (US)
Society of Commercial Teachers Ltd.  (UK)
Society of Community Medicine  (UK)
Society of Cosmetic Chemists  (US)
Society of Critical Care Medicine  (US)
Society of Cryobiology  (US)
Society of Cypriot Studies  (CY)
Society of Dairy Technology  (UK)
Society of Data Educators  (US)
Society of Die Casting Engineers, Inc.  (US)
Society of Dyers and Colourists  (UK)
Society of Economic Paleontologists and Mineralogists (US)
Society of Electronic and Radio Technicians  (UK)
Society of Electronic Engineers  (II)
Society of Electrophoresis  (JA)
Society of Electrophotography of Japan  (JA)
Society of Engineers  (UK)
Society of Engineers of Iran  (IR)
Society of Environmental Engineers  (UK)
Society of Exploration Geophysicists  (US)
Society of Federal Linguists, Inc.  (US)

Society of Fiber Science and Technology (JA)
Society of Film & Television Arts Ltd. (UK)
Society of Finnish Jurists
    see Suomalainen Lakimiesyhdistys (FI)
Society of Fisheries Technologists (India) (II)
Society of Flight Test Engineers (US)
Society of Folk Harpists and Craftsmen (US)
Society of Food Science and Technology (UA)
Society of Forestry in Finland
    see Suomen Metsatieteellinen Seura (FI)
Society of Friends (US)
Society of Genealogists (UK)
Society of General Physiologists (US)
Society of Georgia Archivists (US)
Society of Glass Decorators (US)
Society of Glass Technology (UK)
Society of Harvard Engineers and Scientists (US)
Society of Health of Nigeria (NR)
Society of Heating, Air Conditioning and Sanitary
    Engineers of Japan (JA)
Society of Hospital Pharmacists of Australia (AT)
Society of Illustrators (US)
Society of Independent Professional Earth Scientists
    (US)
Society of Indexers (UK)
Society of Industrial Accountants of Canada (CN)
Society of Industrial Artists & Designers (UK)
Society of Instrument and Control Engineers (JA)
Society of Investment Analysts (UK)
Society of Irish Foresters (IE)
Society of Irreproducible Research (US)
Society of Islamic Studies (UA)
Society of Japanese Virologists (JA)
Society of Jesus (US)
Society of Jesus. English Province (UK)
Society of Jewish Science (US)
Society of Leather Technologists and Chemists (UK)
Society of Licensed Aircraft Engineers and
    Technologists (UK)
Society of Lithographic Artists, Designers, Engravers
    & Process Workers (UK)
Society of Logistics Engineers (US)
Society of Malawi (MW)
Society of Management Science and Applied
    Cybernetics (II)
Society of Manufacturing Engineers (US)
Society of Maritime Arbitrators (US)
Society of Master Saddlers (UK)
Society of Medalists (US)
Society of Medical Aeronautical Engineers of India
    (II)
Society of Medical Friends of Wine (US)
Society of Medical Laboratory Technologists of South
    Africa (SA)
Society of Mining Geologists of Japan (JA)
Society of Motion Picture and Television Engineers
    (US)
Society of Motor Manufacturers and Traders Ltd.
    (UK)
Society of Multivariate Experimental Psychology
    (US)
Society of Mycology and Plant Pathology (II)
Society of Naval Architects and Marine Engineers
    (US)
Society of Nematologists (US)
Society of Nematology (US)
Society of Nippon Dental College (JA)
Society of Nuclear Medicine (US)
Society of Occupational Medicine (UK)
Society of Odontostomatological Research (GR)
Society of Ohio Archivists (US)
Society of Opticians (S.A.) (SA)
Society of Painters in Tempera (UK)
Society of Paper Money Collectors, Inc. (US)
Society of Pharmacological and Environmental
    Pathologists (US)
Society of Pharmacology (KO)
Society of Philatelic Americans (US)
Society of Philaticians (US)
Society of Photo-Optical Instrumentation Engineers
    (US)
Society of Photographic Science and Technology of
    Japan (JA)
Society of Photographic Scientists and Engineers
    (US)
Society of Plant Protection of North Japan (JA)
Society of Plastics Engineers (US)
Society of Political Economy (JA)
Society of Polymer Science (JA)
Society of Population Ecology (JA)
Society of Professional Investigators (US)
Society of Professional Journalists, Sigma Delta Chi
    (US)
Society of Professional Well Log Analysts (US)
Society of Professors of Education (US)
Society of Protozoologists (US)
Society of Public Teachers of Law (UK)
Society of Radiographers (UK)

Society of Real Estate Appraisers (US)
Society of Registered Surveyors (AT)
Society of Registration Officers (UK)
Society of Remedial Gymnasts (UK)
Society of Research Administrators (US)
Society of Rheology (US)
Society of Rubber Industry (JA)
Society of St. Edmund (US)
Society of St. Gregory (UK)
Society of St. John Chrysostom (UK)
Society of St. Paul (PH)
Society of St. Paul (Canfield) (US)
Society of St. Thomas (UK)
Society of St. Vincent de Paul (SA)
Society of Separationists (US)
Society of Servants of God (II)
Society of Shipping Executives (UK)
Society of Soil Science (UA)
Society of Systematic Zoology (US)
Society of Teachers of Speech and Drama (UK)
Society of Terrestrial Magnetism and Electricity of
    Japan (JA)
Society of the Classic Guitar (US)
Society of the Divine Word (US)
Society of the Irish Motor Industry (IE)
Society of the Plastics Industry (US)
Society of the Science of Soil & Manure, Japan (JA)
Society of Thoracic Surgeons (US)
Society of University Cartographers (UK)
Society of Vertebrate Paleontology (UK)
Society of Vertebrate Paleontology (US)
Society of Wireless Pioneers (US)
Society of Women Engineers (US)
Society of Women Writers and Journalists (UK)
Society of Wood Science and Technology (US)
Society of World War 1 Aero Historians (US)
Society Oud Utrecht (NE)
Society Publications Ltd. (UK)
Socijalisticki Savez Leskovacke Opstine (YU)
Socijalisticki Savez Radnog Naroda Backa Palanka
    (YU)
Socijalisticki Savez Radnog Naroda Istre, Hrvatskog
    primorja i Gorskog kotara (YU)
Socijalisticki Savez Radnog Naroda Kosova (YU)
Socijalisticki Savez Radnog Naroda Opcine Bjelovar
    (YU)
Socijalisticki Savez Radnog Naroda Opcine Dubrovnik
    (YU)
Socijalisticki Savez Radnog Naroda Opcine Virovitica
    (YU)
Socijalisticki Savez Radnog Naroda Opstine Ivangrad
    (YU)
Socijalisticki Savez Radnog Naroda Opstine Pozarevac
    (YU)
Socijalisticki Savez Radnog Naroda Opstine Titograd
    (YU)
Socijalisticki Savez Radnog Narodna Opstine Trebinje
    (YU)
Socijalisticki Savez Radnog Naroda Opstine Valjevskog
    Sreza (YU)
Socijalisticki Savez Radnog Naroda Opstine Vranje
    (YU)
Socijalisticki Savez Radnog Naroda Suboticke Opstine
    (YU)
Socijalisticki Savez Radnog Naroda Varazdin (YU)
Socijalisticki Savez Radnog Naroda Vinkovacke
    Komune (YU)
Socijalisticki Savez Radnog Naroda Vukovar (YU)
Socijalisticki Savez Radnog Naroda Zajednice Opcina
    Gospic (YU)
Socijalisticki Svaz Pracujucich Vojvodiny Pre Slovakov
    (YU)
Socijalna Politika (YU)
Socio-Economic Publications, Inc. (US)
Sociological Abstracts, Inc. (US)
Sociological Analysis & Theory (UK)
Sociological Association of Australia and New Zealand
    (NZ)
Sociologists for Women in Society (US)
Sociolosko Drustvo Hrvatske (YU)
A. W. Sockwell (US)
Socorema (BE)
Socpresse-Auto-Journal (FR)
Socpresse Bateaux (FR)
Sod House Society of America (US)
Libreria Editoriale Sodalitas (IT)
Sodalizio Internazionale di Spiritualita Alpina. Ordine
    del Cardo (IT)
Sodedi S.A. (BE)
Editions Sodel (FR)
Soe-Lieutenant-Selskabet (DK)
Soedra Skogsaegarna (SW)
Soelberg Trykk A-S (NO)
Sofia-Press Agency (BU)
Sofiiski Universitet. Biologicheski Fakultet (BU)
Sofiiski Universitet. Fakultet po Matematika i
    Mekhanika (BU)

Sofiiski Universitet. Fakultet po Slavianski Filologii
    (BU)
Sofiiski Universitet. Fakultet po Zapadni Filologii
    (BU)
Sofiiski Universitet. Filosofski Fakultet (BU)
Sofiiski Universitet. Geologo-Geografski Fakultet
    (BU)
Sofiiski Universitet. Iuridicheski Fakultet (BU)
Soft Machine Productions (DK)
Soft Press (CN)
Softball (US)
Soho Weekly News, Inc. (US)
Soil Association (UK)
Soil Association of New Zealand (NZ)
Soil Conservation Society of America (US)
Soil Conservation Society of India (II)
Soil Science Society of America (US)
Soil Science Society of Bangladesh (BG)
Soil Science Society of Ceylon (CE)
Franco Soin Editore (IT)
Sojuz na Istoriskite Drustva na SR Makedonija (YU)
Sojuz na Zdruzenijata na Pravnicite na Makedonija
    (YU)
Sojuz Rusinoh i Ukraincoh Gorvatskej (YU)
Sojuzot na Drustvata na Ekonomistite na SR
    Makedonija (YU)
Sojuzot na Fizicka Kultura na Makedonija (YU)
Sojuzot na Geodetskite Inzeneri i Geometri na
    Makedonija (YU)
Sojuzot na Socijalistickata Mladina na Makedonija
    (YU)
Sojuzot na Trudovite Invalidi na Makedonija (YU)
Sokeritautiliitto r.y. (FI)
Sokka Gakkai (JA)
Sokuedit Ltee (CN)
Sol Quarterly (UK)
Solar Energy Digest (US)
Solar Energy Society of Canada (CN)
Solar Engineering Publishers, Inc. (US)
Solar Vision, Inc. (US)
Der Soldat Zeitungs- und Zeitschriftenverlags-
    Gesellschaft MbH (AU)
Soldecor (FR)
Soldier Shop (US)
Societa Editrice Sole s.r.l. (IT)
SOLEDI (BE)
Soleil (FR)
Soleil de Haute-Volta. (UV)
Solent Cruising & Racing Association (UK)
Solicitors' Law Stationery Society Ltd. (UK)
Solid Waste Management Magazine (US)
Solidaridad Publishing House (PH)
Solidarite des Refugies Israelites (FR)
Editions Solidarite Inc. (CN)
Forlaget Solidaritet (DK)
Solidarity Committee with the People of Palestine
    (CN)
Editions Solin (FR)
Soller Press & Publishing House, Inc. (PH)
Solo Press (US)
Solomon Islands Museum Association (BP)
Solomon Schechter Day School Association (US)
Solon (UK)
Juan Solorzano Gomez, Ed. & Pub. (MX)
Editions Sols-Soils (FR)
Solstice (UK)
Solvay Institute of Chemistry (US)
Solvay Institute of Physics (US)
Solway Publications (UK)

Soma Hellinon Proscopon (GR)

Somali Institute of Public Administration (SO)

Somalia. Ministry of Education. Department of
    Planning (SO)

Somalia National Bank (SO)
Some (US)
Some Friends (US)
Some Hard-to-Locate Sources of Information (US)
Somerset and Dorset Notes and Queries (UK)
Somerset Archaeological & Natural History Society
    (UK)
Somerset Newspapers Inc. (US)
Somerset Ornithological Society (UK)
Somerville Poetry Conspiracy (US)
Something for Everybody Ad Bulletin (US)
Somick Publishing Co. (US)
SONAPRESS
    see Societe Nationale de Presse, d'Edition et de
    Publicite (SG)
Sonda, Juventudes Musicales (SP)
Hamburger Fachverlag Gerhard Sondermann (GW)
Editions Sonedis (FR)
Song (US)
Songwriter's Review (US)
Sonnen-Verlag Bauer und Co. (AU)
Alexander Sonnenschein (US)
Sono Nis Press (CN)

Sonostrips Ltd. (UK)
Sons of Norway (US)
Sons of Temperance of Nova Scotia (CN)
Sons of the American Revolution. Massachusetts
  Society (US)
Sons of the Desert (US)
Soochow University (CH)
Soon (US)
Sophia (AT)
Sophia University (JA)
Sophia University. Brazilian Center (JA)
Soprintendenza Alle Gallerie (IT)
Sopusi (FR)
Sorby Natural History Society (UK)
Sorghum Producers Association (US)
Soroptimist International of the Americas (US)
Sorpasso -CB (IT)
Sosialistinen Aikakauslehti (FI)
Sosialoekonomisk Samfunn (NO)
Sosland Publishing Co. (US)
Sotheby Parke Bernet Inc. (US)
Ettore Sottsass, Ed. & Pub. (IT)
Souffles (MR)
Soul and Jazz Record (US)
Soul in Review Publications (US)
Soul Publications, Inc. (US)
Soumalais-Ugrilainen Seura (FI)
Editions Soumillion (BE)
Sound Image (US)
Sound of Malaysian's Musician (MY)
Sound Publications Co. (US)
Sound Publishing (CN)
Sound Publishing Co., Inc. (US)
Sounding Brass Ltd. (UK)
Sounds Fine (US)
Sounds Verlag (GW)
Soundtracks Publishing Pty. Ltd. (AT)
Source (US)
South Africa. Atomic Energy Board (SA)
South Africa. Bureau of Standards (SA)
South Africa. Deciduous Fruit Board (SA)
South Africa. Department of Agricultural Economics
  and Marketing (SA)
South Africa. Department of Agricultural Economics
  and Marketing. Division of Agricultural Marketing
  Research (SA)
South Africa. Department of Agricultural Technical
  Services (SA)
South Africa. Department of Bantu Education (SA)
South Africa. Department of Customs and Excise
  (SA)
South Africa. Department of Defense (SA)
South Africa. Department of Indian Affairs (SA)
South Africa. Department of Information (SA)
South Africa. Department of Labour (SA)
South Africa. Department of Statistics (SA)
South Africa. Department of Transport. Weather
  Bureau
  see South Africa. Weather Bureau (SA)
South Africa. Directorate of Hydrography (SA)
South Africa. Geological Survey (SA)
South Africa. Government Printer (SA)
South Africa. Livestock and Meat Industries Control
  Board (SA)
South Africa. Maize Board (SA)
South Africa. Milk Board (SA)
South Africa. National Parks Board of Trustees (SA)
South Africa. Office of the Director of Archives (SA)
South Africa. Office of the Scientific Advisor to the
  Prime Minister (SA)
South Africa. State Library (SA)
South Africa. Tobacco Board (SA)
South Africa. Unemployment Insurance Fund (SA)
South Africa. Water Research Commission (SA)
South Africa. Weather Bureau (SA)
South Africa. Wheat Board (SA)
South Africa. Wool Board (SA)
South Africa Foundation (SA)
South Africa National Sunday School Association
  (SA)
South African Academy of Arts and Sciences
  see Suid-Afrikaanse Akademie vir Wetenskap en
  Kuns (SA)
South African Airways (SA)
South African Aloe and Succulent Society (SA)
South African Amateur Athletics Union (SA)
South African Antarctic Association (SA)
South African Archaeological Society (SA)
South African Associated Newspapers (SA)
South African Association for Marine Biological
  Research (SA)
South African Association for Technical and
  Vocational Education (SA)
South African Association for the Advancement of
  Science (SA)
South African Association of Botanists (SA)
South African Association of Business Management
  (SA)

South African Association of Consulting Engineers
  (SA)
South African Association of Municipal Employees.
  Pretoria Branch (SA)
South African Association of Occupational Therapists
  (SA)
South African Bridge Federation (SA)
South African Broadcasting Corporation (SA)
South African Builder (Pty) Ltd. (SA)
South African Bureau of Racial Affairs (SA)
South African Chemical Institute (SA)
South African Chessplayer (SA)
South African Communist Party (UK)
South African Consulate General. Consul
  (Commercial) (US)
South African Copper Development Association (Pty.)
  Ltd. (SA)
South African Corrosion Institute (SA)
South African Council of Churches (SA)
South African Cycling Federation (SA)
South African Defence Force (SA)
South African Dog Breeders and Dog Lovers (SA)
South African Embassy, Lisbon (PO)
South African Esperanto Association (SA)
South African Federation of Beekeepers' Associations
  (SA)
South African Fire Services Institute (SA)
South African Footplate Staff Association (SA)
South African Foreign Trade Organization (SA)
South African Forestry Association (SA)
South African Genetic Society (SA)
South African Geographical Society (SA)
South African Guernsey Cattle Breeders Society
  (SA)
South African Historical Society (SA)
South African Information Service (US)
South African Institute for Public Administration
  (SA)
South African Institute of Assayers and Analysts
  (SA)
South African Institute of Draughtsmen (SA)
South African Institute of Electrical Engineers (SA)
South African Institute of Foundrymen (SA)
South African Institute of International Affairs (SA)
South African Institute of Materials Handling (SA)
South African Institute of Mining and Metallurgy
  (SA)
South African Institute of Organization and Methods
  (SA)
South African Institute of Photographers (SA)
South African Institute of Race Relations (SA)
South African Institute of Refrigeration and Air
  Conditioning (SA)
South African Institution of Chemical Engineers
  (SA)
South African Institution of Civil Engineers (SA)
South African Institution of Mechanical Engineers
  (SA)
South African Iron and Steel Industrial Corp., Ltd.
  (SA)
South African Iron, Steel and Allied Industries Union
  (SA)
South African Jewellery Council (SA)
South African Jewish Board of Deputies (SA)
South African Jewish Ex-Service League (SA)
South African Legion (SA)
South African Library (SA)
South African Library Association (SA)
South African Literary Journal Ltd. (SA)
South African Maize Producers Institute (SA)
South African Market Research Association (SA)
South African Medical & Dental Council (SA)
South African Medical Research Council (SA)
South African Museums Association (SA)
South African National Council for the Aged (SA)
South African National Council for the Blind (SA)
South African National Council for the Deaf (SA)
South African National Museum of Military History
  (SA)
South African National Tuberculosis Association
  (SA)
South African Nursing Association (SA)
South African Optometric Association (SA)
South African Ornithological Society (SA)
South African Photographic Trade Association Ltd.
  (SA)
South African Police Force (SA)
South African Postal Association (SA)
South African Progressive Reform Party (SA)
South African Psychological Association (SA)
South African Radio League (SA)
South African Railways and Harbours Employees'
  Union (SA)
South African Railways and Harbours Magazine
  Association (SA)
South African Red Cross Society (Cape Region) (SA)
South African Reserve Bank (SA)
South African Society of Animal Production (SA)

South African Society of Archivists (SA)
South African Society of Bank Officials (SA)
South African Society of Music Teachers (SA)
South African Society of Obstetricians and
  Gynaecologists (SA)
South African Society of Physiotherapy (SA)
South African Sociological Association (SA)
South African Speech & Hearing Association (SA)
South African Statistical Association (SA)
South African Students' Organization (SA)
South African Sugar Association (SA)
South African Table Tennis Union (SA)
South African Teachers' Association (SA)
South African Typographical Union (SA)
South African Union Conference of Seventh-Day
  Adventists (SA)
South African Union of Jewish Students at Wits (SA)
South African Veterinary Association (SA)
South African Water Information Centre (SA)
South African Wool and Textile Research Institute
  (SA)
South African Zionist Federation (SA)
South American Missionary Society (UK)
South and West, Inc. (US)
South Asia Church Aid Association (UK)
South Asia Studies Association (AT)
South Asian Association of Australia and New
  Zealand (NZ)
South Asian Studies Center
  see University of Rajasthan. South Asian Studies
  Center (II)
South Atlantic Modern Language Association (US)
South Australia. Department of Agriculture (AT)
South Australia. Department of Agriculture and
  Fisheries. Economics Branch (AT)
South Australia. Department of Labour and Industry
  (AT)
South Australia. Department of Mines (AT)
South Australia. Department of Public Health (AT)
South Australia. Department of Woods and Forests
  (AT)
South Australia. Education Department (AT)
South Australia. Education Department. School
  Libraries Branch (AT)
South Australia. Government Printer (AT)
South Australia. Highways Department (AT)
South Australia. State Planning Authority (AT)
South Australia Fruitgrowers & Market Gardeners
  Association Inc. (AT)
South Australian Automobile Chamber of Commerce
  (AT)
South Australian Canine Association (AT)
South Australian Chamber of Commerce and Industry
  (AT)
South Australian Chess Association (AT)
South Australian Dairymen's Association (AT)
South Australian Government Tourist Bureau (AT)
South Australian Institute of Teachers (AT)
South Australian Jockey Club Inc. (AT)
South Australian Motor Pty. Ltd. (AT)
South Australian Museum (AT)
South Australian Numismatic Society (AT)
South Australian Ornithological Association (AT)
South Carolina. Board of Engineering Examiners
  (US)
South Carolina. Board of Health (US)
South Carolina. Budget and Control Board (US)
South Carolina. Commission on Alcoholism and Drug
  Abuse (US)
South Carolina. Department of Archives & History
  (US)
South Carolina. Department of Education (US)
South Carolina. Department of Health and
  Environmental Control. Bureau of Health Facilities
  and Services (US)
South Carolina. Department of Highways and Public
  Transportation (US)
South Carolina. Department of Labor (US)
South Carolina. Department of Mental Health. William
  S. Hall Psychiatric Institute (US)
South Carolina. Division of Vital Records (US)
South Carolina. Employment Security Commission
  (US)
South Carolina. State Board for Technical and
  Comprehensive Education (US)
South Carolina. State Development Board (US)
South Carolina. State Library (US)
South Carolina. Wildlife Resources Department (US)
South Carolina Arts Commission (US)
South Carolina Associations of Young Farmers and
  Future Farmers (US)
South Carolina Dental Journal (US)
South Carolina Education Association (US)
South Carolina Electric Cooperative Association (US)
South Carolina Historical Society (US)
South Carolina Labor News, Inc. (US)

South Carolina Library Association (US)
South Carolina Magazine Corporation (US)
South Carolina Medical Association (US)
South Carolina Political Science Association (US)
South Carolina State College (US)
South Carolina State Ports Authority (US)
South Central Modern Language Association (US)
South Central Research Library Council (US)
South China Morning Post Ltd. (HK)
South Coast Herald (Pty) Ltd. (SA)
South Dakota. Department of Agriculture. Crop &
  Livestock Reporting Service (US)
South Dakota. Department of Economic and Tourism
  Development. Industrial Development Division
  (US)
South Dakota. Department of Game, Fish and Parks
  (US)
South Dakota. Department of Health (US)
South Dakota. Department of Labor (US)
South Dakota. Department of Revenue. Division of
  Property Tax (US)
South Dakota. Division of Highway Safety (US)
South Dakota. Economic Opportunity Office (US)
South Dakota. Employment Security Division (US)
South Dakota. Geological Survey (US)
South Dakota. Rural Manpower Service (US)
South Dakota. State Legislative Research Council
  (US)
South Dakota. State Library (US)
South Dakota Academy of Science (US)
South Dakota Association of County Commissioners
  (US)
South Dakota Dental Association (US)
South Dakota Education Association (US)
South Dakota Indian Recipients of Social Welfare
  (US)
South Dakota Library Association (US)
South Dakota Motor Carriers Association (US)
South Dakota Municipal League (US)
South Dakota Ornithologists' Union (US)
South Dakota Rural Electric Association (US)
South Dakota School of Mines and Technology.
  Geology, Mining & Metallurgy Depts. (US)
South Dakota State Historical Society (US)
South Dakota State Medical Association (US)
South Dakota State Poetry Society (US)
South Dakota State University. Agricultural
  Experiment Station (US)
South Dakota State University. Alumni Association
  (US)
South Dakota Stock Growers Association (US)
South Georgia College (US)
South Georgia Conference Commission on Archives
  and History of the United Methodist Church (US)
South Head Press (AT)
South India Teachers' Union (II)
South India Textile Research Association (II)
South Indian Horticultural Association (II)
South Indian Steam & Fuel Users' Association (II)
South London Field Studies Society (UK)
South of Tuk (CN)
South Pacific Commission (NL)
South Pacific Commission. Publications Bureau (AT)
South Pacific Creative Arts Society (FJ)
South Pacific Electric Railway Co-Operative Society
  Ltd. (AT)
South Pacific Social Sciences Association (FJ)
South Penn Motor Club (US)
South Place Ethical Society (UK)
South Publishing Co. (US)
South Seas Society (SI)
South Shore Publishers, Inc. (US)
South Staffordshire Archaeological and Historical
  Society (UK)
South Street Publications (UK)
South Street Seaport Museum (US)
South Suburban Genealogical and Historical Society
  (US)
South-Swedish Geographical Society (SW)
South Texas College of Law (US)
South Trade Publications, Co. (US)
South Vietnam National Front for Liberation (VN)
South Wales and Monmouthshire Master Printers'
  Alliance (UK)
South Wales Institute of Engineers (UK)
Southam Business Publications Ltd. (CN)
Southam-Murray (CN)
Southdown Press Pty. Ltd. (AT)
Southeast Asia Development Corporation Berhad
  (MY)
South East Asia Iron and Steel Institute (SI)
South East Asia Library Group (UK)
South East Asia Treaty Organization (TH)
Southeast Asia Union Mission of Seventh-Day
  Adventists (SI)
Southeast Asian Fisheries Development Center (PH)
Southeast Asian Fisheries Development Center (SI)

Southeast Asian Ministers of Education Organization.
  Regional Language Centre (SI)
Southeast Asian Research Centre (SI)
Southeast Asian Research Materials Group (AT)
Southeast Asian Society of Soil Engineering (TH)
Southeast Farm Press Inc. (US)
Southeast Georgian, Inc. (US)
South East Hampshire Genealogical Society (UK)
Southeast Louisiana Historical Association (US)
Southeast Michigan Council of Governments (US)
Southeast Missouri State College. Department of
  English (US)
Southeast Missouri State University (US)
South East Peace Newsletter (UK)
Southeast Retail Furniture Association (US)
South East Wind Monthly (HK)
Southeastern Association of Game and Fish
  Commissioners (US)
Southeastern Baptist Theological Seminary (US)
Southeastern Composers' League (US)
Southeastern Conference on Latin American Studies
  (US)
Southeastern Conference on Latin American Studies
  (University) (US)
Southeastern Library Association (US)
Southeastern Library Network (US)
South Eastern Magazines Ltd. (UK)
Southeastern Pennsylvania Theological Library
  Association (US)
Southeastern Poultry and Egg Association (US)
Southeastern Press, Inc. (US)
Southeastern Professional Photographers Association,
  Inc. (US)
Southeastern Renaissance Conference (US)
Southeastern School of Alcohol Studies (US)
South-Eastern State. Ministry of Economic
  Development and Reconstruction (NR)
Southeastern Surgical Congress (US)
Southend Chamber of Trade (UK)
Southern Adirondack Library System (US)
Southern Africa Commercial Travellers' Association
  (SA)
Southern Africa Committee (US)
Southern Africa Stainless Steel Development
  Association (SA)
Southern African Catholic Bishops' Conference (SA)
Southern African Wildlife Management Association
  (SA)
Southern Agricultural Economics Association (US)
Southern Alberta Institute of Technology. Students
  Association (CN)
Southern & Southwestern Railway Club (US)
Southern Anthropological Society (US)
Southern Arts Association (UK)
Southern Association of Colleges and Schools (US)
Southern Baptist Convention (US)
Southern Baptist Convention. Brotherhood
  Commission (US)
Southern Baptist Convention. Foreign Mission Board
  (US)
Southern Baptist Convention. Historical Commission
  (US)
Southern Baptist Convention. Home Mission Board
  (US)
Southern Baptist Convention. Sunday School Board
  (US)
Southern Baptist Convention. Woman's Missionary
  Union (US)
Southern Baptist General Convention of California
  (US)
Southern Baptist Radio and Television Commission
  (US)
Southern Baptist Theological Seminary (US)
Southern Bell Telephone Co. (US)
Southern Beverage Journal, Inc. (US)
Southern Bio-Research Institute (US)
Southern Boating and Yachting Inc. (US)
Southern Building Code Congress (US)
Southern Building Code Publishing Co., Inc. (US)
Southern California Academy of Sciences (US)
Southern California Association of Governments
  (US)
Southern California Dental Hygienists' Association
  (US)
Southern California Dental Laboratory Association
  (US)
Southern California Educational Theatre Association
  (US)
Southern California Genealogical Society Inc. (US)
Southern California Golf Association (US)
Southern California Grocers Association (US)
Southern California Jewish Historical Society (US)
Southern California Local History Council (US)
Southern California Psychiatric Society (US)
Southern California Rapid Transit District (US)
Southern California Retailer (US)
Southern California School of Theology (US)
Southern Caving Society (AT)

Southern Center for Studies in Public Policy (US)
Southern Christian Advocate, Inc. (US)
Southern Christian Leadership Conference (US)
Southern Colorado Horseman's Association (US)
Southern Colorado State College (US)
Southern Comparative Literature Association (US)
Southern Conference Educational Fund (US)
Southern Council of Optometrists (US)
Southern Cross Books (NZ)
Southern Cross Model Railway Association (AT)
Southern Dairy Products Journal (US)
Southern Economic Association (US)
Southern Economist Private Ltd. (II)
Southern Electric Group (UK)
Southern Feminists: the Feminist Newsletter (US)
Southern Florist and Nurseryman (US)
Southern Furniture, Inc. (US)
Southern Historical Association (US)
Southern Host Publishing Corporation (US)
Southern Humanities Conference (US)
Southern Illinois University, Carbondale (US)
Southern Illinois University, Carbondale. Business
  Research Bureau (US)
Southern Illinois University, Carbondale. Center for
  Dewey Studies (US)
Southern Illinois University, Carbondale. Center for
  Soviet & East-European Studies (US)
Southern Illinois University, Carbondale. Center for
  Vietnamese Studies (US)
Southern Illinois University, Carbondale. Department
  of Anthropology (US)
Southern Illinois University, Carbondale. Department
  of Foreign Languages (US)
Southern Illinois University, Carbondale. Department
  of Geography (US)
Southern Illinois University, Carbondale. Department
  of Philosophy (US)
Southern Illinois University, Carbondale. Morris
  Library (US)
Southern Illinois University, Carbondale. University
  Museum (US)
Southern Illinois University, Edwardsville (US)
Southern Illinois University, Edwardsville. Center for
  Urban and Environmental Research and Services
  (US)
Southern Illinois University, Edwardsville. Industrial
  Maps Project (US)
Southern Illinois University, Edwardsville. University
  Graphics and Publications (US)
Southern Illinois University, Latin American Institute
  (US)
Southern Illinois University Press (US)
Southern Jewish Weekly, Inc. (US)
Southern Literary Messenger (US)
Southern Market Preview & Shopping Planner (US)
Southern Medical Association (US)
Southern Methodist University. Department of
  Anthropology (US)
Southern Methodist University. Industrial Information
  Services (US)
Southern Methodist University. Institute for the Study
  of Earth and Man (US)
Southern Methodist University. Perkins School of
  Theology (US)
Southern Methodist University Press (US)
Southern Methodist University. Printing Department
  (US)
Southern Methodist University School of Law (US)
Southern Missions, Inc. (US)
Southern Motorsports Journal (US)
Southern Newspaper Enterprises (US)
Southern Oregon College. English Department (US)
Southern Pacific Transportation Co. (US)
Southern Plastic Industries Association (II)
Southern Political Science Assocaiation (US)
Southern Presbyterian Journal Co., Inc. (US)
Southern Preservation Society, Inc. (US)
Southern Press Ltd (NZ)
Southern Printer & Lithographer (US)
Southern Prison Ministry (US)
Southern Publishers (II)
Southern Publishers, Inc. (US)
Southern Publishing Association (US)
Southern Publishing Co. (UK)
Southern Publishing Co. (US)
Southern Railways (II)
Southern Region School Boards Research and Training
  Center, Inc. (US)
Southern Regional Education Board (US)
Southern Regional Science Association (US)
Southern Research Institute (US)
Southern Sociological Society (US)
Southern Speech Communication Association (US)
Southern States Cooperative, Inc. (US)
Southern Tier Library System (US)
Southern Trade Publications Co. (US)
Southern Universities Nuclear Institute (SA)
Southern University Law Review (US)

Southern Utah News  (US)
Southern Veterinarian, Inc.  (US)
Southern Weed Science Society  (US)
Southland Publishing Co.  (US)
South West Africa. Administration  (SX)
South West Africa. Administration on Nature
  Conservation & Tourism  (SX)
Southwest Africa. Department of National Education.
  State Museum
  see Southwest Africa. State Museum  (SX)
South West Africa. State Museum  (SX)
South West Africa People's Organization  (TZ)
South West Africa Scientific Society
  see S.W.A. Scientific Society  (SX)
Southwest Art Magazine  (US)
South West Arts  (UK)
Southwest Bluegrass Club  (US)
Southwest College Student Government  (US)
Southwest Conference on Asian Studies  (US)
Southwest Homefurnishings Association  (US)
Southwest Jewish Chronicle  (US)
Southwest Minnesota State College  (US)
Southwest Museum  (US)
Southwest New Mexico Council of Governments
  (US)
Southwest Radio Church  (US)
Southwest Research and Information Center  (US)
Southwest Research Institute  (US)
South West Scotland Grassland Society  (UK)
Southwest Society of Periodontists  (US)
Southwest Texas State University. Department of
  English  (US)
Southwestern American Literature  (US)
Southwestern Art, Inc.  (US)
Southwestern Association Inc.  (US)
Southwestern Association of Naturalists. Division of
  Biology  (US)
Southwestern Association on Indian Affairs  (US)
Southwestern at Memphis  (US)
Southwestern Baptist Theological Seminary  (US)
Southwestern Baptist Theological Seminary. Fleming
  Library  (US)
Southwestern Institute of Forensic Sciences  (US)
Southwestern Journal of Philosophy  (US)
Southwestern Legal Foundation. International and
  Comparative Law Center  (US)
Southwestern Library Association  (US)
Southwestern Mission Research Center  (US)
Southwestern Oklahoma Historical Society  (US)
Southwestern Pennsylvania Regional Planning
  Commission  (US)
Southwestern Philosophical Society  (US)
South Western Publishing Co.  (US)
Southwestern Purchaser, Inc.  (US)
Southwestern Retailer  (US)
Southwestern Social Science Association  (US)
Southwestern University  (US)
Souvenir Press Ltd.  (UK)
Souvenir Publishers  (SA)
Souvenir Vendeer  (FR)
Souvenirs and Novelties Publishers, Inc.  (US)
Sovereign Order of Saint John of Jerusalem  (MM)
Sovereign Publishing Co.  (CN)
Izdatel'stvo Sovetskaya Rossiya  (UR)
Izdatel'stvo Sovetskii Khudozhnik  (UR)
Sovetskii Komitet Zashchity Mira  (UR)
Izdatel'stvo Sovetskii Kompozitor  (UR)
Soviet Business and Trade. Porter International  (US)
Soviet Embassy in London  (UK)
Sovremennik Publishing Association Inc.  (CN)
Sovremenost  (YU)
Soyuz Arkhitektorov S.S.S.R.  (UR)
Soyuz Dukhovnykh Obshchin Krista  (CN)
Soyuz Khudozhnikov S. S. S. R.  (UR)
Soyuz Kompozitorov Rossiiskoi S.F.S.R. Folklornaya
  Komissiya  (UR)
Soyuz Kompozitorov S.S.S.R.  (UR)
Soyuz Pisatelei Armyanskoi S. S. R.  (UR)
Soyuz Pisatelei Azerbaidzhanskoi S.S.R.  (UR)
Soyuz Pisatelei Belorusskoi S.S.R.  (UR)
Soyuz Pisatelei Kazakhskoi S.S.R.  (UR)
Soyuz Pisatelei Rossiiskoi S.F.S.R.  (UR)
Soyuz Pisatelei Rossiiskoi S.F.S.R. Rostovskoe
  Oblastnoe Otdelenie  (UR)
Soyuz Pisatelei S.S.S.R.  (UR)
Soyuz Pisatelei Ukrainskoi S.S.R.  (UR)
Soyuz Rabotnikov Kinematografii S.S.S.R.  (UR)
Soyuz Sovetskikh Obshchestv Druzhby i Kul'turnoi
  Svyazi s Zarubezhnymi Stranami  (UR)
Soyuz Sportivnykh Obshchestv i Organizatsii
  Rossiiskoi S.F.S.R.  (UR)
Soyuz Sportivnykh Obshchestv i Organizatsii S. S. S.
  R.  (UR)
Soyuz Sportivnykh Obshchestv i Organizatsii
  Ukrainskoi S.S.R.  (UR)
Soyuz Zhurnalistov S.S.S.R.  (UR)
Sozialdemokratische Partei der Schweiz  (SZ)
Sozialdemokratische Partei Deutschlands  (GW)

Sozialistische Einheitspartei Deutschlands.
  Zentralkomitee  (GE)
Sozialistische Jugend Oesterreichs  (AU)
Sozialistische Partei Oberoesterreichs.
  Landesorganisation  (AU)
Sozialistische Partei Oesterreichs  (AU)
Sozialistische Partei Oesterreichs. Bezirksorganisation
  Linz-Stadt  (AU)
Sozialistische Partei Oesterreichs. Bildungszentrale
  (AU)
Verlag Sozialistische Politik  (GW)
Sozialistischer Hochschulbund  (GW)
Sozialistischer Lehrerverein Oesterreichs  (AU)
Sozialistischer Verlag GmbH  (AU)
Sozialistisches Buero  (GW)
Sozialpaedagogischer Verlag  (GW)
Sozialwissenschaftliche Studiengesellschaft.
  Wissenschaftlicher Beirat  (AU)
Uitgeverij Spaarnestad N.V.  (NE)
Space Age Market Research  (US)
Space Age Publishers  (II)
Space Age Translations  (US)
Space and Time  (US)
Space Propulsion Reports, Inc.  (US)
Space Publications Inc.  (US)
Spaceview Magazine  (US)
Spafaswap  (US)
Grupo Editorial Spagat  (BL)
Spain. Boletin Oficial del Estado  (SP)
Spain. Comisaria General de Excavaciones
  Arqueologicas  (SP)
Spain. Consejo de Estado  (SP)
Spain. Consejo Superior de Investigaciones Cientificas
  (SP)
Spain. Consejo Superior de Investigaciones Cientificas.
  Departamento de Investigaciones Fisiologicas  (SP)
Spain. Consejo Superior de Investigaciones Cientificas.
  Instituto de Investigaciones Pesqueras  (SP)
Spain. Consejo Superior de Investigaciones Cientificas.
  Instituto de Medicine Experimental  (SP)
Spain. Consejo Superior de Investigaciones Cientificas.
  Instituto G. Fernandez de Oviedo  (SP)
Spain. Consejo Superior de Investigaciones Cientificas.
  Patronato Juan de la Cierva  (SP)
Spain. Consejo Superior de Investigaciones Cientificas.
  Patronato Menedez Pelayo  (SP)
Spain. Cortes Espanolas. Grupo Espanol de la Union
  Interparlimentaria  (SP)
Spain. Departamento de Fomento y Difusion
  Internacional  (SP)
Spain. Direccion de Pesca Maritima  (SP)
Spain. Direccion General de Banca, Bolsa e
  Inversiones  (SP)
Spain. Direccion General de Bellas Artes  (SP)
Spain. Direccion General de Cooperacion Tecnica
  Internacional  (SP)
Spain. Direccion General de Correos y
  Telecomunicacion  (SP)
Spain. Direccion General de Empresas y Actividades
  Turisticas  (SP)
Spain. Direccion General de Ensenanza Primaria.
  Campana Nacional de Promocion Cultural de
  Adultos  (SP)
Spain. Direccion General de Sanidad  (SP)
Spain. Direccion General de Trafico. Gabinete de
  Estudios  (SP)
Spain. Gabinete Tecnico  (SP)
Spain. Instituto Geografico y Catastral. Observatorio
  Astronomico Nacional  (SP)
Spain. Instituto Geologico y Minero  (SP)
Spain. Instituto Nacional de Educacion Fisica y
  Deportes  (SP)
Spain. Instituto Nacional de Estadistica  (SP)
Spain. Instituto Nacional de Industria. Direccion
  Financiera  (SP)
Spain. Instituto Nacional de Prevision  (SP)
Spain. Ministerio de Agricultura. Direccion General de
  la Produccion Agraria  (SP)
Spain. Ministerio de Agricultura. Estacion Central de
  Ecologia  (SP)
Spain. Ministerio de Agricultura. Secretaria General
  Tecnica  (SP)
Spain. Ministerio de Agricultura. Servicio de Extension
  Agraria  (SP)
Spain. Ministerio de Comercio  (SP)
Spain. Ministerio de Comercio. Servicio de Estudios
  (SP)
Spain. Ministerio de Comercio. Subsecretaria de la
  Marina Mercante  (SP)
Spain. Ministerio de Educacion y Ciencia  (SP)
Spain. Ministerio de Educacion y Ciencia. Junta
  Nacional Contra el Analfabetismo  (SP)
Spain. Ministerio de Hacienda  (SP)

Spain. Ministerio de Hacienda. Instituto de Credito
  Oficial  (SP)
Spain. Ministerio de Hacienda. Instituto de Estudios
  Fiscales  (SP)
Spain. Ministerio de Industria  (SP)
Spain. Ministerio de Industria. Instituto Geologico y
  Minero  (SP)
Spain. Ministerio de Industria. Registro de la
  Propriedad Industrial  (SP)
Spain. Ministerio de Informacion y Turismo  (SP)
Spain. Ministerio de Justicia. Secretaria General
  Tecnica  (SP)
Spain. Ministerio de la Vivienda  (SP)
Spain. Ministerio de Marina  (SP)
Spain. Ministerio de Marina. Instituto y Observatorio
  de Marina  (SP)
Spain. Ministerio de Obras Publicas  (SP)
Spain. Ministerio de Trabajo  (SP)
Spain. Ministerio de Trabajo. Servicio del Mutualismo
  Laboral  (SP)
Spain. Ministerio del Aire  (SP)
Spain. Ministerio del Aire. Subsecretaria de Aviacion
  Civil  (SP)
Spain. Ministerio del Ejercito  (SP)
Spain. Ministerio Espanol de Asuntos Exteriores  (SP)
Spain. Presidencia del Gobierno  (SP)
Spain. Servicio Central de Organizacion y Metodos
  (SP)
Spain. Servicio de Relaciones Exteriores Sindicals
  (SP)
Spain. Servicio Meteorologico Nacional  (SP)
Spain. Servicio Sindical de Estadisticas  (SP)
Spain. Tribunal Central de Trabajo  (SP)
Spain-U.S. Chamber of Commerce Inc.  (US)
Aldo Spallicci, Ed. & Pub.  (IT)
Spangler, Jennings, Spangler & Dougherty  (US)
Spanish American News Inc.  (US)
Spanish Chamber of Commerce in Great Britain
  (UK)
Spanish Institute, Inc.  (US)
Spanish Petroleum Association  (SP)
Spanish Socialist Labour Party (P.S.O.E.)  (FR)
SPARCO  (SP)
Spare Ribs Ltd.  (UK)
Sparebankforeningen i Norge  (NO)
Sparfraemjandet  (SW)
Robert Spark, Ed. & Pub.  (UK)
Spark Publications Ltd.  (GH)
Sparkassenverlag Ges. m.b.H.  (AU)
Sparrow Press  (US)
Spartacist League  (US)
Spartacist League of Australia & New Zealand  (AT)
Spartacus Press  (US)
Spartacus Youth Publishing Co.  (US)
Spastics International Medical Publications  (UK)
Spastics Society  (UK)
Verlagsgesellschaft Otto Spatz oHG  (GW)
Saverio Spaziani, Ed. & Pub.  (IT)
Speak  (AT)
Speakout Publications  (US)
Spear Publications Ltd.  (CN)
Spearhead Publications  (UK)
Spec Tech Publications, Inc.  (US)
Special Child Publications  (US)
Special Education Instructional Materials Center
  (US)
Special Interest Publications  (US)
Special Interest Publications (Des Moines)  (US)
Special Libraries Association  (US)
Special Libraries Association. Advertising and
  Marketing Division  (US)
Special Libraries Association. Cleveland Chapter
  (US)
Special Libraries Association. Food Librarians Division
  (US)
Special Libraries Association. Geography and Map
  Division  (US)
Special Libraries Association. Indiana Chapter  (US)
Special Libraries Association. Insurance Division
  (US)
Special Libraries Association, Japan  (JA)
Special Libraries Association. Metals-Materials
  Division  (US)
Special Libraries Association, Montreal Chapter
  (CN)
Special Libraries Association. New York Chapter
  (US)
Special Libraries Association. Pacific Northwest
  Chapter  (US)
Special Libraries Association. Upstate New York
  Chapter  (US)
Special Libraries Association, Virginia Chapter  (US)
Special Libraries Association. Washington D.C.
  Chapter  (US)
Special Reports, Inc.  (US)
Specialbladsforlaget  (DK)
Specialist Publications, Inc.  (US)
Specialized Agricultural Publications, Inc.  (US)

Specialized Publications Ltd.   (UK)
Edizioni Specializzate   (IT)
Specialtidningsfoerlaget AB   (SW)
Specialty Bakery Owners of America   (US)
Specialty Publications, Inc.   (US)
Specialty Salesman Magazine, Inc.   (US)
Specific Learning Difficulties Association of New
    South Wales   (AT)
Specific Learning Difficulties Association of Victoria
    (AT)
Specific Learning Difficulties Association of Western
    Australia   (AT)
Specola Vaticana   (VC)
Specom, Inc.   (US)
Spectator   (BE)
Spectator International Inc.   (US)
Spectator Ltd.   (UK)
Spectator Publishing Co.   (US)
Spectroscopical Society of Japan   (JA)
Spectroscopy Society of Canada   (CN)
Uitgeverij Het Spectrum B. V.   (NE)
Spectrum Publications, Inc.   (US)
Speech and Hearing Association of Virginia   (US)
Speech and Theatre Association of Missouri   (US)
Speech Communication Association   (US)
Speech Communication Association of Ohio   (US)
Speech Therapy Clinic   (NZ)
Speed and Sports Publications Ltd.   (UK)
J. B. Speed Art Museum   (US)
Speedo Knitting Mills Pty. Ltd.   (AT)
Speedwriter   (II)
Speeltuinvereniging   (NE)
Spektrum-Verlag   (SZ)
Speleologia Emiliana   (IT)
J. R. Spencer   (US)
Charles D. Spencer & Associates, Inc.   (US)
Spencer Marketing Services   (US)
Sperry New Holland   (US)
Sperry Rand Corporation   (US)
Spertus College of Judaica   (US)
Spertus College of Judaica Press   (US)
Spettatore Musicale   (IT)
Spex Industries Inc.   (US)
Spicebox Books, Ltd.   (UK)
Spices Export Promotion Council   (II)
Spicy Isle   (CE)
Spiegel Grove   (US)
Spiegel-Verlag   (GW)
Spilka arkhitektiv Ukrayiny   (UR)
Spin Publications   (UK)
Spink & Son Ltd.   (UK)
Spirit   (UK)
Spiritual Community Publications   (US)
Spiritual Life Institute of America   (US)
Spiritual Press   (CN)
Spiros Spirou & Son Co.   (GR)
Spitzenorganisation der Filmwirtschaft E.V.   (GW)
SPOFA, Spojene Podniky pro Zdravotnickou Vyrobu.
    Vyzkumny Ustav pro Biofaktory a Veterinarni
    Leciva   (CS)
Spokane. Mayor and City Council of Spokane,
    Washington   (US)
Spokane Chamber of Commerce   (US)
Spokane Public Schools   (US)
Spokane Tribe of Indians Tribal Council   (US)
Spokane Westerners Corral   (US)
Spokesman Books, Etc.   (UK)
Spokesman Press   (US)
Spoldzielnia Wydawnicza "Czytelnik"   (PL)
Spolecnost pro Racionalni Vyzivu   (CS)
Spoleczny Komitet Przecialkoholonego   (PL)
Spolek Ceskych Vcelaru   (CS)
E. & F. N. Spon Ltd.   (UK)
Verlagshaus Sponholz   (GW)
Spoon River Poetry Press   (US)
Spoor en Partners B.V.   (NE)
Sport Bowling   (FR)
Sport Fishing Institute   (US)
Sport Hobbyist   (US)
Sport Italia   (IT)
Sport Lisboa e Benfica   (PO)
Sport, Publishing House of the Central Committee of
    the Slovak Physical Culture Organization   (CS)
Sport- Toto- Gesellschaft   (SZ)
Sport- und Jugend-Verlag GmbH und Co. KG   (GW)
Sporting Chronicle Publications Ltd.   (UK)
Sporting News Publishing Co.   (US)
Sporting Shooters Association of Australia   (AT)
Societa Editrice Sportiva   (IT)
Sports and Medicine Publications   (US)
Sports Car Club of America   (US)
Sports Car Club of America. San Francisco Region
    (US)
Sports Communications, Inc.   (US)
Sports Council   (UK)
Sports Eye, Inc.   (US)
Sports Philatelists International   (US)
Sportshelf   (US)

Sportsko Drustvo Crvena Zvezda   (YU)
Sportsmen's Association of Australia. Western
    Australian Division   (AT)
Sportverlag D D R   (GE)
Sportwatch Inc.   (US)
Spotlight Publications Ltd.   (UK)
Spotlight Publishing Co. Ltd.   (US)
Sprachverband Deutsch fuer Auslaendische
    Arbeitnehmer e.V.   (GW)
Sprechsaal-Verlag   (GW)
Spree Publishing Co.   (US)
Sprenger Institute   (NE)
Spring Arbor College   (US)
Spring Manufacturers Institute   (US)
Spring Rain   (US)
Springer Publishing Co., Inc.   (US)
Springer-Verlag   (US)
Axel Springer Verlag AG   (GW)
Springfield Library and Museums Association   (US)
Springfield Public Schools   (US)
Springs Advertiser (Pty.) Ltd.   (SA)
James Sprunt Press   (US)
Spry Publications, Ltd.   (UK)
Spudman   (US)
Spur Inc.   (US)
Spurgeon's Homes   (UK)
Spurk   (LE)
Squadron Shop   (US)
Square Dance Federation of Manitoba. Eastern
    Division   (CN)
Square Dance Federation of Minnesota   (US)
Squash Rackets Association   (UK)
Squatchberry Press   (CN)
E.R. Squibb & Sons, Inc.   (US)
Srecanja   (YU)
Sredisnji Institut za Tumore i Slicne Bolesti   (YU)
Sri Aurobindo Ashram Trust   (II)
Sri Aurobindo Centenary Committee   (CE)
Sri Aurobindo International Center of Education   (II)
Sri Avinashilingam Home Science College for Women
    (II)
Sri Baktha Samaj   (II)
Sri Birendra Nath Ghosh   (II)
Sri Chinmoy Centre, Inc.   (US)
Sri Guru Singh Sabha   (II)
Sri Lanka. Department of Agriculture   (CE)
Sri Lanka. Department of Archaeology   (CE)
Sri Lanka. Department of Census and Statistics   (CE)
Sri Lanka. Department of Labour   (CE)
Sri Lanka. Department of National Archives. National
    Bibliography Branch   (CE)
Sri Lanka. Department of National Museums   (CE)
Sri Lanka. Forest Department   (CE)
Sri Lanka. Government Information Department
    (CE)
Sri Lanka. Irrigation Department. Hydrology Division
    (CE)
Sri Lanka. Ministry of Commerce and Trade   (CE)
Sri Lanka Academy of Administrative Studies   (CE)
Sri Lanka Historical and Social Studies Publication
    Board   (CE)
Sri Lanka Library Association   (CE)
Sri Lanka Medical Association   (CE)
Sri Lanka Meteorological Society   (CE)
Sri Lanka University Law Review Association   (CE)
Sri Ramakrishna Math   (II)
Sri Ramakrishna Mission Vidyalaya Teachers College
    (II)
Sri Ramanasramam   (II)
Sri Venkateswara University. Department of Sanskrit
    (II)
Sri Venkateswara University. Oriental Research
    Institute   (II)
K. Srinivas, Ed. & Pub.   (II)
Srpska Akademija Nauka i Umetnosti   (YU)
Srpska Akademija Nauka i Umetnosti. Etnografski
    Institut   (YU)
Srpska Akademija Nauka i Umetnosti. Koordinacioni
    Medjuakademski Odbor za Balkanologiju   (YU)
Srpska Akademija Nauka i Umetnosti. Odeljenje
    Literature i Jezika   (YU)
Srpska Patrijarsija   (YU)
Srpske Narodne Odrane u Americi   (US)
Srpsko Hemijsko Drustvo   (YU)
Srpsko Kulturno Drustvo "Prosvjeta"   (YU)
Srpsko Lekarsko Drustvo   (YU)
Srpsko Lekarsko Drustvo. Podruznica u Nisu   (YU)
Srpsko Lekarsko Drustvo. Redakcija za Stomatoloski
    Glasnik Srbije   (YU)
Srpsko Sociolosko Drustvo   (YU)
SS. Cyril & Methodias Seminary   (US)
Ssu Hai Chu Pan Shih Yeh Yu Hsien Kung Ssu   (HK)

Staatlich Genehmigte Gesellschaft der Autoren   (AU)
Staatliche Kunsthalle Karlsruhe   (GW)
Staatliche Kunstsammlungen Bayerns   (GW)
Staatliche Kunstsammlungen Dresden   (GE)
Staatliche Kunstsammlungen in Baden-Wuerttemberg
    (GW)
Staatliche Museen Preussischer Kulturbesitz Berlin
    (GW)
Staatliche Museen zu Berlin   (GE)
Staatlicher Mathematisch-Physikalischer Salon,
    Dresden   (GE)
Staatliches Filmarchiv der DDR. Filmtheater   (GE)
Staatliches Institut fuer Musikforschung   (GW)
Staatliches Museum fuer Mineralogie und Geologie,
    Dresden   (GE)
Staatliches Museum fuer Tierkunde in Dresden   (GE)
Staatliches Museum fuer Voelkerkunde Dresden
    (GE)
Staatsarchiv Bremen   (GW)
Staatsbibliothek Preussischer Kulturbesitz   (GW)
Staatsbibliothek Preussischer Kulturbesitz. Arbeitsstelle
    fuer Bibliothekstechnik   (GW)
Staatsverlag der DDR   (GE)
Ed. & Pub. Olga Stacevich   (US)
Stacey Publications   (UK)
Stackpole Books   (US)
Stadl-Paura. Gemeindeamt   (AU)
Stadsingenioerforeningen i Danmark   (DK)
Stadtarchiv Hildesheim   (GW)
Stadtmuseum Linz   (AU)
Staedtische Sukkulentensammlung   (SZ)
Staedtisches Gymnasium, Wuppertal   (GW)
Buchdruckerei Staefa AG   (SZ)
Staempfli und Cie AG   (SZ)
Staffordshire Development Association   (UK)
Stage and Cinema Newspapers (Pty) Ltd.   (SA)
Stagecast Publications   (IE)
Verlag Stahleisen mbH   (GW)
Stained Glass Association of America   (US)
Stained Glass Club   (US)
Stainer and Bell Ltd.   (UK)
Albert & Rita Stainton, Eds. & Pubs.   (US)
Stalna Konferencija Gradova Jugoslavije   (YU)
Stam-Robijns   (NE)
Stam Tijdschriften B.V.   (NE)
Stamats Publishing Co.   (US)
Lazar Stambovsky, Ed. & Pub.   (US)
Federico Stame, Ed. & Pub.   (IT)
Stamex B.V.   (NE)
Stamford College   (SI)
Stamler Publishing Co.   (US)
Stamm-Verlag GmbH   (GW)
Stamm-Werbung GmbH und Co.   (GW)
Stammer S.p.A.   (IT)
Stamp Collecting Ltd.   (UK)
Stamp Shows, Inc.   (US)
Stamp Wholesaler   (US)
Societa Editrice Stampa Europea   (IT)
Stampa Medica   (IT)
Editrice la Stampa S.p.A.   (IT)
Stamper   (US)
Stamperia Editrice Commerciale   (IT)
Stan Kenton's Creative World   (US)
Stanbiro, Poduzece za Organizaciju Informacije
    Ekonomske i Ostale Usluge   (YU)
Stanborough Press Ltd.   (UK)
Stand Magazine   (UK)
Standaard   (BE)
Standaard-Boekhandel N.V.   (BE)
Standard (1938) Ltd.   (IE)
Standard Abstract Corp.   (US)
Standard & Poor's Corporation   (US)
Standard Catalogue Co. Ltd.   (UK)
Standard Chartered Bank Ltd.   (UK)
Standard Educational Corporation   (US)
Standard Oil Company (Indiana)   (US)
Standard Oil Company (Ohio) Government and Public
    Affairs Department   (US)
Standard Oil Company of California   (US)
Standard Press   (II)
Standard Press   (US)
Standard Press Ltd.   (NZ)
Standard Publishing   (US)
Standard Publishing (Boston)   (US)
Standard Rate and Data Service, Inc.   (US)
Standard Research Consultants   (US)
Standards Association of Australia   (AT)
Standards Engineers Society   (US)
Standards Institution of Israel   (IS)
Standbrook Publications Ltd.   (UK)
Verlag fuer Standesamtswesen GmbH und Co. KG
    (GW)
Standing Conference for Local History   (UK)
Standing Conference of African University Libraries
    (NR)

Standing Conference of Co-Operative Library and Information Services (UK)
Standing Conference of Rectors and Vice-Chancellors of the European Universities (SZ)
Standing Conference on National and University Libraries. Subcommitte on Slavonic and East European Materials (UK)
Standpunkte und Dokumente (AU)
Stanford Museum. Committee for Art at Stanford (US)
Stanford Research Institute (US)
Stanford Research Institute. Chemical Information Services Department (US)
Stanford University (US)
Stanford University. Associated Students (US)
Stanford University. Committee on Linguistics (US)
Stanford University. Department of English (US)
Stanford University. Department of Spanish and Portuguese (US)
Stanford University. Food Research Institute (US)
Stanford University. Graduate School of Business (US)
Stanford University. Hoover Institution on War, Revolution and Peace (US)
Stanford University. Library (US)
Stanford University. School of Earth Sciences (US)
Stanford University. Stanford Alumni Association (US)
Stanford University. Stanford Business School Alumni Association (US)
Stanford University. Stanford Center for Research and Development in Teaching (US)
Stanford University. Stanford Law School (US)
Stanford University. Stanford Medical Alumni Association (US)
Stewart Stanley, Ed. & Pub. (US)
Stanley Foundation (US)
Stanley Gibbons Publications Ltd. (UK)
Stanley Publications, Inc. (US)
Stanley Publishing Co. (US)
Stanley Tools Ltd. (UK)
Stanstead County Historical Society (CN)
Stanton Library (AT)
Elizabeth Cady Stanton Publishing Co. (US)
Staple Cotton Cooperative Association (US)
Staples & Staples Ltd. (UK)
Staples Area Vocational Technical Institute (US)
Star (US)
Star-Advertiser Ltd. (BF)
Star and Garter Home for Disabled Sailors Soldiers and Airmen (UK)
Star Guidance, Inc. (US)
Star Publishing Company (US)
Star Research (Publications) Society (UK)
Star West Publications (US)
Stardance (UK)
Stardock (UK)
Starfish Books Ltd. (UK)
Stark Jewish News (US)
C.-A. Starke Verlag (GW)
Starrucca Valley Publications (US)
Stash (US)
State (US)
State Bank of India
  see India. State Bank of India (II)
State Bank of Pakistan
  see Pakistan. State Bank of Pakistan (PK)
State Bar Association of North Dakota (US)
State Bar of Arizona (US)
State Bar of California (US)
State Bar of California and Conference of California Judges (US)
State Bar of Georgia (US)
State Bar of Michigan (US)
State Bar of Nevada (US)
State Bar of New Mexico (US)
State Bar of Texas (US)
State Bar of Utah (US)
State Bar of Wisconsin (US)
State College of Victoria at Toorak (AT)
State Commerce for Construction in the USSR (US)
State Communities Aid Association (US)
State Education Journal Index (US)
State Education Publications (US)
State Farm Insurance Companies (US)
State Historical Society of Colorado (US)
State Historical Society of Iowa (US)
State Historical Society of Missouri (US)
State Historical Society of North Dakota (US)
State Historical Society of Wisconsin (US)
State Industrial Directories, Inc. (US)
State Institute of Education, Maharashtra
  see Maharashtra. Maharashtra State Institute of Education (II)
State Institute of Education, Rajasthan
  see Rajasthan. State Institute of Education (II)
State Library of Tasmania (AT)
State Medical Society of Wisconsin (US)

State Museum
  see Southwest Africa. State Museum (SX)
State Osteopathic Journal Group (US)
State Pharmaceutical Editorial Association (US)
State Planning Authority of New South Wales (AT)
State Principals Association (US)
State Revenue Society (US)
State Review Publishing Co. (US)
State Rivers and Water Supply Commission (AT)
State School Teachers Union of W.A. (Inc.) (AT)
State Supplies (II)
State University of Ghent
  see Rijksuniversiteit Te Gent (BE)
State University of New York (US)
State University of New York, Agricultural and Technical College at Farmingdale. Social Science Department (US)
State University of New York at Albany (US)
State University of New York at Albany. Department of Art (US)
State University of New York at Albany. Department of Philosophy (US)
State University of New York at Albany. Faculty Senate (US)
State University of New York at Albany. Graduate School of Public Affairs (US)
State University of New York at Albany. School of Library and Information Science (US)
State University of New York at Binghamton (US)
State University of New York at Binghamton. English Department (US)
State University of New York at Binghamton. Max Reinhardt Archive (US)
State University of New York at Binghamton. Medieval Center (US)
State University of New York at Binghamton. School of Management (US)
State University of New York at Buffalo (US)
State University of New York at Buffalo. Center for Immunology (US)
State University of New York at Buffalo. Center for Theoretical Biology (US)
State University of New York at Buffalo. Child Study Center (US)
State University of New York at Buffalo. Department of Classics (US)
State University of New York at Buffalo. Department of Foundational Studies (US)
State University of New York at Buffalo. Department of German and Slavic (US)
State University of New York at Buffalo. Department of Italian, Spanish and Portuguese (US)
State University of New York at Buffalo. Faculty of Law and Jurisprudence (US)
State University of New York at Buffalo. Law Library (US)
State University of New York at Buffalo. Program in East European and Slavic Studies (US)
State University of New York at Stony Brook (US)
State University of New York at Stony Brook. Department of Hispanic Languages and Literatures (US)
State University of New York, College at Brockport (US)
State University of New York, College at Brockport. Department of Foreign Languages and Literatures (US)
State University of New York, College at Buffalo. United Students Government, Inc. (US)
State University of New York, College at Cortland. Department of Sociology and Anthropology (US)
State University of New York, College at Fredonia. Department of Foreign Languages (US)
State University of New York, College at Fredonia. Lake Erie Environmental Studies (US)
State University of New York, College at Fredonia. Office of College Relations (US)
State University of New York, College at Geneseo. School of Library and Information Science (US)
State University of New York, College at New Paltz (US)
State University of New York, College at Oneonta. Department of Political Science (US)
State University of New York, College at Plattsburgh. English Department (US)
State University of New York, College at Potsdam. Department of English (US)
State University of New York, College at Potsdam. Philosophy Department (US)
State University of New York. Downstate Medical Center (US)
State University of New York. Foundations of Education Association (US)
State University of New York Librarians Association (US)
State University of New York Press (US)
State University of New York. Research Foundation (US)

State University of New York, Upstate Medical Center (US)
STATEC
  see Luxembourg. Service Central de la Statistique et des Etudes Economiques (LU)
Staten Island Community College (US)
Staten Island Community College. Department of English (US)
Staten Island Historical Society (US)
Staten Island Institute of Arts and Sciences (US)
Staten Island Zoological Society (US)
Statens Geotekniska Institut (SW)
Statens Humanistiska Forskningsraad (SW)
Statens Humanistiske Forskningsraad (DK)
Statens Naturvetenskapliga Forskningsraad
  see Sweden. Statens Naturvetenskapliga Forskningsraad (SW)
States of Malaya Chamber of Mines (MY)
Statesman & Nation Publishing Co. (UK)
Statesman Ltd. (II)
Statesman Publications (GH)
Statewide Air Pollution Research Center (US)
Statewide Homeowners Association (US)
Harry J. Stathos, Ed. & Pub. (US)
Station Biologique de Roscoff (FR)
Statisical Society of Australia (AT)
Statistical and Social Inquiry Society of Ireland (IE)
Statistical Centre of Iran
  see Iran. Statistical Centre (IR)
Statistical Office of the European Communities (EI)
Statistical Publishing Society (II)
Statistical Record (UK)
Statistical Science Association of Canada (CN)
Statistics Canada
  see Canada. Statistics Canada (CN)
Izdatel'stvo Statistika (UR)
Statisztikai Kiado Vallalat (HU)
Statni Filharmonie Brno (CS)
Statni Nakladatelstvi Technicke Literatury (CS)
Statni Pedagogicke Nakladatelstvi (CS)
Statni Plemenna Stanice (CS)
Statni Ustav Tesnopisny (CS)
Statni Vedecka Knihovna. Universitni Knihovna (CS)
Statni Vyzkumny Ustav Ochrany Materialu G. V. Akinova (CS)
Statni Vyzkumny Ustav Sklarsky (CS)
Statni Zemedelske Nakladatelstvi (CS)
Statni Zidovske Museum (CS)
Statny Drevarsky Vyskumny Ustav (CS)
Stato Maggiore della Marina (IT)
Stato Maggiore Esercito (IT)
Statsanstaelldas Foerbund (SW)
Statsfoeretag AB (SW)
Statsoekonomisk Forening (NO)
Johannes Stauda Verlag GmbH (GW)
Elwin Staude Verlag GmbH (GW)
Stauffer Communications, Inc. (US)
Stavanger Museum (NO)
Stazione Sperimentale del Vetro (IT)
Stazione Sperimentale Oli e Grassi (IT)
Stazione Sperimentale per i Combustibili (IT)
Stazione Sperimentale per l'Industria delle Conserve Alimentari (IT)
Stazione Sperimentale per l'Industria delle Essenze e dei Derivati Agrumari (IT)
Stazione Sperimentale per l'Industria delle Pelli e delle Materie Concianti (IT)
Stazione Zoologica di Napoli (IT)
Steamsi.ip Historical Society of America, Inc. (US)
George R. Stearns, Ed. & Pub. (US)
Peter N. Stearns, Ed. & Pub. (US)
Stechert-Macmillan Publishing Co., Inc. (US)
Stedfast Publishers (UK)
Steel Castings Research and Trade Association (UK)
Steel Company of Canada, Ltd. (CN)
Steel Founders' Society of America (US)
Steel Industry Management Association (UK)
Steel Structures Painting Council (US)
Niels Steensens Forlag (DK)
Steering Wheel Publications Ltd. (UK)
Steiermaerkischer Gemeindebund (AU)
Steiermark. Amt der Steiermaerkischen Landesregierung. Landesamtsdirektion - Referat Statistik (AU)
Steiermark. Landesjugendreferat der Steiermaerkischen Landesregierung (AU)
Steiermark. Landesstelle fuer Brandverhuetung in Steiermark (AU)
Steiermarkische Gebietskrankenkasse fuer Arbeiter und Angestellte (AU)
Steiger-Werbung Verlag GmbH (AU)
Stein and Day Publishers (US)
Stein Collectors International (US)
John A. Stein, Ed. & Pub. (US)
Rudolf Steiner Press (UK)
Steiner Schools Fellowship (UK)
Franz Steiner Verlag GmbH (GW)

Stredisko Technickych Informaci Potravinarskeho
  Prumyslu  (CS)
Street  (US)
Street Cries  (US)
Street Fiction Press  (US)
Street Research  (UK)
Street Singer  (UK)
Strength and Health Publishing Co.  (US)
Streven  (BE)
Stride  (II)
Strike It Rich Publications  (US)
Verlag A. Strobel KG  (GW)
Strode Publications (Holdings) Ltd.  (UK)
Stroembergs Idrottsboecker  (SW)
Ed. & Pub. Eduard Strohmaier  (AU)
Stroiizdat  (UR)
Izdavacki Savjet Casopisa Strojarstvo  (YU)
Alfred Strothe Verlag  (GW)
Strout Realty  (US)
Structur-Verlag  (GW)
Structural Engineering Research Centre  (II)
C. Struik Africana Publishers  (SA)
Stryker-Post Publications Inc.  (US)
Stuart Phillips Publications  (UK)
Stubbs Ltd.  (UK)
Stubs Publications  (US)
Stud & Stable Ltd.  (UK)
Studebaker Family National Association  (US)
Student American Pharmaceutical Association  (US)
Student American Pharmaceutical Association. Ohio
  Northern University Chapter  (US)
Student Association for the Study of Hallucinogens
  (US)
Student Book Co. Ltd.  (CH)
Student Conservation Association  (US)
Student Government Association, SUC at Potsdam
  (US)
Student Mathematics  (CN)
Student National Education Association  (US)
Student National Medical Association  (US)
Student Non-Violent Coordinating Committee  (US)
Student Struggle for Soviet Jewry  (US)
Student Times Publications  (PK)
Student Zionist Organization  (US)
Studentenschaft der Johann Wolfgang Goethe-
  Universitaet Frankfurt  (GW)
Students' Information Centre  (II)
Student's Message  (JO)
Students of Boston University  (US)
Students of Holy Cross College  (US)
Students of Mercer University  (US)
Students of Southern University  (US)
Students of the Brooklyn Law School  (US)
Students Ski Association  (US)
Studi e Problemi di Critica Testuale  (IT)
Casa Editrice Studi Meridionali  (IT)
Studi Urbinati. Serie A: Diritto  (IT)
Studia Germanica Gandensia  (BE)
Studia Slovenica  (US)
Studiecentrum Informatica  (NE)
Studiecentrum voor Jeugdmisdadigheid  (BE)
Studiecentrum voor Kernenergie
  see Centre d'Etude de l'Energie Nucleaire  (BE)
Studiengesellschaft fuer Fragen Mittel - und
  Osteuropaeischer Partnerschaft  (GW)
Studiengesellschaft fuer Holzschwellenoberbau e.V.
  (GW)
Studiengesellschaft zur Foerderung der
  Kernenergieverwertung in Schiffbau und Schiffahrt
  e.V.  (GW)
Studiengruppe fuer Systemsforschung e.V., Heidelberg
  (GW)
Studienstiftung  (GW)
Studies Centre on Polish-German Affairs  (UK)
Studies in Education Ltd.  (UK)
Studies in Philosophy and Education Inc.  (US)
Studieselskapet for Nord-Norsk Naeringsliv  (NO)
Studio di Psicologia del Lavoro  (IT)
Studio di Restauro Strini  (IT)
Studio Domenicano  (IT)
Studio Edizioni  (IT)
Studio International Journal Ltd.  (UK)
Studio Manca  (IT)
Studio Museum in Harlem  (US)
Studio Strini  (IT)
Studio Vista  (UK)
Studiorum Novi Testamenti Societas  (UK)
Studium Christi  (IT)
Verlag fuer das Studium der Arbeiterbewegung  (GW)
Studium Ediciones  (SP)
Study Centre for Religion and Society  (CE)
Study Centre for Yugoslav Affairs  (UK)
Study Group on Eighteenth-Century Russia  (UK)
Verlag Herbert Stuenings  (GW)
Verlag Willi Stuenings GmbH  (GW)
Editions Stuessi Ltd.  (SZ)
P. Adalbert Stummbillig, C. Pp.S.  (AU)
Stump  (US)

Stvaranje  (YU)
Style Auto Editrice  (IT)
Stylus (Brockport)  (US)
Styrelsen Foer Svenska Kyrkan i Utlandet  (SW)
Styret for det Industrielle Rettsvern  (NO)
Styria Verlag  (AU)
Suan Sunautha Teacher College  (TH)
Sub-Normal Children's Welfare Association  (AT)
Subdireccion de Estudios Economicos y Marketing
  (SP)
Subdued Publications Ltd.  (US)
Editions Subervie  (FR)
Vittorio Subilia, Ed. & Pub.  (IT)
Subject Index to Children's Magazines  (US)
V. Subramanian Ed. & Pub.  (II)
Subterrranean Sociological Association  (US)
Suburban Action Institute  (US)
Suburban Home Buys  (US)
Suburban Homes Guide  (US)
Suburban Newspapers, Inc.  (US)
Suburban Publishing Co.  (US)
B. V. Uitgeversmaatschappij Succes  (NE)
Success Magazine  (UK)
Success Publications, Inc.  (US)
Success Publishing Co. Inc.  (US)
Success Unlimited, Inc.  (US)
Successful Meetings. Directory Department  (US)
Sucesores de Rivadeneyra, S.A.  (SP)
Suchasnist  (UR)
Sucro S.A.  (SP)
Suction  (US)
Sud  (FR)
Sud-Regie  (FR)
Asociacion Casa Editrice Sudamericana  (AG)
Sudan. Department of Statistics  (SJ)
Sudan. Idarat al-Bahuth al-Iqtisadiyah Wa-al-Maliyah
    see Sudan. Ministry of Finance and National
    Economy. Economic and Financial Research
    Section  (SJ)
Sudan. Maslahat al-'ihsa
    see Sudan. Department of Statistics  (SJ)
Sudan. Ministry of Finance and National Economy.
    Economic and Financial Research Section  (SJ)
Sudan. Ministry of People's Local Government  (SJ)
Sudan. Mufawadiyat al-Takhtit al-Qawmi. Department
  of Statistics
    see Sudan. Department of Statistics  (SJ)
Sudan. Mufawadiyat al-Takhtit al-Qawmi. National
  Income Division
    see Sudan. National Planning Commission. National
    Income Division  (SJ)
Sudan. National Council for Research  (SJ)
Sudan. National Income Division
    see under Sudan. National Planning Commission
  (SJ)
Sudan. National Planning Commission. Department of
  Statistics
    see Sudan. Department of Statistics  (SJ)
Sudan. National Planning Commission. National
  Income Division  (SJ)
Sudan. Wizarat al-Hukumah al-Mahalliyah
    see Sudan. Ministry of People's Local Government
  (SJ)
Sudan Engineering Society  (SJ)
Sudan Food Research Centre  (SJ)
Sudan Interior Mission  (CN)
Sudan Medical Association  (SJ)
Sudan News Agency  (SJ)
Sudan United Mission  (UK)
Sudanese Socialist Union  (SJ)
Sudetendeutsche Landsmannschaft Oesterreich  (AU)
Sudetendeutscher Presseverein  (AU)
Izdatel'stvo Sudostroenie  (UR)
Suedafrikanischer Germanistenverband  (SA)
Verlag Sueddeutsche Bauwirtschaft  (GW)
Sueddeutscher Verlag GmbH  (GW)
Suedost-Institut  (GW)
Suedostdeutsche Historische Kommission  (GW)
Suedostdeutsches Kulturwerk  (GW)
Suedosteuropa Gesellschaft e.V.  (GW)
Suedtirol Verlag  (AU)
Suedtiroler Haupt Verband GmbH  (IT)
Suedwestdeutsche Verlagsanstalt GmbH  (GW)
Suedwestfaelische Industrie- und Handelskammer zu
  Hagen  (GW)
Suenos  (MX)
Finn Suenson Forlag  (DK)
Suffolk County Community College. English
  Department  (US)
Suffolk County Dental Society  (US)
Suffolk County Library Association  (US)
Suffolk University Law School  (US)
Sugaku Kyoshitsu
    see Rikkyo University. Institute of Mathematics
  (JA)
Suganitam Trust  (II)
Sugar Beet Institute  (JA)
Sugar Journal  (US)

Sugar News Press, Inc.  (PH)
Sugar Publications  (US)
Sugar Technologists' Association of Trinidad & Tobago
  (TR)
Sugarland Publications  (PH)
Sugestoes Literarias  (BL)
Suhrkamp Verlag  (GW)
Suid-Afrikaanse Aalwyn- en Vetplantvereniging
    see South African Aloe and Succulent Society
  (SA)
Suid-Afrikaanse Akademie vir Wetenskap en Kuns
  (SA)
Suid-Afrikaanse Genootskap vir die Bevordering van
  die Wetenskap
    see South African Association for the Advancement
  of Science  (SA)
Suiken Kagaku Kenkyujo
    see Nagoya University. Water Research Institute
  (JA)
Suiker Unie  (NE)
Suikerstichting Nederland  (NE)
Suion Chosakai  (JA)
Suiri Kagaku Kenkyusho
    see Water Utilization Research Institute  (JA)
Suisan-cho Nihonkai-ku Suisan Kenkyusho
    see Japan. Japan Sea Regional Fisheries Research
  Laboratory  (JA)
Suisan-cho Tansui-ku Suisan Kenkyusho
    see Japan. Freshwater Fisheries Research
  Laboratory  (JA)
Suisan-cho Tohoku-ku Suisan Kenkyusho
    see Japan. Tohoku Regional Fisheries Research
  Laboratory  (JA)
Suisan-cho Tokai-ku Suisan Kenkyusho
    see Japan. Tokai Regional Fisheries Research
  Laboratory  (JA)
Suisan Kaiyo Kenkyu-Kai
    see Japanese Society of Fisheries and Oceanography
  (JA)
Suishitsu Kagaku Kenkyu Shisetsu
    see Nagoya University. Water Research Institute
  (JA)
Suiuz na Arkhitektite v Bulgaria  (BU)
Suiuz na Bulgarski Filatelisti  (BU)
Suiuz na Bulgarski Kompozitori  (BU)
Suiuz na Bulgarski Pisateli  (BU)
Suiuz na Nauchni Rabotnitsi v Bulgaria  (BU)
Sujaneshu  (BG)
Sulekha Press  (II)
Victor Sulimovich, Ed. & Pub.  (AG)
Livraria Sulina  (BL)
Sulphide Corporation Pty. Ltd.  (AT)
Sulphur Institute  (US)
Sulzer Brothers Ltd.  (SZ)
Sumarie  (IT)
Sumitomo Bakelite Co. Ltd.  (JA)
Sumitomo Bank, Ltd.  (JA)
Sumitomo Denki Kogyo
    see Sumitomo Electric Industries Ltd.  (JA)
Sumitomo Electric Industries Ltd.  (JA)
Sumitomo Keikinzoku Kogyo K. K.
    see Sumitomo Light Metal Industries Ltd.  (JA)
Sumitomo Light Metal Industries, Ltd.  (JA)
Ediciones Summa  (AG)
Summer Institute of Linguistics
    see also under Peru Instituto Linguistico de Verano
  (US)
Summer Institute of Linguistics  (US)
Summer Institute of Linguistics. Departamento de
  Estudos Tecnicos  (BL)
Murray Summers, Ed. & Pub.  (US)
Summit  (US)
Summit County Labor News  (US)
Summit Publishing Co.  (US)
Sun  (US)
Sun and Moon  (US)
Sun Co., Inc.  (US)
Sun Life Assurance Company of Canada  (CN)
Sun-Lin-Sheng  (CH)
Sun Oil Co.  (US)
Sun Oil Company  (US)
Sun Publishing Co.  (US)
Sun Vale  (UK)
Sun Valley Co.  (US)
Sun Yat-Sen Cultural Foundation  (CH)
Sun Yat-Sen University  (CC)
Sunburst Anthology  (US)
Sunbury  (US)
Sunbury Press  (US)
Suncat Enterprises  (US)
Suncraft International Corp.  (US)
Sundar Homoeo Sadan  (II)
Sunday Post  (PK)
Sunday Publications Inc.  (US)
Sundby Sports Inc.  (US)
Sunderland Polytechnic Students Union  (UK)
Sungravure Pty. Ltd.  (AT)
Sunnhetsbladet Trykkeri  (NO)

Sveriges Exportraad  (SW)
Sveriges Faerghandlares Riksfoerbund  (SW)
Sveriges Farmacevtfoerbund  (SW)
Sveriges Fartygsbefaelsfoerening  (SW)
Sveriges Filatelist-Foerbund  (SW)
Sveriges Fiskares Riksfoerbund  (SW)
Sveriges Foerenade Filmstudios  (SW)
Sveriges Foereningsbankers Foerbund  (SW)
Sveriges Foerfattarfoerbund  (SW)
Sveriges Foerskollaerares Riksfoerbund  (SW)
Sveriges Fritidsfiskares Riksfoerbund  (SW)
Sveriges Froeodlarefoerbund  (SW)
Sveriges Gjuteritekniska Foerening  (SW)
Sveriges Glas- och Porslinshandlarefoerbund  (SW)
Sveriges Grossistfoerbund  (SW)
Sveriges Handelsagenters Foerbund  (SW)
Sveriges Hotell- och Restaurangfoerbund  (SW)
Sveriges Jaernhandlarefoerbund  (SW)
Sveriges Juvelerare- och Guldsmedsfoerbund  (SW)
Sveriges Koepmannafoerbund  (SW)
Sveriges Kontoristfoerening  (SW)
Sveriges Korfoerbund  (SW)
Sveriges Laekarfoerbund  (SW)
Sveriges Laerarfoerbund  (SW)
Sveriges Lantbruksuniversitet. Institutionen Foer
  Vaextskydd  (SW)
Sveriges Lantmaestarfoerbund  (SW)
Sveriges Lantmaetarefoerening  (SW)
Sveriges Leksakshandlares Riksfoerbund  (SW)
Sveriges Livsmedelshandlarefoerbund  (SW)
Sveriges Maestarefoerening  (SW)
Sveriges Marknadsfoerbund  (SW)
Sveriges Moebelhandlares Centralfoerbund  (SW)
Sveriges Ornitologiska Foerening  (SW)
Sveriges Paelsdjursuppfoedares Riksfoerbund  (SW)
Sveriges Radio  (SW)
Sveriges Radiohandlares Riksfoerbund  (SW)
Sveriges Redarefoerening  (SW)
Sveriges Riksbank  (SW)
Sveriges Riksidrottsfoerbund  (SW)
Sveriges Schackfoerbund  (SW)
Sveriges Schaktentreprenoerers Riksfoerbund  (SW)
Sveriges Skogsaegarefoereningars Riksfoerbund  (SW)
Sveriges Skogsvaardsfoerbund  (SW)
Sveriges Skohandlarfoerbund  (SW)
Sveriges Skorstensfejaremaestares Riksfoerbund  (SW)
Sveriges Skraedderiidkarefoerbund  (SW)
Sveriges Socialdemokratiska Arbetareparti  (SW)
Sveriges Socialdemokratiska Kvinnofoerbund  (SW)
Sveriges Socialdemokratiska Ungdomsfoerbund  (SW)
Sveriges Socionomeres Riksfoerbund  (SW)
Sveriges Socionomfoerbund  (SW)
Sveriges Standardiseringskommission  (SW)
Sveriges Tandlaekarfoerbund  (SW)
Sveriges Tapetseraremaestare Centralfoerening  (SW)
Sveriges Tegelindustrifoerening  (SW)
Sveriges Textilhandlarefoerbund  (SW)
Sveriges Trae- och Byggvaruhandlares Centralfoerbund
  (SW)
Sveriges Tvaetterifoerbund  (SW)
Sveriges Universitets och Hoegskoleamanuensers
  Foerbund  (SW)
Sveriges Urmakare- och Optikerfoerbund  (SW)
Sveriges Utsaedesfoerening  (SW)
Sveriges Verkstadsfoerening  (SW)
Sveriges Veterinaerfoerbund  (SW)
Sveriges Yngre Lakares Foerening  (SW)
Sveriges Yrkesfruktodlares Riksfoerbund  (SW)
Sveriges 4H  (SW)
Sveti Arhijerejski Sinod Srpske Pravoslavne Crkve
  (YU)
Svetlost  (YU)
Svetovy Kongres Slovakov  (CN)
Svetstekniska Foereningen  (SW)
Sveuciliste u Rijeci. Medicinski Fakultet  (YU)
Sveuciliste u Zagrebu. Fakultet Politickih Nauka
  (YU)
Sveuciliste u Zagrebu. Fakultet Strojarstva i
  Brodogradaje  (YU)
Sveuciliste u Zagrebu. Fakultet za Defektologiju
  (YU)
Sveuciliste u Zagrebu. Filozofski Fakultet  (YU)
Sveuciliste u Zagrebu. Institut za Drustvena
  Istrazivanja  (YU)
Sveuciliste u Zagrebu. Medicinski Fakultet  (YU)
Sveuciliste u Zagrebu. Referalni Centar  (YU)
Sveuciliste u Zagrebu. Stomatoloski Fakultet  (YU)
Svijet  (YU)
Svisa Esperanto Societo  (SZ)
Izdavacko Preduzece Svjetlost  (YU)
Izdatel'stvo Svyaz'  (UR)
Swain & Co. Ltd.  (UK)
Swami Nirmalananda. Bharat Sevasram Sangha  (II)
Swap  (US)
Swaran Publishing House  (II)
Swarthmore College. Swarthmore College Student
  Council  (US)

Rama Swarup, Ed. & Pub.  (II)
Swati Prakashan  (II)
Swaziland. Central Statistical Office  (SQ)
Swaziland. Economic Planning Office  (SQ)
Swaziland. Geological Survey and Mines Department
  (SQ)
Swaziland. Ministry of Agriculture  (SQ)
Swaziland. Ministry of Education  (SQ)
Swaziland. Ministry of Finance  (SQ)
Swaziland National Centre  (SQ)
Sweden. Arbetsmarknadsstyrelsen  (SW)
Sweden. Byggnadsstyrelsen  (SW)
Sweden. Central Bureau of Statistics
  see Sweden. Statistiska Centralbyraan  (SW)
Sweden. Finansdepartementet  (SW)
Sweden. Finansdepartementet. Budget Department
  (SW)
Sweden. Fiskeristyrelsen. Institute of Marine Research
  (SW)
Sweden. Foersvarets Forskningsanstalt  (SW)
Sweden. Folksams Sociala Raad  (SW)
Sweden. Geological Survey of Sweden
  see Sweden. Sveriges Geologiska Undersoekning
  (SW)
Sweden. Inrikesdepartement  (SW)
Sweden. Institute for Water and Air Pollution
  Research
  see Sweden. Institutet Foer Vatten- och
  Luftvaardsforskning  (SW)
Sweden. Institute of Marine Research
  see Sweden. Fiskeristyrelsen. Institute of Marine
  Research  (SW)
Sweden. Institutet Foer Vatten- och
  Luftvaardsforskning  (SW)
Sweden. Konjunkturinstitutet  (SW)
Sweden. Konsumentverket  (SW)
Sweden. Kungliga Biblioteket  (SW)
Sweden. Kungliga Livrustkammaren  (SW)
Sweden. Kungliga Militaerhoegskolan.
  Militaerhistoriska Avdelningen  (SW)
Sweden. Lantmaeteriverket  (SW)
Sweden. Luftfartsverket  (SW)
Sweden. Ministry of Finance
  see Sweden. Finansdepartementet  (SW)
Sweden. Ministry of Foreign Affairs
  see Sweden. Utrikesdepartementet  (SW)
Sweden. Ministry of Labour and Housing
  see Sweden. Inrikesdepartementet  (SW)
Sweden. National Agricultural Marketing Board
  see Sweden. Statens Jordbruksnaemd  (SW)
Sweden. National Audit Bureau
  see Sweden. Riksrevisionsverket  (SW)
Sweden. National Board of Health and Welfare
  see Sweden. Socialstyrelsen  (SW)
Sweden. National Board of Public Building
  see Sweden. Byggnadsstyrelsen  (SW)
Sweden. National Civil Aviation Administration
  see Sweden. Luftfartsverket  (SW)
Sweden. National Collective Bargaining Office
  see Sweden. Statens Avtalsverk  (SW)
Sweden. National Consumer Institute
  see Sweden. Statens Institut Foer Konsumentfraagor
  (SW)
Sweden. National Council for Consumer Goods and
  Consumer Information
  see Sweden. Statens Konsumentraad  (SW)
Sweden. National Debt Office
  see Sweden. Riksgaeldskontoret  (SW)
Sweden. National Defense Research Institute
  see Sweden. Foersvarets Forskningsanstalt  (SW)
Sweden. National Environment Protection Board
  see Sweden. Statens Naturvaardsverk  (SW)
Sweden. National Labour Market Board
  see Sweden. Arbetsmarknadsstyrelsen  (SW)
Sweden. National Record Office
  see Sweden. Riksarkivet  (SW)
Sweden. National Social Insurance Board
  see Sweden. Riksfoersaekringsverket  (SW)
Sweden. Nationalmuseum  (SW)
Sweden. Office of the Chancellor of the Swedish
  Universities
  see Sweden. Universitetskanslersaembetet  (SW)
Sweden. Patent- och Registreringsverket  (SW)
Sweden. Postverket  (SW)
Sweden. Riksarkivet  (SW)
Sweden. Riksdagen  (SW)
Sweden. Riksfoersaekringsverket  (SW)
Sweden. Riksgaeldskontoret  (SW)
Sweden. Riksrevisionsverket  (SW)
Sweden. Royal Armoury
  see Sweden. Kungliga Livrustkammaren  (SW)
Sweden. Royal Library
  see Sweden. Kungliga Biblioteket  (SW)
Sweden. Royal Patent and Registration Office
  see Sweden. Patent- och Registreringsverket  (SW)
Sweden. Sjukvaardens och Socialvaardens Planerings-
  och Rationaliseringsinstitut  (SW)
Sweden. Socialstyrelsen  (SW)

Sweden. State Railways Central Administration
  see Sweden. Statens Jaernvaegars
  Centralfoervaltning  (SW)
Sweden. Statens Avtalsverk  (SW)
Sweden. Statens Humanistiska Forskningsraad
  see Statens Humanistiska Forskningsraad  (SW)
Sweden. Statens Institut Foer Konsumentfraagor
  (SW)
Sweden. Statens Jaernvaegars Centralfoervaltning
  (SW)
Sweden. Statens Jordbruksnaemd  (SW)
Sweden. Statens Konsumentraad  (SW)
Sweden. Statens Lantmaeteriverk  (SW)
Sweden. Statens Livsmedelsverk  (SW)
Sweden. Statens Naturvaardsverk  (SW)
Sweden. Statens Naturvetenskapliga Forskningsraad
  (SW)
Sweden. Statens Offentliga Utredningar  (SW)
Sweden. Statens Planverk  (SW)
Sweden. Statens Raad Foer Byggnadsforskning  (SW)
Sweden. Statens Vaeg- och Trafikinstitut  (SW)
Sweden. Statistiska Centralbyraan  (SW)
Sweden. Statistiska Centralbyraan. Biblioteket  (SW)
Sweden. Styrelsen Foer Internationell Utveckling
  (SW)
Sweden. Sveriges Geologiska Undersoekning  (SW)
Sweden. Sveriges Geologiska Undersoekning. Section
  of Regional Geophysics  (SW)
Sweden. Swedish Air Staff
  (SW)
Sweden. Swedish Cancer Registry  (SW)
Sweden. Swedish Planning and Rationalization
  Institute of the Health and Social Services  (SW)
Sweden. Telecommunications Administration
  see Sweden. Televerket  (SW)
Sweden. Televerket  (SW)
Sweden. Universitetskanslersaembetet  (SW)
Sweden. Utrikesdepartementet  (SW)
Sweden. Yrksev Agledningsenheten  (SW)
Swedenborg Foundation  (US)
Swedenborg Scientific Association  (US)
Swedenborg Verlag  (SZ)
Swedenborgian Church  (US)
Swedish Academy of Pharmaceutical Sciences  (SW)
Swedish Air Line Pilots Association  (SW)
Swedish Association for Mental Health  (SW)
Swedish Atomic Forum  (SW)
Swedish Cancer Registry
  see Sweden. Swedish Cancer Registry  (SW)
Swedish Cement and Concrete Research Institute
  see Cement- och Betonginstitutet  (SW)
Swedish Collector's Society Northern Star  (SW)
Swedish Cooperative Centre  (SW)
Swedish Council for Building Research
  see Sweden. Statens Raad Foer Byggnadsforskning
  (SW)
Swedish Engineers' Press Ltd.
  see Ingenjoersfoerlaget AB  (SW)
Swedish Furniture Manufacturers Association  (SW)
Swedish Humanistic Research Council
  see Statens Humanistiska Forskningsraad  (SW)
Swedish Industrial Publications  (SW)
Swedish Information Service  (US)
Swedish Institute for Nationwide Concerts  (SW)
Swedish Institute of International Affairs
  see Utrikespolitiska Institutet  (SW)
Swedish International Development Authority
  see Sweden. Styrelsen Foer Internationell
  Utveckling  (SW)
Swedish Jazz Federation  (SW)
Swedish-Korean Society  (SW)
Swedish Literary Society of Finland
  see Svenska Litteratursaellskapet i Finland  (FI)
Swedish Natural Science Research Council
  see Sweden. Statens Naturvetenskapliga
  Forskningsraad  (SW)
Swedish Nutrition Foundation  (SW)
Swedish Pioneer Historical Society, Inc.  (US)
Swedish Plastics and Chemicals Suppliers Association
  (SW)
Swedish Society of Actuaries  (SW)
Swedish Sociological Association  (SW)
Swedish Spiritualistic Federation  (SW)
Swedish Sportdivers Federation  (SW)
Swedish Textile Employers' Association  (SW)
Swedish Theological Institute  (IS)
Swedish University of Aabo
  see Aabo Akademi  (FI)
Swedish Veteran Car Club  (SW)
Sweet & Maxwell (N.Z.) Ltd.  (NZ)
Sweet & Maxwell Stevens Journals  (UK)
Sweet Briar Alumnae Association  (US)
Sweet Home Central School District-Towns of
  Amherst and Tonawanda  (US)
Sweet Publishing Co.  (US)
Swets en Zeitlinger B. V.  (NE)
Swift & Co.  (US)
Swift-Dorr Publications  (US)

Swift Fleet Ltd. (UK)
Swift Ltd (UK)
Swimming Teachers Association (UK)
Swimming Times Ltd. (UK)
Swimming World, Inc. (US)
Swing Journal Co. Ltd. (JA)
Swinton Conservative College (UK)
Swiss Alpine Club
  *see* Club Alpin Suisse (SZ)
Swiss American Historical Society (US)
Swiss Association for Atomic Energy
  *see* Schweizerische Vereinigung fuer Atomenergie
  (SZ)
Swiss Association of Graduate Nurses (SZ)
Swiss Bank Corporation
  *see* Schweizerischer Bankverein (SZ)
Swiss Club Toronto (CN)
Swiss Eastern Institute
  *see* Schweizerisches Ost- Institut (SZ)
Swiss Entomological Society
  *see* Schweizerische Entomologische Gesellschaft
  (SZ)
Swiss Federal Institute of Technology
  *see* Eidgenoessische Technische Hochschule Zuerich
  (SZ)
Swiss Federal Railways
  *see* Switzerland. Chemins de Fer Federaux Suisses
  (SZ)
Swiss Federation of Camping and Caravanning (SZ)
Swiss Federation of Plant Engineers (SZ)
Swiss Federation of Trade Unions
  *see* Schweizerischer Gewerkschaftsbund (SZ)
Swiss Meteorological Institute
  *see* Switzerland. Schweizerische Meteorologische
  Zentralanstalt (SZ)
Swiss National Museum
  *see* Schweizerisches Landesmuseum (SZ)
Swiss Natural History Society
  *see* Schweizerische Naturforschende Gesellschaft
  (SZ)
Swiss Newspaper Publishers Association
  *see* Schweizerischer Zeitungsverleger-Verband (SZ)
Swiss Observer Ltd. (UK)
Swiss Pharmaceutical Society
  *see* Societe Suisse de Pharmacie (SZ)
Swiss Publishing Co., Inc. (US)
Swiss Reinsurance Co. (US)
Swiss Shipping Association
  *see* Schweizerische Schiffahrtsvereinigung (SZ)
Swiss Society of Dermatology and Venerology (SZ)
Swiss Society of Engineers and Architects
  *see* Societe Suisse des Ingenieurs et des Architectes
  (SZ)
Swiss Society of Food Science and Technology
  *see* Schweizerische Gesellschaft fuer
  Lebensmittelwissenschaft und- Technologie (SZ)
Swiss Society of Paediatrics (SZ)
Swiss Society of Plastic and Reconstructive Surgeons
  (SZ)
Swiss Union of Arts and Crafts
  *see* Schweizerischer Gewerbeverband (SZ)
Swiss Watch Fair (SZ)
Swiss Watch Shops Association
  *see* Verband Schweizerischer Uhrenfachgeschaefte
  (SZ)
Swissexport Cooperation Alliance (SZ)
Switzerland. Bibliotheque Nationale Suisse (SZ)
Switzerland. Bundesamt fuer Industrie, Gewerbe und
  Arbeit (SZ)
Switzerland. Bundesamt fuer Sozialversicherung (SZ)
Switzerland. Bundesamt fuer Zivilschutz (SZ)
Switzerland. Bureau Federal de Statistique
  *see* Switzerland. Statistisches Amt. (SZ)
Switzerland. Chemins de Fer Federaux Suisses (SZ)
Switzerland. Commission de Recherches Economiques
  *see* Switzerland. Eidgenoessisches
  Volkswirtschaftsdepartement. Kommission fuer
  Konjunkturfragen (SZ)
Switzerland. Departement Federal de l'Economie
  Publique. Commission de Recherches Economiques
  *see* Switzerland. Eidgenoessisches
  Volkswirtschaftsdepartement. Kommission fuer
  Konjunkturfragen (SZ)
Switzerland. Department Federal de l'Economie
  Publique
  *see* Switzerland. Eidgenoessisches
  Volkswirtschaftsdepartement (SZ)
Switzerland. Direction Generale des Douanes
  *see* Switzerland. Eidgenoessische Oberzolldirektion
  (SZ)
Switzerland. Directorate General of Customs
  *see* Switzerland. Eidgenoessische Oberzolldirektion
  (SZ)
Switzerland. Eidgenoessische Anstalt fuer das
  Forstliche Versuchswesen (SZ)
Switzerland. Eidgenoessische Gesundheitsamt (SZ)
Switzerland. Eidgenoessische Oberzolldirektion (SZ)

Switzerland. Eidgenoessisches Amt fuer Geistiges
  Eigentum (SZ)
Switzerland. Eidgenoessisches Departement des Innern
  (SZ)
Switzerland. Eidgenoessisches
  Volkswirtschaftsdepartement (SZ)
Switzerland. Eidgenoessisches
  Volkswirtschaftsdepartement. Abteilung fuer
  Landwirtschaft (SZ)
Switzerland. Eidgenoessisches
  Volkswirtschaftsdepartement. Kommission fuer
  Konjunkturfragen (SZ)
Switzerland. Kommission fuer Konjunkturfragen
  *see under* Switzerland. Eidgenoessisches
  Volkswirtschaftsdepartement (SZ)
Switzerland. Office d'Orientation et de Formation
  Professionelle (SZ)
Switzerland. Office de la Science et de la Recherche
  (SZ)
Switzerland. Office Federal de la Protection Civile
  *see* Switzerland. Bundesamt fuer Zivilschutz (SZ)
Switzerland. Office Federal du Personnel. Service de
  Placement (SZ)
Switzerland. Schweizerische Landesbibliotek
  *see* Switzerland. Bibliotheque Nationale Suisse
  (SZ)
Switzerland. Schweizerische Meteorologische
  Zentralanstalt (SZ)
Switzerland. Schweizerisches Bundesarchiv (SZ)
Switzerland. Statistisches Amt. (SZ)
Switzerland. Wildlife Information Service (SZ)
Swizzle Stick Enterprises (US)
Sword of the Lord Publishers (US)
Swordsman Publishing Co. (US)
Sydantautiliitto r.y. (FI)
Sydney Bush Walkers (AT)
Sydney County Council. Publicity Section (AT)
Sydney Libertarians (AT)
Sydney Medieval and Renaissance Group (AT)
Sydney Metropolitan Water Sewerage and Drainage
  Board (AT)
Sydney Observatory (AT)
Sydney Rugby Union (AT)
Sydney Speleological Society (AT)
Sydney Stock Exchange (AT)
Sydney Teachers' College (AT)
Sydney University Press (AT)
Sydney University Speleological Society (AT)
Foerlags AB Sydvaestkusten (FI)
Sylip, Gorres, Velayo & Co. (PH)
Symcon Marine Corp (US)
Symcon Publishing Co. (US)
David Syme & Co. (AT)
Symphonette Press (US)
Synagogue Council of America. Institute for Jewish
  Policy Planning and Research (US)
Synapse Inc. (US)
Syndicale Kamer Belgische Tuinbouw (BE)
Syndicale Kamer der Fabrikanten van Confectie van
  Belgie
  *see* Chambre Syndicale des Fabricants de
  Confections de Belgique (BE)
Syndicat de la Librairie Ancienne et Moderne (FR)
Syndicat des Cadres et Agents de Maitrise de
  l'Imprimerie, des Arts Graphiques et du Cartonnage
  (FR)
Syndicat des Cafetiers, Restaurateurs de Paris et
  Banlieues (FR)
Syndicat des Constructeurs de Moteurs a Combustion
  Interne (FR)
Syndicat des Critiques Litteraires (FR)
Syndicat des Exportateurs et Negociants en Bois de
  Cote d'Ivoire (IV)
Syndicat des Femmes Chirugiens-Dentistes (FR)
Syndicat des Grades de la Police Nationale (FR)
Syndicat des Industriels de la Cote d'Ivoire (IV)
Syndicat des Industries du Cameroun (CM)
Syndicat des Industries du Livres (FR)
Syndicat des Journalistes et Ecrivains (FR)
Syndicat des Journalistes Francais C.F.D.T. (FR)
Syndicat des Patissiers de la Region de Paris (FR)
Syndicat des Pisciculteurs-Salmoniculteurs de France
  (FR)
Syndicat Federal des Industries Polygraphiques
  (SYFIP) (FR)
Syndicat General de l'Industrie Cotonniere Francaise
  et Textiles Allies (FR)
Syndicat General de l'Industrie du Jute (FR)
Syndicat General des Fondeurs de France et Industries
  Connexes (FR)
Syndicat General du Caoutchouc et des Plastiques
  (FR)
Syndicat Medecins du Travail (FR)
Syndicat National d'Apiculture (FR)
Syndicat National de Cadres Hospitaliers (FR)
Syndicat National de l'Enseignement Superieur (FR)
Syndicat National de la Distribution pour l'Automobile
  et l'Industrie (FR)

Syndicat National des Agences (FR)
Syndicat National des Anesthesiologistes-Reanimateurs
  Francais (FR)
Syndicat National des Angeiologues (FR)
Syndicat National des Antiquaires (FR)
Syndicat National des Chercheurs Scientifiques (FR)
Syndicat National des Constructeurs de Moules et
  Modeles (FR)
Syndicat National des Courtiers d'Assurances et de
  Reassurances (FR)
Syndicat National des Createurs d'Architectures
  Interieures et de Modeles (C.A.I.M.) (FR)
Syndicat National des Depositaires de Presse (FR)
Syndicat National des Employes Techniciens et Cadres
  de la Publicite C. G. T. (FR)
Syndicat National des Enseignements de Second
  Degre (FR)
Syndicat National des Entreprises du Froid et du
  Conditionnement de l'Air (FR)
Syndicat National des Fabricants de Ciments et de
  Chaux (FR)
Syndicat National des Instituteurs (FR)
Syndicat National des Lycees et Colleges (FR)
Syndicat National des Officers de la Marine
  Marchande C.F.D.T. (FR)
Syndicat National des Pilotes de Ligne Francais (FR)
Syndicat National des Services Veterinaires (FR)
Syndicat National des Techniciens Superieurs en
  Dietetique (FR)
Syndicat National Unifie des Douanes et Droits
  Indirects (FR)
Syndicat Patronal des Cafes (FR)
Syndicate Inc. (US)
Syndicate Magazines Inc. (US)
Syndicate Press Oy (FI)
Synergistic Consultants, Inc. (PH)
Synerjy (US)
Synod of the Diocese of Ontario. Board of Parish
  Services (CN)
Synodalrat der Evangelisch-Reformierten Landeskirche
  des Kantons Bern (SZ)
Synpunkt (SW)
Syntex Brasil S.A., Industria e Comercio (BL)
Syntex Laboratories Inc. (US)
Synthese Editeur (FR)
Synthesis Communications, Inc. (US)
Synthesis Journal (US)
Synthetic Organic Chemical Manufacturers
  Association (US)
Syracuse Peace Council (US)
Syracuse University (US)
Syracuse University. Center on Human Policy (US)
Syracuse University College of Law (US)
Syracuse University. Continuing Education Center for
  the Public Service (US)
Syracuse University. Department of English (US)
Syracuse University. Department of Geography (US)
Syracuse University. Department of Religion (US)
Syracuse University. Department of Romance
  Languages (US)
Syracuse University. Family Planning and Population
  Information Center (US)
Syracuse University. Libraries (US)
Syracuse University Library Associates (US)
Syracuse University. Maxwell Graduate Student
  Association (US)
Syracuse University Press (US)
Syracuse University. Program of East African Studies
  (US)
Syracuse University. Publications in Continuing
  Education (US)
Syracuse University. School of Education (US)
Syracuse University School of Information Studies.
  Subject Access Project (US)
Syria. Central Bureau of Statistics (SY)
Syrian Documentation Papers (LE)
Syrian Documentation Papers (SY)
Editions Syrus (FR)
System Consulting Enterpreneurs (UK)
Systemation, Inc. (US)
Systems Publications Ltd. (UK)
Systems Publishers (Pty) Ltd. (SA)
S. Sytema (NE)
Szakszervezetek Orszagos Tanacsa (HU)
Szakszervezetek Orszagos Tanacsa. Munkavedelmi
  Tudomanyos Kutatointezet (HU)
Szczecinskie Towarzystwo Naukowe (PL)
Szechuan University (CC)
Szefostwo Sluzby Zdrowia MON (PL)
Szilikatipari Tudomanyos Egyesulet (HU)
Szinhazmuveszeti Szovetseg (HU)
Szkola Glowna Planowania i Statystyki. Instytut
  Gospodarstwa Spolecznego (PL)
Wydawnictwa Szkolne i Pedagogiczne (PL)
Szovetkezetek Orszagos Szovetsege (HU)
T A W Publishing Co. (US)
T. and T. Clark (UK)
T B M Publicity Enterprises Ltd. (ZA)

T.C.M. Publishing Co. (Pty) Ltd. (SA)
T. C. Publishing Ltd. (CN)
T E C O L (AG)
T-E Publications, Inc. (US)
Societe T.E.S.T (FR)
T.F.H. Publications, Inc. (US)
T.I.L.L. (US)
T I O Communications Limited (CN)
T. M. C. Asser Institute (NE)
T.M.P. Book Department (TZ)
T.O.P. Verlag GmbH (GW)
T R (US)
T R A Publishing Co. (US)
T R M Publications Inc. (US)
T R Report (US)
T R W. Systems Application Center (US)
T V and Advertising (PK)
T V Digest, Inc. (US)
T V-Film Filebook (CN)
T V Guide Ltd. (CN)
T V News Company, Inc. (US)
T. V. Sports, Inc. (US)
T V Z (NE)
Tab Publishing (CN)
Tabapress S.A. (SP)
Table Ronde Francaise (FR)
Tablet Publishing Co. (UK)
Tablet Publishing Co. (US)
Tabor (IT)
Editions R. Tacoen (BE)
Tacoma Area Chamber of Commerce (US)
N. V. Drukkerij V. H. G. Taconis (NE)
Jean-Pierre Tadros, Ed. & Pub. (CN)
Taehan Sanggong Hoeuiso (KO)
Tafelberg Publishers (SA)
Tafnews Press (US)
Taft Corporation (US)
Taggart Publishing Co. (US)
Tagore Institute of Creative Writing, International
 (II)
Tagore Research Institute (II)
Tagus Poetry (UK)
Taibundo Publishing Co. (JA)
Taikabutsu Gijutsu Kyokai
 see Technical Association of Refractories (JA)
Taiki Osen Kenkyu Zenkoku Kyogikai
 see Japan Society of Air Pollution (JA)
Tail-Waggers' Club (Gt. Britain) Ltd. (UK)
Taipei City Department of Information (CH)
Taipei Public Health Teaching and Demonstration
 Center (CH)
Taipei Tourism Bureau (CH)
Taiseisha Ltd. (JA)
Taishitsu Igaku Kenkyusho
 see Kumamoto University. Institute of
 Constitutional Medicine (JA)
Taishukan Publishing Co. Ltd. (JA)
Taiwan Agricultural Research Institute (CH)
Taiwan Enterprise Press (CH)
Taiwan Fisheries Research Institute (CH)
Taiwan Fisheries Research Institute. Tungkang Marine
 Laboratory (CH)
Taiwan Museum (CH)
Taiwan Pictorial Society (CH)
Taiwan Provincial Labor Force Survey and Research
 Institute (CH)
Taiwan Railway Administration (CH)
Taiwan Sheng Cheng Fu Chiao Tung Chu (CH)
Taiwan Sugar Research Institute. Tai-Wan Tang Yeh
 Yen Chiu So (CH)
Taiwan ta Hsueh Nung Tai Hui (CH)
Taiwan Telecommunications Administration (CH)
Taj Mahal Hotel (II)
Take Over (US)
Takenaka Komuten Co., Ltd. (JA)
Takii Shubyo Co. Ltd. (JA)
Tal (FR)
Tala Publishing Corporation (PH)
Talbot Press Ltd. (IE)
Talcott Communications Corp. (US)
Tales Publishing Co. (US)
Talisman (US)
Talisman Co. (US)
Tall-Taylor Publishing Co. Ltd. (CN)
Talladega College (US)
Tallahassee Tall Timbers Research Station (US)
Librairie Jules Tallandier (FR)
Talleres Graficos Amalevi (AG)
Talonbooks (CN)
Talyllyn Railway Preservation Society (UK)
Tamagawa University. Faculty of Agriculture (JA)
Tamalpais Union High School District (US)
Tamarack Review (CN)
Tamarind Institute (US)
Tamburini Editore S.p.A. (IT)
Tamil Nadu
 see also Madras (II)
Tamil Nadu. Commissioner of Labour (II)

Tamil Nadu. Department of Archaeology (II)
Tamil Nadu. Director of Employment and Training
 (II)
Tamil Nadu. Director of Information and Public
 Relations (II)
Tamil Nadu. Director of Information and Publicity
 (II)
Tamil Nadu. Director of Statistics (II)
Tamil Nadu. Government Museum, Madras (II)
Tamil Nadu. Government Oriental Manuscripts
 Library (II)
Tamil Nadu. Legislative Council (II)
Tamil Nadu Agricultural University (II)
Tamil Nadu Co-operative Union (II)
Tamil Nadu Industrial Development Corporation (II)
Tamil Nadu P. W. D. Workers' Union (II)
Tamil Nadu Tourism Development Corporation (II)
Noel Tamini, Ed. & Pub. (SZ)
Tamkang College of Arts & Sciences (CH)
Tamkang College of Arts & Sciences. Graduate
 Institute of Western Languages and Literature
 (CH)
Tamkang College of Arts & Sciences. Research
 Institute of Mathematics (CH)
Tampere Peace Research Institute (FI)
Tams-Witmark Music Library, Inc. (US)
Tamworth Swine Association (US)
Tan King Publications, Inc (US)
Tanabe Amino Acid Research Foundation (JA)
Tancsics Konyvkiado (HU)
Tandy Corp. (US)
C. K. Tang Ltd. (SI)
Tangent (Estuary Press) (US)
Tanjug Economic Service (YU)
Tanjug News Agency (YU)
Tankian Publishing Corp. (US)
Tanne Advertising Ltd. (IS)
Tanner Publications Co., Inc. (US)
Tanners' Council of America, Inc. (US)
Tanpakushitsu Kenkyusho
 see Osaka University. Institute for Protein Research
 (JA)
Tansy (US)
Tantalus Research Ltd. (CN)
Tantivy Press (UK)
Johan Grundt Tanum Forlag (NO)
Tanzania. Bureau of Statistics (TZ)
Tanzania. Capital Development Authority (TZ)
Tanzania. Geology and Mines Division (TZ)
Tanzania. Government Publications Agency (TZ)
Tanzania. Ministry of Agriculture (TZ)
Tanzania. Ministry of Economic Affairs and
 Development Planning (TZ)
Tanzania. Ministry of National Education (TZ)
Tanzania. Ministry of Water, Energy and Minerals
 (TZ)
Tanzania. Police Force (TZ)
Tanzania. Urban Planning Division (TZ)
Tanzania Library Association (TZ)
Tanzania Library Service (TZ)
Tanzania Publishing House (TZ)
Tanzania Society (TZ)
Tanzania Trade and Industry (TZ)
Verlag das Tanzarchiv (GW)
Tao-Tao Industries (US)
Tapco Ltd. (US)
Tape Deck Quarterly (US)
Tapia House Publishing Co. Ltd. (TR)
Tapicerias Gancedo (SP)
Taplinger Publishing Co. (US)
Ram Ballabh Tapuriah, Pub. (II)
Tara Cultural Trust (II)
Target Communications Corp. (US)
Target Publishers (US)
W. H. Targett and Co. Ltd. (II)
Tariffs and Trade (US)
Tarrant County Hospital District (US)
Tartarino (IT)
Tarter Communications, Inc. (US)
Tasco Publishing Corp. (US)
Tasmania. Department of Agriculture (AT)
Tasmania. Department of Agriculture. Fisheries Div.
 (AT)
Tasmania. Department of Mines (AT)
Tasmania. Department of Tourism and Immigration
 (AT)
Tasmania. Directorate of Industrial Development &
 Trade (AT)
Tasmania. Education Department (AT)
Tasmania. Education Department. Curriculum Branch
 (AT)
Tasmania. Government Printer (AT)
Tasmania. Metropolitan Water Board (AT)
Tasmania. Tasmanian Government Printer (AT)
Tasmania Press, Inc. (US)
Tasmanian Association for the Teaching of English
 (AT)
Tasmanian Automobile Chamber of Commerce (AT)

Tasmanian Caverneering Club (AT)
Tasmanian Chamber of Industries (AT)
Tasmanian Historical Research Association. Dept. of
 History (AT)
Tasmanian Teachers' Federation (AT)
Tasmanian Trade Protective Institute (AT)
Tasmanian Transport Commission (AT)
Tata Economic Consultancy Services (II)
Tata Institute of Fundamental Research. Bombay (II)
Tata Institute of Social Sciences (II)
Tata Iron and Steel Co. Ltd. (II)
Tattersall's Club (AT)
Tattilo Editrice S.p.A. (IT)
Tattler (CH)
Tau Beta Pi Association Inc. (US)
Tau Epsilon Rho Law Fraternity (US)
Taunton Press (US)
Shamseddin Tavakoli, Ed. & Pub. (IR)
Tavistock Institute of Human Relations (UK)
Tavistock Publications Ltd. (UK)
Tavkozlesi Kutato Intezet (HU)
Tax Affairs (II)
Tax Executives Institute (US)
Tax Foundation, Inc. (US)
Tax Foundation of Hawaii (US)
Tax Institute of America
 see National Tax Association-Tax Institute of
 America (US)
Tax Management Inc. (US)
Tax Research Group, Ltd. (US)
Tax Shelter Monitor (US)
Tax Strike News (US)
Tax Times Trust (II)
Taxation (II)
Taxation Institute of Australia (AT)
Taxation Publishers (PK)
Taxation Publishing Co. Ltd. (UK)
Taxation with Representation (US)
Taxation with Representation (Pembroke) (US)
Taxes and Estates (US)
Taxes and Planning (US)
Taxi Council of Queensland (AT)
Taxi News Digest (US)
Taxpayer (Pty.) Ltd. (SA)
Taxpayers Association of New Mexico (US)
Casa Editrice Taylor (IT)
Taylor & Francis Ltd. (UK)
Sally Taylor & Friends (US)
Taylor-Constantine (US)
Taylor County Historical Society (US)
Alister Taylor, Ed. & Pub. (NZ)
Taylor Enterprises (CN)
Taylor Publishing Co. (US)
Taylorix-Fach-Verlag (GW)
Tazpiot, Ltd. (IS)
Tazuke Kofukai Medical Research Institute (JA)
Tbilisi Universitet (UR)
Tchad et Culture (CD)
Bezalel Tcherikover, Pubs., Ltd. (IS)
Tchou Editeur (FR)
Tea and Coffee Trade Journal Co. (US)
Tea Board (II)
Tea Research Association (II)
Tea Research Foundation of Central Africa (MW)
Tea Research Institute of East Africa (KE)
Tea Research Institute of Sri Lanka (CE)
Teach'em, Inc. (US)
Teacher Information Center (US)
Teacher Training College, Teheran. Educational
 Research Institute (IR)
Teacher Travel (II)
Teachers and Writers Collaborative (US)
Teachers Association of Ethiopia (ET)
Teachers Association of Ethiopia. Eritrea Branch
 (ET)
Teachers Association of Long Beach, Inc. (US)
Teachers Central Registry (AT)
Teachers College Press (US)
Teachers' Cooperative Education Journals and
 Publications Ltd. (II)
Teachers Guide to Television (US)
Teachers' Guild of New South Wales (AT)
Teachers of English to Speakers of Other Languages
 (US)
Teachers of Home Economics Specialist Association
 (CN)
Teachers Training College, Shiraz (IR)
Teaching Philosophy (US)
Teakfield Ltd. (UK)
Team Verlag GmbH und Fachzeitschriften KG (GW)
Teamsters Joint Council 13 (US)
Teatro (AG)
Teatro Clasico de Mexico (MX)
TEBROC
 see Institute for Research and Planning in Science
 and Education. Tehran Book Processing Centre
 (IR)
Techni Research Associates (US)

Technic Hebdo  (FR)
Technical and General Press. Engineers' Bureau  (II)
Technical Assistance Information Clearing House  (US)
Technical Association of Graphic Arts of Japan  (JA)
Technical Association of Malaysia  (MY)
Technical Association of Refractories  (JA)
Technical Association of the Australian and New Zealand Pulp and Paper Industry  (AT)
Technical Association of the Graphic Arts  (US)
Technical Association of the Pulp & Paper Industry  (US)
Technical Chamber of Greece  (GR)
Technical Economics Associates  (US)
Technical Economics, Inc.  (US)
Technical Indexes Ltd.  (UK)
Technical Information Co. Ltd.  (UI)
Technical Information-Documentation Consultants Ltd.  (CN)
Technical Information Service (Washington)  (US)
Technical Insights, Inc.  (US)
Technical Journals Ltd.  (UK)
Technical Press Publications  (II)
Technical Publications  (US)
Technical Publications Ltd.  (NZ)
Technical Publications Malaya  (MY)
Technical Publishing Co.  (US)
Technical Publishing Co. (Greenwich)  (US)
Technical Publishing Co. (Los Angeles)  (US)
Technical Reporting Corp.  (US)
Technical Research Centre of Finland
    see Valtion Teknillinen Tutkimuskeskus  (FI)
Technical Teachers Association of Australia  (AT)
Technical Teachers Association of Victoria  (AT)
Technical Teachers' Training Institute  (II)
Technical University of Istanbul. Department of the History of Architecture and Preservation  (TU)
Edizioni Techniche Moderne  (IT)
Edizioni Techniche S.A.S.  (IT)
Technicien Belge en Prothese Dentaire  (BE)
Technicopy Ltd.  (UK)
Technicraft  (US)
Technifax Publications, Inc  (US)
VEB Verlag Technik  (GE)
Verlag fuer Technik und Handwerk  (GW)
Verlag fuer Technik und Wirtschaft Meynen KG  (GW)
Technion-Israel Institute of Technology  (IS)
Editions Technip  (FR)
Technique des Travaux  (BE)
Technique Laitiere  (FR)
Techniques Nouvelles  (BE)
Technisch Film Centrum  (NE)
Technische Akademie Wuppertal  (GW)
Technische Hochschule Carl Schorlemmer Leuna-Merseburg. Wissenschaftliche Zeitschrift.  (GE)
Technische Hochschule, Ilmenau  (GE)
Technische Hochschule Karl-Marx-Stadt. Bibliothek  (GE)
Technische Hochschule Otto von Guericke  (GE)
Technische Hogeschool te Delft. Bibliotheek  (NE)
Technische Hogeschool Te Delft. Department of Civil Engineering  (NE)
Technische Hogeschool Twente. Department of Physics  (NE)
Technische Universitaet Berlin. Institut fuer Sozialoekonomie der Agrarentwicklung  (GW)
Technische Universitaet Berlin. Universitaetsbibliothek  (GW)
Technische Universitaet Braunschweig  (GW)
Technische Universitaet Clausthal  (GW)
Technische Universitaet Dresden  (GE)
Technische Universitaet Hannover  (GW)
Technische Universitaet Hannover. Franzius-Institut fuer Wasserbau und Kuesteningenieurwesen  (GW)
Technische Universitaet Hannover. Institut fuer Siedlungswasserwirtschaft  (GW)
Technische Universitaet Hannover. Institut fuer Statik  (GW)
Technische Universitaet Hannover. Institut fuer Theoretische Geodaesie  (GW)
Technische Universitaet Muenchen  (GW)
Technische Universitaet Muenchen. Institut fuer Wirtschaftslehre des Gartenbaues  (GW)
Technische Universitaet Wien. Institut fuer Eisenbahnwesen, Spezialbahnen und Verkehrswirtschaft  (AU)
Technische Universitaet Wien. Institut fuer Wasserversorgung, Abwassereinigung und Gewaesserschutz  (AU)
Technische Vereinigung der Grosskraftwerksbetreiber e.V.  (GW)
Technischer Verlag Resch KG
    see Resch KG  (GW)

Technisches Museum fuer Industrie und Gewerbe, Vienna  (AU)
Technitrade Journals Ltd.  (UK)
Techno-Loisirs  (FR)
Technocracy Inc.  (CN)
Technocracy, Inc  (US)
Technoinform
    see Hungarian Central Technical Library and Documentation Centre - Technoinform  (HU)
Technological Association  (II)
Technology Clearing House, Inc.  (US)
Technology Marketing Corp.  (US)
Technology News Center Inc.  (US)
Technology Organization Inc.  (US)
Technomic Publishing Co. Inc.  (US)
Technopress Fachzeitschriften Verlagsgesellschaft m.b.H.  (AU)
Editions Technorama  (FR)
Technosdar, Ltd.-International Scientific Publications  (IS)
Tecnica della Scuola  (IT)
Tecnica e Industria  (AG)
Tecnica e Invencion  (SP)
Tecnica e Uomo  (IT)
Editorial Tecnica Espanola, S.A.  (SP)
Editora Tecnica Ltda  (BL)
Editoriale Tecnica Macchine  (IT)
Prensa Tecnica, S.A.  (SP)
Ediciones Tecnicas Doria  (SP)
Ediciones Tecnicas Especializadas  (SP)
Publicaciones Tecnicas Periodicas  (SP)
Ediciones Tecnicas R.E.D.E.  (SP)
Societa Edizioni Tecniche  (IT)
Societa Edizioni Tecniche Arredamento  (IT)
Tecniche Nuove s.r.l.  (IT)
Edizioni Tecniche Publiedi  (IT)
Edizioni Tecniche SIGMA 2  (IT)
Tecnologia Alimentaria  (AG)
TecPress Group  (AT)
Tednik  (YU)
Teen Topics Publications  (NR)
Teenager Monthly  (PK)
Teens' Magazine Publishing Co.  (HK)
Teesside & District-Chamber of Commerce & Industry  (UK)
Tegwar Press  (CN)
Tehnicka Knjiga, Belgrade  (YU)
Tehnicka Knjiga, Zagreb  (YU)
Tehniska Zalozba Slovenije  (YU)
Tehran Book Processing Centre
    see under Institute for Research and Planning in Science and Education  (IR)
Tehran Economist  (IR)
Tehran Poultry Syndicate  (IR)
Teiba Publications Ltd.  (GH)
Peter Teichmann  (US)
Editorial Teide  (SP)
Teilhard Centre for the Future of Man  (UK)
Editions Teintex, S.A.R.L.  (FR)
Oyama Pereira Teixeira e Ronaldo Boucas Teixeira, Eds. and Pubs.  (BL)
Tejidos  (US)
Izdatel'stvo Tekhnika  (UR)
Tekhnolohichnyi Instytut Lehkoy Promyslovosti  (UR)
Aravind Teki, Ed. & Pub.  (II)
Teknillisten Tieteiden Akatemia  (FI)
Teknisk Forlag A-S  (DK)
Teknisk Presse A-S  (NO)
Teknisk Skoleforening  (DK)
Tekniska Litteratursaellskapet  (SW)
Tekniska Museet  (SW)
Tekniska Nomenklaturcentralen  (SW)
Teknologisk Institut. Afdeling for Varme- og Installationsteknik  (DK)
Tekstiilikauppiaiden Liitto r. y.  (FI)
Tektronix, Inc.  (US)
Tel-Aviv University  (IS)
Tel-Aviv University. David Horowitz Institute for the Research of Developing Countries  (IS)
Tel-Aviv University. Diaspora Research Institute  (IS)
Tel-Aviv University. Institute for German History  (IS)
Tel Aviv University. Institute for Zionist Research  (IS)
Tel Aviv University. Institute of Criminology and Criminal Law  (IS)
Tel-Aviv University. Shiloah Center for Middle Eastern and African Studies  (IS)
Tel Aviv-Yafo. Department of Research and Statistics  (IS)
Tel-Aviv Zoological Garden Society  (IS)
Telberg Book Corp.  (US)
Tele-Afrika-Verlagsgesellschaft mbH  (GW)
Tele Magazine  (FR)
Editions Tele Semaine Inc.  (CN)
Telecine  (FR)
Telecommunicacoes do Rio de Janeiro S.A.  (BL)

Telecommunication Authority of Singapore  (SI)
Telecommunication Society of Australia  (AT)
Telecommunications Association (Denki Tsushin Kyokai)  (JA)
Telecommunications Reports  (US)
Telediffusion de France  (FR)
Teleflora, Inc.  (US)
Telefoninraettningarnas Foerbund
    see Puhelinlaitosten Liitto  (FI)
Telefonos de Mexico, S.A.  (MX)
Telefood Magazine  (US)
Telefornaktiebolaget L.M. Ericsson  (SW)
Telegraphic Cable & Radio Registrations, Inc.  (US)
Telephone  (US)
Telephone Report  (US)
Telephony Publishing Corp.  (US)
Teleplan S-A  (BL)
TELEPRESS Servicos de Imprensa, Ltda.  (BL)
Telepro  (BE)
Telepublicaciones  (SP)
Telespazio  (IT)
Television and Electronic Services Associations of Australasia  (AT)
Television Bureau of Advertising  (US)
Television Digest, Inc.  (US)
Television Editorial Corp.  (US)
Television Index, Inc.  (US)
Television International Magazine  (US)
Editorial Television S.A.  (MX)
Telex-Verlag Jaeger und Waldmann oHG  (GW)
Thomas Telford Ltd.  (UK)
Maurice Telleen, Ed. & Pub.  (US)
Christa van Tellingen, Ed. & Pub.  (NE)
Telltale Compass  (US)
Telluride Association  (US)
Alf Teloeken-Verlag KG  (GW)
Telos Press  (US)
Telugu Akademi  (II)
Telugu Bhasha Samiti  (II)
Telva  (SP)
Temas de Orientacion Agropecuaria  (CK)
Temas Economicos  (VE)
Societa Editrice Temi  (IT)
Abdeljelil Temimi, Ed. & Pub.  (TI)
Temko Enterprises Inc.  (US)
Editions du Temoignage Chretien  (FR)
De Tempel  (BE)
Temperance Council of Christian Churches  (UK)
Tempest Publications, Inc.  (US)
Adelberto Tempesta, Ed. & Pub  (IT)
Redazione Tempi Moderni  (IT)
Templar Press  (US)
Temple of Truth  (US)
Temple Publicity Services  (TH)
Temple University  (US)
Temple University. Center for the Study of Communal Societies  (US)
Temple University. Center for the Study of Federalism  (US)
Temple University. Department of English  (US)
Temple University. Department of History  (US)
Temple University. Department of Radio-TV-Film  (US)
Temple University. Laboratory of Anthropology  (US)
Temple University Press  (US)
Temple University. School of Business Administration  (US)
Temple University School of Law  (US)
Temple University School of Pharmacy. Pharmacy Alumni Association  (US)
Tempo  (IO)
Tempo Medico s.r.l.  (IT)
Tempografica, S. A. R. L.  (MZ)
Temprint Press Ltd.  (UK)
Temps Modernes  (FR)
Tendens  (NE)
Tenneco Inc.  (US)
Tennessee. Advisory Council on Vocational Education  (US)
Tennessee. Department of Agriculture. Division of Plant Industries  (US)
Tennessee. Department of Conservation  (US)
Tennessee. Department of Economic and Community Development  (US)
Tennessee. Department of Employment Security  (US)
Tennessee. Department of Human Services  (US)
Tennessee. Department of Revenue. Sales and Use Tax Division  (US)
Tennessee. Department of Safety  (US)
Tennessee. Division of Veterans Affairs  (US)
Tennessee. Division of Water Quality Control  (US)
Tennessee. Division of Water Resources  (US)
Tennessee. Higher Education Commission  (US)
Tennessee. State Board for Vocational Education  (US)
Tennessee. State Library and Archives. Public Libraries Section  (US)

Tennessee. State Planning Office  (US)
Tennessee. State Planning Office. Middle Tennessee Section  (US)
Tennessee. Wildlife Resources Agency  (US)
Tennessee Academy of Science  (US)
Tennessee Association of Plumbing-Heating-Cooling Contractors, Inc.  (US)
Tennessee Association of Realtors  (US)
Tennessee Bankers Association  (US)
Tennessee Congress of Parents and Teachers  (US)
Tennessee Dental Association  (US)
Tennessee Education Association  (US)
Tennessee Electric Cooperative Association  (US)
Tennessee Farm Bureau Federation  (US)
Tennessee Fine Arts Center and Botanical Gardens  (US)
Tennessee Folklore Society  (US)
Tennessee Genealogical Society  (US)
Tennessee Historical Commission  (US)
Tennessee Historical Society  (US)
Tennessee Law Enforcement Officers Association  (US)
Tennessee Law Review Association, Inc.  (US)
Tennessee Library Association  (US)
Tennessee Livestock Association  (US)
Tennessee Medical Association  (US)
Tennessee Municipal League  (US)
Tennessee Music Educators Association  (US)
Tennessee Nurses Association  (US)
Tennessee Ornithological Society  (US)
Tennessee Research Coordinating Unit for Vocational Education  (US)
Tennessee School Boards Association  (US)
Tennessee School for the Blind  (US)
Tennessee State University. Department of Public Relations  (US)
Tennessee Technological University  (US)
Tennessee Valley Authority
    see U.S. Tennessee Valley Authority  (US)
Tennessee Valley Historical Society  (US)
Tennessee Valley Old Time Fiddlers Association  (US)
Tennis de France  (FR)
Tennis Gazette, Inc.  (US)
Tennis News, Inc.  (US)
Tenniswoman  (US)
Tennyson Society  (UK)
Tenri University  (JA)
Tenri University Press  (JA)
Tenrikyo Overseas Mission Department  (JA)
Tensor Society  (JA)
Tensor Society of Great Britain  (UK)
Tentagel, Inc.  (US)
Tenth District Dental Society Headquarters  (US)
Tenth Muse  (US)
Tenth Presbyterian Church  (US)
Teollisuuden Keskusliitto  (FI)
Teologinen Julkaisuseura r.y.  (FI)
Teoloska Fakulteta v Ljubljani  (YU)
Teoria y Praxis  (VE)
Editorial Teosofica  (AG)
C. S. Tepfer Publishing Co., Inc.  (US)
Teratology Society  (US)
Ediciones Tercer Mundo  (CK)
Terminal Publications, Inc.  (US)
Terminus Media  (US)
Termomeccanica Italiana S.p.A.  (IT)
J. Terpstra.  (NE)
Terra-Verlag  (GW)
Librairie "le Terrain Vogue"  (FR)
Terre Africaine  (CX)
Territorial Imperative, Inc.  (US)
Territorio Federal, Venezuela. Direccion de Educacion y Cultura. Departamento de Extension Cultural  (VE)
Terror Fantastic  (SP)
Terry Art Ltd.  (CN)
Terry Art Ltd.  (UK)
Tertulia Edipica  (PO)
Tertulia Flamenca de Ceuta  (SP)
Dott. G. Terzano & Co. S.p.A.  (IT)
Terz'ordine e le Vocazioni Cappuccine Salernitane  (IT)
Dr. Tesdorpf Verlag  (GW)
Tessner-Verlag  (GW)
A. Testa, Ed. & Pub.  (IT)
Testimonianze  (IT)
Ediciones Testimonio  (CK)
Testing, Instruments & Controls  (AT)
Editions Tests  (FR)
Teton  (US)
Tetra Werke  (GW)
Tetsudo Gijutsu Kenkyusho (Railway Technical Research Institute)
    see under Japanese National Railways  (JA)
Tetsudo Tosho Kankai  (JA)
Tetzlaff Verlag GmbH  (GW)
Otto Teubel Verlag  (GW)

Teubner Verlagsgesellschaft  (GE)
Olive Rhodes Teugels, Ed. & Pub.  (UK)
Tevai Jezuitai Cikagoje  (US)
Texaco, Inc.  (US)
Texas. Advisory Council for Technical-Vocational Education  (US)
Texas. Crop and Livestock Reporting Service  (US)
Texas. Department of Agriculture  (US)
Texas. Department of Community Affairs. Office of Early Childhood Development  (US)
Texas. Department of Corrections  (US)
Texas. Department of Health Resources  (US)
Texas. Department of Highways and Public Transportation  (US)
Texas. Employment Commission  (US)
Texas. Farm Bureau  (US)
Texas. Forest Service  (US)
Texas. Forest Service. Forest Products Laboratory  (US)
Texas. Governor's Committee on Aging  (US)
Texas. Industrial Commission  (US)
Texas. Legislative Reference Library  (US)
Texas. Office of Economic Opportunity  (US)
Texas. Office of Minority Business Enterprises  (US)
Texas. Office of the Governor  (US)
Texas. Parks and Wildlife Department  (US)
Texas. Railroad Commission  (US)
Texas. Railroad Commission. Oil and Gas Division  (US)
Texas. Secretary of State  (US)
Texas. State Library  (US)
Texas. State Library. Department of Library Development  (US)
Texas. State Securities Board  (US)
Texas. Water Development Board  (US)
Texas. Water Quality Board  (US)
Texas A & I University  (US)
Texas A & M University  (US)
Texas A & M University. Association of Former Students  (US)
Texas A & M University. Center for Dredging Studies  (US)
Texas A & M University. Center for Energy and Mineral Resources  (US)
Texas A & M University. College of Business Administration  (US)
Texas A & M University. Department of Agricultural Communications  (US)
Texas A & M University. Department of Oceanography  (US)
Texas A & M University Libraries  (US)
Texas A & M University. Sea Grant Program Office  (US)
Texas Academy of Family Physicians  (US)
Texas Academy of Science  (US)
Texas Agricultural Extension Service  (US)
Texas and Southwestern Cattle Raisers Association Inc.  (US)
Texas Archeological Society  (US)
Texas Association of Business  (US)
Texas Association of Secondary School Principals  (US)
Texas Beverage News  (US)
Texas Bluegrass Association  (US)
Texas Books in Review  (US)
Texas Certified Seed Directory  (US)
Texas Christian University. Department of English  (US)
Texas Christian University Press  (US)
Texas Classroom Teachers Association  (US)
Texas College and University System  (US)
Texas Congress of Parents and Teachers  (US)
Texas Cooperative Ginners Association  (US)
Texas Council for Social Studies  (US)
Texas Criminal Defense Lawyers Association  (US)
Texas Dental Assistants Association  (US)
Texas Dental Association  (US)
Texas Dental Hygienists Association  (US)
Texas Education Agency  (US)
Texas Elementary Principals and Supervisors Association  (US)
Texas Fine Arts Society  (US)
Texas Folklore Society  (US)
Texas Heart Institute  (US)
Texas High School Coaches Association  (US)
Texas Hospital Association  (US)
Texas Hotel & Motel Association  (US)
Texas Independent Producers & Royalty Owners Association  (US)
Texas Institute for Educational Development  (US)
Texas International Airlines, Houston, Texas  (US)
Texas International Law Journal  (US)
Texas Jewish Post  (US)
Texas Joint Council of Teachers of English  (US)
Texas Law Review Publications, Inc.  (US)
Texas Library and Historical Commission  (US)
Texas Library Association  (US)
Texas LP-Gas Association  (US)

Texas Medical Association  (US)
Texas Memorial Museum  (US)
Texas Metropolitan Publications  (US)
Texas Motor Transportation Association  (US)
Texas Municipal League  (US)
Texas Music Educators Association  (US)
Texas Numismatic Association  (US)
Texas Nurses Association  (US)
Texas Observer Publishing Co.  (US)
Texas Oil Journal  (US)
Texas Oil Marketers Association  (US)
Texas Optometric Association  (US)
Texas Ornithological Society  (US)
Texas Orthopedic Association  (US)
Texas Outdoor Guide, Inc.  (US)
Texas Parade, Inc.  (US)
Texas Pecan Growers Association  (US)
Texas Personnel and Guidance Association  (US)
Texas Press Association  (US)
Texas Public Employees Association  (US)
Texas Research Foundation, Renner  (US)
Texas Restaurant Association  (US)
Texas Retail Grocers' Association  (US)
Texas School Directory  (US)
Texas Sheep and Goat Raisers' Association  (US)
Texas Slough  (US)
Texas Society of Architects  (US)
Texas Society of Certified Public Accountants.  (US)
Texas Society of Professional Engineers  (US)
Texas Southern University. School of Law  (US)
Texas Spectator Magazines, Inc.  (US)
Texas Speech Communication Association  (US)
Texas Speleological Association  (US)
Texas State Board of Landscape Architects  (US)
Texas State Historical Association  (US)
Texas State Teachers Association  (US)
Texas Student Publications  (US)
Texas Tech University  (US)
Texas Tech University. College of Home Economics  (US)
Texas Tech University. Department of Biology  (US)
Texas Tech University. Ex-Students Association  (US)
Texas Tech University. Friends of the University Library  (US)
Texas Tech University. Institute for Studies in Pragmaticism  (US)
Texas Tech University. Interdepartmental Committee on Comparative Literature  (US)
Texas Transportation Institute  (US)
Texas Veterinary Medical Association  (US)
Texas Watchmakers Association  (US)
Texas Water Resources Institute  (US)
Texas Wesleyan College  (US)
Texas Western Press  (US)
Texian Press  (US)
Textil Vestido  (MX)
Textile Association (India)  (II)
Textile Business Press Ltd.  (UK)
Textile Council of Australia  (AT)
Textile Economics Bureau, Inc.  (US)
Textile Industry Publications  (PK)
Textile Information Sources  (US)
Textile Institute  (UK)
Textile Journal and Book Pub. Co.  (JA)
Textile Machinery Society of Japan  (JA)
Textile Magazine  (BE)
Textile Mercury Ltd.  (UK)
Textile Mills and Manufacturing Association  (II)
Textile Museum  (US)
Textile Research Institute  (US)
Textile Technical Federation of Canada  (CN)
Textile Trade Publications Ltd.  (UK)
Textile Workers Union of America  (CN)
Textile Workers Union of America  (US)
Textile World  (US)
Textilipari Muszaki es Tudomanyos Egyesulet  (HU)
Textilreinigungsverband e.V.  (GW)
Textilyon: Bulletin des Soies et Soicries  (FR)
Texto e Imagen S.A.  (MX)
Textolux AG  (SZ)
Thackrey Publishing Co., Inc.  (US)
Thai Chamber of Commerce.  (TH)
Thai National Documentation Centre  (TH)
Thailand. Bureau of the Budget  (TH)
Thailand. Government House Press  (TH)
Thailand. Government Public Relations Department  (TH)
Thailand. Ministry of Agriculture. Department of Fisheries  (TH)
Thailand. Ministry of Agriculture. Division of Agricultural Chemistry  (TH)
Thailand. Ministry of Agriculture. Division of Agriculture Economics  (TH)
Thailand. Ministry of Foreign Affairs. Department of Information  (TH)
Thailand. National Economic Development Board  (TH)

Tohoku University. Department of Psychology   (JA)
Tohoku University. Faculty of Agriculture   (JA)
Tohoku University. Faculty of Engineering   (JA)
Tohoku University. Faculty of Science   (JA)
Tohoku University. Institute for Agricultural Research
   (JA)
Tohoku University. Institute of Geology and
   Paleontology   (JA)
Tohoku University Mathematical Institute   (JA)
Tohoku University. Research Institute for Scientific
   Measurements   (JA)
Tohoku University. Research Institute for Strength and
   Fracture of Materials   (JA)
Tohoku University. Research Institute for Tuberculosis,
   Leprosy and Cancer   (JA)
Tohoku University. Research Institute of Electrical
   Communication   (JA)
Tohoku University. Research Institute of Mineral
   Dressing and Metallurgy   (JA)
Tohoku University. School of Medicine   (JA)
Toimiupseeriliitto   (FI)
Toison d'Or   (BE)
Tokai Bank Ltd.   (JA)
Tokai Daigaku
   see Tokai University   (JA)
Tokai Daigaku Shuppankai
   see Tokai University Press   (JA)
Tokai Regional Fisheries Research Laboratory
   see Japan. Tokai Regional Fisheries Research
   Laboratory   (JA)
Tokai Research Establishment
   see under Japan Atomic Energy Research Institute
   (JA)
Tokai University. Faculty of Literature   (JA)
Tokai University Press   (JA)
Tokei Kagaku Kenkyukai
   see Kyushu University. Research Association of
   Statistical Sciences   (JA)
Tokei Suri Kenkyusho
   see Japan. Institute of Statistical Mathematics   (JA)
Token and Medal Society   (US)
Tokita Seed Co. Ltd.   (JA)
Tokushima Daigaku
   see Tokushima University   (JA)
Tokushima Medical Association   (JA)
Tokushima University. Faculty of Education   (JA)
Tokushima University. Faculty of Engineering   (JA)
Tokushima University. School of Medicine   (JA)
Tokyo. Bureau of Public Cleansing   (JA)
Tokyo. Council on Liaison with Foreign Cities   (JA)
Tokyo. Port and Harbor Bureau   (JA)
Tokyo Astronomical Observatory   (JA)
Tokyo Ato Direkutazu Kurabu
   see Art Directors Club of Tokyo   (JA)
Tokyo Chigaku Kyokai
   see Tokyo Geographical Society   (JA)
Tokyo College of Domestic Science   (JA)
Tokyo College of Economics. Institute of Industrial
   and Commercial Research   (JA)
Tokyo Consolidated Fire Prevention Association
   (JA)
Tokyo Daigaku
   see University of Tokyo   (JA)
Tokyo Daigaku Bussei Kenkyusho
   see University of Tokyo. Institute for Solid State
   Physics   (JA)
Tokyo Daigaku Genshikaku Kenkyusho
   see University of Tokyo. Institute for Nuclear Study
   (JA)
Tokyo Daigaku Ikagaku Kenkyusho
   see University of Tokyo. Institute of Medical
   Science   (JA)
Tokyo Daigaku Jishin Kenkyusho
   see University of Tokyo. Earthquake Research
   Institute   (JA)
Tokyo Daigaku Kaiyo Kenkyusho
   see University of Tokyo. Ocean Research Institute
   (JA)
Tokyo Daigaku Oyo Biseibutsu Kenkyusho
   see University of Tokyo. Institute of Applied
   Microbiology   (JA)
Tokyo Daigaku Rigakubu Fuzoku Rinkai Jikkensho
   see University of Tokyo. Misaki Marine Biological
   Station   (JA)
Tokyo Daigaku Seisan Gijutsu Kenkyusho
   see University of Tokyo. Institute of Industrial
   Science   (JA)
Tokyo Daigaku Shakai Kagaku Kenkyusho
   see University of Tokyo. Institute of Social Science
   (JA)
Tokyo Daigaku Uchu Koku Kenkyusho
   see University of Tokyo. Institute of Space and
   Aeronautical Science   (JA)
Tokyo Dental College   (JA)
Tokyo Dental College Society   (JA)
Tokyo Economic Information Service Co.   (JA)
Tokyo Gaikogu Daigaku
   see Tokyo University of Foreign Studies   (JA)

Tokyo Geographical Society   (JA)
Tokyo Ika Daigaku
   see Tokyo Medical College   (JA)
Tokyo Ika Shika Daigaku
   see Tokyo Medical and Dental University   (JA)
Tokyo Ika Shika Daigaku Iyo Kizai Kenkyusho
   see Tokyo Medical and Dental University. Institute
   for Medical and Dental Engineering   (JA)
Tokyo Institute of Technology   (JA)
Tokyo Institute of Technology. Research Laboratory of
   Resources Utilization   (JA)
Tokyo Jikekai Ika Daigaku
   see Jikei University School of Medicine   (JA)
Tokyo Joshi Ika Daigaku
   see Tokyo Women's Medical College Society   (JA)
Tokyo Kasei Daigaku
   see Tokyo College of Domestic Science   (JA)
Tokyo Keizai Daigaku Sangyo Boeki Kenkyusho
   see Tokyo College of Economics. Institute of
   Industrial and Commercial Research   (JA)
Tokyo Kogyo Daigaku
   see Tokyo Institute of Technology   (JA)
Tokyo Kokuritsu Hakubutsukan
   see Tokyo National Museum   (JA)
Tokyo Kyoiku Daigaku
   see Tokyo University of Education   (JA)
Tokyo Kyoiku Daigaku Kikogaku Danwakai
   see Tokyo University of Education. Laboratory of
   Climatology   (JA)
Tokyo Kyoiku Daigaku Kikogaku Kyoshitsu
   see Tokyo University of Education. Laboratory of
   Climatology   (JA)
Tokyo Kyoiku Daigaku Kogaku Kenkyusho
   see Tokyo Kyoiku University. Institute for Optical
   Research   (JA)
Tokyo Kyoiku University. Institute for Optical
   Research   (JA)
Tokyo Lincoln Book Center   (JA)
Tokyo Medical and Dental University   (JA)
Tokyo Medical and Dental University. Department of
   Human Genetics   (JA)
Tokyo Medical and Dental University. Institute for
   Medical and Dental Engineering   (JA)
Tokyo Medical and Dental University. School of
   Dentistry   (JA)
Tokyo Medical Association   (JA)
Tokyo Medical College   (JA)
Tokyo Metropolitan Agricultural Experiment Station,
   Itsukaichi Office   (JA)
Tokyo Metropolitan Institute for Neurosciences   (JA)
Tokyo Metropolitan Research Institute for
   Environmental Protection   (JA)
Tokyo Metropolitan Research Laboratory of Public
   Health   (JA)
Tokyo Metropolitan University   (JA)
Tokyo Metropolitan University. Department of
   Geography   (JA)
Tokyo Metropolitan University. Faculty of Technology
   (JA)
Tokyo Metropolitan University. Institute for Social
   Sciences and Humanity   (JA)
Tokyo Metropolitan University. Shakai-jinruigakkai
   (JA)
Tokyo National Museum   (JA)
Tokyo News Service, Ltd.   (JA)
Tokyo Nyusa Tsushinsha
   see Tokyo News Service Ltd.   (JA)
Tokyo Rengo Boka Kyokai
   see Tokyo Consolidated Fire Prevention Association
   (JA)
Tokyo Rinkan Bukka Senta
   see Tokyo Lincoln Book Center   (JA)
Tokyo Shibaura Electric Co., Ltd.   (JA)
Tokyo Shika Daigaku
   see Tokyo Dental College   (JA)
Tokyo Shika Daigaku Gakkai
   see Tokyo Dental College Society   (JA)
Tokyo Shuppan Hanbai Co., Ltd.   (JA)
Tokyo Suisan Daigaku
   see Tokyo University of Fisheries   (JA)
Tokyo Tanabe Co., Ltd.   (JA)
Tokyo Tenmondai
   see Tokyo Astronomical Observatory   (JA)
Tokyo-to Ishikai
   see Tokyo Medical Association   (JA)
Tokyo-to Kogai Kenkyusho
   see Tokyo Metropolitan Research Institute for
   Environmental Protection   (JA)
Tokyo-to Kyoiku Iinkai   (JA)
Tokyo-to Nogyo Shikenjo Itsukaichi Bunjo
   see Tokyo Metropolitan Agricultural Experiment
   Station, Itsukaichi Office   (JA)
Tokyo-to Sangyo Rodo Kaikan   (JA)
Tokyo-to Seihon Kogyo Kumiai   (JA)
Tokyo-to Seiso-kyoku Kikaku-bu
   see Tokyo. Bureau of Public Cleansing   (JA)
Tokyo-to Shinkei Kagaku Sogo Kenkyujo Nempo

   see Tokyo Metropolitan Institute for Neurosciences
   (JA)
Tokyo-toritsu Daigaku
   see Tokyo Metropolitan University   (JA)
Tokyo-toritsu Daigaku Jinbun Gakkai
   see Tokyo Metropolitan University. Institute for
   Social Sciences and Humanity   (JA)
Tokyo-toritsu Eisei Kenkyusho
   see Tokyo Metropolitan Research Laboratory of
   Public Health   (JA)
Tokyo-toritsu Koka Tanki Daigaku Gakujutsu Kenkyu
   Un'Eikai
   see Metropolitan Technical College   (JA)
Tokyo-toritsu Kyoiku Kenkyujo   (JA)
Tokyo University
   see University of Tokyo   (JA)
Tokyo University of Education. Faculty of Science
   (JA)
Tokyo University of Education. Laboratory of
   Climatology   (JA)
Tokyo University of Fisheries   (JA)
Tokyo University of Foreign Studies   (JA)
Tokyo Women's Medical College Society   (JA)
Tolar Creek Syndicate   (US)
Toledo Area Chamber of Commerce   (US)
Toledo Commission of Publicity and Efficiency   (US)
Toledo Dental Society   (US)
Toledo Federation of Art Societies, Inc   (US)
Toledo-Lucas County Port Authority   (US)
Toledo Museum of Art   (US)
Toledo Organization of Psychic Sciences (T O P S)
   (US)
Bernard Tolk Co.   (US)
Tolkien Society   (UK)
Tolkien Society of America   (US)
Tolkien Society. University of Wisconsin   (US)
Toll Free Digest Co.   (US)
Tolley Publishing Co.   (UK)
Tolphus Books   (US)
Tolpolski's Chronicle   (UK)
Tom Chalmers Enterprises Ltd.   (UK)
Tombstone Epitaph   (US)
Francis J. Tominey   (US)
Tomorrow's Business Decisions   (AT)
J. B. Tompkins, Ed. & Pub.   (CN)
Tomskii Meditsinskii Institut. Tsentralnaya Nauchno-
   Issledovatelskaya Laboratoriya   (UR)
Tomskii Universitet   (UR)
Tonatiuh International, Inc.   (US)
Tong-Hsing Culture Press   (CH)
Tong-Tong B.V.   (NE)
Tonga Islands. Government Printer   (TO)
Tongil Chuche Kungmin Hoeui Samucho   (KO)
Tonto Publishing Co.   (US)
Uitgeverij De Toorts   (NE)
Tooth of Time Review   (US)
Toothpaste Press   (US)
Toothpick, Lisbon & the Orcas Islands Press   (US)
Top Art S.A.   (BE)
Top Sellers Ltd.   (UK)
Topeka Public Library   (US)
Topic Publications Pvt. Ltd.   (II)
Erwin Toppelberg   (AG)
Torc   (UK)
Torch Services   (LB)
Michael Torf   (US)
Unione Tipografico Editrice Torinese   (IT)
Torino Motori   (IT)
Toronto Board of Trade   (CN)
Toronto Boys and Girls House   (CN)
Toronto Bureau of Municipal Research   (CN)
Toronto Dominion Bank   (CN)
Toronto Field Naturalists' Club   (CN)
Toronto Free Press Publications Ltd.   (CN)
Toronto Home Builders Association   (CN)
Toronto Jewish Press   (CN)
Toronto Public Library   (CN)
Toronto Railway Club   (CN)
Toronto Ski Club   (CN)
Toronto Stock Exchange   (CN)
Toronto Vegetarian Association   (CN)
Toronto Wages for Housework Committee   (CN)
Torquay Natural History Society   (UK)
Torre   (IT)
Publicaciones Torregrosa   (PR)
Torrey Botanical Club   (US)
Torrington Co.   (US)
Torry Research Station   (UK)
Carlos Tort International, Inc.   (US)
Tortenelmi Leveltar   (YU)
Michele Tosco   (IT)
Casa Editrice la Toscografica   (IT)
Toshi Keikaku Kyokai
   see City Planning Association of Japan   (JA)
Totalcreative Intercontinental Service Ltd   (NE)
Totalisator Agency Board   (NZ)
Totalworld Services of Provincetown, Inc.   (US)

T. Toth, Ed. & Pub. (CN)
Tottel's (US)
Tottori University. Faculty of Agriculture (JA)
Tottori University. School of Medicine (JA)
Tottori University Forests (JA)
Toucan Press (UI)
Touchdown Publications Inc. (US)
Touche Ross & Co. (US)
Tour Arrangements, Inc. (US)
Touring Club de France (FR)
Touring Club Italiano (IT)
Touring Club of Belgium (BE)
Touring-Club of Switzerland (SZ)
Touring Secours (BE)
Tourism Company of Puerto Rico (PR)
Tourism International Press Ltd. (UK)
Tourisme (FR)
Tourist Court Journal Co. (US)
Tourist Information Brussels (BE)
Tourist Organization of Thailand (TH)
Touristenverein Naturfreunde Schweiz (SZ)
Tout Lyon (FR)
Librarie Jean Touzot (FR)
Tovarystvo Ukrayins'kykh Inzheneriv Ameryki (US)
Toward Freedom, Inc. (US)
Towarzystwo Chirurgow Polskich (PL)
Towarzystwo Internistow Polskich (PL)
Towarzystwo Milosnikow Historii i Zabytkow
    Krakowa (PL)
Towarzystwo Milosnikow Historii w Warszawie (PL)
Towarzystwo Milosnikow Jezyka Polskiego (PL)
Towarzystwo Milosnikow Wroclawia (PL)
Towarzystwo Milosnikow Ziemi Klodzkiej (PL)
Towarzystwo Naukowe Plockie (PL)
Towarzystwo Naukowe w Toruniu (PL)
Towarzystwo Przyjaciol Ziemi Jeleniogorskiej (PL)
Towarzystwo Wiedzy Powszechnej (PL)
Tower International TechnoMedical Institute, Inc.
    (US)
Tower Press, Inc. (US)
Town and Country Planning Association (UK)
Town and Country Planning Association of Victoria
    (AT)
Town & Village Inc. (US)
Town Talk Publications (CN)
Township Officials of Illinois (US)
Townsville Writers' Group (AT)
Towson State College. International Studies
    Department (US)
Toyama Mercantile Marine College (JA)
Toyama Prefecture. Welfare Department (JA)
Toyama Shosen Koto Senmon Gakko
    see Toyama Mercantile Marine College (JA)
Toyo Bunko
    see Oriental Library (JA)
Toyo Communication Equipment Company (JA)
Toyo Keizai Shinposha
    see Oriental Economist (JA)
Toyo Soda Kogyo K. K.
    see Toyo Soda Manufacturing Co., Ltd. (JA)
Toyo Soda Manufacturing Co., Ltd. (JA)
Toyo Tsushinki K. K.
    see Toyo Communication Equipment Company
    (JA)
Toyoda Machine Works Ltd. (JA)
Toyota Motor Sales Co. Ltd. (JA)
Toys International Trade News Ltd. (UK)
Trabalho e Seguro Social (BL)
Traces (FR)
Track & Field News, Inc. (US)
Tracommunications (US)
Trade Activities, Inc. (US)
Trade and Industry of Curacao. Monthly Publication
    (NA)
Trade and Industry Publications Limited (PK)
Trade & Investment Publications (II)
Trade & Technical Press Ltd. (UK)
Trade Channel Organisation (NE)
Trade Development Authority (II)
Trade Digest Publications (II)
Trade Directories (AT)
Trade Distributors (UK)
Trade Magazines Ltd. (UK)
Trade Media Ltd. (HK)
Trade Papers (London) Ltd. (UK)
Trade Periodicals Inc. (US)
Trade Press (FMB) Ltd. (UK)
Trade Press Media Ltd. (HK)
Trade Press Publishing Co. (US)
Trade Publications, Inc. (US)
Trade Publications, Inc. (Miami) (US)
Trade Publications Ltd. (NZ)
Trade Publishing Co. Ltd. (US)
Trade Union Education Centre (AT)
Trade Unionists' Defence Committee. Union Publicity
    Council (AT)
Trade Unions International of Agricultural Forestry
    and Plantataion Workers (CS)

Trade Unions International of Chemical, Oil and
    Allied Workers (HU)
Trade Unions International of Transport Workers
    (CS)
Trade Unions International of Workers in Commerce
    (CS)
Trade Unions International of Workers of the Building,
    Wood and Building Materials Industries (FI)
Trade Winds, Inc. (CH)
Trade Winds Publications Pty. Ltd. (AT)
Trader Speaks (US)
Trades and Labor Council of Queensland (AT)
Trades Publishing Co. (US)
Trades Union Congress of Ghana (GH)
Trades Unionist Inc. A F L-C I O (US)
Tradeshow Week, Inc. (US)
Traditional Studies Press (CN)
Trado Publications Pvt. Ltd. (II)
Traeindustriens Fabrikantforening (DK)
Traffic Analysis Service (US)
Traffic Service Corp. (US)
George L. Trager, Ed. & Pub. (US)
Trail Blazer's Publishing Co. (US)
Trail Press Inc. (US)
Trailbeau Publications (US)
Trailer Dealer Publishing Co. (US)
Trailer Life Publishing Co. Inc. (US)
Train Collectors Association (US)
Cino Traina Ed. & Pub. (IT)
Trained Nurses Association of India (II)
Training Centre for Teachers of the Deaf (AT)
Traktor- og Landbrugsbladet (DK)
Tramontane (FR)
Tramway Museum Society (UK)
Trans-Australia Airlines (AT)
Trans-Canada Matchcover Club (CN)
Trans-Global Enterprises Ltd. (CN)
Trans-High Corp. (US)
Trans-High Corporation (US)
Trans-Media Publishing Co. (US)
Trans Mediterranean Airways (US)
Trans Pacific Stamp Co. (US)
Trans-Tasman News Service Ltd. (NZ)
Trans Tech Publications (US)
Trans World Airlines (US)
Transaction Periodicals Consortium (US)
Transafrica Publishers Ltd. (KE)
Transamerican Press, Inc. (US)
Transatlantic Arts, Inc. (US)
Transatlantik Publishing Corp. (US)
Transcommunications International Inc. (US)
Transcripta Press (UK)
Transcription Feature Service Ltd. (UK)
Transflor (FR)
Transgravity Press (UK)
Transient Press (US)
Transit Research Foundation of Los Angeles Inc.
    (US)
Transition Society (CN)
Transkei Teachers Association (SA)
Translation Company of America (US)
Translatoerforeningen (DK)
Translators' Association of India (II)
Translators' Society of Quebec (CN)
Transmedia (US)
Transnational Family Research Institute (US)
Transnational News Co. Inc. (US)
TransPacific (US)
Transpacific Magazines Ltd. (HK)
Transpatent GmbH. (GW)
Transpersonal Institute (US)
Transpharma, Inc. (US)
Transplantation Society (US)
Izdatel'stvo Transport (UR)
Transport and Distribution Press (UK)
Transport & General Workers Union (UK)
Transport and Tourism Journal (II)
Transport Journal of Australia (AT)
Izdatel'stvo Transport. Leningradskoe Otdelenie
    (UR)
Transport-Nytt Foerlags AB (SW)
Transport Press Ltd. (IE)
Transport Publications (US)
Transport Routier du Quebec (CN)
Transport Studies Group (UK)
Transport Ticket Society (UK)
Transport Workers Union of America (US)
Transportation Alternatives (US)
Transportation Engineer (US)
Transportation Guides, Inc. (US)
Transportation Research Forum (US)
Transportation Research Information Service (US)
Transportation Safety Association of Ontario (CN)
Empresa Jornalistica dos Transportes (BL)
Transportoekonomisk Forening (DK)
Transportoekonomisk Institutt (NO)
Transpress VEB Verlag fuer Verkehrswesen (GE)
Transropa Press (DK)

Transvaal. Education Department (SA)
Transvaal. Education Library Service (SA)
Transvaal. Nature Conservation Division (SA)
Transvaal Farmer (SA)
Transvaal High School Teachers' Association (SA)
Transvaal Horticultural Society (SA)
Transvaal Museum (SA)
Transvaal Provincial Golf Association (SA)
Transvaal School Library Association (SA)
Transvaal Teachers' Association (SA)
Transvaal Women's Agricultural Union (SA)
Transvaalse Raad vir die Uitvoerende Kunste
    see Performing Arts Council Transvaal (SA)
Transworld Publishers Ltd. (UK)
Trapani Nuova (IT)
Trapeza Tes Hellados
    see Bank of Greece (GR)
Trasumenus (IT)
Trattamenti dei Metalli (IT)
Rudolf Trauner Verlag (AU)
Travancore-Cochin Chemicals Ltd. (II)
Travcom Inc. (CN)
Travel Aid Services Ltd. (UK)
Travel Alberta (CN)
Travel and Transport Ltd. (UK)
Travel Communications, Inc. (US)
Travel Industry Association of Alberta (CN)
Travel Industry Association of Canada (CN)
Travel International Associates Ltd. (GR)
Travel Magazine, Inc. (US)
Travel Master (US)
Travel Publications, Inc. (US)
Travel Rates and Places (US)
Travel Research Association (US)
Travel Trade Gazette Ltd. (UK)
Travel Trade Publishing Co. (US)
Travelcade Publications, Inc. (US)
Travelers Insurance Companies (US)
Travelers Protective Association of America (US)
Travelers' Research Publishing Co., Inc. (US)
Travelog Publications (US)
Traveltips (US)
TravLtips Inc. (US)
O. Traylor Mercer Publications, Inc. (US)
Treasure Hunting Unlimited (US)
Treasure Search (US)
Tree Books (US)
Tree Club (NR)
Tree of Peace (CN)
Tree-Ring Society (US)
Tree Society of Southern Africa (SA)
Trees (US)
Trefoil Guild (UK)
Trelleborgs Gummifabriks AB (SW)
Trellis Press Association (US)
Tremco News (US)
Trend Publications Inc. (US)
Trendline (US)
Trends Publishing, Inc. (US)
Trendway Advisory Service, Inc. (US)
Trent Polytechnic. National Centre for School
    Technology (UK)
Trent Press (Nottingham) Ltd. (UK)
Trent University (CN)
Trent University. Student Union (CN)
Editions Trente Jours S.A. (SZ)
Giorgio Trentin, Ed. & Pub. (IT)
Trenton-Mercer County Chamber of Commerce (US)
Trenton State College. Department of Geography
    (US)
Ediciones la Trenza Loca (AG)
Editora Tres Ltda. (BL)
Treub Laboratory (IO)
Trevi Editore (IT)
Trevithick Society (UK)
Tri-County Dental Society (US)
Tri County Newspapers Inc. (US)
Tri-County Publications (US)
Tri I - Informatore Immobiliare Italiano (IT)
Tri-State Regional Planning Commission (US)
Tri-State Transportation Commission (US)
Tri-State United Way (US)
Triangle (US)
Triangle Communications Inc. (US)
Triangle Publications (US)
Triangle Publications Inc. (US)
Tribal Press (US)
Tribal Research and Development Institute (II)
Tribe of Many Feathers (Indian Club) (US)
Tribhuvan University (NP)
Tribhuvan University. Centre for Economic
    Development and Administration
    see Centre for Economic Development and
    Administration (NP)
Tribhuvan University History Association (NP)
Tribhuvan University. Institute of Nepal and Asian
    Studies (NP)
Tribune-Verlag (GW)

Tribuna de New Jersey (US)
Tribuna Italiana (CN)
Tribuna Mladih (YU)
Tribuna Odontologica (AG)
Tribuna Politica (IT)
Tribunal de Commerce de Paris (FR)
Tribunal de Justica (BL)
Tribunal de Justica do Estado do Rio Grande do Sul (BL)
Tribunal Federal de Recursos (BL)
Verlag Tribune (GE)
Tribune (CE)
Tribune des Nations (FR)
Tribune Medicale (FR)
Tribune Press Ltd. (CN)
Tribune Publications Ltd. (UK)
Tribune Publishing Co. (US)
Tribune Publishing Co. Ltd. (CN)
Tributi Sugli Affari (IT)
Tricontinental Publications (CU)
Tricots Chics (FR)
Trident Press Ltd. (CN)
Trier. Bezirks-Regierung. Schulabteilung (GW)
Societa Editrice Trieste (IT)
Trilateral Commission (US)
Trilce de Poesia (CL)
Editorial Trillas, S. A. (MX)
Robert Trillo Ltd. (UK)
Michael Triltsch Verlag (GW)
Trimedia N.V. (BE)
Trimurti Prakashan (II)
Trinc Transportation Consultants (US)
Tringale Editore (IT)
Trinidad and Tobago. Auditor General of Trinidad and Tobago (TR)
Trinidad and Tobago. Central Statistical Office (TR)
Trinidad and Tobago. Department of Petroleum and Mines (TR)
Trinidad & Tobago. Management Development Centre. Library (TR)
Trinidad and Tobago. Ministry of Petroleum and Mines (TR)
Trinidad and Tobago Society (UK)
Trinidad Naturalist (TR)
Trinidad Philatelic Society (TR)
Trinidad Publishing Company Ltd. (TR)
Trinitarian Bible Society (UK)
Trinity College (IE)
Trinity College (Hartford) (US)
Trinity College (Washington) (US)
Trinity College. Friends of the Library (IE)
Trinity College, Legon (GH)
Trinity College of Quezon City (PH)
Trinity Evangelical Divinity School (US)
Trinity Lutheran Hospital (US)
Trinity University. Department of Religion (US)
Trinity University Press (US)
Drukkerij Trio (NE)
Trio Publications (US)
Trio-Rand Publishers (SA)
Tripura. Department of Agriculture (II)
Tripura Government Press (II)
TriQuarterly (US)
Abner L. Tritt (US)
TRIUMF (CN)
Triumph Magazine, Inc. (US)
Triveni Press (II)
Trocadero Publishing Co., Inc. (US)
Dr Rudolf Trofenik Verlag (GW)
Editora Trofeu Ltda. (BL)
Tromsoe Museum (NO)
Tropical Agriculture Research Association of Japan (JA)
Tropical Agriculture Research Center
  see Japan. Tropical Agriculture Research Center (JA)
Tropical Grassland Society of Australia (AT)
Tropical Pesticides Research Institute (TZ)
Tropical Products Institute (UK)
Tropical Science Center (CR)
Tros (NE)
Harlan Trott, Ed. & Pub. (US)
Editrice Trotto Italiano (IT)
Trouser Press (US)
Trout Unlimited (US)
Troxler-Verlag (SZ)
Troy Enterprises Co. (US)
Troy State University Press (US)
Truck Press (US)
Truck Tracks Inc. (US)
Truck Trends (US)
Trucking Activities, Inc. (US)
Izdatel'stvo Trud (UR)
Trudbenik (YU)
True Whig Party (LB)
Truly Fine Press (US)
Truman & Knightley Educational Trust Ltd. (UK)
Trust Companies Association of Canada (CN)

Estelle Trust, Ed. & Pub. (US)
Trust for British Archaeology (UK)
Trust Territory Government Printing Office (TT)
Trust Territory of the Pacific Islands (TT)
Trust Territory of the Pacific Islands. Congress of Micronesia. House of Representatives (TT)
Trust Territory of the Pacific Islands. Congress of Micronesia. Joint Committee on Program and Budget Planning (TT)
Trust Territory of the Pacific Islands. Congress of Micronesia Library (TT)
Trust Territory of the Pacific Islands. Congress of Micronesia. Senate (TT)
Trust Territory of the Pacific Islands. Territorial Housing Commission (TT)
Trustee Savings Bank Association (UK)
Truth Seeker Co., Inc. (US)
Try It, You'll like It (US)
Trygdekontorenes Landsforening (NO)
Tsai Cheng Pu Tung Chi Chu (CH)
Tsentral'nyi Nauchno-Issledovatel'skii Institut Patentnoi Informatsii i Tekhniko-Ekonom'cheskikh Issledovanii (UR)
Tsentur za Nauchno-Meditsinska Informatsiia (BU)
John Tsitrian, Ed. & Pub. (US)
Tsuda-Juku Women's College (JA)
Tsumura Junten-do Co. Ltd. (JA)
Tsushin Kikai Kogyokai
  see Communication Industries Association of Japan (JA)
Tsusho Sangyo-cho Kogyo Gijutsu-in Hokkaido Kogyo Kaihatsu Shikenjo
  see Japan. Government Industrial Development Laboratory, Hokkaido (JA)
Tsusho Sangyo-cho Kogyo Gijutsu-in Kogai Shigen Kenkyusho
  see Japan. National Research Institute for Pollution and Resources (JA)
Tsusho Sangyo-sho Gijutsu-in Tokyo Kogyo Shikensho
  see Japan. National Chemical Laboratory for Industry (JA)
Tsusho Sangyo-sho Kogyo Gijutsu-in Chishitsu Chosasho
  see Japan. Geological Survey of Japan (JA)
Tsusho Sangyo-sho Kogyo Gijutsu-in Keiryo Kenkyusho
  see Japan. National Research Laboratory of Metrology (JA)
Tsusho Sangyo-sho Kogyo Gijutsu-in Kyushu Kogyo Gijutsu Shikenjo
  see Japan. Government Industrial Research Institute, Kyushu (JA)
TU: S Foerlags AB (SW)
Tu Sei Me (IT)
Tuatara (CN)
Tube (AT)
Tuberculosis Association of India (II)
Tuberkuloosi ja Keuhkovammaisten Liitto (FI)
Tubists Universal Brotherhood Association (US)
Tubman Teachers College
  see under University of Liberia (LB)
Tucar Ediciones S.A. (SP)
Tucson Educational Association (US)
Tudomanyos Ismeretterjeszto Tarsulat (HU)
Tudor Press Ltd. (UK)
Tuduv-Verlagsgesellschaft (GW)
Tuermer-Verlag (GW)
Tuesday Publications, Inc. (US)
Tufts Kinsmen Association (US)
Tufts New England Medical Center (US)
Tufts University Theater (US)
Tufty Communications, Inc. (US)
Editions des Tuileries (FR)
Tulane Institute of Comparative Law (US)
Tulane Law Review Association (US)
Tulane Medical Center. Alumni Association (US)
Tulane University. Department of Biology (US)
Tulane University. Department of English (US)
Tulane University. Department of Geology (US)
Tulane University. Department of Mechanical Engineering (US)
Tulane University. Department of Philosophy (US)
Tulane University. Department of Political Science (US)
Tulane University. Department of Sociology and Anthropology (US)
Tulane University. Division of Alumni Activities (US)
Tulane University. Library (US)
Tulane University School of Law (US)
Tulika Prakashan-Quill (II)
Tulsa City-County Library System (US)
Tulsa County Bar Association (US)
Tumminelli (IT)
Tunisia. Division des Resources en Eau (TI)
Tunisia. Institut National de la Statistique (TI)
Tunisia. Ministere de l'Equipement (TI)
Tunisia. Ministere du Plan (TI)

Tunisia. Ministere du Plan. Institut National de la Statistique
  see Tunisia. Institut National de la Statistique (TI)
Tunisia. Office des Ports Nationaux (TI)
Tunnell Publications, Inc. (US)
TURDOK
  see Turkish Scientific and Technical Documentation Centre (TU)
Turf and Sport International, Ltd. (US)
Turf Newspapers Ltd. (UK)
Turin, Italy. Comitato Provinciale di Educazione Grafica (IT)
Turismo (MX)
Turisport (SP)
Edizioni Turistampa (IT)
Ediciones Turisticas, S. A. (SP)
Turisticka Stampa (YU)
Turistlena Zveza Slovenije (YU)
Turk Belediyecilik Dernegi (TU)
Turk Dil Kurumu
  see Turkish Linguistic Society (TU)
Turk Folklor Arastirmalari (TU)
Turk Kulturunu Arastirma Enstitusu
  see Turkish Cultural Research Institute (TU)
Turk Sesi Pty. Ltd. (AT)
Turk Sinematek Dernegi (TU)
Turk Tarih Kurumu
  see Turkish Historical Society (TU)
Turkey. Devlet Istatistik Enstitusu
  see Turkey. State Institute of Statistics (TU)
Turkey. Devlet Planlama Teskilati
  see Turkey. State Planning Organization (TU)
Turkey. Electricity Authority (TU)
Turkey. General Directorate of Antiquities and Museums (TU)
Turkey. General Directorate of Highways (TU)
Turkey. Icisleri Bakanligi
  see Turkey. Ministry of Interior (TU)
Turkey. Mili Kutuphane
  see Turkey. National Library (TU)
Turkey. Ministry of Interior (TU)
Turkey. Ministry of Tourism and Information (TU)
Turkey. National Library (TU)
Turkey. National Library. Bibliographical Institute (TU)
Turkey. State Institute of Statistics (TU)
Turkey. State Planning Organization (TU)
Turkey. Turizm ve Tanitma Bakanligi
  see Turkey. Ministry of Tourism and Information (TU)
Turkine Bilimsel ve Teknik Dokumentasyon Merkezi
  see Turkish Scientific and Technical Documentation Centre (TU)
Turkish Chamber of Chemical Engineers (TU)
Turkish Cultural Research Institute (TU)
Turkish Embassy (US)
Turkish Historical Society (TU)
Turkish Librarians' Association (TU)
Turkish Linguistic Society (TU)
Turkish Medical Association (TU)
Turkish Phytopathological Society (TU)
Turkish Scientific and Technical Documentation Centre (TU)
Turkish Teachers' Union of Western Thrace (GR)
Turkiye Elekrik Kurumu
  see Turkey. Electricity Authority (TU)
Turkiye Fitopatoloji Dernegi
  see Turkish Phytopathological Society (TU)
Turkiye Is Bankasi (TU)
Turkiye Kimya Cemiyeti
  see Chemical Society of Turkey (TU)
Turkiye Sinai Kalkinma Bankasi
  see Industrial Development Bank of Turkey (TU)
Turner and Devereux (UK)
R. H. Turner, Ed. & Pub. (CN)
John D. Turrel, Ed. & Pub. (US)
Turret Press Ltd. (UK)
Turtle Bay Association (US)
Turtle Island Foundation (US)
Turun Hammaslaaketieteenkandidaattiseura (FI)
Turun Historiallinen Yhdistys (FI)
Turun Yliopisto (FI)
Turun Yliopisto. Kirjasto (FI)
Turun Yliopisto. Klassillisen Filologian Laitos (FI)
Turun Yliopisto. Poliittisen Historian Laitos (FI)
Turun Yliopisto. Psykologian Laitos (FI)
Tusho Sangiyo Chosakai
  see Research Institute of International Trade and Industry (JA)
Tuskegee Institute (US)
J. Tutching (US)
Tutmonda Esperantista Junulara Organizo (NE)
Tuvoti Books (US)
Twain Associates (US)
Twayne Publishers, Inc. (US)
Tweed (AT)
Tweeddale Press Ltd. (UK)
Twentieth Century Fund (US)

Twentieth Century Publications, Inc. (US)
Twenty-Third Publications (US)
Twickenham Local History Society (UK)
Twilight (US)
Twin Circle Publishing Co. (US)
Twin Cities Media Project Inc. (US)
Twin City Purchasing Management Association (US)
Twin Coast Newspapers, Inc. (US)
Twin Oaks Community (US)
Two Feet of Poetry (US)
Two Hands News (US)
Two Rivers (UK)
Two Thousand (UK)
Two Tone (RH)
Two Worlds Publishing Co. Ltd. (UK)
Tydskrif vir Letterkunde (SA)
Tydskriftemaatskappy van die Nederduitse
  Gereformeerde Kerk (SA)
Tyndale Fellowship for Biblical and Theological
  Research (UK)
Tyne & Wear Chamber of Commerce (UK)
Typewriter (US)
Tyre Industry Publications Ltd. (UK)
Tyrol. Amt der Tiroler Landesregierung (AU)
Tyrol. Institut fuer Verkehr und Tourismus (AU)
Tyrol. Tiroler Landesregierung. Kulturreferat (AU)
W. Tyrrell (CN)
Tyrrell Burgess Associates Ltd. (UK)
U.A.W. & A.F.L.-C.I.O. Local Unions. Capital Area
  Community Action Program (US)
U B O K (CS)
U. E. M (FR)
Editions U F A F (FR)
U.F.W., A.F.L.-C.I.O. (FR)
U H A Publishing (US)
U I E
  see Unesco Institute for Education (UN)
U I T
  see International Telecommunication Union (UN)
U. K. Chemical Information Service (UK)
U.K. Publications Ltd. (UK)
U.N.A.E.D.E. (FR)
U N C H R
  see United Nations High Commissioner for
  Refugees (UN)
U N C I T R A L
  see United Nations. Commission on International
  Trade Law (UN)
U N C R D
  see United Nations Centre for Regional
  Development (UN)
U N C T A D
  see United Nations Conference on Trade and
  Development (UN)
U N C T A D- G A T T
  see General Agreement on Tariffs and Trades.
  International Trade Centre (UN)
U N D P
  see United Nations Development Programme
  (UN)
U N E P
  see United Nations Environment Programme
  (UN)
U N E S C O
  see Unesco (UN)
U N F P A
  see United Nations Fund for Population Activities
  (UN)
U N H C R
  see United Nations High Commissioner for
  Refugees (UN)
U N I C E F
  see Unicef (UN)
U N I D O
  see United Nations Industrial Development
  Organization (UN)
U N I T A R
  see United Nations Institute for Training and
  Research (UN)
U N O R (BE)
U N R I S D
  see United Nations Research Institute for Social
  Development (UN)
U N R W A
  see United Nations Relief and Works Agency for
  Palestine Refugees in the Near East (UN)
U. P. E. M
  see Union de Publications et d'Editions Modernes
  (U.P.E.M.) (FR)
U. P. Irrigation Research Institute (II)
U P R A Maine Anjou (FR)
U P U
  see Universal Postal Union (UN)
U.R.O.G (FR)
U S A-C I O Local Union 1010 (US)
U S A-C I O. Local 1104 (US)
U S A Publishing Co., Inc. (US)
U S - Austrian Chamber of Commerce (US)

U S Capitol Historical Society (US)
U S-China Friendship Association (US)
U S-China Peoples Friendship Association (US)
U S Conference of Mennonite Brethren Churches
  (US)
U S Directory Service (US)
U S Directory Service (Miami) (US)
U..S. Employment and Training Administration (US)
U S Glass Publications, Inc. (US)
U S Handball Association (US)
U S Hang Gliding Association (US)
U S Institute for Theatre Technology, Inc. (US)
U S Jaycees (US)
U S L A Justice Committee (US)
U. S. M. M. A. (US)
U S Medicine, Inc. (US)
U S Metric Association, Inc. (US)
U S Microfilm Sales Corp. (US)
U S Naval Academy Alumni Association, Inc. (US)
U S News and World Report, Inc. (US)
U S News and World Report, Inc. (New York) (US)
U S Park Police (US)
U S Philatelic Classics Society Inc. (US)
U S Pipe and Foundry Co. (US)
U S Racquetball Association (US)
U.S.S.R. Embassy in India (II)
U. S. S. R. Glavnoe Arkhivnoe Upravlenie (UR)
U. S. S. R. Glavnoe Upravlenie Geodezii i Kartografii
  pri Sovete Ministrov (UR)
U. S. S. R. Gosplan (UR)
U. S. S. R. Gosstroi (UR)
U. S. S. R. Gosudarstvennyi Komitet Autotraktornogo
  i Sel'skokhozyaistvennogo Mashinostroeniya pri
  Gosplane (UR)
U. S. S. R. Gosudarstvennyi Komitet Khimicheskogo i
  Neftyanogo Mashinostroeniya pri Gosplane (UR)
U. S. S. R. Gosudarstvennyi Komitet Khimicheskoi
  Promyshlennosti pri Gosplane (UR)
U. S. S. R. Gosudarstvennyi Komitet po Chernoi i
  Tsvetnoi Metallurgii (UR)
U. S. S. R. Gosudarstvennyi Komitet po
  Grazhdanskomu Stroitel'stvu i Arkhitekture (UR)
U. S. S. R. Gosudarstvennyi Komitet po Ispol'zovaniyu
  Atomnoi Energii S. S. R. (UR)
U. S. S. R. Gosudarstvennyi Komitet po Khimii pri
  Sovete Ministrov (UR)
U. S. S. R. Gosudarstvennyi Komitet po
  Kinematografii Soveta Ministrov (UR)
U. S. S. R. Gosudarstvennyi Komitet po Torgovle
  (UR)
U. S. S. R. Gosudarstvennyi Komitet Soveta Ministrov
  po Nauke i Tekhnike (UR)
U. S. S. R. Gosudarstvennyi Komitet Soveta Ministrov
  po Pechati (UR)
U. S. S. R. Gosudarstvennyi Komitet Soveta Ministrov
  po Voprosam Truda i Zarabotnoi Platy (UR)
U. S. S. R. Gosudarstvennyi Komitet Standartov Mer i
  Izmeritel'nykh Priborov (UR)
U. S. S. R. Gosudarstvennyi Komitet Tyazhelogo,
  Energeticheskogo i Transportnogo Mashinostroenie
  pri Gosplane (UR)
U.S.S.R. Komitet po Delam Izobretenii i Otkrytii
  Soveta Ministrov S.S.S.R. (UR)
U.S.S.R. Komitet po Delam Stroitel'stva Soveta
  Ministrov S.S.S.R. (UR)
U. S. S. R. Komitet po Fizicheskoi Kul'ture i Sportu
  pri Sovete Ministrov (UR)
U. S. S. R. Komitet po Pechati Soveta Ministrov
  (UR)
U. S. S. R. Ministerstvo Chernoi Metallurgii (UR)
U. S. S. R. Ministerstvo Derevoobrabatyvayushchei
  Promyshlennosti (UR)
U.S.S.R. Ministerstvo Elektricheskoi Promyshlennosti
  (UR)
U.S.S.R. Ministerstvo Energetiki i Elektrifikatsii
  (UR)
U. S. S. R. Ministerstvo Finansov (UR)
U. S. S. R. Ministerstvo Gazovoi Promyshlennosti
  (UR)
U.S.S.R. Ministerstvo Geologii (UR)
U. S. S. R. Ministerstvo Grazhdanskoi Aviatsii (UR)
U.S.S.R. Ministerstvo Khimicheskoi Promyshlennosti
  (UR)
U.S.S.R. Ministerstvo Kommercheskogo Flota (UR)
U. S. S. R. Ministerstvo Kul'tury (UR)
U.S.S.R. Ministerstvo Legkoi Promyshlennosti (UR)
U.S.S.R. Ministerstvo Meditsinskoi Promyshlennosti
  (UR)
U.S.S.R. Ministerstvo Myasnoi i Molochnoi
  Promyshlennosti (UR)
U.S.S.R. Ministerstvo Neftyanoi Promyshlennosti
  (UR)
U.S.S.R. Ministerstvo Oborony (UR)

U.S.S.R. Ministerstvo Pishchevoi Promyshlennosti
  (UR)
U. S. S. R. Ministerstvo Priborostroeniya (UR)
U.S.S.R. Ministerstvo Promyshlennosti Stroitel'nykh
  Materialov (UR)
U.S.S.R. Ministerstvo Prosveshcheniya (UR)
U.S.S.R. Ministerstvo Putei Soobshcheniya (UR)
U.S.S.R. Ministerstvo Rybnogo Khozyaistva (UR)
U. S. S. R. Ministerstvo Sel'skogo Khozyaistva (UR)
U.S.S.R. Ministerstvo Stankostroitel'noi i
  Instrumental'noi Promyshlennosti (UR)
U.S.S.R. Ministerstvo Stroitel'nogo, Dorozhnogo i
  Kommunal'nogo Mashinostroeniya (UR)
U.S.S.R. Ministerstvo Sudostroeniya (UR)
U.S.S.R. Ministerstvo Svyazi (UR)
U.S.S.R. Ministerstvo Tselyulozno-bumazhnoi
  Promyshlennosti (UR)
U. S. S. R. Ministerstvo Tsvetnoi Metallurgii (UR)
U.S.S.R. Ministerstvo Ugol'noi Promyshlennosti (UR)
U.S.S.R. Ministerstvo Visshego i Srednego
  Spetsialnogo Obrazovaniya (UR)
U.S.S.R. Ministerstvo Vneshnei Torgovli (UR)
U. S. S. R. Ministerstvo Vysshego i Srednego
  Spetsial'nogo Obrazovaniya (UR)
U. S. S. R. Ministerstvo Zdravookhraneniya (UR)
U.S.S.R. Prokuratura (UR)
U.S.S.R. Tsentral'noe Statisticheskoe Upravlenie pri
  Sovete Ministrov (UR)
U. S. S. R. Verkhovnyi Sovet (UR)
U S Servas Committee, Inc. (US)
U S Ski Association. Eastern Division (US)
U S Transportation, Inc. (US)
U S Travel Data Center (US)
U S Yugoslav Economic Council, Inc. (US)
U S 1 Poets' Cooperative (US)
U.V. Spectrometry Group (UK)
Ubezzi & Dones, S.p.A. (IT)
Uchu Koku Kenkyusho
  see University of Tokyo. Institute of Space and
  Aeronautical Science (JA)
Uchusen Boenkyo
  see Nagoya University. Cosmic-Ray Research
  Laboratory (JA)
Udayana State University (IO)
Udbodhan (II)
Udenrigs Handel & Industri Information (DK)
Udenrigspolitiske Selskab (DK)
Udruzena Elektroprivreda SR Hrvatske (YU)
Udruzeni Zavod za Osiguranje i Reosiguranje (YU)
Udruzenje Banka Jugoslavije (YU)
Udruzenje Dermatovenerologa Jugoslavije (YU)
Udruzenje Emajliraca Jugoslavije (YU)
Udruzenje Ginekologa-Opstetricara Jugoslavije (YU)
Udruzenje Hirurga Jugoslavije (YU)
Udruzenje Knjijigovoda Hrvatske (YU)
Udruzenje Knjigovoda Srbije (YU)
Udruzenje Knjizevnih Prevodilaca Srbije (YU)
Udruzenje Komercijalista Jugoslavije (YU)
Udruzenje Mlekarskih Radnika SR Hrvatske (YU)
Udruzenje Muzickih Pedagoga Hrvatske (YU)
Udruzenje Neurologa i Psihijatara Jugoslavije (YU)
Udruzenje Oftalmologa Jugoslavije (YU)
Udruzenje Pravoslavnog Svestenstva SFR Jugoslavije.
  Glavni Savez (YU)
Udruzenje za Tehnologiju Vode (YU)
Ueberparteilicher Aerzteverband Niederoesterreichs
  (AU)
Carl Ueberreuter (AU)
Uebersee-Museum, Bremen (GW)
Uebersee-Post Verlag Dr. Harnisch GmbH und Co.
  KG (GW)
Uebersee-Verlag GmbH (GW)
Ufficio Centrale per l'Emigrazione Italiana (IT)
Ufficio Intercantonale di Controllo dei Medicamenti
  see Interkantonale Kontrollstelle fuer Heilmittel
  (SZ)
Ufficio Moderno (IT)
Uganda. Forest Department (UG)
Uganda. Geological Survey and Mines Department
  (UG)
Uganda. Government Printer (UG)
Uganda. Ministry of Information, Broadcasting and
  Tourism (UG)
Uganda. Ministry of Planning and Economic
  Development. Statistics Division (UG)
Uganda Church Publications (UG)
Uganda Economic Association (UG)
Uganda Geographical Association (UG)
Uganda School Leavers Association (UG)
Uganda Society (UG)
Ugo Ragozzino, Ed. & Pub. (IT)
Uhren und Maschinenkombinat Ruhla (GE)
Uinversidad de Granada. Departamento de Historia
  Medieval (SP)
Uirusu Kenkyusho
  see Kyoto University. Institute for Virus Research
  (JA)
Uitgave M.S.C (NE)

B. V. Uitgeversbedrijf voor de Tuinbouw   (NE)
Ukrainian Academy of Sciences   (US)
Ukrainian Artist's Association in U.S.A. Philadelphia
     Branch   (US)
Ukrainian Canadian Committee   (CN)
Ukrainian Catholic Archdiocese of Winnipeg   (CN)
Ukrainian Catholic Church. Archdiocese of
     Philadelphia   (US)
Ukrainian Catholic Mission of the Most Holy
     Redeemer   (CN)
Ukrainian Congress Committee of America   (US)
Ukrainian Engineers' Society of America   (US)
Ukrainian Evangelical Alliance of North America
     (US)
Ukrainian Evangelical Baptist Convention   (US)
Ukrainian Historian   (US)
Ukrainian Historical Association   (US)
Ukrainian Language Association   (CN)
Ukrainian Medical Association of North America
     (US)
Ukrainian Museum-Archives, Inc.   (US)
Ukrainian National Aid Association of America   (US)
Ukrainian National Association, Inc.   (US)
Ukrainian National Women's League   (US)
Ukrainian News Publishers Ltd.   (CN)
Ukrainian Orthodox Church of the U.S.A.   (US)
Ukrainian Philatelic and Numismatic Society   (US)
Ukrainian Publishers Ltd.   (UK)
Ukrainian Publishing Co.   (US)
Ukrainian Student Organization of Michnowsky,
     T.U.S.M.   (US)
Ukrainian Womens' Association in Australia   (AT)
Ukrainian Workingmen's Association   (US)
Ukrainskaya S.S.R. Ministerstvo Kul'tury   (UR)
Ukrainskaya S.S.R. Ministerstvo Osvity   (UR)
Ukrainskaya S.S.R. Ministerstvo Zdorovya   (UR)
Ukrayins'ke Suspil'no-Kul'turne Tovarystvo   (PL)
Ulkopoliittinen Instituutti   (FI)
Walter E. Ullmann, Editor and Publisher   (AU)
Elinor Ulman, Ed. & Pub.   (US)
Verlag Eugen Ulmer   (GW)
Ulster Archaeological Society   (UK)
Ulster County Extension Association   (US)
Ulster County Genealogical Society   (US)
Ulster Folk and Transport Museum   (UK)
Ulster Journals Ltd.   (UK)
Ulster Link   (AT)
Ulster Medical Society   (UK)
Ulster Motorist   (UK)
Ultra Light Aircraft Association of Australia   (AT)
Ulyanovskii Politekhnicheskii Institut   (UR)
M. Umapathi, Pub.   (II)
Umbra   (US)
Umeaa Universitet   (SW)
Umeaa Universitet. Department of Education   (SW)
VEB Kombinat Umformtechnik "Herbert Warnke"
     Erfort. Forschungszentrum fuer Umformverfahren
     (GE)
Umma Publishing House   (PK)
Umschau Verlag   (GW)
Un'Yu Chosakyoku
     see Institute of Transportation Economics   (JA)
Un'Yu-sho Daijin Kanbo Joho Kanri-bu
     see Japan. Ministry of Transport   (JA)
Un'Yu-sho Kowan Gijutsu Kenkyusho
     see Japan. Port and Harbour Technical Research
     Institute   (JA)
Un'Yu-sho Senpaku Gijutsu Kenkyusho
     see Japan. Ship Research Institute   (JA)
Unabashed Librarian   (US)
Unabhaengiger Arbeitskreis Arzneimittelpolitik   (GW)
Unda-International Catholic Association for Radio & T
     V   (US)
Undena Publications   (US)
Undercurrents Ltd.   (UK)
Underground Alternative Press Service - Europe
     (UK)
Underground Engineering Contractors' Association
     (US)
Underground Officials' Association of South Africa
     (SA)
Underground Teacher   (US)
Undersea Medical Society, Inc.   (US)
Understanding, Inc.   (US)
Undervisnings- og Velferdsoffiserenes Forening   (NO)
Underwater Federation of Australia   (AT)
Underwater Skindivers and Fishermen's Association of
     N.S.W.   (AT)
Underwriter Printing and Publishing Co.   (US)
Underwriters Laboratories, Inc.   (US)
Underwriters' Report   (US)
Underwriters Review   (US)
Unesco
     see also Unesco Press   (UN)
Unesco   (UN)
Unesco. Coordinating Committee for International
     Voluntary Service   (UN)

Unesco Institute for Education   (UN)
Unesco. International Bureau of Education   (UN)
Unesco. International Copyright Information Center
     (UN)
Unesco. International Institute for Educational
     Planning
     see International Institute for Educational Planning
     (UN)
Unesco Press
     see also Unesco   (UN)
Unesco Press   (UN)
Unesco. Regional Cultural Bureau for Latin America
     and the Caribbean   (UN)
Unesco. Regional Office for Culture and Book
     Development in Asia   (UN)
Unesco. Regional Office for Education in Asia   (UN)
Unesco. Regional Office for Education in Latin
     America and the Caribbean   (UN)
Unesco. Regional Office of Science and Technology
     for Africa   (UN)
Unesco. Regional Office of Science and Technology
     for Latin America and the Caribbean   (UN)
Unga Filosofers Foerlag   (SW)
Unga Oernars Riksfoerbund   (SW)
Frederick Ungar Publishing Co., Inc.   (US)
Ungarisches Institut, Muenchen   (GW)
Ungdomen Selvbyggerlag   (NO)
Uniao das Associacoes de Espectaculos e Diversoes
     (PO)
Unicef   (UN)
Unicef Canada   (UN)
Unicef. European Office   (UN)
Unicorn   (US)
Unicorn Press   (US)
Unicorn Publishing Corporation   (CN)
Unicorn Systems Company   (US)
Unidade Executiva de Pesquisa Agropecuaria Estadual-
     RS   (BL)
Unidentified Flying Objects Investigation Centre
     (AT)
Unidroit (International Institute for the Unification of
     Private Law)   (IT)
Unie van Baptisten Gemeenten   (NE)
Unie van Waterschappen   (NE)
Unieboek B.V.   (NE)
Uniespana   (SP)
Unifarm   (CN)
Unification Printers & Publishers Pty. Ltd.   (AT)
Unified Science and Mathematics for Elementary
     Schools   (US)
Unifier   (II)
Uniformed Fire Officers Association. Local 854
     I.A.F.F.-AFL-CIO   (US)
Uniformed Firefighters Association of Greater New
     York. Local 94   (US)
Uniformed Sanitationmen's Association   (US)
Uniformed Services Almanac, Inc.   (US)
Uniforms and Accessories Review   (US)
Unifrance Film   (FR)
Unija Bioloskih Naucnih Drustava Jugoslavije   (YU)
Union Acceptances Ltd.   (SA)
Union Agricultural Cooperative of Syra   (GR)
Union Bank of Finland
     see Suomen Yhdyspankki   (FI)
Union Bank of Switzerland
     see Union de Banques Suisses   (SZ)
Union-Betriebs-Gesellschaft mbH   (GW)
Union Bible Institute   (SA)
Union Carbide Corp.   (US)
Union College   (US)
Union College (Lincoln) Associated Student Body
     (US)
Union College (Schenectady)   (US)
Union College (Schenectady) Character Research
     Project   (US)
Union Confederale des Ingenieurs & Cadres C F D T
     Francaise   (FR)
Union Cultural Organization Ltd.   (HK)
Union Culturelle et Technique de Langue Francaise
     (FR)
Union de Banques Suisses   (SZ)
Union de Escritores y Artistas de Cuba   (CU)
Union de Fabricantes de Conservas de Galicia   (SP)
Union de Jovenes Comunistas. Movimiento de Brigadas
     Tecnicas   (CU)
Union de Jovenes Comunistas. Sector de la
     Construccion   (CU)
Union de la Jeunesse du Travail d'Albanie   (AA)
Union de la Presse Europeenne   (FR)
Union de Periodistas de Cuba   (CU)
Union de Publications et d'Editions Modernes
     (U.P.E.M.)   (FR)
Union de Universidades de America Latina   (MX)
Union Departementale des Societes Mutualistes
     d'Indre-et-Loire   (FR)
Union Departmentale Mutaliste des Travailleurs   (FR)
Union der Leitenden Angestellten   (GW)
Union des Associations Internationales

     see Union of International Associations   (BE)
Union des Aveugles de Guerre   (FR)
Union des Caisses Centrales de la Mutualite Agricole
     (FR)
Union des Ecrivains et Artistes d'Albanie   (AA)
Union des Ecrivains Zairois   (ZR)
Union des Editeurs de Langue Francaise   (FR)
Union des Editeurs Francais   (FR)
Union des Editions Modernes   (FR)
Union des Etudes et Recherches des Sciences
     Odontologiques   (FR)
Union des Etudiants de l'Ichec   (BE)
Union des Exploitations Electriques en Belgique   (BE)
Union des Fabricants pour la Protection de la
     Propriete Industrielle et Artistique   (FR)
Union des Federalistes Polonais   (FR)
Union des Femmes d'Albanie   (AA)
Union des Jeunes Avocats a la Cour de Paris   (FR)
Union des Jeunes pour le Progres   (FR)
Union des Jeunesses Revolutionnaires Congolaises
     (ZR)
Union des Journalistes d'Albanie   (AA)
Union des Libraires d'Art et d'Essai   (FR)
Union des Oeuvres Catholiques de France   (FR)
Union des Organisations Agricoles du Sud-Est   (FR)
Union des Producteurs Agricoles   (CN)
Union des Revues Techniques Belges   (BE)
Union des Societes Bretonnes de l'Ile de France   (FR)
Union des Societes d'Education Physique et de
     Preparation Militaire   (FR)
Union des Societes Francophones pour l'Investigation
     Psychique et l'Etude de la Survivance   (FR)
Union des Superieures Majeures de France.   (FR)
Union des Syndicats d'Interet Economique de
     Madagascar   (MG)
Union des Syndicats de Medecins de Centres de Sante
     (FR)
Union des Syndicats Dentaires de Bourgogne-Franche-
     Comte   (FR)
Union des Vieux de France   (FR)
Union des Villes et Communes Belges   (BE)
Union Druck und Verlag   (SZ)
Union Eglises Evangeliques Libres de France   (FR)
Union Europeenne des Experts Comptables
     Economiques et Financiers   (GW)
Union Federale Francaise de Musique Sacree   (FR)
Union Federaliste Mondiale   (FR)
Union Feminine Civique et Sociale   (FR)
Union Francaise d'Annuaires Professionnels   (FR)
Union Francaise des Centres de Vacances   (FR)
Union Francaise des Oeuvres Laiques d'Education
     Physique   (FR)
Union Francaise pour l'Esperanto   (FR)
Union General des Travailleurs Algeriens   (AE)
Union Geofisica Mexicana. Centro de Ciencias de la
     Atmosfera   (MX)
Union Hospitaliere Privee   (FR)
Union Interlinguiste de France   (FR)
Union International de Interlinguistik Servicie   (NE)
Union International des Avocats
     see International Association of Lawyers   (BE)
Union Internationale Chretienne des Dirigeants
     d'Enterprise. Centre Chretien d'Action pour les
     Dirigeants et Cadres des Enterprise   (ZR)
Union Internationale Contre le Cancer
     see International Union Against Cancer   (SZ)
Union Internationale d'Action Morale et Sociale
     see International Union for Moral and Social Action
     (BE)
Union Internationale d'Histoire des Sciences   (FR)
Union Internationale de la Navigation Fluviale
     see International Union for Inland Navigation
     (BE)
Union Internationale de Protection de l'Enfance
     see International Union for Child Welfare   (SZ)
Union Internationale des Architectes   (FR)
Union Internationale des Associations d'Alpinisme
     see International Union of Alpine Associations
     (SZ)
Union Internationale des Maires   (FR)
Union Internationale des Ouvriers du Vetement pour
     Dames   (CN)
Union Internationale des Producteurs et Distributeurs
     d'Energie Electrique
     see International Union of Producers and
     Distributors of Electrical Energy   (FR)
Union Internationale des Telecommunications
     see International Telecommunication Union   (UN)
Union Internationale des Travailleurs de l'Alimentation
     et des Branches Connexes
     see International Union of Food and Allied
     Workers' Associations   (SZ)
Union Interparlementaire
     see Interparliamentary Union   (SZ)
Union Intersyndicale des Medecins Cinesiologues:
     Sport et Reeducation   (FR)

United Labor Council of Reading and Berks County (US)
United Lodge of Theosophists (II)
United Lutheran Society (US)
United Malayan Banking Corp. Berhad (MY)
United Malays National Organisation (MY)
United Marine Publishing, Inc. (US)
United Media International, Inc. (US)
United Methodist Church (US)
United Methodist Church. Arkansas Area (US)
United Methodist Church. Board of Church and Society (US)
United Methodist Church. Board of Discipleship (US)
United Methodist Church. Board of Global Ministries (US)
United Methodist Church. Commission on Archives and History (US)
United Methodist Church. Division of Education (US)
United Methodist Church. Division of Education. Department of Adult Publications (US)
United Methodist Church. Historical Society (US)
United Methodist Church. North Carolina Conference and Western North Carolina Conference (US)
United Methodist Church. North Mississippi and Mississippi Conference (US)
United Methodist Church. Section of Records and Statistics (US)
United Methodist Church. South Carolina Conference (US)
United Methodist Church. Virginia Conference (US)
United Methodist Church. West Michigan and Detroit Annual Conferences (US)
United Methodist Communications (US)
United Methodist Communications Council (US)
United Methodist Homes of New Jersey (US)
United Methodist Publishing House (US)
United Methodist Publishing House. Graded Press (US)
United Mine Workers (US)
United Missionaries in Higher Education (US)
United National Independence Party. Youth Wing (ZA)
United Nations (UN)
United Nations Association (UK)
United Nations Association of Australia (AT)
United Nations Association of New Zealand (NZ)
United Nations Association of the Republic of China (CH)
United Nations Association of the U.S.A. (US)
United Nations Central American Hydrometeorological Project (UN)
United Nations Central American Hydrometeorological Project. Regional Committee for Water Resources (UN)
United Nations. Centre for Economic and Social Information (UN)
United Nations. Centre for Housing, Building and Planning (UN)
United Nations. Centre for Natural Resources, Energy and Transport (UN)
United Nations Centre for Regional Development (UN)
United Nations. Centro Latinoamericano de Demografia (UN)
United Nations Children's Fund
  see Unicef (UN)
United Nations. Commission on International Trade Law (UN)
United Nations Conference on Trade and Development (UN)
United Nations. Department of Economic and Social Affairs (UN)
United Nations Development Programme (UN)
United Nations Disarmament Commission (UN)
United Nations. Division of Human Rights (UN)
United Nations. Division of Narcotic Drugs (UN)
United Nations Economic and Social Commission for Asia and the Far East
  see United Nations Economic and Social Commission for Asia and the Pacific (UN)
United Nations Economic and Social Commission for Asia and the Pacific (UN)
United Nations Economic and Social Commission for Asia and the Pacific. Asian Development Institute (UN)
United Nations Economic and Social Council (UN)
United Nations Economic Commission for Africa (UN)
United Nations Economic Commission for Europe (UN)
United Nations Economic Commission for Latin America (UN)

United Nations Economic Commission for Western Asia (UN)
United Nations Educational, Scientific and Cultural Organization
  see Unesco (UN)
United Nations Environment Programme (UN)
United Nations Fund for Population Activities (UN)
United Nations. General Assembly (UN)
United Nations High Commissioner for Refugees (UN)
United Nations Industrial Development Organization (UN)
United Nations Institute for Training and Research (UN)
United Nations. Institute of Nutrition of Central American and Panama (UN)
United Nations International Children's Emergency Fund
  see Unicef (UN)
United Nations International Law Commission (UN)
United Nations International Law Seminar (UN)
United Nations Library (UN)
United Nations Library, Geneva (UN)
United Nations. Protocol Section, Geneva Office (UN)
United Nations Publications (UN)
United Nations. Regional Center for Demographic Training and Research in Latin America
  see United Nations. Centro Latinoamericano de Demografia (UN)
United Nations Regional Housing Centre (IO)
United Nations Relief and Works Agency for Palestine Refugees in the Near East (UN)
United Nations Research Institute for Social Development (UN)
United Nations Security Council (UN)
United Nations Social Defense Research Institute (UN)
United Nations Statistical Office (UN)
United Nations Trade and Development Board (UN)
United Nations Trustee Council (UN)
United Nations World (AU)
United Native Americans, Inc. (US)
United Neighborhood Houses of New York (US)
United Newspapers Publications Ltd (UK)
United NFL Groups of Sweden (SW)
United Nurses Inc. (CN)
United Order of True Sisters (US)
United Ostomy Association, Inc. (US)
United Paperworkers International Union (US)
United Parents Associations of New York City (US)
United Planters' Association of Southern India (II)
United Planting Association of Malaysia (MY)
United Presbyterian Church in the U.S.A. (US)
United Presbyterian Church in the U. S. A. United Presbyterian Women (US)
United Presbyterian Health, Education and Welfare Association (US)
United Prospectors Inc. (US)
United Publications, Inc. (US)
United Publicity Services Ltd. (UK)
United Publishers (CM)
United Publishing Corp. (US)
United Radomer Relief for U.S. and Canada (CN)
United Reformed Church in England and Wales (UK)
United Reformed History Society (UK)
United Rubber, Cork, Linoleum and Plastic Workers of America (US)
United Russian Orthodox Brotherhood of America (US)
United Schools Organisation of India (II)
United Secularists of America (US)
United Senior Citizens of Ontario (CN)
United Service Institution of India (II)
United Service Organizations, Inc. (US)
United Sisters (US)
United Slate, Tile and Composition Roofers, Damp and Waterproof Workers' Association (US)
United Society for Christian Literature (UK)
United Society for the Propagation of the Gospel (UK)
United South African National Party (SA)
U. S. ACTION. National Student Volunteer Program
  see U. S. National Student Volunteer Program (US)
U. S. ACTION. Peace Corps
  see U. S. Peace Corps (US)
U.S. Administration on Aging (US)
U.S. Administrative Office of the United States Courts (US)
U. S. Advisory Commission on Intergovernmental Relations (US)
U. S. Advisory Commission on International Educational and Cultural Affairs (US)
U.S. Advisory Council on Historic Preservation (US)
U.S. Agency for International Development (US)
U.S. Agricultural Marketing Service (US)

U.S. Agricultural Marketing Service. Cotton Division (US)
U.S. Agricultural Marketing Service. Grain and Seed Division (US)
U.S. Agricultural Research Service (US)
U.S. Agricultural Research Service. Animal Improvement Programs Laboratory (US)
U. S. Agricultural Research Service. North Central Region (US)
U. S. Agricultural Research Service. Plum Island Animal Disease Center
  see U. S. Plum Island Animal Disease Center (US)
U.S. Agricultural Research Service. Southern Region (US)
U.S. Agricultural Research Service. Western Regional Research Center (US)
U.S. Air Force (US)
United States Air Force Academy (US)
U.S. Air Force Accounting and Finance Center (US)
U.S. Air Force. Air Training Command (US)
U.S. Air Force. Air University (US)
U.S. Air Force. Air University Library (US)
U.S. Air Force Association (US)
U. S. Air Force Cambridge Research Laboratories (US)
U.S. Air Force. Civil Air Patrol (US)
U.S. Air Force Inspection and Safety Center (US)
U.S. Air Force Institute of Technology. Civil Engineering School (US)
U.S. Air Force. Judge Advocate General's School (US)
U.S. Air Force. Military Airlift Command (US)
U.S. Air Force Office of Scientific Research (US)
U.S. Air Force. School of Aerospace Medicine (US)
U.S. Air Force Strategic Air Command (US)
U.S. Air Force Systems Command (US)
U. S. Alcohol, Drug Abuse, and Mental Health Administration. National Institute on Drug Abuse
  see U. S. National Institute on Drug Abuse (US)
U. S. Alcohol, Drug Abuse, and Mental Health Administration. National Institute of Mental Health
  see U. S. National Institute of Mental Health (US)
U.S. Animal and Plant Health Inspection Service (US)
U.S. Appalachian Regional Commission (US)
U. S. Archives of American Art
  see under Smithsonian Institution (US)
U.S. Arms Control and Disarmament Agency (US)
U.S. Army (US)
U. S. Army Administration Center (US)
U.S. Army Air Defense School (US)
U. S. Army Armor School (US)
U.S. Army Aviation School (US)
U.S. Army. Center of Military History (US)
U. S. Army Coastal Engineering Research Center
  see U. S. Coastal Engineering Research Center (US)
U. S. Army Cold Regions Research and Engineering Laboratory (US)
U.S. Army Command and General Staff College (US)
U.S. Army. Corps of Engineers. (US)
U. S. Army Corps of Engineers, Buffalo District (US)
U.S.Army. Corps of Engineers, Detroit District (US)
U.S. Army Electronics Command (US)
U.S. Army. Fitzsimons Army Medical Center (US)
U.S. Army Infantry School (US)
U.S.Army. Judge Advocate General's School (US)
U.S. Army Legal Services Agency (US)
U.S. Army Logistics Management Center (US)
U.S. Army Materiel Development and Readiness Command (US)
U.S. Army Medical Department (US)
U.S. Army Medical Research Institute of Infectious Diseases (US)
U.S. Army Military Police School (US)
U.S. Army. Military Traffic Management Command (US)
U.S. Army Personnel Information Activity (US)
U.S. Army Recruiting Command (US)
U.S. Army Reserve. Office of the Chief Army Reserve (US)
U.S. Army Russian Institute (US)
U.S. Army Security Agency (US)
U. S. Army War College (US)
U.S. Army Warrant Officers Assn. (US)
U.S. Board of Geographic Names (US)
U.S. Bureau of Community Health Service (US)
U. S. Bureau of Domestic Commerce
  see under U. S. Domestic and International Business Administration (US)
U. S. Bureau of East- West Trade
  see under U. S. Domestic and International Business Administration (US)
U.S. Bureau of Economic Analysis (US)
U.S. Bureau of Health Planning and Resources Development. Division of Nursing (US)
U. S. Bureau of Indian Affairs (US)

U.S. Department of Transportation. Federal Highway Administration. Federal Highway Administration
  see U.S. Federal Highway Administration  (US)
U.S. Department of Transportation. Federal Aviation Administration
  see U.S. Federal Aviation Administration  (US)
U.S. Department of Transportation. Federal Railroad Administration
  see U.S. Federal Railroad Administration  (US)
U.S. Department of Transportation. National Highway Traffic Safety Administration
  see U.S. National Highway Traffic Safety Administration  (US)
U.S. Department of Transportation. Saint Lawrence Seaway Development Corporation
  see U.S. Saint Lawrence Seaway Development Corporation  (US)
U.S. Department of Transportation. U.S. Coast Guard
  see U.S. Coast Guard  (US)
U.S. Department of Transportation. Urban Mass Transportation Administration
  see U.S. Urban Mass Transportation Administration  (US)
U. S. District of Columbia
  see District of Columbia  (US)
U.S. Domestic and International Business Administration  (US)
U.S. Domestic and International Business Administration. Bureau of Domestic Commerce  (US)
U.S. Domestic and International Business Administration. Bureau of East-West Trade  (US)
U.S. Domestic and International Business Administration. Bureau of International Commerce  (US)
U.S. Domestic and International Business Administration. Bureau of International Economic Policy and Research  (US)
U.S. Drug Enforcement Administration  (US)
U.S. Economic Development Administration. Office of Economic Research  (US)
U. S. Educational Resources Information Center
  see E R I C  (US)
U. S. Embassy
  see Embassy of the United States in Japan  (JA)
U.S. Embassy  (GY)
U. S. Emergency Loan Guarantee Board  (US)
U.S. Employment and Training Administration  (US)
U.S. Employment and Training Administration. Unemployment Insurance Service
  see U.S. Unemployment Insurance Service  (US)
U.S. Employment Standards Administration  (US)
U.S. Employment Standards Administration. Women's Bureau  (US)
U.S. Energy Research and Development Administration. Technical Information Center  (US)
U.S. Environmental Data Service  (US)
U.S. Environmental Data Service. National Climatic Center
  see U.S. National Climatic Center  (US)
U.S. Environmental Data Service. National Geophyiscal and Solar-Terrestrial Data Center
  see U.S. National Geophysical and Solar-Terrestrial Data Center  (US)
U.S. Environmental Data Service. National Oceanographic Data Center
  see U.S. National Oceanographic Data Center  (US)
U.S. Environmental Data Service. World Data Center A for Glaciology  (US)
U.S. Environmental Protection Agency  (US)
U. S. Environmental Protection Agency. Arctic Environmental Research Laboratory  (US)
U. S. Environmental Protection Agency. Grosse Ile Laboratory  (US)
U. S. Environmental Protection Agency. Gulf Breeze Environmental Research Laboratory  (US)
U. S. Environmental Protection Agency. National Marine Water Quality Laboratory  (US)
U. S. Environmental Protection Agency. National Water Quality Laboratory  (US)
U.S. Environmental Protection Agency. Office of Air Quality Planning and Standards  (US)
U.S. Environmental Protection Agency. Office of Pesticides Programs  (US)
U.S. Environmental Protection Agency. Office of Radiation Programs  (US)
U.S. Environmental Protection Agency. Region V  (US)
U.S. Environmental Protection Agency. Water Planning Division  (US)
U.S. Equal Employment Opportunity Commission  (US)
U. S. Executive Office of the President  (US)

U. S. Executive Office of the President. Central Intelligence Agency
  see U. S. Central Intelligence Agency  (US)
U.S. Executive Office of the President. Council of Economic Advisers  (US)
U.S. Executive Office of the President. Office of Management and Budget
  see U. S. Office of Management and Budget  (US)
U. S. Export- Import Bank
  see Export- Import Bank of the United States  (US)
U.S. Farm Credit Administration.  (US)
U.S. Farmer Cooperative Service  (US)
U. S. Federal Aviation Administration  (US)
U. S. Federal Bureau of Investigation  (US)
U.S. Federal Communications Commission  (US)
U.S. Federal Council for Science and Technology. Interdepartmental Committee for Atmospheric Sciences  (US)
U.S. Federal Crop Insurance Corporation.  (US)
U.S. Federal Deposit Insurance Corporation  (US)
U.S. Federal Energy Administration  (US)
U. S. Federal Fire Council  (US)
U. S. Federal Highway Administration  (US)
U. S. Federal Home Loan Bank Board  (US)
U. S. Federal Housing Administration  (US)
U. S. Federal Judicial Center  (US)
U.S. Federal Maritime Commission.  (US)
U.S. Federal Mediation and Conciliation Service.  (US)
U.S. Federal Power Commission  (US)
U. S. Federal Railroad Administration  (US)
U.S. Federal Reserve System. Board of Governors  (US)
U.S. Federal Trade Commission.  (US)
U. S. Fish and Wildlife Service  (US)
U. S. Food and Drug Administration  (US)
U.S. Food and Drug Administration. Bureau of Radiological Health
  see U.S. Bureau of Radiological Health  (US)
U. S. Food and Drug Administration. National Clearinghouse for Poison Control Centers
  see U. S. National Clearinghouse for Poison Control Centers  (US)
U.S. Foreign Agricultural Service  (US)
U.S. Foreign Broadcast Information Service  (US)
U.S. Forest Products Laboratory
  see under U.S. Forest Service. Forest Products Laboratory  (US)
U. S. Forest Service  (US)
U. S. Forest Service. Forest Products Laboratory  (US)
U. S. Forest Service. Intermountain Forest and Range Experiment Station  (US)
U.S. Forest Service. North Central Forest Experiment Station  (US)
U.S. Forest Service. Northeastern Forest Experiment Station  (US)
U.S. Forest Service. Pacific Northwest Forest and Range Experiment Station  (US)
U. S. Forest Service. Pacific Southwest Forest and Range Experiment Station  (US)
U. S. Forest Service. Rocky Mountain Forest and Range Experiment Station  (US)
U.S. Forest Service. Southern Forest Experiment Station  (US)
U.S. General Accounting Office  (US)
U. S. General Services Administration  (US)
U.S. General Services Administration. Consumer Information Center  (US)
U. S. General Services Administration. National Archives and Records Service
  see U. S. National Archives and Records Service  (US)
U. S. General Services Administration. National Audiovisual Center
  see U.S. National Audiovisual Center  (US)
U.S. General Services Administration. Office of Preparedness  (US)
U.S. General Services Administration. Public Buildings Service  (US)
U. S. Geological Survey  (PR)
U.S. Geological Survey  (US)
U. S. Geological Survey. National Cartographic Information Center
  see U. S. National Cartographic Information Center  (US)
U.S. Geological Survey. National Earthquake Information Center  (US)
U.S. Geological Survey. Seismic Engineering Branch  (US)
U.S. Geological Survey. Water Resources Division (New York)  (US)
U.S. Government Printing Office  (US)

U.S. Health Resources Administration  (US)
U.S. Health Resources Administration. Bureau of Health Planning and Resources Development
  see U.S. Bureau of Health Planning and Resources Development  (US)
U. S. Health Resources Administration. National Center for Health Statistics
  see U. S. National Center for Health Statistics  (US)
U. S. Health Services Administration. Bureau of Community Health Service
  see U. S. Bureau of Community Health Service  (US)
U.S. Health Services Administration. Indian Health Service
  see U.S. Indian Health Service  (US)
U.S. Immigration and Naturalization Service  (US)
U.S. Indian Arts and Crafts Board  (US)
U.S. Indian Health Service  (US)
U.S. Industrial College of the Armed Forces  (US)
U.S. Information Agency  (PH)
U. S. Information Agency  (US)
U.S. Information Service  (NR)
U. S. Information Service  (FR)
U.S. Information Service  (IR)
U.S. Institute of Tropical Forestry  (PR)
U.S. Interagency Arctic Research Coordinating Committee  (US)
U. S. Interim Compliance Panel  (US)
U.S. Intermountain Forest and Range Experiment Station
  see under U.S. Forest Service  (US)
U. S. Internal Revenue Service  (US)
U.S. International Trade Commission  (US)
U.S. Interstate Commerce Commission  (US)
U.S. Labor Management Services Administration  (US)
U.S. Law Enforcement Assistance Administration  (US)
U.S. Law Enforcement Assistance Administration. National Criminal Justice Information and Statistics Service
  see U.S. National Criminal Justice Information and Statistics Service  (US)
U.S. Library of Congress  (US)
U.S. Library of Congress. Copyright Office  (US)
U. S. Library of Congress. Division for the Blind and Physically Handicapped  (US)
U. S. Library of Congress. Federal Library Committee  (US)
U.S. Library of Congress. Overseas Operations Division  (US)
U.S. Marine Corps  (US)
U.S. Marine Corps. History and Museums Division  (US)
U.S. Maritime Administration  (US)
U. S. Military Academy  (US)
U.S. Mining Enforcement and Safety Administration  (US)
U.S. National Advisory Committee on the Handicapped  (US)
U.S. National Advisory Council on Extension and Continuing Education  (US)
U. S. National Advisory Council on Indian Education  (US)
U.S. National Aeronautics and Space Administration  (US)
U. S. National Aeronautics and Space Administration. Goddard Space Flight Center
  see Goddard Space Flight Center  (US)
U.S. National Aeronautics and Space Administration. Jet Propulsion Laboratory  (US)
U. S. National Aeronautics and Space Administration. Technology Utilization Office  (US)
U.S. National Agricultural Library  (US)
U. S. National Archives and Records Service  (US)
U. S. National Archives and Records Service. National Historical Publications and Records Commission
  see U. S. National Historical Publications and Records Commission  (US)
U.S. National Archives and Records Service. Office of the Federal Register
  see U.S. Office of the Federal Register  (US)
U.S. National Audiovisual Center  (US)
U. S. National Bureau of Standards  (US)
U. S. National Bureau of Standards. Cryogenic Data Center  (US)
U. S. National Bureau of Standards. Electromagnetic Metrology Information Center  (US)
U.S. National Bureau of Standards. High Pressure Data Center  (US)
U.S. National Cancer Institute  (US)
U.S. National Capital Planning Commission  (US)
U.S. National Cartographic Information Center  (US)
U.S. National Center for Education Communications  (US)
U. S. National Center for Education Statistics  (US)
U.S. National Center for Health Statistics  (US)

United States Auto Club  (US)
United States Basketball Writers Association  (US)
United States Catholic Conference  (US)
United States Catholic Conference. Department of
  Education  (US)
United States Catholic Mission Council  (US)
United States Chess Federation  (US)
United States Coalition for Life  (US)
United States Committee for Refugees  (US)
United States Committee for UNICEF  (US)
United States Committee on Large Dams  (US)
United States Conference for the World Council of
  Churches  (US)
United States Conference of Mayors  (US)
United States Cross-Country Coaches Association
  (US)
United States Divorce Reform, Inc.  (US)
United States East-West Trade Center  (AU)
United States Educational Foundation in India  (II)
United States Fidelity and Guaranty Co.  (US)
United States Field Hockey Association  (US)
United States Golf Association  (US)
United States Hereditary Register, Inc.  (US)
United States Hockey League  (US)
United States Independent Telephone Association
  (US)
United States Industrial Chemicals Co.  (US)
United States Industrial Publications, Inc.  (US)
United States Information Service  (HK)
United States Information Service  (IT)
United States International University  (US)
United States International University. Doctoral
  Society  (US)
United States - Israel Binational Science Foundation
  (IS)
United States Judicial Reporter  (US)
United States Judo Association, Inc.  (US)
United States Lawn Tennis Association  (US)
United States League of Savings Associations  (US)
United States Olympic Committee  (US)
United States Pharmacopeial Convention, Inc.  (US)
United States Polo Association  (US)
United States Polo Association (Middleburg)  (US)
United States Professional Tennis Association  (US)
United States Review Publishing Co.  (US)
United States Ski Association  (US)
United States Soccer Federation  (US)
United States Squash Racquets Association  (US)
United States Steel Corp.  (US)
United States Table Tennis Association  (US)
United States Tobacco Journal  (US)
United States Track Coaches Association  (US)
United States Trademark Association  (US)
United States Trotting Association  (US)
United States Volleyball Association  (US)
United Steelworkers of America  (CN)
United Steelworkers of America  (US)
United Synagogue of America  (US)
United Synagogue of America. Commission on Jewish
  Education  (US)
United Synagogue of America. Department of Youth
  Activities  (US)
United Synagogue of America. National Academy for
  Adult Jewish Studies  (US)
United Talmudical Academy  (US)
United Teachers of Dade  (US)
United Technical Publications, Inc.  (US)
United Technologies Corp.  (US)
United Telegraph Workers  (US)
United Theological Seminary of the Twin Cities  (US)
United Thoroughbred Trainers of America, Inc.  (US)
United Towns Organization  (FR)
United Trade Press Ltd.  (UK)
United Transportation Union  (US)
United Transvestite Transexual Society  (US)
United Way for the Greater New Orleans Area  (US)
United Way of America  (US)
United Women's Societies of the Adoration of the
  Most Blessed Sacrament  (US)
United Writers Publications  (UK)
Unites s.r.l.  (IT)
Uniti Bundesverband Mittelstaendischer
  Mineraloelunternehmen e.V.  (GW)
Unity Buying Service, Inc.  (US)
Unity Compound  (II)
Unity in Diversity Centers  (US)
Unity of the Brethren  (US)
Unity Publications (Finchley) Ltd  (UK)
Unity School of Christianity  (US)
Uniunea Arhitectilor din Republica Socialista Romania
  (RM)
Uniunea Artistilor Plastici din Republica Socialista
  Romania  (RM)
Uniunea Compozitorilor din Republica Socialista
  Romania  (RM)

Uniunea Generala a Sindicatelor din Romania.
  Consiliul Central  (RM)
Uniunea Scriitorilor din Republica Socialista Romania
  (RM)
Uniunea Scriitorilor din Republica Socialista Romania
  (Timisoara)  (RM)
Uniunea Societatilor De Stiinte Medicale Din
  Republica Socialista Romania  (RM)
Uniunea Ziaristilor din Republica Socialista Romania
  (RM)
Editura Univers  (RM)
Editions Universa  (BE)
Universal Business Directories (Australia) Pty. Ltd.
  (AT)
Universal Business Directories (Vic.) Pty. Ltd.  (AT)
Universal Business Directories (WA) Pty. Ltd.  (AT)
Universal Business Directories Ltd.  (NZ)
Universal Center  (US)
Universal Christian Publications  (US)
Universal Coterie of Pipe Smokers  (US)
Universal Edition AG  (AU)
Universal Edition Sales, Inc.  (US)
Universal Esperanto Association  (US)
Universal Fellowship of Metropolitan Community
  Churches. Board of Institutional Ministry  (US)
Universal Fellowship Press  (US)
Universal Graphics Corp.  (US)
Universal News, Inc.  (US)
Universal Oil Products Co. Johnson Division  (US)
Universal Postal Union  (UN)
Universal Publications Ltd.  (NR)
Universal Publications of America  (US)
Universal Publishing and Distributing Corp.  (US)
Universal Serials and Book Exchange  (US)
Universal Services, Inc.  (US)
Universal Spiritual League in America Inc.  (US)
Universala Esperanto-Asocio  (NE)
Universalist Historical Society  (US)
Universariun Foundation, Inc.  (US)
Universe Press Agency Ltd.  (NZ)
Universidad Austral de Chile. Facultad de Ciencias
  Agrarias  (CL)
Universidad Austral de Chile. Facultad de Filosofia y
  Letras  (CL)
Universidad Austral de Chile. Instituto de Filologica
  (CL)
Universidad Autonoma de Barcelona  (SP)
Universidad Autonoma de Guadalajara  (MX)
Universidad Autonoma de Madrid. Fundacion
  Universidad Empresa  (SP)
Universidad Autonoma de San Luis Potosi  (MX)
Universidad Autonoma de San Luis Potosi. Instituto
  de Geologia y Metalurgia  (MX)
Imprenta de Universidad Autonoma de Santo
  Domingo  (DR)
Universidad Autonoma de Santo Domingo. Biblioteca
  Central  (DR)
Universidad Autonoma de Santo Domingo. Comision
  para el Desarrollo y Reforma Universitarios  (DR)
Universidad Autonoma de Santo Domingo. Direccion
  de Investigaciones  (DR)
Universidad Autonoma de Santo Domingo. Direccion
  de Investigaciones Cientificas  (DR)
Universidad Autonoma de Santo Domingo. Escuela de
  Ciencias de la Informacios Publica  (DR)
Universidad Autonoma de Santo Domingo. Facultad
  de Ciencias Economicas y Sociales  (DR)
Universidad Autonoma de Santo Domingo. Facultad
  de Humanidades  (DR)
Universidad Autonoma de Sinaloa. Escuela de
  Economia  (MX)
Universidad Autonoma del Estado de Mexico.
  Instituto de Investigaciones Historicas  (MX)
Universidad Autonoma Latinoamericana  (CK)
Universidad Boliviana Gabriel Rene Moreno  (BO)
Universidad Boliviana Juan Misael Saracho  (BO)
Universidad Boliviana Mayor de San Andres. Facultad
  de Derecho, Ciencias Politicas y Sociales  (BO)
Universidad Boliviana Mayor de San Andres. Facultad
  de Economia, Juridica y Ciencias Sociales  (BO)
Universidad Boliviana Mayor de "San Simon"  (BO)
Universidad Boliviana Mayor de "San Simon".
  Facultad de Economia, Juridica y Ciencias Sociales
  (BO)
Universidad Boliviana Tecnica de Oruro. Centro de
  Estudiantes de Ciencias Economicas  (BO)
Universidad Boliviana Tecnica de Oruro.
  Departamento de Extension Cultural  (BO)
Universidad Catolica Andres Bello. Centro de Estudios
  del Futuro de Venezuela  (VE)
Universidad Catolica Andres Bello. Facultad de Letras
  (VE)
Universidad Catolica Andres Bello. Instituto de
  Investigaciones Economicas  (VE)
Editorial Universidad Catolica de Chile  (CL)

Universidad Catolica de Chile. Centro de Estudios de
  la Realidad Nacional  (CL)
Universidad Catolica de Chile. Escuela Artes de la
  Comunicacion  (CL)
Universidad Catolica de Chile. Escuela de Teatro, Cine
  y Television  (CL)
Universidad Catolica de Chile. Escuela de Trabajo
  Social  (CL)
Universidad Catolica de Chile. Facultad de Agronomia
  (CL)
Universidad Catolica de Chile. Facultad de Teologia
  (CL)
Universidad Catolica de Chile. Instituto de Economia
  (CL)
Universidad Catolica de Chile. Instituto de Estetica
  (CL)
Universidad Catolica de Chile. Instituto de Historia
  (CL)
Universidad Catolica de Chile. Instituto de
  Matematicas  (CL)
Universidad Catolica de Chile. Instituto de
  Planificacion del Desarrollo Urbano  (CL)
Universidad Catolica de Chile. Seminario
  Latinoamericano  (CL)
Universidad Catolica de Puerto Rico  (PR)
Universidad Catolica de Puerto Rico. School of Law
  (PR)
Universidad Catolica de Valparaiso  (CL)
Universidad Catolica de Valparaiso. Centro de
  Investigaciones del Mar  (CL)
Universidad Catolica de Valparaiso. Instituto de
  Geografia  (CL)
Universidad Catolica de Valparaiso. Instituto de
  Lenguas y Literatura  (CL)
Universidad Catolica. Instituto de Letras  (CL)
Universidad Catolica Madre y Maestra. Centro de
  Estudios Dominicanos  (DR)
Universidad Catolica Nuestra Senora de la Asuncion
  (PY)
Universidad Catolica Nuestra Senora de la Asuncion.
  Centro de Estudios Antropologicos  (PY)
Universidad Central de las Villas. Faculty of
  Humanities  (CU)
Universidad Central de Venezuela  (VE)
Universidad Central de Venezuela. Academia de
  Ciencias Politicas y Sociales  (VE)
Universidad Central de Venezuela. Biblioteca Central
  (VE)
Universidad Central de Venezuela. Consejo de
  Desarrollo Cientifico y Humanistico  (VE)
Universidad Central de Venezuela. Direccion de
  Cultura  (VE)
Universidad Central de Venezuela. Escuela de Biologia
  (VE)
Universidad Central de Venezuela. Facultad de
  Agronomia  (VE)
Universidad Central de Venezuela. Facultad de
  Ciencias Economicas y Sociales  (VE)
Universidad Central de Venezuela. Facultad de
  Ciencias Veterinarias  (VE)
Universidad Central de Venezuela. Facultad de
  Derecho  (VE)
Universidad Central de Venezuela. Facultad de
  Farmacia  (VE)
Universidad Central de Venezuela. Facultad de
  Humanidades y Educacion  (VE)
Universidad Central de Venezuela. Facultad de
  Odontologia  (VE)
Universidad Central de Venezuela. Instituto de
  Antropologia e Historia  (VE)
Universidad Central de Venezuela. Instituto de
  Estudios Hispanoamericanos  (VE)
Universidad Central del Ecuador  (EC)
Universidad Central del Ecuador. Biblioteca General
  (EC)
Universidad Central del Ecuador. Facultad de Ciencias
  Economicas y Administrativas  (EC)
Universidad Central del Ecuador. Instituto de Ciencias
  Naturales  (EC)
Universidad Central del Ecuador. Instituto de
  Criminologia  (EC)
Universidad Central del Ecuador. Instituto de Derecho
  Comparado  (EC)
Universidad Central del Ecuador. Instituto de Estudios
  Administrativos  (EC)
Universidad Central del Ecuador. Instituto de
  Investigaciones Economicas  (EC)
Universidad Central del Ecuador. Instituto Ecuatoriano
  de Derecho Internacional  (EC)
Universidad Centroamericana  (NQ)
Universidad Centroamericana "Jose Simeon Canas"
  (ES)
Universidad Complutense de Madrid  (SP)
Universidad Complutense de Madrid. Centro de
  Calculo  (SP)
Universidad Complutense de Madrid. Consejo Superior
  de Investigaciones Cientificas  (SP)

Universidad de Uruguay. Facultad de Agronomia (UY)

Universidad de Uruguay. Instituto de Matematica y Estadistica (UY)

Universidad de Valencia (SP)

Universidad de Valencia. Facultad de Filosofia y Letras (SP)

Universidad de Valladolid. Facultad de Medicina (SP)

Universidad de Yucatan (MX)

Universidad de Zaragoza. Facultad de Medicina (SP)

Universidad del Atlantico. Instituto de Investigacion Etnologica (CK)

Universidad del Cauca. Archivo Central del Cauca (CK)

Universidad del Museo Social Argentina. Estudiantes Universitarios de Psicologia (AG)

Universidad del Norte. Departamento de Agricultura (CL)

Universidad del Norte. Museo de Arqueologia (CL)

Universidad del Norte "San Tomas de Aquino". Facultad de Agronomia y Zootecnia (AG)

Universidad del Salvador (AG)

Universidad del Salvador. Facultad de Psicopedagogia (AG)

Universidad del Salvador. Facultades de Filosofia y Teologia (AG)

Universidad del Valle. Departamento de Bibliotecas (CK)

Universidad del Valle. Division de Ciencias Sociales y Economicas (CK)

Universidad del Valle. Division de Humanidades (CK)

Universidad del Zulia. Escuela de Comunicacion Social (VE)

Universidad del Zulia. Facultad de Agronomia (VE)

Universidad del Zulia. Facultad de Derecho (VE)

Universidad del Zulia. Facultad de Humanidades y Educacion (VE)

Universidad del Zulia. Facultad de Medicina (VE)

Universidad del Zulia, Instituto de Investigacion Clinica. Facultad de Medicina (VE)

Universidad Externado de Colombia (CK)

Universidad Iberoamericana (MX)

Universidad Industrial de Santander (CK)

Universidad Internacional Menendez Pelayo (SP)

Universidad Javeriana. Facultad de Teologia (CK)

Universidad La Gran Colombia (CK)

Universidad Mayor, Real y Pontificia de San Francisco Xavier de Chuquisaca (BO)

Universidad Nacional Agraria (PE)

Universidad Nacional Autonoma de el Salvador. Instituto de Estudios Economicas (ES)

Universidad Nacional Autonoma de Honduras. Facultad de Ciencias Juridicas y Sociales (HO)

Universidad Nacional Autonoma de Honduras. Instituto de Investigaciones Economicas y Sociales (HO)

Universidad Nacional Autonoma de Mexico (MX)

Universidad Nacional Autonoma de Mexico. Biblioteca Nacional e Instituto de Investigaciones Bibliograficas (MX)

Universidad Nacional Autonoma de Mexico. Centro de Estudios Mayas (MX)

Universidad Nacional Autonoma de Mexico. Direccion General de Difusion Cultural (MX)

Universidad Nacional Autonoma de Mexico. Facultad de Ciencias Politicas y Sociales (MX)

Universidad Nacional Autonoma de Mexico. Facultad de Comercio y Adminstracion (MX)

Universidad Nacional Autonoma de Mexico. Facultad de Contaduria Administracion (MX)

Universidad Nacional Autonoma de Mexico. Facultad de Derecho (MX)

Universidad Nacional Autonoma de Mexico. Facultad de Filosofia y Letras (MX)

Universidad Nacional Autonoma de Mexico. Facultad de Ingenieria (MX)

Universidad Nacional Autonoma de Mexico. Facultad de Medicina (MX)

Universidad Nacional Autonoma de Mexico. Facultad de Medicina Veterinaria y Zootecnia (MX)

Universidad Nacional Autonoma de Mexico. Instituto de Astronomia (MX)

Universidad Nacional Autonoma de Mexico. Instituto de Biologia (MX)

Universidad Nacional Autonoma de Mexico. Instituto de Geofisica (MX)

Universidad Nacional Autonoma de Mexico. Instituto de Geografia (MX)

Universidad Nacional Autonoma de Mexico. Instituto de Geologia (MX)

Universidad Nacional Autonoma de Mexico. Instituto de Investigaciones Antropologicas (MX)

Universidad Nacional Autonoma de Mexico. Instituto de Investigaciones Esteticas (MX)

Universidad Nacional Autonoma de Mexico. Instituto de Investigaciones Filosoficas (MX)

Universidad Nacional Autonoma de Mexico. Instituto de Investigaciones Historicas (MX)

Universidad Nacional Autonoma de Mexico. Instituto de Investigaciones Juridicas (MX)

Universidad Nacional Autonoma de Mexico. Instituto de Investigaciones Sociales (MX)

Universidad Nacional Autonoma de Mexico. Instituto de Matematicas (MX)

Universidad Nacional Autonoma de Mexico. Seminario de Investigaciones Bibliotecologicas (MX)

Universidad Nacional Autonoma de Nicaragua (NQ)

Universidad Nacional Autonoma de Nicaragua. Biblioteca Central (NQ)

Universidad Nacional de Asuncion. Facultad de Ciencias Medicas (PY)

Universidad Nacional de Colombia (CK)

Universidad Nacional de Colombia. Biblioteca Central (CK)

Universidad Nacional de Colombia. Departamento de Farmacia (CK)

Universidad Nacional de Colombia. Dept. de Filosofia y Humanidades (CK)

Universidad Nacional de Colombia. Departamento de Geologia (CK)

Universidad Nacional de Colombia. Facultad de Artes (CK)

Universidad Nacional de Colombia. Facultad de Ciencias (CK)

Universidad Nacional de Colombia. Facultad de Ciencias Agropecuarias (CK)

Universidad Nacional de Colombia. Facultad de Ciencias Humanas (CK)

Universidad Nacional de Colombia. Facultad de Ingenieria (CK)

Universidad Nacional de Colombia. Facultad de Odontologia (CK)

Universidad Nacional de Colombia. Facultad Nacional de Minas (CK)

Universidad Nacional de Colombia. Instituto de Ciencias Naturales (CK)

Universidad Nacional de Cordoba. Division Publicaciones de la Escuela de Ciencias Politicas y Relaciones Internationales (AG)

Universidad Nacional de Cordoba. Facultad de Ciencias Economicas (AG)

Universidad Nacional de Cordoba. Facultad de Ciencias Exactas, Fisicas y Naturales (AG)

Universidad Nacional de Cordoba. Facultad de Ciencias Medicas (AG)

Universidad Nacional de Cordoba. Facultad de Derecho y Ciencias Sociales (AG)

Universidad Nacional de Cordoba. Facultad de Filosofia y Humanidades (AG)

Universidad Nacional de Cordoba. Facultad de Odontologia (AG)

Universidad Nacional de Cordoba. Instituto de Derecho Constitucional (AG)

Universidad Nacional de Cordoba. Instituto de Economia y Finanzas (AG)

Universidad Nacional de Cuyo (AG)

Universidad Nacional de Cuyo. Biblioteca Central (AG)

Universidad Nacional de Cuyo. Facultad de Ciencias Economicas (AG)

Universidad Nacional de Cuyo. Facultad de Ciencias Politicas y Sociales (AG)

Universidad Nacional de Cuyo. Instituto de Arqueologia y Etnologia (AG)

Universidad Nacional de Cuyo. Instituto de Filosofia (AG)

Universidad Nacional de Cuyo. Instituto de Sociologia (AG)

Universidad Nacional de la Plata (AG)

Universidad Nacional de la Plata. Biblioteca Publica (AG)

Universidad Nacional de la Plata. Facultad de Agronomia (AG)

Universidad Nacional de la Plata. Facultad de Ciencias Economicas (AG)

Universidad Nacional de la Plata. Facultad de Ciencias Economicas-Biblioteca (Hemeroteca) (AG)

Universidad Nacional de la Plata. Facultad de Humanidades y Ciencias de la Educacion (AG)

Universidad Nacional de la Plata. Instituto de Filosofia (AG)

Universidad Nacional de la Plata. Instituto de Investigaciones Administrativas (AG)

Universidad Nacional de la Plata. Instituto de la Produccion (AG)

Universidad Nacional de Rosario (AG)

Universidad Nacional de San Agustin (PE)

Universidad Nacional de San Marcos (PE)

Universidad Nacional de Trujillo (PE)

Universidad Nacional de Tucuman. Facultad de Ciencias Exactas y Tecnologia (AG)

Universidad Nacional de Tucuman. Facultad de Filosofia y Letras (AG)

Universidad Nacional de Tucuman. Instituto de Derecho Publico (AG)

Universidad Nacional de Tucuman. Instituto de Ingenieria Electrica (AG)

Universidad Nacional del Centro del Peru. Departamento de Publicaciones e Impresiones (PE)

Universidad Nacional del Cuzco. Sociedad Peruana de Folklore (PE)

Universidad Nacional del Litoral (AG)

Universidad Nacional del Litoral. Facultad de Ciencias de la Administracion (AG)

Universidad Nacional del Litoral. Facultad de Ciencias Economicas Comerciales y Politicas (AG)

Universidad Nacional del Litoral. Facultad de Ciencias Juridicas y Sociales (AG)

Universidad Nacional del Nordeste. Facultad de Humanidades (AG)

Universidad Nacional del Nordeste. Instituto de Geografia (AG)

Universidad Nacional del Nordeste. Instituto de Letras (AG)

Universidad Nacional del Sur. Centro de Documentacion Bibliotecologica (AG)

Universidad Nacional del Sur. Instituto de Economia (AG)

Universidad Nacional del Sur. Instituto de Matematica (AG)

Universidad Nacional Federico Villareal. Departamento de Ciencias Historico Sociales (PE)

Universidad Nacional Federico Villareal. Facultad de Derecho (PE)

Universidad Nacional Mayor de San Marcos. Departamento de Sociologia (PE)

Universidad Nacional Mayor de San Marcos. Facultad de Ciencias Economicas y Comerciales (PE)

Universidad Nacional Mayor de San Marcos. Facultad de Derecho (PE)

Universidad Nacional Mayor de San Marcos. Instituto de Biologia Andina (PE)

Universidad Nacional Mayor de San Marcos. Instituto Veterinario de Investigaciones Tropicales y de Altura (PE)

Universidad Nacional "Pedro Henriquez Urena" (DR)

Universidad Nacional San Luis Gonzaga. Facultad de Odontologia (PE)

Universidad Pedagogica y Tecnologica de Colombia. Fundo Especial de Publicaciones y Ayudas Educativas (CK)

Universidad Politecnica de Barcelona (SP)

Universidad Politecnica de Barcelona. Instituto de Investigacion Textil y de Cooperacion Industrial. (SP)

Universidad Politecnica de Madrid. Escuela Tecnica Superior de Ingenieros de Montes (SP)

Universidad Pontificia Bolivariana. Facultad de Filosifia y Letras (CK)

Universidad Pontificia de Salamanca (SP)

Universidad Pontificia Salamanca. Centro Estudios Orientales y Ecumenicos (SP)

Universidad, Santiago de Compostela. Seminario de Arqueologia (SP)

Universidad Simon Bolivar (VE)

Universidad Simon Bolivar. Departamento de Filosofia (VE)

Universidad Tecnica del Estado (CL)

Universidad Tecnica Federico Santa Maria (CL)

Universidad Tecnologica del Magdalena (CK)

Universidad Veracruzana (MX)

Universidade Catolica de Campinas (BL)

Universidade Catolica de Campinas. Dept. of Geography (BL)

Universidade Catolica de Goias. Gabinete de Arqueologia (BL)

Universidade Catolica de Minas Gerais. Escola de Servico Social (BL)

Universidade Catolica de Pernambuco. Biblioteca Central (BL)

Universidade Catolica do Parana. Departamento de Letras (BL)

Universidade Catolica Portuguesa. Faculdade de Teologia (PO)

Universidade de Brasilia. Departamento de Biblioteconomia (BL)

Universidade de Coimbra. Arquivo (PO)

Universidade de Coimbra. Departamento de Zoologia (PO)

Universidade de Coimbra. Faculdade de Direito (PO)

Universidade de Coimbra. Faculdade de Farmacia (PO)

Universidade de Coimbra. Faculdade de Letras (PO)

Universidade de Coimbra. Faculdade de Medicina (PO)

Universidade de Coimbra. Instituto Botanico (PO)

Universita degli Studi di Palermo. Clinica Tisiologica (IT)
Universita degli Studi di Perugia (IT)
Universita degli Studi di Perugia. Division of Cancer Research (IT)
Universita degli Studi di Perugia. Facolta di Medicina e Chirurgia (IT)
Universita degli Studi di Perugia. Istituto di Anatomia e Istologia Patologica (IT)
Universita degli Studi di Perugia. Istituto di Idrobiologia (IT)
Universita degli Studi di Perugia. Istituto di Igene (IT)
Universita degli Studi di Pisa. Istituto di Glottologia (IT)
Universita degli Studi di Pisa. Rettorato (IT)
Universita degli Studi di Sicilia (IT)
Universita degli Studi di Trieste (IT)
Universita degli Studi di Trieste. Facolta di Scienze Politiche (IT)
Universita degli Studi di Trieste. Istituto di Chimica Farmaceutica (IT)
Universita degli Studi di Trieste. Istituto di Pedagogia (IT)
Universita degli Studi di Trieste. Istituto di Ricerche Economico-Agrarie (IT)
Universita degli Studi di Trieste. Istituto di Storia dell'Arte (IT)
Universita degli Studi di Urbino. Istituto di Storia dell'Arte (IT)
Universita degli Studi di Venezia. Laboratorio di Economia Politica e Servizio Studi Economici "A. de Pietri-Tonelli" (IT)
Universita di Bari. Facolta di Scienza (IT)
Universita di Cagliari (IT)
Universita di Cagliari. Facolta di Magistero (IT)
Universita di Cagliari. Facolta di Medicina Chirurgia (IT)
Universita di Cagliari. Faculta di Scienze (IT)
Universita di Cagliari. Istituto di Storia Medioevale (IT)
Universita di Cagliari. Istituto Economico-Statistico (IT)
Universita di Catania. Facolta di Lettere e Filosofia (IT)
Universita di Catania. Istituto di Storia delle Tradizioni Popolari (IT)
Universita di Catania. Istituto di Storia Economica (IT)
Universita di Ferrara (IT)
Universita di Ferrara. Istituto di Geologia, Paleontologia e Paleontologia Umana (IT)
Universita di Ferrara. Istituto di Mineralogia (IT)
Universita di Genova. Istituto de Filosofia del Diritto (IT)
Universita di Genova. Istituto di Filologia Classica e Medievale (IT)
Universita di Genova. Istituto di Geologia (IT)
Universita di Genova. Istituto di Igiene (IT)
Universita di Genova. Istituto di Paleografia e Storia Medievale (IT)
Universita di Genova. Istituto di Progettazione Architettonica (IT)
Universita di Genova. Istituto di Zoologia (IT)
Universita di Genova. Istituto Scientifico di Medicina Interna (IT)
Universita di Macerata. Facolta di Lettere e Filosofie (IT)
Universita di Modena. Seminario Matematico e Fisico (IT)
Universita di Napoli. Istituto di Medicina del Lavoro (IT)
Universita di Padova (IT)
Universita di Padova. Clinica Ortopedica (IT)
Universita di Padova. Clinica Pediatrica (IT)
Universita di Padova. Facolta di Lettere e Filosofia (IT)
Universita di Padova. Facolta di Medicina e Chirurgia (IT)
Universita di Padova. Istituto di Idraulica (IT)
Universita di Padova. Istituto di Letterature Straniere (IT)
Universita di Padova. Istituto di Pedagogia (IT)
Universita di Padova. Istituto di Storia Antica (IT)
Universita di Padova. Istituto di Storia della Medicina (IT)
Universita di Padova. Scuola di Perfezionamento in Filosofia (IT)
Universita di Palermo. Facolta di Economia e Commercio (IT)
Universita di Palermo. Facolta di Lettere e Filosofia (IT)
Universita di Palermo. Istituto di Filologia Greca (IT)
Universita di Parma (IT)
Universita di Parma. Istituto di Chimica Generale (IT)
Universita di Parma. Istituto di Matematica (IT)

Universita di Pavia. Facolta di Lettere (IT)
Universita di Pavia. Istituto Botanico (IT)
Universita di Pavia. Istituto di Scienze Politiche (IT)
Universita di Pavia. Policlinico (IT)
Universita di Pavia. Scuola Universitaria di Paleografia e Filologia Musicale (IT)
Universita di Roma (IT)
Universita di Roma. Clinica Malattie Infettive (IT)
Universita di Roma. Clinica Odontoiatrica (IT)
Universita di Roma. Facolta di Ingegneria (IT)
Universita di Roma. Facolta di Scienze Statistiche Demografiche Ed Attuariali (IT)
Universita di Roma. Istituti di Archeologia e Storia dell'Arte Greca e Romana e di Etruscologia e Anchichita Italiche (IT)
Universita di Roma. Istituto Botanico (IT)
Universita di Roma. Istituto di Automatica (IT)
Universita di Roma. Istituto di Clinica Pediatrica (IT)
Universita di Roma. Istituto di Economia Politica (IT)
Universita di Roma. Istituto di Lingua e Letteratura Latina (IT)
Universita di Roma. Istituto di Medicina Legale (IT)
Universita di Roma. Istituto di Microbiologia (IT)
Universita di Roma. Istituto di Studi Filosofici (IT)
Universita di Roma. Istituto di Studi Francesi (IT)
Universita di Roma. Istituto Studi Albanesi (IT)
Universita di Roma. Scuola di Filologia Classica (IT)
Universita di Roma. Scuola di Filologia Moderna (IT)
Universita di Roma. Scuola di Studi Storico - Religiosi (IT)
Universita di Roma. Scuola Orientale (IT)
Universita di Sassari. Societa Sassarese per le Scienze Giuridiche (IT)
Universita di Siena (IT)
Universita di Sienna. Istituto di Storia Dell Arte (IT)
Universita di Torino (IT)
Universita di Torino. Clinica Oculista (IT)
Universita di Torino. Facolta di Scienze Agrarie (IT)
Universita di Torino. Istituto dell' Atlante Linguistico Italiano (IT)
Universita di Torino. Istituto di Storia (IT)
Universita di Trieste (IT)
Universita di Udine. Biblioteca Centrale (IT)
Universita Internazionale dell'Arte. Centro di Studi per la Museologia (IT)
Universita J. E. Purkyne (CS)
Universita J. E. Purkyne. Filosoficka Fakulta (CS)
Universita J. E. Purkyne. Lekarska Fakulta (CS)
Universita J. E. Purkyne. Prirodovedecka Fakulta (CS)
Universita Karlova (CS)
Universita Karlova. Centrum Numericke Matematiky (CS)
Universita Karlova. Fakulta Matematiky a Fyziky (CS)
Universita Karlova. Fakulta Vseobecneho Lekarstvi (CS)
Universita Karlova. Filosoficka Fakulta (CS)
Universita Karlova. Matematicky Ustav (CS)
Universita Karlova. Prirodovedecka Fakulta (CS)
Universita Karlova. Psychologicky Ustav (CS)
Universita Karlova. Ustav Geologickych Ved (CS)
Universita' Ospedale Garibaldi. Otorinolaringoiatrica (IT)
Universita Palackeho. Filosoficka Fakulta (CS)
Universita Palackeho. Pedagogicka Fakulta (CS)
Universita Pontificia Salesiana (IT)
Universita Salesiana di Roma. Facolta di Scienze dell'Educazione (IT)
Universitaet Basel. Theologische Fakultaet (SZ)
Universitaet Basel. Wirtschaftswissenschaftliche Institut (SZ)
Universitaet Bern. Forschungsinstitut fuer Fremdenverkehr (SZ)
Universitaet Bern. Institut fuer Betriebswirtschaft (SZ)
Universitaet Bern. Institut fuer Soziologie und Sozio-Oekonomische Entwicklungsfragen (SZ)
Universitaet Bielefeld (GW)
Universitaet Bonn (GW)
Universitaet Bonn. Forschungsstelle fuer Orientalische Kunstgeschichte (GW)
Universitaet Bonn. Franz Joseph Doelger-Institut (GW)
Universitaet Bonn. Geographisches Institut (GW)
Universitaet Bonn. Institut fuer Geschichtliche Landeskunde der Rheinlande (GW)
Universitaet Bonn. Institut fuer Oekonometrie und Operations Research (GW)
Universitaet Bonn. Mathematisches Institut (GW)
Universitaet Bonn. Meteorologisches Institut (GW)
Universitaet Bremen (GW)
Universitaet des Saarlandes (GW)
Universitaet des Saarlandes. Geographisches Institut (GW)

Universitaet des Saarlandes. Musikwissenschaftliches Institut (GW)
Universitaet des Saarlandes. Universitaetsbibliothek (GW)
Universitaet Duesseldorf (GW)
Universitaet Erlangen. Geologisches Institut (GW)
Universitaet Erlangen-Nuernberg (GW)
Universitaet Frankfurt (GW)
Universitaet Frankfurt. Geographisches Institut (GW)
Universitaet Frankfurt. Seminar fuer Sprach- und Kulturwissenschaft Zentralasiens (GW)
Universitaet Frankfurt. Wissenschaftliche Gesellschaft (GW)
Universitaet Freiburg (GW)
Universitaet Freiburg. Geographisches Institut (GW)
Universitaet Giessen (GW)
Universitaet Giessen. Bibliothek (GW)
Universitaet Giessen. Matematisches Institut (GW)
Universitaet Giessen. Zentrum fuer Kontinentale Agrar- und Wirtschaftsforschung (GW)
Universitaet Goettingen (GW)
Universitaet Goettingen. Geographisches Institut (GW)
Universitaet Goettingen. Niedersaechsisches Institut fuer Landeskunde und Landesentwicklung (GW)
Universitaet Hamburg (GW)
Universitaet Hamburg. Finnisch-Ugrisches Seminar (GW)
Universitaet Hamburg. Geologisch-Palaeontologisches Institut (GW)
Universitaet Hamburg. Ibero-Amerikanisches Forschungsinstitut (GW)
Universitaet Hamburg. Institut fuer Internationale Angelegenheiten (GW)
Universitaet Hamburg. Mathematisches Seminar (GW)
Universitaet Hamburg. Seminar fuer Oeffentliches Recht und Staatslehre (GW)
Universitaet Hamburg. Seminar fuer Sprache und Kultur Japans (GW)
Universitaet Heidelberg (GW)
Universitaet Heidelberg. Institut fuer Soziologie und Ethnologie (GW)
Universitaet Heidelberg. Juristische Fakultaet (GW)
Universitaet Heidelberg. Suedasien-Institut (GW)
Universitaet Hohenheim (GW)
Universitaet Hohenheim. Informations- und Pressestelle (GW)
Universitaet Hohenheim. Institut fuer Sozialwissenschaften (GW)
Universitaet Innsbruck (AU)
Universitaet Innsbruck. Arbeitsgemeinschaft fuer Wissenschaft und Politik (AU)
Universitaet Innsbruck. Theologische Fakultaet (AU)
Universitaet Karlsruhe. Zentrum fuer Didaktik der Mathematik (GW)
Universitaet Kiel. Agrarwissenschaftliche Fakultaet (GW)
Universitaet Kiel. Englisches Seminar (GW)
Universitaet Kiel. Geographisches Institut (GW)
Universitaet Kiel. Institut fuer Agrarpolitik und Marktlehre (GW)
Universitaet Kiel. Institut fuer Internationales Recht (GW)
Universitaet Kiel. Institut fuer Meereskunde (GW)
Universitaet Mainz. Institut fuer Geschichtliche Landeskunde (GW)
Universitaet Marburg (GW)
Universitaet Marburg. Institut fuer Medizinisch-biologische Statistik (GW)
Universitaet Muenchen. Geophysikalisches Observatorium (GW)
Universitaet Muenchen. Institut fuer Byzantinistik und Neugriechische Philologie (GW)
Universitaet Muenchen. Institut fuer Geographie (GW)
Universitaet Muenchen. Wirtschaftsgeographisches Institut (GW)
Universitaet Muenster (GW)
Universitaet Muenster. Astronomisches Institut (GW)
Universitaet Muenster. Forschungsstelle fuer Allgemeine und Textile Marktwirtschaft (GW)
Universitaet Muenster. Institut fuer Christliche Sozialwissenschaften (GW)
Universitaet Muenster. Institut fuer Epigraphik (GW)
Universitaet Muenster. Institut fuer Fruehmittelalterforschung (GW)
Universitaet Muenster. Institut fuer Kreditwesen (GW)
Universitaet Muenster. Katholisch-Theologische Fakultaet (GW)
Universitaet Muenster. Sozialforschungsstelle (GW)
Universitaet Rostock (GE)
Universitaet Rostock. Instituto Latinoamericano (GE)
Universitaet Salzburg (AU)

# R.R. BOWKER ORDER DEPARTMENT

D748

P.O. Box 1807, Ann Arbor, Michigan 48106

(Outside Western Hemisphere: Bowker, Erasmus House, Epping, Essex, England.)

Please send:

_____ copy(ies) of BOOKS IN SERIES IN THE U.S. (0-8352-0902-4, 1977, 2,486 pp.) @ $52.50

_____ copy(ies) of BOOKS IN SERIES SUPPLEMENT (0-8352-1031-6, Dec. 1977, c. 2,000 pp.)
@ $34.50 tent.

_____ copy(ies) of IRREGULAR SERIALS AND ANNUALS, 5 e (0-8352-1047-2, 1978, c. 1,400 pp.)
@ $52.50 tent.

_____ copy(ies) of SOURCES OF SERIALS (0-8352-0855-9, Nov. 1977, c. 2,700 pp.) @ $52.50

_____ copy(ies) of ULRICH'S INT'L PERIODICALS DIRECTORY, 17 e (0-8352-0925-3, Sept. 1977,
c. 2,300 pp.) @ $57.50

_____ Please put me on standing order to receive_____ copy(ies) of all subsequent
biennial editions, automatically upon publication.

_____ subscription(s) to ULRICH'S QUARTERLY (ISSN 0000-0507) U.S.A. rate $23.50; Canada &
Mexico rate $24.50; Rest of world $25.50. Airmail rates on request.

Name _____

Address _____

_____

City/State/Zip _____

Purchase Order No._____ ☐Bill me. ☐Check enclosed.

Sales tax will be added where applicable. All prices include shipping and handling charges, and are applicable to the U.S.,
its territories and possessions. Prices are 10% higher in all other Western Hemisphere countries. Prices and publication
dates are subject to change without notice.

First Class Mail
Permit No. 1746
Ann Arbor, Michigan

**Business Reply Mail**  No Postage Necessary if Mailed in the United States

**Postage Will be Paid by**

R.R. Bowker Company
P.O. Box 1807
Ann Arbor, Michigan 48106

First Class Mail
Permit No. 1746
Ann Arbor, Michigan

**Business Reply Mail**  No Postage Necessary if Mailed in the United States

**Postage Will be Paid by**

R.R. Bowker Company
P.O. Box 1807
Ann Arbor, Michigan 48106

**BOWKER**
NEW YORK & LONDON

Universite de Liege. Cercle Scientifique des Anciens Eleves de l'Institut A. Gilkinet (BE)
Universite de Liege. Faculte de Medecine Veterinaire (BE)
Universite de Liege. Faculte de Philosophie et Lettres (BE)
Universite de Liege. Faculte des Sciences Appliquees (BE)
Universite de Liege. Institut de Pharmacie (BE)
Universite de Liege. Institut Superieur des Sciences Pedagogiques (BE)
Universite de Liege. Laboratoire d'Analyse Statistique des Langues Anciennes (BE)
Universite de Lille I (Universite des Sciences et Techniques de Lille) (FR)
Universite de Lille II (Droit et Sante) (FR)
Universite de Lille III (Sciences Humaines, Lettres et Arts) (FR)
Universite de Lyon I. Departement de Mathematiques (FR)
Universite de Lyon I. Departement Sciences de la Terre (FR)
Universite de Lyon II. Centre d'Etudes Gidiennes (FR)
Universite de Lyon III. Faculte de Droit (FR)
Universite de Madagascar. Bibliotheque Universitaire (MG)
Universite de Madagascar. Faculte des Lettres et Sciences Humaines (MG)
Universite de Madagascar. Laboratoire de Geographie (MG)
Universite de Metz. Centre d'Analyse Syntaxique (FR)
Universite de Metz. Centre de Recherches Relations Internationales (FR)
Universite de Moncton (CN)
Universite de Montreal (CN)
Universite de Montreal. Association des Diplomes (CN)
Universite de Montreal. Ecole de Bibliotheconomie (CN)
Universite de Montreal. Ecole de Medecine Veterinaire (CN)
Universite de Montreal. Faculte de Medecine Veterinaire (CN)
Universite de Montreal. Industrialization Forum Team (CN)
Universite de Montreal. Institut Botanique (CN)
Universite de Montreal. Institut d'Etudes Medievales (CN)
Universite de Nancy II (FR)
Universite de Nancy II. Centre Europeen Universitaire (FR)
Universite de Nancy II. Faculte de Droit et des Sciences Economiques (FR)
Universite de Nantes. Centre de Recherches sur l'Histoire de la France Atlantique (FR)
Universite de Neuchatel (SZ)
Universite de Neuchatel. Centre de Recherches en Mathematiques Pures (SZ)
Universite de Neuchatel. Faculte des Lettres (SZ)
Universite de Nice. Centre du Vingtieme Siecle (FR)
Universite de Paris (Pantheon-Sorbonne)
see Universite de Paris I (FR)
Universite de Paris (Paris-Nanterre)
see Universite de Paris X (FR)
Universite de Paris (Paris-Val-de-Marne)
see Universite de Paris XII (FR)
Universite de Paris (Pierre et Marie Curie)
see Universite de Paris VI (FR)
Universite de Paris (Rene Descartes)
see Universite de Paris V (FR)
Universite de Paris I (Pantheon-Sorbonne) Centre d'Etudes Archeologiques de la Mediterranee Occidentale (FR)
Universite de Paris I (Pantheon-Sorbonne) Institut d'Histoire des Relations Internationales Contemporaines (FR)
Universite de Paris I (Paris-Nanterre) Centre d'Etudes Theatrales (FR)
Universite de Paris II (Universite Droit, d'Economie et des Sciences Sociales) Institut de Droit Compare (FR)
Universite de Paris V (Rene Descartes) (FR)
Universite de Paris VI (Pierre et Marie Curie) Institut de Statistique (FR)
Universite de Paris VI (Pierre et Marie Curie) Institut Henri Poincare (FR)
Universite de Paris VI (Pierre et Marie Curie) Laboratoire Arago de Biologie Marine (FR)
Universite de Paris VII. Groupe de Linguistique Japonaise (FR)
Universite de Paris VII. Laboratoire de Psychanalyse et Psychopathologie (FR)
Universite de Paris VIII (Paris-Vincenners) Departement de Linguistique (FR)
Universite de Paris X (Paris-Nanterre) Centre d'Etudes Finno-Ougriennes (FR)

Universite de Paris X. Laboratoire d'Ethnologie et de Sociologie Comparative (FR)
Universite de Paris XII (Paris-Val-de-Marne) Institut d'Urbanisme (FR)
Universite de Poitiers. Centre de Recherches Latino-Americaines (FR)
Universite de Poitiers. Centre d'Etudes Superieures de Civilisation Medievale (FR)
Universite de Poitiers. Departement d'Etudes Portugaises et Bresiliennes (FR)
Universite de Provence
see Universite d'Aix-Marseille I (FR)
Universite de Reims. Institut de Geographie (FR)
Universite de Rennes I. Institut de Geologie (FR)
Universite de Rennes II (Universite de Haute Bretagne) (FR)
Universite de Sherbrooke. Centre d'Etude des Litteratures d'Expression Francaise (CN)
Universite de Sherbrooke. Departement d'Economique (CN)
Universite de Sherbrooke. Faculte de Droit (CN)
Universite de Sherbrooke. Faculte des Arts (CN)
Universite de Strasbourg I (Universite Louis Pasteur) Institut de Geologie (FR)
Universite de Strasbourg II (FR)
Universite de Strasbourg II. Centre de Philologie et de Litteratures Romanes (FR)
Universite de Strasbourg II. Centre de Recherche et de Documentation des Institutions Chretiennes (FR)
Universite de Strasbourg II. Faculte de Theologie Catholique (FR)
Universite de Strasbourg II. Groupe de Recherche d'Histoire Romaine (FR)
Universite de Strasbourg II. Institut de Phonetique (FR)
Universite de Strasbourg. Institut d'Etudes Latino-Americaines (FR)
Universite de Toulouse I (Sciences Sociales) (FR)
Universite de Toulouse I (Sciences Sociales) Institut d'Etudes Internationales et des Pays en Voie de Developpement (FR)
Universite de Toulouse II (le Mirail) (FR)
Universite de Toulouse II (le Mirail) Institut d'Etudes Hispaniques, Hispanoamericaines (FR)
Universite de Tunis. Centre d'Etudes et de Recherches Economiques et Sociales (TI)
Universite de Yaounde (CM)
Universite de Yaounde. Ecole Normale Superieure (CM)
Universite de Yaounde. Faculte des Sciences (CM)
Universite des Langues et Lettres de Grenoble
see Universite de Grenoble III (FR)
Universite des Sciences et Techniques de Lille
see Universite de Lille I (FR)
Universite des Sciences Humaines de Strasbourg
see Universite de Strasbourg II (FR)
Universite des Sciences Humaines, Lettres et Arts de Lille
see Universite de Lille III (FR)
Universite des Sciences Sociales
see Universite de Grenoble III (FR)
Universite du Benin (TG)
Universite du Quebec (CN)
Universite du Quebec a Chicoutimi. Department des Sciences Humaines (CN)
Universite du Quebec a Montreal (CN)
Universite du Quebec a Trois-Rivieres. Centre de Recherches en Histoire des Religions et de la Pensee (CN)
Universite Francois Rabelais, Tours (FR)
Universite Jean Moulin
see Universite de Lyon III (FR)
Universite Laval (CN)
Universite Laval. Association des Etudiants en Sciences (CN)
Universite Laval. Cartotheque, Bibliotheque Generale (CN)
Universite Laval. Centre d'Etudes Nordiques (CN)
Universite Laval. Centre de Recherches sur les Atomes et les Molecules (CN)
Universite Laval. Department de l'Anthropologie (CN)
Universite Laval. Department de Linguistique (CN)
Universite Laval. Department de Sociologie (CN)
Universite Laval. Faculte de Foresterie (CN)
Universite Laval. Faculte de Medecine (CN)
Universite Laval. Faculte des Sciences de l'Administration (CN)
Universite Laval. Fonds de Recherches Forestieres (CN)
Universite Laval. Public Relations Department (CN)
Universite Libre de Bruxelles
see also Vrije Universiteit Brussel (the two universities have been separate institutions since 1970) (BE)

Universite Libre de Bruxelles. Association des Medecins Anciens Etudiants (BE)
Universite Libre de Bruxelles. Centre d'Etude des Pays de l'Est (BE)
Universite Libre de Bruxelles. Centre d'Etudes de Recherche Operationnelle (BE)
Universite Libre de Bruxelles. Cercle des Sciences (BE)
Universite Libre de Bruxelles. Department of Economics (BE)
Universite Libre de Bruxelles. Groupe d'Etude de Dix-Huiteme Siecle (BE)
Universite Libre de Bruxelles. Institut d'Etudes Europeennes (BE)
Universite Libre de Bruxelles. Institut d'Histoire du Christianisme (BE)
Universite Libre de Bruxelles. Institut de Philosophie (BE)
Universite Libre de Bruxelles. Institut de Sociologie (BE)
Universite Louis Pasteur
see Universite de Strasbourg I (Universite Louis Pasteur) (FR)
Universite Moderne (FR)
Universite Mohammed V. Faculte des Lettres et des Sciences Humaines (MR)
Universite Montpellier III (Universite Paul Valery) Centre d'Etudes et de Recherches Elisabethaines (FR)
Universite Montpellier III (Universite Paul Valery) Centre d'Etudes Occitanes (FR)
Universite Nationale du Rwanda (RW)
Universite Nationale du Zaire. Junction des Etudiants (ZR)
Universite Nationale du Zaire, Kinshasa. Centre d'Etudes des Religions Africaines (ZR)
Universite Nationale du Zaire, Kinshasa. Faculte du Droit (ZR)
Universite Nationale du Zaire, Kinshasa. Institut de Recherches Economiques et Sociales (ZR)
Universite Nationale du Zaire, Kisangani. Centre de Recherches Interdisciplinaires pour le Developpement de l'Education (ZR)
Universite Nationale du Zaire, Lubumbashi (ZR)
Universite Nationale du Zaire, Lubumbashi. Centre de Linguistique Theorique et Appliquee (ZR)
Universite Nationale du Zaire, Lubumbashi. Department d'Histoire (ZR)
Universite Nationale du Zaire, Lubumbashi. Department de Philosophie (ZR)
Universite Nationale du Zaire, Lubumbashi. Faculte de Philosophie et Lettres (ZR)
Universite Nationale du Zaire, Lubumbashi. Faculte des Sciences Socials, Politiques et Administratives (ZR)
Universite Paul Sabatier (Toulouse) Station Biologique du Lac d'Oredon (FR)
Universite Paul Valery
see Universite Montpellier III (FR)
Universite Saint Esprit Kaslik (LE)
Universite Saint Joseph (LE)
Universite St. Joseph. Faculte de Droit et des Sciences Economiques (LE)
Universite Saint Joseph. Institut de Lettres Orientales (LE)
Universite Scientifique et Medicale de Grenoble
see Universite de Grenoble I (FR)
Universiteit van Amsterdam. Commissie voor de Artis Bibliotheek (NE)
Universiteit van Amsterdam. Europa Instituut (NE)
Universiteit van Amsterdam. Fysisch Geografish en Bodemkundig Laboratorium (NE)
Universiteit van Amsterdam. Mathematisch Instituut (NE)
Universiteit van Amsterdam. Zoologisch Museum (NE)
Universitet i Uppsala. Institutionen Foer Allmaen och Jaemfoerande Ethnografi (SW)
Universitetet i Bergen (NO)
Universitetet i Bergen. Department of Applied Mathematics (NO)
Universitetet i Bergen. Institute of Psychology (NO)
Universitetet i Bergen. Radiation Observatory (NO)
Universitetet i Oslo. Biblioteket (NO)
Universitetet i Oslo. Britisk Institutt (NO)
Universitetet i Oslo. Etnografiske Museum (NO)
Universitetet i Oslo. Institutett for Statsvitenskap (NO)
Universitetet i Oslo. Institutt for Bibelvitenskap (NO)
Universitetet i Oslo. Institutt for Teoretisk Astrofysikk (NO)
Universitetet i Oslo. Institutt for Teoretisk Fysikk (NO)
Universitetet i Oslo. Slavisk-Baltisk Institutt (NO)
Universitetet i Oslo. Sosialoekonomissie (NO)
Universitetet i Tromsoe (NO)
Universitetet i Trondheim. Norges Laererhoegskole (NO)

University of British Columbia. Department of Geological Sciences (CN)
University of British Columbia. Department of Geophysics and Astronomy (CN)
University of British Columbia. Department of Psychiatry (CN)
University of British Columbia. Electrical Engineering Department (CN)
University of British Columbia. Faculty of Commerce and Business Administration (CN)
University of British Columbia. Faculty of Forestry (CN)
University of British Columbia. Faculty of Law (CN)
University of British Columbia. Library (CN)
University of British Columbia Library. Asian Studies Division (CN)
University of British Columbia Press (CN)
University of British Columbia. School of Community and Regional Planning (CN)
University of British Columbia. Westwater Research Centre (CN)
University of Cairo. Botany Department (UA)
University of Cairo. Faculty of Commerce (UA)
University of Cairo. Faculty of Law (UA)
University of Cairo. Faculty of Medicine (UA)
University of Cairo. Institute of Statistical Studies and Research (UA)
University of Calcutta
  see also Calcutta University Press (II)
University of Calcutta (II)
University of Calcutta. Centre of Advanced Study in Ancient Indian History and Culture (II)
University of Calcutta. Department of Botany (II)
University of Calcutta. Department of Economics (II)
University of Calcutta. Department of English (II)
University of Calcutta. University College of Medicine (II)
University of Calgary (CN)
University of Calgary. Archaeological Association (CN)
University of Calgary. Computer Services (CN)
University of Calgary. Department of Archaeology (CN)
University of Calgary. Department of Civil Engineering (CN)
University of Calgary. Department of English (CN)
University of Calgary. Department of History (CN)
University of Calgary. Department of Mathematics and Computing Science (CN)
University of Calgary. Department of Sociology (CN)
University of Calgary. Faculty of Education (CN)
University of Calicut (II)
University of California, Berkeley (US)
University of California, Berkeley. Agricultural Experiment Station (US)
University of California, Berkeley. Archaeological Research Facility (US)
University of California, Berkeley. Bancroft Library (US)
University of California, Berkeley. Center for Chinese Studies (US)
University of California, Berkeley. Center for Real Estate and Urban Economics (US)
University of California, Berkeley. Center for Research and Development in Higher Education (US)
University of California, Berkeley. Center for South and Southeast Asian Studies (US)
University of California, Berkeley. College of Engineering (US)
University of California, Berkeley. Cooperative Extension (US)
University of California, Berkeley. Department of Anthropology (US)
University of California, Berkeley. Department of Forestry and Conservation (US)
University of California, Berkeley. Design Methods Group (US)
University of California, Berkeley. Division of Agricultural Sciences (US)
University of California, Berkeley. Earthquake Engineering Research Center (US)
University of California, Berkeley. Forest Products Library (US)
University of California, Berkeley. Graduate Sociology Union (US)
University of California, Berkeley. Institute of Business and Economic Research (US)
University of California, Berkeley. Institute of Governmental Studies (US)
University of California, Berkeley. Institute of Human Development (US)
University of California, Berkeley. Institute of Industrial Relations (US)
University of California, Berkeley. Institute of International Studies (US)
University of California, Berkeley. Institute of Race and Community Relations (US)

University of California, Berkeley. Institute of Transportation and Traffic Engineering (US)
University of California, Berkeley. Institute of Transportation Studies Library (US)
University of California, Berkeley. Language Behavior Research Laboratory (US)
University of California, Berkeley. Lawrence Berkeley Laboratory (US)
University of California, Berkeley. Library (US)
University of California, Berkeley. Library School Library (US)
University of California, Berkeley. Music Library (US)
University of California, Berkeley. Office of Institutional Research (US)
University of California, Berkeley. Office of Public Information (US)
University of California, Berkeley. School of Criminology (US)
University of California, Berkeley. School of Law (US)
University of California, Berkeley. Science Curriculum Improvement Study (US)
University of California, Berkeley. Seismographic Station (US)
University of California, Berkeley. Student Engineers' Joint Council (US)
University of California, Berkeley. University Extension (US)
University of California, Berkeley. Vice-President-University Relations (US)
University of California, Berkeley. Visual Science Information Center (US)
University of California, Davis (US)
University of California, Davis. Cooperative Extension (US)
University of California, Davis. Department of Avian Sciences (US)
University of California, Davis. Department of English (US)
University of California, Davis. Food Protection and Toxicology Center (US)
University of California, Davis. Institute of Governmental Affairs (US)
University of California, Davis. Packaging Program (US)
University of California, Davis. School of Law (US)
University of California, Davis. University Library (US)
University of California, Davis. Water Resources Center (US)
University of California, Irvine. Center for Pathobiology (US)
University of California, Irvine. Museum of Systematic Biology (US)
University of California, Irvine. School of Humanities (US)
University of California, Los Angeles (US)
University of California, Los Angeles. African Studies Center (US)
University of California, Los Angeles. Asian American Studies Center (US)
University of California, Los Angeles. Biomedical Library (US)
University of California, Los Angeles, Brain Information Service
  see Brain Information Service-Brain Research Institute (US)
University of California, Los Angeles. Center for Medieval and Renaissance Studies (US)
University of California, Los Angeles. Center for the Study of Comparative Folklore and Mythology (US)
University of California, Los Angeles. Center for the Study of Evaluation (US)
University of California, Los Angeles. Chicano Studies Center (US)
University of California, Los Angeles. Department of Anthropology (US)
University of California, Los Angeles. Department of Geography (US)
University of California, Los Angeles. Department of Linguistics (US)
University of California, Los Angeles. Department of Music (US)
University of California, Los Angeles. Department of Slavic Languages (US)
University of California, Los Angeles. Graduate School of Management (US)
University of California, Los Angeles. Institute of Archaeology (US)
University of California, Los Angeles. Institute of Government and Public Affairs (US)
University of California, Los Angeles. Institute of Industrial Relations (US)
University of California, Los Angeles. Jewish Students (US)

University of California, Los Angeles. Latin American Center (US)
University of California Los Angeles Medical Center. School of Dentistry (US)
University of California, Los Angeles. Musuem of Cultural History (US)
University of California, Los Angeles. Neuropsychiatric Institute (US)
University of California, Los Angeles. School of Dentistry (US)
University of California, Los Angeles. School of Engineering & Applied Science (US)
University of California, Los Angeles. School of Law (US)
University of California, Los Angeles. University Research Library (US)
University of California Press (US)
University of California, Riverside. Department of Anthropology (US)
University of California, Riverside. Spanish Department (US)
University of California, San Diego. Central University Library (US)
University of California, San Diego. Institute of Marine Resources (US)
University of California, San Francisco. Drug Abuse Information Project (US)
University of California, San Francisco. Hastings College of the Law (US)
University of California, San Francisco. Synapse Publication Board (US)
University of California, Santa Barbara. Library (US)
University of California, Santa Cruz. College 5 (US)
University of California, Santa Cruz, Lick Observatory
  see Lick Observatory (US)
University of Canterbury (NZ)
University of Canterbury. Biological Society (NZ)
University of Canterbury. Department of History (NZ)
University of Canterbury. Department of Psychology (NZ)
University of Canterbury. School of Engineering (NZ)
University of Cape Coast (GH)
University of Cape Town (SA)
University of Cape Town. Centre for Intergroup Studies (SA)
University of Cape Town. Department of English (SA)
University of Cape Town. Department of Geology (SA)
University of Cape Town. Department of Obstetrics and Gynaecology (SA)
University of Cape Town. Department of Sociology (SA)
University of Cape Town. Faculty of Law (SA)
University of Cape Town. Science Students' Council (SA)
University of Cape Town. Student Law Society (SA)
University of Cape Town. Students Health and Welfare Centres Organisation (SHAWCO) (SA)
University of Cape Town. Students Representative Council (SA)
University of Chiba
  see Chiba University (JA)
University of Chicago (US)
University of Chicago. A. G. Bush Library (US)
University of Chicago Alumni Association (US)
University of Chicago. Biology Department (US)
University of Chicago. Center for Health Administration Studies (US)
University of Chicago. Center for Studies in Criminal Justice (US)
University of Chicago. Department of Anthropology (US)
University of Chicago. Department of Geography (US)
University of Chicago. Department of Psychology (US)
University of Chicago. Division of Biological Sciences (US)
University of Chicago. Graduate School of Business (US)
University of Chicago. Ida Noyes Hall (US)
University of Chicago. Industrial Relations Center (US)
University of Chicago Law School (US)
University of Chicago. Midwest Administration Center (US)
University of Chicago. Oriental Institute (US)
University of Chicago Press (US)
University of Chicago. Pritzker School of Medicine (US)
University of Chicago. Research Center in Economic Development and Cultural Change (US)
University of Chicago. Vice-President for Public Affairs (US)

University of Cincinnati  (US)
University of Cincinnati. College of Law  (US)
University of Cincinnati. Department of Classics  (US)
University of Cincinnati. Department of English  (US)
University of Cincinnati. Department of Romance Languages and Literature  (US)
University of Cochin. Department of Marine Sciences  (II)
University of Cochin. Foundation for Management Education  (II)
University of Colorado  (US)
University of Colorado. Black Studies Program  (US)
University of Colorado. Bureau of Governmental Research and Service  (US)
University of Colorado. College of Engineering  (US)
University of Colorado Denver Campus  (US)
University of Colorado. Graduate School of Business Administration  (US)
University of Colorado. Institute of Arctic and Alpine Research  (US)
University of Colorado. Institute of Behavioral Science  (US)
University of Colorado Libraries  (US)
University of Colorado Libraries. Interlibrary Loan Service  (US)
University of Colorado. Mountain View Center for Environmental Education  (US)
University of Colorado. Norlin Library  (US)
University of Colorado. School of Law  (US)
University of Colorado. School of Pharmacy  (US)
University of Colorado. Women Studies Program  (US)
University of Connecticut. Center for Real Estate & Urban Economic Studies  (US)
University of Connecticut. College of Agriculture and Natural Resources  (US)
University of Connecticut. Department of History  (US)
University of Connecticut. English Department  (US)
University of Connecticut. Institute of Materials Science  (US)
University of Connecticut. Institute of Public Service  (US)
University of Connecticut. Institute of Urban Research  (US)
University of Connecticut. Institute of Water Resources  (US)
University of Connecticut Library. Special Collections  (US)
University of Connecticut. School of Social Work  (US)
University of Dacca  (BG)
University of Dacca. Department of Library Science  (BG)
University of Dacca. Economics Association  (BG)
University of Dacca. Institute of Education and Research  (BG)
University of Dacca. Institute of Statistical Research and Training  (BG)
University of Dacca. Studies Board  (BG)
University of Dallas  (US)
University of Dar es Salaam  (TZ)
University of Dar es Salaam. Botany Department  (TZ)
University of Dar es Salaam. Bureau of Resource Assessment and Land Use Planning  (TZ)
University of Dar es Salaam. Department of Literature  (TZ)
University of Dar es Salaam. Department of Political Science  (TZ)
University of Dar es Salaam. Economics Association  (TZ)
University of Dar es Salaam. Faculty of Arts and Social Science  (TZ)
University of Dar es Salaam. Faculty of Law  (TZ)
University of Dar es Salaam. Faculty of Medicine  (TZ)
University of Dar es Salaam. Institute of Swahili Research  (TZ)
University of Dar es Salaam. Student's Organization
  see Dar es Salaam University Student's Organization  (TZ)
University of Dayton  (US)
University of Dayton. Law School  (US)
University of Dayton. School of Education  (US)
University of Delaware. College of Agricultural Sciences  (US)
University of Delaware. Department of Anthropology  (US)
University of Delaware. Department of Civil Engineering  (US)
University of Delaware. Water Resources Center  (US)
University of Delhi. Department of African Studies  (II)
University of Delhi. Department of Anthropology  (II)

University of Delhi. Department of Library Science  (II)
University of Delhi. Department of Political Science  (II)
University of Delhi. Department of Sanskrit  (II)
University of Delhi. Faculty of Law  (II)
University of Delhi. Library  (II)
University of Delhi. School of Economics  (II)
University of Denver  (US)
University of Denver. College of Business Administration  (US)
University of Denver. College of Law  (US)
University of Denver. Denver Research Institute  (US)
University of Denver. Department of Chemical Engineering and Metallurgy  (US)
University of Denver. Graduate School of International Studies  (US)
University of Denver. Graduate School of Librarianship  (US)
University of Detroit. School of Dentistry  (US)
University of Detroit. School of Law  (US)
University of Dublin. Trinity College  (IE)
University of Durban-Westville  (SA)
University of Durham  (UK)
University of Durham. Anthropological Society  (UK)
University of Durham. Center for Middle Eastern and Islamic Studies  (UK)
University of Durham. Institute of Education  (UK)
University of Eastern Philippines  (PH)
University of Edinburgh  (UK)
University of Edinburgh. Architecture Research Unit  (UK)
University of Edinburgh. Graduates' Association  (UK)
University of Edinburgh. School of Scottish Studies  (UK)
University of Edinburgh. Student Publications Board  (UK)
University of Electro-Communications  (JA)
University of Esfahan. Faculty of Medicine  (IR)
University of Essex  (UK)
University of Exeter  (UK)
University of Exeter. Agricultural Economics Unit  (UK)
University of Exeter. American Arts Documentation Centre  (UK)
University of Exeter. Department of Politics  (UK)
University of Exeter. Faculty of Social Studies  (UK)
University of Ferdowsi. Faculty of Letters and Humanities  (IR)
University of Ferdowsi. Faculty of Medicine  (IR)
University of Ferdowsi. Faculty of Theology and Islamic Studies  (IR)
University of Florida  (US)
University of Florida. Center for Latin American Studies  (US)
University of Florida. Center for Tropical Agriculture  (US)
University of Florida. College of Business Administration  (US)
University of Florida. College of Dentistry  (US)
University of Florida. College of Education  (US)
University of Florida College of Engineering. Engineering and Industrial Experiment Station  (US)
University of Florida. College of Law  (US)
University of Florida. Communication Sciences Laboratory  (US)
University of Florida. Department of Accounting  (US)
University of Florida. Department of History  (US)
University of Florida. Department of Mathematics  (US)
University of Florida. Department of Zoology  (US)
University of Florida. Growth Conference  (US)
University of Florida. Institute of Food and Agricultural Sciences  (US)
University of Florida. Library  (US)
University of Florida Press
  see University Presses of Florida  (US)
University of Florida. Rehabilitation Research Institute  (US)
University of Florida. School of Forest Resources & Conservation  (US)
University of Florida. University College  (US)
University of Fort Hare. Faculty of Law  (SA)
University of Fukui
  see Fukui University  (JA)
University of Fukuoka
  see Fukuoka University  (JA)
University of Garyounis. Faculty of Economics and Commerce  (LY)
University of Gauhati
  see Gauhati University  (II)
University of Georgia  (US)
University of Georgia Alumni Society  (US)

University of Georgia. Anthropology Curriculum Project  (US)
University of Georgia. Center for Continuing Education  (US)
University of Georgia. College of Agriculture  (US)
University of Georgia. College of Agriculture Experiment Stations  (US)
University of Georgia. College of Business Administration  (US)
University of Georgia. College of Education  (US)
University of Georgia. College of Veterinary Medicine  (US)
University of Georgia. Environmental Education Materials Center  (US)
University of Georgia. Geography Curriculum Project  (US)
University of Georgia. Georgia Museum of Art  (US)
University of Georgia. Graduate School  (US)
University of Georgia. Institute of Community and Area Development  (US)
University of Georgia. Institute of Ecology  (US)
University of Georgia. Institute of Government  (US)
University of Georgia Law School Association  (US)
University of Georgia Libraries  (US)
University of Georgia. Marine Institute  (US)
University of Georgia Press  (US)
University of Georgia School of Law  (US)
University of Georgia. School of Pharmacy  (US)
University of Georgia. School of Social Work  (US)
University of Ghana. Department of Library Studies  (GH)
University of Ghana. Department of Philosophy  (GH)
University of Ghana. Department of Sociology  (GH)
University of Ghana. Faculty of Law  (GH)
University of Ghana. Faculty of Social Studies  (GH)
University of Ghana. Institute of African Studies  (GH)
University of Ghana. Institute of Statistical, Social and Economic Research  (GH)
University of Ghana. School of Administration  (GH)
University of Glasgow  (UK)
University of Glasgow. Department of Psychology  (UK)
University of Glasgow. Institute of Latin American Studies  (UK)
University of Glasgow. Medico-Chirurgical Society  (UK)
University of Glasgow Press  (UK)
University of Glasgow. Students' Representative Council  (UK)
University of Guam. Micronesian Area Research Center  (GU)
University of Guelph. Center for Resources Development  (CN)
University of Guelph. Department of Geography  (CN)
University of Guelph. Department of Land Resource Science  (CN)
University of Guelph. Interdepartmental Committee on Scottish Studies  (CN)
University of Gujarat
  see Gujarat University  (II)
University of Guyana  (GY)
University of Hacettepe  (TU)
University of Hacettepe. Institute of Child Health  (TU)
University of Hacettepe. Institute of Population Studies  (TU)
University of Hartford  (US)
University of Haryana
  see Haryana Agricultural University  (II)
University of Hawaii  (US)
University of Hawaii. Asian Studies Program  (US)
University of Hawaii. Board of Publications  (US)
University of Hawaii. College of Education  (US)
University of Hawaii. College of Tropical Agriculture  (US)
University of Hawaii. Counseling and Testing Center  (US)
University of Hawaii. Department of Electrical Engineering  (US)
University of Hawaii. Department of European Languages & Literature  (US)
University of Hawaii. Graduate School of Library Studies  (US)
University of Hawaii. Hawaii Institute of Geophysics  (US)
University of Hawaii. Industrial Relations Center  (US)
University of Hawaii Library  (US)
University of Hawaii. Office of University Relations and Development  (US)
University of Hawaii. Sea Grant College Program  (US)
University of Hawaii. Social Sciences and Linguistics Institute  (US)

University of Hawaii. Southeast Asian Studies Program (US)
University of Hawaii. Water Resources Research Center (US)
University of Helsinki
see Helsingin Yliopisto (FI)
University of Hirosaki
see Hirosaki University (JA)
University of Hiroshima
see Hiroshima University (JA)
University of Hokkaido
see Hokkaido University (JA)
University of Hong Kong. Centre of Asian Studies (HK)
University of Hong Kong. Department of Economics and Political Science (HK)
University of Hong Kong. English Society (HK)
University of Houston. College of Law (US)
University of Houston. Department of English (US)
University of Houston. Department of Mathematics (US)
University of Houston. Friends of the Library (US)
University of Houston. Graduate School and University Libraries (US)
University of Houston. University News Service and Office of Development (US)
University of Hull. Department of Geography (UK)
University of Hull. Department of German (UK)
University of Hull. Institute of Education (UK)
University of Hull Publications Committee (UK)
University of Ibadan (NR)
University of Ibadan. Department of Agricultural Economics (NR)
University of Ibadan. Department of Education (NR)
University of Ibadan. Department of Linguistics and Nigerian Languages (NR)
University of Ibadan. Department of Religious Studies (NR)
University of Ibadan. Institute of African Studies (NR)
University of Ibadan. Institute of Education (NR)
University of Ibadan. Library (NR)
University of Ibadan Medical Students' Association (NR)
University of Ibadan. Nigerian Institute of Social and Economic Research
see Nigerian Institute of Social and Economic Research (NR)
University of Ibadan. Sociological Society (NR)
University of Ibadan. Student Affairs Office (NR)
University of Idaho. Center for Business Development and Research (US)
University of Idaho. College of Forestry, Wildlife and Range Sciences (US)
University of Idaho. College of Law (US)
University of Idaho. Cooperative Extension Service (US)
University of Idaho. Department of Entomology (US)
University of Idaho. Department of Sociology-Anthropology (US)
University of Idaho. Forest, Wildlife and Range Experiment Station (US)
University of Idaho. Water Resources Research Institute (US)
University of Ife (NR)
University of Ife. Department of Education (NR)
University of Ife. Economics Society (NR)
University of Ife. Faculty of Agriculture (NR)
University of Ife. Faculty of Arts (NR)
University of Ife. Faculty of Law (NR)
University of Ife. Geographical Society (NR)
University of Ife. Historical Society (NR)
University of Ife. Institute of Administration (NR)
University of Ife. Institute of African Studies (NR)
University of Ife Bookshop Ltd. (NR)
University of Ife Press (NR)
University of Illinois at Chicago Circle (US)
University of Illinois at Chicago Circle. College of Urban Sciences (US)
University of Illinois at Urbana-Champaign (US)
University of Illinois at Urbana- Champaign. Agricultural Experiment Station (US)
University of Illinois at Urbana-Champaign. Alumni Association (US)
University of Illinois at Urbana-Champaign. Bureau of Institutional Research (US)
University of Illinois at Urbana-Champaign. Bureau of Urban and Regional Planning Research (US)
University of Illinois at Urbana-Champaign. Center for Advanced Computation (US)
University of Illinois at Urbana-Champaign. Center for International Education and Research in Accounting (US)
University of Illinois at Urbana-Champaign. Classics Department (US)
University of Illinois at Urbana-Champaign. College of Agriculture (US)

University of Illinois at Urbana-Champaign. College of Commerce and Business Administration (US)
University of Illinois at Urbana-Champaign. College of Education (US)
University of Illinois at Urbana-Champaign. College of Law (US)
University of Illinois at Urbana-Champaign. Computing Services Office (US)
University of Illinois at Urbana-Champaign. Cooperative Extension Service (US)
University of Illinois at Urbana-Champaign. Department of Agricultural Economics (US)
University of Illinois at Urbana-Champaign. Department of Anthropology (US)
University of Illinois at Urbana-Champaign. Department of Art (US)
University of Illinois at Urbana-Champaign. Department of Civil Engineering (US)
University of Illinois at Urbana-Champaign. Department of Comparative Literature (US)
University of Illinois at Urbana-Champaign. Department of Electrical Engineering (US)
University of Illinois at Urbana-Champaign. Department of Linguistics (US)
University of Illinois at Urbana-Champaign. Department of Theoretical and Applied Mechanics (US)
University of Illinois at Urbana-Champaign. Division of Home Economics Education (US)
University of Illinois at Urbana-Champaign. Engineering Experiment Station (US)
University of Illinois at Urbana-Champaign. Engineering Publications Office (US)
University of Illinois at Urbana-Champaign. English Department (US)
University of Illinois at Urbana-Champaign. Eta Kappa Nu Association (US)
University of Illinois at Urbana-Champaign. Graduate School of Library Science (US)
University of Illinois at Urbana-Champaign. Institute of Aviation (US)
University of Illinois at Urbana-Champaign. Institute of Government & Public Affairs (US)
University of Illinois at Urbana-Champaign. Institute of Labor and Industrial Relations (US)
University of Illinois at Urbana- Champaign Library Friends (US)
University of Illinois at Urbana-Champaign. Office of Instructional Resources (US)
University of Illinois at Urbana-Champaign. School of Music (US)
University of Illinois at Urbana-Champaign. Small Homes Council - Building Research Council (US)
University of Illinois at Urbana-Champaign. Visual Aids Service (US)
University of Illinois at Urbana-Champaign. Water Resources Center (US)
University of Illinois Press (US)
University of Indiana. Department of Geography (US)
University of Indonesia. Department of Anthropology (IO)
University of Indonesia. Lembaga Demografi (IO)
University of Indore (II)
University of Iowa (US)
University of Iowa. Associated Students of Engineering (US)
University of Iowa. College of Business Administration (US)
University of Iowa College of Dentistry (US)
University of Iowa. College of Law (US)
University of Iowa. Comparative Legislative Research Center (US)
University of Iowa. Department of Botany (US)
University of Iowa. Graduate Program in Hospital and Health Administration (US)
University of Iowa. Institute of Public Affairs (US)
University of Iowa. Laboratory for Political Research(US)
University of Iowa. Libraries (US)
University of Iowa, Lindquist Center for Measurement (US)
University of Iowa. Museum of Art (US)
University of Iowa Press (US)
University of Iowa. Russian Department (US)
University of Iowa. School of Letters (US)
University of Iowa. School of Library Science (US)
University of Iowa. School of Social Work (US)
University of Iwate
see Iwate University (JA)
University of Jadavpur
see Jadavpur University (II)
University of Jammu (II)
University of Jodhpur. Botany Department (II)
University of Jodhpur. Faculty of Commerce (II)
University of Jyvaskyla
see Jyvaskylan Yliopisto (FI)
University of Kagoshima
see Kagoshima University (JA)
University of Kanazawa

see Kanazawa University (JA)
University of Kansas (US)
University of Kansas. American Studies Department (US)
University of Kansas. Center for East Asian Studies (US)
University of Kansas. Center for Latin American Studies (US)
University of Kansas College of Health Sciences and Hospital (US)
University of Kansas. Department of Anthropology (US)
University of Kansas. Department of Geology (US)
University of Kansas. Department of Philosophy (US)
University of Kansas. Department of Sociology (US)
University of Kansas Libraries (US)
University of Kansas Libraries. Director of Libraries (US)
University of Kansas. Library Exchange & Gift Section (US)
University of Kansas. Linguistics Department (US)
University of Kansas. Museum of Art (US)
University of Kansas. Museum of Natural History (US)
University of Kansas. National Sculpture Center (US)
University of Kansas News Bureau (US)
University of Kansas Press (US)
University of Kansas. School of Engineering (US)
University of Kansas. School of Law (US)
University of Kansas. School of Social Welfare (US)
University of Kansas Southwest Center (US)
University of Karachi. Department of English (PK)
University of Karachi. Department of Journalism (PK)
University of Karachi. Department of Library Science (PK)
University of Karachi. Department of Psychology (PK)
University of Karnataka
see Karnatak University (II)
University of Kashmir (II)
University of Keele (UK)
University of Kensington. School of Librarianship (AT)
University of Kentucky (US)
University of Kentucky. College of Agriculture (US)
University of Kentucky. College of Business and Economics (US)
University of Kentucky, College of Business and Economics. Center for Public Affairs (US)
University of Kentucky. College of Engineering (US)
University of Kentucky. College of Law (US)
University of Kentucky. College of Library Science (US)
University of Kentucky. Department of Germanic and Classical Languages (US)
University of Kentucky Libraries. Government Publications Department (US)
University of Kentucky. Office of Development Services and Business Research (US)
University of Kentucky Press (US)
University of Kentucky. Research Foundation (US)
University of Kentucky. Southeast Community College (US)
University of Kerala. Department of History (II)
University of Kerala. Department of Linguistics (II)
University of Kerala. Department of Tamil (II)
University of Khartoum. Faculty of Arts (SJ)
University of Kobe
see Kobe University (JA)
University of Kumamoto
see Kumamoto University (JA)
University of Kurume
see Kurume University (JA)
University of Kuwait. Faculty of Science (KU)
University of Kyoto
see Kyoto University (JA)
University of Lagos (NR)
University of Lagos. Continuing Education Centre (NR)
University of Lagos. Faculty of Law (NR)
University of Lagos. Human Resources Research Unit (NR)
University of Lagos. Law Society (NR)
University of Lagos. Library (NR)
University of Lagos. School of Administration and Social Sciences (NR)
University of Lagos. School of African Studies (NR)
University of Lancaster. Department of Systems (UK)
University of Lancaster. Library (UK)
University of Leeds (UK)
University of Leeds. African Studies Unit (UK)
University of Leeds. Department of Earth Sciences (UK)
University of Leeds. Institute of Education (UK)
University of Leeds. Leeds University Union (UK)

University of Michigan. Museum of Paleontology (US)
University of Michigan. Museum of Zoology (US)
University of Michigan. National Program for the Advancement of Pre-College Russian and East European Studies (US)
University of Michigan Observatories (US)
University of Michigan. Office of University Relations and Development (US)
University of Michigan. Population Studies Center (US)
University of Michigan Press (US)
University of Michigan. School of Dentistry (US)
University of Michigan. School of Education (US)
University of Michigan. School of Public Health (US)
University of Michigan. University Herbarium (US)
University of Michigan-Wayne State University. Institute of Labor & Industrial Relations (US)
University of Michigan. William L. Clements Library of American History (US)
University of Michigan. Women's Studies Program (US)
University of Minnesota. Agricultural Experiment Station (US)
University of Minnesota. Audio Visual Library Service (US)
University of Minnesota. Board of Publications (US)
University of Minnesota. Center for Advanced Studies in Language, Style, and Literary Theory (US)
University of Minnesota. Center for Research in Human Learning (US)
University of Minnesota. Center for Youth Development (US)
University of Minnesota. Cereal Rust Laboratory (US)
University of Minnesota. Department of Agricultural Economics (US)
University of Minnesota. Department of Economics (US)
University of Minnesota. Graduate School Research Center (US)
University of Minnesota. History Department (US)
University of Minnesota. Immigration History Research Center (US)
University of Minnesota. Industrial Relations Center (US)
University of Minnesota. Institute of Child Development (US)
University of Minnesota James Ford Bell Library
see James Ford Bell Library (US)
University of Minnesota. Law School (US)
University of Minnesota. Minnesota Alumni Association (US)
University of Minnesota Press (US)
University of Minnesota. University Student Telecommunications Corp. (US)
University of Minnesota. Water Resources Research Center (US)
University of Minnesota, Duluth. Bureau of Business and Economic Research (US)
University of Minnesota, Duluth. Department of English (US)
University of Minnesota, Morris (US)
University of Mississippi (US)
University of Mississippi. Bureau of Governmental Research (US)
University of Mississippi. Department of Engineering (US)
University of Mississippi. Department of English (US)
University of Mississippi Law Center (US)
University of Mississippi Law School (US)
University of Mississippi. School of Business Administration (US)
University of Missouri-Columbia (US)
University of Missouri-Columbia. Agriculture & Engineering Department (US)
University of Missouri-Columbia. College of Business and Public Administration (US)
University of Missouri-Columbia. College of Education (US)
University of Missouri-Columbia. Department of Agronomy (US)
University of Missouri-Columbia. Department of Psychiatry (US)
University of Missouri-Columbia. Department of Regional & Community Affairs (US)
University of Missouri-Columbia. Department of Sociology and Rural Sociology (US)
University of Missouri-Columbia. Environmental Health Center and Extension Division (US)
University of Missouri-Columbia. Museum of Anthropology (US)
University of Missouri-Columbia. Museum of Art and Archaeology (US)
University of Missouri-Columbia. School of Law (US)

University of Missouri-Columbia. Veterinary Medical Diagnostic Labrary (US)
University of Missouri- Kansas City (US)
University of Missouri-Kansas City. School of Administration (US)
University of Missouri-Kansas City. School of Law (US)
University of Missouri Press (US)
University of Missouri- Rolla (US)
University of Missouri-Rolla. Department of Civil Engineering (US)
University of Missouri- St. Louis. Center for International Studies (US)
University of Montana. Associated Students (US)
University of Montana. Bureau of Business and Economic Research (US)
University of Montana. Bureau of Government Research (US)
University of Montana. Department of Anthropology (US)
University of Montana. Department of Geology (US)
University of Montana. Division of Educational Research and Services (US)
University of Montana. Information Services (US)
University of Montana. Publications in History (US)
University of Montana, School of Education (US)
University of Montana, School of Forestry (US)
University of Montana. School of Journalism (US)
University of Montana. School of Law (US)
University of Montana. Students of School of Law (US)
University of Mysore. Department of Post-Graduate Studies in English (II)
University of Mysore. Post-Graduate Department of Psychology (II)
University of Nagasaki
see Nagasaki University (JA)
University of Nagpur (II)
University of Nairobi. Institute for Development Studies (KE)
University of Nairobi. Library (KE)
University of Natal (SA)
University of Natal. Faculty of Arts (SA)
University of Natal. Faculty of Medicine (SA)
University of Natal. Institute for Social Research (SA)
University of Natal. Oceanographic Research Institute (SA)
University of Natal Press (SA)
University of Natal. Students Engineering Society (SA)
University of Natal. Students Geographical Society (SA)
University of Natal. Students Representative Council (SA)
University of Nebraska-Lincoln (US)
University of Nebraska-Lincoln. Alumni Association (US)
University of Nebraska-Lincoln. Bureau of Business Research (US)
University of Nebraska-Lincoln. College of Business Administration (US)
University of Nebraska-Lincoln. College of Engineering and Technology (US)
University of Nebraska-Lincoln. College of Law (US)
University of Nebraska- Lincoln. Department of Agricultural Education (US)
University of Nebraska-Lincoln. Department of Horticulture and Forestry (US)
University of Nebraska- Lincoln. Department of Publications Services & Control (US)
University of Nebraska-Lincoln. Institute of Agriculture and Natural Resources (US)
University of Nebraska-Lincoln. Libraries (US)
University of Nebraska-Lincoln. School of Journalism (US)
University of Nebraska Medical Center. Clinical Neurology Information Center (US)
University of Nebraska. North Platte Agricultural Experiment Station (US)
University of Nebraska-Omaha. Center for Applied Urban Research (US)
University of Nebraska Press (US)
University of Nebraska State Museum (US)
University of Nevada (US)
University of Nevada. Anthropology Department (US)
University of Nevada. Basque Studies Program (US)
University of Nevada. Bureau of Business and Economic Research (US)
University of Nevada. Bureau of Governmental Research (US)
University of Nevada. Department of Psychology (US)
University of Nevada. Departments of History and Political Science (US)
University of Nevada. Desert Research Institute (US)

University of Nevada Library. Special Collections Department (US)
University of Nevada. Mackay School of Mines (US)
University of Nevada. Max C. Fleischmann College of Agriculture (US)
University of Nevada Press (US)
University of Nevada. Seismological Laboratory (US)
University of New Brunswick (CN)
University of New Brunswick. Department of English (CN)
University of New Brunswick. Department of History (CN)
University of New Brunswick. Faculty of Forestry (CN)
University of New Brunswick. Faculty of Law (CN)
University of New Brunswick. Student Union (CN)
University of New Brunswick. Students Representative Council (CN)
University of New England (AT)
University of New England. Agricultural Business Research Institute (AT)
University of New England. Classical Society (AT)
University of New England. Department of Accounting & Financial Management (AT)
University of New England. Department of Continuing Education (AT)
University of New England. Department of External Studies (AT)
University of New England. Department of Geography (AT)
University of New England. Exploration Society (AT)
University of New England. Faculty of Education (AT)
University of New England. Rural Science Undergraduates' Society (AT)
University of New England. Student's Representative Council (AT)
University of New Hampshire. Agricultural Experiment Station (US)
University of New Hampshire. Alumni Association (US)
University of New Hampshire. Cooperative Extension Service (US)
University of New Hampshire. Department of Music (US)
University of New Hampshire. Institute of Natural and Environmental Resources (US)
University of New Hampshire. Publications Office (US)
University of New Haven (US)
University of New Mexico (US)
University of New Mexico. American Studies Program (US)
University of New Mexico. Art Museum (US)
University of New Mexico. Board of Student Publications (US)
University of New Mexico. Bureau of Business & Economic Research (US)
University of New Mexico. Department of Anthropology (US)
University of New Mexico. Department of Civil Engineering (US)
University of New Mexico. Department of Geology (US)
University of New Mexico. Institute for Applied Research Services (US)
University of New Mexico. Office of Research Administration (US)
University of New Mexico. School of Law (US)
University of New Mexico. Technology Application Center (US)
University of New Mexico. Women's Center (US)
University of New Orleans. College of Business Administration (US)
University of New South Wales (AT)
University of New South Wales. Commerce Society (AT)
University of New South Wales. Democratic Club (AT)
University of New South Wales. Faculty of Law (AT)
University of New South Wales. Library (AT)
University of New South Wales. Metallurgical Society (AT)
University of New South Wales. School of Civil Engineering (AT)
University of New South Wales. School of Health Administration (AT)
University of New South Wales. School of Sociology (AT)
University of New South Wales. School of Surveying (AT)
University of New South Wales. School of Town Planning (AT)
University of New South Wales. Water Reference Library (AT)

University of Rajasthan  (II)
University of Rajasthan. Department of Adult
    Education  (II)
University of Rajasthan. Department of History and
    Indian Culture  (II)
University of Rajasthan. Department of
    Parapsychology  (II)
University of Rajasthan. Department of Political
    Science  (II)
University of Rajasthan. Department of Public
    Administration  (II)
University of Rajasthan. Departments of Sanskrit and
    Hindi  (II)
University of Rajasthan Library
    see Rajasthan University Library  (II)
University of Rajasthan. School of Commerce  (II)
University of Rajasthan. South Asian Studies Centre
    (II)
University of Rajshahi  (BG)
University of Ranchi
    see Ranchi University  (II)
University of Reading. Department of Agricultural
    Economics  (UK)
University of Reading. Department of Agricultural
    Economics & Management  (UK)
University of Reading. Department of Geography
    (UK)
University of Reading. Graduate School of
    Contemporary European Studies  (UK)
University of Redlands Associated Students  (US)
University of Regina  (CN)
University of Regina. Department of English  (CN)
University of Regina. Students' Union  (CN)
University of Rhode Island  (US)
University of Rhode Island. Association of Friends of
    the Library  (US)
University of Rhode Island. Bureau of Government
    Research  (US)
University of Rhode Island. College of Business
    Administration  (US)
University of Rhode Island. College of Pharmacy
    (US)
University of Rhode Island. Cooperative Extension
    Service  (US)
University of Rhode Island. Department of Political
    Science  (US)
University of Rhode Island. Graduate School of
    Oceanography  (US)
University of Rhode Island. Marine Advisory Service
    (US)
University of Rhode Island. Water Resources Center
    (US)
University of Rhodesia  (RH)
University of Rhodesia. Department of Law  (RH)
University of Richmond. Institute for Business and
    Community Development  (US)
University of Richmond. School of Law  (US)
University of Rochester  (US)
University of Rochester. Department of Anthropology
    (US)
University of Rochester. New Zealand Romanian
    Cultural Association  (NZ)
University of Roorkee  (II)
University of St. Andrews  (UK)
University of San Carlos  (PH)
University of San Diego  (US)
University of San Diego. School of Law  (US)
University of San Fernando Valley. College of Law
    (US)
University of San Francisco  (US)
University of San Francisco. Labor Management
    School  (US)
University of San Francisco. School of Law  (US)
University of Santa Clara  (US)
University of Santa Clara. School of Law  (US)
University of Santo Tomas  (PH)
University of Santo Tomas. College of Architecture
    and Fine Arts  (PH)
University of Santo Tomas. College of Nursing  (PH)
University of Santo Tomas. Ecclesiastical Faculties
    (PH)
University of Santo Tomas. Faculty of Civil Law
    (PH)
University of Santo Tomas. Faculty of Medicine
    (PH)
University of Santo Tomas. Graduate School  (PH)
University of Santo Tomas. Institute for the Study of
    Human Reproduction  (PH)
University of Saskatchewan  (CN)
University of Saskatchewan. Alumni Association
    (CN)
University of Saskatchewan. College of Law  (CN)
University of Saskatchewan. Department of
    Anthropology and Archaeology  (CN)
University of Saskatchewan. Extension Division
    (CN)
University of Saskatchewan. Institute for Northern
    Studies  (CN)

University of Saugar. Botanical Society  (II)
University of Science and Technology  (GH)
University of Science and Technology. Students'
    Representative Council  (GH)
University of Science of Malaysia. School of
    Humanities  (MY)
University of Sheffield  (UK)
University of Sierra Leone. Fourah Bay College  (SL)
University of Sierra Leone. Njala University College
    (SL)
University of Sierra Leone Press  (SL)
University of Sind. Faculty of Arts  (PK)
University of Sind. Institute of Education & Research
    (PK)
University of Singapore  (SI)
University of Singapore. Chinese Society  (SI)
University of Singapore. Department of English  (SI)
University of Singapore. Department of Geography
    (SI)
University of Singapore. Department of Sociology  (SI)
University of Singapore. Economic Research Centre
    (SI)
University of Singapore. Economics Society  (SI)
University of Singapore. Faculty of Engineering  (SI)
University of Singapore Historical Society  (SI)
University of Singapore. History Department  (SI)
University of Singapore. Law Society  (SI)
University of Singapore. Muslim Society  (SI)
University of Singapore Political Science Society  (SI)
University of Singapore Science Society  (SI)
University of Singapore Society  (SI)
University of Singapore. Students' Union  (SI)
University of South Africa  (SA)
University of South Africa. Department of Art History
    and Fine Arts  (SA)
University of South Africa. Department of Bantu
    Languages  (SA)
University of South Africa. Department of
    Development Administration and Politics  (SA)
University of South Africa. Department of English
    (SA)
University of South Africa. Department of History
    (SA)
University of South Africa. Department of Library
    Science  (SA)
University of South Africa. Faculty of Education
    (SA)
University of South Africa. Faculty of Law  (SA)
University of South Africa. Institute of Foreign and
    Comparative Law  (SA)
University of South Carolina  (US)
University of South Carolina. Belle W. Baruch Institute
    for Marine Biology & Coastal Research  (US)
University of South Carolina. Bureau of Governmental
    Research  (US)
University of South Carolina. College of Business
    Administration  (US)
University of South Carolina. College of Education
    (US)
University of South Carolina. Department of English
    (US)
University of South Carolina. Department of Foreign
    Languages and Literatures  (US)
University of South Carolina. Graduate School of
    Social Work  (US)
University of South Carolina. Institute of International
    Studies  (US)
University of South Carolina Libraries  (US)
University of South Carolina Press  (US)
University of South Carolina. School of Law  (US)
University of South Dakota. Center for Continuing
    Education  (US)
University of South Dakota. College of Arts and
    Sciences  (US)
University of South Dakota. Governmental Research
    Bureau  (US)
University of South Dakota. Institute of Indian Studies
    (US)
University of South Dakota. School of Business  (US)
University of South Dakota. School of Law  (US)
University of South Florida. College of Arts and
    Letters  (US)
University of South Florida. College of Medicine
    (US)
University of South Florida. Department of English
    (US)
University of Southampton  (UK)
University of Southampton. Library  (UK)
University of Southern California  (US)
University of Southern California. Department of
    History  (US)
University of Southern California. Department of
    Linguistics  (US)
University of Southern California. Department of
    University Affairs  (US)
University of Southern California Law Center  (US)
University of Southern California. Library  (US)
University of Southern California Press  (US)

University of Southern California. School of Education
    (US)
University of Southern California. School of
    International Relations  (US)
University of Southern California. School of
    Philosophy  (US)
University of Southern Mississippi  (US)
University of Southern Mississippi. Alumni Association
    (US)
University of Southern Mississippi. Center for Writers
    (US)
University of Southern Mississippi. Department of
    English  (US)
University of Southern Mississippi. School of
    Education and Psychology  (US)
University of Southwestern Louisiana  (US)
University of Southwestern Louisiana. Center for
    Louisiana Studies  (US)
University of Sri Lanka  (CE)
University of Sri Lanka, Colombo Campus  (CE)
University of Sri Lanka, Peradeniya Campus  (CE)
University of Stellenbosch  (SA)
University of Stellenbosch. Bureau for Economic
    Research  (SA)
University of Stellenbosch. Department of Latin  (SA)
University of Strathclyde. Fraser of Allander Institute
    for Research on the Scottish Economy  (UK)
University of Strathclyde. Politics Department  (UK)
University of Strathclyde. Students' Association  (UK)
University of Surrey  (UK)
University of Sussex. Center for Contemporary
    European Studies  (UK)
University of Sussex. Institute of Development Studies
    (UK)
University of Sussex Union. Unionews Management
    Board  (UK)
University of Sydney  (AT)
University of Sydney. Archives  (AT)
University of Sydney. Arts Association  (AT)
University of Sydney. Arts Society  (AT)
University of Sydney. Australian Society for Classical
    Studies  (AT)
University of Sydney. Basser Department of Computer
    Science  (AT)
University of Sydney. Dental Alumni Society  (AT)
University of Sydney. Dental Health Education and
    Research Foundation  (AT)
University of Sydney. Department of Adult Education
    (AT)
University of Sydney. Department of Agricultural
    Economics  (AT)
University of Sydney. Department of Architectural
    Science  (AT)
University of Sydney. Department of Government and
    Public Administration  (AT)
University of Sydney. Department of History  (AT)
University of Sydney. Department of Indonesian &
    Malayan Studies  (AT)
University of Sydney. Department of Oriental Studies
    (AT)
University of Sydney. Department of Semitic Studies
    (AT)
University of Sydney. Economics Society  (AT)
University of Sydney. Faculty of Law  (AT)
University of Sydney Geographical Society  (AT)
University of Sydney. Institute of Criminology  (AT)
University of Sydney. Law Graduates Association
    (AT)
University of Sydney. Medical Society  (AT)
University of Sydney. Students Representative Council
    (AT)
University of Sydney Union  (AT)
University of Tampa  (US)
University of Tasmania. Law Review  (AT)
University of Teheran  (IR)
University of Teheran. Center for International Studies
    (IR)
University of Teheran. Central Library  (IR)
University of Teheran. Children's Medical Center
    (IR)
University of Teheran. College of Education  (IR)
University of Teheran. Faculty of Agriculture  (IR)
University of Teheran. Faculty of Education  (IR)
University of Teheran. Faculty of Engineering  (IR)
University of Teheran. Faculty of Health  (IR)
University of Teheran. Faculty of Law and Political
    Science  (IR)
Univ. of Teheran. Faculty of Letters and Humanities
    (IR)
University of Teheran. Faculty of Medicine  (IR)
University of Teheran. Faculty of Pharmacy  (IR)
University of Teheran. Faculty of Science  (IR)
University of Teheran. Faculty of Veterinary Medicine
    (IR)
University of Teheran. Institute for Economic
    Research  (IR)
University of Teheran. Institute of Geophysics  (IR)
University of Teheran. Institute of Psychology  (IR)

University of Teheran. School of Dental Medicine   (IR)
University of Tennessee   (US)
University of Tennessee. Agricultural Experiment Station   (US)
University of Tennessee. Center for Business and Economic Research   (US)
University of Tennessee. Center for the Health Sciences   (US)
University of Tennessee. College of Dentistry   (US)
University of Tennessee. College of Engineering   (US)
University of Tennessee. Department of English   (US)
University of Tennessee. Drug and Toxicology Information Center   (US)
University of Tennessee. Institute for Public Service   (US)
University of Tennessee. National Alumni Association   (US)
University of Tennessee at Chattanooga   (US)
University of Texas at Arlington   (US)
University of Texas at Arlington. Department of English   (US)
University of Texas at Austin   (US)
University of Texas at Austin. African and Afro-American Studies and Research Center   (US)
University of Texas at Austin. Bureau of Business Research   (US)
University of Texas at Austin. Bureau of Economic Geology   (US)
University of Texas at Austin. Center for Communication Research   (US)
University of Texas at Austin. Center for Intercultural Studies in Folklore and Ethnomusicology   (US)
University of Texas at Austin. Center for Intercultural Studies in Folklore and Oral History   (US)
University of Texas at Austin. Center for Neo-Hellenic Studies   (US)
University of Texas at Austin. Center for Research in Water Resources   (US)
University of Texas at Austin. Department of Anthropology   (US)
Univ. of Texas at Austin. Department of Astronomy   (US)
University of Texas at Austin. Department of English   (US)
University of Texas at Austin. Department of Germanic Languages   (US)
University of Texas at Austin. Electronics Research Center   (US)
University of Texas at Austin. Ex-Students Association   (US)
University of Texas at Austin. Humanities Research Center   (US)
University of Texas at Austin. Law School Foundation   (US)
University of Texas at Austin. Lyndon B. Johnson School of Public Affairs   (US)
University of Texas at Austin. Natural Fibers Economic Research   (US)
University of Texas at Austin. School of Law   (US)
University of Texas at Austin. Tarlton Law Library   (US)
University of Texas at Dallas   (US)
University of Texas at El Paso   (US)
University of Texas at El Paso. Bureau of Business and Economic Research   (US)
University of Texas at Galveston. Medical Branch   (US)
University of Texas at Port Aransas. Marine Science Institute   (US)
University of Texas at San Antonio. Center for Archeological Research   (US)
University of Texas. M.D. Anderson Hospital and Tumor Institute   (US)
University of Texas Press   (US)
University of the East. College of Business Administration   (PH)
University of the East. Faculty of the Graduate School   (PH)
University of the North. Department of Bantu Languages   (SA)
University of the Orange Free State   (SA)
University of the Orange Free State. Institute for Contemporary History   (SA)
University of the Pacific   (US)
University of the Pacific. Association of Students   (US)
University of the Pacific. McGeorge School of Law   (US)
University of the Pacific. Pacific Marine Station   (US)
University of the Pacific. School of Dentistry   (US)
University of the Pacific. School of Pharmacy   (US)
University of the Philippines   (PH)
University of the Philippines. Asian Centre   (PH)
University of the Philippines. College of Arts and Sciences   (PH)
University of the Philippines. College of Dentistry   (PH)

University of the Philippines. College of Education   (PH)
University of the Philippines. College of Medicine   (PH)
University of the Philippines. College of Public Administration   (PH)
University of the Philippines. College of Veterinary Medicine   (PH)
University of the Philippines. Community Development Research Council   (PH)
University of the Philippines. Institute of Environmental Planning   (PH)
University of the Philippines. Institute of Library Science   (PH)
University of the Philippines. Institute of Mass Communications   (PH)
University of the Philippines. Institute of Public Administration   (PH)
University of the Philippines. Interdepartmental Reference Service   (PH)
University of the Philippines. Law Center   (PH)
University of the Philippines. Library   (PH)
University of the Philippines. Office of Alumni Relations   (PH)
University of the Philippines. Philippine Center for Advanced Studies   (PH)
University of the Philippines Press   (PH)
University of the Philippines. School of Economics   (PH)
University of the Philippines at Los Banos. Agrarian Reform Institute   (PH)
University of the Philippines at Los Banos. College of Agriculture   (PH)
University of the Philippines at Los Banos. College of Forestry   (PH)
University of the Philippines at Los Banos. Rodent Research Center   (PH)
University of the Punjab. Arabic and Persian Society   (PK)
University of the Punjab. Department of Economics   (PK)
University of the Punjab. Department of Geography   (PK)
University of the Punjab. Department of Geology   (PK)
University of the Punjab. Department of Zoology   (PK)
University of the Ryukyus. College of Agriculture   (JA)
University of the Sacred Heart   (JA)
University of the South   (US)
University of the South Pacific   (FJ)
University of the South. School of Theology   (US)
University of the West Indies   (TR)
University of the West Indies   (JM)
University of the West Indies. Caribbean Food & Nutrition Institute   (JM)
University of the West Indies. Department of Extra-Mural Studies   (JM)
University of the West Indies. Department of Geography   (JM)
University of the West Indies. Department of History   (BB)
University of the West Indies. Department of Soil Science   (TR)
University of the West Indies. Faculty of Agriculture   (JM)
University of the West Indies. Imperial College of Tropical Agriculture   (TR)
University of the West Indies. Institute of International Relations   (TR)
University of the West Indies. Institute of Social and Economic Research   (JM)
University of the West Indies. Library   (TR)
University of the West Indies. School of Education   (BB)
University of the West Indies. School of Education   (JM)
University of the Witwatersrand, Johannesburg   (SA)
University of the Witwatersrand, Johannesburg. Bernard Price Institute for Palaeontological Research   (SA)
University of the Witwatersrand, Johannesburg. Faculty of Medicine   (SA)
University of the Witwatersrand, Johannesburg. Library   (SA)
University of the Witwatersrand, Johannesburg. Medical School   (SA)
University of the Witwatersrand, Johannesburg. School of Mechanical Engineering   (SA)
University of the Witwatersrand, Johannesburg. Student Engineers Council   (SA)
University of Tokushima
    see Tokushima University   (JA)
University of Tokyo. Center for American Studies   (JA)
University of Tokyo. College of General Education   (JA)

University of Tokyo. Computer Center   (JA)
University of Tokyo. Department of Geography   (JA)
University of Tokyo. Earthquake Research Institute   (JA)
University of Tokyo. Faculty of Engineering   (JA)
University of Tokyo. Faculty of Medicine   (JA)
University of Tokyo. Faculty of Science   (JA)
University of Tokyo. Institute for Nuclear Study   (JA)
University of Tokyo. Institute for Solid State Physics   (JA)
University of Tokyo. Institute of Applied Microbiology   (JA)
University of Tokyo. Institute of Industrial Science   (JA)
University of Tokyo. Institute of Medical Science   (JA)
University of Tokyo. Institute of Social Science   (JA)
University of Tokyo. Institute of Space and Aeronautical Science   (JA)
University of Tokyo. Misaki Marine Biological Station   (JA)
University of Tokyo. Ocean Research Institute   (JA)
University of Tokyo Press   (JA)
University of Tokyo. Research Institute of Logopedics and Phoniatrics   (JA)
University of Tokyo. School of Medicine   (JA)
University of Tokyo Society of Economics   (JA)
University of Tokyo. Tokyo Astronomical Observatory
    see Tokyo Astronomical Observatory   (JA)
University of Toledo. College of Business Administration   (US)
University of Toledo. College of Education   (US)
University of Toledo. College of Law   (US)
University of Toledo Press   (US)
University of Toronto. Centre for Medieval Studies   (CN)
University of Toronto. Centre of Criminology   (CN)
University of Toronto. Commerce Club   (CN)
University of Toronto. Department of Computer Science   (CN)
University of Toronto. Department of Electrical Engineering   (CN)
University of Toronto. Department of Geography   (CN)
University of Toronto. Department of Information Services   (CN)
University of Toronto. Department of Mathematics   (CN)
University of Toronto. Department of Mechanical Engineering   (CN)
University of Toronto. Department of Romance Languages   (CN)
University of Toronto. Department of Urban & Regional Planning   (CN)
University of Toronto. Engineering Society   (CN)
University of Toronto. Erindale College   (CN)
University of Toronto. Faculty of Education   (CN)
University of Toronto. Faculty of Forestry   (CN)
University of Toronto. Faculty of Law   (CN)
University of Toronto. Faculty of Management Studies   (CN)
University of Toronto. Graduate Centre for Study of Drama   (CN)
University of Toronto. Great Lakes Institute   (CN)
University of Toronto. Guidance Centre   (CN)
University of Toronto. Institute for Aerospace Studies   (CN)
University of Toronto. Institute for Policy Analysis   (CN)
University of Toronto. Library   (CN)
University of Toronto. Medical Society   (CN)
University of Toronto Press   (CN)
University of Toronto. Students Administrative Council   (CN)
University of Toronto. Victoria College   (CN)
University of Toronto-York University Joint Program in Transportation   (CN)
University of Tulsa   (US)
University of Tulsa College of Law   (US)
University of Tulsa. Department of English   (US)
University of Tulsa. Information Services Department   (US)
University of Turku
    see Turun Yliopisto   (FI)
University of Utah   (US)
University of Utah. Bureau of Economic and Business Research   (US)
University of Utah. College of Law   (US)
University of Utah. Department of Economics   (US)
University of Utah. Department of English   (US)
University of Utah. Eccles Medical Sciences Library   (US)
University of Utah. Electrical Engineering Department   (US)
University of Utah. Institute of Industrial Relations   (US)
University of Utah. Office of Institutional Studies   (US)

University of Utah Press  (US)
University of Vermont. Cooperative Extension Service  (US)
University of Vermont. Department of English  (US)
University of Victoria  (CN)
University of Victoria. Alma Mater Society  (CN)
University of Victoria. Department of Geography  (CN)
University of Victoria. McPherson Library  (CN)
University of Virginia  (US)
University of Virginia. Corcoran Department of History  (US)
University of Virginia. Institute of Government  (US)
University of Virginia Library  (US)
University of Virginia. School of Law  (US)
University of Virginia. School of Medicine  (US)
University of Waikato. Antarctic Research Unit  (NZ)
University of Wales. Board of Celtic Studies  (UK)
University of Wales. Institute of Science and Technology  (UK)
University of Wales Press  (UK)
University of Warwick. Centre for Industrial Economic & Business Research  (UK)
University of Warwick. Department of Economics  (UK)
University of Warwick. Department of English  (UK)
University of Warwick. Department of German Studies  (UK)
University of Warwick. Graduate School of Literature  (UK)
University of Warwick Library  (UK)
University of Washington  (US)
University of Washington. Black Student Union  (US)
University of Washington. College of Architecture & Urban Planning  (US)
University of Washington. College of Business Administration  (US)
University of Washington. College of Education  (US)
University of Washington. College of Engineering  (US)
University of Washington. College of Fisheries  (US)
University of Washington. College of Fisheries and Fisheries Institute  (US)
University of Washington. Department of English  (US)
University of Washington. Department of Environmental Health  (US)
University of Washington. Department of Oceanography  (US)
University of Washington. Division of Marine Resources  (US)
University of Washington. Graduate School of Business Administration  (US)
University of Washington. Graduate School of Public Affairs  (US)
University of Washington. Henry Art Gallery  (US)
University of Washington. Institute for Comparative & Foreign Area Studies  (US)
University of Washington. Institute for Environmental Studies  (US)
University of Washington Libraries  (US)
University of Washington Press  (US)
University of Washington. School of Law  (US)
University of Washington School of Medicine. Health Sciences Information Services  (US)
University of Waterloo  (CN)
University of Waterloo. Department of Biology  (CN)
University of Waterloo. Department of Chemistry  (CN)
University of Waterloo. Department of English  (CN)
University of Waterloo. Department of Germanic and Slavic Languages and Literature  (CN)
University of Waterloo. Department of History  (CN)
University of Waterloo. Department of Physics  (CN)
University of Waterloo. Department of Political Science  (CN)
University of Waterloo. Faculty of Environmental Studies  (CN)
University of Waterloo. Faculty of Mathematics  (CN)
University of Waterloo. Information Services Department  (CN)
University of Waterloo. Solid Mechanics Division  (CN)
University of Waterloo. Undergraduate Engineering Society "B"  (CN)
University of West Florida  (US)
University of West Los Angeles  (US)
University of Western Australia  (AT)
University of Western Australia. Centre for Asian Studies  (AT)
University of Western Australia. Centre for South & Southeast Asian Studies  (AT)
University of Western Australia. Department of Agricultural Economics  (AT)
University of Western Australia. Department of Anthropology  (AT)

University of Western Australia. Department of Education  (AT)
University of Western Australia. Department of English  (AT)
University of Western Australia. Department of Music  (AT)
University of Western Australia. Faculty of Economics and Commerce  (AT)
University of Western Australia. Faculty of Law  (AT)
University of Western Australia. Philosophy Department  (AT)
University of Western Australia Press  (AT)
University of Western Ontario  (CN)
University of Western Ontario. D. B. Weldon Library  (CN)
University of Western Ontario. Department of Alumni Affairs  (CN)
University of Western Ontario. Faculty of Education  (CN)
University of Western Ontario. Faculty of Law  (CN)
University of Western Ontario. Library  (CN)
University of Western Ontario. Medical School  (CN)
University of Western Ontario. Office of International Education  (CN)
University of Western Ontario. School of Business Administration  (CN)
University of Western Ontario. School of Library and Information Science  (CN)
University of Windsor  (CN)
University of Windsor. Faculty of Human Kinetics  (CN)
University of Windsor Press  (CN)
University of Windsor. Students' Administrative Council  (CN)
University of Winnipeg. Institute of Urban Studies  (CN)
University of Winnipeg. Students Association  (CN)
University of Wisconsin-La Crosse  (US)
University of Wisconsin-La Crosse. Center for Contemporary Poetry  (US)
University of Wisconsin-La Crosse. Institute for Minority Studies  (US)
University of Wisconsin-Madison  (US)
University of Wisconsin-Madison. African Studies Program  (US)
University of Wisconsin-Madison. Applied Population Laboratory  (US)
University of Wisconsin, Madison. Cartographic Laboratory  (US)
University of Wisconsin, Madison. Center for Women's and Family Living Education  (US)
University of Wisconsin-Madison. Center System Libraries  (US)
University of Wisconsin-Madison. Department of African Languages and Literature  (US)
University of Wisconsin, Madison. Department of Art  (US)
University of Wisconsin-Madison. Department of East Asian Languages and Literature  (US)
University of Wisconsin-Madison. Department of English  (US)
University of Wisconsin-Madison. Department of French & Italian  (US)
University of Wisconsin-Madison. Department of German  (US)
University of Wisconsin-Madison. Engineering Experiment Station  (US)
University of Wisconsin-Madison. Extension Departments of Mathematics  (US)
University of Wisconsin-Madison. Extension Services in Pharmacy  (US)
University of Wisconsin-Madison. Graduate School of Business  (US)
University of Wisconsin-Madison. Institute for Research in the Humanities  (US)
University of Wisconsin-Madison. Institute for Research on Poverty  (US)
University of Wisconsin-Madison. Land Tenure Center  (US)
University of Wisconsin-Madison. Law School  (US)
University of Wisconsin-Madison. Office of Research Publications  (US)
University of Wisconsin-Madison. Program in African Economic History  (US)
University of Wisconsin-Madison. Regional Rehabilitation Research Institute  (US)
University of Wisconsin-Madison. Seminar on the Acquisition of Latin American Library Materials  (US)
University of Wisconsin-Madison. University Center for Cooperatives  (US)
University of Wisconsin-Madison. University-Industry Research Program  (US)

University of Wisconsin. Mathematical Research Center  (US)
University of Wisconsin-Milwaukee. Center for Latin America  (US)
University of Wisconsin-Milwaukee. Institute of World Affairs  (US)
University of Wisconsin-Milwaukee Library  (US)
University of Wisconsin-Oshkosh  (US)
University of Wisconsin-Platteville. Institute of Public Affairs  (US)
University of Wisconsin Press  (US)
University of Wyoming. Agricultural Experiment Station  (US)
University of Wyoming. College of Law  (US)
University of Wyoming. Department of Geology  (US)
University of Wyoming. Division of Adult Education and Community Service  (US)
University of Wyoming Library  (US)
University of Wyoming. Natural Resources Research Institute  (US)
University of Wyoming. Water Resources Research Institute  (US)
University of Wyoming. Wyoming Educational Center  (US)
University of York  (UK)
University of York. Centre for Southern African Studies  (UK)
University of Zambia  (ZA)
University of Zambia. Institute for African Studies  (ZA)
University of Zambia. School of Law  (ZA)
University Park Press  (US)
University Photographers Association of America  (US)
University Press Book Service Inc.  (US)
University Press of Hawaii  (US)
University Press of Kentucky  (US)
University Press of New Brunswick Ltd.  (CN)
University Press of Virginia  (US)
University Presses of Florida  (US)
University Printing  (US)
University Professors for Academic Order  (US)
University Publications  (US)
University Publishing Projects Ltd.  (IS)
Casa Editrice Universo  (IT)
Societa Editrice Universo  (IT)
Universum Sokol Publications Inc  (US)
Universum-Verlagsanstalt GmbH KG  (GW)
Univerza v Ljubljani  (YU)
Univerza v Ljubljani. Fakulteta za Sociologijo, Politicne Vede in Novinarstvo  (YU)
Univerza v Ljubljani. Fakulteta za Strojnistvo  (YU)
Univerza v Ljubljani. Filozofska Fakulteta  (YU)
Univerza v Ljubljani. Medicinska Fakulteta  (YU)
Univerza v Ljubljani. Pravni Fakultet  (YU)
Univerzita Komenskeho. Farmaceuticka Fakulta  (CS)
Univerzita Komenskeho. Filozoficka Fakulta  (CS)
Univerzita Komenskeho. Lekarska Fakulta  (CS)
Univerzita Komenskeho. Oddelenie Liecebnej a Specialnej Pedagogiky  (CS)
Univerzita Komenskeho. Pedagogicka Fakulta v Trnave  (CS)
Univerzita Komenskeho. Ustav Marxizmu-Leninizmu  (CS)
Univerzita Palackeho. Filosoficka Fakulta  (CS)
Univerzita Palackeho. Lekarska Fakulta  (CS)
Univerzita Palackeho. Pedagogicka Fakulta  (CS)
Univerzitet u Beogradu  (YU)
Univerzitet u Beogradu. Elektrotehnicki Fakultet  (YU)
Univerzitet u Beogradu. Filoloski Fakultet  (YU)
Univerzitet u Beogradu. Institut za Botaniku i Botanicke Baste  (YU)
Univerzitet u Beogradu. Pravni Fakultet  (YU)
Univerzitet u Beogradu. Prirodno-Matematicki Fakultet  (YU)
Univerzitet u Beogradu. Tehnicki Fakultet  (YU)
Univerzitet u Nisu  (YU)
Univerzitet u Novom Sadu. Prirodno-Matematicki Fakultet  (YU)
Univerzitet u Sarajevu  (YU)
Univerzitet u Sarajevu. Gradjevinski Fakultet  (YU)
Univerzitet u Sarajevu. Poljoprivredni Fakultet  (YU)
Univerzitet u Zagrebu
   see Sveuciliste u Zagrebu  (YU)
Univerzitet vo Skoplje. Ekonomskiot Fakultet  (YU)
Univerzitet vo Skoplje. Medicinski Fakultet  (YU)
Univerzitna Kniznica  (CS)
Uniwersytet Gdanski  (PL)
Uniwersytet im. Adama Mickiewicza  (PL)
Uniwersytet Jagiellonski  (PL)
Uniwersytet Lodzki  (PL)
Uniwersytet Marii Curie-Sklodowskiej  (PL)
Uniwersytet Mikolaja Kopernika  (PL)
Uniwersytet Slaski w Katowicach  (PL)
Uniwersytet Warszawski  (PL)

Vanderbilt University. W. T. Bandy Center for
    Baudelaire Studies  (US)
Vanderveer B. V.  (NE)
Vanguard Productions  (US)
Vanier Institute of the Family  (CN)
Vanity Fair  (US)
Al Vann  (US)
Vantasy Press  (UK)
Edition et Publicite Jean Vanvert  (FR)
Dan Vap Press  (US)
Var Konst  (SW)
Mariso Varagnolo, Ed. & Pub.  (IT)
Varazdinske Vijesti  (YU)
Editions Varia  (FR)
Variety, Inc.  (US)
Varlik Yayinevi  (TU)
Redaktion VARTA-Fuehrer  (GW)
Vasan, S.L. Ediciones Tecnica  (SP)
Vasantha Vilas  (II)
Vassar College  (US)
Vasudha Publication  (NP)
Vatican. Segretaria di Stato. Ufficio Centrale di
    Statistica della Chiesa  (VC)
Vatican Press  (VC)
Libreria Editrice Vaticana  (VC)
Regitec, J. de Vaubernier et Cie  (FR)
Editions Vauclair S.A.R.L.  (FR)
Vauxhall Motors Ltd.  (UK)
Ve Venezuela  (VE)
Editora Vecchi, S.A.  (BL)
Veda, Publishing House of the Slovak Academy of
    Sciences  (CS)
Vedanta Movement  (UK)
Vedic Publications  (UK)
H. Veenman en Zonen  (NE)
Veer  (SA)
Vega  (IT)
Vegetable Growers Association of New Jersey Inc.
    (US)
Vegetarian Society  (UK)
Vegetarian Society of New York  (US)
Vegetarian Society, South Australia  (AT)
Vegetarian Times  (US)
Vegetarian World  (US)
Vehicle Builders and Repairers Association  (UK)
Veiligheidsinstituut  (NE)
R. Veillith Ed. and Pub.  (FR)
Veljesliitto  (FI)
Vellez Music News  (US)
Velocidad  (AG)
Velser Basketball Club  (NE)
Veltro Editrice  (IT)
Venceremos Brigade. National Office  (US)
Vending Times, Inc.  (US)
Vendre Aujourd'hui  (FR)
Vends Annual Market Data and Directory  (US)
Editrice le Venezie e l'Italia  (IT)
Venezuela. Administracion General del Impuesto
    Sobre la Renta. Division de Coordinacion y
    Supervision Legal y Tecnica  (VE)
Venezuela. Archivo General de la Nacion  (VE)
Venezuela. Biblioteca Nacional  (VE)
Venezuela. Departamento de Hacienda  (VE)
Venezuela. Direccion de Hidrografia y Navegacion.
    Seccion de Climatologia  (VE)
Venezuela. Direccion de Normalizacion y Certificacion
    de Calidad  (VE)
Venezuela. Division de Economica Petrolera  (VE)
Venezuela. Imprimeria Nacional  (VE)
Venezuela. Ministerio de Agricultura y Cria  (VE)
Venezuela. Ministerio de Agricultura y Cria. Direccion
    de Planificacion y Estadistica  (VE)
Venezuela. Ministerio de Agricultura y Cria. Insituto
    Botanico  (VE)
Venezuela. Ministerio de Educacion  (VE)
Venezuela. Ministerio de Educacion. Direccion de
    Cultura y Bellas Artes  (VE)
Venezuela. Ministerio de Educacion Nacional. Museo
    de Ciencias Naturales  (VE)
Venezuela. Ministerio de Energia y Minas  (VE)
Venezuela. Ministerio de Fomento  (VE)
Venezuela. Ministerio de Fomento. Direccion General
    de Estadistica y Censos Nacionales  (VE)
Venezuela. Ministerio de Hacienda. Direccion General
    de Finanzas Publicas  (VE)
Venezuela. Ministerio de Justicia  (VE)
Venezuela. Ministerio de Justicia. Comision Indigenista
    Nacional  (VE)
Venezuela. Ministerio de la Defensa. Las Fuerzas
    Armadas  (VE)
Venezuela. Ministerio de la Defensa. Oficina Tecnica
    (VE)
Venezuela. Ministerio de la Defensa. Servicio de
    Sanidad Militar  (VE)
Venezuela. Ministerio de Minas e Hidrocarburos
    (VE)

Venezuela. Ministerio de Sanidad y Asistencia Social
    (VE)
Venezuela. Ministerio de Sanidad y Assistencia Social.
    Direccion de Salud Publica  (VE)
Venezuela. Ministerio del Trabajo  (VE)
Venezuela. Oficina Central de Informacion  (VE)
Venezuela. Secretaria de la Presidencia  (VE)
Venezuela. Sociedad Venezolana de Ingeniera
    Hidraulica  (VE)
Venezuelan-American Chamber of Commerce and
    Industry  (VE)
Venga Que le Cuento...  (AG)
K. Venkataraman, Ed. & Pub.  (II)
S. Venkatraman, Ed. & Pub.  (II)
W. Venner  (CN)
Venstres Landsorganisation  (DK)
Vent - Art  (BE)
Ventil  (AU)
Publications Georges Ventillard  (FR)
Ventla-Verlag  (GW)
Ventura County Historical Society  (US)
Ver Poets  (UK)
Enrique Vicente de Vera, Ed. & Pub.  (SP)
Veratbrite Ltd.  (UK)
Verband Bayerischer Berufsschullehrer  (GW)
Verband Beratender Ingenieure  (GW)
Verband Bildender Kuenstler der DDR  (GE)
Verband der Agrarjournalisten  (GW)
Verband der Altpfadfindergilden Oesterreichs  (AU)
Verband der Angestellten-Krankenkassen e.V.  (GW)
Verband der Automobilindustrie  (GW)
Verband der Beamten der Bundesanstalt fuer Arbeit
    (GW)
Verband der Bibliotheken des Landes Nordrhein-
    Westfalen  (GW)
Verband der Caritas-Konferenzen Deutschlands
    (GW)
Verband der Chemischen Industrie  (GW)
Verband der Cigarettenindustrie  (GW)
Verband der Deutschen Bundeswehr e.V.  (GW)
Verband der Deutschen Dental-Industrie e.V.  (GW)
Verband der Deutschen Fruchtsaft-Industrie e.V.
    (GW)
Verband der Deutschen Kautschukgesellschaften
    (GW)
Verband der Deutschen Schiffbauindustrie e.V.  (GW)
Verband der Energieabnehmer e.V.  (GW)
Verband der Freien Presse e.V.  (GW)
Verband der Geschichtslehrer Deutschlands  (GW)
Verband der Haftpflicht- , Unfall- und
    Kraftverkehrsversicherer e.V.  (GW)
Verband der Journalisten der DDR  (GE)
Verband der Koeche Deutschlands e.V.  (GW)
Verband der Komponisten und Musikwissenschaftler
    der DDR  (GE)
Verband der Korbwaren-, Korbmoebel- und
    Kinderwagenindustrie e.V.  (GW)
Verband der Kraftfahrzeugteile- und Zweirad-
    Grosshaendler  (GW)
Verband der Kriegs- und Wehrdienstopfer, Behinderten
    und Sozialrentner Deutschlands e.V.  (GW)
Verband der Lebensversicherungsunternehmen e.V.
    (GW)
Verband der Maschinen- und Werkzeughaendler,
    MAWEV  (AU)
Verband der Niedersaechsischen Landvolkes e.V.
    (GW)
Verband der Oesterreichischen Neuphilologen fuer
    Moderne Sprachen, Literatur und Paedagogik
    (AU)
Verband der Parlaments- und
    Verhandlungsstenographen  (GW)
Verband der Privaten Krankenversicherung e.V.
    (GW)
Verband der Professoren Oesterreichs  (AU)
Verband der Rundfunkhoerer und Fernsehteilnehmer
    in Bayern e.V.  (GW)
Verband der Schuhindustrie und dem Schuhhandel
    (AU)
Verband der Taschen- und Armbanduhren Industrie
    e.V.  (GW)
Verband der Teer- und Asphaltmischwerke e.V.
    (GW)
Verband der Theaterschaffenden der DDR  (GE)
Verband der Tropenlandwirte aus Witzenhausen e.V.
    (GW)
Verband der Weiblichen Angestellten e.V.  (GW)
Verband der Wissenschaftlichen Gesellschaften  (AU)
Verband der Versicherungsunternehmungen
    Oesterreichs  (AU)
Verband der Zuechter des Holsteiner Pferdes  (GW)
Verband der Zuechter des Oldenburger Pferdes  (GW)
Verband des Deutschen Blumen-Gross- und
    Importhandels e.V.  (GW)

Verband des Deutschen Fass- und Weinkuefer-
    Handwerks e.V.  (GW)
Verband des Deutschen Gas- und Wasserwerke
    (GW)
Verband des deutschen Tischlerhandwerks  (GW)
Verband des Naehmaschinen-und Fahrradhandels und
    Gewerbes Oesterreichs  (AU)
Verband Deutsche Sportpresse E.V  (GW)
Verband Deutscher Akademiker fuer Landwirtschaft,
    Ernaehrung und Landespflege e.V.  (GW)
Verband Deutscher Badeaerzte  (GW)
Verband Deutscher Badebetriebe e.V.  (GW)
Verband Deutscher Eisenbahningenieure  (GW)
Verband Deutscher Elektrotechniker e.V.  (GW)
Verband Deutscher Flugleiter e.V.  (GW)
Verband Deutscher Hoehlen- und Karstfoerscher e.V.
    (GW)
Verband Deutscher Hopfenpflanzer e.V.  (GW)
Verband Deutscher Mineralbrunnen e.V.  (GW)
Verband Deutscher Postingenieure  (GW)
Verband Deutscher Rentenversicherungstraeger
    (GW)
Verband Deutscher Rotviehzuechter  (GW)
Verband Deutscher Rundfunk- und Fernseh-
    Fachgrosshaendler e.V.  (GW)
Verband Deutscher Schiffswerften e.V.  (GW)
Verband Deutscher Schulmusikerzieher  (GW)
Verband Deutscher Soldaten e.V.  (GW)
Verband Deutscher Sportgeschaefte e.V.  (GW)
Verband Deutscher Sporttaucher e.V.  (GW)
Verband deutscher Stahlwaren-Fachhandler e.V
    (GW)
Verband Deutscher Vereine fuer Aquarien- und
    Terrarienkunde  (GW)
Verband Deutscher Vermessungsingenieure e.V.
    (GW)
Verband Deutscher Zahntechnikerinnungen e.V.
    (GW)
Verband Evangelischer Kirchenchoere Deutschlands
    (GW)
Verband Evangelischer Kirchenmusiker Deutschlands
    (GW)
Verband Evangelischer Missionskonferenzen  (GW)
Verband Freier Wohnungsunternehmen e.V.  (GW)
Verband fuer Arbeitsstudien  (GW)
Verband fuer Cash and Carry Grosshandel e.V.
    (GW)
Verband fuer Heimatschutz und Heimatpflege in Tirol
    (AU)
Verband fuer Ruten- und Pendelkunde (Radiaesthesie)
    (GW)
Verband Hannoverscher Warmblutzuechter e.V.
    (GW)
Verband Kommunaler Stadtreinigungsbetriebe  (GW)
Verband Landwirtschaftlicher Gutsbetriebe in
    Oesterreich  (AU)
Verband Oeffentlicher Verkehrsbetriebe  (GW)
Verband Oesterreichischer Archivare  (AU)
Verband Oesterreichischer Brieftaubenzuechter  (AU)
Verband Oesterreichischer Hoehlenforscher  (AU)
Verband Oesterreichischer Landsmannschaften  (AU)
Verband Oesterreichischer Philatelisten-Vereine  (AU)
Verband Oesterreichischer Zeitungsherausgeber und
    Zeitungsverleger  (AU)
Verband Papier, Buerobedarf, Schreibwaren  (GW)
Verband Schweizer Metzgermeister  (SZ)
Verband Schweizerischer Artillerie-Vereine  (SZ)
Verband Schweizerischer Bildhauer- und
    Steinmetzmeister  (SZ)
Verband Schweizerischer Foerster  (SZ)
Verband Schweizerischer Gaertnermeister  (SZ)
Verband Schweizerischer Heizungs- und
    Leuftungsfirmen  (SZ)
Verband Schweizerischer Lebensmittel-Detaillisten
    (SZ)
Verband Schweizerischer Militaerkuechenchefs  (SZ)
Verband Schweizerischer Papeteristen  (SZ)
Verband Schweizerischer Schreinermeister und
    Moebelfabrikanten  (SZ)
Verband Schweizerischer Tabakhaendler  (SZ)
Verband Schweizerischer Transportunternehmungen
    des Oeffentlichen Verkehrs  (SZ)
Verband Schweizerischer Uhrenfachgeschaefte  (SZ)
Verband Schweizerischer Vogelschutzvereine  (SZ)
Verband Sozialistischer Mittelschueler  (AU)
Verband Sozialistischer Studenten Oesterreichs  (AU)
Buchverlag Verbandsdruckerei AG  (SZ)
Verbond van Nederlandse Ondernemingen  (NE)
Verbond van Wetenschappelijke Onderzoekers  (NE)
Verden og Vi  (NO)
Vereeniging der Antwerpsche Bibliophielen  (BE)
Vereeniging ter Bevordering van de Belangen des
    Boekhandels  (NE)
Vereeniging voor den Katoenhandel, Rotterdam  (NE)
Vereeniging Zuid-Afrikaansche Stichting Moederland
    (NE)
Verein Bayerischer Krippenfreunde  (GW)
Verein Beethoven-Haus Bonn  (GW)

Vermont. Department of Libraries. Law and Document Library  (US)
Vermont. Geological Survey  (US)
Vermont. Office of Statistical Coordination  (US)
Vermont Agricultural Experiment Station  (US)
Vermont Catholic Press Association  (US)
Vermont Education Association  (US)
Vermont Historical Society  (US)
Vermont Industrial Development Authority  (US)
Vermont Library Association  (US)
Vermont Music Educators Association  (US)
Vermont Philatelic Society  (US)
Vermont School Boards Association  (US)
Vernepligtige Officerers Forening  (NO)
Vernice  (IT)
Vernon Directories  (CN)
Verona Fathers-Sons of the Sacred Heart  (US)
Casa Editrice Luigi Veronelli  (IT)
Lawrence Verry, Inc. (U.S. Distrib.)  (US)
Vers la Vie Nouvelle  (FR)
Versatile Publishing Co. Ltd.  (CN)
Verse Writers' Guild of Ohio  (US)
Versicherungsanstalt der Oesterreichischen Eisenbahnen. Unfallverhuetungsdienst  (AU)
Verlag Versicherungswirtschaft e.V.  (GW)
Versoehnungsbund e.V.  (GW)
Verlag Versorgungswirtschaft  (GW)
Versuchs- und Lehranstalt fuer Brauerei in Berlin  (GW)
Versuchs- und Lehranstalt fuer Spiritusfabrikation und Fermentationstechnologie  (GW)
Versuchsstation fuer das Gaerungsgewerbe  (AU)
Vertente Editora Ltda.  (BL)
Vertical  (BO)
Vertical Marketing Inc.  (US)
Vertice  (PO)
Vesihuoltomiitto  (FI)
Vesiyhdistys r.y.  (FI)
Verlag der "Veska"  (SZ)
Vestal Central Schools  (US)
Vestdijkkring  (NE)
Vestlandske Felleskjoep  (NO)
Veszpremi Vegyipari Egyetem  (HU)
Veteran Car Club of Great Britian  (UK)
Veteran Car Club of South Africa  (SA)
Veteran Motor Club of America  (US)
Veterans Information Service  (US)
Veterans of Foreign Wars of the United States  (US)
Veterans of Foreign Wars of the United States. Department of Minnesota  (US)
Veterans of Foreign Wars of the United States. Ladies Auxiliary  (US)
Editorial Veterinaria, S.A.  (SP)
Veterinarians Alliance  (UK)
Veterinary Medicine Association of Iran  (IR)
Veterinary Medicine Publishing Co.  (US)
Veterinary Practice Publishing Co.  (US)
Veterinary Surgeons Board of New Zealand  (NZ)

Vi Bilaegare Med Hem och Hobby  (SW)

Via Femminile  (IT)
Via Libera  (IT)
Editions H. Vial  (FR)
Vianelli Eleganza  (IT)
Viborg Stiftsmuseum  (DK)
Vibration  (US)
Vicariato General Castrense  (SP)
Vichiana  (IT)
Vickers Ltd.  (UK)
Vickers Petroleum Corporation  (US)
Able David Victor, Inc.  (US)
Victoria. Department of Agriculture  (AT)
Victoria. Department of Agriculture. Agricultural Research Unit  (AT)
Victoria. Department of Agriculture. Information Officer  (AT)
Victoria. Department of Education  (AT)
Victoria. Department of Education. Curriculum & Research Branch  (AT)
Victoria. Department of Education. Publications Branch  (AT)
Victoria. Department of Youth, Sport and Recreation  (AT)
Victoria. Forests Commission  (AT)
Victoria. Government Printer  (AT)
Victoria. Ministry for Conservation. Fisheries and Wildlife Division  (AT)
Victoria. Ministry of Fuel and Power  (AT)
Victoria. Ministry of Tourism  (AT)
Victoria. Premier's Department  (AT)
Victoria. State Electricity Commission. Herman Central Scientific Laboratory  (AT)
Victoria. State Rivers & Water Supply Commission  (AT)
Victoria College. School and Old Victorians' Association  (UI)
Victoria Druck-und Verlag Poech und Co. GmbH  (AU)

Victoria Institute  (UK)
Victoria Institute of Colleges  (AT)
Victoria League  (UK)
Victoria Police Force  (AT)
Victoria Promotion Committe  (AT)
Victoria Promotion Committee, Melbourne  (AT)
Victoria State Film Centre  (AT)
Victoria Town and Country Planning Board  (AT)
Victoria University of Wellington  (NZ)
Victoria University of Wellington. Department of Psychology  (NZ)
Victoria University of Wellington. Faculty of Commerce & Administration  (NZ)
Victoria University of Wellington. School of Political Science  (NZ)
Victoria University of Wellington. Zoology Department  (NZ)
Victorian Advisory Committee on the Teaching of Social Sciences in Secondary Schools  (AT)
Victorian Apiarist's Association  (AT)
Victorian Association for the Teaching of English  (AT)
Victorian Association of Social Studies Teachers  (AT)
Victorian Autombile Chamber of Commerce  (AT)
Victorian Bands League  (AT)
Victorian Ceramic Group  (AT)
Victorian Chamber of Manufacturers  (AT)
Victorian Country Press Association  (AT)
Victorian Dairyfarmer Company Pty Ltd.  (AT)
Victorian Dairyfarmers' Association  (AT)
Victorian Farmers Newspapers Pty Ltd.  (AT)
Victorian Farmers Union  (AT)
Victorian Flute Guild  (AT)
Victorian Football League  (AT)
Victorian Historical Association  (AT)
Victorian Institute of Educational Research  (AT)
Victorian Jazz Club  (AT)
Victorian Labor College  (AT)
Victorian Ladies' Bowling Association  (AT)
Victorian Music Teachers Association  (AT)
Victorian Order of Nurses for Canada  (CN)
Victorian Potato Growers Association  (AT)
Victorian Railways Board  (AT)
Victorian Road Transport Association  (AT)
Victorian Secondary Teachers Association  (AT)
Victorian Showmen's Guild  (AT)
Victorian Society  (UK)
Victorian Society in America  (US)
Victorian Speleological Association  (AT)
Victorian Teachers' Union  (AT)
Victorian Tobacco Growers' Association  (AT)
Victorian U.F.O. Research Society  (AT)
Victorians Institute Journal  (US)
Vida de la Piedad  (MX)
Vida Rural e Economica  (BL)
Vidarbha Industries Association  (II)
Video Publishing Co.  (AT)
Vidya  (IT)
Vie au Soleil  (FR)
Editions de la Vie Catholique  (FR)
Vie Collective  (FR)
Vie Communale et Departementale  (FR)
Vie de la Douane  (FR)
Vie des Collectivites Ouvrieres  (FR)
Vie et Travail  (FR)
Vie Judiciaire  (FR)
Editions de la Vie Medicale  (FR)
Vie Medicale Inc.  (CN)
Vie Montante. Edition Canadienne  (CN)
Vie Musicale  (FR)
Vie Publique  (FR)
Vie Theresienne  (FR)
Editions de la Vie Wallonne  (BE)
Nikolajs Vieglais, Ed. & Pub.  (US)
Vienna. Kulturamt der Stadt Wien. Direktion der Staedtischen Buechereien  (AU)
Vienna. Magistrat der Stadt Wien  (AU)
Vienna. Magistrat der Stadt Wien. Statistisches Amt  (AU)
Vienna. Magistrat der Stadt Wien. Verein Wiener Jugendkreis  (AU)
Vienna. Stadtbauamt der Stadt Wien  (AU)
Viens et Vois  (FR)
Vientin S.A.  (AG)
Vienybe  (US)
Vier-Tuerme-Verlag  (GW)
Verlag und Werbung Otto Vieth  (GW)
Vietnam  (VN)
Vietnam. Directorate of Archives and Libraries  (VN)
Vietnam Bulletin  (US)
Vietnam Solidarity Committee  (UK)
Vietnam Women's Hanoi  (VN)
Vietnam Youth Federation  (VN)
Vietnamese Studies  (VN)
Friedr. Vieweg und Sohn Verlagsgesellschaft mbH  (GW)
Viewpoint Aquarius  (UK)

Viewpoints Institute, Inc.  (US)
Viga en el Ojo  (CK)
Vigilancia  (MX)
Vigo County Public Library  (US)
Editions Vigot Freres  (FR)
Richard A. Viguerie Co., Inc.  (US)
Manuel Vijungco, Ed. & Pub.  (PH)
Vikas Publishing House Pvt. Ltd.  (II)
Viking Press, Inc  (US)
Viking Society for Northern Research  (UK)
Vikingens Forlag  (DK)
Vikram University  (II)
Vikram University. Maharaja Jiwajirao Library  (II)
Vikrant Publications  (II)
Vilaggazdasagi Tudomanyos Tanacs  (HU)
Villa Guide Ltd.  (UK)
Foerlags AB Villa och Hem  (SW)
Village Press  (US)
Village Voice  (US)
Periodicos Villagran, S. A.  (MX)
Villanova University Law School  (US)
Angel Villatoro, Ed. & Pub.  (SP)
Vilmy Ricerche  (IT)
Vilnius Universitet  (UR)
Viltis  (US)
Vimal Prasad Jain  (II)
Guy Vinatrel  (FR)
Vincent Press  (UK)
Editions Charles Vincent, S. A.  (FR)
Vincentian Fathers  (IT)
Curt R. Vincentz Verlag  (GW)
Leonardo da Vinci  (IT)
Vinohrad  (CS)
Vintage  (UK)
Vintage Jazz Mart  (UK)
Vintage Magazine Inc.  (US)
Vintage Record Mart  (UK)
Vintage Records  (US)
Vintage Transport Enthusiasts Club  (UK)
Vinzenzgemeinschaft  (AU)
Viola da Gamba Society  (UK)
Viola da Gamba Society of America, Inc.  (US)
Viomichaniki Epitheorissis  (GR)
Viraleinen Lehti  (FI)
Virendra Prasad Jain
  *see* World Jain Mission  (II)
Virgil Society  (UK)
Virgin Islands (U.S.) Department of Commerce. Division of Trade and Industry  (VI)
Virgin Islands Archaeological Society  (VI)
Virgin Islands Nurses Association  (VI)
Virginia. Air Pollution Control Board  (US)
Virginia. Commission for Children and Youth  (US)
Virginia. Commission of Game and Inland Fisheries  (US)
Virginia. Council on the Environment  (US)
Virginia. Department of Agriculture and Commerce  (US)
Virginia. Department of Agriculture and Commerce. Division of Product and Industry Regulation  (US)
Virginia. Department of Conservation and Economic Development. Division of Mineral Resources  (US)
Virginia. Department of Corrections. Bureau of Management Information  (US)
Virginia. Department of Education  (US)
Virginia. Department of Health. Bureau of Health Education  (US)
Virginia. Department of Health. Medical Examiner Division  (US)
Virginia. Department of Highways and Transportation  (US)
Virginia. Department of Labor and Industry. Division of Research and Statistics  (US)
Virginia. Department of Vocational Rehabilitation  (US)
Virginia. Division of Aeronautics  (US)
Virginia. Division of Justice and Crime Prevention  (US)
Virginia. Drug Abuse Advisory Council  (US)
Virginia. Employment Commission  (US)
Virginia. Law Enforcement Officers Training Standards Commission  (US)
Virginia. Office of the Attorney General  (US)
Virginia. Port Authority  (US)
Virginia. State Council of Higher Education  (US)
Virginia. State Library  (US)
Virginia. State Library. Historical Publications Division  (US)
Virginia. State Library. Library Development Branch  (US)
Virginia. State Water Control Board  (US)
Virginia Academy of Science  (US)
Virginia Association of Plumbing-Heating-Cooling Contractors  (US)
Virginia Association of Teachers of English  (US)
Virginia Baptist Historical Society  (US)
Virginia Bar Association  (US)
Virginia-Carolina Peanut Association  (US)

Virginia Commonwealth University. Adult Education
    Program (US)
Virginia Commonwealth University. University
    Computer Center (US)
Virginia Congress of Parents and Teachers (US)
Virginia Education Association (US)
Virginia Education Association. School Librarians
    Department (US)
Virginia Food Dealers Association (US)
Virginia Forests, Inc. (US)
Virginia Gazette Inc. (US)
Virginia Geographical Society (US)
Virginia High School League (US)
Virginia Highway Users Association (US)
Virginia Historical Society (US)
Virginia Institute of Marine Science (US)
Virginia Institute of Pastoral Care, Inc. (US)
Virginia Journal of International Law Association
    (US)
Virginia Law Review Association (US)
Virginia Library Association (US)
Virginia Military Institute (US)
Virginia Municipal League (US)
Virginia Museum of Fine Arts (US)
Virginia Nurses Association (US)
Virginia Pharmaceutical Association (US)
Virginia Place Name Society (US)
Virginia Polytechnic Institute and State University.
    Center for Study of Public Choice (US)
Virginia Polytechnic Institute and State University.
    Department of Sociology (US)
Virginia Polytechnic Institute and State University.
    Department of Geological Sciences (US)
Virginia Polytechnic Institute and State University.
    Extension Division (US)
Virginia Polytechnic Institute and State University.
    News Services (US)
Virginia Polytechnic Institute and State University.
    Research Division (US)
Virginia Polytechnic Institute and State University.
    School of Forestry and Wildlife Resources (US)
Virginia Polytechnic Institute and State University.
    Water Resources Research Center (US)
Virginia Polytechnic Institute and State University.
    Wood Research and Wood Construction Laboratory
    (US)
Virginia Poultry Federation (US)
Virginia Press Association (US)
Virginia Publishers Wing, Inc. (US)
Virginia School Boards Association (US)
Virginia Society of Certified Public Accountants (US)
Virginia Society of Ornithology (US)
Virginia Sports Publications, Inc. (US)
Virginia State Bar. Criminal Law Section (US)
Virginia State Bar. Young Lawyers Conference (US)
Virginia State Chamber of Commerce (US)
Virginia State Dental Association (US)
Virginia State Reading Association (US)
Virginia Wesleyan College. Department of English
    (US)
Virgo Enterprises (US)
Viridian Starfire (US)
M'litograph di Virna Antoni & C. (IT)
Visage Press, Inc. (US)
Visages de l'Ain (FR)
Visao S.A. Editorial (BL)
Verlag Curt Visel (GW)
Vishva Hindu Parishad (II)
Vishveshvaranand Vedic Research Institute (II)
Vishwa Hindu Dharma Sammelan (II)
Visible Language (US)
Visindafelag Islendinga (IC)
Vision Boliviana (BO)
Vision, Inc. (US)
Vision Inc., S.A. (UK)
Vision Publishing Corporation (PH)
Editorial Vision, S. A. (MX)
Visite (GE)
Visiting Nurse Association of Brooklyn. Department of
    Resources Development (US)
Visitors East (US)
Visoka Ekonomsko Komercialna Sola (YU)
Neue Buchdruckerei Visp AG (SZ)
Vissh Finansovo- Stopanski Institut (BU)
Vista Femenina Centroamericana (CR)
Vista Hill Foundation (US)
Visual Arts Research and Resource Center Relating to
    the Caribbean. Phelps Stoke Fund (US)
Visual Dialog (US)
Visual Publications Ltd. (UK)
Visual Resources Inc. (US)
Visual Science Information Center (US)
Visual Studies Workshop (US)
Visual Ventures Publishing (US)
Visva-Bharati (II)
Visva - Bharati University (II)
Viswa Sahiti (II)
Vita e Pensiero (IT)

Luigi Vita, Ed. & Pub. (IT)
Vita et Pax-Foundation for Unity (UK)
Vita Farmaceutici (IT)
Vita Nova S.p.A. (IT)
Edizioni di Vita Sociale (IT)
Vitamin Society of Japan (JA)
Dr. Carlo Alberto Viterbo (IT)
Editions Vitesse Speed (FR)
Viva International Ltd. (US)
Viva-Kollektiv (SZ)
Vivant Univers (BE)
Vivek Trust (II)
Vivekananda Rock Memorial Committee (II)
Viviamo (IT)
Editions Vivienne (FR)
Vivre en Harmonie (FR)
Vivliographike Hetaireia Tes Hellados (GR)
Vjesnik (YU)
Vlaamse Automobilistenbond (BE)
Vlaamse Jeugherbergcentrale (BE)
Vlaamse Pomologische Verenigingen (BE)
Vlaamse Toeristenbond (BE)
Vlaamse Vereniging van Bibliotheek- en
    Archiefpersoneel (BE)
Vlaamse Vereniging voor Familiekunde (BE)
Vlaamse Volksbeweging (BE)
Vneshtorgreklama (UR)
Vocational Guidance Manuals (US)
Vocational Industrial Clubs of America, Inc. (US)
Vocations for Social Change, Inc. (US)
Vocations for Social Change, Inc. (Oakland) (US)
Voce (IT)
Voce Bruzia (IT)
Voce d'Italia in Canada (CN)
Voce di Siracusa (IT)
Voce Editrice s.r.l. (IT)
Edizioni della Voce s.r.l. (IT)
Vochenblatt Association (CN)
Voci del Nostro Tempo (IT)
Voenizdat (UR)
Verlag Heinrich Vogel (GW)
Verlag A. Vogel (SZ)
Vogel-Verlag KG (GW)
Vogel-Verlag. Zweigniederlassung Duesseldorf (GW)
Vogelkundliche Beobachtungsstation Untermain
    (GW)
Vogelzug-Verlag (GW)
Vogt-Schild AG (SZ)
Voice of Brotherhood (US)
Voice of India (US)
Voice of Jamaica (JM)
Voice of Liberty Association (US)
Voice of Malta (AT)
Voice of Methodism Association (UK)
Voice of Prison (US)
Voice of the Basques (US)
Voice of the Black Community (US)
Voice of the Nazarene, Inc. (US)
Voices of North Devon (UK)
Voicespondence Club (US)
Void (AT)
Voie de la Paix (FR)
Voix Dentaire (FR)
Vojensky Historicky Ustav (CS)
Vojna Akademija Rodova Kopnene Vojske i
    Intendantske Sluzbe (YU)
Vojni Muzej, Belgrade (YU)
Vojnoistorijski Institut (YU)
Vojnoizdavacki Zavod (YU)
Vojvodjansko Drustvo za Poljoprivrednu Tehniku
    (YU)
Volcanological Society of Japan (JA)
Julia Voldan, Ed. & Pub. (DK)
VEB Verlag Volk und Gesundheit (GE)
Verlag Volk und Welt (GE)
Verlag Volk und Wissen (GE)
Arno Volk Verlag Hans Gerig KG (GW)
Volksbildungshaus Wiener Urania (AU)
Volksbuchverlag GmbH (AU)
Volksbund Deutsche Kriegsgraeberfuersorge E.V.
    (GW)
Volkshochschule Linz (AU)
Volkskas- Amptenarevereniging (SA)
Volkskas Ltd. (SA)
Volkswagen of America, Inc. (US)
Volkswirtschaftliche Verlagsgesellschaft m.b.H. (AU)
Volkswirtschaftlicher Verlag GmbH (GW)
Volonte du Commerce et de l'Industrie et des
    Prestataires de Services (FR)
Volpe Editore (IT)
Voltaire Foundation (UK)
Voluntary Committee on Overseas Aid and
    Development (UK)
Volunteer Lawyers for the Arts (US)
Volunteer Services for the Blind (US)
Volunteers in Technical Assistance (US)
Volvo Flygmotor AB (SW)

Industrieverlag Von Hernhaussen KG (GW)
Von Kleinsmid Institute of International Affairs (US)
Philipp Von Zabern (GW)
Edward Vondrak (US)
J. Vontobel & Co., Bankers (SZ)
Vooraziatisch-Egyptisch Genootschap "Ex Oriente
    Lux" (NE)
Voorns' Papierwereld (NE)
Vorarlberg. Landesregierung (AU)
Vorarlberger Verlagsanstalt GmbH (AU)
Voronezhskii Gosudarstvennyi Universitet (UR)
Vorosvary Publishing Co. Ltd. (CN)
Vort Works Ink (US)
Vortex Institute, Inc. (US)
Vorwaerts AG (AU)
Voter Education Project Inc. (US)
Votre Opinion (FR)
Vou (JA)
Voyages, Inc. (US)
Voyageur (US)
Voz del Pueblo (AG)
Voz do Operario (PO)
Editora Vozes Ltda. (BL)
Vrije Pers Nederland N.V. (NE)
Vrije Universiteit, Amsterdam (NE)
Vrije Universiteit Brussel
    see also Universite Libre de Bruxelles (the two
    universities have been separate institutions since
    1970) (BE)
Vrije Universiteit Brussel (BE)
Vrije Universiteit Brussel. Centrum voor Studie van de
    Verlichting (BE)
Vrije Universiteit Brussel. Dienst Uitgaven (BE)
Editions Vrille-Copalic (FR)
Librairie Philosophique J. Vrin (FR)
Vrishchik (II)
Vserossiiskoe Teatral'noe Obshchestvo (UR)
Vsesoyuznaya Akademiya Sel'skokhozyaistvennykh
    Nauk im. V. I. Lenina (UR)
Vsesoyuznaya Gosudarstvennaya Biblioteka
    Inostrannoi Literatury (UR)
Vsesoyuznoe Geograficheskoe Obshchestvo (UR)
Vsesoyuznoe Mineralogicheskoe Obshchestvo (UR)
Vsesoyuznoe Nauchnoe Obshchestvo Sudebnykh
    Medikov (UR)
Vsesoyuznoe Obshchestvo Filatelistov (UR)
Vsesoyuznoe Obshchestvo "Znanie" (UR)
Vsesoyuznyi Institut Assortimenta Izdelii Legkoi
    Promyshlennosti i Kul'tury Odezhdy (UR)
Vsesoyuznyi Institut Nauchno-Tekhnicheskoi
    Informatsii (VINITI) (UR)
Vsesoyuznyi Issledovatel'skii Institut Morskoi Geologii
    i Geofiziki (UR)
Vsesoyuznyi Leninskii Kommunisticheskii Soyuz
    Molodezhi. Tsentral'nyi Komitet (UR)
Vsesoyuznyi Nauchno - Issledovatel'skii
    Geologorazvedochnyi Neftyanoi Institut (UR)
Vsesoyuznyi Nauchno-Issledovatelskii Institut
    Prirodnykh Gazov. Tyumenskii Filial (UR)
Vsesoyuznyi Nauchno-issledovatel'skii Institut
    Vagonostroeniya (UR)
Vsesoyuznyi Nauchno-Issledovatelskii Institut
    Zheleznodorozhnogo Transporta (UR)
Vsesoyuznyi Tsentral'nyi Sovet Professional'nykh
    Soyuzov (UR)
Vuga B.V. (NE)
Librairie Vuibert (FR)
N. V. Vuil Afvoer Maatschappij (NE)
Vulkan-Verlag Dr. W. Classen (GW)
Vuorimiesyhdistys (FI)
Uitgeverij De Vuurbaak (NE)
Vyapari-Mitra (II)
Vychodoslovenske Muzeum (CS)
Vychodoslovenske Vydavatelstvo (CS)
Drukkerij-Uitgeverij Vyncke (BE)
Vyskumny Ustav Chemickych Vlaken (CS)
Vyskumny Ustav Ekonomiky a Organizacie
    Stavebnictva (CS)
Vyskumny Ustav Inzinierskych Stavieb (CS)
Vyskumny Ustav Papiera a Celulozy (CS)
Vysoka Skola Banska (CS)
Vysoka Skola Veterinarni, Brno (CS)
Vysoka Skola Veterinarska v Kosiciach (CS)
Vysoka Skola Zemedelska (CS)
Izdatel'stvo Vysshaya Shkola (UR)
Izdatel'stvo Vysshaya Shkola B.S.S.R. (UR)
Vyzkumny a Zkusebni Letecky Ustav (CS)
Vyzkumny Ustav Agrochemicke Technologie (CS)
Vyzkumny Ustav Automacnich Prostredku (CS)
Vyzkumny Ustav Balneologicky (CS)
Vyzkumny Ustav Energeticky (CS)
Vyzkumny Ustav Prumyslu Cukrovarnickeho (CS)
Vyzkumny Ustav Rybarsky a Hydrobiologicky (CS)
Vyzkumny Ustav Spoju (CS)

Vyzkumny Ustav Technicko-Ekonomicky Chemickeho Prumyslu  (CS)
Vyzkumny Ustav Vystavby a Architektury  (CS)
W A G B I for Shooting and Conservation  (UK)
W.A. Sporting Car Club  (AT)
W B  (US)
W.C.C. Publishing Ltd.  (CN)
W. D. & H. O. Wills  (UK)
W F M T, Inc.  (US)
W H O
    see World Health Organization  (UN)
W I P O
    see World Intellectual Property Organization  (UN)
W I S E
    see World Information Systems Exchange (W I S E)  (US)
W M D Publications  (US)
W M O
    see World Meteorological Organization  (UN)
W M S E Publications  (US)
W N Y C  (US)
W T S Pharmcraft  (US)
W. W. Publications  (US)
W W R  (US)
W - W Twentyfirst Corporation  (US)
W W W W W Information Services, Inc.  (US)
W 3 Publishing Co.  (CN)
Waalse Gemeente Nederland  (NE)
Wabash Valley Genealogical Society, Inc.  (US)
Karl Wachholtz Verlag  (GW)
Wachovia Bank and Trust Company, N.A.  (US)
John Waddington Ltd.  (UK)
Wade Publishing Co.  (US)
Wadham Publications Ltd.  (CN)
Wadhera Publications  (II)
Wadley Institutes of Molecular Medicine  (US)
Wadsworth Publishing Co.  (US)
Wagga Wagga & District Historical Society  (AT)
Karl Dieter Wagner (Hamburg)  (GW)
Arnold L. Wagner, Ed. & Pub.  (US)
J. H. Wagner, Ed. & Pub.  (US)
J. Richard Wagner, Ed. & Pub.  (US)
Richard Wagner, Ed. & Pub.  (NE)

Wagner College. Horrmann Library  (US)

Wagon & Star Publishers  (US)

Wagtail  (CN)
Waikiki Aquarium  (US)
Waikiki Publishing Co. Inc.  (US)
Waisenhaus Buchdruckerei und Verlag  (GW)
Arthur Waite Productions  (UK)
Wakatkat al-Sudan Lil-Anba
    see Sudan News Agency  (SJ)
Wakayama Chiho Kishodai
    see Wakayama Local Meteorological Observatory  (JA)
Wakayama Daigaku Keizai Gakkai
    see Wakayama University. Economic Society  (JA)
Wakayama Igakkai
    see Wakayama Medical Society  (JA)
Wakayama-kenritsu Ika Daigaku
    see Wakayama Medical College  (JA)
Wakayama Local Meteorological Observatory  (JA)
Wakayama Medical College  (JA)
Wakayama Medical Society  (JA)
Wakayama University. Economic Society  (JA)
Wake Forest University  (US)
Wake Forest University. Overseas Research Center  (US)
Wake Forest University. School of Law  (US)
Wakeman-Walworth, Inc.  (US)
Wakra Publishing Group  (US)
Waksman Foundation of Japan  (JA)
Walden - Mott Corporation  (US)
Laurie Wale (Pty) Ltd.  (SA)
Wales International  (UK)
Wales Publications Ltd.  (UK)
Walhalla- U. Praetoria-Verlag Georg Zwickenpflug  (GW)
Walker and Co.  (US)
W. Walker & Sons (Otley) Ltd.  (UK)
Walker Art Center  (US)
Walker-Davis Publications, Inc.  (US)
Walker Publishing Co., Inc.  (US)
Walker's Manual Incorporated  (US)
Walkers Publicity  (AT)
Stephen Wall, Christopher Ricks and F. W. Bateson  (UK)
Wall Street Publishing Institute Inc.  (US)
Wall Street Reports Publishing Corp.  (US)
Wall Street Transcript Corp.  (US)
Wallace-Homestead Co.  (US)
Wallace Publishing Co., Inc.  (US)
Wallacia (Sales) Pty.  (AT)
M. A. Walli  (II)
Wallpaper Paint & Wallcovering Retailers Association  (UK)
Walnut Grove Publishing, Inc.  (US)

Walt Disney Production  (US)
David Walter Associates  (US)
Roy W. Walter & Associates  (US)
Walter Eucken Institut  (GW)
Walter Verlag AG  (SZ)
Walter-Verlag GmbH  (GW)
Walters Art Gallery  (US)
Editions Publicitaires Waltz P.R. et M. Puget  (FR)
Wanderer Printing Co.  (US)
Karl Wang, Ed. & Pub  (US)
Wang Laboratories  (US)
Wantok Publications  (PP)
Wapen der Koninklijke Marechaussee  (NE)
Wapiti Regional Library  (CN)
War Resisters' International  (BE)
War Resisters International Society  (AT)
War Resisters League  (US)
War Resisters League, Southeast  (US)
Warburg Institute  (UK)
Alan Ward, Ed. & Pub  (UK)
Jim Ward, Ed. & Pub.  (US)
Ward Lock, Ltd.  (UK)
Ward Publishing Co.  (NZ)
Wardha Press  (II)
Ward's Communications, Inc.  (US)
Ward's Natural Science Establishment  (US)
Waren Einkaufs- und Vertriebs-Gesellschaft mbH  (GW)
Wargamer  (CN)
George Warman Publications (Pty) Ltd.  (SA)
Warner Press, Inc.  (US)
Warner Publicity Ltd.  (UK)
Warp Four  (US)
Warren Burkett  (US)
Warren County Historical Society  (US)
Warren Education Association  (US)
Warren, Gorham and Lamont, Inc.  (US)
Warren Publishing Co.  (US)
Warren Spring Laboratory  (UK)
Warrior  (IT)
Wartburg Verlag Max Kessler  (GE)
Verlag Wartenberg und Soehne  (GW)
Warwick Boyce Publishing Pty. Ltd.  (AT)
Waseda Daigaku
    see Waseda University  (JA)
Waseda Daigaku Imono Kenkyushitsu
    see Waseda University. Casting Research Laboratory  (JA)
Waseda Daigaku Rikogaku Kenkyusho
    see Waseda University. Science and Engineering Research Laboratory  (JA)
Waseda Daigaku Shakaigakkai  (JA)
Waseda University. Casting Research Laboratory  (JA)
Waseda University. Commercial Study Society  (JA)
Waseda University. Graduate Division of Commerce  (JA)
Waseda University. Graduate Division of Political Science  (JA)
Waseda University. Political and Economic Science Society  (JA)
Waseda University. School of Science and Engineering  (JA)
Waseda University. Science and Engineering Research Laboratory  (JA)
Waseda University. Socio-Economic History Society  (JA)
J. H. Waser AG  (SZ)
Washburn University. School of Law  (US)
Robert E. Washer, Ed. & Pub.  (US)
Washington (State) Attorney General's Office  (US)
Washington (State) Department of Commerce and Economic Development  (US)
Washington (State) Department of Commerce and Economic Development. Department of Foreign Trade  (US)
Washington (State) Department of Ecology  (US)
Washington (State) Department of Fisheries  (US)
Washington (State) Department of Highways  (US)
Washington (State) Department of Motor Vehicles  (US)
Washington (State) Department of Motor Vehicles. Information Office  (US)
Washington (State) Department of Natural Resources  (US)
Washington (State) Department of Natural Resources. Division of Geology and Earth Resources  (US)
Washington (State) Department of Revenue  (US)
Washington (State) Department of Social and Health Services  (US)
Washington (State) Department of Social and Health Services. Office on Aging  (US)
Washington (State) Department of Social and Health Services. Office of Community Health Service  (US)
Washington (State) Employment Security Department  (US)
Washington (State) Fruit Commission  (US)

Washington (State) Game Department  (US)
Washington (State) Indian Assistance Division. Office of Community Development  (US)
Washington (State) Law and Justice Planning Office  (US)
Washington (State) Legislature  (US)
Washington (State) Legislature. Transportation Committee  (US)
Washington (State) Real Estate Division  (US)
Washington (State) State Library  (US)
Washington (State) State Office of Program Planning and Fiscal Management  (US)
Washington (State) State Patrol  (US)
Washington (State) Superintendent of Public Instruction  (US)
Washington (State) Utilities and Transportation Commission  (US)
Washington (State) Vocational Rehabilitation Services Division  (US)
Washington (State) Water Research Center  (US)
Washington Academy of Sciences  (US)
Washington Alaska Regional Medical Program  (US)
Washington & Jefferson College  (US)
Washington and Lee University  (US)
Washington and Lee University. Office of Publications  (US)
Washington and Lee University. School of Law  (US)
Washington Archaeologist  (US)
Washington Area Council on Alcoholism & Drug Abuse, Inc.  (US)
Washington Association of Sheriffs and Police Chiefs  (US)
Washington Association of Wheat Growers  (US)
Washington Banktrends  (US)
Washington Board of Realtors, Inc.  (US)
Washington Business Information, Inc.  (US)
Washington Center of Foreign Policy Research  (US)
Washington Community Video Center, Inc.  (US)
Washington Consortium of Universities  (US)
Washington County (Arkansas) Historical Society  (US)
Washington County (Maryland) Board of Education  (US)
Washington County (Ohio) Historical Society  (US)
Washington County World  (US)
Washington Crime News Services  (US)
Washington Criminal Justice Education and Training Center  (US)
Washington Crop and Livestock Reporting Service  (US)
Washington Data Processing Service Center  (US)
Washington Dental Service  (US)
Washington-District of Columbia Pharmaceutical Association, Inc.  (US)
Washington Folk Strums  (US)
Washington Insurance Newsletter, Inc.  (US)
Washington International Arts Letter  (US)
Washington Journalism Center  (US)
Washington Law Reporter Co.  (US)
Washington Library Association. O.P.E.N. Interest Group  (US)
Washington Literary Society  (US)
Washington Magazine Inc.  (US)
Washington Metropolitan Area Transit Authority  (US)
Washington Monitor, Inc.  (US)
Washington Monthly Co.  (US)
Washington Music Educator's Association  (US)
Washington Newspaper Publishers' Association, Inc.  (US)
Washington Performing Arts Society  (US)
Washington Poets Association  (US)
Washington Publishing House  (UK)
Washington Recreation and Park Society, Inc.  (US)
Washington Reports to Africa  (US)
Washington Researchers Information Report  (US)
Washington Review: a Quarterly Review of the Arts  (US)
Washington School of Psychiatry. Forum on Psychiatry and the Humanities  (US)
Washington Science Fiction Association  (US)
Washington Spectator, Inc.  (US)
Washington State Association of Counties  (US)
Washington State Association of School Librarians  (US)
Washington State Coaches Association  (US)
Washington State Dental Association  (US)
Washington State Entomological Society  (US)
Washington State Food Dealers Association  (US)
Washington State Grange  (US)
Washington State Horticultural Association  (US)
Washington State Nurses Association  (US)
Washington State Pharmaceutical Association  (US)
Washington State Research Council  (US)
Washington State School Directors' Association  (US)
Washington State University  (US)
Washington State University. College of Engineering  (US)

Washington State University. Department of English (US)
Washington State University. Department of Pure and Applied Mathematics (US)
Washington State University. Engineering Extension Service (US)
Washington State University Library. Library Staff Association (US)
Washington State University Press (US)
Washington University (US)
Washington University. Institute for Urban & Regional Studies (US)
Washington University. Library (US)
Washington University. School of Law (US)
Washington University. School of Medicine Library (US)
Washington University. Student Union (US)
Washington Watch, Inc. (US)
Washington Women's Art Center (US)
Washington Workshops (US)
Washout Publishing Co. (US)
Washtenaw Community College (US)
Wasser- und Abwasser-Forschung Verlagsgesellschaft MbH und Co. (GW)
Watan Publications Ltd. (UK)
Watauga Association of Genealogists (US)
Watch on the Atomic Energy Commission Citizen's Energy Council (US)
Watch Tower Bible & Tract Society (SA)
Watchtower Bible and Tract Society (UK)
Watchtower Bible & Tract Society, Inc. (US)
Water and Power Development Consultancy Services (India) Ltd. (II)
Water Information Center, Inc. (US)
Water Pollution Control Federation (US)
Water Polo Scoreboard (US)
Water Research Centre (UK)
Water Research Commission (SA)
Water Research Foundation of Australia Ltd. (AT)
Water Research Institute
    see under Nagoya University (JA)
Water Resources Association of the Delaware River Basin (US)
Water Resources Information System (US)
Water Resources Publications (US)
Water Spectrum (US)
Water Utilization Research Institute (JA)
Waterloo Historical Society (CN)
Waterloo-Wellington Flying Club (CN)
Watershed Foundation (US)
Waterside Workers' Federation of Australia (AT)
Watervale Press Pty. Ltd. (AT)
Waterway Productions Ltd. (UK)
Waterways Journal, Inc. (US)
Watford and District Industrial History Society (UK)
Sylvestre C. Watkins, Ed. & Pub. (US)
Watman Educational Services (US)
Watmoughs Ltd. (UK)
Ann Watson (US)
Neale Watson Academic Publications, Inc. (US)
Watson-Guptill Publications, Inc. (US)
Watson Publications (US)
Watt Publishing Co. (US)
Franklin Watts Inc. (US)
Waugh & Josephson Pty. Ltd. (AT)
Waukesha County Historical Society (US)
Wax Publications, Inc. (US)
Way Out West Tent (US)
Way Publications (UK)
Wayfarer Corporation (US)
Wayne State University (US)
Wayne State University. Archives of Labor History and Urban Affairs (US)
Wayne State University. Center for the Study of Cognitive Processes (US)
Wayne State University. College of Engineering (US)
Wayne State University. College of Pharmacy (US)
Wayne State University. Division of University Relations (US)
Wayne State University Law School (US)
Wayne State University. Medical Library (US)
Wayne State University Press (US)
Wayside Gardens (US)
Wayside Press (US)
Wayside Press (Cottonwood) (US)
We Are One (US)
Weald of Kent Publications (Tonbridge) Ltd. (UK)
Wealden Press Ltd. (UK)
Wealth of Nations (IR)
A. Webb & Sons Pty. Ltd. (AT)
Webb Co. (US)
Webb Society (UK)
Webe Mit (GW)
Arthur Weber (US)
J. F. Weber, Ed. & Pub. (US)
Weber Publications Inc. (US)
Webster College (US)
Websters Publications Ltd. (UK)

Wedge Publishing Foundation (CN)
Wedgwood International Seminar (US)
Wedgwood Society (UK)
Wedgwood Society of Australia (AT)
Weed Science Society of America (US)
Weed Society of N.S.W. (AT)
Gerd-Volker Weege (GW)
Week End Publications (FR)
Weekbladpers (NE)
Weekly al-Fatah (PK)
Weekly Analysis of Ecuadorian Issues (EC)
Weekly Bulletin of Leather and Shoe News Co. (US)
Weekly California Citator (US)
Weekly Gayzette (US)
Weekly Guardian Associates Inc. (US)
Weekly Notes Printing Works, Pvt. Ltd. (II)
Verlag Weg zur Gesundheit (GW)
Wegwijs Tijdschriften Exploitatie (NE)
Wehr und Wissen Verlagsgesellschaft GmbH (GW)
Wehrpolitische Information (GW)
Weibullsholm Plant Breeding Institute (SW)
Fr. Weidemann's Buchhandlung (H.Witt) (GW)
Weidenfeld and Nicolson Ltd. (UK)
Weight Watchers of Philadelphia (US)
Van der Weij Periodieken B.V. (NE)
Weimaraner Club of America (US)
Weinberg und Keller Verlag (GW)
Deutscher Weinwirtschaftsverlag Diemer und Meininger KG (GW)
Weis Laboratories (US)
Editeur R. Weiss (FR)
Weizmann Institute of Science (IS)
Weizmann Science Press of Israel (IS)
Robert F. Welch, Ed. & Pub. (US)
Robert Welch, Inc. (US)
Welcome to Malta League (MM)
Welding Institute (UK)
Welding Institute. Surfacing Division (UK)
Welding Research Council (US)
Wellcome Institute for the History of Medicine (UK)
Wellens Publishing (UK)
Wellesley College. Department of Music (US)
Wellington. Department of Education (NZ)
Wellington Publishing Co. Ltd. (NZ)
Wellington Regional Employers Association (Inc.) (NZ)
Wellman Press, Inc. (US)
Ch. Wellmann (GW)
Mark Wells, Jr., Ed. & Pub. (US)
Wells Fargo Bank. Economics Department (US)
Wells Gardner, Darton & Co. Ltd. (UK)
Wels. Magistrat der Stadt Wels (AU)
Welser Kulturring (AU)
Welsh Amateur Swimming Association (UK)
Welsh Arts Council (UK)
Welsh Association of Youth Clubs (UK)
Welsh Bibliographical Society (UK)
Welsh Calvinistic Methodist Book Agency (UK)
Robin Welsh, Ed. & Pub. (UK)
Welsh Medical Press Ltd. (UK)
Welsh Nation Office (UK)
Welsh Pony and Cob Society (UK)
Welsh Secondary Schools Association (UK)
Welsh Soils Discussion Group (UK)
Welshpool Webb-Offset Co. (UK)
Welt Am Sonnabend GmbH (GW)
Welt Publishing Co. (US)
Welt-Spirale (AU)
Verlag Weltarchiv GmbH (GW)
Verlag die Weltbuehne (GE)
Weltfernschachbund (I J C F) (GW)
Weltforum Verlags-Gesellschaft mbH (GW)
Weltfriedensrates (FI)
Weltgewerkschaftsbund (GE)
Welttierschutzbund
    see World Federation for the Protection of Animals (SZ)
Wembley History Society (UK)
Wen i Yueh K'an She (CH)
Wen-Tsal-Lee (CH)
Wenco Enterprises (US)
Wenner-Gren Foundation for Anthropological Research (US)
Karl Wenschow GmbH (GW)
Wentworth Press (AT)
Verlag Werbekreis Werbe und Anzeigen KG (GE)
Werbel Publishing Co., Inc. (US)
Wereldverbond van Bouwvakarbeiders- en Houtbewerkersorganisaties (NE)
Wereldwijd (BE)
Van der Werff en Hubrecht N. V. (NE)
Werk-Verlag Dr. Edmund Banaschewski (GW)
Werkgemeenschap voor Vernieuwing van Opvoeding, Onderwijs en Maatschappij (NE)
Werkschriften- Verlag GmbH (GW)
Werkzeitung der Schweizerischen Industrie (SZ)
Karl Werner (AU)
Werner & Werner Corporation (US)

Werner Management Consultants, Inc. (US)
Werner-Verlag GmbH (GW)
Wertpapierboerse in Stuttgart (GW)
F. W. Wesel (GW)
Weser-Kurier GmbH (GW)
Weserbund e. V. (GW)
Wesfarmers (AT)
Frank D. Wesley (US)
Wesley Historical Society (UK)
Wesley Methodist Church (SI)
Wesley Press (II)
Wesleyan Christian Advocate (US)
Wesleyan Church (US)
Wesleyan Church Youth Department (US)
Wesleyan College (US)
Wesleyan College Alumnae Association (US)
Wesleyan Publishing House (US)
Wesleyan Theological Society (US)
Wesleyan University Press (US)
Wessex Cave Club (UK)
West Africa Rice Development Association (LB)
West African Book Publishers Ltd. (NR)
West African Classical Association (NR)
West African Examinations Council. Test Development and Research Division (NR)
West African Journal of Biological and Applied Chemistry (NR)
West African Modern Languages Association (NR)
West African Science Association (NR)
West African Society for Pharmacology (NR)
West African Technical Review (UK)
West Aurora Public Schools (US)
West Australian Chamber of Manufactures (AT)
West Australian Newspapers Ltd. (AT)
West Australian Petroleum Pty. Ltd. (AT)
West Bend News (US)
West Bengal. Bureau of Applied Economics and Statistics (II)
West Bengal. Commerce & Industries Department (II)
West Bengal. Department of Information and Public Relations (II)
West Bengal. Department of Labour (II)
West Bengal Government Press (II)
West Cameroon. Service Statistique (CM)
West Canadian Research Publications (CN)
West Central Kentucky Family Research Association (US)
West Central Missouri Genealogical Society (US)
West Chester State College (US)
West Coast Dry Kiln Association (US)
West Coast Poetry Review (US)
West Coast Publicity Service (II)
West End (US)
N. V. Drukkerij West-Friesland (NE)
West Georgia College (US)
West Georgia College. Division of Social Sciences (US)
West Highland Publishing Co. Ltd. (UK)
West India Committee (UK)
West Indian Sportsman (JM)
West Indies Sugar Association (TR)
West-Japanese Society of Orthopedics & Traumatology (JA)
West Java Chamber of Commerce and Industry
    see Kamar Dagang dan Industri Jawa-Barat (IO)
West Midland Bird Club (UK)
West Midland Institute of Geriatric Medicine and Gerontology (UK)
West Midlands Arts Association (UK)
West of England Newspapers (UK)
West Pakistan Bar Council (PK)
John West Publications Ltd. (NR)
West Publishing Co. (US)
West Publishing Corp. Pty. Ltd. (AT)
West Side Association of Commerce, Inc. (US)
West Tennessee Historical Society (US)
West Texas Chamber of Commerce (US)
West Texas Geological Society (US)
West Texas Livestock Weekly (US)
West Texas State University. College of Education (US)
West Virginia. Board of Regents (US)
West Virginia. Commission on Aging (US)
West Virginia. Commission on Mental Retardation (US)
West Virginia. Department of Agriculture (US)
West Virginia. Department of Archives and History (US)
West Virginia. Department of Commerce (US)
West Virginia. Department of Education (US)
West Virginia. Department of Employment Security. Research and Statistics Division (US)
West Virginia. Department of Health (US)
West Virginia. Department of Mines (US)
West Virginia. Department of Natural Resources (US)

West Virginia. Division of Vocational Rehabilitation (US)
West Virginia. Geological and Economic Survey (US)
West Virginia. Governor's Committee on Crime, Delinquency, and Corrections (US)
West Virginia. Human Rights Commission (US)
West Virginia. Office of Emergency Services (US)
West Virginia Chamber of Commerce (US)
West Virginia Coal Association (US)
West Virginia Coal Mining Institute (US)
West Virginia Dental Association (US)
West Virginia Echoer (US)
West Virginia Education Association (US)
West Virginia Free Press (US)
West Virginia Highlands Conservancy (US)
West Virginia Hillbilly (US)
West Virginia Hills and Streams, Inc. (US)
West Virginia Library Association (US)
West Virginia Motor Truck Association (US)
West Virginia Music Educators Association, Inc. (US)
West Virginia Nurses Association (US)
West Virginia Record and West Virginia Merchant (US)
West Virginia Research League Inc. (US)
West Virginia School Boards Association (US)
West Virginia Society of Certified Public Accountants (US)
West Virginia State Medical Association (US)
West Virginia University (US)
West Virginia University. Agricultural Experiment Station (US)
West Virginia University. Bureau of Business Research (US)
West Virginia University. Center for Extension and Continuing Education (US)
West Virginia University. College of Agriculture and Forestry (US)
West Virginia University. Department of Biology (US)
West Virginia University. Engineering Experiment Station (US)
West Virginia University Law Center (US)
West Virginia University Library (US)
West Virginia Wildwater Association (US)
Westana Publications (US)
Westart (US)
Westbourne Journals Ltd. (UK)
Westburg Associates, Publishers (US)
Westchester Academy of Medicine (US)
Westchester County Board of Realtors, Inc. (US)
Westchester County Historical Society (US)
Westchester Law Journal Inc. (US)
Westdeutsche Verlagsanstalt GmbH (GW)
Westdeutscher Rundfunk (GW)
Westdeutscher Verlag (GW)
Westdeutscher Verlag GmbH (GW)
Georg Westermann Verlag (GW)
Western Agricultural Economics Association (US)
Western Airlines (US)
Western Association of Africanists (US)
Western Association of Graduate Schools (US)
Western Association of Insurance Brokers (US)
Western Association of Map Libraries (US)
Western Association of Schools and Colleges (US)
Western Association of State Game and Fish Commissioners (US)
Western Australia. Coastal Shipping Commission (AT)
Western Australia. Committee for the Understanding of the Environment (AT)
Western Australia. Crown Law Department (AT)
Western Australia. Department for Community Welfare (AT)
Western Australia. Department of Agriculture (AT)
Western Australia. Department of Agriculture. Animal Division (AT)
Western Australia. Department of Agriculture. Rangeland Management Section (AT)
Western Australia. Department of Agriculture. Rural Economics and Marketing Section (AT)
Western Australia. Department of Agriculture. Western Australian Herbarium (AT)
Western Australia. Department of Agriculture. Wheat and Sheep Division (AT)
Western Australia. Department of Conservation and Environment (AT)
Western Australia. Department of Fisheries and Wildlife (AT)
Western Australia. Department of Industrial Development and Decentralisation (AT)
Western Australia. Department of Tourism (AT)
Western Australia. Director General of Transport (AT)
Western Australia. Education Department (AT)

Western Australia. Education Department. Curriculum Branch (AT)
Western Australia. Forests Department (AT)
Western Australia. Geological Survey (AT)
Western Australia. Government Chemical Laboratories (AT)
Western Australia. Law Reform Commission (AT)
Western Australia. Main Roads Department (AT)
Western Australia. Parliamentary Library of Western Australia (AT)
Western Australia. Public Library, Museum and Art Gallery (AT)
Western Australia. Road Traffic Safety Authority (AT)
Western Australia. State Health Laboratory Services (AT)
Western Australia. Transport Commission (AT)
Western Australia. Western Australia Government Printing Office (AT)
Western Australia Horticultural Council (AT)
Western Australia Seed Board (AT)
Western Australia Vegetable Growers' Association, Inc. (AT)
Western Australian Automobile Chamber of Commerce (AT)
Western Australian Egg Marketing Board (AT)
Western Australian Employers' Federation (AT)
Western Australian Institute of Technology (AT)
Western Australian Museum (AT)
Western Australian Music Teachers Association (AT)
Western Australian Naturalists' Club (AT)
Western Australian Potato Marketing Board (AT)
Western Australian Secondary Teachers' College (AT)
Western Australian Speleological Group (AT)
Western Builder Publishing Co. (US)
Western Business Publications (US)
Western Canada Water and Sewage Conference (CN)
Western Canadian Society for Horticulture (CN)
Western Carolina University. Division of Economic Development (US)
Western Christian Leadership Conference (US)
Western Communications. Ltd. (US)
Western Confectioners and Tobacconist Co. (US)
Western Conservation Journal (US)
Western Construction Magazine, Inc. (US)
Western Counties, Association of Chambers of Commerce (UK)
Western Dental Society (US)
Western Economic Association (US)
Western Educational Society for Telecommunications (US)
Western Electric Co., Inc. (US)
Western Electric Co. Inc. Organization 400 (US)
Western Electronic Manufacturers Association (US)
Western Electronic Show and Convention (US)
Western European Airport Association (FR)
Western Farm Equipment (US)
Western Finance Association (US)
Western Fish & Game Magazine Ltd. (CN)
Western Flyer (US)
Western Forestry and Conservation Association (US)
Western Forestry Center (US)
Western Fraternal Life Association (US)
Western Growers Association (US)
Western Guard Party (CN)
Western Heart Publishing Co. (US)
Western Highway Institute (US)
Western History Association (US)
Western Horseman, Inc. (US)
Western Illinois University (US)
Western Illinois University. Center for Business and Economic Research (US)
Western Illinois University. College of Education (US)
Western Illinois University. Department of English (US)
Western India Automobile Association (II)
Western Industrial Advertisers (US)
Western Institute for the Deaf (CN)
Western Institute of Multivariate Experimental Psychology (US)
Western Interstate Commission for Higher Education (US)
Western Interstate Library Coordinating Organization (US)
Western Interstate Nuclear Board (US)
Western Jewish News (CN)
Western Literature Association (US)
Western Livestock Reporter, Inc. (US)
Western Management Sciences Institute (US)
Western Massachusetts Genealogical Society (US)
Western Merchandise Mart (US)
Western Michigan University (US)
Western Michigan University. Department of English (US)
Western Michigan University. Medieval Institute (US)

Western Michigan University. Office of Research Services (US)
Western Michigan University. School of Librarianship (US)
Western Miner Press Ltd. (CN)
Western Mining News (US)
Western New York Genealogical Society, Inc. (US)
Western News Printing and Publishing (US)
Western Newspaper Publishing Co. (US)
Western Nigeria Development Corporation (NR)
Western Orchestral Society Ltd. (UK)
Western Outdoors Publications (US)
Western Pacific Orthopaedic Association (HK)
Western Pennsylvania Bluegrass Committee (US)
Western Pennsylvania Genealogical Society (US)
Western Pennsylvania School for Blind Children (US)
Western Periodicals Co. (US)
Western Pharmacology Society (US)
Western Plains Library System (US)
Western Plastics News Inc. (US)
Western Poetry Press (US)
Western Political Science Association (US)
Western Printing & Publishing Co. (US)
Western Producer Publications (CN)
Western Psychological Services (US)
Western Publications, Inc. (Austin) (US)
Western Publicity Service (II)
Western Publishers (CN)
Western Publishing Co., Inc. (US)
Western Railway Club (US)
Western Regional Science Association (US)
Western Reserve Historical Society (US)
Western Reserve Magazine (US)
Western Retail Implement & Hardware Association (US)
Western Ski Promotions, Inc. (US)
Western Snow Conference (US)
Western Social Science Association (US)
Western Social Science Association (Boulder) (US)
Western Society of Engineers (US)
Western Society of Malacologists (US)
Western Society of Weed Science (US)
Western Speech Communication Association (US)
Western Sporting Press Ltd. (UK)
Western State. Government Printer (NR)
Western State. Ministry of Economic Planning and Community Development (NR)
Western State. Ministry of Education (NR)
Western State. Ministry of Home Affairs and Information (NR)
Western State. Ministry of Local Government and Chieftancy Affairs (NR)
Western States Publications (US)
Western Sun (AT)
Western Temperance League (UK)
Western Theological Seminary (US)
Western Thoroughbred (CN)
Western Trade Magazine Publishers (US)
Western Washington State College (US)
Western Washington State College. Aquatic Studies Program (US)
Western Washington State College. College of Ethnic Studies (US)
Western Washington State College. Department of English (US)
Western Washington State College. Dept. of History (US)
Western Washington State College. Program in East Asian Studies (US)
Western Wood Products Association (US)
Western World Press (US)
Western World Publishers (US)
Western Writers of America, Inc. (US)
Westerners International (US)
Westerners. Kansas City Posse (US)
Westerners. Kansas Corral (US)
Westerners. Los Angeles Corral (US)
Westerners, San Diego Corral (US)
Westernlore Press (US)
Westfaelische Gesellschaft fuer Genealogie und Familienforschung (GW)
Westfaelische Verlagsgesellschaft MbH (GW)
Westigan Review of Poetry (US)
Westigan Review Press (US)
Westkreuz Druckerei und Verlag (GW)
Westminster Abbey Ltd. (CN)
Westminster Medical School. Student's Union (UK)
Westminster Press (US)
Westminster Press Ltd. (UK)
Westminster Theological Seminary (US)
Westmoreland County Motor Club (US)
Westmorland Historical Society (CN)
Weston School of Theology (US)
Weston Studstock Advertising (AT)
Westview Press (US)
Westworld Publications Ltd. (CN)
Wetenschappelijk Onderwijs Limburg (BE)

Wisconsin Alliance Press, Inc.  (US)
Wisconsin Alumni Association  (US)
Wisconsin American Legion  (US)
Wisconsin Archeological Society  (US)
Wisconsin Association of School Boards  (US)
Wisconsin Audiovisual Association  (US)
Wisconsin Coalition for Education Reform  (US)
Wisconsin Congress of Parents and Teachers Inc. (US)
Wisconsin Council of Teachers of English  (US)
Wisconsin County Boards Association  (US)
Wisconsin County Lands  (US)
Wisconsin Crime Information Bureau  (US)
Wisconsin Dental Association  (US)
Wisconsin Electric Cooperative Association  (US)
Wisconsin Engineering Journal Association  (US)
Wisconsin Evangelical Lutheran Synod  (US)
Wisconsin Farm Bureau Federation  (US)
Wisconsin Farmer Co., Inc.  (US)
Wisconsin Geological Society  (US)
Wisconsin Institute of Certified Public Accountants (US)
Wisconsin Jewish Publications Foundation  (US)
Wisconsin Library Association  (US)
Wisconsin Manufacturers' Association  (US)
Wisconsin Nurses Association  (US)
Wisconsin Optometric Association  (US)
Wisconsin Petroleum Association  (US)
Wisconsin Poetry Magazine Illustrated  (US)
Wisconsin Research and Development Center for Cognitive Learning  (US)
Wisconsin Restaurant Association  (US)
Wisconsin Retailers Review  (US)
Wisconsin School Music Association  (US)
Wisconsin Secondary School Administrators Association  (US)
Wisconsin Sheriffs and Deputy Sheriffs Association (US)
Wisconsin Society for Ornithology, Inc  (US)
Wisconsin Sociological Association  (US)
Wisconsin Sportsman, Inc.  (US)
Wisconsin State Historical Society  (US)
Wisconsin State University  (US)
Wisconsin Tales and Trails, Inc.  (US)
Wisconsin Union Labor News Publishing Co.  (US)
H. Wise & Co. Ltd.  (UK)
Wm. H. Wise & Co., Inc.  (US)
Wiskundig Genootschap  (NE)
Verlag Wissenschaft und Politik Berend von Nottbeck (GW)
Wissenschaft und Werbung  (GW)
Verlag fuer Wissenschaft, Wirtschaft und Technik GmbH und Co.  (GW)
VEB Deutscher Verlag der Wissenschaften  (GE)
Wissenschaftliche Gesellschaft fuer Europarecht (GW)
Wissenschaftliche Gesellschaft fuer Luft- und Raumfahrt e.V  (GW)
Wissenschaftliche Gesellschaft fuer Personenstandswesen und Verwandte Gebiete (GW)
Wissenschaftliche Gesellschaft fuer Veterinaermedizin der DDR  (GE)
Wissenschaftliche Vereinigung fuer Augenoptik und Optometrie E.V.  (GW)
Wissenschaftliche Verlagsgesellschaft mbH  (GW)
Wistar Institute Press  (US)
Witan Publications Ltd  (UK)
Witches International Craft Associaties; Witches Liberation Movement  (US)
Witches Trine  (US)
Witcom Group  (PR)
Universitaets Buchhandlung Dr. J.C. Witsch  (GW)
Wittenborn and Co.  (US)
Dean Witter and Co.  (US)
Wittgensteiner Heimatvereins e.V  (GW)
Dr. Heinrich Wittmann Verlag  (GW)
Witwatersrand University Press  (SA)
Verlag Gerhard Witzstrock  (GW)
Wochenschau-Verlag  (GW)
Wofford College. Sandor Teszler Library  (US)
Gert Wohlfarth KG Verlag Fachtechnik und Mercator-Verlag  (GW)
Verlag Juergen Wohlrabe  (GW)
Wohnungsaktiengesellschaft Linz  (AU)
Wojewodzka i Miejska Biblioteka Publiczna-Biblioteka Glowna im. S. Staszica  (PL)
Wojsko Polskie. Glowny Zarzad Polityczny  (PL)
Wojskowy Instytut Historyczny  (PL)
Woking Muslim Mission and Literary Trust  (UK)
Woking Review Ltd.  (UK)
Woldon Communications, Inc.  (US)
Ed. & Pub. Alois Wolf  (AU)
Wolf House Books  (US)
M. C. Wolf Kg  (GW)
Wolf Verlag GmbH  (GW)

Wolfe Publishing Co., Inc.  (US)
Wolfe Publishing, Inc.  (US)
Wolfenbuetteler Arbeitskreis fuer Geschichte des Buchwesens  (GW)
Wolfer Printing Co., Inc.  (US)
Henry Wolfrath, Ed. & Pub.  (US)
Thom. F. Wolfs  (NE)
Wollongong Teachers College  (AT)
Wollongong University College  (AT)
Wolters-Noordhoff B.V.  (NE)
Woman Activist, Inc.  (US)
Woman Becoming  (US)
Woman Talk  (US)
Womanchild  (US)
Woman's Christian Temperance Union of Australia (AT)
Woman's National Farm & Garden Association, Inc. (US)
Woman's Soul Publishing, Inc  (US)
Woman's World Joint Venture  (US)
Womanspeak Collective  (AT)
WomanSpirit  (US)
Women  (US)
Women Eros  (JA)
Women for Constitutional Government  (US)
Women for Sobriety, Inc.  (US)
Women in Communications, Inc.  (US)
Women in Struggle  (US)
Women Library Workers  (US)
Women - Poems  (US)
Women Strike for Peace  (US)
Women Writing Newsletter  (US)
Women's American ORT  (US)
Women's Center (Venice)  (US)
Women's Circle Home Cooking  (US)
Women's Electoral Lobby  (AT)
Women's Employment Publishing Co., Ltd.  (UK)
Women's Engineering Society  (UK)
Women's Equity Action League. National Capital Chapter  (US)
Women's History Research Center  (US)
Women's International Bowling Congress, Inc.  (US)
Women's International Cultural Federation  (FR)
Women's International Democratic Federation  (GE)
Women's International League for Peace and Freedom (SZ)
Women's International League for Peace and Freedom (UK)
Women's International League for Peace and Freedom (Philadelphia)  (US)
Women's International League for Peace and Freedom. Swedish Section  (SW)
Women's International Network  (US)
Women's International Zionist Organization  (IS)
Women's Law Journal  (US)
Women's League for Conservative Judaism  (US)
Women's Liberation Movement National Information Service  (UK)
Women's Liberation Movement of Montreal  (CN)
Women's Liberation Workshop  (UK)
Women's Lobby, Inc.  (US)
Women's Missionary Society (WD)  (CN)
Women's National Abortion Action Coalition  (US)
Womens' Organization of Iran  (IR)
Women's Poetry Collective  (US)
Women's Press Collective  (US)
Women's Report Collective  (UK)
Women's Rights Law Reporter, Inc.  (US)
Women's Squash Rackets Association  (UK)
Women's Studies Group  (AT)
Women's Track and Field World Publications, Inc. (US)
Women's Work, Inc.  (US)
Women's Zionist Council of South Africa  (SA)
Wonderworld  (US)
Gilbert Woo, Ed. & Pub.  (US)
Wood County Board of Education  (US)
I.J.A. Wood, Pub.  (SA)
Wood Research Institute  (JA)
Wood Technological Association of Japan  (JA)
Wood, Wire and Metal Lathers' International Union (US)
Wood - Woods Family Magazine  (US)
W. C. Woodall, Ed. & Pub.  (US)
Woodall Publishing Co.  (US)
Woodbine Publishers Inc.  (US)
Woodenboat  (US)
Woodland Indian Cultural Educational Centre  (CN)
Woodmen of the World Life Insurance Society  (US)
Woodrow Wilson Foundation  (US)
Woodrow Wilson International Center for Scholars (US)
Woodrow Wilson National Fellowship Foundation (US)
Woods Hole Oceanographic Institution  (US)
Woodson County Historical Society  (US)
Wool & Woollens Export Promotion Council  (II)
Woolhope Club  (UK)

Woolknit Associates, Inc.  (US)
J. Howard Woolmer - Books  (US)
Wootten Publications Ltd.  (UK)
Worcester Art Museum  (US)
Worcester City Museum and Art Gallery  (UK)
Worcester District Medical Society  (US)
Worcester Polytechnic Institute. Alumni Association (US)
Worcestershire Catholic History Society  (UK)
Word, Inc.  (US)
Word of Truth Productions  (US)
Word Smith  (US)
Word to the Wise  (US)
Wordens Weekly Report  (US)
Words News & Interview, Inc.  (US)
Words Unlimited Writers Group  (CN)
Wordsworth Circle  (US)
Work in America Institute, Inc.  (US)
Workers Association in Belfast  (UK)
Workers' Compensation Board of British Columbia (CN)
Workers Defense League  (US)
Workers Educational Association  (FI)
Worker's Northern Publishing Society Ltd.  (UK)
Workers' Party  (SI)
Workers World Party  (US)
Working Craftsman, Inc.  (US)
Working Kelpie Council  (AT)
Working Men's Club and Institute Union Ltd.  (UK)
Working Papers in Sex, Science and Culture  (AT)
Workmen's Benefit Fund of the United States of America  (US)
Workmen's Circle  (US)
Workshop Press Ltd.  (UK)
World Affairs Council of Northern California  (US)
World Airline Record  (US)
World Alliance of Reformed Churches  (SZ)
World Alliance of Young Men's Christian Associations (SZ)
World Anti-Communist League  (KO)
World Archaeological Society  (US)
World Association for Animal Production  (UY)
World Association for Buiatrics  (GW)
World Association for Christian Communication (GW)
World Association for the Advancement of Veterinary Parasitology  (US)
World Association of Estonians, Inc.  (US)
World Association of Girl Guides and Girl Scouts (UK)
World Association of Veterinary Anatomists  (GW)
World Association of World Federalists  (NE)
World Athletics & Sporting Publications Ltd.  (UK)
World Bank
    see International Bank for Reconstruction and Development  (UN)
World Bird Research Station  (UK)
World Book and Travel Report  (US)
World Bureau of Metal Statistics  (UK)
World Chess Federation - FIDE  (YU)
World Co.  (US)
World Collectors Publishers  (NE)
World Community Association  (US)
World Confederation of Labour  (BE)
World Confederation of Organizations of the Teaching Profession  (SZ)
World Confederation of Physical Therapy  (UK)
World Council of Churches  (SZ)
World Council of Credit Unions  (US)
World Council of Young Men's Service Clubs  (AT)
World Council of Young Men's Service Clubs  (UK)
World Crafts Council  (US)
World Crops Publications Ltd.  (UK)
World Cutter and Chariot Racing Association  (US)
World Data Center A for Glaciology
    see under U. S. Environmental Data Service  (US)
World Economic Information Services  (JA)
World Education  (US)
World Education Fellowship  (UK)
World Education Fellowship in Australia, Inc.  (AT)
World Education Markets Inc.  (US)
World Energy Conference  (UK)
World Enterprise  (CH)
World Esperantist Youth Organization
    see Tutmonda Esperantista Junulara Organizo (NE)
World Federalist Educational Fund  (US)
World Federalists, USA  (US)
World Federation for Mental Health  (CN)
World Federation for the Protection of Animals (NE)
World Federation for the Protection of Animals  (SZ)
World Federation of Christian Life Communities  (IT)
World Federation of Democratic Youth  (HU)
World Federation of Diamond Bourses  (IS)
World Federation of Hemophilia  (CN)
World Federation of Hungarian Jews  (US)

World Federation of Islamic Missions  (PK)
World Federation of Jewish Journalists  (IS)
World Federation of Neurological Societies  (NE)
World Federation of Neurology  (NE)
World Federation of Neurology. Groupe de Travail de Neurogenetique  (SZ)
World Federation of Occupational Therapists  (UK)
World Federation of Parasitologists  (IT)
World Federation of Scientific Workers  (UK)
World Federation of Societies of Anaesthesiologists (NE)
World Federation of Societies of Anaesthesiologists (SP)
World Federation of Teachers' Unions  (CS)
World Federation of the Deaf  (IT)
World Federation of Trade Unions  (CS)
World Federation of Trade Unions  (UR)
World Federation of United Nations Associates  (SZ)
World Fellowship of Buddhists  (TH)
World Fertility Survey  (NE)
World Future Society  (US)
World Future Society. Special Studies Division  (US)
World Gift Review  (US)
World Goodwill  (US)
World Health Organization  (UN)
World Health Organization. Centro Pan Americano de Febre Aftosa  (UN)
World Health Organization. International Agency for Research on Cancer
    see International Agency for Research on Cancer (UN)
World Health Organization. Pan American Health Organization  (UN)
World Health Organization. Pan American Health Organization. Caribbean Food and Nutrition Institute  (UN)
World Health Organization. Pan American Health Organization. Institute of Nutrition of Central America and Panama
    see United Nations. Institute of Nutrition of Central America and Panama  (UN)
World Health Organization. Regional Office for Africa (UN)
World Health Organization. Regional Office for Europe  (UN)
World Health Organization. Regional Office for South-East Asia  (UN)
World Health Organization. Regional Office for the Americas
    see World Health Organization. Pan American Health Organization  (UN)
World Health Organization. Regional Office for the Eastern Mediterranean  (UN)
World Health Organization. Regional Office for the Western Pacific  (UN)
World Health Organization. Research and Training Centre on Human Reproduction  (UN)
World Information Systems Exchange (W I S E) (US)
World Information Systems Exchange (W I S E) Library and Information Science Division  (US)
World Institute Council  (US)
World Intellectual Property Organization (WIPO) (UN)
World Jain Mission  (II)
World Jersey Cattle Bureau  (UK)
World Jewish Congress  (AG)
World Jewish Congress  (UK)
World Jewish Congress  (IS)
World Jnana Sadhak Society  (II)
World League Against Vivisection  (UK)
World Leisure and Recreation Association  (US)
World Media Ltd.  (UK)
World Medical Association  (FR)
World Medical Association, Inc.  (US)
World Meetings Information Center, Inc.  (US)
World Meteorological Organization  (UN)
World Methodist Council  (US)
World Methodist Historical Society  (US)
World Muslim Congress  (PK)
World Neighbors  (US)
World News Corporation  (US)
World O R T Union  (SZ)
World of Comic Art Publications  (US)
World Organization of the Scout Movement  (SZ)
World Peace Council  (FI)
World Peace Council. Presidential Committee  (FI)
World Peace Foundation  (US)
World Peace News  (US)
World Peace Through Law Center  (US)
World Pen Pals  (US)
World Pentecostal Conference  (UK)
World Petroleum Congress. Japanese National Committee  (JA)
World Petroleum Congresses  (UK)
World Pictures A-S  (DK)
World Ploughing Federation  (UK)
World Poetry, Inc.  (US)

World Poetry Society Intercontinental  (II)
World Presbyterian Missions, Inc.  (US)
World Printing and Publishing Co. (Pty) Ltd  (SA)
World Products  (US)
World Prohibition Federation  (UK)
World Prophetic Ministry, Inc.  (US)
World Psychiatric Association  (UK)
World Publications  (US)
World Publishing, Inc.  (US)
World Redemption  (US)
World Refrigeration and Air Conditioning  (UK)
World Research, Inc.  (US)
World Science Education  (US)
World Science Fiction Association  (US)
World Scout Bureau  (SZ)
World Scout Bureau. Asia-Pacific Region  (PH)
World Ship Society  (UK)
World Ship Society. Port of New York Branch  (US)
World Ship Society. Queensland Branch  (AT)
World Small Animal Veterinary Association. Deutsche Gruppe  (GW)
World Socialist Party of the United States  (US)
World Society for Stereotactic and Functional Neurosurgery  (SZ)
World Sports Publishers  (US)
World Student Christian Federation  (SZ)
World Team Tennis (Organization)  (US)
World Touring and Automobile Organization  (UK)
World Tourism Organization  (SP)
World Trade Academy Press, Inc.  (US)
World Trade Academy Press, Inc. Technical and Reference Book Division  (US)
World Trade Center of Japan, Inc.  (JA)
World Trade Centers Association of Japan  (JA)
World Trade Magazines Ltd.  (UK)
World Tribune Press  (US)
World Underwater Federation  (FR)
World Union for the Safeguard of Youth  (FR)
World Union International Centre  (II)
World Union of Jewish Students  (UK)
World Union of Liberal Trade Union Organizations (SZ)
World Union of Mapam  (IS)
World Union of National Socialists  (US)
World United Formosans for Independence  (US)
World United Formosans for Independence  (JA)
World University Service  (US)
World Veterinary Association  (SZ)
World Veterinary Congress  (SZ)
World View Publishers, Inc.  (US)
World Vision International  (US)
World Ways  (US)
World Wide Gun Report, Inc.  (US)
World Wide Trade Service  (US)
World Wide Wrestling Federation  (US)
World Zionist Organization  (IS)
World Zionist Organization-American Section Inc. Department of Education and Culture in the Diaspora  (US)
World's Fair Ltd.  (UK)
World's Poultry Science Association  (UK)
World's Poultry Science Association  (US)
World's Woman's Christian Temperance Union  (UK)
Worldwide Culture Society  (US)
Worldwide Evangelization Crusade  (UK)
Worldwide Knitting Publications, Ltd.  (UK)
Wormald International Ltd  (AT)
Worms. Stadtbibliothek  (GW)
Wormsloe Foundation  (US)
Wormwood Review Press  (US)
Worn-out Press  (US)
Verlag Wort und Bild Rolf Becker  (GW)
Verlag Wort und Werk GmbH  (GW)
Worth International Communications Corp.  (US)
Worthington S.p.A.  (IT)
Wotanin Press  (US)
Wrangler's Roost  (UK)
Ron Wray, Ed. & Pub.  (US)
Wrecking & Salvage Journal  (US)
John Wright & Sons Ltd.  (UK)
Wright Investors' Service  (US)
Wright Publishing Co.  (US)
Wright State University  (US)
Wright State University. College of Education  (US)
Wright State University. English Department  (US)
Writ  (CN)
Write on Publishing House, Inc.  (US)
Writer, Inc.  (US)
Writers Digest  (US)
Writers Foundation Favorable Trust  (II)
Writers Guild of America, East  (US)
Writers Guild of America, West  (US)
Writers' Resources  (US)
Writers Workshop  (II)
Wroclawskie Towarzystwo Milosnikow Historii  (PL)
Wroclawskie Towarzystwo Naukowe  (PL)
Wudd Verlag  (GW)
Wuerttemberg. Landesversicherungsanstalt  (GW)

Wuerttembergische Bau-Berufsgenossenschaft  (GW)
Wuerzburger Dioezesangeschichtsverein  (GW)
Verlag Dr. Ruediger Wurth  (AU)
Wyandotte General Hospital  (US)
Wycliffe Bible Translators, Inc.  (US)
Wye College (University of London) School of Rural Economics and Related Studies  (UK)
Wyevern Astronomical Society  (UK)
Wykeham Publications, Ltd., London  (UK)
Wyndham Lewis Society  (UK)
Wyoming. Archives and Historical Department  (US)
Wyoming. Department of Administration and Fiscal Control. Research and Statistics Division  (US)
Wyoming. Department of Economic Planning and Development  (US)
Wyoming. Department of Education  (US)
Wyoming. Department of Environmental Quality (US)
Wyoming. Department of Health and Social Services (US)
Wyoming. Department of Labor and Statistics  (US)
Wyoming. Department of Revenue and Taxation (US)
Wyoming. Division of Educational Data Systems and Statistical Service  (US)
Wyoming. Division of Planning, Evaluation and Information Services  (US)
Wyoming. Division of Public Assistance and Social Services  (US)
Wyoming. Employment Security Commission  (US)
Wyoming. Employment Security Commission. Research and Analysis Section  (US)
Wyoming. Game and Fish Department  (US)
Wyoming. Geological Survey  (US)
Wyoming. Governor's Office of Highway Safety  (US)
Wyoming. Recreation Commission  (US)
Wyoming. State Library  (US)
Wyoming Congress of Parents and Teachers  (US)
Wyoming Education Association  (US)
Wyoming Farm Bureau Federation  (US)
Wyoming Geological Association  (US)
Wyoming Nurses Association  (US)
Wyoming School Board Association  (US)
Wyoming State Medical Society  (US)
Wyoming State Rural Electric Association  (US)
Wyoming Stock Growers Association  (US)
Wyoming Stockman-Farmer Publishing Co.  (US)
Wyoming Wool Growers Association  (US)
Wyrd Publications  (US)
K.J. Wyss Erben AG  (SZ)
Wythe County Historical Review  (US)
Wyzsza Szkola Morska. Instytut Nawigacji  (PL)
Wyzsza Szkola Pedagogiczna, Katowice  (PL)
Wyzsza Szkola Pedagogiczna, Krakow  (PL)
Wyzsza Szkola Pedagogiczna, Opole  (PL)
Xaloc  (MX)
Xaverian Brothers  (US)
Xaverian Missionary Fathers  (US)
Xavier Society for the Blind  (US)
Xavier University  (PH)
Xavier University  (US)
Xavier University of Louisiana  (US)
Xerox Corporation  (US)
Xerox Education Publications  (US)
Xi Psi Phi Fraternity  (US)
Xunhasaba  (VN)
Y W C A Nederland  (NE)
Y. W. Heron Sailing Association of Australia  (AT)
Yacht Racing  (US)
Yachting Italiano-Altomare  (IT)
Yachting News (Pty) Ltd.  (SA)
Yachting Publishing Corporation  (US)
Yad Maimon Research Institute  (IS)
Yad Vashem Martyr's and Heroes Remembrance Authority  (IS)
Yaffa Publishing Group  (AT)
Yakima Tribe  (US)
Yakugaku Kenkyusho
    see Pharmaceutical Research Institute  (JA)
Yakugyo Jiho Co. Ltd.  (JA)
Yakugyo Kenkyukai
    see Pharmaceutical Research Association  (JA)
Yakuji Nippo Ltd.  (JA)
Yakuji Nyususha  (JA)
Richard B. Yale  (US)
Yale Alumni Publications  (US)
Yale Banner Publications  (US)
Yale Book Co. Ltd.  (CN)
Yale Forestry Alumni Association  (US)
Yale Law Journal Co., Inc.  (US)
Yale Law Library  (US)
Yale Scientific Publications, Inc.  (US)
Yale Speleological Society  (US)
Yale Studies in World Public Order, Inc.  (US)
Yale University  (US)
Yale University. Afro- American Cultural Center (US)
Yale University Art Gallery  (US)

Yale University. Department of Anthropology (US)
Yale University. Department of Music (US)
Yale University. Economic Growth Center (US)
Yale University Library (US)
Yale University Press (US)
Yale University. School of Art (US)
Yale University. School of Drama (US)
Yale University. School of Forestry (US)
Yale University. School of Law (US)
Yale University. School of Medicine (US)
Yale University School of Medicine. Department of
  Microbiology (US)
Yale University. School of Music (US)
Yale University. Sears Foundation for Marine
  Research (US)
Yale University. Southeast Asia Studies (US)
Yama-to-Keikoku Sha Co. Ltd. (JA)
Yamagata University (JA)
Yamaguchi Daigaku
  see Yamaguchi University (JA)
Yamaguchi University. Faculty of Engineering (JA)
Yamaguchi University. School of Medicine (JA)
Yamaha International Corp. (US)
Yamaha Music (Asia) Pte. (SI)
Yamanouchi Pharmaceutical Co. Ltd. (JA)
Yamanouchi Seiyaku K. K.
  see Yamanouchi Pharmaceutical Co. (JA)
Yamashina Institute for Ornithology (JA)
Yankee Gardener (US)
Yankee, Inc. (US)
Yankee Milk Inc. (US)
Yanks Abroad (US)
Yaovank-Jeune Breton (FR)
Yardage Publications (US)
Yardbird Pub. Cooperative (US)
Yasodhara Ashram Society (CN)
Yate y Motonautica (SP)
Yavneh (US)
Yayasan Foto Indonesia (IO)
Yayasan Harapan Kita (IO)
Yayasan Idayu (IO)
Yayasan Komunikasi (IO)
Yayasan Media Pembangunan (IO)
Yayasan Perpustakaan Nasional (IO)
Ye Olde Genealogie Shoppe (US)

Year, Inc. (US)

Year Book Medical Publishers, Inc. (US)
Years Press (US)
Robert Yeatman Ltd. (UK)
Julian Yebenes Guerrero (SP)
Yedon le-Tekhnologyah Shel Meda u-Mahshevim
  (IS)
Yellow Press, Inc. (US)
Yellow Seed Center (US)
Yellowknife Publishing Co. Ltd. (CN)
Yelmo (SP)
Yemen. Central Statistical Office (YE)
Yerkes Regional Primate Research Center (US)
Yeshiva University (US)
Yeshiva University. Albert Einstein College of
  Medicine (US)
Yeshiva University. Belfer Graduate School of Science
  (US)
Yeshiva University. Sephardic Studies Program (US)
Yeshiva University. Wurzweiler School of Social Work
  (US)
Yeshiva University. Yeshiva College Student Council
  (US)
Yeshivat Ohr Somayach College of Judaic Studies.
  Joseph and Faye Tanenbaum Centre (IS)
Michael Yessis, Ed. & Pub. (US)
Yhtyneet Kuvalehdet Oy (FI)
Yid Pub Association (US)
Yiddish Press (CN)
Yiddisher Kultur Farband Inc. (US)
Yidishe Shrayber Grupe in Yerusholaim. (IS)
YIVO Institute for Jewish Research (US)
YIVO Institute for Jewish Research. Max Weinreich
  Center for Advanced Jewish Studies (US)
Yliopiston Farmasiakunta r.y. (FI)
Yoga Institute (II)
Yoga Research Association (UK)
Yogyo Kyokai
  see Yamanouchi Pharmaceutical Co., Ltd. (JA)
Yokendo Ltd. (JA)
Yokkaichi. Yokkaichi City Library (JA)
Yokkaichi-shiritsu Toshokan
  see Yokkaichi. Yokkaichi City Library (JA)
Yokohama. Port and Harbor Bureau (JA)
Yokohama City University. Department of
  Mathematics (JA)
Yokohama City University. School of Medicine (JA)
Yokohama Kokuritsu Daigaku
  see Yokohama National University (JA)
Yokohama National University. Department of
  Sociology (JA)

Yokohama National University. Faculty of Education
  (JA)
Yokohama National University. Faculty of Engineering
  (JA)
Yokohama National University. Society for Economics
  and Business Administration (JA)
Yokohama Plant Protection Station
  see Japan. Yokohama Plant Protection Station
  (JA)
Yokohama-shiritsu Daigaku
  see Yokohama City University (JA)
Yokufukai Geriatric Hospital (JA)
Yomtov Bletter (SA)
Yonago Igakkai
  see Yonago Medical Association (JA)
Yonago Medical Association (JA)
Yonsei University College of Medicine (KO)
Yonsei University. Graduate School (KO)
Yonsei University. Industrial Management Research
  Centre (KO)
Yonsei University. Institute of East and West Studies
  (KO)
Yonsei University. Institute of Humanistic Studies
  (KO)
Yonsei University Press (KO)
John W. Yopp Publications, Inc. (US)
York Barbell Co (US)
York College. Department of Foreign Languages
  (US)
York Georgian Society (UK)
York Pioneer and Historical Society (CN)
York Press Ltd. (AT)
York Research Publishing Co. (US)
York Rite Publishing Co. (US)
York University (CN)
York University. Department of Geography (CN)
York University. Department of Sociology (CN)
York University. Faculty of Administrative Studies
  (CN)
York University. Glendon College (CN)
York University. Osgoode Hall Law School (CN)
Yorke Medical Group (US)
Yorkshire Archaeological Society (UK)
Yorkshire Dialect Society (UK)
Yorkshire Naturalists' Union (UK)
Yorktown Printing & Pennysaver Corp. (US)
Yoruba Studies Association of Nigeria (NR)
Thomas Yoseloff, Inc. (US)
Yosetsu Gakkai
  see Japan Welding Society (JA)
You: the Quest (US)
J.R. Young (US)
Young Adult Alternative Newsletter (US)
Young Advertising & Marketing Ltd. (SI)
Young Age (II)
Arthur Young & Co. (US)
Young Athlete Enterprises (US)
Young Calvinist Federation (US)
Young Christian Workers (SA)
Young Communication (US)
Young-Conway Publications, Inc. (US)
Young-Conway Publishing Co (US)
Young East Association (JA)
James Dean Young, Ed. & Pub. (US)
Young Farmers' Association, India (II)
Young Farmers Clubs of Ulster (UK)
Young India (II)
Young Labor Association of South Australia (AT)
Young Lords Party (US)
Young Men's and Young Women's Hebrew
  Association of New York (US)
Young Men's Christian Association of Canada.
  National Council (CN)
Young Men's Institute (US)
Young Mens Muslim Association (MF)
Young Ornithologist's Club (UK)
Young People's Socialist League (US)
Young People's Societies Eastern Ontario League
  (CN)
Young Scientists of America Foundation, Inc. (US)
Young Socialist (CN)
Young Socialist Alliance (US)
Young Way Publishing (US)
Young Women's Christian Association (US)
Young Worker Publishing Co. (CN)
Young Writer Group (UK)
Your Story Magazine (US)
Your Tomorrow (US)
Youth Aliyah (UK)
Youth Correctional Institution (US)
Youth for Christ (NE)
Youth for Christ International (US)
Youth Hostels Association of N.S.W. (AT)
Youth Hostels Association of South Australia (AT)
Youth Hostels Association of Victoria (AT)
Youth Hostels Associations (England & Wales) (UK)
Youth Institute for Peace in the Middle East (US)
Youth International Party (US)

Youth Liberation Press, Inc. (US)
Youth Organization for Black Unity (US)
Youth Science Foundation (CN)
Youth Specialties (US)
Youth's Library (SK)
Youthways Corporation (US)
Yritystieto Oy (FI)
Yugoslav Information Center (US)
Yugoslavia. Beogradska Armijska Oblast (YU)
Yugoslavia. Privredna Komora (YU)
Yugoslavia. Ratna Mornarica (YU)
Yugoslavia. Ratno Vozduhoplovstvo i Protivvazdusne
  Odbrane (YU)
Yugoslavia. Savezna Komisija za Nuklearnu Energiju
  (YU)
Yugoslavia. Savezni Sekretarijat za Inostrane Poslove
  (YU)
Yugoslavia. Savezni Sekretarijat za Narodnu Odbranu
  (YU)
Yugoslavia. Savezni Sekretarijat za Narodnu Odbranu.
  Sanitetska Uprava (YU)
Yugoslavia. Savezni Sekretarijat za Unutresnje Poslove
  (YU)
Yugoslavia. Savezni Zavod za Patente (YU)
Yugoslavia. Savezni Zavod za Statistiku (YU)
Yugoslaviapublic (YU)
Yugyo Hochi Shinbunsha (JA)
Yuhikaku Publishing Co. Ltd. (JA)
Yuki Gosei Kagaku Kyokai
  see Society of Synthetic Organic Chemistry (JA)
Yukijirushi Nyugyo K. K.
  see Snow Brand Milk Products Co. Ltd. (JA)
Yukon News Ltd. (CN)
Yukranda (II)
Yura Bhasati Trust (II)
Yuri Shuppan (JA)
Yusei-sho Denpa Kenkyusho
  see Japan. Ministry of Posts and
  Telecommunications. Radio Research Laboratories
  (JA)
Yushodo Booksellers Ltd. (JA)
Mazhar Yusuf, Ed. & Pub. (PK)
Z (II)
Z Press, Inc. (US)
Za Domovinu (YU)
David Zackin (US)
Zagaglia (IT)
Zagreb Academy of Music. Institute of Musicology
  (YU)
Zagreb Univerzitet
  see Sveuciliste u Zagrebu (YU)
Zahn Techniker-Meisterschule, Halle (GE)
Verlag Zahnaerztlich-Medizinisches Schrifttum (GW)
Zahnaerztlicher Bezirksverband Muenchen Stadt und
  Land (GW)
Zaikeo Shoho Sha (JA)
Zaire. Conseil Legislatif National (ZR)
Zaire. Conseil Permanent de la Comptabilite (ZR)
Zaire. Direction des Archives et Bibliotheques (ZR)
Zaire. Direction Generale des Finances (ZR)
Zaire. Direction Generale et Administration (ZR)
Zaire. Institut National de la Statistique (ZR)
Zaire. Ministere de la Culture et des Arts. Direction
  des Archives et Bibliotheques
  see Zaire. Direction des Archives et Bibliotheques
  (ZR)
Zaire Business (ZR)
Zajednica (YU)
Zajednica Jugoslovenske Elektroprivrede (YU)
Zajednica Jugoslovenskih Posta, Telegrafe i Telefona
  (YU)
Zajednica Jugoslovenskih Univerziteta (YU)
Zajednica Kulturno-Prosvetnih Organizacija Jugoslavije
  (YU)
Zaklad Projektowych Miedzi "Cuprum" (PL)
Zalozba Obzorja Maribor (YU)
Zamana (MF)
Zambia. Central Fisheries Research Institute (ZA)
Zambia. Central Statistical Office (ZA)
Zambia. Commission for Investigation (ZA)
Zambia. Commission for the Preservation of Natural
  and Historical Monuments and Relics (ZA)
Zambia. Geological Survey (ZA)
Zambia. Government Printer (ZA)
Zambia. Health and Welfare Department (ZA)
Zambia. Information Services (ZA)
Zambia. Meteorological Department (ZA)
Zambia. Ministry of Education (ZA)
Zambia. Ministry of Education. Curriculum
  Development Centre (ZA)
Zambia. Ministry of Planning and Finance (ZA)
Zambia. Ministry of Rural Development (ZA)
Zambia. Ministry of Rural Development. Land Use
  Branch (ZA)
Zambia. National Archives (ZA)

Zambia. National Council for Scientific Research (ZA)
Zambia. National Food and Nutrition Commission (ZA)
Zambia. National Museums Board (ZA)
Zambia. National Parks and Wildlife Service (ZA)
Zambia Association for Scientific Education (ZA)
Zambia Congress of Trade Unions (ZA)
Zambia Electricity Supply Corporation (ZA)
Zambia Geographical Association (ZA)
Zambia Industrial and Mining Corp. Ltd. (ZA)
Zambia Library Association (ZA)
Zambia Medical Association (ZA)
Zambia Nurses Association (ZA)
Zambia Publishing Company (ZA)
Zambian Ornithological Society (ZA)
Nicola Zanichelli Editore (IT)
Kristian Zarp, Ed. & Pub. (DK)
Zartaj Publications (PK)
Zastita Rada (YU)
Zauberkreis Verlag (GW)
Zava Misy (MG)
Editorial Zavaleta (ES)
Zavod SR Slovenije za Spomenisko Varstvo (YU)
Zavod SR Slovenije za Statistiko (YU)
Zavod SR Slovenije za Varstvo Pri Delu (YU)
Zavod za Casopisno in Radijsko Dejavnost Murska Sobota (YU)
Zavod za Ekonomske Ekspertize (YU)
Zavod za Javnu Upravu, Belgrade (YU)
Zavod za Mentalno Zdravlje (YU)
Zavod za Novinsko Izdavacku i Propagandnu Delatnost JZ (YU)
Zavod za Organizaciju i Ekonomiku Zdravstva. Centar za Lijekove (YU)
Zavod za Organizaciju i Upravljanje Poslovnim Sistemom u Organizacijama Udruzenog Rada (YU)
Zavod za Pedagoska i Kulturno Prosvjetna Pitanja (YU)
Zavod za Proucavanje i Zastitu Uha i Disnih Organa (YU)
Zavod za Proucavanje Kulturnog Razvitka (YU)
Zavod za Tehnologiju Zita i Brasna (YU)
Zavod za Transfuziju Krvi, Belgrade (YU)
Zavod za Trzisna Istrazivanja (YU)
Zavod za Trzisna Istrazivanja. Centar za Istrazivanje Konjukture (YU)
Zavod za Unapredivanje Osnovnog Obrazovanja SR Hrvatske (YU)
Zavod za Unapredjenje Domacinstva Bosne i Hercegovine (YU)
Zavod za Zdravstvenu Zastitu SR Srbije (YU)
Zbor Lijecnika Hrvatske. Sekcija za Maksilofacijalnu i Plasticnu Kirurgiju (YU)
Zbor Lijecnika u Rijeci (YU)
Izdatel'stvo Zdorovya (UR)
Zdravotnicke Noviny (CS)
Zdruzene PTT Organizacije Slovenije (YU)
Zdruzenie na Smetkovodstveno-Finansiskite Rabotnici na Makedonija (YU)
Zdruzenje Anatomov Jugoslavije (YU)
Zdruzenje Bank SR Slovenije (YU)
Zechner und Huethig Verlag GmbH (GW)
Zeeland. Provinciale Waterstaatsdienst (NE)
Verlag Zeichentechnik (GW)
Zeil-Verlag GmbH (GW)
Zeirei Agudath Israel of America (US)
VEB Carl Zeiss (GE)
Carl Zeiss (GW)
Verlag Zeit im Bild (GE)
Zeitgeist, Inc. (US)
Verlag der Zeitschrift fuer Naturforschung (GW)
Zeitschriftenverlag Austria International GmbH (AU)
Zeitungs- und Zeitschriften-Verlag GmbH (GW)
Zeitungsunternehmen "Sport", GmbH (AU)
Josef Zelger (AU)
Hans Zell Publishers Ltd. (UK)
Fachverlag Erwin P. H. Zellmer (GW)
Zemaljski Muzej Bosne i Hercegovine (YU)
Zemedelska Skola (CS)
Zen Center (Rochester) (US)
Zen Center (San Francisco) (US)
Zen Center of Los Angeles (US)
Zen-chu
   see Central Union of Agricultural Co-operatives (JA)
Zen Kokutetsu Shinshosa Kyokai
   see Handicapped Persons Association of Japan National Railways (JA)
Zena (YU)
Zendingscentrum van de Gereformeerde Kerken in Nederland (NE)
Zendingsgenootschap der Evangelische Broedergemeente (NE)
Tidskriftsforeningen Zenit (SW)
Zenith (CR)
Zenkoku Kensetsu Gyomukai

   see Associated General Contractors of Japan Inc. (JA)
Zenkoku Shakai Fukushi Kyogikai
   see National Council of Social Welfare (JA)
Zenkoku Shinrin Byochu Jugai Bojo Kyokai (JA)
Zentralanstalt fuer Meteorologie und Geodynamik (AU)
Zentralarchiv fuer Hochschulbau (GW)
Zentralausschuss fuer Deutsche Landeskunde (GW)
Zentrale der Caritas-Schwesternschaft e.V. (GW)
Zentrale fuer Gasverwendung e.V. (GW)
Zentrale fuer GmbH Dr. O. Schmidt (GW)
Zentraler Rat fuer Asien-, Afrika- und Lateinamerikawissenschaften in der DDR (GE)
Zentrales Geologisches Institut (GE)
Zentralgenossenschaft fuer Viehverwertung e.V. (GW)
Zentralhaus fuer Kulturarbeit (GE)
Zentralinstitut fuer Bibliothekswesen (GE)
Zentralinstitut fuer Bibliothekswesen. Zentralstelle fuer die Information und Dokumentation Bibliothekswesen (GE)
Zentralinstitut fuer Holztechnologie Dresden (GE)
Zentralinstitut fuer Information und Dokumentation (GE)
Zentralinstitut fuer Kunstgeschichte in Muenchen (GW)
Zentralinstitut fuer Musikforschung (GE)
Zentralinstitut fuer Schweisstechnik der DDR (GE)
Zentralkomitee der Deutschen Katholiken (GW)
Zentralrat der Freien Deutschen Jugend (GE)
Zentralsparkasse der Gemeinde Wien (AU)
Zentralstelle fuer Atomkernenergie-Dokumentation. Kernforschungszentrum (GW)
Zentralstelle fuer die Philosophische Information und Dokumentation (GE)
Zentralstelle fuer Korrosionsschutz (GE)
Zentralstelle fuer Soziologische Information und Dokumentation Am Institut fuer Gesellschaftswissenschaftenbeim ZK der SED (GE)
Zentralverband Demokratischer Widerstandskaempfer und Verfolgtenorganisationen e.V. (GW)
Zentralverband der Aerzte fuer Naturheilverfahren e.V. (GW)
Zentralverband der Deutschen Gefluegelwirtschaft (GW)
Zentralverband der Deutschen Geographen (GW)
Zentralverband der Deutschen Haus, Wohnungs und Grundeigentuemer e.V. (GW)
Zentralverband der Fusspfleger Deutschlands e.V. (GW)
Zentralverband der Kleingaertner, Siedler und Kleintierzuechter Oesterreichs (AU)
Zentralverband der oesterreichischen Aktiengesellschaften (AU)
Zentralverband der Oesterreichischen Konsumgenossenschaften Konsumverband (AU)
Zentralverband der Schweizerischen Milchproduzenten (SZ)
Zentralverband des Dachdeckerhandwerks e.V (GW)
Zentralverband des Deutschen Baugewerbes e.V. (GW)
Zentralverband des Deutschen Elektrohandwerks (GW)
Zentralverband des Deutschen Elektrohandwerks. Bundesfachgruppe Elektromaschinenbau (GW)
Zentralverband des Deutschen Elektrohandwerks. Bundesfachgruppe Radio- und Fernsehtechnik (GW)
Zentralverband des Deutschen Handwerks (GW)
Zentralverband des Deutschen Vulkaniseurhandwerks (GW)
Zentralverband des Kraftfahrzeughandels e.V. (GW)
Zentralverband des Kraftfahrzeughandwerks (GW)
Zentralverband des Kuerschnerhandwerks (GW)
Zentralverband Deutscher Molkereifachleute und Milchwirtschaftler (GW)
Zentralverband Deutscher Photographen (GW)
Zentralverband fuer Sanitaer-, Klima- und Heizungstechnik (GW)
Zentralverband fuer Uhren, Schmuck und Zeitmesstechnik (GW)
Zentralverband Karosserie und Fahrzeugtechnik e. V. (GW)
Zentralverband Krankengymnastik e.V. (GW)
Zentralverband Schweizer Volksbuehnen (SZ)
Zentralverband Schweizerischer Arbeitgeber-Organisationen (SZ)
Zentralverband Schweizerischer Uhrmacher (SZ)
Zentralverband Zoologischer Fachgeschaefte Deutschlands e.V. (GW)
Zentralverein der Wiener Lehrerschaft (AU)
Zentralvereinigung Deutscher Handelsvertreter- und Handelsmaklerverbaende e.V. (GW)
Zephyr Records & Magazines (UK)

Zephyros (US)
Edizioni Suvini Zerboni (IT)
Zero Population Growth, Inc. (US)
Zetetic Press (US)
Zetlan Picture Libraries (US)
Zeugma (US)
Zevende Dags Adventisten (NE)
ZfGW-Verlag GmbH (GW)
Zgodovinsko Drustvo za Slovenijo (YU)
Zien Enterprises, Inc. (US)
Ziff-Davis Publishing Co. (US)
Ziff-Davis Publishing Co. Public Transportation and Travel Division (US)
Zim-Mer Trade Publications, Inc. (US)
Zimbabwe African Peoples Union (ZA)
Harold O. Zimman, Inc. (US)
Donald R. & Robert H. Zimmer, Eds. & Pubs. (US)
Verlag Dieter Zimmerle (GW)
Toni Ortner Zimmerman, Ed. & Pub. (US)
Zimmermann-Verlag (GW)
Izdevnieciba Zinatne (UR)
Zinbum Kagata Kenkynsyo
   see Kyota University. Research Institute for Humanistic Studies (JA)
Zinc Development Association (UK)
Zinc-Lead Library and Abstracts Service (UK)
Zionist Federation of Great Britain and Northern Ireland (UK)
Zionist Organization of America (US)
Zionist Organization of America. Masada Youth Movement (US)
Zionist Record (Pty) Ltd. (SA)
Zionist Review Ltd. (UK)
Zionist Revisionist Organisation of South Africa (SA)
Zisin Gakkai
   see Seismological Society of Japan (JA)
Zjednoczenie Przemyslu Cementowego, Wapienniczego i Gipsowego, Sosnowiec (PL)
Spoleczny Instytut Wydawniczy "Znak" (PL)
Izdatel'stvo Znanie (UR)
Z. I. Zobairy, Ed. & Pub. (PK)
Zollikofer und Co. AG (SZ)
Zomer en Keuning Tijdschriften (NE)
Zona Abierta (SP)
Zona s.r.l (AG)
Zondervan Publishing House (US)
Zoo-Centrum (UK)
Zoological Laboratory and Museum, Athens (GR)
Zoological Society Amsterdam (NE)
Zoological Society, Calcutta (II)
Zoological Society of Bangladesh (BG)
Zoological Society of India (II)
Zoological Society of Japan (JA)
Zoological Society of London (UK)
Zoological Society of Pakistan (PK)
Zoological Society of San Diego (US)
Zoologicka Society of Southern Africa (SA)
Zoologicka Zahrada v Praze (CS)
Zoologisch-Botanische Gesellschaft (AU)
Zoologisch Museum
   see under Universiteit van Amsterdam (NE)
Zoologische Staatssammlung Muenchen (GW)
Zoologisches Forschungsinstitut und Museum A. Koenig (GW)
Zoologisches Museum Hamburg (GW)
Zoologisk Institut (SW)
Mike Zotti (US)
Zrinyi Katonai Kiado (HU)
Zrzeszenie Miedzynarodowych Przewoznikow Drogowych (PL)
Zrzeszenie Polskich Hoteli Turystycznych (PL)
Gerald A. Zucker (US)
Zuercher Boerse (SZ)
Hubert Zuerl (GW)
Werbeagenturen Zuhlke und Scholz KG (GW)
Zuidafrikaanse Ambassade (NE)
Drukkerij Uitgeverij Zuijderduijn (NE)
Zulch and Zulch, Inc. (US)
Zululand Swaziland Association (UK)
Zumstein and Cie (SZ)
Zurich (Canton). Amt fuer Raumplanung (SZ)
Giorgio Zusi Editore (IT)
Zusters Augustinessen van Sint Monica (NE)
Zvaz Slovenskych Architektov (CS)
Zvaz Slovenskych Spisovatelov (CS)
Zveza Arhitektov Slovenije (YU)
Zveza Drustev Glasbenih Pedagogov Slovenije (YU)
Zveza Drustev Pravnikov SR Slovenije (YU)
Zveza Ekonomistov Slovenije (YU)
Zveza Gradbenih Inzenirjev in Tehnikov Slovenije (YU)
Zveza Inzenirjev in Tehnikov Gozdarstva in Lesarstva SR Slovenije (YU)
Zveza Inzenirjev in Tehnikov Slovenije (YU)
Zveza Kulturnih Delavcev v Mariboru (YU)
Zveza Kulturno Prosvetnih Organizacij Slovenije (YU)
Zveza Pedagoskih Drustev Slovenije (YU)

Zveza Prijateljev Mladine Slovenije   (YU)
Zveza Sindikatov Slovenije   (YU)
Zveza Socialisticne Mladine Slovenije. Univerzitetna
   Konferenca   (YU)
Zvezda, Trgovinska i Radna Organizacija   (YU)
Izdatel'stvo Zvyazda   (UR)
Zweckverband Deutscher Apotheker   (GW)
Zwiazek Nauczycielstwa Polskiego   (PL)
Zwiazek Polakow W Austrii   (AU)
Zwiazek Zawodowy Gornikow   (PL)
Zwiazek Zawodowy Pracownikow Sluzby Zdrowia
   (PL)

Barrie Zwicker, Ed. & Pub.   (CN)
Zydowski Instytut Historyczny w Polsce   (PL)
1 del Metal de Valencia   (SP)
Editorial 2 de Octubre   (AG)
3A Editores S.A.   (MX)
3M National Ad. Co.   (US)
3M Oesterreich m.b.h.   (AU)
3M United Kingdom Ltd.   (UK)
Les 4 Points Cardinaux   (CM)
Editions des 4 Seigneurs   (FR)
Editorial 8 de Junio   (CK)
8 X 10 Art Portfolios   (US)

13th Moon, Inc.   (US)
15 Dias en Costa Rica   (CR)
Editrice 18 Karati s.r.l.   (IT)
20th Century Christian, Inc.   (US)
21st Century Communications, Inc.   (US)
73 Inc.   (US)
100 Flowers Bookstore   (US)
613 Magazine   (US)
1745 Association and National Military History
   Society   (UK)
1820 Settler's Association of South Africa   (SA)